P9-BHV-083

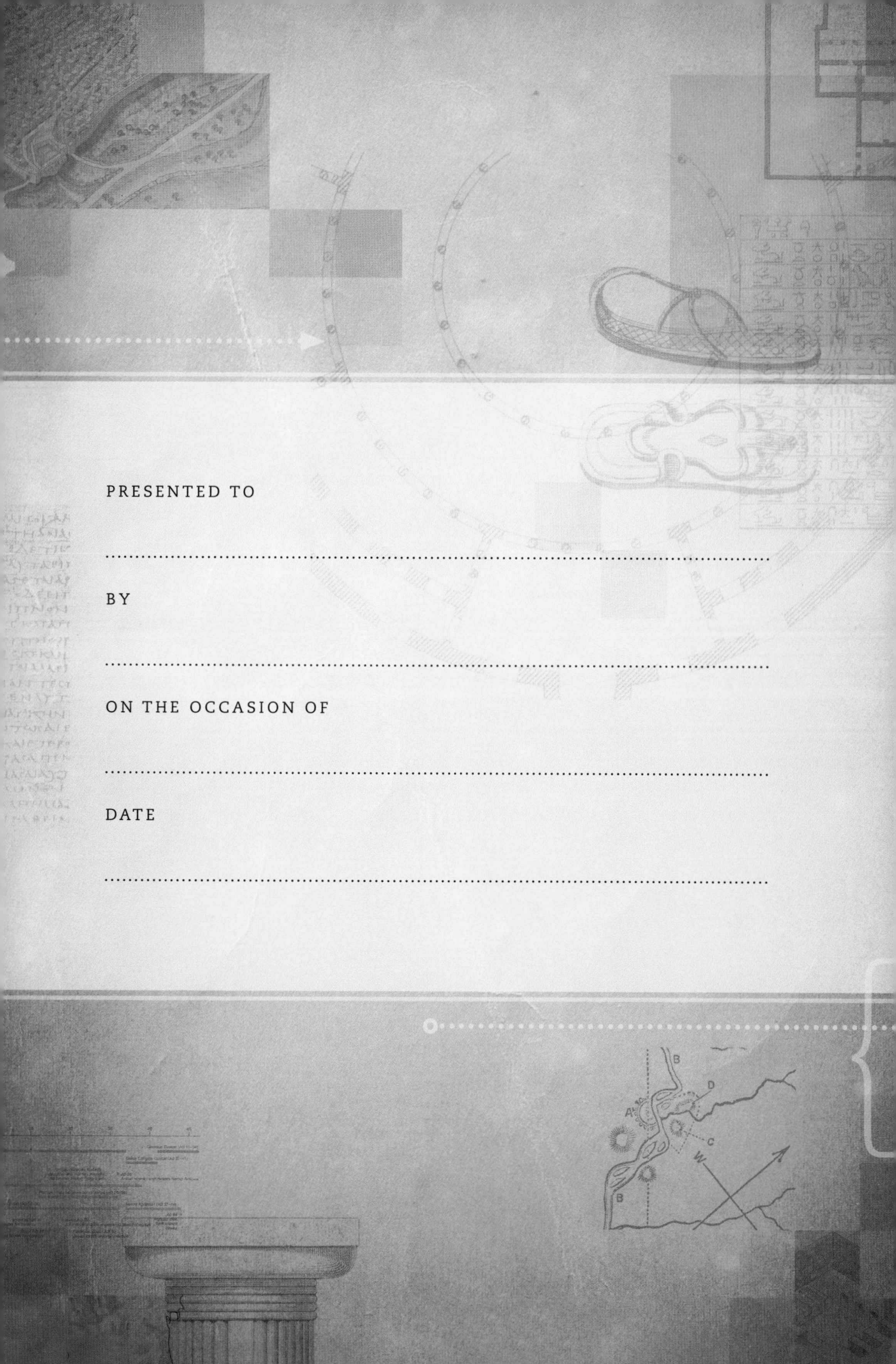

PRESENTED TO

BY

ON THE OCCASION OF

DATE

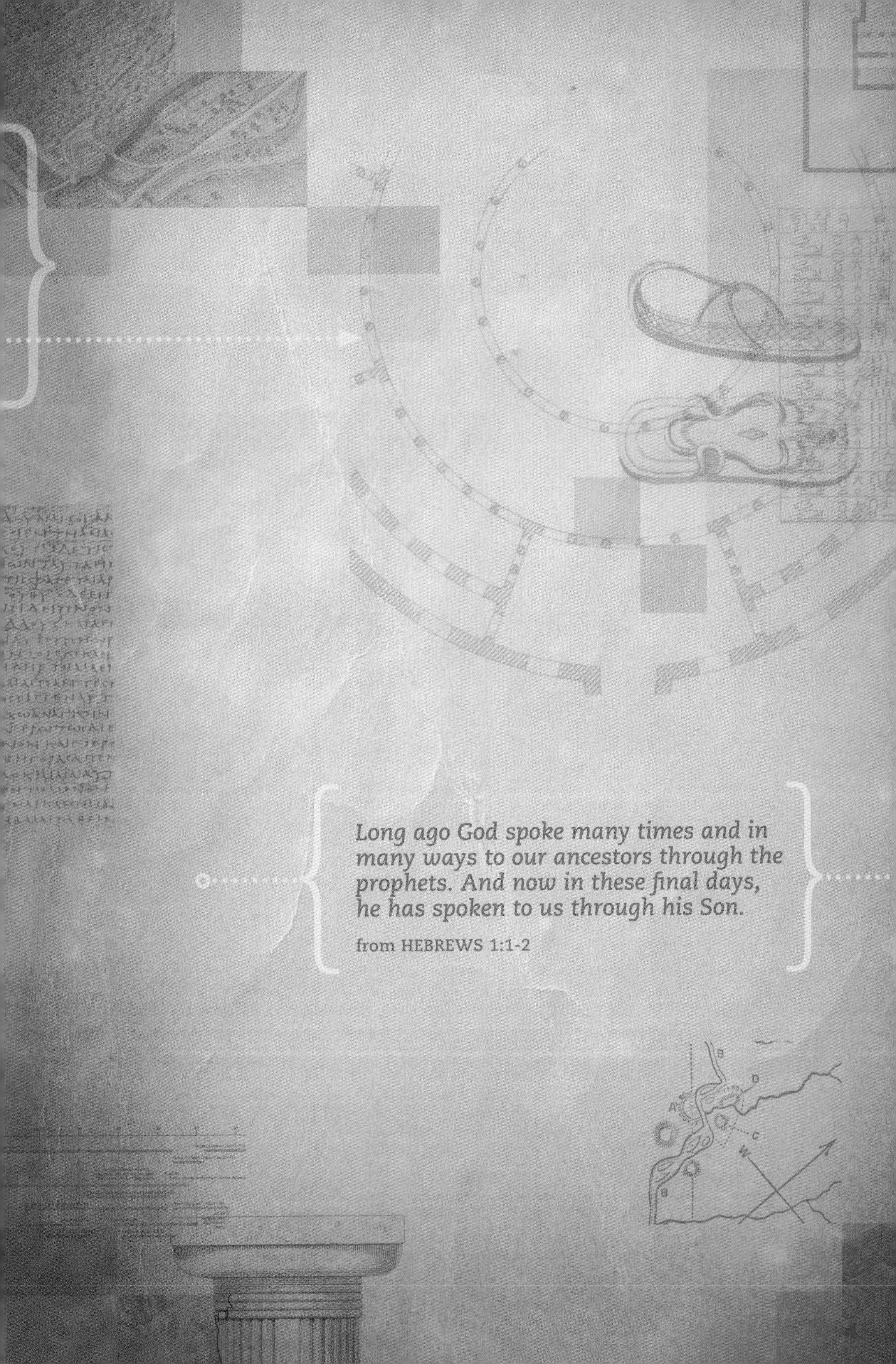

Long ago God spoke many times and in many ways to our ancestors through the prophets. And now in these final days, he has spoken to us through his Son.
from HEBREWS 1:1-2

Chronological
Life Application
Study Bible

Chronological
Life Application®
Study Bible

New Living Translation®
SECOND EDITION

Tyndale House Publishers, Inc.
Carol Stream, Illinois

Visit Tyndale online at www.newlivingtranslation.com and www.tyndale.com.

Tyndale House Publishers gratefully acknowledges the role of Youth for Christ/USA in preparing the Life Application Notes and Bible Helps.

Chronological Life Application Study Bible is an edition of the *Holy Bible,* New Living Translation.

ISBN 978-1-4143-3927-6 Hardcover
ISBN 978-1-4143-3928-3 LeatherLike Brown/Tan
ISBN 978-1-4143-3929-0 LeatherLike Brown/Green/Dark Teal

Printed in Italy

18 17 16 15 14 13 12
7 6 5 4 3 2 1

Tyndale House Publishers and Wycliffe Bible Translators share the vision for an understandable, accurate translation of the Bible for every person in the world. Each sale of the *Holy Bible,* New Living Translation, benefits Wycliffe Bible Translators. Wycliffe is working with partners around the world to accomplish Vision 2025—an initiative to start a Bible translation program in every language group that needs it by the year 2025.

CONTENTS

USING THE CANONICAL TABLE OF CONTENTS

These pages give you quick access to any passage of Scripture in the *Chronological Life Application Study Bible*. Just find the reference you are looking for in this canonically arranged index, and you'll get the precise page where that passage is found. Colored squares indicate which section the passage appears in:

■ Beginnings (Undated–2100 B.C.)

■ God's Chosen Family (2100–1800 B.C.)

■ Birth of Israel (1800–1406 B.C.)

■ Possessing the Land (1406–1050 B.C.)

■ United Monarchy (1050–930 B.C.)

■ Splintered Nation (930–586 B.C.)

■ Exile (586–538 B.C.)

■ Return & Diaspora (538–6 B.C.)

■ Jesus Christ (6 B.C.–A.D. 30)

■ The Church (A.D. 30–Present)

CANONICAL TABLE OF CONTENTS

The Old Testament

1 CHRONICLES

2 CHRONICLES

EZRA

NEHEMIAH

ESTHER

JOB

PSALMS

PROVERBS

ECCLESIASTES

SONG OF SONGS

ISAIAH

JEREMIAH

LAMENTATIONS

EZEKIEL

DANIEL

HOSEA

JOEL

AMOS

OBADIAH

JONAH

MICAH

NAHUM

HABAKKUK

ZEPHANIAH

HAGGAI

ZECHARIAH

MALACHI

The New Testament

MATTHEW

MARK

LUKE

INTRODUCTION TO THE CHRONOLOGICAL LIFE APPLICATION STUDY BIBLE

WHY THE **CHRONOLOGICAL LIFE APPLICATION STUDY BIBLE** IS UNIQUE

Have you ever opened your Bible and asked the following:

- What does this passage really mean?
- How does it apply to my life?
- Why does some of the Bible seem irrelevant?
- What do these ancient cultures have to do with today?
- I love God; why can't I understand what he is saying to me through his Word?
- What's going on in the lives of these Bible people?

Many Christians do not read the Bible regularly. Why? Because in the pressures of daily living, they cannot find a connection between the timeless principles of Scripture and the ever-present problems of day-by-day living.

God urges us to apply his Word (Isa 42:23; 1 Cor 10:11; 2 Thes 3:4), but too often we stop at accumulating Bible knowledge. This is why the *Life Application Study Bible* was originally developed—to show how to put into practice what we have learned.

Applying God's Word is a vital part of one's relationship with God; it is the evidence that we are obeying him. The difficulty in applying the Bible is not with the Bible itself but with the reader's inability to bridge the gap between the past and present, the conceptual and practical. When we don't or can't do this, spiritual dryness, shallowness, and indifference are the results.

The words of Scripture itself cry out to us, "Don't just listen to God's word. You must do what it says. Otherwise, you are only fooling yourselves" (Jas 1:22). The *Life Application Study Bible* does just that. It helps you understand the context of a passage, gives important background and historical information, explains difficult words and phrases, and helps you see the interrelationships within Scripture. But it does much more. The *Life Application Study Bible* goes deeper into God's Word, helping you discover the timeless truths being communicated, see the relevance for your life, and make a personal application. The notes answer the questions, "So what?" and " What does this passage mean to me, my family, my friends, my job, my neighborhood, my church, my country?"

Developed by an interdenominational team of pastors, scholars, family counselors, and a national organization dedicated to promoting God's Word and spreading the gospel, the *Life Application Study Bible* took many years to complete, and all the work was reviewed by renowned theologians.

This edition is the *Chronological Life Application Study Bible*, and it goes even further in helping you to understand the Bible and apply it to your life. Instead of the traditional canonical arrangement, this Bible is arranged so events appear in the order in which they occurred. Although it contains every word of the 66 books of the Bible, this Bible is divided into 10 eras of biblical history, with the books intermingled to help you see how the story actually unfolded. The *Chronological Life Application Study Bible* retains all the features that make the *Life Application Study Bible* so useful, and it adds more features for even greater depth in studying the Bible.

Imagine reading a familiar passage of Scripture and gaining fresh insight, as if it were the first time you had ever read it. How much richer would your life be if you left each Bible reading with a new perspective and a small change for the better? A small change every day adds up to a changed life—and that is the very purpose of Scripture.

WHAT IS **APPLICATION**?

The best way to define *application* is to first determine what it is *not*. Application is *not* just accumulating knowledge. Knowledge helps us discover and understand facts and concepts, but it stops there. History is filled with philosophers who knew what the Bible said but failed to apply it to their lives, keeping them from believing and changing. Many think that understanding is the end goal of Bible study, but it is really only the beginning.

Application is *not* just illustration. Illustration only tells us how someone else handled a similar situation. While we may empathize with that person, we still have little direction for our personal situation.

Application is *not* just making a passage "relevant." Making the Bible relevant only helps us to see that the same lessons that were true in Bible times are true today; it does not show us how to apply them to the problems and pressures of our individual lives.

What, then, is application? Application *begins* by knowing and understanding God's Word and goes further. It focuses on the truth of the particular Scripture text, shows us what to do about what we're reading, and motivates us to respond to what God is teaching. All three are essential.

Application is putting into practice what we already know (see Mark 4:24; Heb 5:14). It answers our question "So what?" by confronting us with the right questions and motivating us to take action (see 1 Jn 2:5-6; Jas 2:17). Application is unique for each individual. It is making a relevant truth a personal truth, and it involves developing a strategy and action plan to live our lives in harmony with the Bible. It is the biblical "how to" of life.

You may ask, "How can your application notes be relevant to *my* life?" Each application note has three parts: (1) an *explanation* that ties the note directly to the Scripture passage and sets up the truth that is being taught, (2) the *bridge* that explains the truth and makes it relevant for today, and (3) the *application* that shows you how to take that truth and apply it to your personal situation. No note, by itself, can apply Scripture directly to your life. It can only teach, direct, lead, guide, inspire, recommend, and urge. It can give you the resources and direction you need to apply the Bible; but only *you* can take these resources and put them into practice.

A good note, therefore, should not only give you knowledge and understanding, but point you to application. Before you buy any kind of resource Bible, you should evaluate the notes and ask the following questions: (1) Does the note contain enough information to help me understand the point of the Scripture passage? (2) Does the note assume I know too much? (3) Does the note avoid denominational bias? (4) Do the notes touch most of life's experiences? (5) Does the note help me *apply* God's Word?

WHAT IS UNIQUE ABOUT A **CHRONOLOGICAL BIBLE**?

The Bible does not proceed in chronological order from beginning to end. Indeed, the 66 books of the Bible do tell a unified story that begins at Genesis 1:1 and ends at Revelation 22:21, but the books are essentially organized by grouping similar kinds of books together (prophets, letters, etc.) rather than proceeding in chronological order. Some books cover the exact same events from different perspectives, like the books of Kings and Chronicles. Others, like the Psalms, are spread over hundreds of years by many different authors. It is often difficult for ordinary readers to put together the little clues throughout the Bible that show how a particular book or chapter fits into the larger story of the Bible. But seeing that larger story is often the key that unlocks understanding for some parts of the Bible that seem obscure.

The *Chronological Life Application Study Bible* helps the reader see the larger story by breaking up the traditional books of the Bible into 10 major eras of biblical history, intermingling the Scriptures into a single, unified story from Creation to the end. This provides readers with a unique viewpoint on the biblical story, and it can give fresh and exciting insight into books of the Bible that might have been difficult to understand apart from knowing where they fall chronologically. For example, see the way the prophets Haggai and Zechariah are interacting with what is happening in the book of Ezra (pp. 1162-1181). Intermingling the prophets with the historical books can give us a new perspective on the issues they were dealing with. In this case, it shows how the people responded to God's call on their life through the prophets: The Temple was rebuilt and proper worship in Jerusalem was restored! This is only one of many examples. In the *Chronological Life Application Study Bible*, you will notice that the prophets are an integral part of the story of Israel, and their writings will pop up right in the middle of the story when they confronted a king or the people. You will read Paul's letters to the Thessalonians right when he wrote them, during a stay in Corinth a few months after his visit to Thessalonica. This new view on the text of Scripture will give you surprising and valuable insights.

Although a chronological Bible gives us a new and exciting outlook on the message of Scripture, we do need to remember that the Bible was not written as a single story. God gave us the Bible as a collection of 66 individual books, not a chronological rearrangement of those books. While helpful as a tool for gaining insight into the meaning, message, and significance of Scripture, a chronological Bible is not a substitute for a traditional Bible. The *Chronological Life Application Study Bible* does contain every word of the Bible, but because it is rearranged and books are often presented out of canonical order or broken up into smaller pieces, we should remember that the books of the Bible are intended to be read as whole books. It is helpful to see the Gospels mingled together in one common narrative, with parallel passages together, but it is not a substitute for reading the book of Matthew as a whole, unbroken story about Jesus' life and his significance. With that in mind, it is our hope that the *Chronological Life Application Study Bible* will be a vital tool in helping you understand the Bible, but it should not replace a traditional Bible in any sense.

Organizing the Bible into chronological order is sometimes tricky, and excellent Christian scholars do not always agree on the order of certain books or passages. The editors of the *Chronological Life Application Study Bible* created the chronological arrangement by consulting several scholarly resources, but it should not be considered the only legitimate way to organize the Bible chronologically. Some books, such as the book of the prophet Joel, are very difficult to place chronologically. In cases like that, we used our best judgment, but ultimately certainty eludes us. In many places, the study notes will mention the possibility of alternative chronologies. We encourage readers to question our decisions and consider alternatives to the arrangement we have provided—the text of Scripture is infallible, but our arrangement of it in this Bible certainly is not!

FEATURES OF THE CHRONOLOGICAL LIFE APPLICATION STUDY BIBLE

Front matter features

- **Canonical Table of Contents** A table of contents listing each passage of Scripture in its canonical order was created in order to give you a quick way to find any passage in this Bible based just on the reference, even if you have no idea what place that book or verse has in the chronological story.

- **Chronological Survey of the Bible** To help you understand the Old and New Testaments from their chronological viewpoint, a quick overview of the whole story, including gaps like the intertestamental period, begins on p. A23.

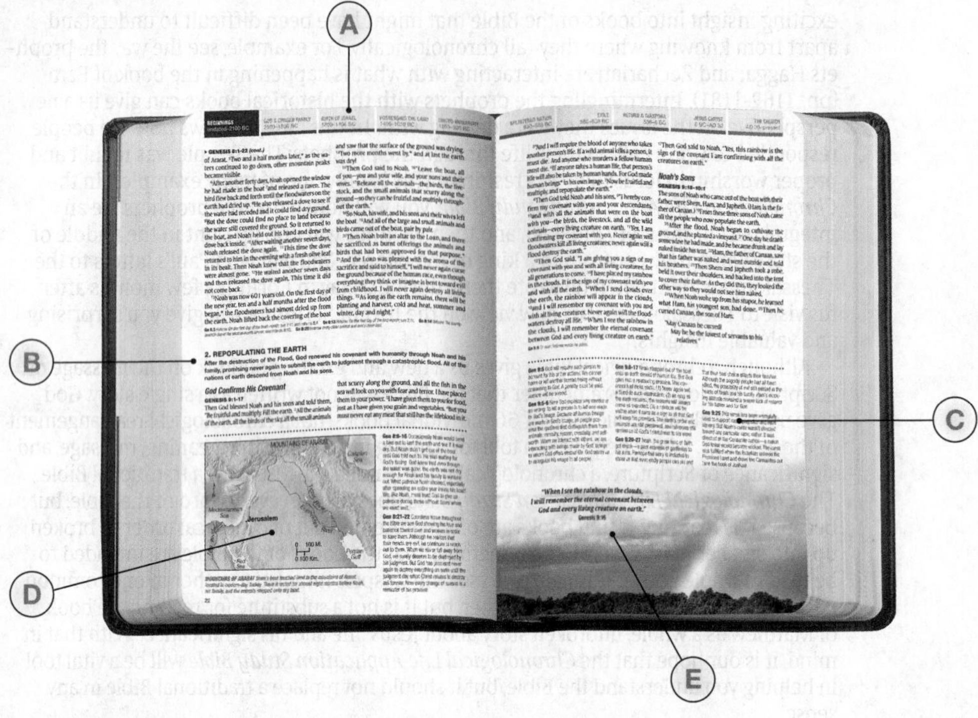

Interior features

A. Chronological Header System You'll never be at a loss for where you are in the story of the Bible. Every page shows the entirety of the historical eras covered with the current era highlighted for quick recognition of where you are in God's story.

B. Outline The *Chronological Life Application Study Bible* has a new, custom-made outline that was designed specifically from an application point of view. Several unique features should be noted:

1. To avoid confusion, each section outline has only three levels of headings. Main outline heads are marked with a capital letter. Subheads are marked by a number. Minor explanatory heads have no letter or number.
2. Brief paragraphs below each main head and subhead summarize the content of the following Bible text and offer important contextual information.

C. Notes In addition to providing the reader with many application notes, the *Chronological Life Application Study Bible* also offers several kinds of explanatory notes that help you understand culture, history, context, difficult-to-understand passages, background, places, theological concepts, and the relationship of various passages in Scripture to other passages. Maps, charts, and diagrams are also found on the same page as the passages to which they relate. For an example of an application note, see the note on John 20:23 (p. 1495). For an example of an explanatory note, see the note on Mark 11:1-2 (p. 1430). The abbreviation ff appears in some notes to indicate that the comments apply not only to the verse referenced but to the following passage as well.

D. Maps The *Chronological Life Application Study Bible* has more maps than any other Bible. A thorough and comprehensive Bible atlas is built right into each Bible section. There are two kinds of maps: (1) A section introduction map, telling the story of that section of Bible history. (2) Thumbnail maps in the notes, plotting most geographic movements in the Bible. In addition to these numerous full-color maps, there is a comprehensive set of color maps and diagrams at the back of this Bible.

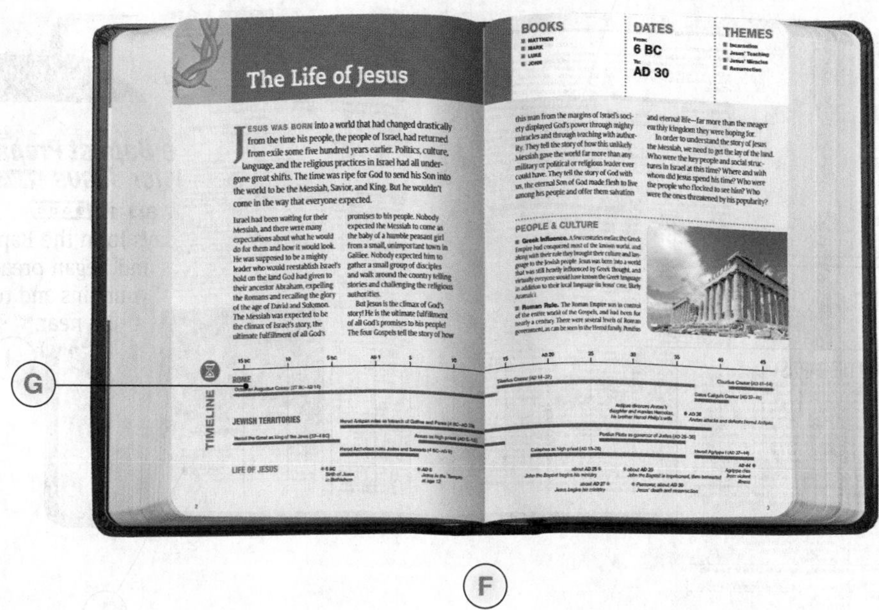

E. Illustrated Verses Many photos appear throughout this Bible that illustrate important verses and bring the Bible to life.

F. Section Introductions The Section Introductions are divided into several easy-to-find parts:

Overview. This is a summary with general lessons and applications that can be drawn from the section as a whole.

Timeline. This puts the Bible books or passages of that section's era into their historical setting. It lists the key events of that era and the dates when they occurred.

People and Culture. This is an overview of the important people and cultural issues that provide background for what is happening historically during that time.

Books in this Section. This is a list of straight facts about each book in the section—those pieces of information you need to know at a glance.

Article. Some introductions include an article that explains an important biblical or theological concept to help in understanding that section.

Megathemes. This feature gives the main themes of the section, explains their significance, and then tells why they are still important for us today.

Map. This shows the key places found in the section and retells the story of the section from a geographical point of view.

G. Timeline Three types of timelines appear in this Bible. There is a master timeline listing all the events that are recorded throughout the Bible (p. A34). There are also more detailed timelines at the beginning of each era of biblical history, showing the events of that section in the context of other major world powers and events. Finally, there is a running timeline of key dates in the margins of the text to indicate when in history that passage took place.

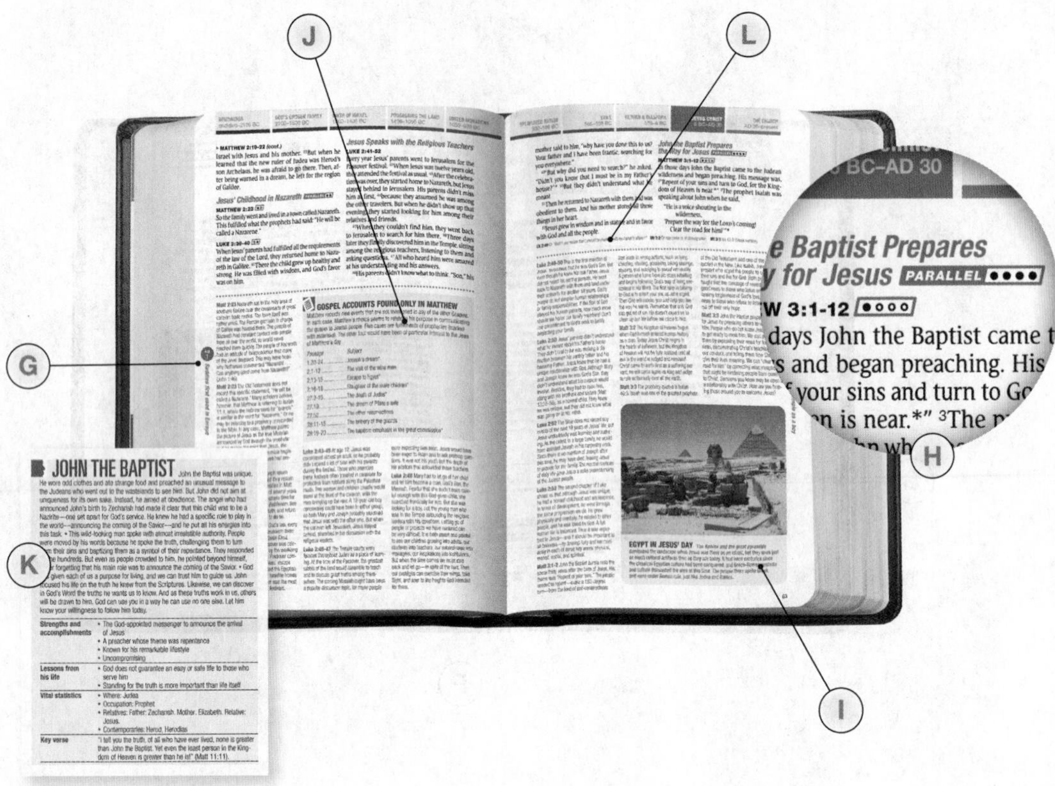

H. **Parallel Passage Indicator** Parallel passages are placed one after another. Each is identified by a bar signifying that it is part of a parallel section. Markers identify how many passages—two, three, or four—are in the parallel. The parallel passages are also marked to indicate which one it is in the parallel: first, second, third, or fourth.

I. **Archaeological Notes** These notes feature full-color images and highlight important places, archaeological discoveries, and historical artifacts that put the Bible into real historical context.

J. **Charts and Diagrams** Hundreds of charts and diagrams are included to help the reader better visualize difficult concepts or relationships. Most charts not only present the needed information but show its significance as well.

K. **Personality Profiles** Another unique feature of this Bible is a collection of profiles of many Bible people, including their strengths and weaknesses, greatest accomplishments and mistakes, and key lessons from their lives.

L. **Textual Notes and Sectional Headings** Directly related to the New Living Translation text, the textual notes examine such things as alternate translations, meaning of Hebrew and Greek terms, Old Testament quotations, and variant readings in the ancient biblical manuscripts. The NLT text also contains sectional headings in order to help you more easily understand the subject and content of each section; these headings appear as the third level of the three-level header system described above.

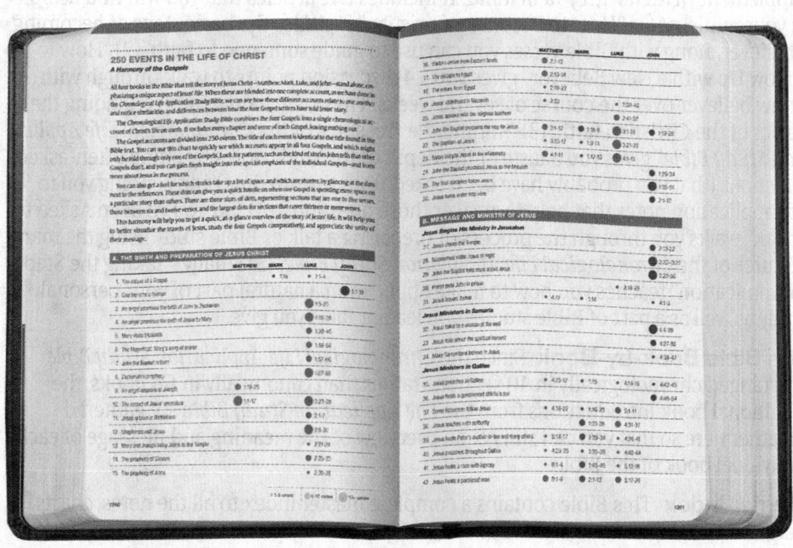

M

M. Harmony of the Gospels A visual harmony of the Gospels was developed specifically for this Bible. It is located on p. 1260 and explained in detail there.

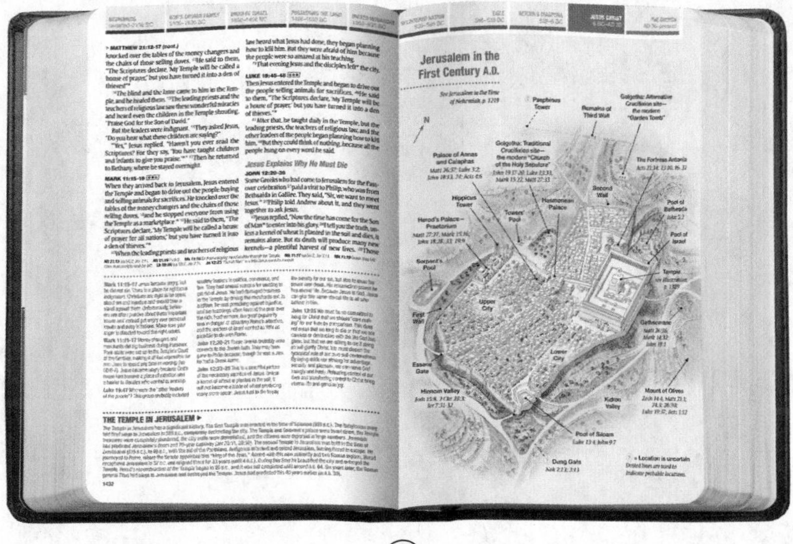

N

N. New Full-Color Illustrations. Eight full-color illustrations were commissioned specifically for the *Chronological Life Application Study Bible*, including four drawings of Jerusalem from various periods in history and detailed illustrations of the Tabernacle and Temple.

Back matter features

- **A Christian Worker's Resource** The Christian Worker's Resource is a special supplement written with you in mind. It includes five articles that you will find useful in your ministry: (1) "How to Become a Christian" includes the basic steps of becoming a believer, along with Bible verses you can use to guide someone to faith. (2) "How to Follow Up with a New Believer" gives you 14 discussion points to walk through with a new believer over the course of several weeks. These will help in understanding the basics of the Christian faith. (3) "Mining the Treasures of the *Chronological Life Application Study Bible*" gives you a taste of the depth of the study notes by citing often-asked questions (that you probably have been asked from time to time) and sending you to life application notes that help to answer those questions. (4) "So You've Been Asked to Speak" walks you through the process of preparing a talk or Bible study using the many features of the *Chronological Life Application Study Bible*. (5) Finally, "Taking the Step to Application" teaches you how to make application a natural part of your personal study as well as a part of Bible studies you lead or talks you give.
- **The Bible Book-by-Book** Since the *Chronological Life Application Study Bible* is arranged chronologically in 10 sections rather than canonically in 66 books, the traditional book introductions from the *Life Application Study Bible* are gathered together here so that you can still get an overview of the meaning and message of each individual book of the Bible.
- **Master Index** This Bible contains a complete master index to all the notes, charts, maps, archaeological notes, illustrations, and personality profiles, as well as separate indexes for each of these.
- **Dictionary/Concordance** A concise concordance identifies terms and proper names of special interest and points to the important occurrences in context. Each word is followed by a brief definition or description.

A CHRONOLOGICAL SURVEY OF THE BIBLE

Biblical history spans the entire course of time from the creation of the world to the era of the early Christian church in the late first century A.D. At its most basic level, it is simply the story of God fashioning a people for himself and redemptively interacting with them throughout history. From the creation of the world and the first human beings to the fall of humanity; to the calling of Abraham and the rise of Israel; to the return of Judah from exile in Babylon; to the incarnation, life, death, and resurrection of Jesus; and finally to the indwelling presence of the Holy Spirit in all believers—God continually works to redeem a people for himself, a people he can lovingly bless with good things as they seek him and find their hope in him, the source of all good things.

■ Beginnings: Creation–2100 B.C. The story begins with the very creation of the world, when God formed the heavens and earth and then all living things to inhabit them. All that he created was "good," but God distinguished human beings from the rest of creation by creating them in his very own image. He abundantly provided for Adam and Eve, the first man and woman, by placing them in a specially prepared garden, and he enjoyed unbroken fellowship with them. But this perfect world was soon poisoned by sin when Adam and Eve sought to be their own masters and disobeyed God. Instead of trusting and obeying God, they swallowed the lie of the serpent, who told them they could be like God. Because of their sin, Adam and Eve were cast out of the garden and from then on suffered pain, sorrow, hardship, and even death. But thankfully, the story of God's people did not end there. In fact, that was just the beginning.

Sadly, the curse of sin brought into the world by Adam and Eve was passed down to all their descendants as well. Every human being is "bent," so to speak, just like their ancestors. This can be seen as early as their first child: Cain killed his brother out of jealousy. The curse of sin continued until the whole world was so wicked that God chose to wipe it all out and start over, in a sense, with a new people, a people descended from a righteous man named Noah.

God instructed Noah to build a giant boat to save his family and pairs of every kind of animal living on the earth. Then God made it rain for 40 days until the whole earth was covered with water, and every living thing that was not on the boat—including human beings—died. After the floodwaters subsided, Noah and his family left the boat to start a new humanity. God told them to multiply and fill the earth, and he promised never again to destroy the earth with a flood.

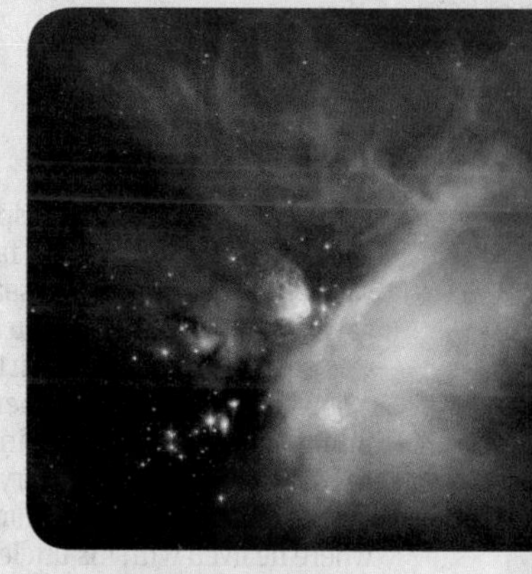

Noah's descendants multiplied. Everyone spoke a single language, enabling them to easily work together. So they decided to build a great tower to the heavens, a testimony to their own greatness. But God chose to confuse them with different languages, making it virtually impossible for them to continue with their great project, since they could no longer understand each other. As a result, the people soon dispersed and spread out over all the earth, which is what God had commanded them to do in the first place.

■ God's Chosen Family: 2100–1800 B.C. It appears that with each generation after Noah, people drifted further and further from God. God chose once again to create a new people for himself *within* the rest of humanity—this time through a man named Abram (eventually renamed Abraham). Through this chosen people, God would ultimately bless all of humanity. Interestingly, the Bible does not mention why God chose Abram. It simply says God told him to leave his family and his home country and go to a new land that God would show him. God promised to bless Abraham and make a great nation from his descendants. And Abraham obeyed God. Thus begins the rest of the story of the Old Testament—the story of God's chosen people.

In obedience and faith, Abraham left his home and traveled to the land of Canaan. God told Abraham that this was the land he was going to give him, and he sealed his promise with a solemn covenant ceremony. God also reaffirmed his promise to give Abraham many descendants. After an agonizing wait, God finally gave Abraham and his wife, Sarah, a son, Isaac. Abraham was 100 and Sarah was 91. Then God tested Abraham's faith by telling him to sacrifice Isaac. This was the ultimate demonstration of Abraham's faithful trust in God since Isaac was the only son born to Abraham and Sarah, the only visible hope that God would fulfill his promise to bless Abraham with many descendants. Abraham obeyed, and God spared Isaac's life.

Isaac lived much like his father, sojourning in various places in Canaan. Isaac's wife, Rebekah, gave birth to twin boys, Esau and Jacob. Esau was older, but he sold his birthright to Jacob for a bowl of stew, and Jacob then tricked his father into granting him the blessings that belonged to Esau. So Esau became very angry with Jacob, and Jacob fled to the homeland of his ancestors, where he lived with his uncle Laban for many years. While working for Laban, Jacob married his daughters Leah and Rachel and began to raise a family. He eventually returned to Canaan and reconciled with Esau. God changed Jacob's name to Israel. His 12 sons became the ancestors of the 12 tribes of Israel. God also reaffirmed to Jacob the covenant he had made with his father, Isaac, and his grandfather Abraham.

One of Jacob's 12 sons was named Joseph, clearly Jacob's favorite. Though one of the youngest, Joseph had dreams (literally) of one day becoming master over his brothers. His brothers became very angry with him because of this and sold him to slave traders headed to Egypt. Yet God blessed Joseph even while a slave in Egypt. Through a complicated interplay of circumstances, Joseph was eventually brought before Pharaoh himself to interpret Pharaoh's dream. God gave Joseph wisdom to understand that the dream foretold of a coming worldwide famine. As a result, Pharaoh made him second in command of all of Egypt in order to prepare. During the famine, Joseph's brothers were forced to travel to Egypt to buy grain from Joseph, though they did not know he was their long-lost brother. Eventually Joseph revealed his identity to them, and they were reconciled. Joseph convinced his entire family, including his father, Jacob, to move to Egypt. And there Jacob's descendants flourished and multiplied.

■ **The Birth of Israel: 1800–1406 B.C.** Many years later, a new leader arose in Egypt who did not know of all that Joseph had done, and he began to oppress the Israelites for fear that they might rebel against him. The Israelites were made slaves, and eventually Pharaoh even ordered all Israelite baby boys to be thrown into the Nile River. One Israelite couple, however, hid their baby boy in a basket in the river to keep him from being killed. Pharaoh's daughter found the baby and adopted him, calling him Moses.

Moses grew up in the Egyptian royal court. One day, he witnessed an Egyptian beating an Israelite, so Moses killed the Egyptian and hid his body in the sand. When Pharaoh found out, Moses fled to the land of Midian. There God spoke to Moses from a burning bush, revealing his name—the LORD—and telling him to go back to Egypt and lead his people out of slavery to the land that God was giving them. Moses was reluctant to go, but the Lord assured him that he would be with him and would give him power to do amazing miracles before Pharaoh. God also sent Moses' brother, Aaron, along with him to Egypt.

When Moses arrived in Egypt, he spoke to Pharaoh, telling him God's command to let the Israelites go out into the wilderness to worship God. Pharaoh refused and then treated the Israelites even more harshly. This set in motion a series of 10 plagues that God inflicted on Egypt. Each plague cycle followed essentially the same pattern: Moses told Pharaoh to let God's people go; Pharaoh refused; the plague was unleashed; Pharaoh recanted and agreed to let the Israelites go; Moses prayed for the plague to be stopped; Pharaoh then changed his mind and refused to let the Israelites go. The final plague was a curse upon the firstborn of all people and animals in Egypt. All homes without the blood of a lamb smeared on the doorframe would be visited by the angel of

death. The firstborn sons of Egypt were killed by the angel that night, including Pharaoh's own son. The annual feast of Passover commemorates this momentous event.

After this 10th plague, Pharaoh allowed the Israelites to leave Egypt; but once they had left, he again changed his mind and set out in pursuit of them. Just as Pharaoh's army was closing in on the Israelites, who were blocked by the Red Sea, the Lord miraculously parted the sea and allowed the Israelites to pass through on dry land. When the Egyptians tried to follow them, the sea closed over them and they drowned. This whole event, the Exodus, became a defining moment in the history of the nation of Israel, when God decisively rescued and redeemed his people for himself. Repeatedly throughout the Old Testament, God would refer to himself as the one who led the Israelites out of bondage in Egypt with strength and miraculous signs.

With the threat of the Egyptians behind them, the Israelites were now free to journey to the place where God wanted them to worship him. They began to grumble for food, so God provided quail for meat, and each morning manna, mysterious bread-like flakes, fell from heaven. At times, God also provided water from a rock.

Finally the Israelites came to Mount Sinai, and God met with Moses there. God gave him the Ten Commandments and other instructions to give to the people. These essentially defined what it meant to live as the people of God. While the Israelites were at Sinai, God also gave Moses instructions for building the Tabernacle, which would serve as a sort of portable temple as the Israelites moved from place to place on their way to the land that God had promised to their ancestors Abraham, Isaac, and Jacob. Even while Moses was receiving God's laws, however, the people demonstrated their persistent unfaithfulness by constructing an idol and worshiping it! And Moses' brother Aaron, who had just been appointed high priest over the Israelites, was the one who instructed them to build it!

After the Israelites had camped at the foot of Mount Sinai for a year, God directed them to begin making their way to the Promised Land. God told Moses to send 12 scouts into Canaan. All but Joshua and Caleb reported that the land was good but that the inhabitants were stronger than them. So the Israelites refused to take possession of the land. Because they failed to trust in God for victory, he condemned them to wander in the wilderness for 40 years until that entire generation had died, except for Joshua and Caleb. God continued to provide for his people during those forty years, despite their repeated instances of grumbling and unfaithfulness to him. At the end of 40 years, the new generation of Israelites came to Kadesh-barnea, and then they began making their way to the Promised Land once again. They set up camp on the plains of Moab. The Promised Land lay just across the Jordan River to the west. Moses reviewed the history of God's dealings with them up to that point and exhorted them to be faithful to God after they conquered the land. Moses died just before the Israelites entered the land, leaving his assistant Joshua to lead the conquest.

Possessing the Land: 1406–1050 B.C.

The first city to be taken was the imposing city of Jericho, which stood just across the Jordan River in Canaan. But the Israelites did not even have to lay siege to the city or attack its gates to capture it, because God miraculously caused the walls of the city to fall down. Joshua then led the Israelites to capture towns throughout the Promised Land. The entire conquest of the land occurred over many years, but they never fully completed it. God had commanded the Israelites to completely drive out the Canaanites, but they were satisfied to simply live alongside the inhabitants. Several areas within the land continued to be controlled by Canaanites even after the conquest period was over, and their idolatry was a snare to the Israelites for centuries to come.

After Joshua died, God repeatedly raised up leaders, called judges, to deliver his people from oppression. This oppression was typically a direct result of the Israelites' sin. This cycle of sin, oppression, and deliverance occurred throughout the period of the judges. During this time the Israelites also experienced conflict among themselves as the tribe of Benjamin was almost completely wiped out by the other tribes in a bloody civil war. The period of the judges was a spiritually dark, chaotic time for Israel, all the people doing whatever seemed right in their own eyes.

The United Monarchy: 1050–930 B.C.

The Israelites asked Samuel, the last of the judges, for a king to rule over them like the kings of the nations around them. God told Samuel to agree to their request but to warn them of the hardships a king would bring upon them. God had been their king, but they had rejected his leadership in favor of being more like the other nations.

God led Samuel to anoint Saul from the tribe of Benjamin as the first king (c. 1050 B.C.). Saul was tall and handsome. He also proved to be an able military leader in many ways. But his spiritual character was lacking. On various occasions, he sacrificed God's ways to ensure military success or personal gain. For these reasons, God rejected Saul as king and chose a man after his own heart to replace him: David.

David was an unlikely choice. The youngest of eight brothers, he was not even considered at first. But soon after Samuel anointed David to be the next king, David demonstrated that he was indeed specially chosen by God; for he slew the Philistine giant Goliath when all Israel's soldiers, including his brothers, were too afraid to face the giant in battle.

David joined Saul's warriors at his palace and became close friends with Saul's son Jonathan. David quickly proved himself to be a very able military leader and gained the favor of the Israelite people. This incited Saul's bitter jealousy, and Saul began trying to kill David. David fled, moving from place to place, at times narrowly escaping Saul and his men. When David heard that Saul and his sons had been killed in a battle with the Philistines, he moved to Hebron and was proclaimed king over Judah. But the commander of Saul's army proclaimed Ishbosheth, one of Saul's sons, king over Israel. Eventually Ishbosheth was assassinated by his own men, and David was proclaimed king over all the Israelite tribes.

After becoming king over all Israel around 1000 B.C., David captured the fortified city of Jerusalem from the Jebusites and moved his capital there. David was extremely successful in battle against virtually all the surrounding nations. He established a treaty with the powerful and wealthy city-state of Tyre. The king of Tyre supplied David with stonemasons and coveted cedar, and David built himself a palace and stockpiled materials for building the Temple.

The high point of David's reign was when God chose to establish a permanent covenant with David and his descendants. David wanted to build a permanent Temple for the Lord in Jerusalem but the Lord had a different plan: God was going to build *David* a "house," that is, he was going to establish David's family line as the ruling dynasty over Israel forever.

Unfortunately, David's reign as king was not without trouble. David himself committed adultery with the wife of Uriah, one of his most valiant warriors, and she became pregnant. Then David sought to cover up his sin by arranging Uriah's death on the battlefield. Later in his reign, David brought a plague upon all Israel because he ordered a census to be taken of all men of military age. Several of David's children brought heartache to him as well. David's son Amnon raped his own half-sister Tamar, and then her full brother Absalom killed Amnon in revenge. Absalom then fled into exile. Years later Absalom returned, but he mounted a rebellion against his father and proclaimed himself king. David was forced to flee Jerusalem for a time and set up his capital in Mahanaim. David's men fought against Absalom's men, and Absalom was killed, so David returned to Jerusalem.

Just before David died in 970 B.C., he appointed his son Solomon as king over Israel. Having received an extensive and powerful kingdom, Solomon was able to focus on tasks such as building a beautiful royal palace and the Temple for the Lord in Jerusalem. At the same time, Solomon capitalized on Israel's strategic position as a land bridge between Egypt and the other major powers of the ancient Near East. Solomon exacted lucrative tolls from those traveling through Israel, and he even engaged in arms dealing, buying horses and chariots from various nations and selling them to others. Solomon expanded his kingdom until it reached as far as the Euphrates River. Solomon's wisdom and riches were renowned throughout the ancient Near East.

However, Solomon's reign was not entirely a success story. He married literally hundreds of wives, primarily to seal political alliances with other nations, and this led to the spread of idolatry in Israel as these wives brought their idolatrous ways with them. Solomon even funded the building of pagan shrines for his wives on the hill across from the Temple of the Lord in Jerusalem. Solomon's extravagant royal court also placed a huge tax burden on the people of Israel, a burden that became difficult to bear.

■ **Splintered Nation: 930–586 B.C.** These cracks in Solomon's kingdom eventually led to outright rebellion. When his son Rehoboam became king in 930 B.C., the people of Israel demanded that he grant some reprieve from the heavy tax burden placed on them by his father. Rehoboam foolishly vowed instead to tax the people even more. So 10 of the 12 tribes of Israel refused to submit to Rehoboam, and they set up their own king instead. Only the tribes of Judah and Benjamin remained loyal. From then on, the kingdom established by the 10 northern tribes was called Israel, and the kingdom in the south that continued to be ruled by Davidic kings was called Judah. The division between these two kingdoms was very real, and they often fought wars against each other.

The northern tribes installed a man named Jeroboam as their king, and he immediately set a wicked precedent of idolatry for Israel. In order to keep his people from traveling to Jerusalem (in Judah) to worship at the Temple, Jeroboam set up calf idols at the northern and southern extremes of his kingdom and encouraged the people to worship there instead. He also appointed priests who were not Levites. His wickedness was so renowned that later wicked kings were said to follow the example of Jeroboam, who led Israel into sin.

The people of Judah continued to worship at the Temple of the Lord in Jerusalem, and their priests were descended from Aaron, as the law of Moses stipulated. Not that idolatry was never a problem in Judah, but for most of Judah's existence, idolatry did not typically receive the same degree of royal backing and widespread acceptance as it did in the northern kingdom.

Another distinction between the two kingdoms was the frequency with which royal dynasties changed. The northern kingdom experienced numerous assassinations and coups, which led to new dynasties taking power. But the southern kingdom always remained loyal to the Davidic dynasty.

Perhaps one of the most significant kings of Israel was Ahab, who took the throne in 874 B.C. Ahab was a skilled military leader. Spiritually, however, Ahab was very wicked, leading the Israelites into idolatry and other sins. Much of his wickedness was due to the influence of his wife Jezebel, the daughter of a pagan king. Jezebel promoted idolatry throughout the land, and she and Ahab were often condemned by the prophet Elijah.

Around this time a number of prophets gained prominence in Israel and Judah, and they spoke out against many sins that had grown rampant in society, including social injustice, idolatry, and general unfaithfulness to the Lord. They also foretold of a day when God would send his deliverer to Israel, a divine ruler who would set all things right once again. This deliverer is sometimes referred to as the Messiah ("anointed one"). The writings of several of these prophets became part of the Old Testament.

Over time, Assyria regained strength and absorbed nation after nation into its vast empire. Israel's territory was repeatedly reduced by Assyrian attacks until it was less than half its original size. Finally in 722 B.C., Israel's capital city of Samaria fell to the Assyrians, and the northern kingdom came to an end. Many Israelites were exiled to faraway lands, and other foreign peoples were brought in to diffuse the possibility of unified revolt. The Bible makes it clear that this exile was a direct result of the wickedness and idolatry of the people of Israel. Long ago when God gave his laws to Moses, he had forewarned the people that they, too, would be cast out of the Promised Land if they became like the wicked Canaanites. Now the day of reckoning had finally come for Israel's many sins of idolatry and injustice.

Several kings of Judah stand out. Jehoshaphat was regarded as a righteous king by the writers of Scripture, and he earnestly sought the Lord when foreign armies threatened Judah. However, he formed an alliance with wicked King Ahab of Israel, which had consequences later.

King Ahaz of Judah was deemed a wicked king by the writers of Scripture. When the northern kingdom of Israel teamed up with the Arameans to attack Judah (733 B.C.), Ahaz made the fateful decision to appeal to Assyria for help, essentially making Judah a vassal (subservient) kingdom to Assyria. He also replaced the altar of the Lord with a replica of a pagan one he saw in Damascus, and he got rid of many other sacred Temple items. Eventually he closed up the Temple entirely and allowed idolatry to flourish in Judah.

Ironically, Ahaz's son Hezekiah was one of the most righteous kings of Israel, and he was also a successful military leader. Hezekiah knew that the Assyrians would soon attempt to conquer Judah. Hezekiah prepared the city for this attack, which kept it from falling for a long time. Finally God sent a plague throughout the Assyrian camp, and the few who survived broke off the siege and returned to Assyria. Hezekiah also restored and purified the Temple and the worship of the Lord, purged idolatry from the land, and reinstituted the festival of Passover.

Just as quickly as Hezekiah had restored

proper worship of the Lord, his wicked son Manasseh corrupted it all once again. Manasseh promoted idolatry throughout Judah like no one else before him. He placed a pagan idol in the Temple of the Lord and even sacrificed his own sons by fire just outside the walls of Jerusalem. Near the end of his life, Manasseh was taken away into exile in Babylon, and he repented of all that he had done. After he was allowed to return to Judah, he strove to undo all the evil that he had done, tearing down pagan altars and restoring worship of the Lord.

By the time Manasseh's grandson Josiah became king of Judah (640 B.C.), Assyria was in decline, and the Babylonians were on the rise in the ancient Near East. Josiah capitalized on the situation, expanding the borders of Judah to include nearly all of the northern kingdom of Israel, whose people had by this time been carried away into exile. Josiah then strove to purge the land of idolatry and restore proper worship of the Lord. He also arranged for extensive repairs to be made to the Temple. Josiah died in 609 B.C. while trying to stop the Egyptians from passing through Judah and Israel to help the Assyrians, who were on the run from the Babylonians and the Medes in the far north.

After Josiah died, the Babylonians essentially took over Judah, installing and quickly deposing several of Josiah's sons as kings of Judah. They also exiled the upper echelon of society to Babylon in several waves (605 B.C., 597 B.C., and 586 B.C.) until finally in 586 B.C. the Babylonians attacked the city of Jerusalem and completely destroyed the Temple, leaving the once-proud nation in ruins.

Exile: 586–538 B.C. Unlike the experience of the northern kingdom of Israel, the Judeans were, for the most part, allowed to maintain their cultural and religious distinctiveness even in exile, and no large-scale effort was made to repopulate the land of Judah with foreigners. It was during the Exile that the people of Judah first came to be referred to as Jews (from the term *Judeans*).

This time of exile had a massive impact on virtually every aspect of Israelite life. Only the poor were left in Judah, and the ritual sacrificial system had essentially ceased. At the same time, many of those taken into exile became somewhat prosperous and even occupied positions of significant political power in the governments of their captors. Daniel and his friends were groomed to be part of the royal court, and Daniel was a close adviser to several Babylonian and Persian rulers.

The Babylonian empire were the ones who conquered Judah and took them off into exile, but the Babylonians soon faced a military threat themselves. The mighty Persian empire from the north was growing, and they eventually conquered Babylon and nearly everything else in the known world at the time. Persia had a different stance towards conquered peoples than Babylon had, which led to the end of this period of exile for the Jews.

Return and Diaspora: 538–6 B.C. King Cyrus of Persia captured Babylon in 539 B.C. and absorbed the Babylonian empire into his vast domain. In order to foster gratitude and loyalty among his subjects, Cyrus quickly decreed that those held captive in Babylon were free to return to their native lands. So around 538 B.C., a small contingent of Jews returned home to the land of Israel and reestablished a semiautonomous state under the dominion of Persia. They repaired the altar, reinstituted the daily sacrifices, and rebuilt the Temple as well. As the memoirs of Ezra and Nehemiah attest, Israel continued to enjoy relative religious freedom under the Persians throughout the remainder of the Old Testament period, despite occasional periods of oppression.

Not all of the Jews returned to the Promised Land, however. Over the decades in exile, many had largely integrated with the societies in which they were living and had built lives for themselves there. Over time the Hebrew language came to be replaced by Aramaic (the dominant language of the land of their exile) as the primary spoken language among Jews, and many Jews began to intermarry with the local foreign peoples and to regard their place of exile as their permanent home. This large population of Jews living permanently outside of the Promised Land while maintaining some degree of religious and cultural distinctiveness is often referred as the *Diaspora* ("scattering"). Some, like Daniel, Mordecai, and Esther continued to serve God faithfully even in prominent positions while far from the land of Israel. Over time, more and more of the Jews chose to return home, even leaving important positions to do so, such as Nehemiah, who was cup-bearer to the king.

The Intertestamental Period

The time between the last recorded events of the Old Testament and the first recorded events of the New Testament are sometimes referred to as the intertestamental period. Christians often think of this period as shrouded in mystery and darkness. In reality, quite a bit is known about this very formative period of biblical history, and understanding these events can help us better understand the New Testament. In a real way, the intertestamental period set the scene for the life and ministry of Jesus and his followers. For example, the Pharisees and Sadducees didn't even exist during Old Testament times; but by the time of Jesus, these two groups were key players in the political and religious life of Israel—so much so that Jesus spent considerable time and energy condemning them and instructing his disciples not to follow their example.

A brief review of a few events from the Old Testament will help us better understand the events that came after them. When the Assyrians exiled the northern kingdom *out* of the land, they brought foreign peoples from other lands *into* Israel in order to diffuse the possibility of unified revolt. Intermarriage among these foreigners and Israelites in Palestine gave rise to a group of people known as Samaritans, who were characterized by their syncretistic blend of Judaism and pagan religious practices. When Babylon conquered and exiled the southern kingdom of Judah, they destroyed the Temple in Jerusalem, bringing a halt to the ritual sacrificial system of Israel. This crisis led to a shift in focus away from the Temple and its rituals to the written word of Scripture, which was still accessible even in exile. Thus, it is likely during this time that synagogues and scribes became more widespread in Israelite society.

It is roughly at this point that we quietly exit the period of the Old Testament and enter the time known as the intertestamental period. Perhaps the single most significant event that occurred during this period was the rise of Alexander the Great. After ascending to the throne at the age of 20 (336 B.C.) and securing his grip over Macedonia and the Greek peninsula, young Alexander launched a series of stunning victories over the Persians that eventually culminated in his complete dominion over virtually all former Persian territory. Just as quickly as he rose to power, however, Alexander succumbed to illness and died in 323 B.C. at the age of 32.

One major effect of Alexander's conquest relates to his promotion of the Greek language and culture throughout his conquered lands. Greek soon came to function as a near universal means of communication and understanding throughout the ancient Near East. The pervasiveness and lasting influence of the Greek language can be seen most clearly in the fact that every single book of the New Testament, over 300 years after Alexander's death, was written in Greek.

Upon Alexander's death, his kingdom was broken up among his generals and other successors. A series of wars followed, with each successor vying for territory controlled by another. In time (around 220 B.C.), the Near East came to be dominated by three primary Greek powers: the Ptolemaic dynasty in Egypt; the Seleucid dynasty in much of Anatolia, Mesopotamia, and Persia; and the Antigonid dynasty in Macedonia. The land of Israel was initially part of the Ptolemaic realm, and Jews typically enjoyed a great deal of religious freedom and even favor at times. During this time a large number of Jews moved to Alexandria in northern Egypt, where they became relatively prosperous and influential. It was in Alexandria that a group of Jewish biblical scholars translated the Old Testament into Greek to make it more accessible to the increasing number of Jews who no longer spoke Hebrew. The translation, known as the Septuagint, would later become the Bible of the early Christian church, and most Old Testament quotations found in the New Testament are drawn from it.

In 198 B.C., the Seleucid ruler Antiochus III seized the land of Israel from the Ptolemies. When his son Antiochus IV Epiphanes took the throne in 175 B.C., everything changed for the Jews. Antiochus held ambitions of conquering the Ptolemaic kingdom in Egypt. In order to shore up his defenses and to prepare for his Egyptian campaign, Antiochus imposed a strict policy of Hellenization upon his subjects, most notably the Jews in Palestine. Compliance was regarded as

loyalty, and refusal was interpreted as rebellion. Jews were required to adopt the beliefs and practices of the Greeks (often abhorrent to pious Jews), and they were forbidden to practice many distinctly Jewish rituals and customs, such as circumcision, observance of the Sabbath, and ritual food laws. Copies of the law of Moses were burned. A pagan idol of Zeus was even placed in the Temple in Jerusalem. Antiochus sold the office of high priest in Israel, restricted to the line of Aaron by Mosaic law, to the highest bidder who would promote Antiochus's policies. Unsurprisingly, these policies caused a crisis of conscience for many Jews. The crisis became even more pronounced in 167 B.C. after Antiochus was forced by the Romans to turn back from certain defeat. He vented his anger mercilessly upon many Jews who refused to give up their religious beliefs, and he banned Judaism altogether. The situation was growing ripe for revolt.

Open revolt by the Jews finally broke out under the leadership of a priest named Mattathias and his five sons, who are often referred to as the Maccabees (meaning "hammers"). By 164 B.C. they had recaptured the Temple and ritually purified and restored it (the event commemorated by Hannukah, the Feast of Dedication). The next several decades were characterized by armed resistance against the Seleucid rulers, and several of Mattathias's sons lost their lives. Over time, they established their dynasty as the permanent political leaders of Israel. They were also granted the office of the high priesthood. This concentration of political and religious power in a single family led to various abuses. Ironically, each succeeding Maccabean ruler also became increasingly enamored with the Hellenistic way of life. All this led to dissension among the Jews, and various sects and parties arose with different views on these issues. The Pharisees largely opposed Hellenization and the singular power of the ruler. The Sadducees favored both. Still others, such as the Qumran community, wholly rejected the Maccabean dynasty and the Temple system as completely corrupt and withdrew into their own communities.

Maccabean rule over Israel continued until 63 B.C., when the rising Roman Empire finally engulfed Israel and Jewish independence came to an end. Around 39 B.C., a young Idumean named Herod was named king of Judea by the Roman Senate. Herod the Great proved to be an extremely shrewd leader, an able builder (including completely refurbishing the Temple in Jerusalem), but fiercely brutal against those who opposed him.

By the end of the intertestamental period, distinct Jewish communities could be found throughout the known world, and each one would have been forced to reconcile how God's people were to continue to live in faithful obedience to God's laws in the midst of their unique cultural setting. In all of this, there also continued to be an ever evolving hope in a Messiah, the anointed one, God's chosen instrument of deliverance and restoration for his people. Various Old Testament passages laid the foundation for this hope, but exactly who the Messiah would be and what he would do were open to about as many interpretations as there were communities of God's people.

Jesus Christ: 6 B.C.–A.D. 30 In the midst of this incredibly complex interplay of religion, political struggle, and social change, God did indeed send his Messiah, the long awaited hope of his people. But God's Messiah would not be quite like any conceived by human minds. The story of the New Testament opens with the shockingly humble birth of the King of kings.

The birth of the Messiah (called the *Christ* in Greek) took place in the final years of Herod the Great, probably around 6 or 5 B.C. (The odd phenomenon of Jesus being born "B.C." is due to a miscalculation by church scholars about 500 years after Jesus' death.) The angel Gabriel appeared to a virgin named Mary and foretold that she would conceive and bear a son by the power of the Holy Spirit and that he would be the Son of God and was to be called Jesus. Her fiancé, Joseph, was also told by an angel that Mary would give birth to the Messiah. Caesar Augustus ordered a census of the entire Roman world, so Joseph traveled with Mary to Bethlehem, the town of his ancestors. There Mary gave birth to Jesus, fulfilling prophecies that the Messiah would be born in Bethlehem. Shepherds came to worship him, as did wise men (royal astrologers) from the East, perhaps as much as two years later.

Herod the Great attempted to eliminate this newborn threat to his reign by killing all baby boys in Bethlehem. Joseph, Mary, and Jesus escaped to Egypt and then returned after an angel informed them of Herod's death. They resettled in Nazareth, and Joseph took up work as a carpenter or perhaps a stone mason. The Bible tells nothing more of Jesus' childhood until he was 12, when he amazed the scribes and teachers of the law with his understanding. As Jesus grew into adulthood, it is likely that he took up Joseph's trade.

At about the age of 30, Jesus began his public ministry. John the Baptist had been drawing great crowds throughout Israel with his declaration that "the Kingdom of Heaven is near" and his baptism of repentance. Jesus was baptized by John, after which God the Father verbally affirmed Jesus' Sonship and the Holy Spirit descended upon him. Soon after this, Jesus also began to preach that "the Kingdom of Heaven is near," a key theme in his teaching and parables. Some of John's own followers began to follow Jesus, apparently with the blessing of John himself, who saw his role as preparing the way for the coming of the Messiah, who had now arrived in the person of Jesus.

Early in his ministry, Jesus based his work in Capernaum on the Sea of Galilee. Using figurative and even somewhat cryptic stories called parables, Jesus captured people's interest and taught them about the Kingdom of Heaven. He also healed many sick people, cast out demons, and performed other miracles that demonstrated his divine power and provided a foretaste of life in the Kingdom of Heaven. He began to draw large crowds of followers. Jesus selected a special group of 12 disciples to follow him everywhere he went. Several of these men were previously fishermen, including Peter, Andrew, James, and John. These men would remain with Jesus throughout his ministry and became privy to his most intimate teaching and deeds.

Jesus' ministry likely lasted at least three years, the initial years marked by increasing popularity, the final year marked by increasing dissent and even animosity. Throughout his ministry, Jesus consistently condemned two particular groups of religious leaders: the Pharisees and the Sadducees. These two groups had very differing views from each other on both religion and politics. Jesus repeatedly castigated the Pharisees for their legalistic adherence to the law of Moses that lacked real love for God and people. Jesus exposed the Sadducees' faulty understanding of Scripture and of God's power. Sometimes he lumped the two groups together in his condemnations. At the same time, Jesus often praised prostitutes, tax collectors, and other "sinners" who repented of their sins and followed him. Over time, the combination of Jesus' growing popularity, his condemnation of the religious leaders, and his claims to be the Son of God proved more than the leaders could stomach, and a plot was hatched to end his life.

By the end of his ministry, Jesus began another journey from Galilee in northern Israel to Jerusalem in the south to celebrate the Passover with his disciples. By now Jesus was extremely well known throughout Israel, and many believed him to be—or at least wondered if he *might* be—the Messiah, as he claimed. No doubt many were hoping for the overthrow of the hated Roman rule. News of Jesus' impending arrival in Jerusalem went ahead of him, and people laid palm branches and cloaks on the road to receive him as king. Jesus, in turn, chose to enter the city on a donkey just as the Old Testament prophet Zechariah had foretold, apparently in recognition of his role as Messiah. Thus, the city was ripe with expectation for the upcoming week of Passover, when Jews celebrated their deliverance from slavery in Egypt many centuries before.

Immediately upon entering the city in triumph, Jesus went up to the Temple and threw out the money changers and merchants, declaring that his Father's house was to be a house of prayer. His actions angered many of the religious leaders, some of whom received a cut of the profits from the Temple sales.

Jesus spent much of the week of Passover teaching in the Temple area and debating with the Pharisees and Sadducees. He also foretold of events to come, including the destruction of the Temple and his eventual return to earth to gather his people. At some point in the week, Judas Iscariot, one of Jesus' 12 closest disciples, agreed to betray Jesus to the religious leaders for 30 pieces of silver.

On Thursday of that week, Jesus shared the Passover meal with his 12 disciples. Judas Iscariot left during the meal to carry out his act of betrayal. Afterward, Jesus and his disciples went just outside the city to Gethsemane, an olive garden where they often relaxed from the busy events of the day in Jerusalem. There Judas carried out his betrayal. The guards arrested Jesus, and most of his disciples fled.

Jesus was interrogated throughout the night in order to find him guilty of a crime worthy of death. Various accusations were made, but none held up to close scrutiny. By morning, they settled on Jesus' own claim to be the Messiah in order to accuse him of treason against Rome. They led him to Pontius Pilate, the Roman governor, who held ultimate power to sentence someone to death, and they accused Jesus of treason. Pilate knew the leaders' true motives had nothing to do with loyalty to Rome, but in the end he acquiesced and condemned Jesus to death by crucifixion.

After Jesus was subjected to various abuses, beatings, and ridicule by Roman soldiers, he was nailed to a cross and put on public display as a deterrent to all who might consider committing the same crime of treason against Rome. Jesus' charge was posted: THIS IS JESUS, THE KING OF THE JEWS. Jesus continued to suffer on the cross until about 3 o'clock in the afternoon, when he cried with a loud voice, "It is finished," and he died.

Pilate granted permission to a rich man named Joseph of Arimathea to bury Jesus' body in his own nearby tomb. Because the Sabbath was fast approaching, Jesus' body was quickly placed in the tomb without being treated with burial spices.

On Sunday, some women who had followed Jesus and cared for his needs went to Jesus' tomb to finish preparing his body for burial. When they reached the tomb, however, they discovered that Jesus' body was gone! Angels at the tomb then told them that Jesus had risen from the dead! The women ran back to tell the other disciples the news. Jesus was alive!

During the 40 days following his resurrection, Jesus appeared to various disciples on different occasions, confirming that he had been raised from the dead, giving them further instructions and teaching, and commanding them to go out and be his witnesses, telling people everywhere about him. He told his disciples to remain in Jerusalem (not their home area of Galilee) until the Holy Spirit came and filled them with power. He then ascended to heaven as his disciples watched, where he remains until he returns in glory for his people.

The Church: A.D. 30–Present During the festival of Pentecost, 50 days after Passover, the promised Holy Spirit finally came upon Jesus' disciples, and they began proclaiming the great works of God in languages they did not even know. Peter spoke to the crowd about Jesus and his resurrection and implored his listeners to repent and follow him. About 3,000 people became believers in Jesus that day, launching the Christian church.

The depth of Jesus' impact upon these new believers became immediately visible by their commitment to love and care for each other. Many believers voluntarily gave their possessions to help provide for the needs of others in the church, and the church made specific arrangements to care for the needs of widows. God also worked many miracles through Peter and the other leaders, confirming their authority and encouraging the believers.

Persecution soon came, however. A believer named Stephen and James, the brother of John, were killed for their faith in Jesus. Many believers fled Jerusalem, but God used even this to spread the Good News across the known world. Eventually new churches were established as far away as Damascus and Antioch in Syria. Some of the leaders in the Jerusalem church moved to Antioch, including a man named Barnabas. James, the brother of Jesus, became a leader in the church in Jerusalem.

One of the persecutors was a zealous young Pharisee named Saul. As Saul was traveling to Damascus from Jerusalem to pursue Christians there, the Lord Jesus appeared to Saul, temporarily blinding him, and asked why he was persecuting him. After this, Saul completed his journey to Damascus, but as a new man: a zealous servant of Jesus Christ. God would eventually use Saul, who became known as Paul, to reach countless others with the message of the gospel.

In the meantime, the church continued to grow, as did the bounds of the gospel itself. What had originally started out essentially as a Jewish sect had expanded to include Samaritans (despised by many Jews as half-breeds), proselytized Jews (Gentiles who had become Jews), and even God-fearing Gentiles. The church received these changes with joy, but they also introduced some questions that would not be fully resolved until several years later at the Jerusalem council.

Over time Barnabas convinced Paul to join him at Antioch, and later they traveled through Cyprus and Galatia preaching the gospel to Jews and Gentiles alike. During this journey, Paul was repeatedly persecuted by Jews, and he eventually decided to begin preaching primarily to Gentiles. This raised a key question: Did these Gentiles need to adhere to the laws of Moses in order to be followers of Jesus? That is, did these Gentiles need to become converts to Judaism (including being circumcised and following strict food laws) before they could become Christians? Soon after Paul and Barnabas returned from their journey, the leaders of the Jerusalem church held a council to decide the issue. After some discussion, the leaders agreed that Gentile believers did not need to be circumcised and become Jewish converts in order to become Christians. They were full-fledged Christians just as they were.

Soon after this Paul embarked on two more missionary journeys. The great distances traveled were made possible in part by Rome's excellent road system and the relative peace ("Pax Romana") due to Rome's unrivalled power in the region. Along the way Paul established churches throughout Asia Minor, Macedonia, and Achaia, and several of his letters to these churches have become part of the canon of the New Testament.

At the end of his third missionary journey, Paul's work among the Gentiles fostered rumor and anger among many Jews who were zealous for the law of Moses. They accused Paul of teaching Gentiles to flout the laws of Moses, and they mistakenly thought he had brought a Gentile into the Jewish section of the Temple courts. A riot erupted, and the Roman commander took Paul into custody for his safety. Paul was then transferred to Caesarea on the coast. He remained in custody for nearly two years until finally he invoked his right as a Roman citizen to appeal his case to Caesar himself. So Paul was sent under guard to Rome.

Paul's journey to Rome proved difficult, as Paul suffered shipwreck off the island of Malta near Sicily. Eventually Paul made it safely to Rome, however, and as he awaited trial in Rome under house arrest, he continued to minister to believers there and probably wrote several other letters of the New Testament. It is not certain exactly what happened to Paul after this, but it appears that he was soon released and embarked on at least one other journey before he was arrested again. Church tradition holds that Paul was finally executed under the emperor Nero.

During these years, other changes were taking place in the church as well. Apparently the apostle Peter moved to Rome, where he, too, suffered martyrdom under Nero. According to tradition, Barnabas's relative John Mark recorded Peter's stories and teachings from Jesus' life and ministry (the Gospel of Mark). Likewise, the apostle John moved to Ephesus (probably along with Mary, the mother of Jesus), where he served as a prominent leader for several churches that had been established in western Asia Minor. John also recorded many stories and teachings of Jesus in the Gospel of John. Eventually John was exiled to the island of Patmos (not far from Ephesus), where he recorded the revelation from Jesus concerning the end of the world. According to church tradition, John died on Patmos. The Gospels of Matthew (another apostle) and Luke (a Gentile companion of Paul's) were also compiled from the testimonies of those who had been eyewitnesses to Jesus' life and ministry.

COMPLETE **BIBLICAL TIMELINE**

Catch a glimpse of the whole sweep of biblical history. The ten historical eras outlined in the *Chronological Life Application Study Bible*, along with the books of the Bible you will find in each, are in the center bar. Significant world events are above the bar, and biblical events are below it.

WORLD EVENTS

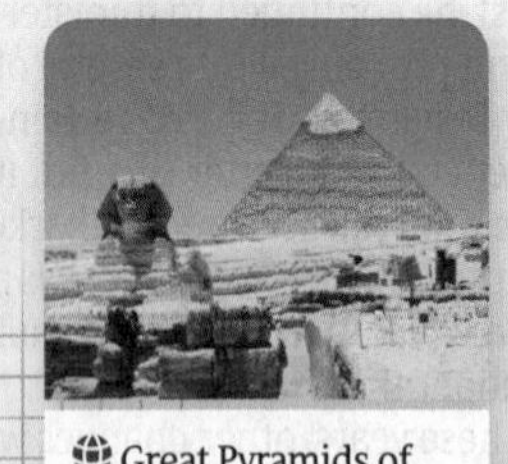

Great Pyramids of Egypt constructed
2630 BC

Iron objects manufactured in the ancient Near East
2500 BC

Egyptians use papyrus and ink for writing
2500 BC

Egyptians import gold from other parts of Africa
2400 BC

Sumerian king, Sargon, becomes first "world conqueror"
2331 BC

Horses domesticated in Egypt
2300 BC

Ziggurats built in Mesopotamia
2100 BC

2600 BC | 2500 BC | 2400 BC | 2300 BC | 2200 BC | 2100 BC

Beginnings

undated–2100 BC

GENESIS, undated–1805 BC

BIBLICAL EVENTS

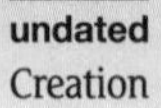

undated
Creation

undated
Noah builds the ark

▲ ***Early Accounts of Creation and the Flood***
Several ancient civilizations wrote down their own stories about origins. These tablets from Babylon record a creation myth and a story about an ancient flood.

2166 BC
Abraham is born

2091 BC
Abraham travels to Canaan

Stonehenge erected in England *estimated*
2000 BC

Spoked wheels invented *estimated*
1900 BC

Hammurabi of Babylon provides first written law code *estimated*
1750 BC

Mexican Sun Pyramid built
1500 BC

First metal-working in South America
1440 BC

2000 BC | 1900 BC | 1800 BC | 1700 BC | 1600 BC | 1500 BC | 1400 BC

God's Chosen Family
2100 BC–1800 BC

JOB, *around* 1900 BC

The Birth of Israel
1800 BC–1406 BC

EXODUS, 1500–1445 BC

LEVITICUS, 1445–1444 BC

NUMBERS, 1445–1406 BC

DEUTERONOMY, 1406 BC

2066 BC
Isaac is born

2006 BC
Jacob and Esau are born

1929 BC
Jacob flees to Haran

1915 BC
Joseph is born

1898 BC
Joseph sold into slavery

1885 BC
Joseph rules Egypt

1876 BC
Jacob moves to Egypt

1805 BC
Joseph dies

around **1800–1446 BC**
Slavery in Egypt

1526 BC
Moses is born

1446 BC
The Exodus

1445 BC
Ten Commandments given

1445 BC
The second Passover

1443 BC
Israel refuses to enter Canaan

1406 BC
Moses dies

1400 BC — Water clock invented in Egypt

1380 BC — Palace of Knossos on island of Crete destroyed by earthquake

King Tutankhamen is buried in Egypt amidst great treasure **1358 BC**

1250 BC — Silk fabrics manufactured in China

1200 BC — First Chinese dictionary

1183 BC — Destruction of Troy during Trojan War

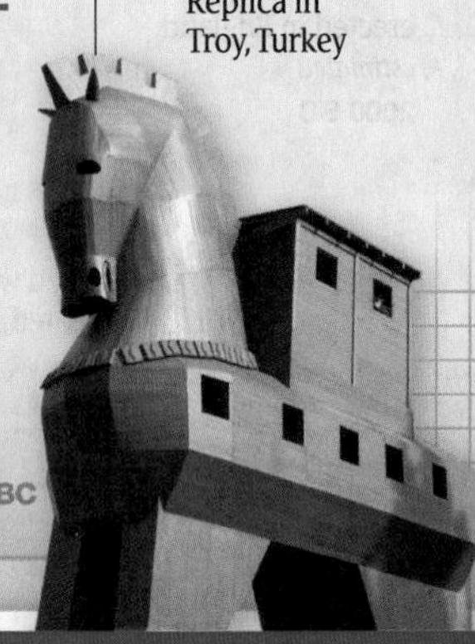

▼ ***Trojan Horse*** Replica in Troy, Turkey

1400 BC · WORLD EVENTS · 1300 BC · 1200 BC

Possessing the Land

1406 BC–1050 BC

JOSHUA, 1406–1376 BC

JUDGES, 1376–1100 BC

BIBLICAL EVENTS

1406 BC Joshua leads Israel into Canaan

1376 BC Judges begin to rule in Israel

Israel Stele 1213 BC ▲ This monument honoring Pharaoh Merneptah is the earliest evidence for the existence of the nation of Israel outside the Bible.

1209 BC Deborah becomes Israel's judge

1162 BC Gideon becomes Israel's judge

1020 BC Philistines land on coast of Canaan

Mayans settle in the Yucatan peninsula
1000 BC

Celts invade Britain
900 BC

Homer's *Iliad* and *Odyssey* written down
800 BC

Native Americans in California build wood-reed houses
1000 BC

Gold vessels and jewelry popular in Northern Europe
950 BC

Evidence of highly developed metal and stone sculptures in Africa
850 BC

Founding of Carthage
814 BC

1100 BC — 1000 BC — 900 BC — 800 BC

United Monarchy

1050 BC–930 BC

Splintered Nation

930 BC–586 BC

1 SAMUEL, 1105–1010 BC

RUTH, *around* 1100 BC

2 SAMUEL & 1 CHRONICLES, 1010–970 BC

SONG OF SONGS & ECCLESIASTES, *around* 950 BC

1 KINGS, 970–853 BC

2 CHRONICLES, 970–538 BC

2 KINGS, 853–561 BC

1105 BC
Samuel is born

1075 BC
Samuel becomes Israel's final judge

1050 BC
Saul becomes king

1025 BC
David anointed as king

1020 BC
David defeats Goliath

1010 BC
David becomes king in Judah

1003 BC
David becomes king over all Israel

997 BC
David sins with Bathsheba

970 BC
Solomon becomes king

970 BC
Solomon begins building the Temple

960 BC
The Temple is completed

930 BC
Israel divides into two nations

910 BC
Asa begins to rule in Judah

885 BC
Omri begins to rule in Israel

875 BC
Elijah begins his ministry

853 BC
Ahab dies in battle

848 BC
Elisha's ministry begins

835 BC
Joash begins to rule in Judah

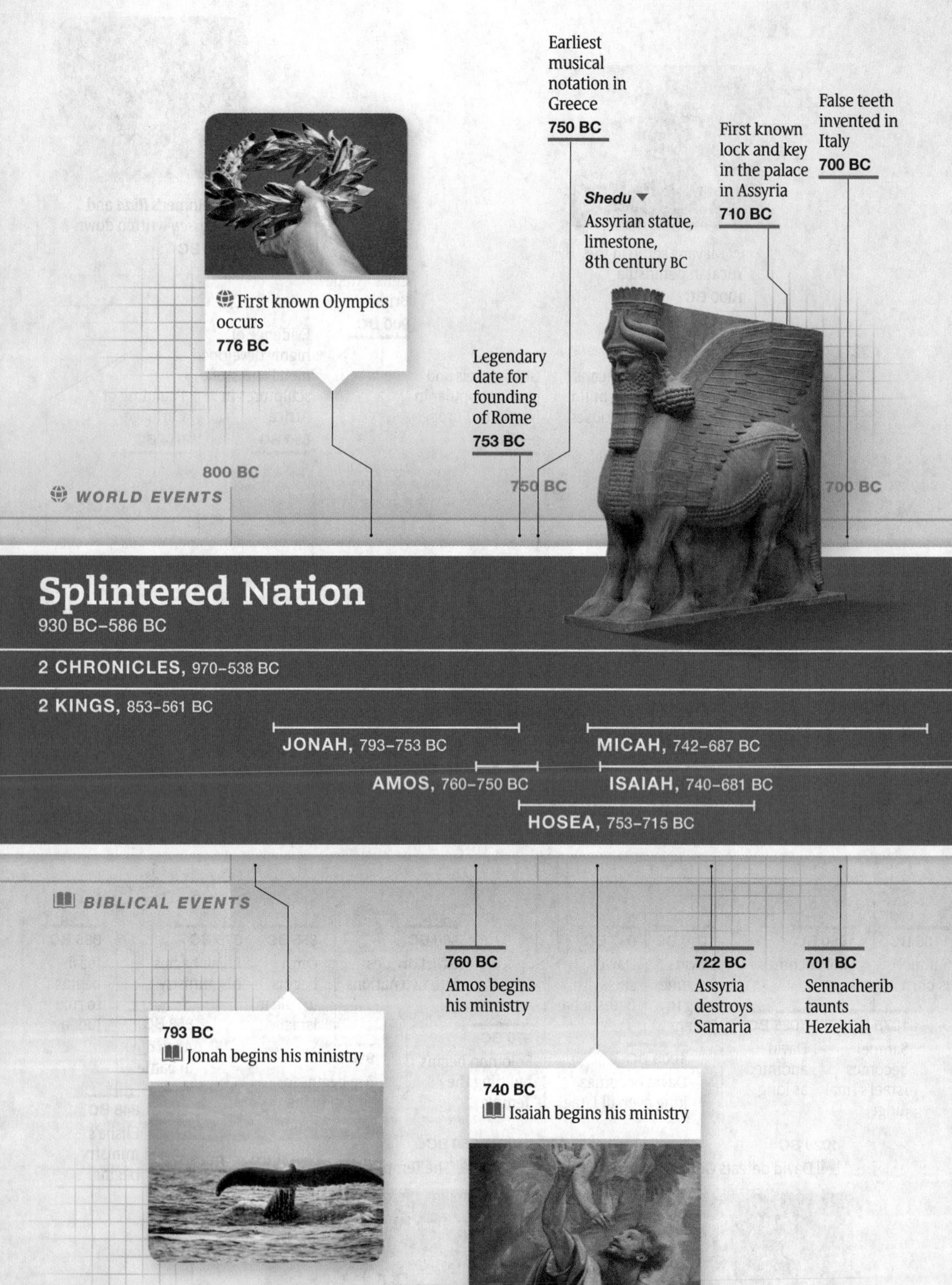

Splintered Nation

930 BC–586 BC

2 CHRONICLES, 970–538 BC

2 KINGS, 853–561 BC

JONAH, 793–753 BC

MICAH, 742–687 BC

AMOS, 760–750 BC

ISAIAH, 740–681 BC

HOSEA, 753–715 BC

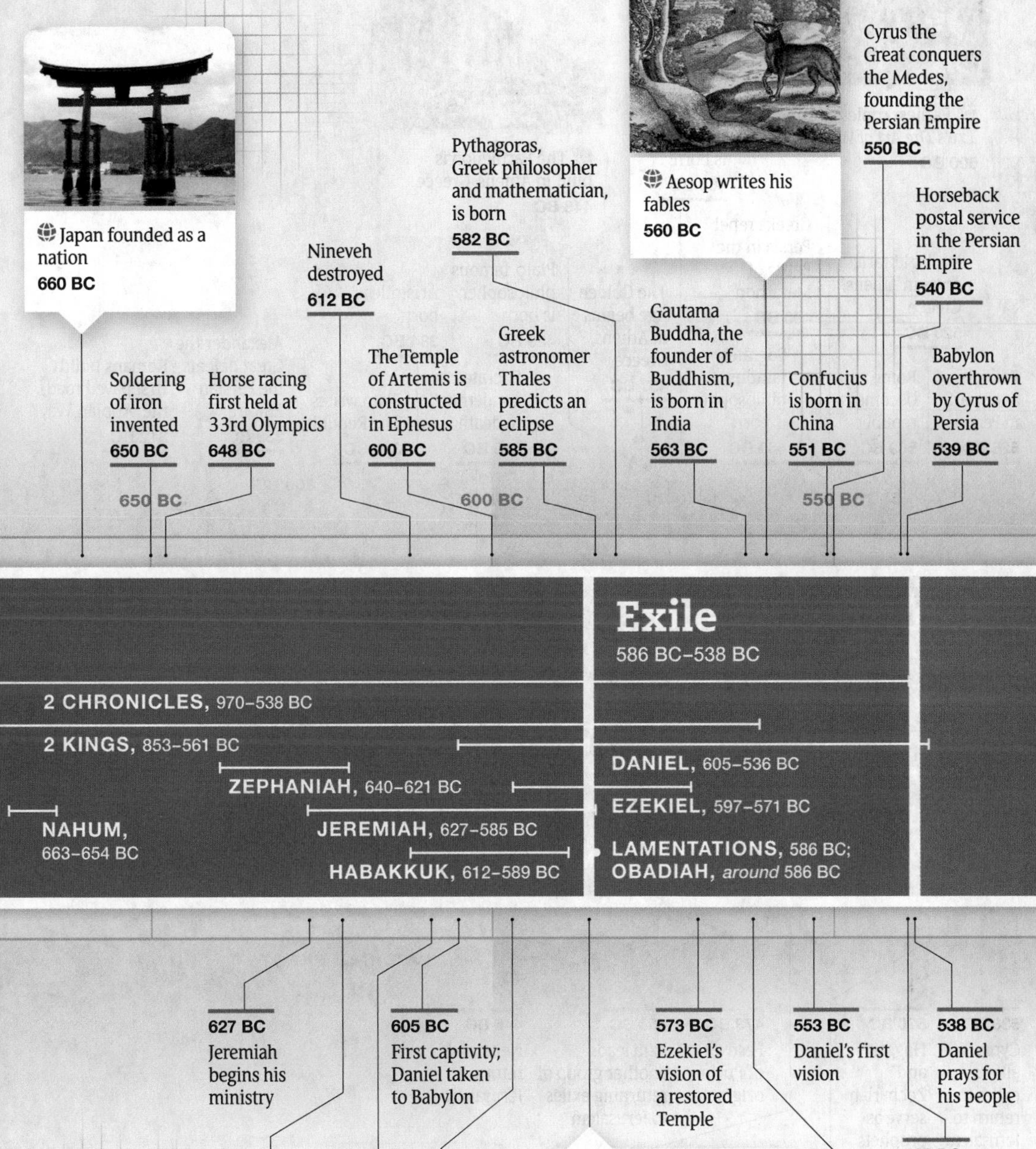
Japan founded as a nation
660 BC
Soldering of iron invented
650 BC
Horse racing first held at 33rd Olympics
648 BC
650 BC
Nineveh destroyed
612 BC
The Temple of Artemis is constructed in Ephesus
600 BC
Pythagoras, Greek philosopher and mathematician, is born
582 BC
Greek astronomer Thales predicts an eclipse
585 BC
600 BC
Aesop writes his fables
560 BC
Gautama Buddha, the founder of Buddhism, is born in India
563 BC
Confucius is born in China
551 BC
Cyrus the Great conquers the Medes, founding the Persian Empire
550 BC
550 BC
Horseback postal service in the Persian Empire
540 BC
Babylon overthrown by Cyrus of Persia
539 BC
Exile
586 BC–538 BC
2 CHRONICLES, 970–538 BC
2 KINGS, 853–561 BC
ZEPHANIAH, 640–621 BC
NAHUM, 663–654 BC
JEREMIAH, 627–585 BC
HABAKKUK, 612–589 BC
DANIEL, 605–536 BC
EZEKIEL, 597–571 BC
LAMENTATIONS, 586 BC;
OBADIAH, *around* 586 BC
627 BC
Jeremiah begins his ministry
622 BC
Law scroll found in the Temple
609 BC
Neco kills Josiah in battle
605 BC
First captivity; Daniel taken to Babylon
597 BC
Second captivity; Ezekiel taken to Babylon
586 BC
Babylon destroys Jerusalem
573 BC
Ezekiel's vision of a restored Temple
562 BC
King Nebuchadnezzar of Babylon dies
553 BC
Daniel's first vision
539 BC
Daniel thrown to the lions
538 BC
Daniel prays for his people

Earliest copies of Sun Tzu's *The Art of War*
500 BC

Hippocrates, the father of modern medicine, is born
460 BC

The Parthenon is built in Athens, Greece
448 BC

Public libraries open in Athens, Greece
520 BC

Greeks repel Persia in the Battle of Marathon
490 BC

The Golden Age begins in Athens, Greece
457 BC

Plato, famous philosopher, is born
429 BC

Aristotle is born
384 BC

Polo played as a sport in Persia
525 BC

Rome becomes a republic
509 BC

Socrates, famous philosopher, is born
469 BC

Socrates condemned to death
399 BC

Plato writes The Republic
370 BC

Alexander the Great defeats the Persian Empire
330 BC

Romans build first paved road, the "Appian Way"
312 BC

500 BC | 450 BC | 400 BC | 350 BC | 300 BC

WORLD EVENTS

Return & Diaspora

538 BC–6 BC

EZRA, 538–450 BC

- **HAGGAI**, 520 BC
- **ZECHARIAH**, 520–518 BC

MALACHI, 430s BC

ESTHER, 483–473 BC

NEHEMIAH, 446–432 BC

BIBLICAL EVENTS

538 BC
Cyrus allows exiles to return to Jerusalem

520 BC
Haggai and Zechariah serve as prophets

473 BC
Festival of Purim originates

458 BC
Ezra leads another group of returning exiles to Jerusalem

445 BC
Nehemiah returns to Jerusalem

538 BC
Zerubbabel leads 50,000 people back to Jerusalem

515 BC
Second Temple completed in Jerusalem

479 BC
Esther becomes queen of Persia

250 BC — 200 BC — 150 BC — 100 BC — 50 BC — AD 1

around **255 BC**
Hebrew Old Testament begins to be translated into Greek (Septuagint)

Romans conquer Sicily
241 BC

Great Wall of China built
215 BC

Antiochus IV plunders Jerusalem Temple
169 BC

Judas Maccabeus begins a revolt against Antiochus IV
165 BC

Jews and astrologers banished from Rome
139 BC

First Chinese ships reach east coast of India
102 BC

Julius Caesar, first emperor of Rome, is born
100 BC

Romans conquer England
55 BC

Cleopatra becomes last independent Egyptian ruler
51 BC

Julius Caesar becomes dictator for life, assassinated 2 years later
46 BC

Romans make Herod the Great king of Judea
37 BC

Cleopatra and Marc Antony commit suicide
30 BC

Sumo wrestling in Japan
23 BC

Herod the Great begins remodeling Temple in Jerusalem
20 BC

20? BC
Mary, Jesus' mother, is born

INTERTESTAMENTAL PERIOD

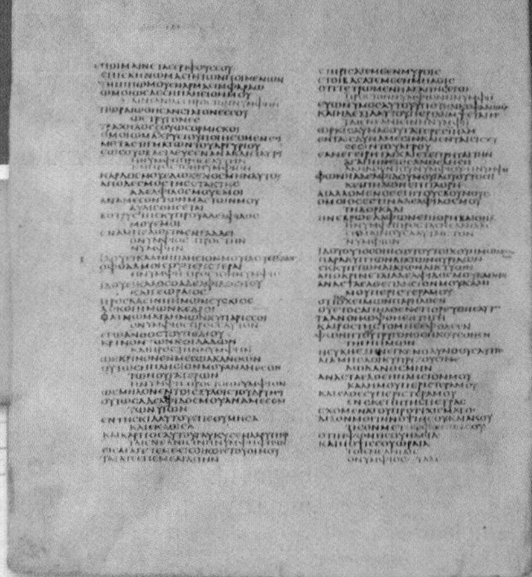

▲ ***The Septuagint***
Jesus and the apostles apparently referred to the Old Testament in translation quite often. This 4th century AD manuscript is particularly well preserved.

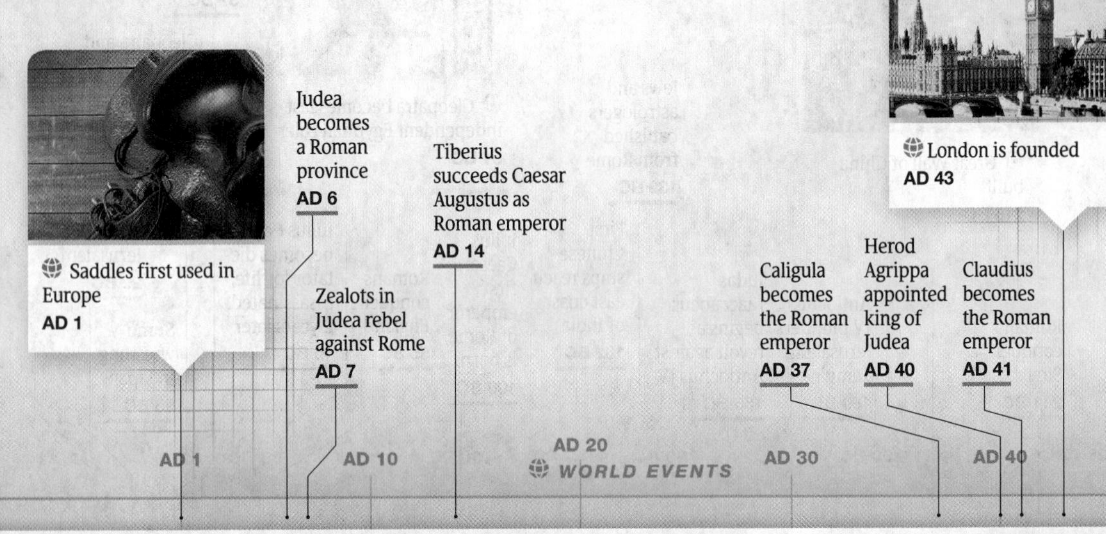

WORLD EVENTS

Saddles first used in Europe
AD 1

Judea becomes a Roman province
AD 6

Zealots in Judea rebel against Rome
AD 7

Tiberius succeeds Caesar Augustus as Roman emperor
AD 14

Caligula becomes the Roman emperor
AD 37

Herod Agrippa appointed king of Judea
AD 40

Claudius becomes the Roman emperor
AD 41

London is founded
AD 43

AD 1 · AD 10 · AD 20 · AD 30 · AD 40

Jesus Christ

6 BC–AD 30

MATTHEW, 6 BC–AD 30

LUKE, 6 BC–AD 30

MARK, AD 26–30

JOHN, AD 26–30

The Church

AD 30–present

ACTS, AD 30–60

BIBLICAL EVENTS

6 BC
Jesus is born

4 BC
Herod the Great dies

AD 5?
Paul is born

AD 6
Jesus visits Temple as a boy

AD 26
John the Baptist begins his ministry

AD 27
Jesus begins his ministry

AD 29
John the Baptist is beheaded

AD 30
Jesus is crucified

AD 30
The Holy Spirit descends on Pentecost

AD 35
Saul's conversion on the Damascus road

AD 40
The conversion of Cornelius

AD 46
Paul begins his first missionary journey

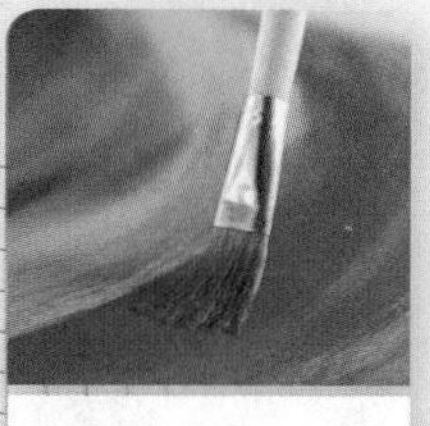

Romans begin using soap
AD 50

Emperor Claudius poisoned by order of his wife
AD 54

Nero becomes the Roman emperor
AD 54

Fire burns Rome, Nero blames Christians
AD 64

Painting on canvas
AD 66

Romans destroy a religious commune at Qumran
AD 68

China opens silk trade with the West
AD 74

Rome begins construction on the Colosseum
AD 75

Mount Vesuvius erupts
AD 79

Domitian becomes the Roman emperor
AD 81

AD 50 | AD 60 | AD 70 | AD 80 | AD 90 | AD 100

- **JAMES,** AD 48
- **GAL,** AD 49
- **1 & 2 THES,** AD 50
- **1 COR,** AD 53
- **2 COR & ROMANS,** AD 54
- **COL, PHLM, & EPH,** AD 60
- **PHIL,** AD 61
- **1 TIM & TITUS,** AD 62
- **2 TIM & 1 PETER,** AD 64
- **2 PETER,** AD 65
- **HEBREWS & JUDE,** *around* AD 66
- **1 JOHN,** *between* AD 80–90
- **2 & 3 JOHN,** *around* AD 90
- **REVELATION,** AD 95

AD 49
The Jerusalem Council

AD 51
Paul begins his third missionary journey

AD 57
Paul in prison in Caesarea

AD 59
Paul's voyage to Rome

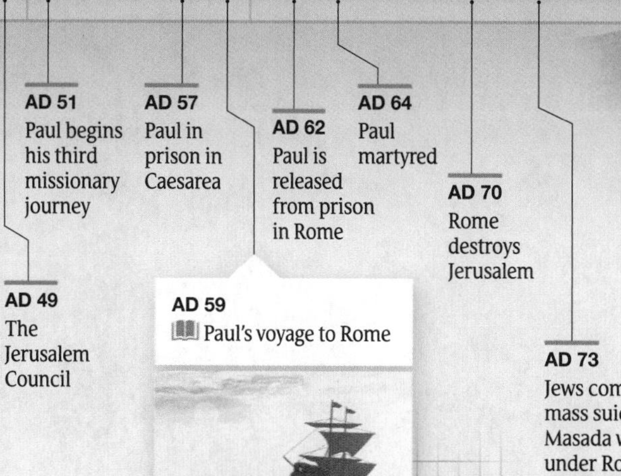

AD 62
Paul is released from prison in Rome

AD 64
Paul martyred

AD 70
Rome destroys Jerusalem

AD 73
Jews commit mass suicide at Masada while under Roman attack

▲ ***Masada***
After Rome destroyed Jerusalem in 70 AD, a small group of Jewish nationalists dug in at the rugged fortress of Masada, where they remained for three years until the Romans' siege finally broke through the stronghold.

A NOTE TO READERS

The *Holy Bible*, New Living Translation, was first published in 1996. It quickly became one of the most popular Bible translations in the English-speaking world. While the NLT's influence was rapidly growing, the Bible Translation Committee determined that an additional investment in scholarly review and text refinement could make it even better. So shortly after its initial publication, the committee began an eight-year process with the purpose of increasing the level of the NLT's precision without sacrificing its easy-to-understand quality. This second-generation text was completed in 2004, with minor changes subsequently introduced in 2007.

The goal of any Bible translation is to convey the meaning and content of the ancient Hebrew, Aramaic, and Greek texts as accurately as possible to contemporary readers. The challenge for our translators was to create a text that would communicate as clearly and powerfully to today's readers as the original texts did to readers and listeners in the ancient biblical world. The resulting translation is easy to read and understand, while also accurately communicating the meaning and content of the original biblical texts. The NLT is a general-purpose text especially good for study, devotional reading, and reading aloud in worship services.

We believe that the New Living Translation—which combines the latest biblical scholarship with a clear, dynamic writing style—will communicate God's word powerfully to all who read it. We publish it with the prayer that God will use it to speak his timeless truth to the church and the world in a fresh, new way.

The Publishers, October 2007

INTRODUCTION TO THE
NEW LIVING TRANSLATION

Translation Philosophy and Methodology

English Bible translations tend to be governed by one of two general translation theories. The first theory has been called "formal-equivalence," "literal," or "word-for-word" translation. According to this theory, the translator attempts to render each word of the original language into English and seeks to preserve the original syntax and sentence structure as much as possible in translation. The second theory has been called "dynamic-equivalence," "functional-equivalence," or "thought-for-thought" translation. The goal of this translation theory is to produce in English the closest natural equivalent of the message expressed by the original-language text, both in meaning and in style.

Both of these translation theories have their strengths. A formal-equivalence translation preserves aspects of the original text—including ancient idioms, term consistency, and original-language syntax—that are valuable for scholars and professional study. It allows a reader to trace formal elements of the original-language text through the English translation. A dynamic-equivalence translation, on the other hand, focuses on translating the message of the original-language text. It ensures that the meaning of the text is readily apparent to the contemporary reader. This allows the message to come through with immediacy, without requiring the reader to struggle with foreign idioms and awkward syntax. It also facilitates serious study of the text's message and clarity in both devotional and public reading.

The pure application of either of these translation philosophies would create translations at opposite ends of the translation spectrum. But in reality, all translations contain a mixture of these two philosophies. A purely formal-equivalence translation would be unintelligible in English, and a purely dynamic-equivalence translation would risk being unfaithful to the original. That is why translations shaped by dynamic-equivalence theory are usually quite literal when the original text is relatively clear, and the translations shaped by formal-equivalence theory are sometimes quite dynamic when the original text is obscure.

The translators of the New Living Translation set out to render the message of the original texts of Scripture into clear, contemporary English. As they did so, they kept the concerns of both formal-equivalence and dynamic-equivalence in mind. On the one hand, they translated as simply and literally as possible when that approach yielded an accurate, clear, and natural English text. Many words and phrases were rendered literally and consistently into English, preserving essential literary and rhetorical devices, ancient metaphors, and word choices that give structure to the text and provide echoes of meaning from one passage to the next.

On the other hand, the translators rendered the message more dynamically when the literal rendering was hard to understand, was misleading, or yielded archaic or foreign wording. They clarified difficult metaphors and terms to aid in the reader's understanding. The translators first struggled with the meaning of the words and phrases in the ancient context; then they rendered the message into clear, natural English. Their goal was to be both faithful to the ancient texts and eminently readable. The result is a translation that is both exegetically accurate and idiomatically powerful.

Translation Process and Team

To produce an accurate translation of the Bible into contemporary English, the translation team needed the skills necessary to enter into the thought patterns of the ancient authors and then to render their ideas, connotations, and effects into clear, contemporary English. To begin this process, qualified biblical scholars were needed to interpret the meaning of the original text and to check it against our base English translation. In order to guard against personal and theological biases, the scholars needed to represent a diverse group of evangelicals who would employ the best exegetical tools. Then to work alongside the scholars, skilled English stylists were needed to shape the text into clear, contemporary English.

With these concerns in mind, the Bible Translation Committee recruited teams of scholars that represented a broad spectrum of denominations, theological perspectives, and backgrounds within the worldwide evangelical community. (These scholars are listed at the end of this introduction.) Each book of the Bible was assigned to three different scholars with proven expertise in the book or group of books to be reviewed. Each of these scholars made a thorough review of a base translation and submitted suggested revisions to the appropriate Senior Translator. The Senior Translator then reviewed and summarized these suggestions and proposed a first-draft revision of the base text. This draft served as the basis for several additional phases of exegetical and stylistic committee review. Then the Bible Translation Committee jointly reviewed and approved every verse of the final translation.

Throughout the translation and editing process, the Senior Translators and their scholar teams were given a chance to review the editing done by the team of stylists. This ensured that exegetical errors would not be introduced late in the process and that the entire Bible Translation Committee was happy with the final result. By choosing a team of qualified scholars and skilled stylists and by setting up a process that allowed their interaction throughout the process, the New Living Translation has been refined to preserve the essential formal elements of the original biblical texts, while also creating a clear, understandable English text.

The New Living Translation was first published in 1996. Shortly after its initial publication, the Bible Translation Committee began a process of further committee review and translation refinement. The purpose of this continued revision was to increase the level of precision without sacrificing the text's easy-to-understand quality. This second-edition text was completed in 2004, with minor changes subsequently introduced in 2007.

Written to Be Read Aloud

It is evident in Scripture that the biblical documents were written to be read aloud, often in public worship (see Nehemiah 8; Luke 4:16-20; 1 Timothy 4:13; Revelation 1:3). It is still the case today that more people will hear the Bible read aloud in church than are likely to read it for themselves. Therefore, a new translation must communicate with clarity and power when it is read publicly. Clarity was a primary goal for the NLT translators, not only to facilitate private reading and understanding, but also to ensure that it would be excellent for public reading and make an immediate and powerful impact on any listener.

The Texts behind the New Living Translation

The Old Testament translators used the Masoretic Text of the Hebrew Bible as represented in *Biblia Hebraica Stuttgartensia* (1977), with its extensive system of textual notes; this is an update of Rudolf Kittel's *Biblia Hebraica* (Stuttgart, 1937). The translators also further compared the Dead Sea Scrolls, the Septuagint and other Greek manuscripts, the Samaritan Pentateuch, the Syriac Peshitta, the Latin Vulgate, and any other versions or manuscripts that shed light on the meaning of difficult passages.

The New Testament translators used the two standard editions of the Greek New Testament: the *Greek New Testament*, published by the United Bible Societies (UBS, fourth revised edition, 1993), and *Novum Testamentum Graece*, edited by Nestle and Aland (NA, twenty-seventh edition, 1993). These two editions, which have the same text but differ in punctuation and textual notes, represent, for the most part, the best in modern textual scholarship. However, in cases where strong textual or other scholarly evidence supported the decision, the translators sometimes chose to differ from the UBS and NA Greek texts and followed variant readings found in other ancient witnesses. Significant textual variants of this sort are always noted in the textual notes of the New Living Translation.

Translation Issues

The translators have made a conscious effort to provide a text that can be easily understood by the typical reader of modern English. To this end, we sought to use only vocabulary and language structures in common use today. We avoided using language likely to become quickly dated or that reflects only a narrow subdialect of English, with the goal of making the New Living Translation as broadly useful and timeless as possible.

But our concern for readability goes beyond the concerns of vocabulary and sentence structure. We are also concerned about historical and cultural barriers to understanding the Bible, and we have sought to translate terms shrouded in history and culture in ways that can be immediately understood. To this end:

- We have converted ancient weights and measures (for example, "ephah" [a unit of dry volume] or "cubit" [a unit of length]) to modern English (American) equivalents, since the ancient measures are not generally meaningful to today's readers. Then in the textual footnotes we offer the literal Hebrew, Aramaic, or Greek measures, along with modern metric equivalents.
- Instead of translating ancient currency values literally, we have expressed them in common terms that communicate the message. For example, in the Old Testament, "ten shekels of silver" becomes "ten pieces of silver" to convey the intended message. In the New Testament, we have often translated the "denarius" as "the normal daily wage" to facilitate understanding. Then a footnote offers: "Greek *a denarius*, the payment for a full day's wage." In general, we give a clear English rendering and then state the literal Hebrew, Aramaic, or Greek in a textual footnote.
- Since the names of Hebrew months are unknown to most contemporary readers, and since the Hebrew lunar calendar fluctuates from year to year in relation to the solar calendar used today, we have looked for clear ways to communicate the time of year the Hebrew months (such as Abib) refer to. When an expanded or interpretive rendering is given in the text, a textual note gives the literal rendering. Where it is possible to define a specific ancient date in terms of our modern calendar, we use modern dates in the text. A textual footnote then gives the literal Hebrew date and states the rationale for our rendering. For example, Ezra 6:15 pinpoints the date when the postexilic Temple was completed in Jerusalem: "the third day of the month Adar." This was during the sixth year of King Darius's reign (that is, 515 B.C.). We have translated that date as March 12, with a footnote giving the Hebrew and identifying the year as 515 B.C.
- Since ancient references to the time of day differ from our modern methods of denoting

time, we have used renderings that are instantly understandable to the modern reader. Accordingly, we have rendered specific times of day by using approximate equivalents in terms of our common "o'clock" system. On occasion, translations such as "at dawn the next morning" or "as the sun was setting" have been used when the biblical reference is more general.

- When the meaning of a proper name (or a wordplay inherent in a proper name) is relevant to the message of the text, its meaning is often illuminated with a textual footnote. For example, in Exodus 2:10 the text reads: "The princess named him Moses, for she explained, 'I lifted him out of the water.'" The accompanying footnote reads: "*Moses* sounds like a Hebrew term that means 'to lift out.'"

  Sometimes, when the actual meaning of a name is clear, that meaning is included in parentheses within the text itself. For example, the text at Genesis 16:11 reads: "You are to name him Ishmael (*which means 'God hears'*), for the LORD has heard your cry of distress." Since the original hearers and readers would have instantly understood the meaning of the name "Ishmael," we have provided modern readers with the same information so they can experience the text in a similar way.
- Many words and phrases carry a great deal of cultural meaning that was obvious to the original readers but needs explanation in our own culture. For example, the phrase "they beat their breasts" (Luke 23:48) in ancient times meant that people were very upset, often in mourning. In our translation we chose to translate this phrase dynamically for clarity: "They went home *in deep sorrow*." Then we included a footnote with the literal Greek, which reads: "Greek *went home beating their breasts*." In other similar cases, however, we have sometimes chosen to illuminate the existing literal expression to make it immediately understandable. For example, here we might have expanded the literal Greek phrase to read: "They went home beating their breasts *in sorrow*." If we had done this, we would not have included a textual footnote, since the literal Greek clearly appears in translation.
- Metaphorical language is sometimes difficult for contemporary readers to understand, so at times we have chosen to translate or illuminate the meaning of a metaphor. For example, the ancient poet writes, "Your neck is *like* the tower of David" (Song of Songs 4:4). We have rendered it "Your neck is *as beautiful as* the tower of David" to clarify the intended positive meaning of the simile. Another example comes in Ecclesiastes 12:3, which can be literally rendered: "Remember him . . . when the grinding women cease because they are few, and the women who look through the windows see dimly." We have rendered it: "Remember him before your teeth—your few remaining servants—stop grinding; and before your eyes—the women looking through the windows—see dimly." We clarified such metaphors only when we believed a typical reader might be confused by the literal text.
- When the content of the original language text is poetic in character, we have rendered it in English poetic form. We sought to break lines in ways that clarify and highlight the relationships between phrases of the text. Hebrew poetry often uses parallelism, a literary form where a second phrase (or in some instances a third or fourth) echoes the initial phrase in some way. In Hebrew parallelism, the subsequent parallel phrases continue, while also furthering and sharpening, the thought expressed in the initial line or phrase. Whenever possible, we sought to represent these parallel phrases in natural poetic English.
- The Greek term *hoi Ioudaioi* is literally translated "the Jews" in many English translations. In the Gospel of John, however, this term doesn't always refer to the Jewish people generally. In some contexts, it refers more particularly to the Jewish religious leaders. We have attempted to capture the meaning in these different contexts by using terms such as "the people" (with a footnote: Greek *the Jewish people*) or "the religious leaders," where appropriate.
- One challenge we faced was how to translate accurately the ancient biblical text that was originally written in a context where male-oriented terms were used to refer to humanity generally. We needed to respect the nature of the ancient context while also trying to make the translation clear to a modern audience that tends to read male-oriented language as applying only to males. Often the original text, though using masculine nouns and pronouns, clearly intends that the message be applied to both men and women. A typical example is found in the New Testament letters, where the believers are called "brothers" (*adelphoi*). Yet it is clear from the content of these letters that they were addressed to all the believers—male and female. Thus, we have usually translated this Greek word as "brothers and sisters" in order to represent the historical situation more accurately.

  We have also been sensitive to passages where the text applies generally to human beings or to the human condition. In some instances we have used plural pronouns (they, them) in place of the masculine singular (he, him). For example, a traditional rendering of Proverbs 22:6 is: "Train up a child in the way he should go, and when he is old he will not turn from it." We have rendered it: "Direct your children onto the right path, and when they are older, they will not leave it." At times, we have also replaced third person pronouns with the second person to ensure clarity. A traditional rendering of Proverbs 26:27 is: "He who digs a pit will fall into it, and he who rolls a stone, it will come back on him." We have rendered it: "If you set a trap for others, you will get caught in it yourself. If you roll a boulder down on others, it will crush you instead."

We should emphasize, however, that all masculine nouns and pronouns used to represent God (for example, "Father") have been maintained without exception. All decisions of this kind have been driven by the concern to reflect accurately the intended meaning of the original texts of Scripture.

Lexical Consistency in Terminology

For the sake of clarity, we have translated certain original-language terms consistently, especially within synoptic passages and for commonly repeated rhetorical phrases, and within certain word categories such as divine names and non-theological technical terminology (e.g., liturgical, legal, cultural, zoological, and botanical terms). For theological terms, we have allowed a greater semantic range of acceptable English words or phrases for a single Hebrew or Greek word. We have avoided some theological terms that are not readily understood by many modern readers. For example, we avoided using words such as "justification" and "sanctification," which are carryovers from Latin translations. In place of these words, we have provided renderings such as "made right with God" and "made holy."

The Spelling of Proper Names

Many individuals in the Bible, especially the Old Testament, are known by more than one name (e.g., Uzziah/Azariah). For the sake of clarity, we have tried to use a single spelling for any one individual, footnoting the literal spelling whenever we differ from it. This is especially helpful in delineating the kings of Israel and Judah. King Joash/Jehoash of Israel has been consistently called Jehoash, while King Joash/Jehoash of Judah is called Joash. A similar distinction has been used to distinguish between Joram/Jehoram of Israel and Joram/Jehoram of Judah. All such decisions were made with the goal of clarifying the text for the reader. When the ancient biblical writers clearly had a theological purpose in their choice of a variant name (e.g., Esh-baal/Ishbosheth), the different names have been maintained with an explanatory footnote.

For the names Jacob and Israel, which are used interchangeably for both the individual patriarch and the nation, we generally render it "Israel" when it refers to the nation and "Jacob" when it refers to the individual. When our rendering of the name differs from the underlying Hebrew text, we provide a textual footnote, which includes this explanation: "The names 'Jacob' and 'Israel' are often interchanged throughout the Old Testament, referring sometimes to the individual patriarch and sometimes to the nation."

The Rendering of Divine Names

In the Old Testament, all appearances of *'el, 'elohim,* or *'eloah* have been translated "God," except where the context demands the translation "god(s)." We have generally rendered the tetragrammaton (*YHWH*) consistently as "the LORD," utilizing a form with small capitals that is common among English translations. This will distinguish it from the name *'adonai,* which we render "Lord." When *'adonai* and *YHWH* appear together, we have rendered it "Sovereign LORD." When *'elohim* and *YHWH* appear together, we have rendered it "LORD God." When *YH* (the short form of *YHWH*) and *YHWH* appear together, we have rendered it "LORD GOD." When *YHWH* appears with the term *tseba'oth,* we have rendered it "LORD of Heaven's Armies" to translate the meaning of the name. In a few cases, we have utilized the transliteration, *Yahweh,* when the personal character of the name is being invoked in contrast to another divine name or the name of some other god (for example, see Exodus 3:15; 6:2-3).

In the Gospels and Acts, the Greek word *christos* has been translated as "Messiah" when the context assumes a Jewish audience. When a Gentile audience can be assumed (which is consistently the case for the Epistles and Revelation), *christos* has been translated as "Christ." The Greek word *kurios* is consistently translated "Lord," except that it is translated "LORD" wherever the New Testament text explicitly quotes from the Old Testament, and the text there has it in small capitals.

Textual Footnotes

The New Living Translation provides several kinds of textual footnotes, all designated in the text with an asterisk:

- When for the sake of clarity the NLT renders a difficult or potentially confusing phrase dynamically, we generally give the literal rendering in a textual footnote. This allows the reader to see the literal source of our dynamic rendering and how our translation relates to other more literal translations. These notes are prefaced with "Hebrew," "Aramaic," or "Greek," identifying the language of the underlying source text. For example, in Acts 2:42 we translated the literal "breaking of bread" (from the Greek) as "the Lord's Supper" to clarify that this verse refers to the ceremonial practice of the church rather than just an ordinary meal. Then we attached a footnote to "the Lord's Supper," which reads: "Greek *the breaking of bread.*"
- Textual footnotes are also used to show alternative renderings, prefaced with the word "Or." These normally occur for passages where an aspect of the meaning is debated. On occasion, we also

provide notes on words or phrases that represent a departure from long-standing tradition. These notes are prefaced with "Traditionally rendered." For example, the footnote to the translation "serious skin disease" at Leviticus 13:2 says: "Traditionally rendered *leprosy*. The Hebrew word used throughout this passage is used to describe various skin diseases."

- When our translators follow a textual variant that differs significantly from our standard Hebrew or Greek texts (listed earlier), we document that difference with a footnote. We also footnote cases when the NLT excludes a passage that is included in the Greek text known as the *Textus Receptus* (and familiar to readers through its translation in the King James Version). In such cases, we offer a translation of the excluded text in a footnote, even though it is generally recognized as a later addition to the Greek text and not part of the original Greek New Testament.
- All Old Testament passages that are quoted in the New Testament are identified by a textual footnote at the New Testament location. When the New Testament clearly quotes from the Greek translation of the Old Testament, and when it differs significantly in wording from the Hebrew text, we also place a textual footnote at the Old Testament location. This note includes a rendering of the Greek version, along with a cross-reference to the New Testament passage(s) where it is cited (for example, see notes on Psalms 8:2; 53:3; Proverbs 3:12).
- Some textual footnotes provide cultural and historical information on places, things, and people in the Bible that are probably obscure to modern readers. Such notes should aid the reader in understanding the message of the text. For example, in Acts 12:1, "King Herod" is named in this translation as "King Herod Agrippa" and is identified in a footnote as being "the nephew of Herod Antipas and a grandson of Herod the Great."
- When the meaning of a proper name (or a wordplay inherent in a proper name) is relevant to the meaning of the text, it is either illuminated with a textual footnote or included within parentheses in the text itself. For example, the footnote concerning the name "Eve" at Genesis 3:20 reads: "*Eve* sounds like a Hebrew term that means 'to give life.'" This wordplay in the Hebrew illuminates the meaning of the text, which goes on to say that Eve "would be the mother of all who live."

Cross-References

There are a number of different cross-referencing tools that appear in New Living Translation Bibles, and each offers a different level of help. All straight-text Bibles have the standard set of textual footnotes that include cross-references connecting New Testament texts to their related Old Testament sources. (See more on this above.)

Many NLT Bibles include an additional concise cross-reference system that places key cross-references at the ends of paragraphs, linking them to the associated verse or verses with a cross symbol within each paragraph. This space-efficient system, while not being obtrusive, offers many important key connections.

Larger study editions include a full-column cross-reference system, which allows space for a more comprehensive listing of cross-references. In this larger system, symbols differentiate between various kinds of cross-references. The parallel marker (//) designates a cross-referenced passage that is parallel in nature to the passage at hand. The asterisk (*) designates a cross-reference whose connection involves a direct quote from the other testament. Standard cross-references in this system appear unmarked.

In some study editions, we utilize an expanded full-column cross-reference system that has been enhanced by adding a system of Hebrew and Greek word studies. This tool, which takes 100 of the most significant Hebrew words in the Old Testament and 100 Greek words from the New Testament, creates a chain reference which points to key instances of these words so they can be studied in context. In the cross-reference system, each word is attached to a modified Strong's number, which points to a helpful key-word glossary at the back of the Bible.

As WE SUBMIT this translation for publication, we recognize that any translation of the Scriptures is subject to limitations and imperfections. Anyone who has attempted to communicate the richness of God's Word into another language will realize it is impossible to make a perfect translation. Recognizing these limitations, we sought God's guidance and wisdom throughout this project. Now we pray that he will accept our efforts and use this translation for the benefit of the church and of all people.

We pray that the New Living Translation will overcome some of the barriers of history, culture, and language that have kept people from reading and understanding God's Word. We hope that readers unfamiliar with the Bible will find the words clear and easy to understand and that readers well versed in the Scriptures will gain a fresh perspective. We pray that readers will gain insight and wisdom for living, but most of all that they will meet the God of the Bible and be forever changed by knowing him.

The Bible Translation Committee
October 2007

BIBLE TRANSLATION TEAM
HOLY BIBLE, **NEW LIVING TRANSLATION**

PENTATEUCH
Daniel I. Block, Senior Translator
Wheaton College

GENESIS
Allen Ross, *Beeson Divinity School, Samford University*
Gordon Wenham, *Trinity College, Bristol*

EXODUS
Robert Bergen, *Hannibal-LaGrange College*
Daniel I. Block, *Wheaton College*
Eugene Carpenter, *Bethel College, Mishawaka, Indiana*

LEVITICUS
David Baker, *Ashland Theological Seminary*
Victor Hamilton, *Asbury College*
Kenneth Mathews, *Beeson Divinity School, Samford University*

NUMBERS
Dale A. Brueggemann, *Assemblies of God Division of Foreign Missions*
R. K. Harrison (deceased), *Wycliffe College*
Paul R. House, *Beeson Divinity School, Samford University*
Gerald L. Mattingly, *Johnson Bible College*

DEUTERONOMY
J. Gordon McConville, *University of Gloucester*
Eugene H. Merrill, *Dallas Theological Seminary*
John A. Thompson (deceased), *University of Melbourne*

HISTORICAL BOOKS
Barry J. Beitzel, Senior Translator
Trinity Evangelical Divinity School

JOSHUA, JUDGES
Carl E. Armerding, *Schloss Mittersill Study Centre*
Barry J. Beitzel, *Trinity Evangelical Divinity School*
Lawson Stone, *Asbury Theological Seminary*

1 & 2 SAMUEL
Robert Gordon, *Cambridge University*
V. Philips Long, *Regent College*
J. Robert Vannoy, *Biblical Theological Seminary*

1 & 2 KINGS
Bill T. Arnold, *Asbury Theological Seminary*
William H. Barnes, *North Central University*
Frederic W. Bush, *Fuller Theological Seminary*

1 & 2 CHRONICLES
Raymond B. Dillard (deceased), *Westminster Theological Seminary*
David A. Dorsey, *Evangelical School of Theology*
Terry Eves, *Erskine College*

RUTH, EZRA—ESTHER
William C. Williams, *Vanguard University*
H. G. M. Williamson, *Oxford University*

WISDOM BOOKS
Tremper Longman III, Senior Translator
Westmont College

JOB
August Konkel, *Providence Theological Seminary*
Tremper Longman III, *Westmont College*
Al Wolters, *Redeemer College*

PSALMS 1–75
Mark D. Futato, *Reformed Theological Seminary*
Douglas Green, *Westminster Theological Seminary*
Richard Pratt, *Reformed Theological Seminary*

PSALMS 76–150
David M. Howard Jr., *Bethel Theological Seminary*
Raymond C. Ortlund Jr., *Immanuel Church, Nashville, Tennessee*
Willem VanGemeren, *Trinity Evangelical Divinity School*

PROVERBS
Ted Hildebrandt, *Gordon College*
Richard Schultz, *Wheaton College*
Raymond C. Van Leeuwen, *Eastern College*

ECCLESIASTES, SONG OF SONGS
Daniel C. Fredericks, *Belhaven College*
David Hubbard (deceased), *Fuller Theological Seminary*
Tremper Longman III, *Westmont College*

PROPHETS
John N. Oswalt, Senior Translator
Asbury Theological Seminary

ISAIAH
John N. Oswalt, *Asbury Theological Seminary*
Gary Smith, *Union University*
John Walton, *Wheaton College*

JEREMIAH, LAMENTATIONS
G. Herbert Livingston, *Asbury Theological Seminary*
Elmer A. Martens, *Mennonite Brethren Biblical Seminary*

EZEKIEL
Daniel I. Block, *Wheaton College*
David H. Engelhard, *Calvin Theological Seminary*
David Thompson, *Asbury Theological Seminary*

DANIEL, HAGGAI—MALACHI
Joyce Baldwin Caine (deceased), *Trinity College, Bristol*
Douglas Gropp, *Catholic University of America*
Roy Hayden, *Oral Roberts School of Theology*
Andrew Hill, *Wheaton College*
Tremper Longman III, *Westmont College*

HOSEA—ZEPHANIAH
Joseph Coleson, *Nazarene Theological Seminary*

Roy Hayden, *Oral Roberts School of Theology*
Andrew Hill, *Wheaton College*
Richard Patterson, *Liberty University*

GOSPELS AND ACTS

Grant R. Osborne, Senior Translator
Trinity Evangelical Divinity School

MATTHEW
Craig Blomberg, *Denver Seminary*
Donald A. Hagner, *Fuller Theological Seminary*
David Turner, *Grand Rapids Baptist Seminary*

MARK
Robert Guelich (deceased), *Fuller Theological Seminary*
George Guthrie, *Union University*
Grant R. Osborne, *Trinity Evangelical Divinity School*

LUKE
Darrell Bock, *Dallas Theological Seminary*
Scot McKnight, *North Park University*
Robert Stein, *The Southern Baptist Theological Seminary*

JOHN
Gary M. Burge, *Wheaton College*
Philip W. Comfort, *Coastal Carolina University*
Marianne Meye Thompson, *Fuller Theological Seminary*

ACTS
D. A. Carson, *Trinity Evangelical Divinity School*
William J. Larkin, *Columbia International University*
Roger Mohrlang, *Whitworth University*

LETTERS AND REVELATION

Norman R. Ericson, Senior Translator
Wheaton College

ROMANS, GALATIANS
Gerald Borchert, *Northern Baptist Theological Seminary*
Douglas J. Moo, *Wheaton College*
Thomas R. Schreiner, *The Southern Baptist Theological Seminary*

1 & 2 CORINTHIANS
Joseph Alexanian, *Trinity International University*
Linda Belleville, *Bethel College, Mishawaka, Indiana*
Douglas A. Oss, *Central Bible College*
Robert Sloan, *Houston Baptist University*

EPHESIANS—PHILEMON
Harold W. Hoehner (deceased), *Dallas Theological Seminary*
Moises Silva, *Gordon-Conwell Theological Seminary*
Klyne Snodgrass, *North Park Theological Seminary*

HEBREWS, JAMES, 1 & 2 PETER, JUDE
Peter Davids, *St. Stephen's University*
Norman R. Ericson, *Wheaton College*
William Lane (deceased), *Seattle Pacific University*
J. Ramsey Michaels, *S. W. Missouri State University*

1–3 JOHN, REVELATION
Greg Beale, *Westminster Theological Seminary*
Robert Mounce, *Whitworth University*
M. Robert Mulholland Jr., *Asbury Theological Seminary*

SPECIAL REVIEWERS

F. F. Bruce (deceased), *University of Manchester*
Kenneth N. Taylor (deceased), *Translator,* The Living Bible

COORDINATING TEAM

Mark D. Taylor, *Director and Chief Stylist*
Ronald A. Beers, *Executive Director and Stylist*
Mark R. Norton, *Managing Editor and O.T. Coordinating Editor*
Philip W. Comfort, *N.T. Coordinating Editor*
Daniel W. Taylor, *Bethel University, Senior Stylist*

CHRONOLOGICAL LIFE APPLICATION STUDY BIBLE **TEAM**

GENERAL EDITOR
Keith Williams

COPY EDITORS
Leanne Rolland, Coordinator
Susan F. Tristano
Carole L. Johnson

PROOFREADING
Peachtree Editorial Services

DESIGN
Timothy R. Botts
Daniel Farrell

TYPESETTING
Gwendolyn Elliott

ILLUSTRATIONS
Dr. Leen Ritmeyer
Luke Daab

TIMELINE AND MAP DESIGN
Ruth Berg

SECTION INTRODUCTIONS
Keith Williams

ARCHAEOLOGICAL NOTES
Philip W. Comfort
Keith Williams

CHRONOLOGICAL SURVEY OF THE BIBLE
David P. Barrett

PUBLISHER
Douglas R. Knox

ASSOCIATE PUBLISHER
Blaine A. Smith

ACQUISITIONS DIRECTOR
Kevin O'Brien

ORIGINAL LIFE APPLICATION STUDY BIBLE **CONTRIBUTORS**

SENIOR EDITORIAL TEAM
Dr. Bruce B. Barton
Ronald A. Beers
Dr. James C. Galvin
LaVonne Neff
Linda Chaffee Taylor
David R. Veerman

GENERAL EDITOR
Ronald A. Beers

TYNDALE HOUSE BIBLE EDITORS
Philip W. Comfort
Mark R. Norton
Robert K. Brown
Virginia Muir
Del Lankford

BOOK INTRODUCTIONS
David R. Veerman

BOOK OUTLINES, BLUEPRINTS
Dr. James C. Galvin

MEGATHEMES
Dr. Bruce B. Barton

MAP CONSULTANT
Dr. Barry Beitzel

CHARTS & DIAGRAMS
Neil S. Wilson
Ronald A. Beers
David R. Veerman
Pamela York

PERSONALITY PROFILES
Neil S. Wilson

DESIGN & DEVELOPMENT TEAM
Dr. Bruce B. Barton
Ronald A. Beers
Dr. James C. Galvin
David R. Veerman

THEOLOGICAL REVIEWERS
Dr. Kenneth S. Kantzer
Dr. V. Gilbert Beers
Dr. Barry Beitzel
Dr. Edwin A. Blum
Dr. Geoffrey W. Bromiley
Dr. George K. Brushaber
Dr. L. Russ Bush
C. Donald Cole
Mrs. Naomi E. Cole
Dr. Walter A. Elwell
Dr. Gerald F. Hawthorne
Dr. Howard G. Hendricks
Dr. Grant R. Osborne

A special thanks to the nationwide staff of Youth for Christ/USA for their suggestions and field testing, and to the following additional contributing writers:

V. Gilbert Beers, Neil Wilson, John Crosby, Joan Young, Jack Crabtree, Philip Craven, Bob Black, Bur Shilling, Arthur Deyo, Annie Lafrentz, Danny Sartin, William Hanawalt, William Bonikowsky, Brian Rathbun, Pamela Barden, Thomas Stobie, Robert Arnold, Greg Monaco, Larry Dunn, Lynn Ziegenfuss, Mitzie Barton, Mari-jean Hamilton, Larry Kreider, Gary Dausey, William Roland, Kathy Howell, Philip Steffeck, James Coleman, Marty Grasley, O'Ann Steere, Julia Amstutz.

A special thanks also to the following people whose personal counsel, encouragement, and determination helped make this product a reality:

Dr. Kenneth N. Taylor
Mark D. Taylor
Dr. Wendell C. Hawley
Virginia Muir
Richard R. Wynn
Dr. Jay L. Kesler

Old
Testament

Beginnings

EVERY STORY has a beginning. The Bible begins with God. At the very beginning of this story, God created the universe and put everything in order, forming all of the planets, stars, and galaxies and setting them in motion. On earth, he created abundant varieties of living creatures. And he made the crown of his creation in his own image, his vice-regents: humans.

Creation isn't the only beginning recorded in the Bible, though. There is also the more tragic story of the beginning of sin and death. Adam and Eve, the humans whom God placed over his creation, chose to disobey him and shattered its perfection. This tragedy soon led to others, such as Cain murdering his brother Abel in a jealous rage. And ultimately, sin became so rampant and pervasive that God decided to begin once again. He chose Noah, the only righteous man left on earth, to be the patriarch of a fresh beginning for humanity. But even Noah was vulnerable to sin, and his descendants showed that the sin problem was still very real and in need of a solution.

How would God continue his rescue plan for humanity? Would he need to begin again after the tower of Babel?

TIMELINE

4000 BC

3500 BC

MESOPOTAMIA

CREATION *(undated)*

GREAT FLOOD *(undated)*

CANAAN

EGYPT

PREDYNASTIC PERIOD (4000–3000 BC)

BOOKS

- GENESIS

DATES

FROM:
Undated
TO:
2100 BC

THEMES

- Creation
- Sin
- Redemption

PEOPLE & CULTURE

■ **Adam and Eve.** God created Adam and Eve and placed them in the Garden of Eden to rule on his behalf. They worked hard at cultivating the ground and managing the affairs of the Garden, and they enjoyed communion with God there. But they chose to disobey God's one command, and through them sin entered the world. They were banished from the Garden, and their fellowship with God was broken. But God immediately set into motion his plan to bring humanity back into fellowship with him—this is the story of the entire Bible.

■ **Noah.** By the time of Noah, sin and wickedness were so rampant that God was actually sorry he had ever created humans (Gen 6:7). But Noah was a righteous man, and God chose to save him from the destruction that was planned for the rest of humanity. Noah and his family became a new beginning for humanity.

■ **Language and Culture.** After Noah's sons populated the earth again, there was a unified language and culture throughout the world. But this unity led to pride and a sense that humans didn't need God. As a result, God caused them to be divided by different languages and to be scattered around the world. Different cultures began to emerge from the different language groups and regions.

Adam and Eve in the Garden of Eden, by Wenzel Peter

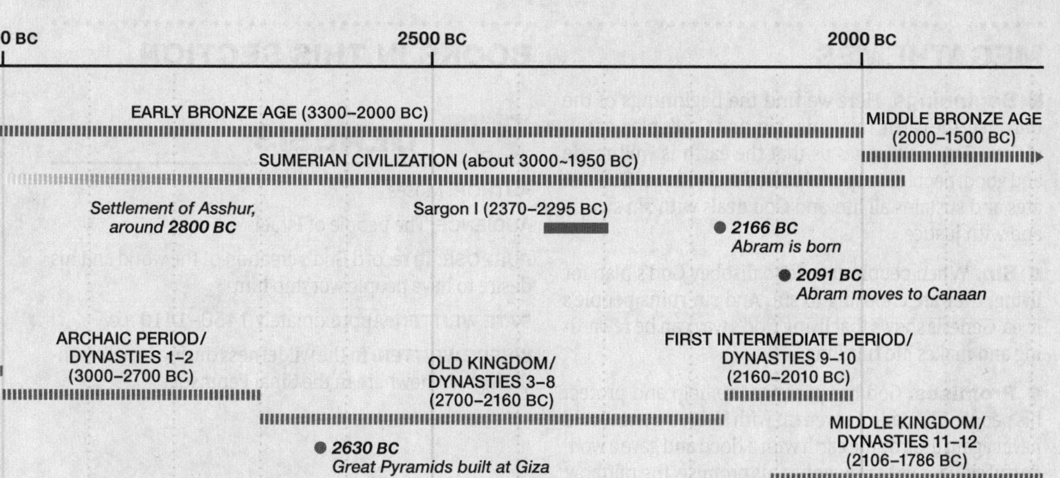

MAP

1 Garden of Eden God placed Adam and Eve in the Garden of Eden when he made them in his image. The Bible doesn't tell us exactly where Eden was located, except for a few clues that are difficult to decipher in Genesis 2:10-14.

2 Mountains of Ararat Noah's boat came to rest on the mountains of Ararat, in modern-day Turkey (Gen 8:4). From here his sons and their descendants spread out to build new nations.

3 Babel The tower of Babel was built in the fertile area between the Tigris and Euphrates Rivers, in modern-day Iraq.

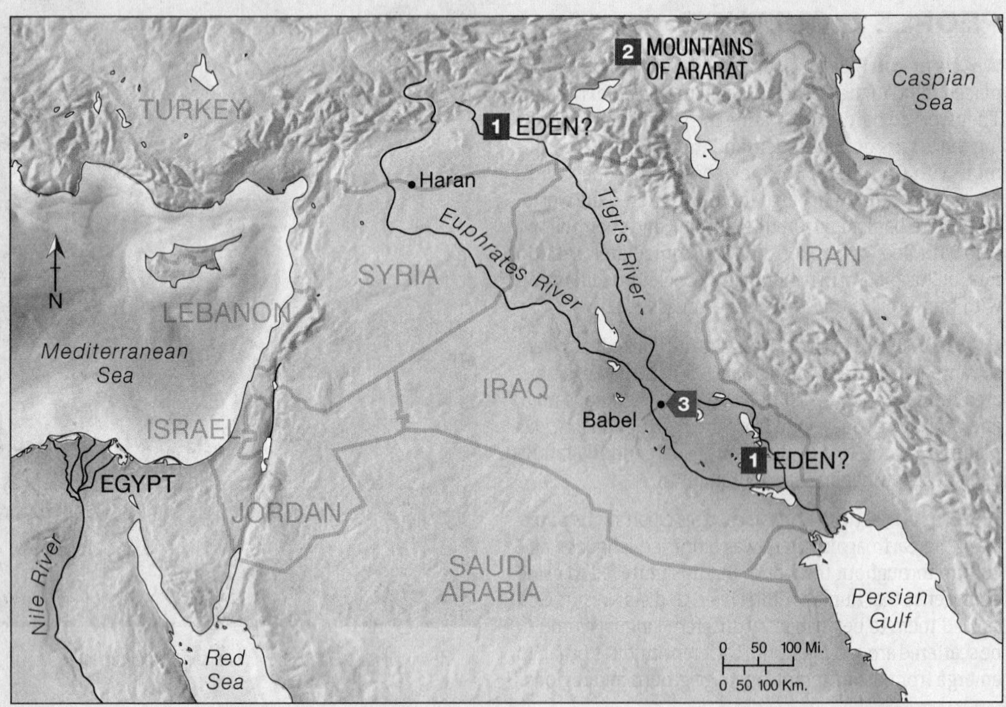

MEGATHEMES

■ **Beginnings.** Here we find the beginnings of the universe, the earth, humanity, sin, and God's plan of salvation. Genesis teaches us that the earth is well-made and good; people are special to God and unique; God creates and sustains all life; and God deals with sin swiftly and with justice.

■ **Sin.** When people choose to disobey God's plan for living, they are choosing to sin. And sin ruins people's lives. Genesis shows that living God's way can be rewarding and makes life fulfilling.

■ **Promises.** God has promised to help and protect his people. He made a covenant with Noah that he would never again destroy the earth with a flood and gave a wonderful sign for us to remember his promise: the rainbow. God always keeps his promises.

BOOKS IN THIS SECTION

GENESIS

AUTHOR: Moses

AUDIENCE: The people of Israel

PURPOSE: To record God's creation of the world and his desire to have people worship him

DATE WRITTEN: Approximately 1450–1410 B.C.

WHERE WRITTEN: In the wilderness during Israel's wanderings, somewhere in the Sinai Peninsula

And God saw that the light was good.
Then he separated the light from the darkness.
Genesis 1:4

A. The Beginning of Creation

We sometimes wonder how our world came to be. But here we find the answer. God created the earth and everything in it, and made humans like himself. Although we may not understand the complexity of just how he did it, it is clear that God did create all life. This shows not only God's authority over humanity, but his deep love for all creation.

The Account of Creation

GENESIS 1:1–2:4a

In the beginning God created the heavens and the
earth.* 2The earth was formless and empty, and darkness covered the deep waters. And the Spirit of God
was hovering over the surface of the waters.

3Then God said, "Let there be light," and there was
light. 4And God saw that the light was good. Then
he separated the light from the darkness. 5God
called the light "day" and the darkness "night."

And evening passed and morning came,
marking the first day.

6Then God said, "Let there be a space between the
waters, to separate the waters of the heavens
from the waters of the earth." 7And that is what
happened. God made this space to separate

Gn 1:1 Or *In the beginning when God created the heavens and the earth, . . .* Or *When God began to create the heavens and the earth, . . .*

Gen 1:1 The simple statement "God created the heavens and the earth" is one of the most challenging concepts confronting the modern mind. The vast galaxy we live in is spinning at the incredible speed of 490,000 miles per hour. But even at this breakneck speed, our galaxy still needs 200 million years to make one rotation. And there are over one billion other galaxies just like ours in the universe.

Some scientists say that the number of stars in creation is equal to all the grains of sand on all the beaches of the world. Yet this complex sea of spinning stars functions with remarkable order and efficiency. To say that the universe "just happened" or "evolved" requires more faith than to believe that God is behind these amazing statistics. God truly did create a wonderful universe.

God did not *need* to create the universe; he *chose* to create it. Why? God is love, and love is best expressed toward something or someone else—so God created the world and people as an expression of his love. We should avoid reducing God's creation to merely scientific terms. Remember that God created the universe because of love.

Gen 1:1ff The creation story teaches us much about God and ourselves. First, we learn about God: (1) He is creative; (2) as the Creator, he is distinct from his creation; (3) he is eternal and in control of the world. We also learn about ourselves: (1) Since God chose to create us, we are valuable in his eyes; (2) we are more important than the animals. (See Gen 1:28 for more on our role in the created order.)

Gen 1:1ff Just how did God create the earth? This is still a subject of great debate. Some say that with a sudden explosion, the universe appeared. Others say God started the process and then the universe evolved over billions of years. Almost every ancient religion has its own story to explain how the earth came to be. And almost every scientist has an opinion on the origin of the universe. But only the Bible shows one supreme God creating the earth out of his great love and giving all people a special place in it. We may never know exactly how God created the earth, but the Bible tells us that God did create it. That fact alone gives worth and dignity to all people.

ORIGIN OF THE UNIVERSE

The Bible does not discuss the subject of evolution, but its worldview assumes God created the world. The biblical view of creation is not in conflict with science; rather, it is in conflict with any worldview that starts without a creator.

Equally committed and sincere Christians have struggled with the subject of beginnings and come to **differing conclusions**. This is to be expected because the evidence is very old and quite fragmented, due to the ravages of the ages. Polarizations and black-and-white thinking should be avoided. Students of the Bible must be careful not to make the Bible say what it doesn't say, and students of science must not make science say what it doesn't say.

The most important aspect of the continuing discussion is not the process of creation, but the origin of creation. **The world is not a product of blind chance and probability; God created it.**

The Bible not only tells us that the world was created by God, but more importantly, it tells us who this God is. It reveals God's personality, his character, and his plan for his creation. It also reveals God's deepest desire—to relate to and fellowship with the people he created. God took the ultimate step toward fellowship with us through his historic visit to this planet in the person of his Son, Jesus Christ. **We can know in a very personal way this God who created the universe.**

The book of Genesis begins with "God created the heavens and the earth." The heavens and the earth are here. We are here. God created all that we see and experience. Here we begin the most exciting and fulfilling journey imaginable.

Gen 1:2 Who created God? To ask that question is to assume there was another creator before God. At some time, however, we are forced to stop asking that question and realize that there has to be something that has always existed. God is that infinite Being who has always been and who was created by no one. This is difficult to understand because finite minds cannot comprehend the infinite. For example, we can try to think of the highest number, but we can't do it. Likewise, we must not limit the infinite God by our finite understanding.

Gen 1:2 The statement "the earth was formless and empty" provides the setting for the creation narrative that follows. During the second and third days of creation, God gave form to the universe; during days four through six, God filled the earth with living beings. The "darkness" was dispelled on the first day, when God created light.

Gen 1:2 The image of the Spirit of God hovering over the surface of the water is similar to a mother bird caring for and protecting its young (see Deut 32:11-12; Isa 31:5). God's Spirit was actively involved in the creation of the world (see Job 33:4; Ps 104:30). God's care and protection are still active.

Gen 1:3–2:7 How long did it take God to create the world? There are two basic views about the days of creation: (1) Each day was a literal 24-hour period; (2) each day represents an indefinite period of time (even millions of years).

the waters of the earth from the waters of the
heavens. 8God called the space "sky."
And evening passed and morning came,
marking the second day.
9Then God said, "Let the waters beneath the sky
flow together into one place, so dry ground may
appear." And that is what happened. 10God called
the dry ground "land" and the waters "seas." And
God saw that it was good. 11Then God said, "Let
the land sprout with vegetation—every sort of
seed-bearing plant, and trees that grow seed-
bearing fruit. These seeds will then produce the
kinds of plants and trees from which they came."
And that is what happened. 12The land produced
vegetation—all sorts of seed-bearing plants,
and trees with seed-bearing fruit. Their seeds
produced plants and trees of the same kind.
And God saw that it was good.
13And evening passed and morning came,
marking the third day.
14Then God said, "Let lights appear in the sky to
separate the day from the night. Let them be
signs to mark the seasons, days, and years. 15Let
these lights in the sky shine down on the earth."
And that is what happened. 16God made two great
lights—the larger one to govern the day, and the
smaller one to govern the night. He also made
the stars. 17God set these lights in the sky to light
the earth, 18to govern the day and night, and to
separate the light from the darkness. And God
saw that it was good.
19And evening passed and morning came,
marking the fourth day.
20Then God said, "Let the waters swarm with fish
and other life. Let the skies be filled with birds of
every kind." 21So God created great sea creatures
and every living thing that scurries and swarms in
the water, and every sort of bird—each producing
offspring of the same kind. And God saw that it
was good. 22Then God blessed them, saying, "Be
fruitful and multiply. Let the fish fill the seas,
and let the birds multiply on the earth."
23And evening passed and morning came,
marking the fifth day.
24Then God said, "Let the earth produce every sort
of animal, each producing offspring of the same
kind—livestock, small animals that scurry along
the ground, and wild animals." And that is what
happened. 25God made all sorts of wild animals,
livestock, and small animals, each able to produce
offspring of the same kind. And God saw that it
was good.

The Bible does not say how long these days were. The real question, however, is not how long God took, but how he did it. God created the earth in an orderly fashion (he did not make plants before light), and he created men and women as unique beings capable of communication with him. No other part of creation can claim that remarkable privilege. It is not important how long it took God to create the world, whether a few days or a few billion years, but that he created it just the way he wanted it.

Gen 1:6 The "space between the waters" was a separation between the sea and the mists of the skies.

Gen 1:25 God saw that his work was good. People sometimes feel guilty for feeling good about an accomplishment. This need not be so. Just as God felt good about his work, we can be pleased with our work when it is well-done. However, we should not feel good about our work if God would not be pleased with it. What are you doing that pleases both you and God?

Animals

Animals are mentioned throughout the Bible from Genesis to Revelation. Animals figured into many important biblical events, including the Creation, the fall of man, the Flood, the ten plagues in Egypt, and the life of Jesus Christ. The people of both the Old and New Testaments lived close to the land and were well acquainted with various animals, which explains why the Scripture writers and Jesus himself frequently used animals as object lessons.

Present-day biologists classify animals based on internal and external structures, but in the creation account animals are classified by habitat. Thus, Genesis 1 speaks of water and air animals (Gen 1:20-21); cattle or domesticated animals—that is, animals that live with humans (Gen 1:24); animals that scurry along the ground (Gen 1:24); and wild animals (Gen 1:24). When God made animals, they became living souls (having nephesh—the Hebrew word translated "life" in Gen 1:20, 30). The same word is used in Genesis 2:7 to describe the human being God made; that is, the man became a living soul (nephesh). Both animals and humans are nephesh—that is, they are living souls. Human beings are different from animals in the sense that we have "spirit" (ruach) and we bear the image of God (Gen 1:27).

▸ **GENESIS 1:1–2:4a *(cont.)***

26Then God said, "Let us make human beings*
in our image, to be like us. They will reign over
the fish in the sea, the birds in the sky, the
livestock, all the wild animals on the earth,
and the small animals that scurry along the
ground."

27 So God created human beings* in his own
image.
In the image of God he created them;
male and female he created them.

28Then God blessed them and said, "Be
fruitful and multiply. Fill the earth and govern
it. Reign over the fish in the sea, the birds in
the sky, and all the animals that scurry along
the ground."
29Then God said, "Look! I have given you every
seed-bearing plant throughout the earth and all

Gn 1:26 Or *man;* Hebrew reads *adam.* **Gn 1:27** Or *the man;* Hebrew reads *ha-adam.*

ADAM

We can hardly imagine what it must have been like to be the first and only person on earth. Adam had to learn to be human on his own. Fortunately, God didn't let him struggle too long before presenting him with an ideal companion and mate, Eve. Theirs was a complete, innocent, and open oneness, without a hint of shame. • One of Adam's first conversations with his delightful new companion must have been about the rules of the garden. They had complete freedom in the garden, with the responsibility to tend and care for it. But one tree was off-limits, the tree of the knowledge of good and evil. Adam would have told Eve all about this. She knew that the tree's fruit was not to be eaten. However, she decided to eat the forbidden fruit. Then she offered some to Adam, and he didn't pause to consider the consequences. He went ahead and ate. • In that moment of rebellion something large, beautiful, and free was shattered . . . God's perfect creation. Adam was separated from God by his desire to act on his own. The effect on a plate-glass window is the same whether a pebble or a boulder is hurled at it—the thousands of fragments can never be regathered. • In the case of Adam's sin, however, God already had a plan in motion to overcome the effects of the rebellion. The entire Bible is the story of how that plan unfolds, ultimately leading to God's own visit to earth through his Son, Jesus Christ. Jesus' sinless life and death made it possible for God to offer forgiveness to all. Our own acts of rebellion—both large and small—prove that we are descendants of Adam. Only by asking forgiveness of Jesus Christ can we become children of God.

Strengths and accomplishments	• First zoologist—named the animals • First landscape architect, placed in the garden to care for it • Father of the human race • First person made in the image of God, and the first human to share an intimate personal relationship with God
Weaknesses and mistakes	• Avoided responsibility and blamed others; chose to hide rather than to confront; made excuses rather than admitting the truth • Greatest mistake: together with Eve, brought sin into the world
Lessons from his life	• As Adam's descendants, we all reflect the image of God • God wants people who, though free to do wrong, choose instead to love him • We should not blame others for our faults • We cannot hide from God
Vital statistics	• Where: Garden of Eden • Occupation: Caretaker, gardener, farmer • Relatives: Wife: Eve. Sons: Cain, Abel, Seth. Numerous other children. The only man who never had an earthly mother or father.
Key verses	"It was the woman you gave me who gave me the fruit, and I ate it" (Gen 3:12). "Just as everyone dies because we all belong to Adam, everyone who belongs to Christ will be given new life" (1 Cor 15:22).

Adam's story is told in Genesis 1:26–5:5. He is also mentioned in Luke 3:38; Romans 5:14; 1 Corinthians 15:22, 45; 1 Timothy 2:13-14.

Gen 1:26 Why does God use the plural form, "Let *us* make human beings in *our* image"? One view says this is a reference to the Trinity—God the Father, Jesus Christ his Son, and the Holy Spirit—all of whom are God. Another view is that the plural wording is used to denote majesty; kings traditionally used the plural form in speaking of themselves. The grammar doesn't decide the matter for us, but in either case it is God who created humans in his image, and God has revealed himself to us as a Trinity clearly through the whole of the Scriptures.

Gen 1:26 In what ways are we made in God's image? God obviously did not create us exactly like himself because God has no physical body. Instead, we are a reflection of God's glory. Some feel that the image of God can be found in one or more of the uniquely human capacities for reason, creativity, speech, or self-determination. More likely, the image of God is something that describes our entire being as humans, not just one aspect. God made humans to be in a special relationship with him and to reign over creation as his ambassadors and administrators on earth. We ought to reflect his character in our love, patience, forgiveness, kindness, and faithfulness.

Knowing that we are made in God's image provides a solid basis for self-worth. Human worth is not based on possessions, achievements, physical attractiveness, or public acclaim. Instead, it is based on being made in God's image. Because we bear God's image, we can feel positive about ourselves. Criticizing or downgrading ourselves is criticizing what God has made and the abilities he has given us. Knowing that you are a person of worth helps you love God, know him personally, and make a valuable contribution to those around you.

Gen 1:27 God made both man and woman in his image. Neither one is made more in the image of God than the other. From the beginning the Bible places both man and woman at the pinnacle of God's creation. Neither gender is exalted over the other nor depreciated.

Gen 1:28 To "reign over" something is to have absolute authority and control over it. God has ultimate rule over the earth, and he exercises his authority with loving care. When God delegated some of his authority to the human race, he expected us to take responsibility for the environment and the other creatures that share our planet. We must not be careless

the fruit trees for your food. [30]And I have given
every green plant as food for all the wild animals,
the birds in the sky, and the small animals that
scurry along the ground—everything that has
life." And that is what happened.
[31]Then God looked over all he had made, and
he saw that it was very good!
And evening passed and morning came,
marking the sixth day.

[2:1]So the creation of the heavens and the earth
and everything in them was completed. [2]On
the seventh day God had finished his work of
creation, so he rested* from all his work. [3]And
God blessed the seventh day and declared it holy,
because it was the day when he rested from all
his work of creation.

[4]This is the account of the creation of the heavens
and the earth.

Gn 2:2 Or *ceased;* also in 2:3.

B. The Beginning of Humanity

Learning about our ancestors often helps us understand ourselves. The stories of Adam and Eve in the Garden, followed by the tragic story of their two sons Cain and Abel, explain the sin and suffering in our world and help us to live our lives in reliance on God and his promises.

1. ADAM AND EVE

Adam and Eve, our first ancestors, were the climax of God's creation—the very reason God made the world. But they didn't always live the way God intended. Through their mistakes, we can learn important lessons about the way God wants us to live. Adam and Eve teach us much about the nature of sin and its consequences.

The Man and Woman in the Garden

GENESIS 2:4b-25

When the LORD God made the earth and the heavens,
[5]neither wild plants nor grains were growing on the
earth. For the LORD God had not yet sent rain to water the earth, and there were no people to cultivate
the soil. [6]Instead, springs* came up from the ground
and watered all the land. [7]Then the LORD God formed
the man from the dust of the ground. He breathed
the breath of life into the man's nostrils, and the man
became a living person.
[8]Then the LORD God planted a garden in Eden in
the east, and there he placed the man he had made.
[9]The LORD God made all sorts of trees grow up from

Gn 2:6 Or *mist.*

DAYS OF CREATION

First Day	Light (so there was light and darkness)
Second Day	Sky and water (waters separated)
Third Day	Land and seas (waters gathered); vegetation
Fourth Day	Sun, moon, and stars (to govern the day and the night and to mark seasons, days, and years)
Fifth Day	Fish and birds (to fill the waters and the sky)
Sixth Day	Animals (to fill the earth) Man and woman (to care for the earth and to commune with God)
Seventh Day	God rested and declared all he had made to be very good

and wasteful as we fulfill this charge. God was careful how he made this earth. We must not be careless about how we take care of it.

Gen 1:31 God saw that all he had created was excellent in every way. You are part of God's creation, and he is pleased with how he made you. If at times you feel worthless, remember that God made you for a good reason. You are valuable to him.

Gen 2:2-3 We live in an action-oriented world! There always seems to be something to do and no time to rest. Yet God demonstrated that rest is appropriate and right. If God himself rested from his work, we should not be surprised that we also need rest. Jesus demonstrated this principle when he and his disciples left in a boat to get away from the crowds (see Mark 6:31-32). Our times of rest refresh us for times of service.

Gen 2:3 That God blessed the seventh day means that he set it apart for holy use. The Ten Commandments emphasize this distinction by commanding the observance of the Sabbath (Exod 20:8-11).

Gen 2:7 "From the dust of the ground" implies that there is nothing fancy about the chemical elements making up our bodies. The body is a lifeless shell until God brings it to life with his "breath of life." When God removes his life-giving breath, our bodies once again return to dust. Our life and worth, therefore, come from God's Spirit. Many boast of their achievements and abilities as though they were the originators of their own strengths. Others feel worthless because their abilities do not stand out. In reality, our worth comes not from our achievements but from the God of the universe, who chooses to give us the mysterious and miraculous gift of life. Value life, as he does.

Gen 2:9, 16-17 Were the tree of life and the tree of the knowledge of good and evil real trees? Two views are often expressed: (1) *The trees were real, but symbolic.* Eternal life with God was pictured as eating from the tree of life. (2) *The trees were real, possessing special properties.* By eating the fruit from the tree of life, Adam and Eve could have had eternal life, enjoying a permanent relationship as God's children.

In either case, Adam and Eve's sin separated them from the tree of life and thus kept them from obtaining eternal life. Interestingly,

▸ **GENESIS 2:4b-25** ***(cont.)***
the ground—trees that were beautiful and that produced delicious fruit. In the middle of the garden he
placed the tree of life and the tree of the knowledge
of good and evil.
[10]A river flowed from the land of Eden, watering
the garden and then dividing into four branches.
[11]The first branch, called the Pishon, flowed around
the entire land of Havilah, where gold is found. [12]The
gold of that land is exceptionally pure; aromatic resin
and onyx stone are also found there. [13]The second
branch, called the Gihon, flowed around the entire
land of Cush. [14]The third branch, called the Tigris,
flowed east of the land of Asshur. The fourth branch
is called the Euphrates.
[15]The LORD God placed the man in the Garden of
Eden to tend and watch over it. [16]But the LORD God
warned him, "You may freely eat the fruit of every tree
in the garden—[17]except the tree of the knowledge of
good and evil. If you eat its fruit, you are sure to die."
[18]Then the LORD God said, "It is not good for the
man to be alone. I will make a helper who is just right
for him." [19]So the LORD God formed from the ground
all the wild animals and all the birds of the sky. He
brought them to the man* to see what he would call
them, and the man chose a name for each one. [20]He
gave names to all the livestock, all the birds of the sky,
and all the wild animals. But still there was no helper
just right for him.
[21]So the LORD God caused the man to fall into a
deep sleep. While the man slept, the LORD God took
out one of the man's ribs* and closed up the opening.
[22]Then the LORD God made a woman from the rib, and
he brought her to the man.
[23]"At last!" the man exclaimed.

"This one is bone from my bone,
and flesh from my flesh!
She will be called 'woman,'
because she was taken from 'man.'"

Gn 2:19 Or *Adam,* and so throughout the chapter. **Gn 2:21** Or *took a part of the man's side.*

the tree of life again appears in a description in Revelation 22 of people enjoying eternal life with God.

Gen 2:15-17 God gave Adam responsibility for the garden and told him not to eat from the tree of the knowledge of good and evil. Rather than physically preventing him from eating, God gave Adam a choice and, thus, the possibility of choosing wrongly. God still gives us choices, and we, too, often choose wrongly. These wrong choices may cause us pain, but they can help us learn and grow and make better choices in the future. Living with the consequences of our choices teaches us to think and choose more carefully.

Gen 2:16-17 Why would God place a tree in the garden and then forbid Adam to eat from it? God wanted Adam to obey, but God gave Adam the freedom to choose. Without choice, Adam would have been like a prisoner, and his obedience would have been hollow. The two trees provided an exercise in choice with rewards for choosing to obey and sad consequences for choosing to disobey. When you are faced with a choice, always choose to obey God.

Gen 2:18-24 God's creative work was not complete until he made woman. He could have made her from the dust of the ground, as he had made man. But God chose to make her from the man's flesh and bone. In so doing, he illustrated for us that in marriage man and woman symbolically are united into one. This is a mystical union of the couple's hearts and lives. Throughout the Bible, God treats this special partnership seriously. If you are married or planning to be married, are you willing to keep the commitment that makes the two of you one? The goal in marriage should be more than friendship; it should be oneness.

Gen 2:21-23 God forms and equips men and women for various tasks, but all these tasks lead to the same goal—honoring God.

WHAT THE BIBLE SAYS ABOUT MARRIAGE

Gen 2:18-24	Marriage is God's idea
Gen 24:58-60	Commitment is essential to a successful marriage
Prov 5:18	Marriage holds times of great joy
Song 4:9-10	Romance is important
Mal 2:14-15	Marriage creates the best environment for raising children
Matt 5:32	Unfaithfulness breaks the bond of trust, the foundation of all relationships
Matt 19:6	Marriage is permanent
Rom 7:2-3	Only death should dissolve marriage
Eph 5:21-33	Marriage is based on the principled practice of love, not on feelings
Eph 5:23-32	Marriage is a living symbol of Christ and the church
Heb 13:4	Marriage is good and honorable

There is no room for thinking that one gender is superior to the other.

Gen 2:24 God gave marriage as a gift to Adam and Eve. They were created perfect for each other. Marriage was not just for convenience, nor was it brought about by any particular culture. It was instituted by God and has three basic aspects: (1) The man leaves his parents and, in a public act, promises himself to his wife; (2) the man and woman are joined together by taking responsibility for each other's welfare and by loving each other above all others; (3) the two are united into one in the intimacy and commitment of sexual union that is reserved for marriage. Strong marriages include all three of these aspects.

Gen 2:25 Have you ever noticed how a little child can run naked through a room full of strangers without embarrassment? He is not aware of his nakedness, just as Adam and Eve were not embarrassed in their innocence. But after Adam and Eve sinned, shame and awkwardness followed, creating barriers between themselves and God. We often experience these same barriers in marriage. Ideally a husband and wife have no barriers, feeling no embarrassment in exposing themselves to each other or to God. But like Adam and Eve we put on fig leaves (barriers) because we have areas we don't want our spouse, or God, to know about (Gen 3:7). Then we hide, just as Adam and Eve hid from God. In marriage, lack of spiritual, emotional, and intellectual intimacy usually precedes a breakdown of physical intimacy. In the same way, when we fail to expose our secret thoughts to God, we break our lines of communication with him.

Gen 3:1 Disguised as a shrewd serpent, Satan came to tempt Eve. At one time, Satan had been a glorious angel. But in pride, he rebelled against God and was cast out of heaven. As a created being, Satan has definite limitations. Although he is trying to tempt

24This explains why a man leaves his father and mother and is joined to his wife, and the two are united into one.
25Now the man and his wife were both naked, but they felt no shame.

The Man and Woman Sin

GENESIS 3:1-19

The serpent was the shrewdest of all the wild animals the LORD God had made. One day he asked the woman, "Did God really say you must not eat the fruit from any of the trees in the garden?"
2"Of course we may eat fruit from the trees in the
garden," the woman replied. 3"It's only the fruit from the tree in the middle of the garden that we are not allowed to eat. God said, 'You must not eat it or even touch it; if you do, you will die.'"
4"You won't die!" the serpent replied to the woman.
5"God knows that your eyes will be opened as soon as you eat it, and you will be like God, knowing both good and evil."
6The woman was convinced. She saw that the tree was beautiful and its fruit looked delicious, and she wanted the wisdom it would give her. So she took

everyone away from God, he will not be the final victor. In Genesis 3:14-15, God promises that Satan will be crushed by one of the woman's offspring, the Messiah.

Gen 3:1-6 Why does Satan tempt us? Temptation is Satan's invitation to give in to his kind of life and give up on God's kind of life. Satan tempted Eve and succeeded in getting her to sin. Ever since then, he's been busy trying to get people to sin. He even tempted Jesus (Matt 4:1-11), but Jesus did not sin!

How could Eve have resisted temptation? By following the same guidelines we can follow. First, we must realize that *being tempted* is not a sin. We have not sinned until we *give in* to the temptation. Second, to resist temptation, we must pray for strength to resist, run from it (sometimes literally), and say no when confronted with what we know is wrong. James 1:12 tells of the blessings and rewards for those who don't give in when tempted.

Gen 3:1-6 The serpent, Satan, tempted Eve by getting her to doubt God's goodness. He implied that God was strict, stingy, and selfish for not wanting Eve to share his knowledge of good and evil. Satan made Eve forget all that God had given her and, instead, focus on what God had forbidden. We fall into trouble, too, when we dwell on what God forbids rather than on the countless blessings and promises God has given us. The next time you are feeling sorry for yourself because of what you don't have, consider all that you *do* have and thank God. Then your doubts won't lead you into sin.

Gen 3:5 Adam and Eve got what they wanted: an intimate knowledge of both good and evil. But they got it by disobeying God, and the results were disastrous. Sometimes we have the illusion that freedom is doing anything we want. But God says that true freedom comes from obedience and knowing what *not* to do. The restrictions he gives us are for our good, helping us avoid evil. We have the freedom to walk in front of a speeding car, but we don't need to be hit to realize it would be foolish to do so. Don't listen to Satan's temptations. You don't have to do evil to gain more experience and learn more about life.

Gen 3:5 Satan used a sincere motive to tempt Eve: "You will be like God." It wasn't wrong of Eve to want to be like God. To become more like God is humanity's highest goal. It is what we are supposed to do. But Satan misled Eve concerning the right way to accomplish this goal. He told her that she could become more like God by defying God's authority, by taking God's place and deciding for herself what was best for her life. In effect, he told her to become her own god.

To become like God is not the same as trying to become God. Rather, it is to reflect his characteristics and to recognize his authority over our lives. Like Eve, we often have a worthy goal but try to achieve it the wrong way. We act like a political candidate who pays off an election judge to be "voted" into office; serving the people is no longer his highest goal.

Self-exaltation leads to rebellion against God. As soon as we begin to leave God out of our plans, we are placing ourselves above him. This is exactly what Satan wants us to do.

Gen 3:6 Satan tried to make Eve think that sin is good, pleasant, and desirable. A knowledge of both good and evil seemed harmless to her. People usually choose wrong things because they have become convinced that those things are good, at least for themselves. Our sins do not always appear ugly to us, and the pleasant sins are the hardest to avoid. So prepare yourself for the attractive temptations that may come your way. We cannot always prevent temptation, but there is always a way of escape (1 Cor 10:13). Use God's Word and God's people to help you stand against it.

Gen 3:6-7 Notice what Eve did: She looked, she took, she ate, and she gave. The battle is often lost at the first look. Temptation often begins by simply seeing something you want. Are you struggling with temptation because you have not learned that looking is the first step toward sin? You would win over temptation more often if you followed Paul's advice to run from those things that produce evil thoughts (2 Tim 2:22).

Gen 3:6-7 One of the realities of sin is that its effects spread. After Eve sinned, she involved Adam in her wrongdoing. When we do something wrong, often we try to relieve our guilt by involving someone else. Like toxic waste spilled into a river, sin swiftly spreads. Recognize and confess your sin to God before you are tempted to pollute those around you.

Creation Stories

Several ancient civilizations wrote down their own accounts of how the world was created. The best known of these extra-biblical creation myths is a Babylonian adaptation of the Sumerian story called Enuma Elish. The gods Tiamat and Apsu existed from the beginning, but after other gods were born Apsu tried to do away with them. One of the gods, Ea, killed Apsu; then Tiamat was herself killed by Ea's son Marduk, the god of Babylon in whose honor the poem was composed. Marduk used the two halves of Tiamat's body to create the foundation for both heaven and earth. He then set in order the stars, sun, and moon. Lastly, to free the gods from menial tasks, with Ea's help he created mankind from clay mingled with the blood of Kingu, the rebel god who had led Tiamat's forces. Other creation stories are found in Babylonian records. The Epic of Atrahasis describes the creation of man as a solution to relieve the gods of the work of cultivating the land.

In contrast to these stories from the surrounding cultures, Israel's creation story shows that God is completely in control. He is not one of many gods, and his creation of humanity was not a matter of convenience but an act of love. God created humans to rule his creation and have relationship with him, not simply to do the hard work that he didn't want to do.

▸ **GENESIS 3:1-19 *(cont.)***
some of the fruit and ate it. Then she gave some to her
husband, who was with her, and he ate it, too. 7At that
moment their eyes were opened, and they suddenly
felt shame at their nakedness. So they sewed fig leaves
together to cover themselves.
8When the cool evening breezes were blowing,
the man* and his wife heard the LORD God walking
about in the garden. So they hid from the LORD God
among the trees. 9Then the LORD God called to the
man, "Where are you?"
10He replied, "I heard you walking in the garden, so
I hid. I was afraid because I was naked."
11"Who told you that you were naked?" the LORD
God asked. "Have you eaten from the tree whose fruit
I commanded you not to eat?"
12The man replied, "It was the woman you gave me
who gave me the fruit, and I ate it."
13Then the LORD God asked the woman, "What have
you done?"
"The serpent deceived me," she replied. "That's
why I ate it."

Gn 3:8 Or *Adam*, and so throughout the chapter.

Gen 3:7-8 After sinning, Adam and Eve felt guilt and embarrassment over their nakedness. Their guilty feelings made them try to hide from God. A guilty conscience is a warning signal God has placed inside of you that goes off when you've done wrong. The worst step you can take is to try to stifle or eliminate those guilty feelings without eliminating the cause. That would be like using a painkiller but not treating the disease that is causing the pain. Be glad those guilty feelings are there. They make you aware of your sin so you can ask God's forgiveness and then correct your wrongdoing.

Gen 3:8 The thought of two humans covered with fig leaves trying to hide from the all-seeing, all-knowing God is humorous. How could they be so silly as to think they could actually hide? Yet we do the same, acting as though God doesn't know what we're doing. Have the courage to share all you do and think with him. And don't try to hide—it can't be done. Honesty will strengthen your relationship with God.

Gen 3:8-9 These verses show God's desire to have fellowship with us. They also show why we are afraid to have fellowship with him. Adam and Eve hid from God when they heard him approaching. God wanted to be with them, but because of their sin, they were afraid to show themselves. Sin had broken their close relationship with God, just as it has broken ours. But Jesus Christ, God's Son, opens the way for us to renew our fellowship with him. God longs to be with us. He actively offers us his unconditional love. Our natural response is fear because we feel we can't live up to his standards. But understanding that he loves us, regardless of our faults, can help remove that dread.

Gen 3:11-13 Adam and Eve failed to heed God's warning recorded in Genesis 2:16-17. They did not understand the reasons for his command, so they chose to act in another way that looked better to them. All of God's commands are for our own good, but we may not always understand the reasons behind them. People who trust God will obey because God asks them to, whether or not they understand why God commands it.

EVE

We know very little about Eve, yet she is the mother of us all. She was the final piece in the intricate and amazing puzzle of God's creation. Adam now had another human being with whom to fellowship—someone equally made in God's image. Here was someone alike enough for companionship, yet different enough for relationship. Together they were greater than either could have been alone. • Satan approached Eve in the Garden of Eden, where she and Adam lived. He questioned her contentment. How could she be happy when she was not allowed to eat from one of the fruit trees? Satan helped Eve shift her focus from all that God had done and given to the one thing he had withheld. And Eve was willing to accept Satan's viewpoint without checking with God. • Sound familiar? How often is our attention drawn from all that is ours to the little that isn't? We get that "I've got to have it" feeling. Eve was typical of us all, and we consistently show we are her descendants by repeating her mistakes. Our desires, like Eve's, can be quite easily manipulated. They are not the best basis for actions. We need to keep God central in our decision-making process. His Word, the Bible, is our guidebook in decision making.

Strengths and accomplishments	• First wife and mother • First female. As such she shared a special relationship with God, had coresponsibility with Adam over creation, and displayed certain characteristics of God
Weaknesses and mistakes	• Allowed her contentment to be undermined by Satan • Acted impulsively without talking either to God or to her mate • Not only sinned, but shared her sin with Adam • When confronted, blamed others
Lessons from her life	• Women bear the image of God fully • The necessary ingredients for a strong marriage are commitment to each other, companionship with each other, complete oneness, absence of shame (Gen 2:24-25) • The basic human tendency to sin goes back to the beginning of the human race
Vital statistics	• Where: Garden of Eden • Occupation: Wife, companion, co-manager of Eden • Relatives: Husband: Adam. Sons: Cain, Abel, Seth. Numerous other children.
Key verse	"'At last!' the man exclaimed. 'This one is bone from my bone, and flesh from my flesh! She will be called "woman," because she was taken from "man"'" (Gen 2:23).

Eve's story is told in Genesis 2:18–4:26. Her death is not mentioned in Scripture.

Gen 3:11-13 When God asked Adam about his sin, Adam blamed Eve. Then Eve blamed the serpent. How easy it is to excuse our sins by blaming someone else or our circumstances. But God knows the truth, and he holds each of us responsible for what we do (see Gen 3:14-19). Admit your wrong attitudes and actions to God. Don't try to get away with sin by placing blame.

14Then the LORD God said to the serpent,

"Because you have done this, you are cursed
more than all animals, domestic
and wild.
You will crawl on your belly,
groveling in the dust as long as you live.
15 And I will cause hostility between you and
the woman,
and between your offspring and her
offspring.
He will strike* your head,
and you will strike his heel."

16Then he said to the woman,

"I will sharpen the pain of your pregnancy,
and in pain you will give birth.
And you will desire to control your husband,
but he will rule over you.*"

17And to the man he said,

"Since you listened to your wife and ate
from the tree
whose fruit I commanded you not to eat,
the ground is cursed because of you.
All your life you will struggle to scratch
a living from it.
18 It will grow thorns and thistles for you,
though you will eat of its grains.
19 By the sweat of your brow
will you have food to eat
until you return to the ground
from which you were made.
For you were made from dust,
and to dust you will return."

Paradise Lost: God's Judgment

GENESIS 3:20-24

Then the man—Adam—named his wife Eve, because
she would be the mother of all who live.* 21And the
LORD God made clothing from animal skins for Adam
and his wife.
22Then the LORD God said, "Look, the human beings* have become like us, knowing both good and
evil. What if they reach out, take fruit from the tree
of life, and eat it? Then they will live forever!" 23So the
LORD God banished them from the Garden of Eden,
and he sent Adam out to cultivate the ground from
which he had been made. 24After sending them out,
the LORD God stationed mighty cherubim to the east
of the Garden of Eden. And he placed a flaming sword
that flashed back and forth to guard the way to the
tree of life.

Gn 3:15 Or *bruise;* also in 3:15b. **Gn 3:16** Or *And though you will have desire for your husband, / he will rule over you.* **Gn 3:20** *Eve* sounds like a Hebrew term that means "to give life." **Gn 3:22** Or *the man;* Hebrew reads *ha-adam.*

SATAN'S PLAN AGAINST US

Doubt	Makes you question God's Word and his goodness
Discouragement	Makes you look at your problems rather than at God
Diversion	Makes the wrong things seem attractive so that you will want them more than the right things
Defeat	Makes you feel like a failure so that you don't even try
Delay	Makes you put off doing something so that it never gets done

Gen 3:14ff Adam and Eve chose their course of action (disobedience), and then God chose his. As a holy God, he could only respond in a way consistent with his perfect moral nature. He could not allow sin to go unchecked; he had to punish it. If the consequences of Adam and Eve's sin seem extreme, remember that their sin set in motion the world's tendency toward disobeying God. That is why we sin today. Every human being ever born, with the exception of Jesus, has inherited the sinful nature of Adam and Eve (Rom 5:12-21). Adam and Eve's punishment reflects how seriously God views sin of any kind.

Gen 3:14-19 Adam and Eve learned by painful experience that because God is holy and hates sin, he must punish sinners. The rest of the book of Genesis recounts painful stories of lives ruined as a result of the Fall. Disobedience is sin, and it breaks our fellowship with God. But fortunately, God is willing to forgive us and to restore our relationship with him when we admit our sin.

Gen 3:15 Satan is our enemy. He will do anything he can to get us to follow his evil, deadly path. The phrase "you will strike his heel" refers to Satan's repeated attempts to defeat Christ during his life on earth. "He will strike your head" foreshadows Satan's defeat when Christ rose from the dead. A strike on the heel is not deadly, but a blow to the head is. Already God was revealing his plan to defeat Satan and offer salvation to the world through his Son, Jesus Christ.

Gen 3:17-19 Adam and Eve's disobedience and fall from God's gracious presence affected all creation, including the environment. Years ago people thought nothing of polluting streams and rivers with chemical waste and garbage. The amount dumped seemed so insignificant, so small compared to these large water sources. Now we know that just two or three parts per million of certain chemicals can damage human health. Sin in our lives is similar to pollution in streams. Even small amounts are deadly, and the consequences reach far beyond ourselves.

Gen 3:22-24 Life in the Garden of Eden was perfect, and if Adam and Eve had obeyed God, they could have lived there forever. But after disobeying, Adam and Eve no longer deserved paradise, and God told them to leave. If they had continued to live in the garden and eat from the tree of life, they would have lived forever. But eternal life in a state of sin would mean forever trying to hide from God. Like Adam and Eve, all of us have sinned and are separated from fellowship with God. But we do not have to stay separated. And God is also preparing a new earth as an eternal paradise for his people (see Rev 21–22).

Gen 3:24 This is how Adam and Eve broke their relationship with God: (1) They became convinced their way was better than God's and acted on that choice; (2) they became self-conscious and hid; and (3) they tried to excuse and defend themselves. To build a relationship with God we must reverse those steps: (1) We must drop our excuses and self-defenses; (2) we must stop trying to hide from God; (3) we must become convinced that God's way is better than our way.

2. CAIN AND ABEL

The tragic story of Cain and Abel shows how dramatically sin had affected humanity. Less than a generation after being banished from the Garden of Eden, jealousy leads to murder.

Cain Murders Abel

GENESIS 4:1-16

Now Adam* had sexual relations with his wife, Eve, and she became pregnant. When she gave birth to Cain, she said, "With the LORD's help, I have produced* a man!" [2]Later she gave birth to his brother and named him Abel.

When they grew up, Abel became a shepherd, while Cain cultivated the ground. [3]When it was time for the harvest, Cain presented some of his crops as a gift to the LORD. [4]Abel also brought a gift—the best of the firstborn lambs from his flock. The LORD accepted Abel and his gift, [5]but he did not accept Cain and his gift. This made Cain very angry, and he looked dejected.

[6]"Why are you so angry?" the LORD asked Cain. "Why do you look so dejected? [7]You will be accepted if you do what is right. But if you refuse to do what is right, then watch out! Sin is crouching at the door, eager to control you. But you must subdue it and be its master."

[8]One day Cain suggested to his brother, "Let's go out

Gn 4:1a Or *the man;* also in 4:25. **Gn 4:1b** Or *I have acquired. Cain* sounds like a Hebrew term that can mean "produce" or "acquire."

ABEL

Abel was the second child born into the world, but the first one to obey God. All we know about this man is that his parents were Adam and Eve, he was a shepherd, he presented pleasing offerings to God, and his life was ended at the hands of his jealous older brother, Cain. • The Bible doesn't tell us why God liked Abel's gift and disliked Cain's, but both Cain and Abel knew what God expected. Only Abel obeyed. Throughout history, Abel is remembered for his obedience and faith (Heb 11:4), and he is called "righteous" (Matt 23:35). • The Bible is filled with God's general guidelines and expectations for our lives. It is also filled with more specific directions. Like Abel, we must obey regardless of the cost and trust God to make things right.

Strengths and accomplishments	• Mentioned in the Hall of Faith in Hebrews 11 • First shepherd • First martyr for truth (Matt 23:35)
Lessons from his life	• God hears those who come to him • God recognizes the innocent person and sooner or later punishes the guilty
Vital statistics	• Where: Just outside of Eden • Occupation: Shepherd • Relatives: Parents: Adam and Eve. Brother: Cain.
Key verse	"It was by faith that Abel brought a more acceptable offering to God than Cain did. Abel's offering gave evidence that he was a righteous man, and God showed his approval of his gifts. Although Abel is long dead, he still speaks to us by his example of faith" (Heb 11:4).

Abel's story is told in Genesis 4:1-8. He is also mentioned in Matthew 23:35; Luke 11:51; Hebrews 11:4; 12:24.

Gen 4:1 Sexual union means oneness and total knowledge of the other person. Sexual intercourse is the most intimate of acts, sealing a social, physical, and spiritual relationship. That is why God has reserved it for marriage alone.

Gen 4:2 No longer was everything provided for Adam and Eve as it had been in the Garden of Eden, where their daily tasks were refreshing and delightful. Now they had to struggle against the elements in order to provide food, clothing, and shelter for themselves and their family. Cain became a farmer, while Abel became a shepherd. In parts of the Middle East today, these ancient occupations are still practiced much as they were in Cain and Abel's time.

Gen 4:3-5 The Bible doesn't say why God did not accept Cain's gift. Perhaps Cain's attitude was improper, or perhaps his gift was not up to God's standards. Proverbs 21:27 says, "The sacrifice of an evil person is detestable, especially when it is offered with wrong motives." God evaluates both our motives and the quality of what we offer him. When we give to God and others, we should have a joyful heart because of what we are able to give. We should not worry about how much we are giving up, for all things are God's in the first place. Instead, we should joyfully give to God our best in time, money, possessions, and talents.

Gen 4:6-7 How do you react when someone suggests you have done something wrong? Do you move to correct the mistake or deny that you need to correct it? After Cain's gift was rejected, God gave him the chance to right his wrong and try again. God even encouraged him to do this! But Cain refused, and the rest of his life is a startling example of what happens to those who refuse to admit their mistakes. The next time someone suggests you are wrong, take an honest look at yourself and choose God's way instead of Cain's.

Gen 4:7 For Cain to subdue the sin that was waiting to attack and destroy him, he would have to give up his jealous anger so that sin would not find a foothold in his life. Sin is still waiting to attack and destroy us today. Like Cain, we will be victims of sin if we do not master it. But we cannot master sin in our own strength. Instead, we must turn to God to receive faith for ourselves and turn to other believers to receive encouragement and strength. The Holy Spirit will help us master sin. This will be a lifelong battle, but it will be over when we are face to face with Christ.

Gen 4:8-10 This is the first murder—taking a life by shedding human blood. Blood represents life (Lev 17:10-14). If blood is removed from a living creature, it will die. Because God created human life in his image, only God should take life away.

Gen 4:8-10 Adam and Eve's disobedience brought sin into the human race. They may have thought their sin—eating a piece of fruit—wasn't very bad, but notice how quickly their sinful nature developed in their children. Simple disobedience quickly degenerated into outright murder. Adam and Eve acted only against God, but Cain acted against both God and other people. A small

into the fields."* And while they were in the field, Cain attacked his brother, Abel, and killed him.

[9]Afterward the LORD asked Cain, "Where is your brother? Where is Abel?"

"I don't know," Cain responded. "Am I my brother's guardian?"

[10]But the LORD said, "What have you done? Listen! Your brother's blood cries out to me from the ground! [11]Now you are cursed and banished from the ground, which has swallowed your brother's blood. [12]No longer will the ground yield good crops for you, no matter how hard you work! From now on you will be a homeless wanderer on the earth."

[13]Cain replied to the LORD, "My punishment* is too great for me to bear! [14]You have banished me from the land and from your presence; you have made me a homeless wanderer. Anyone who finds me will kill me!"

[15]The LORD replied, "No, for I will give a sevenfold punishment to anyone who kills you." Then the LORD put a mark on Cain to warn anyone who might try to kill him. [16]So Cain left the LORD's presence and settled in the land of Nod,* east of Eden.

The Descendants of Cain

GENESIS 4:17-24

Cain had sexual relations with his wife, and she became pregnant and gave birth to Enoch. Then Cain founded a city, which he named Enoch, after his son. [18]Enoch had a son named Irad. Irad became the father of* Mehujael. Mehujael became the father of Methushael. Methushael became the father of Lamech.

[19]Lamech married two women. The first was named Adah, and the second was Zillah. [20]Adah gave birth to

Gn 4:8 As in Samaritan Pentateuch, Greek and Syriac versions, and Latin Vulgate; Masoretic Text lacks *"Let's go out into the fields."* **Gn 4:13** Or *My sin.* **Gn 4:16** *Nod* means "wandering." **Gn 4:18** Or *the ancestor of,* and so throughout the verse.

sin has a way of growing out of control. Let God help you with your "little" sins before they turn into tragedies.

Gen 4:11-15 Cain was severely punished for this murder. God judges all sins and punishes appropriately, not out of vengeance, but because he desires to correct us and restore our fellowship with him. When you're corrected, don't resent it. Instead, renew your fellowship with God.

Gen 4:14 We have heard about only four people so far—Adam, Eve, Cain, and Abel. Two questions arise: Why was Cain worried about being killed by others, and where did he get his wife (see Gen 4:17)?

Adam and Eve had numerous children; they had been told to "fill the earth" (Gen 1:28). Cain's guilt and fear over killing his brother was heavy, and he probably feared repercussions from his family. If he was capable of murder, so were they. The wife Cain chose may have been one of his sisters or a niece. The human race was still genetically pure, and there was no fear of side effects from marrying relatives.

Gen 4:15 The expression "sevenfold punishment" means that the person's punishment would be complete, thorough, and much worse than that received by Cain for his sin.

Gen 4:19-26 Unfortunately, when left to themselves, people tend to get worse instead of better. This short summary of Lamech's family shows us the variety of talent and ability God gives humans. It also presents the continuous development of sin as time passes. Another killing occurred, presumably in self-defense. Violence was on the rise. Two distinct groups were emerging: those who showed indifference to sin and evil, and those who worshiped the Lord—the descendants of Seth (Gen 4:26). Seth would take Abel's place as leader of a line of God's faithful people.

CAIN

In spite of parents' efforts and worries, conflicts between children in a family seem inevitable. Sibling relationships allow both competition and cooperation. In most cases, the mixture of loving and fighting eventually creates a strong bond between brothers and sisters. But for Cain, the conflict and jealousy overcame whatever love he had for Abel. And while we don't know many details of this first child's life, his story can still teach us. • Cain was angry. Furious. Both he and his brother Abel had given offerings to God, and his had been rejected. Cain's reaction gives us a clue that his attitude was probably wrong from the start. Cain had a choice to make. He could correct his attitude about his offering to God, or he could take his anger out on his brother. His decision is a clear reminder of how often we are aware of opposite choices, yet choose the wrong one. We may not be choosing to murder, but we are still intentionally choosing what we shouldn't. • The feelings motivating our behavior can't always be changed by simple thought-power. But here we can begin to experience God's willingness to help. Asking for his help to do what is right can prevent us from setting into motion actions that we will later regret.

Strengths and accomplishments	• First human child • First to follow in father's profession, farming
Weaknesses and mistakes	• When disappointed, reacted in anger • Took the negative option even when a positive possibility was offered • Was the first murderer
Lessons from his life	• Anger is not necessarily a sin, but actions motivated by anger can be sinful. Anger should be the energy behind good action, not evil action • What we offer to God must be from the heart—the best we are and have • The consequences of sin may last a lifetime
Vital statistics	• Where: Near Eden • Occupation: Farmer, then wanderer • Relatives: Parents: Adam and Eve. Brothers: Abel, Seth, and others not mentioned by name.
Key verse	"You will be accepted if you do what is right. But if you refuse to do what is right, then watch out! Sin is crouching at the door, eager to control you. But you must subdue it and be its master" (Gen 4:7).

Cain's story is told in Genesis 4:1-17. He is also mentioned in Hebrews 11:4; 1 John 3:12; Jude 1:11.

▸ **GENESIS 4:17-24 *(cont.)***

Jabal, who was the first of those who raise livestock and live in tents. [21]His brother's name was Jubal, the first of all who play the harp and flute. [22]Lamech's other wife, Zillah, gave birth to a son named Tubal-cain. He became an expert in forging tools of bronze and iron. Tubal-cain had a sister named Naamah. [23]One day Lamech said to his wives,

"Adah and Zillah, hear my voice;
listen to me, you wives of Lamech.
I have killed a man who attacked me,
a young man who wounded me.
[24] If someone who kills Cain is punished
seven times,
then the one who kills me will be punished
seventy-seven times!"

The Birth of Seth

GENESIS 4:25-26

Adam had sexual relations with his wife again, and she gave birth to another son. She named him Seth,* for she said, "God has granted me another son in place of Abel, whom Cain killed." [26]When Seth grew up, he had a son and named him Enosh. At that time people first began to worship the LORD by name.

Gn 4:25 *Seth* probably means "granted"; the name may also mean "appointed."

3. ADAM'S DESCENDANTS

Beginning with Adam and Eve, humanity grew to become independent families and tribes.

From Adam to Noah

GENESIS 5:1-32

This is the written account of the descendants of Adam. When God created human beings,* he made them to be like himself. [2]He created them male and female, and he blessed them and called them "human."

[3]When Adam was 130 years old, he became the father of a son who was just like him—in his very image. He named his son Seth. [4]After the birth of Seth, Adam lived another 800 years, and he had other sons and daughters. [5]Adam lived 930 years, and then he died.

[6]When Seth was 105 years old, he became the father of* Enosh. [7]After the birth of* Enosh, Seth lived another 807 years, and he had other sons and daughters. [8]Seth lived 912 years, and then he died.

[9]When Enosh was 90 years old, he became the father of Kenan. [10]After the birth of Kenan, Enosh lived another 815 years, and he had other sons and daughters. [11]Enosh lived 905 years, and then he died.

[12]When Kenan was 70 years old, he became the father of Mahalalel. [13]After the birth of Mahalalel, Kenan lived another 840 years, and he had other sons and daughters. [14]Kenan lived 910 years, and then he died.

[15]When Mahalalel was 65 years old, he became the father of Jared. [16]After the birth of Jared, Mahalalel lived another 830 years, and he had other sons and daughters. [17]Mahalalel lived 895 years, and then he died.

[18]When Jared was 162 years old, he became the father of Enoch. [19]After the birth of Enoch, Jared lived another 800 years, and he had other sons and daughters. [20]Jared lived 962 years, and then he died.

[21]When Enoch was 65 years old, he became the father of Methuselah. [22]After the birth of Methuselah, Enoch lived in close fellowship with God for another 300 years, and he had other sons and daughters. [23]Enoch lived 365 years, [24]walking in close fellowship with God. Then one day he disappeared, because God took him.

[25]When Methuselah was 187 years old, he became the father of Lamech. [26]After the birth of Lamech, Methuselah lived another 782 years, and he had other sons and daughters. [27]Methuselah lived 969 years, and then he died.

Gn 5:1 Or *man;* Hebrew reads *adam;* similarly in 5:2. **Gn 5:6** Or *the ancestor of;* also in 5:9, 12, 15, 18, 21, 25. **Gn 5:7** Or *the birth of this ancestor of;* also in 5:10, 13, 16, 19, 22, 26.

Gen 5:1ff The Bible contains several lists of ancestors, called genealogies. They are not intended to be exhaustive and may include only famous people or the heads of families. "He became the father of" could refer not just to a son, but also to a more distant descendant.

Why are genealogies included in the Bible? The Hebrew people passed on their beliefs through oral tradition. For many years in many places, writing was primitive or nonexistent. Stories were told to children who passed them on to their children. Genealogies gave a skeletal outline that helped people remember the stories. For centuries these genealogies were added to and passed down from family to family. Even more important than preserving family tradition, genealogies were included to confirm the Bible's promise that the coming Messiah, Jesus Christ, would be born into the line of Abraham.

Genealogies point out that people are important to God as individuals. Therefore, God refers to people by name, mentioning their life span and descendants. The next time you feel overwhelmed in a vast crowd, remember that the focus of God's attention and love is on the individual—on you!

Gen 5:3-5 All human beings are related, going back to Adam and Eve. All people form a family that shares one flesh and blood. Remember this when prejudice enters your mind or hatred invades your feelings. Each person is a valuable and unique creation of God.

Gen 5:25-27 How did these people live so long? Some believe that the ages listed here were lengths of family dynasties rather than ages of individual men. Those who think these were actual ages offer three explanations: (1) The human race was more

[28]When Lamech was 182 years old, he became the father of a son. [29]Lamech named his son Noah, for he said, "May he bring us relief* from our work and the painful labor of farming this ground that the LORD has cursed." [30]After the birth of Noah, Lamech lived another 595 years, and he had other sons and daughters. [31]Lamech lived 777 years, and then he died.

[32]By the time Noah was 500 years old, he was the father of Shem, Ham, and Japheth.

Gn 5:29 *Noah* sounds like a Hebrew term that can mean "relief" or "comfort."

C. A New Beginning for Humanity

Earth was no longer the perfect paradise that God had intended. It is frightening to see how quickly all of humanity forgot about God. Incredibly, in all the world, only one man and his family still worshiped God. That man was Noah. Because of his faithfulness and obedience, God saved him and his family from a vast flood that destroyed every other human being on earth. This section shows us how God hates sin and judges those who enjoy it.

1. THE FLOOD

The Flood was God's judgment of the world's pervasive sin, cleansing his creation and creating a new beginning with Noah and his family.

A World Gone Wrong

GENESIS 6:1-8

Then the people began to multiply on the earth, and daughters were born to them. [2]The sons of God saw the beautiful women* and took any they wanted as their wives. [3]Then the LORD said, "My Spirit will not put up with* humans for such a long time, for they are only mortal flesh. In the future, their normal lifespan will be no more than 120 years."

[4]In those days, and for some time after, giant Nephilites lived on the earth, for whenever the sons of God had intercourse with women, they gave birth to children who became the heroes and famous warriors of ancient times.

[5]The LORD observed the extent of human wickedness on the earth, and he saw that everything they thought or imagined was consistently and totally evil.

[6]So the LORD was sorry he had ever made them and put them on the earth. It broke his heart. [7]And the LORD said, "I will wipe this human race I have created from the face of the earth. Yes, and I will destroy every living thing—all the people, the large animals, the small animals that scurry along the ground, and even the birds of the sky. I am sorry I ever made them." [8]But Noah found favor with the LORD.

The Story of Noah

GENESIS 6:9-22

This is the account of Noah and his family. Noah was a righteous man, the only blameless person living on earth at the time, and he walked in close fellowship with God. [10]Noah was the father of three sons: Shem, Ham, and Japheth.

[11]Now God saw that the earth had become corrupt

Gn 6:2 Hebrew *daughters of men;* also in 6:4. **Gn 6:3** Greek version reads *will not remain in.*

genetically pure in this early time period with less disease to shorten life spans; (2) no rain had yet fallen on the earth, and the expanse of "the waters of the heavens" (Gen 1:7) kept out harmful cosmic rays and shielded people from environmental factors that hasten aging; (3) God gave people longer lives so they would have time to "fill the earth" (Gen 1:28).

Gen 6:1-4 Some people have thought that the "sons of God" were fallen angels. But the "sons of God" were probably not angels because angels do not marry or reproduce (Matt 22:30; Mark 12:25). Some scholars believe this phrase refers to the descendants of Seth who intermarried with Cain's evil descendants. This would have weakened the good influence of the faithful and increased moral depravity in the world, resulting in an explosion of evil.

Gen 6:3 "Their normal lifespan will be no more than 120 years" has been interpreted by some commentators to mean that God was allowing the people of Noah's day 120 years to change their sinful ways. God shows his great patience with us as well (2 Pet 3:8-9). He is giving us time to quit living our way and begin living his way, the way he shows us in his Word. While 120 years may seem like a long time, eventually the time ran out, and the floodwaters swept across the earth. Your time also may be running out (2 Pet 3:10-14). Turn to God to forgive your sins. You don't know how much time God will give you to turn to him, and once that time comes there will be no more opportunities.

Gen 6:4 These "giant Nephilites" were people probably nine or ten feet tall. This same Hebrew term was used to name a tall race of people in Numbers 13:33. Goliath, who was nine feet tall, appears in 1 Samuel 17. The giants used their physical advantage to oppress the people around them.

Gen 6:6-7 Does this mean that God regretted creating humanity? Was he admitting he made a mistake? No, God does not change his mind (1 Sam 15:29). Instead, he was expressing sorrow for what the people had done to themselves, as a parent might express sorrow over a rebellious child. God was sorry that the people chose sin and death instead of a relationship with him.

Gen 6:6-8 The people's sin grieved God. Our sins break God's heart as much as sin did in Noah's day. Noah, however, pleased God, although he was far from perfect. We can follow Noah's example and find "favor with the LORD" in spite of the sin that surrounds us.

Gen 6:9 Saying that Noah was "righteous" and "blameless" does not mean that he never sinned (the Bible records one of his sins in Gen 9:20ff). Rather, it means that Noah wholeheartedly loved and obeyed God. For a lifetime he walked step by step in faith as a living example to his generation. Like Noah, we live in a world filled with evil. Are we influencing others or being influenced by them?

▸ **GENESIS 6:9-22** ***(cont.)***

and was filled with violence. 12God observed all this
corruption in the world, for everyone on earth was
corrupt. 13So God said to Noah, "I have decided to
destroy all living creatures, for they have filled the
earth with violence. Yes, I will wipe them all out along
with the earth!

14"Build a large boat* from cypress wood* and
waterproof it with tar, inside and out. Then construct
decks and stalls throughout its interior. 15Make the
boat 450 feet long, 75 feet wide, and 45 feet high.*
16Leave an 18-inch opening* below the roof all the way
around the boat. Put the door on the side, and build
three decks inside the boat—lower, middle, and upper.

17"Look! I am about to cover the earth with a flood
that will destroy every living thing that breathes.
Everything on earth will die. 18But I will confirm my
covenant with you. So enter the boat—you and your
wife and your sons and their wives. 19Bring a pair of
every kind of animal—a male and a female—into the
boat with you to keep them alive during the flood.
20Pairs of every kind of bird, and every kind of animal,
and every kind of small animal that scurries along the
ground, will come to you to be kept alive. 21And be sure
to take on board enough food for your family and for
all the animals."

22So Noah did everything exactly as God had commanded him.

The Flood Covers the Earth

GENESIS 7:1-24

When everything was ready, the LORD said to Noah,
"Go into the boat with all your family, for among all
the people of the earth, I can see that you alone are
righteous. 2Take with you seven pairs—male and female—of each animal I have approved for eating and
for sacrifice,* and take one pair of each of the others.
3Also take seven pairs of every kind of bird. There must
be a male and a female in each pair to ensure that all
life will survive on the earth after the flood. 4Seven
days from now I will make the rains pour down on the
earth. And it will rain for forty days and forty nights,
until I have wiped from the earth all the living things
I have created."

5So Noah did everything as the LORD commanded
him.

6Noah was 600 years old when the flood covered
the earth. 7He went on board the boat to escape
the flood—he and his wife and his sons and their
wives. 8With them were all the various kinds of
animals—those approved for eating and for sacrifice and those that were not—along with all the
birds and the small animals that scurry along the
ground. 9They entered the boat in pairs, male and
female, just as God had commanded Noah. 10After
seven days, the waters of the flood came and covered the earth.

Gn 6:14a Traditionally rendered *an ark.* **Gn 6:14b** Or *gopher wood.* **Gn 6:15** Hebrew *300 cubits* [138 meters] *long, 50 cubits* [23 meters] *wide, and 30 cubits* [13.8 meters] *high.* **Gn 6:16** Hebrew *an opening of 1 cubit* [46 centimeters]. **Gn 7:2** Hebrew *of each clean animal;* similarly in 7:8.

Epic of Gilgamesh

The Bible isn't the only ancient document that tells about a great flood with a lone surviving family and pairs of animals on board; in fact, there are several flood stories from many different cultures that have strikingly similar details to Noah's story in Genesis. A Sumerian story called Eridu Genesis tells how king Ziusudra was warned that the gods had decreed a deluge to destroy mankind and was told to build a great boat in which to escape. An Akkadian story called the Atrahasis Epic describes a flood sent by the gods to destroy humanity after earlier attempts to control them had failed. The pious Atrahasis was warned by the creator god Ea to build a boat and escape with his family, treasure, and animals. The most famous of these flood stories is the Babylonian Story of the Flood, which is pictured on tablet 11 of the longer Epic of Gilgamesh. This story, focused on the hero Gilgamesh, tells of the boat coming to rest on a mountain and the dispatch in succession of a dove, a swallow, and a raven—the occupants of the boat disembarking when the raven did not return.

The fact that all of these different cultures trace their lineage back to a great hero who survived a great flood in a boat filled with animals, and who left only after sending birds out from the top of a mountain, is interesting confirmation of the claim in Genesis 6–9 that there was indeed a great flood in ancient times.

Gen 6:15 The boat Noah built was no canoe! Picture yourself building a boat the length of one and a half football fields and as high as a four-story building. The boat was exactly six times longer than it was wide—the same ratio used by modern shipbuilders. This huge boat was probably built miles from any body of water, but Noah was motivated by God's promises and obeyed his commands.

Gen 6:18 When God said, "I will confirm my covenant," he was making a promise. This is a familiar theme in Scripture—God making covenants with his people. How reassuring it is to know God's covenant is established with us. He is still our salvation, and we are kept safe through our relationship with him. (For more on covenants, see Gen 9:8-17; 12:1-3; 15:17-21.)

Gen 6:22 Noah got right to work when God told him to build the huge boat. Other people must have been warned by Noah about the coming disaster (2 Pet 2:5), but apparently they did not expect it to happen. Things haven't changed much. Each day thousands of people are warned of God's inevitable judgment, yet most of them don't really believe it will happen. Don't expect people to welcome or accept your message of God's coming judgment on sin. Those who don't believe in God will deny his judgment and try to get you to deny God as well. But

[11]When Noah was 600 years old, on the seventeenth day of the second month, all the underground waters erupted from the earth, and the rain fell in mighty torrents from the sky. [12]The rain continued to fall for forty days and forty nights.

[13]That very day Noah had gone into the boat with his wife and his sons—Shem, Ham, and Japheth—and their wives. [14]With them in the boat were pairs of every kind of animal—domestic and wild, large and small—along with birds of every kind. [15]Two by two they came into the boat, representing every living thing that breathes. [16]A male and female of each kind entered, just as God had commanded Noah. Then the LORD closed the door behind them.

[17]For forty days the floodwaters grew deeper, covering the ground and lifting the boat high above the earth. [18]As the waters rose higher and higher above the ground, the boat floated safely on the surface. [19]Finally, the water covered even the highest mountains on the earth, [20]rising more than twenty-two feet* above the highest peaks. [21]All the living things on earth died—birds, domestic animals, wild animals, small animals that scurry along the ground, and all the people. [22]Everything that breathed and lived on dry land died. [23]God wiped out every living thing on the earth—people, livestock, small animals that scurry along the ground, and the birds of the sky. All were destroyed. The only people who survived were Noah and those with him in the boat. [24]And the floodwaters covered the earth for 150 days.

The Flood Recedes

GENESIS 8:1-22

But God remembered Noah and all the wild animals and livestock with him in the boat. He sent a wind to blow across the earth, and the floodwaters began to recede. [2]The underground waters stopped flowing, and the torrential rains from the sky were stopped. [3]So the floodwaters gradually receded from the earth. After 150 days, [4]exactly five months from the time the flood began,* the boat came to rest on the mountains

Gn 7:20 Hebrew *15 cubits* [6.9 meters]. **Gn 8:4** Hebrew *on the seventeenth day of the seventh month;* see 7:11.

NOAH

The story of Noah's life involves not one but two great and tragic floods. The world in Noah's day was flooded with evil. The number of those who remembered the God of creation, perfection, and love had dwindled to one. Only Noah still worshiped God. God's response to the severe situation was a 120-year-long last chance, during which he had Noah build a graphic illustration of the message of his life. Nothing like a huge boat on dry land to make a point! For Noah, obedience meant a long-term commitment to a project. • Many of us have trouble sticking to any project, whether or not it is directed by God. It is interesting that the length of Noah's obedience was greater than the life span of people today. The only comparable long-term project is our very lives. But perhaps this is one great challenge Noah's life gives us—to live, in acceptance of God's grace, an entire lifetime of obedience and gratitude.

Strengths and accomplishments	• Only follower of God left in his generation • Second father of the human race • Man of patience, consistency, and obedience
Weakness and mistake	• Got drunk and embarrassed himself in front of his sons
Lessons from his life	• God is faithful to those who obey him • God does not always protect us from trouble, but cares for us in spite of trouble • Obedience is a long-term commitment • We may be faithful, but our sinful nature always travels with us
Vital statistics	• Where: We're not told how far from the Garden of Eden people had settled • Occupation: Farmer, shipbuilder, preacher • Relatives: Grandfather: Methuselah. Father: Lamech. Sons: Ham, Shem, and Japheth.
Key verse	"So Noah did everything exactly as God had commanded him" (Gen 6:22).

Noah's story is told in Genesis 5:28–10:32. He is also mentioned in Isaiah 54:9; Ezekiel 14:14, 20; Matthew 24:37-38; Luke 3:36; 17:26-27; Hebrews 11:7; 1 Peter 3:20; 2 Peter 2:5.

remember God's promise to Noah to keep him safe. This can inspire you to trust God for deliverance in the judgment that is sure to come.

Gen 7:1ff Pairs of every animal joined Noah in the boat; seven pairs were taken of those animals used for sacrifice. It has been estimated that almost 45,000 animals could have fit into the boat.

Gen 7:16 Many have wondered how this animal-kingdom roundup happened. Did Noah and his sons spend years collecting all the animals? But the Creation, along with Noah, was doing just as God had commanded. There seemed to be no problem gathering the animals—God took care of the details of that job while Noah was doing his part by building the boat. Often we do just the opposite of Noah. We worry about details over which we have no control, while neglecting specific areas (such as attitudes, relationships, responsibilities) that *are* under our control. Like Noah, concentrate on what God has given you to do, and leave the rest to God.

Gen 7:17-24 Was the Flood a local event, or did it cover the entire earth? A universal flood was certainly possible. Enough water exists in the oceans to cover all dry land (the earth began that way; see Gen 1:9-10). Afterward God promised never again to destroy the earth with a flood. Thus, this flood must have either covered the entire earth or destroyed all the inhabitants of the earth. Remember, God's reason for sending the Flood was to destroy all the earth's wickedness. It would have taken a major flood to accomplish this.

▸ **GENESIS 8:1-22 *(cont.)***
of Ararat. 5Two and a half months later,* as the waters continued to go down, other mountain peaks
became visible.
6After another forty days, Noah opened the window
he had made in the boat 7and released a raven. The
bird flew back and forth until the floodwaters on the
earth had dried up. 8He also released a dove to see if
the water had receded and it could find dry ground.
9But the dove could find no place to land because
the water still covered the ground. So it returned to
the boat, and Noah held out his hand and drew the
dove back inside. 10After waiting another seven days,
Noah released the dove again. 11This time the dove
returned to him in the evening with a fresh olive leaf
in its beak. Then Noah knew that the floodwaters
were almost gone. 12He waited another seven days
and then released the dove again. This time it did
not come back.
13Noah was now 601 years old. On the first day of
the new year, ten and a half months after the flood
began,* the floodwaters had almost dried up from
the earth. Noah lifted back the covering of the boat
and saw that the surface of the ground was drying.
14Two more months went by,* and at last the earth
was dry!
15Then God said to Noah, 16"Leave the boat, all
of you—you and your wife, and your sons and their
wives. 17Release all the animals—the birds, the livestock, and the small animals that scurry along the
ground—so they can be fruitful and multiply throughout the earth."
18So Noah, his wife, and his sons and their wives left
the boat. 19And all of the large and small animals and
birds came out of the boat, pair by pair.
20Then Noah built an altar to the LORD, and there
he sacrificed as burnt offerings the animals and
birds that had been approved for that purpose.*
21And the LORD was pleased with the aroma of the
sacrifice and said to himself, "I will never again curse
the ground because of the human race, even though
everything they think or imagine is bent toward evil
from childhood. I will never again destroy all living
things. 22As long as the earth remains, there will be
planting and harvest, cold and heat, summer and
winter, day and night."

Gn 8:5 Hebrew *On the first day of the tenth month;* see 7:11 and note on 8:4. **Gn 8:13** Hebrew *On the first day of the first month;* see 7:11. **Gn 8:14** Hebrew *The twenty-seventh day of the second month arrived;* see note on 8:13. **Gn 8:20** Hebrew *every clean animal and every clean bird.*

2. REPOPULATING THE EARTH

After the destruction of the Flood, God renewed his covenant with humanity through Noah and his family, promising never again to submit the earth to judgment through a catastrophic flood. All of the nations of earth descend from Noah and his sons.

God Confirms His Covenant

GENESIS 9:1-17
Then God blessed Noah and his sons and told them,
"Be fruitful and multiply. Fill the earth. 2All the animals
of the earth, all the birds of the sky, all the small animals
that scurry along the ground, and all the fish in the
sea will look on you with fear and terror. I have placed
them in your power. 3I have given them to you for food,
just as I have given you grain and vegetables. 4But you
must never eat any meat that still has the lifeblood in it.

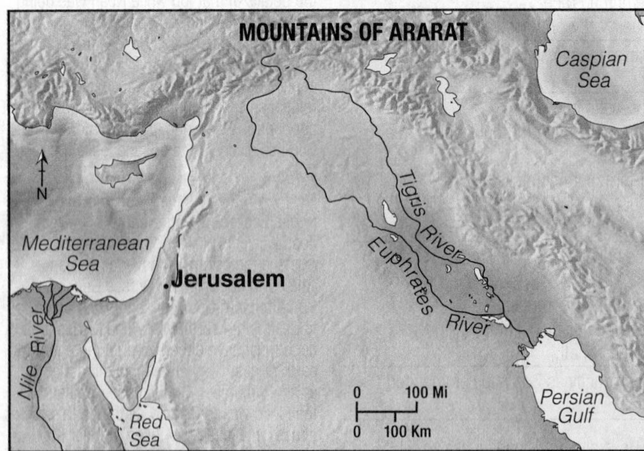

***MOUNTAINS OF ARARAT** Noah's boat touched land in the mountains of Ararat, located in modern-day Turkey. There it rested for almost eight months before Noah, his family, and the animals stepped onto dry land.*

Gen 8:6-16 Occasionally Noah would send a bird out to test the earth and see if it was dry. But Noah didn't get out of the boat until God told him to. He was waiting for God's timing. God knew that even though the water was gone, the earth was not dry enough for Noah and his family to venture out. What patience Noah showed, especially after spending an entire year inside his boat! We, like Noah, must trust God to give us patience during those difficult times when we must wait.

Gen 8:21-22 Countless times throughout the Bible we see God showing his love and patience toward men and women in order to save them. Although he realizes that their hearts are evil, he continues to reach out to them. When we sin or fall away from God, we surely deserve to be destroyed by his judgment. But God has promised never again to destroy everything on earth until the judgment day when Christ returns to destroy evil forever. Now every change of season is a reminder of his promise.

[5]"And I will require the blood of anyone who takes another person's life. If a wild animal kills a person, it must die. And anyone who murders a fellow human must die. [6]If anyone takes a human life, that person's life will also be taken by human hands. For God made human beings* in his own image. [7]Now be fruitful and multiply, and repopulate the earth."

[8]Then God told Noah and his sons, [9]"I hereby confirm my covenant with you and your descendants, [10]and with all the animals that were on the boat with you—the birds, the livestock, and all the wild animals—every living creature on earth. [11]Yes, I am confirming my covenant with you. Never again will floodwaters kill all living creatures; never again will a flood destroy the earth."

[12]Then God said, "I am giving you a sign of my covenant with you and with all living creatures, for all generations to come. [13]I have placed my rainbow in the clouds. It is the sign of my covenant with you and with all the earth. [14]When I send clouds over the earth, the rainbow will appear in the clouds, [15]and I will remember my covenant with you and with all living creatures. Never again will the floodwaters destroy all life. [16]When I see the rainbow in the clouds, I will remember the eternal covenant between God and every living creature on earth."

Gn 9:6 Or *man;* Hebrew reads *ha-adam.*

[17]Then God said to Noah, "Yes, this rainbow is the sign of the covenant I am confirming with all the creatures on earth."

Noah's Sons

GENESIS 9:18–10:1

The sons of Noah who came out of the boat with their father were Shem, Ham, and Japheth. (Ham is the father of Canaan.) [19]From these three sons of Noah came all the people who now populate the earth.

[20]After the flood, Noah began to cultivate the ground, and he planted a vineyard. [21]One day he drank some wine he had made, and he became drunk and lay naked inside his tent. [22]Ham, the father of Canaan, saw that his father was naked and went outside and told his brothers. [23]Then Shem and Japheth took a robe, held it over their shoulders, and backed into the tent to cover their father. As they did this, they looked the other way so they would not see him naked.

[24]When Noah woke up from his stupor, he learned what Ham, his youngest son, had done. [25]Then he cursed Canaan, the son of Ham:

"May Canaan be cursed!
May he be the lowest of servants to his
relatives."

Gen 9:5 God will require each person to account for his or her actions. We cannot harm or kill another human being without answering to God. A penalty must be paid. Justice will be served.

Gen 9:5-6 Here God explains why murder is so wrong: To kill a person is to kill one made in God's image. Because all human beings are made in God's image, all people possess the qualities that distinguish them from animals: morality, reason, creativity, and self-worth. When we interact with others, we are interacting with beings made by God, beings to whom God offers eternal life. God wants us to recognize his image in all people.

Gen 9:8-17 Noah stepped out of the boat onto an earth devoid of human life. But God gave him a reassuring promise. This covenant had three parts: (1) Never again will a flood do such destruction; (2) as long as the earth remains, the seasons will always come as expected; (3) a rainbow will be visible when it rains as a sign to all that God will keep his promises. The earth's order and seasons are still preserved, and rainbows still remind us of God's faithfulness to his word.

Gen 9:20-27 Noah, the great hero of faith, got drunk—a poor example of godliness to his sons. Perhaps this story is included to show us that even godly people can sin and that their bad choice affects their families. Although the ungodly people had all been killed, the possibility of evil still existed in the hearts of Noah and his family. Ham's mocking attitude revealed a severe lack of respect for his father and for God.

Gen 9:25 This verse has been wrongfully used to support racial prejudice and even slavery. But Noah's curse wasn't directed toward any particular race; rather, it was directed at the Canaanite nation—a nation God knew would become wicked. The curse was fulfilled when the Israelites entered the Promised Land and drove the Canaanites out (see the book of Joshua).

"When I see the rainbow in the clouds, I will remember the eternal covenant between God and every living creature on earth."
Genesis 9:16

▸ **GENESIS 9:18–10:1 *(cont.)***
26 Then Noah said,

"May the Lord, the God of Shem, be blessed,
and may Canaan be his servant!
27 May God expand the territory of Japheth!
May Japheth share the prosperity of Shem,*
and may Canaan be his servant."

28 Noah lived another 350 years after the great
flood. 29 He lived 950 years, and then he died.

10:1 This is the account of the families of Shem, Ham,
and Japheth, the three sons of Noah. Many children
were born to them after the great flood.

Descendants of Japheth

GENESIS 10:2-5
2 The descendants of Japheth were Gomer, Magog,
Madai, Javan, Tubal, Meshech, and Tiras.
3 The descendants of Gomer were Ashkenaz,
Riphath, and Togarmah.
4 The descendants of Javan were Elishah, Tarshish,
Kittim, and Rodanim.* 5 Their descendants
became the seafaring peoples that spread out
to various lands, each identified by its own
language, clan, and national identity.

2630 BC

Great Pyramid of Egypt constructed

Descendants of Ham

GENESIS 10:6-20
6 The descendants of Ham were Cush, Mizraim, Put,
and Canaan.
7 The descendants of Cush were Seba, Havilah,
Sabtah, Raamah, and Sabteca. The descendants
of Raamah were Sheba and Dedan.
8 Cush was also the ancestor of Nimrod, who
was the first heroic warrior on earth. 9 Since
he was the greatest hunter in the world,* his
name became proverbial. People would say,
"This man is like Nimrod, the greatest hunter
in the world." 10 He built his kingdom in the
land of Babylonia,* with the cities of Babylon,
Erech, Akkad, and Calneh. 11 From there he
expanded his territory to Assyria,* building
the cities of Nineveh, Rehoboth-ir, Calah, 12 and
Resen (the great city located between Nineveh
and Calah).
13 Mizraim was the ancestor of the Ludites,
Anamites, Lehabites, Naphtuhites, 14 Pathrusites,
Casluhites, and the Caphtorites, from whom the
Philistines came.*
15 Canaan's oldest son was Sidon, the ancestor of
the Sidonians. Canaan was also the ancestor of
the Hittites,* 16 Jebusites, Amorites, Girgashites,
17 Hivites, Arkites, Sinites, 18 Arvadites, Zemarites,
and Hamathites. The Canaanite clans eventually
spread out, 19 and the territory of Canaan
extended from Sidon in the north to Gerar and
Gaza in the south, and east as far as Sodom,
Gomorrah, Admah, and Zeboiim, near Lasha.
20 These were the descendants of Ham, identified by
clan, language, territory, and national identity.

Descendants of Shem

GENESIS 10:21-31
21 Sons were also born to Shem, the older brother
of Japheth.* Shem was the ancestor of all the
descendants of Eber.
22 The descendants of Shem were Elam, Asshur,
Arphaxad, Lud, and Aram.
23 The descendants of Aram were Uz, Hul, Gether,
and Mash.
24 Arphaxad was the father of Shelah,* and Shelah
was the father of Eber.
25 Eber had two sons. The first was named Peleg
(which means "division"), for during his lifetime
the people of the world were divided into
different language groups. His brother's name
was Joktan.
26 Joktan was the ancestor of Almodad, Sheleph,
Hazarmaveth, Jerah, 27 Hadoram, Uzal, Diklah,
28 Obal, Abimael, Sheba, 29 Ophir, Havilah, and

Gn 9:27 Hebrew *May he live in the tents of Shem.* **Gn 10:4** As in some Hebrew manuscripts and Greek version (see also 1 Chr 1:7); most Hebrew manuscripts read *Dodanim.* **Gn 10:9** Hebrew *a great hunter before the Lord;* also in 10:9b. **Gn 10:10** Hebrew *Shinar.* **Gn 10:11** Or *From that land Assyria went out.* **Gn 10:14** Hebrew *Casluhites, from whom the Philistines came, and Caphtorites.* Compare Jer 47:4; Amos 9:7. **Gn 10:15** Hebrew *ancestor of Heth.* **Gn 10:21** Or *Shem, whose older brother was Japheth.* **Gn 10:24** Greek version reads *Arphaxad was the father of Cainan, Cainan was the father of Shelah.* Compare Luke 3:36.

Gen 10:8-9 Who was Nimrod? Not much is known about him except that he was a heroic warrior. But people with great gifts can become proud, and that is probably what happened to Nimrod. Some consider him the founder of the great, godless Babylonian Empire.

BIBLE NATIONS DESCENDED FROM NOAH'S SONS

Shem's descendants were called Semites. Abraham, David, and Jesus descended from Shem. Ham's descendants settled in Canaan, Egypt, and the rest of Africa. Japheth's descendants settled for the most part in Europe and Asia Minor.

Shem	*Ham*	*Japheth*
Hebrews	Canaanites	Greeks
Chaldeans	Egyptians	Thracians
Assyrians	Philistines	Scythians
Persians	Hittites	
Arameans (Syrians)	Amorites	

Jobab. All these were descendants of Joktan.
30The territory they occupied extended from
Mesha all the way to Sephar in the eastern
mountains.
31These were the descendants of Shem, identified by clan, language, territory, and national identity.

Conclusion

GENESIS 10:32

These are the clans that descended from Noah's sons, arranged by nation according to their lines of descent. All the nations of the earth descended from these clans after the great flood.

3. SCATTERING THE PEOPLE

People continued to rebel against God, but their efforts were thwarted by the confusion of their languages. This marks the beginning of different languages and cultures as the people scattered all over the world and began to develop their own customs.

The Tower of Babel

GENESIS 11:1-9

At one time all the people of the world spoke the same language and used the same words. 2As the people migrated to the east, they found a plain in the land of Babylonia* and settled there.

3They began saying to each other, "Let's make bricks and harden them with fire." (In this region bricks were used instead of stone, and tar was used for mortar.) 4Then they said, "Come, let's build a great city for ourselves with a tower that reaches into the sky. This will make us famous and keep us from being scattered all over the world."

5But the LORD came down to look at the city and the tower the people were building. 6"Look!" he said. "The people are united, and they all speak the same language. After this, nothing they set out to do will be impossible for them! 7Come, let's go down and confuse the people with different languages. Then they won't be able to understand each other."

8In that way, the LORD scattered them all over the world, and they stopped building the city. 9That is why the city was called Babel,* because that is where the LORD confused the people with different languages. In this way he scattered them all over the world.

From Shem to Abram

GENESIS 11:10-26

This is the account of Shem's family.

Two years after the great flood, when Shem
was 100 years old, he became the father of*
Arphaxad. 11After the birth of* Arphaxad, Shem
lived another 500 years and had other sons
and daughters.
12When Arphaxad was 35 years old, he became
the father of Shelah. 13After the birth of Shelah,

Gn 11:2 Hebrew *Shinar.* **Gn 11:9** Or *Babylon. Babel* sounds like a Hebrew term that means "confusion." **Gn 11:10** Or *the ancestor of;* also in 11:12, 14, 16, 18, 20, 22, 24. **Gn 11:11** Or *the birth of this ancestor of;* also in 11:13, 15, 17, 19, 21, 23, 25.

Gen 11:3 The brick used to build this tower was man-made and not as hard as stone.

Gen 11:3-4 The tower of Babel was most likely a ziggurat, a common structure in Babylonia at this time. Most often built as temples, ziggurats looked like pyramids with steps or ramps leading up the sides. Ziggurats stood as high as 300 feet and were often just as wide; thus they were the focal point of the city. The people in this story built their tower as a monument to their own greatness, something for the whole world to see.

Gen 11:4 The tower of Babel was a great human achievement, a wonder of the world. But it was a monument to the people themselves rather than to God. We may build monuments to ourselves (expensive clothes, big house, fancy car, important job) to call attention to our achievements. These may not be wrong in themselves, but when we use them to give ourselves identity and self-worth, they take God's place in our lives. We are free to develop in many areas, but we are not free to think we have replaced God. What "towers" have you built in your life?

Gen 11:10-27 Here, and in Genesis 10:22-31, appears a list of Shem's descendants, who were blessed (Gen 9:26). Because of that blessing, from Shem's line came Abram and the entire Jewish nation, which would eventually conquer the land of Canaan in the days of Joshua.

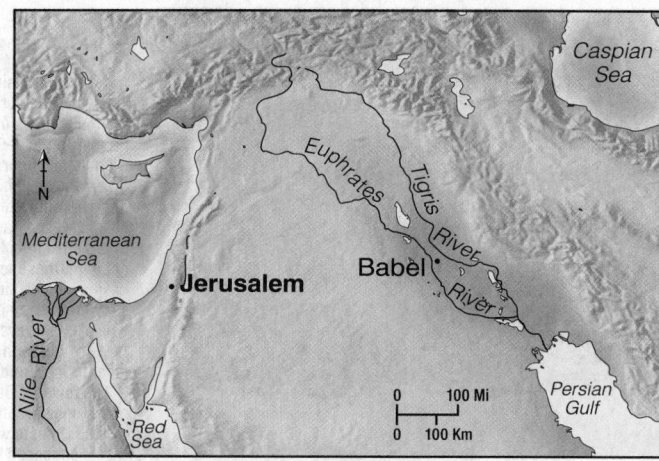

THE TOWER OF BABEL *The plain between the Tigris and Euphrates rivers offered a perfect location for the city and tower "that reaches into the sky" (Gen 11:4).*

▸ **GENESIS 11:10-26** ***(cont.)***

Arphaxad lived another 403 years and had other
sons and daughters.*
14When Shelah was 30 years old, he became the
father of Eber. 15After the birth of Eber, Shelah
lived another 403 years and had other sons
and daughters.
16When Eber was 34 years old, he became the
father of Peleg. 17After the birth of Peleg, Eber
lived another 430 years and had other sons
and daughters.
18When Peleg was 30 years old, he became the
father of Reu. 19After the birth of Reu, Peleg
lived another 209 years and had other sons
and daughters.
20When Reu was 32 years old, he became the
father of Serug. 21After the birth of Serug, Reu
lived another 207 years and had other sons
and daughters.
22When Serug was 30 years old, he became the
father of Nahor. 23After the birth of Nahor, Serug
lived another 200 years and had other sons
and daughters.
24When Nahor was 29 years old, he became the
father of Terah. 25After the birth of Terah, Nahor
lived another 119 years and had other sons and
daughters.
26After Terah was 70 years old, he became the father
of Abram, Nahor, and Haran.

The Family of Terah

GENESIS 11:27-32

This is the account of Terah's family. Terah was the
father of Abram, Nahor, and Haran; and Haran was the
father of Lot. 28But Haran died in Ur of the Chaldeans,
the land of his birth, while his father, Terah, was still
living. 29Meanwhile, Abram and Nahor both married.
The name of Abram's wife was Sarai, and the name of
Nahor's wife was Milcah. (Milcah and her sister Iscah
were daughters of Nahor's brother Haran.) 30But Sarai
was unable to become pregnant and had no children.
31One day Terah took his son Abram, his daughter-
in-law Sarai (his son Abram's wife), and his grandson
Lot (his son Haran's child) and moved away from
Ur of the Chaldeans. He was headed for the land
of Canaan, but they stopped at Haran and settled
there. 32Terah lived for 205 years* and died while
still in Haran.

Gn 11:12-13 Greek version reads *12When Arphaxad was 135 years old, he became the father of Cainan. 13After the birth of Cainan, Arphaxad lived another 430 years and had other sons and daughters, and then he died. When Cainan was 130 years old, he became the father of Shelah. After the birth of Shelah, Cainan lived another 330 years and had other sons and daughters, and then he died.* Compare Luke 3:35-36. **Gn 11:32** Some ancient versions read *145 years;* compare 11:26 and 12:4.

Gen 11:27-28 Abram grew up in Ur of the Chaldeans, an important city in the ancient world. Archaeologists have discovered evidence of a flourishing civilization there in Abram's day. The city carried on an extensive trade with its neighbors and had a vast library. Growing up in Ur, Abram was probably well educated.

Gen 11:31 Terah left Ur to go to Canaan but settled in Haran instead. Why did he stop halfway? It may have been his health, the climate, or even fear. But this did not change Abram's calling ("the LORD had said to Abram," Gen 12:1). He had respect for his father's leadership, but when Terah died, Abram moved on to Canaan. God's will may come in stages. Just as the time in Haran was a transition period for Abram, so God may give us transition periods and times of waiting to help us depend on him and trust his timing. If we patiently do his will during the transition times, we will be better prepared to serve him as we should when he calls us.

Ziggurat

A ziggurat was similar to the step pyramid of Egypt and was used for worship. Ziggurats were often built in the major cities of ancient Mesopotamia. The tower of Babel (Gen 11:1-9) is thought to have been a particularly prominent ziggurat. It was widely believed that deities dwelt above, in high places. Therefore, worship was more appropriate on hills or mountains. There are no hills in Mesopotamia, so the people there built ziggurats to provide high places to worship. Like the pyramids of Egypt, these temple towers were square. Instead of having sloping sides, there was a succession of terraces, each smaller than the one below. Access to each level was by stairways or ramps. The shrine or altar was at the top, where the priests would officiate at sacrifices, incantations, and prayers.

The tower of Babel, however, was built as a monument to the greatness of the people who were building it rather than to worship God. It is easy to turn something that is supposed to be about God into a celebration of ourselves. How can we ensure that we are truly worshiping God rather than doing great things for our own glory?

NAMES OF GOD

Name of God	*Meaning*	*Reference*	*Significance*
Elohim	God	Gen 1:1; Num 23:19; Ps 19:1	Refers to God's power and might. He is the only supreme and true God.
Yahweh	The LORD	Gen 2:4; Exod 6:2-3	The proper name of the divine person.
El Elyon	God Most High	Gen 14:17-20; Num 24:16; Ps 7:17; Isa 14:13-14	He is above all gods; nothing in life is more sacred.
El Roi	God Who Sees	Gen 16:13	God oversees all creation and the affairs of people.
El Shaddai	God Almighty	Gen 17:1; Ps 91:1	God is all-powerful.
Yahweh Yireh	The LORD Will Provide	Gen 22:13-14	God will provide our real needs.
Yahweh Nissi	The LORD Is My Banner	Exod 17:15	We should remember God for helping us.
Adonai	Lord	Gen 18:27	God alone is the head over all.
Yahweh Elohe Yisrael	LORD God of Israel	Judg 5:3; Ps 59:5; Isa 17:6; Zeph 2:9	He is the God of the nation.
Yahweh Shalom	The LORD Is Peace	Judg 6:24	God gives us peace so we need not fear.
Qedosh Yisrael	Holy One of Israel	Isa 1:4	God is morally perfect.
Yahweh Sabaoth	LORD of Hosts (*Hosts* refers to armies but also to all the heavenly powers.)	1 Sam 1:3; Isa 6:1-3	God is our savior and protector.
El Olam	The Everlasting God	Isa 40:28-31	God is eternal. He will never die.
Yahweh Tsidkenu	The LORD Our Righteousness	Jer 23:6; 33:16	God is our standard for right behavior. He alone can make us righteous.
Yahweh Shammah	The LORD Is There	Ezek 48:35	God is always present with us.
Attiq Yomin	Ancient of Days	Dan 7:9, 13	God is the ultimate authority. He will one day judge all nations.

God's Chosen Family

GOD'S PERFECT CREATION had been marred by sin. Even with a new beginning after the Flood, humanity continued to rebel against God. The incident with the tower of Babel is just one example of how people were following other gods and pursuing their own glory.

God broke into his creation once again and spoke to one man, asking him to leave the things that the world was offering him behind and go to a new place in complete reliance on God. God promised Abram that he would make him into a great nation and that he would use him to bless the entire world. Abram heard the voice of God and responded in faith. He left the city where he had grown up and traveled across the known world to settle in the land that God showed him.

Abram received a new name, Abraham, and in his story we discover the beginning of God's covenant people and the broad strokes of his salvation plan: Salvation comes by faith, Abraham's descendants will be God's people, and the Savior of the world will come through this chosen nation. The stories of Isaac, Jacob, and Joseph that follow are more than interesting biographies. They emphasize the promises of God and the proof that he is faithful. The people we meet in Genesis are simple, ordinary people; yet through them, God did great things. Their lives are vivid pictures of how God uses all kinds of people to accomplish his good purposes—even people like you.

TIMELINE

2200 BC | 2100 BC | 2000 BC | 1900 BC

MESOPOTAMIA

EARLY BRONZE AGE (3300–2000 BC)

2166 BC — *Abram is born*

1950 BC — *Amorite invasion of lower Mesopotamia (end of Sumerian civilization)*

CANAAN

2091 BC — *Abram travels to Canaan*

1876 BC — *Jacob moves to Egypt*

EGYPT

OLD KINGDOM/ DYNASTIES 3–8 (2700–2160 BC)

FIRST INTERMEDIATE PERIOD/ DYNASTIES 9–10 (2160–2010 BC)

MIDDLE KINGDOM/ DYNASTIES 11–12 (2106–1786 BC)

BOOKS

- GENESIS
- JOB

DATES

FROM:

2100 BC

TO:

1800 BC

THEMES

- Promises
- God's Faithfulness
- Suffering

PEOPLE & CULTURE

■ **Nomadic Culture.** Although there were some great cities in the early world (such as Ur, where Abraham was born), most of the people we meet early on in the pages of the Bible were nomadic. They lived in tents, measured their wealth in livestock, and settled down temporarily in areas that were fertile enough to support their herds and family. The family was the primary social unit, and large extended families would travel together along with their servants, effectively forming tribes and villages when they settled. Sometimes families would be forced to move to a new area due to famine, seasonal weather changes, or simply because they outgrew their land.

■ **Abraham.** Born as Abram in the cultural center of Ur, he followed God's command to move to the land of Canaan. Although God promised to make him into a great nation, Abraham and his wife Sarah were childless until a very old age, when God miraculously provided a son for them. Abraham was faithful to God, but he was far from perfect. He lied at least twice about the identity of his wife, he had a child with his wife's servant in an effort to speed up God's plan, and his later treatment of Ishmael and Hagar was less than admirable. In spite of these failures, God chose Abraham to be the father of his chosen nation.

■ **Jacob.** Jacob was one of two grandsons of Abraham. Working with his mother, Rebekah, he deceived his father, Isaac, into giving the blessing of the firstborn to him instead of his twin brother, Esau. But like his grandfather Abraham, and in spite of his flaws, Jacob was the one God chose to fulfill his promise to bless the entire world. His twelve sons became the leaders of the twelve tribes of Israel, and his son Joseph was used by God to save the people of Egypt as well as his own family from a devastating famine.

■ **Job.** Job was a prosperous farmer living in the land of Uz. We don't know the precise location of Uz or when Job may have lived. But the way Job's family, wealth, and religious practices are described seem to indicate that he lived around the time of the patriarchs (Abraham, Isaac, and Jacob). He lost everything that mattered to him and was struck with painful sores, but he remained faithful to God in spite of his suffering.

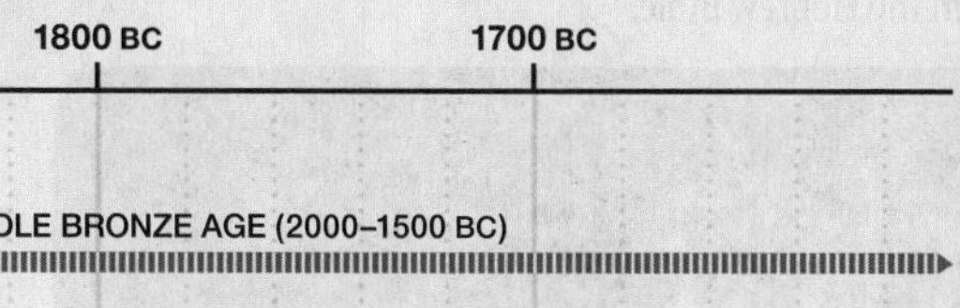

MEGATHEMES

■ **Promises.** God makes promises to help and protect people. This kind of promise is called a "covenant." God's covenant with Abraham involved making him into a great nation that would become a blessing to all nations. God kept his promises then, and he keeps them now. He promises to love us, accept us, and forgive us.

■ **Obedience and Disobedience.** Disobedience separates us from God, but obeying him restores our relationship with him. God uses sinful people in his plan, but the only way to enjoy the benefits of God's promises is to turn from sin and obey him.

■ **Israel.** God founded the nation of Israel in order to have a dedicated people who would teach the world about him and prepare the world for the birth of his Son, Jesus. God is looking for people today to follow him as well. We are to proclaim God's truth and love to all nations. We must be faithful to carry out the mission God has given us.

■ **Suffering.** Through no fault of his own, Job lost his wealth, children, and health. Even his friends were convinced that Job had brought this suffering upon himself. For Job, the greatest trial was not the pain of the loss; rather, it was not being able to understand why God allowed him to suffer. Those who love God are not exempt from trouble. Although we may not be able to understand fully the reasons for the pain we experience, it can lead us to rediscover God.

■ **God's Goodness.** God is all-wise, all-powerful, and all-loving. His will is perfect, yet he doesn't always act in ways that we understand. Abraham and Sarah didn't understand why they weren't able to have children when they were of normal child-bearing age, but they trusted God's promise and were blessed with a son. Job's suffering didn't make sense to him; but when God spoke to him, he saw God's power and wisdom. God is never insensitive to our suffering, even if it feels like we are alone and he is far away. Because God is sufficient, we must hold on to him.

BOOKS IN THIS SECTION

GENESIS

AUTHOR: Moses

AUDIENCE: The people of Israel

PURPOSE: To record God's creation of the world and his desire to have people worship him

DATE WRITTEN: Approximately 1450–1410 B.C.

WHERE WRITTEN: In the wilderness during Israel's wanderings, somewhere in the Sinai Peninsula

JOB

AUTHOR: Unknown

PURPOSE: To demonstrate God's sovereignty. It addresses the question, "Why do the righteous suffer?"

DATE WRITTEN: Unknown. Seems to record events that take place around the time of the patriarchs, approximately 2000–1800 B.C.

SETTING: The land of Uz, possibly located northeast of Palestine, near the desert land between Damascus and the Euphrates River

SPECIAL FEATURES: Job is the first of the poetic books in the Hebrew Bible.

An early engraving by William Blake for the Book of Job

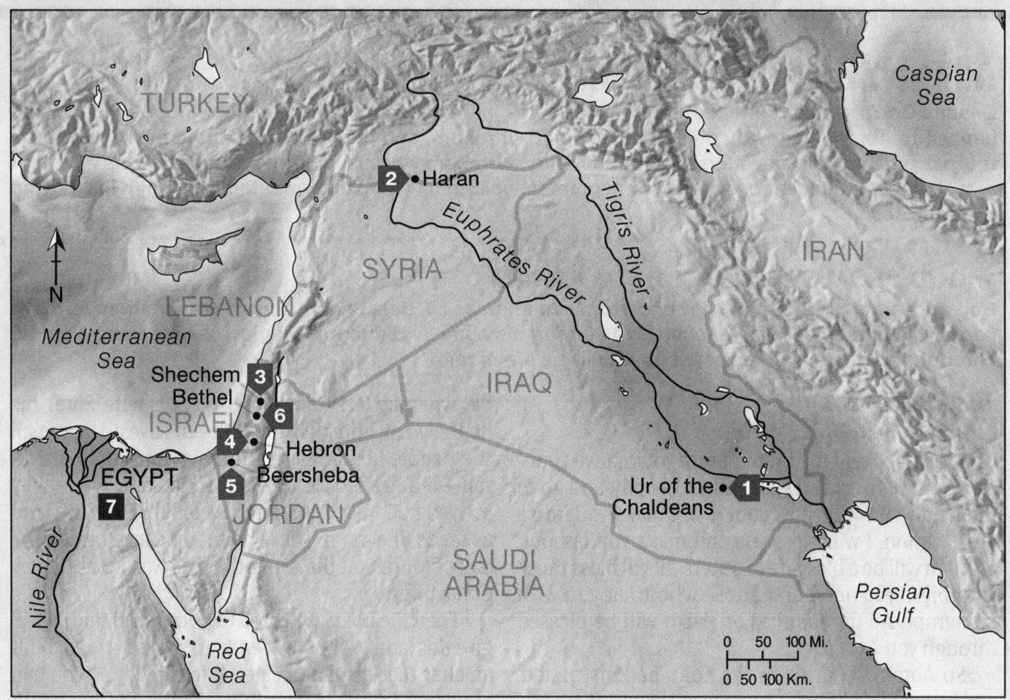

MAP

1 Ur of the Chaldeans Abram, a descendant of Shem and the father of the Hebrew nation, was born in this great city (Gen 11:27-28).

2 Haran Terah, Abram, Lot, and Sarai left Ur and, following the fertile crescent of the Euphrates River, headed toward the land of Canaan. Along the way, they settled in the village of Haran for a while (Gen 11:31).

3 Shechem God urged Abram to leave Haran and go to a place where he would become the father of a great nation (Gen 12:1-2). So Abram, Lot, and Sarai traveled to the land of Canaan and settled near a city called Shechem (Gen 12:6).

4 Hebron Abram moved on to Hebron where he put down his deepest roots (Gen 13:18). Abraham, Isaac, and Jacob all lived and were buried here.

5 Beersheba The well at Beersheba was a source of conflict between Abraham and King Abimelech and later became a sign of the oath that they swore here (Gen 21:31). Years later, as Isaac was moving from place to place, God appeared to him here and passed on to him the covenant he had made with his father, Abraham (Gen 26:23-25).

6 Bethel After deceiving his brother, Jacob left Beersheba and fled to Haran. Along the way, God revealed himself to Jacob in a dream and passed on the covenant he had made with Abraham and Isaac (Gen 28:10-22). Jacob lived in Haran, worked for Laban, and married Leah and Rachel (Gen 29:15-30). After a tense meeting with his brother, Esau, Jacob returned to Bethel (Gen 35:1).

7 Egypt Jacob had 12 sons, including Joseph, Jacob's favorite. Joseph's 10 older brothers grew jealous, until one day the brothers sold him to Ishmaelite traders going to Egypt. Eventually, Joseph rose from Egyptian slave to Pharaoh's right-hand man, saving Egypt from famine. His entire family moved from Canaan to Egypt and settled here (Gen 46:3-7).

A. The Story of Abraham

Despite God's swift judgment of sin, most people ignored him and continued to sin. But God revealed himself to Abram, who would later be renamed Abraham, and chose to use Abraham's family to be the instrument of his salvation plan for humanity. Abraham was not chosen because he was a perfect man; in fact, his life demonstrated some great flaws. But he also demonstrated great faith in God and his promises.

1. GOD PROMISES A NATION TO ABRAM

God appeared to Abram one day and promised to make his descendants into a great nation. Abram's part of the agreement was to obey God, leaving his homeland and traveling across the known world. Through this section we discover how to live a life of faith.

The Call of Abram

GENESIS 12:1-9

The LORD had said to Abram, "Leave your native country, your relatives, and your father's family, and go to
the land that I will show you. 2I will make you into a
great nation. I will bless you and make you famous,
and you will be a blessing to others. 3I will bless those
who bless you and curse those who treat you with
contempt. All the families on earth will be blessed
through you."
4So Abram departed as the LORD had instructed,
and Lot went with him. Abram was seventy-five years
old when he left Haran. 5He took his wife, Sarai, his
nephew Lot, and all his wealth—his livestock and all
the people he had taken into his household at Haran—and headed for the land of Canaan. When they
arrived in Canaan, 6Abram traveled through the land
as far as Shechem. There he set up camp beside the
oak of Moreh. At that time, the area was inhabited by
Canaanites.
7Then the LORD appeared to Abram and said, "I will
give this land to your descendants.*" And Abram built
an altar there and dedicated it to the LORD, who had
appeared to him. 8After that, Abram traveled south

Gn 12:7 Hebrew *seed.*

Abram travels to Canaan

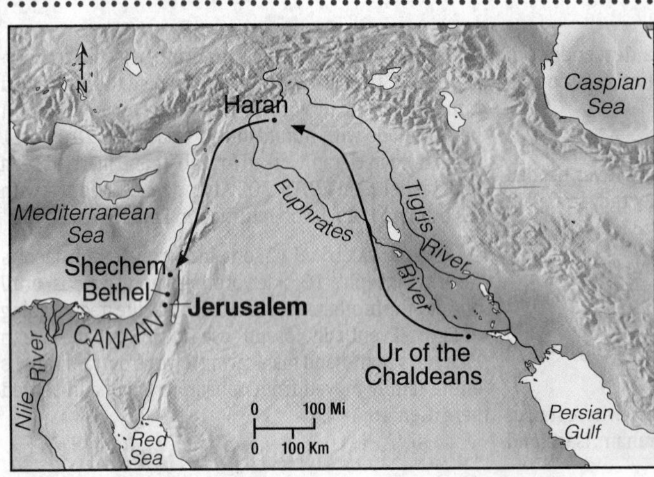

ABRAM'S JOURNEY TO CANAAN *Abram, Sarai, and Lot traveled from Ur of the Chaldeans to Canaan by way of Haran. Though indirect, this route followed the rivers rather than attempting to cross the vast desert.*

Gen 12:1-3 When God called him, Abram moved out in faith from Ur to Haran and finally to Canaan. God then established a covenant with Abram, telling him that he would be the founder of a great nation. Not only would this nation be blessed, God said, but the other nations of the earth would be blessed through Abram's descendants. Israel, the nation that would come from Abram, was to follow God and influence those with whom it came in contact. Through Abram's family tree, Jesus Christ was born to save humanity. Through Christ, people can have a personal relationship with God and be blessed beyond measure.

Gen 12:2 God promised to bless Abram and make him famous, but God had one condition: Abram had to do what God wanted him to do. This meant leaving his home and friends and traveling to a new land where God promised to build a great nation from Abram's family. Abram obeyed, walking away from his home for God's promise of even greater blessings in the future. God may be trying to lead you to a place of greater service and usefulness for him. Don't let the comfort and security of your present position make you miss God's plan for you.

Gen 12:5 God planned to develop a nation of people he would call his own. He called Abram from the godless, self-centered city of Ur to a fertile region called Canaan, where a God-centered, moral nation could be established. Though small in dimension, the land of Canaan was the focal point for most of the history of Israel as well as for the rise of Christianity. This small land given to one man, Abram, has had a tremendous impact on world history.

Gen 12:7 Abram built an altar to the Lord. Altars were used in many religions, but for God's people, altars were more than places of sacrifice; they symbolized communion with God and commemorated notable encounters with him. Built of rough stones and earth, altars often remained in place for years as continual reminders of God's protection and promises.

Abram regularly built altars to God for two reasons: (1) for prayer and worship, and (2) as reminders of God's promise to bless him. Abram couldn't survive spiritually without regularly renewing his love and loyalty to God. Building altars helped Abram remember that God was at the center of his life. Regular worship helps us remember what God desires and motivates us to obey him.

and set up camp in the hill country, with Bethel to the west and Ai to the east. There he built another altar and dedicated it to the LORD, and he worshiped the LORD. 9Then Abram continued traveling south by stages toward the Negev.

Abram and Sarai in Egypt

GENESIS 12:10-20

At that time a severe famine struck the land of Canaan, forcing Abram to go down to Egypt, where he lived as a foreigner. 11As he was approaching the border of Egypt, Abram said to his wife, Sarai, "Look, you are a very beautiful woman. 12When the Egyptians see you, they will say, 'This is his wife. Let's kill him; then we can have her!' 13So please tell them you are my sister. Then they will spare my life and treat me well because of their interest in you."

14And sure enough, when Abram arrived in Egypt, everyone noticed Sarai's beauty. 15When the palace officials saw her, they sang her praises to Pharaoh, their king, and Sarai was taken into his palace. 16Then Pharaoh gave Abram many gifts because of her—sheep, goats, cattle, male and female donkeys, male and female servants, and camels.

17But the LORD sent terrible plagues upon Pharaoh and his household because of Sarai, Abram's wife. 18So Pharaoh summoned Abram and accused him sharply. "What have you done to me?" he demanded.

ABRAHAM

We all know that there are consequences to our actions. What we do can set into motion a series of events that may continue long after we're gone. Unfortunately, when we are making a decision, most of us think only of the immediate consequences. These are often misleading because they are short-lived. • Abraham had a choice to make. His decision was between setting out with his family and belongings for parts unknown or staying right where he was. He had to decide between the security of what he already had and the uncertainty of traveling under God's direction. All he had to go on was God's promise to guide and bless him. Abraham could hardly have been expected to visualize how much of the future was resting on his decision of whether to go or stay, but his obedience affected the history of the world. His decision to follow God set into motion the development of the nation that God would eventually use as his own when he visited earth himself. When Jesus Christ came to earth, God's promise was fulfilled; through Abraham the entire world was blessed. • You probably don't know the long-term effects of most decisions you make. But shouldn't the fact that there will be long-term results cause you to think carefully and seek God's guidance as you make choices and take action today?

Strengths and accomplishments	• His faith pleased God • Became the founder of the Jewish nation • Was not only a caring father to his own family, but practiced hospitality to others • Was a successful and wealthy rancher • Usually avoided conflicts, but when they were unavoidable, he allowed his opponent to set the rules for settling the dispute
Weakness and mistake	• Under direct pressure, he distorted the truth
Lessons from his life	• God desires dependence, trust, and faith in him—not faith in our ability to please him • God's plan from the beginning has been to make himself known to all people
Vital statistics	• Where: Born in Ur of the Chaldeans; spent most of his life in the land of Canaan • Occupation: Wealthy livestock owner • Relatives: Brothers: Nahor and Haran. Father: Terah. Wife: Sarah. Nephew: Lot. Sons: Ishmael and Isaac. • Contemporaries: Abimelech, Melchizedek
Key verse	"And Abram believed the LORD, and the LORD counted him as righteous because of his faith" (Gen 15:6).

Abraham's story is told in Genesis 11–25. He is also mentioned in Exodus 2:24; Matthew 1:1-2; Luke 3:34; Acts 7:2-8; Romans 4; Galatians 3; Hebrews 2; 6–7; 11.

Gen 12:10 When famine struck, Abram went to Egypt where there was food. Why would God allow a famine in the land where he had just called Abram? This was a test of Abram's faith, and Abram passed. He didn't question God's leading when facing this difficulty. Many believers find that when they determine to follow God, they immediately encounter great obstacles. The next time you face such a test, don't try to second-guess what God is doing. Use the intelligence God has given you, as Abram did when he temporarily moved to Egypt, and wait for new opportunities.

Gen 12:11-13 Abram, acting out of fear, asked Sarai to tell a half-truth by saying she was his sister. She *was* his half sister (see Gen 20:12), but she was also his wife.

Abram's intent was to deceive the Egyptians. He feared that if they knew the truth, they would kill him to get Sarai. She would have been a desirable addition to Pharaoh's harem because of her wealth, beauty, and potential for political alliance. As Sarai's brother, Abram would have been given a place of honor. But as her husband, his life would be in danger because Sarai could not enter Pharaoh's harem unless Abram was dead. So Abram lost faith in God's protection, even after all God had promised him, and told a half-truth. When he lied, Abram's problems multiplied. Lying usually compounds the effects of sin.

▸ **GENESIS 12:10-20** ***(cont.)***

"Why didn't you tell me she was your wife? 19Why did you say, 'She is my sister,' and allow me to take her as my wife? Now then, here is your wife. Take her and get out of here!" 20Pharaoh ordered some of his men to escort them, and he sent Abram out of the country, along with his wife and all his possessions.

2. ABRAM AND LOT

When Abram went to Canaan, his entire family came with him—including his nephew Lot. When their families grew too large to stay together, they had to separate, and when Lot got himself in trouble God helped Abram to rescue Lot and his family.

Abram and Lot Separate

GENESIS 13:1-18

So Abram left Egypt and traveled north into the Negev, along with his wife and Lot and all that they owned. 2(Abram was very rich in livestock, silver, and gold.) 3From the Negev, they continued traveling by stages toward Bethel, and they pitched their tents between Bethel and Ai, where they had camped before. 4This was the same place where Abram had built the altar, and there he worshiped the LORD again.

5Lot, who was traveling with Abram, had also become very wealthy with flocks of sheep and goats, herds of cattle, and many tents. 6But the land could not support both Abram and Lot with all their flocks and herds living so close together. 7So disputes broke out between the herdsmen of Abram and Lot. (At that time Canaanites and Perizzites were also living in the land.)

8Finally Abram said to Lot, "Let's not allow this conflict to come between us or our herdsmen. After all, we are close relatives! 9The whole countryside is open to you. Take your choice of any section of the land you want, and we will separate. If you want the land to the left, then I'll take the land on the right. If you prefer the land on the right, then I'll go to the left."

10Lot took a long look at the fertile plains of the Jordan Valley in the direction of Zoar. The whole area was well watered everywhere, like the garden of the LORD or the beautiful land of Egypt. (This was before the LORD destroyed Sodom and Gomorrah.) 11Lot chose for himself the whole Jordan Valley to the east of them. He went there with his flocks and servants and parted company with his uncle Abram. 12So Abram settled in the land of Canaan, and Lot moved his tents to a place near Sodom and settled among the cities of the plain. 13But the people of this area were extremely wicked and constantly sinned against the LORD.

14After Lot had gone, the LORD said to Abram, "Look as far as you can see in every direction—north and south, east and west. 15I am giving all this land, as far as you can see, to you and your descendants* as a

Gn 13:15 Hebrew *seed;* also in 13:16.

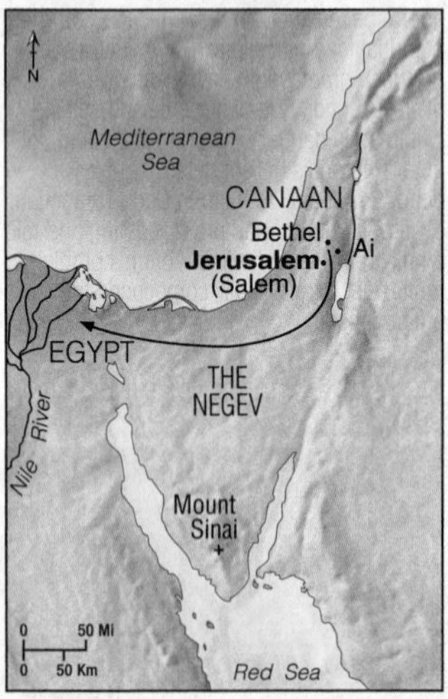

ABRAM'S JOURNEY TO EGYPT *A famine could cause the loss of a shepherd's wealth. So Abram traveled through the Negev to Egypt, where there was plenty of food and good land for his flocks.*

Gen 13:1-2 In Abram's day, sheep and cattle owners could acquire great wealth. Abram's wealth not only included silver and gold, but also livestock. These animals were a valuable commodity used for food, clothing, tent material, and sacrifices. They were often traded for other goods and services. Abram was able to watch his wealth grow and multiply daily.

Gen 13:5-9 Facing a potential conflict with his nephew Lot, Abram took the initiative in settling the dispute. He gave Lot first choice, even though Abram, being older, had the right to choose first. Abram also showed a willingness to risk being cheated. Abram's example shows us how to respond to difficult family situations: Take the initiative in resolving conflicts; let others have first choice, even if that means not getting what we want; and put family peace above personal desires.

Gen 13:7-8 Surrounded by hostile neighbors, the herdsmen of Abram and Lot should have pulled together. Instead, they let petty jealousy tear them apart. Similar situations exist today. Christians often bicker while Satan is at work all around them.

Rivalries, arguments, and disagreements among believers can be destructive in three ways: (1) They damage goodwill, trust, and peace—the foundations of good human relations; (2) they hamper progress toward important goals; (3) they make us self-centered rather than love-centered. Jesus understood how destructive arguments among brothers could be. In his prayer on the night he was betrayed and arrested, Jesus asked God that his followers be "one" (John 17:21).

Gen 13:10-11 Lot's character is revealed by his choices. He took the best share of the land even though it meant living near Sodom, a city known for its sin. He was greedy, wanting the best for himself, without thinking about his uncle Abram's needs or what was fair.

Life presents a series of choices. We, too, can choose the best while ignoring the needs and feelings of others. But this kind of choice, as Lot's life shows, leads to problems. When we stop making choices in God's direction, our only option is to make choices in the wrong direction.

Gen 13:12-13 Good pasture and available water seemed like a wise choice to Lot at first. But he failed to recognize that wicked Sodom could provide temptations strong enough to destroy his family. Have you chosen to live or work in a "Sodom"? Even though you may be strong enough to resist the temptations, other members of your family may not. While God

permanent possession. 16And I will give you so many descendants that, like the dust of the earth, they cannot be counted! 17Go and walk through the land in every direction, for I am giving it to you."

18So Abram moved his camp to Hebron and settled near the oak grove belonging to Mamre. There he built another altar to the LORD.

Abram Rescues Lot

GENESIS 14:1-16

About this time war broke out in the region. King Amraphel of Babylonia,* King Arioch of Ellasar, King Kedorlaomer of Elam, and King Tidal of Goiim 2fought against King Bera of Sodom, King Birsha of Gomorrah, King Shinab of Admah, King Shemeber of Zeboiim, and the king of Bela (also called Zoar).

3This second group of kings joined forces in Siddim Valley (that is, the valley of the Dead Sea*). 4For twelve years they had been subject to King Kedorlaomer, but in the thirteenth year they rebelled against him.

5One year later Kedorlaomer and his allies arrived and defeated the Rephaites at Ashteroth-karnaim, the Zuzites at Ham, the Emites at Shaveh-kiriathaim, 6and the Horites at Mount Seir, as far as El-paran at the edge of the wilderness. 7Then they turned back and came to En-mishpat (now called Kadesh) and conquered all the territory of the Amalekites, and also the Amorites living in Hazazon-tamar.

8Then the rebel kings of Sodom, Gomorrah, Admah, Zeboiim, and Bela (also called Zoar) prepared for battle in the valley of the Dead Sea.* 9They fought against King Kedorlaomer of Elam, King Tidal of Goiim, King Amraphel of Babylonia, and King Arioch of Ellasar—four kings against five. 10As it happened, the valley of the Dead Sea was filled with tar pits. And as the army of the kings of Sodom and Gomorrah fled, some fell into the tar pits, while the rest escaped into the mountains. 11The victorious invaders then plundered Sodom and Gomorrah and headed for home, taking with them all the spoils of war and the food supplies. 12They also captured Lot—Abram's nephew who lived in Sodom—and carried off everything he owned.

13But one of Lot's men escaped and reported everything to Abram the Hebrew, who was living near the oak grove belonging to Mamre the Amorite. Mamre and his relatives, Eshcol and Aner, were Abram's allies.

14When Abram heard that his nephew Lot had been

Gn 14:1 Hebrew *Shinar;* also in 14:9. **Gn 14:3** Hebrew *Salt Sea.* **Gn 14:8** Hebrew *Siddim Valley* (see 14:3); also in 14:10.

commands us to reach people in the "Sodom" near us, we must be careful not to become like the very people we are trying to reach.

Gen 14:4-16 Who was Kedorlaomer, and why was he important? In Abram's time, most cities had their own kings. Wars and rivalries among kings were common. A conquered city paid tribute to the victorious king. Nothing is known about Kedorlaomer except what we read in the Bible, but apparently he was quite powerful. Five cities including Sodom had paid tribute to him for 12 years. These cities formed an alliance and rebelled by withholding tribute. Kedorlaomer reacted swiftly and reconquered them all. When he defeated Sodom, he captured Lot, his family, and his possessions. Abram, with only 318 men, chased Kedorlaomer's army and attacked him near Damascus. With God's help, he defeated them and recovered Lot, his family, and their possessions.

Gen 14:12 Lot's greedy desire for the best of everything led him into sinful surroundings. His burning desire for possessions and success cost him his freedom and enjoyment. As a captive to Kedorlaomer, he faced torture, slavery, or death. In much the same way, we can be enticed into doing things or going places we shouldn't. The prosperity we long for is captivating; it can both entice us and enslave us if our motives are not in line with God's desires.

Gen 14:14-16 These incidents portray two of Abram's characteristics: (1) He had courage that came from God; facing a powerful foe, he attacked. (2) He was prepared; he had taken time to train his men for a potential conflict. We never know when we will be called upon to complete difficult tasks. Like Abram, we should prepare for those times and take courage from God when they come.

Gen 14:14-16 When Abram learned that Lot was a captive, he immediately tried to rescue his nephew. It would have been easier and safer not to become involved. But with Lot in serious trouble, Abram acted at once. Sometimes we must get involved in a messy or painful situation in order to help others. We should be willing to act immediately when others need our help.

Hebron

Hebron is still standing today, about 25 miles southwest of Jerusalem. Abraham spent much of his life in this area. It was here that Abraham built an altar to the Lord after parting from Lot (Gen 13:18). And years later, he entertained three angels in his tent here and was told of the judgment soon to fall on Sodom and Gomorrah (Gen 18). Sarah died in Hebron, and Abraham purchased the cave at Machpelah from Ephron the Hittite (Gen 23:8-9, 17-20) so that she would be buried in the land God had promised to give to Abraham and his descendants. The building in the photograph is the traditional site of the cave at Mamre in Hebron, the burial location for Abraham, Isaac, and Jacob.

Abraham trusted God's promise that this land would be given to him and his ancestors, and he took the bold step of purchasing a parcel of land to bury his wife here, rather than bringing her body back to Ur. Abraham was fully confident that God would fulfill his promise, and he wasn't afraid to act. How can you demonstrate this kind of faith in God's promises in your life?

▸ **GENESIS 14:1-16 *(cont.)***

captured, he mobilized the 318 trained men who had been born into his household. Then he pursued Kedorlaomer's army until he caught up with them at Dan. [15]There he divided his men and attacked during the night. Kedorlaomer's army fled, but Abram chased them as far as Hobah, north of Damascus. [16]Abram recovered all the goods that had been taken, and he brought back his nephew Lot with his possessions and all the women and other captives.

Melchizedek Blesses Abram

GENESIS 14:17-24

After Abram returned from his victory over Kedorlaomer and all his allies, the king of Sodom went out to meet him in the valley of Shaveh (that is, the King's Valley).

[18]And Melchizedek, the king of Salem and a priest of God Most High,* brought Abram some bread and wine. [19]Melchizedek blessed Abram with this blessing:

"Blessed be Abram by God Most High,
Creator of heaven and earth.
20 And blessed be God Most High,
who has defeated your enemies
for you."

Then Abram gave Melchizedek a tenth of all the goods he had recovered.

[21]The king of Sodom said to Abram, "Give back my people who were captured. But you may keep for yourself all the goods you have recovered."

[22]Abram replied to the king of Sodom, "I solemnly swear to the LORD, God Most High, Creator of heaven and earth, [23]that I will not take so much as a single thread or sandal thong from what belongs to you. Otherwise you might say, 'I am the one who made Abram rich.' [24]I will accept only what my young warriors have already eaten, and I request that you give a fair share of the goods to my allies—Aner, Eshcol, and Mamre."

Gn 14:18 Hebrew *El-Elyon;* also in 14:19, 20, 22.

3. GOD PROMISES A SON TO ABRAM

God had promised to make Abram into a great nation, but that could never happen if Abram died childless. Abram was getting old, and he wondered if God had another plan, but God confirmed to Abram that he would have a son to carry on the promise that God had made to him.

The LORD's Covenant Promise to Abram

GENESIS 15:1-21

Some time later, the LORD spoke to Abram in a vision and said to him, "Do not be afraid, Abram, for I will protect you, and your reward will be great."

[2]But Abram replied, "O Sovereign LORD, what good are all your blessings when I don't even have a son? Since you've given me no children, Eliezer of Damascus, a servant in my household, will inherit all my wealth. [3]You have given me no descendants of my own, so one of my servants will be my heir."

[4]Then the LORD said to him, "No, your servant will not

Gen 14:18 Who was Melchizedek? He was obviously a God-fearing man, for his name means "king of righteousness," and *king of Salem* means "king of peace." He was a "priest of God Most High" (Heb 7:1-2). He recognized God as creator of heaven and earth. What else is known about him? Four main theories have been suggested: (1) Melchizedek was a respected king of that region. Abram was simply showing him the respect he deserved. (2) The name Melchizedek may have been a standing title for all the kings of Salem. (3) Melchizedek was a "type" of Christ (Heb 7:3). A type is an Old Testament event or teaching that so closely resembles what Christ did that it illustrates a lesson about Christ. (4) Melchizedek was an appearance on earth of the preincarnate Christ in a temporary bodily form.

Gen 14:20ff Abram gave a tenth of the goods he recovered to Melchizedek. Even in some pagan religions, it was traditional to give a tenth of one's earnings to the gods. Abram followed accepted tradition; however, he refused to take any of the recovered goods from the king of Sodom. Even though this huge amount would significantly increase what he could have given to God, he chose to reject it for more important reasons—he didn't want the ungodly king of Sodom to say, "I am the one who made Abram rich." Instead, Abram wanted him to say, "God has made Abram rich." In this case, accepting the gifts would have focused everyone's attention on Abram or the king of Sodom rather than on God, the giver of victory. When people look at us, they need to see what God has accomplished in our lives.

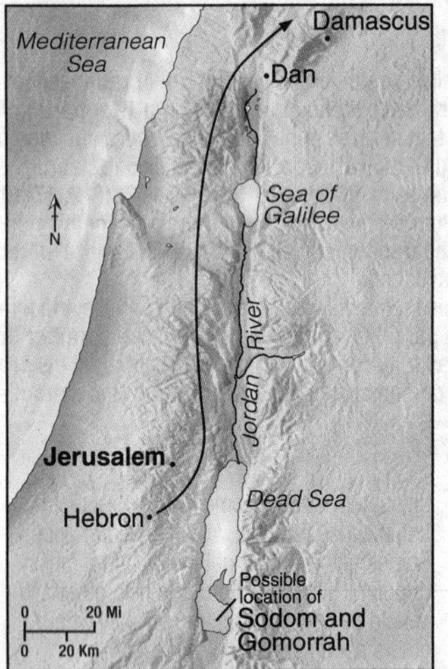

◀ ***LOT'S RESCUE** Having conquered Sodom, Kedorlaomer left for his home country, taking many captives with him. Abram learned what had happened and chased Kedorlaomer past Dan and beyond Damascus. There he defeated the king and rescued the captives, among them Lot.*

Gen 15:1 Why would Abram be afraid? Perhaps he feared revenge from the kings he had just defeated (Gen 14:15). God gave him two good reasons for courage: He promised to protect Abram, and he promised a great reward to Abram. When you fear what lies ahead, remember that God will stay with you through difficult times and that he has promised you great blessings.

Gen 15:2-3 Eliezer was Abram's most

be your heir, for you will have a son of your own who will
be your heir." 5Then the LORD took Abram outside and
said to him, "Look up into the sky and count the stars if
you can. That's how many descendants you will have!"
6And Abram believed the LORD, and the LORD
counted him as righteous because of his faith.
7Then the LORD told him, "I am the LORD who brought
you out of Ur of the Chaldeans to give you this land as
your possession."
8But Abram replied, "O Sovereign LORD, how can I
be sure that I will actually possess it?"
9The LORD told him, "Bring me a three-year-old
heifer, a three-year-old female goat, a three-year-old
ram, a turtledove, and a young pigeon." 10So Abram
presented all these to him and killed them. Then he
cut each animal down the middle and laid the halves
side by side; he did not, however, cut the birds in half.
11Some vultures swooped down to eat the carcasses,
but Abram chased them away.
12As the sun was going down, Abram fell into a deep
sleep, and a terrifying darkness came down over him.
13Then the LORD said to Abram, "You can be sure that
your descendants will be strangers in a foreign land,
where they will be oppressed as slaves for 400 years.
14But I will punish the nation that enslaves them, and
in the end they will come away with great wealth. 15(As
for you, you will die in peace and be buried at a ripe old
age.) 16After four generations your descendants will

MELCHIZEDEK

Do you like a good mystery? One of the most mysterious people in the Bible is the king of Salem, Melchizedek. He appeared one day in the life of Abraham (then Abram) and was never heard from again. But what happened that day was to be remembered throughout history and was even a subject of discussion in the New Testament letter of Hebrews. • This meeting between Abram and Melchizedek was most unusual. Although the two men were strangers, they shared a most important characteristic: Both worshiped and served the one God who made heaven and earth. • This was a great moment of triumph for Abram. He had just defeated an army and regained the freedom of his nephew Lot and many other captives. If there was any doubt about whose victory it was, Melchizedek reminded Abram, "And blessed be God Most High, who has defeated your enemies for you" (Gen 14:20). • Melchizedek was one of a small group of God-honoring people throughout the Old Testament who came in contact with the Jews (Israelites) but were not Jews themselves. This indicates that the requirement to be a follower of God is not genetic but is based on recognizing his greatness and faithfully obeying his teachings. • Do you let God speak to you through other people? In evaluating others, do you consider God's impact on their lives? Are you aware of the similarities between yourself and others who worship God, even if their form of worship is different? Do you know the God of the Bible well enough to know if you truly worship him? Allow Melchizedek, Abraham, David, and Jesus, along with many other persons in the Bible, to show you this great God, Creator of heaven and earth. He wants you to know how much he loves you; he wants you to know him personally.

Strengths and accomplishments	• The first priest/king of Scripture • Good at encouraging others to serve God wholeheartedly • His character reflected his love for God
Lesson from his life	• Live for God and you're likely to be at the right place at the right time. Examine your heart: To whom or what is your greatest loyalty? If you can honestly answer *God*, you are living for him
Vital statistics	• Where: Ruled in Salem, site of the future Jerusalem • Occupation: King of Salem and priest of God Most High
Key verses	"This Melchizedek was king of the city of Salem and also a priest of God Most High. . . . Consider then how great this Melchizedek was. Even Abraham, the great patriarch of Israel, recognized this by giving him a tenth of what he had taken in battle" (Heb 7:1, 4).

Melchizedek's story is told in Genesis 14:17-20. He is also mentioned in Psalm 110:4; Hebrews 5–7.

trusted servant, acting as household administrator. According to custom, if Abram were to die without a son, his eldest servant would become his heir. Although Abram loved his servant, he wanted a son to carry on the family line.

Gen 15:5 Abram wasn't promised wealth or fame; he already had that. Instead, God promised descendants like the stars in the sky or the grains of sand on the seashore (Gen 22:17), too numerous to count. To appreciate the vast number of stars scattered through the sky, you need to be, like Abram, away from any distractions. Or pick up a handful of sand and try to count the grains—it can't be done! Just when Abram was despairing of ever having an heir, God promised descendants too numerous to imagine. God's blessings are beyond our imagination!

Gen 15:6 Although Abram had been demonstrating his faith through his actions, it was his belief in the Lord, not his actions, that made Abram right with God (Rom 4:1-5). We, too, can have a right relationship with God by trusting him. Our outward actions—church attendance, prayer, good deeds—will not by themselves make us right with God. A right relationship is based on faith—the heartfelt inner confidence that God is who he says he is and does what he says he will do. Right actions will follow naturally as by-products.

Gen 15:8 Abram was looking for confirmation and assurance that he was doing God's will. We also want assurance when we ask for guidance. But we can know for sure that what we are doing is right if we do what the Bible says. Abram didn't have the Bible—we do.

Gen 15:13-14 The book of Exodus tells the story of the enslavement and miraculous deliverance of Abram's descendants.

Gen 15:16 The Amorites were one of the nations living in Canaan, the land God promised Abram. God knew the people would grow more wicked and would someday need to be punished. Part of that punishment would involve taking away their land and giving it to Abram's descendants. God in his mercy was giving the Amorites plenty of time to repent, but he already knew they would not. At the right time, they would have to be punished. Everything God does is true to his character. He is merciful, knows all, and acts justly—and his timing is perfect.

▸ **GENESIS 15:1-21 *(cont.)***
return here to this land, for the sins of the Amorites
do not yet warrant their destruction."
17After the sun went down and darkness fell, Abram
saw a smoking firepot and a flaming torch pass between the halves of the carcasses. 18So the LORD made
a covenant with Abram that day and said, "I have given
this land to your descendants, all the way from the
border of Egypt* to the great Euphrates River—19the
land now occupied by the Kenites, Kenizzites, Kad-
monites, 20Hittites, Perizzites, Rephaites, 21Amorites,
Canaanites, Girgashites, and Jebusites."

The Birth of Ishmael

GENESIS 16:1-16
Now Sarai, Abram's wife, had not been able to bear
children for him. But she had an Egyptian servant
named Hagar. 2So Sarai said to Abram, "The LORD has
prevented me from having children. Go and sleep with
my servant. Perhaps I can have children through her."
And Abram agreed with Sarai's proposal. 3So Sarai,
Abram's wife, took Hagar the Egyptian servant and
gave her to Abram as a wife. (This happened ten years
after Abram had settled in the land of Canaan.)
4So Abram had sexual relations with Hagar, and
she became pregnant. But when Hagar knew she was
pregnant, she began to treat her mistress, Sarai, with
contempt. 5Then Sarai said to Abram, "This is all your
fault! I put my servant into your arms, but now that
she's pregnant she treats me with contempt. The LORD
will show who's wrong—you or me!"
6Abram replied, "Look, she is your servant, so deal
with her as you see fit." Then Sarai treated Hagar so
harshly that she finally ran away.
7The angel of the LORD found Hagar beside a spring
of water in the wilderness, along the road to Shur. 8The
angel said to her, "Hagar, Sarai's servant, where have
you come from, and where are you going?"
"I'm running away from my mistress, Sarai," she
replied.

Gn 15:18 Hebrew *the river of Egypt,* referring either to an eastern branch of the Nile River or to the Brook of Egypt in the Sinai (see Num 34:5).

Gen 15:17 Why did God send this strange vision to Abram? God's covenant with Abram was serious business. It represented an incredible promise from God and a huge responsibility for Abram. To confirm his promise, God gave Abram a sign—the smoking firepot and a flaming torch. The fire and smoke suggest God's holiness, his zeal for righteousness, and his judgment on all the nations. God took the initiative, gave the confirmation, and followed through on his promises. God's passing through the pieces was a visible assurance to Abram that the covenant God had made was real.

Gen 16:1-3 Sarai gave Hagar to Abram as a substitute wife, a common practice of that time. A married woman who could not have children was shamed by her peers and was often required to give a female servant to her husband in order to produce heirs. The children born to the servant woman were considered the children of the wife. Abram was acting in line with the custom of the day, but his action showed a lack of faith that God would fulfill his promise.

Gen 16:3 Sarai took matters into her own hands by giving Hagar to Abram. Like Abram she had trouble believing God's promise, which was directed specifically toward Abram and Sarai. Out of this lack of faith came a series of problems. This invariably happens when we take over for God, trying to make his promise come true through efforts that are not in line with his specific directions. In this case, time was the greatest test of Abram and Sarai's willingness to let God work in their lives. Sometimes we, too, must simply wait. When we ask God for something and have to wait, we can be tempted to take matters into our own hands and interfere with God's plans.

Gen 16:5 Although Sarai arranged for Hagar to have a child by Abram, she later blamed Abram for the results. It is often easier to strike out in frustration and accuse someone else than to admit an error and ask forgiveness. (Adam and Eve did the same thing in Gen 3:12-13.)

Gen 16:6 Sarai was angry with Abram, but she took it out on Hagar, and her treatment was harsh enough to cause Hagar to run away. Anger, especially when it arises from our own shortcomings, can be dangerous.

Gen 16:8 Hagar was running away from her mistress and her problem. The angel of the Lord gave her this advice: Return and face Sarai, the cause of the problem, and submit to her. Hagar needed to work on her attitude toward Sarai, no matter how justified it may have been. Running away from problems rarely solves them. It is wise to return to our

Ur of the Chaldeans

Abraham came from a culturally sophisticated and powerful city. The landscape was dominated by a massive ziggurat (temple tower), and the life of the city was controlled by a religion with a multiplicity of gods. The chief deity was Nannar, the moon god, who was also worshiped at Haran.

Many clay tablets found at Ur tell of the business life of the city, which focused on the temples and their income. Other tablets deal with religion, history, law, and education. Students were instructed in reading and writing in cuneiform script. Some clay religious figures (*teraphim* or household idols) have been discovered in Ur, along with many art objects made of precious metals and other costly materials, especially in the royal tombs. But Abraham left this prosperous cultural center to follow the Lord on the basis of his promise. What are you willing to leave behind for God?

9The angel of the LORD said to her, "Return to your
mistress, and submit to her authority." 10Then he
added, "I will give you more descendants than you
can count."

11And the angel also said, "You are now pregnant
and will give birth to a son. You are to name him Ishmael (which means 'God hears'), for the LORD has
heard your cry of distress. 12This son of yours will be
a wild man, as untamed as a wild donkey! He will raise his fist against everyone, and everyone will be against him. Yes, he will live in open hostility against all his relatives."

13Thereafter, Hagar used another name to refer to
the LORD, who had spoken to her. She said, "You are
the God who sees me."* She also said, "Have I truly
seen the One who sees me?" 14So that well was named
Beer-lahai-roi (which means "well of the Living One who sees me"). It can still be found between Kadesh and Bered.

15So Hagar gave Abram a son, and Abram named
him Ishmael. 16Abram was eighty-six years old when
Ishmael was born.

Gn 16:13 Hebrew *El-roi.*

Abram Is Named Abraham

GENESIS 17:1-8

When Abram was ninety-nine years old, the LORD appeared to him and said, "I am El-Shaddai—'God Almighty.' Serve me faithfully and live a blameless

---

ISHMAEL

Have you ever wondered if you were born into the wrong family? We don't know much about how Ishmael viewed life, but that question must have haunted him at times. His life, his name, and his position were bound up in a conflict between two jealous women. Sarah (then Sarai), impatient with God's timetable, had taken matters into her own hands, deciding to have a child through another woman. Hagar, servant that she was, submitted to being used this way, but her pregnancy gave birth to strong feelings of superiority toward Sarai. Into this tense atmosphere, Ishmael was born. • For 13 years Abraham thought Ishmael's birth had fulfilled God's promise. He was surprised to hear God say that the promised child would be Abraham and Sarah's very own. Sarah's pregnancy and Isaac's birth must have had a devastating impact on Ishmael. Until then he had been treated as a son and heir, but this late arrival made his future uncertain. During Isaac's weaning celebration, Sarah caught Ishmael teasing his half brother. As a result, Hagar and Ishmael were permanently expelled from Abraham's family. • Much of what happened throughout his life cannot be blamed on Ishmael. He was caught in a mess that wasn't his doing. However, his own actions showed that he had chosen to become part of the problem and not part of the solution. He chose to live under his circumstances rather than above them. • The choice he faced is one we must all face. There are circumstances over which we have no control, but there are others that we can control (decisions we make). At the heart of the matter is the sin-oriented nature we have all inherited. It can be partly controlled—although not overcome—by human effort. In the context of history, Ishmael's life represents the mess we make when we don't try to change the things we can change. God has offered a solution. His answer is not control but a changed life. To have a changed life, turn to God, trust him to forgive your sinful past, and ask him for help in changing your attitude toward him and others.

Strengths and accomplishments	• Known for his ability as an archer and hunter • Fathered 12 sons who became leaders of warrior tribes
Weakness and mistake	• Failed to recognize the place of his half brother, Isaac
Lesson from his life	• God's plans incorporate people's mistakes
Vital statistics	• Where: Canaan and Egypt • Occupation: Hunter, archer, warrior • Relatives: Parents: Hagar and Abraham. Half brother: Isaac.
Key verses	"But God heard the boy crying, and the angel of God called to Hagar from heaven, 'Hagar, what's wrong? Do not be afraid! God has heard the boy crying as he lies there. Go to him and comfort him, for I will make a great nation from his descendants'" (Gen 21:17-18).

Ishmael's story is told in Genesis 16–17; 21:8-20; 25:12-18; 28:8-9; 36:1-3.
He is also mentioned in Romans 9:7-9; Galatians 4:21-31.

problems, face them squarely, accept God's promise of help, correct our attitudes, and act as we should.

Gen 16:13 We have watched three people make serious mistakes: Sarai, who took matters into her own hands and gave her servant to Abram; Abram, who went along with the plan but, when circumstances began to go wrong, refused to help solve the problem; and Hagar, who ran away from the problem. In spite of this messy situation, God demonstrated his ability to work in all things for good (Rom 8:28). Sarai and Abram still received the son they so desperately wanted, and God solved Hagar's problem despite Abram's refusal to get involved. No problem is too complicated for God if you are willing to let him help you.

Gen 17:1 The Lord told Abram, "I am El-Shaddai—'God Almighty.' Serve me faithfully and live a blameless life." God has the same message for us today. We are to obey the Lord in every respect because he is God—that is reason enough. If you don't think the benefits of obedience are worth it, consider who God is—the only one with the power and ability to meet your every need.

Gen 17:2-8 Why did God repeat his covenant to Abram? Twice before, he had mentioned this agreement (Gen 12; 15). Here, however, God was bringing it into focus and preparing to carry it out. He revealed to Abram several specific parts of his covenant: (1) God would give Abram many descendants; (2) many nations would descend from him; (3) God would maintain his covenant with Abram's descendants; (4) God would give Abram's descendants the land of Canaan.

▸ **GENESIS 17:1-8** ***(cont.)***
life. [2]I will make a covenant with you, by which I will
guarantee to give you countless descendants."
[3]At this, Abram fell face down on the ground. Then
God said to him, [4]"This is my covenant with you: I will
make you the father of a multitude of nations! [5]What's
more, I am changing your name. It will no longer be
Abram. Instead, you will be called Abraham,* for you
will be the father of many nations. [6]I will make you extremely fruitful. Your descendants will become many
nations, and kings will be among them!
[7]"I will confirm my covenant with you and your
descendants* after you, from generation to generation. This is the everlasting covenant: I will always
be your God and the God of your descendants after you. [8]And I will give the entire land of Canaan,
where you now live as a foreigner, to you and your
descendants. It will be their possession forever, and
I will be their God."

The Mark of the Covenant

GENESIS 17:9-14
Then God said to Abraham, "Your responsibility is
to obey the terms of the covenant. You and all your
descendants have this continual responsibility. [10]This
is the covenant that you and your descendants must
keep: Each male among you must be circumcised.
[11]You must cut off the flesh of your foreskin as a
sign of the covenant between me and you. [12]From
generation to generation, every male child must be
circumcised on the eighth day after his birth. This
applies not only to members of your family but also to
the servants born in your household and the foreign-
born servants whom you have purchased. [13]All must

Gn 17:5 *Abram* means "exalted father"; *Abraham* sounds like a Hebrew term that means "father of many." **Gn 17:7** Hebrew *seed;* also in 17:7b, 8, 9, 10, 19.

SARAH

There probably isn't anything harder to do than wait, whether we are expecting something good, something bad, or an unknown. • One way we often cope with waiting is to begin helping God get his plan into action. Sarah tried this approach. She was too old to expect to have a child of her own, so she thought God must have something else in mind. From Sarah's limited point of view, this could only be to give Abraham a son through another woman—a common practice in her day. The plan seemed harmless enough. Abraham would sleep with Sarah's servant, who would then give birth to a child. Sarah would take the child as her own. The plan seemed flawless. But as you read about the events that followed, you will be struck by how often Sarah must have regretted the day she decided to push God's timetable ahead. • Another way we cope with a long wait is to gradually conclude that what we're waiting for is never going to happen. Sarah waited until about age 90 for a baby! When God told her she would finally have one of her own, she laughed. When confronted about her laughter, she lied—as she had seen her husband do from time to time. • What parts of your life seem to be on hold right now? Do you understand that this may be part of God's plan for you? The Bible has more than enough clear direction to keep us busy while we're waiting for some particular part of life to move ahead.

Strengths and accomplishments	• Became the mother of a nation and an ancestor of Jesus • Was a woman of faith, the first woman listed in the Hall of Faith in Hebrews 11
Weaknesses and mistakes	• Had trouble believing God's promises to her • Attempted to work problems out on her own, without consulting God • Tried to cover her faults by blaming others
Lessons from her life	• God responds to faith even in the midst of failure • God is not bound by what usually happens; he can stretch the limits and cause unheard-of events to occur
Vital statistics	• Where: Married Abram in Ur of the Chaldeans, then moved with him to Canaan • Occupation: Wife, mother, household manager • Relatives: Father: Terah. Husband: Abraham. Half brothers: Nahor and Haran. Nephew: Lot. Son: Isaac.
Key verse	"It was by faith that even Sarah was able to have a child, though she was barren and was too old. She believed that God would keep his promise" (Heb 11:11).

Sarah's story is told in Genesis 11–25. She is also mentioned in Isaiah 51:2; Romans 4:19; 9:9; Hebrews 11:11; 1 Peter 3:6.

Gen 17:5 In the Bible, people's names were very important—a name described a person's character or experience. Therefore, shortly before the promised son was conceived, God changed Abram's name (which meant "exalted father") to Abraham (which meant "father of many"). From this point on, the Bible calls him Abraham.

Gen 17:5-14 God was making a covenant, or contract, between himself and Abraham. The terms were simple: Abraham would obey God and circumcise all the males in his household; God's part was to give Abraham heirs, property, power, and wealth. Most contracts are even trades: We give something and, in turn, receive something of equal value. But when we become part of God's covenant family, the blessings we receive far outweigh what we must give up.

Gen 17:9-10 Why did God require circumcision? (1) As a sign of obedience to him in all matters. (2) As a sign of belonging to his covenant people. Once circumcised, the man would be identified as one of God's chosen people (eventually the Jews) forever. (3) As a symbol of "cutting off" the old life of sin, purifying one's heart, and dedicating oneself to God. (4) Possibly as a health measure.

Circumcision more than any other practice separated God's people from their pagan neighbors. In Abraham's day, this was essential in order to develop the pure worship of the one true God.

Gen 17:17-27 How could Abraham doubt God? It seemed incredible that he and Sarah in their advanced years could have a child. Abraham, the man God considered righteous because of his faith, had trouble believing God's promise to him. But despite his doubts, Abraham followed God's commands (Gen 17:22-27). Even people of great faith may have doubts. When God seems to want the impossible and you begin to doubt his leading, be like Abraham. Focus on God's commitment to fulfill his promises to you, and then continue to obey.

be circumcised. Your bodies will bear the mark of my everlasting covenant. [14]Any male who fails to be circumcised will be cut off from the covenant family for breaking the covenant."

Sarai Is Named Sarah

GENESIS 17:15-27

Then God said to Abraham, "Regarding Sarai, your wife—her name will no longer be Sarai. From now on her name will be Sarah.* [16]And I will bless her and give you a son from her! Yes, I will bless her richly, and she will become the mother of many nations. Kings of nations will be among her descendants."

[17]Then Abraham bowed down to the ground, but he laughed to himself in disbelief. "How could I become a father at the age of 100?" he thought. "And how can Sarah have a baby when she is ninety years old?" [18]So Abraham said to God, "May Ishmael live under your special blessing!"

[19]But God replied, "No—Sarah, your wife, will give birth to a son for you. You will name him Isaac,* and I will confirm my covenant with him and his descendants as an everlasting covenant. [20]As for Ishmael, I will bless him also, just as you have asked. I will make him extremely fruitful and multiply his descendants. He will become the father of twelve princes, and I will make him a great nation. [21]But my covenant will be confirmed with Isaac, who will be born to you and Sarah about this time next year." [22]When God had finished speaking, he left Abraham.

[23]On that very day Abraham took his son, Ishmael, and every male in his household, including those born there and those he had bought. Then he circumcised them, cutting off their foreskins, just as God had told him. [24]Abraham was ninety-nine years old when he was circumcised, [25]and Ishmael, his son, was thirteen. [26]Both Abraham and his son, Ishmael, were circumcised on that same day, [27]along with all the other men and boys of the household, whether they were born there or bought as servants. All were circumcised with him.

Gn 17:15 *Sarai* and *Sarah* both mean "princess"; the change in spelling may reflect the difference in dialect between Ur and Canaan. **Gn 17:19** *Isaac* means "he laughs."

4. SODOM AND GOMORRAH

Sin was still rampant in the world, and Abraham's family was stuck in the middle of it. His nephew Lot was living in a city that was desperately wicked, and only he and his daughters escaped the fire of God's judgment there.

A Son Is Promised to Sarah

GENESIS 18:1-15

The Lord appeared again to Abraham near the oak grove belonging to Mamre. One day Abraham was sitting at the entrance to his tent during the hottest part of the day. [2]He looked up and noticed three men standing nearby. When he saw them, he ran to meet them and welcomed them, bowing low to the ground.

[3]"My lord," he said, "if it pleases you, stop here for a while. [4]Rest in the shade of this tree while water is brought to wash your feet. [5]And since you've honored your servant with this visit, let me prepare some food to refresh you before you continue on your journey."

"All right," they said. "Do as you have said."

[6]So Abraham ran back to the tent and said to Sarah, "Hurry! Get three large measures* of your best flour, knead it into dough, and bake some bread." [7]Then Abraham ran out to the herd and chose a tender calf and gave it to his servant, who quickly prepared it. [8]When the food was ready, Abraham took some yogurt and milk and the roasted meat, and he served it to the men. As they ate, Abraham waited on them in the shade of the trees.

[9]"Where is Sarah, your wife?" the visitors asked.

"She's inside the tent," Abraham replied.

[10]Then one of them said, "I will return to you about this time next year, and your wife, Sarah, will have a son!"

Sarah was listening to this conversation from the tent. [11]Abraham and Sarah were both very old by this time, and Sarah was long past the age of having children. [12]So she laughed silently to herself and said, "How could a worn-out woman like me enjoy such pleasure, especially when my master—my husband—is also so old?"

[13]Then the Lord said to Abraham, "Why did Sarah laugh? Why did she say, 'Can an old woman like me

Gn 18:6 Hebrew *3 seahs,* about half a bushel or 18 liters.

Gen 17:20 God did not forget Ishmael. Although he was not to be Abraham's heir, he would also be the father of a great nation. Regardless of your circumstances, God has not forgotten you. Obey him and trust in his plan.

Gen 18:2-5 Abraham was eager to show hospitality to these three visitors, as was Lot (Gen 19:2). In Abraham's day, a person's reputation was largely connected to his hospitality—the sharing of home and food. Even strangers were to be treated as highly honored guests. Meeting another's need for food or shelter was and still is one of the most immediate and practical ways to obey God. It is also a time-honored relationship builder. Hebrews 13:2 suggests that we, like Abraham, might actually entertain angels. This thought should be on our minds the next time we have the opportunity to meet a stranger's needs.

▸ **GENESIS 18:1-15** ***(cont.)***
have a baby?' [14]Is anything too hard for the LORD? I will return about this time next year, and Sarah will have a son."

[15]Sarah was afraid, so she denied it, saying, "I didn't laugh."

But the LORD said, "No, you did laugh."

Abraham Intercedes for Sodom

GENESIS 18:16-33

Then the men got up from their meal and looked out toward Sodom. As they left, Abraham went with them to send them on their way.

[17]"Should I hide my plan from Abraham?" the LORD asked. [18]"For Abraham will certainly become a great and mighty nation, and all the nations of the earth will be blessed through him. [19]I have singled him out so that he will direct his sons and their families to keep the way of the LORD by doing what is right and just. Then I will do for Abraham all that I have promised."

[20]So the LORD told Abraham, "I have heard a great outcry from Sodom and Gomorrah, because their sin is so flagrant. [21]I am going down to see if their actions are as wicked as I have heard. If not, I want to know."

[22]The other men turned and headed toward Sodom, but the LORD remained with Abraham. [23]Abraham approached him and said, "Will you sweep away both the righteous and the wicked? [24]Suppose you find fifty righteous people living there in the city—will you still sweep it away and not spare it for their sakes? [25]Surely you wouldn't do such a thing, destroying the righteous along with the wicked. Why, you would be treating the righteous and the wicked exactly the same! Surely you wouldn't do that! Should not the Judge of all the earth do what is right?"

[26]And the LORD replied, "If I find fifty righteous people in Sodom, I will spare the entire city for their sake."

[27]Then Abraham spoke again. "Since I have begun, let me speak further to my Lord, even though I am but dust and ashes. [28]Suppose there are only forty-five righteous people rather than fifty? Will you destroy the whole city for lack of five?"

And the LORD said, "I will not destroy it if I find forty-five righteous people there."

[29]Then Abraham pressed his request further. "Suppose there are only forty?"

And the LORD replied, "I will not destroy it for the sake of the forty."

[30]"Please don't be angry, my Lord," Abraham pleaded. "Let me speak—suppose only thirty righteous people are found?"

And the LORD replied, "I will not destroy it if I find thirty."

[31]Then Abraham said, "Since I have dared to speak to the Lord, let me continue—suppose there are only twenty?"

And the LORD replied, "Then I will not destroy it for the sake of the twenty."

[32]Finally, Abraham said, "Lord, please don't be angry with me if I speak one more time. Suppose only ten are found there?"

And the LORD replied, "Then I will not destroy it for the sake of the ten."

[33]When the LORD had finished his conversation with Abraham, he went on his way, and Abraham returned to his tent.

Gen 18:14 "Is anything too hard for the LORD?" The obvious answer is, "Of course not!" This question reveals much about God. Make it a habit to insert your specific needs into the question. "Is this day in my life too hard for the Lord?" "Is this habit I'm trying to break too hard for him?" "Is the communication problem I'm having too hard for him?" Asking the question this way reminds you that God is personally involved in your life and nudges you to ask for his power to help you.

Gen 18:15 Sarah lied because she was afraid of being discovered. Fear is the most common motive for lying. We are afraid that our inner thoughts and emotions will be exposed or our wrongdoings discovered. But lying causes greater complications than telling the truth and brings even more problems. You will be far better off telling the truth right from the start.

Gen 18:20-33 Did Abraham change God's mind? Of course not. The more likely answer is that God changed Abraham's mind. Abraham knew that God is just and that he punishes sin, but he may have wondered about God's mercy. Abraham seemed to be probing God's mind to see how merciful he really was. He left his conversation with God convinced that God was both kind and fair. Our prayers won't change God's mind, but they may change ours just as Abraham's prayer changed his. Prayer helps us better understand the mind of God.

Gen 18:20-33 Why did God let Abraham question his justice and intercede for a wicked city? Abraham knew that God must punish sin, but he also knew from experience that God is merciful to sinners. God knew there were not 10 innocent people in the city, but he was merciful enough to allow Abraham to intercede. He was also merciful enough to help Lot, Abraham's nephew, get out of Sodom before it was destroyed. God does not take pleasure in destroying the wicked, but he must punish sin. He is both just and merciful. We should be thankful that God's mercy extends to us.

Gen 18:21 God gave the men of Sodom a fair test. He was not ignorant of the city's wicked practices, but in his fairness and patience he gave the people of Sodom one last chance to repent. God is still waiting, giving people the opportunity to turn to him (2 Pet 3:9). Those who are wise will turn to him without delay.

Gen 18:25 Was God being unfair to the people of Sodom? Did he really plan to destroy the innocent with the guilty? On the contrary, God's fairness stood out. (1) He agreed to spare the entire city if only 10 innocent people lived there. (2) He showed great mercy toward Lot, apparently the only man in the city who had any kind of relationship with him (and even that was questionable). (3) He showed great patience toward Lot, almost forcing him to leave Sodom before it was destroyed. Remember God's patience when you are tempted to think he is unfair. Even the most godly people deserve his justice. We should be glad God doesn't direct his justice toward us as he did toward Sodom.

Gen 18:33 God showed Abraham that asking for anything is allowed, with the understanding that God's answers come from God's perspective. They are not always in harmony with our expectations, for only he knows the whole story. Are you missing God's answer to a prayer because you haven't considered any possible answers other than the one you expect?

Sodom and Gomorrah Destroyed

GENESIS 19:1-29

That evening the two angels came to the entrance of the city of Sodom. Lot was sitting there, and when he saw them, he stood up to meet them. Then he welcomed them and bowed with his face to the ground. 2"My lords," he said, "come to my home to wash your feet, and be my guests for the night. You may then get up early in the morning and be on your way again."

"Oh no," they replied. "We'll just spend the night out here in the city square."

3But Lot insisted, so at last they went home with him. Lot prepared a feast for them, complete with fresh bread made without yeast, and they ate. 4But before they retired for the night, all the men of Sodom, young and old, came from all over the city and surrounded the house. 5They shouted to Lot, "Where are the men who came to spend the night with you? Bring them out to us so we can have sex with them!"

6So Lot stepped outside to talk to them, shutting the door behind him. 7"Please, my brothers," he begged, "don't do such a wicked thing. 8Look, I have two virgin daughters. Let me bring them out to you, and you can do with them as you wish. But please, leave these men alone, for they are my guests and are under my protection."

9"Stand back!" they shouted. "This fellow came to town as an outsider, and now he's acting like our judge! We'll treat you far worse than those other men!" And they lunged toward Lot to break down the door.

10But the two angels* reached out, pulled Lot into the house, and bolted the door. 11Then they blinded all the men, young and old, who were at the door of the house, so they gave up trying to get inside.

12Meanwhile, the angels questioned Lot. "Do you have any other relatives here in the city?" they asked. "Get them out of this place—your sons-in-law, sons, daughters, or anyone else. 13For we are about to destroy this city completely. The outcry against this place is so great it has reached the LORD, and he has sent us to destroy it."

14So Lot rushed out to tell his daughters' fiancés, "Quick, get out of the city! The LORD is about to destroy it." But the young men thought he was only joking.

15At dawn the next morning the angels became insistent. "Hurry," they said to Lot. "Take your wife and your two daughters who are here. Get out right now, or you will be swept away in the destruction of the city!"

16When Lot still hesitated, the angels seized his hand and the hands of his wife and two daughters and rushed them to safety outside the city, for the LORD was merciful. 17When they were safely out of the city, one of the angels ordered, "Run for your lives! And don't look back or stop anywhere in the valley! Escape to the mountains, or you will be swept away!"

18"Oh no, my lord!" Lot begged. 19"You have been so gracious to me and saved my life, and you have shown such great kindness. But I cannot go to the mountains. Disaster would catch up to me there, and I would soon die. 20See, there is a small village nearby. Please let me go there instead; don't you see how small it is? Then my life will be saved."

21"All right," the angel said, "I will grant your request. I will not destroy the little village. 22But hurry! Escape to it, for I can do nothing until you arrive there." (This explains why that village was known as Zoar, which means "little place.")

Gn 19:10 Hebrew *men;* also in 19:12, 16.

Gen 19:1 The entrance of the city was the meeting place for city officials and other men to discuss current events and transact business. It was a place of authority and status where a person could see and be seen. Evidently Lot held an important position in the government or associated with those who did because the angels found him at the city's entrance. Perhaps Lot's status in Sodom was one reason he was so reluctant to leave (Gen 19:16, 18-22).

Gen 19:8 How could any father give his daughters to be ravished by a mob of perverts, just to protect two strangers? Possibly Lot was scheming to save both the girls and the visitors, hoping the girls' fiancés would rescue them or that the homosexual men would be disinterested in the girls and simply go away. Although it was the custom of the day to protect guests at any cost, this terrible suggestion reveals how deeply sin had been absorbed into Lot's life. He had become hardened to evil acts in an evil city. Whatever Lot's motives were, we see here an illustration of Sodom's terrible wickedness—a wickedness so great that God had to destroy the entire city.

Gen 19:13 God promised to spare Sodom if only 10 innocent people lived there (Gen 18:32). Obviously not even 10 could be found, because the angels arrived to destroy the city. Archaeological evidence points to an advanced civilization in this area during Abraham's day. Most researchers also confirm some kind of sudden and devastating destruction. It is now widely thought that the buried city lies beneath the waters of the southern end of the Dead Sea. The story of Sodom reveals that the people of Lot's day had to deal with the same kinds of repulsive sins the world faces today. We should follow Abraham's example of trusting God. His selfless faith contrasts with the self-gratifying people of Sodom.

Gen 19:14 Lot had lived so long and was so contented among ungodly people that he was no longer a believable witness for God. He had allowed his environment to shape him, rather than he shaping his environment. Do those who know you see you as a witness for God, or are you just one of the crowd, blending in unnoticed? Lot had compromised to the point that he was almost useless to God. When he finally made a stand, nobody listened. Have you, too, become useless to God because you are too much like your environment? To make a difference, you must first decide to be different in your faith and your conduct.

Gen 19:16 Lot hesitated, so the angel seized his hand and rushed him to safety. Lot did not want to abandon the wealth, position, and comfort he enjoyed in Sodom. It is easy to criticize Lot for being hypnotized by Sodom when the choice seems so clear to us. To be wiser than Lot, we must see that our hesitation to obey may stem from the false attractions of our culture's pleasures.

Gen 19:16-29 Notice how God's mercy toward Abraham extended to Lot and his family. Because Abraham pleaded for Lot, God was merciful and saved Lot from the fiery destruction of Sodom. A righteous person can often affect others for good. James says, "The earnest prayer of a righteous person has great power" (Jas 5:16). All Christians should follow Abraham's example and pray for others to be saved.

▸ **GENESIS 19:1-29 *(cont.)***

23Lot reached the village just as the sun was rising over the horizon. 24Then the LORD rained down fire and burning sulfur from the sky on Sodom and Gomorrah. 25He utterly destroyed them, along with the other cities and villages of the plain, wiping out all the people and every bit of vegetation. 26But Lot's wife looked back as she was following behind him, and she turned into a pillar of salt.

27Abraham got up early that morning and hurried out to the place where he had stood in the LORD's presence. 28He looked out across the plain toward Sodom and Gomorrah and watched as columns of smoke rose from the cities like smoke from a furnace.

29But God had listened to Abraham's request and kept Lot safe, removing him from the disaster that engulfed the cities on the plain.

Lot and His Daughters

GENESIS 19:30-38

Afterward Lot left Zoar because he was afraid of the people there, and he went to live in a cave in the mountains with his two daughters. 31One day the older daughter said to her sister, "There are no men left anywhere in this entire area, so we can't get married like everyone else. And our father will soon be too old to have children. 32Come, let's get him drunk with wine, and then we will have sex with him. That way we will preserve our family line through our father."

33So that night they got him drunk with wine, and the older daughter went in and had intercourse with her father. He was unaware of her lying down or getting up again.

34The next morning the older daughter said to her younger sister, "I had sex with our father last night. Let's get him drunk with wine again tonight, and you go in and have sex with him. That way we will preserve our family line through our father." 35So that night they got him drunk with wine again, and the younger daughter went in and had intercourse with him. As before, he was unaware of her lying down or getting up again.

36As a result, both of Lot's daughters became pregnant by their own father. 37When the older daughter gave birth to a son, she named him Moab.* He became the ancestor of the nation now known as the Moabites. 38When the younger daughter gave birth to a son, she named him Ben-ammi.* He became the ancestor of the nation now known as the Ammonites.

Abraham Deceives Abimelech

GENESIS 20:1-18

Abraham moved south to the Negev and lived for a while between Kadesh and Shur, and then he moved on to Gerar. While living there as a foreigner, 2Abraham introduced his wife, Sarah, by saying, "She is my sister." So King Abimelech of Gerar sent for Sarah and had her brought to him at his palace.

3But that night God came to Abimelech in a dream and told him, "You are a dead man, for that woman you have taken is already married!"

4But Abimelech had not slept with her yet, so he said, "Lord, will you destroy an innocent nation? 5Didn't Abraham tell me, 'She is my sister'? And she herself said, 'Yes, he is my brother.' I acted in complete innocence! My hands are clean."

6In the dream God responded, "Yes, I know you are innocent. That's why I kept you from sinning against me, and why I did not let you touch her. 7Now return

Gn 19:37 *Moab* sounds like a Hebrew term that means "from father." **Gn 19:38** *Ben-ammi* means "son of my kinsman."

Gen 19:24 In the story of Sodom and Gomorrah, we see two facets of God's character: his great patience (agreeing to spare a wicked city for 10 good people) and his fierce anger (destroying both cities). As we grow spiritually, we should find ourselves developing not only a deeper respect for God because of his anger toward sin but also a deeper love for God because of his patience when we sin.

Gen 19:26 Lot's wife turned back to look at the smoldering city of Sodom. Clinging to the past, she was unwilling to turn completely away. Are you looking back longingly at sin while trying to move forward with God? You can't make progress with God as long as you are holding on to pieces of your old life. Jesus said it this way in Matthew 6:24: "No one can serve two masters."

Gen 19:30-38 In this pitiful sequel to the story of the destruction of Sodom, we see two women compelled to preserve their family line. They were driven not by lust but by desperation—they feared they would never marry. Lot's tendency to compromise and refusal to act reached its peak. He should have found right partners for his daughters long before this; Abraham's family wasn't far away. Now the two daughters stooped to incest, showing their acceptance of the morals of Sodom. We are most likely to sin when we are desperate for what we feel we must have.

Gen 19:30-38 Why doesn't the Bible openly condemn these sisters for what they did? In many cases, the Bible doesn't judge people for their actions. It simply reports the events. However, incest is clearly condemned in other parts of Scripture (Lev 18:6-18; 20:11-12, 17, 19-21; Deut 22:30; 27:20-23; Ezek 22:11; 1 Cor 5:1). Perhaps the consequence of their action—Moab and Ammon became enemies of Israel—was God's way of judging their sin.

Gen 19:37-38 Moab and Ben-ammi were the products of incest. They became the fathers of two of Israel's greatest enemies, the Moabites and the Ammonites. These nations settled east of the Jordan River, and Israel never conquered them. Because of the family connection, Moses was forbidden to attack them (Deut 2:9). Ruth, great-grandmother of David and an ancestor of Jesus, was from Moab.

Gen 20:2 Abraham had used this same trick before to protect himself (Gen 12:11-13). Although Abraham is one of our heroes of faith, he did not learn his lesson well enough the first time. In fact, by giving in to the temptation again, he risked turning a sinful act into a sinful pattern of lying whenever he suspected his life was in danger.

No matter how much we love God, certain temptations are especially difficult to resist. These are the vulnerable spots in our spiritual armor. As we struggle with these weaknesses, we can be encouraged to know that God is watching out for us just as he did for Abraham.

Gen 20:6 Abimelech had unknowingly taken a married woman to be his wife and was about to commit adultery. But God somehow prevented him from touching Sarah and held him back from sinning. What mercy on God's part! How many times has God done

the woman to her husband, and he will pray for you, for he is a prophet. Then you will live. But if you don't return her to him, you can be sure that you and all your people will die."

[8]Abimelech got up early the next morning and quickly called all his servants together. When he told them what had happened, his men were terrified. [9]Then Abimelech called for Abraham. "What have you done to us?" he demanded. "What crime have I committed that deserves treatment like this, making me and my kingdom guilty of this great sin? No one should ever do what you have done! [10]Whatever possessed you to do such a thing?"

[11]Abraham replied, "I thought, 'This is a godless place. They will want my wife and will kill me to get her.' [12]And she really is my sister, for we both have the same father, but different mothers. And I married her. [13]When God called me to leave my father's home and to travel from place to place, I told her, 'Do me a favor. Wherever we go, tell the people that I am your brother.'"

[14]Then Abimelech took some of his sheep and goats, cattle, and male and female servants, and he presented them to Abraham. He also returned his wife, Sarah, to him. [15]Then Abimelech said, "Look over my land and choose any place where you would like to live." [16]And he said to Sarah, "Look, I am giving your 'brother' 1,000 pieces of silver* in the presence of all these witnesses. This is to compensate you for any wrong I may have done to you. This will settle any claim against me, and your reputation is cleared."

[17]Then Abraham prayed to God, and God healed Abimelech, his wife, and his female servants, so they could have children. [18]For the LORD had caused all the women to be infertile because of what happened with Abraham's wife, Sarah.

Gn 20:16 Hebrew *1,000 [shekels] of silver,* about 25 pounds or 11.4 kilograms in weight.

5. BIRTH AND NEAR SACRIFICE OF ISAAC

God was faithful to his promise to give Abraham and Sarah a son of their own who would carry on the covenant blessings that God had given to this chosen family. But when Isaac was a young man, Abraham faced an unthinkable test of his faith in God's promise.

The Birth of Isaac

GENESIS 21:1-7

The LORD kept his word and did for Sarah exactly what he had promised. [2]She became pregnant, and she gave birth to a son for Abraham in his old age. This happened at just the time God had said it would. [3]And Abraham named their son Isaac. [4]Eight days after Isaac was born, Abraham circumcised him as God had commanded. [5]Abraham was 100 years old when Isaac was born.

[6]And Sarah declared, "God has brought me laughter.* All who hear about this will laugh with me. [7]Who would have said to Abraham that Sarah would nurse a baby? Yet I have given Abraham a son in his old age!"

Hagar and Ishmael Are Sent Away

GENESIS 21:8-21

2066 BC — *Isaac is born*

When Isaac grew up and was about to be weaned, Abraham prepared a huge feast to celebrate the occasion. [9]But Sarah saw Ishmael—the son of Abraham and her Egyptian servant Hagar—making fun of her son, Isaac.* [10]So she turned to Abraham and demanded, "Get rid of that slave woman and her son. He is not going to share the inheritance with my son, Isaac. I won't have it!"

[11]This upset Abraham very much because Ishmael was his son. [12]But God told Abraham, "Do not be upset over the boy and your servant. Do whatever Sarah tells you, for Isaac is the son through whom your descendants will be counted. [13]But I will also make a nation

Gn 21:6 The name *Isaac* means "he laughs." **Gn 21:9** As in Greek version and Latin Vulgate; Hebrew lacks *of her son, Isaac.*

the same for us, holding us back from sin in ways we can't even detect? We have no way of knowing—we just know from this story that he can. God works just as often in ways we *can't* see as in ways we can.

Gen 20:11-13 Because Abraham mistakenly assumed that Abimelech was a wicked man, he made a quick decision to tell a half-truth. Abraham thought it would be more effective to deceive Abimelech than to trust God to work in the king's life. Don't assume that God will not work in a situation that has potential problems. You may not completely understand the situation, and God may intervene when you least expect it.

Gen 20:17-18 Why did God punish Abimelech when he had no idea Sarah was married? (1) Even though Abimelech's intentions were good, as long as Sarah was living in his harem he was in danger of sinning. A person who eats a poisonous toadstool, thinking it's a harmless mushroom, no doubt has perfectly good intentions—but will still suffer. Sin is a poison that damages us and those around us, whatever our intentions. (2) The punishment, striking all the women of Abimelech's household with infertility, lasted only as long as Abimelech was in danger of sleeping with Sarah. It was meant to change the situation, not to harm Abimelech. (3) The punishment clearly showed that Abraham was in league with almighty God. This incident may have made Abimelech respect and fear Abraham's God.

Gen 21:1-7 Who could have believed that Abraham would have a son at 100 years of age—and live to raise him to adulthood? But doing the impossible is everyday business for God. Our big problems won't seem so impossible if we let God handle them.

Gen 21:7 After repeated promises, a visit by two angels, and the appearance of the Lord himself, Sarah finally cried out with surprise and joy at the birth of her son. Because of her doubt, worry, and fear, she had forfeited the peace she could have felt in God's wonderful promise to her. The way to bring peace to a troubled heart is to focus on God's promises. Trust him to do what he says.

▶ **GENESIS 21:8-21** ***(cont.)***
of the descendants of Hagar's son because he is your
son, too."
14So Abraham got up early the next morning, prepared food and a container of water, and strapped
them on Hagar's shoulders. Then he sent her away
with their son, and she wandered aimlessly in the
wilderness of Beersheba.
15When the water was gone, she put the boy in the
shade of a bush. 16Then she went and sat down by
herself about a hundred yards* away. "I don't want
to watch the boy die," she said, as she burst into tears.
17But God heard the boy crying, and the angel
of God called to Hagar from heaven, "Hagar, what's
wrong? Do not be afraid! God has heard the boy crying as he lies there. 18Go to him and comfort him, for
I will make a great nation from his descendants."
19Then God opened Hagar's eyes, and she saw a well
full of water. She quickly filled her water container
and gave the boy a drink.
20And God was with the boy as he grew up in the
wilderness. He became a skillful archer, 21and he
settled in the wilderness of Paran. His mother arranged for him to marry a woman from the land
of Egypt.

Abraham's Covenant with Abimelech

GENESIS 21:22-34
About this time, Abimelech came with Phicol, his army
commander, to visit Abraham. "God is obviously with
you, helping you in everything you do," Abimelech
said. 23"Swear to me in God's name that you will never
deceive me, my children, or any of my descendants. I
have been loyal to you, so now swear that you will be
loyal to me and to this country where you are living
as a foreigner."
24Abraham replied, "Yes, I swear to it!" 25Then Abraham complained to Abimelech about a well that Abimelech's servants had taken by force from Abraham's
servants.
26"This is the first I've heard of it," Abimelech answered. "I have no idea who is responsible. You have
never complained about this before."
27Abraham then gave some of his sheep, goats, and
cattle to Abimelech, and they made a treaty. 28But
Abraham also took seven additional female lambs
and set them off by themselves. 29Abimelech asked,
"Why have you set these seven apart from the others?"
30Abraham replied, "Please accept these seven
lambs to show your agreement that I dug this well."
31Then he named the place Beersheba (which means
"well of the oath"), because that was where they had
sworn the oath.
32After making their covenant at Beersheba, Abimelech left with Phicol, the commander of his army,
and they returned home to the land of the Philistines.
33Then Abraham planted a tamarisk tree at Beersheba,
and there he worshiped the LORD, the Eternal God.*
34And Abraham lived as a foreigner in Philistine country for a long time.

Gn 21:16 Hebrew *a bowshot.* **Gn 21:33** Hebrew *El-Olam.*

ISAAC

In a family of forceful initiators, Isaac was the quiet, mind-my-own-business type unless he was specifically called on to take action. He was the protected only child from the time Sarah got rid of Ishmael until Abraham arranged his marriage to Rebekah. • In his own family, Isaac had the patriarchal position, but Rebekah had the power. And rather than stand his ground, Isaac found it easier to compromise or lie to avoid confrontations. • In spite of these shortcomings, Isaac was part of God's plan. The model his father gave him included a priceless gift of faith in the one true God. God's promise to create a great nation through which he would bless the world was passed on by Isaac to his son Jacob. • It is usually not hard to identify with Isaac in his weaknesses. But consider for a moment that God works through people in spite of and often through their shortcomings. As you pray, put into words your desire to be available to God. You will discover that his willingness to use you is even greater than your desire to be used.

Strengths and accomplishments	• He was the first descendant in fulfillment of God's promise to Abraham • He demonstrated great patience
Weaknesses and mistakes	• Under pressure he tended to lie • In conflict he sought to avoid confrontation • He played favorites between his sons and alienated his wife
Lessons from his life	• Patience often brings rewards • God keeps his promises! He remains faithful though we are often faithless • Playing favorites is sure to bring family conflict
Vital statistics	• Where: Various places in the southern part of Palestine, including Beersheba (Gen 26:23) • Occupation: Wealthy livestock owner • Relatives: Parents: Abraham and Sarah. Half brother: Ishmael. Wife: Rebekah. Twin sons: Jacob and Esau.
Key verse	"But God replied, 'No—Sarah, your wife, will give birth to a son for you. You will name him Isaac, and I will confirm my covenant with him and his descendants as an everlasting covenant'" (Gen 17:19).

Isaac's story is told in Genesis 17:15–35:29. He is also mentioned in Romans 9:7-10; Hebrews 11:17-20; James 2:21.

Abraham's Faith Tested

GENESIS 22:1-24

Some time later, God tested Abraham's faith. "Abraham!" God called.
"Yes," he replied. "Here I am."
2"Take your son, your only son—yes, Isaac, whom
you love so much—and go to the land of Moriah. Go
and sacrifice him as a burnt offering on one of the
mountains, which I will show you."
3The next morning Abraham got up early. He saddled his donkey and took two of his servants with him,
along with his son, Isaac. Then he chopped wood for a
fire for a burnt offering and set out for the place God
had told him about. 4On the third day of their journey,
Abraham looked up and saw the place in the distance.
5"Stay here with the donkey," Abraham told the servants. "The boy and I will travel a little farther. We
will worship there, and then we will come right back."
6So Abraham placed the wood for the burnt offering
on Isaac's shoulders, while he himself carried the fire
and the knife. As the two of them walked on together,
7Isaac turned to Abraham and said, "Father?"
"Yes, my son?" Abraham replied.
"We have the fire and the wood," the boy said, "but
where is the sheep for the burnt offering?"
8"God will provide a sheep for the burnt offering,
my son," Abraham answered. And they both walked
on together.
9When they arrived at the place where God had
told him to go, Abraham built an altar and arranged

Gen 21:18 What happened to Ishmael, and who are his descendants? Ishmael became the founder of a large tribe or nation. The Ishmaelites were nomads living in the wilderness of Sinai and Paran, south of Israel. One of Ishmael's daughters married Esau, Ishmael's nephew (Gen 28:9). The Bible pictures the Ishmaelites as hostile to Israel and to God (Ps 83:5-6).

Gen 21:31 Beersheba, the southernmost city of Israel, lay on the edge of a vast desert that stretched as far as Egypt to the southwest and Mount Sinai to the south. The area described as being from Dan in the north to Beersheba in the south was often used to describe the traditional boundaries of the Promised Land (2 Chr 30:5). Beersheba's southern location and the presence of several wells in the area may explain why Abraham settled there. Beersheba was also the home of Isaac, Abraham's son.

Gen 22:1 God tested Abraham, not to trip him and watch him fall, but to deepen his capacity to obey God and thus to develop his character. Just as fire refines ore to extract precious metals, God refines us through difficult circumstances. When we are tested, we can complain, or we can try to see how God is stretching us to develop our character.

Gen 22:3 That morning Abraham began one of the greatest acts of obedience in recorded history. He traveled 50 miles to Mount Moriah near the site of Jerusalem. Over the years he had learned many tough lessons about the importance of obeying God. This time his obedience was prompt and complete. Obeying God is often a struggle because it may mean giving up something we truly want. We should not expect our obedience to God to be easy or to come naturally.

Gen 22:6 We don't know how Abraham carried the fire. Perhaps he carried a live coal or a flint to start a fire.

Gen 22:7-8 Why did God ask Abraham to perform human sacrifice? Pagan nations practiced human sacrifice, but God condemned this as a terrible sin (Lev 20:1-5). God did not want Isaac to die, but he wanted Abraham to sacrifice Isaac in his heart so it would be clear that Abraham loved God more than he loved his promised, long-awaited son. God was testing Abraham. The purpose of testing is to strengthen our character and deepen our commitment to God and his perfect timing. Through this difficult experience, Abraham strengthened his commitment to obey God. He also learned about God's ability to provide.

HAGAR

Escape of some kind is usually the most tempting solution to our problems. Hagar was a person who used that approach. When the going got tough, she got going—in the other direction. • However, it is worthwhile to note that the biggest challenges Hagar faced were brought on by other people's choices. Sarah chose her to bear Abraham's child, and Hagar probably had little to say in the matter. • It isn't hard to understand how Hagar's pregnancy caused her to look down on Sarah. But that brought on hard feelings, and Sarah consequently punished Hagar. This motivated her first escape. When she returned to the family and gave birth to Ishmael, Sarah's continued barrenness must have contributed to bitterness on both sides. • When Isaac was finally born, Sarah looked for any excuse to have Hagar and Ishmael sent away. She found it when she caught Ishmael teasing Isaac. In the wilderness, out of water and facing the death of her son, Hagar once again tried to escape. She walked away so she wouldn't have to watch her son die. Once again, God graciously intervened. • Have you noticed how patiently God operates to make our escape attempts fail? Have you begun to learn that escape is only a temporary solution? God's continual desire is for us to face our problems with his help. We experience his help most clearly in and through conflicts and difficulties, not away from them. Are there problems in your life for which you've been using the "Hagar solution"? Choose one of those problems, ask for God's help, and begin to face it today.

Strength and accomplishment	• Mother of Abraham's first child, Ishmael, who became the founder of the Arab nations
Weaknesses and mistakes	• When faced with problems, she tended to run away • Her pregnancy brought out strong feelings of pride and arrogance
Lessons from her life	• God is faithful to his plan and promises, even when humans complicate the process • God shows himself as one who knows us and wants to be known by us
Vital statistics	• Where: Canaan and Egypt • Occupation: Servant, mother • Relatives: Son: Ishmael.
Key verse	"The angel of the LORD said to her, 'Return to your mistress, and submit to her authority'" (Gen 16:9).

Hagar's story is told in Genesis 16; 21. She is also mentioned in Galatians 4:21-31.

▸ **GENESIS 22:1-24 *(cont.)***

the wood on it. Then he tied his son, Isaac, and laid
him on the altar on top of the wood. 10And Abraham
picked up the knife to kill his son as a sacrifice. 11At
that moment the angel of the LORD called to him from
heaven, "Abraham! Abraham!"

"Yes," Abraham replied. "Here I am!"

12"Don't lay a hand on the boy!" the angel said. "Do
not hurt him in any way, for now I know that you truly
fear God. You have not withheld from me even your
son, your only son."

13Then Abraham looked up and saw a ram caught
by its horns in a thicket. So he took the ram and
sacrificed it as a burnt offering in place of his son.
14Abraham named the place Yahweh-Yireh (which
means "the LORD will provide"). To this day, people
still use that name as a proverb: "On the mountain of
the LORD it will be provided."

15Then the angel of the LORD called again to Abraham from heaven. 16"This is what the LORD says: Because you have obeyed me and have not withheld even
your son, your only son, I swear by my own name that
17I will certainly bless you. I will multiply your descendants* beyond number, like the stars in the sky
and the sand on the seashore. Your descendants will
conquer the cities of their enemies. 18And through
your descendants all the nations of the earth will be
blessed—all because you have obeyed me."

19Then they returned to the servants and traveled
back to Beersheba, where Abraham continued to live.

20Soon after this, Abraham heard that Milcah, his
brother Nahor's wife, had borne Nahor eight sons.
21The oldest was named Uz, the next oldest was Buz,
followed by Kemuel (the ancestor of the Arameans),
22Kesed, Hazo, Pildash, Jidlaph, and Bethuel. 23(Bethuel
became the father of Rebekah.) In addition to these
eight sons from Milcah, 24Nahor had four other children from his concubine Reumah. Their names were
Tebah, Gaham, Tahash, and Maacah.

The Burial of Sarah

GENESIS 23:1-20

When Sarah was 127 years old, 2she died at Kiriath-
arba (now called Hebron) in the land of Canaan. There
Abraham mourned and wept for her.

3Then, leaving her body, he said to the Hittite elders,
4"Here I am, a stranger and a foreigner among you.
Please sell me a piece of land so I can give my wife a
proper burial."

5The Hittites replied to Abraham, 6"Listen, my lord,
you are an honored prince among us. Choose the finest of our tombs and bury her there. No one here will
refuse to help you in this way."

7Then Abraham bowed low before the Hittites
8and said, "Since you are willing to help me in this
way, be so kind as to ask Ephron son of Zohar 9to let
me buy his cave at Machpelah, down at the end of
his field. I will pay the full price in the presence of
witnesses, so I will have a permanent burial place
for my family."

10Ephron was sitting there among the others, and
he answered Abraham as the others listened, speaking

Gn 22:17 Hebrew *seed;* also in 22:17b, 18.

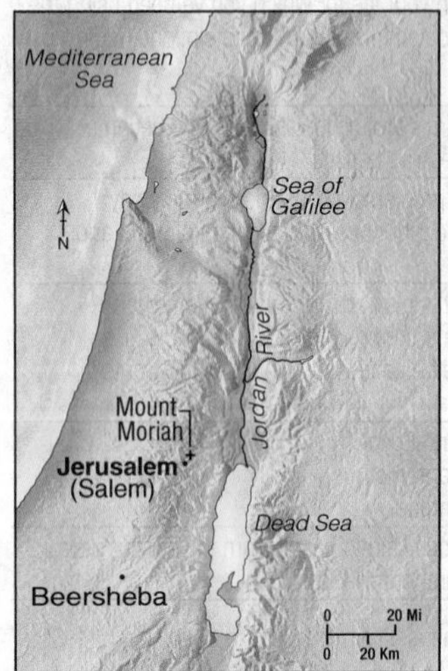

ABRAHAM'S TRIP TO MOUNT MORIAH
Abraham and Isaac traveled the 50 or 60 miles from Beersheba to Mount Moriah in about three days. This was a very difficult time for Abraham, who was on his way to sacrifice his beloved son, Isaac.

Gen 22:12 It is difficult to let go of what we deeply love. What could be more proper than to love your only child? Yet when we do give to God what he asks, he returns to us far more than we could dream. The spiritual benefits of his blessings far outweigh our sacrifices. Have you withheld your love, your children, or your time from him? Trust him to provide (Gen 22:8).

Gen 22:13 Notice the parallel between the ram offered on the altar as a substitute for Isaac and Christ offered on the cross as a substitute for us. Whereas God stopped Abraham from sacrificing his son, God did not spare his own Son, Jesus, from dying on the cross. If Jesus had lived, the rest of humankind would have died. God sent his only Son to die for us so that we could be spared from the eternal death we deserve and instead receive eternal life (John 3:16).

Gen 22:15-18 Abraham received abundant blessings because he obeyed God. God promised to give Abraham's descendants the ability to conquer their enemies. In addition, God promised Abraham children and grandchildren who would in turn bless the whole earth. People's lives would be changed as a result of knowing of the faith of Abraham and his descendants. We often think of blessings as gifts that we will enjoy. But when God blesses us, he also wants us to share our blessings in overflow to others—today and into eternity.

Gen 23:1-4 In Abraham's day, death and burial were steeped in ritual and traditions. Failing to honor a dead person demonstrated the greatest possible lack of respect. An improper burial was the equivalent of a curse. Mourning was an essential part of the death ritual. Friends and relatives would cry loudly for the whole neighborhood to hear. Because there were no funeral homes or undertakers, these same friends and relatives would help prepare the body for burial, which usually would take place on the same day because of the warm climate.

Gen 23:4-6 Abraham was in a foreign land looking for a place to bury his wife. Strangers offered to help him because he was "an honored prince," and they respected him. Although Abraham had not put down roots in the area, his reputation was above reproach. Those who invest their time and money in serving God often earn a pleasant return on their investment—a good reputation and the respect of others.

Gen 23:10-16 The polite interchange between Abraham and Ephron was typical

publicly before all the Hittite elders of the town. [11]"No, my lord," he said to Abraham, "please listen to me. I will give you the field and the cave. Here in the presence of my people, I give it to you. Go and bury your dead."

[12]Abraham again bowed low before the citizens of the land, [13]and he replied to Ephron as everyone listened. "No, listen to me. I will buy it from you. Let me pay the full price for the field so I can bury my dead there."

[14]Ephron answered Abraham, [15]"My lord, please listen to me. The land is worth 400 pieces* of silver, but what is that between friends? Go ahead and bury your dead."

[16]So Abraham agreed to Ephron's price and paid the amount he had suggested—400 pieces of silver, weighed according to the market standard. The Hittite elders witnessed the transaction.

[17]So Abraham bought the plot of land belonging to Ephron at Machpelah, near Mamre. This included the field itself, the cave that was in it, and all the surrounding trees. [18]It was transferred to Abraham as his permanent possession in the presence of the Hittite elders at the city gate. [19]Then Abraham buried his wife, Sarah, there in Canaan, in the cave of Machpelah, near Mamre (also called Hebron). [20]So the field and the cave were transferred from the Hittites to Abraham for use as a permanent burial place.

Gn 23:15 Hebrew *400 shekels,* about 10 pounds or 4.6 kilograms in weight; also in 23:16.

6. ISAAC AND REBEKAH

Abraham didn't want his son Isaac to marry a woman from the Canaanite peoples, so he sent his servant back to where his family had come from to find a suitable wife for his son.

A Wife for Isaac

GENESIS 24:1-67

Abraham was now a very old man, and the LORD had blessed him in every way. [2]One day Abraham said to his oldest servant, the man in charge of his household, "Take an oath by putting your hand under my thigh. [3]Swear by the LORD, the God of heaven and earth, that you will not allow my son to marry one of these local Canaanite women. [4]Go instead to my homeland, to my relatives, and find a wife there for my son Isaac."

[5]The servant asked, "But what if I can't find a young woman who is willing to travel so far from home? Should I then take Isaac there to live among your relatives in the land you came from?"

[6]"No!" Abraham responded. "Be careful never to take my son there. [7]For the LORD, the God of heaven, who took me from my father's house and my native land, solemnly promised to give this land to my descendants.* He will send his angel ahead of you, and he will see to it that you find a wife there for my son. [8]If she

Gn 24:7 Hebrew *seed;* also in 24:60.

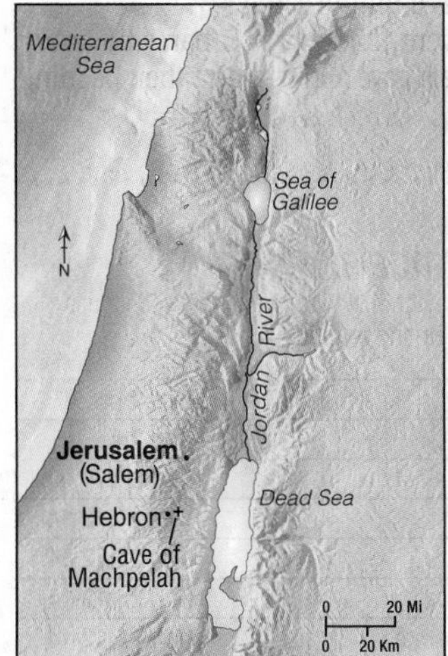

***CAVE OF MACHPELAH** Sarah died in Hebron. Abraham bought the cave of Machpelah, near Hebron, as her burial place. Later, Abraham was also buried there, as were his son and grandson, Isaac and Jacob.*

of bargaining at that time. Ephron graciously offered to give his land to Abraham at no charge; Abraham insisted on paying for it; Ephron politely mentioned the price but said, in effect, that it wasn't important; Abraham paid the 400 shekels of silver. Both men knew what was going on as they went through the bargaining process. If Abraham had accepted the land as a gift when it was offered, he would have insulted Ephron, who then would have rescinded his offer. Many Middle Eastern shopkeepers still follow this bargaining ritual with their customers.

Gen 23:16 For the piece of property Abraham bought, 400 pieces of silver was an outrageous price. The Hittites weren't thrilled about foreigners buying their property, so Abraham had little bargaining leverage.

The custom of the day was to ask double the fair-market value of the land, fully expecting the buyer to offer half the stated price. But Abraham didn't even bargain. He simply paid the initial price. He was not trying to take anything he didn't deserve. Even though God had promised the land to Abraham, he did not just take it away from Ephron.

Gen 24:4 Abraham wanted Isaac to marry within the family. This was a common and acceptable practice at this time that had the added advantage of avoiding intermarriage with pagan neighbors. A son's wife was usually chosen by the parents. It was common for a woman to be married in her early teens, although Rebekah was probably older.

Gen 24:6 Abraham wanted Isaac to stay in Canaan, but he didn't want him to marry one of the local girls. To have Isaac stay and marry a woman from Canaan would have been easier. But Abraham wanted to obey God in the *who* as well as in the *where.* Make your obedience full and complete.

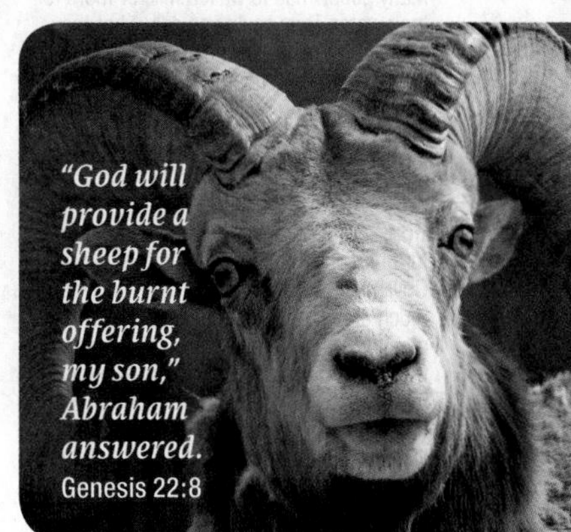

"God will provide a sheep for the burnt offering, my son," Abraham answered.
Genesis 22:8

▸ **GENESIS 24:1-67** ***(cont.)***

is unwilling to come back with you, then you are free from this oath of mine. But under no circumstances are you to take my son there."

9So the servant took an oath by putting his hand under the thigh of his master, Abraham. He swore to follow Abraham's instructions. 10Then he loaded ten of Abraham's camels with all kinds of expensive gifts from his master, and he traveled to distant Aram-naharaim. There he went to the town where Abraham's brother Nahor had settled. 11He made the camels kneel beside a well just outside the town. It was evening, and the women were coming out to draw water.

12"O LORD, God of my master, Abraham," he prayed. "Please give me success today, and show unfailing love to my master, Abraham. 13See, I am standing here beside this spring, and the young women of the town are coming out to draw water. 14This is my request. I will ask one of them, 'Please give me a drink from your jug.' If she says, 'Yes, have a drink, and I will water your camels, too!'—let her be the one you have selected as Isaac's wife. This is how I will know that you have shown unfailing love to my master."

15Before he had finished praying, he saw a young woman named Rebekah coming out with her water jug on her shoulder. She was the daughter of Bethuel, who was the son of Abraham's brother Nahor and his wife, Milcah. 16Rebekah was very beautiful and old enough to be married, but she was still a virgin. She went down to the spring, filled her jug, and came up again. 17Running over to her, the servant said, "Please give me a little drink of water from your jug."

18"Yes, my lord," she answered, "have a drink." And she quickly lowered her jug from her shoulder and gave him a drink. 19When she had given him a drink, she said, "I'll draw water for your camels, too, until they have had enough to drink." 20So she quickly emptied her jug into the watering trough and ran back to the well to draw water for all his camels.

21The servant watched her in silence, wondering whether or not the LORD had given him success in his mission. 22Then at last, when the camels had finished drinking, he took out a gold ring for her nose and two large gold bracelets* for her wrists.

23"Whose daughter are you?" he asked. "And please tell me, would your father have any room to put us up for the night?"

24"I am the daughter of Bethuel," she replied. "My grandparents are Nahor and Milcah. 25Yes, we have plenty of straw and feed for the camels, and we have room for guests."

26The man bowed low and worshiped the LORD. 27"Praise the LORD, the God of my master, Abraham," he said. "The LORD has shown unfailing love and faithfulness to my master, for he has led me straight to my master's relatives."

28The young woman ran home to tell her family everything that had happened. 29Now Rebekah had a brother named Laban, who ran out to meet the man at the spring. 30He had seen the nose-ring and the bracelets on his sister's wrists, and had heard Rebekah tell what the man had said. So he rushed out to the spring, where the man was still standing beside his camels. 31Laban said to him, "Come and stay with us, you who are blessed by the LORD! Why are you standing here outside the town when I have a room all ready for you and a place prepared for the camels?"

32So the man went home with Laban, and Laban unloaded the camels, gave him straw for their bedding,

Gn 24:22 Hebrew *a gold nose-ring weighing a half shekel* [0.2 ounces or 6 grams] *and two gold bracelets weighing 10 shekels* [4 ounces or 114 grams].

Gen 24:11 The well, the chief source of water for an entire village, was usually located outside town along the main road. Many people had to walk a mile or more for their water. They could use only what they could carry home. Farmers and shepherds would come from nearby fields to draw water for their animals. The well was a good place to meet new friends or to chat with old ones. Rebekah would have visited the well twice daily to draw water for her family.

Gen 24:12 Abraham's servant asked God for guidance in this very important task. Obviously Eliezer (see Gen 15:2) had learned much about faith and about God from his master. What are your family members, friends, and associates learning about God from watching you? Be like Abraham, setting an example of dependent faith. And be like Eliezer, asking God for guidance before any venture.

Gen 24:14 Was it right for Abraham's servant to ask God for such a specific sign? The sign he requested was only slightly out

ELIEZER: PROFILE OF A TRUE SERVANT

Have you ever approached a responsibility with this kind of single-mindedness and careful planning, while ultimately depending on God?

Accepted the challenge	**Gen 24:3, 9**
Examined alternatives	**Gen 24:5**
Promised to follow instructions	**Gen 24:9**
Made a plan	**Gen 24:12-14**
Submitted the plan to God	**Gen 24:12-14**
Prayed for guidance	**Gen 24:12-14**
Devised a strategy with room for God to operate	**Gen 24:12-14**
Waited	**Gen 24:21**
Watched closely	**Gen 24:21**
Accepted the answer thankfully	**Gen 24:26**
Explained the situation to concerned parties	**Gen 24:34-49**
Refused unnecessary delay	**Gen 24:56**
Followed through with entire plan	**Gen 24:66**

fed them, and provided water for the man and the
camel drivers to wash their feet. 33Then food was
served. But Abraham's servant said, "I don't want to
eat until I have told you why I have come."
"All right," Laban said, "tell us."
34"I am Abraham's servant," he explained. 35"And the
LORD has greatly blessed my master; he has become a
wealthy man. The LORD has given him flocks of sheep
and goats, herds of cattle, a fortune in silver and gold,
and many male and female servants and camels and
donkeys.
36"When Sarah, my master's wife, was very old, she
gave birth to my master's son, and my master has given
him everything he owns. 37And my master made me
take an oath. He said, 'Do not allow my son to marry
one of these local Canaanite women. 38Go instead to
my father's house, to my relatives, and find a wife there
for my son.'
39"But I said to my master, 'What if I can't find a
young woman who is willing to go back with me?'
40He responded, 'The LORD, in whose presence I have
lived, will send his angel with you and will make your
mission successful. Yes, you must find a wife for my
son from among my relatives, from my father's family. 41Then you will have fulfilled your obligation. But
if you go to my relatives and they refuse to let her go
with you, you will be free from my oath.'
42"So today when I came to the spring, I prayed this
prayer: 'O LORD, God of my master, Abraham, please
give me success on this mission. 43See, I am standing
here beside this spring. This is my request. When a
young woman comes to draw water, I will say to her,
"Please give me a little drink of water from your jug."
44If she says, "Yes, have a drink, and I will draw water
for your camels, too," let her be the one you have selected to be the wife of my master's son.'
45"Before I had finished praying in my heart, I
saw Rebekah coming out with her water jug on her

of the ordinary. The hospitality of the day required women at the well to offer water to weary travelers, but not to their animals. Eliezer was simply asking God to show him a woman with an attitude of service—someone who would go beyond the expected. An offer to water his camels would indicate that kind of attitude. Eliezer did not ask for a woman with good looks or wealth. He knew the importance of finding a woman with the right heart, and he asked God to help him with this task.

Gen 24:15-16 Rebekah had physical beauty, but the servant was looking for a sign of inner beauty. Appearance is important to us, and we spend time and money improving it. But how much effort do we put into developing our inner beauty? Patience, kindness, and joy are the beauty treatments that help us become truly lovely—on the inside.

Gen 24:18-21 Rebekah's servant spirit was clearly demonstrated as she willingly and quickly drew water for Eliezer and his camels. The pots used for carrying water were large and heavy. A thirsty camel drinks a lot of water—up to 25 gallons after a week's travel. Seeing Rebekah go to work, Eliezer knew this was a woman with a heart for doing far more than the bare minimum. Do you have a servant spirit? When asked to help or when you see a need, go beyond the minimum.

Gen 24:26-27 As soon as Abraham's servant knew that God had answered his prayer, he thanked God for his goodness and guidance. God will also use and lead us if we are available like Eliezer. Our first response should be praise and thanksgiving that God would choose to work in and through us.

Gen 24:42, 48 When Eliezer told his story to Laban, he spoke openly of God and his goodness. Often we do the opposite, afraid that we will be misunderstood, rejected, or seen as too religious. Instead, we should share openly what God is doing for us.

REBEKAH

Some people are initiators. They help get the ball rolling. Rebekah's life was characterized by initiative. When she saw a need, she took action, even though the action was not always right. • It was Rebekah's initiative that first caught the attention of Eliezer, the servant Abraham sent to find a wife for Isaac. It was common courtesy to give a drink to a stranger, but it took added character to also fetch water for ten thirsty camels. • Several later events help us see how initiative can be misdirected. Rebekah was aware that God's plan would be channeled through Jacob, not Esau (Gen 25:23). So not only did Jacob become her favorite; she actually planned ways to ensure that he would overshadow his older twin. Meanwhile, Isaac preferred Esau. This created a conflict between the couple. She felt justified in deceiving her husband when the time came to bless the sons, and her ingenious plan was carried out to perfection. • Most of the time we try to justify the things we choose to do. When thinking about a course of action, are you simply seeking God's stamp of approval on something you've already decided to do? Or are you willing to set the plan aside if the principles and commands of God's Word are against the action? Initiative and action are admirable and right when they are controlled by God's wisdom.

Strengths and accomplishments	• When confronted with a need, she took immediate action • She was accomplishment oriented
Weaknesses and mistakes	• Her initiative was not always balanced by wisdom • She favored one of her sons • She deceived her husband
Lessons from her life	• Our actions must be guided by God's Word • God even makes use of our mistakes in his plan • Parental favoritism hurts a family
Vital statistics	• Where: Haran, Canaan • Occupation: Wife, mother, household manager • Relatives: Grandparents: Nahor and Milcah. Father: Bethuel. Brother: Laban. Husband: Isaac. Twin sons: Esau and Jacob.
Key verses	"And Isaac brought Rebekah into his mother Sarah's tent, and she became his wife. He loved her deeply, and she was a special comfort to him after the death of his mother" (Gen 24:67). "Isaac loved Esau because he enjoyed eating the wild game Esau brought home, but Rebekah loved Jacob" (Gen 25:28).

Rebekah's story is told in Genesis 24–27. She is also mentioned in Romans 9:10.

▸ **GENESIS 24:1-67** ***(cont.)***

shoulder. She went down to the spring and drew water. So I said to her, 'Please give me a drink.' 46She quickly lowered her jug from her shoulder and said, 'Yes, have a drink, and I will water your camels, too!' So I drank, and then she watered the camels.

47"Then I asked, 'Whose daughter are you?' She replied, 'I am the daughter of Bethuel, and my grandparents are Nahor and Milcah.' So I put the ring on her nose, and the bracelets on her wrists.

48"Then I bowed low and worshiped the LORD. I praised the LORD, the God of my master, Abraham, because he had led me straight to my master's niece to be his son's wife. 49So tell me—will you or won't you show unfailing love and faithfulness to my master? Please tell me yes or no, and then I'll know what to do next."

50Then Laban and Bethuel replied, "The LORD has obviously brought you here, so there is nothing we can say. 51Here is Rebekah; take her and go. Yes, let her be the wife of your master's son, as the LORD has directed."

52When Abraham's servant heard their answer, he bowed down to the ground and worshiped the LORD. 53Then he brought out silver and gold jewelry and clothing and presented them to Rebekah. He also gave expensive presents to her brother and mother. 54Then they ate their meal, and the servant and the men with him stayed there overnight.

But early the next morning, Abraham's servant said, "Send me back to my master."

55"But we want Rebekah to stay with us at least ten days," her brother and mother said. "Then she can go."

56But he said, "Don't delay me. The LORD has made my mission successful; now send me back so I can return to my master."

57"Well," they said, "we'll call Rebekah and ask her what she thinks." 58So they called Rebekah. "Are you willing to go with this man?" they asked her.

And she replied, "Yes, I will go."

59So they said good-bye to Rebekah and sent her away with Abraham's servant and his men. The woman who had been Rebekah's childhood nurse went along with her. 60They gave her this blessing as she parted:

"Our sister, may you become
 the mother of many millions!
May your descendants be strong
 and conquer the cities of their enemies."

61Then Rebekah and her servant girls mounted the camels and followed the man. So Abraham's servant took Rebekah and went on his way.

62Meanwhile, Isaac, whose home was in the Negev, had returned from Beer-lahai-roi. 63One evening as he was walking and meditating in the fields, he looked up and saw the camels coming. 64When Rebekah looked up and saw Isaac, she quickly dismounted from her camel. 65"Who is that man walking through the fields to meet us?" she asked the servant.

And he replied, "It is my master." So Rebekah covered her face with her veil. 66Then the servant told Isaac everything he had done.

67And Isaac brought Rebekah into his mother Sarah's tent, and she became his wife. He loved her deeply, and she was a special comfort to him after the death of his mother.

7. ABRAHAM DIES

When Abraham died, he could rest secure that he had been faithful to God, and God was certain to be faithful to the promises he made to Abraham.

The Death of Abraham

GENESIS 25:1-11

Abraham married another wife, whose name was Keturah. 2She gave birth to Zimran, Jokshan, Medan, Midian, Ishbak, and Shuah. 3Jokshan was the father of Sheba and Dedan. Dedan's descendants were the Asshurites, Letushites, and Leummites. 4Midian's sons were Ephah, Epher, Hanoch, Abida, and Eldaah. These were all descendants of Abraham through Keturah.

5Abraham gave everything he owned to his son Isaac. 6But before he died, he gave gifts to the sons of his concubines and sent them off to a land in the east, away from Isaac.

7Abraham lived for 175 years, 8and he died at a ripe old age, having lived a long and satisfying life. He breathed his last and joined his ancestors in death. 9His sons Isaac and Ishmael buried him in the cave of Machpelah, near Mamre, in the field of Ephron son of Zohar the Hittite. 10This was the field Abraham had purchased from the Hittites and where he had buried his wife Sarah. 11After Abraham's death, God blessed his son Isaac, who settled near Beer-lahai-roi in the Negev.

Ishmael's Descendants

GENESIS 25:12-18

This is the account of the family of Ishmael, the son of Abraham through Hagar, Sarah's Egyptian servant.

Gen 24:64-65 When Rebekah learned that the man coming to greet them was Isaac, her husband-to-be, she followed two Oriental customs. She dismounted from her camel to show respect, and she placed a veil over her face as a bride.

Gen 25:1-6 Abraham took another wife, Keturah, after Sarah died. Although the sons and grandsons of Abraham and Keturah received many gifts from Abraham, all his property and authority went to Isaac, his principal heir.

[13]Here is a list, by their names and clans, of Ishmael's descendants: The oldest was Nebaioth, followed by Kedar, Adbeel, Mibsam, [14]Mishma, Dumah, Massa, [15]Hadad, Tema, Jetur, Naphish, and Kedemah. [16]These twelve sons of Ishmael became the founders of twelve tribes named after them, listed according to the places they settled and camped. [17]Ishmael lived for 137 years. Then he breathed his last and joined his ancestors in death. [18]Ishmael's descendants occupied the region from Havilah to Shur, which is east of Egypt in the direction of Asshur. There they lived in open hostility toward all their relatives.*

Gn 25:18 The meaning of the Hebrew is uncertain.

B. The Story of Isaac

Isaac inherited everything from his father, including God's promise to make his descendants into a great nation. As a young man, Isaac did not resist as his father prepared to sacrifice him, and as a man, he gladly accepted the wife that others chose for him. Through Isaac, we learn how to let God guide our life and place his will ahead of our own.

1. ISAAC'S SONS

Although they were twins, Isaac's sons, Jacob and Esau, couldn't have been more different. They spent much of their lives struggling with one another—beginning in the womb!

The Births of Esau and Jacob

GENESIS 25:19-26

This is the account of the family of Isaac, the son of Abraham. [20]When Isaac was forty years old, he married Rebekah, the daughter of Bethuel the Aramean from Paddan-aram and the sister of Laban the Aramean.

[21]Isaac pleaded with the LORD on behalf of his wife, because she was unable to have children. The LORD answered Isaac's prayer, and Rebekah became pregnant with twins. [22]But the two children struggled with each other in her womb. So she went to ask the LORD about it. "Why is this happening to me?" she asked.

[23]And the LORD told her, "The sons in your womb will become two nations. From the very beginning, the two nations will be rivals. One nation will be stronger than the other; and your older son will serve your younger son."

[24]And when the time came to give birth, Rebekah discovered that she did indeed have twins! [25]The first one was very red at birth and covered with thick hair like a fur coat. So they named him Esau.* [26]Then the other twin was born with his hand grasping Esau's heel. So they named him Jacob.* Isaac was sixty years old when the twins were born.

Esau Sells His Birthright

GENESIS 25:27-34

2006 BC

Jacob and Esau are born

As the boys grew up, Esau became a skillful hunter. He was an outdoorsman, but Jacob had a quiet temperament, preferring to stay at home. [28]Isaac loved Esau because he enjoyed eating the wild game Esau brought home, but Rebekah loved Jacob.

[29]One day when Jacob was cooking some stew, Esau arrived home from the wilderness exhausted and hungry. [30]Esau said to Jacob, "I'm starved! Give me some of that red stew!" (This is how Esau got his other name, Edom, which means "red.")

[31]"All right," Jacob replied, "but trade me your rights as the firstborn son."

Gn 25:25 *Esau* sounds like a Hebrew term that means "hair." **Gn 25:26** *Jacob* sounds like the Hebrew words for "heel" and "deceiver."

Gen 25:21 As Isaac pleaded with God for children, so the Bible encourages us to ask and even plead for our most personal and important requests. God wants to grant our requests, but he wants us to ask him. Even then, as Isaac learned, God may decide to withhold his answer for a while in order to deepen our insight into what we really need, broaden our appreciation for his answers, or allow us to mature so we can use his gifts more wisely.

Gen 25:31 A birthright was a special honor given to the firstborn son. It included a double portion of the family inheritance along with the honor of one day becoming the family's leader. The oldest son could sell his birthright or give it away if he chose, but in so doing, he would lose both material goods and his leadership position. By trading his birthright, Esau showed complete disregard for the spiritual blessings that would have come his way if he had kept it.

Gen 25:32-33 Esau traded the lasting benefits of his birthright for the immediate pleasure of food. He acted on impulse, satisfying his immediate desires without pausing to consider the long-range consequences of what he was about to do. We can fall into the same trap. When we see something we want, our first impulse is to get it. At first we feel intensely satisfied and sometimes even powerful because we have obtained what we set out to get. But immediate pleasure often loses sight of the future. We can avoid making Esau's mistake by comparing the short-term satisfaction with its long-range consequences before we act.

Esau exaggerated his hunger. "I'm dying of starvation!" he said. This thought made his choice much easier because if he died of starvation, what good was an inheritance anyway? The pressure of the moment distorted his perspective and made his decision seem urgent. We often experience similar pressures. For example, when we feel sexual pressure, a marriage vow may seem unimportant. We might feel such great pressure in one area that nothing else seems to matter, and we lose our perspective. Getting through that short, pressure-filled moment is often the most difficult part of overcoming a temptation.

▸ **GENESIS 25:27-34 *(cont.)***

32“Look, I'm dying of starvation!” said Esau. “What
good is my birthright to me now?”
33But Jacob said, “First you must swear that your
birthright is mine.” So Esau swore an oath, thereby
selling all his rights as the firstborn to his brother,
Jacob.
34Then Jacob gave Esau some bread and lentil stew.
Esau ate the meal, then got up and left. He showed
contempt for his rights as the firstborn.

2. ISAAC AND ABIMELECH

Isaac learned a lot from his father, Abraham. He learned about faith in God and the permanence of God's promises, but unfortunately he didn't learn from some of Abraham's mistakes. Like his father before him, Isaac lied to a powerful foreign ruler about the identity of his wife.

Isaac Deceives Abimelech

GENESIS 26:1-11

A severe famine now struck the land, as had happened before in Abraham's time. So Isaac moved to
Gerar, where Abimelech, king of the Philistines, lived.
2The Lord appeared to Isaac and said, “Do not
go down to Egypt, but do as I tell you. 3Live here as
a foreigner in this land, and I will be with you and
bless you. I hereby confirm that I will give all these
lands to you and your descendants,* just as I solemnly promised Abraham, your father. 4I will cause
your descendants to become as numerous as the
stars of the sky, and I will give them all these lands.
And through your descendants all the nations of the
earth will be blessed. 5I will do this because Abraham listened to me and obeyed all my requirements,

Gn 26:3 Hebrew *seed;* also in 26:4, 24.

Gen 26:1 The Philistines would become some of Israel's fiercest enemies. The Philistines were one group of a number of migrating sea peoples from the Aegean Sea who had settled in Palestine. They arrived by way of Crete and Cyprus and were used as mercenaries by Canaanite rulers. These people, living along the southwest coast, were few but ferocious in battle. Although friendly to Isaac, this small group was the forerunner of the nation that would plague Israel during the time of Joshua, the judges, and David. This King Abimelech was not the same Abimelech that Abraham encountered (Gen 20–21). *Abimelech* may have been a dynastic name of the Philistine rulers.

Gen 26:7-11 Isaac was afraid that the men in Gerar would kill him to get his beautiful wife, Rebekah. So he lied, claiming that Rebekah was his sister. Where did he learn that trick? He may have known about the actions of his father, Abraham (see Gen 12:10-13; 20:1-5). Parents help shape the world's future by the way they shape their children's values. The first step toward helping children live right is for the parents to live right. Your actions are often copied by those closest to you. What kind of example are you setting for your children?

Gen 26:12-16 God kept his promise to bless Isaac. The neighboring Philistines grew jealous because everything Isaac did seemed to go right. So they filled his wells with dirt and tried to get rid of him. Jealousy is a dividing force strong enough to tear apart the mightiest of nations or the closest of friends. It forces you to separate yourself from what you were longing for in the first place. When you find yourself becoming jealous of others, try thanking God for their good fortune. Before striking out in anger, consider what you could lose—a friend, a job, a spouse?

2000 BC ***Stonehenge erected in England (estimated)***

ESAU

Common sense isn't all that common. In fact, the common thread in many decisions is that they don't make sense. Esau's life was filled with choices he must have regretted bitterly. He appears to have been a person who found it hard to consider consequences, reacting to the need of the moment without realizing what he was giving up to meet that need. Trading his birthright for a bowl of stew was the clearest example of this weakness. He also chose wives in direct opposition to his parents' wishes. He learned the hard way. • What are you willing to trade for the things you want? Do you ever find yourself willing to negotiate anything for what you feel you need now? Does your family, spouse, integrity, body, or soul get included in these deals? Do you sometimes feel that the important parts of life escaped while you were grabbing for something else? • If so, your initial response, like Esau's, may be deep anger. In itself that isn't wrong, as long as you direct the energy of that anger toward a solution and not toward yourself or others as the cause of the problem. Your greatest need is to find a focal point other than “what I need now.” The only worthy focal point is God. A relationship with him will not only give an ultimate purpose to your life, it will also be a daily guideline for living.

Strengths and accomplishments	• Ancestor of the Edomites • Known for his archery skill • Able to forgive after explosive anger
Weaknesses and mistakes	• Tended to choose according to the immediate need rather than the long-range effect when faced with important decisions • Upset his parents by poor marriage choices
Lessons from his life	• God allows certain events in our lives to accomplish his overall purposes, but we are still responsible for our actions • Consequences are important to consider
Vital statistics	• Where: Canaan • Occupation: Skillful hunter • Relatives: Parents: Isaac and Rebekah. Brother: Jacob. Wives: Judith, Basemath, and Mahalath.
Key verse	“Esau pleaded, ‘But do you have only one blessing? Oh my father, bless me, too!’ Then Esau broke down and wept.” (Gen 27:38).

Esau's story is told in Genesis 25–36. He is also mentioned in Malachi 1:2-3; Romans 9:13; Hebrews 12:16-17.

commands, decrees, and instructions." [6]So Isaac stayed in Gerar.

[7]When the men who lived there asked Isaac about his wife, Rebekah, he said, "She is my sister." He was afraid to say, "She is my wife." He thought, "They will kill me to get her, because she is so beautiful." [8]But some time later, Abimelech, king of the Philistines, looked out his window and saw Isaac caressing Rebekah.

[9]Immediately, Abimelech called for Isaac and exclaimed, "She is obviously your wife! Why did you say, 'She is my sister'?"

"Because I was afraid someone would kill me to get her from me," Isaac replied.

[10]"How could you do this to us?" Abimelech exclaimed. "One of my people might easily have taken your wife and slept with her, and you would have made us guilty of great sin."

[11]Then Abimelech issued a public proclamation: "Anyone who touches this man or his wife will be put to death!"

Conflict over Water Rights

GENESIS 26:12-25

When Isaac planted his crops that year, he harvested a hundred times more grain than he planted, for the LORD blessed him. [13]He became a very rich man, and his wealth continued to grow. [14]He acquired so many flocks of sheep and goats, herds of cattle, and servants that the Philistines became jealous of him. [15]So the Philistines filled up all of Isaac's wells with dirt. These were the wells that had been dug by the servants of his father, Abraham.

[16]Finally, Abimelech ordered Isaac to leave the country. "Go somewhere else," he said, "for you have become too powerful for us."

[17]So Isaac moved away to the Gerar Valley, where he set up their tents and settled down. [18]He reopened the wells his father had dug, which the Philistines had filled in after Abraham's death. Isaac also restored the names Abraham had given them.

[19]Isaac's servants also dug in the Gerar Valley and discovered a well of fresh water. [20]But then the shepherds from Gerar came and claimed the spring. "This is our water," they said, and they argued over it with Isaac's herdsmen. So Isaac named the well Esek (which means "argument"). [21]Isaac's men then dug another well, but again there was a dispute over it. So Isaac named it Sitnah (which means "hostility"). [22]Abandoning that one, Isaac moved on and dug another well. This time there was no dispute over it, so Isaac named the place Rehoboth (which means "open space"), for he said, "At last the LORD has created enough space for us to prosper in this land."

[23]From there Isaac moved to Beersheba, [24]where the LORD appeared to him on the night of his arrival. "I am the God of your father, Abraham," he said. "Do not be afraid, for I am with you and will bless you. I will multiply your descendants, and they will become a great nation. I will do this because of my promise to Abraham, my servant." [25]Then Isaac built an altar there and worshiped the LORD. He set up his camp at that place, and his servants dug another well.

Isaac's Covenant with Abimelech

GENESIS 26:26-35

One day King Abimelech came from Gerar with his adviser, Ahuzzath, and also Phicol, his army commander. [27]"Why have you come here?" Isaac asked. "You obviously hate me, since you kicked me off your land."

[28]They replied, "We can plainly see that the LORD is with you. So we want to enter into a sworn treaty with you. Let's make a covenant. [29]Swear that you will not harm us, just as we have never troubled you. We have always treated you well, and we sent you away

Gen 26:17-18 The desolate Gerar area was located on the edge of a desert. Water was as precious as gold. A person who dug a well was staking a claim to the land. Some wells had locks to keep thieves from stealing the water. To fill in someone's well with dirt was an act of war; it was one of the most serious crimes in the land. Isaac had every right to fight back when the Philistines ruined his wells, yet he chose to keep the peace. In the end, the Philistines respected him for his patience.

Gen 26:17-22 Three times Isaac and his men dug new wells. When the first two disputes arose, Isaac moved on. Finally room was available for everyone. Rather than start a huge conflict, Isaac compromised for the sake of peace. Would you be willing to forsake an important position or valuable possession to keep peace? Ask God for the wisdom to know when to withdraw and when to stand and fight.

Gen 26:26-31 With his enemies wanting to make a peace treaty, Isaac was quick to respond, turning the occasion into a celebration. We should be just as receptive to those who want to make peace with us. When God's influence in our lives attracts people—even enemies—we must take the opportunity to reach out to them with God's love.

ISAAC'S MOVE TO GERAR ▶

Isaac had settled near Beer-lahai-roi ("the well of the Living One who sees me"), where his sons, Jacob and Esau, were born. A famine drove him to Gerar. But when he became wealthy, his jealous neighbors asked him to leave. From Gerar he moved to Beersheba (Gen 26:23).

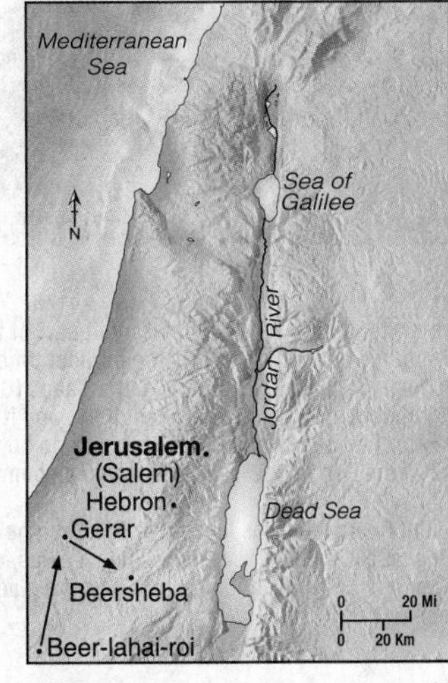

▸ **GENESIS 26:26-35 *(cont.)***
from us in peace. And now look how the LORD has
blessed you!"
30So Isaac prepared a covenant feast to celebrate
the treaty, and they ate and drank together. 31Early
the next morning, they each took a solemn oath not to
interfere with each other. Then Isaac sent them home
again, and they left him in peace.
32That very day Isaac's servants came and told him
about a new well they had dug. "We've found water!"
they exclaimed. 33So Isaac named the well Shibah
(which means "oath"). And to this day the town that
grew up there is called Beersheba (which means "well
of the oath").
34At the age of forty, Esau married two Hittite
wives: Judith, the daughter of Beeri, and Basemath,
the daughter of Elon. 35But Esau's wives made life
miserable for Isaac and Rebekah.

3. ISAAC'S BLESSING

Jacob was the son that God chose to inherit his covenant promises to Abraham and Isaac, but he and his mother, Rebekah, decided to scheme and deceive Isaac rather than trusting in God to work his way. As a result, Jacob had to flee his home and family for fear of his brother.

Jacob Steals Esau's Blessing

GENESIS 27:1-40
One day when Isaac was old and turning blind, he
called for Esau, his older son, and said, "My son."
"Yes, Father?" Esau replied.
2"I am an old man now," Isaac said, "and I don't
know when I may die. 3Take your bow and a quiver full
of arrows, and go out into the open country to hunt
some wild game for me. 4Prepare my favorite dish,
and bring it here for me to eat. Then I will pronounce
the blessing that belongs to you, my firstborn son,
before I die."
5But Rebekah overheard what Isaac had said to his
son Esau. So when Esau left to hunt for the wild game,
6she said to her son Jacob, "Listen. I overheard your
father say to Esau, 7'Bring me some wild game and

Gen 26:34-35 Esau married pagan women, and this upset his parents greatly. Most parents can be a storehouse of good advice because they have a lifetime of insight into their children's character. You may not agree with everything your parents say, but at least talk with them and listen carefully. This will help avoid the hard feelings Esau experienced.

Gen 27:5-10 When Rebekah learned that Isaac was preparing to bless Esau, she quickly devised a plan to trick him into blessing Jacob instead. Although God had already told her that Jacob would become the family leader (Gen 25:23), Rebekah took matters into her own hands. She resorted to doing something wrong to try to bring about what God had already said would happen. For Rebekah, the end justified the means. No matter how good we think our goals are, we should not attempt to achieve them by doing what is wrong. Would God approve of the methods you are using to accomplish your goals?

Gen 27:11-12 How we react to a moral dilemma often exposes our real motives. Frequently we are more worried about getting caught than about doing what is right. Jacob did not seem concerned about the deceitfulness of his mother's plan; instead he was afraid of getting in trouble while carrying it out. If you are worried about getting caught, you are probably in a position that is less than honest. Let your fear of getting caught be a warning to do right. Jacob paid a huge price for carrying out this dishonest plan.

Gen 27:11-13 Jacob hesitated when he heard Rebekah's deceitful plan. Although he questioned it for the wrong reason (fear of getting caught), he protested and thus gave her one last chance to reconsider. But Rebekah had become so wrapped up in her plan that she no longer saw clearly what she was doing. Sin had trapped her and was degrading her character. Correcting yourself in the middle of doing wrong may bring hurt and disappointment, but it also will bring freedom from sin's control.

Beersheba

Beersheba is a town in the southernmost part of the Promised Land, 28 miles southwest of Hebron. It was important from the earliest times in Israel's history. Hagar wandered with Ishmael in this area (Gen 21). Later, Isaac (Gen 26) and Jacob (Gen 46:1-5) both had significant spiritual experiences there, and it was important in the lives of numerous other Hebrews. Beersheba was considered to be the extreme south of the land, and the phrase "from Dan to Beersheba" became a common way to refer to all of Israel (e.g., Judg 20:1; 1 Kgs 4:25).

Ancient Beersheba was located at Tell Beersheba, two miles northeast of the modern city. Recent excavations reveal that the city was founded by the Hebrews in the twelfth or eleventh century B.C. and probably was the place where the sons of Samuel judged the people (1 Sam 8:2).

prepare me a delicious meal. Then I will bless you in
the LORD's presence before I die.' 8Now, my son, listen
to me. Do exactly as I tell you. 9Go out to the flocks, and
bring me two fine young goats. I'll use them to prepare
your father's favorite dish. 10Then take the food to your
father so he can eat it and bless you before he dies."
11"But look," Jacob replied to Rebekah, "my brother,
Esau, is a hairy man, and my skin is smooth. 12What if
my father touches me? He'll see that I'm trying to trick
him, and then he'll curse me instead of blessing me."
13But his mother replied, "Then let the curse fall
on me, my son! Just do what I tell you. Go out and get
the goats for me!"
14So Jacob went out and got the young goats for his
mother. Rebekah took them and prepared a delicious
meal, just the way Isaac liked it. 15Then she took Esau's
favorite clothes, which were there in the house, and
gave them to her younger son, Jacob. 16She covered his
arms and the smooth part of his neck with the skin of
the young goats. 17Then she gave Jacob the delicious
meal, including freshly baked bread.
18So Jacob took the food to his father. "My father?"
he said.
"Yes, my son," Isaac answered. "Who are you—Esau
or Jacob?"
19Jacob replied, "It's Esau, your firstborn son. I've
done as you told me. Here is the wild game. Now sit
up and eat it so you can give me your blessing."
20Isaac asked, "How did you find it so quickly,
my son?"
"The LORD your God put it in my path!" Jacob replied.
21Then Isaac said to Jacob, "Come closer so I can
touch you and make sure that you really are Esau." 22So
Jacob went closer to his father, and Isaac touched him.
"The voice is Jacob's, but the hands are Esau's," Isaac
said. 23But he did not recognize Jacob, because Jacob's
hands felt hairy just like Esau's. So Isaac prepared to
bless Jacob. 24"But are you really my son Esau?" he asked.

JACOB

Abraham, Isaac, and Jacob are among the most significant people in the Old Testament. This isn't based upon their personal character but rather upon the character of God. They were all men who earned the grudging respect and even fear of their peers. They were wealthy and powerful. And yet each was capable of lying, deceit, and selfishness. They were not the perfect heroes we might have expected; instead, they were just like us, trying to please God, but often falling short. • Jacob was the third link in God's plan to start a nation from Abraham. The success of that plan was more often in spite of than because of Jacob's life. Before Jacob was born, God promised that his plan would be worked out through Jacob and not his twin brother, Esau. Although Jacob's methods were not always respectable, his skill, determination, and patience have to be admired. • Jacob's life had four stages, each marked by a personal encounter with God. In the first stage, Jacob lived up to his name, which means "he grasps the heel" (figuratively, "he deceives"). He grabbed Esau's heel at birth, and by the time he fled from home, he had also grabbed his brother's birthright and blessing. It was during his flight that God first appeared to him. Not only did God confirm to Jacob his blessing, but he awakened in Jacob a personal knowledge of God. In the second stage, Jacob experienced life from the other side, being manipulated and deceived by Laban. But there is a curious change: The Jacob of stage one would simply have left Laban, whereas the Jacob of stage two, after deciding to leave, waited six years for God's permission. In the third stage, Jacob was in a new role as grabber. This time, by the Jordan River, he grabbed on to God and wouldn't let go. He realized his dependence on the God who had continued to bless him. His relationship to God became essential to his life, and his name was changed to Israel, "he struggles with God." Jacob's last stage of life was to be grabbed—God achieved a firm hold on him. In responding to Joseph's invitation to come to Egypt, Jacob was clearly unwilling to make a move without God's approval. • Can you think of times when God has made himself known to you? Do you allow yourself to meet him as you study his Word? What difference have these experiences made in your life? Are you more like the young Jacob, forcing God to track you down in the desert of your own plans and mistakes? Or are you more like the older Jacob, who presented his desires and plans to God for his approval before taking any action?

Strengths and accomplishments	• Father of the 12 tribes of Israel • Determined and willing to work long and hard for what he wanted • Good businessman
Weaknesses and mistakes	• When faced with conflict, relied on his own resources rather than going to God for help • Relied on deception
Lessons from his life	• Security does not lie in the accumulation of goods • All human intentions and actions—for good or evil—are woven by God into his ongoing plan
Vital statistics	• Where: Canaan • Occupation: Shepherd, livestock owner • Relatives: Parents: Isaac and Rebekah. Brother: Esau. Father-in-law: Laban. Wives: Rachel and Leah. Offspring: Twelve sons and one daughter are mentioned in the Bible.
Key verse	"What's more, I am with you, and I will protect you wherever you go. One day I will bring you back to this land. I will not leave you until I have finished giving you everything I have promised you" (Gen 28:15).

Jacob's story is told in Genesis 25–50. He is also mentioned in Hosea 12:2-5; Matthew 22:32; Acts 7:8-16; Romans 9:11-13; Hebrews 11:9, 20-21.

▸ **GENESIS 27:1-40** ***(cont.)***

"Yes, I am," Jacob replied.
25Then Isaac said, "Now, my son, bring me the wild
game. Let me eat it, and then I will give you my blessing." So Jacob took the food to his father, and Isaac
ate it. He also drank the wine that Jacob served him.
26Then Isaac said to Jacob, "Please come a little closer
and kiss me, my son."
27So Jacob went over and kissed him. And when
Isaac caught the smell of his clothes, he was finally
convinced, and he blessed his son. He said, "Ah! The
smell of my son is like the smell of the outdoors, which
the LORD has blessed!

28 "From the dew of heaven
and the richness of the earth,
may God always give you abundant harvests
of grain
and bountiful new wine.
29 May many nations become your servants,
and may they bow down to you.
May you be the master over your brothers,
and may your mother's sons bow down
to you.
All who curse you will be cursed,
and all who bless you will be blessed."

30As soon as Isaac had finished blessing Jacob,
and almost before Jacob had left his father, Esau returned from his hunt. 31Esau prepared a delicious
meal and brought it to his father. Then he said, "Sit
up, my father, and eat my wild game so you can give
me your blessing."
32But Isaac asked him, "Who are you?"
Esau replied, "It's your son, your firstborn son,
Esau."
33Isaac began to tremble uncontrollably and said,
"Then who just served me wild game? I have already
eaten it, and I blessed him just before you came. And
yes, that blessing must stand!"
34When Esau heard his father's words, he let out
a loud and bitter cry. "Oh my father, what about me?
Bless me, too!" he begged.
35But Isaac said, "Your brother was here, and he
tricked me. He has taken away your blessing."
36Esau exclaimed, "No wonder his name is Jacob,
for now he has cheated me twice.* First he took my
rights as the firstborn, and now he has stolen my
blessing. Oh, haven't you saved even one blessing
for me?"
37Isaac said to Esau, "I have made Jacob your master and have declared that all his brothers will be
his servants. I have guaranteed him an abundance
of grain and wine—what is left for me to give you,
my son?"
38Esau pleaded, "But do you have only one blessing? Oh my father, bless me, too!" Then Esau broke
down and wept.
39Finally, his father, Isaac, said to him,

"You will live away from the richness of the earth,
and away from the dew of the heaven above.
40 You will live by your sword,
and you will serve your brother.
But when you decide to break free,
you will shake his yoke from your neck."

Jacob Flees to Paddan-Aram

GENESIS 27:41–28:9

From that time on, Esau hated Jacob because their
father had given Jacob the blessing. And Esau began
to scheme: "I will soon be mourning my father's death.
Then I will kill my brother, Jacob."
42But Rebekah heard about Esau's plans. So she
sent for Jacob and told him, "Listen, Esau is consoling himself by plotting to kill you. 43So listen carefully,
my son. Get ready and flee to my brother, Laban, in
Haran. 44Stay there with him until your brother cools
off. 45When he calms down and forgets what you have
done to him, I will send for you to come back. Why
should I lose both of you in one day?"
46Then Rebekah said to Isaac, "I'm sick and tired of

Gn 27:36 *Jacob* sounds like the Hebrew words for "heel" and "deceiver."

Gen 27:24 Although Jacob got the blessing he wanted, deceiving his father cost him dearly. These are some of the consequences of that deceit: (1) He never saw his mother again; (2) his brother wanted to kill him; (3) he was deceived by his uncle Laban; (4) his family became torn by strife; (5) Esau became the founder of an enemy nation; (6) he was exiled from his family for years. Ironically, Jacob would have received the birthright and blessing anyway (Gen 25:23). Imagine how different his life would have been had he and his mother waited for God to work his way, in his time!

Gen 27:33 In ancient times, a person's word was binding (much like a written contract today), especially when it was a formal oath. This is why Isaac's blessing was irrevocable.

Gen 27:33-37 Before the father died, he performed a ceremony of blessing in which he officially handed over the birthright to the rightful heir. Although the firstborn son was entitled to the birthright, it was not actually his until the blessing was pronounced. Before the blessing was given, the father could take the birthright away from the oldest son and give it to a more deserving son. But after the blessing was given, the birthright could no longer be taken away. This is why fathers usually waited until late in life to pronounce the blessing. Although Jacob had been given the birthright by his older brother years before (Gen 25:27-34), he still needed his father's blessing to make it binding.

Gen 27:41 Esau was so angry at Jacob that he failed to see his own wrong in giving away the birthright in the first place. Jealous anger blinds us from seeing the benefits we have and makes us dwell on what we don't have.

Gen 27:41 When Esau lost the valuable family blessing, his future suddenly changed. Reacting in anger, he decided to kill Jacob. When you lose something of great value, or if others conspire against you and succeed, anger is the first and most natural reaction. But you can control your feelings by recognizing your reaction for what it is, praying for strength, and asking God for help to see the benefits you do have and the opportunities present even in bad situations.

Gen 28:9 Ishmael was Isaac's half brother, the son of Abraham and Hagar, Sarah's maidservant (Gen 16:1-4, 15). After marrying two foreign girls (Gen 26:34), Esau hoped his

these local Hittite women! I would rather die than see
Jacob marry one of them."
28:1 So Isaac called for Jacob, blessed him, and said,
"You must not marry any of these Canaanite women.
2Instead, go at once to Paddan-aram, to the house of
your grandfather Bethuel, and marry one of your uncle
Laban's daughters. 3May God Almighty* bless you and
give you many children. And may your descendants
multiply and become many nations! 4May God pass
on to you and your descendants* the blessings he
promised to Abraham. May you own this land where
you are now living as a foreigner, for God gave this
land to Abraham."

5So Isaac sent Jacob away, and he went to Paddan-
aram to stay with his uncle Laban, his mother's brother,
the son of Bethuel the Aramean.
6Esau knew that his father, Isaac, had blessed Jacob
and sent him to Paddan-aram to find a wife, and that
he had warned Jacob, "You must not marry a Canaanite woman." 7He also knew that Jacob had obeyed his
parents and gone to Paddan-aram. 8It was now very
clear to Esau that his father did not like the local Canaanite women. 9So Esau visited his uncle Ishmael's
family and married one of Ishmael's daughters, in
addition to the wives he already had. His new wife's
name was Mahalath. She was the sister of Nebaioth
and the daughter of Ishmael, Abraham's son.

Gn 28:3 Hebrew *El-Shaddai.* **Gn 28:4** Hebrew *seed;* also in 28:13, 14.

C. The Story of Jacob

Jacob did everything, both right and wrong, with great zeal. He deceived his own brother, Esau, and his father, Isaac. He wrestled with God and worked fourteen years to marry the woman he loved. Through Jacob we learn how a strong leader can also be a servant. We also see how wrong actions will always come back to haunt us.

1. JACOB STARTS A FAMILY

Jacob had to flee from his brother and live with his mother's family in Haran, but on his way God appeared to him in a dream and confirmed the covenant promises that he had made to Abraham. While in Haran, Jacob suffered the consequences of being on the other side of family deception, but he was also blessed with many children and great wealth.

Jacob flees to Haran

Jacob's Dream at Bethel

GENESIS 28:10-22

Meanwhile, Jacob left Beersheba and traveled toward Haran. 11At sundown he arrived at a good place
to set up camp and stopped there for the night.
Jacob found a stone to rest his head against and
lay down to sleep. 12As he slept, he dreamed of a
stairway that reached from the earth up to heaven.
And he saw the angels of God going up and down
the stairway.
13At the top of the stairway stood the LORD, and he
said, "I am the LORD, the God of your grandfather Abraham, and the God of your father, Isaac. The ground
you are lying on belongs to you. I am giving it to you
and your descendants. 14Your descendants will be as
numerous as the dust of the earth! They will spread

marriage into Ishmael's family would please his parents, Isaac and Rebekah.

Gen 28:10-15 God's covenant promise to Abraham and Isaac was offered to Jacob as well. But it was not enough to be Abraham's grandson; Jacob had to establish his own personal relationship with God. God has no grandchildren; each person must have a personal relationship with him. It is not enough to hear wonderful stories about Christians in your family. You need to become part of the story yourself (see Gal 3:6-7).

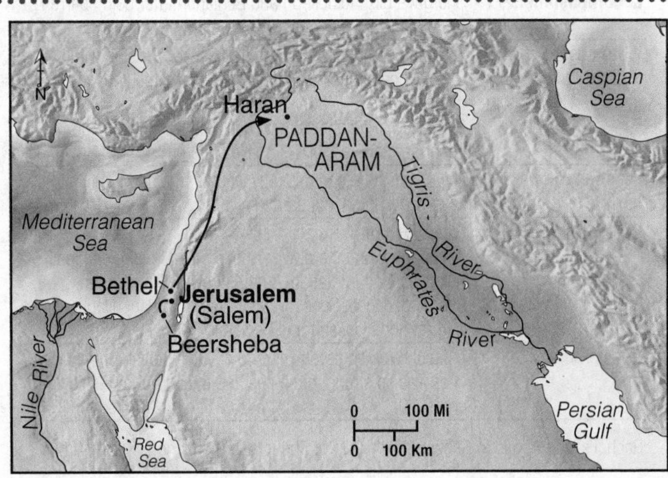

JACOB'S TRIP TO HARAN ▶
After deceiving Esau, Jacob ran for his life, traveling more than 400 miles to Haran, where his uncle Laban lived. On his way, he received a message from the Lord in a dream and named that place Bethel. In Haran, Jacob married and started a family.

▸ **GENESIS 28:10-22** ***(cont.)***

out in all directions—to the west and the east, to the
north and the south. And all the families of the earth
will be blessed through you and your descendants.
15What's more, I am with you, and I will protect you
wherever you go. One day I will bring you back to this
land. I will not leave you until I have finished giving
you everything I have promised you."
16Then Jacob awoke from his sleep and said, "Surely
the LORD is in this place, and I wasn't even aware of it!"
17But he was also afraid and said, "What an awesome
place this is! It is none other than the house of God,
the very gateway to heaven!"
18The next morning Jacob got up very early. He
took the stone he had rested his head against, and
he set it upright as a memorial pillar. Then he poured
olive oil over it. 19He named that place Bethel (which
means "house of God"), although it was previously
called Luz.
20Then Jacob made this vow: "If God will indeed
be with me and protect me on this journey, and if
he will provide me with food and clothing, 21and if I
return safely to my father's home, then the LORD will
certainly be my God. 22And this memorial pillar I have
set up will become a place for worshiping God, and I
will present to God a tenth of everything he gives me."

RACHEL

History seems to repeat itself here. Twice a town well at Haran was the site of significant events in one family's story. It was here that Rebekah met Eliezer, Abraham's servant, who had come to find a wife for Isaac. Some 40 years later, Rebekah's son Jacob returned the favor by serving his cousin Rachel and her sheep from the same well. The relationship that developed between them not only reminds us that romance is not a modern invention but also teaches us a few lessons about patience and love. • Jacob's love for Rachel was both patient and practical. Jacob had the patience to wait seven years for her, but he kept busy in the meantime. His commitment to Rachel kindled a strong loyalty within her. In fact, her loyalty to Jacob got out of hand and became self-destructive. She was frustrated by her barrenness and desperate to compete with her sister for Jacob's affection. She was trying to gain from Jacob what he had already given: devoted love. • Rachel's error can be instructive for us. Like her, we find ourselves trying somehow to earn love—God's love. But apart from his Word, we end up with one of two false ideas. Either we think we've been good enough to deserve his love or we recognize that we aren't able to earn his love and assume that it cannot be ours. If the Bible makes no other point, it shouts this one: God loves us! His love had no beginning and is incredibly patient. All we need to do is respond, not try to earn what is freely offered. God has said in many ways, "I love you. I have demonstrated that love to you by all I've done for you. I have even sacrificed my Son, Jesus, to pay the price for your sin. Now, live because of my love. Respond to me; love me with your whole being; give yourself to me in thanksgiving, not as payment." Live life fully, in the freedom of knowing you are loved.

Strengths and accomplishments	• She showed great loyalty to her family • She gave birth to Joseph and Benjamin after being barren for many years
Weaknesses and mistakes	• Envy and competitiveness marred her relationship with Leah • She was capable of dishonesty when she took her loyalty too far • She failed to recognize that Jacob's devotion was not dependent on her ability to have children
Lessons from her life	• Loyalty must be controlled by what is true and right • Love is accepted, not earned
Vital statistics	• Where: Haran • Occupation: Shepherd, wife, mother, household manager • Relatives: Father: Laban. Aunt: Rebekah. Sister: Leah. Husband: Jacob. Sons through Bilhah: Dan and Naphtali. Natural Sons: Joseph and Benjamin.
Key verse	"So Jacob worked seven years to pay for Rachel. But his love for her was so strong that it seemed to him but a few days" (Gen 29:20).

Rachel's story is told in Genesis 29:1–35:20. She is also mentioned in Ruth 4:11.

Gen 28:19 Bethel was about 10 miles north of Jerusalem and 60 miles north of Beersheba, where Jacob left his family. This was where Abraham made one of his first sacrifices to God when he entered the land. At first, Bethel became an important center for worship; later it was a center of idol worship. The prophet Hosea condemned its evil practices, which began when Jeroboam set up calf idols there when the northern kingdom of Israel first split from Judah (1 Kgs 12:25-33).

Gen 28:20-22 Was Jacob trying to bargain with God? It is possible that he, in his ignorance of how to worship and serve God, treated God like a servant who would perform a service for a tip. More likely, Jacob was not bargaining but pledging his future to God. He may have been saying, in effect, "Because you have blessed me, I will follow you." Whether Jacob was bargaining or pledging, God blessed him. But God also had some difficult lessons for Jacob to learn.

Gen 29:18-27 It was the custom of the day for a man to present a dowry, or substantial gift, to the family of his future wife. This was to compensate the family for the loss of the girl. Jacob's dowry was not a material possession, for he had none to offer. Instead, he agreed to work seven years for Laban. But there was another custom of the land that Laban did not tell Jacob. The older daughter had to be married first. By giving Jacob Leah and not Rachel, Laban tricked him into promising another seven years of hard work.

Gen 29:20-28 People often wonder if working a long time for something they desire is worth it. Jacob worked seven years to marry Rachel. After being tricked, he agreed to work seven more years for her (although he did get to marry Rachel shortly after he married Leah)! The most important goals and desires are worth working and waiting for. Movies and television have created the illusion that people have to wait only about an hour to solve their problems or get what they want. Don't be trapped into thinking the same is true in real life. Patience is hardest when we need it the most, but it is the key to achieving our goals.

Jacob Arrives at Paddan-Aram

GENESIS 29:1-14a

Then Jacob hurried on, finally arriving in the land of
the east. 2He saw a well in the distance. Three flocks of
sheep and goats lay in an open field beside it, waiting
to be watered. But a heavy stone covered the mouth
of the well.

3It was the custom there to wait for all the flocks
to arrive before removing the stone and watering
the animals. Afterward the stone would be placed
back over the mouth of the well. 4Jacob went over
to the shepherds and asked, "Where are you from,
my friends?"

"We are from Haran," they answered.

5"Do you know a man there named Laban, the
grandson of Nahor?" he asked.

"Yes, we do," they replied.

6"Is he doing well?" Jacob asked.

"Yes, he's well," they answered. "Look, here comes
his daughter Rachel with the flock now."

7Jacob said, "Look, it's still broad daylight—too early
to round up the animals. Why don't you water the
sheep and goats so they can get back out to pasture?"

8"We can't water the animals until all the flocks
have arrived," they replied. "Then the shepherds move
the stone from the mouth of the well, and we water all
the sheep and goats."

9Jacob was still talking with them when Rachel arrived with her father's flock, for she was a shepherd.
10And because Rachel was his cousin—the daughter of
Laban, his mother's brother—and because the sheep
and goats belonged to his uncle Laban, Jacob went
over to the well and moved the stone from its mouth
and watered his uncle's flock. 11Then Jacob kissed
Rachel, and he wept aloud. 12He explained to Rachel
that he was her cousin on her father's side—the son
of her aunt Rebekah. So Rachel quickly ran and told
her father, Laban.

13As soon as Laban heard that his nephew Jacob
had arrived, he ran out to meet him. He embraced and
kissed him and brought him home. When Jacob had
told him his story, 14Laban exclaimed, "You really are
my own flesh and blood!"

Jacob Marries Leah and Rachel

GENESIS 29:14b-30

After Jacob had stayed with Laban for about a month,
15Laban said to him, "You shouldn't work for me without pay just because we are relatives. Tell me how
much your wages should be."

16Now Laban had two daughters. The older daughter was named Leah, and the younger one was Rachel.
17There was no sparkle in Leah's eyes,* but Rachel had
a beautiful figure and a lovely face. 18Since Jacob was
in love with Rachel, he told her father, "I'll work for you
for seven years if you'll give me Rachel, your younger
daughter, as my wife."

19"Agreed!" Laban replied. "I'd rather give her to you
than to anyone else. Stay and work with me." 20So Jacob
worked seven years to pay for Rachel. But his love for
her was so strong that it seemed to him but a few days.

21Finally, the time came for him to marry her. "I have

Gn 29:17 Or *Leah had dull eyes,* or *Leah had soft eyes.* The meaning of the Hebrew is uncertain.

As he slept, he dreamed of a stairway that reached from the earth up to heaven. And he saw the angels of God going up and down the stairway.

Genesis 28:12

▸ **GENESIS 29:14b-30** ***(cont.)***

fulfilled my agreement," Jacob said to Laban. "Now
give me my wife so I can sleep with her."
22So Laban invited everyone in the neighborhood
and prepared a wedding feast. 23But that night, when
it was dark, Laban took Leah to Jacob, and he slept
with her. 24(Laban had given Leah a servant, Zilpah,
to be her maid.)
25But when Jacob woke up in the morning—it was
Leah! "What have you done to me?" Jacob raged at
Laban. "I worked seven years for Rachel! Why have
you tricked me?"
26"It's not our custom here to marry off a younger
daughter ahead of the firstborn," Laban replied. 27"But
wait until the bridal week is over, then we'll give you
Rachel, too—provided you promise to work another
seven years for me."
28So Jacob agreed to work seven more years. A week
after Jacob had married Leah, Laban gave him Rachel,
too. 29(Laban gave Rachel a servant, Bilhah, to be her
maid.) 30So Jacob slept with Rachel, too, and he loved
her much more than Leah. He then stayed and worked
for Laban the additional seven years.

LEAH

How do we respond when life seems set against us? Leah faced a blunt and painful world. She observed it with sad eyes. Women in her day were considered property. Daughters were traded by their fathers in business deals. Leah's father, Laban, gave her to a man who did not love her. But God loved her. • Leah was given to a man who loved her younger sister, Rachel. In fact, Jacob agreed to work seven years for Rachel's hand in marriage. Jacob kept his end of the contract, but Laban deceived his future son-in-law. He substituted Leah for Rachel under the wedding veil. By the time Jacob knew a switch had been made, he was already married. Laban excused his deception by citing a local custom that a younger daughter could not marry ahead of an older one. After a brief confrontation, Laban agreed to give Rachel to Jacob in exchange for another seven years of work. And although Leah was not his first choice, Jacob accepted her as his wife. • Leah revealed how she felt toward Jacob in the name she gave their first son, Reuben. The name expressed her desire to be noticed by her husband. Because Leah and Rachel competed for Jacob's attention, there was constant friction in the family. They measured their worth by their ability to bear children. Leah was winning the fertility contest handily when Rachel died bearing her second child, Benjamin. But Leah's victory carried little satisfaction, and the Scriptures mention no more children born to Jacob. Ironically, the greatest honor Jacob finally gave Leah was to bury her with his parents and grandparents in the cave at Machpelah (Gen 49:31). • When we fail to live at peace with the important people in our lives, we leave a tragic legacy. When we struggle to love others, we can be helped by reflecting on the fact that God loves us. If God's love doesn't free us, we need to think again!

Strengths and accomplishments	• Bore Jacob six sons and one daughter • Collaborated with Jacob and Rachel to outwit Laban's ruthless manipulation • Is honored as one of the mothers of Israel (Ruth 4:11) • Stands in the lineage of Jesus through her son Judah
Weaknesses and mistakes	• Envied her sister Rachel over Jacob's love • Competed with Rachel for Jacob's attention and respect
Lessons from her life	• Opportunities for joy can be missed through wrong motives toward others • God has a way of using unexpected people to accomplish his purposes and plans
Vital statistics	• Where: Paddan-aram • Occupation: Wife and mother • Relatives: Father: Laban. Sister: Rachel. Husband: Jacob. Daughter: Dinah. Sons through Zilpah: Gad and Asher. Natural Sons: Reuben, Simeon, Levi, Judah, Issachar, and Zebulun.
Key verse	"She named him Zebulun, for she said, 'God has given me a good reward. Now my husband will treat me with respect, for I have given him six sons'" (Gen 30:20).

Leah's story is told in Genesis 29–35. She is also mentioned in Genesis 46:15, 18, 31; Ruth 4:11.

Gen 29:23-25 Jacob was enraged when he learned that Laban had tricked him. The deceiver was now deceived himself. How natural it is for us to become upset at an injustice done to us while closing our eyes to the injustices we do to others. Sin has a way of coming back to haunt us.

Gen 29:28-30 Although Jacob was tricked by Laban, he kept his part of the bargain. There was more at stake than just Jacob's hurt. There was Rachel to think about, as well as God's plan for his life. When we are tricked by others, keeping our part of the bargain may still be wise. Nursing our wounds or plotting revenge makes us unable to see from God's perspective.

Gen 29:32 Today parents usually give their children names that sound good or have sentimental appeal. But the Old Testament portrays a more dynamic use of names. Parents often chose names that reflected the situation at the time of the birth. They sometimes hoped their children would fulfill the meaning of the names given them. Later the parents could look back and see if their grown children had lived up to their names. Sometimes a person's name was changed because his or her character and name did not match. This happened to Jacob ("he grasps the heel," figuratively, "he deceives"), whose name was changed to Israel ("one who struggles with God"). Jacob's character had changed to the point that he was no longer seen as a deceiver, but as a God-honoring man.

Gen 30:3 Each of the three great patriarchs (Abraham, Isaac, and Jacob) had wives who had difficulty conceiving children. It is interesting to note how each man reacted to his wife's predicament. Abraham had relations with Sarah's servant in order to have his own child, thus introducing bitterness and jealousy into his family. Isaac, by contrast, prayed to God when his wife was barren. God eventually answered his prayers, and Rebekah had twin sons. Jacob, however, followed his grandfather's example and had children by his wives' servants, leading to sad and sometimes bitter consequences.

Jacob's Many Children

GENESIS 29:31–30:24

When the LORD saw that Leah was unloved, he enabled
her to have children, but Rachel could not conceive.
32 So Leah became pregnant and gave birth to a son.
She named him Reuben,* for she said, "The LORD has
noticed my misery, and now my husband will love me."
33 She soon became pregnant again and gave birth
to another son. She named him Simeon,* for she said,
"The LORD heard that I was unloved and has given me
another son."
34 Then she became pregnant a third time and gave
birth to another son. She named him Levi,* for she
said, "Surely this time my husband will feel affection
for me, since I have given him three sons!"
35 Once again Leah became pregnant and gave birth
to another son. She named him Judah,* for she said,
"Now I will praise the LORD!" And then she stopped
having children.

30:1 When Rachel saw that she wasn't having any children for Jacob, she became jealous of her sister. She
pleaded with Jacob, "Give me children, or I'll die!"
2 Then Jacob became furious with Rachel. "Am I
God?" he asked. "He's the one who has kept you from
having children!"
3 Then Rachel told him, "Take my maid, Bilhah, and
sleep with her. She will bear children for me,* and
through her I can have a family, too." 4 So Rachel gave
her servant, Bilhah, to Jacob as a wife, and he slept with
her. 5 Bilhah became pregnant and presented him with
a son. 6 Rachel named him Dan,* for she said, "God has
vindicated me! He has heard my request and given me
a son." 7 Then Bilhah became pregnant again and gave
Jacob a second son. 8 Rachel named him Naphtali,*
for she said, "I have struggled hard with my sister,
and I'm winning!"
9 Meanwhile, Leah realized that she wasn't getting
pregnant anymore, so she took her servant, Zilpah, and
gave her to Jacob as a wife. 10 Soon Zilpah presented
him with a son. 11 Leah named him Gad,* for she said,
"How fortunate I am!" 12 Then Zilpah gave Jacob a second son. 13 And Leah named him Asher,* for she said,
"What joy is mine! Now the other women will celebrate
with me."
14 One day during the wheat harvest, Reuben found
some mandrakes growing in a field and brought them
to his mother, Leah. Rachel begged Leah, "Please give
me some of your son's mandrakes."
15 But Leah angrily replied, "Wasn't it enough that
you stole my husband? Now will you steal my son's
mandrakes, too?"

Gn 29:32 *Reuben* means "Look, a son!" It also sounds like the Hebrew for "He has seen my misery." **Gn 29:33** *Simeon* probably means "one who hears." **Gn 29:34** *Levi* sounds like a Hebrew term that means "being attached" or "feeling affection for." **Gn 29:35** *Judah* is related to the Hebrew term for "praise." **Gn 30:3** Hebrew *bear children on my knees.* **Gn 30:6** *Dan* means "he judged" or "he vindicated." **Gn 30:8** *Naphtali* means "my struggle." **Gn 30:11** *Gad* means "good fortune." **Gn 30:13** *Asher* means "happy."

JACOB'S CHILDREN

This chart shows from left to right Jacob's children in the order in which they were born.

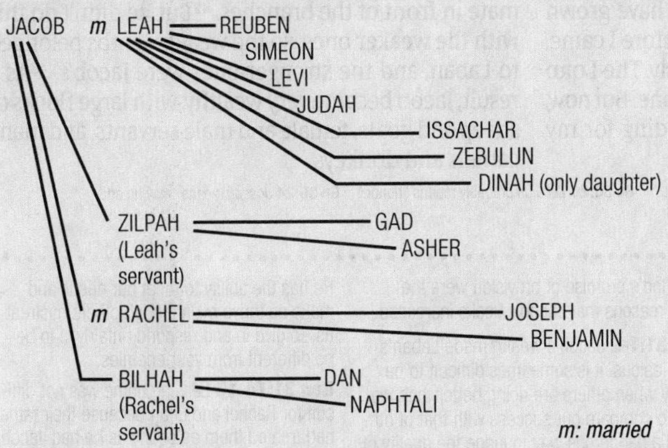

Jacob's many wives (two wives and two "substitute" wives) led to sad and bitter consequences among the children. Anger, resentment, and jealousy were common among Jacob's sons. It is interesting to note that the worst fighting and rivalry occurred between Leah's children and Rachel's children, and among the tribes that descended from them.

Gen 30:4-13 Rachel and Leah were locked in a cruel contest. In their race to have more children, they both gave their servants to Jacob as concubines. Jacob would have been wise to refuse, even though this was an accepted custom of the day. The fact that a custom is socially acceptable does not mean it is wise or right. You will be spared much heartbreak if you look at the potential consequences, for you or others, of your actions. Are you doing anything now that might cause future problems?

▸ **GENESIS 29:31–30:24** ***(cont.)***

Rachel answered, "I will let Jacob sleep with you tonight if you give me some of the mandrakes."

16So that evening, as Jacob was coming home from the fields, Leah went out to meet him. "You must come and sleep with me tonight!" she said. "I have paid for you with some mandrakes that my son found." So that night he slept with Leah. 17And God answered Leah's prayers. She became pregnant again and gave birth to a fifth son for Jacob. 18She named him Issachar,* for she said, "God has rewarded me for giving my servant to my husband as a wife." 19Then Leah became pregnant again and gave birth to a sixth son for Jacob. 20She named him Zebulun,* for she said, "God has given me a good reward. Now my husband will treat me with respect, for I have given him six sons." 21Later she gave birth to a daughter and named her Dinah.

22Then God remembered Rachel's plight and answered her prayers by enabling her to have children. 23She became pregnant and gave birth to a son. "God has removed my disgrace," she said. 24And she named him Joseph,* for she said, "May the LORD add yet another son to my family."

Jacob's Wealth Increases

GENESIS 30:25-43

1915 BC Soon after Rachel had given birth to Joseph, Jacob said to Laban, "Please release me so I can go home to my own country. 26Let me take my wives and children, for I have earned them by serving you, and let me be on my way. You certainly know how hard I have worked for you."

Joseph is born

27"Please listen to me," Laban replied. "I have become wealthy, for* the LORD has blessed me because of you. 28Tell me how much I owe you. Whatever it is, I'll pay it."

29Jacob replied, "You know how hard I've worked for you, and how your flocks and herds have grown under my care. 30You had little indeed before I came, but your wealth has increased enormously. The LORD has blessed you through everything I've done. But now, what about me? When can I start providing for my own family?"

31"What wages do you want?" Laban asked again.

Jacob replied, "Don't give me anything. Just do this one thing, and I'll continue to tend and watch over your flocks. 32Let me inspect your flocks today and remove all the sheep and goats that are speckled or spotted, along with all the black sheep. Give these to me as my wages. 33In the future, when you check on the animals you have given me as my wages, you'll see that I have been honest. If you find in my flock any goats without speckles or spots, or any sheep that are not black, you will know that I have stolen them from you."

34"All right," Laban replied. "It will be as you say." 35But that very day Laban went out and removed the male goats that were streaked and spotted, all the female goats that were speckled and spotted or had white patches, and all the black sheep. He placed them in the care of his own sons, 36who took them a three-days' journey from where Jacob was. Meanwhile, Jacob stayed and cared for the rest of Laban's flock.

37Then Jacob took some fresh branches from poplar, almond, and plane trees and peeled off strips of bark, making white streaks on them. 38Then he placed these peeled branches in the watering troughs where the flocks came to drink, for that was where they mated. 39And when they mated in front of the white-streaked branches, they gave birth to young that were streaked, speckled, and spotted. 40Jacob separated those lambs from Laban's flock. And at mating time he turned the flock to face Laban's animals that were streaked or black. This is how he built his own flock instead of increasing Laban's.

41Whenever the stronger females were ready to mate, Jacob would place the peeled branches in the watering troughs in front of them. Then they would mate in front of the branches. 42But he didn't do this with the weaker ones, so the weaker lambs belonged to Laban, and the stronger ones were Jacob's. 43As a result, Jacob became very wealthy, with large flocks of sheep and goats, female and male servants, and many camels and donkeys.

Gn 30:18 *Issachar* sounds like a Hebrew term that means "reward." **Gn 30:20** *Zebulun* probably means "honor." **Gn 30:24** *Joseph* means "may he add." **Gn 30:27** Or *I have learned by divination that.*

Gen 30:22-24 Eventually God answered Rachel's prayers and gave her a child of her own. But in the meantime, she had given her servant to Jacob. Trusting God when nothing seems to happen is difficult. But it is harder still to live with the consequences of taking matters into our own hands. Resist the temptation to think God has forgotten you. Have patience and courage to wait for God to act.

Gen 30:37-43 It is unclear what this method was or how it worked. Some say that there was a belief among herdsmen that vivid impressions at mating time influenced the offspring. Most likely, the selective breeding and God's promise of provision were the main reasons that Jacob's flocks increased.

Gen 31:1-2 Jacob's wealth made Laban's sons jealous. It is sometimes difficult to be happy when others are doing better than we are. To compare our success with that of others is a dangerous way to judge the quality of our lives. By comparing ourselves to others, we may be giving jealousy a foothold. We can avoid jealousy by rejoicing in others' successes (see Rom 12:15).

Gen 31:4-13 Although Laban treated Jacob unfairly, God still increased Jacob's wealth. God's power is not limited by lack of fair play. He has the ability to meet our needs and make us thrive even though others mistreat us. To give in and respond unfairly is to be no different from your enemies.

Gen 31:14-15 Leaving home was not difficult for Rachel and Leah because their father had treated them as poorly as he had Jacob. According to custom, they were supposed to receive the benefits of the dowry Jacob paid for them, which was 14 years of hard work. When Laban did not give them what was rightfully theirs, they knew they would never inherit anything from their father. Thus, they wholeheartedly approved of Jacob's plan to take the wealth he had gained and leave.

2. JACOB RETURNS HOME

God told Jacob it was time for him to return to Canaan, so he packed up his family and went home—even though he was still deathly afraid of his brother, Esau. On his way, he had an amazing encounter with God and received a new name, just like his grandfather Abraham had. And when he finally met Esau, the reunion was better than he had expected.

Jacob Flees from Laban

GENESIS 31:1-21

But Jacob soon learned that Laban's sons were grumbling about him. "Jacob has robbed our father of
everything!" they said. "He has gained all his wealth
at our father's expense." 2And Jacob began to notice
a change in Laban's attitude toward him.
3Then the LORD said to Jacob, "Return to the land
of your father and grandfather and to your relatives
there, and I will be with you."
4So Jacob called Rachel and Leah out to the field
where he was watching his flock. 5He said to them, "I
have noticed that your father's attitude toward me has
changed. But the God of my father has been with me.
6You know how hard I have worked for your father,
7but he has cheated me, changing my wages ten times.
But God has not allowed him to do me any harm.
8For if he said, 'The speckled animals will be your
wages,' the whole flock began to produce speckled
young. And when he changed his mind and said, 'The
striped animals will be your wages,' then the whole
flock produced striped young. 9In this way, God has
taken your father's animals and given them to me.
10"One time during the mating season, I had a
dream and saw that the male goats mating with the
females were streaked, speckled, and spotted. 11Then
in my dream, the angel of God said to me, 'Jacob!' And
I replied, 'Yes, here I am.'
12"The angel said, 'Look up, and you will see that
only the streaked, speckled, and spotted males are
mating with the females of your flock. For I have seen
how Laban has treated you. 13I am the God who appeared to you at Bethel,* the place where you anointed
the pillar of stone and made your vow to me. Now get
ready and leave this country and return to the land
of your birth.'"
14Rachel and Leah responded, "That's fine with
us! We won't inherit any of our father's wealth anyway. 15He has reduced our rights to those of foreign
women. And after he sold us, he wasted the money
you paid him for us. 16All the wealth God has given
you from our father legally belongs to us and our

Gn 31:13 As in Greek version and an Aramaic Targum; Hebrew reads *the God of Bethel.*

LABAN

We're all selfish, but some of us are particularly accomplished at it. Laban's whole life was stamped by self-centeredness. His chief goal was to look out for himself. The way he treated others was controlled by that goal. He made profitable arrangements for his sister Rebekah's marriage to Isaac and used his daughters' lives as bargaining chips. Jacob eventually outmaneuvered Laban, but the older man was unwilling to admit defeat. His hold on Jacob was broken, but he still tried to maintain some kind of control by getting Jacob to promise to be gone for good. He realized that Jacob and Jacob's God were more than he could handle. • On the surface, we may find it difficult to identify with Laban. But his selfishness is one point we have in common. Like him, we often have a strong tendency to want to control people and events to our benefit. Our "good" reasons for treating others the way we do may simply be a thin cover on our self-centered motives. We may not even recognize our own selfishness. One way to discover it is to examine our willingness to admit we're wrong. Laban could not bring himself to do this. If you ever amaze yourself by what you say and do to avoid facing up to wrong actions, you are getting a glimpse of your selfishness in action. Recognizing selfishness is painful, but it is the first step on the road back to God.

Strengths and accomplishments	• Arranged two generations of marriages in the Abrahamic family (Rebekah, Leah, Rachel) • Quick-witted
Weaknesses and mistakes	• Manipulated others for his own benefit • Unwilling to admit wrongdoing • Benefited financially by using Jacob, but never fully benefited spiritually by knowing and worshiping Jacob's God
Lessons from his life	• Those who set out to use people will eventually find themselves being used • God's plan cannot be blocked
Vital statistics	• Where: Haran • Occupation: Wealthy sheep breeder • Relatives: Father: Bethuel. Sister: Rebekah. Brother-in-law: Isaac. Daughters: Rachel and Leah. Son-in-law: Jacob.
Key verse	"In fact, if the God of my father had not been on my side—the God of Abraham and the fearsome God of Isaac—you would have sent me away empty-handed. But God has seen your abuse and my hard work. That is why he appeared to you last night and rebuked you!" (Gen 31:42).

Laban's story is told in Genesis 24:1–31:55.

▸ **GENESIS 31:1-21** *(cont.)*

children. So go ahead and do whatever God has told you."

[17]So Jacob put his wives and children on camels, [18]and he drove all his livestock in front of him. He packed all the belongings he had acquired in Paddan-aram and set out for the land of Canaan, where his father, Isaac, lived. [19]At the time they left, Laban was some distance away, shearing his sheep. Rachel stole her father's household idols and took them with her. [20]Jacob outwitted Laban the Aramean, for they set out secretly and never told Laban they were leaving. [21]So Jacob took all his possessions with him and crossed the Euphrates River,* heading for the hill country of Gilead.

Laban Pursues Jacob

GENESIS 31:22-42

Three days later, Laban was told that Jacob had fled. [23]So he gathered a group of his relatives and set out in hot pursuit. He caught up with Jacob seven days later in the hill country of Gilead. [24]But the previous night God had appeared to Laban the Aramean in a dream and told him, "I'm warning you—leave Jacob alone!"

[25]Laban caught up with Jacob as he was camped in the hill country of Gilead, and he set up his camp not far from Jacob's. [26]"What do you mean by deceiving me like this?" Laban demanded. "How dare you drag my daughters away like prisoners of war? [27]Why did you slip away secretly? Why did you deceive me? And why didn't you say you wanted to leave? I would have given you a farewell feast, with singing and music, accompanied by tambourines and harps. [28]Why didn't you let me kiss my daughters and grandchildren and tell them good-bye? You have acted very foolishly! [29]I could destroy you, but the God of your father appeared to me last night and warned me, 'Leave Jacob alone!' [30]I can understand your feeling that you must go, and your intense longing for your father's home. But why have you stolen my gods?"

[31]"I rushed away because I was afraid," Jacob answered. "I thought you would take your daughters from me by force. [32]But as for your gods, see if you can find them, and let the person who has taken them die! And if you find anything else that belongs to you, identify it before all these relatives of ours, and I will give it back!" But Jacob did not know that Rachel had stolen the household idols.

[33]Laban went first into Jacob's tent to search there, then into Leah's, and then the tents of the two servant wives—but he found nothing. Finally, he went into Rachel's tent. [34]But Rachel had taken the household idols and hidden them in her camel saddle, and now she was sitting on them. When Laban had thoroughly searched her tent without finding them, [35]she said to her father, "Please, sir, forgive me if I don't get up for you. I'm having my monthly period." So Laban continued his search, but he could not find the household idols.

[36]Then Jacob became very angry, and he challenged Laban. "What's my crime?" he demanded. "What have I done wrong to make you chase after me as though I were a criminal? [37]You have rummaged through everything I own. Now show me what you found that belongs to you! Set it out here in front of us, before our relatives, for all to see. Let them judge between us!

[38]"For twenty years I have been with you, caring for your flocks. In all that time your sheep and goats never

Gn 31:21 Hebrew *the river.*

Gen 31:19 Many people kept small wooden or metal idols ("household idols") in their homes. These idols were called *teraphim*, and they were thought to protect the home and offer advice in times of need. They had legal significance as well, for when they were passed on to an heir, the person who received them could rightfully claim the greatest part of the family inheritance. No wonder Laban was concerned when he realized his idols were missing (Gen 31:30). Most likely Rachel stole her father's idols because she was afraid Laban would consult them and learn where she and Jacob had gone, or perhaps she wanted to claim the family inheritance.

Gen 31:32 Do you remember feeling absolutely sure about something? Jacob was so sure that no one had stolen Laban's idols that he vowed to kill the offender. Because Rachel took them, this statement put her safety in serious jeopardy. Even when you are absolutely sure about a matter, avoid rash statements. Someone may hold you to them.

Gen 31:38-42 Jacob made it a habit to do more than was expected of him. When his flocks were attacked, he took the losses rather than splitting them with Laban. He worked hard even after several pay cuts. His diligence eventually paid off; his flocks began to multiply. Making a habit of doing

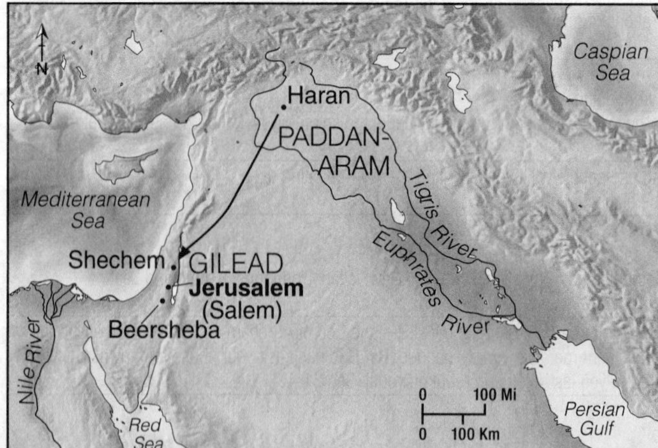

◀ ***JACOB'S RETURN TO CANAAN***
God told Jacob to leave Haran and return to his homeland. Jacob took his family, crossed the Euphrates River, and headed first for the hill country of Gilead. Laban caught up with him there.

miscarried. In all those years I never used a single ram of yours for food. 39If any were attacked and killed by wild animals, I never showed you the carcass and asked you to reduce the count of your flock. No, I took the loss myself! You made me pay for every stolen animal, whether it was taken in broad daylight or in the dark of night.

40"I worked for you through the scorching heat of the day and through cold and sleepless nights. 41Yes, for twenty years I slaved in your house! I worked for fourteen years earning your two daughters, and then six more years for your flock. And you changed my wages ten times! 42In fact, if the God of my father had not been on my side—the God of Abraham and the fearsome God of Isaac*—you would have sent me away empty-handed. But God has seen your abuse and my hard work. That is why he appeared to you last night and rebuked you!"

Jacob's Treaty with Laban

GENESIS 31:43–32:2

Then Laban replied to Jacob, "These women are my daughters, these children are my grandchildren, and these flocks are my flocks—in fact, everything you see is mine. But what can I do now about my daughters and their children? 44So come, let's make a covenant, you and I, and it will be a witness to our commitment."

45So Jacob took a stone and set it up as a monument. 46Then he told his family members, "Gather some stones." So they gathered stones and piled them in a heap. Then Jacob and Laban sat down beside the pile of stones to eat a covenant meal. 47To commemorate the event, Laban called the place Jegar-sahadutha (which means "witness pile" in Aramaic), and Jacob called it Galeed (which means "witness pile" in Hebrew).

48Then Laban declared, "This pile of stones will stand as a witness to remind us of the covenant we have made today." This explains why it was called Galeed—"Witness Pile." 49But it was also called Mizpah (which means "watchtower"), for Laban said, "May the LORD keep watch between us to make sure that we keep this covenant when we are out of each other's sight. 50If you mistreat my daughters or if you marry other wives, God will see it even if no one else does. He is a witness to this covenant between us.

51"See this pile of stones," Laban continued, "and see this monument I have set between us. 52They stand between us as witnesses of our vows. I will never pass this pile of stones to harm you, and you must never pass these stones or this monument to harm me. 53I call on the God of our ancestors—the God of your grandfather Abraham and the God of my grandfather Nahor—to serve as a judge between us."

So Jacob took an oath before the fearsome God of his father, Isaac,* to respect the boundary line. 54Then Jacob offered a sacrifice to God there on the mountain and invited everyone to a covenant feast. After they had eaten, they spent the night on the mountain.

55*Laban got up early the next morning, and he kissed his grandchildren and his daughters and blessed them. Then he left and returned home.

32:1*As Jacob started on his way again, angels of God came to meet him. 2When Jacob saw them, he exclaimed, "This is God's camp!" So he named the place Mahanaim.*

Jacob Sends Gifts to Esau

GENESIS 32:3-21

Then Jacob sent messengers ahead to his brother, Esau, who was living in the region of Seir in the land of Edom. 4He told them, "Give this message to my master Esau: 'Humble greetings from your servant Jacob. Until now I have been living with Uncle Laban, 5and now I own cattle, donkeys, flocks of sheep and goats, and many servants, both men and women. I have sent these messengers to inform my lord of my coming, hoping that you will be friendly to me.'"

Spoked wheels invented (estimated)

6After delivering the message, the messengers returned to Jacob and reported, "We met your brother, Esau, and he is already on his way to meet you—with an army of 400 men!" 7Jacob was terrified at the news. He divided his household, along with the flocks and herds and camels, into two groups. 8He thought, "If Esau meets one group and attacks it, perhaps the other group can escape."

9Then Jacob prayed, "O God of my grandfather Abraham, and God of my father, Isaac—O LORD, you told

Gn 31:42 Or *and the Fear of Isaac.* **Gn 31:53** Or *the Fear of his father, Isaac.* **Gn 31:55** Verse 31:55 is numbered 32:1 in Hebrew text. **Gn 32:1** Verses 32:1-32 are numbered 32:2-33 in Hebrew text. **Gn 32:2** *Mahanaim* means "two camps."

more than expected can pay off. It pleases God, earns recognition and advancement, enhances your reputation, builds others' confidence in you, gives you more experience and knowledge, and develops your spiritual maturity.

Gen 31:49 To be binding, an agreement had to be witnessed by a third party. In this case, Jacob and Laban used God as their witness that they would keep their word.

Gen 32:1 Although angels often would appear in human form, these angels must have looked different, for Jacob recognized them at once. Why did angels of God meet Jacob? The reason is unclear; but because of their visit, Jacob knew God was with him.

Gen 32:3 The last time Jacob had seen Esau, his older brother had been ready to kill him for stealing the family blessing (Gen 25:29–27:42). Esau was so angry that he had vowed to kill Jacob as soon as their father, Isaac, died (Gen 27:41). Fearing their reunion, Jacob sent a messenger ahead with gifts. He hoped to buy Esau's favor.

Gen 32:9-12 How would you feel if you knew you were about to meet the person you had cheated out of his most precious possession? Jacob had taken Esau's birthright (Gen 25:33) and his blessing (Gen 27:27-40). Now he was about to meet this brother for the first time in 20 years, and he was frantic with fear. But he collected his thoughts and decided to pray. When we face a difficult conflict, we can run about frantically or we can pause to pray. Which approach will be more effective?

▸ **GENESIS 32:3-21 *(cont.)***

me, 'Return to your own land and to your relatives.' And you promised me, 'I will treat you kindly.' [10]I am not worthy of all the unfailing love and faithfulness you have shown to me, your servant. When I left home and crossed the Jordan River, I owned nothing except a walking stick. Now my household fills two large camps! [11]O LORD, please rescue me from the hand of my brother, Esau. I am afraid that he is coming to attack me, along with my wives and children. [12]But you promised me, 'I will surely treat you kindly, and I will multiply your descendants until they become as numerous as the sands along the seashore—too many to count.'"

[13]Jacob stayed where he was for the night. Then he selected these gifts from his possessions to present to his brother, Esau: [14]200 female goats, 20 male goats, 200 ewes, 20 rams, [15]30 female camels with their young, 40 cows, 10 bulls, 20 female donkeys, and 10 male donkeys. [16]He divided these animals into herds and assigned each to different servants. Then he told his servants, "Go ahead of me with the animals, but keep some distance between the herds."

[17]He gave these instructions to the men leading the first group: "When my brother, Esau, meets you, he will ask, 'Whose servants are you? Where are you going? Who owns these animals?' [18]You must reply, 'They belong to your servant Jacob, but they are a gift for his master Esau. Look, he is coming right behind us.'"

[19]Jacob gave the same instructions to the second and third herdsmen and to all who followed behind the herds: "You must say the same thing to Esau when you meet him. [20]And be sure to say, 'Look, your servant Jacob is right behind us.'"

Jacob thought, "I will try to appease him by sending gifts ahead of me. When I see him in person, perhaps he will be friendly to me." [21]So the gifts were sent on ahead, while Jacob himself spent that night in the camp.

Jacob Wrestles with God

GENESIS 32:22-32

During the night Jacob got up and took his two wives, his two servant wives, and his eleven sons and crossed the Jabbok River with them. [23]After taking them to the other side, he sent over all his possessions.

[24]This left Jacob all alone in the camp, and a man came and wrestled with him until the dawn began to break. [25]When the man saw that he would not win the match, he touched Jacob's hip and wrenched it out of its socket. [26]Then the man said, "Let me go, for the dawn is breaking!"

But Jacob said, "I will not let you go unless you bless me."

[27]"What is your name?" the man asked.

He replied, "Jacob."

[28]"Your name will no longer be Jacob," the man told him. "From now on you will be called Israel,* because you have fought with God and with men and have won."

[29]"Please tell me your name," Jacob said.

"Why do you want to know my name?" the man replied. Then he blessed Jacob there.

[30]Jacob named the place Peniel (which means "face of God"), for he said, "I have seen God face to face, yet my life has been spared." [31]The sun was rising as Jacob left Peniel,* and he was limping because of the injury to his hip. [32](Even today the people of Israel

Gn 32:28 *Jacob* sounds like the Hebrew words for "heel" and "deceiver." *Israel* means "God fights." **Gn 32:31** Hebrew *Penuel,* a variant spelling of Peniel.

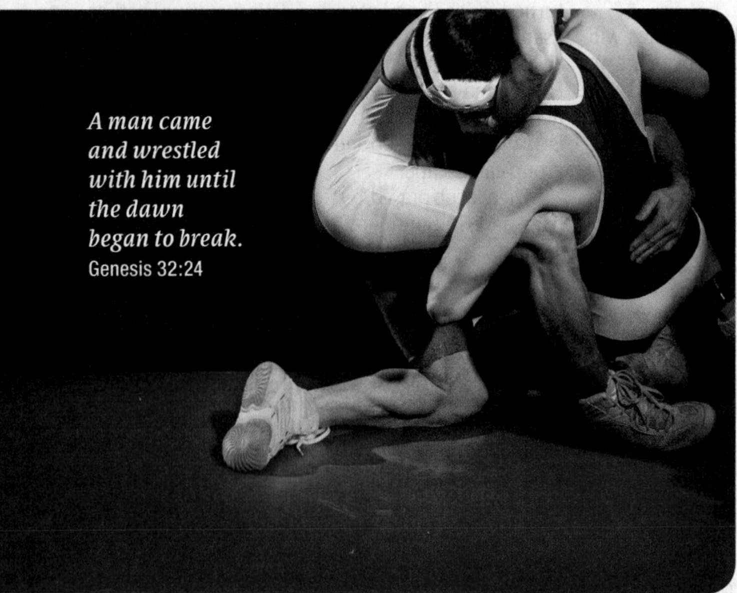

A man came and wrestled with him until the dawn began to break.
Genesis 32:24

Gen 32:26 Jacob continued this wrestling match all night just to be blessed. He was persistent. God encourages persistence in all areas of our lives, including the spiritual. Where in your spiritual life do you need more persistence? Strong character develops as you struggle through tough conditions.

Gen 32:27-29 God gave many Bible people new names (Abraham, Sarah, Peter). Their new names were symbols of how God had changed their lives. Here we see how Jacob's character had changed. Jacob, the ambitious deceiver, became Israel, the one who struggles with God and overcomes.

Gen 33:1-11 Jacob must have been amazed to see Esau's change of heart when the two brothers met again (Gen 33:10). Esau was no longer bitter over losing his birthright and blessing (Gen 27:36-41); instead, he was content with what he had.

Life can bring us some bad situations. We can feel cheated, as Esau did, but we don't have to remain bitter. We can remove bitterness from our lives by honestly expressing our feelings to God, forgiving those who have wronged us, and being content with what we have.

don't eat the tendon near the hip socket because of what happened that night when the man strained the tendon of Jacob's hip.)

Jacob and Esau Make Peace

GENESIS 33:1-20

Then Jacob looked up and saw Esau coming with his 400 men. So he divided the children among Leah, Rachel, and his two servant wives. 2He put the servant wives and their children at the front, Leah and her children next, and Rachel and Joseph last. 3Then Jacob went on ahead. As he approached his brother, he bowed to the ground seven times before him. 4Then Esau ran to meet him and embraced him, threw his arms around his neck, and kissed him. And they both wept.

5Then Esau looked at the women and children and asked, "Who are these people with you?"

"These are the children God has graciously given to me, your servant," Jacob replied. 6Then the servant wives came forward with their children and bowed before him. 7Next came Leah with her children, and they bowed before him. Finally, Joseph and Rachel came forward and bowed before him.

8"And what were all the flocks and herds I met as I came?" Esau asked.

Jacob replied, "They are a gift, my lord, to ensure your friendship."

9"My brother, I have plenty," Esau answered. "Keep what you have for yourself."

10But Jacob insisted, "No, if I have found favor with you, please accept this gift from me. And what a relief to see your friendly smile. It is like seeing the face of God! 11Please take this gift I have brought you, for God has been very gracious to me. I have more than enough." And because Jacob insisted, Esau finally accepted the gift.

12"Well," Esau said, "let's be going. I will lead the way."

13But Jacob replied, "You can see, my lord, that some of the children are very young, and the flocks and herds have their young, too. If they are driven too hard, even for one day, all the animals could die. 14Please, my lord, go ahead of your servant. We will follow slowly, at a pace that is comfortable for the livestock and the children. I will meet you at Seir."

15"All right," Esau said, "but at least let me assign some of my men to guide and protect you."

Jacob responded, "That's not necessary. It's enough that you've received me warmly, my lord!"

16So Esau turned around and started back to Seir that same day. 17Jacob, on the other hand, traveled on to Succoth. There he built himself a house and made shelters for his livestock. That is why the place was named Succoth (which means "shelters").

18Later, having traveled all the way from Paddan-aram, Jacob arrived safely at the town of Shechem, in the land of Canaan. There he set up camp outside the town. 19Jacob bought the plot of land where he camped from the family of Hamor, the father of Shechem, for 100 pieces of silver.* 20And there he built an altar and named it El-Elohe-Israel.*

Revenge against Shechem

GENESIS 34:1-31

One day Dinah, the daughter of Jacob and Leah, went to visit some of the young women who lived in

Gn 33:19 Hebrew *100 kesitahs;* the value or weight of the kesitah is no longer known. **Gn 33:20** *El-Elohe-Israel* means "God, the God of Israel."

Gen 33:3 Bowing to the ground seven times was the sign of respect given to a king. Jacob was taking every precaution as he met Esau, hoping to dispel any thoughts of revenge.

Gen 33:4 Esau greeted his brother, Jacob, with a great hug. Imagine how difficult this must have been for a man who once had actually plotted his brother's death (Gen 27:41). But time away from each other allowed the bitter wounds to heal. With the passing of time, each brother was able to see that their relationship was more important than their real estate.

Gen 33:11 Why did Jacob send gifts ahead for Esau? In Bible times, gifts were given for several reasons. (1) This may have been a bribe. Gifts are still given to win over or buy someone's support. Esau may first have refused Jacob's gifts (Gen 33:9) because he didn't want or need a bribe. He had already forgiven Jacob, and he had ample wealth of his own. (2) This may have been an expression of affection. (3) It may have been the customary way of greeting someone before an important meeting. Such gifts were often related to a person's occupation. This explains why Jacob sent Esau (a herdsman) sheep, goats, and cattle.

Gen 33:14-17 Why did Jacob imply that he was going to Seir but then stop at Succoth? We don't know the answer, but perhaps Jacob decided to stop there as they journeyed because Succoth is a beautiful site on the eastern side of the Jordan River. Whatever the reason, Jacob and Esau parted in peace. Then they lived fairly close to each other until after their father's death (Gen 36:6-8).

Gen 34:1-4 Shechem may have been a victim of "love at first sight," but his actions were impulsive and evil. Not only did he sin against Dinah, he sinned against the entire family (Gen 34:6-7). The consequences of his deed were severe both for his family and for Jacob's (Gen 34:25-31). Even Shechem's declared love for Dinah could not excuse the evil he did by raping her.

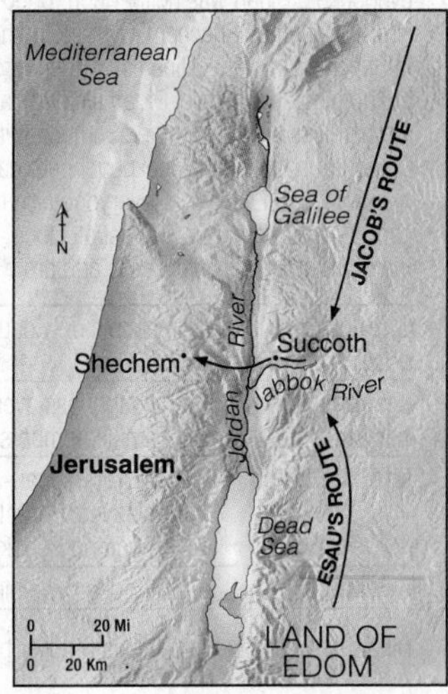

JACOB'S JOURNEY TO SHECHEM ▶ ***After a joyful reunion with his brother, Esau (who journeyed from Edom), Jacob set up camp in Succoth. Later he moved on to Shechem where his daughter, Dinah, was raped and two of his sons took revenge on the city.***

▸ **GENESIS 34:1-31** ***(cont.)***
the area. 2But when the local prince, Shechem son
of Hamor the Hivite, saw Dinah, he seized her and
raped her. 3But then he fell in love with her, and he
tried to win her affection with tender words. 4He said
to his father, Hamor, "Get me this young girl. I want
to marry her."
5Soon Jacob heard that Shechem had defiled his
daughter, Dinah. But since his sons were out in the
fields herding his livestock, he said nothing until they
returned. 6Hamor, Shechem's father, came to discuss
the matter with Jacob. 7Meanwhile, Jacob's sons had
come in from the field as soon as they heard what
had happened. They were shocked and furious that
their sister had been raped. Shechem had done a disgraceful thing against Jacob's family,* something that
should never be done.
8Hamor tried to speak with Jacob and his sons. "My
son Shechem is truly in love with your daughter," he
said. "Please let him marry her. 9In fact, let's arrange
other marriages, too. You give us your daughters for
our sons, and we will give you our daughters for your
sons. 10And you may live among us; the land is open
to you! Settle here and trade with us. And feel free to
buy property in the area."
11Then Shechem himself spoke to Dinah's father
and brothers. "Please be kind to me, and let me marry
her," he begged. "I will give you whatever you ask. 12No
matter what dowry or gift you demand, I will gladly
pay it—just give me the girl as my wife."
13But since Shechem had defiled their sister, Dinah,
Jacob's sons responded deceitfully to Shechem and
his father, Hamor. 14They said to them, "We couldn't
possibly allow this, because you're not circumcised.
It would be a disgrace for our sister to marry a man
like you! 15But here is a solution. If every man among
you will be circumcised like we are, 16then we will give
you our daughters, and we'll take your daughters for
ourselves. We will live among you and become one
people. 17But if you don't agree to be circumcised, we
will take her and be on our way."
18Hamor and his son Shechem agreed to their proposal. 19Shechem wasted no time in acting on this
request, for he wanted Jacob's daughter desperately.
Shechem was a highly respected member of his family,
20and he went with his father, Hamor, to present this
proposal to the leaders at the town gate.
21"These men are our friends," they said. "Let's
invite them to live here among us and trade freely.
Look, the land is large enough to hold them. We can
take their daughters as wives and let them marry
ours. 22But they will consider staying here and becoming one people with us only if all of our men are
circumcised, just as they are. 23But if we do this, all

Gn 34:7 Hebrew *a disgraceful thing in Israel.*

DINAH

As far as we know, Dinah was Jacob's only daughter. She lived among ten older and two younger brothers. She grew up in a family rocked by struggle between two sisters married to the same man. Dinah's mother, Leah, knew that Jacob loved her sister and rival, Rachel. We don't know how the bitterness and jealousy between these women affected Dinah. By the time she was a teenager, her family was living in Shechem, a town north of Bethel and Jerusalem in the Promised Land. • One day, Dinah went out for a walk in town. She was noticed and raped by Shechem, the son of the ruler of the city. Violated and shamed, Dinah found herself in the center of a family crisis. Shechem asked his father to arrange a marriage with Dinah. But in Jacob's and his sons' eyes, Dinah had been wronged and their family had been insulted. Jacob failed to provide any fatherly leadership in this situation and his sons took matters into their own hands. The results were treacherous and bloody. • In all of this, the victim was overlooked. Dinah was neither comforted nor consulted. Instead, she was treated with almost as much disrespect by her family as she had been by Shechem. By handing her over to Shechem, they used Dinah as bait in a trap that led to the murder of all the men in Shechem's village. Dinah's brothers profited from the massacre of Shechem. Jacob was angry at his sons for their actions, but did nothing. Meanwhile, Dinah slipped back into oblivion. Her story reminds us of the tragedies that occur when family members are careless with each other. Someone ends up paying a high price. • You probably know someone who can identify closely with Dinah. Perhaps you have experienced that same anonymity as a victim who was unnoticed or forgotten. Remember several glimmers of hope: Even when everyone else forgets, God doesn't; when no one seems to notice, God sees; when no one seems to care, God cares; when you feel all alone, you aren't. And one of the first lessons God will teach you as you depend on him is that there are others who also care and are willing to help. Begin to speak to God today in prayer about your past.

Strength and accomplishment	• Jacob's only daughter
Lessons from her life	• Thoughtless avengers often hurt the original victims a second time • Family members can be trampled in the rush for family honor
Vital statistics	• Where: Paddan-aram • Relatives: Parents: Jacob and Leah. Siblings: Twelve brothers. Aunt: Rachel. Uncle: Esau. Grandparents: Isaac and Rebekah, Laban.
Key verse	"Later she gave birth to a daughter and named her Dinah" (Gen 30:21).

Dinah's story is told in Genesis 34. Her birth is mentioned in Genesis 30:21; she is last mentioned in Genesis 46:15.

their livestock and possessions will eventually be ours. Come, let's agree to their terms and let them settle here among us."

24So all the men in the town council agreed with
Hamor and Shechem, and every male in the town was
circumcised. 25But three days later, when their wounds
were still sore, two of Jacob's sons, Simeon and Levi,
who were Dinah's full brothers, took their swords
and entered the town without opposition. Then they
slaughtered every male there, 26including Hamor and
his son Shechem. They killed them with their swords,
then took Dinah from Shechem's house and returned
to their camp.
27Meanwhile, the rest of Jacob's sons arrived. Finding
the men slaughtered, they plundered the town because
their sister had been defiled there. 28They seized all the
flocks and herds and donkeys—everything they could
lay their hands on, both inside the town and outside in
the fields. 29They looted all their wealth and plundered
their houses. They also took all their little children and
wives and led them away as captives.
30Afterward Jacob said to Simeon and Levi, "You
have ruined me! You've made me stink among all the
people of this land—among all the Canaanites and
Perizzites. We are so few that they will join forces and
crush us. I will be ruined, and my entire household
will be wiped out!"
31"But why should we let him treat our sister like a
prostitute?" they retorted angrily.

Jacob's Return to Bethel

GENESIS 35:1-15

Then God said to Jacob, "Get ready and move to Bethel
and settle there. Build an altar there to the God who
appeared to you when you fled from your brother,
Esau."
2So Jacob told everyone in his household, "Get rid
of all your pagan idols, purify yourselves, and put on
clean clothing. 3We are now going to Bethel, where I
will build an altar to the God who answered my prayers
when I was in distress. He has been with me wherever
I have gone."
4So they gave Jacob all their pagan idols and earrings, and he buried them under the great tree near
Shechem. 5As they set out, a terror from God spread
over the people in all the towns of that area, so no one
attacked Jacob's family.
6Eventually, Jacob and his household arrived at Luz
(also called Bethel) in Canaan. 7Jacob built an altar
there and named the place El-bethel (which means
"God of Bethel"), because God had appeared to him
there when he was fleeing from his brother, Esau.
8Soon after this, Rebekah's old nurse, Deborah,
died. She was buried beneath the oak tree in the valley below Bethel. Ever since, the tree has been called
Allon-bacuth (which means "oak of weeping").
9Now that Jacob had returned from Paddan-aram,
God appeared to him again at Bethel. God blessed
him, 10saying, "Your name is Jacob, but you will not be

Gen 34:25-31 Why did Simeon and Levi take such harsh action against the city of Shechem? Jacob's family saw themselves as set apart from others. God wanted them to remain separate from their pagan neighbors. But the brothers wrongly thought that being set apart also meant being better. This arrogant attitude led to the terrible slaughter of innocent people.

Gen 34:27-29 When Shechem raped Dinah, the consequences were far greater than he could have imagined. Dinah's brothers were outraged and took revenge. Pain, deceit, and murder followed. Don't allow sexual passion to boil over into evil actions. Passion must be controlled. Sexual sin is devastating because its consequences are so far-reaching.

Gen 34:30-31 In seeking revenge against Shechem, Simeon and Levi lied, stole, and murdered. Their desire for justice was right, but their ways of achieving it were wrong. Because of their sin, their father cursed them with his dying breath (Gen 49:5-7). Generations later, their descendants lost the part of the Promised Land allotted to them. When tempted to return evil for evil, leave revenge to God and spare yourself the dreadful consequences of sin.

Gen 35:2 Why did the people have these idols? Idols were sometimes seen more as good luck charms than as gods. But Jacob rightly believed that idols should have no place in his household. He wanted nothing to divert his family's spiritual focus.

Jacob ordered his household to get rid of their idols. Unless we, too, remove idols from our lives, they can ruin our faith. What idols do we have? An idol is anything we put before God. Idols don't have to be physical objects; they can be thoughts or desires. Like Jacob, we should get rid of anything that could stand between us and God.

Gen 35:4 Why did the people give Jacob their earrings? Jewelry in itself was not evil, but in Jacob's day earrings were often worn as good luck charms to ward off evil. The people in his family had to cleanse themselves of all pagan influences, including reminders of foreign gods.

Gen 35:10 God reminded Jacob of his new name, Israel, which means "one who struggles with God." Although Jacob's life was littered with difficulties and trials, his new name was a tribute to his desire to stay close to God despite life's disappointments.

Many people believe that Christianity should offer a problem-free life. Consequently, as life gets tough, they draw back disappointed. Instead, they should determine to prevail with God through life's storms. Problems and difficulties are painful but inevitable; you might as well see them as opportunities for growth. You can't prevail with God unless you have troubles to prevail over.

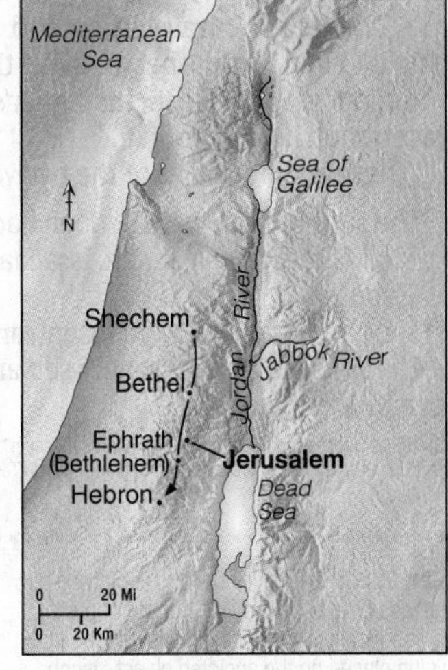

JACOB'S JOURNEY BACK TO HEBRON
After Jacob's sons Simeon and Levi destroyed Shechem, God told Jacob to move to Bethel, where God reminded him that his name had been changed to Israel. He then traveled to Hebron, but along the way his wife Rachel died near Ephrath (Bethlehem).

▶ **GENESIS 35:1-15** ***(cont.)***

called Jacob any longer. From now on your name will be Israel."* So God renamed him Israel.

11Then God said, "I am El-Shaddai—'God Almighty.' Be fruitful and multiply. You will become a great nation, even many nations. Kings will be among your descendants! 12And I will give you the land I once gave to Abraham and Isaac. Yes, I will give it to you and your descendants after you." 13Then God went up from the place where he had spoken to Jacob.

14Jacob set up a stone pillar to mark the place where God had spoken to him. Then he poured wine over it as an offering to God and anointed the pillar with olive oil. 15And Jacob named the place Bethel (which means "house of God"), because God had spoken to him there.

The Deaths of Rachel and Isaac

GENESIS 35:16-29

Leaving Bethel, Jacob and his clan moved on toward Ephrath. But Rachel went into labor while they were still some distance away. Her labor pains were intense. 17After a very hard delivery, the midwife finally exclaimed, "Don't be afraid—you have another son!" 18Rachel was about to die, but with her last breath she named the baby Ben-oni (which means "son of my sorrow"). The baby's father, however, called him Benjamin (which means "son of my right hand"). 19So Rachel died and was buried on the way to Ephrath (that is, Bethlehem). 20Jacob set up a stone monument over Rachel's grave, and it can be seen there to this day.

21Then Jacob* traveled on and camped beyond Migdal-eder. 22While he was living there, Reuben had intercourse with Bilhah, his father's concubine, and Jacob soon heard about it.

These are the names of the twelve sons of Jacob:

23The sons of Leah were Reuben (Jacob's oldest son), Simeon, Levi, Judah, Issachar, and Zebulun.

24The sons of Rachel were Joseph and Benjamin.

25The sons of Bilhah, Rachel's servant, were Dan and Naphtali.

26The sons of Zilpah, Leah's servant, were Gad and Asher.

These are the names of the sons who were born to Jacob at Paddan-aram.

27So Jacob returned to his father, Isaac, in Mamre, which is near Kiriath-arba (now called Hebron), where Abraham and Isaac had both lived as foreigners. 28Isaac lived for 180 years. 29Then he breathed his last and died at a ripe old age, joining his ancestors in death. And his sons, Esau and Jacob, buried him.

Descendants of Esau

GENESIS 36:1-19

This is the account of the descendants of Esau (also known as Edom). 2Esau married two young women from Canaan: Adah, the daughter of Elon the Hittite; and Oholibamah, the daughter of Anah and granddaughter of Zibeon the Hivite. 3He also married his cousin Basemath, who was the daughter of Ishmael and the sister of Nebaioth. 4Adah gave birth to a son named Eliphaz for Esau. Basemath gave birth to a son named Reuel. 5Oholibamah gave birth to sons named Jeush, Jalam, and Korah. All these sons were born to Esau in the land of Canaan.

6Esau took his wives, his children, and his entire household, along with his livestock and cattle—all the wealth he had acquired in the land of Canaan—and moved away from his brother, Jacob. 7There was not enough land to support them both because of all the livestock and possessions they had acquired. 8So Esau (also known as Edom) settled in the hill country of Seir.

9This is the account of Esau's descendants, the Edomites, who lived in the hill country of Seir.

10These are the names of Esau's sons: Eliphaz, the son of Esau's wife Adah; and Reuel, the son of Esau's wife Basemath.

11The descendants of Eliphaz were Teman, Omar, Zepho, Gatam, and Kenaz. 12Timna, the concubine of Esau's son Eliphaz, gave birth to a son named Amalek. These are the descendants of Esau's wife Adah.

Gn 35:10 *Jacob* sounds like the Hebrew words for "heel" and "deceiver." *Israel* means "God fights." **Gn 35:21** Hebrew *Israel;* also in 35:22a. The names "Jacob" and "Israel" are often interchanged throughout the Old Testament, referring sometimes to the individual patriarch and sometimes to the nation.

Gen 35:13-14 The oil used to anoint the pillar was olive oil of the finest grade of purity. It was expensive, so using it showed the high value placed on the anointed object. Jacob was showing the greatest respect for the place where he had met with God.

Gen 35:22 Reuben's sin was costly, although not right away. As the oldest son, he stood to receive a double portion of the family inheritance and a place of leadership among his people. Reuben may have thought he had gotten away with his sin. No more is mentioned of it until Jacob, on his deathbed, assembled his family for the final blessing. Suddenly Jacob took away Reuben's double portion and gave it to someone else. The reason? "You went to bed with my wife; you defiled my marriage couch" (Gen 49:4).

Sin's consequences can plague us long after the sin is committed. When we do something wrong, we may think we can escape unnoticed, only to discover later that the sin has been quietly breeding serious consequences.

Gen 36:9 The Edomites were descendants of Esau who lived south and east of the Dead Sea. The country featured rugged mountains and desolate wilderness. Several major roads led through Edom because it was rich in natural resources. During the Exodus, God told Israel to leave the Edomites alone (Deut 2:4-5) because they were "relatives." But Edom refused to let them enter the land, and later they became bitter enemies of King David. The nations of Edom and Israel shared the same ancestor, Isaac, and the same border. But the Israelites looked down on the Edomites because they had intermarried with the Canaanites.

13The descendants of Reuel were Nahath,
Zerah, Shammah, and Mizzah. These are the
descendants of Esau's wife Basemath.
14Esau also had sons through Oholibamah, the
daughter of Anah and granddaughter of Zibeon.
Their names were Jeush, Jalam, and Korah.

15These are the descendants of Esau who became the
leaders of various clans:

The descendants of Esau's oldest son, Eliphaz,
became the leaders of the clans of Teman, Omar,
Zepho, Kenaz, 16Korah, Gatam, and Amalek.
These are the clan leaders in the land of Edom
who descended from Eliphaz. All these were
descendants of Esau's wife Adah.
17The descendants of Esau's son Reuel became the
leaders of the clans of Nahath, Zerah, Shammah,
and Mizzah. These are the clan leaders in the land
of Edom who descended from Reuel. All these
were descendants of Esau's wife Basemath.
18The descendants of Esau and his wife Oholibamah
became the leaders of the clans of Jeush, Jalam,
and Korah. These are the clan leaders who
descended from Esau's wife Oholibamah, the
daughter of Anah.
19These are the clans descended from Esau (also
known as Edom), identified by their clan leaders.

Original Peoples of Edom

GENESIS 36:20-30

These are the names of the tribes that descended from
Seir the Horite. They lived in the land of Edom: Lotan,
Shobal, Zibeon, Anah, 21Dishon, Ezer, and Dishan.
These were the Horite clan leaders, the descendants
of Seir, who lived in the land of Edom.

22The descendants of Lotan were Hori and Hemam.
Lotan's sister was named Timna.
23The descendants of Shobal were Alvan, Manahath,
Ebal, Shepho, and Onam.
24The descendants of Zibeon were Aiah and Anah.
(This is the Anah who discovered the hot springs
in the wilderness while he was grazing his
father's donkeys.)
25The descendants of Anah were his son, Dishon,
and his daughter, Oholibamah.
26The descendants of Dishon* were Hemdan,
Eshban, Ithran, and Keran.
27The descendants of Ezer were Bilhan, Zaavan,
and Akan.
28The descendants of Dishan were Uz and Aran.
29So these were the leaders of the Horite clans: Lotan,
Shobal, Zibeon, Anah, 30Dishon, Ezer, and Dishan. The
Horite clans are named after their clan leaders, who
lived in the land of Seir.

Gn 36:26 Hebrew *Dishan,* a variant spelling of Dishon; compare 36:21, 28.

JOSEPH

As a youngster, Joseph was overconfident. His natural self-assurance—increased by being Jacob's favorite son and by knowing of God's designs on his life—was unbearable to his ten older brothers, who eventually conspired against him. But this self-assurance, molded by pain and combined with a personal knowledge of God, allowed him to survive and prosper where most would have failed. He added quiet wisdom to his confidence and won the hearts of everyone he met—Potiphar, the prison warden, other prisoners, the pharaoh, and, after many years, even those ten brothers. • Perhaps you can identify with one or more of these hardships Joseph experienced: He was betrayed and deserted by his family, exposed to sexual temptation, and punished for doing the right thing; he endured a long imprisonment and was forgotten by those he helped. As you read his story, note what Joseph did in each case. His positive response transformed each setback into a step forward. He didn't spend much time asking why. His approach was "What shall I do now?" Those who met Joseph were aware that wherever he went and whatever he did, God was with him. When you're facing a setback, the beginning of a Joseph-like attitude is to acknowledge that God is with you. There is nothing like his presence to shed new light on a dark situation.

Strengths and accomplishments	• Rose in power from slave to ruler of Egypt • Was known for his personal integrity • Was a man of spiritual sensitivity • Prepared a nation to survive a famine
Weakness and mistake	• His youthful pride caused friction with his brothers
Lessons from his life	• What matters is not so much the events or circumstances of life, but our response to them • With God's help, any situation can be used for good, even when others intend it for evil
Vital statistics	• Where: Canaan, Egypt • Occupation: Shepherd, slave, convict, ruler • Relatives: Parents: Jacob and Rachel. Siblings: Eleven brothers and one sister. Wife: Asenath. Sons: Manasseh and Ephraim.
Key verse	"So Pharaoh asked his officials, 'Can we find anyone else like this man so obviously filled with the spirit of God?'" (Gen 41:38).

Joseph's story is told in Genesis 30–50. He is also mentioned in Hebrews 11:22.

Rulers of Edom

GENESIS 36:31-43

These are the kings who ruled in the land of Edom before any king ruled over the Israelites*:

32Bela son of Beor, who ruled in Edom from his city of Dinhabah.

33When Bela died, Jobab son of Zerah from Bozrah became king in his place.

34When Jobab died, Husham from the land of the Temanites became king in his place.

35When Husham died, Hadad son of Bedad became king in his place and ruled from the city of Avith. He was the one who defeated the Midianites in the land of Moab.

36When Hadad died, Samlah from the city of Masrekah became king in his place.

37When Samlah died, Shaul from the city of Rehoboth-on-the-River became king in his place.

38When Shaul died, Baal-hanan son of Acbor became king in his place.

39When Baal-hanan son of Acbor died, Hadad* became king in his place and ruled from the city of Pau. His wife was Mehetabel, the daughter of Matred and granddaughter of Me-zahab.

40These are the names of the leaders of the clans
descended from Esau, who lived in the places named
for them: Timna, Alvah, Jetheth, 41Oholibamah, Elah,
Pinon, 42Kenaz, Teman, Mibzar, 43Magdiel, and Iram.
These are the leaders of the clans of Edom, listed according to their settlements in the land they occupied. They all descended from Esau, the ancestor of the Edomites.

Gn 36:31 Or *before an Israelite king ruled over them.* **Gn 36:39** As in some Hebrew manuscripts, Samaritan Pentateuch, and Syriac version (see also 1 Chr 1:50); most Hebrew manuscripts read *Hadar.*

D. The Story of Joseph

Joseph, one of Jacob's 12 sons, was obviously the favorite. Hated by his brothers for this, Joseph was sold to slave traders only to emerge as ruler of all Egypt. Through Joseph, we learn how suffering, no matter how unfair, develops strong character and deep wisdom.

1. JOSEPH IS SOLD INTO SLAVERY

Joseph enjoyed being his father's favorite son, and he didn't seem to care about how that made his brothers feel. He never could have imagined that they would sell him to slave traders, but that is exactly what they did.

Joseph's Dreams

GENESIS 37:1-17

So Jacob settled again in the land of Canaan, where his father had lived as a foreigner.

2This is the account of Jacob and his family. When Joseph was seventeen years old, he often tended his father's flocks. He worked for his half brothers, the sons of his father's wives Bilhah and Zilpah. But Joseph reported to his father some of the bad things his brothers were doing.

3Jacob* loved Joseph more than any of his other children because Joseph had been born to him in his

Gn 37:3a Hebrew *Israel;* also in 37:13. See note on 35:21.

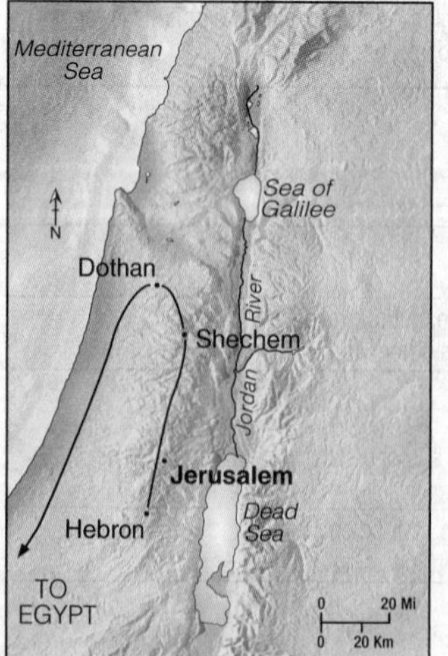

◀ ***JOSEPH GOES TO MEET HIS BROTHERS** Jacob asked Joseph to go find his brothers, who were grazing their flocks near Shechem. When Joseph arrived, he learned that his brothers had gone on to Dothan, which lay along a major trade route to Egypt. There the jealous brothers sold Joseph as a slave to a group of Ishmaelite traders on their way to Egypt.*

Gen 37:3 In Joseph's day, everyone had a robe or cloak. Robes were used for warmth, to bundle up belongings for a trip, to wrap babies, to sit on, or even to serve as security for a loan. Most robes were knee length, short sleeved, and plain. In contrast, Joseph's robe was probably of the kind worn by royalty—long sleeved, ankle length, and colorful. The robe became a symbol of Jacob's favoritism toward Joseph, and it aggravated the already strained relations between Joseph and his brothers. Favoritism in families may be unavoidable, but its divisive effects should be minimized. Parents may not be able to change their feelings toward a favorite child, but they can change their actions toward the others.

Gen 37:6-11 Joseph's brothers were already angry over the possibility of being ruled by their little brother. Joseph then fueled the fire with his immature attitude and boastful manner. No one enjoys a braggart. Joseph learned this the hard way. His angry brothers sold him into slavery to get rid of him. After several years of hardship, Joseph learned an important lesson: Because our talents and knowledge come from God, it is more appropriate to thank him for them than to brag about them. Later Joseph gave God the credit (Gen 41:16).

old age. So one day Jacob had a special gift made for
Joseph—a beautiful robe.* 4But his brothers hated
Joseph because their father loved him more than the
rest of them. They couldn't say a kind word to him.
5One night Joseph had a dream, and when he told
his brothers about it, they hated him more than ever.
6"Listen to this dream," he said. 7"We were out in the
field, tying up bundles of grain. Suddenly my bundle
stood up, and your bundles all gathered around and
bowed low before mine!"
8His brothers responded, "So you think you will be
our king, do you? Do you actually think you will reign
over us?" And they hated him all the more because of
his dreams and the way he talked about them.
9Soon Joseph had another dream, and again he
told his brothers about it. "Listen, I have had another
dream," he said. "The sun, moon, and eleven stars
bowed low before me!"
10This time he told the dream to his father as well as
to his brothers, but his father scolded him. "What kind
of dream is that?" he asked. "Will your mother and I
and your brothers actually come and bow to the ground
before you?" 11But while his brothers were jealous of
Joseph, his father wondered what the dreams meant.
12Soon after this, Joseph's brothers went to pasture
their father's flocks at Shechem. 13When they had
been gone for some time, Jacob said to Joseph, "Your
brothers are pasturing the sheep at Shechem. Get
ready, and I will send you to them."
"I'm ready to go," Joseph replied.
14"Go and see how your brothers and the flocks
are getting along," Jacob said. "Then come back and
bring me a report." So Jacob sent him on his way, and
Joseph traveled to Shechem from their home in the
valley of Hebron.
15When he arrived there, a man from the area noticed him wandering around the countryside. "What
are you looking for?" he asked.
16"I'm looking for my brothers," Joseph replied. "Do
you know where they are pasturing their sheep?"
17"Yes," the man told him. "They have moved on
from here, but I heard them say, 'Let's go on to Dothan.'" So Joseph followed his brothers to Dothan and
found them there.

Joseph Sold into Slavery

GENESIS 37:18-36

When Joseph's brothers saw him coming, they recognized him in the distance. As he approached, they
made plans to kill him. 19"Here comes the dreamer!"
they said. 20"Come on, let's kill him and throw him into
one of these cisterns. We can tell our father, 'A wild

Gn 37:3b Traditionally rendered *a coat of many colors.* The exact meaning of the Hebrew is uncertain.

1898 BC

Joseph sold into slavery

Gen 37:19-20 Could jealousy ever make you feel like killing someone? Before saying, "Of course not!" look at what happened in this story. Ten men were willing to kill their younger brother over a robe and a few reported dreams. Their deep jealousy had grown into ugly rage, completely blinding them to what was right. Jealousy can be difficult to recognize because our reasons for it seem to make sense. But left unchecked, jealousy grows quickly and leads to serious sins. The longer you cultivate jealous feelings, the harder it is to uproot them. The time to deal with jealousy is when you notice yourself keeping score of others' recognition, awards, and achievements.

REUBEN

Parents are usually the best judges of their children's character. Jacob summarized the personality of his son Reuben by comparing him to water. Except when frozen, water has no stable shape of its own. It always shapes itself to its container or environment. Reuben usually had good intentions, but he seemed unable to stand against a crowd. His instability made him hard to trust. He had both private and public values, but these contradicted each other. He went along with his brothers in their action against Joseph while hoping to counteract the evil in private. The plan failed. Compromise has a way of destroying convictions. Without convictions, lack of direction will destroy life. Reuben's sleeping with one of his father's wives showed how little he had left of the integrity he had displayed earlier in life. • How consistent are your public and private lives? We may want to think they are separate, but we can't deny that they affect each other. What convictions are present in your life at all times? How closely does Jacob's description of his son—"unruly as a flood"—describe your life?

Strengths and accomplishments	• Saved Joseph's life by talking the other brothers out of murder • Offered his own sons as a guarantee that he would protect Benjamin's life
Weaknesses and mistakes	• Did not directly protect Joseph from his brothers, although as oldest son he had the authority to do so • Slept with one of his father's wives
Lessons from his life	• Public and private integrity must be the same, or one will destroy the other • Punishment for sin may not be immediate, but it is certain
Vital statistics	• Where: Canaan, Egypt • Occupation: Shepherd • Relatives: Parents: Jacob and Leah. Siblings: Eleven brothers, one sister.
Key verses	"Reuben, you are my firstborn, my strength, the child of my vigorous youth. You are first in rank and first in power. But you are as unruly as a flood, and you will be first no longer. For you went to bed with my wife; you defiled my marriage couch" (Gen 49:3-4).

Reuben's story is told in Genesis 29–50.

▶ **GENESIS 37:18-36** ***(cont.)***

animal has eaten him.' Then we'll see what becomes of his dreams!"

[21]But when Reuben heard of their scheme, he came to Joseph's rescue. "Let's not kill him," he said. [22]"Why should we shed any blood? Let's just throw him into this empty cistern here in the wilderness. Then he'll die without our laying a hand on him." Reuben was secretly planning to rescue Joseph and return him to his father.

[23]So when Joseph arrived, his brothers ripped off the beautiful robe he was wearing. [24]Then they grabbed him and threw him into the cistern. Now the cistern was empty; there was no water in it. [25]Then, just as they were sitting down to eat, they looked up and saw a caravan of camels in the distance coming toward them. It was a group of Ishmaelite traders taking a load of gum, balm, and aromatic resin from Gilead down to Egypt.

[26]Judah said to his brothers, "What will we gain by killing our brother? We'd have to cover up the crime.* [27]Instead of hurting him, let's sell him to those Ishmaelite traders. After all, he is our brother—our own flesh and blood!" And his brothers agreed. [28]So when the Ishmaelites, who were Midianite traders, came by, Joseph's brothers pulled him out of the cistern and sold him to them for twenty pieces* of silver. And the traders took him to Egypt.

[29]Some time later, Reuben returned to get Joseph out of the cistern. When he discovered that Joseph was missing, he tore his clothes in grief. [30]Then he went back to his brothers and lamented, "The boy is gone! What will I do now?"

[31]Then the brothers killed a young goat and dipped Joseph's robe in its blood. [32]They sent the beautiful robe to their father with this message: "Look at what we found. Doesn't this robe belong to your son?"

[33]Their father recognized it immediately. "Yes," he said, "it is my son's robe. A wild animal must have eaten him. Joseph has clearly been torn to pieces!" [34]Then Jacob tore his clothes and dressed himself in burlap. He mourned deeply for his son for a long time. [35]His family all tried to comfort him, but he refused to be comforted. "I will go to my grave* mourning for my son," he would say, and then he would weep.

[36]Meanwhile, the Midianite traders* arrived in Egypt, where they sold Joseph to Potiphar, an officer of Pharaoh, the king of Egypt. Potiphar was captain of the palace guard.

Gn 37:26 Hebrew *cover his blood.* **Gn 37:28** Hebrew *20 shekels,* about 8 ounces or 228 grams in weight. **Gn 37:35** Hebrew *go down to Sheol.* **Gn 37:36** Hebrew *the Medanites.* The relationship between the Midianites and Medanites is unclear; compare 37:28. See also 25:2.

2. JUDAH AND TAMAR

This story about Judah interrupts the story of Joseph, but it is important because it shows how much Jacob's family was becoming more and more connected to the people and culture in Canaan. This helps to explain why God sent Jacob and his family to Egypt, where they would be better able to build their own identity separate from the Canaanites.

Judah and Tamar

GENESIS 38:1-30

About this time, Judah left home and moved to Adullam, where he stayed with a man named Hirah. [2]There he saw a Canaanite woman, the daughter of Shua, and he married her. When he slept with her, [3]she became pregnant and gave birth to a son, and he named the boy Er. [4]Then she became pregnant again and gave birth to another son, and she named him Onan. [5]And when she gave birth to a third son, she named him

Gen 37:26-27 The brothers were worried about bearing the guilt of Joseph's death. Judah suggested an option that was not right but would leave them innocent of murder. Sometimes we jump at a solution because it is the lesser of two evils but still is not the right action to take. When someone proposes a seemingly workable solution, first ask, "Is it right?"

Gen 37:28 Although Joseph's brothers didn't kill him outright, they wouldn't expect him to survive for long as a slave. They were quite willing to let cruel slave traders do their dirty work for them. Joseph faced a 30-day journey through the desert, probably chained and on foot. He would be treated like baggage and, once in Egypt, would be sold as a piece of merchandise. His brothers thought they would never see him again. But God was in control of Joseph's life and had other plans.

Gen 37:29-30 Reuben returned to the cistern to find Joseph, but his little brother was gone. His first response, in effect, was "What will happen to me?" rather than "What will happen to Joseph?" In a tough situation, are you usually concerned first about yourself? Consider the person most affected by the problem, and you will be more likely to find a solution for it.

Gen 37:31-35 To cover their evil action, Jacob's sons deceived their father into thinking Joseph was dead. Jacob himself had deceived others many times (including his own father; Gen 27:35). Even though he didn't know it at this point, Jacob was learning by hard experience the painfulness and destructive consequences of deceit.

Gen 37:34 Tearing one's clothes and wearing burlap (sometimes called sackcloth) were signs of mourning, much like wearing black today.

Gen 37:36 Imagine the culture shock Joseph experienced upon arriving in Egypt. Joseph had lived as a nomad, traveling the countryside with his family, caring for sheep. Suddenly he was thrust into the world's most advanced civilization with great pyramids, beautiful homes, sophisticated people, and a new language. While Joseph saw Egypt's skill and intelligence at their best, he also saw the Egyptians' spiritual blindness. They worshiped countless gods related to every aspect of life.

Gen 38:1ff This chapter vividly contrasts the immoral character of Judah with the moral character of Joseph. Judah's lack of integrity resulted in family strife and deception. Genesis 39 shows how Joseph's integrity and wise choices reflected his godly character. His faithfulness was rewarded with blessings greater than he could imagine, both for himself and for his family.

Shelah. At the time of Shelah's birth, they were living at Kezib.

6In the course of time, Judah arranged for his firstborn son, Er, to marry a young woman named Tamar. 7But Er was a wicked man in the LORD's sight, so the LORD took his life. 8Then Judah said to Er's brother Onan, "Go and marry Tamar, as our law requires of the brother of a man who has died. You must produce an heir for your brother."

9But Onan was not willing to have a child who would not be his own heir. So whenever he had intercourse with his brother's wife, he spilled the semen on the ground. This prevented her from having a child who would belong to his brother. 10But the LORD considered it evil for Onan to deny a child to his dead brother. So the LORD took Onan's life, too.

11Then Judah said to Tamar, his daughter-in-law, "Go back to your parents' home and remain a widow until my son Shelah is old enough to marry you." (But Judah didn't really intend to do this because he was afraid Shelah would also die, like his two brothers.) So Tamar went back to live in her father's home.

12Some years later Judah's wife died. After the time of mourning was over, Judah and his friend Hirah the Adullamite went up to Timnah to supervise the shearing of his sheep. 13Someone told Tamar, "Look, your father-in-law is going up to Timnah to shear his sheep."

14Tamar was aware that Shelah had grown up, but no arrangements had been made for her to come and marry him. So she changed out of her widow's clothing and covered herself with a veil to disguise herself. Then she sat beside the road at the entrance to the village of Enaim, which is on the road to Timnah. 15Judah noticed her and thought she was a prostitute, since she had covered her face. 16So he stopped and propositioned her. "Let me have sex with you," he said, not realizing that she was his own daughter-in-law.

"How much will you pay to have sex with me?" Tamar asked.

17"I'll send you a young goat from my flock," Judah promised.

"But what will you give me to guarantee that you will send the goat?" she asked.

18"What kind of guarantee do you want?" he replied.

She answered, "Leave me your identification seal and its cord and the walking stick you are carrying." So Judah gave them to her. Then he had intercourse with her, and she became pregnant. 19Afterward she went back home, took off her veil, and put on her widow's clothing as usual.

20Later Judah asked his friend Hirah the Adullamite to take the young goat to the woman and to pick up the things he had given her as his guarantee. But Hirah couldn't find her. 21So he asked the men who lived there, "Where can I find the shrine prostitute who was sitting beside the road at the entrance to Enaim?"

WOMEN IN JESUS' FAMILY TREE

Tamar	Canaanite	**Gen 38:1-30**
Rahab	Canaanite	**Josh 6:22-25**
Ruth	Moabite	**Ruth 4:13-22**
Bathsheba	Israelite	**2 Sam 12:24-25**

Gen 38:8-10 This law about marrying a widow in the family is explained in Deuteronomy 25:5-10. Its purpose was to ensure that a childless widow would have a son who would receive her late husband's inheritance and who, in turn, would care for her. Because Judah's son (Tamar's husband) had no children, there was no family line through which the inheritance and the blessing of the covenant could continue. God killed Onan because he refused to fulfill his obligation to his brother and to Tamar.

Gen 38:15-23 It may seem strange that prostitution is written about in such a matter-of-fact way here. Prostitutes were common in pagan cultures such as Canaan. Public prostitutes served Canaanite goddesses and were common elements of the religious cults. Fornication was encouraged to improve fertility in crops and flocks. Public prostitutes were more highly respected than private prostitutes, who were sometimes punished when caught. Tamar was driven to seduce Judah because of her intense desire to have children and be the matriarch of Judah's line; Judah was driven by his lust. Neither case was justified.

Gen 38:15-24 Why was Judah so open about his relations with a prostitute, yet ready to execute his daughter-in-law for being one? To understand this apparent contradiction, we must understand the place of women in Canaan. A woman's most important function was bearing children who would perpetuate the family line. To ensure that children belonged to the husband, the bride was expected to be a virgin, and the wife was expected to have relations only with him. If a wife committed adultery, she could be executed. Some women, however, did not belong to families. They might serve as shrine prostitutes supported by offerings or common prostitutes supported by the men who used their services. Their children were nobody's heirs, and men who hired them adulterated no one's bloodlines.

Judah saw no harm in hiring a prostitute for a night; after all, he was more than willing to pay. But he was ready to execute Tamar because if she was pregnant as a result of prostitution, his grandchild would not be part of his family line. Apparently the question of sexual morality never entered Judah's mind; his concern was for keeping his inheritance in the family. Ironically, it was Tamar, not Judah, who acted to provide him with legal heirs. By seducing him, she acted more in the spirit of the law than he did when he refused to send his third son to her.

This event in no way implies that God thinks lightly of prostitution. Throughout Scripture, prostitution is condemned as a serious sin. If the story has a moral, it is that faithfulness to family obligations is important. Incidentally, Judah and Tamar are direct ancestors of Jesus Christ (see Matt 1:1-6).

Gen 38:18 This identification seal was used to authenticate legal documents. Usually a unique design carved in stone and worn on a ring or necklace inseparable from its owner, the seal was used by the wealthy and powerful to mark clay or wax. Because Tamar had Judah's seal, she could prove beyond a doubt that he had been with her.

▶ **GENESIS 38:1-30 *(cont.)***

"We've never had a shrine prostitute here," they replied.

[22]So Hirah returned to Judah and told him, "I couldn't find her anywhere, and the men of the village claim they've never had a shrine prostitute there."

[23]"Then let her keep the things I gave her," Judah said. "I sent the young goat as we agreed, but you couldn't find her. We'd be the laughingstock of the village if we went back again to look for her."

[24]About three months later, Judah was told, "Tamar, your daughter-in-law, has acted like a prostitute. And now, because of this, she's pregnant."

"Bring her out, and let her be burned!" Judah demanded.

[25]But as they were taking her out to kill her, she sent this message to her father-in-law: "The man who owns these things made me pregnant. Look closely. Whose seal and cord and walking stick are these?"

[26]Judah recognized them immediately and said, "She is more righteous than I am, because I didn't arrange for her to marry my son Shelah." And Judah never slept with Tamar again.

[27]When the time came for Tamar to give birth, it was discovered that she was carrying twins. [28]While she was in labor, one of the babies reached out his hand. The midwife grabbed it and tied a scarlet string around the child's wrist, announcing, "This one came out first." [29]But then he pulled back his hand, and out came his brother! "What!" the midwife exclaimed. "How did you break out first?" So he was named Perez.* [30]Then the baby with the scarlet string on his wrist was born, and he was named Zerah.*

Gn 38:29 *Perez* means "breaking out." **Gn 38:30** *Zerah* means "scarlet" or "brightness."

3. JOSEPH IS THROWN INTO PRISON

Joseph made the best of his situation as a slave in Egypt, earning the trust of his master—until his master's wife accused him falsely of assaulting her, and he was quickly thrown into prison. In spite of his worsening situation, Joseph continued to rely on God and succeeded in whatever situation he found himself.

Joseph in Potiphar's House

GENESIS 39:1-18

When Joseph was taken to Egypt by the Ishmaelite traders, he was purchased by Potiphar, an Egyptian officer. Potiphar was captain of the guard for Pharaoh, the king of Egypt.

[2]The LORD was with Joseph, so he succeeded in everything he did as he served in the home of his Egyptian master. [3]Potiphar noticed this and realized that the LORD was with Joseph, giving him success in everything he did. [4]This pleased Potiphar, so he soon made Joseph his personal attendant. He put him

Slaves in Egypt

Joseph wasn't the only person from his area that was carried off to become a slave in Egypt. This papyrus contains a list of 79 servants from an Egyptian household c. 1750 B.C. At least 45 of these slaves were not Egyptians but foreigners like Joseph. Many of the names are very similar to biblical names—such as Jacob, Issachar, Asher, Job, and Menahem. This indicates that they were likely from the same general area as Joseph and probably spoke either the same or a closely related language. Some were domestic servants like Joseph (Gen 39:2). Such lists are important in telling us that Semites were in Egypt during the time of Joseph and thereafter, thereby confirming the biblical record.

Gen 38:24-26 When Tamar revealed she was pregnant, Judah, who unknowingly had gotten her pregnant, moved to have her killed. Judah had concealed his own sin, yet he came down harshly on Tamar. Often the sins we try to cover up are the ones that anger us most when we see them in others. If you become indignant at the sins of others, you may have a similar tendency to sin that you don't wish to face. When we admit our sins and ask God to forgive us, forgiving others becomes easier.

Gen 39:1 The date of Joseph's arrival in Egypt is debatable. Many believe he arrived during the period of the Hyksos rulers, foreigners who came from the region of Canaan. They invaded Egypt and controlled the land for almost 150 years. If Joseph arrived during their rule, it is easy to see why he was rapidly promoted up the royal ladder. Because the Hyksos were foreigners themselves, they would not hold this brilliant young foreigner's ancestry against him.

Gen 39:1 *Pharaoh* was the general name for all the kings of Egypt. It was a title like "king" or "president" used to address the country's leader. The pharaoh who placed Joseph in charge of Egypt was a different person from the pharaoh who turned against the Hebrews in the book of Exodus.

Gen 39:1 Ancient Egypt was a land of great contrasts. People were either rich beyond measure or poverty stricken. There wasn't much middle ground. Joseph found himself serving Potiphar, an extremely rich officer in Pharaoh's service. Rich families like Potiphar's had elaborate homes two or three stories tall with beautiful gardens and balconies. They enjoyed live entertainment at home as they chose delicious fruit from expensive bowls. They surrounded themselves with alabaster vases, paintings, beautiful rugs, and hand-carved chairs. Dinner was served on golden tableware, and the rooms were lighted with gold lampstands. Servants, like Joseph, worked on the first floor, while the family occupied the upper stories.

in charge of his entire household and everything he
owned. [5]From the day Joseph was put in charge of his
master's household and property, the LORD began to
bless Potiphar's household for Joseph's sake. All his
household affairs ran smoothly, and his crops and
livestock flourished. [6]So Potiphar gave Joseph complete administrative responsibility over everything
he owned. With Joseph there, he didn't worry about
a thing—except what kind of food to eat!

Joseph was a very handsome and well-built young
man, [7]and Potiphar's wife soon began to look at him
lustfully. "Come and sleep with me," she demanded.

[8]But Joseph refused. "Look," he told her, "my master
trusts me with everything in his entire household. [9]No
one here has more authority than I do. He has held
back nothing from me except you, because you are his
wife. How could I do such a wicked thing? It would be
a great sin against God."

[10]She kept putting pressure on Joseph day after day,
but he refused to sleep with her, and he kept out of
her way as much as possible. [11]One day, however, no
one else was around when he went in to do his work.
[12]She came and grabbed him by his cloak, demanding,
"Come on, sleep with me!" Joseph tore himself away, but
he left his cloak in her hand as he ran from the house.

[13]When she saw that she was holding his cloak and
he had fled, [14]she called out to her servants. Soon all
the men came running. "Look!" she said. "My husband
has brought this Hebrew slave here to make fools of
us! He came into my room to rape me, but I screamed.
[15]When he heard me scream, he ran outside and got
away, but he left his cloak behind with me."

POTIPHAR & HIS WIFE

Potiphar, the captain of Pharaoh's royal guard, had a large household and a wife with too much time on her hands. One day he purchased Joseph from some Midianite slave traders and put him to work in his home. This was the best decision Potiphar ever made. Joseph was very talented, and God was with him. Because of Joseph, Potiphar began to prosper greatly. • While Potiphar was benefiting from Joseph's good work ethic, Potiphar's wife was noticing Joseph's good looks. Soon she moved from looking to seducing, but Joseph continually resisted her advances. Denied the thrill of chasing and capturing her prey, of feeling a few moments of illicit pleasure, Potiphar's wife became angry and hurt. One day, after she had been scorned again, she accused Joseph of attempted rape. Since she couldn't have Joseph, she decided to punish him. • Potiphar had Joseph thrown into prison. We don't know if Potiphar ever realized what was going on in his house, but he sided with his wife. Because he listened to a faithless woman, Potiphar jailed an innocent man and got rid of the best household overseer in all of Egypt. Had Potiphar been more observant, he would have seen that Joseph was not merely an administrative windfall but also a young man of integrity. Perhaps he did see Joseph's character but didn't have enough himself to face the truth. • Although Potiphar recognized talent when he saw it, he wasn't quite as good a judge of character. Both qualities are important, but character matters far more in the long run. Selfishness, faithlessness, and deceit have no place in a person who wants to develop character. Potiphar and his wife show us that anyone can be a judge of talent, but it takes insight and courage to be a judge of character.

Strengths and accomplishments	• Potiphar reached a high rank in Pharaoh's court • Both enjoyed the temporary blessing of having Joseph, God's servant, as their slave • Potiphar was a good judge of talent
Weaknesses and mistakes	• Both failed in judging character—Potiphar toward his wife and Joseph, his wife toward Joseph • Falsely accused and imprisoned Joseph, their faithful servant
Lessons from their lives	• God can accomplish his purposes through other's mistakes and sins • One person with character stands out among those who possess little of it
Vital statistics	• Where: Egypt • Occupation: Potiphar: Palace official. Potiphar's wife: Wife.
Key verse	"From the day Joseph was put in charge of his master's household and property, the LORD began to bless Potiphar's household for Joseph's sake. All his household affairs ran smoothly, and his crops and livestock flourished" (Gen 39:5).

The story of Potiphar and his wife is told in Genesis 37:36; 39:1-20.

Gen 39:9 Potiphar's wife failed to seduce Joseph, who resisted this temptation by saying it would be a sin against God. Joseph didn't say, "I'd be hurting you," or "I'd be sinning against Potiphar," or "I'd be sinning against myself." Under pressure, such excuses are easily rationalized away. Remember that sexual sin is not just between two consenting adults. It is an act of disobedience against God.

Gen 39:10-15 Joseph avoided Potiphar's wife as much as possible. He refused her advances and finally *ran* from her. Sometimes merely trying to avoid temptation is not enough. We must turn and run from it, especially when the temptation seems very strong, as is often the case in sexual temptation.

▸ **GENESIS 39:1-18** ***(cont.)***

16She kept the cloak with her until her husband came home. 17Then she told him her story. "That Hebrew slave you've brought into our house tried to come in and fool around with me," she said. 18"But when I screamed, he ran outside, leaving his cloak with me!"

Joseph Put in Prison

GENESIS 39:19-23

Potiphar was furious when he heard his wife's story about how Joseph had treated her. 20So he took Joseph and threw him into the prison where the king's prisoners were held, and there he remained. 21But the LORD was with Joseph in the prison and showed him his faithful love. And the LORD made Joseph a favorite with the prison warden. 22Before long, the warden put Joseph in charge of all the other prisoners and over everything that happened in the prison. 23The warden had no more worries, because Joseph took care of everything. The LORD was with him and caused everything he did to succeed.

Joseph Interprets Two Dreams

GENESIS 40:1-23

Some time later, Pharaoh's chief cup-bearer and chief baker offended their royal master. 2Pharaoh became angry with these two officials, 3and he put them in the prison where Joseph was, in the palace of the captain of the guard. 4They remained in prison for quite some time, and the captain of the guard assigned them to Joseph, who looked after them.

5While they were in prison, Pharaoh's cup-bearer and baker each had a dream one night, and each dream had its own meaning. 6When Joseph saw them the next morning, he noticed that they both looked upset. 7"Why do you look so worried today?" he asked them.

8And they replied, "We both had dreams last night, but no one can tell us what they mean."

"Interpreting dreams is God's business," Joseph replied. "Go ahead and tell me your dreams."

9So the chief cup-bearer told Joseph his dream first. "In my dream," he said, "I saw a grapevine in front of me. 10The vine had three branches that began to bud and blossom, and soon it produced clusters of ripe grapes. 11I was holding Pharaoh's wine cup in my hand, so I took a cluster of grapes and squeezed the juice into the cup. Then I placed the cup in Pharaoh's hand."

12"This is what the dream means," Joseph said. "The three branches represent three days. 13Within three days Pharaoh will lift you up and restore you to your position as his chief cup-bearer. 14And please remember me and do me a favor when things go well for you. Mention me to Pharaoh, so he might let me out of this place. 15For I was kidnapped from my homeland, the land of the Hebrews, and now I'm here in prison, but I did nothing to deserve it."

16When the chief baker saw that Joseph had given the first dream such a positive interpretation, he said to Joseph, "I had a dream, too. In my dream there were three baskets of white pastries stacked on my head. 17The top basket contained all kinds of pastries for Pharaoh, but the birds came and ate them from the basket on my head."

18"This is what the dream means," Joseph told him. "The three baskets also represent three days. 19Three days from now Pharaoh will lift you up and impale your body on a pole. Then birds will come and peck away at your flesh."

20Pharaoh's birthday came three days later, and he prepared a banquet for all his officials and staff. He summoned* his chief cup-bearer and chief baker to join the other officials. 21He then restored the chief cup-bearer to his former position, so he could again hand Pharaoh his cup. 22But Pharaoh impaled the chief baker, just as Joseph had predicted when he interpreted his dream. 23Pharaoh's chief cup-bearer, however, forgot all about Joseph, never giving him another thought.

Gn 40:20 Hebrew *He lifted up the head of.*

Gen 39:20 Prisons were grim places with vile conditions. They were used to house forced laborers or, like Joseph, the accused who were awaiting trial. Prisoners were guilty until proven innocent, and there was no right to a speedy trial. Many prisoners never made it to court because trials were held at the whim of the ruler. Joseph was in prison a long time before he appeared before Pharaoh, and then he was called out to interpret a dream, not to stand trial.

Gen 39:21-23 As a prisoner and slave, Joseph could have seen his situation as hopeless. Instead, he did his best with each small task given him. His diligence and positive attitude were soon noticed by the warden, who promoted him to prison administrator. Are you facing a seemingly hopeless predicament? At work, at home, or at school, follow Joseph's example by taking each small task and doing your best. Remember how God turned Joseph's situation around. He will see your efforts and can reverse even overwhelming odds.

Gen 40:1-3 The cup-bearer and the chief baker were two of the most trusted men in Pharaoh's kingdom. The baker was in charge of making the Pharaoh's food, and the cup-bearer tasted all of Pharaoh's food and drink before giving it to him, in case any of it was contaminated or poisoned. These trusted men must have been suspected of a serious wrong, perhaps of conspiring against Pharaoh. Later the cup-bearer was released and the baker executed.

Gen 40:8 When the subject of dreams came up, Joseph focused everyone's attention on God. Rather than using the situation to make himself look good, he turned it into a powerful witness for the Lord. One secret of effective witnessing is to recognize opportunities to relate God to the other person's experience. When the opportunity arises, we must have the courage to speak, as Joseph did.

Gen 40:23 When Pharaoh's cup-bearer was freed from prison, he forgot about Joseph. Two full years passed before Joseph had another opportunity to be freed (Gen 41:1). Yet Joseph's faith was deep, and he would be ready when the next chance came. When we feel passed by, overlooked, or forgotten, we shouldn't be surprised that people are often forgetful. In similar situations, we should trust

4. JOSEPH IS PLACED IN CHARGE OF EGYPT

God was with Joseph through all of his difficulties, and eventually God created an opportunity for Joseph to rise to a place of great influence and prestige. He was also able to help Egypt prepare for a great famine, saving many lives—including the lives of his own family hundreds of miles away.

Pharaoh's Dreams

GENESIS 41:1-36

Two full years later, Pharaoh dreamed that he was standing on the bank of the Nile River. 2In his dream he saw seven fat, healthy cows come up out of the river and begin grazing in the marsh grass. 3Then he saw seven more cows come up behind them from the Nile, but these were scrawny and thin. These cows stood beside the fat cows on the riverbank. 4Then the scrawny, thin cows ate the seven healthy, fat cows! At this point in the dream, Pharaoh woke up.

5But he fell asleep again and had a second dream. This time he saw seven heads of grain, plump and beautiful, growing on a single stalk. 6Then seven more heads of grain appeared, but these were shriveled and withered by the east wind. 7And these thin heads swallowed up the seven plump, well-formed heads! Then Pharaoh woke up again and realized it was a dream.

8The next morning Pharaoh was very disturbed by the dreams. So he called for all the magicians and wise men of Egypt. When Pharaoh told them his dreams, not one of them could tell him what they meant.

9Finally, the king's chief cup-bearer spoke up. "Today I have been reminded of my failure," he told Pharaoh. 10"Some time ago, you were angry with the chief baker and me, and you imprisoned us in the palace of the captain of the guard. 11One night the chief baker and I each had a dream, and each dream had its own meaning. 12There was a young Hebrew man with us in the prison who was a slave of the captain of the guard. We told him our dreams, and he told us what each of our dreams meant. 13And everything happened just as he had predicted. I was restored to my position as cup-bearer, and the chief baker was executed and impaled on a pole."

14Pharaoh sent for Joseph at once, and he was quickly brought from the prison. After he shaved and changed his clothes, he went in and stood before Pharaoh. 15Then Pharaoh said to Joseph, "I had a dream last night, and no one here can tell me what it means. But I have heard that when you hear about a dream you can interpret it."

16"It is beyond my power to do this," Joseph replied. "But God can tell you what it means and set you at ease."

17So Pharaoh told Joseph his dream. "In my dream," he said, "I was standing on the bank of the Nile River, 18and I saw seven fat, healthy cows come up out of the river and begin grazing in the marsh grass. 19But then I saw seven sick-looking cows, scrawny and

PARALLELS BETWEEN JOSEPH AND JESUS

Joseph	*Parallels*	*Jesus*
Gen 37:3	Their fathers loved them dearly	**Matt 3:17**
Gen 37:2	Shepherds of their fathers' sheep	**John 10:11, 27**
Gen 37:13-14	Sent by father to brothers	**Heb 2:11**
Gen 37:4	Hated by brothers	**John 7:5**
Gen 37:20	Others plotted to harm them	**John 11:53**
Gen 39:7	Tempted	**Matt 4:1**
Gen 37:25	Taken to Egypt	**Matt 2:14-15**
Gen 37:23	Robes taken from them	**John 19:23**
Gen 37:28	Sold for the price of a slave	**Matt 26:15**
Gen 39:20	Bound in chains	**Matt 27:2**
Gen 39:16-18	Falsely accused	**Matt 26:59-60**
Gen 40:2-3	Placed with two other prisoners, one who was saved and the other lost	**Luke 23:32**
Gen 41:46	Both 30 years old at the beginning of public recognition	**Luke 3:23**
Gen 41:41	Exalted after suffering	**Phil 2:9-11**
Gen 45:1-15	Forgave those who wronged them	**Luke 23:34**
Gen 45:7	Saved their nation	**Matt 1:21**
Gen 50:20	What people did to hurt them God turned to good	**1 Cor 2:7-8**

God as Joseph did. More opportunities may be waiting.

Gen 41:8 Magicians and wise men were common in the palaces of ancient rulers. Their job description included studying sacred arts and sciences, reading the stars, interpreting dreams, predicting the future, and performing magic. These men had power (see Exod 7:11-12), but their power was satanic. They were unable to interpret Pharaoh's dream, but God had revealed it to Joseph in prison.

Gen 41:14 Our most important opportunities may come when we least expect them. Joseph was brought hastily from the dungeon and pushed before Pharaoh. Did he have time to prepare? Yes and no. He had no warning that he would be suddenly pulled from prison and questioned by the king. Yet Joseph was ready for almost anything because of his right relationship with God. It was not Joseph's knowledge of dreams that helped him interpret their meaning. It was his knowledge of God. Be ready for opportunities by staying close to God. Then, when he calls you to a task, you'll be ready.

Gen 41:16 Joseph made sure that he gave the credit to God. We should be careful to do the same. To take the honor for ourselves is a form of stealing God's honor. Don't be silent when you know you should be giving glory and credit to God.

▸ **GENESIS 41:1-36** ***(cont.)***
thin, come up after them. I've never seen such sorry-
looking animals in all the land of Egypt. 20These thin,
scrawny cows ate the seven fat cows. 21But afterward
you wouldn't have known it, for they were still as thin
and scrawny as before! Then I woke up.
22"Then I fell asleep again, and I had another dream.
This time I saw seven heads of grain, full and beautiful,
growing on a single stalk. 23Then seven more heads
of grain appeared, but these were blighted, shriveled,
and withered by the east wind. 24And the shriveled
heads swallowed the seven healthy heads. I told these
dreams to the magicians, but no one could tell me what
they mean."
25Joseph responded, "Both of Pharaoh's dreams
mean the same thing. God is telling Pharaoh in advance
what he is about to do. 26The seven healthy cows and
the seven healthy heads of grain both represent seven
years of prosperity. 27The seven thin, scrawny cows that
came up later and the seven thin heads of grain, withered by the east wind, represent seven years of famine.
28"This will happen just as I have described it, for
God has revealed to Pharaoh in advance what he is
about to do. 29The next seven years will be a period of
great prosperity throughout the land of Egypt. 30But
afterward there will be seven years of famine so great
that all the prosperity will be forgotten in Egypt. Famine will destroy the land. 31This famine will be so severe that even the memory of the good years will be
erased. 32As for having two similar dreams, it means
that these events have been decreed by God, and he
will soon make them happen.
33"Therefore, Pharaoh should find an intelligent and
wise man and put him in charge of the entire land of
Egypt. 34Then Pharaoh should appoint supervisors
over the land and let them collect one-fifth of all the
crops during the seven good years. 35Have them gather
all the food produced in the good years that are just
ahead and bring it to Pharaoh's storehouses. Store it
away, and guard it so there will be food in the cities.
36That way there will be enough to eat when the seven
years of famine come to the land of Egypt. Otherwise
this famine will destroy the land."

Joseph Made Ruler of Egypt

GENESIS 41:37-57
Joseph's suggestions were well received by Pharaoh
and his officials. 38So Pharaoh asked his officials, "Can
we find anyone else like this man so obviously filled
with the spirit of God?" 39Then Pharaoh said to Joseph,
"Since God has revealed the meaning of the dreams
to you, clearly no one else is as intelligent or wise as

1885 BC

Joseph rules Egypt

Joseph in Egyptian Dress
When Joseph was called from the prison to appear before Pharaoh, he first had to be shaved and properly clothed (Gen 41:14). But Joseph's God-given ability to tell Pharaoh all about his dream and how Egypt needed to prepare for the coming famine impressed the pharaoh so much that he assigned Joseph a high office in the traditional Egyptian way, giving him a signet ring, fine linen, and a gold chain. Joseph's rank was probably vizier, second only to the pharaoh. This drawing from an Egyptian tomb illustrates the ceremony when Paser was installed as vizier of Sethos I (from the tomb of Paser, c. 1300 B.C.). In a matter of hours, God brought Joseph from prison rags to the glorious outfit of a high government official. Joseph was faithful to God through his difficult circumstances, and God never abandoned him. He will never abandon you, either!

Gen 41:28-36 After interpreting Pharaoh's dream, Joseph gave the king a survival plan for the next 14 years. The only way to prevent starvation was through careful planning; without a famine plan, Egypt would have turned from prosperity to ruin. Many find detailed planning boring and unnecessary. But planning is a responsibility, not an option. Joseph was able to save a nation by translating God's plan for Egypt into practical action.

Gen 41:38 Pharaoh recognized that Joseph was a man "filled with the spirit of God." You probably won't get to interpret dreams for a king, but those who know you should be able to see God in you, through your kind words, merciful acts, and wise advice. Do your relatives, neighbors, and coworkers see you as a person in whom the Spirit of God lives?

Gen 41:39-40 Joseph rose quickly to the top, from prison walls to Pharaoh's palace. His training for this important position involved being first a slave and then a prisoner. In each situation he learned the importance of serving God and others. Whatever your situation, no matter how undesirable, consider it part of your training program for serving God.

Gen 41:45 Pharaoh may have been trying to make Joseph more acceptable by giving him an Egyptian name and wife. He probably wanted to (1) play down the fact that Joseph was a nomadic shepherd, an occupation disliked by the Egyptians, (2) make Joseph's name easier for Egyptians to pronounce and

you are. 40You will be in charge of my court, and all my people will take orders from you. Only I, sitting on my throne, will have a rank higher than yours."

41Pharaoh said to Joseph, "I hereby put you in charge of the entire land of Egypt." 42Then Pharaoh removed his signet ring from his hand and placed it on Joseph's finger. He dressed him in fine linen clothing and hung a gold chain around his neck. 43Then he had Joseph ride in the chariot reserved for his second-in-command. And wherever Joseph went, the command was shouted, "Kneel down!" So Pharaoh put Joseph in charge of all Egypt. 44And Pharaoh said to him, "I am Pharaoh, but no one will lift a hand or foot in the entire land of Egypt without your approval."

45Then Pharaoh gave Joseph a new Egyptian name, Zaphenath-paneah.* He also gave him a wife, whose name was Asenath. She was the daughter of Potiphera, the priest of On.* So Joseph took charge of the entire land of Egypt. 46He was thirty years old when he began serving in the court of Pharaoh, the king of Egypt. And when Joseph left Pharaoh's presence, he inspected the entire land of Egypt.

47As predicted, for seven years the land produced bumper crops. 48During those years, Joseph gathered all the crops grown in Egypt and stored the grain from the surrounding fields in the cities. 49He piled up huge amounts of grain like sand on the seashore. Finally, he stopped keeping records because there was too much to measure.

50During this time, before the first of the famine years, two sons were born to Joseph and his wife, Asenath, the daughter of Potiphera, the priest of On. 51Joseph named his older son Manasseh,* for he said, "God has made me forget all my troubles and everyone in my father's family." 52Joseph named his second son Ephraim,* for he said, "God has made me fruitful in this land of my grief."

53At last the seven years of bumper crops throughout the land of Egypt came to an end. 54Then the seven years of famine began, just as Joseph had predicted. The famine also struck all the surrounding countries, but throughout Egypt there was plenty of food. 55Eventually, however, the famine spread throughout the land of Egypt as well. And when the people cried out to Pharaoh for food, he told them, "Go to Joseph, and do whatever he tells you." 56So with severe famine everywhere, Joseph opened up the storehouses and distributed grain to the Egyptians, for the famine was severe throughout the land of Egypt. 57And people from all around came to Egypt to buy grain from Joseph because the famine was severe throughout the world.

Gn 41:45a *Zaphenath-paneah* probably means "God speaks and lives." **Gn 41:45b** Greek version reads *of Heliopolis;* also in 41:50. **Gn 41:51** *Manasseh* sounds like a Hebrew term that means "causing to forget." **Gn 41:52** *Ephraim* sounds like a Hebrew term that means "fruitful."

5. JOSEPH AND HIS BROTHERS MEET IN EGYPT

The last time Joseph saw his brothers, they were sending him away with slave traders for a few pieces of silver. Now, the tables were completely turned. Joseph was able to provide food for his brothers and invite his entire family to join him in Egypt.

Joseph's Brothers Go to Egypt

GENESIS 42:1-38

When Jacob heard that grain was available in Egypt, he said to his sons, "Why are you standing around looking at one another? 2I have heard there is grain in Egypt. Go down there, and buy enough grain to keep us alive. Otherwise we'll die."

3So Joseph's ten older brothers went down to Egypt to buy grain. 4But Jacob wouldn't let Joseph's younger brother, Benjamin, go with them, for fear some harm might come to him. 5So Jacob's* sons arrived in Egypt along with others to buy food, for the famine was in Canaan as well.

6Since Joseph was governor of all Egypt and in charge of selling grain to all the people, it was to him that his brothers came. When they arrived, they bowed before him with their faces to the ground. 7Joseph recognized his brothers instantly, but he pretended to be

Gn 42:5 Hebrew *Israel's.* See note on 35:21.

remember, and (3) show how highly he was honored by giving him the daughter of a prominent Egyptian official.

Gen 41:46 Joseph was 30 years old when he became second-in-command in Egypt. At age 17, he had been sold into slavery by his brothers. Thus he had spent 13 years as an Egyptian slave and as a prisoner.

Gen 41:54 Famine was a catastrophe because ancient peoples relied almost exclusively on their own crops for food. Almost perfect conditions were needed to produce good crops because there were no chemical fertilizers or pesticides. Any variances in rainfall or insect activity could cause crop failure and great hunger. Lack of storage, refrigeration, or transportation turned a moderate famine into a desperate situation. The famine Joseph prepared for was especially severe because seven years of famine came one right after the other. Without God's intervention, the Egyptian nation would have crumbled.

Gen 42:1-2 Why was grain so valuable in those days? As a food source it was universal and used in nearly everything eaten. It could be dried and stored much longer than any vegetables, milk products, or meat. It was so important that it was even used as money.

Gen 42:4 Jacob was especially fond of Benjamin because he was Joseph's only full brother and—as far as Jacob knew—the only surviving son of his beloved wife, Rachel. Benjamin was also Jacob's youngest son and a child of his old age.

Gen 42:7 Joseph could have revealed his identity to his brothers at once. But Joseph's last memory of them may well have been staring at their faces in horror as slave traders carried him away. Were his brothers still evil and treacherous, or had they changed over the years? Joseph decided to put them through a few tests to find out.

▸ **GENESIS 42:1-38** ***(cont.)***
a stranger and spoke harshly to them. "Where are you
from?" he demanded.
"From the land of Canaan," they replied. "We have
come to buy food."
8Although Joseph recognized his brothers, they
didn't recognize him. 9And he remembered the
dreams he'd had about them many years before. He
said to them, "You are spies! You have come to see how
vulnerable our land has become."
10"No, my lord!" they exclaimed. "Your servants have
simply come to buy food. 11We are all brothers—members of the same family. We are honest men, sir! We
are not spies!"
12"Yes, you are!" Joseph insisted. "You have come to
see how vulnerable our land has become."
13"Sir," they said, "there are actually twelve of us. We,
your servants, are all brothers, sons of a man living in
the land of Canaan. Our youngest brother is back there
with our father right now, and one of our brothers is
no longer with us."
14But Joseph insisted, "As I said, you are spies! 15This
is how I will test your story. I swear by the life of Pharaoh that you will never leave Egypt unless your youngest brother comes here! 16One of you must go and get
your brother. I'll keep the rest of you here in prison.
Then we'll find out whether or not your story is true.
By the life of Pharaoh, if it turns out that you don't
have a younger brother, then I'll know you are spies."
17So Joseph put them all in prison for three days. 18On
the third day Joseph said to them, "I am a God-fearing
man. If you do as I say, you will live. 19If you really are
honest men, choose one of your brothers to remain in
prison. The rest of you may go home with grain for your
starving families. 20But you must bring your youngest
brother back to me. This will prove that you are telling
the truth, and you will not die." To this they agreed.
21Speaking among themselves, they said, "Clearly
we are being punished because of what we did to Joseph long ago. We saw his anguish when he pleaded
for his life, but we wouldn't listen. That's why we're
in this trouble."
22"Didn't I tell you not to sin against the boy?" Reuben asked. "But you wouldn't listen. And now we have
to answer for his blood!"
23Of course, they didn't know that Joseph understood them, for he had been speaking to them through
an interpreter. 24Now he turned away from them and
began to weep. When he regained his composure,
he spoke to them again. Then he chose Simeon from
among them and had him tied up right before their
eyes.
25Joseph then ordered his servants to fill the men's
sacks with grain, but he also gave secret instructions
to return each brother's payment at the top of his sack.
He also gave them supplies for their journey home.
26So the brothers loaded their donkeys with the grain
and headed for home.
27But when they stopped for the night and one of
them opened his sack to get grain for his donkey, he
found his money in the top of his sack. 28"Look!" he exclaimed to his brothers. "My money has been returned;
it's here in my sack!" Then their hearts sank. Trembling,
they said to each other, "What has God done to us?"
29When the brothers came to their father, Jacob, in
the land of Canaan, they told him everything that had
happened to them. 30"The man who is governor of
the land spoke very harshly to us," they told him. "He
accused us of being spies scouting the land. 31But we
said, 'We are honest men, not spies. 32We are twelve
brothers, sons of one father. One brother is no longer
with us, and the youngest is at home with our father
in the land of Canaan.'
33"Then the man who is governor of the land told
us, 'This is how I will find out if you are honest men.
Leave one of your brothers here with me, and take
grain for your starving families and go on home. 34But
you must bring your youngest brother back to me.
Then I will know you are honest men and not spies.
Then I will give you back your brother, and you may
trade freely in the land.'"
35As they emptied out their sacks, there in each
man's sack was the bag of money he had paid for the
grain! The brothers and their father were terrified
when they saw the bags of money. 36Jacob exclaimed,
"You are robbing me of my children! Joseph is gone!
Simeon is gone! And now you want to take Benjamin,
too. Everything is going against me!"
37Then Reuben said to his father, "You may kill my
two sons if I don't bring Benjamin back to you. I'll be
responsible for him, and I promise to bring him back."
38But Jacob replied, "My son will not go down with
you. His brother Joseph is dead, and he is all I have
left. If anything should happen to him on your journey, you would send this grieving, white-haired man
to his grave.*"

Gn 42:38 Hebrew *to Sheol.*

Gen 42:8-9 Joseph remembered his dreams about his brothers bowing down to him (Gen 37:6-9). Those dreams were coming true! As a young boy, Joseph had been boastful about his dreams. As a man, he no longer flaunted his superior status. He did not feel the need to say, "I told you so." It was not yet time to reveal his identity, so he kept quiet. Sometimes it is best to remain quiet, even when we would like to have the last word.

Gen 42:15 Joseph was testing his brothers to make sure they had not been as cruel to Benjamin as they had been to him. Benjamin was his only full brother, and he wanted to see him face to face.

Gen 42:22 Reuben couldn't resist saying, "I told you so." He thought they were being punished by God for what they had done to Joseph. Apparently the intervening years had not lessened their guilt. Selling Joseph into slavery amounted to death in their minds, for they surely never expected to see him again.

The Brothers Return to Egypt

GENESIS 43:1-18

But the famine continued to ravage the land of Canaan. 2When the grain they had brought from Egypt
was almost gone, Jacob said to his sons, "Go back and
buy us a little more food."
3But Judah said, "The man was serious when he
warned us, 'You won't see my face again unless your
brother is with you.' 4If you send Benjamin with us,
we will go down and buy more food. 5But if you don't
let Benjamin go, we won't go either. Remember, the
man said, 'You won't see my face again unless your
brother is with you.'"
6"Why were you so cruel to me?" Jacob* moaned.
"Why did you tell him you had another brother?"
7"The man kept asking us questions about our family," they replied. "He asked, 'Is your father still alive?
Do you have another brother?' So we answered his
questions. How could we know he would say, 'Bring
your brother down here'?"
8Judah said to his father, "Send the boy with me,
and we will be on our way. Otherwise we will all die of
starvation—and not only we, but you and our little ones.
9I personally guarantee his safety. You may hold me
responsible if I don't bring him back to you. Then let
me bear the blame forever. 10If we hadn't wasted all this
time, we could have gone and returned twice by now."
11So their father, Jacob, finally said to them, "If it
can't be avoided, then at least do this. Pack your bags
with the best products of this land. Take them down
to the man as gifts—balm, honey, gum, aromatic resin,
pistachio nuts, and almonds. 12Also take double the
money that was put back in your sacks, as it was probably someone's mistake. 13Then take your brother,
and go back to the man. 14May God Almighty* give
you mercy as you go before the man, so that he will
release Simeon and let Benjamin return. But if I must
lose my children, so be it."
15So the men packed Jacob's gifts and double the
money and headed off with Benjamin. They finally
arrived in Egypt and presented themselves to Joseph.
16When Joseph saw Benjamin with them, he said to
the manager of his household, "These men will eat
with me this noon. Take them inside the palace. Then
go slaughter an animal, and prepare a big feast." 17So
the man did as Joseph told him and took them into
Joseph's palace.
18The brothers were terrified when they saw that
they were being taken into Joseph's house. "It's because of the money someone put in our sacks last
time we were here," they said. "He plans to pretend
that we stole it. Then he will seize us, make us slaves,
and take our donkeys."

A Feast at Joseph's Palace

GENESIS 43:19-34

The brothers approached the manager of Joseph's
household and spoke to him at the entrance to the
palace. 20"Sir," they said, "we came to Egypt once before to buy food. 21But as we were returning home, we

Gn 43:6 Hebrew *Israel;* also in 43:11. See note on 35:21. **Gn 43:14** Hebrew *El-Shaddai.*

Gen 43:1 Jacob and his sons had no relief from the famine. They could not see God's overall plan of sending them to Egypt to be reunited with Joseph and fed from Egypt's storehouses. If you are praying for relief from suffering or pressure and God is not bringing it as quickly as you would like, remember that God may be leading you to special treasures.

Gen 43:9 Judah accepted full responsibility for Benjamin's safety. He did not know what that might mean for him, but he was determined to do his duty. In the end, Judah's stirring words (Gen 44:18-34) caused Joseph to break down with emotion and reveal himself to his brothers. Accepting responsibilities is difficult, but it builds character and confidence, earns others' respect, and motivates us to complete our work. When you have been given an assignment to complete or a responsibility to fulfill, commit yourself to seeing it through.

Ancient Visitors to Egypt

This Egyptian wall painting, c. 1900 B.C., provides an interesting glimpse at what the patriarchs might have looked like. This scene was painted on the wall of an Egyptian nobleman's tomb, showing a group of people from the region of Shut in southern Canaan or the Sinai peninsula, who had traveled to Egypt for trade. The darker-skinned man at the front of the line is an Egyptian scribe announcing their arrival.

Gen 43:11 These gifts of balm, honey, gum, aromatic resin, pistachio nuts, and almonds were highly valuable specialty items not common in Egypt. Because of the famine, they were even more rare.

Gen 43:12 Joseph's brothers arrived home from Egypt only to find in their grain sacks the money they had used to pay for the grain (Gen 42:35). Some months later, when it was time to return to Egypt for more food, Jacob instructed them to take extra money so they could pay for the previous purchase as well as for additional grain. Jacob did not try to get away with anything. He was a man of integrity who paid for what he bought, whether he had to or not. We should follow his example and guard our integrity. A reputation for honesty is worth far more than the money we might gain by compromising it.

▸ **GENESIS 43:19-34** ***(cont.)***

stopped for the night and opened our sacks. Then we discovered that each man's money—the exact amount paid—was in the top of his sack! Here it is; we have brought it back with us. 22We also have additional money to buy more food. We have no idea who put our money in our sacks."

23"Relax. Don't be afraid," the household manager told them. "Your God, the God of your father, must have put this treasure into your sacks. I know I received your payment." Then he released Simeon and brought him out to them.

24The manager then led the men into Joseph's palace. He gave them water to wash their feet and provided food for their donkeys. 25They were told they would be eating there, so they prepared their gifts for Joseph's arrival at noon.

26When Joseph came home, they gave him the gifts they had brought him, then bowed low to the ground before him. 27After greeting them, he asked, "How is your father, the old man you spoke about? Is he still alive?"

28"Yes," they replied. "Our father, your servant, is alive and well." And they bowed low again.

29Then Joseph looked at his brother Benjamin, the son of his own mother. "Is this your youngest brother, the one you told me about?" Joseph asked. "May God be gracious to you, my son." 30Then Joseph hurried from the room because he was overcome with emotion for his brother. He went into his private room, where he broke down and wept. 31After washing his face, he came back out, keeping himself under control. Then he ordered, "Bring out the food!"

32The waiters served Joseph at his own table, and his brothers were served at a separate table. The Egyptians who ate with Joseph sat at their own table, because Egyptians despise Hebrews and refuse to eat with them. 33Joseph told each of his brothers where to sit, and to their amazement, he seated them according to age, from oldest to youngest. 34And Joseph filled their plates with food from his own table, giving Benjamin five times as much as he gave the others. So they feasted and drank freely with him.

Joseph's Silver Cup

GENESIS 44:1-17

When his brothers were ready to leave, Joseph gave these instructions to his palace manager: "Fill each of their sacks with as much grain as they can carry, and put each man's money back into his sack. 2Then put my personal silver cup at the top of the youngest brother's sack, along with the money for his grain." So the manager did as Joseph instructed him.

3The brothers were up at dawn and were sent on their journey with their loaded donkeys. 4But when they had gone only a short distance and were barely out of the city, Joseph said to his palace manager, "Chase after them and stop them. When you catch up with them, ask them, 'Why have you repaid my kindness with such evil? 5Why have you stolen my master's silver cup,* which he uses to predict the future? What a wicked thing you have done!'"

6When the palace manager caught up with the men, he spoke to them as he had been instructed.

7"What are you talking about?" the brothers responded. "We are your servants and would never do such a thing! 8Didn't we return the money we found in our sacks? We brought it back all the way from the land of Canaan. Why would we steal silver or gold from your master's house? 9If you find his cup with any one of us, let that man die. And all the rest of us, my lord, will be your slaves."

10"That's fair," the man replied. "But only the one who stole the cup will be my slave. The rest of you may go free."

11They all quickly took their sacks from the backs of their donkeys and opened them. 12The palace manager searched the brothers' sacks, from the oldest to the youngest. And the cup was found in Benjamin's sack! 13When the brothers saw this, they tore their clothing in despair. Then they loaded their donkeys again and returned to the city.

14Joseph was still in his palace when Judah and his brothers arrived, and they fell to the ground before him. 15"What have you done?" Joseph demanded. "Don't you know that a man like me can predict the future?"

16Judah answered, "Oh, my lord, what can we say to you? How can we explain this? How can we prove our innocence? God is punishing us for our sins. My lord, we have all returned to be your slaves—all of us, not just our brother who had your cup in his sack."

17"No," Joseph said. "I would never do such a thing! Only the man who stole the cup will be my slave. The rest of you may go back to your father in peace."

Gn 44:5 As in Greek version; Hebrew lacks this phrase.

Gen 43:23 How did the money get into the sacks? Most likely, Joseph instructed his household manager to replace the money and then explain it with this response. Note that the household manager credited their God, not some Egyptian deity.

Gen 43:32 Joseph ate by himself because he was following the laws of the Egyptians' caste system. Egyptians considered themselves highly intelligent and sophisticated. They looked upon shepherds and nomads as uncultured and even vulgar. As a Hebrew, Joseph could not eat with Egyptians even though he outranked them. As foreigners and shepherds, his brothers were lower in rank than any Egyptian citizens, so they had to eat separately too.

Gen 44:2 Joseph's silver cup was a symbol of his authority. It was thought to have supernatural powers, and to steal it would be a serious crime. Such goblets were used for predicting the future. A person poured water into the cup and interpreted the reflections, ripples, and bubbles. Joseph wouldn't have needed his cup since God told him everything he needed to know about the future.

Gen 44:13 Tearing clothes was an expression of deep sorrow, a customary manner of showing grief. The brothers were terrified that Benjamin might be harmed.

Judah Speaks for His Brothers

GENESIS 44:18-34

Then Judah stepped forward and said, "Please, my lord, let your servant say just one word to you. Please, do not be angry with me, even though you are as powerful as Pharaoh himself.

19"My lord, previously you asked us, your servants, 'Do you have a father or a brother?' 20And we responded, 'Yes, my lord, we have a father who is an old man, and his youngest son is a child of his old age. His full brother is dead, and he alone is left of his mother's children, and his father loves him very much.'

21"And you said to us, 'Bring him here so I can see him with my own eyes.' 22But we said to you, 'My lord, the boy cannot leave his father, for his father would die.' 23But you told us, 'Unless your youngest brother comes with you, you will never see my face again.'

24"So we returned to your servant, our father, and told him what you had said. 25Later, when he said, 'Go back again and buy us more food,' 26we replied, 'We can't go unless you let our youngest brother go with us. We'll never get to see the man's face unless our youngest brother is with us.'

27"Then my father said to us, 'As you know, my wife had two sons, 28and one of them went away and never returned. Doubtless he was torn to pieces by some wild animal. I have never seen him since. 29Now if you take his brother away from me, and any harm comes to him, you will send this grieving, white-haired man to his grave.*'

30"And now, my lord, I cannot go back to my father

Gn 44:29 Hebrew *to Sheol;* also in 44:31.

JUDAH

People who are leaders stand out. They don't necessarily look or act a certain way until the need for their action is apparent. Among their skills are outspokenness, decisiveness, action, and control. These skills can be used for great good or great evil. Jacob's fourth son, Judah, was a natural leader. The events of his life provided many opportunities to exercise those skills. Unfortunately Judah's decisions were often shaped more by the pressures of the moment than by a conscious desire to cooperate with God's plan. But when he did recognize his mistakes, he was willing to admit them. His experience with Tamar and the final confrontation with Joseph are both examples of Judah's willingness to bear the blame when confronted. It is a quality we also see in his descendant David. • Whether or not we have Judah's natural leadership qualities, we share with him a tendency to be blind toward our own sin. But too often we don't share his willingness to admit mistakes. From Judah we can learn that it is not wise to wait until our errors force us to admit to wrongdoing. It is far better to admit our mistakes openly, to shoulder the blame, and to seek forgiveness.

Strengths and accomplishments	• Was a natural leader—outspoken and decisive • Thought clearly and took action in high-pressure situations • Was willing to stand by his word and put himself on the line when necessary • Ancestor of David and Jesus, the Messiah
Weaknesses and mistakes	• Suggested to his brothers they sell Joseph into slavery • Failed miserably in the matter with his daughter-in-law, Tamar
Lessons from his life	• God is in control, far beyond the immediate situation • Procrastination often makes matters worse
Vital statistics	• Where: Canaan and Egypt • Occupation: Shepherd • Relatives: Parents: Jacob and Leah. Siblings: Eleven brothers and one sister. Wife: Bathshua (1 Chr 2:3). Daughter-in-law: Tamar. Sons: At least five.
Key verses	"Judah, your brothers will praise you. You will grasp your enemies by the neck. All your relatives will bow before you. Judah, my son, is a young lion that has finished eating its prey. Like a lion he crouches and lies down; like a lioness—who dares to rouse him? The scepter will not depart from Judah, nor the ruler's staff from his descendants, until the coming of the one to whom it belongs, the one whom all nations will honor" (Gen 49:8-10).

Judah's story is told in Genesis 29:35–50:26. He is also mentioned in 1 Chronicles 2–4.

Gen 44:16-34 When Judah was younger, he had shown no regard for his brother Joseph or his father, Jacob. First he had convinced his brothers to sell Joseph as a slave (Gen 37:27); then he had joined his brothers in lying to his father about Joseph's fate (Gen 37:32). But what a change had taken place in Judah! The man who had sold one favored little brother into slavery now offered to become a slave himself to save another favored little brother. He was so concerned for his father and younger brother that he was willing to die for them. When you are ready to give up hope on yourself or someone else, remember that God can work a complete change in even the most selfish personality.

Gen 44:18-34 Judah finally could take no more and stepped forward to plead their case. This was risky because Joseph could have had him killed. But Judah courageously defended himself and his brothers and pleaded for mercy. And he offered to put himself in Benjamin's place. At times we should be silent, but at times we should speak up, even if there could be serious repercussions. When faced with a situation that needs a strong voice and courageous action, remember Judah and speak up.

▸ **GENESIS 44:18-34** ***(cont.)***
without the boy. Our father's life is bound up in the
boy's life. [31]If he sees that the boy is not with us, our
father will die. We, your servants, will indeed be responsible for sending that grieving, white-haired man
to his grave. [32]My lord, I guaranteed to my father that I
would take care of the boy. I told him, 'If I don't bring
him back to you, I will bear the blame forever.'
[33]"So please, my lord, let me stay here as a slave
instead of the boy, and let the boy return with his
brothers. [34]For how can I return to my father if the
boy is not with me? I couldn't bear to see the anguish
this would cause my father!"

Joseph Reveals His Identity

GENESIS 45:1-15
Joseph could stand it no longer. There were many
people in the room, and he said to his attendants, "Out,
all of you!" So he was alone with his brothers when he
told them who he was. [2]Then he broke down and wept.
He wept so loudly the Egyptians could hear him, and
word of it quickly carried to Pharaoh's palace.
[3]"I am Joseph!" he said to his brothers. "Is my father
still alive?" But his brothers were speechless! They were
stunned to realize that Joseph was standing there in
front of them. [4]"Please, come closer," he said to them.
So they came closer. And he said again, "I am Joseph,
your brother, whom you sold into slavery in Egypt. [5]But
don't be upset, and don't be angry with yourselves for
selling me to this place. It was God who sent me here
ahead of you to preserve your lives. [6]This famine that
has ravaged the land for two years will last five more
years, and there will be neither plowing nor harvesting.
[7]God has sent me ahead of you to keep you and your
families alive and to preserve many survivors.* [8]So it
was God who sent me here, not you! And he is the one
who made me an adviser* to Pharaoh—the manager of
his entire palace and the governor of all Egypt.
[9]"Now hurry back to my father and tell him, 'This
is what your son Joseph says: God has made me master over all the land of Egypt. So come down to me
immediately! [10]You can live in the region of Goshen,
where you can be near me with all your children and
grandchildren, your flocks and herds, and everything
you own. [11]I will take care of you there, for there are
still five years of famine ahead of us. Otherwise you,
your household, and all your animals will starve.'"
[12]Then Joseph added, "Look! You can see for yourselves, and so can my brother Benjamin, that I really
am Joseph! [13]Go tell my father of my honored position
here in Egypt. Describe for him everything you have
seen, and then bring my father here quickly." [14]Weep-
ing with joy, he embraced Benjamin, and Benjamin did
the same. [15]Then Joseph kissed each of his brothers
and wept over them, and after that they began talking
freely with him.

Pharaoh Invites Jacob to Egypt

GENESIS 45:16-28
The news soon reached Pharaoh's palace: "Joseph's
brothers have arrived!" Pharaoh and his officials were
all delighted to hear this.

Gn 45:7 Or *and to save you with an extraordinary rescue.* The meaning of the Hebrew is uncertain. **Gn 45:8** Hebrew *a father.*

Granary

Along with herding animals, grain farming was one of the most important agricultural and economic activities of early civilization. Archaeologists date the existence of grain farming to around 6800 B.C. in the Near East. Isaac sowed in Gerar (Gen 26:12), and Joseph's dream centered around sheaves of grain (Gen 37:6-7). Joseph learned even more about farming grain from the Egyptians, who raised it on the fertile soils of the Nile floodplain. The picture shows an ancient model of an Egyptian granary, found in the tomb of an Egyptian official. Joseph, foreseeing the years of famine ahead, had wheat stored in granaries much like this one. Jacob's family needed the grain from Egypt in order to stave off starvation.

Gen 44:32-33 Judah had promised Jacob that he would guarantee young Benjamin's safety (Gen 43:9). Now Judah had a chance to keep that promise. Becoming a slave was a terrible fate, but Judah was determined to keep his word to his father. He showed great courage in carrying out his promise. Accepting a responsibility means carrying it out with determination and courage, regardless of the personal sacrifice.

Gen 44:33 Joseph wanted to see if his brothers' attitudes had changed for the better, so he tested the way they treated each other. Judah, the brother who had stepped forward with the plan to sell Joseph (Gen 37:27), now stepped forward to take Benjamin's punishment so that Benjamin could return to their father. This courageous act convinced Joseph that his brothers had dramatically changed for the better.

Gen 45:4-8 Although Joseph's brothers had wanted to get rid of him, God used even their evil actions to fulfill his ultimate plan. He had sent Joseph ahead to preserve their lives, save Egypt, and prepare the way for the beginning of the nation of Israel. God is sovereign. His plans are not dictated by human actions. When others intend evil toward you, remember that they are only God's tools. As

17Pharaoh said to Joseph, "Tell your brothers, 'This is
what you must do: Load your pack animals, and hurry
back to the land of Canaan. 18Then get your father and
all of your families, and return here to me. I will give
you the very best land in Egypt, and you will eat from
the best that the land produces.'"
19Then Pharaoh said to Joseph, "Tell your brothers,
'Take wagons from the land of Egypt to carry your little
children and your wives, and bring your father here.
20Don't worry about your personal belongings, for the
best of all the land of Egypt is yours.'"
21So the sons of Jacob* did as they were told. Joseph
provided them with wagons, as Pharaoh had commanded, and he gave them supplies for the journey.
22And he gave each of them new clothes—but to Benjamin he gave five changes of clothes and 300 pieces*
of silver. 23He also sent his father ten male donkeys
loaded with the finest products of Egypt, and ten female donkeys loaded with grain and bread and other
supplies he would need on his journey.
24So Joseph sent his brothers off, and as they left, he
called after them, "Don't quarrel about all this along
the way!" 25And they left Egypt and returned to their
father, Jacob, in the land of Canaan.
26"Joseph is still alive!" they told him. "And he is
governor of all the land of Egypt!" Jacob was stunned
at the news—he couldn't believe it. 27But when they
repeated to Jacob everything Joseph had told them,
and when he saw the wagons Joseph had sent to carry
him, their father's spirits revived.
28Then Jacob exclaimed, "It must be true! My son
Joseph is alive! I must go and see him before I die."

Gn 45:21 Hebrew *Israel;* also in 45:28. See note on 35:21. **Gn 45:22** Hebrew *300 shekels,* about 7.5 pounds or 3.4 kilograms in weight.

6. JACOB'S FAMILY MOVES TO EGYPT

Jacob's entire family went to live with Joseph in Egypt. This took them out of the land of Canaan, which God promised to Abraham and his descendants, but it also took them away from the influence of the Canaanites who were turning their hearts away from God. After 400 years in Egypt, the nation of Israel would return to Canaan as God promised.

Jacob's Journey to Egypt

GENESIS 46:1-27

So Jacob* set out for Egypt with all his possessions.
And when he came to Beersheba, he offered sacrifices
to the God of his father, Isaac. 2During the night God
spoke to him in a vision. "Jacob! Jacob!" he called.
"Here I am," Jacob replied.
3"I am God,* the God of your father," the voice said.
"Do not be afraid to go down to Egypt, for there I will
make your family into a great nation. 4I will go with
you down to Egypt, and I will bring you back again.
You will die in Egypt, but Joseph will be with you to
close your eyes."
5So Jacob left Beersheba, and his sons took him to

Gn 46:1 Hebrew *Israel;* also in 46:29, 30. See note on 35:21. **Gn 46:3** Hebrew *I am El.*

1876 BC

Jacob moves to Egypt

Joseph said to his brothers, "You intended to harm me, but God intended it all for good. He brought me to this position so I could save the lives of many people" (Gen 50:20).

Gen 45:17-20 Joseph had been rejected, kidnapped, enslaved, and imprisoned. Although his brothers had been unfaithful to him, he graciously forgave them and shared his prosperity. Joseph demonstrated how God forgives us and showers us with goodness even though we have sinned against him. The same forgiveness and blessings are ours if we ask for them.

Gen 45:26-27 Jacob needed some evidence before he could believe the incredible news that Joseph was alive. Similarly, Thomas refused to believe that Jesus had risen from the dead until he could see and touch him (John 20:25). It is hard to change what you believe without all the facts—or sometimes even with the facts. Good news can be difficult to believe. Don't ever give up hope that God has a wonderful future in store for you.

Gen 46:3-4 The Israelites did become a great nation, and Jacob's descendants eventually returned to Canaan. The book of Exodus recounts the story of Israel's slavery in Egypt for 400 years (fulfilling God's words to Abraham in Gen 15:13-16), and the book of Joshua gives an exciting account of the Israelites entering and conquering Canaan, the Promised Land.

Gen 46:3-4 God told Jacob to leave his home and travel to a strange and faraway land. But God reassured him by promising to go with him and take care of him. When new situations or surroundings frighten you, recognize that experiencing fear is normal. But to be paralyzed by fear is an indication that you question God's ability to take care of you.

Gen 46:4 Jacob never returned to Canaan, but God promised that his descendants would return. That Jacob would die in Egypt with Joseph at his side was God's promise to Jacob that he would never know the pain of being lonely again.

JACOB MOVES TO EGYPT ▶
After hearing the joyful news that Joseph was alive, Jacob packed up and moved his family to Egypt. Stopping first in Beersheba, Jacob offered sacrifices and received assurance from God that Egypt was where he should go. Jacob and his family settled in the region of Goshen, in the northeastern part of Egypt.

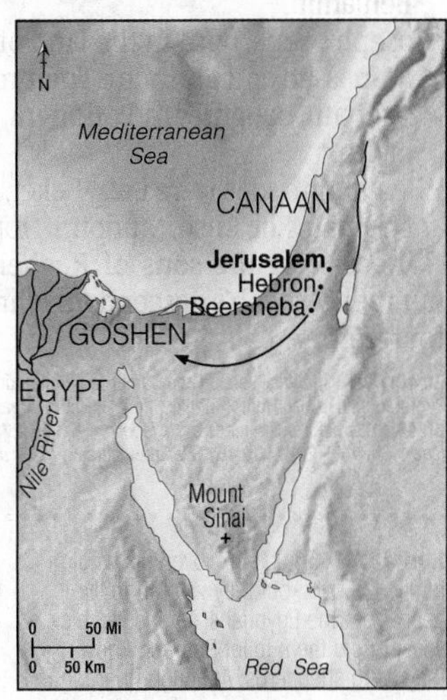

▸ **GENESIS 46:1-27** ***(cont.)***

Egypt. They carried him and their little ones and their wives in the wagons Pharaoh had provided for them. 6They also took all their livestock and all the personal belongings they had acquired in the land of Canaan. So Jacob and his entire family went to Egypt—7sons and grandsons, daughters and granddaughters—all his descendants.

8These are the names of the descendants of Israel—the sons of Jacob—who went to Egypt:

Reuben was Jacob's oldest son. 9The sons of Reuben were Hanoch, Pallu, Hezron, and Carmi.

10The sons of Simeon were Jemuel, Jamin, Ohad, Jakin, Zohar, and Shaul. (Shaul's mother was a Canaanite woman.)

11The sons of Levi were Gershon, Kohath, and Merari.

12The sons of Judah were Er, Onan, Shelah, Perez, and Zerah (though Er and Onan had died in the land of Canaan). The sons of Perez were Hezron and Hamul.

13The sons of Issachar were Tola, Puah,* Jashub,* and Shimron.

14The sons of Zebulun were Sered, Elon, and Jahleel.

15These were the sons of Leah and Jacob who were born in Paddan-aram, in addition to their daughter, Dinah. The number of Jacob's descendants (male and female) through Leah was thirty-three.

16The sons of Gad were Zephon,* Haggi, Shuni, Ezbon, Eri, Arodi, and Areli.

17The sons of Asher were Imnah, Ishvah, Ishvi, and Beriah. Their sister was Serah. Beriah's sons were Heber and Malkiel.

18These were the sons of Zilpah, the servant given to Leah by her father, Laban. The number of Jacob's descendants through Zilpah was sixteen.

19The sons of Jacob's wife Rachel were Joseph and Benjamin.

20Joseph's sons, born in the land of Egypt, were Manasseh and Ephraim. Their mother was Asenath, daughter of Potiphera, the priest of On.*

21Benjamin's sons were Bela, Beker, Ashbel, Gera, Naaman, Ehi, Rosh, Muppim, Huppim, and Ard.

22These were the sons of Rachel and Jacob. The number of Jacob's descendants through Rachel was fourteen.

23The son of Dan was Hushim.

24The sons of Naphtali were Jahzeel, Guni, Jezer, and Shillem.

25These were the sons of Bilhah, the servant given to Rachel by her father, Laban. The number of Jacob's descendants through Bilhah was seven.

26The total number of Jacob's direct descendants who went with him to Egypt, not counting his sons' wives, was sixty-six. 27In addition, Joseph had two sons* who were born in Egypt. So altogether, there were seventy* members of Jacob's family in the land of Egypt.

Jacob's Family Arrives in Goshen

GENESIS 46:28-34

As they neared their destination, Jacob sent Judah ahead to meet Joseph and get directions to the region of Goshen. And when they finally arrived there, 29Joseph prepared his chariot and traveled to Goshen to meet his father, Jacob. When Joseph arrived, he embraced his father and wept, holding him for a long time. 30Finally, Jacob said to Joseph, "Now I am ready to die, since I have seen your face again and know you are still alive."

31And Joseph said to his brothers and to his father's entire family, "I will go to Pharaoh and tell him, 'My brothers and my father's entire family have come to me from the land of Canaan. 32These men are shepherds, and they raise livestock. They have brought with them their flocks and herds and everything they own.'"

33Then he said, "When Pharaoh calls for you and asks you about your occupation, 34you must tell him, 'We, your servants, have raised livestock all our lives, as our ancestors have always done.' When you tell him this, he will let you live here in the region of Goshen, for the Egyptians despise shepherds."

Jacob Blesses Pharaoh

GENESIS 47:1-12

Then Joseph went to see Pharaoh and told him, "My father and my brothers have arrived from the land of Canaan. They have come with all their flocks and herds and possessions, and they are now in the region of Goshen."

2Joseph took five of his brothers with him and presented them to Pharaoh. 3And Pharaoh asked the brothers, "What is your occupation?"

Gn 46:13a As in Syriac version and Samaritan Pentateuch (see also 1 Chr 7:1); Hebrew reads *Puvah*. **Gn 46:13b** As in some Greek manuscripts and Samaritan Pentateuch (see also Num 26:24; 1 Chr 7:1); Hebrew reads *Iob*. **Gn 46:16** As in Greek version and Samaritan Pentateuch (see also Num 26:15); Hebrew reads *Ziphion*. **Gn 46:20** Greek version reads *of Heliopolis*. **Gn 46:27a** Greek version reads *nine sons*, probably including Joseph's grandsons through Ephraim and Manasseh (see 1 Chr 7:14-20). **Gn 46:27b** Greek version reads *seventy-five*; see note on Exod 1:5.

Gen 46:31-34 Jacob moved his whole family to Egypt, but they wanted to live apart from the Egyptians. To ensure this, Joseph told them to let Pharaoh know they were shepherds. Although Pharaoh may have been sympathetic to shepherds (for he was probably descended from the nomadic Hyksos line), the Egyptian culture would not willingly accept shepherds among them. The strategy worked, and Jacob's family was able to benefit from Pharaoh's generosity as well as from the Egyptians' prejudice.

They replied, "We, your servants, are shepherds, just like our ancestors. [4]We have come to live here in Egypt for a while, for there is no pasture for our flocks in Canaan. The famine is very severe there. So please, we request permission to live in the region of Goshen."

[5]Then Pharaoh said to Joseph, "Now that your father and brothers have joined you here, [6]choose any place in the entire land of Egypt for them to live. Give them the best land of Egypt. Let them live in the region of Goshen. And if any of them have special skills, put them in charge of my livestock, too."

[7]Then Joseph brought in his father, Jacob, and presented him to Pharaoh. And Jacob blessed Pharaoh.

[8]"How old are you?" Pharaoh asked him.

[9]Jacob replied, "I have traveled this earth for 130 hard years. But my life has been short compared to the lives of my ancestors." [10]Then Jacob blessed Pharaoh again before leaving his court.

[11]So Joseph assigned the best land of Egypt—the region of Rameses—to his father and his brothers, and he settled them there, just as Pharaoh had commanded. [12]And Joseph provided food for his father and his brothers in amounts appropriate to the number of their dependents, including the smallest children.

Joseph's Leadership in the Famine

GENESIS 47:13-26

Meanwhile, the famine became so severe that all the food was used up, and people were starving throughout the lands of Egypt and Canaan. [14]By selling grain to the people, Joseph eventually collected all the money in Egypt and Canaan, and he put the money in Pharaoh's treasury. [15]When the people of Egypt and Canaan ran out of money, all the Egyptians came to Joseph. "Our money is gone!" they cried. "But please give us food, or we will die before your very eyes!"

[16]Joseph replied, "Since your money is gone, bring me your livestock. I will give you food in exchange for your livestock." [17]So they brought their livestock to Joseph in exchange for food. In exchange for their horses, flocks of sheep and goats, herds of cattle, and donkeys, Joseph provided them with food for another year.

[18]But that year ended, and the next year they came again and said, "We cannot hide the truth from you, my lord. Our money is gone, and all our livestock and cattle are yours. We have nothing left to give but our bodies and our land. [19]Why should we die before your very eyes? Buy us and our land in exchange for food; we offer our land and ourselves as slaves for Pharaoh. Just give us grain so we may live and not die, and so the land does not become empty and desolate."

[20]So Joseph bought all the land of Egypt for Pharaoh. All the Egyptians sold him their fields because the famine was so severe, and soon all the land belonged to Pharaoh. [21]As for the people, he made them all slaves,* from one end of Egypt to the other. [22]The only land he did not buy was the land belonging to the priests. They received an allotment of food directly from Pharaoh, so they didn't need to sell their land.

[23]Then Joseph said to the people, "Look, today I have bought you and your land for Pharaoh. I will provide you with seed so you can plant the fields. [24]Then when you harvest it, one-fifth of your crop will belong to Pharaoh. You may keep the remaining four-fifths as seed for your fields and as food for you, your households, and your little ones."

[25]"You have saved our lives!" they exclaimed. "May it please you, my lord, to let us be Pharaoh's servants." [26]Joseph then issued a decree still in effect in the land of Egypt, that Pharaoh should receive one-fifth of all the crops grown on his land. Only the land belonging to the priests was not given to Pharaoh.

Gn 47:21 As in Greek version and Samaritan Pentateuch; Hebrew reads *he moved them all into the towns.*

7. JACOB AND JOSEPH DIE IN EGYPT

Jacob and Joseph both died in Egypt, but before they died they made sure that their bones would be returned to the land that God had promised to them and their descendants.

Joseph Makes a Promise to Jacob

GENESIS 47:27-31

Meanwhile, the people of Israel settled in the region of Goshen in Egypt. There they acquired property, and they were fruitful, and their population grew rapidly. [28]Jacob lived for seventeen years after his arrival in Egypt, so he lived 147 years in all.

[29]As the time of his death drew near, Jacob* called for his son Joseph and said to him, "Please do me this favor. Put your hand under my thigh and swear that you will treat me with unfailing love by honoring this last request: Do not bury me in Egypt. [30]When I die, please take my body out of Egypt and bury me with my ancestors."

So Joseph promised, "I will do as you ask."

[31]"Swear that you will do it," Jacob insisted. So

Gn 47:29 Hebrew *Israel;* also in 47:31b. See note on 35:21.

Gen 47:1-6 Joseph's faithfulness affected his entire family. When he was in the pit and in prison, Joseph must have wondered about his future. Instead of despairing, he faithfully obeyed God and did what was right. Here we see one of the exciting results. We may not always see the effects of our faith, but we can be sure that God will honor faithfulness.

▸ **GENESIS 47:27-31** ***(cont.)***
Joseph gave his oath, and Jacob bowed humbly at the head of his bed.*

Jacob Blesses Manasseh and Ephraim

GENESIS 48:1-22
One day not long after this, word came to Joseph, "Your father is failing rapidly." So Joseph went to visit his father, and he took with him his two sons, Manasseh and Ephraim.
[2]When Joseph arrived, Jacob was told, "Your son Joseph has come to see you." So Jacob* gathered his strength and sat up in his bed.
[3]Jacob said to Joseph, "God Almighty* appeared to me at Luz in the land of Canaan and blessed me. [4]He said to me, 'I will make you fruitful, and I will multiply your descendants. I will make you a multitude of nations. And I will give this land of Canaan to your descendants* after you as an everlasting possession.'
[5]"Now I am claiming as my own sons these two boys of yours, Ephraim and Manasseh, who were born here in the land of Egypt before I arrived. They will be my sons, just as Reuben and Simeon are. [6]But any children born to you in the future will be your own, and they will inherit land within the territories of their brothers Ephraim and Manasseh.
[7]"Long ago, as I was returning from Paddan-aram, Rachel died in the land of Canaan. We were still on the way, some distance from Ephrath (that is, Bethlehem). So with great sorrow I buried her there beside the road to Ephrath."
[8]Then Jacob looked over at the two boys. "Are these your sons?" he asked.
[9]"Yes," Joseph told him, "these are the sons God has given me here in Egypt."
And Jacob said, "Bring them closer to me, so I can bless them."
[10]Jacob was half blind because of his age and could hardly see. So Joseph brought the boys close to him, and Jacob kissed and embraced them. [11]Then Jacob said to Joseph, "I never thought I would see your face again, but now God has let me see your children, too!"
[12]Joseph moved the boys, who were at their grandfather's knees, and he bowed with his face to the ground. [13]Then he positioned the boys in front of Jacob. With his right hand he directed Ephraim toward Jacob's left hand, and with his left hand he put Manasseh at Jacob's right hand. [14]But Jacob crossed his arms as he reached out to lay his hands on the boys' heads. He put his right hand on the head of Ephraim, though he was the younger boy, and his left hand on the head of Manasseh, though he was the firstborn.
[15]Then he blessed Joseph and said,

"May the God before whom my grandfather
    Abraham
  and my father, Isaac, walked—
the God who has been my shepherd
  all my life, to this very day,
[16] the Angel who has redeemed me from all harm—
  may he bless these boys.
May they preserve my name
  and the names of Abraham and Isaac.
And may their descendants multiply greatly
  throughout the earth."

[17]But Joseph was upset when he saw that his father placed his right hand on Ephraim's head. So Joseph lifted it to move it from Ephraim's head to Manasseh's head. [18]"No, my father," he said. "This one is the firstborn. Put your right hand on his head."
[19]But his father refused. "I know, my son; I know," he replied. "Manasseh will also become a great people, but his younger brother will become even greater. And his descendants will become a multitude of nations."
[20]So Jacob blessed the boys that day with this blessing: "The people of Israel will use your names when they give a blessing. They will say, 'May God make you as prosperous as Ephraim and Manasseh.'" In this way, Jacob put Ephraim ahead of Manasseh.
[21]Then Jacob said to Joseph, "Look, I am about to

Gn 47:31 Greek version reads *and Israel bowed in worship as he leaned on his staff.* Compare Heb 11:21. **Gn 48:2** Hebrew *Israel;* also in 48:8, 10, 11, 13, 14, 21. See note on 35:21. **Gn 48:3** Hebrew *El-Shaddai.* **Gn 48:4** Hebrew *seed;* also in 48:19.

Gen 47:29-31 Jacob had Joseph promise to bury him in his homeland. Few things were written in this culture, so a person's word carried as much force as a written contract does today. People today seem to find it easy to say, "I didn't mean that." God's people, however, are to speak the truth and live the truth. Let your words be as binding as a written contract.

Gen 48:8-20 Jacob gave Ephraim, instead of his older brother Manasseh, the greater blessing. When Joseph objected, Jacob refused to listen because God had told him that Ephraim would become greater. God often works in unexpected ways. When he chooses people to fulfill his plans, he always goes deeper than appearance, tradition, or position. He sometimes surprises us by choosing the less obvious person, at least by human reasoning. God can use you to carry out his plans, even if you don't think you have all the qualifications.

Gen 48:11 When Joseph became a slave, Jacob thought he was dead and wept in despair (Gen 37:34). But eventually God's plan allowed Jacob to regain not only his son but his grandchildren as well. Circumstances are never so bad that they are beyond God's help. Jacob regained his son. Job got a new family (Job 42:10-17). Mary regained her brother, Lazarus (John 11:1-44). We need never despair because we belong to a loving God. We don't yet know what good he may bring out of a seemingly hopeless situation.

Gen 48:15 Jacob spoke of God as his shepherd throughout his life. In his old age, he could clearly see his dependence upon God. This marks a total attitude change from that of his scheming and dishonest youth. To develop an attitude like Jacob's, let God shepherd you as you trust in his provision and care. When people chase after what they want with no thought of God, they are willing to do anything, even what is wrong, in order to get it. It is far better to trust God and realize that all good things come from his hand.

Gen 48:20-22 Jacob was giving these young boys land occupied by the Philistines and Canaanites. His gift became reality when the tribes of Ephraim and Manasseh occupied the east and west sides of the Jordan River (Josh 16).

die, but God will be with you and will take you back to Canaan, the land of your ancestors. [22]And beyond what I have given your brothers, I am giving you an extra portion of the land* that I took from the Amorites with my sword and bow."

Jacob's Last Words to His Sons

GENESIS 49:1-28

Then Jacob called together all his sons and said, "Gather around me, and I will tell you what will happen to each of you in the days to come.

2 "Come and listen, you sons of Jacob;
listen to Israel, your father.
3 "Reuben, you are my firstborn, my strength,
the child of my vigorous youth.
You are first in rank and first in power.
4 But you are as unruly as a flood,
and you will be first no longer.
For you went to bed with my wife;
you defiled my marriage couch.
5 "Simeon and Levi are two of a kind;
their weapons are instruments of violence.
6 May I never join in their meetings;
may I never be a party to their plans.
For in their anger they murdered men,
and they crippled oxen just for sport.
7 A curse on their anger, for it is fierce;
a curse on their wrath, for it is cruel.
I will scatter them among the descendants
of Jacob;
I will disperse them throughout Israel.
8 "Judah, your brothers will praise you.
You will grasp your enemies by the neck.
All your relatives will bow before you.
9 Judah, my son, is a young lion
that has finished eating its prey.
Like a lion he crouches and lies down;
like a lioness—who dares to rouse him?
10 The scepter will not depart from Judah,
nor the ruler's staff from his descendants,*
until the coming of the one to whom
it belongs,*
the one whom all nations will honor.
11 He ties his foal to a grapevine,
the colt of his donkey to a choice vine.
He washes his clothes in wine,
his robes in the blood of grapes.
12 His eyes are darker than wine,
and his teeth are whiter than milk.
13 "Zebulun will settle by the seashore
and will be a harbor for ships;
his borders will extend to Sidon.
14 "Issachar is a sturdy donkey,
resting between two saddlepacks.*
15 When he sees how good the countryside is
and how pleasant the land,

Gn 48:22 Or *an extra ridge of land.* The meaning of the Hebrew is uncertain. **Gn 49:10a** Hebrew *from between his feet.* **Gn 49:10b** Or *until tribute is brought to him and the peoples obey;* traditionally rendered *until Shiloh comes.* **Gn 49:14** Or *sheepfolds,* or *hearths.*

JACOB'S SONS AND THEIR NOTABLE DESCENDANTS

Jacob's 12 sons were the ancestors of the 12 tribes of Israel. The entire nation of Israel came from these men.

Son	Notable descendants
REUBEN	none
SIMEON	none
LEVI	Aaron, Moses, Eli, John the Baptist
JUDAH	David, Jesus
DAN	Samson
NAPHTALI	Barak, Elijah
GAD	Jephthah (?)
ASHER	none
ISSACHAR	none
ZEBULUN	none
JOSEPH	Joshua, Gideon, Samuel
BENJAMIN	Saul, Esther, Paul

Gen 49:3-28 Jacob blessed each of his sons and then made a prediction about each one's future. The way the men had lived played an important part in Jacob's blessing and prophecy. Our past also affects our present and future. By sunrise tomorrow, our actions of today will have become part of the past. Yet they will already have begun to shape the future. What actions can you choose or avoid that will positively shape your future?

Gen 49:4 The oldest son was supposed to receive a double inheritance, but Reuben lost his special honor. Unruly and untrustworthy, especially in his younger days, he had gone so far as to sleep with one of his father's concubines. Jacob could not give the birthright blessing to such a dishonorable son.

Gen 49:8-12 Judah had sold Joseph into slavery and tried to defraud his daughter-in-law. So why did Jacob grant him this blessing? God had chosen Judah to be the ancestor of Israel's line of kings (that is the meaning of "the scepter will not depart from Judah"). This may have been due to Judah's dramatic change of character (Gen 44:33-34). Judah's line would produce the promised Messiah, Jesus.

Gen 49:10 "Until the coming of the one to whom it belongs" may also be translated, "until Shiloh comes." What is *Shiloh*? The meaning of this difficult passage is disputed. *Shiloh* may be another name for the Messiah because its literal meaning is "sent." *Shiloh* might also refer to the Tabernacle set up at the city of Shiloh (Josh 18:1).

▸ **GENESIS 49:1-28** ***(cont.)***

he will bend his shoulder to the load
and submit himself to hard labor.

16 "Dan will govern his people,
like any other tribe in Israel.
17 Dan will be a snake beside the road,
a poisonous viper along the path
that bites the horse's hooves
so its rider is thrown off.
18 I trust in you for salvation, O LORD!
19 "Gad will be attacked by marauding bands,
but he will attack them when they retreat.

20 "Asher will dine on rich foods
and produce food fit for kings.

21 "Naphtali is a doe set free
that bears beautiful fawns.

22 "Joseph is the foal of a wild donkey,
the foal of a wild donkey at a spring—
one of the wild donkeys on the ridge.*
23 Archers attacked him savagely;
they shot at him and harassed him.
24 But his bow remained taut,
and his arms were strengthened
by the hands of the Mighty One of Jacob,
by the Shepherd, the Rock of Israel.
25 May the God of your father help you;
may the Almighty bless you
with the blessings of the heavens above,
and blessings of the watery depths below,
and blessings of the breasts and womb.
26 May the blessings of your father
surpass the blessings of the ancient
mountains,*
reaching to the heights of the eternal hills.
May these blessings rest on the head of Joseph,
who is a prince among his brothers.

27 "Benjamin is a ravenous wolf,
devouring his enemies in the morning
and dividing his plunder in the evening."

28These are the twelve tribes of Israel, and this is
what their father said as he told his sons good-bye.
He blessed each one with an appropriate message.

Jacob's Death and Burial

GENESIS 49:29–50:13

Then Jacob instructed them, "Soon I will die and join
my ancestors. Bury me with my father and grandfather
in the cave in the field of Ephron the Hittite. 30This
is the cave in the field of Machpelah, near Mamre in
Canaan, that Abraham bought from Ephron the Hittite
as a permanent burial site. 31There Abraham and his
wife Sarah are buried. There Isaac and his wife, Rebekah, are buried. And there I buried Leah. 32It is the
plot of land and the cave that my grandfather Abraham
bought from the Hittites."

33When Jacob had finished this charge to his sons,
he drew his feet into the bed, breathed his last, and
joined his ancestors in death.

50:1 Joseph threw himself on his father and wept over
him and kissed him. 2Then Joseph told the physicians
who served him to embalm his father's body; so Jacob*
was embalmed. 3The embalming process took the
usual forty days. And the Egyptians mourned his death
for seventy days.

4When the period of mourning was over, Joseph
approached Pharaoh's advisers and said, "Please do
me this favor and speak to Pharaoh on my behalf. 5Tell
him that my father made me swear an oath. He said to
me, 'Listen, I am about to die. Take my body back to the
land of Canaan, and bury me in the tomb I prepared for
myself.' So please allow me to go and bury my father.
After his burial, I will return without delay."

6Pharaoh agreed to Joseph's request. "Go and bury

Gn 49:22 Or *Joseph is a fruitful tree, / a fruitful tree beside a spring. / His branches reach over the wall.* The meaning of the Hebrew is uncertain. **Gn 49:26** Or *of my ancestors.* **Gn 50:2** Hebrew *Israel.* See note on 35:21.

Gen 49:18 In the middle of his prophecy to Dan, Jacob exclaimed, "I trust in you for salvation, O LORD!" He was emphasizing to Dan that he would be a strong leader only if he trusted in God, not in his natural strength or ability. Those who are strong, attractive, or talented often find it easier to trust in themselves than in God, who gave them their gifts. Remember to thank God for what you are and have so that your trust does not become misplaced.

Gen 49:22 Joseph would have some heroic descendants. Among them were Joshua, who would lead the Israelites into the Promised Land (Josh 1:10-11), and Deborah and Gideon, judges of Israel (Judg 4:4; 6:11-12).

Gen 49:23-24 These verses celebrate the times God rescued Joseph when his enemies attacked him. So often we struggle by ourselves, forgetting that God is able to help us fight our battles, whether they are against people with weapons or against spiritual forces. Joseph was able to draw closer to God as adversity mounted. To trust God to rescue you shows great faith. Can you trust him when injury or persecution is directed at you? Such spiritual battles require teamwork between courageous, faithful people and a mighty God.

Gen 50:1-11 When Jacob died at the age of 147, Joseph wept and mourned for months. When someone close to us dies, we need a long period of time to work through our grief. Crying and sharing our feelings with others helps us recover and go on with life. Allow yourself and others the freedom to grieve over the loss of a loved one, and give yourself time enough to complete your grieving process.

Gen 50:2-3 Embalming was typical for Egyptians but unusual for nomadic shepherds. Believing that the dead went to the next world in their physical bodies, the Egyptians embalmed bodies to preserve them so they could function in the world to come. Jacob's family allowed him to be embalmed as a sign of courtesy and respect to the Egyptians.

Gen 50:5 Joseph had proven himself trustworthy as Pharaoh's adviser. Because of his good record, Pharaoh had little doubt that he would return to Egypt as promised after burying his father in Canaan. Privileges and freedom often result when we have demonstrated our trustworthiness. Since trust must be built gradually over time, take every opportunity to prove your reliability even in minor matters.

your father, as he made you promise," he said. 7So Joseph went up to bury his father. He was accompanied by all of Pharaoh's officials, all the senior members of Pharaoh's household, and all the senior officers of Egypt. 8Joseph also took his entire household and his brothers and their households. But they left their little children and flocks and herds in the land of Goshen. 9A great number of chariots and charioteers accompanied Joseph.

10When they arrived at the threshing floor of Atad, near the Jordan River, they held a very great and solemn memorial service, with a seven-day period of mourning for Joseph's father. 11The local residents, the Canaanites, watched them mourning at the threshing floor of Atad. Then they renamed that place (which is near the Jordan) Abel-mizraim,* for they said, "This is a place of deep mourning for these Egyptians."

12So Jacob's sons did as he had commanded them. 13They carried his body to the land of Canaan and buried him in the cave in the field of Machpelah, near Mamre. This is the cave that Abraham had bought as a permanent burial site from Ephron the Hittite.

Joseph Reassures His Brothers

GENESIS 50:14-21

After burying Jacob, Joseph returned to Egypt with his brothers and all who had accompanied him to his father's burial. 15But now that their father was dead, Joseph's brothers became fearful. "Now Joseph will show his anger and pay us back for all the wrong we did to him," they said.

16So they sent this message to Joseph: "Before your father died, he instructed us 17to say to you: 'Please forgive your brothers for the great wrong they did to you—for their sin in treating you so cruelly.' So we, the servants of the God of your father, beg you to forgive our sin." When Joseph received the message, he broke down and wept. 18Then his brothers came and threw themselves down before Joseph. "Look, we are your slaves!" they said.

19But Joseph replied, "Don't be afraid of me. Am I God, that I can punish you? 20You intended to harm me, but God intended it all for good. He brought me to this position so I could save the lives of many people. 21No, don't be afraid. I will continue to take care of you and your children." So he reassured them by speaking kindly to them.

The Death of Joseph

GENESIS 50:22-26

22So Joseph and his brothers and their families continued to live in Egypt. Joseph lived to the age of 110. 23He lived to see three generations of descendants of his son Ephraim, and he lived to see the birth of the children of Manasseh's son Makir, whom he claimed as his own.*

24"Soon I will die," Joseph told his brothers, "but God will surely come to help you and lead you out of this land of Egypt. He will bring you back to the land he solemnly promised to give to Abraham, to Isaac, and to Jacob."

Joseph dies

25Then Joseph made the sons of Israel swear an oath, and he said, "When God comes to help you and lead you back, you must take my bones with you." 26So Joseph died at the age of 110. The Egyptians embalmed him, and his body was placed in a coffin in Egypt.

Gn 50:11 *Abel-mizraim* means "mourning of the Egyptians." **Gn 50:23** Hebrew *who were born on Joseph's knees.*

Gen 50:12-13 Abraham had purchased the cave in the field of Machpelah as a burial place for his wife Sarah (Gen 23:1-9). It was to be a burial place for his entire family. Jacob was Abraham's grandson, and Jacob's sons returned to Canaan to bury him in this cave along with Abraham and Isaac. Their desire to be buried in this cave expressed their faith in God's promise to give their descendants the land of Canaan.

Gen 50:15-21 Now that Jacob (or Israel) was dead, the brothers feared revenge from Joseph. Could he really have forgiven them for selling him into slavery? But to their surprise, Joseph not only forgave them but reassured them, offering to care for them and their families. Joseph's forgiveness was complete. He demonstrated how God graciously accepts us even though we don't deserve it. Because God forgives us even when we have ignored or rejected him, we should graciously forgive others.

Gen 50:20 God brought good from the brothers' evil deed, Potiphar's wife's false accusation, the cup-bearer's neglect, and seven years of famine. The experiences in Joseph's life taught him that God brings good from evil for those who trust him. Do you trust God enough to wait patiently for him to bring good out of bad situations? You can trust him because, as Joseph learned, God can overrule people's evil intentions to bring about his intended results.

Gen 50:24 Joseph was ready to die. He had no doubts that God would keep his promise and one day bring the Israelites back to their homeland. What a tremendous example! The secret of that kind of faith is a lifetime of trusting God. Your faith is like a muscle—it grows with exercise, gaining strength over time. After a lifetime of exercising trust, your faith can be as strong as Joseph's. Then at your death, you can be confident that God will fulfill all his promises to you and to all those faithful to him who may live after you.

Gen 50:24 This verse sets the stage for what would begin to happen in Exodus and come to completion in Joshua. God was going to make Jacob's family into a great nation, lead them out of Egypt, and bring them into the land he had promised them. The nation would rely heavily on this promise, and Joseph emphasized his belief that God would do what he had promised.

Gen 50:26 The book of Genesis gives us rich descriptions of the lives of many great men and women who walked with God. They sometimes succeeded and often failed. Yet we learn much by reading the biographies of these people. Where did they get their motivation and courage? They got it by realizing God was with them despite their inadequacies. Knowing this should encourage us to be faithful to God, to rely on him for guidance, and to utilize the gifts and abilities he has given us.

E. The Story of Job

Job doesn't seem to be a member of God's chosen family line, but he is portrayed as a man who knew the true God and worshiped him. He probably lived around the same time as Abraham, Isaac, and Jacob because of the way his life is described, but certainty isn't possible.

1. JOB IS TESTED

Job is portrayed as a wealthy man of upright character who loves God. Yet God allows Satan to destroy his flocks, his possessions, his children, and his health. Job refuses to give up on God, even though he does not understand why this is happening to him. We, too, must trust God when we do not understand why we face difficulties.

Prologue

JOB 1:1-5

There once was a man named Job who lived in the land of Uz. He was blameless—a man of complete integrity. He feared God and stayed away from evil. [2]He had seven sons and three daughters. [3]He owned 7,000 sheep, 3,000 camels, 500 teams of oxen, and 500 female donkeys. He also had many servants. He was, in fact, the richest person in that entire area.

[4]Job's sons would take turns preparing feasts in their homes, and they would also invite their three sisters to celebrate with them. [5]When these celebrations ended—sometimes after several days—Job would purify his children. He would get up early in the morning and offer a burnt offering for each of them. For Job said to himself, "Perhaps my children have sinned and have cursed God in their hearts." This was Job's regular practice.

Job's First Test

JOB 1:6-22

One day the members of the heavenly court* came to present themselves before the LORD, and the Accuser, Satan,* came with them. [7]"Where have you come from?" the LORD asked Satan.

Jb 1:6a Hebrew *the sons of God.* **Jb 1:6b** Hebrew *and the satan;* similarly throughout this chapter.

Job 1:1 As we read the book of Job, we have inside information that the characters of the story do not have. Job, the main character of the book, lost everything through no fault of his own. As he struggled to understand why all this was happening to him, it became clear that he was not meant to know the reasons. He would have to face life with no answers or explanations.

We must experience life as Job did—one day at a time and without complete answers to all of life's questions. Will we, like Job, trust God no matter what? Or will we give in to the temptation to say that God doesn't really care?

Job 1:1 The location of the land of Uz is uncertain. We only know that Uz had plentiful pastures and crops (Job 1:3), was located near a wilderness area (Job 1:19), and was close enough to the Sabeans and Chaldeans to be raided (Job 1:14-17). Uz is also mentioned in Jeremiah 25:19-20. Some scholars believe Uz was located east of the Jordan River near Canaan (Israel), where the Jews (those to whom God first revealed himself) eventually lived.

Job 1:1ff As we see calamity and suffering in the book of Job, we must remember that we live in a fallen world where good behavior is not always rewarded and bad behavior is not always punished. When we see a notorious criminal prospering or an innocent child in pain, we say, "That's wrong." And it is. Sin has twisted justice and made our world unpredictable and ugly.

The book of Job shows a good man suffering for no apparent reason. Sadly, our world is like that. But Job's story does not end in despair. Through Job's life we can see that faith in God is justified even when our situations look hopeless. Faith based on rewards or prosperity is hollow. To be unshakable, faith must be built on the confidence that God's ultimate purpose will come to pass.

Job 1:5 It is not known for sure, but Job probably lived around the time of the patriarchs (Abraham, Isaac, Jacob) before God gave his written law or appointed priests to be religious leaders. During Job's day, the father was the family's religious leader. Because there were no priests to instruct him in God's laws, Job acted as the priest and offered sacrifices to God to ask for forgiveness for sins he and his family had committed. This demonstrated that Job did not consider himself sinless. Job did this out of conviction and love for God, not just because it was his role as head of the house. Do you carry out your spiritual duties because they are expected or spontaneously from a heart of devotion?

Job 1:5 Job showed deep concern for the spiritual welfare of his children. Fearful that they might have sinned unknowingly, he offered sacrifices for them. Parents today can show the same concern by praying for their children. This means "sacrificing" some time each day to ask God to forgive them, to help them grow, to protect them, and to help them please him.

Job 1:6 The Bible speaks of other heavenly councils where God and the angels plan their activities on earth and where angels are required to give account of themselves (e.g., 1 Kgs 22:19-23). Because God is creator of all angels—both those who serve him and those who rebelled—he has complete power and authority over them.

Job 1:6-7 Satan, originally an angel of God, had become corrupt through his own pride. He has been evil since his rebellion against God (1 Jn 3:8). Satan considers God his enemy. He tries to hinder God's work in people, but he is limited by God's power and can do only what he is permitted (Luke 22:31-32; 1 Tim 1:19-20; 2 Tim 2:23-26). Satan is our enemy because he actively looks for people to attack with temptation (1 Pet 5:8-9) and because he wants to make people hate God. He does this through lies and deception (Gen 3:1-6). Job, a blameless and upright man who had been greatly blessed, was a perfect target for Satan. Any person who is committed to God should expect Satan's attacks.

Job 1:6-12 From this conversation, we learn a great deal about Satan. (1) He is accountable to God. All angelic beings, good and evil, are compelled to present themselves before God (Job 1:6). God knew that Satan was intent on attacking Job. (2) Satan can be at only one place at a time (Job 1:6-7). His demons aid him in his work; but as a created being, he is limited. (3) Satan cannot see into our minds or foretell the future (Job 1:9-11). If he could, he would have known that Job would not break under pressure. (4) Because Satan can do nothing without God's permission (Job 1:12), God's people can overcome his attacks through God's power. (5) God puts

Satan answered the LORD, "I have been patrolling
the earth, watching everything that's going on."
[8]Then the LORD asked Satan, "Have you noticed my
servant Job? He is the finest man in all the earth. He is
blameless—a man of complete integrity. He fears God
and stays away from evil."
[9]Satan replied to the LORD, "Yes, but Job has good
reason to fear God. [10]You have always put a wall of
protection around him and his home and his property. You have made him prosper in everything he
does. Look how rich he is! [11]But reach out and take
away everything he has, and he will surely curse you
to your face!"
[12]"All right, you may test him," the LORD said to Satan. "Do whatever you want with everything he pos-
sesses, but don't harm him physically." So Satan left
the LORD's presence.
[13]One day when Job's sons and daughters were
feasting at the oldest brother's house, [14]a messenger arrived at Job's home with this news: "Your oxen
were plowing, with the donkeys feeding beside them,
[15]when the Sabeans raided us. They stole all the animals and killed all the farmhands. I am the only one
who escaped to tell you."
[16]While he was still speaking, another messenger
arrived with this news: "The fire of God has fallen
from heaven and burned up your sheep and all the
shepherds. I am the only one who escaped to tell you."
[17]While he was still speaking, a third messenger
arrived with this news: "Three bands of Chaldean
raiders have stolen your camels and killed your servants. I am the only one who escaped to tell you."
[18]While he was still speaking, another messenger
arrived with this news: "Your sons and daughters were
feasting in their oldest brother's home. [19]Suddenly, a
powerful wind swept in from the wilderness and hit
the house on all sides. The house collapsed, and all
your children are dead. I am the only one who escaped
to tell you."
[20]Job stood up and tore his robe in grief. Then he

THE SOURCES OF SUFFERING

When suffering or troubles happen, do they always come from Satan? In Job's story, his series of tragedies did come from Satan, but this is not always the case. This chart shows four major causes of suffering. Any one of these or a combination of them may create suffering. If knowing why we are suffering will teach us to avoid the cause, then the causes are worth knowing. However, it is most important to know how to respond during suffering.

Source	Who Is Responsible	Who Is Affected	Needed Response
My sin	I am	Myself and others	Repentance and confession to God
Others' sin	Person who sinned and others who allowed the sin	Probably many people, including those who sinned	Active resistance to the sinful behavior, while accepting the sinner
Avoidable physical (or natural) disaster	Persons who ignore the facts or refuse to take precautions	Most of those exposed to the cause	Prevent them if possible; be prepared if they can't be prevented
Unavoidable physical (or natural) disaster	God, Satan	Most of those present	Ongoing trust in God's faithfulness

limitations on what Satan can do (Job 1:12; 2:6). Satan's response to the Lord's question (Job 1:7) tells us that Satan is real and active on earth. Knowing this about Satan should cause us to remain close to the one who is greater than Satan—God himself.

Job 1:7ff Could this conversation between God and Satan really have happened? Other Bible passages tell us that Satan does indeed have access to God (see Rev 12:10). He even went into God's presence to make accusations against Joshua the high priest (Zech 3:1-2). Apart from this conversation, the reasons for Job's suffering become meaningless, and the book of Job loses its force.

Job 1:8, 12 Job was a model of trust in and obedience to God, yet God permitted Satan to attack him in an especially harsh manner. Although God loves us, believing and obeying him do not shelter us from life's calamities. Setbacks, tragedies, and sorrows strike Christians and non-Christians alike. But in our tests and trials, God expects us to express our faith to the world. How do you respond to your troubles? Do you ask God, "Why me?" or do you say, "Use me!"?

Job 1:9 Satan attacked Job's motives, saying that Job was blameless and had integrity only because he had no reason to turn against God. Ever since he had started following God, everything had gone well for Job. Satan wanted to prove that Job worshiped God not out of love but because God had given him so much.

Satan accurately analyzed why many people trust God. They are fair-weather believers, following God only when everything is going well or for what they can get. Adversity destroys this superficial faith. But adversity strengthens real faith by causing believers to dig their roots deeper into God in order to withstand the storms. How deep does your faith go? Put the roots of your faith down deep into God so that you can withstand any storm you may face.

Job 1:12 This conversation between God and Satan teaches us an important fact about God—he is fully aware of every attempt by Satan to bring suffering and difficulty upon us. While God may allow us to suffer for a reason beyond our understanding, he is never caught off-guard by our troubles and is always compassionate.

Job 1:15-17 The Sabeans were from southwest Arabia, while the Chaldeans were from the region north of the Persian Gulf.

Job 1:20-22 Job did not hide his overwhelming grief. He had not lost his faith in God; instead, his emotions showed that he was human and that he loved his family. God created our emotions, and it is not sinful or inappropriate to express them as Job did. If you have experienced a deep loss, a disappointment, or a heartbreak, admit your feelings to yourself and others, and grieve.

Job 1:20-22 Job had lost his possessions and family in the first of Satan's tests, but he reacted rightly toward God by acknowledging God's sovereign authority over everything God had given him. Satan lost this first round. Job passed the test and proved that people can love God for who he is, not for what he gives.

▸ **JOB 1:6-22** ***(cont.)***

shaved his head and fell to the ground to worship. [21]He said,

"I came naked from my mother's womb,
and I will be naked when I leave.
The LORD gave me what I had,
and the LORD has taken it away.
Praise the name of the LORD!"

[22]In all of this, Job did not sin by blaming God.

Job's Second Test

JOB 2:1-10

One day the members of the heavenly court* came again to present themselves before the LORD, and the Accuser, Satan,* came with them. [2]"Where have you come from?" the LORD asked Satan.

Satan answered the LORD, "I have been patrolling the earth, watching everything that's going on."

[3]Then the LORD asked Satan, "Have you noticed my servant Job? He is the finest man in all the earth. He is blameless—a man of complete integrity. He fears God and stays away from evil. And he has maintained his integrity, even though you urged me to harm him without cause."

[4]Satan replied to the LORD, "Skin for skin! A man will give up everything he has to save his life. [5]But reach out and take away his health, and he will surely curse you to your face!"

[6]"All right, do with him as you please," the LORD said to Satan. "But spare his life." [7]So Satan left the LORD's presence, and he struck Job with terrible boils from head to foot.

[8]Job scraped his skin with a piece of broken pottery as he sat among the ashes. [9]His wife said to him, "Are you still trying to maintain your integrity? Curse God and die."

[10]But Job replied, "You talk like a foolish woman. Should we accept only good things from the hand of God and never anything bad?" So in all this, Job said nothing wrong.

Job's Three Friends Share His Anguish

JOB 2:11-13

When three of Job's friends heard of the tragedy he had suffered, they got together and traveled from their homes to comfort and console him. Their names were Eliphaz the Temanite, Bildad the Shuhite, and Zophar the Naamathite. [12]When they saw Job from a distance, they scarcely recognized him. Wailing loudly, they tore their robes and threw dust into the air over their heads to show their grief. [13]Then they sat on the ground with him for seven days and nights. No one said a word to Job, for they saw that his suffering was too great for words.

Jb 2:1a Hebrew *the sons of God.* **Jb 2:1b** Hebrew *and the satan;* similarly throughout this chapter.

Job 2:3-6 Can Satan persuade God to change his plans? At first God said he did not want Job harmed physically, but then he decided to allow it. Satan is unable to persuade God to go against his character—God is completely and eternally good. But God was willing to go along with Satan's plan because God knew the eventual outcome of Job's story. God cannot be fooled by Satan. Job's suffering was a test for Job, Satan, and us—not God.

Job 2:4-5 "Skin for skin" was Satan's comment concerning Job's response to the loss of his family. Satan still held to his opinion that Job was faithful only because of God's blessings. Satan believed that Job was willing to accept the loss of family and property as long as his own skin was safe. Satan's next step was to inflict physical suffering upon Job to prove his original accusation (Job 1:9).

Job 2:6 Again Satan had to seek permission from God to inflict pain upon Job. God limits Satan, and in this case he did not allow Satan to destroy Job.

Job 2:9 Why was Job's wife spared when the rest of his family was killed? It is possible that her very presence caused Job even more suffering through her chiding and sorrow over all they had lost.

Job 2:10 Many people think that believing in God protects them from trouble, so when calamity comes, they question God's goodness and justice. But the message of Job is that you should not give up on God because he allows you to have bad experiences. Faith in God does not guarantee personal prosperity, and lack of faith does not guarantee troubles in this life. If this were so, people would believe in God simply to get rich or avoid pain. God is capable of rescuing us from suffering, but he may also allow suffering to come for reasons we cannot understand. It is Satan's strategy to get us to doubt God at exactly this moment. Here Job shows a perspective broader than seeking his own personal comfort.

Job 2:11 Eliphaz, Bildad, and Zophar were not only Job's friends, they were also known for their wisdom. But in the end, their wisdom was shown to be narrow-minded and incomplete.

Job 2:11 Upon learning of Job's difficulties, three of his friends came to sympathize with him and comfort him. Later we learn that their words of comfort were not helpful—but at least they came. While God rebuked them for what they had said (Job 42:7), he did not rebuke them for making the effort to come to their friend in need. Unfortunately, they did a poor job of comforting Job because they were proud of their own advice and insensitive to Job's needs. When someone is in need, go to that person, but be sensitive about how you give comfort.

Job 2:13 Why did the friends arrive and then just sit quietly? According to Jewish tradition, people who come to comfort someone in mourning should not speak until the mourner speaks. Often the best response to another person's suffering is silence. Job's friends realized that his pain was too deep to be healed with mere words, so they said nothing. (If only they had continued to sit quietly!) Often we feel we must say something spiritual and insightful to a hurting friend. Perhaps what a friend needs most is just our presence, showing that we care. Pat answers and trite quotations say much less than empathetic silence and loving companionship.

Job 3:1ff Job's response to his second test—physical affliction—contrasts greatly to his attitude after the first test (Job 1:20-22). Job still did not curse God, but he cursed the day of his birth. He felt it would be better never to have been born than to be forsaken by God. Job was struggling emotionally, physically, and spiritually; his misery was pervasive and deep. Never underestimate how vulnerable we are during times of suffering and pain. We must hold on to God even if there is no relief.

Job 3:8 In Job's day, people were hired to pronounce curses. Job desired that the experts at cursing would call up the sea monster, Leviathan, to swallow up the day of his birth.

2. THREE FRIENDS ANSWER JOB

Job agonizes over his situation. His three friends explain that he must be suffering because of some terrible sin he committed. They try to persuade Job to repent of his sin. When Job argues that he has not sinned enough to deserve such suffering, his friends respond with even harsher accusations. While there are elements of truth in the speeches of Job's three friends, they are based on wrong assumptions. We must be careful what we assume to be true in the lives of others. We cannot assume that suffering is their own fault or a result of their sin.

Job's First Speech

JOB 3:1-26

At last Job spoke, and he cursed the day of his birth.
2He said:

3 "Let the day of my birth be erased,
and the night I was conceived.
4 Let that day be turned to darkness.
Let it be lost even to God on high,
and let no light shine on it.
5 Let the darkness and utter gloom claim that day
for its own.
Let a black cloud overshadow it,
and let the darkness terrify it.
6 Let that night be blotted off the calendar,
never again to be counted among the days
of the year,
never again to appear among the months.
7 Let that night be childless.
Let it have no joy.
8 Let those who are experts at cursing—
whose cursing could rouse Leviathan*—
curse that day.

Jb 3:8 The identification of Leviathan is disputed, ranging from an earthly creature to a mythical sea monster in ancient literature.

JOB

Children never tire of asking *why.* Yet the question produces a bitter taste the older we get. Children wonder about everything; adults wonder about suffering. We would expect Job's wealth and family to give him a very happy life, and for a while, they did. But the loss and pain he experienced, and his immediate response, are shocking. To those so quick to ask *why* at the smallest misfortune, Job's faithfulness seems incredible. But even Job had something to learn. We can learn with him. • Our age of "instant" everything has caused us to lose the ability to wait. We expect to learn patience instantly, and in our hurry, we miss the contradiction. Of all that we want now, relief from pain is at the top of our list. We want an instant cure for everything from toothaches to heartbreaks. • Although some pains have been cured, we still live in a world where many people suffer. Job was not expecting instant answers for the intense emotional and physical pain he endured. But in the end, what broke Job's patience was not the suffering but rather not knowing *why* he suffered. • When Job expressed his frustration, his friends were ready with their answers. They believed that the law of cause and effect applied to all people's experiences. Their view of life boiled down to this: Good things happen to good people, and bad things happen to bad people. Because of this, they felt their role was to help Job admit to whatever sin was causing his suffering. • Job actually looked at life almost the same way as his friends. What he couldn't understand was why he was suffering so much when he was sure he had done nothing to deserve such punishment. When God finally spoke, he didn't offer Job an answer. Instead, he drove home the point that it is better to know God than to know answers. • Often we suffer consequences for bad decisions and actions. Sometimes suffering shapes us for special service to others. Sometimes suffering is an attack by Satan on our lives. And sometimes we don't know why we suffer. At those times, are we willing to trust God in spite of unanswered questions?

Strengths and accomplishments	• A man of faith, patience, and endurance • Known as a generous and caring person • Very wealthy
Weakness and mistake	• Allowed his desire to understand why he was suffering to overwhelm him and make him question God
Lessons from his life	• Knowing God is better than knowing answers • Pain is not always punishment
Vital statistics	• Where: Uz • Occupation: Wealthy landowner and livestock owner • Relatives: Wife and first 10 children not named. Daughters from the second set of 10 children are named: Jemimah, Keziah, Keren-happuch. • Contemporaries: Eliphaz, Bildad, Zophar, Elihu
Key verses	"For examples of patience in suffering, dear brothers and sisters, look at the prophets who spoke in the name of the Lord. We give great honor to those who endure under suffering. For instance, you know about Job, a man of great endurance. You can see how the Lord was kind to him at the end, for the Lord is full of tenderness and mercy" (Jas 5:10-11).

Job's story is told in the book of Job. He is also referred to in Ezekiel 14:14, 20; James 5:11.

▸ **JOB 3:1-26** ***(cont.)***

9 Let its morning stars remain dark.
Let it hope for light, but in vain;
may it never see the morning light.
10 Curse that day for failing to shut my mother's womb,
for letting me be born to see all this trouble.

11 "Why wasn't I born dead?
Why didn't I die as I came from the womb?
12 Why was I laid on my mother's lap?
Why did she nurse me at her breasts?
13 Had I died at birth, I would now be at peace.
I would be asleep and at rest.
14 I would rest with the world's kings and prime ministers,
whose great buildings now lie in ruins.
15 I would rest with princes, rich in gold,
whose palaces were filled with silver.
16 Why wasn't I buried like a stillborn child,
like a baby who never lives to see the light?
17 For in death the wicked cause no trouble,
and the weary are at rest.
18 Even captives are at ease in death,
with no guards to curse them.
19 Rich and poor are both there,
and the slave is free from his master.
20 "Oh, why give light to those in misery,
and life to those who are bitter?
21 They long for death, and it won't come.
They search for death more eagerly than for hidden treasure.
22 They're filled with joy when they finally die,
and rejoice when they find the grave.
23 Why is life given to those with no future,
those God has surrounded with difficulties?
24 I cannot eat for sighing;
my groans pour out like water.
25 What I always feared has happened to me.
What I dreaded has come true.
26 I have no peace, no quietness.
I have no rest; only trouble comes."

Eliphaz's First Response to Job

JOB 4:1-21

Then Eliphaz the Temanite replied to Job:

2 "Will you be patient and let me say a word?
For who could keep from speaking out?

3 "In the past you have encouraged many people;
you have strengthened those who were weak.
4 Your words have supported those who were falling;
you encouraged those with shaky knees.
5 But now when trouble strikes, you lose heart.
You are terrified when it touches you.
6 Doesn't your reverence for God give you confidence?
Doesn't your life of integrity give you hope?

7 "Stop and think! Do the innocent die?
When have the upright been destroyed?
8 My experience shows that those who plant trouble
and cultivate evil will harvest the same.
9 A breath from God destroys them.
They vanish in a blast of his anger.
10 The lion roars and the wildcat snarls,
but the teeth of strong lions will be broken.

Job 3:11 Job was experiencing extreme physical pain as well as grief over the loss of his family and possessions. He can't be blamed for wishing he were dead. Job's grief placed him at the crossroads of his faith, shattering many misconceptions about God (e.g., he makes you rich, always keeps you from trouble and pain, or protects your loved ones). Job was driven back to the basics of his faith in God. He had only two choices: (1) He could curse God and give up, or (2) he could trust God and draw strength from him to continue.

Job 3:23-26 Job had been careful not to worship material possessions but to worship God alone. Here he was overwhelmed by calamities that mocked his caution, and he complained about trials that came despite his right living. All the principles by which he had lived were crumbling, and Job began to lose his perspective. Trials and grief, whether temporary or enduring, do not destroy the real purpose of life. Life is not given merely for happiness and personal fulfillment but for us to serve and honor God. The worth and meaning of life is not based on what we feel but on the one reality no one can take away—God's love for us. Don't assume that because God truly loves you he will always prevent suffering. The opposite may be true. God's love cannot be measured or limited by how great or how little we may suffer. Romans 8:38-39 teaches us that nothing can separate us from God's love.

Job 4:1ff Eliphaz claimed to have been given secret knowledge through a special revelation from God (Job 4:12-16) and that he had learned much from personal experience (Job 4:8). He argued that suffering is a direct result of sin, so if Job would only confess his sin, his suffering would end. Eliphaz saw suffering as God's punishment, which should be welcomed in order to bring a person back to God. In some cases, of course, this may be true (Gal 6:7-8), but it was not true with Job. Although Eliphaz had many good and true comments, he made three wrong assumptions: (1) A good and innocent person never suffers; (2) those who suffer are being punished for their past sins; and (3) Job, because he was suffering, had done something wrong in God's eyes. (For more about Eliphaz, see the Profile on p. 105 and the chart on p. 100.) Teman was a trading city in Edom, noted as a place of wisdom; see Jer 49:7.)

Job 4:7-8 Part of what Eliphaz said is true, and part is false. It is true that those who promote sin and trouble eventually will be punished; it is false that anyone who is good and innocent will never suffer.

All the material recorded in the Bible is here by God's choice. Some is a record of what people said and did but is not an example to follow. The sins, the defeats, the evil thoughts, and the misconceptions about God are all recorded in God's divinely inspired Word, but we should not follow those wrong examples just because they are in the Bible. The Bible gives us teachings and examples of what we *should* do as well as what we *should not* do. Eliphaz's comments are an example of what we should try to avoid—making false assumptions about others based on our own experiences.

11 The fierce lion will starve for lack of prey,
and the cubs of the lioness will be scattered.

12 "This truth was given to me in secret,
as though whispered in my ear.
13 It came to me in a disturbing vision at night,
when people are in a deep sleep.
14 Fear gripped me,
and my bones trembled.
15 A spirit* swept past my face,
and my hair stood on end.*
16 The spirit stopped, but I couldn't see its shape.
There was a form before my eyes.
In the silence I heard a voice say,
17 'Can a mortal be innocent before God?
Can anyone be pure before the Creator?'

18 "If God does not trust his own angels
and has charged his messengers with foolishness,
19 how much less will he trust people made of clay!
They are made of dust, crushed as easily as a moth.
20 They are alive in the morning but dead by evening,
gone forever without a trace.
21 Their tent-cords are pulled and the tent collapses,
and they die in ignorance.

Eliphaz's Response Continues

JOB 5:1-27

1 "Cry for help, but will anyone answer you?
Which of the angels* will help you?
2 Surely resentment destroys the fool,
and jealousy kills the simple.
3 I have seen that fools may be successful for the moment,
but then comes sudden disaster.
4 Their children are abandoned far from help;
they are crushed in court with no one to defend them.
5 The hungry devour their harvest,
even when it is guarded by brambles.*
The thirsty pant after their wealth.
6 But evil does not spring from the soil,
and trouble does not sprout from the earth.
7 People are born for trouble
as readily as sparks fly up from a fire.

8 "If I were you, I would go to God
and present my case to him.
9 He does great things too marvelous to understand.
He performs countless miracles.
10 He gives rain for the earth
and water for the fields.
11 He gives prosperity to the poor
and protects those who suffer.
12 He frustrates the plans of schemers
so the work of their hands will not succeed.
13 He traps the wise in their own cleverness
so their cunning schemes are thwarted.
14 They find it is dark in the daytime,
and they grope at noon as if it were night.
15 He rescues the poor from the cutting words of the strong,
and rescues them from the clutches of the powerful.
16 And so at last the poor have hope,
and the snapping jaws of the wicked are shut.

17 "But consider the joy of those corrected by God!
Do not despise the discipline of the Almighty when you sin.

Jb 4:15a Or *wind;* also in 4:16. **Jb 4:15b** Or *its wind sent shivers up my spine.* **Jb 5:1** Hebrew *the holy ones.* **Jb 5:5** The meaning of the Hebrew for this phrase is uncertain.

Job 4:12-13 Although Eliphaz claimed that his vision was divinely inspired, it is doubtful that it came from God because later God criticized Eliphaz for misrepresenting him (Job 42:7). Whatever the vision's source, it is summarized in Job 4:17. On the surface, this statement is completely true—a mere mortal cannot compare to God and should not try to question God's motives and actions. But Eliphaz took this thought and expounded on it later, expressing his own opinions. His conclusion (Job 5:8) reveals a very shallow understanding of Job and his suffering. It is easy for teachers, counselors, and well-meaning friends to begin with a portion of God's truth but then go off on a tangent. Don't limit God to your perspective and finite understanding of life.

Job 4:18-19 Do angels really make errors? Remember that Eliphaz was speaking, not God, so we must be careful about building our knowledge of the spiritual world from Eliphaz's opinions. In addition, the word translated "foolishness" is used only here, and its meaning is unclear. We could save Eliphaz's credibility by saying he meant fallen angels, but this passage is not meant to teach about angels. Eliphaz was saying that sinful human beings are far beneath God and the angels. He was right about God's greatness but did not understand God's greater purposes concerning suffering.

Job 5:8 All three of Job's friends made the mistake of assuming that Job had committed some great sin that caused his suffering. Neither they nor Job knew of Satan's conversation with God (Job 1:6–2:6). It is human nature to blame people for their own troubles, but Job's story makes it clear that blame cannot always be attached to those whom trouble strikes.

Job 5:13 Paul later quoted part of this verse (1 Cor 3:19)—the only time Job is clearly quoted in the New Testament. Although God rebuked Eliphaz for being wrong in his advice to Job (Job 42:7), not all he said was in error. The part Paul quoted was correct—people are often caught in their own traps. This illustrates how Scripture must be used to explain and comment on itself. We must be familiar with the entire scope of God's Word to properly understand the difficult portions of it.

Job 5:17 Eliphaz was correct—it is a joy to be disciplined by God when we do wrong. Eliphaz's advice, however, did not apply to Job. As we know from the beginning of the book, Job's suffering was not a result of some great sin. We sometimes give people

▸ **JOB 5:1-27 *(cont.)***

18 For though he wounds, he also bandages.
He strikes, but his hands also heal.
19 From six disasters he will rescue you;
even in the seventh, he will keep you from evil.
20 He will save you from death in time of famine,
from the power of the sword in time of war.
21 You will be safe from slander
and have no fear when destruction comes.
22 You will laugh at destruction and famine;
wild animals will not terrify you.
23 You will be at peace with the stones of the field,
and its wild animals will be at peace with you.
24 You will know that your home is safe.
When you survey your possessions, nothing will be missing.
25 You will have many children;
your descendants will be as plentiful as grass!
26 You will go to the grave at a ripe old age,
like a sheaf of grain harvested at the proper time!

27 "We have studied life and found all this to be true.
Listen to my counsel, and apply it to yourself."

ADVICE FROM JOB'S FRIENDS

Overwhelmed by suffering, Job was not comforted but rather condemned by his friends. Each of their views represents a well-known way to understand suffering. God proves that each explanation given by Job's friends has less than the whole answer.

Who They Were	Reference	How They Helped	Their Reasoning	Their Advice	Job's Response	God's Response
Eliphaz the Temanite	Job 4–5; 15; 22	They sat in silence with Job for seven days. (Job 2:11-13)	Job is suffering because he has sinned.	Go to God and present your case to him. (Job 5:8)	Stop assuming my guilt. (Job 6:29)	God rebukes Job's friends. (Job 42:7)
Bildad the Shuhite	Job 8; 18; 25		Job won't admit he sinned, so he's still suffering.	How long will you go on like this? (Job 8:2)	I will say to God, "Tell me the charge you are bringing against me." (Job 10:2)	
Zophar the Naamathite	Job 11; 20		Job's sin deserves even more suffering than he's experienced.	Get rid of your sins. (Job 11:13-14)	I will be proved innocent. (Job 13:18)	
Elihu the Buzite	Job 32–37	Confronted Job with the need to be content even though he didn't know why he was suffering.	God is using suffering to mold and train Job.	Keep silent and I will teach you wisdom. (Job 33:33)	No response	God does not directly address Elihu.
God	Job 38–41		Did not explain the reason for the pain	Do you still want to argue with the Almighty? (Job 40:2)	I was talking about things I did not understand. (Job 42:3-5)	

excellent advice only to learn that it does not apply to them and is therefore not very helpful. All who offer counsel from God's Word should take care to thoroughly understand a person's situation *before* giving advice.

Job 5:17-26 Eliphaz's words in Job 5:17-18 show a view of discipline that has been almost forgotten: Pain can help us grow. These are good words to remember when we face hardship and loss. Because Job did not understand why he suffered, his faith in God had a chance to grow. On the other hand, we must not make Eliphaz's mistake. God does not eliminate all hardship when we are following him closely, and good behavior is not always rewarded by prosperity. Rewards for good and punishment for evil are in God's hands and given out according to his timetable. Satan's ploy is to get us to doubt God's love and faithfulness toward us.

Job's Second Speech: A Response to Eliphaz

JOB 6:1–7:5

Then Job spoke again:

2 "If my misery could be weighed
and my troubles be put on the scales,
3 they would outweigh all the sands of the sea.
That is why I spoke impulsively.
4 For the Almighty has struck me down with his arrows.
Their poison infects my spirit.
God's terrors are lined up against me.
5 Don't I have a right to complain?
Don't wild donkeys bray when they find no grass,
and oxen bellow when they have no food?
6 Don't people complain about unsalted food?
Does anyone want the tasteless white of an egg?*
7 My appetite disappears when I look at it;
I gag at the thought of eating it!

8 "Oh, that I might have my request,
that God would grant my desire.
9 I wish he would crush me.
I wish he would reach out his hand and kill me.
10 At least I can take comfort in this:
Despite the pain,
I have not denied the words of the Holy One.
11 But I don't have the strength to endure.
I have nothing to live for.
12 Do I have the strength of a stone?
Is my body made of bronze?
13 No, I am utterly helpless,
without any chance of success.

14 "One should be kind to a fainting friend,
but you accuse me without any fear of the Almighty.*
15 My brothers, you have proved as unreliable
as a seasonal brook
that overflows its banks in the spring
16 when it is swollen with ice and melting snow.
17 But when the hot weather arrives, the water disappears.
The brook vanishes in the heat.
18 The caravans turn aside to be refreshed,
but there is nothing to drink, so they die.
19 The caravans from Tema search for this water;
the travelers from Sheba hope to find it.
20 They count on it but are disappointed.
When they arrive, their hopes are dashed.
21 You, too, have given no help.
You have seen my calamity, and you are afraid.
22 But why? Have I ever asked you for a gift?
Have I begged for anything of yours for myself?
23 Have I asked you to rescue me from my enemies,
or to save me from ruthless people?
24 Teach me, and I will keep quiet.
Show me what I have done wrong.
25 Honest words can be painful,
but what do your criticisms amount to?
26 Do you think your words are convincing
when you disregard my cry of desperation?
27 You would even send an orphan into slavery*
or sell a friend.
28 Look at me!
Would I lie to your face?
29 Stop assuming my guilt,
for I have done no wrong.
30 Do you think I am lying?
Don't I know the difference between right and wrong?

7:1 "Is not all human life a struggle?
Our lives are like that of a hired hand,
2 like a worker who longs for the shade,
like a servant waiting to be paid.
3 I, too, have been assigned months of futility,
long and weary nights of misery.
4 Lying in bed, I think, 'When will it be morning?'
But the night drags on, and I toss till dawn.
5 My body is covered with maggots and scabs.
My skin breaks open, oozing with pus.

Jb 6:6 Or *the tasteless juice of the mallow plant?* **Jb 6:14** Or *friend, / or he might lose his fear of the Almighty.* **Jb 6:27** Hebrew *even gamble over an orphan.*

Job 6:6-7 Job said that Eliphaz's advice was like eating the tasteless white of an egg. When people are going through severe trials, ill-advised counsel is distasteful. They may listen politely, but inside they are upset. Be slow to give advice to those who are hurting. They often need compassion more than they need advice.

Job 6:8-9 In his grief, Job wanted to give in, to be freed from his discomfort, and to die. But God did not grant Job's request. He had a greater plan for him. Our tendency, like Job's, is to want to give up and get out when the going gets rough. To trust God in the good times is commendable, but to trust him during the difficult times tests us to our limits and exercises our faith. In your struggles, large or small, trust that God is in control and that he will take care of you (Rom 8:28).

Job 6:29-30 Job referred to his own righteousness, not because he was sinless, but because he had a right relationship with God. He was not guilty of the sins his friends accused him of (see Job 31 for his summary of the life he had led). When Job said, "I have done no wrong," he was not claiming to be sinless. No one but Jesus Christ has ever been sinless—free from all wrong thoughts and actions. Even Job needed to make some changes in his attitude toward God, as we will see by the end of the book. Nevertheless Job was blameless (Job 1:8). He carefully obeyed God to the best of his ability in all aspects of his life.

Job Cries Out to God

JOB 7:6-21

6 "My days fly faster than a weaver's shuttle.
They end without hope.
7 O God, remember that my life is but a breath,
and I will never again feel happiness.
8 You see me now, but not for long.
You will look for me, but I will be gone.
9 Just as a cloud dissipates and vanishes,
those who die* will not come back.
10 They are gone forever from their home—
never to be seen again.

11 "I cannot keep from speaking.
I must express my anguish.
My bitter soul must complain.
12 Am I a sea monster or a dragon
that you must place me under guard?
13 I think, 'My bed will comfort me,
and sleep will ease my misery,'
14 but then you shatter me with dreams
and terrify me with visions.
15 I would rather be strangled—
rather die than suffer like this.
16 I hate my life and don't want to go on living.
Oh, leave me alone for my few
remaining days.

17 "What are people, that you should make
so much of us,
that you should think of us so often?
18 For you examine us every morning
and test us every moment.
19 Why won't you leave me alone,
at least long enough for me to swallow!
20 If I have sinned, what have I done to you,
O watcher of all humanity?
Why make me your target?
Am I a burden to you?
21 Why not just forgive my sin
and take away my guilt?
For soon I will lie down in the dust and die.
When you look for me, I will be gone."

Jb 7:9 Hebrew *who go down to Sheol.*

Bildad's First Response to Job

JOB 8:1-22

Then Bildad the Shuhite replied to Job:

2 "How long will you go on like this?
You sound like a blustering wind.
3 Does God twist justice?
Does the Almighty twist what is right?
4 Your children must have sinned against him,
so their punishment was well deserved.
5 But if you pray to God
and seek the favor of the Almighty,
6 and if you are pure and live with integrity,
he will surely rise up and restore your
happy home.
7 And though you started with little,
you will end with much.

8 "Just ask the previous generation.
Pay attention to the experience of our
ancestors.
9 For we were born but yesterday and know
nothing.
Our days on earth are as fleeting as a shadow.
10 But those who came before us will teach you.
They will teach you the wisdom of old.

11 "Can papyrus reeds grow tall without a marsh?
Can marsh grass flourish without water?
12 While they are still flowering, not ready
to be cut,
they begin to wither more quickly
than grass.
13 The same happens to all who forget God.
The hopes of the godless evaporate.
14 Their confidence hangs by a thread.
They are leaning on a spider's web.
15 They cling to their home for security, but it
won't last.
They try to hold it tight, but it will not endure.
16 The godless seem like a lush plant growing
in the sunshine,
its branches spreading across the garden.

Job 7:11 Job felt deep anguish and bitterness, and he spoke honestly to God about his feelings to let out his frustrations. If we express our feelings to God, we can deal with them without exploding into harsh words and actions, possibly hurting ourselves and others. The next time strong emotions threaten to overwhelm you, express them openly to God in prayer. This will help you gain an eternal perspective on the situation and give you greater ability to deal with it constructively.

Job 7:12 Job stopped talking to Eliphaz and spoke directly to God. Although Job had lived a blameless life, he was beginning to doubt the value of living in such a way. By doing this, he was coming dangerously close to suggesting that God didn't care about him and was not being fair. Later God reproved Job for this attitude (Job 38:2). Satan always exploits these thoughts to get us to forsake God. Our suffering, like Job's, may not be the result of our sin, but we must be careful not to sin as a result of our suffering.

Job 7:20 Job referred to God as a watcher or observer of humanity. He was expressing his feeling that God seemed like an enemy to him—someone who mercilessly watched him squirm in his misery. We know that God does watch over everything that happens to us, but we must never forget that he sees us with compassion, not merely with critical scrutiny. His eyes are eyes of love.

Job 8:1ff Bildad was upset that Job still claimed innocence while questioning God's justice. The basis of Bildad's argument (the justice of God) was correct, but his idea of God's justice was not. Bildad's argument went like this: God could not be unjust, and God would not punish a just man; therefore, Job must be unjust. Bildad felt there were no exceptions to his theory. Like Eliphaz, Bildad wrongly assumed that people suffer only as a result of their sins. Bildad was even less sensitive and compassionate, saying that Job's children died because of *their* wickedness.

Job 8:14-15 Bildad wrongly assumed that Job was trusting in something other than God for security, so he pointed out that such

17 Its roots grow down through a pile of stones;
it takes hold on a bed of rocks.
18 But when it is uprooted,
it's as though it never existed!
19 That's the end of its life,
and others spring up from the earth
to replace it.
20 "But look, God will not reject a person of integrity,
nor will he lend a hand to the wicked.
21 He will once again fill your mouth with laughter
and your lips with shouts of joy.
22 Those who hate you will be clothed with shame,
and the home of the wicked will be destroyed."

Job's Third Speech: A Response to Bildad

JOB 9:1-35

Then Job spoke again:

2 "Yes, I know all this is true in principle.
But how can a person be declared innocent
in God's sight?
3 If someone wanted to take God to court,*
would it be possible to answer him even once
in a thousand times?
4 For God is so wise and so mighty.
Who has ever challenged him successfully?

5 "Without warning, he moves the mountains,
overturning them in his anger.
6 He shakes the earth from its place,
and its foundations tremble.
7 If he commands it, the sun won't rise
and the stars won't shine.
8 He alone has spread out the heavens
and marches on the waves of the sea.
9 He made all the stars—the Bear and Orion,
the Pleiades and the constellations of the
southern sky.
10 He does great things too marvelous
to understand.
He performs countless miracles.

11 "Yet when he comes near, I cannot see him.
When he moves by, I do not see him go.
12 If he snatches someone in death, who can
stop him?
Who dares to ask, 'What are you doing?'
13 And God does not restrain his anger.
Even the monsters of the sea* are crushed
beneath his feet.

14 "So who am I, that I should try to answer God
or even reason with him?
15 Even if I were right, I would have no defense.
I could only plead for mercy.
16 And even if I summoned him and he
responded,
I'm not sure he would listen to me.
17 For he attacks me with a storm
and repeatedly wounds me without cause.
18 He will not let me catch my breath,
but fills me instead with bitter sorrows.
19 If it's a question of strength, he's the strong one.
If it's a matter of justice, who dares to summon
him to court?
20 Though I am innocent, my own mouth would
pronounce me guilty.
Though I am blameless, it* would prove
me wicked.

21 "I am innocent,
but it makes no difference to me—
I despise my life.
22 Innocent or wicked, it is all the same to God.
That's why I say, 'He destroys both the
blameless and the wicked.'
23 When a plague* sweeps through,
he laughs at the death of the innocent.

Jb 9:3 Or *If God wanted to take someone to court.* **Jb 9:13** Hebrew *the helpers of Rahab,* the name of a mythical sea monster that represents chaos in ancient literature. **Jb 9:20** Or *he.* **Jb 9:23** Or *disaster.*

supports will collapse. One of people's basic needs is security, and many will do almost anything to feel secure. But eventually our money, possessions, knowledge, and relationships will fail or be gone. Only God can give lasting security. What have you trusted for your security? How lasting is it? If you have a secure foundation with God, feelings of insecurity will not undermine you.

Job 9:1ff Bildad said nothing new to Job. Job knew that the wicked ultimately perish, but his situation confused him. Why, then, was *he* perishing? Job didn't think his life warranted such suffering, so he wanted his case presented before God (Job 9:32-35). He recognized, however, that arguing with God would be futile and unproductive (Job 9:4). Job didn't claim to be perfect (Job 7:20-21; 9:20), but he did claim to be good and faithful (Job 6:29-30). While Job showed impatience toward God, he did not reject or curse God.

Job 9:9 The Bear, Orion, and Pleiades are constellations.

Job 9:20-21 "Though I am innocent, my own mouth would pronounce me guilty." Job was saying, in effect, "In spite of my good life, God is determined to condemn me." As his suffering continued, he became more impatient. Although Job remained loyal to God, he made statements he would later regret. In times of extended sickness or prolonged pain, it is natural for people to doubt, to despair, or to become impatient. During those times, people need someone to listen to them, to help them work through their feelings and frustrations. Your patience with their impatience will help them.

"Their confidence hangs by a thread. They are leaning on a spider's web."
Job 8:14

▸ **JOB 9:1-35 *(cont.)***

24 The whole earth is in the hands of the wicked,
and God blinds the eyes of the judges.
If he's not the one who does it, who is?

25 "My life passes more swiftly than a runner.
It flees away without a glimpse of happiness.
26 It disappears like a swift papyrus boat,
like an eagle swooping down on its prey.
27 If I decided to forget my complaints,
to put away my sad face and be cheerful,
28 I would still dread all the pain,
for I know you will not find me innocent,
O God.
29 Whatever happens, I will be found guilty.
So what's the use of trying?
30 Even if I were to wash myself with soap
and clean my hands with lye,
31 you would plunge me into a muddy ditch,
and my own filthy clothing would hate me.

32 "God is not a mortal like me,
so I cannot argue with him or take him to trial.
33 If only there were a mediator between us,
someone who could bring us together.
34 The mediator could make God stop beating me,
and I would no longer live in terror of his
punishment.
35 Then I could speak to him without fear,
but I cannot do that in my own strength.

Job Frames His Plea to God

JOB 10:1-22

1 "I am disgusted with my life.
Let me complain freely.
My bitter soul must complain.
2 I will say to God, 'Don't simply condemn me—
tell me the charge you are bringing against me.
3 What do you gain by oppressing me?
Why do you reject me, the work of your
own hands,
while smiling on the schemes of the wicked?
4 Are your eyes like those of a human?
Do you see things only as people see them?
5 Is your lifetime only as long as ours?
Is your life so short
6 that you must quickly probe for my guilt
and search for my sin?
7 Although you know I am not guilty,
no one can rescue me from your hands.

8 "'You formed me with your hands; you
made me,
yet now you completely destroy me.
9 Remember that you made me from dust—
will you turn me back to dust so soon?
10 You guided my conception
and formed me in the womb.*
11 You clothed me with skin and flesh,
and you knit my bones and sinews together.
12 You gave me life and showed me your unfailing
love.
My life was preserved by your care.

13 "'Yet your real motive—
your true intent—
14 was to watch me, and if I sinned,
you would not forgive my guilt.
15 If I am guilty, too bad for me;
and even if I'm innocent, I can't hold my
head high,
because I am filled with shame and misery.
16 And if I hold my head high, you hunt me like
a lion
and display your awesome power
against me.
17 Again and again you witness against me.
You pour out your growing anger on me
and bring fresh armies against me.

18 "'Why, then, did you deliver me from my
mother's womb?
Why didn't you let me die at birth?
19 It would be as though I had never existed,
going directly from the womb to the grave.
20 I have only a few days left, so leave me alone,
that I may have a moment of comfort
21 before I leave—never to return—
for the land of darkness and utter gloom.
22 It is a land as dark as midnight,
a land of gloom and confusion,
where even the light is dark as midnight.'"

Jb 10:10 Hebrew *You poured me out like milk / and curdled me like cheese.*

Job 10:1 Job began to wallow in self-pity. When we face baffling affliction, our pain lures us toward feeling sorry for ourselves. At this point we are only one step from self-righteousness, where we keep track of life's injustices and say, "Look what happened to me; how unfair it is!" We may feel like blaming God. Remember that life's trials, whether allowed by God or sent by God, can be the means for development and refinement. When facing trials, ask "What can I learn and how can I grow?" rather than "Who did this to me and how can I get out of it?"

Job 10:13-14 In frustration, Job jumped to the false conclusion that God was out to get him. Wrong assumptions lead to wrong conclusions. We dare not jump to conclusions about life in general based on our limited experiences. If you find yourself doubting God, remember that you don't have all the facts. God wants only the very best for your life. Many people endure great pain, but ultimately they find some greater good has come from it. When you're struggling, don't assume the worst.

Job 10:20-22 Job was expressing the view of death common in Old Testament times—the belief that the dead went to a joyless, dark place. There was no punishment or reward there and no escape from it. (See the note on Job 19:25-27, p. 112, for a broader picture of Job's view of death.)

Zophar's First Response to Job

JOB 11:1-20

Then Zophar the Naamathite replied to Job:

2 "Shouldn't someone answer this torrent of words?
Is a person proved innocent just by a lot of talking?
3 Should I remain silent while you babble on?
When you mock God, shouldn't someone make you ashamed?
4 You claim, 'My beliefs are pure,'
and 'I am clean in the sight of God.'
5 If only God would speak;
if only he would tell you what he thinks!
6 If only he would tell you the secrets of wisdom,
for true wisdom is not a simple matter.
Listen! God is doubtless punishing you
far less than you deserve!
7 "Can you solve the mysteries of God?
Can you discover everything about the Almighty?
8 Such knowledge is higher than the heavens—
and who are you?
It is deeper than the underworld*—
what do you know?
9 It is broader than the earth
and wider than the sea.
10 If God comes and puts a person in prison
or calls the court to order, who can stop him?

Jb 11:8 Hebrew *than Sheol.*

Job 11:1ff Zophar was the third of Job's friends to speak and the least courteous. Full of anger, he lashed out at Job, saying that Job deserved more punishment, not less. Zophar took the same position as Eliphaz (Job 4–5) and Bildad (Job 8)—that Job was suffering because of sin—but his speech was by far the most arrogant. Zophar was the kind of person who has an answer for everything; he was totally insensitive to Job's unique situation. (For more on Zophar, see the Profile below and the chart on p. 100.)

ELIPHAZ/BILDAD/ZOPHAR

Few people in history have experienced the kind of tragedy that crushed Job. He lost everything. His children were killed, his possessions and wealth were taken, his wife turned her back on him, and his health was broken—all in a matter of days. • Upon learning of Job's difficulties, some of his friends came to help. Eliphaz, Bildad, and Zophar were shocked when they found Job. They wept for him. They tore their clothes and put dust on their heads in acts of sorrow. Then they sat in silence with Job for seven days. • Why did his friends remain silent for so long? One ancient Jewish tradition teaches that people who come to comfort someone in mourning should not speak until the mourner speaks. That is a wise tradition, for often the best response to another person's suffering is to say nothing. • If Job's losses were his first test and his painful boils his second, then his friends provided a third and perhaps most frustrating test. When Job finally vented his grief, each of the friends took turns attempting to explain Job's agony. They heard Job's questions as arrogant claims of not deserving such suffering rather than expressions of deep grief and misunderstanding. They offered answers that only served to make Job's pain go deeper. Eliphaz appealed to personal experience; Bildad pointed to universal wisdom; and Zophar declared what he felt was common sense. They all agreed that Job's problems were his own doing and that he needed to repent. • The harder Eliphaz, Bildad, and Zophar tried to explain Job's suffering, the less they helped. Consolation turned to condemnation as the grief-stricken Job rejected their reasoning and demanded a hearing with God. When God finally did speak, he never answered Job's questions. He simply challenged Job to trust, even beyond understanding. • Friendship in grief requires patience. Friends in need don't have to have all their questions answered as much as they need to have someone listen. Some questions are so deep that their best response is silence. Make it a point to be with those in pain, but let your physical presence be your strongest statement of support. Pray for patience. When in doubt about a question, wait. Sit quietly and be the best friend you can be during difficult times.

Strengths and accomplishments	• Understood the importance of personal contact in sharing grief • Approached Job with silence rather than immediate conversation
Weaknesses and mistakes	• Assumed that tragedy and suffering invariably represent some kind of punishment for sin • Decided to try to explain Job's suffering rather than help him endure it • Heard Job's questions as challenges rather than expressions of grief • Took offense and became abusive when Job did not agree with their assessments or answers
Lessons from their lives	• Those who wish to comfort people in sorrow should consider silence before speech, empathy before explanations, and patience with their pain • Even the hardest questions that come out of grief do not require instant answers • Genuine friendship includes attentive, compassionate presence in times of sorrow and loss
Vital statistics	• Where: Uz • Contemporaries: Job, Elihu
Key verse	"When three of Job's friends heard of the tragedy he had suffered, they got together and traveled from their homes to comfort and console him. Their names were Eliphaz the Temanite, Bildad the Shuhite, and Zophar the Naamathite" (Job 2:11).

Job's interaction with his three friends is found in the Old Testament book of Job.

▸ **JOB 11:1-20** ***(cont.)***

11 For he knows those who are false,
and he takes note of all their sins.
12 An empty-headed person won't become wise
any more than a wild donkey can bear
a human child.*
13 "If only you would prepare your heart
and lift up your hands to him in prayer!
14 Get rid of your sins,
and leave all iniquity behind you.
15 Then your face will brighten with innocence.
You will be strong and free of fear.
16 You will forget your misery;
it will be like water flowing away.
17 Your life will be brighter than the noonday.
Even darkness will be as bright as morning.
18 Having hope will give you courage.
You will be protected and will rest in safety.
19 You will lie down unafraid,
and many will look to you for help.
20 But the wicked will be blinded.
They will have no escape.
Their only hope is death."

Job's Fourth Speech: A Response to Zophar

JOB 12:1-25

Then Job spoke again:

2 "You people really know everything, don't you?
And when you die, wisdom will die
with you!
3 Well, I know a few things myself—
and you're no better than I am.
Who doesn't know these things you've
been saying?
4 Yet my friends laugh at me,
for I call on God and expect an answer.
I am a just and blameless man,
yet they laugh at me.
5 People who are at ease mock those in trouble.
They give a push to people who are stumbling.
6 But robbers are left in peace,
and those who provoke God live in safety—
though God keeps them in his power.
7 "Just ask the animals, and they will teach you.
Ask the birds of the sky, and they will tell you.
8 Speak to the earth, and it will instruct you.
Let the fish in the sea speak to you.
9 For they all know
that my disaster* has come from the hand
of the LORD.
10 For the life of every living thing is in his hand,
and the breath of every human being.
11 The ear tests the words it hears
just as the mouth distinguishes between foods.
12 Wisdom belongs to the aged,
and understanding to the old.

13 "But true wisdom and power are found in God;
counsel and understanding are his.
14 What he destroys cannot be rebuilt.
When he puts someone in prison, there
is no escape.
15 If he holds back the rain, the earth becomes
a desert.
If he releases the waters, they flood the earth.
16 Yes, strength and wisdom are his;
deceivers and deceived are both in his power.
17 He leads counselors away, stripped of good
judgment;
wise judges become fools.
18 He removes the royal robe of kings.
They are led away with ropes around
their waist.
19 He leads priests away, stripped of status;
he overthrows those with long years in power.
20 He silences the trusted adviser
and removes the insight of the elders.
21 He pours disgrace upon princes
and disarms the strong.
22 "He uncovers mysteries hidden in darkness;
he brings light to the deepest gloom.
23 He builds up nations, and he destroys them.
He expands nations, and he abandons them.
24 He strips kings of understanding
and leaves them wandering in a pathless
wasteland.
25 They grope in the darkness without a light.
He makes them stagger like drunkards.

Jb 11:12 Or *than a wild male donkey can bear a tame colt.* **Jb 12:9** Hebrew *that this.*

Job 11:11 By calling Job "false," Zophar was accusing Job of hiding secret faults and sins. Although Zophar's assumption was wrong, he explained quite accurately that God knows and sees everything. We are often tempted by the thought "No one will ever know!" Perhaps we can hide some sin from others, but we can do *nothing* without God knowing about it. Because our very thoughts are known to God, of course he will notice our sins. Job understood this as well as Zophar did, but it didn't apply to his current dilemma.

Job 12:1ff Job answered Zophar's argument with great sarcasm: "Wisdom will die with you!" He went on to say that his three friends didn't need to explain God to him—they were saying nothing he didn't already know (Job 12:7-9; 13:1-2). Job continued to maintain that his friends had completely misunderstood the reason for his suffering; Job did not know it either, but he was certain that their reasons were both narrow-minded and incorrect. Once again Job appealed to God to give him an answer (Job 13:3).

Job 12:24-25 Job affirmed that no leader has any real wisdom apart from God. No research or report can outweigh God's opinion. No scientific discovery or medical advance takes him by surprise. When we look for guidance for our decisions, we must recognize that God's wisdom is superior to any the world has to offer. Don't let earthly advisers dampen your desire to know God better.

Job Wants to Argue His Case with God

JOB 13:1-19

1 "Look, I have seen all this with my own eyes
and heard it with my own ears, and now I understand.
2 I know as much as you do.
You are no better than I am.
3 As for me, I would speak directly to the Almighty.
I want to argue my case with God himself.
4 As for you, you smear me with lies.
As physicians, you are worthless quacks.
5 If only you could be silent!
That's the wisest thing you could do.
6 Listen to my charge;
pay attention to my arguments.

7 "Are you defending God with lies?
Do you make your dishonest arguments for his sake?
8 Will you slant your testimony in his favor?
Will you argue God's case for him?
9 What will happen when he finds out what you are doing?
Can you fool him as easily as you fool people?
10 No, you will be in trouble with him
if you secretly slant your testimony in his favor.
11 Doesn't his majesty terrify you?
Doesn't your fear of him overwhelm you?
12 Your platitudes are as valuable as ashes.
Your defense is as fragile as a clay pot.

13 "Be silent now and leave me alone.
Let me speak, and I will face the consequences.
14 Yes, I will take my life in my hands
and say what I really think.
15 God might kill me, but I have no other hope.*
I am going to argue my case with him.
16 But this is what will save me—I am not godless.
If I were, I could not stand before him.

17 "Listen closely to what I am about to say.
Hear me out.
18 I have prepared my case;
I will be proved innocent.
19 Who can argue with me over this?
And if you prove me wrong, I will remain silent and die.

Job Asks How He Has Sinned

JOB 13:20–14:22

20 "O God, grant me these two things,
and then I will be able to face you.
21 Remove your heavy hand from me,
and don't terrify me with your awesome presence.
22 Now summon me, and I will answer!
Or let me speak to you, and you reply.
23 Tell me, what have I done wrong?
Show me my rebellion and my sin.
24 Why do you turn away from me?
Why do you treat me as your enemy?
25 Would you terrify a leaf blown by the wind?
Would you chase dry straw?

26 "You write bitter accusations against me
and bring up all the sins of my youth.
27 You put my feet in stocks.
You examine all my paths.
You trace all my footprints.
28 I waste away like rotting wood,
like a moth-eaten coat.

Jb 13:15 An alternate reading in the Masoretic Text reads *God might kill me, but I hope in him.*

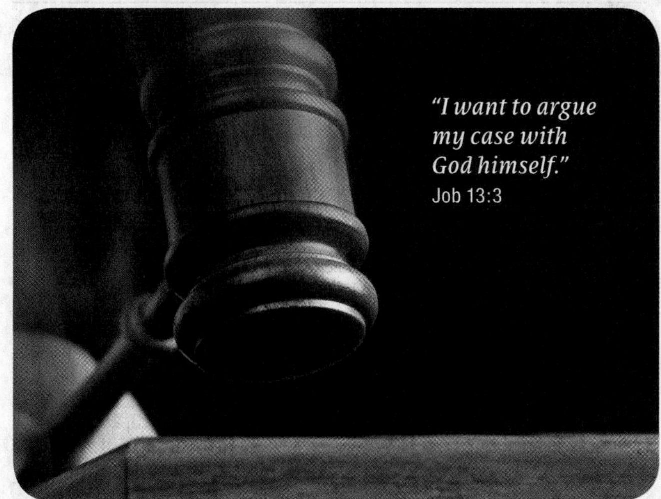
"I want to argue my case with God himself."
Job 13:3

Job 13:4 Job compared his three friends to physicians who don't know what they are doing. They were like eye surgeons trying to perform open-heart surgery. Many of their ideas about God were true, but they did not apply to Job's situation. They were right to say that God is just. They were right to say God punishes sin. But they were wrong to assume that Job's suffering was a just punishment for his sin. They took a true principle and applied it wrongly, ignoring the vast differences in human circumstances. We must be careful and compassionate in how we apply biblical condemnations to others; we must be slow to judge.

▶ **JOB 13:20–14:22** ***(cont.)***

14:1"How frail is humanity!
How short is life, how full of trouble!
2 We blossom like a flower and then wither.
Like a passing shadow, we quickly disappear.
3 Must you keep an eye on such a frail creature
and demand an accounting from me?
4 Who can bring purity out of an impure person?
No one!
5 You have decided the length of our lives.
You know how many months we will live,
and we are not given a minute longer.
6 So leave us alone and let us rest!
We are like hired hands, so let us finish our
work in peace.

7 "Even a tree has more hope!
If it is cut down, it will sprout again
and grow new branches.
8 Though its roots have grown old in the earth
and its stump decays,
9 at the scent of water it will bud
and sprout again like a new seedling.
10 "But when people die, their strength is gone.
They breathe their last, and then where
are they?
11 As water evaporates from a lake
and a river disappears in drought,
12 people are laid to rest and do not rise again.
Until the heavens are no more, they will not
wake up
nor be roused from their sleep.

13 "I wish you would hide me in the grave*
and forget me there until your anger has passed.
But mark your calendar to think of me again!
14 Can the dead live again?
If so, this would give me hope through all my
years of struggle,
and I would eagerly await the release of death.
15 You would call and I would answer,
and you would yearn for me, your handiwork.
16 For then you would guard my steps,
instead of watching for my sins.
17 My sins would be sealed in a pouch,
and you would cover my guilt.

18 "But instead, as mountains fall and crumble
and as rocks fall from a cliff,
19 as water wears away the stones
and floods wash away the soil,
so you destroy people's hope.
20 You always overpower them, and they pass from
the scene.
You disfigure them in death and send
them away.
21 They never know if their children grow up
in honor
or sink to insignificance.

Jb 14:13 Hebrew *in Sheol.*

Job 14:1ff In his closing remarks to this first round of conversation, Job lamented that life is short and full of trouble. Sickness, loneliness, disappointment, and death caused Job to say that life is not fair. Some understand verses 14 and 15 to mean that, even in his gloom, Job hoped for the resurrection of the dead. If this is true, then Job understood the one truth that could put his suffering in perspective. God's solution for believers who live in an unfair world is to guarantee life with him forever. No matter how unfair your present world seems, God offers the hope of being in his presence eternally. Have you accepted this offer?

Job 14:7-22 The Old Testament does not say much about the resurrection of the dead. This is not surprising because Jesus had not yet conquered death. Job's pessimism about death is understandable. What is remarkable is his budding hope (Job 14:14). If only God would hide him with the dead and then bring him out again! If only he could die and live again! When we must endure suffering, we have an advantage over Job. We *know* that the dead will rise. Christ arose, and we have hope based on Christ's promise in John 14:19.

BIBLE "WAITERS"

In the Bible we find many people who had to "wait on the Lord," just as believers today must patiently wait for Christ's return. We can learn a lesson in patience from these Bible waiters.

Noah waited for God's timing before leaving the ark	**Gen 8:10, 12**
Moses waited on God on the mountain	**Exod 24:12**
Job waited for God's answers	**Job 14:14**
Isaiah waited for God to work in Israel	**Isa 8:17; 25:9; 26:8; 30:18; 33:2; 40:31; 49:23; 59:9, 11; 64:4**
Jeremiah understood the need to wait quietly for God's salvation	**Lam 3:25**
Hosea warned the people to return to God and wait for him to work	**Hos 12:6**
Micah waited for the God of his salvation	**Mic 7:7**
Zephaniah explained that the Lord wanted his people to wait for him	**Zeph 3:8**
Joseph of Arimathea was waiting for God's Kingdom	**Luke 23:51**
The disciples were ordered by Jesus to wait in Jerusalem for the coming of the Holy Spirit	**Acts 1:4**
Believers are called to wait for heaven, for the promise is sure	**Rom 8:23, 25; Gal 5:5; 1 Thess 1:10; Titus 2:13; 2 Pet 3:12-14**

22 They suffer painfully;
their life is full of trouble."

Eliphaz's Second Response to Job

JOB 15:1-35

Then Eliphaz the Temanite replied:

2 "A wise man wouldn't answer with such empty talk!
You are nothing but a windbag.
3 The wise don't engage in empty chatter.
What good are such words?
4 Have you no fear of God,
no reverence for him?
5 Your sins are telling your mouth what to say.
Your words are based on clever deception.
6 Your own mouth condemns you, not I.
Your own lips testify against you.

7 "Were you the first person ever born?
Were you born before the hills were made?
8 Were you listening at God's secret council?
Do you have a monopoly on wisdom?
9 What do you know that we don't?
What do you understand that we do not?
10 On our side are aged, gray-haired men
much older than your father!

11 "Is God's comfort too little for you?
Is his gentle word not enough?
12 What has taken away your reason?
What has weakened your vision,*
13 that you turn against God
and say all these evil things?
14 Can any mortal be pure?
Can anyone born of a woman be just?
15 Look, God does not even trust the angels.*
Even the heavens are not absolutely pure in his sight.
16 How much less pure is a corrupt and sinful person
with a thirst for wickedness!

17 "If you will listen, I will show you.
I will answer you from my own experience.
18 And it is confirmed by the reports of wise men
who have heard the same thing from their fathers—
19 from those to whom the land was given
long before any foreigners arrived.

20 "The wicked writhe in pain throughout their lives.
Years of trouble are stored up for the ruthless.
21 The sound of terror rings in their ears,
and even on good days they fear the attack of the destroyer.
22 They dare not go out into the darkness
for fear they will be murdered.
23 They wander around, saying, 'Where can I find bread?'*
They know their day of destruction is near.
24 That dark day terrifies them.
They live in distress and anguish,
like a king preparing for battle.
25 For they shake their fists at God,
defying the Almighty.
26 Holding their strong shields,
they defiantly charge against him.

27 "These wicked people are heavy and prosperous;
their waists bulge with fat.
28 But their cities will be ruined.
They will live in abandoned houses
that are ready to tumble down.
29 Their riches will not last,
and their wealth will not endure.
Their possessions will no longer spread across the horizon.

30 "They will not escape the darkness.
The burning sun will wither their shoots,
and the breath of God will destroy them.
31 Let them no longer fool themselves by trusting in empty riches,
for emptiness will be their only reward.
32 Like trees, they will be cut down in the prime of life;
their branches will never again be green.
33 They will be like a vine whose grapes are harvested too early,
like an olive tree that loses its blossoms before the fruit can form.

Jb 15:12 Or *Why do your eyes flash with anger;* Hebrew reads *Why do your eyes blink.* **Jb 15:15** Hebrew *the holy ones.* **Jb 15:23** Greek version reads *He is appointed to be food for a vulture.*

Job 14:22 Job's profound speech in this chapter illustrates a great truth: To have a right set of doctrines is not enough. To know what to believe is not all that is required to please God. Truth untested by life's experiences may become static and stagnant. Suffering can bring a dynamic quality to life. Just as drought drives the roots of a tree deeper to find water, so suffering can drive us beyond superficial acceptance of truth to dependence on God for hope and life.

Job 15:1ff With the first round of talks concluded, each friend, in the same order, pressed the argument further. Again Job answered each argument (Job 15–31). This time Eliphaz was more rude, more intense, and more threatening, but he said nothing new. (See his first speech in Job 4–5.) He began by saying that Job's words were empty and useless; then he restated his opinion that Job must be a great sinner. According to Eliphaz, the experience and wisdom of their ancestors were more valuable than Job's individual thoughts. Eliphaz assumed that his words were as true as God's. It is easy to spot his arrogance.

Job 15:15-16 "Even the heavens are not absolutely pure in his sight." Eliphaz was repeating his argument that anything created, whether angels or people, is not a sufficient basis for trust and hope. Only in God can we be sure. (See the note on Job 4:18-19, p. 99.)

▸ **JOB 15:1-35** ***(cont.)***

34 For the godless are barren.
Their homes, enriched through bribery,
will burn.
35 They conceive trouble and give birth to evil.
Their womb produces deceit."

Job's Fifth Speech: A Response to Eliphaz

JOB 16:1-22

Then Job spoke again:

2 "I have heard all this before.
What miserable comforters you are!
3 Won't you ever stop blowing hot air?
What makes you keep on talking?
4 I could say the same things if you were
in my place.
I could spout off criticism and shake
my head at you.
5 But if it were me, I would encourage you.
I would try to take away your grief.
6 Instead, I suffer if I defend myself,
and I suffer no less if I refuse to speak.

7 "O God, you have ground me down
and devastated my family.
8 As if to prove I have sinned, you've reduced
me to skin and bones.
My gaunt flesh testifies against me.
9 God hates me and angrily tears me apart.
He snaps his teeth at me
and pierces me with his eyes.
10 People jeer and laugh at me.
They slap my cheek in contempt.
A mob gathers against me.
11 God has handed me over to sinners.
He has tossed me into the hands
of the wicked.

12 "I was living quietly until he shattered me.
He took me by the neck and broke me
in pieces.
Then he set me up as his target,
13 and now his archers surround me.
His arrows pierce me without mercy.
The ground is wet with my blood.*
14 Again and again he smashes against me,
charging at me like a warrior.
15 I wear burlap to show my grief.
My pride lies in the dust.
16 My eyes are red with weeping;
dark shadows circle my eyes.
17 Yet I have done no wrong,
and my prayer is pure.

18 "O earth, do not conceal my blood.
Let it cry out on my behalf.
19 Even now my witness is in heaven.
My advocate is there on high.
20 My friends scorn me,
but I pour out my tears to God.
21 I need someone to mediate between
God and me,
as a person mediates between friends.
22 For soon I must go down that road
from which I will never return.

Job Continues to Defend His Innocence

JOB 17:1-16

1 "My spirit is crushed,
and my life is nearly snuffed out.
The grave is ready to receive me.
2 I am surrounded by mockers.
I watch how bitterly they taunt me.

3 "You must defend my innocence, O God,
since no one else will stand up for me.
4 You have closed their minds to understanding,
but do not let them triumph.
5 They betray their friends for their own
advantage,
so let their children faint with hunger.

6 "God has made a mockery of me among the
people;
they spit in my face.
7 My eyes are swollen with weeping,
and I am but a shadow of my former self.
8 The virtuous are horrified when they see me.
The innocent rise up against the ungodly.
9 The righteous keep moving forward,
and those with clean hands become stronger
and stronger.

Jb 16:13 Hebrew *my gall.*

Job 16:1ff Job's friends were supposed to be comforting him in his grief. Instead, they condemned him for causing his own suffering. Job began his reply to Eliphaz by calling all of them "miserable comforters." Job's words reveal several ways to become a better comforter to those in pain: Don't talk just for the sake of talking; don't sermonize by giving pat answers; don't accuse or criticize; put yourself in the other person's place; and offer help and encouragement. Try Job's suggestions, knowing that they are given by a person who needed great comfort. The best comforters are those who know something about personal suffering.

Job 16:19 Job was afraid that God had abandoned him. Yet he appealed directly to God (his witness and advocate) and to God's knowledge of his innocence. A *witness* is someone who has seen what has happened, and an *advocate* is like a lawyer who speaks on behalf of the plaintiff. By using these terms, Job showed he had cast all his hope for any fair defense upon God in heaven because he would probably die before it happened on earth. In the New Testament we learn that Jesus Christ intercedes on our behalf (Heb 7:25; 1 Jn 2:1); therefore, we have nothing to fear.

10 "As for all of you, come back with a better
argument,
though I still won't find a wise man
among you.
11 My days are over.
My hopes have disappeared.
My heart's desires are broken.
12 These men say that night is day;
they claim that the darkness is light.
13 What if I go to the grave*
and make my bed in darkness?
14 What if I call the grave my father,
and the maggot my mother or my sister?
15 Where then is my hope?
Can anyone find it?
16 No, my hope will go down with me to the grave.
We will rest together in the dust!"

Bildad's Second Response to Job

JOB 18:1-21

Then Bildad the Shuhite replied:

2 "How long before you stop talking?
Speak sense if you want us to answer!
3 Do you think we are mere animals?
Do you think we are stupid?
4 You may tear out your hair in anger,
but will that destroy the earth?
Will it make the rocks tremble?

5 "Surely the light of the wicked will be
snuffed out.
The sparks of their fire will not glow.
6 The light in their tent will grow dark.
The lamp hanging above them will be
quenched.
7 The confident stride of the wicked will be
shortened.
Their own schemes will be their downfall.
8 The wicked walk into a net.
They fall into a pit.
9 A trap grabs them by the heel.
A snare holds them tight.
10 A noose lies hidden on the ground.
A rope is stretched across their path.

11 "Terrors surround the wicked
and trouble them at every step.
12 Hunger depletes their strength,
and calamity waits for them to stumble.
13 Disease eats their skin;
death devours their limbs.
14 They are torn from the security of their homes
and are brought down to the king of terrors.
15 The homes of the wicked will burn down;
burning sulfur rains on their houses.
16 Their roots will dry up,
and their branches will wither.
17 All memory of their existence will fade from
the earth;
no one will remember their names.
18 They will be thrust from light into darkness,
driven from the world.
19 They will have neither children nor
grandchildren,
nor any survivor in the place where they lived.
20 People in the west are appalled at their fate;
people in the east are horrified.
21 They will say, 'This was the home of a wicked
person,
the place of one who rejected God.'"

Job's Sixth Speech: A Response to Bildad

JOB 19:1-29

Then Job spoke again:

2 "How long will you torture me?
How long will you try to crush me with
your words?
3 You have already insulted me ten times.
You should be ashamed of treating me so badly.

Jb 17:13 Hebrew *to Sheol;* also in 17:16.

Job 17:10 Job's three friends had a reputation for being wise, but Job could not find wisdom in any of them. Later (in Job 42:7) God backs up Job's claim when he condemns these men for their false portrayal of him. They assumed that because they were prosperous and successful, God must be pleased with the way they were living and thinking. Job, however, told his friends that they were starting with the wrong idea because earthly success and prosperity are not a reward for faith in God. Likewise, trouble and affliction do not prove faithlessness. The truly wise man knows that wisdom comes from God alone. And the truly wise man never forsakes God. God's wisdom proved superior to Job's and to all his friends' wisdom.

Job 17:15 Job was giving up hope of any future restoration of wealth and family and wrapping himself in thoughts of death and the rest from grief and pain it promised. The rewards that Job's friends described were all related to this present life. They were silent about the possibility of life after death. We must not evaluate life only in terms of this present world because God promises a never-ending, wonderful future to those who are faithful to him.

Job 18:1ff Bildad thought he knew how the universe should be run, and he saw Job as an illustration of the consequences of sin. Bildad rejected Job's side of the story because it did not fit in with his outlook on life. It is easy to condemn Bildad because his errors are obvious; unfortunately, we often act the same way when our ideas are threatened.

Job 18:14 The "king of terrors" is a figure of speech referring to death. Bildad viewed death as a great devourer (Job 18:13), but the Bible teaches that God has the power to devour even death (Ps 49:15; Isa 25:8; 1 Cor 15:54-56).

Job 19:3-5 It is easy to point out someone else's faults or sins. Job's friends accused him of sin to make him feel guilty, not to encourage or correct him. If we feel we must admonish someone, we should be sure we are confronting that person out of love, not because we are annoyed, inconvenienced, or seeking to fix blame.

▶ **JOB 19:1-29 *(cont.)***

4 Even if I have sinned,
that is my concern, not yours.
5 You think you're better than I am,
using my humiliation as evidence of my sin.
6 But it is God who has wronged me,
capturing me in his net.*

7 "I cry out, 'Help!' but no one answers me.
I protest, but there is no justice.
8 God has blocked my way so I cannot move.
He has plunged my path into darkness.
9 He has stripped me of my honor
and removed the crown from my head.
10 He has demolished me on every side, and I am
finished.
He has uprooted my hope like a fallen tree.
11 His fury burns against me;
he counts me as an enemy.
12 His troops advance.
They build up roads to attack me.
They camp all around my tent.

13 "My relatives stay far away,
and my friends have turned against me.
14 My family is gone,
and my close friends have forgotten me.
15 My servants and maids consider me a stranger.
I am like a foreigner to them.
16 When I call my servant, he doesn't come;
I have to plead with him!
17 My breath is repulsive to my wife.
I am rejected by my own family.
18 Even young children despise me.
When I stand to speak, they turn their backs
on me.
19 My close friends detest me.
Those I loved have turned against me.
20 I have been reduced to skin and bones
and have escaped death by the skin
of my teeth.

21 "Have mercy on me, my friends, have mercy,
for the hand of God has struck me.
22 Must you also persecute me, like God does?
Haven't you chewed me up enough?

23 "Oh, that my words could be recorded.
Oh, that they could be inscribed on a
monument,
24 carved with an iron chisel and filled with lead,
engraved forever in the rock.

25 "But as for me, I know that my Redeemer lives,
and he will stand upon the earth at last.
26 And after my body has decayed,
yet in my body I will see God!*
27 I will see him for myself.
Yes, I will see him with my own eyes.
I am overwhelmed at the thought!

28 "How dare you go on persecuting me,
saying, 'It's his own fault'?
29 You should fear punishment yourselves,
for your attitude deserves punishment.
Then you will know that there is indeed
a judgment."

Jb 19:6 Or *for I am like a city under siege.* **Jb 19:26** Or *without my body I will see God.* The meaning of the Hebrew is uncertain.

Job 19:6 Job felt that God was treating him as an enemy when, in fact, God was his friend and thought highly of him (Job 1:8; 2:3). In his difficulty, Job pointed at the wrong person. It was Satan, not God, who was Job's enemy. Because they stressed ultimate causes, most Israelites believed that both good and evil came from God; they also thought people were responsible for their own destinies. But the evil power loose in this world also accounts for much of the suffering we experience. In verse 7, Job continued to cry out for God to hear him.

Job 19:25-27 At the heart of the book of Job comes his ringing affirmation of confidence: "I know that my Redeemer lives." In ancient Israel a *redeemer* was a family member who bought a slave's way to freedom or who took care of a widow (see the note on Ruth 3:1-9, p. 413). What tremendous faith Job had, especially since he was unaware of the conference between God and Satan. Job thought that God had brought all these disasters upon him! Faced with death and decay, Job still expected to see God—and he expected to do so in his body. When the book of Job was written, Israel did not have a well-developed doctrine of the resurrection. Although Job struggled with the idea that God was presently against him, he firmly believed that in the end God would be on his side. This belief was so strong that Job became one of the first to talk about the resurrection of the body (see also Ps 16:10; Isa 26:19; Dan 12:2, 13).

Job 19:26 Job said, "In my body I will see God." In Job's situation, it seemed unlikely to him that he would, in his body, see God. And that's just the point of Job's faith! He was confident that God's justice would triumph, even if it would take a miracle like resurrection to accomplish this.

JOB AND JESUS

The book of Job is intimately tied to the New Testament because Job's questions and problems are answered perfectly in Jesus Christ.

Subject/Reference in Job	How Jesus Is the Answer
Someone must help us approach God. (Job 9:32-33)	1 Tim 2:5
Is there life after death? (Job 14:14)	John 11:25
There is one in heaven working on our behalf. (Job 16:19)	Heb 9:24
There is one who can save us from judgment. (Job 19:25)	Heb 7:24-25
What is important in life? (Job 21:7-15)	Matt 16:26; John 3:16
Where do we find God? (Job 23:3-5)	John 14:9

Zophar's Second Response to Job

JOB 20:1-29

Then Zophar the Naamathite replied:

2 "I must reply
because I am greatly disturbed.
3 I've had to endure your insults,
but now my spirit prompts me to reply.

4 "Don't you realize that from the beginning
of time,
ever since people were first placed on
the earth,
5 the triumph of the wicked has been short lived
and the joy of the godless has been only
temporary?
6 Though the pride of the godless reaches
to the heavens
and their heads touch the clouds,
7 yet they will vanish forever,
thrown away like their own dung.
Those who knew them will ask,
'Where are they?'
8 They will fade like a dream and not be found.
They will vanish like a vision in the night.
9 Those who once saw them will see them
no more.
Their families will never see them again.
10 Their children will beg from the poor,
for they must give back their stolen riches.
11 Though they are young,
their bones will lie in the dust.

12 "They enjoyed the sweet taste of wickedness,
letting it melt under their tongue.
13 They savored it,
holding it long in their mouths.
14 But suddenly the food in their bellies turns sour,
a poisonous venom in their stomach.
15 They will vomit the wealth they swallowed.
God won't let them keep it down.
16 They will suck the poison of cobras.
The viper will kill them.
17 They will never again enjoy streams of olive oil
or rivers of milk and honey.
18 They will give back everything they worked for.
Their wealth will bring them no joy.
19 For they oppressed the poor and left them
destitute.
They foreclosed on their homes.
20 They were always greedy and never satisfied.
Nothing remains of all the things they dreamed
about.
21 Nothing is left after they finish gorging
themselves.
Therefore, their prosperity will not endure.

22 "In the midst of plenty, they will run into trouble
and be overcome by misery.
23 May God give them a bellyful of trouble.
May God rain down his anger upon them.
24 When they try to escape an iron weapon,
a bronze-tipped arrow will pierce them.
25 The arrow is pulled from their back,
and the arrowhead glistens with blood.*
The terrors of death are upon them.
26 Their treasures will be thrown into deepest
darkness.
A wildfire will devour their goods,
consuming all they have left.
27 The heavens will reveal their guilt,
and the earth will testify against them.
28 A flood will sweep away their house.
God's anger will descend on them in torrents.
29 This is the reward that God gives the wicked.
It is the inheritance decreed by God."

Job's Seventh Speech: A Response to Zophar

JOB 21:1-34

Then Job spoke again:

2 "Listen closely to what I am saying.
That's one consolation you can give me.
3 Bear with me, and let me speak.
After I have spoken, you may resume
mocking me.

4 "My complaint is with God, not with people.
I have good reason to be so impatient.

Jb 20:25 Hebrew *with gall.*

Job 20:1ff Zophar's speech again revealed his false assumption, because he based his arguments purely on the idea that Job was an evil hypocrite. Zophar said that although Job had had it good for a while, he didn't live righteously, so God took his wealth from him. According to Zophar, Job's calamities *proved* his wickedness.

Job 20:6-7 Although Zophar was wrong in directing this tirade against Job, he was correct in talking about the final end of evil people. At first, sin seems enjoyable and attractive. Lying, stealing, or oppressing others often brings temporary gain to those who practice these sins. Some live a long time with ill-gotten gain. Judgment for these sins may not come in the lifetime of the sinner. But in the end, God's justice will prevail. Punishment may be deferred until the very end— the Last Judgment, when sinners will be eternally cut off from God. We should not be impressed with or misled by the success and power of evil people. God's judgment on them is certain.

Job 21:1ff Job refuted Zophar's idea that evil people never experience wealth and happiness, pointing out that in the real world the wicked do indeed prosper. (See Ps 73 for more on the apparent prosperity of evil people.) God does as he wills to individuals (Job 21:22-25), and people cannot use their circumstances to measure their own goodness or God's—they are sometimes (but not always) related. To Job's friends, success was based on outward performance; to God, however, success is based on a person's heart.

▸ **JOB 21:1-34 *(cont.)***

5 Look at me and be stunned.
Put your hand over your mouth in shock.
6 When I think about what I am saying, I shudder.
My body trembles.

7 "Why do the wicked prosper,
growing old and powerful?
8 They live to see their children grow up and settle down,
and they enjoy their grandchildren.
9 Their homes are safe from every fear,
and God does not punish them.
10 Their bulls never fail to breed.
Their cows bear calves and never miscarry.
11 They let their children frisk about like lambs.
Their little ones skip and dance.
12 They sing with tambourine and harp.
They celebrate to the sound of the flute.
13 They spend their days in prosperity,
then go down to the grave* in peace.
14 And yet they say to God, 'Go away.
We want no part of you and your ways.
15 Who is the Almighty, and why should we obey him?
What good will it do us to pray?'
16 (They think their prosperity is of their own doing,
but I will have nothing to do with that kind of thinking.)

17 "Yet the light of the wicked never seems to be extinguished.
Do they ever have trouble?
Does God distribute sorrows to them in anger?
18 Are they driven before the wind like straw?
Are they carried away by the storm like chaff?
Not at all!

19 "'Well,' you say, 'At least God will punish their children!'
But I say he should punish the ones who sin,
so that they understand his judgment.
20 Let them see their destruction with their own eyes.
Let them drink deeply of the anger of the Almighty.
21 For they will not care what happens to their family
after they are dead.

22 "But who can teach a lesson to God,
since he judges even the most powerful?
23 One person dies in prosperity,
completely comfortable and secure,
24 the picture of good health,
vigorous and fit.
25 Another person dies in bitter poverty,
never having tasted the good life.
26 But both are buried in the same dust,
both eaten by the same maggots.

27 "Look, I know what you're thinking.
I know the schemes you plot against me.
28 You will tell me of rich and wicked people
whose houses have vanished because of their sins.
29 But ask those who have been around,
and they will tell you the truth.
30 Evil people are spared in times of calamity
and are allowed to escape disaster.
31 No one criticizes them openly
or pays them back for what they have done.
32 When they are carried to the grave,
an honor guard keeps watch at their tomb.
33 A great funeral procession goes to the cemetery.
Many pay their respects as the body is laid to rest,
and the earth gives sweet repose.

34 "How can your empty clichés comfort me?
All your explanations are lies!"

Eliphaz's Third Response to Job

JOB 22:1-30

Then Eliphaz the Temanite replied:

2 "Can a person do anything to help God?
Can even a wise person be helpful to him?
3 Is it any advantage to the Almighty if you are righteous?
Would it be any gain to him if you were perfect?

Jb 21:13 Hebrew *to Sheol.*

Job 21:22 Although baffled by the reasons for his suffering, Job affirmed God's superior understanding by asking, "Who can teach a lesson to God?" The way you respond to your personal struggles shows your attitude toward God. Rather than becoming angry with God, continue to trust him, no matter what your circumstances may be. Although it is sometimes difficult to see, God *is* in control. We must commit ourselves to him so we will not resent his timing.

Job 21:29-33 If wicked people become wealthy despite their sin, why should we try to be good? The wicked may *seem* to get away with sin, but there is a higher Judge and a future judgment (Rev 20:11-15). The final settlement of justice will come not in this life but in the next. What is important is how a person views *God* in prosperity or poverty, not the condition of prosperity or poverty itself.

Job 22:1ff This is Eliphaz's third and final speech to Job. When he first spoke to Job (Job 4–5), he commended Job's good deeds and gently suggested that Job might need to repent of some sin. While he said nothing new in this speech, he did get more specific. He couldn't shake his belief that suffering is God's punishment for evil deeds, so he suggested several possible sins that Job might have committed. Eliphaz wasn't trying to destroy Job; at the end of his speech he promised that Job would receive peace and restoration if he would only admit his sin and repent.

4 Is it because you're so pious that he accuses you
and brings judgment against you?
5 No, it's because of your wickedness!
There's no limit to your sins.

6 "For example, you must have lent money
to your friend
and demanded clothing as security.
Yes, you stripped him to the bone.
7 You must have refused water for the thirsty
and food for the hungry.
8 You probably think the land belongs to the
powerful
and only the privileged have a right to it!
9 You must have sent widows away empty-handed
and crushed the hopes of orphans.
10 That is why you are surrounded by traps
and tremble from sudden fears.
11 That is why you cannot see in the darkness,
and waves of water cover you.

12 "God is so great—higher than the heavens,
higher than the farthest stars.
13 But you reply, 'That's why God can't see what
I am doing!
How can he judge through the thick darkness?
14 For thick clouds swirl about him, and he cannot
see us.
He is way up there, walking on the vault
of heaven.'

15 "Will you continue on the old paths
where evil people have walked?
16 They were snatched away in the prime of life,
the foundations of their lives washed away.
17 For they said to God, 'Leave us alone!
What can the Almighty do to us?'
18 Yet he was the one who filled their homes with
good things,
so I will have nothing to do with that kind of
thinking.

19 "The righteous will be happy to see the wicked
destroyed,
and the innocent will laugh in contempt.
20 They will say, 'See how our enemies have been
destroyed.
The last of them have been consumed
in the fire.'

21 "Submit to God, and you will have peace;
then things will go well for you.
22 Listen to his instructions,
and store them in your heart.
23 If you return to the Almighty, you will be
restored—
so clean up your life.
24 If you give up your lust for money
and throw your precious gold into the river,
25 the Almighty himself will be your treasure.
He will be your precious silver!

26 "Then you will take delight in the Almighty
and look up to God.
27 You will pray to him, and he will hear you,
and you will fulfill your vows to him.
28 You will succeed in whatever you choose to do,
and light will shine on the road ahead of you.
29 If people are in trouble and you say, 'Help them,'
God will save them.
30 Even sinners will be rescued;
they will be rescued because your hands
are pure."

Job's Eighth Speech: A Response to Eliphaz

JOB 23:1-17

Then Job spoke again:

2 "My complaint today is still a bitter one,
and I try hard not to groan aloud.
3 If only I knew where to find God,
I would go to his court.
4 I would lay out my case
and present my arguments.
5 Then I would listen to his reply
and understand what he says to me.
6 Would he use his great power to argue with me?
No, he would give me a fair hearing.
7 Honest people can reason with him,
so I would be forever acquitted by my judge.
8 I go east, but he is not there.
I go west, but I cannot find him.

Job 22:12-14 Eliphaz declared that Job's view of God was too small, and he criticized Job for thinking that God was too far removed from earth to care about him. If Job knew of God's intense, personal interest in him, Eliphaz said, he wouldn't dare take his sins so lightly. Eliphaz had a point—some people do take sin lightly because they think God is far away and doesn't notice all we do. But his point did not apply to Job.

Job 22:21-30 Several times Job's friends showed a partial knowledge of God's truth and character, but they had trouble accurately applying this truth to life. Such was the case with Eliphaz, who gave a beautiful summary of repentance. He was correct in saying that we must ask for God's forgiveness when we sin, but his statement did not apply to Job, who had already sought God's forgiveness (Job 7:20-21; 9:20; 13:23) and had lived closely in touch with God all along.

Job 23:1–24:25 Job continued his questioning, saying that his suffering would be more bearable if only he knew why it was happening. If there was sin for which he could repent, he would! He knew about the wicked and the fact that they would be punished; he knew God could vindicate him if he so chose. In all his examples of the wicked in the world, his overriding desire was for God to clear his name, prove his righteousness, and explain why he was chosen to receive all this calamity. Job tried to make his friends see that questions about God, life, and justice are not as simple as they assumed.

▶ **JOB 23:1-17 *(cont.)***

9 I do not see him in the north, for he is hidden.
I look to the south, but he is concealed.
10 "But he knows where I am going.
And when he tests me, I will come out
as pure as gold.
11 For I have stayed on God's paths;
I have followed his ways and not turned aside.
12 I have not departed from his commands,
but have treasured his words more than
daily food.
13 But once he has made his decision, who can
change his mind?
Whatever he wants to do, he does.
14 So he will do to me whatever he has
planned.
He controls my destiny.
15 No wonder I am so terrified in his presence.
When I think of it, terror grips me.
16 God has made me sick at heart;
the Almighty has terrified me.
17 Darkness is all around me;
thick, impenetrable darkness is everywhere.

Job Asks Why the Wicked Are Not Punished

JOB 24:1-25

1 "Why doesn't the Almighty bring the wicked
to judgment?
Why must the godly wait for him in vain?
2 Evil people steal land by moving the boundary
markers.
They steal livestock and put them in their
own pastures.
3 They take the orphan's donkey
and demand the widow's ox as security
for a loan.
4 The poor are pushed off the path;
the needy must hide together for safety.
5 Like wild donkeys in the wilderness,
the poor must spend all their time looking
for food,
searching even in the desert for food for
their children.
6 They harvest a field they do not own,
and they glean in the vineyards of the
wicked.
7 All night they lie naked in the cold,
without clothing or covering.
8 They are soaked by mountain showers,
and they huddle against the rocks for want
of a home.
9 "The wicked snatch a widow's child from
her breast,
taking the baby as security for a loan.
10 The poor must go about naked, without any
clothing.
They harvest food for others while they
themselves are starving.
11 They press out olive oil without being allowed
to taste it,
and they tread in the winepress as they suffer
from thirst.
12 The groans of the dying rise from the city,
and the wounded cry for help,
yet God ignores their moaning.
13 "Wicked people rebel against the light.
They refuse to acknowledge its ways
or stay in its paths.
14 The murderer rises in the early dawn
to kill the poor and needy;
at night he is a thief.
15 The adulterer waits for the twilight,
saying, 'No one will see me then.'
He hides his face so no one will know him.
16 Thieves break into houses at night
and sleep in the daytime.
They are not acquainted with the light.
17 The black night is their morning.
They ally themselves with the terrors of the
darkness.
18 "But they disappear like foam down a river.
Everything they own is cursed,

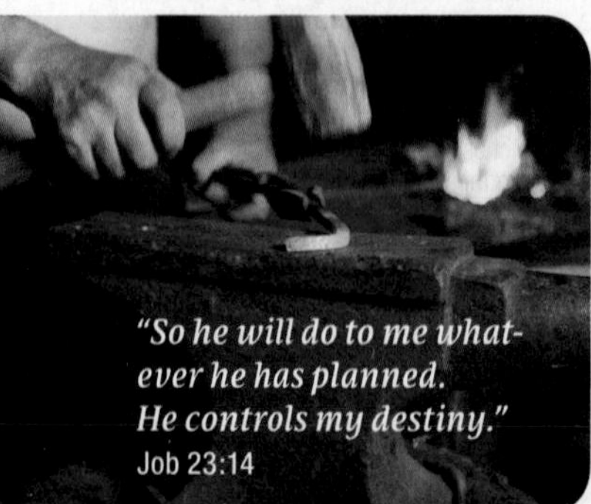
"So he will do to me whatever he has planned. He controls my destiny."
Job 23:14

Job 23:10 In Job 22, Eliphaz had tried to condemn Job by identifying some secret sin that he may have committed. Here Job declares his confidence in his integrity and God's justice. We are always likely to have hidden sin in our lives, sin we don't even know about because God's standards are so high and our performance is so imperfect. But if we are true believers, all our sins are forgiven because of what Christ did on the cross on our behalf (Rom 5:1; 8:1). The Bible also teaches that even if we feel guilty, God is greater than our feelings (1 Jn 3:20). His forgiveness and cleansing are sufficient; they overrule our nagging doubts. The Holy Spirit in us is our proof that we are forgiven in God's eyes even though we may *feel* guilty. If we, like Job, are truly seeking God, we can stand up to others' accusations as well as our own nagging doubts. If God has forgiven and accepted us, we are forgiven indeed.

Job 24:18-21 Job suddenly seemed to be arguing on his friends' side. For this reason, some commentators think one of Job's friends said these words. But we shouldn't expect Job to present a unified argument. He was confused. He was not arguing that, in every case, God rewards the wicked and punishes the righteous; he was simply asserting that in his case, a righteous man was suffering.

and they are afraid to enter their own
vineyards.
19 The grave* consumes sinners
just as drought and heat consume snow.
20 Their own mothers will forget them.
Maggots will find them sweet to eat.
No one will remember them.
Wicked people are broken like a tree
in the storm.
21 They cheat the woman who has no son to help her.
They refuse to help the needy widow.

22 "God, in his power, drags away the rich.
They may rise high, but they have no assurance
of life.
23 They may be allowed to live in security,
but God is always watching them.
24 And though they are great now,
in a moment they will be gone like all others,
cut off like heads of grain.
25 Can anyone claim otherwise?
Who can prove me wrong?"

Bildad's Third Response to Job

JOB 25:1-6

Then Bildad the Shuhite replied:

2 "God is powerful and dreadful.
He enforces peace in the heavens.
3 Who is able to count his heavenly army?
Doesn't his light shine on all the earth?
4 How can a mortal be innocent before God?
Can anyone born of a woman be pure?
5 God is more glorious than the moon;
he shines brighter than the stars.
6 In comparison, people are maggots;
we mortals are mere worms."

Job's Ninth Speech: A Response to Bildad

JOB 26:1-14

Then Job spoke again:

2 "How you have helped the powerless!
How you have saved the weak!
3 How you have enlightened my stupidity!
What wise advice you have offered!
4 Where have you gotten all these wise sayings?
Whose spirit speaks through you?

5 "The dead tremble—
those who live beneath the waters.
6 The underworld* is naked in God's presence.
The place of destruction* is uncovered.
7 God stretches the northern sky over
empty space
and hangs the earth on nothing.
8 He wraps the rain in his thick clouds,
and the clouds don't burst with the weight.
9 He covers the face of the moon,*
shrouding it with his clouds.
10 He created the horizon when he separated
the waters;
he set the boundary between day and night.
11 The foundations of heaven tremble;
they shudder at his rebuke.
12 By his power the sea grew calm.
By his skill he crushed the great sea monster.*
13 His Spirit made the heavens beautiful,
and his power pierced the gliding serpent.
14 These are just the beginning of all that he does,
merely a whisper of his power.
Who, then, can comprehend the thunder
of his power?"

Job's Final Speech

JOB 27:1-23

Job continued speaking:

2 "I vow by the living God, who has taken away
my rights,
by the Almighty who has embittered
my soul—
3 As long as I live,
while I have breath from God,
4 my lips will speak no evil,
and my tongue will speak no lies.
5 I will never concede that you are right;
I will defend my integrity until I die.

Jb 24:19 Hebrew *Sheol.* **Jb 26:6a** Hebrew *Sheol.* **Jb 26:6b** Hebrew *Abaddon.* **Jb 26:9** Or *covers his throne.* **Jb 26:12** Hebrew *Rahab,* the name of a mythical sea monster that represents chaos in ancient literature.

Job 25:1ff Bildad's final reply was weak. It ignored Job's examples of the prosperity of the wicked. Instead of attempting to refute Job, Bildad accused Job of pride because he was claiming that his suffering was not the result of sin. Job never claimed to be without sin, but only that his sin could not have caused his present trouble.

Job 25:6 It is important to understand that Bildad, not God, was calling people worms. Human beings are created in God's image (Gen 1:26-27). Psalm 8:5 says that people are "a little lower than God." Bildad may have simply been using a poetic description to contrast our worth to the worth and power of God. To come to God, we need not crawl like worms. We can approach him boldly in faith (Heb 4:16).

Job 26:1ff Job has the distinction of giving the longest speech in the book—six chapters—weaving together pictures of God's mystery and power in a beautiful poem of trust. Beginning by brushing off Bildad's latest reply as irrelevant (Job 25), Job then told Bildad and his friends that they could not possibly know everything about God. Wisdom does not originate from this life or from the human mind—it comes from God (Job 28:27-28). Job then defended his upright and honest life. He had effectively sought to follow God's way of living. While admitting that he was not perfect, Job maintained that his motives were right.

Job 26:2-4 With great sarcasm, Job attacked Bildad's comments. Job's friends' theological explanations failed to bring any relief because they were unable to turn their knowledge into helpful counsel. When dealing with people, it is more important to love and understand them than to analyze them or give advice. Compassion produces greater results than criticism or blame.

▸ **JOB 27:1-23 *(cont.)***

6 I will maintain my innocence without wavering.
My conscience is clear for as long as I live.
7 "May my enemy be punished like the wicked,
my adversary like those who do evil.
8 For what hope do the godless have when God
cuts them off
and takes away their life?
9 Will God listen to their cry
when trouble comes upon them?
10 Can they take delight in the Almighty?
Can they call to God at any time?
11 I will teach you about God's power.
I will not conceal anything concerning
the Almighty.
12 But you have seen all this,
yet you say all these useless things to me.
13 "This is what the wicked will receive
from God;
this is their inheritance from the Almighty.
14 They may have many children,
but the children will die in war or starve
to death.
15 Those who survive will die of a plague,
and not even their widows will mourn them.
16 "Evil people may have piles of money
and may store away mounds of clothing.
17 But the righteous will wear that clothing,
and the innocent will divide that money.
18 The wicked build houses as fragile as a
spider's web,*
as flimsy as a shelter made of branches.
19 The wicked go to bed rich
but wake to find that all their wealth is gone.
20 Terror overwhelms them like a flood,
and they are blown away in the storms
of the night.
21 The east wind carries them away, and they
are gone.
It sweeps them away.
22 It whirls down on them without mercy.
They struggle to flee from its power.
23 But everyone jeers at them
and mocks them.

Job Speaks of Wisdom and Understanding

JOB 28:1-28

1 "People know where to mine silver
and how to refine gold.
2 They know where to dig iron from the earth
and how to smelt copper from rock.
3 They know how to shine light in the darkness
and explore the farthest regions of the earth
as they search in the dark for ore.
4 They sink a mine shaft into the earth
far from where anyone lives.
They descend on ropes, swinging back
and forth.
5 Food is grown on the earth above,
but down below, the earth is melted as by fire.
6 Here the rocks contain precious lapis lazuli,
and the dust contains gold.
7 These are treasures no bird of prey can see,
no falcon's eye observe.
8 No wild animal has walked upon these treasures;
no lion has ever set his paw there.
9 People know how to tear apart flinty rocks
and overturn the roots of mountains.

Jb 27:18 As in Greek and Syriac versions (see also 8:14); Hebrew reads *a moth.*

Job 27:6 In the midst of all the accusations, Job was able to declare that his conscience was clear. Only God's forgiveness and the determination to live right before God can bring a clear conscience. How important Job's record became as he was being accused. Like Job, we can't claim sinless lives, but we *can* claim forgiven lives. When we confess our sins to God, he forgives us. Then we can live with clear consciences.

Job 27:13-23 Job agreed with his friends that the end of the wicked will be disaster, but he did not agree that *he* was wicked and deserving of punishment. Most of the punishments Job listed never happened to him. So he wasn't including himself as one of the wicked. On the contrary, he continually pleaded for God to vindicate him.

WHERE CAN WISDOM BE FOUND?

Job and his friends differed in their ideas of how people become wise.

Person	*His Source of Wisdom*	*Attitude toward God*
Eliphaz	Wisdom is learned by observing and experiencing life. He based his advice to Job on his confident, firsthand knowledge (Job 4:7-8; 5:3, 27).	I have personally observed how God works and have figured him out.
Bildad	Wisdom is inherited from the past. Trustworthy knowledge is secondhand. He based his advice to Job on traditional proverbs and sayings that he frequently quoted (Job 8:8-9; 18:5-21).	Those who have gone before us figured God out, and all we have to do is use that knowledge.
Zophar	Wisdom belongs to the wise. He based his advice on his wisdom that had no other source than himself (Job 11:6; 20:1-29).	The wise know what God is like, but there aren't many of us around.
Job	God is the source of wisdom, and the first step toward wisdom is to fear God (Job 28:20-28).	God reveals his wisdom to those who humbly trust him.

10 They cut tunnels in the rocks
and uncover precious stones.
11 They dam up the trickling streams
and bring to light the hidden treasures.

12 "But do people know where to find wisdom?
Where can they find understanding?
13 No one knows where to find it,
for it is not found among the living.
14 'It is not here,' says the ocean.
'Nor is it here,' says the sea.
15 It cannot be bought with gold.
It cannot be purchased with silver.
16 It's worth more than all the gold of Ophir,
greater than precious onyx or lapis lazuli.
17 Wisdom is more valuable than gold and
crystal.
It cannot be purchased with jewels
mounted in fine gold.
18 Coral and jasper are worthless in trying
to get it.
The price of wisdom is far above rubies.
19 Precious peridot from Ethiopia* cannot be
exchanged for it.
It's worth more than the purest gold.

20 "But do people know where to find wisdom?
Where can they find understanding?
21 It is hidden from the eyes of all humanity.
Even the sharp-eyed birds in the sky cannot
discover it.
22 Destruction* and Death say,
'We've heard only rumors of where wisdom
can be found.'

23 "God alone understands the way to wisdom;
he knows where it can be found,
24 for he looks throughout the whole earth
and sees everything under the heavens.
25 He decided how hard the winds should blow
and how much rain should fall.
26 He made the laws for the rain
and laid out a path for the lightning.
27 Then he saw wisdom and evaluated it.
He set it in place and examined it thoroughly.
28 And this is what he says to all humanity:
'The fear of the Lord is true wisdom;
to forsake evil is real understanding.'"

Job Speaks of His Former Blessings

JOB 29:1-25

Job continued speaking:

2 "I long for the years gone by
when God took care of me,
3 when he lit up the way before me
and I walked safely through the darkness.
4 When I was in my prime,
God's friendship was felt in my home.
5 The Almighty was still with me,
and my children were around me.
6 My cows produced milk in abundance,
and my groves poured out streams of olive oil.

7 "Those were the days when I went to the
city gate
and took my place among the honored
leaders.
8 The young stepped aside when they saw me,
and even the aged rose in respect at my
coming.
9 The princes stood in silence
and put their hands over their mouths.
10 The highest officials of the city stood quietly,
holding their tongues in respect.

11 "All who heard me praised me.
All who saw me spoke well of me.
12 For I assisted the poor in their need
and the orphans who required help.
13 I helped those without hope, and they blessed me.
And I caused the widows' hearts to sing for joy.

Jb 28:19 Hebrew *from Cush.* **Jb 28:22** Hebrew *Abaddon.*

Job 28:13 Job stated that wisdom cannot be found among the living. It is natural for people who do not understand the importance of God's Word to seek wisdom here on earth. They look to philosophers and other leaders to give them direction for living. Yet Job said that wisdom is not found there. No leader or group of leaders can produce enough knowledge or insight to explain the totality of human experience. The ultimate interpretation of life, of who we are and where we are going, must come from outside and above our mortal life. When looking for guidance, seek God's wisdom as revealed in the Bible. To be lifted above and beyond the boundaries of life, we must know and trust the Lord of life.

Job 28:16 Gold of Ophir was considered the finest gold available. Ophir may have been located in Africa, along the Arabian coast, or in India. Wherever it was, it was a good distance from Israel, for it took Solomon's ships three years to make the voyage (1 Kgs 9:28; 10:22).

Job 28:28 "The fear of the Lord" is a key theme in the wisdom literature of the Bible (Job, Psalms, Proverbs, Ecclesiastes, and Song of Songs). It means to have respect and reverence for God and to be in awe of his majesty and power. This is the starting point to finding real wisdom (see Prov 1:7-9).

Job 29:6 Milk and olive oil were symbols of material prosperity in an agricultural society. Job's flocks and olive trees were so plentiful that everything seemed to overflow.

Job 29:7ff Job was walking a fine line between bragging about past accomplishments and recalling good deeds in order to answer the charges against him. Job's one weakness throughout his conversations is that he came dangerously close to pride. Pride is especially deceptive when we are doing right. But it separates us from God by making us think we're better than we really are. Then comes the tendency to trust our own opinions, which leads to other kinds of sin. While it is not wrong to recount past deeds, it is far better to recount God's blessings to us. This will help keep us from inadvertently falling into pride.

Job 29:7-17 Because of this description of Job's work, many commentators believe that Job was a judge. In Job's day, a judge served as both a city councilman and a magistrate, helping to manage the community and settle disputes. In most cases, this was not a full-time position but a part-time post held on the basis of one's respect and standing in the area.

▸ **JOB 29:1-25** ***(cont.)***

14 Everything I did was honest.
Righteousness covered me like a robe,
and I wore justice like a turban.
15 I served as eyes for the blind
and feet for the lame.
16 I was a father to the poor
and assisted strangers who needed help.
17 I broke the jaws of godless oppressors
and plucked their victims from their teeth.

18 "I thought, 'Surely I will die surrounded
by my family
after a long, good life.*
19 For I am like a tree whose roots reach
the water,
whose branches are refreshed with the dew.
20 New honors are constantly bestowed on me,
and my strength is continually renewed.'

21 "Everyone listened to my advice.
They were silent as they waited for me
to speak.
22 And after I spoke, they had nothing to add,
for my counsel satisfied them.
23 They longed for me to speak as people long
for rain.
They drank my words like a refreshing
spring rain.
24 When they were discouraged, I smiled at them.
My look of approval was precious to them.
25 Like a chief, I told them what to do.
I lived like a king among his troops
and comforted those who mourned.

Job Speaks of His Anguish

JOB 30:1-31

1 "But now I am mocked by people younger
than I,
by young men whose fathers are not worthy
to run with my sheepdogs.
2 A lot of good they are to me—
those worn-out wretches!
3 They are gaunt with hunger
and flee to the deserts,
to desolate and gloomy wastelands.
4 They pluck wild greens from among the bushes
and eat from the roots of broom trees.
5 They are driven from human society,
and people shout at them as if they were
thieves.
6 So now they live in frightening ravines,
in caves and among the rocks.
7 They sound like animals howling among
the bushes,
huddled together beneath the nettles.
8 They are nameless fools,
outcasts from society.

9 "And now they mock me with vulgar songs!
They taunt me!
10 They despise me and won't come near me,
except to spit in my face.
11 For God has cut my bowstring.
He has humbled me,
so they have thrown off all restraint.
12 These outcasts oppose me to my face.
They send me sprawling
and lay traps in my path.
13 They block my road
and do everything they can to destroy me.
They know I have no one to help me.
14 They come at me from all directions.
They jump on me when I am down.
15 I live in terror now.
My honor has blown away in the wind,
and my prosperity has vanished like
a cloud.

16 "And now my life seeps away.
Depression haunts my days.
17 At night my bones are filled with pain,
which gnaws at me relentlessly.
18 With a strong hand, God grabs my shirt.
He grips me by the collar of my coat.
19 He has thrown me into the mud.
I'm nothing more than dust and ashes.

20 "I cry to you, O God, but you don't answer.
I stand before you, but you don't even look.
21 You have become cruel toward me.
You use your power to persecute me.
22 You throw me into the whirlwind
and destroy me in the storm.
23 And I know you are sending me to my death—
the destination of all who live.

24 "Surely no one would turn against the needy
when they cry for help in their trouble.
25 Did I not weep for those in trouble?
Was I not deeply grieved for the needy?
26 So I looked for good, but evil came instead.
I waited for the light, but darkness fell.
27 My heart is troubled and restless.
Days of suffering torment me.
28 I walk in gloom, without sunlight.
I stand in the public square and cry for help.

Jb 29:18 Hebrew *after I have counted my days like sand.*

Job 30:1ff To suffer extreme loss, as Job did, was humiliating. But to face abuse at the hands of young upstarts added insult to injury. Job had lost his family, possessions, health, position, and good name. He was not even respected for suffering bravely. Unfortunately, young people sometimes mock and take advantage of older people and those who are limited in some way. Instead, they should realize that their own physical abilities and attributes are short-lived and that God loves all people equally.

29 Instead, I am considered a brother to jackals
and a companion to owls.
30 My skin has turned dark,
and my bones burn with fever.
31 My harp plays sad music,
and my flute accompanies those who weep.

Job's Final Protest of Innocence

JOB 31:1-40

1 "I made a covenant with my eyes
not to look with lust at a young woman.
2 For what has God above chosen for us?
What is our inheritance from the Almighty
on high?
3 Isn't it calamity for the wicked
and misfortune for those who do evil?
4 Doesn't he see everything I do
and every step I take?

5 "Have I lied to anyone
or deceived anyone?
6 Let God weigh me on the scales of justice,
for he knows my integrity.
7 If I have strayed from his pathway,
or if my heart has lusted for what my eyes
have seen,
or if I am guilty of any other sin,
8 then let someone else eat the crops I have
planted.
Let all that I have planted be uprooted.
9 "If my heart has been seduced by a woman,
or if I have lusted for my neighbor's wife,
10 then let my wife belong to* another man;
let other men sleep with her.
11 For lust is a shameful sin,
a crime that should be punished.
12 It is a fire that burns all the way to hell.*
It would wipe out everything I own.

13 "If I have been unfair to my male or female
servants
when they brought their complaints to me,
14 how could I face God?
What could I say when he questioned me?
15 For God created both me and my servants.
He created us both in the womb.

16 "Have I refused to help the poor,
or crushed the hopes of widows?
17 Have I been stingy with my food
and refused to share it with orphans?
18 No, from childhood I have cared for orphans
like a father,
and all my life I have cared for widows.
19 Whenever I saw the homeless without clothes
and the needy with nothing to wear,
20 did they not praise me
for providing wool clothing to keep
them warm?

21 "If I raised my hand against an orphan,
knowing the judges would take my side,
22 then let my shoulder be wrenched out of place!
Let my arm be torn from its socket!
23 That would be better than facing God's judgment.
For if the majesty of God opposes me, what
hope is there?

24 "Have I put my trust in money
or felt secure because of my gold?
25 Have I gloated about my wealth
and all that I own?

26 "Have I looked at the sun shining in the skies,
or the moon walking down its silver pathway,

Jb 31:10 Hebrew *grind for.* **Jb 31:12** Hebrew *to Abaddon.*

HOW SUFFERING AFFECTS US

Suffering is helpful when:	Suffering is harmful when:
We turn to God for understanding, endurance, and deliverance	We become hardened and reject God
We ask important questions we might not take time to think about in our normal routine	We refuse to ask any questions and miss any lessons that might be good for us
We are prepared by it to identify with and comfort others who suffer	We allow it to make us self-centered and selfish
We are open to being helped by others who are obeying God	We withdraw from the help others can give
We are ready to learn from a trustworthy God	We reject the fact that God can bring good out of calamity
We realize we can identify with what Christ suffered on the cross for us	We accuse God of being unjust and perhaps lead others to reject him
We are sensitized to the amount of suffering in the world	We refuse to be open to any changes in our lives

Job 31:1-4 Job had not only avoided committing the great sin of adultery, he had not even taken the first step toward that sin by looking at a woman with lust. Job said he was innocent of both outward and inward sins. In Job 29, Job reviewed his good deeds. Here in Job 31 he listed sins he had *not* committed—in his heart (Job 31:1-12), against his neighbors (Job 31:13-23), or against God (Job 31:24-34).

Job 31:24-28 Job affirmed that depending on wealth for happiness is idolatry and denies the God of heaven. We excuse our society's obsession with money and possessions as a necessary evil or "the way it works" in the modern world. But every society in every age has valued the power and prestige that money brings. True believers must purge themselves of the deep-seated desire for more power, prestige, and possessions. They must also not withhold their resources from neighbors near and far who have desperate physical needs.

▸ **JOB 31:1-40 *(cont.)***

27 and been secretly enticed in my heart
to throw kisses at them in worship?
28 If so, I should be punished by the judges,
for it would mean I had denied the God
of heaven.

29 "Have I ever rejoiced when disaster struck
my enemies,
or become excited when harm came
their way?
30 No, I have never sinned by cursing anyone
or by asking for revenge.

31 "My servants have never said,
'He let others go hungry.'
32 I have never turned away a stranger
but have opened my doors to everyone.

33 "Have I tried to hide my sins like other people do,
concealing my guilt in my heart?
34 Have I feared the crowd
or the contempt of the masses,
so that I kept quiet and stayed indoors?

35 "If only someone would listen to me!
Look, I will sign my name to my defense.
Let the Almighty answer me.
Let my accuser write out the charges against
me.
36 I would face the accusation proudly.
I would wear it like a crown.
37 For I would tell him exactly what I have done.
I would come before him like a prince.

38 "If my land accuses me
and all its furrows cry out together,
39 or if I have stolen its crops
or murdered its owners,
40 then let thistles grow on that land instead
of wheat,
and weeds instead of barley."

Job's words are ended.

3. A YOUNG MAN ANSWERS JOB

Young Elihu rebukes the three friends for being unable to give Job a reasonable answer for why he was suffering. But he only gives a partial answer to Job's question by saying that people cannot understand all that God allows but must trust him. This was the best answer that a human could give, yet it was incomplete. Often the best human answers are incomplete because we do not have all the facts.

Elihu Responds to Job's Friends

JOB 32:1-22

Job's three friends refused to reply further to him because he kept insisting on his innocence.
2Then Elihu son of Barakel the Buzite, of the clan of
Ram, became angry. He was angry because Job refused
to admit that he had sinned and that God was right
in punishing him. 3He was also angry with Job's three
friends, for they made God* appear to be wrong by
their inability to answer Job's arguments. 4Elihu had
waited for the others to speak to Job because they
were older than he. 5But when he saw that they had
no further reply, he spoke out angrily. 6Elihu son of
Barakel the Buzite said,

"I am young and you are old,
so I held back from telling you what I think.
7 I thought, 'Those who are older should speak,
for wisdom comes with age.'
8 But there is a spirit* within people,
the breath of the Almighty within them,
that makes them intelligent.

Jb 32:3 As in ancient Hebrew scribal tradition; the Masoretic Text reads *Job.* **Jb 32:8** Or *Spirit;* also in 32:18.

Job 31:33-34 Job declared that he did not try to hide his sin as people often do. The fear that our sins will be discovered leads us to patterns of deception. We cover up with lies so that we will appear good to others. But we cannot hide from God. Do you try to keep people from seeing the real you? When you acknowledge your sins, you free yourself to receive forgiveness and a new life.

Job 32:1 If Job's friends believed he was really a good man, they would have to drop their theory that suffering is always God's punishment for evil actions. Instead of considering another viewpoint, however, they cut off the discussion. They were convinced that Job had some hidden fault or sin, so there was no point in continuing if Job would not confess it. But Job knew he had lived uprightly before God and others (Job 29) and had avoided wrong thoughts and actions (Job 31). He wasn't about to invent a sin to satisfy his friends!

Job 32:2ff When Eliphaz, Bildad, and Zophar had nothing more to say, Elihu became the fourth person to speak to Job. This was the first and only time he spoke. Apparently he was a bystander and much younger than the others (Job 32:6-7), but he introduced a new viewpoint. While Job's three friends said he was suffering from some past sins, Elihu said Job's suffering would not go away until he realized his *present* sin. He maintained that Job wasn't suffering because of sin; he was sinning because of suffering. Elihu pointed out that Job's attitude had become arrogant as he tried to defend his innocence. Elihu also said that suffering is not meant to punish us as much as it is meant to correct and restore us, to keep us on the right path.

There is much truth in Elihu's speech. He was urging Job to look at his suffering from a different perspective and with a greater purpose in mind. While his speech is on a higher spiritual plateau than the others, Elihu still wrongly assumed that a correct response to suffering always brings healing and restoration (Job 33:23-30) and that suffering is always in some way connected to sin (Job 34:11).

Job 32:7-9 "The breath of the Almighty within them . . . makes them intelligent." It is not enough to recognize a great truth; it must be lived out each day. Elihu recognized the truth that God was the only source of real wisdom, but he did not use God's wisdom to help Job. While he recognized where wisdom

9 Sometimes the elders are not wise.
Sometimes the aged do not understand justice.
10 So listen to me,
and let me tell you what I think.

11 "I have waited all this time,
listening very carefully to your arguments,
listening to you grope for words.
12 I have listened,
but not one of you has refuted Job
or answered his arguments.
13 And don't tell me, 'He is too wise for us.
Only God can convince him.'
14 If Job had been arguing with me,
I would not answer with your kind of logic!
15 You sit there baffled,
with nothing more to say.
16 Should I continue to wait, now that you are silent?
Must I also remain silent?
17 No, I will say my piece.
I will speak my mind.
18 For I am full of pent-up words,
and the spirit within me urges me on.
19 I am like a cask of wine without a vent,
like a new wineskin ready to burst!
20 I must speak to find relief,
so let me give my answers.
21 I won't play favorites
or try to flatter anyone.
22 For if I tried flattery,
my Creator would soon destroy me.

Elihu Presents His Case against Job

JOB 33:1-33

1 "Listen to my words, Job;
pay attention to what I have to say.
2 Now that I have begun to speak,
let me continue.
3 I speak with all sincerity;
I speak the truth.
4 For the Spirit of God has made me,
and the breath of the Almighty gives me life.
5 Answer me, if you can;
make your case and take your stand.
6 Look, you and I both belong to God.
I, too, was formed from clay.
7 So you don't need to be afraid of me.
I won't come down hard on you.

8 "You have spoken in my hearing,
and I have heard your very words.
9 You said, 'I am pure; I am without sin;
I am innocent; I have no guilt.
10 God is picking a quarrel with me,
and he considers me his enemy.
11 He puts my feet in the stocks
and watches my every move.'

12 "But you are wrong, and I will show you why.
For God is greater than any human being.
13 So why are you bringing a charge against him?
Why say he does not respond to people's
complaints?
14 For God speaks again and again,
though people do not recognize it.
15 He speaks in dreams, in visions of the night,
when deep sleep falls on people
as they lie in their beds.
16 He whispers in their ears
and terrifies them with warnings.
17 He makes them turn from doing wrong;
he keeps them from pride.
18 He protects them from the grave,
from crossing over the river of death.

19 "Or God disciplines people with pain on their
sickbeds,
with ceaseless aching in their bones.
20 They lose their appetite
for even the most delicious food.
21 Their flesh wastes away,
and their bones stick out.
22 They are at death's door;
the angels of death wait for them.

23 "But if an angel from heaven appears—
a special messenger to intercede for a person
and declare that he is upright—
24 he will be gracious and say,
'Rescue him from the grave,
for I have found a ransom for his life.'
25 Then his body will become as healthy
as a child's,
firm and youthful again.

---

came from, he did not seek to acquire it. Becoming wise is an ongoing, lifelong pursuit. Don't be content just to know *about* wisdom; make it a part of your life.

Job 33:13 Being informed brings a sense of security. It's natural to want to know what's happening in our lives. Job wanted to know what was going on and why he was suffering. In previous chapters, we sense his frustration. Elihu claimed to have the answer for Job's biggest question, "Why doesn't God tell me what is happening?" Elihu told Job that God was trying to answer him, but he was not listening. Elihu misjudged God on this point. If God were to answer all our questions, we would not be adequately tested. What if God had said, "Job, Satan's going to test you and afflict you, but in the end you'll be healed and get everything back"? Job's greatest test was not the pain but rather that he didn't know *why* he was suffering. Our greatest test may be that we must trust God's goodness even though we don't understand why our lives are going a certain way. We must learn to trust in *God*, who is good, and not in the goodness of life.

Job 33:14-24 Elihu's point was that God had spoken again and again. He spoke in dreams and visions (Job 33:15-18), through suffering (Job 33:19-22), and by mediating angels (Job 33:23-24). Job already knew that. Elihu accused Job of not listening to God, which was not true.

▶ **JOB 33:1-33 *(cont.)***

26 When he prays to God,
he will be accepted.
And God will receive him with joy
and restore him to good standing.
27 He will declare to his friends,
'I sinned and twisted the truth,
but it was not worth it.*
28 God rescued me from the grave,
and now my life is filled with light.'

29 "Yes, God does these things
again and again for people.
30 He rescues them from the grave
so they may enjoy the light of life.
31 Mark this well, Job. Listen to me,
for I have more to say.
32 But if you have anything to say, go ahead.
Speak, for I am anxious to see you justified.
33 But if not, then listen to me.
Keep silent and I will teach you wisdom!"

Elihu Accuses Job of Arrogance

JOB 34:1-37

Then Elihu said:

2 "Listen to me, you wise men.
Pay attention, you who have knowledge.
3 Job said, 'The ear tests the words it hears
just as the mouth distinguishes between foods.'
4 So let us discern for ourselves what is right;
let us learn together what is good.
5 For Job also said, 'I am innocent,
but God has taken away my rights.
6 I am innocent, but they call me a liar.
My suffering is incurable, though I have not sinned.'
7 "Tell me, has there ever been a man like Job,
with his thirst for irreverent talk?
8 He chooses evil people as companions.
He spends his time with wicked men.
9 He has even said, 'Why waste time
trying to please God?'

10 "Listen to me, you who have understanding.
Everyone knows that God doesn't sin!
The Almighty can do no wrong.
11 He repays people according to their deeds.
He treats people as they deserve.
12 Truly, God will not do wrong.
The Almighty will not twist justice.
13 Did someone else put the world in his care?
Who set the whole world in place?
14 If God were to take back his spirit
and withdraw his breath,
15 all life would cease,
and humanity would turn again to dust.

16 "Now listen to me if you are wise.
Pay attention to what I say.
17 Could God govern if he hated justice?
Are you going to condemn the almighty judge?
18 For he says to kings, 'You are wicked,'
and to nobles, 'You are unjust.'
19 He doesn't care how great a person may be,
and he pays no more attention to the rich than to the poor.
He made them all.
20 In a moment they die.
In the middle of the night they pass away;
the mighty are removed without human hand.

21 "For God watches how people live;
he sees everything they do.
22 No darkness is thick enough
to hide the wicked from his eyes.

Jb 33:27 Greek version reads *but he* [God] *did not punish me as my sin deserved.*

Job 34:10-15 God doesn't sin and is never unjust, Elihu claimed. Throughout this book, Eliphaz, Bildad, Zophar, and Elihu all have elements of truth in their speeches. Unfortunately, the nuggets of truth are buried under layers of false assumptions and incorrect conclusions. Although we might have a wealth of Bible knowledge and life experiences, we must make sure our conclusions are consistent with all of God's Word, not just parts of it.

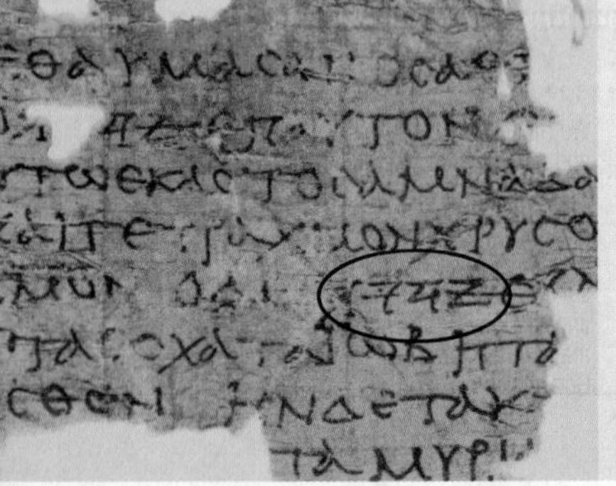

Ancient Manuscript of Job

This manuscript is fascinating because it is a Greek Old Testament text with the name of Yahweh written in Hebrew (see the middle of the fifth line). In English, this reads "And they consoled him and comforted him because of all the trials the LORD [YHWH] had brought against him" (Job 42:11). The scribe filled in the Hebrew tetragrammaton YHWH where the name would normally have been *kurios* in Greek.

Why the difference? The name of God was considered so holy that it wasn't to be spoken at all—in fact, even in Hebrew the vowels were never attached to the name of God. When the name of God would appear in the text, readers would say *adonay*, the Hebrew word meaning "my Lord, my master," instead. So the scribe of this manuscript wanted to highlight the importance of God's name by refusing to even translate it into Greek. This kind of special treatment of God's name in writing can also be seen in New Testament manuscripts, where the names Jesus, Christ, Lord, God, and Spirit were written in a special way.

23 We don't set the time
when we will come before God in judgment.
24 He brings the mighty to ruin without asking
anyone,
and he sets up others in their place.
25 He knows what they do,
and in the night he overturns and
destroys them.
26 He strikes them down because they are wicked,
doing it openly for all to see.
27 For they turned away from following him.
They have no respect for any of his ways.
28 They cause the poor to cry out, catching God's
attention.
He hears the cries of the needy.
29 But if he chooses to remain quiet,
who can criticize him?
When he hides his face, no one can find him,
whether an individual or a nation.
30 He prevents the godless from ruling
so they cannot be a snare to the people.
31 "Why don't people say to God, 'I have sinned,
but I will sin no more'?
32 Or 'I don't know what evil I have done—tell me.
If I have done wrong, I will stop at once'?
33 "Must God tailor his justice to your demands?
But you have rejected him!
The choice is yours, not mine.
Go ahead, share your wisdom with us.
34 After all, bright people will tell me,
and wise people will hear me say,
35 'Job speaks out of ignorance;
his words lack insight.'
36 Job, you deserve the maximum penalty
for the wicked way you have talked.
37 For you have added rebellion to your sin;
you show no respect,
and you speak many angry words against God."

Elihu Reminds Job of God's Justice

JOB 35:1-36:21

Then Elihu said:

2 "Do you think it is right for you to claim,
'I am righteous before God'?
3 For you also ask, 'What's in it for me?
What's the use of living a righteous life?'

4 "I will answer you
and all your friends, too.
5 Look up into the sky,
and see the clouds high above you.
6 If you sin, how does that affect God?
Even if you sin again and again,
what effect will it have on him?
7 If you are good, is this some great gift to him?
What could you possibly give him?
8 No, your sins affect only people like yourself,
and your good deeds also affect only humans.

9 "People cry out when they are oppressed.
They groan beneath the power of the mighty.
10 Yet they don't ask, 'Where is God my Creator,
the one who gives songs in the night?
11 Where is the one who makes us smarter than
the animals
and wiser than the birds of the sky?'
12 And when they cry out, God does not answer
because of their pride.
13 But it is wrong to say God doesn't listen,
to say the Almighty isn't concerned.
14 You say you can't see him,
but he will bring justice if you will only wait.*
15 You say he does not respond to sinners with anger
and is not greatly concerned about wickedness.*
16 But you are talking nonsense, Job.
You have spoken like a fool."

36:1 Elihu continued speaking:

2 "Let me go on, and I will show you the truth.
For I have not finished defending God!
3 I will present profound arguments
for the righteousness of my Creator.
4 I am telling you nothing but the truth,
for I am a man of great knowledge.

5 "God is mighty, but he does not despise anyone!
He is mighty in both power and
understanding.
6 He does not let the wicked live
but gives justice to the afflicted.
7 He never takes his eyes off the innocent,
but he sets them on thrones with kings
and exalts them forever.
8 If they are bound in chains
and caught up in a web of trouble,
9 he shows them the reason.
He shows them their sins of pride.
10 He gets their attention
and commands that they turn from evil.

11 "If they listen and obey God,
they will be blessed with prosperity
throughout their lives.
All their years will be pleasant.

Jb 35:13-14 These verses can also be translated as follows: [13]*Indeed, God doesn't listen to their empty plea; / the Almighty is not concerned. /* [14]*How much less will he listen when you say you don't see him, / and that your case is before him and you're waiting for justice.* **Jb 35:15** As in Greek and Latin versions; the meaning of this Hebrew word is uncertain.

Job 35:1ff Sometimes we wonder if being faithful to our convictions really does any good at all. Elihu spoke to this very point. His conclusion was that God is still concerned even though he doesn't intervene immediately in every situation. In the broad scope of time, God executes justice. We have his promise on that. Don't lose hope. Wait upon God. He notices your right living and your faith.

▸ **JOB 35:1–36:21** ***(cont.)***

12 But if they refuse to listen to him,
they will be killed by the sword*
and die from lack of understanding.
13 For the godless are full of resentment.
Even when he punishes them,
they refuse to cry out to him for help.
14 They die when they are young,
after wasting their lives in immoral living.
15 But by means of their suffering, he rescues
those who suffer.
For he gets their attention through adversity.

16 "God is leading you away from danger, Job,
to a place free from distress.
He is setting your table with the best food.
17 But you are obsessed with whether the godless
will be judged.
Don't worry, judgment and justice will be
upheld.
18 But watch out, or you may be seduced by wealth.*
Don't let yourself be bribed into sin.
19 Could all your wealth*
or all your mighty efforts
keep you from distress?
20 Do not long for the cover of night,
for that is when people will be destroyed.*
21 Be on guard! Turn back from evil,
for God sent this suffering
to keep you from a life of evil.

Elihu Reminds Job of God's Power

JOB 36:22–37:24

22 "Look, God is all-powerful.
Who is a teacher like him?
23 No one can tell him what to do,
or say to him, 'You have done wrong.'
24 Instead, glorify his mighty works,
singing songs of praise.
25 Everyone has seen these things,
though only from a distance.

26 "Look, God is greater than we can understand.
His years cannot be counted.
27 He draws up the water vapor
and then distills it into rain.
28 The rain pours down from the clouds,
and everyone benefits.
29 Who can understand the spreading of the clouds
and the thunder that rolls forth from heaven?
30 See how he spreads the lightning around him
and how it lights up the depths of the sea.
31 By these mighty acts he nourishes* the people,
giving them food in abundance.
32 He fills his hands with lightning bolts
and hurls each at its target.
33 The thunder announces his presence;
the storm announces his indignant anger.*

37:1"My heart pounds as I think of this.
It trembles within me.

Jb 36:12 Or *they will cross the river* [of death]. **Jb 36:18** Or *But don't let your anger lead you to mockery.* **Jb 36:19** Or *Could all your cries for help.* **Jb 36:16-20** The meaning of the Hebrew in this passage is uncertain. **Jb 36:31** Or *he governs.* **Jb 36:33** Or *even the cattle know when a storm is coming.* The meaning of the Hebrew is uncertain.

GOD SPEAKS

On various occasions in the Old Testament, God chose to communicate audibly with individuals. God will always find a way to make contact with those who want to know him. Some of those occasions are listed here.

Whom He Spoke To	*What He Said*	*Reference*
Adam and Eve	Confronted them about sin	Gen 3:8-13
Noah	Gave him directions about building the boat	Gen 6:13-22; 7:1; 8:15-17
Abraham	Commanded him to follow God's leading and promised to bless him	Gen 12:1-9
	Tested his obedience by commanding him to sacrifice his son	Gen 22:1-14
Jacob	Permitted him to go to Egypt	Gen 46:1-4
Moses	Sent him to lead the people out of Egypt	Exod 3:1-10
	Gave him the Ten Commandments	Exod 19:1–20:20
Moses, Aaron, Miriam	Pronounced judgment on a family conflict	Num 12:1-15
Joshua	Promised to be with him as he was with Moses	Josh 1:1-9
Samuel	Chose him to be his spokesman	1 Sam 3:1-18
Isaiah	Sent him to the people with his message	Isa 6:1-13
Jeremiah	Encouraged him to be his prophet	Jer 1:4-10
Ezekiel	Sent him to Israel to warn them of coming judgment	Ezek 2:1-8

Job 36:26 One theme in the poetic literature of the Bible is that God is incomprehensible; we cannot know him completely. We can have some knowledge about him, for the Bible is full of details about who God is, how we can know him, and how we can have an eternal relationship with him. But we can never know enough to answer all of life's questions (Eccl 3:11), to predict our own future, or to manipulate God for our own ends. Life always creates more questions than answers, and we must constantly go to God for fresh insights into life's dilemmas. (See Job 37:19-24.)

2 Listen carefully to the thunder of
God's voice
as it rolls from his mouth.
3 It rolls across the heavens,
and his lightning flashes in every
direction.
4 Then comes the roaring of the thunder—
the tremendous voice of his majesty.
He does not restrain it when he speaks.
5 God's voice is glorious in the thunder.
We can't even imagine the greatness
of his power.

6 "He directs the snow to fall on the earth
and tells the rain to pour down.
7 Then everyone stops working
so they can watch his power.
8 The wild animals take cover
and stay inside their dens.
9 The stormy wind comes from its chamber,
and the driving winds bring the cold.
10 God's breath sends the ice,
freezing wide expanses of water.
11 He loads the clouds with moisture,
and they flash with his lightning.
12 The clouds churn about at his direction.
They do whatever he commands throughout
the earth.
13 He makes these things happen either
to punish people
or to show his unfailing love.

14 "Pay attention to this, Job.
Stop and consider the wonderful miracles
of God!
15 Do you know how God controls the storm
and causes the lightning to flash from his
clouds?
16 Do you understand how he moves the clouds
with wonderful perfection and skill?
17 When you are sweltering in your clothes
and the south wind dies down and everything
is still,
18 he makes the skies reflect the heat like a
bronze mirror.
Can you do that?

19 "So teach the rest of us what to say to God.
We are too ignorant to make our own arguments.
20 Should God be notified that I want to speak?
Can people even speak when they are
confused?*
21 We cannot look at the sun,
for it shines brightly in the sky
when the wind clears away the clouds.
22 So also, golden splendor comes from the
mountain of God.*
He is clothed in dazzling splendor.
23 We cannot imagine the power of the Almighty;
but even though he is just and righteous,
he does not destroy us.
24 No wonder people everywhere fear him.
All who are wise show him reverence."

Jb 37:20 Or *speak without being swallowed up?* **Jb 37:22** Or *from the north;* or *from the abode.*

4. GOD ANSWERS JOB

Instead of answering Job's question directly, God asks Job a series of questions which no human could possibly answer. Job responds by recognizing that God's ways are best. During difficult times, we, too, must humbly remember our position before the eternal, holy, incomprehensible God.

The Lord Challenges Job

JOB 38:1-41

Then the Lord answered Job from the whirlwind:
2 "Who is this that questions my
wisdom
with such ignorant words?
3 Brace yourself like a man,
because I have some questions for you,
and you must answer them.

4 "Where were you when I laid the foundations
of the earth?
Tell me, if you know so much.

Job 37:2 Nothing can compare to God. His power and presence are awesome, and when he speaks, we must listen. Too often we presume to speak for God (as did Job's friends), to put words in his mouth, to take him for granted, or to interpret his silence to mean that he is absent or unconcerned. But God cares. He is in control, and he will speak. Be ready to hear his message—in the Bible, through the Holy Spirit, through prayer, and through circumstances and relationships.

Job 37:21-24 Elihu concluded his speech with the tremendous truth that faith in God is far more important than Job's desire for an explanation for his suffering. He came so close to helping Job but then went down the wrong path. Significantly, it is here that God himself broke into the discussion to draw the right conclusions from this important truth (Job 38:1ff).

Job 37:23 Elihu stressed God's sovereignty over all of nature as a reminder of his sovereignty over our lives. God is in control—he directs, preserves, and maintains his created order. Although we can't see it, God is divinely governing the moral and political affairs of people as well. By spending time observing the majestic and intricate parts of God's creation, we can be reminded of his power in every aspect of our lives.

Job 38:1ff Out of a whirlwind, God spoke. Surprisingly, he didn't answer any of Job's questions; Job's questions were not at the heart of the issue. Instead, God used Job's ignorance of the earth's natural order to reveal his ignorance of God's moral order. If Job did not understand the workings of God's physical creation, how could he possibly understand God's mind and character? There is no standard or criterion higher than God himself by which to judge. God himself is the standard. Our only option is to submit to his authority and rest in his care.

▸ **JOB 38:1-41 *(cont.)***

5 Who determined its dimensions
and stretched out the surveying line?
6 What supports its foundations,
and who laid its cornerstone
7 as the morning stars sang together
and all the angels* shouted for joy?

8 "Who kept the sea inside its boundaries
as it burst from the womb,
9 and as I clothed it with clouds
and wrapped it in thick darkness?
10 For I locked it behind barred gates,
limiting its shores.
11 I said, 'This far and no farther will you come.
Here your proud waves must stop!'

12 "Have you ever commanded the morning
to appear
and caused the dawn to rise in the east?
13 Have you made daylight spread to the ends
of the earth,
to bring an end to the night's wickedness?
14 As the light approaches,
the earth takes shape like clay pressed
beneath a seal;
it is robed in brilliant colors.*
15 The light disturbs the wicked
and stops the arm that is raised in violence.

16 "Have you explored the springs from which
the seas come?
Have you explored their depths?
17 Do you know where the gates of death are located?
Have you seen the gates of utter gloom?
18 Do you realize the extent of the earth?
Tell me about it if you know!

19 "Where does light come from,
and where does darkness go?
20 Can you take each to its home?
Do you know how to get there?
21 But of course you know all this!
For you were born before it was all created,
and you are so very experienced!

22 "Have you visited the storehouses of the snow
or seen the storehouses of hail?
23 (I have reserved them as weapons for the time
of trouble,
for the day of battle and war.)
24 Where is the path to the source of light?
Where is the home of the east wind?

25 "Who created a channel for the torrents of rain?
Who laid out the path for the lightning?
26 Who makes the rain fall on barren land,
in a desert where no one lives?
27 Who sends rain to satisfy the parched ground
and make the tender grass spring up?

28 "Does the rain have a father?
Who gives birth to the dew?
29 Who is the mother of the ice?
Who gives birth to the frost from
the heavens?
30 For the water turns to ice as hard as rock,
and the surface of the water freezes.

31 "Can you direct the movement of the stars—
binding the cluster of the Pleiades
or loosening the cords of Orion?
32 Can you direct the sequence of the seasons
or guide the Bear with her cubs across the
heavens?
33 Do you know the laws of the universe?
Can you use them to regulate the earth?

34 "Can you shout to the clouds
and make it rain?

Jb 38:7 Hebrew *the sons of God.* **Jb 38:14** Or *its features stand out like folds in a robe.*

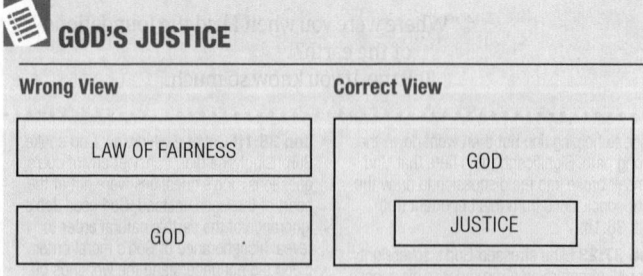

GOD'S JUSTICE

Wrong View	Correct View
LAW OF FAIRNESS	GOD
GOD	JUSTICE
There is a law of fairness or justice that is higher and more absolute than God. It is binding even for God. God must act in response to that law in order to be fair. Our response is to appeal to that law.	God himself is the standard of justice. He uses his power according to his own moral perfection. Thus, whatever he does is fair, even if we don't understand it. Our response is to appeal directly to him.

Job 38:22-23 God said he was reserving the storehouses of the snow and hail for times of trouble. God used hail to help Joshua and the Israelites win a battle (Josh 10:11). Just as armies keep weapons in the armory, God has all the forces of nature in his control. Sometimes he uses them to confound those opposed to him or his people. Job couldn't even begin to know all of God's resources.

Job 38:22-35 God stated that he has all the forces of nature at his command and that he can unleash or restrain them at will. No one completely understands such common occurrences as rain or snow, and no one can command them—only God who created them has that power. God's point was that if Job could not explain such common events in nature, how could he possibly explain or question God? And if nature is beyond our grasp, God's moral purposes may not be what we imagine either.

35 Can you make lightning appear
and cause it to strike as you direct?
36 Who gives intuition to the heart
and instinct to the mind?
37 Who is wise enough to count all the clouds?
Who can tilt the water jars of heaven
38 when the parched ground is dry
and the soil has hardened into clods?

39 "Can you stalk prey for a lioness
and satisfy the young lions' appetites
40 as they lie in their dens
or crouch in the thicket?
41 Who provides food for the ravens
when their young cry out to God
and wander about in hunger?

The Lord's Challenge Continues

JOB 39:1–40:2

1 "Do you know when the wild goats give birth?
Have you watched as deer are born in the wild?
2 Do you know how many months they carry
their young?
Are you aware of the time of their delivery?
3 They crouch down to give birth to their young
and deliver their offspring.
4 Their young grow up in the open fields,
then leave home and never return.

5 "Who gives the wild donkey its freedom?
Who untied its ropes?
6 I have placed it in the wilderness;
its home is the wasteland.
7 It hates the noise of the city
and has no driver to shout at it.
8 The mountains are its pastureland,
where it searches for every blade of grass.

9 "Will the wild ox consent to being tamed?
Will it spend the night in your stall?
10 Can you hitch a wild ox to a plow?
Will it plow a field for you?
11 Given its strength, can you trust it?
Can you leave and trust the ox to do your work?
12 Can you rely on it to bring home your grain
and deliver it to your threshing floor?

13 "The ostrich flaps her wings grandly,
but they are no match for the feathers
of the stork.
14 She lays her eggs on top of the earth,
letting them be warmed in the dust.
15 She doesn't worry that a foot might crush them
or a wild animal might destroy them.
16 She is harsh toward her young,
as if they were not her own.
She doesn't care if they die.
17 For God has deprived her of wisdom.
He has given her no understanding.
18 But whenever she jumps up to run,
she passes the swiftest horse with its rider.

19 "Have you given the horse its strength
or clothed its neck with a flowing mane?
20 Did you give it the ability to leap like a locust?
Its majestic snorting is terrifying!
21 It paws the earth and rejoices in its strength
when it charges out to battle.
22 It laughs at fear and is unafraid.
It does not run from the sword.
23 The arrows rattle against it,
and the spear and javelin flash.
24 It paws the ground fiercely
and rushes forward into battle when
the ram's horn blows.
25 It snorts at the sound of the horn.
It senses the battle in the distance.
It quivers at the captain's commands
and the noise of battle.

Job 38:31-32 These are constellations, and they are all under God's control.

Job 39:1ff God asked Job several questions about the animal kingdom in order to demonstrate how limited Job's knowledge really was. God was not seeking answers from Job. Instead, he was getting Job to recognize and submit to God's power and sovereignty. Only then could he hear what God was really saying to him.

"Can you make lightning appear and cause it to strike as you direct?"
Job 38:35

▸ **JOB 39:1–40:2 *(cont.)***

26 "Is it your wisdom that makes the hawk soar
and spread its wings toward the south?
27 Is it at your command that the eagle rises
to the heights to make its nest?
28 It lives on the cliffs,
making its home on a distant, rocky crag.
29 From there it hunts its prey,
keeping watch with piercing eyes.
30 Its young gulp down blood.
Where there's a carcass, there you'll find it."

40:1 Then the LORD said to Job,

2 "Do you still want to argue with the Almighty?
You are God's critic, but do you have the answers?"

Job Responds to the LORD

JOB 40:3-5

Then Job replied to the LORD,

4 "I am nothing—how could I ever find the answers?
I will cover my mouth with my hand.
5 I have said too much already.
I have nothing more to say."

The LORD Challenges Job Again

JOB 40:6-24

Then the LORD answered Job from the whirlwind:

7 "Brace yourself like a man,
because I have some questions for you,
and you must answer them.

8 "Will you discredit my justice
and condemn me just to prove you are right?
9 Are you as strong as God?
Can you thunder with a voice like his?
10 All right, put on your glory and splendor,
your honor and majesty.
11 Give vent to your anger.
Let it overflow against the proud.
12 Humiliate the proud with a glance;
walk on the wicked where they stand.
13 Bury them in the dust.
Imprison them in the world of the dead.
14 Then even I would praise you,
for your own strength would save you.

15 "Take a look at Behemoth,*
which I made, just as I made you.
It eats grass like an ox.
16 See its powerful loins
and the muscles of its belly.
17 Its tail is as strong as a cedar.
The sinews of its thighs are knit tightly together.
18 Its bones are tubes of bronze.
Its limbs are bars of iron.
19 It is a prime example of God's handiwork,
and only its Creator can threaten it.
20 The mountains offer it their best food,
where all the wild animals play.
21 It lies under the lotus plants,*
hidden by the reeds in the marsh.
22 The lotus plants give it shade
among the willows beside the stream.
23 It is not disturbed by the raging river,
not concerned when the swelling Jordan rushes around it.
24 No one can catch it off guard
or put a ring in its nose and lead it away.

Jb 40:15 The identification of Behemoth is disputed, ranging from an earthly creature to a mythical sea monster in ancient literature. **Jb 40:21** Or *bramble bushes;* also in 40:22.

Job 40:2-5 How do you argue with or criticize almighty God? Do you demand answers when things don't go your way, you lose a job, someone close to you is ill or dies, finances are tight, you fail, or unexpected changes occur? The next time you are tempted to complain to God, consider how much he loves you. And remember Job's reaction when he had his chance to speak. Are you worse off than Job or more righteous than he? Give God a chance to reveal his greater purposes for you, but remember that they may unfold over the course of your life and not at the moment you desire.

Job 40:4 Throughout his time of suffering, Job longed to have an opportunity to plead his innocence before God. Here God appeared to Job and gave him that opportunity. But Job decided to remain quiet because it was no longer necessary for him to speak. God had shown Job that, as a limited human being, he had neither the ability to judge the God who created the universe nor the right to ask why. God's actions do not depend on ours. He will do what he knows is best, regardless of what we think is fair. It is important to note, however, that God came to Job, demonstrating his love and care for him.

FOUR VIEWS OF SUFFERING

Satan's view	People believe in God only when they are prospering and not suffering. This is wrong.
The view of Job's three friends	Suffering is God's judgment for sin. This is not always true.
Elihu's view	Suffering is God's way to teach, discipline, and refine. This is true, but an incomplete explanation.
God's view	Suffering causes us to trust God for who he is, not what he does.

Job 41:9-11 It is foolish for people to think they can stand up against God when they are afraid to confront even a crocodile. How much more powerful is God!

The LORD's Challenge Continues

JOB 41:1-34

1* "Can you catch Leviathan* with a hook
or put a noose around its jaw?
2 Can you tie it with a rope through the nose
or pierce its jaw with a spike?
3 Will it beg you for mercy
or implore you for pity?
4 Will it agree to work for you,
to be your slave for life?
5 Can you make it a pet like a bird,
or give it to your little girls to play with?
6 Will merchants try to buy it
to sell it in their shops?
7 Will its hide be hurt by spears
or its head by a harpoon?
8 If you lay a hand on it,
you will certainly remember the battle
that follows.
You won't try that again!
9*No, it is useless to try to capture it.
The hunter who attempts it will be
knocked down.
10 And since no one dares to disturb it,
who then can stand up to me?
11 Who has given me anything that I need
to pay back?
Everything under heaven is mine.
12 "I want to emphasize Leviathan's limbs
and its enormous strength and
graceful form.
13 Who can strip off its hide,
and who can penetrate its double layer
of armor?*
14 Who could pry open its jaws?
For its teeth are terrible!
15 Its scales are like rows of shields
tightly sealed together.
16 They are so close together
that no air can get between them.
17 Each scale sticks tight to the next.
They interlock and cannot be penetrated.

18 "When it sneezes, it flashes light!
Its eyes are like the red of dawn.
19 Lightning leaps from its mouth;
flames of fire flash out.
20 Smoke streams from its nostrils
like steam from a pot heated over burning
rushes.
21 Its breath would kindle coals,
for flames shoot from its mouth.

22 "The tremendous strength in Leviathan's neck
strikes terror wherever it goes.
23 Its flesh is hard and firm
and cannot be penetrated.
24 Its heart is hard as rock,
hard as a millstone.
25 When it rises, the mighty are afraid,
gripped by terror.
26 No sword can stop it,
no spear, dart, or javelin.
27 Iron is nothing but straw to that creature,
and bronze is like rotten wood.
28 Arrows cannot make it flee.
Stones shot from a sling are like bits
of grass.
29 Clubs are like a blade of grass,
and it laughs at the swish of javelins.
30 Its belly is covered with scales as sharp as glass.
It plows up the ground as it drags through
the mud.

Jb 41:1a Verses 41:1-8 are numbered 40:25-32 in Hebrew text. **Jb 41:1b** The identification of Leviathan is disputed, ranging from an earthly creature to a mythical sea monster in ancient literature. **Jb 41:9** Verses 41:9-34 are numbered 41:1-26 in Hebrew text. **Jb 41:13** As in Greek version; Hebrew reads *its bridle?*

WHEN WE SUFFER

Here are six questions to ask ourselves when we suffer, and what to do if the answer is yes.

Questions	Our Response
Am I being punished by God for sin?	Confess known sin.
Is Satan attacking me as I try to survive as a Christian?	Call on God for strength.
Am I being prepared for a special service, learning to be compassionate to those who suffer?	Resist self-pity. Ask God to open up doors of opportunity and help you discover others who suffer as you do.
Am I specifically selected for testing, like Job?	Accept help from the body of believers. Trust God to work his purpose through you.
Is my suffering a result of natural consequences for which I am not directly responsible?	Recognize that in a sinful world, both good and evil people will suffer. But the good person has a promise from God that those sufferings will one day come to an end.
Is my suffering due to some unknown reason?	Don't draw inward from the pain. Proclaim your faith in God, know that he cares, and wait patiently for his aid.

▸ **JOB 41:1-34 *(cont.)***

31 "Leviathan makes the water boil with
its commotion.
It stirs the depths like a pot
of ointment.
32 The water glistens in its wake,
making the sea look white.
33 Nothing on earth is its equal,
no other creature so fearless.
34 Of all the creatures, it is the
proudest.
It is the king of beasts."

5. JOB IS RESTORED

In response to God's speech, Job humbles himself. God rebukes his three friends for adding to Job's suffering by their false assumptions and critical attitudes. Job's material possessions and family are restored, and he receives even greater blessings than he had before. Those who persist in trusting God will be rewarded.

Job Responds to the Lord

JOB 42:1-6

Then Job replied to the Lord:

2 "I know that you can do anything,
and no one can stop you.
3 You asked, 'Who is this that questions my wisdom
with such ignorance?'
It is I—and I was talking about things I knew
nothing about,
things far too wonderful for me.
4 You said, 'Listen and I will speak!
I have some questions for you,
and you must answer them.'
5 I had only heard about you before,
but now I have seen you with my own eyes.
6 I take back everything I said,
and I sit in dust and ashes to show my
repentance."

Conclusion: The Lord Blesses Job

JOB 42:7-17

After the Lord had finished speaking to Job, he said to
Eliphaz the Temanite: "I am angry with you and your
two friends, for you have not spoken accurately about
me, as my servant Job has. 8So take seven bulls and
seven rams and go to my servant Job and offer a burnt
offering for yourselves. My servant Job will pray for
you, and I will accept his prayer on your behalf. I will
not treat you as you deserve, for you have not spoken
accurately about me, as my servant Job has." 9So Eliphaz the Temanite, Bildad the Shuhite, and Zophar
the Naamathite did as the Lord commanded them,
and the Lord accepted Job's prayer.
10When Job prayed for his friends, the Lord restored
his fortunes. In fact, the Lord gave him twice as much
as before! 11Then all his brothers, sisters, and former
friends came and feasted with him in his home. And
they consoled him and comforted him because of all
the trials the Lord had brought against him. And each
of them brought him a gift of money* and a gold ring.
12So the Lord blessed Job in the second half of his
life even more than in the beginning. For now he had
14,000 sheep, 6,000 camels, 1,000 teams of oxen, and
1,000 female donkeys. 13He also gave Job seven more
sons and three more daughters. 14He named his first
daughter Jemimah, the second Keziah, and the third

Jb 42:11 Hebrew *a kesitah;* the value or weight of the kesitah is no longer known.

Job 42:1ff Throughout the book, Job's friends had asked him to admit his sin and ask for forgiveness, and eventually Job did indeed repent. Ironically, Job's repentance was not the kind called for by his friends. He asked for forgiveness, not for committing secret sins, but for questioning God's sovereignty and justice. Job repented of his attitude and acknowledged God's great power and perfect justice. We sin when we angrily ask, "If God is in control, how could he let this happen?" Because we are locked into time, unable to see beyond today, we cannot know the reasons for everything that happens. Thus, we must often choose between doubt and trust. Will you trust God with your unanswered questions?

Job 42:2-4 Job was quoting the Lord's earlier questions to him (Job 38:2-3). He openly and honestly faced God and admitted that he was the one who had been foolish. Are you using what you can't understand as an excuse for your lack of trust? Admit to God that you don't even have enough faith to trust him. True faith begins in such humility.

Job 42:7-8 God made it clear that Job's friends were wrong. The fact that God did not mention any specific sins shows that God confirmed Job's claim to have led a devout and obedient life. Job's friends had made the error of assuming that Job's suffering was caused by some great sin. They were judging Job without knowing what God was doing. We must be careful to avoid making judgments about a person because God may be working in ways we know nothing about.

Job 42:8-10 After receiving much criticism, Job was still able to pray for his three friends. It is difficult to forgive someone who has accused us of wrongdoing, but Job did. Are you praying for those who have hurt you? Can you forgive them? Follow the actions of Job and pray for those who have wronged you.

Job 42:10-11 Would the message of the book of Job change if God had not restored to Job his former blessings? No. God is still sovereign. Jesus said that anyone who gives up something for the Kingdom of God will be repaid (Luke 18:29-30). Our restoration may or may not be the same kind as Job's, which was both spiritual and material. Our complete restoration may not be in this life—but it *will* happen. God loves us, and he is just. He not only will restore whatever we have lost unjustly, but he also will give us more than we can imagine as we live with him in eternity. Cling tightly to your faith through all your trials, and you, too, will be rewarded by God—if not now, then in the life to come.

Keren-happuch. 15In all the land no women were as lovely as the daughters of Job. And their father put them into his will along with their brothers.

16Job lived 140 years after that, living to see four generations of his children and grandchildren. 17Then
he died, an old man who had lived a long, full life.

Job 42:17 The main question in the book of Job is timeless: Why do believers experience troubles and suffering? Through a long debate, Job's supposedly wise friends were unable to answer this question. They made a serious error, for which God rebuked them. They assumed that trouble comes only because people sin. People make the same mistake today when they assert that sickness or lack of material blessing is a sign of unconfessed sin or a lack of faith. Though following God normally leads to a happier life (but not always), and rebelling against God normally leads to an unhappy life (but not always), *God is in control*. In a world invaded by the tragic consequences of sin, calamity and suffering come to both believers and unbelievers alike.

This does not mean that God is indifferent, uncaring, unjust, or powerless to protect us. Bad things happen because we live in a fallen world, where both believers and unbelievers are hit with the tragic consequences of sin. God allows evil for a time, and he actually turns it around for our good (Rom 8:28). We may have no answers as to our *whys*, but we can be sure that God is all-powerful and knows what he is doing. The next time you face trials and dilemmas, see them as opportunities to turn to God for strength. You will find a God who only desires to show his love and compassion to you. If you can trust him in pain, confusion, and loneliness, you will win the victory and eliminate doubt, one of Satan's greatest footholds in your life. Make God your foundation. You can never be separated from his love.

So the LORD blessed Job
in the second half of his life
even more than in the beginning.
Job 42:12

The Birth of Israel

GOD'S CHOSEN FAMILY grew into a large nation in the land of Egypt, but it wasn't long after Joseph died that a new pharaoh decided to turn them into a nation of slaves for building his kingdom. For 400 years the Hebrews multiplied quickly as a people, but they also suffered under an increasingly oppressive yoke of slavery. Eventually the burden was so great that they cried out to God for deliverance, and he chose to act by freeing them from their slavery and fulfilling all of his covenant promises to Abraham, Isaac, and Jacob.

The Lord raised up Moses to lead his people out of slavery. After a dramatic and miraculous exit from Egypt, God revealed himself to them at Mount Sinai through the Ten Commandments and the rest of the law at Mount Sinai. God wanted to set his people apart so that the entire world would recognize them as his people and would want to follow him as well. But while Moses was meeting with God on Mount Sinai, the people began acting just like the other nations: creating their own idol to worship! This was not a great beginning for God's new nation.

The people of Israel were grateful to be delivered from slavery in Egypt, but it didn't take long for them to begin complaining about the

1900 BC — 1800 BC — 1700 BC

MESOPOTAMIA

MIDDLE BRONZE AGE (2000–1500 BC)

ISRAEL

- *1876 BC* — *Jacob moves to Egypt*
- *1805 BC* — *Joseph dies*

EGYPT

MIDDLE KINGDOM/DYNASTIES 11–12 (2106–1786 BC)

SECOND INTERMEDIATE PERIOD/DYNASTIES 13–17 (1786–1550 BC)

BOOKS	DATES	THEMES
■ EXODUS ■ LEVITICUS ■ NUMBERS ■ DEUTERONOMY ■ PSALMS	FROM: **1800 BC** TO: **1406 BC**	■ Redemption ■ Law ■ Disobedience ■ Wandering ■ Covenant Renewal

difficulty of traveling through the wilderness. God responded to their complaints with gracious, miraculous provision of water and food. Even after this, when their travels through the wilderness were about to be over, this young nation refused to trust God to give them the land that he had promised them in Canaan. Ten of the 12 scouts that were sent to look over the Promised Land were convinced that the people there were too powerful to be defeated; listening to them, the nation rebelled against God and refused to follow Moses into the land that had been promised to Abraham and Jacob. As a result, God punished them by forcing them to wander in the wilderness for 40 years, until nearly the entire generation of adults who had been delivered from Egypt died.

In spite of his people's consistent rebellion and grumbling, God remained faithful. He remembered his covenant promises to Abraham and Jacob, and he created a great and powerful nation from their descendants. God led the nation a second time to the border of the Promised Land. Moses then taught the law to a new generation of Israelites and entrusted Joshua, one of only two adults from the first generation who was allowed to enter the Promised Land, with leading the nation forward.

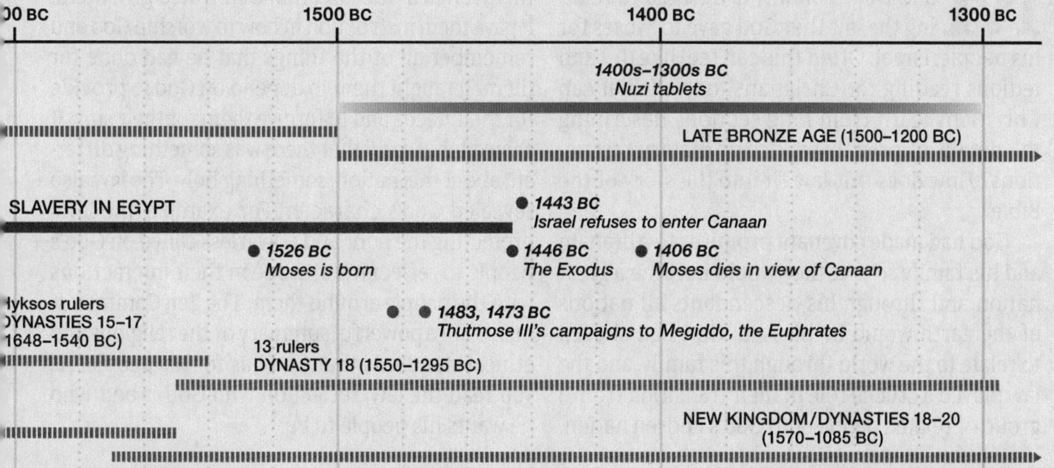

PEOPLE & CULTURE

■ **Slavery in Egypt.** A few centuries earlier, Joseph had risen from the depths of an Egyptian prison to become the second most powerful man in Egypt. He had saved the entire nation from the effects of a devastating famine, but within a few decades of his death his entire family was enslaved by a new pharaoh. The Hebrews were slaves for 400 years—long enough that they grew from a family of 70 people into a nation of nearly two million. The life of a Hebrew slave was difficult: long hours of back-breaking work, building cities in the hot sun. The slaves cried out to God for deliverance, and he heard them!

■ **Canaan.** While the Hebrews were in Egypt, many powerful peoples rose up and filled the land of Canaan. It was a fruitful and abundant land and did not just lie empty waiting for Israel to return. God was preparing his people to come back and claim the land that he had promised them, but in the meantime, other nations were thriving there. These people frightened most of the Hebrew spies when they surveyed the land after God had rescued them from Egypt.

■ **Pharaoh.** The pharaoh who put Joseph in charge of Egypt died, and the pharaohs after him did not have any loyalty to the Hebrew people. The Hebrews were cast into slavery and forced to do hard labor, yet they continued to multiply at a rapid pace. Pharaoh was afraid that his slave nation was becoming too powerful, so he issued the order that all of their male babies be slaughtered at birth. This cruel and monstrous edict was probably a major factor in the Hebrews' crying out to God for deliverance, and he heard their cries.

■ **Moses.** Pharaoh's edict to control the Hebrew population should have killed Moses. But God preserved his life through his mother's brave scheme, and even placed him in the Egyptian palace as an adopted son of Pharaoh's daughter. Moses ultimately became the leader that God chose to speak to the Hebrews and Pharaoh on his behalf, and through Moses God saved his people from their bondage. Later, Moses received the law directly from God and led the stubborn, grumbling Israelites through the wilderness to the edge of the Promised Land.

■ **Aaron and Miriam.** Moses' brother and sister were also key leaders in the birth of the nation of Israel. Miriam played an important role in saving Moses' life when he was a baby. She became a prominent leader during the Exodus period; she led the nation in praising God, and she was known as a prophet. Aaron stood alongside Moses as they confronted Pharaoh in Egypt, and he became the first high priest of the nation of Israel. The entire priesthood descended from Aaron and his sons.

■ **Joshua.** Joshua was one of only two people from the first generation of Israelites to enter the Promised Land. He was one of the 12 scouts sent to investigate the land of Canaan, and only he and Caleb came back convinced that the Lord would give this abundant land to his people, as he had promised. As a result, Joshua became the next great leader of God's people, succeeding Moses after his death east of the Jordan River.

The Law in the Birth of Israel

Much in the books of Exodus, Leviticus, and Deuteronomy is devoted to relating the law that God gave to Moses for his people, Israel. Often this can feel like dry and tedious reading for Christians today. What can Christians learn from long sections describing the details of priestly service or dietary restrictions? How does this law fit into the story of the Bible?

God had made covenant promises to Abraham and his family so that they would become a great nation and through his descendants all nations of the earth would be blessed. God had chosen to relate to the world through this family, and the law played a crucial role in their transition from a group of related people into God's chosen nation. The law gave them a structure for organizing themselves in the land that God would give them. It gave them instruction in how to worship God and remember all of the things that he had done for them. It taught them to depend on God to provide for their needs and to forgive them for their sins. It showed the world that there was something different about this nation, something holy. The law also revealed God's character. For example, the laws protecting the poor and powerless called on God's people to reflect his attitude in their interactions with the people around them. The Ten Commandments are a powerful summary of the religious and ethical standards that God has for his people. As you read the law, reflect on who God is and who he wants his people to be.

BOOKS IN THIS SECTION

EXODUS

AUTHOR: Moses

AUDIENCE: The people of Israel

PURPOSE: To record the events of Israel's deliverance from Egypt and development as a nation

DATE WRITTEN: 1450–1410 B.C.

WHERE WRITTEN: In the wilderness during Israel's wanderings

SPECIAL FEATURES: Exodus relates more miracles than any other Old Testament book and is noted for containing the Ten Commandments

LEVITICUS

AUTHOR: Moses

AUDIENCE: The people of Israel

PURPOSE: A handbook for the priests and Levites to outline their duties in worship, and a guidebook of holy living for the Hebrew people

DATE WRITTEN: 1450–1410 B.C.

WHERE WRITTEN: In the wilderness during Israel's wanderings

SPECIAL FEATURES: Holiness is mentioned more times (152) than in any other book of the Bible

For book information on **PSALMS**, see the introduction to the United Monarchy, p. 430.

NUMBERS

AUTHOR: Moses

AUDIENCE: The people of Israel

PURPOSE: To tell the story of how Israel prepared to enter the Promised Land, how they sinned and were punished, and how they prepared to try again

DATE WRITTEN: 1450–1410 B.C.

WHERE WRITTEN: In the wilderness during Israel's wanderings

SPECIAL FEATURES: It contains stories related to Israel's wilderness wanderings and a beautiful priestly blessing, often used in worship (Num 6:24-26).

DEUTERONOMY

AUTHOR: Moses (except for the final summary, which was probably written by Joshua after Moses' death)

AUDIENCE: The new generation of Israel entering the Promised Land

PURPOSE: To remind the people of what God had done and encourage them to rededicate their lives to him

DATE WRITTEN: 1406 B.C.

WHERE WRITTEN: The east side of the Jordan River, in view of Canaan

SPECIAL FEATURES: It includes many reminders to the Israelites (and to all God's people) of the blessings that come from following God's instructions.

MEGATHEMES

■ **Redemption.** God rescued Israel through their leader Moses and through mighty miracles. The Passover celebration was an annual reminder of their escape from slavery. God delivers us from the slavery of sin. Jesus Christ celebrated the Passover with his disciples at the Last Supper and then rescued all of us from sin by dying in our place.

■ **Guidance.** God guided Israel out of Egypt by using the plagues, Moses' heroic courage, the miracle of the Red Sea, and the Ten Commandments. He also guided them through the wilderness with a pillar of cloud by day and a pillar of fire by night. God is a trustworthy guide. His Word gives us the wisdom to make daily decisions and govern our lives well.

■ **Worship.** God laid out the rules for worshiping him, including a sacrificial system for praise and forgiveness along with annual festivals to remember God's provision. Seven festivals were designated as religious and national holidays. They were often celebrated in family settings. These practices teach us much about worshiping God in both celebration and quiet dedication. Our worship should demonstrate our deep devotion to God and the joy we find in serving him.

■ **Holiness.** Holy means "set apart" or "devoted." God first removed his people from Egypt; then he had to remove Egypt from the people. He showed them how to exchange Egyptian ways of living and thinking for his ways. We must devote every area of our lives to God. God desires absolute obedience in motives as well as in practices. Though we no longer observe all the worship practices of Israel, we are to have the same spirit of preparation and devotion.

■ **Rebellion.** When Moses sent scouts into the land of Canaan to survey the land, 10 of them returned to say that Israel should give up and go back to Egypt. As a result, the people refused to enter the land. Faced with a choice, Israel rebelled against God. Rebellion did not start with an uprising but with griping and murmuring against Moses and God. Rebellion against God is always a serious matter. It is not something to take lightly, for God's punishment is often severe. Our rebellion does not usually begin with all-out warfare; it starts in subtle ways—with griping and criticizing. Make sure your negative comments are not the product of a rebellious spirit.

■ **Wandering.** Because they rebelled, the Israelites wandered 40 years in the wilderness. This shows how seriously God takes sin. That was enough time for all those who had held on to Egypt's customs and values to die off. It gave time to train up a new generation in the ways of God. God judges sin because he is holy. The wanderings in the wilderness demonstrate how seriously God considers flagrant disobedience of his commands and forgetting his faithfulness to his promises. Purging our lives of sin is vital to God's purpose.

■ **Renewal.** After the older generation had died in the wilderness, Moses reviewed the mighty acts of God whereby God had liberated Israel from slavery in Egypt, and he recounted how God had helped them in spite of their disobedience. He also reviewed the law for this new generation of Israelites who would be entering the Promised Land in fulfillment of God's promises. By reviewing God's promises, mighty acts, and laws, we can learn about his character. We come to know God more intimately through understanding how he has acted in the past. We can also avoid mistakes in our own lives through learning from Israel's past failures.

■ **The Nation.** God founded the nation of Israel to be the source of truth and salvation to the whole world. His relationship to his people was loving yet firm. The Israelites had no structure when they left Egypt. God had to instruct them in their constitutional laws and daily practices. He showed them how to worship and how to have national holidays. Israel's newly formed nation had all the behavioral characteristics of Christians today. We are often disorganized, sometimes rebellious, and sometimes victorious. God's Person and Word are still our only guides. If our churches reflect his leadership, they will be effective in serving him.

MAP ▶

1 Goshen This area was given to Jacob and his family when they moved to Egypt (Gen 47:5-6). It was the Hebrews' homeland for 400 years as they grew from a family into a powerful people (Exod 1:7). Here they became enslaved by the Egyptians, who forced them to build the cities of Pithom and Rameses (Exod 1:11).

2 Midian Moses fled to Midian after killing an Egyptian who was mistreating a fellow Hebrew (Exod 2:11-15). Here he became a shepherd, married Zipporah, and received a call from God to lead the Hebrews out of Egypt.

3 Baal-zephon Pharaoh decided to let the Hebrews leave Egypt after a series of devastating plagues from the Lord, but he quickly changed his mind and chased them to their camp near Baal-zephon (Exod 14:9). It was there that God led the Hebrews through the Red Sea, drowning the Egyptian army behind them.

4 Elim Moses led the people south, through Marah (where the Lord gave them fresh water, Exod 15:22-25) and on to the oasis of Elim (Exod 15:27).

5 Wilderness of Sin After leaving Elim, the Israelites became hungry in the wilderness of Sin. God provided them with manna that came down from heaven and covered the ground each morning (Exod 16:1, 4, 13-15). The Lord continued to provide manna for his people until they finally entered the Promised Land.

6 Rephidim Moses led the people to Rephidim, where they found no water. But God miraculously provided water from a rock (Exod 17:1, 5-6). The Israelites had their first test in battle here, clashing with the Amalekites (Exod 17:9-13).

7 Mount Sinai God had previously appeared to Moses on this mountain and commissioned him to lead Israel (Exod 3:1-10). Moses returned with the people God had asked him to lead. For almost a year the people camped at the foot of Mount Sinai. During this time God gave them the Ten Commandments and the rest of the law (Exod 19–40; Leviticus). He was forging a holy nation, prepared to live and serve him alone.

8 Wilderness of Paran After their year at Mount Sinai, the Israelites broke camp and began their march toward the Promised Land by moving into the wilderness of Paran. From there, one leader from each tribe was sent to scout out the new land. After 40 days they returned, and all but Joshua and Caleb were too afraid to enter. Because of their lack of faith, the Israelites were made to wander in the wilderness for 40 years (Num 12:16–19:22).

9 Kadesh Toward the end of their wanderings, the Israelites headed to Kadesh, where Miriam died. It was also here that Moses angrily struck a rock, which kept him from entering the Promised Land (Num 20).

10 Arad When the king in Arad heard that Israel was on the move, he attacked, but he was soundly defeated. Moses then led the people southeast around the Dead Sea (Num 21:1-3).

11 Edom The Israelites wanted to travel through Edom, but the king of Edom refused them passage (Num 20:14-22), so they had to travel around this region instead.

12 Bashan Moses led the nation north toward Bashan, defeating the Amorites (Num 21:21-32) and the occupants of Bashan (Num 21:33-35) along the way.

13 Plains of Moab The people camped on the plains of Moab, east of the Jordan River across from Jericho (Num 22:1). They were on the verge of the Promised Land, and it was here that Moses taught God's law to a new generation of Israelites (Deuteronomy) before he died, turning the nation over to Joshua's leadership (Deut 34:1-9).

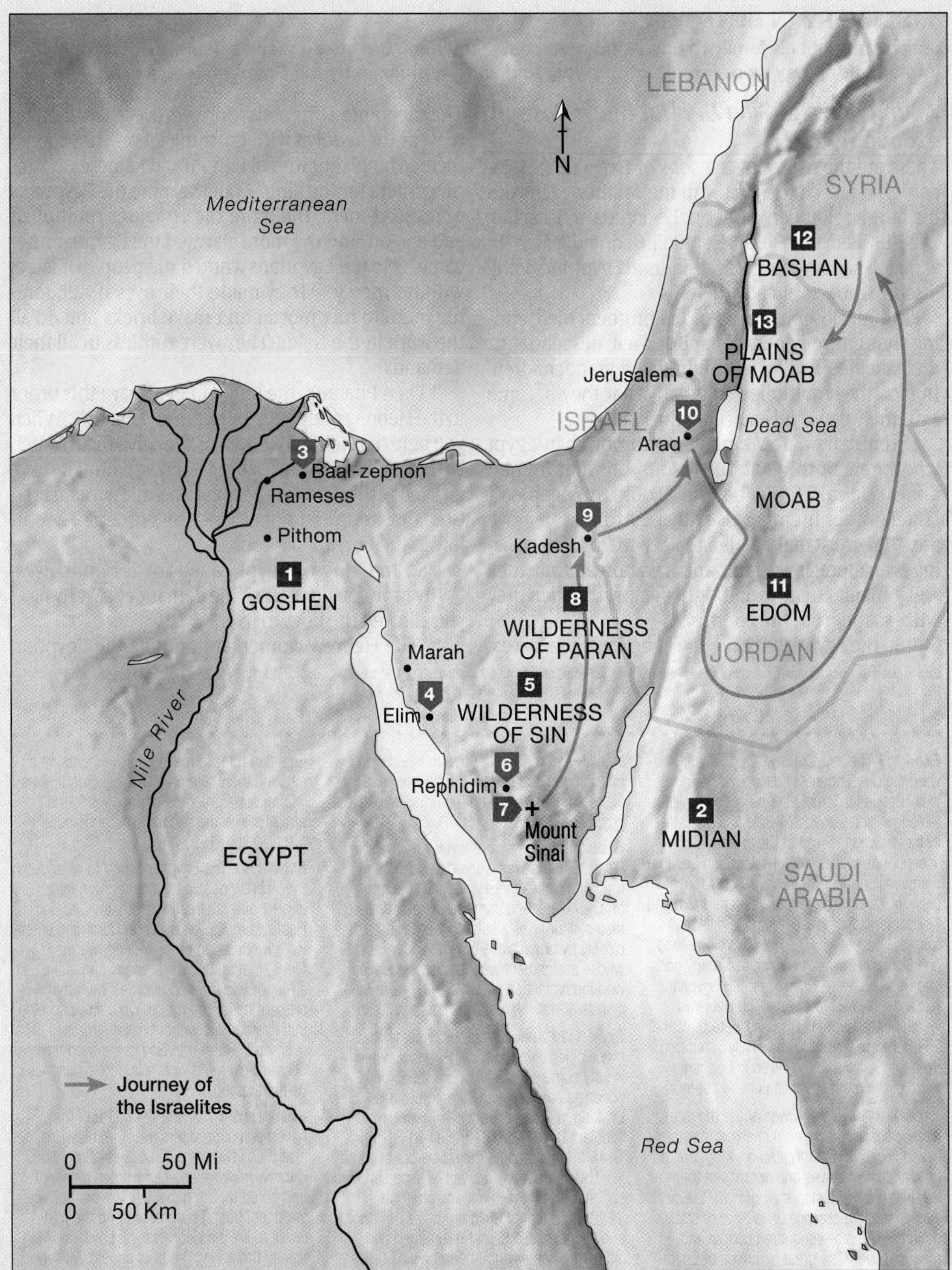

A. Israel in Egypt

When Joseph died, Israel was still a large extended family, settled in the region of Goshen in Egypt. But as time went on, they grew into a large nation and were enslaved by the Egyptians. After four hundred years in the land, there were nearly two million Hebrews living in Egypt, waiting for God to make them into the nation he had promised to their ancestor Abraham.

1. SLAVERY IN EGYPT

Joseph brought his family to Egypt and protected them there. But after Joseph's death, as they multiplied into a nation, they were forced into slavery and were brutalized by the Egyptian leaders.

A King in Egypt Who Did Not Know Joseph

EXODUS 1:1-22

These are the names of the sons of Israel (that is, Jacob) who moved to Egypt with their father, each with his family: 2Reuben, Simeon, Levi, Judah, 3Issachar, Zebulun, Benjamin, 4Dan, Naphtali, Gad, and Asher. 5In all, Jacob had seventy* descendants in Egypt, including Joseph, who was already there.

6In time, Joseph and all of his brothers died, ending that entire generation. 7But their descendants, the Israelites, had many children and grandchildren. In fact, they multiplied so greatly that they became extremely powerful and filled the land.

8Eventually, a new king came to power in Egypt who knew nothing about Joseph or what he had done. 9He said to his people, "Look, the people of Israel now outnumber us and are stronger than we are. 10We must make a plan to keep them from growing even more. If we don't, and if war breaks out, they will join our enemies and fight against us. Then they will escape from the country.*"

11So the Egyptians made the Israelites their slaves. They appointed brutal slave drivers over them, hoping to wear them down with crushing labor. They forced them to build the cities of Pithom and Rameses as supply centers for the king. 12But the more the Egyptians oppressed them, the more the Israelites multiplied and spread, and the more alarmed the Egyptians became. 13So the Egyptians worked the people of Israel without mercy. 14They made their lives bitter, forcing them to mix mortar and make bricks and do all the work in the fields. They were ruthless in all their demands.

15Then Pharaoh, the king of Egypt, gave this order to the Hebrew midwives, Shiphrah and Puah: 16"When you help the Hebrew women as they give birth, watch as they deliver.* If the baby is a boy, kill him; if it is a girl, let her live." 17But because the midwives feared God, they refused to obey the king's orders. They allowed the boys to live, too.

18So the king of Egypt called for the midwives. "Why have you done this?" he demanded. "Why have you allowed the boys to live?"

19"The Hebrew women are not like the Egyptian

Ex 1:5 Dead Sea Scrolls and Greek version read *seventy-five;* see notes on Gen 46:27. **Ex 1:10** Or *will take the country.* **Ex 1:16** Hebrew *look upon the two stones;* perhaps the reference is to a birthstool.

1750 BC *Hammurabi of Babylon provides first written law code (estimated)*

Exod 1:1 The "sons of Israel" (or Israelites) were the descendants of Jacob, whose name was changed to Israel after he wrestled with the angel (see Gen 32:24-30). Jacob's family had moved to Egypt at the invitation of Joseph, one of Jacob's sons who had become a great ruler under Pharaoh. Jacob's family grew into a large nation. But as foreigners and newcomers, their lives were quite different from the Egyptians'. The Hebrews worshiped one God; the Egyptians worshiped many gods. The Hebrews were wanderers; the Egyptians had a deeply rooted culture. The Hebrews were shepherds; the Egyptians were builders. The Hebrews were also physically separated from the Egyptians: They lived in Goshen, north of the great Egyptian cultural centers.

Exod 1:9-10 Pharaoh was afraid the Israelites were becoming so numerous that they would organize and threaten his kingdom, so he made them slaves and oppressed them to kill their spirit and stop their growth. Slavery was an ancient practice used by almost all nations to employ conquered people and other captives. The great pyramids of Egypt were built with slave labor, long before the Israelites were there. Although Israel was not a conquered nation, the people were foreigners and thus lacked the rights of native Egyptians.

Exod 1:11 There were levels of slavery in Egypt. Some slaves worked long hours in mud pits while others were skilled carpenters, jewelers, and craftsmen. Regardless of their skill or level, all slaves were watched closely by brutal slave drivers, supervisors whose assignment was to keep the slaves working as fast as possible. They were specialists at making a slave's life miserable.

Exod 1:11 Ancient records indicate that these cities were built in 1290 B.C., which is why some scholars believe the Exodus occurred early in the 13th century B.C. Looking at other evidence, however, other scholars believe the Hebrews left Egypt in 1446 B.C. How could they have built two cities 150 years after they left? These scholars suggest that Rameses II, the pharaoh in 1290 B.C., did not build the cities of Pithom and Rameses. Instead, he renamed two cities that actually had been built 150 years previously. It was a common practice for an Egyptian ruler to make improvements on a city and then take credit for building it, thus wiping out all records of previous founders. Also see the second note on Exodus 13:17-18, p. 159.

Exod 1:12 The Egyptians tried to wear down the Hebrew people by forcing them into slavery and mistreating them. Instead, the Hebrews multiplied and grew stronger. When we are burdened or mistreated, we may feel defeated. But our burdens can make us stronger and develop qualities in us that will prepare us for the future. We cannot develop into overcomers without having troubles to overcome. Be true to God in the hard times because even the worst situations can make us better people.

Exod 1:15-17 Shiphrah and Puah may have been supervisors over the midwives, or else these two were given special mention. Hebrew midwives helped women give birth and cared for the baby until the mother was stronger. When Pharaoh ordered the midwives to kill the Hebrew baby boys, he was asking the wrong group of people. Midwives were committed to helping babies be born,

women," the midwives replied. "They are more vigorous and have their babies so quickly that we cannot get there in time."

[20]So God was good to the midwives, and the Israelites continued to multiply, growing more and more powerful. [21]And because the midwives feared God, he gave them families of their own.

[22]Then Pharaoh gave this order to all his people: "Throw every newborn Hebrew boy into the Nile River. But you may let the girls live."

2. GOD CHOOSES MOSES

Eventually, the burden of slavery and the threat of death for their children became too much for the Hebrews to bear. They cried out to God for rescue, and God chose Moses for the task. God then prepared Moses to free his people from slavery and lead them out of Egypt.

The Birth of Moses

EXODUS 2:1-10

About this time, a man and woman from the tribe of Levi got married. [2]The woman became pregnant and gave birth to a son. She saw that he was a special baby and kept him hidden for three months. [3]But when she could no longer hide him, she got a basket made of papyrus reeds and waterproofed it with tar and pitch. She put the baby in the basket and laid it among the reeds along the bank of the Nile River. [4]The baby's sister then stood at a distance, watching to see what would happen to him.

not to killing them. These women showed great courage and love for God by risking their lives to disobey Pharaoh's command.

Exod 1:17-21 Against Pharaoh's orders, the midwives spared the Hebrew babies. Their faith in God gave them the courage to take a stand for what they knew was right. In this situation, disobeying the authority was proper. God does not expect us to obey those in authority when they ask us to disobey him or his Word. The Bible is filled with examples of those who were willing to sacrifice their very lives in order to obey God or save others. Esther and Mordecai (Esth 3:2; 4:13-16) and Shadrach, Meshach, and Abednego (Dan 3:16-18) are some of the people who took a bold stand for what was right. Whole nations can be caught up in immorality (racial hatred, slavery, prison cruelty); thus, following the majority or the ruling authority is not always right. Whenever we are ordered to disobey God's Word, "we must obey God rather than any human authority" (Acts 5:29).

Exod 1:19-21 Did God bless the Hebrew midwives for lying to Pharaoh? God blessed them not because they lied, but because they saved the lives of innocent children. This doesn't mean that a lie was necessarily the best way to answer Pharaoh. The midwives were blessed, however, for not violating the higher law of God that forbids the senseless slaughter of innocent lives.

Exod 2:1-2 Although a name is not mentioned yet, the baby in this story was Moses. Moses' mother and father were named Jochebed and Amram. His brother was Aaron and his sister, Miriam.

Exod 2:3 This tiny boat made of papyrus reeds was fashioned by a woman who knew what she was doing. Egyptian riverboats were made with these same reeds and waterproofed with tar. The reeds, which grew as tall as 16 feet, could be gathered in swampy areas along the Nile. Thus, a small basket hidden among the reeds would be well insulated from the weather and difficult to see.

The Nile River

This ancient Egyptian illustration shows how important the Nile River was in so many areas of Egyptian life. In the ancient world, the nation of Egypt was sometimes referred to as the gift of the Nile, without which it would not have been able to thrive. The Nile would deposit a thin layer of rich silt each year as it overflowed its banks. Then, having deposited this soil, the Nile also provided water for irrigation. On its banks, ancient farmers raised grain, such as barley and wheat. Onions, leeks, beans, and lentils were common vegetables. Dates, figs, and grapes were the most commonly grown fruits. Oil came from castor oil plants and the seeds of sesame plants rather than from the olive, as in other Mediterranean lands. Flax provided linen for clothing. Along the river grew papyrus reeds, from which writing material could be made. Many copies of the Bible, especially the New Testament, were written on papyrus. And many of these copies survived in Egypt for nearly 2,000 years.

The Nile River was also an all-weather highway for ancient Egypt. Boats could float northward with the current or sail southward by means of the prevailing northerly winds. Land routes normally conducted traffic to the river's edge, ferry boats then taking passengers and cargo from shore to shore.

Exod 2:3ff Moses' mother knew how wrong it would be to destroy her child. But there was little she could do to change Pharaoh's new law. Her only alternative was to hide the child and later place him in a tiny papyrus basket on the river. God used her courageous act to place her son, the Hebrew of his choice, in the house of Pharaoh. Do you sometimes feel surrounded by evil and frustrated by how little you can do about it? When faced with evil, look for ways to act against it. Then trust God to use your effort, however small it seems, in his war against evil.

▸ **EXODUS 2:1-10** ***(cont.)***

5 Soon Pharaoh's daughter came down to bathe in the river, and her attendants walked along the riverbank. When the princess saw the basket among the reeds, she sent her maid to get it for her. 6 When the princess opened it, she saw the baby. The little boy was crying, and she felt sorry for him. "This must be one of the Hebrew children," she said.

7 Then the baby's sister approached the princess. "Should I go and find one of the Hebrew women to nurse the baby for you?" she asked.

8 "Yes, do!" the princess replied. So the girl went and called the baby's mother.

9 "Take this baby and nurse him for me," the princess told the baby's mother. "I will pay you for your help." So the woman took her baby home and nursed him.

10 Later, when the boy was older, his mother brought him back to Pharaoh's daughter, who adopted him as her own son. The princess named him Moses,* for she explained, "I lifted him out of the water."

Moses Escapes to Midian

EXODUS 2:11-25

Many years later, when Moses had grown up, he went out to visit his own people, the Hebrews, and he saw how hard they were forced to work. During his visit, he saw an Egyptian beating one of his fellow Hebrews. 12 After looking in all directions to make sure no one was watching, Moses killed the Egyptian and hid the body in the sand.

13 The next day, when Moses went out to visit his people again, he saw two Hebrew men fighting. "Why are you beating up your friend?" Moses said to the one who had started the fight.

14 The man replied, "Who appointed you to be our prince and judge? Are you going to kill me as you killed that Egyptian yesterday?"

Then Moses was afraid, thinking, "Everyone knows what I did." 15 And sure enough, Pharaoh heard what had happened, and he tried to kill Moses. But Moses fled from Pharaoh and went to live in the land of Midian.

When Moses arrived in Midian, he sat down beside a well. 16 Now the priest of Midian had seven daughters who came as usual to draw water and fill the water troughs for their father's flocks. 17 But some other shepherds came and chased them away. So Moses jumped up and rescued the girls from the shepherds. Then he drew water for their flocks.

18 When the girls returned to Reuel, their father, he asked, "Why are you back so soon today?"

Ex 2:10 *Moses* sounds like a Hebrew term that means "to lift out."

1526 BC

Moses is born

Exod 2:5 Who was Pharaoh's daughter? There are two popular explanations. (1) Some think that Hatshepsut was the woman who pulled Moses from the river. Her husband was Pharaoh Thutmose II. (This would match the earlier Exodus date.) Apparently Hatshepsut could not have children, so Thutmose had a son by another woman, and this son became heir to the throne. Hatshepsut would have considered Moses a gift from the gods because now she had her own son who would be the legal heir to the throne. (2) Some think the princess who rescued baby Moses was the daughter of Rameses II, an especially cruel Pharaoh who would have made life miserable for the Hebrew slaves. (This would match the later Exodus date, but not the chronology used in this Bible.)

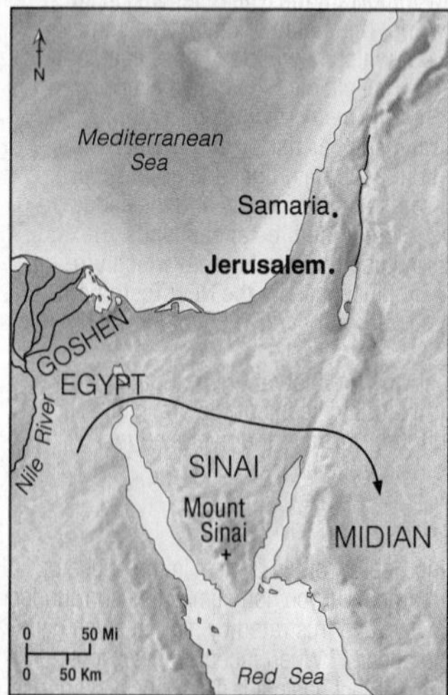

MOSES FLEES TO MIDIAN *After murdering an Egyptian, Moses escaped into Midian. There he married Zipporah and became a shepherd.*

Exod 2:7-8 Miriam, the baby's sister, saw that Pharaoh's daughter had discovered Moses. Quickly she took the initiative to suggest a nurse (her mother) who might care for the baby. The Bible doesn't say if Miriam was afraid to approach the Egyptian princess or if the princess was suspicious of the Hebrew girl. But Miriam did approach her, and the princess bought the services of Miriam and her mother. Their family was reunited. Special opportunities may come our way unexpectedly. Don't let the fear of what might happen cause you to miss an opportunity. Be alert for the opportunities God gives you, and take full advantage of them.

Exod 2:9 Moses' mother was reunited with her baby! God used her courageous act of saving and hiding her baby to begin his plan to rescue his people from Egypt. God doesn't need much from us to accomplish his plan for our lives. Focusing on our human predicament may paralyze us because the situation may appear humanly impossible. But concentrating on God and his power will help us see the way out. Right now you may feel unable to see through your troubles. Focus instead on God, and trust him for the way out. That is all he needs to begin his work in you.

Exod 2:12-14 Moses tried to make sure no one was watching before he killed the Egyptian. But as it turned out, someone did see, and Moses had to flee the country. Sometimes we mistakenly think we can get away with doing wrong if no one sees or catches us. But sooner or later doing wrong will catch up with us as it did with Moses. Even if we are not caught in this life, we will still have to face God and his evaluation of our actions.

Exod 2:15 To escape punishment for killing the Egyptian, Moses ran away to Midian. He became a stranger in a strange land, separated from his home and family. It took many years after this incident for Moses to be ready to serve God. But he trusted God instead of fearing the king (Heb 11:27). We may feel abandoned or isolated because of something we have done. But though we feel afraid and separated, we should not give up. Moses didn't. He trusted God to deliver him, no matter how dark his past or how bleak his future.

Exod 2:17 How did Moses handle these shepherds so easily? As an Egyptian prince, Moses would have been well trained in the Egyptian military, the most advanced army in the world. Even a large group of shepherds would have been no match for the sophisticated fighting techniques of this trained warrior.

Exod 2:18 Reuel is also called Jethro in Exodus 3:1.

19"An Egyptian rescued us from the shepherds,"
they answered. "And then he drew water for us and
watered our flocks."
20"Then where is he?" their father asked. "Why did
you leave him there? Invite him to come and eat with us."
21Moses accepted the invitation, and he settled
there with him. In time, Reuel gave Moses his daughter Zipporah to be his wife. 22Later she gave birth
to a son, and Moses named him Gershom,* for he
explained, "I have been a foreigner in a foreign land."
23Years passed, and the king of Egypt died. But the
Israelites continued to groan under their burden of
slavery. They cried out for help, and their cry rose up to
God. 24God heard their groaning, and he remembered
his covenant promise to Abraham, Isaac, and Jacob.
25He looked down on the people of Israel and knew
it was time to act.*

Moses and the Burning Bush

EXODUS 3:1-22

One day Moses was tending the flock of his
father-in-law, Jethro,* the priest of Midian. He led the
flock far into the wilderness and came to Sinai,* the
mountain of God. 2There the angel of the LORD appeared to him in a blazing fire from the middle of a
bush. Moses stared in amazement. Though the bush
was engulfed in flames, it didn't burn up. 3"This is
amazing," Moses said to himself. "Why isn't that bush
burning up? I must go see it."
4When the LORD saw Moses coming to take a closer
look, God called to him from the middle of the bush,
"Moses! Moses!"
"Here I am!" Moses replied.
5"Do not come any closer," the LORD warned. "Take
off your sandals, for you are standing on holy ground.

Ex 2:22 *Gershom* sounds like a Hebrew term that means "a foreigner there." **Ex 2:25** Or *and acknowledged his obligation to help them.* **Ex 3:1a** Moses' father-in-law went by two names, Jethro and Reuel. **Ex 3:1b** Hebrew *Horeb,* another name for Sinai.

Exod 2:23-25 God's rescue doesn't always come the moment we want it. God had promised to bring the Hebrew slaves out of Egypt (Gen 15:16; 46:3-4). The people had waited a long time for that promise to be kept, but God rescued them when he knew the right time had come. God knows the best time to act. When you feel that God has forgotten you in your troubles, remember that God has a time schedule we can't see.

Exod 3:1 What a contrast between Moses' life as an Egyptian prince and his life as a Midianite shepherd! As a prince he had everything done for him; he was the famous son of an Egyptian princess. As a shepherd he had to do everything for himself; he was holding the very job he had been taught to despise (Gen 43:32; 46:33-34), and he lived as an unknown foreigner. What a humbling experience this must have been for Moses! But God was preparing him for leadership. Living the life of a shepherd and nomad, Moses learned about the ways of the people he would be leading and also about life in the wilderness. Moses couldn't appreciate this lesson yet, but God was getting him ready to free Israel from Pharaoh's grasp.

Exod 3:1 Mount Sinai is the place where God would give the people his revealed law, known today as the Ten Commandments (Exod 3:12; 19:1–20:21).

Exod 3:2 God spoke to Moses from an unexpected source: a burning bush. When Moses saw it, he went to investigate. God may use unexpected sources when communicating to us, too, whether people, thoughts, or experiences. Be willing to investigate, and be open to God's surprises.

Exod 3:2-4 Moses saw a burning bush and spoke with God. Many people in the Bible experienced God in visible (not necessarily human) form. Abraham saw the smoking firepot and flaming torch (Gen 15:17); Jacob wrestled with a man (Gen 32:24-29). When the slaves were freed from Egypt, God led them by pillars of cloud and fire (Exod 13:17-22). God made such appearances to encourage his new nation, to guide them, and to prove the reliability of his verbal message.

Exod 3:5-6 At God's command, Moses removed his sandals and covered his face. Taking off his shoes was an act of reverence, conveying his own unworthiness before God. God is our friend, but he is also our sovereign Lord. To approach him frivolously shows a lack of respect and sincerity. When you come to God in worship, do you approach him casually, or do you come as though you were an invited guest before a king? If necessary, adjust your attitude so it is suitable for approaching a holy God.

The Tetragrammaton

Tetragrammaton refers to the primary Hebrew name for God, represented by four Hebrew consonants (from the Greek *tetra,* "four," and *gramma,* "letter"), shown in both an ancient Hebrew style (above) and with contemporary style (below). These letters are the equivalent of English YHWH, and they are usually translated as "LORD," and occasionally "Yahweh." The most widely accepted meaning of the name is "the one who is, that is, the absolute and unchangeable one." This is the name the Lord revealed to Moses (Exod 3:13-15). According to the Ten Commandments, the Jews were not to take this name in vain (Exod 20:2, 7). The Jews, therefore, regarded the name as so holy that they would not pronounce it but said *Adonai*—the Hebrew word meaning "Lord." Originally the text was written only with consonants, but when vowel points were added, they used the vowels for *Adonai* as a reminder not to read the sacred name. This is why most English translations render it "LORD," using small capital letters to distinguish it from places where the Hebrew actually uses the word *Adonai,* which is translated "Lord."

Christians, unlike Jews, are encouraged to call on the name of the Lord Jesus Christ and to pray in the name of the Lord Jesus Christ. And there will come a time that at the name of Jesus every knee will bow and every tongue confess that he is Lord (Phil 2:9-11).

▸ **EXODUS 3:1-22 *(cont.)***

6I am the God of your father*—the God of Abraham,
the God of Isaac, and the God of Jacob." When Moses
heard this, he covered his face because he was afraid
to look at God.
7Then the LORD told him, "I have certainly seen the
oppression of my people in Egypt. I have heard their
cries of distress because of their harsh slave drivers.
Yes, I am aware of their suffering. 8So I have come
down to rescue them from the power of the Egyptians and lead them out of Egypt into their own fertile
and spacious land. It is a land flowing with milk and
honey—the land where the Canaanites, Hittites, Amorites, Perizzites, Hivites, and Jebusites now live. 9Look!
The cry of the people of Israel has reached me, and
I have seen how harshly the Egyptians abuse them.
10Now go, for I am sending you to Pharaoh. You must
lead my people Israel out of Egypt."
11But Moses protested to God, "Who am I to appear
before Pharaoh? Who am I to lead the people of Israel
out of Egypt?"
12God answered, "I will be with you. And this is your
sign that I am the one who has sent you: When you
have brought the people out of Egypt, you will worship
God at this very mountain."
13But Moses protested, "If I go to the people of Israel
and tell them, 'The God of your ancestors has sent me
to you,' they will ask me, 'What is his name?' Then what
should I tell them?"
14God replied to Moses, "I AM WHO I AM.* Say this
to the people of Israel: I AM has sent me to you." 15God
also said to Moses, "Say this to the people of Israel:
Yahweh,* the God of your ancestors—the God of Abraham, the God of Isaac, and the God of Jacob—has sent
me to you.

This is my eternal name,
my name to remember for all generations.

16"Now go and call together all the elders of Israel.
Tell them, 'The LORD, the God of your ancestors—the
God of Abraham, Isaac, and Jacob—has appeared to
me. He told me, "I have been watching closely, and I
see how the Egyptians are treating you. 17I have promised to rescue you from your oppression in Egypt. I will
lead you to a land flowing with milk and honey—the
land where the Canaanites, Hittites, Amorites, Perizzites, Hivites, and Jebusites now live."'
18"The elders of Israel will accept your message.
Then you and the elders must go to the king of Egypt
and tell him, 'The LORD, the God of the Hebrews, has
met with us. So please let us take a three-day journey
into the wilderness to offer sacrifices to the LORD,
our God.'
19"But I know that the king of Egypt will not let you
go unless a mighty hand forces him.* 20So I will raise
my hand and strike the Egyptians, performing all kinds
of miracles among them. Then at last he will let you go.
21And I will cause the Egyptians to look favorably on
you. They will give you gifts when you go so you will not
leave empty-handed. 22Every Israelite woman will ask
for articles of silver and gold and fine clothing from
her Egyptian neighbors and from the foreign women
in their houses. You will dress your sons and daughters
with these, stripping the Egyptians of their wealth."

Ex 3:6 Greek version reads *your fathers.* **Ex 3:14** Or *I WILL BE WHAT I WILL BE.* **Ex 3:15** *Yahweh* is a transliteration of the proper name *YHWH* that is sometimes rendered "Jehovah"; in this translation it is usually rendered "the LORD" (note the use of small capitals). **Ex 3:19** As in Greek and Latin versions; Hebrew reads *will not let you go, not by a mighty hand.*

Exod 3:8 This "land flowing with milk and honey" is the land of Israel and Jordan today. This was a poetic word picture expressing the beauty and productivity of the Promised Land.

Exod 3:10ff Moses made excuses because he felt inadequate for the job God asked him to do. It was natural for him to feel that way. He was inadequate all by himself. But God wasn't asking Moses to work alone. He offered other resources to help (God himself, Aaron, and the ability to do miracles). God often calls us to do tasks that seem too difficult, but he doesn't ask us to do them alone. God offers us his resources, just as he did to Moses. We should not hide behind our inadequacies, as Moses did, but look beyond ourselves to the great resources available. Then we can allow God to use our unique contributions.

Exod 3:13-15 The Egyptians had many gods by many different names. Moses wanted to know God's name so the Hebrew people would know exactly who had sent him to them. God called himself I AM, a name describing his eternal power and unchangeable character. In a world where values, morals, and laws change constantly, we can find stability and security in our unchanging God. The God who appeared to Moses is the same God who can live in us today. Hebrews 13:8 says, "Jesus Christ is the same yesterday, today, and forever." Because God's nature is stable and trustworthy, we are free to follow and enjoy him rather than spend our time trying to figure him out.

Exod 3:14-15 God reminded Moses of his covenant promises to Abraham (Gen 12:1-3; 15; 17), Isaac (Gen 26:2-5), and Jacob (Gen 28:13-15), and he used the name I AM to show his unchanging nature. What God promised to the great patriarchs hundreds of years earlier he would fulfill through Moses. His wisdom spans the ages, and his promises give meaning and direction to our lives.

Exod 3:16-17 God told Moses to tell the people what he saw and heard at the burning bush. Our God is a God who acts and speaks. One of the most convincing ways to tell others about him is to describe what he has done and how he has spoken to his people. If you are trying to explain God to others, talk about what he has done for you, for people you know, or for people whose stories are told in the Bible.

Exod 3:18-20 The elders (leaders) of Israel would accept God's message, and the leaders of Egypt would reject it. God knew what both reactions would be before they happened. This is more than good psychology—God knows the future. Believers can trust their futures to God because he already knows what is going to happen.

Exod 3:22 The jewelry and clothing were not merely borrowed—they were asked for and easily acquired. The Egyptians were so glad to see the Israelites go that they sent them out with gifts. These items were used later in building the Tabernacle (Exod 35:5, 22). The promise of being able to strip the Egyptians of their wealth seemed impossible to Moses at this time.

Signs of the Lord's Power

EXODUS 4:1-17

But Moses protested again, "What if they won't believe me or listen to me? What if they say, 'The LORD never appeared to you'?"

2Then the LORD asked him, "What is that in your hand?"

"A shepherd's staff," Moses replied.

3"Throw it down on the ground," the LORD told him. So Moses threw down the staff, and it turned into a snake! Moses jumped back.

4Then the LORD told him, "Reach out and grab its tail." So Moses reached out and grabbed it, and it turned back into a shepherd's staff in his hand.

5"Perform this sign," the LORD told him. "Then they will believe that the LORD, the God of their ancestors—the God of Abraham, the God of Isaac, and the God of Jacob—really has appeared to you."

6Then the LORD said to Moses, "Now put your hand inside your cloak." So Moses put his hand inside his cloak, and when he took it out again, his hand was white as snow with a severe skin disease.* 7"Now put your hand back into your cloak," the LORD said. So Moses put his hand back in, and when he took it out again, it was as healthy as the rest of his body.

8The LORD said to Moses, "If they do not believe you and are not convinced by the first miraculous sign, they will be convinced by the second sign. 9And if they don't believe you or listen to you even after these two signs, then take some water from the Nile River and pour it out on the dry ground. When you do, the water from the Nile will turn to blood on the ground."

10But Moses pleaded with the LORD, "O Lord, I'm not very good with words. I never have been, and I'm not now, even though you have spoken to me. I get tongue-tied, and my words get tangled."

11Then the LORD asked Moses, "Who makes a person's mouth? Who decides whether people speak or do not speak, hear or do not hear, see or do not see? Is it not I, the LORD? 12Now go! I will be with you as you speak, and I will instruct you in what to say."

13But Moses again pleaded, "Lord, please! Send anyone else."

14Then the LORD became angry with Moses. "All right," he said. "What about your brother, Aaron the Levite? I know he speaks well. And look! He is on his way to meet you now. He will be delighted to see you. 15Talk to him, and put the words in his mouth. I will be with both of you as you speak, and I will instruct you both in what to do. 16Aaron will be your spokesman to the people. He will be your mouthpiece, and you will stand in the place of God for him, telling him what to say. 17And take your shepherd's staff with you, and use it to perform the miraculous signs I have shown you."

Moses Returns to Egypt

EXODUS 4:18-31

So Moses went back home to Jethro, his father-in-law. "Please let me return to my relatives in Egypt," Moses said. "I don't even know if they are still alive."

"Go in peace," Jethro replied.

19Before Moses left Midian, the LORD said to him, "Return to Egypt, for all those who wanted to kill you have died."

20So Moses took his wife and sons, put them on a

Ex 4:6 Or *with leprosy.* The Hebrew word used here can describe various skin diseases.

Exod 4:1 Moses' reluctance and fear were caused by overanticipation. He was worried about how the people might respond to him. We often build up events in our minds and then panic over what might go wrong. God does not ask us to go where he has not provided the means to help. Go where he leads, trusting him to supply courage, confidence, and resources at the right moment.

Exod 4:2-4 A shepherd's staff was commonly a three- to six-foot wooden rod with a curved hook at the top. The shepherd used it for walking, guiding his sheep, killing snakes, and many other tasks. Still, it was just a stick. But God used the simple shepherd's staff Moses carried as a sign to teach him an important lesson. God sometimes takes joy in using ordinary things for extraordinary purposes. What are the ordinary things in your life—your voice, a pen, a hammer, a broom, a musical instrument, a computer? While it is easy to assume God can use only special skills, you must not hinder his use of the everyday contributions you can make. Little did Moses imagine the power his simple staff would wield when it became the staff of God.

Exod 4:6-7 This severe skin disease was leprosy, one of the most feared diseases of this time. There was no cure, and a great deal of suffering preceded eventual death. Through this experience, Moses learned that God could cause or cure any kind of disease. He saw that God indeed had all power and was commissioning him to exercise that power to lead the Hebrews out of Egypt.

Exod 4:10-13 Moses pleaded with God to let him out of his mission. After all, he was not a good speaker and would probably embarrass both himself and God. But God looked at Moses' problem quite differently. All Moses needed was some help, and who better than God could help him say and do the right things. God had made his mouth and would give him the words to say. It is easy for us to focus on our weaknesses, but if God asks us to do something, then he will help us get the job done. If the job involves some of our weak areas, then we can trust that he will provide words, strength, courage, and ability where needed.

Exod 4:14 God finally agreed to let Aaron speak for Moses. Moses' feelings of inadequacy were so strong that he could not trust even God's ability to help him. Moses had to deal with his deep sense of inadequacy many times. When we face difficult or frightening situations, we must be willing to let God help us.

Exod 4:16 The phrase "you will stand in the place of God for him" means that Moses would tell Aaron what to say as God was telling him.

Exod 4:17-20 Moses clung tightly to the shepherd's staff as he left for Egypt to face the greatest challenge of his life. The staff was his assurance of God's presence and power. When feeling uncertain, some people need something to stabilize and reassure them. For assurance when facing great trials, God has given promises from his Word and examples from great heroes of faith. Any Christian may cling tightly to these. As we grow in faith, we will outgrow our need for physical or temporary assurances and be able to trust God's Word alone.

▶ **EXODUS 4:18-31** ***(cont.)***

donkey, and headed back to the land of Egypt. In his
hand he carried the staff of God.
21And the LORD told Moses, "When you arrive back
in Egypt, go to Pharaoh and perform all the miracles
I have empowered you to do. But I will harden his
heart so he will refuse to let the people go. 22Then you
will tell him, 'This is what the LORD says: Israel is my
firstborn son. 23I commanded you, "Let my son go, so
he can worship me." But since you have refused, I will
now kill your firstborn son!'"
24On the way to Egypt, at a place where Moses and
his family had stopped for the night, the LORD confronted him and was about to kill him. 25But Moses'
wife, Zipporah, took a flint knife and circumcised her
son. She touched his feet* with the foreskin and said,
"Now you are a bridegroom of blood to me." 26(When
she said "a bridegroom of blood," she was referring to
the circumcision.) After that, the LORD left him alone.
27Now the LORD had said to Aaron, "Go out into
the wilderness to meet Moses." So Aaron went and
met Moses at the mountain of God, and he embraced
him. 28Moses then told Aaron everything the LORD
had commanded him to say. And he told him about
the miraculous signs the LORD had commanded him
to perform.
29Then Moses and Aaron returned to Egypt and
called all the elders of Israel together. 30Aaron told
them everything the LORD had told Moses, and Moses
performed the miraculous signs as they watched.
31Then the people of Israel were convinced that the
LORD had sent Moses and Aaron. When they heard
that the LORD was concerned about them and had
seen their misery, they bowed down and worshiped.

Ex 4:25 The Hebrew word for "feet" may refer here to the male sex organ.

3. GOD SENDS MOSES TO PHARAOH

Moses and Aaron went to Pharaoh as God's representatives, asking for the release of his people from slavery so that they could go to the land he had promised to their ancestors. In spite of the powerful signs Moses and Aaron were able to perform by God's power, Pharaoh refused to let the Hebrews go.

Moses and Aaron Speak to Pharaoh

EXODUS 5:1-5

1500 BC

After this presentation to Israel's leaders, Moses and
Aaron went and spoke to Pharaoh. They told him,
"This is what the LORD, the God of Israel, says: Let my
people go so they may hold a festival in my honor in
the wilderness."
2"Is that so?" retorted Pharaoh. "And who is the
LORD? Why should I listen to him and let Israel go?
I don't know the LORD, and I will not let Israel go."
3But Aaron and Moses persisted. "The God of the
Hebrews has met with us," they declared. "So let us
take a three-day journey into the wilderness so we can
offer sacrifices to the LORD our God. If we don't, he
will kill us with a plague or with the sword."
4Pharaoh replied, "Moses and Aaron, why are you

Mexican Sun Pyramid built

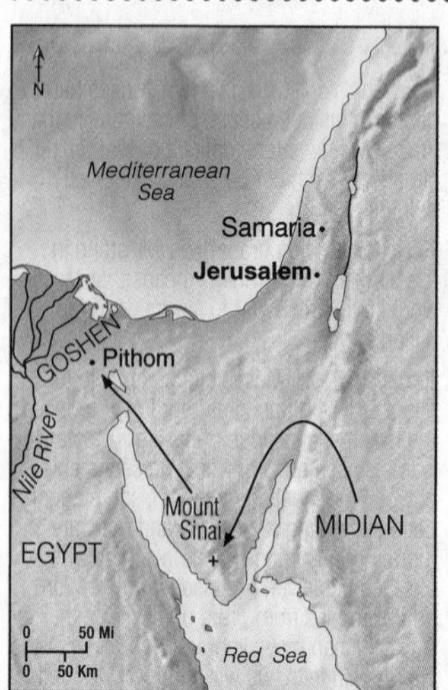

MOSES RETURNS TO EGYPT *God appeared to Moses in a mysterious burning bush on Mount Sinai. Later Aaron met Moses at the mountain, and together they returned to Egypt, a 200-mile trip.*

Exod 4:24-26 God was about to kill Moses because Moses had not circumcised his son. Why hadn't Moses done this? Remember that Moses had spent half his life in Pharaoh's palace and half his life in the Midianite wilderness. He might not have been too familiar with God's laws, especially since all the requirements of God's covenant with Israel (Gen 17) had not been actively carried out for over 400 years. In addition, Moses' wife, due to her Midianite background, may have opposed circumcision. But Moses could not effectively serve as deliverer of God's people until he had fulfilled the conditions of God's covenant, and one of those conditions was circumcision. Before they could go any farther, Moses and his family had to follow God's commands completely. Under Old Testament law, failing to circumcise your son was to remove yourself and your family from God's blessings. Moses learned that disobeying God was even more dangerous than tangling with an Egyptian pharaoh.

Exod 4:25-26 Why did Zipporah perform the circumcision? It may have been Zipporah who, as a Midianite unfamiliar with the circumcision requirement, had persuaded Moses not to circumcise their son. If she had prevented the action, now she would have to perform it. It is also possible that Moses became ill as a result of permitting disobedience, and so Zipporah had to perform the circumcision herself to save both her husband and son. This would not have made her happy—hence, her unflattering comment to Moses.

Exod 5:1-2 Pharaoh was familiar with many gods (Egypt was filled with them), but he had never heard of the God of Israel. Pharaoh assumed that the God of the Hebrew slaves couldn't be very powerful. At first, Pharaoh was not at all worried about Moses' message, for he had not yet seen any evidence of the Lord's power.

Exod 5:3 Pharaoh would not listen to Moses and Aaron because he did not know or respect God. People who do not know God may not listen to his Word or his messengers. Like Moses and Aaron, we need to persist. When others reject you or your faith, don't be surprised or discouraged. Continue to tell them about God, trusting him to open minds and soften stubborn hearts.

Exod 5:4-9 Moses and Aaron took their message to Pharaoh just as God directed. The unhappy result was harder work and more oppression for the Hebrews. Sometimes hardship comes because of obeying God.

distracting the people from their tasks? Get back to
work! 5Look, there are many of your people in the land,
and you are stopping them from their work."

Making Bricks without Straw

EXODUS 5:6-23

That same day Pharaoh sent this order to the Egyptian
slave drivers and the Israelite foremen: 7"Do not supply any more straw for making bricks. Make the people
get it themselves! 8But still require them to make the
same number of bricks as before. Don't reduce the
quota. They are lazy. That's why they are crying out,
'Let us go and offer sacrifices to our God.' 9Load them
down with more work. Make them sweat! That will
teach them to listen to lies!"

10So the slave drivers and foremen went out and
told the people: "This is what Pharaoh says: I will not
provide any more straw for you. 11Go and get it yourselves. Find it wherever you can. But you must produce
just as many bricks as before!" 12So the people scattered throughout the land of Egypt in search of stubble
to use as straw.

13Meanwhile, the Egyptian slave drivers continued
to push hard. "Meet your daily quota of bricks, just
as you did when we provided you with straw!" they
demanded. 14Then they whipped the Israelite foremen they had put in charge of the work crews. "Why
haven't you met your quotas either yesterday or today?" they demanded.

15So the Israelite foremen went to Pharaoh and
pleaded with him. "Please don't treat your servants
like this," they begged. 16"We are given no straw, but
the slave drivers still demand, 'Make bricks!' We are
being beaten, but it isn't our fault! Your own people
are to blame!"

17But Pharaoh shouted, "You're just lazy! Lazy! That's
why you're saying, 'Let us go and offer sacrifices to
the LORD.' 18Now get back to work! No straw will be
given to you, but you must still produce the full quota
of bricks."

19The Israelite foremen could see that they were
in serious trouble when they were told, "You must
not reduce the number of bricks you make each day."
20As they left Pharaoh's court, they confronted Moses
and Aaron, who were waiting outside for them. 21The
foremen said to them, "May the LORD judge and punish you for making us stink before Pharaoh and his
officials. You have put a sword into their hands, an
excuse to kill us!"

22Then Moses went back to the LORD and protested,

Are you following God but still suffering—or suffering even worse than before? If your life is miserable, don't assume you have fallen out of God's favor. You may be suffering for doing good in an evil world.

Exod 5:7-8 Mixing straw with mud made bricks stronger and more durable. Pharaoh had supplied the slaves with straw, but now he made them find their own straw and keep up their production quota as well.

Exod 5:15-21 The foremen were caught in the middle. First they tried to get the people to produce the same amount; then they complained to Pharaoh; finally they turned on Moses. Perhaps you have felt caught in the middle at work or in relationships in your family or church. Complaining or turning on the leadership does not solve the problem. In the case of these supervisors, God had a larger purpose in mind, just as he might have in your situation. So rather than turning on the leadership when you feel pressured by both sides, turn to God to see what else he might be doing in this situation.

Exod 5:22-23 Pharaoh had just increased the Hebrews' workload, and Moses protested that God had not rescued his people. Moses expected faster results and fewer problems. When God is at work, suffering, setbacks, and hardship may still occur. In James 1:2-4, we are encouraged to be happy when difficulties come our way. Problems develop our patience and character by teaching us to trust God to do what is best for us, look for ways to honor God in our present situation, remember that God will not abandon us, and watch for God's plan for us.

Great Pyramids

The Egyptians achieved the most lasting architectural forms ever attempted by any civilization, and much of their architecture has been preserved. The most outstanding examples of Egyptian architecture are the pyramids, virtually all of which were constructed in the Old Kingdom period (c. 2700–2200 B.C.), before Joseph and Jacob (and their descendants) arrived in Egypt. (This, by the way, dispels the myth that the Hebrews worked as slaves building the pyramids.) In building the pyramids, the Sumerian principle of the recessed niche was employed to accommodate the enormous stresses of stone masonry. Without that technique it would have been impossible to construct anything as huge as the Great Pyramid, which weighs an estimated six million tons. The Great Pyramid is one of the most perfectly oriented buildings on earth, being just a few seconds of one degree short of true north–south orientation. Many of the huge blocks of stone were cut and fitted together so accurately that it is impossible to insert the edge of a sheet of paper between them. The pyramids were meant to serve as tombs, but the structures themselves have become monuments to human creativity.

Many pharaohs built pyramids as places whereby they could enter the next life. They believed they would resurrect from the pyramid and go into the afterlife. But only faith in Jesus can bring real resurrection. Believe in him and you will have resurrection and eternal life (John 11:25).

▸ **EXODUS 5:6-23** ***(cont.)***
"Why have you brought all this trouble on your own
people, Lord? Why did you send me? 23 Ever since I
came to Pharaoh as your spokesman, he has been even
more brutal to your people. And you have done nothing
to rescue them!"

Promises of Deliverance

EXODUS 6:1-13
Then the LORD told Moses, "Now you will see what
I will do to Pharaoh. When he feels the force of my
strong hand, he will let the people go. In fact, he will
force them to leave his land!"
2 And God said to Moses, "I am Yahweh—'the LORD.'*
3 I appeared to Abraham, to Isaac, and to Jacob as El-
Shaddai—'God Almighty'*—but I did not reveal my
name, Yahweh, to them. 4 And I reaffirmed my covenant with them. Under its terms, I promised to give
them the land of Canaan, where they were living as
foreigners. 5 You can be sure that I have heard the
groans of the people of Israel, who are now slaves to
the Egyptians. And I am well aware of my covenant
with them.
6 "Therefore, say to the people of Israel: 'I am the
LORD. I will free you from your oppression and will
rescue you from your slavery in Egypt. I will redeem
you with a powerful arm and great acts of judgment.
7 I will claim you as my own people, and I will be your
God. Then you will know that I am the LORD your God
who has freed you from your oppression in Egypt. 8 I
will bring you into the land I swore to give to Abraham,
Isaac, and Jacob. I will give it to you as your very own
possession. I am the LORD!'"
9 So Moses told the people of Israel what the LORD
had said, but they refused to listen anymore. They had
become too discouraged by the brutality of their slavery.

Ex 6:2 *Yahweh* is a transliteration of the proper name *YHWH* that is sometimes rendered "Jehovah"; in this translation it is usually rendered "the LORD" (note the use of small capitals). **Ex 6:3** *El-Shaddai,* which means "God Almighty," is the name for God used in Gen 17:1; 28:3; 35:11; 43:14; 48:3.

MOSES

Some people can't stay out of trouble. When conflict breaks out, they always manage to be nearby. Reaction is their favorite action. This was Moses. He seemed drawn to what needed to be righted. Throughout his life, he was at his finest and his worst responding to the conflicts around him. Whether jumping into a fight to defend a Hebrew slave or trying to referee a struggle between two kinsmen, when Moses saw conflict, he reacted. • Over the years, however, an amazing thing happened to Moses. He didn't stop reacting; rather, he learned to react correctly. With each day's events shifting like a kaleidoscope, leading two million people in the wilderness was more than enough challenge for Moses' reacting ability. Much of the time he served as a buffer between God and the people. At one moment he had to respond to God's anger at the people's stubbornness and forgetfulness. At another moment he had to react to the people's bickering and complaining. At still another moment he had to react to their unjustified attacks on his character. • Leadership often involves reaction. If we want to react with instincts consistent with God's will, we must develop habits of obedience to God. Consistent obedience to God is best developed in times of less stress. Then when stress comes, our natural reaction will be to obey God. • In our age of lowering moral standards, we find it almost impossible to believe that God would punish Moses for the one time he outright disobeyed. What we fail to see, however, is that God did not reject Moses; Moses simply disqualified himself to enter the Promised Land. Personal greatness does not make a person immune to error or its consequences. • In Moses we see an outstanding personality shaped by God. But we must not misunderstand what God did. He did not change who or what Moses was; he did not give Moses new abilities and strengths. Instead, he took Moses' characteristics and molded them until they were suited to his purposes. Does knowing this make a difference in your understanding of God's purpose in your life? He is trying to take what he created in the first place and use it for its intended purposes. The next time you talk with God, don't ask, "What should I change into?" Instead ask, "How should I use my own abilities and strengths to do your will?"

Strengths and accomplishments	• Egyptian education; wilderness training • Greatest Jewish leader; led the Exodus • Prophet and lawgiver • Author of the Pentateuch
Weakness and mistake	• Failed to enter the Promised Land because of disobedience to God
Lessons from his life	• God prepares, then uses. His timetable is life-sized • God does his greatest work through frail people
Vital statistics	• Where: Egypt, Midian, wilderness of Sinai • Occupations: Prince, shepherd, leader of the Israelites • Relatives: Sister: Miriam. Brother: Aaron. Wife: Zipporah. Sons: Gershom and Eliezer.
Key verses	"It was by faith that Moses, when he grew up, refused to be called the son of Pharaoh's daughter. He chose to share the oppression of God's people instead of enjoying the fleeting pleasures of sin" (Heb 11:24-25).

Moses' story is told in the books of Exodus, Leviticus, Numbers, and Deuteronomy. He is also mentioned in Acts 7:20-44; Hebrews 11:23-29.

10Then the LORD said to Moses, 11"Go back to Pharaoh, the king of Egypt, and tell him to let the people of Israel leave his country."

12"But LORD!" Moses objected. "My own people won't listen to me anymore. How can I expect Pharaoh to listen? I'm such a clumsy speaker!*"

13But the LORD spoke to Moses and Aaron and gave them orders for the Israelites and for Pharaoh, the king of Egypt. The LORD commanded Moses and Aaron to lead the people of Israel out of Egypt.

The Ancestors of Moses and Aaron

EXODUS 6:14-30

These are the ancestors of some of the clans of Israel:

The sons of Reuben, Israel's oldest son, were Hanoch, Pallu, Hezron, and Carmi. Their descendants became the clans of Reuben.

15The sons of Simeon were Jemuel, Jamin, Ohad, Jakin, Zohar, and Shaul. (Shaul's mother was a Canaanite woman.) Their descendants became the clans of Simeon.

16These are the descendants of Levi, as listed in their family records: The sons of Levi were Gershon, Kohath, and Merari. (Levi lived to be 137 years old.)

17The descendants of Gershon included Libni and Shimei, each of whom became the ancestor of a clan.

18The descendants of Kohath included Amram, Izhar, Hebron, and Uzziel. (Kohath lived to be 133 years old.)

19The descendants of Merari included Mahli and Mushi.

These are the clans of the Levites, as listed in their family records.

20Amram married his father's sister Jochebed, and she gave birth to his sons, Aaron and Moses. (Amram lived to be 137 years old.)

21The sons of Izhar were Korah, Nepheg, and Zicri.

22The sons of Uzziel were Mishael, Elzaphan, and Sithri.

23Aaron married Elisheba, the daughter of Amminadab and sister of Nahshon, and she gave birth to his sons, Nadab, Abihu, Eleazar, and Ithamar.

24The sons of Korah were Assir, Elkanah, and Abiasaph. Their descendants became the clans of Korah.

25Eleazar son of Aaron married one of the daughters of Putiel, and she gave birth to his son, Phinehas.

These are the ancestors of the Levite families, listed according to their clans.

26The Aaron and Moses named in this list are the same ones to whom the LORD said, "Lead the people of Israel out of the land of Egypt like an army." 27It was Moses and Aaron who spoke to Pharaoh, the king of Egypt, about leading the people of Israel out of Egypt.

28When the LORD spoke to Moses in the land of Egypt, 29he said to him, "I am the LORD! Tell Pharaoh, the king of Egypt, everything I am telling you." 30But Moses argued with the LORD, saying, "I can't do it! I'm such a clumsy speaker! Why should Pharaoh listen to me?"

Aaron's Staff Becomes a Serpent

EXODUS 7:1-13

Then the LORD said to Moses, "Pay close attention to this. I will make you seem like God to Pharaoh, and your brother, Aaron, will be your prophet. 2Tell Aaron everything I command you, and Aaron must command

Ex 6:12 Hebrew *I have uncircumcised lips;* also in 6:30.

Exod 6:6 Small problems need only small solutions. But when we face great problems, God has an opportunity to exercise his great power. As the Hebrews' troubles grew steadily worse, God planned to intervene with his mighty power and perform great miracles to deliver them. How big are your problems? Big problems put you in a perfect position to watch God provide big solutions.

Exod 6:6-8 God's promises in these verses were fulfilled to the letter when the Hebrews left Egypt. He freed them from slavery, became their God, and accepted them as his people. Then he led them toward the land he had promised. When the Hebrews were rescued from slavery, they portrayed the drama of salvation for all of us. When God redeems us from sin, he delivers us, accepts us, and becomes our God. Then he leads us to a new life as we follow him.

Exod 6:9-12 When Moses gave God's message to the people, they were too discouraged to listen. The Hebrews didn't want to hear any more about God and his promises because the last time they listened to Moses, all they got was more work and greater suffering. Sometimes a clear message from God is followed by a period when no change in the situation is apparent. During that time, seeming setbacks may turn people away from wanting to hear more about God. If you are a leader, don't give up. Keep bringing people God's message as Moses did. By focusing on God, who must be obeyed, rather than on the results to be achieved, good leaders see beyond temporary setbacks and reversals.

Exod 6:10-12 Think how hard it must have been for Moses to bring God's message to Pharaoh when his own people had trouble believing it. Eventually the Hebrews believed that God had sent Moses, but for a time he must have felt very alone. Moses obeyed God, however, and what a difference it made! When the chances for success appear slim, remember that anyone can obey God when the task is easy and everyone is behind it. Only those with persistent faith can obey when the task seems impossible.

Exod 6:14-25 This genealogy, or family tree, was placed here to identify more firmly Moses and Aaron. Genealogies were used to establish credentials and authority as well as to outline the history of a family.

Exod 6:26 To bring the Israelites out of Egypt like an army means that they would be brought out in tribes, clans, or family groups.

Exod 7:1 God made Moses "seem like God to Pharaoh"—in other words, a powerful person who deserved to be listened to. Pharaoh himself was considered a god, so he recognized Moses as one of his peers. But his refusal to give in to Moses shows that he did not feel inferior to Moses.

▸ **EXODUS 7:1-13** ***(cont.)***
Pharaoh to let the people of Israel leave his country.
3But I will make Pharaoh's heart stubborn so I can
multiply my miraculous signs and wonders in the land
of Egypt. 4Even then Pharaoh will refuse to listen to
you. So I will bring down my fist on Egypt. Then I will
rescue my forces—my people, the Israelites—from the
land of Egypt with great acts of judgment. 5When I
raise my powerful hand and bring out the Israelites,
the Egyptians will know that I am the LORD."
6So Moses and Aaron did just as the LORD had commanded them. 7Moses was eighty years old, and Aaron
was eighty-three when they made their demands to
Pharaoh.
8Then the LORD said to Moses and Aaron, 9"Pharaoh will demand, 'Show me a miracle.' When he does
this, say to Aaron, 'Take your staff and throw it down
in front of Pharaoh, and it will become a serpent.*'"
10So Moses and Aaron went to Pharaoh and did
what the LORD had commanded them. Aaron threw
down his staff before Pharaoh and his officials, and it
became a serpent! 11Then Pharaoh called in his own
wise men and sorcerers, and these Egyptian magicians
did the same thing with their magic. 12They threw
down their staffs, which also became serpents! But
then Aaron's staff swallowed up their staffs. 13Pha-
raoh's heart, however, remained hard. He still refused
to listen, just as the LORD had predicted.

Ex 7:9 Hebrew *tannin*, which elsewhere refers to a sea monster. Greek version translates it "dragon."

4. PLAGUES STRIKE EGYPT

To help Moses and Aaron deal with the stubborn Pharaoh, God unleashed ten plagues upon the land of Egypt. After the tenth plague, Pharaoh finally let the people go. On the night before the great Exodus, God's new nation celebrated the Passover. Just as God delivered Israel from Egypt, he delivers us from sin, death, and evil.

A Plague of Blood

EXODUS 7:14-25
Then the LORD said to Moses, "Pharaoh's heart is
stubborn,* and he still refuses to let the people go.
15So go to Pharaoh in the morning as he goes down
to the river. Stand on the bank of the Nile and meet
him there. Be sure to take along the staff that turned
into a snake. 16Then announce to him, 'The LORD, the
God of the Hebrews, has sent me to tell you, "Let my
people go, so they can worship me in the wilderness."
Until now, you have refused to listen to him. 17So this
is what the LORD says: "I will show you that I am the
LORD." Look! I will strike the water of the Nile with
this staff in my hand, and the river will turn to blood.
18The fish in it will die, and the river will stink. The
Egyptians will not be able to drink any water from
the Nile.'"
19Then the LORD said to Moses: "Tell Aaron, 'Take
your staff and raise your hand over the waters of
Egypt—all its rivers, canals, ponds, and all the reservoirs. Turn all the water to blood. Everywhere in Egypt
the water will turn to blood, even the water stored in
wooden bowls and stone pots.'"
20So Moses and Aaron did just as the LORD commanded them. As Pharaoh and all of his officials
watched, Aaron raised his staff and struck the water
of the Nile. Suddenly, the whole river turned to blood!
21The fish in the river died, and the water became
so foul that the Egyptians couldn't drink it. There
was blood everywhere throughout the land of Egypt.
22But again the magicians of Egypt used their magic,
and they, too, turned water into blood. So Pharaoh's
heart remained hard. He refused to listen to Moses
and Aaron, just as the LORD had predicted. 23Pharaoh
returned to his palace and put the whole thing out
of his mind. 24Then all the Egyptians dug along the
riverbank to find drinking water, for they couldn't
drink the water from the Nile.
25Seven days passed from the time the LORD struck
the Nile.

Ex 7:14 Hebrew *heavy.*

Exod 7:11 How were these wise men and sorcerers able to duplicate Moses' miracles? Some of their feats involved trickery or illusion, and some may have used satanic power since worshiping gods of the underworld was part of their religion. Ironically, whenever they duplicated one of Moses' plagues, it only made matters worse. If the magicians had been as powerful as God, they would have reversed the plagues, not added to them.

Exod 7:12 God performed a miracle by turning Aaron's staff into a serpent, and Pharaoh's magicians did the same through trickery or sorcery. Although miracles can help us believe, it is dangerous to rely on them alone. Satan can imitate some parts of God's work and lead people astray. Pharaoh focused on the miracle rather than the message. We can avoid this error by letting the Word of God be the basis of our faith. No miracle from God would endorse any message that is contrary to the teachings of his Word.

Exod 7:17 God dramatically turned the water of the Nile into blood to show Pharaoh who he was. Do you sometimes wish for miraculous signs so you can be sure about God? God has given you the miracle of eternal life through your faith in him, something Pharaoh never obtained. This is a quiet miracle and, though less evident right now, just as extraordinary as water turned to blood. The desire for spectacular signs may cause us to ignore the more subtle miracles God is working every day.

Exod 7:20 Egypt was a large country, but most of the population lived along the banks of the Nile River. This 3,000-mile waterway was truly a river of life for the Egyptians. It made life possible in a land that was mostly desert by providing water for drinking, farming, bathing, and fishing. Egyptian society was a ribbon of civilization lining the banks of this life source, rarely reaching very far into the surrounding desert. Without the Nile's water, Egypt could not have existed. Imagine Pharaoh's dismay when Moses turned this sacred river to blood!

A Plague of Frogs

EXODUS 8:1-15

1*Then the LORD said to Moses, "Go back to Pharaoh
and announce to him, 'This is what the LORD says: Let
my people go, so they can worship me. 2If you refuse
to let them go, I will send a plague of frogs across your
entire land. 3The Nile River will swarm with frogs.
They will come up out of the river and into your palace, even into your bedroom and onto your bed! They
will enter the houses of your officials and your people.
They will even jump into your ovens and your kneading bowls. 4Frogs will jump on you, your people, and
all your officials.'"
5*Then the LORD said to Moses, "Tell Aaron, 'Raise
the staff in your hand over all the rivers, canals, and
ponds of Egypt, and bring up frogs over all the land.'"
6So Aaron raised his hand over the waters of Egypt, and
frogs came up and covered the whole land! 7But the magicians were able to do the same thing with their magic.
They, too, caused frogs to come up on the land of Egypt.
8Then Pharaoh summoned Moses and Aaron and
begged, "Plead with the LORD to take the frogs away
from me and my people. I will let your people go, so
they can offer sacrifices to the LORD."
9"You set the time!" Moses replied. "Tell me when
you want me to pray for you, your officials, and your
people. Then you and your houses will be rid of the
frogs. They will remain only in the Nile River."
10"Do it tomorrow," Pharaoh said.
"All right," Moses replied, "it will be as you have said.
Then you will know that there is no one like the LORD
our God. 11The frogs will leave you and your houses,
your officials, and your people. They will remain only
in the Nile River."
12So Moses and Aaron left Pharaoh's palace, and
Moses cried out to the LORD about the frogs he had
inflicted on Pharaoh. 13And the LORD did just what
Moses had predicted. The frogs in the houses, the
courtyards, and the fields all died. 14The Egyptians
piled them into great heaps, and a terrible stench filled

Ex 8:1 Verses 8:1-4 are numbered 7:26-29 in Hebrew text. **Ex 8:5** Verses 8:5-32 are numbered 8:1-28 in Hebrew text.

Exod 8:3ff Moses predicted that every house in Egypt would be infested with frogs. The poor of Egypt lived in small, mud-brick houses of one or two rooms with palm-trunk roofs. The homes of the rich were often two or three stories high, surrounded by landscaped gardens and enclosed by a high wall. Servants lived and worked on the first floor while the family occupied the upper floors. Thus, if the frogs got into the royal bedrooms, they had infiltrated even the upper floors. No place in Egypt would be safe from them.

THE PLAGUES ON EGYPT

Reference	*Plague*	*What Happened*	*Result*
Exod 7:14-24	Blood	Fish die, the river smells, the people are without water	Pharaoh's magicians duplicate the miracle by "their magic," and Pharaoh is unmoved
Exod 8:1-15	Frogs	Frogs come up from the water and completely cover the land	Again Pharaoh's magicians duplicate the miracle by sorcery, and Pharaoh is unmoved
Exod 8:16-19	Gnats	All the dust of Egypt becomes a massive swarm of gnats	Magicians are unable to duplicate this; they say it is "the finger of God," but Pharaoh's heart remains hard
Exod 8:20-32	Flies	Swarms of flies cover the land	Pharaoh promises to let the Hebrews go but then becomes stubborn and refuses
Exod 9:1-7	Livestock	All the Egyptian livestock die—but none of Israelites' are even sick	Pharaoh still refuses to let the people go
Exod 9:8-12	Boils	Horrible boils break out on everyone in Egypt	Magicians cannot respond because they are struck with boils as well—Pharaoh refuses to listen
Exod 9:13-35	Hail	Hailstorms kill all the slaves and animals left out or unprotected and strip or destroy almost every plant	Pharaoh admits his sin but then changes his mind and refuses to let Israel go
Exod 10:1-20	Locusts	Locusts cover Egypt and eat everything left after the hail	Everyone advises Pharaoh to let the Hebrews go, but God hardens Pharaoh's heart and he refuses
Exod 10:21-29	Darkness	Total darkness covers Egypt for three days so no one can even move—except the Hebrews, who have light as usual	Pharaoh again promises to let Israel go but again changes his mind
Exod 11:1–12:33	Death of Firstborn	The firstborn of all the people and cattle of Egypt die—but Israel is spared	Pharaoh and the Egyptians urge Israel to leave quickly; after they are gone, Pharaoh again changes his mind and chases after them

▶ **EXODUS 8:1-15 *(cont.)***
the land. [15]But when Pharaoh saw that relief had come,
he became stubborn.* He refused to listen to Moses
and Aaron, just as the LORD had predicted.

A Plague of Gnats

EXODUS 8:16-19
So the LORD said to Moses, "Tell Aaron, 'Raise your staff
and strike the ground. The dust will turn into swarms
of gnats throughout the land of Egypt.'" [17]So Moses
and Aaron did just as the LORD had commanded them.
When Aaron raised his hand and struck the ground
with his staff, gnats infested the entire land, covering
the Egyptians and their animals. All the dust in the
land of Egypt turned into gnats. [18]Pharaoh's magicians
tried to do the same thing with their secret arts, but
this time they failed. And the gnats covered everyone,
people and animals alike.
[19]"This is the finger of God!" the magicians exclaimed to Pharaoh. But Pharaoh's heart remained
hard. He wouldn't listen to them, just as the LORD had
predicted.

A Plague of Flies

EXODUS 8:20-32
Then the LORD told Moses, "Get up early in the morning and stand in Pharaoh's way as he goes down to the
river. Say to him, 'This is what the LORD says: Let my
people go, so they can worship me. [21]If you refuse,
then I will send swarms of flies on you, your officials,
your people, and all the houses. The Egyptian homes
will be filled with flies, and the ground will be covered
with them. [22]But this time I will spare the region of
Goshen, where my people live. No flies will be found
there. Then you will know that I am the LORD and that
I am present even in the heart of your land. [23]I will
make a clear distinction between* my people and your
people. This miraculous sign will happen tomorrow.'"
[24]And the LORD did just as he had said. A thick
swarm of flies filled Pharaoh's palace and the houses
of his officials. The whole land of Egypt was thrown
into chaos by the flies.
[25]Pharaoh called for Moses and Aaron. "All right! Go
ahead and offer sacrifices to your God," he said. "But
do it here in this land."
[26]But Moses replied, "That wouldn't be right. The
Egyptians detest the sacrifices that we offer to the
LORD our God. Look, if we offer our sacrifices here
where the Egyptians can see us, they will stone us.
[27]We must take a three-day trip into the wilderness
to offer sacrifices to the LORD our God, just as he has
commanded us."
[28]"All right, go ahead," Pharaoh replied. "I will let
you go into the wilderness to offer sacrifices to the
LORD your God. But don't go too far away. Now hurry
and pray for me."
[29]Moses answered, "As soon as I leave you, I will
pray to the LORD, and tomorrow the swarms of flies
will disappear from you and your officials and all your
people. But I am warning you, Pharaoh, don't lie to
us again and refuse to let the people go to sacrifice
to the LORD."
[30]So Moses left Pharaoh's palace and pleaded with
the LORD to remove all the flies. [31]And the LORD did
as Moses asked and caused the swarms of flies to disappear from Pharaoh, his officials, and his people. Not
a single fly remained. [32]But Pharaoh again became
stubborn and refused to let the people go.

A Plague against Livestock

EXODUS 9:1-7
"Go back to Pharaoh," the LORD commanded Moses.
"Tell him, 'This is what the LORD, the God of the Hebrews, says: Let my people go, so they can worship
me. [2]If you continue to hold them and refuse to let
them go, [3]the hand of the LORD will strike all your
livestock—your horses, donkeys, camels, cattle, sheep,
and goats—with a deadly plague. [4]But the LORD will
again make a distinction between the livestock of the
Israelites and that of the Egyptians. Not a single one
of Israel's animals will die! [5]The LORD has already set
the time for the plague to begin. He has declared that
he will strike the land tomorrow.'"
[6]And the LORD did just as he had said. The next

Ex 8:15 Hebrew *made his heart heavy;* also in 8:32. **Ex 8:23** As in Greek and Latin versions; Hebrew reads *I will set redemption between.*

Exod 8:15 After repeated warnings, Pharaoh still refused to obey God. He hardened his heart every time there was a break in the plagues. His stubborn disobedience brought suffering upon himself and his entire country. While persistence is good, stubbornness is usually self-centered. Stubbornness toward God amounts to rebellion against him. Rebellion will not only bring you grief, but it also may affect those who stand with you.

Exod 8:19 Some people think, *If only I could see a miracle, I could believe in God.* God gave Pharaoh just such an opportunity. When gnats infested Egypt, even the magicians agreed that this was God's work ("the finger of God")—but still Pharaoh refused to believe. He was stubborn, and stubbornness can blind a person to the truth. When you rid yourself of stubbornness, you may be surprised by abundant evidence of God's work in your life.

Exod 8:25-29 Pharaoh wanted a compromise. He would allow the Hebrews to sacrifice, but only if they would do it nearby. But God's requirement was firm: The Hebrews had to leave Egypt. Sometimes people urge believers to compromise and give only partial obedience to God's commands. But commitment and obedience to God cannot be negotiated. When it comes to obeying God, half measures won't do.

Exod 8:26 The Israelites would be sacrificing animals that the Egyptians regarded as sacred, and this would be offensive to them. Moses was concerned about a violent reaction to sacrificing these animals near the Egyptians.

Exod 9:1 This was the fifth time God sent Moses back to Pharaoh with the demand "Let my people go." By this time, Moses may have been tired and discouraged, but he continued to obey. Is there a difficult conflict you must face again and again? Don't give up when you know what is right to do. As Moses discovered, persistence is rewarded.

morning all the livestock of the Egyptians died, but the Israelites didn't lose a single animal. [7]Pharaoh sent his officials to investigate, and they discovered that the Israelites had not lost a single animal! But even so, Pharaoh's heart remained stubborn,* and he still refused to let the people go.

A Plague of Festering Boils

EXODUS 9:8-12

Then the LORD said to Moses and Aaron, "Take handfuls of soot from a brick kiln, and have Moses toss it into the air while Pharaoh watches. [9]The ashes will spread like fine dust over the whole land of Egypt, causing festering boils to break out on people and animals throughout the land."

[10]So they took soot from a brick kiln and went and stood before Pharaoh. As Pharaoh watched, Moses threw the soot into the air, and boils broke out on people and animals alike. [11]Even the magicians were unable to stand before Moses, because the boils had broken out on them and all the Egyptians. [12]But the LORD hardened Pharaoh's heart, and just as the LORD had predicted to Moses, Pharaoh refused to listen.

A Plague of Hail

EXODUS 9:13-35

Then the LORD said to Moses, "Get up early in the morning and stand before Pharaoh. Tell him, 'This is what the LORD, the God of the Hebrews, says: Let my people go, so they can worship me. [14]If you don't, I will send more plagues on you* and your officials and your people. Then you will know that there is no one like me in all the earth. [15]By now I could have lifted my hand and struck you and your people with a plague to wipe you off the face of the earth. [16]But I have spared you for a purpose—to show you my power* and to spread my fame throughout the earth. [17]But you still lord it over my people and refuse to let them go. [18]So tomorrow at this time I will send a hailstorm more devastating than any in all the history of Egypt. [19]Quick! Order your livestock and servants to come in from the fields to find shelter. Any person or animal left outside will die when the hail falls.'"

[20]Some of Pharaoh's officials were afraid because of what the LORD had said. They quickly brought their servants and livestock in from the fields. [21]But those who paid no attention to the word of the LORD left theirs out in the open.

[22]Then the LORD said to Moses, "Lift your hand toward the sky so hail may fall on the people, the livestock, and all the plants throughout the land of Egypt."

[23]So Moses lifted his staff toward the sky, and the LORD sent thunder and hail, and lightning flashed toward the earth. The LORD sent a tremendous hailstorm against all the land of Egypt. [24]Never in all the history of Egypt had there been a storm like that, with such devastating hail and continuous lightning. [25]It left all of Egypt in ruins. The hail struck down everything in the open field—people, animals, and plants alike. Even the trees were destroyed. [26]The only place without hail was the region of Goshen, where the people of Israel lived.

[27]Then Pharaoh quickly summoned Moses and Aaron. "This time I have sinned," he confessed. "The LORD is the righteous one, and my people and I are wrong. [28]Please beg the LORD to end this terrifying thunder and hail. We've had enough. I will let you go; you don't need to stay any longer."

[29]"All right," Moses replied. "As soon as I leave the city, I will lift my hands and pray to the LORD. Then the thunder and hail will stop, and you will know that the earth belongs to the LORD. [30]But I know that you and your officials still do not fear the LORD God."

[31](All the flax and barley were ruined by the hail, because the barley had formed heads and the flax was budding. [32]But the wheat and the emmer wheat were spared, because they had not yet sprouted from the ground.)

[33]So Moses left Pharaoh's court and went out of the city. When he lifted his hands to the LORD, the thunder and hail stopped, and the downpour ceased. [34]But when Pharaoh saw that the rain, hail, and thunder had stopped, he and his officials sinned again, and Pharaoh again became stubborn.* [35]Because his heart was hard, Pharaoh refused to let the people leave, just as the LORD had predicted through Moses.

A Plague of Locusts

EXODUS 10:1-20

Then the LORD said to Moses, "Return to Pharaoh and make your demands again. I have made him and his officials stubborn* so I can display my miraculous

Ex 9:7 Hebrew *heavy.* **Ex 9:14** Hebrew *on your heart.* **Ex 9:16** Greek version reads *to display my power in you;* compare Rom 9:17. **Ex 9:34** Hebrew *made his heart heavy.* **Ex 10:1** Hebrew *have made his heart and his officials' hearts heavy.*

Exod 9:12 God gave Pharaoh many opportunities to heed Moses' warnings. But finally God seemed to say, "All right, Pharaoh, have it your way," and Pharaoh's heart became permanently hardened. Did God intentionally harden Pharaoh's heart and overrule his free will? No, he simply confirmed that Pharaoh freely chose a life of resisting God. Similarly, after a lifetime of resisting God, you may find it impossible to turn to him. Don't wait until just the right time before turning to God. Do it now while you still have the chance. If you continually ignore God's voice, eventually you will be unable to hear it at all.

Exod 9:20-21 If all the Egyptians' livestock were killed in the earlier plague (Exod 9:6), how could the slaves of Pharaoh bring their livestock in from the fields? The answer is probably that the earlier plague killed all the animals in the fields (Exod 9:3) but not those in the shelters.

Exod 9:27-34 After promising to let the Hebrews go, Pharaoh immediately broke his promise and brought even more trouble upon the land. His actions reveal that his repentance was not real. We do damage to ourselves and to others if we pretend to change but don't mean it.

▸ **EXODUS 10:1-20** ***(cont.)***
signs among them. 2I've also done it so you can tell
your children and grandchildren about how I made
a mockery of the Egyptians and about the signs I displayed among them—and so you will know that I am
the LORD."

3So Moses and Aaron went to Pharaoh and said,
"This is what the LORD, the God of the Hebrews, says:
How long will you refuse to submit to me? Let my people go, so they can worship me. 4If you refuse, watch
out! For tomorrow I will bring a swarm of locusts on
your country. 5They will cover the land so that you
won't be able to see the ground. They will devour what
little is left of your crops after the hailstorm, including
all the trees growing in the fields. 6They will overrun
your palaces and the homes of your officials and all
the houses in Egypt. Never in the history of Egypt have
your ancestors seen a plague like this one!" And with
that, Moses turned and left Pharaoh.

7Pharaoh's officials now came to Pharaoh and appealed to him. "How long will you let this man hold
us hostage? Let the men go to worship the LORD their
God! Don't you realize that Egypt lies in ruins?"

8So Moses and Aaron were brought back to Pharaoh.
"All right," he told them, "go and worship the LORD your
God. But who exactly will be going with you?"

9Moses replied, "We will all go—young and old, our
sons and daughters, and our flocks and herds. We must
all join together in celebrating a festival to the LORD."

10Pharaoh retorted, "The LORD will certainly need
to be with you if I let you take your little ones! I can
see through your evil plan. 11Never! Only the men may
go and worship the LORD, since that is what you requested." And Pharaoh threw them out of the palace.

12Then the LORD said to Moses, "Raise your hand
over the land of Egypt to bring on the locusts. Let them
cover the land and devour every plant that survived
the hailstorm."

13So Moses raised his staff over Egypt, and the
LORD caused an east wind to blow over the land all
that day and through the night. When morning arrived, the east wind had brought the locusts. 14And
the locusts swarmed over the whole land of Egypt,
settling in dense swarms from one end of the country
to the other. It was the worst locust plague in Egyptian
history, and there has never been another one like
it. 15For the locusts covered the whole country and
darkened the land. They devoured every plant in the
fields and all the fruit on the trees that had survived
the hailstorm. Not a single leaf was left on the trees
and plants throughout the land of Egypt.

16Pharaoh quickly summoned Moses and Aaron.
"I have sinned against the LORD your God and against
you," he confessed. 17"Forgive my sin, just this once,
and plead with the LORD your God to take away this
death from me."

18So Moses left Pharaoh's court and pleaded with
the LORD. 19The LORD responded by shifting the wind,
and the strong west wind blew the locusts into the Red
Sea.* Not a single locust remained in all the land of
Egypt. 20But the LORD hardened Pharaoh's heart again,
so he refused to let the people go.

A Plague of Darkness

EXODUS 10:21-29

Then the LORD said to Moses, "Lift your hand toward
heaven, and the land of Egypt will be covered with a
darkness so thick you can feel it." 22So Moses lifted
his hand to the sky, and a deep darkness covered the
entire land of Egypt for three days. 23During all that
time the people could not see each other, and no one
moved. But there was light as usual where the people
of Israel lived.

24Finally, Pharaoh called for Moses. "Go and worship
the LORD," he said. "But leave your flocks and herds
here. You may even take your little ones with you."

Ex 10:19 Hebrew *sea of reeds*.

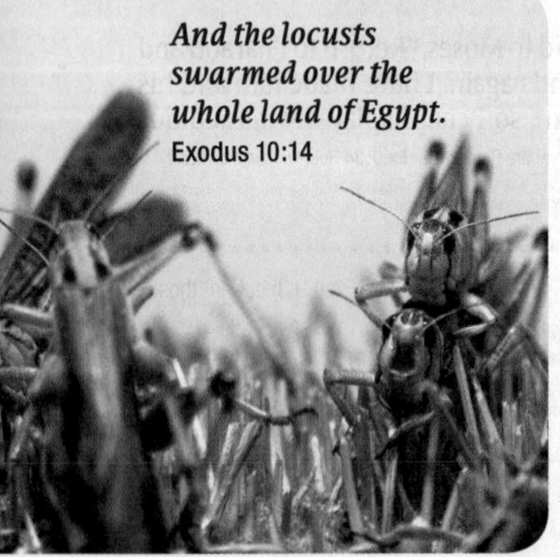

And the locusts swarmed over the whole land of Egypt.
Exodus 10:14

Exod 10:2 God told Moses that his miraculous experiences with Pharaoh should be retold to his descendants. What stories Moses had to tell! Living out one of the greatest dramas in biblical history, he witnessed events few people would ever see. It is important to tell our children about God's work in our past and to help them see what he is doing right now. What are the turning points in your life where God intervened? What is God doing for you now? Your stories will form the foundations of your children's belief in God.

Exod 10:22 As each plague descended upon the land, the Egyptian people realized how powerless their own gods were to stop it. Hapi, the god of the Nile River, could not prevent the waters from turning to blood (Exod 7:20). Hathor, the crafty cow-goddess, was helpless as Egyptian livestock died in droves (Exod 9:6). Amon-Re, the sun-god and chief of the Egyptian gods, could not stop an eerie darkness from covering the land for three full days (Exod 10:21-22). The Egyptian gods were (1) not personal, centering around images like the sun or the river; (2) numerous; and (3) not exclusive (any and all could be worshiped). By contrast, the God of the Hebrews was (1) a living, personal Being; (2) the only true God; and (3) the only God who should be worshiped. God was proving to both the Hebrews and the Egyptians that he alone is the living and all-powerful God.

Exod 10:27-28 Why was Pharaoh so reluctant to let the people go? The Hebrews were Egypt's free labor—the builders of their great cities. As Egypt's leader, Pharaoh would not easily let such a great resource go.

25"No," Moses said, "you must provide us with animals for sacrifices and burnt offerings to the LORD our
God. 26All our livestock must go with us, too; not a hoof
can be left behind. We must choose our sacrifices for
the LORD our God from among these animals. And
we won't know how we are to worship the LORD until
we get there."
27But the LORD hardened Pharaoh's heart once
more, and he would not let them go. 28"Get out of
here!" Pharaoh shouted at Moses. "I'm warning you.
Never come back to see me again! The day you see my
face, you will die!"
29"Very well," Moses replied. "I will never see your
face again."

Death for Egypt's Firstborn

EXODUS 11:1-10

Then the LORD said to Moses, "I will strike Pharaoh
and the land of Egypt with one more blow. After that,
Pharaoh will let you leave this country. In fact, he will
be so eager to get rid of you that he will force you all to
leave. 2Tell all the Israelite men and women to ask their
Egyptian neighbors for articles of silver and gold."
3(Now the LORD had caused the Egyptians to look favorably on the people of Israel. And Moses was considered a very great man in the land of Egypt, respected
by Pharaoh's officials and the Egyptian people alike.)
4Moses had announced to Pharaoh, "This is what
the LORD says: At midnight tonight I will pass through
the heart of Egypt. 5All the firstborn sons will die in
every family in Egypt, from the oldest son of Pharaoh, who sits on his throne, to the oldest son of his
lowliest servant girl who grinds the flour. Even the
firstborn of all the livestock will die. 6Then a loud
wail will rise throughout the land of Egypt, a wail
like no one has heard before or will ever hear again.
7But among the Israelites it will be so peaceful that
not even a dog will bark. Then you will know that the
LORD makes a distinction between the Egyptians and
the Israelites. 8All the officials of Egypt will run to
me and fall to the ground before me. 'Please leave!'
they will beg. 'Hurry! And take all your followers with
you.' Only then will I go!" Then, burning with anger,
Moses left Pharaoh.
9Now the LORD had told Moses earlier, "Pharaoh will
not listen to you, but then I will do even more mighty
miracles in the land of Egypt." 10Moses and Aaron
performed these miracles in Pharaoh's presence, but
the LORD hardened Pharaoh's heart, and he wouldn't
let the Israelites leave the country.

The First Passover

EXODUS 12:1-30

While the Israelites were still in the land of Egypt, the
LORD gave the following instructions to Moses and
Aaron: 2"From now on, this month will be the first
month of the year for you. 3Announce to the whole
community of Israel that on the tenth day of this
month each family must choose a lamb or a young
goat for a sacrifice, one animal for each household.
4If a family is too small to eat a whole animal, let them
share with another family in the neighborhood. Divide
the animal according to the size of each family and
how much they can eat. 5The animal you select must
be a one-year-old male, either a sheep or a goat, with
no defects.

Exod 11:7 Moses told Pharaoh that God made a distinction between Egypt and Israel. At this time the distinction was very clear in God's mind: He knew the Hebrews would become his chosen people. The distinction was taking shape in Moses' mind also. But the Hebrews still saw the distinction only in terms of slave and free. Later, when they were in the wilderness, God would teach them the laws, principles, and values that would make them distinct as his people. Remember that God sees us in terms of what we will become and not just what we are right now.

Exod 11:9-10 You may wonder how Pharaoh could be so foolish as to see God's miraculous power and still not listen to Moses. But Pharaoh had his mind made up long before the plagues began. He couldn't believe that someone was greater than him. This stubborn unbelief led to a heart so hard that even a major catastrophe couldn't soften it. Finally, it took the greatest of all calamities, the loss of his son, to force him to recognize God's authority. But even then he wanted God to leave, not to rule his country. We must not wait for great calamities to drive us to God but must open our hearts and minds to his direction now.

Exod 11:10 Did God really harden Pharaoh's heart and force him to do wrong? Before the 10 plagues began, Moses and Aaron announced what God would do if Pharaoh didn't let the people go. But their message only made Pharaoh stubborn—he was hardening his own heart. In so doing, Pharaoh defied both God and God's messengers. Through the first six plagues, Pharaoh's heart grew even more stubborn. After the sixth plague, God passed judgment. Sooner or later, evil people will be punished for their sins. When it became evident that Pharaoh wouldn't change, God confirmed Pharaoh's prideful decision and set the painful consequences of his actions in motion. God didn't force Pharaoh to reject him; rather, he gave him every opportunity to change his mind. In Ezekiel 33:11, God says, "I take no pleasure in the death of wicked people."

Exod 12:1-3 Certain holidays were instituted by God himself. Passover was a holiday designed to celebrate Israel's deliverance from Egypt and to remind the people of what God had done. Holidays can be important today, too, as annual reminders of what God has done for us. Develop traditions in your family to highlight the religious significance of certain holidays. These serve as reminders to the older people and learning experiences for the younger ones.

Exod 12:3ff For the Israelites to be spared from the plague of death, a lamb with no defects had to be killed and its blood placed on the doorframes of each home. What was the significance of the lamb? In killing the lamb, the Israelites shed innocent blood. The lamb was a sacrifice, a substitute for the person who would have died in the plague. From this point on, the Hebrew people would clearly understand that for them to be spared from death, an innocent life had to be sacrificed in their place.

▸ **EXODUS 12:1-30 *(cont.)***

6“Take special care of this chosen animal until the evening of the fourteenth day of this first month. Then the whole assembly of the community of Israel must slaughter their lamb or young goat at twilight. 7They are to take some of the blood and smear it on the sides and top of the doorframes of the houses where they eat the animal. 8That same night they must roast the meat over a fire and eat it along with bitter salad greens and bread made without yeast. 9Do not eat any of the meat raw or boiled in water. The whole animal—including the head, legs, and internal organs—must be roasted over a fire. 10Do not leave any of it until the next morning. Burn whatever is not eaten before morning.

11“These are your instructions for eating this meal: Be fully dressed,* wear your sandals, and carry your walking stick in your hand. Eat the meal with urgency, for this is the LORD's Passover. 12On that night I will pass through the land of Egypt and strike down every firstborn son and firstborn male animal in the land of Egypt. I will execute judgment against all the gods of Egypt, for I am the LORD! 13But the blood on your doorposts will serve as a sign, marking the houses where you are staying. When I see the blood, I will pass over you. This plague of death will not touch you when I strike the land of Egypt.

14“This is a day to remember. Each year, from generation to generation, you must celebrate it as a special festival to the LORD. This is a law for all time. 15For seven days the bread you eat must be made without yeast. On the first day of the festival, remove every trace of yeast from your homes. Anyone who eats bread made with yeast during the seven days of the festival will be cut off from the community of Israel. 16On the first day of the festival and again on the seventh day, all the people must observe an official day for holy assembly. No work of any kind may be done on these days except in the preparation of food.

17“Celebrate this Festival of Unleavened Bread, for it will remind you that I brought your forces out of the land of Egypt on this very day. This festival will be a permanent law for you; celebrate this day from generation to generation. 18The bread you eat must be made without yeast from the evening of the fourteenth day of the first month until the evening of the twenty-first day of that month. 19During those seven days, there must be no trace of yeast in your homes. Anyone who eats anything made with yeast during this week will be cut off from the community of Israel. These regulations apply both to the foreigners living among you and to the native-born Israelites. 20During those days you must not eat anything made with yeast. Wherever you live, eat only bread made without yeast.”

21Then Moses called all the elders of Israel together and said to them, “Go, pick out a lamb or young goat for each of your families, and slaughter the Passover animal. 22Drain the blood into a basin. Then take a bundle of hyssop branches and dip it into the blood. Brush the hyssop across the top and sides of the doorframes of your houses. And no one may go out through the door until morning. 23For the LORD will pass through the land to strike down the Egyptians. But when he sees the blood on the top and sides of the doorframe, the LORD will pass over your home. He will not permit his death angel to enter your house and strike you down.

24“Remember, these instructions are a permanent law that you and your descendants must observe forever. 25When you enter the land the LORD has promised to give you, you will continue to observe this ceremony. 26Then your children will ask, ‘What does this ceremony mean?’ 27And you will reply, ‘It is the Passover sacrifice to the LORD, for he passed over the houses of the Israelites in Egypt. And though he struck the

Ex 12:11 Hebrew *Bind up your loins.*

Exod 12:6-11 The Festival of Passover was to be an annual holiday in honor of the night when the Lord “passed over” the homes of the Israelites. The Hebrews followed God's instructions by smearing the blood of a lamb on the doorframes of their homes. That night the firstborn son of every family that did not have blood on the doorframes was killed. The lamb had to be killed in order to get the blood that would protect them. (This foreshadowed the blood of Christ, the Lamb of God, who gave his blood for the sins of all people.) Inside their homes, the Israelites ate a meal of roast lamb, bitter herbs, and bread made without yeast. Unleavened bread could be made quickly because the dough did not have to rise. Thus, they could leave at any time. Bitter herbs signified the bitterness of slavery.

Exod 12:11 Eating the Passover feast while dressed for travel was a sign of the Hebrews' faith. Although they were not yet free, they were to prepare themselves, for God had said he would lead them out of Egypt. Their preparation was an act of faith. Preparing ourselves for the fulfillment of God's promises, however unlikely they may seem, demonstrates our faith.

Exod 12:17, 23-25 Passover and the Festival of Unleavened Bread became an annual remembrance of how God delivered the Hebrews from Egypt. Each year the people would pause to remember the day when the death angel passed over their homes. They gave thanks to God for saving them from death and bringing them out of a land of slavery and sin. Believers today have experienced a day of deliverance as well—the day we were delivered from spiritual death and slavery to sin. The Lord's Supper is our Passover remembrance of new life and freedom from sin. The next time struggles and trials come, remember how God has delivered you in the past and focus on his promise of new life with him.

Exod 12:29-30 Every firstborn child of the Egyptians died, but the Israelite children were spared because the blood of the lamb had been smeared on their doorframes. So begins the story of redemption, the central theme of the Bible.

Redemption means “to buy back” or “to save from captivity by paying a ransom.” One way to buy back a slave was to offer an equivalent or superior slave in exchange. That is the way God chose to buy us back—he offered his Son in exchange for us.

In Old Testament times, God accepted symbolic offerings. Jesus had not yet been sacrificed, so God accepted the life of an animal in place of the life of the sinner. When Jesus came, he substituted his perfect life for our sinful lives, taking the penalty for sin that

Egyptians, he spared our families.'" When Moses had
finished speaking, all the people bowed down to the
ground and worshiped.
28So the people of Israel did just as the LORD had
commanded through Moses and Aaron. 29And that
night at midnight, the LORD struck down all the firstborn sons in the land of Egypt, from the firstborn son
of Pharaoh, who sat on his throne, to the firstborn son
of the prisoner in the dungeon. Even the firstborn of
their livestock were killed. 30Pharaoh and all his officials and all the people of Egypt woke up during the
night, and loud wailing was heard throughout the land
of Egypt. There was not a single house where someone
had not died.

B. Israel Is Rescued from Egypt

The most powerful nation in the world was not enough to keep God from fulfilling his covenant promises to Abraham and the Hebrew people. He broke the bonds of slavery in Egypt and led his people through the Red Sea and into the wilderness to meet with him in preparation for becoming a great nation to represent him to the entire world. God is always faithful to his promises, no matter how difficult the situation might seem.

1. THE EXODUS

As Egypt buried its dead, the Hebrew slaves left the country, a free people at last.

Israel's Exodus from Egypt

EXODUS 12:31-42

Pharaoh sent for Moses and Aaron during the night.
"Get out!" he ordered. "Leave my people—and take
the rest of the Israelites with you! Go and worship
the LORD as you have requested. 32Take your flocks
and herds, as you said, and be gone. Go, but bless me
as you leave." 33All the Egyptians urged the people of
Israel to get out of the land as quickly as possible, for
they thought, "We will all die!"
34The Israelites took their bread dough before yeast
was added. They wrapped their kneading boards in

THE HEBREW CALENDAR

A Hebrew month began in what is the middle of a month on our modern-day calendar. Crops were planted in November and December and harvested in March and April.

Month	Today's Calendar	Bible Reference	Israel's Holidays
1 Abib (Nisan)	March–April	Exod 13:4; 23:15; 34:18; Deut 16:1	Passover (Lev 23:5) Unleavened Bread (Lev 23:6) First Harvest (Lev 23:10)
2 Ziv (Iyyar)	April–May	1 Kgs 6:1, 37	Second Passover (Num 9:10-11)
3 Sivan	May–June		Harvest (Pentecost) (Lev 23:16)
4 Tammuz	June–July		
5 Ab	July–August		
6 Elul	August–September		
7 Ethanaim (Tishri)	September–October	1 Kgs 8:2	Trumpets (Num 29:1; Lev 23:24) Day of Atonement (Lev 23:27) Shelters (Lev 23:34)
8 Bul (Marchesh-van)	October–November	1 Kgs 6:38	
9 Kislev	November–December	Neh 1:1	Dedication (Hanukkah) (John 10:22)
10 Tebeth	December–January		
11 Shebat	January–February		
12 Adar	February–March		Purim (Esth 9:24-32)

we deserve. Thus he redeemed us from the power of sin and restored us to God. Jesus' sacrifice was the reality that animal sacrifices were pointing toward, so after Jesus' death and resurrection, there is no longer any need to sacrifice animals.

We must recognize that if we want to be freed from the deadly consequences of our sins, a tremendous price must be paid. But we don't have to pay it. Jesus Christ, our substitute, has already redeemed us by his death on the cross. Our part is to trust him and accept his gift of eternal life. Our sins have been paid for, and the way has been cleared for us to begin a relationship with God (Titus 2:14; Heb 9:13-15, 23-26).

Exod 12:34 A kneading board was made of wood, bronze, or pottery and used for kneading dough. Bread was made by mixing water and flour with a small piece of leavened dough saved from the previous day's batch. Bread was the primary food in the Hebrews' diet, and thus it was vital to bring the board along. It could be easily carried on the shoulder.

▸ **EXODUS 12:31-42 *(cont.)***
their cloaks and carried them on their shoulders.
[35]And the people of Israel did as Moses had instructed;
they asked the Egyptians for clothing and articles of
silver and gold. [36]The LORD caused the Egyptians to
look favorably on the Israelites, and they gave the
Israelites whatever they asked for. So they stripped
the Egyptians of their wealth!

[37]That night the people of Israel left Rameses and
started for Succoth. There were about 600,000 men,*
plus all the women and children. [38]A rabble of non-
Israelites went with them, along with great flocks and
herds of livestock. [39]For bread they baked flat cakes
from the dough without yeast they had brought from
Egypt. It was made without yeast because the people
were driven out of Egypt in such a hurry that they had
no time to prepare the bread or other food.

[40]The people of Israel had lived in Egypt* for 430
years. [41]In fact, it was on the last day of the 430th
year that all the LORD's forces left the land. [42]On this
night the LORD kept his promise to bring his people
out of the land of Egypt. So this night belongs to him,
and it must be commemorated every year by all the
Israelites, from generation to generation.

Instructions for the Passover

EXODUS 12:43-51

Then the LORD said to Moses and Aaron, "These are the
instructions for the festival of Passover. No outsiders
are allowed to eat the Passover meal. [44]But any slave
who has been purchased may eat it if he has been circumcised. [45]Temporary residents and hired servants
may not eat it. [46]Each Passover lamb must be eaten in
one house. Do not carry any of its meat outside, and do
not break any of its bones. [47]The whole community of
Israel must celebrate this Passover festival.

[48]"If there are foreigners living among you who
want to celebrate the LORD's Passover, let all their
males be circumcised. Only then may they celebrate
the Passover with you like any native-born Israelite.
But no uncircumcised male may ever eat the Passover
meal. [49]This instruction applies to everyone, whether
a native-born Israelite or a foreigner living among
you."

[50]So all the people of Israel followed all the LORD's
commands to Moses and Aaron. [51]On that very day
the LORD brought the people of Israel out of the land
of Egypt like an army.

Dedication of the Firstborn

EXODUS 13:1-16

Then the LORD said to Moses, [2]"Dedicate to me every
firstborn among the Israelites. The first offspring to
be born, of both humans and animals, belongs to me."

[3]So Moses said to the people, "This is a day to remember forever—the day you left Egypt, the place
of your slavery. Today the LORD has brought you out
by the power of his mighty hand. (Remember, eat no
food containing yeast.) [4]On this day in early spring,
in the month of Abib,* you have been set free. [5]You
must celebrate this event in this month each year after
the LORD brings you into the land of the Canaanites,
Hittites, Amorites, Hivites, and Jebusites. (He swore
to your ancestors that he would give you this land—a
land flowing with milk and honey.) [6]For seven days
the bread you eat must be made without yeast. Then
on the seventh day, celebrate a feast to the LORD. [7]Eat
bread without yeast during those seven days. In fact,
there must be no yeast bread or any yeast at all found
within the borders of your land during this time.

[8]"On the seventh day you must explain to your
children, 'I am celebrating what the LORD did for me
when I left Egypt.' [9]This annual festival will be a visible sign to you, like a mark branded on your hand or
your forehead. Let it remind you always to recite this
teaching of the LORD: 'With a strong hand, the LORD
rescued you from Egypt.'* [10]So observe the decree of
this festival at the appointed time each year.

[11]"This is what you must do when the LORD fulfills
the promise he swore to you and to your ancestors.
When he gives you the land where the Canaanites
now live, [12]you must present all firstborn sons and
firstborn male animals to the LORD, for they belong
to him. [13]A firstborn donkey may be bought back

Ex 12:37 Or *fighting men;* Hebrew reads *men on foot.* **Ex 12:40** Samaritan Pentateuch reads *in Canaan and Egypt;* Greek version reads *in Egypt and Canaan.*
Ex 13:4 Hebrew *On this day in the month of Abib.* This first month of the ancient Hebrew lunar calendar usually occurs within the months of March and April.
Ex 13:9 Or *Let it remind you always to keep the instructions of the LORD on the tip of your tongue, because with a strong hand, the LORD rescued you from Egypt.*

Exod 12:37-38 The total number of people leaving Egypt is estimated to have been about two million. The "rabble of non-Israelites" may have been Egyptians and others who were drawn to the Hebrews by God's mighty works and who decided to leave Egypt with them.

Exod 13:2 *Dedicate* means to sacrifice or to consider something as belonging to God. This dedication practice described in Exodus 13:11-16 was to remind the people of their deliverance through God.

Exod 13:6-9 The Festival of Unleavened Bread marked the Hebrews as a unique people—as though they were branded on their hands and foreheads. What do you do that marks you as a follower of God? The way you raise your children, demonstrate love for others, show concern for the poor, and live in devotion to God—these actions will leave visible marks for all to see. While national groups are marked by customs and traditions, Christians are marked by loving one another (John 13:34-35).

Exod 13:12-14 What did it mean to "buy back every firstborn son"? During the night the Hebrews escaped from Egypt, God spared the oldest son of every house marked with blood on the doorframe. Because God saved the lives of the firstborn, he had a rightful claim to them. But God commanded the Israelites to buy their sons back from him. This ritual served three main purposes: (1) It was a reminder to the people of how God had spared their sons from death and freed them all from slavery; (2) it showed God's high respect for human life in contrast to the pagan gods who, their worshipers believed, demanded human sacrifice; and (3) it looked forward to the day when Jesus Christ would buy us back by paying the price for our sin once and for all.

from the LORD by presenting a lamb or young goat in its place. But if you do not buy it back, you must break its neck. However, you must buy back every firstborn son.

14"And in the future, your children will ask you, 'What does all this mean?' Then you will tell them, 'With the power of his mighty hand, the LORD brought us out of Egypt, the place of our slavery. 15Pharaoh stubbornly refused to let us go, so the LORD killed all the firstborn males throughout the land of Egypt, both people and animals. That is why I now sacrifice all the firstborn males to the LORD—except that the firstborn sons are always bought back.' 16This ceremony will be like a mark branded on your hand or your forehead. It is a reminder that the power of the LORD's mighty hand brought us out of Egypt."

2. CROSSING THE SEA

Pharaoh made one last attempt to bring them back, but the people escaped when God miraculously parted the waters of the Red Sea.

Israel's Wilderness Detour

EXODUS 13:17–14:4

When Pharaoh finally let the people go, God did not lead them along the main road that runs through Philistine territory, even though that was the shortest route to the Promised Land. God said, "If the people are faced with a battle, they might change their minds and return to Egypt." 18So God led them in a roundabout way through the wilderness toward the Red Sea.* Thus the Israelites left Egypt like an army ready for battle.*

19Moses took the bones of Joseph with him, for Joseph had made the sons of Israel swear to do this. He said, "God will certainly come to help you. When he does, you must take my bones with you from this place."

20The Israelites left Succoth and camped at Etham on the edge of the wilderness. 21The LORD went ahead of them. He guided them during the day with a pillar of cloud, and he provided light at night with a pillar of fire. This allowed them to travel by day or by night. 22And the LORD did not remove the pillar of cloud or pillar of fire from its place in front of the people.

14:1Then the LORD gave these instructions to Moses: 2"Order the Israelites to turn back and camp by Pi-hahiroth between Migdol and the sea. Camp there along the shore, across from Baal-zephon. 3Then Pharaoh will think, 'The Israelites are confused. They are trapped in the wilderness!' 4And once again I will harden Pharaoh's heart, and he will chase after you.* I have planned this in order to display my glory through Pharaoh and his whole army. After this the Egyptians will know that I am the LORD!" So the Israelites camped there as they were told.

Ex 13:18a Hebrew *sea of reeds.* **Ex 13:18b** Greek version reads *left Egypt in the fifth generation.* **Ex 14:4** Hebrew *after them.*

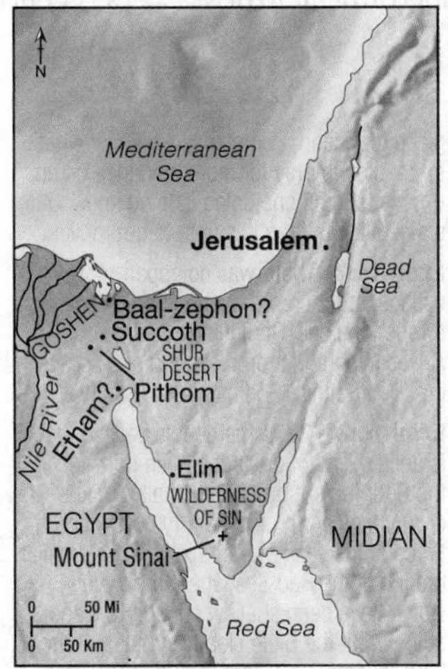

***THE EXODUS** The Israelites left Succoth and camped first at Etham before going toward Baal-zephon to camp by the sea (Exod 14:2). God miraculously brought them across the sea, into the desert of Shur (Exod 15:22). After stopping at the oasis of Elim, the people moved into the wilderness of Sin (Exod 16:1).*

Exod 13:17-18 God doesn't always work in the way that seems best to us. Instead of guiding the Hebrews along the direct route from Egypt to the Promised Land, he took them by a longer route to avoid fighting with the Philistines. If God does not lead you along the shortest path to your goal, don't complain or resist. Follow him willingly and trust him to lead you safely around unseen obstacles. He can see the end of your journey from the beginning, and he knows the safest and best route.

Exod 13:17-18 When did the Hebrews leave Egypt? There are two theories. The early theory says the Exodus occurred around 1446–1445 B.C. The late theory suggests the Exodus happened between 1300 and 1200 B.C. Those who hold to the earlier date point to 1 Kings 6:1, where the Bible clearly states that Solomon began building the Temple 480 years after the Hebrews left Egypt. Since almost all scholars agree that Solomon began building the Temple in 966, this puts the Exodus in the year 1446. But those who hold to the later date suggest that the 480 years cannot be taken literally. They point to Exodus 1:11, which says that the Hebrews built the store cities of Pithom and Rameses, named after Pharaoh Rameses II, who reigned around 1290 B.C. This Bible follows the earlier dating, but regardless of which date is correct, the fact is that God led the Hebrews out of Egypt, just as he had promised. This showed his great power and his great love for his people.

Exod 13:21-22 God gave the Hebrews a pillar of cloud and a pillar of fire so they would know day and night that God was with them on their journey to the Promised Land. What has God given us so that we can have the same assurance? The Bible—something the Israelites did not have. He also has given us the Holy Spirit to remind us of what the Bible says and to guide us each day (John 14:26). Look to God's Word for reassurance of his presence. As the Hebrews looked to the pillars of cloud and fire, we can look to God's Word day and night to know he is with us, helping us on our journey.

Exod 13:21-22 The pillars of fire and cloud were examples of *theophany*—God appearing in a physical form. In this form, God lighted Israel's path, protected them from their enemies, provided reassurance, controlled their movements, and inspired the burning zeal that Israel should have for their God.

The Egyptians Pursue Israel

EXODUS 14:5-14

When word reached the king of Egypt that the Israelites had fled, Pharaoh and his officials changed their minds. "What have we done, letting all those Israelite slaves get away?" they asked. 6So Pharaoh harnessed his chariot and called up his troops. 7He took with him 600 of Egypt's best chariots, along with the rest of the chariots of Egypt, each with its commander. 8The LORD hardened the heart of Pharaoh, the king of Egypt, so he chased after the people of Israel, who had left with fists raised in defiance. 9The Egyptians chased after them with all the forces in Pharaoh's army—all his horses and chariots, his charioteers, and his troops. The Egyptians caught up with the people of Israel as they were camped beside the shore near Pi-hahiroth, across from Baal-zephon.

10As Pharaoh approached, the people of Israel looked up and panicked when they saw the Egyptians overtaking them. They cried out to the LORD, 11and they said to Moses, "Why did you bring us out here to die in the wilderness? Weren't there enough graves for us in Egypt? What have you done to us? Why did you make us leave Egypt? 12Didn't we tell you this would happen while we were still in Egypt? We said, 'Leave us alone! Let us be slaves to the Egyptians. It's better to be a slave in Egypt than a corpse in the wilderness!'"

13But Moses told the people, "Don't be afraid. Just stand still and watch the LORD rescue you today. The Egyptians you see today will never be seen again. 14The LORD himself will fight for you. Just stay calm."

Escape through the Red Sea

EXODUS 14:15-31

Then the LORD said to Moses, "Why are you crying out to me? Tell the people to get moving! 16Pick up your staff and raise your hand over the sea. Divide the water so the Israelites can walk through the middle of the sea on dry ground. 17And I will harden the hearts of the Egyptians, and they will charge in after the Israelites. My great glory will be displayed through Pharaoh and his troops, his chariots, and his charioteers. 18When my glory is displayed through them, all Egypt will see my glory and know that I am the LORD!"

19Then the angel of God, who had been leading the people of Israel, moved to the rear of the camp. The pillar of cloud also moved from the front and stood behind them. 20The cloud settled between the Egyptian and Israelite camps. As darkness fell, the cloud turned to fire, lighting up the night. But the Egyptians and Israelites did not approach each other all night.

21Then Moses raised his hand over the sea, and the LORD opened up a path through the water with a strong east wind. The wind blew all that night, turning the seabed into dry land. 22So the people of Israel walked through the middle of the sea on dry ground, with walls of water on each side!

23Then the Egyptians—all of Pharaoh's horses, chariots, and charioteers—chased them into the middle of the sea. 24But just before dawn the LORD looked down on the Egyptian army from the pillar of fire and cloud, and he threw their forces into total confusion. 25He twisted* their chariot wheels, making their chariots difficult to drive. "Let's get out

Ex 14:25 As in Greek version, Samaritan Pentateuch, and Syriac version; Hebrew reads *He removed.*

Exod 14:6-9 Six hundred Egyptian war chariots were bearing down on the helpless Israelites, who were trapped between the mountains and the sea. The war chariots each carried two people—one to drive and one to fight. These chariots were made of a wood or leather cab placed over two wheels, and they were pulled by horses. These were the armored tanks of Bible times. But even their power was no match for God, who destroyed both the chariots and their soldiers.

Exod 14:10-11 Trapped against the sea, the Israelites faced the Egyptian army sweeping in for the kill. The Israelites thought they were doomed. After watching God's powerful hand deliver them from Egypt, their only response was fear, whining, and despair. Where was their trust in God? Israel had to learn from repeated experience that God was able to provide for them. God has preserved these examples in the Bible so that we can learn to trust him the first time. By focusing on God's faithfulness in the past, we can face crises with confidence rather than with fear and complaining.

Exod 14:11-12 This is the first instance of grumbling and complaining by the Israelites during their journey to the Promised Land. Grumbling would become a major problem for the people on this journey. Their lack of faith in God is startling. Yet how often do we find ourselves doing the same thing—complaining over inconveniences or discomforts? The Israelites were about to learn some tough lessons. Had they trusted God, they would have been spared much grief.

Exod 14:13-14 The people were hostile and despairing, but Moses encouraged them to watch the wonderful way God would rescue them. Moses had a positive attitude! When it looked as if they were trapped, Moses called upon God to intervene. We may not be chased by an army, but we may still feel trapped. Instead of giving in to despair, we should adopt Moses' attitude to "stand still and watch the LORD rescue" us.

Exod 14:15 The Lord told Moses to stop praying and get moving! Prayer must have a vital place in our lives, but there is also a place for action. Sometimes we know what to do, but we pray for more guidance as an excuse to postpone doing it. If we know what we should do, then it is time to get moving.

Exod 14:21 There was no apparent way of escape, but the Lord opened up a dry path through the sea. Sometimes we find ourselves caught in a problem and see no way out. Don't panic; God can open up a way.

Exod 14:21-22 Some people believe the Israelites did not cross the main body of the Red Sea but one of the shallow lakes or marshes north of it that dry up at certain times of the year, or perhaps it was a smaller branch of the Red Sea where the water would have been shallow enough to wade across. But the Bible clearly states that the Lord "opened up a path through the water with a strong east wind . . . turning the seabed into dry land" (Exod 14:21; see also Josh 3:15-16; 2 Kgs 2:13-14). Also, the water was deep enough to cover the chariots (Exod 14:28). The God who created the earth and water performed a mighty miracle at exactly the right time to demonstrate his great power and love for his people.

of here—away from these Israelites!" the Egyptians shouted. "The LORD is fighting for them against Egypt!"

26 When all the Israelites had reached the other side, the LORD said to Moses, "Raise your hand over the sea again. Then the waters will rush back and cover the Egyptians and their chariots and charioteers."
27 So as the sun began to rise, Moses raised his hand over the sea, and the water rushed back into its usual place. The Egyptians tried to escape, but the LORD swept them into the sea.
28 Then the waters returned and covered all the chariots and charioteers—the entire army of Pharaoh. Of all the Egyptians who had chased the Israelites into the sea, not a single one survived.

29 But the people of Israel had walked through the middle of the sea on dry ground, as the water stood up like a wall on both sides.
30 That is how the LORD rescued Israel from the hand of the Egyptians that day. And the Israelites saw the bodies of the Egyptians washed up on the seashore.
31 When the people of Israel saw the mighty power that the LORD had unleashed against the Egyptians, they were filled with awe before him. They put their faith in the LORD and in his servant Moses.

A Song of Deliverance

EXODUS 15:1-21

Then Moses and the people of Israel sang this song to the LORD:

1 "I will sing to the LORD,
for he has triumphed gloriously;
he has hurled both horse and rider
into the sea.
2 The LORD is my strength and my song;
he has given me victory.
This is my God, and I will praise him—
my father's God, and I will exalt him!
3 The LORD is a warrior;
Yahweh* is his name!
4 Pharaoh's chariots and army
he has hurled into the sea.
The finest of Pharaoh's officers
are drowned in the Red Sea.*
5 The deep waters gushed over them;
they sank to the bottom like a stone.

6 "Your right hand, O LORD,
is glorious in power.

Ex 15:3 *Yahweh* is a transliteration of the proper name *YHWH* that is sometimes rendered "Jehovah"; in this translation it is usually rendered "the LORD" (note the use of small capitals). **Ex 15:4** Hebrew *sea of reeds;* also in 15:22.

Exod 14:27-28 No evidence of this great Exodus has been discovered in Egyptian historical records. This was because it was a common practice for Egyptian pharaohs not to record their defeats. They even went so far as to take existing records and delete the names of traitors and political adversaries. Pharaoh would have been especially anxious not to record that his great army was destroyed chasing a band of runaway slaves. Since either the Egyptians failed to record the Exodus or the record has not yet been found, it is impossible to place a precise date on the event.

Exod 15:1ff Music played an important part in Israel's worship and celebration. Singing was an expression of love and thanks, and it was a creative way to pass down oral traditions. This song of Moses was a festive epic poem celebrating God's victory, lifting the hearts and voices of the people outward and upward. After having been delivered from great danger, they sang with joy! Psalms and hymns can be great ways to express relief, praise, and thanks when you have been through trouble.

The Red Sea

In modern times, the Red Sea refers to an arm of the Indian Ocean, lying between Africa and the Middle East. It is a long, narrow body of water, about 1,350 miles long and averaging 180 miles wide. In the Hebrew Old Testament the Red Sea is called the "Sea of Reeds," but English translations ordinarily render it "Red Sea," following the Septuagint. This body of water could be different from what is known today as the Red Sea.

The crossing of the Red Sea by the Israelites at the time of the Exodus is one of the most celebrated events of Hebrew history. The place of this crossing is much debated. Wherever it occurred, it is evident that the water was too deep to wade across and the distance too far to swim—it was wide enough to engulf the whole Egyptian army and deep enough to drown them. Confronted by the sea and closely pursued by the troops and chariots of the best army in the world at that time, the Israelites were delivered by the direct intervention of the Lord, who used an east wind to make a channel for their passage upon the seabed (Exod 14:10-31).

In the New Testament, Paul likens the crossing of the Red Sea to baptism (1 Cor 10:1-2). The crossing was a mighty symbol of God's saving work on behalf of his people, an event that the Hebrews always looked back on to remember the salvation of their God. How do you remind yourself of God's great saving work in your life?

▸ **EXODUS 15:1-21** ***(cont.)***

Your right hand, O Lord,
smashes the enemy.
7 In the greatness of your majesty,
you overthrow those who rise against you.
You unleash your blazing fury;
it consumes them like straw.
8 At the blast of your breath,
the waters piled up!
The surging waters stood straight like a wall;
in the heart of the sea the deep waters
became hard.
9 "The enemy boasted, 'I will chase them
and catch up with them.
I will plunder them
and consume them.
I will flash my sword;
my powerful hand will destroy them.'
10 But you blew with your breath,
and the sea covered them.
They sank like lead
in the mighty waters.
11 "Who is like you among the gods,
O Lord—
glorious in holiness,
awesome in splendor,
performing great wonders?
12 You raised your right hand,
and the earth swallowed our enemies.
13 "With your unfailing love you lead
the people you have redeemed.
In your might, you guide them
to your sacred home.
14 The peoples hear and tremble;
anguish grips those who live in Philistia.
15 The leaders of Edom are terrified;
the nobles of Moab tremble.
All who live in Canaan melt away;
16 terror and dread fall upon them.
The power of your arm
makes them lifeless as stone
until your people pass by, O Lord,
until the people you purchased pass by.
17 You will bring them in and plant them on your
own mountain—
the place, O Lord, reserved for your own
dwelling,
the sanctuary, O Lord, that your hands have
established.
18 The Lord will reign forever and ever!"

19When Pharaoh's horses, chariots, and charioteers
rushed into the sea, the Lord brought the water crashing down on them. But the people of Israel had walked
through the middle of the sea on dry ground!
20Then Miriam the prophet, Aaron's sister, took
a tambourine and led all the women as they played
their tambourines and danced. 21And Miriam sang
this song:

"Sing to the Lord,
for he has triumphed gloriously;
he has hurled both horse and rider
into the sea."

3. COMPLAINING IN THE WILDERNESS

Once they had been rescued from Egypt, the people quickly became dissatisfied and complained bitterly to Moses and Aaron about their trek through the wilderness. It is so easy to forget the things God has saved us from and complain about the problems we still face.

Bitter Water at Marah

EXODUS 15:22-27

Then Moses led the people of Israel away from the Red
Sea, and they moved out into the desert of Shur. They
traveled in this desert for three days without finding
any water. 23When they came to the oasis of Marah,
the water was too bitter to drink. So they called the
place Marah (which means "bitter").
24Then the people complained and turned against
Moses. "What are we going to drink?" they demanded.
25So Moses cried out to the Lord for help, and the
Lord showed him a piece of wood. Moses threw it
into the water, and this made the water good to drink.
It was there at Marah that the Lord set before them
the following decree as a standard to test their faithfulness to him. 26He said, "If you will listen carefully

Exod 15:20 Miriam was called a prophet not only because she received revelations from God (Num 12:1-2; Mic 6:4) but also because of her musical skill. Prophecy and music were often closely related in the Bible (1 Sam 10:5; 1 Chr 25:1).

Exod 15:23, 27 The water in the oasis of Marah is contrasted with the springs in the oasis of Elim. Marah stands for the unbelieving, grumbling attitude of the people who would not trust God. Elim stands for God's bountiful provision. How easy it is to grumble and complain too quickly, only to be embarrassed by God's help! We must be patient for God's kindness and help. Don't let your negative attitude erode your trust in God.

Exod 15:26 God promised that if the people obeyed him, they would not suffer from the diseases that plagued the Egyptians. Little did they know that many of the moral laws he later gave them were designed to keep them free from sickness. For example, following God's law against prostitution would keep them free of venereal disease. God's laws for us are often designed to keep us from harm. Men and women are complex beings. Our physical, emotional, and spiritual lives are intertwined. Modern medicine is now acknowledging what these laws assumed. If we want God to care for us, we need to submit to his directions for living.

to the voice of the LORD your God and do what is right in his sight, obeying his commands and keeping all his decrees, then I will not make you suffer any of the diseases I sent on the Egyptians; for I am the LORD who heals you."

[27]After leaving Marah, the Israelites traveled on to the oasis of Elim, where they found twelve springs and seventy palm trees. They camped there beside the water.

Manna and Quail from Heaven

EXODUS 16:1-36

Then the whole community of Israel set out from Elim and journeyed into the wilderness of Sin,* between Elim and Mount Sinai. They arrived there on the fifteenth day of the second month, one month after leaving the land of Egypt.* [2]There, too, the whole community of Israel complained about Moses and Aaron.

[3]"If only the LORD had killed us back in Egypt," they moaned. "There we sat around pots filled with meat and ate all the bread we wanted. But now you have brought us into this wilderness to starve us all to death."

[4]Then the LORD said to Moses, "Look, I'm going to rain down food from heaven for you. Each day the people can go out and pick up as much food as they need for that day. I will test them in this to see whether or not they will follow my instructions. [5]On the sixth day they will gather food, and when they prepare it, there will be twice as much as usual."

[6]So Moses and Aaron said to all the people of Israel, "By evening you will realize it was the LORD who brought you out of the land of Egypt. [7]In the morning you will see the glory of the LORD, because he has heard your complaints, which are against him, not against us. What have we done that you should complain about us?" [8]Then Moses added, "The LORD will give you meat to eat in the evening and bread to satisfy you in the morning, for he has heard all your complaints against him. What have we done? Yes, your complaints are against the LORD, not against us."

[9]Then Moses said to Aaron, "Announce this to the entire community of Israel: 'Present yourselves before the LORD, for he has heard your complaining.'" [10]And as Aaron spoke to the whole community of Israel, they looked out toward the wilderness. There they could see the awesome glory of the LORD in the cloud.

[11]Then the LORD said to Moses, [12]"I have heard the Israelites' complaints. Now tell them, 'In the evening you will have meat to eat, and in the morning you will

Ex 16:1a The geographical name *Sin* is related to *Sinai* and should not be confused with the English word *sin*. **Ex 16:1b** The Exodus had occurred on the fifteenth day of the first month (see Num 33:3).

FAMOUS SONGS IN THE BIBLE

Where	*Purpose of Song*
Exod 15:1-21	Moses' song of deliverance and praise after God led Israel out of Egypt and saved them by parting the Red Sea; Miriam joined in the singing too
Num 21:17-18	Israel's song of praise to God for giving them water in the wilderness
Deut 32:1-43	Moses' song of Israel's history with thanksgiving and praise as the Hebrews were about to enter the Promised Land
Judg 5:2-31	Deborah and Barak's song of praise thanking God for Israel's victory over King Jabin's army at Mount Tabor
2 Sam 22:2-51	David's song of thanks and praise to God for rescuing him from Saul and his other enemies
Song of Songs	Solomon's song of love celebrating the union of husband and wife
Isa 26:1-21	Isaiah's prophetic song about how the redeemed will sing in the new Jerusalem
Ezra 3:11	Israel's song of praise at the completion of the Temple's foundation
Luke 1:46-55	Mary's song of praise to God for the conception of Jesus
Luke 1:68-79	Zechariah's song of praise for the birth of his son
Acts 16:25	Paul and Silas sang hymns in prison
Rev 5:9-10	The "new song" of the 24 elders acclaiming Christ as worthy to break the seven seals of God's scroll
Rev 14:3	The song of the 144,000 redeemed from the earth
Rev 15:3-4	The song of all the redeemed in praise of the Lamb who has redeemed them

Exod 16:1 The wilderness of Sin was a vast, hostile environment of sand and stone. Its barren surroundings provided the perfect place for God to test and shape the character of his people.

Exod 16:2-3 It happened again. As the Israelites encountered danger, shortages, and inconvenience, they complained bitterly and longed to be back in Egypt. But as always, God provided for their needs. Difficult circumstances often lead to stress, and complaining is a natural response. The Israelites didn't really want to be back in Egypt; they just wanted life to get a little easier. In the pressure of the moment, they could not focus on the cause of their stress (in this case, lack of trust in God); they could only think about the quickest way of escape. When pressure comes your way, resist the temptation to make a quick escape. Instead, focus on God's power and wisdom to help you deal with the cause of your stress.

Exod 16:4-5 God promised to meet the Hebrews' need for food in the desert, but he decided to test their obedience. God wanted to see if they would obey his detailed instructions. We can learn to trust him as our Lord only by following. We can learn to obey by taking small steps of obedience.

▶ **EXODUS 16:1-36 *(cont.)***

have all the bread you want. Then you will know that I am the LORD your God.'"

13 That evening vast numbers of quail flew in and covered the camp. And the next morning the area around the camp was wet with dew. 14 When the dew evaporated, a flaky substance as fine as frost blanketed the ground. 15 The Israelites were puzzled when they saw it. "What is it?" they asked each other. They had no idea what it was.

And Moses told them, "It is the food the LORD has given you to eat. 16 These are the LORD's instructions: Each household should gather as much as it needs. Pick up two quarts* for each person in your tent."

17 So the people of Israel did as they were told. Some gathered a lot, some only a little. 18 But when they measured it out,* everyone had just enough. Those who gathered a lot had nothing left over, and those who gathered only a little had enough. Each family had just what it needed.

19 Then Moses told them, "Do not keep any of it until morning." 20 But some of them didn't listen and kept some of it until morning. But by then it was full of maggots and had a terrible smell. Moses was very angry with them.

21 After this the people gathered the food morning by morning, each family according to its need. And as the sun became hot, the flakes they had not picked up melted and disappeared. 22 On the sixth day, they gathered twice as much as usual—four quarts* for each person instead of two. Then all the leaders of the community came and asked Moses for an explanation. 23 He told them, "This is what the LORD commanded: Tomorrow will be a day of complete rest, a holy Sabbath day set apart for the LORD. So bake or boil as much as you want today, and set aside what is left for tomorrow."

24 So they put some aside until morning, just as Moses had commanded. And in the morning the leftover food was wholesome and good, without maggots or odor. 25 Moses said, "Eat this food today, for today is a Sabbath day dedicated to the LORD. There will be no food on the ground today. 26 You may gather the food for six days, but the seventh day is the Sabbath. There will be no food on the ground that day."

27 Some of the people went out anyway on the seventh day, but they found no food. 28 The LORD asked Moses, "How long will these people refuse to obey my commands and instructions? 29 They must realize that the Sabbath is the LORD's gift to you. That is why he gives you a two-day supply on the sixth day, so there will be enough for two days. On the Sabbath day you must each stay in your place. Do not go out to pick up food on the seventh day." 30 So the people did not gather any food on the seventh day.

31 The Israelites called the food manna.* It was white like coriander seed, and it tasted like honey wafers.

32 Then Moses said, "This is what the LORD has commanded: Fill a two-quart container with manna to preserve it for your descendants. Then later generations will be able to see the food I gave you in the wilderness when I set you free from Egypt."

33 Moses said to Aaron, "Get a jar and fill it with two quarts of manna. Then put it in a sacred place before the LORD to preserve it for all future generations." 34 Aaron did just as the LORD had commanded Moses. He eventually placed it in the Ark of the Covenant—in front of the stone tablets inscribed with the terms of the covenant.* 35 So the people of Israel ate manna for forty years until they arrived at the land where they would settle. They ate manna until they came to the border of the land of Canaan.

36 The container used to measure the manna was an omer, which was one-tenth of an ephah; it held about two quarts.*

Ex 16:16 Hebrew *1 omer* [2 liters]; also in 16:32, 33. **Ex 16:18** Hebrew *measured it with an omer.* **Ex 16:22** Hebrew *2 omers* [4 liters]. **Ex 16:31** *Manna* means "What is it?" See 16:15. **Ex 16:34** Hebrew *He placed it in front of the Testimony;* see note on 25:16. **Ex 16:36** Hebrew *An omer is one-tenth of an ephah.*

Exod 16:14-16 Manna (Exod 16:31) appeared on the ground each day as thin flakes like frost. The people gathered it, ground it like grain, and made it into honey-tasting pancakes. For the Israelites, manna was a gift—it came every day and was just what they needed. It satisfied their temporary physical need. In John 6:48-51 Jesus compares himself to manna. Christ is our daily bread who satisfies our eternal, spiritual need.

Exod 16:23 The Israelites were not to work on the Sabbath—not even to cook food. Why? God knew that the busy routine of daily living could distract people from worshiping him. It is so easy to let work, family responsibilities, and recreation crowd our schedules so tightly that we don't take time to worship. Carefully guard your time with God.

Exod 16:32 The Hebrews put some manna in a special jar as a reminder of the way God provided for them in the wilderness. Symbols have always been an important part of Christian worship as well. We use special objects as symbols to remind us of God's work. Such symbols can be valuable aids to our worship as long as we are careful to keep them from becoming objects of worship.

***JOURNEY TO MOUNT SINAI* ▶**
God miraculously supplied food and water in the wilderness for the Israelites. In the wilderness of Sin, he provided manna (Exod 16). At Rephidim, he provided water from a rock (Exod 17:1-7). Finally God brought them to the foot of Mount Sinai, where he gave them his holy laws.

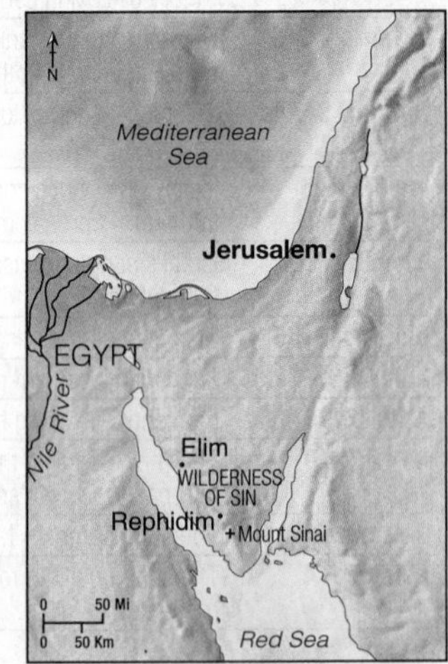

Water from the Rock

EXODUS 17:1-7

At the LORD's command, the whole community of Israel left the wilderness of Sin* and moved from place
to place. Eventually they camped at Rephidim, but
there was no water there for the people to drink. 2So
once more the people complained against Moses.
"Give us water to drink!" they demanded.
"Quiet!" Moses replied. "Why are you complaining
against me? And why are you testing the LORD?"
3But tormented by thirst, they continued to argue
with Moses. "Why did you bring us out of Egypt? Are
you trying to kill us, our children, and our livestock
with thirst?"
4Then Moses cried out to the LORD, "What should
I do with these people? They are ready to stone me!"
5The LORD said to Moses, "Walk out in front of the
people. Take your staff, the one you used when you
struck the water of the Nile, and call some of the elders
of Israel to join you. 6I will stand before you on the rock
at Mount Sinai.* Strike the rock, and water will come
gushing out. Then the people will be able to drink."
So Moses struck the rock as he was told, and water
gushed out as the elders looked on.
7Moses named the place Massah (which means
"test") and Meribah (which means "arguing") because
the people of Israel argued with Moses and tested the
LORD by saying, "Is the LORD here with us or not?"

Israel Defeats the Amalekites

EXODUS 17:8-16

While the people of Israel were still at Rephidim,
the warriors of Amalek attacked them. 9Moses commanded Joshua, "Choose some men to go out and
fight the army of Amalek for us. Tomorrow, I will
stand at the top of the hill, holding the staff of God
in my hand."
10So Joshua did what Moses had commanded and
fought the army of Amalek. Meanwhile, Moses, Aaron,
and Hur climbed to the top of a nearby hill. 11As long
as Moses held up the staff in his hand, the Israelites
had the advantage. But whenever he dropped his hand,
the Amalekites gained the advantage. 12Moses' arms
soon became so tired he could no longer hold them
up. So Aaron and Hur found a stone for him to sit
on. Then they stood on each side of Moses, holding
up his hands. So his hands held steady until sunset.
13As a result, Joshua overwhelmed the army of Amalek in battle.
14After the victory, the LORD instructed Moses,
"Write this down on a scroll as a permanent reminder,
and read it aloud to Joshua: I will erase the memory
of Amalek from under heaven." 15Moses built an altar
there and named it Yahweh-Nissi (which means "the
LORD is my banner"). 16He said, "They have raised their
fist against the LORD's throne, so now* the LORD will
be at war with Amalek generation after generation."

Ex 17:1 The geographical name *Sin* is related to *Sinai* and should not be confused with the English word *sin.* **Ex 17:6** Hebrew *Horeb,* another name for Sinai. **Ex 17:16** Or *Hands have been lifted up to the LORD's throne, and now.*

Exod 17:2 Again the people complained about their problem instead of praying. Some problems can be solved by careful thought or by rearranging our priorities. Some can be solved by discussion and good counsel. But some problems can be solved only by prayer. We should make a determined effort to pray when we feel like complaining because complaining only raises our level of stress. Prayer quiets our thoughts and emotions and prepares us to listen.

Exod 17:8 The Amalekites were descendants of Amalek, a grandson of Esau. They were a fierce nomadic tribe that lived in the desert region of the Dead Sea. They made part of their livelihood by conducting frequent raids on other settlements and carrying off plundered goods. They killed for pleasure. One of the greatest insults in Israelite culture was to call someone "a friend of Amalek." When the Israelites entered the region, the warriors of Amalek saw this as a perfect opportunity for both pleasure and profit. But this hostile tribe was moving in on the wrong group—a people led by God. For the Israelite slaves to defeat such a warlike nation was more than enough proof that God was with them as he had promised to be.

Exod 17:9 Here we meet Joshua for the first time. Later he would become the great leader who would bring God's people into the Promised Land. As a general of the Israelite army, he was gaining valuable experience for the greater battles to come.

Exod 17:10-13 Aaron and Hur stood by Moses' side and held up his arms to ensure victory against Amalek. We need to "hold up the hands" of our spiritual leaders as well. Shouldering some responsibility, lending a word of encouragement, or offering a prayer are ways of refreshing spiritual leaders in their work.

Desert of Sinai

After passing through the Red Sea, the Israelites traveled through the Sinai Desert, which was a wilderness. A wilderness is usually a place with no settled population (Num 14:33; Deut 32:10) and is the dwelling place of wildlife: wild donkeys (Job 24:5), jackals (Mal 1:3), and ostriches (Lam 4:3). The wilderness is also a desert—an infertile, desolate, bare place. In such a harsh environment the Israelites needed God's miraculous supply to keep them alive. Sometimes we Christians have a "wilderness" experience where we feel dry and destitute. Stay steadfast in your faith. Believe in God to supply you with everything you need.

Jethro's Visit to Moses

EXODUS 18:1-12

Moses' father-in-law, Jethro, the priest of Midian, heard about everything God had done for Moses and his people, the Israelites. He heard especially about how the LORD had rescued them from Egypt.

2Earlier, Moses had sent his wife, Zipporah, and his two sons back to Jethro, who had taken them in. 3(Moses' first son was named Gershom,* for Moses had said when the boy was born, "I have been a foreigner in a foreign land." 4His second son was named Eliezer,* for Moses had said, "The God of my ancestors was my helper; he rescued me from the sword of Pharaoh.") 5Jethro, Moses' father-in-law, now came to visit Moses in the wilderness. He brought Moses' wife and two sons with him, and they arrived while Moses and the people were camped near the mountain of God. 6Jethro had sent a message to Moses, saying, "I, Jethro, your father-in-law, am coming to see you with your wife and your two sons."

7So Moses went out to meet his father-in-law. He bowed low and kissed him. They asked about each other's welfare and then went into Moses' tent. 8Moses told his father-in-law everything the LORD had done to Pharaoh and Egypt on behalf of Israel. He also told about all the hardships they had experienced along the way and how the LORD had rescued his people from all their troubles. 9Jethro was delighted when he heard about all the good things the LORD had done for Israel as he rescued them from the hand of the Egyptians.

10"Praise the LORD," Jethro said, "for he has rescued you from the Egyptians and from Pharaoh. Yes, he has rescued Israel from the powerful hand of Egypt! 11I know now that the LORD is greater than all other gods, because he rescued his people from the oppression of the proud Egyptians."

12Then Jethro, Moses' father-in-law, brought a burnt offering and sacrifices to God. Aaron and all the elders of Israel came out and joined him in a sacrificial meal in God's presence.

Jethro's Wise Advice

EXODUS 18:13-27

The next day, Moses took his seat to hear the people's disputes against each other. They waited before him from morning till evening.

14When Moses' father-in-law saw all that Moses was doing for the people, he asked, "What are you really accomplishing here? Why are you trying to do all this alone while everyone stands around you from morning till evening?"

15Moses replied, "Because the people come to me to get a ruling from God. 16When a dispute arises, they come to me, and I am the one who settles the case between the quarreling parties. I inform the people of God's decrees and give them his instructions."

17"This is not good!" Moses' father-in-law exclaimed. 18"You're going to wear yourself out—and the people, too. This job is too heavy a burden for you to handle all by yourself. 19Now listen to me, and let me give you a word of advice, and may God be with you.

Ex 18:3 *Gershom* sounds like a Hebrew term that means "a foreigner there." **Ex 18:4** *Eliezer* means "God is my helper."

JETHRO

People such as Jethro and Melchizedek—not Israelites, but nevertheless worshipers of the one true God—play an important role in the Old Testament. They remind us of God's commitment to the world. God chose one nation through which to work, but his love and concern are for all nations! • Jethro's religious background prepared him for, rather than prevented him from, responding in faith to God. When he saw and heard what God had done for the Israelites, he worshiped God wholeheartedly. We can guess that for 40 years as Moses' father-in-law, Jethro had been watching God at work, molding a leader. Moses' and Jethro's relationship must have been close, for Moses readily accepted his father-in-law's advice. Each benefited from knowing the other. Jethro met God through Moses, and Moses received hospitality, his wife, and wisdom from Jethro. • The greatest gift one person can give another is an introduction to God. But real friends give to and receive from each other. The importance of introducing a friend to God does not make the friend's gifts to us insignificant. Rather, the believer is doubly blessed—first by receiving the gifts the friend wishes to give; then by growing in knowledge of the Lord. As we give God away, he gives himself even more to us. • Only by having a vital relationship with God can you pass on to others the excitement of allowing God to guide your life. Have you reached the point of saying, with Jethro, "I know now that the LORD is greater than all other gods" (Exod 18:11)?

Strengths and accomplishments	• As father-in-law to Moses, he came to recognize the one true God • He was a practical troubleshooter and organizer
Lessons from his life	• Supervision and administration are team efforts • God's plan includes all nations
Vital statistics	• Where: The land of Midian and the wilderness of Sinai • Occupations: Shepherd, priest • Relatives: Daughter: Zipporah. Son-in-law: Moses. Son: Hobab.
Key verse	"Jethro was delighted when he heard about all the good things the LORD had done for Israel as he rescued them from the hand of the Egyptians" (Exod 18:9).

Jethro's story is told in Exodus 2:15–3:1; 18:1-27. He is also mentioned in Judges 1:16.

You should continue to be the people's representative before God, bringing their disputes to him. [20]Teach them God's decrees, and give them his instructions. Show them how to conduct their lives. [21]But select from all the people some capable, honest men who fear God and hate bribes. Appoint them as leaders over groups of one thousand, one hundred, fifty, and ten. [22]They should always be available to solve the people's common disputes, but have them bring the major cases to you. Let the leaders decide the smaller matters themselves. They will help you carry the load, making the task easier for you. [23]If you follow this advice, and if God commands you to do so, then you will be able to endure the pressures, and all these people will go home in peace."

[24]Moses listened to his father-in-law's advice and followed his suggestions. [25]He chose capable men from all over Israel and appointed them as leaders over the people. He put them in charge of groups of one thousand, one hundred, fifty, and ten. [26]These men were always available to solve the people's common disputes. They brought the major cases to Moses, but they took care of the smaller matters themselves.

[27]Soon after this, Moses said good-bye to his father-in-law, who returned to his own land.

C. Israel at Sinai

After escaping through the Red Sea, the Hebrews traveled through the wilderness and arrived at Sinai, God's holy mountain. There they received the Ten Commandments, as well as instructions for building a Tabernacle as a center of worship. These laws, and their acceptance of God's covenant promises, marked the formal transition from being God's chosen people to becoming his holy nation. Through Israel's experiences at Mount Sinai, we learn about the importance of obedience in our relationship with God. His laws help expose sin, and they give standards for righteous living.

1. GIVING THE LAW

Having rescued the Hebrews from slavery in Egypt, God further revealed himself to his people by giving them a body of instructions for worshiping him and life as a nation. The people accepted God's covenant and agreed to worship him alone and follow him.

The Lord Reveals Himself at Sinai

EXODUS 19:1-25

Exactly two months after the Israelites left Egypt,* they arrived in the wilderness of Sinai. [2]After breaking camp at Rephidim, they came to the wilderness of Sinai and set up camp there at the base of Mount Sinai.

[3]Then Moses climbed the mountain to appear before God. The Lord called to him from the mountain and said, "Give these instructions to the family of Jacob; announce it to the descendants of Israel: [4]'You have seen what I did to the Egyptians. You know how I carried you on eagles' wings and brought you to myself. [5]Now

Ex 19:1 Hebrew *In the third month after the Israelites left Egypt, on the very day*, i.e., two lunar months to the day after leaving Egypt. Compare Num 33:3.

Exod 18:7 Jethro entered Moses' tent where the two talked. Tents were the homes of shepherds. In shape and design, they resembled the tents of today, but they were very large and made of a thick cloth woven from goat or camel hair. This fabric breathed in warm weather and contracted in stormy weather to offer protection from the winter winds and rains. The floor was often covered with animal-skin rugs, while curtains divided the inside space into rooms.

Exod 18:8-11 Moses told his father-in-law all that God had done, convincing him that the Lord was greater than any other god. Our relatives are often the hardest people to tell about God. Yet we should look for opportunities to tell them what God is doing in our lives because we can have an important influence on them.

Exod 18:12 This reunion turned into a large celebration. The Israelites frequently shared a sacrificial meal among themselves. A burnt offering was sacrificed to God, and then the meal taken from the sacrifice was dedicated to God and eaten ceremonially as a fellowship dinner.

Exod 18:13-26 Moses was spending so much time and energy hearing the Hebrews' complaints that he could not get to other important work. Jethro suggested that Moses delegate most of this work to others and focus his efforts on jobs only he could do. People in positions of responsibility sometimes feel they are the only ones who can do necessary tasks; but others are capable of handling part of the load. Delegation relieved Moses' stress and improved the quality of governance. It helped prepare the Israelites for the system of government set up in Canaan. Proper delegation can multiply your effectiveness while giving others a chance to grow.

Exod 18:16 Moses not only decided these cases, but he also taught the people God's laws. Whenever we help others settle disputes or resolve conflicts, we should also look for opportunities to teach about God.

Exod 19:2-3 Mount Sinai is one of the most sacred locations in Israel's history. Located in the south-central Sinai Peninsula, this mountain is where Moses met God in a burning bush, God made his covenant with Israel, and Elijah heard God in the gentle whisper. Here God gave his people the laws and guidelines for right living. They learned the potential blessings of obedience (Exod 34:4-28) and the tragic consequences of disobedience (Exod 34:7).

Exod 19:4-6 God had a reason for rescuing the Israelites from slavery. Now he was ready to tell them what it was: Israel was to become a kingdom of priests and a holy nation where anyone could approach God freely and they would represent God to the rest of the world. It didn't take long, however, for the people to corrupt God's plan. God then established Aaron's descendants from the tribe of Levi as priests (Lev 8–9), representing what the entire nation should have been. But with the coming of Jesus Christ, God has once again extended his plan to all believers. We are to become holy, "royal priests" (1 Pet 2:9). The death and resurrection of Christ has allowed each of us to approach God freely.

▸ **EXODUS 19:1-25** ***(cont.)***

if you will obey me and keep my covenant, you will be my own special treasure from among all the peoples on earth; for all the earth belongs to me. 6And you will be my kingdom of priests, my holy nation.' This is the message you must give to the people of Israel."

7So Moses returned from the mountain and called together the elders of the people and told them everything the LORD had commanded him. 8And all the people responded together, "We will do everything the LORD has commanded." So Moses brought the people's answer back to the LORD.

9Then the LORD said to Moses, "I will come to you in a thick cloud, Moses, so the people themselves can hear me when I speak with you. Then they will always trust you."

Moses told the LORD what the people had said. 10Then the LORD told Moses, "Go down and prepare the people for my arrival. Consecrate them today and tomorrow, and have them wash their clothing. 11Be sure they are ready on the third day, for on that day the LORD will come down on Mount Sinai as all the people watch. 12Mark off a boundary all around the mountain. Warn the people, 'Be careful! Do not go up on the mountain or even touch its boundaries. Anyone who touches the mountain will certainly be put to death. 13No hand may touch the person or animal that crosses the boundary; instead, stone them or shoot them with arrows. They must be put to death.' However, when the ram's horn sounds a long blast, then the people may go up on the mountain.*"

14So Moses went down to the people. He consecrated them for worship, and they washed their clothes. 15He told them, "Get ready for the third day, and until then abstain from having sexual intercourse."

16On the morning of the third day, thunder roared and lightning flashed, and a dense cloud came down on the mountain. There was a long, loud blast from a ram's horn, and all the people trembled. 17Moses led them out from the camp to meet with God, and they stood at the foot of the mountain. 18All of Mount Sinai was covered with smoke because the LORD had descended on it in the form of fire. The smoke billowed into the sky like smoke from a brick kiln, and the whole mountain shook violently. 19As the blast of the ram's horn grew louder and louder, Moses spoke, and God thundered his reply. 20The LORD came down on the top of Mount Sinai and called Moses to the top of the mountain. So Moses climbed the mountain.

21Then the LORD told Moses, "Go back down and warn the people not to break through the boundaries to see the LORD, or they will die. 22Even the priests who regularly come near to the LORD must purify themselves so that the LORD does not break out and destroy them."

23"But LORD," Moses protested, "the people cannot come up to Mount Sinai. You already warned us. You told me, 'Mark off a boundary all around the mountain to set it apart as holy.'"

24But the LORD said, "Go down and bring Aaron back up with you. In the meantime, do not let the priests or the people break through to approach the LORD, or he will break out and destroy them."

25So Moses went down to the people and told them what the LORD had said.

Ten Commandments for the Covenant Community

EXODUS 20:1-21

Then God gave the people all these instructions*:

2"I am the LORD your God, who rescued you from the land of Egypt, the place of your slavery.

3"You must not have any other god but me.

4"You must not make for yourself an idol of any kind or an image of anything in the heavens or on the earth or in the sea. 5You must not bow down

Ex 19:13 Or *up to the mountain.* **Ex 20:1** Hebrew *all these words.*

Exod 19:5 Why did God choose Israel as his nation? God knew that no nation on earth was good enough to deserve to be called his people, his "special treasure." He chose Israel, not because of anything they had done, but in his love and mercy he chose Israel in spite of the wrong the nation had done and would do. Why did he want to have a special nation on earth? To represent his way of life, to teach his Word, and to be an agent of salvation to the world. "All the nations of the earth" would be blessed through Abraham's descendants (Gen 18:18). Gentiles and kings would come to the Lord through Israel, predicted Isaiah (Isa 60:3). Through the nation of Israel, the Messiah, God's chosen Son, would be born. God chose one nation and put it through a rigorous training program, so that one day it could be a channel for his blessings to the whole world.

Exod 19:5-8 In Genesis 15 and 17, God made a covenant with Abraham, promising to make his descendants into a great nation. Now that promise was being realized as God restated his agreement with the Israelite nation, the descendants of Abraham. God promised to bless and care for them. The people promised to obey him. The covenant was thus sealed. But the good intentions of the people quickly wore off. Have you made a commitment to God? How are you holding up your end of the bargain?

Exod 19:9-11 Moses was told to consecrate the people. This meant getting them physically and spiritually ready to meet God. The people were to set themselves apart from sin and even ordinary daily routine in order to dedicate themselves to God. The act of washing and preparing served to get their minds and hearts ready. When we meet God for worship, we should set aside the cares and preoccupations of everyday life. Use your time of physical preparation to get your mind ready to meet God.

Exod 19:23 Because God's glory and power were so strong, and because God is completely holy, the people could not come to him. God did this to show that he was not like the idols of Egypt that could be seen and touched. Today we are invited to approach God because of what Christ has done for us (Heb 12:18-24). Jesus is superior to Moses because Jesus opens the way for us to come to God with great joy.

Exod 20:1ff Why were the Ten Commandments necessary for God's new nation? At the foot of Mount Sinai, God showed his people the true function and beauty of his laws. The commandments were designed to lead Israel to a life of practical holiness.

to them or worship them, for I, the LORD your
God, am a jealous God who will not tolerate your
affection for any other gods. I lay the sins of the
parents upon their children; the entire family is
affected—even children in the third and fourth
generations of those who reject me. 6 But I lavish
unfailing love for a thousand generations on
those* who love me and obey my commands.
7 "You must not misuse the name of the LORD your
God. The LORD will not let you go unpunished if
you misuse his name.
8 "Remember to observe the Sabbath day by keeping
it holy. 9 You have six days each week for your
ordinary work, 10 but the seventh day is a Sabbath
day of rest dedicated to the LORD your God. On
that day no one in your household may do any
work. This includes you, your sons and daughters,
your male and female servants, your livestock,
and any foreigners living among you. 11 For in six
days the LORD made the heavens, the earth, the
sea, and everything in them; but on the seventh
day he rested. That is why the LORD blessed the
Sabbath day and set it apart as holy.
12 "Honor your father and mother. Then you will live
a long, full life in the land the LORD your God is
giving you.

Ex 20:6 Hebrew *for thousands of those.*

THE TEN COMMANDMENTS AND THE WORDS OF JESUS

The Ten Commandments said . . .	Jesus said . . .
Exod 20:3 "You must not have any other god but me."	Matt 4:10 "You must worship the LORD your God and serve only him."
Exod 20:4 "You must not make for yourself an idol."	Luke 16:13 "No one can serve two masters."
Exod 20:7 "You must not misuse the name of the LORD your God."	Matt 5:34 "Do not make any vows! Do not say, 'By heaven!' because heaven is God's throne."
Exod 20:8 "Remember to observe the Sabbath day by keeping it holy."	Mark 2:27-28 "The Sabbath was made to meet the needs of people, and not people to meet the requirements of the Sabbath. So the Son of Man is Lord, even over the Sabbath!"
Exod 20:12 "Honor your father and mother."	Matt 10:37 "If you love your father or mother more than you love me, you are not worthy of being mine."
Exod 20:13 "You must not murder."	Matt 5:22 "If you are even angry with someone, you are subject to judgment!"
Exod 20:14 "You must not commit adultery."	Matt 5:28 "Anyone who even looks at a woman with lust has already committed adultery with her in his heart."
Exod 20:15 "You must not steal."	Matt 5:40 "If you are sued in court and your shirt is taken from you, give your coat, too."
Exod 20:16 "You must not testify falsely against your neighbor."	Matt 12:36 "You must give an account on judgment day for every idle word you speak."
Exod 20:17 "You must not covet."	Luke 12:15 "Guard against every kind of greed."

In them, people could see the nature of God and his plan for how they should live. The commands and guidelines were intended to direct the community to meet the needs of each individual in a loving and responsible manner. But many people looked at the law the wrong way. They saw it as a means to prosperity in both this world and the next. And they thought that to obey every law was the way to earn God's protection from foreign invasion and natural disaster. Keeping the law became an end in itself, not the means to fulfill God's ultimate law of love.

Exod 20:1-6 The Israelites had just come from Egypt, a land of many idols and many gods. Because each god represented a different aspect of life, it was common to worship many gods in order to get the maximum number of blessings. When God told his people to worship and believe in him, that wasn't so hard for them—he was just one more god to add to the list. But when he said, "You must not have any other god but me," that was difficult for the people to accept. But if they didn't learn that the God who led them out of Egypt was the only true God, they could not be his people—no matter how faithfully they kept the other nine commandments. Thus, God made this his first commandment. Today we can allow many things to become gods to us. Money, fame, work, or pleasure can become gods when we concentrate too much on them for personal identity, meaning, and security. No one sets out with the intention of worshiping these things. But by the amount of time we devote to them, they can grow into gods that ultimately control our thoughts and energies. Letting God hold the central place in our lives keeps these things from turning into gods.

Exod 20:7 God's name is special because it carries his personal identity. Using it frivolously or in a curse is so common today that we may fail to realize how serious it is. The way we use God's name conveys how we really feel about him. We should respect his name and use it appropriately, speaking it in praise or worship rather than in curse or in jest. We should not take lightly the abuse or dishonor of his name.

Exod 20:8-11 The Sabbath was a day set aside for rest and worship. God commanded a Sabbath because human beings need to spend unhurried time in worship and rest each week. A God who is concerned enough to provide a day each week for us to rest is indeed wonderful. To observe a regular time of rest and worship in our fast-paced world demonstrates how important God is to us, and it gives us the extra benefit of refreshing our spirits. Don't neglect God's provision.

Exod 20:12 This is the first commandment with a promise attached. To live in peace for generations in the Promised Land, the Israelites would need to respect authority and build strong families. But what does it mean to "honor" parents? Partly, it means speaking well of them and politely to them. It also means acting in a way that shows them courtesy and respect (but not to obey them if this means disobedience to God). It means following their teaching and example of putting God first. Parents have a special place in God's sight. Even those who find it difficult to get along with their parents are still commanded to honor them.

▸ **EXODUS 20:1-21** ***(cont.)***

13"You must not murder.
14"You must not commit adultery.
15"You must not steal.
16"You must not testify falsely against your neighbor.
17"You must not covet your neighbor's house. You must not covet your neighbor's wife, male or female servant, ox or donkey, or anything else that belongs to your neighbor."

18When the people heard the thunder and the loud
blast of the ram's horn, and when they saw the flashes
of lightning and the smoke billowing from the mountain, they stood at a distance, trembling with fear.
19And they said to Moses, "You speak to us, and we
will listen. But don't let God speak directly to us, or
we will die!"
20"Don't be afraid," Moses answered them, "for God
has come in this way to test you, and so that your fear
of him will keep you from sinning!"
21As the people stood in the distance, Moses approached the dark cloud where God was.

Proper Use of Altars

EXODUS 20:22-26

And the LORD said to Moses, "Say this to the people of
Israel: You saw for yourselves that I spoke to you from
heaven. 23Remember, you must not make any idols of
silver or gold to rival me.
24"Build for me an altar made of earth, and offer
your sacrifices to me—your burnt offerings and peace
offerings, your sheep and goats, and your cattle. Build
my altar wherever I cause my name to be remembered,
and I will come to you and bless you. 25If you use stones
to build my altar, use only natural, uncut stones. Do
not shape the stones with a tool, for that would make
the altar unfit for holy use. 26And do not approach
my altar by going up steps. If you do, someone might
look up under your clothing and see your nakedness.

Fair Treatment of Slaves

EXODUS 21:1-11

"These are the regulations you must present to Israel.
2"If you buy a Hebrew slave, he may serve for no
more than six years. Set him free in the seventh year,
and he will owe you nothing for his freedom. 3If he

Mount Sinai

Mount Sinai is the mountain where God met Moses and gave him the Ten Commandments and the rest of the law. The traditional location is among the mountains at the southern end of the Sinai Peninsula. Since at least the fourth century, many Christians have identified Jebel Musa ("Mount Moses" in Arabic) as the site where God molded the families of Jacob into the nation of Israel. The Greek monastery of Saint Catherine at the base of the 7,500-foot peak has been there for over 1,500 years. Israel was camped for two years on the plains adjacent to this mountain. This is the site of one of the most significant events in human history: the giving of God's law. This law has endured for thousands of years as God's revelation to his people.

Exod 20:16 To testify falsely means lying in court. God knew that Israel could not survive unless its system of justice was incorruptible. We should be honest in our private dealings as well as in our public statements. In either situation, we "testify falsely" by leaving something out of a story, telling a half-truth, twisting the facts, or inventing a falsehood. God warns us against deception. Even though deception is a way of life for many people, God's people must not give in to it!

Exod 20:17 To covet is to wish to have the possessions of others. It goes beyond simply admiring someone else's possessions or thinking, "I'd like to have one of those." Coveting includes envy—resenting the fact that others have what you don't. God knows that possessions never make anyone happy for long. Since only God can supply all our needs, true contentment is found only in him. When you begin to covet, try to determine if a more basic need is leading you to envy. For example, you may covet someone's success, not because you want to take it away, but because you would like to feel as appreciated by others as that person is. If this is the case, pray that God will help you deal with your resentment and meet your basic needs.

Exod 20:18 Sometimes God speaks to his people with a majestic display of power; at other times he speaks quietly. Why the difference? God speaks in the way that best accomplishes his purposes. At Sinai, the awesome display of light and sound was necessary to show Israel God's great power and authority. Only then would they listen to Moses and Aaron.

Exod 20:20 Throughout the Bible we find this phrase: "Don't be afraid." God wasn't trying to scare the people. He was showing his mighty power so the Israelites would know he was the true God and would therefore obey him. If they would do this, he would make his power available to them. God wants us to follow him out of love rather than fear. To overcome fear, we must think more about his love. "Perfect love expels all fear" (1 Jn 4:18).

Exod 20:24-26 Why were specific directions given for building altars? God's people had no Bible and few religious traditions to learn from. God had to start from scratch and teach them how to worship him. God gave specific instructions about building altars because he wanted to control the way sacrifices were offered. To prevent idolatry from creeping into worship, God did not allow the altar stones to be cut or shaped into any form. Nor did God let the people build an altar just anywhere. This was designed to prevent them from starting their own religions or making changes in the way God wanted things done. God is not against creativity, but he is against us creating our own religion.

was single when he became your slave, he shall leave single. But if he was married before he became a slave, then his wife must be freed with him.

4"If his master gave him a wife while he was a slave and they had sons or daughters, then only the man will be free in the seventh year, but his wife and children will still belong to his master. 5But the slave may declare, 'I love my master, my wife, and my children. I don't want to go free.' 6If he does this, his master must present him before God.* Then his master must take him to the door or doorpost and publicly pierce his ear with an awl. After that, the slave will serve his master for life.

7"When a man sells his daughter as a slave, she will not be freed at the end of six years as the men are. 8If she does not satisfy her owner, he must allow her to be bought back again. But he is not allowed to sell her to foreigners, since he is the one who broke the contract with her. 9But if the slave's owner arranges for her to marry his son, he may no longer treat her as a slave but as a daughter.

10"If a man who has married a slave wife takes another wife for himself, he must not neglect the rights of the first wife to food, clothing, and sexual intimacy. 11If he fails in any of these three obligations, she may leave as a free woman without making any payment.

Cases of Personal Injury

EXODUS 21:12-36

"Anyone who assaults and kills another person must be put to death. 13But if it was simply an accident permitted by God, I will appoint a place of refuge where the slayer can run for safety. 14However, if someone deliberately kills another person, then the slayer must be dragged even from my altar and be put to death.

15"Anyone who strikes father or mother must be put to death.

16"Kidnappers must be put to death, whether they are caught in possession of their victims or have already sold them as slaves.

17"Anyone who dishonors* father or mother must be put to death.

18"Now suppose two men quarrel, and one hits the other with a stone or fist, and the injured person does not die but is confined to bed. 19If he is later able to walk outside again, even with a crutch, the assailant will not be punished but must compensate his victim for lost wages and provide for his full recovery.

20"If a man beats his male or female slave with a club and the slave dies as a result, the owner must be punished. 21But if the slave recovers within a day or two, then the owner shall not be punished, since the slave is his property.

22"Now suppose two men are fighting, and in the process they accidentally strike a pregnant woman so she gives birth prematurely.* If no further injury results, the man who struck the woman must pay the amount of compensation the woman's husband demands and the judges approve. 23But if there is further injury, the punishment must match the injury: a life for a life, 24an eye for an eye, a tooth for a tooth, a hand for a hand, a foot for a foot, 25a burn for a burn, a wound for a wound, a bruise for a bruise.

26"If a man hits his male or female slave in the eye and the eye is blinded, he must let the slave go free to compensate for the eye. 27And if a man knocks out the tooth of his male or female slave, he must let the slave go free to compensate for the tooth.

28"If an ox* gores a man or woman to death, the ox must be stoned, and its flesh may not be eaten. In such a case, however, the owner will not be held liable. 29But suppose the ox had a reputation for goring, and the owner had been informed but failed to keep it under control. If the ox then kills someone, it must be stoned, and the owner must also be put to death. 30However, the dead person's relatives may accept payment to compensate for the loss of life. The owner of the ox may redeem his life by paying whatever is demanded.

31"The same regulation applies if the ox gores a boy or a girl. 32But if the ox gores a slave, either male or female, the animal's owner must pay the slave's owner thirty silver coins,* and the ox must be stoned.

33"Suppose someone digs or uncovers a pit and fails to cover it, and then an ox or a donkey falls into it. 34The owner of the pit must pay full compensation to the owner of the animal, but then he gets to keep the dead animal.

35"If someone's ox injures a neighbor's ox and the injured ox dies, then the two owners must sell the live ox and divide the price equally between them. They

Ex 21:6 Or *before the judges.* **Ex 21:17** Greek version reads *Anyone who speaks disrespectfully of.* Compare Matt 15:4; Mark 7:10. **Ex 21:22** Or *so she has a miscarriage;* Hebrew reads *so her children come out.* **Ex 21:28** Or *bull,* or *cow;* also in 21:29-36. **Ex 21:32** Hebrew *30 shekels of silver,* about 12 ounces or 342 grams in weight.

Exod 21:1ff These laws were given because everything we do has consequences. It is vital to think before acting, to consider the effects of our choices. Think of your plans for today and consider what their long-range results will be. As we deal with others, we should keep the principles of these laws in mind. We should act responsibly and justly with all people—friends and enemies alike.

Exod 21:2 The Hebrews, though freed from slavery, had slaves (or servants) themselves. A person could become a slave because of poverty, debt, or even crime. But Hebrew slaves were treated as humans, not property, and were allowed to work their way to freedom. The Bible acknowledges the existence of slavery but never encourages it.

Exod 21:24-25 The "eye for an eye" rule was instituted as a guide for judges, not as a rule for personal relationships or to justify revenge. This rule made the punishment fit the crime, thereby preventing the cruel and barbaric punishments that characterized many ancient countries. Jesus used this principle to teach us not to retaliate (Matt 5:38-48). Judges, parents, teachers, and others who work with people must make wise decisions in order for discipline to be effective. A punishment too harsh is unfair, and one too lenient is powerless to teach. Ask God for wisdom before you judge.

▸ **EXODUS 21:12-36** ***(cont.)***

must also divide the dead animal. 36But if the ox had a reputation for goring, yet its owner failed to keep it under control, he must pay full compensation—a live ox for the dead one—but he may keep the dead ox.

Protection of Property

EXODUS 22:1-15

1*"If someone steals an ox* or sheep and then kills or sells it, the thief must pay back five oxen for each ox stolen, and four sheep for each sheep stolen.

2*"If a thief is caught in the act of breaking into a house and is struck and killed in the process, the person who killed the thief is not guilty of murder. 3But if it happens in daylight, the one who killed the thief is guilty of murder.

"A thief who is caught must pay in full for everything he stole. If he cannot pay, he must be sold as a slave to pay for his theft. 4If someone steals an ox or a donkey or a sheep and it is found in the thief's possession, then the thief must pay double the value of the stolen animal.

5"If an animal is grazing in a field or vineyard and the owner lets it stray into someone else's field to graze, then the animal's owner must pay compensation from the best of his own grain or grapes.

6"If you are burning thornbushes and the fire gets out of control and spreads into another person's field, destroying the sheaves or the uncut grain or the whole crop, the one who started the fire must pay for the lost crop.

7"Suppose someone leaves money or goods with a neighbor for safekeeping, and they are stolen from the neighbor's house. If the thief is caught, the compensation is double the value of what was stolen. 8But if the thief is not caught, the neighbor must appear before God,* who will determine if he stole the property.

9"Suppose there is a dispute between two people who both claim to own a particular ox, donkey, sheep, article of clothing, or any lost property. Both parties must come before God, and the person whom God declares* guilty must pay double compensation to the other.

10"Now suppose someone leaves a donkey, ox, sheep, or any other animal with a neighbor for safekeeping, but it dies or is injured or gets away, and no one sees what happened. 11The neighbor must then take an oath in the presence of the LORD. If the LORD confirms that the neighbor did not steal the property, the owner must accept the verdict, and no payment will be required. 12But if the animal was indeed stolen, the guilty person must pay compensation to the owner. 13If it was torn to pieces by a wild animal, the remains of the carcass must be shown as evidence, and no compensation will be required.

14"If someone borrows an animal from a neighbor and it is injured or dies when the owner is absent, the person who borrowed it must pay full compensation. 15But if the owner was present, no compensation is required. And no compensation is required if the animal was rented, for this loss is covered by the rental fee.

Social Responsibility

EXODUS 22:16-31

"If a man seduces a virgin who is not engaged to anyone and has sex with her, he must pay the customary bride price and marry her. 17But if her father refuses to let him marry her, the man must still pay him an amount equal to the bride price of a virgin.

18"You must not allow a sorceress to live.

19"Anyone who has sexual relations with an animal must certainly be put to death.

20"Anyone who sacrifices to any god other than the LORD must be destroyed.*

21"You must not mistreat or oppress foreigners in any way. Remember, you yourselves were once foreigners in the land of Egypt.

22"You must not exploit a widow or an orphan. 23If you exploit them in any way and they cry out to me, then I will certainly hear their cry. 24My anger will blaze against you, and I will kill you with the sword.

Ex 22:1a Verse 22:1 is numbered 21:37 in Hebrew text. **Ex 22:1b** Or *bull,* or *cow;* also in 22:4, 9, 10. **Ex 22:2** Verses 22:2-31 are numbered 22:1-30 in Hebrew text. **Ex 22:8** Or *before the judges.* **Ex 22:9** Or *before the judges, and the person whom the judges declare.* **Ex 22:20** The Hebrew term used here refers to the complete consecration of things or people to the LORD, either by destroying them or by giving them as an offering.

Exod 22:1ff These are not a collection of picky laws but are case studies of God's principles in action. God was taking potential situations and showing how his laws would work in the Israelites' everyday lives. These case studies had several objectives: to protect the nation, to organize the nation, and to focus the nation's attention on God. The laws listed here do not cover every possible situation but give practical examples that make it easier to decide what God wants.

Exod 22:3ff Throughout Exodus 22 we find examples of the principle of restitution—making wrongs right. For example, if a man stole an animal, he had to repay double the beast's market value. If you have done someone wrong, perhaps you should go beyond what is expected to make things right. This will help ease any pain you've caused, help the other person be more forgiving, and make you more likely to think before you do it again.

Exod 22:18 Why did God's laws speak so strongly against sorcery (Lev 19:31; 20:6, 27; Deut 18:10-12)? Sorcery was punishable by death because it was a crime against God himself. To invoke evil powers violated the first commandment to not worship any other god. Sorcery was rebellion against God and his authority. In essence, it was teaming up with Satan instead of with God.

Exod 22:21 God warned the Israelites not to treat foreigners unfairly because they themselves were once foreigners in Egypt. It is not easy coming into a new environment where you feel alone and out of place. Are there foreigners in your corner of the world—refugees, new arrivals at school, immigrants from another country? Be sensitive to their struggles, and express God's love by your kindness and generosity.

Exod 22:22-27 The Hebrew law code is noted for its fairness and social responsibility toward the poor. God insisted that the poor and powerless be well treated and given the chance to restore their fortunes. We should reflect God's concern for the poor by giving

Then your wives will be widows and your children fatherless.

25"If you lend money to any of my people who are in need, do not charge interest as a money lender would. 26If you take your neighbor's cloak as security for a loan, you must return it before sunset. 27This coat may be the only blanket your neighbor has. How can a person sleep without it? If you do not return it and your neighbor cries out to me for help, then I will hear, for I am merciful.

28"You must not dishonor God or curse any of your rulers.

29"You must not hold anything back when you give me offerings from your crops and your wine.

"You must give me your firstborn sons.

30"You must also give me the firstborn of your cattle, sheep, and goats. But leave the newborn animal with its mother for seven days; then give it to me on the eighth day.

31"You must be my holy people. Therefore, do not eat any animal that has been torn up and killed by wild animals. Throw it to the dogs.

A Call for Justice

EXODUS 23:1-13

"You must not pass along false rumors. You must not cooperate with evil people by lying on the witness stand.

2"You must not follow the crowd in doing wrong. When you are called to testify in a dispute, do not be swayed by the crowd to twist justice. 3And do not slant your testimony in favor of a person just because that person is poor.

4"If you come upon your enemy's ox or donkey that has strayed away, take it back to its owner. 5If you see that the donkey of someone who hates you has collapsed under its load, do not walk by. Instead, stop and help.

6"In a lawsuit, you must not deny justice to the poor.

7"Be sure never to charge anyone falsely with evil. Never sentence an innocent or blameless person to death, for I never declare a guilty person to be innocent.

8"Take no bribes, for a bribe makes you ignore something that you clearly see. A bribe makes even a righteous person twist the truth.

9"You must not oppress foreigners. You know what it's like to be a foreigner, for you yourselves were once foreigners in the land of Egypt.

10"Plant and harvest your crops for six years, 11but let the land be renewed and lie uncultivated during the seventh year. Then let the poor among you harvest whatever grows on its own. Leave the rest for wild animals to eat. The same applies to your vineyards and olive groves.

12"You have six days each week for your ordinary work, but on the seventh day you must stop working. This gives your ox and your donkey a chance to rest. It also allows your slaves and the foreigners living among you to be refreshed.

13"Pay close attention to all my instructions. You must not call on the name of any other gods. Do not even speak their names.

Three Annual Festivals

EXODUS 23:14-19

"Each year you must celebrate three festivals in my honor. 15First, celebrate the Festival of Unleavened Bread. For seven days the bread you eat must be made without yeast, just as I commanded you. Celebrate this festival annually at the appointed time in early spring, in the month of Abib,* for that is the anniversary of your departure from Egypt. No one may appear before me without an offering.

16"Second, celebrate the Festival of Harvest,* when you bring me the first crops of your harvest.

"Finally, celebrate the Festival of the Final Harvest*

Ex 23:15 Hebrew *appointed time in the month of Abib.* This first month of the ancient Hebrew lunar calendar usually occurs within the months of March and April. **Ex 23:16a** Or *Festival of Weeks.* This was later called the Festival of Pentecost (see Acts 2:1). It is celebrated today as Shavuot (or Shabuoth). **Ex 23:16b** Or *Festival of Ingathering.* This was later called the Festival of Shelters or Festival of Tabernacles (see Lev 23:33-36). It is celebrated today as Sukkot (or Succoth).

and by helping those less fortunate than ourselves.

Exod 22:26 Why did the law insist on returning a person's cloak before sunset? The cloak was one of an Israelite's most valuable possessions. Making clothing was difficult and time-consuming. As a result, cloaks were expensive, and most people owned only one. The cloak was used as a blanket, a sack to carry things in, a place to sit, a pledge for a debt, and, of course, clothing.

Exod 22:29 The Israelites were to be prompt in giving God their offerings and not hold anything back. The first of the harvest was to be dedicated to him. Since God doesn't send payment overdue notices, it is easy to take care of other financial responsibilities while letting our gifts to him slide. Giving to God first out of what he has allowed you to have demonstrates that he has first priority in your life.

Exod 23:1 Making up or spreading rumors was strictly forbidden by God. Gossip, slander, and false witnessing would undermine families, strain neighborhood cooperation, and make chaos of the justice system. Destructive gossip still causes problems. Even if you do not initiate a lie, you become responsible if you pass it along. Don't circulate rumors; squelch them.

Exod 23:2-3 Justice is often perverted in favor of the rich. Here the people are warned against twisting justice in favor of the poor. Justice should be impartial, treating rich and poor alike. Giving special privileges to either rich or poor only makes justice for everyone more unlikely. Withstand the pressure of the crowd to sway your decision about a person. Let the fairness God shows to each of us guide your judgment.

Exod 23:4-5 The thought of being kind to enemies was new and startling in a world where revenge was the common form of justice. God not only introduced this idea to the Israelites, but he made it law! If a man found a lost animal owned by his enemy, he was to return it at once, even if his enemy might use it to harm him. Jesus clearly taught in Luke 10:30-37 to reach out to all people in need, even our enemies. Following the laws of right living is hard enough with friends. When we apply God's laws of fairness and kindness to our enemies, we show how different we are from the world.

▸ **EXODUS 23:14-19 *(cont.)***

at the end of the harvest season, when you have harvested all the crops from your fields. 17At these three times each year, every man in Israel must appear before the Sovereign, the LORD.

18"You must not offer the blood of my sacrificial offerings together with any baked goods containing yeast. And do not leave the fat from the festival offerings until the next morning.

19"As you harvest your crops, bring the very best of the first harvest to the house of the LORD your God.

"You must not cook a young goat in its mother's milk.

A Promise of the LORD's Presence

EXODUS 23:20-33

"See, I am sending an angel before you to protect you on your journey and lead you safely to the place I have prepared for you. 21Pay close attention to him, and obey his instructions. Do not rebel against him, for he is my representative, and he will not forgive your rebellion. 22But if you are careful to obey him, following all my instructions, then I will be an enemy to your enemies, and I will oppose those who oppose you. 23For my angel will go before you and bring you into the land of the Amorites, Hittites, Perizzites, Canaanites, Hivites, and Jebusites, so you may live there. And I will destroy them completely. 24You must not worship the gods of these nations or serve them in any way or imitate their evil practices. Instead, you must utterly destroy them and smash their sacred pillars.

25"You must serve only the LORD your God. If you do, I* will bless you with food and water, and I will protect you from illness. 26There will be no miscarriages or infertility in your land, and I will give you long, full lives.

27"I will send my terror ahead of you and create panic among all the people whose lands you invade. I will make all your enemies turn and run. 28I will send terror* ahead of you to drive out the Hivites, Canaanites, and Hittites. 29But I will not drive them out in a single year, because the land would become desolate and the wild animals would multiply and threaten you. 30I will drive them out a little at a time until your population has increased enough to take possession of the land. 31And I will fix your boundaries from the Red Sea to the Mediterranean Sea,* and from the eastern wilderness to the Euphrates River.* I will hand over to you the people now living in the land, and you will drive them out ahead of you.

32"Make no treaties with them or their gods. 33They must not live in your land, or they will cause you to sin against me. If you serve their gods, you will be caught in the trap of idolatry."

Israel Accepts the LORD's Covenant

EXODUS 24:1-18

Then the LORD instructed Moses: "Come up here to me, and bring along Aaron, Nadab, Abihu, and seventy of Israel's elders. All of you must worship from a distance. 2Only Moses is allowed to come near to the LORD. The others must not come near, and none of the other people are allowed to climb up the mountain with him."

3Then Moses went down to the people and repeated all the instructions and regulations the LORD had given him. All the people answered with one voice, "We will do everything the LORD has commanded."

4Then Moses carefully wrote down all the LORD's instructions. Early the next morning Moses got up and built an altar at the foot of the mountain. He also set up twelve pillars, one for each of the twelve tribes of Israel. 5Then he sent some of the young Israelite men to present burnt offerings and to sacrifice bulls as peace offerings to the LORD. 6Moses drained half the blood from these animals into basins. The other half he splattered against the altar.

7Then he took the Book of the Covenant and read it

Ex 23:25 As in Greek and Latin versions; Hebrew reads *he.* **Ex 23:28** Often rendered *the hornet.* The meaning of the Hebrew is uncertain. **Ex 23:31a** Hebrew *from the sea of reeds to the sea of the Philistines.* **Ex 23:31b** Hebrew *from the wilderness to the river.*

Exod 23:20-21 Who was this angel that went with the Israelites? Most likely the angel was a manifestation of God. God is not present in all the angels in this way. Angels are God's created messengers (Heb 1:14). God chose to make himself known in this special way for a special purpose. God was in the angel in the same way he was present in the pillars of cloud and fire (Exod 13:21-22). "He is my representative" means the essential nature and power of God were made known in this angel.

Exod 23:24-25 If you're in the furnace, it's easy to catch on fire. God warned the Israelites about their neighbors whose beliefs and actions could turn them away from him. We also live among neighbors whose values may be completely different from ours. We are called to maintain a lifestyle that shows our faith. This can be a struggle, especially if our Christian lifestyle differs from the norm. Our lives should demonstrate that obeying God takes precedence over conforming to our neighbors' way of life. God's Word, not society, dictates how we should live.

Exod 23:29 Not all of God's solutions are instantaneous. Nor does delay justify inaction. In this case, God's cause would require constant cooperation, persistence, and effort by the Israelites. Success would come step by step.

Exod 23:32-33 God continually warned the people to avoid false religions and false gods. In Egypt they had been surrounded by idols and sorcerers, but leaving that land did not mean they were free from pagan religious influences. The land of Canaan was just as infested with idol worship. God knew his people needed extra strength, so he continually emphasized guarding against the influence of pagan religions.

Exod 24:6-8 To understand this unusual covenant ratification ceremony, we need to understand the Bible's view of sin and forgiveness. God is the sovereign Judge of the universe. He is also absolutely holy. As the holy Judge of all, he condemns sin and judges it worthy of death. In the Old Testament God accepted the death of an animal as a substitute for the sinner. The animal's shed blood was proof that one life had been given for another. So blood symbolized the death of the animal, but it also symbolized the life that was spared as a result. Of course the death of the animal that brought forgiveness in the Old Testament was only a temporary provision, looking forward to the death of Jesus Christ (Heb 9:9–10:28).

In the ceremony described here, Moses sprinkled half the blood from the sacrificed animals on the altar to show that the sinner could once again approach God because

aloud to the people. Again they all responded, "We will do everything the LORD has commanded. We will obey."
[8]Then Moses took the blood from the basins and splattered it over the people, declaring, "Look, this blood confirms the covenant the LORD has made with you in giving you these instructions."
[9]Then Moses, Aaron, Nadab, Abihu, and the seventy elders of Israel climbed up the mountain. [10]There they saw the God of Israel. Under his feet there seemed to be a surface of brilliant blue lapis lazuli, as clear as the sky itself. [11]And though these nobles of Israel gazed upon God, he did not destroy them. In fact, they ate a covenant meal, eating and drinking in his presence!
[12]Then the LORD said to Moses, "Come up to me on the mountain. Stay there, and I will give you the tablets of stone on which I have inscribed the instructions and commands so you can teach the people." [13]So Moses and his assistant Joshua set out, and Moses climbed up the mountain of God.
[14]Moses told the elders, "Stay here and wait for us until we come back. Aaron and Hur are here with you. If anyone has a dispute while I am gone, consult with them."
[15]Then Moses climbed up the mountain, and the cloud covered it. [16]And the glory of the LORD settled down on Mount Sinai, and the cloud covered it for six days. On the seventh day the LORD called to Moses from inside the cloud. [17]To the Israelites at the foot of the mountain, the glory of the LORD appeared at the summit like a consuming fire. [18]Then Moses disappeared into the cloud as he climbed higher up the mountain. He remained on the mountain forty days and forty nights.

2. TABERNACLE INSTRUCTIONS

Israel needed a place for their formal worship of God, so he instructed them to build the Tabernacle, a mobile center for worship. These instructions would later form the basis for building the Temple when they were settled in the Promised Land.

Offerings for the Tabernacle

EXODUS 25:1-9

The LORD said to Moses, [2]"Tell the people of Israel to bring me their sacred offerings. Accept the contributions from all whose hearts are moved to offer them. [3]Here is a list of sacred offerings you may accept from them:

gold, silver, and bronze;
[4] blue, purple, and scarlet thread;
fine linen and goat hair for cloth;
[5] tanned ram skins and fine goatskin leather;
acacia wood;
[6] olive oil for the lamps;
spices for the anointing oil and the fragrant incense;
[7] onyx stones, and other gemstones to be set in the ephod and the priest's chestpiece.

[8]"Have the people of Israel build me a holy sanctuary so I can live among them. [9]You must build this Tabernacle and its furnishings exactly according to the pattern I will show you.

THEOPHANIES IN SCRIPTURE

Appearances of God

At the foot of Mount Sinai, God appeared to the people of Israel in a physical form. This is called a *theophany*. Here are some of the other times God appeared to Bible people.

Verse	*Theophany*
Gen 16:7	The angel of the Lord appeared to Sarah's servant, Hagar, announcing the birth of Abraham's son Ishmael
Gen 18:1-11	The Lord appeared to Abraham, foretelling Isaac's birth
Gen 22:11-12	The angel of the Lord stopped Abraham from sacrificing Isaac
Exod 3:2	The angel of the Lord appeared to Moses as a blazing fire in a bush
Exod 13:21-22	God appeared to Israel in pillars of cloud and fire to guide them through the wilderness
Exod 33:11	The Lord spoke to Moses face to face
Dan 3:25	One "like a god" appeared as the fourth man with Shadrach, Meshach, and Abednego in the fiery furnace

something had died in his place. He sprinkled the other half of the blood on the people to show that the penalty for their sin had been paid and they could be reunited with God. Through this symbolic act God's promises to Israel were reaffirmed, and lessons are taught to us about the future sacrificial death (or atonement) of Jesus Christ.

Exod 25:1ff Exodus 25–31 records God's directions for building the Tabernacle, and Exodus 35–39 tells how these instructions were carried out. But what can all these ancient, complicated construction details show us today? First, the high quality of the precious materials making up the Tabernacle shows God's greatness and transcendence. Second, the curtain surrounding the Most Holy Place shows God's moral perfection as symbolized by his separation from the common and unclean. Third, the portable nature of the Tabernacle shows God's desire to be with his people as they traveled. Fourth, the Tabernacle, its furnishings, and the service performed there provide a picture of the atonement that would one day come through Jesus Christ.

Plans for the Ark of the Covenant

EXODUS 25:10-22

"Have the people make an Ark of acacia wood—a sacred chest 45 inches long, 27 inches wide, and 27 inches high.* [11]Overlay it inside and outside with pure gold, and run a molding of gold all around it. [12]Cast four gold rings and attach them to its four feet, two rings on each side. [13]Make poles from acacia wood, and overlay them with gold. [14]Insert the poles into the rings at the sides of the Ark to carry it. [15]These carrying poles must stay inside the rings; never remove them. [16]When the Ark is finished, place inside it the stone tablets inscribed with the terms of the covenant,* which I will give to you.

[17]"Then make the Ark's cover—the place of atonement—from pure gold. It must be 45 inches long and 27 inches wide.* [18]Then make two cherubim from hammered gold, and place them on the two ends of the atonement cover. [19]Mold the cherubim on each end of the atonement cover, making it all of one piece of gold. [20]The cherubim will face each other and look down on the atonement cover. With their wings spread above it, they will protect it. [21]Place inside the Ark the stone tablets inscribed with the terms of the covenant, which I will give to you. Then put the atonement cover on top of the Ark. [22]I will meet with you there and talk to you from above the atonement cover between the gold cherubim that hover over the Ark of the Covenant.* From there I will give you my commands for the people of Israel.

Plans for the Table of the Presence

EXODUS 25:23-30

"Then make a table of acacia wood, 36 inches long, 18 inches wide, and 27 inches high.* [24]Overlay it with pure gold and run a gold molding around the edge. [25]Decorate it with a 3-inch border* all around, and run a gold molding along the border. [26]Make four gold rings for the table and attach them at the four corners next to the four legs. [27]Attach the rings near the border to hold the poles that are used to carry the table. [28]Make these poles from acacia wood, and overlay them with gold. [29]Make special containers of pure gold for the table—bowls, pans, pitchers, and jars—to be used in pouring out liquid offerings. [30]Place the Bread of the Presence on the table to remain before me at all times.

Plans for the Lampstand

EXODUS 25:31-40

"Make a lampstand of pure, hammered gold. Make the entire lampstand and its decorations of one piece—the base, center stem, lamp cups, buds, and petals. [32]Make it with six branches going out from the center stem, three on each side. [33]Each of the six branches will have three lamp cups shaped like almond blossoms, complete with buds and petals. [34]Craft the center stem of the lampstand with four lamp cups shaped like almond blossoms, complete with buds and petals. [35]There will also be an almond bud beneath each pair of branches where the six branches extend from the center stem. [36]The almond buds and branches must all be of one piece with the center stem, and they must be hammered from pure gold. [37]Then make the seven lamps for the lampstand, and set them so they reflect their light forward. [38]The lamp snuffers and trays must also be made of pure gold. [39]You will need seventy-five pounds* of pure gold for the lampstand and its accessories.

[40]"Be sure that you make everything according to the pattern I have shown you here on the mountain.

Ex 25:10 Hebrew *2.5 cubits* [115 centimeters] *long, 1.5 cubits* [69 centimeters] *wide, and 1.5 cubits high.* **Ex 25:16** Hebrew *Place inside the Ark the Testimony;* similarly in 25:21. The Hebrew word for "testimony" refers to the terms of the LORD's covenant with Israel as written on stone tablets, and also to the covenant itself. **Ex 25:17** Hebrew *2.5 cubits* [115 centimeters] *long and 1.5 cubits* [69 centimeters] *wide.* **Ex 25:22** Or *Ark of the Testimony.* **Ex 25:23** Hebrew *2 cubits* [92 centimeters] *long, 1 cubit* [46 centimeters] *wide, and 1.5 cubits* [69 centimeters] *high.* **Ex 25:25** Hebrew *a border of a handbreadth* [8 centimeters]. **Ex 25:39** Hebrew *1 talent* [34 kilograms].

Exod 25:10 Much of the Tabernacle and its furniture was made of acacia wood. Acacia trees flourished in barren regions and were fairly common in Old Testament times. The wood was brownish-orange and very hard, making it an excellent material for furniture. Acacia wood is still used in furniture making today.

Exod 25:17 The cover of the Ark of the Covenant was called the atonement cover. This was where, between the two golden cherubim (mighty angels), the presence of God would dwell in a cloud above their outstretched wings. The atonement cover was where the highest and most perfect act of atonement would be made when the high priest would enter the Most Holy Place on the Day of Atonement to atone for the sins of all the people (Exod 30:10).

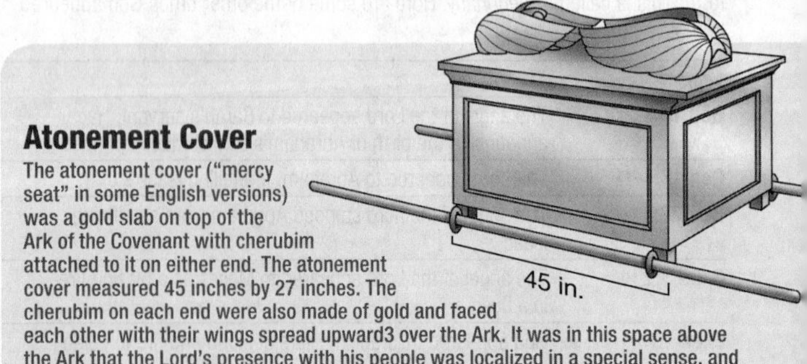

Atonement Cover

The atonement cover ("mercy seat" in some English versions) was a gold slab on top of the Ark of the Covenant with cherubim attached to it on either end. The atonement cover measured 45 inches by 27 inches. The cherubim on each end were also made of gold and faced each other with their wings spread upward3 over the Ark. It was in this space above the Ark that the Lord's presence with his people was localized in a special sense, and from here the Lord made his commands known to Moses (Exod 25:22; Lev 16:2).

The atonement cover points forward to Jesus, who is termed by Paul as "the sacrifice for sin." For it is through faith in Jesus' shed blood that we, having sinned and fallen short of God's glorious standard, are saved (Rom 3:23-25). Have you put your faith in the shed blood of Jesus Christ?

Plans for the Tabernacle

EXODUS 26:1-37

"Make the Tabernacle from ten curtains of finely woven linen. Decorate the curtains with blue, purple, and scarlet thread and with skillfully embroidered cherubim. 2These ten curtains must all be exactly the same size—42 feet long and 6 feet wide.* 3Join five of these curtains together to make one long curtain, then join the other five into a second long curtain. 4Put loops of blue yarn along the edge of the last curtain in each set. 5The fifty loops along the edge of one curtain are to match the fifty loops along the edge of the other curtain. 6Then make fifty gold clasps and fasten the long curtains together with the clasps. In this way, the Tabernacle will be made of one continuous piece.

7"Make eleven curtains of goat-hair cloth to serve as a tent covering for the Tabernacle. 8These eleven curtains must all be exactly the same size—45 feet long and 6 feet wide.* 9Join five of these curtains together to make one long curtain, and join the other six into a second long curtain. Allow 3 feet of material from the second set of curtains to hang over the front* of the sacred tent. 10Make fifty loops for one edge of each large curtain. 11Then make fifty bronze clasps, and fasten the loops of the long curtains with the clasps. In this way, the tent covering will be made of one continuous piece. 12The remaining 3 feet* of this tent covering will be left to hang over the back of the Tabernacle. 13Allow 18 inches* of remaining material to hang down over each side, so the Tabernacle is completely covered. 14Complete the tent covering with a protective layer of tanned ram skins and a layer of fine goatskin leather.

15"For the framework of the Tabernacle, construct frames of acacia wood. 16Each frame must be 15 feet high and 27 inches wide,* 17with two pegs under each frame. Make all the frames identical. 18Make twenty of these frames to support the curtains on the south side of the Tabernacle. 19Also make forty silver bases—two bases under each frame, with the pegs fitting securely into the bases. 20For the north side of the Tabernacle, make another twenty frames, 21with their forty silver bases, two bases under each frame. 22Make six frames for the rear—the west side of the Tabernacle—23along with two additional frames to reinforce the rear corners of the Tabernacle. 24These corner frames will be matched at the bottom and firmly attached at the top with a single ring, forming a single corner unit. Make both of these corner units the same way. 25So there will be eight frames at the rear of the Tabernacle, set in sixteen silver bases—two bases under each frame.

26"Make crossbars of acacia wood to link the frames, five crossbars for the north side of the Tabernacle 27and five for the south side. Also make five crossbars for the rear of the Tabernacle, which will face west. 28The middle crossbar, attached halfway up the frames, will run all the way from one end of the Tabernacle to the other. 29Overlay the frames with gold, and make gold rings to hold the crossbars. Overlay the crossbars with gold as well.

30"Set up this Tabernacle according to the pattern you were shown on the mountain.

31"For the inside of the Tabernacle, make a special curtain of finely woven linen. Decorate it with blue, purple, and scarlet thread and with skillfully embroidered cherubim. 32Hang this curtain on gold hooks attached to four posts of acacia wood. Overlay the posts with gold, and set them in four silver bases. 33Hang the inner curtain from clasps, and put the Ark of the Covenant* in the room behind it. This curtain will separate the Holy Place from the Most Holy Place.

34"Then put the Ark's cover—the place of atonement—on top of the Ark of the Covenant inside the Most Holy Place. 35Place the table outside the inner curtain on the north side of the Tabernacle, and place the lampstand across the room on the south side.

36"Make another curtain for the entrance to the sacred tent. Make it of finely woven linen and embroider it with exquisite designs, using blue, purple, and scarlet thread. 37Craft five posts from acacia wood. Overlay them with gold, and hang the curtain from them with gold hooks. Cast five bronze bases for the posts.

Plans for the Altar of Burnt Offering

EXODUS 27:1-8

"Using acacia wood, construct a square altar 7½ feet wide, 7½ feet long, and 4½ feet high.* 2Make horns

Ex 26:2 Hebrew *28 cubits* [12.9 meters] *long and 4 cubits* [1.8 meters] *wide.* **Ex 26:8** Hebrew *30 cubits* [13.8 meters] *long and 4 cubits* [1.8 meters] *wide.* **Ex 26:9** Hebrew *Double over the sixth sheet at the front.* **Ex 26:12** Hebrew *The half sheet that is left over.* **Ex 26:13** Hebrew *1 cubit* [46 centimeters]. **Ex 26:16** Hebrew *10 cubits* [4.6 meters] *high and 1.5 cubits* [69 centimeters] *wide.* **Ex 26:33** Or *Ark of the Testimony;* also in 26:34. **Ex 27:1** Hebrew *5 cubits* [2.3 meters] *wide, 5 cubits long, a square, and 3 cubits* [1.4 meters] *high.*

Exod 26:31-33 This curtain separated the two sacred rooms in the Tabernacle—the Holy Place and the Most Holy Place. The priest entered the Holy Place each day to commune with God and to tend to the incense altar, the lampstand, and the table with the Bread of the Presence. The Most Holy Place was where God himself dwelt, his presence resting on the atonement cover, which covered the Ark of the Covenant. Only the high priest could enter the Most Holy Place. Even he could do so only once a year (on the Day of Atonement) to make atonement for the sins of the nation as a whole. When Jesus Christ died on the cross, the curtain in the Temple (which had replaced the Tabernacle) tore from top to bottom (Mark 15:38), symbolizing our free access to God because of Jesus' death. No longer did people have to approach God only on special days through priests and sacrifices.

Exod 27:1 The altar of burnt offering was the first thing the Israelites saw as they entered the Tabernacle courtyard. Here sacrifices were continually made. Its vivid presence constantly reminded the people that they could only come to God by means of the sacrifice. It was the only way their sins could be forgiven and taken away. In Hebrews 10:1-18, Jesus Christ is portrayed as the ultimate sacrifice. This teaches that we are not to seek any other means of having a personal relationship with God. No counseling theory, Eastern mysticism, or modern ideas of spirituality can remove our sin. Jesus is our only High Priest today. Put all your confidence in him.

▸ **EXODUS 27:1-8 *(cont.)***
for each of its four corners so that the horns and altar
are all one piece. Overlay the altar with bronze. 3 Make
ash buckets, shovels, basins, meat forks, and firepans,
all of bronze. 4 Make a bronze grating for it, and attach four bronze rings at its four corners. 5 Install the
grating halfway down the side of the altar, under the
ledge. 6 For carrying the altar, make poles from acacia
wood, and overlay them with bronze. 7 Insert the poles
through the rings on the two sides of the altar. 8 The
altar must be hollow, made from planks. Build it just
as you were shown on the mountain.

Plans for the Courtyard

EXODUS 27:9-19
"Then make the courtyard for the Tabernacle, enclosed
with curtains made of finely woven linen. On the south
side, make the curtains 150 feet long.* 10 They will
be held up by twenty posts set securely in twenty
bronze bases. Hang the curtains with silver hooks
and rings. 11 Make the curtains the same on the north
side—150 feet of curtains held up by twenty posts set
securely in bronze bases. Hang the curtains with silver
hooks and rings. 12 The curtains on the west end of the
courtyard will be 75 feet long,* supported by ten posts
set into ten bases. 13 The east end of the courtyard, the
front, will also be 75 feet long. 14 The courtyard entrance will be on the east end, flanked by two curtains.
The curtain on the right side will be 22½ feet long,*
supported by three posts set into three bases. 15 The
curtain on the left side will also be 22½ feet long, supported by three posts set into three bases.

16 "For the entrance to the courtyard, make a curtain that is 30 feet long.* Make it from finely woven
linen, and decorate it with beautiful embroidery in
blue, purple, and scarlet thread. Support it with four
posts, each securely set in its own base. 17 All the posts
around the courtyard must have silver rings and hooks
and bronze bases. 18 So the entire courtyard will be
150 feet long and 75 feet wide, with curtain walls
7½ feet high,* made from finely woven linen. The
bases for the posts will be made of bronze.

19 "All the articles used in the rituals of the Tabernacle, including all the tent pegs used to support the
Tabernacle and the courtyard curtains, must be made
of bronze.

Light for the Tabernacle

EXODUS 27:20-21
"Command the people of Israel to bring you pure oil of
pressed olives for the light, to keep the lamps burning
continually. 21 The lampstand will stand in the Tabernacle, in front of the inner curtain that shields the Ark
of the Covenant.* Aaron and his sons must keep the
lamps burning in the LORD's presence all night. This is
a permanent law for the people of Israel, and it must
be observed from generation to generation.

Clothing for the Priests

EXODUS 28:1-5
"Call for your brother, Aaron, and his sons, Nadab,
Abihu, Eleazar, and Ithamar. Set them apart from the
rest of the people of Israel so they may minister to me
and be my priests. 2 Make sacred garments for Aaron
that are glorious and beautiful. 3 Instruct all the skilled
craftsmen whom I have filled with the spirit of wisdom. Have them make garments for Aaron that will
distinguish him as a priest set apart for my service.
4 These are the garments they are to make: a chestpiece, an ephod, a robe, a patterned tunic, a turban,
and a sash. They are to make these sacred garments for
your brother, Aaron, and his sons to wear when they
serve me as priests. 5 So give them fine linen cloth, gold
thread, and blue, purple, and scarlet thread.

Design of the Ephod

EXODUS 28:6-14
"The craftsmen must make the ephod of finely woven linen and skillfully embroider it with gold and
with blue, purple, and scarlet thread. 7 It will consist
of two pieces, front and back, joined at the shoulders
with two shoulder-pieces. 8 The decorative sash will
be made of the same materials: finely woven linen
embroidered with gold and with blue, purple, and
scarlet thread.

9 "Take two onyx stones, and engrave on them the

Ex 27:9 Hebrew *100 cubits* [46 meters]; also in 27:11. **Ex 27:12** Hebrew *50 cubits* [23 meters]; also in 27:13. **Ex 27:14** Hebrew *15 cubits* [6.9 meters]; also in 27:15. **Ex 27:16** Hebrew *20 cubits* [9.2 meters]. **Ex 27:18** Hebrew *100 cubits* [46 meters] *long and 50 by 50* [23 meters] *wide and 5 cubits* [2.3 meters] *high.* **Ex 27:21** Hebrew *in the Tent of Meeting, outside the inner curtain that is in front of the Testimony.* See note on 25:16.

Exod 28:1ff God was teaching his people how to worship him. To do so, he needed ministers to oversee the operations of the Tabernacle and to help the people maintain their relationship with God. These men were called priests and Levites, and they could only come from the tribe of Levi. Exodus 28–29 gives some details about priests. Not only was a priest from the tribe of Levi, but he also was a descendant of Aaron, Israel's first high priest. Priests had more responsibilities than Levites. As high priest, Aaron was in charge of all the priests and Levites. The priests performed the daily sacrifices, maintained the Tabernacle, and counseled the people on how to follow God. They were the people's representatives before God and thus were required to live worthy of their office. Jesus is now our High Priest (Heb 8). Daily sacrifices are no longer required because he sacrificed himself on the cross for our sins. Today ministers no longer sacrifice animals. Instead, ministers lead us in prayer and teach us about both the benefits and the commandments that characterize our new life as Christians.

Exod 28:3 The tailors who made Aaron's garments were given wisdom by God in order to do their task. All of us have special skills. God wants to fill us with his Spirit so we will use those skills for his glory. Think about your special talents and abilities and the ways you could use them for God's work in the world. As you focus on helping and giving to others, God will show you the best ways to do it and give you wisdom to accomplish the task.

Exod 28:6-13 The ephod was a kind of apron elaborately embroidered with two pieces, back and front, joined at the

names of the tribes of Israel. [10]Six names will be on each stone, arranged in the order of the births of the original sons of Israel. [11]Engrave these names on the two stones in the same way a jeweler engraves a seal. Then mount the stones in settings of gold filigree. [12]Fasten the two stones on the shoulder-pieces of the ephod as a reminder that Aaron represents the people of Israel. Aaron will carry these names on his shoulders as a constant reminder whenever he goes before the LORD. [13]Make the settings of gold filigree, [14]then braid two cords of pure gold and attach them to the filigree settings on the shoulders of the ephod.

Design of the Chestpiece

EXODUS 28:15-30

"Then, with great skill and care, make a chestpiece to be worn for seeking a decision from God.* Make it to match the ephod, using finely woven linen embroidered with gold and with blue, purple, and scarlet thread. [16]Make the chestpiece of a single piece of cloth folded to form a pouch nine inches* square. [17]Mount four rows of gemstones* on it. The first row will contain a red carnelian, a pale-green peridot, and an emerald. [18]The second row will contain a turquoise, a blue lapis lazuli, and a white moonstone. [19]The third row will contain an orange jacinth, an agate, and a purple amethyst. [20]The fourth row will contain a blue-green beryl, an onyx, and a green jasper. All these stones will be set in gold filigree. [21]Each stone will represent one of the twelve sons of Israel, and the name of that tribe will be engraved on it like a seal.

[22]"To attach the chestpiece to the ephod, make braided cords of pure gold thread. [23]Then make two gold rings and attach them to the top corners of the chestpiece. [24]Tie the two gold cords to the two rings on the chestpiece. [25]Tie the other ends of the cords to the gold settings on the shoulder-pieces of the ephod. [26]Then make two more gold rings and attach them to the inside edges of the chestpiece next to the ephod. [27]And make two more gold rings and attach them to the front of the ephod, below the shoulder-pieces, just above the knot where the decorative sash is fastened to the ephod. [28]Then attach the bottom rings of the chestpiece to the rings on the ephod with blue cords. This will hold the chestpiece securely to the ephod above the decorative sash.

[29]"In this way, Aaron will carry the names of the tribes of Israel on the sacred chestpiece* over his heart when he goes into the Holy Place. This will be a continual reminder that he represents the people when he comes before the LORD. [30]Insert the Urim and Thummim into the sacred chestpiece so they will be carried over Aaron's heart when he goes into the LORD's presence. In this way, Aaron will always carry over his heart the objects used to determine the LORD's will for his people whenever he goes in before the LORD.

Additional Clothing for the Priests

EXODUS 28:31-43

"Make the robe that is worn with the ephod from a single piece of blue cloth, [32]with an opening for Aaron's head in the middle of it. Reinforce the opening with a woven collar* so it will not tear. [33]Make pomegranates out of blue, purple, and scarlet yarn, and attach them to the hem of the robe, with gold bells between them. [34]The gold bells and pomegranates are to alternate all around the hem. [35]Aaron will wear this robe whenever he ministers before the LORD, and the bells will tinkle as he goes in and out of the LORD's presence in the Holy Place. If he wears it, he will not die.

[36]"Next make a medallion of pure gold, and engrave it like a seal with these words: HOLY TO THE LORD. [37]Attach the medallion with a blue cord to the front of Aaron's turban, where it must remain. [38]Aaron must

Ex 28:15 Hebrew *a chestpiece for decision.* **Ex 28:16** Hebrew *1 span* [23 centimeters]. **Ex 28:17** The identification of some of these gemstones is uncertain. **Ex 28:29** Hebrew *the chestpiece for decision;* also in 28:30. See 28:15. **Ex 28:32** The meaning of the Hebrew is uncertain.

shoulder and with a band at the waist. On each shoulder strap was a stone, and each stone had the names of 6 of the 12 tribes of Israel engraved on it. The priest symbolically carried the burden of the whole nation on his shoulders as he represented them before God.

Exod 28:30 The Urim and the Thummim were used by the priest to make decisions. These names mean "Curses" and "Perfections" and refer to the nature of God whose will they revealed. They were kept in a pocket and taken out or shaken out to get either a yes or no decision.

The High Priest's Chestpiece

The chestpiece worn by the high priest was symbolic of the nature and importance of his office. There are three major themes in the symbolism. The first is beauty. The Hebrew word translated as "chestpiece" has within its basic meaning the idea of beauty or excellence. The second theme is the role of the priest as the representative of the entire nation of Israel before God. This aspect is seen in the names of the 12 tribes of Israel engraved on the two onyx stones of the ephod and in the 12 precious stones attached to the chestpiece. The third theme is the role of the high priest as the representative of God to Israel. This dimension is seen in the Urim and Thummim, kept in the chestpiece, by which God made his will known to Israel.

▸ **EXODUS 28:31-43** ***(cont.)***

wear it on his forehead so he may take on himself any guilt of the people of Israel when they consecrate their sacred offerings. He must always wear it on his forehead so the LORD will accept the people.

[39]"Weave Aaron's patterned tunic from fine linen cloth. Fashion the turban from this linen as well. Also make a sash, and decorate it with colorful embroidery.

[40]"For Aaron's sons, make tunics, sashes, and special head coverings that are glorious and beautiful. [41]Clothe your brother, Aaron, and his sons with these garments, and then anoint and ordain them. Consecrate them so they can serve as my priests. [42]Also make linen undergarments for them, to be worn next to their bodies, reaching from their hips to their thighs. [43]These must be worn whenever Aaron and his sons enter the Tabernacle* or approach the altar in the Holy Place to perform their priestly duties. Then they will not incur guilt and die. This is a permanent law for Aaron and all his descendants after him.

Dedication of the Priests

EXODUS 29:1-46

"This is the ceremony you must follow when you consecrate Aaron and his sons to serve me as priests: Take a young bull and two rams with no defects. [2]Then, using choice wheat flour and no yeast, make loaves of bread, thin cakes mixed with olive oil, and wafers spread with oil. [3]Place them all in a single basket, and present them at the entrance of the Tabernacle, along with the young bull and the two rams.

[4]"Present Aaron and his sons at the entrance of the Tabernacle,* and wash them with water. [5]Dress Aaron in his priestly garments—the tunic, the robe worn with the ephod, the ephod itself, and the chestpiece. Then wrap the decorative sash of the ephod around him. [6]Place the turban on his head, and fasten the sacred medallion to the turban. [7]Then anoint him by pouring the anointing oil over his head. [8]Next present his sons, and dress them in their tunics. [9]Wrap the sashes around the waists of Aaron and his sons, and put their special head coverings on them. Then the right to the priesthood will be theirs by law forever. In this way, you will ordain Aaron and his sons.

[10]"Bring the young bull to the entrance of the Tabernacle, where Aaron and his sons will lay their hands on its head. [11]Then slaughter the bull in the LORD's presence at the entrance of the Tabernacle. [12]Put some of its blood on the horns of the altar with your finger, and pour out the rest at the base of the altar. [13]Take all the fat around the internal organs, the long lobe of the liver, and the two kidneys and the fat around them, and burn it all on the altar. [14]Then take the rest of the bull, including its hide, meat, and dung, and burn it outside the camp as a sin offering.

[15]"Next Aaron and his sons must lay their hands on the head of one of the rams. [16]Then slaughter the ram, and splatter its blood against all sides of the altar. [17]Cut the ram into pieces, and wash off the internal organs and the legs. Set them alongside the head and the other pieces of the body, [18]then burn the entire animal on the altar. This is a burnt offering to the LORD; it is a pleasing aroma, a special gift presented to the LORD.

[19]"Now take the other ram, and have Aaron and his sons lay their hands on its head. [20]Then slaughter it, and apply some of its blood to the right earlobes of Aaron and his sons. Also put it on the thumbs of their right hands and the big toes of their right feet. Splatter the rest of the blood against all sides of the altar. [21]Then take some of the blood from the altar and some of the anointing oil, and sprinkle it on Aaron and his sons and on their garments. In this way, they and their garments will be set apart as holy.

[22]"Since this is the ram for the ordination of Aaron and his sons, take the fat of the ram, including the fat of the broad tail, the fat around the internal organs, the long lobe of the liver, and the two kidneys and the fat around them, along with the right thigh. [23]Then take one round loaf of bread, one thin cake mixed with olive oil, and one wafer from the basket of bread without yeast that was placed in the LORD's presence. [24]Put all these in the hands of Aaron and his sons to be lifted up as a special offering to the LORD. [25]Afterward take the various breads from their hands, and burn them on the altar along with the burnt offering. It is a pleasing aroma to the LORD, a special gift for him. [26]Then take the breast of Aaron's ordination ram, and lift it up in the LORD's presence as a special offering to him. Then keep it as your own portion.

[27]"Set aside the portions of the ordination ram that

Ex 28:43 Hebrew *Tent of Meeting.* **Ex 29:4** Hebrew *Tent of Meeting;* also in 29:10, 11, 30, 32, 42, 44.

Exod 29:1ff Why did God set up the priesthood? God had originally intended that his chosen people be a "kingdom of priests" with both the nation as a whole and each individual dealing directly with God. But the people's sin prevented this from happening because a sinful person is not worthy to approach a perfect God. God then appointed priests from the tribe of Levi and set up the system of sacrifices to help the people approach him. He promised to forgive the people's sins if they would offer certain sacrifices administered by the priests on behalf of the people. Through these priests and their work, God wished to prepare all people for the coming of Jesus Christ, who would once again offer a direct relationship with God for anyone who would come to him. But until Christ came, the priests were the people's representatives before God. Through this Old Testament system, we can better understand the significance of what Christ did for us (see Heb 10:1-14).

Exod 29:10-41 Why were there such detailed rituals in connection with these sacrifices? A centralized, standardized form of worship prevented problems of belief which could arise from individuals creating their own worship practices. Also, it differentiated the Hebrews from the pagan Canaanites they would meet in the Promised Land. By closely following God's instructions, the Hebrews could not possibly join the Canaanites in their immoral religious practices. Finally, it showed Israel that God was serious about his relationship with them.

belong to Aaron and his sons. This includes the breast and the thigh that were lifted up before the LORD as a special offering. 28In the future, whenever the people of Israel lift up a peace offering, a portion of it must be set aside for Aaron and his descendants. This is their permanent right, and it is a sacred offering from the Israelites to the LORD.

29"Aaron's sacred garments must be preserved for his descendants who succeed him, and they will wear them when they are anointed and ordained. 30The descendant who succeeds him as high priest will wear these clothes for seven days as he ministers in the Tabernacle and the Holy Place.

31"Take the ram used in the ordination ceremony, and boil its meat in a sacred place. 32Then Aaron and his sons will eat this meat, along with the bread in the basket, at the Tabernacle entrance. 33They alone may eat the meat and bread used for their purification* in the ordination ceremony. No one else may eat them, for these things are set apart and holy. 34If any of the ordination meat or bread remains until the morning, it must be burned. It may not be eaten, for it is holy.

35"This is how you will ordain Aaron and his sons to their offices, just as I have commanded you. The ordination ceremony will go on for seven days. 36Each day you must sacrifice a young bull as a sin offering to purify them, making them right with the LORD.* Afterward, cleanse the altar by purifying it*; make it holy by anointing it with oil. 37Purify the altar, and consecrate it every day for seven days. After that, the altar will be absolutely holy, and whatever touches it will become holy.

38"These are the sacrifices you are to offer regularly on the altar. Each day, offer two lambs that are a year old, 39one in the morning and the other in the evening. 40With one of them, offer two quarts of choice flour mixed with one quart of pure oil of pressed olives; also, offer one quart of wine* as a liquid offering. 41Offer the other lamb in the evening, along with the same offerings of flour and wine as in the morning. It will be a pleasing aroma, a special gift presented to the LORD.

42"These burnt offerings are to be made each day from generation to generation. Offer them in the LORD's presence at the Tabernacle entrance; there I will meet with you and speak with you. 43I will meet the people of Israel there, in the place made holy by my glorious presence. 44Yes, I will consecrate the Tabernacle and the altar, and I will consecrate Aaron and his sons to serve me as priests. 45Then I will live among the people of Israel and be their God, 46and they will know that I am the LORD their God. I am the one who brought them out of the land of Egypt so that I could live among them. I am the LORD their God.

Plans for the Incense Altar

EXODUS 30:1-10

"Then make another altar of acacia wood for burning incense. 2Make it 18 inches square and 36 inches high,* with horns at the corners carved from the same piece of wood as the altar itself. 3Overlay the top, sides, and horns of the altar with pure gold, and run a gold molding around the entire altar. 4Make two gold rings, and attach them on opposite sides of the altar below the gold molding to hold the carrying poles. 5Make the poles of acacia wood and overlay them with gold. 6Place the incense altar just outside the inner curtain that shields the Ark of the Covenant,* in front of the Ark's cover—the place of atonement—that covers the tablets inscribed with the terms of the covenant.* I will meet with you there.

7"Every morning when Aaron maintains the lamps, he must burn fragrant incense on the altar. 8And each evening when he lights the lamps, he must again burn incense in the LORD's presence. This must be done

Ex 29:33 Or *their atonement.* **Ex 29:36a** Or *to make atonement.* **Ex 29:36b** Or *by making atonement for it;* similarly in 29:37. **Ex 29:40** Hebrew *1/10 of an ephah* [2.2 liters] *of choice flour . . . ¼ of a hin* [1 liter] *of pure oil . . . ¼ of a hin of wine.* **Ex 30:2** Hebrew *1 cubit* [46 centimeters] *long and 1 cubit wide, a square, and 2 cubits* [92 centimeters] *high.* **Ex 30:6a** Or *Ark of the Testimony;* also in 30:26. **Ex 30:6b** Hebrew *that covers the Testimony;* see note on 25:16.

Exod 29:37 Notice the overwhelming emphasis on the holiness of God. The priests, the clothes, the Tabernacle, and the sacrifices had to be clean and consecrated, prepared to meet God. In contrast, today we tend to take God for granted, rushing into worship and treating him with almost casual disregard. But we worship the almighty Creator and Sustainer of the universe. Remember that profound truth when you pray or worship, and come before him with reverence and repentance.

Exod 29:45-46 God's action in bringing the Israelites out of Egypt showed his great desire to be with them and protect them. Throughout the Bible, God shows that he is not an absentee landlord. He wants to live among us, even in our hearts. Don't exclude God from your life. Allow him to be your God as you obey his Word and communicate with him in prayer. Let him be your resident landlord.

The Incense Altar

The Tabernacle and Temple contained two altars: one for burning sacrifices and one for burning incense. The incense altar was placed in front of the veil between the Holy Place and Most Holy Place (the inner sanctuary). The incense altar was made of cedar wood and overlaid with gold (1 Kgs 6:20-22); it was about 18 inches square and 3 feet high. This altar was used to burn incense before the veil. The burning incense symbolized the prayers of God's people ascending to God (Luke 1:10-11; Rev 8:3-4). The heavenly temple also has an incense altar (Rev 6:9; 8:5; 9:13). The next time you pray, think of your prayers as ascending to God like incense.

18 IN

▸ **EXODUS 30:1-10 *(cont.)***
from generation to generation. [9]Do not offer any unholy incense on this altar, or any burnt offerings, grain offerings, or liquid offerings.

[10]"Once a year Aaron must purify* the altar by smearing its horns with blood from the offering made to purify the people from their sin. This will be a regular, annual event from generation to generation, for this is the LORD's most holy altar."

Money for the Tabernacle

EXODUS 30:11-16

Then the LORD said to Moses, [12]"Whenever you take a census of the people of Israel, each man who is counted must pay a ransom for himself to the LORD. Then no plague will strike the people as you count them. [13]Each person who is counted must give a small piece of silver as a sacred offering to the LORD. (This payment is half a shekel,* based on the sanctuary shekel, which equals twenty gerahs.) [14]All who have reached their twentieth birthday must give this sacred offering to the LORD. [15]When this offering is given to the LORD to purify your lives, making you right with him,* the rich must not give more than the specified amount, and the poor must not give less. [16]Receive this ransom money from the Israelites, and use it for the care of the Tabernacle.* It will bring the Israelites to the LORD's attention, and it will purify your lives."

Plans for the Washbasin

EXODUS 30:17-21

Then the LORD said to Moses, [18]"Make a bronze washbasin with a bronze stand. Place it between the Tabernacle and the altar, and fill it with water. [19]Aaron and his sons will wash their hands and feet there. [20]They must wash with water whenever they go into the Tabernacle to appear before the LORD and when they approach the altar to burn up their special gifts to the LORD—or they will die! [21]They must always wash their hands and feet, or they will die. This is a permanent law for Aaron and his descendants, to be observed from generation to generation."

The Anointing Oil

EXODUS 30:22-33

Then the LORD said to Moses, [23]"Collect choice spices—12½ pounds of pure myrrh, 6¼ pounds of fragrant cinnamon, 6¼ pounds of fragrant calamus,* [24]and 12½ pounds of cassia*—as measured by the weight of the sanctuary shekel. Also get one gallon of olive oil.* [25]Like a skilled incense maker, blend these ingredients to make a holy anointing oil. [26]Use this sacred oil to anoint the Tabernacle, the Ark of the Covenant, [27]the table and all its utensils, the lampstand and all its accessories, the incense altar, [28]the altar of burnt offering and all its utensils, and the washbasin with its stand. [29]Consecrate them to make them absolutely holy. After this, whatever touches them will also become holy.

[30]"Anoint Aaron and his sons also, consecrating them to serve me as priests. [31]And say to the people of Israel, 'This holy anointing oil is reserved for me from generation to generation. [32]It must never be used to anoint anyone else, and you must never make any blend like it for yourselves. It is holy, and you must treat it as holy. [33]Anyone who makes a blend like it or anoints someone other than a priest will be cut off from the community.'"

The Incense

EXODUS 30:34-38

Then the LORD said to Moses, "Gather fragrant spices—resin droplets, mollusk shell, and galbanum—and mix these fragrant spices with pure frankincense, weighed

Ex 30:10 Or *make atonement for;* also in 30:10b. **Ex 30:13** Or *0.2 ounces,* or *6 grams.* **Ex 30:15** Or *to make atonement for your lives;* similarly in 30:16. **Ex 30:16** Hebrew *Tent of Meeting;* also in 30:18, 20, 26, 36. **Ex 30:23** Hebrew *500 shekels* [5.7 kilograms] *of pure myrrh, 250 shekels* [2.9 kilograms] *of fragrant cinnamon, 250 shekels of fragrant calamus.* **Ex 30:24a** Hebrew *500 shekels* [5.7 kilograms] *of cassia.* **Ex 30:24b** Hebrew *1 hin* [3.8 liters] *of olive oil.*

The Washbasin

This basin was filled with water that the priests used to wash their hands and feet before entering the Holy Place and before returning to serve at the altar (Exod 30:17-21). In Solomon's Temple a large laver called "the molten sea" was placed between the altar of burnt offerings in the courtyard and the entrance to the inner sanctuary. This consisted of the large basin and the pedestal on which it sat (Exod 30:18). It was made of bronze or brass, melted and shaped from mirrors of highly polished metal given by the Israelite women (Exod 38:8). Many Bible scholars picture the washbasin as symbolizing the washing of the Holy Spirit that Christians receive at their new birth (Titus 3:5). Ask God to thoroughly cleanse you by means of his indwelling Spirit.

Exod 30:10 This once-a-year ceremony was called the Day of Atonement. On this day a sacrifice was made for the sins of the entire Israelite nation. This was the only day the high priest could enter the Most Holy Place, the innermost room of the Tabernacle. Here he asked God to forgive the people. The Day of Atonement served as a reminder that the daily, weekly, and monthly sacrifices could cover sins only temporarily. It pointed toward Jesus Christ, the perfect atonement, who would remove sins forever.

Exod 30:11-16 This money was like a census tax. It continued the principle that all the people belonged to God and therefore needed to be redeemed by a sacrifice. Whenever a census took place, everyone, both rich and poor, was required to pay a ransom. God does not discriminate between people (see Acts 10:34; Gal 3:28). All of

out in equal amounts. [35]Using the usual techniques of the incense maker, blend the spices together and sprinkle them with salt to produce a pure and holy incense. [36]Grind some of the mixture into a very fine powder and put it in front of the Ark of the Covenant,* where I will meet with you in the Tabernacle. You must treat this incense as most holy. [37]Never use this formula to make this incense for yourselves. It is reserved for the LORD, and you must treat it as holy. [38]Anyone who makes incense like this for personal use will be cut off from the community."

Craftsmen: Bezalel and Oholiab

EXODUS 31:1-11

Then the LORD said to Moses, [2]"Look, I have specifically chosen Bezalel son of Uri, grandson of Hur, of the tribe of Judah. [3]I have filled him with the Spirit of God, giving him great wisdom, ability, and expertise in all kinds of crafts. [4]He is a master craftsman, expert in working with gold, silver, and bronze. [5]He is skilled in engraving and mounting gemstones and in carving wood. He is a master at every craft!

[6]"And I have personally appointed Oholiab son of Ahisamach, of the tribe of Dan, to be his assistant. Moreover, I have given special skill to all the gifted craftsmen so they can make all the things I have commanded you to make:

7 the Tabernacle;*
the Ark of the Covenant;*
the Ark's cover—the place of atonement;
all the furnishings of the Tabernacle;
8 the table and its utensils;
the pure gold lampstand with all its accessories;
the incense altar;
9 the altar of burnt offering with all its utensils;
the washbasin with its stand;
10 the beautifully stitched garments—the sacred garments for Aaron the priest, and the garments for his sons to wear as they minister as priests;
11 the anointing oil;
the fragrant incense for the Holy Place.

The craftsmen must make everything as I have commanded you."

Instructions for the Sabbath

EXODUS 31:12-18

The LORD then gave these instructions to Moses: [13]"Tell the people of Israel: 'Be careful to keep my Sabbath day, for the Sabbath is a sign of the covenant between me and you from generation to generation. It is given so you may know that I am the LORD, who makes you holy. [14]You must keep the Sabbath day, for it is a holy day for you. Anyone who desecrates it must be put to death; anyone who works on that day will be cut off from the community. [15]You have six days each week for your ordinary work, but the seventh day must be a Sabbath day of complete rest, a holy day dedicated to the LORD. Anyone who works on the Sabbath must be put to death. [16]The people of Israel must keep the Sabbath day by observing it from generation to generation. This is a covenant obligation for all time. [17]It is a permanent sign of my covenant with the people of Israel. For in six days the LORD made heaven and earth, but on the seventh day he stopped working and was refreshed.'"

[18]When the LORD finished speaking with Moses on Mount Sinai, he gave him the two stone tablets inscribed with the terms of the covenant,* written by the finger of God.

Ex 30:36 Hebrew *in front of the Testimony;* see note on 25:16. **Ex 31:7a** Hebrew *the Tent of Meeting.* **Ex 31:7b** Hebrew *the Ark of the Testimony.* **Ex 31:18** Hebrew *the two tablets of the Testimony;* see note on 25:16.

us need mercy and forgiveness because of our sinful thoughts and actions. There is no way the rich person can buy off God, and no way the poor person can avoid paying. God's demand is that all of us come humbly before him to be forgiven and brought into his family.

Exod 30:34-38 The Israelites often burned incense, but this holy incense could be burned only in the Tabernacle. Here God gave the recipe for this special incense. The sweet-smelling incense was burned in shallow dishes called incense burners and was used to show honor and reverence to God. It was like prayer lifting up to God. It was also a vital part of the sacred ceremony on the Day of Atonement, when the high priest carried his smoking censer into the Most Holy Place. This incense, like the sacred anointing oil, was so holy that the people were strictly forbidden to copy it for personal use.

Exod 31:1-11 God regards all the skills of his people, not merely those with theological or ministerial abilities. Our tendency is to regard only those who are up front and in leadership roles. God gave Bezalel and Oholiab Spirit-filled abilities in artistic craftsmanship. Take notice of all the abilities God gives his people. Don't diminish your skills if they are not like Moses' and Aaron's.

Exod 31:12-17 The Sabbath had two purposes: It was a time to rest and a time to remember what God had done. We need rest. Without time off from the bustle, life loses its meaning. In our day, as in Moses' day, taking time off is not easy. But God reminds us that without Sabbaths we will forget the purpose for all of our activity and lose the balance crucial to a faithful life. Make sure your Sabbath provides a time of both refreshment and remembrance of God.

Exod 31:18 The two stone tablets contained the Ten Commandments. These were not the only code of laws in the ancient world. Other law codes had come into existence when cities or nations decided that there must be standards of judgment, ways to correct specific wrongs. But God's laws for Israel were unique: (1) They alleviated the harsh judgments typical of the day; (2) they were egalitarian—the poor and the powerful received the same punishment; and (3) they did not separate religious and social law. All law rested on God's authority.

3. BREAKING THE LAW

It didn't take long for Israel to violate their commitment to God. While Moses was still on Mount Sinai with God, they insisted on building an idol for worship, in direct violation of the Ten Commandments they had already received from God.

The Gold Calf

EXODUS 32:1-29

When the people saw how long it was taking Moses to come back down the mountain, they gathered around Aaron. "Come on," they said, "make us some gods who can lead us. We don't know what happened to this fellow Moses, who brought us here from the land of Egypt."

2So Aaron said, "Take the gold rings from the ears of your wives and sons and daughters, and bring them to me."

3All the people took the gold rings from their ears
and brought them to Aaron. 4Then Aaron took the gold,
melted it down, and molded it into the shape of a calf.
When the people saw it, they exclaimed, "O Israel, these
are the gods who brought you out of the land of Egypt!"
5Aaron saw how excited the people were, so he built
an altar in front of the calf. Then he announced, "Tomorrow will be a festival to the LORD!"
6The people got up early the next morning to sacrifice burnt offerings and peace offerings. After this,
they celebrated with feasting and drinking, and they
indulged in pagan revelry.
7The LORD told Moses, "Quick! Go down the moun-

Exod 32:1-10 Idols again! Even though Israel had seen the invisible God in action, they still wanted the familiar gods they could see and shape into whatever image they desired. How much like them we are! Our great temptation is still to shape God to our liking, to make him convenient to obey or ignore. God responds in great anger when his mercy is trampled on. The gods we create blind us to the love that our loving God wants to shower on us. God cannot work in us when we elevate anyone or anything above him. What false gods in your life are preventing the true God from living in you?

Exod 32:4-5 Two popular Egyptian gods, Hapi (Apis) and Hathor, were thought of as a bull and a heifer. The Canaanites around them worshiped Baal, thought of as a bull. Baal was their sacred symbol of power and fertility and was closely connected to immoral sexual practices. No doubt the Israelites, fresh from Egypt, found it quite natural to make a gold calf to represent the God that had just delivered them from their oppressors. They were weary of a god without a face. But in doing so, they were ignoring the command he had just given them: "You must not make for yourself an idol of any kind" (Exod 20:4). They may even have thought they were worshiping God. Their apparent sincerity was no substitute for obedience or excuse for disobedience.

Even if we do not make idols, we are often guilty of trying to make God in our image, molding him to fit our expectations, desires, and circumstances. When we do this, we end up worshiping ourselves rather than the God who created us—and self-worship, today as in the Israelites' time, leads to all kinds of immorality. What is your favorite image of God? Is it biblical? Is it adequate? Do you need to destroy it in order to worship the immeasurably powerful God who delivered you from bondage to sin?

AARON

Effective teamwork happens when all team members use their special skills. Ideally each member's strengths will contribute something important to the team effort. In this way, members make up for one another's weaknesses. Aaron made a good team with Moses. He provided Moses with one skill Moses lacked—effective public speaking. But while Aaron was necessary to Moses, he needed Moses as well. Without a guide, Aaron had little direction of his own. There was never any doubt as to who God's chosen and trained leader was. The pliability that made Aaron a good follower made him a weak leader. His major failures were caused by his inability to stand alone. His yielding to public pressure and making an idol was a good example of this weakness. • Most of us have more of the follower than the leader in us. We may even be good followers if we are following a good leader. But no leader is perfect, and no human deserves our complete and unquestioning allegiance. Only God deserves our complete loyalty and obedience. We need to be effective team members in using the skills and abilities God has given us. But if the team or the leader goes against God's Word, we must be willing to stand alone.

Strengths and accomplishments	• First high priest of God in Israel • Effective communicator; Moses' mouthpiece
Weaknesses and mistakes	• Pliable personality; gave in to the people's demands for a gold calf • Joined with Moses in disobeying God's orders about the water-giving rock • Joined sister Miriam in complaining against Moses
Lessons from his life	• God gives individuals special abilities, which he weaves together for his use • The very skills that make a good team player sometimes also make a poor leader
Vital statistics	• Where: Egypt, wilderness of Sinai • Occupations: High priest, Moses' second in command • Relatives: Brother: Moses. Sister: Miriam. Sons: Nadab, Abihu, Eleazar, and Ithamar.
Key verses	"Then the LORD became angry with Moses. 'All right,' he said. 'What about your brother, Aaron the Levite? I know he speaks well. And look! He is on his way to meet you now. He will be delighted to see you. . . . Aaron will be your spokesman to the people. He will be your mouthpiece, and you will stand in the place of God for him, telling him what to say'" (Exod 4:14, 16).

Aaron's story is told in Exodus—Deuteronomy 10:6. He is also mentioned in Hebrews 7:11.

tain! Your people whom you brought from the land of Egypt have corrupted themselves. 8How quickly they have turned away from the way I commanded them to live! They have melted down gold and made a calf, and they have bowed down and sacrificed to it. They are saying, 'These are your gods, O Israel, who brought you out of the land of Egypt.'"

9Then the LORD said, "I have seen how stubborn and rebellious these people are. 10Now leave me alone so my fierce anger can blaze against them, and I will destroy them. Then I will make you, Moses, into a great nation."

11But Moses tried to pacify the LORD his God. "O LORD!" he said. "Why are you so angry with your own people whom you brought from the land of Egypt with such great power and such a strong hand? 12Why let the Egyptians say, 'Their God rescued them with the evil intention of slaughtering them in the mountains and wiping them from the face of the earth'? Turn away from your fierce anger. Change your mind about this terrible disaster you have threatened against your people! 13Remember your servants Abraham, Isaac, and Jacob.* You bound yourself with an oath to them, saying, 'I will make your descendants as numerous as the stars of heaven. And I will give them all of this land that I have promised to your descendants, and they will possess it forever.'"

14So the LORD changed his mind about the terrible disaster he had threatened to bring on his people.

15Then Moses turned and went down the mountain. He held in his hands the two stone tablets inscribed with the terms of the covenant.* They were inscribed on both sides, front and back. 16These tablets were God's work; the words on them were written by God himself.

17When Joshua heard the boisterous noise of the people shouting below them, he exclaimed to Moses, "It sounds like war in the camp!"

18But Moses replied, "No, it's not a shout of victory nor the wailing of defeat. I hear the sound of a celebration."

19When they came near the camp, Moses saw the calf and the dancing, and he burned with anger. He threw the stone tablets to the ground, smashing them at the foot of the mountain. 20He took the calf they had made and burned it. Then he ground it into powder, threw it into the water, and forced the people to drink it.

21Finally, he turned to Aaron and demanded, "What did these people do to you to make you bring such terrible sin upon them?"

22"Don't get so upset, my lord," Aaron replied. "You yourself know how evil these people are. 23They said to me, 'Make us gods who will lead us. We don't know what happened to this fellow Moses, who brought us here from the land of Egypt.' 24So I told them, 'Whoever has gold jewelry, take it off.' When they brought it to me, I simply threw it into the fire—and out came this calf!"

25Moses saw that Aaron had let the people get completely out of control, much to the amusement of their enemies.* 26So he stood at the entrance to the camp and shouted, "All of you who are on the LORD's side, come here and join me." And all the Levites gathered around him.

27Moses told them, "This is what the LORD, the God of Israel, says: Each of you, take your swords and go back and forth from one end of the camp to the other. Kill everyone—even your brothers, friends, and neighbors." 28The Levites obeyed Moses' command, and about 3,000 people died that day.

29Then Moses told the Levites, "Today you have ordained yourselves* for the service of the LORD, for you obeyed him even though it meant killing your own sons and brothers. Today you have earned a blessing."

Moses Intercedes for Israel

EXODUS 32:30–33:11

The next day Moses said to the people, "You have committed a terrible sin, but I will go back up to the LORD on the mountain. Perhaps I will be able to obtain forgiveness* for your sin."

31So Moses returned to the LORD and said, "Oh, what a terrible sin these people have committed. They have

Ex 32:13 Hebrew *Israel.* The names "Jacob" and "Israel" are often interchanged throughout the Old Testament, referring sometimes to the individual patriarch and sometimes to the nation. **Ex 32:15** Hebrew *the two tablets of the Testimony;* see note on 25:16. **Ex 32:25** Or *out of control, and they mocked anyone who opposed them.* The meaning of the Hebrew is unclear. **Ex 32:29** As in Greek and Latin versions; Hebrew reads *Today ordain yourselves.* **Ex 32:30** Or *to make atonement.*

Exod 32:9-14 God was ready to destroy the whole nation because of their sin. But Moses pleaded for mercy, and God spared them. This is one of the countless examples in the Bible of God's mercy. Although we deserve his anger, he is willing to forgive and restore us to himself. We can receive God's forgiveness from sin by asking him. Like Moses, we can pray that he will forgive others and use us to bring them the message of his mercy.

Exod 32:14 How could God relent? God did not change his mind in the same way that a parent decides not to discipline a child. Instead, God changed his behavior to remain consistent with his nature. When God first wanted to destroy the people, he was acting consistently with his justice. When Moses interceded for the people, God relented in order to act consistently with his mercy. God had often told the people that if they changed their ways, he would not condemn them. They changed, and God forgave them as he had promised.

Exod 32:19-20 Overwhelmed by the actual sight of the blatant idolatry and revelry, Moses broke the tablets containing the commandments which had already been broken in the hearts and actions of the people. There is a place for righteous anger. However angry Moses might have been, God was angrier still—he wanted to kill all the people. Anger at sin is a sign of spiritual vitality. Don't squelch this kind of anger. But when you are justifiably angry at sin, be careful not to do anything that you will regret later.

Exod 32:21-24 Aaron's decision nearly cost him his life. His absurd excuse shows the spiritual decline in his leadership and in the people. Those who function as spokespersons and assistants need to be doubly sure their theology and morality are in tune with God so they will not be influenced by pressure from people.

▸ **EXODUS 32:30–33:11** ***(cont.)***

made gods of gold for themselves. 32But now, if you will only forgive their sin—but if not, erase my name from the record you have written!"

33But the LORD replied to Moses, "No, I will erase the name of everyone who has sinned against me. 34Now go, lead the people to the place I told you about. Look! My angel will lead the way before you. And when I come to call the people to account, I will certainly hold them responsible for their sins."

35Then the LORD sent a great plague upon the people because they had worshiped the calf Aaron had made.

33:1 The LORD said to Moses, "Get going, you and the people you brought up from the land of Egypt. Go up to the land I swore to give to Abraham, Isaac, and Jacob. I told them, 'I will give this land to your descendants.' 2And I will send an angel before you to drive out the Canaanites, Amorites, Hittites, Perizzites, Hivites, and Jebusites. 3Go up to this land that flows with milk and honey. But I will not travel among you, for you are a stubborn and rebellious people. If I did, I would surely destroy you along the way."

4When the people heard these stern words, they went into mourning and stopped wearing their jewelry and fine clothes. 5For the LORD had told Moses to tell them, "You are a stubborn and rebellious people. If I were to travel with you for even a moment, I would destroy you. Remove your jewelry and fine clothes while I decide what to do with you." 6So from the time they left Mount Sinai,* the Israelites wore no more jewelry or fine clothes.

7It was Moses' practice to take the Tent of Meeting* and set it up some distance from the camp. Everyone who wanted to make a request of the LORD would go to the Tent of Meeting outside the camp.

8Whenever Moses went out to the Tent of Meeting, all the people would get up and stand in the entrances of their own tents. They would all watch Moses until he disappeared inside. 9As he went into the tent, the pillar of cloud would come down and hover at its entrance while the LORD spoke with Moses. 10When the people saw the cloud standing at the entrance of the tent, they would stand and bow down in front of their own tents. 11Inside the Tent of Meeting, the LORD would speak to Moses face to face, as one speaks to a friend. Afterward Moses would return to the camp, but the young man who assisted him, Joshua son of Nun, would remain behind in the Tent of Meeting.

Moses Sees the LORD's Glory

EXODUS 33:12-23

One day Moses said to the LORD, "You have been telling me, 'Take these people up to the Promised Land.' But you haven't told me whom you will send with me. You have told me, 'I know you by name, and I look favorably on you.' 13If it is true that you look favorably on me, let me know your ways so I may understand you more fully and continue to enjoy your favor. And remember that this nation is your very own people."

14The LORD replied, "I will personally go with you, Moses, and I will give you rest—everything will be fine for you."

15Then Moses said, "If you don't personally go with us, don't make us leave this place. 16How will anyone know that you look favorably on me—on me and on your people—if you don't go with us? For your presence among us sets your people and me apart from all other people on the earth."

17The LORD replied to Moses, "I will indeed do what you have asked, for I look favorably on you, and I know you by name."

18Moses responded, "Then show me your glorious presence."

19The LORD replied, "I will make all my goodness pass before you, and I will call out my name, Yahweh,* before you. For I will show mercy to anyone I choose, and I will show compassion to anyone I choose. 20But you may not look directly at my face, for no one may see me and live." 21The LORD continued, "Look, stand near me on this rock. 22As my glorious presence passes by, I will hide you in the crevice of the rock and cover you with my hand until I have passed by. 23Then I will remove my hand and let you see me from behind. But my face will not be seen."

Ex 33:6 Hebrew *Horeb,* another name for Sinai. **Ex 33:7** This "Tent of Meeting" is different from the Tabernacle described in chapters 26 and 36. **Ex 33:19** *Yahweh* is a transliteration of the proper name *YHWH* that is sometimes rendered "Jehovah"; in this translation it is usually rendered "the LORD" (note the use of small capitals).

Exod 33:5-6 This was not a permanent ban on all jewelry. It was a temporary sign of repentance and mourning. In Exodus 35:22 we read that the people still had jewelry.

Exod 33:11 God and Moses talked face to face in the Tent of Meeting, just as friends do. Why did Moses find such favor with God? It certainly was not because he was perfect, gifted, or powerful. Rather, it was because God chose Moses, and Moses in turn relied wholeheartedly on God's wisdom and direction. Friendship with God was a true privilege for Moses, out of reach for the other Hebrews. But it is not out of reach for us today. Jesus called his disciples—and, by extension, all of his followers—his friends (John 15:15). He has called you to be his friend. Will you accept his invitation to openly communicate with him? He desires this kind of relationship with you.

Exod 33:11 Joshua, Moses' aide, did not leave the Tent of Meeting, probably because he was guarding it. No doubt there were curious people who would have dared to go inside.

Exod 33:18-23 Moses wanted to see God's glory. He wanted assurance of God's presence with him, Aaron, and Joshua; and he desired to know that presence experientially. Because we are finite and morally imperfect, we cannot see God as he is and live. We cannot comprehend God as he really is apart from Jesus Christ (John 14:9). Jesus promised to show himself to those who love him (John 14:21).

A New Copy of the Covenant

EXODUS 34:1-35

Then the LORD told Moses, "Chisel out two stone tablets like the first ones. I will write on them the same
words that were on the tablets you smashed. [2]Be ready
in the morning to climb up Mount Sinai and present
yourself to me on the top of the mountain. [3]No one
else may come with you. In fact, no one is to appear
anywhere on the mountain. Do not even let the flocks
or herds graze near the mountain."

[4]So Moses chiseled out two tablets of stone like the
first ones. Early in the morning he climbed Mount Sinai as the LORD had commanded him, and he carried
the two stone tablets in his hands.

[5]Then the LORD came down in a cloud and stood
there with him; and he called out his own name, Yahweh.* [6]The LORD passed in front of Moses, calling out,

"Yahweh!* The LORD!
The God of compassion and mercy!
I am slow to anger
and filled with unfailing love and
faithfulness.
[7] I lavish unfailing love to a thousand generations.*
I forgive iniquity, rebellion, and sin.
But I do not excuse the guilty.
I lay the sins of the parents upon their children
and grandchildren;
the entire family is affected—
even children in the third and fourth
generations."

[8]Moses immediately threw himself to the ground
and worshiped. [9]And he said, "O Lord, if it is true that
I have found favor with you, then please travel with
us. Yes, this is a stubborn and rebellious people, but
please forgive our iniquity and our sins. Claim us as
your own special possession."

[10]The LORD replied, "Listen, I am making a covenant with you in the presence of all your people. I
will perform miracles that have never been performed
anywhere in all the earth or in any nation. And all the
people around you will see the power of the LORD—the
awesome power I will display for you. [11]But listen carefully to everything I command you today. Then I will go
ahead of you and drive out the Amorites, Canaanites,
Hittites, Perizzites, Hivites, and Jebusites.

[12]"Be very careful never to make a treaty with the
people who live in the land where you are going. If
you do, you will follow their evil ways and be trapped.

Ex 34:5 *Yahweh* is a transliteration of the proper name *YHWH* that is sometimes rendered "Jehovah"; in this translation it is usually rendered "the LORD" (note the use of small capitals). **Ex 34:6** See note on 34:5. **Ex 34:7** Hebrew *for thousands.*

Exod 34:6-7 Moses had asked to see God's glorious presence (Exod 33:18), and this was God's response. What is God's glory? It is his character, his nature, his way of relating to his creatures. Notice that God did not give Moses a vision of his power and majesty, but rather of his love. God's glory is revealed in his mercy, grace, compassion, faithfulness, forgiveness, and justice. God's love and mercy are truly wonderful, and we benefit from them. We can respond and give glory to God when our characters resemble his.

Exod 34:6-7 Many people think the God of the Old Testament is a God of wrath, only to be feared. These words from God revealed to Moses the very heart or essence of God's nature (Exod 33:19). What do we learn from these assurances to Moses? God is merciful, gracious, loving, forgiving. Don't accept anyone's argument that the God of the Old Testament is merely vengeful. Instead, remember that God is "slow to anger," and his love cannot be diminished.

Exod 34:7 Why would sins affect children and grandchildren? This is no arbitrary punishment. Children still suffer for the sins of their parents. Consider child abuse or alcoholism, for example. While these sins are obvious, sins like selfishness and greed can be passed along as well. The dire consequences of sin are not limited to the individual family member. Be careful not to treat sin casually, but repent and turn from it. Your sin may cause you little pain now, but it could sting you in a most tender area of your life later—in the lives of your children and grandchildren.

Exod 34:12-14 God told the Israelites not to join in religious rites with the sinful people around them, but to give their absolute loyalty and exclusive devotion to him. Pagan worship simply cannot be mixed with the worship of the holy God. As Jesus pointed out, "No one can serve two masters. . . . You cannot serve both God and money" (Luke 16:13). Love of money is the god of this age, and many Christians attempt to make a treaty with this enslaving god. Are you trying to worship two gods at once? Where is your first allegiance?

"As my glorious presence passes by, I will hide you in the crevice of the rock."

Exodus 33:22

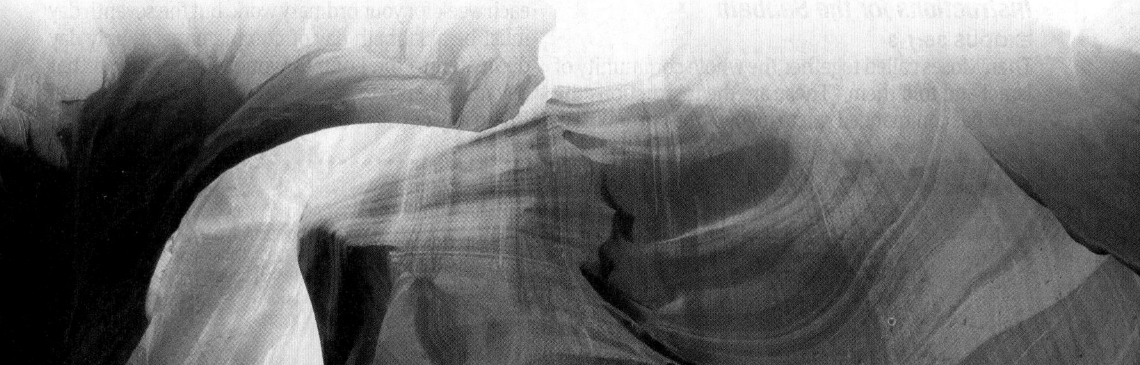

▸ **EXODUS 34:1-35** ***(cont.)***

[13]Instead, you must break down their pagan altars, smash their sacred pillars, and cut down their Asherah poles. [14]You must worship no other gods, for the Lord, whose very name is Jealous, is a God who is jealous about his relationship with you.

[15]"You must not make a treaty of any kind with the people living in the land. They lust after their gods, offering sacrifices to them. They will invite you to join them in their sacrificial meals, and you will go with them. [16]Then you will accept their daughters, who sacrifice to other gods, as wives for your sons. And they will seduce your sons to commit adultery against me by worshiping other gods. [17]You must not make any gods of molten metal for yourselves.

[18]"You must celebrate the Festival of Unleavened Bread. For seven days the bread you eat must be made without yeast, just as I commanded you. Celebrate this festival annually at the appointed time in early spring, in the month of Abib,* for that is the anniversary of your departure from Egypt.

[19]"The firstborn of every animal belongs to me, including the firstborn males from your herds of cattle and your flocks of sheep and goats. [20]A firstborn donkey may be bought back from the Lord by presenting a lamb or young goat in its place. But if you do not buy it back, you must break its neck. However, you must buy back every firstborn son.

"No one may appear before me without an offering.

[21]"You have six days each week for your ordinary work, but on the seventh day you must stop working, even during the seasons of plowing and harvest.

[22]"You must celebrate the Festival of Harvest* with the first crop of the wheat harvest, and celebrate the Festival of the Final Harvest* at the end of the harvest season. [23]Three times each year every man in Israel must appear before the Sovereign, the Lord, the God of Israel. [24]I will drive out the other nations ahead of you and expand your territory, so no one will covet and conquer your land while you appear before the Lord your God three times each year.

[25]"You must not offer the blood of my sacrificial offerings together with any baked goods containing yeast. And none of the meat of the Passover sacrifice may be kept over until the next morning.

[26]"As you harvest your crops, bring the very best of the first harvest to the house of the Lord your God.

"You must not cook a young goat in its mother's milk."

[27]Then the Lord said to Moses, "Write down all these instructions, for they represent the terms of the covenant I am making with you and with Israel."

[28]Moses remained there on the mountain with the Lord forty days and forty nights. In all that time he ate no bread and drank no water. And the Lord* wrote the terms of the covenant—the Ten Commandments*—on the stone tablets.

[29]When Moses came down Mount Sinai carrying the two stone tablets inscribed with the terms of the covenant,* he wasn't aware that his face had become radiant because he had spoken to the Lord. [30]So when Aaron and the people of Israel saw the radiance of Moses' face, they were afraid to come near him.

[31]But Moses called out to them and asked Aaron and all the leaders of the community to come over, and he talked with them. [32]Then all the people of Israel approached him, and Moses gave them all the instructions the Lord had given him on Mount Sinai. [33]When Moses finished speaking with them, he covered his face with a veil. [34]But whenever he went into the Tent of Meeting to speak with the Lord, he would remove the veil until he came out again. Then he would give the people whatever instructions the Lord had given him, [35]and the people of Israel would see the radiant glow of his face. So he would put the veil over his face until he returned to speak with the Lord.

Ex 34:18 Hebrew *appointed time in the month of Abib.* This first month of the ancient Hebrew lunar calendar usually occurs within the months of March and April. **Ex 34:22a** Hebrew *Festival of Weeks;* compare 23:16. This was later called the Festival of Pentecost. It is celebrated today as Shavuot (or Shabuoth). **Ex 34:22b** Or *Festival of Ingathering.* This was later called the Festival of Shelters or Festival of Tabernacles (see Lev 23:33-36). It is celebrated today as Sukkot (or Succoth). **Ex 34:28a** Hebrew *he.* **Ex 34:28b** Hebrew *the ten words.* **Ex 34:29** Hebrew *the two tablets of the Testimony;* see note on 25:16.

4. TABERNACLE CONSTRUCTION

The people of Israel gave willingly for the construction of the Tabernacle, and God blessed the nation with talented builders and craftsmen to complete the work.

Instructions for the Sabbath

EXODUS 35:1-3

Then Moses called together the whole community of Israel and told them, "These are the instructions the Lord has commanded you to follow. [2]You have six days each week for your ordinary work, but the seventh day must be a Sabbath day of complete rest, a holy day dedicated to the Lord. Anyone who works on that day must be put to death. [3]You must not even light a fire in any of your homes on the Sabbath."

Exod 34:13 Sacred pillars were wooden poles that stood by Baal's altar (see Judg 6:25). Also called "Asherah poles," they were used to worship the goddess who was the consort (wife) of Baal. She represented fertility and good luck in agriculture.

Exod 34:28-35 Moses' face was radiant after he spent time with God. The people could clearly see God's presence in him. How often do you spend time alone with God? Although your face may not light up a room, time spent in prayer, reading the Bible, and meditating should have such an effect on your life that people will know you have been with God.

Offerings for the Tabernacle

EXODUS 35:4–36:7

Then Moses said to the whole community of Israel, "This is what the LORD has commanded: 5 Take a sacred offering for the LORD. Let those with generous hearts present the following gifts to the LORD:

gold, silver, and bronze;
6 blue, purple, and scarlet thread;
fine linen and goat hair for cloth;
7 tanned ram skins and fine goatskin leather;
acacia wood;
8 olive oil for the lamps;
spices for the anointing oil and the fragrant incense;
9 onyx stones, and other gemstones to be set in the ephod and the priest's chestpiece.

10 "Come, all of you who are gifted craftsmen. Construct everything that the LORD has commanded:

11 the Tabernacle and its sacred tent, its covering, clasps, frames, crossbars, posts, and bases;
12 the Ark and its carrying poles;
the Ark's cover—the place of atonement;
the inner curtain to shield the Ark;
13 the table, its carrying poles, and all its utensils;
the Bread of the Presence;
14 for light, the lampstand, its accessories, the lamp cups, and the olive oil for lighting;
15 the incense altar and its carrying poles;
the anointing oil and fragrant incense;
the curtain for the entrance of the Tabernacle;
16 the altar of burnt offering;
the bronze grating of the altar and its carrying poles and utensils;
the washbasin with its stand;
17 the curtains for the walls of the courtyard;
the posts and their bases;
the curtain for the entrance to the courtyard;
18 the tent pegs of the Tabernacle and courtyard and their ropes;
19 the beautifully stitched garments for the priests to wear while ministering in the Holy Place—
the sacred garments for Aaron the priest,
and the garments for his sons to wear as they minister as priests."

20 So the whole community of Israel left Moses and
returned to their tents. 21 All whose hearts were stirred
and whose spirits were moved came and brought
their sacred offerings to the LORD. They brought all
the materials needed for the Tabernacle,* for the performance of its rituals, and for the sacred garments.
22 Both men and women came, all whose hearts were
willing. They brought to the LORD their offerings of
gold—brooches, earrings, rings from their fingers,
and necklaces. They presented gold objects of every
kind as a special offering to the LORD. 23 All those who
owned the following items willingly brought them:
blue, purple, and scarlet thread; fine linen and goat
hair for cloth; and tanned ram skins and fine goatskin
leather. 24 And all who had silver and bronze objects
gave them as a sacred offering to the LORD. And those
who had acacia wood brought it for use in the project.
25 All the women who were skilled in sewing and
spinning prepared blue, purple, and scarlet thread,
and fine linen cloth. 26 All the women who were willing
used their skills to spin the goat hair into yarn. 27 The
leaders brought onyx stones and the special gemstones to be set in the ephod and the priest's chestpiece. 28 They also brought spices and olive oil for the
light, the anointing oil, and the fragrant incense. 29 So
the people of Israel—every man and woman who was
eager to help in the work the LORD had given them
through Moses—brought their gifts and gave them
freely to the LORD.
30 Then Moses told the people of Israel, "The LORD
has specifically chosen Bezalel son of Uri, grandson of
Hur, of the tribe of Judah. 31 The LORD has filled Bezalel with the Spirit of God, giving him great wisdom,
ability, and expertise in all kinds of crafts. 32 He is a
master craftsman, expert in working with gold, silver,

Ex 35:21 Hebrew *Tent of Meeting.*

Exod 35:5-21 God did not require these special offerings, but he appealed to people with generous hearts. Only those who were willing to give were invited to participate. God loves people who give cheerfully (2 Cor 9:7). Our giving should be from love and generosity, not from a guilty conscience. Review what God has done for you. Has he blessed you with enough to meet your daily needs? Thank him, and then cheerfully give so others' needs can be met. Learn the joy of giving wholeheartedly to God.

Exod 35:10-19 Moses asked people with various abilities to help with the Tabernacle. Every one of God's people has been given special abilities. We are responsible to develop these abilities—even the ones not considered religious—and to use them for God's glory. We can become skilled through study, by watching others, and through practice. Work on your skills or abilities that could help your church or community.

Exod 35:20-24 Where did the Israelites, who were once Egyptian slaves, get all this gold and jewelry? When the Hebrews left Egypt, they took with them items they requested from the Egyptians. The Egyptians had been so glad for them to go that they readily gave these valuables to the Hebrews (Exod 3:22; 12:35-36). This included gold, silver, jewels, linen, skins, and other valuables.

Exod 35:21-22 Those whose hearts were stirred gave willingly to the Tent of Meeting (also called the Tabernacle). With great enthusiasm they gave because they knew how important their giving was to the completion of God's house. Moses had carefully explained the need and the plans for the Tabernacle, and so many people responded generously. For God to stir our hearts, we must be informed. If your church has a stewardship campaign, get involved and learn all you can. Find out about evangelistic missions and ministries to the poor. God will use this knowledge to stir your heart.

Exod 35:26 Those who spun cloth made a beautiful contribution to the Tabernacle. Good workers take pride in the quality and beauty of their work. God is concerned with the quality and beauty of what you do. Whether you are a corporate executive or a drugstore cashier, your work should reflect the creative abilities God has given you.

▸ EXODUS 35:4–36:7 *(cont.)*

and bronze. 33He is skilled in engraving and mounting gemstones and in carving wood. He is a master at every craft. 34And the LORD has given both him and Oholiab son of Ahisamach, of the tribe of Dan, the ability to teach their skills to others. 35The LORD has given them special skills as engravers, designers, embroiderers in blue, purple, and scarlet thread on fine linen cloth, and weavers. They excel as craftsmen and as designers.

36:1"The LORD has gifted Bezalel, Oholiab, and the other skilled craftsmen with wisdom and ability to perform any task involved in building the sanctuary. Let them construct and furnish the Tabernacle, just as the LORD has commanded."

2So Moses summoned Bezalel and Oholiab and all the others who were specially gifted by the LORD and were eager to get to work. 3Moses gave them the materials donated by the people of Israel as sacred offerings for the completion of the sanctuary. But the people continued to bring additional gifts each morning. 4Finally the craftsmen who were working on the sanctuary left their work. 5They went to Moses and reported, "The people have given more than enough materials to complete the job the LORD has commanded us to do!"

6So Moses gave the command, and this message was sent throughout the camp: "Men and women, don't prepare any more gifts for the sanctuary. We have enough!" So the people stopped bringing their sacred offerings. 7Their contributions were more than enough to complete the whole project.

Building the Tabernacle

EXODUS 36:8-38

The skilled craftsmen made ten curtains of finely woven linen for the Tabernacle. Then Bezalel* decorated the curtains with blue, purple, and scarlet thread and with skillfully embroidered cherubim. 9All ten curtains were exactly the same size—42 feet long and 6 feet wide.* 10Five of these curtains were joined together to make one long curtain, and the other five were joined to make a second long curtain. 11He made fifty loops of blue yarn and put them along the edge of the last curtain in each set. 12The fifty loops along the edge of one curtain matched the fifty loops along the edge of the other curtain. 13Then he made fifty gold clasps and fastened the long curtains together with the clasps. In this way, the Tabernacle was made of one continuous piece.

14He made eleven curtains of goat-hair cloth to serve as a tent covering for the Tabernacle. 15These eleven curtains were all exactly the same size—45 feet long and 6 feet wide.* 16Bezalel joined five of these curtains together to make one long curtain, and the other six were joined to make a second long curtain. 17He made fifty loops for the edge of each large curtain. 18He also made fifty bronze clasps to fasten the long curtains together. In this way, the tent covering was made of one continuous piece. 19He completed the tent covering with a layer of tanned ram skins and a layer of fine goatskin leather.

20For the framework of the Tabernacle, Bezalel constructed frames of acacia wood. 21Each frame was 15 feet high and 27 inches wide,* 22with two pegs under each frame. All the frames were identical. 23He made twenty of these frames to support the curtains on the south side of the Tabernacle. 24He also made forty silver bases—two bases under each frame, with the pegs fitting securely into the bases. 25For the north side of the Tabernacle, he made another twenty frames, 26with their forty silver bases, two bases under each frame. 27He made six frames for the rear—the west side of the Tabernacle—28along with two additional frames to reinforce the rear corners of the Tabernacle. 29These corner frames were matched at the bottom and firmly attached at the top with a single ring, forming a single corner unit. Both of these corner units were made the same way. 30So there were eight frames at the rear of the Tabernacle, set in sixteen silver bases—two bases under each frame.

31Then he made crossbars of acacia wood to link the frames, five crossbars for the north side of the Tabernacle 32and five for the south side. He also made five crossbars for the rear of the Tabernacle, which faced west. 33He made the middle crossbar to attach halfway up the frames; it ran all the way from one end of the Tabernacle to the other. 34He overlaid the frames with gold and made gold rings to hold the crossbars. Then he overlaid the crossbars with gold as well.

35For the inside of the Tabernacle, Bezalel made a special curtain of finely woven linen. He decorated it with blue, purple, and scarlet thread and with skillfully embroidered cherubim. 36For the curtain, he made four posts of acacia wood and four gold hooks. He overlaid the posts with gold and set them in four silver bases.

37Then he made another curtain for the entrance to the sacred tent. He made it of finely woven linen

Ex 36:8 Hebrew *he;* also in 36:16, 20, 35. See 37:1. **Ex 36:9** Hebrew *28 cubits* [12.9 meters] *long and 4 cubits* [1.8 meters] *wide.* **Ex 36:15** Hebrew *30 cubits* [13.8 meters] *long and 4 cubits* [1.8 meters] *wide.* **Ex 36:21** Hebrew *10 cubits* [4.6 meters] *high and 1.5 cubits* [69 centimeters] *wide.*

Exod 36:8-9 Making cloth (spinning and weaving) took a great deal of time in Moses' day. To own more than two or three changes of clothes was a sign of wealth. The effort involved in making enough cloth for the Tabernacle was staggering. The Tabernacle would never have been built without tremendous community involvement. Today, churches and neighborhoods often require this same kind of pulling together. Without it, many essential services wouldn't get done.

Exod 36:35 Cherubim are mighty angels.

and embroidered it with exquisite designs using blue, purple, and scarlet thread. [38]This curtain was hung on gold hooks attached to five posts. The posts with their decorated tops and hooks were overlaid with gold, and the five bases were cast from bronze.

Building the Ark of the Covenant

EXODUS 37:1-9

Next Bezalel made the Ark of acacia wood—a sacred chest 45 inches long, 27 inches wide, and 27 inches high.* [2]He overlaid it inside and outside with pure gold, and he ran a molding of gold all around it. [3]He cast four gold rings and attached them to its four feet, two rings on each side. [4]Then he made poles from acacia wood and overlaid them with gold. [5]He inserted the poles into the rings at the sides of the Ark to carry it.

[6]Then he made the Ark's cover—the place of atonement—from pure gold. It was 45 inches long and 27 inches wide.* [7]He made two cherubim from hammered gold and placed them on the two ends of the atonement cover. [8]He molded the cherubim on each end of the atonement cover, making it all of one piece of gold. [9]The cherubim faced each other and looked down on the atonement cover. With their wings spread above it, they protected it.

Building the Table of the Presence

EXODUS 37:10-16

Then Bezalel* made the table of acacia wood, 36 inches long, 18 inches wide, and 27 inches high.* [11]He overlaid it with pure gold and ran a gold molding around the edge. [12]He decorated it with a 3-inch border* all around, and he ran a gold molding along the border. [13]Then he cast four gold rings for the table and attached them at the four corners next to the four legs. [14]The rings were attached near the border to hold the poles that were used to carry the table. [15]He made these poles from acacia wood and overlaid them with gold. [16]Then he made special containers of pure gold for the table—bowls, pans, jars, and pitchers—to be used in pouring out liquid offerings.

Ex 37:1 Hebrew *2.5 cubits* [115 centimeters] *long, 1.5 cubits* [69 centimeters] *wide, and 1.5 cubits high.* **Ex 37:6** Hebrew *2.5 cubits* [115 centimeters] *long and 1.5 cubits* [69 centimeters] *wide.* **Ex 37:10a** Hebrew *he;* also in 37:17, 25. **Ex 37:10b** Hebrew *2 cubits* [92 centimeters] *long, 1 cubit* [46 centimeters] *wide, and 1.5 cubits* [69 centimeters] *high.* **Ex 37:12** Hebrew *a border of a handbreadth* [8 centimeters].

KEY TABERNACLE PIECES

Name	Function and Significance
Ark of the Covenant	• A golden rectangular box that contained the Ten Commandments • Symbolized God's covenant with the people of Israel • Located in the Most Holy Place
Atonement Cover	• The lid to the Ark of the Covenant • Symbolized the presence of God among his people
Curtain	• The curtain that divided the two sacred rooms of the Tabernacle —the Holy Place and the Most Holy Place • Symbolized how the people were separated from God because of sin
Table	• A wooden table located in the Holy Place of the Tabernacle. The Bread of the Presence and various utensils were kept on this table
Bread of the Presence	• Twelve loaves of baked bread, one for each tribe of Israel • Symbolized the spiritual nourishment God offers his people
Lampstands and Lamps	• A golden lampstand located in the Holy Place, which held seven burning oil lamps • The lampstand lit the Holy Place for the priests
Incense Altar	• An altar in the Holy Place in front of the curtain • Used for burning God's special incense and symbolic of acceptable prayer
Anointing Oil	• A special oil used to anoint the priests and all the pieces in the Tabernacle • A sign of being set apart for God
Altar of Burnt Offering	• The bronze altar outside the Tabernacle used for the sacrifices • Symbolized how sacrifice restored one's relationship with God
Washbasin	• A large washbasin outside the Tabernacle used by the priests to cleanse themselves before performing their duties • Symbolized the need for spiritual cleansing

Exod 37:1 The Ark (also called the Ark of the Covenant) was built to hold the Ten Commandments. It symbolized God's covenant with his people. Two gold angels called cherubim were placed on its top. The Ark was Israel's most sacred object and was kept in the Most Holy Place in the Tabernacle. Only once each year, the high priest entered the Most Holy Place to sprinkle blood on the top of the Ark (called the atonement cover) to atone for the sins of the entire nation.

Building the Lampstand

EXODUS 37:17-24

Then Bezalel made the lampstand of pure, hammered gold. He made the entire lampstand and its decorations of one piece—the base, center stem, lamp cups, buds, and petals. [18]The lampstand had six branches going out from the center stem, three on each side. [19]Each of the six branches had three lamp cups shaped like almond blossoms, complete with buds and petals. [20]The center stem of the lampstand was crafted with four lamp cups shaped like almond blossoms, complete with buds and petals. [21]There was an almond bud beneath each pair of branches where the six branches extended from the center stem, all made of one piece. [22]The almond buds and branches were all of one piece with the center stem, and they were hammered from pure gold.

[23]He also made seven lamps for the lampstand, lamp snuffers, and trays, all of pure gold. [24]The entire lampstand, along with its accessories, was made from seventy-five pounds* of pure gold.

Building the Incense Altar

EXODUS 37:25-29

Then Bezalel made the incense altar of acacia wood. It was 18 inches square and 36 inches high,* with horns at the corners carved from the same piece of wood as the altar itself. [26]He overlaid the top, sides, and horns of the altar with pure gold, and he ran a gold molding around the entire altar. [27]He made two gold rings and attached them on opposite sides of the altar below the gold molding to hold the carrying poles. [28]He made the poles of acacia wood and overlaid them with gold.

[29]Then he made the sacred anointing oil and the fragrant incense, using the techniques of a skilled incense maker.

Building the Altar of Burnt Offering

EXODUS 38:1-7

Next Bezalel* used acacia wood to construct the square altar of burnt offering. It was 7½ feet wide, 7½ feet long, and 4½ feet high.* [2]He made horns for each of its four corners so that the horns and altar were all one piece. He overlaid the altar with bronze. [3]Then he made all the altar utensils of bronze—the ash buckets, shovels, basins, meat forks, and firepans. [4]Next he made a bronze grating and installed it halfway down the side of the altar, under the ledge. [5]He cast four rings and attached them to the corners of the bronze grating to hold the carrying poles. [6]He made the poles from acacia wood and overlaid them with bronze. [7]He inserted the poles through the rings on the sides of the altar. The altar was hollow and was made from planks.

Building the Washbasin

EXODUS 38:8

Bezalel made the bronze washbasin and its bronze stand from bronze mirrors donated by the women who served at the entrance of the Tabernacle.*

Building the Courtyard

EXODUS 38:9-20

Then Bezalel made the courtyard, which was enclosed with curtains made of finely woven linen. On the south side the curtains were 150 feet long.* [10]They were held up by twenty posts set securely in twenty bronze bases. He hung the curtains with silver hooks and rings. [11]He made a similar set of curtains for the north side—150 feet of curtains held up by twenty posts set securely in bronze bases. He hung the curtains with silver hooks and rings. [12]The curtains on the west end of the courtyard were 75 feet long,* hung with silver hooks and rings and supported by ten posts set into ten bases. [13]The east end, the front, was also 75 feet long.

[14]The courtyard entrance was on the east end, flanked by two curtains. The curtain on the right side was 22½ feet long* and was supported by three posts set into three bases. [15]The curtain on the left side was also 22½ feet long and was supported by three posts set into three bases. [16]All the curtains used in the courtyard were made of finely woven linen. [17]Each post had a bronze base, and all the hooks and rings were silver. The tops of the posts of the courtyard were overlaid

Ex 37:24 Hebrew *1 talent* [34 kilograms]. **Ex 37:25** Hebrew *1 cubit* [46 centimeters] *long and 1 cubit wide, a square, and 2 cubits* [92 centimeters] *high.* **Ex 38:1a** Hebrew *he;* also in 38:8, 9. **Ex 38:1b** Hebrew *5 cubits* [2.3 meters] *wide, 5 cubits long, a square, and 3 cubits* [1.4 meters] *high.* **Ex 38:8** Hebrew *Tent of Meeting;* also in 38:30. **Ex 38:9** Hebrew *100 cubits* [46 meters]; also in 38:11. **Ex 38:12** Hebrew *50 cubits* [23 meters]; also in 38:13. **Ex 38:14** Hebrew *15 cubits* [6.9 meters]; also in 38:15.

The Lampstand

The lampstand used in the Tabernacle and the Temple is sometimes called a *menorah* today. In Solomon's Temple there were 10 such lampstands, five on each side before the Most Holy Place (1 Kgs 7:49). The design of the original lampstand was conceived by Bezalel, a man filled with God's Spirit who was an excellent craftsman (Exod 31:1-4). According to Josephus (a Jewish historian), the central shaft was fixed to a base, and from it extended slender branches placed like prongs of a trident—with the end of each one forged into a lamp. Josephus's account of the Temple lampstand tallies well with that of Zechariah's in his vision of the restored Temple after the Exile (Zech 4:2-3).

The lampstand symbolized God's light present among his people. Jesus Christ told us that he is the light of the world. If we follow him, we will have the light that leads to life (John 8:12).

with silver, and the rings to hold up the curtains were made of silver.

18He made the curtain for the entrance to the courtyard of finely woven linen, and he decorated it with beautiful embroidery in blue, purple, and scarlet thread. It was 30 feet long, and its height was 7½ feet,* just like the curtains of the courtyard walls. 19It was supported by four posts, each set securely in its own bronze base. The tops of the posts were overlaid with silver, and the hooks and rings were also made of silver.

20All the tent pegs used in the Tabernacle and courtyard were made of bronze.

Inventory of Materials

EXODUS 38:21-31

This is an inventory of the materials used in building the Tabernacle of the Covenant.* The Levites compiled the figures, as Moses directed, and Ithamar son of Aaron the priest served as recorder. 22Bezalel son of Uri, grandson of Hur, of the tribe of Judah, made everything just as the LORD had commanded Moses. 23He was assisted by Oholiab son of Ahisamach, of the tribe of Dan, a craftsman expert at engraving, designing, and embroidering with blue, purple, and scarlet thread on fine linen cloth.

24The people brought special offerings of gold totaling 2,193 pounds,* as measured by the weight of the sanctuary shekel. This gold was used throughout the Tabernacle.

25The whole community of Israel gave 7,545 pounds* of silver, as measured by the weight of the sanctuary shekel. 26This silver came from the tax collected from each man registered in the census. (The tax is one beka, which is half a shekel,* based on the sanctuary shekel.) The tax was collected from 603,550 men who had reached their twentieth birthday. 27The hundred bases for the frames of the sanctuary walls and for the posts supporting the inner curtain required 7,500 pounds of silver, about 75 pounds for each base.* 28The remaining 45 pounds* of silver was used to make the hooks and rings and to overlay the tops of the posts.

29The people also brought as special offerings 5,310 pounds* of bronze, 30which was used for casting the bases for the posts at the entrance to the Tabernacle, and for the bronze altar with its bronze grating and all the altar utensils. 31Bronze was also used to make the bases for the posts that supported the curtains around the courtyard, the bases for the curtain at the entrance of the courtyard, and all the tent pegs for the Tabernacle and the courtyard.

Clothing for the Priests

EXODUS 39:1

The craftsmen made beautiful sacred garments of blue, purple, and scarlet cloth—clothing for Aaron to wear while ministering in the Holy Place, just as the LORD had commanded Moses.

Making the Ephod

EXODUS 39:2-7

Bezalel* made the ephod of finely woven linen and embroidered it with gold and with blue, purple, and scarlet thread. 3He made gold thread by hammering out thin sheets of gold and cutting it into fine strands. With great skill and care, he worked it into the fine linen with the blue, purple, and scarlet thread.

4The ephod consisted of two pieces, front and back, joined at the shoulders with two shoulder-pieces. 5The decorative sash was made of the same materials: finely woven linen embroidered with gold and with blue, purple, and scarlet thread, just as the LORD had commanded Moses. 6They mounted the two onyx stones in settings of gold filigree. The stones were engraved with the names of the tribes of Israel, just as a seal is engraved. 7He fastened these stones on the shoulder-pieces of the ephod as a reminder that the priest represents the people of Israel. All this was done just as the LORD had commanded Moses.

Making the Chestpiece

EXODUS 39:8-21

Bezalel made the chestpiece with great skill and care. He made it to match the ephod, using finely woven linen embroidered with gold and with blue, purple, and scarlet thread. 9He made the chestpiece of a single piece of cloth folded to form a pouch nine inches* square. 10They mounted four rows of gemstones* on

Ex 38:18 Hebrew *20 cubits* [9.2 meters] *long and 5 cubits* [2.3 meters] *high.* **Ex 38:21** Hebrew *the Tabernacle, the Tabernacle of the Testimony.* **Ex 38:24** Hebrew *29 talents and 730 shekels* [994 kilograms]. Each shekel weighed about 0.4 ounces. **Ex 38:25** Hebrew *100 talents and 1,775 shekels* [3,420 kilograms]. **Ex 38:26** Or *0.2 ounces,* or *6 grams.* **Ex 38:27** Hebrew *100 talents* [3,400 kilograms] *of silver, 1 talent* [34 kilograms] *for each base.* **Ex 38:28** Hebrew *1,775 shekels* [20.2 kilograms]. **Ex 38:29** Hebrew *70 talents and 2,400 shekels* [2,407 kilograms]. **Ex 39:2** Hebrew *He;* also in 39:8, 22. **Ex 39:9** Hebrew *1 span* [23 centimeters]. **Ex 39:10** The identification of some of these gemstones is uncertain.

Exod 38:21 In the building of the Tabernacle, Moses laid out the steps, but Ithamar supervised the project. We all have different talents and abilities. God didn't ask Moses to build the Tabernacle himself but to motivate the experts to do it. Look for the areas where God has gifted you and then seek opportunities to allow God to use your gifts.

Exod 39:1-21 The priests wore a uniform to the Tabernacle each day. Some of the pieces of their uniform were not only beautiful but also significant. Two parts of the high priest's uniform were the ephod and chestpiece. The ephod looked like a vest and was worn over the outer clothing. The chestpiece was fitted to the ephod (and sometimes was called the ephod). The chestpiece was made of colored linens about nine inches square. On its front were attached 12 gemstones, each inscribed with the name of a tribe of Israel. This symbolized how the high priest represented all the people before God. The chestpiece also contained pockets that held two stones or plates called the Urim and Thummim. The high priest could determine God's will for the nation by consulting the Urim and Thummim. (See the notes on Exod 28:30, p. 179, and Lev 8:8, p. 210.)

▶ **EXODUS 39:8-21 *(cont.)***

it. The first row contained a red carnelian, a pale-green peridot, and an emerald. [11]The second row contained a turquoise, a blue lapis lazuli, and a white moonstone. [12]The third row contained an orange jacinth, an agate, and a purple amethyst. [13]The fourth row contained a blue-green beryl, an onyx, and a green jasper. All these stones were set in gold filigree. [14]Each stone represented one of the twelve sons of Israel, and the name of that tribe was engraved on it like a seal.

[15]To attach the chestpiece to the ephod, they made braided cords of pure gold thread. [16]They also made two settings of gold filigree and two gold rings and attached them to the top corners of the chestpiece. [17]They tied the two gold cords to the rings on the chestpiece. [18]They tied the other ends of the cords to the gold settings on the shoulder-pieces of the ephod. [19]Then they made two more gold rings and attached them to the inside edges of the chestpiece next to the ephod. [20]Then they made two more gold rings and attached them to the front of the ephod, below the shoulder-pieces, just above the knot where the decorative sash was fastened to the ephod. [21]They attached the bottom rings of the chestpiece to the rings on the ephod with blue cords. In this way, the chestpiece was held securely to the ephod above the decorative sash. All this was done just as the LORD had commanded Moses.

Additional Clothing for the Priests

EXODUS 39:22-31

Bezalel made the robe that is worn with the ephod from a single piece of blue woven cloth, [23]with an opening for Aaron's head in the middle of it. The opening was reinforced with a woven collar* so it would not tear. [24]They made pomegranates of blue, purple, and scarlet yarn, and attached them to the hem of the robe. [25]They also made bells of pure gold and placed them between the pomegranates along the hem of the robe, [26]with bells and pomegranates alternating all around the hem. This robe was to be worn whenever the priest ministered before the LORD, just as the LORD had commanded Moses.

[27]They made tunics for Aaron and his sons from fine linen cloth. [28]The turban and the special head coverings were made of fine linen, and the undergarments were also made of finely woven linen. [29]The sashes were made of finely woven linen and embroidered with blue, purple, and scarlet thread, just as the LORD had commanded Moses.

[30]Finally, they made the sacred medallion—the badge of holiness—of pure gold. They engraved it like a seal with these words: HOLY TO THE LORD. [31]They attached the medallion with a blue cord to Aaron's turban, just as the LORD had commanded Moses.

Moses Inspects the Work

EXODUS 39:32-43

And so at last the Tabernacle* was finished. The Israelites had done everything just as the LORD had commanded Moses. [33]And they brought the entire Tabernacle to Moses:

the sacred tent with all its furnishings, clasps, frames, crossbars, posts, and bases;
34 the tent coverings of tanned ram skins and fine goatskin leather;
the inner curtain to shield the Ark;
35 the Ark of the Covenant* and its carrying poles;
the Ark's cover—the place of atonement;
36 the table and all its utensils;
the Bread of the Presence;
37 the pure gold lampstand with its symmetrical lamp cups, all its accessories, and the olive oil for lighting;
38 the gold altar;
the anointing oil and fragrant incense;
the curtain for the entrance of the sacred tent;
39 the bronze altar;
the bronze grating and its carrying poles and utensils;
the washbasin with its stand;
40 the curtains for the walls of the courtyard;
the posts and their bases;
the curtain for the entrance to the courtyard;
the ropes and tent pegs;
all the furnishings to be used in worship at the Tabernacle;
41 the beautifully stitched garments for the priests to wear while ministering in the Holy Place—
the sacred garments for Aaron the priest, and the garments for his sons to wear as they minister as priests.

[42]So the people of Israel followed all of the LORD's instructions to Moses. [43]Then Moses inspected all their work. When he found it had been done just as the LORD had commanded him, he blessed them.

Ex 39:23 The meaning of the Hebrew is uncertain. **Ex 39:32** Hebrew *the Tabernacle, the Tent of Meeting;* also in 39:40. **Ex 39:35** Or *Ark of the Testimony.*

Exod 39:32 The Tabernacle was finally complete to the last detail. God was keenly interested in every minute part. The Creator of the universe was concerned about even the little things. Matthew 10:30 says that God knows the number of hairs on our heads. This shows that God is greatly interested in you. Don't be afraid to talk with him about any of your concerns—no matter how small or unimportant they might seem.

Exod 39:42 Moses had learned his management lesson well. He gave important responsibilities to others and then trusted them to do the job. Great leaders, like Moses, give plans and direction while letting others participate on the team. If you are a leader, trust your assistants with key responsibilities.

Exod 39:43 Moses inspected the finished work, saw that it was done the way God wanted, and then blessed the people. A good leader follows up on assigned tasks and

5. THE DEDICATION OF THE TABERNACLE

After the work on the Tabernacle was completed, Israel celebrated with a huge dedication ceremony followed by the observance of Passover. This was the second Passover, one year after their exodus from Egypt.

The Tabernacle Completed

EXODUS 40:1-33

Then the LORD said to Moses, [2]"Set up the Tabernacle* on the first day of the new year.* [3]Place the Ark of the Covenant* inside, and install the inner curtain to enclose the Ark within the Most Holy Place. [4]Then bring in the table, and arrange the utensils on it. And bring in the lampstand, and set up the lamps.

[5]"Place the gold incense altar in front of the Ark of the Covenant. Then hang the curtain at the entrance of the Tabernacle. [6]Place the altar of burnt offering in front of the Tabernacle entrance. [7]Set the washbasin between the Tabernacle* and the altar, and fill it with water. [8]Then set up the courtyard around the outside of the tent, and hang the curtain for the courtyard entrance.

[9]"Take the anointing oil and anoint the Tabernacle and all its furnishings to consecrate them and make them holy. [10]Anoint the altar of burnt offering and its utensils to consecrate them. Then the altar will become absolutely holy. [11]Next anoint the washbasin and its stand to consecrate them.

[12]"Present Aaron and his sons at the entrance of the Tabernacle, and wash them with water. [13]Dress Aaron with the sacred garments and anoint him, consecrating him to serve me as a priest. [14]Then present his sons and dress them in their tunics. [15]Anoint them as you did their father, so they may also serve me as priests. With their anointing, Aaron's descendants are set apart for the priesthood forever, from generation to generation."

[16]Moses proceeded to do everything just as the LORD had commanded him. [17]So the Tabernacle was set up on the first day of the first month of the second year. [18]Moses erected the Tabernacle by setting down its bases, inserting the frames, attaching the crossbars, and setting up the posts. [19]Then he spread the coverings over the Tabernacle framework and put on the protective layers, just as the LORD had commanded him.

[20]He took the stone tablets inscribed with the terms of the covenant and placed them* inside the Ark. Then he attached the carrying poles to the Ark, and he set the Ark's cover—the place of atonement—on top of it. [21]Then he brought the Ark of the Covenant into the Tabernacle and hung the inner curtain to shield it from view, just as the LORD had commanded him.

[22]Next Moses placed the table in the Tabernacle, along the north side of the Holy Place, just outside the inner curtain. [23]And he arranged the Bread of the Presence on the table before the LORD, just as the LORD had commanded him.

[24]He set the lampstand in the Tabernacle across from the table on the south side of the Holy Place. [25]Then he lit the lamps in the LORD's presence, just as the LORD had commanded him. [26]He also placed the gold incense altar in the Tabernacle, in the Holy Place in front of the inner curtain. [27]On it he burned the fragrant incense, just as the LORD had commanded him.

[28]He hung the curtain at the entrance of the Tabernacle, [29]and he placed the altar of burnt offering near the Tabernacle entrance. On it he offered a burnt offering and a grain offering, just as the LORD had commanded him.

[30]Next Moses placed the washbasin between the Tabernacle and the altar. He filled it with water so the priests could wash themselves. [31]Moses and Aaron and Aaron's sons used water from it to wash their hands and feet. [32]Whenever they approached the altar and entered the Tabernacle, they washed themselves, just as the LORD had commanded Moses.

[33]Then he hung the curtains forming the courtyard around the Tabernacle and the altar. And he set up the curtain at the entrance of the courtyard. So at last Moses finished the work.

Ex 40:2a Hebrew *the Tabernacle, the Tent of Meeting;* also in 40:6, 29. **Ex 40:2b** Hebrew *the first day of the first month.* This day of the ancient Hebrew lunar calendar occurred in March or April. **Ex 40:3** Or *Ark of the Testimony;* also in 40:5, 21. **Ex 40:7** Hebrew *Tent of Meeting;* also in 40:12, 22, 24, 26, 30, 32, 34, 35. **Ex 40:20** Hebrew *He placed the Testimony;* see note on 25:16.

gives rewards for good work. In whatever responsible position you find yourself, follow up to make sure that tasks are completed as intended, and show your appreciation to the people who have helped.

Exod 40:1ff Moses was careful to obey God's instructions in the smallest detail. Notice that he didn't make a reasonable facsimile of God's description, but an exact copy. We should follow Moses' example and be fastidious about our obedience. If God has told you to do something, do it, do it right, and do it completely.

Exod 40:16 God told Moses how to build the Tabernacle, and Moses delegated jobs in order to do it. God allows people to participate with him in carrying out his will. Your task is not just to sit and watch God work but to give your best effort when work needs to be done.

Exod 40:17-33 The physical care of the Tabernacle required a long list of tasks, and each was important to the work of God's house. This principle is important to remember today when God's house is the church. There are many seemingly unimportant tasks that must be done to keep your church building maintained. Washing dishes, painting walls, or shoveling snow may not seem very spiritual; but they are vital to the ministry of the church and are an important part of our worship of God.

The LORD's Glory Fills the Tabernacle

EXODUS 40:34-38

Then the cloud covered the Tabernacle, and the glory of the LORD filled the Tabernacle. [35]Moses could no longer enter the Tabernacle because the cloud had settled down over it, and the glory of the LORD filled the Tabernacle.

[36]Now whenever the cloud lifted from the Tabernacle, the people of Israel would set out on their journey, following it. [37]But if the cloud did not rise, they remained where they were until it lifted. [38]The cloud of the LORD hovered over the Tabernacle during the day, and at night fire glowed inside the cloud so the whole family of Israel could see it. This continued throughout all their journeys.

Offerings of Dedication

NUMBERS 7:1-89

On the day Moses set up the Tabernacle, he anointed it and set it apart as holy. He also anointed and set apart all its furnishings and the altar with its utensils. [2]Then the leaders of Israel—the tribal leaders who had registered the troops—came and brought their offerings. [3]Together they brought six large wagons and twelve oxen. There was a wagon for every two leaders and an ox for each leader. They presented these to the LORD in front of the Tabernacle.

[4]Then the LORD said to Moses, [5]"Receive their gifts, and use these oxen and wagons for transporting the Tabernacle.* Distribute them among the Levites according to the work they have to do." [6]So Moses took the wagons and oxen and presented them to the Levites. [7]He gave two wagons and four oxen to the Gershonite division for their work, [8]and he gave four wagons and eight oxen to the Merarite division for their work. All their work was done under the leadership of Ithamar son of Aaron the priest. [9]But he gave none of the wagons or oxen to the Kohathite division, since they were required to carry the sacred objects of the Tabernacle on their shoulders.

[10]The leaders also presented dedication gifts for the altar at the time it was anointed. They each placed their gifts before the altar. [11]The LORD said to Moses, "Let one leader bring his gift each day for the dedication of the altar."

[12]On the first day Nahshon son of Amminadab, leader of the tribe of Judah, presented his offering.

[13]His offering consisted of a silver platter weighing 3¼ pounds and a silver basin weighing 1¾ pounds* (as measured by the weight of the sanctuary shekel). These were both filled with grain offerings of choice flour moistened with olive oil. [14]He also brought a gold container weighing four ounces,* which was filled with incense. [15]He brought a young bull, a ram, and a one-year-old male lamb for a burnt offering, [16]and a male goat for a sin offering. [17]For a peace offering he brought two bulls, five rams, five male goats, and five one-year-old male lambs. This was the offering brought by Nahshon son of Amminadab.

[18]On the second day Nethanel son of Zuar, leader of the tribe of Issachar, presented his offering.

[19]His offering consisted of a silver platter

Nm 7:5 Hebrew *the Tent of Meeting;* also in 7:89. **Nm 7:13** Hebrew *silver platter weighing 130 shekels* [1.5 kilograms] *and a silver basin weighing 70 shekels* [800 grams]; also in 7:19, 25, 31, 37, 43, 49, 55, 61, 67, 73, 79, 85. **Nm 7:14** Hebrew *10 shekels* [114 grams]; also in 7:20, 26, 32, 38, 44, 50, 56, 62, 68, 74, 80, 86.

Exod 40:34 The Tabernacle was God's home on earth. He filled it with his glory—the overpowering sense of his presence. Almost 500 years later, Solomon built the Temple, which replaced the Tabernacle as the central place of worship. God also filled the Temple with his glory (2 Chr 5:13-14). But when Israel turned from God, his glory and presence departed from the Temple, and the Temple was destroyed by invading armies (2 Kgs 25). The Temple was rebuilt in 515 B.C., and God's glory returned in even greater splendor nearly five centuries later when Jesus Christ, God's Son, entered it and taught. When Jesus was crucified, God's glory again left the Temple. But God no longer needed a physical building after Jesus rose from the dead. God's temple now is his church, the body of believers.

Exod 40:38 The Israelites were once Egyptian slaves making bricks without straw. Here they were following the pillar of cloud and the pillar of fire, carrying the Tabernacle they had built for God. Exodus begins in gloom and ends in glory. This parallels our progress through the Christian life. We begin as slaves to sin, are redeemed by God, and end our pilgrimage living with God forever. The lessons the Israelites learned along the way are ones we also need to learn.

Num 7:1ff After the Tabernacle was set up, anointed, and consecrated, the leaders of the 12 tribes brought gifts and offerings for its use and maintenance. All of the people participated—it was everyone's Tabernacle.

The Tabernacle ▶

The Tabernacle was the precursor of the Temple during most of the period between the formation of Israel as a nation at Mt. Sinai and its final establishment in the Promised Land in the early period of Israel's monarchy. A portable sanctuary for easy mobility, it was the symbol of God's presence with and availability for his people, as well as a place where his will was communicated.

The three-part construction of the Tabernacle, with one general area and two restricted areas, was not unique. In other developed religions that included a priesthood there were three main levels of approach: one for all members of the community; one for the priests generally; and one for the chief religious leaders, which was an inner sanctuary thought of as the dwelling place of the deity. Excavations of heathen sanctuaries in Palestine and Syria in the pre-Israelite period have revealed this type of divided sanctuary. There is also widespread evidence of the use of portable, often complex, prefabricated structures during the second millennium B.C., usually as either staterooms for kings and other high dignitaries, or as sanctuaries.

The Tabernacle symbolizes God's presence with his people. The Gospel of John tells us that Jesus "made his home among us" (John 1:14), using a word that is closely related to the word for the Tabernacle. Through Jesus, God is always present with believers today.

The Tabernacle

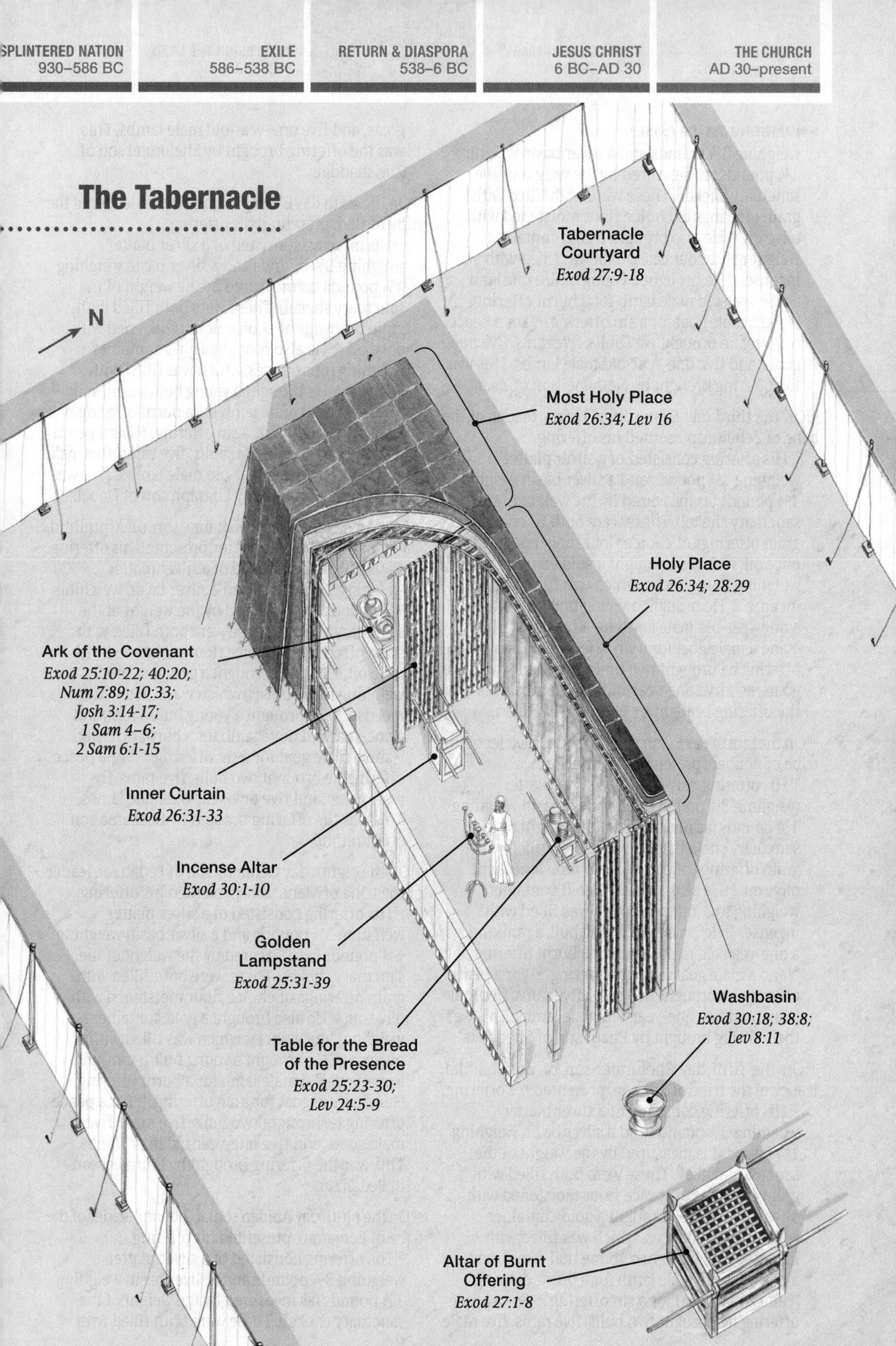

N
Tabernacle Courtyard
Exod 27:9-18
Most Holy Place
Exod 26:34; Lev 16
Holy Place
Exod 26:34; 28:29
Ark of the Covenant
Exod 25:10-22; 40:20; Num 7:89; 10:33; Josh 3:14-17; 1 Sam 4–6; 2 Sam 6:1-15
Inner Curtain
Exod 26:31-33
Incense Altar
Exod 30:1-10
Golden Lampstand
Exod 25:31-39
Table for the Bread of the Presence
Exod 25:23-30; Lev 24:5-9
Washbasin
Exod 30:18; 38:8; Lev 8:11
Altar of Burnt Offering
Exod 27:1-8

▸ **NUMBERS 7:1-89** ***(cont.)***

weighing 3¼ pounds and a silver basin weighing
1¾ pounds (as measured by the weight of the
sanctuary shekel). These were both filled with
grain offerings of choice flour moistened with
olive oil. 20He also brought a gold container
weighing four ounces, which was filled with
incense. 21He brought a young bull, a ram, and
a one-year-old male lamb for a burnt offering,
22and a male goat for a sin offering. 23For a peace
offering he brought two bulls, five rams, five male
goats, and five one-year-old male lambs. This was
the offering brought by Nethanel son of Zuar.

24On the third day Eliab son of Helon, leader of the
tribe of Zebulun, presented his offering.
25His offering consisted of a silver platter
weighing 3¼ pounds and a silver basin weighing
1¾ pounds (as measured by the weight of the
sanctuary shekel). These were both filled with
grain offerings of choice flour moistened with
olive oil. 26He also brought a gold container
weighing four ounces, which was filled with
incense. 27He brought a young bull, a ram, and
a one-year-old male lamb for a burnt offering,
28and a male goat for a sin offering. 29For a peace
offering he brought two bulls, five rams, five male
goats, and five one-year-old male lambs. This was
the offering brought by Eliab son of Helon.

30On the fourth day Elizur son of Shedeur, leader of the
tribe of Reuben, presented his offering.
31His offering consisted of a silver platter
weighing 3¼ pounds and a silver basin weighing
1¾ pounds (as measured by the weight of the
sanctuary shekel). These were both filled with
grain offerings of choice flour moistened with
olive oil. 32He also brought a gold container
weighing four ounces, which was filled with
incense. 33He brought a young bull, a ram, and
a one-year-old male lamb for a burnt offering,
34and a male goat for a sin offering. 35For a peace
offering he brought two bulls, five rams, five male
goats, and five one-year-old male lambs. This was
the offering brought by Elizur son of Shedeur.

36On the fifth day Shelumiel son of Zurishaddai,
leader of the tribe of Simeon, presented his offering.
37His offering consisted of a silver platter
weighing 3¼ pounds and a silver basin weighing
1¾ pounds (as measured by the weight of the
sanctuary shekel). These were both filled with
grain offerings of choice flour moistened with
olive oil. 38He also brought a gold container
weighing four ounces, which was filled with
incense. 39He brought a young bull, a ram, and
a one-year-old male lamb for a burnt offering,
40and a male goat for a sin offering. 41For a peace
offering he brought two bulls, five rams, five male
goats, and five one-year-old male lambs. This
was the offering brought by Shelumiel son of
Zurishaddai.

42On the sixth day Eliasaph son of Deuel, leader of the
tribe of Gad, presented his offering.
43His offering consisted of a silver platter
weighing 3¼ pounds and a silver basin weighing
1¾ pounds (as measured by the weight of the
sanctuary shekel). These were both filled with
grain offerings of choice flour moistened with
olive oil. 44He also brought a gold container
weighing four ounces, which was filled with
incense. 45He brought a young bull, a ram, and
a one-year-old male lamb for a burnt offering,
46and a male goat for a sin offering. 47For a peace
offering he brought two bulls, five rams, five male
goats, and five one-year-old male lambs. This was
the offering brought by Eliasaph son of Deuel.

48On the seventh day Elishama son of Ammihud,
leader of the tribe of Ephraim, presented his offering.
49His offering consisted of a silver platter
weighing 3¼ pounds and a silver basin weighing
1¾ pounds (as measured by the weight of the
sanctuary shekel). These were both filled with
grain offerings of choice flour moistened with
olive oil. 50He also brought a gold container
weighing four ounces, which was filled with
incense. 51He brought a young bull, a ram, and
a one-year-old male lamb for a burnt offering,
52and a male goat for a sin offering. 53For a peace
offering he brought two bulls, five rams, five
male goats, and five one-year-old male lambs.
This was the offering brought by Elishama son
of Ammihud.

54On the eighth day Gamaliel son of Pedahzur, leader
of the tribe of Manasseh, presented his offering.
55His offering consisted of a silver platter
weighing 3¼ pounds and a silver basin weighing
1¾ pounds (as measured by the weight of the
sanctuary shekel). These were both filled with
grain offerings of choice flour moistened with
olive oil. 56He also brought a gold container
weighing four ounces, which was filled with
incense. 57He brought a young bull, a ram, and
a one-year-old male lamb for a burnt offering,
58and a male goat for a sin offering. 59For a peace
offering he brought two bulls, five rams, five
male goats, and five one-year-old male lambs.
This was the offering brought by Gamaliel son
of Pedahzur.

60On the ninth day Abidan son of Gideoni, leader of the
tribe of Benjamin, presented his offering.
61His offering consisted of a silver platter
weighing 3¼ pounds and a silver basin weighing
1¾ pounds (as measured by the weight of the
sanctuary shekel). These were both filled with

grain offerings of choice flour moistened with
olive oil. 62He also brought a gold container
weighing four ounces, which was filled with
incense. 63He brought a young bull, a ram, and
a one-year-old male lamb for a burnt offering,
64and a male goat for a sin offering. 65For a peace
offering he brought two bulls, five rams, five male
goats, and five one-year-old male lambs. This was
the offering brought by Abidan son of Gideoni.

66On the tenth day Ahiezer son of Ammishaddai,
leader of the tribe of Dan, presented his offering.
67His offering consisted of a silver platter
weighing 3¼ pounds and a silver basin weighing
1¾ pounds (as measured by the weight of the
sanctuary shekel). These were both filled with
grain offerings of choice flour moistened with
olive oil. 68He also brought a gold container
weighing four ounces, which was filled with
incense. 69He brought a young bull, a ram, and
a one-year-old male lamb for a burnt offering,
70and a male goat for a sin offering. 71For a peace
offering he brought two bulls, five rams, five
male goats, and five one-year-old male lambs.
This was the offering brought by Ahiezer son
of Ammishaddai.

72On the eleventh day Pagiel son of Ocran, leader of the
tribe of Asher, presented his offering.
73His offering consisted of a silver platter
weighing 3¼ pounds and a silver basin weighing
1¾ pounds (as measured by the weight of the
sanctuary shekel). These were both filled with
grain offerings of choice flour moistened with
olive oil. 74He also brought a gold container
weighing four ounces, which was filled with
incense. 75He brought a young bull, a ram, and
a one-year-old male lamb for a burnt offering,
76and a male goat for a sin offering. 77For a peace
offering he brought two bulls, five rams, five male
goats, and five one-year-old male lambs. This was
the offering brought by Pagiel son of Ocran.

78On the twelfth day Ahira son of Enan, leader of the
tribe of Naphtali, presented his offering.
79His offering consisted of a silver platter
weighing 3¼ pounds and a silver basin weighing
1¾ pounds (as measured by the weight of the
sanctuary shekel). These were both filled with
grain offerings of choice flour moistened with
olive oil. 80He also brought a gold container
weighing four ounces, which was filled with
incense. 81He brought a young bull, a ram, and
a one-year-old male lamb for a burnt offering,
82and a male goat for a sin offering. 83For a
peace offering he brought two bulls, five rams,
five male goats, and five one-year-old male
lambs. This was the offering brought by Ahira
son of Enan.

84So this was the dedication offering brought by
the leaders of Israel at the time the altar was anointed:
twelve silver platters, twelve silver basins, and twelve
gold incense containers. 85Each silver platter weighed
3¼ pounds, and each silver basin weighed 1¾ pounds.
The total weight of the silver was 60 pounds* (as measured by the weight of the sanctuary shekel). 86Each of
the twelve gold containers that was filled with incense
weighed four ounces (as measured by the weight of
the sanctuary shekel). The total weight of the gold
was three pounds.* 87Twelve young bulls, twelve rams,
and twelve one-year-old male lambs were donated for
the burnt offerings, along with their prescribed grain
offerings. Twelve male goats were brought for the sin
offerings. 88Twenty-four bulls, sixty rams, sixty male
goats, and sixty one-year-old male lambs were donated
for the peace offerings. This was the dedication offering for the altar after it was anointed.
89Whenever Moses went into the Tabernacle to
speak with the LORD, he heard the voice speaking to
him from between the two cherubim above the Ark's
cover—the place of atonement—that rests on the Ark
of the Covenant.* The LORD spoke to him from there.

Preparing the Lamps

NUMBERS 8:1-4

The LORD said to Moses, 2"Give Aaron the following
instructions: When you set up the seven lamps in the
lampstand, place them so their light shines forward in
front of the lampstand." 3So Aaron did this. He set up
the seven lamps so they reflected their light forward,
just as the LORD had commanded Moses. 4The entire
lampstand, from its base to its decorative blossoms,
was made of beaten gold. It was built according to the
exact design the LORD had shown Moses.

The Levites Dedicated

NUMBERS 8:5-26

Then the LORD said to Moses, 6"Now set the Levites
apart from the rest of the people of Israel and make
them ceremonially clean. 7Do this by sprinkling them

Nm 7:85 Hebrew *2,400 shekels* [27.6 kilograms]. **Nm 7:86** Hebrew *120 shekels* [1.4 kilograms]. **Nm 7:89** Or *Ark of the Testimony.*

Num 7:89 Imagine hearing the very voice of God! Moses must have trembled at the sound. Yet we have God's words recorded for us in the Bible, and we should have no less reverence and awe for them. God sometimes spoke directly to his people to tell them the proper way to live. The Bible records these conversations to give us insights into God's character. How tragic when we take the words of God lightly. Like Moses, we have the privilege of talking to God, but God answers us differently—through his written Word and the guidance of his Holy Spirit. To receive this guidance, we need to seek to know God as Moses did.

Num 8:1-4 The lamps provided light for the priests as they carried out their duties. The light was also an expression of God's presence. Jesus said, "I am the light of the world" (John 8:12). The golden lampstand is still one of the major symbols of the Jewish faith.

1445 BC

The second Passover

▶ **NUMBERS 8:5-26 *(cont.)***

with the water of purification, and have them shave their entire body and wash their clothing. Then they will be ceremonially clean. 8Have them bring a young bull and a grain offering of choice flour moistened with olive oil, along with a second young bull for a sin offering. 9Then assemble the whole community of Israel, and present the Levites at the entrance of the Tabernacle.* 10When you present the Levites before the LORD, the people of Israel must lay their hands on them. 11Raising his hands, Aaron must then present the Levites to the LORD as a special offering from the people of Israel, thus dedicating them to the LORD's service.

12"Next the Levites will lay their hands on the heads of the young bulls. Present one as a sin offering and the other as a burnt offering to the LORD, to purify the Levites and make them right with the LORD.* 13Then have the Levites stand in front of Aaron and his sons, and raise your hands and present them as a special offering to the LORD. 14In this way, you will set the Levites apart from the rest of the people of Israel, and the Levites will belong to me. 15After this, they may go into the Tabernacle to do their work, because you have purified them and presented them as a special offering.

16"Of all the people of Israel, the Levites are reserved for me. I have claimed them for myself in place of all the firstborn sons of the Israelites; I have taken the Levites as their substitutes. 17For all the firstborn males among the people of Israel are mine, both of people and of animals. I set them apart for myself on the day I struck down all the firstborn sons of the Egyptians. 18Yes, I have claimed the Levites in place of all the firstborn sons of Israel. 19And of all the Israelites, I have assigned the Levites to Aaron and his sons. They will serve in the Tabernacle on behalf of the Israelites and make sacrifices to purify* the people so no plague will strike them when they approach the sanctuary."

20So Moses, Aaron, and the whole community of Israel dedicated the Levites, carefully following all the LORD's instructions to Moses. 21The Levites purified themselves from sin and washed their clothes, and Aaron lifted them up and presented them to the LORD as a special offering. He then offered a sacrifice to purify them and make them right with the LORD.* 22After that the Levites went into the Tabernacle to perform their duties, assisting Aaron and his sons. So they carried out all the commands that the LORD gave Moses concerning the Levites.

23The LORD also instructed Moses, 24"This is the rule the Levites must follow: They must begin serving in the Tabernacle at the age of twenty-five, 25and they must retire at the age of fifty. 26After retirement they may assist their fellow Levites by serving as guards at the Tabernacle, but they may not officiate in the service. This is how you must assign duties to the Levites."

The Second Passover

NUMBERS 9:1-14

A year after Israel's departure from Egypt, the LORD spoke to Moses in the wilderness of Sinai. In the first month* of that year he said, 2"Tell the Israelites to celebrate the Passover at the prescribed time, 3at twilight on the fourteenth day of the first month.* Be sure to follow all my decrees and regulations concerning this celebration."

4So Moses told the people to celebrate the Passover 5in the wilderness of Sinai as twilight fell on the fourteenth day of the month. And they celebrated the festival there, just as the LORD had commanded Moses. 6But some of the men had been ceremonially defiled by touching a dead body, so they could not celebrate the Passover that day. They came to Moses and Aaron that day 7and said, "We have become ceremonially unclean by touching a dead body. But why should we be prevented from presenting the LORD's offering at the proper time with the rest of the Israelites?"

8Moses answered, "Wait here until I have received instructions for you from the LORD."

9This was the LORD's reply to Moses. 10"Give the following instructions to the people of Israel: If any of the people now or in future generations are ceremonially unclean at Passover time because of touching a dead body, or if they are on a journey and cannot be present at the ceremony, they may still celebrate the LORD's

Nm 8:9 Hebrew *the Tent of Meeting;* also in 8:15, 19, 22, 24, 26. **Nm 8:12** Or *to make atonement for the Levites.* **Nm 8:19** Or *make atonement for.* **Nm 8:21** Or *then made atonement for them to purify them.* **Nm 9:1** The first month of the ancient Hebrew lunar calendar usually occurs within the months of March and April. **Nm 9:3** This day in the ancient Hebrew lunar calendar occurred in late March, April, or early May.

Num 8:25-26 Why were the Levites supposed to retire at age 50? The reasons were probably more practical than theological. Moving the Tabernacle and its furniture through the wilderness required strength. The younger men were more suited for the work of lifting the heavy articles. The Levites over 50 did not stop working altogether. They were allowed to assist with various light duties in the Tabernacle. This helped the younger men assume more responsibilities, and it allowed the older men to be in a position to advise and counsel them.

Num 9:2 This is the second Passover. The first was instituted in Egypt and recorded in Exodus 12. Passover and the Festival of Unleavened Bread were an eight-day religious observance (Lev 23:5-6) commemorating the Israelites' escape from slavery in Egypt by God's power.

Num 9:6-12 Several men came to Moses because of a predicament they faced: They were "ceremonially defiled" because of contact with a dead body (or entering the home of a person who had died), and this prevented them from participating in the Passover meal. Notice that God did not adjust the requirements of the Passover. The standards of holiness were maintained, and the men were not allowed to participate. But God did make an exception and allowed the men to celebrate the Passover at a later date. This upheld the sacred requirements while allowing the men to participate in the feast—a duty for all Israelite men. Sometimes we face predicaments where the most obvious solution might cause us to compromise God's standards. Like Moses, we should use wisdom and prayer to reach a workable solution.

Passover. [11]They must offer the Passover sacrifice one
month later, at twilight on the fourteenth day of the
second month.* They must eat the Passover lamb at
that time with bitter salad greens and bread made
without yeast. [12]They must not leave any of the lamb
until the next morning, and they must not break any of
its bones. They must follow all the normal regulations
concerning the Passover.

[13]"But those who neglect to celebrate the Passover
at the regular time, even though they are ceremonially
clean and not away on a trip, will be cut off from the
community of Israel. If they fail to present the LORD's
offering at the proper time, they will suffer the consequences of their guilt. [14]And if foreigners living among
you want to celebrate the Passover to the LORD, they
must follow these same decrees and regulations. The
same laws apply both to native-born Israelites and to
the foreigners living among you."

Nm 9:11 This day in the ancient Hebrew lunar calendar occurred in late April, May, or early June.

6. RECEIVING GUIDANCE FOR THE JOURNEY

God provided guidance for his people at every step on their journey through the wilderness toward the Promised Land. While we can't always see a cloud like the Israelites did, God still guides his people today through the Spirit, the Word of God, and the church.

The Fiery Cloud

NUMBERS 9:15-23

On the day the Tabernacle was set up, the cloud covered it.* But from evening until morning the cloud
over the Tabernacle looked like a pillar of fire. [16]This
was the regular pattern—at night the cloud that
covered the Tabernacle had the appearance of fire.
[17]Whenever the cloud lifted from over the sacred
tent, the people of Israel would break camp and follow it. And wherever the cloud settled, the people of
Israel would set up camp. [18]In this way, they traveled
and camped at the LORD's command wherever he
told them to go. Then they remained in their camp
as long as the cloud stayed over the Tabernacle. [19]If
the cloud remained over the Tabernacle for a long
time, the Israelites stayed and performed their duty

Nm 9:15 Hebrew *covered the Tabernacle, the Tent of the Testimony.*

Num 9:14 God said regarding foreigners and the Passover, "They must follow these same decrees and regulations." This principle designed for foreigners doesn't mean we mandate our religion to our neighbors, but in our homes we should live out our convictions. When we have guests in our homes, whether visitors or family, we may be tempted to change or water down our Christian practices. If family devotions, attending church, and mealtime prayers are your practices, don't change these when you have guests. Holidays such as Christmas and Easter should not be reduced to nothing more than society's expressions. Further, you should maintain your family standards even when guests visit—for example, unmarried couples who are guests should not be allowed to sleep together. Maintain your Christian standards and principles. You never know what influence you may have on the guests in your home.

Num 9:15-22 A pillar of cloud by day and a pillar of fire by night guided and protected the Israelites as they traveled across the wilderness. Some have said this pillar may have been a burning bowl of pitch whose smoke was visible during the day and whose fire could be seen at night. However, a bowl of pitch would not have lifted itself up and moved ahead of the people, and the Bible is clear that the cloud and fire moved in accordance with the will of God. The cloud and the fire were not merely natural phenomena; they were the vehicle of God's presence and the visible evidence of his moving and directing his people.

At night the cloud that covered the Tabernacle had the appearance of fire. Whenever the cloud lifted from over the sacred tent, the people of Israel would break camp and follow it.

Numbers 9:16-17

▶ **NUMBERS 9:15-23** ***(cont.)***
to the LORD. 20Sometimes the cloud would stay over the Tabernacle for only a few days, so the people would stay for only a few days, as the LORD commanded. Then at the LORD's command they would break camp and move on. 21Sometimes the cloud stayed only overnight and lifted the next morning. But day or night, when the cloud lifted, the people broke camp and moved on. 22Whether the cloud stayed above the Tabernacle for two days, a month, or a year, the people of Israel stayed in camp and did not move on. But as soon as it lifted, they broke camp and moved on. 23So they camped or traveled at the LORD's command, and they did whatever the LORD told them through Moses.

The Silver Trumpets

NUMBERS 10:1-10
Now the LORD said to Moses, 2"Make two trumpets of hammered silver for calling the community to assemble and for signaling the breaking of camp. 3When both trumpets are blown, everyone must gather before you at the entrance of the Tabernacle.*

Nm 10:3 Hebrew *Tent of Meeting.*

4But if only one trumpet is blown, then only the leaders—the heads of the clans of Israel—must present themselves to you.

5"When you sound the signal to move on, the tribes camped on the east side of the Tabernacle must break camp and move forward. 6When you sound the signal a second time, the tribes camped on the south will follow. You must sound short blasts as the signal for moving on. 7But when you call the people to an assembly, blow the trumpets with a different signal. 8Only the priests, Aaron's descendants, are allowed to blow the trumpets. This is a permanent law for you, to be observed from generation to generation.

9"When you arrive in your own land and go to war against your enemies who attack you, sound the alarm with the trumpets. Then the LORD your God will remember you and rescue you from your enemies. 10Blow the trumpets in times of gladness, too, sounding them at your annual festivals and at the beginning of each month. And blow the trumpets over your burnt offerings and peace offerings. The trumpets will remind the LORD your God of his covenant with you. I am the LORD your God."

D. Laws for Worshiping a Holy God

The Israelites are camped at the foot of Mount Sinai, and the Tabernacle has been completed. The people will spend a great deal of time here as God shows them a new way of life with clear instructions on how sinful people can relate to a holy God. These instructions also help us avoid taking our relationship with the same holy God too lightly. We learn about the holiness and majesty of the God with whom we are allowed to have a personal relationship.

1. INSTRUCTIONS FOR THE OFFERINGS

Offerings were a central part of Israel's worship. The various offerings remind us of the many ways that God provides for our needs and forgives us for our failings, and they point to Christ—the ultimate sacrifice.

Procedures for the Burnt Offering

LEVITICUS 1:1-17
The LORD called to Moses from the Tabernacle* and said to him, 2"Give the following instructions to the people of Israel. When you present an animal as an offering to the LORD, you may take it from your herd of cattle or your flock of sheep and goats.

3"If the animal you present as a burnt offering is

Lv 1:1 Hebrew *Tent of Meeting;* also in 1:3, 5.

Num 9:23 The Israelites traveled and camped as God guided. When you follow God's guidance, you know you are where God wants you, whether you're moving or staying in one place. You are physically somewhere right now. Instead of praying, "God, what do you want me to do next?" ask, "God, what do you want me to do while I'm right here?" Direction from God is not just for your next big move. He has a purpose in placing you where you are right now. Begin to understand God's purpose for your life by discovering what he wants you to do now!

Num 10:1-10 The two silver trumpets were used to coordinate the tribes as they moved through the wilderness. To keep so many people in tight formations required clear communication and control. Trumpet blasts also reminded Israel of God's protection over them.

Lev 1:1 The "Tabernacle" where God met with Moses was actually the Tent of Meeting, a smaller structure inside the larger Tabernacle. The Tent of Meeting contained the sanctuary in one part and the Most Holy Place with the Ark in another part. These two sections were separated by a curtain. God revealed himself to Moses in the Most Holy Place. Exodus 33:7 mentions a "Tent of Meeting" where Moses met God before the Tabernacle was constructed. Many believe it served the same function as the one described here.

Lev 1:1ff We may be tempted to dismiss Leviticus as a record of bizarre rituals of a different age. But its practices made sense to the people of the day and offer important insights for us into God's nature and character. Animal sacrifice seems obsolete and repulsive to many people today, but animal sacrifices were practiced in many cultures in the Middle East. God used the form of

from the herd, it must be a male with no defects. Bring it to the entrance of the Tabernacle so you* may be accepted by the LORD. 4Lay your hand on the animal's head, and the LORD will accept its death in your place to purify you, making you right with him.* 5Then slaughter the young bull in the LORD's presence, and Aaron's sons, the priests, will present the animal's blood by splattering it against all sides of the altar that stands at the entrance to the Tabernacle. 6Then skin the animal and cut it into pieces. 7The sons of Aaron the priest will build a wood fire on the altar. 8They will arrange the pieces of the offering, including the head and fat, on the wood burning on the altar. 9But the internal organs and the legs must first be washed with water. Then the priest will burn the entire sacrifice on the altar as a burnt offering. It is a special gift, a pleasing aroma to the LORD.

10"If the animal you present as a burnt offering

Lv 1:3 Or *it.* **Lv 1:4** Or *to make atonement for you.*

sacrifice to teach his people about faith. Sin needed to be taken seriously. When people saw the sacrificial animals being killed, they were sensitized to the importance of their sin and guilt. Our culture's casual attitude toward sin ignores the cost of sin and the need for repentance and restoration. Although many of the rituals of Leviticus were designed for the culture of the day, their purpose was to reveal a high and holy God who should be loved, obeyed, and worshiped. God's laws and sacrifices were intended to bring out true devotion of the heart. The ceremonies and rituals were the best way for the Israelites to focus their lives on God.

Lev 1:2 Was there any difference between a sacrifice and an offering? In Leviticus the words are interchanged. Usually a specific sacrifice is called an offering (burnt offering, grain offering, peace offering). Offerings in general are called sacrifices. The point is that each person offered a gift to God by sacrificing it on the altar. In the Old Testament, the sacrifice was the only way to approach God and restore a relationship with him. There was more than one kind of offering or sacrifice. The variety of sacrifices made them more meaningful because each one related to a specific life situation. Sacrifices were given in praise, worship, and thanksgiving, as well as for forgiveness and fellowship. The first seven chapters of Leviticus describe the variety of offerings and how they were to be used.

Lev 1:2 When God taught his people to worship him, he placed great emphasis on sacrifices. Why? Sacrifices were God's Old Testament way for people to ask forgiveness for their sins. Since Creation, God has made it clear that sin separates people from him, and that those who sin deserve to die. Because "everyone has sinned" (Rom 3:23), God designed sacrifice as a way to seek forgiveness and restore a relationship with him. Because he is a God of love and mercy, God decided from the very first that he would come into our world and die to pay the penalty for all humans. This he did in his Son, who, while still God, became a human being. In the meantime, before God made this ultimate sacrifice of his Son, he instructed people to kill animals as sacrifices for sin.

Animal sacrifice accomplished two purposes: (1) The animal symbolically took the sinner's place and paid the penalty for sin, and (2) the animal's death represented one life given so that another life could be saved. This method of sacrifice continued throughout Old Testament times. It was effective in teaching and guiding the people and bringing them back to God. But after Christ's death, no more sacrifices were needed. He took our punishment once and for all. Animal sacrifice is no longer required. Now any person can be freed from the penalty of sin by simply believing in Jesus, acknowledging Jesus' sacrifice in exchange, and accepting the forgiveness Jesus offers.

Lev 1:3-4 The first offering God describes is the burnt offering. A person who had sinned brought an animal with no defects to a priest. The unblemished animal symbolized the moral perfection demanded by a holy God and the perfect nature of the real sacrifice to come—Jesus Christ. The person laid a hand on the head of the animal—symbolizing complete identification with the animal as substitute—and then killed the animal. The priest then sprinkled the blood. The person's sins were symbolically transferred to the animal, and thus they were taken away (atonement). Finally the animal (except for the blood and skin) was burned on the altar, signifying the person's complete dedication to God. God required more than a sacrifice, of course. He also asked the sinner to have an attitude of repentance. The outward symbol (the sacrifice) and the inner change (repentance) were to work together. But it is important to remember that neither sacrifice nor repentance actually caused the sin to be taken away. God alone forgives sin. Fortunately for us, forgiveness is part of God's loving nature. Have you responded to God's offer to forgive you?

Lev 1:3ff What did sacrifices teach the people? (1) By requiring perfect animals and holy priests, they taught reverence for a holy God. (2) By demanding exact obedience, they taught total submission to God's laws. (3) By requiring an animal of great value, they showed the high cost of sin and demonstrated the sincerity of the people's commitment to God. (4) By their nature, sacrifices required the use of all the senses in worship, encouraging a whole-person response to God. Some sacrifices were voluntary while others were required. The sacrificial system taught a combination of requirements before God, but also presented opportunities for heartfelt voluntary response to God.

Lev 1:3-13 Why are there such detailed regulations for each offering? God had a purpose in giving these commands. Starting from scratch, he was teaching his people a whole new way of life, cleansing them from the many pagan practices they had learned in Egypt and restoring true worship of himself. The strict details kept Israel from slipping back into their old lifestyle. In addition, each law painted a graphic picture of the seriousness of sin and of God's great mercy in forgiving sinners.

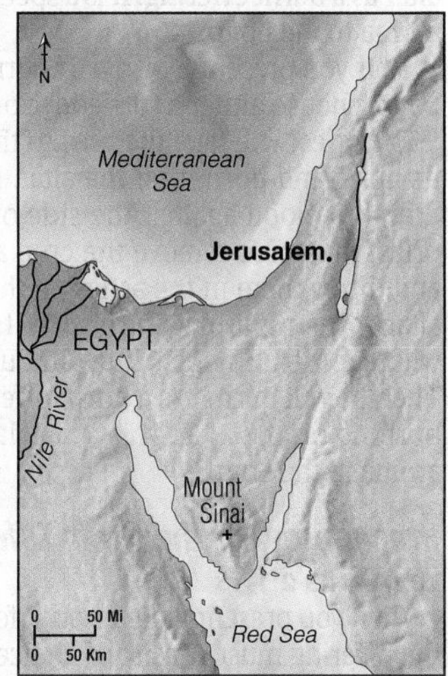

THE ISRAELITES AT MOUNT SINAI *Throughout the book of Leviticus, the Israelites were camped at the foot of Mount Sinai. It was time to regroup as a nation and learn the importance of following God as they prepared to march toward the Promised Land.*

Lev 1:4ff Israel was not the only nation to sacrifice animals. Many other religions did it as well to try to please their gods. Some cultures even included human sacrifice, which was strictly forbidden by God. However, the meaning of Israel's animal sacrifices was clearly different from that of their pagan neighbors' sacrifices. Israelites sacrificed animals not just to appease God's wrath, but also as a substitute for the punishment they deserved for their sins. A sacrifice showed faith in God and commitment to his laws. Most important, this system foreshadowed the day when the Lamb of God (Jesus Christ) would die and conquer sin once and for all.

▸ **LEVITICUS 1:1-17** ***(cont.)***

is from the flock, it may be either a sheep or a goat, but it must be a male with no defects. [11]Slaughter the animal on the north side of the altar in the LORD's presence, and Aaron's sons, the priests, will splatter its blood against all sides of the altar. [12]Then cut the animal in pieces, and the priests will arrange the pieces of the offering, including the head and fat, on the wood burning on the altar. [13]But the internal organs and the legs must first be washed with water. Then the priest will burn the entire sacrifice on the altar as a burnt offering. It is a special gift, a pleasing aroma to the LORD.

[14]"If you present a bird as a burnt offering to the LORD, choose either a turtledove or a young pigeon. [15]The priest will take the bird to the altar, wring off its head, and burn it on the altar. But first he must drain its blood against the side of the altar. [16]The priest must also remove the crop and the feathers* and throw them in the ashes on the east side of the altar. [17]Then, grasping the bird by its wings, the priest will tear the bird open, but without tearing it apart. Then he will burn it as a burnt offering on the wood burning on the altar. It is a special gift, a pleasing aroma to the LORD.

Procedures for the Grain Offering

LEVITICUS 2:1-16

"When you present grain as an offering to the LORD, the offering must consist of choice flour. You are to pour olive oil on it, sprinkle it with frankincense, [2]and bring it to Aaron's sons, the priests. The priest will scoop out a handful of the flour moistened with oil, together with all the frankincense, and burn this representative portion on the altar. It is a special gift, a pleasing aroma to the LORD. [3]The rest of the grain offering will then be given to Aaron and his sons. This offering will be considered a most holy part of the special gifts presented to the LORD.

[4]"If your offering is a grain offering baked in an oven, it must be made of choice flour, but without any yeast. It may be presented in the form of thin cakes mixed with olive oil or wafers spread with olive oil. [5]If your grain offering is cooked on a griddle, it must be made of choice flour mixed with olive oil but without any yeast. [6]Break it in pieces and pour olive oil on it; it is a grain offering. [7]If your grain offering is prepared in a pan, it must be made of choice flour and olive oil.

[8]"No matter how a grain offering for the LORD has been prepared, bring it to the priest, who will present it at the altar. [9]The priest will take a representative portion of the grain offering and burn it on the altar. It is a special gift, a pleasing aroma to the LORD. [10]The rest of the grain offering will then be given to Aaron and his sons as their food. This offering will be considered a most holy part of the special gifts presented to the LORD.

[11]"Do not use yeast in preparing any of the grain offerings you present to the LORD, because no yeast or honey may be burned as a special gift presented to the LORD. [12]You may add yeast and honey to an offering of the first crops of your harvest, but these must never be offered on the altar as a pleasing aroma to the LORD. [13]Season all your grain offerings with salt to remind you of God's eternal covenant. Never forget to add salt to your grain offerings.

[14]"If you present a grain offering to the LORD from the first portion of your harvest, bring fresh grain that is coarsely ground and roasted on a fire. [15]Put olive oil on this grain offering, and sprinkle it with frankincense. [16]The priest will take a representative portion of the grain moistened with oil, together with all the frankincense, and burn it as a special gift presented to the LORD.

Lv 1:16 Or *the crop and its contents.* The meaning of the Hebrew is uncertain.

Lev 1:13 The "pleasing aroma" is a way of saying that God accepted the sacrifice because of the attitude of the people.

Lev 2:1ff The grain offering accompanied all burnt offerings and was a gift of thanks to God. It reminded the people that their food came from God and that they therefore owed their lives to him. Three kinds of grain offerings are listed: (1) fine flour with oil and incense, (2) baked cakes or wafers of fine flour and oil, and (3) roasted kernels of grain (corn) with oil and incense. The absence of yeast symbolized the absence of sin, and the oil symbolized God's presence. Part of the grain offering was burned on the altar as a gift to God, and the rest was eaten by the priests. The offerings helped support them in their work.

Lev 2:11 Why was no yeast allowed in the grain offerings? Yeast is a bacterial fungus or mold and is, therefore, an appropriate symbol for sin. It grows in bread dough just as sin grows in a life. A little yeast will affect the whole loaf, just as a little sin can ruin a whole life. Jesus expanded this analogy by warning about the "yeast of the Pharisees and Sadducees" (Matt 16:6; Mark 8:15). How do you visualize the effects of sin in your life? What do you do to eliminate sin from your attitudes and actions?

Lev 2:13 The offerings were seasoned with salt as a reminder of the people's covenant (contract) with God. Salt is a good symbol of God's activity in a person's life because it penetrates, preserves, and aids in healing. God wants to be active in your life. Let him become part of you, penetrating every aspect of your life, preserving you from the evil all around, and healing you of your sins and shortcomings.

Lev 2:13 In ancient Middle Eastern lands, an agreement was sealed with a gift of salt to show the strength and permanence of the contract. Salt also points to the effects of a truthful agreement—it changes behavior. In Matthew 5:13 believers are called "the salt of the earth." Let the salt you use each day remind you that you are now one of God's covenant people, who actively helps preserve and purify the world.

Lev 2:14-15 Coarsely ground heads of new grain mixed with oil and baked was typical food for the average person. This offering was a token presentation of a person's daily food. In this way, people acknowledged God as provider of their food. Even a poor person could fulfill this offering. God was pleased by the motivation and the dedication of the persons making it.

Lev 3:1ff A person gave a peace offering as an expression of gratitude and a means of maintaining fellowship with God. The animal's sacrificed life emphasized the value of that gratitude and harmony. Neither peace with God nor thanks to God was to be considered a cheap or unimportant gift.

Procedures for the Peace Offering

LEVITICUS 3:1-17

"If you present an animal from the herd as a peace offering to the LORD, it may be a male or a female, but it must have no defects. [2]Lay your hand on the animal's head, and slaughter it at the entrance of the Tabernacle.* Then Aaron's sons, the priests, will splatter its blood against all sides of the altar. [3]The priest must present part of this peace offering as a special gift to the LORD. This includes all the fat around the internal organs, [4]the two kidneys and the fat around them near the loins, and the long lobe of the liver. These must be removed with the kidneys, [5]and Aaron's sons will burn them on top of the burnt offering on the wood burning on the altar. It is a special gift, a pleasing aroma to the LORD.

[6]"If you present an animal from the flock as a peace offering to the LORD, it may be a male or a female, but it must have no defects. [7]If you present a sheep as your offering, bring it to the LORD, [8]lay your hand on its head, and slaughter it in front of the Tabernacle. Aaron's sons will then splatter the sheep's blood against all sides of the altar. [9]The priest must present the fat of this peace offering as a special gift to the LORD. This includes the fat of the broad tail cut off near the backbone, all the fat around the internal organs, [10]the two kidneys and the fat around them near the loins, and the long lobe of the liver. These must be removed with the kidneys, [11]and the priest will burn them on the altar. It is a special gift of food presented to the LORD.

[12]"If you present a goat as your offering, bring it to the LORD, [13]lay your hand on its head, and slaughter it in front of the Tabernacle. Aaron's sons will then splatter the goat's blood against all sides of the altar. [14]The priest must present part of this offering as a special gift to the LORD. This includes all the fat around the internal organs, [15]the two kidneys and the fat around them near the loins, and the long lobe of the liver. These must be removed with the kidneys, [16]and the priest will burn them on the altar. It is a special gift of food, a pleasing aroma to the LORD. All the fat belongs to the LORD.

[17]"You must never eat any fat or blood. This is a permanent law for you, and it must be observed from generation to generation, wherever you live."

Procedures for the Sin Offering

LEVITICUS 4:1-35

Then the LORD said to Moses, [2]"Give the following instructions to the people of Israel. This is how you are to deal with those who sin unintentionally by doing anything that violates one of the LORD's commands.

[3]"If the high priest* sins, bringing guilt upon the

Lv 3:2 Hebrew *Tent of Meeting;* also in 3:8, 13. **Lv 4:3** Hebrew *the anointed priest;* also in 4:5, 16.

THE OFFERINGS

Listed here are the five key offerings the Israelites made to God. They made these offerings in order to have their sins forgiven and to restore their fellowship with God. The death of Jesus Christ made these sacrifices unnecessary. Because of his death, our sins are completely forgiven, and fellowship with God has been restored.

Offering	*Purpose*	*Significance*	*Christ, the Perfect Offering*
Burnt Offering (Lev 1—voluntary)	To make payment for sins in general	Showed a person's devotion to God	Christ's death was the perfect offering
Grain Offering (Lev 2—voluntary)	To show honor and respect to God in worship	Acknowledged that all we have belongs to God	Christ was the perfect man, who gave all of himself to God and others
Peace Offering (Lev 3—voluntary)	To express gratitude to God	Symbolized peace and fellowship with God	Christ is the only way to fellowship with God
Sin Offering (Lev 4—required)	To make payment for unintentional sins of uncleanness, neglect, or thoughtlessness	Restored the sinner to fellowship with God; showed seriousness of sin	Christ's death restores our fellowship with God
Guilt Offering (Lev 5—required)	To make payment for sins against God and others. A sacrifice was made to God, and the injured person was repaid or compensated.	Provided compensation for injured parties	Christ's death takes away the deadly consequences of sin

Because it symbolized peace with God, part of the offering could be eaten by the person presenting it.

Lev 4:1ff Have you ever done something wrong without realizing it until later? Although your sin was unintentional, it was still sin. God's commands served to make the Israelites aware of their sins (even the unintentional ones) so they could be forgiven for them, and to keep the people from repeating those sins. Leviticus 4–5 mentions some of these unintentional sins and the way the Israelites could be forgiven for them. As you read more of God's laws, keep in mind that they were meant to teach and guide the people. Let them help you become more aware of sin in your life.

Lev 4:3 The sin offering was for those who (1) committed a sin without realizing it or (2) committed a sin out of weakness or negligence as opposed to outright rebellion against God. Both individuals and groups could be guilty of unintentional sin. Different animals were sacrificed for the different kinds of sin. The death of Jesus Christ was the final sin offering in the Bible (Heb 9:25-28 tells why).

▶ **LEVITICUS 4:1-35 *(cont.)***
entire community, he must give a sin offering for the
sin he has committed. He must present to the LORD a
young bull with no defects. [4]He must bring the bull
to the LORD at the entrance of the Tabernacle,* lay his
hand on the bull's head, and slaughter it before the
LORD. [5]The high priest will then take some of the bull's
blood into the Tabernacle, [6]dip his finger in the blood,
and sprinkle it seven times before the LORD in front
of the inner curtain of the sanctuary. [7]The priest will
then put some of the blood on the horns of the altar
for fragrant incense that stands in the LORD's presence inside the Tabernacle. He will pour out the rest
of the bull's blood at the base of the altar for burnt
offerings at the entrance of the Tabernacle. [8]Then the
priest must remove all the fat of the bull to be offered
as a sin offering. This includes all the fat around the
internal organs, [9]the two kidneys and the fat around
them near the loins, and the long lobe of the liver. He
must remove these along with the kidneys, [10]just as he
does with cattle offered as a peace offering, and burn
them on the altar of burnt offerings. [11]But he must
take whatever is left of the bull—its hide, meat, head,
legs, internal organs, and dung—[12]and carry it away to
a place outside the camp that is ceremonially clean,
the place where the ashes are dumped. There, on the
ash heap, he will burn it on a wood fire.

[13]"If the entire Israelite community sins by violating
one of the LORD's commands, but the people don't realize it, they are still guilty. [14]When they become aware
of their sin, the people must bring a young bull as an
offering for their sin and present it before the Tabernacle. [15]The elders of the community must then lay
their hands on the bull's head and slaughter it before
the LORD. [16]The high priest will then take some of
the bull's blood into the Tabernacle, [17]dip his finger
in the blood, and sprinkle it seven times before the
LORD in front of the inner curtain. [18]He will then put
some of the blood on the horns of the altar for fragrant
incense that stands in the LORD's presence inside the
Tabernacle. He will pour out the rest of the blood at
the base of the altar for burnt offerings at the entrance
of the Tabernacle. [19]Then the priest must remove all
the animal's fat and burn it on the altar, [20]just as he
does with the bull offered as a sin offering for the high
priest. Through this process, the priest will purify the
people, making them right with the LORD,* and they
will be forgiven. [21]Then the priest must take what is
left of the bull and carry it outside the camp and burn
it there, just as is done with the sin offering for the
high priest. This offering is for the sin of the entire
congregation of Israel.

[22]"If one of Israel's leaders sins by violating one of
the commands of the LORD his God but doesn't realize it, he is still guilty. [23]When he becomes aware of
his sin, he must bring as his offering a male goat with
no defects. [24]He must lay his hand on the goat's head
and slaughter it at the place where burnt offerings are
slaughtered before the LORD. This is an offering for his
sin. [25]Then the priest will dip his finger in the blood
of the sin offering and put it on the horns of the altar
for burnt offerings. He will pour out the rest of the
blood at the base of the altar. [26]Then he must burn
all the goat's fat on the altar, just as he does with the
peace offering. Through this process, the priest will
purify the leader from his sin, making him right with
the LORD, and he will be forgiven.

[27]"If any of the common people sin by violating
one of the LORD's commands, but they don't realize
it, they are still guilty. [28]When they become aware of
their sin, they must bring as an offering for their sin
a female goat with no defects. [29]They must lay a hand
on the head of the sin offering and slaughter it at the
place where burnt offerings are slaughtered. [30]Then
the priest will dip his finger in the blood and put it
on the horns of the altar for burnt offerings. He will
pour out the rest of the blood at the base of the altar.
[31]Then he must remove all the goat's fat, just as he
does with the fat of the peace offering. He will burn
the fat on the altar, and it will be a pleasing aroma
to the LORD. Through this process, the priest will purify the people, making them right with the LORD, and
they will be forgiven.

[32]"If the people bring a sheep as their sin offering,
it must be a female with no defects. [33]They must lay
a hand on the head of the sin offering and slaughter

Lv 4:4 Hebrew *Tent of Meeting;* also in 4:5, 7, 14, 16, 18. **Lv 4:20** Or *will make atonement for the people;* similarly in 4:26, 31, 35.

The Sin Offering

The Israelites, like many nations in the Middle East, offered animal sacrifices to God. The sin offering was their primary sacrifice. Different animals were specified depending on who was bringing the offering. A high priest had to bring a young bull (Lev 4:3), as did the congregation as a whole (Lev 4:14). A ruler would bring a male goat (Lev 4:23), but a commoner could provide a female goat (Lev 4:28). If a person was poor, they could offer two turtledoves or two young pigeons (one of which would be a burnt offering, Lev 5:7), and the extremely poor could even substitute a tenth of an ephah of fine flour (Lev 5:11-13). We who live after the death and resurrection of Jesus know that Christ is the final sin offering. We must look to him for salvation from sin.

it at the place where burnt offerings are slaughtered. 34Then the priest will dip his finger in the blood of the sin offering and put it on the horns of the altar for burnt offerings. He will pour out the rest of the blood at the base of the altar. 35Then he must remove all the sheep's fat, just as he does with the fat of a sheep presented as a peace offering. He will burn the fat on the altar on top of the special gifts presented to the LORD. Through this process, the priest will purify the people from their sin, making them right with the LORD, and they will be forgiven.

Sins Requiring a Sin Offering

LEVITICUS 5:1-13

"If you are called to testify about something you have seen or that you know about, it is sinful to refuse to testify, and you will be punished for your sin.

2"Or suppose you unknowingly touch something that is ceremonially unclean, such as the carcass of an unclean animal. When you realize what you have done, you must admit your defilement and your guilt. This is true whether it is a wild animal, a domestic animal, or an animal that scurries along the ground.

3"Or suppose you unknowingly touch something that makes a person unclean. When you realize what you have done, you must admit your guilt.

4"Or suppose you make a foolish vow of any kind, whether its purpose is for good or for bad. When you realize its foolishness, you must admit your guilt.

5"When you become aware of your guilt in any of these ways, you must confess your sin. 6Then you must bring to the LORD as the penalty for your sin a female from the flock, either a sheep or a goat. This is a sin offering with which the priest will purify you from your sin, making you right with the LORD.*

7"But if you cannot afford to bring a sheep, you may bring to the LORD two turtledoves or two young pigeons as the penalty for your sin. One of the birds will be for a sin offering, and the other for a burnt offering. 8You must bring them to the priest, who will present the first bird as the sin offering. He will wring its neck but without severing its head from the body. 9Then he will sprinkle some of the blood of the sin offering against the sides of the altar, and the rest of the blood will be drained out at the base of the altar. This is an offering for sin. 10The priest will then prepare the second bird as a burnt offering, following all the procedures that have been prescribed. Through this process the priest will purify you from your sin, making you right with the LORD, and you will be forgiven.

11"If you cannot afford to bring two turtledoves or two young pigeons, you may bring two quarts* of choice flour for your sin offering. Since it is an offering for sin, you must not moisten it with olive oil or put any frankincense on it. 12Take the flour to the priest, who will scoop out a handful as a representative portion. He will burn it on the altar on top of the special gifts presented to the LORD. It is an offering for sin. 13Through this process, the priest will purify those who are guilty of any of these sins, making them right with the LORD, and they will be forgiven. The rest of the flour will belong to the priest, just as with the grain offering."

Procedures for the Guilt Offering

LEVITICUS 5:14-19

Then the LORD said to Moses, 15"If one of you commits a sin by unintentionally defiling the LORD's sacred property, you must bring a guilt offering to the LORD. The offering must be your own ram with no defects, or you may buy one of equal value with silver, as measured by the weight of the sanctuary shekel.* 16You must make restitution for the sacred property you have harmed by paying for the loss, plus an additional 20 percent. When you give the payment to the priest, he will purify you with the ram sacrificed as a guilt offering, making you right with the LORD, and you will be forgiven.

17"Suppose you sin by violating one of the LORD's commands. Even if you are unaware of what you have done, you are guilty and will be punished for your sin. 18For a guilt offering, you must bring to the priest your own ram with no defects, or you may buy one of equal value. Through this process the priest will purify you from your unintentional sin, making you right with the LORD, and you will be forgiven. 19This is a guilt offering, for you have been guilty of an offense against the LORD."

Lv 5:6 Or *will make atonement for you for your sin;* similarly in 5:10, 13, 16, 18. **Lv 5:11** Hebrew *1/10 of an ephah* [2.2 liters]. **Lv 5:15** Each shekel was about 0.4 ounces or 11 grams in weight.

Lev 5:4 Have you ever sworn to do or not do something and then realized how foolish your promise was? God's people are called to keep their word, even if they make promises that are tough to keep. Jesus was warning against swearing (in the sense of making vows or oaths) when he said, "Just say a simple, 'Yes, I will,' or 'No, I won't.' Anything beyond this is from the evil one" (Matt 5:37). Our word should be enough. If we feel we have to strengthen it with an oath, something is wrong with our sincerity. The only promises we ought not to keep are promises that lead to sin. A wise and self-controlled person avoids making rash promises.

Lev 5:5 The entire system of sacrifices could not help a sinner unless he brought his offering with an attitude of repentance and a willingness to confess sin. Because of Christ's death on the cross, we do not have to sacrifice animals today. But it is still vital to confess sin because genuine confession shows realization of sin, awareness of God's holiness, humility before God, and willingness to turn from the sin (Ps 51:16-17). Even Jesus' death will be of little value to us if we do not repent and follow him. It is like a vaccine for a dangerous disease—it won't help unless it enters the bloodstream.

Lev 5:14-19 The guilt offering was a way of taking care of sin committed unintentionally. It was for those who sinned in some way against "sacred property"—the Tabernacle or the priesthood—as well as for those who unintentionally sinned against someone. In either case, a ram with no defects had to be sacrificed, and those harmed by the sin had to be compensated for their loss plus a 20 percent penalty. Even though Christ's death has made guilt offerings unnecessary for us today, we still need to make things right with those we hurt.

Sins Requiring a Guilt Offering

LEVITICUS 6:1-7

1*Then the LORD said to Moses, 2"Suppose one of you sins against your associate and is unfaithful to the LORD. Suppose you cheat in a deal involving a security deposit, or you steal or commit fraud, 3or you find lost property and lie about it, or you lie while swearing to tell the truth, or you commit any other such sin. 4If you have sinned in any of these ways, you are guilty. You must give back whatever you stole, or the money you took by extortion, or the security deposit, or the lost property you found, 5or anything obtained by swearing falsely. You must make restitution by paying the full price plus an additional 20 percent to the person you have harmed. On the same day you must present a guilt offering. 6As a guilt offering to the LORD, you must bring to the priest your own ram with no defects, or you may buy one of equal value. 7Through this process, the priest will purify you before the LORD, making you right with him,* and you will be forgiven for any of these sins you have committed."

Further Instructions for the Burnt Offering

LEVITICUS 6:8-13

8*Then the LORD said to Moses, 9"Give Aaron and his sons the following instructions regarding the burnt offering. The burnt offering must be left on top of the altar until the next morning, and the fire on the altar must be kept burning all night. 10In the morning, after the priest on duty has put on his official linen clothing and linen undergarments, he must clean out the ashes of the burnt offering and put them beside the altar. 11Then he must take off these garments, change back into his regular clothes, and carry the ashes outside the camp to a place that is ceremonially clean. 12Meanwhile, the fire on the altar must be kept burning; it must never go out. Each morning the priest will add fresh wood to the fire and arrange the burnt offering on it. He will then burn the fat of the peace offerings on it. 13Remember, the fire must be kept burning on the altar at all times. It must never go out.

Further Instructions for the Grain Offering

LEVITICUS 6:14-18

"These are the instructions regarding the grain offering. Aaron's sons must present this offering to the LORD in front of the altar. 15The priest on duty will take from the grain offering a handful of the choice flour moistened with olive oil, together with all the frankincense. He will burn this representative portion on the altar as a pleasing aroma to the LORD. 16Aaron and his sons may eat the rest of the flour, but it must be baked without yeast and eaten in a sacred place within the courtyard of the Tabernacle.* 17Remember, it must never be prepared with yeast. I have given it to the priests as their share of the special gifts presented to me. Like the sin offering and the guilt offering, it is most holy. 18Any of Aaron's male descendants may eat from the special gifts presented to the LORD. This is their permanent right from generation to generation. Anyone or anything that touches these offerings will become holy."

Procedures for the Ordination Offering

LEVITICUS 6:19-23

Then the LORD said to Moses, 20"On the day Aaron and his sons are anointed, they must present to the LORD a grain offering of two quarts* of choice flour, half to be offered in the morning and half to be offered in the evening. 21It must be carefully mixed with olive oil and cooked on a griddle. Then slice* this grain offering and present it as a pleasing aroma to the LORD. 22In each generation, the high priest* who succeeds Aaron must prepare this same offering. It belongs to the LORD and must be burned up completely. This is a permanent law. 23All such grain offerings of a priest must be burned up entirely. None of it may be eaten."

Further Instructions for the Sin Offering

LEVITICUS 6:24-30

Then the LORD said to Moses, 25"Give Aaron and his sons the following instructions regarding the sin offering. The animal given as an offering for sin is a most holy offering, and it must be slaughtered in the LORD's presence at the place where the burnt offerings are slaughtered. 26The priest who offers the sacrifice as a sin offering must eat his portion in a sacred place within the courtyard of the Tabernacle. 27Anyone or anything that touches the sacrificial meat will become holy. If any of the sacrificial blood spatters on a person's clothing, the soiled garment must be washed in a sacred place. 28If a clay pot is used to boil the sacrificial

Lv 6:1 Verses 6:1-7 are numbered 5:20-26 in Hebrew text. **Lv 6:7** Or *will make atonement for you before the LORD.* **Lv 6:8** Verses 6:8-30 are numbered 6:1-23 in Hebrew text. **Lv 6:16** Hebrew *Tent of Meeting;* also in 6:26, 30. **Lv 6:20** Hebrew *1/10 of an ephah* [2.2 liters]. **Lv 6:21** The meaning of this Hebrew term is uncertain. **Lv 6:22** Hebrew *the anointed priest.*

Lev 6:1-7 Here we discover that stealing involves more than just taking from someone. Finding something and not returning it or failing to return something borrowed are other forms of stealing. These are sins against God and not just your neighbor, a stranger, or a large business. If you have gotten something deceitfully, then confess your sin to God, apologize to the owner, and return the stolen items—with interest.

Lev 6:12-13 While the previous offerings and sacrifices were ones that the people did, the section from Leviticus 6:8–7:38 deals with general and continual priestly duties. The burnt offering was presented in the morning and evening for the whole nation (see Exod 29:38-43). The holy fire on the altar had to keep burning because God had started it. This represented God's continual presence in the sacrificial system. It showed the people that only by God's gracious favor could their sacrifices be acceptable. God's fire is present in each believer's life today. He lights the fire when the Holy Spirit comes to live in us, and he tends it so that we will grow in grace as we walk with him. When we are aware that God lives in us, we have confidence to come to him for forgiveness and restoration. We can carry out our work with strength and enthusiasm.

meat, it must then be broken. If a bronze pot is used, it must be scoured and thoroughly rinsed with water. [29]Any male from a priest's family may eat from this offering; it is most holy. [30]But the offering for sin may not be eaten if its blood was brought into the Tabernacle as an offering for purification* in the Holy Place. It must be completely burned with fire.

Further Instructions for the Guilt Offering

LEVITICUS 7:1-10

"These are the instructions for the guilt offering. It is most holy. [2]The animal sacrificed as a guilt offering must be slaughtered at the place where the burnt offerings are slaughtered, and its blood must be splattered against all sides of the altar. [3]The priest will then offer all its fat on the altar, including the fat of the broad tail, the fat around the internal organs, [4]the two kidneys and the fat around them near the loins, and the long lobe of the liver. These are to be removed with the kidneys, [5]and the priests will burn them on the altar as a special gift presented to the LORD. This is the guilt offering. [6]Any male from a priest's family may eat the meat. It must be eaten in a sacred place, for it is most holy.

[7]"The same instructions apply to both the guilt offering and the sin offering. Both belong to the priest who uses them to purify someone, making that person right with the LORD.* [8]In the case of the burnt offering, the priest may keep the hide of the sacrificed animal. [9]Any grain offering that has been baked in an oven, prepared in a pan, or cooked on a griddle belongs to the priest who presents it. [10]All other grain offerings, whether made of dry flour or flour moistened with olive oil, are to be shared equally among all the priests, the descendants of Aaron.

Further Instructions for the Peace Offering

LEVITICUS 7:11-21

"These are the instructions regarding the different kinds of peace offerings that may be presented to the LORD. [12]If you present your peace offering as an expression of thanksgiving, the usual animal sacrifice must be accompanied by various kinds of bread made without yeast—thin cakes mixed with olive oil, wafers spread with oil, and cakes made of choice flour mixed with olive oil. [13]This peace offering of thanksgiving must also be accompanied by loaves of bread made with yeast. [14]One of each kind of bread must be presented as a gift to the LORD. It will then belong to the priest who splatters the blood of the peace offering against the altar. [15]The meat of the peace offering of thanksgiving must be eaten on the same day it is offered. None of it may be saved for the next morning.

[16]"If you bring an offering to fulfill a vow or as a voluntary offering, the meat must be eaten on the same day the sacrifice is offered, but whatever is left over may be eaten on the second day. [17]Any meat left over until the third day must be completely burned up. [18]If any of the meat from the peace offering is eaten on the third day, the person who presented it will not be accepted by the LORD. You will receive no credit for offering it. By then the meat will be contaminated; if you eat it, you will be punished for your sin.

[19]"Meat that touches anything ceremonially unclean may not be eaten; it must be completely burned up. The rest of the meat may be eaten, but only by people who are ceremonially clean. [20]If you are ceremonially unclean and you eat meat from a peace offering that was presented to the LORD, you will be cut off from the community. [21]If you touch anything that is unclean (whether it is human defilement or an unclean animal or any other unclean, detestable thing) and then eat meat from a peace offering presented to the LORD, you will be cut off from the community."

The Forbidden Blood and Fat

LEVITICUS 7:22-27

Then the LORD said to Moses, [23]"Give the following instructions to the people of Israel. You must never eat fat, whether from cattle, sheep, or goats. [24]The fat of an animal found dead or torn to pieces by wild animals must never be eaten, though it may be used for any other purpose. [25]Anyone who eats fat from an animal presented as a special gift to the LORD will be cut off from the community. [26]No matter where you live, you must never consume the blood of any bird or animal. [27]Anyone who consumes blood will be cut off from the community."

A Portion for the Priests

LEVITICUS 7:28-38

Then the LORD said to Moses, [29]"Give the following instructions to the people of Israel. When you

Lv 6:30 Or *an offering to make atonement.* **Lv 7:7** Or *to make atonement.*

Lev 7:11-18 The peace offering was divided into three kinds according to purpose: thanksgiving offering, vow offering, and voluntary offering. A thanksgiving offering was appropriate whenever one wished to show thanks to God, as when recovering from a serious illness or surviving a dangerous calamity (Ps 107). A vow offering was given in fulfillment of a vow (2 Sam 15:7-8). The voluntary offering, however, needed no special occasion or reason.

Lev 7:22-27 The fat portions were regarded as the best portions; therefore, it was appropriate to dedicate them only to God. Because blood was the river of life, and life was God's gift and his alone, blood had to be returned to God and not used by people.

Lev 7:28-30 God told the people of Israel to bring their peace offerings personally, with their own hands. They were to take time and effort to express thanks to God. You are the best person to express your thankfulness to God and to others. Do you leave it to others to express thanks to someone who has been helpful? Do you rely on the one leading in prayer to thank God for you? Take time to communicate your personal gratitude both to God and to others who have helped and blessed you.

▸ **LEVITICUS 7:28-38 *(cont.)***

present a peace offering to the LORD, bring part of it as a gift to the LORD. 30Present it to the LORD with your own hands as a special gift to the LORD. Bring the fat of the animal, together with the breast, and lift up the breast as a special offering to the LORD. 31Then the priest will burn the fat on the altar, but the breast will belong to Aaron and his descendants. 32Give the right thigh of your peace offering to the priest as a gift. 33The right thigh must always be given to the priest who offers the blood and the fat of the peace offering. 34For I have reserved the breast of the special offering and the right thigh of the sacred offering for the priests. It is the permanent right of Aaron and his descendants to share in the peace offerings brought by the people of Israel. 35This is their rightful share. The special gifts presented to the LORD have been reserved for Aaron and his descendants from the time they were set apart to serve the LORD as priests. 36On the day they were anointed, the LORD commanded the Israelites to give these portions to the priests as their permanent share from generation to generation."

37These are the instructions for the burnt offering, the grain offering, the sin offering, and the guilt offering, as well as the ordination offering and the peace offering. 38The LORD gave these instructions to Moses on Mount Sinai when he commanded the Israelites to present their offerings to the LORD in the wilderness of Sinai.

2. ORDINATION FOR THE PRIESTS

The priesthood represented God to the people, and represented the people to God. The descendants of Aaron were set apart for this special work, and they were quickly reminded of the seriousness of their task when two of Aaron's sons died for offering improper worship.

Ordination of the Priests

LEVITICUS 8:1-36

Then the LORD said to Moses, 2"Bring Aaron and his sons, along with their sacred garments, the anointing oil, the bull for the sin offering, the two rams, and the basket of bread made without yeast, 3and call the entire community of Israel together at the entrance of the Tabernacle.*"

4So Moses followed the LORD's instructions, and the whole community assembled at the Tabernacle entrance. 5Moses announced to them, "This is what the LORD has commanded us to do!" 6Then he presented Aaron and his sons and washed them with water. 7He put the official tunic on Aaron and tied the sash around his waist. He dressed him in the robe, placed the ephod on him, and attached the ephod securely with its decorative sash. 8Then Moses placed the chestpiece on Aaron and put the Urim and the Thummim inside it. 9He placed the turban on Aaron's head and attached the gold medallion—the badge of

Lv 8:3 Hebrew *Tent of Meeting;* also in 8:4, 31, 33, 35.

Lev 7:31-36 Part of the offering was designated for the priests. This food helped to care for the priests, who cared for God's house. The New Testament teaches that ministers should be paid by the people they serve (1 Cor 9:14). We should give generously to those who minister to us.

Lev 7:37 The ordination offering refers to the offering given at the ceremony when priests were inducted into office (Lev 8:22).

Lev 7:38 God gave his people many rituals and instructions to follow. All the rituals in Leviticus were meant to teach the people valuable lessons. But over time, the people became indifferent to the meanings of these rituals, and they began to lose touch with God. When your church appears to be conducting dry, meaningless rituals, instead of criticizing or becoming discouraged, try rediscovering the original meaning and purpose behind each. Your worship will be revitalized.

Lev 8:1ff Why did Aaron and his sons need to be cleansed and set apart? Although all the men from the tribe of Levi were dedicated for service to God, only Aaron's descendants could be priests. They alone had the honor and responsibility of performing the sacrifices. These priests had to cleanse and dedicate themselves before they could help the people do the same.

The ceremony described in Leviticus 8–9 was their ordination ceremony. Aaron and his sons were washed with water (Lev 8:6), clothed with special garments (Lev 8:7-9, 13), and anointed with oil (Lev 8:12). They placed their hands on a young bull as it was killed (Lev 8:14-15), and on two rams as they were killed (Lev 8:18-19, 22-23). This showed that holiness came from God alone, not from the priestly role. Similarly, we are not spiritually cleansed because we have a religious position, reputation, or title. Spiritual cleansing comes only from God. No matter how high our position or how long we have held it, we must depend on God for spiritual vitality.

Lev 8:2-3 Why were priests needed in Israel? In Exodus 19:6, the Israelites were instructed to be a kingdom of priests; ideally they would all be holy and relate to God. But from the time of Adam's fall, sin has separated humans and God, and people have needed mediators to help them find forgiveness. At first, the patriarchs—heads of households like Abraham and Job—were priests of the house or clan and made sacrifices for the family. When the Israelites left Egypt, the descendants of Aaron from the tribe of Levi were chosen to serve as priests for the nation. The priests stood in the gap between God and the people. They were the full-time spiritual leaders and overseers of offerings. The priestly system was a concession to the people's inability, because of sin, to confront and relate to God individually and corporately. In Christ, this imperfect system was transformed. Jesus Christ himself is our High Priest. Now all believers can approach God through him.

Lev 8:8 What were the Urim and Thummim? Little is known about them, but they were probably precious stones or flat objects that God used to give guidance to his people. The high priest kept them in a pocket attached to his chestpiece. Some scholars think the Urim may have been the *no* answer and the Thummim the *yes* answer. After a time of prayer for guidance, the priest would shake the stones and God would cause the proper one to fall out. Another view is that the Urim and Thummim were small flat objects, each with a *yes* side and a *no* side. The priest spilled both from his pouch. If both landed on their *yes* sides, God's answer was positive. Two *no* sides were negative. A *yes* and a *no* meant no reply. God had a specific purpose for using

holiness—to the front of the turban, just as the LORD had commanded him.

10 Then Moses took the anointing oil and anointed the Tabernacle and everything in it, making them holy. 11 He sprinkled the oil on the altar seven times, anointing it and all its utensils, as well as the washbasin and its stand, making them holy. 12 Then he poured some of the anointing oil on Aaron's head, anointing him and making him holy for his work. 13 Next Moses presented Aaron's sons. He clothed them in their tunics, tied their sashes around them, and put their special head coverings on them, just as the LORD had commanded him.

14 Then Moses presented the bull for the sin offering. Aaron and his sons laid their hands on the bull's head, 15 and Moses slaughtered it. Moses took some of the blood, and with his finger he put it on the four horns of the altar to purify it. He poured out the rest of the blood at the base of the altar. Through this process, he made the altar holy by purifying it.* 16 Then Moses took all the fat around the internal organs, the long lobe of the liver, and the two kidneys and the fat around them, and he burned it all on the altar. 17 He took the rest of the bull, including its hide, meat, and dung, and burned it on a fire outside the camp, just as the LORD had commanded him.

18 Then Moses presented the ram for the burnt offering. Aaron and his sons laid their hands on the ram's head, 19 and Moses slaughtered it. Then Moses took the ram's blood and splattered it against all sides of the altar. 20 Then he cut the ram into pieces, and he burned the head, some of its pieces, and the fat on the altar. 21 After washing the internal organs and the legs with water, Moses burned the entire ram on the altar as a burnt offering. It was a pleasing aroma, a special gift presented to the LORD, just as the LORD had commanded him.

22 Then Moses presented the other ram, which was the ram of ordination. Aaron and his sons laid their hands on the ram's head, 23 and Moses slaughtered it. Then Moses took some of its blood and applied it to the lobe of Aaron's right ear, the thumb of his right hand, and the big toe of his right foot. 24 Next Moses presented Aaron's sons and applied some of the blood to the lobes of their right ears, the thumbs of their right hands, and the big toes of their right feet. He then splattered the rest of the blood against all sides of the altar.

25 Next Moses took the fat, including the fat of the broad tail, the fat around the internal organs, the long lobe of the liver, and the two kidneys and the fat around them, along with the right thigh. 26 On top of these he placed a thin cake of bread made without yeast, a cake of bread mixed with olive oil, and a wafer spread with olive oil. All these were taken from the basket of bread made without yeast that was placed in the LORD's presence. 27 He put all these in the hands of Aaron and his sons, and he lifted them up as a special offering to the LORD. 28 Moses then took all the offerings back from them and burned them on the altar on top of the burnt offering. This was the ordination offering. It was a pleasing aroma, a special gift presented to the LORD. 29 Then Moses took the breast and lifted it up as a special offering to the LORD. This was Moses' portion of the ram of ordination, just as the LORD had commanded him.

30 Next Moses took some of the anointing oil and some of the blood that was on the altar, and he sprinkled them on Aaron and his garments and on his sons and their garments. In this way, he made Aaron and his sons and their garments holy.

31 Then Moses said to Aaron and his sons, "Boil the remaining meat of the offerings at the Tabernacle entrance, and eat it there, along with the bread that is in the basket of offerings for the ordination, just as I commanded when I said, 'Aaron and his sons will eat it.' 32 Any meat or bread that is left over must then be burned up. 33 You must not leave the Tabernacle entrance for seven days, for that is when the ordination ceremony will be completed. 34 Everything we have done today was commanded by the LORD in order to purify you, making you right with him.* 35 Now stay at the entrance of the Tabernacle day and night for seven days, and do everything the LORD requires. If you fail to do this, you will die, for this is what the LORD has commanded." 36 So Aaron and his sons did everything the LORD had commanded through Moses.

The Priests Begin Their Work

LEVITICUS 9:1-24

After the ordination ceremony, on the eighth day, Moses called together Aaron and his sons and the elders of Israel. 2 He said to Aaron, "Take a young bull for a sin offering and a ram for a burnt offering, both without defects, and present them to the LORD. 3 Then tell the Israelites, 'Take a male goat for a sin offering, and take a calf and a lamb, both a year old and without

Lv 8:15 Or *by making atonement for it;* or *that offerings for purification might be made on it.* **Lv 8:34** Or *to make atonement for you.*

this method of guidance—he was teaching a nation the principles of following him. But our situation is not the same, so we must not invent ways like this for God to guide us.

Lev 8:12 What was the significance of anointing Aaron as high priest? The high priest had special duties that no other priest had. He alone could enter the Most Holy Place in the Tabernacle on the annual Day of Atonement to atone for the sins of the nation. Therefore, he was in charge of all the other priests. The high priest was a picture of Jesus Christ, who is our High Priest (Heb 7:26-28).

Lev 8:36 Aaron and his sons did "everything the LORD had commanded." Considering the many detailed lists of Leviticus, that was a remarkable feat. They knew what God wanted, how he wanted it done, and with what attitude it was to be carried out. This can serve as a model for how carefully we ought to obey God. God wants us to be thoroughly holy people, not a rough approximation of the way his followers should be.

▶ **LEVITICUS 9:1-24 *(cont.)***
defects, for a burnt offering. 4Also take a bull* and a
ram for a peace offering and flour moistened with olive
oil for a grain offering. Present all these offerings to
the LORD because the LORD will appear to you today.'"
5So the people presented all these things at the
entrance of the Tabernacle,* just as Moses had commanded. Then the whole community came forward
and stood before the LORD. 6And Moses said, "This is
what the LORD has commanded you to do so that the
glory of the LORD may appear to you."
7Then Moses said to Aaron, "Come to the altar and
sacrifice your sin offering and your burnt offering to
purify yourself and the people. Then present the offerings of the people to purify them, making them right
with the LORD,* just as he has commanded."
8So Aaron went to the altar and slaughtered the calf
as a sin offering for himself. 9His sons brought him
the blood, and he dipped his finger in it and put it on
the horns of the altar. He poured out the rest of the
blood at the base of the altar. 10Then he burned on the
altar the fat, the kidneys, and the long lobe of the liver
from the sin offering, just as the LORD had commanded
Moses. 11The meat and the hide, however, he burned
outside the camp.
12Next Aaron slaughtered the animal for the burnt
offering. His sons brought him the blood, and he
splattered it against all sides of the altar. 13Then they
handed him each piece of the burnt offering, including
the head, and he burned them on the altar. 14Then he
washed the internal organs and the legs and burned
them on the altar along with the rest of the burnt
offering.
15Next Aaron presented the offerings of the people.
He slaughtered the people's goat and presented it as an
offering for their sin, just as he had first done with the
offering for his own sin. 16Then he presented the burnt
offering and sacrificed it in the prescribed way. 17He
also presented the grain offering, burning a handful of
the flour mixture on the altar, in addition to the regular
burnt offering for the morning.
18Then Aaron slaughtered the bull and the ram for
the people's peace offering. His sons brought him the
blood, and he splattered it against all sides of the altar.
19Then he took the fat of the bull and the ram—the fat
of the broad tail and from around the internal organs—
along with the kidneys and the long lobes of the livers.
20He placed these fat portions on top of the breasts of
these animals and burned them on the altar. 21Aaron
then lifted up the breasts and right thighs as a special
offering to the LORD, just as Moses had commanded.
22After that, Aaron raised his hands toward the
people and blessed them. Then, after presenting the
sin offering, the burnt offering, and the peace offering,
he stepped down from the altar. 23Then Moses and
Aaron went into the Tabernacle, and when they came
back out, they blessed the people again, and the glory
of the LORD appeared to the whole community. 24Fire
blazed forth from the LORD's presence and consumed
the burnt offering and the fat on the altar. When the
people saw this, they shouted with joy and fell face
down on the ground.

The Sin of Nadab and Abihu

LEVITICUS 10:1-7
Aaron's sons Nadab and Abihu put coals of fire in their
incense burners and sprinkled incense over them.
In this way, they disobeyed the LORD by burning before him the wrong kind of fire, different than he had
commanded. 2So fire blazed forth from the LORD's
presence and burned them up, and they died there
before the LORD.
3Then Moses said to Aaron, "This is what the LORD
meant when he said,

Lv 9:4 Or *cow;* also in 9:18, 19. **Lv 9:5** Hebrew *Tent of Meeting;* also in 9:23. **Lv 9:7** Or *to make atonement for them.*

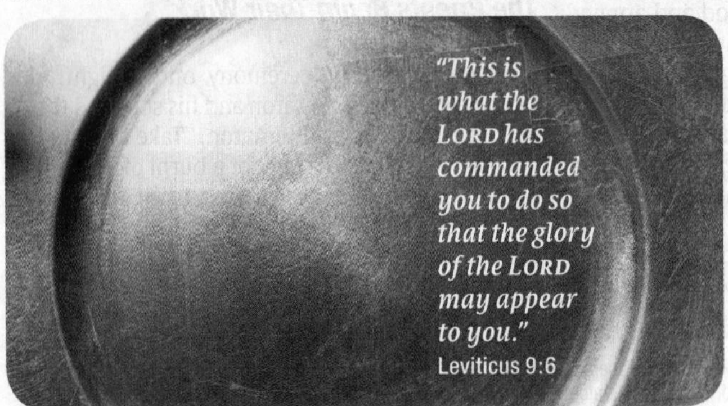
"This is what the LORD has commanded you to do so that the glory of the LORD may appear to you."
Leviticus 9:6

Lev 9:22-23 In Leviticus 9:6 Moses said to the people, "This is what the LORD has commanded you to do so that the glory of the LORD may appear to you." Moses, Aaron, and the people then got to work and followed God's instructions. Soon after, the glory of the Lord appeared. Often we look for God's glorious acts without concern for following his instructions. Do you serve God in the daily routines of life, or do you wait for him to do a mighty act? If you depend on his glorious acts, you may find yourself sidestepping your everyday duty to obey.

Lev 9:24 As a display of his mighty power, God sent fire from the sky to consume Aaron's offering. The people fell to the ground in awe. Some people wonder if God really exists because they don't see his activity in the world. But God is at work in today's world just as he was in Moses' world. Where a large body of believers is active for him, God tends not to display his power in the form of mighty physical acts. Instead, he works to change the world through the work of these believers. When you realize that, you will begin to see acts of love and faith that are just as supernatural.

Lev 10:1 What was the "wrong kind of fire" that Nadab and Abihu offered before the Lord? The fire on the altar of burnt offering was never to go out (Lev 6:12-13), implying that it was holy. It is possible that Nadab and

'I will display my holiness
through those who come near me.
I will display my glory
before all the people.'"

And Aaron was silent.

4Then Moses called for Mishael and Elzaphan,
Aaron's cousins, the sons of Aaron's uncle Uzziel. He
said to them, "Come forward and carry away the bodies of your relatives from in front of the sanctuary to a
place outside the camp." 5So they came forward and
picked them up by their garments and carried them
out of the camp, just as Moses had commanded.

6Then Moses said to Aaron and his sons Eleazar and
Ithamar, "Do not show grief by leaving your hair uncombed* or by tearing your clothes. If you do, you will
die, and the LORD's anger will strike the whole community of Israel. However, the rest of the Israelites,
your relatives, may mourn because of the LORD's fiery
destruction of Nadab and Abihu. 7But you must not
leave the entrance of the Tabernacle* or you will die,
for you have been anointed with the LORD's anointing
oil." So they did as Moses commanded.

Instructions for Priestly Conduct

LEVITICUS 10:8-20

Then the LORD said to Aaron, 9"You and your descendants must never drink wine or any other alcoholic
drink before going into the Tabernacle. If you do, you
will die. This is a permanent law for you, and it must
be observed from generation to generation. 10You
must distinguish between what is sacred and what is

Lv 10:6 Or *by uncovering your heads.* **Lv 10:7** Hebrew *Tent of Meeting;* also in 10:9.

NADAB/ABIHU

Some brothers, like Cain and Abel or Jacob and Esau, get each other in trouble. The brothers Nadab and Abihu got in trouble together. • Although little is known of their early years, the Bible gives us an abundance of information about the environment in which they grew up. Born in Egypt, they were eyewitnesses of God's mighty acts of the Exodus. They saw their father, Aaron, their uncle, Moses, and their aunt, Miriam, in action many times. They had firsthand knowledge of God's holiness as few men have ever had, and for a while at least, they followed God wholeheartedly (Lev 8:36). But at a crucial moment they chose to treat with indifference the clear instructions from God. The consequence of their sin was fiery, instant, and shocking to all. • We are in danger of making the same mistake as these brothers when we treat lightly the justice and holiness of God. We must draw near to God while realizing that there is a proper fear of God. Don't forget that the opportunity to know God personally is based on his gracious invitation to an always unworthy people; it is not a gift to be taken for granted. Do your thoughts about God include a humble recognition of his great holiness?

Strengths and accomplishments	• Primary candidates to become high priest after their father • Involved with the original consecration of the Tabernacle • Commended for doing "everything the LORD had commanded" (Lev 8:36)
Weakness and mistake	• Treated God's direct commands lightly
Lesson from their lives	• Sin has deadly consequences
Vital statistics	• Where: The Sinai peninsula • Occupation: Priests-in-training • Relatives: Father: Aaron. Uncle: Moses. Aunt: Miriam. Brothers: Eleazar and Ithamar.
Key verses	"Aaron's sons Nadab and Abihu put coals of fire in their incense burners and sprinkled incense over them. In this way, they disobeyed the LORD by burning before him the wrong kind of fire, different than he had commanded. So fire blazed forth from the LORD's presence and burned them up, and they died there before the LORD" (Lev 10:1-2).

The story of Nadab and Abihu is told in Leviticus 8–10. They are also mentioned in Exodus 24:1, 9; 28:1; Numbers 3:2-4; 26:60-61.

Abihu brought coals of fire to the altar from another source, making the sacrifice unholy. It has also been suggested that the two priests gave an offering at an unprescribed time. Whatever explanation is correct, the point is that Nadab and Abihu abused their office as priests in a flagrant act of disrespect to God, who had just reviewed with them precisely how they were to conduct worship. As leaders, they had special responsibility to obey God. In their position, they could easily lead many people astray. If God has commissioned you to lead or teach others, never take that role for granted or abuse it. Stay faithful to God and follow his instructions.

Lev 10:2 Aaron's sons were careless about following the laws for sacrifices. In response, God destroyed them with a blast of fire. Performing the sacrifices was an act of obedience. Doing them correctly showed respect for God. It is easy for us to grow careless about obeying God, to live our way instead of God's. But if one way were just as good as another, God would not have commanded us to live his way. He always has good reasons for his commands, and we always place ourselves in danger when we consciously or carelessly disobey them.

Lev 10:8-11 The priests were not to drink wine or other alcoholic beverages before going into the Tabernacle. If their senses were dulled by alcohol, they might repeat Nadab and Abihu's sin and bring something unholy into the worship ceremony. In addition, drinking would disqualify them to teach the people God's requirements of self-discipline. Drunkenness was associated with pagan practices and the Jewish priests were supposed to be distinctively different.

Lev 10:10-11 This passage (along with Lev 19:1-2) shows the focus of Leviticus. The Ten Commandments recorded in Exodus 20 were God's fundamental laws. Leviticus explained and supplemented those laws with many other guidelines and principles that helped the Israelites put them into practice. The purpose of God's laws was to teach people how to distinguish right from wrong, the sacred from the common, the clean from the unclean. The nation who lived by God's laws would be set apart, dedicated to his service.

▶ **LEVITICUS 10:8-20 *(cont.)***

common, between what is ceremonially unclean and what is clean. 11And you must teach the Israelites all the decrees that the LORD has given them through Moses."

12Then Moses said to Aaron and his remaining sons, Eleazar and Ithamar, "Take what is left of the grain offering after a portion has been presented as a special gift to the LORD, and eat it beside the altar. Make sure it contains no yeast, for it is most holy. 13You must eat it in a sacred place, for it has been given to you and your descendants as your portion of the special gifts presented to the LORD. These are the commands I have been given. 14But the breast and thigh that were lifted up as a special offering may be eaten in any place that is ceremonially clean. These parts have been given to you and your descendants as your portion of the peace offerings presented by the people of Israel. 15You must lift up the thigh and breast as a special offering to the LORD, along with the fat of the special gifts. These parts will belong to you and your descendants as your permanent right, just as the LORD has commanded."

16Moses then asked them what had happened to the goat of the sin offering. When he discovered it had been burned up, he became very angry with Eleazar and Ithamar, Aaron's remaining sons. 17"Why didn't you eat the sin offering in the sacred area?" he demanded. "It is a holy offering! The LORD has given it to you to remove the guilt of the community and to purify the people, making them right with the LORD.* 18Since the animal's blood was not brought into the Holy Place, you should have eaten the meat in the sacred area as I ordered you."

19Then Aaron answered Moses, "Today my sons presented both their sin offering and their burnt offering to the LORD. And yet this tragedy has happened to me. If I had eaten the people's sin offering on such a tragic day as this, would the LORD have been pleased?" 20And when Moses heard this, he was satisfied.

Lv 10:17 Or *to make atonement for the people before the LORD.*

3. INSTRUCTIONS FOR THE PEOPLE

The law isn't all about worship and priestly service. There are also many instructions about mundane things like healthcare and eating habits. God cares about the details of daily life as well as our worship habits.

Ceremonially Clean and Unclean Animals

LEVITICUS 11:1-47

Then the LORD said to Moses and Aaron, 2"Give the following instructions to the people of Israel.

"Of all the land animals, these are the ones you may use for food. 3You may eat any animal that has completely split hooves and chews the cud. 4You may not, however, eat the following animals* that have split hooves or that chew the cud, but not both. The camel chews the cud but does not have split hooves, so it is ceremonially unclean for you. 5The hyrax* chews the cud but does not have split hooves, so it is unclean. 6The hare chews the cud but does not have split hooves, so it is unclean. 7The pig has evenly split hooves but does not chew the cud, so it is unclean. 8You may not eat the meat of these animals or even touch their carcasses. They are ceremonially unclean for you.

9"Of all the marine animals, these are ones you may use for food. You may eat anything from the water if it has both fins and scales, whether taken from salt water or from streams. 10But you must never eat animals from the sea or from rivers that do not have both fins and scales. They are detestable to you. This applies both to little creatures that live in shallow water and to all creatures that live in deep water. 11They will always be detestable to you. You must never eat their meat or even touch their dead bodies. 12Any marine animal that does not have both fins and scales is detestable to you.

13"These are the birds that are detestable to you. You must never eat them: the griffon vulture, the bearded vulture, the black vulture, 14the kite, falcons of all kinds, 15ravens of all kinds, 16the eagle owl, the short-eared owl, the seagull, hawks of all kinds, 17the little owl, the cormorant, the great owl, 18the barn owl, the desert owl, the Egyptian vulture, 19the stork, herons of all kinds, the hoopoe, and the bat.

Lv 11:4 The identification of some of the animals, birds, and insects in this chapter is uncertain. **Lv 11:5** Or *coney*, or *rock badger.*

Lev 10:16-20 The priest who offered the sin offering was supposed to eat a portion of the animal and then burn the rest (Lev 6:24-30). Moses was angry because Eleazar and Ithamar burned the sin offering but did not eat any of it. Aaron explained to Moses that his two sons did not feel it appropriate to eat the sacrifice after their two brothers, Nadab and Abihu, had just been killed for sacrificing wrongly. Moses then understood that Eleazar and Ithamar were not trying to disobey God. They were simply afraid and upset over what had just happened to their brothers.

Lev 11:8 God had strictly forbidden eating the meat of certain "unclean" animals; to make sure, he forbade even touching them. He wanted the people to be totally separated from those things he had forbidden. So often we flirt with temptation, rationalizing that at least we are technically keeping the commandment not to commit the sin. But God wants us to separate ourselves completely from all sin and tempting situations. Perhaps this passage has made you aware of areas of your life where you have "technical" innocence but in which you have actually been involved in sin. It's time to cross back over the line and stay there.

20“You must not eat winged insects that walk along
the ground; they are detestable to you. 21You may, however, eat winged insects that walk along the ground
and have jointed legs so they can jump. 22The insects
you are permitted to eat include all kinds of locusts,
bald locusts, crickets, and grasshoppers. 23All other
winged insects that walk along the ground are detestable to you.

24“The following creatures will make you ceremonially unclean. If any of you touch their carcasses, you
will be defiled until evening. 25If you pick up their
carcasses, you must wash your clothes, and you will
remain defiled until evening.

26“Any animal that has split hooves that are not
evenly divided or that does not chew the cud is unclean for you. If you touch the carcass of such an animal, you will be defiled. 27Of the animals that walk
on all fours, those that have paws are unclean. If you
touch the carcass of such an animal, you will be defiled
until evening. 28If you pick up its carcass, you must
wash your clothes, and you will remain defiled until
evening. These animals are unclean for you.

29“Of the small animals that scurry along the
ground, these are unclean for you: the mole rat, the
rat, large lizards of all kinds, 30the gecko, the monitor lizard, the common lizard, the sand lizard, and
the chameleon. 31All these small animals are unclean
for you. If any of you touch the dead body of such an
animal, you will be defiled until evening. 32If such an
animal dies and falls on something, that object will
be unclean. This is true whether the object is made of
wood, cloth, leather, or burlap. Whatever its use, you
must dip it in water, and it will remain defiled until
evening. After that, it will be ceremonially clean and
may be used again.

33“If such an animal falls into a clay pot, everything in the pot will be defiled, and the pot must
be smashed. 34If the water from such a container
spills on any food, the food will be defiled. And any
beverage in such a container will be defiled. 35Any
object on which the carcass of such an animal falls
will be defiled. If it is an oven or hearth, it must be
destroyed, for it is defiled, and you must treat it accordingly.

36“However, if the carcass of such an animal falls
into a spring or a cistern, the water will still be clean.
But anyone who touches the carcass will be defiled.
37If the carcass falls on seed grain to be planted in the
field, the seed will still be considered clean. 38But if
the seed is wet when the carcass falls on it, the seed
will be defiled.

39“If an animal you are permitted to eat dies and you
touch its carcass, you will be defiled until evening. 40If
you eat any of its meat or carry away its carcass, you
must wash your clothes, and you will remain defiled
until evening.

41“All small animals that scurry along the ground
are detestable, and you must never eat them. 42This
includes all animals that slither along on their bellies,
as well as those with four legs and those with many
feet. All such animals that scurry along the ground are
detestable, and you must never eat them. 43Do not defile yourselves by touching them. You must not make
yourselves ceremonially unclean because of them.
44For I am the LORD your God. You must consecrate
yourselves and be holy, because I am holy. So do not
defile yourselves with any of these small animals that
scurry along the ground. 45For I, the LORD, am the one
who brought you up from the land of Egypt, that I
might be your God. Therefore, you must be holy because I am holy.

46“These are the instructions regarding land animals, birds, marine creatures, and animals that scurry
along the ground. 47By these instructions you will
know what is unclean and clean, and which animals
may be eaten and which may not be eaten.”

Lev 11:25 In order to worship, people need to be prepared. Some acts of disobedience, some natural acts (such as childbirth, menstruation, or sex), or some accidents (such as touching a dead or diseased body) would make people ceremonially unclean (defiled) and thus forbidden to participate in worship. This did not imply that they had sinned or were rejected by God, but it insured that all worship was done decently and in order. This chapter describes many of the intentional or accidental occurrences that would disqualify people from worship until they were "cleansed" or straightened out. Similarly, we need to be prepared for worship. We cannot live any way we want during the week and then rush into God's presence on Sunday. We should prepare ourselves through repentance, correction of errors where possible, and thoughtful anticipation of what it will mean to be in God's presence with other believers.

Lev 11:44-45 There is more to this chapter than eating right. These verses provide a key to understanding all the laws and regulations in Leviticus. God wanted his people to be holy (set apart, different, unique), just as he is holy. He knew they had only two options: to be separate and holy, or to compromise with their pagan neighbors and become corrupt. That is why he called them out of idolatrous Egypt and set them apart as a unique nation, dedicated to worshiping him alone and leading moral lives. That is also why he designed laws and restrictions to help them remain separate—both socially and spiritually—from the wicked pagan nations they would encounter in Canaan. Christians also are called to be holy (1 Pet 1:15). Like the Israelites, we should remain spiritually separate from the world's wickedness, even though—unlike them—we rub shoulders with unbelievers every day. It is no easy task to be holy in an unholy world, but God doesn't ask you to accomplish this on your own. He has provided help. Through the death of his Son, "you are holy and blameless as you stand before him without a single fault" (Col 1:22). With Christ, you can live *in* the world without having to be *of* the world.

Lev 11:47 The designations *clean* and *unclean* were used to define the kinds of animals the Israelites could and could not eat. There were several reasons for this restricted diet: (1) To ensure the health of the nation. The forbidden foods were usually scavenging animals that fed on dead animals; thus disease could be transmitted through them. (2) To visibly distinguish Israel from other nations. The pig, for example, was a common sacrifice of pagan religions. (3) To avoid objectionable associations. The creatures that move about on the ground, for example, were reminiscent of serpents, which often symbolized sin.

Purification after Childbirth

LEVITICUS 12:1-8

The LORD said to Moses, 2"Give the following instructions to the people of Israel. If a woman becomes pregnant and gives birth to a son, she will be ceremonially unclean for seven days, just as she is unclean during her menstrual period. 3On the eighth day the boy's foreskin must be circumcised. 4After waiting thirty-three days, she will be purified from the bleeding of childbirth. During this time of purification, she must not touch anything that is set apart as holy. And she must not enter the sanctuary until her time of purification is over. 5If a woman gives birth to a daughter, she will be ceremonially unclean for two weeks, just as she is unclean during her menstrual period. After waiting sixty-six days, she will be purified from the bleeding of childbirth.

6"When the time of purification is completed for either a son or a daughter, the woman must bring a one-year-old lamb for a burnt offering and a young pigeon or turtledove for a purification offering. She must bring her offerings to the priest at the entrance of the Tabernacle.* 7The priest will then present them to the LORD to purify her.* Then she will be ceremonially clean again after her bleeding at childbirth. These are the instructions for a woman after the birth of a son or a daughter.

8"If a woman cannot afford to bring a lamb, she must bring two turtledoves or two young pigeons. One will be for the burnt offering and the other for the purification offering. The priest will sacrifice them to purify her, and she will be ceremonially clean."

Serious Skin Diseases

LEVITICUS 13:1-46

The LORD said to Moses and Aaron, 2"If anyone has a swelling or a rash or discolored skin that might develop into a serious skin disease,* that person must be brought to Aaron the priest or to one of his sons.* 3The priest will examine the affected area of the skin. If the hair in the affected area has turned white and the problem appears to be more than skin-deep, it is a serious skin disease, and the priest who examines it must pronounce the person ceremonially unclean.

4"But if the affected area of the skin is only a white discoloration and does not appear to be more than skin-deep, and if the hair on the spot has not turned white, the priest will quarantine the person for seven days. 5On the seventh day the priest will make another examination. If he finds the affected area has not changed and the problem has not spread on the skin, the priest will quarantine the person for seven more days. 6On the seventh day the priest will make another examination. If he finds the affected area has faded and has not spread, the priest will pronounce the person ceremonially clean. It was only a rash. The person's clothing must be washed, and the person will be ceremonially clean. 7But if the rash continues to spread after the person has been examined by the priest and has been pronounced clean, the infected person must return to be examined again. 8If the priest finds that the rash has spread, he must pronounce the person ceremonially unclean, for it is indeed a skin disease.

9"Anyone who develops a serious skin disease must go to the priest for an examination. 10If the priest finds a white swelling on the skin, and some hair on the spot has turned white, and there is an open sore in the affected area, 11it is a chronic skin disease, and the priest must pronounce the person ceremonially unclean. In such cases the person need not be quarantined, for it is obvious that the skin is defiled by the disease.

12"Now suppose the disease has spread all over the person's skin, covering the body from head to foot. 13When the priest examines the infected person and finds that the disease covers the entire body, he will pronounce the person ceremonially clean. Since the skin has turned completely white, the person is clean. 14But if any open sores appear, the infected person will be pronounced ceremonially unclean. 15The priest must make this pronouncement as soon as he sees an open sore, since open sores indicate the presence of a skin disease. 16However, if the open sores heal and turn white like the rest of the skin, the person must return to the priest 17for another examination. If the affected areas have indeed turned white, the priest will then pronounce the person ceremonially clean by declaring, 'You are clean!'

18"If anyone has a boil on the skin that has started to heal, 19but a white swelling or a reddish white spot

Lv 12:6 Hebrew *Tent of Meeting.* **Lv 12:7** Or *to make atonement for her;* also in 12:8. **Lv 13:2a** Traditionally rendered *leprosy.* The Hebrew word used throughout this passage is used to describe various skin diseases. **Lv 13:2b** Or *one of his descendants.*

Lev 12:1-4 Why was a woman considered "ceremonially unclean" after the wonderful miracle of birth? It was due to the bodily emissions and secretions occurring during and after childbirth. These were considered unclean and made the woman unprepared to enter the pure surroundings of the Tabernacle. Her temporary status highlighted her role as a young mother and relieved her of certain duties that probably made the early days with a new baby easier.

Lev 12:1-4 *Unclean* did not mean sinful or dirty. God created us male and female, and he ordered us to be fruitful and multiply (Gen 1:27-28). He did not change his mind and say that sex and procreation were now somehow unclean. Instead, he made a distinction between his worship and the popular worship of fertility gods and goddesses. Canaanite religions incorporated prostitution and immoral rites as the people begged their gods to make their crops, herds, and families increase. By contrast, Israel's religion avoided all sexual connotations. By keeping worship and sex entirely separate, God helped the Israelites avoid confusion with pagan rites. The Israelites worshiped God as their loving Creator and Provider, and they thanked him for bountiful crops, marital love, and safe childbirth.

Lev 13:1ff Leprosy (here called "a serious skin disease") is a name applied to several different diseases and was greatly feared in

develops in its place, that person must go to the priest to be examined. 20If the priest examines it and finds it to be more than skin-deep, and if the hair in the affected area has turned white, the priest must pronounce the person ceremonially unclean. The boil has become a serious skin disease. 21But if the priest finds no white hair on the affected area and the problem appears to be no more than skin-deep and has faded, the priest must quarantine the person for seven days. 22If during that time the affected area spreads on the skin, the priest must pronounce the person ceremonially unclean, because it is a serious disease. 23But if the area grows no larger and does not spread, it is merely the scar from the boil, and the priest will pronounce the person ceremonially clean.

24"If anyone has suffered a burn on the skin and the burned area changes color, becoming either reddish white or shiny white, 25the priest must examine it. If he finds that the hair in the affected area has turned white and the problem appears to be more than skin-deep, a skin disease has broken out in the burn. The priest must then pronounce the person ceremonially unclean, for it is clearly a serious skin disease. 26But if the priest finds no white hair on the affected area and the problem appears to be no more than skin-deep and has faded, the priest must quarantine the infected person for seven days. 27On the seventh day the priest must examine the person again. If the affected area has spread on the skin, the priest must pronounce that person ceremonially unclean, for it is clearly a serious skin disease. 28But if the affected area has not changed or spread on the skin and has faded, it is simply a swelling from the burn. The priest will then pronounce the person ceremonially clean, for it is only the scar from the burn.

29"If anyone, either a man or woman, has a sore on the head or chin, 30the priest must examine it. If he finds it is more than skin-deep and has fine yellow hair on it, the priest must pronounce the person ceremonially unclean. It is a scabby sore of the head or chin. 31If the priest examines the scabby sore and finds that it is only skin-deep but there is no black hair on it, he must quarantine the person for seven days. 32On the seventh day the priest must examine the sore again. If he finds that the scabby sore has not spread, and there is no yellow hair on it, and it appears to be only skin-deep, 33the person must shave off all hair except the hair on the affected area. Then the priest must quarantine the person for another seven days. 34On the seventh day he will examine the sore again. If it has not spread and appears to be no more than skin-deep, the priest will pronounce the person ceremonially clean. The person's clothing must be washed, and the person will be ceremonially clean. 35But if the scabby sore begins to spread after the person is pronounced clean, 36the priest must do another examination. If he finds that the sore has spread, the priest does not need to look for yellow hair. The infected person is ceremonially unclean. 37But if the color of the scabby sore does not change and black hair has grown on it, it has healed. The priest will then pronounce the person ceremonially clean.

38"If anyone, either a man or woman, has shiny white patches on the skin, 39the priest must examine the affected area. If he finds that the shiny patches are only pale white, this is a harmless skin rash, and the person is ceremonially clean.

40"If a man loses his hair and his head becomes bald, he is still ceremonially clean. 41And if he loses hair on his forehead, he simply has a bald forehead; he is still clean. 42However, if a reddish white sore appears on the bald area at the top or back of his head, this is a skin disease. 43The priest must examine him, and if he finds swelling around the reddish white sore anywhere on the man's head and it looks like a skin disease, 44the man is indeed infected with a skin disease and is unclean. The priest must pronounce him ceremonially unclean because of the sore on his head.

45"Those who suffer from a serious skin disease must tear their clothing and leave their hair uncombed.* They must cover their mouth and call out, 'Unclean! Unclean!' 46As long as the serious disease lasts, they will be ceremonially unclean. They must live in isolation in their place outside the camp.

Lv 13:45 Or *and uncover their heads.*

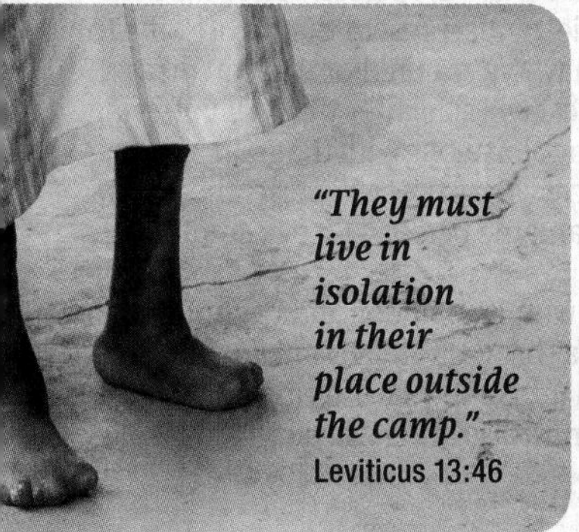
"They must live in isolation in their place outside the camp."
Leviticus 13:46

Bible times. Some of these diseases, unlike the disease we call leprosy or Hansen's disease today, were highly contagious. The worst of them slowly ruined the body and, in most cases, were fatal. Lepers were separated from family and friends and confined outside the camp. Since priests were responsible for the health of the camp, it was their duty to expel and readmit lepers. If someone's leprosy appeared to go away, only the priest could decide if that person was truly cured. Leprosy is often used in the Bible as an illustration of sin because sin is contagious and destructive and leads to separation.

Lev 13:45-46 A person with a serious skin disease had to perform this strange ritual to protect others from coming too near. Because the disease described in Leviticus was highly contagious, it was important that people stay away from those who had it.

Treatment of Contaminated Clothing

LEVITICUS 13:47-59

"Now suppose mildew* contaminates some woolen or linen clothing, 48woolen or linen fabric, the hide of an animal, or anything made of leather. 49If the contaminated area in the clothing, the animal hide, the fabric, or the leather article has turned greenish or reddish, it is contaminated with mildew and must be shown to the priest. 50After examining the affected spot, the priest will put the article in quarantine for seven days. 51On the seventh day the priest must inspect it again. If the contaminated area has spread, the clothing or fabric or leather is clearly contaminated by a serious mildew and is ceremonially unclean. 52The priest must burn the item—the clothing, the woolen or linen fabric, or piece of leather—for it has been contaminated by a serious mildew. It must be completely destroyed by fire.

53"But if the priest examines it and finds that the contaminated area has not spread in the clothing, the fabric, or the leather, 54the priest will order the object to be washed and then quarantined for seven more days. 55Then the priest must examine the object again. If he finds that the contaminated area has not changed color after being washed, even if it did not spread, the object is defiled. It must be completely burned up, whether the contaminated spot* is on the inside or outside. 56But if the priest examines it and finds that the contaminated area has faded after being washed, he must cut the spot from the clothing, the fabric, or the leather. 57If the spot later reappears on the clothing, the fabric, or the leather article, the mildew is clearly spreading, and the contaminated object must be burned up. 58But if the spot disappears from the clothing, the fabric, or the leather article after it has been washed, it must be washed again; then it will be ceremonially clean.

59"These are the instructions for dealing with mildew that contaminates woolen or linen clothing or fabric or anything made of leather. This is how the priest will determine whether these items are ceremonially clean or unclean."

Cleansing from Skin Diseases

LEVITICUS 14:1-32

And the LORD said to Moses, 2"The following instructions are for those seeking ceremonial purification from a skin disease.* Those who have been healed must be brought to the priest, 3who will examine them at a place outside the camp. If the priest finds that someone has been healed of a serious skin disease, 4he will perform a purification ceremony, using two live birds that are ceremonially clean, a stick of cedar,* some scarlet yarn, and a hyssop branch. 5The priest will order that one bird be slaughtered over a clay pot filled with fresh water. 6He will take the live bird, the cedar stick, the scarlet yarn, and the hyssop branch, and dip them into the blood of the bird that was slaughtered over the fresh water. 7The priest will then sprinkle the blood of the dead bird seven times on the person being purified of the skin disease. When the priest has purified the person, he will release the live bird in the open field to fly away.

8"The persons being purified must then wash their clothes, shave off all their hair, and bathe themselves in water. Then they will be ceremonially clean and may return to the camp. However, they must remain outside their tents for seven days. 9On the seventh day they must again shave all the hair from their heads, including the hair of the beard and eyebrows. They must also wash their clothes and bathe themselves in water. Then they will be ceremonially clean.

10"On the eighth day each person being purified must bring two male lambs and a one-year-old female lamb, all with no defects, along with a grain offering of six quarts* of choice flour moistened with olive oil, and a cup* of olive oil. 11Then the officiating priest will present that person for purification, along with the offerings, before the LORD at the entrance of the Tabernacle.* 12The priest will take one of the male lambs and the olive oil and present them as a guilt offering, lifting them up as a special offering before the LORD. 13He will then slaughter the male lamb in the sacred area where sin offerings and burnt offerings are slaughtered. As with the sin offering, the guilt offering belongs to the priest. It is a most holy offering. 14The priest will then take some of the blood of the guilt offering and apply it to the lobe of the right ear, the thumb of the right hand, and the big toe of the right foot of the person being purified.

15"Then the priest will pour some of the olive oil into the palm of his own left hand. 16He will dip his right finger into the oil in his palm and sprinkle some of it with his finger seven times before the LORD. 17The priest will then apply some of the oil in his palm over the blood from the guilt offering that is on the lobe of the right ear, the thumb of the right hand, and the big toe of the right foot of the person being purified. 18The priest will apply the oil remaining in his hand to the head of the person being purified. Through this process, the priest will purify* the person before the LORD.

19"Then the priest must present the sin offering to purify the person who was cured of the skin disease. After that, the priest will slaughter the burnt offering 20and offer it on the altar along with the grain offering. Through this process, the priest will purify the person who was healed, and the person will be ceremonially clean.

21"But anyone who is too poor and cannot afford these offerings may bring one male lamb for a guilt offering, to be lifted up as a special offering for purification. The person must also bring two quarts* of choice

Lv 13:47 Traditionally rendered *leprosy.* The Hebrew term used throughout this passage is the same term used for the various skin diseases described in 13:1-46. **Lv 13:55** The meaning of the Hebrew is uncertain. **Lv 14:2** Traditionally rendered *leprosy;* see note on 13:2a. **Lv 14:4** Or *juniper;* also in 14:6, 49, 51. **Lv 14:10a** Hebrew *3/10 of an ephah* [6.6 liters]. **Lv 14:10b** Hebrew *1 log* [0.3 liters]; also in 14:21. **Lv 14:11** Hebrew *Tent of Meeting;* also in 14:23. **Lv 14:18** Or *will make atonement for;* similarly in 14:19, 20, 21, 29, 31, 53. **Lv 14:21** Hebrew *1/10 of an ephah* [2.2 liters].

flour moistened with olive oil for the grain offering and a cup of olive oil. 22 The offering must also include two turtledoves or two young pigeons, whichever the person can afford. One of the pair must be used for the sin offering and the other for a burnt offering. 23 On the eighth day of the purification ceremony, the person being purified must bring the offerings to the priest in the LORD's presence at the entrance of the Tabernacle. 24 The priest will take the lamb for the guilt offering, along with the olive oil, and lift them up as a special offering to the LORD. 25 Then the priest will slaughter the lamb for the guilt offering. He will take some of its blood and apply it to the lobe of the right ear, the thumb of the right hand, and the big toe of the right foot of the person being purified.

26 "The priest will also pour some of the olive oil into the palm of his own left hand. 27 He will dip his right finger into the oil in his palm and sprinkle some of it seven times before the LORD. 28 The priest will then apply some of the oil in his palm over the blood from the guilt offering that is on the lobe of the right ear, the thumb of the right hand, and the big toe of the right foot of the person being purified. 29 The priest will apply the oil remaining in his hand to the head of the person being purified. Through this process, the priest will purify the person before the LORD.

30 "Then the priest will offer the two turtledoves or the two young pigeons, whichever the person can afford. 31 One of them is for a sin offering and the other for a burnt offering, to be presented along with the grain offering. Through this process, the priest will purify the person before the LORD. 32 These are the instructions for purification for those who have recovered from a serious skin disease but who cannot afford to bring the offerings normally required for the ceremony of purification."

Treatment of Contaminated Houses

LEVITICUS 14:33-57

Then the LORD said to Moses and Aaron, 34 "When you arrive in Canaan, the land I am giving you as your own possession, I may contaminate some of the houses in your land with mildew.* 35 The owner of such a house must then go to the priest and say, 'It appears that my house has some kind of mildew.' 36 Before the priest goes in to inspect the house, he must have the house emptied so nothing inside will be pronounced ceremonially unclean. 37 Then the priest will go in and examine the mildew on the walls. If he finds greenish or reddish streaks and the contamination appears to go deeper than the wall's surface, 38 the priest will step outside the door and put the house in quarantine for seven days. 39 On the seventh day the priest must return for another inspection. If he finds that the mildew on the walls of the house has spread, 40 the priest must order that the stones from those areas be removed. The contaminated material will then be taken outside the town to an area designated as ceremonially unclean. 41 Next the inside walls of the entire house must be scraped thoroughly and the scrapings dumped in the unclean place outside the town. 42 Other stones will be brought in to replace the ones that were removed, and the walls will be replastered.

43 "But if the mildew reappears after all the stones have been replaced and the house has been scraped and replastered, 44 the priest must return and inspect the house again. If he finds that the mildew has spread, the walls are clearly contaminated with a serious mildew, and the house is defiled. 45 It must be torn down, and all its stones, timbers, and plaster must be carried out of town to the place designated as ceremonially unclean. 46 Those who enter the house during the period of quarantine will be ceremonially unclean until evening, 47 and all who sleep or eat in the house must wash their clothing.

48 "But if the priest returns for his inspection and finds that the mildew has not reappeared in the house after the fresh plastering, he will pronounce it clean because the mildew is clearly gone. 49 To purify the house the priest must take two birds, a stick of cedar, some scarlet yarn, and a hyssop branch. 50 He will slaughter one of the birds over a clay pot filled with fresh water. 51 He will take the cedar stick, the hyssop branch, the scarlet yarn, and the live bird, and dip them into the blood of the slaughtered bird and into the fresh water. Then he will sprinkle the house seven times. 52 When the priest has purified the house in exactly this way, 53 he will release the live bird in the open fields outside the town. Through this process, the priest will purify the house, and it will be ceremonially clean.

54 "These are the instructions for dealing with serious skin diseases,* including scabby sores; 55 and

Lv 14:34 Traditionally rendered *leprosy;* see note on 13:47. **Lv 14:54** Traditionally rendered *leprosy;* see note on 13:2a.

Lev 14:34-35 This mildew was dry rot or mineral crystals affecting stone walls. These specific cleansing procedures designated for mildewed clothing and buildings were fully required by the law (Lev 14:44-57). Why was mildew so dangerous? This fungus could spread rapidly and promote disease. It was therefore important to check its spread as soon as possible. In extreme cases, if the fungus had done enough damage, the clothing was burned or the house destroyed.

Lev 14:54-57 God told the Israelites how to diagnose serious skin diseases and mildew so they could avoid them or treat them. These laws were given for the people's health and protection. They helped the Israelites avoid diseases that were serious threats in that time and place. Although they wouldn't have understood the medical reasons for some of these laws, their obedience to them made them healthier. Many of God's laws must have seemed strange to the Israelites. But his laws helped them avoid not only physical contamination but also moral and spiritual infection.

The Word of God still provides a pattern for physically, spiritually, and morally healthy living. We may not always understand the wisdom of God's laws, but if we obey them, we will thrive. Does this mean we are to follow the Old Testament health and dietary restrictions? In general, the basic principles of health and cleanliness are still healthful

▶ **LEVITICUS 14:33-57 *(cont.)***

mildew,* whether on clothing or in a house; [56]and a swelling on the skin, a rash, or discolored skin. [57]This procedure will determine whether a person or object is ceremonially clean or unclean.

"These are the instructions regarding skin diseases and mildew."

Bodily Discharges

LEVITICUS 15:1-33

The LORD said to Moses and Aaron, [2]"Give the following instructions to the people of Israel.

"Any man who has a bodily discharge is ceremonially unclean. [3]This defilement is caused by his discharge, whether the discharge continues or stops. In either case the man is unclean. [4]Any bed on which the man with the discharge lies and anything on which he sits will be ceremonially unclean. [5]So if you touch the man's bed, you must wash your clothes and bathe yourself in water, and you will remain unclean until evening. [6]If you sit where the man with the discharge has sat, you must wash your clothes and bathe yourself in water, and you will remain unclean until evening. [7]If you touch the man with the discharge, you must wash your clothes and bathe yourself in water, and you will remain unclean until evening. [8]If the man spits on you, you must wash your clothes and bathe yourself in water, and you will remain unclean until evening. [9]Any saddle blanket on which the man rides will be ceremonially unclean. [10]If you touch anything that was under the man, you will be unclean until evening. You must wash your clothes and bathe yourself in water, and you will remain unclean until evening. [11]If the man touches you without first rinsing his hands, you must wash your clothes and bathe yourself in water, and you will remain unclean until evening. [12]Any clay pot the man touches must be broken, and any wooden utensil he touches must be rinsed with water.

[13]"When the man with the discharge is healed, he must count off seven days for the period of purification. Then he must wash his clothes and bathe himself in fresh water, and he will be ceremonially clean. [14]On the eighth day he must get two turtledoves or two young pigeons and come before the LORD at the entrance of the Tabernacle* and give his offerings to the priest. [15]The priest will offer one bird for a sin offering and the other for a burnt offering. Through this process, the priest will purify* the man before the LORD for his discharge.

[16]"Whenever a man has an emission of semen, he must bathe his entire body in water, and he will remain ceremonially unclean until the next evening.* [17]Any clothing or leather with semen on it must be washed in water, and it will remain unclean until evening. [18]After a man and a woman have sexual intercourse, they must each bathe in water, and they will remain unclean until the next evening.

[19]"Whenever a woman has her menstrual period, she will be ceremonially unclean for seven days. Anyone who touches her during that time will be unclean until evening. [20]Anything on which the woman lies or sits during the time of her period will be unclean. [21]If any of you touch her bed, you must wash your clothes and bathe yourself in water, and you will remain unclean until evening. [22]If you touch any object she has sat on, you must wash your clothes and bathe yourself in water, and you will remain unclean until evening. [23]This includes her bed or any other object she has sat on; you will be unclean until evening if you touch it. [24]If a man has sexual intercourse with her and her blood touches him, her menstrual impurity will be transmitted to him. He will remain unclean for seven days, and any bed on which he lies will be unclean.

[25]"If a woman has a flow of blood for many days that is unrelated to her menstrual period, or if the blood continues beyond the normal period, she is ceremonially unclean. As during her menstrual period, the woman will be unclean as long as the discharge continues. [26]Any bed she lies on and any object she sits on during that time will be unclean, just as during her normal menstrual period. [27]If any of you touch these things, you will be ceremonially unclean. You must wash your clothes and bathe yourself in water, and you will remain unclean until evening.

[28]"When the woman's bleeding stops, she must count off seven days. Then she will be ceremonially clean. [29]On the eighth day she must bring two turtledoves or two young pigeons and present them to the priest at the entrance of the Tabernacle. [30]The priest will offer one for a sin offering and the other

Lv 14:55 Traditionally rendered *leprosy;* see note on 13:47. **Lv 15:14** Hebrew *Tent of Meeting;* also in 15:29. **Lv 15:15** Or *will make atonement for;* also in 15:30. **Lv 15:16** Hebrew *until evening;* also in 15:18.

practices, but it would be legalistic, if not wrong, to adhere to each specific restriction today. Some of these regulations were intended to mark the Israelites as different from the wicked people around them. Others were given to prevent God's people from becoming involved in pagan religious practices, one of the most serious problems of the day. Still others related to quarantines in a culture where exact medical diagnosis was impossible. Today, for example, physicians can diagnose the different forms of leprosy, and they know which ones are contagious. Treatment methods have greatly improved, and quarantine for leprosy is rarely necessary.

Lev 15:18 The verses in this section are not implying that sex is dirty or disgusting. God created sex for (1) the enjoyment of married couples, (2) the continuation of the race, and (3) the preservation of the covenant. Everything must be seen and done with a view toward God's love and ultimate authority. Sex is not separate from spirituality and God's care. God is concerned about our sexual habits. He designed us, including our sexuality, as wonderfully complex and unified creations. We tend to try to separate our physical and spiritual lives, but they are intertwined. God must be Lord over our whole selves—

for a burnt offering. Through this process, the priest will purify her before the LORD for the ceremonial impurity caused by her bleeding.

[31]"This is how you will guard the people of Israel from ceremonial uncleanness. Otherwise they would die, for their impurity would defile my Tabernacle that stands among them. [32]These are the instructions for dealing with anyone who has a bodily discharge—a man who is unclean because of an emission of semen [33]or a woman during her menstrual period. It applies to any man or woman who has a bodily discharge, and to a man who has sexual intercourse with a woman who is ceremonially unclean."

The Day of Atonement

LEVITICUS 16:1-34

The LORD spoke to Moses after the death of Aaron's two sons, who died after they entered the LORD's presence and burned the wrong kind of fire before him. [2]The LORD said to Moses, "Warn your brother, Aaron, not to enter the Most Holy Place behind the inner curtain whenever he chooses; if he does, he will die. For the Ark's cover—the place of atonement—is there, and I myself am present in the cloud above the atonement cover.

[3]"When Aaron enters the sanctuary area, he must follow these instructions fully. He must bring a young bull for a sin offering and a ram for a burnt offering. [4]He must put on his linen tunic and the linen undergarments worn next to his body. He must tie the linen sash around his waist and put the linen turban on his head. These are sacred garments, so he must bathe himself in water before he puts them on. [5]Aaron must take from the community of Israel two male goats for a sin offering and a ram for a burnt offering.

[6]"Aaron will present his own bull as a sin offering to purify himself and his family, making them right with the LORD.* [7]Then he must take the two male goats and present them to the LORD at the entrance of the Tabernacle.* [8]He is to cast sacred lots to determine which goat will be reserved as an offering to the LORD and which will carry the sins of the people to the wilderness of Azazel. [9]Aaron will then present as a sin offering the goat chosen by lot for the LORD. [10]The other goat, the scapegoat chosen by lot to be sent away, will be kept alive, standing before the LORD. When it is sent away to Azazel in the wilderness, the people will be purified and made right with the LORD.*

[11]"Aaron will present his own bull as a sin offering to purify himself and his family, making them right with the LORD. After he has slaughtered the

Lv 16:6 Or *to make atonement for himself and his family;* similarly in 16:11, 17b, 24, 34. **Lv 16:7** Hebrew *Tent of Meeting;* also in 16:16, 17, 20, 23, 33. **Lv 16:10** Or *wilderness, it will make atonement for the people.*

OLD/NEW SYSTEMS OF SACRIFICE

Old System of Sacrifice	*New System of Sacrifice*
Was temporary (Heb 8:13)	Is permanent (Heb 7:21)
Aaron the first high priest (Lev 16:32)	Jesus our High Priest (Heb 4:14)
From tribe of Levi (Heb 7:5)	From tribe of Judah (Heb 7:14)
Ministered on earth (Heb 8:4)	Ministers in heaven (Heb 8:1-2)
Used blood of animals (Lev 16:15)	Uses blood of Christ (Heb 10:4-12)
Required many sacrifices (Heb 10:1-3)	Requires one sacrifice (Heb 9:28)
Needed perfect animals (Lev 22:19)	Needs a perfect life (Heb 5:9)
Required careful approach to Tabernacle (Lev 16:2)	Encourages confident approach to throne (Heb 4:16)
Looked forward to new system (Heb 10:1)	Sets aside old system (Heb 10:9)

including our private lives. In what ways do you acknowledge your relationship with God in your sexuality?

Lev 15:32-33 God is concerned about health. He upholds the dignity of the person, the dignity of the body, and the dignity of the sexual experience. His commands call the people to avoid unhealthy practices and promote healthy ones with practical instructions. Washing was a God-directed means to maintain physical health; acts of purification or cleansing were God-directed means to preserve spiritual dignity. Millennia before the rise of the AIDS epidemic, God's directions already preserved people from known and unknown dangers. This shows God's high regard for sex and sexuality. In our day, sex has been degraded by shocking media exposure. It has become public domain, not private celebration. We are called to have a high regard for sex, both in good health and in purity. Our deepest form of gratitude to God for the gift of sex is expressed in how we use the gift.

Lev 16:1ff The Day of Atonement was the greatest day of the year for Israel. The Hebrew word for *atone* means "to cover." Old Testament sacrifices could not actually remove sins, only cover them. On this day, the people confessed their sins as a nation, and the high priest went into the Most Holy Place to make atonement for them. Sacrifices were made and blood was shed so that the people's sins could be "covered" until Christ's sacrifice on the cross would give people the opportunity to have their sins removed forever.

Lev 16:1-25 Aaron had to spend hours preparing himself to meet God. But we can approach God anytime (Heb 4:16). What a privilege! We are offered easier access to God than the high priests of Old Testament times! Still, we must never forget that God is holy nor let this privilege cause us to approach God carelessly. The way to God has been opened to us by Christ. But easy access to God does not eliminate our need to prepare our hearts as we draw near in prayer.

Lev 16:5-28 This event with the two goats occurred on the Day of Atonement. The two goats represented the two ways God was dealing with the Israelites' sin: (1) He was forgiving their sin through the first goat, which was sacrificed, and (2) he was removing their guilt through the second goat, the scapegoat, that was sent into the wilderness. The same ritual had to be repeated every year. Jesus Christ's death replaced this system once and for all. We can have our sins forgiven and guilt removed by placing our trust in Christ (Heb 10:1-18).

▸ **LEVITICUS 16:1-34** ***(cont.)***

bull as a sin offering, 12he will fill an incense burner
with burning coals from the altar that stands before the LORD. Then he will take two handfuls of fragrant powdered incense and will carry the burner
and the incense behind the inner curtain. 13There
in the LORD's presence he will put the incense on
the burning coals so that a cloud of incense will rise
over the Ark's cover—the place of atonement—that
rests on the Ark of the Covenant.* If he follows these
instructions, he will not die. 14Then he must take
some of the blood of the bull, dip his finger in it, and
sprinkle it on the east side of the atonement cover.
He must sprinkle blood seven times with his finger
in front of the atonement cover.

15"Then Aaron must slaughter the first goat as a
sin offering for the people and carry its blood behind
the inner curtain. There he will sprinkle the goat's
blood over the atonement cover and in front of it,
just as he did with the bull's blood. 16Through this
process, he will purify* the Most Holy Place, and he
will do the same for the entire Tabernacle, because
of the defiling sin and rebellion of the Israelites.
17No one else is allowed inside the Tabernacle when
Aaron enters it for the purification ceremony in the
Most Holy Place. No one may enter until he comes
out again after purifying himself, his family, and all
the congregation of Israel, making them right with
the LORD.

18"Then Aaron will come out to purify the altar that
stands before the LORD. He will do this by taking some
of the blood from the bull and the goat and putting
it on each of the horns of the altar. 19Then he must
sprinkle the blood with his finger seven times over
the altar. In this way, he will cleanse it from Israel's
defilement and make it holy.

20"When Aaron has finished purifying the Most
Holy Place and the Tabernacle and the altar, he must
present the live goat. 21He will lay both of his hands
on the goat's head and confess over it all the wickedness, rebellion, and sins of the people of Israel. In this
way, he will transfer the people's sins to the head of
the goat. Then a man specially chosen for the task
will drive the goat into the wilderness. 22As the goat
goes into the wilderness, it will carry all the people's
sins upon itself into a desolate land.

23"When Aaron goes back into the Tabernacle, he
must take off the linen garments he was wearing when
he entered the Most Holy Place, and he must leave the
garments there. 24Then he must bathe himself with
water in a sacred place, put on his regular garments,
and go out to sacrifice a burnt offering for himself and
a burnt offering for the people. Through this process,
he will purify himself and the people, making them
right with the LORD. 25He must then burn all the fat
of the sin offering on the altar.

26"The man chosen to drive the scapegoat into the
wilderness of Azazel must wash his clothes and bathe
himself in water. Then he may return to the camp.

27"The bull and the goat presented as sin offerings,
whose blood Aaron takes into the Most Holy Place for
the purification ceremony, will be carried outside the
camp. The animals' hides, internal organs, and dung
are all to be burned. 28The man who burns them must
wash his clothes and bathe himself in water before
returning to the camp.

29"On the tenth day of the appointed month in early
autumn,* you must deny yourselves.* Neither native-
born Israelites nor foreigners living among you may
do any kind of work. This is a permanent law for you.
30On that day offerings of purification will be made
for you,* and you will be purified in the LORD's presence from all your sins. 31It will be a Sabbath day of
complete rest for you, and you must deny yourselves.
This is a permanent law for you. 32In future generations, the purification* ceremony will be performed
by the priest who has been anointed and ordained to
serve as high priest in place of his ancestor Aaron. He

Lv 16:13 Hebrew *that is above the Testimony.* The Hebrew word for "testimony" refers to the terms of the LORD's covenant with Israel as written on stone tablets, which were kept in the Ark, and also to the covenant itself. **Lv 16:16** Or *make atonement for;* similarly in 16:17a, 18, 20, 27, 33. **Lv 16:29a** Hebrew *On the tenth day of the seventh month.* This day in the ancient Hebrew lunar calendar occurred in September or October. **Lv 16:29b** Or *must fast;* also in 16:31. **Lv 16:30** Or *atonement will be made for you, to purify you.* **Lv 16:32** Or *atonement.*

Lev 16:12 An incense burner was a dish or shallow bowl that hung by a chain or was carried with tongs. Inside the burner were placed incense (a combination of sweet-smelling spices) and burning coals from the altar. On the Day of Atonement, the high priest entered the Most Holy Place carrying a smoking incense burner. The smoke shielded him from the Ark of the Covenant and the presence of God—otherwise he would die. Incense may also have had a very practical purpose. The sweet smell drew the people's attention to the morning and evening sacrifices and helped cover the sometimes foul smell of the camp.

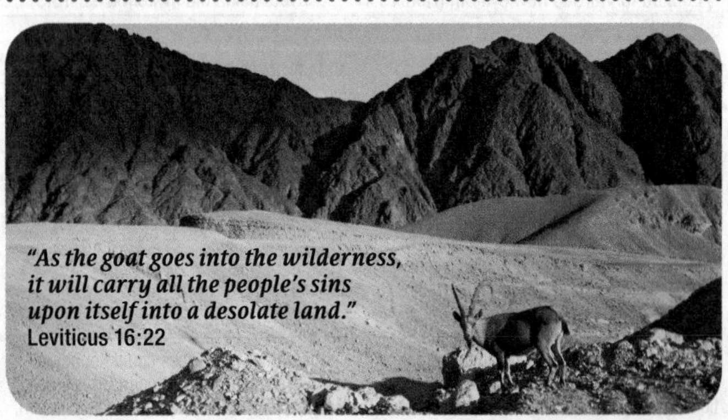
"As the goat goes into the wilderness, it will carry all the people's sins upon itself into a desolate land."
Leviticus 16:22

will put on the holy linen garments [33]and purify the Most Holy Place, the Tabernacle, the altar, the priests, and the entire congregation. [34]This is a permanent law for you, to purify the people of Israel from their sins, making them right with the LORD once each year."

Moses followed all these instructions exactly as the LORD had commanded him.

Prohibitions against Eating Blood

LEVITICUS 17:1-16

Then the LORD said to Moses, [2]"Give the following instructions to Aaron and his sons and all the people of Israel. This is what the LORD has commanded.

[3]"If any native Israelite sacrifices a bull* or a lamb or a goat anywhere inside or outside the camp [4]instead of bringing it to the entrance of the Tabernacle* to present it as an offering to the LORD, that person will be as guilty as a murderer.* Such a person has shed blood and will be cut off from the community. [5]The purpose of this rule is to stop the Israelites from sacrificing animals in the open fields. It will ensure that they bring their sacrifices to the priest at the entrance of the Tabernacle, so he can present them to the LORD as peace offerings. [6]Then the priest will be able to splatter the blood against the LORD's altar at the entrance of the Tabernacle, and he will burn the fat as a pleasing aroma to the LORD. [7]The people must no longer be unfaithful to the LORD by offering sacrifices to the goat idols.* This is a permanent law for them, to be observed from generation to generation.

[8]"Give them this command as well. If any native Israelite or foreigner living among you offers a burnt offering or a sacrifice [9]but does not bring it to the entrance of the Tabernacle to offer it to the LORD, that person will be cut off from the community.

[10]"And if any native Israelite or foreigner living among you eats or drinks blood in any form, I will turn against that person and cut him off from the community of your people, [11]for the life of the body is in its blood. I have given you the blood on the altar to purify you, making you right with the LORD.* It is the blood, given in exchange for a life, that makes purification possible. [12]That is why I have said to the people of Israel, 'You must never eat or drink blood—neither you nor the foreigners living among you.'

[13]"And if any native Israelite or foreigner living among you goes hunting and kills an animal or bird that is approved for eating, he must drain its blood and cover it with earth. [14]The life of every creature is in its blood. That is why I have said to the people of Israel, 'You must never eat or drink blood, for the life of any creature is in its blood.' So whoever consumes blood will be cut off from the community.

[15]"And if any native-born Israelites or foreigners eat the meat of an animal that died naturally or was torn up by wild animals, they must wash their clothes and bathe themselves in water. They will remain ceremonially unclean until evening, but then they will be clean. [16]But if they do not wash their clothes and bathe themselves, they will be punished for their sin."

Lv 17:3 Or *cow.* **Lv 17:4a** Hebrew *Tent of Meeting;* also in 17:5, 6, 9. **Lv 17:4b** Hebrew *will be guilty of blood.* **Lv 17:7** Or *goat demons.* **Lv 17:11** Or *to make atonement for you.*

Lev 17:1ff Leviticus 17–26 is sometimes called the "holiness code" because these chapters focus on what it means to live a holy life. The central verse is Leviticus 19:2, "You must be holy because I, the LORD your God, am holy."

Lev 17:3-9 Why were the Israelites prohibited from sacrificing outside the Tabernacle area? God had established specific times and places for sacrifices, and each occasion was permeated with symbolism. If people sacrificed on their own, they might easily add to or subtract from God's laws to fit their own lifestyles. Many pagan religions allowed individual priests to set their own rules; God's command helped the Israelites resist the temptation to follow the pagan pattern. When the Israelites slipped into idolatry, it was because "all the people did whatever seemed right in their own eyes" (Judg 17:6).

Lev 17:7 The "goat idols" were objects of worship and sacrifice in ancient times, particularly in Egypt from which they had recently escaped. God did not want the people to make this kind of sacrifice in the wilderness or in the Promised Land, where they were heading.

Lev 17:11-14 How does blood make atonement for sin? When offered with the right attitude, the sacrifice and the blood shed from it made forgiveness of sin possible. On the one hand, blood represented the sinner's life, infected by his sin and headed for death. On the other hand, the blood represented the innocent life of the animal that was sacrificed in place of the guilty person making the offering. The death of the animal (of which the blood was proof) fulfilled the penalty of death. God therefore granted forgiveness to the sinner based on the faith of the person doing the sacrificing.

Lev 17:14 Why was eating or drinking blood prohibited? The prohibition against eating blood can be traced all the way back to Noah (Gen 9:4). God prohibited eating or drinking blood for several reasons: (1) To discourage pagan practices. Israel was to be separate and distinct from the foreign nations around them. Eating blood was a common pagan practice. It was often done in hopes of gaining the characteristics of the slain animal (strength, speed, etc.). God's people were to rely on him, not on ingested blood, for their strength. (2) To preserve the symbolism of the sacrifice. Blood symbolized the life of the animal that was sacrificed in the sinner's place. To drink it would change the symbolism of the sacrificial penalty and destroy the evidence of the sacrifice. (3) To protect the people from infection, because many deadly diseases are transmitted through the blood. The Jews took this prohibition seriously, and that is why Jesus' hearers were so upset when Jesus told them to drink his blood (John 6:53-56). However, Jesus, as God himself and the last sacrifice ever needed for sins, was asking believers to identify with him completely. He wants us to take his life into us, and he wants to participate in our lives as well.

E. Laws for Living a Holy Life

After the sacrificial system for forgiving sins was in place, the people were instructed on how to live as forgiven people. Applying these standards to our lives helps us grow in obedience and please God.

1. STANDARDS FOR THE PEOPLE

God gave the people of Israel instructions on many areas of their lives, especially in the way they treated other people. The consequences for disobedience of these commands were also made very clear.

Forbidden Sexual Practices

LEVITICUS 18:1-30

Then the LORD said to Moses, [2]"Give the following instructions to the people of Israel. I am the LORD your God. [3]So do not act like the people in Egypt, where you used to live, or like the people of Canaan, where I am taking you. You must not imitate their way of life. [4]You must obey all my regulations and be careful to obey my decrees, for I am the LORD your God. [5]If you obey my decrees and my regulations, you will find life through them. I am the LORD.

[6]"You must never have sexual relations with a close relative, for I am the LORD.

[7]"Do not violate your father by having sexual relations with your mother. She is your mother; you must not have sexual relations with her.

[8]"Do not have sexual relations with any of your father's wives, for this would violate your father.

[9]"Do not have sexual relations with your sister or half sister, whether she is your father's daughter or your mother's daughter, whether she was born into your household or someone else's.

[10]"Do not have sexual relations with your granddaughter, whether she is your son's daughter or your daughter's daughter, for this would violate yourself.

[11]"Do not have sexual relations with your stepsister, the daughter of any of your father's wives, for she is your sister.

[12]"Do not have sexual relations with your father's sister, for she is your father's close relative.

[13]"Do not have sexual relations with your mother's sister, for she is your mother's close relative.

[14]"Do not violate your uncle, your father's brother, by having sexual relations with his wife, for she is your aunt.

[15]"Do not have sexual relations with your daughter-in-law; she is your son's wife, so you must not have sexual relations with her.

[16]"Do not have sexual relations with your brother's wife, for this would violate your brother.

[17]"Do not have sexual relations with both a woman and her daughter. And do not take* her granddaughter, whether her son's daughter or her daughter's daughter, and have sexual relations with her. They are close relatives, and this would be a wicked act.

[18]"While your wife is living, do not marry her sister and have sexual relations with her, for they would be rivals.

[19]"Do not have sexual relations with a woman during her period of menstrual impurity.

[20]"Do not defile yourself by having sexual intercourse with your neighbor's wife.

[21]"Do not permit any of your children to be offered as a sacrifice to Molech, for you must not bring shame on the name of your God. I am the LORD.

[22]"Do not practice homosexuality, having sex with another man as with a woman. It is a detestable sin.

[23]"A man must not defile himself by having sex with an animal. And a woman must not offer herself

Lv 18:17 Or *do not marry.*

Lev 18:3 The Israelites moved from one idol-infested country (Egypt) to another (Canaan). They also had contact with other cultures (Moab). As God helped them form a new culture, he warned them to leave all aspects of their pagan background and surroundings behind. He also warned them how easy it would be to slip into the pagan culture of Canaan, where they were going. Canaan's society and religions appealed to worldly desires, especially sexual immorality and drunkenness. The Israelites were to keep themselves pure and set apart for God. God did not want his people absorbed into the surrounding culture and environment. Society may pressure us to conform to its way of life and thought, but yielding to that pressure will create confusion as to which side we should be on and eliminate our effectiveness in serving God. Follow God by obeying his Word, and don't let the culture around you mold your thoughts and actions (see Rom 12:2).

Lev 18:6-18 Marrying relatives was prohibited by God for physical, social, and moral reasons. Children born to near relatives may experience serious health problems. Without these specific laws, sexual promiscuity would have been more likely, first in families, then outside. Improper sexual relations destroy family life.

Lev 18:6-27 Several detestable activities are listed here: (1) having sexual relations with close relatives, (2) committing adultery, (3) offering children as sacrifices, (4) having homosexual relations, and (5) having sexual relations with animals. These practices were common in pagan religions and cultures, and it is easy to see why God dealt harshly with those who began to follow them. Such practices lead to disease, deformity, and death. They disrupt family life and society and reveal a low regard for the value of oneself and of others. Society today takes some of these practices lightly, even trying to make them acceptable. But they are still sins in God's eyes. If you consider them acceptable, you are not living by God's standards.

to a male animal to have intercourse with it. This is a perverse act.

24"Do not defile yourselves in any of these ways, for the people I am driving out before you have defiled themselves in all these ways. 25Because the entire land has become defiled, I am punishing the people who live there. I will cause the land to vomit them out. 26You must obey all my decrees and regulations. You must not commit any of these detestable sins. This applies both to native-born Israelites and to the foreigners living among you.

27"All these detestable activities are practiced by the people of the land where I am taking you, and this is how the land has become defiled. 28So do not defile the land and give it a reason to vomit you out, as it will vomit out the people who live there now. 29Whoever commits any of these detestable sins will be cut off from the community of Israel. 30So obey my instructions, and do not defile yourselves by committing any of these detestable practices that were committed by the people who lived in the land before you. I am the LORD your God."

Holiness in Personal Conduct

LEVITICUS 19:1-37

The LORD also said to Moses, 2"Give the following instructions to the entire community of Israel. You must be holy because I, the LORD your God, am holy.

3"Each of you must show great respect for your mother and father, and you must always observe my Sabbath days of rest. I am the LORD your God.

4"Do not put your trust in idols or make metal images of gods for yourselves. I am the LORD your God.

5"When you sacrifice a peace offering to the LORD, offer it properly so you* will be accepted by God. 6The sacrifice must be eaten on the same day you offer it or on the next day. Whatever is left over until the third day must be completely burned up. 7If any of the sacrifice is eaten on the third day, it will be contaminated, and I will not accept it. 8Anyone who eats it on the third day will be punished for defiling what is holy to the LORD and will be cut off from the community.

9"When you harvest the crops of your land, do not harvest the grain along the edges of your fields, and do not pick up what the harvesters drop. 10It is the same with your grape crop—do not strip every last bunch of grapes from the vines, and do not pick up the grapes that fall to the ground. Leave them for the poor and the foreigners living among you. I am the LORD your God.

11"Do not steal.

"Do not deceive or cheat one another.

12"Do not bring shame on the name of your God by using it to swear falsely. I am the LORD.

13"Do not defraud or rob your neighbor.

"Do not make your hired workers wait until the next day to receive their pay.

14"Do not insult the deaf or cause the blind to stumble. You must fear your God; I am the LORD.

15"Do not twist justice in legal matters by favoring the poor or being partial to the rich and powerful. Always judge people fairly.

16"Do not spread slanderous gossip among your people.*

"Do not stand idly by when your neighbor's life is threatened. I am the LORD.

17"Do not nurse hatred in your heart for any of your relatives.* Confront people directly so you will not be held guilty for their sin.

18"Do not seek revenge or bear a grudge against a fellow Israelite, but love your neighbor as yourself. I am the LORD.

19"You must obey all my decrees.

"Do not mate two different kinds of animals. Do not plant your field with two different kinds of seed. Do not wear clothing woven from two different kinds of thread.

20"If a man has sex with a slave girl whose freedom has never been purchased but who is committed to become another man's wife, he must pay full compensation to her master. But since she is not a free woman, neither the man nor the woman will be put to death. 21The man, however, must bring a ram as a guilt offering and present it to the LORD at the entrance of the Tabernacle.* 22The priest will then purify him* before the LORD with the ram of the guilt offering, and the man's sin will be forgiven.

23"When you enter the land and plant fruit trees, leave the fruit unharvested for the first three years and consider it forbidden.* Do not eat it. 24In the fourth year the entire crop must be consecrated to the LORD as a celebration of praise. 25Finally, in the fifth year you may eat the fruit. If you follow this pattern, your harvest will increase. I am the LORD your God.

Lv 19:5 Or *it.* **Lv 19:16** Hebrew *Do not act as a merchant toward your own people.* **Lv 19:17** Hebrew *for your brother.* **Lv 19:21** Hebrew *Tent of Meeting.* **Lv 19:22** Or *make atonement for him.* **Lv 19:23** Hebrew *consider it uncircumcised.*

Lev 19:9-10 This law was a protection for the poor and the foreigner and a reminder that God owned the land; the people were only caretakers. Laws such as this showed God's generosity and liberality. As people of God, the Israelites were to reflect his nature and characteristics in their attitudes and actions. Ruth and Naomi were two people who benefited from this merciful law (Ruth 2:2).

Lev 19:9-10 God instructed the Hebrews to provide for those in need. He required that the people leave the edges of their fields unharvested, providing food for travelers and the poor. It is easy to ignore the poor or forget about those who have less than we do. But God desires generosity. In what ways can you leave the "edges of your fields" for those in need?

Lev 19:10-35 "Do not . . ." Some people think the Bible is nothing but a book of *don'ts*. But Jesus neatly summarized all these rules when he said to love God with all your heart and your neighbor as yourself. He called these the greatest commandments (or rules) of all (Matt 22:34-40). By carrying out Jesus' simple commands, we find ourselves following all of God's other laws as well.

▸ **LEVITICUS 19:1-37** ***(cont.)***

26"Do not eat meat that has not been drained of its blood.

"Do not practice fortune-telling or witchcraft.

27"Do not trim off the hair on your temples or trim your beards.

28"Do not cut your bodies for the dead, and do not mark your skin with tattoos. I am the LORD.

29"Do not defile your daughter by making her a prostitute, or the land will be filled with prostitution and wickedness.

30"Keep my Sabbath days of rest, and show reverence toward my sanctuary. I am the LORD.

31"Do not defile yourselves by turning to mediums or to those who consult the spirits of the dead. I am the LORD your God.

32"Stand up in the presence of the elderly, and show respect for the aged. Fear your God. I am the LORD.

33"Do not take advantage of foreigners who live among you in your land. 34Treat them like native-born Israelites, and love them as you love yourself. Remember that you were once foreigners living in the land of Egypt. I am the LORD your God.

35"Do not use dishonest standards when measuring length, weight, or volume. 36Your scales and weights must be accurate. Your containers for measuring dry materials or liquids must be accurate.* I am the LORD your God who brought you out of the land of Egypt.

37"You must be careful to keep all of my decrees and regulations by putting them into practice. I am the LORD."

Punishments for Disobedience

LEVITICUS 20:1-27

The LORD said to Moses, 2"Give the people of Israel these instructions, which apply both to native Israelites and to the foreigners living in Israel.

"If any of them offer their children as a sacrifice to Molech, they must be put to death. The people of the community must stone them to death. 3I myself will turn against them and cut them off from the community, because they have defiled my sanctuary and brought shame on my holy name by offering their children to Molech. 4And if the people of the community ignore those who offer their children to Molech and refuse to execute them, 5I myself will turn against them and their families and will cut them off from the community. This will happen to all who commit spiritual prostitution by worshiping Molech.

6"I will also turn against those who commit spiritual prostitution by putting their trust in mediums or in those who consult the spirits of the dead. I will cut them off from the community. 7So set yourselves apart to be holy, for I am the LORD your God. 8Keep all my decrees by putting them into practice, for I am the LORD who makes you holy.

9"Anyone who dishonors* father or mother must

Lv 19:36 Hebrew *Use an honest ephah* [a dry measure] *and an honest hin* [a liquid measure]. **Lv 20:9** Greek version reads *Anyone who speaks disrespectfully of.* Compare Matt 15:4; Mark 7:10.

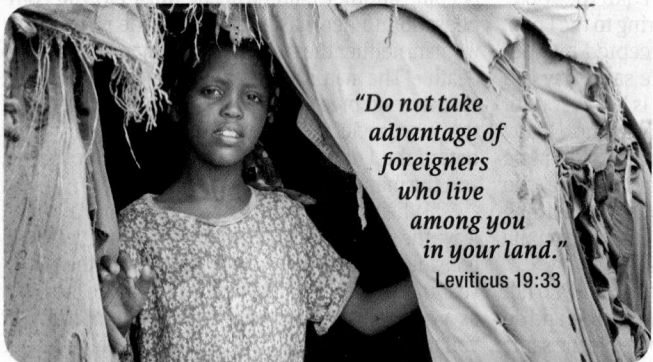

"Do not take advantage of foreigners who live among you in your land."
Leviticus 19:33

Lev 19:32 People often find it easy to dismiss the opinions of the elderly and avoid taking time to visit with them. But the fact that God commanded the Israelites to show respect for the elderly shows how seriously we should take the responsibility of respecting those older than we are. Their wisdom gained from experience can save us from many pitfalls. How do you show respect and honor to your elders?

Lev 19:33-34 How do you feel when you encounter foreigners, especially those who don't speak your language? Are you impatient? Do you think or act as if they should go back where they came from? Are you tempted to take advantage of them? God says to treat foreigners as you'd treat fellow countrymen, to love them as you love yourself. In reality, we are all foreigners in this world because it is only our temporary home. View strangers, newcomers, and foreigners as opportunities to demonstrate God's love.

Lev 20:1-3 Sacrificing children to the gods was a common practice in ancient religions. The Ammonites, Israel's neighbors, sacrificed children to Molech (their national god) a vital part of their religion. They saw this as the greatest gift they could offer to ward off evil or appease angry gods. God made it clear that this practice was detestable and strictly forbidden. In both Old and New Testament times, his character made human sacrifice unthinkable. Unlike the pagan gods, he is a God of love, who does not need to be appeased (Exod 34:6). He is a God of life, who prohibits murder and encourages practices that lead to health and happiness (Deut 30:15-16). He is a God of the helpless, who shows special concern for children (Ps 72:4). He is a God of unselfishness who, instead of demanding human sacrifices, sacrificed himself for us (Isa 53:4-5).

Lev 20:6 Everyone is interested in what the future holds, and we often look to others for guidance. But God warned about looking to the occult for advice. Mediums and psychics were outlawed because God was not the source of their information. At best, occult practitioners are fakes whose predictions cannot be trusted. At worst, they are in contact with evil spirits and are thus extremely dangerous. We don't need to look to the occult for information about the future. God has given us the Bible so that we may obtain all the information we need—and the Bible's teaching is trustworthy.

be put to death. Such a person is guilty of a capital offense.

10 "If a man commits adultery with his neighbor's wife, both the man and the woman who have committed adultery must be put to death.

11 "If a man violates his father by having sex with one of his father's wives, both the man and the woman must be put to death, for they are guilty of a capital offense.

12 "If a man has sex with his daughter-in-law, both must be put to death. They have committed a perverse act and are guilty of a capital offense.

13 "If a man practices homosexuality, having sex with another man as with a woman, both men have committed a detestable act. They must both be put to death, for they are guilty of a capital offense.

14 "If a man marries both a woman and her mother, he has committed a wicked act. The man and both women must be burned to death to wipe out such wickedness from among you.

15 "If a man has sex with an animal, he must be put to death, and the animal must be killed.

16 "If a woman presents herself to a male animal to have intercourse with it, she and the animal must both be put to death. You must kill both, for they are guilty of a capital offense.

17 "If a man marries his sister, the daughter of either his father or his mother, and they have sexual relations, it is a shameful disgrace. They must be publicly cut off from the community. Since the man has violated his sister, he will be punished for his sin.

18 "If a man has sexual relations with a woman during her menstrual period, both of them must be cut off from the community, for together they have exposed the source of her blood flow.

19 "Do not have sexual relations with your aunt, whether your mother's sister or your father's sister. This would dishonor a close relative. Both parties are guilty and will be punished for their sin.

20 "If a man has sex with his uncle's wife, he has violated his uncle. Both the man and woman will be punished for their sin, and they will die childless.

21 "If a man marries his brother's wife, it is an act of impurity. He has violated his brother, and the guilty couple will remain childless.

22 "You must keep all my decrees and regulations by putting them into practice; otherwise the land to which I am bringing you as your new home will vomit you out. 23 Do not live according to the customs of the people I am driving out before you. It is because they do these shameful things that I detest them. 24 But I have promised you, 'You will possess their land because I will give it to you as your possession—a land flowing with milk and honey.' I am the LORD your God, who has set you apart from all other people.

25 "You must therefore make a distinction between ceremonially clean and unclean animals, and between clean and unclean birds. You must not defile yourselves by eating any unclean animal or bird or creature that scurries along the ground. I have identified them as being unclean for you. 26 You must be holy because I, the LORD, am holy. I have set you apart from all other people to be my very own.

27 "Men and women among you who act as mediums or who consult the spirits of the dead must be put to death by stoning. They are guilty of a capital offense."

2. RULES FOR THE PRIESTS

The priests were set apart for service to God, and so they had special rules about how to live and interact with others.

Instructions for the Priests

LEVITICUS 21:1–22:16

The LORD said to Moses, "Give the following instructions to the priests, the descendants of Aaron.

"A priest must not make himself ceremonially unclean by touching the dead body of a relative. 2 The only exceptions are his closest relatives—his mother or father, son or daughter, brother, 3 or his virgin sister who

---

Lev 20:10-21 The detestable acts listed here were very common in the pagan nations of Canaan; their religions were rampant with sex goddesses, temple prostitution, and other gross sins. The Canaanites' immoral religious practices reflected a decadent culture that tended to corrupt whoever came in contact with it. By contrast, God was building a nation to make a positive influence on the world. He did not want the Israelites to adopt the Canaanites' practices and slide into debauchery. So he prepared the people for what they would face in the Promised Land by commanding them to steer clear of sexual sins.

Lev 20:10-21 This list of commands against sexual sins includes extremely harsh punishments. Why? God has no tolerance for such acts: (1) They shatter the mutual commitment of married partners; (2) they destroy the sanctity of the family; (3) they twist people's mental well-being; and (4) they spread disease. Sexual sin has always been widely available, but the glorification of sex between people who are not married to each other often hides deep tragedy and hurt behind the scenes. When society portrays sexual sins as attractive, it is easy to forget the dark side. God has good reasons for prohibiting sexual sins: He loves us and wants the very best for us. God still expects those who worship him to maintain sexual purity in their lives.

Lev 20:22-23 God gave many rules to his people—but not without reason. He did not withhold good from them; he only prohibited those acts that would bring them to ruin. All of us understand God's physical laws of nature. For example, jumping off of a 10-story building means death because of the law of gravity. But some of us don't understand how God's spiritual laws work. God forbids us to do certain things because he wants to keep us from self-destruction. The next time you are drawn to a forbidden physical or emotional pleasure, remind yourself that the consequences might be suffering and separation from God, who is trying to help you.

▸ **LEVITICUS 21:1–22:16 *(cont.)***

depends on him because she has no husband. [4]But a priest must not defile himself and make himself unclean for someone who is related to him only by marriage.

[5]"The priests must not shave their heads or trim their beards or cut their bodies. [6]They must be set apart as holy to their God and must never bring shame on the name of God. They must be holy, for they are the ones who present the special gifts to the LORD, gifts of food for their God.

[7]"Priests may not marry a woman defiled by prostitution, and they may not marry a woman who is divorced from her husband, for the priests are set apart as holy to their God. [8]You must treat them as holy because they offer up food to your God. You must consider them holy because I, the LORD, am holy, and I make you holy.

[9]"If a priest's daughter defiles herself by becoming a prostitute, she also defiles her father's holiness, and she must be burned to death.

[10]"The high priest has the highest rank of all the priests. The anointing oil has been poured on his head, and he has been ordained to wear the priestly garments. He must never leave his hair uncombed* or tear his clothing. [11]He must not defile himself by going near a dead body. He may not make himself ceremonially unclean even for his father or mother. [12]He must not defile the sanctuary of his God by leaving it to attend to a dead person, for he has been made holy by the anointing oil of his God. I am the LORD.

[13]"The high priest may marry only a virgin. [14]He may not marry a widow, a woman who is divorced, or a woman who has defiled herself by prostitution. She must be a virgin from his own clan, [15]so that he will not dishonor his descendants among his clan, for I am the LORD who makes him holy."

[16]Then the LORD said to Moses, [17]"Give the following instructions to Aaron: In all future generations, none of your descendants who has any defect will qualify to offer food to his God. [18]No one who has a defect qualifies, whether he is blind, lame, disfigured, deformed, [19]or has a broken foot or arm, [20]or is hunchbacked or dwarfed, or has a defective eye, or skin sores or scabs, or damaged testicles. [21]No descendant of Aaron who has a defect may approach the altar to present special gifts to the LORD. Since he has a defect, he may not approach the altar to offer food to his God. [22]However, he may eat from the food offered to God, including the holy offerings and the most holy offerings. [23]Yet because of his physical defect, he may not enter the room behind the inner curtain or approach the altar, for this would defile my holy places. I am the LORD who makes them holy."

[24]So Moses gave these instructions to Aaron and his sons and to all the Israelites.

22:1 The LORD said to Moses, [2]"Tell Aaron and his sons to be very careful with the sacred gifts that the Israelites set apart for me, so they do not bring shame on my holy name. I am the LORD. [3]Give them the following instructions.

"In all future generations, if any of your descendants is ceremonially unclean when he approaches the sacred offerings that the people of Israel consecrate to the LORD, he must be cut off from my presence. I am the LORD.

[4]"If any of Aaron's descendants has a skin disease* or any kind of discharge that makes him ceremonially unclean, he may not eat from the sacred offerings until he has been pronounced clean. He also becomes unclean by touching a corpse, or by having an emission of semen, [5]or by touching a small animal that is unclean, or by touching someone who is ceremonially unclean for any reason. [6]The man who is defiled in any of these ways will remain unclean until evening. He may not eat from the sacred offerings until he has bathed himself in water. [7]When the sun goes down, he will be ceremonially clean again and may eat from the sacred offerings, for this is his food. [8]He may not eat an animal that has died a natural death or has been torn apart by wild animals, for this would defile him. I am the LORD.

[9]"The priests must follow my instructions carefully. Otherwise they will be punished for their sin and will die for violating my instructions. I am the LORD who makes them holy.

[10]"No one outside a priest's family may eat the sacred offerings. Even guests and hired workers in a priest's home are not allowed to eat them. [11]However, if the priest buys a slave for himself, the slave may eat from the sacred offerings. And if his slaves have children, they also may share his food. [12]If a priest's daughter marries someone outside the priestly family,

Lv 21:10 Or *never uncover his head.* **Lv 22:4** Traditionally rendered *leprosy;* see note on 13:2a.

Lev 21:16-23 Was God unfairly discriminating against handicapped people when he said they were unqualified to offer sacrifices? Just as God demanded that no imperfect animals be used for sacrifice, he required that no handicapped priests offer sacrifices. This was not meant as an insult; rather, it had to do with the fact that the priest must match as closely as possible the perfect God he served. Of course, such perfection was not fully realized until Jesus Christ came. Because they were Levites, the handicapped priests were protected and supported with food from the sacrifices. They were not abandoned; they still had opportunity to perform many essential services within the Tabernacle.

Lev 22:1-9 Why were there so many specific guidelines for the priests? The Israelites would have been quite familiar with priests from Egypt. Egyptian priests were mainly interested in politics. They viewed religion as a way to gain power. Thus, the Israelites would have been suspicious of the establishment of a new priestly order. But God wanted his priests to serve him and the people. Their duties were religious—to help people draw near to God and worship him. They could not use their position to gain power because they were not allowed to own land or take money from anyone. All these guidelines reassured the people and helped the priests accomplish their purpose.

she may no longer eat the sacred offerings. 13But if she becomes a widow or is divorced and has no children to support her, and she returns to live in her father's home as in her youth, she may eat her father's food again. Otherwise, no one outside a priest's family may eat the sacred offerings.

14"Any such person who eats the sacred offerings without realizing it must pay the priest for the amount eaten, plus an additional 20 percent. 15The priests must not let the Israelites defile the sacred offerings brought to the LORD 16by allowing unauthorized people to eat them. This would bring guilt upon them and require them to pay compensation. I am the LORD who makes them holy."

Worthy and Unworthy Offerings

LEVITICUS 22:17-33

And the LORD said to Moses, 18"Give Aaron and his sons and all the Israelites these instructions, which apply both to native Israelites and to the foreigners living among you.

"If you present a gift as a burnt offering to the LORD, whether it is to fulfill a vow or is a voluntary offering, 19you* will be accepted only if your offering is a male animal with no defects. It may be a bull, a ram, or a male goat. 20Do not present an animal with defects, because the LORD will not accept it on your behalf.

21"If you present a peace offering to the LORD from the herd or the flock, whether it is to fulfill a vow or is a voluntary offering, you must offer a perfect animal. It may have no defect of any kind. 22You must not offer an animal that is blind, crippled, or injured, or that has a wart, a skin sore, or scabs. Such animals must never be offered on the altar as special gifts to the LORD. 23If a bull* or lamb has a leg that is too long or too short, it may be offered as a voluntary offering, but it may not be offered to fulfill a vow. 24If an animal has damaged testicles or is castrated, you may not offer it to the LORD. You must never do this in your own land, 25and you must not accept such an animal from foreigners and then offer it as a sacrifice to your God. Such animals will not be accepted on your behalf, for they are mutilated or defective."

26And the LORD said to Moses, 27"When a calf or lamb or goat is born, it must be left with its mother for seven days. From the eighth day on, it will be acceptable as a special gift to the LORD. 28But you must not slaughter a mother animal and her offspring on the same day, whether from the herd or the flock. 29When you bring a thanksgiving offering to the LORD, sacrifice it properly so you will be accepted. 30Eat the entire sacrificial animal on the day it is presented. Do not leave any of it until the next morning. I am the LORD.

31"You must faithfully keep all my commands by putting them into practice, for I am the LORD. 32Do not bring shame on my holy name, for I will display my holiness among the people of Israel. I am the LORD who makes you holy. 33It was I who rescued you from the land of Egypt, that I might be your God. I am the LORD."

Lv 22:19 *Or it.* **Lv 22:23** *Or cow.*

3. SEASONS AND FESTIVALS

Israel had several annual festivals that were designed to remind them of the goodness of God and the need to worship him alone. These were times of somber reflection, but they were also times for great celebration. The people of Israel organized their time around these festivals, so they were always reminded of God's presence in their lives.

The Religious Festivals

LEVITICUS 23:1-4

The LORD said to Moses, 2"Give the following instructions to the people of Israel. These are the LORD's appointed festivals, which you are to proclaim as official days for holy assembly.

3"You have six days each week for your ordinary work, but the seventh day is a Sabbath day of complete rest, an official day for holy assembly. It is the LORD's Sabbath day, and it must be observed wherever you live.

4"In addition to the Sabbath, these are the LORD's appointed festivals, the official days for holy assembly that are to be celebrated at their proper times each year.

Lev 22:19-25 Animals with defects were not acceptable as sacrifices because they did not represent God's holy nature. Furthermore, the animal had to be without defect in order to foreshadow the perfect, sinless life of Jesus Christ. When we give our best time, talent, and treasure to God rather than what is tarnished or common, we demonstrate the true meaning of worship and testify to God's supreme worth. What kind of quality can people see in your service and giving?

Lev 23:1ff Festivals played a major role in Israel's culture. Israel's festivals were different from those of any other nation because, being ordained by God, they were times of celebrating with him, not times of moral depravity. God wanted to set aside special days for the people to come together for rest, refreshment, and remembering with thanksgiving all he had done for them.

Lev 23:1-4 God established several national holidays each year for celebration, fellowship, and worship. Much can be learned about people by observing the holidays they celebrate and the way they celebrate them. Take note of your holiday traditions. What do they say about your values? In what ways do your celebrations and holidays reflect your relationship with God?

Passover and the Festival of Unleavened Bread

LEVITICUS 23:5-8

"The LORD's Passover begins at sundown on the fourteenth day of the first month.* 6On the next day, the
fifteenth day of the month, you must begin celebrating
the Festival of Unleavened Bread. This festival to the
LORD continues for seven days, and during that time
the bread you eat must be made without yeast. 7On the
first day of the festival, all the people must stop their
ordinary work and observe an official day for holy assembly. 8For seven days you must present special gifts
to the LORD. On the seventh day the people must again
stop all their ordinary work to observe an official day
for holy assembly."

Celebration of First Harvest

LEVITICUS 23:9-14

Then the LORD said to Moses, 10"Give the following
instructions to the people of Israel. When you enter
the land I am giving you and you harvest its first crops,
bring the priest a bundle of grain from the first cutting
of your grain harvest. 11On the day after the Sabbath,
the priest will lift it up before the LORD so it may be
accepted on your behalf. 12On that same day you must
sacrifice a one-year-old male lamb with no defects as a
burnt offering to the LORD. 13With it you must present
a grain offering consisting of four quarts* of choice
flour moistened with olive oil. It will be a special gift,
a pleasing aroma to the LORD. You must also offer one
quart* of wine as a liquid offering. 14Do not eat any
bread or roasted grain or fresh kernels on that day until
you bring this offering to your God. This is a permanent
law for you, and it must be observed from generation
to generation wherever you live.

The Festival of Harvest

LEVITICUS 23:15-22

"From the day after the Sabbath—the day you bring
the bundle of grain to be lifted up as a special offering—count off seven full weeks. 16Keep counting until the day after the seventh Sabbath, fifty days later.
Then present an offering of new grain to the LORD.
17From wherever you live, bring two loaves of bread
to be lifted up before the LORD as a special offering.
Make these loaves from four quarts of choice flour,
and bake them with yeast. They will be an offering to
the LORD from the first of your crops. 18Along with the
bread, present seven one-year-old male lambs with
no defects, one young bull, and two rams as burnt offerings to the LORD. These burnt offerings, together
with the grain offerings and liquid offerings, will be
a special gift, a pleasing aroma to the LORD. 19Then
you must offer one male goat as a sin offering and two
one-year-old male lambs as a peace offering.

20"The priest will lift up the two lambs as a special
offering to the LORD, together with the loaves representing the first of your crops. These offerings, which
are holy to the LORD, belong to the priests. 21That same
day will be proclaimed an official day for holy assembly, a day on which you do no ordinary work. This is a
permanent law for you, and it must be observed from
generation to generation wherever you live.*

22"When you harvest the crops of your land, do not
harvest the grain along the edges of your fields, and
do not pick up what the harvesters drop. Leave it for

Lv 23:5 This day in the ancient Hebrew lunar calendar occurred in late March, April, or early May. **Lv 23:13a** Hebrew *2/10 of an ephah* [4.4 liters]; also in 23:17. **Lv 23:13b** Hebrew *1/4 of a hin* [1 liter]. **Lv 23:21** This celebration, called the Festival of Harvest or the Festival of Weeks, was later called the Festival of Pentecost (see Acts 2:1). It is celebrated today as Shavuot (or Shabuoth).

"These are the LORD's appointed festivals, the official days for holy assembly that are to be celebrated at their proper times each year."
Leviticus 23:4

Lev 23:6 The Festival of Unleavened Bread reminded Israel of their escape from Egypt. For seven days they ate unleavened bread, just as they had eaten it back then (Exod 12:14-15). The symbolism of this bread made without yeast was important to the Israelites. First, because the bread was unique, it illustrated Israel's uniqueness as a nation. Second, because yeast was a symbol of sin, the yeastless bread represented Israel's moral purity. Third, the baking method reminded them to obey quickly. Their ancestors left the yeast out of their dough so they could leave Egypt quickly without waiting for the dough to rise.

Lev 23:9-14 The Festival of First Harvest required that the first crops harvested be offered to God. The Israelites could not eat the food from their harvest until they had made this offering. Today God still expects us to set aside his portion first, not last. Giving leftovers to God is no way to express thanks. What does the "first harvest" represent in your life?

Lev 23:15-22 The Festival of Harvest was a festival praising God for a bountiful harvest.

the poor and the foreigners living among you. I am
the Lord your God."

The Festival of Trumpets

LEVITICUS 23:23-25

The Lord said to Moses, 24"Give the following instructions to the people of Israel. On the first day of the
appointed month in early autumn,* you are to observe
a day of complete rest. It will be an official day for holy
assembly, a day commemorated with loud blasts of a
trumpet. 25You must do no ordinary work on that day.
Instead, you are to present special gifts to the Lord."

The Day of Atonement

LEVITICUS 23:26-32

Then the Lord said to Moses, 27"Be careful to celebrate
the Day of Atonement on the tenth day of that same
month—nine days after the Festival of Trumpets.* You
must observe it as an official day for holy assembly, a
day to deny yourselves* and present special gifts to the
Lord. 28Do no work during that entire day because it is
the Day of Atonement, when offerings of purification
are made for you, making you right with* the Lord
your God. 29All who do not deny themselves that day
will be cut off from God's people. 30And I will destroy
anyone among you who does any work on that day.
31You must not do any work at all! This is a permanent
law for you, and it must be observed from generation
to generation wherever you live. 32This will be a Sabbath day of complete rest for you, and on that day you
must deny yourselves. This day of rest will begin at
sundown on the ninth day of the month and extend
until sundown on the tenth day."

The Festival of Shelters

LEVITICUS 23:33-44

And the Lord said to Moses, 34"Give the following instructions to the people of Israel. Begin celebrating
the Festival of Shelters* on the fifteenth day of the
appointed month—five days after the Day of Atonement.* This festival to the Lord will last for seven days.
35On the first day of the festival you must proclaim an
official day for holy assembly, when you do no ordinary work. 36For seven days you must present special
gifts to the Lord. The eighth day is another holy day
on which you present your special gifts to the Lord.
This will be a solemn occasion, and no ordinary work
may be done that day.

37("These are the Lord's appointed festivals. Celebrate them each year as official days for holy assembly by presenting special gifts to the Lord—burnt
offerings, grain offerings, sacrifices, and liquid offerings—each on its proper day. 38These festivals must
be observed in addition to the Lord's regular Sabbath
days, and the offerings are in addition to your personal gifts, the offerings you give to fulfill your vows,
and the voluntary offerings you present to the Lord.)

39"Remember that this seven-day festival to the
Lord—the Festival of Shelters—begins on the fifteenth day of the appointed month,* after you have
harvested all the produce of the land. The first day and
the eighth day of the festival will be days of complete
rest. 40On the first day gather branches from magnificent trees*—palm fronds, boughs from leafy trees, and
willows that grow by the streams. Then celebrate with
joy before the Lord your God for seven days. 41You
must observe this festival to the Lord for seven days
every year. This is a permanent law for you, and it must
be observed in the appointed month* from generation
to generation. 42For seven days you must live outside
in little shelters. All native-born Israelites must live in
shelters. 43This will remind each new generation of
Israelites that I made their ancestors live in shelters
when I rescued them from the land of Egypt. I am the
Lord your God."

44So Moses gave the Israelites these instructions
regarding the annual festivals of the Lord.

Pure Oil and Holy Bread

LEVITICUS 24:1-9

The Lord said to Moses, 2"Command the people of
Israel to bring you pure oil of pressed olives for the
light, to keep the lamps burning continually. 3This is
the lampstand that stands in the Tabernacle, in front of

Lv 23:24 Hebrew *On the first day of the seventh month.* This day in the ancient Hebrew lunar calendar occurred in September or October. This festival is celebrated today as Rosh Hashanah, the Jewish new year. **Lv 23:27a** Hebrew *on the tenth day of the seventh month;* see 23:24 and the note there. This day in the ancient Hebrew lunar calendar occurred in September or October. It is celebrated today as Yom Kippur. **Lv 23:27b** Or *to fast;* similarly in 23:29, 32. **Lv 23:28** Or *when atonement is made for you before.* **Lv 23:34a** Or *Festival of Booths,* or *Festival of Tabernacles.* This was earlier called the Festival of the Final Harvest or Festival of Ingathering (see Exod 23:16b). It is celebrated today as Sukkot (or Succoth). **Lv 23:34b** Hebrew *on the fifteenth day of the seventh month;* see 23:27a and the note there. **Lv 23:39** Hebrew *on the fifteenth day of the seventh month.* **Lv 23:40** Or *gather fruit from majestic trees.* **Lv 23:41** Hebrew *the seventh month.*

Lev 23:23-24 Most of the trumpets used were rams' horns, although some of the more special trumpets were made of beaten silver. Trumpets were blown to announce the beginning of each month as well as the start of festivals.

Lev 23:33-43 The Festival of Shelters was a special celebration involving the whole family (see Lev 23:34; Exod 23:16; Deut 16:13-14). Like Passover, this festival taught family members of all ages about God's nature and what he had done for them, and it was a time of renewed commitment to God. Our families also need rituals of celebration to renew our faith and to pass it on to our children. In addition to Christmas and Easter, we should select other special days to commemorate God's goodness.

Lev 23:44 Worship involves both celebration and confession. But in Israel's national holidays, the balance seems heavily tipped in favor of celebration—five joyous occasions to two solemn ones. The God of the Bible encourages joy! God does not intend for religion to be only meditation and introspection. He also wants us to celebrate. Serious reflection and immediate confession of sin are essential. But this should be balanced by celebrating who God is and what he has done for his people. What special occasions on your calendar would you describe as times for joy? Which would be times for confession? How are you doing with the five-to-two balance?

▶ **LEVITICUS 24:1-9** ***(cont.)***

the inner curtain that shields the Ark of the Covenant.* Aaron must keep the lamps burning in the LORD's presence all night. This is a permanent law for you, and it must be observed from generation to generation. 4Aaron and the priests must tend the lamps on the pure gold lampstand continually in the LORD's presence.

5"You must bake twelve loaves of bread from choice flour, using four quarts* of flour for each loaf. 6Place the bread before the LORD on the pure gold table, and arrange the loaves in two rows, with six loaves in each row. 7Put some pure frankincense near each row to serve as a representative offering, a special gift presented to the LORD. 8Every Sabbath day this bread must be laid out before the LORD. The bread is to be received from the people of Israel as a requirement of the eternal covenant. 9The loaves of bread will belong to Aaron and his descendants, who must eat them in a sacred place, for they are most holy. It is the permanent right of the priests to claim this portion of the special gifts presented to the LORD."

An Example of Just Punishment

LEVITICUS 24:10-23

One day a man who had an Israelite mother and an Egyptian father came out of his tent and got into a fight with one of the Israelite men. 11During the fight, this son of an Israelite woman blasphemed the Name of the LORD* with a curse. So the man was brought to Moses for judgment. His mother was Shelomith, the daughter of Dibri of the tribe of Dan. 12They kept the man in custody until the LORD's will in the matter should become clear to them.

13Then the LORD said to Moses, 14"Take the blasphemer outside the camp, and tell all those who heard the curse to lay their hands on his head. Then let the entire community stone him to death. 15Say to the people of Israel: Those who curse their God will be punished for their sin. 16Anyone who blasphemes the Name of the LORD must be stoned to death by the whole community of Israel. Any native-born Israelite or foreigner among you who blasphemes the Name of the LORD must be put to death.

17"Anyone who takes another person's life must be put to death.

18"Anyone who kills another person's animal must pay for it in full—a live animal for the animal that was killed.

19"Anyone who injures another person must be dealt with according to the injury inflicted—20a fracture for a fracture, an eye for an eye, a tooth for a tooth. Whatever anyone does to injure another person must be paid back in kind.

21"Whoever kills an animal must pay for it in full, but whoever kills another person must be put to death.

22"This same standard applies both to native-born Israelites and to the foreigners living among you. I am the LORD your God."

23After Moses gave all these instructions to the Israelites, they took the blasphemer outside the camp and stoned him to death. The Israelites did just as the LORD had commanded Moses.

The Sabbath Year

LEVITICUS 25:1-7

While Moses was on Mount Sinai, the LORD said to him, 2"Give the following instructions to the people of Israel. When you have entered the land I am giving you, the land itself must observe a Sabbath rest before the LORD every seventh year. 3For six years you may plant your fields and prune your vineyards and harvest your crops, 4but during the seventh year the land must have a Sabbath year of complete rest. It is the LORD's Sabbath. Do not plant your fields or prune your vineyards during that year. 5And don't store away the crops that grow on their own or gather the grapes from your unpruned vines. The land must have a year of complete rest. 6But you may eat whatever the land produces on its own during its Sabbath. This applies to you, your male and female servants, your hired workers, and the temporary residents who live with you. 7Your livestock and the wild animals in your land will also be allowed to eat what the land produces.

The Year of Jubilee

LEVITICUS 25:8-22

"In addition, you must count off seven Sabbath years, seven sets of seven years, adding up to forty-nine years in all. 9Then on the Day of Atonement in the fiftieth year,* blow the ram's horn loud and long throughout the land. 10Set this year apart as holy, a time to proclaim freedom throughout the land for all who live there. It will be a jubilee year for you, when each of you may return to the land that belonged to your ancestors and return to your own clan. 11This fiftieth year will be a jubilee for you. During that year you must not plant

Lv 24:3 Hebrew *in the Tent of Meeting, outside the inner curtain of the Testimony;* see note on 16:13. **Lv 24:5** Hebrew *2/10 of an ephah* [4.4 liters]. **Lv 24:11** Hebrew *the Name;* also in 24:16b. **Lv 25:9** Hebrew *on the tenth day of the seventh month, on the Day of Atonement;* see 23:27a and the note there.

Lev 24:14 This punishment for blasphemy (cursing God) seems extreme by modern standards. But it shows how seriously God expects us to take our relationship with him. Often we use his name in swearing, or we act as though he doesn't exist. We should be careful how we speak and act, treating God with reverence. Eventually he will have the last word.

Lev 24:17-22 This was a code for judges, not an endorsement of personal vengeance. In effect, it was saying that the punishment should fit the crime, but it should not go beyond.

Lev 25:1-7 The Sabbath year provided one year in seven for the fields to lay fallow (unplowed). This was good management of natural resources and reminded the people of God's control and provision for them.

Lev 25:8-17 The Year of Jubilee was meant to be celebrated every 50 years. It included canceling all debts, freeing all slaves, and returning to its original owners all land that had been sold. There is no indication in the Bible that the Year of Jubilee was ever carried

your fields or store away any of the crops that grow on their own, and don't gather the grapes from your unpruned vines. [12]It will be a jubilee year for you, and you must keep it holy. But you may eat whatever the land produces on its own. [13]In the Year of Jubilee each of you may return to the land that belonged to your ancestors.

[14]"When you make an agreement with your neighbor to buy or sell property, you must not take advantage of each other. [15]When you buy land from your neighbor, the price you pay must be based on the number of years since the last jubilee. The seller must set the price by taking into account the number of years remaining until the next Year of Jubilee. [16]The more years until the next jubilee, the higher the price; the fewer years, the lower the price. After all, the person selling the land is actually selling you a certain number of harvests. [17]Show your fear of God by not taking advantage of each other. I am the Lord your God.

[18]"If you want to live securely in the land, follow my decrees and obey my regulations. [19]Then the land will yield large crops, and you will eat your fill and live securely in it. [20]But you might ask, 'What will we eat during the seventh year, since we are not allowed to plant or harvest crops that year?' [21]Be assured that I will send my blessing for you in the sixth year, so the land will produce a crop large enough for three years. [22]When you plant your fields in the eighth year, you will still be eating from the large crop of the sixth year. In fact, you will still be eating from that large crop when the new crop is harvested in the ninth year.

Redemption of Property

LEVITICUS 25:23-34

"The land must never be sold on a permanent basis, for the land belongs to me. You are only foreigners and tenant farmers working for me.

[24]"With every purchase of land you must grant the seller the right to buy it back. [25]If one of your fellow Israelites falls into poverty and is forced to sell some family land, then a close relative should buy it back for him. [26]If there is no close relative to buy the land, but the person who sold it gets enough money to buy it back, [27]he then has the right to redeem it from the one who bought it. The price of the land will be discounted according to the number of years until the next Year of Jubilee. In this way the original owner can then return to the land. [28]But if the original owner cannot afford to buy back the land, it will remain with the new owner until the next Year of Jubilee. In the jubilee year, the land must be returned to the original owners so they can return to their family land.

[29]"Anyone who sells a house inside a walled town has the right to buy it back for a full year after its sale. During that year, the seller retains the right to buy it back. [30]But if it is not bought back within a year, the sale of the house within the walled town cannot be reversed. It will become the permanent property of the buyer. It

THE FESTIVALS

Besides enjoying one Sabbath day of rest each week, the Israelites also enjoyed 19 days when national holidays were celebrated.

Festival	*What It Celebrated*	*Its Importance*
Passover One day (Lev 23:5)	When God spared the lives of Israel's firstborn children in Egypt and freed the Hebrews from slavery	Reminded the people of God's deliverance
Unleavened Bread Seven days (Lev 23:6-8)	The exodus from Egypt	Reminded the people they were leaving the old life behind and entering a new way of living
First Harvest One day (Lev 23:9-14)	The first crops of the barley harvest	Reminded the people how God provided for them
Harvest (Pentecost) One day (Lev 23:15-22)	The end of the barley harvest and beginning of the wheat harvest	Showed joy and thanksgiving over the bountiful harvest
Trumpets One day (Lev 23:23-25)	The beginning of the seventh month (civil new year)	Expressed joy and thanksgiving to God
Day of Atonement One day (Lev 23:26-32)	The removal of sin from the people and the nation	Restored fellowship with God
Shelters Seven days (Lev 23:33-43)	God's protection and guidance in the wilderness	Renewed Israel's commitment to God and trust in his guidance and protection

out. If Israel had followed this practice faithfully, they would have been a society without permanent poverty.

Lev 25:23 The people would one day possess land in Canaan, but in God's plan, only God's ownership was absolute. He wanted his people to avoid greed and materialism. If you have the attitude that you are taking care of the Lord's property, you will make what you have more available to others. This is difficult to do if you have an attitude of ownership. Think of yourself as a manager of all that is under your care, not as an owner.

▸ **LEVITICUS 25:23-34 *(cont.)***
will not be returned to the original owner in the Year
of Jubilee. 31 But a house in a village—a settlement without fortified walls—will be treated like property in the
countryside. Such a house may be bought back at any
time, and it must be returned to the original owner in
the Year of Jubilee.

32"The Levites always have the right to buy back
a house they have sold within the towns allotted to
them. 33 And any property that is sold by the Levites—
all houses within the Levitical towns—must be returned in the Year of Jubilee. After all, the houses in
the towns reserved for the Levites are the only property they own in all Israel. 34 The open pastureland
around the Levitical towns may never be sold. It is
their permanent possession.

Redemption of the Poor and Enslaved

LEVITICUS 25:35-55

"If one of your fellow Israelites falls into poverty and
cannot support himself, support him as you would a
foreigner or a temporary resident and allow him to live
with you. 36 Do not charge interest or make a profit at
his expense. Instead, show your fear of God by letting
him live with you as your relative. 37 Remember, do
not charge interest on money you lend him or make a
profit on food you sell him. 38 I am the LORD your God,
who brought you out of the land of Egypt to give you
the land of Canaan and to be your God.

39"If one of your fellow Israelites falls into poverty
and is forced to sell himself to you, do not treat him
as a slave. 40 Treat him instead as a hired worker or as
a temporary resident who lives with you, and he will
serve you only until the Year of Jubilee. 41 At that time
he and his children will no longer be obligated to you,
and they will return to their clans and go back to the
land originally allotted to their ancestors. 42 The people
of Israel are my servants, whom I brought out of the
land of Egypt, so they must never be sold as slaves.
43 Show your fear of God by not treating them harshly.

44"However, you may purchase male and female
slaves from among the nations around you. 45 You
may also purchase the children of temporary residents who live among you, including those who have
been born in your land. You may treat them as your
property, 46 passing them on to your children as a permanent inheritance. You may treat them as slaves, but
you must never treat your fellow Israelites this way.

47"Suppose a foreigner or temporary resident becomes rich while living among you. If any of your fellow
Israelites fall into poverty and are forced to sell themselves to such a foreigner or to a member of his family,
48 they still retain the right to be bought back, even after
they have been purchased. They may be bought back by
a brother, 49 an uncle, or a cousin. In fact, anyone from
the extended family may buy them back. They may also
redeem themselves if they have prospered. 50 They will
negotiate the price of their freedom with the person
who bought them. The price will be based on the number of years from the time they were sold until the next
Year of Jubilee—whatever it would cost to hire a worker
for that period of time. 51 If many years still remain
until the jubilee, they will repay the proper proportion
of what they received when they sold themselves. 52 If
only a few years remain until the Year of Jubilee, they
will repay a small amount for their redemption. 53 The
foreigner must treat them as workers hired on a yearly
basis. You must not allow a foreigner to treat any of
your fellow Israelites harshly. 54 If any Israelites have
not been bought back by the time the Year of Jubilee
arrives, they and their children must be set free at that
time. 55 For the people of Israel belong to me. They are
my servants, whom I brought out of the land of Egypt.
I am the LORD your God.

4. RECEIVING GOD'S BLESSING

The law was very clear about the consequences for obedience or disobedience to God's commands. Israel had every incentive to obey God's law, and they knew what would result if they chose to disobey.

Blessings for Obedience

LEVITICUS 26:1-13

"Do not make idols or set up carved images, or sacred
pillars, or sculptured stones in your land so you may
worship them. I am the LORD your God. 2 You must
keep my Sabbath days of rest and show reverence for
my sanctuary. I am the LORD.

3"If you follow my decrees and are careful to obey
my commands, 4 I will send you the seasonal rains.
The land will then yield its crops, and the trees of the

Lev 25:35ff The Bible places great emphasis on assisting the poor and helpless, especially orphans, widows, and the handicapped. In Israelite society, no paid work was available to women; thus, a widow and her children had no livelihood. Neither was there work available for the seriously handicapped in this nation of farmers and shepherds. The poor were to be helped without charging any interest. Individual and family responsibility for the poor was crucial since there was no government aid.

Lev 25:35-37 God said that neglecting the poor was a sin. Permanent poverty was not allowed in Israel. Financially secure families were responsible to help and house those in need. Many times we do nothing, not because we lack compassion, but because we are overwhelmed by the size of the problem and don't know where to begin. God doesn't expect you to eliminate poverty, nor does he expect you to neglect your family while providing for others. He does, however, expect that when you see an individual in need, you will reach out with whatever help you can offer, including hospitality.

Lev 25:44 Why did God allow the Israelites to purchase slaves? Under Hebrew laws, slaves were treated differently from slaves

field will produce their fruit. [5]Your threshing season will overlap with the grape harvest, and your grape harvest will overlap with the season of planting grain. You will eat your fill and live securely in your own land.

[6]"I will give you peace in the land, and you will be able to sleep with no cause for fear. I will rid the land of wild animals and keep your enemies out of your land. [7]In fact, you will chase down your enemies and slaughter them with your swords. [8]Five of you will chase a hundred, and a hundred of you will chase ten thousand! All your enemies will fall beneath your sword.

[9]"I will look favorably upon you, making you fertile and multiplying your people. And I will fulfill my covenant with you. [10]You will have such a surplus of crops that you will need to clear out the old grain to make room for the new harvest! [11]I will live among you, and I will not despise you. [12]I will walk among you; I will be your God, and you will be my people. [13]I am the LORD your God, who brought you out of the land of Egypt so you would no longer be their slaves. I broke the yoke of slavery from your neck so you can walk with your heads held high.

Punishments for Disobedience

LEVITICUS 26:14-46

"However, if you do not listen to me or obey all these commands, [15]and if you break my covenant by rejecting my decrees, treating my regulations with contempt, and refusing to obey my commands, [16]I will punish you. I will bring sudden terrors upon you—wasting diseases and burning fevers that will cause your eyes to fail and your life to ebb away. You will plant your crops in vain because your enemies will eat them. [17]I will turn against you, and you will be defeated by your enemies. Those who hate you will rule over you, and you will run even when no one is chasing you!

[18]"And if, in spite of all this, you still disobey me, I will punish you seven times over for your sins. [19]I will break your proud spirit by making the skies as unyielding as iron and the earth as hard as bronze. [20]All your work will be for nothing, for your land will yield no crops, and your trees will bear no fruit.

[21]"If even then you remain hostile toward me and refuse to obey me, I will inflict disaster on you seven times over for your sins. [22]I will send wild animals that will rob you of your children and destroy your livestock. Your numbers will dwindle, and your roads will be deserted.

[23]"And if you fail to learn the lesson and continue your hostility toward me, [24]then I myself will be hostile toward you. I will personally strike you with calamity seven times over for your sins. [25]I will send armies against you to carry out the curse of the covenant you have broken. When you run to your towns for safety, I will send a plague to destroy you there, and you will be handed over to your enemies. [26]I will destroy your food supply, so that ten women will need only one oven to bake bread for their families. They will ration your food by weight, and though you have food to eat, you will not be satisfied.

[27]"If in spite of all this you still refuse to listen and still remain hostile toward me, [28]then I will give full vent to my hostility. I myself will punish you seven times over for your sins. [29]Then you will eat the flesh of your own sons and daughters. [30]I will destroy your pagan shrines and knock down your places of worship. I will leave your lifeless corpses piled on top of your lifeless idols,* and I will despise you. [31]I will make your cities desolate and destroy your places of pagan worship. I will take no pleasure in your offerings that should be a pleasing aroma to me. [32]Yes, I myself will devastate your land, and your enemies who come to occupy it will be appalled at what they see. [33]I will scatter you among the nations and bring

Lv 26:30 The Hebrew term (literally *round things*) probably alludes to dung.

---

in other nations. They were seen as human beings with dignity, and not as animals. Hebrew slaves, for example, took part in the religious festivals and rested on the Sabbath. Nowhere does the Bible condone slavery, but it recognizes its existence. God's laws offered many guidelines for treating slaves properly.

Lev 26:1ff This chapter presents the two paths of obedience and disobedience that God set before the people (see also Deut 28). The people of the Old Testament were warned over and over against worshiping idols. We wonder how they could deceive themselves with these objects of wood and stone. Yet God could well give us the same warning, for we are prone to put idols before him. Idolatry is making anything more important than God, and our lives are full of that temptation. Money, looks, success, reputation, security—these are today's idols. As you look at these false gods that promise everything you want but nothing you need, does idolatry seem so far removed from your experience?

Lev 26:13 Imagine the joy of a slave set free. God took the children of Israel out of bitter slavery and gave them freedom and dignity. We, too, are set free when we accept Christ's payment that redeems us from sin's slavery. We no longer need to be bogged down in shame over our past sins; we can walk with dignity because God has forgiven us and forgotten them. But just as the Israelites were still in danger of returning to a slave mentality, we need to beware of the temptation to return to our former sinful patterns.

Lev 26:18 If the Israelites obeyed, there would be peace in the land. If they disobeyed, disaster would follow. God used sin's consequences to draw them to repentance, not to get back at them. Today, sin's consequences are not always so apparent. When calamity strikes us, we may not know the reason. It may be the result of our own disobedience, the result of someone else's sin, or the result of natural disaster. Because we don't know, we should search our hearts and be sure we are at peace with God. His Spirit, like a great searchlight, will reveal those areas we need to deal with. Because calamity is not always the result of wrongdoing, we must guard against assigning or accepting blame for every tragedy we encounter. Misplaced guilt is one of Satan's favorite weapons against believers.

Lev 26:33-35 In 2 Kings 17 and 25 the warning pronounced in these verses came true. The people persistently disobeyed, and eventually they were conquered and carried off to the lands of Assyria and Babylonia. The nation was held in captivity for 70 years, making up for all of the years that the Israelites did not observe the law of the Sabbath year (2 Chr 36:21).

▸ **LEVITICUS 26:14-46** ***(cont.)***

out my sword against you. Your land will become desolate, and your cities will lie in ruins. [34]Then at last the land will enjoy its neglected Sabbath years as it lies desolate while you are in exile in the land of your enemies. Then the land will finally rest and enjoy the Sabbaths it missed. [35]As long as the land lies in ruins, it will enjoy the rest you never allowed it to take every seventh year while you lived in it.

[36]"And for those of you who survive, I will demoralize you in the land of your enemies. You will live in such fear that the sound of a leaf driven by the wind will send you fleeing. You will run as though fleeing from a sword, and you will fall even when no one pursues you. [37]Though no one is chasing you, you will stumble over each other as though fleeing from a sword. You will have no power to stand up against your enemies. [38]You will die among the foreign nations and be devoured in the land of your enemies. [39]Those of you who survive will waste away in your enemies' lands because of their sins and the sins of their ancestors.

[40]"But at last my people will confess their sins and the sins of their ancestors for betraying me and being hostile toward me. [41]When I have turned their hostility back on them and brought them to the land of their enemies, then at last their stubborn hearts will be humbled, and they will pay for their sins. [42]Then I will remember my covenant with Jacob and my covenant with Isaac and my covenant with Abraham, and I will remember the land. [43]For the land must be abandoned to enjoy its years of Sabbath rest as it lies deserted. At last the people will pay for their sins, for they have continually rejected my regulations and despised my decrees.

[44]"But despite all this, I will not utterly reject or despise them while they are in exile in the land of their enemies. I will not cancel my covenant with them by wiping them out, for I am the LORD their God. [45]For their sakes I will remember my ancient covenant with their ancestors, whom I brought out of the land of Egypt in the sight of all the nations, that I might be their God. I am the LORD."

[46]These are the decrees, regulations, and instructions that the LORD gave through Moses on Mount Sinai as evidence of the relationship between himself and the Israelites.

Redemption of Gifts Offered to the LORD

LEVITICUS 27:1-34

The LORD said to Moses, [2]"Give the following instructions to the people of Israel. If anyone makes a special vow to dedicate someone to the LORD by paying the value of that person, [3]here is the scale of values to be used. A man between the ages of twenty and sixty is valued at fifty shekels* of silver, as measured by the sanctuary shekel. [4]A woman of that age is valued at thirty shekels* of silver. [5]A boy between the ages of five and twenty is valued at twenty shekels of silver; a girl of that age is valued at ten shekels* of silver. [6]A boy between the ages of one month and five years is valued at five shekels of silver; a girl of that age is valued at three shekels* of silver. [7]A man older than sixty is valued at fifteen shekels of silver; a woman of that age is valued at ten shekels* of silver. [8]If you desire to make such a vow but cannot afford to pay the required amount, take the person to the priest. He will determine the amount for you to pay based on what you can afford.

[9]"If your vow involves giving an animal that is acceptable as an offering to the LORD, any gift to the LORD will be considered holy. [10]You may not exchange or substitute it for another animal—neither a good animal for a bad one nor a bad animal for a good one. But if you do exchange one animal for another, then both the original animal and its substitute will be considered holy. [11]If your vow involves an unclean animal—one that is not acceptable as an offering to the LORD—then you must bring the animal to the priest. [12]He will assess its value, and his assessment will be

Lv 27:3 Or *20 ounces* [570 grams]. **Lv 27:4** Or *12 ounces* [342 grams]. **Lv 27:5** Or *A boy . . . 8 ounces* [228 grams] *of silver; a girl . . . 4 ounces* [114 grams]. **Lv 27:6** Or *A boy . . . 2 ounces* [57 grams] *of silver; a girl . . . 1.2 ounces* [34 grams]. **Lv 27:7** Or *A man . . . 6 ounces* [171 grams] *of silver; a woman . . . 4 ounces* [114 grams].

Lev 26:40-45 These verses show what God meant when he said he is slow to anger (Exod 34:6). Even if the Israelites chose to disobey and were scattered among their enemies, God would still give them the opportunity to repent and return to him. His purpose was not to destroy them, but to help them grow. Our day-to-day experiences and hardships are sometimes overwhelming; unless we can see that God's purpose is to bring about continual growth in us, we may despair. The hope we need is well expressed in Jeremiah 29:11-12: "'For I know the plans I have for you,' says the LORD. 'They are plans for good and not for disaster, to give you a future and a hope. In those days when you pray, I will listen.'" To retain hope while we suffer shows we understand God's merciful ways of relating to his people.

Lev 27:1ff The Israelites were required to give or dedicate certain things to the Lord and to his service: the first portion of their harvests, their firstborn animals, their firstborn sons, a tithe of their increase. Many wished to go beyond this and dedicate themselves or another family member, additional animals, a house, or a field to God. In these cases, it was possible to donate money instead of the actual person, animal, or property. Some people made rash or unrealistic vows. To urge them to think about it first, a 20-percent penalty was put on those items purchased back by money. This chapter explains how valuations were to be made and what to do if a donor later wished to buy back what had been donated to God.

Lev 27:3-7 This section reflects social rank in ancient Near Eastern cultures. An adult *man* of working age had the hightest rank, followed by an adult *woman* of working age. A *boy* ranked higher than a *girl*, and both ranked higher than toddlers. Senior citizens, who were past prime working age, ranked comparably to boys and girls

The amount of *fifthy shekels* would have represented about 20 ounces of silver, a significant amount. Comparisons with other literature of the time indicates that the

final, whether high or low. 13If you want to buy back
the animal, you must pay the value set by the priest,
plus 20 percent.

14"If someone dedicates a house to the LORD, the
priest will come to assess its value. The priest's assessment will be final, whether high or low. 15If the
person who dedicated the house wants to buy it back,
he must pay the value set by the priest, plus 20 percent. Then the house will again be his.

16"If someone dedicates to the LORD a piece of his
family property, its value will be assessed according to
the amount of seed required to plant it—fifty shekels
of silver for a field planted with five bushels of barley
seed.* 17If the field is dedicated to the LORD in the
Year of Jubilee, then the entire assessment will apply.
18But if the field is dedicated after the Year of Jubilee,
the priest will assess the land's value in proportion to
the number of years left until the next Year of Jubilee.
Its assessed value is reduced each year. 19If the person
who dedicated the field wants to buy it back, he must
pay the value set by the priest, plus 20 percent. Then
the field will again be legally his. 20But if he does not
want to buy it back, and it is sold to someone else, the
field can no longer be bought back. 21When the field
is released in the Year of Jubilee, it will be holy, a field
specially set apart* for the LORD. It will become the
property of the priests.

22"If someone dedicates to the LORD a field he
has purchased but which is not part of his family
property, 23the priest will assess its value based on
the number of years left until the next Year of Jubilee.
On that day he must give the assessed value of the
land as a sacred donation to the LORD. 24In the Year
of Jubilee the field must be returned to the person
from whom he purchased it, the one who inherited
it as family property. 25(All the payments must be
measured by the weight of the sanctuary shekel,*
which equals twenty gerahs.)

26"You may not dedicate a firstborn animal to
the LORD, for the firstborn of your cattle, sheep, and
goats already belong to him. 27However, you may buy
back the firstborn of a ceremonially unclean animal
by paying the priest's assessment of its worth, plus
20 percent. If you do not buy it back, the priest will
sell it at its assessed value.

28"However, anything specially set apart for
the LORD—whether a person, an animal, or family
property—must never be sold or bought back. Anything devoted in this way has been set apart as holy,
and it belongs to the LORD. 29No person specially
set apart for destruction may be bought back. Such
a person must be put to death.

30"One-tenth of the produce of the land, whether
grain from the fields or fruit from the trees, belongs
to the LORD and must be set apart to him as holy. 31If
you want to buy back the LORD's tenth of the grain or
fruit, you must pay its value, plus 20 percent. 32Count
off every tenth animal from your herds and flocks
and set them apart for the LORD as holy. 33You may
not pick and choose between good and bad animals,
and you may not substitute one for another. But if you
do exchange one animal for another, then both the
original animal and its substitute will be considered
holy and cannot be bought back."

34These are the commands that the LORD gave
through Moses on Mount Sinai for the Israelites.

Lv 27:16 Hebrew *50 shekels* [20 ounces, or 570 grams] *of silver for a homer* [182 liters] *of barley seed.* **Lv 27:21** The Hebrew term used here refers to the complete consecration of things or people to the LORD, either by destroying them or by giving them as an offering; also in 27:28, 29. **Lv 27:25** Each shekel was about 0.4 ounces [11 grams] in weight.

biblical valuation is quite high and would have been out of reach for most people.

Lev 27:9-10 God taught the Israelites that when they made a vow to him, they must not go back on their promise even if it turned out to cost more than expected. (This applied to animals; humans could be redeemed or purchased back.) God takes our promises seriously. If you vow to give 10 percent of your income and suddenly some unexpected bills come along, your faithful stewardship will be costly. God still expects you to fulfill your vow even if it is difficult to do so.

Lev 27:14-25 Real estate could be given as a voluntary offering in much the same way that people today give property through a will or donate the proceeds from the sale of property to a church or Christian organization.

Lev 27:28-29 Things set apart (devoted) applies to personal property or persons placed under God's ban, such as captured plunder from idol worshipers or idols themselves. These were to be destroyed and could not be redeemed.

The context here is the war for the conquest of Canaan, when cities, animals, and people deemed holy to some other god were set apart to be destroyed.

Lev 27:30 *One-tenth* (the "tithe") of the harvest belonged to the Lord (Deut 14:22-26; cp. Lev 23:10-14). Members of the tribe of Levi, the priests and Levites, received no tribal lands. Accordingly, they were allotted one tenth of all produce from those who did own land (Num 18:21-29). This tithe was set aside every year (Deut 14:22) and was taken to the sanctuary; part of it was eaten there in a ritual meal (Deut 14:23-26). A second tithe was paid locally every third year to the local Levites and the poor (Deut 14:27-29; 26:12; contrast Amos 4:4). The Levites then paid a tithe of what they received to the Tabernacle priests (Num 18:26), who used it to support themselves and maintain the sanctuary.

Lev 27:33 Many of the principles regarding sacrifices and tithes were intended to encourage inward attitudes as well as outward actions. If a person gives grudgingly, he shows that he has a stingy heart. God wants us to be cheerful givers (2 Cor 9:7), who give with gratitude to him.

Lev 27:34 The book of Leviticus is filled with the commands God gave his people at the foot of Mount Sinai. From these commands we can learn much about God's nature and character. At first glance, Leviticus seems irrelevant to our high-tech world. But digging a little deeper, we realize that the book still speaks to us today—God has not changed, and his principles are for all times. As people and society change, we need constantly to search for ways to apply the principles of God's law to our present circumstances. God was the same in Leviticus as he is today and will be forever (Heb 13:8).

F. Preparing for the Journey to the Promised Land

At Mount Sinai, the Israelites received specific directions for their lifestyle in the new land God would give to them. The people were now prepared to continue their journey to the Promised Land, just over one year from when they were rescued from slavery in Egypt. Just as the Lord prepared the Israelites, he prepares us for our journey through life.

1. THE FIRST CENSUS OF THE NATION

Before the people set out from Sinai, they had a census to determine the size of their armies and organize themselves for the move to the Promised Land.

Registration of Israel's Troops

NUMBERS 1:1-54

A year after Israel's departure from Egypt, the LORD
spoke to Moses in the Tabernacle* in the wilderness of
Sinai. On the first day of the second month* of that year
he said, 2"From the whole community of Israel, record
the names of all the warriors by their clans and families.
List all the men 3twenty years old or older who are able to
go to war. You and Aaron must register the troops, 4and
you will be assisted by one family leader from each tribe.
5"These are the tribes and the names of the leaders
who will assist you:

Tribe	*Leader*
Reuben	Elizur son of Shedeur
6 Simeon	Shelumiel son of Zurishaddai
7 Judah	Nahshon son of Amminadab
8 Issachar	Nethanel son of Zuar
9 Zebulun	Eliab son of Helon
10 Ephraim son of Joseph	Elishama son of Ammihud
Manasseh son of Joseph	Gamaliel son of Pedahzur
11 Benjamin	Abidan son of Gideoni
12 Dan	Ahiezer son of Ammishaddai
13 Asher	Pagiel son of Ocran
14 Gad	Eliasaph son of Deuel
15 Naphtali	Ahira son of Enan

16These are the chosen leaders of the community, the
leaders of their ancestral tribes, the heads of the clans
of Israel."
17So Moses and Aaron called together these chosen
leaders, 18and they assembled the whole community
of Israel on that very day.* All the people were registered according to their ancestry by their clans and
families. The men of Israel who were twenty years old
or older were listed one by one, 19just as the LORD had
commanded Moses. So Moses recorded their names
in the wilderness of Sinai.
20-21This is the number of men twenty years old or
older who were able to go to war, as their names were
listed in the records of their clans and families*:

Tribe	*Number*
Reuben (Jacob's* oldest son)	46,500
22-23 Simeon	59,300
24-25 Gad	45,650
26-27 Judah	74,600
28-29 Issachar	54,400
30-31 Zebulun	57,400
32-33 Ephraim son of Joseph	40,500
34-35 Manasseh son of Joseph	32,200
36-37 Benjamin	35,400
38-39 Dan	62,700
40-41 Asher	41,500
42-43 Naphtali	53,400

Nm 1:1a Hebrew *the Tent of Meeting.* **Nm 1:1b** This day in the ancient Hebrew lunar calendar occurred in April or May. **Nm 1:18** Hebrew *on the first day of the second month;* see 1:1. **Nm 1:20-21a** In the Hebrew text, this sentence (*This is the number of men twenty years old or older who were able to go to war, as their names were listed in the records of their clans and families*) is repeated in 1:22, 24, 26, 28, 30, 32, 34, 36, 38, 40, 42. **Nm 1:20-21b** Hebrew *Israel's.* The names "Jacob" and "Israel" are often interchanged throughout the Old Testament, referring sometimes to the individual patriarch and sometimes to the nation.

Num 1:1 As the book of Numbers opens, the Israelites had been camped near Mount Sinai for more than a year. There they had received all the laws and regulations recorded in the book of Leviticus. They had been transformed into a new nation and equipped for their task. At this time, they were ready to move out and receive their land. In preparation, Moses and Aaron were told to number all the men who were able to serve in the army. This book is named for this census, or numbering, of the people.

Num 1:1 The Tabernacle contained the sanctuary (or Holy Place) in one part, and the Most Holy Place with the Ark in another part. These two parts were separated by a curtain. God revealed himself to Moses in the Most Holy Place. Exodus 33:7 mentions the "Tent of Meeting" as the place where Moses met with God before the Tabernacle was constructed. Many believe that the Tent of Meeting in Exodus served the same function as the Tabernacle described here.

Num 1:2-15 Taking a census was long and tedious, but it was an important task. The fighting men had to be counted to determine Israel's military strength before entering the Promised Land. In addition, the tribes had to be organized to determine the amount of land each would need, as well as to provide genealogical records. Without such a census, the task of conquering and organizing the Promised Land would have been more difficult. Whenever we are at a crossroads, it is important to take inventory of our resources. We will serve more effectively if, before plunging in, we set aside time to take a "census" of all we have—possessions, relationships, spiritual condition, time, goals.

Num 1:20-46 If there were 603,550 men, not counting the Levites or women and children, the total population must have numbered more than two million Israelites. How could such a large population have grown from Jacob's family of 70 who originally moved down to Egypt? The book of Exodus tells us that the Israelites who descended from Jacob's family "multiplied so greatly that they became extremely powerful and filled the land" (Exod 1:7). Because they remained in Egypt more than 400 years, they had plenty of time to grow into

44These were the men registered by Moses and Aaron
and the twelve leaders of Israel, all listed according
to their ancestral descent. 45They were registered by
families—all the men of Israel who were twenty years
old or older and able to go to war. 46The total number
was 603,550.
47But this total did not include the Levites. 48For the
LORD had said to Moses, 49"Do not include the tribe
of Levi in the registration; do not count them with
the rest of the Israelites. 50Put the Levites in charge
of the Tabernacle of the Covenant,* along with all its
furnishings and equipment. They must carry the Tabernacle and all its furnishings as you travel, and they
must take care of it and camp around it. 51Whenever
it is time for the Tabernacle to move, the Levites will
take it down. And when it is time to stop, they will set
it up again. But any unauthorized person who goes
too near the Tabernacle must be put to death. 52Each
tribe of Israel will camp in a designated area with its
own family banner. 53But the Levites will camp around
the Tabernacle of the Covenant to protect the community of Israel from the LORD's anger. The Levites are
responsible to stand guard around the Tabernacle."
54So the Israelites did everything just as the LORD
had commanded Moses.

Organization for Israel's Camp

NUMBERS 2:1-34

Then the LORD gave these instructions to Moses and
Aaron: 2"When the Israelites set up camp, each tribe
will be assigned its own area. The tribal divisions will
camp beneath their family banners on all four sides of
the Tabernacle,* but at some distance from it.
3-4"The divisions of Judah, Issachar, and Zebulun
are to camp toward the sunrise on the east side of the
Tabernacle, beneath their family banners. These are
the names of the tribes, their leaders, and the numbers
of their registered troops:

Tribe	*Leader*	*Number*
Judah	Nahshon son of Amminadab	74,600
5-6 Issachar	Nethanel son of Zuar	54,400
7-8 Zebulun	Eliab son of Helon	57,400

9So the total of all the troops on Judah's side of the
camp is 186,400. These three tribes are to lead the
way whenever the Israelites travel to a new campsite.
10-11"The divisions of Reuben, Simeon, and Gad are
to camp on the south side of the Tabernacle, beneath
their family banners. These are the names of the tribes,
their leaders, and the numbers of their registered troops:

Tribe	*Leader*	*Number*
Reuben	Elizur son of Shedeur	46,500
12-13 Simeon	Shelumiel son of Zurishaddai	59,300
14-15 Gad	Eliasaph son of Deuel*	45,650

16So the total of all the troops on Reuben's side of the
camp is 151,450. These three tribes will be second in
line whenever the Israelites travel.

Nm 1:50 Or *Tabernacle of the Testimony;* also in 1:53. **Nm 2:2** Hebrew *the Tent of Meeting;* also in 2:17. **Nm 2:14-15** As in many Hebrew manuscripts, Samaritan Pentateuch, and Latin Vulgate (see also 1:14); most Hebrew manuscripts read *son of Reuel.*

ARRANGEMENT OF THE TRIBES AROUND THE TABERNACLE WHILE IN THE WILDERNESS

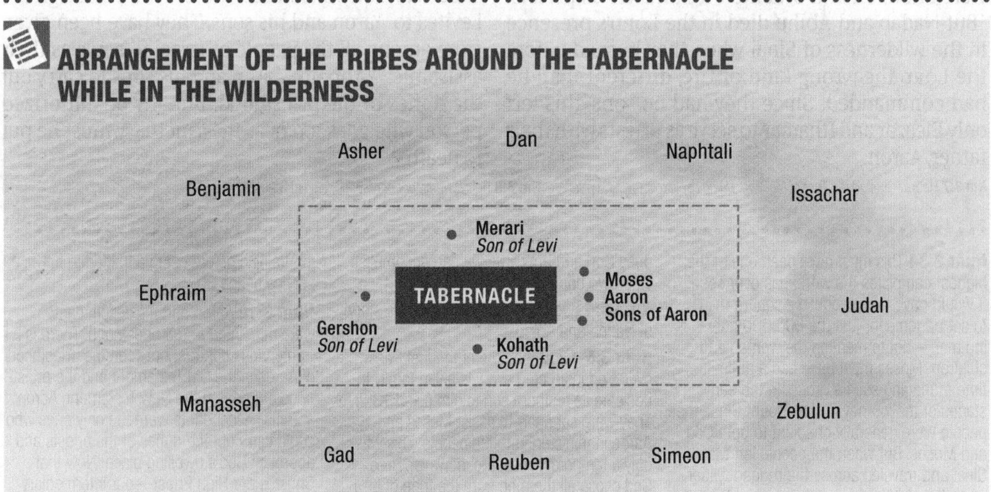

a large group of people. After leaving Egypt, they were able to survive in the wilderness because God miraculously provided the food and water they needed. The leaders of Moab were terrified because of the large number of Israelites (Num 22:3).

Num 2:2 The nation of Israel was organized according to tribes for several reasons. (1) It was an effective way to manage and govern a large group. (2) It made dividing the Promised Land easier. (3) It was part of their culture and heritage (people were not known by a last name, but by their family, clan, and tribe). (4) It was easier to keep detailed genealogies, which was the only way to prove membership in God's chosen nation. (5) It made travel much more efficient. The people followed the tribe's standard (a kind of flag) and thus stayed together and kept from getting lost.

▸ **NUMBERS 2:1-34 *(cont.)***

17"Then the Tabernacle, carried by the Levites, will set out from the middle of the camp. All the tribes are to travel in the same order that they camp, each in position under the appropriate family banner.

18-19"The divisions of Ephraim, Manasseh, and Benjamin are to camp on the west side of the Tabernacle, beneath their family banners. These are the names of the tribes, their leaders, and the numbers of their registered troops:

Tribe	*Leader*	*Number*
Ephraim	Elishama son of Ammihud	40,500
20-21 Manasseh	Gamaliel son of Pedahzur	32,200
22-23 Benjamin	Abidan son of Gideoni	35,400

24So the total of all the troops on Ephraim's side of the camp is 108,100. These three tribes will be third in line whenever the Israelites travel.

25-26"The divisions of Dan, Asher, and Naphtali are to camp on the north side of the Tabernacle, beneath their family banners. These are the names of the tribes, their leaders, and the numbers of their registered troops:

Tribe	*Leader*	*Number*
Dan	Ahiezer son of Ammishaddai	62,700
27-28 Asher	Pagiel son of Ocran	41,500
29-30 Naphtali	Ahira son of Enan	53,400

31So the total of all the troops on Dan's side of the camp is 157,600. These three tribes will be last, marching under their banners whenever the Israelites travel."

32In summary, the troops of Israel listed by their families totaled 603,550. 33But as the LORD had commanded, the Levites were not included in this registration. 34So the people of Israel did everything as the LORD had commanded Moses. Each clan and family set up camp and marched under their banners exactly as the LORD had instructed them.

2. THE ROLE OF THE LEVITES

The Levites were a special tribe in Israel, set apart for service to God and his people. The priests came from this tribe, but not all Levites were priests. Here God details the roles of the other Levites in the life of his people.

Levites Appointed for Service

NUMBERS 3:1-13

This is the family line of Aaron and Moses as it was
recorded when the LORD spoke to Moses on Mount
Sinai: 2The names of Aaron's sons were Nadab (the oldest), Abihu, Eleazar, and Ithamar. 3These sons of Aaron
were anointed and ordained to minister as priests.
4But Nadab and Abihu died in the LORD's presence
in the wilderness of Sinai when they burned before
the LORD the wrong kind of fire, different than he
had commanded. Since they had no sons, this left
only Eleazar and Ithamar to serve as priests with their
father, Aaron.

5Then the LORD said to Moses, 6"Call forward the
tribe of Levi, and present them to Aaron the priest to
serve as his assistants. 7They will serve Aaron and the
whole community, performing their sacred duties in
and around the Tabernacle.* 8They will also maintain
all the furnishings of the sacred tent,* serving in the
Tabernacle on behalf of all the Israelites. 9Assign the
Levites to Aaron and his sons. They have been given
from among all the people of Israel to serve as their
assistants. 10Appoint Aaron and his sons to carry out
the duties of the priesthood. But any unauthorized
person who goes too near the sanctuary must be put
to death."

Nm 3:7 Hebrew *around the Tent of Meeting, doing service at the Tabernacle.* **Nm 3:8** Hebrew *the Tent of Meeting;* also in 3:25.

Num 2:34 This must have been one of the biggest campsites the world has ever seen! It would have taken about 12 square miles to set up tents for just the 600,000 fighting men—not to mention the women and children. Moses must have had a difficult time managing such a group. In the early stages of the journey and at Mount Sinai, the people were generally obedient to both God and Moses. But when the people left Mount Sinai and traveled across the rugged wilderness, they began to complain, grumble, and disobey. Soon problems erupted, and Moses could no longer effectively manage the Israelites. The books of Exodus, Leviticus, and Numbers present a striking contrast between how much we can accomplish when we obey God and how little we can accomplish when we don't.

Num 3:4 See Leviticus 10:1-2 for the story of Nadab and Abihu.

Num 3:5-13 At the time of the first Passover, God instructed every Israelite family to dedicate its firstborn son to him (Exod 13:2). They were set apart to assist Moses and Aaron in ministering to the people. This was only a temporary measure, however. Here God chose all the men from the tribe of Levi to replace the firstborn sons from every Israelite tribe (Num 3:40-51; 8:16). These men, called Levites, were set apart to care for the Tabernacle and minister to the people. All the priests had to belong to the tribe of Levi, but not all Levites were priests. The Levites were to be 25 years old before entering service. They probably received five years of on-the-job training before being admitted to full service at age 30.

Num 3:10 Aaron and his descendants were appointed to the priesthood. There is a tremendous contrast between the priesthood of Aaron in the Old Testament and the priesthood of Christ in the New Testament. Aaron and his descendants were the only ones who could carry out the duties of the priests and approach God's dwelling place. Now that Christ is our High Priest—our intermediary with God—anyone who follows him is also called a priest (1 Pet 2:5, 9). Now all Christians may come into God's presence without fear because God's own Son encourages his followers to do so. We can put guilt behind us and experience forgiveness when we have a special relationship with God based on what Christ has done for us.

11 And the LORD said to Moses, 12 "Look, I have chosen the Levites from among the Israelites to serve as substitutes for all the firstborn sons of the people of Israel. The Levites belong to me, 13 for all the firstborn males are mine. On the day I struck down all the firstborn sons of the Egyptians, I set apart for myself all the firstborn in Israel, both of people and of animals. They are mine; I am the LORD."

Registration of the Levites

NUMBERS 3:14-39

The LORD spoke again to Moses in the wilderness of Sinai. He said, 15 "Record the names of the members of the tribe of Levi by their families and clans. List every male who is one month old or older." 16 So Moses listed them, just as the LORD had commanded.

17 Levi had three sons, whose names were Gershon, Kohath, and Merari.
18 The clans descended from Gershon were named after two of his descendants, Libni and Shimei.
19 The clans descended from Kohath were named after four of his descendants, Amram, Izhar, Hebron, and Uzziel.
20 The clans descended from Merari were named after two of his descendants, Mahli and Mushi.

These were the Levite clans, listed according to their family groups.

21 The descendants of Gershon were composed of the clans descended from Libni and Shimei. 22 There were 7,500 males one month old or older among these Gershonite clans. 23 They were assigned the area to the west of the Tabernacle for their camp. 24 The leader of the Gershonite clans was Eliasaph son of Lael. 25 These two clans were responsible to care for the Tabernacle, including the sacred tent with its layers of coverings, the curtain at its entrance, 26 the curtains of the courtyard that surrounded the Tabernacle and altar, the curtain at the courtyard entrance, the ropes, and all the equipment related to their use.

27 The descendants of Kohath were composed of the clans descended from Amram, Izhar, Hebron, and Uzziel. 28 There were 8,600* males one month old or older among these Kohathite clans. They were responsible for the care of the sanctuary, 29 and they were assigned the area south of the Tabernacle for their camp. 30 The leader of the Kohathite clans was Elizaphan son of Uzziel. 31 These four clans were responsible for the care of the Ark, the table, the lampstand, the altars, the various articles used in the sanctuary, the inner curtain, and all the equipment related to their use. 32 Eleazar, son of Aaron the priest, was the chief administrator over all the Levites, with special responsibility for the oversight of the sanctuary.

33 The descendants of Merari were composed of the clans descended from Mahli and Mushi. 34 There were 6,200 males one month old or older among these Merarite clans. 35 They were assigned the area north of the Tabernacle for their camp. The leader of the Merarite clans was Zuriel son of Abihail. 36 These two clans were responsible for the care of the frames supporting the Tabernacle, the crossbars, the pillars, the bases, and all the equipment related to their use. 37 They were also responsible for the posts of the courtyard and all their bases, pegs, and ropes.

38 The area in front of the Tabernacle, in the east toward the sunrise,* was reserved for the tents of Moses and of Aaron and his sons, who had the final responsibility for the sanctuary on behalf of the people of Israel. Anyone other than a priest or Levite who went too near the sanctuary was to be put to death.

39 When Moses and Aaron counted the Levite clans at the LORD's command, the total number was 22,000 males one month old or older.

Redeeming the Firstborn Sons

NUMBERS 3:40-51

Then the LORD said to Moses, "Now count all the firstborn sons in Israel who are one month old or older, and make a list of their names. 41 The Levites must be reserved for me as substitutes for the firstborn sons of Israel; I am the LORD. And the Levites' livestock must be reserved for me as substitutes for the firstborn livestock of the whole nation of Israel."

42 So Moses counted the firstborn sons of the people of Israel, just as the LORD had commanded. 43 The number of firstborn sons who were one month old or older was 22,273.

44 Then the LORD said to Moses, 45 "Take the Levites as substitutes for the firstborn sons of the people of Israel. And take the livestock of the Levites as substitutes for the firstborn livestock of the people of Israel. The Levites belong to me; I am the LORD. 46 There are 273 more firstborn sons of Israel than there are Levites. To redeem these extra firstborn sons, 47 collect five pieces of silver* for each of them (each piece weighing the same as the sanctuary shekel, which equals twenty gerahs). 48 Give the silver to Aaron and his sons as the redemption price for the extra firstborn sons."

49 So Moses collected the silver for redeeming the firstborn sons of Israel who exceeded the number of Levites. 50 He collected 1,365 pieces of silver* on behalf of these firstborn sons of Israel (each piece weighing the same as the sanctuary shekel). 51 And Moses gave the silver for the redemption to Aaron and his sons, just as the LORD had commanded.

Nm 3:28 Some Greek manuscripts read *8,300;* see total in 3:39. **Nm 3:38** Hebrew *toward the sunrise, in front of the Tent of Meeting.* **Nm 3:47** Hebrew *5 shekels* [2 ounces or 57 grams]. **Nm 3:50** Hebrew *1,365 shekels* [34 pounds or 15.5 kilograms].

Duties of the Kohathite Clan

NUMBERS 4:1-20

Then the LORD said to Moses and Aaron, 2"Record the names of the members of the clans and families of the Kohathite division of the tribe of Levi. 3List all the men between the ages of thirty and fifty who are eligible to serve in the Tabernacle.*

4"The duties of the Kohathites at the Tabernacle will relate to the most sacred objects. 5When the camp moves, Aaron and his sons must enter the Tabernacle first to take down the inner curtain and cover the Ark of the Covenant* with it. 6Then they must cover the inner curtain with fine goatskin leather and spread over that a single piece of blue cloth. Finally, they must put the carrying poles of the Ark in place.

7"Next they must spread a blue cloth over the table where the Bread of the Presence is displayed, and on the cloth they will place the bowls, pans, jars, pitchers, and the special bread. 8They must spread a scarlet cloth over all of this, and finally a covering of fine goatskin leather on top of the scarlet cloth. Then they must insert the carrying poles into the table.

9"Next they must cover the lampstand with a blue cloth, along with its lamps, lamp snuffers, trays, and special jars of olive oil. 10Then they must cover the lampstand and its accessories with fine goatskin leather and place the bundle on a carrying frame.

11"Next they must spread a blue cloth over the gold incense altar and cover this cloth with fine goatskin leather. Then they must attach the carrying poles to the altar. 12They must take all the remaining furnishings of the sanctuary and wrap them in a blue cloth, cover them with fine goatskin leather, and place them on the carrying frame.

13"They must remove the ashes from the altar for sacrifices and cover the altar with a purple cloth. 14All the altar utensils—the firepans, meat forks, shovels, basins, and all the containers—must be placed on the cloth, and a covering of fine goatskin leather must be spread over them. Finally, they must put the carrying poles in place. 15The camp will be ready to move when Aaron and his sons have finished covering the sanctuary and all the sacred articles. The Kohathites will come and carry these things to the next destination. But they must not touch the sacred objects, or they will die. So these are the things from the Tabernacle that the Kohathites must carry.

16"Eleazar son of Aaron the priest will be responsible for the oil of the lampstand, the fragrant incense, the daily grain offering, and the anointing oil. In fact, Eleazar will be responsible for the entire Tabernacle and everything in it, including the sanctuary and its furnishings."

17Then the LORD said to Moses and Aaron, 18"Do not let the Kohathite clans be destroyed from among the Levites! 19This is what you must do so they will live and not die when they approach the most sacred objects. Aaron and his sons must always go in with them and assign a specific duty or load to each person. 20The Kohathites must never enter the sanctuary to look at the sacred objects for even a moment, or they will die."

Duties of the Gershonite Clan

NUMBERS 4:21-28

And the LORD said to Moses, 22"Record the names of the members of the clans and families of the Gershonite division of the tribe of Levi. 23List all the men between the ages of thirty and fifty who are eligible to serve in the Tabernacle.

24"These Gershonite clans will be responsible for general service and carrying loads. 25They must carry the curtains of the Tabernacle, the Tabernacle itself with its coverings, the outer covering of fine goatskin leather, and the curtain for the Tabernacle entrance. 26They are also to carry the curtains for the courtyard walls that surround the Tabernacle and altar, the curtain across the courtyard entrance, the ropes, and all the equipment related to their use. The Gershonites are responsible for all these items. 27Aaron and his sons will direct the Gershonites regarding all their duties, whether it involves moving the equipment or doing other work. They must assign the Gershonites responsibility for the loads they are to carry. 28So these are the duties assigned to the Gershonite clans at the Tabernacle. They will be directly responsible to Ithamar son of Aaron the priest.

Duties of the Merarite Clan

NUMBERS 4:29-33

"Now record the names of the members of the clans and families of the Merarite division of the tribe of Levi. 30List all the men between the ages of thirty and fifty who are eligible to serve in the Tabernacle.

31"Their only duty at the Tabernacle will be to carry loads. They will carry the frames of the Tabernacle, the crossbars, the posts, and the bases; 32also the posts for

Nm 4:3 Hebrew *the Tent of Meeting;* also in 4:4, 15, 23, 25, 28, 30, 31, 33, 35, 37, 39, 41, 43, 47. **Nm 4:5** Or *Ark of the Testimony.*

Num 4:2ff The Kohathites, Gershonites (Num 4:21), and Merarites (Num 4:29) were families of Levites who were assigned special tasks in Israel's worship. For the jobs described in this chapter, a Levite had to be between 30 and 50 years old. He was expected to carry out his duties as described here in every detail. In fact, failure to do so would mean death (Num 4:20). This contrasted greatly from the religious practices of the Egyptians, who could purchase amulets and potions. Their idols could be handled. The God of the Hebrews was not to be handled or reduced to common elements. He is greater than anything in his creation. Worshiping our holy God must not be taken lightly.

Num 4:27-28 The Gershonites could receive directions from any of Aaron's sons, but they were directly responsible to Ithamar only. The lines of authority and accountability were clearly communicated to all. As you function with others in service to God, make sure the lines of authority between you and those you work with are clearly understood. Good communication builds good relationships.

the courtyard walls with their bases, pegs, and ropes; and all the accessories and everything else related to their use. Assign the various loads to each man by name. [33]So these are the duties of the Merarite clans at the Tabernacle. They are directly responsible to Ithamar son of Aaron the priest."

Summary of the Registration

NUMBERS 4:34-49

So Moses, Aaron, and the other leaders of the community listed the members of the Kohathite division by their clans and families. [35]The list included all the men between thirty and fifty years of age who were eligible for service in the Tabernacle, [36]and the total number came to 2,750. [37]So this was the total of all those from the Kohathite clans who were eligible to serve at the Tabernacle. Moses and Aaron listed them, just as the LORD had commanded through Moses.

[38]The Gershonite division was also listed by its clans and families. [39]The list included all the men between thirty and fifty years of age who were eligible for service in the Tabernacle, [40]and the total number came to 2,630. [41]So this was the total of all those from the Gershonite clans who were eligible to serve at the Tabernacle. Moses and Aaron listed them, just as the LORD had commanded.

[42]The Merarite division was also listed by its clans and families. [43]The list included all the men between thirty and fifty years of age who were eligible for service in the Tabernacle, [44]and the total number came to 3,200. [45]So this was the total of all those from the Merarite clans who were eligible for service. Moses and Aaron listed them, just as the LORD had commanded through Moses.

[46]So Moses, Aaron, and the leaders of Israel listed all the Levites by their clans and families. [47]All the men between thirty and fifty years of age who were eligible for service in the Tabernacle and for its transportation [48]numbered 8,580. [49]When their names were recorded, as the LORD had commanded through Moses, each man was assigned his task and told what to carry.

And so the registration was completed, just as the LORD had commanded Moses.

3. THE PURITY OF THE CAMP

It was absolutely vital that God's people remain pure so that they could represent him well to the world. This meant that they needed to deal with sin and maintain God's standards within their camp, which essentially represented their borders while they were traveling through the wilderness.

Purity in Israel's Camp

NUMBERS 5:1-10

The LORD gave these instructions to Moses: [2]"Command the people of Israel to remove from the camp anyone who has a skin disease* or a discharge, or who has become ceremonially unclean by touching a dead person. [3]This command applies to men and women alike. Remove them so they will not defile the camp in which I live among them." [4]So the Israelites did as the LORD had commanded Moses and removed such people from the camp.

[5]Then the LORD said to Moses, [6]"Give the following instructions to the people of Israel: If any of the people—men or women—betray the LORD by doing wrong to another person, they are guilty. [7]They must confess their sin and make full restitution for what they have done, adding an additional 20 percent and returning it to the person who was wronged. [8]But if the person who was wronged is dead, and there are no near relatives to whom restitution can be made, the payment belongs to the LORD and must be given to the priest. Those who are guilty must also bring a ram as a sacrifice, and they will be purified and made right with the LORD.* [9]All the sacred offerings that the Israelites bring to a priest will belong to him. [10]Each priest may keep all the sacred donations that he receives."

Protecting Marital Faithfulness

NUMBERS 5:11-31

And the LORD said to Moses, [12]"Give the following instructions to the people of Israel.

"Suppose a man's wife goes astray, and she is unfaithful to her husband [13]and has sex with another man, but neither her husband nor anyone else knows about it. She has defiled herself, even though there was no witness and she was not caught in the act. [14]If

Nm 5:2 Traditionally rendered *leprosy.* The Hebrew word used here describes various skin diseases. **Nm 5:8** Or *bring a ram for atonement, which will make atonement for them.*

Num 5:5-8 God included restitution, a unique concept for that day, as part of his law for Israel. When someone was robbed, the guilty person was required to restore the loss to the victim and pay an additional interest penalty. When we have wronged others, we ought to do more than apologize. We should look for ways to set matters right and, if possible, leave the victim even better off than before. When we have been wronged, we should seek restoration rather than striking out in revenge.

Num 5:11-31 This test for adultery served to remove a jealous husband's suspicion. Trust between husband and wife had to be completely eroded for a man to bring his wife to the priest for this type of test. Today priests and pastors help restore marriages by counseling couples who have lost faith in each other. Men and women should strengthen the bond of trust in marriage. Flirtatious and intimate communication with someone you're not married to can build suspicion and weaken trust. Guard your heart and guard your marriage in order to maintain trust and strengthen your bond with your spouse.

▸ NUMBERS 5:11-31 *(cont.)*

her husband becomes jealous and is suspicious of his wife and needs to know whether or not she has defiled herself, [15]the husband must bring his wife to the priest. He must also bring an offering of two quarts* of barley flour to be presented on her behalf. Do not mix it with olive oil or frankincense, for it is a jealousy offering—an offering to prove whether or not she is guilty.

[16]"The priest will then present her to stand trial before the LORD. [17]He must take some holy water in a clay jar and pour into it dust he has taken from the Tabernacle floor. [18]When the priest has presented the woman before the LORD, he must unbind her hair and place in her hands the offering of proof—the jealousy offering to determine whether her husband's suspicions are justified. The priest will stand before her, holding the jar of bitter water that brings a curse to those who are guilty. [19]The priest will then put the woman under oath and say to her, 'If no other man has had sex with you, and you have not gone astray and defiled yourself while under your husband's authority, may you be immune from the effects of this bitter water that brings on the curse. [20]But if you have gone astray by being unfaithful to your husband, and have defiled yourself by having sex with another man—'

[21]"At this point the priest must put the woman under oath by saying, 'May the people know that the LORD's curse is upon you when he makes you infertile, causing your womb to shrivel* and your abdomen to swell. [22]Now may this water that brings the curse enter your body and cause your abdomen to swell and your womb to shrivel.*' And the woman will be required to say, 'Yes, let it be so.' [23]And the priest will write these curses on a piece of leather and wash them off into the bitter water. [24]He will make the woman drink the bitter water that brings on the curse. When the water enters her body, it will cause bitter suffering if she is guilty.

[25]"The priest will take the jealousy offering from the woman's hand, lift it up before the LORD, and carry it to the altar. [26]He will take a handful of the flour as a token portion and burn it on the altar, and he will require the woman to drink the water. [27]If she has defiled herself by being unfaithful to her husband, the water that brings on the curse will cause bitter suffering. Her abdomen will swell and her womb will shrink,* and her name will become a curse among her people. [28]But if she has not defiled herself and is pure, then she will be unharmed and will still be able to have children.

[29]"This is the ritual law for dealing with suspicion. If a woman goes astray and defiles herself while under her husband's authority, [30]or if a man becomes jealous and is suspicious that his wife has been unfaithful, the husband must present his wife before the LORD, and the priest will apply this entire ritual law to her. [31]The husband will be innocent of any guilt in this matter, but his wife will be held accountable for her sin."

Nazirite Laws

NUMBERS 6:1-21

Then the LORD said to Moses, [2]"Give the following instructions to the people of Israel.

"If any of the people, either men or women, take the special vow of a Nazirite, setting themselves apart to the LORD in a special way, [3]they must give up wine and other alcoholic drinks. They must not use vinegar made from wine or from other alcoholic drinks, they must not drink fresh grape juice, and they must not eat grapes or raisins. [4]As long as they are bound by their Nazirite vow, they are not allowed to eat or drink anything that comes from a grapevine—not even the grape seeds or skins.

[5]"They must never cut their hair throughout the time of their vow, for they are holy and set apart to the LORD. Until the time of their vow has been fulfilled, they must let their hair grow long. [6]And they must not go near a dead body during the entire period of their vow to the LORD. [7]Even if the dead person is their own father, mother, brother, or sister, they must not defile themselves, for the hair on their head is the symbol of their separation to God. [8]This requirement applies as long as they are set apart to the LORD.

[9]"If someone falls dead beside them, the hair they have dedicated will be defiled. They must wait for seven days and then shave their heads. Then they will be cleansed from their defilement. [10]On the eighth day they must bring two turtledoves or two young pigeons to the priest at the entrance of the Tabernacle.* [11]The priest will offer one of the birds for a sin offering and the other for a burnt offering. In this way, he will purify them* from the guilt they incurred through contact with the dead body. Then they must reaffirm their commitment and let their hair begin to grow again. [12]The days of their vow that were completed before their defilement no longer count. They must rededicate themselves to the LORD as a Nazirite for the full term of their vow, and each must bring a one-year-old male lamb for a guilt offering.

Nm 5:15 Hebrew *1/10 of an ephah* [2.2 liters]. **Nm 5:21** Hebrew *when he causes your thigh to waste away.* **Nm 5:22** Hebrew *and your thigh to waste away.* **Nm 5:27** Hebrew *and her thigh will waste away.* **Nm 6:10** Hebrew *the Tent of Meeting;* also in 6:13, 18. **Nm 6:11** Or *make atonement for them.*

Num 6:1-2 In Moses' day, a personal vow was as binding as a written contract. It was one thing to say you would do something, but it was considered much more serious when you made a solemn vow to do it. God instituted the Nazirite vow for people who wanted to devote some time exclusively to serving him. This vow could be taken for as little as 30 days or as long as a lifetime. It was voluntary, with one exception—parents could take the vow for their young children, making them Nazirites for life. The vow included three distinct restrictions: (1) The person must abstain from wine and fermented drink; (2) the hair could not be cut, and the beard could not be shaved; (3) touching a dead body was prohibited. The purpose of the Nazirite vow was to raise up a group of leaders devoted completely to God. Samson, Samuel, and John the Baptist were probably Nazirites for life.

13"This is the ritual law for Nazirites. At the conclusion of their time of separation as Nazirites, they must
each go to the entrance of the Tabernacle 14and offer
their sacrifices to the LORD: a one-year-old male lamb
without defect for a burnt offering, a one-year-old
female lamb without defect for a sin offering, a ram
without defect for a peace offering, 15a basket of bread
made without yeast—cakes of choice flour mixed with
olive oil and wafers spread with olive oil—along with
their prescribed grain offerings and liquid offerings.
16The priest will present these offerings before the
LORD: first the sin offering and the burnt offering;
17then the ram for a peace offering, along with the
basket of bread made without yeast. The priest must
also present the prescribed grain offering and liquid
offering to the LORD.

18"Then the Nazirites will shave their heads at the
entrance of the Tabernacle. They will take the hair that
had been dedicated and place it on the fire beneath
the peace-offering sacrifice. 19After the Nazirite's
head has been shaved, the priest will take for each
of them the boiled shoulder of the ram, and he will
take from the basket a cake and a wafer made without
yeast. He will put them all into the Nazirite's hands.
20Then the priest will lift them up as a special offering
before the LORD. These are holy portions for the priest,
along with the breast of the special offering and the
thigh of the sacred offering that are lifted up before
the LORD. After this ceremony the Nazirites may again
drink wine.

21"This is the ritual law of the Nazirites, who vow
to bring these offerings to the LORD. They may also
bring additional offerings if they can afford it. And
they must be careful to do whatever they vowed when
they set themselves apart as Nazirites."

The Priestly Blessing

NUMBERS 6:22-27

Then the LORD said to Moses, 23"Tell Aaron and his
sons to bless the people of Israel with this special
blessing:

24 'May the LORD bless you
and protect you.
25 May the LORD smile on you
and be gracious to you.
26 May the LORD show you his favor
and give you his peace.'

27Whenever Aaron and his sons bless the people of
Israel in my name, I myself will bless them."

Num 6:24-26 A blessing was one way of asking for God's divine favor to rest upon others. The ancient blessing in these verses helps us understand what a blessing was supposed to do. Its five parts conveyed hope that God would (1) bless and protect them; (2) smile on them (be pleased); (3) be gracious (merciful and compassionate); (4) show his favor toward them (give his approval); (5) give peace. When you ask God to bless others or yourself, you are asking him to do these five things. The blessing you offer will not only help the one receiving it, but it will also demonstrate love, encourage others, and provide a model of caring for others.

"May the LORD bless you and protect you.
May the LORD smile on you and be gracious to you.
May the LORD show you his favor and give you his peace."
Numbers 6:24-26

G. The First Approach to the Promised Land

As the Israelites approached the Promised Land, Moses sent leaders to scout out the land and its people. But the scouts returned with a discouraging report—"It is indeed a bountiful country. . . . But the people living there are powerful. . . . We can't go up against them!" Although Joshua and Caleb disagreed, the Israelites had already made up their minds and began to complain. As punishment for their lack of faith, God condemned them to wander in the wilderness for 40 years. Our obedience must be complete and timely.

1. THE PEOPLE COMPLAIN

In spite of all the amazing things God had done for the people of Israel, they regularly complained to Moses about the difficulties they faced and rebelled against God's plan for them. Even Aaron and Miriam, Moses' siblings and fellow leaders of the nation, complained about his leadership. It is easy to overlook God's blessings and only see the things we wish were different.

The Israelites Leave Sinai

NUMBERS 10:11-36

In the second year after Israel's departure from
Egypt—on the twentieth day of the second month*—
the cloud lifted from the Tabernacle of the Covenant.*
12 So the Israelites set out from the wilderness of Sinai
and traveled on from place to place until the cloud
stopped in the wilderness of Paran.
13 When the people set out for the first time, following the instructions the LORD had given through Moses,
14 Judah's troops led the way. They marched behind their
banner, and their leader was Nahshon son of Amminadab. 15 They were joined by the troops of the tribe of
Issachar, led by Nethanel son of Zuar, 16 and the troops
of the tribe of Zebulun, led by Eliab son of Helon.
17 Then the Tabernacle was taken down, and the Gershonite and Merarite divisions of the Levites were next
in the line of march, carrying the Tabernacle with them.
18 Reuben's troops went next, marching behind their
banner. Their leader was Elizur son of Shedeur. 19 They
were joined by the troops of the tribe of Simeon, led by
Shelumiel son of Zurishaddai, 20 and the troops of the
tribe of Gad, led by Eliasaph son of Deuel.
21 Next came the Kohathite division of the Levites,
carrying the sacred objects from the Tabernacle. Before they arrived at the next camp, the Tabernacle
would already be set up at its new location. 22 Ephraim's troops went next, marching behind their banner.
Their leader was Elishama son of Ammihud. 23 They
were joined by the troops of the tribe of Manasseh,
led by Gamaliel son of Pedahzur, 24 and the troops of
the tribe of Benjamin, led by Abidan son of Gideoni.
25 Dan's troops went last, marching behind their
banner and serving as the rear guard for all the tribal
camps. Their leader was Ahiezer son of Ammishaddai.
26 They were joined by the troops of the tribe of Asher,
led by Pagiel son of Ocran, 27 and the troops of the tribe
of Naphtali, led by Ahira son of Enan.
28 This was the order in which the Israelites
marched, division by division.
29 One day Moses said to his brother-in-law, Hobab
son of Reuel the Midianite, "We are on our way to the

Nm 10:11a This day in the ancient Hebrew lunar calendar occurred in late April, May, or early June. **Nm 10:11b** Or *Tabernacle of the Testimony.*

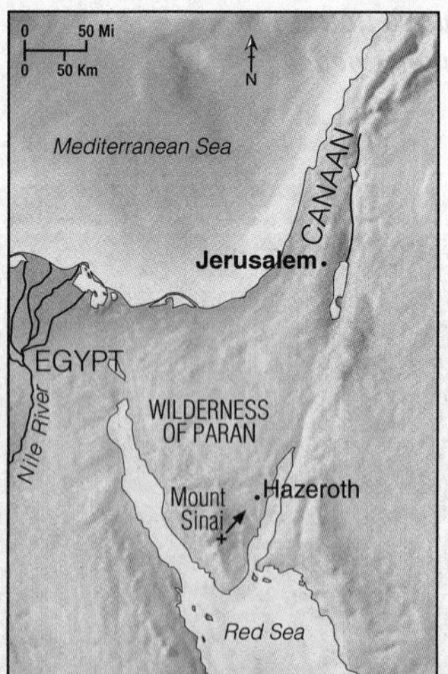

◀ ***ISRAEL'S DEPARTURE FROM SINAI***
Two years have passed since Israel left Egypt. Having received God's travel instructions through Moses, Israel set out from Mount Sinai into the wilderness of Paran on their way toward the Promised Land.

Num 10:21 Those who travel, move, or face new challenges know what it is to be uprooted. Life is full of changes, and few things remain stable. The Israelites were constantly moving through the wilderness. They were able to handle change only because God's presence in the Tabernacle was always with them. The portable Tabernacle signified God and his people moving together. For us, stability does not mean lack of change; it means moving with God in every circumstance.

Num 10:29-32 By complimenting Hobab's wilderness skills, Moses let him know he was needed. People cannot know you appreciate them if you do not tell them they are important to you. Complimenting those who deserve it builds lasting relationships and helps people know they are valued. Think about those who have helped you this month. What can you do to let them know how much you need and appreciate them?

Num 11:1, 6-15 The Israelites complained, and then Moses complained. But God responded positively to Moses and negatively to the rest of the people. Why? The people complained to one another, and nothing was accomplished. Moses took his complaint to God, who could solve any problem. Many of us are good at complaining to each other. We need to learn to take our problems to the One who can do something about them.

place the LORD promised us, for he said, 'I will give it
to you.' Come with us and we will treat you well, for
the LORD has promised wonderful blessings for Israel!"
30 But Hobab replied, "No, I will not go. I must return
to my own land and family."
31 "Please don't leave us," Moses pleaded. "You know
the places in the wilderness where we should camp.
Come, be our guide. 32 If you do, we'll share with you
all the blessings the LORD gives us."
33 They marched for three days after leaving the
mountain of the LORD, with the Ark of the LORD's Covenant moving ahead of them to show them where to
stop and rest. 34 As they moved on each day, the cloud
of the LORD hovered over them. 35 And whenever the
Ark set out, Moses would shout, "Arise, O LORD, and
let your enemies be scattered! Let them flee before
you!" 36 And when the Ark was set down, he would say,
"Return, O LORD, to the countless thousands of Israel!"

The People Complain to Moses

NUMBERS 11:1-15

Soon the people began to complain about their hardship, and the LORD heard everything they said. Then
the LORD's anger blazed against them, and he sent a
fire to rage among them, and he destroyed some of the
people in the outskirts of the camp. 2 Then the people
screamed to Moses for help, and when he prayed to
the LORD, the fire stopped. 3 After that, the area was
known as Taberah (which means "the place of burning"), because fire from the LORD had burned among
them there.
4 Then the foreign rabble who were traveling with

ISRAEL'S COMPLAINING

Reference	Complaint	Sin	Result
Num 11:1	About their hardships	Complained about their problems instead of praying to God about them	Thousands of people were destroyed when God sent a plague of fire to punish them
Num 11:4	About the lack of meat	Lusted after things they didn't have	God sent quail; but as the people began to eat, God struck them with a plague that killed many
Num 14:1-4	About being stuck in the wilderness, facing the giants of the Promised Land, and wishing to return to Egypt	Openly rebelled against God's leaders and failed to trust in his promises	All who complained were not allowed to enter the Promised Land, being doomed to wander in the wilderness until they died
Num 16:3	About Moses' and Aaron's authority and leadership	Were greedy for more power and authority	The families, friends, and possessions of Korah, Dathan, and Abiram were swallowed up by the earth. Fire then burned up the 250 other men who rebelled
Num 16:41	That Moses and Aaron caused the deaths of Korah and his conspirators	Blamed others for their own troubles	God began to destroy Israel with a plague. Moses and Aaron made atonement for the people, but 14,700 of them were killed
Num 20:2-3	About the lack of water	Refused to believe that God would provide as he had promised	Moses sinned along with the people. For this he was barred from entering the Promised Land
Num 21:5	That God and Moses brought them into the wilderness to die	Failed to recognize that their problems were brought on by their own disobedience	God sent poisonous snakes that killed many people and seriously injured many others

Num 11:4 The "foreign rabble" refers to a mixed crowd of Egyptians and others who had followed Israel out of Egypt (Exod 12:38).

Num 11:4-6 Dissatisfaction comes when our attention shifts from what we have to what we don't have. The people of Israel didn't seem to notice what God was doing for them—setting them free, making them a nation, giving them a new land—because they were so wrapped up in what God wasn't doing for them. They could think of nothing but the delicious Egyptian food they had left behind. Somehow they forgot that the brutal whip of Egyptian slavery was the cost of eating that food. Before we judge the Israelites too harshly, it's helpful to think about what occupies our attention most of the time. Are we grateful for what God has given us, or are we always thinking about what we would like to have? We should not allow our unfulfilled desires to cause us to forget God's gifts of life, food, health, work, and friends.

Num 11:4-9 Every morning the Israelites drew back their tent doors and witnessed a miracle. Covering the ground was pale-yellow, fluffy manna—food from heaven. But soon that wasn't enough. Feeling it was their right to have more, they forgot what they already had. They didn't ask God to fill their need; instead, they demanded meat, and they stopped trusting God to care for them. "Give us meat to eat!" (Num 11:13) they demanded of Moses as they reminisced about the good food they had in Egypt. God gave them what they asked for, but they paid dearly for it when a plague struck the camp (see Num 11:18-20, 31-34). When you ask God for something, he may grant your request. But if you approach him with a sinful attitude, getting what you want may prove costly.

▶ **NUMBERS 11:1-15** ***(cont.)***

the Israelites began to crave the good things of Egypt. And the people of Israel also began to complain. "Oh, for some meat!" they exclaimed. 5"We remember the fish we used to eat for free in Egypt. And we had all the cucumbers, melons, leeks, onions, and garlic we wanted. 6But now our appetites are gone. All we ever see is this manna!"

7The manna looked like small coriander seeds, and it was pale yellow like gum resin. 8The people would go out and gather it from the ground. They made flour by grinding it with hand mills or pounding it in mortars. Then they boiled it in a pot and made it into flat cakes. These cakes tasted like pastries baked with olive oil. 9The manna came down on the camp with the dew during the night.

10Moses heard all the families standing in the doorways of their tents whining, and the LORD became extremely angry. Moses was also very aggravated. 11And Moses said to the LORD, "Why are you treating me, your servant, so harshly? Have mercy on me! What did I do to deserve the burden of all these people? 12Did I give birth to them? Did I bring them into the world? Why did you tell me to carry them in my arms like a mother carries a nursing baby? How can I carry them to the land you swore to give their ancestors? 13Where am I supposed to get meat for all these people? They keep whining to me, saying, 'Give us meat to eat!' 14I can't carry all these people by myself! The load is far too heavy! 15If this is how you intend to treat me, just go ahead and kill me. Do me a favor and spare me this misery!"

Moses Chooses Seventy Leaders

NUMBERS 11:16-30

Then the LORD said to Moses, "Gather before me seventy men who are recognized as elders and leaders of Israel. Bring them to the Tabernacle* to stand there with you. 17I will come down and talk to you there. I will take some of the Spirit that is upon you, and I will put the Spirit upon them also. They will bear the burden of the people along with you, so you will not have to carry it alone.

18"And say to the people, 'Purify yourselves, for tomorrow you will have meat to eat. You were whining, and the LORD heard you when you cried, "Oh, for some meat! We were better off in Egypt!" Now the LORD will give you meat, and you will have to eat it. 19And it won't be for just a day or two, or for five or ten or even twenty. 20You will eat it for a whole month until you gag and are sick of it. For you have rejected the LORD, who is here among you, and you have whined to him, saying, "Why did we ever leave Egypt?"'"

21But Moses responded to the LORD, "There are 600,000 foot soldiers here with me, and yet you say, 'I will give them meat for a whole month!' 22Even if we butchered all our flocks and herds, would that satisfy them? Even if we caught all the fish in the sea, would that be enough?"

23Then the LORD said to Moses, "Has my arm lost its power? Now you will see whether or not my word comes true!"

24So Moses went out and reported the LORD's words to the people. He gathered the seventy elders and stationed them around the Tabernacle.* 25And the LORD came down in the cloud and spoke to Moses. Then he gave the seventy elders the same Spirit that was upon Moses. And when the Spirit rested upon them, they prophesied. But this never happened again.

26Two men, Eldad and Medad, had stayed behind in the camp. They were listed among the elders, but they had not gone out to the Tabernacle. Yet the Spirit rested upon them as well, so they prophesied there in the camp. 27A young man ran and reported to Moses, "Eldad and Medad are prophesying in the camp!"

28Joshua son of Nun, who had been Moses' assistant since his youth, protested, "Moses, my master, make them stop!"

29But Moses replied, "Are you jealous for my sake? I wish that all the LORD's people were prophets and that the LORD would put his Spirit upon them all!" 30Then Moses returned to the camp with the elders of Israel.

Nm 11:16 Hebrew *the Tent of Meeting.* **Nm 11:24** Hebrew *the tent;* also in 11:26.

Num 11:21-22 Moses had witnessed God's power in spectacular miracles, yet at this time he questioned God's ability to feed the wandering Israelites. If even Moses doubted God's power, how much easier it is for us to do the same. But completely depending upon God is essential, regardless of our level of spiritual maturity. When we begin to rely on our own understanding, we are in danger of ignoring God's assessment of the situation. By remembering his past works and his present power, we can be sure that we are not cutting off his potential help.

Num 11:23 How strong is God? It is easy to trust God when we see his mighty acts (the Israelites saw many), but after a while, in the routine of daily life, his strength may appear to diminish. God doesn't change, but our view of him often does. The monotony of day-by-day living lulls us into forgetting how powerful God can be. As Moses learned, God's strength is always available.

Num 11:26-29 This incident is similar to a story told in Mark 9:38-41. The disciples wanted Jesus to forbid others to drive out demons because they were not part of the disciples' group. But this type of narrow attitude was condemned by both Moses and Jesus. Beware of putting limits on God—he can work through whomever he chooses.

Num 11:29 Moses was looking forward to the day when all God's people would experience the pouring out of God's Spirit. The prophet Joel recorded God's promise to pour out his Spirit on all believers (Joel 2:28-29), and this was fulfilled at Pentecost (Acts 2:16-21). Believers today can be sure that they have the Holy Spirit when they become Christians (Rom 8:9). We also can pray to live by the Holy Spirit's power (Gal 5:16-26). If you wish to have the Holy Spirit's power, pray for him to fill your life with his presence and strengthen you to follow Christ.

The LORD Sends Quail

NUMBERS 11:31-35

Now the LORD sent a wind that brought quail from the
sea and let them fall all around the camp. For miles
in every direction there were quail flying about three
feet above the ground.* 32So the people went out and
caught quail all that day and throughout the night and
all the next day, too. No one gathered less than fifty
bushels*! They spread the quail all around the camp
to dry. 33But while they were gorging themselves on
the meat—while it was still in their mouths—the anger
of the LORD blazed against the people, and he struck
them with a severe plague. 34So that place was called
Kibroth-hattaavah (which means "graves of gluttony") because there they buried the people who had
craved meat from Egypt. 35From Kibroth-hattaavah
the Israelites traveled to Hazeroth, where they stayed
for some time.

The Complaints of Miriam and Aaron against Moses

NUMBERS 12:1-16

While they were at Hazeroth, Miriam and Aaron criticized Moses because he had married a Cushite woman.
2They said, "Has the LORD spoken only through Moses?
Hasn't he spoken through us, too?" But the LORD heard
them. 3(Now Moses was very humble—more humble
than any other person on earth.)
4So immediately the LORD called to Moses, Aaron,
and Miriam and said, "Go out to the Tabernacle,* all
three of you!" So the three of them went to the Tabernacle. 5Then the LORD descended in the pillar of cloud

Nm 11:31 Or *there were quail 3 feet* [2 cubits or 92 centimeters] *deep on the ground.* **Nm 11:32** Hebrew *10 homers* [1.8 kiloliters]. **Nm 12:4** Hebrew *the Tent of Meeting.*

MIRIAM

Ask older brothers or sisters what their greatest trial in life is and they will often answer, "My younger brother [or sister]!" This is especially true when the younger sibling is more successful than the older. • When we first meet Miriam, she is involved in one of history's most unusual baby-sitting jobs. She is watching her infant brother float on the Nile River in a waterproof cradle. Miriam's quick thinking allowed Moses to be raised by his own mother. Her protective superiority, reinforced by that event, must have been hard to give up as she watched her little brother rise to greatness. • Moses' choice of a wife gave Miriam an opportunity to criticize. The real issue, however, was not the kind of woman Moses had married. It was the fact that he was the most important man in Israel. "Has the LORD spoken only through Moses? Hasn't he spoken through us, too?" (Num 12:2). No mention is made of Moses' response, but God had a quick answer for Miriam and Aaron. Without denying their role in his plan, God clearly pointed out his special relationship with Moses. Miriam was stricken with leprosy, as punishment for her insubordination. But Moses, true to his character, intervened for his sister so that God healed Miriam. • Before criticizing someone else, we need to pause long enough to discover our own motives. Failing to do this can bring disastrous results. What is often labeled as constructive criticism may actually be destructive jealousy, since the easiest way to raise our own status is to bring someone else down. Are you willing to question your motives before you offer criticism? Does the critical finger you point need to be pointed first toward yourself?

Strengths and accomplishments	• Quick thinker under pressure • Led the people alongside Moses and Aaron • Led the people in praises to God • God's prophet
Weaknesses and mistakes	• Was jealous of Moses' authority • Openly criticized Moses' leadership
Lesson from her life	• The motives behind criticism are often more important to deal with than the criticism itself
Vital statistics	• Where: Egypt, Sinai peninsula • Occupations: Able leader, songwriter, prophet • Relatives: Brothers: Aaron and Moses.
Key verses	"Then Miriam the prophet, Aaron's sister, took a tambourine and led all the women as they played their tambourines and danced. And Miriam sang this song: 'Sing to the LORD, for he has triumphed gloriously; he has hurled both horse and rider into the sea'" (Exod 15:20-21).

Miriam's story is told in Exodus 2; 15; and Numbers 12; 20:1. She is also mentioned in Deuteronomy 24:9; 1 Chronicles 6:3; Micah 6:4.

Num 11:34 Craving or lusting is more than inappropriate sexual desire. It can be an unnatural or greedy desire for anything (sports, knowledge, possessions, influence over others). In this circumstance, God punished the Israelites for craving good food! Their desire was not wrong; the sin was in allowing that desire to turn into greed. They felt it was their right to have fine food, and they could think of nothing else. When you become preoccupied with something until it affects your perspective on everything else, you have moved from desire to lust.

Num 12:1 Moses didn't have a Jewish wife because he had lived with the Egyptians the first 40 years of his life, and he was in the wilderness the next 40 years. The woman is probably not Zipporah, his first wife, who was a Midianite (see Exod 2:21). A Cushite was an Ethiopian. There is no explanation given for why Miriam and Aaron objected to this woman.

Num 12:1 People often argue over minor disagreements, leaving the real issue untouched. Such was the case when Miriam and Aaron criticized Moses. They represented the priests and the prophets, the two most powerful groups next to Moses. The real issue was their growing jealousy of Moses' position and influence. Since they could not find fault with the way Moses was leading the people, they chose to criticize his wife. Rather than face the problem squarely by dealing with their envy and pride, they chose to create a diversion from the real issue. When you are in a disagreement, stop and ask yourself if you are arguing over the real issue or if you have introduced a smoke screen by attacking someone's character. If you are unjustly criticized, remember that your critics may be afraid to face the real problem. Don't take this type of criticism personally. Ask God to help you identify the real issue and deal with it.

▸ **NUMBERS 12:1-16** ***(cont.)***
and stood at the entrance of the Tabernacle.* "Aaron
and Miriam!" he called, and they stepped forward.
6 And the LORD said to them, "Now listen to what I say:

"If there were prophets among you,
I, the LORD, would reveal myself in visions.
I would speak to them in dreams.
7 But not with my servant Moses.
Of all my house, he is the one I trust.
8 I speak to him face to face,
clearly, and not in riddles!
He sees the LORD as he is.
So why were you not afraid
to criticize my servant Moses?"

9 The LORD was very angry with them, and he departed. 10 As the cloud moved from above the Tabernacle, there stood Miriam, her skin as white as snow
from leprosy.* When Aaron saw what had happened
to her, 11 he cried out to Moses, "Oh, my master! Please
don't punish us for this sin we have so foolishly committed. 12 Don't let her be like a stillborn baby, already
decayed at birth."

13 So Moses cried out to the LORD, "O God, I beg you,
please heal her!"

14 But the LORD said to Moses, "If her father had
done nothing more than spit in her face, wouldn't
she be defiled for seven days? So keep her outside
the camp for seven days, and after that she may be
accepted back."

15 So Miriam was kept outside the camp for seven
days, and the people waited until she was brought
back before they traveled again. 16 Then they left
Hazeroth and camped in the wilderness of Paran.

Nm 12:5 Hebrew *the tent;* also in 12:10. **Nm 12:10** Or *with a skin disease.* The Hebrew word used here can describe various skin diseases.

2. THE SCOUTS INCITE REBELLION

Israel had followed God's lead from Egypt all the way to the edge of the Promised Land. But when the scouts came back with a report of the strength of the people living in Canaan, the people were afraid and rebelled against God—refusing to enter the Promised Land. Because they failed to trust in God's promise, that generation of Israelites was forced to wander in the wilderness for 40 years.

1443 BC

Israel refuses to enter Canaan

Twelve Scouts Explore Canaan

NUMBERS 13:1-24
The LORD now said to Moses, 2 "Send out men to explore the land of Canaan, the land I am giving to the
Israelites. Send one leader from each of the twelve
ancestral tribes." 3 So Moses did as the LORD commanded him. He sent out twelve men, all tribal leaders of Israel, from their camp in the wilderness of
Paran. 4 These were the tribes and the names of their
leaders:

Tribe	*Leader*
Reuben	Shammua son of Zaccur
5 Simeon	Shaphat son of Hori
6 Judah	Caleb son of Jephunneh
7 Issachar	Igal son of Joseph
8 Ephraim	Hoshea son of Nun
9 Benjamin	Palti son of Raphu
10 Zebulun	Gaddiel son of Sodi
11 Manasseh son of Joseph	Gaddi son of Susi
12 Dan	Ammiel son of Gemalli
13 Asher	Sethur son of Michael
14 Naphtali	Nahbi son of Vophsi
15 Gad	Geuel son of Maki

16 These are the names of the men Moses sent out to
explore the land. (Moses called Hoshea son of Nun by
the name Joshua.)

17 Moses gave the men these instructions as he sent
them out to explore the land: "Go north through the
Negev into the hill country. 18 See what the land is like,
and find out whether the people living there are strong
or weak, few or many. 19 See what kind of land they live
in. Is it good or bad? Do their towns have walls, or are
they unprotected like open camps? 20 Is the soil fertile
or poor? Are there many trees? Do your best to bring
back samples of the crops you see." (It happened to
be the season for harvesting the first ripe grapes.)

21 So they went up and explored the land from the
wilderness of Zin as far as Rehob, near Lebo-hamath.

Num 12:11 Aaron asked that he and Miriam not be punished for their sin. It is easy to look back at our mistakes and recognize their foolishness. It is much harder to recognize foolish plans while we are carrying them out because they seem appropriate at the time. To get rid of foolish ideas before they turn into foolish actions requires eliminating our wrong thoughts and motives. Failing to do this caused Miriam and Aaron much grief.

Num 12:14 Spitting in someone's face was considered the ultimate insult and a sign of shame imposed on wrongdoers. The religious leaders spat in Jesus' face to insult him (Matt 26:67). God punished Miriam for her smug attitude not only toward Moses' authority but also God's. He struck her with leprosy, then ordered her out of the camp for a week. This punishment was actually quite lenient. A week was the length of time she would have been excluded if her father had spit in her face. How much more she deserved for wronging God! Once again, God was merciful while exercising effective discipline.

Num 13:17-20 Moses decided what information was needed before the people could enter the Promised Land, and he took careful steps to get that information. When you are making decisions or assuming new responsibilities, remember these two important steps. Ask yourself what you need to know about the opportunity, and then obtain that knowledge. Common sense is a valuable aid in accomplishing God's purposes. See Proverbs 12:15; 15:22.

[22]Going north, they passed through the Negev and arrived at Hebron, where Ahiman, Sheshai, and Talmai—all descendants of Anak—lived. (The ancient town of Hebron was founded seven years before the Egyptian city of Zoan.) [23]When they came to the valley of Eshcol, they cut down a branch with a single cluster of grapes so large that it took two of them to carry it on a pole between them! They also brought back samples of the pomegranates and figs. [24]That place was called the valley of Eshcol (which means "cluster"), because of the cluster of grapes the Israelite men cut there.

The Scouting Report

NUMBERS 13:25-33

After exploring the land for forty days, the men returned [26]to Moses, Aaron, and the whole community of Israel at Kadesh in the wilderness of Paran. They reported to the whole community what they had seen and showed them the fruit they had taken from the land. [27]This was their report to Moses: "We entered the land you sent us to explore, and it is indeed a bountiful country—a land flowing with milk and honey. Here is the kind of fruit it produces. [28]But the people living there are powerful, and their towns are large and fortified. We even saw giants there, the descendants of Anak! [29]The Amalekites live in the Negev, and the Hittites, Jebusites, and Amorites live in the hill country. The Canaanites live along the coast of the Mediterranean Sea* and along the Jordan Valley."

[30]But Caleb tried to quiet the people as they stood before Moses. "Let's go at once to take the land," he said. "We can certainly conquer it!"

[31]But the other men who had explored the land with him disagreed. "We can't go up against them! They are stronger than we are!" [32]So they spread this bad report about the land among the Israelites: "The land we traveled through and explored will devour anyone who goes to live there. All the people we saw were huge. [33]We even saw giants* there, the descendants of Anak. Next to them we felt like grasshoppers, and that's what they thought, too!"

The People Rebel

NUMBERS 14:1-12

Then the whole community began weeping aloud, and they cried all night. [2]Their voices rose in a great

Nm 13:29 Hebrew *the sea.* **Nm 13:33** Hebrew *nephilim.*

Num 13:25-29 God told the Israelites that the Promised Land was rich and fertile. Not only that, he promised that this bountiful land would be theirs. When the scouts reported back to Moses, they gave plenty of good reasons for entering the land, but they couldn't stop focusing on their fear. Talk of giants (descendants of Anak) and fortified cities made it easy to forget about God's promise to help. When facing a tough decision, don't let the negatives cause you to lose sight of the positives. Weigh both sides carefully. Don't let potential difficulties blind you to God's power to help and his promise to guide.

Num 13:26 Although Kadesh was only an oasis in the wilderness, it was a crossroads in Israel's history. When the scouts returned to Kadesh from their mission, the people had to decide either to enter the land or to retreat. They chose to retreat and were condemned to wander 40 years in the wilderness. It was also at Kadesh that Moses disobeyed God (Num 20:7-12). For this he, too, was denied entrance into the Promised Land. Aaron and Miriam died there, for they could not enter the new land either. Kadesh was near Canaan's southern borders, but because of the Israelites' lack of faith, they needed more than a lifetime to go from Kadesh to the Promised Land.

Num 13:27 The Promised Land, also called the land of Canaan, was indeed bountiful, as the 12 scouts discovered. The Bible often calls it the land flowing with milk and honey. Although the land was relatively small—150 miles long and 60 miles wide—its lush hillsides were covered with fig, date, and nut trees. It was the land God had promised to Abraham, Isaac, and Jacob.

Num 13:28 The "descendants of Anak" were a race of abnormally large people. The family of Goliath may have been descended from these people (see 2 Sam 21:16-22).

Num 13:28-29 The fortified cities the scouts talked about were surrounded by high walls as much as 20 feet thick and 25 feet tall. Guards were often stationed on top, where there was a commanding view of the countryside. Some of the inhabitants, said the scouts, were formidable men—from seven to nine feet tall—so that the Israelites felt like grasshoppers next to them (Num 13:33). The fortified cities and the giants struck fear into the hearts of most of the scouts.

Num 13:30-32 Imagine standing before a crowd and loudly voicing an unpopular opinion! Caleb was willing to take the unpopular stand to do as God had commanded. To be effective when you go against the crowd, you must have the facts (Caleb had seen the land himself); have the right attitude (Caleb trusted God's promise to give Israel the land); and state clearly what you believe (Caleb said, "We can certainly conquer it!").

Num 13:33–14:4 The negative opinion of 10 men caused a great rebellion among the people. Because it is human nature to accept opinion as fact, we must be especially careful when voicing our negative opinions. What we say may heavily influence the actions of those who trust us to give sound advice.

Num 14:1-4 When the chorus of despair went up, everyone joined in. Their greatest fears were being realized. Losing their perspective, the people were caught up in the emotion of the moment, forgetting what they knew about God's character. What if the people had spent as much energy moving forward as they did moving backward? They could have enjoyed their land—instead, they never even entered it. When a cry of despair goes up around you, consider the larger perspective before you join in. You have better ways to use your energy than to complain.

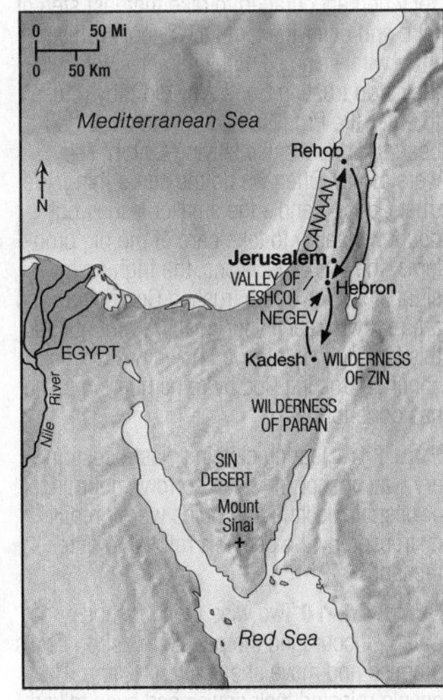

***ROUTE OF THE SCOUTS** The scouts traveled from Kadesh at the southernmost edge of the wilderness of Zin to Rehob at the northernmost edge and back, a round trip of about 500 miles.*

▶ **NUMBERS 14:1-12** ***(cont.)***

chorus of protest against Moses and Aaron. "If only
we had died in Egypt, or even here in the wilderness!"
they complained. 3"Why is the LORD taking us to this
country only to have us die in battle? Our wives and
our little ones will be carried off as plunder! Wouldn't
it be better for us to return to Egypt?" 4Then they plotted among themselves, "Let's choose a new leader and
go back to Egypt!"
5Then Moses and Aaron fell face down on the
ground before the whole community of Israel. 6Two
of the men who had explored the land, Joshua son of
Nun and Caleb son of Jephunneh, tore their clothing.
7They said to all the people of Israel, "The land we traveled through and explored is a wonderful land! 8And
if the LORD is pleased with us, he will bring us safely
into that land and give it to us. It is a rich land flowing
with milk and honey. 9Do not rebel against the LORD,
and don't be afraid of the people of the land. They are
only helpless prey to us! They have no protection, but
the LORD is with us! Don't be afraid of them!"
10But the whole community began to talk about
stoning Joshua and Caleb. Then the glorious presence
of the LORD appeared to all the Israelites at the Tabernacle.* 11And the LORD said to Moses, "How long will
these people treat me with contempt? Will they never
believe me, even after all the miraculous signs I have
done among them? 12I will disown them and destroy
them with a plague. Then I will make you into a nation
greater and mightier than they are!"

Moses Intercedes for the People

NUMBERS 14:13-25

But Moses objected. "What will the Egyptians think
when they hear about it?" he asked the LORD. "They
know full well the power you displayed in rescuing
your people from Egypt. 14Now if you destroy them,
the Egyptians will send a report to the inhabitants of

Nm 14:10 Hebrew *the Tent of Meeting.*

Num 14:5-9 With great miracles, God had led the Israelites out of slavery, through the desolate wilderness, and up to the very edge of the Promised Land. He had protected them, fed them, and fulfilled every promise. Yet when encouraged to take that last step of faith and enter the land, the people refused. After witnessing so many miracles, why did they stop trusting God? Why did they refuse to enter the Promised Land when that had been their goal since leaving Egypt? They were afraid. Often we do the same thing. We trust God to handle the smaller issues but doubt his ability to take care of the big problems, the tough decisions, the frightening situations. Don't stop trusting God just as you are ready to reach your goal. He brought you this far and won't let you down now. We can continue trusting God by remembering all he has done for us.

Num 14:6 Tearing clothing was a customary way of showing deep sorrow, mourning, or despair. Joshua and Caleb were greatly distressed by the people's refusal to enter the land.

Num 14:6-10 Two wise men, Joshua and Caleb, encouraged the people to act on God's promise and move ahead into the land. The people rejected their advice and even talked of stoning them. Don't be too quick to reject advice you don't like. Evaluate it carefully, comparing it to the teaching in God's Word. The advice may be God's message.

CALEB

The voice of the minority is not often given a hearing. Nevertheless, truth cannot be measured by numbers. On the contrary, it often stands against majority opinion. Truth remains unchanged because it is guaranteed by the character of God. God is truth; what he says is the last word. At times, a person must even stand alone on the side of truth. • Caleb was not so much a man of great faith as a man of faith in a great God! His boldness rested on his understanding of God, not on his confidence in Israel's abilities to conquer the land. He could not agree with the majority, for that would be to disagree with God. • We, on the other hand, often base our decisions on what everyone else is doing. Few of us are first-order cowards like the 10 scouts. We are more like the people of Israel, getting our cowardice secondhand. Our search for right and wrong usually starts with questions such as "What do the experts say?" or "What do my friends say?" The question we most often avoid is "What does God say?" The principles we learn as we study the Bible provide a dependable road map for life. They draw us into a personal relationship with the God whose Word is the Bible. The God who gave Caleb his boldness is the same God who offers us the gift of eternal life through his Son, Jesus. That's truth worth believing!

Strengths and accomplishments	• One of the 12 scouts sent by Moses to survey the land of Canaan • One of the only two adults who left Egypt to enter the Promised Land • Expressed faith in God's promises, in spite of apparent obstacles
Lessons from his life	• Majority opinion is not an accurate measurement of right and wrong • Boldness based on God's faithfulness is appropriate • For courage and faith to be effective, they must combine words and actions
Vital statistics	• Where: From Egypt to the Sinai peninsula to the Promised Land, specifically Hebron • Occupations: Scout, soldier, shepherd
Key verse	"But my servant Caleb has a different attitude than the others have. He has remained loyal to me, so I will bring him into the land he explored. His descendants will possess their full share of that land" (Num 14:24).

Caleb's story is told in Numbers 13–14 and Joshua 14–15. He is also mentioned in Judges 1; 1 Chronicles 4:15.

this land, who have already heard that you live among
your people. They know, LORD, that you have appeared
to your people face to face and that your pillar of cloud
hovers over them. They know that you go before them
in the pillar of cloud by day and the pillar of fire by
night. [15]Now if you slaughter all these people with a
single blow, the nations that have heard of your fame
will say, [16]'The LORD was not able to bring them into
the land he swore to give them, so he killed them in
the wilderness.'
[17]"Please, Lord, prove that your power is as great as
you have claimed. For you said, [18]'The LORD is slow to
anger and filled with unfailing love, forgiving every
kind of sin and rebellion. But he does not excuse the
guilty. He lays the sins of the parents upon their children; the entire family is affected—even children in
the third and fourth generations.' [19]In keeping with
your magnificent, unfailing love, please pardon the
sins of this people, just as you have forgiven them ever
since they left Egypt."
[20]Then the LORD said, "I will pardon them as you
have requested. [21]But as surely as I live, and as surely
as the earth is filled with the LORD's glory, [22]not one
of these people will ever enter that land. They have all
seen my glorious presence and the miraculous signs
I performed both in Egypt and in the wilderness, but
again and again they have tested me by refusing to
listen to my voice. [23]They will never even see the land I
swore to give their ancestors. None of those who have
treated me with contempt will ever see it. [24]But my
servant Caleb has a different attitude than the others
have. He has remained loyal to me, so I will bring him
into the land he explored. His descendants will possess their full share of that land. [25]Now turn around,
and don't go on toward the land where the Amalekites
and Canaanites live. Tomorrow you must set out for
the wilderness in the direction of the Red Sea.*"

The LORD Punishes the Israelites

NUMBERS 14:26-45

Then the LORD said to Moses and Aaron, [27]"How long
must I put up with this wicked community and its
complaints about me? Yes, I have heard the complaints the Israelites are making against me. [28]Now tell
them this: 'As surely as I live, declares the LORD, I will
do to you the very things I heard you say. [29]You will all
drop dead in this wilderness! Because you complained
against me, every one of you who is twenty years old
or older and was included in the registration will die.
[30]You will not enter and occupy the land I swore to
give you. The only exceptions will be Caleb son of Jephunneh and Joshua son of Nun.
[31]"'You said your children would be carried off as
plunder. Well, I will bring them safely into the land,
and they will enjoy what you have despised. [32]But as
for you, you will drop dead in this wilderness. [33]And
your children will be like shepherds, wandering in the
wilderness for forty years. In this way, they will pay
for your faithlessness, until the last of you lies dead
in the wilderness.
[34]"'Because your men explored the land for forty
days, you must wander in the wilderness for forty
years—a year for each day, suffering the consequences
of your sins. Then you will discover what it is like to
have me for an enemy.' [35]I, the LORD, have spoken! I
will certainly do these things to every member of the
community who has conspired against me. They will
be destroyed here in this wilderness, and here they
will die!"
[36]The ten men Moses had sent to explore the

Nm 14:25 Hebrew *sea of reeds.*

Num 14:17-20 Moses pleaded with God, asking him to forgive his people. His plea reveals several characteristics of God: (1) God is immensely patient; (2) God's love is one promise we can always count on; (3) God forgives again and again; (4) God is merciful, listening to and answering our requests. God has not changed since Moses' day. Like Moses, we can rely on God's patience, love, forgiveness, and mercy.

Num 14:20-23 The people of Israel had a clearer view of God than any people before them, for they had both his laws and his physical presence. Their refusal to follow God after witnessing his miraculous deeds and listening to his words made the judgment against them more severe. Increased opportunity brings increased responsibility. As Jesus said: "When someone has been given much, much will be required in return" (Luke 12:48). How much greater is our responsibility to obey and serve God—we have the whole Bible, and we know God's Son, Jesus Christ.

Num 14:22 God wasn't exaggerating when he said that the Israelites had "again and again" failed to trust and obey him. Here is a list of their failures: (1) lacking trust at the crossing of the Red Sea (Exod 14:11-12); (2) complaining over bitter water at Marah (Exod 15:24); (3) complaining in the wilderness of Sin (Exod 16:3); (4) collecting more than the daily quota of manna (Exod 16:20); (5) trying to collect manna on the Sabbath (Exod 16:27-29); (6) complaining over lack of water at Rephidim (Exod 17:2-3); (7) engaging in idolatry with a golden calf (Exod 32:7-10); (8) complaining at Taberah (Num 11:1-2); (9) more complaining over the lack of delicious food (Num 11:4); (10) failing to trust God and enter the Promised Land (Num 14:1-4).

Num 14:24 The fulfillment of this verse is recorded in Joshua 14:6-15 when Caleb received his inheritance in the Promised Land. Caleb followed God with all his heart and was rewarded for his obedience. Are you wholehearted in your commitment to obey God?

Num 14:34 God's judgment came in the form the people feared most. The people were afraid of dying in the wilderness, so God punished them by making them wander in the wilderness until they died. Now they wished they had the problem of facing the giants and the fortified cities of the Promised Land. Failing to trust God often brings even greater problems than those we originally faced. When we run from God, we inevitably run into problems.

Num 14:35 Was this judgment—wandering 40 years in the wilderness—too harsh? Not compared to the instant death that God first threatened (Num 14:12). Instead, God allowed the people to live. God had brought his people to the edge of the Promised Land, just as he said he would. He was ready to give them the rich land, but the people didn't want it (Num 14:1-2). By this time, God had put up with a lot. Again and again the people had refused to trust and obey him (Num 14:22). The whole nation (except for Joshua, Caleb, Moses, and Aaron) showed contempt for and distrust of God. But God's punishment was not permanent. In 40 years, a new generation would have a chance to enter Canaan (Josh 1–3).

▸ **NUMBERS 14:26-45 *(cont.)***

land—the ones who incited rebellion against the LORD with their bad report—[37]were struck dead with a plague before the LORD. [38]Of the twelve who had explored the land, only Joshua and Caleb remained alive.

[39]When Moses reported the LORD's words to all the Israelites, the people were filled with grief. [40]Then they got up early the next morning and went to the top of the range of hills. "Let's go," they said. "We realize that we have sinned, but now we are ready to enter the land the LORD has promised us."

[41]But Moses said, "Why are you now disobeying the LORD's orders to return to the wilderness? It won't work. [42]Do not go up into the land now. You will only be crushed by your enemies because the LORD is not with you. [43]When you face the Amalekites and Canaanites in battle, you will be slaughtered. The LORD will abandon you because you have abandoned the LORD."

[44]But the people defiantly pushed ahead toward the hill country, even though neither Moses nor the Ark of the LORD's Covenant left the camp. [45]Then the Amalekites and the Canaanites who lived in those hills came down and attacked them and chased them back as far as Hormah.

H. Israel Wandering in the Wilderness

After their disobedience and unsuccessful attempt to enter the Promised Land, the Israelites were condemned to wander 40 years in the wilderness. Even in the midst of this punishment, the people continued to rebel, and thus God continued to punish them. But the hearts of the people remained hard and rebellious. Hard hearts toward God may bring similar calamity to us.

1. ADDITIONAL REGULATIONS

The Lord continued to give his people instruction during their journey, revealing himself to them more and more.

Laws concerning Offerings

NUMBERS 15:1-31

Then the LORD told Moses, [2]"Give the following instructions to the people of Israel.

"When you finally settle in the land I am giving you, [3]you will offer special gifts as a pleasing aroma to the LORD. These gifts may take the form of a burnt offering, a sacrifice to fulfill a vow, a voluntary offering, or an offering at any of your annual festivals, and they may be taken from your herds of cattle or your flocks of sheep and goats. [4]When you present these offerings, you must also give the LORD a grain offering of two quarts* of choice flour mixed with one quart* of olive oil. [5]For each lamb offered as a burnt offering or a special sacrifice, you must also present one quart of wine as a liquid offering.

[6]"If the sacrifice is a ram, give a grain offering of four quarts* of choice flour mixed with a third of a gallon* of olive oil, [7]and give a third of a gallon of wine as a liquid offering. This will be a pleasing aroma to the LORD.

[8]"When you present a young bull as a burnt offering or as a sacrifice to fulfill a vow or as a peace offering to the LORD, [9]you must also give a grain offering of six quarts* of choice flour mixed with two quarts* of olive oil, [10]and give two quarts of wine as a liquid offering. This will be a special gift, a pleasing aroma to the LORD.

[11]"Each sacrifice of a bull, ram, lamb, or young goat should be prepared in this way. [12]Follow these instructions with each offering you present. [13]All of you native-born Israelites must follow these instructions when you offer a special gift as a pleasing aroma to the LORD. [14]And if any foreigners visit you or live among you and want to present a special gift as a pleasing aroma to the LORD, they must follow these same procedures. [15]Native-born Israelites and foreigners are equal before the LORD and are subject to the same decrees. This is a permanent law for you, to be observed from generation to generation. [16]The same instructions and regulations will apply both to you and to the foreigners living among you."

[17]Then the LORD said to Moses, [18]"Give the following instructions to the people of Israel.

"When you arrive in the land where I am taking you, [19]and you eat the crops that grow there, you must set some aside as a sacred offering to the LORD. [20]Present a cake from the first of the flour you grind, and set it aside as a sacred offering, as you do with the first grain from the threshing floor. [21]Throughout the generations to come, you are to present a sacred offering to the LORD each year from the first of your ground flour.

Nm 15:4a Hebrew *1⁄10 of an ephah* [2.2 liters]. **Nm 15:4b** Hebrew *1⁄4 of a hin* [1 liter]; also in 15:5. **Nm 15:6a** Hebrew *2⁄10 of an ephah* [4.4 liters]. **Nm 15:6b** Hebrew *1⁄3 of a hin* [1.3 liters]; also in 15:7. **Nm 15:9a** Hebrew *3⁄10 of an ephah* [6.6 liters]. **Nm 15:9b** Hebrew *1⁄2 of a hin* [2 liters]; also in 15:10.

Num 14:40-44 When the Israelites realized their foolish mistake, they were suddenly ready to return to God. But God didn't confuse their admission of guilt with true repentance because he knew their hearts. Sure enough, they soon went their own way again. Sometimes right actions or good intentions come too late. We must not only do what is right but also do it at the right time. God wants complete and instant obedience.

22 “But suppose you unintentionally fail to carry out all these commands that the LORD has given you through Moses. 23 And suppose your descendants in the future fail to do everything the LORD has commanded through Moses. 24 If the mistake was made unintentionally, and the community was unaware of it, the whole community must present a young bull for a burnt offering as a pleasing aroma to the LORD. It must be offered along with its prescribed grain offering and liquid offering and with one male goat for a sin offering. 25 With it the priest will purify the whole community of Israel, making them right with the LORD,* and they will be forgiven. For it was an unintentional sin, and they have corrected it with their offerings to the LORD—the special gift and the sin offering. 26 The whole community of Israel will be forgiven, including the foreigners living among you, for all the people were involved in the sin.

27 “If one individual commits an unintentional sin, the guilty person must bring a one-year-old female goat for a sin offering. 28 The priest will sacrifice it to purify* the guilty person before the LORD, and that person will be forgiven. 29 These same instructions apply both to native-born Israelites and to the foreigners living among you.

30 “But those who brazenly violate the LORD’s will, whether native-born Israelites or foreigners, have blasphemed the LORD, and they must be cut off from the community. 31 Since they have treated the LORD’s word with contempt and deliberately disobeyed his command, they must be completely cut off and suffer the punishment for their guilt.”

Penalty for Breaking the Sabbath

NUMBERS 15:32-36

One day while the people of Israel were in the wilderness, they discovered a man gathering wood on the Sabbath day. 33 The people who found him doing this took him before Moses, Aaron, and the rest of the community. 34 They held him in custody because they did not know what to do with him. 35 Then the LORD said to Moses, “The man must be put to death! The whole community must stone him outside the camp.” 36 So the whole community took the man outside the camp and stoned him to death, just as the LORD had commanded Moses.

Tassels on Clothing

NUMBERS 15:37-41

Then the LORD said to Moses, 38 “Give the following instructions to the people of Israel: Throughout the generations to come you must make tassels for the hems of your clothing and attach them with a blue cord. 39 When you see the tassels, you will remember and obey all the commands of the LORD instead of following your own desires and defiling yourselves, as you are prone to do. 40 The tassels will help you remember that you must obey all my commands and be holy to your God. 41 I am the LORD your God who brought you out of the land of Egypt that I might be your God. I am the LORD your God!”

First metalworking in South America

Nm 15:25 Or *will make atonement for the whole community of Israel.* **Nm 15:28** Or *to make atonement for.*

2. MANY LEADERS REBEL AGAINST MOSES

Rebellion wasn’t limited to the masses in Israel; even some leading Levites chose to question God’s choice of Moses and Aaron as their leaders and decided to assert themselves as leaders of the nation. But God confirmed his choice of Moses and Aaron in dramatic fashion.

Korah, Dathan, and Abiram

NUMBERS 16:1-50

One day Korah son of Izhar, a descendant of Kohath son of Levi, conspired with Dathan and Abiram, the sons of Eliab, and On son of Peleth, from the tribe of Reuben. 2 They incited a rebellion against Moses, along with 250 other leaders of the community, all prominent members of the assembly. 3 They united against Moses and Aaron and said, “You have gone too far! The whole community of Israel has been set

Num 15:30-31 God was willing to forgive those who made unintentional errors if they realized their mistakes quickly and corrected them. However, those who brazenly and deliberately sinned received a harsher judgment. Intentional sin grows out of an improper attitude toward God. A child who knowingly disobeys his parents challenges their authority and dares them to respond. Both the act and the attitude have to be dealt with.

Num 15:32-36 Stoning a man for gathering wood on the Sabbath seems like a severe punishment, and it was. This act was a deliberate sin, defying God’s law against working on the Sabbath. Perhaps the man was taking advantage of everyone else while they were at home resting, in addition to breaking the Sabbath.

Num 15:39 The tassels were to remind people not to seek after their own lustful desires but to seek the Lord. Idol worship is self-centered, focusing on what a person can get from serving an idol. Good luck, prosperity, long life, and success in battle were expected from the gods. So were power and prestige. The worship of God is the opposite. Believers are to be selfless rather than self-centered. Instead of expecting God to serve us, we are to serve him, expecting nothing in return. We serve God for who he is, not for what we get from him.

Num 16:1-3 Korah and his associates had seen the advantages of the priesthood in Egypt. Egyptian priests had great wealth and political influence, something Korah wanted for himself. Korah may have assumed that Moses, Aaron, and his sons were trying to make the Israelite priesthood the same kind of political machine, and he wanted to be a part of it. He did not understand that Moses’ main ambition was to serve God rather than to control others.

▸ **NUMBERS 16:1-50** ***(cont.)***

apart by the LORD, and he is with all of us. What right
do you have to act as though you are greater than the
rest of the LORD's people?"
[4]When Moses heard what they were saying, he
fell face down on the ground. [5]Then he said to Korah and his followers, "Tomorrow morning the LORD
will show us who belongs to him* and who is holy.
The LORD will allow only those whom he selects to
enter his own presence. [6]Korah, you and all your
followers must prepare your incense burners. [7]Light
fires in them tomorrow, and burn incense before
the LORD. Then we will see whom the LORD chooses
as his holy one. You Levites are the ones who have
gone too far!"
[8]Then Moses spoke again to Korah: "Now listen,
you Levites! [9]Does it seem insignificant to you that
the God of Israel has chosen you from among all
the community of Israel to be near him so you can
serve in the LORD's Tabernacle and stand before the
people to minister to them? [10]Korah, he has already
given this special ministry to you and your fellow
Levites. Are you now demanding the priesthood as
well? [11]The LORD is the one you and your followers
are really revolting against! For who is Aaron that
you are complaining about him?"
[12]Then Moses summoned Dathan and Abiram, the
sons of Eliab, but they replied, "We refuse to come
before you! [13]Isn't it enough that you brought us out
of Egypt, a land flowing with milk and honey, to kill us
here in this wilderness, and that you now treat us like
your subjects? [14]What's more, you haven't brought
us into another land flowing with milk and honey.
You haven't given us a new homeland with fields
and vineyards. Are you trying to fool these men?*
We will not come."
[15]Then Moses became very angry and said to
the LORD, "Do not accept their grain offerings! I
have not taken so much as a donkey from them,
and I have never hurt a single one of them." [16]And
Moses said to Korah, "You and all your followers
must come here tomorrow and present yourselves

Nm 16:5 Greek version reads *God has visited and knows those who are his.* Compare 2 Tim 2:19. **Nm 16:14** Hebrew *Are you trying to put out the eyes of these men?*

Num 16:8-10 Moses saw through their charge to their true motivation—some of the Levites wanted the power of the priesthood. Like Korah, we often desire the special qualities God has given others. Korah had significant, worthwhile abilities and responsibilities of his own. But in the end, his ambition for more caused him to lose everything. Inappropriate ambition is greed in disguise. Concentrate on finding the special purpose God has for you instead of wishing you were in someone else's shoes.

Num 16:13-14 One of the easiest ways to fall away from following God is to look at our present problems and exaggerate them. Dathan and Abiram did just that when they began to long for better food and more pleasant surroundings. Egypt, the place they had longed to leave, was now looking better and better—not because of slavery and taskmasters, of course, but because of its mouthwatering food! These two men and their followers had completely lost their perspective. When we take our eyes off God and start looking at ourselves and our problems, we begin to lose our perspective as well. Overrating problems can hinder our relationship with God. Don't let difficulties make you lose sight of God's direction for your life.

KORAH

Korah was a Levite who assisted in the daily functions of the Tabernacle. Shortly after Israel's great rebellion against God (Num 13–14), Korah instigated his own mini-rebellion. He recruited a grievance committee and confronted Moses and Aaron. Their list of complaints: (1) You are no better than anyone else; (2) everyone in Israel has been chosen of the Lord; (3) we don't need to obey you. It is amazing to see how Korah twisted the first two statements—both true—to reach the wrong conclusion. • Moses would have agreed that he was no better than anyone else. He would also have agreed that all Israelites were God's chosen people. But Korah's application of these truths was wrong. Not all Israelites were chosen to lead. Korah's hidden claim was this: "I have as much right to lead as Moses does." • Korah's story gives us numerous warnings: (1) Don't let desire for what someone else has make you discontent with what you already have. (2) Don't try to raise your own self-esteem by attacking someone else's. (3) Don't use part of God's Word to support what you want, rather than allowing its entirety to shape your wants. (4) Don't expect to find satisfaction in power and position; God may want to work through you in the position you are now in.

Strengths and accomplishments	• Popular leader; influential figure during the Exodus • Mentioned among the chief men of Israel (Exod 6)
Weaknesses and mistakes	• Allowed greed to blind his common sense
Lessons from his life	• There is a fine line between goals and greed • If we are discontent with what we have, we may lose it without gaining anything better
Vital statistics	• Where: Egypt, Sinai peninsula • Occupation: Levite (Tabernacle assistant)
Key verses	"Then Moses spoke again to Korah: 'Now listen, you Levites! Does it seem insignificant to you that the God of Israel has chosen you from among all the community of Israel to be near him so you can serve in the LORD's Tabernacle and stand before the people to minister to them? Korah, he has already given this special ministry to you and your fellow Levites. Are you now demanding the priesthood as well?'" (Num 16:8-10).

Korah's story is told in Numbers 16:1-40. He is also mentioned in Numbers 26:9; Jude 1:11.

before the LORD. Aaron will also be here. 17You and each of your 250 followers must prepare an incense burner and put incense on it, so you can all present them before the LORD. Aaron will also bring his incense burner."

18So each of these men prepared an incense burner, lit the fire, and placed incense on it. Then they all stood at the entrance of the Tabernacle* with Moses and Aaron. 19Meanwhile, Korah had stirred up the entire community against Moses and Aaron, and they all gathered at the Tabernacle entrance. Then the glorious presence of the LORD appeared to the whole community, 20and the LORD said to Moses and Aaron, 21"Get away from all these people so that I may instantly destroy them!"

22But Moses and Aaron fell face down on the ground. "O God," they pleaded, "you are the God who gives breath to all creatures. Must you be angry with all the people when only one man sins?"

23And the LORD said to Moses, 24"Then tell all the people to get away from the tents of Korah, Dathan, and Abiram."

25So Moses got up and rushed over to the tents of Dathan and Abiram, followed by the elders of Israel. 26"Quick!" he told the people. "Get away from the tents of these wicked men, and don't touch anything that belongs to them. If you do, you will be destroyed for their sins." 27So all the people stood back from the tents of Korah, Dathan, and Abiram. Then Dathan and Abiram came out and stood at the entrances of their tents, together with their wives and children and little ones.

28And Moses said, "This is how you will know that the LORD has sent me to do all these things that I have done—for I have not done them on my own. 29If these men die a natural death, or if nothing unusual happens, then the LORD has not sent me. 30But if the LORD does something entirely new and the ground opens its mouth and swallows them and all their belongings, and they go down alive into the grave,* then you will know that these men have shown contempt for the LORD."

31He had hardly finished speaking the words when the ground suddenly split open beneath them. 32The earth opened its mouth and swallowed the men, along with their households and all their followers who were standing with them, and everything they owned. 33So they went down alive into the grave, along with all their belongings. The earth closed over them, and they all vanished from among the people of Israel. 34All the people around them fled when they heard their screams. "The earth will swallow us, too!" they cried. 35Then fire blazed forth from the LORD and burned up the 250 men who were offering incense.

36*And the LORD said to Moses, 37"Tell Eleazar son of Aaron the priest to pull all the incense burners from the fire, for they are holy. Also tell him to scatter the burning coals. 38Take the incense burners of these men who have sinned at the cost of their lives, and hammer the metal into a thin sheet to overlay the altar. Since these burners were used in the LORD's presence, they have become holy. Let them serve as a warning to the people of Israel."

39So Eleazar the priest collected the 250 bronze incense burners that had been used by the men who died in the fire, and he hammered them into a thin sheet to overlay the altar. 40This would warn the Israelites that no unauthorized person—no one who

Nm 16:18 Hebrew *the Tent of Meeting;* also in 16:19, 42, 43, 50. **Nm 16:30** Hebrew *into Sheol;* also in 16:33. **Nm 16:36** Verses 16:36-50 are numbered 17:1-15 in Hebrew text.

Num 16:26 The Israelites were told to not even touch the belongings of the wicked rebels. In this case, doing so would have shown sympathy to their cause and agreement with their principles. Korah, Dathan, and Abiram were directly challenging Moses and God. Moses clearly stated what God intended to do to the rebels (Num 16:28-30). He did this so that everyone would have to choose between following Korah or following Moses, God's chosen leader. When God asks us to make a fundamental choice between siding with wicked people or siding with him, we should not hesitate but commit ourselves to be 100 percent on the Lord's side.

Num 16:27-35 Although the families of Dathan and Abiram were swallowed up, the sons of Korah were not wiped out (see Num 26:11).

Incense

Incense offerings were common throughout the ancient Near East from the earliest times of organized worship. Egyptian paintings and reliefs show men holding censers of burning incense. Incense seems to have been used as well in the rituals of Assyria, Babylonia, and Arabia. Canaanite altars found at Megiddo and Tell Beit Mirsim have large limestone horns (10th century B.C.) that were designed to hold a bowl of incense. Hence, it is reasonable to assume that the Israelites would have been familiar with the practice of incense offerings in worship even before it was described to them in the law. But in spite of some common practices, worshiping the true God was very different from worshiping the Canaanite deities, and the law had very strict requirements for the kind of incense to use and how it would be offered. Incense symbolizes continuous prayer (Luke 1:8-10; Rev 8:3-4). Paul says to pray without ceasing (1 Thes 5:17). How often do you pray each day?

▸ NUMBERS 16:1-50 *(cont.)*

was not a descendant of Aaron—should ever enter the LORD's presence to burn incense. If anyone did, the same thing would happen to him as happened to Korah and his followers. So the LORD's instructions to Moses were carried out.

[41]But the very next morning the whole community of Israel began muttering again against Moses and Aaron, saying, "You have killed the LORD's people!" [42]As the community gathered to protest against Moses and Aaron, they turned toward the Tabernacle and saw that the cloud had covered it, and the glorious presence of the LORD appeared.

[43]Moses and Aaron came and stood in front of the Tabernacle, [44]and the LORD said to Moses, [45]"Get away from all these people so that I can instantly destroy them!" But Moses and Aaron fell face down on the ground.

[46]And Moses said to Aaron, "Quick, take an incense burner and place burning coals on it from the altar. Lay incense on it, and carry it out among the people to purify them and make them right with the LORD.* The LORD's anger is blazing against them—the plague has already begun."

[47]Aaron did as Moses told him and ran out among the people. The plague had already begun to strike down the people, but Aaron burned the incense and purified* the people. [48]He stood between the dead and the living, and the plague stopped. [49]But 14,700 people died in that plague, in addition to those who had died in the affair involving Korah. [50]Then because the plague had stopped, Aaron returned to Moses at the entrance of the Tabernacle.

The Budding of Aaron's Staff

NUMBERS 17:1-13

[1]*Then the LORD said to Moses, [2]"Tell the people of Israel to bring you twelve wooden staffs, one from each leader of Israel's ancestral tribes, and inscribe each leader's name on his staff. [3]Inscribe Aaron's name on the staff of the tribe of Levi, for there must be one staff for the leader of each ancestral tribe. [4]Place these staffs in the Tabernacle in front of the Ark containing the tablets of the Covenant,* where I meet with you. [5]Buds will sprout on the staff belonging to the man I choose. Then I will finally put an end to the people's murmuring and complaining against you."

[6]So Moses gave the instructions to the people of Israel, and each of the twelve tribal leaders, including Aaron, brought Moses a staff. [7]Moses placed the staffs in the LORD's presence in the Tabernacle of the Covenant.* [8]When he went into the Tabernacle of the Covenant the next day, he found that Aaron's staff, representing the tribe of Levi, had sprouted, budded, blossomed, and produced ripe almonds!

[9]When Moses brought all the staffs out from the LORD's presence, he showed them to the people. Each man claimed his own staff. [10]And the LORD said to Moses: "Place Aaron's staff permanently before the Ark of the Covenant* to serve as a warning to rebels. This should put an end to their complaints against me and prevent any further deaths." [11]So Moses did as the LORD commanded him.

[12]Then the people of Israel said to Moses, "Look, we are doomed! We are dead! We are ruined! [13]Everyone who even comes close to the Tabernacle of the LORD dies. Are we all doomed to die?"

Nm 16:46 Or *to make atonement for them.* **Nm 16:47** Or *and made atonement for.* **Nm 17:1** Verses 17:1-13 are numbered 17:16-28 in Hebrew text. **Nm 17:4** Hebrew *in the Tent of Meeting before the Testimony.* The Hebrew word for "testimony" refers to the terms of the LORD's covenant with Israel as written on stone tablets, which were kept in the Ark, and also to the covenant itself. **Nm 17:7** Or *Tabernacle of the Testimony;* also in 17:8. **Nm 17:10** Hebrew *before the Testimony;* see note on 17:4.

3. RESPONSIBILITIES OF THE PRIESTS AND LEVITES

After confirming Aaron and his decendants as the rightful priests in Israel, God gave them further instruction on how to serve him as priests and Levites.

Duties of Priests and Levites

NUMBERS 18:1-7

Then the LORD said to Aaron: "You, your sons, and your relatives from the tribe of Levi will be held responsible for any offenses related to the sanctuary. But you and your sons alone will be held responsible for violations connected with the priesthood.

[2]"Bring your relatives of the tribe of Levi—your

Num 16:41 Just one day after Korah and his followers were executed for grumbling and complaining against God, the Israelites started all over with more muttering and complaining. Their negative attitude only caused them to rebel even more and to bring about even greater trouble. It eroded their faith in God and encouraged thoughts of giving up and turning back. The path to open rebellion against God begins with dissatisfaction and skepticism, then moves to grumbling about both God and present circumstances. Next come bitterness and resentment, followed finally by rebellion and open hostility. If you are often dissatisfied, skeptical, complaining, or bitter—beware! These attitudes lead to rebellion and separation from God. Any choice to side against God is a step in the direction of letting go of him completely and making your own way through life.

Num 17:5, 10 After witnessing spectacular miracles, seeing the Egyptians punished by the plagues, and experiencing the actual presence of God, the Israelites still complained and rebelled. We wonder how they could be so blind and ignorant, and yet we often repeat this same pattern. We have centuries of evidence, the Bible in many translations, and the convincing results of archaeological and historical studies. But people today continue to disobey God and go their own way. Like the Israelites, we are more concerned about our physical condition than our spiritual condition. We can escape this pattern only by paying attention to all the signs of God's presence that we have been given. Has God guided and protected you? Has he answered your prayers? Do you know people who have experienced

ancestral tribe—to assist you and your sons as you perform the sacred duties in front of the Tabernacle of the Covenant.* 3But as the Levites go about all their assigned duties at the Tabernacle, they must be careful not to go near any of the sacred objects or the altar. If they do, both you and they will die. 4The Levites must join you in fulfilling their responsibilities for the care and maintenance of the Tabernacle,* but no unauthorized person may assist you.

5"You yourselves must perform the sacred duties inside the sanctuary and at the altar. If you follow these instructions, the LORD's anger will never again blaze against the people of Israel. 6I myself have chosen your fellow Levites from among the Israelites to be your special assistants. They are a gift to you, dedicated to the LORD for service in the Tabernacle. 7But you and your sons, the priests, must personally handle all the priestly rituals associated with the altar and with everything behind the inner curtain. I am giving you the priesthood as your special privilege of service. Any unauthorized person who comes too near the sanctuary will be put to death."

Support for the Priests and Levites

NUMBERS 18:8-32

The LORD gave these further instructions to Aaron: "I myself have put you in charge of all the holy offerings that are brought to me by the people of Israel. I have given all these consecrated offerings to you and your sons as your permanent share. 9You are allotted the portion of the most holy offerings that is not burned on the fire. This portion of all the most holy offerings—including the grain offerings, sin offerings, and guilt offerings—will be most holy, and it belongs to you and your sons. 10You must eat it as a most holy offering. All the males may eat of it, and you must treat it as most holy.

11"All the sacred offerings and special offerings presented to me when the Israelites lift them up before the altar also belong to you. I have given them to you and to your sons and daughters as your permanent share. Any member of your family who is ceremonially clean may eat of these offerings.

12"I also give you the harvest gifts brought by the people as offerings to the LORD—the best of the olive oil, new wine, and grain. 13All the first crops of their land that the people present to the LORD belong to you. Any member of your family who is ceremonially clean may eat this food.

14"Everything in Israel that is specially set apart for the LORD* also belongs to you.

15"The firstborn of every mother, whether human or animal, that is offered to the LORD will be yours. But you must always redeem your firstborn sons and the firstborn of ceremonially unclean animals. 16Redeem them when they are one month old. The redemption price is five pieces of silver* (as measured by the weight of the sanctuary shekel, which equals twenty gerahs).

17"However, you may not redeem the firstborn of cattle, sheep, or goats. They are holy and have been set apart for the LORD. Sprinkle their blood on the altar, and burn their fat as a special gift, a pleasing aroma to the LORD. 18The meat of these animals will be yours, just like the breast and right thigh that are presented by lifting them up as a special offering before the altar. 19Yes, I am giving you all these holy offerings that the people of Israel bring to the LORD. They are for you and your sons and daughters, to be eaten as your permanent share. This is an eternal and unbreakable covenant* between the LORD and you, and it also applies to your descendants."

20And the LORD said to Aaron, "You priests will receive no allotment of land or share of property among the people of Israel. I am your share and your allotment. 21As for the tribe of Levi, your relatives, I will compensate them for their service in the Tabernacle. Instead of an allotment of land, I will give them the tithes from the entire land of Israel.

22"From now on, no Israelites except priests or Levites may approach the Tabernacle. If they come too near, they will be judged guilty and will die. 23Only the Levites may serve at the Tabernacle, and they will be held responsible for any offenses against it. This is a permanent law for you, to be observed from generation to generation. The Levites will receive no allotment of land among the Israelites, 24because I have given them the Israelites' tithes, which have been presented as sacred offerings to the LORD. This will be the Levites' share. That is why I said they would receive no allotment of land among the Israelites."

25The LORD also told Moses, 26"Give these instructions to the Levites: When you receive from the people of Israel the tithes I have assigned as your allotment,

Nm 18:2 Or *Tabernacle of the Testimony.* **Nm 18:4** Hebrew *the Tent of Meeting;* also in 18:6, 21, 22, 23, 31. **Nm 18:14** The Hebrew term used here refers to the complete consecration of things or people to the LORD, either by destroying them or by giving them as an offering. **Nm 18:16** Hebrew *5 shekels* [2 ounces or 57 grams] *of silver.* **Nm 18:19** Hebrew *a covenant of salt.*

remarkable blessings and healings? Do you know Bible stories about the way God has led his people? Focus your thoughts on what God has done, and rebellion will become unthinkable.

Num 18:25-26 Even the Levites, who were ministers, had to tithe to support the Lord's work. No one was exempt from returning to God a portion of what was received. Though the Levites owned no land and operated no great enterprises, they were to treat their income the same as everyone else did by giving a portion to care for the needs of the other Levites and of the Tabernacle. The tithing principle is still relevant. God expects all his followers to supply the material needs of those who devote themselves to meeting the spiritual needs of the community of faith. Ask God to direct you about what you should give and to help you give generously.

▸ **NUMBERS 18:8-32 *(cont.)***

give a tenth of the tithes you receive—a tithe of the
tithe—to the LORD as a sacred offering. 27The LORD will
consider this offering to be your harvest offering, as
though it were the first grain from your own threshing floor or wine from your own winepress. 28You
must present one-tenth of the tithe received from
the Israelites as a sacred offering to the LORD. This is
the LORD's sacred portion, and you must present it to
Aaron the priest. 29Be sure to give to the LORD the best
portions of the gifts given to you.

30"Also, give these instructions to the Levites:
When you present the best part as your offering, it
will be considered as though it came from your own
threshing floor or winepress. 31You Levites and your
families may eat this food anywhere you wish, for it
is your compensation for serving in the Tabernacle.
32You will not be considered guilty for accepting
the LORD's tithes if you give the best portion to the
priests. But be careful not to treat the holy gifts of
the people of Israel as though they were common.
If you do, you will die."

Nm 19:4 Hebrew *the Tent of Meeting.* **Nm 19:6** Or *juniper.*

The Water of Purification

NUMBERS 19:1-22

The LORD said to Moses and Aaron, 2"Here is another
legal requirement commanded by the LORD: Tell the
people of Israel to bring you a red heifer, a perfect
animal that has no defects and has never been yoked
to a plow. 3Give it to Eleazar the priest, and it will be
taken outside the camp and slaughtered in his presence. 4Eleazar will take some of its blood on his finger
and sprinkle it seven times toward the front of the
Tabernacle.* 5As Eleazar watches, the heifer must
be burned—its hide, meat, blood, and dung. 6Eleazar
the priest must then take a stick of cedar,* a hyssop
branch, and some scarlet yarn and throw them into
the fire where the heifer is burning.

7"Then the priest must wash his clothes and bathe
himself in water. Afterward he may return to the camp,
though he will remain ceremonially unclean until evening. 8The man who burns the animal must also wash
his clothes and bathe himself in water, and he, too, will
remain unclean until evening. 9Then someone who is
ceremonially clean will gather up the ashes of the heifer

Num 19:9-10 What is the significance of the red heifer's ashes? When a person touched a dead body, he was considered unclean (i.e., unable to approach God in worship). This ritual purified the unclean person so that once again he could offer sacrifices to and worship God. Death was the strongest of defilements because it was the final result of sin. Thus, a special sacrifice—a red heifer—was required. It had to be offered by someone who was not unclean. When it had been burned on the altar, its ashes were used to purify water for ceremonial cleansing—not so much physically as symbolically. The unclean person then washed himself, and often his clothes and belongings, with this purified water as an act of becoming clean again.

ELEAZAR

An understudy must know the lead role completely and be willing to step into it at a moment's notice. Eleazar was an excellent understudy, well trained for his eventual leading role. However, his moments in the spotlight were painful. On one occasion, he watched his two older brothers burn to death for failing to take God's holiness seriously. Later, as his father was dying, he was made high priest, surely one of the most responsible—and therefore potentially most stressful—positions in Israel. • An understudy benefits from having both the script and a human model of the role. Ever since childhood, Eleazar had been able to observe Moses and Aaron. Now he could learn from watching Joshua. In addition, he had God's laws to guide him as he worked as priest and adviser to Joshua.

Strengths and accomplishments	• Succeeded his father, Aaron, as high priest • Completed his father's work by helping lead the people into the Promised Land • Teamed up with Joshua • Acted as God's spokesman to the people
Lessons from his life	• Concentrating on our present challenges and responsibilities is the best way to prepare for what God has planned for our future • God's desire is consistent obedience throughout our lives
Vital statistics	• Where: Wilderness of Sinai, Promised Land • Occupations: Priest and high priest • Relatives: Father: Aaron. Brothers: Nadab, Abihu, and Ithamar. Aunt: Miriam. Uncle: Moses. • Contemporaries: Joshua, Caleb
Key verses	"There, on the border of the land of Edom, the LORD said to Moses and Aaron, 'The time has come for Aaron to join his ancestors in death. . . . Now take Aaron and his son Eleazar up Mount Hor. There you will remove Aaron's priestly garments and put them on Eleazar, his son'" (Num 20:23-26).

Eleazar is mentioned in Exodus 6:23; Leviticus 10:16-20; Numbers 3:1-4; 4:16; 16:36-40; 20:25-29; 26:1-4, 63; 27:2, 15-23; 32:2; 34:17; Deuteronomy 10:6; Joshua 14:1; 17:4; 24:33.

and deposit them in a purified place outside the camp. They will be kept there for the community of Israel to use in the water for the purification ceremony. This ceremony is performed for the removal of sin. [10]The man who gathers up the ashes of the heifer must also wash his clothes, and he will remain ceremonially unclean until evening. This is a permanent law for the people of Israel and any foreigners who live among them.

[11]"All those who touch a dead human body will be ceremonially unclean for seven days. [12]They must purify themselves on the third and seventh days with the water of purification; then they will be purified. But if they do not do this on the third and seventh days, they will continue to be unclean even after the seventh day. [13]All those who touch a dead body and do not purify themselves in the proper way defile the LORD's Tabernacle, and they will be cut off from the community of Israel. Since the water of purification was not sprinkled on them, their defilement continues.

[14]"This is the ritual law that applies when someone dies inside a tent: All those who enter that tent and those who were inside when the death occurred will be ceremonially unclean for seven days. [15]Any open container in the tent that was not covered with a lid is also defiled. [16]And if someone in an open field touches the corpse of someone who was killed with a sword or who died a natural death, or if someone touches a human bone or a grave, that person will be defiled for seven days.

[17]"To remove the defilement, put some of the ashes from the burnt purification offering in a jar, and pour fresh water over them. [18]Then someone who is ceremonially clean must take a hyssop branch and dip it into the water. That person must sprinkle the water on the tent, on all the furnishings in the tent, and on the people who were in the tent; also on the person who touched a human bone, or touched someone who was killed or who died naturally, or touched a grave. [19]On the third and seventh days the person who is ceremonially clean must sprinkle the water on those who are defiled. Then on the seventh day the people being cleansed must wash their clothes and bathe themselves, and that evening they will be cleansed of their defilement.

[20]"But those who become defiled and do not purify themselves will be cut off from the community, for they have defiled the sanctuary of the LORD. Since the water of purification has not been sprinkled on them, they remain defiled. [21]This is a permanent law for the people. Those who sprinkle the water of purification must afterward wash their clothes, and anyone who then touches the water used for purification will remain defiled until evening. [22]Anything and anyone that a defiled person touches will be ceremonially unclean until evening."

4. THE NEW GENERATION

The 40 years of wandering was coming to an end, and a new generation of Israelites were growing to adulthood and preparing themselves to finally enter the Promised Land. Miriam and Aaron died, and God led the nation in a series of military victories over nations that were opposed to seeing Israel move into the area permanently.

Moses Strikes the Rock

NUMBERS 20:1-13

In the first month of the year,* the whole community of Israel arrived in the wilderness of Zin and camped at Kadesh. While they were there, Miriam died and was buried.

[2]There was no water for the people to drink at that place, so they rebelled against Moses and Aaron. [3]The people blamed Moses and said, "If only we had died in the LORD's presence with our brothers! [4]Why have you brought the congregation of the LORD's people into this wilderness to die, along with all our livestock? [5]Why did you make us leave Egypt and bring us here to this terrible place? This land has no grain, no figs, no grapes, no pomegranates, and no water to drink!"

[6]Moses and Aaron turned away from the people and went to the entrance of the Tabernacle,* where they fell face down on the ground. Then the glorious presence of the LORD appeared to them, [7]and the LORD said to Moses, [8]"You and Aaron must take the staff and assemble the entire community. As the people watch, speak to the rock over there, and it will pour out its water. You will provide enough water from the rock to satisfy the whole community and their livestock."

[9]So Moses did as he was told. He took the staff from the place where it was kept before the LORD. [10]Then he

Nm 20:1 The first month of the ancient Hebrew lunar calendar usually occurs within the months of March and April. The number of years since leaving Egypt is not specified. **Nm 20:6** Hebrew *the Tent of Meeting.*

Num 20:1 It had been 37 years since Israel's first scouting mission into the Promised Land (Num 13–14) and 40 years since the Exodus from Egypt. The Bible is virtually silent about those 37 years of aimless wandering. The generation of those who had lived in Egypt had almost died off, and the new generation would soon be ready to enter the land. Moses, Aaron, Joshua, and Caleb were among the few who remained from those who had left Egypt. Once again they camped at Kadesh, the site of the first scouting mission that had ended in disaster. Moses hoped the people were ready for a fresh start.

Num 20:3-5 After 37 years in the wilderness, the Israelites forgot that their wanderings were a result of their parents' and their own sin. They could not accept the fact that they brought their problems upon themselves, so they blamed Moses for their condition. Often our troubles result from our own disobedience or lack of faith. We cannot blame God for our sins. Until we face this reality, we will have little peace and no spiritual growth.

▶ **NUMBERS 20:1-13 *(cont.)***

and Aaron summoned the people to come and gather at the rock. "Listen, you rebels!" he shouted. "Must we bring you water from this rock?" [11]Then Moses raised his hand and struck the rock twice with the staff, and water gushed out. So the entire community and their livestock drank their fill.

[12]But the LORD said to Moses and Aaron, "Because you did not trust me enough to demonstrate my holiness to the people of Israel, you will not lead them into the land I am giving them!" [13]This place was known as the waters of Meribah (which means "Arguing") because there the people of Israel argued with the LORD, and there he demonstrated his holiness among them.

Edom Refuses Israel Passage

NUMBERS 20:14-21

While Moses was at Kadesh, he sent ambassadors to the king of Edom with this message:

"This is what your relatives, the people of Israel, say: You know all the hardships we have been through. [15]Our ancestors went down to Egypt, and we lived there a long time, and we and our ancestors were brutally mistreated by the Egyptians. [16]But when we cried out to the LORD, he heard us and sent an angel who brought us out of Egypt. Now we are camped at Kadesh, a town on the border of your land. [17]Please let us travel through your land. We will be careful not to go through your fields and vineyards. We won't even drink water from your wells. We will stay on the king's road and never leave it until we have passed through your territory."

[18]But the king of Edom said, "Stay out of my land, or I will meet you with an army!"

[19]The Israelites answered, "We will stay on the main road. If our livestock drink your water, we will pay for it. Just let us pass through your country. That's all we ask."

[20]But the king of Edom replied, "Stay out! You may not pass through our land." With that he mobilized his army and marched out against them with an imposing force. [21]Because Edom refused to allow Israel to pass through their country, Israel was forced to turn around.

The Death of Aaron

NUMBERS 20:22-29

The whole community of Israel left Kadesh and arrived at Mount Hor. [23]There, on the border of the land of Edom, the LORD said to Moses and Aaron, [24]"The time has come for Aaron to join his ancestors in death. He will not enter the land I am giving the people of Israel, because the two of you rebelled against my instructions concerning the water at Meribah. [25]Now take Aaron and his son Eleazar up

Num 20:12 The Lord had told Moses to *speak* to the rock; however, Moses struck it—not once, but twice. God did the miracle; yet Moses was taking credit for it when he shouted, "Must we bring you water from this rock?" (Num 20:10). For this he was forbidden to enter the Promised Land. Was God's punishment of Moses too harsh? After all, the people had nagged him, slandered him, and rebelled against both him and God. Now they were at it again (Num 20:5). But Moses was the leader and model for the entire nation. Because of this great responsibility to the people, he could not be let off lightly. By striking the rock, Moses disobeyed God's direct command and dishonored God in the presence of his people.

Num 20:14 Two brothers became the ancestors of two nations. The Edomites descended from Esau, the Israelites from Jacob. Thus, the Edomites were "relatives" to the Israelites. Israel sent a brotherly message to Edom requesting passage through their land on the main road, a well-traveled trade route. Israel promised to stay on the road, thus harmlessly bypassing Edom's fields, vineyards, and wells. The Edomites refused, however, because they did not trust Israel's word. They were afraid that this great horde of people would either attack them or devour their crops (Deut 2:4-5). Because brothers should not fight, God told the Israelites to turn back and travel by a different route to the Promised Land.

Num 20:17 The king's road was an old caravan route. Long before this time it was used as a major public road.

Num 20:21 Moses tried to negotiate and reason with the Edomite king. When nothing worked, he was left with two choices—force a conflict or avoid it. Moses knew there

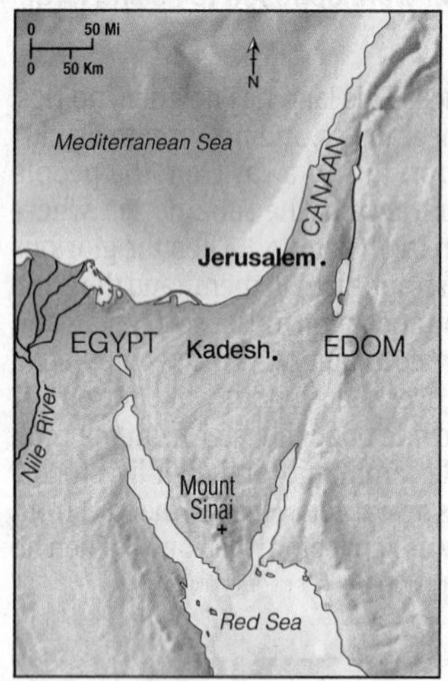

***EVENTS AT KADESH** After wandering in the wilderness for 40 years, Israel arrived at Kadesh, where Miriam died. There was not enough water, and the people complained bitterly. Moses struck a rock, and it gave enough water for everyone. The king of Edom refused Israel passage through his land, forcing them to travel around his country.*

THE SNAKE IN THE WILDERNESS

Compare the texts for yourself: Numbers 21:7-9 and John 3:14-15.

Israelites	Christians
Bitten by snakes	Bitten by sin
Little initial pain, then intense suffering	Little initial pain, then intense suffering
Physical death from snakes' poison	Spiritual death from sin's poison
Bronze snake lifted up in the wilderness	Christ lifted up on the cross
Looking to the snake spared one's life	Looking to Christ saves one from eternal death

Mount Hor. 26There you will remove Aaron's priestly garments and put them on Eleazar, his son. Aaron will die there and join his ancestors."

27So Moses did as the LORD commanded. The three of them went up Mount Hor together as the whole community watched. 28At the summit, Moses removed the priestly garments from Aaron and put them on Eleazar, Aaron's son. Then Aaron died there on top of the mountain, and Moses and Eleazar went back down. 29When the people realized that Aaron had died, all Israel mourned for him thirty days.

Victory over the Canaanites

NUMBERS 21:1-3

The Canaanite king of Arad, who lived in the Negev, heard that the Israelites were approaching on the road through Atharim. So he attacked the Israelites and took some of them as prisoners. 2Then the people of Israel made this vow to the LORD: "If you will hand these people over to us, we will completely destroy* all their towns." 3The LORD heard the Israelites' request and gave them victory over the Canaanites. The Israelites completely destroyed them and their towns, and the place has been called Hormah* ever since.

The Bronze Snake

NUMBERS 21:4-9

Then the people of Israel set out from Mount Hor, taking the road to the Red Sea* to go around the land of Edom. But the people grew impatient with the long journey, 5and they began to speak against God and Moses. "Why have you brought us out of Egypt to die here in the wilderness?" they complained. "There is nothing to eat here and nothing to drink. And we hate this horrible manna!"

6So the LORD sent poisonous snakes among the people, and many were bitten and died. 7Then the people came to Moses and cried out, "We have sinned by speaking against the LORD and against you. Pray that the LORD will take away the snakes." So Moses prayed for the people.

8Then the LORD told him, "Make a replica of a poisonous snake and attach it to a pole. All who are bitten will live if they simply look at it!" 9So Moses made a snake out of bronze and attached it to a pole. Then anyone who was bitten by a snake could look at the bronze snake and be healed!

Israel's Journey to Moab

NUMBERS 21:10-20

The Israelites traveled next to Oboth and camped there. 11Then they went on to Iye-abarim, in the wilderness on the eastern border of Moab. 12From there they traveled to the valley of Zered Brook and set up camp. 13Then they moved out and camped on the far side of the Arnon River, in the wilderness adjacent to the territory of the Amorites. The Arnon is the boundary line between the Moabites and the Amorites. 14For this reason *The Book of the Wars of the LORD* speaks of "the town of Waheb in the area of Suphah, and the ravines of the Arnon River, 15and the ravines that extend as far as the settlement of Ar on the border of Moab."

Nm 21:2 The Hebrew term used here refers to the complete consecration of things or people to the LORD, either by destroying them or by giving them as an offering; also in 21:3. **Nm 21:3** *Hormah* means "destruction." **Nm 21:4** Hebrew *sea of reeds.*

would be enough barriers in the days and months ahead. There was no point in adding another one unnecessarily. Sometimes conflict is unavoidable. But sometimes it isn't worth the consequences. Open warfare may seem heroic, courageous, and even righteous, but it is not always the best choice. At times, we should follow Moses' example and find another way to solve our problems, even if it is harder for us to do.

Num 20:28 Aaron died just before entering the Promised Land, as punishment for his sin of rebellion (Exod 32; Num 12:1-9). This was the first time that a new high priest was appointed. The priestly clothing was removed from Aaron and placed on his son Eleazar, following the commands recorded in the book of Leviticus.

Num 21:5 In Psalm 78, we learn the sources of Israel's complaining: (1) Their spirits were not faithful to God (Ps 78:8); (2) they refused to obey God's law (Ps 78:10); (3) they forgot the miracles God had done for them (Ps 78:11). Our complaining often has its roots in one of these thoughtless actions and attitudes. If we can deal with the cause of our complaining, it will not take hold and grow in our lives.

Num 21:6 God used poisonous snakes to punish the people for their unbelief and complaining. The wilderness where they traveled has a variety of snakes. Some hide in the sand and attack without warning. Both the Israelites and the Egyptians had a great fear of snakes. A bite by a poisonous snake often meant a slow death with intense suffering.

Num 21:8-9 When the bronze snake was hung on the pole, the Israelites didn't know the fuller meaning Jesus Christ would bring to this event (see John 3:14-15). Jesus explained that just as the Israelites were healed of their sickness by looking at the snake on the pole, all believers today can be saved from the sickness of sin by looking to Jesus' death on the cross. It was not the snake that healed the people but their belief that God could heal them. This belief was demonstrated by their obedience to God's instructions. In the same way, we should continue to look to Christ (see Heb 12:2).

Num 21:14 There is no other existing record of *The Book of the Wars of the LORD.* Most likely, it was a collection of victory songs or poems.

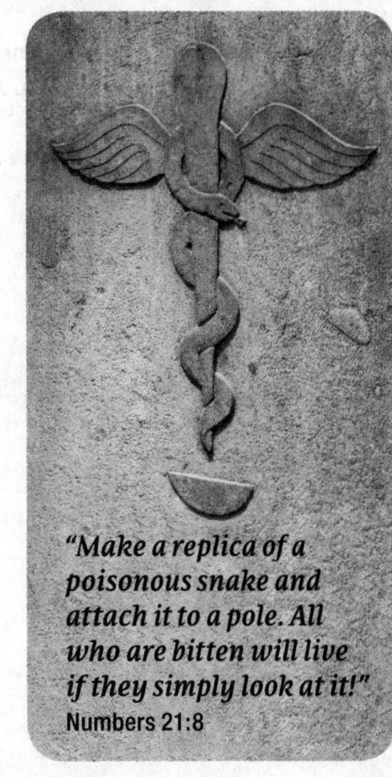

"Make a replica of a poisonous snake and attach it to a pole. All who are bitten will live if they simply look at it!"
Numbers 21:8

▶ **NUMBERS 21:10-20** ***(cont.)***

16From there the Israelites traveled to Beer,* which
is the well where the LORD said to Moses, "Assemble
the people, and I will give them water." 17There the
Israelites sang this song:

"Spring up, O well!
Yes, sing its praises!
18 Sing of this well,
which princes dug,
which great leaders hollowed out
with their scepters and staffs."

Then the Israelites left the wilderness and proceeded on through Mattanah, 19Nahaliel, and Bamoth.
20After that they went to the valley in Moab where
Pisgah Peak overlooks the wasteland.*

Victory over Sihon and Og

NUMBERS 21:21-35

The Israelites sent ambassadors to King Sihon of the
Amorites with this message:

22"Let us travel through your land. We will
be careful not to go through your fields and
vineyards. We won't even drink water from your
wells. We will stay on the king's road until we
have passed through your territory."

23But King Sihon refused to let them cross his
territory. Instead, he mobilized his entire army and
attacked Israel in the wilderness, engaging them in
battle at Jahaz. 24But the Israelites slaughtered them
with their swords and occupied their land from the
Arnon River to the Jabbok River. They went only as far
as the Ammonite border because the boundary of the
Ammonites was fortified.*
25So Israel captured all the towns of the Amorites
and settled in them, including the city of Heshbon
and its surrounding villages. 26Heshbon had been the
capital of King Sihon of the Amorites. He had defeated
a former Moabite king and seized all his land as far as
the Arnon River. 27Therefore, the ancient poets wrote
this about him:

"Come to Heshbon and let it be rebuilt!
Let the city of Sihon be restored.
28 A fire flamed forth from Heshbon,
a blaze from the city of Sihon.
It burned the city of Ar in Moab;
it destroyed the rulers of the Arnon
heights.
29 What sorrow awaits you, O people of Moab!
You are finished, O worshipers of Chemosh!
Chemosh has left his sons as refugees,
his daughters as captives of Sihon,
the Amorite king.
30 We have utterly destroyed them,
from Heshbon to Dibon.
We have completely wiped them out
as far away as Nophah and Medeba.*"

31So the people of Israel occupied the territory of
the Amorites. 32After Moses sent men to explore the
Jazer area, they captured all the towns in the region
and drove out the Amorites who lived there. 33Then
they turned and marched up the road to Bashan, but
King Og of Bashan and all his people attacked them
at Edrei. 34The LORD said to Moses, "Do not be afraid
of him, for I have handed him over to you, along with
all his people and his land. Do the same to him as
you did to King Sihon of the Amorites, who ruled in
Heshbon." 35And Israel killed King Og, his sons, and
all his subjects; not a single survivor remained. Then
Israel occupied their land.

Nm 21:16 *Beer* means "well." **Nm 21:20** Or *overlooks Jeshimon.* **Nm 21:24** Or *because the terrain of the Ammonite frontier was rugged;* Hebrew reads *because the boundary of the Ammonites was strong.* **Nm 21:30** Or *until fire spread to Medeba.* The meaning of the Hebrew is uncertain.

Num 21:27-30 Chemosh, the national god of Moab, was worshiped as a god of war. This false god was no help to this nation when it fought against Israel. Israel's God was stronger than any of Canaan's war gods.

Num 21:34 God assured Moses that Israel's enemy was conquered even before the battle began! God wants to give us victory over our enemies (which are usually problems related to sin rather than armed soldiers). But first we must believe that he can help us. Second, we must trust him to help us. Third, we must take the steps he shows us.

EVENTS IN THE WILDERNESS ▶
Israel next met resistance from the king of Arad but soundly defeated him. The next stop was Mount Hor (where Aaron died); then they traveled south and east around Edom. After camping at Oboth, they moved toward the Arnon River and on to the plains of Moab near Pisgah Peak.

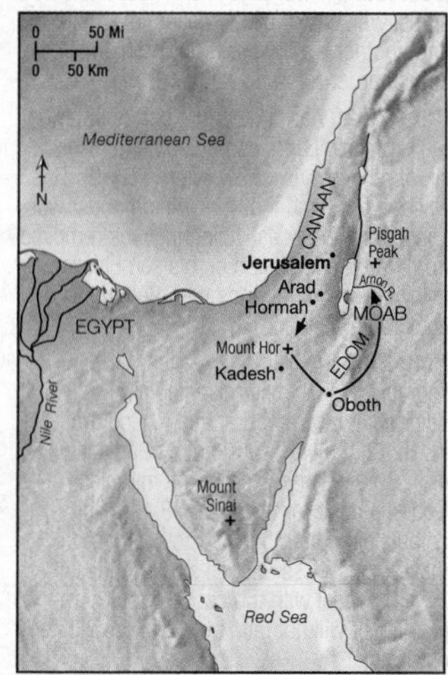

I. Second Approach to the Promised Land

Now the old generation has died and a new generation stands poised at the border, ready to enter the Promised Land. Neighboring nations, however, cause Israel to begin worshiping other gods. Without Moses' quick action, the nation may never have entered Canaan. We must never let down our guard in resisting sin.

1. THE STORY OF BALAAM

The king in Moab didn't want Israel anywhere near his land, so he hired a prophet named Balaam to curse them and send them away. But God spoke to Balaam and blessed Israel rather than cursing them. God cannot be manipulated out of keeping his promises.

Balak Sends for Balaam

NUMBERS 22:1-20

Then the people of Israel traveled to the plains of Moab
and camped east of the Jordan River, across from Jericho. [2]Balak son of Zippor, the Moabite king, had seen
everything the Israelites did to the Amorites. [3]And
when the people of Moab saw how many Israelites
there were, they were terrified. [4]The king of Moab said
to the elders of Midian, "This mob will devour everything in sight, like an ox devours grass in the field!"
So Balak, king of Moab, [5]sent messengers to call Balaam son of Beor, who was living in his native land of
Pethor* near the Euphrates River.* His message said:

> "Look, a vast horde of people has arrived from
> Egypt. They cover the face of the earth and are
> threatening me. [6]Please come and curse these
> people for me because they are too powerful
> for me. Then perhaps I will be able to conquer
> them and drive them from the land. I know that
> blessings fall on any people you bless, and curses
> fall on people you curse."

[7]Balak's messengers, who were elders of Moab and
Midian, set out with money to pay Balaam to place a
curse upon Israel.* They went to Balaam and delivered
Balak's message to him. [8]"Stay here overnight," Balaam
said. "In the morning I will tell you whatever the LORD
directs me to say." So the officials from Moab stayed
there with Balaam.
[9]That night God came to Balaam and asked him,
"Who are these men visiting you?"
[10]Balaam said to God, "Balak son of Zippor, king of
Moab, has sent me this message: [11]'Look, a vast horde
of people has arrived from Egypt, and they cover the
face of the earth. Come and curse these people for
me. Then perhaps I will be able to stand up to them
and drive them from the land.'"
[12]But God told Balaam, "Do not go with them. You are
not to curse these people, for they have been blessed!"
[13]The next morning Balaam got up and told Balak's
officials, "Go on home! The LORD will not let me go
with you."
[14]So the Moabite officials returned to King Balak and reported, "Balaam refused to come with us."
[15]Then Balak tried again. This time he sent a larger
number of even more distinguished officials than
those he had sent the first time. [16]They went to Balaam and delivered this message to him:

> "This is what Balak son of Zippor says: Please
> don't let anything stop you from coming to help

Nm 22:5a Or *who was at Pethor in the land of the Amavites.* **Nm 22:5b** Hebrew *the river.* **Nm 22:7** Hebrew *set out with the money of divination in their hand.*

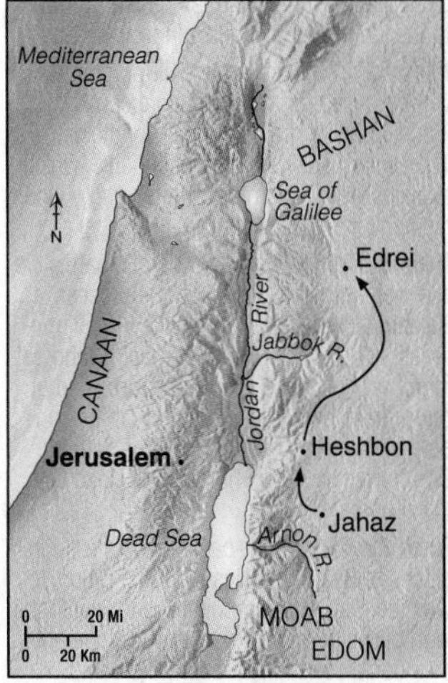

Num 22:4-6 Balaam was a sorcerer, one called upon to place curses on others. Belief in curses and blessings was common in Old Testament times. Sorcerers were thought to have power with the gods. Thus, the king of Moab wanted Balaam to use his powers with the God of Israel to place a curse on Israel—hoping that, by magic, God would turn against his people. Neither Balaam nor Balak had any idea whom they were dealing with!

◀ ***BATTLES WITH SIHON AND OG***
King Sihon refused passage to the Israelites through his land, and he attacked Israel at Jahaz. Israel defeated him, occupying the land between the Arnon and Jabbok Rivers, including the capital city, Heshbon. As they moved north, they defeated King Og of Bashan at Edrei.

Num 22:9 Why would God speak through a sorcerer like Balaam? God wanted to give a message to the Moabites, and they had already chosen to employ Balaam. So Balaam was available for God to use, much as he used the wicked pharaoh to accomplish his will in Egypt (Exod 10:1). Balaam entered into his prophetic role seriously, but his heart was mixed. He had some knowledge of God, but not enough to forsake his magic and turn wholeheartedly to God. Although this story leads us to believe he turned completely to God, later passages in the Bible show that Balaam couldn't resist the tempting pull of money and idolatry (Num 31:16; 2 Pet 2:15; Jude 1:11).

▸ **NUMBERS 22:1-20** ***(cont.)***

me. 17I will pay you very well and do whatever you tell me. Just come and curse these people for me!"

18But Balaam responded to Balak's messengers, "Even if Balak were to give me his palace filled with silver and gold, I would be powerless to do anything against the will of the LORD my God. 19But stay here one more night, and I will see if the LORD has anything else to say to me."

20That night God came to Balaam and told him, "Since these men have come for you, get up and go with them. But do only what I tell you to do."

Balaam and His Donkey

NUMBERS 22:21-41

So the next morning Balaam got up, saddled his donkey, and started off with the Moabite officials. 22But God was angry that Balaam was going, so he sent the angel of the LORD to stand in the road to block his way. As Balaam and two servants were riding along, 23Balaam's donkey saw the angel of the LORD standing in the road with a drawn sword in his hand. The donkey bolted off the road into a field, but Balaam beat it and turned it back onto the road. 24Then the angel of the LORD stood at a place where the road narrowed between two vineyard walls. 25When the donkey saw the angel of the LORD, it tried to squeeze by and crushed Balaam's foot against the wall. So Balaam beat the donkey again. 26Then the angel of the LORD moved farther down the road and stood in a place too narrow for the donkey to get by at all. 27This time when the donkey saw the angel, it lay down under Balaam. In a fit of rage Balaam beat the animal again with his staff.

28Then the LORD gave the donkey the ability to speak. "What have I done to you that deserves your beating me three times?" it asked Balaam.

29"You have made me look like a fool!" Balaam shouted. "If I had a sword with me, I would kill you!"

30"But I am the same donkey you have ridden all your life," the donkey answered. "Have I ever done anything like this before?"

"No," Balaam admitted.

31Then the LORD opened Balaam's eyes, and he saw the angel of the LORD standing in the roadway with a drawn sword in his hand. Balaam bowed his head and fell face down on the ground before him.

32"Why did you beat your donkey those three times?" the angel of the LORD demanded. "Look, I have come to block your way because you are stubbornly resisting me. 33Three times the donkey saw me and shied away; otherwise, I would certainly have killed you by now and spared the donkey."

34Then Balaam confessed to the angel of the LORD, "I have sinned. I didn't realize you were standing in the road to block my way. I will return home if you are against my going."

35But the angel of the LORD told Balaam, "Go with these men, but say only what I tell you to say." So Balaam went on with Balak's officials. 36When King Balak heard that Balaam was on the way, he went out to meet him at a Moabite town on the Arnon River at the farthest border of his land.

37"Didn't I send you an urgent invitation? Why didn't you come right away?" Balak asked Balaam. "Didn't you believe me when I said I would reward you richly?"

38Balaam replied, "Look, now I have come, but I have no power to say whatever I want. I will speak only the message that God puts in my mouth." 39Then Balaam accompanied Balak to Kiriath-huzoth, 40where the king sacrificed cattle and sheep. He sent portions of the meat to Balaam and the officials who were with him. 41The next morning Balak took Balaam up to Bamoth-baal. From there he could see some of the people of Israel spread out below him.

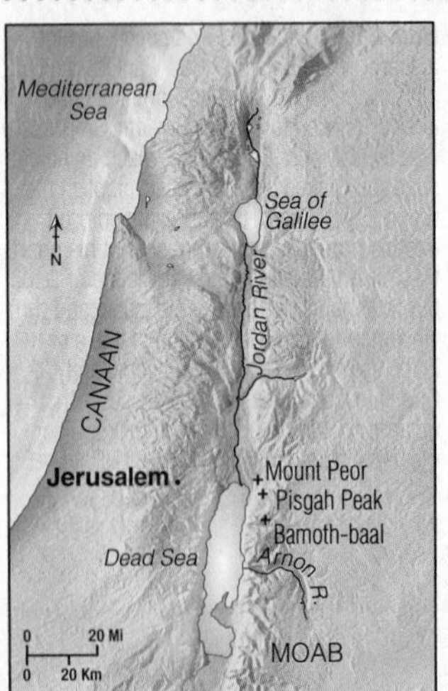

◂ ***THE STORY OF BALAAM***
At King Balak's request, Balaam traveled nearly 400 miles to curse Israel. Balak took Balaam to Bamoth-baal ("the high places of Baal"), then to Pisgah Peak, and finally to Mount Peor. Each place looked over the plains of Moab, where the Israelites were camped. But to the king's dismay, Balaam blessed, not cursed, Israel.

Num 22:20-23 God let Balaam go with Balak's messengers, but he was angry about Balaam's greedy attitude. Balaam claimed that he would not go against God just for money, but his resolve was beginning to slip. His greed for the wealth offered by the king blinded him so that he could not see how God was trying to stop him. Though we may know what God wants us to do, we can become blinded by the desire for money, possessions, or prestige. We can avoid Balaam's mistake by looking past the allure of fame or fortune to the long-range benefits of following God.

Num 22:27 Donkeys were all-purpose vehicles used for transportation, carrying loads, grinding grain, and plowing fields. They were usually highly dependable, which explains why Balaam became so angry when his donkey refused to move.

Num 22:29 The donkey saved Balaam's life but made him look foolish in the process, so Balaam lashed out at the donkey. We sometimes strike out at blameless people who get in our way because we are embarrassed or our pride is hurt. Lashing out at others can be a sign that something is wrong with us. Don't allow your own hurt pride to lead you to hurt others.

Num 22:41 *Bamoth-baal* means the "high places of Baal" near Heshbon and Dibon. It was the first stopping point on the way to the high plains of Moab. From this vantage point, they could see the entire Israelite camp.

Balaam Blesses Israel

NUMBERS 23:1-12

Then Balaam said to King Balak, "Build me seven altars here, and prepare seven young bulls and seven rams for me to sacrifice." [2]Balak followed his instructions, and the two of them sacrificed a young bull and a ram on each altar.

[3]Then Balaam said to Balak, "Stand here by your burnt offerings, and I will go to see if the LORD will respond to me. Then I will tell you whatever he reveals to me." So Balaam went alone to the top of a bare hill, [4]and God met him there. Balaam said to him, "I have prepared seven altars and have sacrificed a young bull and a ram on each altar."

[5]The LORD gave Balaam a message for King Balak. Then he said, "Go back to Balak and give him my message."

[6]So Balaam returned and found the king standing beside his burnt offerings with all the officials of Moab. [7]This was the message Balaam delivered:

"Balak summoned me to come from Aram;
the king of Moab brought me from the eastern hills.
'Come,' he said, 'curse Jacob for me!
Come and announce Israel's doom.'
8 But how can I curse those
whom God has not cursed?
How can I condemn those
whom the LORD has not condemned?
9 I see them from the cliff tops;
I watch them from the hills.
I see a people who live by themselves,
set apart from other nations.
10 Who can count Jacob's descendants,
as numerous as dust?
Who can count even a fourth of Israel's people?
Let me die like the righteous;
let my life end like theirs."

[11]Then King Balak demanded of Balaam, "What have you done to me? I brought you to curse my enemies. Instead, you have blessed them!"

[12]But Balaam replied, "I will speak only the message that the LORD puts in my mouth."

Balaam's Second Message

NUMBERS 23:13-26

Then King Balak told him, "Come with me to another place. There you will see another part of the nation of Israel, but not all of them. Curse at least that many!" [14]So Balak took Balaam to the plateau of Zophim on Pisgah Peak. He built seven altars there and offered a young bull and a ram on each altar.

[15]Then Balaam said to the king, "Stand here by your burnt offerings while I go over there to meet the LORD."

[16]And the LORD met Balaam and gave him a message. Then he said, "Go back to Balak and give him my message."

[17]So Balaam returned and found the king standing beside his burnt offerings with all the officials of Moab. "What did the LORD say?" Balak asked eagerly.

[18]This was the message Balaam delivered:

"Rise up, Balak, and listen!
Hear me, son of Zippor.
19 God is not a man, so he does not lie.
He is not human, so he does not change his mind.
Has he ever spoken and failed to act?
Has he ever promised and not carried it through?
20 Listen, I received a command to bless;
God has blessed, and I cannot reverse it!
21 No misfortune is in his plan for Jacob;
no trouble is in store for Israel.
For the LORD their God is with them;
he has been proclaimed their king.
22 God brought them out of Egypt;
for them he is as strong as a wild ox.
23 No curse can touch Jacob;
no magic has any power against Israel.
For now it will be said of Jacob,
'What wonders God has done for Israel!'
24 These people rise up like a lioness,
like a majestic lion rousing itself.
They refuse to rest
until they have feasted on prey,
drinking the blood of the slaughtered!"

[25]Then Balak said to Balaam, "Fine, but if you won't curse them, at least don't bless them!"

[26]But Balaam replied to Balak, "Didn't I tell you that I can do only what the LORD tells me?"

Balaam's Third Message

NUMBERS 23:27–24:14

Then King Balak said to Balaam, "Come, I will take you to one more place. Perhaps it will please God to let you curse them from there."

[28]So Balak took Balaam to the top of Mount Peor, overlooking the wasteland.* [29]Balaam again told Balak, "Build me seven altars, and prepare seven young bulls and seven rams for me to sacrifice." [30]So Balak

Nm 23:28 Or *overlooking Jeshimon.*

Num 23:1-3 The number seven was sacred among many of the nations and religions at this time.

Num 23:27 Balak took Balaam to several places to try to entice him to curse the Israelites. He thought a change of scenery might help change Balaam's mind. But changing locations won't change God's will. We must learn to face the source of our problems. Moving to escape problems only makes solving them more difficult. Problems rooted in us are not solved by a change of scenery. A change in location or job may only distract us from the need for us to change our heart.

▶ **NUMBERS 23:27–24:14 *(cont.)***
did as Balaam ordered and offered a young bull and
a ram on each altar.

24:1 By now Balaam realized that the LORD was determined to bless Israel, so he did not resort to divination
as before. Instead, he turned and looked out toward
the wilderness, 2where he saw the people of Israel
camped, tribe by tribe. Then the Spirit of God came
upon him, 3and this is the message he delivered:

"This is the message of Balaam son of Beor,
the message of the man whose eyes see clearly,
4 the message of one who hears the words of God,
who sees a vision from the Almighty,
who bows down with eyes wide open:
5 How beautiful are your tents, O Jacob;
how lovely are your homes, O Israel!
6 They spread before me like palm groves,*
like gardens by the riverside.
They are like tall trees planted by the LORD,
like cedars beside the waters.
7 Water will flow from their buckets;
their offspring have all they need.
Their king will be greater than Agag;
their kingdom will be exalted.
8 God brought them out of Egypt;
for them he is as strong as a wild ox.
He devours all the nations that oppose him,
breaking their bones in pieces,
shooting them with arrows.
9 Like a lion, Israel crouches and lies down;
like a lioness, who dares to arouse her?
Blessed is everyone who blesses you, O Israel,
and cursed is everyone who curses you."

10King Balak flew into a rage against Balaam. He
angrily clapped his hands and shouted, "I called you
to curse my enemies! Instead, you have blessed them
three times. 11Now get out of here! Go back home!
I promised to reward you richly, but the LORD has kept
you from your reward."

12Balaam told Balak, "Don't you remember what I
told your messengers? I said, 13'Even if Balak were to
give me his palace filled with silver and gold, I would be
powerless to do anything against the will of the LORD.'
told you that I could say only what the LORD says! 14Now
I am returning to my own people. But first let me tell you
what the Israelites will do to your people in the future."

Balaam's Final Messages

NUMBERS 24:15-25
This is the message Balaam delivered:

"This is the message of Balaam son of Beor,
the message of the man whose eyes see clearly,
16 the message of one who hears the words of God,
who has knowledge from the Most High,
who sees a vision from the Almighty,
who bows down with eyes wide open:
17 I see him, but not here and now.
I perceive him, but far in the distant future.
A star will rise from Jacob;
a scepter will emerge from Israel.
It will crush the foreheads of Moab's people,
cracking the skulls of the people of Sheth.
18 Edom will be taken over,
and Seir, its enemy, will be conquered,
while Israel marches on in triumph.
19 A ruler will rise in Jacob
who will destroy the survivors of Ir."

20Then Balaam looked over toward the people of
Amalek and delivered this message:

"Amalek was the greatest of nations,
but its destiny is destruction!"

21Then he looked over toward the Kenites and delivered this message:

"Your home is secure;
your nest is set in the rocks.
22 But the Kenites will be destroyed
when Assyria* takes you captive."

23Balaam concluded his messages by saying:

"Alas, who can survive
unless God has willed it?
24 Ships will come from the coasts of Cyprus*;
they will oppress Assyria and afflict Eber,
but they, too, will be utterly destroyed."

25Then Balaam and Balak returned to their homes.

Nm 24:6 Or *like a majestic valley.* **Nm 24:22** Hebrew *Asshur;* also in 24:24. **Nm 24:24** Hebrew *Kittim.*

Num 24:1 Because Balaam was a sorcerer, he would look for omens or signs to help him tell the future. In this situation, it was clear that God himself was speaking, so Balaam needed no other signs, real or imagined.

Num 24:7 Who was Agag? *Agag* was the title for the king of the Amalekites, just as *pharaoh* was the title for the ruler of Egypt. Saul, the first king of Israel, defeated Agag (1 Sam 15:8). Balaam prophesied correctly the ruin of Israel's oldest enemy (Exod 17:14-16).

Num 24:11 Although Balaam's motives were not correct, in blessing Israel he acted with integrity. God's message had so filled him that Balaam spoke the truth. In so doing, he forfeited the reward that had lured him to speak in the first place. Staying true to God's Word may cost us promotions and advantages in the short run, but those who choose God over money will one day acquire heavenly wealth beyond measure (Matt 6:19-21).

Num 24:15-19 The star that will rise from Jacob is often thought to refer to the coming Messiah. It was probably this prophecy that convinced the astrologers to travel to Israel to search for the baby Jesus (see Matt 2:1-2). It seems strange that God would use a sorcerer like Balaam to foretell the coming of the Messiah. But this teaches us that God can use anything or anyone to accomplish his plans. By using a sorcerer, God did not make sorcery acceptable; in fact, the Bible condemns it in several places (Exod 22:18; 2 Chr 33:6; Rev 18:23). Rather, God showed his ultimate sovereignty over good and evil.

Num 25:1 This verse shows the great challenge Israel had to face. The most dangerous problem for Moses and Joshua was not Jericho's hostile army, but the ever-present

Moab Seduces Israel

NUMBERS 25:1-18

While the Israelites were camped at Acacia Grove,*
some of the men defiled themselves by having* sexual
relations with local Moabite women. 2These women
invited them to attend sacrifices to their gods, so the
Israelites feasted with them and worshiped the gods
of Moab. 3In this way, Israel joined in the worship of
Baal of Peor, causing the LORD's anger to blaze against
his people.
4The LORD issued the following command to Moses:
"Seize all the ringleaders and execute them before the
LORD in broad daylight, so his fierce anger will turn
away from the people of Israel."
5So Moses ordered Israel's judges, "Each of you
must put to death the men under your authority who
have joined in worshiping Baal of Peor."
6Just then one of the Israelite men brought a Midianite woman into his tent, right before the eyes of
Moses and all the people, as everyone was weeping
at the entrance of the Tabernacle.* 7When Phinehas
son of Eleazar and grandson of Aaron the priest saw
this, he jumped up and left the assembly. He took a
spear 8and rushed after the man into his tent. Phinehas thrust the spear all the way through the man's
body and into the woman's stomach. So the plague
against the Israelites was stopped, 9but not before
24,000 people had died.
10Then the LORD said to Moses, 11"Phinehas son of
Eleazar and grandson of Aaron the priest has turned

Nm 25:1a Hebrew *Shittim.* **Nm 25:1b** As in Greek version; Hebrew reads *some of the men began having.* **Nm 25:6** Hebrew *the Tent of Meeting.*

BALAAM

Balaam was one of those noteworthy Old Testament characters who, though not one of God's chosen people, was willing to acknowledge that Yahweh (the LORD) was indeed a powerful God. But he did not believe in the Lord as the only true God. His story exposes the deception of maintaining an outward facade of spirituality over a corrupt inward life. Balaam was a man ready to obey God's command as long as he could profit from doing so. This mixture of motives—obedience and profit—eventually led to Balaam's death. Although he realized the awesome power of Israel's God, his heart was occupied with the wealth he could gain in Moab. There he returned to die when the armies of Israel invaded.

• Eventually, each of us lives through the same process. Who and what we are will somehow come to the surface, destroying any masks we may have put on to cover up our true selves. Efforts spent on keeping up appearances would be much better spent on finding the answer to sin in our lives. We can avoid Balaam's mistake by facing ourselves and realizing that God is willing to accept us, forgive us, and literally make us over from within. Don't miss this great discovery that eluded Balaam.

Strengths and accomplishments	• Widely known for his effective curses and blessings • Obeyed God and blessed Israel, in spite of Balak's bribe
Weaknesses and mistakes	• Encouraged the Israelites to worship idols (Num 31:16) • Returned to Moab and was killed in war
Lessons from his life	• Motives are just as important as actions • Your treasure is where your heart is
Vital statistics	• Where: Lived near the Euphrates River, traveled to Moab • Occupations: Sorcerer, prophet • Relative: Father: Beor • Contemporaries: Balak (king of Moab), Moses, Aaron
Key verses	"They have wandered off the right road and followed the footsteps of Balaam son of Beor, who loved to earn money by doing wrong. But Balaam was stopped from his mad course when his donkey rebuked him with a human voice" (2 Pet 2:15-16).

Balaam's story is told in Numbers 22:1–24:25. He is also mentioned in Numbers 31:7-8, 16; Deuteronomy 23:4-5; Joshua 24:9-10; Nehemiah 13:2; Micah 6:5; 2 Peter 2:15-16; Jude 1:11; Revelation 2:14.

temptation to compromise with the pagan Canaanite religions and cultures.

Num 25:1-2 The Bible doesn't say how the Israelite men got involved in sexual immorality. We do know that sacred prostitution was a common practice among Canaanite religions. At first, they didn't think about worshiping idols; they were just interested in sex. Before long they started attending local feasts and family celebrations that involved idol worship. Soon they were in over their heads, absorbed into the practices of the pagan culture. Their desire for fun and pleasure caused them to loosen their spiritual commitment. Have you relaxed your standards in order to justify your desires?

Num 25:1-3 This combination of sexual sin and idolatry, it turns out, was Balaam's idea (see Num 31:16; Rev 2:14)—the same Balaam who had just blessed Israel and who appeared to be on their side. It is easy to see how the Israelites were misled, for Balaam seemed to say and do all the right things—at least for a while (Num 22–24). Not until Balaam had inflicted great damage on them did the Israelites realize that he was greedy, used sorcery, and was deeply involved in pagan religious practices. We must be careful to weigh both the words and the deeds of those who claim to offer spiritual help.

Num 25:3 Baal was the most popular god in Canaan, the land Israel was about to enter. Represented by a bull, symbol of strength and fertility, he was the god of the rains and harvest. The Israelites were continually attracted to Baal worship, in which prostitution played a large part, throughout their years in Canaan. Because Baal was so popular, his name was often used as a generic title for all the local gods.

Num 25:6 That this man "brought a Midianite woman into his tent" meant that she was brought into his tent for sex. Zimri (Num 25:14) so disregarded the law of God that he brought the woman right into the camp.

Num 25:10-11 It is clear from Phinehas's story that some anger is proper and justified. Phinehas was angry because of his zeal for the Lord. But how can we know when our anger is appropriate and when it should be restrained? Ask these questions when you become angry: (1) Why am I angry? (2) Whose rights are being violated (mine or another's)? (3) Is the truth (a principle of God) being violated? If only your rights are at stake, it may be wiser to keep angry feelings under control. But if the truth is at stake, anger is often justified, although violence and retaliation are usually the wrong way to express it (Phinehas's case was unique). If we are becoming more and more like God, we should be angered by sin.

▸ **NUMBERS 25:1-18 *(cont.)***
my anger away from the Israelites by being as zealous among them as I was. So I stopped destroying all
Israel as I had intended to do in my zealous anger.
12Now tell him that I am making my special covenant
of peace with him. 13In this covenant, I give him and
his descendants a permanent right to the priesthood,
for in his zeal for me, his God, he purified the people
of Israel, making them right with me.*"
14The Israelite man killed with the Midianite
woman was named Zimri son of Salu, the leader of a
family from the tribe of Simeon. 15The woman's name
was Cozbi; she was the daughter of Zur, the leader of
a Midianite clan.
16Then the LORD said to Moses, 17"Attack the Midianites and destroy them, 18because they assaulted
you with deceit and tricked you into worshiping Baal
of Peor, and because of Cozbi, the daughter of a Midianite leader, who was killed at the time of the plague
because of what happened at Peor."

Nm 25:13 Or *he made atonement for the people of Israel.*

2. THE SECOND CENSUS OF THE NATION

Israel had done a census when they first left Sinai, and after 40 years in the wilderness and the death of nearly everyone from that generation it was time to do another one. This generation would be ready to follow God into the land he had promised their ancestors.

The Second Registration of Israel's Troops

NUMBERS 26:1-4

After the plague had ended, the LORD said to Moses
and to Eleazar son of Aaron the priest, 2"From the
whole community of Israel, record the names of all
the warriors by their families. List all the men twenty
years old or older who are able to go to war."
3So there on the plains of Moab beside the Jordan
River, across from Jericho, Moses and Eleazar the
priest issued these instructions to the leaders of Israel: 4"List all the men of Israel twenty years old and
older, just as the LORD commanded Moses."

This is the record of all the descendants of Israel who came out of Egypt.

The Tribe of Reuben

NUMBERS 26:5-11

These were the clans descended from the sons of Reuben, Jacob's* oldest son:

The Hanochite clan, named after their ancestor Hanoch.
The Palluite clan, named after their ancestor Pallu.
6 The Hezronite clan, named after their ancestor Hezron.
The Carmite clan, named after their ancestor Carmi.

7These were the clans of Reuben. Their registered
troops numbered 43,730.
8Pallu was the ancestor of Eliab, 9and Eliab was the
father of Nemuel, Dathan, and Abiram. This Dathan
and Abiram are the same community leaders who conspired with Korah against Moses and Aaron, rebelling
against the LORD. 10But the earth opened up its mouth
and swallowed them with Korah, and fire devoured
250 of their followers. This served as a warning to the
entire nation of Israel. 11However, the sons of Korah
did not die that day.

The Tribe of Simeon

NUMBERS 26:12-14

These were the clans descended from the sons of Simeon:

The Jemuelite clan, named after their ancestor Jemuel.*
The Jaminite clan, named after their ancestor Jamin.
The Jakinite clan, named after their ancestor Jakin.
13 The Zoharite clan, named after their ancestor Zohar.*
The Shaulite clan, named after their ancestor Shaul.

14These were the clans of Simeon. Their registered
troops numbered 22,200.

The Tribe of Gad

NUMBERS 26:15-18

These were the clans descended from the sons of Gad:

The Zephonite clan, named after their ancestor Zephon.
The Haggite clan, named after their ancestor Haggi.
The Shunite clan, named after their ancestor Shuni.
16 The Oznite clan, named after their ancestor Ozni.
The Erite clan, named after their ancestor Eri.

Nm 26:5 Hebrew *Israel's;* see note on 1:20-21b. **Nm 26:12** As in Syriac version (see also Gen 46:10; Exod 6:15); Hebrew reads *Nemuelite . . . Nemuel.* **Nm 26:13** As in parallel texts at Gen 46:10 and Exod 6:15; Hebrew reads *Zerahite . . . Zerah.*

Num 25:12-13 Phinehas's act made atonement for the nation of Israel; in effect, what he did averted God's judgment. Because of this, his descendants would become the high priests of Israel. They continued so throughout the history of the Tabernacle and the Temple.

17 The Arodite clan, named after their ancestor Arodi.*
The Arelite clan, named after their ancestor Areli.

18 These were the clans of Gad. Their registered troops numbered 40,500.

The Tribe of Judah

NUMBERS 26:19-22

Judah had two sons, Er and Onan, who had died in the
land of Canaan. 20 These were the clans descended
from Judah's surviving sons:

The Shelanite clan, named after their ancestor Shelah.
The Perezite clan, named after their ancestor Perez.
The Zerahite clan, named after their ancestor Zerah.

21 These were the subclans descended from the Perezites:

The Hezronites, named after their ancestor Hezron.
The Hamulites, named after their ancestor Hamul.

22 These were the clans of Judah. Their registered troops numbered 76,500.

The Tribe of Issachar

NUMBERS 26:23-25

These were the clans descended from the sons of Issachar:

The Tolaite clan, named after their ancestor Tola.
The Puite clan, named after their ancestor Puah.*
24 The Jashubite clan, named after their ancestor Jashub.
The Shimronite clan, named after their ancestor Shimron.

25 These were the clans of Issachar. Their registered troops numbered 64,300.

The Tribe of Zebulun

NUMBERS 26:26-27

These were the clans descended from the sons of Zebulun:

The Seredite clan, named after their ancestor Sered.
The Elonite clan, named after their ancestor Elon.
The Jahleelite clan, named after their ancestor Jahleel.

27 These were the clans of Zebulun. Their registered troops numbered 60,500.

The Tribe of Manasseh

NUMBERS 26:28-34

Two clans were descended from Joseph through Manasseh and Ephraim.

29 These were the clans descended from Manasseh:

The Makirite clan, named after their ancestor Makir.
The Gileadite clan, named after their ancestor Gilead, Makir's son.

30 These were the subclans descended from the Gileadites:

The Iezerites, named after their ancestor Iezer.
The Helekites, named after their ancestor Helek.
31 The Asrielites, named after their ancestor Asriel.
The Shechemites, named after their ancestor Shechem.
32 The Shemidaites, named after their ancestor Shemida.
The Hepherites, named after their ancestor Hepher.
33 (One of Hepher's descendants, Zelophehad, had no sons, but his daughters' names were Mahlah, Noah, Hoglah, Milcah, and Tirzah.)

34 These were the clans of Manasseh. Their registered troops numbered 52,700.

The Tribe of Ephraim

NUMBERS 26:35-37

These were the clans descended from the sons of Ephraim:

The Shuthelahite clan, named after their ancestor Shuthelah.
The Bekerite clan, named after their ancestor Beker.
The Tahanite clan, named after their ancestor Tahan.

36 This was the subclan descended from the Shuthelahites:

The Eranites, named after their ancestor Eran.

37 These were the clans of Ephraim. Their registered troops numbered 32,500.

These clans of Manasseh and Ephraim were all descendants of Joseph.

The Tribe of Benjamin

NUMBERS 26:38-41

These were the clans descended from the sons of Benjamin:

The Belaite clan, named after their ancestor Bela.
The Ashbelite clan, named after their ancestor Ashbel.
The Ahiramite clan, named after their ancestor Ahiram.
39 The Shuphamite clan, named after their ancestor Shupham.*

Nm 26:17 As in Samaritan Pentateuch and Greek and Syriac versions (see also Gen 46:16); Hebrew reads *Arod.* **Nm 26:23** As in Samaritan Pentateuch, Greek and Syriac versions, and Latin Vulgate (see also 1 Chr 7:1); Hebrew reads *The Punite clan, named after its ancestor Puvah.* **Nm 26:39** As in some Hebrew manuscripts, Samaritan Pentateuch, Greek and Syriac versions, and Latin Vulgate; most Hebrew manuscripts read *Shephupham.*

▸ NUMBERS 26:38-41 *(cont.)*

The Huphamite clan, named after their ancestor Hupham.

40These were the subclans descended from the Belaites:

The Ardites, named after their ancestor Ard.*
The Naamites, named after their ancestor Naaman.

41These were the clans of Benjamin. Their registered troops numbered 45,600.

The Tribe of Dan

NUMBERS 26:42-43

These were the clans descended from the sons of Dan:

The Shuhamite clan, named after their ancestor Shuham.

43These were the Shuhamite clans of Dan. Their registered troops numbered 64,400.

The Tribe of Asher

NUMBERS 26:44-47

These were the clans descended from the sons of Asher:

The Imnite clan, named after their ancestor Imnah.
The Ishvite clan, named after their ancestor Ishvi.
The Beriite clan, named after their ancestor Beriah.

45These were the subclans descended from the Beriites:

The Heberites, named after their ancestor Heber.
The Malkielites, named after their ancestor Malkiel.

46Asher also had a daughter named Serah.

47These were the clans of Asher. Their registered troops numbered 53,400.

The Tribe of Naphtali

NUMBERS 26:48-50

These were the clans descended from the sons of Naphtali:

The Jahzeelite clan, named after their ancestor Jahzeel.
The Gunite clan, named after their ancestor Guni.
49 The Jezerite clan, named after their ancestor Jezer.
The Shillemite clan, named after their ancestor Shillem.

50These were the clans of Naphtali. Their registered troops numbered 45,400.

Results of the Registration

NUMBERS 26:51-56

In summary, the registered troops of all Israel numbered 601,730.

52Then the LORD said to Moses, 53"Divide the land
among the tribes, and distribute the grants of land
in proportion to the tribes' populations, as indicated
by the number of names on the list. 54Give the larger
tribes more land and the smaller tribes less land, each
group receiving a grant in proportion to the size of
its population. 55But you must assign the land by lot,
and give land to each ancestral tribe according to the
number of names on the list. 56Each grant of land
must be assigned by lot among the larger and smaller
tribal groups."

The Tribe of Levi

NUMBERS 26:57-65

This is the record of the Levites who were counted according to their clans:

The Gershonite clan, named after their ancestor Gershon.
The Kohathite clan, named after their ancestor Kohath.
The Merarite clan, named after their ancestor Merari.

58The Libnites, the Hebronites, the Mahlites, the
Mushites, and the Korahites were all subclans of the
Levites.

Now Kohath was the ancestor of Amram, 59and
Amram's wife was named Jochebed. She also was a descendant of Levi, born among the Levites in the land
of Egypt. Amram and Jochebed became the parents
of Aaron, Moses, and their sister, Miriam. 60To Aaron
were born Nadab, Abihu, Eleazar, and Ithamar. 61But
Nadab and Abihu died when they burned before the
LORD the wrong kind of fire, different than he had
commanded.

62The men from the Levite clans who were one
month old or older numbered 23,000. But the Levites
were not included in the registration of the rest of the
people of Israel because they were not given an allotment of land when it was divided among the Israelites.

63So these are the results of the registration of the
people of Israel as conducted by Moses and Eleazar
the priest on the plains of Moab beside the Jordan
River, across from Jericho. 64Not one person on this
list had been among those listed in the previous registration taken by Moses and Aaron in the wilderness
of Sinai. 65For the LORD had said of them, "They will

Nm 26:40 As in Samaritan Pentateuch, some Greek manuscripts, and Latin Vulgate; Hebrew lacks *named after their ancestor Ard.*

Num 26:64 A new census for a new generation. Thirty-eight years had elapsed since the first great census recorded in Numbers (see Num 1:1–2:33). During that time, every Israelite man and woman 20 years old and over—except Caleb, Joshua, and Moses—had died, and yet God's laws and the spiritual character of the nation were still intact. Numbers records some dramatic miracles. This is a quiet but powerful miracle often overlooked: A whole nation moved from one land to another, lost its entire adult population, yet managed to maintain its spiritual direction. Sometimes it may feel like God isn't working dramatic miracles in our lives. But God often works in quiet ways to bring about his long-range purposes.

Num 27:3 "Died because of his own sin" means that he died a natural death. His death

all die in the wilderness." Not one of them survived except Caleb son of Jephunneh and Joshua son of Nun.

The Daughters of Zelophehad

NUMBERS 27:1-11

One day a petition was presented by the daughters of Zelophehad—Mahlah, Noah, Hoglah, Milcah, and Tirzah. Their father, Zelophehad, was a descendant of Hepher son of Gilead, son of Makir, son of Manasseh, son of Joseph. 2These women stood before Moses, Eleazar the priest, the tribal leaders, and the entire community at the entrance of the Tabernacle.* 3"Our father died in the wilderness," they said. "He was not among Korah's followers, who rebelled against the LORD; he died because of his own sin. But he had no sons. 4Why should the name of our father disappear from his clan just because he had no sons? Give us property along with the rest of our relatives."

5So Moses brought their case before the LORD. 6And the LORD replied to Moses, 7"The claim of the daughters of Zelophehad is legitimate. You must give them a grant of land along with their father's relatives. Assign them the property that would have been given to their father.

8"And give the following instructions to the people of Israel: If a man dies and has no son, then give his inheritance to his daughters. 9And if he has no daughter either, transfer his inheritance to his brothers. 10If he has no brothers, give his inheritance to his father's brothers. 11But if his father has no brothers, give his inheritance to the nearest relative in his clan. This is a legal requirement for the people of Israel, just as the LORD commanded Moses."

Joshua Chosen to Lead Israel

NUMBERS 27:12-23

One day the LORD said to Moses, "Climb one of the mountains east of the river,* and look out over the land I have given the people of Israel. 13After you have seen it, you will die like your brother, Aaron, 14for you both rebelled against my instructions in the wilderness of Zin. When the people of Israel rebelled, you failed to demonstrate my holiness to them at the waters." (These are the waters of Meribah at Kadesh* in the wilderness of Zin.)

15Then Moses said to the LORD, 16"O LORD, you are the God who gives breath to all creatures. Please appoint a new man as leader for the community. 17Give them someone who will guide them wherever they go and will lead them into battle, so the community of the LORD will not be like sheep without a shepherd."

18The LORD replied, "Take Joshua son of Nun, who has the Spirit in him, and lay your hands on him. 19Present him to Eleazar the priest before the whole community, and publicly commission him to lead the people. 20Transfer some of your authority to him so the whole community of Israel will obey him. 21When direction from the LORD is needed, Joshua will stand before Eleazar the priest, who will use the Urim—one of the sacred lots cast before the LORD—to determine his will. This is how Joshua and the rest of the community of Israel will determine everything they should do."

22So Moses did as the LORD commanded. He presented Joshua to Eleazar the priest and the whole community. 23Moses laid his hands on him and commissioned him to lead the people, just as the LORD had commanded through Moses.

Nm 27:2 Hebrew *the Tent of Meeting.* **Nm 27:12** Or *the mountains of Abarim.* **Nm 27:14** Hebrew *waters of Meribath-kadesh.*

3. INSTRUCTIONS CONCERNING OFFERINGS

God gave the new generation additional instructions about the offerings that they should bring as part of their regular worship. We often need reminders of the proper ways to acknowledge God's reign in our lives.

The Daily Offerings

NUMBERS 28:1-8

The LORD said to Moses, 2"Give these instructions to the people of Israel: The offerings you present as special gifts are a pleasing aroma to me; they are my food. See to it that they are brought at the appointed times and offered according to my instructions.

3"Say to the people: This is the special gift you must

fell under the judgment of the entire nation for believing the faithless scouts.

Num 27:3-4 Up to this point, the Hebrew law gave sons alone the right to inherit. The daughters of Zelophehad, having no brothers, came to Moses to ask for their father's possessions. God told Moses that if a man died without sons, his inheritance would go to his daughters (Num 27:8). But the daughters could keep it only if they married within their own tribe, probably so the territorial lines would remain intact (Num 36:5-12).

Num 27:15-17 Moses asked God to appoint a leader who was capable of directing both external and internal affairs—one who could lead them in battle but who would also care for their needs. The Lord responded by appointing Joshua. Many people want to be known as leaders. Some are very capable of reaching their goals, while others care deeply for the people in their charge. The best leaders are both goal-oriented and people-oriented.

Num 27:15-21 Moses did not want to leave his work without making sure a new leader was ready to replace him. First, he asked God to help him find a replacement. Then, when Joshua was selected, Moses gave him a variety of tasks to ease the transition into his new position. Moses also clearly told the people that Joshua had the authority and the ability to lead the nation. His display of confidence in Joshua was good for both Joshua and the people. To minimize leadership gaps, anyone in a leadership position should train others to carry on the duties should he or she suddenly or eventually have to leave. While you have the opportunity, follow Moses' pattern: pray, select, develop, and commission.

Num 28:1-2 Offerings had to be brought regularly and presented according to prescribed rituals under the priests' supervision. Following these rituals took time, and this gave the people the opportunity to prepare their hearts for worship. Unless our hearts are ready, worship is meaningless. By contrast, God is delighted, and we get more from it, when our hearts are prepared to come before him in a spirit of thankfulness.

▸ **NUMBERS 28:1-8 *(cont.)***

present to the Lord as your daily burnt offering. You must offer two one-year-old male lambs with no defects. [4]Sacrifice one lamb in the morning and the other in the evening. [5]With each lamb you must offer a grain offering of two quarts* of choice flour mixed with one quart* of pure oil of pressed olives. [6]This is the regular burnt offering instituted at Mount Sinai as a special gift, a pleasing aroma to the LORD. [7]Along with it you must present the proper liquid offering of one quart of alcoholic drink with each lamb, poured out in the Holy Place as an offering to the LORD. [8]Offer the second lamb in the evening with the same grain offering and liquid offering. It, too, is a special gift, a pleasing aroma to the LORD.

The Sabbath Offerings

NUMBERS 28:9-10

"On the Sabbath day, sacrifice two one-year-old male lambs with no defects. They must be accompanied by a grain offering of four quarts* of choice flour moistened with olive oil, and a liquid offering. [10]This is the burnt offering to be presented each Sabbath day, in addition to the regular burnt offering and its accompanying liquid offering.

The Monthly Offerings

NUMBERS 28:11-15

"On the first day of each month, present an extra burnt offering to the LORD of two young bulls, one ram, and seven one-year-old male lambs, all with no defects. [12]These must be accompanied by grain offerings of choice flour moistened with olive oil—six quarts* with each bull, four quarts with the ram, [13]and two quarts with each lamb. This burnt offering will be a special gift, a pleasing aroma to the LORD. [14]You must also present a liquid offering with each sacrifice: two quarts* of wine for each bull, a third of a gallon* for the ram, and one quart* for each lamb. Present this monthly burnt offering on the first day of each month throughout the year.

[15]"On the first day of each month, you must also offer one male goat for a sin offering to the LORD. This is in addition to the regular burnt offering and its accompanying liquid offering.

Offerings for the Passover

NUMBERS 28:16-25

"On the fourteenth day of the first month,* you must celebrate the LORD's Passover. [17]On the following day—the fifteenth day of the month—a joyous, seven-day festival will begin, but no bread made with yeast may be eaten. [18]The first day of the festival will be an official day for holy assembly, and no ordinary work may be done on that day. [19]As a special gift you must present a burnt offering to the LORD—two young bulls, one ram, and seven one-year-old male lambs, all with no defects. [20]These will be accompanied by grain offerings of choice flour moistened with olive oil—six quarts with each bull, four quarts with the ram, [21]and two quarts with each of the seven lambs. [22]You must also offer a male goat as a sin offering to purify yourselves and make yourselves right with the LORD.* [23]Present these offerings in addition to your regular

Nm 28:5a Hebrew *1/10 of an ephah* [2.2 liters]; also in 28:13, 21, 29. **Nm 28:5b** Hebrew *1/4 of a hin* [1 liter]; also in 28:7. **Nm 28:9** Hebrew *2/10 of an ephah* [4.4 liters]; also in 28:12, 20, 28. **Nm 28:12** Hebrew *3/10 of an ephah* [6.6 liters]; also in 28:20, 28. **Nm 28:14a** Hebrew *1/2 of a hin* [2 liters]. **Nm 28:14b** Hebrew *1/3 of a hin* [1.3 liters]. **Nm 28:14c** Hebrew *1/4 of a hin* [1 liter]. **Nm 28:16** This day in the ancient Hebrew lunar calendar occurred in late March, April, or early May. **Nm 28:22** Or *to make atonement for yourselves;* also in 28:30.

Num 28:9-10 Why were extra offerings made on the Sabbath day? The Sabbath was a special day of rest and worship commemorating both creation (Exod 20:8-11) and the deliverance from Egypt (Deut 5:12-15). Because of the significance of this special day, it was only natural to offer extra sacrifices on it.

Altar for Burnt Offerings

An altar was a platform upon which offerings were made to God. The Hebrew word for "altar" and the verb meaning "to slaughter" are closely related; they are both used in connection with the ritual of sacrificing animals to God as a covering for sin. The practice was widely known in the ancient Near East as well as in other parts of the world. Israel's immediate neighbors, the Canaanites, had their own altars of sacrifice and rituals.

In Exodus 20:24-26, instructions were given to Israel to make an altar of earth or of uncut stones, upon which burnt offerings and peace offerings were to be made, in every place where God caused his name to dwell. This allowed various individuals to erect an altar from time to time. Joshua built an altar on Mt. Ebal (Josh 8:30-31); the Reubenites, Gadites, and half-tribe of Manasseh built one at Geliloth (Josh 22:10-16); Gideon built one in Ophrah (Judg 6:24); David on the threshing floor of Araunah (2 Sam 24:18-25); and Elijah on Mt. Carmel (1 Kgs 18:19-30). Finally, Solomon built an altar for the Temple. Though we, as Christians, aren't required to build altars, we are to present our bodies as living sacrifices to God (Rom 12:1).

7.5 ft.

morning burnt offering. 24On each of the seven days
of the festival, this is how you must prepare the food
offering that is presented as a special gift, a pleasing
aroma to the LORD. These will be offered in addition to
the regular burnt offerings and liquid offerings. 25The
seventh day of the festival will be another official day
for holy assembly, and no ordinary work may be done
on that day.

Offerings for the Festival of Harvest

NUMBERS 28:26-31

"At the Festival of Harvest,* when you present the first
of your new grain to the LORD, you must call an official
day for holy assembly, and you may do no ordinary
work on that day. 27Present a special burnt offering
on that day as a pleasing aroma to the LORD. It will
consist of two young bulls, one ram, and seven one-
year-old male lambs. 28These will be accompanied by
grain offerings of choice flour moistened with olive
oil—six quarts with each bull, four quarts with the
ram, 29and two quarts with each of the seven lambs.
30Also, offer one male goat to purify yourselves and
make yourselves right with the LORD. 31Prepare these
special burnt offerings, along with their liquid offerings, in addition to the regular burnt offering and
its accompanying grain offering. Be sure that all the
animals you sacrifice have no defects.

Offerings for the Festival of Trumpets

NUMBERS 29:1-6

"Celebrate the Festival of Trumpets each year on the
first day of the appointed month in early autumn.*
You must call an official day for holy assembly, and
you may do no ordinary work. 2On that day you must
present a burnt offering as a pleasing aroma to the
LORD. It will consist of one young bull, one ram, and
seven one-year-old male lambs, all with no defects.
3These must be accompanied by grain offerings of
choice flour moistened with olive oil—six quarts*
with the bull, four quarts* with the ram, 4and two
quarts* with each of the seven lambs. 5In addition,
you must sacrifice a male goat as a sin offering to
purify yourselves and make yourselves right with the
LORD.* 6These special sacrifices are in addition to
your regular monthly and daily burnt offerings, and
they must be given with their prescribed grain offerings and liquid offerings. These offerings are given
as a special gift to the LORD, a pleasing aroma to him.

Offerings for the Day of Atonement

NUMBERS 29:7-11

"Ten days later, on the tenth day of the same month,*
you must call another holy assembly. On that day, the
Day of Atonement, the people must go without food
and must do no ordinary work. 8You must present a
burnt offering as a pleasing aroma to the LORD. It will
consist of one young bull, one ram, and seven one-
year-old male lambs, all with no defects. 9These offerings must be accompanied by the prescribed grain
offerings of choice flour moistened with olive oil—six
quarts of choice flour with the bull, four quarts of
choice flour with the ram, 10and two quarts of choice
flour with each of the seven lambs. 11You must also
sacrifice one male goat for a sin offering. This is in addition to the sin offering of atonement and the regular
daily burnt offering with its grain offering, and their
accompanying liquid offerings.

Offerings for the Festival of Shelters

NUMBERS 29:12-40

"Five days later, on the fifteenth day of the same
month,* you must call another holy assembly of all
the people, and you may do no ordinary work on that
day. It is the beginning of the Festival of Shelters,* a
seven-day festival to the LORD. 13On the first day of the
festival, you must present a burnt offering as a special
gift, a pleasing aroma to the LORD. It will consist of
thirteen young bulls, two rams, and fourteen one-year-
old male lambs, all with no defects. 14Each of these
offerings must be accompanied by a grain offering of
choice flour moistened with olive oil—six quarts for
each of the thirteen bulls, four quarts for each of the
two rams, 15and two quarts for each of the fourteen
lambs. 16You must also sacrifice a male goat as a sin

Nm 28:26 Hebrew *Festival of Weeks.* This was later called the Festival of Pentecost (see Acts 2:1). It is celebrated today as Shavuot (or Shabuoth). **Nm 29:1** Hebrew *the first day of the seventh month.* This day in the ancient Hebrew lunar calendar occurred in September or October. This festival is celebrated today as Rosh Hashanah, the Jewish new year. **Nm 29:3a** Hebrew *3/10 of an ephah* [6.6 liters]; also in 29:9, 14. **Nm 29:3b** Hebrew *2/10 of an ephah* [4.4 liters]; also in 29:9, 14. **Nm 29:4** Hebrew *1/10 of an ephah* [2.2 liters]; also in 29:10, 15. **Nm 29:5** Or *to make atonement for yourselves.* **Nm 29:7** Hebrew *On the tenth day of the seventh month;* see 29:1 and the note there. This day in the ancient Hebrew lunar calendar occurred in September or October. It is celebrated today as Yom Kippur. **Nm 29:12a** Hebrew *On the fifteenth day of the seventh month;* see 29:1, 7 and the notes there. This day in the ancient Hebrew lunar calendar occurred in late September, October, or early November. **Nm 29:12b** Or *Festival of Booths,* or *Festival of Tabernacles.* This was earlier called the Festival of the Final Harvest or Festival of Ingathering (see Exod 23:16b). It is celebrated today as Sukkot (or Succoth).

Num 29:1ff God placed many holidays on Israel's calendar. The Festival of Trumpets was one of three great holidays celebrated in the seventh month (the Festival of Shelters and Day of Atonement were the other two). These holidays provided a time to refresh the mind and body and to renew one's commitment to God. If you feel tired or far from God, try taking a "spiritual holiday." Separate yourself from your daily routine and concentrate on renewing your commitment to God.

Num 29:1-2 The Festival of Trumpets demonstrated three important principles that we should follow in our worship today: (1) The people gathered together to celebrate and worship. There is an extra benefit to be gained from worshiping with other believers. (2) The normal daily routine was suspended, and no hard work was done. It takes time to worship, and setting aside the time allows us to adjust our attitudes before and reflect afterward. (3) The people gave God something of value by sacrificing animals as burnt offerings to him. We show our commitment to God when we give something of value to him. God desires wholehearted worship. Our gift of money presented generously to God's work also demonstrates our thanks to him. The best gift, of course, is ourselves.

▶ **NUMBERS 29:12-40** ***(cont.)***

offering, in addition to the regular burnt offering with its accompanying grain offering and liquid offering.

17"On the second day of this seven-day festival, sacrifice twelve young bulls, two rams, and fourteen one-year-old male lambs, all with no defects. 18Each of these offerings of bulls, rams, and lambs must be accompanied by its prescribed grain offering and liquid offering. 19You must also sacrifice a male goat as a sin offering, in addition to the regular burnt offering with its accompanying grain offering and liquid offering.

20"On the third day of the festival, sacrifice eleven young bulls, two rams, and fourteen one-year-old male lambs, all with no defects. 21Each of these offerings of bulls, rams, and lambs must be accompanied by its prescribed grain offering and liquid offering. 22You must also sacrifice a male goat as a sin offering, in addition to the regular burnt offering with its accompanying grain offering and liquid offering.

23"On the fourth day of the festival, sacrifice ten young bulls, two rams, and fourteen one-year-old male lambs, all with no defects. 24Each of these offerings of bulls, rams, and lambs must be accompanied by its prescribed grain offering and liquid offering. 25You must also sacrifice a male goat as a sin offering, in addition to the regular burnt offering with its accompanying grain offering and liquid offering.

26"On the fifth day of the festival, sacrifice nine young bulls, two rams, and fourteen one-year-old male lambs, all with no defects. 27Each of these offerings of bulls, rams, and lambs must be accompanied by its prescribed grain offering and liquid offering. 28You must also sacrifice a male goat as a sin offering, in addition to the regular burnt offering with its accompanying grain offering and liquid offering.

29"On the sixth day of the festival, sacrifice eight young bulls, two rams, and fourteen one-year-old male lambs, all with no defects. 30Each of these offerings of bulls, rams, and lambs must be accompanied by its prescribed grain offering and liquid offering. 31You must also sacrifice a male goat as a sin offering, in addition to the regular burnt offering with its accompanying grain offering and liquid offering.

32"On the seventh day of the festival, sacrifice seven young bulls, two rams, and fourteen one-year-old male lambs, all with no defects. 33Each of these offerings of bulls, rams, and lambs must be accompanied by its prescribed grain offering and liquid offering. 34You must also sacrifice one male goat as a sin offering, in addition to the regular burnt offering with its accompanying grain offering and liquid offering.

35"On the eighth day of the festival, proclaim another holy day. You must do no ordinary work on that day. 36You must present a burnt offering as a special gift, a pleasing aroma to the LORD. It will consist of one young bull, one ram, and seven one-year-old male lambs, all with no defects. 37Each of these offerings must be accompanied by its prescribed grain offering and liquid offering. 38You must also sacrifice one male goat as a sin offering, in addition to the regular burnt offering with its accompanying grain offering and liquid offering.

39"You must present these offerings to the LORD at your annual festivals. These are in addition to the sacrifices and offerings you present in connection with vows, or as voluntary offerings, burnt offerings, grain offerings, liquid offerings, or peace offerings."

40*So Moses gave all of these instructions to the people of Israel as the LORD had commanded him.

Laws concerning Vows

NUMBERS 30:1-16

1*Then Moses summoned the leaders of the tribes of Israel and told them, "This is what the LORD has commanded: 2A man who makes a vow to the LORD or makes a pledge under oath must never break it. He must do exactly what he said he would do.

3"If a young woman makes a vow to the LORD or a pledge under oath while she is still living at her father's home, 4and her father hears of the vow or pledge and does not object to it, then all her vows and pledges will stand. 5But if her father refuses to let her fulfill the vow or pledge on the day he hears of it, then all her vows and pledges will become invalid. The LORD will forgive her because her father would not let her fulfill them.

6"Now suppose a young woman makes a vow or binds herself with an impulsive pledge and later marries. 7If her husband learns of her vow or pledge and does not object on the day he hears of it, her vows and pledges will stand. 8But if her husband refuses to accept her vow or impulsive pledge on the day he hears of it, he nullifies her commitments, and the LORD will forgive her. 9If, however, a woman is a widow or is divorced, she must fulfill all her vows and pledges.

Nm 29:40 Verse 29:40 is numbered 30:1 in Hebrew text. **Nm 30:1** Verses 30:1-16 are numbered 30:2-17 in Hebrew text.

Num 30:1-2 Moses reminded the people that their promises to God and others must be kept. In ancient times, people did not sign written contracts. A person's word was as binding as a signature. To make a vow even more binding, an offering was given along with it. No one was forced by law to make a vow; but once made, vows had to be fulfilled. Breaking a vow meant a broken trust and a broken relationship. Trust is still the basis of our relationships with God and others. A broken promise today is just as harmful as it was in Moses' day.

Num 30:3-8 Under Israelite law, parents could overrule their children's vows. This helped young people avoid the consequences of making foolish promises or costly commitments. From this law comes an important principle for both parents and children. Young people still living at home should seek their parents' help when they make decisions. A parent's experience could save a child from a serious mistake. Parents, however, should exercise their authority with caution and grace. They should let children learn from their mistakes while protecting them from disaster.

10"But suppose a woman is married and living in her husband's home when she makes a vow or binds herself with a pledge. 11If her husband hears of it and does not object to it, her vow or pledge will stand. 12But if her husband refuses to accept it on the day he hears of it, her vow or pledge will be nullified, and the LORD will forgive her. 13So her husband may either confirm or nullify any vows or pledges she makes to deny herself. 14But if he does not object on the day he hears of it, then he is agreeing to all her vows and pledges. 15If he waits more than a day and then tries to nullify a vow or pledge, he will be punished for her guilt."

16These are the regulations the LORD gave Moses concerning relationships between a man and his wife, and between a father and a young daughter who still lives at home.

4. VENGEANCE ON THE MIDIANITES

In preparation for their conquest of the Promised Land, God led the Israelites to conquer the Midianites for their attempts to get Israel to worship other gods.

Conquest of the Midianites

NUMBERS 31:1-24

Then the LORD said to Moses, 2"On behalf of the people of Israel, take revenge on the Midianites for leading them into idolatry. After that, you will die and join your ancestors."

3So Moses said to the people, "Choose some men, and arm them to fight the LORD's war of revenge against Midian. 4From each tribe of Israel, send 1,000 men into battle." 5So they chose 1,000 men from each tribe of Israel, a total of 12,000 men armed for battle. 6Then Moses sent them out, 1,000 men from each tribe, and Phinehas son of Eleazar the priest led them into battle. They carried along the holy objects of the sanctuary and the trumpets for sounding the charge. 7They attacked Midian as the LORD had commanded Moses, and they killed all the men. 8All five of the Midianite kings—Evi, Rekem, Zur, Hur, and Reba—died in the battle. They also killed Balaam son of Beor with the sword.

9Then the Israelite army captured the Midianite women and children and seized their cattle and flocks and all their wealth as plunder. 10They burned all the towns and villages where the Midianites had lived. 11After they had gathered the plunder and captives, both people and animals, 12they brought them all to Moses and Eleazar the priest, and to the whole community of Israel, which was camped on the plains of Moab beside the Jordan River, across from Jericho. 13Moses, Eleazar the priest, and all the leaders of the community went to meet them outside the camp. 14But Moses was furious with all the generals and captains* who had returned from the battle.

15"Why have you let all the women live?" he demanded. 16"These are the very ones who followed Balaam's advice and caused the people of Israel to rebel against the LORD at Mount Peor. They are the ones who caused the plague to strike the LORD's people. 17So kill all the boys and all the women who have had intercourse with a man. 18Only the young girls who are virgins may live; you may keep them for yourselves. 19And all of you who have killed anyone or touched a dead body must stay outside the camp for seven days. You must purify yourselves and your captives on the third and seventh days. 20Purify all your clothing, too, and everything made of leather, goat hair, or wood."

21Then Eleazar the priest said to the men who were in the battle, "The LORD has given Moses this legal requirement: 22Anything made of gold, silver, bronze, iron, tin, or lead—23that is, all metals that do not burn—must be passed through fire in order to be made ceremonially pure. These metal objects must then be further purified with the water of purification. But everything that burns must be purified by the water alone. 24On the seventh day you must wash your clothes and be purified. Then you may return to the camp."

Nm 31:14 Hebrew *the commanders of thousands, and the commanders of hundreds;* also in 31:48, 52, 54.

Num 31:1ff The Midianites were a nomadic people who descended from Abraham and his second wife, Keturah. The land of Midian lay far to the south of Canaan, but large bands of Midianites roamed many miles from their homeland, searching for grazing areas for their flocks. Such a group was near the Promised Land when the Israelites arrived. When Moses fled from Egypt (Exod 2), he took refuge in the land of Midian. His wife and father-in-law were Midianites. Despite this alliance, the Israelites and Midianites were always bitter enemies.

Num 31:14-16 Because Midianites were responsible for enticing Israel into Baal worship, God commanded Israel to destroy them (Num 25:16-18). But Israel took the women as captives, rather than killing them, probably because of the tempting enticements of the Midianites' sinful lifestyle. When we discover sin in our lives, we must deal with it completely. When the Israelites later entered the Promised Land, it was their indifferent attitude to sin that eventually ruined them. Moses dealt with the sin promptly and completely. When God points out sin, move quickly to remove it from your life.

Num 31:16 Balaam's story (Num 22:1–24:25) taken alone would lead us to believe that Balaam was an honest and God-fearing man. But here is the first of much biblical evidence that Balaam was not the good man he might appear to be. For more on Balaam, see the notes on Numbers 22:9, p. 265, and Numbers 25:1-3, p. 269, and Balaam's Profile on p. 269.

Division of the Plunder

NUMBERS 31:25-54

And the LORD said to Moses, 26"You and Eleazar the priest and the family leaders of each tribe are to make a list of all the plunder taken in the battle, including the people and animals. 27Then divide the plunder into two parts, and give half to the men who fought the battle and half to the rest of the people. 28From the army's portion, first give the LORD his share of the plunder—one of every 500 of the prisoners and of the cattle, donkeys, sheep, and goats. 29Give this share of the army's half to Eleazar the priest as an offering to the LORD. 30From the half that belongs to the people of Israel, take one of every fifty of the prisoners and of the cattle, donkeys, sheep, goats, and other animals. Give this share to the Levites, who are in charge of maintaining the LORD's Tabernacle." 31So Moses and Eleazar the priest did as the LORD commanded Moses.

32The plunder remaining from everything the fighting men had taken totaled 675,000 sheep and goats, 3372,000 cattle, 3461,000 donkeys, 35and 32,000 virgin girls.

36Half of the plunder was given to the fighting men. It totaled 337,500 sheep and goats, 37of which 675 were the LORD's share; 3836,000 cattle, of which 72 were the LORD's share; 3930,500 donkeys, of which 61 were the LORD's share; 40and 16,000 virgin girls, of whom 32 were the LORD's share. 41Moses gave all the LORD's share to Eleazar the priest, just as the LORD had directed him.

42Half of the plunder belonged to the people of Israel, and Moses separated it from the half belonging to the fighting men. 43It totaled 337,500 sheep and goats, 4436,000 cattle, 4530,500 donkeys, 46and 16,000 virgin girls. 47From the half-share given to the people, Moses took one of every fifty prisoners and animals and gave them to the Levites, who maintained the LORD's Tabernacle. All this was done as the LORD had commanded Moses.

48Then all the generals and captains came to Moses 49and said, "We, your servants, have accounted for all the men who went out to battle under our command; not one of us is missing! 50So we are presenting the items of gold we captured as an offering to the LORD from our share of the plunder—armbands, bracelets, rings, earrings, and necklaces. This will purify our lives before the LORD and make us right with him.*"

51So Moses and Eleazar the priest received the gold from all the military commanders—all kinds of jewelry and crafted objects. 52In all, the gold that the generals and captains presented as a gift to the LORD weighed about 420 pounds.* 53All the fighting men had taken some of the plunder for themselves. 54So Moses and Eleazar the priest accepted the gifts from the generals and captains and brought the gold to the Tabernacle* as a reminder to the LORD that the people of Israel belong to him.

Nm 31:50 Or *will make atonement for our lives before the LORD.* **Nm 31:52** Hebrew *16,750 shekels* [191 kilograms]. **Nm 31:54** Hebrew *the Tent of Meeting.*

5. THE TRANSJORDAN TRIBES

Israel had grown quite large, and some of the tribes chose to settle in the land east of the Jordan River rather than cross into the Promised Land with the rest of the nation. They agreed to help the rest of the nation conquer the land before returning to their new homes.

Some Tribes Settle East of the Jordan River

NUMBERS 32:1-42

The tribes of Reuben and Gad owned vast numbers of livestock. So when they saw that the lands of Jazer and Gilead were ideally suited for their flocks and herds, 2they came to Moses, Eleazar the priest, and the other leaders of the community. They said, 3"Notice the towns of Ataroth, Dibon, Jazer, Nimrah, Heshbon, Elealeh, Sibmah,* Nebo, and Beon. 4The LORD has conquered this whole area for the community of Israel, and it is ideally suited for all our livestock. 5If we have found favor with you, please let us have this land as our property instead of giving us land across the Jordan River."

6"Do you intend to stay here while your brothers go across and do all the fighting?" Moses asked the men of Gad and Reuben. 7"Why do you want to discourage the rest of the people of Israel from going across to the land the LORD has given them? 8Your ancestors did the same thing when I sent them from Kadesh-barnea to explore the land. 9After they went

Nm 32:3 As in Samaritan Pentateuch and Greek version (see also 32:38); Hebrew reads *Sebam.*

Num 31:25-30 Moses told the Israelites to give a portion of the war plunder to God. Another portion was to go to the people who remained behind. Similarly, the money we earn is not ours alone. Everything we possess comes directly or indirectly from God and ultimately belongs to him. We should return a portion to him and also share a portion with those in need.

Num 31:48-50 After carefully accounting for all their men, the officers discovered that not one soldier had been lost in battle. At once they thanked God. After going through tough times, we should be quick to thank God for delivering us and protecting us.

Num 32:1ff Three tribes (Reuben, Gad, and the half-tribe of Manasseh) wanted to live east of the Jordan River (sometimes referred to as the Transjordan area) on land they had already conquered. Moses immediately assumed they had selfish motives and were trying to avoid helping the others fight for the land across the river. But Moses jumped to the wrong conclusion. In dealing with people, we must find out all the facts before making up our minds. We shouldn't automatically assume that their motives are wrong, even if their plans sound suspicious.

up to the valley of Eshcol and explored the land, they discouraged the people of Israel from entering the land the LORD was giving them. [10]Then the LORD was very angry with them, and he vowed, [11]'Of all those I rescued from Egypt, no one who is twenty years old or older will ever see the land I swore to give to Abraham, Isaac, and Jacob, for they have not obeyed me wholeheartedly. [12]The only exceptions are Caleb son of Jephunneh the Kenizzite and Joshua son of Nun, for they have wholeheartedly followed the LORD.'

[13]"The LORD was angry with Israel and made them wander in the wilderness for forty years until the entire generation that sinned in the LORD's sight had died. [14]But here you are, a brood of sinners, doing exactly the same thing! You are making the LORD even angrier with Israel. [15]If you turn away from him like this and he abandons them again in the wilderness, you will be responsible for destroying this entire nation!"

[16]But they approached Moses and said, "We simply want to build pens for our livestock and fortified towns for our wives and children. [17]Then we will arm ourselves and lead our fellow Israelites into battle until we have brought them safely to their land. Meanwhile, our families will stay in the fortified towns we build here, so they will be safe from any attacks by the local people. [18]We will not return to our homes until all the people of Israel have received their portions of land. [19]But we do not claim any of the land on the other side of the Jordan. We would rather live here on the east side and accept this as our grant of land."

[20]Then Moses said, "If you keep your word and arm yourselves for the LORD's battles, [21]and if your troops cross the Jordan and keep fighting until the LORD has driven out his enemies, [22]then you may return when the LORD has conquered the land. You will have fulfilled your duty to the LORD and to the rest of the people of Israel. And the land on the east side of the Jordan will be your property from the LORD. [23]But if you fail to keep your word, then you will have sinned against the LORD, and you may be sure that your sin will find you out. [24]Go ahead and build towns for your families and pens for your flocks, but do everything you have promised."

[25]Then the men of Gad and Reuben replied, "We, your servants, will follow your instructions exactly. [26]Our children, wives, flocks, and cattle will stay here in the towns of Gilead. [27]But all who are able to bear arms will cross over to fight for the LORD, just as you have said."

[28]So Moses gave orders to Eleazar the priest, Joshua son of Nun, and the leaders of the clans of Israel. [29]He said, "The men of Gad and Reuben who are armed for battle must cross the Jordan with you to fight for the LORD. If they do, give them the land of Gilead as their property when the land is conquered. [30]But if they refuse to arm themselves and cross over with you, then they must accept land with the rest of you in the land of Canaan."

[31]The tribes of Gad and Reuben said again, "We are your servants, and we will do as the LORD has commanded! [32]We will cross the Jordan into Canaan fully armed to fight for the LORD, but our property will be here on this side of the Jordan."

[33]So Moses assigned land to the tribes of Gad, Reuben, and half the tribe of Manasseh son of Joseph. He gave them the territory of King Sihon of the Amorites and the land of King Og of Bashan—the whole land with its cities and surrounding lands.

[34]The descendants of Gad built the towns of Dibon, Ataroth, Aroer, [35]Atroth-shophan, Jazer, Jogbehah, [36]Beth-nimrah, and Beth-haran. These were all fortified towns with pens for their flocks.

[37]The descendants of Reuben built the towns of Heshbon, Elealeh, Kiriathaim, [38]Nebo, Baal-meon, and Sibmah. They changed the names of some of the towns they conquered and rebuilt.

[39]Then the descendants of Makir of the tribe of Manasseh went to Gilead and conquered it, and they drove out the Amorites living there. [40]So Moses gave Gilead to the Makirites, descendants of Manasseh, and they settled there. [41]The people of Jair, another clan of the tribe of Manasseh, captured many of the towns in Gilead and changed the name of that region to the Towns of Jair.* [42]Meanwhile, a man named Nobah captured the town of Kenath and its surrounding villages, and he renamed that area Nobah after himself.

Nm 32:41 Hebrew *Havvoth-jair.*

Num 32:16 A simple fold for livestock had four roughly built stone walls, high enough to keep wild animals out. Sometimes the top of the wall was lined with thorns to further discourage predators and thieves. The fold's single entrance made it easier for a shepherd to guard his flock. Often several shepherds used a single fold and took turns guarding the entrance. Mingling the animals was no problem since each flock responded readily to its own shepherd's voice. The three tribes who chose to remain east of the Jordan River wanted to build sheepfolds to protect their flocks, and cities to protect their families before the men crossed the river to help the rest of the tribes conquer the Promised Land.

Num 32:16-19 The land on the east side of the Jordan had been conquered. The hard work was done by all of the tribes together. But the tribes of Reuben and Gad and the half-tribe of Manasseh did not stop after their land was cleared. They promised to keep working with the others until everyone's land was conquered. After others have helped you, do you make excuses to escape helping them? Finish the whole job, even those parts that may not benefit you directly.

6. CAMPED ON THE PLAINS OF MOAB

Israel made their final camp before entering the Promised Land, and they recounted how God had led them all the way from slavery in Egypt to the verge of the land that Abraham, Isaac, and Jacob had lived in and that God had promised them.

Remembering Israel's Journey

NUMBERS 33:1-56

This is the route the Israelites followed as they
marched out of Egypt under the leadership of Moses
and Aaron. 2At the LORD's direction, Moses kept a written record of their progress. These are the stages of
their march, identified by the different places where
they stopped along the way.
3They set out from the city of Rameses in early
spring—on the fifteenth day of the first month*—on
the morning after the first Passover celebration. The
people of Israel left defiantly, in full view of all the
Egyptians. 4Meanwhile, the Egyptians were burying
all their firstborn sons, whom the LORD had killed the
night before. The LORD had defeated the gods of Egypt
that night with great acts of judgment!

5After leaving Rameses, the Israelites set up camp at Succoth.
6Then they left Succoth and camped at Etham on the edge of the wilderness.
7They left Etham and turned back toward Pi-hahiroth, opposite Baal-zephon, and camped near Migdol.
8They left Pi-hahiroth and crossed the Red Sea* into the wilderness beyond. Then they traveled for three days into the Etham wilderness and camped at Marah.
9They left Marah and camped at Elim, where there were twelve springs of water and seventy palm trees.
10They left Elim and camped beside the Red Sea.*
11They left the Red Sea and camped in the wilderness of Sin.*
12They left the wilderness of Sin and camped at Dophkah.
13They left Dophkah and camped at Alush.
14They left Alush and camped at Rephidim, where there was no water for the people to drink.
15They left Rephidim and camped in the wilderness of Sinai.
16They left the wilderness of Sinai and camped at Kibroth-hattaavah.
17They left Kibroth-hattaavah and camped at Hazeroth.
18They left Hazeroth and camped at Rithmah.
19They left Rithmah and camped at Rimmon-perez.
20They left Rimmon-perez and camped at Libnah.
21They left Libnah and camped at Rissah.
22They left Rissah and camped at Kehelathah.
23They left Kehelathah and camped at Mount Shepher.
24They left Mount Shepher and camped at Haradah.
25They left Haradah and camped at Makheloth.
26They left Makheloth and camped at Tahath.
27They left Tahath and camped at Terah.
28They left Terah and camped at Mithcah.
29They left Mithcah and camped at Hashmonah.
30They left Hashmonah and camped at Moseroth.
31They left Moseroth and camped at Bene-jaakan.
32They left Bene-jaakan and camped at Hor-haggidgad.
33They left Hor-haggidgad and camped at Jotbathah.

Nm 33:3 This day in the ancient Hebrew lunar calendar occurred in late March, April, or early May. **Nm 33:8** Hebrew *the sea.* **Nm 33:10** Hebrew *sea of reeds;* also in 33:11. **Nm 33:11** The geographical name *Sin* is related to *Sinai* and should not be confused with the English word *sin.*

Num 33:1ff Look at the map in the introduction to this section (p. 139) to see the travels of the Israelites.

Num 33:1ff The itinerary contains features that reflect detailed record keeping. This is the only place where Numbers says that Moses kept a record of Israel's history (cp. Exod 24:4). It does not provide enough data to plot an accurate, specific route because it is partial or selective, omitting some of the place-names mentioned earlier in the journey.

Num 33:2 Moses recorded the Israelites' journeys as God instructed him, providing a record of their spiritual as well as geographic progress. In their travels between Rameses in Egypt (Num 33:3) and Acacia on the plains of Moab (Num 33:49). Israel finally became the people who could invade the land of Canaan and claim the promises God made to Abraham. Have you made spiritual progress lately? Recording your thoughts about God and lessons you have learned over a period of time can be a valuable aid to spiritual growth. A record of your spiritual pilgrimage will let you check up on your progress and avoid repeating past mistakes.

Num 33:4 God "defeated the gods of Egypt" by sending the plagues. See the note on Exodus 10:22, p. 154, for a further explanation.

PREPARING TO ENTER THE PROMISED LAND ▶
The Israelites had been camped in the plains of Moab, across from Jericho. From this position, they were ready to enter the Promised Land.

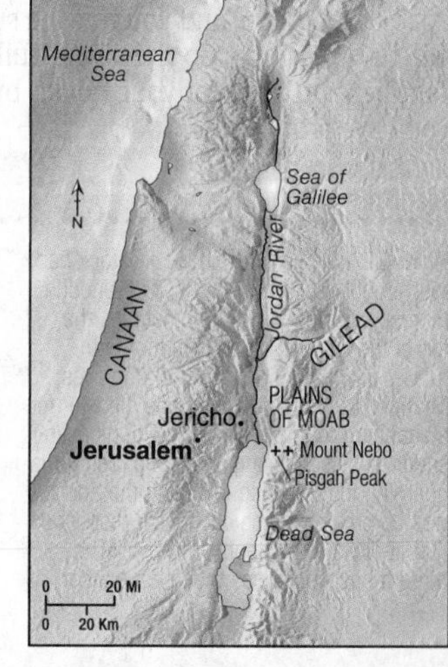

34 They left Jotbathah and camped at Abronah.
35 They left Abronah and camped at Ezion-geber.
36 They left Ezion-geber and camped at Kadesh in the wilderness of Zin.
37 They left Kadesh and camped at Mount Hor, at the border of Edom. 38 While they were at the foot of Mount Hor, Aaron the priest was directed by the LORD to go up the mountain, and there he died. This happened in midsummer, on the first day of the fifth month* of the fortieth year after Israel's departure from Egypt. 39 Aaron was 123 years old when he died there on Mount Hor.
40 At that time the Canaanite king of Arad, who lived in the Negev in the land of Canaan, heard that the people of Israel were approaching his land.
41 Meanwhile, the Israelites left Mount Hor and camped at Zalmonah.
42 Then they left Zalmonah and camped at Punon.
43 They left Punon and camped at Oboth.
44 They left Oboth and camped at Iye-abarim on the border of Moab.
45 They left Iye-abarim* and camped at Dibon-gad.
46 They left Dibon-gad and camped at Almon-diblathaim.
47 They left Almon-diblathaim and camped in the mountains east of the river,* near Mount Nebo.
48 They left the mountains east of the river and camped on the plains of Moab beside the Jordan River, across from Jericho. 49 Along the Jordan River they camped from Beth-jeshimoth as far as the meadows of Acacia* on the plains of Moab.

50 While they were camped near the Jordan River on the plains of Moab opposite Jericho, the LORD said to Moses, 51 "Give the following instructions to the people of Israel: When you cross the Jordan River into the land of Canaan, 52 you must drive out all the people living there. You must destroy all their carved and molten images and demolish all their pagan shrines. 53 Take possession of the land and settle in it, because I have given it to you to occupy. 54 You must distribute the land among the clans by sacred lot and in proportion to their size. A larger portion of land will be allotted to each of the larger clans, and a smaller portion will be allotted to each of the smaller clans. The decision of the sacred lot is final. In this way, the portions of land will be divided among your ancestral tribes. 55 But if you fail to drive out the people who live in the land, those who remain will be like splinters in your eyes and thorns in your sides. They will harass you in the land where you live. 56 And I will do to you what I had planned to do to them."

Boundaries of the Land

NUMBERS 34:1-15

Then the LORD said to Moses, 2 "Give these instructions to the Israelites: When you come into the land of Canaan, which I am giving you as your special possession, these will be the boundaries. 3 The southern portion of your country will extend from the wilderness of Zin, along the edge of Edom. The southern boundary will begin on the east at the Dead Sea.* 4 It will then run south past Scorpion Pass* in the direction of Zin. Its southernmost point will be Kadesh-barnea, from which it will go to Hazar-addar, and on to Azmon. 5 From Azmon the boundary will turn toward the Brook of Egypt and end at the Mediterranean Sea.*

6 "Your western boundary will be the coastline of the Mediterranean Sea.

7 "Your northern boundary will begin at the Mediterranean Sea and run east to Mount Hor, 8 then to Lebo-hamath, and on through Zedad 9 and Ziphron to Hazar-enan. This will be your northern boundary.

Nm 33:38 This day in the ancient Hebrew lunar calendar occurred in July or August. **Nm 33:45** As in 33:44; Hebrew reads *Iyim,* another name for Iye-abarim. **Nm 33:47** Or *the mountains of Abarim;* also in 33:48. **Nm 33:49** Hebrew *as far as Abel-shittim.* **Nm 34:3** Hebrew *Salt Sea;* also in 34:12. **Nm 34:4** Or *the ascent of Akrabbim.* **Nm 34:5** Hebrew *the sea;* also in 34:6, 7.

Num 33:50-53 God told Moses that before the Israelites settled in the Promised Land they should drive out the wicked inhabitants and destroy their idols. In Colossians 3, Paul encourages us to live as Christians in the same manner: throwing away our old way of living and moving ahead into our new life of obedience to God and faith in Jesus Christ. Like the Israelites moving into the Promised Land, we can destroy the wickedness in our lives, or we can settle down and live with it. To move in and possess the new life, we must drive out the sinful thoughts and practices to make room for the new.

Num 33:50-56 Why were the Israelites told to destroy the people living in Canaan? God had several compelling reasons for giving this command: (1) God was stamping out the wickedness of an extremely sinful group of nations. The Canaanites brought on their own punishment. Idol worship expressed their deepest evil desires. It ultimately led to the worship of Satan and the total rejection of God. (2) God was using Moses and Israel to judge Canaan for its sins in fulfillment of the prophecy in Genesis 9:25. (3) God wanted to remove all trace of pagan beliefs and practices from the land. He did not want his people to mix or compromise with idolatry in any way. The Israelites did not fully understand God's reasons, and they did not carry out his command. This eventually led them to compromise and corruption. In all areas of life, we should obey God's Word without question because we know he is just, even if we cannot fully understand his overall purposes.

Num 33:55 If you don't do the job right the first time, it often becomes much more difficult to accomplish. God warned that if the Israelites did not drive the wicked inhabitants out of the Promised Land, later these people would become a source of great irritation. That is exactly what happened. Just as the Israelites were hesitant to clear out all the wicked people, we are sometimes hesitant to clear out all the sin in our lives, either because we are afraid of it (as the Israelites feared the giants), or because it seems harmless and attractive (as sexual sin seemed). But Hebrews 12:1 tells us to strip off "the sin that so easily trips us up." We all have "idols" we don't want to let go of (a bad habit, an unhealthy relationship, a certain lifestyle). If we allow these idols to dominate us, they will cause serious problems later.

Num 34:1ff The land was given by God as an inheritance; no tribe was to claim its own land. The boundaries declared by God are larger than the area actually occupied by the Hebrews. The boundaries correspond more to the land conquered by David and to the ideal territory portrayed by Ezekiel (Ezek 47–48). The size of the land portrays God's generosity. He always gives us more than we could ask or think.

▶ **NUMBERS 34:1-15** ***(cont.)***

10"The eastern boundary will start at Hazar-enan
and run south to Shepham, 11then down to Riblah on
the east side of Ain. From there the boundary will run
down along the eastern edge of the Sea of Galilee,*
12and then along the Jordan River to the Dead Sea.
These are the boundaries of your land."

13Then Moses told the Israelites, "This territory is
the homeland you are to divide among yourselves by
sacred lot. The LORD has commanded that the land be
divided among the nine and a half remaining tribes.
14The families of the tribes of Reuben, Gad, and half
the tribe of Manasseh have already received their
grants of land 15on the east side of the Jordan River,
across from Jericho toward the sunrise."

Leaders to Divide the Land

NUMBERS 34:16-29

And the LORD said to Moses, 17"Eleazar the priest and
Joshua son of Nun are the men designated to divide
the grants of land among the people. 18Enlist one
leader from each tribe to help them with the task.
19These are the tribes and the names of the leaders:

Tribe	*Leader*
Judah	Caleb son of Jephunneh
20 Simeon	Shemuel son of Ammihud
21 Benjamin	Elidad son of Kislon
22 Dan	Bukki son of Jogli
23 Manasseh son of Joseph	Hanniel son of Ephod
24 Ephraim son of Joseph	Kemuel son of Shiphtan
25 Zebulun	Elizaphan son of Parnach
26 Issachar	Paltiel son of Azzan
27 Asher	Ahihud son of Shelomi
28 Naphtali	Pedahel son of Ammihud

29These are the men the LORD has appointed to divide
the grants of land in Canaan among the Israelites."

Towns for the Levites

NUMBERS 35:1-8

While Israel was camped beside the Jordan on the
plains of Moab across from Jericho, the LORD said
to Moses, 2"Command the people of Israel to give to
the Levites from their property certain towns to live
in, along with the surrounding pasturelands. 3These
towns will be for the Levites to live in, and the surrounding lands will provide pasture for their cattle,
flocks, and other livestock. 4The pastureland assigned
to the Levites around these towns will extend 1,500
feet* from the town walls in every direction. 5Measure
off 3,000 feet* outside the town walls in every direction—east, south, west, north—with the town at the
center. This area will serve as the larger pastureland
for the towns.

6"Six of the towns you give the Levites will be cities of refuge, where a person who has accidentally
killed someone can flee for safety. In addition, give
them forty-two other towns. 7In all, forty-eight towns
with the surrounding pastureland will be given to the
Levites. 8These towns will come from the property of
the people of Israel. The larger tribes will give more
towns to the Levites, while the smaller tribes will give
fewer. Each tribe will give property in proportion to
the size of its land."

Cities of Refuge

NUMBERS 35:9-34

The LORD said to Moses, 10"Give the following instructions to the people of Israel.

"When you cross the Jordan into the land of

Nm 34:11 Hebrew *Sea of Kinnereth.* **Nm 35:4** Hebrew *1,000 cubits* [460 meters]. **Nm 35:5** Hebrew *2,000 cubits* [920 meters].

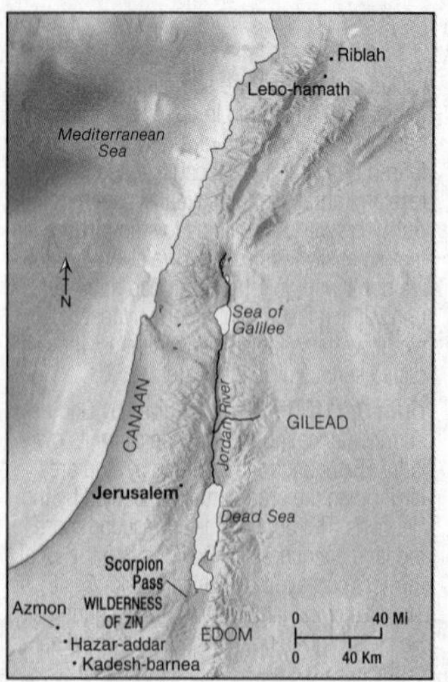

◀ ***THE BORDERS OF THE PROMISED LAND***
The borders of the Promised Land stretched from the wilderness of Zin and Kadesh-barnea in the south to Lebo-hamath and Riblah in the north, and from the Mediterranean seacoast on the west to the Jordan River on the east. The land of Gilead was also included.

Num 34:16-29 In God's plan for settling the land, he explained what to do, communicated this clearly to Moses, and assigned specific people to oversee the apportionment of the land. No plan is complete until each job is assigned and everyone understands their responsibilities. When you have a job to do, determine what must be done, give clear instructions, and put people in charge of each part.

Num 35:2-3 The Levites were ministers. They were supported by the tithes of the people who gave them homes, flocks, and pasturelands. Likewise, we are responsible to provide for the needs of our ministers and missionaries so they can be free to do their God-ordained work.

Num 35:6 Of the 48 cities given to the Levites, six were cities of refuge. These six cities were probably put under the Levites' supervision because they would be the most impartial judges. Such cities were needed because the ancient customs of justice called for revenge in the event of the death of a relative or loved one (2 Sam 14:7). The Levites would hold a preliminary hearing outside the gates while the accused person was kept in the city until the time of his trial. If the killing was judged accidental, the person would stay in the city until the death of the high priest. At that time, he would be allowed to go free, and he could start a new life without worrying about avengers. If it was not accidental, the person would be delivered to the slain person's avengers. This system of justice shows how God's law and his mercy go hand in hand.

Canaan, [11]designate cities of refuge to which people can flee if they have killed someone accidentally. [12]These cities will be places of protection from a dead person's relatives who want to avenge the death. The slayer must not be put to death before being tried by the community. [13]Designate six cities of refuge for yourselves, [14]three on the east side of the Jordan River and three on the west in the land of Canaan. [15]These cities are for the protection of Israelites, foreigners living among you, and traveling merchants. Anyone who accidentally kills someone may flee there for safety.

[16]"But if someone strikes and kills another person with a piece of iron, it is murder, and the murderer must be executed. [17]Or if someone with a stone in his hand strikes and kills another person, it is murder, and the murderer must be put to death. [18]Or if someone strikes and kills another person with a wooden object, it is murder, and the murderer must be put to death. [19]The victim's nearest relative is responsible for putting the murderer to death. When they meet, the avenger must put the murderer to death. [20]So if someone hates another person and pushes him or throws a dangerous object at him and he dies, it is murder. [21]Or if someone hates another person and hits him with a fist and he dies, it is murder. In such cases, the avenger must put the murderer to death when they meet.

[22]"But suppose someone pushes another person without having shown previous hostility, or throws something that unintentionally hits another person, [23]or accidentally drops a huge stone on someone, though they were not enemies, and the person dies. [24]If this should happen, the community must follow these regulations in making a judgment between the slayer and the avenger, the victim's nearest relative: [25]The community must protect the slayer from the avenger and must escort the slayer back to live in the city of refuge to which he fled. There he must remain until the death of the high priest, who was anointed with the sacred oil.

[26]"But if the slayer ever leaves the limits of the city of refuge, [27]and the avenger finds him outside the city and kills him, it will not be considered murder. [28]The slayer should have stayed inside the city of refuge until the death of the high priest. But after the death of the high priest, the slayer may return to his own property. [29]These are legal requirements for you to observe from generation to generation, wherever you may live.

[30]"All murderers must be put to death, but only if evidence is presented by more than one witness. No one may be put to death on the testimony of only one witness. [31]Also, you must never accept a ransom payment for the life of someone judged guilty of murder and subject to execution; murderers must always be put to death. [32]And never accept a ransom payment from someone who has fled to a city of refuge, allowing a slayer to return to his property before the death of the high priest. [33]This will ensure that the land where you live will not be polluted, for murder pollutes the land. And no sacrifice except the execution of the murderer can purify the land from murder.* [34]You must not defile the land where you live, for I live there myself. I am the LORD, who lives among the people of Israel."

Nm 35:33 Or *can make atonement for murder.*

The Dead Sea

The Dead Sea is a large saltwater lake into which the Jordan River empties. The sea lies in the great trough of the Jordan Valley, also known as the Rift Valley. Since the Greek era, Western civilization has referred to this body of water as the Dead Sea. However, the frequent Old Testament term for this sea is the "Salt Sea" (see textual notes on Gen 14:3; Num 34:3, 12; Deut 3:17; Josh 3:16; 12:3; 15:2, 5; 18:19), the name deriving from that most important and valuable commodity traded in antiquity. The Dead Sea is also designated the sea of the Arabah (see textual notes on Deut 3:17; 4:49; Josh 3:16; 12:3; 2 Kgs 14:25) and the eastern sea (see textual notes on Ezek 47:18; Joel 2:20; Zech 14:8), since it was on the eastern edge of the Promised Land (Num 34:12).

Num 35:11-28 If anyone died because of violence, murder was assumed, but the murder suspect was not automatically assumed guilty. The cities of refuge assured the accused that justice would be served. But if that person left the city, then he or she would be assumed guilty and able to be killed by the avenging party. The people were to be intolerant of the sin yet impartial to the accused so as to have a fair trial. The cities of refuge represented God's concern for justice in a culture that did not always protect the innocent. It is unjust both to overlook wrongdoing and to jump to conclusions about guilt. When someone is accused of wrongdoing, stand up for justice, protect those not yet proven guilty, and listen carefully to all sides of the story.

Women Who Inherit Property

NUMBERS 36:1-13

Then the heads of the clans of Gilead—descendants of Makir, son of Manasseh, son of Joseph—came to Moses and the family leaders of Israel with a petition. 2They said, "Sir, the LORD instructed you to divide the land by sacred lot among the people of Israel. You were told by the LORD to give the grant of land owned by our brother Zelophehad to his daughters. 3But if they marry men from another tribe, their grants of land will go with them to the tribe into which they marry. In this way, the total area of our tribal land will be reduced. 4Then when the Year of Jubilee comes, their portion of land will be added to that of the new tribe, causing it to be lost forever to our ancestral tribe."

5So Moses gave the Israelites this command from the LORD: "The claim of the men of the tribe of Joseph is legitimate. 6This is what the LORD commands concerning the daughters of Zelophehad: Let them marry anyone they like, as long as it is within their own ancestral tribe. 7None of the territorial land may pass from tribe to tribe, for all the land given to each tribe must remain within the tribe to which it was first allotted. 8The daughters throughout the tribes of Israel who are in line to inherit property must marry within their tribe, so that all the Israelites will keep their ancestral property. 9No grant of land may pass from one tribe to another; each tribe of Israel must keep its allotted portion of land."

10The daughters of Zelophehad did as the LORD commanded Moses. 11Mahlah, Tirzah, Hoglah, Milcah, and Noah all married cousins on their father's side. 12They married into the clans of Manasseh son of Joseph. Thus, their inheritance of land remained within their ancestral tribe.

13These are the commands and regulations that the LORD gave to the people of Israel through Moses while they were camped on the plains of Moab beside the Jordan River across from Jericho.

J. Moses' First Address on the Plains of Moab

God has led his people out of Egypt and through the great wilderness for 40 years. Now they stand ready to enter the Promised Land. But before the Israelites go into the land, Moses has some important advice to give them. He delivers his advice in three parts. In the first, Moses reviews the history of God's previous care for the people of Israel.

1. WHAT GOD HAS DONE FOR US

With a new generation poised to enter the Promised Land, Moses reviewed their history so that they would not forget how greatly God had blessed them. It is very important for us to remember what God has done for us and for others before us to build our faith and help us to follow him through rough times. Through God's actions in the past, we can learn about the God we serve today.

Introduction to Moses' First Address

DEUTERONOMY 1:1-5

These are the words that Moses spoke to all the people of Israel while they were in the wilderness east of the Jordan River. They were camped in the Jordan Valley* near Suph, between Paran on one side and Tophel, Laban, Hazeroth, and Di-zahab on the other.

2Normally it takes only eleven days to travel from Mount Sinai* to Kadesh-barnea, going by way of Mount Seir. 3But forty years after the Israelites left

Dt 1:1 Hebrew *the Arabah;* also in 1:7. **Dt 1:2** Hebrew *Horeb,* another name for Sinai; also in 1:6, 19.

Num 36:1-9 Zelophehad had five daughters but no sons. After he died, the daughters made an appeal to Moses. Because the inheritance normally passed only through the male line, the family line of Zelophehad would have disappeared. God told Moses that if a man died without sons, then the inheritance would go to his daughters (Num 27:8). But the question of marriage arose. If the daughters were to marry outside of their tribe, the land would belong to another tribe at the Year of Jubilee. So Moses commanded that in such cases the women should marry men in their own clan and tribe so that each tribe would retain its original inheritance. Later, when the tribes received their land under Joshua, the daughters of Zelophehad received their inheritance as God had instructed (Josh 17:3-6).

We don't have to look far to find those who want to be considered "special cases" and "exceptions to the rule," but wise leaders will sort out those who have legitimate concerns and make sure that justice is done in these special situations.

Num 36:13 The book of Numbers covers 39 years and closes with the Israelites poised near the banks of the Jordan River with the Promised Land in sight. The wanderings in the wilderness had come to an end, and the people were preparing for their next big move—the conquest of the land. The apostle Paul says that the events described in Numbers are examples that warn us and help us avoid the Israelites' mistakes (1 Cor 10:1-12). From their experiences we learn that unbelief is disastrous. We also learn not to long for the sinful pleasures of the past, to avoid complaining, and to stay away from all forms of sexual sin. We must not weaken our biblical beliefs by compromising them with our culture's values. If we choose to let God lead our lives, we should not ignore his message in the book of Numbers.

Deut 1:1-2 The Israelites spent 40 years on a journey that should have lasted 11 days. It wasn't distance that stood between them and the Promised Land. It was the condition of their hearts. God's purpose went deeper than simply transporting a huge group of people to a new land. He was preparing them to live in obedience to him once they arrived. What good was the Promised Land if the Israelites

Egypt, on the first day of the eleventh month,* Moses
addressed the people of Israel, telling them everything
the LORD had commanded him to say. [4]This took place
after he had defeated King Sihon of the Amorites, who
had ruled in Heshbon, and King Og of Bashan, who
had ruled in Ashtaroth and Edrei.

[5]While the Israelites were in the land of Moab east
of the Jordan River, Moses carefully explained the
LORD's instructions as follows.

The Command to Leave Sinai

DEUTERONOMY 1:6-8

"When we were at Mount Sinai, the LORD our God said
to us, 'You have stayed at this mountain long enough.
[7]It is time to break camp and move on. Go to the hill
country of the Amorites and to all the neighboring regions—the Jordan Valley, the hill country, the western
foothills,* the Negev, and the coastal plain. Go to the
land of the Canaanites and to Lebanon, and all the way
to the great Euphrates River. [8]Look, I am giving all this
land to you! Go in and occupy it, for it is the land the
LORD swore to give to your ancestors Abraham, Isaac,
and Jacob, and to all their descendants.'"

Moses Appoints Leaders from Each Tribe

DEUTERONOMY 1:9-18

Moses continued, "At that time I told you, 'You are
too great a burden for me to carry all by myself. [10]The
LORD your God has increased your population, making
you as numerous as the stars! [11]And may the LORD,
the God of your ancestors, multiply you a thousand
times more and bless you as he promised! [12]But you
are such a heavy load to carry! How can I deal with all
your problems and bickering? [13]Choose some well-
respected men from each tribe who are known for
their wisdom and understanding, and I will appoint
them as your leaders.'

[14]"Then you responded, 'Your plan is a good one.'
[15]So I took the wise and respected men you had selected from your tribes and appointed them to serve as
judges and officials over you. Some were responsible
for a thousand people, some for a hundred, some for
fifty, and some for ten.

[16]"At that time I instructed the judges, 'You must
hear the cases of your fellow Israelites and the foreigners living among you. Be perfectly fair in your
decisions [17]and impartial in your judgments. Hear the
cases of those who are poor as well as those who are
rich. Don't be afraid of anyone's anger, for the decision you make is God's decision. Bring me any cases
that are too difficult for you, and I will handle them.'

[18]"At that time I gave you instructions about everything you were to do.

Scouts Explore the Land

DEUTERONOMY 1:19-25

"Then, just as the LORD our God commanded us, we
left Mount Sinai and traveled through the great and
terrifying wilderness, as you yourselves remember,
and headed toward the hill country of the Amorites.
When we arrived at Kadesh-barnea, [20]I said to you,
'You have now reached the hill country of the Amorites that the LORD our God is giving us. [21]Look! He
has placed the land in front of you. Go and occupy it

Dt 1:3 Hebrew *In the fortieth year, on the first day of the eleventh month.* This day in the ancient Hebrew lunar calendar occurred in January or February. **Dt 1:7** Hebrew *the Shephelah.*

were just as wicked as the nations already living there? The journey was a painful but necessary part of their preparation. Through it God taught the Israelites who he was: the living God, the Leader of their nation. He also taught them who they were: people who were fallen, sinful, prone to rebellion and doubt. He gave his rebellious people the law to help them understand how to relate to God and to other people. Your spiritual pilgrimage may be lengthy, and you may face pain, discouragement, and difficulties. But remember that God isn't just trying to keep you alive. He wants to prepare you to live for service and devotion to him.

Deut 1:1-5 The 40 years of wilderness wandering had come to an end. The events of Deuteronomy cover only a week or two of the 11th month of the 40th year (Deut 1:3). The 12th and last month was spent in mourning for Moses (Deut 34:8). Then the Israelites entered the Promised Land the first month of the 41st year after the Exodus (Josh 4:19).

Deut 1:6-7 Notice that Moses' summary of Israel's 40-year journey begins at Mount Sinai, not in Egypt. Why did Moses leave out the first part of the Exodus? Moses was not giving an itinerary—he was summarizing the nation's development. In Moses' mind the nation of Israel began at the base of Mount Sinai, not in Egypt, for it was at Mount Sinai that God gave his covenant to the people (Exod 19–20). Along with this covenant came knowledge and responsibility. After the people chose to follow God, they had to know how to follow him. Therefore, God gave them a comprehensive set of laws and guidelines that stated how he wanted them to live (these are found in the books of Exodus, Leviticus, and Numbers). The people could no longer say they didn't know the difference between right and wrong. Now that the people had promised to follow God and knew how to follow him, they had a responsibility to do it. When God tells you to break camp and move out to face a challenge he gives you, will you be ready to obey?

Deut 1:9-13 It was a tremendous burden for Moses to lead the nation by himself. He could not accomplish the task single-handedly. As nations, organizations, and churches grow, they become increasingly complex. Conflicting needs and quarrels arise. No longer can one leader make all the decisions. Like Moses, you may have a natural tendency to try to do all the work alone. You may be afraid or embarrassed to ask for help. Moses made a wise decision to share the leadership with others. Rather than trying to handle larger responsibilities alone, look for ways of sharing the load so that others may exercise their God-given gifts and abilities.

Deut 1:13-18 Moses identified some of the inner qualities of good leaders: wisdom, experience, and understanding. These characteristics differ markedly from the ones that often help elect leaders today: good looks, wealth, popularity, willingness to do anything to get to the top. The qualities Moses identified should be evident in us as we lead, and we should look for them in those we elect to positions of leadership.

▸ **DEUTERONOMY 1:19-25 *(cont.)***

as the LORD, the God of your ancestors, has promised you. Don't be afraid! Don't be discouraged!'

22"But you all came to me and said, 'First, let's send out scouts to explore the land for us. They will advise us on the best route to take and which towns we should enter.'

23"This seemed like a good idea to me, so I chose twelve scouts, one from each of your tribes. 24They headed for the hill country and came to the valley of Eshcol and explored it. 25They picked some of its fruit and brought it back to us. And they reported, 'The land the LORD our God has given us is indeed a good land.'

Israel's Rebellion against the LORD

DEUTERONOMY 1:26-46

"But you rebelled against the command of the LORD your God and refused to go in. 27You complained in your tents and said, 'The LORD must hate us. That's why he has brought us here from Egypt—to hand us over to the Amorites to be slaughtered. 28Where can we go? Our brothers have demoralized us with their report. They tell us, "The people of the land are taller and more powerful than we are, and their towns are large, with walls rising high into the sky! We even saw giants there—the descendants of Anak!"'

29"But I said to you, 'Don't be shocked or afraid of them! 30The LORD your God is going ahead of you. He will fight for you, just as you saw him do in Egypt. 31And you saw how the LORD your God cared for you all along the way as you traveled through the wilderness, just as a father cares for his child. Now he has brought you to this place.'

32"But even after all he did, you refused to trust the LORD your God, 33who goes before you looking for the best places to camp, guiding you with a pillar of fire by night and a pillar of cloud by day.

34"When the LORD heard your complaining, he became very angry. So he solemnly swore, 35'Not one of you from this wicked generation will live to see the good land I swore to give your ancestors, 36except Caleb son of Jephunneh. He will see this land because he has followed the LORD completely. I will give to him and his descendants some of the very land he explored during his scouting mission.'

37"And the LORD was also angry with me because of you. He said to me, 'Moses, not even you will enter the Promised Land! 38Instead, your assistant, Joshua son of Nun, will lead the people into the land. Encourage him, for he will lead Israel as they take possession of it. 39I will give the land to your little ones—your innocent children. You were afraid they would be captured, but they will be the ones who occupy it. 40As for you, turn around now and go on back through the wilderness toward the Red Sea.*'

41"Then you confessed, 'We have sinned against the LORD! We will go into the land and fight for it, as the LORD our God has commanded us.' So your men strapped on their weapons, thinking it would be easy to attack the hill country.

42"But the LORD told me to tell you, 'Do not attack, for I am not with you. If you go ahead on your own, you will be crushed by your enemies.'

43"This is what I told you, but you would not listen. Instead, you again rebelled against the LORD's command and arrogantly went into the hill country to fight. 44But the Amorites who lived there came out against you like a swarm of bees. They chased and battered you all the way from Seir to Hormah. 45Then you returned and wept before the LORD, but he refused to listen. 46So you stayed there at Kadesh for a long time.

Remembering Israel's Wanderings

DEUTERONOMY 2:1-25

"Then we turned around and headed back across the wilderness toward the Red Sea,* just as the LORD had instructed me, and we wandered around in the region of Mount Seir for a long time.

2"Then at last the LORD said to me, 3'You have been wandering around in this hill country long enough; turn to the north. 4Give these orders to the people:

Dt 1:40 Hebrew *sea of reeds.* **Dt 2:1** Hebrew *sea of reeds.*

Deut 1:22 The scouts had been sent into the land to determine not *whether* they should enter, but *where* they should enter. But upon returning, most of the scouts concluded that the land was not worth the obstacles. God would give the Israelites the power to conquer the land, but they were afraid of the risk and decided not to enter. God gives us the power to overcome our obstacles, but just as the Israelites were filled with fear and skepticism, we often let difficulties control our lives. When we follow God regardless of the difficulties, we demonstrate courageous, overcoming faith.

Deut 1:23-40 Moses retold the story of the scouting mission into the Promised Land (Num 13–14). When the scouts returned with reports of giants and walled cities, the people were afraid to move ahead and began to complain about their predicament. But the minority report of Joshua and Caleb pointed out that the land was fertile, the enemy was vulnerable, and God was on their side. We become fearful and immobile when we focus on the negative aspects of a situation. How much better it is to focus on the positive—God's direction and promises. When you are confronted with an important decision and know what you should do, move out in faith. Focus on the positives while trusting God to overcome the negatives. Problems don't have to rob you of the victory.

Deut 1:28 Canaan was a land with giants and imposing fortresses. The "descendants of Anak" may have been seven to nine feet tall. Many of the land's fortified cities had walls as high as 30 feet. The Israelites' fear was understandable but not justified, for the all-powerful God had already promised them victory.

Deut 2:4-6 When the Israelites passed through Seir, God advised them to be careful. The Israelites were known as warriors, and the descendants of Esau—the Edomites—would be understandably nervous as the great crowd passed through their land. God warned the Israelites not to start a fight, to respect the Edomites' territory, and to pay for whatever they used. God wanted the Israelites to deal justly with these neighbors. We must also act justly in dealing with others.

"You will pass through the country belonging to your relatives the Edomites, the descendants of Esau, who live in Seir. The Edomites will feel threatened, so be careful. 5Do not bother them, for I have given them all the hill country around Mount Seir as their property, and I will not give you even one square foot of their land. 6If you need food to eat or water to drink, pay them for it. 7For the LORD your God has blessed you in everything you have done. He has watched your every step through this great wilderness. During these forty years, the LORD your God has been with you, and you have lacked nothing.'"

8"So we bypassed the territory of our relatives, the descendants of Esau, who live in Seir. We avoided the road through the Arabah Valley that comes up from Elath and Ezion-geber.

"Then as we turned north along the desert route through Moab, 9the LORD warned us, 'Do not bother the Moabites, the descendants of Lot, or start a war with them. I have given them Ar as their property, and I will not give you any of their land.'"

10(A race of giants called the Emites had once lived in the area of Ar. They were as strong and numerous and tall as the Anakites, another race of giants. 11Both the Emites and the Anakites are also known as the Rephaites, though the Moabites call them Emites. 12In earlier times the Horites had lived in Seir, but they were driven out and displaced by the descendants of Esau, just as Israel drove out the people of Canaan when the LORD gave Israel their land.)

13Moses continued, "Then the LORD said to us, 'Get moving. Cross the Zered Brook.' So we crossed the brook.

14"Thirty-eight years passed from the time we first left Kadesh-barnea until we finally crossed the Zered Brook! By then, all the men old enough to fight in battle had died in the wilderness, as the LORD had vowed would happen. 15The LORD struck them down until they had all been eliminated from the community.

16"When all the men of fighting age had died, 17the LORD said to me, 18'Today you will cross the border of Moab at Ar 19and enter the land of the Ammonites, the descendants of Lot. But do not bother them or start a war with them. I have given the land of Ammon to them as their property, and I will not give you any of their land.'"

20(That area was once considered the land of the Rephaites, who had lived there, though the Ammonites call them Zamzummites. 21They were also as strong and numerous and tall as the Anakites. But the LORD destroyed them so the Ammonites could occupy their land. 22He had done the same for the descendants of Esau who lived in Seir, for he destroyed the Horites so they could settle there in their place. The descendants of Esau live there to this day. 23A similar thing happened when the Caphtorites from Crete* invaded and destroyed the Avvites, who had lived in villages in the area of Gaza.)

24Moses continued, "Then the LORD said, 'Now get moving! Cross the Arnon Gorge. Look, I will hand over to you Sihon the Amorite, king of Heshbon, and I will give you his land. Attack him and begin to occupy the land. 25Beginning today I will make people throughout the earth terrified because of you. When they hear reports about you, they will tremble with dread and fear.'"

Victory over Sihon of Heshbon

DEUTERONOMY 2:26-37

Moses continued, "From the wilderness of Kedemoth I sent ambassadors to King Sihon of Heshbon with this proposal of peace:

Dt 2:23 Hebrew *from Caphtor.*

Recognize the rights of others, even your opponents. By behaving wisely and justly you may be able to establish or restore a relationship.

Deut 2:11 Both Moab and Ammon had removed a tall Anakim-like people usually known as the Rephaites, but called Emites by the Moabites and Zamzummites by the Ammonites (Deut 2:20). If our enemies seem overwhelming, we must remember that God can deliver us as he did the Israelites.

Deut 2:14-15 Israel did not have to spend 40 years on the way to the Promised Land. God sentenced them to wilderness wanderings because they rejected his love, rebelled against his authority, ignored his commands for right living, and willfully broke their end of the agreement made in Exodus 19:8; 24:3-8. In short, they disobeyed God. We often make life's journey more difficult than necessary by disobedience. Accept God's love, read and follow his commands in the Bible, and make a promise to stick with God whatever your situation. You will find that your life will be less complicated and more rewarding.

Deut 2:25 God told Moses he would make the enemy nations terrified of Israel. By worldly standards, Israel's army was not intimidating, but Israel had God on its side. Moses no longer had to worry about his enemies because his enemies were worried about him. God often goes before us in our daily battles, preparing the way and overcoming barriers. We need to follow him wholeheartedly and be alert to his leading.

EVENTS IN DEUTERONOMY ▶

The book of Deuteronomy opens with Israel camped east of the Jordan River in the land of Moab. Just before the people crossed the river into the Promised Land, Moses delivered an inspirational speech indicating how they were to live.

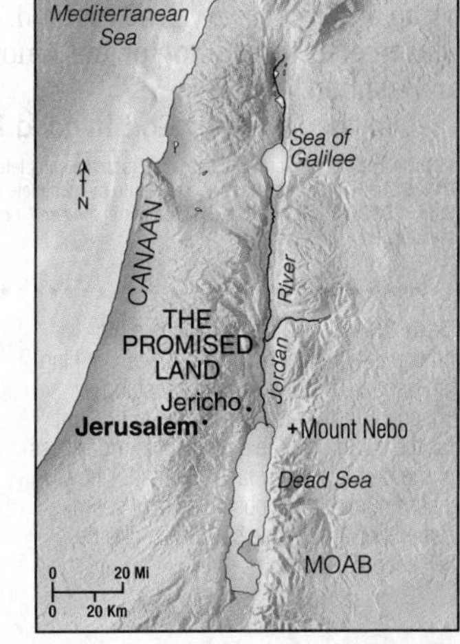

▸ **DEUTERONOMY 2:26-37 *(cont.)***
27'Let us travel through your land. We will stay
on the main road and won't turn off into the
fields on either side. 28Sell us food to eat and
water to drink, and we will pay for it. All we want
is permission to pass through your land. 29The
descendants of Esau who live in Seir allowed
us to go through their country, and so did the
Moabites, who live in Ar. Let us pass through until
we cross the Jordan into the land the LORD our
God is giving us.'

30"But King Sihon of Heshbon refused to allow us to
pass through, because the LORD your God made Sihon
stubborn and defiant so he could help you defeat him,
as he has now done.

31"Then the LORD said to me, 'Look, I have begun to
hand King Sihon and his land over to you. Begin now
to conquer and occupy his land.'

32"Then King Sihon declared war on us and mobilized his forces at Jahaz. 33But the LORD our God
handed him over to us, and we crushed him, his sons,
and all his people. 34We conquered all his towns and
completely destroyed* everyone—men, women, and
children. Not a single person was spared. 35We took
all the livestock as plunder for ourselves, along with
anything of value from the towns we ransacked.

36"The LORD our God also helped us conquer Aroer
on the edge of the Arnon Gorge, and the town in the
gorge, and the whole area as far as Gilead. No town had
walls too strong for us. 37However, we avoided the land
of the Ammonites all along the Jabbok River and the
towns in the hill country—all the places the LORD our
God had commanded us to leave alone.

Victory over Og of Bashan

DEUTERONOMY 3:1-11
"Next we turned and headed for the land of Bashan,
where King Og and his entire army attacked us at Edrei. 2But the LORD told me, 'Do not be afraid of him,
for I have given you victory over Og and his entire
army, and I will give you all his land. Treat him just as
you treated King Sihon of the Amorites, who ruled
in Heshbon.'

3"So the LORD our God handed King Og and all
his people over to us, and we killed them all. Not a
single person survived. 4We conquered all sixty of
his towns—the entire Argob region in his kingdom
of Bashan. Not a single town escaped our conquest.
5These towns were all fortified with high walls and
barred gates. We also took many unwalled villages at
the same time. 6We completely destroyed* the kingdom of Bashan, just as we had destroyed King Sihon
of Heshbon. We destroyed all the people in every town
we conquered—men, women, and children alike. 7But
we kept all the livestock for ourselves and took plunder
from all the towns.

8"So we took the land of the two Amorite kings east
of the Jordan River—all the way from the Arnon Gorge
to Mount Hermon. 9(Mount Hermon is called Sirion
by the Sidonians, and the Amorites call it Senir.) 10We
had now conquered all the cities on the plateau and
all Gilead and Bashan, as far as the towns of Salecah
and Edrei, which were part of Og's kingdom in Bashan.
11(King Og of Bashan was the last survivor of the giant
Rephaites. His bed was made of iron and was more
than thirteen feet long and six feet wide.* It can still
be seen in the Ammonite city of Rabbah.)

Land Division East of the Jordan

DEUTERONOMY 3:12-20
"When we took possession of this land, I gave to the
tribes of Reuben and Gad the territory beyond Aroer
along the Arnon Gorge, plus half of the hill country of
Gilead with its towns. 13Then I gave the rest of Gilead
and all of Bashan—Og's former kingdom—to the half-
tribe of Manasseh. (This entire Argob region of Bashan used to be known as the land of the Rephaites.
14Jair, a leader from the tribe of Manasseh, conquered
the whole Argob region in Bashan, all the way to the
border of the Geshurites and Maacathites. Jair renamed this region after himself, calling it the Towns
of Jair,* as it is still known today.) 15I gave Gilead to
the clan of Makir. 16But I also gave part of Gilead to
the tribes of Reuben and Gad. The area I gave them
extended from the middle of the Arnon Gorge in the
south to the Jabbok River on the Ammonite frontier.
17They also received the Jordan Valley, all the way
from the Sea of Galilee down to the Dead Sea,* with

Dt 2:34 The Hebrew term used here refers to the complete consecration of things or people to the LORD, either by destroying them or by giving them as an offering. **Dt 3:6** The Hebrew term used here refers to the complete consecration of things or people to the LORD, either by destroying them or by giving them as an offering; also in 3:6b. **Dt 3:11** Hebrew *9 cubits* [4.1 meters] *long and 4 cubits* [1.8 meters] *wide.* **Dt 3:14** Hebrew *Havvoth-jair.* **Dt 3:17** Hebrew *from Kinnereth to the Sea of the Arabah, the Salt Sea.*

Deut 3:1-3 The Israelites faced a big problem—the well-trained army of Og, king of Bashan. The Israelites hardly stood a chance. But they won because God fought for them. God can help his people regardless of the problems they face. No matter how insurmountable the obstacles may seem, remember that God is sovereign, and he will keep his promises.

Deut 3:21-22 What encouraging news for Joshua, who was to lead his men against the persistent forces of evil in the Promised Land! Since God promised to help him win every battle, he had nothing to fear. Our battles may not be against godless armies, but they are just as real as Joshua's. Whether we are resisting temptation or battling fear, God has promised to fight with and for us as we place our hope and confidence in him.

Deut 3:26-28 God had made it clear that Moses would not enter the Promised Land (Num 20:12). So God told Moses to commission Joshua as the new leader and encourage him in this new role. This is a good example to churches and organizations who must eventually replace their leaders. Good leaders prepare their people to function without them by discovering those with leadership potential, providing the training they need, and looking for ways to encourage them.

the Jordan River serving as the western boundary. To the east were the slopes of Pisgah.

[18]"At that time I gave this command to the tribes that would live east of the Jordan: 'Although the LORD your God has given you this land as your property, all your fighting men must cross the Jordan ahead of your Israelite relatives, armed and ready to assist them. [19]Your wives, children, and numerous livestock, however, may stay behind in the towns I have given you. [20]When the LORD has given security to the rest of the Israelites, as he has to you, and when they occupy the land the LORD your God is giving them across the Jordan River, then you may all return here to the land I have given you.'

Moses Forbidden to Enter the Land

DEUTERONOMY 3:21-29

"At that time I gave Joshua this charge: 'You have seen for yourself everything the LORD your God has done to these two kings. He will do the same to all the kingdoms on the west side of the Jordan. [22]Do not be afraid of the nations there, for the LORD your God will fight for you.'

[23]"At that time I pleaded with the LORD and said, [24]'O Sovereign LORD, you have only begun to show your greatness and the strength of your hand to me, your servant. Is there any god in heaven or on earth who can perform such great and mighty deeds as you do? [25]Please let me cross the Jordan to see the wonderful land on the other side, the beautiful hill country and the Lebanon mountains.'

[26]"But the LORD was angry with me because of you, and he would not listen to me. 'That's enough!' he declared. 'Speak of it no more. [27]But go up to Pisgah Peak, and look over the land in every direction. Take a good look, but you may not cross the Jordan River. [28]Instead, commission Joshua and encourage and strengthen him, for he will lead the people across the Jordan. He will give them all the land you now see before you as their possession.' [29]So we stayed in the valley near Beth-peor.

Moses Urges Israel to Obey

DEUTERONOMY 4:1-14

"And now, Israel, listen carefully to these decrees and regulations that I am about to teach you. Obey them so that you may live, so you may enter and occupy the land that the LORD, the God of your ancestors, is giving you. [2]Do not add to or subtract from these commands I am giving you. Just obey the commands of the LORD your God that I am giving you.

[3]"You saw for yourself what the LORD did to you at Baal-peor. There the LORD your God destroyed everyone who had worshiped Baal, the god of Peor. [4]But all of you who were faithful to the LORD your God are still alive today—every one of you.

[5]"Look, I now teach you these decrees and regulations just as the LORD my God commanded me, so

EIGHT WORDS FOR LAW

Hebrew law served as the personal and national guide for living under God's authority. It directed the moral, spiritual, and social life. Its purpose was to produce better understanding of God and greater commitment to him.

Word	Meaning	Examples	Significance
Torah	Direction, Guidance, Instruction	Exod 24:12	Need for law in general; a command from a higher person to a lower person
Mitswah	Commandment, Command	Gen 26:5; Exod 15:26; 20:2-17	God's specific instruction to be obeyed rather than a general law; used of the Ten Commandments
Mishpat	Regulations, Judgment, Ordinance	Gen 18:19; Deut 16:18; 17:9	Refers to the civil, social, and sanitation laws
Eduth	Testimony, Truth	Exod 25:22	Refers to God's law as he deals with his people
Huqqim	Statutes, Laws	Lev 18:4; Deut 4:1	Dealt with the royal pronouncements; mainly connected to worship and feasts
Piqqudim	Orders, Commandments	Pss 19:8; 103:18	Used often in the Psalms to describe God's orders and assignments
Dabar	Word, Terms	Exod 34:28; Deut 4:13	Used to indicate divine oracles or revelations of God
Dath	Royal Edict, Public Law	Ezek 7:26; Dan 6:8, 12	Refers to a public law or Jewish religious tradition

Deut 4:2 What is meant by adding to or subtracting from God's commands? These laws were the word of God, and they were complete. How could any human being, with limited wisdom and knowledge, edit God's perfect laws? To add to the laws would make them a burden; to subtract from the laws would make them incomplete. Thus the laws were to remain unchanged. To presume to make changes in God's law is to assume a position of authority over God, who gave the laws (Matt 5:17-19; 15:3-9; Rev 22:18-19). The religious leaders at the time of Christ did exactly this; they elevated their own laws to the same level as God's. Jesus rebuked them for this (Matt 23:1-4).

▸ **DEUTERONOMY 4:1-14 *(cont.)***

that you may obey them in the land you are about to enter and occupy. [6]Obey them completely, and you will display your wisdom and intelligence among the surrounding nations. When they hear all these decrees, they will exclaim, 'How wise and prudent are the people of this great nation!' [7]For what great nation has a god as near to them as the LORD our God is near to us whenever we call on him? [8]And what great nation has decrees and regulations as righteous and fair as this body of instructions that I am giving you today?

[9]"But watch out! Be careful never to forget what you yourself have seen. Do not let these memories escape from your mind as long as you live! And be sure to pass them on to your children and grandchildren. [10]Never forget the day when you stood before the LORD your God at Mount Sinai,* where he told me, 'Summon the people before me, and I will personally instruct them. Then they will learn to fear me as long as they live, and they will teach their children to fear me also.'

[11]"You came near and stood at the foot of the mountain, while flames from the mountain shot into the sky. The mountain was shrouded in black clouds and deep darkness. [12]And the LORD spoke to you from the heart of the fire. You heard the sound of his words but didn't see his form; there was only a voice. [13]He proclaimed his covenant—the Ten Commandments*—which he commanded you to keep, and which he wrote on two stone tablets. [14]It was at that time that the LORD commanded me to teach you his decrees and regulations so you would obey them in the land you are about to enter and occupy.

A Warning against Idolatry

DEUTERONOMY 4:15-31

"But be very careful! You did not see the LORD's form on the day he spoke to you from the heart of the fire at Mount Sinai. [16]So do not corrupt yourselves by making an idol in any form—whether of a man or a woman, [17]an animal on the ground, a bird in the sky, [18]a small animal that scurries along the ground, or a fish in the deepest sea. [19]And when you look up into the sky and see the sun, moon, and stars—all the forces of heaven—don't be seduced into worshiping them. The LORD your God gave them to all the peoples of the earth. [20]Remember that the LORD rescued you from the iron-smelting furnace of Egypt in order to make you his very own people and his special possession, which is what you are today.

[21]"But the LORD was angry with me because of you. He vowed that I would not cross the Jordan River into the good land the LORD your God is giving you as your special possession. [22]You will cross the Jordan to occupy the land, but I will not. Instead, I will die here on the east side of the river. [23]So be careful not to break the covenant the LORD your God has made with you. Do not make idols of any shape or form, for the LORD your God has forbidden this. [24]The LORD your God is a devouring fire; he is a jealous God.

[25]"In the future, when you have children and grand-

Dt 4:10 Hebrew *Horeb,* another name for Sinai; also in 4:15. **Dt 4:13** Hebrew *the ten words.*

Deut 4:8 Do the laws God gave to the Israelites still apply to Christians today? God's laws are designed to guide all people toward lifestyles that are healthy, upright, and devoted to God. Their purpose is to point out sin (or potential sin) and show the proper way to deal with that sin. The Ten Commandments, the heart of God's law, are just as applicable today as they were 3,000 years ago because they proclaim a lifestyle endorsed by God. They are the perfect expression of who God is and how he wants people to live.

But God gave other laws besides the Ten Commandments. Are these just as important? God never issued a law that didn't have a purpose. However, many of the laws we read in the Pentateuch were directed specifically to people of that time and culture. Although a specific law may not apply to us, the timeless truth or principle behind the law does.

For example, Christians do not practice animal sacrifice in worship. But the principles behind the sacrifices—forgiveness for sin and thankfulness to God—still apply. The sacrifices point to the ultimate sacrifice made for us by Jesus Christ. The New Testament says that with the death and resurrection of Jesus Christ the Old Testament laws were fulfilled. This means that while the Old Testament laws help us recognize our sins and correct our wrongdoings, it is Jesus Christ who takes our sins away. Jesus is our primary example to follow because he alone perfectly obeyed the law and modeled its true intent.

Deut 4:9 Moses wanted to make sure that the people did not forget all they had seen God do, so he urged parents to teach their children about God's great miracles. This helped parents remember God's faithfulness and provided the means for passing on from one generation to the next the stories recounting God's great acts. It is easy to forget the wonderful ways God has worked in the lives of his people. But you can remember God's great acts of faithfulness by telling your children, friends, or associates what you have seen him do.

Deut 4:19 God was not excusing the other nations for their idol worship. He was simply saying that while judgment might be delayed for those other nations, it would be swift and complete for Israel because Israel knew God's laws. We must remember that idol worship was not just keeping statues around the house—harmless lumps of clay, wood, or iron. It was the commitment to the other evil qualities and practices the idol represented (such as murder, prostitution, cruelty in war, or self-centeredness). When the strengths and attributes of powerful humans or animals are revered or the cycles of nature are honored without reference to God who created them, this is idolatry. Because God had so clearly revealed himself in Israel's history, the Israelites had no excuse for worshiping any person or power but the one true God.

Deut 4:24 God is a devouring fire. Because he is morally perfect, he hates sin and cannot accept those who practice it. Moses' sin kept him from entering the Promised Land, and no sacrifice could remove that judgment. Sin kept us from entering God's presence, but Jesus Christ paid the penalty for our sin and removed God's judgment forever by Jesus' death. Trusting in Jesus Christ will save you from God's anger and allow you to begin a personal relationship with him.

Deut 4:24 Jealousy is a demand for someone else's exclusive affection or loyalty. Some jealousy is bad. It is destructive for a person to get upset when his or her spouse talks to someone of the opposite sex. But other jealousy is good. It is right for a man to demand that his wife treat him, and only him, as her husband. Usually we use the word *jealousy* only for the bad reaction. But God's kind of jealousy is appropriate and good. He is defending his word and guarding his high honor. He makes a strong, exclusive demand on us: We must treat only the Lord—and no one else in all the universe—as God.

children and have lived in the land a long time, do not corrupt yourselves by making idols of any kind. This is evil in the sight of the LORD your God and will arouse his anger.
[26]"Today I call on heaven and earth as witnesses against you. If you break my covenant, you will quickly disappear from the land you are crossing the Jordan to occupy. You will live there only a short time; then you will be utterly destroyed. [27]For the LORD will scatter you among the nations, where only a few of you will survive. [28]There, in a foreign land, you will worship idols made from wood and stone—gods that neither see nor hear nor eat nor smell. [29]But from there you will search again for the LORD your God. And if you search for him with all your heart and soul, you will find him.
[30]"In the distant future, when you are suffering all these things, you will finally return to the LORD your God and listen to what he tells you. [31]For the LORD your God is a merciful God; he will not abandon you or destroy you or forget the solemn covenant he made with your ancestors.

There Is Only One God

DEUTERONOMY 4:32-40

"Now search all of history, from the time God created people on the earth until now, and search from one end of the heavens to the other. Has anything as great as this ever been seen or heard before? [33]Has any nation ever heard the voice of God* speaking from fire—as you did—and survived? [34]Has any other god dared to take a nation for himself out of another nation by means of trials, miraculous signs, wonders, war, a strong hand, a powerful arm, and terrifying acts? Yet that is what the LORD your God did for you in Egypt, right before your eyes.
[35]"He showed you these things so you would know that the LORD is God and there is no other. [36]He let you hear his voice from heaven so he could instruct you. He let you see his great fire here on earth so he could speak to you from it. [37]Because he loved your ancestors, he chose to bless their descendants, and he personally brought you out of Egypt with a great display of power. [38]He drove out nations far greater than you, so he could bring you in and give you their land as your special possession, as it is today.
[39]"So remember this and keep it firmly in mind: The LORD is God both in heaven and on earth, and there is no other. [40]If you obey all the decrees and commands I am giving you today, all will be well with you and your children. I am giving you these instructions so you will enjoy a long life in the land the LORD your God is giving you for all time."

Dt 4:33 Or *voice of a god.*

Eastern Cities of Refuge

DEUTERONOMY 4:41-43

Then Moses set apart three cities of refuge east of the Jordan River. [42]Anyone who killed another person unintentionally, without previous hostility, could flee there to live in safety. [43]These were the cities: Bezer on the wilderness plateau for the tribe of Reuben; Ramoth in Gilead for the tribe of Gad; Golan in Bashan for the tribe of Manasseh.

K. Moses' Second Address on the Plains of Moab

After reviewing the history of Israel's journey, Moses recounts the Ten Commandments and the other laws given to the Israelites at Mount Sinai. He urges them to obey the law and reminds them of the consequences of disobeying God's laws. The Ten Commandments and all of God's laws point out to us where we fall short and show us how we should act as God's people.

Introduction to Moses' Second Address

DEUTERONOMY 4:44-49

This is the body of instruction that Moses presented to the Israelites. [45]These are the laws, decrees, and regulations that Moses gave to the people of Israel when they left Egypt, [46]and as they camped in the valley near Beth-peor east of the Jordan River. (This land was formerly occupied by the Amorites under King Sihon,

Deut 4:29 Do you want to know God? God promised the Israelites that they would find him when they searched with all their hearts and souls. God is knowable and wants to be known—but we have to want to know him. Acts of service and worship must be accompanied by sincere devotion of the heart. As Hebrews 11:6 says, "Anyone who wants to come to him must believe that God exists and that he rewards those who sincerely seek him." God will reward those who pursue a relationship with him.

Deut 4:32 How tempted we are to look everywhere else but to God for our guidance and leadership! We trust medical doctors, financial advisers, and news commentators, but do we trust God? Get God's advice first (Deut 4:39-40), and recognize his authority over every dimension of life.

Deut 4:40 Was Israel guaranteed prosperity for obeying God's laws? Yes—but we have to look carefully at what that means. God's laws were designed to make his chosen nation devout, healthy, just, and merciful. When the people followed those laws, they prospered. This does not mean that no sickness, sadness, or misunderstandings existed among them. Rather, it means that as a nation they prospered and that individuals' problems were handled as fairly as possible. Today God's promise of prosperity—his constant presence, comfort, and the resources to live as we should—extends to all believers. We will face trials; Jesus told us that. But we will avoid the misery that directly results from intentional sin, and we will know that a great treasure awaits us in heaven.

▸ **DEUTERONOMY 4:44-49** ***(cont.)***
who ruled from Heshbon. But Moses and the Israelites
destroyed him and his people when they came up from
Egypt. 47 Israel took possession of his land and that
of King Og of Bashan—the two Amorite kings east of
the Jordan. 48 So Israel conquered the entire area from
Aroer at the edge of the Arnon Gorge all the way to
Mount Sirion,* also called Mount Hermon. 49 And they
conquered the eastern bank of the Jordan River as far
south as the Dead Sea,* below the slopes of Pisgah.)

Dt 4:48 As in Syriac version (see also 3:9); Hebrew reads *Mount Sion.* **Dt 4:49** Hebrew *took the Arabah on the east side of the Jordan as far as the sea of the Arabah.*

1. SUMMARY OF THE LAW

The general principles behind God's law are laid out in summary form, most notably through the Ten Commandments.

The Ten Commandments

DEUTERONOMY 5:1-33
Moses called all the people of Israel together and said,
"Listen carefully, Israel. Hear the decrees and regulations I am giving you today, so you may learn them
and obey them!
2 "The LORD our God made a covenant with us at
Mount Sinai.* 3 The LORD did not make this covenant
with our ancestors, but with all of us who are alive
today. 4 At the mountain the LORD spoke to you face
to face from the heart of the fire. 5 I stood as an intermediary between you and the LORD, for you were
afraid of the fire and did not want to approach the
mountain. He spoke to me, and I passed his words on
to you. This is what he said:

6 "I am the LORD your God, who rescued you from
the land of Egypt, the place of your slavery.
7 "You must not have any other god but me.
8 "You must not make for yourself an idol of any
kind, or an image of anything in the heavens or
on the earth or in the sea. 9 You must not bow
down to them or worship them, for I, the LORD
your God, am a jealous God who will not tolerate
your affection for any other gods. I lay the sins of
the parents upon their children; the entire family
is affected—even children in the third and fourth
generations of those who reject me. 10 But I lavish
unfailing love for a thousand generations on
those* who love me and obey my commands.
11 "You must not misuse the name of the LORD your

Dt 5:2 Hebrew *Horeb,* another name for Sinai. **Dt 5:10** Hebrew *for thousands of those.*

BROKEN COMMANDMENTS

The Ten Commandments were God's standard for right living. To obey them was to obey God (Deut 5:6-21). Yet throughout the Old Testament, we can see how each commandment was broken. As you read the stories, notice the tragic consequences that occurred as a result of violating God's law.

Ten Commandments	Notable Violations
"You must not have any other god but me."	Solomon (1 Kgs 11)
"You must not make for yourself an idol of any kind. . . . You must not bow down to them or worship them."	The gold calf-idol incident (Exod 32); generations after Joshua (Judg 2:10-14; 2 Kgs 21:1-15; Jer 1:16)
"You must not misuse the name of the LORD your God."	Zedekiah (Ezek 17:15-21)
"Observe the Sabbath day by keeping it holy."	Judah (2 Chr 36:21)
"Honor your father and mother."	Eli's sons—Hophni and Phinehas (1 Sam 2:12, 23-25)
"You must not murder."	Hazael (2 Kgs 8:15)
"You must not commit adultery."	David (2 Sam 11:2-5)
"You must not steal."	Ahab (1 Kgs 21:1-19)
"You must not testify falsely against your neighbor."	Saul (1 Sam 15:13-25)
"You must not covet your neighbor's wife. You must not covet your neighbor's house or land, . . . or anything else that belongs to your neighbor."	Achan (Josh 7:19-26)

Deut 5:1 The people had entered into a covenant with God, and Moses commanded them to hear, learn, and obey his regulations. Christians also have entered into a covenant with God through Jesus Christ and should be responsive to what God expects. Moses' threefold command to the Israelites provides excellent advice for all God's followers. *Listening* is absorbing and accepting information about God. *Learning* is understanding its meaning and implications. *Obeying* is putting into action all we have learned and understood. All three parts are essential to a growing relationship with God.

Deut 5:7 A *god* is whatever people use as a driving force in their lives. Some people literally worship other gods by joining cults or strange religions. In a more subtle way, many of us worship other gods by building our lives around something other than the one true God. If your greatest desire is for popularity, power, or money, you are devoting yourself to something other than God. To put God first, (1) recognize what is taking his place in your life; (2) renounce this substitute god as unworthy of your devotion; (3) ask God for forgiveness; (4) restructure your priorities so that love for God is the motive for everything you do; (5) examine yourself daily to be sure you are giving God first place.

Deut 5:8-9 How would you feel if someone took a picture of you, framed it, stared at it a lot, showed it to others, but completely ignored the real you? God does not want to

God. The LORD will not let you go unpunished if
you misuse his name.
12"Observe the Sabbath day by keeping it holy, as
the LORD your God has commanded you. 13You
have six days each week for your ordinary work,
14but the seventh day is a Sabbath day of rest
dedicated to the LORD your God. On that day no
one in your household may do any work. This
includes you, your sons and daughters, your male
and female servants, your oxen and donkeys and
other livestock, and any foreigners living among
you. All your male and female servants must rest
as you do. 15Remember that you were once slaves
in Egypt, but the LORD your God brought you out
with his strong hand and powerful arm. That is
why the LORD your God has commanded you to
rest on the Sabbath day.
16"Honor your father and mother, as the LORD
your God commanded you. Then you will live
a long, full life in the land the LORD your God
is giving you.
17"You must not murder.
18"You must not commit adultery.
19"You must not steal.
20"You must not testify falsely against your
neighbor.
21"You must not covet your neighbor's wife. You
must not covet your neighbor's house or land,
male or female servant, ox or donkey, or anything
else that belongs to your neighbor.

22"The LORD spoke these words to all of you assembled there at the foot of the mountain. He spoke with
a loud voice from the heart of the fire, surrounded by
clouds and deep darkness. This was all he said at that
time, and he wrote his words on two stone tablets and
gave them to me.
23"But when you heard the voice from the heart of
the darkness, while the mountain was blazing with
fire, all your tribal leaders and elders came to me.
24They said, 'Look, the LORD our God has shown us
his glory and greatness, and we have heard his voice
from the heart of the fire. Today we have seen that
God can speak to us humans, and yet we live! 25But

be treated this way either. He wants a genuine relationship with us, not mere ritual. He wants us to know him. God knows that if we put anything other than him at the center of our lives, we will not reach our potential and become all that he wants us to be.

Deut 5:11 We are familiar with the sin to be avoided in this commandment: we should not misuse the name of the Lord by saying it in an empty or worthless way. But there is a good work that is implied as well: to use God's name to praise him and ascribe to him glory. This is the opposite of misusing his name. While you might be able to keep yourself from swearing, how have you done at finding time to praise God and honor his name?

Deut 5:16 Obeying our parents is our main task when we are young, but honoring them should continue even beyond their death. One way to honor parents is to provide for them in times of financial need or when they are ill and unable to care for themselves. Perhaps the best way to honor them is to pass on their Christ-honoring values to our children. Honoring involves all that sons and daughters do with their lives—the way they work and talk, the values they hold, and the morals they practice. What are you doing to show respect to your parents? Are you living in a way that brings honor to them?

Deut 5:17 "But I don't murder people," you may say. Good. That fulfills the letter of the law. But Jesus explained that even hateful anger breaks this commandment (Matt 5:21-22). Have you ever been so angry with someone who mistreated you that for a moment you wished that person were dead? Have you ever fantasized that you could get rid of someone? Jesus' teaching concerning this law demonstrates that we are capable of murder in our hearts. Even if we are legally innocent, we are all morally guilty of murder and need to ask God's forgiveness. We need to commit ourselves to the opposite of hatred and anger—love and reconciliation.

Deut 5:21 To *covet* means to ardently desire another person's prosperity. We are not to set our desires on anything that belongs to someone else. Not only can such cravings make us miserable, but they can also lead us to other sins such as adultery and stealing. Envying others is a useless exercise because God is able to provide everything we really need, even if he does not always give us everything we want. To stop coveting, we need to practice being content with what we have. The apostle Paul emphasizes the significance of contentment in Philippians 4:11-12. It's a matter of perspective. Instead of thinking about what we don't have, we should thank God for what he has given and strive to be content. After all, our most important possession is free and available to everyone—eternal life through Christ.

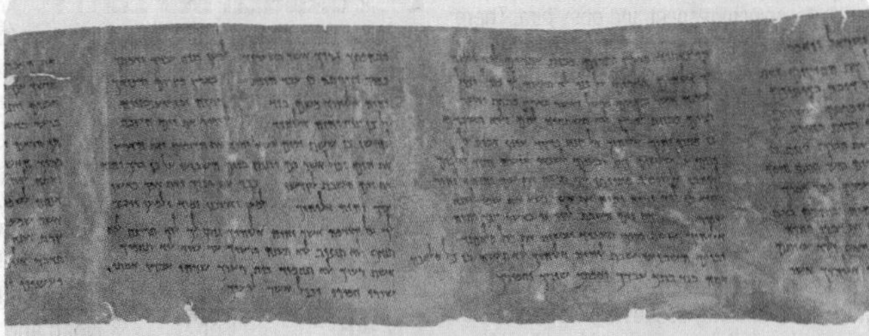

Dead Sea Scroll of Deuteronomy

One of the most amazing archaeological discoveries of the 20th century was the finding of over 600 manuscripts in the Qumran caves overlooking the Dead Sea. These manuscripts, dated between 200 B.C. and A.D. 100, provide the text of the Old Testament 1,000 years earlier than the manuscripts that were available to scholars before 1947. Of the 600 manuscripts, 200 preserve portions of the Old Testament. The books that are most represented are Genesis, Deuteronomy, Psalms, and Isaiah. In this photograph of 4QDeut[n] the text contains Deuteronomy 5:1–6:1. This is one of the oldest copies of the Ten Commandments, a sacred document that is revered by Jews and Christians alike. Take time to read the Ten Commandments again. They are a precious revelation of God's will for his people.

▸ **DEUTERONOMY 5:1-33 *(cont.)***
now, why should we risk death again? If the LORD our
God speaks to us again, we will certainly die and be
consumed by this awesome fire. 26Can any living thing
hear the voice of the living God from the heart of the
fire as we did and yet survive? 27Go yourself and listen
to what the LORD our God says. Then come and tell us
everything he tells you, and we will listen and obey.'
28"The LORD heard the request you made to me.
And he said, 'I have heard what the people said to you,
and they are right. 29Oh, that they would always have
hearts like this, that they might fear me and obey all
my commands! If they did, they and their descendants
would prosper forever. 30Go and tell them, "Return to
your tents." 31But you stand here with me so I can give
you all my commands, decrees, and regulations. You
must teach them to the people so they can obey them
in the land I am giving them as their possession.'"
32So Moses told the people, "You must be careful to obey all the commands of the LORD your God,
following his instructions in every detail. 33Stay on the
path that the LORD your God has commanded you to
follow. Then you will live long and prosperous lives in
the land you are about to enter and occupy.

Love the LORD Your God

DEUTERONOMY 6:1-25
"These are the commands, decrees, and regulations
that the LORD your God commanded me to teach you.
You must obey them in the land you are about to enter
and occupy, 2and you and your children and grandchildren must fear the LORD your God as long as you
live. If you obey all his decrees and commands, you
will enjoy a long life. 3Listen closely, Israel, and be
careful to obey. Then all will go well with you, and you
will have many children in the land flowing with milk
and honey, just as the LORD, the God of your ancestors,
promised you.
4"Listen, O Israel! The LORD is our God, the LORD
alone.* 5And you must love the LORD your God with

Dt 6:4 Or *The LORD our God is one LORD;* or *The LORD our God, the LORD is one;* or *The LORD is our God, the LORD is one.*

Deut 5:29 God told Moses that he wanted the people to incline their hearts to fear him—to *want* to respect and obey him. There is a difference between doing something because it is required and doing something because we want to. God is not interested in forced religious exercises and rule keeping. He wants our hearts and lives completely dedicated to him. If we love him, obedience will follow.

Deut 6:3 For a nation that had wandered 40 years in a parched wilderness, a land flowing with milk and honey sounded like paradise. It brought to mind rich crops, rushing streams, gentle rains, and lush fields filled with livestock. The Israelites could have had all that 40 years earlier. Numbers 13–14 explains how the people missed their chance. Now Moses was determined to help the people avoid the same mistake by whetting their appetite for the beautiful land and then clearly explaining the conditions for entering it.

Deut 6:4 Monotheism—belief in only one God—was a distinctive feature of the Hebrew religion. Many ancient religions believed in many gods. But the God of Abraham, Isaac, and Jacob is the God of the whole earth, the only true God. This was an important insight for the nation of Israel because they were about to enter a land filled with people who believed in many gods. Both then and today, there are people who prefer to place their trust in many different values, belief systems, and "gods." But the day is coming when God will be recognized as the only one. He will be the king over the whole earth (Zech 14:9).

Deut 6:4-9 This passage provides the central theme of Deuteronomy. It sets a pattern that helps us relate the Word of God to our daily lives. We are to love God, think constantly about his commandments, teach his commandments to our children, and live each day by the guidelines in his Word. God emphasized the importance of parents teaching the Bible to their children. The church and Christian schools cannot be used to escape from this responsibility. The Bible provides so many opportunities for object lessons and practical teaching that it would be a shame to study it only one day a week. Eternal truths are most effectively learned in the loving environment of a God-fearing home.

Deut 6:5 Jesus said that loving God with all of yourself is the first and greatest commandment (Matt 22:37-39). This command, combined with the command to love your neighbor (Lev 19:18), encompasses all the other Old Testament laws.

DANGER IN PLENTY

"When you have eaten your fill in this land, be careful not to forget the LORD" (Deut 6:11-12). It is often most difficult to follow God when life is easy—we can fall prey to temptation and fall away from God. Here are some notable examples of this truth.

Person	*Reference*	*Comment*
ADAM	Gen 3	Adam lived in a perfect world and had a perfect relationship with God. His needs were met; he had everything. But he fell to Satan's deception.
NOAH	Gen 9	Noah and his family had survived the Flood, and the whole world was theirs. They were prosperous, and life was easy. Noah shamed himself by becoming drunk, and then he cursed Canaan, the son of Ham.
THE NATION OF ISRAEL	Judg 2	God had given Israel the Promised Land—rest at last with no more wandering. But as soon as brave and faithful Joshua died, the Israelites fell into the idolatrous practices of the Canaanites.
DAVID	2 Sam 11	David ruled well, and Israel was a dominant nation politically, economically, and militarily. In the midst of prosperity and success, he committed adultery with Bathsheba and had her husband, Uriah, murdered.
SOLOMON	1 Kgs 11	Solomon truly had it all: power, wealth, fame, and wisdom. But his very abundance was the source of his downfall. He loved his pagan, idolatrous wives so much that he allowed himself and Israel to copy their detestable religious rites.

all your heart, all your soul, and all your strength. 6And you must commit yourselves wholeheartedly to these commands that I am giving you today. 7Repeat them again and again to your children. Talk about them when you are at home and when you are on the road, when you are going to bed and when you are getting up. 8Tie them to your hands and wear them on your forehead as reminders. 9Write them on the doorposts of your house and on your gates.

10"The LORD your God will soon bring you into the land he swore to give you when he made a vow to your ancestors Abraham, Isaac, and Jacob. It is a land with large, prosperous cities that you did not build. 11The houses will be richly stocked with goods you did not produce. You will draw water from cisterns you did not dig, and you will eat from vineyards and olive trees you did not plant. When you have eaten your fill in this land, 12be careful not to forget the LORD, who rescued you from slavery in the land of Egypt. 13You must fear the LORD your God and serve him. When you take an oath, you must use only his name.

14"You must not worship any of the gods of neighboring nations, 15for the LORD your God, who lives among you, is a jealous God. His anger will flare up against you, and he will wipe you from the face of the earth. 16You must not test the LORD your God as you did when you complained at Massah. 17You must diligently obey the commands of the LORD your God—all the laws and decrees he has given you. 18Do what is right and good in the LORD's sight, so all will go well with you. Then you will enter and occupy the good land that the LORD swore to give your ancestors. 19You will drive out all the enemies living in the land, just as the LORD said you would.

20"In the future your children will ask you, 'What is the meaning of these laws, decrees, and regulations that the LORD our God has commanded us to obey?'

21"Then you must tell them, 'We were Pharaoh's slaves in Egypt, but the LORD brought us out of Egypt with his strong hand. 22The LORD did miraculous signs and wonders before our eyes, dealing terrifying blows against Egypt and Pharaoh and all his people. 23He brought us out of Egypt so he could give us this land he had sworn to give our ancestors. 24And the LORD our God commanded us to obey all these decrees and to fear him so he can continue to bless us and preserve our lives, as he has done to this day. 25For we will be counted as righteous when we obey all the commands the LORD our God has given us.'

The Privilege of Holiness

DEUTERONOMY 7:1-26

"When the LORD your God brings you into the land you are about to enter and occupy, he will clear away many nations ahead of you: the Hittites, Girgashites, Amorites, Canaanites, Perizzites, Hivites, and Jebusites. These seven nations are greater and more numerous than you. 2When the LORD your God hands these

Deut 6:7 The Hebrews were extremely successful at making religion an integral part of life. The reason for their success was that religious education was life-oriented, not information-oriented. They used the context of daily life to teach about God. The key to teaching your children to love God is stated simply and clearly in these verses. If you want your children to follow God, you must make God a part of your everyday experiences. You must teach your children diligently to see God in all aspects of life, not just those that are church related.

Deut 6:10-13 Moses warned the people not to forget God when they entered the Promised Land and became prosperous. Prosperity, more than poverty, can dull our spiritual vision because it tends to make us self-sufficient and eager to acquire still more of everything—except God. The same thing can happen in our church. Once we become successful in terms of numbers, programs, and buildings, we can easily become self-sufficient and less sensitive to our need for God. This leads us to concentrate on self-preservation rather than thankfulness and service to God.

Deut 6:24 Does the phrase "so he can continue to bless us and preserve our lives" mean that we can expect only good things and no suffering when we obey God? What is promised here is a right relationship with God for all those who love him with all their hearts. It speaks of a good relationship with God and the ultimate benefit of knowing him. It is not blanket protection against poverty, adversity, or suffering. We can have this right relationship with God by obeying his command to love him with all that we are.

Deut 7:2 God told the Israelites to completely destroy their enemies. How can a God of love and mercy wipe out everyone, even children? Although God is loving and merciful, he is also just. These enemy nations were as much a part of God's creation as Israel was, and God does not allow evil to continue unchecked. God had punished Israel by keeping out of the Promised Land all those who had disobeyed. The command to destroy these nations was both a judgment (Deut 9:4-6) and a safety measure. On one hand, the people living in the land were being judged for their sin, and Israel was God's instrument of judgment—just as God would one day use other nations to judge Israel for its sin (2 Chr 36:17; Isa 10:12). On the other hand, God's command was designed to protect the nation of Israel from being ruined by the idolatry and immorality of its enemies. To think that God is too nice to judge sin would be to underestimate him.

"Write them on the doorposts of your house and on your gates."
Deuteronomy 6:9

▸ **DEUTERONOMY 7:1-26 *(cont.)***
nations over to you and you conquer them, you must
completely destroy* them. Make no treaties with them
and show them no mercy. 3You must not intermarry
with them. Do not let your daughters and sons marry
their sons and daughters, 4for they will lead your children away from me to worship other gods. Then the
anger of the LORD will burn against you, and he will
quickly destroy you. 5This is what you must do. You
must break down their pagan altars and shatter their
sacred pillars. Cut down their Asherah poles and burn
their idols. 6For you are a holy people, who belong to
the LORD your God. Of all the people on earth, the
LORD your God has chosen you to be his own special
treasure.
7"The LORD did not set his heart on you and choose
you because you were more numerous than other nations, for you were the smallest of all nations! 8Rather,
it was simply that the LORD loves you, and he was keeping the oath he had sworn to your ancestors. That is
why the LORD rescued you with such a strong hand
from your slavery and from the oppressive hand of
Pharaoh, king of Egypt. 9Understand, therefore, that
the LORD your God is indeed God. He is the faithful
God who keeps his covenant for a thousand generations and lavishes his unfailing love on those who
love him and obey his commands. 10But he does not
hesitate to punish and destroy those who reject him.
11Therefore, you must obey all these commands, decrees, and regulations I am giving you today.
12"If you listen to these regulations and faithfully
obey them, the LORD your God will keep his covenant
of unfailing love with you, as he promised with an
oath to your ancestors. 13He will love you and bless
you, and he will give you many children. He will give
fertility to your land and your animals. When you arrive in the land he swore to give your ancestors, you
will have large harvests of grain, new wine, and olive
oil, and great herds of cattle, sheep, and goats. 14You
will be blessed above all the nations of the earth. None
of your men or women will be childless, and all your
livestock will bear young. 15And the LORD will protect
you from all sickness. He will not let you suffer from
the terrible diseases you knew in Egypt, but he will
inflict them on all your enemies!
16"You must destroy all the nations the LORD your
God hands over to you. Show them no mercy, and do
not worship their gods, or they will trap you. 17Perhaps
you will think to yourselves, 'How can we ever conquer
these nations that are so much more powerful than
we are?' 18But don't be afraid of them! Just remember
what the LORD your God did to Pharaoh and to all the
land of Egypt. 19Remember the great terrors the LORD
your God sent against them. You saw it all with your
own eyes! And remember the miraculous signs and
wonders, and the strong hand and powerful arm with
which he brought you out of Egypt. The LORD your God
will use this same power against all the people you
fear. 20And then the LORD your God will send terror*
to drive out the few survivors still hiding from you!
21"No, do not be afraid of those nations, for the LORD
your God is among you, and he is a great and awesome
God. 22The LORD your God will drive those nations out
ahead of you little by little. You will not clear them
away all at once, otherwise the wild animals would
multiply too quickly for you. 23But the LORD your God
will hand them over to you. He will throw them into
complete confusion until they are destroyed. 24He will
put their kings in your power, and you will erase their
names from the face of the earth. No one will be able
to stand against you, and you will destroy them all.
25"You must burn their idols in fire, and you must
not covet the silver or gold that covers them. You
must not take it or it will become a trap to you, for it
is detestable to the LORD your God. 26Do not bring any
detestable objects into your home, for then you will be
destroyed, just like them. You must utterly detest such
things, for they are set apart for destruction.

A Call to Remember and Obey

DEUTERONOMY 8:1-20
"Be careful to obey all the commands I am giving you
today. Then you will live and multiply, and you will enter and occupy the land the LORD swore to give your

Dt 7:2 The Hebrew term used here refers to the complete consecration of things or people to the LORD, either by destroying them or by giving them as an offering; also in 7:26. **Dt 7:20** Often rendered *the hornet.* The meaning of the Hebrew is uncertain.

Deut 7:5 Asherah was a Canaanite fertility goddess associated with Baal. Baal was the most worshiped god of the Canaanites. Most often cast in the form of a bull, he symbolized strength and fertility and was considered the god of agriculture. Asherah was Baal's female consort. She was worshiped by means of wooden pillars (here called "poles").

Deut 7:6-8 How did Israel deserve to be chosen above all of the other nations at that time? It was not a matter of Israel's merit, but of God keeping his promise to their ancestors. Just as God chose the nation of Israel, he has chosen all believers today to be his treasured possession. Similarly, it is not because of our merit that we have come to faith in Christ. Instead, God chose us out of his goodness and grace.

Deut 7:21-24 Moses told the Israelites that God would destroy Israel's enemies, but not all at once. God had the power to destroy those nations instantly, but he chose to do it in stages, "little by little." In the same way and with the same power, God could miraculously and instantaneously change your life. Usually he chooses to help you gradually, teaching you one lesson at a time. Rather than expecting instant spiritual maturity and solutions to all your problems, slow down and work one step at a time, trusting God to make up the difference between where you should be and where you are now. You'll soon look back and see that a miraculous transformation has occurred.

Deut 7:25-26 Moses warned Israel against becoming ensnared by the idols of the defeated nations by desiring the silver or gold on them. We may think it's all right to be close to sin as long as we don't participate. "After all," we say, "I won't do anything wrong!" But being close can hurt us as we become attracted and finally give in. Avoid the snare of sin by first reigning in your desires. Then stay as far away from sin as you can.

ancestors. 2Remember how the LORD your God led you
through the wilderness for these forty years, humbling
you and testing you to prove your character, and to find
out whether or not you would obey his commands.
3Yes, he humbled you by letting you go hungry and then
feeding you with manna, a food previously unknown
to you and your ancestors. He did it to teach you that
people do not live by bread alone; rather, we live by
every word that comes from the mouth of the LORD.
4For all these forty years your clothes didn't wear out,
and your feet didn't blister or swell. 5Think about it:
Just as a parent disciplines a child, the LORD your God
disciplines you for your own good.
6"So obey the commands of the LORD your God by
walking in his ways and fearing him. 7For the LORD
your God is bringing you into a good land of flowing streams and pools of water, with fountains and
springs that gush out in the valleys and hills. 8It is
a land of wheat and barley; of grapevines, fig trees,
and pomegranates; of olive oil and honey. 9It is a land
where food is plentiful and nothing is lacking. It is a
land where iron is as common as stone, and copper
is abundant in the hills. 10When you have eaten your
fill, be sure to praise the LORD your God for the good
land he has given you.
11"But that is the time to be careful! Beware that in
your plenty you do not forget the LORD your God and
disobey his commands, regulations, and decrees that
I am giving you today. 12For when you have become
full and prosperous and have built fine homes to live
in, 13and when your flocks and herds have become
very large and your silver and gold have multiplied
along with everything else, be careful! 14Do not become proud at that time and forget the LORD your God,
who rescued you from slavery in the land of Egypt.
15Do not forget that he led you through the great and
terrifying wilderness with its poisonous snakes and
scorpions, where it was so hot and dry. He gave you
water from the rock! 16He fed you with manna in the
wilderness, a food unknown to your ancestors. He did
this to humble you and test you for your own good.
17He did all this so you would never say to yourself, 'I
have achieved this wealth with my own strength and
energy.' 18Remember the LORD your God. He is the
one who gives you power to be successful, in order to
fulfill the covenant he confirmed to your ancestors
with an oath.
19"But I assure you of this: If you ever forget the
LORD your God and follow other gods, worshiping and
bowing down to them, you will certainly be destroyed.
20Just as the LORD has destroyed other nations in your
path, you also will be destroyed if you refuse to obey
the LORD your God.

Victory by God's Grace

DEUTERONOMY 9:1-6

"Listen, O Israel! Today you are about to cross the Jordan River to take over the land belonging to nations

OBEDIENCE

Deuteronomy 8:1 tells us to obey God's commandments. We do this by obeying God with . . .

OUR HEARTS	By loving him more than any relationship, activity, achievement, or possession
OUR WILLS	By committing ourselves completely to him
OUR MINDS	By seeking to know him and his Word, so his principles and values form the foundation of all we think and do
OUR BODIES	By recognizing that our strengths, talents, and sexuality are given to us by God to be used for pleasure and fulfillment according to his rules, not ours
OUR FINANCES	By deciding that all of the resources we have ultimately come from God, and that we are to be managers of them and not owners
OUR FUTURES	By deciding to make service to God and man the main purpose of our life's work

Deut 8:3 Jesus quoted this verse when the devil tempted him to turn stones into bread (Matt 4:4). Many people think that life is based on satisfying their appetites. If they can earn enough money to dress, eat, and play in high style, they think they are living "the good life." But such things do not satisfy our deepest longings. In the end they leave us empty and dissatisfied. Real life, according to Moses, comes from total commitment to God and living by every word that comes from him. How can we live by his every word? (1) Recognize our need for it. (2) Agree that God alone can truly satisfy us. (3) Pray for God's presence, wisdom, and direction as we read his Word. (4) Savor the relationship we have with him through Christ. (5) Practice what he teaches us.

Deut 8:4 It's easy for us to take God's protection for granted. We seldom take notice or thank God when our car doesn't break down, our clothes don't rip, or our tools don't break. The people of Israel also failed to take notice, it seems, for they didn't even notice that in 40 years of wandering in the wilderness, their clothes didn't wear out and their feet didn't blister or swell. Thus, they did not remember to give thanks to God for these blessings. What has been working well for you? What has been giving you good service? What has been lasting for a long time without breaking? Remember to thank God for these quiet blessings.

Deut 8:10 This verse is traditionally cited as the reason we say grace before or after meals. Its purpose, however, was to warn the Israelites not to forget God when their needs and wants were satisfied. Let your table prayers serve as a constant reminder of the Lord's goodness to you and your duty to those who are less fortunate.

Deut 8:11-20 In times of plenty, we often take credit for our prosperity and become proud that our own hard work and cleverness have made us rich. It is easy to get so busy collecting and managing wealth that we push God right out of our lives. But it is God who gives us everything we have, and it is God who asks us to manage it for him.

▶ **DEUTERONOMY 9:1-6 *(cont.)***

much greater and more powerful than you. They live in cities with walls that reach to the sky! 2The people are strong and tall—descendants of the famous Anakite giants. You've heard the saying, 'Who can stand up to the Anakites?' 3But recognize today that the LORD your God is the one who will cross over ahead of you like a devouring fire to destroy them. He will subdue them so that you will quickly conquer them and drive them out, just as the LORD has promised.

4"After the LORD your God has done this for you, don't say in your hearts, 'The LORD has given us this land because we are such good people!' No, it is because of the wickedness of the other nations that he is pushing them out of your way. 5It is not because you are so good or have such integrity that you are about to occupy their land. The LORD your God will drive these nations out ahead of you only because of their wickedness, and to fulfill the oath he swore to your ancestors Abraham, Isaac, and Jacob. 6You must recognize that the LORD your God is not giving you this good land because you are good, for you are not—you are a stubborn people.

Remembering the Gold Calf

DEUTERONOMY 9:7-29

"Remember and never forget how angry you made the LORD your God out in the wilderness. From the day you left Egypt until now, you have been constantly rebelling against him. 8Even at Mount Sinai* you made the LORD so angry he was ready to destroy you. 9This happened when I was on the mountain receiving the tablets of stone inscribed with the words of the covenant that the LORD had made with you. I was there for forty days and forty nights, and all that time I ate no food and drank no water. 10The LORD gave me the two tablets on which God had written with his own finger all the words he had spoken to you from the heart of the fire when you were assembled at the mountain.

11"At the end of the forty days and nights, the LORD handed me the two stone tablets inscribed with the words of the covenant. 12Then the LORD said to me, 'Get up! Go down immediately, for the people you brought out of Egypt have corrupted themselves. How quickly they have turned away from the way I commanded them to live! They have melted gold and made an idol for themselves!'

13"The LORD also said to me, 'I have seen how stubborn and rebellious these people are. 14Leave me alone so I may destroy them and erase their name from under heaven. Then I will make a mighty nation of your descendants, a nation larger and more powerful than they are.'

15"So while the mountain was blazing with fire I turned and came down, holding in my hands the two stone tablets inscribed with the terms of the covenant. 16There below me I could see that you had sinned against the LORD your God. You had melted gold and made a calf idol for yourselves. How quickly you had turned away from the path the LORD had commanded you to follow! 17So I took the stone tablets and threw them to the ground, smashing them before your eyes.

18"Then, as before, I threw myself down before the LORD for forty days and nights. I ate no bread and drank no water because of the great sin you had committed by doing what the LORD hated, provoking him to anger. 19I feared that the furious anger of the LORD, which turned him against you, would drive him to destroy you. But again he listened to me. 20The LORD was so angry with Aaron that he wanted to destroy him, too. But I prayed for Aaron, and the LORD spared him. 21I took your sin—the calf you had made—and I melted it down in the fire and ground it into fine dust. Then I threw the dust into the stream that flows down the mountain.

22"You also made the LORD angry at Taberah,* Massah,* and Kibroth-hattaavah.* 23And at Kadesh-barnea the LORD sent you out with this command: 'Go up and take over the land I have given you.' But you rebelled against the command of the LORD your God and refused to put your trust in him or obey him. 24Yes, you have been rebelling against the LORD as long as I have known you.

25"That is why I threw myself down before the LORD for forty days and nights—for the LORD said he would destroy you. 26I prayed to the LORD and said, 'O Sovereign LORD, do not destroy them. They are your own people. They are your special possession, whom

Dt 9:8 Hebrew *Horeb,* another name for Sinai. **Dt 9:22a** *Taberah* means "place of burning." See Num 11:1-3. **Dt 9:22b** *Massah* means "place of testing." See Exod 17:1-7. **Dt 9:22c** *Kibroth-hattaavah* means "graves of gluttony." See Num 11:31-34.

Deut 9:2-3 The Anakites were enormous people, some seven to nine feet tall. Goliath, probably a descendant of this race, was over nine feet tall (1 Sam 17:4-7). Unfortunately, these great men used their stature as a means of intimidation rather than for noble causes. Their appearance alone frightened most of the Israelite scouts (Num 13:28), and their bad reputation may have been the deciding factor that kept the Israelites out of the land 40 years earlier (Num 13–14). Moses used all his persuasive power to convince the people that God could handle these bullies. He used the illustration of God as a devouring fire, for not even a giant could stand up to that.

Deut 9:18 From the record of this event in Exodus 32, it seems as though Moses acted immediately, grinding the gold calf into powder and forcing the people to drink water mixed with it. But evidently, Moses first spent 40 days and nights interceding for the people.

Deut 9:23 Moses was reminding the people of the nation's unbelief 40 years earlier, when they had been afraid to enter Canaan. The Israelites had not believed God would be able to help them in spite of all he had already done. They refused to follow because they looked only to their own limited resources instead of to God. Unbelief is the root of many sins and problems. When you feel lost, it may be because you're looking everywhere but to God for your help and guidance. (See Pss 81:6-12; 95:8; 106:13-20; Heb 3.)

you redeemed from Egypt by your mighty power and your strong hand. [27]Please overlook the stubbornness and the awful sin of these people, and remember instead your servants Abraham, Isaac, and Jacob. [28]If you destroy these people, the Egyptians will say, "The Israelites died because the LORD wasn't able to bring them to the land he had promised to give them." Or they might say, "He destroyed them because he hated them; he deliberately took them into the wilderness to slaughter them." [29]But they are your people and your special possession, whom you brought out of Egypt by your great strength and powerful arm.'

A New Copy of the Covenant

DEUTERONOMY 10:1-11

"At that time the LORD said to me, 'Chisel out two stone tablets like the first ones. Also make a wooden Ark—a sacred chest to store them in. Come up to me on the mountain, [2]and I will write on the tablets the same words that were on the ones you smashed. Then place the tablets in the Ark.'

[3]"So I made an Ark of acacia wood and cut two stone tablets like the first two. Then I went up the mountain with the tablets in my hand. [4]Once again the LORD wrote the Ten Commandments* on the tablets and gave them to me. They were the same words the LORD had spoken to you from the heart of the fire on the day you were assembled at the foot of the mountain. [5]Then I turned and came down the mountain and placed the tablets in the Ark of the Covenant, which I had made, just as the LORD commanded me. And the tablets are still there in the Ark."

[6](The people of Israel set out from the wells of the people of Jaakan* and traveled to Moserah, where Aaron died and was buried. His son Eleazar ministered as high priest in his place. [7]Then they journeyed to Gudgodah, and from there to Jotbathah, a land with many brooks and streams. [8]At that time the LORD set apart the tribe of Levi to carry the Ark of the LORD's Covenant, and to stand before the LORD as his ministers, and to pronounce blessings in his name. These are their duties to this day. [9]That is why the Levites have no share of property or possession of land among the other Israelite tribes. The LORD himself is their special possession, as the LORD your God told them.)

[10]"As for me, I stayed on the mountain in the LORD's presence for forty days and nights, as I had done the first time. And once again the LORD listened to my pleas and agreed not to destroy you. [11]Then the LORD said to me, 'Get up and resume the journey, and lead the people to the land I swore to give to their ancestors, so they may take possession of it.'

Dt 10:4 Hebrew *the ten words.* **Dt 10:6** Or *set out from Beeroth of Bene-jaakan.*

PRIESTS IN ISRAEL'S HISTORY

Deuteronomy 10:6 mentions the death of Aaron, the first high priest. Each new high priest had to come from the lineage of Aaron. Listed here are the ones whose stories are told elsewhere in the Bible.

Priest	*Importance*	*Reference*
Aaron	Moses' brother and first high priest	Exod 28:1-3
Eleazar	Watched two of his brothers die in a fire from God because they did not follow God's instructions. He obeyed God and became chief leader of the Tabernacle.	Lev 10 Num 3:32
Phinehas	Executed a young Israelite idol worshiper and his Midianite mistress to end a plague. He was then promised that his priestly line would never end.	Num 25:1-15
Ahijah	A priest during King Saul's reign	1 Sam 14:3
Zadok	A faithful high priest under King David. He and Nathan anointed Solomon as the next king.	2 Sam 8:17 1 Kgs 1:38-39
Ahimaaz	Carried the message of Absalom's death to King David but was apparently afraid to tell about it.	2 Sam 18:19-29
Azariah	High priest under King Solomon	1 Kgs 4:2
Azariah	High priest under Uzziah. He rebuked the king for burning incense himself.	2 Chr 26:17-21
	When Hezekiah became king, he reopened the Temple. Azariah again served as high priest.	2 Chr 31:10-13
Amariah	King Jehoshaphat appointed him to judge religious disputes.	2 Chr 19:11
Hilkiah	Found the Book of the Law during Josiah's reign	2 Kgs 22:3-13 2 Chr 34:14-21
Azariah	Probably one of the first to return to Israel from Babylon	1 Chr 9:10-11
Seraiah	The father of Ezra	Ezra 7:1-5

Deut 10:5 The tablets of the law were still in the Ark about 500 years later when Solomon put it in his newly built Temple (1 Kgs 8:9). The Ark last appears in the Israelites' history during the reign of Josiah, about 300 years after Solomon (2 Chr 35:3).

A Call to Love and Obedience

DEUTERONOMY 10:12–11:7

"And now, Israel, what does the LORD your God require of you? He requires only that you fear the LORD your God, and live in a way that pleases him, and love him and serve him with all your heart and soul. [13]And you must always obey the LORD's commands and decrees that I am giving you today for your own good.

[14]"Look, the highest heavens and the earth and everything in it all belong to the LORD your God. [15]Yet the LORD chose your ancestors as the objects of his love. And he chose you, their descendants, above all other nations, as is evident today. [16]Therefore, change your hearts* and stop being stubborn.

[17]"For the LORD your God is the God of gods and Lord of lords. He is the great God, the mighty and awesome God, who shows no partiality and cannot be bribed. [18]He ensures that orphans and widows receive justice. He shows love to the foreigners living among you and gives them food and clothing. [19]So you, too, must show love to foreigners, for you yourselves were once foreigners in the land of Egypt. [20]You must fear the LORD your God and worship him and cling to him. Your oaths must be in his name alone. [21]He alone is your God, the only one who is worthy of your praise, the one who has done these mighty miracles that you have seen with your own eyes. [22]When your ancestors went down into Egypt, there were only seventy of them. But now the LORD your God has made you as numerous as the stars in the sky!

11:1"You must love the LORD your God and obey all his requirements, decrees, regulations, and commands. [2]Keep in mind that I am not talking now to your children, who have never experienced the discipline of the LORD your God or seen his greatness and his strong hand and powerful arm. [3]They didn't see the miraculous signs and wonders he performed in Egypt against Pharaoh and all his land. [4]They didn't see what the LORD did to the armies of Egypt and to their horses and chariots—how he drowned them in the Red Sea* as they were chasing you. He destroyed them, and they have not recovered to this very day!

[5]"Your children didn't see how the LORD cared for you in the wilderness until you arrived here. [6]They didn't see what he did to Dathan and Abiram (the sons of Eliab, a descendant of Reuben) when the earth opened its mouth in the Israelite camp and swallowed them, along with their households and tents and every living thing that belonged to them. [7]But you have seen the LORD perform all these mighty deeds with your own eyes!

The Blessings of Obedience

DEUTERONOMY 11:8-32

"Therefore, be careful to obey every command I am giving you today, so you may have strength to go in and take over the land you are about to enter. [9]If you obey, you will enjoy a long life in the land the LORD swore to give to your ancestors and to you, their descendants—a land flowing with milk and honey! [10]For the land you are about to enter and take over is not like the land of Egypt from which you came, where you planted your seed and made irrigation ditches with your foot as in a vegetable garden. [11]Rather, the land you will soon take over is a land of hills and valleys with plenty of rain—[12]a land that the LORD your God cares for. He watches over it through each season of the year!

[13]"If you carefully obey all the commands I am giving you today, and if you love the LORD your God and serve him with all your heart and soul, [14]then he will send the rains in their proper seasons—the early and late rains—so you can bring in your harvests of grain, new wine, and olive oil. [15]He will give you lush pastureland for your livestock, and you yourselves will have all you want to eat.

[16]"But be careful. Don't let your heart be deceived so that you turn away from the LORD and serve and

Dt 10:16 Hebrew *circumcise the foreskin of your hearts.* **Dt 11:4** Hebrew *sea of reeds.*

Deut 10:12-13 Often we ask, What does God expect of me? Here Moses gives a summary that is simple in form and easy to remember. Here are the essentials: (1) Fear God (have reverence for him). (2) Live in a way that pleases him. (3) Love him. (4) Serve him with all your heart and soul. (5) Obey his commands. How often we complicate faith with man-made rules, regulations, and requirements. Are you frustrated and burned out from trying hard to please God? Concentrate on his real requirements and find peace: respect, follow, love, serve, and obey.

Deut 10:16-19 God required all male Israelites to be circumcised, but he wanted them to go beyond performing the surgery to understanding its meaning. They needed to submit to God inside, in their hearts, as well as outside, in their bodies. Then they could begin to imitate God's love and justice in their relationships with others. If our hearts are right with God, then our relationships with other people can be made right too. When your heart has been cleansed and you have been reconciled to God, you will begin to see a difference in the way you treat others.

Deut 10:17 In saying that the Lord is God of gods and Lord of lords, Moses was distinguishing the true God from all the local gods worshiped throughout the land. Then Moses went a step further, calling God "mighty and awesome." He has such awesome power and justice that people cannot stand before him without his mercy. Fortunately, his mercy toward his people is unlimited. When we begin to grasp the extent of God's mercy toward us, we see what true love is and how deeply God loves us. Although our sins deserve severe judgment, God has chosen to show love and mercy to all who seek him.

Deut 10:20 "Your oaths must be in his name alone" means that God alone should have their allegiance.

Deut 11:7 Israel had strong reasons to believe in God and obey his commands. They had witnessed a parade of mighty miracles that demonstrated God's love and care for them. Incredibly, they still had trouble remaining faithful. Because few of us have seen such dramatic miracles, it may seem even more difficult for us to obey God and remain faithful. But we have the Bible, the written record of God's acts throughout history. Reading God's Word gives us a panoramic view of both the miracles Israel saw and others they didn't see. The lessons from the past, the instructions for the present, and the glimpses into the future give us many opportunities to strengthen our faith in God.

worship other gods. 17If you do, the LORD's anger will burn against you. He will shut up the sky and hold back the rain, and the ground will fail to produce its harvests. Then you will quickly die in that good land the LORD is giving you.

18"So commit yourselves wholeheartedly to these words of mine. Tie them to your hands and wear them on your forehead as reminders. 19Teach them to your children. Talk about them when you are at home and when you are on the road, when you are going to bed and when you are getting up. 20Write them on the doorposts of your house and on your gates, 21so that as long as the sky remains above the earth, you and your children may flourish in the land the LORD swore to give your ancestors.

22"Be careful to obey all these commands I am giving you. Show love to the LORD your God by walking in his ways and holding tightly to him. 23Then the LORD will drive out all the nations ahead of you, though they are much greater and stronger than you, and you will take over their land. 24Wherever you set foot, that land will be yours. Your frontiers will stretch from the wilderness in the south to Lebanon in the north, and from the Euphrates River in the east to the Mediterranean Sea in the west.* 25No one will be able to stand against you, for the LORD your God will cause the people to fear and dread you, as he promised, wherever you go in the whole land.

26"Look, today I am giving you the choice between a blessing and a curse! 27You will be blessed if you obey the commands of the LORD your God that I am giving you today. 28But you will be cursed if you reject the commands of the LORD your God and turn away from him and worship gods you have not known before.

29"When the LORD your God brings you into the land and helps you take possession of it, you must pronounce the blessing at Mount Gerizim and the curse at Mount Ebal. 30(These two mountains are west of the Jordan River in the land of the Canaanites who live in the Jordan Valley,* near the town of Gilgal, not far from the oaks of Moreh.) 31For you are about to cross the Jordan River to take over the land the LORD your God is giving you. When you take that land and are living in it, 32you must be careful to obey all the decrees and regulations I am giving you today.

Dt 11:24 Hebrew *to the western sea.* **Dt 11:30** Hebrew *the Arabah.*

2. LAWS FOR PROPER WORSHIP

After summarizing the principles behind all of the law, Moses continues by detailing some of the specific laws concerning Israel's worship when they are in the land.

The LORD's Chosen Place for Worship

DEUTERONOMY 12:1-32

"These are the decrees and regulations you must be careful to obey when you live in the land that the LORD, the God of your ancestors, is giving you. You must obey them as long as you live.

2"When you drive out the nations that live there, you must destroy all the places where they worship their gods—high on the mountains, up on the hills, and under every green tree. 3Break down their altars and smash their sacred pillars. Burn their Asherah poles and cut down their carved idols. Completely erase the names of their gods!

4"Do not worship the LORD your God in the way these pagan peoples worship their gods. 5Rather, you must seek the LORD your God at the place of worship he himself will choose from among all the tribes—the place where his name will be honored. 6There you will bring your burnt offerings, your sacrifices, your tithes, your sacred offerings, your offerings to fulfill a vow, your voluntary offerings, and your offerings of the firstborn animals of your herds and flocks. 7There you and your families will feast in the presence of the LORD your God, and you will rejoice in all you have accomplished because the LORD your God has blessed you.

8"Your pattern of worship will change. Today all of you are doing as you please, 9because you have not yet arrived at the place of rest, the land the LORD your God is giving you as your special possession. 10But you will soon cross the Jordan River and live in the

Deut 11:26 What is God's curse? It is not a magician's spell. To understand it, we must remember the conditions of the covenant between God and Israel. Both parties had agreed to the terms. The blessings would benefit Israel if they kept their part of the covenant; they would receive the land, live there forever, have fruitful crops, and expel their enemies. The curse would fall on Israel only if they broke their agreement; they would forfeit God's blessing and be in danger of crop failure, invasion, and expulsion from their land. Joshua later reviewed these blessings and curses with the entire nation (Josh 8:34).

Deut 11:26 It is amazing that God set before the Israelites a choice between a blessing and a curse. It is even more amazing that most of them, through their disobedience, chose the curse. We have the same fundamental choice today. We can live for ourselves or live in service to God. To choose our own way is to travel on a dead-end road, but to choose God's way is to receive eternal life (John 5:24).

Deut 12:2-3 When taking over a nation, the Israelites were supposed to destroy every pagan altar and idol in the land. God knew it would be easy for them to change their beliefs if they started using those altars, so nothing was to remain that might tempt them to worship idols. We, too, should ruthlessly find and remove any centers of false worship in our lives. These may be activities, attitudes, possessions, relationships, places, or habits—anything that tempts us to turn our hearts from God and do wrong. We should never flatter ourselves by thinking we're too strong to be tempted. Israel learned that lesson the hard way.

▸ **DEUTERONOMY 12:1-32 *(cont.)***

land the LORD your God is giving you. When he gives you rest from all your enemies and you're living safely in the land, [11]you must bring everything I command you—your burnt offerings, your sacrifices, your tithes, your sacred offerings, and your offerings to fulfill a vow—to the designated place of worship, the place the LORD your God chooses for his name to be honored.

[12]"You must celebrate there in the presence of the LORD your God with your sons and daughters and all your servants. And remember to include the Levites who live in your towns, for they will receive no allotment of land among you. [13]Be careful not to sacrifice your burnt offerings just anywhere you like. [14]You may do so only at the place the LORD will choose within one of your tribal territories. There you must offer your burnt offerings and do everything I command you.

[15]"But you may butcher your animals and eat their meat in any town whenever you want. You may freely eat the animals with which the LORD your God blesses you. All of you, whether ceremonially clean or unclean, may eat that meat, just as you now eat gazelle and deer. [16]But you must not consume the blood. You must pour it out on the ground like water.

[17]"But you may not eat your offerings in your hometown—neither the tithe of your grain and new wine and olive oil, nor the firstborn of your flocks and herds, nor any offering to fulfill a vow, nor your voluntary offerings, nor your sacred offerings. [18]You must eat these in the presence of the LORD your God at the place he will choose. Eat them there with your children, your servants, and the Levites who live in your towns, celebrating in the presence of the LORD your God in all you do. [19]And be very careful never to neglect the Levites as long as you live in your land.

[20]"When the LORD your God expands your territory as he has promised, and you have the urge to eat meat, you may freely eat meat whenever you want. [21]It might happen that the designated place of worship—the place the LORD your God chooses for his name to be honored—is a long way from your home. If so, you may butcher any of the cattle, sheep, or goats the LORD has given you, and you may freely eat the meat in your hometown, as I have commanded you. [22]Anyone, whether ceremonially clean or unclean, may eat that meat, just as you do now with gazelle and deer. [23]But never consume the blood, for the blood is the life, and you must not consume the lifeblood with the meat. [24]Instead, pour out the blood on the ground like water. [25]Do not consume the blood, so that all may go well with you and your children after you, because you will be doing what pleases the LORD.

[26]"Take your sacred gifts and your offerings given to fulfill a vow to the place the LORD chooses. [27]You must offer the meat and blood of your burnt offerings on the altar of the LORD your God. The blood of your other sacrifices must be poured out on the altar of the LORD your God, but you may eat the meat. [28]Be careful to obey all my commands, so that all will go well with you and your children after you, because you will be doing what is good and pleasing to the LORD your God.

[29]"When the LORD your God goes ahead of you and destroys the nations and you drive them out and live in their land, [30]do not fall into the trap of following their customs and worshiping their gods. Do not inquire about their gods, saying, 'How do these nations worship their gods? I want to follow their example.' [31]You must not worship the LORD your God the way the other nations worship their gods, for they perform for their gods every detestable act that the LORD hates. They even burn their sons and daughters as sacrifices to their gods.

[32]*"So be careful to obey all the commands I give you. You must not add anything to them or subtract anything from them.

A Warning against Idolatry

DEUTERONOMY 13:1-18

[1]*"Suppose there are prophets among you or those who dream dreams about the future, and they promise

Dt 12:32 Verse 12:32 is numbered 13:1 in Hebrew text. **Dt 13:1** Verses 13:1-18 are numbered 13:2-19 in Hebrew text.

Deut 12:12, 18 The Hebrews placed great emphasis on family worship. Whether offering a sacrifice or attending a great festival, the family was often together. This gave the children a healthy attitude toward worship, and it put extra meaning into it for the adults. Watching a family member confess a sin was just as important as celebrating a great holiday together. Although there are appropriate times to separate people by ages, some of the most meaningful worship can be experienced only when shared by old and young.

Deut 12:13-14 The pagans offered sacrifices to their gods in many places. In contrast, the Israelites were only to offer sacrifices in the prescribed manner and in the prescribed places. This restriction was meant to ensure purity of worship for the nation of Israel. Later, they would neglect this injunction and offer sacrifices at the high places where pagan deities were worshiped. (See, for example, 2 Kgs 23 where Josiah destroyed the other altars.) We should take steps to safeguard the purity of worship in our congregations. If we all individualized and customized worship to suit our own preferences, we would lose the benefit of worshiping as a body of believers.

Deut 12:16 Eating blood was forbidden for several reasons: (1) It was an integral part of the pagan practices of the land the Israelites were about to enter; (2) it represented life, which is sacred to God; (3) it reminded the people that life and strength come from God, not from drinking or eating blood; (4) it was a symbol of the sacrifice that had to be made for sin. (For more on why eating blood was prohibited, see the note on Lev 17:14, p. 223.)

Deut 12:30-31 God did not want the Israelites to even ask about the pagan religions surrounding them. Idolatry completely permeated the land of Canaan. It was too easy to get drawn into the subtle temptations of seemingly harmless practices. Sometimes curiosity can cause us to stumble. Knowledge of evil is harmful if the evil becomes too tempting to resist. To resist curiosity about harmful practices shows discretion and obedience.

Deut 13:1-3 Attractive leaders are not always led by God. Moses warned the Israelites against false prophets who encour-

you signs or miracles, 2and the predicted signs or miracles occur. If they then say, 'Come, let us worship other
gods'—gods you have not known before—3do not listen
to them. The LORD your God is testing you to see if you
truly love him with all your heart and soul. 4Serve only
the LORD your God and fear him alone. Obey his commands, listen to his voice, and cling to him. 5The false
prophets or visionaries who try to lead you astray must
be put to death, for they encourage rebellion against
the LORD your God, who redeemed you from slavery
and brought you out of the land of Egypt. Since they
try to lead you astray from the way the LORD your God
commanded you to live, you must put them to death.
In this way you will purge the evil from among you.
6"Suppose someone secretly entices you—even your
brother, your son or daughter, your beloved wife, or
your closest friend—and says, 'Let us go worship other
gods'—gods that neither you nor your ancestors have
known. 7They might suggest that you worship the gods
of peoples who live nearby or who come from the
ends of the earth. 8But do not give in or listen. Have
no pity, and do not spare or protect them. 9You must
put them to death! Strike the first blow yourself, and
then all the people must join in. 10Stone the guilty
ones to death because they have tried to draw you
away from the LORD your God, who rescued you from
the land of Egypt, the place of slavery. 11Then all Israel
will hear about it and be afraid, and no one will act so
wickedly again.
12"When you begin living in the towns the LORD
your God is giving you, you may hear 13that scoundrels
among you are leading their fellow citizens astray by
saying, 'Let us go worship other gods'—gods you have
not known before. 14In such cases, you must examine
the facts carefully. If you find that the report is true
and such a detestable act has been committed among
you, 15you must attack that town and completely destroy* all its inhabitants, as well as all the livestock.
16Then you must pile all the plunder in the middle
of the open square and burn it. Burn the entire town
as a burnt offering to the LORD your God. That town
must remain a ruin forever; it may never be rebuilt.
17Keep none of the plunder that has been set apart for
destruction. Then the LORD will turn from his fierce
anger and be merciful to you. He will have compassion
on you and make you a large nation, just as he swore
to your ancestors.
18"The LORD your God will be merciful only if you
listen to his voice and keep all his commands that I
am giving you today, doing what pleases him.

Ceremonially Clean and Unclean Animals

DEUTERONOMY 14:1-21

"Since you are the people of the LORD your God, never
cut yourselves or shave the hair above your foreheads
in mourning for the dead. 2You have been set apart
as holy to the LORD your God, and he has chosen you
from all the nations of the earth to be his own special
treasure.
3"You must not eat any detestable animals that
are ceremonially unclean. 4These are the animals*
you may eat: the ox, the sheep, the goat, 5the deer, the

Dt 13:15 The Hebrew term used here refers to the complete consecration of things or people to the LORD, either by destroying them or by giving them as an offering; similarly in 13:17. **Dt 14:4** The identification of some of the animals and birds listed in this chapter is uncertain.

aged worship of other gods. New ideas from inspiring people may sound good, but we must judge them by whether or not they are consistent with God's Word. When people claim to speak for God today, check them in these areas: Are they telling the truth? Is their focus on God? Are their words consistent with what you already know to be true? Some people speak the truth while directing you toward God, but others speak persuasively while directing you toward themselves. It is even possible to say the right words but still lead people in the wrong direction. God is not against new ideas, but he is for discernment. When you hear a new, attractive idea, examine it carefully before getting too excited. False prophets are still around today. The wise person will carefully test ideas against the truth of God's Word.

Deut 13:2-11 The Israelites were warned not to listen to false prophets or to anyone else who tried to get them to worship other gods—even if this person was a close friend or family member. The temptation to abandon God's commands often sneaks up on us. It may come not with a loud shout but in a whispering doubt. And whispers can be very persuasive, especially if they come from loved ones. But love for relatives should not take precedence over devotion to God. We can overcome whispered temptations by pouring out our hearts to God in prayer and by diligently studying his Word.

Deut 13:12-16 A town that completely rejected God was to be destroyed so as not to lead the rest of the nation astray. But Israel was not to take action against a town until the rumor about its rejection of God was proven true. This guideline saved many lives when the leaders of Israel wrongly accused three tribes of falling away from their faith (Josh 22). If we hear of friends who have wandered from the Lord or of entire congregations that have fallen away, we should check the facts and find the truth before doing or saying anything that could prove harmful. There are times, of course, when God wants us to take action—to rebuke a wayward friend, to discipline a child, to reject false teaching—but first we must be sure we have all the facts straight.

Deut 14:1 The actions described here refer to a cult of the dead. Many other religions today have some kind of worship of or service to the dead. But Christianity and Judaism are very different from other religions because they focus on serving God in this life. Don't let concern or worry over the dead distract you from the tasks that God has for you while you are still alive.

Deut 14:3-21 Why was Israel forbidden to eat certain foods? There are several reasons: (1) Predatory animals ate the blood of other animals, and scavengers ate dead animals. Because the people could not eat blood or animals they found dead, they could not eat animals that did these things either. (2) Some forbidden animals had bad associations in the Israelite culture just as bats, snakes, and spiders do for some people today. Some may have been used in pagan religious practices (Isa 66:17). To the Israelites, the unclean animals represented sin or unhealthy habits. (3) Perhaps some restrictions were given to Israel just to remind them continually that they were a different and separate people committed to God. Although we no longer must follow these laws about food (Acts 10:9-16), we can still learn from them the lesson that holiness is to be carried into all parts of life. We can't restrict holiness only to the spiritual side; we must be holy in the everyday practical part of life as well. Health practices, finances, use of leisure—all provide opportunities to put holy living into daily living.

▸ **DEUTERONOMY 14:1-21** ***(cont.)***
gazelle, the roe deer, the wild goat, the addax, the antelope, and the mountain sheep.
6"You may eat any animal that has completely split hooves and chews the cud, 7but if the animal doesn't have both, it may not be eaten. So you may not eat the camel, the hare, or the hyrax.* They chew the cud but do not have split hooves, so they are ceremonially unclean for you. 8And you may not eat the pig. It has split hooves but does not chew the cud, so it is ceremonially unclean for you. You may not eat the meat of these animals or even touch their carcasses.
9"Of all the marine animals, you may eat whatever has both fins and scales. 10You may not, however, eat marine animals that do not have both fins and scales. They are ceremonially unclean for you.
11"You may eat any bird that is ceremonially clean.
12These are the birds you may not eat: the griffon vulture, the bearded vulture, the black vulture, 13the kite,
the falcon, buzzards of all kinds, 14ravens of all kinds,
15the eagle owl, the short-eared owl, the seagull, hawks
of all kinds, 16the little owl, the great owl, the barn owl,
17the desert owl, the Egyptian vulture, the cormorant,
18the stork, herons of all kinds, the hoopoe, and the bat.
19"All winged insects that walk along the ground are ceremonially unclean for you and may not be eaten.
20But you may eat any winged bird or insect that is ceremonially clean.
21"You must not eat anything that has died a natural death. You may give it to a foreigner living in your town, or you may sell it to a stranger. But do not eat it yourselves, for you are set apart as holy to the LORD your God.
"You must not cook a young goat in its mother's milk.

The Giving of Tithes

DEUTERONOMY 14:22-29
"You must set aside a tithe of your crops—one-tenth of all the crops you harvest each year. 23Bring this tithe to the designated place of worship—the place the LORD your God chooses for his name to be honored—and eat it there in his presence. This applies to your tithes of grain, new wine, olive oil, and the firstborn males of your flocks and herds. Doing this will teach you always to fear the LORD your God.
24"Now when the LORD your God blesses you with a good harvest, the place of worship he chooses for his name to be honored might be too far for you to bring the tithe. 25If so, you may sell the tithe portion of your crops and herds, put the money in a pouch, and go to the place the LORD your God has chosen.
26When you arrive, you may use the money to buy any kind of food you want—cattle, sheep, goats, wine, or other alcoholic drink. Then feast there in the presence of the LORD your God and celebrate with your household. 27And do not neglect the Levites in your town, for they will receive no allotment of land among you.
28"At the end of every third year, bring the entire tithe of that year's harvest and store it in the nearest town. 29Give it to the Levites, who will receive no allotment of land among you, as well as to the foreigners living among you, the orphans, and the widows in your towns, so they can eat and be satisfied. Then the LORD your God will bless you in all your work.

Dt 14:7 *Or coney, or rock badger.*

The Kite

The kite is a large bird of prey; it is listed among the unclean birds in the Mosaic law (Lev 11:14; Deut 14:13). Its average length is about 19 inches. Its upper part is generally dark, but its belly is often white. Kites make their homes high in the trees, building nests of sticks and other vegetation. They rarely have more than two or three young, to which they feed snakes and grasshoppers. Sometimes kites are called snake hawks. The kite is a migratory bird that stays in Israel during the summer, especially in the mountains of southern Judea, in the trackless wasteland west of the Dead Sea, and in the wilderness of Beersheba.

Deut 14:21 This prohibition against cooking a young goat in its mother's milk may reflect a Canaanite fertility rite. Or it may just mean that the Israelites were not to take what was intended to promote life and use it to kill or destroy life. This commandment is also given in Exodus 23:19.

Deut 14:22-23 The Bible makes the purpose of tithing very clear—to teach us to fear the Lord and to put him first in our lives. We are to give God the first and best of what we earn. For example, what we do first with our money shows what we value most. Giving the first part of our paycheck to God immediately focuses our attention on him. It also reminds us that all we have belongs to him. A habit of regular tithing can keep God at the top of our priority list and give us a proper perspective on everything else we have.

Deut 14:28-29 The Bible supports an organized system of caring for the poor. God told his people to use their tithe every third year for those who were helpless, hungry, or poor. These regulations were designed to prevent the country from sinking under crushing poverty and oppression. It was everyone's responsibility to care for those less fortunate. Families were to help other family members, and towns were to help members of their community. National laws protected the rights of the poor, but helping the poor was also an active part of religious life. God counts on believers to provide for the needy, and we should use what God has given us to aid those less fortunate. Look beyond your regular giving and think of ways to help the needy. This will help you show your regard for God as Creator of all people, share God's goodness with others, and draw them to him. It is a practical and essential way to make faith work in everyday life.

Release for Debtors

DEUTERONOMY 15:1-11

"At the end of every seventh year you must cancel the debts of everyone who owes you money. 2This is how it must be done. Everyone must cancel the loans they have made to their fellow Israelites. They must not demand payment from their neighbors or relatives, for the LORD's time of release has arrived. 3This release from debt, however, applies only to your fellow Israelites—not to the foreigners living among you.

4"There should be no poor among you, for the LORD your God will greatly bless you in the land he is giving you as a special possession. 5You will receive this blessing if you are careful to obey all the commands of the LORD your God that I am giving you today. 6The LORD your God will bless you as he has promised. You will lend money to many nations but will never need to borrow. You will rule many nations, but they will not rule over you.

7"But if there are any poor Israelites in your towns when you arrive in the land the LORD your God is giving you, do not be hard-hearted or tightfisted toward them. 8Instead, be generous and lend them whatever they need. 9Do not be mean-spirited and refuse someone a loan because the year for canceling debts is close at hand. If you refuse to make the loan and the needy person cries out to the LORD, you will be considered guilty of sin. 10Give generously to the poor, not grudgingly, for the LORD your God will bless you in everything you do. 11There will always be some in the land who are poor. That is why I am commanding you to share freely with the poor and with other Israelites in need.

Release for Hebrew Slaves

DEUTERONOMY 15:12-18

"If a fellow Hebrew sells himself or herself to be your servant* and serves you for six years, in the seventh year you must set that servant free.

13"When you release a male servant, do not send him away empty-handed. 14Give him a generous farewell gift from your flock, your threshing floor, and your winepress. Share with him some of the bounty with which the LORD your God has blessed you. 15Remember that you were once slaves in the land of Egypt and the LORD your God redeemed you! That is why I am giving you this command.

16"But suppose your servant says, 'I will not leave you,' because he loves you and your family, and he has done well with you. 17In that case, take an awl and push it through his earlobe into the door. After that, he will be your servant for life. And do the same for your female servants.

18"You must not consider it a hardship when you release your servants. Remember that for six years they have given you services worth double the wages of hired workers, and the LORD your God will bless you in all you do.

Sacrificing Firstborn Male Animals

DEUTERONOMY 15:19-23

"You must set aside for the LORD your God all the firstborn males from your flocks and herds. Do not use the firstborn of your herds to work your fields, and do not shear the firstborn of your flocks. 20Instead, you and your family must eat these animals in the presence of the LORD your God each year at the place he chooses. 21But if this firstborn animal has any defect, such as lameness or blindness, or if anything else is wrong with it, you must not sacrifice it to the LORD your God. 22Instead, use it for food for your family in your hometown. Anyone, whether ceremonially clean or unclean, may eat it, just as anyone may eat a gazelle or deer. 23But you must not consume the blood. You must pour it out on the ground like water.

Passover and the Festival of Unleavened Bread

DEUTERONOMY 16:1-8

"In honor of the LORD your God, celebrate the Passover each year in the early spring, in the month of Abib,* for that was the month in which the LORD your God brought you out of Egypt by night. 2Your Passover sacrifice may be from either the flock or the herd, and it must be sacrificed to the LORD your God at the designated place of worship—the place he chooses for his name to be honored. 3Eat it with bread made without yeast. For seven days the bread you eat must be made without yeast, as when you escaped from Egypt in such a hurry. Eat this bread—the bread of

Dt 15:12 Or *If a Hebrew man or woman is sold to you.* **Dt 16:1** Hebrew *Observe the month of Abib, and keep the Passover unto the LORD your God.* Abib, the first month of the ancient Hebrew lunar calendar, usually occurs within the months of March and April.

Deut 15:7-11 God told the Israelites to help the poor among them when they arrived in the Promised Land. This was an important part of possessing the land. Many people conclude that people are poor through some fault of their own. This kind of reasoning makes it easy to close their hearts and hands to the needy. But we are not to invent reasons for ignoring the poor. We are to respond to their needs no matter who or what was responsible for their condition. Who are the poor in your community? How could your church help them? If your church does not have a program to identify the poor and assist in fulfilling their needs, why not help start one? What can you do to help someone in need?

Deut 15:12-15 The Israelites were to release their servants after six years, sending them away with enough food so that they would be amply supplied until their needs could be met by some other means. This humanitarian act recognized that God created each person with dignity and worth. It also reminded the Israelites that they, too, had once been slaves in Egypt, and that their present freedom was a gift from God. We do not have servants such as these today, but God's instructions still apply to us: We must still be sure to treat our employees with respect and economic fairness.

▸ **DEUTERONOMY 16:1-8 *(cont.)***
suffering—so that as long as you live you will remember the day you departed from Egypt. [4]Let no yeast be found in any house throughout your land for those seven days. And when you sacrifice the Passover lamb on the evening of the first day, do not let any of the meat remain until the next morning.

[5]"You may not sacrifice the Passover in just any of the towns that the LORD your God is giving you. [6]You must offer it only at the designated place of worship—the place the LORD your God chooses for his name to be honored. Sacrifice it there in the evening as the sun goes down on the anniversary of your exodus from Egypt. [7]Roast the lamb and eat it in the place the LORD your God chooses. Then you may go back to your tents the next morning. [8]For the next six days you may not eat any bread made with yeast. On the seventh day proclaim another holy day in honor of the LORD your God, and no work may be done on that day.

The Festival of Harvest

DEUTERONOMY 16:9-12

"Count off seven weeks from when you first begin to cut the grain at the time of harvest. [10]Then celebrate the Festival of Harvest* to honor the LORD your God. Bring him a voluntary offering in proportion to the blessings you have received from him. [11]This is a time to celebrate before the LORD your God at the designated place of worship he will choose for his name to be honored. Celebrate with your sons and daughters, your male and female servants, the Levites from your towns, and the foreigners, orphans, and widows who live among you. [12]Remember that you were once slaves in Egypt, so be careful to obey all these decrees.

The Festival of Shelters

DEUTERONOMY 16:13-17

"You must observe the Festival of Shelters* for seven days at the end of the harvest season, after the grain has been threshed and the grapes have been pressed. [14]This festival will be a happy time of celebrating with your sons and daughters, your male and female servants, and the Levites, foreigners, orphans, and widows from your towns. [15]For seven days you must celebrate this festival to honor the LORD your God at the place he chooses, for it is he who blesses you with bountiful harvests and gives you success in all your work. This festival will be a time of great joy for all.

[16]"Each year every man in Israel must celebrate these three festivals: the Festival of Unleavened Bread, the Festival of Harvest, and the Festival of Shelters. On each of these occasions, all men must appear before the LORD your God at the place he chooses, but they must not appear before the LORD without a gift for him. [17]All must give as they are able, according to the blessings given to them by the LORD your God.

Dt 16:10 Hebrew *Festival of Weeks;* also in 16:16. This was later called the Festival of Pentecost (see Acts 2:1). It is celebrated today as Shavuot (or Shabuoth).
Dt 16:13 Or *Festival of Booths,* or *Festival of Tabernacles;* also in 16:16. This was earlier called the Festival of the Final Harvest or Festival of Ingathering (see Exod 23:16b). It is celebrated today as Sukkot (or Succoth).

3. LAWS FOR RULING THE NATION

Moses continues his address to the people by giving them the specific laws about governing the nation when they are in the Promised Land.

Justice for the People

DEUTERONOMY 16:18–17:13

"Appoint judges and officials for yourselves from each of your tribes in all the towns the LORD your God is giving you. They must judge the people fairly. [19]You must never twist justice or show partiality. Never accept a bribe, for bribes blind the eyes of the wise and corrupt the decisions of the godly. [20]Let true justice prevail, so you may live and occupy the land that the LORD your God is giving you.

[21]"You must never set up a wooden Asherah pole beside the altar you build for the LORD your God. [22]And never set up sacred pillars for worship, for the LORD your God hates them.

17:1"Never sacrifice sick or defective cattle, sheep, or goats to the LORD your God, for he detests such gifts.

Deut 16:16-17 Three times a year every male was to make a journey to the sanctuary in the city that would be designated as Israel's religious capital. At these festivals, each participant was encouraged to give what he could in proportion to what God had given him. God does not expect us to give more than we can, but we will be blessed when we give cheerfully. For some, 10 percent may be a burden. For most of us, that would be far too little. Look at what you have and then give in proportion to what you have been given.

Deut 16:18-20 These verses anticipated a great problem the Israelites would face when they arrived in the Promised Land. Although they had Joshua as their national leader, they failed to complete the task and choose other spiritual leaders who would lead the tribes, districts, and cities with justice and God's wisdom. Because they did not appoint wise judges and faithful administrators, rebellion and injustice plagued their communities. It is a serious responsibility to appoint or elect wise and just officials. In your sphere of influence—home, church, school, job—are you ensuring that justice and godliness prevail? Failing to choose leaders who uphold justice can lead to much trouble, as Israel would discover.

Deut 17:1 The fact that this command was included probably indicates that some Israelites were sacrificing imperfect or deformed animals to God. Then, as now, it is difficult and expensive to offer God our best (i.e., the first part of what we earn). It is always tempting to shortchange God because we think we won't get caught. But our giving shows our real priorities. When we give God the leftovers, it is obvious that he is not at the center of our lives. Give God the honor of having first claim on your money, time, and talents.

2"When you begin living in the towns the LORD
your God is giving you, a man or woman among you
might do evil in the sight of the LORD your God and
violate the covenant. 3For instance, they might serve
other gods or worship the sun, the moon, or any of
the stars—the forces of heaven—which I have strictly
forbidden. 4When you hear about it, investigate the
matter thoroughly. If it is true that this detestable
thing has been done in Israel, 5then the man or woman
who has committed such an evil act must be taken to
the gates of the town and stoned to death. 6But never
put a person to death on the testimony of only one
witness. There must always be two or three witnesses.
7The witnesses must throw the first stones, and then
all the people may join in. In this way, you will purge
the evil from among you.

8"Suppose a case arises in a local court that is too
hard for you to decide—for instance, whether someone is guilty of murder or only of manslaughter, or a
difficult lawsuit, or a case involving different kinds
of assault. Take such legal cases to the place the LORD
your God will choose, 9and present them to the Levitical priests or the judge on duty at that time. They
will hear the case and declare the verdict. 10You must
carry out the verdict they announce and the sentence
they prescribe at the place the LORD chooses. You must
do exactly what they say. 11After they have interpreted
the law and declared their verdict, the sentence they
impose must be fully executed; do not modify it in any
way. 12Anyone arrogant enough to reject the verdict
of the judge or of the priest who represents the LORD
your God must die. In this way you will purge the evil
from Israel. 13Then everyone else will hear about it
and be afraid to act so arrogantly.

Guidelines for a King

DEUTERONOMY 17:14-20

"You are about to enter the land the LORD your God
is giving you. When you take it over and settle there,
you may think, 'We should select a king to rule over
us like the other nations around us.' 15If this happens,
be sure to select as king the man the LORD your God
chooses. You must appoint a fellow Israelite; he may
not be a foreigner.

16"The king must not build up a large stable of
horses for himself or send his people to Egypt to buy
horses, for the LORD has told you, 'You must never
return to Egypt.' 17The king must not take many wives
for himself, because they will turn his heart away from
the LORD. And he must not accumulate large amounts
of wealth in silver and gold for himself.

18"When he sits on the throne as king, he must copy
for himself this body of instruction on a scroll in the
presence of the Levitical priests. 19He must always
keep that copy with him and read it daily as long as
he lives. That way he will learn to fear the LORD his
God by obeying all the terms of these instructions
and decrees. 20This regular reading will prevent him
from becoming proud and acting as if he is above his
fellow citizens. It will also prevent him from turning
away from these commands in the smallest way. And
it will ensure that he and his descendants will reign
for many generations in Israel.

Gifts for the Priests and Levites

DEUTERONOMY 18:1-8

"Remember that the Levitical priests—that is, the
whole of the tribe of Levi—will receive no allotment
of land among the other tribes in Israel. Instead, the

Deut 17:6-7 A person was not put to death on the testimony of only one witness. On the witness of two or three, a man or woman could be condemned and then sentenced to death by stoning. The condemned individual would be taken outside the city gates, and the witnesses would be the first to throw heavy stones down upon the offender. Bystanders would then pelt the dying person with stones. This system would "purge the evil" by putting the idolater to death. At the same time, it protected the rights of accused persons two ways. First, by requiring several witnesses, it prevented any angry individual from giving false testimony. Second, by requiring the accusers to throw the first stones, it made them think twice about accusing unjustly. They were responsible to finish what they had started.

Deut 17:14-20 God was not encouraging Israel to appoint a king to rule their nation. He was actually against the idea because he was their King, and the people were to obey and follow him. But God knew that the people would one day demand a king for selfish reasons—they would want to be like the nations around them (1 Sam 8). If they insisted on having a king, he wanted to make sure they chose the right person. That is why he included these instructions both for the people's benefit as they chose their king and for the king himself as he sought to lead the nation according to God's laws.

Deut 17:16-17 Israel's kings did not heed this warning, and their behavior led to their downfall. Solomon had everything going for him, but when he became rich, built up a large army, and married many wives, his heart turned from God (1 Kgs 11). Out of Solomon's sin came Israel's disobedience, division, and captivity.

Deut 17:18-20 The king was to be a man of God's Word. He was to (1) make for himself a copy of the law, (2) keep it with him all the time, (3) read from it every day, and (4) obey it completely. Through this process he would learn respect for God, keep himself from feeling more important than others, and avoid neglecting God in times of prosperity. We can't know what God wants except through his Word, and his Word won't affect our lives unless we read and think about it regularly. With the abundant availability of the Bible today, it is not difficult to gain access to the source of the king's wisdom. What is more of a challenge is following its directives.

Deut 18:1-8 The priests and Levites served much the same function as our ministers today. Their duties included teaching the people about God, setting an example of godly living, caring for the sanctuary and its workers, and distributing the offerings. Because priests and Levites could not own property or pursue outside business interests, God made special arrangements so that people would not take advantage of them. Often churches take advantage of the men and women God has brought to lead them. For example, ministers may not be paid in accordance with their skills or the time they put in. Or pastors may be expected to attend every evening meeting, even if this continual absence is harmful to the family. As you look at your own church in light of God's Word, what ways do you see to honor the leaders God has given you?

▶ **DEUTERONOMY 18:1-8 *(cont.)***
priests and Levites will eat from the special gifts given
to the LORD, for that is their share. 2They will have
no land of their own among the Israelites. The LORD
himself is their special possession, just as he promised them.
3"These are the parts the priests may claim as their
share from the cattle, sheep, and goats that the people
bring as offerings: the shoulder, the cheeks, and the
stomach. 4You must also give to the priests the first
share of the grain, the new wine, the olive oil, and the
wool at shearing time. 5For the LORD your God chose
the tribe of Levi out of all your tribes to minister in
the LORD's name forever.
6"Suppose a Levite chooses to move from his town
in Israel, wherever he is living, to the place the LORD
chooses for worship. 7He may minister there in the
name of the LORD his God, just like all his fellow Levites
who are serving the LORD there. 8He may eat his share
of the sacrifices and offerings, even if he also receives
support from his family.

A Call to Holy Living

DEUTERONOMY 18:9-14
"When you enter the land the LORD your God is giving
you, be very careful not to imitate the detestable customs of the nations living there. 10For example, never
sacrifice your son or daughter as a burnt offering.*
And do not let your people practice fortune-telling,
or use sorcery, or interpret omens, or engage in witchcraft, 11or cast spells, or function as mediums or psychics, or call forth the spirits of the dead. 12Anyone
who does these things is detestable to the LORD. It
is because the other nations have done these detestable things that the LORD your God will drive them
out ahead of you. 13But you must be blameless before
the LORD your God. 14The nations you are about to
displace consult sorcerers and fortune-tellers, but the
LORD your God forbids you to do such things."

True and False Prophets

DEUTERONOMY 18:15-22
Moses continued, "The LORD your God will raise up
for you a prophet like me from among your fellow
Israelites. You must listen to him. 16For this is what
you yourselves requested of the LORD your God when
you were assembled at Mount Sinai.* You said, 'Don't
let us hear the voice of the LORD our God anymore or
see this blazing fire, for we will die.'
17"Then the LORD said to me, 'What they have
said is right. 18I will raise up a prophet like you from
among their fellow Israelites. I will put my words in
his mouth, and he will tell the people everything I
command him. 19I will personally deal with anyone
who will not listen to the messages the prophet proclaims on my behalf. 20But any prophet who falsely
claims to speak in my name or who speaks in the
name of another god must die.'

Dt 18:10 Or *never make your son or daughter pass through the fire.* **Dt 18:16** Hebrew *Horeb,* another name for Sinai.

The Messiah in the Dead Sea Scrolls

Archaeological evidence has shown that Qumran was the headquarters of a Jewish sect called the Essenes. The Qumran sect had a strong messianic hope. They believed that they were living in the last days before the coming of the Messiah (or Messiahs) and the final battle with wickedness. The "Damascus Document" discovered at Qumran used the expression "the anointed ones [messiahs] of Aaron and Israel." Many scholars see in this expression a reference to two messiahs: a superior, priestly messiah (descended from Aaron) and a lesser, kingly messiah (descended from Israel). Some scholars even see three messianic figures: one descended from David, a messianic king; one from Aaron, a messianic priest; and one from Moses, a messianic prophet (Deut 18:18). The "Teacher of Righteousness" (found in some Dead Sea Scrolls) may even have had the role of the anticipated prophet. For Christians, Jesus fulfills all three roles: He is the kingly Messiah (John 1:41), the Prophet (Acts 3:22-25), and the High Priest (Heb 9:11). He is the fulfillment of all the prophecies.

Deut 18:10 Child sacrifice and occult practices were strictly forbidden by God. These practices were common among pagan religions. Israel's own neighbors actually sacrificed their children to the god Molech (Lev 20:2-5). Other neighboring religions used supernatural means, such as contacting the spirit world, to foretell the future and gain guidance. Because of these wicked practices, God would drive out the pagan nations (Deut 18:12). The Israelites were to replace their evil practices with the worship of the one true God.

Deut 18:10-13 The Israelites were naturally curious about the occult practices of the Canaanite religions. But Satan is behind the occult, and God flatly forbade Israel to have anything to do with it. Today people are still fascinated by horoscopes, fortune-telling, witchcraft, and bizarre cults. Often their interest comes from a desire to know and control the future. But Satan is no less dangerous today than he was in Moses' time. In the Bible, God tells us all we need to know about what is going to happen. The information Satan offers is likely to be distorted or completely false. With the trustworthy guidance of the Holy Spirit through the Bible and the church, we don't need to turn to occult sources for faulty information.

Deut 18:15 Who is this prophet? Stephen used this verse to support his claim that Jesus Christ is God's Son, the Messiah (Acts 7:37). The coming of Jesus Christ to earth was not an afterthought, but part of God's original plan.

[21]“But you may wonder, ‘How will we know whether or not a prophecy is from the LORD?’ [22]If the prophet speaks in the LORD’s name but his prediction does not happen or come true, you will know that the LORD did not give that message. That prophet has spoken without my authority and need not be feared.

Cities of Refuge

DEUTERONOMY 19:1-13

“When the LORD your God destroys the nations whose land he is giving you, you will take over their land and settle in their towns and homes. [2]Then you must set apart three cities of refuge in the land the LORD your God is giving you. [3]Survey the territory,* and divide the land the LORD your God is giving you into three districts, with one of these cities in each district. Then anyone who has killed someone can flee to one of the cities of refuge for safety.

[4]“If someone kills another person unintentionally, without previous hostility, the slayer may flee to any of these cities to live in safety. [5]For example, suppose someone goes into the forest with a neighbor to cut wood. And suppose one of them swings an ax to chop down a tree, and the ax head flies off the handle, killing the other person. In such cases, the slayer may flee to one of the cities of refuge to live in safety.

[6]“If the distance to the nearest city of refuge is too far, an enraged avenger might be able to chase down and kill the person who caused the death. Then the slayer would die unfairly, since he had never shown hostility toward the person who died. [7]That is why I am commanding you to set aside three cities of refuge.

[8]“And if the LORD your God enlarges your territory, as he swore to your ancestors, and gives you all the land he promised them, [9]you must designate three additional cities of refuge. (He will give you this land if you are careful to obey all the commands I have given you—if you always love the LORD your God and walk in his ways.) [10]That way you will prevent the death of innocent people in the land the LORD your God is giving you as your special possession. You will not be held responsible for the death of innocent people.

[11]“But suppose someone is hostile toward a neighbor and deliberately ambushes and murders him and then flees to one of the cities of refuge. [12]In that case, the elders of the murderer’s hometown must send agents to the city of refuge to bring him back and hand him over to the dead person’s avenger to be put to death. [13]Do not feel sorry for that murderer! Purge from Israel the guilt of murdering innocent people; then all will go well with you.

Concern for Justice

DEUTERONOMY 19:14-21

“When you arrive in the land the LORD your God is giving you as your special possession, you must never steal anyone’s land by moving the boundary markers your ancestors set up to mark their property.

[15]“You must not convict anyone of a crime on the testimony of only one witness. The facts of the case must be established by the testimony of two or three witnesses.

[16]“If a malicious witness comes forward and accuses someone of a crime, [17]then both the accuser and accused must appear before the LORD by coming to the priests and judges in office at that time. [18]The judges must investigate the case thoroughly. If the accuser has brought false charges against his fellow Israelite, [19]you must impose on the accuser the sentence he intended for the other person. In this way, you will purge such evil from among you. [20]Then the rest of the people will hear about it and be afraid to do such

Dt 19:3 Or *Keep the roads in good repair.*

Deut 18:21-22 As in the days of ancient Israel, some people today claim to have messages from God. God still speaks to his people, but we must be cautious before saying that someone is God’s spokesman. How can we tell when people are speaking for the Lord? (1) We can see whether or not their prophecies come true—the ancient test for judging prophets. (2) We can check their words against the Bible. God never contradicts himself, so if someone says something contrary to the Bible, we can know that what they say is not from God (see Deut 13:1-11).

Deut 19:2-7 Every society must deal with the problem of murder. But how should society treat those who have accidentally killed someone? God had an answer for the Israelites. Since revenge was common and swift in Moses’ day, God had the Israelites set apart several cities of refuge. Anyone who claimed to have accidentally killed someone could flee to one of these cities until he could have a fair trial. If he was found innocent of intentional murder, he could remain in that city and be safe from those seeking revenge. This is a beautiful example of how God blended his justice and mercy toward his people. (For more information on cities of refuge, see the note on Num 35:6, p. 282.)

Deut 19:12 The “avenger” was the nearest male relative to the person killed. He acted as the family protector (see Num 35:19).

CITIES OF REFUGE ▶
Six of the Levites’ cities were designated as cities of refuge (Num 35:6). They were spaced throughout the land and protected those who had accidentally committed a crime or who were awaiting trial.

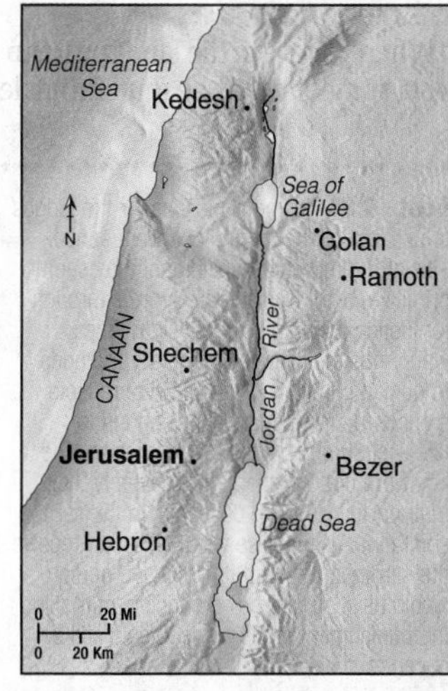

▸ **DEUTERONOMY 19:14-21** ***(cont.)***

an evil thing. 21You must show no pity for the guilty! Your rule should be life for life, eye for eye, tooth for tooth, hand for hand, foot for foot.

Regulations concerning War

DEUTERONOMY 20:1-20

"When you go out to fight your enemies and you face horses and chariots and an army greater than your own, do not be afraid. The LORD your God, who brought you out of the land of Egypt, is with you! 2When you prepare for battle, the priest must come forward to speak to the troops. 3He will say to them, 'Listen to me, all you men of Israel! Do not be afraid as you go out to fight your enemies today! Do not lose heart or panic or tremble before them. 4For the LORD your God is going with you! He will fight for you against your enemies, and he will give you victory!'

5"Then the officers of the army must address the troops and say, 'Has anyone here just built a new house but not yet dedicated it? If so, you may go home! You might be killed in the battle, and someone else would dedicate your house. 6Has anyone here just planted a vineyard but not yet eaten any of its fruit? If so, you may go home! You might die in battle, and someone else would eat the first fruit. 7Has anyone here just become engaged to a woman but not yet married her? Well, you may go home and get married! You might die in the battle, and someone else would marry her.'

8"Then the officers will also say, 'Is anyone here afraid or worried? If you are, you may go home before you frighten anyone else.' 9When the officers have finished speaking to their troops, they will appoint the unit commanders.

10"As you approach a town to attack it, you must first offer its people terms for peace. 11If they accept your terms and open the gates to you, then all the people inside will serve you in forced labor. 12But if they refuse to make peace and prepare to fight, you must attack the town. 13When the LORD your God hands the town over to you, use your swords to kill every man in the town. 14But you may keep for yourselves all the women, children, livestock, and other plunder. You may enjoy the plunder from your enemies that the LORD your God has given you.

15"But these instructions apply only to distant towns, not to the towns of the nations in the land you will enter. 16In those towns that the LORD your God is giving you as a special possession, destroy every living thing. 17You must completely destroy* the Hittites, Amorites, Canaanites, Perizzites, Hivites, and Jebusites, just as the LORD your God has commanded you. 18This will prevent the people of the land from teaching you to imitate their detestable customs in the worship of their gods, which would cause you to sin deeply against the LORD your God.

19"When you are attacking a town and the war drags on, you must not cut down the trees with your axes. You may eat the fruit, but do not cut down the trees. Are the trees your enemies, that you should attack them? 20You may only cut down trees that you know are not valuable for food. Use them to make the equipment you need to attack the enemy town until it falls.

Dt 20:17 The Hebrew term used here refers to the complete consecration of things or people to the LORD, either by destroying them or by giving them as an offering.

4. LAWS FOR HUMAN RELATIONSHIPS

God is concerned about more than just the worship and government of his people. The law continues with specifics for how to live in a way that honors him in our relationships with other people.

Cleansing for Unsolved Murder

DEUTERONOMY 21:1-9

"When you are in the land the LORD your God is giving you, someone may be found murdered in a field, and you don't know who committed the murder. 2In such a case, your elders and judges must measure the distance from the site of the crime to the nearby towns. 3When the nearest town has been determined, that

Deut 19:21 This principle was for the judges to use, not a plan for personal vengeance. This attitude toward punishment may seem primitive, but it was actually a breakthrough for justice and fairness in ancient times when most nations used arbitrary methods to punish criminals. This guideline reflects a concern for evenhandedness and justice—ensuring that those who violated the law were not punished more severely than their particular crime deserved. In the same spirit of justice, a false witness was to receive the same punishment the accused person would have suffered. The principle of making the punishment fit the crime should still be observed today.

Deut 20:1 Just like the Israelites, we sometimes face overwhelming opposition. Whether at school, at work, or even at home, we can feel outnumbered and helpless. God bolstered the Israelites' confidence by reminding them that he was always with them and that he had already saved them from the potential danger. We, too, can feel secure when we consider that God is able to overcome even the most difficult odds.

Deut 20:13-18 How could a merciful and just God order the destruction of entire population centers? He did this to protect his people from idol worship, which was certain to bring ruin to Israel (Deut 20:18). In fact, because Israel did not completely destroy these evil people as God commanded, Israel was constantly oppressed by them and experienced greater bloodshed and destruction than if they had followed God's instructions in the first place (see Deut 7:2-6).

Deut 20:20 Archaeologists have uncovered the remnants of many well-fortified cities in Canaan. Some had tall walls (up to 30 feet high), ramparts, moats, and towers. Accustomed to fighting on the open plains, the Israelites were going to have to learn new battle strategies to conquer these massive fortresses.

Deut 21:1-9 When a crime was committed and the criminal got away, the whole town's elders must select from the herd a young cow that has never been trained or yoked to a plow. [4]They must lead it down to a valley that has not been plowed or planted and that has a stream running through it. There in the valley they must break the young cow's neck. [5]Then the Levitical priests must step forward, for the LORD your God has chosen them to minister before him and to pronounce blessings in the LORD's name. They are to decide all legal and criminal cases.

[6]"The elders of the town must wash their hands over the young cow whose neck was broken. [7]Then they must say, 'Our hands did not shed this person's blood, nor did we see it happen. [8]O LORD, forgive your people Israel whom you have redeemed. Do not charge your people with the guilt of murdering an innocent person.' Then they will be absolved of the guilt of this person's blood. [9]By following these instructions, you will do what is right in the LORD's sight and will cleanse the guilt of murder from your community.

Marriage to a Captive Woman

DEUTERONOMY 21:10-14

"Suppose you go out to war against your enemies and the LORD your God hands them over to you, and you take some of them as captives. [11]And suppose you see among the captives a beautiful woman, and you are attracted to her and want to marry her. [12]If this happens, you may take her to your home, where she must shave her head, cut her nails, [13]and change the clothes she was wearing when she was captured. She will stay in your home, but let her mourn for her father and mother for a full month. Then you may marry her, and you will be her husband and she will be your wife. [14]But if you marry her and she does not please you, you must let her go free. You may not sell her or treat her as a slave, for you have humiliated her.

Rights of the Firstborn

DEUTERONOMY 21:15-17

"Suppose a man has two wives, but he loves one and not the other, and both have given him sons. And suppose the firstborn son is the son of the wife he does not love. [16]When the man divides his inheritance, he may not give the larger inheritance to his younger son, the son of the wife he loves, as if he were the firstborn son. [17]He must recognize the rights of his oldest son, the son of the wife he does not love, by giving him a double portion. He is the first son of his father's virility, and the rights of the firstborn belong to him.

Dealing with a Rebellious Son

DEUTERONOMY 21:18-21

"Suppose a man has a stubborn and rebellious son who will not obey his father or mother, even though they discipline him. [19]In such a case, the father and mother must take the son to the elders as they hold court at the town gate. [20]The parents must say to the elders, 'This son of ours is stubborn and rebellious and refuses to obey. He is a glutton and a drunkard.' [21]Then all the men of his town must stone him to death. In this way, you will purge this evil from among you, and all Israel will hear about it and be afraid.

Various Regulations

DEUTERONOMY 21:22–22:12

"If someone has committed a crime worthy of death and is executed and hung on a tree,* [23]the body must not remain hanging from the tree overnight. You must bury the body that same day, for anyone who is hung* is cursed in the sight of God. In this way, you will prevent the defilement of the land the LORD your God is giving you as your special possession.

22:1"If you see your neighbor's ox or sheep or goat wandering away, don't ignore your responsibility.* Take it back to its owner. [2]If its owner does not live nearby or you don't know who the owner is, take it to your place and keep it until the owner comes looking for it. Then you must return it. [3]Do the same if you find your neighbor's donkey, clothing, or anything else your neighbor loses. Don't ignore your responsibility.

[4]"If you see that your neighbor's donkey or ox has collapsed on the road, do not look the other way. Go and help your neighbor get it back on its feet!

Dt 21:22 Or *impaled on a pole;* similarly in 21:23. **Dt 21:23** Greek version reads *for everyone who is hung on a tree.* Compare Gal 3:13. **Dt 22:1** Hebrew *don't hide yourself;* similarly in 22:3.

community was held responsible. In much the same way, if a city has a dangerous intersection and someone is killed there, the community may be held responsible for both damages and repairs. God was pointing to the need for the whole community to feel a keen sense of responsibility for what was going on around them and to move to correct any situations that were potentially harmful—physically, socially, or morally.

Deut 21:18-21 Disobedient and rebellious children were to be brought before the elders of the city and stoned to death. There is no biblical or archaeological evidence that this punishment was ever carried out, but the point was that disobedience and rebellion were not to be tolerated in the home or allowed to continue unchecked. These principles must never be used to justify or overlook abuse or harsh treatment of children. While firm guidance may be needed with strong consequences for disobedience, the Bible does not condone physical, verbal, or emotional abuse of children.

Deut 22:1-4 The Hebrews were to care for and return lost animals or possessions to their rightful owners. The way of the world, by contrast, is "Finders keepers, losers weepers." To go beyond the finders-keepers rule by protecting and returning the property of others keeps us from being envious and greedy.

▶ **DEUTERONOMY 21:22–22:12** ***(cont.)***
5“A woman must not put on men's clothing, and
a man must not wear women's clothing. Anyone
who does this is detestable in the sight of the LORD
your God.
6“If you happen to find a bird's nest in a tree or on
the ground, and there are young ones or eggs in it with
the mother sitting in the nest, do not take the mother
with the young. 7You may take the young, but let the
mother go, so that you may prosper and enjoy a long life.
8“When you build a new house, you must build a
railing around the edge of its flat roof. That way you
will not be considered guilty of murder if someone
falls from the roof.
9“You must not plant any other crop between the
rows of your vineyard. If you do, you are forbidden to
use either the grapes from the vineyard or the other
crop.
10“You must not plow with an ox and a donkey harnessed together.
11“You must not wear clothing made of wool and
linen woven together.
12“You must put four tassels on the hem of the cloak
with which you cover yourself—on the front, back,
and sides.

Regulations for Sexual Purity

DEUTERONOMY 22:13-30
“Suppose a man marries a woman, but after sleeping with her, he turns against her 14and publicly
accuses her of shameful conduct, saying, ‘When
I married this woman, I discovered she was not a
virgin.’ 15Then the woman's father and mother must
bring the proof of her virginity to the elders as they
hold court at the town gate. 16Her father must say to
them, ‘I gave my daughter to this man to be his wife,
and now he has turned against her. 17He has accused
her of shameful conduct, saying, “I discovered that
your daughter was not a virgin.” But here is the proof
of my daughter's virginity.’ Then they must spread
her bed sheet before the elders. 18The elders must
then take the man and punish him. 19They must also
fine him 100 pieces of silver,* which he must pay
to the woman's father because he publicly accused

Dt 22:19 Hebrew *100 shekels of silver,* about 2.5 pounds or 1.1 kilograms in weight.

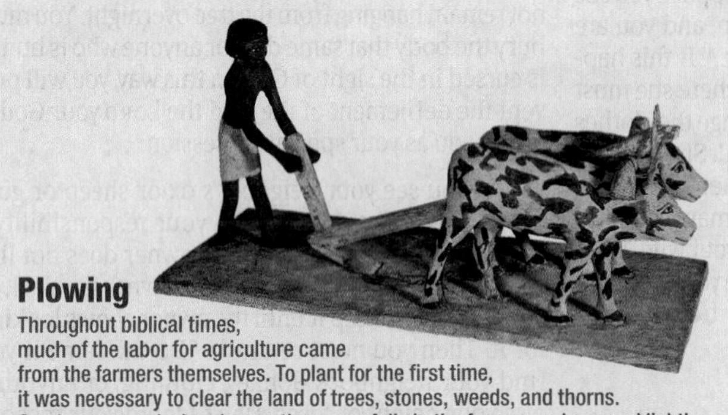

Plowing

Throughout biblical times, much of the labor for agriculture came from the farmers themselves. To plant for the first time, it was necessary to clear the land of trees, stones, weeds, and thorns. Seed was sown by hand, sometimes carefully in the furrow, and covered lightly, other times by scattering the seed. Sometimes irrigation was employed, and sometimes thin soil on hillsides was terraced. Such tasks limited the size of farms so that only the very wealthy, such as Job and Boaz, had large holdings.

To till the land, farmers used oxen or cows to pull very primitive plows (Deut 22:10). The plow consisted of an upright J-shaped piece of hardwood and attachments, drawn by oxen at one end and held by the driver at the other. Such a primitive device could break up the soil only to a depth of four or five inches. This image is from an ancient Egyptian tomb, but implements did not change much during Bible times. After the Exodus, iron became available for the tip of the plow. It is possible that Jesus, as a carpenter, made many of these farm implements as a young adult (Mark 6:3).

Deut 22:5 This verse commands men and women not to reverse their sexual roles. It is not a statement about clothing styles. Today, role rejections are common—there are men who want to become women and women who want to become men. It's not the clothing style that offends God, but using the style to act out a different sex role. God had a purpose in making us uniquely male and female.

Deut 22:8-11 These are practical laws, helpful for establishing good habits for everyday living. Verse 8: Since people used their flat roofs as porches, a railing was a wise safety precaution. Verse 9: If you plant two different crops side by side, one of them will not survive, since the stronger, taller one will block the sunlight and take most of the vital nutrients from the soil. Verse 10: A donkey and an ox, due to differences in strength and size, cannot pull a plow evenly. Verse 11: Two different kinds of thread wear unevenly and wash differently. Combining them reduces the life of the garment. Don't think of God's laws as arbitrary restrictions. Look for the reasons behind the laws. They are made not just to teach or restrict but also to protect and help us.

Deut 22:13-30 Why did God include all these laws about sexual sins? Instructions about sexual behavior would have been vital for three million people on a 40-year camping trip. But they would be equally important when they entered the Promised Land and settled down as a nation. In Colossians 3:5-8, Paul recognizes the importance of strong rules about sex for believers because sexual sins have the power to disrupt and destroy the church. Sins involving sex are not innocent dabblings in forbidden pleasures, as is so often portrayed, but powerful destroyers of relationships. They confuse and tear down the climate of respect, trust, and credibility that is so essential for solid marriages and secure children.

Deut 23:17-18 Prostitution was not overlooked in God's law—it was strictly forbidden. To forbid this practice may seem obvious to us, but it may not have been so obvious to the Israelites. Almost every other religion known to them included prostitution as an integral part of its worship services. Prostitution makes a mockery of God's original idea for sex, treating it as an isolated physical act rather than an act of commitment to another. Outside of marriage, sex destroys relationships. Within marriage, if approached with the right attitude, it can be a relationship builder. God frequently had to warn the people against the practice of extramarital sex. Today we still need to hear his warnings.

a virgin of Israel of shameful conduct. The woman will then remain the man's wife, and he may never divorce her.

[20]"But suppose the man's accusations are true, and he can show that she was not a virgin. [21]The woman must be taken to the door of her father's home, and there the men of the town must stone her to death, for she has committed a disgraceful crime in Israel by being promiscuous while living in her parents' home. In this way, you will purge this evil from among you.

[22]"If a man is discovered committing adultery, both he and the woman must die. In this way, you will purge Israel of such evil.

[23]"Suppose a man meets a young woman, a virgin who is engaged to be married, and he has sexual intercourse with her. If this happens within a town, [24]you must take both of them to the gates of that town and stone them to death. The woman is guilty because she did not scream for help. The man must die because he violated another man's wife. In this way, you will purge this evil from among you.

[25]"But if the man meets the engaged woman out in the country, and he rapes her, then only the man must die. [26]Do nothing to the young woman; she has committed no crime worthy of death. She is as innocent as a murder victim. [27]Since the man raped her out in the country, it must be assumed that she screamed, but there was no one to rescue her.

[28]"Suppose a man has intercourse with a young woman who is a virgin but is not engaged to be married. If they are discovered, [29]he must pay her father fifty pieces of silver.* Then he must marry the young woman because he violated her, and he may never divorce her as long as he lives.

[30]*"A man must not marry his father's former wife, for this would violate his father.

Regulations concerning Worship

DEUTERONOMY 23:1-8

[1]*"If a man's testicles are crushed or his penis is cut off, he may not be admitted to the assembly of the LORD.

[2]"If a person is illegitimate by birth, neither he nor his descendants for ten generations may be admitted to the assembly of the LORD.

[3]"No Ammonite or Moabite or any of their descendants for ten generations may be admitted to the assembly of the LORD. [4]These nations did not welcome you with food and water when you came out of Egypt. Instead, they hired Balaam son of Beor from Pethor in distant Aram-naharaim to curse you. [5]But the LORD your God refused to listen to Balaam. He turned the intended curse into a blessing because the LORD your God loves you. [6]As long as you live, you must never promote the welfare and prosperity of the Ammonites or Moabites.

[7]"Do not detest the Edomites or the Egyptians, because the Edomites are your relatives and you lived as foreigners among the Egyptians. [8]The third generation of Edomites and Egyptians may enter the assembly of the LORD.

Miscellaneous Regulations

DEUTERONOMY 23:9–25:19

"When you go to war against your enemies, be sure to stay away from anything that is impure.

[10]"Any man who becomes ceremonially defiled because of a nocturnal emission must leave the camp and stay away all day. [11]Toward evening he must bathe himself, and at sunset he may return to the camp.

[12]"You must have a designated area outside the camp where you can go to relieve yourself. [13]Each of you must have a spade as part of your equipment. Whenever you relieve yourself, dig a hole with the spade and cover the excrement. [14]The camp must be holy, for the LORD your God moves around in your camp to protect you and to defeat your enemies. He must not see any shameful thing among you, or he will turn away from you.

[15]"If slaves should escape from their masters and take refuge with you, you must not hand them over to their masters. [16]Let them live among you in any town they choose, and do not oppress them.

[17]"No Israelite, whether man or woman, may become a temple prostitute. [18]When you are bringing an offering to fulfill a vow, you must not bring to the house of the LORD your God any offering from the earnings of a prostitute, whether a man* or a woman, for both are detestable to the LORD your God.

[19]"Do not charge interest on the loans you make to a fellow Israelite, whether you loan money, or food, or anything else. [20]You may charge interest to foreigners, but you may not charge interest to Israelites, so that the LORD your God may bless you in everything you do in the land you are about to enter and occupy.

[21]"When you make a vow to the LORD your God, be prompt in fulfilling whatever you promised him. For the LORD your God demands that you promptly fulfill all your vows, or you will be guilty of sin. [22]However, it is not a sin to refrain from making a vow. [23]But once you have voluntarily made a vow, be careful to fulfill your promise to the LORD your God.

[24]"When you enter your neighbor's vineyard, you may eat your fill of grapes, but you must not carry any

Dt 22:29 Hebrew *50 shekels of silver,* about 1.25 pounds or 570 grams in weight. **Dt 22:30** Verse 22:30 is numbered 23:1 in Hebrew text. **Dt 23:1** Verses 23:1-25 are numbered 23:2-26 in Hebrew text. **Dt 23:18** Hebrew *a dog.*

Deut 23:24-25 This commandment guarded against selfishly holding on to one's possessions. It also ensured that no one had to go hungry. It was not, however, an excuse for taking advantage of one's neighbor. The Pharisees did not interpret this appropriately when they accused Jesus and the disciples of harvesting on the Sabbath (Matt 12:1-2).

▶ DEUTERONOMY 23:9–25:19 *(cont.)*

away in a basket. 25 And when you enter your neighbor's field of grain, you may pluck the heads of grain with your hand, but you must not harvest it with a sickle.

24:1 "Suppose a man marries a woman but she does not please him. Having discovered something wrong with her, he writes her a letter of divorce, hands it to her, and sends her away from his house. 2 When she leaves his house, she is free to marry another man. 3 But if the second husband also turns against her and divorces her, or if he dies, 4 the first husband may not marry her again, for she has been defiled. That would be detestable to the LORD. You must not bring guilt upon the land the LORD your God is giving you as a special possession.

5 "A newly married man must not be drafted into the army or be given any other official responsibilities. He must be free to spend one year at home, bringing happiness to the wife he has married.

6 "It is wrong to take a set of millstones, or even just the upper millstone, as security for a loan, for the owner uses it to make a living.

7 "If anyone kidnaps a fellow Israelite and treats him as a slave or sells him, the kidnapper must die. In this way, you will purge the evil from among you.

8 "In all cases involving serious skin diseases,* be careful to follow the instructions of the Levitical priests; obey all the commands I have given them. 9 Remember what the LORD your God did to Miriam as you were coming from Egypt.

10 "If you lend anything to your neighbor, do not enter his house to pick up the item he is giving as security. 11 You must wait outside while he goes in and brings it out to you. 12 If your neighbor is poor and gives you his cloak as security for a loan, do not keep the cloak overnight. 13 Return the cloak to its owner by sunset so he can stay warm through the night and bless you, and the LORD your God will count you as righteous.

14 "Never take advantage of poor and destitute laborers, whether they are fellow Israelites or foreigners living in your towns. 15 You must pay them their wages each day before sunset because they are poor and are counting on it. If you don't, they might cry out to the LORD against you, and it would be counted against you as sin.

16 "Parents must not be put to death for the sins of their children, nor children for the sins of their parents. Those deserving to die must be put to death for their own crimes.

17 "True justice must be given to foreigners living among you and to orphans, and you must never accept a widow's garment as security for her debt. 18 Always remember that you were slaves in Egypt and that the LORD your God redeemed you from your slavery. That is why I have given you this command.

19 "When you are harvesting your crops and forget to bring in a bundle of grain from your field, don't go back to get it. Leave it for the foreigners, orphans, and widows. Then the LORD your God will bless you in all you do. 20 When you beat the olives from your olive trees, don't go over the boughs twice. Leave the remaining olives for the foreigners, orphans, and widows. 21 When you gather the grapes in your vineyard, don't glean the vines after they are picked. Leave the remaining grapes for the foreigners, orphans, and widows. 22 Remember that you were slaves in the land of Egypt. That is why I am giving you this command.

25:1 "Suppose two people take a dispute to court, and the judges declare that one is right and the other is wrong. 2 If the person in the wrong is sentenced to be

Dt 24:8 Traditionally rendered *leprosy.* The Hebrew word used here can describe various skin diseases.

Deut 24:1-4 Some think this passage supports divorce, but that is not the case. It simply recognizes a practice that already existed in Israel. All four verses must be read to understand the point of the passage; it certainly is not suggesting that a man divorce his wife on a whim. Divorce was a permanent and final act for the couple. Once divorced and remarried to others, they could never be remarried to each other (Deut 24:4). This restriction was to prevent casual remarriage after a frivolous separation. The intention was to make people think twice before divorcing.

Deut 24:5 Newly married couples were to remain together their first year. This was to avoid placing an excessive burden upon a new, unproven relationship and to give it a chance to mature and strengthen before confronting it with numerous responsibilities. A gardener starts a tiny seedling in a small pot and allows it to take root before planting it in the field. Let your marriage grow strong by protecting your relationship from too many outside pressures and distractions—especially in the beginning. And don't expect or demand so much from newlyweds that they have inadequate time or energy to establish their marriage.

Deut 24:10-22 Throughout the Old Testament God told his people to treat the poor with justice. The powerless and poverty-stricken are often looked upon by some people as incompetent or lazy when, in fact, those facing that situation may be victims of oppression and circumstance. God says we must do all we can to help those who are needy. His justice did not permit the Israelites to insist on profits or quick payment from those who were less fortunate. Instead, his laws gave the poor every opportunity to better their situation, while providing humane options for those who couldn't. None of us is completely isolated from the poor; many of us face needs at one time or another. God wants us to treat each other fairly and do our part to help meet one another's needs.

Deut 24:19-21 God's people were instructed to leave some of their harvest in the fields so travelers and the poor could gather it. This second gathering, called gleaning, was a way for them to provide food for themselves. Years later, Ruth obtained food for herself and Naomi by gleaning behind the reapers in Boaz's field, picking up the leftovers (Ruth 2:2). Because this law was being obeyed years after it was written, Ruth, a woman in Christ's lineage, was able to find food.

Deut 25:1-3 At first glance these verses appear irrelevant today. But a closer look reveals some important principles about discipline. Are you responsible for the discipline of a child, a student, or an employee? Three important points will help you carry out your responsibility: (1) Let the punishment follow quickly after the offense; (2) let the degree of punishment reflect the seriousness of the offense; and (3) don't overdo the punishment. Discipline that is swift, just, and restrained

flogged, the judge must command him to lie down and
be beaten in his presence with the number of lashes
appropriate to the crime. 3But never give more than
forty lashes; more than forty lashes would publicly
humiliate your neighbor.

4"You must not muzzle an ox to keep it from eating
as it treads out the grain.

5"If two brothers are living together on the same
property and one of them dies without a son, his
widow may not be married to anyone from outside the
family. Instead, her husband's brother should marry
her and have intercourse with her to fulfill the duties
of a brother-in-law. 6The first son she bears to him will
be considered the son of the dead brother, so that his
name will not be forgotten in Israel.

7"But if the man refuses to marry his brother's
widow, she must go to the town gate and say to the
elders assembled there, 'My husband's brother refuses
to preserve his brother's name in Israel—he refuses
to fulfill the duties of a brother-in-law by marrying
me.' 8The elders of the town will then summon him
and talk with him. If he still refuses and says, 'I don't
want to marry her,' 9the widow must walk over to him
in the presence of the elders, pull his sandal from his
foot, and spit in his face. Then she must declare, 'This
is what happens to a man who refuses to provide his
brother with children.' 10Ever afterward in Israel his
family will be referred to as 'the family of the man
whose sandal was pulled off'!

11"If two Israelite men get into a fight and the wife
of one tries to rescue her husband by grabbing the
testicles of the other man, 12you must cut off her hand.
Show her no pity.

13"You must use accurate scales when you weigh out
merchandise, 14and you must use full and honest measures. 15Yes, always use honest weights and measures,
so that you may enjoy a long life in the land the LORD
your God is giving you. 16All who cheat with dishonest weights and measures are detestable to the LORD
your God.

17"Never forget what the Amalekites did to you as
you came from Egypt. 18They attacked you when you
were exhausted and weary, and they struck down
those who were straggling behind. They had no fear
of God. 19Therefore, when the LORD your God has given
you rest from all your enemies in the land he is giving
you as a special possession, you must destroy the Amalekites and erase their memory from under heaven.
Never forget this!

Harvest Offerings and Tithes

DEUTERONOMY 26:1-15

"When you enter the land the LORD your God is giving
you as a special possession and you have conquered it
and settled there, 2put some of the first produce from
each crop you harvest into a basket and bring it to the
designated place of worship—the place the LORD your
God chooses for his name to be honored. 3Go to the
priest in charge at that time and say to him, 'With this
gift I acknowledge to the LORD your God that I have
entered the land he swore to our ancestors he would
give us.' 4The priest will then take the basket from your
hand and set it before the altar of the LORD your God.

5"You must then say in the presence of the LORD
your God, 'My ancestor Jacob was a wandering Aramean who went to live as a foreigner in Egypt. His family arrived few in number, but in Egypt they became
a large and mighty nation. 6When the Egyptians oppressed and humiliated us by making us their slaves,
7we cried out to the LORD, the God of our ancestors.
He heard our cries and saw our hardship, toil, and
oppression. 8So the LORD brought us out of Egypt with
a strong hand and powerful arm, with overwhelming
terror, and with miraculous signs and wonders. 9He
brought us to this place and gave us this land flowing with milk and honey! 10And now, O LORD, I have
brought you the first portion of the harvest you have
given me from the ground.' Then place the produce
before the LORD your God, and bow to the ground
in worship before him. 11Afterward you may go and

makes its point while preserving the dignity of the offender.

Deut 25:4 What is the point of this Old Testament regulation? Oxen were often used to tread out the grain on a threshing floor. The animal was attached by poles to a large millstone. As it walked around the millstone, its hooves trampled the grain, separating the kernels from the chaff. At the same time, the millstone ground the grain into flour. To muzzle the ox would prevent it from eating while it was working. Paul used this as an illustration in the New Testament to argue that people productive in Christian work should not be denied its benefits—they should receive financial support (1 Cor 9:9-12; 1 Tim 5:17-18) and be fairly paid. There is also a broader application: Don't be stingy with those who work for you.

Deut 25:5-10 This law describes a "levirate" marriage, the marriage of a widow to the brother of her dead husband. The purpose of such a marriage was to carry on the dead man's name and inheritance. Family ties were an important aspect of Israelite culture. The best way to be remembered was through your line of descendants. If a widow married someone outside the family, her first husband's line would come to an end. Tamar fought for this right in Genesis 38.

Deut 26:5-10 This recitation of God's dealings with his people helped the people remember what God had done for them. What is the history of your relationship with God? Can you put into clear and concise words what God has done for you? Find a friend with whom you can share your spiritual journey. Telling your stories to each other will help you clearly understand your personal spiritual history, as well as encouraging and inspiring you both. Note: *Wandering* can mean lost or dying. Also, Arameans were the people of northern Syria and among the ancestors of Abraham. This is also used as a reference to Jacob, who spent many years there (Gen 29–31) and got his two wives in Aram.

▸ **DEUTERONOMY 26:1-15 *(cont.)***

celebrate because of all the good things the LORD your
God has given to you and your household. Remember
to include the Levites and the foreigners living among
you in the celebration.
12“Every third year you must offer a special tithe of
your crops. In this year of the special tithe you must
give your tithes to the Levites, foreigners, orphans, and
widows, so that they will have enough to eat in your
towns. 13Then you must declare in the presence of
the LORD your God, ‘I have taken the sacred gift from
my house and have given it to the Levites, foreigners,
orphans, and widows, just as you commanded me. I
have not violated or forgotten any of your commands.
14I have not eaten any of it while in mourning; I have
not handled it while I was ceremonially unclean;
and I have not offered any of it to the dead. I have
obeyed the LORD my God and have done everything
you commanded me. 15Now look down from your holy
dwelling place in heaven and bless your people Israel
and the land you swore to our ancestors to give us—a
land flowing with milk and honey.’

A Call to Obey the LORD's Commands

DEUTERONOMY 26:16-19

“Today the LORD your God has commanded you to
obey all these decrees and regulations. So be careful to
obey them wholeheartedly. 17You have declared today
that the LORD is your God. And you have promised to
walk in his ways, and to obey his decrees, commands,
and regulations, and to do everything he tells you.
18The LORD has declared today that you are his people,
his own special treasure, just as he promised, and that
you must obey all his commands. 19And if you do, he
will set you high above all the other nations he has
made. Then you will receive praise, honor, and renown.
You will be a nation that is holy to the LORD your God,
just as he promised.”

5. CONSEQUENCES OF OBEDIENCE AND DISOBEDIENCE

Moses concluded his second address to Israel on the Plains of Moab with a reminder of the promises God had made for blessings if they obeyed him and for curses if they rebelled.

The Altar on Mount Ebal

DEUTERONOMY 27:1-10

Then Moses and the leaders of Israel gave this charge
to the people: “Obey all these commands that I am
giving you today. 2When you cross the Jordan River
and enter the land the LORD your God is giving you,
set up some large stones and coat them with plaster.
3Write this whole body of instruction on them when
you cross the river to enter the land the LORD your
God is giving you—a land flowing with milk and honey,
just as the LORD, the God of your ancestors, promised
you. 4When you cross the Jordan, set up these stones
at Mount Ebal and coat them with plaster, as I am
commanding you today.
5“Then build an altar there to the LORD your God,
using natural, uncut stones. You must not shape the
stones with an iron tool. 6Build the altar of uncut
stones, and use it to offer burnt offerings to the LORD
your God. 7Also sacrifice peace offerings on it, and
celebrate by feasting there before the LORD your God.
8You must clearly write all these instructions on the
stones coated with plaster.”
9Then Moses and the Levitical priests addressed all
Israel as follows: “O Israel, be quiet and listen! Today
you have become the people of the LORD your God.
10So you must obey the LORD your God by keeping all
these commands and decrees that I am giving you
today.”

Curses from Mount Ebal

DEUTERONOMY 27:11-26

That same day Moses also gave this charge to the people: 12“When you cross the Jordan River, the tribes of
Simeon, Levi, Judah, Issachar, Joseph, and Benjamin
must stand on Mount Gerizim to proclaim a blessing over the people. 13And the tribes of Reuben, Gad,
Asher, Zebulun, Dan, and Naphtali must stand on
Mount Ebal to proclaim a curse.
14“Then the Levites will shout to all the people of
Israel:
15‘Cursed is anyone who carves or casts an idol
and secretly sets it up. These idols, the work
of craftsmen, are detestable to the LORD.’
And all the people will reply, ‘Amen.’

Deut 26:12 This law is repeated from Deuteronomy 14:28-29. The people were to give their tithe to the needy every third year. This amounts to one-third of their giving on a three-year cycle. Though we are not under this law today, the New Testament reminds us not to forget the poor. Consider giving one-third of your annual contribution to overseas ministries or to relief of the poor, orphans, and widows.

Deut 27:5-6 The Lord had specified an altar made of natural, uncut stones so that the people would not begin worshiping the altars as idols. To use an iron tool on a stone of the altar would be to profane it (Exod 20:24-25). Additionally, because the Israelites did not have the capacity to work with iron at this time, using iron tools might mean using the cooperation and expertise of other nations.

Deut 27:9-10 Moses was reviewing the law with the new generation of people. When we decide to believe in God, we must also decide to follow his ways. What we do shows what we really believe. Can people tell that you are a member of God's family?

Deut 27:15-26 These curses were a series of oaths, spoken by the priests and affirmed by the people, by which the people promised to stay away from wrong actions. By saying *Amen*, “So be it,” the people took responsibility for their actions. Sometimes looking at a list of curses like this gives us the idea that God has a bad temper and

16'Cursed is anyone who dishonors father
or mother.'
And all the people will reply, 'Amen.'

17'Cursed is anyone who steals property from
a neighbor by moving a boundary marker.'
And all the people will reply, 'Amen.'

18'Cursed is anyone who leads a blind person astray
on the road.'
And all the people will reply, 'Amen.'

19'Cursed is anyone who denies justice to foreigners,
orphans, or widows.'
And all the people will reply, 'Amen.'

20'Cursed is anyone who has sexual intercourse with
one of his father's wives, for he has violated his
father.'
And all the people will reply, 'Amen.'

21'Cursed is anyone who has sexual intercourse
with an animal.'
And all the people will reply, 'Amen.'

22'Cursed is anyone who has sexual intercourse
with his sister, whether she is the daughter of
his father or his mother.'
And all the people will reply, 'Amen.'

23'Cursed is anyone who has sexual intercourse
with his mother-in-law.'
And all the people will reply, 'Amen.'

24'Cursed is anyone who attacks a neighbor
in secret.'
And all the people will reply, 'Amen.'

25'Cursed is anyone who accepts payment to kill
an innocent person.'
And all the people will reply, 'Amen.'

26'Cursed is anyone who does not affirm and obey
the terms of these instructions.'
And all the people will reply, 'Amen.'

Blessings for Obedience

DEUTERONOMY 28:1-14

"If you fully obey the LORD your God and carefully keep
all his commands that I am giving you today, the LORD
your God will set you high above all the nations of the
world. 2You will experience all these blessings if you
obey the LORD your God:

3 Your towns and your fields
will be blessed.
4 Your children and your crops
will be blessed.
The offspring of your herds and flocks
will be blessed.
5 Your fruit baskets and breadboards
will be blessed.
6 Wherever you go and whatever you do,
you will be blessed.

7"The LORD will conquer your enemies when they
attack you. They will attack you from one direction,
but they will scatter from you in seven!
8"The LORD will guarantee a blessing on everything you do and will fill your storehouses with grain.
The LORD your God will bless you in the land he is
giving you.

is out to crush anyone who steps out of line. We need to see these restrictions not as threats, but rather as loving warnings about the plain facts of life. Just as we warn children to stay away from hot stoves and busy streets, God warns us to stay away from dangerous actions. The natural law of his universe makes it clear that wrongdoing toward others or God has tragic consequences. God is merciful enough to tell us this truth plainly. Motivated by love and not anger, his strong words help us avoid the serious consequences that result from neglecting God or wronging others. But God does not leave us with only curses (negative consequences). Immediately following these curses, we discover the great blessings (positive consequences) that come from living for God (Deut 28:1-14). These give us extra incentive to obey God's laws. While all these blessings may not come in our lifetime on earth, those who obey God will experience the fullness of his blessing when he establishes the new heaven and the new earth.

Mount Ebal and Mount Gerizim

Years before the Israelites' entrance into the Promised Land, God, through Moses, designated the twin mountains Ebal and Gerizim as the place for the recitation of the curses and blessings of Deuteronomy 27–28. According to Deuteronomy 27:12-13, six tribes of Israel were to stand on Gerizim and shout the blessings. These were Simeon, Levi, Judah, Issachar, Joseph, and Benjamin. The tribe of Joseph mentioned here would actually mean the tribes of Ephraim and Manasseh (Joseph's sons) in whose territories these two mountains belonged. The other six tribes—Reuben, Gad, Asher, Zebulun, Dan, and Naphtali—were to recite the curses from Ebal.

▸ **DEUTERONOMY 28:1-14 *(cont.)***

9 "If you obey the commands of the LORD your God and walk in his ways, the LORD will establish you as his holy people as he swore he would do. 10 Then all the nations of the world will see that you are a people claimed by the LORD, and they will stand in awe of you.

11 "The LORD will give you prosperity in the land he swore to your ancestors to give you, blessing you with many children, numerous livestock, and abundant crops. 12 The LORD will send rain at the proper time from his rich treasury in the heavens and will bless all the work you do. You will lend to many nations, but you will never need to borrow from them. 13 If you listen to these commands of the LORD your God that I am giving you today, and if you carefully obey them, the LORD will make you the head and not the tail, and you will always be on top and never at the bottom. 14 You must not turn away from any of the commands I am giving you today, nor follow after other gods and worship them.

Curses for Disobedience

DEUTERONOMY 28:15–29:1

"But if you refuse to listen to the LORD your God and do not obey all the commands and decrees I am giving you today, all these curses will come and overwhelm you:

16 Your towns and your fields
will be cursed.
17 Your fruit baskets and breadboards
will be cursed.
18 Your children and your crops
will be cursed.
The offspring of your herds and flocks
will be cursed.
19 Wherever you go and whatever you do,
you will be cursed.

20 "The LORD himself will send on you curses, confusion, and frustration in everything you do, until at last you are completely destroyed for doing evil and abandoning me. 21 The LORD will afflict you with diseases until none of you are left in the land you are about to enter and occupy. 22 The LORD will strike you with wasting diseases, fever, and inflammation, with scorching heat and drought, and with blight and mildew. These disasters will pursue you until you die. 23 The skies above will be as unyielding as bronze, and the earth beneath will be as hard as iron. 24 The LORD will change the rain that falls on your land into powder, and dust will pour down from the sky until you are destroyed.

25 "The LORD will cause you to be defeated by your enemies. You will attack your enemies from one direction, but you will scatter from them in seven! You will be an object of horror to all the kingdoms of the earth. 26 Your corpses will be food for all the scavenging birds and wild animals, and no one will be there to chase them away.

27 "The LORD will afflict you with the boils of Egypt and with tumors, scurvy, and the itch, from which you cannot be cured. 28 The LORD will strike you with madness, blindness, and panic. 29 You will grope around in broad daylight like a blind person groping in the darkness, but you will not find your way. You will be oppressed and robbed continually, and no one will come to save you.

30 "You will be engaged to a woman, but another man will sleep with her. You will build a house, but someone else will live in it. You will plant a vineyard, but you will never enjoy its fruit. 31 Your ox will be butchered before your eyes, but you will not eat a single bite of the meat. Your donkey will be taken from you, never to be returned. Your sheep and goats will be given to your enemies, and no one will be there to help you. 32 You will watch as your sons and daughters are taken away as slaves. Your heart will break for them, but you won't be able to help them. 33 A foreign nation you have never heard about will eat the crops you worked so hard to grow. You will suffer under constant oppression and harsh treatment. 34 You will go mad because of all the tragedy you see around you. 35 The LORD will cover your knees and legs with incurable boils. In fact, you will be covered from head to foot.

36 "The LORD will exile you and your king to a nation unknown to you and your ancestors. There in exile you will worship gods of wood and stone! 37 You will become an object of horror, ridicule, and mockery among all the nations to which the LORD sends you.

38 "You will plant much but harvest little, for locusts will eat your crops. 39 You will plant vineyards and care for them, but you will not drink the wine or eat the grapes, for worms will destroy the vines. 40 You will grow olive trees throughout your land, but you will never use the olive oil, for the fruit will drop before it ripens. 41 You will have sons and daughters, but you will lose them, for they will be led away into captivity. 42 Swarms of insects will destroy your trees and crops.

43 "The foreigners living among you will become stronger and stronger, while you become weaker and weaker. 44 They will lend money to you, but you will not lend to them. They will be the head, and you will be the tail!

Deut 28:23-24 This curse is referring to a drought.

Deut 28:34 One of the curses for those who rejected God was that they would go mad from seeing all the tragedy around them. Do you ever feel that you will go crazy if you hear about one more rape, kidnapping, murder, or war? Much of the world's evil is a result of people's failure to acknowledge and serve God. When you hear bad news, don't groan helplessly as do unbelievers who have no hope for the future. Remind yourself that in spite of it all, God has ultimate control and will one day come back to make everything right.

45"If you refuse to listen to the LORD your God and to obey the commands and decrees he has given you, all these curses will pursue and overtake you until you are destroyed. 46These horrors will serve as a sign and warning among you and your descendants forever. 47If you do not serve the LORD your God with joy and enthusiasm for the abundant benefits you have received, 48you will serve your enemies whom the LORD will send against you. You will be left hungry, thirsty, naked, and lacking in everything. The LORD will put an iron yoke on your neck, oppressing you harshly until he has destroyed you.

49"The LORD will bring a distant nation against you from the end of the earth, and it will swoop down on you like a vulture. It is a nation whose language you do not understand, 50a fierce and heartless nation that shows no respect for the old and no pity for the young. 51Its armies will devour your livestock and crops, and you will be destroyed. They will leave you no grain, new wine, olive oil, calves, or lambs, and you will starve to death. 52They will attack your cities until all the fortified walls in your land—the walls you trusted to protect you—are knocked down. They will attack all the towns in the land the LORD your God has given you.

53"The siege and terrible distress of the enemy's attack will be so severe that you will eat the flesh of your own sons and daughters, whom the LORD your God has given you. 54The most tenderhearted man among you will have no compassion for his own brother, his beloved wife, and his surviving children. 55He will refuse to share with them the flesh he is devouring—the flesh of one of his own children—because he has nothing else to eat during the siege and terrible distress that your enemy will inflict on all your towns. 56The most tender and delicate woman among you—so delicate she would not so much as touch the ground with her foot—will be selfish toward the husband she loves and toward her own son or daughter. 57She will hide from them the afterbirth and the new baby she has borne, so that she herself can secretly eat them. She will have nothing else to eat during the siege and terrible distress that your enemy will inflict on all your towns.

58"If you refuse to obey all the words of instruction that are written in this book, and if you do not fear the glorious and awesome name of the LORD your God, 59then the LORD will overwhelm you and your children with indescribable plagues. These plagues will be intense and without relief, making you miserable and unbearably sick. 60He will afflict you with all the diseases of Egypt that you feared so much, and you will have no relief. 61The LORD will afflict you with every sickness and plague there is, even those not mentioned in this Book of Instruction, until you are destroyed. 62Though you become as numerous as the stars in the sky, few of you will be left because you would not listen to the LORD your God.

63"Just as the LORD has found great pleasure in causing you to prosper and multiply, the LORD will find pleasure in destroying you. You will be torn from the land you are about to enter and occupy. 64For the LORD will scatter you among all the nations from one end of the earth to the other. There you will worship foreign gods that neither you nor your ancestors have known, gods made of wood and stone! 65There among those nations you will find no peace or place to rest. And the LORD will cause your heart to tremble, your eyesight to fail, and your soul to despair. 66Your life will constantly hang in the balance. You will live night and day in fear, unsure if you will survive. 67In the morning you will say, 'If only it were night!' And in the evening you will say, 'If only it were morning!' For you will be terrified by the awful horrors you see around you. 68Then the LORD will send you back to Egypt in ships, to a destination I promised you would never see again. There you will offer to sell yourselves to your enemies as slaves, but no one will buy you."

29:1*These are the terms of the covenant the LORD commanded Moses to make with the Israelites while they were in the land of Moab, in addition to the covenant he had made with them at Mount Sinai.*

Dt 29:1a Verse 29:1 is numbered 28:69 in Hebrew text. **Dt 29:1b** Hebrew *Horeb*, another name for Sinai.

Deut 28:36 This happened when Assyria and Babylonia took the Israelites captive to their lands (2 Kgs 17:23; 25:11).

Deut 28:64 This severe warning tragically came true when Israel was defeated and carried away into captivity by Assyria (722 B.C.), and Judah by Babylon (586 B.C.). Later, in A.D. 70, Roman oppression forced many Jews to flee their homeland. Thus, the people were scattered throughout the various nations.

Deut 29:1ff At Mount Sinai, 40 years earlier, God and Israel had made a covenant (Exod 19–20). Although there were many parts to the covenant (read the books of Exodus, Leviticus, and Numbers), its purpose can be summed up in two sentences: God promised to bless the Israelites by making them the nation through whom the rest of the world could know God. In return, the Israelites promised to love and obey God in order to receive physical and spiritual blessings. Here Moses reviewed this covenant. God was still keeping his part of the bargain (and he always would), but the Israelites were already neglecting their part. Moses restated the covenant to warn the people that if they did not keep their part of the agreement, they would experience severe discipline.

L. Moses' Third Address on the Plains of Moab

After reviewing God's laws for the new generation, Moses addresses the people for a third and final time to remind them that they have the choice to follow God or reject him.

1. A CALL FOR COMMITMENT TO GOD

Moses calls for commitment, urging the people to honor the contract they had previously made with God. Knowing God's Word is not enough; we must obey it.

Moses Reviews the Covenant

DEUTERONOMY 29:2-29

2*Moses summoned all the Israelites and said to them, "You have seen with your own eyes everything the LORD did in the land of Egypt to Pharaoh and to all his servants and to his whole country—3all the great tests of strength, the miraculous signs, and the amazing wonders. 4But to this day the LORD has not given you minds that understand, nor eyes that see, nor ears that hear! 5For forty years I led you through the wilderness, yet your clothes and sandals did not wear out. 6You ate no bread and drank no wine or other alcoholic drink, but he gave you food so you would know that he is the LORD your God.

7"When we came here, King Sihon of Heshbon and King Og of Bashan came out to fight against us, but we defeated them. 8We took their land and gave it to the tribes of Reuben and Gad and to the half-tribe of Manasseh as their grant of land.

9"Therefore, obey the terms of this covenant so that you will prosper in everything you do. 10All of you—tribal leaders, elders, officers, all the men of Israel—are standing today in the presence of the LORD your God. 11Your little ones and your wives are with you, as well as the foreigners living among you who chop your wood and carry your water. 12You are standing here today to enter into the covenant of the LORD your God. The LORD is making this covenant, including the curses. 13By entering into the covenant today, he will establish you as his people and confirm that he is your God, just as he promised you and as he swore to your ancestors Abraham, Isaac, and Jacob.

14"But you are not the only ones with whom I am making this covenant with its curses. 15I am making this covenant both with you who stand here today in the presence of the LORD our God, and also with the future generations who are not standing here today.

16"You remember how we lived in the land of Egypt and how we traveled through the lands of enemy nations as we left. 17You have seen their detestable practices and their idols* made of wood, stone, silver, and gold. 18I am making this covenant with you so that no one among you—no man, woman, clan, or tribe—will turn away from the LORD our God to worship these gods of other nations, and so that no root among you bears bitter and poisonous fruit.

19"Those who hear the warnings of this curse should not congratulate themselves, thinking, 'I am safe, even though I am following the desires of my own stubborn heart.' This would lead to utter ruin! 20The LORD will never pardon such people. Instead his anger and jealousy will burn against them. All the curses written in this book will come down on them, and the LORD will erase their names from under heaven. 21The LORD will separate them from all the tribes of Israel, to pour out on them all the curses of the covenant recorded in this Book of Instruction.

22"Then the generations to come, both your own descendants and the foreigners who come from distant lands, will see the devastation of the land and the diseases the LORD inflicts on it. 23They will exclaim, 'The whole land is devastated by sulfur and salt. It is a wasteland with nothing planted and nothing growing, not even a blade of grass. It is like the cities of Sodom and Gomorrah, Admah and Zeboiim, which the LORD destroyed in his intense anger.'

24"And all the surrounding nations will ask, 'Why has the LORD done this to this land? Why was he so angry?'

25"And the answer will be, 'This happened because the people of the land abandoned the covenant that the LORD, the God of their ancestors, made with them when he brought them out of the land of Egypt. 26Instead, they turned away to serve and worship gods they had not known before, gods that were not from the LORD. 27That is why the LORD's anger has burned against this

Dt 29:2 Verses 29:2-29 are numbered 29:1-28 in Hebrew text. **Dt 29:17** The Hebrew term (literally *round things*) probably alludes to dung.

Deut 29:5 Just as the people of Israel did not notice God's care for them along their journey, we sometimes do not notice all of the ways that God takes care of us—that all of our daily needs have been supplied and we have been well fed and well clothed. Worse yet, we mistakenly take the credit ourselves for being good providers instead of recognizing God's hand in the process.

Deut 29:9 What is the best way to prosper in life? For the Israelites, their first step was to keep their part of the covenant. They were to love God with all of their heart, soul, and strength (Deut 6:4-5). We, too, are to seek first the Kingdom of God and his righteousness (Matt 6:33); then true success in life will follow as a blessing from the hand of God.

Deut 29:18 Moses cautioned that the day the Hebrews chose to turn from God, a root would be planted that would produce bitter and poisonous fruit (see Heb 12:15). When we decide to do what we know is wrong, we plant an evil seed that begins to grow out of control, eventually yielding a crop of sorrow and pain. But we can prevent those seeds of sin from taking root. If you have done something wrong, confess it to God and others immediately. If the seed never finds fertile soil, its bitter fruit will never ripen.

land, bringing down on it every curse recorded in this book. 28In great anger and fury the LORD uprooted his people from their land and banished them to another land, where they still live today!'

29"The LORD our God has secrets known to no one. We are not accountable for them, but we and our children are accountable forever for all that he has revealed to us, so that we may obey all the terms of these instructions.

A Call to Return to the LORD

DEUTERONOMY 30:1-10

"In the future, when you experience all these blessings and curses I have listed for you, and when you are living among the nations to which the LORD your God has exiled you, take to heart all these instructions. 2If at that time you and your children return to the LORD your God, and if you obey with all your heart and all your soul all the commands I have given you today, 3then the LORD your God will restore your fortunes. He will have mercy on you and gather you back from all the nations where he has scattered you. 4Even though you are banished to the ends of the earth, the LORD your God will gather you from there and bring you back again. 5The LORD your God will return you to the land that belonged to your ancestors, and you will possess that land again. Then he will make you even more prosperous and numerous than your ancestors!

6"The LORD your God will change your heart* and the hearts of all your descendants, so that you will love him with all your heart and soul and so you may live! 7The LORD your God will inflict all these curses on your enemies and on those who hate and persecute you. 8Then you will again obey the LORD and keep all his commands that I am giving you today.

9"The LORD your God will then make you successful in everything you do. He will give you many children and numerous livestock, and he will cause your fields to produce abundant harvests, for the LORD will again delight in being good to you as he was to your ancestors. 10The LORD your God will delight in you if you obey his voice and keep the commands and decrees written in this Book of Instruction, and if you turn to the LORD your God with all your heart and soul.

The Choice of Life or Death

DEUTERONOMY 30:11-20

"This command I am giving you today is not too difficult for you to understand, and it is not beyond your reach. 12It is not kept in heaven, so distant that you must ask, 'Who will go up to heaven and bring it down so we can hear it and obey?' 13It is not kept beyond the sea, so far away that you must ask, 'Who will cross the sea to bring it to us so we can hear it and obey?' 14No, the message is very close at hand; it is on your lips and in your heart so that you can obey it.

15"Now listen! Today I am giving you a choice between life and death, between prosperity and disaster. 16For I command you this day to love the LORD your God and to keep his commands, decrees, and regulations by walking in his ways. If you do this, you will live and multiply, and the LORD your God will bless you and the land you are about to enter and occupy.

17"But if your heart turns away and you refuse to listen, and if you are drawn away to serve and worship other gods, 18then I warn you now that you will certainly be destroyed. You will not live a long, good life in the land you are crossing the Jordan to occupy.

19"Today I have given you the choice between life and death, between blessings and curses. Now I call on heaven and earth to witness the choice you make. Oh, that you would choose life, so that you and your descendants might live! 20You can make this choice by loving the LORD your God, obeying him, and committing yourself firmly to him. This* is the key to your life. And if you love and obey the LORD, you will live long in the land the LORD swore to give your ancestors Abraham, Isaac, and Jacob."

Dt 30:6 Hebrew *circumcise your heart.* **Dt 30:20** Or *He.*

Deut 29:29 There are some secrets God has chosen not to reveal to us, possibly for the following reasons: (1) Our finite minds cannot fully understand the infinite aspects of God's nature and the universe (Eccl 3:11); (2) some things are unnecessary for us to know until we are more mature; (3) God is infinite and all-knowing, and we do not have the capacity to know everything he does. This verse shows that although God has not told us everything there is to know about obeying him, he has told us enough. Thus, disobedience comes from an act of the will, not a lack of knowledge. Through God's Word we know enough about him to be saved by faith and to serve him. We must not use the limitation of our knowledge as an excuse to reject his claim on our life.

Deut 30:1-6 Moses told the Hebrews that when they were ready to return to God, he would be ready to receive them. God's mercy is unbelievable. It goes far beyond what we can imagine. Even if the Jews deliberately walked away from him and ruined their lives, God would still take them back. God would give them inward spiritual renewal. God wants to forgive us and bring us back to himself too. Some people will not learn this until their world has crashed in around them. The sorrow and pain they have gone through provide new insight into what God has been saying to them all along. Are you separated from God by sin? No matter how far you have wandered, God promises a fresh beginning if only you will turn to him.

Deut 30:11-14 God has called us to keep his commands, while reminding us that his laws are not hidden from us or beyond our reach. Have you ever said you would obey God if you knew what he wanted? Have you ever complained that obedience is too difficult for a mere human? These are unacceptable excuses. God's laws are written in the Bible and are clearly evident in the world around us. Obeying them is reasonable, sensible, and beneficial. The most difficult part of obeying God's laws is simply deciding to start now. Paul refers to this passage in Romans 10:5-8.

Deut 30:19-20 Moses challenged Israel to choose life, to obey God, and therefore to continue to experience his blessings. God doesn't force his will on anyone. He lets us decide whether to follow him or reject him. This decision is a life-or-death matter. God wants us to realize this, for he would like us all to choose life. Daily, in each new situation, we must affirm and reinforce this commitment.

M. A Change in Leadership: Moses' Last Days

Realizing that he is about to die, Moses commissions Joshua, records the laws in a permanent form, and teaches a special song to the Israelites. Thus, Moses prepared the people for his departure. Similarly, we should not allow others to become dependent upon us for their spiritual growth but help them to become dependent upon God.

Joshua Becomes Israel's Leader

DEUTERONOMY 31:1-8

When Moses had finished giving these instructions* to all the people of Israel, [2]he said, "I am now 120 years old, and I am no longer able to lead you. The LORD has told me, 'You will not cross the Jordan River.' [3]But the LORD your God himself will cross over ahead of you. He will destroy the nations living there, and you will take possession of their land. Joshua will lead you across the river, just as the LORD promised.

[4]"The LORD will destroy the nations living in the land, just as he destroyed Sihon and Og, the kings of the Amorites. [5]The LORD will hand over to you the people who live there, and you must deal with them as I have commanded you. [6]So be strong and courageous! Do not be afraid and do not panic before them. For the LORD your God will personally go ahead of you. He will neither fail you nor abandon you."

[7]Then Moses called for Joshua, and as all Israel watched, he said to him, "Be strong and courageous! For you will lead these people into the land that the LORD swore to their ancestors he would give them. You are the one who will divide it among them as their grants of land. [8]Do not be afraid or discouraged, for the LORD will personally go ahead of you. He will be with you; he will neither fail you nor abandon you."

Public Reading of the Book of Instruction

DEUTERONOMY 31:9-13

So Moses wrote this entire body of instruction in a book and gave it to the priests, who carried the Ark of the LORD's Covenant, and to the elders of Israel. [10]Then Moses gave them this command: "At the end of every seventh year, the Year of Release, during the Festival of Shelters, [11]you must read this Book of Instruction to all the people of Israel when they assemble before the LORD your God at the place he chooses. [12]Call them all together—men, women, children, and the foreigners living in your towns—so they may hear this Book of Instruction and learn to fear the LORD your God and carefully obey all the terms of these instructions. [13]Do this so that your children who have not known these instructions will hear them and will learn to fear the LORD your God. Do this as long as you live in the land you are crossing the Jordan to occupy."

Israel's Disobedience Predicted

DEUTERONOMY 31:14-29

Then the LORD said to Moses, "The time has come for you to die. Call Joshua and present yourselves at the Tabernacle,* so that I may commission him there." So Moses and Joshua went and presented themselves at the Tabernacle. [15]And the LORD appeared to them in a pillar of cloud that stood at the entrance to the sacred tent.

[16]The LORD said to Moses, "You are about to die and join your ancestors. After you are gone, these people will begin to worship foreign gods, the gods of the land where they are going. They will abandon me and break my covenant that I have made with them. [17]Then my anger will blaze forth against them. I will abandon them, hiding my face from them, and they will be devoured. Terrible trouble will come down on them, and on that day they will say, 'These disasters have come down on us because God is no longer among us!' [18]At that time I will hide my face from them on account of all the evil they commit by worshiping other gods.

[19]"So write down the words of this song, and teach it to the people of Israel. Help them learn it, so it may serve as a witness for me against them. [20]For I will bring them into the land I swore to give their ancestors—a land flowing with milk and honey. There they will become prosperous, eat all the food they want, and become fat. But they will begin to worship other gods; they will despise me and break my covenant. [21]And when great disasters come down on them, this song will stand as evidence against them, for it will never be forgotten by their descendants. I know the intentions of these people, even now before they have entered the land I swore to give them."

[22]So that very day Moses wrote down the words of the song and taught it to the Israelites.

Dt 31:1 As in Dead Sea Scrolls and Greek version; Masoretic Text reads *Moses went and spoke.* **Dt 31:14** Hebrew *Tent of Meeting;* also in 31:14b.

Deut 31:10-13 The laws were to be read to the whole assembly so that everyone, including the children, could hear them. Every seven years the entire nation would gather together and listen as a priest read the law to them. There were no books, Bibles, or websites to spread God's Word, so the people had to rely on word of mouth and an accurate memory. Memorization was an important part of worship because if everyone knew the law, ignorance would be no excuse for breaking it. To fulfill God's purpose and will in our lives, we need the content and substance of his Word in our hearts and minds. For the Hebrews, this process began in childhood. Teaching our children and new believers should be one of our top priorities. Our finest teachers, best resources, and most careful thought should be directed toward showing young believers how to follow God in all life's situations.

23 Then the LORD commissioned Joshua son of Nun
with these words: "Be strong and courageous, for you
must bring the people of Israel into the land I swore
to give them. I will be with you."
24 When Moses had finished writing this entire body
of instruction in a book, 25 he gave this command to the
Levites who carried the Ark of the LORD's Covenant:
26 "Take this Book of Instruction and place it beside
the Ark of the Covenant of the LORD your God, so it
may remain there as a witness against the people of
Israel. 27 For I know how rebellious and stubborn you
are. Even now, while I am still alive and am here with
you, you have rebelled against the LORD. How much
more rebellious will you be after my death!
28 "Now summon all the elders and officials of your
tribes, so that I can speak to them directly and call
heaven and earth to witness against them. 29 I know
that after my death you will become utterly corrupt
and will turn from the way I have commanded you to
follow. In the days to come, disaster will come down
on you, for you will do what is evil in the LORD's sight,
making him very angry with your actions."

The Song of Moses

DEUTERONOMY 31:30–32:47

So Moses recited this entire song publicly to the assembly of Israel:

32:1 "Listen, O heavens, and I will speak!
Hear, O earth, the words that I say!
2 Let my teaching fall on you like rain;
let my speech settle like dew.
Let my words fall like rain on tender grass,
like gentle showers on young plants.
3 I will proclaim the name of the LORD;
how glorious is our God!
4 He is the Rock; his deeds are perfect.
Everything he does is just and fair.
He is a faithful God who does no wrong;
how just and upright he is!

5 "But they have acted corruptly toward him;
when they act so perversely,
are they really his children?*
They are a deceitful and twisted generation.
6 Is this the way you repay the LORD,
you foolish and senseless people?
Isn't he your Father who created you?
Has he not made you and established you?
7 Remember the days of long ago;
think about the generations past.
Ask your father, and he will inform you.
Inquire of your elders, and they will
tell you.
8 When the Most High assigned lands to the
nations,
when he divided up the human race,
he established the boundaries of the peoples
according to the number in his heavenly
court.*

Dt 32:5 The meaning of the Hebrew is uncertain. **Dt 32:8** As in Dead Sea Scrolls, which read *the number of the sons of God,* and Greek version, which reads *the number of the angels of God;* Masoretic Text reads *the number of the sons of Israel.*

Deut 31:23 Joshua had been appointed to take over the leadership of Israel and guide the people into the Promised Land (Moses could not enter the land due to his disobedience—Num 20:12). Joshua, first mentioned in Exodus 17:9, had been Moses' assistant for many years (Josh 1:1). One of his key qualifications was his faith. As one of the 12 scouts to first enter Canaan, only he and Caleb believed that God could help Israel conquer the land (Num 13:1–14:30). Moses told Joshua to be strong and courageous twice in this chapter (Deut 31:7, 23). Indeed, this was a frightening task, with three million people to care for, settle disputes for, and lead into battle. Finding courage would be Joshua's greatest test. He was strong and courageous because he knew God was with him and because he had faith that God would do all he had promised Israel.

So Moses recited this entire song publicly to the assembly of Israel.
Deuteronomy 31:30

Deut 31:27-29 Moses knew that the Israelites, in spite of all they had seen of God's work, were rebellious at heart. They deserved God's punishment, although they often received his mercy instead. We, too, are stubborn and rebellious by nature. Throughout our lives we struggle with sin. Repentance once a month or once a week is not enough. We must constantly turn from our sins to God and let him, in his mercy, save us.

Deut 32:1ff Moses was not only a great prophet but also a song leader. After three sermons, he changed the form of his message to singing. Sometimes reciting something in a different form makes it easier to remember. This song gives a brief history of Israel. It reminds the people of their mistakes, warns them to avoid repetition of those mistakes, and offers the hope that comes only by trusting God.

▶ **DEUTERONOMY 31:30–32:47 *(cont.)***

9 "For the people of Israel belong to the LORD;
Jacob is his special possession.
10 He found them in a desert land,
in an empty, howling wasteland.
He surrounded them and watched over them;
he guarded them as he would guard his
own eyes.*
11 Like an eagle that rouses her chicks
and hovers over her young,
so he spread his wings to take them up
and carried them safely on his pinions.
12 The LORD alone guided them;
they followed no foreign gods.
13 He let them ride over the highlands
and feast on the crops of the fields.
He nourished them with honey from the rock
and olive oil from the stony ground.
14 He fed them yogurt from the herd
and milk from the flock,
together with the fat of lambs.
He gave them choice rams from Bashan,
and goats,
together with the choicest wheat.
You drank the finest wine,
made from the juice of grapes.

15 "But Israel* soon became fat and unruly;
the people grew heavy, plump, and stuffed!
Then they abandoned the God who had
made them;
they made light of the Rock of their salvation.
16 They stirred up his jealousy by worshiping
foreign gods;
they provoked his fury with detestable
deeds.
17 They offered sacrifices to demons, which are
not God,
to gods they had not known before,
to new gods only recently arrived,
to gods their ancestors had never feared.
18 You neglected the Rock who had fathered you;
you forgot the God who had given you birth.

19 "The LORD saw this and drew back,
provoked to anger by his own sons and
daughters.
20 He said, 'I will abandon them;
then see what becomes of them.
For they are a twisted generation,
children without integrity.
21 They have roused my jealousy by worshiping
things that are not God;
they have provoked my anger with their
useless idols.
Now I will rouse their jealousy through people
who are not even a people;
I will provoke their anger through the foolish
Gentiles.
22 For my anger blazes forth like fire
and burns to the depths of the grave.*
It devours the earth and all its crops
and ignites the foundations of the mountains.
23 I will heap disasters upon them
and shoot them down with my arrows.
24 I will weaken them with famine,
burning fever, and deadly disease.
I will send the fangs of wild beasts
and poisonous snakes that glide in the dust.
25 Outside, the sword will bring death,
and inside, terror will strike
both young men and young women,
both infants and the aged.
26 I would have annihilated them,
wiping out even the memory of them.
27 But I feared the taunt of Israel's enemy,
who might misunderstand and say,
"Our own power has triumphed!
The LORD had nothing to do with this!"'

28 "But Israel is a senseless nation;
the people are foolish, without
understanding.

Dt 32:10 Hebrew *as the pupil of his eye.* **Dt 32:15** Hebrew *Jeshurun*, a term of endearment for Israel. **Dt 32:22** Hebrew *of Sheol.*

Deut 32:10-11 The Israelites had no excuse for abandoning God. He had shielded them like a kindly shepherd. He had guarded them like a person protects the pupil (apple) of his eye. He had been the encircling protector, like a mother eagle who protects her young. The Lord alone had led them. And he alone leads us. Let us remember to trust in him.

VARIETY IN WORSHIP

Israel's worship used all of the senses; each reinforced the meaning of the ceremony. Every sense can be used to worship God.

SIGHT	The beauty and symbolism of the Tabernacle; every color and hue had a meaning
HEARING	The use of music; there were instructions for the use of a variety of instruments, and the Bible records many songs
TOUCH	The head of the animal to be sacrificed was touched, symbolizing the fact that it was taking their place
SMELL	The sacrifices were burned, emitting a familiar aroma
TASTE	The festivals were celebrations and memorials—much of the food was symbolic

29 Oh, that they were wise and could understand
this!
Oh, that they might know their fate!
30 How could one person chase a thousand of them,
and two people put ten thousand to flight,
unless their Rock had sold them,
unless the LORD had given them up?
31 But the rock of our enemies is not like our Rock,
as even they recognize.*
32 Their vine grows from the vine of Sodom,
from the vineyards of Gomorrah.
Their grapes are poison,
and their clusters are bitter.
33 Their wine is the venom of serpents,
the deadly poison of cobras.

34 "The LORD says, 'Am I not storing up these things,
sealing them away in my treasury?
35 I will take revenge; I will pay them back.
In due time their feet will slip.
Their day of disaster will arrive,
and their destiny will overtake them.'

36 "Indeed, the LORD will give justice to his people,
and he will change his mind about* his
servants,
when he sees their strength is gone
and no one is left, slave or free.
37 Then he will ask, 'Where are their gods,
the rocks they fled to for refuge?
38 Where now are those gods,
who ate the fat of their sacrifices
and drank the wine of their offerings?
Let those gods arise and help you!
Let them provide you with shelter!
39 Look now; I myself am he!
There is no other god but me!
I am the one who kills and gives life;
I am the one who wounds and heals;
no one can be rescued from my powerful
hand!
40 Now I raise my hand to heaven
and declare, "As surely as I live,
41 when I sharpen my flashing sword
and begin to carry out justice,
I will take revenge on my enemies
and repay those who reject me.
42 I will make my arrows drunk with blood,
and my sword will devour flesh—
the blood of the slaughtered and the captives,
and the heads of the enemy leaders."'

43 "Rejoice with him, you heavens,
and let all of God's angels worship him.*
Rejoice with his people, you nations,
and let all the angels be strengthened in him.*
For he will avenge the blood of his servants;
he will take revenge against his enemies.
He will repay those who hate him*
and cleanse the land for his people."

44 So Moses came with Joshua* son of Nun and recited all the words of this song to the people.
45 When Moses had finished reciting all these words
to the people of Israel, 46 he added: "Take to heart all
the words of warning I have given you today. Pass them
on as a command to your children so they will obey
every word of these instructions. 47 These instructions
are not empty words—they are your life! By obeying
them you will enjoy a long life in the land you will occupy when you cross the Jordan River."

Moses' Death Foretold

DEUTERONOMY 32:48-52

That same day the LORD said to Moses, 49 "Go to Moab,
to the mountains east of the river,* and climb Mount
Nebo, which is across from Jericho. Look out across
the land of Canaan, the land I am giving to the people
of Israel as their own special possession. 50 Then you
will die there on the mountain. You will join your ancestors, just as Aaron, your brother, died on Mount Hor
and joined his ancestors. 51 For both of you betrayed
me with the Israelites at the waters of Meribah at Kadesh* in the wilderness of Zin. You failed to demonstrate my holiness to the people of Israel there. 52 So
you will see the land from a distance, but you may
not enter the land I am giving to the people of Israel."

Psalm 90

THEME: God's eternal nature is contrasted with people's frailty. Our time on earth is limited and we are to use it wisely, not living for the moment, but with our eternal home in mind.

AUTHOR: Moses, making this the oldest of the psalms

A prayer of Moses, the man of God.

1 Lord, through all the generations
you have been our home!
2 Before the mountains were born,
before you gave birth to the earth and the world,
from beginning to end, you are God.

Dt 32:31 The meaning of the Hebrew is uncertain. Greek version reads *our enemies are fools.* **Dt 32:36** Or *will take revenge for.* **Dt 32:43a** As in Dead Sea Scrolls and Greek version; Masoretic Text lacks the first two lines. Compare Heb 1:6. **Dt 32:43b** As in Greek version; Hebrew text lacks this line. **Dt 32:43c** As in Dead Sea Scrolls and Greek version; Masoretic Text lacks this line. **Dt 32:44** Hebrew *Hoshea,* a variant name for Joshua. **Dt 32:49** Hebrew *the mountains of Abarim.* **Dt 32:51** Hebrew *waters of Meribah-kadesh.*

Deut 32:46-47 Moses urged the people to think about God's word and teach it to their children. The Bible can sit on your bookshelf and gather dust, or you can make it a vital part of your life by regularly setting aside time to study it. When you discover the wisdom of God's message, you will want to apply it to your life and pass it on to your family and others. The Bible is not merely good reading—it's real help for real life.

▸ **PSALM 90 *(cont.)***

3 You turn people back to dust, saying,
"Return to dust, you mortals!"
4 For you, a thousand years are as a passing day,
as brief as a few night hours.
5 You sweep people away like dreams that disappear.
They are like grass that springs up in the morning.
6 In the morning it blooms and flourishes,
but by evening it is dry and withered.
7 We wither beneath your anger;
we are overwhelmed by your fury.
8 You spread out our sins before you—
our secret sins—and you see them all.
9 We live our lives beneath your wrath,
ending our years with a groan.
10 Seventy years are given to us!
Some even live to eighty.
But even the best years are filled with pain and trouble;
soon they disappear, and we fly away.
11 Who can comprehend the power of your anger?
Your wrath is as awesome as the fear you deserve.
12 Teach us to realize the brevity of life,
so that we may grow in wisdom.
13 O LORD, come back to us!
How long will you delay?
Take pity on your servants!
14 Satisfy us each morning with your unfailing love,
so we may sing for joy to the end of our lives.
15 Give us gladness in proportion to our former misery!
Replace the evil years with good.
16 Let us, your servants, see you work again;
let our children see your glory.
17 And may the Lord our God show us his approval
and make our efforts successful.
Yes, make our efforts successful!

Moses Blesses the People

DEUTERONOMY 33:1-29

This is the blessing that Moses, the man of God, gave to the people of Israel before his death:

2 "The LORD came from Mount Sinai
and dawned upon us* from Mount Seir;
he shone forth from Mount Paran
and came from Meribah-kadesh
with flaming fire at his right hand.*
3 Indeed, he loves his people;*
all his holy ones are in his hands.
They follow in his steps
and accept his teaching.
4 Moses gave us the LORD's instruction,
the special possession of the people of Israel.*
5 The LORD became king in Israel*—
when the leaders of the people assembled,
when the tribes of Israel gathered as one."

6 Moses said this about the tribe of Reuben:*

"Let the tribe of Reuben live and not die out,
though they are few in number."

7 Moses said this about the tribe of Judah:

"O LORD, hear the cry of Judah
and bring them together as a people.
Give them strength to defend their cause;
help them against their enemies!"

8 Moses said this about the tribe of Levi:

"O LORD, you have given your Thummim and Urim—the sacred lots—
to your faithful servants the Levites.*

Dt 33:2a As in Greek and Syriac versions; Hebrew reads *upon them.* **Dt 33:2b** Or *came from myriads of holy ones, from the south, from his mountain slopes.* The meaning of the Hebrew is uncertain. **Dt 33:3** As in Greek version; Hebrew reads *Indeed, lover of the peoples.* **Dt 33:4** Hebrew *of Jacob.* The names "Jacob" and "Israel" are often interchanged throughout the Old Testament, referring sometimes to the individual patriarch and sometimes to the nation. **Dt 33:5** Hebrew *in Jeshurun,* a term of endearment for Israel. **Dt 33:6** Hebrew lacks *Moses said this about the tribe of Reuben.* **Dt 33:8** As in Greek version; Hebrew lacks *the Levites.*

Ps 90:4 Moses reminds us that a thousand years are like a day to the Lord. God is not limited by time. It's easy to get discouraged when years pass and the world doesn't get better. We sometimes wonder if God is able to see the future. But don't assume that God has our limitations. God is completely unrestricted by time. Because he is eternal, we can depend on him.

Ps 90:8 God knows all our sins as if they were spread out before him, even the secret ones. We don't need to cover up our sins before him because we can talk openly and honestly with him. But while he knows all that terrible information about us, God still loves us and wants to forgive us. This should encourage us to come to him rather than frighten us into covering up our sin.

Ps 90:12 Realizing that life is short helps us use the little time we have more wisely and for eternal good. Take time to number your days by asking yourself these question: What do I want to see happen in my life before I die? What small step can I take toward that purpose today?

Ps 90:17 Because our days are numbered, we want our work to count, to be effective and productive. We desire to see God's eternal plan revealed now and for our work to reflect his permanence. If we feel dissatisfied with this life and all its imperfections, we must remember that our desire to see our work established is placed there by God (see the note on Eccl 3:11, p. 675). But our desire can only be satisfied in eternity. Until then we must apply ourselves to loving and serving God.

Deut 33:6-25 Note the difference in the blessings God gave each tribe. To one he gave the best land, to another strength, to another safety. Too often we see someone with a particular blessing and think that God must love that person more than others. Think rather that God draws out in all people their unique talents. All these gifts are needed to complete his plan. Don't be envious of the gifts others have. Instead, look for the gifts God has given you, and resolve to do the tasks he has uniquely qualified you to do.

You put them to the test at Massah
and struggled with them at the waters
of Meribah.
9 The Levites obeyed your word
and guarded your covenant.
They were more loyal to you
than to their own parents.
They ignored their relatives
and did not acknowledge their own children.
10 They teach your regulations to Jacob;
they give your instructions to Israel.
They present incense before you
and offer whole burnt offerings on the altar.
11 Bless the ministry of the Levites, O LORD,
and accept all the work of their hands.
Hit their enemies where it hurts the most;
strike down their foes so they never rise
again."

12 Moses said this about the tribe of Benjamin:

"The people of Benjamin are loved by the LORD
and live in safety beside him.
He surrounds them continuously
and preserves them from every harm."

13 Moses said this about the tribes of Joseph:

"May their land be blessed by the LORD
with the precious gift of dew from the heavens
and water from beneath the earth;
14 with the rich fruit that grows in the sun,
and the rich harvest produced each month;
15 with the finest crops of the ancient mountains,
and the abundance from the everlasting hills;
16 with the best gifts of the earth and its bounty,
and the favor of the one who appeared in the
burning bush.
May these blessings rest on Joseph's head,
crowning the brow of the prince among his
brothers.
17 Joseph has the majesty of a young bull;
he has the horns of a wild ox.
He will gore distant nations,
driving them to the ends of the earth.
This is my blessing for the multitudes of Ephraim
and the thousands of Manasseh."

18 Moses said this about the tribes of Zebulun and
Issachar*:

"May the people of Zebulun prosper in their
travels.
May the people of Issachar prosper at home
in their tents.
19 They summon the people to the mountain
to offer proper sacrifices there.
They benefit from the riches of the sea
and the hidden treasures in the sand."

20 Moses said this about the tribe of Gad:

"Blessed is the one who enlarges Gad's territory!
Gad is poised there like a lion
to tear off an arm or a head.
21 The people of Gad took the best land for
themselves;
a leader's share was assigned to them.
When the leaders of the people were assembled,
they carried out the LORD's justice
and obeyed his regulations for Israel."

22 Moses said this about the tribe of Dan:

"Dan is a lion's cub,
leaping out from Bashan."

23 Moses said this about the tribe of Naphtali:

"O Naphtali, you are rich in favor
and full of the LORD's blessings;
may you possess the west and the south."

24 Moses said this about the tribe of Asher:

"May Asher be blessed above other sons;
may he be esteemed by his brothers;
may he bathe his feet in olive oil.
25 May the bolts of your gates be of iron and bronze;
may you be secure all your days."
26 "There is no one like the God of Israel.*
He rides across the heavens to help you,
across the skies in majestic splendor.
27 The eternal God is your refuge,
and his everlasting arms are under you.
He drives out the enemy before you;
he cries out, 'Destroy them!'

Dt 33:18 Hebrew lacks *and Issachar.* **Dt 33:26** Hebrew *of Jeshurun,* a term of endearment for Israel.

Deut 33:20-21 The people of the tribe of Gad received the best of the new land because they obeyed God by punishing Israel's wicked enemies. Punishment is unpleasant for both the giver and the receiver, but it is a necessary part of growth. If you are in a position that sometimes requires you to correct others, don't hold back from fulfilling your task. Understand that realistic discipline is important to character development. Always strive to be both just and merciful, keeping in mind the best interests of the person who must receive the punishment.

Deut 33:24 Bathing the feet in oil was a sign of prosperity.

Deut 33:27 Moses' song declares that God is our refuge, our only true security. How often we entrust our lives to other things—perhaps money, career, a noble cause, or a lifelong dream. But our only true refuge is the eternal God, who always holds out his arms to catch us when the shaky supports that we trust collapse and we fall. No storm can destroy us when we take refuge in him. Those without God, however, must forever be cautious. One mistake may wipe them out. Living for God in this world may look like risky business. But it is the godless who are on shaky ground. Because God is our refuge, we can dare to be bold.

▸ **DEUTERONOMY 33:1-29** ***(cont.)***

28 So Israel will live in safety,
prosperous Jacob in security,
in a land of grain and new wine,
while the heavens drop down dew.
29 How blessed you are, O Israel!
Who else is like you, a people saved
by the LORD?
He is your protecting shield
and your triumphant sword!
Your enemies will cringe before you,
and you will stomp on their backs!"

The Death of Moses

DEUTERONOMY 34:1-12

Then Moses went up to Mount Nebo from the plains of
Moab and climbed Pisgah Peak, which is across from
Jericho. And the LORD showed him the whole land,
from Gilead as far as Dan; 2all the land of Naphtali; the
land of Ephraim and Manasseh; all the land of Judah,
extending to the Mediterranean Sea*; 3the Negev; the
Jordan Valley with Jericho—the city of palms—as far as
Zoar. 4Then the LORD said to Moses, "This is the land I
promised on oath to Abraham, Isaac, and Jacob when
I said, 'I will give it to your descendants.' I have now
allowed you to see it with your own eyes, but you will
not enter the land."

5So Moses, the servant of the LORD, died there in
the land of Moab, just as the LORD had said. 6The
LORD buried him* in a valley near Beth-peor in Moab,
but to this day no one knows the exact place. 7Moses
was 120 years old when he died, yet his eyesight was
clear, and he was as strong as ever. 8The people of Israel
mourned for Moses on the plains of Moab for thirty
days, until the customary period of mourning was over.

9Now Joshua son of Nun was full of the spirit of
wisdom, for Moses had laid his hands on him. So the
people of Israel obeyed him, doing just as the LORD
had commanded Moses.

10There has never been another prophet in Israel
like Moses, whom the LORD knew face to face. 11The
LORD sent him to perform all the miraculous signs
and wonders in the land of Egypt against Pharaoh,
and all his servants, and his entire land. 12With mighty
power, Moses performed terrifying acts in the sight
of all Israel.

Dt 34:2 Hebrew *the western sea.* **Dt 34:6** Hebrew *He buried him;* Samaritan Pentateuch and some Greek manuscripts read *They buried him.*

Moses dies

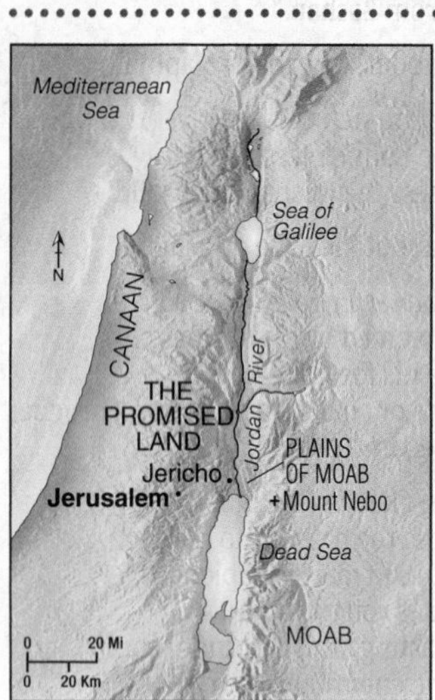

◀ ***THE DEATH OF MOSES***
Just before Moses died, he climbed Mount Nebo. Although he could not enter the Promised Land, God showed him its beauty from Mount Nebo's peak.

Deut 34:4, 10 Moses was the only person who ever spoke with God face to face (Exod 33:11; Num 12:8). He was called Israel's greatest prophet. Yet even this great man was not allowed to enter the Promised Land because he had disobeyed God (Num 20:12). No matter how good we are or how much we've done for God, we sometimes disobey him. The result of our disobedience is that we will be disciplined. God disciplined Moses severely but still called him his friend. When you experience the sting of God's discipline, respond as Moses did. Don't turn away in anger, embarrassment, or resentment. Instead, turn toward God with love, openness, and a desire to do better.

Deut 34:10-12 Moses, the man who did not want to be sent to Egypt because he was "not very good with words" (Exod 4:10), delivered the three addresses to Israel that make up the book of Deuteronomy. God gave him the power to develop from a stuttering shepherd into a national leader and powerful orator. His courage, humility, and wisdom molded the Hebrew slaves into a nation. But Moses was one person who did not let success go to his head. In the end, God was still Moses' best friend. His love, respect, and awe for God had grown daily throughout his life. Moses knew that it was not any greatness in himself that made him successful; it was the greatness of the all-powerful God in whom he trusted. There were many great and powerful prophets during the time of the kings, but it would be more than a thousand years before one greater than Moses would appear—Jesus.

Then Moses went up to Mount Nebo from the plains of Moab and climbed Pisgah Peak, which is across from Jericho. And the LORD showed him the whole land, from Gilead as far as Dan; all the land of Naphtali; the land of Ephraim and Manasseh; all the land of Judah, extending to the Mediterranean Sea; the Negev; the Jordan Valley with Jericho—the city of palms—as far as Zoar. Then the LORD said to Moses, "This is the land I promised on oath to Abraham, Isaac, and Jacob when I said, 'I will give it to your descendants.' I have now allowed you to see it with your own eyes, but you will not enter the land."

Deuteronomy 34:1-4

Possessing the Land

GOD BROUGHT HIS PEOPLE to the edge of the land he had promised to their ancestors, and Moses handed over leadership of the nation to Joshua. After 40 years of wandering in the wilderness, finally the people of God were ready to realize the promise of living in the land of Canaan.

Joshua began by reminding the people that they needed to serve God and depend on him fully in order to succeed in possessing the land, and they agreed. Things started out gloriously, with a miraculous entry into the land through the Jordan River and a victory over the city of Jericho that was clearly the result of God's power. But it didn't take long for Israel to find out that they were completely dependent on God in their conquest of the Promised Land. An Israelite man named Achan kept some things that were supposed to be devoted to God, and as a result Israel was routed in their battle with Ai. Israel would not succeed until they returned to following God and depending on him fully.

Joshua's strong leadership kept the nation focused on God, and they were indeed successful in taking over the Promised Land and distributing the land among the twelve tribes. God did not drive out all of the inhabitants of the land under Joshua, leaving some of the people behind to be driven out by individual tribes as they grew into the land they had been given. But the people's devotion to God didn't outlast

1450 BC | 1400 BC | 1350 BC | 1300 BC | 1250 BC

MESOPOTAMIA

LATE BRONZE AGE (1500–1200 BC)

ISRAEL

TIME OF THE JUDGES (1376–1050 BC

Israel's conquest of Canaan (1406–1376 BC)

- ***1446 BC*** *The Exodus*
- ***1406 BC*** *Moses dies*
- ***1376 BC*** *Joshua dies*

EGYPT

DYNASTY 18 (1550–1295 BC)

DYNASTY 19 (1295–1186 BC)

NEW KINGDOM/DYNASTIES 18–20 (1550–1069 BC)

BOOKS

- JOSHUA
- JUDGES
- RUTH
- 1 SAMUEL

DATES

FROM:
1406 BC
TO:
1050 BC

THEMES

- Obedience
- Rebellion
- Repentance
- Deliverance
- Leadership

Joshua's leadership. After his death many tribes simply gave up trying to conquer the land, or they tried to defeat the Canaanites in their own strength rather than God's.

God continued to be faithful to his people despite their constant failings. He raised up leaders (judges) who would rescue Israel from their oppressors, but almost as soon as they were rescued the people would again forget about the Lord and turn toward selfish and destructive living. They followed the gods of the surrounding nations and ignored the commands of God that they had promised to keep.

But there were some who clung to God and called the people back to him, either through their words or their silent example. Ehud, Deborah, Boaz, Ruth, and Samuel are a few of those people who served as shining lights in the midst of this dark time in Israel's history. Ultimately, God was faithful to his people and gave them possession of the land he had promised to Abraham, Isaac, and Jacob. But the fractured and disobedient nation needed to be brought together by focusing on God. They looked forward to having a king, thinking that would solve their problems.

Joshua Commanding the Sun to Stand Still upon Gibeon, by John Martin.

1200 BC — 1150 BC — 1100 BC — 1050 BC — 1000 BC — 950 BC

- IRON AGE (1200–500 BC)
- UNITED MONARCHY (1050–931 BC)
- about **1200 BC** *The Philistines arrive in Canaan*
- about **1100 BC** *The events of Ruth*
- Eli as priest (1100~1070 BC)
- Samuel's ministry (1075~1040 BC)
- Saul (1050–1011 BC)
- David (1011–971 BC)
- Solomon (971–931 BC)
- DYNASTY 20 (1186–1069 BC)
- DYNASTY 21 (1069–945 BC)
- THIRD INTERMEDIATE PERIOD (1069–664 BC)

PEOPLE & CULTURE

■ **Canaan.** God had promised Abraham, Isaac, and Jacob that their descendants would dwell in the land of Canaan and worship him there, but there were many powerful nations living in the land when Joshua finally led the people of Israel to take possession of it. The Ammonites, Perizzites, Jebusites, Hittites, and Philistines were just a few of the nations that would stand in the way of Israel as they struggled to settle in the land, but God was able to provide victory for his people even though they were not strong enough on their own. The Canaanite nations worshiped other gods, and over time influenced the people of Israel to worship other gods as well.

■ **Tribal Confederation.** Israel was always separated into tribes, but after the military conquest under Joshua their unity was even more fractured than before. The independent tribes were sent to the land that had been assigned to them to take possession of it and drive out the remaining Canaanites, but many of them were satisfied to live with the surrounding nations, or even to move somewhere else that was easier to conquer. The unity among these twelve tribes was so loose that on more than one occasion they went to war against one another.

■ **Joshua.** Joshua was one of only two adults from the first generation of Israelites to enter the Promised Land. He was Moses' close companion and successor, and he led the nation in their military conquest of the land. Joshua reminded the people that they needed to rely on God and obey him in order to take possession of the land. His strong leadership helped keep the nation together and made it clear that God had given this land to his people, just as he had promised generations earlier.

■ **A Series of Judges.** God raised up a series of judges to lead and rescue his people, who continually rebelled against God and followed after the practices of the Canaanites. These men, along with one woman, provided military leadership as well as spiritual renewal for Israel. God empowered them to drive out the oppressors and to call the people of Israel back to worshiping the Lord. Many of these leaders were flawed, and some of them even led Israel away from God after their initial deliverance, but they were God's chosen people to rescue his people and remind them of his power.

■ **Ruth and Boaz.** Ruth was a Moabite woman who married an Israelite from the tribe of Judah, but was widowed at a young age. Boaz was an influential man in Judah who clearly followed God and his law in spite of the prevailing culture of his day. When Ruth accompanied her mother-in-law back to Judah, she met Boaz and they married. They would become the great-grandparents of David, Israel's greatest king. Their story shines a bright light in this dark period and looks forward to better days when Israel would be unified and following God.

■ **Samuel.** Samuel was the last and greatest judge. He was also the first great prophet of the nation of Israel. As the miracle child of a barren woman, he was dedicated to God's service from birth. He became a great leader in Israel and was chosen by God to help the nation navigate the transition from a tribal confederation to a unified kingdom.

BOOKS IN THIS SECTION

JOSHUA

AUTHOR: Unknown. Some parts may have been written by Joshua or Phinehas, the high priest.

AUDIENCE: The people of Israel

PURPOSE: To give the history of Israel's conquest of the Promised Land

SETTING: Canaan, also called the Promised Land, which occupied the same general geographical territory of modern-day Israel

SPECIAL FEATURES: Out of over a million people, Joshua and Caleb were the only two adults who left Egypt and entered the Promised Land.

JUDGES

AUTHOR: Unknown. Possibly Samuel.

AUDIENCE: The people of Israel

PURPOSE: To show that God's judgment against sin is certain, and his forgiveness of sin and restoration to relationship are just as certain for those who repent

SETTING: The land of Canaan

SPECIAL FEATURES: Records Israel's first civil war

RUTH

AUTHOR: Unknown

AUDIENCE: The people of Israel

PURPOSE: To show how three people remained strong in character and true to God even when the society around them was collapsing

SETTING: A dark time in Israel's history when people lived to please themselves, not God (Judg 17:6)

For book information on **1 SAMUEL**, see the introduction to the United Monarchy, p. 430.

MEGATHEMES

■ **Success.** God gave success to the Israelites when they obeyed his master plan, not when they followed their own desires. Victory came when they trusted in him rather than in their military power, money, muscle, or mental capacity. God's work done in God's way will bring his success, but we must adjust our minds to God's way of thinking in order to pursue his standard for success rather than the world's.

■ **Leadership.** Excellent leaders are confident in God's strength, courageous in the face of opposition, and willing to seek God's advice. God's instructions to Israel extended to every aspect of their lives, and his guidance was followed by Israel's greatest leaders. Strong leaders are led by God, who guides us by his Word. By staying in touch with God through the Bible and prayer, we will have the needed wisdom to meet the great challenges of life.

■ **Compromise and Decay.** Again and again the people of Israel faced decline and failure because they compromised their spiritual and religious life. Everyone did what was right in their own eyes, and that inevitably led them farther and farther from God. Idol worship and man-made religion resulted, leading the people to completely abandon their faith in God. We can expect the same result if we allow ourselves to compromise our faith in God to be more like the people around us who don't know him. We must keep our eyes on Christ and allow him to have the first claim on our lives and all our desires.

■ **Defeat and Oppression.** God used evil oppressors to punish the Israelites for their sin, to bring them to the point of repentance, and to test their allegiance to him. Rebellion against God like this leads to disaster. God may use defeat to bring wandering hearts back to him. When all else is stripped away, we recognize the importance of serving only him.

Ruth in the Fields, by Hugues Merle

■ **Repentance and Deliverance.** God used evil oppressors to punish the Israelites for their sin, to bring them to the point of repentance, and to test their allegiance to him. Rebellion against God like this leads to disaster. God may use defeat to bring wandering hearts back to him. When all else is stripped away, we recognize the importance of serving only him.

■ **Faithfulness.** There are several stories of faithfulness to God in the midst of this dark time. Ruth, Naomi, and Boaz were found faithful to God, as was Samuel. One constant throughout Israel's history is that God is faithful to his people and his promises. When people are guided by faithfulness toward God, it reveals itself through loyalty, love, and refusal to give in to the values of the world. To have this kind of faithfulness in our lives, we must imitate God's faithfulness to us in our relationships with others and in our relationship with him.

MAP ▶

1 Acacia This section begins with the Israelites camping at Acacia. The Israelites under Joshua were ready to enter and conquer Canaan. But before the nation moved out, Joshua received instructions from God (Josh 1:1-18).

2 Jordan River The nation needed to cross this river, which was swollen from spring rains. The priests carried the Ark into the Jordan River, the water stopped flowing, and the entire nation crossed on dry ground into the Promised Land (Josh 2:1–4:24).

3 Gilgal After crossing the Jordan River, the Israelites camped at Gilgal, where they renewed their commitment to God and celebrated the Passover. As Joshua made plans for the attack on Jericho, an angel appeared to him (Josh 5:1-15).

4 Jericho The walled city of Jericho seemed a formidable enemy. But when Joshua followed God's plans, the great walls were no obstacle. The city was conquered with only the obedient marching of the people (Josh 6:1-27). Later, Moab's King Eglon conquered much of Israel—including the city of Jericho—and forced the people to pay unreasonable taxes. But Ehud killed the Moabite king by trickery and escaped, only to return with an army that chased out the Moabites and freed Israel from its oppressors (Judg 3:12-31).

5 Ai Victory was contingent on obedience to God. That is why the disobedience of one man, Achan, brought defeat to the entire nation in the first battle against Ai. But once the sin was recognized and punished, God told Joshua to take heart and try Ai once again. This time the city was taken (Josh 7:1–8:29).

6 Mount Ebal and Mount Gerizim After the defeat of Ai, Joshua built an altar at Mount Ebal. Then the people divided themselves, half at the foot of Mount Ebal, half at the foot of Mount Gerizim. The priests stood between the mountains holding the Ark of the Covenant as Joshua read God's law to all the people (Josh 8:30–35).

7 Gibeon Israel's leaders were tricked into making a peace treaty with the city of Gibeon. The leaders made the agreement without consulting God. The trick was soon discovered, but because the treaty had been made, Israel could not go back on its word. As a result, the Gibeonites saved their own lives, but they were forced to become Israel's slaves (Josh 9:1-27).

8 Hazor Up north in Hazor, King Jabin mobilized the kings of the surrounding cities to unite and crush Israel. But God gave Joshua and Israel victory (Josh 11:1-23). Later, another King Jabin of Hazor conquered Israel and oppressed the people for 20 years. Together Deborah and Barak led Israel's army into battle against Jabin's forces in the land between Mount Tabor and the Kishon River and conquered them (Judg 4:1–5:31).

9 Shiloh After the armies of Canaan were conquered, Israel gathered at Shiloh to set up the Tabernacle (Josh 18:1), where it stayed throughout the period of the judges. This is where Samuel served God faithfully, and God blessed him as he grew (1 Sam 2:12–3:21).

10 Shechem Before Joshua died he called the entire nation together at Shechem to remind them that it was God who had given them their land and that only with God's help could they keep it. The people vowed to follow God. As long as Joshua was alive, the land was at rest from war and trouble (Josh 24:1-33).

11 Hill of Moreh Gideon was chosen by God to deliver Israel from the oppression of the Midianites. Filled with the Spirit of God, he attacked the vast army of Midian, which was camped near the Hill of Moreh. With just a handful of men he sent the enemy running away in confusion (Judg 6:1–7:25).

12 Ammon Again Israel turned completely from God; so God turned from them. But when the Ammonites mobilized their army to attack, Israel threw away her idols and called upon God again. Jephthah, a prostitute's son who had been run out of Israel, was asked to return and lead Israel's forces against the enemy. After defeating the Ammonites, Jephthah became involved in a war with the tribe of Ephraim over a misunderstanding (Judg 10:1–12:15).

13 Timnah Samson fell in love with a Philistine girl in Timnah and asked to marry her. Before the wedding, Samson held a party for some men in the city, using a riddle to place a bet with them. The men, however, forced Samson's fiancée into giving the answer. Furious at being tricked, Samson paid his bet with the lives of 30 Philistines who lived in the nearby city of Ashkelon (Judg 13:1–14:20).

14 Gaza After being tricked by Delilah, Samson was blinded and led captive to a prison in Gaza. There the Philistines held a great festival to celebrate Samson's imprisonment and to humiliate him before the crowds. When he was brought out as the entertainment, he literally brought down the house when he pushed on the main pillars of the banquet hall and killed the thousands trapped inside. The prophecy that he would begin to free Israel from the Philistines had come true (Judg 16:21-31).

15 Dan The tribe of Dan migrated north in order to find new territory. They came upon the city of Laish and slaughtered the unarmed and innocent citizens, renaming the conquered city Dan. Micah's idols were then set up in the city and became the focal point of the tribe's worship for many years (Judg 18:1-31).

16 Gibeah The extent to which many people had fallen away from God became clear in Gibeah. A man and his concubine were traveling and stopped for the night in Gibeah. But some people in the city demanded that the man come out to have sexual relations with them. Instead, the man and his host pushed the concubine out the door. She was raped and abused all night. When the man found her lifeless body the next morning, he cut it into 12 pieces and sent the parts to each tribe. This tragic event showed that the nation had sunk to its lowest level (Judg 19:1-30).

17 Moab Naomi moved to Moab with her sons during a famine in Israel (Ruth 1:1-2), and there one of her sons married a Moabite girl name Ruth. After Naomi's sons died, Ruth followed her mother-in-law to Israel.

18 Bethlehem Ruth and Naomi went back to Naomi's home in Israel, Bethlehem (Ruth 1:6-22). There Ruth met and married Boaz.

19 Ramah Samuel was born in Ramah. Before his birth, Samuel's mother, Hannah, made a promise to God that she would dedicate her son to serve God alongside the priests in the Tabernacle at Shiloh (1 Sam 1:1–2:11).

20 Ebenezer Israel was constantly at odds with the Philistines, and another battle was brewing. Hophni and Phinehas brought the Ark of the Covenant from Shiloh to the battlefield, believing that its mere presence would bring the Israelites victory. The Israelites were defeated by the Philistines at Ebenezer, and the Ark was captured. However, the Philistines soon found out that the Ark was not quite the great battle trophy they had expected, for God sent plagues upon every Philistine city into which the Ark was brought. Finally, the Philistines sent it back to Kiriath-jearim in Israel (1 Sam 4:1–7:1).

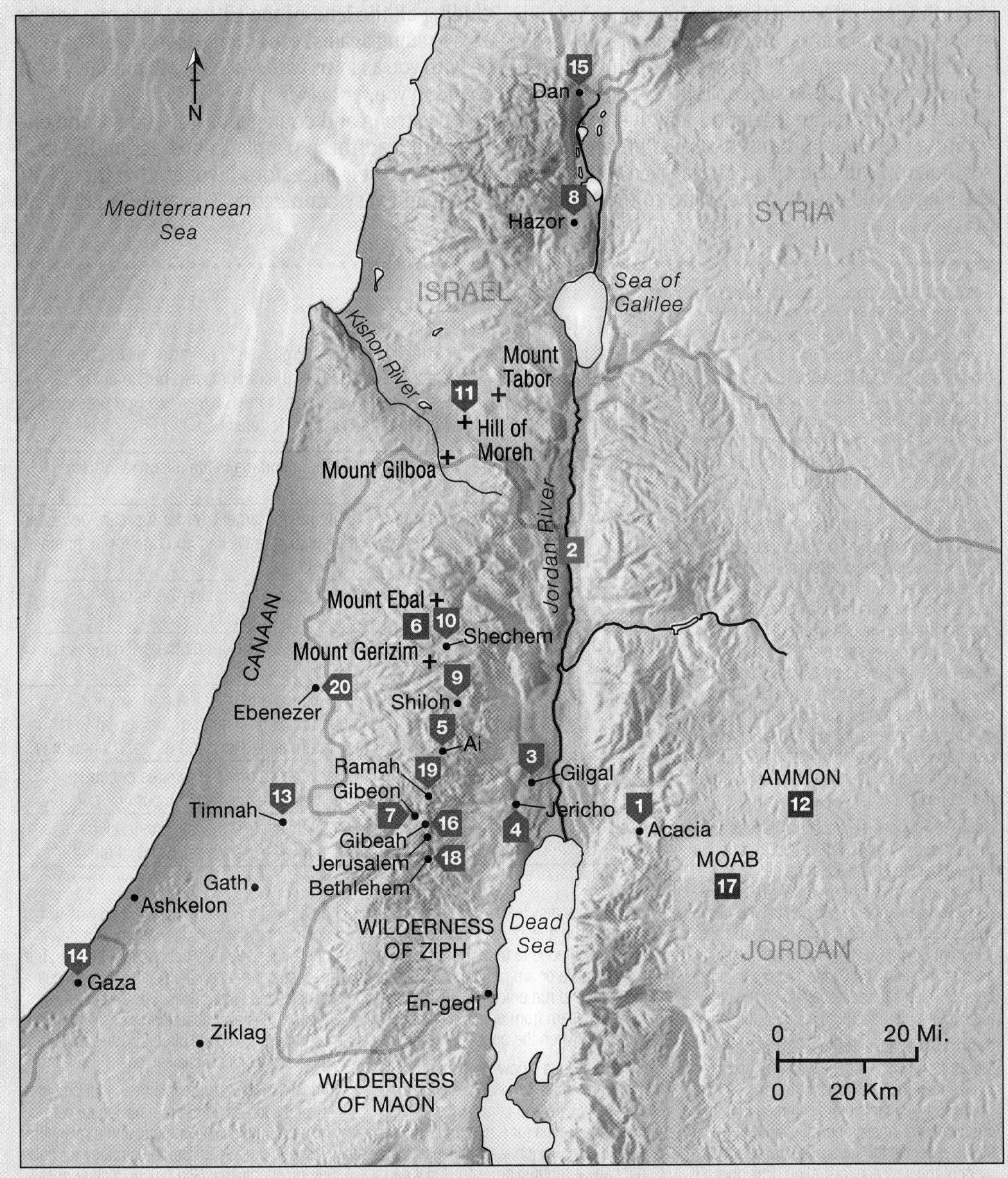

A. Israel Enters the Promised Land

After wandering for 40 years in the wilderness, a new generation is ready to enter Canaan. But first God prepares both Joshua and the nation by teaching them the importance of courageous and consistent faith. The nation then miraculously crosses the Jordan River to begin the long-awaited conquest of the Promised Land. Like Joshua, we, too, need faith to begin and continue living the Christian life.

1. JOSHUA LEADS THE NATION

Joshua's leadership showed the people that they needed to obey God and put their trust in him in order to take possession of the land he had promised them.

The LORD's Charge to Joshua

JOSHUA 1:1-9

After the death of Moses the LORD's servant, the LORD spoke to Joshua son of Nun, Moses' assistant. He said, 2"Moses my servant is dead. Therefore, the time has come for you to lead these people, the Israelites, across the Jordan River into the land I am giving them. 3I promise you what I promised Moses: 'Wherever you set foot, you will be on land I have given you—4from the Negev wilderness in the south to the Lebanon mountains in the north, from the Euphrates River in the east to the Mediterranean Sea* in the west, including all the land of the Hittites.' 5No one will be able to stand against you as long as you live. For I will be with you as I was with Moses. I will not fail you or abandon you.

6"Be strong and courageous, for you are the one who will lead these people to possess all the land I swore to their ancestors I would give them. 7Be strong and very courageous. Be careful to obey all

Jo 1:4 Hebrew *the Great Sea.*

Josh 1:1 As the book of Joshua opens, the Israelites are camped along the east bank of the Jordan River at the very edge of the Promised Land, and they are completing the mourning period for Moses, who has just died (Deut 34:7-8). The Israelites had an opportunity to enter the Promised Land 39 years earlier (after spending a year at Mount Sinai receiving God's law), but they failed to trust God to give them victory. As a result, God did not allow them to enter the land but made them wander in the wilderness until the disobedient generation had died out.

During their wilderness wanderings, the Israelites obeyed God's laws. They also taught the new generation to obey God's laws so that they might enter the Promised Land (Canaan). As the children grew, they were often reminded that faith and obedience to God brought victory, while unbelief and disobedience brought tragedy. When the last of the older generation had died and the new generation had become adults, the Israelites prepared to make their long-awaited claim on the Promised Land.

Josh 1:1-5 Joshua succeeded Moses as Israel's leader. What qualifications did he have to become the leader of a nation? (1) God appointed him (Num 27:18-23). (2) He was one of only two adults who had witnessed the Egyptian plagues and the exodus from Egypt. (3) He was Moses' personal aide for 40 years. (4) Of the 12 scouts, only he and Caleb showed complete confidence that God would help them conquer the land.

Josh 1:2 Because Joshua had assisted Moses for many years, he was well prepared to take over the leadership of the nation. Changes in leadership are common in many organizations. At such times, a smooth transition is essential for the successful establishment of the new administration. This doesn't happen unless new leaders are trained. If you are currently in a leadership position, begin preparing someone to take your place. Then, when you leave or are promoted, operations can continue to run efficiently. If you want to be a leader, learn from others so that you will be prepared when the opportunity comes.

Josh 1:5 Joshua's new job consisted of leading more than 2 million people into a strange new land and conquering it. What a challenge—even for a man of Joshua's caliber! Every new job is a challenge. Without God it can be frightening; with God it can be a great adventure. Just as God was with Joshua, he is with us as we face our new challenges. We may not conquer nations, but every day we face tough situations, difficult people, and temptations. But God promises that he will never abandon us or fail to help us. By asking God to direct us, we can conquer many of life's challenges.

Josh 1:6-8 Many people think that prosperity and success come from having power, influential personal contacts, and a relentless desire to get ahead. But the strategy for gaining prosperity that God taught Joshua goes

TAKE THE LAND

God told Joshua to lead the Israelites into the Promised Land (also called Canaan) and conquer it. This was not an act of imperialism or aggression but an act of judgment. Here are some of the earlier passages in the Bible where God promised to give this land to the Israelites and the reasons for doing so.

Gen 12:1-3	God promised to bless Abraham and make his descendants into a great nation
Gen 15:16	God would choose the right time for Israel to enter Canaan, because the nations living there then would be wicked and ripe for judgment (their sin would run its course)
Gen 17:7-8	God promised to give all the land of Canaan to Abraham's descendants
Exod 33:1-3	God promised to help the Israelites drive out all the evil nations from Canaan
Deut 4:5-8	The Israelites were to be an example of right living, their wisdom amazing the surrounding nations and pointing to their great God; this would not work if they intermingled with the wicked Canaanites
Deut 7:1-5	The Israelites were to utterly wipe out the Canaanites because of their wickedness and because of Israel's call to purity
Deut 12:2	The Israelites were to completely destroy the Canaanite altars so nothing would tempt them away from worshiping God alone

the instructions Moses gave you. Do not deviate from
them, turning either to the right or to the left. Then
you will be successful in everything you do. 8 Study
this Book of Instruction continually. Meditate on it
day and night so you will be sure to obey everything
written in it. Only then will you prosper and succeed
in all you do. 9 This is my command—be strong and
courageous! Do not be afraid or discouraged. For the
LORD your God is with you wherever you go."

Joshua's Charge to the Israelites

JOSHUA 1:10-18

Joshua then commanded the officers of Israel, 11 "Go
through the camp and tell the people to get their provisions ready. In three days you will cross the Jordan
River and take possession of the land the LORD your
God is giving you."
12 Then Joshua called together the tribes of Reuben,
Gad, and the half-tribe of Manasseh. He told them,
13 "Remember what Moses, the servant of the LORD,
commanded you: 'The LORD your God is giving you a
place of rest. He has given you this land.' 14 Your wives,
children, and livestock may remain here in the land
Moses assigned to you on the east side of the Jordan
River. But your strong warriors, fully armed, must lead
the other tribes across the Jordan to help them conquer their territory. Stay with them 15 until the LORD
gives them rest, as he has given you rest, and until they,
too, possess the land the LORD your God is giving them.
Only then may you return and settle here on the east
side of the Jordan River in the land that Moses, the
servant of the LORD, assigned to you."
16 They answered Joshua, "We will do whatever you
command us, and we will go wherever you send us.
17 We will obey you just as we obeyed Moses. And may
the LORD your God be with you as he was with Moses.
18 Anyone who rebels against your orders and does not
obey your words and everything you command will be
put to death. So be strong and courageous!"

Rahab Protects the Spies

JOSHUA 2:1-24

Then Joshua secretly sent out two spies from the
Israelite camp at Acacia Grove.* He instructed them,
"Scout out the land on the other side of the Jordan
River, especially around Jericho." So the two men set
out and came to the house of a prostitute named Ra-
hab and stayed there that night.
2 But someone told the king of Jericho, "Some
Israelites have come here tonight to spy out the land."

Jo 2:1 Hebrew *Shittim.*

against such criteria. He said that to succeed Joshua must (1) be strong and courageous because the task ahead would not be easy, (2) obey God's law, and (3) constantly read and study the Book of Instruction—God's Word. To be successful, follow God's words to Joshua. You may not succeed by the world's standards, but you will be a success in God's eyes—and his opinion is the most important.

Josh 1:12-15 During the previous year, the tribes of Reuben and Gad and the half-tribe of Manasseh had asked Moses if they could settle just east of the Promised Land. The area was excellent pastureland for their large flocks. Moses agreed to give them the land on one condition—that they help their fellow tribes enter and conquer the Promised Land. Only after the land was conquered could they return to their homes. Now it was time for these three tribes to live up to their agreement.

Josh 1:13 God was giving the people rest. This was wonderful news to these people who had been on the move for their entire lives. The people who had no land would be given a land of their own, and they would be able to settle and to "rest."

Josh 1:16 If everyone had tried to conquer the Promised Land their own way, chaos would have ensued. In order to complete the enormous task of conquering the land, everyone had to agree to Joshua's plan and be willing to support and obey him. If we are going to complete the tasks God has given us, we must fully agree to his plan, pledge ourselves to obey it, and put his principles into action. Agreeing to God's plan means both knowing what the plan is (as found in the Bible) and carrying it out daily.

Josh 1:18 When God commissioned Joshua, he was told three times to be strong and courageous (see Josh 1:6-7, 9). Here, Joshua was given the same kind of encouragement from the people. Apparently, he took God's message to heart and found the strength and courage he needed in his relationship with God. The next time you are afraid to do what you know is right, remember that strength and courage are readily available from God.

Josh 2:1 Why did Joshua send the spies secretly? As far as he knew, he would be attacking a heavily fortified city using conventional warfare tactics. He needed strategic information about the city for the upcoming battle. But he also knew that this might draw criticism from the other leaders. After all, the last time spies were sent, the report they brought back caused disastrous problems (see Num 13:1–14:4). While he did not want to move ahead without information, he also did not want to cause the people to stumble and question his wisdom and ability to lead the nation.

Josh 2:1 Why would the spies stop at the house of Rahab, a prostitute? (1) It was a good place to gather information and have no questions asked in return. (2) Rahab's house was in an ideal location for a quick escape because it was built into the city wall (Josh 2:15). (3) God directed the spies to Rahab's house because he knew her heart was open to him and that she would be instrumental in the Israelite victory over Jericho. God often uses people with simple faith to accomplish his great purposes, no matter what kind of past they have had or how insignificant they seem to be. Rahab didn't allow her past to keep her from the new role God had for her.

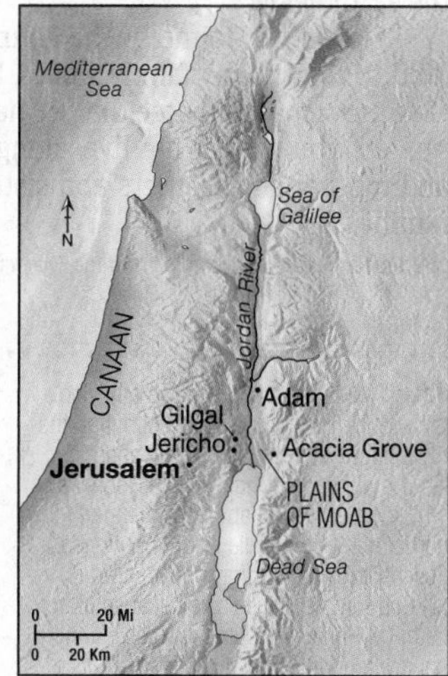

***SPY MISSION TO JERICHO** Two spies left the Israelite camp at Acacia Grove, crossed the Jordan River, and slipped into Jericho. Jericho was the first major city the Israelites set out to conquer. The city was built around an oasis in the midst of a hot and desolate valley 840 feet below sea level.*

▸ **JOSHUA 2:1-24 *(cont.)***

3So the king of Jericho sent orders to Rahab: "Bring out the men who have come into your house, for they have come here to spy out the whole land."

4Rahab had hidden the two men, but she replied, "Yes, the men were here earlier, but I didn't know where they were from. 5They left the town at dusk, as the gates were about to close. I don't know where they went. If you hurry, you can probably catch up with them." 6(Actually, she had taken them up to the roof and hidden them beneath bundles of flax she had laid out.) 7So the king's men went looking for the spies along the road leading to the shallow crossings of the Jordan River. And as soon as the king's men had left, the gate of Jericho was shut.

8Before the spies went to sleep that night, Rahab went up on the roof to talk with them. 9"I know the LORD has given you this land," she told them. "We are all afraid of you. Everyone in the land is living in terror. 10For we have heard how the LORD made a dry path for you through the Red Sea* when you left Egypt. And we know what you did to Sihon and Og, the two Amorite kings east of the Jordan River, whose people you completely destroyed.* 11No wonder our hearts have melted in fear! No one has the courage to fight after hearing such things. For the LORD your God is the supreme God of the heavens above and the earth below.

1406 BC

Joshua leads Israel into Canaan

12"Now swear to me by the LORD that you will be kind to me and my family since I have helped you. Give me some guarantee that 13when Jericho is conquered, you will let me live, along with my father and mother, my brothers and sisters, and all their families."

14"We offer our own lives as a guarantee for your safety," the men agreed. "If you don't betray us, we will keep our promise and be kind to you when the LORD gives us the land."

15Then, since Rahab's house was built into the town wall, she let them down by a rope through the window. 16"Escape to the hill country," she told them. "Hide there for three days from the men searching for you. Then, when they have returned, you can go on your way."

17Before they left, the men told her, "We will be bound by the oath we have taken only if you follow these instructions. 18When we come into the land, you must leave this scarlet rope hanging from the window through which you let us down. And all your family members—your father, mother, brothers, and all your relatives—must be here inside the house. 19If they go out into the street and are killed, it will not be our fault. But if anyone lays a hand on people inside this house, we will accept the responsibility for their death. 20If you betray us, however, we are not bound by this oath in any way."

21"I accept your terms," she replied. And she sent them on their way, leaving the scarlet rope hanging from the window.

22The spies went up into the hill country and stayed there three days. The men who were chasing them searched everywhere along the road, but they finally returned without success.

23Then the two spies came down from the hill country, crossed the Jordan River, and reported to Joshua all that had happened to them. 24"The LORD has given us the whole land," they said, "for all the people in the land are terrified of us."

Jo 2:10a Hebrew *sea of reeds.* **Jo 2:10b** The Hebrew term used here refers to the complete consecration of things or people to the LORD, either by destroying them or by giving them as an offering.

Josh 2:4-5 Was Rahab justified in lying to save the lives of the spies? Although the Bible does not speak negatively about her lie, it is clear that lying is sin. In Hebrews 11:31, however, Rahab is commended for her faith in God. Her lie is not mentioned. Several explanations have been offered: (1) God forgave Rahab's lie because of her faith; (2) Rahab was simply deceiving the enemy, a normal and acceptable practice in wartime; (3) Rahab was not a Jew, so she could not be held responsible for keeping the moral standards set forth in God's law; (4) Rahab broke a lesser principle—telling the truth—to uphold a higher principle—protecting God's people.

There may have been another way to save the lives of the Israelite spies. But under the pressure of the moment, Rahab had to make a choice. Most of us will face dilemmas at one time or another. We may feel that there is no perfect solution to our problem. Fortunately, God does not demand that our judgment be perfect in all situations. He simply asks us to put our trust in him and to do the best we know how. Rahab did that and was commended for her faith.

Josh 2:6 Flax was harvested in the fields and piled high on the rooftops to dry. It was then made into yarn, which was used to make linen cloth. Flax grows to a height of three or four feet. Stacked on the roof, it made an excellent hiding place for the spies.

Josh 2:8-13 Many would assume that Rahab—a pagan, a Canaanite, and a prostitute—would never be interested in God. Yet Rahab was willing to risk everything she had for a God she barely knew. We must not gauge a person's interest in God based on background, lifestyle, or appearance. We should let nothing get in the way of our telling people the Good News.

Josh 2:11 Rahab recognized something that many of the Israelites did not—the God of heaven is not an ordinary god! He is all-powerful. The people of Jericho were afraid because they had heard the news of God's extraordinary power in defeating the armies across the Jordan River. Today we can worship this same powerful, miracle-working God. He is powerful enough to destroy mighty, wicked armies, as he did in Jericho. He is also powerful enough to save us from certain death, as he did with Rahab.

Josh 2:15 In Joshua's day it was common to build houses on city walls. Many cities had two walls about 12 to 15 feet apart. Houses were built on wooden logs laid across the tops of the two walls. Rahab may have lived in such a house with a window that looked out over the outside wall.

2. CROSSING THE JORDAN

When the Israelites finally entered the Promised Land, there was no question that God was with them. Joshua was careful to make sure that the people recognized this, and they constructed memorials so that they wouldn't forget.

The Israelites Cross the Jordan

JOSHUA 3:1-17

Early the next morning Joshua and all the Israelites left Acacia Grove* and arrived at the banks of the Jordan River, where they camped before crossing. [2]Three days later the Israelite officers went through the camp, [3]giving these instructions to the people: "When you see the Levitical priests carrying the Ark of the Covenant of the LORD your God, move out from your positions and follow them. [4]Since you have never traveled this way before, they will guide you. Stay about a half mile* behind them, keeping a clear distance between you and the Ark. Make sure you don't come any closer."

[5]Then Joshua told the people, "Purify yourselves, for tomorrow the LORD will do great wonders among you."

[6]In the morning Joshua said to the priests, "Lift up the Ark of the Covenant and lead the people across the river." And so they started out and went ahead of the people.

Jo 3:1 Hebrew *Shittim.* **Jo 3:4** Hebrew *about 2,000 cubits* [920 meters].

JOSHUA

One of the greatest challenges facing leaders is to replace themselves, training others to become leaders. One of the best tests of our leadership is our willingness and ability to train another for our position. • Moses made an excellent decision when he chose Joshua as his assistant. That choice was later confirmed by God himself when he instructed Moses to commission Joshua as his successor (Num 27:15-23). Joshua had played a key role in the exodus from Egypt. Introduced as the field general of Israel's army, he was the only person allowed to accompany Moses partway up the mountain when Moses received the law. Joshua and Caleb were the only 2 among the 12 scouts to bring back an encouraging report after being sent into the Promised Land the first time. Other references show him to have been Moses' constant shadow. His basic training was living with Moses—experiencing firsthand what it meant to lead God's people. This was modeling at its best! • Who is your Moses? Who is your Joshua? You are part of the chain of God's ongoing work in the world. You are modeling yourself after others, and others are patterning their lives after you. How important is God to those you want to be like? Do those who are watching you see God reflected in every area of your life? Ask God to lead you to a trustworthy Moses. Ask him to make you a good Joshua.

Strengths and accomplishments	• Moses' assistant and successor • One of only two scouts who trusted God to deliver the Promised Land to his people • Led the Israelites into their God-given homeland • Faithful to ask God's direction in the challenges he faced
Lessons from his life	• Effective leadership is often the product of good preparation and encouragement • The persons after whom we pattern ourselves will have a definite effect on us • A person committed to God provides the best model for us
Vital statistics	• Where: Egypt, the wilderness of Sinai, Canaan (the Promised Land) • Occupations: Special assistant to Moses, warrior, leader • Relative: Father: Nun. • Contemporaries: Moses, Caleb, Miriam, Aaron
Key verses	"So Moses did as the LORD commanded. He presented Joshua to Eleazar the priest and the whole community. Moses laid his hands on him and commissioned him to lead the people, just as the LORD had commanded through Moses" (Num 27:22-23).

Joshua is also mentioned in Exodus 17:9-14; 24:13; 32:17; 33:11; Numbers 11:28; 13–14; 26:65; 27:18-23; 32:11-28; 34:17; Deuteronomy 1:38; 3:21-28; 31:3-23; 34:9; the book of Joshua; Judges 2:6-9; 1 Kings 16:34.

Josh 3:2-4 The Ark of the Covenant was Israel's most sacred treasure. It was a symbol of God's presence and power. The Ark was a gold rectangular box with two cherubim (angels) facing each other on the lid. Inside the Ark were the tablets of the Ten Commandments Moses had received from God, a jar of manna (the bread God miraculously sent from heaven during the wilderness wanderings), and Aaron's staff (the symbol of the high priest's authority). According to God's law, only the Levites could carry the Ark. The Ark was constructed at the same time as the Tabernacle (Exod 37:1-9) and placed in the sanctuary's most sacred room.

Josh 3:5 Before entering the Promised Land, the Israelites were to perform a purification ceremony. This was often done before making a sacrifice or, as in this case, before witnessing a great act of God. God's law stated that a person could become unclean for many reasons—eating certain foods (Lev 11), giving birth (Lev 12), dealing with disease (Lev 13–14), touching a dead person (Num 19:11-22). God used these various outward signs of uncleanness to illustrate a person's inward uncleanness that comes as a result of sin. The purification ceremony pictured the importance of approaching God with a pure heart. Like the Israelites, we need God's forgiveness before we approach him.

▸ **JOSHUA 3:1-17** ***(cont.)***

7The LORD told Joshua, "Today I will begin to make
you a great leader in the eyes of all the Israelites. They
will know that I am with you, just as I was with Moses.
8Give this command to the priests who carry the Ark
of the Covenant: 'When you reach the banks of the
Jordan River, take a few steps into the river and stop
there.'"
9So Joshua told the Israelites, "Come and listen
to what the LORD your God says. 10Today you will
know that the living God is among you. He will surely
drive out the Canaanites, Hittites, Hivites, Perizzites,
Girgashites, Amorites, and Jebusites ahead of you.
11Look, the Ark of the Covenant, which belongs to
the Lord of the whole earth, will lead you across the
Jordan River! 12Now choose twelve men from the
tribes of Israel, one from each tribe. 13The priests
will carry the Ark of the LORD, the Lord of all the
earth. As soon as their feet touch the water, the flow
of water will be cut off upstream, and the river will
stand up like a wall."
14So the people left their camp to cross the Jordan,
and the priests who were carrying the Ark of the Covenant went ahead of them. 15It was the harvest season,
and the Jordan was overflowing its banks. But as soon
as the feet of the priests who were carrying the Ark
touched the water at the river's edge, 16the water above
that point began backing up a great distance away at
a town called Adam, which is near Zarethan. And the
water below that point flowed on to the Dead Sea*
until the riverbed was dry. Then all the people crossed
over near the town of Jericho.
17Meanwhile, the priests who were carrying the
Ark of the LORD's Covenant stood on dry ground in
the middle of the riverbed as the people passed by.
They waited there until the whole nation of Israel had
crossed the Jordan on dry ground.

Memorials to the Jordan Crossing

JOSHUA 4:1–5:1

When all the people had crossed the Jordan, the LORD
said to Joshua, 2"Now choose twelve men, one from
each tribe. 3Tell them, 'Take twelve stones from the
very place where the priests are standing in the middle
of the Jordan. Carry them out and pile them up at the
place where you will camp tonight.'"
4So Joshua called together the twelve men he had
chosen—one from each of the tribes of Israel. 5He
told them, "Go into the middle of the Jordan, in front
of the Ark of the LORD your God. Each of you must
pick up one stone and carry it out on your shoulder—
twelve stones in all, one for each of the twelve tribes of
Israel. 6We will use these stones to build a memorial.
In the future your children will ask you, 'What do
these stones mean?' 7Then you can tell them, 'They remind us that the Jordan River stopped flowing when
the Ark of the LORD's Covenant went across.' These
stones will stand as a memorial among the people of
Israel forever."
8So the men did as Joshua had commanded them.

Jo 3:16 Hebrew *the sea of the Arabah, the Salt Sea.*

Josh 3:9 Just before crossing over into the Promised Land, Joshua gathered the people to hear the words of the Lord. Their excitement was high. No doubt they wanted to rush on, but Joshua made them stop and listen. We live in a fast-paced age where everyone rushes just to keep up. It is easy to get caught up in our tasks, becoming too busy for what God says is most important—listening to his words. Before making your schedule, take time to focus on what God wants from all your activities. Knowing what God has said before you rush into your day can help you avoid foolish mistakes.

Josh 3:10 Why would God help the Israelites drive out these nations from their native land? God had punished Israel first for its disobedience. He then turned to the rest of the nations. Genesis 15:16 implies that the people of Canaan were wicked and deserved to be punished for their terrible sins. Israel was to be a vehicle for this punishment. More important was the fact that Israel, as a holy nation, could not live among such evil and idolatrous people. To do so would be to invite sin into their lives. The only way to prevent Israel from being infected by evil religions was to drive out those who practiced them. But Israel failed to drive everyone out as God had told them to do. It wasn't long before Israel—the nation God chose to be his holy people—began following the evil practices of the Canaanites.

Josh 3:13-14 The Israelites were eager to enter the Promised Land, conquer nations, and live peacefully. But first they had to cross the flood-level waters of the Jordan River. God gave them specific instructions: In order to cross, the priests had to step into the water. What if these priests had been afraid to take that first step? Often God provides no solution to our problems until we trust him and move ahead with what we know we should do. What are the rivers, or obstacles, in your life? In obedience to God, take that first step.

Josh 3:13-17 God had parted the waters of the Red Sea to let the people out of Egypt (Exod 14), and here he parted the Jordan River to let them enter Canaan. These miracles showed Israel that God keeps his promises. God's presence among his people and his faithfulness to them made the entire journey from Egypt to the Promised Land possible. He was with them at the end of their wanderings just as he had been with them in the beginning.

Josh 3:15-16 The Israelites crossed the Jordan River in the spring, when it was overflowing its banks. God chose the time when the river was at its highest to demonstrate his power—parting the waters so that the entire nation could cross on dry ground. Some say that God used a natural occurrence (such as a landslide) to stop the waters of the Jordan; others say he did it by a direct act. In either case, God showed his great power by working a miracle of timing and location to allow his people to cross the river on dry ground. This testimony of God's supernatural power served to build the Israelites' hope in God and to give them a great reputation among their enemies, who greatly outnumbered them.

Josh 4:1ff After the people safely crossed the river, what would be next? Conquering the land? Not yet. First, God directed them to build a memorial from 12 stones drawn from the river by 12 men, one from each tribe. This may seem like an insignificant step in their mission of conquering the land, but God did not want his people to plunge into their task unprepared. They were to focus on him and remember who was guiding them. As you are busy doing your God-given tasks, set aside quiet moments to build your own memorial to God's power. Too much activity may shift your focus away from God.

They took twelve stones from the middle of the Jordan River, one for each tribe, just as the LORD had told Joshua. They carried them to the place where they camped for the night and constructed the memorial there.

9Joshua also set up another pile of twelve stones in the middle of the Jordan, at the place where the priests who carried the Ark of the Covenant were standing. And they are there to this day.

10The priests who were carrying the Ark stood in the
middle of the river until all of the LORD's commands that Moses had given to Joshua were carried out. Meanwhile, the people hurried across the riverbed.
11And when everyone was safely on the other side, the priests crossed over with the Ark of the LORD as the people watched.

12The armed warriors from the tribes of Reuben, Gad, and the half-tribe of Manasseh led the Israelites
across the Jordan, just as Moses had directed. 13These
armed men—about 40,000 strong—were ready for battle, and the LORD was with them as they crossed over to the plains of Jericho.

14That day the LORD made Joshua a great leader in the eyes of all the Israelites, and for the rest of his life they revered him as much as they had revered Moses.

15The LORD had said to Joshua, 16"Command the
priests carrying the Ark of the Covenant* to come up out of the riverbed." 17So Joshua gave the com-
mand. 18As soon as the priests carrying the Ark of the LORD's Covenant came up out of the riverbed and their feet were on high ground, the water of the Jordan returned and overflowed its banks as before.

19The people crossed the Jordan on the tenth day of the first month.* Then they camped at Gilgal, just east of Jericho. 20It was there at Gilgal that Joshua piled up the twelve stones taken from the Jordan River.

21Then Joshua said to the Israelites, "In the future your children will ask, 'What do these stones mean?'
22Then you can tell them, 'This is where the Israelites crossed the Jordan on dry ground.' 23For the LORD
your God dried up the river right before your eyes, and he kept it dry until you were all across, just as he did at the Red Sea* when he dried it up until we had all crossed over. 24He did this so all the nations of the earth might know that the LORD's hand is powerful, and so you might fear the LORD your God forever."

Jo 4:16 Hebrew *Ark of the Testimony.* **Jo 4:19** This day in the ancient Hebrew lunar calendar occurred in late March, April, or early May. **Jo 4:23** Hebrew *sea of reeds.*

Josh 4:14 The Israelites revered Joshua for his role in leading them across the Jordan River. He, like Moses, would receive Israel's praises generation after generation. Although Israel was not a world power at that time, Joshua's reputation for handling his responsibilities God's way brought him greater glory than if he had been a hero in a "superpower" nation. Doing right is more important than doing well.

Josh 4:21-24 The memorial of 12 stones was to be a constant reminder of the day the Israelites crossed the Jordan River on dry ground. Their children would see the stones, hear the story, and learn about God. Do you have traditions—special dates or special places—to help your children learn about God's work in your life? Do you take time to tell them what God has done for you—forgiving and saving you, answering your prayers, supplying your needs? Retelling your story will help keep memories of God's faithfulness alive in your family.

The Jordan River

The Jordan River connects the Sea of Galilee to the Dead Sea, a distance of 65 miles; but the river snakes back and forth, taking a circuitous 135-mile path between these two bodies of water. As the eastern border of the Promised Land, the Jordan River played a significant role in several biblical events. The Israelites crossed through the Jordan upon entry into the Promised Land (Josh 3:14-17). The fords of the Jordan were the sites of conflict in the war of Jephthah and the men of Gilead against Ephraim (Judg 12:1-6). Elijah was translated to heaven in a whirlwind after having crossed the Jordan (2 Kgs 2:6-12). Naaman, the Syrian general, bathed in the Jordan at the command of the prophet Elisha and his leprosy was cured (2 Kgs 5:8-14). Elisha made an ax head float on the Jordan River (2 Kgs 6:1-7). And in the New Testament, John the Baptist used the Jordan River to baptize many people, including Jesus (Matt 3:13).

▸ **JOSHUA 4:1–5:1** ***(cont.)***

5:1 When all the Amorite kings west of the Jordan and
all the Canaanite kings who lived along the Mediterranean coast* heard how the LORD had dried up the Jordan River so the people of Israel could cross, they lost
heart and were paralyzed with fear because of them.

Israel Reestablishes Covenant Ceremonies

JOSHUA 5:2-12

At that time the LORD told Joshua, "Make flint knives
and circumcise this second generation of Israelites.*"
3 So Joshua made flint knives and circumcised the
entire male population of Israel at Gibeath-haaraloth.*
4 Joshua had to circumcise them because all the
men who were old enough to fight in battle when they
left Egypt had died in the wilderness. 5 Those who left
Egypt had all been circumcised, but none of those
born after the Exodus, during the years in the wilderness, had been circumcised. 6 The Israelites had traveled in the wilderness for forty years until all the men
who were old enough to fight in battle when they left
Egypt had died. For they had disobeyed the LORD, and
the LORD vowed he would not let them enter the land
he had sworn to give us—a land flowing with milk and
honey. 7 So Joshua circumcised their sons—those who
had grown up to take their fathers' places—for they
had not been circumcised on the way to the Promised
Land. 8 After all the males had been circumcised, they
rested in the camp until they were healed.
9 Then the LORD said to Joshua, "Today I have rolled
away the shame of your slavery in Egypt." So that place
has been called Gilgal* to this day.
10 While the Israelites were camped at Gilgal on the
plains of Jericho, they celebrated Passover on the evening of the fourteenth day of the first month.* 11 The
very next day they began to eat unleavened bread and
roasted grain harvested from the land. 12 No manna
appeared on the day they first ate from the crops of
the land, and it was never seen again. So from that
time on the Israelites ate from the crops of Canaan.

Jo 5:1 Hebrew *along the sea.* **Jo 5:2** Or *circumcise the Israelites a second time.* **Jo 5:3** *Gibeath-haaraloth* means "hill of foreskins." **Jo 5:9** *Gilgal* sounds like the Hebrew word *galal,* meaning "to roll." **Jo 5:10** This day in the ancient Hebrew lunar calendar occurred in late March, April, or early May.

B. Israel Begins Conquering the Promised Land

After crossing the Jordan River, the Israelites begin to conquer Canaan. Jericho is the first to fall. Then Israel suffers its first defeat because of one man's disobedience. After the people remove the sin from their community, they strike again—this time with success. Soon great kings attack from the north and south, but they are defeated because God is with Israel. Evil could not be tolerated in the Promised Land, nor can it be tolerated in our lives. We, like Israel, must ruthlessly remove sin from our lives before it takes control of us.

1. JOSHUA ATTACKS THE CENTER OF THE LAND

Jericho and Ai both served as valuable lessons to the people of Israel as they began to take possession of the land God had given them. When they trusted God and obeyed him completely, they were assured of victory. But disobedience and self-reliance were a recipe for defeat.

The LORD's Commander Confronts Joshua

JOSHUA 5:13-15

When Joshua was near the town of Jericho, he looked
up and saw a man standing in front of him with sword
in hand. Joshua went up to him and demanded, "Are
you friend or foe?"
14 "Neither one," he replied. "I am the commander
of the LORD's army."

Josh 5:1 The Amorites and Canaanites were the two major groups living in Canaan at the time of Israel's invasion. The Canaanites worshiped a variety of gods, but Baal was the most prominent. Canaanite culture was materialistic, and their religion was sensual. The Israelites continually turned to Baal after entering Canaan. The Amorite gods also infected Israel's worship and turned people away from worshiping the true God. Worshiping these false gods eventually brought about Israel's downfall.

Josh 5:1 The Israelites spent 39 years in the wilderness unnecessarily because they were terrified of the Canaanites. They underestimated God's ability. The Israelites' first attempt to enter the Promised Land had failed (Num 13–14). Here Israel saw that the Canaanites were terrified of their army. The Canaanites had heard about Israel's great victories through God (Josh 2:9-11), and they hoped that the Jordan River would slow Israel down or discourage them from entering Canaan. But news that the Israelites had crossed the Jordan on dry land caused any courage the Canaanites still had to melt away.

Don't underestimate God. If we are faithful to God, he will cause even great opposition to disappear. God can change the attitudes of those who oppose him.

Josh 5:2-3 The rite of circumcision marked Israel's position as God's covenant people. When God made the original covenant with Abraham, he required that each male be circumcised as a sign of cutting off the old life and beginning a new life with God (Gen 17:13). Other cultures at that time used circumcision as a sign of entry into adulthood, but only Israel used it as a sign of following God.

Josh 5:8-9 Located about two miles northeast of Jericho, Gilgal was Israel's base camp and their temporary center of government and worship during their invasion of Canaan. Here the people renewed their commitment to God and covenant with him before attempting to conquer the new land. At Gilgal the angelic commander of the Lord's army appeared to Joshua with further instructions for battle and encouragement for the conquest (Josh 5:13-15). After the conquest, Gilgal continued to be an important place in Israel. It was here that Israel's first king, Saul, was crowned (1 Sam 11:14-15).

At this, Joshua fell with his face to the ground in reverence. "I am at your command," Joshua said. "What do you want your servant to do?"
15The commander of the LORD's army replied, "Take off your sandals, for the place where you are standing is holy." And Joshua did as he was told.

The Fall of Jericho

JOSHUA 6:1-27

Now the gates of Jericho were tightly shut because
the people were afraid of the Israelites. No one was
allowed to go out or in. 2But the LORD said to Joshua,
"I have given you Jericho, its king, and all its strong
warriors. 3You and your fighting men should march
around the town once a day for six days. 4Seven
priests will walk ahead of the Ark, each carrying a
ram's horn. On the seventh day you are to march
around the town seven times, with the priests blowing the horns. 5When you hear the priests give one
long blast on the rams' horns, have all the people
shout as loud as they can. Then the walls of the town
will collapse, and the people can charge straight into
the town."
6So Joshua called together the priests and said,
"Take up the Ark of the LORD's Covenant, and assign
seven priests to walk in front of it, each carrying a

Jericho

Jericho is an ancient city located on the west side of the Jordan River about 5 miles from the southernmost fords and 10 miles northwest of the Dead Sea. Being in the broad part of the plain of Jordan, it lies nearly 1,000 feet below sea level and about 3,500 feet below Jerusalem, which was just 17 miles away. It was the first city that Joshua and the Israelites conquered when they entered Canaan, and the city was rebuilt and destroyed by conquering armies several times over the centuries. Jesus visited Jericho where he healed the blind beggar Bartimaeus (Mark 10:46-52) and brought salvation to Zacchaeus (Luke 19:1-10).

Josh 5:10 This joyous Passover was the first to be celebrated in the Promised Land and only the third celebrated by Israel since the exodus from Egypt. The last time was at the foot of Mount Sinai, 39 years earlier. This celebration reminded Israel of God's mighty miracles that brought them out of Egypt. There they had to eat in fear and haste; here they ate in celebration of God's blessings and promises. (See Exod 12 for a description of the night the angel "passed over" the Israelites' homes.)

Josh 5:11-12 God supplied manna to the hungry Israelites during their 40 years in the wilderness (Exod 16:14-31). In the bountiful Promised Land they no longer needed this daily food supply because the land was ready for planting and harvesting. God had miraculously provided food for the Israelites while they were in the wilderness; here he provided food from the land itself. Prayer is not an alternative to preparation, and faith is not a substitute for hard work. God can and does provide miraculously for his people as needed, but he also expects them to use their God-given talents and resources to provide for themselves. If your prayers have gone unanswered, perhaps what you need is within your reach. Pray instead for the wisdom to see it and the energy and motivation to do it.

Josh 5:14-15 This was an angel of superior rank, the commander of the Lord's army. Some say he was an appearance of God in human form. As a sign of respect, Joshua took off his sandals. Although Joshua was Israel's leader, he was still subordinate to God, the absolute Leader. Awe and respect are the responses due to our holy God. How can we show respect for him? By our attitudes and actions. We should recognize God's power, authority, and deep love, and our actions must model our absolute reverence for God. Respect for God is just as important today as it was in Joshua's day, even though removing shoes is no longer our cultural way of showing it.

Josh 6:1 The city of Jericho, built thousands of years before Joshua was born, was one of the oldest cities in the world. In some places it had fortified walls up to 25 feet high and 20 feet thick. Soldiers standing guard on top of the walls could see for miles. Jericho was a symbol of military power and strength—the Canaanites considered it invincible.

Israel would attack this city first, and its destruction would put the fear of Israel into the heart of every person in Canaan. The Canaanites saw Israel's God as a nature god because he parted the Jordan and as a war god because he defeated Sihon and Og. But the Canaanites did not consider him a fortress god—one who could prevail against a walled city. The defeat of Jericho showed not only that Israel's God was superior to the Canaanite gods but also that he was invincible.

Josh 6:2-5 God told Joshua that Jericho was already delivered into his hands—the enemy was already defeated! What confidence Joshua must have had as he went into battle! Christians also fight against a defeated enemy. Our enemy, Satan, has been defeated by Christ (Rom 8:37-39; Heb 2:14-15; 1 Jn 3:8). Although we still fight battles every day and sin runs rampant in the world, we have the assurance that the war has already been won. We do not have to be paralyzed by the power of a defeated enemy; we can overcome him through Christ's power.

Josh 6:3-5 Why did God give Joshua all these complicated instructions for the battle? Several answers are possible: (1) God was making it undeniably clear that the battle would depend upon him, and not upon Israel's weapons and expertise. This is why priests carrying the Ark, not soldiers, led the Israelites into battle. (2) God's method of taking the city accentuated the terror already felt in Jericho (Josh 2:9). (3) This strange military maneuver was a test of the Israelites' faith and their willingness to follow God completely. The blowing of the horns had a special significance. The same horns used in their religious festivals were to be blown in their battles to remind them that their victory would come from the Lord, not their own military might (Num 10:9).

▸ **JOSHUA 6:1-27** ***(cont.)***

ram's horn." [7]Then he gave orders to the people:
"March around the town, and the armed men will lead
the way in front of the Ark of the LORD."
[8]After Joshua spoke to the people, the seven priests
with the rams' horns started marching in the presence of the LORD, blowing the horns as they marched.
And the Ark of the LORD's Covenant followed behind
them. [9]Some of the armed men marched in front of
the priests with the horns and some behind the Ark,
with the priests continually blowing the horns. [10]"Do
not shout; do not even talk," Joshua commanded. "Not
a single word from any of you until I tell you to shout.
Then shout!" [11]So the Ark of the LORD was carried
around the town once that day, and then everyone
returned to spend the night in the camp.
[12]Joshua got up early the next morning, and the
priests again carried the Ark of the LORD. [13]The seven
priests with the rams' horns marched in front of the
Ark of the LORD, blowing their horns. Again the armed
men marched both in front of the priests with the
horns and behind the Ark of the LORD. All this time
the priests were blowing their horns. [14]On the second
day they again marched around the town once and
returned to the camp. They followed this pattern for
six days.
[15]On the seventh day the Israelites got up at dawn
and marched around the town as they had done before. But this time they went around the town seven
times. [16]The seventh time around, as the priests
sounded the long blast on their horns, Joshua commanded the people, "Shout! For the LORD has given
you the town! [17]Jericho and everything in it must be
completely destroyed* as an offering to the LORD. Only
Rahab the prostitute and the others in her house will
be spared, for she protected our spies.
[18]"Do not take any of the things set apart for
destruction, or you yourselves will be completely destroyed, and you will bring trouble on the camp of
Israel. [19]Everything made from silver, gold, bronze,
or iron is sacred to the LORD and must be brought
into his treasury."
[20]When the people heard the sound of the rams'
horns, they shouted as loud as they could. Suddenly,
the walls of Jericho collapsed, and the Israelites
charged straight into the town and captured it.
[21]They completely destroyed everything in it with
their swords—men and women, young and old, cattle,
sheep, goats, and donkeys.
[22]Meanwhile, Joshua said to the two spies, "Keep
your promise. Go to the prostitute's house and bring
her out, along with all her family."
[23]The men who had been spies went in and brought
out Rahab, her father, mother, brothers, and all the
other relatives who were with her. They moved her
whole family to a safe place near the camp of Israel.
[24]Then the Israelites burned the town and everything in it. Only the things made from silver, gold,
bronze, or iron were kept for the treasury of the LORD's
house. [25]So Joshua spared Rahab the prostitute and
her relatives who were with her in the house, because
she had hidden the spies Joshua sent to Jericho. And
she lives among the Israelites to this day.
[26]At that time Joshua invoked this curse:

"May the curse of the LORD fall on anyone
who tries to rebuild the town of Jericho.
At the cost of his firstborn son,
he will lay its foundation.
At the cost of his youngest son,
he will set up its gates."

[27]So the LORD was with Joshua, and his reputation
spread throughout the land.

Ai Defeats the Israelites

JOSHUA 7:1-15

But Israel violated the instructions about the things
set apart for the LORD.* A man named Achan had stolen some of these dedicated things, so the LORD was
very angry with the Israelites. Achan was the son of
Carmi, a descendant of Zimri* son of Zerah, of the
tribe of Judah.
[2]Joshua sent some of his men from Jericho to spy
out the town of Ai, east of Bethel, near Beth-aven.

Jo 6:17 The Hebrew term used here refers to the complete consecration of things or people to the LORD, either by destroying them or by giving them as an offering; similarly in 6:18, 21. **Jo 7:1a** The Hebrew term used here refers to the complete consecration of things or people to the LORD, either by destroying them or by giving them as an offering; similarly in 7:11, 12, 13, 15. **Jo 7:1b** As in parallel text at 1 Chr 2:6; Hebrew reads *Zabdi.* Also in 7:17, 18.

Josh 6:21 Why did God demand that the Israelites destroy almost everyone and everything in Jericho? He was carrying out severe judgment against the wickedness of the Canaanites. This judgment, or ban, usually required that everything be destroyed (Deut 12:2-3; 13:12-18). Because of their evil practices and intense idolatry, the Canaanites were a stronghold of rebellion against God. This threat to the right kind of living that God required had to be removed. If not, it would affect all Israel like a cancerous growth (as it did in the sad story told in the book of Judges). A few people and some items in Jericho were not destroyed, but these were special cases. Rahab and her household were saved because she had faith in God and because she had helped the Israelite spies. The silver and gold and articles of bronze and iron were kept, not to enrich the people, but to beautify the Tabernacle and its services (Josh 6:24).

God's purpose in all this was to keep the people's faith and religion uncontaminated. He did not want the plunder to remind Israel of Canaanite practices.

God also wants us to be pure. He wants us to clean up our behavior when we begin a new life with him. We must not let the desire for personal gain distract us from our spiritual purpose. We must also reject any objects that are reminders of a life of rebellion against God. (For more information on how Israel handled its plunder, see the note on Num 31:25-30, p. 278.)

Josh 6:26 This curse was fulfilled in 1 Kings 16:34 when a man, Hiel, rebuilt Jericho and consequently lost his oldest and youngest sons.

Josh 7:1 The things to be "set apart" refers to all the clothing, cattle, and other plunder

3 When they returned, they told Joshua, "There's no
need for all of us to go up there; it won't take more
than two or three thousand men to attack Ai. Since
there are so few of them, don't make all our people
struggle to go up there."
4 So approximately 3,000 warriors were sent, but
they were soundly defeated. The men of Ai 5 chased
the Israelites from the town gate as far as the quar-
ries,* and they killed about thirty-six who were re-
treating down the slope. The Israelites were paralyzed
with fear at this turn of events, and their courage
melted away.
6 Joshua and the elders of Israel tore their clothing
in dismay, threw dust on their heads, and bowed face
down to the ground before the Ark of the LORD until
evening. 7 Then Joshua cried out, "Oh, Sovereign LORD,
why did you bring us across the Jordan River if you are
going to let the Amorites kill us? If only we had been
content to stay on the other side! 8 Lord, what can I say
now that Israel has fled from its enemies? 9 For when
the Canaanites and all the other people living in the
land hear about it, they will surround us and wipe our
name off the face of the earth. And then what will
happen to the honor of your great name?"

Jo 7:5 Or *as far as Shebarim.*

RAHAB

Rahab was a prostitute in the city of Jericho. As a prostitute, she lived on the edge of society, one stop short of rejection. Her house, built right into the city wall, provided both lodging and favors to travelers. It was a natural place for the Israelite spies to stay, as they would be mistaken for Rahab's customers. • Stories about the Israelites had been circulating for some time, but now it was evident that the Israelites were about to invade. Living on the wall, Rahab felt especially vulnerable. Yet while she shared the general mood of fear with the rest of Jericho's population, she alone turned to the Lord for her salvation. Her faith gave her the courage to hide the spies and lie to the authorities. Rahab knew her position was dangerous; she could have been killed if she had been caught harboring the Israelites. Rahab took the risk because she sensed that the Israelites relied on a God worth trusting. And God rewarded Rahab by promising safety for her and her family. • God works through people—like Rahab—whom we are inclined to reject. God remembered her because of her faith, not her profession. If at times you feel like a failure, remember that Rahab rose above her situation through her trust in God. You can do the same!

Strengths and accomplishments	• Relative of Boaz, and thus an ancestor of David and Jesus • One of only two women listed in the Hall of Faith in Hebrews 11 • Resourceful, willing to help others at great cost to herself
Weakness and mistake	• She was a prostitute
Lesson from her life	• Do not let fear affect your faith in God's ability to deliver
Vital statistics	• Where: Jericho • Occupations: Prostitute/innkeeper, later became a wife • Relatives: Ancestor of David and Jesus (Matt 1:5) • Contemporary: Joshua
Key verse	"It was by faith that Rahab the prostitute was not destroyed with the people in her city who refused to obey God. For she had given a friendly welcome to the spies" (Heb 11:31).

Rahab's story is told in Joshua 2; 6:22-23. She is also mentioned in Matthew 1:5; Hebrews 11:31; James 2:25.

that God said Israel should destroy when they conquered Jericho (see Josh 6:17-19). It was not that Achan found a good use for something that was going to be thrown out anyway. This was a serious offense because it was in direct defiance of an explicit command of God (see Deut 20:16-18).

Josh 7:1ff Notice the results of Achan's sin: Many men died (Josh 7:5); Israel's army melted in fear (Josh 7:5); Joshua questioned God (Josh 7:7-9); God threatened to withdraw his presence from the people (Josh 7:12); and Achan and his family had to be destroyed (Josh 7:24-26).

When Israel eliminated the sin from their community, these were the results: God's encouragement (Josh 8:1); God's presence in battle (Josh 8:1); God's guidance and promise of victory (Josh 8:2); and God's permission to keep the plunder and livestock from the battle for themselves (Josh 8:2). Throughout Israel's history, blessings came when the people got rid of their sin. You will also experience blessings when you turn from your sin and follow God's plan wholeheartedly.

Josh 7:6 Joshua and the leaders tore their clothing and threw dust on their heads as signs of deep mourning before God. They were confused by their defeat at the small city of Ai after the spectacular Jericho victory, so they went before God in deep humility and sorrow to receive his instructions. When our lives fall apart, we also should turn to God for direction and help. Like Joshua and the leaders, we should humble ourselves so that we will be able to hear God's words.

Josh 7:7 When Joshua first went against Ai (Josh 7:3), he did not consult God but relied on the strength of his army to defeat the small city. Only after Israel was defeated did they turn to God and ask what happened.

Too often we rely on our own skills and strength, especially when the task before us seems easy. We go to God only when the obstacles seem too great. However, only God knows what lies ahead. Consulting him, even when we are on a winning streak, may save us from grave mistakes or misjudgments. God may want us to learn lessons, remove pride, or consult others before he will work through us.

Josh 7:7-9 Imagine praying this way to God. This is not a formal church prayer; it is the prayer of a man who is afraid and confused by what is happening around him. Joshua poured out his real thoughts to God. Hiding your needs from God is ignoring the only one who can really help. God welcomes your honest prayers and wants you to express your true feelings to him. Any believer can become more honest in prayer by remembering that God is all-knowing and all-powerful and that his love is everlasting.

▸ **JOSHUA 7:1-15 *(cont.)***

[10]But the LORD said to Joshua, "Get up! Why are you lying on your face like this? [11]Israel has sinned and broken my covenant! They have stolen some of the things that I commanded must be set apart for me. And they have not only stolen them but have lied about it and hidden the things among their own belongings. [12]That is why the Israelites are running from their enemies in defeat. For now Israel itself has been set apart for destruction. I will not remain with you any longer unless you destroy the things among you that were set apart for destruction.

[13]"Get up! Command the people to purify themselves in preparation for tomorrow. For this is what the LORD, the God of Israel, says: Hidden among you, O Israel, are things set apart for the LORD. You will never defeat your enemies until you remove these things from among you.

[14]"In the morning you must present yourselves by tribes, and the LORD will point out the tribe to which the guilty man belongs. That tribe must come forward with its clans, and the LORD will point out the guilty clan. That clan will then come forward, and the LORD will point out the guilty family. Finally, each member of the guilty family must come forward one by one. [15]The one who has stolen what was set apart for destruction will himself be burned with fire, along with everything he has, for he has broken the covenant of the LORD and has done a horrible thing in Israel."

Achan's Sin

JOSHUA 7:16-26

Early the next morning Joshua brought the tribes of Israel before the LORD, and the tribe of Judah was singled out. [17]Then the clans of Judah came forward, and the clan of Zerah was singled out. Then the families of Zerah came forward, and the family of Zimri was singled out. [18]Every member of Zimri's family was brought forward person by person, and Achan was singled out.

[19]Then Joshua said to Achan, "My son, give glory to the LORD, the God of Israel, by telling the truth. Make your confession and tell me what you have done. Don't hide it from me."

[20]Achan replied, "It is true! I have sinned against the LORD, the God of Israel. [21]Among the plunder I saw a beautiful robe from Babylon,* 200 silver coins,* and a bar of gold weighing more than a pound.* I wanted them so much that I took them. They are hidden in the ground beneath my tent, with the silver buried deeper than the rest."

[22]So Joshua sent some men to make a search. They ran to the tent and found the stolen goods hidden there, just as Achan had said, with the silver buried beneath the rest. [23]They took the things from the tent and brought them to Joshua and all the Israelites. Then they laid them on the ground in the presence of the LORD.

[24]Then Joshua and all the Israelites took Achan, the silver, the robe, the bar of gold, his sons, daughters, cattle, donkeys, sheep, goats, tent, and everything he had, and they brought them to the valley of Achor. [25]Then Joshua said to Achan, "Why have you brought trouble on us? The LORD will now bring trouble on you." And all the Israelites stoned Achan and his family and burned their bodies. [26]They piled a great heap of stones over Achan, which remains to this day. That is why the place has been called the Valley of Trouble* ever since. So the LORD was no longer angry.

Jo 7:21a Hebrew *Shinar.* **Jo 7:21b** Hebrew *200 shekels of silver,* about 5 pounds or 2.3 kilograms in weight. **Jo 7:21c** Hebrew *50 shekels,* about 20 ounces or 570 grams in weight. **Jo 7:26** Hebrew *valley of Achor.*

Josh 7:10-12 Why did Achan's sin bring judgment on the entire nation? Although it was one man's failure, God saw it as national disobedience to a national law. God needed the entire nation to be committed to the job they had agreed to do—conquer the land. Thus, when one person failed, everyone failed. If Achan's sin went unpunished, unlimited looting could break out. The nation as a whole had to take responsibility for preventing this undisciplined disobedience.

Achan's sin was not merely his keeping some of the captured goods (God allowed it in some cases), but more importantly it was his disobeying God's explicit command to destroy everything connected with Jericho. Achan's sin was indifference to the evil and idolatry of the city, not just a desire for money and clothes. God would not protect Israel's army again until the sin was removed and the army returned to obeying him without reservation. God is not content with our doing what is right some of the time. He wants us to do what is right all the time. We are under his orders to eliminate any thoughts, practices, or possessions that hinder our devotion to him.

Josh 7:13 The Israelites had to undergo purification rites (like those mentioned in Josh 3:5) when they were preparing to cross the Jordan River. Such rites prepared the people to approach God and constantly reminded them of their sinfulness and his holiness.

Josh 7:24-25 Achan underestimated God and didn't take his commands seriously (Josh 6:18). Taking a robe, along with some silver and gold, may have seemed a small thing to Achan, but the effects of his sin were felt by the entire nation, especially his family. Like Achan, our actions affect more people than just ourselves. Beware of the temptation to rationalize your sins by saying they are too small or too personal to hurt anyone but you.

Josh 7:24-26 Why did Achan's entire family pay for his sin? The biblical record does not tell us if they were accomplices to his crime, but in the ancient world, the family was treated as a whole. Achan, as the head of his family, was like a tribal chief. If he prospered, the family prospered with him. If he suffered, so did they. Many Israelites had already died in battle because of Achan's sin. Now he was to be completely cut off from Israel.

Achan's entire family was to be stoned along with him so that no trace of the sin would remain in Israel. In our permissive and individualistic culture we have a hard time understanding such a decree, but in ancient cultures this punishment fit the crime: Achan had disobeyed God's command to destroy everything in Jericho; thus, everything that belonged to Achan had to be destroyed. Sin has drastic consequences, so we should take drastic measures to avoid it.

The Israelites Defeat Ai

JOSHUA 8:1-29

Then the LORD said to Joshua, "Do not be afraid or
discouraged. Take all your fighting men and attack Ai,
for I have given you the king of Ai, his people, his town,
and his land. 2 You will destroy them as you destroyed
Jericho and its king. But this time you may keep the
plunder and the livestock for yourselves. Set an ambush behind the town."
3 So Joshua and all the fighting men set out to attack Ai. Joshua chose 30,000 of his best warriors and
sent them out at night 4 with these orders: "Hide in
ambush close behind the town and be ready for action. 5 When our main army attacks, the men of Ai will
come out to fight as they did before, and we will run
away from them. 6 We will let them chase us until we
have drawn them away from the town. For they will say,
'The Israelites are running away from us as they did
before.' Then, while we are running from them, 7 you
will jump up from your ambush and take possession
of the town, for the LORD your God will give it to you.
8 Set the town on fire, as the LORD has commanded.
You have your orders."
9 So they left and went to the place of ambush
between Bethel and the west side of Ai. But Joshua
remained among the people in the camp that night.
10 Early the next morning Joshua roused his men and
started toward Ai, accompanied by the elders of Israel.
11 All the fighting men who were with Joshua marched
in front of the town and camped on the north side of
Ai, with a valley between them and the town. 12 That
night Joshua sent 5,000 men to lie in ambush between
Bethel and Ai, on the west side of the town. 13 So they
stationed the main army north of the town and the
ambush west of the town. Joshua himself spent that
night in the valley.
14 When the king of Ai saw the Israelites across
the valley, he and all his army hurried out early in the
morning and attacked the Israelites at a place overlooking the Jordan Valley.* But he didn't realize there
was an ambush behind the town. 15 Joshua and the
Israelite army fled toward the wilderness as though
they were badly beaten. 16 Then all the men in the town
were called out to chase after them. In this way, they
were lured away from the town. 17 There was not a
man left in Ai or Bethel* who did not chase after the
Israelites, and the town was left wide open.
18 Then the LORD said to Joshua, "Point the spear in
your hand toward Ai, for I will hand the town over to
you." Joshua did as he was commanded. 19 As soon as
Joshua gave this signal, all the men in ambush jumped
up from their position and poured into the town. They
quickly captured it and set it on fire.
20 When the men of Ai looked behind them, smoke
from the town was filling the sky, and they had nowhere to go. For the Israelites who had fled in the
direction of the wilderness now turned on their
pursuers. 21 When Joshua and all the other Israelites
saw that the ambush had succeeded and that smoke
was rising from the town, they turned and attacked

Jo 8:14 Hebrew *the Arabah.* **Jo 8:17** Some manuscripts lack *or Bethel.*

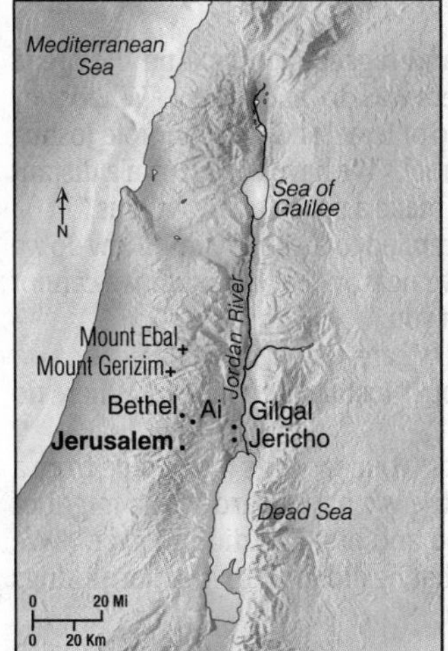

***THE BATTLE FOR AI** During the night, Joshua sent one detachment of soldiers to the west of Ai to lie in wait. The next morning he led a second group north of Ai. When the army of Ai attacked, the Israelites to the north pretended to scatter, only to turn on the enemy as the men lying in ambush moved in and burned the city.*

Josh 8:1 After Israel had been cleansed from Achan's sin, Joshua prepared to attack Ai again—this time to win. Joshua had learned some lessons that we can follow: (1) Confess your sins when God reveals them to you (Josh 7:19-21); (2) when you fail, refocus on God, deal with the problem, and move on (Josh 7:22-25; 8:1). God wants the cycle of sin, repentance, and forgiveness to strengthen us, not weaken us. The lessons we learn from our failures should make us better able to handle the same situation the second time around. Because God is eager to give us cleansing, forgiveness, and strength, the only way to lose is to give up. We can tell what kind of people we are by what we do on the second and third attempts.

Josh 8:2 Why did God allow the Israelites to keep the plunder and cattle (livestock) this time? Israel's laws for handling the spoils of war covered two situations: (1) Cities like Jericho which were under God's ban (judgment for idolatry) could not be looted (see Deut 20:16-18). God's people were to be kept holy and separate from every influence of idolatry. (2) The distribution of captured goods from cities not under the ban was a normal part of warfare. It provided the army and the nation with the necessary food, flocks, and weapons needed to sustain itself in wartime. Ai was not under the ban. The conquering army needed the food and equipment. Because soldiers were not paid, the plunder was part of their incentive and reward for going to war.

Josh 8:3 The conquest of Ai was very important to the Israelites. Only 11 miles away from Jericho, Ai was a key stronghold for the Canaanites and a buffer fortress for Bethel (Josh 8:12). If the Canaanite kings got wind of an Israelite defeat at Ai, they could unite in a coordinated attack. They did not know that God had restored his power and protection to Joshua's troops. We must depend on God with absolute obedience to be sure of the victory he has promised.

Josh 8:18-19 The Lord gave Joshua the city. Yesterday's defeat became today's victory. Once sin is dealt with, forgiveness and victory lie ahead. With God's direction we need not stay discouraged or burdened with guilt. No matter how difficult a setback sin may bring, we must renew our efforts to carry out God's will.

▸ **JOSHUA 8:1-29** ***(cont.)***

the men of Ai. [22]Meanwhile, the Israelites who were inside the town came out and attacked the enemy from the rear. So the men of Ai were caught in the middle, with Israelite fighters on both sides. Israel attacked them, and not a single person survived or escaped. [23]Only the king of Ai was taken alive and brought to Joshua.

[24]When the Israelite army finished chasing and killing all the men of Ai in the open fields, they went back and finished off everyone inside. [25]So the entire population of Ai, including men and women, was wiped out that day—12,000 in all. [26]For Joshua kept holding out his spear until everyone who had lived in Ai was completely destroyed.* [27]Only the livestock and the treasures of the town were not destroyed, for the Israelites kept these as plunder for themselves, as the LORD had commanded Joshua. [28]So Joshua burned the town of Ai,* and it became a permanent mound of ruins, desolate to this very day.

[29]Joshua impaled the king of Ai on a sharpened pole and left him there until evening. At sunset the Israelites took down the body, as Joshua commanded, and threw it in front of the town gate. They piled a great heap of stones over him that can still be seen today.

The LORD's Covenant Renewed

JOSHUA 8:30-35

Then Joshua built an altar to the LORD, the God of Israel, on Mount Ebal. [31]He followed the commands that Moses the LORD's servant had written in the Book of Instruction: "Make me an altar from stones that are uncut and have not been shaped with iron tools."* Then on the altar they presented burnt offerings and peace offerings to the LORD. [32]And as the Israelites watched, Joshua copied onto the stones of the altar* the instructions Moses had given them.

[33]Then all the Israelites—foreigners and native-born alike—along with the elders, officers, and judges, were divided into two groups. One group stood in front of Mount Gerizim, the other in front of Mount Ebal. Each group faced the other, and between them stood the Levitical priests carrying the Ark of the LORD's Covenant. This was all done according to the commands that Moses, the servant of the LORD, had previously given for blessing the people of Israel.

[34]Joshua then read to them all the blessings and curses Moses had written in the Book of Instruction. [35]Every word of every command that Moses had ever given was read to the entire assembly of Israel, including the women and children and the foreigners who lived among them.

Jo 8:26 The Hebrew term used here refers to the complete consecration of things or people to the LORD, either by destroying them or by giving them as an offering. **Jo 8:28** *Ai* means "ruin." **Jo 8:31** Exod 20:25; Deut 27:5-6. **Jo 8:32** Hebrew *onto the stones.*

2. JOSHUA ATTACKS THE SOUTHERN KINGS

Joshua and the rest of Israel's leaders failed to consult God, and they were tricked into making a peace treaty with the Gibeonites. This led to a great confrontation with a coalition of kings from the southern regions of the Promised Land.

The Gibeonites Deceive Israel

JOSHUA 9:1-27

Now all the kings west of the Jordan River heard about what had happened. These were the kings of the Hittites, Amorites, Canaanites, Perizzites, Hivites, and Jebusites, who lived in the hill country, in the western foothills,* and along the coast of the Mediterranean Sea* as far north as the Lebanon mountains. [2]These kings combined their armies to fight as one against Joshua and the Israelites.

[3]But when the people of Gibeon heard what Joshua had done to Jericho and Ai, [4]they resorted to deception to save themselves. They sent ambassadors to Joshua, loading their donkeys with weathered saddlebags and old, patched wineskins. [5]They put on worn-out, patched sandals and ragged clothes. And the bread they took with them was dry and moldy. [6]When they arrived at the camp of Israel at Gilgal, they told Joshua and the men of Israel, "We have come from a distant land to ask you to make a peace treaty with us."

[7]The Israelites replied to these Hivites, "How do we know you don't live nearby? For if you do, we cannot make a treaty with you."

[8]They replied, "We are your servants."

"But who are you?" Joshua demanded. "Where do you come from?"

[9]They answered, "Your servants have come from a very distant country. We have heard of the might of the LORD your God and of all he did in Egypt. [10]We have also heard what he did to the two Amorite kings

Jo 9:1a Hebrew *the Shephelah.* **Jo 9:1b** Hebrew *the Great Sea.*

Josh 8:30-31 The altar was to be built out of uncut stones so it would be holy (see Exod 20:25). This would prevent the people from worshiping altars like idols, or worshiping the craftsmanship of the workers rather than the great works of God.

Josh 8:32 It was most likely the Ten Commandments (recorded in Exod 20) that Joshua copied on the stones. These were the heart of all God's laws.

Josh 9:1-6 As the news about their victory became widespread, the Israelites experienced opposition in two forms: direct (kings in the area began to unite against them) and indirect (the Gibeonites resorted to deception). We can expect similar opposition as we obey God's commands. To guard against these pressures, we must rely on God and communicate daily with him. He will give us strength to endure the direct and indirect pressures and wisdom to see through deception.

east of the Jordan River—King Sihon of Heshbon and King Og of Bashan (who lived in Ashtaroth). 11 So our elders and all our people instructed us, 'Take supplies for a long journey. Go meet with the people of Israel and tell them, "We are your servants; please make a treaty with us."'

12 "This bread was hot from the ovens when we left our homes. But now, as you can see, it is dry and moldy. 13 These wineskins were new when we filled them, but now they are old and split open. And our clothing and sandals are worn out from our very long journey."

14 So the Israelites examined their food, but they did not consult the LORD. 15 Then Joshua made a peace treaty with them and guaranteed their safety, and the leaders of the community ratified their agreement with a binding oath.

16 Three days after making the treaty, they learned that these people actually lived nearby! 17 The Israelites set out at once to investigate and reached their towns in three days. The names of these towns were Gibeon, Kephirah, Beeroth, and Kiriath-jearim. 18 But the Israelites did not attack the towns, for the Israelite leaders had made a vow to them in the name of the LORD, the God of Israel.

The people of Israel grumbled against their leaders because of the treaty. 19 But the leaders replied, "Since we have sworn an oath in the presence of the LORD, the God of Israel, we cannot touch them. 20 This is what we must do. We must let them live, for divine anger would come upon us if we broke our oath. 21 Let them live." So they made them woodcutters and water carriers for the entire community, as the Israelite leaders directed.

22 Joshua called together the Gibeonites and said, "Why did you lie to us? Why did you say that you live in a distant land when you live right here among us? 23 May you be cursed! From now on you will always be servants who cut wood and carry water for the house of my God."

24 They replied, "We did it because we—your servants—were clearly told that the LORD your God commanded his servant Moses to give you this entire land and to destroy all the people living in it. So we feared greatly for our lives because of you. That is why we have done this. 25 Now we are at your mercy—do to us whatever you think is right."

26 So Joshua did not allow the people of Israel to kill them. 27 But that day he made the Gibeonites the woodcutters and water carriers for the community of Israel and for the altar of the LORD—wherever the LORD would choose to build it. And that is what they do to this day.

Israel Defeats the Southern Armies

JOSHUA 10:1-15

Adoni-zedek, king of Jerusalem, heard that Joshua had captured and completely destroyed* Ai and killed its king, just as he had destroyed the town of Jericho and killed its king. He also learned that the Gibeonites had made peace with Israel and were now their allies. 2 He and his people became very afraid when they heard all this because Gibeon was a large town—as large as

Jo 10:1 The Hebrew term used here refers to the complete consecration of things or people to the LORD, either by destroying them or by giving them as an offering; also in 10:28, 35, 37, 39, 40.

Josh 9:14-17 When the leaders sampled these men's provisions, they saw that the bread was dry and moldy, the wineskins were split open, and the clothes and sandals were worn out. But they did not see through the deception. After the promise had been made and the treaty ratified, the facts came out—Israel's leaders had been deceived. God had specifically instructed Israel to make no treaties with the inhabitants of Canaan (Exod 23:32; 34:12; Num 33:55; Deut 7:2; 20:17-18). As a strategist, Joshua knew enough to talk to God before leading his troops into battle. But the peace treaty seemed innocent enough, so Joshua and the leaders made this decision on their own. By failing to seek God's guidance and rushing ahead with their own plans, they had to deal with angry people and an awkward alliance. Once again, they had forgotten to go to God; yet how often we do the same. A new situation arises, and we forget to seek God's wisdom and guidance. When we learn the lessons of the past and apply them to today, we save ourselves a lot of trouble.

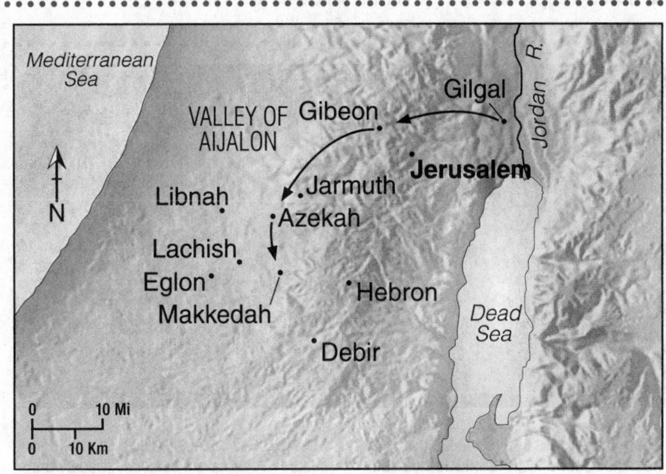

***THE BATTLE FOR GIBEON** Five Amorite kings conspired to destroy Gibeon. Israel came to the aid of the Gibeonites. The Israelites attacked the enemy armies outside of Gibeon and chased them through the valley of Aijalon as far as Azekah and Makkedah.*

Josh 9:19-20 Joshua and his advisers had made a mistake. But because they had given an oath to protect the Gibeonites, they would keep their word. The oath was not nullified by the Gibeonites' trickery. God had commanded that oaths be kept (Lev 5:4; 27:2, 28), and breaking an oath was serious. This encourages us not to take our promises lightly.

▸ **JOSHUA 10:1-15 *(cont.)***
the royal cities and larger than Ai. And the Gibeonite
men were strong warriors.
3 So King Adoni-zedek of Jerusalem sent messengers to several other kings: Hoham of Hebron, Piram of
Jarmuth, Japhia of Lachish, and Debir of Eglon. 4 "Come
and help me destroy Gibeon," he urged them, "for they
have made peace with Joshua and the people of Israel."
5 So these five Amorite kings combined their armies
for a united attack. They moved all their troops into
place and attacked Gibeon.
6 The men of Gibeon quickly sent messengers to
Joshua at his camp in Gilgal. "Don't abandon your
servants now!" they pleaded. "Come at once! Save us!
Help us! For all the Amorite kings who live in the hill
country have joined forces to attack us."
7 So Joshua and his entire army, including his best
warriors, left Gilgal and set out for Gibeon. 8 "Do not
be afraid of them," the LORD said to Joshua, "for I have
given you victory over them. Not a single one of them
will be able to stand up to you."
9 Joshua traveled all night from Gilgal and took the
Amorite armies by surprise. 10 The LORD threw them
into a panic, and the Israelites slaughtered great numbers of them at Gibeon. Then the Israelites chased the
enemy along the road to Beth-horon, killing them all
along the way to Azekah and Makkedah. 11 As the Amorites retreated down the road from Beth-horon, the
LORD destroyed them with a terrible hailstorm from
heaven that continued until they reached Azekah. The
hail killed more of the enemy than the Israelites killed
with the sword.
12 On the day the LORD gave the Israelites victory
over the Amorites, Joshua prayed to the LORD in front
of all the people of Israel. He said,

> "Let the sun stand still over Gibeon,
> and the moon over the valley
> of Aijalon."

13 So the sun stood still and the moon stayed in place
until the nation of Israel had defeated its enemies.
Is this event not recorded in *The Book of Jashar**?
The sun stayed in the middle of the sky, and it did
not set as on a normal day.* 14 There has never been
a day like this one before or since, when the LORD
answered such a prayer. Surely the LORD fought for
Israel that day!
15 Then Joshua and the Israelite army returned to
their camp at Gilgal.

Joshua Kills the Five Southern Kings

JOSHUA 10:16-27
During the battle the five kings escaped and hid in
a cave at Makkedah. 17 When Joshua heard that they
had been found, 18 he issued this command: "Cover the
opening of the cave with large rocks, and place guards
at the entrance to keep the kings inside. 19 The rest of
you continue chasing the enemy and cut them down
from the rear. Don't give them a chance to get back
to their towns, for the LORD your God has given you
victory over them."
20 So Joshua and the Israelite army continued the
slaughter and completely crushed the enemy. They
totally wiped out the five armies except for a tiny
remnant that managed to reach their fortified towns.
21 Then the Israelites returned safely to Joshua in the

Jo 10:13a Or *The Book of the Upright.* **Jo 10:13b** Or *did not set for about a whole day.*

So the sun stood still and the moon stayed in place until the nation of Israel had defeated its enemies.
Joshua 10:13

Josh 10:5-8 This alliance of enemy kings from the south actually helped Joshua and his army. Because the enemies had united to attack Gibeon, Joshua didn't have to spend the time and resources required to wage separate campaigns against each fortified city represented in the coalition. Joshua confidently confronted this coalition of armies and defeated them in a single battle because he trusted God to give Israel the victory.

Josh 10:6-7 Joshua's response shows his integrity. After having been deceived by the Gibeonites, Joshua and the leaders could have been slow about their attempt to rescue them. Instead, they immediately responded to their call for help. How willing would you be to help someone who had deceived you, even though you had forgiven that person? We should take our word just as seriously as Joshua did.

Josh 10:12-14 How did the sun stand still? Of course, in relation to the earth the sun always stands still—it is the earth that travels around the sun. But the terminology used in Joshua should not cause us to doubt the miracle. After all, we are not confused when someone tells us the sun rises or sets. The point is that the day was prolonged, not that God used a particular method to prolong it. Two explanations have been given for how this event occurred: (1) A slowing of the earth's normal rotation gave Joshua more time. (2) Some unusual refraction of the sun's rays gave additional hours of light. Regardless of God's chosen method, the Bible is clear that the day was prolonged by a miracle, and that God's intervention turned the tide of the battle for his people.

Josh 10:13 *The Book of Jashar* (also mentioned in 2 Sam 1:18) was probably a collection of historical events put to music. Many parts of the Bible contain quotations from previous books, songs, poems, or other spoken and written materials. Because God guided the writer of this book to select this material, his message comes with divine authority.

camp at Makkedah. After that, no one dared to speak even a word against Israel.

[22]Then Joshua said, "Remove the rocks covering the opening of the cave, and bring the five kings to me." [23]So they brought the five kings out of the cave—the kings of Jerusalem, Hebron, Jarmuth, Lachish, and Eglon. [24]When they brought them out, Joshua told the commanders of his army, "Come and put your feet on the kings' necks." And they did as they were told.

[25]"Don't ever be afraid or discouraged," Joshua told his men. "Be strong and courageous, for the LORD is going to do this to all of your enemies." [26]Then Joshua killed each of the five kings and impaled them on five sharpened poles, where they hung until evening.

[27]As the sun was going down, Joshua gave instructions for the bodies of the kings to be taken down from the poles and thrown into the cave where they had been hiding. Then they covered the opening of the cave with a pile of large rocks, which remains to this very day.

Israel Destroys the Southern Towns

JOSHUA 10:28-43

That same day Joshua captured and destroyed the town of Makkedah. He killed everyone in it, including the king, leaving no survivors. He destroyed them all, and he killed the king of Makkedah as he had killed the king of Jericho. [29]Then Joshua and the Israelites went to Libnah and attacked it. [30]There, too, the LORD gave them the town and its king. He killed everyone in it, leaving no survivors. Then Joshua killed the king of Libnah as he had killed the king of Jericho.

[31]From Libnah, Joshua and the Israelites went to Lachish and attacked it. [32]Here again, the LORD gave them Lachish. Joshua took it on the second day and killed everyone in it, just as he had done at Libnah. [33]During the attack on Lachish, King Horam of Gezer arrived with his army to help defend the town. But Joshua's men killed him and his army, leaving no survivors.

[34]Then Joshua and the Israelite army went on to Eglon and attacked it. [35]They captured it that day and killed everyone in it. He completely destroyed everyone, just as he had done at Lachish. [36]From Eglon, Joshua and the Israelite army went up to Hebron and attacked it. [37]They captured the town and killed everyone in it, including its king, leaving no survivors. They did the same thing to all of its surrounding villages. And just as he had done at Eglon, he completely destroyed the entire population.

[38]Then Joshua and the Israelites turned back and attacked Debir. [39]He captured the town, its king, and all of its surrounding villages. He completely destroyed everyone in it, leaving no survivors. He did to Debir and its king just what he had done to Hebron and to Libnah and its king.

[40]So Joshua conquered the whole region—the kings and people of the hill country, the Negev, the western foothills,* and the mountain slopes. He completely destroyed everyone in the land, leaving no survivors, just as the LORD, the God of Israel, had commanded. [41]Joshua slaughtered them from Kadesh-barnea to Gaza and from the region around the town of Goshen up to Gibeon. [42]Joshua conquered all these kings and their land in a single campaign, for the LORD, the God of Israel, was fighting for his people.

[43]Then Joshua and the Israelite army returned to their camp at Gilgal.

Jo 10:40 Hebrew *the Shephelah.*

1400 BC **Water clock invented in Egypt**

Josh 10:24 Placing a foot on the neck of a captive was a common military practice in the ancient Near East. It symbolized the victor's domination over his captives. These proud kings had boasted of their power. Now all Israel could see that God was superior to any earthly army.

Josh 10:25 With God's help, Israel won the battle against five Amorite armies. Such a triumph was part of God's daily business as he worked with his people for victory. Joshua told his men never to be afraid because God would give them similar victories over all their enemies. God has often protected us and won victories for us. The same God who empowered Joshua and who has led us in the past will help us with our present and future needs. Reminding ourselves of his help in the past will give us hope for the struggles that lie ahead.

Josh 10:32 Notice that in every Israelite victory, the text gives the credit to the Lord. All of Israel's victories came from God. When we are successful, we may be tempted to take all the credit and glory as though we succeeded by ourselves, in our own strength. In reality, God gives us the victories, and he alone delivers us from our enemies. We should give him the credit and praise him for his goodness.

Josh 10:40-43 God had commanded Joshua to take the leadership in ridding the land of sin so God's people could occupy it. Joshua did his part thoroughly—leading the united army to weaken the inhabitants. When God orders us to stop sinning, we must not pause to debate, consider the options, negotiate a compromise, or rationalize. Instead, like Joshua, our response must be swift and complete. We must be ruthless in avoiding relationships and activities that can lead us into sin.

3. JOSHUA ATTACKS THE NORTHERN KINGS

After completing the conquest of the southern regions of the Promised Land, Joshua led Israel north to defeat the kings in the north, led by King Jabin of Hazor.

Israel Defeats the Northern Armies

JOSHUA 11:1-15

When King Jabin of Hazor heard what had happened,
he sent messages to the following kings: King Jobab of
Madon; the king of Shimron; the king of Acshaph; 2 all
the kings of the northern hill country; the kings in the
Jordan Valley south of Galilee*; the kings in the Galilean foothills*; the kings of Naphoth-dor on the west;
3 the kings of Canaan, both east and west; the kings of
the Amorites, the Hittites, the Perizzites, the Jebusites
in the hill country, and the Hivites in the towns on
the slopes of Mount Hermon in the land of Mizpah.
4 All these kings came out to fight. Their combined
armies formed a vast horde. And with all their horses
and chariots, they covered the landscape like the sand
on the seashore. 5 The kings joined forces and established their camp around the water near Merom to
fight against Israel.
6 Then the LORD said to Joshua, "Do not be afraid of
them. By this time tomorrow I will hand all of them
over to Israel as dead men. Then you must cripple their
horses and burn their chariots."
7 So Joshua and all his fighting men traveled to
the water near Merom and attacked suddenly. 8 And
the LORD gave them victory over their enemies. The
Israelites chased them as far as Greater Sidon and
Misrephoth-maim, and eastward into the valley of
Mizpah, until not one enemy warrior was left alive.
9 Then Joshua crippled the horses and burned all the
chariots, as the LORD had instructed.
10 Joshua then turned back and captured Hazor and
killed its king. (Hazor had at one time been the capital
of all these kingdoms.) 11 The Israelites completely
destroyed* every living thing in the city, leaving no
survivors. Not a single person was spared. And then
Joshua burned the city.
12 Joshua slaughtered all the other kings and their
people, completely destroying them, just as Moses,
the servant of the LORD, had commanded. 13 But the
Israelites did not burn any of the towns built on
mounds except Hazor, which Joshua burned. 14 And
the Israelites took all the plunder and livestock of
the ravaged towns for themselves. But they killed
all the people, leaving no survivors. 15 As the LORD
had commanded his servant Moses, so Moses commanded Joshua. And Joshua did as he was told, carefully obeying all the commands that the LORD had
given to Moses.

Jo 11:2a Hebrew *in the Arabah south of Kinnereth.* **Jo 11:2b** Hebrew *the Shephelah;* also in 11:16. **Jo 11:11** The Hebrew term used here refers to the complete consecration of things or people to the LORD, either by destroying them or by giving them as an offering; also in 11:12, 20, 21.

Josh 11:1-5 Two kings of Hazor were named Jabin. The other, apparently a weak ruler, is mentioned in Judges 4:2-3. The Jabin of this story was quite powerful because he was able to build an alliance with dozens of kings. By all appearances, Jabin had a clear advantage over Joshua and his outnumbered forces. But those who honor God can be victorious regardless of the odds.

Josh 11:10-13 Victorious invaders usually kept captured cities intact, moving into them and making them centers of commerce and defense. For example, Moses predicted in Deuteronomy 6:10-12 that Israel would occupy cities they themselves had not built. Joshua, however, burned Hazor. As a former capital of the land, Hazor symbolized the wicked culture that Israel had come to destroy. In addition, its capture and destruction broke the backbone of the federation and weakened the will of the Canaanite people to resist.

Josh 11:15 Joshua carefully obeyed all the instructions given by God. This theme of obedience is repeated frequently in the book of Joshua, partly because obedience is one aspect of life that each individual believer can control. We can't always control our understanding because we may not have all the facts. We can't control what other people do or how they treat us. However, we can control our choice to obey God. Whatever new challenges we may face, the Bible contains relevant instructions that we can choose to ignore or choose to follow.

Josh 11:15 Joshua followed every detail of God's commands to Moses. It is usually difficult to complete someone else's project, but Joshua stepped into Moses' job, building upon what Moses had started, and brought it to completion. A new person starting a new job usually brings a new style and personality to that job. But the church or any other organization cannot work effectively if every change of personnel means starting from scratch.

***THE BATTLE FOR HAZOR** Kings from the north joined together to battle the Israelites, who controlled the southern half of Canaan. They gathered by the water near Merom, but Joshua attacked them by surprise—the enemies' chariots were useless in the dense forests. Hazor, the largest Canaanite center in Galilee, was destroyed.*

4. SUMMARY OF JOSHUA'S CONQUESTS

God was with Israel as they were conquering the land he had promised, and he gave them success in defeating many different kings throughout the land.

Summary of Conquests

JOSHUA 11:16-23

So Joshua conquered the entire region—the hill country, the entire Negev, the whole area around the town
of Goshen, the western foothills, the Jordan Valley,*
the mountains of Israel, and the Galilean foothills.
17 The Israelite territory now extended all the way from
Mount Halak, which leads up to Seir in the south, as
far north as Baal-gad at the foot of Mount Hermon
in the valley of Lebanon. Joshua killed all the kings
of those territories, 18 waging war for a long time to
accomplish this. 19 No one in this region made peace
with the Israelites except the Hivites of Gibeon. All
the others were defeated. 20 For the LORD hardened
their hearts and caused them to fight the Israelites.
So they were completely destroyed without mercy, as
the LORD had commanded Moses.
21 During this period Joshua destroyed all the descendants of Anak, who lived in the hill country of Hebron, Debir, Anab, and the entire hill country of Judah
and Israel. He killed them all and completely destroyed
their towns. 22 None of the descendants of Anak were
left in all the land of Israel, though some still remained
in Gaza, Gath, and Ashdod.
23 So Joshua took control of the entire land, just
as the LORD had instructed Moses. He gave it to the
people of Israel as their special possession, dividing
the land among the tribes. So the land finally had rest
from war.

Kings Defeated East of the Jordan

JOSHUA 12:1-6

These are the kings east of the Jordan River who had
been killed by the Israelites and whose land was taken.
Their territory extended from the Arnon Gorge to
Mount Hermon and included all the land east of the
Jordan Valley.*
2 King Sihon of the Amorites, who lived in Heshbon, was defeated. His kingdom included Aroer, on
the edge of the Arnon Gorge, and extended from the
middle of the Arnon Gorge to the Jabbok River, which
serves as a border for the Ammonites. This territory
included the southern half of the territory of Gilead.
3 Sihon also controlled the Jordan Valley and regions
to the east—from as far north as the Sea of Galilee to
as far south as the Dead Sea,* including the road to
Beth-jeshimoth and southward to the slopes of Pisgah.
4 King Og of Bashan, the last of the Rephaites, lived

Jo 11:16 Hebrew *the Shephelah, the Arabah.* **Jo 12:1** Hebrew *the Arabah;* also in 12:3, 8. **Jo 12:3** Hebrew *from the Sea of Kinnereth to the Sea of the Arabah, which is the Salt Sea.*

Hazor

Hazor was by far the largest Canaanite settlement with a population of perhaps 40,000 at its peak. Archaeological digs at Hazor are particularly interesting for the light they have shed on the conquest of Canaan described in the book of Joshua. Excavations clearly show that the great city was destroyed by fire in the last half of the 13th century B.C., just like the biblical picture of these events during the conquest under Joshua. The meager Israelite occupation in the 12th and 11th centuries B.C. was replaced by a well-fortified city during Solomon's reign as king, and this fortified city remained in use by the northern kingdom until it was destroyed by Tiglath-Pileser III in about 732 B.C. (2 Kgs 15:29). Located 10 miles north of the Sea of Galilee, it is known as Tell el-Qedah today.

Josh 11:18 The conquest of much of the land of Canaan seems to have happened quickly (we can read about it in one sitting), but it actually took seven years. We often expect quick changes in our lives and quick victories over sin. But our journey with God is a lifelong process, and the changes and victories may take time. It is easy to grow impatient with God and feel like giving up hope because things are moving too slowly. When we are close to a situation, it is difficult to see progress. But when we look back, we can see that God never stopped working.

Josh 11:21-22 The descendants of Anak were the tribes of giants the Israelite scouts described when they gave their negative report on the Promised Land (Num 13–14). This time the people did not let their fear of the giants prevent them from engaging in battle and claiming the land God had promised.

Josh 12:1ff Chapter 12 is a summary of the first half of the book of Joshua. It lists the kings and nations conquered by Joshua both east and west of the Jordan River. As long as the people trusted and obeyed God, one evil nation after another fell in defeat.

▸ **JOSHUA 12:1-6** ***(cont.)***

at Ashtaroth and Edrei. [5]He ruled a territory stretching from Mount Hermon to Salecah in the north and to all of Bashan in the east, and westward to the borders of the kingdoms of Geshur and Maacah. This territory included the northern half of Gilead, as far as the boundary of King Sihon of Heshbon.

[6]Moses, the servant of the LORD, and the Israelites had destroyed the people of King Sihon and King Og. And Moses gave their land as a possession to the tribes of Reuben, Gad, and the half-tribe of Manasseh.

Kings Defeated West of the Jordan

JOSHUA 12:7-24

The following is a list of the kings that Joshua and the Israelite armies defeated on the west side of the Jordan, from Baal-gad in the valley of Lebanon to Mount Halak, which leads up to Seir. (Joshua gave this land to the tribes of Israel as their possession, [8]including the hill country, the western foothills,* the Jordan Valley, the mountain slopes, the Judean wilderness, and the Negev. The people who lived in this region were the Hittites, the Amorites, the Canaanites, the Perizzites, the Hivites, and the Jebusites.) These are the kings Israel defeated:

[9] The king of Jericho
The king of Ai, near Bethel
[10] The king of Jerusalem
The king of Hebron
[11] The king of Jarmuth
The king of Lachish
[12] The king of Eglon
The king of Gezer
[13] The king of Debir

Jo 12:8 Hebrew *the Shephelah.*

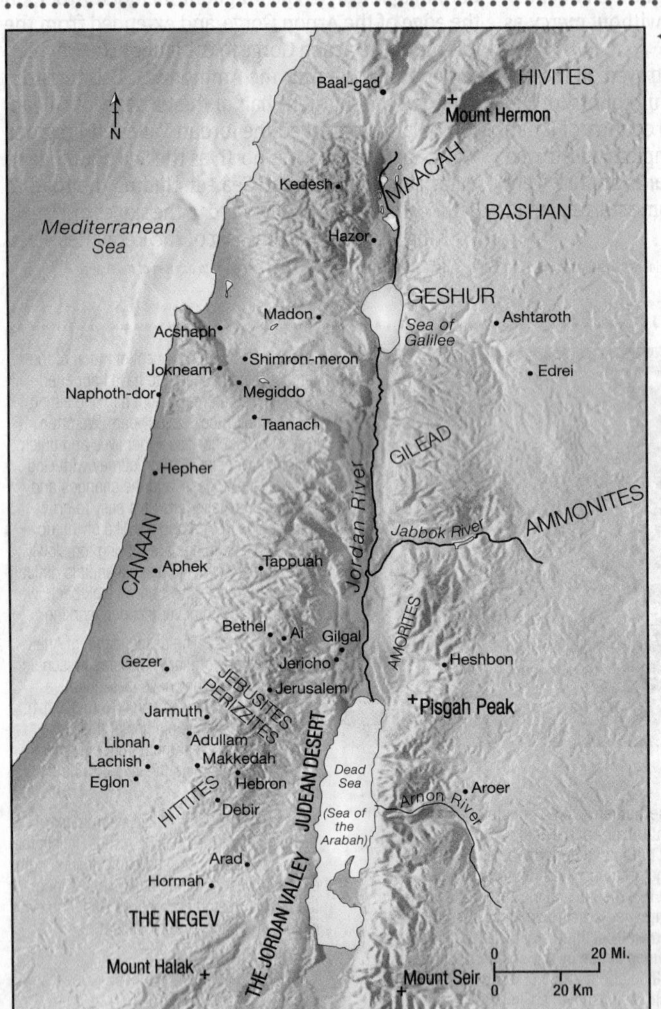

◀ ***THE CONQUERED LAND***
Joshua displayed brilliant military strategy in the way he went about conquering the land of Canaan. He first captured well-fortified Jericho to gain a foothold in Canaan and to demonstrate the awesome might of the God of Israel. Then he gained the hill country around Bethel. From there he subdued towns in the lowlands. Then his army conquered important cities in the north, such as Hazor. In all, Israel conquered land both east (Josh 12:1-6) and west (Josh 12:7-24) of the Jordan River—from Mount Hermon in the north to Mount Halak beyond the Negev in the south. Thirty-one kings and their cities had been defeated. The Israelites had overpowered the Hittites, the Amorites, the Canaanites, the Perizzites, the Hivites, and the Jebusites. Other peoples living in Canaan were yet to be conquered.

Josh 13–19 These chapters describe how the Promised Land was to be divided among the 12 tribes. First, the tribe of Levi was not to have any land because they were to spend all their energies serving the people, not their own interests (Josh 13:14, 33; 18:7). Second, the tribes of Reuben and Gad and the half-tribe of Manasseh had already received land east of the Jordan River, which had been given to them by Moses (Num 32). Third, the tribes of Judah and Joseph (Ephraim and the other half-tribe of Manasseh) had received land that their ancestor Jacob had promised them 450 years earlier (Gen 48:22; Josh 15–17). The rest of the tribes divided up the remaining land by casting sacred lots (Josh 18–19).

Through Jacob's original blessing of his sons (Gen 49) and Moses' blessing of the 12 tribes (Deut 33), the type of land each tribe would receive was already known. The two blessings were prophetic, for although Joshua cast lots to determine the land to be given to each of the remaining tribes, the allotments came out just as Jacob and Moses had predicted.

The king of Geder
14 The king of Hormah
The king of Arad
15 The king of Libnah
The king of Adullam
16 The king of Makkedah
The king of Bethel
17 The king of Tappuah
The king of Hepher
18 The king of Aphek
The king of Lasharon
19 The king of Madon
The king of Hazor
20 The king of Shimron-meron
The king of Acshaph
21 The king of Taanach
The king of Megiddo
22 The king of Kedesh
The king of Jokneam in Carmel
23 The king of Dor in the town of Naphoth-dor*
The king of Goyim in Gilgal*
24 The king of Tirzah.

In all, thirty-one kings were defeated.

Jo 12:23a Hebrew *Naphath-dor,* a variant spelling of Naphoth-dor. **Jo 12:23b** Greek version reads *Goyim in Galilee.*

C. Dividing the Promised Land

After seven years of battle, Israel gained control of the land, which was then divided and allotted to the tribes. Joshua dismissed the army, for it was now each tribe's responsibility to clear out the remaining enemies from their own areas. Joshua continued to encourage the people to remain faithful to God so they could remain in the land. The Promised Land was Israel's earthly inheritance. But Israel also had a spiritual inheritance in which we can share when we live a life of faithfulness to God.

1. THE TRIBES RECEIVE THEIR LAND

Each of the twelve tribes was given their own land. They were to finish the job of driving out the Canaanites and take complete possession of the Promised Land on their own, after God has used Joshua to secure the borders and clearly establish God's control over the land.

The Land Yet to Be Conquered

JOSHUA 13:1-7

When Joshua was an old man, the LORD said to him,
"You are growing old, and much land remains to be
conquered. 2 This is the territory that remains: all the
regions of the Philistines and the Geshurites, 3 and
the larger territory of the Canaanites, extending
from the stream of Shihor on the border of Egypt,

Josh 13:1 Joshua was getting old—he was between 85 and 100 years of age at this time. God, however, still had work for him to do. Our culture often glorifies the young and strong and sets aside those who are older. Yet older people are filled with the wisdom that comes with experience. They are very capable of serving if given the chance and should be encouraged to do so. Believers are never allowed to retire from God's service. Those past retirement age should not assume that age disqualifies or excuses them from serving God.

Mount Hermon

Mount Hermon is about 13 miles long and rises to a height of 9,166 feet. It is the mountain often mentioned as the northern extremity of the territory conquered by Joshua. It is also the northern boundary of the inheritance of the half-tribe of Manasseh, as well as of Israel in general (Deut 3:8; 4:48; Josh 11:17; 12:1, 5; 13:11; 1 Chr 5:23). Mount Hermon towers over the valley of Lebanon (Josh 11:17; 13:5) and over the valley of Mizpah, to which Joshua pursued the kings of Canaan after his victory over them at the waters of Merom (Josh 11:3, 8). Biblical poetry praises Hermon for its height and for sending dew to Zion (Ps 133:3); it was famed for its wildlife (Song 4:8). Mountains, such as Hermon, inspire praise of the Creator. Take the time to see God in the creation around you and you will find that praising him comes naturally.

▸ **JOSHUA 13:1-7** ***(cont.)***
northward to the boundary of Ekron. It includes the territory of the five Philistine rulers of Gaza, Ashdod, Ashkelon, Gath, and Ekron. The land of the Avvites
4in the south also remains to be conquered. In the north, the following area has not yet been conquered: all the land of the Canaanites, including Mearah (which belongs to the Sidonians), stretching northward to Aphek on the border of the Amorites;
5the land of the Gebalites and all of the Lebanon mountain area to the east, from Baal-gad below Mount Hermon to Lebo-hamath;
6and all the hill country from Lebanon to Misrephoth-maim, including all the land of the Sidonians.

"I myself will drive these people out of the land ahead of the Israelites. So be sure to give this land to Israel as a special possession, just as I have commanded you.
7Include all this territory as Israel's possession when you divide this land among the nine tribes and the half-tribe of Manasseh."

The Land Divided East of the Jordan

JOSHUA 13:8-13

Half the tribe of Manasseh and the tribes of Reuben and Gad had already received their grants of land on the east side of the Jordan, for Moses, the servant of the Lord, had previously assigned this land to them.

9Their territory extended from Aroer on the edge of the Arnon Gorge (including the town in the middle of the gorge) to the plain beyond Medeba, as far as Dibon.
10It also included all the towns of King Sihon of the Amorites, who had reigned in Heshbon, and extended as far as the borders of Ammon.
11It included Gilead, the territory of the kingdoms of Geshur and Maacah, all of Mount Hermon, all of Bashan as far as Salecah,
12and all the territory of King Og of Bashan, who had reigned in Ashtaroth and Edrei. King Og was the last of the Rephaites, for Moses had attacked them and driven them out.
13But the Israelites failed to drive out the people of Geshur and Maacah, so they continue to live among the Israelites to this day.

An Allotment for the Tribe of Levi

JOSHUA 13:14

Moses did not assign any allotment of land to the tribe of Levi. Instead, as the Lord had promised them, their allotment came from the offerings burned on the altar to the Lord, the God of Israel.

The Land Given to the Tribe of Reuben

JOSHUA 13:15-23

Moses had assigned the following area to the clans of the tribe of Reuben.

16Their territory extended from Aroer on the edge of the Arnon Gorge (including the town in the middle of the gorge) to the plain beyond Medeba.
17It included Heshbon and the other towns on the plain—Dibon, Bamoth-baal, Beth-baal-meon,
18Jahaz, Kedemoth, Mephaath,

Josh 13:7 Much of the land was unconquered at this point, but God's plan was to go ahead and include it in the divisions among the tribes. God's desire was that it would eventually be conquered by the Israelites. God knows the future, and as he leads you he already knows about the victories that lie ahead. But just as the Israelites still had to go to battle and fight, we must still face the trials and fight the battles of our unconquered land.

What are our unconquered lands? They may be overseas missionary territories, new languages in which to translate the Bible, new missionary areas in our neighborhoods, interest groups or institutions that need redemptive work, unchallenged public problems or ethical issues, unconfessed sin in our lives, or underdeveloped talents and resources. What territory has God given you to conquer? Our inheritance will be a new heaven and a new earth (Rev 21:1) if we fulfill the mission God has given us to do.

Josh 13:13 One reason the Israelites encountered so many problems as they settled the land was that they failed to fully conquer the land and drive out *all* its inhabitants. The cancer-like presence of the remaining Canaanites caused unending difficulties for the Israelites, as the book of Judges records. Just as they failed to remove completely the sin from the land, believers today often fail to remove completely the sin from their lives—also with disastrous results. As a self-test, reread the Ten Commandments (Exod 20:1-17). Ask yourself: Am I tolerating sinful practices or thoughts? Have I accepted half-measures as good enough? Do I condemn the faults of others but condone my own?

Josh 13:15-23 Because of Joseph's godly character (Gen 49:22-26), the tribes descended from him—Ephraim and Manasseh—were given the richest, most fertile land in all of Canaan. Judah, who offered himself in exchange for his brother Benjamin's safety (Gen 44:18-34), received the largest portion of land, which eventually became the southern kingdom and the seat of David's dynasty. Reuben, who slept with one of his father's wives (Gen 49:4), was given desert land, the region described here. The blessings Jacob gave to his sons according to their character seem also to be reflected in the characteristics of the land each tribe later received.

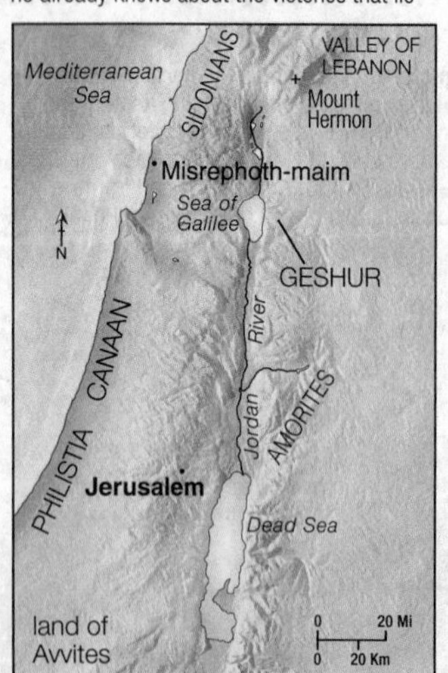

◂ ***THE LAND YET TO BE CONQUERED***
Canaan was now controlled by the Israelites, although much land and several cities still needed to be conquered. Joshua told the people to include both conquered and unconquered lands in the territorial allotments (Josh 13:7). He was certain the people would complete the conquest as God had commanded.

19 Kiriathaim, Sibmah, Zereth-shahar on the
hill above the valley, 20 Beth-peor, the slopes of
Pisgah, and Beth-jeshimoth.
21 The land of Reuben also included all the
towns of the plain and the entire kingdom of
Sihon. Sihon was the Amorite king who had
reigned in Heshbon and was killed by Moses
along with the leaders of Midian—Evi, Rekem,
Zur, Hur, and Reba—princes living in the region
who were allied with Sihon. 22 The Israelites had
also killed Balaam son of Beor, who used magic
to tell the future. 23 The Jordan River marked
the western boundary for the tribe of Reuben.
The towns and their surrounding villages in this
area were given as a homeland to the clans of the
tribe of Reuben.

The Land Given to the Tribe of Gad

JOSHUA 13:24-28

Moses had assigned the following area to the clans of
the tribe of Gad.

25 Their territory included Jazer, all the towns
of Gilead, and half of the land of Ammon, as far
as the town of Aroer just west of* Rabbah. 26 It
extended from Heshbon to Ramath-mizpeh and
Betonim, and from Mahanaim to the territory
of Lo-debar.* 27 In the valley were Beth-haram,
Beth-nimrah, Succoth, Zaphon, and the rest of
the kingdom of King Sihon of Heshbon. The
western boundary ran along the Jordan River,
extended as far north as the tip of the Sea
of Galilee,* and then turned eastward. 28 The
towns and their surrounding villages in this
area were given as a homeland to the clans of
the tribe of Gad.

The Land Given to the Half-Tribe of Manasseh

JOSHUA 13:29-33

Moses had assigned the following area to the clans of
the half-tribe of Manasseh.

30 Their territory extended from Mahanaim,
including all of Bashan, all the former kingdom
of King Og, and the sixty towns of Jair in Bashan.
31 It also included half of Gilead and King Og's
royal cities of Ashtaroth and Edrei. All this was
given to the clans of the descendants of Makir,
who was Manasseh's son.

32 These are the allotments Moses had made while
he was on the plains of Moab, across the Jordan River,
east of Jericho. 33 But Moses gave no allotment of land
to the tribe of Levi, for the LORD, the God of Israel, had
promised that he himself would be their allotment.

The Land Divided West of the Jordan

JOSHUA 14:1-5

The remaining tribes of Israel received land in Canaan as allotted by Eleazar the priest, Joshua son of
Nun, and the tribal leaders. 2 These nine and a half
tribes received their grants of land by means of sacred
lots, in accordance with the LORD's command through
Moses. 3 Moses had already given a grant of land to the
two and a half tribes on the east side of the Jordan
River, but he had given the Levites no such allotment.
4 The descendants of Joseph had become two separate tribes—Manasseh and Ephraim. And the Levites
were given no land at all, only towns to live in with
surrounding pasturelands for their livestock and all
their possessions. 5 So the land was distributed in strict
accordance with the LORD's commands to Moses.

Jo 13:25 Hebrew *in front of.* **Jo 13:26** Hebrew *Li-debir,* apparently a variant spelling of Lo-debar (compare 2 Sam 9:4; 17:27; Amos 6:13). **Jo 13:27** Hebrew *Sea of Kinnereth.*

Josh 13:29 The tribe of Manasseh was divided into two half-tribes. This occurred when many people from the tribe wanted to settle east of the Jordan River in an area that was especially suited for their flocks (Num 32:33). The rest of the tribe preferred to settle west of the Jordan River in the land of Canaan.

Josh 13:33 The tribe of Levi was dedicated to serving God. The Levites needed more time and mobility than a landowner could possibly have. Giving them land would mean saddling them with responsibilities and loyalties that would hinder their service to God. Instead, God arranged for the other tribes to meet the Levites' needs through donations. (See Num 35:2-4 for how the Levites were to receive cities within each tribal territory.)

Josh 14:5 The land was divided exactly as God had instructed Moses years before. Joshua did not change a word. He followed God's commands precisely. Often we believe that *almost* is close enough, and this idea can carry over into our spiritual lives. For example, we may follow God's Word as long as we agree with it, but we ignore it when the demands seem harsh. But God is looking for people who follow instructions thoroughly.

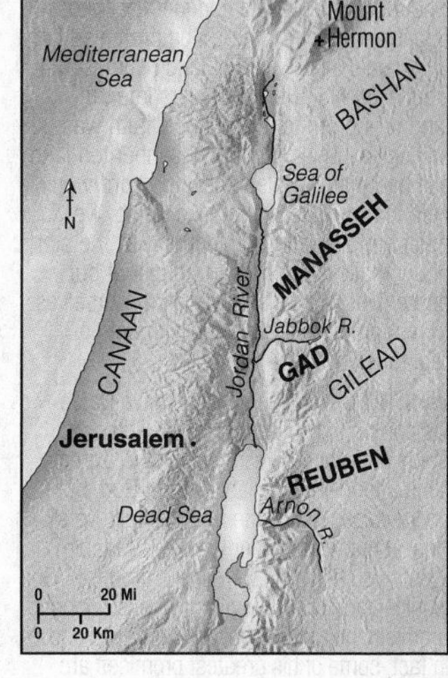

THE TRIBES EAST OF THE JORDAN ▶
Joshua assigned territory to the tribes of Reuben, Gad, and the half-tribe of Manasseh on the east side of the Jordan where they had chosen to remain because it was country ideally suited for livestock (Num 32:1-5).

Caleb Requests His Land

JOSHUA 14:6-15

A delegation from the tribe of Judah, led by Caleb son
of Jephunneh the Kenizzite, came to Joshua at Gilgal.
Caleb said to Joshua, "Remember what the LORD said
to Moses, the man of God, about you and me when we
were at Kadesh-barnea. 7 I was forty years old when
Moses, the servant of the LORD, sent me from Kadesh-
barnea to explore the land of Canaan. I returned and
gave an honest report, 8 but my brothers who went with
me frightened the people from entering the Promised
Land. For my part, I wholeheartedly followed the LORD
my God. 9 So that day Moses solemnly promised me,
'The land of Canaan on which you were just walking
will be your grant of land and that of your descendants forever, because you wholeheartedly followed
the LORD my God.'

10 "Now, as you can see, the LORD has kept me alive
and well as he promised for all these forty-five years
since Moses made this promise—even while Israel
wandered in the wilderness. Today I am eighty-five
years old. 11 I am as strong now as I was when Moses
sent me on that journey, and I can still travel and fight
as well as I could then. 12 So give me the hill country
that the LORD promised me. You will remember that as
scouts we found the descendants of Anak living there
in great, walled towns. But if the LORD is with me, I
will drive them out of the land, just as the LORD said."

13 So Joshua blessed Caleb son of Jephunneh and
gave Hebron to him as his portion of land. 14 Hebron
still belongs to the descendants of Caleb son of Jephunneh the Kenizzite because he wholeheartedly followed
the LORD, the God of Israel. 15 (Previously Hebron had
been called Kiriath-arba. It had been named after Arba,
a great hero of the descendants of Anak.)

And the land had rest from war.

The Land Given to the Tribe of Judah

JOSHUA 15:1-12

The allotment for the clans of the tribe of Judah reached southward to the border of Edom, as far south as the wilderness of Zin.

2 The southern boundary began at the south bay
of the Dead Sea,* 3 ran south of Scorpion Pass*
into the wilderness of Zin, and then went south
of Kadesh-barnea to Hezron. Then it went up
to Addar, where it turned toward Karka. 4 From
there it passed to Azmon until it finally reached
the Brook of Egypt, which it followed to the
Mediterranean Sea.* This was their* southern
boundary.

5 The eastern boundary extended along the
Dead Sea to the mouth of the Jordan River.

The northern boundary began at the bay where
the Jordan River empties into the Dead Sea, 6 went
up from there to Beth-hoglah, then proceeded
north of Beth-arabah to the Stone of Bohan.
(Bohan was Reuben's son.) 7 From that point it
went through the valley of Achor to Debir, turning
north toward Gilgal, which is across from the
slopes of Adummim on the south side of the
valley. From there the boundary extended to
the springs at En-shemesh and on to En-rogel.
8 The boundary then passed through the valley
of Ben-Hinnom, along the southern slopes
of the Jebusites, where the city of Jerusalem

Jo 15:2 Hebrew *the Salt Sea;* also in 15:5. **Jo 15:3** Hebrew *Akrabbim.* **Jo 15:4a** Hebrew *the sea;* also in 15:11. **Jo 15:4b** Hebrew *your.*

Josh 14:6-12 Caleb was faithful from the start. As one of the original scouts sent into the Promised Land (Num 13:30-33), he saw great cities and giants, yet he knew God would help the people conquer the land. Because of Caleb's faith, God promised him a personal inheritance of land (Num 14:24; Deut 1:34-36). Here, 45 years later, the land was given to him. Caleb's faith was still unwavering. Although his inherited land still had giants, Caleb knew the Lord would help him conquer them. Like Caleb, we must be faithful to God, not only at the start of our walk with him but throughout our entire lives. We must never allow ourselves to rest on our past accomplishments or reputations.

Josh 14:6-12 When Joshua gave Caleb his portion, it fulfilled a promise God had made to Caleb 45 years earlier. We expect such integrity and reliability from God, but do we expect the same from his followers? How about you? Is your word this reliable? Would you honor a 45-year-old promise? God would—and does. Even today he is honoring promises he made thousands of years ago. In fact, some of his greatest promises are yet to be fulfilled. This gives us much to look forward to. Let your faith grow as you realize that God keeps his word.

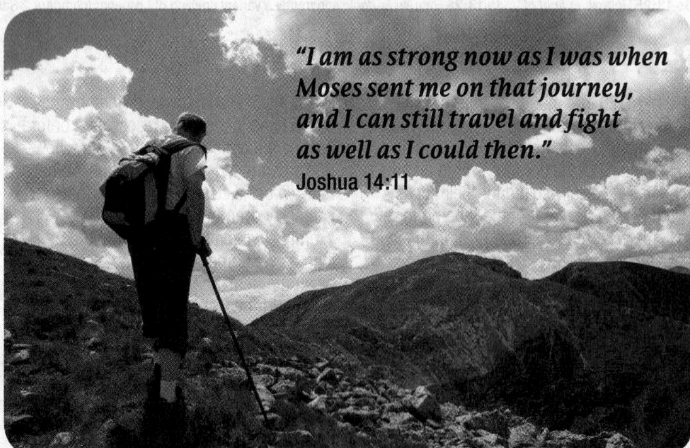
"I am as strong now as I was when Moses sent me on that journey, and I can still travel and fight as well as I could then."
Joshua 14:11

Josh 14:15 The descendants of Anak were a race of giants who inhabited parts of the land before Joshua's conquest.

Josh 15:4 Notice that these boundaries and descriptions of the Promised Land are very specific. God was telling Israel exactly what to do, and he was giving them just what they needed. They had no excuse for disobedience.

is located. Then it went west to the top of the mountain above the valley of Hinnom, and on up to the northern end of the valley of Rephaim. 9From there the boundary extended from the top of the mountain to the spring at the waters of Nephtoah,* and from there to the towns on Mount Ephron. Then it turned toward Baalah (that is, Kiriath-jearim). 10The boundary circled west of Baalah to Mount Seir, passed along to the town of Kesalon on the northern slope of Mount Jearim, and went down to Beth-shemesh and on to Timnah. 11The boundary then proceeded to the slope of the hill north of Ekron, where it turned toward Shikkeron and Mount Baalah. It passed Jabneel and ended at the Mediterranean Sea.

12The western boundary was the shoreline of the Mediterranean Sea.*

These are the boundaries for the clans of the tribe of Judah.

The Land Given to Caleb

JOSHUA 15:13-19

The LORD commanded Joshua to assign some of Judah's territory to Caleb son of Jephunneh. So Caleb was given the town of Kiriath-arba (that is, Hebron), which had been named after Anak's ancestor. 14Caleb drove out the three groups of Anakites—the descendants of Sheshai, Ahiman, and Talmai, the sons of Anak.

15From there he went to fight against the people living in the town of Debir (formerly called Kiriath-sepher). 16Caleb said, "I will give my daughter Acsah in marriage to the one who attacks and captures Kiriath-sepher." 17Othniel, the son of Caleb's brother Kenaz, was the one who conquered it, so Acsah became Othniel's wife.

18When Acsah married Othniel, she urged him* to ask her father for a field. As she got down off her donkey, Caleb asked her, "What's the matter?"

19She said, "Give me another gift. You have already given me land in the Negev; now please give me springs of water, too." So Caleb gave her the upper and lower springs.

The Towns Allotted to Judah

JOSHUA 15:20-63

This was the homeland allocated to the clans of the tribe of Judah.

21The towns of Judah situated along the borders of Edom in the extreme south were Kabzeel, Eder, Jagur, 22Kinah, Dimonah, Adadah, 23Kedesh, Hazor, Ithnan, 24Ziph, Telem, Bealoth, 25Hazor-hadattah, Kerioth-hezron (that is, Hazor), 26Amam, Shema, Moladah, 27Hazar-gaddah, Heshmon, Beth-pelet, 28Hazar-shual, Beersheba, Biziothiah, 29Baalah, Iim, Ezem, 30Eltolad, Kesil, Hormah, 31Ziklag, Madmannah, Sansannah, 32Lebaoth, Shilhim, Ain, and Rimmon—twenty-nine towns with their surrounding villages.

33The following towns situated in the western foothills* were also given to Judah: Eshtaol, Zorah, Ashnah, 34Zanoah, En-gannim, Tappuah, Enam, 35Jarmuth, Adullam, Socoh, Azekah, 36Shaaraim, Adithaim, Gederah, and Gederothaim—fourteen towns with their surrounding villages.

37Also included were Zenan, Hadashah, Migdal-gad, 38Dilean, Mizpeh, Joktheel, 39Lachish, Bozkath, Eglon, 40Cabbon, Lahmam, Kitlish, 41Gederoth, Beth-dagon, Naamah, and Makkedah—sixteen towns with their surrounding villages.

42Besides these, there were Libnah, Ether, Ashan, 43Iphtah, Ashnah, Nezib, 44Keilah, Aczib, and Mareshah—nine towns with their surrounding villages.

45The territory of the tribe of Judah also included Ekron and its surrounding settlements and villages. 46From Ekron the boundary extended west and included the towns near Ashdod with their surrounding villages. 47It also included Ashdod with its surrounding settlements and villages and Gaza with its settlements and villages, as far as the Brook of Egypt and along the coast of the Mediterranean Sea.

48Judah also received the following towns in the hill country: Shamir, Jattir, Socoh, 49Dannah, Kiriath-sannah (that is, Debir), 50Anab, Eshtemoh, Anim, 51Goshen, Holon, and Giloh—eleven towns with their surrounding villages.

52Also included were the towns of Arab, Dumah, Eshan, 53Janim, Beth-tappuah, Aphekah, 54Humtah, Kiriath-arba (that is, Hebron), and Zior—nine towns with their surrounding villages.

55Besides these, there were Maon, Carmel, Ziph, Juttah, 56Jezreel, Jokdeam, Zanoah, 57Kain, Gibeah, and Timnah—ten towns with their surrounding villages.

58In addition, there were Halhul, Beth-zur, Gedor, 59Maarath, Beth-anoth, and Eltekon—six towns with their surrounding villages.

60There were also Kiriath-baal (that is,

Jo 15:9 Or *the spring at Me-nephtoah.* **Jo 15:12** Hebrew *the Great Sea;* also in 15:47. **Jo 15:18** Some Greek manuscripts read *he urged her.* **Jo 15:33** Hebrew *the Shephelah.*

Josh 15:16-19 Othniel became Israel's first judge after Joshua's death (Judg 1:13; 3:9-11). He played an important role in reforming Israel by chasing away an oppressive enemy army and bringing peace back to the land. Thus Caleb's legacy of faithfulness continued to the next generation.

Josh 15:19 Acsah asked Caleb for springs of water because her land was in the south and was very arid. Caleb probably granted her request as a wedding present (see Josh 15:17).

▸ **JOSHUA 15:20-63** ***(cont.)***

Kiriath-jearim) and Rabbah—two towns with their surrounding villages.

[61]In the wilderness there were the towns of Beth-arabah, Middin, Secacah, [62]Nibshan, the City of Salt, and En-gedi—six towns with their surrounding villages.

[63]But the tribe of Judah could not drive out the Jebusites, who lived in the city of Jerusalem, so the Jebusites live there among the people of Judah to this day.

The Land Given to Ephraim and West Manasseh

JOSHUA 16:1-4

The allotment for the descendants of Joseph extended from the Jordan River near Jericho, east of the springs of Jericho, through the wilderness and into the hill country of Bethel. [2]From Bethel (that is, Luz)* it ran over to Ataroth in the territory of the Arkites. [3]Then it descended westward to the territory of the Japhletites as far as Lower Beth-horon, then to Gezer and over to the Mediterranean Sea.*

[4]This was the homeland allocated to the families of Joseph's sons, Manasseh and Ephraim.

The Land Given to Ephraim

JOSHUA 16:5-10

The following territory was given to the clans of the tribe of Ephraim.

The boundary of their homeland began at Ataroth-addar in the east. From there it ran to Upper Beth-horon, [6]then on to the Mediterranean Sea. From Micmethath on the north, the boundary curved eastward past Taanath-shiloh to the east of Janoah. [7]From Janoah it turned southward to Ataroth and Naarah, touched Jericho, and ended at the Jordan River. [8]From Tappuah the boundary extended westward, following the Kanah Ravine to the Mediterranean Sea. This is the homeland allocated to the clans of the tribe of Ephraim.

[9]In addition, some towns with their surrounding villages in the territory allocated to the half-tribe of Manasseh were set aside for the tribe of Ephraim. [10]They did not drive the Canaanites out of Gezer, however, so the people of Gezer live as slaves among the people of Ephraim to this day.

The Land Given to West Manasseh

JOSHUA 17:1-18

The next allotment of land was given to the half-tribe of Manasseh, the descendants of Joseph's older son. Makir, the firstborn son of Manasseh, was the father of Gilead. Because his descendants were experienced soldiers, the regions of Gilead and Bashan on the east side of the Jordan had already been given to them. [2]So the allotment on the west side of the Jordan was for the remaining families within the clans of the tribe of Manasseh: Abiezer, Helek, Asriel, Shechem, Hepher, and Shemida. These clans represent the male descendants of Manasseh son of Joseph.

[3]However, Zelophehad, a descendant of Hepher son of Gilead, son of Makir, son of Manasseh, had no sons. He had only daughters, whose names were Mahlah, Noah, Hoglah, Milcah, and Tirzah. [4]These women came to Eleazar the priest, Joshua son of Nun, and the Israelite leaders and said, "The LORD commanded Moses to give us a grant of land along with the men of our tribe."

So Joshua gave them a grant of land along with their uncles, as the LORD had commanded. [5]As a result, Manasseh's total allocation came to ten parcels of land, in addition to the land of Gilead and Bashan across the Jordan River, [6]because the female descendants of Manasseh received a grant of land along with the male descendants. (The land of Gilead was given to the rest of the male descendants of Manasseh.)

[7]The boundary of the tribe of Manasseh extended from the border of Asher to Micmethath, near Shechem. Then the boundary went south from Micmethath to the settlement near the spring of Tappuah. [8]The land surrounding Tappuah belonged to Manasseh, but the town of Tappuah itself, on the border of Manasseh's territory, belonged to the tribe of Ephraim. [9]From the spring of Tappuah, the boundary of Manasseh

Jo 16:2 As in Greek version (also see 18:13); Hebrew reads *From Bethel to Luz.* **Jo 16:3** Hebrew *the sea;* also in 16:6, 8.

Josh 16:1ff Although Joseph was one of Jacob's 12 sons, he did not have a tribe named after him. This was because Joseph, as the oldest son of Jacob's wife Rachel, received a double portion of the inheritance. Joseph's double portion was divided between his two sons, Ephraim and Manasseh, whom Jacob considered as his own (Gen 48:5). The largest territory and the greatest influence in the northern half of Israel belonged to their tribes.

Josh 16:10 Occasionally this short phrase appears: "They did not drive out" the people of the land (see also Josh 15:63; 17:12). This was contrary to God's explicit desire and command (Josh 13:1-6). The failure to completely remove the pagan people and their gods from the land would cause many problems for the nation. The book of Judges records many of these struggles.

Josh 17:3-4 Although women did not traditionally inherit property in Israelite society, Moses put justice ahead of tradition and gave these five women the land they deserved (see Num 27:1-11). In fact, God told Moses to add a law that would help other women in similar circumstances inherit property as well. Joshua was now carrying out this law. It is easy to refuse to honor a reasonable request because "we have never done it that way before." But, like Moses and Joshua, we should look carefully at the purpose of the law and the merits of each case before deciding.

followed the Kanah Ravine to the Mediterranean
Sea.* Several towns south of the ravine were
inside Manasseh's territory, but they actually
belonged to the tribe of Ephraim. 10 In general,
however, the land south of the ravine belonged
to Ephraim, and the land north of the ravine
belonged to Manasseh. Manasseh's boundary ran
along the northern side of the ravine and ended
at the Mediterranean Sea. North of Manasseh
was the territory of Asher, and to the east was the
territory of Issachar.
11 The following towns within the territory
of Issachar and Asher, however, were given to
Manasseh: Beth-shan,* Ibleam, Dor (that is,
Naphoth-dor),* Endor, Taanach, and Megiddo,
each with their surrounding settlements.

12 But the descendants of Manasseh were unable
to occupy these towns. They could not drive out the
Canaanites who continued to live there. 13 Later, however, when the Israelites became strong enough, they
forced the Canaanites to work as slaves. But they did
not drive them out of the land.
14 The descendants of Joseph came to Joshua and
asked, "Why have you given us only one portion of
land as our homeland when the LORD has blessed us
with so many people?"
15 Joshua replied, "If there are so many of you, and
if the hill country of Ephraim is not large enough for
you, clear out land for yourselves in the forest where
the Perizzites and Rephaites live."
16 The descendants of Joseph responded, "It's
true that the hill country is not large enough for
us. But all the Canaanites in the lowlands have iron
chariots, both those in Beth-shan and its surrounding
settlements and those in the valley of Jezreel. They are
too strong for us."
17 Then Joshua said to the tribes of Ephraim and
Manasseh, the descendants of Joseph, "Since you are
so large and strong, you will be given more than one
portion. 18 The forests of the hill country will be yours
as well. Clear as much of the land as you wish, and take
possession of its farthest corners. And you will drive
out the Canaanites from the valleys, too, even though
they are strong and have iron chariots."

The Allotments of the Remaining Land

JOSHUA 18:1-10

Now that the land was under Israelite control, the entire community of Israel gathered at Shiloh and set up
the Tabernacle.* 2 But there remained seven tribes who
had not yet been allotted their grants of land.
3 Then Joshua asked them, "How long are you going to wait before taking possession of the remaining
land the LORD, the God of your ancestors, has given
to you? 4 Select three men from each tribe, and I will
send them out to explore the land and map it out.
They will then return to me with a written report of
their proposed divisions of their new homeland. 5 Let
them divide the land into seven sections, excluding
Judah's territory in the south and Joseph's territory in
the north. 6 And when you record the seven divisions
of the land and bring them to me, I will cast sacred
lots in the presence of the LORD our God to assign
land to each tribe.
7 "The Levites, however, will not receive any allotment of land. Their role as priests of the LORD is their
allotment. And the tribes of Gad, Reuben, and the half-
tribe of Manasseh won't receive any more land, for
they have already received their grant of land, which

Jo 17:9 Hebrew *the sea;* also in 17:10. **Jo 17:11a** Hebrew *Beth-shean,* a variant spelling of Beth-shan; also in 17:16. **Jo 17:11b** The meaning of the Hebrew here is uncertain. **Jo 18:1** Hebrew *Tent of Meeting.*

Josh 17:14-15 Notice the two contrasting attitudes toward settling the Promised Land: Caleb took what God gave him and moved ahead to fulfill God's plan for him (Josh 14:12). He was confident that God would help him drive out the wicked inhabitants and that he would soon fully occupy his land (Josh 15:14-15). In contrast, the two tribes of Joseph were given rich land and lots of it, but they were afraid to drive out the inhabitants and take full possession. Instead, they begged for more land. But Joshua asked them to prove their sincerity first by clearing the unclaimed forest areas. They agreed, but they failed to carry through (Judg 1:27).

Josh 18:1-2 With most of the conquest behind them, Israel moved its religious center from Gilgal (see the note on Josh 5:8-9, p. 342) to Shiloh. This was probably the first permanent location for the Tabernacle. Its central location in the land made it easier for the people to attend the special worship services and yearly festivals.

Later, the family of Samuel, a great priest and prophet, would often travel to Shiloh, and Samuel would be left there when a small boy (1 Sam 1:3, 22). The Tabernacle would remain in Shiloh through the period of the judges (about 300 years). Apparently the city was destroyed by the Philistines when the Ark of the Covenant was captured (1 Sam 4–5). Shiloh never lived up to its reputation as Israel's religious center, for later references in the Bible point to the wickedness and idolatry in the city (Ps 78:56-60; Jer 7:12-15).

Josh 18:2ff Seven of the tribes had not yet been assigned their land. They gathered at Shiloh, where Joshua cast lots to determine which areas would be given to them. Using the sacred lottery, God would make the choice, not Joshua or any other human leader.

By this time the Canaanites were, in most places, so weakened that they were no longer a threat. Instead of fulfilling God's command to destroy the remaining Canaanites, however, these seven tribes would often take the path of least resistance. As nomadic people, they may have been reluctant to settle down, preferring to depend economically on the people they were supposed to eliminate. Others may have feared the high cost of continued warfare. Trading for goods was easier and more profitable than destroying the suppliers and having to provide for themselves.

Josh 18:3-6 Joshua asked why some of the tribes were putting off the job of possessing the land. Often we delay doing jobs that seem large, difficult, boring, or disagreeable. Jobs we don't enjoy require concentration, teamwork, twice as much time, lots of encouragement, and accountability. But to continue putting them off shows lack of discipline, poor stewardship of time, and, in some cases, disobedience to God. Remember this when you are tempted to procrastinate.

▸ **JOSHUA 18:1-10** ***(cont.)***

Moses, the servant of the LORD, gave them on the east
side of the Jordan River."
8 As the men started on their way to map out the
land, Joshua commanded them, "Go and explore the
land and write a description of it. Then return to
me, and I will assign the land to the tribes by casting
sacred lots here in the presence of the LORD at Shiloh."
9 The men did as they were told and mapped the entire
territory into seven sections, listing the towns in each
section. They made a written record and then returned
to Joshua in the camp at Shiloh. 10 And there at Shiloh,
Joshua cast sacred lots in the presence of the LORD to
determine which tribe should have each section.

The Land Given to Benjamin

JOSHUA 18:11-20

The first allotment of land went to the clans of the
tribe of Benjamin. It lay between the territory assigned
to the tribes of Judah and Joseph.
12 The northern boundary of Benjamin's land
began at the Jordan River, went north of the slope
of Jericho, then west through the hill country and
the wilderness of Beth-aven. 13 From there the
boundary went south to Luz (that is, Bethel) and
proceeded down to Ataroth-addar on the hill that
lies south of Lower Beth-horon.
14 The boundary then made a turn and swung
south along the western edge of the hill facing
Beth-horon, ending at the village of Kiriath-
baal (that is, Kiriath-jearim), a town belonging
to the tribe of Judah. This was the western
boundary.
15 The southern boundary began at the outskirts
of Kiriath-jearim. From that western point it
ran* to the spring at the waters of Nephtoah,*
16 and down to the base of the mountain beside
the valley of Ben-Hinnom, at the northern end
of the valley of Rephaim. From there it went
down the valley of Hinnom, crossing south of the
slope where the Jebusites lived, and continued
down to En-rogel. 17 From En-rogel the boundary
proceeded in a northerly direction and came to
En-shemesh and on to Geliloth (which is across
from the slopes of Adummim). Then it went
down to the Stone of Bohan. (Bohan was Reuben's
son.) 18 From there it passed along the north side
of the slope overlooking the Jordan Valley.* The
border then went down into the valley, 19 ran past
the north slope of Beth-hoglah, and ended at the
north bay of the Dead Sea,* which is the southern
end of the Jordan River. This was the southern
boundary.
20 The eastern boundary was the Jordan River.
These were the boundaries of the homeland allocated
to the clans of the tribe of Benjamin.

The Towns Given to Benjamin

JOSHUA 18:21-28

These were the towns given to the clans of the tribe
of Benjamin.

Jericho, Beth-hoglah, Emek-keziz, 22 Beth-arabah,
Zemaraim, Bethel, 23 Avvim, Parah, Ophrah,
24 Kephar-ammoni, Ophni, and Geba—twelve
towns with their surrounding villages. 25 Also
Gibeon, Ramah, Beeroth, 26 Mizpah, Kephirah,
Mozah, 27 Rekem, Irpeel, Taralah, 28 Zela, Haeleph,
Jebus (that is, Jerusalem), Gibeah, and Kiriath*—
fourteen towns with their surrounding villages.

This was the homeland allocated to the clans of the
tribe of Benjamin.

Jo 18:15a Or *From there it went to Mozah.* The meaning of the Hebrew is uncertain. **Jo 18:15b** Or *the spring at Me-nephtoah.* **Jo 18:18** Hebrew *overlooking the Arabah,* or *overlooking Beth-arabah.* **Jo 18:19** Hebrew *Salt Sea.* **Jo 18:28** Some Greek manuscripts read *Kiriath-jearim.*

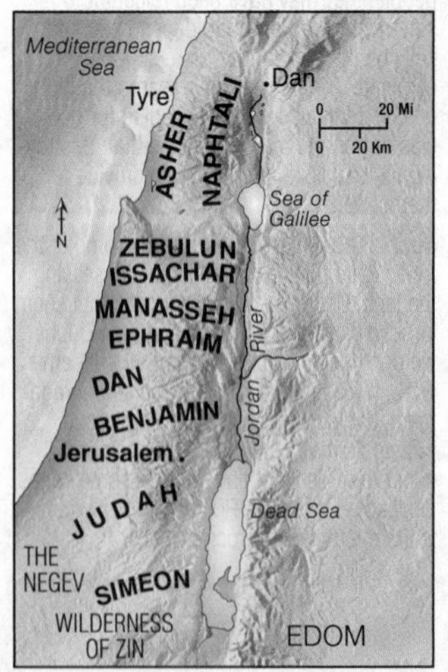

◀ ***THE TRIBES WEST OF THE JORDAN*** *Judah, Ephraim, and the other half-tribe of Manasseh were the first tribes to receive land west of the Jordan because of their past acts of faith. The remaining seven tribes—Benjamin, Zebulun, Issachar, Asher, Naphtali, Simeon, and Dan—were slow to conquer and possess the land allotted to them.*

Josh 18:8 Making decisions by casting lots was a common practice among the Hebrews. Little is known about the actual method used in Joshua's day. A type of dice may have been used. Another possibility is that two urns were used: one containing tribal names and the other, the divisions of the land. Drawing one name from each urn matched a tribe to a region. The Urim and Thummim (explained in the note on Lev 8:8, p. 210) may also have been used. No matter how it was done, the process removed human choice from the decision-making process and allowed God to match tribes and lands as he saw fit.

Josh 18:11 The tribe of Benjamin was given a narrow strip of land that served as a buffer zone between Judah and Ephraim, the two tribes that would later dominate the land.

Josh 18:16 The valley of Hinnom became associated with the worship of Molech (the Ammonite god) in Jeremiah's time. These terrible rites involved sacrificing children. Later the valley was used for burning garbage and the corpses of criminals and animals. Thus, the name became a synonym for hell.

The Land Given to Simeon

JOSHUA 19:1-9

The second allotment of land went to the clans of the tribe of Simeon. Their homeland was surrounded by Judah's territory.

[2]Simeon's homeland included Beersheba, Sheba,
Moladah, [3]Hazar-shual, Balah, Ezem, [4]Eltolad,
Bethul, Hormah, [5]Ziklag, Beth-marcaboth, Hazar-
susah, [6]Beth-lebaoth, and Sharuhen—thirteen
towns with their surrounding villages. [7]It also
included Ain, Rimmon, Ether, and Ashan—four
towns with their villages, [8]including all the
surrounding villages as far south as Baalath-beer
(also known as Ramah of the Negev).

This was the homeland allocated to the clans of the
tribe of Simeon. [9]Their allocation of land came from
part of what had been given to Judah because Judah's territory was too large for them. So the tribe of Simeon received an allocation within the territory of Judah.

The Land Given to Zebulun

JOSHUA 19:10-16

The third allotment of land went to the clans of the tribe of Zebulun.

The boundary of Zebulun's homeland started
at Sarid. [11]From there it went west, going past
Maralah, touching Dabbesheth, and proceeding
to the brook east of Jokneam. [12]In the other
direction, the boundary went east from Sarid to
the border of Kisloth-tabor, and from there to
Daberath and up to Japhia. [13]Then it continued
east to Gath-hepher, Eth-kazin, and Rimmon and
turned toward Neah. [14]The northern boundary
of Zebulun passed Hannathon and ended at the
valley of Iphtah-el. [15]The towns in these areas
included Kattath, Nahalal, Shimron, Idalah, and
Bethlehem—twelve towns with their surrounding
villages.

[16]The homeland allocated to the clans of the tribe of
Zebulun included these towns and their surrounding
villages.

The Land Given to Issachar

JOSHUA 19:17-23

The fourth allotment of land went to the clans of the tribe of Issachar.

[18]Its boundaries included the following towns:
Jezreel, Kesulloth, Shunem, [19]Hapharaim, Shion,
Anaharath, [20]Rabbith, Kishion, Ebez, [21]Remeth,
En-gannim, En-haddah, and Beth-pazzez. [22]The
boundary also touched Tabor, Shahazumah, and
Beth-shemesh, ending at the Jordan River—
sixteen towns with their surrounding villages.

[23]The homeland allocated to the clans of the tribe of
Issachar included these towns and their surrounding
villages.

The Land Given to Asher

JOSHUA 19:24-31

The fifth allotment of land went to the clans of the tribe of Asher.

[25]Its boundaries included these towns: Helkath,
Hali, Beten, Acshaph, [26]Allammelech, Amad,
and Mishal. The boundary on the west touched
Carmel and Shihor-libnath, [27]then it turned east
toward Beth-dagon, and ran as far as Zebulun
in the valley of Iphtah-el, going north to Beth-
emek and Neiel. It then continued north to
Cabul, [28]Abdon,* Rehob, Hammon, Kanah, and
as far as Greater Sidon. [29]Then the boundary
turned toward Ramah and the fortress of Tyre,
where it turned toward Hosah and came to the
Mediterranean Sea.* The territory also included
Mehebel, Aczib, [30]Ummah, Aphek, and Rehob—
twenty-two towns with their surrounding villages.

[31]The homeland allocated to the clans of the tribe of
Asher included these towns and their surrounding
villages.

The Land Given to Naphtali

JOSHUA 19:32-39

The sixth allotment of land went to the clans of the tribe of Naphtali.

[33]Its boundary ran from Heleph, from the oak
at Zaanannim, and extended across to Adami-
nekeb, Jabneel, and as far as Lakkum, ending at
the Jordan River. [34]The western boundary ran
past Aznoth-tabor, then to Hukkok, and touched
the border of Zebulun in the south, the border
of Asher on the west, and the Jordan River* on
the east. [35]The fortified towns included in this
territory were Ziddim, Zer, Hammath, Rakkath,
Kinnereth, [36]Adamah, Ramah, Hazor, [37]Kedesh,
Edrei, En-hazor, [38]Yiron, Migdal-el, Horem, Beth-
anath, and Beth-shemesh—nineteen towns with
their surrounding villages.

[39]The homeland allocated to the clans of the tribe of
Naphtali included these towns and their surrounding villages.

The Land Given to Dan

JOSHUA 19:40-48

The seventh allotment of land went to the clans of the tribe of Dan.

[41]The land allocated as their homeland included
the following towns: Zorah, Eshtaol, Ir-shemesh,
[42]Shaalabbin, Aijalon, Ithlah, [43]Elon, Timnah,

Jo 19:28 As in some Hebrew manuscripts (see also 21:30); most Hebrew manuscripts read *Ebron.* **Jo 19:29** Hebrew *the sea.* **Jo 19:34** Hebrew *and Judah at the Jordan River.*

▸ **JOSHUA 19:40-48 *(cont.)***

Ekron, 44Eltekeh, Gibbethon, Baalath, 45Jehud,
Bene-berak, Gath-rimmon, 46Me-jarkon, Rakkon,
and the territory across from Joppa.
47But the tribe of Dan had trouble taking
possession of their land,* so they attacked the
town of Laish.* They captured it, slaughtered its
people, and settled there. They renamed the town
Dan after their ancestor.

48The homeland allocated to the clans of the tribe
of Dan included these towns and their surrounding
villages.

The Land Given to Joshua

JOSHUA 19:49-51

After all the land was divided among the tribes, the
Israelites gave a piece of land to Joshua as his allocation. 50For the LORD had said he could have any town
he wanted. He chose Timnath-serah in the hill country
of Ephraim. He rebuilt the town and lived there.
51These are the territories that Eleazar the priest,
Joshua son of Nun, and the tribal leaders allocated as
grants of land to the tribes of Israel by casting sacred
lots in the presence of the LORD at the entrance of
the Tabernacle* at Shiloh. So the division of the land
was completed.

Jo 19:47a Or *had trouble holding on to their land.* **Jo 19:47b** Hebrew *Leshem,* a variant spelling of Laish. **Jo 19:51** Hebrew *Tent of Meeting.*

2. SPECIAL CITIES ARE SET ASIDE

The Levites were not given any land to possess, since they were set aside to serve God and to be his own. Instead, they were given cities within the boundaries of the land given to other tribes. Some of these cities were also designated as cities of refuge, where those accused of murder could flee and remain safe while awaiting trial.

The Cities of Refuge

JOSHUA 20:1-9

The LORD said to Joshua, 2"Now tell the Israelites to
designate the cities of refuge, as I instructed Moses.
3Anyone who kills another person accidentally and
unintentionally can run to one of these cities; they will
be places of refuge from relatives seeking revenge for
the person who was killed.
4"Upon reaching one of these cities, the one who
caused the death will appear before the elders at the
city gate and present his case. They must allow him
to enter the city and give him a place to live among
them. 5If the relatives of the victim come to avenge
the killing, the leaders must not release the slayer to
them, for he killed the other person unintentionally
and without previous hostility. 6But the slayer must
stay in that city and be tried by the local assembly,
which will render a judgment. And he must continue
to live in that city until the death of the high priest
who was in office at the time of the accident. After

Josh 19:47-48 The tribe of Dan found that some of their land was difficult to conquer, so they chose to migrate to Laish, where they knew victory would be easier. Anyone can trust God when the going is easy. It is when everything looks impossible that our faith and courage are put to the test. Have faith that God is great enough to tackle your most difficult situations.

Josh 19:49 There were several good reasons for establishing these well-set boundaries instead of turning the Promised Land into a single undivided nation. (1) The boundaries gave each tribe ownership of an area, promoting loyalty and unity that would strengthen each tribe. (2) The boundaries delineated areas of responsibility and privilege, which would help each tribe develop and mature. (3) The boundaries reduced conflicts that might have broken out if everyone had wanted to live in the choicest areas. (4) The boundaries fulfilled the promised inheritances for each tribe, some of which were promised as early as the days of Jacob (Gen 48:21-22).

Josh 20:6 A new nation in a new land needed a new government. Many years earlier God had told Moses how this government should function. One of the tasks God wanted the Israelites to do when they entered the Promised Land was to designate certain cities as "cities of refuge." These were to be scattered throughout the land. Their purpose was to prevent injustice, especially in cases of revenge. For example, if someone accidentally killed another person, he could flee to a city of refuge where he was safe until he could have a fair trial. The Levites were in charge of these cities. They were to ensure that God's principles of justice and fairness were kept. (For more on cities of refuge, see the notes on Num 35:6, p. 282 and Num 35:11-28, p. 283.)

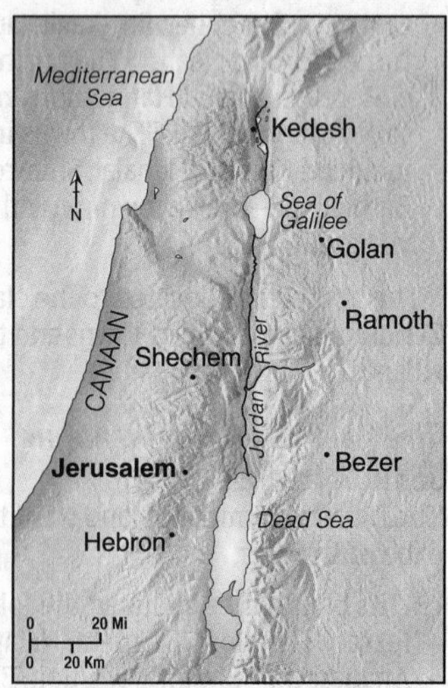

***THE CITIES OF REFUGE** A city of refuge was just that—refuge for someone who committed an unintentional murder that would evoke revenge from the victim's friends and relatives. The six cities of refuge were spaced throughout the land so that a person was never too far from one.*

that, he is free to return to his own home in the town from which he fled."

7 The following cities were designated as cities of refuge: Kedesh of Galilee, in the hill country of Naphtali; Shechem, in the hill country of Ephraim; and Kiriath-arba (that is, Hebron), in the hill country of Judah. 8 On the east side of the Jordan River, across from Jericho, the following cities were designated: Bezer, in the wilderness plain of the tribe of Reuben; Ramoth in Gilead, in the territory of the tribe of Gad; and Golan in Bashan, in the land of the tribe of Manasseh. 9 These cities were set apart for all the Israelites as well as the foreigners living among them. Anyone who accidentally killed another person could take refuge in one of these cities. In this way, they could escape being killed in revenge prior to standing trial before the local assembly.

The Towns Given to the Levites

JOSHUA 21:1-45

Then the leaders of the tribe of Levi came to consult with Eleazar the priest, Joshua son of Nun, and the leaders of the other tribes of Israel. 2 They came to them at Shiloh in the land of Canaan and said, "The Lord commanded Moses to give us towns to live in and pasturelands for our livestock." 3 So by the command of the Lord the people of Israel gave the Levites the following towns and pasturelands out of their own grants of land.

4 The descendants of Aaron, who were members of the Kohathite clan within the tribe of Levi, were allotted thirteen towns that were originally assigned to the tribes of Judah, Simeon, and Benjamin. 5 The other families of the Kohathite clan were allotted ten towns from the tribes of Ephraim, Dan, and the half-tribe of Manasseh.

6 The clan of Gershon was allotted thirteen towns from the tribes of Issachar, Asher, Naphtali, and the half-tribe of Manasseh in Bashan.

7 The clan of Merari was allotted twelve towns from the tribes of Reuben, Gad, and Zebulun.

8 So the Israelites obeyed the Lord's command to Moses and assigned these towns and pasturelands to the Levites by casting sacred lots.

9 The Israelites gave the following towns from the tribes of Judah and Simeon 10 to the descendants of Aaron, who were members of the Kohathite clan within the tribe of Levi, since the sacred lot fell to them first: 11 Kiriath-arba (that is, Hebron), in the hill country of Judah, along with its surrounding pasturelands. (Arba was an ancestor of Anak.) 12 But the open fields beyond the town and the surrounding villages were given to Caleb son of Jephunneh as his possession.

13 The following towns with their pasturelands were given to the descendants of Aaron the priest: Hebron (a city of refuge for those who accidentally killed someone), Libnah, 14 Jattir, Eshtemoa, 15 Holon, Debir, 16 Ain, Juttah, and Beth-shemesh—nine towns from these two tribes.

17 From the tribe of Benjamin the priests were given the following towns with their pasturelands: Gibeon, Geba, 18 Anathoth, and Almon—four towns. 19 So in all, thirteen towns with their pasturelands were given to the priests, the descendants of Aaron.

20 The rest of the Kohathite clan from the tribe of Levi was allotted the following towns and pasturelands from the tribe of Ephraim: 21 Shechem in the hill country of Ephraim (a city of refuge for those who

Josh 21:2 The Levites were to minister on behalf of all the people, so they were given cities scattered throughout the land. Although Jerusalem was far away from the homes of many Israelites, almost no one lived more than a day's journey from a Levitical city.

Beth-shemesh

Beth-shemesh was a Canaanite city on the northern border of Judah's territory (Josh 15:10) and the southern border of Dan's territory. Beth-shemesh was one of the towns of Judah granted to the Levites (Josh 21:16). When the Philistines decided to dispose of the captured Ark of the Covenant because plagues were breaking out in their cities, they sent it out and it came to Beth-shemesh (1 Sam 6:1-14). The area was also the scene of a great victory by King Joash (Jehoash) of Israel over King Amaziah of Judah (2 Chr 25:21-23). About a century later, the Philistines captured Beth-shemesh from King Ahaz of Judah (2 Chr 28:16-20). After that, the settlement fell into decline and was finally destroyed by Nebuchadnezzar in 586 B.C. Beth-shemesh's best moment in history was when it housed the Ark of God because God was present with them (1 Sam 6:9-20). In your spiritual history, think about the best moments you have had with God.

▸ **JOSHUA 21:1-45** ***(cont.)***
accidentally killed someone), Gezer, 22Kibzaim, and
Beth-horon—four towns.
23The following towns and pasturelands were allotted to the priests from the tribe of Dan: Eltekeh,
Gibbethon, 24Aijalon, and Gath-rimmon—four towns.
25The half-tribe of Manasseh allotted the following
towns with their pasturelands to the priests: Taanach
and Gath-rimmon—two towns. 26So in all, ten towns
with their pasturelands were given to the rest of the
Kohathite clan.
27The descendants of Gershon, another clan within
the tribe of Levi, received the following towns with
their pasturelands from the half-tribe of Manasseh:
Golan in Bashan (a city of refuge for those who accidentally killed someone) and Be-eshterah—two
towns.
28From the tribe of Issachar they received the following towns with their pasturelands: Kishion, Daberath, 29Jarmuth, and En-gannim—four towns.
30From the tribe of Asher they received the following towns with their pasturelands: Mishal, Abdon,
31Helkath, and Rehob—four towns.
32From the tribe of Naphtali they received the following towns with their pasturelands: Kedesh in Galilee (a city of refuge for those who accidentally killed
someone), Hammoth-dor, and Kartan—three towns.
33So in all, thirteen towns with their pasturelands were
allotted to the clan of Gershon.
34The rest of the Levites—the Merari clan—were
given the following towns with their pasturelands
from the tribe of Zebulun: Jokneam, Kartah, 35Dimnah,
and Nahalal—four towns.
36From the tribe of Reuben they received the following towns with their pasturelands: Bezer, Jahaz,*
37Kedemoth, and Mephaath—four towns.
38From the tribe of Gad they received the following
towns with their pasturelands: Ramoth in Gilead (a city
of refuge for those who accidentally killed someone),
Mahanaim, 39Heshbon, and Jazer—four towns. 40So
in all, twelve towns were allotted to the clan of Merari.
41The total number of towns and pasturelands
within Israelite territory given to the Levites came
to forty-eight. 42Every one of these towns had
pasturelands surrounding it.
43So the LORD gave to Israel all the land he had
sworn to give their ancestors, and they took possession of it and settled there. 44And the LORD gave them
rest on every side, just as he had solemnly promised
their ancestors. None of their enemies could stand
against them, for the LORD helped them conquer all
their enemies. 45Not a single one of all the good promises the LORD had given to the family of Israel was
left unfulfilled; everything he had spoken came true.

Jo 21:36 Hebrew *Jahzah*, a variant spelling of Jahaz.

3. THE EASTERN TRIBES RETURN TO THEIR LAND

The tribes that had been granted land east of the Jordan River had fulfilled their promise to accompany the rest of the nation in their conquest of the Promised Land, so Joshua sent them back to their families across the Jordan.

The Eastern Tribes Go Home

JOSHUA 22:1-9
Then Joshua called together the tribes of Reuben,
Gad, and the half-tribe of Manasseh. 2He told them,
"You have done as Moses, the servant of the LORD,
commanded you, and you have obeyed every order
I have given you. 3During all this time you have not
deserted the other tribes. You have been careful to
obey the commands of the LORD your God right up
to the present day. 4And now the LORD your God has
given the other tribes rest, as he promised them. So go
back home to the land that Moses, the servant of the
LORD, gave you as your possession on the east side of
the Jordan River. 5But be very careful to obey all the
commands and the instructions that Moses gave to
you. Love the LORD your God, walk in all his ways, obey
his commands, hold firmly to him, and serve him with
all your heart and all your soul." 6So Joshua blessed
them and sent them away, and they went home.
7Moses had given the land of Bashan, east of the

Josh 21:43-45 God proved faithful in fulfilling every promise he had given to Israel. Fulfillment of some promises took several years, but "not a single one of all the good promises the LORD had given to the family of Israel was left unfulfilled." God's promises will be fulfilled according to his timetable, not ours, but we know that his word is sure. The more we learn of those promises God has fulfilled and continues to fulfill, the easier it is to hope for those yet to come. Sometimes we become impatient, wanting God to act in a certain way now. Instead, we should faithfully do what we know he wants us to do and trust him for the future.

Josh 22:2-4 Before the conquest had begun, these tribes were given land on the east side of the Jordan River. But before they could settle down, they had to first promise to help the other tribes conquer the land on the west side (Num 32:20-22). They had patiently and diligently carried out their promised duties. Joshua commended them for doing just that. At last they were permitted to return to their families and build their cities. Follow-through is vital in God's work. Beware of the temptation to quit early and leave God's work undone.

Josh 22:5 Here Joshua briefly restated the central message Moses gave the people in Deuteronomy: Obedience should be based on love for God. Although the Israelites had completed their military responsibility, Joshua reminded them of their spiritual responsibility. Sometimes we think so much about what we are to do that we neglect thinking about who we are to be. If we know we are God's children, we will love him and joyfully serve him. We must not let daily service take away from our love for God.

Jordan River, to the half-tribe of Manasseh. (The other
half of the tribe was given land west of the Jordan.) As
Joshua sent them away and blessed them, [8]he said to
them, "Go back to your homes with the great wealth
you have taken from your enemies—the vast herds of
livestock, the silver, gold, bronze, and iron, and the
large supply of clothing. Share the plunder with your
relatives."

[9]So the men of Reuben, Gad, and the half-tribe of
Manasseh left the rest of Israel at Shiloh in the land
of Canaan. They started the journey back to their own
land of Gilead, the territory that belonged to them
according to the LORD's command through Moses.

The Eastern Tribes Build an Altar

JOSHUA 22:10-34

But while they were still in Canaan, and when they
came to a place called Geliloth* near the Jordan River,
the men of Reuben, Gad, and the half-tribe of Manasseh stopped to build a large and imposing altar.

[11]The rest of Israel heard that the people of Reuben, Gad, and the half-tribe of Manasseh had built
an altar at Geliloth at the edge of the land of Canaan,
on the west side of the Jordan River. [12]So the whole
community of Israel gathered at Shiloh and prepared
to go to war against them. [13]First, however, they sent a
delegation led by Phinehas son of Eleazar, the priest,
to talk with the tribes of Reuben, Gad, and the half-
tribe of Manasseh. [14]In this delegation were ten leaders of Israel, one from each of the ten tribes, and each
the head of his family within the clans of Israel.

[15]When they arrived in the land of Gilead, they
said to the tribes of Reuben, Gad, and the half-tribe
of Manasseh, [16]"The whole community of the LORD
demands to know why you are betraying the God of
Israel. How could you turn away from the LORD and
build an altar for yourselves in rebellion against him?
[17]Was our sin at Peor not enough? To this day we are
not fully cleansed of it, even after the plague that
struck the entire community of the LORD. [18]And yet
today you are turning away from following the LORD.
If you rebel against the LORD today, he will be angry
with all of us tomorrow.

[19]"If you need the altar because the land you possess
is defiled, then join us in the LORD's land, where the
Tabernacle of the LORD is situated, and share our land
with us. But do not rebel against the LORD or against
us by building an altar other than the one true altar
of the LORD our God. [20]Didn't divine anger fall on the
entire community of Israel when Achan, a member
of the clan of Zerah, sinned by stealing the things set
apart for the LORD*? He was not the only one who died
because of his sin."

[21]Then the people of Reuben, Gad, and the half-
tribe of Manasseh answered the heads of the clans
of Israel: [22]"The LORD, the Mighty One, is God! The
LORD, the Mighty One, is God! He knows the truth,
and may Israel know it, too! We have not built the
altar in treacherous rebellion against the LORD. If
we have done so, do not spare our lives this day. [23]If
we have built an altar for ourselves to turn away
from the LORD or to offer burnt offerings or grain
offerings or peace offerings, may the LORD himself
punish us.

[24]"The truth is, we have built this altar because we
fear that in the future your descendants will say to
ours, 'What right do you have to worship the LORD,
the God of Israel? [25]The LORD has placed the Jordan
River as a barrier between our people and you people
of Reuben and Gad. You have no claim to the LORD.'
So your descendants may prevent our descendants
from worshiping the LORD.

[26]"So we decided to build the altar, not for burnt
offerings or sacrifices, [27]but as a memorial. It will
remind our descendants and your descendants that
we, too, have the right to worship the LORD at his
sanctuary with our burnt offerings, sacrifices, and
peace offerings. Then your descendants will not be
able to say to ours, 'You have no claim to the LORD.'

[28]"If they say this, our descendants can reply,
'Look at this copy of the LORD's altar that our ancestors made. It is not for burnt offerings or sacrifices;
it is a reminder of the relationship both of us have
with the LORD.' [29]Far be it from us to rebel against
the LORD or turn away from him by building our
own altar for burnt offerings, grain offerings, or

Jo 22:10 Or *to the circle of stones;* similarly in 22:11. **Jo 22:20** The Hebrew term used here refers to the complete consecration of things or people to the LORD, either by destroying them or by giving them as an offering.

Josh 22:11-34 When the tribes of Reuben and Gad and the half-tribe of Manasseh built an altar near the Jordan River, the rest of Israel feared that these tribes were starting their own religion and rebelling against God. But before beginning an all-out war, Phinehas led a delegation to learn the truth, following the principle taught in Deuteronomy 13:12-18. He was prepared to negotiate rather than fight if a battle was not necessary. When he learned that the altar was for a memorial rather than for pagan sacrifice, war was averted and unity restored. As nations and as individuals, we would benefit from a similar approach to resolving conflicts. Assuming the worst about the intentions of others only brings trouble. Israel averted the threat of civil war by asking before assaulting. Beware of reacting before you hear the whole story.

Josh 22:17 For the story of how Israel turned away from God and began to worship Baal at Peor, see Numbers 25:1-18.

Josh 22:20 For the story of Achan, a man who allowed greed to get the best of him, see Joshua 7.

Josh 22:26-28 The tribes were concerned that, without some visible sign of unity between the people on the two sides of the Jordan, future generations might see conflict between them. The altar, patterned after the altar of the Lord, was to remind these people that they all worshiped the same God. Often we need to be reminded of the faith of our fathers. What actions demonstrate to your children your reliance on God and remind them of what he has done? Take the time to establish family traditions that will help your children remember.

▸ **JOSHUA 22:10-34 *(cont.)***
sacrifices. Only the altar of the LORD our God that
stands in front of the Tabernacle may be used for
that purpose."
30 When Phinehas the priest and the leaders of the
community—the heads of the clans of Israel—heard
this from the tribes of Reuben, Gad, and the half-tribe
of Manasseh, they were satisfied. 31 Phinehas son of
Eleazar, the priest, replied to them, "Today we know
the LORD is among us because you have not committed
this treachery against the LORD as we thought. Instead,
you have rescued Israel from being destroyed by the
hand of the LORD."
32 Then Phinehas son of Eleazar, the priest, and the
other leaders left the tribes of Reuben and Gad in
Gilead and returned to the land of Canaan to tell the
Israelites what had happened. 33 And all the Israelites
were satisfied and praised God and spoke no more of
war against Reuben and Gad.
34 The people of Reuben and Gad named the altar
"Witness,"* for they said, "It is a witness between us
and them that the LORD is our God, too."

Jo 22:34 Some manuscripts lack this word.

4. JOSHUA'S FAREWELL TO THE LEADERS

Joshua again reminded the people of Israel that they needed to remain faithful to God, and they renewed their covenant with God by promising to serve and obey him alone. Then Joshua died and was buried in the Promised Land.

Joshua's Final Words to Israel

JOSHUA 23:1-16

The years passed, and the LORD had given the people
of Israel rest from all their enemies. Joshua, who was
now very old, 2 called together all the elders, leaders,
judges, and officers of Israel. He said to them, "I am
now a very old man. 3 You have seen everything the
LORD your God has done for you during my lifetime.
The LORD your God has fought for you against your
enemies. 4 I have allotted to you as your homeland all
the land of the nations yet unconquered, as well as the
land of those we have already conquered—from the
Jordan River to the Mediterranean Sea* in the west.
5 This land will be yours, for the LORD your God will
himself drive out all the people living there now. You
will take possession of their land, just as the LORD your
God promised you.
6 "So be very careful to follow everything Moses
wrote in the Book of Instruction. Do not deviate from
it, turning either to the right or to the left. 7 Make sure
you do not associate with the other people still remaining in the land. Do not even mention the names
of their gods, much less swear by them or serve them
or worship them. 8 Rather, cling tightly to the LORD
your God as you have done until now.
9 "For the LORD has driven out great and powerful
nations for you, and no one has yet been able to defeat
you. 10 Each one of you will put to flight a thousand of
the enemy, for the LORD your God fights for you, just
as he has promised. 11 So be very careful to love the
LORD your God.
12 "But if you turn away from him and cling to the
customs of the survivors of these nations remaining
among you, and if you intermarry with them, 13 then
know for certain that the LORD your God will no longer drive them out of your land. Instead, they will be

Jo 23:4 Hebrew *the Great Sea.*

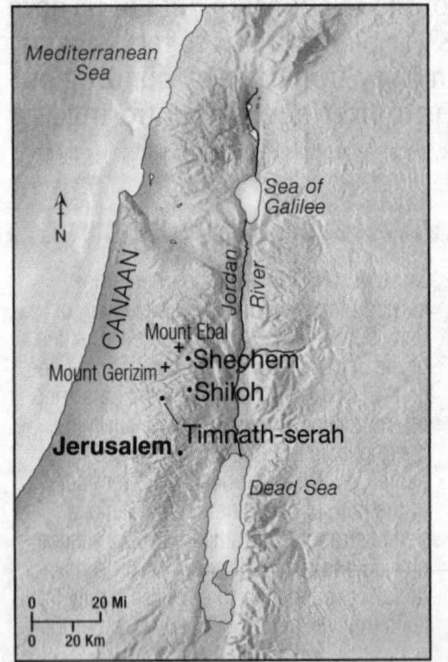

◀ ***JOSHUA'S FINAL SPEECH** Joshua called all the Israelites to Shechem to hear his final words. He challenged the people to make a conscious choice to always serve God. Soon afterward, Joshua died and was buried in his hometown of Timnath-serah.*

Josh 22:33 Both the eastern and western tribes were relieved that the crisis had been averted, and they joyfully praised God to renew their affirmation of national unity in faithfulness to God.

Josh 23:4-5 Some of the land that Joshua had assigned to the various tribes remained unconquered. Israel's gradual occupation of the land had an ecological reason (see Exod 23:29-30), a military reason (see Judg 1:19), and a theological reason (see Judg 2:20–3:4). Israel's ensuing unfaithfulness delayed the settlement process by several centuries; instead of driving out the remaining Canaanites, Israel absorbed them, bringing God's people even greater temptations to unfaithfulness. Joshua knew this to be a real danger. (Josh 23:15-16). We need to root out sinful influences in our life rather than allow them to become sinful practices.

Josh 23:6-13 Joshua knew the nation's weak spots. Before dying, he called the people together and gave commands to help them where they were most likely to slip: (1) Follow all that is written in the Book of Instruction without turning aside; (2) don't associate with the pagan nations or worship their gods; (3) don't intermarry with the pagan nations. These temptations were right in their backyard. Our associations and relationships can be temptations to us as well. It's wise to identify our weak spots *before* we break down. Then we can develop strategies to overcome these temptations instead of being overcome by them.

a snare and a trap to you, a whip for your backs and
thorny brambles in your eyes, and you will vanish from
this good land the LORD your God has given you.
14"Soon I will die, going the way of everything on
earth. Deep in your hearts you know that every promise of the LORD your God has come true. Not a single
one has failed! 15But as surely as the LORD your God
has given you the good things he promised, he will
also bring disaster on you if you disobey him. He will
completely destroy you from this good land he has
given you. 16If you break the covenant of the LORD your
God by worshiping and serving other gods, his anger
will burn against you, and you will quickly vanish from
the good land he has given you."

The LORD's Covenant Renewed

JOSHUA 24:1-28

Then Joshua summoned all the tribes of Israel to Shechem, including their elders, leaders, judges, and officers. So they came and presented themselves to God.
2Joshua said to the people, "This is what the LORD,
the God of Israel, says: Long ago your ancestors, including Terah, the father of Abraham and Nahor, lived
beyond the Euphrates River,* and they worshiped
other gods. 3But I took your ancestor Abraham from
the land beyond the Euphrates and led him into the
land of Canaan. I gave him many descendants through
his son Isaac. 4To Isaac I gave Jacob and Esau. To Esau
I gave the mountains of Seir, while Jacob and his children went down into Egypt.
5"Then I sent Moses and Aaron, and I brought terrible plagues on Egypt; and afterward I brought you
out as a free people. 6But when your ancestors arrived
at the Red Sea,* the Egyptians chased after you with
chariots and charioteers. 7When your ancestors cried
out to the LORD, I put darkness between you and the
Egyptians. I brought the sea crashing down on the
Egyptians, drowning them. With your very own eyes
you saw what I did. Then you lived in the wilderness
for many years.
8"Finally, I brought you into the land of the Amorites
on the east side of the Jordan. They fought against
you, but I destroyed them before you. I gave you victory over them, and you took possession of their land.
9Then Balak son of Zippor, king of Moab, started a war
against Israel. He summoned Balaam son of Beor to
curse you, 10but I would not listen to him. Instead, I
made Balaam bless you, and so I rescued you from
Balak.
11"When you crossed the Jordan River and came to
Jericho, the men of Jericho fought against you, as did
the Amorites, the Perizzites, the Canaanites, the Hittites, the Girgashites, the Hivites, and the Jebusites. But
I gave you victory over them. 12And I sent terror* ahead
of you to drive out the two kings of the Amorites. It
was not your swords or bows that brought you victory.

Jo 24:2 Hebrew *the river;* also in 24:3, 14, 15. **Jo 24:6** Hebrew *sea of reeds.* **Jo 24:12** Often rendered *the hornet.* The meaning of the Hebrew is uncertain.

Josh 23:8 Joshua was dying, and so he called all the leaders of the nation together to give them his final words of encouragement and instruction. His whole message can be summarized in this verse: "Cling tightly to the LORD your God." Joshua had been a living example of those words, and he wanted that to be his legacy. For what do you want to be remembered, and what do you want to pass on to your children and associates? You can leave them nothing better than the admonition to hold on to God and to the memory of a person who did.

Josh 23:12-16 This chilling prediction about the consequences of intermarriage with the Canaanite nations eventually became a reality. Numerous stories in the book of Judges show what Israel had to suffer because of failure to follow God wholeheartedly. God was supremely loving and patient with Israel, just as he is today. But we must not confuse his patience with us as approval of or indifference to our sin. Beware of demanding your own way because eventually you may get it—along with all its painful consequences.

Israel Stele

Israel has now been established as a people with their own land (Josh 23:1-5; 24:13). The earliest evidence for the existence of the nation of Israel outside the Bible comes from a monument (or *stele*) found in 1896. It honored the Pharaoh Merneptah, who reigned in Egypt around 1213 B.C. The end of the inscription reads: "Canaan has been plundered in every evil way, Ashkelon has been brought away captive, Gezer has been seized, Yanoam has been destroyed. Israel is devastated, having no seed." It has been called the "Israel stele" because of the appearance of "Israel" in the inscription. The conflict spoken of is in the period when Israel was settling the Promised Land after the death of Joshua. The expression "devastated, having no seed" is a way of claiming a complete victory; it should not be interpreted literally. This evidence of Israel's early history silences the critics of the Bible who say that Israel could not have been a nation that early. We can trust the reliability of the Bible.

▸ **JOSHUA 24:1-28 *(cont.)***

13 I gave you land you had not worked on, and I gave you towns you did not build—the towns where you are now living. I gave you vineyards and olive groves for food, though you did not plant them.

14 "So fear the LORD and serve him wholeheartedly. Put away forever the idols your ancestors worshiped when they lived beyond the Euphrates River and in Egypt. Serve the LORD alone. 15 But if you refuse to serve the LORD, then choose today whom you will serve. Would you prefer the gods your ancestors served beyond the Euphrates? Or will it be the gods of the Amorites in whose land you now live? But as for me and my family, we will serve the LORD."

16 The people replied, "We would never abandon the LORD and serve other gods. 17 For the LORD our God is the one who rescued us and our ancestors from slavery in the land of Egypt. He performed mighty miracles before our very eyes. As we traveled through the wilderness among our enemies, he preserved us. 18 It was the LORD who drove out the Amorites and the other nations living here in the land. So we, too, will serve the LORD, for he alone is our God."

19 Then Joshua warned the people, "You are not able to serve the LORD, for he is a holy and jealous God. He will not forgive your rebellion and your sins. 20 If you abandon the LORD and serve other gods, he will turn against you and destroy you, even though he has been so good to you."

1380 BC *Palace of Knossos on island of Crete destroyed by earthquake*

21 But the people answered Joshua, "No, we will serve the LORD!"

22 "You are a witness to your own decision," Joshua said. "You have chosen to serve the LORD."

"Yes," they replied, "we are witnesses to what we have said."

23 "All right then," Joshua said, "destroy the idols among you, and turn your hearts to the LORD, the God of Israel."

24 The people said to Joshua, "We will serve the LORD our God. We will obey him alone."

25 So Joshua made a covenant with the people that day at Shechem, committing them to follow the decrees and regulations of the LORD. 26 Joshua recorded these things in the Book of God's Instructions. As a reminder of their agreement, he took a huge stone and rolled it beneath the terebinth tree beside the Tabernacle of the LORD.

27 Joshua said to all the people, "This stone has heard everything the LORD said to us. It will be a witness to testify against you if you go back on your word to God."

28 Then Joshua sent all the people away to their own homelands.

Leaders Buried in the Promised Land PARALLEL

JOSHUA 24:29-33

After this, Joshua son of Nun, the servant of the LORD, died at the age of 110. 30 They buried him in the land he had been allocated, at Timnath-serah in the hill country of Ephraim, north of Mount Gaash.

31 The people of Israel served the LORD throughout the lifetime of Joshua and of the elders who outlived him—those who had personally experienced all that the LORD had done for Israel.

32 The bones of Joseph, which the Israelites had brought along with them when they left Egypt, were buried at Shechem, in the parcel of ground Jacob had bought from the sons of Hamor for 100 pieces of silver.* This land was located in the territory allotted to the descendants of Joseph.

Jo 24:32 Hebrew *100 kesitahs;* the value or weight of the kesitah is no longer known.

Josh 24:15 The people had to decide whether they would obey the Lord, who had proven his trustworthiness, or obey the local gods, which were only hand-made idols. It's easy to slip into a quiet rebellion—going about life in your own way. But the time comes when you have to choose who or what will control you. The choice is yours. Will it be God, your own limited personality, or another imperfect substitute? Once you have chosen to be controlled by God's Spirit, reaffirm your choice every day.

Josh 24:15 In taking a definite stand for the Lord, Joshua again displayed his spiritual leadership. Because Joshua had made a commitment to God, he was determined to set an example of living by that decision, regardless of what others decided. The way we live shows others the strength of our commitment to serving God.

Josh 24:16-18, 21 All the people boldly claimed that they would never forsake the Lord. But they did not keep that promise. Very soon God would charge them with breaking their contract with him (Judg 2:2-3). Talk is cheap. It is easy to say we will follow God, but it is much more important to live like it. Yet the nation followed God throughout Joshua's lifetime, a great tribute to Joshua's faith in God and powerful leadership.

Josh 24:23 Joshua told the Israelites to destroy their foreign gods—their idols. To follow God requires destroying whatever gets in the way of worshiping him. We have our own form of idols—greed, wrong priorities, jealousy, prejudice—that get in the way of worshiping God. God is not satisfied if we merely hide these idols. We must completely remove them from our lives.

Josh 24:24-26 The covenant between Israel and God was that the people would worship and obey the Lord alone. Their purpose was to become a holy nation that would influence the rest of the world for God. The conquest of Canaan was a means to achieve this purpose, but Israel became preoccupied with the land and lost sight of God.

The same can happen in our lives. We can spend so much time on the means that we forget the end—to glorify God. Churches may make this mistake as well. For example, the congregation may pour all of its energies into a new facility, only to become self-satisfied or fearful of letting certain groups use it. If this happens, they have focused on the building and lost sight of its purpose—to bring others to God.

Josh 24:29-31 The book of Joshua opens with a new leader being handed a seemingly impossible task—to lead the nation in taking over the land of Canaan. By following God closely, Joshua led the people through military victories and faithful spiritual obedience. In Joshua 24:16 we read that the people were sure they would never forsake the Lord. The response of the whole nation during these many years is a tribute both to Joshua's leadership and to the God he faithfully served.

Josh 24:33 Joshua and Eleazar died, but not before laying before the people the fundamentals of what it means to have faith in God. We are to honor and serve the

33 Eleazar son of Aaron also died. He was buried in
the hill country of Ephraim, in the town of Gibeah,
which had been given to his son Phinehas.

JUDGES 2:6-9

After Joshua sent the people away, each of the tribes
left to take possession of the land allotted to them.
7 And the Israelites served the LORD throughout the
lifetime of Joshua and the leaders who outlived him—
those who had seen all the great things the LORD had
done for Israel.
8 Joshua son of Nun, the servant of the LORD, died at
the age of 110. 9 They buried him in the land he had
been allocated, at Timnath-serah* in the hill country
of Ephraim, north of Mount Gaash.

Jgs 2:9 As in parallel text at Josh 24:30; Hebrew reads *Timnath-heres*, a variant spelling of Timnath-serah.

D. The Military Failure of Israel

By faithfully obeying the Lord, Joshua led the Israelites to military victory. After his death, however, the tribes failed to clear the inhabitants from the land, so the Lord withdrew his promise to help drive the people out and bless the Israelites in battle. The new generation abandoned God and worshiped idols. This shows what can happen when we neglect to teach our children to follow the Lord.

1. INCOMPLETE CONQUEST OF THE LAND

Israel failed to complete the task that God had given them. They were satisfied with partial success, and did not obey God by trusting him to complete the conquest of the land.

Judah and Simeon Conquer the Land

JUDGES 1:1-18

After the death of Joshua, the Israelites asked the LORD,
"Which tribe should go first to attack the Canaanites?"
2 The LORD answered, "Judah, for I have given them
victory over the land."
3 The men of Judah said to their relatives from the
tribe of Simeon, "Join with us to fight against the
Canaanites living in the territory allotted to us. Then
we will help you conquer your territory." So the men
of Simeon went with Judah.
4 When the men of Judah attacked, the LORD gave
them victory over the Canaanites and Perizzites, and
they killed 10,000 enemy warriors at the town of Bezek. 5 While at Bezek they encountered King Adoni-
bezek and fought against him, and the Canaanites

Lord alone (Josh 24:14). This is based on a choice: to obey him instead of following other gods (Josh 24:15). We are incapable of properly worshiping him because of our rebellion and sins (Josh 24:19). By choosing God as Lord, we enter into a covenant with him (Josh 24:25) whereby he promises not only to forgive and love us but also to enable us by his Spirit to do his work here on earth. This covenant requires us to renounce the principles and practices of the culture around us that are hostile to God's plan (Josh 24:23). This is not to be done alone but by binding ourselves together with others who have faith in God. (See Deut 30:15-20 for a similar message from Moses.)

Judg 1:1 The people of Israel had finally entered and taken control of the land promised to their ancestors (Gen 12:7; Exod 3:16-17). The book of Judges continues the story of this conquest that began in the book of Joshua. Through God's strength, the Israelites had conquered many enemies and overcome many difficulties, but their work was not yet finished. They had effectively met many political and military challenges, but facing spiritual challenges was more difficult. The unholy but attractive lifestyle of the Canaanites proved more dangerous than their military might. The Israelites gave in to the pressure and compromised their faith. If we attempt to meet life's challenges with human effort alone, we will find the pressures and temptations around us too great to resist.

Judg 1:1 Soon after Joshua died, Israel began to lose its firm grip on the land. Although Joshua was a great commander, the people missed his spiritual leadership even more than his military skill, for he had kept the people focused on God and his purposes. Joshua had been the obvious successor to Moses, but there was no obvious successor to Joshua. During this crisis of leadership, Israel had to learn that no matter how powerful and wise the current leader was, their real leader was God. We often focus our hope and confidence on some influential leader, failing to realize that in reality it is God who is in command. Acknowledge God as your commander in chief, and avoid the temptation of relying too heavily on human leaders, regardless of their spiritual wisdom.

Judg 1:1 The Canaanites were all the people who lived in Canaan (the Promised Land). They lived in city-states where each city had its own government, army, and laws. One reason Canaan was so difficult to conquer was that each city had to be defeated individually. There was no single king who could surrender the entire country into the hands of the Israelites.

Canaan's greatest threat to Israel was not its army but its religion. Canaanite religion idealized evil traits: cruelty in war, sexual immorality, selfish greed, and materialism. It was a "me first, anything goes" society. Obviously, the religions of Israel and Canaan could not coexist.

Judg 1:2 The book of Joshua tells of a swift and thorough conquest of enemy armies and cities, while the book of Judges seems to suggest a more lengthy and gradual conquest. When the Israelites first entered the Promised Land (Josh 1–12), they united as one army to crush the inhabitants until they were too weak to retaliate. Then, after the land was divided among the 12 tribes (Josh 13–24), each tribe was responsible for driving out the remaining enemy from its own territory. The book of Judges tells of their failure to do this.

Some tribes were more successful than others. Under Joshua, they all began strong, but soon most were sidetracked by fear, weariness, lack of discipline, or the pursuit of their own interests. As a result, their faith began to fade away, and "All the people did whatever seemed right in their own eyes" (Judg 17:6). In order for our faith to survive, it must be practiced day by day. It must penetrate every aspect of our lives. Beware of starting out strong and then getting sidetracked from your real purpose—loving God and living for him.

▸ **JUDGES 1:1-18 *(cont.)***
and Perizzites were defeated. 6 Adoni-bezek escaped,
but the Israelites soon captured him and cut off his
thumbs and big toes.
7 Adoni-bezek said, "I once had seventy kings with
their thumbs and big toes cut off, eating scraps from
under my table. Now God has paid me back for what
I did to them." They took him to Jerusalem, and he
died there.
8 The men of Judah attacked Jerusalem and captured it, killing all its people and setting the city on
fire. 9 Then they went down to fight the Canaanites
living in the hill country, the Negev, and the western
foothills.* 10 Judah marched against the Canaanites in
Hebron (formerly called Kiriath-arba), defeating the
forces of Sheshai, Ahiman, and Talmai.
11 From there they went to fight against the people
living in the town of Debir (formerly called Kiriath-
sepher). 12 Caleb said, "I will give my daughter Acsah in marriage to the one who attacks and captures
Kiriath-sepher." 13 Othniel, the son of Caleb's younger
brother, Kenaz, was the one who conquered it, so Acsah became Othniel's wife.
14 When Acsah married Othniel, she urged him*
to ask her father for a field. As she got down off her
donkey, Caleb asked her, "What's the matter?"
15 She said, "Let me have another gift. You have already given me land in the Negev; now please give me
springs of water, too." So Caleb gave her the upper and
lower springs.
16 When the tribe of Judah left Jericho—the city of
palms—the Kenites, who were descendants of Moses'
father-in-law, traveled with them into the wilderness
of Judah. They settled among the people there, near
the town of Arad in the Negev.
17 Then Judah joined with Simeon to fight against
the Canaanites living in Zephath, and they completely
destroyed* the town. So the town was named Hormah.* 18 In addition, Judah captured the towns of Gaza,
Ashkelon, and Ekron, along with their surrounding
territories.

Israel Fails to Conquer the Land

JUDGES 1:19-36
The LORD was with the people of Judah, and they
took possession of the hill country. But they failed to
drive out the people living in the plains, who had iron
chariots. 20 The town of Hebron was given to Caleb as
Moses had promised. And Caleb drove out the people
living there, who were descendants of the three sons
of Anak.
21 The tribe of Benjamin, however, failed to drive

Jgs 1:9 Hebrew *the Shephelah.* **Jgs 1:14** Greek version and Latin Vulgate read *he urged her.* **Jgs 1:17a** The Hebrew term used here refers to the complete consecration of things or people to the LORD, either by destroying them or by giving them as an offering. **Jgs 1:17b** *Hormah* means "destruction."

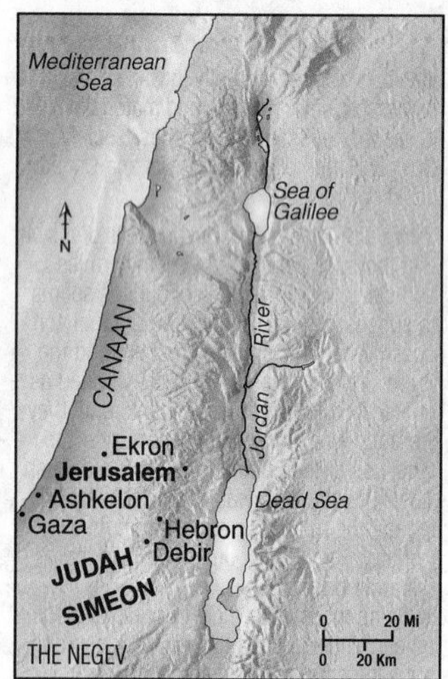

***JUDAH FIGHTS FOR ITS LAND** The tribe of Judah wasted no time beginning the conquest of its allotted territory. With help from the tribe of Simeon, Jerusalem was conquered, as were the Canaanites in the Negev and along the coast. Hebron and Debir fell to Judah, and later Gaza, Ashkelon, and Ekron.*

Judg 1:6 The maiming of Adoni-bezek was one example in a long string of actions that demonstrated Israel's tendency to disobey God's instructions by only giving partial obedience. Enemy kings were supposed to be executed, not humiliated. This defeated king recognized God's righteous punishment more clearly than God's people acknowledged God's commands. When we understand what God tells us to do, we run great danger if we don't carry out both the letter and the spirit of his commands.

Judg 1:8 Although the Israelites conquered Jerusalem, they did not occupy the city until the days of David (2 Sam 5:6-10).

Judg 1:12-15 This same event is recorded in Joshua 15:16-19. Caleb was one of the original men who scouted out the Promised Land (Num 13–14) and, with Joshua, encouraged the people to conquer it. For his faithfulness, he was given the land of his choice.

Judg 1:17 Why did God order the Israelites to drive the Canaanites from their land? Although the command seems cruel, the Israelites were under God's order to execute judgment on those wicked people. The other nations were to be judged for their sin as God had judged Israel by forcing them to wander for 40 years before they were allowed to enter the Promised Land. Over 700 years earlier, God had told Abraham that when the Israelites entered the Promised Land, the gross evil of the native people would be ready for judgment (Gen 15:16). But God wasn't playing favorites. Eventually the Israelites would also be severely punished for becoming as evil as the people they were ordered to drive out (2 Kgs 17; 25; Jer 6:18-19; Ezek 8). God is not partial; all people are eligible for God's gracious forgiveness as well as for his firm justice.

Judg 1:19 Canaanite chariots pulled by horses were among the most sophisticated weapons of the day. Israelite foot soldiers were absolutely powerless when a speeding iron chariot bore down upon them. This is why Israel preferred to fight in the hills where chariots couldn't venture.

Judg 1:21ff Tribe after tribe failed to drive the evil Canaanites from their land. Why didn't they follow through and completely obey God's commands? (1) They had been fighting for a long time and were tired. Although the goal was in sight, they lacked the discipline and energy to reach it. (2) They were afraid the enemy was too strong—the iron chariots seemed invincible. (3) After Joshua's death, power and authority were decentralized to the tribal leaders, and the tribes were no longer unified in purpose. (4) Spiritual decay had infected them from within. They thought they could handle the temptation and be more prosperous by doing business with the Canaanites.

We, too, often choose to tolerate sin rather than drive it from our lives. We may know what to do but just don't follow through. This results in a gradual deterioration of our relationship with God. In our battles, we may grow tired and want rest, but we need

out the Jebusites, who were living in Jerusalem. So
to this day the Jebusites live in Jerusalem among the
people of Benjamin.
22 The descendants of Joseph attacked the town of
Bethel, and the LORD was with them. 23 They sent men
to scout out Bethel (formerly known as Luz). 24 They
confronted a man coming out of the town and said to
him, "Show us a way into the town, and we will have
mercy on you." 25 So he showed them a way in, and they
killed everyone in the town except that man and his
family. 26 Later the man moved to the land of the Hittites, where he built a town. He named it Luz, which
is its name to this day.
27 The tribe of Manasseh failed to drive out the
people living in Beth-shan,* Taanach, Dor, Ibleam,
Megiddo, and all their surrounding settlements,
because the Canaanites were determined to stay
in that region. 28 When the Israelites grew stronger,
they forced the Canaanites to work as slaves, but they
never did drive them completely out of the land.
29 The tribe of Ephraim failed to drive out the
Canaanites living in Gezer, so the Canaanites continued to live there among them.
30 The tribe of Zebulun failed to drive out the residents of Kitron and Nahalol, so the Canaanites continued to live among them. But the Canaanites were
forced to work as slaves for the people of Zebulun.
31 The tribe of Asher failed to drive out the residents of Acco, Sidon, Ahlab, Aczib, Helbah, Aphik,
and Rehob. 32 Instead, the people of Asher moved in
among the Canaanites, who controlled the land, for
they failed to drive them out.
33 Likewise, the tribe of Naphtali failed to drive
out the residents of Beth-shemesh and Beth-anath.
Instead, they moved in among the Canaanites, who
controlled the land. Nevertheless, the people of Beth-
shemesh and Beth-anath were forced to work as slaves
for the people of Naphtali.
34 As for the tribe of Dan, the Amorites forced
them back into the hill country and would not let
them come down into the plains. 35 The Amorites
were determined to stay in Mount Heres, Aijalon,
and Shaalbim, but when the descendants of Joseph
became stronger, they forced the Amorites to work
as slaves. 36 The boundary of the Amorites ran from
Scorpion Pass* to Sela and continued upward from
there.

The LORD's Messenger Comes to Bokim

JUDGES 2:1-5

The angel of the LORD went up from Gilgal to Bokim
and said to the Israelites, "I brought you out of Egypt
into this land that I swore to give your ancestors, and
I said I would never break my covenant with you. 2 For
your part, you were not to make any covenants with
the people living in this land; instead, you were to destroy their altars. But you disobeyed my command.
Why did you do this? 3 So now I declare that I will no

Jgs 1:27 Hebrew *Beth-shean,* a variant spelling of Beth-shan. **Jgs 1:36** Hebrew *Akrabbim.*

Arad

In Judges 1:16, Arad is used as a reference point for the land settled by the Kenites. Arad had been a large, important city during the early Bronze Age, but after being destroyed around 2600 B.C., it was not reoccupied until shortly before 1000 B.C. From the time of King Solomon (970–930 B.C.) until the Jews were taken into exile, Arad served as a fortified citadel on Judah's southern border.

Several interesting discoveries were made during the excavation of Tell Arad. An Israelite sanctuary was uncovered that is very similar in plan to the Tabernacle and the Temple, with an altar that has the same dimensions as described in Exodus 27:1. It has been suggested that this sanctuary might have served as the worship center of the Kenite clan. Tell Arad has also provided us with a number of inscribed potsherds, one of which contains a reference to the "house of Yahweh," likely meaning the Temple in Jerusalem, the place where Yahweh (the LORD God) chose to reveal himself.

more than a break from our work. We need to know that God loves us and has given us a purpose for life. Victory comes from living according to his purpose and from being willing to fully obey him.

Judg 2:1-3 This event marks a significant change in Israel's relationship with God. At Mount Sinai, God made a sacred and binding agreement with the Israelites called a covenant (Exod 19:5-8). God's part was to make Israel a special nation (see the note on Gen 12:1-3, p. 30), to protect them, and to give them unique blessings for following him. Israel's part was to love God and obey his laws. But because they rejected and disobeyed God, the agreement to protect them was no longer in effect. But God wasn't going to abandon his people. They would receive wonderful blessings if they asked God to forgive them and sincerely followed him again.

Although God's agreement to help Israel conquer the land was no longer in effect, his covenant to make Israel a nation through whom the whole world would be blessed (fulfilled in the Messiah's coming) remained valid. God still wanted the Israelites to be a holy people (just as he wants us to be holy), and he often used oppression to bring them back to him, just as he warned he would (Lev 26; Deut 28). The book of Judges records a number of instances where God allowed his people to be oppressed so that they would repent of their sins and return to him.

Too often people want God to fulfill his promises while excusing themselves from their responsibilities. Before you think that you deserve the fruits of God's promises, ask, "Have I done my part?"

▸ **JUDGES 2:1-5** ***(cont.)***

longer drive out the people living in your land. They will be thorns in your sides,* and their gods will be a constant temptation to you."

4 When the angel of the LORD finished speaking to all the Israelites, the people wept loudly. 5 So they called the place Bokim (which means "weeping"), and they offered sacrifices there to the LORD.

Jgs 2:3 Hebrew *They will be in your sides;* compare Num 33:55.

2. DISOBEDIENCE AND DEFEAT

This is now the third generation of Israel. The first one failed to trust God to give them the Promised Land, and they died in the wilderness. The second one failed to complete the task of conquering the land, and they died defeated. The third generation did not even remember the mighty things God had done for Israel.

Israel Disobeys the LORD

JUDGES 2:10-15

After that generation died, another generation grew up who did not acknowledge the LORD or remember the mighty things he had done for Israel.

11 The Israelites did evil in the LORD's sight and
served the images of Baal. 12 They abandoned the LORD,
the God of their ancestors, who had brought them out of Egypt. They went after other gods, worshiping the gods of the people around them. And they angered the

THE JUDGES OF ISRAEL

Judge	*Years of Judging*	*Memorable Act(s)*	*Reference*
OTHNIEL	40	He was victorious over the king of Aram	Judg 3:7-11
EHUD	80	He killed Eglon and defeated the Moabites	Judg 3:12-30
SHAMGAR	unrecorded	He killed 600 Philistines with an ox goad	Judg 3:31
DEBORAH (w/Barak)	40	She defeated Sisera and the Canaanites and later sang a victory song with Barak	Judg 4–5
GIDEON	40	He destroyed his family idols, used a fleece to determine God's will, raised an army of 10,000, and defeated 135,000 Midianites with 300 soldiers	Judg 6–8
TOLA	23	Unrecorded	Judg 10:1-2
JAIR	22	He had 30 sons	Judg 10:3-5
JEPHTHAH	6	He made a rash vow, defeated the Ammonites, and later battled jealous Ephraim	Judg 10:6–12:7
IBZAN	7	He had 30 sons and 30 daughters	Judg 12:8-10
ELON	10	Unrecorded	Judg 12:11-12
ABDON	8	He had 40 sons and 30 grandsons, who rode on donkeys	Judg 12:13-15
SAMSON	20	He was a Nazirite, killed a lion with his bare hands, burned Philistine wheat fields, killed 1,000 Philistines with a donkey's jawbone, tore off an iron gate, was betrayed by Delilah, and destroyed thousands of Philistines in one last mighty act	Judg 13–16

Judg 2:4 The people of Israel knew they had sinned, and they wept loudly, responding with deep sorrow. Because we have a tendency to sin, only repentance is the true measure of spiritual sensitivity. Repentance means not only confessing sins and asking God to forgive us but also abandoning our sinful ways. But we cannot do this sincerely unless we are truly sorry for our sinful actions. Tears alone are not enough. When we are aware that we have done wrong, we should admit it plainly to God rather than try to cover it up or hope we can get away with it.

Judg 2:10ff One generation died, and the next did not follow God. Judges 2:10–3:7 is a brief preview of the cycle of sin, judgment, and repentance that Israel experienced again and again. Each generation failed to teach the next generation to love and follow God. Yet this was at the very center of God's law (Deut 6:4-9). It is tempting to leave the job of teaching the Christian faith to the church or Christian school. Yet God says that the responsibility for this task belongs primarily to the family. Because children learn so much by our example, the home offers the most effective place to pass on the faith to the next generation.

Judg 2:11-15 Baal was a god of storms and rains; therefore, he was thought to control vegetation and agriculture. Ashtoreth was the mother goddess of love, war, and fertility (she was also called Astarte or Ishtar). Temple prostitution and child sacrifice were a part of the worship of these Canaanite idols. This generation of Israelites abandoned the faith of their parents and began worshiping the gods of their neighbors. Many things can tempt us to abandon what we know is right. The desire to be accepted by our neighbors can lead us into behavior that is unacceptable to God. Don't be lulled into compromise or pressured into disobedience.

Judg 2:12-15 God often delivered his harshest criticism and punishment to those who worshiped idols. Why were idols so bad in God's sight? To worship an idol violated the first two of the Ten Commandments (Exod 20:3-6). The Canaanites had gods for almost every season, activity, or place.

LORD. 13 They abandoned the LORD to serve Baal and
the images of Ashtoreth. 14 This made the LORD burn
with anger against Israel, so he handed them over to
raiders who stole their possessions. He turned them
over to their enemies all around, and they were no
longer able to resist them. 15 Every time Israel went
out to battle, the LORD fought against them, causing
them to be defeated, just as he had warned. And the
people were in great distress.

The LORD Rescues His People

JUDGES 2:16-23

Then the LORD raised up judges to rescue the Israelites
from their attackers. 17 Yet Israel did not listen to the
judges but prostituted themselves by worshiping
other gods. How quickly they turned away from the
path of their ancestors, who had walked in obedience
to the LORD's commands.
18 Whenever the LORD raised up a judge over Israel,
he was with that judge and rescued the people from
their enemies throughout the judge's lifetime. For the
LORD took pity on his people, who were burdened by
oppression and suffering. 19 But when the judge died,
the people returned to their corrupt ways, behaving
worse than those who had lived before them. They
went after other gods, serving and worshiping them.
And they refused to give up their evil practices and
stubborn ways.
20 So the LORD burned with anger against Israel. He
said, "Because these people have violated my covenant,
which I made with their ancestors, and have ignored
my commands, 21 I will no longer drive out the nations
that Joshua left unconquered when he died. 22 I did
this to test Israel—to see whether or not they would
follow the ways of the LORD as their ancestors did."
23 That is why the LORD left those nations in place.
He did not quickly drive them out or allow Joshua to
conquer them all.

To them, the Lord was just another god to add to their collection of gods. Israel, by contrast, was to worship only the Lord. They could not possibly believe that God was the one true God and at the same time bow to an idol. Idol worshipers could not see their god as their creator because they created it. These idols represented sensual, carnal, and immoral aspects of human nature. But God's nature is spiritual and moral. Adding the worship of idols to the worship of God could not be tolerated.

Judg 2:15-16 Despite Israel's disobedience, God showed his great mercy by raising up judges to save the people from their oppressors. Mercy has been defined as "not giving a person what he or she deserves." This is exactly what God did for Israel and what he does for us. Our disobedience demands judgment! But God shows mercy toward us by providing an escape from sin's penalty through Jesus Christ, who alone saves us from sin. When we pray for forgiveness, we are asking for what we do not deserve. Yet when we take this step and trust in Christ's saving work on our behalf, we can experience God's forgiveness.

Judg 2:16-19 Throughout this stage of history, Israel went through seven cycles of (1) rebelling against God, (2) being overrun by enemy nations, (3) being delivered by a God-fearing judge, (4) remaining loyal to God under that judge, and (5) again forgetting God when the judge died. We tend to follow the same cycle—remaining loyal to God as long as we are near those who are devoted to him. But when we are on our own, the pressure to be drawn away from God increases. Determine to be faithful to God despite the difficult situations you encounter. Recognize the importance of maintaining contact with other believers.

Judg 2:17 Why would the people of Israel turn away so quickly from their faith in God? Simply put, the Canaanite religion appeared more attractive to the sensual nature and offered more short-range benefits (sexual permissiveness and the promise of increased fertility in childbearing and farming). One of its most attractive features was that people could remain selfish and yet fulfill their religious requirements. They could do almost anything they wished and still be obeying at least one of the many Canaanite gods. Male and female prostitution was not only allowed but was encouraged as a form of worship.

Faith in the one true God does not offer short-range benefits that appeal to our sinful human nature. The essence of sin is selfishness; the essence of God's way of life is selflessness. We must seek Christ's help to live God's way.

WHY DID ISRAEL WANT TO WORSHIP IDOLS?

The temptation to follow false gods because of short-term benefits, good feelings, easy "rules," or convenience was always present. But the benefits were deceptive because the gods were false. We worship God because he is the one and only true God.

Worshiping God	Worshiping Idols
Long-range benefits	Short-range benefits
Gratification postponed	Self-gratification immediate
Morality required	Sensuality encouraged
High ethical standards demanded	Low ethical standards tolerated
Neighbors' sins disapproved	Neighbors' sins approved
Unseen God worshiped	Visible idols worshiped
Unselfishness expected	Selfishness condoned
Business relations hindered	Business relations improved
Strict religious practices maintained	Religious practices loosely regulated
Changed life demanded	Changed life not demanded
Ethical stand expected	Compromise and cooperation practiced
Concern for others taught	No concern for others expected

The Nations Left in Canaan

JUDGES 3:1-6

These are the nations that the LORD left in the land to test those Israelites who had not experienced the wars of Canaan. [2]He did this to teach warfare to generations of Israelites who had no experience in battle. [3]These are the nations: the Philistines (those living under the five Philistine rulers), all the Canaanites, the Sidonians, and the Hivites living in the mountains of Lebanon from Mount Baal-hermon to Lebo-hamath. [4]These people were left to test the Israelites—to see whether they would obey the commands the LORD had given to their ancestors through Moses.

[5]So the people of Israel lived among the Canaanites, Hittites, Amorites, Perizzites, Hivites, and Jebusites, [6]and they intermarried with them. Israelite sons married their daughters, and Israelite daughters were given in marriage to their sons. And the Israelites served their gods.

E. The Rescue of Israel by the Judges

The Israelites began a series of cycles of disobedience: worshiping idols, being punished, crying out for help, being rescued by a judge sent from God, obeying God for a while, then falling back into idolatry. They were conquered by Aram, Moab, Canaan, Midian, Ammon, and Philistia. They even faced the threat of civil war. Just as God sent help to the people when they cried out to him, he will deliver us when we call on him.

1. FIRST PERIOD: OTHNIEL

The first cycle was relatively brief, with only 8 years of servitude to Aram before God raised up a judge to save Israel.

Othniel Becomes Israel's Judge

JUDGES 3:7-11

The Israelites did evil in the LORD's sight. They forgot about the LORD their God, and they served the images of Baal and the Asherah poles. [8]Then the LORD burned with anger against Israel, and he turned them over to King Cushan-rishathaim of Aram-naharaim.* And the Israelites served Cushan-rishathaim for eight years.

[9]But when the people of Israel cried out to the LORD for help, the LORD raised up a rescuer to save them. His name was Othniel, the son of Caleb's younger brother, Kenaz. [10]The Spirit of the LORD came upon him, and he became Israel's judge. He went to war against King Cushan-rishathaim of Aram, and the LORD gave Othniel victory over him. [11]So there was peace in the land for forty years. Then Othniel son of Kenaz died.

Jgs 3:8 *Aram-naharaim* means "Aram of the two rivers," thought to have been located between the Euphrates and Balih Rivers in northwestern Mesopotamia.

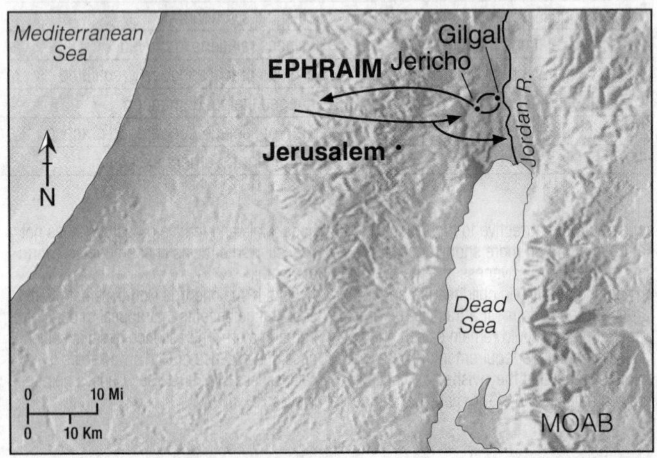

***EHUD FREES ISRAEL FROM MOAB** When King Eglon of Moab conquered part of Israel, he set up his throne in the city of Jericho. Ehud was chosen to take Israel's tribute there. After delivering Israel's tribute, Ehud killed King Eglon and escaped into the hill country of Ephraim. From there he gathered together an army to cut off any Moabites trying to escape across the Jordan River.*

Judg 3:1-4 We learn from Judges 1 that these enemy nations were still in the land because the Israelites had failed to obey God and drive them out. Now God would allow the enemies to remain in order to "test" the Israelites; that is, to give them an opportunity to exercise faith and obedience. By now the younger generation that had not fought in the great battles of conquest was coming of age. It was their job to complete the conquest of the land. There were many obstacles yet to be overcome in their new homeland. How they would handle these obstacles would be a test of their faith.

Perhaps God has left obstacles in your life—hostile people, difficult situations, baffling problems—to allow you to develop faith and obedience.

Judg 3:5-7 The Israelites discovered that relationships affect faith. The men and women of the surrounding nations were attractive to the Israelites. Soon they intermarried, and the Israelites accepted their pagan gods. This was clearly forbidden by God (Exod 34:15-17; Deut 7:1-4). By accepting these gods into their homes, the Israelites gradually began to accept the immoral practices associated with them. Most Israelites

2. SECOND PERIOD: EHUD AND SHAMGAR

The second cycle of disobedience led to 18 years of servitude to Moab and oppression by the Philistines. God used Ehud and Shamgar to rescue his people.

Ehud Becomes Israel's Judge

JUDGES 3:12-30

Once again the Israelites did evil in the LORD's sight, and the LORD gave King Eglon of Moab control over Israel because of their evil. 13 Eglon enlisted the Ammonites and Amalekites as allies, and then he went out and defeated Israel, taking possession of Jericho, the city of palms. 14 And the Israelites served Eglon of Moab for eighteen years.

15 But when the people of Israel cried out to the LORD for help, the LORD again raised up a rescuer to save them. His name was Ehud son of Gera, a left-handed man of the tribe of Benjamin. The Israelites sent Ehud to deliver their tribute money to King Eglon of Moab.

EHUD

At first glance, Ehud's career as a judge in Israel may not seem relevant to us. He clearly lived in another time. He took radical and violent action to free his people. His murder of Eglon shocks us. His war on Moab was swift and deadly. His life is difficult to relate to. But our commitment to God's Word challenges us not to ignore this leader. As we read about his life, some questions come to mind: When was the last time God showed me something wrong in my life and I took immediate and painful action to correct the error? When was the last time I asked God to show me how he could use something unique about me (as he used Ehud's left-handedness)? When was the last time I made a plan to obey God in some specific area of my life and then followed through on that plan? When was the last time my life was an example to others of obedience to God? • The enemies we face are as real as Ehud's, but they are most often within ourselves. The battles we fight are not against other people but against the power of sin. We need God's help in doing battle against sin. We also need to remember that he has already won the war. He has defeated sin by Jesus' death and resurrection. His help is the cause of each success, and his forgiveness is sufficient for each failure.

Strengths and accomplishments	• Second judge of Israel • A man of direct action, a frontline leader • Led the revolt against Moabite domination and gave Israel 80 years of peace
Lessons from his life	• Some conditions call for radical action • God responds to the cry of repentance • God is ready to use our unique qualities to accomplish his work
Vital statistics	• Where: Born during the last years of the wilderness wanderings or during Israel's early years in the Promised Land • Occupations: Messenger, judge • Relative: Father: Gera. • Contemporary: Eglon of Moab
Key verse	"But when the people of Israel cried out to the LORD for help, the LORD again raised up a rescuer to save them. His name was Ehud son of Gera, a left-handed man of the tribe of Benjamin" (Judg 3:15).

Ehud's story is told in Judges 3:12-30.

didn't start out determined to be idolaters; they just added the idols to the worship of God. But before long they found themselves absorbed in pagan worship.

A similar danger faces us. We want to befriend those who don't know God, but through those friendships we can become entangled in unhealthy practices. Friendships with unbelievers are important, but we must accept people without compromising our beliefs or adopting their patterns of behavior.

Judg 3:7 Baal was the most worshiped god of the Canaanites. Most often cast in the form of a bull, he symbolized strength and fertility and was considered the god of agriculture. Asherah was Baal's female consort, mother goddess of the sea, who was worshiped by means of wooden pillars that substituted for sacred trees. In times of famine, the Canaanites believed Baal was angry with them and was withholding rain as punishment. Archaeologists have uncovered many Baal idols in Israel. It is difficult to imagine the people of Israel trading worship of the Lord for worship of idols of wood, stone, and iron, but we do the same when we forsake worshiping God for other activities, hobbies, or priorities. Our idols are not made of wood or stone, but they are every bit as sinful.

Judg 3:9 Othniel was Israel's first judge. Judges 1:13 records that he volunteered to lead an attack against a fortified city. Here he was to lead the nation back to God. Othniel had a rich spiritual heritage—his uncle was Caleb, a man with unwavering faith in God (Num 13:30; 14:24). Othniel's leadership brought the people back to God and freed them from oppression. But after Othniel's death, it didn't take the Israelites long to fall back into their neighbors' comfortable but sinful ways.

Judg 3:10 This phrase, "The Spirit of the LORD came upon him," was also spoken of the judges Gideon, Jephthah, and Samson, among others. It expresses a temporary and spontaneous increase of physical, spiritual, or mental strength. This was an extraordinary and supernatural occurrence to prepare a person for a special task. Today, the Holy Spirit is available to all believers, but for special tasks he may come upon believers in an extraordinary way. We should ask the Holy Spirit's help as we face our daily problems as well as life's major challenges.

Judg 3:12-13 The Moabites, Ammonites, and Amalekites were nomadic tribes that lived near each other east and southeast of Canaan. These tribes were notorious raiders, possessing great military skill. This was the first time nations outside Canaan attacked the Israelites in their own land.

Judg 3:15-30 This unusual story demonstrates how God can use us just the way he made us. Being left-handed in Ehud's day was considered an exceptional ability. Many Benjaminites were left-handed (see Judg 20:16), making them highly specialized troops, able to use a sling or bow with tactics designed to repel right-handed warriors. Eglon's bodyguard never checked Israel's messengers for left-handed weapons. But God used Ehud's overlooked ability to give Israel victory. Let God use you the way you are to accomplish his work.

King Tutankhamen is buried in Egypt amidst great treasure

▸ **JUDGES 3:12-30** ***(cont.)***

16So Ehud made a double-edged dagger that was about a foot* long, and he strapped it to his right thigh, keeping it hidden under his clothing. 17He brought the tribute money to Eglon, who was very fat.

18After delivering the payment, Ehud started home with those who had helped carry the tribute. 19But when Ehud reached the stone idols near Gilgal, he turned back. He came to Eglon and said, "I have a secret message for you."

So the king commanded his servants, "Be quiet!" and he sent them all out of the room.

20Ehud walked over to Eglon, who was sitting alone in a cool upstairs room. And Ehud said, "I have a message from God for you!" As King Eglon rose from his seat, 21Ehud reached with his left hand, pulled out the dagger strapped to his right thigh, and plunged it into the king's belly. 22The dagger went so deep that the handle disappeared beneath the king's fat. So Ehud did not pull out the dagger, and the king's bowels emptied.* 23Then Ehud closed and locked the doors of the room and escaped down the latrine.*

24After Ehud was gone, the king's servants returned and found the doors to the upstairs room locked. They thought he might be using the latrine in the room, 25so they waited. But when the king didn't come out after a long delay, they became concerned and got a key. And when they opened the doors, they found their master dead on the floor.

26While the servants were waiting, Ehud escaped, passing the stone idols on his way to Seirah. 27When he arrived in the hill country of Ephraim, Ehud sounded a call to arms. Then he led a band of Israelites down from the hills.

28"Follow me," he said, "for the LORD has given you victory over Moab your enemy." So they followed him. And the Israelites took control of the shallow crossings of the Jordan River across from Moab, preventing anyone from crossing.

29They attacked the Moabites and killed about 10,000 of their strongest and most able-bodied warriors. Not one of them escaped. 30So Moab was conquered by Israel that day, and there was peace in the land for eighty years.

Shamgar Becomes Israel's Judge

JUDGES 3:31

After Ehud, Shamgar son of Anath rescued Israel. He once killed 600 Philistines with an ox goad.

Jgs 3:16 Hebrew *gomed,* the length of which is uncertain. **Jgs 3:22** Or *and it came out behind.* **Jgs 3:23** Or *and went out through the porch;* the meaning of the Hebrew is uncertain.

3. THIRD PERIOD: DEBORAH AND BARAK

Israel's third cycle of disobedience led to a period of dominance by a Canaanite, King Jabin of Hazor. After twenty years of ruthless oppression, Israel cried out to God and he used Deborah and Barak to rescue them.

Deborah Becomes Israel's Judge

JUDGES 4:1-24

After Ehud's death, the Israelites again did evil in the LORD's sight. 2So the LORD turned them over to King Jabin of Hazor, a Canaanite king. The commander of his army was Sisera, who lived in Harosheth-haggoyim. 3Sisera, who had 900 iron chariots, ruthlessly oppressed the Israelites for twenty

Judg 3:31 To kill 600 Philistines with an ox goad was quite a feat. An ox goad was a long stick with a small flat piece of iron on one side and a sharp point on the other. The sharp side was used to drive the oxen during the times of plowing, and the flat end was used to clean the mud off the plow. Eight-foot-long ancient ox goads have been found. In times of crisis they could easily have been used as spears, as in Shamgar's case. Ox goads are still used in the Middle East to drive oxen.

Judg 4:1 Israel sinned "in the LORD's sight." Our sins harm both ourselves and others, but all sin is ultimately against God because it disregards his commands and his authority over us. When confessing his sin, David prayed, "Against you, and you alone, have I sinned; I have done what is evil in your sight" (Ps 51:4). Recognizing the seriousness of sin is the first step toward removing it from our lives.

Judg 4:2-3 Nothing more is known about Jabin. Joshua had defeated a king by that name years earlier and burned the city of Hazor to the ground (Josh 11:1-11). Either the city was now rebuilt, or this Jabin was hoping to rebuild it.

This is the only time during the period of the judges when the Israelites' enemies came from within their land. The Israelites had failed to drive out all the Canaanites. These Canaanites had regrouped and were attempting to restore their lost power. If the Israelites had obeyed God in the first place and had driven the Canaanites from the land, this incident would not have happened.

THE JUDGES' FUNCTIONS

Regardless of an individual judge's leadership style, each one demonstrated that God's judgment follows apostasy, while repentance brings restoration.

Judges of Israel could be		
saviors (deliverers) and redeemers (Gideon)	*or*	mediators and administrators (Tola)
providers of rest and peace (Ehud and Jair)	*or*	rude, petty dictators (Jephthah)
famous and powerful (Samson)	*or*	hardworking yet unsung (Elon and Abdon)
leaders of the nation (Othniel and Deborah)	*or*	local heroes (Shamgar and Ibzan)

years. Then the people of Israel cried out to the LORD for help.

4 Deborah, the wife of Lappidoth, was a prophet who was judging Israel at that time. 5 She would sit under the Palm of Deborah, between Ramah and Bethel in the hill country of Ephraim, and the Israelites would go to her for judgment. 6 One day she sent for Barak son of Abinoam, who lived in Kedesh in the land of Naphtali. She said to him, "This is what the LORD, the God of Israel, commands you: Call out 10,000 warriors from the tribes of Naphtali and Zebulun at Mount Tabor. 7 And I will call out Sisera, commander of Jabin's army, along with his chariots and warriors, to the Kishon River. There I will give you victory over him."

8 Barak told her, "I will go, but only if you go with me."

9 "Very well," she replied, "I will go with you. But you will receive no honor in this venture, for the LORD's victory over Sisera will be at the hands of a woman." So Deborah went with Barak to Kedesh. 10 At Kedesh, Barak called together the tribes of Zebulun and Naphtali, and 10,000 warriors went up with him. Deborah also went with him.

11 Now Heber the Kenite, a descendant of Moses' brother-in-law* Hobab, had moved away from the other members of his tribe and pitched his tent by the oak of Zaanannim near Kedesh.

12 When Sisera was told that Barak son of Abinoam had gone up to Mount Tabor, 13 he called for all 900 of his iron chariots and all of his warriors, and they marched from Harosheth-haggoyim to the Kishon River.

14 Then Deborah said to Barak, "Get ready! This is the day the LORD will give you victory over Sisera, for the LORD is marching ahead of you." So Barak led his 10,000 warriors down the slopes of Mount Tabor into battle. 15 When Barak attacked, the LORD threw Sisera and all his chariots and warriors into a panic. Sisera leaped down from his chariot and escaped on foot. 16 Then Barak chased the chariots and the enemy army all the way to Harosheth-haggoyim, killing all of Sisera's warriors. Not a single one was left alive.

17 Meanwhile, Sisera ran to the tent of Jael, the wife of Heber the Kenite, because Heber's family was on friendly terms with King Jabin of Hazor. 18 Jael went

Jgs 4:11 Or *father-in-law.*

Judg 4:2-3 Chariots were the tanks of the ancient world. Made of iron or wood, they were pulled by one or two horses and were the most feared and powerful weapons of the day. Some chariots even had razor-sharp knives extending from the wheels designed to mutilate helpless foot soldiers. The Canaanite army had 900 iron chariots. Israel was not powerful enough to defeat such an invincible army. Therefore, Jabin and Sisera had no trouble oppressing the people—until a faithful woman named Deborah called upon God.

Judg 4:3 After 20 years of unbearable circumstances, the Israelites finally cried to the Lord for help. But God should be the first one we turn to when facing struggles or dilemmas. The Israelites chose to go their own way and got into a mess. We often do the same. Trying to control our own lives without God's help leads to struggle and confusion. By contrast, when we stay in daily contact with the Lord, we are less likely to create painful circumstances for ourselves. This is a lesson the Israelites never fully learned. When struggles come our way, God wants us to come to him first, seeking his strength and guidance.

Judg 4:4ff The Bible records several women who held national leadership positions, and Deborah was an exceptional woman. Obviously she was the best person for the job, and God chose her to lead Israel. God can choose anyone to lead his people, young or old, man or woman. Don't let your prejudices get in the way of those God may have chosen to lead you.

Judg 4:6-8 Was Barak cowardly or just in need of support? We don't know Barak's character, but we see the character of a great leader in Deborah, who took charge as God directed. Deborah told Barak that God would be with him in battle, but that was not enough for Barak. He wanted Deborah to go with him. Barak's request shows that at heart he trusted human strength more than God's promise. A person of real faith steps out at God's command, even if having to do so alone.

Judg 4:9 How did Deborah command such respect? She was responsible for leading the people into battle, but more than that, she influenced them to live for God after the battle was over. Her personality drew people together and commanded the respect of even Barak, a military general. She was also a prophet, whose main role was to encourage the people to obey God. Those who lead must not forget about the spiritual condition of those being led. A true leader is concerned for the people themselves, not just success.

Judg 4:11 Heber was Jael's husband (Judg 4:17). He was from the Kenite tribe, descendants of Moses' father-in-law, and longtime allies of Israel. But for some reason, Heber decided to remain neutral in this war (maybe because Jabin's army appeared to have the military advantage). It was probably Heber who told Sisera that the Israelites were camped near Mount Tabor (Judg 4:12). Although Heber threw in his lot with Jabin and his forces, his wife, Jael, did not (Judg 4:21).

Judg 4:18-21 Sisera couldn't have been more pleased when Jael offered him her tent as a hiding place. First, because Jael was the wife of Heber, a man friendly to Sisera's forces (see the note on Judg 4:11, above), he thought she could be trusted. Second, because men were never allowed to enter a woman's tent, no one would think to look for Sisera there.

Even though her husband, Heber, apparently sided with Sisera's forces, Jael certainly did not. Because women of that day were in charge of pitching the tents, Jael had no problem driving the tent peg into Sisera's head while he slept. Deborah's prediction was thus fulfilled: The honor of conquering Sisera went to a brave and resourceful woman (Judg 4:9).

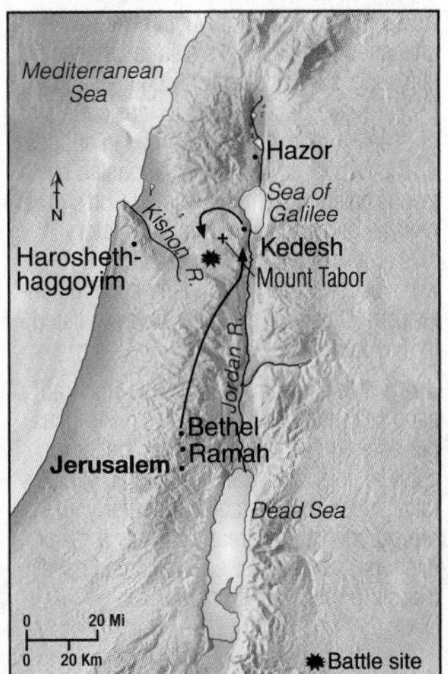

KING JABIN IS DEFEATED *Deborah traveled from her home between Ramah and Bethel to march with Barak and the Israelite army against Hazor. Sisera, commander of Hazor's army, had assembled his men at Harosheth-haggoyim. Sisera had 900 chariots and an expertly trained army, but when they met below Mount Tabor, Israel was victorious.*

▸ **JUDGES 4:1-24 *(cont.)***
out to meet Sisera and said to him, "Come into my
tent, sir. Come in. Don't be afraid." So he went into
her tent, and she covered him with a blanket.
19 "Please give me some water," he said. "I'm thirsty."
So she gave him some milk from a leather bag and
covered him again.
20 "Stand at the door of the tent," he told her. "If
anybody comes and asks you if there is anyone here,
say no."
21 But when Sisera fell asleep from exhaustion, Jael
quietly crept up to him with a hammer and tent peg
in her hand. Then she drove the tent peg through his
temple and into the ground, and so he died.
22 When Barak came looking for Sisera, Jael went
out to meet him. She said, "Come, and I will show you
the man you are looking for." So he followed her into
the tent and found Sisera lying there dead, with the
tent peg through his temple.
23 So on that day Israel saw God defeat Jabin, the
Canaanite king. 24 And from that time on Israel became
stronger and stronger against King Jabin until they
finally destroyed him.

The Song of Deborah

JUDGES 5:1-31

On that day Deborah and Barak son of Abinoam sang this song:

2 "Israel's leaders took charge,
and the people gladly followed.
Praise the LORD!

3 "Listen, you kings!
Pay attention, you mighty rulers!
For I will sing to the LORD.
I will make music to the LORD, the God of Israel.

4 "LORD, when you set out from Seir
and marched across the fields of Edom,
the earth trembled,
and the cloudy skies poured down rain.
5 The mountains quaked in the presence of the LORD,
the God of Mount Sinai—
in the presence of the LORD,
the God of Israel.

Judg 5:1ff Music and singing were a cherished part of Israel's culture. Judges 5 is a song, sung and possibly composed by Deborah and Barak. It sets to music the story of Israel's great victory described in Judges 4. This victory song was accompanied by joyous celebration. It proclaimed God's greatness by giving him credit for the victory. It was an excellent way to preserve and retell this wonderful story from generation to generation. (Other songs in the Bible are listed in the chart on p. 163.)

Judg 5:1ff In victory, Barak and Deborah sang praises to God. Songs of praise focus our attention on God, give us an outlet for spiritual celebration, and remind us of God's faithfulness and character. Whether you are experiencing a great victory or a major dilemma, singing praises to God can have a positive effect on your attitude.

DEBORAH

Wise leaders are rare. They accomplish great amounts of work without direct involvement because they know how to work through other people. They are able to see the big picture that often escapes those directly involved, so they make good mediators, advisers, and planners. Deborah fit this description perfectly. She had all these leadership skills, and she had a remarkable relationship with God. The insight and confidence God gave this woman placed her in a unique position in the Old Testament. Deborah is among the outstanding women of history. • Her story shows that she was not power hungry. She wanted to serve God. Whenever praise came her way, she gave God the credit. She didn't deny or resist her position in the culture as a woman and wife, but she never allowed herself to be hindered by it either. Her story shows that God can accomplish great things through people who are willing to be led by him. • Deborah's life challenges us in several ways: She reminds us of the need to be available both to God and to others; she encourages us to spend our efforts on what we can do rather than on worrying about what we can't do; she challenges us to be wise leaders. Deborah's life demonstrates what a person can accomplish when God is in control.

Strengths and accomplishments	• Only female judge of Israel • Special abilities as a mediator, adviser, and counselor • When called on to lead, was able to plan, direct, and delegate • Known for her prophetic power
Lessons from her life	• God chooses leaders by his standards, not ours • Wise leaders choose good helpers
Vital statistics	• Where: Canaan • Occupations: Prophet, judge • Relative: Husband: Lappidoth. • Contemporaries: Barak, Jael, Jabin of Hazor, Sisera
Key verse	"Deborah, the wife of Lappidoth, was a prophet who was judging Israel at that time" (Judg 4:4).

Deborah's story is told in Judges 4–5.

6 "In the days of Shamgar son of Anath,
and in the days of Jael,
people avoided the main roads,
and travelers stayed on winding pathways.
7 There were few people left in the villages
of Israel*—
until Deborah arose as a mother for Israel.
8 When Israel chose new gods,
war erupted at the city gates.
Yet not a shield or spear could be seen
among forty thousand warriors in Israel!
9 My heart is with the commanders of Israel,
with those who volunteered for war.
Praise the LORD!

10 "Consider this, you who ride on fine donkeys,
you who sit on fancy saddle blankets,
and you who walk along the road.
11 Listen to the village musicians*
gathered at the watering holes.
They recount the righteous victories
of the LORD
and the victories of his villagers in Israel.
Then the people of the LORD
marched down to the city gates.

12 "Wake up, Deborah, wake up!
Wake up, wake up, and sing a song!
Arise, Barak!
Lead your captives away, son of Abinoam!

13 "Down from Tabor marched the few against
the nobles.
The people of the LORD marched down against
mighty warriors.
14 They came down from Ephraim—
a land that once belonged to the Amalekites;
they followed you, Benjamin, with your troops.
From Makir the commanders marched down;
from Zebulun came those who carry a
commander's staff.
15 The princes of Issachar were with Deborah
and Barak.
They followed Barak, rushing into the valley.
But in the tribe of Reuben
there was great indecision.
16 Why did you sit at home among the sheepfolds—
to hear the shepherds whistle for their flocks?
Yes, in the tribe of Reuben
there was great indecision.
17 Gilead remained east of the Jordan.
And why did Dan stay home?
Asher sat unmoved at the seashore,
remaining in his harbors.
18 But Zebulun risked his life,
as did Naphtali, on the heights of the battlefield.

19 "The kings of Canaan came and fought,
at Taanach near Megiddo's springs,
but they carried off no silver treasures.
20 The stars fought from heaven.
The stars in their orbits fought against Sisera.
21 The Kishon River swept them away—
that ancient torrent, the Kishon.
March on with courage, my soul!

Jgs 5:7 The meaning of the Hebrew is uncertain. **Jgs 5:11** The meaning of the Hebrew is uncertain.

Judg 5:8 War was the inevitable result when Israel chose to follow false gods. Although God had given Israel clear directions, the people failed to put his words into practice. Without God at the center of their national life, pressure from the outside soon became greater than the power from within, and they were an easy prey for their enemies. If you are letting a desire for recognition, craving for power, or love of money rule your life, you may find yourself besieged by enemies—stress, anxiety, illness, fatigue. Keep God at the center of your life, and you will have the power you need to fight these destroyers.

Judg 5:15-17 Four tribes—Reuben, Gilead (either Gad or Manasseh), Dan, and Asher—were accused of not lending a helping hand in the battle. No reasons are given for their refusal to help their fellow Israelites, but they may be the same ones that stopped them from driving out the Canaanites in the first place: lack of reliance on God for help, lack of effort, fear of the enemy, and fear of antagonizing those whom they did business with and thus prospered from. This disobedience showed both a lack of commitment to God's plan and a weak faith in God's power.

Mount Gilboa

Mount Gilboa is on the east side of the plain of Esdraelon between Galilee on the north and Samaria on the south (modern Jebel Fuqu'ah). Mount Gilboa towers over the valley of Jezreel. It is a weathered limestone ridge reaching 1,700 feet above sea level.

Many battles were fought in the area, including Deborah's defeat of Sisera. At that time the flooding of the Kishon River, which has its source in the Gilboa ridge, greatly helped in the victory (Judg 5:21). This region was the probable location of Gideon's camp when he attacked the Midianites (Judg 6:33; 7:7-9). Gilboa is mentioned by name only in connection with Saul's defense of the area against the Philistines. It was here that his sons were killed, and where he himself committed suicide (1 Sam 31:1, 8; 2 Sam 1:6, 21; 21:12; 1 Chr 10:1, 8).

▸ **JUDGES 5:1-31** ***(cont.)***

22 Then the horses' hooves hammered the ground,
the galloping, galloping of Sisera's mighty steeds.
23 'Let the people of Meroz be cursed,' said the angel of the LORD.
'Let them be utterly cursed,
because they did not come to help the LORD—
to help the LORD against the mighty warriors.'

24 "Most blessed among women is Jael,
the wife of Heber the Kenite.
May she be blessed above all women who live in tents.
25 Sisera asked for water,
and she gave him milk.
In a bowl fit for nobles,
she brought him yogurt.
26 Then with her left hand she reached for a tent peg,
and with her right hand for the workman's hammer.
She struck Sisera with the hammer, crushing his head.
With a shattering blow, she pierced his temples.
27 He sank, he fell,
he lay still at her feet.
And where he sank,
there he died.

28 "From the window Sisera's mother looked out.
Through the window she watched for his return, saying,
'Why is his chariot so long in coming?
Why don't we hear the sound of chariot wheels?'

29 "Her wise women answer,
and she repeats these words to herself:
30 'They must be dividing the captured plunder—
with a woman or two for every man.
There will be colorful robes for Sisera,
and colorful, embroidered robes for me.
Yes, the plunder will include
colorful robes embroidered on both sides.'

31 "LORD, may all your enemies die like Sisera!
But may those who love you rise like the sun in all its power!"

Then there was peace in the land for forty years.

4. FOURTH PERIOD: GIDEON, TOLA, AND JAIR

The fourth cycle of disobedience led to a period of oppression at the hands of the Midianites. After God used Gideon to free Israel from their foreign oppressors, they fell into a period of inner turmoil. One of Gideon's sons proclaimed himself king, and this led to a bloody internal conflict.

Gideon Becomes Israel's Judge

JUDGES 6:1-32

The Israelites did evil in the LORD's sight. So the LORD
handed them over to the Midianites for seven years.
2 The Midianites were so cruel that the Israelites made
hiding places for themselves in the mountains, caves,
and strongholds. 3 Whenever the Israelites planted
their crops, marauders from Midian, Amalek, and
the people of the east would attack Israel, 4 camping
in the land and destroying crops as far away as Gaza.
They left the Israelites with nothing to eat, taking all
the sheep, goats, cattle, and donkeys. 5 These enemy
hordes, coming with their livestock and tents, were
as thick as locusts; they arrived on droves of camels
too numerous to count. And they stayed until the land
was stripped bare. 6 So Israel was reduced to starvation
by the Midianites. Then the Israelites cried out to the
LORD for help.
7 When they cried out to the LORD because of Midian, 8 the LORD sent a prophet to the Israelites. He
said, "This is what the LORD, the God of Israel, says:
I brought you up out of slavery in Egypt. 9 I rescued
you from the Egyptians and from all who oppressed
you. I drove out your enemies and gave you their land.
10 I told you, 'I am the LORD your God. You must not
worship the gods of the Amorites, in whose land you
now live.' But you have not listened to me."
11 Then the angel of the LORD came and sat beneath
the great tree at Ophrah, which belonged to Joash of
the clan of Abiezer. Gideon son of Joash was threshing

Judg 6:2 The Midianites were desert people descended from Abraham's second wife, Keturah (Gen 25:1-2). From this relationship came a nation that was always in conflict with Israel. Years earlier, while still wandering in the wilderness, the Israelites battled the Midianites and almost destroyed them (Num 31:1-20). Because of their failure to completely destroy them, the tribe repopulated. Here they were once again oppressing Israel.

Judg 6:6 Again the Israelites hit rock bottom before turning back to God. How much suffering they could have avoided if they had trusted him! Turning to God shouldn't be a last resort; we should look to him for help each day. This isn't to say life will always be easy. There will be struggles, but God will give us the strength to live through them. Don't wait until you're at the end of your rope. Call on God first in every situation.

Judg 6:11 The Old Testament records several appearances of the angel of the Lord: Genesis 16:7; 22:11; 31:11; Exodus 3:2; 14:19; Judges 2:1; 13:3; Zechariah 3:1-6. It is not known whether the same angel appeared in each case. The angel mentioned here appears to be separate from God in one place (Judg 6:12) and yet the same as God in another place (Judg 6:14). This has led some to believe that the angel was a special appearance of Jesus Christ prior to his mission on earth as recorded in the New Testament. It is also possible that as a special messenger from God, the angel had authority to speak for God. In either case, God sent a special messenger to deliver an important message to Gideon.

wheat at the bottom of a winepress to hide the grain
from the Midianites. 12 The angel of the LORD appeared
to him and said, "Mighty hero, the LORD is with you!"
13 "Sir," Gideon replied, "if the LORD is with us, why
has all this happened to us? And where are all the miracles our ancestors told us about? Didn't they say, 'The
LORD brought us up out of Egypt'? But now the LORD has
abandoned us and handed us over to the Midianites."
14 Then the LORD turned to him and said, "Go with
the strength you have, and rescue Israel from the
Midianites. I am sending you!"
15 "But Lord," Gideon replied, "how can I rescue
Israel? My clan is the weakest in the whole tribe of
Manasseh, and I am the least in my entire family!"
16 The LORD said to him, "I will be with you. And
you will destroy the Midianites as if you were fighting
against one man."
17 Gideon replied, "If you are truly going to help me,
show me a sign to prove that it is really the LORD speaking to me. 18 Don't go away until I come back and bring
my offering to you."

He answered, "I will stay here until you return."
19 Gideon hurried home. He cooked a young goat,
and with a basket* of flour he baked some bread without yeast. Then, carrying the meat in a basket and the
broth in a pot, he brought them out and presented
them to the angel, who was under the great tree.
20 The angel of God said to him, "Place the meat
and the unleavened bread on this rock, and pour the
broth over it." And Gideon did as he was told. 21 Then
the angel of the LORD touched the meat and bread
with the tip of the staff in his hand, and fire flamed
up from the rock and consumed all he had brought.
And the angel of the LORD disappeared.

Jgs 6:19 Hebrew *an ephah* [20 quarts or 22 liters].

GOD USES COMMON PEOPLE

God uses all sorts of people to do his work—like you and me!

Person	*Known as*	*Task*	*Reference*
JACOB	A deceiver	To father the Israelite nation	Gen 27–28
JOSEPH	A slave	To save his family	Gen 39–50
MOSES	Shepherd in exile (and murderer)	To lead Israel out of bondage, to the Promised Land	Exod 3
GIDEON	A farmer	To deliver Israel from Midian	Judg 6:11-14
JEPHTHAH	Son of a prostitute	To deliver Israel from the Ammonites	Judg 11
HANNAH	A homemaker	To be the mother of Samuel	1 Sam 1
DAVID	A shepherd boy and last-born of the family	To be Israel's greatest king	1 Sam 16
EZRA	A scribe	To lead the return to Judah and to write some of the Bible	Ezra, Nehemiah
ESTHER	A girl from among the exiles of Judah	To save her people from massacre	Esther
MARY	A peasant girl	To be the mother of Christ	Luke 1:27-38
MATTHEW	A tax collector	To be an apostle and Gospel writer	Matt 9:9
LUKE	A Greek physician	To be a companion of Paul and a Gospel writer	Col 4:14
PETER	A fisherman	To be an apostle, a leader of the early church, and a writer of two New Testament letters	Matt 4:18-20

Judg 6:11 Threshing was the process of separating the grains of wheat from the useless outer shell called chaff. This was normally done in a large area, often on a hill, where the wind could blow away the lighter chaff when the farmer tossed the beaten wheat into the air. But if Gideon had done this, he would have been an easy target for the bands of raiders who were overrunning the land. Therefore, he was forced to thresh his wheat in a winepress, a pit that was probably hidden from view and that would not be suspected as a place to find a farmer's crops.

Judg 6:13 Gideon questioned God about the problems he and his nation faced and about God's apparent lack of help. What he didn't acknowledge was the fact that the people had brought calamity upon themselves when they decided to disobey and neglect God. How easy it is to overlook personal accountability and blame our problems on God and others. Unfortunately, this does not solve our problems. It brings us no closer to God, and it escorts us to the very edge of rebellion and backsliding.

When problems come, the first place to look is within. Our immediate response should be confession to God of sins that may have created our problems.

Judg 6:14-16 God promised to give Gideon the strength he needed to overcome the opposition, and God told him, "I will be with you." In spite of this clear promise for strength, Gideon made excuses. Seeing only his limitations and weaknesses, he failed to see how God could work through him.

Like Gideon, we are called to serve God in specific ways. Although God promises us the tools and strength we need, we often make excuses. But reminding God of our limitations only implies that he does not know all about us or that he has made a mistake in evaluating our character. Don't spend time making excuses. Instead, spend it doing what God wants.

▸ **JUDGES 6:1-32** ***(cont.)***

22 When Gideon realized that it was the angel of the
LORD, he cried out, "Oh, Sovereign LORD, I'm doomed!
I have seen the angel of the LORD face to face!"
23 "It is all right," the LORD replied. "Do not be afraid.
You will not die." 24 And Gideon built an altar to the
LORD there and named it Yahweh-Shalom (which
means "the LORD is peace"). The altar remains in
Ophrah in the land of the clan of Abiezer to this day.
25 That night the LORD said to Gideon, "Take the
second bull from your father's herd, the one that is
seven years old. Pull down your father's altar to Baal,
and cut down the Asherah pole standing beside it.
26 Then build an altar to the LORD your God here on
this hilltop sanctuary, laying the stones carefully.
Sacrifice the bull as a burnt offering on the altar,
using as fuel the wood of the Asherah pole you cut
down."
27 So Gideon took ten of his servants and did as the
LORD had commanded. But he did it at night because
he was afraid of the other members of his father's
household and the people of the town.
28 Early the next morning, as the people of the town
began to stir, someone discovered that the altar of
Baal had been broken down and that the Asherah pole
beside it had been cut down. In their place a new altar
had been built, and on it were the remains of the bull
that had been sacrificed. 29 The people said to each
other, "Who did this?" And after asking around and
making a careful search, they learned that it was Gideon, the son of Joash.
30 "Bring out your son," the men of the town demanded of Joash. "He must die for destroying the altar
of Baal and for cutting down the Asherah pole."
31 But Joash shouted to the mob that confronted
him, "Why are you defending Baal? Will you argue his
case? Whoever pleads his case will be put to death by
morning! If Baal truly is a god, let him defend himself and destroy the one who broke down his altar!"
32 From then on Gideon was called Jerub-baal, which
means "Let Baal defend himself," because he broke
down Baal's altar.

Gideon Asks for a Sign

JUDGES 6:33-40

33 Soon afterward the armies of Midian, Amalek, and the
people of the east formed an alliance against Israel
and crossed the Jordan, camping in the valley of Jezreel. 34 Then the Spirit of the LORD took possession of
Gideon. He blew a ram's horn as a call to arms, and the
men of the clan of Abiezer came to him. 35 He also sent
messengers throughout Manasseh, Asher, Zebulun,
and Naphtali, summoning their warriors, and all of
them responded.
36 Then Gideon said to God, "If you are truly going to
use me to rescue Israel as you promised, 37 prove it to
me in this way. I will put a wool fleece on the threshing
floor tonight. If the fleece is wet with dew in the morning but the ground is dry, then I will know that you are
going to help me rescue Israel as you promised." 38 And
that is just what happened. When Gideon got up early
the next morning, he squeezed the fleece and wrung
out a whole bowlful of water.
39 Then Gideon said to God, "Please don't be angry
with me, but let me make one more request. Let me use
the fleece for one more test. This time let the fleece
remain dry while the ground around it is wet with
dew." 40 So that night God did as Gideon asked. The
fleece was dry in the morning, but the ground was
covered with dew.

Judg 6:22-23 Why was Gideon afraid of seeing an angel? The Israelites believed that no one could see God and live (see God's words to Moses in Exod 33:20). Evidently Gideon thought this also applied to angels.

Judg 6:25-30 After God called Gideon to be Israel's deliverer, he immediately asked him to tear down the altar of the pagan god Baal—an act that would test Gideon's faith and commitment. Canaanite religion was very political, so an attack on a god was often seen as an attack on the local government supporting that god. If caught, Gideon would face serious social problems and probable physical attack. (For more on Baal and Asherah, see the notes on Judg 2:11-15, p. 374, and Judg 3:7, p. 377.)

Gideon took a great risk by following God's higher law, which specifically forbids idol worship (Exod 20:1-5). After learning what Gideon had done, the townspeople wanted to kill him. Many of those people were fellow Israelites. This shows how immoral God's people had become. God said in Deuteronomy 13:6-11 that idolaters must be stoned to death, but these Israelites wanted to stone Gideon for tearing down an idol and worshiping God! When you begin to accomplish something for God, you may be criticized by the very people who should support you.

Judg 6:33 The armies of Midian and Amalek camped in the valley of Jezreel, the agricultural center for the area. Whoever controlled the valley's rich and fertile land controlled the people who lived in and around it. Because of the valley's vast resources, many major trade routes converged at the pass which led into it. This made it the site of many great battles. Gideon's men attacked the enemy armies from the hills, and the only escape route was through the pass toward the Jordan River. That is why Gideon urged some of his troops to take control of the river's crossing points (Judg 7:24).

Judg 6:37-39 Was Gideon testing God, or was he simply asking God for more encouragement? In either case, though his motive was right (to obey God and defeat the enemy), his method was less than ideal. Gideon seems to have known that his requests might displease God (Judg 6:39), and yet he demanded two miracles (Judg 6:37, 39) even after witnessing the miraculous fire from the rock (Judg 6:21). It is true that to make good decisions, we need facts. Gideon had all the facts, but still he hesitated. He delayed obeying God because he wanted even more proof.

Demanding extra signs was an indication of unbelief. Fear often makes us wait for more confirmation when we should be taking action. Visible signs are unnecessary if they only confirm what we already know is true.

Today the greatest means of God's guidance is his Word, the Bible. Unlike Gideon, we have God's complete, revealed Word. If you want to have more of God's guidance, don't ask for signs; study the Bible (2 Tim 3:16-17).

Judg 6:39 After seeing the miracle of the wet fleece, why did Gideon ask for another miracle? Perhaps he thought the results of

Gideon Defeats the Midianites

JUDGES 7:1-25

So Jerub-baal (that is, Gideon) and his army got up early and went as far as the spring of Harod. The armies of Midian were camped north of them in the valley near the hill of Moreh. [2]The LORD said to Gideon, "You have too many warriors with you. If I let all of you fight the Midianites, the Israelites will boast to me that they saved themselves by their own strength. [3]Therefore, tell the people, 'Whoever is timid or afraid may leave this mountain* and go home.'" So 22,000 of them went home, leaving only 10,000 who were willing to fight.

[4]But the LORD told Gideon, "There are still too many! Bring them down to the spring, and I will test them to determine who will go with you and who will not." [5]When Gideon took his warriors down to the water, the LORD told him, "Divide the men into two groups. In one group put all those who cup water in their hands and lap it up with their tongues like dogs. In the other group put all those who kneel down and drink with their mouths in the stream." [6]Only 300 of the men drank from their hands. All the others got down on their knees and drank with their mouths in the stream.

[7]The LORD told Gideon, "With these 300 men I will rescue you and give you victory over the Midianites. Send all the others home." [8]So Gideon collected the provisions and rams' horns of the other warriors and sent them home. But he kept the 300 men with him.

The Midianite camp was in the valley just below Gideon. [9]That night the LORD said, "Get up! Go down into the Midianite camp, for I have given you victory over them! [10]But if you are afraid to attack, go down to the camp with your servant Purah. [11]Listen to what the Midianites are saying, and you will be greatly encouraged. Then you will be eager to attack."

So Gideon took Purah and went down to the edge of the enemy camp. [12]The armies of Midian, Amalek, and the people of the east had settled in the valley like a swarm of locusts. Their camels were like grains of sand on the seashore—too many to count! [13]Gideon crept up just as a man was telling his companion about a dream. The man said, "I had this dream, and in my dream a loaf of barley bread came tumbling down into the Midianite camp. It hit a tent, turned it over, and knocked it flat!"

[14]His companion answered, "Your dream can mean only one thing—God has given Gideon son of Joash, the Israelite, victory over Midian and all its allies!"

[15]When Gideon heard the dream and its interpretation, he bowed in worship before the LORD.* Then he returned to the Israelite camp and shouted, "Get up! For the LORD has given you victory over the Midianite hordes!" [16]He divided the 300 men into three groups and gave each man a ram's horn and a clay jar with a torch in it.

[17]Then he said to them, "Keep your eyes on me. When I come to the edge of the camp, do just as I do. [18]As soon as I and those with me blow the rams' horns, blow your horns, too, all around the entire camp, and shout, 'For the LORD and for Gideon!'"

[19]It was just after midnight,* after the changing of

Jgs 7:3 Hebrew *may leave Mount Gilead.* The identity of Mount Gilead is uncertain in this context. It is perhaps used here as another name for Mount Gilboa. **Jgs 7:15** As in Greek version; Hebrew reads *he bowed.* **Jgs 7:19** Hebrew *at the beginning of the second watch.*

the first test could have happened naturally. A thick fleece could retain moisture long after the sun had dried the surrounding ground. "Putting out fleeces" is a poor decision-making method. Those who do this put limitations on God. They ask him to fit their expectations. The results of such experiments are usually inconclusive and thus fail to make us any more confident about our choices. Don't let a "fleece" become a substitute for God's wisdom that comes through Bible study and prayer.

Judg 7:2 Self-sufficiency is a handicap when it causes us to believe we can do what needs to be done in our own strength. To prevent this attitude among Gideon's soldiers, God reduced their number from 32,000 to 300. With an army this vastly outnumbered, there could be no doubt that victory was from God. The men could not take the credit. Like Gideon, we must recognize the danger of fighting in our own strength. We can be confident of victory against life's challenges and temptations only if we put our confidence in God and not ourselves.

Judg 7:10-11 Facing overwhelming odds, Gideon was afraid. God understood his fear, but he didn't excuse Gideon from his task. Instead, he allowed Gideon to slip into the enemy camp and overhear a conversation that would give him courage (Judg 7:12-15). Are you facing a battle with internal or external foes that have defeated you in the past or appear invincible today? God can give you the strength you need for any situation. And don't be startled by the way he helps you. Like Gideon, you must listen to God and be ready to take the first step. Only after you begin to obey God will you find the courage to move ahead.

Judg 7:12 Midianites were camel-riding marauders composed of the descendants of five families linked to Abraham through Midian, the son of Abraham's second wife, Keturah. They inhabited the desert regions from the Dead Sea to the Red Sea.

Judg 7:13 An enemy soldier dreamed of a loaf of barley bread tumbling into camp. Barley grain had only half the value of wheat, and the bread made from it was considered inferior. In the same way, Israel's tiny band of men was considered inferior to the vast forces of Midian and Amalek. But God would make the underdog Israelites seem invincible.

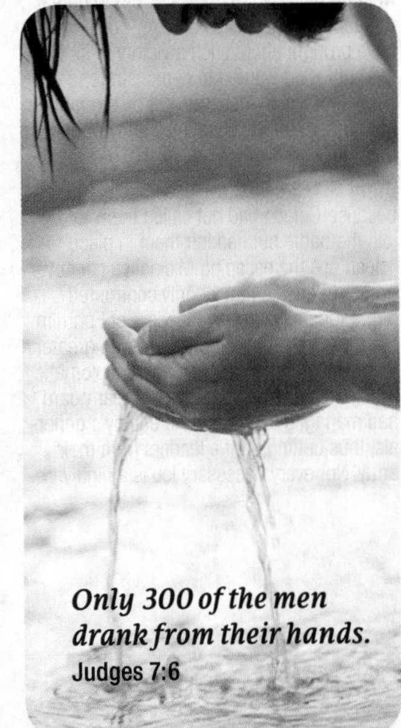
Only 300 of the men drank from their hands.
Judges 7:6

▸ **JUDGES 7:1-25 *(cont.)***

the guard, when Gideon and the 100 men with him
reached the edge of the Midianite camp. Suddenly,
they blew the rams' horns and broke their clay jars.
20 Then all three groups blew their horns and broke
their jars. They held the blazing torches in their left
hands and the horns in their right hands, and they
all shouted, "A sword for the LORD and for Gideon!"
21 Each man stood at his position around the camp
and watched as all the Midianites rushed around
in a panic, shouting as they ran to escape. 22 When
the 300 Israelites blew their rams' horns, the LORD
caused the warriors in the camp to fight against each
other with their swords. Those who were not killed
fled to places as far away as Beth-shittah near Zererah and to the border of Abel-meholah near Tabbath.
23 Then Gideon sent for the warriors of Naphtali,
Asher, and Manasseh, who joined in chasing the army
of Midian. 24 Gideon also sent messengers throughout
the hill country of Ephraim, saying, "Come down to
attack the Midianites. Cut them off at the shallow
crossings of the Jordan River at Beth-barah."
So all the men of Ephraim did as they were told.
25 They captured Oreb and Zeeb, the two Midianite
commanders, killing Oreb at the rock of Oreb, and
Zeeb at the winepress of Zeeb. And they continued to
chase the Midianites. Afterward the Israelites brought
the heads of Oreb and Zeeb to Gideon, who was by
the Jordan River.

Gideon Kills Zebah and Zalmunna

JUDGES 8:1-21

Then the people of Ephraim asked Gideon, "Why have
you treated us this way? Why didn't you send for us
when you first went out to fight the Midianites?" And
they argued heatedly with Gideon.
2 But Gideon replied, "What have I accomplished
compared to you? Aren't even the leftover grapes of
Ephraim's harvest better than the entire crop of my
little clan of Abiezer? 3 God gave you victory over Oreb
and Zeeb, the commanders of the Midianite army.
What have I accomplished compared to that?" When
the men of Ephraim heard Gideon's answer, their anger subsided.
4 Gideon then crossed the Jordan River with his
300 men, and though exhausted, they continued to
chase the enemy. 5 When they reached Succoth, Gideon asked the leaders of the town, "Please give my
warriors some food. They are very tired. I am chasing
Zebah and Zalmunna, the kings of Midian."
6 But the officials of Succoth replied, "Catch Zebah
and Zalmunna first, and then we will feed your army."
7 So Gideon said, "After the LORD gives me victory
over Zebah and Zalmunna, I will return and tear your
flesh with the thorns and briers from the wilderness."
8 From there Gideon went up to Peniel* and again
asked for food, but he got the same answer. 9 So he
said to the people of Peniel, "After I return in victory,
I will tear down this tower."

Jgs 8:8 Hebrew *Penuel,* a variant spelling of Peniel; also in 8:9, 17.

Judg 7:21 Gideon's warriors simply watched as the army of Midian fell into panic, confusion, and disorderly retreat. Not one man had to draw a sword to defeat the enemy. Gideon's small army could never have brought about such a victory in its own strength. God wanted to demonstrate to Israel that victory depends not on strength or numbers but on obedience and commitment to him.

Judg 8:1-3 Ephraim's leaders felt left out because Gideon had not called them to join the battle but had left them in place to "clean up" the escaping Midianites ("leftover grapes"), and so they angrily confronted him. Gideon assured the leaders of Ephraim that their accomplishment was even greater than his own clan's (Abiezer). His diplomatic explanation pointed out that this rear guard had managed to capture the enemy's generals, thus cutting off the leaders from their army. Not every necessary job is a highly visible leadership role. Much of the necessary labor of any effective enterprise is considered by many to be dirty work. But such work is vital to getting any big task done. Engineers and millionaires may design and finance an elegant building, but it is the bricklayers who get the work done. Pride causes us to want recognition. Are you content to be God's bricklayer, or do you resent the work God has given you?

Judg 8:5-9 The leaders of Succoth and Peniel refused to help Gideon, probably fearing Midian's revenge should he fail (Gideon's army was 300 men chasing 15,000). They should have realized that victory was certain because God was with Gideon. But they were so worried about saving themselves that they never thought about God's power to save.

Because of fear for ourselves, we may not recognize God's presence in other people and therefore miss God's victory. Then we must face the often bitter consequences of failing to join forces with those God has chosen to do his work. Because God will prevail with or without you, be quick to join others who are engaged in his work. Lend support with your time, money, talents, and prayers.

Judg 8:11 The Midianites, tent-dwelling nomads, were trying to escape back into the desert where they lived. They didn't expect Gideon to follow them that far.

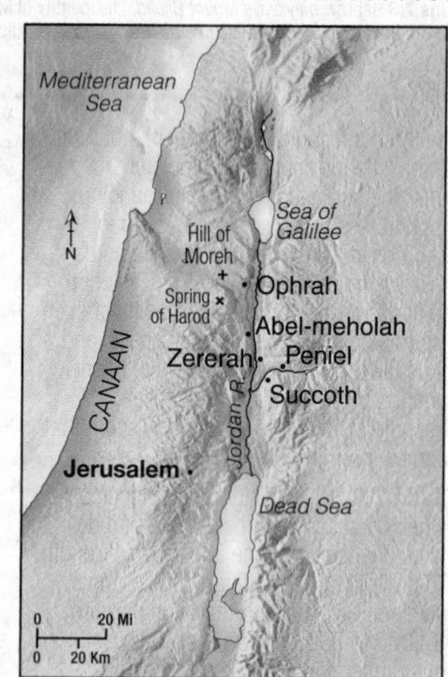

GIDEON'S BATTLE *In spite of Deborah and Barak's victory, the Canaanites still caused trouble in this fertile region. God appeared to Gideon at Ophrah and called him to defeat them. With only 300 fighting men, Gideon routed thousands of Midianites, chasing them to Zererah and Abel-meholah.*

10 By this time Zebah and Zalmunna were in Karkor
with 15,000 warriors—all that remained of the allied armies of the east, for 120,000 had already been
killed. 11 Gideon circled around by the caravan route
east of Nobah and Jogbehah, taking the Midianite
army by surprise. 12 Zebah and Zalmunna, the two
Midianite kings, fled, but Gideon chased them down
and captured all their warriors.
13 After this, Gideon returned from the battle by way
of Heres Pass. 14 There he captured a young man from
Succoth and demanded that he write down the names
of all the seventy-seven officials and elders in the town.
15 Gideon then returned to Succoth and said to the leaders, "Here are Zebah and Zalmunna. When we were
here before, you taunted me, saying, 'Catch Zebah and
Zalmunna first, and then we will feed your exhausted
army.'" 16 Then Gideon took the elders of the town and
taught them a lesson, punishing them with thorns and
briers from the wilderness. 17 He also tore down the
tower of Peniel and killed all the men in the town.
18 Then Gideon asked Zebah and Zalmunna, "The
men you killed at Tabor—what were they like?"
"Like you," they replied. "They all had the look of
a king's son."
19 "They were my brothers, the sons of my own
mother!" Gideon exclaimed. "As surely as the LORD
lives, I wouldn't kill you if you hadn't killed them."
20 Turning to Jether, his oldest son, he said, "Kill
them!" But Jether did not draw his sword, for he was
only a boy and was afraid.

GIDEON

Gideon had a limited vision, but he was committed to it. His challenge was to obtain food for his family even though hostile invaders were making the growing, gathering, and preparation of the food almost impossible. Gideon was resourceful; his winepress doubled as a sunken threshing floor. It lacked ventilation to blow the chaff away, but at least it was hidden from the Midianites. Gideon was working there when God sent him a messenger with a challenge. • Gideon was surprised by what God told him to do. He did not want to jump into a task for which he was ill prepared. The angel had to overcome three objections before Gideon was convinced: (1) Gideon's feelings of responsibility for his family's welfare, (2) his doubts about the call itself, and (3) his feelings of inadequacy for the job. Once Gideon was convinced, he obeyed with zest, resourcefulness, and speed. He dedicated those personality traits to God, with whom he was now personally acquainted. • Gideon had his weak moments and failures, but he was still God's servant. If you can easily relate to Gideon's weakness, can you also see yourself being willing to serve? Remember Gideon as a man who obeyed God by giving his attention to the task at hand. Then give your full attention to believing that God will prepare you for tomorrow when it comes.

Strengths and accomplishments	• Israel's fifth judge. • A member of the Hall of Faith in Hebrews 11 • Defeated the Midianite army • Was offered a hereditary kingship by the men of Israel • Though slow to be convinced, acted on his convictions
Weaknesses and mistakes	• Feared that his own limitations would prevent God from working through him • Collected Midianite gold and made a symbol that became an evil object of worship • Through a concubine, fathered a son who would bring great grief and tragedy to both Gideon's family and the nation of Israel • Failed to establish the nation in God's ways; after he died, they all went back to idol worship
Lessons from his life	• God calls in the middle of our present obedience. As we are faithful, he gives us more responsibility • God uses us in spite of our limitations and failures • Even those who make great spiritual progress can easily fall into sin if they don't consistently follow God
Vital statistics	• Where: Ophrah, valley of Jezreel, spring of Harod • Occupations: Farmer, warrior, judge • Relatives: Father: Joash. Son: Abimelech. • Contemporaries: Zebah, Zalmunna
Key verses	"'But Lord,' Gideon replied, 'how can I rescue Israel? My clan is the weakest in the whole tribe of Manasseh, and I am the least in my entire family!' The LORD said to him, 'I will be with you. And you will destroy the Midianites as if you were fighting against one man'" (Judg 6:15-16).

Gideon's story is told in Judges 6–8. He is also mentioned in Hebrews 11:32.

Judg 8:15-17 Gideon carried out the threats he had made in Judges 8:7, 9. It is difficult to determine whether this act of revenge was justified or whether he should have left the punishment up to God. Gideon was God's appointed leader, but the officials of Succoth and Peniel refused to help him in any way because they feared the enemy. They showed neither faith nor respect for God or the man God had chosen to save them. We should help others because it is right, regardless of whether we will benefit personally.

Judg 8:20-21 For a king to be killed by a boy was humiliating because it would look as though he was no match for a boy. The two men wanted to avoid that disgrace as well as the slower and more painful death that an inexperienced swordsman might inflict.

▸ **JUDGES 8:1-21 *(cont.)***

21 Then Zebah and Zalmunna said to Gideon, "Be a man! Kill us yourself!" So Gideon killed them both and took the royal ornaments from the necks of their camels.

Gideon's Sacred Ephod

JUDGES 8:22-35

Then the Israelites said to Gideon, "Be our ruler! You and your son and your grandson will be our rulers, for you have rescued us from Midian."

23 But Gideon replied, "I will not rule over you, nor will my son. The LORD will rule over you! 24 However, I do have one request—that each of you give me an earring from the plunder you collected from your fallen enemies." (The enemies, being Ishmaelites, all wore gold earrings.)

25 "Gladly!" they replied. They spread out a cloak, and each one threw in a gold earring he had gathered from the plunder. 26 The weight of the gold earrings was forty-three pounds,* not including the royal ornaments and pendants, the purple clothing worn by the kings of Midian, or the chains around the necks of their camels.

27 Gideon made a sacred ephod from the gold and put it in Ophrah, his hometown. But soon all the Israelites prostituted themselves by worshiping it, and it became a trap for Gideon and his family.

28 That is the story of how the people of Israel defeated Midian, which never recovered. Throughout the rest of Gideon's lifetime—about forty years—there was peace in the land.

29 Then Gideon* son of Joash returned home. 30 He had seventy sons born to him, for he had many wives. 31 He also had a concubine in Shechem, who gave birth to a son, whom he named Abimelech. 32 Gideon died when he was very old, and he was buried in the grave of his father, Joash, at Ophrah in the land of the clan of Abiezer.

33 As soon as Gideon died, the Israelites prostituted themselves by worshiping the images of Baal, making Baal-berith their god. 34 They forgot the LORD their God, who had rescued them from all their enemies surrounding them. 35 Nor did they show any loyalty to the family of Jerub-baal (that is, Gideon), despite all the good he had done for Israel.

Abimelech Rules over Shechem

JUDGES 9:1-6

One day Gideon's* son Abimelech went to Shechem to visit his uncles—his mother's brothers. He said to them and to the rest of his mother's family, 2 "Ask the leading citizens of Shechem whether they want to be ruled by all seventy of Gideon's sons or by one man. And remember that I am your own flesh and blood!"

3 So Abimelech's uncles gave his message to all the citizens of Shechem on his behalf. And after listening to this proposal, the people of Shechem decided in favor of Abimelech because he was their relative. 4 They gave him seventy silver coins from the temple of Baal-berith, which he used to hire some reckless troublemakers who agreed to follow him. 5 He went to his father's home at Ophrah, and there, on one stone, they killed all seventy of his half brothers, the sons of Gideon.* But the youngest brother, Jotham, escaped and hid.

6 Then all the leading citizens of Shechem and Beth-

Jgs 8:26 Hebrew *1,700 shekels* [19.4 kilograms]. **Jgs 8:29** Hebrew *Jerub-baal;* see 6:32. **Jgs 9:1** Hebrew *Jerub-baal's* (see 6:32); also in 9:2, 24. **Jgs 9:5** Hebrew *Jerub-baal* (see 6:32); also in 9:16, 19, 28, 57.

Judg 8:23 The people wanted to make Gideon their king, but Gideon stressed that the Lord was to rule over them. Despite his inconsistencies, Gideon recognized the importance of putting God first, for both a nation and an individual. Is God first in your life? If he is, he must affect every dimension of your life, not just what you do in church.

Judg 8:26-27 Those who were very wealthy put ornaments on their camels as a way of displaying their riches. Women wore vast amounts of jewelry as well, often up to 15 pairs of earrings. Jewelry was also worn for good luck. After Gideon's rise to power, he seems to have become carried away with this accumulation of wealth. Eventually it led the Israelites to idolatry.

Judg 8:27 An ephod was a linen garment worn by priests over their chests. It was considered holy (Exod 28:6-35; 39:2-24; Lev 8:7-8). Gideon probably had good motives for making the ephod (a visible remembrance commemorating the victory). Unfortunately, the people began to worship the ephod as an idol. Sadly, many decisions that stem from good motives produce negative results. Perhaps no one stops to ask, "What might go wrong?" or "Is there a possibility of negative consequences?" In your plans and decisions, take time to anticipate how a good idea might lead to potential problems and take steps to avoid them.

Judg 8:31 This relationship between Gideon and a concubine produced a son who tore apart Gideon's family and caused tragedy for the nation. Gideon's story illustrates the fact that heroes in battle are not always heroes in daily life. Gideon led the nation but could not lead his family. No matter who you are, moral laxness will cause problems. Just because you have won a single battle with temptation does not mean you will automatically win the next one. We need to be constantly watchful against temptation. Sometimes Satan's strongest attacks come after a victory.

Judg 8:33 Baal-berith means "Baal (lord) of the covenant." Worship of the idol may have combined elements of both the Israelite and Canaanite religions.

Judg 9:1-3 With Gideon dead, Abimelech wanted to take his father's place. To set his plan in motion he went to the city of Shechem, his mother's hometown, to drum up support. There he felt kinship with the residents. These relatives were Canaanites and would be glad to unite against Israel. Shechem was an important city, a crossroads for trade routes and a natural link between the coastal plain and the Jordan Valley. Whoever controlled Shechem would dominate the countryside.

Judg 9:2-5 Israel's king was to be the Lord and not a man. But Abimelech wanted to usurp the position reserved for God alone. In his selfish quest, he killed all but one of his 70 half brothers. people with selfish desires often seek to fulfill them in ruthless ways. Examine your ambitions to see if they are self-centered or God-centered. Be sure you always fulfill your desires in ways that God would approve.

Judg 9:4 Politics played a major part in pagan religions such as the worship of Baal-berith. Governments often went so far as to hire temple prostitutes to bring in additional money. In many cases a religious system was set up and supported by the government so the offerings could fund community projects. Religion became a profit-making business. In Israel's religion, this was strictly forbidden. God's system of religion was designed to

millo called a meeting under the oak beside the pillar* at Shechem and made Abimelech their king.

Jotham's Parable

JUDGES 9:7-21

When Jotham heard about this, he climbed to the top of Mount Gerizim and shouted,

"Listen to me, citizens of Shechem!
Listen to me if you want God to listen to you!
8 Once upon a time the trees decided to choose
a king.
First they said to the olive tree,
'Be our king!'
9 But the olive tree refused, saying,
'Should I quit producing the olive oil
that blesses both God and people,
just to wave back and forth over the trees?'
10 "Then they said to the fig tree,
'You be our king!'
11 But the fig tree also refused, saying,
'Should I quit producing my sweet fruit
just to wave back and forth over the trees?'
12 "Then they said to the grapevine,
'You be our king!'
13 But the grapevine also refused, saying,
'Should I quit producing the wine
that cheers both God and people,
just to wave back and forth over the trees?'
14 "Then all the trees finally turned to the
thornbush and said,
'Come, you be our king!'
15 And the thornbush replied to the trees,
'If you truly want to make me your king,
come and take shelter in my shade.
If not, let fire come out from me
and devour the cedars of Lebanon.'"

16 Jotham continued, "Now make sure you have
acted honorably and in good faith by making

Jgs 9:6 The meaning of the Hebrew is uncertain.

ABIMELECH

People who desire power always outnumber those who are able to use power wisely. Perhaps this is because power has a way of taking over and controlling the person using it. This is especially true in cases of inherited but unmerited power. Abimelech's life shows us what happens when hunger for power corrupts judgment. • Abimelech's position in Gideon's family as the son of a concubine must have created great tension between him and Gideon's many other sons. One against 70: Such odds can either crush a person or make him ruthless. It is obvious which direction Abimelech chose. Gideon's position as warrior and judge had placed Abimelech in an environment of power; Gideon's death provided an opportunity for this son to seize power. Once the process began, the disastrous results were inevitable. A person's thirst for power is not satisfied when he gets power—it only becomes more intense. Abimelech's life was consumed by that thirst. Eventually, he could not tolerate any threat to his power. • By this time Abimelech no longer had power—power had him. One lesson we can learn from his life is that our goals control our actions. The amount of control is related to the importance of the goal. Abimelech's most important goal was to have power. His lust for power led him to wipe out not only his brothers but also whole cities that refused to submit to him. Nothing but death could stop his bloodthirsty drive to conquer. How ironic that he was fatally injured by a woman with a farm implement! The contrast between Abimelech and the godly people of the Bible is great. He wanted to control the nation; they were willing to be controlled by God.

Strengths and accomplishments	• The first self-declared king in Israel • Qualified tactical planner and organizer
Weaknesses and mistakes	• Power hungry and ruthless • Overconfident • Had 69 of his 70 half brothers killed
Vital statistics	• Where: Shechem, Arumah, Thebez • Occupations: Self-acclaimed king, judge, political troublemaker • Relatives: Father: Gideon. Only surviving half brother: Jotham.
Key verses	"In this way, God punished Abimelech for the evil he had done against his father by murdering his seventy brothers. God also punished the men of Shechem for all their evil. So the curse of Jotham son of Gideon was fulfilled" (Judg 9:56-57).

Abimelech's story is told in Judges 8:31–9:57.

---

come from an attitude of the heart, not from calculated plans and business opportunities. It was also designed to serve people and help those in need, not to oppress them. Is your faith genuine and sincere, or is it based on convenience, comfort, and availability?

Judg 9:6 Abimelech was declared ruler of Israel at Shechem, the site of other key Bible events. It was one of Abraham's first stops upon arriving in Canaan (Gen 12:6-7). When Jacob lived there, two of his sons killed all the men in Shechem because the prince's son had raped their sister (Gen 34). Joseph's bones were buried in Shechem (Josh 24:32); Israel renewed its covenant with God there (Josh 24); and the kingdom of Israel would split apart at this same city (1 Kgs 12).

Judg 9:7-15 In Jotham's parable the trees represented Gideon's 70 sons, and the thornbush represented Abimelech. Jotham's point was this: A productive person would be too busy doing good to want to bother with power politics. A worthless person, on the other hand, would be glad to accept the honor—but he would destroy the people he ruled. Abimelech, like a thornbush, could offer Israel no real protection or security. Jotham's parable came true when Abimelech destroyed the city of Shechem (Judg 9:45), burned "the tower of Shechem" (Judg 9:46-49; also known as the city of Beth-millo [Judg 9:20]), and was finally killed at Thebez (Judg 9:53-54).

Judg 9:16 Jotham told the story about the trees in order to help the people set good priorities. He did not want them to appoint a leader of low character. As we serve in leadership positions, we should examine our motives. Do we just want praise, prestige, or power? In the parable, the good trees chose to be productive and to provide benefits to people. Make sure these are your priorities as you aspire to leadership.

▸ **JUDGES 9:7-21** ***(cont.)***

Abimelech your king, and that you have done right by Gideon and all of his descendants. Have you treated him with the honor he deserves for all he accomplished? 17For he fought for you and risked his life when he rescued you from the Midianites. 18But today you have revolted against my father and his descendants, killing his seventy sons on one stone. And you have chosen his slave woman's son, Abimelech, to be your king just because he is your relative.

19"If you have acted honorably and in good faith toward Gideon and his descendants today, then may you find joy in Abimelech, and may he find joy in you. 20But if you have not acted in good faith, then may fire come out from Abimelech and devour the leading citizens of Shechem and Beth-millo; and may fire come out from the citizens of Shechem and Beth-millo and devour Abimelech!"

21Then Jotham escaped and lived in Beer because he was afraid of his brother Abimelech.

Shechem Rebels against Abimelech

JUDGES 9:22-57

After Abimelech had ruled over Israel for three years, 23God sent a spirit that stirred up trouble between Abimelech and the leading citizens of Shechem, and they revolted. 24God was punishing Abimelech for murdering Gideon's seventy sons, and the citizens of Shechem for supporting him in this treachery of murdering his brothers. 25The citizens of Shechem set an ambush for Abimelech on the hilltops and robbed everyone who passed that way. But someone warned Abimelech about their plot.

26One day Gaal son of Ebed moved to Shechem with his brothers and gained the confidence of the leading citizens of Shechem. 27During the annual harvest festival at Shechem, held in the temple of the local god, the wine flowed freely, and everyone began cursing Abimelech. 28"Who is Abimelech?" Gaal shouted. "He's not a true son of Shechem,* so why should we be his servants? He's merely the son of Gideon, and this Zebul is merely his deputy. Serve the true sons of Hamor, the founder of Shechem. Why should we serve Abimelech? 29If I were in charge here, I would get rid of Abimelech. I would say* to him, 'Get some soldiers, and come out and fight!'"

30But when Zebul, the leader of the city, heard what Gaal was saying, he was furious. 31He sent messengers to Abimelech in Arumah,* telling him, "Gaal son of Ebed and his brothers have come to live in Shechem, and now they are inciting the city to rebel against you. 32Come by night with an army and hide out in the fields. 33In the morning, as soon as it is daylight, attack the city. When Gaal and those who are with him come out against you, you can do with them as you wish."

34So Abimelech and all his men went by night and split into four groups, stationing themselves around Shechem. 35Gaal was standing at the city gates when Abimelech and his army came out of hiding. 36When Gaal saw them, he said to Zebul, "Look, there are people coming down from the hilltops!"

Zebul replied, "It's just the shadows on the hills that look like men."

37But again Gaal said, "No, people are coming down from the hills.* And another group is coming down the road past the Diviners' Oak.*"

38Then Zebul turned on him and asked, "Now where is that big mouth of yours? Wasn't it you that said, 'Who is Abimelech, and why should we be his

Jgs 9:28 Hebrew *Who is Shechem?* **Jgs 9:29** As in Greek version; Hebrew reads *And he said.* **Jgs 9:31** Or *in secret;* Hebrew reads *in Tormah;* compare 9:41. **Jgs 9:37a** Or *the center of the land.* **Jgs 9:37b** Hebrew *Elon-meonenim.*

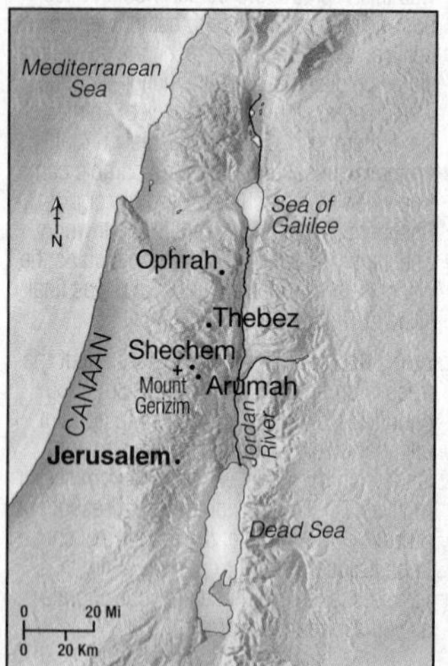

Judg 9:22-24 Abimelech was the opposite of what God wanted in a judge, but it was three years before God moved against him, fulfilling Jotham's parable. Those three years must have seemed like forever to Jotham. Why wasn't Abimelech punished sooner for his evil ways?

◀ ***ABIMELECH'S FALL***
Gideon's illegitimate son killed 69 of his 70 half brothers in Ophrah and returned to Shechem to be proclaimed king. But three years later, Shechem rebelled. From Arumah, Abimelech attacked Shechem, Beth-millo ("the tower at Shechem"), and Thebez, where he was killed.

We are not alone when we wonder why evil seems to prevail (Job 10:3; 21:1-18; Jer 12:1; Hab 1:2-4, 12-17). God promises to deal with sin—but in his time, not ours. Actually it is good news that God doesn't punish us immediately because we all have sinned and deserve God's punishment. God, in his mercy, often spares us from immediate punishment and allows us time to turn from our sins and turn to him in repentance. Trusting God for justice means (1) we must first recognize our own sins and repent, and (2) we may face a difficult time of waiting for the wicked to be punished. But in God's time, all evil will be destroyed.

Judg 9:23 This "trouble" stirred up was not just an attitude of strife—it was a demon. It was not Satan himself, but one of the fallen angels under Satan's influence. God used this evil spirit to bring about judgment on Shechem. God judged King Saul in a similar way (1 Sam 16:14).

servants?' The men you mocked are right outside the
city! Go out and fight them!"
39 So Gaal led the leading citizens of Shechem into
battle against Abimelech. 40 But Abimelech chased
him, and many of Shechem's men were wounded and
fell along the road as they retreated to the city gate.
41 Abimelech returned to Arumah, and Zebul drove
Gaal and his brothers out of Shechem.
42 The next day the people of Shechem went out
into the fields to battle. When Abimelech heard about
it, 43 he divided his men into three groups and set
an ambush in the fields. When Abimelech saw the
people coming out of the city, he and his men jumped
up from their hiding places and attacked them.
44 Abimelech and his group stormed the city gate to
keep the men of Shechem from getting back in, while
Abimelech's other two groups cut them down in the
fields. 45 The battle went on all day before Abimelech
finally captured the city. He killed the people, leveled
the city, and scattered salt all over the ground.
46 When the leading citizens who lived in the tower
of Shechem heard what had happened, they ran and
hid in the temple of Baal-berith.* 47 Someone reported to Abimelech that the citizens had gathered
in the temple, 48 so he led his forces to Mount Zalmon.
He took an ax and chopped some branches from a
tree, then put them on his shoulder. "Quick, do as I
have done!" he told his men. 49 So each of them cut
down some branches, following Abimelech's example. They piled the branches against the walls of the
temple and set them on fire. So all the people who
had lived in the tower of Shechem died—about 1,000
men and women.
50 Then Abimelech attacked the town of Thebez
and captured it. 51 But there was a strong tower inside
the town, and all the men and women—the entire
population—fled to it. They barricaded themselves in
and climbed up to the roof of the tower. 52 Abimelech
followed them to attack the tower. But as he prepared
to set fire to the entrance, 53 a woman on the roof
dropped a millstone that landed on Abimelech's head
and crushed his skull.
54 He quickly said to his young armor bearer, "Draw
your sword and kill me! Don't let it be said that a
woman killed Abimelech!" So the young man ran him
through with his sword, and he died. 55 When Abimelech's men saw that he was dead, they disbanded and
returned to their homes.
56 In this way, God punished Abimelech for the
evil he had done against his father by murdering his
seventy brothers. 57 God also punished the men of
Shechem for all their evil. So the curse of Jotham son
of Gideon was fulfilled.

Tola Becomes Israel's Judge

JUDGES 10:1-2

After Abimelech died, Tola son of Puah, son of Dodo,
was the next person to rescue Israel. He was from
the tribe of Issachar but lived in the town of Shamir
in the hill country of Ephraim. 2 He judged Israel for
twenty-three years. When he died, he was buried
in Shamir.

Silk fabrics manufactured in China

Jair Becomes Israel's Judge

JUDGES 10:3-5

After Tola died, Jair from Gilead judged Israel for
twenty-two years. 4 His thirty sons rode around on
thirty donkeys, and they owned thirty towns in the
land of Gilead, which are still called the Towns of Jair.*
5 When Jair died, he was buried in Kamon.

Jgs 9:46 Hebrew *El-berith,* another name for Baal-berith; compare 9:4. **Jgs 10:4** Hebrew *Havvoth-jair.*

Judg 9:45 To scatter salt over a conquered city was a ritual to symbolize the perpetual desolation of the city. It would not be rebuilt for 150 years.

Judg 9:53 In times of battle, women were sometimes asked to join the men at the city wall to drop heavy objects on the soldiers below. A millstone would have been an ideal object for this purpose. It was a heavy, round stone about 18 inches in diameter with a hole in the center. Millstones were used to grind grain into flour. The grain was placed between two millstones. The top millstone was turned, crushing the grain.

Abimelech's death was especially humiliating: He was killed by a woman, not by fighting; and he was killed by a farm implement instead of a weapon. Abimelech, therefore, asked his armor bearer to stab him with his sword before he died from the blow of the millstone.

Judg 9:56-57 Gideon, Abimelech's father, succeeded in military battles but sometimes failed in his personal struggles. Gideon was not condemned for taking a concubine (Judg 8:31), but the family problems that resulted from this relationship are clearly stated.

In the end, Abimelech killed 69 of his 70 half brothers, tore apart a nation, and then was killed himself. From Gideon's life we learn that no matter how much good we do for God's Kingdom, sin in our lives will still produce powerful, damaging consequences.

Judg 9:56-57 Jotham's curse is found in Judges 9:16-20.

Judg 10:1-5 In five verses we read about two men who judged Israel for a total of 45 years, yet all we know about them besides the length of their rules is that one had 30 sons who rode around on 30 donkeys. God often uses otherwise unknown people to do great things for him. Are you willing to serve God even in obscurity?

5. FIFTH PERIOD: JEPHTHAH, IBZAN, ELON, AND ABDON

The fifth cycle of disobedience led to a period of oppression by the Philistines and the Ammonites. God used Jephthah to rescue Israel from Ammonite oppression, but again they were plagued by internal strife and civil war.

The Ammonites Oppress Israel

JUDGES 10:6-18

Again the Israelites did evil in the LORD's sight. They served the images of Baal and Ashtoreth, and the gods of Aram, Sidon, Moab, Ammon, and Philistia. They abandoned the LORD and no longer served him at all. 7 So the LORD burned with anger against Israel, and he turned them over to the Philistines and the Ammonites, 8 who began to oppress them that year. For eighteen years they oppressed all the Israelites east of the Jordan River in the land of the Amorites (that is, in Gilead). 9 The Ammonites also crossed to the west side of the Jordan and attacked Judah, Benjamin, and Ephraim.

The Israelites were in great distress. 10 Finally, they cried out to the LORD for help, saying, "We have sinned against you because we have abandoned you as our God and have served the images of Baal."

11 The LORD replied, "Did I not rescue you from the Egyptians, the Amorites, the Ammonites, the Philistines, 12 the Sidonians, the Amalekites, and the Maonites? When they oppressed you, you cried out to me for help, and I rescued you. 13 Yet you have abandoned me and served other gods. So I will not rescue you anymore. 14 Go and cry out to the gods you have chosen! Let them rescue you in your hour of distress!"

15 But the Israelites pleaded with the LORD and said, "We have sinned. Punish us as you see fit, only rescue us today from our enemies." 16 Then the Israelites put aside their foreign gods and served the LORD. And he was grieved by their misery.

17 At that time the armies of Ammon had gathered for war and were camped in Gilead, and the people of Israel assembled and camped at Mizpah. 18 The leaders of Gilead said to each other, "Whoever attacks the Ammonites first will become ruler over all the people of Gilead."

Jephthah Becomes Israel's Judge

JUDGES 11:1-28

Now Jephthah of Gilead was a great warrior. He was the son of Gilead, but his mother was a prostitute. 2 Gilead's wife also had several sons, and when these half brothers grew up, they chased Jephthah off the land. "You will not get any of our father's inheritance," they said, "for you are the son of a prostitute." 3 So Jephthah fled from his brothers and lived in the land of Tob. Soon he had a band of worthless rebels following him.

4 At about this time, the Ammonites began their war against Israel. 5 When the Ammonites attacked, the elders of Gilead sent for Jephthah in the land of Tob. The elders said, 6 "Come and be our commander! Help us fight the Ammonites!"

7 But Jephthah said to them, "Aren't you the ones who hated me and drove me from my father's house? Why do you come to me now when you're in trouble?"

8 "Because we need you," the elders replied. "If you

Judg 10:6 The gods of Aram and Sidon were very similar to Baal and Ashtoreth (explained in the notes on Judg 2:11-15, p. 374, and Judg 3:7, p. 377). The gods of Moab and Ammon were Chemosh and Molech. The Philistine gods were Dagon, Ashtoreth, Asherah, and Baal-zebul.

Judg 10:9-10 Once again the Israelites suffered for many years before they gave up their sinful ways and called out to God for help (see Judg 4:1-3; 6:1-6). Notice that when they were at the end of their rope they finally looked to the only one who was really able to help, not to their pagan gods.

Is God your last resort? So much unnecessary suffering takes place because we don't call on God until we've used up all other resources. Rather than waiting until the situation becomes desperate, turn to God first. He has the necessary resources to meet every kind of problem.

Judg 10:11-16 These verses show how difficult it can be to follow God over the long haul. The Israelites always seemed to forget God when all was well. But despite being rejected by his own people, God never failed to rescue them when they called out to him in repentance. God never fails to rescue us, either. We act just like the Israelites when we put God outside our daily events instead of at the center of them. Just as a loving parent feels rejected when a child rebels, so God feels great rejection when we ignore or neglect him (1 Sam 8:4-9; 10:17-19; John 12:44-50). We should strive to stay close to God rather than see how far we can go before judgment comes.

Judg 10:17-18 The power of the Ammonite nation was at its peak during the period of the judges. The people were descendants of Ammon, conceived when Lot's daughter slept with her drunk father (Gen 19:30-38). The land of Ammon was located just east of the Jordan River across from Jerusalem. South of Ammon lay the land of Moab, the nation conceived when Lot's other daughter slept with her father. Moab and Ammon were usually allies. It was a formidable task to defeat these nations.

Judg 11:1-2 Jephthah, an illegitimate son of Gilead, was chased out of the country by his half brothers. He suffered as a result of another's decision and not for any wrong he had done. Yet in spite of his brothers' rejection, God used him. If you are suffering from unfair rejection, don't blame others and become discouraged. Remember how God used Jephthah despite his unjust circumstances, and realize that he is able to use you even if you feel rejected by some.

Judg 11:3 Circumstances beyond his control forced Jephthah away from his people and into life as an outcast. Today, both believers and nonbelievers may drive away those who do not fit the norms dictated by our society, neighborhoods, or churches. Often, as in Jephthah's case, great potential is wasted because of prejudice—a refusal to look beyond ill-conceived stereotypes. Look around you to see if there are potential Jephthahs being kept out due to factors beyond their control. As a Christian, you know that everyone can have a place in God's family. Can you do anything to help these people gain acceptance for their character and abilities?

lead us in battle against the Ammonites, we will make you ruler over all the people of Gilead."

9 Jephthah said to the elders, "Let me get this straight. If I come with you and if the LORD gives me victory over the Ammonites, will you really make me ruler over all the people?"

10 "The LORD is our witness," the elders replied. "We promise to do whatever you say."

11 So Jephthah went with the elders of Gilead, and the people made him their ruler and commander of the army. At Mizpah, in the presence of the LORD, Jephthah repeated what he had said to the elders.

12 Then Jephthah sent messengers to the king of Ammon, asking, "Why have you come out to fight against my land?"

13 The king of Ammon answered Jephthah's messengers, "When the Israelites came out of Egypt, they stole my land from the Arnon River to the Jabbok River and all the way to the Jordan. Now then, give back the land peaceably."

14 Jephthah sent this message back to the Ammonite king:

15 "This is what Jephthah says: Israel did not
steal any land from Moab or Ammon. 16 When
the people of Israel arrived at Kadesh on their
journey from Egypt after crossing the Red Sea,*
17 they sent messengers to the king of Edom
asking for permission to pass through his land.
But their request was denied. Then they asked
the king of Moab for similar permission, but he
wouldn't let them pass through either. So the
people of Israel stayed in Kadesh.

18 "Finally, they went around Edom and Moab
through the wilderness. They traveled along
Moab's eastern border and camped on the other
side of the Arnon River. But they never once
crossed the Arnon River into Moab, for the Arnon
was the border of Moab.

19 "Then Israel sent messengers to King Sihon

Jgs 11:16 Hebrew *sea of reeds.*

JEPHTHAH

It's hard not to admire people whose word can be depended on completely and whose actions are consistent with their words. For such people, talking is not avoiding action—it is the beginning of action. People like this can make excellent negotiators. They approach a conflict with the full intention of settling issues verbally, but they do not hesitate to use other means if verbal attempts fail. Jephthah was this kind of person. • In most of his conflicts, Jephthah's first move was to talk. In the war with the Ammonites, his strategy was negotiation. He clarified the issues so that everyone knew the cause of the conflict. His opponent's response determined his next action. • The fate of Jephthah's daughter is difficult to understand. We are not sure what Jephthah meant by his vow recorded in Judges 11:31. In any case, his vow was unnecessary. We do not know what actually happened to his daughter—whether she was burned as an offering or set apart as a virgin, thus denying Jephthah any hope of descendants since she was his only child. What we do know is that Jephthah was a person of his word, even when it was a word spoken in haste, and even when keeping his word caused him great pain. • How do you approach conflicts? There is a big difference between trying to settle a conflict through words and simply counterattacking someone verbally. How dependable are the statements you make? Do your children, friends, and fellow workers know you to be a person of your word? The measure of your trustworthiness is your willingness to take responsibility, even if you must pay a painful price because of something you said.

Strengths and accomplishments	• Listed in the Hall of Faith in Hebrews 11 • Controlled by God's Spirit • Brilliant military strategist who negotiated before fighting
Weaknesses and mistakes	• Was bitter over the treatment he received from his half brothers • Made a rash and foolish vow
Lesson from his life	• One's background does not prevent God from working powerfully
Vital statistics	• Where: Gilead • Occupations: Warrior, judge • Relative: Father: Gilead.
Key verse	"So Jephthah led his army against the Ammonites, and the LORD gave him victory" (Judg 11:32).

Jephthah's story is told in Judges 11:1–12:7. He is also mentioned in 1 Samuel 12:11; Hebrews 11:32.

Judg 11:11 What does it mean that Jephthah repeated what he had said, in the presence of the Lord? Those making covenants in ancient times often made them at shrines so that they would be witnessed by deities. Often a written copy was also deposited at the shrine. This was much like a coronation ceremony for Jephthah.

Judg 11:14ff Jephthah sent messengers to the Ammonite king wanting to know why the Israelites in the land of Gilead were being attacked (Judg 11:12). The king replied that Israel had stolen this land and he wanted it back (Judg 11:13).

Jephthah's reply to the king (Judg 11:14-27) contained three arguments against the king's claim: (1) Gilead was never the king's land in the first place because Israel took it from the Amorites, not the Ammonites (Judg 11:16-22); (2) Israel should possess land given by Israel's God, and Ammon should possess land given by Ammon's god; (3) no one had contested Israel's ownership of the land since its conquest 300 years earlier (Judg 11:25-26).

To Jephthah's credit, he tried to solve the problem without bloodshed. But the king of Ammon ignored his message and prepared his troops for battle.

1200 BC

First Chinese dictionary

▸ **JUDGES 11:1-28** ***(cont.)***

of the Amorites, who ruled from Heshbon, asking
for permission to cross through his land to get
to their destination. 20 But King Sihon didn't
trust Israel to pass through his land. Instead, he
mobilized his army at Jahaz and attacked them.
21 But the LORD, the God of Israel, gave his people
victory over King Sihon. So Israel took control
of all the land of the Amorites, who lived in that
region, 22 from the Arnon River to the Jabbok River,
and from the eastern wilderness to the Jordan.

23 "So you see, it was the LORD, the God of Israel,
who took away the land from the Amorites and
gave it to Israel. Why, then, should we give it back
to you? 24 You keep whatever your god Chemosh
gives you, and we will keep whatever the LORD our
God gives us. 25 Are you any better than Balak son
of Zippor, king of Moab? Did he try to make a case
against Israel for disputed land? Did he go to war
against them?

26 "Israel has been living here for 300 years,
inhabiting Heshbon and its surrounding
settlements, all the way to Aroer and its
settlements, and in all the towns along the Arnon
River. Why have you made no effort to recover
it before now? 27 Therefore, I have not sinned
against you. Rather, you have wronged me by
attacking me. Let the LORD, who is judge, decide
today which of us is right—Israel or Ammon."

28 But the king of Ammon paid no attention to Jephthah's message.

Jephthah's Vow

JUDGES 11:29-40

At that time the Spirit of the LORD came upon Jephthah, and he went throughout the land of Gilead and
Manasseh, including Mizpah in Gilead, and from there
he led an army against the Ammonites. 30 And Jephthah
made a vow to the LORD. He said, "If you give me victory
over the Ammonites, 31 I will give to the LORD whatever

Judg 11:27 Over the years, Israel had many judges to lead them. But Jephthah recognized the Lord as the people's true Judge, the only one who could really lead them and help them conquer the invading enemies.

Judg 11:30-31 In God's law, a vow was a promise to God that was not to be broken (Num 30:1-2; Deut 23:21-23). It carried as much force as a written contract. Many people made vows in biblical times. Some, like Jephthah's, were very foolish.

Judg 11:30-31 Before Jephthah made his vow, had he stopped to consider that a person, not a sheep or goat, might come out to meet him? Scholars are divided over the issue. Those who say Jephthah was considering human sacrifice use the following arguments: (1) He was from an area where pagan religion and human sacrifice were common. In his eyes, it may not have seemed like a sin. (2) Jephthah may not have had a background in religious law. Perhaps he was ignorant of God's command against human sacrifice.

Those who say Jephthah could not have been thinking about human sacrifice point to other evidence: (1) As leader of the people, Jephthah must have been familiar with God's laws; human sacrifice was clearly forbidden (Lev 18:21; 20:1-5). (2) No legitimate priest would have helped Jephthah carry out his vow if a person was to be the sacrifice.

Whatever Jephthah had in mind when he made the vow, did he or did he not sacrifice his daughter? Some think he did, because his vow was to make a burnt offering. Some think he did not, and they offer these two reasons: (1) If the girl was to die, she would not have spent her last two months in the hills. (2) God would not have honored a vow based on a wicked practice.

RASH VOWS

Ecclesiastes 5:2 says: "Don't make rash promises, and don't be hasty in bringing matters before God. After all, God is in heaven, and you are here on earth. So let your words be few." Scripture records the vows of many men and women. Some of these vows proved to be rash and unwise, and others, though extreme, were kept to the letter by those who made them. Let us learn from the examples in God's Word not to make rash vows.

Person	*Vow*	*Result*	*Reference*
JACOB	To "choose" the true God and to give back a tenth to him if he kept him safe	God protected Jacob, who kept his vow to follow God	Gen 28:20
JEPHTHAH	To offer to the Lord whatever came out to meet him after battle (turned out to be his daughter)	He lost his daughter	Judg 11:30-31
HANNAH	To give her son back to God if God would give her a son	When Samuel was born, she dedicated him to God	1 Sam 1:9-11
SAUL	To kill anyone who ate before evening (Jonathan, his son, had not heard the command and broke it)	Saul would have killed Jonathan if soldiers had not intervened	1 Sam 14:24-45
DAVID	To be kind to Jonathan's family	David treated Mephibosheth, Jonathan's son, royally	2 Sam 9:7
ITTAI	To remain loyal to David	He became one of the great men in David's army	2 Sam 15:21
MICAIAH	To say only what God told him to say	He was put in prison	1 Kgs 22:14
JOB	That he was not rebelling against God	His fortunes were restored	Job 42:10
HEROD ANTIPAS	To give Herodias's daughter anything she requested	Herod was forced to order John the Baptist's death	Mark 6:22-23
PAUL	To offer a sacrifice of thanksgiving in Jerusalem	He made the sacrifice despite the danger	Acts 18:18

comes out of my house to meet me when I return in
triumph. I will sacrifice it as a burnt offering."
32 So Jephthah led his army against the Ammonites,
and the LORD gave him victory. 33 He crushed the
Ammonites, devastating about twenty towns from
Aroer to an area near Minnith and as far away as Abel-
keramim. In this way Israel defeated the Ammonites.
34 When Jephthah returned home to Mizpah, his
daughter came out to meet him, playing on a tambourine and dancing for joy. She was his one and only
child; he had no other sons or daughters. 35 When he
saw her, he tore his clothes in anguish. "Oh, my daughter!" he cried out. "You have completely destroyed me!
You've brought disaster on me! For I have made a vow
to the LORD, and I cannot take it back."
36 And she said, "Father, if you have made a vow to
the LORD, you must do to me what you have vowed,
for the LORD has given you a great victory over your
enemies, the Ammonites. 37 But first let me do this
one thing: Let me go up and roam in the hills and
weep with my friends for two months, because I will
die a virgin."
38 "You may go," Jephthah said. And he sent her away
for two months. She and her friends went into the
hills and wept because she would never have children.
39 When she returned home, her father kept the vow
he had made, and she died a virgin.
So it has become a custom in Israel 40 for young
Israelite women to go away for four days each year to
lament the fate of Jephthah's daughter.

Ephraim Fights with Jephthah

JUDGES 12:1-7

Then the people of Ephraim mobilized an army and
crossed over the Jordan River to Zaphon. They sent
this message to Jephthah: "Why didn't you call for us
to help you fight against the Ammonites? We are going
to burn down your house with you in it!"
2 Jephthah replied, "I summoned you at the beginning of the dispute, but you refused to come! You
failed to help us in our struggle against Ammon. 3 So
when I realized you weren't coming, I risked my life
and went to battle without you, and the LORD gave me
victory over the Ammonites. So why have you now
come to fight me?"
4 The people of Ephraim responded, "You men of
Gilead are nothing more than fugitives from Ephraim
and Manasseh." So Jephthah gathered all the men of
Gilead and attacked the men of Ephraim and defeated
them.
5 Jephthah captured the shallow crossings of the Jordan River, and whenever a fugitive from Ephraim tried
to go back across, the men of Gilead would challenge
him. "Are you a member of the tribe of Ephraim?"
they would ask. If the man said, "No, I'm not," 6 they
would tell him to say "Shibboleth." If he was from
Ephraim, he would say "Sibboleth," because people
from Ephraim cannot pronounce the word correctly.
Then they would take him and kill him at the shallow
crossings of the Jordan. In all, 42,000 Ephraimites
were killed at that time.
7 Jephthah judged Israel for six years. When he died,
he was buried in one of the towns of Gilead.

1183 BC

Destruction of Troy during Trojan War

Ibzan Becomes Israel's Judge

JUDGES 12:8-10

After Jephthah died, Ibzan from Bethlehem judged
Israel. 9 He had thirty sons and thirty daughters. He
sent his daughters to marry men outside his clan, and
he brought in thirty young women from outside his

Judg 11:34-35 Jephthah's rash vow brought him unspeakable grief. In the heat of emotion or personal turmoil it is easy to make foolish promises to God. These promises may sound very spiritual when we make them, but they may produce only guilt and frustration when we are forced to fulfill them. Making spiritual "deals" only brings disappointment. God does not want promises for the future, but obedience for today.

Judg 12:1ff Israel had just won a great battle, but instead of joy, there was pettiness and quarreling. The tribe of Ephraim was angry and jealous that they had not been invited to join in the fighting (although Jephthah said he had invited them). The insults of the Ephraimites enraged Jephthah, who called out his troops and killed 42,000 men from Ephraim.

Jephthah usually spoke before he acted, but this time his revenge was swift. It cost Israel dearly, and it might have been avoided. Insulting others and being jealous are not right responses when we feel left out. But seeking revenge for an insult is just as wrong and very costly.

Judg 12:4-7 The men of the tribe of Ephraim caused Jephthah trouble just as they had Gideon (Judg 8:1-3). Jephthah captured the shallow crossings of the Jordan, the boundary of Ephraim, and was able to defeat his countrymen as they crossed the river. He used a pronunciation test. *Shibboleth* is the word for "stream." The Ephraimites pronounced "sh" as "s," so Jephthah's army could easily identify them.

Judg 12:8-15 There is little else known about these three judges or their importance. The large number of children and donkeys are an indication of the wealth of these men.

JEPHTHAH'S VICTORY ▶
The Ephraimites mobilized an army because they were angry at not being included in the battle against Ammon. They planned to attack Jephthah at his home in Gilead. Jephthah captured the shallows of the Jordan at the Jabbok River and killed the Ephraimites who tried to cross.

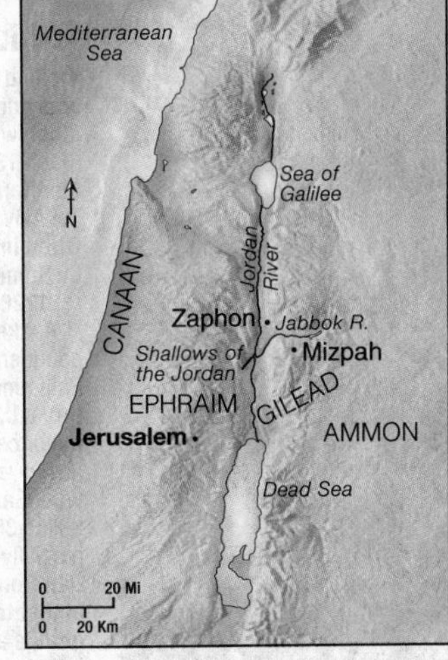

▸ **JUDGES 12:8-10 *(cont.)***

clan to marry his sons. Ibzan judged Israel for seven years. [10]When he died, he was buried at Bethlehem.

Elon Becomes Israel's Judge

JUDGES 12:11-12

After Ibzan died, Elon from the tribe of Zebulun judged Israel for ten years. [12]When he died, he was buried at Aijalon in Zebulun.

Abdon Becomes Israel's Judge

JUDGES 12:13-15

After Elon died, Abdon son of Hillel, from Pirathon, judged Israel. [14]He had forty sons and thirty grandsons, who rode on seventy donkeys. He judged Israel for eight years. [15]When he died, he was buried at Pirathon in Ephraim, in the hill country of the Amalekites.

6. SIXTH PERIOD: SAMSON

The sixth cycle of disobedience led to 40 years of oppression at the hands of the Philistines. God used Samson to save Israel from the Philistines, but his leadership was marked by moral and spiritual failure as much as it was by military success. Israel continued their steady decline away from God.

The Birth of Samson

JUDGES 13:1-25

Again the Israelites did evil in the LORD's sight, so the LORD handed them over to the Philistines, who oppressed them for forty years.

[2]In those days a man named Manoah from the tribe of Dan lived in the town of Zorah. His wife was unable to become pregnant, and they had no children. [3]The angel of the LORD appeared to Manoah's wife and said, "Even though you have been unable to have children, you will soon become pregnant and give birth to a son. [4]So be careful; you must not drink wine or any other alcoholic drink nor eat any forbidden food.* [5]You will become pregnant and give birth to a son, and his hair must never be cut. For he will be dedicated to God as a Nazirite from birth. He will begin to rescue Israel from the Philistines."

[6]The woman ran and told her husband, "A man of God appeared to me! He looked like one of God's angels, terrifying to see. I didn't ask where he was from, and he didn't tell me his name. [7]But he told me, 'You will become pregnant and give birth to a son. You must not drink wine or any other alcoholic drink nor eat any forbidden food. For your son will be dedicated to God as a Nazirite from the moment of his birth until the day of his death.'"

[8]Then Manoah prayed to the LORD, saying, "Lord, please let the man of God come back to us again and give us more instructions about this son who is to be born."

[9]God answered Manoah's prayer, and the angel of God appeared once again to his wife as she was sitting in the field. But her husband, Manoah, was not with her. [10]So she quickly ran and told her husband, "The man who appeared to me the other day is here again!"

Jgs 13:4 Hebrew *any unclean thing;* also in 13:7, 14.

Ashkelon

A city dating back to ancient times, Ashkelon was one of the Philistines' five main cities, along with Gaza, Ashdod, Gath, and Ekron (Josh 13:3). Ashkelon was located on the Mediterranean coast 30 miles south of modern Tel Aviv, and was always an important port. Often in conflict with Egypt, it was captured by Rameses II (c. 1286 B.C.) and by Merneptah (c. 1220 B.C.).

Ashkelon is mentioned as one of the cities conquered by Judah (Judg 1:18). After the Philistine invasion of Canaan in the 12th century B.C., the city became one of the invaders' major centers. When Samson's riddle was answered through the duplicity of his Philistine wife, Samson vented his rage at Ashkelon, killing 30 men (Judg 14:19). Ashkelon was partially responsible for pushing the tribe of Dan from its allotment; so Samson, a member of that tribe, probably had a long-standing grudge against the city. Ashkelon also figures into the story of the Philistines' possession of the Ark (1 Sam 4–6).

Judg 13:1 The Philistines lived on the west side of Canaan, along the Mediterranean seacoast. From Samson's day until the time of David they were the major enemy force in the land and a constant threat to Israel. The Philistines were fierce warriors; they had the advantage over Israel in numbers, tactical expertise, and technology. They knew the secret of making weapons out of iron (1 Sam 13:19-22). But none of that mattered when God was fighting for Israel.

Judg 13:1ff Once again the cycle of sin, judgment, and repentance began (Judg 3:8-9, 14-15; 4:1-4; 6:1-14; 10:6–11:11). The Israelites would not turn to God unless they had been stunned by suffering, oppression, and death. This suffering was not caused by God but resulted from the fact that the people ignored God, their Judge and Ruler. What will it take for you to follow God? The warnings in God's Word are clear: If we continue to harden our hearts against God, we can expect the same fate as Israel.

Judg 13:5 Samson was to be a Nazirite—a person who took a vow to be set apart for God's service. Samson's parents made the

11 Manoah ran back with his wife and asked, "Are
you the man who spoke to my wife the other day?"
"Yes," he replied, "I am."
12 So Manoah asked him, "When your words come
true, what kind of rules should govern the boy's life
and work?"
13 The angel of the LORD replied, "Be sure your wife
follows the instructions I gave her. 14 She must not eat
grapes or raisins, drink wine or any other alcoholic
drink, or eat any forbidden food."
15 Then Manoah said to the angel of the LORD,
"Please stay here until we can prepare a young goat
for you to eat."
16 "I will stay," the angel of the LORD replied, "but
I will not eat anything. However, you may prepare a
burnt offering as a sacrifice to the LORD." (Manoah
didn't realize it was the angel of the LORD.)
17 Then Manoah asked the angel of the LORD, "What
is your name? For when all this comes true, we want
to honor you."
18 "Why do you ask my name?" the angel of the LORD
replied. "It is too wonderful for you to understand."
19 Then Manoah took a young goat and a grain offering and offered it on a rock as a sacrifice to the LORD.
And as Manoah and his wife watched, the LORD did
an amazing thing. 20 As the flames from the altar shot
up toward the sky, the angel of the LORD ascended in
the fire. When Manoah and his wife saw this, they fell
with their faces to the ground.
21 The angel did not appear again to Manoah and

SAMSON

It is sad to be remembered for what one might have been. Samson had tremendous potential. Not many people have started life with credentials like his. Born as a result of God's plan in the lives of Manoah and his wife, Samson was to do a great work for God—to rescue Israel from the Philistines. To help him accomplish God's plan, he was given enormous physical strength.

• Because Samson wasted his strength on practical jokes and getting out of scrapes, and because he eventually gave it up altogether to satisfy the woman he loved, we tend to see him as a failure. We remember him as the judge in Israel who spent his last days grinding grain in an enemy prison, and we say, "What wasted potential!"

• Yes, Samson could have strengthened his nation. He could have returned his people to the worship of God. He could have wiped out the Philistines. But even though he did none of those things, Samson still accomplished the purpose announced by the angel who visited his parents before his birth. In his final act, Samson began to rescue Israel from the Philistines. • Interestingly, the New Testament does not mention Samson's failures or his heroic feats of strength. In Hebrews 11:33, he is simply listed with others who "overthrew kingdoms, ruled with justice, and received what God had promised them." In the end, Samson recognized his dependence on God. When he died, God turned his failures and defeats into victory. Samson's story teaches us that it is never too late to start over. However badly we may have failed in the past, today is not too late for us to put our complete trust in God.

Strengths and accomplishments	• Dedicated to God from birth as a Nazirite • Known for his feats of strength • Listed in the Hall of Faith in Hebrews 11 • Began to free Israel from Philistine oppression
Weaknesses and mistakes	• Violated God's laws on many occasions • Was controlled by sensuality • Confided in the wrong people • Used his gifts and abilities unwisely
Lessons from his life	• Great strength in one area of life does not make up for great weaknesses in other areas • God's presence does not overwhelm a person's will • God can use a person of faith in spite of past mistakes
Vital statistics	• Where: Zorah, Timnah, Ashkelon, Gaza, valley of Sorek • Occupation: Judge • Relative: Father: Manoah. • Contemporaries: Delilah
Key verse	"You will become pregnant and give birth to a son, and his hair must never be cut. For he will be dedicated to God as a Nazirite from birth. He will begin to rescue Israel from the Philistines" (Judg 13:5).

Samson's story is told in Judges 13–16. He is also mentioned in Hebrews 11:32.

vow for him. A Nazirite vow was sometimes temporary but in Samson's case it was for life. As a Nazirite, Samson could not cut his hair, touch a dead body, or drink anything containing alcohol.

Although Samson often used poor judgment and sinned terribly, he accomplished much when he determined to be set apart for God. In this way he was like the nation Israel. As long as the Israelites remained set apart for God, the nation thrived. But when they ignored God, they fell into terrible sin.

Philistines land on coast of Canaan

Judg 13:18 Why did the angel keep his name a secret? In those days people believed that if they knew someone's name, they knew his character and how to control him. By not giving his name, the angel was not allowing himself to be controlled by Manoah. He was also saying that his name was a mystery beyond understanding and too wonderful to imagine. Manoah asked the angel for an answer that he wouldn't have understood. Sometimes we ask God questions and then receive no answer. This may not be because God is saying *no.* We may have asked for knowledge beyond our ability to understand or accept.

Judg 13:19 Manoah sacrificed a grain offering to the Lord. A grain offering was grain, oil, and flour shaped into a cake and burned on the altar along with the burnt offering (the young goat). The grain offering (described in Lev 2) was offered to God as a sign of honor, respect, and worship. It was an acknowledgment that because the Israelites' food came from God, they owed their lives to him. With the grain offering, Manoah showed his desire to serve God and demonstrated his respect.

▸ **JUDGES 13:1-25** ***(cont.)***
his wife. Manoah finally realized it was the angel of
the LORD, 22 and he said to his wife, "We will certainly
die, for we have seen God!"
23 But his wife said, "If the LORD were going to kill
us, he wouldn't have accepted our burnt offering and
grain offering. He wouldn't have appeared to us and
told us this wonderful thing and done these miracles."
24 When her son was born, she named him Samson.
And the LORD blessed him as he grew up. 25 And the
Spirit of the LORD began to stir him while he lived in
Mahaneh-dan, which is located between the towns of
Zorah and Eshtaol.

Samson's Riddle

JUDGES 14:1-20
One day when Samson was in Timnah, one of the
Philistine women caught his eye. 2 When he returned
home, he told his father and mother, "A young Philistine woman in Timnah caught my eye. I want to marry
her. Get her for me."
3 His father and mother objected. "Isn't there even
one woman in our tribe or among all the Israelites you
could marry?" they asked. "Why must you go to the
pagan Philistines to find a wife?"
But Samson told his father, "Get her for me! She
looks good to me." 4 His father and mother didn't
realize the LORD was at work in this, creating an opportunity to work against the Philistines, who ruled
over Israel at that time.
5 As Samson and his parents were going down to
Timnah, a young lion suddenly attacked Samson near
the vineyards of Timnah. 6 At that moment the Spirit
of the LORD came powerfully upon him, and he ripped
the lion's jaws apart with his bare hands. He did it
as easily as if it were a young goat. But he didn't tell
his father or mother about it. 7 When Samson arrived
in Timnah, he talked with the woman and was very
pleased with her.
8 Later, when he returned to Timnah for the wedding, he turned off the path to look at the carcass of
the lion. And he found that a swarm of bees had made
some honey in the carcass. 9 He scooped some of the
honey into his hands and ate it along the way. He also
gave some to his father and mother, and they ate it.
But he didn't tell them he had taken the honey from
the carcass of the lion.
10 As his father was making final arrangements for
the marriage, Samson threw a party at Timnah, as was
the custom for elite young men. 11 When the bride's
parents* saw him, they selected thirty young men
from the town to be his companions.
12 Samson said to them, "Let me tell you a riddle.
If you solve my riddle during these seven days of the
celebration, I will give you thirty fine linen robes and
thirty sets of festive clothing. 13 But if you can't solve
it, then you must give me thirty fine linen robes and
thirty sets of festive clothing."
"All right," they agreed, "let's hear your riddle."
14 So he said:

"Out of the one who eats came something to eat;
out of the strong came something sweet."

Three days later they were still trying to figure it out.
15 On the fourth* day they said to Samson's wife, "Entice your husband to explain the riddle for us, or we
will burn down your father's house with you in it. Did
you invite us to this party just to make us poor?"

Jgs 14:11 Hebrew *they.* **Jgs 14:15** As in Greek version; Hebrew reads *seventh.*

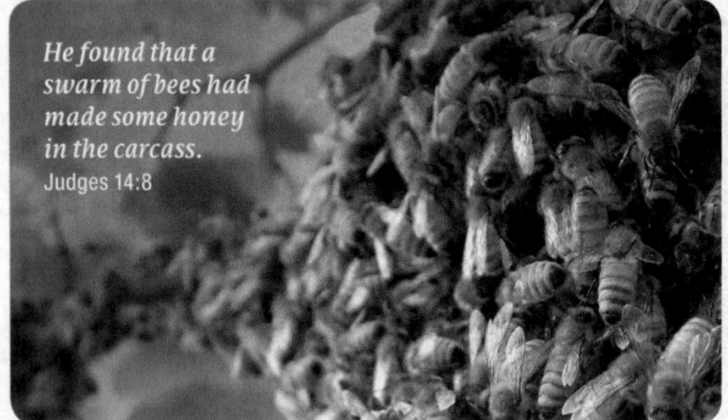

He found that a swarm of bees had made some honey in the carcass.
Judges 14:8

Judg 13:25 Samson's tribe, Dan, continued to wander in their inherited land (Judg 18:1), which was yet unconquered (Josh 19:47-48). Samson must have grown up with his warlike tribe's yearnings for a permanent and settled territory. Thus, his visits to the tribal army camp stirred his heart, and God's Spirit began preparing him for his role as judge and leader against the Philistines.

Perhaps there are things that stir your heart. These may indicate areas where God wants to use you. God uses a variety of means to develop and prepare us: hereditary traits, environmental influences, and personal experiences. As with Samson, this preparation often begins long before adulthood. Work at being sensitive to the Holy Spirit's leading and the tasks God has prepared for you. Your past may be more useful to you than you imagine.

Judg 14:3 Samson's parents objected to his marrying the Philistine woman for several reasons: (1) It was against God's law (Exod 34:15-17; Deut 7:1-4). A stark example of what happened when the Israelites married pagans is in Judges 3:5-7. (2) The Philistines were Israel's greatest enemies. Marriage to a hated Philistine would be a disgrace to Samson's family. But Samson's father gave in to Samson's demand and allowed the marriage, even though he had the right to refuse his son.

Judg 14:6 "The Spirit of the LORD came powerfully upon him" refers to the unusual physical strength given him by the Spirit of the Lord. Samson did not seem to be affected in any way other than increased physical strength.

[16]So Samson's wife came to him in tears and said, "You don't love me; you hate me! You have given my people a riddle, but you haven't told me the answer."

"I haven't even given the answer to my father or mother," he replied. "Why should I tell you?" [17]So she cried whenever she was with him and kept it up for the rest of the celebration. At last, on the seventh day he told her the answer because she was tormenting him with her nagging. Then she explained the riddle to the young men.

[18]So before sunset of the seventh day, the men of the town came to Samson with their answer:

"What is sweeter than honey?
What is stronger than a lion?"

Samson replied, "If you hadn't plowed with my heifer, you wouldn't have solved my riddle!"

[19]Then the Spirit of the Lord came powerfully upon him. He went down to the town of Ashkelon, killed thirty men, took their belongings, and gave their clothing to the men who had solved his riddle. But Samson was furious about what had happened, and he went back home to live with his father and mother. [20]So his wife was given in marriage to the man who had been Samson's best man at the wedding.

Samson's Vengeance on the Philistines

JUDGES 15:1-20

Later on, during the wheat harvest, Samson took a young goat as a present to his wife. He said, "I'm going into my wife's room to sleep with her," but her father wouldn't let him in.

[2]"I truly thought you must hate her," her father explained, "so I gave her in marriage to your best man. But look, her younger sister is even more beautiful than she is. Marry her instead."

[3]Samson said, "This time I cannot be blamed for everything I am going to do to you Philistines." [4]Then he went out and caught 300 foxes. He tied their tails together in pairs, and he fastened a torch to each pair of tails. [5]Then he lit the torches and let the foxes run through the grain fields of the Philistines. He burned all their grain to the ground, including the sheaves and the uncut grain. He also destroyed their vineyards and olive groves.

[6]"Who did this?" the Philistines demanded.

"Samson," was the reply, "because his father-in-law from Timnah gave Samson's wife to be married to his best man." So the Philistines went and got the woman and her father and burned them to death.

[7]"Because you did this," Samson vowed, "I won't rest until I take my revenge on you!" [8]So he attacked the Philistines with great fury and killed many of them. Then he went to live in a cave in the rock of Etam.

[9]The Philistines retaliated by setting up camp in Judah and spreading out near the town of Lehi. [10]The men of Judah asked the Philistines, "Why are you attacking us?"

The Philistines replied, "We've come to capture Samson. We've come to pay him back for what he did to us."

[11]So 3,000 men of Judah went down to get Samson at the cave in the rock of Etam. They said to Samson, "Don't you realize the Philistines rule over us? What are you doing to us?"

But Samson replied, "I only did to them what they did to me."

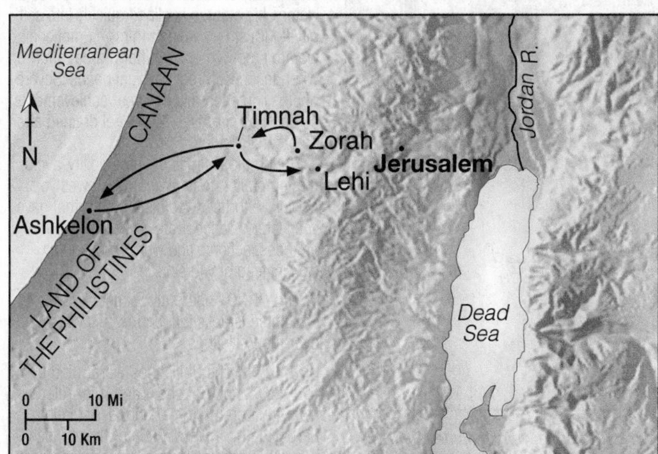

SAMSON'S VENTURES *Samson grew up in Zorah and wanted to marry a Philistine girl from Timnah. Tricked at his own wedding feast, he went to Ashkelon and killed some Philistine men and stole their clothes to pay off a bet. Samson then let himself be captured and brought to Lehi, where he snapped his ropes and killed 1,000 people.*

Judg 14:18 "If you hadn't plowed with my heifer" means "If you had not manipulated my wife." If they hadn't threatened his wife, they wouldn't have learned the answer to his riddle.

Judg 14:19 Samson impulsively used the special gift God gave him for selfish purposes. Today, God distributes abilities and skills throughout the church (1 Cor 12:1ff). The apostle Paul states that these gifts are to be used "to do his work and build up the church, the body of Christ" (Eph 4:12). To use these abilities for selfish purposes is to rob the church and fellow believers of strength. As you use the gifts God has given you, be sure you are helping others, not just yourself.

Judg 15:1ff Samson's reply in Judges 15:11 tells the story of this chapter: "I only did to them what they did to me." Revenge is an uncontrollable monster. Each act of retaliation brings another. The revenge cycle can be halted only by forgiveness.

▸ **JUDGES 15:1-20 *(cont.)***
12But the men of Judah told him, "We have come
to tie you up and hand you over to the Philistines."
"All right," Samson said. "But promise that you won't
kill me yourselves."
13"We will only tie you up and hand you over to the
Philistines," they replied. "We won't kill you." So they
tied him up with two new ropes and brought him up
from the rock.
14As Samson arrived at Lehi, the Philistines came
shouting in triumph. But the Spirit of the LORD came
powerfully upon Samson, and he snapped the ropes
on his arms as if they were burnt strands of flax, and
they fell from his wrists. 15Then he found the jawbone
of a recently killed donkey. He picked it up and killed
1,000 Philistines with it. 16Then Samson said,

"With the jawbone of a donkey,
I've piled them in heaps!
With the jawbone of a donkey,
I've killed a thousand men!"

17When he finished his boasting, he threw away the
jawbone; and the place was named Jawbone Hill.*
18Samson was now very thirsty, and he cried out to
the LORD, "You have accomplished this great victory by
the strength of your servant. Must I now die of thirst
and fall into the hands of these pagans?" 19So God
caused water to gush out of a hollow in the ground at
Lehi, and Samson was revived as he drank. Then he
named that place "The Spring of the One Who Cried
Out,"* and it is still in Lehi to this day.
20Samson judged Israel for twenty years during the
period when the Philistines dominated the land.

Samson Carries Away Gaza's Gates

JUDGES 16:1-3
One day Samson went to the Philistine town of Gaza
and spent the night with a prostitute. 2Word soon
spread* that Samson was there, so the men of Gaza
gathered together and waited all night at the town
gates. They kept quiet during the night, saying to
themselves, "When the light of morning comes, we
will kill him."
3But Samson stayed in bed only until midnight.
Then he got up, took hold of the doors of the town
gate, including the two posts, and lifted them up, bar
and all. He put them on his shoulders and carried
them all the way to the top of the hill across from
Hebron.

Samson and Delilah

JUDGES 16:4-22
Some time later Samson fell in love with a woman
named Delilah, who lived in the valley of Sorek. 5The
rulers of the Philistines went to her and said, "Entice
Samson to tell you what makes him so strong and how
he can be overpowered and tied up securely. Then
each of us will give you 1,100 pieces* of silver."
6So Delilah said to Samson, "Please tell me what
makes you so strong and what it would take to tie you
up securely."
7Samson replied, "If I were tied up with seven new

Jgs 15:17 Hebrew *Ramath-lehi.* **Jgs 15:19** Hebrew *En-hakkore.* **Jgs 16:2** As in Greek and Syriac versions and Latin Vulgate; Hebrew lacks *Word soon spread.* **Jgs 16:5** Hebrew *1,100 shekels,* about 28 pounds or 12.5 kilograms in weight.

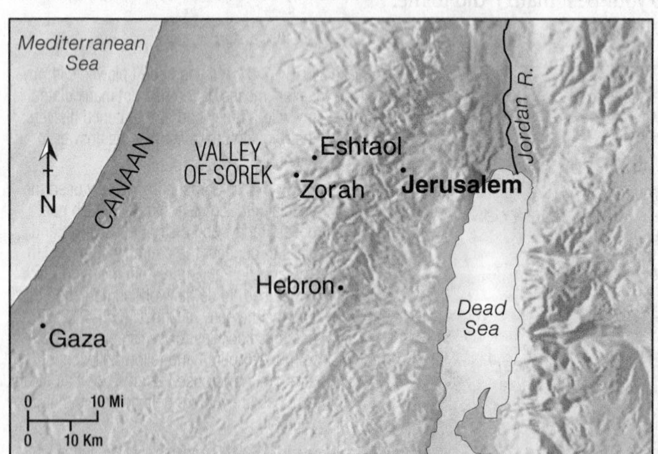

***SAMSON AND DELILAH** Samson was seduced by a Philistine woman named Delilah who lived in the valley of Sorek. She betrayed the secret of his strength to the Philistines, who captured him and led him away in chains to Gaza. There he died. His relatives buried him between Zorah and Eshtaol.*

Judg 15:14-17 The Lord's strength came upon Samson, but he was proud and boasted only of his own strength: "With the jawbone of a donkey . . . I've killed a thousand men!" Pride can cause us to take credit for work we've done only because of God's strength.

Judg 15:18 Samson was physically and emotionally exhausted. After a great personal victory, his attitude declined quickly into self-pity—"Must I now die of thirst?" Emotionally, we are most vulnerable after a great effort or when faced with real physical needs. Severe depression often follows great achievements, so don't be surprised if you feel drained after a personal victory.

During these times of vulnerability, avoid the temptation to think that God owes you for your efforts. It was his strength that gave you victory. Concentrate on keeping your attitudes, actions, and words focused on God instead of yourself.

Judg 15:20 Apparently Samson was appointed Israel's judge after this victory over the Philistines.

Judg 16:5 The Philistines were ruled by five rulers, not just one. Each ruler ruled from a different city—Ashdod, Ashkelon, Ekron, Gath, or Gaza. Each of these cities was an important center for trade and commerce. Given Delilah's character, it is little wonder that she betrayed Samson when these rich and powerful men paid her a personal visit.

bowstrings that have not yet been dried, I would become as weak as anyone else."
8 So the Philistine rulers brought Delilah seven new
bowstrings, and she tied Samson up with them. 9 She
had hidden some men in one of the inner rooms of her
house, and she cried out, "Samson! The Philistines have
come to capture you!" But Samson snapped the bowstrings as a piece of string snaps when it is burned by
a fire. So the secret of his strength was not discovered.
10 Afterward Delilah said to him, "You've been making fun of me and telling me lies! Now please tell me
how you can be tied up securely."
11 Samson replied, "If I were tied up with brand-new
ropes that had never been used, I would become as
weak as anyone else."
12 So Delilah took new ropes and tied him up with
them. The men were hiding in the inner room as before,
and again Delilah cried out, "Samson! The Philistines
have come to capture you!" But again Samson snapped
the ropes from his arms as if they were thread.
13 Then Delilah said, "You've been making fun of
me and telling me lies! Now tell me how you can be
tied up securely."
Samson replied, "If you were to weave the seven
braids of my hair into the fabric on your loom and
tighten it with the loom shuttle, I would become as
weak as anyone else."
So while he slept, Delilah wove the seven braids of
his hair into the fabric. 14 Then she tightened it with
the loom shuttle.* Again she cried out, "Samson! The
Philistines have come to capture you!" But Samson
woke up, pulled back the loom shuttle, and yanked
his hair away from the loom and the fabric.
15 Then Delilah pouted, "How can you tell me, 'I
love you,' when you don't share your secrets with
me? You've made fun of me three times now, and you
still haven't told me what makes you so strong!" 16 She
tormented him with her nagging day after day until
he was sick to death of it.
17 Finally, Samson shared his secret with her. "My
hair has never been cut," he confessed, "for I was
dedicated to God as a Nazirite from birth. If my head
were shaved, my strength would leave me, and I would
become as weak as anyone else."
18 Delilah realized he had finally told her the truth,
so she sent for the Philistine rulers. "Come back one
more time," she said, "for he has finally told me his secret." So the Philistine rulers returned with the money
in their hands. 19 Delilah lulled Samson to sleep with
his head in her lap, and then she called in a man to

Jgs 16:13-14 As in Greek version and Latin Vulgate; Hebrew lacks *I would become as weak as anyone else. / So while he slept, Delilah wove the seven braids of his hair into the fabric.* [14]*Then she tightened it with the loom shuttle.*

DELILAH

A person's greatest accomplishment may well be helping others accomplish great things. Likewise, a person's greatest failure may be preventing others from achieving greatness. Delilah played a minor role in Samson's life but her effect was devastating, for she influenced him to betray his special calling from God. Motivated by greed, Delilah used her persistence to wear down Samson. His infatuation with her made Samson a vulnerable target. For all his physical strength, he was no match for her nagging and her beauty, and he paid a great price for giving in to her. Delilah is never mentioned again in the Bible. Her unfaithfulness to Samson brought ruin to him and to her people. • Are people helped by knowing you? Do they find that knowing you challenges them to be the best they can be? Even more important, does knowing you help their relationship with God? What do your demands for their time and attention tell them about your real care for them? Are you willing to be God's instrument in the lives of others?

Strength and accomplishment	• Persistent when faced with obstacles
Weaknesses and mistakes	• Valued money more than relationships • Betrayed the man who trusted her
Lesson from her life	• We need to be careful to place our trust only in people who are trustworthy
Vital statistics	• Where: Valley of Sorek • Contemporary: Samson
Key verses	"She tormented him with her nagging day after day until he was sick to death of it. Finally, Samson shared his secret with her" (Judg 16:16-17).

Delilah's story is told in Judges 16.

Judg 16:15 Samson was deceived because he wanted to believe Delilah's lies. Although he could strangle a lion, he could not smother his burning lust and see Delilah for who she really was. How can you keep your desire for love and sexual pleasure from deceiving you? (1) You must decide what kind of a person you will love before passion takes over. Determine whether a person's character and faith in God are as desirable as physical appearance. (2) Because most of the time you spend with your spouse will not involve sex, your companion's personality, temperament, and commitment to solve problems must be as gratifying as the kisses. (3) Be patient. Time and observation often reveal what is beneath the pleasant appearance and attentive touch.

Judg 16:16-17 Delilah kept asking Samson for the secret of his strength until he finally grew tired of hearing her nagging and gave in. This was the second time that Samson allowed himself to be worn down by constant nagging (Judg 14:17). What a pitiful excuse for disobedience. Don't allow anyone—no matter how attractive, persuasive, or persistent—to talk you into doing wrong.

Judg 16:19 Delilah was a deceitful woman with honey on her lips and poison in her heart. Cold and calculating, she toyed with Samson, pretending to love him while looking for personal gain. How could Samson be so foolish? Four times Delilah took advantage of him. If he didn't realize what was happening after the first or second experience, surely he should have understood the situation by the fourth time! We think Samson is foolish, but how many times do we allow ourselves to be deceived by flattery and give in to temptation and wrong beliefs? Avoid falling prey to deceit by asking God to help you distinguish between deception and truth.

▸ **JUDGES 16:4-22** ***(cont.)***
shave off the seven locks of his hair. In this way she
began to bring him down,* and his strength left him.
20 Then she cried out, "Samson! The Philistines have
come to capture you!"

When he woke up, he thought, "I will do as before and shake myself free." But he didn't realize the LORD had left him.
21 So the Philistines captured him and gouged out his
eyes. They took him to Gaza, where he was bound with
bronze chains and forced to grind grain in the prison.
22 But before long, his hair began to grow back.

Samson's Final Victory

JUDGES 16:23-31

The Philistine rulers held a great festival, offering sacrifices and praising their god, Dagon. They said, "Our god has given us victory over our enemy Samson!"
24 When the people saw him, they praised their god,
saying, "Our god has delivered our enemy to us! The
one who killed so many of us is now in our power!"
25 Half drunk by now, the people demanded, "Bring
out Samson so he can amuse us!" So he was brought
from the prison to amuse them, and they had him
stand between the pillars supporting the roof.
26 Samson said to the young servant who was leading
him by the hand, "Place my hands against the pillars
that hold up the temple. I want to rest against them."
27 Now the temple was completely filled with people.
All the Philistine rulers were there, and there were
about 3,000 men and women on the roof who were
watching as Samson amused them.
28 Then Samson prayed to the LORD, "Sovereign
LORD, remember me again. O God, please strengthen
me just one more time. With one blow let me pay back
the Philistines for the loss of my two eyes." 29 Then
Samson put his hands on the two center pillars that
held up the temple. Pushing against them with both
hands, 30 he prayed, "Let me die with the Philistines."
And the temple crashed down on the Philistine rulers
and all the people. So he killed more people when he
died than he had during his entire lifetime.
31 Later his brothers and other relatives went down to
get his body. They took him back home and buried him
between Zorah and Eshtaol, where his father, Manoah,
was buried. Samson had judged Israel for twenty years.

Jgs 16:19 Or *she began to torment him.* Greek version reads *He began to grow weak.*

F. The Moral Failure of Israel

This section shows Israel falling into idolatry, moral decline, and petty fighting. Israel, the nation that was to set the example for spiritual living, had instead become morally depraved. When Israel did serve God during the period of the judges, and that was seldom, it was often from selfish motives. Selfish obedience does not bring us far. Genuine obedience is motivated by a love and reverence for God himself.

1. MICAH AND THE TRIBE OF DAN

Israel was so far away from God. A wealthy Israelite hired a Levite to be his personal priest in a shrine for idols of his own making. The tribe of Dan refused to settle in the land they were given by God, and they stole both the idols and the priest from this man. Everyone was simply doing what seemed right in their own eyes.

Micah's Idols

JUDGES 17:1-13

There was a man named Micah, who lived in the hill
country of Ephraim. 2 One day he said to his mother, "I
heard you place a curse on the person who stole 1,100
pieces* of silver from you. Well, I have the money. I
was the one who took it."

"The LORD bless you for admitting it," his mother

Jgs 17:2 Hebrew *1,100 shekels,* about 28 pounds or 12.5 kilograms in weight.

Judg 16:21 Samson, the mighty warrior, became a slave. Rather than kill him, the Philistines preferred to humiliate him by gouging out his eyes and making him grind grain. Samson now had plenty of time to wonder if Delilah's charms were worth spending the rest of his life in humiliation.

Although God did not completely abandon Samson (Judg 16:28-30), he allowed Samson's decision to stand, and the consequences of his decision followed naturally. We may choose to be close to God or to go our own way, but there are consequences resulting from our choice. Samson didn't choose to be captured, but he chose to be with Delilah, and he could not escape the consequences of his decision.

Judg 16:21 Blinded and without strength, Samson was taken to Gaza where he would spend the rest of his short life. Gaza was one of the five capital cities of the Philistines. Known for its many wells, Gaza was a vital stop along a great caravan route that connected Egypt to the south with Aram to the north. The Philistines probably showed off their prize captive, Samson, to many dignitaries passing through.

Ironically, it was in Gaza that Samson had earlier demonstrated his great strength by uprooting the city gates (Judg 16:1-3). Now he was an example of weakness.

Judg 16:23-24 Dagon was the chief god of the Philistines, the god of grain and harvest. Many temples were built to Dagon, and the worship there included human sacrifice. The temples were also the local entertainment centers. Just as people today crowd into theaters, Philistine townspeople crowded into the local temple. They sat on the flat temple roof and looked into the courtyard below. What they often saw was the torture and humiliation of prisoners.

replied. [3]He returned the money to her, and she said, "I
now dedicate these silver coins to the LORD. In honor
of my son, I will have an image carved and an idol cast."
[4]So when he returned the money to his mother, she
took 200 silver coins and gave them to a silversmith,
who made them into an image and an idol. And these
were placed in Micah's house. [5]Micah set up a shrine
for the idol, and he made a sacred ephod and some
household idols. Then he installed one of his sons as
his personal priest.
[6]In those days Israel had no king; all the people did
whatever seemed right in their own eyes.
[7]One day a young Levite, who had been living in
Bethlehem in Judah, arrived in that area. [8]He had left
Bethlehem in search of another place to live, and as he
traveled, he came to the hill country of Ephraim. He
happened to stop at Micah's house as he was traveling
through. [9]"Where are you from?" Micah asked him.

He replied, "I am a Levite from Bethlehem in Judah, and I am looking for a place to live."

[10]"Stay here with me," Micah said, "And you can be
a father and priest to me. I will give you ten pieces* of
silver a year, plus a change of clothes and your food."
[11]The Levite agreed to this, and the young man became
like one of Micah's sons.
[12]So Micah installed the Levite as his personal
priest, and he lived in Micah's house. [13]"I know the
LORD will bless me now," Micah said, "because I have
a Levite serving as my priest."

Idolatry in the Tribe of Dan

JUDGES 18:1-31

Now in those days Israel had no king. And the tribe of Dan was trying to find a place where they could settle, for they had not yet moved into the land assigned to them when the land was divided among the tribes of
Israel. [2]So the men of Dan chose from their clans five
capable warriors from the towns of Zorah and Eshtaol to scout out a land for them to settle in.

When these warriors arrived in the hill country of Ephraim, they came to Micah's house and spent the
night there. [3]While at Micah's house, they recognized
the young Levite's accent, so they went over and asked him, "Who brought you here, and what are you doing

Jgs 17:10 Hebrew *10 shekels,* about 4 ounces or 114 grams in weight.

Since the Philistines had control over the Israelites, they thought their god was stronger. But when the Ark of God was placed before Dagon in a similar temple, the idol fell over and broke into pieces (1 Sam 5:1-7). God's strength goes beyond numbers or physical might.

Judg 16:28-30 In spite of Samson's past, God still answered his prayer and destroyed the pagan temple and worshipers. God still loved him. He was willing to hear Samson's prayer of confession and repentance and use him this final time. One of the effects of sin in our lives is to keep us from feeling like praying. But perfect moral behavior is not a condition for prayer. Don't let guilt feelings over sin keep you from your only means of restoration. No matter how long you have been away from God, he is ready to hear from you and restore you to a right relationship. Every situation can be salvaged if you are willing to turn again to him. If God could still work in Samson's situation, he can certainly make something worthwhile out of yours.

Judg 17:2 Micah and his mother seemed to be good and moral and may have sincerely desired to worship God, but they disobeyed God by following their own desires instead of doing what God wanted. The attitude that prevailed in Micah's day was this: "The people did whatever seemed right in their own eyes" (Judg 17:6). This is remarkably similar to today's prevailing attitudes. But God has given us standards. He has not left our conduct up to us and our opinions. We can avoid conforming to society's low standards by taking God's commands seriously and applying them to life. Independence and self-reliance are positive traits, but only within the framework of God's standards.

Judg 17:6 Today, as in Micah's day, everyone seems to put self-interest first. Time has not changed human nature. Most people still reject God's right way of living. The people in Micah's time replaced the true worship of God with a homemade version of worship. As a result, justice was soon replaced by revenge and chaos. Ignoring God's direction led to confusion and destruction. Anyone who has not submitted to God will end up doing whatever seems right at the time. This tendency is present in all of us. To know what is really right and to have the strength to do it, we need to draw closer to God and his Word.

Judg 17:7-12 Apparently the Israelites no longer supported the priests and Levites with their tithes because so many of the people no longer worshiped God. The young Levite in this story probably left his home in Bethlehem because the money he had been receiving from the people there was not enough to live on. But Israel's moral decay affected even the priests and Levites. This man accepted money (Judg 17:10-11), idols (Judg 18:20), and position (Judg 17:12) in a way that was inconsistent with God's laws. While Micah revealed the religious downfall of individual Israelites, this priest illustrated the religious downfall of priests and Levites.

Judg 18:1 The Danites had been assigned enough land to meet their needs (Josh 19:40-48). But because they had failed to trust God to help them conquer their territory, the Amorites forced them into the hill country and wouldn't let them settle in the plains (Judg 1:34). Rather than fight for their allotted territory, they preferred to look for new land in the north where resistance from the enemy wouldn't be so tough. It was while they were traveling north that some of their men passed Micah's home and stole some of his idols.

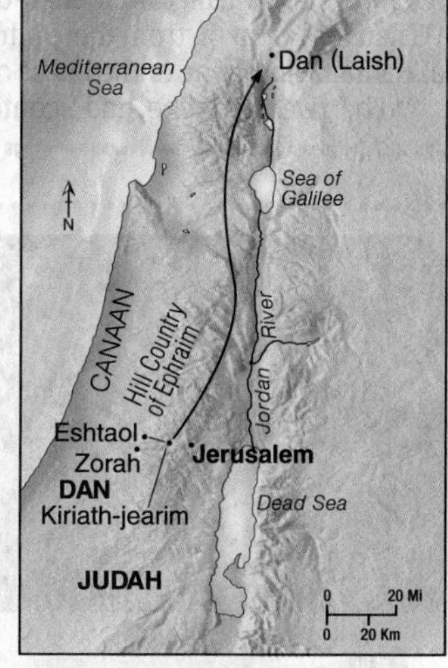

THE TRIBE OF DAN MOVES NORTH
Troops from the tribe of Dan traveled from Zorah and Eshtaol into the hill country of Ephraim, where they persuaded Micah's priest to come with them. They continued north to Laish, where they ruthlessly butchered its citizens. The city was renamed Dan, and the priest's idols became the focus of their worship.

▸ **JUDGES 18:1-31** ***(cont.)***
in this place? Why are you here?" 4He told them about
his agreement with Micah and that he had been hired
as Micah's personal priest.
5Then they said, "Ask God whether or not our journey will be successful."
6"Go in peace," the priest replied. "For the LORD is
watching over your journey."
7So the five men went on to the town of Laish, where
they noticed the people living carefree lives, like the
Sidonians; they were peaceful and secure.* The people
were also wealthy because their land was very fertile.
And they lived a great distance from Sidon and had
no allies nearby.
8When the men returned to Zorah and Eshtaol,
their relatives asked them, "What did you find?"
9The men replied, "Come on, let's attack them! We
have seen the land, and it is very good. What are you
waiting for? Don't hesitate to go and take possession
of it. 10When you get there, you will find the people
living carefree lives. God has given us a spacious and
fertile land, lacking in nothing!"
11So 600 men from the tribe of Dan, armed with
weapons of war, set out from Zorah and Eshtaol.
12They camped at a place west of Kiriath-jearim in
Judah, which is called Mahaneh-dan* to this day.
13Then they went on from there into the hill country
of Ephraim and came to the house of Micah.
14The five men who had scouted out the land
around Laish explained to the others, "These buildings contain a sacred ephod, as well as some household idols, a carved image, and a cast idol. What do
you think you should do?" 15Then the five men turned
off the road and went over to Micah's house, where
the young Levite lived, and greeted him kindly. 16As
the 600 armed warriors from the tribe of Dan stood
at the entrance of the gate, 17the five scouts entered
the shrine and removed the carved image, the sacred ephod, the household idols, and the cast idol.
Meanwhile, the priest was standing at the gate with
the 600 armed warriors.
18When the priest saw the men carrying all the sacred objects out of Micah's shrine, he said, "What are
you doing?"
19"Be quiet and come with us," they said. "Be a father and priest to all of us. Isn't it better to be a priest
for an entire tribe and clan of Israel than for the household of just one man?"
20The young priest was quite happy to go with them,
so he took along the sacred ephod, the household
idols, and the carved image. 21They turned and started
on their way again, placing their children, livestock,
and possessions in front of them.
22When the people from the tribe of Dan were quite
a distance from Micah's house, the people who lived
near Micah came chasing after them. 23They were
shouting as they caught up with them. The men of Dan
turned around and said to Micah, "What's the matter?

Jgs 18:7 The meaning of the Hebrew is uncertain. **Jgs 18:12** *Mahaneh-dan* means "the camp of Dan."

Dan

Dan was a Phoenician city originally named Laish (Josh 19:47; Judg 18:7), which was conquered by the tribe of Dan when it migrated northward. A day's journey from Sidon (on the Mediterranean coast), the city lay in the valley at the southern base of Mount Hermon. The site of Dan guarded a major trading route running between Damascus and Tyre, and was therefore an important commercial center.

One of the principal sources of the Jordan River rose in the area, making the valley below Dan lush and fertile even in the heat of summer. Consequently, the territory around the city produced grain and vegetable crops in abundance and supplied the needs of flocks and herds adequately. In the early Iron Age, Dan was a prosperous city (as indicated in Judg 18:7), but by the middle of the 11th century B.C., it had been destroyed, evidently as a result of occupation by the Danites.

Throughout its history, Dan was known as the most northerly point of the Israelite kingdom, and it was used as a topographical marker in the phrase "from Dan . . . to Beersheba" (Judg 20:1; 2 Sam 3:10). As such, it designated the extent of Israel's inheritance. As Christians, our inheritance is much greater: We have inherited Christ, who is the fullness of God (Eph 1:14; Col 2:9-10).

Judg 18:4-6 Priests and their assistants were all members of the tribe of Levi (Num 3:5-13). They were to serve the people, teach them how to worship God, and perform the rituals involved in the worship services both at the Tabernacle in Shiloh and in the designated cities throughout the land. But this disobedient priest showed disrespect for God in several ways: (1) He performed his duties in a house. Priestly duties were to be performed only in the Tabernacle or a designated city (Deut 12:4-14). (2) He used idols (Exod 20:4; Lev 19:4). (3) He claimed to speak for God when God had not spoken through him (Deut 18:15-22).

Judg 18:11-26 Through this entire incident, no one desired to worship God; instead, they wanted to use God for selfish gain. Today some people go to church to feel better, be accepted, relieve guilt, and gain business contacts or friends. Beware of following God for selfish gain rather than selfless service.

Judg 18:14 An ephod was a ceremonial vest worn by a priest.

Judg 18:24 Micah had made idols and hired a priest to run his personal religion. When the men of Dan took his idols and priest, nothing remained. What an empty spiritual condition! An idol is anything that takes God's place in a person's life. Some people invest all their energy in pursuit of

Why have you called these men together and chased after us like this?"

24 "What do you mean, 'What's the matter?'" Micah replied. "You've taken away all the gods I have made, and my priest, and I have nothing left!"

25 The men of Dan said, "Watch what you say! There are some short-tempered men around here who might get angry and kill you and your family." 26 So the men of Dan continued on their way. When Micah saw that there were too many of them for him to attack, he turned around and went home.

27 Then, with Micah's idols and his priest, the men of Dan came to the town of Laish, whose people were peaceful and secure. They attacked with swords and burned the town to the ground. 28 There was no one to rescue the people, for they lived a great distance from Sidon and had no allies nearby. This happened in the valley near Beth-rehob.

Then the people of the tribe of Dan rebuilt the town and lived there. 29 They renamed the town Dan after their ancestor, Israel's son, but it had originally been called Laish.

30 Then they set up the carved image, and they appointed Jonathan son of Gershom, son of Moses,* as their priest. This family continued as priests for the tribe of Dan until the Exile. 31 So Micah's carved image was worshiped by the tribe of Dan as long as the Tabernacle of God remained at Shiloh.

Jgs 18:30 As in an ancient Hebrew tradition, some Greek manuscripts, and Latin Vulgate; Masoretic Text reads *son of Manasseh.*

2. WAR AGAINST THE TRIBE OF BENJAMIN

Things keep going from bad to worse in Israel. Neglecting to follow God, Israel spiraled down into a story of rape, murder, and civil war. It seems as though nobody in all of Israel remembers God at all.

The Levite and His Concubine

JUDGES 19:1-30

Now in those days Israel had no king. There was a man from the tribe of Levi living in a remote area of the hill country of Ephraim. One day he brought home a woman from Bethlehem in Judah to be his concubine. 2 But she became angry with him* and returned to her father's home in Bethlehem.

Jgs 19:2 Or *she was unfaithful to him.*

money, success, possessions, or a career. If these idols are taken away, only an empty shell is left. The only way to protect yourself against such loss is to invest your life in the living God, whom you can never lose.

Judg 18:27 Did the tribe of Dan have the right to kill the citizens of Laish? No. God had commanded Israel to clean out and destroy certain cities because of their idolatry and wickedness (Deut 13:12-15), but Laish did not fall under that judgment. The Danites themselves were guilty of this sin. Further, Laish was not within the assigned boundaries of Dan (Josh 19:40-48), and its people were peaceful in contrast to the warlike Canaanites. But the tribe of Dan had no regard for God's law. This story shows how far some of the tribes had wandered away from God.

Judg 18:27 Just because the Danites successfully defeated Laish doesn't mean their actions were right. Their idolatry showed that God was not guiding them. Today many justify their wrong actions by outward signs of success. They think that wealth, popularity, or lack of suffering is an indication of God's blessing. But many stories in the Bible indicate that evil and earthly success can go hand in hand (e.g., 2 Kgs 14:23-29). Success doesn't indicate God's approval. Don't allow personal success to become a measuring rod of whether or not you are pleasing God.

Judg 18:30-31 The tribe of Dan had stolen Micah's idols, and now they set them up in Laish. Although the Danites might have assumed they were worshiping God through these images (see the note on Exod 32:4-5, p. 184), they were actually denying God (Exod 20:1-5). Worshiping images of God is *not* worshiping God, even if it resembles true worship in some ways. people repeat the same mistake today when they claim to be Christians without really believing in God's power or changing their conduct to conform to his expectations. Godliness cannot be merely a claim. It must be a reality in our motives and in our actions.

Judg 18:31 Shiloh was probably destroyed during the events reported in 1 Samuel 4–5, not long after the time described here. Because Shiloh was the religious center for Israel, all adult males were required to travel there for certain religious feasts. But the tribe of Dan set up idols and priests in the new territory they had conquered. The fact that they were over 80 miles away from Shiloh may have been their excuse for not fulfilling the law's requirements. This act was a further demonstration of their disregard for God.

Judg 18:31 The true worship of God should have been maintained by the Levitical priests scattered throughout the land and the influence of the Tabernacle in Shiloh. This story shows how pagan influences and moral depravity had crept into every corner of Israelite culture. Although 300 years had passed since entering the Promised Land, they still had not destroyed the idolatry and evil practices within it.

There may be a tendency in your life to allow "harmless" habits to have their own small corners, but they can become dominating forces. The values, attitudes, and practices you have adopted from the world's system can be exposed by applying the light of God's truth to them. Once you see them for what they are, you can begin to uproot them.

Judg 19:1–21:25 What is the significance of this tragic story? When the Israelites' faith in God disintegrated, their unity as a nation also disintegrated. They could have taken complete possession of the land if they had obeyed God and trusted him to keep his promises. But when they forgot him, they lost their purpose, and soon "the people did whatever seemed right in their own eyes" (Judg 21:25). When they stopped letting God lead them, they became no better than the evil people around them. When they made laws for their own benefit, they set standards far below God's. When you leave God out of your life, you may be shocked at what you are capable of doing (Judg 19:29-30).

Judg 19:1 Having concubines was an accepted part of Israelite society although this is not what God intended (Gen 2:24). A concubine had most of the duties but only some of the privileges of a wife. Although she was legally attached to one man, she and her children usually did not have the inheritance rights of the legal wife and legitimate children. Her primary purpose was giving the man sexual pleasure, bearing additional children, and contributing more help to the household or estate. Concubines were often foreign prisoners of war. But they could also be Israelites, as was probably the case in this story.

▸ **JUDGES 19:1-30 *(cont.)***

After about four months, 3her husband set out for Bethlehem to speak personally to her and persuade her to come back. He took with him a servant and a pair of donkeys. When he arrived at* her father's house, her father saw him and welcomed him. 4Her father urged him to stay awhile, so he stayed three days, eating, drinking, and sleeping there.

5On the fourth day the man was up early, ready to leave, but the woman's father said to his son-in-law, "Have something to eat before you go." 6So the two men sat down together and had something to eat and drink. Then the woman's father said, "Please stay another night and enjoy yourself." 7The man got up to leave, but his father-in-law kept urging him to stay, so he finally gave in and stayed the night.

8On the morning of the fifth day he was up early again, ready to leave, and again the woman's father said, "Have something to eat; then you can leave later this afternoon." So they had another day of feasting. 9Later, as the man and his concubine and servant were preparing to leave, his father-in-law said, "Look, it's almost evening. Stay the night and enjoy yourself. Tomorrow you can get up early and be on your way."

10But this time the man was determined to leave. So he took his two saddled donkeys and his concubine and headed in the direction of Jebus (that is, Jerusalem). 11It was late in the day when they neared Jebus, and the man's servant said to him, "Let's stop at this Jebusite town and spend the night there."

12"No," his master said, "we can't stay in this foreign town where there are no Israelites. Instead, we will go on to Gibeah. 13Come on, let's try to get as far as Gibeah or Ramah, and we'll spend the night in one of those towns." 14So they went on. The sun was setting as they came to Gibeah, a town in the land of Benjamin, 15so they stopped there to spend the night. They rested in the town square, but no one took them in for the night.

16That evening an old man came home from his work in the fields. He was from the hill country of Ephraim, but he was living in Gibeah, where the people were from the tribe of Benjamin. 17When he saw the travelers sitting in the town square, he asked them where they were from and where they were going.

18"We have been in Bethlehem in Judah," the man replied. "We are on our way to a remote area in the hill country of Ephraim, which is my home. I traveled to Bethlehem, and now I'm returning home.* But no one has taken us in for the night, 19even though we have everything we need. We have straw and feed for our donkeys and plenty of bread and wine for ourselves."

20"You are welcome to stay with me," the old man said. "I will give you anything you might need. But whatever you do, don't spend the night in the square." 21So he took them home with him and fed the donkeys. After they washed their feet, they ate and drank together.

22While they were enjoying themselves, a crowd of troublemakers from the town surrounded the house. They began beating at the door and shouting to the old man, "Bring out the man who is staying with you so we can have sex with him."

23The old man stepped outside to talk to them. "No, my brothers, don't do such an evil thing. For this man is a guest in my house, and such a thing would be shameful. 24Here, take my virgin daughter and this man's concubine. I will bring them out to you, and you can abuse them and do whatever you like. But don't do such a shameful thing to this man."

25But they wouldn't listen to him. So the Levite took hold of his concubine and pushed her out the door. The men of the town abused her all night, taking turns raping her until morning. Finally, at dawn they let her go. 26At daybreak the woman returned to the house where her husband was staying. She collapsed at the door of the house and lay there until it was light.

27When her husband opened the door to leave, there lay his concubine with her hands on the threshold. 28He said, "Get up! Let's go!" But there was no answer.* So he put her body on his donkey and took her home.

29When he got home, he took a knife and cut his concubine's body into twelve pieces. Then he sent one piece to each tribe throughout all the territory of Israel.

Jgs 19:3 As in Greek version; Hebrew reads *When she brought him to.* **Jgs 19:18** As in Greek version (see also 19:29); Hebrew reads *now I'm going to the Tabernacle of the LORD.* **Jgs 19:28** Greek version adds *for she was dead.*

Judg 19:24 Nowhere is the unwritten law of hospitality stronger than in the Middle East. Protecting a guest at any cost ranked at the top of a man's code of honor. But here the hospitality code turned to fanaticism. The rape and abuse of a daughter and a concubine were preferable to the possibility of a conflict between a guest and a neighbor. The two men were selfish (they didn't want to get hurt themselves); they lacked courage (they didn't want to face a conflict even when lives were at stake); and they disobeyed God's law (they allowed deliberate abuse and murder). What drastic consequences can result when social protocol carries more authority than moral convictions!

Judg 19:29-30 Although this was an appalling way to spread the news, it effectively communicated the horror of the crime and called the people to action. (Saul used a similar method in 1 Sam 11:7.) Ironically, the man who alerted Israel to the murder of his concubine was just as guilty for her death as the men who actually killed her.

Judg 19:30 The horrible crime described in this chapter wasn't Israel's primary offense; it was a result of the nation's failure to establish a government based upon God's moral principles, where the law of God was the law of the land. As a result, laws were usually not enforced and crime was ignored. Sexual perversion and lawlessness were by-products of Israel's disobedience to God. The Israelites weren't willing to speak up until events had gone too far.

Whenever we get away from God and his Word, all sorts of evil can follow. Our drifting away from God may be slow and almost imperceptible, with the ultimate results affecting a future generation. We must continually call people back to God and work toward the establishment of God's moral and spiritual reign in the heart of every person.

30Everyone who saw it said, "Such a horrible crime has not been committed in all the time since Israel left Egypt. Think about it! What are we going to do? Who's going to speak up?"

Israel's War with Benjamin

JUDGES 20:1-48

Then all the Israelites were united as one man, from Dan in the north to Beersheba in the south, including those from across the Jordan in the land of Gilead. The entire community assembled in the presence of the LORD at Mizpah. 2The leaders of all the people and all the tribes of Israel—400,000 warriors armed with swords—took their positions in the assembly of the people of God. 3(Word soon reached the land of Benjamin that the other tribes had gone up to Mizpah.) The Israelites then asked how this terrible crime had happened.

4The Levite, the husband of the woman who had been murdered, said, "My concubine and I came to spend the night in Gibeah, a town that belongs to the people of Benjamin. 5That night some of the leading citizens of Gibeah surrounded the house, planning to kill me, and they raped my concubine until she was dead. 6So I cut her body into twelve pieces and sent the pieces throughout the territory assigned to Israel, for these men have committed a terrible and shameful crime. 7Now then, all of you—the entire community of Israel—must decide here and now what should be done about this!"

8And all the people rose to their feet in unison and declared, "None of us will return home! No, not even one of us! 9Instead, this is what we will do to Gibeah; we will draw lots to decide who will attack it. 10One-tenth of the men* from each tribe will be chosen to supply the warriors with food, and the rest of us will take revenge on Gibeah* of Benjamin for this shameful thing they have done in Israel." 11So all the Israelites were completely united, and they gathered together to attack the town.

12The Israelites sent messengers to the tribe of Benjamin, saying, "What a terrible thing has been done among you! 13Give up those evil men, those troublemakers from Gibeah, so we can execute them and purge Israel of this evil."

But the people of Benjamin would not listen. 14Instead, they came from their towns and gathered at Gibeah to fight the Israelites. 15In all, 26,000 of their warriors armed with swords arrived in Gibeah to join the 700 elite troops who lived there. 16Among Benjamin's elite troops, 700 were left-handed, and each of them could sling a rock and hit a target within a hairsbreadth without missing. 17Israel had 400,000 experienced soldiers armed with swords, not counting Benjamin's warriors.

18Before the battle the Israelites went to Bethel and asked God, "Which tribe should go first to attack the people of Benjamin?"

The LORD answered, "Judah is to go first."

19So the Israelites left early the next morning and camped near Gibeah. 20Then they advanced toward Gibeah to attack the men of Benjamin. 21But Benjamin's warriors, who were defending the town, came out and killed 22,000 Israelites on the battlefield that day.

22But the Israelites encouraged each other and took their positions again at the same place they had fought the previous day. 23For they had gone up to Bethel and wept in the presence of the LORD until evening. They had asked the LORD, "Should we fight against our relatives from Benjamin again?"

And the LORD had said, "Go out and fight against them."

24So the next day they went out again to fight against the men of Benjamin, 25but the men of Benjamin killed another 18,000 Israelites, all of whom were experienced with the sword.

26Then all the Israelites went up to Bethel and wept in the presence of the LORD and fasted until evening. They also brought burnt offerings and peace offerings to the LORD. 27The Israelites went up seeking direction from the LORD. (In those days the Ark of the Covenant of God was in Bethel, 28and Phinehas son of Eleazar and grandson of Aaron was the priest.) The Israelites asked the LORD, "Should we fight against our relatives from Benjamin again, or should we stop?"

Jgs 20:10a Hebrew *10 men from every hundred, 100 men from every thousand, and 1,000 men from every 10,000.* **Jgs 20:10b** Hebrew *Geba,* in this case a variant spelling of Gibeah; also in 20:33.

Judg 20:1 Dan was the northernmost city in Israel, and Beersheba, the southernmost. The two were often mentioned together as a reference to the entire nation.

Judg 20:5 In reporting the events in Gibeah, the man conveniently left out the fact that he had handed over his concubine to satisfy the mob's demands. He wanted justice for the threats made against himself rather than placing any value on the life of the woman or holding himself partly responsible for her death. How easy it is to give only partial facts or twist events to remove our own culpability when we are seeking to shift blame to someone else. This incident reveals the depths of perversion and violence that develop when a culture abandons God's ways.

Judg 20:13 Perhaps the leaders of the tribe of Benjamin had been given distorted facts about the serious crime in their territory, or perhaps they were too proud to admit that some of their people had stooped so low. In either case, they would not listen to the rest of Israel and hand over the accused criminals. They were more loyal to their own tribe than to God's law.

By covering for their kinsmen, the entire tribe of Benjamin sank to a level of immorality as low as that of the criminals. Through this act, we get a glimpse of how thoroughly the nation's moral fabric had unraveled. The time period of the judges ends in a bloody civil war that sets the stage for the spiritual renewal to come under Samuel (see 1 Samuel).

Judg 20:27-28 This is the only place in Judges where the Ark of the Covenant is mentioned. This probably indicates how seldom the people consulted God.

Phinehas the high priest was also the high priest under Joshua (Josh 22:13). The reference to Phinehas as high priest and the location of the Tabernacle in Bethel instead of Shiloh may indicate that the events of this story occurred during the early years of the judges.

▸ **JUDGES 20:1-48 *(cont.)***

The Lord said, "Go! Tomorrow I will hand them over to you."

29So the Israelites set an ambush all around Gibeah. 30They went out on the third day and took their positions at the same place as before. 31When the men of Benjamin came out to attack, they were drawn away from the town. And as they had done before, they began to kill the Israelites. About thirty Israelites died in the open fields and along the roads, one leading to Bethel and the other leading back to Gibeah.

32Then the warriors of Benjamin shouted, "We're defeating them as we did before!" But the Israelites had planned in advance to run away so that the men of Benjamin would chase them along the roads and be drawn away from the town.

33When the main group of Israelite warriors reached Baal-tamar, they turned and took up their positions. Meanwhile, the Israelites hiding in ambush to the west* of Gibeah jumped up to fight. 34There were 10,000 elite Israelite troops who advanced against Gibeah. The fighting was so heavy that Benjamin didn't realize the impending disaster. 35So the Lord helped Israel defeat Benjamin, and that day the Israelites killed 25,100 of Benjamin's warriors, all of whom were experienced swordsmen. 36Then the men of Benjamin saw that they were beaten.

The Israelites had retreated from Benjamin's warriors in order to give those hiding in ambush more room to maneuver against Gibeah. 37Then those who were hiding rushed in from all sides and killed everyone in the town. 38They had arranged to send up a large cloud of smoke from the town as a signal. 39When the Israelites saw the smoke, they turned and attacked Benjamin's warriors.

By that time Benjamin's warriors had killed about thirty Israelites, and they shouted, "We're defeating them as we did in the first battle!" 40But when the warriors of Benjamin looked behind them and saw the smoke rising into the sky from every part of the town, 41the men of Israel turned and attacked. At this point the men of Benjamin became terrified, because they realized disaster was close at hand. 42So they turned around and fled before the Israelites toward the wilderness. But they couldn't escape the battle, and the people who came out of the nearby towns were also killed.* 43The Israelites surrounded the men of Benjamin and chased them relentlessly, finally overtaking them east of Gibeah.* 44That day 18,000 of Benjamin's strongest warriors died in battle. 45The survivors fled into the wilderness toward the rock of Rimmon, but Israel killed 5,000 of them along the road. They continued the chase until they had killed another 2,000 near Gidom.

46So that day the tribe of Benjamin lost 25,000 strong warriors armed with swords, 47leaving only 600 men who escaped to the rock of Rimmon, where they lived for four months. 48And the Israelites returned and slaughtered every living thing in all the towns—the people, the livestock, and everything they found. They also burned down all the towns they came to.

Israel Provides Wives for Benjamin

JUDGES 21:1-25

The Israelites had vowed at Mizpah, "We will never give our daughters in marriage to a man from the tribe of Benjamin." 2Now the people went to Bethel and sat in the presence of God until evening, weeping loudly and bitterly. 3"O Lord, God of Israel," they cried out, "why has this happened in Israel? Now one of our tribes is missing from Israel!"

4Early the next morning the people built an altar and presented their burnt offerings and peace offerings on it. 5Then they said, "Who among the tribes of Israel did not join us at Mizpah when we held our assembly in the presence of the Lord?" At that time they had taken a solemn oath in the Lord's presence, vowing that anyone who refused to come would be put to death.

6The Israelites felt sorry for their brother Benjamin and said, "Today one of the tribes of Israel has been cut off. 7How can we find wives for the few who remain, since we have sworn by the Lord not to give them our daughters in marriage?"

8So they asked, "Who among the tribes of Israel did not join us at Mizpah when we assembled in the presence of the Lord?" And they discovered that no one from Jabesh-gilead had attended the assembly.

Jgs 20:33 As in Greek and Syriac versions and Latin Vulgate; Hebrew reads *hiding in the open space.* **Jgs 20:42** Or *battle, for the people from the nearby towns also came out and killed them.* **Jgs 20:43** The meaning of the Hebrew is uncertain.

Judg 20:46-48 The effects of the horrible rape and murder should never have been felt outside the community where the crime happened. The local people should have brought the criminals to justice and corrected the laxness that originally permitted the crime. Instead, first the town and then the entire tribe defended this wickedness, even going to war over it.

To prevent unresolved problems from turning into major conflicts, firm action must be taken quickly, wisely, and forcefully before a situation gets out of hand.

Judg 20:48 The tribe of Benjamin eventually recovered from this slaughter. Saul, Israel's first king, was from this tribe (1 Sam 9:21). So were Queen Esther (Esth 2:5-7) and the apostle Paul (Rom 11:1). But the tribe was always known for being smaller than the rest (as in Ps 68:27).

Judg 21:8-12 The Israelites moved from one mess to another. Because of a rash vow made in the heat of emotion (Judg 21:5), here they destroyed another town. The Israelites probably justified their action with the following arguments: (1) An oath could not be broken, and they had vowed that anyone who did not help them fight the tribe of Benjamin would be killed. (2) Because all the women from Benjamin had been killed, the few remaining men needed wives to prevent the tribe from disappearing. To spare the unmarried women from Jabesh-gilead seemed the right solution.

We do not know all the circumstances behind the brutal massacre at Jabesh-gilead, but it seems that the rest of Israel followed Benjamin's pattern. They put tribal loyalties above God's commands, and they justified wrong actions to correct past mistakes.

9For after they counted all the people, no one from Jabesh-gilead was present.
10So the assembly sent 12,000 of their best warriors to Jabesh-gilead with orders to kill everyone there, including women and children. 11"This is what you are to do," they said. "Completely destroy* all the males and every woman who is not a virgin." 12Among the residents of Jabesh-gilead they found 400 young virgins who had never slept with a man, and they brought them to the camp at Shiloh in the land of Canaan.

13The Israelite assembly sent a peace delegation to the remaining people of Benjamin who were living at the rock of Rimmon. 14Then the men of Benjamin returned to their homes, and the 400 women of Jabesh-gilead who had been spared were given to them as wives. But there were not enough women for all of them.

15The people felt sorry for Benjamin because the LORD had made this gap among the tribes of Israel.
16So the elders of the assembly asked, "How can we find wives for the few who remain, since the women of the tribe of Benjamin are dead? 17There must be heirs for the survivors so that an entire tribe of Israel is not wiped out. 18But we cannot give them our own daughters in marriage because we have sworn with a solemn oath that anyone who does this will fall under God's curse."

19Then they thought of the annual festival of the LORD held in Shiloh, south of Lebonah and north of Bethel, along the east side of the road that goes from Bethel to Shechem. 20They told the men of Benjamin who still needed wives, "Go and hide in the vineyards.
21When you see the young women of Shiloh come out for their dances, rush out from the vineyards, and each of you can take one of them home to the land of Benjamin to be your wife! 22And when their fathers and brothers come to us in protest, we will tell them, 'Please be sympathetic. Let them have your daughters, for we didn't find wives for all of them when we destroyed Jabesh-gilead. And you are not guilty of breaking the vow since you did not actually give your daughters to them in marriage.'"

23So the men of Benjamin did as they were told. Each man caught one of the women as she danced in the celebration and carried her off to be his wife. They returned to their own land, and they rebuilt their towns and lived in them.

24Then the people of Israel departed by tribes and families, and they returned to their own homes.

25In those days Israel had no king; all the people did whatever seemed right in their own eyes.

Jgs 21:11 The Hebrew term used here refers to the complete consecration of things or people to the LORD, either by destroying them or by giving them as an offering.

G. The Story of Ruth: A Light in the Darkness

The period of the judges was not a time completely devoid of people who trusted God and followed him wholeheartedly. The book of Ruth gives us a glimpse into the lives of a few people who loved God and serve as a bright shining light in the midst of the darkness of this period of history. It might seem like nobody around you is following God, but you can be sure that he is active, even if you don't see it at first.

1. RUTH REMAINS LOYAL TO NAOMI

Ruth was from Moab, yet she showed her love for Naomi and the God of Israel by remaining faithful to her mother-in-law after the death of her husband. Ruth vowed to stay with Naomi and worship God alone.

Elimelech Moves His Family to Moab

RUTH 1:1-5

In the days when the judges ruled in Israel, a severe famine came upon the land. So a man from Bethlehem in Judah left his home and went to live in the country of Moab, taking his wife and two sons with him. 2The man's name was Elimelech, and his wife was Naomi. Their two sons were Mahlon and Kilion. They were

Judg 21:25 During the time of the judges, the people of Israel experienced trouble because they became their own authority and acted on their individual opinions of right and wrong. This produced horrendous results. Our world is similar. Individuals, groups, and societies have made themselves the final authorities without reference to God. When people selfishly satisfy their personal desires at all costs, everyone pays the price.

It is the ultimate heroic act to submit all our plans, desires, and motives to God. Men like Gideon, Jephthah, and Samson are known for their heroism in battle. But their personal lives were far from heroic.

To be truly heroic, we must go into battle each day—in the home, job, church, and society—to make God's Kingdom a reality. Our weapons are the standards, morals, truths, and convictions we receive from God's Word. We will lose the battle if we gather the spoils of earthly treasures rather than seeking the treasures of heaven.

Ruth 1:1 The story of Ruth takes place toward the end of the period of the rule of the judges. These were dark days for Israel, when "All the people did whatever seemed right in their own eyes" (Judg 17:6; 21:25). But during those dark and evil times, there were still some who followed God. Naomi and Ruth are beautiful examples of loyalty, friendship, and commitment—to God and to each other.

Ruth 1:1-2 Moab was the land east of the Dead Sea. It was one of the nations that oppressed Israel during the period of the judges (Judg 3:12ff), so there was hostility between the two nations. The famine must have been quite severe in Israel for Elimelech to move his family there. They were called Ephrathites because Ephrath was an earlier name for Bethlehem. Even if Israel had already defeated Moab, there still would have been tensions between them.

▸ **RUTH 1:1-5 *(cont.)***
Ephrathites from Bethlehem in the land of Judah. And
when they reached Moab, they settled there.
3 Then Elimelech died, and Naomi was left with her
two sons. 4 The two sons married Moabite women.
One married a woman named Orpah, and the other a
woman named Ruth. But about ten years later, 5 both
Mahlon and Kilion died. This left Naomi alone, without
her two sons or her husband.

Naomi and Ruth Return

RUTH 1:6-22
Then Naomi heard in Moab that the LORD had blessed
his people in Judah by giving them good crops again.
So Naomi and her daughters-in-law got ready to
leave Moab to return to her homeland. 7 With her two
daughters-in-law she set out from the place where she
had been living, and they took the road that would
lead them back to Judah.
8 But on the way, Naomi said to her two daughters-
in-law, "Go back to your mothers' homes. And may the
LORD reward you for your kindness to your husbands
and to me. 9 May the LORD bless you with the security
of another marriage." Then she kissed them good-bye,
and they all broke down and wept.
10 "No," they said. "We want to go with you to your
people."
11 But Naomi replied, "Why should you go on with
me? Can I still give birth to other sons who could grow
up to be your husbands? 12 No, my daughters, return to
your parents' homes, for I am too old to marry again.
And even if it were possible, and I were to get married
tonight and bear sons, then what? 13 Would you wait
for them to grow up and refuse to marry someone
else? No, of course not, my daughters! Things are far
more bitter for me than for you, because the LORD
himself has raised his fist against me."
14 And again they wept together, and Orpah kissed
her mother-in-law good-bye. But Ruth clung tightly
to Naomi. 15 "Look," Naomi said to her, "your sister-in-
law has gone back to her people and to her gods. You
should do the same."
16 But Ruth replied, "Don't ask me to leave you and
turn back. Wherever you go, I will go; wherever you
live, I will live. Your people will be my people, and
your God will be my God. 17 Wherever you die, I will
die, and there I will be buried. May the LORD punish
me severely if I allow anything but death to separate
us!" 18 When Naomi saw that Ruth was determined to
go with her, she said nothing more.
19 So the two of them continued on their journey.
When they came to Bethlehem, the entire town was
excited by their arrival. "Is it really Naomi?" the women
asked.

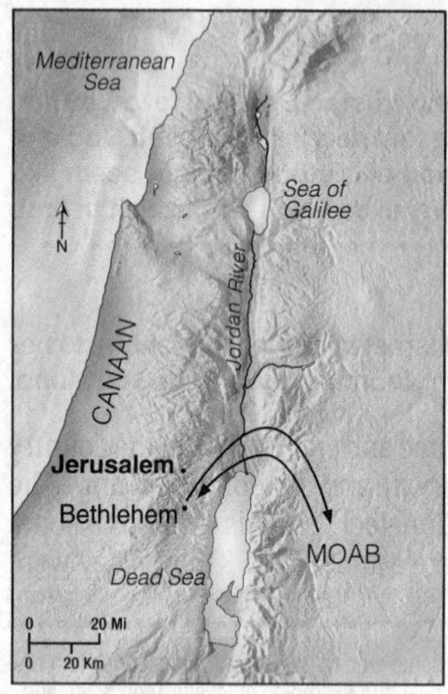

SETTING FOR THE STORY OF RUTH
Elimelech, Naomi, and their sons traveled from Bethlehem to Moab because of a famine. After her husband and sons died, Naomi returned to Bethlehem with her daughter-in-law Ruth.

Ruth 1:4-5 Friendly relations with the Moabites were discouraged (Deut 23:3-6) but probably not forbidden, since the Moabites lived outside the Promised Land. Marrying a Canaanite (or someone from any of the nations who previously lived within the borders of the Promised Land) was against God's law (Deut 7:1-4). Moabites were not allowed to worship at the Tabernacle because they had not let the Israelites pass through their land during the exodus from Egypt.

As God's chosen nation, Israel should have set the standards of high moral living for the other nations. Ironically it was Ruth, a Moabite, whom God used as an example of genuine spiritual character. This shows just how bleak life had become in Israel during those days.

Ruth 1:8-9 There was almost nothing worse than being a widow in the ancient world. Widows were taken advantage of or ignored. They were almost always poverty stricken. God's law, therefore, provided that the nearest relative of the dead husband should care for the widow. But Naomi had no relatives in Moab, and she didn't know if any of her husband's relatives were alive in Israel.

Even in her desperate situation, Naomi had a selfless attitude. Although she had decided to return to Israel, she encouraged Ruth and Orpah to stay in Moab and start their lives over, even though this would mean hardship for her. Like Naomi, we must consider the needs of others and not just our own. As Naomi discovered, when we act selflessly, others are encouraged to follow our example.

Ruth 1:11 Naomi's comment here ("sons who could grow up to be your husbands") refers to *levirate marriage,* the obligation of a dead man's brother to care for the widow (Deut 25:5-10). This law kept the widow from poverty and provided a way for the family name of the dead husband to continue.

Naomi had no other sons for Ruth or Orpah to marry, so she encouraged them to remain in their homeland and remarry. Orpah agreed, which was her right. But Ruth was willing to give up the possibility of security and children in order to care for Naomi.

Ruth 1:16 Ruth was a Moabite, but that didn't stop her from worshiping the true God, nor did it stop God from accepting her worship and blessing her greatly. The Jews were not the only people God loved. God chose the Jews to be the people through whom the rest of the world would come to know him. This was fulfilled when Jesus Christ was born as a Jew. Through him, the entire world can come to know God. Acts 10:35 says that "in every nation he accepts those who fear him and do what is right." God accepts all who worship him; he works through people regardless of their race, gender, or nationality. The book of Ruth is a perfect example of God's impartiality. Although Ruth belonged to a race often despised by Israel, she was blessed because of her faithfulness. She became a great-grandmother of King David and a direct ancestor of Jesus. No one should feel disqualified to serve God because of race, gender, or nationality. And God can use every circumstance to build his Kingdom.

Ruth 1:20-21 Naomi had experienced severe hardships. She had left Israel married and secure; she returned widowed and poor. Naomi changed her name to express the bitterness and pain she felt. Naomi was not rejecting God by openly expressing her pain. However, it seems she lost sight of the

20"Don't call me Naomi," she responded. "Instead, call me Mara,* for the Almighty has made life very bitter for me. 21 I went away full, but the LORD has brought me home empty. Why call me Naomi when the LORD has caused me to suffer* and the Almighty has sent such tragedy upon me?"

22So Naomi returned from Moab, accompanied by her daughter-in-law Ruth, the young Moabite woman. They arrived in Bethlehem in late spring, at the beginning of the barley harvest.

Ru 1:20 *Naomi* means "pleasant"; *Mara* means "bitter." **Ru 1:21** Or *has testified against me.*

2. RUTH AND BOAZ

God showed himself faithful by providing Boaz to keep the family line of Elimelech intact. Boaz treated Ruth with compassion when she and Naomi needed food, and he took her as his wife. Their marriage resulted in a child, who would be the grandfather of David—Israel's greatest king.

Ruth Gleans in Boaz's Field

RUTH 2:1-23

Now there was a wealthy and influential man in Bethlehem named Boaz, who was a relative of Naomi's husband, Elimelech.

2One day Ruth the Moabite said to Naomi, "Let me go out into the harvest fields to pick up the stalks of grain left behind by anyone who is kind enough to let me do it."

Naomi replied, "All right, my daughter, go ahead."

RUTH & NAOMI

The stories of several people in the Bible are woven together so closely that they are almost inseparable. We know more about their relationship than we know about them as individuals. And in an age that worships individualism, their stories become helpful models of good relationships. Naomi and Ruth are a beautiful example of this blending of lives. Their cultures, family backgrounds, and ages were very different. As mother-in-law and daughter-in-law, they probably had as many opportunities for tension as for tenderness. And yet they were bound to each other. • They shared deep sorrow, great affection for each other, and an overriding commitment to the God of Israel. And yet, as much as they depended on each other, they also gave each other freedom in their commitment to one another. Naomi was willing to let Ruth return to her family. Ruth was willing to leave her homeland to go to Israel. Naomi even helped arrange Ruth's marriage to Boaz although it would change their relationship. • God was at the center of their intimate communication. Ruth came to know the God of Israel through Naomi. The older woman allowed Ruth to see, hear, and feel all the joy and anguish of her relationship with God. How often do you feel that your thoughts and questions about God should be left out of a close relationship? How often do you share your unedited thoughts about God with your spouse or friends? Sharing openly about our relationship with God can bring depth and intimacy to our relationships with others.

Strengths and accomplishments	• Had a relationship where the greatest bond was faith in God • Had a relationship of strong mutual commitment • Had a relationship in which each person tried to do what was best for the other
Lesson from their lives	• God's living presence in a relationship overcomes differences that might otherwise create division and disharmony
Vital statistics	• Where: Moab, Bethlehem • Occupation: Wives, widows • Relatives: Naomi's husband: Elimelech. Naomi's sons: Mahlon, Kilion. Naomi's other daughter-in-law: Orpah. Ruth's second husband: Boaz. Ruth's son: Obed.
Key verses	"But Ruth replied, 'Don't ask me to leave you and turn back. Wherever you go, I will go; wherever you live, I will live. Your people will be my people, and your God will be my God. Wherever you die, I will die, and there I will be buried. May the LORD punish me severely if I allow anything but death to separate us!'" (Ruth 1:16-17).

Their story is told in the book of Ruth. Ruth is also mentioned in Matthew 1:5.

tremendous resources she had in her relationship with Ruth and with God. When you face bitter times, God welcomes your honest prayers, but be careful not to overlook the love, strength, and resources that he provides in your present relationships. And don't allow bitterness and disappointment to blind you to your opportunities.

Ruth 1:22 Bethlehem was about five miles southwest of Jerusalem. The town was surrounded by lush fields and olive groves. Its harvests were abundant.

Ruth and Naomi's return to Bethlehem was certainly part of God's plan because in this town David would be born (1 Sam 16:1). As predicted by the prophet Micah (Mic 5:2), Jesus Christ would also be born there. This move, then, was more than mere convenience for Ruth and Naomi. It led to the fulfillment of Scripture.

Ruth 1:22 Because Israel's climate is moderate, there are two harvests each year, in the spring and in the fall. The barley harvest took place in the spring, and it was during this time of hope and plenty that Ruth and Naomi returned to Bethlehem. Bethlehem was a farming community, and because it was the time of the harvest, there was plenty of leftover grain in the fields. This grain could be collected, or gleaned, and then made into food.

Ruth 2:2 When the wheat and barley were ready to be harvested, harvesters were hired to cut down the stalks and tie them into bundles. Israelite law demanded that the corners of the fields not be harvested. In addition, any grain that was dropped was to be left for poor people, who picked it up (this was called *gleaning*) and used it for food (Lev 19:9; 23:22; Deut 24:19). The purpose of this law was to feed the poor and to prevent the owners from hoarding. This law served as a type of welfare program in Israel. Because she was a widow with no means of providing for herself, Ruth went into the fields to glean the grain.

▸ **RUTH 2:1-23 *(cont.)***

3 So Ruth went out to gather grain behind the harvesters. And as it happened, she found herself working in a field that belonged to Boaz, the relative of her father-in-law, Elimelech.

4 While she was there, Boaz arrived from Bethlehem and greeted the harvesters. "The LORD be with you!" he said.

"The LORD bless you!" the harvesters replied.

5 Then Boaz asked his foreman, "Who is that young woman over there? Who does she belong to?"

6 And the foreman replied, "She is the young woman from Moab who came back with Naomi.
7 She asked me this morning if she could gather grain behind the harvesters. She has been hard at work ever since, except for a few minutes' rest in the shelter."

8 Boaz went over and said to Ruth, "Listen, my daughter. Stay right here with us when you gather grain; don't go to any other fields. Stay right behind the young women working in my field.
9 See which part of the field they are harvesting, and then follow them. I have warned the young men not to treat you roughly. And when you are thirsty, help yourself to the water they have drawn from the well."

10 Ruth fell at his feet and thanked him warmly. "What have I done to deserve such kindness?" she asked. "I am only a foreigner."

11 "Yes, I know," Boaz replied. "But I also know about everything you have done for your mother-in-law since the death of your husband. I have heard how you left your father and mother and your own land to live here among complete strangers.
12 May the LORD, the God of Israel, under whose wings you have come to take refuge, reward you fully for what you have done."

13 "I hope I continue to please you, sir," she replied. "You have comforted me by speaking so kindly to me, even though I am not one of your workers."

14 At mealtime Boaz called to her, "Come over here, and help yourself to some food. You can dip your bread in the sour wine." So she sat with his harvesters, and Boaz gave her some roasted grain to eat. She ate all she wanted and still had some left over.

Ruth 2:2-3 Ruth made her home in a foreign land. Instead of depending on Naomi or waiting for good fortune to happen, she took the initiative. She went to work. She was not afraid of admitting her need or working hard to supply it. When Ruth went out to the fields, God provided for her. If you are waiting for God to provide, consider this: He may be waiting for you to take the first step to demonstrate just how important your need is.

Ruth 2:7 Ruth's task, though menial, tiring, and perhaps degrading, was done faithfully. What is your attitude when the task you have been given is not up to your true potential? The task at hand may be all you can do, or it may be the work God wants you to do. Or, as in Ruth's case, it may be a test of your character that can open up new doors of opportunity.

Ruth 2:10-12 Ruth's life exhibited admirable qualities: She was hardworking, loving, kind, faithful, and brave. These qualities gained for her a good reputation, but only because she displayed them consistently in all areas of her life. Wherever Ruth went or whatever she did, her character remained the same.

Your reputation is formed by the people who watch you at work, in town, at home, in church. A good reputation comes by consistently living out the qualities you believe in—no matter what group of people or surroundings you are in.

BOAZ

Heroes are easier to admire than to define. They are seldom conscious of their moments of heroism, and others may not recognize their acts as heroic. Heroes simply do the right thing at the right time, whether or not they realize the impact their action will have. Perhaps the one quality they share is a tendency to think of others before they think of themselves. • Boaz was a hero. • In his dealings with other people, he was always sensitive to their needs. His words to his employees, relatives, and others were colored with kindness. He offered help openly, not grudgingly. When he discovered who Ruth was, he took several steps to help her because she had been faithful to his relative Naomi. When Naomi advised Ruth to request his protection, he was ready to marry her if the legal complications could be worked out. • Boaz not only did what was right, he also did it right away. Of course he could not foresee all that his actions would accomplish. He could not have known that the child he would have by Ruth would be an ancestor of both David and Jesus. He only met the challenge of taking the right action in the situation facing him. • We are faced with this challenge in our daily choices. Like Naomi's nearer relative, we are often more concerned with making the easy choice than with making the right one. Yet more often than not, the right choice is clear. Ask God to give you a special awareness in your choices today as well as renewed commitment to make the right ones.

Strengths and accomplishments	• A man of his word • Sensitive to those in need, caring for his workers • A keen sense of responsibility, integrity • A successful and shrewd businessman
Lessons from his life	• It can be heroic to do what must be done and to do it right • God often uses little decisions to carry out his big plan
Vital statistics	• Where: Bethlehem • Occupation: Wealthy farmer • Relatives: Distant cousins: Elimelech, Naomi. Wife: Ruth. Son: Obed.
Key verse:	"I have acquired Ruth, the Moabite widow of Mahlon, to be my wife. This way she can have a son to carry on the family name of her dead husband and to inherit the family property here in his hometown. You are all witnesses today" (Ruth 4:10).

Boaz's story is told in the book of Ruth. He is also mentioned in Matthew 1:5.

15 When Ruth went back to work again, Boaz ordered his young men, "Let her gather grain right
among the sheaves without stopping her. 16 And pull
out some heads of barley from the bundles and drop
them on purpose for her. Let her pick them up, and
don't give her a hard time!"

17 So Ruth gathered barley there all day, and when
she beat out the grain that evening, it filled an entire
basket.* 18 She carried it back into town and showed
it to her mother-in-law. Ruth also gave her the roasted
grain that was left over from her meal.

19 "Where did you gather all this grain today?" Naomi asked. "Where did you work? May the LORD bless
the one who helped you!"

So Ruth told her mother-in-law about the man in
whose field she had worked. She said, "The man I
worked with today is named Boaz."

20 "May the LORD bless him!" Naomi told her
daughter-in-law. "He is showing his kindness to us
as well as to your dead husband.* That man is one of
our closest relatives, one of our family redeemers."

21 Then Ruth* said, "What's more, Boaz even told
me to come back and stay with his harvesters until
the entire harvest is completed."

22 "Good!" Naomi exclaimed. "Do as he said, my
daughter. Stay with his young women right through
the whole harvest. You might be harassed in other
fields, but you'll be safe with him."

23 So Ruth worked alongside the women in Boaz's
fields and gathered grain with them until the end of
the barley harvest. Then she continued working with
them through the wheat harvest in early summer. And
all the while she lived with her mother-in-law.

Ruth Follows Naomi's Plan

RUTH 3:1-18

One day Naomi said to Ruth, "My daughter, it's time
that I found a permanent home for you, so that you will

Ru 2:17 Hebrew *it was about an ephah* [20 quarts or 22 liters]. **Ru 2:20** Hebrew *to the living and to the dead.* **Ru 2:21** Hebrew *Ruth the Moabite.*

Ruth 2:15-16 The characters in the book of Ruth are classic examples of good people in action. Boaz went far beyond the intent of the gleaners' law in demonstrating his kindness and generosity. Not only did he let Ruth glean in his field, he also told his workers to let some of the grain fall in her path. Out of his abundance he provided for the needy. How often do you go beyond the accepted patterns of providing for those less fortunate? Do more than the minimum for others.

Ruth 2:19-20 Naomi had felt bitter (Ruth 1:20-21), but her faith in God was still alive, and she praised God for Boaz's kindness to Ruth. In her sorrows she still trusted God and acknowledged his goodness. We may feel bitter about a situation, but we must never despair. Today is always a new opportunity for experiencing God's care. (For more on a family redeemer, see the note on Ruth 3:1-9, below.)

Ruth 2:20 Though Ruth may not have always recognized God's guidance, he had been with her every step of the way. She went to glean and "just happened" to end up in the field owned by Boaz who "just happened" to be a close relative. This was more than mere coincidence. As you go about your daily tasks, God is working in your life in ways you may not even notice. We must not close the door on what God can do. Events do not occur by luck or coincidence. We should have faith that God is directing our lives for his purpose.

Ruth 3:1-9 As widows, Ruth and Naomi could only look forward to difficult times. (For more on a widow's life, see the note on Ruth 1:8-9, p. 410.) But when Naomi heard the news about Boaz, her hope for the future was renewed. Typical of her character, she thought first of Ruth, encouraging her to see if Boaz would take the responsibility of being the "family redeemer" (Ruth 2:20).

A family redeemer was a relative who volunteered to take responsibility for the extended family. When a woman's husband died, the law (Deut 25:5-10) provided that she could marry a brother of her dead husband. But Naomi had no more sons. In such a case, the nearest relative to the deceased husband could become a family redeemer and marry the widow. The nearest relative did not have to marry the widow. If he chose not to, the next nearest relative could take his place. If no one chose to help the widow, she would probably live in poverty the rest of her life, because in Israelite culture the inheritance was passed on to the son or nearest male relative, not to the wife. The laws for gleaning and family redeemers helped to take the sting out of these inheritance rules.

We have a family redeemer in Jesus Christ who, though he was God, came to earth as a man in order to save us. By his death on the cross, he has redeemed us from sin and hopelessness and has thereby purchased us to be his own possession (1 Pet 1:18-19). This guarantees our eternal inheritance.

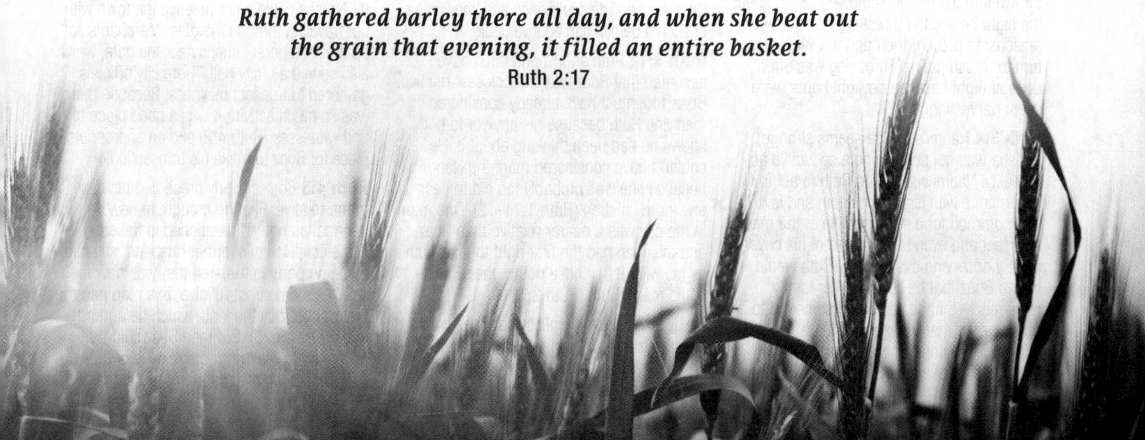

Ruth gathered barley there all day, and when she beat out the grain that evening, it filled an entire basket.
Ruth 2:17

▸ **RUTH 3:1-18** ***(cont.)***

be provided for. 2 Boaz is a close relative of ours, and he's been very kind by letting you gather grain with his young women. Tonight he will be winnowing barley at the threshing floor. 3 Now do as I tell you—take a bath and put on perfume and dress in your nicest clothes. Then go to the threshing floor, but don't let Boaz see you until he has finished eating and drinking. 4 Be sure to notice where he lies down; then go and uncover his feet and lie down there. He will tell you what to do."

5 "I will do everything you say," Ruth replied. 6 So she went down to the threshing floor that night and followed the instructions of her mother-in-law.

7 After Boaz had finished eating and drinking and was in good spirits, he lay down at the far end of the pile of grain and went to sleep. Then Ruth came quietly, uncovered his feet, and lay down. 8 Around midnight Boaz suddenly woke up and turned over. He was surprised to find a woman lying at his feet! 9 "Who are you?" he asked.

"I am your servant Ruth," she replied. "Spread the corner of your covering over me, for you are my family redeemer."

10 "The LORD bless you, my daughter!" Boaz exclaimed. "You are showing even more family loyalty now than you did before, for you have not gone after a younger man, whether rich or poor. 11 Now don't worry about a thing, my daughter. I will do what is necessary, for everyone in town knows you are a virtuous woman. 12 But while it's true that I am one of your family redeemers, there is another man who is more closely related to you than I am. 13 Stay here tonight, and in the morning I will talk to him. If he is willing to redeem you, very well. Let him marry you. But if he is not willing, then as surely as the LORD lives, I will redeem you myself! Now lie down here until morning."

14 So Ruth lay at Boaz's feet until the morning, but she got up before it was light enough for people to recognize each other. For Boaz had said, "No one must know that a woman was here at the threshing floor." 15 Then Boaz said to her, "Bring your cloak and spread it out." He measured six scoops* of barley into the cloak and placed it on her back. Then he* returned to the town.

16 When Ruth went back to her mother-in-law, Naomi asked, "What happened, my daughter?"

Ruth told Naomi everything Boaz had done for her, 17 and she added, "He gave me these six scoops of barley and said, 'Don't go back to your mother-in-law empty-handed.'"

18 Then Naomi said to her, "Just be patient, my daughter, until we hear what happens. The man won't rest until he has settled things today."

Boaz Arranges to Marry Ruth

RUTH 4:1-12

Boaz went to the town gate and took a seat there. Just then the family redeemer he had mentioned came by, so Boaz called out to him, "Come over here and sit down, friend. I want to talk to you." So they sat down together. 2 Then Boaz called ten leaders from the town and asked them to sit as witnesses. 3 And Boaz said to the family redeemer, "You know Naomi, who came back from Moab. She is selling the land

Ru 3:15a Hebrew *six measures*, an unknown quantity. **Ru 3:15b** Most Hebrew manuscripts read *he;* many Hebrew manuscripts, Syriac version, and Latin Vulgate read *she.*

Ruth 3:2 The threshing floor was the place where the grain was separated from the harvested stalks. The stalks were crushed, either by hand or by oxen, and the valuable grain (inner kernels) then separated from the worthless chaff (the outside shell). The floor was made from rock or soil and located outside the village, usually on an elevated site where the winds would blow away the lighter chaff when the crushed wheat was thrown into the air (or winnowed). Boaz spent the night beside the threshing floor for two reasons: to prevent theft and to wait for his turn to thresh grain. (Threshing was often done at night because daylight hours were spent harvesting.)

Ruth 3:4 Naomi's advice seems strange, but she was not suggesting a seductive act. In reality, Naomi was telling Ruth to act in accordance with Israelite custom and law. It was common for a servant to lie at the master's feet and even share a part of his covering. By observing this custom, Ruth would inform Boaz that he could be her family redeemer—that he could find someone to marry her or marry her himself. It was family business, nothing romantic. But the story later became beautifully romantic as Ruth and Boaz developed an unselfish love and deep respect for each other.

Ruth 3:5 As a foreigner, Ruth may have thought that Naomi's advice was odd. But Ruth followed the advice because she knew Naomi was kind, trustworthy, and filled with moral integrity. Each of us knows a parent, older friend, or relative who is always looking out for our best interests. Be willing to listen to the advice of a person who is older and wiser than you are. The experience and knowledge of such a person can be invaluable.

Ruth 3:12 Ruth and Naomi must have assumed that Boaz was their closest relative. Boaz, too, must have already considered marrying Ruth because his answer to her shows he had been thinking about it. He couldn't have considered marrying Naomi because she was probably too old to bear any more children (Ruth 1:11-12). One man in the city was a nearer relative than Boaz, and this man had the first right to take Ruth as his wife. If he chose not to, then Boaz could marry Ruth (Ruth 3:13).

Ruth 3:18 Naomi implied that Boaz would follow through with his promise at once. He obviously had a reputation for keeping his word and would not rest until his task was completed. Such reliable people stand out in any age and culture. Do others regard you as one who will do what you say? Keeping your word and following through on assignments should be high on anyone's priority list. But building a reputation for integrity must be done one brick—one act—at a time.

Ruth 4:1 Boaz knew he could find his relative at the town gate. This was the center of activity. No one could enter or leave the town without traveling through the gate. Merchants set up their temporary shops near the gate, which also served as "city hall." Here city officials gathered to transact business. Because there was so much activity, it was a good place to find witnesses (Ruth 4:2) and an appropriate place for Boaz to make his transaction.

Ruth 4:3 Boaz cleverly presented his case to the relative. First he brought in new information not yet mentioned in the story—Elimelech, Naomi's former husband, still had some property in the area that was now for sale. As the nearest relative, this man had the first right to buy the land, which he agreed to do (Lev 25:25). But then Boaz said that according to the law, if the relative bought the property he also had to marry the widow

that belonged to our relative Elimelech. 4I thought I
should speak to you about it so that you can redeem
it if you wish. If you want the land, then buy it here in
the presence of these witnesses. But if you don't want
it, let me know right away, because I am next in line to
redeem it after you."
The man replied, "All right, I'll redeem it."
5Then Boaz told him, "Of course, your purchase
of the land from Naomi also requires that you marry
Ruth, the Moabite widow. That way she can have children who will carry on her husband's name and keep
the land in the family."
6"Then I can't redeem it," the family redeemer replied, "because this might endanger my own estate.
You redeem the land; I cannot do it."
7Now in those days it was the custom in Israel for
anyone transferring a right of purchase to remove
his sandal and hand it to the other party. This publicly validated the transaction. 8So the other family
redeemer drew off his sandal as he said to Boaz, "You
buy the land."
9Then Boaz said to the elders and to the crowd
standing around, "You are witnesses that today I have
bought from Naomi all the property of Elimelech, Kilion, and Mahlon. 10And with the land I have acquired
Ruth, the Moabite widow of Mahlon, to be my wife.
This way she can have a son to carry on the family
name of her dead husband and to inherit the family
property here in his hometown. You are all witnesses
today."
11Then the elders and all the people standing in
the gate replied, "We are witnesses! May the LORD
make this woman who is coming into your home like
Rachel and Leah, from whom all the nation of Israel
descended! May you prosper in Ephrathah and be famous in Bethlehem. 12And may the LORD give you descendants by this young woman who will be like those
of our ancestor Perez, the son of Tamar and Judah."

The Descendants of Boaz

RUTH 4:13-22

So Boaz took Ruth into his home, and she became
his wife. When he slept with her, the LORD enabled
her to become pregnant, and she gave birth to a son.
14Then the women of the town said to Naomi, "Praise
the LORD, who has now provided a redeemer for your
family! May this child be famous in Israel. 15May he
restore your youth and care for you in your old age. For
he is the son of your daughter-in-law who loves you
and has been better to you than seven sons!"
16Naomi took the baby and cuddled him to her
breast. And she cared for him as if he were her own.
17The neighbor women said, "Now at last Naomi has
a son again!" And they named him Obed. He became
the father of Jesse and the grandfather of David.
18This is the genealogical record of their ancestor
Perez:

Perez was the father of Hezron.
19 Hezron was the father of Ram.
Ram was the father of Amminadab.
20 Amminadab was the father of Nahshon.
Nahshon was the father of Salmon.*
21 Salmon was the father of Boaz.
Boaz was the father of Obed.
22 Obed was the father of Jesse.
Jesse was the father of David.

Ru 4:20 As in some Greek manuscripts (see also 4:21); Hebrew reads *Salma*.

(probably because Mahlon, Ruth's former husband and Elimelech's son, had inherited the property). At this stipulation, the relative backed down. He did not want to complicate his inheritance. Whatever his reason, the way was now clear for Boaz to marry Ruth.

Ruth 4:15 Ruth's love for her mother-in-law was known and recognized throughout the town. From the beginning of the book of Ruth to the end, Ruth's kindness toward others remained unchanged.

Ruth 4:15 God brought great blessings out of Naomi's tragedy, even greater than "seven sons." Throughout her tough times, Naomi continued to trust God. And God, in his time, blessed her greatly. Even in our sorrow and calamity, God can bring great blessings. Instead of asking, "How can God allow this to happen to me?"—trust him. He will be with you in the hard times.

Ruth 4:16-17 To some, the book of Ruth may be just a nice story about a girl who was fortunate. But in reality, the events recorded in Ruth were part of God's preparations for the births of David and of Jesus, the promised Messiah. Just as Ruth was unaware of this larger purpose in her life, we will not know the full purpose and importance of our lives until we are able to look back from the perspective of eternity. We must make our choices with God's eternal values in mind. Taking moral shortcuts and living for short-range pleasures are not good ways to move ahead. Because of Ruth's faithful obedience, her life and legacy were significant even though she couldn't see all the results. Live in faithfulness to God, knowing that the significance of your life will extend beyond your lifetime. The rewards will outweigh any sacrifice you may have made.

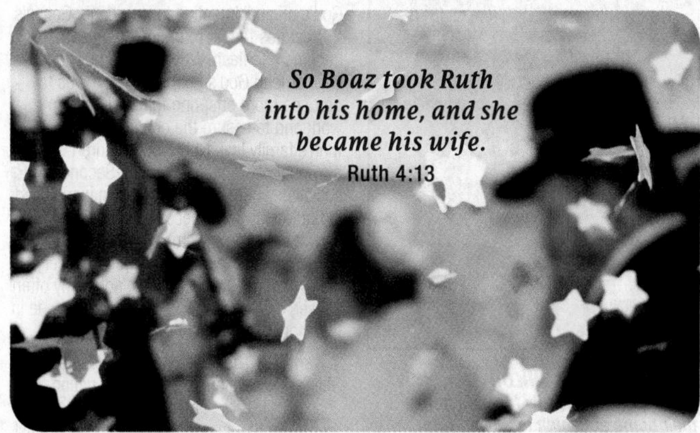
So Boaz took Ruth
into his home, and she
became his wife.
Ruth 4:13

H. Samuel: Israel's Final Judge

Israel has been ruled by judges for around 300 years. Samuel was the last of those judges. Samuel grew up in the Tabernacle as a priest-in-training under Eli and was well qualified to serve Israel as both a priest and a judge. Although the nation had fallen away from God, it is clear that God is preparing Samuel from the very beginning to lead the nation back to right living. God is always in control; he is able to bring his people back to him.

1. SAMUEL'S BIRTH AND CHILDHOOD

Samuel was a special child, a gift from God to a barren woman who was set apart to serve God from the time he was just a child. He showed himself to be more faithful even than the high priest and his sons, so God spoke with him directly.

Elkanah and His Family

1 SAMUEL 1:1-8

There was a man named Elkanah who lived in Ramah
in the region of Zuph* in the hill country of Ephraim.
He was the son of Jeroham, son of Elihu, son of Tohu,
son of Zuph, of Ephraim. [2]Elkanah had two wives,
Hannah and Peninnah. Peninnah had children, but
Hannah did not.
[3]Each year Elkanah would travel to Shiloh to worship and sacrifice to the LORD of Heaven's Armies at
the Tabernacle. The priests of the LORD at that time
were the two sons of Eli—Hophni and Phinehas. [4]On
the days Elkanah presented his sacrifice, he would
give portions of the meat to Peninnah and each of
her children. [5]And though he loved Hannah, he would
give her only one choice portion* because the LORD
had given her no children. [6]So Peninnah would taunt
Hannah and make fun of her because the LORD had
kept her from having children. [7]Year after year it was
the same—Peninnah would taunt Hannah as they went
to the Tabernacle.* Each time, Hannah would be reduced to tears and would not even eat.
[8]"Why are you crying, Hannah?" Elkanah would
ask. "Why aren't you eating? Why be downhearted
just because you have no children? You have me—isn't
that better than having ten sons?"

1 Sm 1:1 As in Greek version; Hebrew reads *in Ramathaim-zophim;* compare 1:19. The meaning of the Hebrew is uncertain. **1 Sm 1:5** Or *And because he loved Hannah, he would give her a choice portion.* **1 Sm 1:7** Hebrew *the house of the LORD;* also in 1:24.

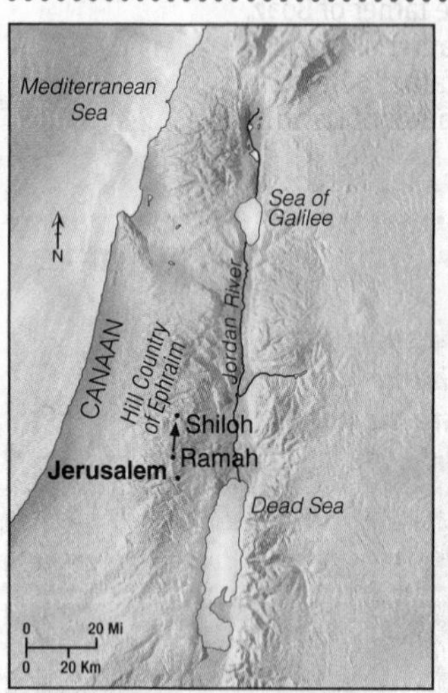

***THE JOURNEY TO SHILOH** Each year Elkanah and his family traveled from their home at Ramah to Shiloh, where they worshiped and sacrificed at God's Tabernacle.*

1 Sam 1:1 The book of 1 Samuel begins in the days when the judges still ruled Israel. Samuel was Israel's last judge and the first priest and prophet to serve during the time of a king. He was the best example of what a good judge should be, governing the people by God's word and not by his own impulses. Samuel was the man who anointed Saul as Israel's first king.

1 Sam 1:2 Although many great Old Testament leaders (such as Abraham, Jacob, and David) had more than one wife, this was not God's original intention for marriage. Genesis 2:24 states that in marriage, two people become one flesh. Why then did polygamy exist among God's people? First, it was to produce more offspring to help in a man's work and to assure the continuation of a man's family line. Numerous children were a symbol of status and wealth. Second, in societies where many young men were killed in battle, polygamy became an accepted way of supporting women who otherwise would have remained unmarried and, very likely, destitute. Nevertheless, polygamy often caused serious family problems, as we see in this story of Hannah and Peninnah.

1 Sam 1:3 The Tabernacle was located at Shiloh, the religious center of the nation (see Josh 18:1). Three times a year all Israelite men were required to attend a religious feast held at the Tabernacle: the Passover with the Festival of Unleavened Bread, the Festival of Harvest, and the Festival of Shelters (Deut 16:16). Elkanah made this pilgrimage regularly to fulfill God's commands. (See Exod 23:14-17 for the regulations concerning the pilgrimage, and see the note on Exodus 40:34, p. 196, for more on the Tabernacle.)

1 Sam 1:6 Hannah had been unable to conceive children, and in Old Testament times, a childless woman was considered a failure. Her barrenness was a social embarrassment for her husband. Children were a very important part of the society's economic structure. They were a source of labor for the family, and it was their duty to care for their parents in their old age. If a wife could not bear children, she was often obligated by ancient Middle Eastern custom to give one of her servant girls to her husband to bear children for her. Although Elkanah could have left Hannah (a husband was permitted to divorce a barren wife), he remained lovingly devoted to her despite social criticism and his rights under civil law.

1 Sam 1:7 Part of God's plan for Hannah involved postponing her years of childbearing. While Peninnah and Elkanah looked at Hannah's outward circumstances, God was moving ahead with his plan. Think of those in your world who are struggling with God's timing in answering their prayers and who need your love and help. By supporting those who are struggling, you may help them remain steadfast in their faith and confident in his timing to bring fulfillment to their lives.

1 Sam 1:8 Hannah knew her husband loved her, but even his encouragement could not comfort her. She could not keep from listening to Peninnah's jeers and letting the words erode her self-confidence. Although we cannot keep others from unjustly criticizing us,

Hannah's Prayer for a Son

1 SAMUEL 1:9-18

Once after a sacrificial meal at Shiloh, Hannah got up and went to pray. Eli the priest was sitting at his customary place beside the entrance of the Tabernacle.*
10 Hannah was in deep anguish, crying bitterly as she prayed to the LORD. 11 And she made this vow: "O LORD of Heaven's Armies, if you will look upon my sorrow and answer my prayer and give me a son, then I will give him back to you. He will be yours for his entire lifetime, and as a sign that he has been dedicated to the LORD, his hair will never be cut.*"
12 As she was praying to the LORD, Eli watched her.
13 Seeing her lips moving but hearing no sound, he thought she had been drinking. 14 "Must you come here drunk?" he demanded. "Throw away your wine!"
15 "Oh no, sir!" she replied. "I haven't been drinking wine or anything stronger. But I am very discouraged, and I was pouring out my heart to the LORD. 16 Don't think I am a wicked woman! For I have been praying out of great anguish and sorrow."
17 "In that case," Eli said, "go in peace! May the God of Israel grant the request you have asked of him."
18 "Oh, thank you, sir!" she exclaimed. Then she went back and began to eat again, and she was no longer sad.

1 Sm 1:9 Hebrew *the Temple of the LORD.* **1 Sm 1:11** Some manuscripts add *He will drink neither wine nor intoxicants.*

ELKANAH & PENINNAH

Husbands can be insensitive for many reasons, but often they simply suffer from ignorance. Elkanah had two wives, which doubled his opportunities to be insensitive. His wife Peninnah was able to give Elkanah many children. His other wife, Hannah, owned Elkanah's heart but was unable to get pregnant. Peninnah, jealous that providing Elkanah with heirs didn't turn his affections toward her, treated Hannah with disdain. Yet Elkanah seemed oblivious to the turmoil around him. Elkanah didn't realize that maybe a little attention toward Peninnah could have cooled the simmering emotions in his home. Nor did he understand that his love for Hannah didn't make up for the emptiness of her womb. • Although the events leading up to the birth of Samuel primarily involved Hannah, both Elkanah and Peninnah played significant roles. Peninnah's competitiveness and derision drove Hannah to prayer; Elkanah's simple love allowed Hannah to entrust their child Samuel into God's care. • The glimpse God gives us of that tense household provides a helpful backdrop for God's purposes, which are not thwarted by human shortcomings. He worked within the strain and stress of those relationships to bring Samuel into the world—one of the most significant figures in the Old Testament. When our relational systems seem too gnarled to be unraveled or salvaged, we need to remember that God is able to bring order and beauty out of even the biggest messes.

Strengths and accomplishments	• Elkanah supported Hannah's decision to leave Samuel in Shiloh to be raised as a priest • Regular trips to Shiloh acknowledged God's importance to the entire family
Weaknesses and mistakes	• Elkanah did not understand what would have helped each of his wives • Peninnah made things worse by taking out her disappointment and anger on Hannah
Lessons from their lives	• Ignorance is not an excuse for insensitivity • Jealousy is not an excuse for bad behavior • God works in the middle of family messes
Vital statistics	• Where: Ramah • Occupation: Unknown • Relatives: Elkanah and Peninnah had an unknown number of children; Elkanah and Hannah bore two daughters and four sons, including Samuel • Contemporary: Eli the priest
Key verse	"'Why are you crying, Hannah?' Elkanah would ask. 'Why aren't you eating? Why be downhearted just because you have no children? You have me—isn't that better than having ten sons?'" (1 Sam 1:8).

Their story is told in 1 Samuel 1–2.

we can choose how we will respond to their hurtful words. Rather than dwelling upon our problems, we can enjoy the loving relationships God has given us. By so doing, we can exchange self-pity for hope.

1 Sam 1:10 Hannah had good reason to feel discouraged and bitter. She was unable to bear children; she shared her husband with a woman who ridiculed her (1 Sam 1:7); her loving husband could not solve her problem (1 Sam 1:8); and even the high priest misunderstood her motives (1 Sam 1:14). But instead of retaliating or giving up hope, Hannah prayed. She brought her problem honestly before God.

Each of us may face times of barrenness when nothing "comes to birth" in our work, service, or relationships. It is difficult to pray in faith when we feel so ineffective. But, as Hannah discovered, prayer opens the way for God to work (1 Sam 1:19-20).

1 Sam 1:11 Be careful what you promise in prayer because God may take you up on it. Hannah so desperately wanted a child that she was willing to strike a bargain with God. God took her up on her promise, and to Hannah's credit, she did her part, even though it was painful (1 Sam 1:27-28).

Although we are not in a position to barter with God, he may still choose to answer a prayer that has an attached promise. When you pray, ask yourself, *Will I follow through on any promises I make to God if he grants my request?* It is dishonest and dangerous to ignore a promise, especially to God. God keeps his promises, and he expects you to keep yours.

1 Sam 1:18 Earlier Hannah had been discouraged to the point of being physically sick and unable to eat. At this point, she returned home well and happy. The change in her attitude may be attributed to three factors: She honestly prayed to God (1 Sam 1:11); she received encouragement from Eli (1 Sam 1:17); and she resolved to leave the problem with God (1 Sam 1:18). This is the cure for discouragement: Tell God how you really feel and leave your problems with him. Then rely upon the support of good friends and counselors.

Samuel is born

Samuel's Birth and Dedication

1 SAMUEL 1:19-28

The entire family got up early the next morning and
went to worship the LORD once more. Then they returned home to Ramah. When Elkanah slept with
Hannah, the LORD remembered her plea, 20 and in due
time she gave birth to a son. She named him Samuel,*
for she said, "I asked the LORD for him."
21 The next year Elkanah and his family went on
their annual trip to offer a sacrifice to the LORD. 22 But
Hannah did not go. She told her husband, "Wait until
the boy is weaned. Then I will take him to the Tabernacle and leave him there with the LORD permanently.*"
23 "Whatever you think is best," Elkanah agreed.
"Stay here for now, and may the LORD help you keep
your promise." So she stayed home and nursed the
boy until he was weaned.
24 When the child was weaned, Hannah took him
to the Tabernacle in Shiloh. They brought along a
three-year-old bull* for the sacrifice and a basket* of
flour and some wine. 25 After sacrificing the bull, they
brought the boy to Eli. 26 "Sir, do you remember me?"
Hannah asked. "I am the woman who stood here several years ago praying to the LORD. 27 I asked the LORD
to give me this boy, and he has granted my request.
28 Now I am giving him to the LORD, and he will belong
to the LORD his whole life." And they* worshiped the
LORD there.

Hannah's Prayer of Praise

1 SAMUEL 2:1-11

Then Hannah prayed:

"My heart rejoices in the LORD!
The LORD has made me strong.*
Now I have an answer for my enemies;
I rejoice because you rescued me.
2 No one is holy like the LORD!
There is no one besides you;
there is no Rock like our God.
3 "Stop acting so proud and haughty!
Don't speak with such arrogance!
For the LORD is a God who knows what
you have done;
he will judge your actions.
4 The bow of the mighty is now broken,
and those who stumbled are now strong.
5 Those who were well fed are now starving,
and those who were starving are now full.
The childless woman now has seven children,
and the woman with many children
wastes away.
6 The LORD gives both death and life;
he brings some down to the grave* but raises
others up.
7 The LORD makes some poor and others rich;
he brings some down and lifts others up.

1 Sm 1:20 *Samuel* sounds like the Hebrew term for "asked of God" or "heard by God." **1 Sm 1:22** Some manuscripts add *I will offer him as a Nazirite for all time.* **1 Sm 1:24a** As in Dead Sea Scrolls, Greek and Syriac versions; Masoretic Text reads *three bulls.* **1 Sm 1:24b** Hebrew *and an ephah* [20 quarts or 22 liters]. **1 Sm 1:28** Hebrew *he.* **1 Sm 2:1** Hebrew *has exalted my horn.* **1 Sm 2:6** Hebrew *to Sheol.*

"I asked the LORD to give me this boy, and he has granted my request. Now I am giving him to the LORD, and he will belong to the LORD his whole life."
1 Samuel 1:27-28

1 Sam 1:26-28 To do what she promised (1 Sam 1:11), Hannah gave up what she wanted most—her son—and presented him to Eli to serve in the house of the Lord. In dedicating her only son to God, Hannah was dedicating her entire life and future to God. Because Samuel's life was from God, Hannah was not really giving him up. Rather, she was returning him to God, who had given Samuel to Hannah in the first place. These verses illustrate the kinds of gifts we should give to God. Do your gifts cost you little (Sunday mornings, a comfortable tithe), or are they gifts of sacrifice? Are you presenting God with tokens, or are you presenting him with your entire life?

1 Sam 1:28 Samuel was probably three years old—the customary age for weaning—when his mother left him at the Tabernacle. By saying, "I am giving him to the LORD," Hannah meant that she was dedicating Samuel to God for lifetime service. She did not, of course, forget her much-wanted son. She visited him regularly, and each year she brought him a robe just like Eli's (1 Sam 2:19). In later years, Samuel lived in Ramah (1 Sam 7:17), his parents' hometown (1 Sam 1:19-20).

1 Sam 2:1-10 Hannah praised God for his answer to her prayer for a son. The theme of her poetic prayer is her confidence in God's sovereignty and her thankfulness for everything he had done. Mary the mother of Jesus modeled her own praise song, called the Magnificat, after Hannah's prayer (Luke 1:46-55). Like Hannah and Mary, we should be confident of God's ultimate control over the events in our lives and thankful for the ways he has blessed us. By praising God for all good gifts, we acknowledge his ultimate control over all the affairs of life.

1 Sam 2:2 Hannah praised God for being a Rock—firm, strong, and unchanging. In our fast-paced world, friends come and go, and circumstances change. It's difficult to find a solid foundation that will not change. Those who devote their lives to achievements, causes, or possessions have as their security that which is finite and changeable. The possessions that we work so hard to obtain will all pass away. But God is always present. Hope in him. He will never fail.

1 Sam 2:3 No doubt as Hannah said these words, she was thinking of Peninnah's arrogance and chiding. Hannah did not have to get even with Peninnah. She knew that God is all-knowing and that he will judge all sin and pride. Hannah wisely left judgment up to God. Resist the temptation to take justice into your own hands. God will weigh your deeds as well as the deeds of those who have wronged you.

1 Sam 2:10 Because we live in a world where evil abounds and where war and terrorism always threaten, we may forget that God is in control. Hannah saw God as (1) a solid rock (1 Sam 2:2), (2) the one who knows what we do (1 Sam 2:3), (3) sovereign over all the affairs of people (1 Sam 2:4-8), and (4) the Supreme Judge who administers perfect justice (1 Sam 2:10). Remembering God's sovereign control helps us put both world and personal events in perspective.

8 He lifts the poor from the dust
and the needy from the garbage dump.
He sets them among princes,
placing them in seats of honor.
For all the earth is the LORD's,
and he has set the world in order.

9 "He will protect his faithful ones,
but the wicked will disappear
in darkness.
No one will succeed by strength alone.
10 Those who fight against the LORD
will be shattered.
He thunders against them from heaven;
the LORD judges throughout the earth.
He gives power to his king;
he increases the strength* of his anointed one."

11 Then Elkanah returned home to Ramah without
Samuel. And the boy served the LORD by assisting Eli
the priest.

Eli's Wicked Sons

1 SAMUEL 2:12-26

Now the sons of Eli were scoundrels who had no
respect for the LORD 13 or for their duties as priests.
Whenever anyone offered a sacrifice, Eli's sons would
send over a servant with a three-pronged fork. While
the meat of the sacrificed animal was still boiling,
14 the servant would stick the fork into the pot and

1 Sm 2:10 Hebrew *he exalts the horn.*

HANNAH

Hannah's prayer shows us that all we have and receive is on loan from God. Hannah might have had many excuses for being a possessive mother. But when God answered her prayer, she followed through on her promise to dedicate Samuel to God's service. She discovered that the greatest joy in having a child is to give that child fully and freely back to God. She entered motherhood prepared to do what all mothers must eventually do—let go of their children. • When children are born, they are completely dependent upon their parents for all their basic necessities. This causes some parents to forget that those same children will grow toward independence within the span of a few short years. Being sensitive to the different stages of that healthy process will greatly strengthen family relationships; resisting or denying that process will cause great pain. We must gradually let go of our children in order to allow them to become mature, independent adults.

Strengths and accomplishments	• Mother of Samuel, Israel's greatest judge • Fervent in worship; effective in prayer • Willing to follow through on even a costly commitment
Weakness and mistake	• Struggled with her sense of self-worth because she had initially been unable to have children
Lessons from her life	• God hears and answers prayer • Our children are gifts from God • God is concerned for the oppressed and afflicted
Vital statistics	• Where: Ephraim • Occupation: Wife and mother • Relatives: Husband: Elkanah. Children: First, Samuel. Later, three other sons and two daughters. • Contemporary: Eli the priest
Key verses	"'Sir, do you remember me?' Hannah asked. 'I am the woman who stood here several years ago praying to the LORD. I asked the LORD to give me this boy, and he has granted my request. Now I am giving him to the LORD, and he will belong to the LORD his whole life.' And they worshiped the LORD there" (1 Sam 1:26-28).

Hannah's story is told in 1 Samuel 1–2.

1 Sam 2:11, 18 Samuel assisted Eli the priest. In this role, Samuel's responsibilities would have included opening the Tabernacle doors each morning (1 Sam 3:15), cleaning the furniture, and sweeping the floors. As he grew older, Samuel would have assisted Eli in offering sacrifices. The fact that he was wearing a linen garment (like the clothing worn only by priests) shows that he was a priest-in-training. Because Samuel was Eli's helper, he was God's helper too. When you serve others—even in carrying out ordinary tasks—you are serving God. Because ultimately we are serving God, every job we do for his glory has dignity.

1 Sam 2:12ff The law stipulated that the needs of all the Levites were to be met through the people's tithes (Num 18:20-24; Josh 13:14, 33). Because Eli's sons were priests, they were to be taken care of this way. But Eli's sons took advantage of their position to satisfy their lust for power, possessions, and control. Their contempt and arrogance toward both people and worship undermined the integrity of the whole priesthood.

Eli knew that his sons were evil, but he did little to correct or stop them, even when the integrity of God's sanctuary was threatened. As the high priest, Eli should have responded by executing his sons (Num 15:22-31). No wonder he chose not to confront the situation. But by ignoring their selfish actions, Eli let his sons ruin their own lives and the lives of many others. There are times when serious problems must be confronted, even if the process and consequences could be painful.

1 Sam 2:13-14 This fork was a utensil used in the Tabernacle for offering sacrifices. Made of bronze (Exod 27:3), it usually had three prongs to hook the meat that was to be offered on the altar. Eli's sons used the fork to take more meat from the pot than was due them.

1 Sam 2:13-17 What were Eli's sons doing wrong? They were taking parts of the sacrifices before they were offered to God on the altar. They were also eating meat before the fat was burned off. This was against God's laws (Lev 3:3-5). In effect, Eli's sons were treating God's offerings with contempt. Offerings were given to show honor and respect to God while seeking forgiveness for sins, but through their irreverence, Eli's sons were actually sinning while making the offerings. To add to their sins, they were also sleeping with the women who served there (1 Sam 2:22).

Like Eli's sons, some religious leaders look down on the faith of ordinary people and treat their offerings to God casually or even with contempt. God harshly judges those who lead his people astray or scorn what is devoted to him (Num 18:32).

▸ **1 SAMUEL 2:12-26 *(cont.)***
demand that whatever it brought up be given to Eli's
sons. All the Israelites who came to worship at Shiloh
were treated this way. 15 Sometimes the servant would
come even before the animal's fat had been burned
on the altar. He would demand raw meat before it
had been boiled so that it could be used for roasting.
16 The man offering the sacrifice might reply, "Take
as much as you want, but the fat must be burned
first." Then the servant would demand, "No, give it
to me now, or I'll take it by force." 17 So the sin of these
young men was very serious in the LORD's sight, for
they treated the LORD's offerings with contempt.
18 But Samuel, though he was only a boy, served the
LORD. He wore a linen garment like that of a priest.*
19 Each year his mother made a small coat for him and
brought it to him when she came with her husband for
the sacrifice. 20 Before they returned home, Eli would
bless Elkanah and his wife and say, "May the LORD
give you other children to take the place of this one
she gave to the LORD.*" 21 And the LORD gave Hannah
three sons and two daughters. Meanwhile, Samuel
grew up in the presence of the LORD.
22 Now Eli was very old, but he was aware of what
his sons were doing to the people of Israel. He knew,
for instance, that his sons were seducing the young
women who assisted at the entrance of the Tabernacle.* 23 Eli said to them, "I have been hearing reports
from all the people about the wicked things you are
doing. Why do you keep sinning? 24 You must stop, my
sons! The reports I hear among the LORD's people are
not good. 25 If someone sins against another person,
God* can mediate for the guilty party. But if someone
sins against the LORD, who can intercede?" But Eli's
sons wouldn't listen to their father, for the LORD was
already planning to put them to death.
26 Meanwhile, the boy Samuel grew taller and grew
in favor with the LORD and with the people.

A Warning for Eli's Family

1 SAMUEL 2:27-36
One day a man of God came to Eli and gave him this
message from the LORD: "I revealed myself* to your
ancestors when the people of Israel were slaves in
Egypt. 28 I chose your ancestor Aaron* from among all
the tribes of Israel to be my priest, to offer sacrifices
on my altar, to burn incense, and to wear the priestly
vest* as he served me. And I assigned the sacrificial
offerings to you priests. 29 So why do you scorn my sacrifices and offerings? Why do you give your sons more
honor than you give me—for you and they have become fat from the best offerings of my people Israel!
30 "Therefore, the LORD, the God of Israel, says: I
promised that your branch of the tribe of Levi* would
always be my priests. But I will honor those who honor
me, and I will despise those who think lightly of me.
31 The time is coming when I will put an end to your
family, so it will no longer serve as my priests. All the
members of your family will die before their time.
None will reach old age. 32 You will watch with envy as
I pour out prosperity on the people of Israel. But no
members of your family will ever live out their days.
33 Those who survive will live in sadness and grief, and
their children will die a violent death.* 34 And to prove
that what I have said will come true, I will cause your
two sons, Hophni and Phinehas, to die on the same day!

1 Sm 2:18 Hebrew *He wore a linen ephod.* **1 Sm 2:20** As in Dead Sea Scrolls and Greek version; Masoretic Text reads *this one he requested of the LORD.* **1 Sm 2:22** Hebrew *Tent of Meeting.* Some manuscripts lack this entire sentence. **1 Sm 2:25** Or *the judges.* **1 Sm 2:27** As in Greek and Syriac versions; Hebrew reads *Did I reveal myself.* **1 Sm 2:28a** Hebrew *your father.* **1 Sm 2:28b** Hebrew *an ephod.* **1 Sm 2:30** Hebrew *that your house and your father's house.* **1 Sm 2:33** As in Dead Sea Scrolls, which read *die by the sword;* Masoretic Text reads *die like mortals.*

---

1 Sam 2:18 Samuel wore a linen garment (also called an *ephod*). Ephods, long sleeveless vests made of plain linen, were worn by all priests. The high priest's ephod carried special significance. It was embroidered with a variety of bright colors. Attached to it was the chestpiece, a bib-like garment with gold embroidered shoulder straps. Twelve precious gemstones were attached to the chestpiece, each stone representing one of the tribes of Israel. A pouch on the ephod held the Urim and the Thummim, two small objects used to determine God's will in certain national matters.

1 Sam 2:21 God honored the desires of faithful Hannah. We never hear about Peninnah or her children again, but Samuel was used mightily by God. God also gave Hannah *five children in addition to Samuel. God often* blesses us in ways we do not expect. Hannah never expected to have a child at her age, much less six children! Don't resent God's timing. His blessings might not be immediate, but they will come if we are faithful to do what he says in his Word.

1 Sam 2:23-25 Eli's sons knew better, but they continued to disobey God deliberately by cheating, seducing, and robbing the people. Therefore, God planned to kill them. Any sin is wrong, but sin carried out deliberately and deceitfully is the worst kind. When we sin out of ignorance, we deserve punishment. But when we sin intentionally, the consequences will be more severe. Don't ignore God's warnings about sin. Abandon sin before it becomes a way of life.

1 Sam 2:25 Does a loving God really will or want to put people to death? Consider the situation in the Tabernacle. A person made an offering in order to have his sins forgiven, and Eli's sons stole the offering and made a sham of the person's repentant attitude. God, in his love for Israel, could not permit *this situation to continue.* He allowed Eli's sons to die as a result of their own boastful presumption. They took the Ark into battle, thinking it would protect them. But God withdrew his protection, and the wicked sons of Eli were killed (1 Sam 4:10-11).

1 Sam 2:29 Eli had a difficult time rearing his sons. He apparently did not take any strong disciplinary action with them when he became aware of their wrongdoing. But Eli was not just a father trying to handle his rebellious sons; he was the high priest ignoring the sins of priests under his jurisdiction. As a result, the Lord took the necessary disciplinary action that Eli would not.

Eli was guilty of honoring his sons above God by letting them continue in their sinful ways. Is there a situation in your life, family, or work that you allow to continue even though you know it is wrong? If so, you may become as guilty as those engaged in the wrong act.

1 Sam 2:31, 35-36 For the fulfillment of this prediction see 1 Kings 2:26-27. This is where Solomon removed Abiathar from his position, thus ending Eli's line. Then God raised up Zadok, a priest under David and then high priest under Solomon. Zadok's line was probably still in place as late as the days of Ezra.

35"Then I will raise up a faithful priest who will serve me and do what I desire. I will establish his family, and they will be priests to my anointed kings forever. 36Then all of your surviving family will bow before him, begging for money and food. 'Please,' they will say, 'give us jobs among the priests so we will have enough to eat.'"

The Lord Speaks to Samuel

1 SAMUEL 3:1-14

Meanwhile, the boy Samuel served the LORD by assisting Eli. Now in those days messages from the LORD were very rare, and visions were quite uncommon.

2One night Eli, who was almost blind by now, had gone to bed. 3The lamp of God had not yet gone out, and Samuel was sleeping in the Tabernacle* near the Ark of God. 4Suddenly the LORD called out, "Samuel!"

"Yes?" Samuel replied. "What is it?" 5He got up and ran to Eli. "Here I am. Did you call me?"

"I didn't call you," Eli replied. "Go back to bed." So he did.

6Then the LORD called out again, "Samuel!"

Again Samuel got up and went to Eli. "Here I am. Did you call me?"

"I didn't call you, my son," Eli said. "Go back to bed."

1 Sm 3:3 Hebrew *the Temple of the LORD.*

ELI

Eli was one Old Testament person with a very modern problem. The recognition and respect he earned in public did not extend to his handling of his private affairs. He may have been an excellent priest, but he was a poor parent. His sons brought him grief and ruin. He lacked two important qualities needed for effective parental discipline: firm resolve and corrective action. • Eli responded to situations rather than solving them. But even his responses were weak. God pointed out his sons' errors, but Eli did little to correct them. The contrast between God's dealing with Eli and Eli's dealing with his sons is clear—God gave warning, spelled out the consequences of disobedience, and then acted. Eli only warned. Children need to learn that their parents' words and actions go together. Both love and discipline must be spoken as well as acted out. • But Eli had another problem. He was more concerned with the symbols of his religion than with the God they represented. For Eli, the Ark of the Covenant had become a relic to be protected rather than a reminder of the Protector. His faith shifted from the Creator to the created. • It may be easier to worship things we can see, whether buildings, people, or Scripture itself, but such tangible things have no power in themselves. This book you hold is not merely a respectable religious relic; it is the sharp and effective Word of God. Your attitude toward it is largely shaped by your relationship to the God from whom it comes. A relic or antique has to be carefully stored away; God's Word has to be used and obeyed. Which attitude accurately describes your approach to the Word of God?

Strengths and accomplishments	• Judged Israel for 40 years • Spoke with Hannah, the mother of Samuel, and assured her of God's blessing • Reared and trained Samuel, the greatest judge of Israel
Weaknesses and mistakes	• Failed to discipline his sons or correct them when they sinned • Tended to react to situations rather than take decisive action • Saw the Ark of the Covenant as a relic to be cherished rather than as a symbol of God's presence with Israel
Lessons from his life	• Parents need to discipline their children responsibly • Life is more than simply reacting; it demands action • Past victories cannot substitute for present trust
Vital statistics	• Where: Shiloh • Occupations: High priest, judge of Israel • Relatives: Sons: Hophni and Phinehas. • Contemporary: Samuel
Key verses	"Then the LORD said to Samuel, 'I am about to do a shocking thing in Israel. I am going to carry out all my threats against Eli and his family, from beginning to end. I have warned him that judgment is coming upon his family forever, because his sons are blaspheming God and he hasn't disciplined them. So I have vowed that the sins of Eli and his sons will never be forgiven by sacrifices or offerings'" (1 Sam 3:11-14).

Eli's story is told in 1 Samuel 1–4. He is also mentioned in 1 Kings 2:26-27.

1 Sam 3:1-5 Although God had spoken directly and audibly with Moses and Joshua, his word became rare during the three centuries of rule by judges. By Eli's time, no prophets were speaking God's messages to Israel. Why? Look at the attitude of Eli's sons. They either refused to listen to God or allowed greed to get in the way of any communication with him.

Listening and responding is vital in a relationship with God. Although God does not always use the sound of a human voice, he always speaks clearly through his Word. To receive his messages, we must be ready to listen and to act upon what he tells us. Like Samuel, be ready to say "Here I am" when God calls you to action.

1 Sam 3:2-3 The Ark of God was kept in the Most Holy Place, the innermost room of the Tabernacle where only the high priest could enter once a year. In front of the Most Holy Place was the Holy Place, a small room where the other sacred furniture of the Tabernacle was kept (the incense altar, the Bread of the Presence, the lampstand). Just outside the Holy Place was a court with small rooms where the priests were to stay. Samuel probably slept here with the other priests, only a few yards away from the Ark.

▸ 1 SAMUEL 3:1-14 *(cont.)*

7 Samuel did not yet know the LORD because he had
never had a message from the LORD before. 8 So the
LORD called a third time, and once more Samuel got up
and went to Eli. "Here I am. Did you call me?"

Then Eli realized it was the LORD who was calling
the boy. 9 So he said to Samuel, "Go and lie down again,
and if someone calls again, say, 'Speak, LORD, your servant is listening.'" So Samuel went back to bed.
10 And the LORD came and called as before, "Samuel! Samuel!"

And Samuel replied, "Speak, your servant is listening."
11 Then the LORD said to Samuel, "I am about to do
a shocking thing in Israel. 12 I am going to carry out
all my threats against Eli and his family, from beginning to end. 13 I have warned him that judgment is
coming upon his family forever, because his sons are
blaspheming God* and he hasn't disciplined them.
14 So I have vowed that the sins of Eli and his sons will
never be forgiven by sacrifices or offerings."

Samuel Speaks for the LORD

1 SAMUEL 3:15–4:1a

Samuel stayed in bed until morning, then got up and
opened the doors of the Tabernacle* as usual. He was
afraid to tell Eli what the LORD had said to him. 16 But
Eli called out to him, "Samuel, my son."

"Here I am," Samuel replied.

17 "What did the LORD say to you? Tell me everything. And may God strike you and even kill you if you
hide anything from me!" 18 So Samuel told Eli everything; he didn't hold anything back. "It is the LORD's
will," Eli replied. "Let him do what he thinks best."

19 As Samuel grew up, the LORD was with him, and
everything Samuel said proved to be reliable. 20 And
all Israel, from Dan in the north to Beersheba in the
south, knew that Samuel was confirmed as a prophet
of the LORD. 21 The LORD continued to appear at Shiloh
and gave messages to Samuel there at the Tabernacle.
4:1 And Samuel's words went out to all the people of
Israel.

1 Sm 3:13 As in Greek version; Hebrew reads *his sons have made themselves contemptible.* **1 Sm 3:15** Hebrew *the house of the LORD.*

ISRAELITES VERSUS PHILISTINES

The Israelites and the Philistines were archenemies and constantly fought. Here are some of their confrontations, found in 1 and 2 Samuel. When the Israelites trusted God for the victory, they always won.

Location of the Battle	*Winner*	*Comments*	*Reference*
Aphek to Ebenezer	Philistines	The Ark was captured and Eli's sons killed	**1 Sam 4:1-11**
Mizpah	Israelites	After the Ark was returned, the Philistines planned to attack again, but God confused them. Israel chased the Philistines back to Beth-car	**1 Sam 7:7-14**
Geba	Israelites under Jonathan	One detachment destroyed	**1 Sam 13:3-4**
Gilgal	A standoff	The Israelites lost their nerve and hid	**1 Sam 13:6-17**
Micmash	Israelites	Jonathan and his armor bearer said it didn't matter how many enemies there were. If God was with them, they would win. They began the battle, and the army completed it	**1 Sam 13:23–14:23**
Valley of Elah	Israelites	David and Goliath	**1 Sam 17:1-58**
?	Israelites	David killed 200 Philistines to earn a wife	**1 Sam 18:17-30**
Keilah	Israelites under David	David protected the threshing floors from Philistine looters	**1 Sam 23:1-5**
Aphek, Jezreel, to Mount Gilboa	Philistines	Saul and Jonathan killed	**1 Sam 29:1; 31:1-13**
Baal-perazim	Israelites	The Philistines tried to capture King David	**2 Sam 5:17-25**
Gath	Israelites	There was very little trouble with the Philistines after this defeat	**2 Sam 8:1**
?	Israelites	Abishai saved David from a Philistine giant	**2 Sam 21:15-17**
Gob	Israelites	Other giants were killed, including Goliath's brother	**2 Sam 21:18-22**

1 Sam 3:8-9 One would naturally expect an audible message from God to be given to the priest Eli and not to the child Samuel. Eli was older and more experienced, and he held the proper position. But God's chain of command is based on faith, not on age or position. In finding faithful followers, God may use unexpected channels. Be prepared for the Lord to work at any place, at any time, and through anyone he chooses.

1 Sam 3:13 Eli had spent his entire life in service to God. His responsibility was to oversee all the worship in Israel. But in pursuing this great mission he neglected the responsibilities in his own home. Don't let your desire

2. WAR WITH THE PHILISTINES

The Philistines continued to plague the Israelites, and the poor leadership in Israel continued to show itself as the sons of Eli brought the Ark into battle, only to have it captured by the enemy. God brought the Ark safely home to Israel, and he used Samuel to subdue the Philistines and restore peace to Israel.

The Philistines Capture the Ark

1 SAMUEL 4:1b-11

At that time Israel was at war with the Philistines. The Israelite army was camped near Ebenezer, and the Philistines were at Aphek. [2]The Philistines attacked and defeated the army of Israel, killing 4,000 men. [3]After the battle was over, the troops retreated to their camp, and the elders of Israel asked, "Why did the LORD allow us to be defeated by the Philistines?" Then they said, "Let's bring the Ark of the Covenant of the LORD from Shiloh. If we carry it into battle with us, it* will save us from our enemies."

[4]So they sent men to Shiloh to bring the Ark of the Covenant of the LORD of Heaven's Armies, who is enthroned between the cherubim. Hophni and Phinehas, the sons of Eli, were also there with the Ark of the Covenant of God. [5]When all the Israelites saw the Ark of the Covenant of the LORD coming into the camp, their shout of joy was so loud it made the ground shake!

[6]"What's going on?" the Philistines asked. "What's all the shouting about in the Hebrew camp?" When they were told it was because the Ark of the LORD had arrived, [7]they panicked. "The gods have* come into their camp!" they cried. "This is a disaster! We have never had to face anything like this before! [8]Help! Who can save us from these mighty gods of Israel? They are the same gods who destroyed the Egyptians with plagues when Israel was in the wilderness. [9]Fight as never before, Philistines! If you don't, we will become the Hebrews' slaves just as they have been ours! Stand up like men and fight!"

[10]So the Philistines fought desperately, and Israel was defeated again. The slaughter was great; 30,000 Israelite soldiers died that day. The survivors turned and fled to their tents. [11]The Ark of God was captured, and Hophni and Phinehas, the two sons of Eli, were killed.

The Death of Eli

1 SAMUEL 4:12-22

A man from the tribe of Benjamin ran from the battlefield and arrived at Shiloh later that same day. He had torn his clothes and put dust on his head to show his grief. [13]Eli was waiting beside the road to hear the news of the battle, for his heart trembled for the safety of the Ark of God. When the messenger arrived and told what had happened, an outcry resounded throughout the town.

[14]"What is all the noise about?" Eli asked.

The messenger rushed over to Eli, [15]who was ninety-eight years old and blind. [16]He said to Eli, "I have just come from the battlefield—I was there this very day."

"What happened, my son?" Eli demanded.

[17]"Israel has been defeated by the Philistines," the messenger replied. "The people have been slaughtered, and your two sons, Hophni and Phinehas, were also killed. And the Ark of God has been captured."

1 Sm 4:3 Or *he.* **1 Sm 4:7** Or *A god has.*

---

to do God's work cause you to neglect your family. If you do, your mission may degenerate into a quest for personal importance, and your family will suffer the consequences of your neglect.

1 Sam 4:1 The Philistines, descendants of Noah's son Ham, settled along the southeastern Mediterranean coast between Egypt and Gaza. They were originally one of the "Sea peoples" who had migrated to the Middle East in ships from Greece and Crete. By Samuel's time, these warlike people were well established in five of Gaza's cities in southwest Canaan and were constantly pressing inland against the Israelites. Throughout this time, the Philistines were Israel's major enemy.

1 Sam 4:3 The Ark of the Covenant contained the Ten Commandments given by God to Moses. The Ark was supposed to be kept in the Most Holy Place, a sacred part of the Tabernacle that only the high priest could enter once a year. Hophni and Phinehas desecrated the room by unlawfully entering it and removing the Ark.

The Israelites rightly recognized the great holiness of the Ark, but they thought that the Ark itself—the wood and metal box—was their source of power. They began to use it as a good-luck charm, expecting it to protect them from their enemies. A symbol of God does not guarantee his presence and power. Their attitude toward the Ark came perilously close to idol worship. When the Ark was captured by their enemies, they thought that Israel's glory was gone (1 Sam 4:19-22) and that God had deserted them (1 Sam 7:1-2). God uses his power according to his own wisdom and will. He responds to the faith of those who seek him.

1 Sam 4:4 "The LORD of Heaven's Armies, who is enthroned between the cherubim," conveys that God's presence rested on the Ark of the Covenant between the two gold cherubim (or angels) attached to its lid. The people believed that the Ark would bring victory when Hophni and Phinehas carried it into battle.

1 Sam 4:5-8 The Philistines were afraid because they remembered stories about God's intervention for Israel when they left Egypt. But Israel had turned away from God and was clinging to only a form of godliness, a symbol of former victories.

People (and churches) often try to live on the memories of God's blessings. The Israelites wrongly assumed that because God had given them victory in the past, he would do it again, even though they had strayed far from him. Today, as in Bible times, spiritual victories come through a continually renewed relationship with God. Don't live off the past. Keep your relationship with God new and fresh.

1 Sam 4:11 This event fulfills the prophecy in 1 Samuel 2:34 stating that Eli's sons, Hophni and Phinehas, would die "on the same day."

1 Sam 4:12 At this time, the city of Shiloh was Israel's religious center (Josh 18:1; 1 Sam 4:3). The Tabernacle was permanently set up there. Because Israel did not have a civil capital—a seat of national government—Shiloh was the natural place for a messenger to deliver the sad news from the battle. Many scholars believe that it was during this battle that Shiloh was destroyed (Jer 7:12; 26:2-6; also see the note on 1 Sam 7:1, p. 426).

▸ **1 SAMUEL 4:12-22 *(cont.)***

[18]When the messenger mentioned what had happened to the Ark of God, Eli fell backward from his seat beside the gate. He broke his neck and died, for he was old and overweight. He had been Israel's judge for forty years.

[19]Eli's daughter-in-law, the wife of Phinehas, was pregnant and near her time of delivery. When she heard that the Ark of God had been captured and that her father-in-law and husband were dead, she went into labor and gave birth. [20]She died in childbirth, but before she passed away the midwives tried to encourage her. "Don't be afraid," they said. "You have a baby boy!" But she did not answer or pay attention to them.

[21]She named the child Ichabod (which means "Where is the glory?"), for she said, "Israel's glory is gone." She named him this because the Ark of God had been captured and because her father-in-law and husband were dead. [22]Then she said, "The glory has departed from Israel, for the Ark of God has been captured."

The Ark in Philistia

1 SAMUEL 5:1-12

After the Philistines captured the Ark of God, they took it from the battleground at Ebenezer to the town of Ashdod. [2]They carried the Ark of God into the temple of Dagon and placed it beside an idol of Dagon. [3]But when the citizens of Ashdod went to see it the next morning, Dagon had fallen with his face to the ground in front of the Ark of the LORD! So they took Dagon and put him in his place again. [4]But the next morning the same thing happened—Dagon had fallen face down before the Ark of the LORD again. This time his head and hands had broken off and were lying in the doorway. Only the trunk of his body was left intact. [5]That is why to this day neither the priests of Dagon nor anyone who enters the temple of Dagon in Ashdod will step on its threshold.

[6]Then the LORD's heavy hand struck the people of Ashdod and the nearby villages with a plague of tumors.* [7]When the people realized what was happening, they cried out, "We can't keep the Ark of the God of Israel here any longer! He is against us! We will all be destroyed along with Dagon, our god." [8]So they called together the rulers of the Philistine towns and asked, "What should we do with the Ark of the God of Israel?"

The rulers discussed it and replied, "Move it to the town of Gath." So they moved the Ark of the God of Israel to Gath. [9]But when the Ark arrived at Gath, the LORD's heavy hand fell on its men, young and old; he

1 Sm 5:6 Greek version and Latin Vulgate read *tumors; and rats appeared in their land, and death and destruction were throughout the city.*

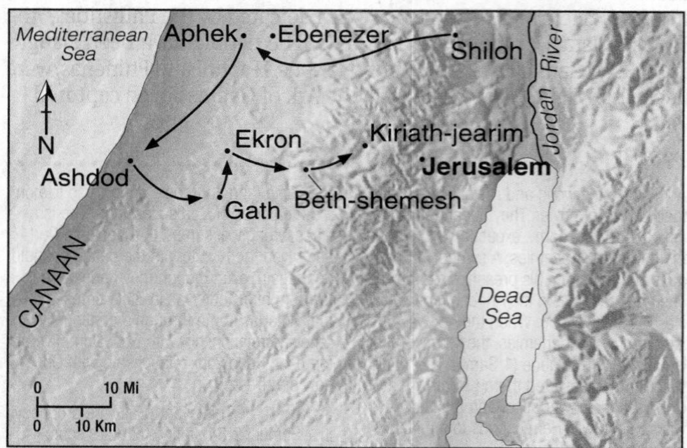

***THE ARK'S TRAVELS** Eli's sons took the Ark from Shiloh to the battlefield on the lower plains at Ebenezer and Aphek. The Philistines captured the Ark and took it to Ashdod, Gath, and Ekron. Plagues forced the people to send the Ark back to Israel, where it finally was taken by cattle-drawn carts to Beth-shemesh and on to the home of Eleazar in Kiriath-jearim.*

1 Sam 4:18 Eli was Israel's judge and high priest. His death marked the end of the dark period of the judges when most of the nation ignored God. Although Samuel was also a judge, his career spanned the transition from Israel's rule by judges to the nation's monarchy. He began the great revival that Israel would experience for the next century. The Bible does not say who became the next high priest (Samuel was not eligible because he was not a direct descendant of Aaron), but Samuel acted as high priest at this time by offering the important sacrifices throughout Israel.

1 Sam 4:19-22 This incident illustrates the spiritual darkness and decline of Israel. This young boy, Ichabod, was supposed to succeed his father, Phinehas, in the priesthood, but his father had been killed because he was an evil man who desecrated the Tabernacle. The terror of God's leaving his people overshadowed the joy of childbirth. When sin dominates our lives, even God-given joys and pleasures seem empty.

1 Sam 5:1ff Dagon was the chief god of the Philistines, who they believed sent rain and assured a bountiful harvest. But the Philistines, like most of their pagan neighbors, worshiped many gods. The more gods they could have on their side, the more secure they felt. That was why they wanted the Ark, thinking that if it helped the Israelites, it could help them, too. But when the people living nearby began to get sick and die, the Philistines realized that the Ark was not a good omen. It was a source of greater power than they had ever seen—power they could not control.

1 Sam 5:6-7 Although the Philistines had just witnessed a great victory by Israel's God over their god Dagon, they didn't act upon that insight until they were afflicted with tumors. Today many people don't respond to biblical truth until they experience pain. Are you willing to listen to God for truth's sake, or do you turn to him only when you are hurting?

1 Sam 5:8 The Philistines were governed by five rulers. Each ruler lived in a different city—Gath, Ekron, Ashdod, Ashkelon, Gaza. The Ark was taken to three of these capital cities, and each time it brought great trouble and chaos to the citizens.

struck them with a plague of tumors, and there was
a great panic.
10 So they sent the Ark of God to the town of Ekron,
but when the people of Ekron saw it coming they cried
out, "They are bringing the Ark of the God of Israel
here to kill us, too!" 11 The people summoned the Philistine rulers again and begged them, "Please send the
Ark of the God of Israel back to its own country, or it*
will kill us all." For the deadly plague from God had
already begun, and great fear was sweeping across
the town. 12 Those who didn't die were afflicted with
tumors; and the cry from the town rose to heaven.

The Philistines Return the Ark

1 SAMUEL 6:1-18

The Ark of the LORD remained in Philistine territory
seven months in all. 2 Then the Philistines called in
their priests and diviners and asked them, "What
should we do about the Ark of the LORD? Tell us how
to return it to its own country."
3 "Send the Ark of the God of Israel back with a gift,"
they were told. "Send a guilt offering so the plague will
stop. Then, if you are healed, you will know it was his
hand that caused the plague."
4 "What sort of guilt offering should we send?" they
asked.
And they were told, "Since the plague has struck
both you and your five rulers, make five gold tumors
and five gold rats, just like those that have ravaged your
land. 5 Make these things to show honor to the God of
Israel. Perhaps then he will stop afflicting you, your
gods, and your land. 6 Don't be stubborn and rebellious
as Pharaoh and the Egyptians were. By the time God
was finished with them, they were eager to let Israel go.
7 "Now build a new cart, and find two cows that have
just given birth to calves. Make sure the cows have
never been yoked to a cart. Hitch the cows to the cart,
but shut their calves away from them in a pen. 8 Put
the Ark of the LORD on the cart, and beside it place a
chest containing the gold rats and gold tumors you
are sending as a guilt offering. Then let the cows go
wherever they want. 9 If they cross the border of our
land and go to Beth-shemesh, we will know it was the
LORD who brought this great disaster upon us. If they
don't, we will know it was not his hand that caused the
plague. It came simply by chance."
10 So these instructions were carried out. Two cows
were hitched to the cart, and their newborn calves
were shut up in a pen. 11 Then the Ark of the LORD and
the chest containing the gold rats and gold tumors
were placed on the cart. 12 And sure enough, without
veering off in other directions, the cows went straight

1 Sm 5:11 Or *he.*

1 Sam 6:3 What was this guilt offering supposed to accomplish? In the Canaanite religions, this was a normal reaction to trouble. The Philistines thought their problems were the result of their gods being angry. They recognized their guilt in taking the Ark and now were trying everything they could to placate Israel's God. The diviners (1 Sam 6:2) probably helped choose the gift they thought would placate Yahweh. But the offering consisted of images of tumors and rats, not the kind of guilt offering prescribed in God's laws (Lev 5:14–6:7; 7:1-10). How easy it is to design our own methods of acknowledging God rather than serving him in the way he requires.

1 Sam 6:7-12 The Philistine priests and diviners devised a test to see if God was really the one who had caused all their recent troubles. Two cows who had just given birth and had never been yoked were hitched to a cart and sent toward Israel's border carrying the Ark of the Covenant. For a cow to leave her nursing calf, she would have to go against all her motherly instincts. Only God, who has power over the natural order, could cause this to happen. God sent the cows to Israel, not to pass the Philistines' test but to show them his mighty power.

1 Sam 6:9 The Philistines acknowledged the existence of the Hebrew God, but only as one of many deities whose favor they sought. Thinking of God in this way made it easy for them to ignore his demand that people worship him alone. Many people "worship" God this way. They see God as just one ingredient in a successful life. But God is far more than an ingredient—he is the source of life itself. Are you a "Philistine," seeing God's favor as only an ingredient of the good life?

Dagon

Until the early part of the 20th century, almost all of what was known about the Canaanite religion came from the Bible. But in 1928 many clay tablets were found at a site called Ras Shamra, which was the ancient Syrian city of Ugarit. They contained abundant new information about the religious life of Canaan. Most of them were in a cuneiform alphabet and written in a previously unknown language quite similar to Hebrew, Aramaic, and Arabic. The documents are often called the Ugaritic texts or the Ras Shamra tablets.

Discovery of these texts opened doors of understanding that had long been closed. The texts provided scholars with important mythological literature that gave the names and functions of the gods. Canaanite deities had two striking features: an extraordinary fluidity of personality and function, and names whose meanings and sources could be easily traced. For example, Dagon, meaning "fish," was the chief god of the city of Ashdod (Judg 16:23; 1 Sam 5:1-7). To this day, certain people groups believe in a "sea god" or "fish god" and pay homage to him, but idolatry can take many different forms in modern culture. We must remember that the Bible warns against all forms of idolatry (1 Jn 5:21), whatever form it may take for an individual.

▸ **1 SAMUEL 6:1-18 *(cont.)***

along the road toward Beth-shemesh, lowing as they
went. The Philistine rulers followed them as far as the
border of Beth-shemesh.
13 The people of Beth-shemesh were harvesting
wheat in the valley, and when they saw the Ark, they
were overjoyed! 14 The cart came into the field of a
man named Joshua and stopped beside a large rock.
So the people broke up the wood of the cart for a fire
and killed the cows and sacrificed them to the LORD
as a burnt offering. 15 Several men of the tribe of Levi
lifted the Ark of the LORD and the chest containing the
gold rats and gold tumors from the cart and placed
them on the large rock. Many sacrifices and burnt offerings were offered to the LORD that day by the people
of Beth-shemesh. 16 The five Philistine rulers watched
all this and then returned to Ekron that same day.
17 The five gold tumors sent by the Philistines as a
guilt offering to the LORD were gifts from the rulers of
Ashdod, Gaza, Ashkelon, Gath, and Ekron. 18 The five
gold rats represented the five Philistine towns and
their surrounding villages, which were controlled by
the five rulers. The large rock at Beth-shemesh, where
they set the Ark of the LORD, still stands in the field of
Joshua as a witness to what happened there.

The Ark Moved to Kiriath-Jearim

1 SAMUEL 6:19–7:2

But the LORD killed seventy men* from Beth-shemesh
because they looked into the Ark of the LORD. And the

1 Sm 6:19 As in a few Hebrew manuscripts; most Hebrew manuscripts read *70 men, 50,000 men.* Perhaps the text should be understood to read *the LORD killed 70 men and 50 oxen.*

1 Sam 6:19 Why were people killed for looking into the Ark? The Israelites had made an idol of the Ark. They had tried to harness God's power, to use it for their own purposes (victory in battle). But the Lord of the universe cannot be controlled by humans. To protect the Israelites from his power, he had warned them not even to look at the sacred sanctuary objects in the Most Holy Place or they would die (Num 4:20). Only Levites were allowed to move the Ark. Because of their disobedience, God carried out his promised judgment.

God could not allow the people to think they could use his power for their own ends. He could not permit them to disregard his warnings and come into his presence lightly. He did not want the cycle of disrespect, disobedience, and defeat to start all over again. God did not kill the men of Beth-shemesh to be cruel. He killed them because overlooking their presumptuous sin would encourage the whole nation of Israel to ignore God.

1 Sam 7:1 The Ark was taken to Kiriath-jearim, a city near the battlefield, for safekeeping, and Eleazar was given the task of caring for it. Why wasn't it taken back to the Tabernacle at Shiloh? Shiloh had probably been defeated and destroyed by the Philistines in an earlier battle (1 Sam 4:1-18; Jer 26:2-6) because of the evil deeds of its priests (1 Sam 2:12-17). Apparently, the Tabernacle and its furniture were saved because we read that the Tabernacle was set up in Nob during Saul's reign (1 Sam 21:1-6) and in Gibeon during the reigns of David and Solomon (1 Chr 16:39; 21:29, 30; 2 Chr 1). Shiloh is never again mentioned in the historical books of the Old Testament. Further evidence of Shiloh's destruction is that Samuel's new home became Ramah (1 Sam 7:15-17; 8:4), his birthplace.

1 Sam 7:2-3 Israel mourned, and sorrow gripped the nation for 20 years. The Ark was put away like an unwanted box in an attic, and it seemed as if the Lord had abandoned his people. Samuel, now a grown man, roused them to action by saying that if they

SAMUEL

We often wonder about the childhoods of great people. We have little information about the early years of most of the people mentioned in the Bible. One delightful exception is Samuel—he came as a result of God's answer to Hannah's fervent prayer for a child. (In fact, the name Samuel comes from the Hebrew expression "heard of God.") God shaped Samuel from the start. Like Moses, Samuel was called to fill many different roles: judge, priest, prophet, counselor, and God's man at a turning point in the history of Israel. God worked through Samuel because Samuel was willing to be one thing: God's servant. • Samuel showed that those whom God finds faithful in small things will be trusted with greater things. He grew up assisting the high priest (Eli) in the Tabernacle until God directed him to other responsibilities. God was able to use Samuel because he was genuinely dedicated to God. • Samuel moved ahead because he was listening to God's directions. Too often we ask God to control our lives without making us give up the goals for which we strive; we ask him to help us get where we want to go. The first step in correcting this tendency is to turn over both the control and destination of our lives to him. The second step is to do what we already know God requires of us. The third step is to listen for further direction from his Word—God's map for life.

Strengths and accomplishments	• Used by God to assist Israel's transition from a loosely governed tribal people to a monarchy • Anointed the first two kings of Israel • Was the last and most effective of Israel's judges • Listed in the Hall of Faith in Hebrews 11
Weakness and mistake	• Was unable to lead his sons into a close relationship with God
Lessons from his life	• The significance of what people accomplish is directly related to their relationship with God • The kind of person we are is more important than anything we might do
Vital statistics	• Where: Ephraim • Occupations: Judge, prophet, priest • Relatives: Mother: Hannah. Father: Elkanah. Sons: Joel and Abijah. • Contemporaries: Eli, Saul, David
Key verses	"As Samuel grew up, the LORD was with him, and everything Samuel said proved to be reliable. And all Israel, from Dan in the north to Beersheba in the south, knew that Samuel was confirmed as a prophet of the LORD" (1 Sam 3:19-20).

Samuel's story is told in 1 Samuel 1–28. He is also mentioned in Psalm 99:6; Jeremiah 15:1; Acts 3:24; 13:20; Hebrews 11:32.

people mourned greatly because of what the LORD had
done. 20 "Who is able to stand in the presence of the
LORD, this holy God?" they cried out. "Where can we
send the Ark from here?"
21 So they sent messengers to the people at Kiriath-
jearim and told them, "The Philistines have returned
the Ark of the LORD. Come here and get it!"

7:1 So the men of Kiriath-jearim came to get the Ark of
the LORD. They took it to the hillside home of Abinadab and ordained Eleazar, his son, to be in charge of it.
2 The Ark remained in Kiriath-jearim for a long time—
twenty years in all. During that time all Israel mourned
because it seemed the LORD had abandoned them.

Samuel Leads Israel to Victory

1 SAMUEL 7:3-17

Then Samuel said to all the people of Israel, "If you are
really serious about wanting to return to the LORD, get
rid of your foreign gods and your images of Ashtoreth.
Determine to obey only the LORD; then he will rescue
you from the Philistines." 4 So the Israelites got rid of
their images of Baal and Ashtoreth and worshiped
only the LORD.
5 Then Samuel told them, "Gather all of Israel to
Mizpah, and I will pray to the LORD for you." 6 So they
gathered at Mizpah and, in a great ceremony, drew
water from a well and poured it out before the LORD.
They also went without food all day and confessed that
they had sinned against the LORD. (It was at Mizpah
that Samuel became Israel's judge.)
7 When the Philistine rulers heard that Israel had
gathered at Mizpah, they mobilized their army and
advanced. The Israelites were badly frightened when
they learned that the Philistines were approaching.
8 "Don't stop pleading with the LORD our God to save us
from the Philistines!" they begged Samuel. 9 So Samuel took a young lamb and offered it to the LORD as
a whole burnt offering. He pleaded with the LORD to
help Israel, and the LORD answered him.
10 Just as Samuel was sacrificing the burnt offering,
the Philistines arrived to attack Israel. But the LORD
spoke with a mighty voice of thunder from heaven
that day, and the Philistines were thrown into such
confusion that the Israelites defeated them. 11 The
men of Israel chased them from Mizpah to a place
below Beth-car, slaughtering them all along the way.
12 Samuel then took a large stone and placed it between the towns of Mizpah and Jeshanah.* He named
it Ebenezer (which means "the stone of help"), for he
said, "Up to this point the LORD has helped us!"
13 So the Philistines were subdued and didn't invade
Israel again for some time. And throughout Samuel's
lifetime, the LORD's powerful hand was raised against
the Philistines. 14 The Israelite villages near Ekron and
Gath that the Philistines had captured were restored
to Israel, along with the rest of the territory that the
Philistines had taken. And there was peace between
Israel and the Amorites in those days.
15 Samuel continued as Israel's judge for the rest of
his life. 16 Each year he traveled around, setting up his
court first at Bethel, then at Gilgal, and then at Mizpah.
He judged the people of Israel at each of these places.
17 Then he would return to his home at Ramah, and he
would hear cases there, too. And Samuel built an altar
to the LORD at Ramah.

Samuel becomes Israel's final judge

1 Sm 7:12 As in Greek and Syriac versions; Hebrew reads *Shen.*

were truly sorry, they should do something about it. How easy it is for us to complain about our problems, even to God, while we refuse to act, change, and do what he requires. We don't even take the advice he has already given us. Do you ever feel as if God has abandoned you? Check to see if there is anything he has already told you to do. You may not receive new guidance from God until you have acted on his previous directions.

1 Sam 7:3 Samuel urged the Israelites to get rid of their foreign gods. Idols today are much more subtle than gods of wood and stone, but they are just as dangerous. Whatever holds first place in our lives or controls us is our god. Money, success, material goods, pride, or anything else can be an idol if it takes the place of God in our lives. The Lord alone is worthy of our service and worship, and we must let nothing rival him. If we have "foreign gods," we need to ask God to help us dethrone them, making the true God our first priority.

1 Sam 7:4 Baal was believed to be the son of El, chief deity of the Canaanites. Baal was regarded as the god of thunder and rain; thus, he controlled vegetation and agriculture. Ashtoreth was a goddess of love and war (she was called Ishtar in Babylon and Astarte or Aphrodite in Greece). She represented fertility. The Canaanites believed that by the sexual union of Baal and Ashtoreth, the earth would be magically rejuvenated and made fertile.

1 Sam 7:5 Mizpah held special significance for the Israelite nation. It was there that the Israelites had gathered to mobilize against the tribe of Benjamin (Judg 20:1); Samuel was appointed as judge there (1 Sam 7:6); and Saul, Israel's first king, would be identified and presented to the people there (1 Sam 10:17ff).

1 Sam 7:6 Pouring water on the ground "before the LORD" was a sign of repenting from sin, turning from idols, and determining to obey God alone.

1 Sam 7:6 Samuel became the last in the long line of Israel's judges (leaders). (For a list of these judges, see the chart on p. 374.) A judge was both a political and a religious leader. God was Israel's true leader, while the judge was to be God's spokesperson to the people and administrator of justice throughout the land. While some of Israel's judges relied more on their own judgment than on God's, Samuel's obedience and dedication to God made him one of the greatest judges in Israel's history. (For more on Samuel as a judge, see the note on 1 Sam 4:18, p. 424.)

1 Sam 7:12 The Israelites had great difficulty with the Philistines, but God rescued them. In response, the people set up a large stone as a memorial of God's great help and deliverance. During tough times, we may need to remember the crucial turning points in our past to help us through the present. Memorials can help us remember God's past victories and gain confidence and strength for the present.

1 Sam 7:14 In Joshua's time, the Amorites were a powerful tribe scattered throughout the hill country on both sides of the Jordan with a heavy concentration occupying the east side of the Jordan River opposite the Dead Sea. In the context of this verse, however, Amorites is another general name for all the inhabitants of Canaan who were not Israelites.

United Monarchy

GOD'S PEOPLE were settled in the land he had promised them, but they wanted to have a king like the nations around them. God granted their request and chose Saul to be the first king of Israel. He was precisely the kind of king that the people were looking for: tall, good looking, and wealthy. He was the kind of leader that they could rally around to unify the tribal confederation under a single ruler, protecting them from the nations that they had displaced and strengthening their position.

Saul might have been just the king the people had asked for, but unfortunately, he was not the kind of king that God wanted for his people. He was arrogant, impulsive, and jealous. And, although he tried to keep up appearances, he cared more about personal and national success than about honoring God and being faithful to him. Because of these things, God rejected Saul as the king of Israel and decided to anoint another to take his place. Saul served as king as long as he lived, but Samuel told him that God had rejected him as king, and Saul continued to spiral further and further away from being the kind of leader Israel needed.

David proved himself to be an exceptional military leader and a shining example of faith in God and reliance on him. The famous story of young David's confrontation with the Philistine Goliath introduced him to

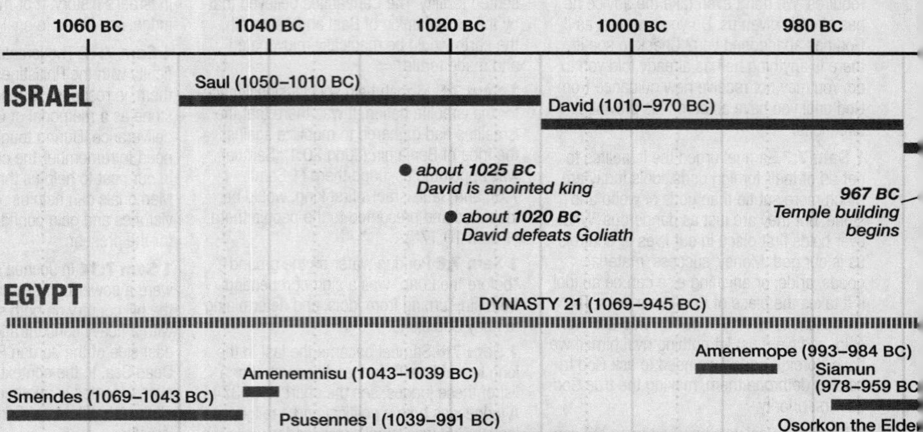

BOOKS

- 1 SAMUEL
- 2 SAMUEL
- 1 KINGS
- 1 CHRONICLES
- 2 CHRONICLES
- PSALMS
- PROVERBS
- ECCLESIASTES
- SONG OF SONGS

DATES

FROM:
1050 BC
TO:
930 BC

THEMES

- Kingdom
- Worship
- Obedience
- Leadership
- Wisdom

the nation, but his fame grew very quickly for his military prowess. This made Saul intensely jealous of David, sending David into exile for the last several years of Saul's reign. After Saul's death and a brief struggle for power with Saul's surviving son, Ishbosheth, David was confirmed as king over the entire nation.

David expanded the kingdom and made worship of God central to his leadership, with elaborate ceremonies to bring the Ark of the Covenant to Jerusalem. David wasn't a perfect king—the incident with Bathsheba and Uriah the Hittite reminds us of that quite clearly—but he was the king God had chosen. God promised to secure the family of David as the ruler over his people for all time. That promise was ultimately fulfilled in Jesus Christ.

Solomon rose to the throne after David's death, and the nation continued to thrive under his rule. The kingdom was completely at peace, became extremely wealthy, and secured the widest borders in its history under Solomon's leadership. Solomon also built a magnificent Temple in Jerusalem, as God had promised David. Israel's worship would center around that Temple until its destruction in 586 B.C. But Solomon was not like his father David in wholehearted devotion to God. He married many foreign women, and worshiped their gods in addition to the Lord. He led the people away from serving God with all their hearts, and set up the kingdom for a great fall after his death.

David, by Jozef Israëls

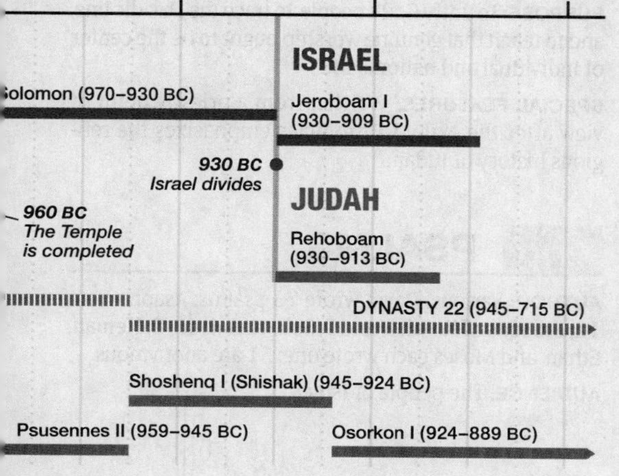

PEOPLE & CULTURE

■ **National Transition.** Samuel was the last judge to lead Israel, and he was instrumental in the transition from a tribal confederation to a united nation under a central monarchy. He was the first prophet of God to anoint and advise the king of the nation. The transition from tribal loyalties to a national identity was not a simple matter. Tribal jealousies and infighting continued well into David's reign, when worship and government were finally unified under his leadership in Jerusalem. This national unity was tenuous, and ultimately didn't even outlast his son Solomon's reign.

■ **Saul.** Israel asked for a king like the nations around them, and Saul fit the bill perfectly. He was imposing physically, a head taller than anybody else in the nation. He came from a prominent family and led the nation to some decisive military victories over their neighbors. He leaned heavily on God's prophet, Samuel, for guidance and support in leading the nation. But beneath the surface, Saul was not the kind of king God wanted for his people. He cared more about appearances than truly following God and doing what was right. He was filled with insecurity and jealousy toward David because of his successes. As time wore on, his flaws became more and more apparent.

■ **David.** Relatively early in Saul's reign, God told Samuel that he had rejected Saul as king of his people. He sent Samuel to anoint a new king for Israel—one that would be the kind of king God wanted for his people. David, though still a boy, would be that man. He showed the strength of his faith and dependence on God early on in his confrontation with Goliath, and continued to serve God faithfully as a soldier in Saul's army even though he knew he had been chosen to be the next king. Once his time came to serve God and the nation, he led them well and brought the nation together. He expanded the borders of the nation, subdued their enemies all around them, and prepared for the building of the Temple. David had some major personal and family problems, but his repentance, dependence on God, and responsiveness to God's prophets demonstrated the kind of faith God wanted in the leader of his people.

■ **Solomon.** David's son and successor got off to a glorious start as king over Israel, expanding the city of Jerusalem with a huge palace complex and building the Temple as a permanent center for national worship. The nation found great prosperity under Solomon's rule and had peace in the land. God offered Solomon the opportunity to ask for anything he wanted, and Solomon's humble request for wisdom to lead the nation was granted in abundance. His wisdom was world-renowned, and some of it has been recorded for us in Scripture. But Solomon did not follow God with his whole heart, as his father had. He married many foreign women and added the worship of their gods to his halfhearted worship of the true God. This set the stage for the tragic division of the nation after his death, and set a tone of disobedience and idolatry that Israel struggled with for generations.

■ **The Temple.** David wanted to build a permanent place for the worship of God to replace the Tabernacle, which was a tent designed for a nation on the move. God said the honor of building a Temple for his name to dwell on the earth would go to David's son Solomon. The Temple was a monumental building project, towering over the city of Jerusalem from the highest point in the city and built with the best materials by the best craftsmen. It was a testament to the central place God had in creating and sustaining the nation, but unfortunately the people (and kings) didn't always give God and his Temple their rightful place at the center of their lives.

BOOKS IN THIS SECTION

1 SAMUEL

AUTHOR: Unknown

AUDIENCE: The people of Israel

PURPOSE: To record the life of Samuel, Israel's last judge; the reign and decline of Saul, Israel's first king; and the choice and preparation of David, Israel's greatest king

SETTING: Israel, during its transition from a theocracy (led by God) to a monarchy (led by a king)

2 SAMUEL

AUTHOR: Unknown

AUDIENCE: The people of Israel

PURPOSE: To record the history of David's reign, showing what effective leadership under God looks like

SETTING: The land of Israel under David's rule

DATE WRITTEN: c. 930 B.C.; shortly after David's reign

1 CHRONICLES

AUTHOR: Ezra, according to Jewish tradition

AUDIENCE: The exiles who returned from captivity

DATE WRITTEN: c. 430 B.C., recording events that occurred from much earlier

PURPOSE: To unify God's people, to trace the Davidic line, and to teach that genuine worship ought to be the center of individual and national life

SPECIAL FEATURES: Written from a priestly point of view after the exile, 1 Chronicles emphasizes the religious history of Judah.

PSALMS

AUTHOR: Various. David wrote 73 psalms; Asaph wrote 12; the sons of Korah wrote 9; Solomon wrote 2; Heman, Ethan, and Moses each wrote one; 51 are anonymous.

AUDIENCE: The people of Israel

PURPOSE: To provide poetry for the expression of praise, worship, confession, and prayer to God

SETTING: Each psalm is unique; many have specific events identified as the background, but most are generic and applicable to many settings.

PROVERBS

AUTHOR: Solomon wrote or collected most of the book, with Agur and Lemuel contributing.

AUDIENCE: The people of Israel

PURPOSE: To teach people how to attain wisdom, discipline, and a prudent life, and how to do what is right, just, and fair—in short, to apply divine wisdom to daily life and to provide moral instruction

DATE WRITTEN: Solomon wrote and compiled most of these proverbs during his reign.

SPECIAL FEATURES: The book used a variety of literary forms: poems, brief parables, pointed questions, and couplets. Other literary devices include antithesis, comparison, and personification.

ECCLESIASTES

AUTHOR: Solomon

AUDIENCE: Solomon's subjects in particular, and all people in general

PURPOSE: To spare future generations the bitterness of learning through their own experience that life is meaningless apart from God

SETTING: Solomon was looking back on his life, much of which was lived apart from God.

SONG OF SONGS

AUTHOR: Solomon

AUDIENCE: The people of Israel

PURPOSE: To tell of the love between a bridegroom and his bride, to affirm the sanctity of marriage, and possibly to picture God's love for his people

For book information on **1 KINGS** and **2 CHRONICLES**, see the introduction to Splintered Nations, p. 687.

MEGATHEMES

■ **King.** The people of Israel wanted a king. They wanted to be organized like the surrounding nations. Though it was against his original purpose for them, God chose a king for his people. But establishing a monarchy didn't solve Israel's problems. What God wants is the genuine devotion of each person's mind and heart to him. No government or set of laws can substitute for the rule of God in your heart and life.

■ **Leadership.** God guided his people using different forms of leadership: judges, priests, prophets, kings. There were many different leadership styles among the leaders of Israel, but their success depended on their devotion to God, not external factors like age, wisdom, or strength. When Saul, David, and Solomon disobeyed God, they faced tragic consequences. Sin affected what they accomplished for God. Being a real leader means letting God guide all aspects of your activities, values, and goals.

■ **The Temple.** Solomon's Temple was a beautiful place of worship and prayer. It was the center of Jewish religion, the place of God's special presence. But a beautiful house of worship doesn't guarantee heartfelt worship of God. God wants to live in our hearts, not just meet us in a sanctuary.

■ **Praise.** The psalms, many of which are sprinkled throughout this section, are songs of praise to God as our Creator, Sustainer, and Redeemer. Praise is recognizing, appreciating, and expressing God's greatness. Focusing our thoughts on God moves us to praise him. The more we know him, the more we can appreciate what he has done for us.

■ **Forgiveness.** Many psalms are intense prayers asking God for forgiveness. God forgives us when we confess our sins and turn from them. Because God forgives us, we can pray to him honestly and directly. When we receive his forgiveness, we move from alienation to intimacy, from guilt to love.

■ **Wisdom.** God wants his people to be wise. Two kinds of people portray two contrasting paths of life. The fool is the wicked, stubborn person who hates or ignores God. The wise person seeks to know and love God. When we choose God's way, he grants us wisdom. His Word, the Bible, leads us to live right, have right relationships, and make right decisions.

■ **Love.** Song of Songs portrays a relationship of intense love. As the relationship developed, the beauty and wonder of a romance unfolded between Solomon and his bride. The power of love affected the hearts, minds, and bodies of the two lovers. Because love is such a powerful expression of feeling and commitment between a man and a woman, it is not to be regarded casually. We are not to manipulate others into loving us, and love should not be prematurely encouraged in a relationship.

MAP ▶

1 Mizpah As Samuel grew old, the people came to him demanding a king in order to be like the other nations. At Mizpah, Saul was chosen by sacred appointment to be Israel's first king with the blessing, though not the approval, of God and Samuel (1 Sam 8:1–10:27).

2 Gilgal A battle with the Ammonites proved Saul's leadership abilities to the people of Israel. He protected the people of Jabesh-gilead and scattered the Ammonite army. Samuel and the people crowned Saul as king of Israel at Gilgal (1 Sam 11:1-15).

3 Valley of Elah Saul won many other battles, but over time he proved to be arrogant, sinful, and rebellious, so God finally rejected him as king. David was anointed to be Israel's next king, but it would be many years before he sat upon the throne. In one battle with the Philistines in the valley of Elah, David killed Goliath, the Philistines' mightiest soldier. But this victory was the beginning of the end of Saul's love for David. Saul became so jealous that he plotted to kill David (1 Sam 12:1–22:23).

4 The Wilderness Even anointed kings are not exempt from troubles. David literally ran for his life from King Saul, hiding with his band of followers in the wilderness of Ziph (where the men of Ziph constantly betrayed him), the wilderness of Maon, and the wilderness of En-gedi. Though he had opportunities to kill Saul, David refused to do so because Saul was God's anointed king (1 Sam 23:1–26:25).

5 Gath David moved his men and family to Gath, the Philistine city where King Achish lived. Saul then stopped chasing him. The Philistines seemed to welcome this famous fugitive from Israel (1 Sam 27:1-4).

6 Ziklag Desiring privacy in return for his pretended loyalty to King Achish, David asked for a city in which to house his men and family. Achish gave him Ziklag. From there David conducted raids against the cities of the Geshurites, Girzites, and Amalekites, making sure no one escaped to tell the tale (1 Sam 27:5-12). David later conquered the Amalekites after they raided Ziklag (1 Sam 30:1-31).

7 Mount Gilboa War with the Philistines broke out again in the north, near Mount Gilboa. Saul, who no longer relied on God, consulted a medium in a desperate attempt to contact Samuel, who had died, for help. The Philistines slaughtered the Israelites on Mount Gilboa, killing King Saul and three of his sons, including David's loyal friend, Jonathan. (1 Sam 28:1–31:13).

8 Hebron After Saul's death, David moved to Hebron, where the tribe of Judah crowned him king. But the rest of Israel's tribes backed Saul's son, Ishbosheth, and crowned him king at Mahanaim. As a result, there was war between Judah and the rest of the tribes of Israel until Ishbosheth was assassinated. Then all of Israel pledged loyalty to David as their king (2 Sam 1:1–5:5).

9 Jerusalem One of David's first battles as king over the entire nation occurred at the fortress of Zion (Jerusalem). David and his troops took the city by surprise, and it became his capital. It was here that David brought the Ark of the Covenant and made a special covenant with God (2 Sam 5:6–7:29).

10 Baal-perazim David was not very popular with the Philistines because he had slain Goliath, one of their greatest warriors (1 Sam 17). When David began to rule over a united Israel, the Philistines set out to capture him. But as David and his army approached Jerusalem, they attacked the Philistines at Baal-perazim. His army defeated the mighty Philistines twice, causing all the surrounding nations to fear David's power (1 Chr 14:11-17).

11 Kiriath-jearim The Ark of the Covenant, which had been captured by the Philistines in battle and returned (1 Sam 4–6), was in safekeeping in Kiriath-jearim. David summoned all Israel to this city to join in bringing the Ark to Jerusalem. Unfortunately, it was not moved according to God's instructions, and as a result, one man died. David left the Ark in the home of Obed-edom until he could discover how to transport it correctly (1 Chr 13:1-14).

12 Moab During the time of the judges, Moab controlled many cities in Israel and demanded heavy taxes (Judg 3:12-30). David conquered Moab and, in turn, levied tribute from them (2 Sam 8:2).

13 Edom Though the Edomites and the Israelites traced their ancestry back to the same man, Isaac (Gen 25:19-23), they were long-standing enemies. David defeated Edom and also forced them to pay tribute (2 Sam 8:14).

14 Rabbah The Ammonites insulted David's delegation and turned a peacemaking mission into angry warfare. The Ammonites called troops from Aram, but David defeated this alliance first at Helam, then at Rabbah, the capital city (2 Sam 10:1–12:31).

15 Mahanaim David had victory in the field but problems at home. His son Absalom incited a rebellion and crowned himself king at Hebron. David and his men fled to Mahanaim. Acting on bad advice, Absalom mobilized his army to fight David (2 Sam 13:1–17:29).

16 Forest of Ephraim The armies of Absalom and David fought in the forest of Ephraim. Absalom's hair got caught in a tree, and Joab, David's general, found and killed him. With Absalom's death the rebellion died, and David was welcomed back to Jerusalem (2 Sam 18:1–19:43).

17 Abel-beth-maacah A man named Sheba also incited a rebellion against David. He fled to Abel-beth-maacah, but Joab and a small company of troops besieged the city. The citizens of Abel-beth-maacah killed Sheba themselves (2 Sam 20:1-26). David's victories laid the foundation for the peaceful reign of his son Solomon.

18 Tyre David and Solomon did much building in Jerusalem. King Hiram of Tyre sent workers and supplies to help build David's palace, and many supplies for the construction of the Temple under Solomon. Cedar, abundant in the mountains north of Israel, was a valuable and hardy wood for the beautiful buildings in Jerusalem.

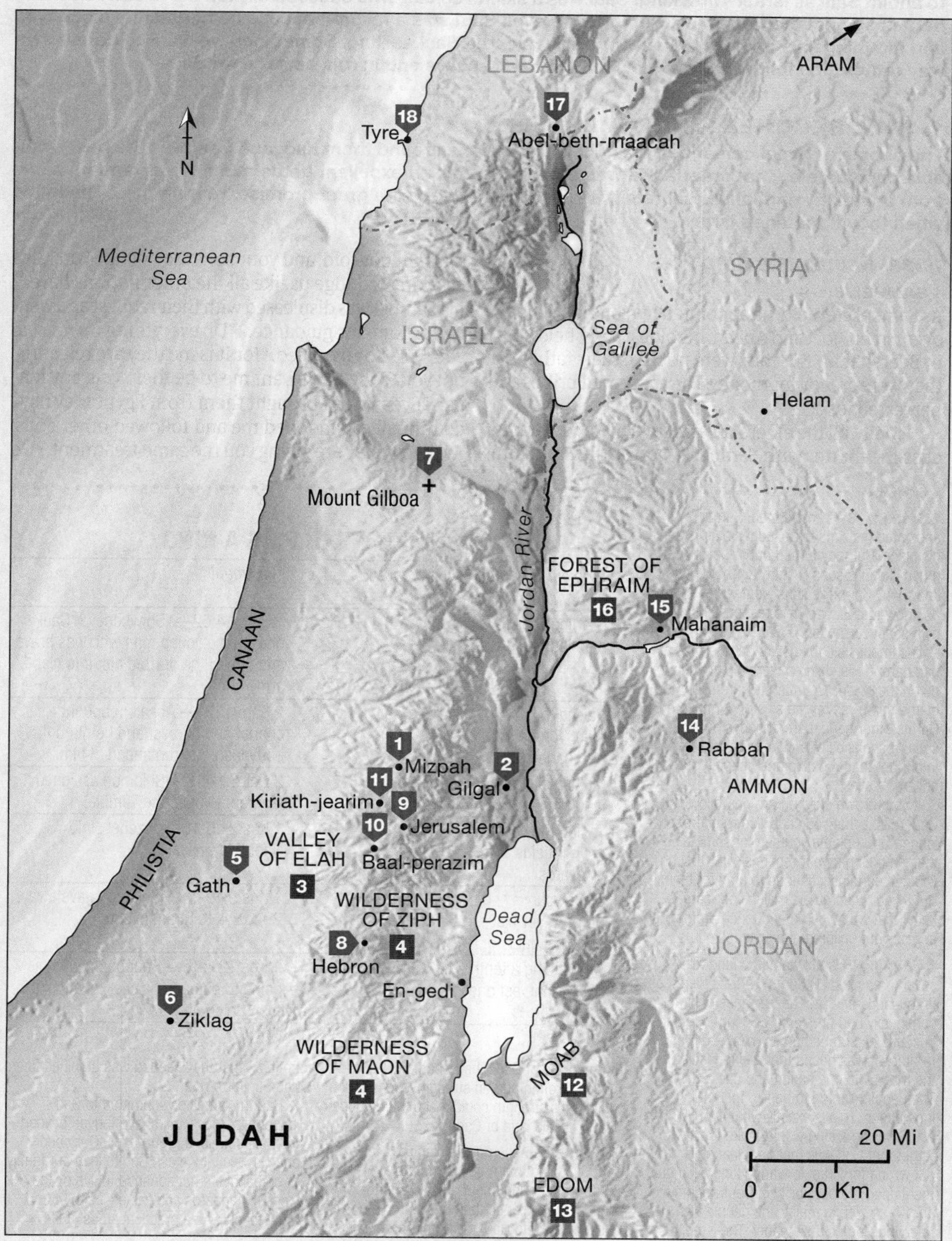

A. Samuel and Saul

Samuel had judged Israel well, saving them from the Philistines and leading them back to God. But when he retired, the nation did not want another judge. Instead, they demanded to be given a king in order to be like the nations around them. Although God was unhappy with their request, he told Samuel to anoint Saul as Israel's first king. Saul was a skillful soldier who successfully led the nation into many battles against their enemies. But in God's eyes Saul was a failure because he constantly disobeyed and did things his own way. God eventually rejected Saul as king. Sometimes we want to go our own way rather than follow the ways of God. This will always end in ruin as it did for Saul.

1. SAUL BECOMES KING OF ISRAEL

The people of Israel demanded a king like the nations around them had, and Saul was the best available candidate by that criteria. He was handsome, tall, an excellent battle commander, and he came from a wealthy and influential family. He began his reign with great promise, routing the Ammonites when they threatened Israel.

Israel Requests a King

1 SAMUEL 8:1-9

As Samuel grew old, he appointed his sons to be judges over Israel. 2Joel and Abijah, his oldest sons, held court in Beersheba. 3But they were not like their father, for they were greedy for money. They accepted bribes and perverted justice.

4Finally, all the elders of Israel met at Ramah to discuss the matter with Samuel. 5"Look," they told him, "you are now old, and your sons are not like you. Give us a king to judge us like all the other nations have."

6Samuel was displeased with their request and went to the LORD for guidance. 7"Do everything they say to you," the LORD replied, "for it is me they are rejecting, not you. They don't want me to be their king any longer. 8Ever since I brought them from Egypt they have continually abandoned me and followed other gods. And now they are giving you the same treatment. 9Do

1 Sam 8:1-3 As an old man, Samuel appointed his sons to be judges over Israel in his place. But they turned out to be corrupt, much like Eli's sons (1 Sam 2:12). We don't know why Samuel's sons went wrong, but we do know that Eli was held responsible for his own sons' corruption (1 Sam 2:29-34).

It is impossible to know if Samuel was a bad parent. His children were old enough to be on their own. We must be careful not to blame ourselves for the sins of our children. On the other hand, parenthood is an awesome responsibility, and nothing is more important than molding and shaping our children's lives.

If your grown children are not following God, realize that you can't control them any longer. Don't blame yourself for something that is no longer your responsibility, though you can certainly continue to pray for them. But if your children are still in your care, know that what you do and teach profoundly affects your children and lasts a lifetime.

1 Sam 8:4-9 Israel wanted a king for several reasons: (1) Samuel's sons were not fit to lead Israel. (2) The 12 tribes of Israel continually had problems working together because each tribe had its own leader and territory. It was hoped that a king would unite the tribes into one nation and one army. (3) The people wanted to be like the neighboring nations. This is exactly what God didn't want. Having a king would make it easy to forget that God was their real leader. It was not wrong for Israel to want a king; God had mentioned the possibility in Deuteronomy 17:14-20. Yet, in reality, the people were rejecting God as their leader. The Israelites wanted laws, an army, and a human monarch in the place of God. They wanted to run the nation through human strength, even though only God's strength could make them flourish in the hostile land of Canaan.

1 Sam 8:5-6 The people clamored for a king, thinking that a new system of government would bring about a change in the nation. But because their basic problem was disobedience to God, their other problems would only continue under the new administration. What they needed was a unified faith, not a uniform rule.

Had the Israelites submitted to God's leadership, they would have thrived beyond their expectations (Deut 28:1). Our obedience is weak if we ask God to lead our family or personal life but continue to live by the world's standards and values. Faith in God must touch all the practical areas of life.

THE PROBLEMS WITH HAVING A KING

Problems (warned by Samuel)	*Reference*	*Fulfillment*
Drafting young men into the army	**1 Sam 8:11-12**	1 Sam 14:52—"So whenever Saul observed a young man who was brave and strong, he drafted him into his army."
Having the young men "run before his chariots"	**1 Sam 8:11**	2 Sam 15:1—"Absalom bought a chariot and horses, and he hired fifty bodyguards to run ahead of him."
Making slave laborers	**1 Sam 8:12, 17**	2 Chr 2:17-18—Solomon assigned laborers to build the Temple.
Taking the best of your fields and vineyards	**1 Sam 8:14**	1 Kgs 21:5-16—Jezebel stole Naboth's vineyard.
Using your property for his personal gain	**1 Sam 8:14-16**	1 Kgs 9:10-14—Solomon gave away 20 towns to Hiram of Tyre.
Demanding a tenth of your harvest and flocks	**1 Sam 8:15, 17**	1 Kgs 12:1-16—Rehoboam was going to demand heavier taxation than Solomon.

as they ask, but solemnly warn them about the way a king will reign over them."

Samuel Warns against a Kingdom

1 SAMUEL 8:10-22

So Samuel passed on the LORD's warning to the people who were asking him for a king. 11"This is how a king will reign over you," Samuel said. "The king will draft your sons and assign them to his chariots and his charioteers, making them run before his chariots. 12Some will be generals and captains in his army,* some will be forced to plow in his fields and harvest his crops, and some will make his weapons and chariot equipment. 13The king will take your daughters from you and force them to cook and bake and make perfumes for him. 14He will take away the best of your fields and vineyards and olive groves and give them to his own officials. 15He will take a tenth of your grain and your grape harvest and distribute it among his officers and attendants. 16He will take your male and female slaves and demand the finest of your cattle* and donkeys for his own use. 17He will demand a tenth of your flocks, and you will be his slaves. 18When that day comes, you will beg for relief from this king you are demanding, but then the LORD will not help you."

19But the people refused to listen to Samuel's warning. "Even so, we still want a king," they said. 20"We want to be like the nations around us. Our king will judge us and lead us into battle."

21So Samuel repeated to the LORD what the people had said, 22and the LORD replied, "Do as they say, and give them a king." Then Samuel agreed and sent the people home.

Saul Meets Samuel

1 SAMUEL 9:1-27

There was a wealthy, influential man named Kish from the tribe of Benjamin. He was the son of Abiel, son of Zeror, son of Becorath, son of Aphiah, of the tribe of Benjamin. 2His son Saul was the most handsome man in Israel—head and shoulders taller than anyone else in the land.

3One day Kish's donkeys strayed away, and he told Saul, "Take a servant with you, and go look for the donkeys." 4So Saul took one of the servants and traveled through the hill country of Ephraim, the land of Shalishah, the Shaalim area, and the entire land of Benjamin, but they couldn't find the donkeys anywhere.

5Finally, they entered the region of Zuph, and Saul

1 Sm 8:12 Hebrew *commanders of thousands and commanders of fifties.* **1 Sm 8:16** As in Greek version; Hebrew reads *young men.*

1 Sam 8:19-20 Samuel carefully explained all the negative consequences of having a king, but the Israelites refused to listen. When you have an important decision to make, weigh the positives and negatives carefully, considering everyone who might be affected by your choice. When you want something badly enough, it is difficult to see the potential problems. But don't discount the negatives. Unless you have a plan to handle each one, they will cause you great difficulty later.

1 Sam 8:19-20 Israel was called to be a holy nation, separate from and unique among all others (Lev 20:26). The Israelites' motive in asking for a king was to be like the nations around them. This was in total opposition to God's original plan. It was not their desire for a king that was wrong, but their reasons for wanting a king.

Often we let others' values and actions dictate our attitudes and behavior. Have you ever made a wrong choice because you wanted to be like everyone else? Be careful that the values of your friends or "heroes" don't pull you away from what God says is right. When God's people want to be like unbelievers, they are heading for spiritual disaster.

1 Sam 9:3 Saul's father sent him on an important mission—to find their stray donkeys. Donkeys were all-purpose animals, the "pickup trucks" of Bible times. Used for transportation, hauling, and farming, they were considered necessities. Even the poorest family owned one. To own many donkeys was a sign of wealth, and to lose them was a disaster. Saul's father was wealthy, and his many donkeys were evidence of that wealth.

1 Sam 9:3ff Often we think that events "just happen" to us, but as we learn from this story about Saul, God may use common occurrences to lead us where he wants. It is important to evaluate all situations as potential "divine appointments" designed to shape our lives. Think of all the good and bad circumstances that have affected you lately. Can you see God's purpose in them? Perhaps he is building a certain quality in you or leading you to serve him in a new area.

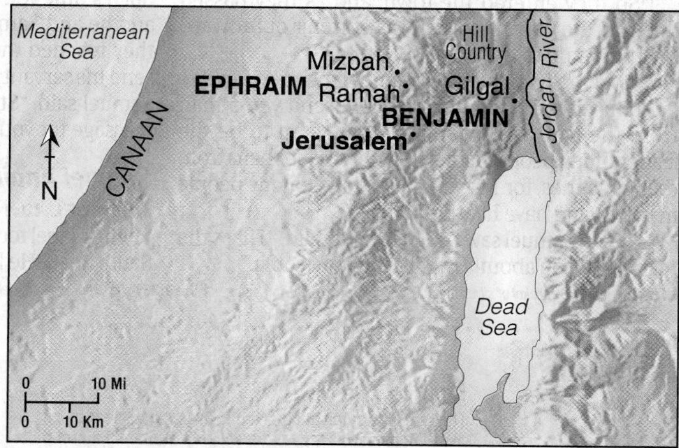

***SAUL CHOSEN AS KING** Saul and a servant searched for their lost donkeys in the hill country of Ephraim and the territory of Benjamin. They went to Ramah looking for help from Samuel the prophet. While Saul was there, he found himself unexpectedly anointed by Samuel as Israel's first king. Samuel called Israel together at Mizpah to tell them God's choice for their king.*

▸ 1 SAMUEL 9:1-27 *(cont.)*
said to his servant, "Let's go home. By now my father
will be more worried about us than about the donkeys!"
6But the servant said, "I've just thought of something! There is a man of God who lives here in this
town. He is held in high honor by all the people because everything he says comes true. Let's go find him.
Perhaps he can tell us which way to go."
7"But we don't have anything to offer him," Saul
replied. "Even our food is gone, and we don't have a
thing to give him."
8"Well," the servant said, "I have one small silver
piece.* We can at least offer it to the man of God and
see what happens!" 9(In those days if people wanted
a message from God, they would say, "Let's go and ask
the seer," for prophets used to be called seers.)
10"All right," Saul agreed, "let's try it!" So they started
into the town where the man of God lived.
11As they were climbing the hill to the town, they
met some young women coming out to draw water. So
Saul and his servant asked, "Is the seer here today?"
12"Yes," they replied. "Stay right on this road. He is
at the town gates. He has just arrived to take part in a
public sacrifice up at the place of worship. 13Hurry and
catch him before he goes up there to eat. The guests
won't begin eating until he arrives to bless the food."
14So they entered the town, and as they passed
through the gates, Samuel was coming out toward
them to go up to the place of worship.
15Now the LORD had told Samuel the previous day,
16"About this time tomorrow I will send you a man
from the land of Benjamin. Anoint him to be the
leader of my people, Israel. He will rescue them from
the Philistines, for I have looked down on my people
in mercy and have heard their cry."
17When Samuel saw Saul, the LORD said, "That's the
man I told you about! He will rule my people."
18Just then Saul approached Samuel at the gateway
and asked, "Can you please tell me where the seer's
house is?"
19"I am the seer!" Samuel replied. "Go up to the
place of worship ahead of me. We will eat there together, and in the morning I'll tell you what you want
to know and send you on your way. 20And don't worry
about those donkeys that were lost three days ago, for
they have been found. And I am here to tell you that
you and your family are the focus of all Israel's hopes."
21Saul replied, "But I'm only from the tribe of Benjamin, the smallest tribe in Israel, and my family is the
least important of all the families of that tribe! Why
are you talking like this to me?"
22Then Samuel brought Saul and his servant into
the hall and placed them at the head of the table, honoring them above the thirty special guests. 23Samuel
then instructed the cook to bring Saul the finest cut of
meat, the piece that had been set aside for the guest of
honor. 24So the cook brought in the meat and placed it
before Saul. "Go ahead and eat it," Samuel said. "I was
saving it for you even before I invited these others!"
So Saul ate with Samuel that day.
25When they came down from the place of worship
and returned to town, Samuel took Saul up to the roof
of the house and prepared a bed for him there.* 26At
daybreak the next morning, Samuel called to Saul, "Get
up! It's time you were on your way." So Saul got ready,
and he and Samuel left the house together. 27When
they reached the edge of town, Samuel told Saul to
send his servant on ahead. After the servant was gone,
Samuel said, "Stay here, for I have received a special
message for you from God."

Samuel Anoints Saul as King

1 SAMUEL 10:1-8
Then Samuel took a flask of olive oil and poured it over
Saul's head. He kissed Saul and said, "I am doing this

1 Sm 9:8 Hebrew *¼ shekel of silver,* about 0.1 ounces or 3 grams in weight. **1 Sm 9:25** As in Greek version; Hebrew reads *and talked with him there.*

Lyre

The lyre was small and portable, as is made clear by its mention as one of the four musical instruments a group of prophets carried around with them while prophesying (1 Sam 10:5). The lyre was made of wood, David's probably being made of cypress (2 Sam 6:5). Those that Solomon made for the Temple were constructed of sandalwood (1 Kgs 10:12) and were evidently very valuable. The lyre was used in the worship of God much in the same way guitars are used in modern worship. If God has gifted you musically, use your gift in your local church.

1 Sam 9:6 The city where the servant said the prophet lived was probably Ramah, where Samuel moved after the Philistine battle near Shiloh (1 Sam 7:17). Saul's lack of knowledge about Samuel showed his ignorance of spiritual matters. Saul and Samuel even lived in the same tribal territory—Benjamin.

1 Sam 9:21 "Why are you talking like this to me?" Saul's outburst reveals a problem he would face repeatedly—feeling inferior. Like a leaf tossed about by the wind, Saul vacillated between his feelings and his convictions. Everything he said and did was selfish because he was worried about himself. For example, Saul said his clan was "the least important" in the smallest tribe in Israel, but 1 Samuel 9:1 says his father was "a wealthy, influential man." (The tribe of Benjamin was the smallest because they were nearly wiped out as punishment for their immorality—see Judg 19–21.) Saul didn't want to face the responsibility God had given him. Later, Saul kept some war plunder that he shouldn't have and then tried to blame his soldiers (1 Sam 15:21) while claiming that they had really taken it to sacrifice to God (1 Sam 15:15).

Although Saul had been called by God and had a mission in life, he struggled constantly with jealousy, insecurity, arrogance, impulsiveness, and deceit. He did not decide to be wholeheartedly committed to God. Because Saul would not let God's love give rest to his heart, he never became God's man.

because the LORD has appointed you to be the ruler
over Israel, his special possession.* 2When you leave
me today, you will see two men beside Rachel's tomb
at Zelzah, on the border of Benjamin. They will tell you
that the donkeys have been found and that your father
has stopped worrying about them and is now worried
about you. He is asking, 'Have you seen my son?'
3"When you get to the oak of Tabor, you will see
three men coming toward you who are on their way
to worship God at Bethel. One will be bringing three
young goats, another will have three loaves of bread,
and the third will be carrying a wineskin full of wine.
4They will greet you and offer you two of the loaves,
which you are to accept.
5"When you arrive at Gibeah of God,* where the
garrison of the Philistines is located, you will meet
a band of prophets coming down from the place of
worship. They will be playing a harp, a tambourine,
a flute, and a lyre, and they will be prophesying. 6At
that time the Spirit of the LORD will come powerfully
upon you, and you will prophesy with them. You will
be changed into a different person. 7After these signs
take place, do what must be done, for God is with you.
8Then go down to Gilgal ahead of me. I will join you
there to sacrifice burnt offerings and peace offerings.
You must wait for seven days until I arrive and give you
further instructions."

Samuel's Signs Are Fulfilled

1 SAMUEL 10:9-16

As Saul turned and started to leave, God gave him a
new heart, and all Samuel's signs were fulfilled that
day. 10When Saul and his servant arrived at Gibeah,
they saw a group of prophets coming toward them.
Then the Spirit of God came powerfully upon Saul,
and he, too, began to prophesy. 11When those who
knew Saul heard about it, they exclaimed, "What? Is
even Saul a prophet? How did the son of Kish become
a prophet?"
12And one of those standing there said, "Can anyone
become a prophet, no matter who his father is?"* So
that is the origin of the saying "Is even Saul a prophet?"
13When Saul had finished prophesying, he went
up to the place of worship. 14"Where have you been?"
Saul's uncle asked him and his servant.
"We were looking for the donkeys," Saul replied,

1 Sm 10:1 Greek version reads *over Israel. And you will rule over the LORD's people and save them from their enemies around them. This will be the sign to you that the LORD has appointed you to be leader over his special possession.* **1 Sm 10:5** Hebrew *Gibeath-elohim.* **1 Sm 10:12** Hebrew *said, "Who is their father?"*

RELIGIOUS AND POLITICAL CENTERS OF ISRAEL

During the period of the judges, Israel may have had more than one capital. This may explain why the Scriptures overlap with reference to some cities.

Gilgal	Josh 4:19; Judg 2:1; Hos 4:15; Mic 6:5
Shiloh	Josh 18:1-10; 19:51; Judg 18:31; 1 Sam 1:3; Jer 7:12-14
Shechem	Josh 24:1
Ramah	1 Sam 7:17; 8:4
Mizpah	Judg 11:11; 20:1; 1 Sam 10:17
Bethel	Judg 20:18, 26; 1 Sam 10:3
Gibeah (political center only)	1 Sam 10:26
Gibeon (religious center only)	1 Kgs 3:4; 2 Chr 1:2-3
Jerusalem	1 Kgs 8:1ff; Ps 51:16-19

Samuel called the Israelites together at Mizpah, where he anointed Saul as their first king. Up to this point, the political seat of the nation seems to have been the religious center of the nation as well. Above are the cities which probably served as both the religious and political centers of Israel since the days of Joshua. Saul may have been the first Israelite leader to separate the nation's religious center (probably Mizpah at this time) from its political center (Gibeah—1 Sam 11:4; 26:1). Politically, the nation grew strong for a while. But when Saul and his officials stopped seeking God's will, internal jealousies and strife soon began to decay the nation from within. When David became king, he brought the Ark of the Covenant back to Jerusalem, his capital. King Solomon then completely united the religious and political centers at Jerusalem.

1 Sam 10:1 When an Israelite king took office, he was not only crowned, he was also anointed. The coronation was the political act of establishing the king as ruler; the anointing was the religious act of making the king God's representative to the people. A king was always anointed by a priest or prophet. The special anointing oil was a mixture of olive oil, myrrh, and other expensive spices. It was poured over the king's head to symbolize the presence and power of the Holy Spirit of God in his life. This anointing ceremony was to remind the king of his great responsibility to lead his people by God's wisdom and not his own.

Saul becomes king

1 Sam 10:6 How could Saul be so filled with the Spirit and yet later commit such evil acts? Throughout the Old Testament, God's Spirit "came upon" individuals temporarily so that God could use them for great acts. This happened frequently to Israel's judges when they were called by God to rescue the nation (Judg 3:8-10). This was not a permanent, abiding influence, but a temporary manifestation of the Holy Spirit. At times in the Old Testament, the Spirit even came upon unbelievers to enable them to do unusual tasks (Num 24; 2 Chr 36:22-23). The Holy Spirit gave the person power to do what God asked, but this did not always produce the other fruits of the Spirit, such as self-control. In his early years as king, Saul was a different person as a result of the Holy Spirit's work in him (1 Sam 10:1-10). But as his power grew, so did his pride. After a while he refused to seek God; the Spirit left him (1 Sam 16:14), and his good attitude melted away.

1 Sam 10:10-11 A prophet is someone who speaks God's words. While God told many prophets to predict certain events, what God wanted most was for them to instruct and inspire people to live in faithfulness to God. When Saul's friends heard inspired words coming from Saul, they exclaimed, "Is even Saul a prophet?" An expression of surprise at worldly Saul becoming religious, it is equivalent to "What? Has he got religion?"

▶ **1 SAMUEL 10:9-16** ***(cont.)***

"but we couldn't find them. So we went to Samuel to ask him where they were."
15"Oh? And what did he say?" his uncle asked.
16"He told us that the donkeys had already been found," Saul replied. But Saul didn't tell his uncle what Samuel said about the kingdom.

Saul Is Acclaimed King

1 SAMUEL 10:17-27

Later Samuel called all the people of Israel to meet
before the LORD at Mizpah. 18And he said, "This is what
the LORD, the God of Israel, has declared: I brought you
from Egypt and rescued you from the Egyptians and
from all of the nations that were oppressing you. 19But
though I have rescued you from your misery and distress, you have rejected your God today and have said, 'No, we want a king instead!' Now, therefore, present yourselves before the LORD by tribes and clans."
20So Samuel brought all the tribes of Israel before
the LORD, and the tribe of Benjamin was chosen by lot.
21Then he brought each family of the tribe of Benjamin before the LORD, and the family of the Matrites was chosen. And finally Saul son of Kish was chosen from among them. But when they looked for him, he
had disappeared! 22So they asked the LORD, "Where
is he?"
And the LORD replied, "He is hiding among the baggage." 23So they found him and brought him out, and
he stood head and shoulders above anyone else.
24Then Samuel said to all the people, "This is the
man the LORD has chosen as your king. No one in all Israel is like him!"
And all the people shouted, "Long live the king!"
25Then Samuel told the people what the rights and
duties of a king were. He wrote them down on a scroll and placed it before the LORD. Then Samuel sent the people home again.

1 Sam 10:19 Israel's true king was God, but the nation demanded another. Imagine wanting a human being instead of God as guide and leader! Throughout history, men and women have rejected God, and they continue to do it today. Are you rejecting God by pushing him aside and acknowledging someone or something else as your "king" or top priority? Learn from these stories of Israel's kings, and don't push God aside.

1 Sam 10:20 The Israelites chose their first king by casting lots—perhaps by using the Urim and Thummim, two plates or flat stones carried by the high priest. The fact that Saul was chosen may seem like luck, but it was really the opposite. God had instructed the Israelites to make the Urim and Thummim for the specific purpose of consulting him in times such as this (Exod 28:30; Num 27:12-21). By using the Urim and Thummim, the Israelites were taking the decision out of their own hands and turning it over to God. Only the high priest could use the Urim and Thummim, which were designed to give only *yes* or *no* answers.

1 Sam 10:22 When the Israelites assembled to choose a king, Saul already knew he was the one (1 Sam 10:1). Instead of coming forward, he hid among the baggage. Often we hide from important responsibilities because we are afraid of failure, afraid of what others will think, or perhaps unsure about how to proceed. Prepare now to step up to your future responsibilities. Count on God's provision rather than your feelings of adequacy.

1 Sam 10:25 The kings of Israel, unlike kings of other nations, had specific regulations outlined for them (Deut 17:14-20). Pagan kings were considered gods; they made their own laws and answered to no one. By contrast, Israel's king had to answer to a higher authority—the Lord of heaven and earth. The Israelites now had a king like everyone else, just as they wanted. But

SAUL

First impressions can be deceiving. Saul presented the ideal visual image of a king, but his character often went contrary to God's commands for a king. Saul was the king God gave to fulfill Israel's request, but this did not mean he was capable of being king on his own. • During his reign, Saul had his greatest successes when he obeyed God. His greatest failures resulted from acting on his own. Saul had the raw materials to be a good leader—appearance, courage, and action. Even his weaknesses could have been used by God if Saul had recognized them and left them in God's hands. His own choices cut him off from God and eventually led to his downfall. • From Saul we learn that while our strengths and abilities make us useful, it is our weaknesses that make us usable. Our skills and talents make us tools, but our failures and shortcomings remind us that we need a Craftsman in control of our lives. Whatever we accomplish on our own is only a hint of what God could do through our lives. Does he control your life?

Strengths and accomplishments	• First king of Israel • Stood tall, with a striking appearance
Weaknesses and mistakes	• His leadership abilities did not match the expectations created by his appearance • Impulsive by nature, he tended to overstep his bounds • Allowed jealousy to overcome him • Directly disobeyed God on several occasions
Lessons from his life	• God wants obedience from the heart, not mere acts of religious ritual • God wants to make use of our strengths and weaknesses • Weaknesses should help us remember our need for God's guidance and help
Vital statistics	• Occupation: King of Israel • Relatives: Father: Kish. Wife: Ahinoam. Sons: Jonathan, Malkishua, Abinadab, Ishbosheth (and possibly Ishvi). Daughters: Merab, Michal.
Key verses	"But Samuel replied, 'What is more pleasing to the LORD: your burnt offerings and sacrifices or your obedience to his voice? Listen! Obedience is better than sacrifice, and submission is better than offering the fat of rams. Rebellion is as sinful as witchcraft, and stubbornness as bad as worshiping idols. So because you have rejected the command of the LORD, he has rejected you as king'" (1 Sam 15:22-23).

Saul's story is told in 1 Samuel 9–31. He is also mentioned in Acts 13:21.

26When Saul returned to his home at Gibeah, a group of men whose hearts God had touched went with him. 27But there were some scoundrels who complained, "How can this man save us?" And they scorned him and refused to bring him gifts. But Saul ignored them.

[Nahash, king of the Ammonites, had been grievously oppressing the people of Gad and Reuben who lived east of the Jordan River. He gouged out the right eye of each of the Israelites living there, and he didn't allow anyone to come and rescue them. In fact, of all the Israelites east of the Jordan, there wasn't a single one whose right eye Nahash had not gouged out. But there were 7,000 men who had escaped from the Ammonites, and they had settled in Jabesh-gilead.]*

Saul Defeats the Ammonites

1 SAMUEL 11:1-15

About a month later,* King Nahash of Ammon led his army against the Israelite town of Jabesh-gilead. But all the citizens of Jabesh asked for peace. "Make a treaty with us, and we will be your servants," they pleaded.

2"All right," Nahash said, "but only on one condition. I will gouge out the right eye of every one of you as a disgrace to all Israel!"

3"Give us seven days to send messengers throughout Israel!" replied the elders of Jabesh. "If no one comes to save us, we will agree to your terms."

4When the messengers came to Gibeah of Saul and told the people about their plight, everyone broke into tears. 5Saul had been plowing a field with his oxen, and when he returned to town, he asked, "What's the matter? Why is everyone crying?" So they told him about the message from Jabesh.

6Then the Spirit of God came powerfully upon Saul, and he became very angry. 7He took two oxen and cut them into pieces and sent the messengers to carry them throughout Israel with this message: "This is what will happen to the oxen of anyone who refuses to follow Saul and Samuel into battle!" And the LORD made the people afraid of Saul's anger, and all of them came out together as one. 8When Saul mobilized them at Bezek, he found that there were 300,000 men from Israel and 30,000* men from Judah.

9So Saul sent the messengers back to Jabesh-gilead to say, "We will rescue you by noontime tomorrow!" There was great joy throughout the town when that message arrived!

10The men of Jabesh then told their enemies, "Tomorrow we will come out to you, and you can do to us whatever you wish." 11But before dawn the next morning, Saul arrived, having divided his army into three detachments. He launched a surprise attack against the Ammonites and slaughtered them the whole morning. The remnant of their army was so badly scattered that no two of them were left together.

12Then the people exclaimed to Samuel, "Now where are those men who said, 'Why should Saul rule over us?' Bring them here, and we will kill them!"

1 Sm 10:27 This paragraph, which is not included in the Masoretic Text, is found in Dead Sea Scroll 4QSam[a]. **1 Sm 11:1** As in Greek version; Hebrew lacks *About a month later.* **1 Sm 11:8** Dead Sea Scrolls and Greek version read *70,000.*

Samuel, in his charge to both the king and the people, wanted to make sure that the rule of Israel's king would be different from that of his pagan counterparts. "Placed it before the LORD" means that Samuel put the scroll, as a witness to the agreement, in a special place at Mizpah.

1 Sam 10:26-27 Some men became Saul's constant companions, while others despised him. Criticism will always be directed toward those who lead because they are out in front. At this time, Saul took no notice of those who seemed to be against him, although later he would become consumed with jealousy (1 Sam 19:1-3; 26:17-21). As you lead, listen to constructive criticism, but don't spend valuable time and energy worrying about those who may oppose you. Instead, focus your attention on those who are ready and willing to help.

1 Sam 11:1ff At this time, Israel was very susceptible to invasion by marauding tribes such as these Ammonites from east of the Jordan River. Saul's leadership in battle against this warlike tribe helped unify the nation and proved that he was a worthy military ruler. Saul's kingship was solidified when he saved the nation from disgrace and spared the people who had criticized him.

1 Sam 11:3 Why would Nahash give the city of Jabesh-gilead seven days to find an army to help them? Because Israel was still disorganized, Nahash was betting that no one would come to the city's aid. He was hoping to take the city without a fight and avoid a battle. He also may not have been prepared to attack the city because a siege against its walls could last weeks or months.

1 Sam 11:6 Anger is a powerful emotion. Often it may drive people to hurt others with words or physical violence. But anger directed at sin and the mistreatment of others is not wrong. Saul was angered by the Ammonites' threat to humiliate and mistreat his fellow Israelites. The Holy Spirit used Saul's anger to bring justice and freedom. When injustice or sin makes you angry, ask God how you can channel that anger in constructive ways to help bring about a positive change.

1 Sam 11:8 Judah, one of the 12 tribes of Israel, is often mentioned separately from the other 11. There are several reasons for this: Judah was the largest tribe (Num 1:20-46), it was the tribe from which most of Israel's kings would come (Gen 49:8-12), and Judah would also be the tribe through which the Messiah would come (Mic 5:2).

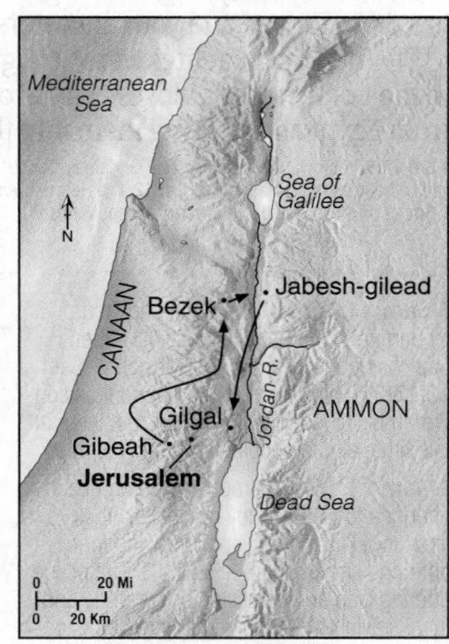

SAUL DEFEATS THE AMMONITES
The Ammonites prepared to attack Jabesh-gilead. The people of Jabesh sent messengers to Saul in Gibeah asking for help. Saul mobilized an army at Bezek and then attacked the Ammonites. After the battle, the Israelites returned to Gilgal to crown Saul as king.

▸ **1 SAMUEL 11:1-15 *(cont.)***

13But Saul replied, "No one will be executed today, for today the LORD has rescued Israel!"

14Then Samuel said to the people, "Come, let us all go to Gilgal to renew the kingdom." 15So they all went to Gilgal, and in a solemn ceremony before the LORD they made Saul king. Then they offered peace offerings to the LORD, and Saul and all the Israelites were filled with joy.

Samuel's Farewell Address

1 SAMUEL 12:1-25

Then Samuel addressed all Israel: "I have done as you asked and given you a king. 2Your king is now your leader. I stand here before you—an old, gray-haired man—and my sons serve you. I have served as your leader from the time I was a boy to this very day. 3Now testify against me in the presence of the LORD and before his anointed one. Whose ox or donkey have I stolen? Have I ever cheated any of you? Have I ever oppressed you? Have I ever taken a bribe and perverted justice? Tell me and I will make right whatever I have done wrong."

4"No," they replied, "you have never cheated or oppressed us, and you have never taken even a single bribe."

5"The LORD and his anointed one are my witnesses today," Samuel declared, "that my hands are clean."

"Yes, he is a witness," they replied.

6"It was the LORD who appointed Moses and Aaron," Samuel continued. "He brought your ancestors out of the land of Egypt. 7Now stand here quietly before the LORD as I remind you of all the great things the LORD has done for you and your ancestors.

8"When the Israelites were* in Egypt and cried out to the LORD, he sent Moses and Aaron to rescue them from Egypt and to bring them into this land. 9But the people soon forgot about the LORD their God, so he handed them over to Sisera, the commander of Hazor's army, and also to the Philistines and to the king of Moab, who fought against them.

10"Then they cried to the LORD again and confessed, 'We have sinned by turning away from the LORD and worshiping the images of Baal and Ashtoreth. But we will worship you and you alone if you will rescue us from our enemies.' 11Then the LORD sent Gideon,* Bedan,* Jephthah, and Samuel* to save you, and you lived in safety.

12"But when you were afraid of Nahash, the king of Ammon, you came to me and said that you wanted a king to reign over you, even though the LORD your God was already your king. 13All right, here is the king you have chosen. You asked for him, and the LORD has granted your request.

14"Now if you fear and worship the LORD and listen to his voice, and if you do not rebel against the LORD's commands, then both you and your king will show that you recognize the LORD as your God. 15But if you rebel against the LORD's commands and refuse to listen to him, then his hand will be as heavy upon you as it was upon your ancestors.

16"Now stand here and see the great thing the LORD is about to do. 17You know that it does not rain at this time of the year during the wheat harvest. I will ask the LORD to send thunder and rain today. Then you will realize how wicked you have been in asking the LORD for a king!"

18So Samuel called to the LORD, and the LORD sent thunder and rain that day. And all the people were terrified of the LORD and of Samuel. 19"Pray to the LORD your God for us, or we will die!" they all said to Samuel. "For now we have added to our sins by asking for a king."

20"Don't be afraid," Samuel reassured them. "You

1 Sm 12:8 Hebrew *When Jacob was.* The names "Jacob" and "Israel" are often interchanged throughout the Old Testament, referring sometimes to the individual patriarch and sometimes to the nation. **1 Sm 12:11a** Hebrew *Jerub-baal,* another name for Gideon; see Judg 6:32. **1 Sm 12:11b** Greek and Syriac versions read *Barak.* **1 Sm 12:11c** Greek and Syriac versions read *Samson.*

1 Sam 11:14 Saul had been anointed by Samuel at Ramah (1 Sam 10:1); then Saul was publicly chosen at Mizpah (1 Sam 10:17-27); his defeat of the Ammonites confirmed his kingship in the people's minds; at this time, all the people confirmed his rule.

1 Sam 11:15 The Israelites offered peace offerings to God as they made Saul their first king. The instructions for giving these offerings are found in Leviticus 3. The peace offering was an expression of gratitude and thanksgiving to God, symbolizing the peace that comes to those who know him and who live in accordance with his commands. Although God did not want his people to have a human king, the people were demonstrating through their offerings that he was still their true King. Unfortunately, this attitude did not last, just as God had predicted (1 Sam 8:7-19).

1 Sam 12:1ff Samuel continued to serve the people as their priest, prophet, and judge, but Saul exercised more and more political and military control over the tribes (see 1 Sam 7:15).

1 Sam 12:1-3 In his farewell speech, Samuel asked the Israelites to point out any wrongs he had committed during his time as Israel's judge. By doing so, Samuel was reminding them that he could be trusted to tell the truth. He was also reminding them that having a king was their idea, not his. Samuel was setting the stage for the miraculous thunderstorm recorded in 1 Samuel 12:16-19, so that the people could not blame him when God punished them for their selfish motives.

1 Sam 12:10 "The images of Baal and Ashtoreth" were pagan gods. (See the note on 1 Sam 7:4, p. 427.)

1 Sam 12:12-15 God granted the nation's request for a king, but his commands and requirements remained the same. God was to be their true King, and both Saul and the people were to be subject to his laws. No person is ever exempt from God's laws. No human action is outside his jurisdiction. God is the true King of every area of life. We must recognize his kingship and pattern our relationships, work life, and home life according to his principles.

1 Sam 12:17 The wheat harvest came near the end of the dry season during the months of May and June. Because rain rarely fell during this period, a great thunderstorm was considered a miraculous event. But it was not a beneficial miracle; rain during the wheat harvest could damage the crops and cause them to rot quickly. This unusual occurrence showed

have certainly done wrong, but make sure now that you worship the LORD with all your heart, and don't turn your back on him. 21 Don't go back to worshiping worthless idols that cannot help or rescue you—they are totally useless! 22 The LORD will not abandon his people, because that would dishonor his great name. For it has pleased the LORD to make you his very own people.

23 "As for me, I will certainly not sin against the LORD by ending my prayers for you. And I will continue to teach you what is good and right. 24 But be sure to fear the LORD and faithfully serve him. Think of all the wonderful things he has done for you. 25 But if you continue to sin, you and your king will be swept away."

2. GOD REJECTS SAUL FOR DISOBEDIENCE

It didn't take long for Saul to show his true colors as Israel's king. He was more concerned about appearances than actually obeying God's commands, and so God rejected him as king of Israel. God allowed him to continue to serve as king as long as he lived, but he would not be able to pass his crown on to his sons when he died. We need to obey God whole-heartedly, because he sees beyond appearances to the motivation of our hearts.

Continued War with Philistia

1 SAMUEL 13:1-7a

Saul was thirty* years old when he became king, and he reigned for forty-two years.*

2 Saul selected 3,000 special troops from the army of Israel and sent the rest of the men home. He took 2,000 of the chosen men with him to Micmash and the hill country of Bethel. The other 1,000 went with Saul's son Jonathan to Gibeah in the land of Benjamin.

3 Soon after this, Jonathan attacked and defeated the garrison of Philistines at Geba. The news spread quickly among the Philistines. So Saul blew the ram's horn throughout the land, saying, "Hebrews, hear this! Rise up in revolt!" 4 All Israel heard the news that Saul had destroyed the Philistine garrison at Geba and that the Philistines now hated the Israelites more than ever. So the entire Israelite army was summoned to join Saul at Gilgal.

5 The Philistines mustered a mighty army of 3,000* chariots, 6,000 charioteers, and as many warriors as the grains of sand on the seashore! They camped at Micmash east of Beth-aven. 6 The men of Israel saw what a tight spot they were in; and because they were hard pressed by the enemy, they tried to hide in caves, thickets, rocks, holes, and cisterns. 7 Some of them crossed the Jordan River and escaped into the land of Gad and Gilead.

Saul's Disobedience and Samuel's Rebuke

1 SAMUEL 13:7b-14

Meanwhile, Saul stayed at Gilgal, and his men were trembling with fear. 8 Saul waited there seven days for Samuel, as Samuel had instructed him earlier, but Samuel still didn't come. Saul realized that his troops were rapidly slipping away. 9 So he demanded, "Bring me the burnt offering and the peace

1 Sm 13:1a As in a few Greek manuscripts; the number is missing in the Hebrew. **1 Sm 13:1b** Hebrew *reigned . . . and two;* the number is incomplete in the Hebrew. Compare Acts 13:21. **1 Sm 13:5** As in Greek and Syriac versions; Hebrew reads *30,000.*

God's displeasure with Israel's demand for a king.

1 Sam 12:22 Why did God make Israel "his very own people"? God did not choose them because they deserved it (Deut 7:7-8) but in order that they might become his channel of blessing to all people (Gen 12:1-3). Because God chose the people of Israel, he would never abandon them; but because they were his special nation, he would often punish them for their disobedience in order to bring them back to a right relationship with him.

1 Sam 12:23 Is failing to pray for others a sin? Samuel's words seem to indicate that it is. His actions illustrate two of God's people's responsibilities: (1) They should pray consistently for others (Eph 6:18), and (2) they should teach others the right way to God (2 Tim 2:2). Samuel disagreed with the Israelites' demand for a king, but he assured them that he would continue to pray for them and teach them. We may disagree with others, but we shouldn't stop praying for them.

1 Sam 12:24 This is the second time in his farewell speech that Samuel reminded the people to take time to consider what great things God had done for them (see 1 Sam 12:7). Taking time for reflection allows us to focus our attention upon God's goodness and strengthens our faith. Sometimes we are so progress- and future-oriented that we fail to take time to recall all that God has already done. Remember what God has done for you so that you may move ahead with gratitude.

1 Sam 13:3-4 Jonathan attacked and destroyed the Philistine outpost, but Saul took all the credit for it. Although this was normal in that culture, it didn't make his action right. Saul's growing pride started out small—taking credit for a battle that was won by his son. Left unchecked, his pride grew into an ugly obsession; thus, it destroyed him, tore his family apart, and threatened the well-being of the nation. Taking credit for the accomplishments of others indicates that pride is controlling your life. When you notice pride taking a foothold, take immediate steps to put it in check by giving credit to those who deserve it.

1 Sam 13:6 When we forget who is on our side or see only our own resources, we tend to panic at the sight of the opposition. The Israelites became terrified and hid when they saw the mighty Philistine army. They forgot that God was on their side and that he couldn't be defeated. As you face problems and temptations, focus your attention on God and his resources, trusting him to help you (Rom 8:31-37).

1 Sam 13:9 Rather than waiting for a priest, Saul offered the sacrifice himself. This was against God's laws (Deut 12:5-14) and against the specific instructions of Samuel (1 Sam 10:8). Under pressure from the approaching Philistines, he took matters into his own hands and disobeyed God. He was doing a good thing (offering a sacrifice to God before a crucial battle), but he did it in the wrong way. Like Saul, our true spiritual character is revealed under pressure. The methods we use to accomplish our goals are as important as the attainment of those goals.

▶ **1 SAMUEL 13:7b-14** ***(cont.)***
offerings!" And Saul sacrificed the burnt offering
himself.
10Just as Saul was finishing with the burnt offering,
Samuel arrived. Saul went out to meet and welcome
him, 11but Samuel said, "What is this you have done?"
Saul replied, "I saw my men scattering from me,
and you didn't arrive when you said you would, and
the Philistines are at Micmash ready for battle. 12So I
said, 'The Philistines are ready to march against us at
Gilgal, and I haven't even asked for the LORD's help!'
So I felt compelled to offer the burnt offering myself
before you came."
13"How foolish!" Samuel exclaimed. "You have not
kept the command the LORD your God gave you. Had
you kept it, the LORD would have established your
kingdom over Israel forever. 14But now your kingdom
must end, for the LORD has sought out a man after his
own heart. The LORD has already appointed him to be
the leader of his people, because you have not kept the
LORD's command."

Israel's Military Disadvantage

1 SAMUEL 13:15-23
Samuel then left Gilgal and went on his way, but the
rest of the troops went with Saul to meet the army.
They went up from Gilgal to Gibeah in the land of
Benjamin.* When Saul counted the men who were still
with him, he found only 600 were left! 16Saul and Jonathan and the troops with them were staying at Geba
in the land of Benjamin. The Philistines set up their
camp at Micmash. 17Three raiding parties soon left
the camp of the Philistines. One went north toward
Ophrah in the land of Shual, 18another went west to
Beth-horon, and the third moved toward the border
above the valley of Zeboim near the wilderness.
19There were no blacksmiths in the land of Israel in
those days. The Philistines wouldn't allow them for fear
they would make swords and spears for the Hebrews.
20So whenever the Israelites needed to sharpen their
plowshares, picks, axes, or sickles,* they had to take
them to a Philistine blacksmith. 21(The charges were
as follows: a quarter of an ounce of silver* for sharpening a plowshare or a pick, and an eighth of an ounce*
for sharpening an ax, a sickle, or an ox goad.) 22So on
the day of the battle none of the people of Israel had a
sword or spear, except for Saul and Jonathan.
23The pass at Micmash had meanwhile been secured by a contingent of the Philistine army.

Jonathan's Daring Plan

1 SAMUEL 14:1-15
One day Jonathan said to his armor bearer, "Come
on, let's go over to where the Philistines have their
outpost." But Jonathan did not tell his father what
he was doing.

1 Sm 13:15 As in Greek version; Hebrew reads *Samuel then left Gilgal and went to Gibeah in the land of Benjamin.* **1 Sm 13:20** As in Greek version; Hebrew reads *or plowshares.* **1 Sm 13:21a** Hebrew *1 pim* [8 grams]. **1 Sm 13:21b** Hebrew *⅓ of a shekel* [4 grams].

1 Sam 13:11-12 It is difficult to trust God when you feel your resources slipping away. When Saul felt that time was running out, he became impatient with God's timing. In thinking that the ritual was all he needed, he substituted the ritual for faith in God.

When faced with a difficult decision, don't allow impatience to drive you to disobey God. When you know what God wants, follow his plan regardless of the consequences. God often uses delays to test our obedience and patience.

1 Sam 13:12-13 Saul had plenty of excuses for his disobedience. But Samuel zeroed in on the real issue: "You have not kept the command the LORD your God gave you." Like Saul, we often gloss over our mistakes and sins, trying to justify our actions because of our "special" circumstances. But our excuses are nothing more than disobedience. God knows our true motives. He forgives, restores, and blesses only when we are honest about our sins. By trying to hide his sins behind excuses, Saul lost his kingship (1 Sam 13:14).

1 Sam 13:19-22 Israel was in no position to conquer anyone. The army had no iron weapons, and there were no facilities for turning their tools into weapons. In fact, if an Israelite wanted to sharpen his tools, he had to pay a Philistine blacksmith to do it because the Philistines had a carefully guarded monopoly on iron and blacksmithing. And they charged high prices for sharpening farm implements. The Philistines' tight control over the technology, along with their surprise raids, demoralized the Israelites and kept them in subjection.

Against such superiority, the Israelites were at a serious disadvantage. How could they hope to rout their oppressors? Only with God's help. God wanted to give Israel victory without swords so they would realize their true source of strength.

GLOOM AND DOOM

Samuel's messages to Israel

Reference	*Message*
1 Sam 3:11-14	Judgment will come to the house of Eli.
1 Sam 7:1-4	The nation must turn from idol worship.
1 Sam 8:10-22	Your kings will bring you nothing but trouble.
1 Sam 12:25	If you continue in sin, you will be destroyed by God.
1 Sam 13:13-14	Saul's kingdom will not continue.
1 Sam 15:17-31	Saul, you have sinned before God.

It wasn't easy being a prophet. Most of the messages prophets had to give were very unpleasant to hear. They preached of repentance, judgment, impending destruction, sin, and in general, how displeased God was over the behavior of his people. Prophets were not the most popular people in town (unless they were false prophets and said just what the people wanted to hear). But popularity was not the bottom line for true prophets of God—it was obedience to God and faithfully proclaiming his word. Samuel is a good example of a faithful prophet.

God has words for us to proclaim as well. And although his messages are loaded with "good news," there is also "bad news" to give. May we, like true prophets, faithfully deliver all God's words, regardless of their popularity or lack of it.

[2]Meanwhile, Saul and his 600 men were camped on the outskirts of Gibeah, around the pomegranate tree* at Migron. [3]Among Saul's men was Ahijah the priest, who was wearing the ephod, the priestly vest. Ahijah was the son of Ichabod's brother Ahitub, son of Phinehas, son of Eli, the priest of the LORD who had served at Shiloh.

No one realized that Jonathan had left the Israelite camp. [4]To reach the Philistine outpost, Jonathan had to go down between two rocky cliffs that were called Bozez and Seneh. [5]The cliff on the north was in front of Micmash, and the one on the south was in front of Geba. [6]"Let's go across to the outpost of those pagans," Jonathan said to his armor bearer. "Perhaps the LORD will help us, for nothing can hinder the LORD. He can win a battle whether he has many warriors or only a few!"

[7]"Do what you think is best," the armor bearer replied. "I'm with you completely, whatever you decide."

[8]"All right then," Jonathan told him. "We will cross over and let them see us. [9]If they say to us, 'Stay where you are or we'll kill you,' then we will stop and not go up to them. [10]But if they say, 'Come on up and fight,' then we will go up. That will be the LORD's sign that he will help us defeat them."

[11]When the Philistines saw them coming, they shouted, "Look! The Hebrews are crawling out of their holes!" [12]Then the men from the outpost shouted to Jonathan, "Come on up here, and we'll teach you a lesson!"

"Come on, climb right behind me," Jonathan said to his armor bearer, "for the LORD will help us defeat them!"

[13]So they climbed up using both hands and feet, and the Philistines fell before Jonathan, and his armor bearer killed those who came behind them. [14]They killed some twenty men in all, and their bodies were scattered over about half an acre.*

[15]Suddenly, panic broke out in the Philistine army, both in the camp and in the field, including even the outposts and raiding parties. And just then an earthquake struck, and everyone was terrified.

Israel Defeats the Philistines

1 SAMUEL 14:16-23

Saul's lookouts in Gibeah of Benjamin saw a strange sight—the vast army of Philistines began to melt away in every direction. [17]"Call the roll and find out who's missing," Saul ordered. And when they checked, they found that Jonathan and his armor bearer were gone.

[18]Then Saul shouted to Ahijah, "Bring the ephod here!" For at that time Ahijah was wearing the ephod in front of the Israelites.* [19]But while Saul was talking

1 Sm 14:2 Or *around the rock of Rimmon;* compare Judg 20:45, 47; 21:13. **1 Sm 14:14** Hebrew *half a yoke;* a "yoke" was the amount of land plowed by a pair of yoked oxen in one day. **1 Sm 14:18** As in some Greek manuscripts; Hebrew reads *"Bring the Ark of God." For at that time the Ark of God was with the Israelites.*

1 Sam 14:1ff In this chapter we read about the miserable job Saul did as leader: He had no communication with Jonathan (1 Sam 14:1, 17), he made a foolish curse (1 Sam 14:24), and he ignored the well-being of his own soldiers (1 Sam 14:31). Saul's poor leadership was not a result of personality traits but of decaying spiritual character. What we do is often a direct result of our spiritual condition. We cannot ignore the importance of spiritual character in effective leadership.

1 Sam 14:1 Why would Jonathan go alone to attack the Philistines? Jonathan may have been weary of the long, hopeless standoff in the battle; he trusted God to give the victory and wanted to act on that trust. He also knew that the number of Philistines was no problem for God. Perhaps he didn't tell his father about his mission because he thought Saul would not let him go.

1 Sam 14:6 Jonathan and his armor bearer weren't much of a force to attack the huge Philistine army. But while everyone else was afraid, they trusted God, knowing that the size of the enemy army would not restrict God's ability to help them. God honored the faith and brave action of these two men with a tremendous victory.

Have you ever felt surrounded by the "enemy" or faced overwhelming odds? God is never intimidated by the size of the enemy or the complexity of a problem. With him, there are always enough resources to resist the pressures and win the battle. If God has called you to action, then bravely commit what resources you have to God, and rely upon him to lead you to victory.

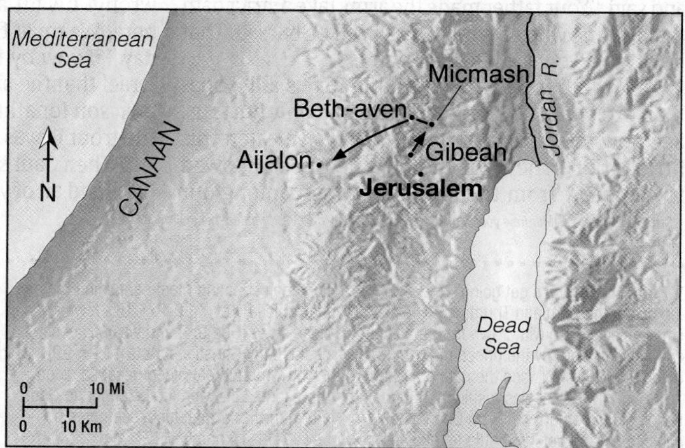

***JONATHAN'S BRAVERY** Saul's son Jonathan left the camp at Gibeah and crept to the Philistine camp at Micmash. With God's help, Jonathan and his armor bearer surprised the Philistines, who panicked and began killing each other! Saul's army heard the commotion and chased the Philistines as far as Beth-aven and Aijalon.*

1 Sam 14:12 Jonathan did not have the authority to lead all the troops into battle, but he could start a small skirmish in one corner of the enemy camp. When he did, panic broke out among the Philistines; the Hebrews who had been drafted into the Philistine army revolted; and the men who were hiding in the hills regained their courage and returned to fight.

When you are facing a difficult situation that is beyond your control, ask yourself, What steps can I take now to work toward a solution? A few small steps may be just what is needed to begin the chain of events leading to eventual victory.

▶ **1 SAMUEL 14:16-23** ***(cont.)***
to the priest, the confusion in the Philistine camp grew louder and louder. So Saul said to the priest, "Never mind; let's get going!"*
[20]Then Saul and all his men rushed out to the battle and found the Philistines killing each other. There was terrible confusion everywhere. [21]Even the Hebrews who had previously gone over to the Philistine army revolted and joined in with Saul, Jonathan, and the rest of the Israelites. [22]Likewise, the men of Israel who were hiding in the hill country of Ephraim joined the chase when they saw the Philistines running away. [23]So the LORD saved Israel that day, and the battle continued to rage even beyond Beth-aven.

Saul's Foolish Oath

1 SAMUEL 14:24-46
Now the men of Israel were pressed to exhaustion that day, because Saul had placed them under an oath, saying, "Let a curse fall on anyone who eats before evening—before I have full revenge on my enemies." So no one ate anything all day, [25]even though they had all found honeycomb on the ground in the forest. [26]They didn't dare touch the honey because they all feared the oath they had taken.

[27]But Jonathan had not heard his father's command, and he dipped the end of his stick into a piece of honeycomb and ate the honey. After he had eaten it, he felt refreshed.* [28]But one of the men saw him and said, "Your father made the army take a strict oath that anyone who eats food today will be cursed. That is why everyone is weary and faint."

[29]"My father has made trouble for us all!" Jonathan exclaimed. "A command like that only hurts us. See how refreshed I am now that I have eaten this little bit of honey. [30]If the men had been allowed to eat freely from the food they found among our enemies, think how many more Philistines we could have killed!"

[31]They chased and killed the Philistines all day from Micmash to Aijalon, growing more and more faint. [32]That evening they rushed for the battle plunder and butchered the sheep, goats, cattle, and calves, but they ate them without draining the blood. [33]Someone reported to Saul, "Look, the men are sinning against the LORD by eating meat that still has blood in it."

"That is very wrong," Saul said. "Find a large stone and roll it over here. [34]Then go out among the troops and tell them, 'Bring the cattle, sheep, and goats here to me. Kill them here, and drain the blood before you eat them. Do not sin against the LORD by eating meat with the blood still in it.'"

So that night all the troops brought their animals and slaughtered them there. [35]Then Saul built an altar to the LORD; it was the first of the altars he built to the LORD.

[36]Then Saul said, "Let's chase the Philistines all night and plunder them until sunrise. Let's destroy every last one of them."

His men replied, "We'll do whatever you think is best."

But the priest said, "Let's ask God first."

[37]So Saul asked God, "Should we go after the Philistines? Will you help us defeat them?" But God made no reply that day.

[38]Then Saul said to the leaders, "Something's wrong! I want all my army commanders to come here. We must find out what sin was committed today. [39]I vow by the name of the LORD who rescued Israel that the sinner will surely die, even if it is my own son Jonathan!" But no one would tell him what the trouble was.

[40]Then Saul said, "Jonathan and I will stand over here, and all of you stand over there."

1 Sm 14:19 Hebrew *Withdraw your hand.* **1 Sm 14:27** Or *his eyes brightened;* similarly in 14:29.

1 Sam 14:19 "Let's get going" refers to the use of the Urim and Thummim. These small objects were withdrawn from the linen ephod (vest) worn by the priest and used to determine God's will (see the note on 1 Sam 10:20, p. 438). Saul was rushing the formalities of getting an answer from God so he could hurry and get into battle to take advantage of the Philistines' confusion.

1 Sam 14:24 Saul made an oath without thinking through the implications. The results? (1) His men were too tired to fight; (2) they were so hungry they ate meat that still contained blood, which was against God's law (1 Sam 14:32); (3) Saul almost killed his own son (1 Sam 14:42-45).

Saul's impulsive oath sounded heroic, but it had disastrous side effects. If you are in the middle of a conflict, guard against impulsive statements that you may be forced to honor.

1 Sam 14:32-34 One of the oldest and strongest Hebrew food laws was the prohibition against eating meat containing the animal's blood (Lev 7:26-27). This law began in Noah's day (Gen 9:4) and was still observed by the early Christians (Acts 15:27-29). It was wrong to eat blood because blood represented life, and life belonged to God. (For a further explanation, see notes on Lev 17:11-14 and Lev 17:14, p. 223.)

1 Sam 14:35-36 After being king for several years, Saul finally built his first altar to God, but only as a last resort. Throughout Saul's reign he consistently approached God only after he had tried everything else. This was in sharp contrast to the priest, who suggested that God be consulted first. How much better if Saul had gone to God first, building an altar as his first official act as king. God is too great to be an afterthought. When we turn to him first, we will never have to turn to him as a last resort.

1 Sam 14:39 This is the second of Saul's foolish vows. Saul made the first of his two oaths (1 Sam 14:24-26) because he was overly anxious to defeat the Philistines and wanted to give his soldiers an incentive to finish the battle quickly. In the Bible, God never asked people to make oaths or vows; but if they did, he expected them to keep them (Lev 5:4; Num 30).

Saul's vow was not something God would have condoned, but still it was an oath. And Jonathan, although he didn't know about Saul's oath, was nevertheless guilty of breaking it. Like Jephthah (Judg 11), Saul made an oath that risked the life of his own child. Fortunately, the people intervened and spared Jonathan's life.

1 Sam 14:39 Saul had issued a ridiculous command and had driven his men to sin, but still he wouldn't back down even if he had to kill his son. When we make ridiculous statements, it is difficult to admit we are wrong. Sticking to the story, just to save face, only compounds the problem. It takes more cour-

And the people responded to Saul, "Whatever you think is best."
41Then Saul prayed, "O LORD, God of Israel, please show us who is guilty and who is innocent.*" Then they cast sacred lots, and Jonathan and Saul were chosen as the guilty ones, and the people were declared innocent.
42Then Saul said, "Now cast lots again and choose between me and Jonathan." And Jonathan was shown to be the guilty one.
43"Tell me what you have done," Saul demanded of Jonathan.

"I tasted a little honey," Jonathan admitted. "It was only a little bit on the end of my stick. Does that deserve death?"
44"Yes, Jonathan," Saul said, "you must die! May God strike me and even kill me if you do not die for this."
45But the people broke in and said to Saul, "Jonathan has won this great victory for Israel. Should he die? Far from it! As surely as the LORD lives, not one hair on his head will be touched, for God helped him do a great deed today." So the people rescued Jonathan, and he was not put to death.
46Then Saul called back the army from chasing the Philistines, and the Philistines returned home.

Saul's Military Successes

1 SAMUEL 14:47-52

Now when Saul had secured his grasp on Israel's throne, he fought against his enemies in every direction—against Moab, Ammon, Edom, the kings of Zobah, and the Philistines. And wherever he turned, he was victorious.* 48He performed great deeds and conquered the Amalekites, saving Israel from all those who had plundered them.
49Saul's sons included Jonathan, Ishbosheth,* and Malkishua. He also had two daughters: Merab, who was older, and Michal. 50Saul's wife was Ahinoam, the daughter of Ahimaaz. The commander of Saul's army was Abner, the son of Saul's uncle Ner. 51Saul's father, Kish, and Abner's father, Ner, were both sons of Abiel.
52The Israelites fought constantly with the Philistines throughout Saul's lifetime. So whenever Saul observed a young man who was brave and strong, he drafted him into his army.

Saul Destroys the Amalekites

1 SAMUEL 15:1-9

One day Samuel said to Saul, "It was the LORD who told me to anoint you as king of his people, Israel. Now listen to this message from the LORD! 2This is what the LORD of Heaven's Armies has declared: I have decided to settle accounts with the nation of Amalek for opposing Israel when they came from Egypt. 3Now go and completely destroy* the entire Amalekite nation—men, women, children, babies, cattle, sheep, goats, camels, and donkeys."
4So Saul mobilized his army at Telaim. There were 200,000 soldiers from Israel and 10,000 men from Judah. 5Then Saul and his army went to a town of the Amalekites and lay in wait in the valley. 6Saul sent this warning to the Kenites: "Move away from where the Amalekites live, or you will die with them. For you showed kindness to all the people of Israel when they came up from Egypt." So the Kenites packed up and left.
7Then Saul slaughtered the Amalekites from Havilah all the way to Shur, east of Egypt. 8He captured Agag, the Amalekite king, but completely destroyed

1 Sm 14:41 Greek version adds *If the fault is with me or my son Jonathan, respond with Urim; but if the men of Israel are at fault, respond with Thummim.* **1 Sm 14:47** As in Greek version; Hebrew reads *he acted wickedly.* **1 Sm 14:49** Hebrew *Ishvi,* a variant name for Ishbosheth; also known as Esh-baal. **1 Sm 15:3** The Hebrew term used here refers to the complete consecration of things or people to the LORD, either by destroying them or by giving them as an offering; also in 15:8, 9, 15, 18, 20, 21.

age to admit a mistake than to hold resolutely to an error.

1 Sam 14:43 Jonathan's spiritual character was in striking contrast to Saul's. Jonathan admitted what he had done; he did not try to make excuses. Even though he was unaware of Saul's oath, Jonathan was willing to accept the consequences of his actions. When you do wrong, even unintentionally, respond like Jonathan, not like Saul.

1 Sam 14:44-45 Saul made another foolish statement, this time because he was more concerned about saving face than being right. To spare Jonathan's life would require him to admit he had acted foolishly, an embarrassment for a king. Saul was really more interested in protecting his image than in enforcing his vow. Fortunately, the people came to Jonathan's rescue. Don't be like Saul. Admit your mistakes, and show that you are more interested in doing what is right than in looking good.

1 Sam 14:47 Why was Saul so successful right after he had disobeyed God and been told that his reign would end (1 Sam 13:13-14)? Sometimes ungodly people win battles. Victory is neither guaranteed nor limited to the righteous. God provides according to his will. God might have given Saul success for the sake of the people, not for Saul. He might have left Saul on the throne for a while to utilize his military talents so that David, Israel's next king, could spend more time focusing on the nation's spiritual battles. Regardless of God's reasons for delaying Saul's demise, his reign ended exactly the way God had foretold. The timing of God's plans and promises is known only to him. Our task is to commit our ways to God and then trust him for the outcome.

1 Sam 15:2-3 Why did God command such utter destruction? The Amalekites were a band of guerrilla terrorists. They lived by attacking other nations and carrying off their wealth and their families. They were the first to attack the Israelites as they entered the Promised Land, and they continued to raid Israelite camps at every opportunity. God knew that the Israelites could never live peacefully in the Promised Land as long as the Amalekites existed. He also knew that their corrupt, idolatrous religious practices threatened Israel's relationship with him. The only way to protect the Israelites' bodies and souls was to utterly destroy the people of this warlike nation and all their possessions, including their idols.

▶ **1 SAMUEL 15:1-9** ***(cont.)***

everyone else. 9Saul and his men spared Agag's life and kept the best of the sheep and goats, the cattle, the fat calves, and the lambs—everything, in fact, that appealed to them. They destroyed only what was worthless or of poor quality.

The Lord Rejects Saul

1 SAMUEL 15:10-23

Then the LORD said to Samuel, 11"I am sorry that I ever made Saul king, for he has not been loyal to me and has refused to obey my command." Samuel was so deeply moved when he heard this that he cried out to the LORD all night.

12Early the next morning Samuel went to find Saul. Someone told him, "Saul went to the town of Carmel to set up a monument to himself; then he went on to Gilgal."

13When Samuel finally found him, Saul greeted him cheerfully. "May the LORD bless you," he said. "I have carried out the LORD's command!"

14"Then what is all the bleating of sheep and goats and the lowing of cattle I hear?" Samuel demanded.

15"It's true that the army spared the best of the sheep, goats, and cattle," Saul admitted. "But they are going to sacrifice them to the LORD your God. We have destroyed everything else."

16Then Samuel said to Saul, "Stop! Listen to what the LORD told me last night!"

"What did he tell you?" Saul asked.

17And Samuel told him, "Although you may think little of yourself, are you not the leader of the tribes of Israel? The LORD has anointed you king of Israel.
18And the LORD sent you on a mission and told you, 'Go and completely destroy the sinners, the Amalekites, until they are all dead.' 19Why haven't you obeyed the LORD? Why did you rush for the plunder and do what was evil in the LORD's sight?"

20"But I did obey the LORD," Saul insisted. "I carried out the mission he gave me. I brought back King Agag, but I destroyed everyone else. 21Then my troops brought in the best of the sheep, goats, cattle, and plunder to sacrifice to the LORD your God in Gilgal."

22But Samuel replied,

"What is more pleasing to the LORD:
your burnt offerings and sacrifices
or your obedience to his voice?
Listen! Obedience is better than sacrifice,
and submission is better than offering the fat of rams.
23 Rebellion is as sinful as witchcraft,
and stubbornness as bad as worshiping idols.
So because you have rejected the command of the LORD,
he has rejected you as king."

"What is more pleasing to the LORD: your burnt offerings and sacrifices or your obedience to his voice?"
1 Samuel 15:22

1 Sam 15:9 Saul and his men did not destroy all the plunder from the battle as God had commanded (1 Sam 15:3). The law of devoting something—setting it aside—entirely for destruction was well known to the Israelites. Anything under God's ban was to be completely destroyed (Deut 20:16-18). This was set up in order to prevent idolatry from taking hold in Israel because many of the valuables were idols. To break this law was punishable by death (Josh 7). It showed disrespect and disregard for God because it directly violated his command.

When we gloss over sin in order to protect what we have or for material gain, we aren't being shrewd; we are disobeying God's law. Selective obedience is just another form of disobedience.

1 Sam 15:11 When God said he was sorry that he had made Saul king, was he saying he had made a mistake? God's comment was an expression of sorrow, not an admission of error (Gen 6:5-7). An omniscient God cannot make a mistake (1 Sam 15:29); therefore, God did not change his mind in the same way humans change their minds. He did, however, change his attitude toward Saul when Saul changed. Saul's heart no longer belonged to God but to his own interests.

1 Sam 15:12 Saul built a monument in honor of himself. What a contrast to Moses and Joshua, who gave all the credit to God.

1 Sam 15:13-14 Saul thought he had won a great victory over the Amalekites, but God saw it as a great failure because Saul had disobeyed him and then lied to Samuel about the results of the battle. Saul may have thought his lie wouldn't be detected, or that what he did wasn't wrong. Saul was deceiving himself.

Dishonest people soon begin to believe the lies they construct around themselves. Then they lose the ability to tell the difference between truth and lies. By believing your own lies, you deceive yourself, alienate yourself from God, and lose credibility in all your relationships. In the long run, honesty wins out.

1 Sam 15:22-23 This is the first of numerous places in the Bible where the theme "obedience is better than sacrifice" is stated (Ps 40:6-8; 51:16-17; Prov 21:3; Isa 1:11-17; Jer 7:21-23; Hos 6:6; Mic 6:6-8; Matt 12:7; Mark 12:33; Heb 10:8-9). Was Samuel saying that sacrifice is unimportant? No, he was urging Saul to look at his reasons for making the sacrifice rather than at the sacrifice itself. A sacrifice was a ritual trans-

Saul Pleads for Forgiveness

1 SAMUEL 15:24-31

Then Saul admitted to Samuel, "Yes, I have sinned.
I have disobeyed your instructions and the LORD's
command, for I was afraid of the people and did
what they demanded. 25But now, please forgive my
sin and come back with me so that I may worship
the LORD."
26But Samuel replied, "I will not go back with you!
Since you have rejected the LORD's command, he has
rejected you as king of Israel."
27As Samuel turned to go, Saul tried to hold him
back and tore the hem of his robe. 28And Samuel said
to him, "The LORD has torn the kingdom of Israel from
you today and has given it to someone else—one who
is better than you. 29And he who is the Glory of Israel
will not lie, nor will he change his mind, for he is not
human that he should change his mind!"
30Then Saul pleaded again, "I know I have sinned.
But please, at least honor me before the elders of my
people and before Israel by coming back with me so
that I may worship the LORD your God." 31So Samuel finally agreed and went back with him, and Saul
worshiped the LORD.

Samuel Executes King Agag

1 SAMUEL 15:32-35

Then Samuel said, "Bring King Agag to me." Agag arrived full of hope, for he thought, "Surely the worst is
over, and I have been spared!"* 33But Samuel said, "As
your sword has killed the sons of many mothers, now
your mother will be childless." And Samuel cut Agag
to pieces before the LORD at Gilgal.
34Then Samuel went home to Ramah, and Saul returned to his house at Gibeah of Saul. 35Samuel never
went to meet with Saul again, but he mourned constantly for him. And the LORD was sorry he had ever
made Saul king of Israel.

1 Sm 15:32 Dead Sea Scrolls and Greek version read *Agag arrived hesitantly, for he thought, "Surely this is the bitterness of death."*

B. Saul and David

While Saul is still on the throne, Samuel anoints David as Israel's next king. Young David then bravely conquers Goliath, the Philistine champion, and establishes a lifelong friendship with Jonathan, Saul's son. When Saul realizes that David will become king one day, he grows very jealous and tries to kill David on several occasions. David escapes into Philistine territory until Saul is killed in battle. When treated unjustly, we should not take matters into our own hands. God, who is faithful and just, sees all that is happening and will judge all evil.

1. SAMUEL ANOINTS DAVID

God rejected Saul for his disobedience and called on Samuel to anoint Israel's next king while Saul still sat on the throne. Unlike Saul, the next king would be chosen for the quality of his heart rather than for his outward appearance. David was the one God chose to be king for his people.

God Selects David as King

1 SAMUEL 16:1-13

Now the LORD said to Samuel, "You have mourned
long enough for Saul. I have rejected him as
king of Israel, so fill your flask with olive oil and
go to Bethlehem. Find a man named Jesse who lives
there, for I have selected one of his sons to be my
king."
2But Samuel asked, "How can I do that? If Saul hears
about it, he will kill me."
"Take a heifer with you," the LORD replied, "And say
that you have come to make a sacrifice to the LORD.
3Invite Jesse to the sacrifice, and I will show you which
of his sons to anoint for me."
4So Samuel did as the LORD instructed. When he
arrived at Bethlehem, the elders of the town came

action between a person and God that physically demonstrated a relationship between them. But if the person's heart was not truly repentant or if he did not truly love God, the sacrifice was a hollow ritual. Religious ceremonies or rituals are empty unless they are performed with an attitude of love and obedience. "Being religious" (going to church, serving on a committee, giving to charity) is not enough if we do not act out of devotion and obedience to God.

1 Sam 15:23 Rebellion and stubbornness are serious sins. They involve far more than being independent and strong-minded. Scripture equates them with witchcraft and idolatry, sins worthy of death (Exod 22:18; Lev 20:6; Deut 13:12-15; 18:10; Mic 5:10-14).

Saul became both rebellious and stubborn, so it is little wonder that God finally rejected him and took away his kingdom. Rebellion against God is perhaps the most serious sin of all because a person who rebels closes the door to forgiveness and restoration with God.

1 Sam 15:26 Saul's excuses had come to an end. It was the time of reckoning. God wasn't rejecting Saul as a person; the king could still seek forgiveness and restore his relationship with God, but it was too late to get his kingdom back. If you do not act responsibly with what God has entrusted to you, eventually you will run out of excuses. All of us must one day give an account for our actions (Rom 14:12; Rev 22:12).

1 Sam 15:30 Saul was more concerned about what others would think of him than he was about the status of his relationship with God (1 Sam 15:24). He begged Samuel to go with him to worship as a public demonstration that Samuel still supported him. If Samuel had refused, the people probably would have lost all confidence in Saul.

▶ **1 SAMUEL 16:1-13 *(cont.)***
trembling to meet him. "What's wrong?" they asked.
"Do you come in peace?"
5"Yes," Samuel replied. "I have come to sacrifice to
the LORD. Purify yourselves and come with me to the
sacrifice." Then Samuel performed the purification
rite for Jesse and his sons and invited them to the
sacrifice, too.
6When they arrived, Samuel took one look at Eliab
and thought, "Surely this is the LORD's anointed!"
7But the LORD said to Samuel, "Don't judge by his
appearance or height, for I have rejected him. The
LORD doesn't see things the way you see them. People
judge by outward appearance, but the LORD looks at
the heart."
8Then Jesse told his son Abinadab to step forward
and walk in front of Samuel. But Samuel said, "This is
not the one the LORD has chosen." 9Next Jesse summoned Shimea,* but Samuel said, "Neither is this
the one the LORD has chosen." 10In the same way all
seven of Jesse's sons were presented to Samuel. But
Samuel said to Jesse, "The LORD has not chosen any
of these." 11Then Samuel asked, "Are these all the
sons you have?"
"There is still the youngest," Jesse replied. "But he's
out in the fields watching the sheep and goats."
"Send for him at once," Samuel said. "We will not
sit down to eat until he arrives."
12So Jesse sent for him. He was dark and handsome,
with beautiful eyes.
And the LORD said, "This is the one; anoint him."
13So as David stood there among his brothers,
Samuel took the flask of olive oil he had brought and
anointed David with the oil. And the Spirit of the LORD
came powerfully upon David from that day on. Then
Samuel returned to Ramah.

1025 BC

David anointed as king

David Serves in Saul's Court

1 SAMUEL 16:14-23
Now the Spirit of the LORD had left Saul, and the LORD
sent a tormenting spirit* that filled him with depression and fear.
15Some of Saul's servants said to him, "A tormenting
spirit from God is troubling you. 16Let us find a good
musician to play the harp whenever the tormenting
spirit troubles you. He will play soothing music, and
you will soon be well again."
17"All right," Saul said. "Find me someone who plays
well, and bring him here."
18One of the servants said to Saul, "One of Jesse's
sons from Bethlehem is a talented harp player. Not
only that—he is a brave warrior, a man of war, and has
good judgment. He is also a fine-looking young man,
and the LORD is with him."
19So Saul sent messengers to Jesse to say, "Send me
your son David, the shepherd." 20Jesse responded by
sending David to Saul, along with a young goat, a donkey loaded with bread, and a wineskin full of wine.
21So David went to Saul and began serving him.
Saul loved David very much, and David became his
armor bearer.
22Then Saul sent word to Jesse asking, "Please let
David remain in my service, for I am very pleased with
him."
23And whenever the tormenting spirit from God
troubled Saul, David would play the harp. Then Saul
would feel better, and the tormenting spirit would
go away.

1 Sm 16:9 Hebrew *Shammah*, a variant spelling of Shimea; compare 1 Chr 2:13; 20:7.

1 Sm 16:14 Or *an evil spirit;* also in 16:15, 16, 23.

1 Sam 16:5 Samuel performed the purification rite for Jesse and his sons to prepare them to come before God in worship or to offer a sacrifice. (For more on this ceremony, see Gen 35:2; Exod 19:10, 14; and the note on Josh 3:5, p. 339.)

1 Sam 16:7 Saul was tall and handsome; he was an impressive-looking man. Samuel may have been trying to find someone who looked like Saul to be Israel's next king, but God warned him against judging by appearance alone. When people judge by outward appearance, they may overlook quality individuals who lack the particular physical qualities society currently admires. Appearance doesn't reveal what people are really like or what their true value is.

Fortunately, God judges by faith and character, not appearances. And because only God can see on the inside, only he can accurately judge people. Most people spend hours each week maintaining their outward appearance; they should do even more to develop their inner character. While everyone can see your face, only you and God know what your heart really looks like. What steps are you taking to improve your heart's attitude?

1 Sam 16:13 David was anointed king, but it was done in secret; he was not publicly anointed until much later (2 Sam 2:4; 5:3). Saul was still legally the king, but God was preparing David for his future responsibilities. The anointing oil poured over David's head stood for holiness. It was used to set people or objects apart for God's service. Each king and high priest of Israel was anointed with oil. This commissioned him as God's representative to the nation. Although God rejected Saul's kingship by not allowing any of his descendants to sit on Israel's throne, Saul himself remained in his position until his death.

1 Sam 16:14 What was this tormenting spirit the Lord sent? Perhaps Saul was simply depressed. Or perhaps the Holy Spirit had left Saul, and God allowed an evil spirit (a demon) to torment him as judgment for his disobedience (this would demonstrate God's power over the spirit world—1 Kgs 22:19-23). Either way, Saul was driven to insanity, which led him to attempt to murder David.

1 Sam 16:15-16 Harps were popular musical instruments in Saul's day, and their music is still known for its soothing qualities. The simplest harps were merely two pieces of wood fastened at right angles to each other. The strings were stretched across the wood to give the harp a triangular shape. Simple strings could be made of twisted grasses, but better strings were made of dried animal intestine. Harps could have up to 40 strings and were louder than the smaller three- or four-stringed instruments called lyres. David, known for his shepherding skills and bravery, was also an accomplished harpist and musician and would eventually write many of the psalms found in the Bible.

1 Sam 16:19-21 When Saul asked David to be in his service, he obviously didn't know that David had been secretly anointed king (1 Sam 16:12). Saul's invitation presented an excellent opportunity for the young man and future king to gain firsthand information about leading a nation.

2. DAVID AND GOLIATH

Before it was widely known that David had been anointed to be Israel's next king, he dramatically illustrated why he was God's choice. When the Philistine giant, Goliath, threatened the army of Israel, Saul and his army cowered in fear. But David trusted in God to defeat the Philistine and was successful. True power doesn't come from size and strength, but from reliance on God.

Goliath Challenges the Israelites

1 SAMUEL 17:1-11

The Philistines now mustered their army for battle and camped between Socoh in Judah and Azekah at Ephes-dammim. 2Saul countered by gathering his Israelite troops near the valley of Elah. 3So the Philistines and Israelites faced each other on opposite hills, with the valley between them.

4Then Goliath, a Philistine champion from Gath, came out of the Philistine ranks to face the forces of Israel. He was over nine feet* tall! 5He wore a bronze helmet, and his bronze coat of mail weighed 125 pounds.* 6He also wore bronze leg armor, and he carried a bronze javelin on his shoulder. 7The shaft of his spear was as heavy and thick as a weaver's beam, tipped with an iron spearhead that weighed 15 pounds.* His armor bearer walked ahead of him carrying a shield.

8Goliath stood and shouted a taunt across to the Israelites. "Why are you all coming out to fight?" he called. "I am the Philistine champion, but you are only the servants of Saul. Choose one man to come down here and fight me! 9If he kills me, then we will be your slaves. But if I kill him, you will be our slaves! 10I defy the armies of Israel today! Send me a man who will fight me!" 11When Saul and the Israelites heard this, they were terrified and deeply shaken.

1 Sm 17:4 Hebrew *6 cubits and 1 span* [which totals about 9.75 feet or 3 meters]; Dead Sea Scrolls and Greek version read *4 cubits and 1 span* [which totals about 6.75 feet or 2 meters]. **1 Sm 17:5** Hebrew *5,000 shekels* [57 kilograms]. **1 Sm 17:7** Hebrew *600 shekels* [6.8 kilograms].

GOLIATH

Goliath was a giant with an attitude. As champion of the Philistines, he immobilized an entire army of Israelites by challenging one of them to duel with him. He made them forget they had an absolute champion in the Lord their God. It took a bold shepherd boy named David to remind them all they were the armies of the living God. • Goliath was a problem to be faced on his terms but not with his weapons. Goliath's strengths were so obvious (size, armor, weapons) that others missed his vulnerability. For Goliath had a glaring weakness that never occurred to him until David's stone struck him down. When David was given Goliath's kind of weapons, he quickly concluded he couldn't even function—much less fight—with those tools. Goliath's strengths would have been David's handicaps. Armor plating and heavy weapons were of little use to the shepherd boy. So David went with the two weapons he knew he could rely on: his trust in God and his shepherd's sling. When others looked at Goliath, they saw an opponent too powerful to defeat; when David looked at Goliath, he saw a target too big to miss! • David had armor to match Goliath's, but it was invisible. He was spiritually equipped. Ephesians 6:10-18 describes in detail the resources that God places at our disposal. How unfortunate that we face our world each day on its terms and too often try to wield its weapons. God's weapons are not as obvious, but they never fail us! How much of your spiritual armor are you wearing today?

Strengths and accomplishments	• Designated champion of the Philistine army • Held the entire army of Israel at bay by intimidation and derision
Weaknesses and mistakes	• Defied the armies of the living God • Failed to take David seriously
Lessons from his life	• Strengths often conceal weaknesses • God will not be mocked • God equips those who trust him with spiritual armor
Vital statistics	• Where: Gath • Occupation: Soldier • Relatives: At least one brother • Contemporaries: Saul, Jonathan, David
Key verse	"Who is this pagan Philistine anyway, that he is allowed to defy the armies of the living God?" (1 Sam 17:26).

Goliath's story is told in 1 Samuel 17.

Sometimes our plans—even the ones we think God has approved—have to be put on hold indefinitely. Like David, we can use this waiting time profitably. We can choose to learn and grow in our present circumstances, whatever they may be.

1 Sam 17:4-7 When they had first approached the Promised Land, most of the Israelites had been afraid to enter because of the giants living there (Num 13:32-33). King Og of Bashan needed a bed over 13 feet long (Deut 3:11). Now Goliath, over 9 feet tall, taunted Israel's soldiers and appeared invincible to them. Saul, the tallest of the Israelites, may have been especially worried because he was obviously the best match for Goliath. In God's eyes, however, Goliath was no different than anyone else.

1 Sam 17:9 An army often avoided the high cost of battle by pitting its strongest warrior against the strongest warrior of the enemy. This avoided great bloodshed because the winner of the fight was considered the winner of the battle. Goliath had the definite advantage against David from a human standpoint. But Goliath didn't realize that in fighting David, he was actually facing the power of God.

Jesse Sends David to Saul's Camp

1 SAMUEL 17:12-31

Now David was the son of a man named Jesse, an
Ephrathite from Bethlehem in the land of Judah.
Jesse was an old man at that time, and he had eight
sons. [13]Jesse's three oldest sons—Eliab, Abinadab, and
Shimea*—had already joined Saul's army to fight the
Philistines. [14]David was the youngest son. David's three
oldest brothers stayed with Saul's army, [15]but David
went back and forth so he could help his father with
the sheep in Bethlehem.
[16]For forty days, every morning and evening, the
Philistine champion strutted in front of the Israelite
army.
[17]One day Jesse said to David, "Take this basket* of
roasted grain and these ten loaves of bread, and carry
them quickly to your brothers. [18]And give these ten
cuts of cheese to their captain. See how your brothers are getting along, and bring back a report on how
they are doing.*" [19]David's brothers were with Saul
and the Israelite army at the valley of Elah, fighting
against the Philistines.
[20]So David left the sheep with another shepherd
and set out early the next morning with the gifts, as
Jesse had directed him. He arrived at the camp just
as the Israelite army was leaving for the battlefield
with shouts and battle cries. [21]Soon the Israelite and
Philistine forces stood facing each other, army against
army. [22]David left his things with the keeper of supplies and hurried out to the ranks to greet his brothers.
[23]As he was talking with them, Goliath, the Philistine
champion from Gath, came out from the Philistine
ranks. Then David heard him shout his usual taunt to
the army of Israel.
[24]As soon as the Israelite army saw him, they began
to run away in fright. [25]"Have you seen the giant?" the
men asked. "He comes out each day to defy Israel. The
king has offered a huge reward to anyone who kills
him. He will give that man one of his daughters for
a wife, and the man's entire family will be exempted
from paying taxes!"
[26]David asked the soldiers standing nearby, "What
will a man get for killing this Philistine and ending
his defiance of Israel? Who is this pagan Philistine
anyway, that he is allowed to defy the armies of the
living God?"
[27]And these men gave David the same reply. They
said, "Yes, that is the reward for killing him."
[28]But when David's oldest brother, Eliab, heard
David talking to the men, he was angry. "What are
you doing around here anyway?" he demanded. "What
about those few sheep you're supposed to be taking
care of? I know about your pride and deceit. You just
want to see the battle!"
[29]"What have I done now?" David replied. "I was
only asking a question!" [30]He walked over to some others and asked them the same thing and received the
same answer. [31]Then David's question was reported
to King Saul, and the king sent for him.

David Kills Goliath

1 SAMUEL 17:32-51a

"Don't worry about this Philistine," David told Saul.
"I'll go fight him!"
[33]"Don't be ridiculous!" Saul replied. "There's no
way you can fight this Philistine and possibly win!
You're only a boy, and he's been a man of war since
his youth."

1 Sm 17:13 Hebrew *Shammah*, a variant spelling of Shimea; compare 1 Chr 2:13; 20:7. **1 Sm 17:17** Hebrew *ephah* [20 quarts or 22 liters]. **1 Sm 17:18** Hebrew *and take their pledge.*

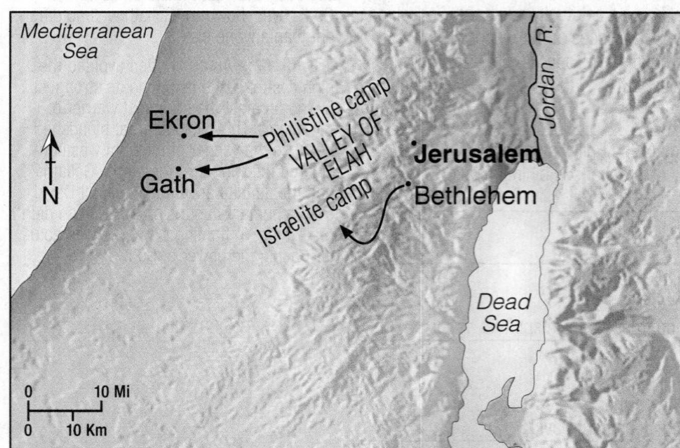

***DAVID AND GOLIATH** The armies of Israel and Philistia faced each other across the valley of Elah. David arrived from Bethlehem and offered to fight the giant Goliath. After David defeated Goliath, the Israelite army chased the Philistines to Ekron and Gath (Goliath's hometown).*

1 Sam 17:16 Why would this go on for 40 days without one side attacking the other? They were camped on opposite sides of a valley with steep walls. Whoever would rush down the valley and up the steep cliffs would be at a disadvantage at the beginning of the battle and probably suffer great casualties. Each side was waiting for the other to attack first.

1 Sam 17:26 What a difference perspective can make. Most of the onlookers saw only a giant. David saw a mortal man defying almighty God. Goliath was a target too big to miss. David knew he would not be alone when he faced Goliath; God would fight with him. He looked at his situation from God's point of view. Who or what are the "giants" you are facing? Viewing impossible situations from God's point of view helps us put giant problems in perspective. Once we see clearly, we can fight more effectively.

1 Sam 17:28-32 Criticism couldn't stop David. While the rest of the army stood around, he knew the importance of taking action. With God to fight for him, there was

34 But David persisted. "I have been taking care of
my father's sheep and goats," he said. "When a lion or
a bear comes to steal a lamb from the flock, 35 I go after
it with a club and rescue the lamb from its mouth. If
the animal turns on me, I catch it by the jaw and club
it to death. 36 I have done this to both lions and bears,
and I'll do it to this pagan Philistine, too, for he has
defied the armies of the living God! 37 The LORD who
rescued me from the claws of the lion and the bear
will rescue me from this Philistine!"
Saul finally consented. "All right, go ahead," he said.
"And may the LORD be with you!"
38 Then Saul gave David his own armor—a bronze
helmet and a coat of mail. 39 David put it on, strapped
the sword over it, and took a step or two to see what
it was like, for he had never worn such things before.
"I can't go in these," he protested to Saul. "I'm not
used to them." So David took them off again. 40 He
picked up five smooth stones from a stream and put
them into his shepherd's bag. Then, armed only with
his shepherd's staff and sling, he started across the
valley to fight the Philistine.
41 Goliath walked out toward David with his shield
bearer ahead of him, 42 sneering in contempt at this
ruddy-faced boy. 43 "Am I a dog," he roared at David,
"that you come at me with a stick?" And he cursed
David by the names of his gods. 44 "Come over here,
and I'll give your flesh to the birds and wild animals!"
Goliath yelled.
45 David replied to the Philistine, "You come to me
with sword, spear, and javelin, but I come to you in
the name of the LORD of Heaven's Armies—the God
of the armies of Israel, whom you have defied. 46 Today
the LORD will conquer you, and I will kill you and cut
off your head. And then I will give the dead bodies
of your men to the birds and wild animals, and the
whole world will know that there is a God in Israel!
47 And everyone assembled here will know that the
LORD rescues his people, but not with sword and spear.
This is the LORD's battle, and he will give you to us!"
48 As Goliath moved closer to attack, David quickly
ran out to meet him. 49 Reaching into his shepherd's
bag and taking out a stone, he hurled it with his sling
and hit the Philistine in the forehead. The stone sank
in, and Goliath stumbled and fell face down on the
ground.
50 So David triumphed over the Philistine with only
a sling and a stone, for he had no sword. 51 Then David
ran over and pulled Goliath's sword from its sheath.
David used it to kill him and cut off his head.

Israel Routs the Philistines

1 SAMUEL 17:51b-58

When the Philistines saw that their champion was
dead, they turned and ran. 52 Then the men of Israel and
Judah gave a great shout of triumph and rushed after
the Philistines, chasing them as far as Gath* and the
gates of Ekron. The bodies of the dead and wounded
Philistines were strewn all along the road from Shaaraim, as far as Gath and Ekron. 53 Then the Israelite
army returned and plundered the deserted Philistine
camp. 54 (David took the Philistine's head to Jerusalem,
but he stored the man's armor in his own tent.)
55 As Saul watched David go out to fight the Philistine, he asked Abner, the commander of his army,
"Abner, whose son is this young man?"
"I really don't know," Abner declared.
56 "Well, find out who he is!" the king told him.
57 As soon as David returned from killing Goliath,
Abner brought him to Saul with the Philistine's head
still in his hand. 58 "Tell me about your father, young
man," Saul said.
And David replied, "His name is Jesse, and we live
in Bethlehem."

1020 BC

David defeats Goliath

1 Sm 17:52 As in some Greek manuscripts; Hebrew reads *a valley.*

no reason to wait. People may try to discourage you with negative comments or mockery, but continue to do what you know is right. By doing what is right, you will be pleasing God, whose opinion matters most.

1 Sam 17:48-49 David was able to move faster than Goliath because David carried no heavy weapons or armor. David was an expert marksman with a sling, and as he advanced on Goliath, he stayed out of range of Goliath's huge weapons. What made David effective was more than his ability with a sling; it was his courage and his faith in God. To fight like David we need David's kind of fearlessness. David's confident trust in God had grown strong in his encounters with wild animals while guarding his father's sheep (1 Sam 17:34-37). When you face towering problems, recall how God has helped you in the past. Take heart because God will give you strength. Use the skills God has already given you and move forward.

He picked up five smooth stones from a stream and put them into his shepherd's bag. Then, armed only with his shepherd's staff and sling, he started across the valley to fight the Philistine.
1 Samuel 17:40

1 Sam 17:55-58 Although David had played his harp many times in front of Saul, Saul's question to Abner seems to show he didn't know David very well. Perhaps, since David was scheduled to marry Saul's daughter if he was successful (1 Sam 17:25), Saul wanted to know more about his family. Or possibly Saul's unstable mental condition (1 Sam 16:14) may have prevented him from recognizing David.

3. DAVID AND JONATHAN BECOME FRIENDS

Despite Saul's bitter jealousy, Saul's son Jonathan developed a close friendship with David. They were closer than brothers, even though Jonathan knew that David would eventually sit on the throne that would otherwise have been his. Their friendship is a model of how godly relationships can transcend worldly allegiances.

Saul Becomes Jealous of David

1 SAMUEL 18:1-16

After David had finished talking with Saul, he met
Jonathan, the king's son. There was an immediate
bond between them, for Jonathan loved David. 2From
that day on Saul kept David with him and wouldn't
let him return home. 3And Jonathan made a solemn
pact with David, because he loved him as he loved
himself. 4Jonathan sealed the pact by taking off his
robe and giving it to David, together with his tunic,
sword, bow, and belt.
5Whatever Saul asked David to do, David did it successfully. So Saul made him a commander over the
men of war, an appointment that was welcomed by
the people and Saul's officers alike.
6When the victorious Israelite army was returning
home after David had killed the Philistine, women
from all the towns of Israel came out to meet King
Saul. They sang and danced for joy with tambourines
and cymbals.* 7This was their song:

"Saul has killed his thousands,
and David his ten thousands!"

8This made Saul very angry. "What's this?" he said.
"They credit David with ten thousands and me with
only thousands. Next they'll be making him their
king!" 9So from that time on Saul kept a jealous eye
on David.
10The very next day a tormenting spirit* from God
overwhelmed Saul, and he began to rave in his house
like a madman. David was playing the harp, as he did
each day. But Saul had a spear in his hand, 11and he
suddenly hurled it at David, intending to pin him to
the wall. But David escaped him twice.
12Saul was then afraid of David, for the LORD was
with David and had turned away from Saul. 13Finally,

1 Sm 18:6 The type of instrument represented by the word *cymbals* is uncertain. **1 Sm 18:10** *Or an evil spirit.*

1 Sam 18:1-4 When David and Jonathan met, they became close friends at once. Their friendship is one of the deepest and closest recorded in the Bible: (1) They based their friendship on commitment to God, not just each other; (2) they let nothing come between them, not even career or family problems; (3) they drew closer together when their friendship was tested; (4) they remained friends to the end.

Jonathan, the prince of Israel, later realized that David, and not he, would be the next king (1 Sam 23:17). But that did not weaken his love for David. Jonathan would much rather lose the throne of Israel than lose his closest friend.

1 Sam 18:8 Saul's appreciation for David turned to jealousy as people began to applaud David's exploits. In a jealous rage, Saul attempted to murder David by hurling his spear at him (1 Sam 18:11-12).

Jealousy may not seem to be a major sin, but in reality, it is one step short of murder. Jealousy starts as you resent a rival; it leads to your wishing that rival removed; then it manifests itself in your seeking ways to harm that person in word or action. Beware of letting jealousy get a foothold in your life.

1 Sam 18:10 The note on 1 Samuel 16:14, p. 448, explains what this tormenting spirit might have been.

1 Sam 18:11-12 Saul tried to kill David because he was jealous of David's popularity, yet David continued to protect and comfort Saul. Perhaps people have been jealous of you and have even attacked you in some way. They may be intimidated by your strengths, which make them conscious of their own shortcomings. It would be natural to strike back or to avoid them. A better response is to befriend them (Matt 5:43-44) and to ask God for the strength to continue loving them, as David kept on loving Saul.

GOD USES SIMPLE OBJECTS

God often uses simple, ordinary objects to accomplish his tasks in the world. It is important only that they be dedicated to him for his use. What do you have that God can use? Anything and everything is a possible "instrument" for him.

Object	*Reference*	*Who Used It?*	*How Was It Used?*
A staff	Exod 4:2-4	Moses	To work miracles before Pharaoh
Horns	Josh 6:3-5	Joshua	To flatten the walls of Jericho
A fleece	Judg 6:36-40	Gideon	To confirm God's will
Horns, jars, and torches	Judg 7:19-22	Gideon	To defeat the Midianites
Jawbone	Judg 15:15	Samson	To kill 1,000 Philistines
Smooth stone	1 Sam 17:40	David	To kill Goliath
Olive oil	2 Kgs 4:1-7	Elisha	To demonstrate God's power to provide
A river	2 Kgs 5:9-14	Elisha	To heal a man of leprosy
Linen loincloth	Jer 13:1-11	Jeremiah	As an object lesson of God's wrath
Clay jar	Jer 19:1-13	Jeremiah	As an object lesson of God's wrath
Iron griddle, water, and food	Ezek 4:1-17	Ezekiel	As an object lesson of judgment
Five loaves and two fish	Mark 6:30-44	Jesus	To feed a crowd of over 5,000 people

Saul sent him away and appointed him commander over 1,000 men, and David faithfully led his troops into battle.
14David continued to succeed in everything he did, for the LORD was with him. 15When Saul recognized this, he became even more afraid of him. 16But all Israel and Judah loved David because he was so successful at leading his troops into battle.

David Marries Saul's Daughter

1 SAMUEL 18:17-30

One day Saul said to David, "I am ready to give you my older daughter, Merab, as your wife. But first you must prove yourself to be a real warrior by fighting the LORD's battles." For Saul thought, "I'll send him out against the Philistines and let them kill him rather than doing it myself."
18"Who am I, and what is my family in Israel that I should be the king's son-in-law?" David exclaimed. "My father's family is nothing!" 19So* when the time came for Saul to give his daughter Merab in marriage to David, he gave her instead to Adriel, a man from Meholah.
20In the meantime, Saul's daughter Michal had fallen in love with David, and Saul was delighted when he heard about it. 21"Here's another chance to see him killed by the Philistines!" Saul said to himself. But to David he said, "Today you have a second chance to become my son-in-law!"
22Then Saul told his men to say to David, "The king really likes you, and so do we. Why don't you accept the king's offer and become his son-in-law?"
23When Saul's men said these things to David, he replied, "How can a poor man from a humble family afford the bride price for the daughter of a king?"
24When Saul's men reported this back to the king,
25he told them, "Tell David that all I want for the bride price is 100 Philistine foreskins! Vengeance on my enemies is all I really want." But what Saul had in mind was that David would be killed in the fight.
26David was delighted to accept the offer. Before the time limit expired, 27he and his men went out and killed 200 Philistines. Then David fulfilled the king's requirement by presenting all their foreskins to him. So Saul gave his daughter Michal to David to be his wife.
28When Saul realized that the LORD was with David and how much his daughter Michal loved him, 29Saul became even more afraid of him, and he remained David's enemy for the rest of his life.
30Every time the commanders of the Philistines attacked, David was more successful against them than all the rest of Saul's officers. So David's name became very famous.

Saul Tries to Kill David

1 SAMUEL 19:1-10

Saul now urged his servants and his son Jonathan to assassinate David. But Jonathan, because of his strong affection for David, 2told him what his father was planning. "Tomorrow morning," he warned him, "you must find a hiding place out in the fields. 3I'll ask my father to go out there with me, and I'll talk to him about you. Then I'll tell you everything I can find out."
4The next morning Jonathan spoke with his father about David, saying many good things about him. "The king must not sin against his servant David," Jonathan said. "He's never done anything to harm you. He has always helped you in any way he could. 5Have you forgotten about the time he risked his life to kill the Philistine giant and how the LORD brought a great victory to all Israel as a result? You were certainly happy about it then. Why should you murder an innocent man like David? There is no reason for it at all!"
6So Saul listened to Jonathan and vowed, "As surely as the LORD lives, David will not be killed."
7Afterward Jonathan called David and told him what had happened. Then he brought David to Saul, and David served in the court as before.
8War broke out again after that, and David led his troops against the Philistines. He attacked them with such fury that they all ran away.
9But one day when Saul was sitting at home, with spear in hand, the tormenting spirit* from the LORD suddenly came upon him again. As David played his harp, 10Saul hurled his spear at David. But David dodged out of the way, and leaving the spear stuck in the wall, he fled and escaped into the night.

Michal Saves David's Life

1 SAMUEL 19:11-17

Then Saul sent troops to watch David's house. They were told to kill David when he came out the next morning. But Michal, David's wife, warned him, "If you don't escape tonight, you will be dead by morning."
12So she helped him climb out through a window, and

1 Sm 18:19 Or *But.* **1 Sm 19:9** Or *evil spirit.*

1 Sam 18:15-18 While Saul's popularity made him proud and arrogant, David remained humble (1 Sam 18:23), even when the entire nation praised him. Although David succeeded in almost everything he tried and became famous throughout the land, he refused to use his popular support to his advantage against Saul. Don't allow popularity to twist your perception of your own importance. It's comparatively easy to be humble when you're not on center stage, but how will you react to praise and honor?

1 Sam 19:1-2 Is it ever right to disobey your father, as Jonathan did here? It is clearly a principle of Scripture that when a father instructs a son to break God's laws, the son should obey God rather than man. This principle assumes that the son is old enough to be accountable and to see through any deception. A son's role is to be respectful, helpful, and obedient to his father (Eph 6:1-3), but not to follow commands or advice that violate God's laws.

▶ **1 SAMUEL 19:11-17 *(cont.)***
he fled and escaped. 13Then she took an idol* and
put it in his bed, covered it with blankets, and put a
cushion of goat's hair at its head.
14When the troops came to arrest David, she told
them he was sick and couldn't get out of bed.
15But Saul sent the troops back to get David. He
ordered, "Bring him to me in his bed so I can kill him!"
16But when they came to carry David out, they discovered that it was only an idol in the bed with a cushion
of goat's hair at its head.
17"Why have you betrayed me like this and let my
enemy escape?" Saul demanded of Michal.

"I had to," Michal replied. "He threatened to kill me if I didn't help him."

Psalm 59

THEME: Prayer and praise for God's saving help. God's constant love is our place of safety in a wicked world.
AUTHOR: David

For the choir director: A psalm of David, regarding the time Saul sent soldiers to watch David's house in order to kill him. To be sung to the tune "Do Not Destroy!"*

1 Rescue me from my enemies, O God.
Protect me from those who have come to destroy me.
2 Rescue me from these criminals;
save me from these murderers.
3 They have set an ambush for me.
Fierce enemies are out there waiting, LORD,
though I have not sinned or offended them.
4 I have done nothing wrong,
yet they prepare to attack me.
Wake up! See what is happening and help me!
5 O LORD God of Heaven's Armies, the God of Israel,
wake up and punish those hostile nations.
Show no mercy to wicked traitors. *Interlude*

6 They come out at night,
snarling like vicious dogs
as they prowl the streets.
7 Listen to the filth that comes from their mouths;
their words cut like swords.
"After all, who can hear us?" they sneer.
8 But LORD, you laugh at them.
You scoff at all the hostile nations.
9 You are my strength; I wait for you to rescue me,
for you, O God, are my fortress.
10 In his unfailing love, my God will stand with me.
He will let me look down in triumph on all my enemies.

11 Don't kill them, for my people soon forget such lessons;
stagger them with your power, and bring them to their knees,
O Lord our shield.
12 Because of the sinful things they say,
because of the evil that is on their lips,
let them be captured by their pride,
their curses, and their lies.
13 Destroy them in your anger!
Wipe them out completely!
Then the whole world will know
that God reigns in Israel.* *Interlude*
14 My enemies come out at night,
snarling like vicious dogs
as they prowl the streets.
15 They scavenge for food
but go to sleep unsatisfied.*

16 But as for me, I will sing about your power.
Each morning I will sing with joy about your unfailing love.
For you have been my refuge,
a place of safety when I am in distress.
17 O my Strength, to you I sing praises,
for you, O God, are my refuge,
the God who shows me unfailing love.

1 Sm 19:13 Hebrew *teraphim;* also in 19:16. **Ps 59:TITLE** Hebrew *miktam.* This may be a literary or musical term. **Ps 59:13** Hebrew *in Jacob.* See note on 44:4. **Ps 59:15** Or *and growl if they don't get enough.*

My enemies come out at night, snarling like vicious dogs as they prowl the streets.
Psalm 59:14

Ps 59:7-8 Vile men curse God as if he cannot hear or will not respond. But God scoffs at them. Evil people live as if God cannot see them or will not punish them. But God watches patiently until that day when their deeds will rise up to accuse them. As believers we must be careful not to follow the same foolish practices as evil people. We must remember that God hears and sees all we do.

Ps 59:10 David was hunted by those whose love had turned to jealousy, driving them to try to murder him. Trusted friends and even his mentor, the king, had turned against him. What changeable love! But David knew that God's love for him was changeless. "His unfailing love continues forever" (Ps 100:5). God's mercy to all who trust him is just as permanent as his mercy to David. When the love of others fails or disappoints us, we can rest in God's unfailing love.

Ps 59:16 Throughout this psalm, David describes in grim detail the behavior of his enemies. He contrasts his own feelings of dread with the desperation and despair that he sees in the lives of those who want to harm him. What a delight, then, in these final verses to read about God's role in David's life as a refuge, a place of safety, and a source of unfailing love. David had learned to turn negative circumstances into reminders of God's faithful presence. What stresses in your life might be transformed today if you made them a starting point for praising God?

David Flees to Ramah

1 SAMUEL 19:18-24

So David escaped and went to Ramah to see Samuel, and he told him all that Saul had done to him. Then Samuel took David with him to live at Naioth. [19]When the report reached Saul that David was at Naioth in Ramah, [20]he sent troops to capture him. But when they arrived and saw Samuel leading a group of prophets who were prophesying, the Spirit of God came upon Saul's men, and they also began to prophesy. [21]When Saul heard what had happened, he sent other troops, but they, too, prophesied! The same thing happened a third time. [22]Finally, Saul himself went to Ramah and arrived at the great well in Secu. "Where are Samuel and David?" he demanded.

"They are at Naioth in Ramah," someone told him.

[23]But on the way to Naioth in Ramah the Spirit of God came even upon Saul, and he, too, began to prophesy all the way to Naioth! [24]He tore off his clothes and lay naked on the ground all day and all night, prophesying in the presence of Samuel. The people who were watching exclaimed, "What? Is even Saul a prophet?"

Jonathan Helps David

1 SAMUEL 20:1-42

David now fled from Naioth in Ramah and found Jonathan. "What have I done?" he exclaimed. "What is my crime? How have I offended your father that he is so determined to kill me?"

[2]"That's not true!" Jonathan protested. "You're not going to die. He always tells me everything he's going to do, even the little things. I know my father wouldn't hide something like this from me. It just isn't so!"

[3]Then David took an oath before Jonathan and said, "Your father knows perfectly well about our friendship, so he has said to himself, 'I won't tell Jonathan—why should I hurt him?' But I swear to you that I am only a step away from death! I swear it by the LORD and by your own soul!"

[4]"Tell me what I can do to help you," Jonathan exclaimed.

[5]David replied, "Tomorrow we celebrate the new moon festival. I've always eaten with the king on this occasion, but tomorrow I'll hide in the field and stay there until the evening of the third day. [6]If your father asks where I am, tell him I asked permission to go

JONATHAN

Loyalty is one of life's most precious qualities; it is the most selfless part of love. To be loyal, you cannot live only for yourself. Loyal people not only stand by their commitments, they are willing to suffer for them. Jonathan is a shining example of loyalty. Sometimes he was forced to deal with conflicting loyalties: to his father, Saul, and to his friend David. His solution to that conflict teaches us both how to be loyal and what must guide loyalty. In Jonathan, truth always guided loyalty. • Jonathan realized that the source of truth was God, who demanded his ultimate loyalty. It was his relationship with God that gave Jonathan the ability to deal effectively with the complicated situations in his life. He was loyal to Saul because Saul was his father and the king. He was loyal to David because David was his friend. His loyalty to God guided him through the conflicting demands of his human relationships. • The conflicting demands of our relationships challenge us as well. If we attempt to settle these conflicts only at the human level, we will be constantly dealing with a sense of betrayal. But if we communicate to our friends that our ultimate loyalty is to God and his truth, many of our choices will be much clearer. The truth in his Word, the Bible, will bring light to our decisions. Do those closest to you know who has your greatest loyalty?

Strengths and accomplishments	• Brave, loyal, and a natural leader • The closest friend David ever had • Depended on God
Lessons from his life	• Loyalty is one of the strongest parts of courage • An allegiance to God puts all other relationships in perspective • Great friendships are costly
Vital statistics	• Occupation: Military leader • Relatives: Father: Saul. Mother: Ahinoam. Brothers: Malkishua, Abinadab, Ishbosheth (and possibly Ishvi). Sisters: Merab, Michal. Son: Mephibosheth.
Key verse	"How I weep for you, my brother Jonathan! Oh, how much I loved you! And your love for me was deep, deeper than the love of women!" (2 Sam 1:26).

Jonathan's story is told in 1 Samuel 13–31. He is also mentioned in 2 Samuel 9.

1 Sam 19:20-24 This was the second time that Saul surprised everyone by joining a group of prophets and prophesying. This seems to be a group of people in Spirit-filled ecstasy. It was very powerful and contagious to anyone who found them. We do not know if they were speaking messages from God or merely joining in ecstatic expression. The first time this happened to Saul (1 Sam 10) was right after he was anointed king and did not want to accept the responsibility. This time Saul was consumed with jealousy over David's growing popularity, but the Spirit of God immobilized him so he was unable to harm David. Although Saul was receptive to the Spirit of God and was caught up in prophesying, his heart and mind were far from loving God and thinking God's thoughts.

1 Sam 20:5 At the beginning of each month, the Israelites gathered to celebrate the new moon festival. While this was mainly a time to be enjoyed, it was also a way to dedicate the next month to God. Other nations had celebrations during the full moon and worshiped the moon itself. The Israelites, however, celebrated their festival at the time of the new moon, when the moon was not visible in the sky. This was an added precaution against false worship. Nothing in the creation is to be worshiped—only the Creator.

▸ **1 SAMUEL 20:1-42 *(cont.)***

home to Bethlehem for an annual family sacrifice. 7If he says, 'Fine!' you will know all is well. But if he is angry and loses his temper, you will know he is determined to kill me. 8Show me this loyalty as my sworn friend—for we made a solemn pact before the LORD—or kill me yourself if I have sinned against your father. But please don't betray me to him!"

9"Never!" Jonathan exclaimed. "You know that if I had the slightest notion my father was planning to kill you, I would tell you at once."

10Then David asked, "How will I know whether or not your father is angry?"

11"Come out to the field with me," Jonathan replied. And they went out there together. 12Then Jonathan told David, "I promise by the LORD, the God of Israel, that by this time tomorrow, or the next day at the latest, I will talk to my father and let you know at once how he feels about you. If he speaks favorably about you, I will let you know. 13But if he is angry and wants you killed, may the LORD strike me and even kill me if I don't warn you so you can escape and live. May the LORD be with you as he used to be with my father. 14And may you treat me with the faithful love of the LORD as long as I live. But if I die, 15treat my family with this faithful love, even when the LORD destroys all your enemies from the face of the earth."

16So Jonathan made a solemn pact with David,* saying, "May the LORD destroy all your enemies!" 17And Jonathan made David reaffirm his vow of friendship again, for Jonathan loved David as he loved himself.

18Then Jonathan said, "Tomorrow we celebrate the new moon festival. You will be missed when your place at the table is empty. 19The day after tomorrow, toward evening, go to the place where you hid before, and wait there by the stone pile.* 20I will come out and shoot three arrows to the side of the stone pile as though I were shooting at a target. 21Then I will send a boy to bring the arrows back. If you hear me tell him, 'They're on this side,' then you will know, as surely as the LORD lives, that all is well, and there is no trouble. 22But if I tell him, 'Go farther—the arrows are still ahead of you,' then it will mean that you must leave immediately, for the LORD is sending you away. 23And may the LORD make us keep our promises to each other, for he has witnessed them."

24So David hid himself in the field, and when the new moon festival began, the king sat down to eat. 25He sat at his usual place against the wall, with Jonathan sitting opposite him* and Abner beside him. But David's place was empty. 26Saul didn't say anything about it that day, for he said to himself, "Something must have made David ceremonially unclean." 27But when David's place was empty again the next day, Saul asked Jonathan, "Why hasn't the son of Jesse been here for the meal either yesterday or today?"

28Jonathan replied, "David earnestly asked me if he could go to Bethlehem. 29He said, 'Please let me go, for we are having a family sacrifice. My brother demanded that I be there. So please let me get away to see my brothers.' That's why he isn't here at the king's table."

30Saul boiled with rage at Jonathan. "You stupid son of a whore!"* he swore at him. "Do you think I don't know that you want him to be king in your place, shaming yourself and your mother? 31As long as that son of Jesse is alive, you'll never be king. Now go and get him so I can kill him!"

32"But why should he be put to death?" Jonathan asked his father. "What has he done?" 33Then Saul hurled his spear at Jonathan, intending to kill him. So at last Jonathan realized that his father was really determined to kill David.

34Jonathan left the table in fierce anger and refused to eat on that second day of the festival, for he was crushed by his father's shameful behavior toward David.

35The next morning, as agreed, Jonathan went out into the field and took a young boy with him to gather his arrows. 36"Start running," he told the boy, "so you can find the arrows as I shoot them." So the boy ran, and Jonathan shot an arrow beyond him. 37When the boy had almost reached the arrow, Jonathan shouted, "The arrow is still ahead of you. 38Hurry, hurry, don't wait." So the boy quickly gathered up the arrows and ran back to his master. 39He, of course, suspected nothing; only Jonathan and David understood the signal. 40Then Jonathan gave his bow and arrows to the boy and told him to take them back to town.

1 Sm 20:16 Hebrew *with the house of David.* **1 Sm 20:19** Hebrew *the stone Ezel.* The meaning of the Hebrew is uncertain. **1 Sm 20:25** As in Greek version; Hebrew reads *with Jonathan standing.* **1 Sm 20:30** Hebrew *You son of a perverse and rebellious woman.*

1 Sam 20:15 Jonathan asked David to keep a promise to treat his children kindly in the future. Years later David took great pains to fulfill this promise: He invited Jonathan's son Mephibosheth into his palace to live (2 Sam 9).

1 Sam 20:26 Because the new moon festival involved making a sacrifice to God (Num 28:11-15), those attending the festival had to be ceremonially clean according to God's laws (Exod 19:10; Lev 15; Num 19:11-22; also see the note on Josh 3:5, p. 339). This cleansing involved washing the body and clothes before approaching God to offer a sacrifice. The outward cleansing was a symbol of the inward desire for a purified heart and right relationship with God. Today our hearts are purified by faith in God through the death of Jesus Christ on our behalf (Heb 10:10, 22) and by reading and heeding God's Word (John 17:17).

1 Sam 20:31-32 Saul was still trying to secure his throne for future generations even though he had already been told his dynasty would end with him (1 Sam 13:13-14). Even worse, he was trying to do this by sinful human means because he knew he would get no help from God. Jonathan could have made a move to become the next king by killing his rival, but he bypassed this opportunity because of his love for both God and David (1 Sam 23:16-18).

41 As soon as the boy was gone, David came out from
where he had been hiding near the stone pile.* Then
David bowed three times to Jonathan with his face to
the ground. Both of them were in tears as they embraced each other and said good-bye, especially David.

42 At last Jonathan said to David, "Go in peace, for we
have sworn loyalty to each other in the LORD's name.
The LORD is the witness of a bond between us and
our children forever." Then David left, and Jonathan
returned to the town.*

1 Sm 20:41 As in Greek version; Hebrew reads *near the south edge.* **1 Sm 20:42** This sentence is numbered 21:1 in Hebrew text.

4. SAUL PURSUES DAVID

David and Saul both knew that David would be the next king of Israel, and this led to Saul's attempts to kill David on multiple occasions. David fled to safety outside of Israel, but in spite of several opportunities to harm Saul and take the throne that he had been promised, David honored God by refusing to lay a hand on the anointed king of Israel. Instead, David waited patiently on God's timing.

David Runs from Saul

1 SAMUEL 21:1-15

1 *David went to the town of Nob to see Ahimelech the
priest. Ahimelech trembled when he saw him. "Why
are you alone?" he asked. "Why is no one with you?"
2 "The king has sent me on a private matter," David
said. "He told me not to tell anyone why I am here. I
have told my men where to meet me later. 3 Now, what
is there to eat? Give me five loaves of bread or anything
else you have."
4 "We don't have any regular bread," the priest replied. "But there is the holy bread, which you can have
if your young men have not slept with any women
recently."
5 "Don't worry," David replied. "I never allow my men
to be with women when they are on a campaign. And
since they stay clean even on ordinary trips, how much
more on this one!"
6 Since there was no other food available, the priest
gave him the holy bread—the Bread of the Presence
that was placed before the LORD in the Tabernacle.
It had just been replaced that day with fresh bread.
7 Now Doeg the Edomite, Saul's chief herdsman,
was there that day, having been detained before the
LORD.*
8 David asked Ahimelech, "Do you have a spear or
sword? The king's business was so urgent that I didn't
even have time to grab a weapon!"
9 "I only have the sword of Goliath the Philistine,
whom you killed in the valley of Elah," the priest replied. "It is wrapped in a cloth behind the ephod. Take
that if you want it, for there is nothing else here."
"There is nothing like it!" David replied. "Give it
to me!"
10 So David escaped from Saul and went to King
Achish of Gath. 11 But the officers of Achish were unhappy about his being there. "Isn't this David, the king
of the land?" they asked. "Isn't he the one the people
honor with dances, singing,

'Saul has killed his thousands,
and David his ten thousands'?"

12 David heard these comments and was very afraid
of what King Achish of Gath might do to him. 13 So
he pretended to be insane, scratching on doors and
drooling down his beard.

1 Sm 21:1 Verses 21:1-15 are numbered 21:2-16 in Hebrew text. **1 Sm 21:7** The meaning of the Hebrew is uncertain.

---

1 Sam 21:1ff This is the first time Ahimelech is mentioned. Either he was the Ahijah mentioned in 1 Samuel 14:3, 18, or more likely, he was Ahijah's successor. In either case, Ahimelech had to go against the law to give the holy bread to David because the bread was supposed to be given only to the priests (Lev 24:5-9). But Ahimelech put David's need and life ahead of religious ceremony and fed him the holy food. This upheld a higher law of love (Lev 19:18). Centuries later, Jesus would refer to this incident to show that God's laws should be applied with compassion. To do good and to save life is God's greater law (Matt 12:1-8; Luke 6:1-5).

1 Sam 21:2 David lied to protect himself from Saul (1 Sam 21:10). Some excuse this lie because a war was going on, and it is the duty of a good soldier to deceive the enemy. But nowhere is David's lie condoned. In fact, the opposite is true because his lie led to the death of 85 priests (1 Sam 22:9-19). David's small lie seemed harmless enough, but it led to tragedy. The Bible makes it very clear that lying is wrong (Lev 19:11). Lying, like every other sin, is serious in God's sight and may lead to all sorts of harmful consequences. Don't minimize or categorize sins. All sins must be avoided whether or not we can foresee their potential consequences.

1 Sam 21:5 The men's bodies were ceremonially clean because they had not had sexual intercourse during this journey. Therefore, the priest allowed them to eat the holy bread.

1 Sam 21:6 Once a week on the Sabbath, a priest entered the Holy Place in the Tabernacle and placed 12 freshly baked loaves of bread on a small table. This bread, called the Bread of the Presence, symbolized God's presence among his people as well as his loving care that met their physical needs. The bread that was replaced was to be eaten only by the priests on duty.

1 Sam 21:9 An ephod was a vest worn by the priest (see the note on 1 Sam 2:18, p. 420). David didn't know Goliath's sword was there, probably because David was a young man when he killed the giant and he had spent much of his time at home.

1 Sam 21:10-15 Gath was one of the five major Philistine cities. Why did the Philistines allow their archenemy, David, into their camp? The Philistines may have been initially happy to accept a defector who was a high military leader. Any enemy of Saul would have been a friend of theirs. They could not have known that David had been anointed Israel's next king (1 Sam 16:13). Soon, however, the Philistines became nervous about David's presence. After all, he had slain thousands of their people (1 Sam 18:7). David then protected himself by acting insane because it was the custom not to harm mentally unstable people.

▸ **1 SAMUEL 21:1-15 *(cont.)***

14Finally, King Achish said to his men, "Must you bring me a madman? 15We already have enough of them around here! Why should I let someone like this be my guest?"

*Psalm 34**

THEME: God pays attention to those who call on him. Whether God offers escape from trouble or help in times of trouble, we can be certain that he always hears and acts on behalf of those who love him.

AUTHOR: David, after pretending to be insane in order to escape from King Achish (1 Samuel 21:10-15)

A psalm of David, regarding the time he pretended to be insane in front of Abimelech, who sent him away.

1 I will praise the LORD at all times.
I will constantly speak his praises.
2 I will boast only in the LORD;
let all who are helpless take heart.
3 Come, let us tell of the LORD's greatness;
let us exalt his name together.
4 I prayed to the LORD, and he answered me.
He freed me from all my fears.
5 Those who look to him for help will be radiant with joy;
no shadow of shame will darken their faces.
6 In my desperation I prayed, and the LORD listened;
he saved me from all my troubles.
7 For the angel of the LORD is a guard;
he surrounds and defends all who fear him.

8 Taste and see that the LORD is good.
Oh, the joys of those who take refuge in him!
9 Fear the LORD, you his godly people,
for those who fear him will have all they need.
10 Even strong young lions sometimes go hungry,
but those who trust in the LORD will lack no good thing.
11 Come, my children, and listen to me,
and I will teach you to fear the LORD.

Ps 34 This psalm is a Hebrew acrostic poem; each verse begins with a successive letter of the Hebrew alphabet.

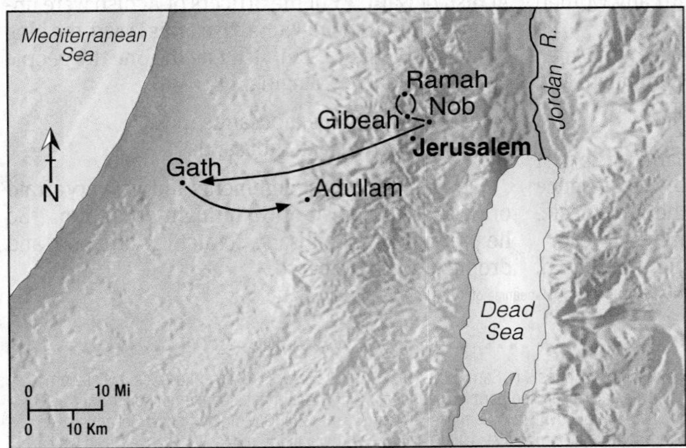

***DAVID'S ESCAPE** David learned of Saul's plans to kill him and fled to Samuel at Ramah. Returning to Gibeah to say good-bye to Jonathan, he then escaped to Nob, where he received food and a sword from the priest. He then fled to Gath in Philistine territory. When the Philistines became suspicious, he escaped to the cave of Adullam, where many men joined him.*

Ps 34:1ff God promises great blessings to his people, but many of these blessings require active participation. He will set us free from our fears (Ps 34:4, 6), guard and defend us (Ps 34:7), show us goodness (Ps 34:8), supply our needs (Ps 34:9), listen when we call to him (Ps 34:15), and redeem us (Ps 34:22), but we must do our part. We can appropriate his blessings when we trust him (Ps 34:4, 10); cry out to him (Ps 34:6, 17); take refuge in him (Ps 34:8); fear him (Ps 34:9); refrain from lying (Ps 34:13); turn from evil, do good, and search for peace (Ps 34:14); are brokenhearted (Ps 34:18); and serve him (Ps 34:22).

Ps 34:8 "Taste and see" does not mean, "Check out God's credentials." Instead, it is a warm invitation: "Try this; I know you'll like it." When we take that first step of obedience in following God, we will discover that he is good and kind. When we begin the Christian life, our knowledge of God is partial and incomplete. As we trust him daily, we experience how good he is.

Ps 34:9 You say you belong to the Lord, but do you fear him? To fear the Lord means to show him deep respect, reverence, and honor. We demonstrate this attitude by humility and genuine worship. Abraham (Gen 17:2-4), Moses (Exod 3:5-6), and the Israelites (Exod 19:16-24) showed this kind of fear of the Lord.

Ps 34:9-10 At first we may question David's statement because we seem to lack many good things. But this is not a blanket promise that all Christians will have everything they want. Instead, this is David's praise for God's goodness—all those who call upon God in their need will be answered, sometimes in unexpected ways.

Remember, God knows what we need, and our deepest needs are spiritual. Even though many Christians face unbearable poverty and hardship, they still have enough spiritual nourishment to live for God. David was saying that if you have God, you have all you really need. God is enough.

If you feel you don't have everything you need, ask: (1) Is this really a need? (2) Is this really good for me? (3) Is this the best time for me to have what I desire? Even if you answer *yes* to all three questions, God may allow you to go without to help you grow more dependent on him. He may want you to learn that you need *him* more than having your immediate desires met.

Ps 34:11-14 The Bible often connects the fear of the Lord (love and reverence for him) with obedience. "Fear God and obey his commands" (Eccl 12:13); "All who love me will do what I say" (John 14:23). David said that a person who fears the Lord doesn't lie, turns from evil, does good, and promotes peace.

12 Does anyone want to live a life
that is long and prosperous?
13 Then keep your tongue from speaking evil
and your lips from telling lies!
14 Turn away from evil and do good.
Search for peace, and work to maintain it.

15 The eyes of the LORD watch over those who
do right;
his ears are open to their cries for help.
16 But the LORD turns his face against those who
do evil;
he will erase their memory from the earth.
17 The LORD hears his people when they call to him
for help.
He rescues them from all their troubles.
18 The LORD is close to the brokenhearted;
he rescues those whose spirits are crushed.

19 The righteous person faces many troubles,
but the LORD comes to the rescue each time.
20 For the LORD protects the bones of the righteous;
not one of them is broken!

21 Calamity will surely overtake the wicked,
and those who hate the righteous will be
punished.
22 But the LORD will redeem those who serve him.
No one who takes refuge in him will be
condemned.

David at the Cave of Adullam

1 SAMUEL 22:1-2

So David left Gath and escaped to the cave of Adullam.
Soon his brothers and all his other relatives joined him
there. 2Then others began coming—men who were
in trouble or in debt or who were just discontented—
until David was the captain of about 400 men.

Psalm 57

THEME: God's faithful help and love in times of trouble. When we face trials, God will quiet our hearts and give us confidence.

AUTHOR: David

For the choir director: A psalm of David, regarding the time he fled from Saul and went into the cave. To be sung to the tune "Do Not Destroy!"*

1 Have mercy on me, O God, have mercy!
I look to you for protection.
I will hide beneath the shadow of your wings
until the danger passes by.
2 I cry out to God Most High,*
to God who will fulfill his purpose for me.
3 He will send help from heaven to rescue me,
disgracing those who hound me. *Interlude*
My God will send forth his unfailing love and
faithfulness.

4 I am surrounded by fierce lions
who greedily devour human prey—
whose teeth pierce like spears and arrows,
and whose tongues cut like swords.

5 Be exalted, O God, above the highest heavens!
May your glory shine over all the earth.

6 My enemies have set a trap for me.
I am weary from distress.
They have dug a deep pit in my path,
but they themselves have fallen into it.
Interlude

Ps 57:TITLE Hebrew *miktam.* This may be a literary or musical term. **Ps 57:2** Hebrew *Elohim-Elyon.*

Reverence is much more than sitting quietly in church. It includes obeying God in the way we speak and the way we treat others.

Ps 34:14 Some may think that peace should come with no effort. But David explained that we are to work hard at peace. Paul echoed this thought in Romans 12:18. A person who wants peace cannot be argumentative and contentious. Because peaceful relationships come from our efforts at peacemaking, work hard at living in peace with others each day.

Ps 34:18-19 We often wish we could escape troubles—the pain of grief, loss, sorrow, and failure, or even the small daily frustrations that constantly wear us down. God promises to be "close to the brokenhearted" and to be our source of power, courage, and wisdom, helping us through our problems. Sometimes he chooses to deliver us from those problems. When trouble strikes, don't get frustrated with God. Instead, admit that you need God's help and thank him for being by your side.

Ps 34:20 This is a prophecy about Christ when he was crucified. Although it was the Roman custom to break the legs of the victim to speed death, not one of Jesus' bones was broken (John 19:32-37). In addition to the prophetic meaning, David was pleading for God's protection in times of crisis.

1 Sam 22:2 Those who were discontented, in trouble, or in debt joined David, who himself was an outlaw. These people were outcasts and could only improve their lot by helping David become king. David's control over this band of men again shows his resourcefulness and ability to lead and motivate others. It is difficult enough to build an army out of good men, but it takes even greater leadership to build one out of the kind of men that followed David. This group eventually formed the core of his military leadership (2 Sam 23:8ff).

Taste and see that the LORD is good.
Psalm 34:8

Ps 57:4 At times we may be surrounded by people who gossip about us or criticize us. Verbal cruelty can damage us as badly as physical abuse. Rather than answering with hateful words, we, like David, can talk with God about the problem.

▸ **PSALM 57 *(cont.)***

7 My heart is confident in you, O God;
my heart is confident.
No wonder I can sing your praises!
8 Wake up, my heart!
Wake up, O lyre and harp!
I will wake the dawn with my song.
9 I will thank you, Lord, among all the people.
I will sing your praises among the nations.
10 For your unfailing love is as high as the heavens.
Your faithfulness reaches to the clouds.
11 Be exalted, O God, above the highest heavens.
May your glory shine over all the earth.

Psalm 142

THEME: A prayer when overwhelmed and desperate. When we feel cornered by our enemies, only God can keep us safe.

AUTHOR: David

A psalm of David, regarding his experience in the cave. A prayer.*

1 I cry out to the LORD;
I plead for the LORD's mercy.
2 I pour out my complaints before him
and tell him all my troubles.
3 When I am overwhelmed,
you alone know the way I should turn.
Wherever I go,
my enemies have set traps for me.
4 I look for someone to come and help me,
but no one gives me a passing thought!
No one will help me;
no one cares a bit what happens to me.
5 Then I pray to you, O LORD.
I say, "You are my place of refuge.
You are all I really want in life.
6 Hear my cry,
for I am very low.
Rescue me from my persecutors,
for they are too strong for me.
7 Bring me out of prison
so I can thank you.
The godly will crowd around me,
for you are good to me."

Ps 142:TITLE Hebrew *maskil.* This may be a literary or musical term.

Warriors Join David

1 CHRONICLES 12:8-18

Some brave and experienced warriors from the tribe
of Gad also defected to David while he was at the
stronghold in the wilderness. They were expert with
both shield and spear, as fierce as lions and as swift
as deer on the mountains.

9 Ezer was their leader.
Obadiah was second.
Eliab was third.
10 Mishmannah was fourth.
Jeremiah was fifth.
11 Attai was sixth.
Eliel was seventh.
12 Johanan was eighth.
Elzabad was ninth.
13 Jeremiah was tenth.
Macbannai was eleventh.

14 These warriors from Gad were army commanders. The weakest among them could take on a hundred regular troops, and the strongest could take
on a thousand! 15 These were the men who crossed
the Jordan River during its seasonal flooding at the
beginning of the year and drove out all the people
living in the lowlands on both the east and west
banks.

16 Others from Benjamin and Judah came to David at the stronghold. 17 David went out to meet them
and said, "If you have come in peace to help me, we
are friends. But if you have come to betray me to my
enemies when I am innocent, then may the God of our
ancestors see it and punish you."

Ps 57:7 David's firm faith in God contrasts sharply with his enemies' loud lying and boasting. When confronted with verbal attacks, the best defense is simply to be quiet and praise God, realizing that our confidence is in his love and faithfulness (Ps 57:10). In times of suffering, don't turn inward to self-pity or outward to revenge, but turn upward to God.

Ps 57:8 David calls out to his soul and his instruments to prepare for praise. Before a new day begins, he wants to "wake the dawn" with his song honoring God's faithfulness. Instead of spending a sleepless night worrying about what he cannot change, he uses those wakeful hours to meditate on an expression suitable for all people, all nations. David's example shows us how to turn times of stress into times of blessing by considering God's faithfulness in comparison with our fleeting problems. Why worry when you can invest that time in praise?

Ps 142:6 Have you ever felt that no one cared what happened to you? David had good reason to feel that way, and he wrote, "Hear my cry, for I am very low." Through prayer we can pull out of our tailspin and be reminded that God cares for us deeply.

Ps 142:7 This psalm was written when David was hiding from Saul in caves like the ones at Adullam (1 Sam 22) or En-gedi (1 Sam 24). These may have seemed like prisons to him because of the confinement.

1 Chr 12:8 While the men of Benjamin were expert archers and slingers, the warriors of Gad were experts with the shield and spear. Israelite spears had wood shafts with spearheads of bone or stone and were often thrown through the air toward their mark. Philistine spears had bronze shafts and iron spearheads, and their shields were made of wood and overlaid with leather. Large shields were often carried by an armor bearer, whose main task was to protect the warrior.

1 Chr 12:18 How did the Holy Spirit work in Old Testament times? When there was an important job to be done, God chose a person to do it, and the Spirit gave that person the needed power and ability. The Spirit gave Bezalel artistic ability (Exod 31:1-5), Jephthah military prowess (Judg 11:29), David power to rule (1 Sam 16:13), and Zechariah an authoritative word of

18 Then the Spirit came upon Amasai, the leader of the Thirty, and he said,

"We are yours, David!
We are on your side, son of Jesse.
Peace and prosperity be with you,
and success to all who help you,
for your God is the one who helps you."

So David let them join him, and he made them officers over his troops.

David Flees from Saul

1 SAMUEL 22:3-10

Later David went to Mizpeh in Moab, where he asked the king, "Please allow my father and mother to live here with you until I know what God is going to do for me." 4 So David's parents stayed in Moab with the king during the entire time David was living in his stronghold.

5 One day the prophet Gad told David, "Leave the stronghold and return to the land of Judah." So David went to the forest of Hereth.

6 The news of his arrival in Judah soon reached Saul. At the time, the king was sitting beneath the tamarisk tree on the hill at Gibeah, holding his spear and surrounded by his officers.

7 "Listen here, you men of Benjamin!" Saul shouted to his officers when he heard the news. "Has that son of Jesse promised every one of you fields and vineyards? Has he promised to make you all generals and captains in his army?* 8 Is that why you have conspired against me? For not one of you told me when my own son made a solemn pact with the son of Jesse. You're not even sorry for me. Think of it! My own son—encouraging him to kill me, as he is trying to do this very day!"

9 Then Doeg the Edomite, who was standing there with Saul's men, spoke up. "When I was at Nob," he said, "I saw the son of Jesse talking to the priest, Ahimelech son of Ahitub. 10 Ahimelech consulted the LORD for him. Then he gave him food and the sword of Goliath the Philistine."

The Slaughter of the Priests

1 SAMUEL 22:11-23

King Saul immediately sent for Ahimelech and all his family, who served as priests at Nob. 12 When they arrived, Saul shouted at him, "Listen to me, you son of Ahitub!"

"What is it, my king?" Ahimelech asked.

13 "Why have you and the son of Jesse conspired against me?" Saul demanded. "Why did you give him food and a sword? Why have you consulted God for him? Why have you encouraged him to kill me, as he is trying to do this very day?"

14 "But sir," Ahimelech replied, "is anyone among all your servants as faithful as David, your son-in-law? Why, he is the captain of your bodyguard and a highly honored member of your household! 15 This was certainly not the first time I had consulted God for him! May the king not accuse me and my family in this matter, for I knew nothing at all of any plot against you."

16 "You will surely die, Ahimelech, along with your entire family!" the king shouted. 17 And he ordered his bodyguards, "Kill these priests of the LORD, for they are allies and conspirators with David! They knew he was running away from me, but they didn't tell me!" But Saul's men refused to kill the LORD's priests.

1 Sm 22:7 Hebrew *commanders of thousands and commanders of hundreds?*

prophecy (2 Chr 24:20). Here the Holy Spirit came upon Amasai, one of David's warriors. The Spirit came upon individuals in order to accomplish specific goals. Beginning at Pentecost, the Spirit came upon all believers, not only to empower them to do God's will, but also to dwell in them day by day (Acts 2:14-21). If you are a believer in Jesus Christ, you will experience the Holy Spirit's ongoing work in your life as well as special times of filling for God's purposes. Expect God's Spirit to work in and through you.

1 Sam 22:7-8 Apparently Saul's key officers were from the tribe of Benjamin, just as he was. David was from the neighboring tribe of Judah. Saul was appealing to tribal loyalty to maintain his hold on the throne.

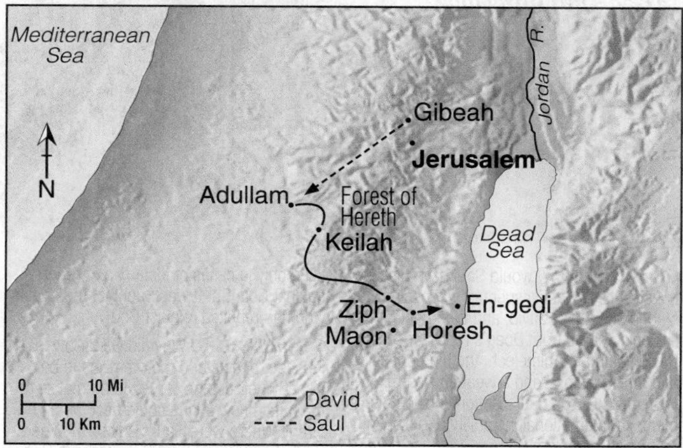

***DAVID FLEES FROM SAUL** David and his men attacked the Philistines at Keilah from the forest of Hereth. Saul came from Gibeah to attack David, but David escaped into the wilderness of Ziph. At Horesh he met Jonathan, who encouraged him. Then he fled into the wilderness of Maon and into the strongholds of En-gedi.*

▸ **1 SAMUEL 22:11-23 *(cont.)***

[18]Then the king said to Doeg, "You do it." So Doeg
the Edomite turned on them and killed them that day,
eighty-five priests in all, still wearing their priestly garments. [19]Then he went to Nob, the town of the priests,
and killed the priests' families—men and women, children and babies—and all the cattle, donkeys, sheep,
and goats.
[20]Only Abiathar, one of the sons of Ahimelech, escaped and fled to David. [21]When he told David that
Saul had killed the priests of the LORD, [22]David exclaimed, "I knew it! When I saw Doeg the Edomite
there that day, I knew he was sure to tell Saul. Now I
have caused the death of all your father's family. [23]Stay
here with me, and don't be afraid. I will protect you with
my own life, for the same person wants to kill us both."

Psalm 52

THEME: God will judge the evildoer. Our anger must not block our confidence in God's ability to defeat evil.

AUTHOR: David

For the choir director: A psalm of David, regarding the time Doeg the Edomite said to Saul, "David has gone to see Ahimelech."*

1 Why do you boast about your crimes, great
warrior?
Don't you realize God's justice continues
forever?
2 All day long you plot destruction.
Your tongue cuts like a sharp razor;
you're an expert at telling lies.
3 You love evil more than good
and lies more than truth. *Interlude*
4 You love to destroy others with your words,
you liar!
5 But God will strike you down once and for all.
He will pull you from your home
and uproot you from the land of the living. *Interlude*
6 The righteous will see it and be amazed.
They will laugh and say,
7 "Look what happens to mighty warriors
who do not trust in God.
They trust their wealth instead
and grow more and more bold in their
wickedness."
8 But I am like an olive tree, thriving in the house
of God.
I will always trust in God's unfailing love.
9 I will praise you forever, O God,
for what you have done.
I will trust in your good name
in the presence of your faithful people.

Ps 52:TITLE Hebrew *maskil.* This may be a literary or musical term.

But I am like an olive tree, thriving in the house of God. I will always trust in God's unfailing love.
Psalm 52:8

1 Sam 22:18 Why would Saul have his own priests killed? Saul suspected a conspiracy among Jonathan, David, and the priests. His suspicion came from Doeg's report of seeing David talking to Ahimelech, the high priest, and receiving food and a weapon from him (1 Sam 22:9-10). Saul's action showed his mental and emotional instability and how far he had strayed from God.

By destroying everything in Nob, Saul was placing the city under the ban (declaring it to be utterly destroyed) described in Deuteronomy 13:12-17, which was supposed to be used only in cases of idolatry and rebellion against God. But it was Saul, not the priests, who had rebelled against God.

1 Sam 22:18-19 Why did God allow 85 innocent priests and their families to be killed? Their deaths served to dramatize to the nation how a king could become an evil tyrant. Where were Saul's advisers? Where were the elders of Israel? Sometimes God allows evil to develop to teach us not to let evil systems flourish. Serving God is not a ticket to wealth, success, or health. God does not promise to protect good people from evil in this world, but he does promise that ultimately all evil will be abolished. Those who have remained faithful through their trials will experience great rewards in the age to come (Matt 5:11-12; Rev 21:1-7; 22:1-21).

1 Sam 22:20 Abiathar escaped to David with an ephod (1 Sam 23:6), a priestly garment containing the Urim and Thummim, two objects David used to consult God. The ephod was probably the only symbol of the priesthood that survived Saul's raid and made it into David's camp (1 Sam 23:6). Saul destroyed Israel's priesthood, but when David became king, he installed Abiathar as the new high priest. Abiathar remained in that position during David's entire reign.

Ps 52:1 This psalm was written about Doeg the Edomite, who had betrayed Ahimelech and David and then killed God's priests (see 1 Sam 21:7; 22:9-23). Doeg thought he was a great warrior—even boasting about his deed. In reality, his deed was evil, an offense to God. It is easy to mistake "accomplishment" for goodness. Just because something is done well or thoroughly doesn't mean it is good (for example, someone may be a great gambler or a skillful liar). Measure all you do by the rule of God's Word, not by how proficiently you do it.

Ps 52:8 With God by his side, David compared himself to an olive tree flourishing in the house of God. Not only is an olive tree a

David Protects the Town of Keilah

1 SAMUEL 23:1-12

One day news came to David that the Philistines were at Keilah stealing grain from the threshing floors.
2David asked the LORD, "Should I go and attack them?"
"Yes, go and save Keilah," the LORD told him.
3But David's men said, "We're afraid even here in Judah. We certainly don't want to go to Keilah to fight the whole Philistine army!"
4So David asked the LORD again, and again the LORD replied, "Go down to Keilah, for I will help you conquer the Philistines."
5So David and his men went to Keilah. They slaughtered the Philistines and took all their livestock and
rescued the people of Keilah. 6Now when Abiathar son of Ahimelech fled to David at Keilah, he brought the ephod with him.
7Saul soon learned that David was at Keilah. "Good!" he exclaimed. "We've got him now! God has handed him over to me, for he has trapped himself in a walled
town!" 8So Saul mobilized his entire army to march to Keilah and besiege David and his men.
9But David learned of Saul's plan and told Abiathar the priest to bring the ephod and ask the LORD what
he should do. 10Then David prayed, "O LORD, God of Israel, I have heard that Saul is planning to come and
destroy Keilah because I am here. 11Will the leaders of Keilah betray me to him?* And will Saul actually come as I have heard? O LORD, God of Israel, please tell me."
And the LORD said, "He will come."
12Again David asked, "Will the leaders of Keilah betray me and my men to Saul?"
And the LORD replied, "Yes, they will betray you."

David Hides in the Wilderness

1 SAMUEL 23:13-29

So David and his men—about 600 of them now—left Keilah and began roaming the countryside. Word soon reached Saul that David had escaped, so he didn't go to
Keilah after all. 14David now stayed in the strongholds of the wilderness and in the hill country of Ziph. Saul hunted him day after day, but God didn't let Saul find him.
15One day near Horesh, David received the news that Saul was on the way to Ziph to search for him and
kill him. 16Jonathan went to find David and encouraged him to stay strong in his faith in God. 17"Don't be afraid," Jonathan reassured him. "My father will never find you! You are going to be the king of Israel, and I will be next to you, as my father, Saul, is well aware."
18So the two of them renewed their solemn pact before the LORD. Then Jonathan returned home, while David stayed at Horesh.
19But now the men of Ziph went to Saul in Gibeah and betrayed David to him. "We know where David is hiding," they said. "He is in the strongholds of Horesh on the hill of Hakilah, which is in the southern part
of Jeshimon. 20Come down whenever you're ready, O king, and we will catch him and hand him over to you!"
21"The LORD bless you," Saul said. "At last someone is concerned about me! 22Go and check again to be sure of where he is staying and who has seen
him there, for I know that he is very crafty. 23Discover his hiding places, and come back when you are sure. Then I'll go with you. And if he is in the area at all, I'll track him down, even if I have to search every hiding
place in Judah!" 24So the men of Ziph returned home ahead of Saul.
Meanwhile, David and his men had moved into the wilderness of Maon in the Arabah Valley south of Je-
shimon. 25When David heard that Saul and his men were searching for him, he went even farther into the wilderness to the great rock, and he remained there in the wilderness of Maon. But Saul kept after him in the wilderness.

1 Sm 23:11 Some manuscripts lack the first sentence of 23:11.

---

thriving tree, but it is also one of the longest-living trees. David was contrasting God's eternal protection of his faithful servants with the sudden destruction of the wicked (Ps 52:5-7).

1 Sam 23:1 Threshing floors were open circular areas where the grain kernels were separated from their husks. (In order to separate the grain from the husk, farmers would toss their grain into the air. The wind would blow the husks away, leaving only the grain. This process is called *winnowing*.) By looting the threshing floors, the Philistines were robbing Keilah's citizens of all their food supplies. (For more on threshing, see the note on Ruth 3:2, p. 414.)

1 Sam 23:2 Through the Urim and Thummim that Abiathar the priest brought (1 Sam 23:6), David sought the Lord's guidance before he took action. He listened to God's directions and then proceeded accordingly. Rather than trying to find God's will after the fact or having to ask God to undo the results of our hasty decisions, we should take time to discern God's will beforehand. We can hear him speak through the counsel of others, his Word, and the leading of his Spirit in our heart, as well as through circumstances.

1 Sam 23:6 An ephod was a sleeveless linen vest worn by priests. The high priest's ephod was brightly colored and had a breastplate with 12 gemstones, each stone representing one of the 12 tribes. The Urim and Thummim were kept in a pouch of the high priest's ephod. (See the note on 1 Sam 2:18, p. 420.)

1 Sam 23:7 When Saul heard that David was trapped in a walled city (one with gates and bars), he thought God was putting David at his mercy. Saul wanted to kill David so badly that he would have interpreted any sign as God's approval to move ahead with his plan. Had Saul known God better, he would have known what God wanted and would not have misread the situation as God's approval for murder.

Not every opportunity is sent from God. We may want something so much that we assume any opportunity to obtain it is of divine origin. As we see from Saul's case, this may not be true. An opportunity to do something against God's will can never be from God because God does not tempt us. When opportunities come your way, double-check your motives. Make sure you are following God's desires and not just your own.

1 Sam 23:16-18 This may have been the last time David and Jonathan were together. As true friends they were more than just companions who enjoyed each other's company. They encouraged each other's faith in God and trusted each other with their deepest thoughts and closest confidences. These are the marks of true friendship.

▸ **1 SAMUEL 23:13-29 *(cont.)***

[26]Saul and David were now on opposite sides of a
mountain. Just as Saul and his men began to close in
on David and his men, [27]an urgent message reached
Saul that the Philistines were raiding Israel again.
[28]So Saul quit chasing David and returned to fight
the Philistines. Ever since that time, the place where
David was camped has been called the Rock of Escape.* [29]*David then went to live in the strongholds
of En-gedi.

Psalm 54

THEME: A call for God to overcome enemies. God is our helper, even in times of hurt and betrayal.

AUTHOR: David

For the choir director: A psalm of David, regarding the time the Ziphites came and said to Saul, "We know where David is hiding." To be accompanied by stringed instruments.*

1 Come with great power, O God, and rescue me!
  Defend me with your might.
2 Listen to my prayer, O God.
  Pay attention to my plea.
3 For strangers are attacking me;
  violent people are trying to kill me.
  They care nothing for God. *Interlude*
4 But God is my helper.
  The Lord keeps me alive!
5 May the evil plans of my enemies be turned
    against them.
  Do as you promised and put an end to them.

6 I will sacrifice a voluntary offering to you;
  I will praise your name, O LORD,
    for it is good.
7 For you have rescued me from my troubles
  and helped me to triumph over my
    enemies.

David Spares Saul's Life

1 SAMUEL 24:1-22

[1]*After Saul returned from fighting the Philistines,
he was told that David had gone into the wilderness
of En-gedi. [2]So Saul chose 3,000 elite troops from all
Israel and went to search for David and his men near
the rocks of the wild goats.
[3]At the place where the road passes some sheepfolds, Saul went into a cave to relieve himself. But as
it happened, David and his men were hiding farther
back in that very cave!
[4]"Now's your opportunity!" David's men whispered
to him. "Today the LORD is telling you, 'I will certainly
put your enemy into your power, to do with as you
wish.'" So David crept forward and cut off a piece of
the hem of Saul's robe.
[5]But then David's conscience began bothering him
because he had cut Saul's robe. [6]"The LORD knows I
shouldn't have done that to my lord the king," he said
to his men. "The LORD forbid that I should do this
to my lord the king and attack the LORD's anointed
one, for the LORD himself has chosen him." [7]So David restrained his men and did not let them kill Saul.
After Saul had left the cave and gone on his way,
[8]David came out and shouted after him, "My lord the
king!" And when Saul looked around, David bowed
low before him.
[9]Then he shouted to Saul, "Why do you listen to the
people who say I am trying to harm you? [10]This very
day you can see with your own eyes it isn't true. For the
LORD placed you at my mercy back there in the cave.
Some of my men told me to kill you, but I spared you.
For I said, 'I will never harm the king—he is the LORD's
anointed one.' [11]Look, my father, at what I have in my
hand. It is a piece of the hem of your robe! I cut it off,
but I didn't kill you. This proves that I am not trying
to harm you and that I have not sinned against you,
even though you have been hunting for me to kill me.
[12]"May the LORD judge between us. Perhaps the

1 Sm 23:28 Hebrew *Sela-hammahlekoth.* **1 Sm 23:29** Verse 23:29 is numbered 24:1 in Hebrew text. **Ps 54:TITLE** Hebrew *maskil.* This may be a literary or musical term. **1 Sm 24:1** Verses 24:1-22 are numbered 24:2-23 in Hebrew text.

Ps 54:3-4 Many of David's psalms follow the pattern found in these two verses—a transition from prayer to praise. David was not afraid to come to God and express his true feelings and needs. Thus, his spirit was lifted, and he praised God—his helper, protector, and friend.

Ps 54:5 David asked God to repay evil to his enemies. He simply stated his confidence in God's promise. Proverbs 26:27 warns that those who cause trouble will reap trouble. What we have intended for others may blow up in our own face. To be honest and straightforward before God and others is simpler, easier, and safer in the long run.

1 Sam 24:3 David and his 600 men found the wilderness of En-gedi a good place to hide because of the many caves in the area. These caves were used by local people for housing and as tombs. For David's men they were places of refuge. These caves can still be seen today. Some are large enough to hold thousands of people.

1 Sam 24:4 Scripture does not record that God made any such statement to David or his men. The men were probably offering their own interpretation of some previous event, such as David's anointing (1 Sam 16:13) or Jonathan's prediction that David would become king (1 Sam 23:17). When David's men saw Saul entering their cave, they wrongly assumed that this was an indication from God that they should act.

1 Sam 24:5-6 David had great respect for Saul, in spite of the fact that Saul was trying to kill him. Although Saul was sinning and rebelling against God, David still respected the position he held as God's anointed king. David knew he would one day be king, and he also knew it was not right to strike down the man God had placed on the throne. If he assassinated Saul, he would be setting a precedent for his own opponents to remove him some day.

Romans 13:1-7 teaches that God has placed the government and its leaders in power. We may not know why, but like David, we are to respect the positions and roles of those to whom God has given authority. There is one exception. Because God is our highest authority, we should

LORD will punish you for what you are trying to do to
me, but I will never harm you. 13As that old proverb
says, 'From evil people come evil deeds.' So you can
be sure I will never harm you. 14Who is the king of
Israel trying to catch anyway? Should he spend his
time chasing one who is as worthless as a dead dog or
a single flea? 15May the LORD therefore judge which of
us is right and punish the guilty one. He is my advocate, and he will rescue me from your power!"
16When David had finished speaking, Saul called
back, "Is that really you, my son David?" Then he
began to cry. 17And he said to David, "You are a better man than I am, for you have repaid me good for
evil. 18Yes, you have been amazingly kind to me today, for when the LORD put me in a place where you
could have killed me, you didn't do it. 19Who else
would let his enemy get away when he had him in
his power? May the LORD reward you well for the
kindness you have shown me today. 20And now I
realize that you are surely going to be king, and that
the kingdom of Israel will flourish under your rule.
21Now swear to me by the LORD that when that happens you will not kill my family and destroy my line
of descendants!"
22So David promised this to Saul with an oath. Then
Saul went home, but David and his men went back to
their stronghold.

The Death of Samuel

1 SAMUEL 25:1a

Now Samuel died, and all Israel gathered for his funeral. They buried him at his house in Ramah.

Nabal Angers David

1 SAMUEL 25:1b-22

Then David moved down to the wilderness of Maon.*
2There was a wealthy man from Maon who owned
property near the town of Carmel. He had 3,000 sheep
and 1,000 goats, and it was sheep-shearing time. 3This
man's name was Nabal, and his wife, Abigail, was a
sensible and beautiful woman. But Nabal, a descendant of Caleb, was crude and mean in all his dealings.
4When David heard that Nabal was shearing his
sheep, 5he sent ten of his young men to Carmel with
this message for Nabal: 6"Peace and prosperity to you,
your family, and everything you own! 7I am told that it
is sheep-shearing time. While your shepherds stayed
among us near Carmel, we never harmed them, and
nothing was ever stolen from them. 8Ask your own
men, and they will tell you this is true. So would you
be kind to us, since we have come at a time of celebration? Please share any provisions you might have on
hand with us and with your friend David." 9David's
young men gave this message to Nabal in David's
name, and they waited for a reply.

1 Sm 25:1 As in Greek version (see also 25:2); Hebrew reads *Paran*.

LIFE OF DAVID VERSUS LIFE OF SAUL

Life of David	Life of Saul
David was God's kind of king (2 Sam 7:8-16)	Saul was man's kind of king (1 Sam 10:23-24)
David was a man after God's heart (Acts 13:22)	Saul needed people's praise (1 Sam 18:6-8)
David's kingship was eternal (through Jesus) (2 Sam 7:29)	Saul's kingship was rejected (1 Sam 15:23)
David was kind and benevolent (2 Sam 9; 1 Chr 19:2)	Saul was cruel (1 Sam 20:30-34; 22:11-19)
David was forgiving (1 Sam 26)	Saul was unforgiving (1 Sam 14:44; 18:9)
David repented (2 Sam 12:13; 24:10)	When confronted, Saul lied (1 Sam 15:10-31)
David was courageous (1 Sam 17; 1 Chr 18)	Saul was fearful (1 Sam 17:11; 18:12)
David was at peace with God (Pss 4:8; 37:11)	Saul was separated from God (1 Sam 16:14)

not allow a leader to pressure us to violate God's law.

1 Sam 24:16-19 The means we use to accomplish a goal are just as important as the goal we are trying to accomplish. David's goal was to become king, so his men urged him to kill Saul when he had the chance. David's refusal was not an example of cowardice but of courage—the courage to stand against the group and do what he knew was right. Don't compromise your moral standards by giving in to group pressure or taking the easy way out.

1 Sam 24:21-22 David kept his promise—he never took revenge on Saul's family or descendants. Most of Saul's sons were eventually killed by the Philistines (1 Sam 31:2) and the Gibeonites (2 Sam 21:1-14). David had promised to be kind to the descendants of Saul's son Jonathan (1 Sam 20:14-15), and he kept this promise when he invited Mephibosheth to live in his palace (2 Sam 9).

1 Sam 25:1 Saul was king, but Samuel had been the nation's spiritual leader. As a young boy and as an older man, Samuel was always careful to listen to (1 Sam 3:10; 9:14-17) and obey (1 Sam 3:21; 10:1-2) the Lord. With Samuel gone, Israel would be without this spiritual leadership until David became king. (For more on Samuel, read his Profile on p. 426.)

1 Sam 25:2-11 Nabal rudely refused David's request to feed his 600 men. If we sympathize with Nabal, it is because customs are so different today. First, simple hospitality demanded that travelers—any number of them—be fed. Nabal was very rich and could have easily afforded to meet David's request. Second, David wasn't asking for a handout. He and his men had been protecting Nabal's workforce, and part of Nabal's prosperity was due to David's vigilance. We should be generous with those who protect us and help us prosper, even if we are not obligated to do so by law or custom.

▶ **1 SAMUEL 25:1b-22** ***(cont.)***

10"Who is this fellow David?" Nabal sneered to the
young men. "Who does this son of Jesse think he is?
There are lots of servants these days who run away
from their masters. 11Should I take my bread and my
water and my meat that I've slaughtered for my shearers and give it to a band of outlaws who come from
who knows where?"
12So David's young men returned and told him what
Nabal had said. 13"Get your swords!" was David's reply
as he strapped on his own. Then 400 men started off
with David, and 200 remained behind to guard their
equipment.
14Meanwhile, one of Nabal's servants went to Abigail and told her, "David sent messengers from the
wilderness to greet our master, but he screamed insults
at them. 15These men have been very good to us, and
we never suffered any harm from them. Nothing was
stolen from us the whole time they were with us. 16In
fact, day and night they were like a wall of protection
to us and the sheep. 17You need to know this and figure
out what to do, for there is going to be trouble for our
master and his whole family. He's so ill-tempered that
no one can even talk to him!"
18Abigail wasted no time. She quickly gathered
200 loaves of bread, two wineskins full of wine, five
sheep that had been slaughtered, nearly a bushel*
of roasted grain, 100 clusters of raisins, and 200 fig
cakes. She packed them on donkeys 19and said to her
servants, "Go on ahead. I will follow you shortly." But
she didn't tell her husband Nabal what she was doing.
20As she was riding her donkey into a mountain
ravine, she saw David and his men coming toward her.
21David had just been saying, "A lot of good it did to
help this fellow. We protected his flocks in the wilderness, and nothing he owned was lost or stolen. But he
has repaid me evil for good. 22May God strike me and
kill me* if even one man of his household is still alive
tomorrow morning!"

Abigail Intercedes for Nabal

1 SAMUEL 25:23-38

When Abigail saw David, she quickly got off her donkey and bowed low before him. 24She fell at his feet
and said, "I accept all blame in this matter, my lord.
Please listen to what I have to say. 25I know Nabal is
a wicked and ill-tempered man; please don't pay any
attention to him. He is a fool, just as his name suggests.* But I never even saw the young men you sent.
26"Now, my lord, as surely as the LORD lives and you

1 Sm 25:18 Hebrew *5 seahs* [30 liters]. **1 Sm 25:22** As in Greek version; Hebrew reads *May God strike and kill the enemies of David.* **1 Sm 25:25** The name *Nabal* means "fool."

ABIGAIL

Some men don't deserve their wives. Abigail was probably the best woman Nabal could afford, and he got even more than he bargained for when he arranged to marry her. She was beautiful and more suited than he was to manage his wealth. But Nabal took his wife for granted. • In spite of his shortcomings, Nabal's household did what they could to keep him out of trouble. This loyalty must have been inspired by Abigail. Although her culture and her husband placed a low value on her, she made the most of her skills and opportunities. David was impressed with her abilities, and when Nabal died, he married her. • Abigail was an effective counselor to both of the men in her life, working hard to prevent them from making rash moves. By her swift action and skillful negotiation, she kept David from taking vengeance upon Nabal. She saw the big picture and left plenty of room for God to get involved. • Do you look beyond the present crisis to the big picture? Do you use your skills to promote peace? Are you loyal without being blind? What challenge or responsibility do you face today that requires you to be a person under God's control?

Strengths and accomplishments	• Sensible and capable • A persuasive speaker, able to see beyond herself
Lessons from her life	• Life's tough situations can bring out the best in people • One does not need a prestigious title to be significant
Vital statistics	• Where: Carmel • Occupation: Homemaker • Relatives: First husband: Nabal. Second husband: David. Son: Kileab (Daniel). • Contemporaries: Saul, Michal, Ahinoam
Key verses	"David replied to Abigail, 'Praise the LORD, the God of Israel, who has sent you to meet me today! Thank God for your good sense! Bless you for keeping me from murder and from carrying out vengeance with my own hands'" (1 Sam 25:32-33).

Abigail's story is told in 1 Samuel 25—2 Samuel 2. She is also mentioned in 1 Chronicles 3:1.

1 Sam 25:24 David was in no mood to listen when he set out for Nabal's property (1 Sam 25:13, 22). Nevertheless, he stopped to hear what Abigail had to say. If he had ignored her, he would have been guilty of taking vengeance into his own hands. No matter how right we think we are, we must always be careful to stop and listen to others. The extra time and effort can save us pain and trouble in the long run.

1 Sam 25:36 Because Nabal was drunk, Abigail waited until morning to tell him what she had done. Abigail knew that Nabal, in his drunkenness, may not have understood her or may have reacted foolishly. When discussing difficult matters with people, especially family members, timing is everything. Ask God for wisdom to know the best time for confrontation and for bringing up touchy subjects.

1 Sam 25:44 The story of David and Michal does not end here. (See 2 Sam 3:12-16 for the next episode.)

1 Sam 26:5-9 Abishai showed great courage when he volunteered to go into Saul's camp with David. In the heat of emotion, Abishai wanted to kill Saul, but David restrained him. Although Abishai was only trying to protect David, his leader, David could not hurt Saul because of his respect for Saul's authority and position as God's anointed king. Abishai may have disagreed with David, but he also respected the one in authority over him. Eventually he became the greatest warrior in David's army (2 Sam 23:18-19).

yourself live, since the LORD has kept you from murdering and taking vengeance into your own hands, let
all your enemies and those who try to harm you be as
cursed as Nabal is. 27And here is a present that I, your
servant, have brought to you and your young men.
28Please forgive me if I have offended you in any way.
The LORD will surely reward you with a lasting dynasty,
for you are fighting the LORD's battles. And you have
not done wrong throughout your entire life.

29"Even when you are chased by those who seek to
kill you, your life is safe in the care of the LORD your
God, secure in his treasure pouch! But the lives of your
enemies will disappear like stones shot from a sling!
30When the LORD has done all he promised and has
made you leader of Israel, 31don't let this be a blemish
on your record. Then your conscience won't have to
bear the staggering burden of needless bloodshed and
vengeance. And when the LORD has done these great
things for you, please remember me, your servant!"

32David replied to Abigail, "Praise the LORD, the God
of Israel, who has sent you to meet me today! 33Thank
God for your good sense! Bless you for keeping me
from murder and from carrying out vengeance with
my own hands. 34For I swear by the LORD, the God of
Israel, who has kept me from hurting you, that if you
had not hurried out to meet me, not one of Nabal's
men would still be alive tomorrow morning." 35Then
David accepted her present and told her, "Return home
in peace. I have heard what you said. We will not kill
your husband."

36When Abigail arrived home, she found that Nabal
was throwing a big party and was celebrating like a
king. He was very drunk, so she didn't tell him anything about her meeting with David until dawn the
next day. 37In the morning when Nabal was sober,
his wife told him what had happened. As a result he
had a stroke,* and he lay paralyzed on his bed like a
stone. 38About ten days later, the LORD struck him,
and he died.

David Marries Abigail

1 SAMUEL 25:39-44

When David heard that Nabal was dead, he said,
"Praise the LORD, who has avenged the insult I received
from Nabal and has kept me from doing it myself.
Nabal has received the punishment for his sin." Then
David sent messengers to Abigail to ask her to become
his wife.

40When the messengers arrived at Carmel, they
told Abigail, "David has sent us to take you back to
marry him."

41She bowed low to the ground and responded,
"I, your servant, would be happy to marry David. I
would even be willing to become a slave, washing
the feet of his servants!" 42Quickly getting ready, she
took along five of her servant girls as attendants,
mounted her donkey, and went with David's messengers. And so she became his wife. 43David also
married Ahinoam from Jezreel, making both of them
his wives. 44Saul, meanwhile, had given his daughter
Michal, David's wife, to a man from Gallim named
Palti son of Laish.

David Spares Saul Again

1 SAMUEL 26:1-25

Now some men from Ziph came to Saul at Gibeah to
tell him, "David is hiding on the hill of Hakilah, which
overlooks Jeshimon."

2So Saul took 3,000 of Israel's elite troops and
went to hunt him down in the wilderness of Ziph.
3Saul camped along the road beside the hill of Hakilah, near Jeshimon, where David was hiding. When
David learned that Saul had come after him into the
wilderness, 4he sent out spies to verify the report of
Saul's arrival.

5David slipped over to Saul's camp one night to look
around. Saul and Abner son of Ner, the commander
of his army, were sleeping inside a ring formed by the
slumbering warriors. 6"Who will volunteer to go in
there with me?" David asked Ahimelech the Hittite
and Abishai son of Zeruiah, Joab's brother.

"I'll go with you," Abishai replied. 7So David and
Abishai went right into Saul's camp and found him
asleep, with his spear stuck in the ground beside
his head. Abner and the soldiers were lying asleep
around him.

8"God has surely handed your enemy over to you
this time!" Abishai whispered to David. "Let me pin
him to the ground with one thrust of the spear; I won't
need to strike twice!"

1 Sm 25:37 Hebrew *his heart failed him.*

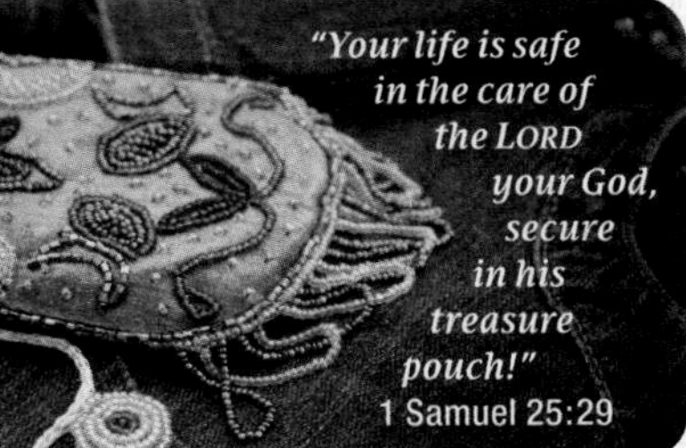
"Your life is safe
in the care of
the LORD
your God,
secure
in his
treasure
pouch!"
1 Samuel 25:29

1 Sam 26:8ff The strongest moral decisions are the ones we make before temptation strikes. David was determined to follow God, and this carried over into his decision not to murder God's anointed king, Saul, even when his men and the circumstances seemed to make it a feasible option. Who would you have been like in such a situation—David or David's men? To be like David and follow God, we must realize that we can't do wrong in order to execute justice. Even when our closest friends counsel us to do something that seems right, we must always put God's commands first.

▸ **1 SAMUEL 26:1-25** ***(cont.)***

9"No!" David said. "Don't kill him. For who can remain innocent after attacking the LORD's anointed one? 10Surely the LORD will strike Saul down someday, or he will die of old age or in battle. 11The LORD forbid that I should kill the one he has anointed! But take his spear and that jug of water beside his head, and then let's get out of here!"

12So David took the spear and jug of water that were near Saul's head. Then he and Abishai got away without anyone seeing them or even waking up, because the LORD had put Saul's men into a deep sleep.

13David climbed the hill opposite the camp until he was at a safe distance. 14Then he shouted down to the soldiers and to Abner son of Ner, "Wake up, Abner!"

"Who is it?" Abner demanded.

15"Well, Abner, you're a great man, aren't you?" David taunted. "Where in all Israel is there anyone as mighty? So why haven't you guarded your master the king when someone came to kill him? 16This isn't good at all! I swear by the LORD that you and your men deserve to die, because you failed to protect your master, the LORD's anointed! Look around! Where are the king's spear and the jug of water that were beside his head?"

17Saul recognized David's voice and called out, "Is that you, my son David?"

And David replied, "Yes, my lord the king. 18Why are you chasing me? What have I done? What is my crime? 19But now let my lord the king listen to his servant. If the LORD has stirred you up against me, then let him accept my offering. But if this is simply a human scheme, then may those involved be cursed by the LORD. For they have driven me from my home, so I can no longer live among the LORD's people, and they have said, 'Go, worship pagan gods.' 20Must I die on foreign soil, far from the presence of the LORD? Why has the king of Israel come out to search for a single flea? Why does he hunt me down like a partridge on the mountains?"

21Then Saul confessed, "I have sinned. Come back home, my son, and I will no longer try to harm you, for you valued my life today. I have been a fool and very, very wrong."

22"Here is your spear, O king," David replied. "Let one of your young men come over and get it. 23The LORD gives his own reward for doing good and for being loyal, and I refused to kill you even when the LORD placed you in my power, for you are the LORD's anointed one. 24Now may the LORD value my life, even as I have valued yours today. May he rescue me from all my troubles."

25And Saul said to David, "Blessings on you, my son David. You will do many heroic deeds, and you will surely succeed." Then David went away, and Saul returned home.

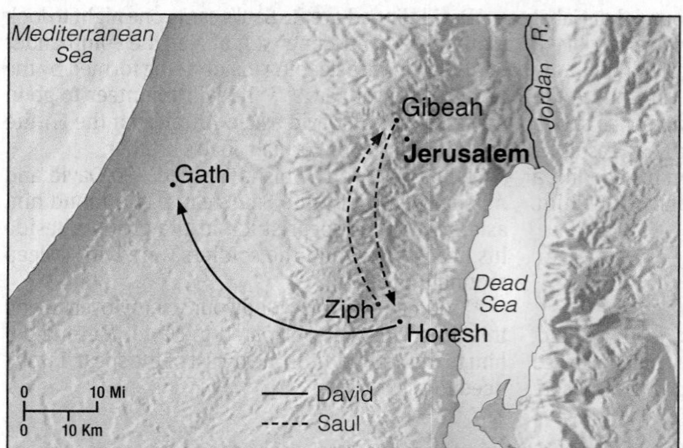

SAUL CHASES DAVID *The men of Ziph again betrayed David to Saul, who was in his palace in Gibeah. Saul took 3,000 troops to the area around Horesh in order to find David. David could have killed Saul, but he refused. Saul, feeling foolish at David's kindness, returned to Gibeah, and David went to Gath.*

1 Sam 26:9 Why did David refuse to kill Saul? God had placed Saul in power and had not yet removed him. David did not want to run ahead of God's timing. We are in similar situations when we have leaders in church or government who are unfaithful or incompetent. It may be easy for us to criticize or move against a leader oblivious to God's hidden purposes and timing. Determining not to do wrong, David left Saul's destiny in God's hands. While we should not ignore sin or sit back and allow evil leaders to carry on their wickedness, neither should we take actions that are against God's laws. We should work for righteousness while trusting God.

1 Sam 26:15-16 David could have killed Saul and Abner, but he would have disobeyed God and possibly set into motion cycles of vengeance and assassination. Instead, he took a spear and water jug, showing that he could have killed the king but had not done it. And he made the point that he had great respect for both God and God's anointed king. When you need to make a point, look for creative, God-honoring ways to do so. It will have a more significant impact.

1 Sam 26:25 Saul had opportunities to kill David, but he never did. Why? First, every time David and Saul were face to face, David did something generous for Saul. The king did not want to respond to David's kindness with cruelty in front of all his men. Second, David had a large following in Israel. By killing him, Saul would risk his hold on the kingdom.

5. SAUL'S DEFEAT AND DEATH

Saul continued to deteriorate as the leader of Israel, even going so far as to consult a medium in a misguided attempt to hear from God through Samuel's spirit from beyond the grave. Ultimately, his rejection as king of Israel culminated in his death during a battle with the Philistines.

David among the Philistines

1 SAMUEL 27:1-7

But David kept thinking to himself, "Someday Saul is going to get me. The best thing I can do is escape to the Philistines. Then Saul will stop hunting for me in Israelite territory, and I will finally be safe."
[2]So David took his 600 men and went over and
joined Achish son of Maoch, the king of Gath. [3]David
and his men and their families settled there with
Achish at Gath. David brought his two wives along
with him—Ahinoam from Jezreel and Abigail, Nabal's widow from Carmel. [4]Word soon reached Saul
that David had fled to Gath, so he stopped hunting
for him.
[5]One day David said to Achish, "If it is all right with
you, we would rather live in one of the country towns
instead of here in the royal city."
[6]So Achish gave him the town of Ziklag (which still
belongs to the kings of Judah to this day), [7]and they
lived there among the Philistines for a year and four
months.

Warriors Join David's Army

1 CHRONICLES 12:1-7

The following men joined David at Ziklag while he
was hiding from Saul son of Kish. They were among
the warriors who fought beside David in battle. [2]All
of them were expert archers, and they could shoot
arrows or sling stones with their left hand as well as
their right. They were all relatives of Saul from the
tribe of Benjamin. [3]Their leader was Ahiezer son of
Shemaah from Gibeah; his brother Joash was second-
in-command. These were the other warriors:

Jeziel and Pelet, sons of Azmaveth;
Beracah;
Jehu from Anathoth;
4 Ishmaiah from Gibeon, a famous warrior and leader among the Thirty;
*Jeremiah, Jahaziel, Johanan, and Jozabad from Gederah;
5 Eluzai, Jerimoth, Bealiah, Shemariah, and Shephatiah from Haruph;
6 Elkanah, Isshiah, Azarel, Joezer, and Jashobeam, who were Korahites;
7 Joelah and Zebadiah, sons of Jeroham from Gedor.

1 Chr 12:4 Verses 12:4b-40 are numbered 12:5-41 in Hebrew text.

David's Army Raids Foreign Lands

1 SAMUEL 27:8-12

David and his men spent their time raiding the
Geshurites, the Girzites, and the Amalekites—people
who had lived near Shur, toward the land of Egypt,
since ancient times. [9]David did not leave one person
alive in the villages he attacked. He took the sheep,
goats, cattle, donkeys, camels, and clothing before
returning home to see King Achish.

Third, God had appointed David to become king of Israel and was protecting him.

1 Sam 27:4 Saul finally stopped pursuing David. His army was not strong enough to invade Philistine territory just to seek one man. Besides, the immediate threat to Saul's throne was gone while David was out of the country.

1 Sam 27:5-7 Gath was one of five principal cities in Philistia, and Achish was one of five co-rulers. David may have wanted to move out of this important city to avoid potential skirmishes or attacks upon his family. He may also have wanted to escape the close scrutiny of the Philistine officials. Achish let David move to Ziklag, where he lived until Saul's death (2 Sam 2:1).

1 Chr 12:1 Ziklag was a city in Philistia to which David had escaped to hide from Saul. Achish, the Philistine ruler of the area, was happy to have a famous Israelite warrior defect to his land. He did not know that David was only pretending loyalty. Achish gave the city of Ziklag to David, his family, and his army (1 Sam 27:5-7). David's whereabouts were not a great secret, and many loyal followers joined him there.

1 Chr 12:1ff David surrounded himself with great warriors, the best of the Israelite army. What qualities made them worthy to be David's warriors and servants? (1) They had practiced long and hard to perfect their skills (with bow, sling, and spear); (2) they were mentally tough and determined ("as fierce as lions," 1 Chr 12:8); (3) they were physically in shape ("as swift as deer," 1 Chr 12:8); (4) they were dedicated to serving God and David. Weak leaders are easily threatened by competent subordinates, but strong leaders surround themselves with the best. They are not intimidated by able followers.

1 Chr 12:1-7 All the warriors mentioned here were from the tribe of Benjamin. Even members of Saul's own tribe (1 Sam 9:1-2) were deserting him to help David become king over all Israel. It was clear to them that God had chosen David to be Israel's next leader.

1 Chr 12:2 Archers and slingers had special weapons. The sling was unassuming in appearance but deadly in battle. A shallow leather pouch with a cord of leather or goats' hair attached to each side, the sling was whirled around the head. When one side was released, it sent a stone to its target. The bow and arrow had been in use for thousands of years. Arrowheads were made of stone, wood, or bone because the Philistines still had a monopoly on metalworking (1 Sam 13:19-20). Arrow shafts were made of reed or wood, and bowstrings were made of animal gut.

1 Sam 27:8-9 David probably conducted these guerrilla-style raids because these three tribes were known for their surprise attacks and cruel treatment of innocent people. These desert tribes were a danger, not just to the Philistines, but especially to the Israelites, the people David would one day lead.

▶ **1 SAMUEL 27:8-12** ***(cont.)***

10"Where did you make your raid today?" Achish would ask.

And David would reply, "Against the south of Judah, the Jerahmeelites, and the Kenites."

11No one was left alive to come to Gath and tell where he had really been. This happened again and again while he was living among the Philistines. 12Achish believed David and thought to himself, "By now the people of Israel must hate him bitterly. Now he will have to stay here and serve me forever!"

Saul Consults a Medium

1 SAMUEL 28:1-25

About that time the Philistines mustered their armies for another war with Israel. King Achish told David, "You and your men will be expected to join me in battle."

2"Very well!" David agreed. "Now you will see for yourself what we can do."

Then Achish told David, "I will make you my personal bodyguard for life."

3Meanwhile, Samuel had died, and all Israel had mourned for him. He was buried in Ramah, his hometown. And Saul had banned from the land of Israel all mediums and those who consult the spirits of the dead.

4The Philistines set up their camp at Shunem, and Saul gathered all the army of Israel and camped at Gilboa. 5When Saul saw the vast Philistine army, he became frantic with fear. 6He asked the LORD what he should do, but the LORD refused to answer him, either by dreams or by sacred lots* or by the prophets. 7Saul then said to his advisers, "Find a woman who is a medium, so I can go and ask her what to do."

His advisers replied, "There is a medium at Endor."

8So Saul disguised himself by wearing ordinary clothing instead of his royal robes. Then he went to the woman's home at night, accompanied by two of his men.

"I have to talk to a man who has died," he said. "Will you call up his spirit for me?"

9"Are you trying to get me killed?" the woman demanded. "You know that Saul has outlawed all the mediums and all who consult the spirits of the dead. Why are you setting a trap for me?"

10But Saul took an oath in the name of the LORD and promised, "As surely as the LORD lives, nothing bad will happen to you for doing this."

11Finally, the woman said, "Well, whose spirit do you want me to call up?"

"Call up Samuel," Saul replied.

12When the woman saw Samuel, she screamed, "You've deceived me! You are Saul!"

13"Don't be afraid!" the king told her. "What do you see?"

"I see a god* coming up out of the earth," she said.

14"What does he look like?" Saul asked.

"He is an old man wrapped in a robe," she replied. Saul realized it was Samuel, and he fell to the ground before him.

15"Why have you disturbed me by calling me back?" Samuel asked Saul.

"Because I am in deep trouble," Saul replied. "The Philistines are at war with me, and God has left me and

1 Sm 28:6 Hebrew *by Urim.* **1 Sm 28:13** Or *gods.*

---

1 Sam 27:10-12 Was David wrong in falsely reporting his activities to Achish? No doubt David was lying, but he may have felt his strategy was justified in a time of war against a pagan enemy. David knew he would one day be Israel's king. The Philistines were still his enemies, but this was an excellent place to hide from Saul. When Achish asked David to go into battle against Israel, David agreed, once again pretending loyalty to the Philistines (1 Sam 28:1ff). Whether he would have actually fought Saul's army we can't know, but we can be sure that his ultimate loyalty was to God, not to Achish or Saul.

1 Sam 28:1-2 Achish's request put David in a difficult position. To refuse to help Achish fight the Israelites would give away David's loyalty to Israel and endanger the lives of his soldiers and family. But to fight his own people would hurt the very people he loved and would soon lead. David never had to solve his dilemma because God protected him. The other Philistine leaders objected to his presence in battle; thus, he did not have to fight his countrymen.

1 Sam 28:3-8 Saul had banned all mediums and spiritists from Israel, but in desperation he turned to one for counsel. Although he had removed the sin of witchcraft from the land, he did not remove it from his heart. We may make a great show of denouncing sin, but if our hearts do not change, the sins will return. Knowing what is right and condemning what is wrong do not take the place of doing what is right.

1 Sam 28:5-6 Casting sacred lots meant using the Urim and Thummim to determine God's guidance in certain matters. (See the notes on 1 Sam 2:18, p. 420, and 1 Sam 10:20, p. 438.)

1 Sam 28:5-7 Saul was overwhelmed at the sight of the Philistine army, and so he turned to the occult. Regard life's difficulties and obstacles as reminders to turn you in God's direction and cause you to depend upon him. Turning to anything or anyone else leads only to disaster.

1 Sam 28:7-8 God had strictly forbidden the Israelites to have anything to do with divination, sorcery, witchcraft, mediums, spiritists, or anyone who consults the dead (Deut 18:9-14). In fact, sorcerers were to be put to death (Exod 22:18). Occult practices were carried on in the name of pagan gods, and people turned to the occult for answers that God would not give.

Practitioners of the occult have Satan and demons as the source of their information; God does not reveal his will to them. Instead, he speaks through his own channels: the Bible, Jesus Christ, the Holy Spirit.

1 Sam 28:12 Did Samuel really come back from the dead at the medium's call? The medium shrieked at the appearance of Samuel—she knew too well that the spirits she usually contacted were either contrived or satanic. Somehow Samuel's appearance revealed to her that she was dealing with a far greater power. She did not call up Samuel by the power of Satan; God brought Samuel back to give Saul a prediction regarding his fate, which Saul already knew. This in no way justifies efforts to contact the dead or communicate with spirits. God is against all such practices (Gal 5:19-21).

1 Sam 28:15 God did not answer Saul's appeals because Saul had not followed God's previous directions. Sometimes people wonder why their prayers are not answered. But if they don't fulfill the responsibilities God has already given them, they should not be surprised when he does not give further guidance.

won't reply by prophets or dreams. So I have called for
you to tell me what to do."
16But Samuel replied, "Why ask me, since the LORD
has left you and has become your enemy? 17The LORD
has done just as he said he would. He has torn the
kingdom from you and given it to your rival, David.
18The LORD has done this to you today because you
refused to carry out his fierce anger against the Amalekites. 19What's more, the LORD will hand you and
the army of Israel over to the Philistines tomorrow,
and you and your sons will be here with me. The LORD
will bring down the entire army of Israel in defeat."
20Saul fell full length on the ground, paralyzed with
fright because of Samuel's words. He was also faint with
hunger, for he had eaten nothing all day and all night.
21When the woman saw how distraught he was, she
said, "Sir, I obeyed your command at the risk of my
life. 22Now do what I say, and let me give you a little
something to eat so you can regain your strength for
the trip back."
23But Saul refused to eat anything. Then his advisers
joined the woman in urging him to eat, so he finally
yielded and got up from the ground and sat on the
couch.
24The woman had been fattening a calf, so she hurried out and killed it. She took some flour, kneaded
it into dough and baked unleavened bread. 25She
brought the meal to Saul and his advisers, and they
ate it. Then they went out into the night.

The Philistines Reject David

1 SAMUEL 29:1-11

The entire Philistine army now mobilized at Aphek,
and the Israelites camped at the spring in Jezreel. 2As
the Philistine rulers were leading out their troops in
groups of hundreds and thousands, David and his
men marched at the rear with King Achish. 3But the
Philistine commanders demanded, "What are these
Hebrews doing here?"

And Achish told them, "This is David, the servant of
King Saul of Israel. He's been with me for years, and
I've never found a single fault in him from the day he
arrived until today."
4But the Philistine commanders were angry. "Send
him back to the town you've given him!" they demanded. "He can't go into the battle with us. What
if he turns against us in battle and becomes our adversary? Is there any better way for him to reconcile
himself with his master than by handing our heads
over to him? 5Isn't this the same David about whom
the women of Israel sing in their dances,

'Saul has killed his thousands,
and David his ten thousands'?"

6So Achish finally summoned David and said to
him, "I swear by the LORD that you have been a trustworthy ally. I think you should go with me into battle,
for I've never found a single flaw in you from the day
you arrived until today. But the other Philistine rulers won't hear of it. 7Please don't upset them, but go
back quietly."
8"What have I done to deserve this treatment?" David demanded. "What have you ever found in your
servant, that I can't go and fight the enemies of my
lord the king?"
9But Achish insisted, "As far as I'm concerned,
you're as perfect as an angel of God. But the Philistine commanders are afraid to have you with them
in the battle. 10Now get up early in the morning, and
leave with your men as soon as it gets light."

1 Sam 29:4 The other Philistine commanders knew that David was the one who, as a young man, had killed their champion, Goliath (1 Sam 17:32-54), had killed hundreds of Philistine soldiers (1 Sam 18:27), and was the hero of Israelite victory songs (1 Sam 21:11). They were afraid that, in the heat of battle, David might turn against them. Although David was upset at this at first, God used the commanders' suspicion to keep him from having to fight against Saul and his countrymen.

Jezreel Valley

The Jezreel Valley is the largest and richest valley in Israel. It was named after the town of Jezreel, which was the only town on the plain where the Israelites had gained a foothold in the early stages of their conquest. The Midianites camped there, between the hill of Moreh and Mount Tabor (Judg 6:33; 7:1). Barak defeated the army of Sisera and Jabin there, near Endor (Ps 83:9-10). Now, the Philistines gathered there to oppose Saul (1 Sam 29:1, 11; 2 Sam 4:4).

When Hosea was preaching to Israel about their impending exile from the land, God told him to name his child "Jezreel" (a name that means "God plants") because God promised to "again plant his people in his land" (see Hos 1:4-5, 11). Even when we are facing God's discipline for our sin, we can look forward with hope because God promises that renewal will follow repentance.

▶ **1 SAMUEL 29:1-11** ***(cont.)***

[11]So David and his men headed back into the land of the Philistines, while the Philistine army went on to Jezreel.

Some Israelites Join David's Army

1 CHRONICLES 12:19

Some men from Manasseh defected from the Israelite army and joined David when he set out with the Philistines to fight against Saul. But as it turned out, the Philistine rulers refused to let David and his men go with them. After much discussion, they sent them back, for they said, "It will cost us our heads if David switches loyalties to Saul and turns against us."

Psalm 56

THEME: Trusting in God's care in the midst of fear. When all seems dark, one truth still shines bright: When God is for us, those against us will never succeed.

AUTHOR: David

For the choir director: A psalm of David, regarding the time the Philistines seized him in Gath. To be sung to the tune "Dove on Distant Oaks."*

1 O God, have mercy on me,
for people are hounding me.
My foes attack me all day long.
2 I am constantly hounded by those who slander me,
and many are boldly attacking me.
3 But when I am afraid,
I will put my trust in you.
4 I praise God for what he has promised.
I trust in God, so why should I be afraid?
What can mere mortals do to me?

5 They are always twisting what I say;
they spend their days plotting to harm me.
6 They come together to spy on me—
watching my every step, eager to kill me.
7 Don't let them get away with their wickedness;
in your anger, O God, bring them down.
8 You keep track of all my sorrows.*
You have collected all my tears in your bottle.
You have recorded each one in your book.
9 My enemies will retreat when I call to you for help.
This I know: God is on my side!
10 I praise God for what he has promised;
yes, I praise the LORD for what he has promised.
11 I trust in God, so why should I be afraid?
What can mere mortals do to me?

12 I will fulfill my vows to you, O God,
and will offer a sacrifice of thanks for your help.
13 For you have rescued me from death;
you have kept my feet from slipping.
So now I can walk in your presence, O God,
in your life-giving light.

David Destroys the Amalekites

1 SAMUEL 30:1-31

Three days later, when David and his men arrived home at their town of Ziklag, they found that the Amalekites had made a raid into the Negev and Ziklag; they had crushed Ziklag and burned it to the ground.
[2]They had carried off the women and children and everyone else but without killing anyone.
[3]When David and his men saw the ruins and realized what had happened to their families, [4]they wept until they could weep no more. [5]David's two wives, Ahinoam from Jezreel and Abigail, the widow of Nabal from Carmel, were among those captured. [6]David was now in great danger because all his men were very bitter about losing their sons and daughters, and they began to talk of stoning him. But David found strength in the LORD his God.
[7]Then he said to Abiathar the priest, "Bring me the ephod!" So Abiathar brought it. [8]Then David asked the LORD, "Should I chase after this band of raiders? Will I catch them?"

And the LORD told him, "Yes, go after them. You will surely recover everything that was taken from you!"

Ps 56:TITLE Hebrew *miktam*. This may be a literary or musical term. **Ps 56:8** Or *my wanderings*.

Ps 56:3-4 David asked, "What can mere mortals do to me?" How much harm can people do to us? They can inflict pain, suffering, and death. But no person can rob us of our souls or our future beyond this life. How much harm can we do to ourselves? The worst thing we can do is to reject God and lose our eternal life. Jesus said, "Don't be afraid of those who want to kill your body; they cannot touch your soul" (Matt 10:28). Instead, we should fear God, who controls this life and the next.

Ps 56:8 Even in our deepest sorrow, God cares! Jesus reminded us further of how much God understands us—even the hairs on our head are all numbered (Matt 10:30). Often we waver between faith and fear. When you feel so discouraged that you are sure no one understands, remember that God knows every problem and sees every tear.

1 Sam 30:6 Faced with the tragedy of losing their families, David's soldiers began to turn against him and even talked about killing him. Instead of planning a rescue, they looked for someone to blame. But David found his strength in God and began looking for a solution instead of a scapegoat. When facing problems, remember that it is useless to look for someone to blame or criticize. Instead, consider how you can help find a solution.

1 Sam 30:7 David couldn't go to the Tabernacle to ask the Lord for guidance because it was in Saul's territory. Therefore, he called for the ephod, the only Tabernacle-related object he possessed. In the presence of the priest and this priestly garment, he asked God for direction. When David called for the ephod, he was really asking the priest to bring him the Urim and Thummim, which were kept in a pouch attached to the ephod. Only the high priest could carry and use the Urim and Thummim. (See the note on Exod 39:1-21, p. 193.)

9 So David and his 600 men set out, and they came to the brook Besor. 10 But 200 of the men were too exhausted to cross the brook, so David continued the pursuit with 400 men.

11 Along the way they found an Egyptian man in a field and brought him to David. They gave him some bread to eat and water to drink. 12 They also gave him part of a fig cake and two clusters of raisins, for he hadn't had anything to eat or drink for three days and nights. Before long his strength returned.

13 "To whom do you belong, and where do you come from?" David asked him.

"I am an Egyptian—the slave of an Amalekite," he replied. "My master abandoned me three days ago because I was sick. 14 We were on our way back from raiding the Kerethites in the Negev, the territory of Judah, and the land of Caleb, and we had just burned Ziklag."

15 "Will you lead me to this band of raiders?" David asked.

The young man replied, "If you take an oath in God's name that you will not kill me or give me back to my master, then I will guide you to them."

16 So he led David to them, and they found the Amalekites spread out across the fields, eating and drinking and dancing with joy because of the vast amount of plunder they had taken from the Philistines and the land of Judah. 17 David and his men rushed in among them and slaughtered them throughout that night and the entire next day until evening. None of the Amalekites escaped except 400 young men who fled on camels. 18 David got back everything the Amalekites had taken, and he rescued his two wives. 19 Nothing was missing: small or great, son or daughter, nor anything else that had been taken. David brought everything back. 20 He also recovered all the flocks and herds, and his men drove them ahead of the other livestock. "This plunder belongs to David!" they said.

21 Then David returned to the brook Besor and met up with the 200 men who had been left behind because they were too exhausted to go with him. They went out to meet David and his men, and David greeted them joyfully. 22 But some evil troublemakers among David's men said, "They didn't go with us, so they can't have any of the plunder we recovered. Give them their wives and children, and tell them to be gone."

23 But David said, "No, my brothers! Don't be selfish with what the LORD has given us. He has kept us safe and helped us defeat the band of raiders that attacked us. 24 Who will listen when you talk like this? We share and share alike—those who go to battle and those who guard the equipment." 25 From then on David made this a decree and regulation for Israel, and it is still followed today.

26 When he arrived at Ziklag, David sent part of the plunder to the elders of Judah, who were his friends. "Here is a present for you, taken from the LORD's enemies," he said.

27 The gifts were sent to the people of the following towns David had visited: Bethel, Ramoth-negev, Jattir, 28 Aroer, Siphmoth, Eshtemoa, 29 Racal,* the towns of the Jerahmeelites, the towns of the Kenites, 30 Hormah, Bor-ashan, Athach, 31 Hebron, and all the other places David and his men had visited.

More Israelites Join David's Army

1 CHRONICLES 12:20-22

Here is a list of the men from Manasseh who defected to David as he was returning to Ziklag: Adnah, Jozabad, Jediael, Michael, Jozabad, Elihu, and Zillethai. Each commanded 1,000 troops from the tribe of Manasseh. 21 They helped David chase down bands of raiders,

1 Sm 30:29 Greek version reads *Carmel.*

1 Sam 30:11-15 The Amalekites cruelly left this slave to die, but God used him to lead David and his men to the Amalekite camp. David and his men treated the young man kindly, and he returned the kindness by leading them to the enemy. Treat those you meet with respect and dignity no matter how insignificant they may seem. You never know how God will use them in your life.

1 Sam 30:24-25 David made a law that those who guarded the equipment were to be treated equally with those who fought in battle. Today it takes several people to provide the support services needed for every soldier in battle. In the church and other organizations, we need to treat those who provide support services equally with those on the front lines. Without bookkeepers, secretaries, trainers, and administrators, those with a public ministry would be unable to do their jobs. Are you on the front lines? Don't forget those who are backing you up. Are you in the support group? Realize that your position, although it may be less glamorous or exciting, is vital to the work of the entire group.

THE BATTLE AT GILBOA ▶
David pretended loyalty to Achish, but when war broke out with Israel, he was sent to Ziklag from Aphek. The Philistines defeated the Israelites at Mount Gilboa. David returned to Ziklag to find that the Amalekites had destroyed Ziklag. So David and his men pursued the Amalekite raiders and slaughtered them, recovering all that was taken.

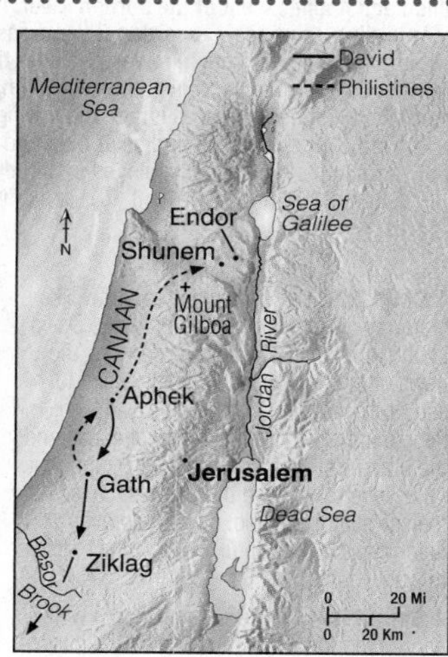

▸ **1 CHRONICLES 12:20-22** ***(cont.)***
for they were all brave and able warriors who became
commanders in his army. 22Day after day more men
joined David until he had a great army, like the army
of God.

The Death of Saul PARALLEL

1 SAMUEL 31:1-13
Now the Philistines attacked Israel, and the men of
Israel fled before them. Many were slaughtered on
the slopes of Mount Gilboa. 2The Philistines closed
in on Saul and his sons, and they killed three of his
sons—Jonathan, Abinadab, and Malkishua. 3The
fighting grew very fierce around Saul, and the Philistine archers caught up with him and wounded
him severely.
4Saul groaned to his armor bearer, "Take your sword
and kill me before these pagan Philistines come to run
me through and taunt and torture me."
But his armor bearer was afraid and would not do
it. So Saul took his own sword and fell on it. 5When
his armor bearer realized that Saul was dead, he fell
on his own sword and died beside the king. 6So Saul,
his three sons, his armor bearer, and his troops all died
together that same day.
7When the Israelites on the other side of the Jezreel
Valley and beyond the Jordan saw that the Israelite
army had fled and that Saul and his sons were dead,
they abandoned their towns and fled. So the Philistines moved in and occupied their towns.
8The next day, when the Philistines went out to strip
the dead, they found the bodies of Saul and his three
sons on Mount Gilboa. 9So they cut off Saul's head and
stripped off his armor. Then they proclaimed the good
news of Saul's death in their pagan temple and to the
people throughout the land of Philistia. 10They placed
his armor in the temple of the Ashtoreths, and they
fastened his body to the wall of the city of Beth-shan.
11But when the people of Jabesh-gilead heard what
the Philistines had done to Saul, 12all their mighty
warriors traveled through the night to Beth-shan and
took the bodies of Saul and his sons down from the

Beth-shan

Beth-shan was a strategic town located in the Jordan Valley 15 miles south of the Sea of Galilee and 4 miles west of the Jordan River. It stood at the eastern end of the Jezreel Valley, guarding an important Jordan River crossing. It was also at the junction of two trade routes, one leading north toward Galilee, the other leading from the mountains of Gilead west through the Jezreel Valley and the hills of Samaria.

When the Philistines defeated Israel under King Saul at the battle of Gilboa, Beth-shan was a Philistine city. The slain bodies of Saul and his sons were hung in disgrace on the city wall, and Saul's head was displayed in the temple of Dagon, a Philistine deity (1 Sam 31:8-13; 2 Sam 21:12-14; 1 Chr 10:8-10). The city later became a part of David's kingdom.

1 Chr 12:22 David "had a great army, like the army of God." Men were drawn to David by the reputation of his great warriors, the news of their victories, and their desire to see God's will done in making David king. People are often drawn to a great cause and the brave, determined people who support it. As believers, we have the greatest cause—the salvation of people. If we are brave, determined, and faithful, others will be drawn to work with us.

1 Sam 31:3-4 The Philistines had a well-earned reputation for torturing their captives. Saul no doubt knew about Samson's fate (Judg 16:18-31) and did not want to risk physical mutilation or other abuse. When his armor bearer refused to kill him, he took his own life.

1 Sam 31:3-4 Saul was tall, handsome, strong, rich, and powerful, but all of this was not enough to make him someone we should emulate. He was tall physically, but he was small in God's eyes. He was handsome, but his sin made him ugly. He was strong, but his lack of faith made him weak. He was rich, but he was spiritually bankrupt. He could give orders to many, but he couldn't command their respect or allegiance. Saul looked good on the outside, but he was decaying on the inside. A right relationship with God and a strong character are much more valuable than a good-looking exterior.

1 Sam 31:3-4 Saul's armor bearer faced a moral dilemma—should he carry out a sinful order from a man he was supposed to obey? He knew he should obey his master, the king, but he also knew murder was wrong. He decided not to kill Saul.

There is a difference between following an order with which you don't agree and following one you know is wrong. It is never right or ethical to carry out a wrong act, no matter who gives the order or what the consequences for disobedience may be. What shapes your choice when you face a moral dilemma? Have the courage to follow God's law above human commands.

1 Sam 31:4 Saul faced death the same way he faced life. He took matters into his own hands without thinking of God or asking for his guidance. If our lives aren't the way we would like them to be now, we can't assume that change will come more easily later. When nearing death, we will respond to God the same way we have been responding all along. Coming face to face with death only shows us what we are really like. How do you want to face death? Start facing life that way right now.

1 Sam 31:10 To put Saul's armor in the Philistine temple gave credit to a pagan goddess for victory over Saul. Ashtoreth was a goddess of fertility and sex. Beth-shan was a town on the eastern slopes of Mount Gilboa, overlooking the Jordan Valley.

wall. They brought them to Jabesh, where they burned
the bodies. 13 Then they took their bones and buried
them beneath the tamarisk tree at Jabesh, and they
fasted for seven days.

1 CHRONICLES 10:1-14

Now the Philistines attacked Israel, and the men of
Israel fled before them. Many were slaughtered on
the slopes of Mount Gilboa. 2 The Philistines closed
in on Saul and his sons, and they killed three of his
sons—Jonathan, Abinadab, and Malkishua. 3 The fighting grew very fierce around Saul, and the Philistine
archers caught up with him and wounded him.

4 Saul groaned to his armor bearer, "Take your sword
and kill me before these pagan Philistines come to
taunt and torture me."

But his armor bearer was afraid and would not do
it. So Saul took his own sword and fell on it. 5 When
his armor bearer realized that Saul was dead, he fell
on his own sword and died. 6 So Saul and his three
sons died there together, bringing his dynasty to
an end.

7 When all the Israelites in the Jezreel Valley saw
that their army had fled and that Saul and his sons
were dead, they abandoned their towns and fled. So
the Philistines moved in and occupied their towns.

8 The next day, when the Philistines went out to
strip the dead, they found the bodies of Saul and his
sons on Mount Gilboa. 9 So they stripped off Saul's
armor and cut off his head. Then they proclaimed
the good news of Saul's death before their idols and
to the people throughout the land of Philistia. 10 They
placed his armor in the temple of their gods, and they
fastened his head to the temple of Dagon.

11 But when everyone in Jabesh-gilead heard about
everything the Philistines had done to Saul, 12 all their
mighty warriors brought the bodies of Saul and his
sons back to Jabesh. Then they buried their bones
beneath the great tree at Jabesh, and they fasted for
seven days.

13 So Saul died because he was unfaithful to the
LORD. He failed to obey the LORD's command, and he
even consulted a medium 14 instead of asking the LORD
for guidance. So the LORD killed him and turned the
kingdom over to David son of Jesse.

---

1 Sam 31:13 Consider the difference between the last judge of Israel and its first king. Samuel, the judge, was characterized by consistency, obedience, and a deep desire for God's will. He had a genuine desire for God. Saul, the king, was characterized by inconsistency, disobedience, and self-will. He did not have a heart for God.

When God called Samuel, Samuel said, "Speak, your servant is listening" (1 Sam 3:10). But when God, through Samuel, called Saul, Saul replied, "Why are you talking like this to me?" (1 Sam 9:21). Saul was dedicated to himself; Samuel was dedicated to God.

1 Sam 31:13 Saul's death was also the death of an ideal—Israel could no longer believe that having a king like the other nations would solve all their troubles. The real problem was not the form of government but the sinful king. Saul tried to please God by spurts of religiosity, but real spirituality takes a lifetime of consistent obedience.

Heroic spiritual lives are built by stacking days of obedience one on top of the other. Like a brick, each obedient act is small in itself, but in time the acts will pile up, and a huge wall of strong character will be built—a great defense against temptation. We should strive for consistent obedience each day.

1 Chr 10:10 Dagon, the most important god of the Philistines, was believed to bring rain and provide rich harvests. The Philistines built temples to him when they settled in the grain-producing land of Canaan. In times of drought, people begged Dagon for pity, even to the point of sacrificing their children in his temples. In times of plenty, the temples were used for twisted forms of entertainment, such as the humiliation of captives (see Judg 16:23-30). But Dagon, like the other pagan gods, was powerless against the one true God (1 Sam 5:1-7).

1 Chr 10:11-12 The actions of the valiant warriors who brought back and buried the bodies of King Saul and his sons should encourage us to respect our God-given leaders. David showed respect for Saul's position, even when Saul was chasing him to kill him (1 Sam 26). How easy it is to be critical of those in authority over us, focusing only on their weaknesses. We cannot excuse sin, but we should respect the positions of those in authority, whether at work, at church, or in government. Romans 13:1ff gives instructions for relating to government leaders and 1 Thessalonians 5:12-13 for honoring church leaders.

1 Chr 10:13-14 Saul's unfaithfulness was both active and passive; he not only did wrong, but he also failed to do right. He actively disobeyed by attempting murder, ignoring God's instructions, and seeking guidance from a medium. He passively disobeyed by neglecting to ask God for guidance as he ran the kingdom. Obedience, too, is both passive and active. It is not enough just to avoid what is wrong; we need to actively pursue what is right.

1 Chr 10:13-14 In the account in 1 Samuel 28, Saul asked the Lord for guidance but received no answer; this account implies that he did not ask God for help. The answer to this apparent contradiction lies in understanding Saul's motives and the timing of his request to God. His frantic requests came only when he had tried everything his own way. He never went to God unless there was nowhere else to turn. When he finally asked, God refused to answer. Saul sought God only when it suited him, and God rejected him for his constant stubbornness and rebellion.

1 Chr 10:14 Throughout much of Saul's reign, David was forced to hide from him (1 Sam 19–30). During this time David had opportunities to kill Saul (1 Sam 24; 26) and to assume the throne that God had promised him (1 Sam 16:1-13). But David trusted in God's promise that he would be king in God's good timing. It was not up to David to decide when Saul's reign would end. During the battle, God ended Saul's reign just as he had promised.

1 Chr 10:14 Why does this verse say that the Lord killed Saul, when Saul took his own life (1 Sam 31:3-4)? God had rejected Saul because of his stubbornness and rebellion (1 Sam 15:22-26) and had judged him for his sins (1 Sam 28:16-19). God arranged a defeat in battle so that Saul would die and his kingdom would be taken from his family. If Saul had not taken his own life, the Philistine soldiers would have killed him.

C. David's Successes

David's reign over God's people began as king over only his tribe of Judah, while the other tribes followed Ishbosheth, Saul's son. After a few years Ishbosheth was assassinated, and the rest of the tribes finally put their support behind David. David moved the capital to Jerusalem, defeated the surrounding nations, and even showed kindness to Saul's family. We may not understand why God seems to move slowly at times, but we must trust him and be faithful with what he has given us.

1. DAVID BECOMES KING OVER JUDAH

After years of running from Saul, David was finally crowned king over the tribe of Judah. The rest of Israel, however, followed Ishbosheth, Saul's son. David did not attempt to take the tribes by force but placed the matter in God's hands.

David Learns of Saul's Death

2 SAMUEL 1:1-16

After the death of Saul, David returned from his victory over the Amalekites and spent two days in Ziklag. 2On the third day a man arrived from Saul's army
camp. He had torn his clothes and put dirt on his head
to show that he was in mourning. He fell to the ground
before David in deep respect.
3"Where have you come from?" David asked.
"I escaped from the Israelite camp," the man replied.
4"What happened?" David demanded. "Tell me how
the battle went."
The man replied, "Our entire army fled from the
1010 BC battle. Many of the men are dead, and Saul and his
son Jonathan are also dead."
5"How do you know Saul and Jonathan are dead?"
David demanded of the young man.
6The man answered, "I happened to be on Mount
Gilboa, and there was Saul leaning on his spear with
the enemy chariots and charioteers closing in on him.
7When he turned and saw me, he cried out for me to
come to him. 'How can I help?' I asked him.
8"He responded, 'Who are you?'
"'I am an Amalekite,' I told him.
9"Then he begged me, 'Come over here and put me
out of my misery, for I am in terrible pain and want
to die.'
10"So I killed him," the Amalekite told David, "for
I knew he couldn't live. Then I took his crown and
his armband, and I have brought them here to you,
my lord."
11David and his men tore their clothes in sorrow
when they heard the news. 12They mourned and wept
and fasted all day for Saul and his son Jonathan, and
for the LORD's army and the nation of Israel, because
they had died by the sword that day.

David becomes king in Judah

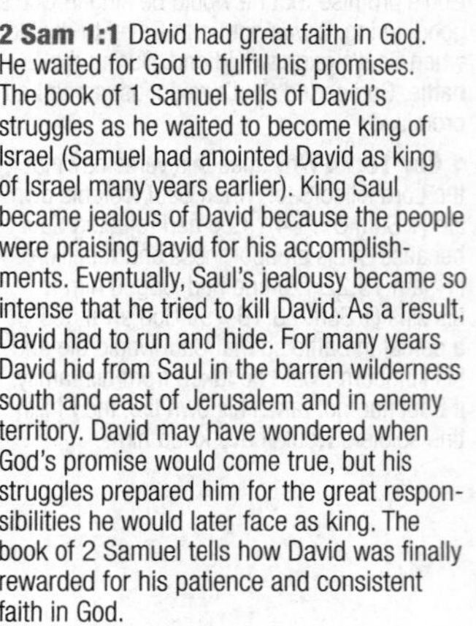

2 Sam 1:1 David had great faith in God. He waited for God to fulfill his promises. The book of 1 Samuel tells of David's struggles as he waited to become king of Israel (Samuel had anointed David as king of Israel many years earlier). King Saul became jealous of David because the people were praising David for his accomplishments. Eventually, Saul's jealousy became so intense that he tried to kill David. As a result, David had to run and hide. For many years David hid from Saul in the barren wilderness south and east of Jerusalem and in enemy territory. David may have wondered when God's promise would come true, but his struggles prepared him for the great responsibilities he would later face as king. The book of 2 Samuel tells how David was finally rewarded for his patience and consistent faith in God.

2 Sam 1:1 When Saul died, David and his men were still living in Ziklag, a Philistine city. Because Saul had driven him out of Israel, David had pretended to be loyal to Achish, a Philistine ruler (1 Sam 27). There he was safe from Saul.

2 Sam 1:11-12 "They mourned and wept and fasted all day." David and his men were visibly shaken over Saul's death. Their actions showed their genuine sorrow over the loss of their king, their friend Jonathan, and the other soldiers of Israel who died that day. They were not ashamed to grieve. Today, some people consider expressing emotions to be a sign of weakness. Those who wish to appear strong try to hide their feelings. But expressing our grief can help us deal with our intense sorrow when a loved one dies.

PEOPLE IN THE DRAMA OF DAVID AND SAUL

It can be confusing to keep track of all the people introduced in the first few chapters of 2 Samuel. Here is some help.

Character	*Relation*	*Position*	*Whose Side?*
Joab	Son of Zeruiah, David's half sister	One of David's military leaders and, later, commander in chief	David's
Abner	Saul's cousin	Saul's commander in chief	Saul and Ishbosheth's, but made overtures to David
Abishai	Joab's brother	High officer in David's army—Commander of "the Thirty"	Joab and David's
Asahel	Joab and Abishai's brother	High officer—one of David's 30 select warriors ("mighty men")	Joab and David's
Ishbosheth	Saul's son	Saul and Abner's selection as king	Saul's

13 Then David said to the young man who had brought the news, "Where are you from?"

And he replied, "I am a foreigner, an Amalekite, who lives in your land."

14 "Why were you not afraid to kill the LORD's anointed one?" David asked.

15 Then David said to one of his men, "Kill him!" So the man thrust his sword into the Amalekite and killed him. 16 "You have condemned yourself," David said, "for you yourself confessed that you killed the LORD's anointed one."

David's Song for Saul and Jonathan

2 SAMUEL 1:17-27

Then David composed a funeral song for Saul and
Jonathan, 18 and he commanded that it be taught to the people of Judah. It is known as the Song of the Bow, and it is recorded in *The Book of Jashar.**

19 Your pride and joy, O Israel, lies dead on the hills!
Oh, how the mighty heroes have fallen!
20 Don't announce the news in Gath,
don't proclaim it in the streets of Ashkelon,
or the daughters of the Philistines will rejoice
and the pagans will laugh in triumph.
21 O mountains of Gilboa,
let there be no dew or rain upon you,
nor fruitful fields producing offerings
of grain.*
For there the shield of the mighty heroes
was defiled;
the shield of Saul will no longer be anointed
with oil.
22 The bow of Jonathan was powerful,
and the sword of Saul did its mighty work.
They shed the blood of their enemies
and pierced the bodies of mighty heroes.
23 How beloved and gracious were Saul and
Jonathan!
They were together in life and in death.
They were swifter than eagles,
stronger than lions.
24 O women of Israel, weep for Saul,
for he dressed you in luxurious scarlet
clothing,
in garments decorated with gold.
25 Oh, how the mighty heroes have fallen
in battle!
Jonathan lies dead on the hills.
26 How I weep for you, my brother Jonathan!
Oh, how much I loved you!
And your love for me was deep,
deeper than the love of women!
27 Oh, how the mighty heroes have fallen!
Stripped of their weapons, they
lie dead.

2 Sm 1:18 Or *The Book of the Upright.* **2 Sm 1:21** The meaning of the Hebrew is uncertain.

2 Sam 1:13 The man identified himself as an Amalekite from Saul's camp (2 Sam 1:2). He may have been an Amalekite under Israelite jurisdiction, but more likely he was a battlefield scavenger. Obviously the man was lying both about his identity and about what had happened on the battlefield. (Compare his story with the account in 1 Sam 31:3-4.) Because he had Saul's crown with him, something the Philistines wouldn't have left behind, we can infer that he found Saul dead on the battlefield before the Philistines arrived (1 Sam 31:8).

A life of deceit leads to disaster. The man lied to gain some personal reward for killing David's rival, but he misread David's character. If David had rewarded him for murdering the king, David would have shared his guilt. Instead, David had the messenger killed. Lying can bring disaster upon the liar, even for something he or she has not done.

2 Sam 1:13 The Amalekites were a fierce nomadic tribe that frequently conducted surprise raids on Canaanite villages. They had been Israel's enemies since Moses' time. David had just destroyed an Amalekite band of raiders who had burned his city and kidnapped its women and children (1 Sam 30:1-20). This man was probably unaware of David's recent confrontations with the Amalekites; if he had been, he might not have come. Instead, he incurred David's wrath by posing as an enemy of Israel and claiming to have killed God's chosen king.

2 Sam 1:15-16 Why did David consider it a crime to kill the king, even though Saul was his enemy? David believed that God had anointed Saul, and only God could remove him from office. If it became casual or commonplace to assassinate the king, the whole society would become chaotic. It was God's job, not David's, to judge Saul's sins (Lev 19:18). We must realize that God has placed rulers in authority over us, and we should respect their positions (Rom 13:1-7).

2 Sam 1:17-18 David was a talented musician. He played the harp (1 Sam 16:23), he brought music into the worship services of the Temple (1 Chr 25), and he wrote many of the psalms. Here we are told that he wrote a funeral song in memory of Saul and his son Jonathan, David's closest friend. Music played an important role in Israel's history. (For other famous songs in the Bible, see the chart on p. 163.)

2 Sam 1:17-27 Saul had caused much trouble for David, but when he died, David composed a song in memory of the king and his son. David had every reason to hate Saul, but he chose not to. Instead, he chose to look at the good Saul had done and to ignore the times when Saul had attacked him. It takes courage to lay aside hatred and hurt and to respect the positive side of another person, especially an enemy.

2 Sam 1:26 By saying that Jonathan's love was "deeper than the love of women," David was not implying that he had a sexual relationship with Jonathan. Homosexual acts were absolutely forbidden in Israel. Leviticus 18:22 calls practicing homosexuality "detestable," and Leviticus 20:13 decrees the death penalty for those who practice homosexuality. David was simply restating the deep brotherhood and faithful friendship he had with Jonathan. (For more on their friendship, see the note on 1 Sam 18:1-4, p. 452.)

David Anointed King of Judah

2 SAMUEL 2:1-7

After this, David asked the LORD, "Should I move back to one of the towns of Judah?"

"Yes," the LORD replied.

Then David asked, "Which town should I go to?"

"To Hebron," the LORD answered.

[2]David's two wives were Ahinoam from Jezreel and Abigail, the widow of Nabal from Carmel. So David and his wives [3]and his men and their families all moved to Judah, and they settled in the villages near Hebron. [4]Then the men of Judah came to David and anointed him king over the people of Judah.

When David heard that the men of Jabesh-gilead had buried Saul, [5]he sent them this message: "May the LORD bless you for being so loyal to your master Saul and giving him a decent burial. [6]May the LORD be loyal to you in return and reward you with his unfailing love! And I, too, will reward you for what you have done. [7]Now that Saul is dead, I ask you to be my strong and loyal subjects like the people of Judah, who have anointed me as their new king."

Ishbosheth Proclaimed King of Israel

2 SAMUEL 2:8-11

But Abner son of Ner, the commander of Saul's army, had already gone to Mahanaim with Saul's son Ishbosheth.* [9]There he proclaimed Ishbosheth king over Gilead, Jezreel, Ephraim, Benjamin, the land of the Ashurites, and all the rest of Israel.

[10]Ishbosheth, Saul's son, was forty years old when he became king, and he ruled from Mahanaim for two years. Meanwhile, the people of Judah remained loyal to David. [11]David made Hebron his capital, and he ruled as king of Judah for seven and a half years.

2 Sm 2:8 *Ishbosheth* is another name for Esh-baal.

2 Sam 2:1 Although David knew he would become king (1 Sam 16:13; 23:17; 24:20), and although the time seemed right now that Saul was dead, David still asked God if he should move back to Judah, the home territory of his tribe. Before moving ahead with what seems obvious, first bring the matter to God, who alone knows the best timing.

2 Sam 2:1 God told David to return to Hebron, where he would soon be crowned king of Judah. David made Hebron his capital because (1) it was the largest city in Judah at that time; (2) it was secure against attack; (3) it was located near the center of Judah's territory, an ideal location for a capital city; and (4) many key trade routes converged at Hebron, making it difficult for supply lines to be cut off in wartime.

2 Sam 2:4 The men of Judah publicly anointed David as their king. David had been anointed king by Samuel years earlier (1 Sam 16:13), but that ceremony had taken place in private. This one was like inaugurating a public official who has already been elected to office. The rest of Israel, however, didn't accept David's kingship for seven and a half years (2 Sam 2:10-11).

2 Sam 2:4-7 David sent a message thanking the men of Jabesh-gilead who had risked their lives to bury Saul's body (1 Sam 31:11-13). Saul had rescued Jabesh-gilead from certain defeat when Nahash the Ammonite had surrounded the city (1 Sam 11), so these citizens showed their gratitude and kindness. In his message, David also suggested that they follow Judah's lead and acknowledge him as their king. Jabesh-gilead was to the north in the land of Gilead, and David was seeking to gain support among the 10 remaining tribes who had not yet recognized him as king.

2 Sam 2:10-11 David ruled over Judah for seven and a half years, while Ishbosheth reigned in Israel for only two years. The five-year gap may be due to Ishbosheth's not assuming the throne immediately after

ABNER

The honest compliments of an opponent are often the best measure of someone's greatness. Although Abner and David frequently saw each other across battle lines, the Bible gives a glimpse of the respect they had for each other. As a young man, David had served under Abner. But later, Abner carried out Saul's campaign to kill David. After Saul's death, Abner temporarily upheld the power of Saul's family. But the struggle between Abner and Saul's heir, Ishbosheth, brought about Abner's decision to support David's claim to the throne. It was during his efforts to unite the kingdom that Abner was murdered by Joab to avenge his brother's death several years earlier. • Abner realized Saul's family was doomed to defeat and that David would be the next king, so he decided to change sides. He hoped that in exchange for his delivering Saul's kingdom, David would make him commander in chief of his army. David's willingness to accept this proposal was probably another reason for Joab's action. • Abner lived by his wits and his will. To him, God was someone with whom he would cooperate if it suited his plans. Otherwise he did what seemed best for him at the time. We can identify with Abner's tendency to give God conditional cooperation. Obedience is easy when the instructions in God's Word fit in with our plans. But our allegiance to God is tested when his plans are contrary to ours. What action should you take today in obedience to God's Word?

Strengths and accomplishments	• Commander in chief of Saul's army and a capable military leader • Recognized and accepted God's plan to make David king over both Israel and Judah
Weaknesses and mistakes	• He had selfish motives in his effort to reunite Judah and Israel rather than godly conviction • He slept with one of the royal concubines after Saul's death
Lesson from his life	• God requires more than conditional, halfhearted cooperation
Vital statistics	• Where: Territory of Benjamin • Occupation: Commander of the armies under Saul and Ishbosheth • Relatives: Father: Ner. Cousin: Saul. Son: Jaasiel. • Contemporaries: David, Asahel, Joab, Abishai
Key verse	"Then King David said to his officials, 'Don't you realize that a great commander has fallen today in Israel?'" (2 Sam 3:38).

Abner's story is told in 1 Samuel 14:50—2 Samuel 4:12. He is also mentioned in 1 Kings 2:5, 32; 1 Chronicles 26:28; 27:16-22.

War between Israel and Judah

2 SAMUEL 2:12-17

One day Abner led Ishbosheth's troops from Mahanaim to Gibeon. 13 About the same time, Joab son of
Zeruiah led David's troops out and met them at the
pool of Gibeon. The two groups sat down there, facing
each other from opposite sides of the pool.
14 Then Abner suggested to Joab, "Let's have a few of
our warriors fight hand to hand here in front of us."
"All right," Joab agreed. 15 So twelve men were chosen to fight from each side—twelve men of Benjamin
representing Ishbosheth son of Saul, and twelve representing David. 16 Each one grabbed his opponent by
the hair and thrust his sword into the other's side so
that all of them died. So this place at Gibeon has been
known ever since as the Field of Swords.*
17 A fierce battle followed that day, and Abner and
the men of Israel were defeated by the forces of David.

The Death of Asahel

2 SAMUEL 2:18-3:1

Joab, Abishai, and Asahel—the three sons of Zeruiah—were among David's forces that day. Asahel could
run like a gazelle, 19 and he began chasing Abner. He
pursued him relentlessly, not stopping for anything.
20 When Abner looked back and saw him coming, he
called out, "Is that you, Asahel?"
"Yes, it is," he replied.
21 "Go fight someone else!" Abner warned. "Take on
one of the younger men, and strip him of his weapons." But Asahel kept right on chasing Abner.
22 Again Abner shouted to him, "Get away from here!
I don't want to kill you. How could I ever face your
brother Joab again?"
23 But Asahel refused to turn back, so Abner thrust
the butt end of his spear through Asahel's stomach,
and the spear came out through his back. He stumbled
to the ground and died there. And everyone who came
by that spot stopped and stood still when they saw
Asahel lying there.
24 When Joab and Abishai found out what had happened, they set out after Abner. The sun was just going
down as they arrived at the hill of Ammah near Giah,
along the road to the wilderness of Gibeon. 25 Abner's
troops from the tribe of Benjamin regrouped there at
the top of the hill to take a stand.
26 Abner shouted down to Joab, "Must we always be
killing each other? Don't you realize that bitterness is
the only result? When will you call off your men from
chasing their Israelite brothers?"
27 Then Joab said, "God only knows what would have
happened if you hadn't spoken, for we would have
chased you all night if necessary." 28 So Joab blew the
ram's horn, and his men stopped chasing the troops
of Israel.
29 All that night Abner and his men retreated
through the Jordan Valley.* They crossed the Jordan
River, traveling all through the morning,* and didn't
stop until they arrived at Mahanaim.
30 Meanwhile, Joab and his men also returned home.
When Joab counted his casualties, he discovered that
only 19 men were missing in addition to Asahel. 31 But

2 Sm 2:16 Hebrew *Helkath-hazzurim.* **2 Sm 2:29a** Hebrew *the Arabah.* **2 Sm 2:29b** Or *continued on through the Bithron.* The meaning of the Hebrew is uncertain.

Saul's death. Because of constant danger from the Philistines in the northern part of Israel, five years may have passed before Ishbosheth could begin his reign. During that time, Abner, commander of his army, probably played a principal role in driving out the Philistines and leading the northern confederacy. Regardless of when Ishbosheth began to rule, his control was weak and limited. The Philistines still dominated the area, and Ishbosheth was intimidated by Abner (2 Sam 3:11).

2 Sam 2:12ff With Israel divided, there was constant tension between north and south. David's true rival in the north was not Ishbosheth, but Abner. In this incident, Abner suggested hand-to-hand combat between the champions of his army and the champions of David's army, led by Joab. The fact that this confrontation occurred at the pool of Gibeon (located in Saul's home territory of Benjamin) suggests that Joab's men were pushing northward, gaining more territory. Abner may have suggested this confrontation in hopes of stopping Joab's advance.

Twelve men from each side were supposed to fight each other, and the side with the most survivors would be declared the winner. The confrontation between David and Goliath (1 Sam 17) was a similar battle strategy—a way to avoid terrible bloodshed from an all-out war. In this case, however, all 24 champions were killed before either side could claim victory. Nothing was accomplished, and the civil war continued.

2 Sam 2:21-23 Abner repeatedly warned Asahel to turn back or risk losing his life, but Asahel refused to turn from his self-imposed duty. Persistence is a good trait if it is for a worthy cause. But if the goal is only personal honor or gain, persistence may be no more than stubbornness. Asahel's stubbornness not only cost him his life, but it also spurred unfortunate disunity in David's army for years to come (2 Sam 3:26-27; 1 Kgs 2:28-35). Before you decide to pursue a goal, make sure it is worthy of your devotion.

2 Sam 2:28 This battle ended with a victory for Joab's troops (2 Sam 2:17), but war in the divided nation continued until David was finally crowned king over all Israel (2 Sam 5:1-5).

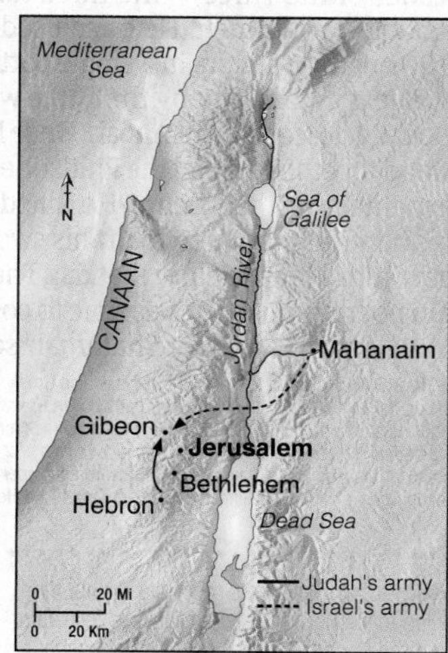

***JOAB VERSUS ABNER** David was crowned king of Judah in Hebron; Ishbosheth was crowned king of Israel in Mahanaim. The opposing armies of Judah and Israel met at Gibeon for battle—Judah under Joab, Israel under Abner.*

▸ **2 SAMUEL 2:18–3:1** ***(cont.)***

360 of Abner's men had been killed, all from the tribe
of Benjamin. 32 Joab and his men took Asahel's body to
Bethlehem and buried him there in his father's tomb.
Then they traveled all night and reached Hebron at
daybreak.

3:1 That was the beginning of a long war between
those who were loyal to Saul and those loyal to David.
As time passed David became stronger and stronger,
while Saul's dynasty became weaker and weaker.

David's Sons Born in Hebron

2 SAMUEL 3:2-5

These are the sons who were born to David in Hebron:

The oldest was Amnon, whose mother was
Ahinoam from Jezreel.
3 The second was Daniel,* whose mother was
Abigail, the widow of Nabal from Carmel.
The third was Absalom, whose mother was
Maacah, the daughter of Talmai, king of Geshur.
4 The fourth was Adonijah, whose mother was
Haggith.
The fifth was Shephatiah, whose mother was
Abital.
5 The sixth was Ithream, whose mother was Eglah,
David's wife.

These sons were all born to David in Hebron.

David's Mightiest Warriors PARALLEL

2 SAMUEL 23:8-17

These are the names of David's mightiest warriors.
The first was Jashobeam the Hacmonite,* who was
leader of the Three*—the three mightiest warriors
among David's men. He once used his spear to kill
800 enemy warriors in a single battle.*
9 Next in rank among the Three was Eleazar son of
Dodai, a descendant of Ahoah. Once Eleazar and David
stood together against the Philistines when the entire
Israelite army had fled. 10 He killed Philistines until
his hand was too tired to lift his sword, and the LORD
gave him a great victory that day. The rest of the army
did not return until it was time to collect the plunder!
11 Next in rank was Shammah son of Agee from
Harar. One time the Philistines gathered at Lehi and
attacked the Israelites in a field full of lentils. The
Israelite army fled, 12 but Shammah* held his ground
in the middle of the field and beat back the Philistines.
So the LORD brought about a great victory.
13 Once during the harvest, when David was at the
cave of Adullam, the Philistine army was camped in
the valley of Rephaim. The Three (who were among the
Thirty—an elite group among David's fighting men)
went down to meet him there. 14 David was staying in
the stronghold at the time, and a Philistine detachment had occupied the town of Bethlehem.
15 David remarked longingly to his men, "Oh, how I
would love some of that good water from the well by
the gate in Bethlehem." 16 So the Three broke through
the Philistine lines, drew some water from the well
by the gate in Bethlehem, and brought it back to David. But he refused to drink it. Instead, he poured it
out as an offering to the LORD. 17 "The LORD forbid that
I should drink this!" he exclaimed. "This water is as
precious as the blood of these men* who risked their
lives to bring it to me." So David did not drink it. These
are examples of the exploits of the Three.

1 CHRONICLES 11:10-19

These are the leaders of David's mighty warriors. Together with all Israel, they decided to make David their
king, just as the LORD had promised concerning Israel.
11 Here is the record of David's mightiest warriors:
The first was Jashobeam the Hacmonite, who was
leader of the Three—the mightiest warriors among
David's men.* He once used his spear to kill 300 enemy warriors in a single battle.
12 Next in rank among the Three was Eleazar son of
Dodai,* a descendant of Ahoah. 13 He was with David
in the battle against the Philistines at Pas-dammim.
The battle took place in a field full of barley, and the
Israelite army fled. 14 But Eleazar and David* held their
ground in the middle of the field and beat back the
Philistines. So the LORD saved them by giving them a
great victory.
15 Once when David was at the rock near the cave
of Adullam, the Philistine army was camped in the
valley of Rephaim. The Three (who were among the
Thirty—an elite group among David's fighting men)

2 Sm 3:3 As in parallel text at 1 Chr 3:1 (see also Greek version, which reads *Daluia,* and Dead Sea Scrolls, which read *Dan[iel]*); Hebrew reads *Kileab.* **2 Sm 23:8a** As in parallel text at 1 Chr 11:11; Hebrew reads *Josheb-basshebeth the Tahkemonite.* **2 Sm 23:8b** As in Greek and Latin versions (see also 1 Chr 11:11); the meaning of the Hebrew is uncertain. **2 Sm 23:8c** As in some Greek manuscripts (see also 1 Chr 11:11); the meaning of the Hebrew is uncertain, though it might be rendered *the Three. It was Adino the Eznite who killed 800 men at one time.* **2 Sm 23:12** Hebrew *he.* **2 Sm 23:17** Hebrew *Shall I drink the blood of these men?* **1 Chr 11:11** As in some Greek manuscripts (see also 2 Sam 23:8); Hebrew reads *leader of the Thirty,* or *leader of the captains.* **1 Chr 11:12** As in parallel text at 2 Sam 23:9 (see also 1 Chr 27:4); Hebrew reads *Dodo,* a variant spelling of Dodai. **1 Chr 11:14** Hebrew *they.*

2 Sam 3:1 The events recorded in chapter 2 led to a long war between David's followers and the troops loyal to Abner and Ishbosheth. Civil war rocked the country at great cost to both sides. This war occurred because Israel and Judah had lost sight of God's vision and purpose: to settle the land (Gen 12:7), to drive out the Canaanites (Deut 7:1-4), and to obey God's laws (Deut 8:1). Instead of uniting to accomplish these goals, they fought each other. When you face conflict, step back from the hostilities and consider whether you and your enemy have common goals that are bigger than your differences. Appeal to those interests as you work for a settlement.

2 Sam 3:2-5 David suffered much heartache because of his many wives. Polygamy was a socially acceptable practice for kings at this time, although God specifically warned against it (Deut 17:14-17). Sadly, the numerous sons born to David's wives caused him great trouble. Rape (2 Sam 13:14), murder (2 Sam 13:28), rebellion (2 Sam 15:13), and greed (1 Kgs 1:5-6) all resulted from the jealous rivalries among the half brothers. Solomon, one of David's sons and his successor to the throne, also took many wives

went down to meet him there. 16David was staying in
the stronghold at the time, and a Philistine detachment had occupied the town of Bethlehem.
17David remarked longingly to his men, "Oh, how
I would love some of that good water from the well
by the gate in Bethlehem." 18So the Three broke
through the Philistine lines, drew some water from the well by the gate in Bethlehem, and brought it back to David. But David refused to drink it. Instead, he poured it out as an offering to the LORD. 19"God forbid that
I should drink this!" he exclaimed. "This water is as precious as the blood of these men* who risked their lives to bring it to me." So David did not drink it. These are examples of the exploits of the Three.

David's Thirty Mighty Men PARALLEL

2 SAMUEL 23:18-39

Abishai son of Zeruiah, the brother of Joab, was the leader of the Thirty.* He once used his spear to kill 300 enemy warriors in a single battle. It was by such feats that he became as famous as the Three. 19Abishai
was the most famous of the Thirty* and was their commander, though he was not one of the Three.
20There was also Benaiah son of Jehoiada, a valiant warrior* from Kabzeel. He did many heroic deeds, which included killing two champions* of Moab. Another time, on a snowy day, he chased a lion down into a pit and killed it. 21Once, armed only with a club, he
killed a great Egyptian warrior who was armed with a spear. Benaiah wrenched the spear from the Egyptian's hand and killed him with it. 22Deeds like these made
Benaiah as famous as the Three mightiest warriors.
23He was more honored than the other members of
the Thirty, though he was not one of the Three. And David made him captain of his bodyguard.
24Other members of the Thirty included:

Asahel, Joab's brother;
Elhanan son of Dodo from Bethlehem;
25 Shammah from Harod;
Elika from Harod;

1 Chr 11:19 Hebrew *Shall I drink the lifeblood of these men?* **2 Sm 23:18** As in a few Hebrew manuscripts and Syriac version; most Hebrew manuscripts read *the Three.* **2 Sm 23:19** As in Syriac version; Hebrew reads *the Three.* **2 Sm 23:20a** Or *son of Jehoiada, son of Ish-hai.* **2 Sm 23:20b** Hebrew *two of Ariel.*

who eventually turned him away from God (1 Kgs 11:3-4).

2 Sam 23:8-39 These verses tell of some of the exploits that the special corps of David's army carried out. There were two elite groups of men: "the Thirty" and "the Three" (2 Sam 23:18, 23; 1 Chr 11:11-25). To become a member of such a group a man had to show unparalleled courage in battle as well as wisdom in leadership. "The Three" was the most elite group. The list of "the Thirty" actually contains 37 names, but it mentions some warriors known to be dead (Uriah, for example, in 2 Sam 23:39). Apparently, new members were appointed to replace those who had fallen in battle.

2 Sam 23:16 David poured out the water as an offering to God because he was so moved by the sacrifice it represented. When Hebrews offered sacrifices, they never consumed the blood. It represented life, and they poured it out before God. David would not drink this water that represented the lives of his soldiers. Instead, he offered it to God. Just as these men gave of themselves to serve David, we should put aside our own interests to serve other Christians (Rom 12:10). When we serve others, we are also serving God.

1 Chr 11:12-14 Eleazar's action changed the course of a battle. When everyone around him ran, he held his ground alongside David and was saved by the Lord. In any struggle, fear can keep us from taking a stand for God and from participating in God's victories. Face your fear head-on. Find other believers along the way who are worth standing beside through thick and thin. If you are grounded in God, victory will come when you hold that ground.

DAVID'S MIGHTY MEN

One way to understand David's success is to notice the kind of men who followed him. During the time Saul was hunting him, David gradually built a fighting force of several hundred men. Some were relatives, others were outcasts of society, many were in trouble with the law. But they all had one trait in common—complete devotion to David. Their achievements made them famous. Among these men were elite military groups like "the Three" and "the Thirty." They were true heroes. • Scripture gives the impression that these men were motivated to greatness by the personal qualities of their leader. David inspired them to achieve beyond their goals and meet their true potential. Likewise, the leaders we follow and the causes to which we commit ourselves will affect our lives. David's effectiveness was clearly connected with his awareness of God's leading. He was a good leader when he was following *his* Leader. Do you know whom the people you respect most are following? Your answer should help you decide whether they deserve your loyalty. Do you also recognize God's leading in your life? No one can lead you to excellence the way your Creator can.

Strengths and accomplishments	• Able soldiers and military leaders • Shared many special skills • Though frequently outnumbered, were consistently victorious • Loyal to David
Lessons from their lives	• Greatness is often inspired by the quality and character of the leadership • Even a small force of able and loyal men can accomplish great feats
Vital statistics	• Where: They came from all over Israel (primarily the tribes of Judah and Benjamin) and from the surrounding nations • Occupations: Various backgrounds—almost all were fugitives
Key verses	"So David left Gath and escaped to the cave of Adullam. Soon his brothers and all his other relatives joined him there. Then others began coming—men who were in trouble or in debt or who were just discontented—until David was the captain of about 400 men" (1 Sam 22:1-2).

Their stories are told in 1 Samuel 22—2 Samuel 23:39. They are also mentioned in 1 Chronicles 11–12.

▸ 2 SAMUEL 23:18-39 *(cont.)*

26 Helez from Pelon*;
Ira son of Ikkesh from Tekoa;
27 Abiezer from Anathoth;
Sibbecai* from Hushah;
28 Zalmon from Ahoah;
Maharai from Netophah;
29 Heled* son of Baanah from Netophah;
Ithai* son of Ribai from Gibeah (in the land of Benjamin);
30 Benaiah from Pirathon;
Hurai* from Nahale-gaash*;
31 Abi-albon from Arabah;
Azmaveth from Bahurim;
32 Eliahba from Shaalbon;
the sons of Jashen;
Jonathan 33 son of Shagee* from Harar;
Ahiam son of Sharar from Harar;
34 Eliphelet son of Ahasbai from Maacah;
Eliam son of Ahithophel from Giloh;
35 Hezro from Carmel;
Paarai from Arba;
36 Igal son of Nathan from Zobah;
Bani from Gad;
37 Zelek from Ammon;
Naharai from Beeroth, Joab's armor bearer;
38 Ira from Jattir;
Gareb from Jattir;
39 Uriah the Hittite.

There were thirty-seven in all.

1 CHRONICLES 11:20-47

Abishai, the brother of Joab, was the leader of the
Thirty.* He once used his spear to kill 300 enemy
warriors in a single battle. It was by such feats that
he became as famous as the Three. 21 Abishai was the
most famous of the Thirty and was their commander,
though he was not one of the Three.

22 There was also Benaiah son of Jehoiada, a valiant
warrior from Kabzeel. He did many heroic deeds,
which included killing two champions* of Moab. Another time, on a snowy day, he chased a lion down into
a pit and killed it. 23 Once, armed only with a club, he
killed an Egyptian warrior who was 7½ feet* tall and
whose spear was as thick as a weaver's beam. Benaiah
wrenched the spear from the Egyptian's hand and
killed him with it. 24 Deeds like these made Benaiah
as famous as the three mightiest warriors. 25 He was
more honored than the other members of the Thirty,
though he was not one of the Three. And David made
him captain of his bodyguard.

26 David's mighty warriors also included:
Asahel, Joab's brother;
Elhanan son of Dodo from Bethlehem;
27 Shammah from Harod;*
Helez from Pelon;
28 Ira son of Ikkesh from Tekoa;
Abiezer from Anathoth;
29 Sibbecai from Hushah;
Zalmon* from Ahoah;
30 Maharai from Netophah;
Heled son of Baanah from Netophah;
31 Ithai son of Ribai from Gibeah (in the land of Benjamin);
Benaiah from Pirathon;
32 Hurai from near Nahale-gaash*;
Abi-albon* from Arabah;
33 Azmaveth from Bahurim*;
Eliahba from Shaalbon;
34 the sons of Jashen* from Gizon;
Jonathan son of Shagee from Harar;
35 Ahiam son of Sharar* from Harar;
Eliphal son of Ur;
36 Hepher from Mekerah;
Ahijah from Pelon;
37 Hezro from Carmel;
Paarai* son of Ezbai;
38 Joel, the brother of Nathan;
Mibhar son of Hagri;
39 Zelek from Ammon;
Naharai from Beeroth, Joab's armor bearer;
40 Ira from Jattir;
Gareb from Jattir;
41 Uriah the Hittite;
Zabad son of Ahlai;
42 Adina son of Shiza, the Reubenite leader who had thirty men with him;
43 Hanan son of Maacah;
Joshaphat from Mithna;
44 Uzzia from Ashtaroth;
Shama and Jeiel, the sons of Hotham, from Aroer;
45 Jediael son of Shimri;
Joha, his brother, from Tiz;
46 Eliel from Mahavah;
Jeribai and Joshaviah, the sons of Elnaam;
Ithmah from Moab;
47 Eliel and Obed;
Jaasiel from Zobah.*

Abner Joins Forces with David

2 SAMUEL 3:6-21

As the war between the house of Saul and the house
of David went on, Abner became a powerful leader
among those loyal to Saul. 7 One day Ishbosheth,*

2 Sm 23:26 As in parallel text at 1 Chr 11:27 (see also 1 Chr 27:10); Hebrew reads *from Palti.* **2 Sm 23:27** As in some Greek manuscripts (see also 1 Chr 11:29); Hebrew reads *Mebunnai.* **2 Sm 23:29a** As in some Hebrew manuscripts (see also 1 Chr 11:30); most Hebrew manuscripts read *Heleb.* **2 Sm 23:29b** As in parallel text at 1 Chr 11:31; Hebrew reads *Ittai.* **2 Sm 23:30a** As in some Greek manuscripts (see also 1 Chr 11:32); Hebrew reads *Hiddai.* **2 Sm 23:30b** Or *from the ravines of Gaash.* **2 Sm 23:33** As in parallel text at 1 Chr 11:34; Hebrew reads *Jonathan, Shammah;* some Greek manuscripts read *Jonathan son of Shammah.* **1 Chr 11:20** As in Syriac version; Hebrew reads *the Three;* also in 11:21. **1 Chr 11:22** Or *two sons of Ariel.* **1 Chr 11:23** Hebrew *5 cubits* [2.3 meters]. **1 Chr 11:27** As in parallel text at 2 Sam 23:25; Hebrew reads *Shammoth from Haror.* **1 Chr 11:29** As in parallel text at 2 Sam 23:28; Hebrew reads *Ilai.* **1 Chr 11:32a** Or *from the ravines of Gaash.* **1 Chr 11:32b** As in parallel text at 2 Sam 23:31; Hebrew reads *Abiel.* **1 Chr 11:33** As in parallel text at 2 Sam 23:31; Hebrew reads *Baharum.* **1 Chr 11:34** As in parallel text at 2 Sam 23:32; Hebrew reads *sons of Hashem.* **1 Chr 11:35** As in parallel text at 2 Sam 23:33; Hebrew reads *son of Sacar.* **1 Chr 11:37** As in parallel text at 2 Sam 23:35; Hebrew reads *Naarai.* **1 Chr 11:47** Or *the Mezobaite.* **2 Sm 3:7** *Ishbosheth* is another name for Esh-baal.

Saul's son, accused Abner of sleeping with one of his
father's concubines, a woman named Rizpah, daughter of Aiah.
8Abner was furious. "Am I some Judean dog to be
kicked around like this?" he shouted. "After all I have
done for your father, Saul, and his family and friends by
not handing you over to David, is this my reward—that
you find fault with me about this woman? 9May God
strike me and even kill me if I don't do everything I can
to help David get what the LORD has promised him!
10I'm going to take Saul's kingdom and give it to David.
I will establish the throne of David over Israel as well as
Judah, all the way from Dan in the north to Beersheba
in the south." 11Ishbosheth didn't dare say another
word because he was afraid of what Abner might do.
12Then Abner sent messengers to David, saying,
"Doesn't the entire land belong to you? Make a solemn pact with me, and I will help turn over all of
Israel to you."
13"All right," David replied, "but I will not negotiate
with you unless you bring back my wife Michal, Saul's
daughter, when you come."
14David then sent this message to Ishbosheth, Saul's
son: "Give me back my wife Michal, for I bought her
with the lives* of 100 Philistines."
15So Ishbosheth took Michal away from her husband, Palti* son of Laish. 16Palti followed along behind
her as far as Bahurim, weeping as he went. Then Abner
told him, "Go back home!" So Palti returned.
17Meanwhile, Abner had consulted with the elders
of Israel. "For some time now," he told them, "you have
wanted to make David your king. 18Now is the time!
For the LORD has said, 'I have chosen David to save my
people Israel from the hands of the Philistines and
from all their other enemies.'" 19Abner also spoke with
the men of Benjamin. Then he went to Hebron to tell
David that all the people of Israel and Benjamin had
agreed to support him.
20When Abner and twenty of his men came to
Hebron, David entertained them with a great feast.
21Then Abner said to David, "Let me go and call an
assembly of all Israel to support my lord the king. They
will make a covenant with you to make you their king,
and you will rule over everything your heart desires."
So David sent Abner safely on his way.

Joab Murders Abner

2 SAMUEL 3:22-30

But just after David had sent Abner away in safety,
Joab and some of David's troops returned from a raid,
bringing much plunder with them. 23When Joab arrived, he was told that Abner had just been there visiting the king and had been sent away in safety.
24Joab rushed to the king and demanded, "What
have you done? What do you mean by letting Abner
get away? 25You know perfectly well that he came to
spy on you and find out everything you're doing!"
26Joab then left David and sent messengers to catch
up with Abner, asking him to return. They found him
at the well of Sirah and brought him back, though
David knew nothing about it. 27When Abner arrived
back at Hebron, Joab took him aside at the gateway
as if to speak with him privately. But then he stabbed
Abner in the stomach and killed him in revenge for
killing his brother Asahel.
28When David heard about it, he declared, "I
vow by the LORD that I and my kingdom are forever
innocent of this crime against Abner son of Ner.

2 Sm 3:14 Hebrew *the foreskins.* **2 Sm 3:15** As in 1 Sam 25:44; Hebrew reads *Paltiel,* a variant spelling of Palti.

2 Sam 3:6-7 To sleep with any of the king's wives or concubines was to make a claim to the throne, and it was considered treason. Because Ishbosheth was a weak ruler, Abner was running the country; thus, he may have felt justified in sleeping with Saul's concubine. Ishbosheth, however, saw that Abner's power was becoming too great.

2 Sam 3:7 Ishbosheth may have been right to speak out against Abner's behavior, but he didn't have the moral strength to maintain his authority (2 Sam 3:11). Lack of moral backbone became the root of Israel's troubles over the next four centuries. Only 4 of the next 40 kings of Israel were called "good." It takes courage and strength to stand firm in your convictions and to confront wrongdoing in the face of opposition. When you believe something is wrong, do not let yourself be talked out of your position. Firmly attack the wrong and uphold the right.

2 Sam 3:8 By saying, "Am I some Judean dog to be kicked around?" Abner meant, "Am I a traitor for Judah?" He may have been refuting the accusation that he was trying to take over the throne, or he may have been angry that Ishbosheth scolded him after Abner had helped put him on the throne in the first place. Prior to this conversation, Abner realized that he could not keep David from eventually taking over Israel. Because he was angry at Ishbosheth, Abner devised a plan to turn the kingdom of Israel over to David.

2 Sam 3:13-14 Michal had been married to David. Saul had arranged the marriage as a reward for David's acts of bravery (1 Sam 17:25; 18:24-27). Later, in one of his jealous fits, Saul took Michal away from David and forced her to marry Palti (1 Sam 25:44). Now David wanted his wife back before he would begin to negotiate peace with the northern tribes. Perhaps David still loved her (but see 2 Sam 6:20-23 for the tension in their relationship). More likely, he thought that marriage to Saul's daughter would strengthen his claim to rule all Israel and demonstrate that he had no animosity toward Saul's house. Palti was an unfortunate victim caught in the web of Saul's jealousy.

2 Sam 3:19 Because Saul, Ishbosheth, and Abner were all from the tribe of Benjamin, the support of the elders of that tribe meant that Abner was serious about his offer. There was a strong possibility of overcoming tribal jealousies and uniting the kingdom.

2 Sam 3:26-29 Joab took revenge for the death of his brother instead of leaving justice to God. But that revenge backfired on him (1 Kgs 2:31-34). God will repay those who deserve it (Rom 12:19). Refuse to rejoice when your enemies suffer, and don't try to get revenge. Seeking revenge will ruin your own peace of mind and increase the chances of further retaliation.

2 Sam 3:27 Abner killed Joab's brother Asahel in self-defense. Joab then killed Abner to avenge his brother's death and also to save his position of military leadership. People who killed in self-defense were supposed to be safe in cities of refuge (Num 35:22-25). Joab showed his disrespect for God's laws by killing Abner out of revenge in Hebron, a city of refuge (Josh 20:7).

▶ **2 SAMUEL 3:22-30** ***(cont.)***

29Joab and his family are the guilty ones. May the
family of Joab be cursed in every generation with a
man who has open sores or leprosy* or who walks
on crutches* or dies by the sword or begs for food!"
30So Joab and his brother Abishai killed Abner because Abner had killed their brother Asahel at the
battle of Gibeon.

David Mourns Abner's Death

2 SAMUEL 3:31-39

Then David said to Joab and all those who were with
him, "Tear your clothes and put on burlap. Mourn for
Abner." And King David himself walked behind the
procession to the grave. 32They buried Abner in Hebron, and the king and all the people wept at his grave-
side. 33Then the king sang this funeral song for Abner:

"Should Abner have died as fools die?
34 Your hands were not bound;
your feet were not chained.
No, you were murdered—
the victim of a wicked plot."

All the people wept again for Abner. 35David had
refused to eat anything on the day of the funeral, and
now everyone begged him to eat. But David had made
a vow, saying, "May God strike me and even kill me if I
eat anything before sundown."
36This pleased the people very much. In fact, everything the king did pleased them! 37So everyone in
Judah and all Israel understood that David was not
responsible for Abner's murder.
38Then King David said to his officials, "Don't you
realize that a great commander has fallen today in
Israel? 39And even though I am the anointed king,
these two sons of Zeruiah—Joab and Abishai—are too
strong for me to control. So may the LORD repay these
evil men for their evil deeds."

The Murder of Ishbosheth

2 SAMUEL 4:1-12

When Ishbosheth,* Saul's son, heard about Abner's
death at Hebron, he lost all courage, and all Israel
became paralyzed with fear. 2Now there were two
brothers, Baanah and Recab, who were captains of
Ishbosheth's raiding parties. They were sons of Rimmon, a member of the tribe of Benjamin who lived in
Beeroth. The town of Beeroth is now part of Benjamin's
territory 3because the original people of Beeroth fled
to Gittaim, where they still live as foreigners.
4(Saul's son Jonathan had a son named Mephibosheth,* who was crippled as a child. He was five years
old when the report came from Jezreel that Saul and
Jonathan had been killed in battle. When the child's
nurse heard the news, she picked him up and fled.
But as she hurried away, she dropped him, and he
became crippled.)
5One day Recab and Baanah, the sons of Rimmon
from Beeroth, went to Ishbosheth's house around
noon as he was taking his midday rest. 6The door-
keeper, who had been sifting wheat, became drowsy
and fell asleep. So Recab and Baanah slipped past
her.* 7They went into the house and found Ishbosheth sleeping on his bed. They struck and killed him
and cut off his head. Then, taking his head with them,
they fled across the Jordan Valley* through the night.
8When they arrived at Hebron, they presented Ishbosheth's head to David. "Look!" they exclaimed to the
king. "Here is the head of Ishbosheth, the son of your
enemy Saul who tried to kill you. Today the LORD has
given my lord the king revenge on Saul and his entire
family!"
9But David said to Recab and Baanah, "The LORD,
who saves me from all my enemies, is my witness.
10Someone once told me, 'Saul is dead,' thinking
he was bringing me good news. But I seized him and

2 Sm 3:29a Or *or a contagious skin disease.* The Hebrew word used here can describe various skin diseases. **2 Sm 3:29b** Or *who is effeminate;* Hebrew reads *who handles a spindle.* **2 Sm 4:1** *Ishbosheth* is another name for Esh-baal. **2 Sm 4:4** *Mephibosheth* is another name for Merib-baal. **2 Sm 4:6** As in Greek version; Hebrew reads *So they went into the house pretending to fetch wheat, but they stabbed him in the stomach. Then Recab and Baanah escaped.* **2 Sm 4:7** Hebrew *the Arabah.*

2 Sam 3:29 David was saying that Joab's descendants would be unclean, unhealthy, and in want. Why did David say such harsh words about Joab? David was upset over Abner's death for several reasons. (1) He was grieved over the loss of a skilled military officer. (2) He wanted to place the guilt of Abner's murder on Joab, not himself. (3) He was on the verge of becoming king over the entire nation, and utilizing Abner was the key to winning over the northern tribes. Abner's death could have revived the civil war. (4) Joab violated David's agreement to protect Abner. Joab's murderous act ruined David's plans, and David was especially angry that his own commander had committed the crime.

2 Sam 3:31 By walking behind the procession (that is, behind the casket), David was leading the mourning.

2 Sam 3:31ff David ordered Joab to mourn, possibly because few people were aware that Joab had committed the crime and because David did not want any further trouble. If this is true, David was thinking more about strengthening his kingdom than about justice.

2 Sam 3:39 Joab and Abishai were the two sons of Zeruiah David mentioned. David had an especially hard time controlling Joab because, although he was intensely loyal, he was strong willed, preferring to do things his own way. In exchange for his loyalty, however, David was willing to give him the flexibility he craved.

Joab's murder of Abner is an example of his fierce independence. While David opposed the murder, he allowed it to remain unpunished because (1) to punish Joab could cause the troops to rebel; (2) Joab was David's nephew, and any harsh treatment could cause family problems; (3) Joab was from the tribe of Judah, and David didn't want rebellion from his own tribe; (4) to get rid of Joab would mean losing a skilled and competent commander who had been invaluable in strengthening his army.

2 Sam 4:1 Ishbosheth was a man who took his courage from another man (Abner) rather than from God. When Abner died, Ishbosheth was left with nothing. In crisis and under pressure, he collapsed in fear. Fear can paralyze us, but faith and trust in God can overcome fear (2 Tim 1:6-8; Heb 13:6). If we trust in God, we will be free to respond boldly to the events around us.

2 Sam 4:4 The rest of Mephibosheth's story is told in 2 Samuel 9; 16:1-4; 19:24-30.

2 Sam 4:11 David called Ishbosheth an "innocent man." As Saul's son, Ishbosheth had reason to think he was in line for the

killed him at Ziklag. That's the reward I gave him for
his news! 11How much more should I reward evil men
who have killed an innocent man in his own house and
on his own bed? Shouldn't I hold you responsible for
his blood and rid the earth of you?"

12So David ordered his young men to kill them, and
they did. They cut off their hands and feet and hung
their bodies beside the pool in Hebron. Then they
took Ishbosheth's head and buried it in Abner's tomb
in Hebron.

2. DAVID BECOMES KING OVER ALL ISRAEL

The nation of Israel was unified once again, under David's leadership. David immediately captured the city of Jerusalem and made it the nation's capital, moving the Ark there and establishing it as the center of worship. God was at the center of the nation from the beginning of David's reign, and God blessed David greatly. Is God at the center of your life?

David Anointed King in Hebron PARALLEL

2 SAMUEL 5:1-5

Then all the tribes of Israel went to David at Hebron
and told him, "We are your own flesh and blood. 2In
the past,* when Saul was our king, you were the one
who really led the forces of Israel. And the LORD told
you, 'You will be the shepherd of my people Israel. You
will be Israel's leader.'"

2 Sm 5:2 Or *For some time.*

DAVID

When we think of David, we think: shepherd, poet, giant-killer, king, ancestor of Jesus—in short, one of the greatest men in the Old Testament. But alongside that list stands another: betrayer, liar, adulterer, murderer. The first list gives qualities we all might like to have; the second, qualities that might be true of any one of us. The Bible makes no effort to hide David's failures. Yet he is remembered and respected for his heart for God. Knowing how much more we share in David's failures than in his greatness, we should be curious to find out what made God refer to David as "a man after my own heart" (Acts 13:22). • David, more than anything else, had an unchangeable belief in the faithful and forgiving nature of God. He was a man who lived with great zest. He sinned, but he was quick to confess his sins. His confessions were from the heart, and his repentance was genuine. David never took God's forgiveness lightly or his blessing for granted. In return, God never held back from David either his forgiveness or the consequences of his actions. David experienced the joy of forgiveness even when he had to suffer the consequences of his sins. • We tend to get these two reversed. Too often we would rather avoid the consequences than experience forgiveness. Another big difference between us and David is that while he sinned greatly, he did not sin repeatedly. He learned from his mistakes because he accepted the suffering they brought. Often we don't seem to learn from our mistakes or the consequences that result from those mistakes. What changes would it take for God to find this kind of obedience in you?

Strengths and accomplishments	• Greatest king of Israel • Ancestor of Jesus Christ • A man described by God himself as a man after his own heart
Weaknesses and mistakes	• Committed adultery with Bathsheba • Arranged the murder of Uriah, Bathsheba's husband • Directly disobeyed God in taking a census of the people • Did not deal decisively with the sins of his children
Lessons from his life	• Willingness to honestly admit our mistakes is the first step in dealing with them • Forgiveness does not remove the consequences of sin • God greatly desires our complete trust and worship
Vital statistics	• Where: Bethlehem, Jerusalem • Occupations: Shepherd, musician, poet, soldier, king • Relatives: Father: Jesse. Wives: included Michal, Ahinoam, Bathsheba, Abigail. Sons: included Absalom, Amnon, Solomon, Adonijah. Daughters: included Tamar. • Contemporaries: Saul, Jonathan, Samuel, Nathan
Key verses	"For you are God, O Sovereign LORD. Your words are truth, and you have promised these good things to your servant. And now, may it please you to bless the house of your servant, so that it may continue forever before you. For you have spoken, and when you grant a blessing to your servant, O Sovereign LORD, it is an eternal blessing!" (2 Sam 7:28-29).

David's story is told in 1 Samuel 16—1 Kings 2. He is also mentioned in Amos 6:5; Matthew 1:1, 6; 22:43-45; Luke 1:32; Acts 13:22; Romans 1:3; Hebrews 11:32.

throne. He was not wicked for wanting to be king; rather, he was simply too weak to stand against injustice. Although David knew Ishbosheth was not the strong leader needed to unite Israel, he had no intention of killing him. God had promised the kingdom to David, and he knew that God would fulfill his promise.

When David learned of Ishbosheth's death, he was angry. He had never harmed Saul, and he thought the assassins' method was cowardly. David wanted to unite Israel, not drive a permanent wedge between him and Ishbosheth's supporters. To show that he had nothing to do with the extermination of Saul's royal line, he ordered the assassins

▸ **2 SAMUEL 5:1-5** ***(cont.)***

3So there at Hebron, King David made a covenant
before the LORD with all the elders of Israel. And they
anointed him king of Israel.

4David was thirty years old when he began to reign,
and he reigned forty years in all. 5He had reigned over
Judah from Hebron for seven years and six months,
and from Jerusalem he reigned over all Israel and Judah for thirty-three years.

1 CHRONICLES 11:1-3

Then all Israel gathered before David at Hebron and
told him, "We are your own flesh and blood. 2In the
past,* even when Saul was king, you were the one who
really led the forces of Israel. And the LORD your God
told you, 'You will be the shepherd of my people Israel.
You will be the leader of my people Israel.'"

3So there at Hebron, David made a covenant before the LORD with all the elders of Israel. And they
anointed him king of Israel, just as the LORD had promised through Samuel.

Warriors Join David's Army

1 CHRONICLES 12:23-40

These are the numbers of armed warriors who joined
David at Hebron. They were all eager to see David
become king instead of Saul, just as the LORD had
1003 BC promised.

24From the tribe of Judah, there were 6,800 warriors
armed with shields and spears.

25From the tribe of Simeon, there were 7,100 brave
warriors.

26From the tribe of Levi, there were 4,600 warriors.
27This included Jehoiada, leader of the family
of Aaron, who had 3,700 under his command.
28This also included Zadok, a brave young
warrior, with 22 members of his family who were
all officers.

29From the tribe of Benjamin, Saul's relatives, there
were 3,000 warriors. Most of the men from
Benjamin had remained loyal to Saul until this
time.

30From the tribe of Ephraim, there were 20,800
brave warriors, each highly respected in his
own clan.

31From the half-tribe of Manasseh west of the
Jordan, 18,000 men were designated by name
to help David become king.

32From the tribe of Issachar, there were 200 leaders
of the tribe with their relatives. All these men
understood the signs of the times and knew the
best course for Israel to take.

33From the tribe of Zebulun, there were 50,000
skilled warriors. They were fully armed and
prepared for battle and completely loyal to David.

34From the tribe of Naphtali, there were 1,000
officers and 37,000 warriors armed with shields
and spears.

35From the tribe of Dan, there were 28,600
warriors, all prepared for battle.

36From the tribe of Asher, there were 40,000 trained
warriors, all prepared for battle.

37From the east side of the Jordan River—where
the tribes of Reuben and Gad and the half-tribe
of Manasseh lived—there were 120,000 troops
armed with every kind of weapon.

38All these men came in battle array to Hebron
with the single purpose of making David the king
over all Israel. In fact, everyone in Israel agreed that
David should be their king. 39They feasted and drank
with David for three days, for preparations had been
made by their relatives for their arrival. 40And people

1 Chr 11:2 Or *For some time.*

David becomes king over all Israel

killed and gave Ishbosheth a proper burial. All the tribes of Israel, recognizing in David the strong leader they needed, pledged their loyalty to him. No doubt the Philistine threat and David's military reputation (1 Sam 18:7) also helped unify the people.

2 Sam 5:3-5 This was the third time David was anointed king. First he was privately anointed by Samuel (1 Sam 16:13). Then he was made king over the tribe of Judah (2 Sam 2:4). Finally he was crowned king over all Israel. David's life as an outlaw had looked bleak, but God's promise to make him king over all Israel was now being fulfilled. Although the kingdom would be divided again in less than 75 years, David's dynasty would reign over Judah, the southern kingdom, for over 400 years.

2 Sam 5:4-5 David did not become king over all Israel until he was 37 years old, although he had been promised the kingdom many years earlier (1 Sam 16:13). During those years, David had to wait patiently for the fulfillment of God's promise. If you feel pressured to achieve instant results and success, remember David's patience. Just as his time of waiting prepared him for his important task, a waiting period may help prepare you by strengthening your character.

1 Chr 11:1-2 The book of 2 Samuel details *how* David came to power while Chronicles emphasizes that *God* declared David to be the ruler; God was working through the efforts of many people, even some of Saul's own family. God is still sovereign over history, directing events to accomplish his will. The books of Chronicles demonstrate that no matter what people may do to try to hinder God's work, God still controls all events and works his will in them.

1 Chr 11:3 When David was finally anointed king over all Israel, 20 years had passed since Samuel had anointed him (1 Sam 16:1-13). God's promises are worth waiting for, even when his timetable doesn't match our expectations or desires.

1 Chr 12:26-29 In Numbers 1:47-50, God said that the Levites were to be exempt from military service. Why then are they listed as part of David's army? Although they were exempt from the draft, they strongly supported David and volunteered their services to help install him as king.

1 Chr 12:32 The 200 leaders from the tribe of Issachar "understood the signs of the times." As a result, their knowledge and judgment provided needed help in making decisions for the nation. For church leaders today, it is equally necessary to know what is happening in society in order to plan the best course of action for the church. Knowledge of current events, trends, and needs helps us understand people's thoughts and attitudes. This gives leaders information to help them make wise decisions for the church and make God's message relevant to people's lives.

1 Chr 12:40 The people were ready for change. They had suffered under Saul's leadership because of his disobedience to

from as far away as Issachar, Zebulun, and Naphtali brought food on donkeys, camels, mules, and oxen. Vast supplies of flour, fig cakes, clusters of raisins, wine, olive oil, cattle, sheep, and goats were brought to the celebration. There was great joy throughout the land of Israel.

David Captures Jerusalem PARALLEL

2 SAMUEL 5:6-16

David then led his men to Jerusalem to fight against the Jebusites, the original inhabitants of the land who were living there. The Jebusites taunted David, saying, "You'll never get in here! Even the blind and lame could keep you out!" For the Jebusites thought they were safe. [7]But David captured the fortress of Zion, which is now called the City of David.

[8]On the day of the attack, David said to his troops, "I hate those 'lame' and 'blind' Jebusites.* Whoever attacks them should strike by going into the city through the water tunnel.*" That is the origin of the saying, "The blind and the lame may not enter the house."*

[9]So David made the fortress his home, and he called it the City of David. He extended the city, starting at the supporting terraces* and working inward. [10]And David became more and more powerful, because the LORD God of Heaven's Armies was with him.

[11]Then King Hiram of Tyre sent messengers to David, along with cedar timber and carpenters and stonemasons, and they built David a palace. [12]And David realized that the LORD had confirmed him as king over Israel and had blessed his kingdom for the sake of his people Israel.

[13]After moving from Hebron to Jerusalem, David married more concubines and wives, and they had more sons and daughters. [14]These are the names of David's sons who were born in Jerusalem: Shammua, Shobab, Nathan, Solomon, [15]Ibhar, Elishua, Nepheg, Japhia, [16]Elishama, Eliada, and Eliphelet.

1 CHRONICLES 11:4-9

Then David and all Israel went to Jerusalem (or Jebus, as it used to be called), where the Jebusites, the original inhabitants of the land, were living. [5]The people of Jebus taunted David, saying, "You'll never get in here!" But David captured the fortress of Zion, which is now called the City of David.

[6]David had said to his troops, "Whoever is first to attack the Jebusites will become the commander of my armies!" And Joab, the son of David's sister Zeruiah, was first to attack, so he became the commander of David's armies.

[7]David made the fortress his home, and that is why it is called the City of David. [8]He extended the city from the supporting terraces* to the surrounding area, while Joab rebuilt the rest of Jerusalem. [9]And David became more and more powerful, because the LORD of Heaven's Armies was with him.

David Attempts to Move the Ark PARALLEL

2 SAMUEL 6:1-11

Then David again gathered all the elite troops in Israel, 30,000 in all. [2]He led them to Baalah of Judah* to bring back the Ark of God, which bears the name of the LORD of Heaven's Armies,* who is enthroned between the cherubim. [3]They placed the Ark of God on a new cart and brought it from Abinadab's house, which was on a hill. Uzzah and Ahio, Abinadab's sons,

2 Sm 5:8a Or *Those 'lame' and 'blind' Jebusites hate me.* **2 Sm 5:8b** Or *with scaling hooks.* The meaning of the Hebrew is uncertain. **2 Sm 5:8c** The meaning of this saying is uncertain. **2 Sm 5:9** Hebrew *the millo.* The meaning of the Hebrew is uncertain. **1 Chr 11:8** Hebrew *the millo.* The meaning of the Hebrew is uncertain. **2 Sm 6:2a** *Baalah of Judah* is another name for Kiriath-jearim; compare 1 Chr 13:6. **2 Sm 6:2b** Or *the Ark of God where the Name is proclaimed—the name of the LORD of Heaven's Armies.*

God (see 1 Chr 10:13). They were so overjoyed with David's coronation that they contributed lavishly to the celebration. It is right and proper to give generously for celebration and joyous worship. God is the author of joy, and he will join us in our celebrations.

2 Sam 5:6 The fortress of Zion (which became the city of Jerusalem) was located on a high ridge near the center of the united Israelite kingdom. David chose Jerusalem as his capital for both political and military reasons. It was considered neutral territory because it stood on the border of the territory of the tribes of Benjamin and Judah, and it was still occupied by the Jebusites, a Canaanite tribe that had never been expelled from the land (Judg 1:21). Jerusalem also sat on a high ridge, making it difficult to attack.

2 Sam 5:6-7 The Jebusites had a clear military advantage, and they boasted of their security behind the impregnable walls of Zion. But they soon discovered that their walls would not protect them. David caught them by surprise by entering the city through the water tunnel.

Only in God are we truly safe and secure. Anything else is false security. Whether you are surrounded by mighty walls of stone, a comfortable home, or a secure job, no one can predict what tomorrow may bring. Our relationship with God is the only security that cannot be taken away.

2 Sam 5:12 "David realized that the LORD had confirmed him as king. . . ." Although the pagan kingdoms based their greatness on conquest, power, armies, and wealth, David knew that his greatness came only from God. To be great means keeping a close relationship with God personally and nationally. To do this, David had to keep his ambition under control. Although he was famous, successful, and well liked, he gave God first place in his life and served the people according to God's purposes. Do you seek greatness from God or from people? In the drive for success, remember to keep your ambition under God's control.

1 Chr 11:9 David's power increased as a direct result of his consistent trust in God. In contrast, Saul's power decreased because he wanted all the credit for himself and ignored God (1 Sam 15:17-26). Those who are concerned about building a name for themselves risk losing the very recognition they crave. Like David, we should be concerned for righteousness, honesty, and excellence and leave the results to God.

2 Sam 6:3 The Ark of God was Israel's national treasure and was ordinarily kept in the Tabernacle. When the Ark was returned to Israel after a brief Philistine captivity (1 Sam 4:1–7:2), it was kept in Abinadab's home for 20 years. David saw how God blessed Abinadab, and he wanted to bring the Ark to Jerusalem to ensure God's blessing on the entire nation. (See the notes on Exod 37:1, p. 191, and Josh 3:2-4, p. 339.)

▸ 2 SAMUEL 6:1-11 *(cont.)*

were guiding the cart as it left the house, [4]carrying the Ark of God. Ahio walked in front of the Ark. [5]David and all the people of Israel were celebrating before the LORD, singing songs* and playing all kinds of musical instruments—lyres, harps, tambourines, castanets, and cymbals.

[6]But when they arrived at the threshing floor of Nacon, the oxen stumbled, and Uzzah reached out his hand and steadied the Ark of God. [7]Then the LORD's anger was aroused against Uzzah, and God struck him dead because of this.* So Uzzah died right there beside the Ark of God.

[8]David was angry because the LORD's anger had burst out against Uzzah. He named that place Perez-uzzah (which means "to burst out against Uzzah"), as it is still called today.

[9]David was now afraid of the LORD, and he asked, "How can I ever bring the Ark of the LORD back into my care?" [10]So David decided not to move the Ark of the LORD into the City of David. Instead, he took it to the house of Obed-edom of Gath. [11]The Ark of the LORD remained there in Obed-edom's house for three months, and the LORD blessed Obed-edom and his entire household.

1 CHRONICLES 13:1-14

David consulted with all his officials, including the generals and captains of his army.* [2]Then he addressed the entire assembly of Israel as follows: "If you approve and if it is the will of the LORD our God, let us send messages to all the Israelites throughout the land, including the priests and Levites in their towns and pasturelands. Let us invite them to come and join us. [3]It is time to bring back the Ark of our God, for we neglected it during the reign of Saul."

[4]The whole assembly agreed to this, for the people could see it was the right thing to do. [5]So David summoned all Israel, from the Shihor Brook of Egypt in the south all the way to the town of Lebo-hamath in the north, to join in bringing the Ark of God from Kiriath-jearim. [6]Then David and all Israel went to Baalah of Judah (also called Kiriath-jearim) to bring back the Ark of God, which bears the name* of the LORD who is enthroned between the cherubim. [7]They placed the Ark of God on a new cart and brought it from Abinadab's house. Uzzah and Ahio were guiding the cart. [8]David and all Israel were celebrating before God with all their might, singing songs and playing all kinds of musical instruments—lyres, harps, tambourines, cymbals, and trumpets.

[9]But when they arrived at the threshing floor of Nacon,* the oxen stumbled, and Uzzah reached out his hand to steady the Ark. [10]Then the LORD's anger was aroused against Uzzah, and he struck him dead because he had laid his hand on the Ark. So Uzzah died there in the presence of God.

2 Sm 6:5 As in Dead Sea Scrolls and Greek version (see also 1 Chr 13:8); Masoretic Text reads *before the LORD with all manner of cypress wood.* **2 Sm 6:7** As in Dead Sea Scrolls; Masoretic Text reads *because of his irreverence.* **1 Chr 13:1** Hebrew *the commanders of thousands and of hundreds.* **1 Chr 13:6** Or *the Ark of God, where the Name is proclaimed—the name.* **1 Chr 13:9** As in parallel text at 2 Sam 6:6; Hebrew reads *Kidon.*

---

2 Sam 6:6-7 Uzzah was only trying to protect the Ark, so was God's anger against Uzzah just? According to Numbers 4:5-15, the Ark was to be moved only by the Levites, who were to carry it using the carrying poles—they were never to touch the Ark itself. To touch it was a capital offense under Hebrew law (Num 4:15). God's action was directed against both David and Uzzah. David placed the Ark on a cart, following the Philistines' example (1 Sam 6:7-8) rather than God's commands. Uzzah, though sincere in his desire to protect the Ark, had to face the consequences of the sin of touching it. Also, Uzzah may not have been a Levite. As David sought to bring Israel back into a relationship with God, God had to remind the nation dramatically that enthusiasm must be accompanied by obedience to his laws. Also, David had "consulted with all his officials" (1 Chr 13:1), but he neglected to ask God. The advice of our friends and colleagues is no substitute for God's direction. The next time David tried to bring the Ark to Jerusalem, he was careful to handle it correctly (1 Chr 15:1-15).

2 Sam 6:8-11 David was angry at both God and himself. He was angry that a well-meaning man had been killed and that his plans for a joyous return of the Ark had been spoiled (2 Sam 6:8). He undoubtedly knew that the fault was his own for transporting the Ark carelessly. After cooling down, he had the Ark put into temporary storage while he waited to see if the Lord would allow him to bring it to Jerusalem. This also gave David time to consider the right way to transport the Ark. The fact that God blessed the home of Obed-edom was a sign to David that he could try once again to move the Ark to Jerusalem.

1 Chr 13:1 David took time to confer with all his officials. As king, he had ultimate authority and could have given orders on his own, but he chose to involve others in leadership. Perhaps this is why there was unanimous support for his decisions (1 Chr 13:1-5). When we are in charge, it is tempting to make unilateral decisions, pushing through our own opinions. But effective leaders listen carefully to others' opinions, and they encourage others to participate in making decisions. Of course, we should always consult God first. We can run into big problems if we don't talk to him (see the note on 2 Sam 6:6-7, above).

1 Chr 13:3 The Ark of our God is also called the Ark of the Covenant. The most sacred object of the Hebrew faith, it was a large box containing the stone tablets on which God had written the Ten Commandments (Exod 25:10-22). David had already made Jerusalem his political capital (1 Chr 11:4-9). At this time, David brought the Ark there in order to make Jerusalem the nation's center for worship as well.

1 Chr 13:3 The Ark of God had been in Kiriath-jearim for many years. The neglect of the Ark symbolized Israel's neglect of God. Bringing the Ark back to the center of Israel's life reflected David's desire to remind the nation of its true foundation—God. Neglecting those things that remind us of God—the Bible, the church, and contact with Christians—will cause us also to neglect God. How would an observer know that God is at the center of your life?

1 Chr 13:6 Cherubim are mighty angels.

1 Chr 13:8 Worship in the Old Testament was more than a sober religious exercise. David's exuberance as he worshiped God with dancing and music is approved in Scripture. Our worship should reflect a healthy balance: Sometimes we should be reflective and serious (see Exod 19:14ff), and sometimes we should show enthusiasm and jubilation. What do you need—more serious reflection or more joyous celebration?

1 Chr 13:10-14 Uzzah died instantly for touching the Ark, but God blessed Obed-edom's home where the Ark was stored. This demonstrates the two-edged aspect of God's character: He is perfectly loving and

11David was angry because the LORD's anger had burst out against Uzzah. He named that place Perez-uzzah (which means "to burst out against Uzzah"), as it is still called today.
12David was now afraid of God, and he asked, "How can I ever bring the Ark of God back into my care?"
13So David did not move the Ark into the City of David. Instead, he took it to the house of Obed-edom of Gath.
14The Ark of God remained there in Obed-edom's house for three months, and the LORD blessed the household of Obed-edom and everything he owned.

David's Palace and Family

1 CHRONICLES 14:1-7

Then King Hiram of Tyre sent messengers to David, along with cedar timber, and stonemasons and carpenters to build him a palace. 2And David realized that the LORD had confirmed him as king over Israel and had greatly blessed his kingdom for the sake of his people Israel.
3Then David married more wives in Jerusalem, and they had more sons and daughters. 4These are the names of David's sons who were born in Jerusalem: Shammua, Shobab, Nathan, Solomon, 5Ibhar, Elishua, Elpelet, 6Nogah, Nepheg, Japhia, 7Elishama, Eliada,* and Eliphelet.

David Conquers the Philistines PARALLEL

2 SAMUEL 5:17-25

When the Philistines heard that David had been anointed king of Israel, they mobilized all their forces to capture him. But David was told they were coming, so he went into the stronghold. 18The Philistines arrived and spread out across the valley of Rephaim. 19So David asked the LORD, "Should I go out to fight the Philistines? Will you hand them over to me?"

The LORD replied to David, "Yes, go ahead. I will certainly hand them over to you."

20So David went to Baal-perazim and defeated the Philistines there. "The LORD did it!" David exclaimed. "He burst through my enemies like a raging flood!" So he named that place Baal-perazim (which means

1 Chr 14:7 Hebrew *Beeliada,* a variant spelling of Eliada; compare 3:8 and parallel text at 2 Sam 5:16.

perfectly just. Great blessings come to those who obey his commands, but severe punishment comes to those who disobey him. This punishment may come swiftly or over time, but it will come. Sometimes we focus only on the blessings God gives us, while forgetting that when we sin, "It is a terrible thing to fall into the hands of the living God" (Heb 10:31). At other times, however, we concentrate so much on judgment that we miss his blessings. Don't fall into a one-sided view of God. Along with God's blessings comes the responsibility to live up to his demands for fairness, honesty, and justice.

1 Chr 14:1 King Hiram also sent lumber and craftsmen to help Solomon build the Temple (2 Chr 2:1ff).

1 Chr 14:2 God gave David honor and success, but not simply for David's personal gain. David realized that God had prospered him for a special reason—for the sake of God's people! Often we are tempted to use our position or possessions only for our own good. Instead, we must remember that God has placed us where we are and given us all we have so that we may encourage others and give to those in need.

1 Chr 14:3 Accumulating wives and concubines in a harem was the custom of the day among Middle Eastern royalty, but it was not God's ideal (Gen 2:24). David's marriages brought him greater power and influence, but they also caused strife, jealousy, and even murder within his family. (See the chart on p. 503 for other consequences of polygamy.)

2 Sam 5:17 "The stronghold" is the mountain stronghold in the wilderness of Judah that David used when defending himself against Saul (see 2 Sam 23:14 and 1 Chr 12:8).

***DAVID DEFEATS THE PHILISTINES** The Philistines camped in the valley of Rephaim. David defeated them at Baal-perazim, but they remained in the valley. He attacked again and chased them from Gibeon to Gezer.*

2 Sam 5:17 The Philistine oppression of Israel had begun in the days of Samson (Judg 13–16). The Philistines were still Israel's most powerful enemy, although David was once considered a friend and ally (1 Sam 27; 29). They apparently did not bother David while he was king of Judah alone. But when they learned that David was planning to unite all Israel, they tried to stop him.

2 Sam 5:19 How could David get such a clear message from God? He may have prayed and been urged to action by the Holy Spirit. He may have asked God through a prophet. Most likely he went to the high priest, who consulted God through the Urim and Thummim that God had told the Israelites to use for just such a purpose. (For more on the Urim and Thummim, see the notes on Lev 8:8, p. 210, and 1 Sam 10:20, p. 438.)

2 Sam 5:19-25 David fought his battles the way God instructed him. In each instance he (1) asked if he should fight or not, (2) followed instructions carefully, and (3) gave God the glory. We can err in our "battles" if we ignore these steps and instead (1) do what we want without considering God's will, (2) do things our way and ignore advice in the Bible or from other wise people, and (3) take the glory ourselves or give it to someone else without acknowledging the help we received from God. All these responses are sinful.

▸ 2 SAMUEL 5:17-25 *(cont.)*
"the Lord who bursts through"). 21 The Philistines had abandoned their idols there, so David and his men confiscated them.

22 But after a while the Philistines returned and again spread out across the valley of Rephaim. 23 And again David asked the LORD what to do. "Do not attack them straight on," the LORD replied. "Instead, circle around behind and attack them near the poplar* trees. 24 When you hear a sound like marching feet in the tops of the poplar trees, be on the alert! That will be the signal that the LORD is moving ahead of you to strike down the Philistine army." 25 So David did what the LORD commanded, and he struck down the Philistines all the way from Gibeon* to Gezer.

1 CHRONICLES 14:8-17
When the Philistines heard that David had been anointed king over all Israel, they mobilized all their forces to capture him. But David was told they were coming, so he marched out to meet them. 9 The Philistines arrived and made a raid in the valley of Rephaim. 10 So David asked God, "Should I go out to fight the Philistines? Will you hand them over to me?"

The LORD replied, "Yes, go ahead. I will hand them over to you."

11 So David and his troops went up to Baal-perazim and defeated the Philistines there. "God did it!" David exclaimed. "He used me to burst through my enemies like a raging flood!" So they named that place Baal-perazim (which means "the Lord who bursts through"). 12 The Philistines had abandoned their gods there, so David gave orders to burn them.

13 But after a while the Philistines returned and raided the valley again. 14 And once again David asked God what to do. "Do not attack them straight on," God replied. "Instead, circle around behind and attack them near the poplar* trees. 15 When you hear a sound like marching feet in the tops of the poplar trees, go out and attack! That will be the signal that God is moving ahead of you to strike down the Philistine army." 16 So David did what God commanded, and they struck down the Philistine army all the way from Gibeon to Gezer.

17 So David's fame spread everywhere, and the LORD caused all the nations to fear David.

Preparing to Move the Ark to Jerusalem

1 CHRONICLES 15:1-24
David now built several buildings for himself in the City of David. He also prepared a place for the Ark of God and set up a special tent for it. 2 Then he commanded, "No one except the Levites may carry the Ark of God. The LORD has chosen them to carry the Ark of the LORD and to serve him forever."

3 Then David summoned all Israel to Jerusalem to bring the Ark of the LORD to the place he had prepared

2 Sm 5:23 Or *aspen,* or *balsam;* also in 5:24. The exact identification of this tree is uncertain. **2 Sm 5:25** As in Greek version (see also 1 Chr 14:16); Hebrew reads *Geba.* **1 Chr 14:14** Or *aspen,* or *balsam;* also in 14:15. The exact identification of this tree is uncertain.

Philistine Soldier

Pharaoh Rameses III (c. 12th century B.C.) defeated many Philistines attempting to invade Egypt. Desiring a record of his triumphs, he had pictures of the battles carved on the walls of a temple. They can still be seen today in Medinet Habu, on the bank of the Nile opposite to the city of Luxor, Egypt. In one scene depicting a land battle, many Philistines lie dead or dying as they vainly fought the Egyptian forces. Pharaoh's artists took care to make the differences between the Egyptian soldiers and their foes clear: Egyptian soldiers carry oblong, round-topped shields; heavy-tipped clubs; and short daggers. Their chariots carry archers. In contrast, the Philistines have spears; long, tapering swords; round shields; and headdresses of feathers or hair standing straight up on their heads.

The Philistines were also long-time enemies of Israel; there was constant warfare between the two peoples. The Philistines were a constant "thorn in the flesh" to the Israelites. We also have thorns in the flesh, whether physical ailments, financial problems, or troublesome people in our lives. We need to rely on God to deal with these "Philistines."

2 Sam 5:25 After David became king, his first order of business was to subdue his enemies—a task the nation had failed to complete when they first entered the land (Judg 2:1-4). David knew this had to be done in order to protect the nation, unify the kingdom, and prepare for building the Temple (which would unify religion under God and help abolish idolatrous influences).

1 Chr 14:10 Before David went to battle, he inquired of God first, asking for his presence and guidance. Too often we wait until we are in trouble before turning to God. By then the consequences of our actions are already unfolding. Do you ask for God's help only as a desperate last resort? Instead, go to him first! Like David, you may receive incredible help and avoid serious trouble. Then give God the credit when you see what he does on your behalf.

1 Chr 14:12 David's quick and decisive action against idols helped unify his kingdom and focus the people on worshiping the one true God. He was obeying the law that said, "You must break down their pagan altars and shatter their sacred pillars. Cut down their Asherah poles and burn their idols" (Deut 7:5). Most of David's successors failed to destroy idols, and this led to unbelievable moral corruption in Israel.

1 Chr 14:12 Often the soldiers wanted to keep souvenirs from their battles, but David ordered them to burn the idols. The only proper response to sin is to get rid of it completely. You cannot be a follower of God while continuing to hold on to parts of your life where God is not the center of your thoughts and actions. Eliminate whatever takes God's rightful place in your life, and follow him with complete devotion.

for it. [4]This is the number of the descendants of Aaron (the priests) and the Levites who were called together:

[5]From the clan of Kohath, 120, with Uriel as their leader.

[6]From the clan of Merari, 220, with Asaiah as their leader.

[7]From the clan of Gershon,* 130, with Joel as their leader.

[8]From the descendants of Elizaphan, 200, with Shemaiah as their leader.

[9]From the descendants of Hebron, 80, with Eliel as their leader.

[10]From the descendants of Uzziel, 112, with Amminadab as their leader.

[11]Then David summoned the priests, Zadok and Abiathar, and these Levite leaders: Uriel, Asaiah, Joel, Shemaiah, Eliel, and Amminadab. [12]He said to them, "You are the leaders of the Levite families. You must purify yourselves and all your fellow Levites, so you can bring the Ark of the LORD, the God of Israel, to the place I have prepared for it. [13]Because you Levites did not carry the Ark the first time, the anger of the LORD our God burst out against us. We failed to ask God how to move it properly." [14]So the priests and the Levites purified themselves in order to bring the Ark of the LORD, the God of Israel, to Jerusalem. [15]Then the Levites carried the Ark of God on their shoulders with its carrying poles, just as the LORD had instructed Moses.

[16]David also ordered the Levite leaders to appoint a choir of Levites who were singers and musicians to sing joyful songs to the accompaniment of harps, lyres, and cymbals. [17]So the Levites appointed Heman son of Joel along with his fellow Levites: Asaph son of Berekiah, and Ethan son of Kushaiah from the clan of Merari. [18]The following men were chosen as their assistants: Zechariah, Jaaziel,* Shemiramoth, Jehiel, Unni, Eliab, Benaiah, Maaseiah, Mattithiah, Eliphelehu, Mikneiah, and the gatekeepers—Obed-edom and Jeiel.

[19]The musicians Heman, Asaph, and Ethan were chosen to sound the bronze cymbals. [20]Zechariah, Aziel, Shemiramoth, Jehiel, Unni, Eliab, Maaseiah, and Benaiah were chosen to play the harps.* [21]Mattithiah, Eliphelehu, Mikneiah, Obed-edom, Jeiel, and Azaziah were chosen to play the lyres.* [22]Kenaniah, the head Levite, was chosen as the choir leader because of his skill.

[23]Berekiah and Elkanah were chosen to guard* the Ark. [24]Shebaniah, Joshaphat, Nethanel, Amasai, Zechariah, Benaiah, and Eliezer—all of whom were priests—were chosen to blow the trumpets as they marched in front of the Ark of God. Obed-edom and Jehiah were chosen to guard the Ark.

Moving the Ark to Jerusalem PARALLEL

2 SAMUEL 6:12-16

Then King David was told, "The LORD has blessed Obed-edom's household and everything he has because of the Ark of God." So David went there and brought the Ark of God from the house of Obed-edom to the City of David with a great celebration. [13]After the men who were carrying the Ark of the LORD had gone six steps, David sacrificed a bull and a fattened calf. [14]And David danced before the LORD with all his might, wearing a priestly garment.* [15]So David and all the people of Israel brought up the Ark of the LORD with shouts of joy and the blowing of rams' horns.

[16]But as the Ark of the LORD entered the City of David, Michal, the daughter of Saul, looked down from

1000 BC Native Americans in California build wood-reed houses

1 Chr 15:7 Hebrew *Gershom,* a variant spelling of Gershon. **1 Chr 15:18** As in several Hebrew manuscripts and Greek version (see also parallel lists in 15:20; 16:5); Masoretic Text reads *Zechariah ben Jaaziel.* **1 Chr 15:20** Hebrew adds *according to Alamoth,* which is probably a musical term. The meaning of the Hebrew is uncertain. **1 Chr 15:21** Hebrew adds *according to the Sheminith,* which is probably a musical term. The meaning of the Hebrew is uncertain. **1 Chr 15:23** Hebrew *chosen as gatekeepers for;* also in 15:24. **2 Sm 6:14** Hebrew *a linen ephod.*

1 Chr 15:12 The priests purified themselves so they would be prepared to carry the Ark. To *purify* literally means "to separate," to set apart for sacred purposes, to consecrate. The priests symbolically separated themselves from sin and evil. This was done by washing themselves and their clothing in a special ceremony (Num 8:5-8). While we are not required to carry out such ceremonies today, we can purify ourselves by reading God's Word, thoughtfully applying it to our lives, and preparing our hearts to participate in worship through anticipation, self-examination, and meditation. Just as we "set apart" time for worship, we also "set apart" ourselves to be in God's presence.

1 Chr 15:13 "The first time" refers to the incident recorded in 1 Chronicles 13:8-11 and 2 Samuel 6:1-11. As the Ark was being brought back to Israel on an oxcart, the oxen stumbled. Uzzah, trying to steady the Ark with his hand, was killed instantly for touching it. The mistake was not in David's desire to move the Ark but in his method for its return. David either ignored or was unaware of the specific instructions in God's law about how the Ark was to be moved. Obviously he had discovered his mistake and was now preparing to correct it. This incident was a divine object lesson to all Israel that God governed the king and not the other way around. If David had been allowed to handle the Ark of God carelessly, what would that have said to the people about their faith?

1 Chr 15:13-15 When David's first attempt to move the Ark failed (1 Chr 13:8-14), he learned an important lesson: When God gives specific instructions, it is wise to follow them precisely. This time David saw to it that the Levites carried the Ark (Num 4:5-15). We may not fully understand the reasons behind God's instructions, but we do know that his wisdom is complete and his judgment infallible. The way to know God's instructions is to know his Word. But just as children do not understand the reasons for all their parents' instructions until they are older, we may not understand all of God's reasons in this life. It is far better to obey God first and then discover the reasons. We are never free to disobey God just because we don't understand.

1 Chr 15:16-24 The great musical procession was designed as a worthy accompaniment to this great occasion. It heightened the excitement, elevated the people's hearts and minds, and focused their attention on the event. It also helped seal it in their memory for years to come. Beginning any task by praising God can inspire us to give him our best. Develop the practice of giving praise to God, and you will experience greater joy and strength to face anything.

2 Sam 6:14 David wore a priestly garment, possibly because it was a religious celebration.

▸ **2 SAMUEL 6:12-16** ***(cont.)***

her window. When she saw King David leaping and dancing before the LORD, she was filled with contempt for him.

1 CHRONICLES 15:25-29

Then David and the elders of Israel and the generals of the army* went to the house of Obed-edom to bring the Ark of the LORD's Covenant up to Jerusalem with a great celebration. [26]And because God was clearly helping the Levites as they carried the Ark of the LORD's Covenant, they sacrificed seven bulls and seven rams.

[27]David was dressed in a robe of fine linen, as were all the Levites who carried the Ark, and also the singers, and Kenaniah the choir leader. David was also wearing a priestly garment.* [28]So all Israel brought up the Ark of the LORD's Covenant with shouts of joy, the blowing of rams' horns and trumpets, the crashing of cymbals, and loud playing on harps and lyres.

[29]But as the Ark of the LORD's Covenant entered the City of David, Michal, the daughter of Saul, looked down from her window. When she saw King David skipping about and laughing with joy, she was filled with contempt for him.

Placing the Ark in the Tabernacle PARALLEL

2 SAMUEL 6:17-19a

They brought the Ark of the LORD and set it in its place inside the special tent David had prepared for it. And David sacrificed burnt offerings and peace offerings to the LORD. [18]When he had finished his sacrifices, David blessed the people in the name of the LORD of Heaven's Armies. [19]Then he gave to every Israelite man and woman in the crowd a loaf of bread, a cake of dates,* and a cake of raisins.

1 CHRONICLES 16:1-6

They brought the Ark of God and placed it inside the special tent David had prepared for it. And they presented burnt offerings and peace offerings to God. [2]When he had finished his sacrifices, David blessed the people in the name of the LORD. [3]Then he gave to every man and woman in all Israel a loaf of bread, a cake of dates,* and a cake of raisins.

[4]David appointed the following Levites to lead the people in worship before the Ark of the LORD—to invoke his blessings, to give thanks, and to praise the LORD, the God of Israel. [5]Asaph, the leader of this group, sounded the cymbals. Second to him was Zechariah, followed by Jeiel, Shemiramoth, Jehiel, Mattithiah, Eliab, Benaiah, Obed-edom, and Jeiel. They played the harps and lyres. [6]The priests, Benaiah and Jahaziel, played the trumpets regularly before the Ark of God's Covenant.

David's Song of Praise

1 CHRONICLES 16:7-36

On that day David gave to Asaph and his fellow Levites this song of thanksgiving to the LORD:

1 Chr 15:25 Hebrew *the commanders of thousands.* **1 Chr 15:27** Hebrew *a linen ephod.* **2 Sm 6:19** Or *a portion of meat.* The meaning of the Hebrew is uncertain.
1 Chr 16:3 Or *a portion of meat.* The meaning of the Hebrew is uncertain.

1 Chr 15:29 David was willing to look foolish in the eyes of some people in order to express his thankfulness to God fully and honestly. In contrast, Michal was so disgusted by his undignified actions that she could not rejoice in the Ark's return to Jerusalem. Michal could accept David as a military conqueror and as a king, but she could not accept his free and spontaneous expression of praise to God. Some devoted people may look foolish to us in their heartfelt expressions of worship, but we must accept them. In the same way, we should not be afraid to worship God with whatever expressions seem appropriate.

2 Sam 6:17 Only a priest could place the sacrifices on the altar. Leviticus 1:2-13 indicates that anyone who was ceremonially clean could assist a priest in offering the sacrifice (see the notes on Josh 3:5, p. 339, and 1 Sam 20:26, p. 456). So David probably offered these sacrifices to God with the aid of a priest. Solomon did the same (1 Kgs 8:62-65).

1 Chr 16:4 Certain Levites were appointed to give continual praise and thanks to God. Praise and thanksgiving should be a regular part of our routine, not reserved only for celebrations. Praise God continually, and you will find that you won't take his blessings for granted.

CRITICIZING GOD'S LEADERS

It is dangerous to criticize God's leaders. Consider the consequences for these men and women.

Person/Situation	*Result*	*Reference*
Miriam: Mocked Moses because he had a Cushite wife	Stricken with leprosy	**Num 12**
Korah and followers: Led the people of Israel to rebel against Moses' leadership	Swallowed by the earth	**Num 16**
Michal: Despised David because he danced before the Lord	Remained childless	**2 Sam 6**
Shimei: Cursed and threw stones at David	Executed at Solomon's order	**2 Sam 16; 1 Kgs 2**
Youths: Mocked Elisha and laughed at his baldness	Killed by bears	**2 Kgs 2**
Sanballat and Tobiah: Spread rumors and lies to stop the building of Jerusalem's walls	Frightened and humiliated	**Neh 2; 4; 6**
Hananiah: Contradicted Jeremiah's prophecies with false predictions	Died two months later	**Jer 28**
Bar-Jesus, a sorcerer: Lied about Paul in an attempt to turn the governor against him	Stricken with blindness	**Acts 13**

1 Chr 16:7-36 Four elements of true thanksgiving are found in this song (psalm): (1) *remembering* what God has done, (2) *telling* others about it, (3) *showing* God's

8 Give thanks to the LORD and proclaim his
greatness.
Let the whole world know what he has done.
9 Sing to him; yes, sing his praises.
Tell everyone about his wonderful deeds.
10 Exult in his holy name;
rejoice, you who worship the LORD.
11 Search for the LORD and for his strength;
continually seek him.
12 Remember the wonders he has performed,
his miracles, and the rulings he has given,
13 you children of his servant Israel,
you descendants of Jacob, his chosen ones.

14 He is the LORD our God.
His justice is seen throughout the land.
15 Remember his covenant forever—
the commitment he made to a thousand
generations.
16 This is the covenant he made with Abraham
and the oath he swore to Isaac.
17 He confirmed it to Jacob as a decree,
and to the people of Israel as a never-ending
covenant:
18 "I will give you the land of Canaan
as your special possession."
19 He said this when you were few in number,
a tiny group of strangers in Canaan.
20 They wandered from nation to nation,
from one kingdom to another.
21 Yet he did not let anyone oppress them.
He warned kings on their behalf:
22 "Do not touch my chosen people,
and do not hurt my prophets."
23 Let the whole earth sing to the LORD!
Each day proclaim the good news that
he saves.
24 Publish his glorious deeds among the nations.
Tell everyone about the amazing things
he does.
25 Great is the LORD! He is most worthy of praise!
He is to be feared above all gods.
26 The gods of other nations are mere idols,
but the LORD made the heavens!
27 Honor and majesty surround him;
strength and joy fill his dwelling.

28 O nations of the world, recognize the LORD,
recognize that the LORD is glorious and strong.
29 Give to the LORD the glory he deserves!
Bring your offering and come into his
presence.
Worship the LORD in all his holy splendor.
30 Let all the earth tremble before him.
The world stands firm and cannot be shaken.

31 Let the heavens be glad, and the earth rejoice!
Tell all the nations, "The LORD reigns!"
32 Let the sea and everything in it shout his praise!
Let the fields and their crops burst out
with joy!
33 Let the trees of the forest rustle with praise,
for the LORD is coming to judge the earth.

34 Give thanks to the LORD, for he is good!
His faithful love endures forever.
35 Cry out, "Save us, O God of our salvation!
Gather and rescue us from among the nations,
so we can thank your holy name
and rejoice and praise you."

36 Praise the LORD, the God of Israel,
who lives from everlasting to everlasting!

And all the people shouted "Amen!" and praised the LORD.

Worship at Jerusalem and Gibeon

1 CHRONICLES 16:37-42

David arranged for Asaph and his fellow Levites to
serve regularly before the Ark of the LORD's Covenant,
doing whatever needed to be done each day. 38This
group included Obed-edom (son of Jeduthun), Hosah,
and sixty-eight other Levites as gatekeepers.
39Meanwhile, David stationed Zadok the priest and
his fellow priests at the Tabernacle of the LORD at the
place of worship in Gibeon, where they continued

glory to others, and (4) *offering* gifts of self, time, and resources. If you are truly thankful, your life will show it.

1 Chr 16:8ff Several parts of this psalm are parallel to songs in the book of Psalms: 1 Chronicles 16:8-22 with Psalm 105:1-15; 1 Chronicles 16:23-33 with Psalm 96; 1 Chronicles 16:34-36 with Psalm 106:1, 47-48.

1 Chr 16:15-18 This covenant was given to Abraham (Gen 15:18-21) and then passed on to Isaac (Gen 26:24-25) and Jacob (Gen 28:13-15). God promised to give the land of Canaan (present-day Israel) to their descendants. He also promised that the Messiah would come from their line.

1 Chr 16:25 Genuine praise results when we declare God's character and attributes in the presence of others. When we recognize and affirm his goodness, we are holding up his perfect moral nature for all to see. Praise benefits us because it takes our mind off our problems and needs and focuses on God's power, mercy, majesty, and love.

1 Chr 16:29 Genuine praise also involves ascribing glory to God. This means that we give credit where credit is due. Remember this in your worship and give God all the glory.

1 Chr 16:37 Asaph and his fellow Levites ministered in the Tabernacle, doing whatever was needed each day. To carry out God's work is not merely to engage in religious exercises. It includes other necessary tasks. Even if you don't have the opportunity to teach or preach, God can use you in the ministry. What needs to be done—cleaning, serving, singing, planning, administering? Look for ways to minister each day.

1 Chr 16:39 David brought the Ark to Jerusalem although the Tabernacle was still at Gibeon. His plan was to reunite the Tabernacle and Ark in a new Temple at Jerusalem that would then become Israel's only worship center. The Temple, however, was not built until Solomon's time. In the meantime, Israel had two worship centers and two high priests (1 Chr 15:11), one at Gibeon and one at Jerusalem.

▸ **1 CHRONICLES 16:37-42 *(cont.)***

to minister before the LORD. 40They sacrificed the
regular burnt offerings to the LORD each morning
and evening on the altar set aside for that purpose,
obeying everything written in the Law of the LORD,
as he had commanded Israel. 41David also appointed
Heman, Jeduthun, and the others chosen by name to
give thanks to the LORD, for "his faithful love endures
forever." 42They used their trumpets, cymbals, and
other instruments to accompany their songs of praise
to God.* And the sons of Jeduthun were appointed as
gatekeepers.

1 Chr 16:42 Or *to accompany the sacred music;* or *to accompany singing to God.*

David Returns Home PARALLEL ●●

2 SAMUEL 6:19b-23 ●●

Then all the people returned to their homes.
20When David returned home to bless his own family, Michal, the daughter of Saul, came out to meet
him. She said in disgust, "How distinguished the king
of Israel looked today, shamelessly exposing himself
to the servant girls like any vulgar person might do!"
21David retorted to Michal, "I was dancing before
the LORD, who chose me above your father and all his
family! He appointed me as the leader of Israel, the
people of the LORD, so I celebrate before the LORD.

MICHAL

Sometimes love is not enough—especially if that love is little more than the strong emotional attraction that grows between a hero and an admirer. To Michal, Saul's daughter, the courageous young David must have seemed like a dream come true. Her feelings about this hero gradually became obvious to others, and eventually, her father heard about her love for David. He saw this as an opportunity to get rid of his rival for the people's loyalty. He promised Michal's hand in marriage in exchange for David's success in the impossible task of killing 100 Philistines. But David was victorious, and so Saul lost a daughter and saw his rival become even more popular with the people. • Michal's love for David did not have time to be tested by the realities of marriage. Instead, she became involved in saving David's life. Her quick thinking helped him escape, but it resulted in Saul's anger and her separation from David. Her father gave her to another man, Palti, but David eventually took her back. • Unlike her brother Jonathan, Michal did not have the kind of deep relationship with God that would have helped her through the difficulties in her life. Instead, she became bitter. She could not share David's joyful worship of God, so she hated it. As a result, she never bore David any children. • Beyond feeling sorry for her, we need to see Michal as a person mirroring our own tendencies. How quickly and easily we become bitter with life's unexpected turns. But bitterness cannot remove or change the bad things that have happened. Often bitterness only makes a bad situation worse. On the other hand, a willingness to respond to God gives him the opportunity to bring good out of the difficult situations. That willingness has two parts: asking God for his guidance and looking for that guidance in his Word.

Strengths and accomplishments	• Loved David and became his first wife • Saved David's life • Could think and act quickly when it was needed
Weaknesses and mistakes	• Lied under pressure • Allowed herself to become bitter over her circumstances • In her unhappiness, she hated David for loving God
Lessons from her life	• We are not as responsible for what happens to us as we are for how we respond to our circumstances • Disobedience to God almost always harms others as well as harming us
Vital statistics	• Occupations: Daughter of King Saul, wife of King David • Relatives: Parents: Saul and Ahinoam. Brothers: Jonathan, Malkishua, Abinadab, Ishbosheth (and possibly Ishvi). Sister: Merab. Husbands: David, Palti.
Key verse	"But as the Ark of the LORD entered the City of David, Michal, the daughter of Saul, looked down from her window. When she saw King David leaping and dancing before the LORD, she was filled with contempt for him" (2 Sam 6:16).

Michal's story is told in 1 Samuel 14—2 Samuel 6. She is also mentioned in 1 Chronicles 15:29.

2 Sam 6:20ff Michal was David's first wife, but here she is called daughter of Saul, possibly to show how similar her attitude was to her father's. Her contempt for David probably did not start with David's grand entrance into the city (2 Sam 6:16). Perhaps she thought it was undignified to be so concerned with public worship at a time when it was so unimportant in the kingdom. Or maybe she thought it was not fitting for a king to display such emotion. She may have resented David's taking her from Palti (see the note on 2 Sam 3:13-14, p. 483). Whatever the reason, this contempt she felt toward her husband escalated into a difficult confrontation, and Michal ended up childless for life. Feelings of bitterness and resentment that go unchecked will destroy a relationship. Deal with your feelings before they escalate into open warfare.

2 Sam 7:1ff This chapter records the covenant God made with David, promising to carry on David's line forever. This promise would be fully realized in the birth of Jesus Christ. Although the word *covenant* is not specifically stated in the Bible text here, it is used elsewhere to describe this occasion (2 Sam 23:5; Ps 89:28, 34).

2 Sam 7:2 This is the first time Nathan the prophet is mentioned. God made certain that a prophet was living during the reign of each of the kings of Israel. The prophet's main tasks were to urge the people to follow God and to communicate God's laws and plans to the king. Most of the kings rejected the prophets God sent. But at least God had given them the opportunity to listen and obey. In earlier years, judges and priests had the role of prophets. Samuel served as judge, priest, and prophet, bridging the gap between the period of the judges and the monarchy.

2 Sam 7:5 In this message from Nathan, God is saying that he doesn't want David to build a temple for him. God told David that his job was to unify and lead Israel and to destroy its enemies. Therefore, David made the plans and collected the materials so that his son Solomon could begin work on the Temple as soon as he became king (1 Kgs 5–7). David accepted his part in God's plan and did not try to go beyond it. Sometimes

[22]Yes, and I am willing to look even more foolish than
this, even to be humiliated in my own eyes! But those
servant girls you mentioned will indeed think I am
distinguished!" [23]So Michal, the daughter of Saul, remained childless throughout her entire life.

1 CHRONICLES 16:43
Then all the people returned to their homes, and David
turned and went home to bless his own family.

The LORD's Covenant Promise to David PARALLEL

2 SAMUEL 7:1-17
When King David was settled in his palace and the
LORD had given him rest from all the surrounding
enemies, [2]the king summoned Nathan the prophet.
"Look," David said, "I am living in a beautiful cedar
palace,* but the Ark of God is out there in a tent!"
[3]Nathan replied to the king, "Go ahead and do
whatever you have in mind, for the LORD is with you."
[4]But that same night the LORD said to Nathan,

[5]"Go and tell my servant David, 'This is what the
LORD has declared: Are you the one to build a
house for me to live in? [6]I have never lived in
a house, from the day I brought the Israelites
out of Egypt until this very day. I have always
moved from one place to another with a tent
and a Tabernacle as my dwelling. [7]Yet no matter
where I have gone with the Israelites, I have never
once complained to Israel's tribal leaders, the
shepherds of my people Israel. I have never asked
them, "Why haven't you built me a beautiful
cedar house?"'

[8]"Now go and say to my servant David, 'This is
what the LORD of Heaven's Armies has declared:
I took you from tending sheep in the pasture and
selected you to be the leader of my people Israel.
[9]I have been with you wherever you have gone,
and I have destroyed all your enemies before your
eyes. Now I will make your name as famous as
anyone who has ever lived on the earth! [10]And
I will provide a homeland for my people Israel,
planting them in a secure place where they will
never be disturbed. Evil nations won't oppress
them as they've done in the past, [11]starting from
the time I appointed judges to rule my people
Israel. And I will give you rest from all your
enemies.

"'Furthermore, the LORD declares that he will
make a house for you—a dynasty of kings! [12]For
when you die and are buried with your ancestors,
I will raise up one of your descendants, your own
offspring, and I will make his kingdom strong.
[13]He is the one who will build a house—a temple—
for my name. And I will secure his royal throne
forever. [14]I will be his father, and he will be my
son. If he sins, I will correct and discipline him
with the rod, like any father would do. [15]But my

2 Sm 7:2 Hebrew *a house of cedar.*

1000 BC *Mayans settle in the Yucatan peninsula*

God says no to our plans. When he does, we should utilize the other opportunities he gives us.

2 Sam 7:8-16 David's request was good, but God said no. This does not mean that God rejected David. In fact, God was planning to do something even greater in David's life than allowing him the prestige of building the Temple. Although God turned down David's request, he promised to continue the house (or dynasty) of David forever. David's earthly dynasty ended four centuries later, but Jesus Christ, a direct descendant of David, was the ultimate fulfillment of this promise (Acts 2:22-36). Christ will reign for eternity: now—in his spiritual kingdom and in heaven; and later—on earth, in the new Jerusalem (Luke 1:30-33; Rev 21). Have you prayed with good intentions, only to have God say no? This might be God's way of directing you to a greater purpose in your life. Accepting God's no requires as great a faith as carrying out his yes.

COVENANTS

A covenant is a legally binding obligation (promise). Throughout history God has made covenants with his people—he would keep his side if they would keep theirs. Here are seven covenants found in the Bible.

Name and Reference	*God's Promise*	*Sign*
In Eden Gen 3:15	Satan and mankind will be enemies.	Pain of childbirth
Noah Gen 9:8-17	God would never again destroy the earth with a flood.	Rainbow
Abraham Gen 15:12-21; 17:1-14	Abraham's descendants would become a great nation if they obeyed God. God would be their God forever.	Smoking firepot and flaming torch
At Mount Sinai Exod 19:5-6	Israel would be God's special people, a holy nation. But they would have to keep their part of the covenant—obedience.	The Exodus
The Priesthood Num 25:10-13	Aaron's descendants would be priests forever.	The Aaronic priesthood
David 2 Sam 7:13; 23:5	Salvation would come through David's line through the birth of the Messiah.	David's line continued, and the Messiah was born a descendant of David
New Covenant Heb 8:6-13	Forgiveness and salvation are available through faith in Christ.	Christ's resurrection

▶ **2 SAMUEL 7:1-17 *(cont.)***
favor will not be taken from him as I took it from
Saul, whom I removed from your sight. [16]Your
house and your kingdom will continue before
me* for all time, and your throne will be secure
forever.'"

[17]So Nathan went back to David and told him everything the LORD had said in this vision.

1 CHRONICLES 17:1-15
When David was settled in his palace, he summoned
Nathan the prophet. "Look," David said, "I am living
in a beautiful cedar palace,* but the Ark of the LORD's
Covenant is out there under a tent!"

[2]Nathan replied to David, "Do whatever you have in
mind, for God is with you."

[3]But that same night God said to Nathan,

[4]"Go and tell my servant David, 'This is what the
LORD has declared: You are not the one to build
a house for me to live in. [5]I have never lived in a
house, from the day I brought the Israelites out
of Egypt until this very day. My home has always
been a tent, moving from one place to another in
a Tabernacle. [6]Yet no matter where I have gone
with the Israelites, I have never once complained
to Israel's leaders,* the shepherds of my people.
I have never asked them, "Why haven't you built
me a beautiful cedar house?"'

[7]"Now go and say to my servant David, 'This is
what the LORD of Heaven's Armies has declared:
I took you from tending sheep in the pasture and
selected you to be the leader of my people Israel.
[8]I have been with you wherever you have gone,
and I have destroyed all your enemies before
your eyes. Now I will make your name as famous
as anyone who has ever lived on the earth! [9]And
I will provide a homeland for my people Israel,
planting them in a secure place where they will
never be disturbed. Evil nations won't oppress
them as they've done in the past, [10]starting from
the time I appointed judges to rule my people
Israel. And I will defeat all your enemies.

"'Furthermore, I declare that the LORD will
build a house for you—a dynasty of kings! [11]For
when you die and join your ancestors, I will raise
up one of your descendants, one of your sons,
and I will make his kingdom strong. [12]He is the
one who will build a house—a temple—for me.
And I will secure his throne forever. [13]I will be
his father, and he will be my son. I will never take
my favor from him as I took it from the one who
ruled before you. [14]I will confirm him as king
over my house and my kingdom for all time, and
his throne will be secure forever.'"

[15]So Nathan went back to David and told him everything the LORD had said in this vision.

David's Prayer of Thanks

PARALLEL

2 SAMUEL 7:18-29
Then King David went in and sat before the LORD and
prayed,

"Who am I, O Sovereign LORD, and what is my
family, that you have brought me this far? [19]And
now, Sovereign LORD, in addition to everything
else, you speak of giving your servant a lasting
dynasty! Do you deal with everyone this way,
O Sovereign LORD?*

[20]"What more can I say to you? You know
what your servant is really like, Sovereign LORD.
[21]Because of your promise and according to your
will, you have done all these great things and have
made them known to your servant.

[22]"How great you are, O Sovereign LORD! There
is no one like you. We have never even heard
of another God like you! [23]What other nation
on earth is like your people Israel? What other
nation, O God, have you redeemed from slavery
to be your own people? You made a great name
for yourself when you redeemed your people
from Egypt. You performed awesome miracles

2 Sm 7:16 As in Greek version and some Hebrew manuscripts; Masoretic Text reads *before you.* **1 Chr 17:1** Hebrew *a house of cedar.* **1 Chr 17:6** As in Greek version (see also 2 Sam 7:7); Hebrew reads *judges.* **2 Sm 7:19** Or *This is your instruction for all humanity, O Sovereign LORD.*

1 Chr 17:1 David felt disturbed that the Ark, the symbol of God's presence, sat in a tent while he lived in a beautiful palace. David's desire was right, but his timing was wrong. God told David not to build his Temple (1 Chr 17:3-4), and David was willing to abide by God's timing. If you live in comparative luxury while God's work, house, or ministers are lacking, perhaps God wants you to change the situation. Like David, take action to correct the imbalance, but be willing to move according to God's timing and direction.

1 Chr 17:3-14 God did not want a warrior to build his Temple (1 Chr 28:3; 1 Kgs 5:3), and David had shed much blood in unifying the nation. So the honor of building the Temple would go to David's son Solomon. David would pass on to Solomon a peaceful and united kingdom, ready to begin work on a beautiful Temple.

1 Chr 17:10 God promised to subdue David's enemies. First Chronicles 18–20 tells how God kept that promise.

1 Chr 17:12-14 Why, after this eternal promise, were the Israelites eventually taken from the Promised Land into captivity? The promise to David had two parts. The first part was conditional: As long as David's descendants followed God's laws and honored him, they would continually be on the throne of Israel. The second part was unconditional: A son of David would occupy his throne forever. This was Jesus the Messiah. The first part of the promise was based on the faithful obedience of David's descendants. The second part would come true regardless of the way his descendants acted.

2 Sam 7:18ff This section records David's prayer expressing his humble acceptance of God's promise to extend his dynasty forever. David realized that these blessings were given to him and his descendants in order that Israel might benefit from them. They would help fulfill God's greater purpose and promises that through the nation the whole world would be blessed (Gen 12:1-3).

and drove out the nations and gods that stood
in their way.* 24You made Israel your very
own people forever, and you, O LORD, became
their God.

25"And now, O LORD God, I am your servant;
do as you have promised concerning me and
my family. Confirm it as a promise that will
last forever. 26And may your name be honored
forever so that everyone will say, 'The LORD of
Heaven's Armies is God over Israel!' And may
the house of your servant David continue before
you forever.

27"O LORD of Heaven's Armies, God of Israel, I
have been bold enough to pray this prayer to you
because you have revealed all this to your servant,
saying, 'I will build a house for you—a dynasty of
kings!' 28For you are God, O Sovereign LORD. Your
words are truth, and you have promised these
good things to your servant. 29And now, may it
please you to bless the house of your servant, so
that it may continue forever before you. For you
have spoken, and when you grant a blessing to
your servant, O Sovereign LORD, it is an eternal
blessing!"

1 CHRONICLES 17:16-27

Then King David went in and sat before the LORD and
prayed,

"Who am I, O LORD God, and what is my family,
that you have brought me this far? 17And now,
O God, in addition to everything else, you speak
of giving your servant a lasting dynasty! You
speak as though I were someone very great,*
O LORD God!

18"What more can I say to you about the way
you have honored me? You know what your
servant is really like. 19For the sake of your
servant, O LORD, and according to your will, you
have done all these great things and have made
them known.

20"O LORD, there is no one like you. We have
never even heard of another God like you!
21What other nation on earth is like your people
Israel? What other nation, O God, have you
redeemed from slavery to be your own people?
You made a great name for yourself when
you redeemed your people from Egypt. You
performed awesome miracles and drove out the
nations that stood in their way. 22You chose Israel
to be your very own people forever, and you,
O LORD, became their God.

23"And now, O LORD, I am your servant; do as
you have promised concerning me and my family.
May it be a promise that will last forever. 24And
may your name be established and honored
forever so that everyone will say, 'The LORD of
Heaven's Armies, the God of Israel, is Israel's
God!' And may the house of your servant David
continue before you forever.

25"O my God, I have been bold enough to
pray to you because you have revealed to your
servant that you will build a house for him—a
dynasty of kings! 26For you are God, O LORD. And
you have promised these good things to your
servant. 27And now, it has pleased you to bless
the house of your servant, so that it will continue
forever before you. For when you grant a blessing,
O LORD, it is an eternal blessing!"

2 Sm 7:23 As in Greek version (see also 1 Chr 17:21); Hebrew reads *You made a great name for yourself and performed awesome miracles for your land. You did this in the sight of your people, whom you redeemed from Egypt, from nations and their gods.* **1 Chr 17:17** The meaning of the Hebrew is uncertain.

1 Chr 17:16-20 God told David that Solomon would be given the honor of building the Temple. David responded with deep humility, not resentment. This king who had conquered his enemies and was loved by his people said, "Who am I . . . that you have brought me this far?" David recognized that *God* was the true king. God has done just as much for us, and he plans to do even more! We should humble ourselves and give glory to God, saying like David, "O LORD, there is no one like you." When God chooses someone else to implement your ideas, will you respond with such humility?

1 Chr 17:16-27 David prayed by humbling himself (1 Chr 17:16-18), praising God (1 Chr 17:19-20), recognizing God's blessings (1 Chr 17:21-22), and accepting God's decisions, promises, and commands (1 Chr 17:23-24). Sometimes we are quick to make requests to God and to tell him our troubles, but these other dimensions of prayer can deepen our spiritual life. Take time to praise God, to count his blessings, and to affirm your commitment to do what he has already said to do.

1 Chr 17:21 David's reference to Israel's exodus from Egypt would have had special significance to the original readers of 1 Chronicles, who were either beginning or had just completed a second great exodus back to Israel from captivity in Babylon. Remembering God's promises, mercy, and protection during the first Exodus would have encouraged the exiles returning once again to Israel, just as God had promised.

3. DAVID CONQUERS THE SURROUNDING NATIONS

God gave David and the armies of Israel swift victory over the nations that were threatening Israel. Under David's leadership, the nation was finally completing the mission that God had given them centuries earlier: to possess the land he had promised them by driving out the Canaanite nations.

David's Military Victories PARALLEL

2 SAMUEL 8:1-18

After this, David defeated and subdued the Philistines by conquering Gath, their largest town.* 2David also conquered the land of Moab. He made the people lie down on the ground in a row, and he measured them off in groups with a length of rope. He measured off two groups to be executed for every one group to be spared. The Moabites who were spared became David's subjects and paid him tribute money.

3David also destroyed the forces of Hadadezer son of Rehob, king of Zobah, when Hadadezer marched out to strengthen his control along the Euphrates River. 4David captured 1,000 chariots, 7,000 charioteers,* and 20,000 foot soldiers. He crippled all the chariot horses except enough for 100 chariots.

5When Arameans from Damascus arrived to help King Hadadezer, David killed 22,000 of them. 6Then he placed several army garrisons in Damascus, the Aramean capital, and the Arameans became David's subjects and paid him tribute money. So the LORD made David victorious wherever he went.

7David brought the gold shields of Hadadezer's officers to Jerusalem, 8along with a large amount of bronze from Hadadezer's towns of Tebah* and Berothai.

9When King Toi of Hamath heard that David had destroyed the entire army of Hadadezer, 10he sent his son Joram to congratulate King David for his successful campaign. Hadadezer and Toi had been enemies and were often at war. Joram presented David with many gifts of silver, gold, and bronze.

11King David dedicated all these gifts to the LORD, as he did with the silver and gold from the other nations he had defeated—12from Edom,* Moab, Ammon, Philistia, and Amalek—and from Hadadezer son of Rehob, king of Zobah.

13So David became even more famous when he returned from destroying 18,000 Edomites* in the Valley of Salt. 14He placed army garrisons throughout Edom, and all the Edomites became David's subjects. In fact, the LORD made David victorious wherever he went.

15So David reigned over all Israel and did what was just and right for all his people. 16Joab son of Zeruiah was commander of the army. Jehoshaphat son of Ahilud was the royal historian. 17Zadok son of Ahitub and

2 Sm 8:1 Hebrew *by conquering Metheg-ammah,* a name that means "the bridle," possibly referring to the size of the town or the tribute money taken from it. Compare 1 Chr 18:1. **2 Sm 8:4** As in Dead Sea Scrolls and Greek version (see also 1 Chr 18:4); Masoretic Text reads *captured 1,700 charioteers.* **2 Sm 8:8** As in some Greek manuscripts (see also 1 Chr 18:8); Hebrew reads *Betah.* **2 Sm 8:12** As in a few Hebrew manuscripts and Greek and Syriac versions (see also 8:14; 1 Chr 18:11); most Hebrew manuscripts read *Aram.* **2 Sm 8:13** As in a few Hebrew manuscripts and Greek and Syriac versions (see also 8:14; 1 Chr 18:12); most Hebrew manuscripts read *Arameans.*

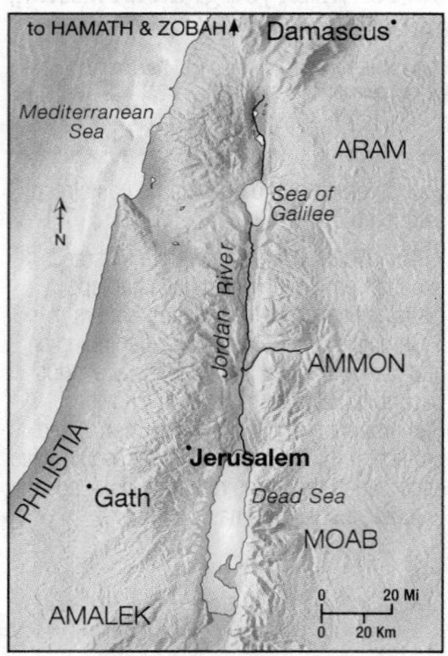

***DAVID'S ENEMIES** David wanted to complete the conquest of Canaan begun by Joshua. He defeated the Jebusites at Jerusalem and the Philistines in the vicinity of Gath. The Ammonites, Arameans, and Moabites became his subjects. He put garrisons in Edom and levied a tax upon them.*

2 Sam 8:1-5 Part of God's covenant with David included the promise that the Israelites' enemies would be defeated and would no longer oppress them (2 Sam 7:10-11). God fulfilled this promise by helping David defeat the opposing nations. Several enemies are listed in this chapter: (1) The Moabites, descendants of Lot who lived east of the Dead Sea. They posed a constant military and religious threat to Israel (Num 25:1-3; Judg 3:12-30; 1 Sam 14:47). David seemed to have a good relationship with the Moabites at one time; David's great-grandmother Ruth had been from Moab. (2) King Hadadezer of Zobah. His defeat at David's hands fulfilled God's promise to Abraham that Israel would control the land as far north as the Euphrates River (Gen 15:18). (3) The Edomites, descendants of Esau (Gen 36:1), were also archenemies of Israel (see 2 Kgs 8:20; Jer 49:7-22; Ezek 25:12-14; and the note on Gen 36:9, p. 70).

2 Sam 8:6 The *tribute money* was the tax levied on conquered nations. The tax helped to support Israel's government and demonstrated that the conquered nation was under Israel's control.

2 Sam 8:15 David pleased the people (2 Sam 3:36) not because he tried to please them but because he tried to please God. Often those who try the hardest to become popular never make it. But the praise of people is not that important. Don't spend your time devising ways to become accepted in the public eye. Instead, strive to do what is right, and both God and people will respect your convictions.

2 Sam 8:15 King David's reign was characterized by doing what was "just and right." David was fair in interpreting the law, administering punishment with mercy, respecting people's rights, and recognizing people's duty toward God. Is it any wonder that almost everyone trusted and followed David? Why was it good for David to pursue justice? (1) It was God's command (Deut 16:18-20) and in keeping with his character (Deut 32:4). God's laws were meant to establish a just society. (2) It was in the nation's best interest because times would arise when each individual would need justice. Justice should characterize the way you relate to people. Make sure you are fair in the way you treat them.

1 Chr 18:2 According to 2 Samuel 8:1-2, David killed two-thirds of the people of Moab. His ancestor Ruth was originally from the land of Moab.

1 Chr 18:6, 14 David was a victorious and fair ruler. We see in David's glowing success

Ahimelech son of Abiathar were the priests. Seraiah
was the court secretary. 18Benaiah son of Jehoiada was
captain of the king's bodyguard.* And David's sons
served as priestly leaders.*

1 CHRONICLES 18:1-17

After this, David defeated and subdued the Philistines
by conquering Gath and its surrounding towns. 2David
also conquered the land of Moab, and the Moabites
who were spared became David's subjects and paid
him tribute money.

3David also destroyed the forces of Hadadezer,
king of Zobah, as far as Hamath,* when Hadadezer
marched out to strengthen his control along the Euphrates River. 4David captured 1,000 chariots, 7,000
charioteers, and 20,000 foot soldiers. He crippled all
the chariot horses except enough for 100 chariots.

5When Arameans from Damascus arrived to help
King Hadadezer, David killed 22,000 of them. 6Then
he placed several army garrisons* in Damascus, the
Aramean capital, and the Arameans became David's
subjects and paid him tribute money. So the LORD
made David victorious wherever he went.

7David brought the gold shields of Hadadezer's
officers to Jerusalem, 8along with a large amount of
bronze from Hadadezer's towns of Tebah* and Cun.
Later Solomon melted the bronze and molded it into
the great bronze basin called the Sea, the pillars, and
the various bronze articles used at the Temple.

9When King Toi* of Hamath heard that David had
destroyed the entire army of King Hadadezer of Zobah,
10he sent his son Joram* to congratulate King David for
his successful campaign. Hadadezer and Toi had been
enemies and were often at war. Joram presented David
with many gifts of gold, silver, and bronze.

11King David dedicated all these gifts to the LORD,
along with the silver and gold he had taken from the
other nations—from Edom, Moab, Ammon, Philistia,
and Amalek.

12Abishai son of Zeruiah destroyed 18,000 Edomites
in the Valley of Salt. 13He placed army garrisons in
Edom, and all the Edomites became David's subjects. In
fact, the LORD made David victorious wherever he went.

14So David reigned over all Israel and did what was
just and right for all his people. 15Joab son of Zeruiah
was commander of the army. Jehoshaphat son of Ahilud was the royal historian. 16Zadok son of Ahitub and
Ahimelech* son of Abiathar were the priests. Seraiah*
was the court secretary. 17Benaiah son of Jehoiada was
captain of the king's bodyguard.* And David's sons
served as the king's chief assistants.

Psalm 60

THEME: Real help comes from God alone. When a situation seems out of control, we can trust God to do mighty things.

AUTHOR: David, when Israel was away at war with Aram in the north, and Edom invaded Judah from the south

For the choir director: A psalm of David useful for teaching, regarding the time David fought Aram-naharaim and Aram-zobah, and Joab returned and killed 12,000 Edomites in the Valley of Salt. To be sung to the tune "Lily of the Testimony."*

1 You have rejected us, O God, and broken our
defenses.
You have been angry with us; now restore
us to your favor.
2 You have shaken our land and split it open.
Seal the cracks, for the land trembles.
3 You have been very hard on us,
making us drink wine that sent us reeling.
4 But you have raised a banner for those who
fear you—
a rallying point in the face of attack.
Interlude
5 Now rescue your beloved people.
Answer and save us by your power.

2 Sm 8:18a Hebrew *of the Kerethites and Pelethites.* **2 Sm 8:18b** Hebrew *David's sons were priests;* compare parallel text at 1 Chr 18:17. **1 Chr 18:3** The meaning of the Hebrew is uncertain. **1 Chr 18:6** As in Greek version and Latin Vulgate (see also 2 Sam 8:6); Hebrew lacks *several army garrisons.* **1 Chr 18:8** Hebrew reads *Tibhath,* a variant spelling of Tebah; compare parallel text at 2 Sam 8:8. **1 Chr 18:9** As in parallel text at 2 Sam 8:9; Hebrew reads *Tou;* also in 18:10. **1 Chr 18:10** As in parallel text at 2 Sam 8:10; Hebrew reads *Hadoram,* a variant spelling of Joram. **1 Chr 18:16a** As in some Hebrew manuscripts, Syriac version, and Latin Vulgate (see also 2 Sam 8:17); most Hebrew manuscripts read *Abimelech.* **1 Chr 18:16b** As in parallel text at 2 Sam 8:17; Hebrew reads *Shavsha.* **1 Chr 18:17** Hebrew *of the Kerethites and Pelethites.* **Ps 60:TITLE** Hebrew *miktam.* This may be a literary or musical term.

a hint of what Christ's reign will be like—complete victory and justice. If David's glory was great, how much greater will Christ's glory be! The great news for us is that we can be rightly related to Jesus Christ through faith. One day we will share in his glory as we reign with him.

1 Chr 18:9-11 When David received gifts from King Toi, he dedicated them to God, realizing that they had come from God and were to be used for him. It is easy to think that our financial and material blessings are the result of our own skill and hard work rather than coming from a loving God (Jas 1:17). What has God given you? Dedicate all your gifts and resources to him, and use them for his service. He will lead you in the method you should use. The first step is to be willing. The second step is to follow up your willingness with action.

1 Chr 18:13 The list of battles in this chapter shows how God gave David victory after victory. Unbelieving people think that victory comes from their own skill plus a little luck. Just as David acknowledged God's role in his success, so should we. Don't take credit for the work God does.

Ps 60:1ff This psalm gives us information about David's reign not found in the books of 1 and 2 Samuel or 1 and 2 Chronicles. Although the setting of the psalm is found in 2 Samuel 8, that passage makes no reference to the fact that David's forces had met stiff resistance (Ps 60:1-3) and apparently even a temporary defeat (Ps 60:9-10). The closer we get to God, the more our enemies will attack us because we threaten their evil and selfish way of living.

Ps 60:3 Instead of the wine of blessing, God had given them the cup of his judgment. God's rejection was intended to bring them back to himself.

▸ **PSALM 60** ***(cont.)***

6 God has promised this by his holiness*:
"I will divide up Shechem with joy.
I will measure out the valley of Succoth.
7 Gilead is mine,
and Manasseh, too.
Ephraim, my helmet, will produce my warriors,
and Judah, my scepter, will produce my kings.
8 But Moab, my washbasin, will become my servant,
and I will wipe my feet on Edom
and shout in triumph over Philistia."

9 Who will bring me into the fortified city?
Who will bring me victory over Edom?
10 Have you rejected us, O God?
Will you no longer march with our armies?
11 Oh, please help us against our enemies,
for all human help is useless.
12 With God's help we will do mighty things,
for he will trample down our foes.

David's Kindness to Mephibosheth

2 SAMUEL 9:1-13

One day David asked, "Is anyone in Saul's family still
alive—anyone to whom I can show kindness for Jonathan's sake?" 2He summoned a man named Ziba,
who had been one of Saul's servants. "Are you Ziba?"
the king asked.

"Yes sir, I am," Ziba replied.

3The king then asked him, "Is anyone still alive from
Saul's family? If so, I want to show God's kindness to
them."

Ziba replied, "Yes, one of Jonathan's sons is still
alive. He is crippled in both feet."

4"Where is he?" the king asked.

"In Lo-debar," Ziba told him, "At the home of Makir
son of Ammiel."

5So David sent for him and brought him from
Makir's home. 6His name was Mephibosheth*; he was
Jonathan's son and Saul's grandson. When he came to
David, he bowed low to the ground in deep respect.
David said, "Greetings, Mephibosheth."

Mephibosheth replied, "I am your servant."

7"Don't be afraid!" David said. "I intend to show
kindness to you because of my promise to your father,
Jonathan. I will give you all the property that once
belonged to your grandfather Saul, and you will eat
here with me at the king's table!"

8Mephibosheth bowed respectfully and exclaimed,
"Who is your servant, that you should show such kindness to a dead dog like me?"

9Then the king summoned Saul's servant Ziba and
said, "I have given your master's grandson everything
that belonged to Saul and his family. 10You and your
sons and servants are to farm the land for him to produce food for your master's household.* But Mephibosheth, your master's grandson, will eat here at my
table." (Ziba had fifteen sons and twenty servants.)

11Ziba replied, "Yes, my lord the king; I am your
servant, and I will do all that you have commanded."
And from that time on, Mephibosheth ate regularly at
David's table,* like one of the king's own sons.

12Mephibosheth had a young son named Mica.
From then on, all the members of Ziba's household
were Mephibosheth's servants. 13And Mephibosheth,
who was crippled in both feet, lived in Jerusalem and
ate regularly at the king's table.

David Defeats the Ammonites PARALLEL

2 SAMUEL 10:1-19

Some time after this, King Nahash* of the Ammonites
died, and his son Hanun became king. 2David said, "I
am going to show loyalty to Hanun just as his father,
Nahash, was always loyal to me." So David sent ambassadors to express sympathy to Hanun about his
father's death.

Ps 60:6 Or *in his sanctuary.* **2 Sm 9:6** *Mephibosheth* is another name for Merib-baal. **2 Sm 9:10** As in Greek version; Hebrew reads *your master's grandson.* **2 Sm 9:11** As in Greek version; Hebrew reads *my table.* **2 Sm 10:1** As in parallel text at 1 Chr 19:1; Hebrew reads *the king.*

Ps 60:6-10 God said the cities and territories of Israel were his, and he knew the future of each of the nations. When the world seems out of control, we must remind ourselves that God owns the cities and knows the future of every nation. God is in control. With God's help, we will gain the victory.

Ps 60:8 David mentioned the enemy nations that surrounded Israel: Moab lay directly to the east, Edom to the south, and Philistia to the west. At the time this psalm was written, David was fighting Aram to the north. Although he was surrounded by enemies, David remembered that God had promised triumph over those nations. He knew that Israel's future was closely tied to God's reputation of keeping his promises.

2 Sam 9:1ff Most kings in David's day tried to wipe out the families of their rivals in order to prevent any descendants from seeking the throne. But David showed kindness to Mephibosheth, whose father was Jonathan and whose grandfather was King Saul. David was kind, partly because of his loyalty to God's previously anointed king (see the note on 1 Sam 24:5-6, p. 464); partly for political reasons—to unite Judah and Israel (see the notes on 2 Sam 3:13-14, p. 483, and 2 Sam 3:29, p. 484); and mainly because of his vow to show kindness to all of Jonathan's descendants (1 Sam 20:14-17).

2 Sam 9:3 How Mephibosheth became crippled is recorded in 2 Samuel 4:4. Mephibosheth was five years old when Saul and Jonathan died.

2 Sam 9:5-6 Mephibosheth was afraid to visit the king, who wanted to treat him like a prince. Although Mephibosheth feared for his life and may have felt unworthy, that didn't mean he should refuse David's gifts. When God graciously offers us forgiveness of sins and a place in heaven, we may feel unworthy, but we will receive these gifts if we accept them. A reception even warmer than the one David gave Mephibosheth awaits for all who receive God's gifts through trusting Jesus Christ—not because we deserve it but because of God's promise (Eph 2:8-9).

2 Sam 9:7 His treatment of Mephibosheth shows David's integrity as a leader who accepted his obligation to show love and mercy. His generous provision for Jonathan's son goes beyond any political benefit he might have received. Are you able to forgive those who have wronged you? Can you be generous to those less deserving? Each time we show compassion, our character is strengthened.

But when David's ambassadors arrived in the land
of Ammon, 3the Ammonite commanders said to Hanun, their master, "Do you really think these men are
coming here to honor your father? No! David has sent
them to spy out the city so they can come in and conquer it!" 4So Hanun seized David's ambassadors and
shaved off half of each man's beard, cut off their robes
at the buttocks, and sent them back to David in shame.
5When David heard what had happened, he sent
messengers to tell the men, "Stay at Jericho until your
beards grow out, and then come back." For they felt
deep shame because of their appearance.
6When the people of Ammon realized how seriously
they had angered David, they sent and hired 20,000
Aramean foot soldiers from the lands of Beth-rehob
and Zobah, 1,000 from the king of Maacah, and 12,000
from the land of Tob. 7When David heard about this,
he sent Joab and all his warriors to fight them. 8The
Ammonite troops came out and drew up their battle
lines at the entrance of the city gate, while the Arameans
from Zobah and Rehob and the men from Tob and Maacah positioned themselves to fight in the open fields.
9When Joab saw that he would have to fight on both
the front and the rear, he chose some of Israel's elite
troops and placed them under his personal command
to fight the Arameans in the fields. 10He left the rest of
the army under the command of his brother Abishai,
who was to attack the Ammonites. 11"If the Arameans
are too strong for me, then come over and help me,"
Joab told his brother. "And if the Ammonites are too
strong for you, I will come and help you. 12Be courageous! Let us fight bravely for our people and the cities
of our God. May the LORD's will be done."
13When Joab and his troops attacked, the Arameans
began to run away. 14And when the Ammonites saw
the Arameans running, they ran from Abishai and
retreated into the city. After the battle was over, Joab
returned to Jerusalem.
15The Arameans now realized that they were no
match for Israel. So when they regrouped, 16they were
joined by additional Aramean troops summoned by
Hadadezer from the other side of the Euphrates River.*
These troops arrived at Helam under the command
of Shobach, the commander of Hadadezer's forces.
17When David heard what was happening, he mobilized all Israel, crossed the Jordan River, and led the
army to Helam. The Arameans positioned themselves
in battle formation and fought against David. 18But
again the Arameans fled from the Israelites. This time
David's forces killed 700 charioteers and 40,000 foot
soldiers,* including Shobach, the commander of their
army. 19When all the kings allied with Hadadezer saw
that they had been defeated by Israel, they surrendered to Israel and became their subjects. After that,
the Arameans were afraid to help the Ammonites.

1 CHRONICLES 19:1-19

Some time after this, King Nahash of the Ammonites
died, and his son Hanun* became king. 2David said,
"I am going to show loyalty to Hanun because his

2 Sm 10:16 Hebrew *the river.* **2 Sm 10:18** As in some Greek manuscripts (see also 1 Chr 19:18); Hebrew reads *charioteers.* **1 Chr 19:1** As in parallel text at 2 Sam 10:1; Hebrew lacks *Hanun.*

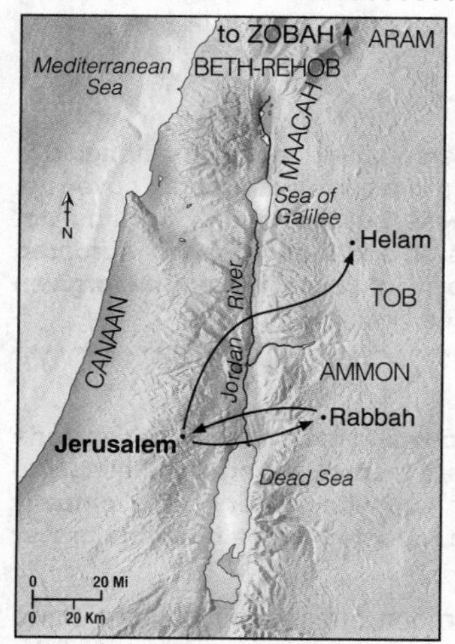

DAVID AND THE AMMONITES *Ammon gathered together its troops from the north; Joab brought the Israelite army to attack them near Rabbah. Joab returned to Jerusalem victorious, but the enemy recruited additional forces and regrouped at Helam. David himself led the next victorious attack.*

2 Sam 10:4-5 In Israelite culture, all men wore full beards. It was a sign of maturity and authority. To be forcibly shaven was embarrassing enough, but these men were also left half naked. Hanun's actions humiliated these men and insulted Israel.

2 Sam 10:6 Because Hanun listened to the wrong advice, he suspected the motives of the ambassadors and humiliated them. Then he realized that David was angry and immediately marshaled his forces for battle. Hanun should have thought through the advice more carefully; but even if he had not, he should have tried to negotiate with David. Instead, he refused to admit any fault and got ready for war. Often we respond angrily and defensively rather than admitting our mistakes, apologizing, and trying to defuse the other person's anger. Instead of fighting, we should seek peace.

2 Sam 10:12 There must be a balance in life between our actions and our faith in God. Joab said, "Let us fight bravely." In other words, they should do what they could, using their minds to figure out the best techniques and using their resources. But he also said, "May the LORD's will be done." He knew that the outcome was in God's hands. We should use our minds and our resources to obey God, while at the same time trusting God for the outcome.

1 Chr 19:1 The land of Ammon bordered Israel to the east. The nation had a sordid beginning: Its founding ancestor, Ben-ammi, was conceived through incest between Lot and his daughter (Gen 19:30-38). The Ammonites, who were constant enemies of Israel, reached their greatest strength in the days of the judges. David was the first military leader of Israel to crush them. They were unable to cause further trouble for many years.

1 Chr 19:2-3 Hanun misread David's intentions. He was overly suspicious and brought disaster upon himself. Because of past experiences, it is easy to be overly suspicious of others, questioning every move and second-guessing their motives. While we should be cautious and wise as we deal with people, we should not assume their every action is ill-intended.

▶ **1 CHRONICLES 19:1-19** ***(cont.)***
father, Nahash, was always loyal to me." So David sent messengers to express sympathy to Hanun about his father's death.

But when David's ambassadors arrived in the land of Ammon, [3]the Ammonite commanders said to Hanun, "Do you really think these men are coming here to honor your father? No! David has sent them to spy out the land so they can come in and conquer it!" [4]So Hanun seized David's ambassadors and shaved them, cut off their robes at the buttocks, and sent them back to David in shame.

[5]When David heard what had happened to the men, he sent messengers to tell them, "Stay at Jericho until your beards grow out, and then come back." For they felt deep shame because of their appearance.

[6]When the people of Ammon realized how seriously they had angered David, Hanun and the Ammonites sent 75,000 pounds* of silver to hire chariots and charioteers from Aram-naharaim, Aram-maacah, and Zobah. [7]They also hired 32,000 chariots and secured the support of the king of Maacah and his army. These forces camped at Medeba, where they were joined by the Ammonite troops that Hanun had recruited from his own towns. [8]When David heard about this, he sent Joab and all his warriors to fight them. [9]The Ammonite troops came out and drew up their battle lines at the entrance of the city, while the other kings positioned themselves to fight in the open fields.

[10]When Joab saw that he would have to fight on both the front and the rear, he chose some of Israel's elite troops and placed them under his personal command to fight the Arameans in the fields. [11]He left the rest of the army under the command of his brother Abishai, who was to attack the Ammonites. [12]"If the Arameans are too strong for me, then come over and help me," Joab told his brother. "And if the Ammonites are too strong for you, I will help you. [13]Be courageous! Let us fight bravely for our people and the cities of our God. May the LORD's will be done."

[14]When Joab and his troops attacked, the Arameans began to run away. [15]And when the Ammonites saw the Arameans running, they also ran from Abishai and retreated into the city. Then Joab returned to Jerusalem.

[16]The Arameans now realized that they were no match for Israel, so they sent messengers and summoned additional Aramean troops from the other side of the Euphrates River.* These troops were under the command of Shobach,* the commander of Hadadezer's forces.

[17]When David heard what was happening, he mobilized all Israel, crossed the Jordan River, and positioned his troops in battle formation. Then David engaged the Arameans in battle, and they fought against him. [18]But again the Arameans fled from the Israelites. This time David's forces killed 7,000 charioteers and 40,000 foot soldiers, including Shobach, the commander of their army. [19]When Hadadezer's allies saw that they had been defeated by Israel, they surrendered to David and became his subjects. After that, the Arameans were no longer willing to help the Ammonites.

1 Chr 19:6 Hebrew *1,000 talents* [34,000 kilograms]. **1 Chr 19:16a** Hebrew *the river.* **1 Chr 19:16b** As in parallel text at 2 Sam 10:16; Hebrew reads *Shophach;* also in 19:18.

D. David's Struggles

After restoring the nation to peace and great military power, David's personal life becomes entangled in sin. He commits adultery with Bathsheba and then orders her husband killed in an attempted cover-up. David deeply regretted what he had done and sought God's forgiveness, but the child of his sinful act died. Further, his sons were out of control: Amnon raped his half-sister, and then Absalom murdered Amnon before briefly taking the throne from his father and sending David into exile. We may be forgiven by God for our sins, but we will often experience harsh consequences.

1. DAVID AND BATHSHEBA

David seemed like the perfect king for Israel, following God and succeeding in battle. But the episode with Bathsheba is a wake-up call that even godly leaders need to guard themselves against falling into temptation. David compounded his sin of adultery by trying to cover it up with trickery and eventually murder. The prophet Nathan confronted David about his sin, and he repented with a beautiful prayer recorded in Psalm 51.

David Sins with Bathsheba PARALLEL

2 SAMUEL 11:1-13
In the spring of the year,* when kings normally go out to war, David sent Joab and the Israelite army to fight the Ammonites. They destroyed the Ammonite army and laid siege to the city of Rabbah. However, David stayed behind in Jerusalem.

[2]Late one afternoon, after his midday rest, David got out of bed and was walking on the roof of the palace. As he looked out over the city, he noticed a woman of unusual beauty taking a bath. [3]He sent someone to find out who she was, and he was told, "She is Bathsheba, the daughter of Eliam and the wife of Uriah the Hittite." [4]Then David sent messengers

2 Sm 11:1 Hebrew *At the turn of the year.* The first day of the year in the ancient Hebrew lunar calendar occurred in March or April.

to get her; and when she came to the palace, he slept
with her. She had just completed the purification rites
after having her menstrual period. Then she returned
home. 5Later, when Bathsheba discovered that she
was pregnant, she sent David a message, saying, "I'm
pregnant."
6Then David sent word to Joab: "Send me Uriah
the Hittite." So Joab sent him to David. 7When Uriah
arrived, David asked him how Joab and the army were
getting along and how the war was progressing. 8Then
he told Uriah, "Go on home and relax.*" David even
sent a gift to Uriah after he had left the palace. 9But
Uriah didn't go home. He slept that night at the palace
entrance with the king's palace guard.
10When David heard that Uriah had not gone home,
he summoned him and asked, "What's the matter?
Why didn't you go home last night after being away
for so long?"
11Uriah replied, "The Ark and the armies of Israel
and Judah are living in tents,* and Joab and my master's men are camping in the open fields. How could
I go home to wine and dine and sleep with my wife? I
swear that I would never do such a thing."
12"Well, stay here today," David told him, "And tomorrow you may return to the army." So Uriah stayed
in Jerusalem that day and the next. 13Then David invited him to dinner and got him drunk. But even then
he couldn't get Uriah to go home to his wife. Again
he slept at the palace entrance with the king's palace
guard.

2 Sm 11:8 Hebrew *and wash your feet*, an expression that may also have a connotation of ritualistic washing. **2 Sm 11:11** Or *at Succoth*.

1 Chr 19:6 Rather than admit his mistake and seek forgiveness and reconciliation, Hanun spent an enormous amount of money to cover up his error. His cover-up cost him dearly (1 Chr 20:1-3). It often costs more to cover up an error than to admit it honestly. Rather than compound an error through defensiveness, seek forgiveness and reconciliation as soon as you realize your mistake. You will save yourself and others a lot of pain and trouble.

2 Sam 11:1 Winter is the rainy season in Israel, the time when crops are planted. Spring was a good time to go to war because the roads were dry, making travel easier for troops, supply wagons, and chariots. In Israel, wheat and barley were ready to be harvested in the spring. These crops were an important food source for traveling armies.

2 Sam 11:1 This successful siege (see 2 Sam 12:26-27) put an end to the Ammonites' power. From this time on, the Ammonites were subject to Israel.

2 Sam 11:1ff In the episode with Bathsheba, David allowed himself to fall deeper and deeper into sin. (1) David abandoned his purpose by staying home from war (2 Sam 11:1). (2) He focused on his own desires (2 Sam 11:2). (3) When temptation came, he looked into it instead of turning away from it (2 Sam 11:3). (4) He sinned deliberately (2 Sam 11:4). (5) He tried to cover up his sin by deceiving others (2 Sam 11:6-15). (6) He committed murder to continue the cover-up (2 Sam 11:15, 17). Eventually David's sin was exposed (2 Sam 12:9) and punished (2 Sam 12:10-14). (7) The consequences of David's sin were far-reaching, affecting many others (2 Sam 11:17; 12:11, 14-15).

David could have chosen to stop and turn from evil at any stage along the way. But once sin gets started, it is difficult to stop (Jas 1:14-15). The deeper the mess, the less we want to admit having caused it. It's much easier to stop sliding down a hill when you are near the top than when you are halfway down. The best solution is to stop sin before it starts.

DAVID'S FAMILY TROUBLES

David's many wives caused him much grief. And as a result of David's sin with Bathsheba, God said that murder would be a constant threat in his family, his family would rebel, and someone else would sleep with his wives. All this happened as the prophet Nathan had predicted. The consequences of sin affect not only us but those we know and love. Remember that the next time you are tempted to sin.

Wife	Children	What Happened
Michal (Saul's daughter)	She was childless	David gave her five nephews to the Gibeonites to be killed because of Saul's sins.
Ahinoam (from Jezreel)	Amnon, David's firstborn	He raped Tamar, his half sister, and was later murdered by Absalom in revenge.
Maacah (daughter of King Talmai of Geshur)	Absalom, third son; Tamar, the only daughter mentioned by name	Absalom killed Amnon for raping Tamar and then fled to Geshur. Later he returned, only to rebel against David. He set up a tent on the roof and slept with 10 of his father's concubines there. His pride led to his death.
Haggith	Adonijah, fourth son. He was very handsome, but it is recorded that he was never disciplined	He set himself up as king before David's death. His plot was exposed, and David spared his life, but his half brother Solomon later had him executed.
Bathsheba	Unnamed infant son	The child died in fulfillment of God's punishment for David and Bathsheba's adultery.
Bathsheba	Solomon	He became the next king of Israel. Ironically Solomon's many wives caused his downfall.

2 Sam 11:3 See Bathsheba's Profile on p. 544.

2 Sam 11:3-4 As David looked from the roof of the palace, he saw a beautiful woman bathing, and he was filled with lust. David should have left the roof and fled the temptation. Instead, he entertained the temptation by inquiring about Bathsheba. The results were devastating.

To flee temptation, (1) ask God in earnest prayer to help you stay away from people, places, and situations that may tempt you. (2) Memorize and meditate on portions of Scripture that combat your specific weaknesses. At the root of most temptation is a real need or desire that God can fill, but we must trust in his timing. (3) Find another believer with whom you can openly share your struggles, and call this person for help when temptation strikes.

2 Sam 11:4 That Bathsheba had just completed the purification rites following menstruation means that she could not have already been pregnant by her own husband when David slept with her. Leviticus 15:19-30 gives more information on the purification rites Bathsheba had to perform.

1 CHRONICLES 20:1

In the spring of the year,* when kings normally go out to war, Joab led the Israelite army in successful attacks against the land of the Ammonites. In the process he laid siege to the city of Rabbah. However, David stayed behind in Jerusalem.

David Arranges for Uriah's Death

2 SAMUEL 11:14-27

So the next morning David wrote a letter to Joab and gave it to Uriah to deliver. [15]The letter instructed Joab, "Station Uriah on the front lines where the battle is fiercest. Then pull back so that he will be killed." [16]So Joab assigned Uriah to a spot close to the city wall where he knew the enemy's strongest men were fighting. [17]And when the enemy soldiers came out of the city to fight, Uriah the Hittite was killed along with several other Israelite soldiers.

[18]Then Joab sent a battle report to David. [19]He told his messenger, "Report all the news of the battle to the king. [20]But he might get angry and ask, 'Why did the troops go so close to the city? Didn't they know there would be shooting from the walls? [21]Wasn't Abimelech son of Gideon* killed at Thebez by a woman who threw a millstone down on him from the wall? Why would you get so close to the wall?' Then tell him, 'Uriah the Hittite was killed, too.'"

[22]So the messenger went to Jerusalem and gave a complete report to David. [23]"The enemy came out against us in the open fields," he said. "And as we chased them back to the city gate, [24]the archers on the wall shot arrows at us. Some of the king's men were killed, including Uriah the Hittite."

[25]"Well, tell Joab not to be discouraged," David said. "The sword devours this one today and that one tomorrow! Fight harder next time, and conquer the city!"

1 Chr 20:1 Hebrew *At the turn of the year.* The first day of the year in the ancient Hebrew lunar calendar occurred in March or April. **2 Sm 11:21** Hebrew *son of Jerub-besheth.* Jerub-besheth is a variation on the name Jerub-baal, which is another name for Gideon; see Judg 6:32.

1 Chr 20:1 David's adultery occurred at this time while he remained in Jerusalem instead of going to battle (2 Sam 11–12). This story may have been excluded from 1 Chronicles because the book was written to focus on God's long-term interest in Israel and on the Temple as a symbol of God's presence among them. The story of David and Bathsheba did not fit this purpose. The story of Absalom's rebellion, which occurred between this chapter and the next, was probably omitted for the same reason (2 Samuel 15–18).

1 Chr 20:1 Kings went out to battle following the spring harvest. At this time, farm work eased off, and the armies could live off the land. During the winter, they plotted and planned future conquests. Then, when fair weather permitted, their armies went to war. But David ignored this opportunity. He stayed home and sent Joab out to lead the army. It was during this time of inactivity that he sinned with Bathsheba. Look for the "springs" in your life, the times when God wants you to respond, take the initiative, and move out to do his will. It is during these critical times that we may be most sensitive to temptation. Resolve to take the action God has prescribed. Don't give temptation a foothold in your inactivity.

1 Chr 20:1 Rabbah was the capital of the Ammonites and is the site of modern Amman in Jordan.

2 Sam 11:15 David put both Bathsheba and Joab in difficult situations. Bathsheba knew it was wrong to commit adultery, but to refuse a king's request could mean punishment or death. Joab did not know why Uriah had to die, but it was obvious the king wanted him killed. We sometimes face situations with only two apparent choices, and both seem wrong. When that happens, we must not lose sight of what God wants. The answer may be to seek out more choices. By doing this, we are likely to find a choice that honors God.

NATHAN

This prophet lived up to the meaning of his name, "He [God] has given." He was a necessary and helpful gift from God to David. He served as God's spokesman to David and proved himself a fearless friend and counselor, always willing to speak the truth, even when he knew great pain would result. • In confronting David's multiple sin of coveting, adultery, and murder in his affair with Bathsheba, Nathan was able to help David see his own wrongdoing by showing that he would not have tolerated such actions from anyone else. David's repentance allowed Nathan to comfort him with the reality of God's forgiveness and at the same time remind him of the painful consequences his sin would bring. • Nathan's approach helps us judge our actions. How often do we make choices that we would condemn others for making? It is helpful to ask ourselves how God and others see our actions. Unfortunately, we have a huge capacity to lie to ourselves. God still provides two safeguards against self-deception: his Word and true friends. In each case, we get a view beyond ourselves. You are holding God's Word. Let it speak to you about yourself, even if the truth is painful. If you don't have a friend like Nathan, ask God for one. And ask God to use you as a suitable Nathan for someone else.

Strengths and accomplishments	• A trusted adviser to David • A prophet of God • A fearless but careful confronter • One of God's controls in David's life
Weakness and mistake	• His eagerness to see David build a temple for God in Jerusalem made him speak without God's instruction
Lessons from his life	• Don't be afraid to tell the truth to those we care about • A trustworthy companion is one of God's greatest gifts • God cares enough to find a way to communicate to us when we are in the wrong
Vital statistics	• Occupations: Prophet, royal adviser • Contemporaries: David, Bathsheba, Solomon, Zadok, Adonijah
Key verse	"So Nathan went back to David and told him everything the LORD had said" (2 Sam 7:17).

Nathan's story is told in 2 Samuel 7—1 Kings 1. He is also mentioned in 1 Chronicles 17:15; 2 Chronicles 9:29; 29:25.

2 Sam 11:25 David's response to Uriah's death seems flippant and insensitive. While he grieved deeply for Saul and Abner, his rivals (2 Sam 1; 3:31-39), he showed no

26 When Uriah's wife heard that her husband was
dead, she mourned for him. 27 When the period of
mourning was over, David sent for her and brought her
to the palace, and she became one of his wives. Then
she gave birth to a son. But the LORD was displeased
with what David had done.

Nathan Rebukes David

2 SAMUEL 12:1-12

So the LORD sent Nathan the prophet to tell David this
story: "There were two men in a certain town. One was
rich, and one was poor. 2 The rich man owned a great
many sheep and cattle. 3 The poor man owned nothing
but one little lamb he had bought. He raised that little
lamb, and it grew up with his children. It ate from the
man's own plate and drank from his cup. He cuddled
it in his arms like a baby daughter. 4 One day a guest arrived at the home of the rich man. But instead of killing
an animal from his own flock or herd, he took the poor
man's lamb and killed it and prepared it for his guest."
5 David was furious. "As surely as the LORD lives," he
vowed, "Any man who would do such a thing deserves
to die! 6 He must repay four lambs to the poor man for
the one he stole and for having no pity."
7 Then Nathan said to David, "You are that man! The
LORD, the God of Israel, says: I anointed you king of Israel and saved you from the power of Saul. 8 I gave you
your master's house and his wives and the kingdoms
of Israel and Judah. And if that had not been enough,
I would have given you much, much more. 9 Why, then,
have you despised the word of the LORD and done
this horrible deed? For you have murdered Uriah the
Hittite with the sword of the Ammonites and stolen
his wife. 10 From this time on, your family will live by
the sword because you have despised me by taking
Uriah's wife to be your own.
11 "This is what the LORD says: Because of what you
have done, I will cause your own household to rebel
against you. I will give your wives to another man before your very eyes, and he will go to bed with them in
public view. 12 You did it secretly, but I will make this
happen to you openly in the sight of all Israel."

Psalm 51

THEME: David's plea for mercy, forgiveness, and cleansing. God wants our hearts to be right with him.

AUTHOR: David

For the choir director: A psalm of David, regarding the time Nathan the prophet came to him after David had committed adultery with Bathsheba.

1 Have mercy on me, O God,
 because of your unfailing love.
Because of your great compassion,
 blot out the stain of my sins.
2 Wash me clean from my guilt.
 Purify me from my sin.
3 For I recognize my rebellion;
 it haunts me day and night.

David sins with Bathsheba

grief for Uriah, a good man with strong spiritual character. Why? David had become callous to his own sin. The only way he could cover up his first sin (adultery) was to sin again, and soon he no longer felt guilty for what he had done. Feelings are not reliable guides for determining right and wrong. Deliberate, repeated sinning had dulled David's sensitivity to God's laws and others' rights. The more you try to cover up a sin, the more insensitive you become toward it. Don't become hardened to sin, as David did. Confess your wrong actions to God before you forget they are sins.

2 Sam 12:1ff As a prophet, Nathan was required to confront sin, even the sin of a king. It took great courage, skill, and tact to speak to David in a way that would make him aware of his wrong actions. When you have to confront someone with unpleasant news, pray for courage, skill, and tact. If you want that person to respond constructively, think through what you are going to say. How you present your message may be as important as what you say. Season your words with wisdom.

2 Sam 12:5-6 It was a year later, and by then David had become so insensitive to his own sins that he didn't realize he was the villain in Nathan's story. The qualities we condemn in others are often our own character flaws. Which friends, associates, or family members do you find easy to criticize and hard to accept? Instead of trying to change them, ask God to help you understand their feelings and see your own flaws more clearly. You may discover that in condemning others, you have been condemning yourself.

2 Sam 12:10-12 The predictions in these verses came true. Because David murdered Uriah and stole his wife, murder was a constant threat in his family (2 Sam 13:26-30; 18:14-15; 1 Kgs 2:23-25); his household rebelled against him (2 Sam 15:13); and his wives were given to another in public view (2 Sam 16:20-23). Further, his first child by Bathsheba died (2 Sam 12:14, 18). If David had known the painful consequences of his sin, he might not have pursued the pleasures of the moment.

Ps 51:1ff This psalm expresses one of the clearest examples of repentance in all of Scripture. Countless broken sinners have found in these words an exquisite expression of their deeply felt need for God's mercy and forgiveness. David's confession has helped people examine excuses, halfhearted repentance, and lack of sorrow over sin that can keep them from experiencing pardon. David's words also demonstrate the place of hope within confession. Use this psalm as a starting point when dealing with a sense of distance or with guilt that is affecting your relationship with God. It will help you identify and rectify sin in your life through confession and repentance.

Ps 51:1-7 David was truly sorry for his adultery with Bathsheba and for murdering her husband to cover it up. He knew that his actions had hurt many people. But because David repented of those sins, God mercifully forgave him. No sin is too great to be forgiven! Do you feel that you could never come close to God because you have done something terrible? God can and will forgive you of any sin. While God forgives us, he does not always erase the natural consequences of our sin. David's life and family were never the same as a result of what he had done (see 2 Sam 12:1-23).

▸ **PSALM 51** ***(cont.)***

4 Against you, and you alone, have I sinned;
I have done what is evil in your sight.
You will be proved right in what you say,
and your judgment against me is just.*
5 For I was born a sinner—
yes, from the moment my mother
conceived me.
6 But you desire honesty from the womb,*
teaching me wisdom even there.
7 Purify me from my sins,* and I will
be clean;
wash me, and I will be whiter than
snow.
8 Oh, give me back my joy again;
you have broken me—
now let me rejoice.
9 Don't keep looking at my sins.
Remove the stain of my guilt.
10 Create in me a clean heart, O God.
Renew a loyal spirit within me.
11 Do not banish me from your presence,
and don't take your Holy Spirit* from me.
12 Restore to me the joy of your salvation,
and make me willing to obey you.
13 Then I will teach your ways to rebels,
and they will return to you.
14 Forgive me for shedding blood, O God
who saves;
then I will joyfully sing of your forgiveness.
15 Unseal my lips, O Lord,
that my mouth may praise you.

16 You do not desire a sacrifice, or I would
offer one.
You do not want a burnt offering.
17 The sacrifice you desire is a broken spirit.
You will not reject a broken and repentant
heart, O God.
18 Look with favor on Zion and help her;
rebuild the walls of Jerusalem.
19 Then you will be pleased with sacrifices offered
in the right spirit—
with burnt offerings and whole burnt
offerings.
Then bulls will again be sacrificed on
your altar.

Ps 51:4 Greek version reads *and you will win your case in court.* Compare Rom 3:4. **Ps 51:6** Or *from the heart;* Hebrew reads *in the inward parts.* **Ps 51:7** Hebrew *Purify me with the hyssop branch.* **Ps 51:11** Or *your spirit of holiness.*

Hyssop

In Psalm 51:7, David cries out to God to be purified from his sins, and he uses the metaphor of being cleansed with a hyssop branch (see NLT textual note). There is little agreement among botanists about which plant is to be identified as the biblical "hyssop." Some have suggested the well-known garden herb now called hyssop. However, this plant is not native either to the Holy Land or to Egypt, being found only in southern Europe. Moreover, it does not fit the description of the biblical plant. The "hyssop" of the Old Testament (see Exod 12:22; Lev 14:4-6; Num 19:6, 18; Ps 51:7) is likely either the Syrian or Egyptian marjoram. These marjoram varieties are minty herbs that can grow two to three feet tall, though usually they are dwarfed when growing in rock crevices and walls (1 Kgs 4:33). If gathered together in a bunch with leaves and flowers, the hairy stems of the marjoram will hold liquid very well and make an excellent sprinkler. The "hyssop" of the crucifixion passage in the New Testament (John 19:29) is probably sorghum, a tall cereal plant grown primarily for food but also used for brushes and mops.

Ps 51:4 Although David had sinned with Bathsheba, David said that he had sinned against God. When someone steals, murders, or slanders, it is against someone else—a victim. According to the world's standards, extramarital sex between two consenting adults is acceptable if nobody gets hurt. But people do get hurt—in David's case, a man was murdered, and a baby died. All sin hurts us and others, but ultimately it offends God because sin in any form is rebellion against God's way of living. When you are tempted to do wrong, remember that you will be sinning against God. That may help you avoid the danger.

Ps 51:10 Because we are born sinners (Ps 51:5), our natural inclination is to please ourselves rather than God. David followed that inclination when he took another man's wife. Like David, we must ask God to cleanse us from within (Ps 51:7), filling our hearts and spirits with new thoughts and desires. Right conduct can come only from a clean heart and spirit. Ask God to create a pure heart and spirit in you.

Ps 51:12 Do you ever feel stagnant in your faith, as though you are just going through the motions? Has sin ever driven a wedge between you and God, making him seem distant? David felt this way. He had sinned with Bathsheba and had just been confronted by Nathan the prophet. In his prayer he cried, "Restore to me the joy of your salvation." God wants us to be close to him and to experience his full and complete life. But sin that remains unconfessed makes such intimacy impossible. Confess your sin to God. You may still have to face earthly consequences, as David did, but God will give back the joy of your relationship with him.

Ps 51:13 When God forgives our sin and restores our fellowship with him, we want to reach out to others who need this forgiveness and reconciliation. The more you have felt God's forgiveness, the more you will desire to tell others about it.

Ps 51:17 God wants a broken spirit and a broken and repentant heart. You can never please God by outward actions—no matter how good—if your heart attitude is not right. Are you sorry for your sin? Do you genuinely intend to stop? God is pleased by this kind of repentance.

2 Sam 12:13 During this incident, David wrote Psalm 51, giving valuable insight into his character and offering hope for us as well. No matter how miserable guilt makes you feel or how terribly you have sinned, you can pour out your heart to God and seek his forgiveness as David did. There is forgiveness for us when we sin.

2 Sam 12:14 David confessed and repented

David Confesses His Guilt

2 SAMUEL 12:13-25

Then David confessed to Nathan, "I have sinned against the LORD."

Nathan replied, "Yes, but the LORD has forgiven you, and you won't die for this sin. 14Nevertheless, because you have shown utter contempt for the LORD* by doing this, your child will die."

15After Nathan returned to his home, the LORD sent a deadly illness to the child of David and Uriah's wife. 16David begged God to spare the child. He went without food and lay all night on the bare ground. 17The elders of his household pleaded with him to get up and eat with them, but he refused.

18Then on the seventh day the child died. David's advisers were afraid to tell him. "He wouldn't listen to reason while the child was ill," they said. "What drastic thing will he do when we tell him the child is dead?"

19When David saw them whispering, he realized what had happened. "Is the child dead?" he asked.

"Yes," they replied, "he is dead."

20Then David got up from the ground, washed himself, put on lotions,* and changed his clothes. He went to the Tabernacle and worshiped the LORD. After that, he returned to the palace and was served food and ate.

21His advisers were amazed. "We don't understand you," they told him. "While the child was still living, you wept and refused to eat. But now that the child is dead, you have stopped your mourning and are eating again."

22David replied, "I fasted and wept while the child was alive, for I said, 'Perhaps the LORD will be gracious to me and let the child live.' 23But why should I fast when he is dead? Can I bring him back again? I will go to him one day, but he cannot return to me."

24Then David comforted Bathsheba, his wife, and slept with her. She became pregnant and gave birth to a son, and David* named him Solomon. The LORD loved the child 25and sent word through Nathan the prophet that they should name him Jedidiah (which means "beloved of the LORD"), as the LORD had commanded.*

David Captures Rabbah PARALLEL

2 SAMUEL 12:26-31

Meanwhile, Joab was fighting against Rabbah, the capital of Ammon, and he captured the royal fortifications.* 27Joab sent messengers to tell David, "I have fought against Rabbah and captured its water supply.* 28Now bring the rest of the army and capture the city. Otherwise, I will capture it and get credit for the victory."

29So David gathered the rest of the army and went to Rabbah, and he fought against it and captured it. 30David removed the crown from the king's head,* and it was placed on his own head. The crown was made of gold and set with gems, and it weighed seventy-five pounds.* David took a vast amount of plunder from the city. 31He also made slaves of the people of Rabbah and forced them to labor with* saws, iron picks, and iron axes, and to work in the brick kilns.* That is how he dealt with the people of all the Ammonite towns. Then David and all the army returned to Jerusalem.

1 CHRONICLES 20:2-3

When David arrived at Rabbah, he removed the crown from the king's head,* and it was placed on his own head. The crown was made of gold and set with gems, and he found that it weighed seventy-five pounds.* David took a vast amount of plunder from the city. 3He also made slaves of the people of Rabbah and forced them to labor with saws, iron picks, and iron axes.* That is how David dealt with the people of all the Ammonite towns. Then David and all the army returned to Jerusalem.

2 Sm 12:14 As in Dead Sea Scrolls; Masoretic Text reads *the LORD's enemies.* **2 Sm 12:20** Hebrew *anointed himself.* **2 Sm 12:24** Hebrew *he;* an alternate Hebrew reading and some Hebrew manuscripts read *she.* **2 Sm 12:25** As in Greek version; Hebrew reads *because of the LORD.* **2 Sm 12:26** Or *the royal city.* **2 Sm 12:27** Or *captured the city of water.* **2 Sm 12:30a** Or *from the head of Milcom* (as in Greek version). Milcom, also called Molech, was the god of the Ammonites. **2 Sm 12:30b** Hebrew *1 talent* [34 kilograms]. **2 Sm 12:31a** Or *He also brought out the people of Rabbah and put them under.* **2 Sm 12:31b** Or *and he made them pass through the brick kilns.* **1 Chr 20:2a** Or *from the head of Milcom* (as in Greek version and Latin Vulgate). Milcom, also called Molech, was the god of the Ammonites. **1 Chr 20:2b** Hebrew *1 talent* [34 kilograms]. **1 Chr 20:3** As in parallel text at 2 Sam 12:31; Hebrew reads *and cut them with saws, iron picks, and saws.*

---

of his sin (2 Sam 12:13), but God's judgment was that his child would die. The consequences of David's sin were irreversible. Sometimes an apology isn't enough. When God forgives us and restores our relationship with him, he doesn't eliminate all the consequences of our wrongdoing. We may be tempted to say, "If this is wrong, I can always apologize to God," but we must remember that we may set into motion events with irreversible consequences.

2 Sam 12:14 Why did this child have to die? This was not a judgment on the child for being conceived out of wedlock, but a judgment on David for his sin. David and Bathsheba deserved to die, but God spared their lives and took the child instead. God still had work for David to do in building the kingdom. The child's death was a horrible punishment for David and Bathsheba to bear.

It is also possible that had the child lived, God's name would have been dishonored among Israel's pagan neighbors. What would they have thought of a God who rewards murder and adultery by giving a king a new heir? A baby's death is tragic, but despising God brings death to entire nations. While God readily forgave David's sin, he did not negate all its consequences.

2 Sam 12:20-24 David did not continue to dwell on his sin. He returned to God, and God forgave him, opening the way to begin life anew. Even the name God gave Solomon, Jedidiah ("beloved of the LORD," 2 Sam 12:25) was a reminder of God's grace. When we return to God, accept his forgiveness, and change our ways, he gives us a fresh start. To feel forgiven as David did, admit your sins to God and turn to him. Then move ahead with a new and fresh approach to life.

2 Sam 12:22-23 Perhaps the most bitter experience in life is the death of one's child. For comfort in such difficult circumstances, see Psalms 16:9-11; 17:15; 139; and Isaiah 40:11.

2 Sam 12:24 Solomon was the fourth son of David and Bathsheba (1 Chr 3:5). Therefore, several years passed between the death of their first child and Solomon's birth. Bathsheba may still have been grieving over the child's death.

2. TURMOIL IN DAVID'S FAMILY

David's family had more than it's share of dysfunction. David had several wives and many children, and his son Amnon became infatuated with the beauty of his half-sister Tamar. With the help of his cousin, Amnon hatched a scheme to rape Tamar. This enraged Absalom, Tamar's brother, and he murdered Amnon and fled the country. No family is immune to dysfunction, but there are things that we can and should be doing to set our family members on a godly path.

The Rape of Tamar

2 SAMUEL 13:1-22

Now David's son Absalom had a beautiful sister named
Tamar. And Amnon, her half brother, fell desperately
in love with her. 2Amnon became so obsessed with
Tamar that he became ill. She was a virgin, and Amnon
thought he could never have her.
3But Amnon had a very crafty friend—his cousin
Jonadab. He was the son of David's brother Shimea.*
4One day Jonadab said to Amnon, "What's the trouble?
Why should the son of a king look so dejected morning after morning?"
So Amnon told him, "I am in love with Tamar, my brother Absalom's sister."
5"Well," Jonadab said, "I'll tell you what to do. Go
back to bed and pretend you are ill. When your father

2 Sm 13:3 Hebrew *Shimeah* (also in 13:32), a variant spelling of Shimea; compare 1 Chr 2:13.

2 Sam 13:3-5 Amnon was encouraged by his cousin Jonadab to commit sexual sin. e may be more vulnerable to the advice of our relatives because we are close to them. However, we must make sure to evaluate every piece of advice by God's standards, even when it comes from relatives.

2 Sam 13:14-15 Love and lust are very different. After Amnon raped his half sister, his "love" turned to hate. Although he had claimed to be in love, he was actually overcome by lust. Love is patient; lust requires immediate satisfaction. Love is kind; lust is harsh. Love does not demand its own way; lust does. You can read about the characteristics of real love in 1 Corinthians 13. Lust may feel like love at first, but when physically expressed, it results in self-disgust and hatred of the other person. If you just can't wait, what you feel is not truly love.

2 Sam 13:16 Rape was strictly forbidden by God (Deut 22:28-29). Why was sending Tamar away an even greater crime? By throwing her out, Amnon made it look as if Tamar had made a shameful proposition to him, and there were no witnesses on her behalf because he had gotten rid of the servants. His crime destroyed her chances of marriage—because she was no longer a virgin, she could not be given in marriage.

2 Sam 13:20 Absalom tried to comfort Tamar and persuade her not to turn the incident into a public scandal. Secretly, he planned to take revenge against Amnon himself. This he did two years later (2 Sam 13:23-33). Absalom told Tamar the crime was only a family matter. But God's standards for moral conduct are not suspended when we deal with family matters.

2 Sam 13:21-24 David was angry with Amnon for raping Tamar, but David did not punish him. David probably hesitated because (1) he didn't want to cross Amnon, who was his firstborn son (1 Chr 3:1)

AMNON

Amnon was king David's firstborn son, born and raised during the years between David's rise to fame and his rise to power. He grew into a prince with too much time on his hands and too little control over his thoughts. Amnon set in motion one of the most shameful and destructive series of actions in the royal family. He allowed himself to become obsessed with sexual desire for his half sister, Tamar. When his attempt to seduce Tamar failed, he raped her. Then his "desire" for her became loathing, and he humiliated her. He even made it look like the incest was his sister's fault. Tamar's full brother Absalom later avenged her shame by killing Amnon. • David was an ineffective father. He failed to train or discipline his children. Although he found out and was furious about Amnon's actions, he did nothing. Amnon, like the rest of his siblings, was a child out of control. He was frustrated when he couldn't have his way, yet was disgusted when he did get his way. Without direction, his actions led to self-destruction. The Bible records not even a hint of remorse for what he had done to Tamar. • Family relationships can be sources of strength or systems of dysfunction. We can think about childhood by counting scars and nightmares or by remembering security and dreams. We may be creating in our own children one or the other of these histories. In what specific ways have you been settling the painful issues of the past in your own life? In what ways are you contributing to a better future for your children?

Weaknesses and mistakes	• Allowed lustful desires to dominate his life • Listened to his cousin Jonadab's bad advice • Raped and then rejected his half sister, Tamar
Lessons from his life	• Children who have everything often lack purpose and direction in their lives • Thoughts and impulses turn self-destructive if not controlled or channeled • Parents contribute good or evil by action or inaction in their children's lives • The distance between lust and hatred is very short
Vital statistics	• Where: Hebron • Occupation: Prince • Relatives: Father: David. Mother: Ahinoam. Many half brothers including Absalom, Adonijah, and Solomon. Half sister: Tamar. • Contemporaries: Nathan, Jonadab, Joab, Ahithophel, Hushai
Key verse	"Then suddenly Amnon's love turned to hate, and he hated her even more than he had loved her. 'Get out of here!' he snarled at her" (2 Sam 13:15).

Amnon's story is told in 2 Samuel 13:1-39. He is also mentioned in 2 Samuel 3:2; 1 Chronicles 3:1.

comes to see you, ask him to let Tamar come and prepare some food for you. Tell him you'll feel better if
she prepares it as you watch and feeds you with her
own hands."
6So Amnon lay down and pretended to be sick. And
when the king came to see him, Amnon asked him,
"Please let my sister Tamar come and cook my favorite dish* as I watch. Then I can eat it from her own
hands." 7So David agreed and sent Tamar to Amnon's
house to prepare some food for him.
8When Tamar arrived at Amnon's house, she went to
the place where he was lying down so he could watch
her mix some dough. Then she baked his favorite dish
for him. 9But when she set the serving tray before him,
he refused to eat. "Everyone get out of here," Amnon
told his servants. So they all left.
10Then he said to Tamar, "Now bring the food into
my bedroom and feed it to me here." So Tamar took
his favorite dish to him. 11But as she was feeding him,
he grabbed her and demanded, "Come to bed with me,
my darling sister."
12"No, my brother!" she cried. "Don't be foolish! Don't
do this to me! Such wicked things aren't done in Israel.
13Where could I go in my shame? And you would be
called one of the greatest fools in Israel. Please, just
speak to the king about it, and he will let you marry me."
14But Amnon wouldn't listen to her, and since he
was stronger than she was, he raped her. 15Then suddenly Amnon's love turned to hate, and he hated her
even more than he had loved her. "Get out of here!"
he snarled at her.
16"No, no!" Tamar cried. "Sending me away now is
worse than what you've already done to me."
But Amnon wouldn't listen to her. 17He shouted for
his servant and demanded, "Throw this woman out,
and lock the door behind her!"
18So the servant put her out and locked the door
behind her. She was wearing a long, beautiful robe,*
as was the custom in those days for the king's virgin
daughters. 19But now Tamar tore her robe and put
ashes on her head. And then, with her face in her
hands, she went away crying.
20Her brother Absalom saw her and asked, "Is it
true that Amnon has been with you? Well, my sister,
keep quiet for now, since he's your brother. Don't you
worry about it." So Tamar lived as a desolate woman
in her brother Absalom's house.
21When King David heard what had happened, he
was very angry.* 22And though Absalom never spoke
to Amnon about this, he hated Amnon deeply because
of what he had done to his sister.

Absalom's Revenge on Amnon

2 SAMUEL 13:23-39

Two years later, when Absalom's sheep were being
sheared at Baal-hazor near Ephraim, Absalom invited
all the king's sons to come to a feast. 24He went to the
king and said, "My sheep-shearers are now at work.
Would the king and his servants please come to celebrate the occasion with me?"
25The king replied, "No, my son. If we all came, we
would be too much of a burden on you." Absalom
pressed him, but the king would not come, though
he gave Absalom his blessing.
26"Well, then," Absalom said, "if you can't come, how
about sending my brother Amnon with us?"
"Why Amnon?" the king asked. 27But Absalom kept
on pressing the king until he finally agreed to let all his
sons attend, including Amnon. So Absalom prepared
a feast fit for a king.*
28Absalom told his men, "Wait until Amnon gets
drunk; then at my signal, kill him! Don't be afraid. I'm
the one who has given the command. Take courage
and do it!" 29So at Absalom's signal they murdered
Amnon. Then the other sons of the king jumped on
their mules and fled.
30As they were on the way back to Jerusalem, this
report reached David: "Absalom has killed all the
king's sons; not one is left alive!" 31The king got up,
tore his robe, and threw himself on the ground. His
advisers also tore their clothes in horror and sorrow.
32But just then Jonadab, the son of David's brother
Shimea, arrived and said, "No, don't believe that all
the king's sons have been killed! It was only Amnon!
Absalom has been plotting this ever since Amnon
raped his sister Tamar. 33No, my lord the king, your
sons aren't all dead! It was only Amnon." 34Meanwhile
Absalom escaped.
Then the watchman on the Jerusalem wall saw a
great crowd coming down the hill on the road from
the west. He ran to tell the king, "I see a crowd of
people coming from the Horonaim road along the
side of the hill."*
35"Look!" Jonadab told the king. "There they are
now! The king's sons are coming, just as I said."
36They soon arrived, weeping and sobbing, and the
king and all his servants wept bitterly with them. 37And
David mourned many days for his son Amnon.
Absalom fled to his grandfather, Talmai son of
Ammihud, the king of Geshur. 38He stayed there in
Geshur for three years. 39And King David,* now reconciled to Amnon's death, longed to be reunited with
his son Absalom.*

2 Sm 13:6 Or *a couple of cakes;* also in 13:8, 10. **2 Sm 13:18** Or *a robe with sleeves,* or *an ornamented robe.* The meaning of the Hebrew is uncertain. **2 Sm 13:21** Dead Sea Scrolls and Greek version add *But he did not punish his son Amnon, because he loved him, for he was his firstborn.* **2 Sm 13:27** As in Greek and Latin versions (compare also Dead Sea Scrolls); the Hebrew text lacks this sentence. **2 Sm 13:34** As in Greek version; Hebrew lacks this sentence. **2 Sm 13:39a** Dead Sea Scrolls and Greek version read *And the spirit of the king.* **2 Sm 13:39b** Or *no longer felt a need to go out after Absalom.*

and therefore next in line to be king, and (2) David was guilty of a similar sin himself in his adultery with Bathsheba. While David was unsurpassed as a king and military leader, he lacked skill and sensitivity as a husband and father.

2 Sam 13:37-39 Absalom fled to Geshur because King Talmai was his grandfather (1 Chr 3:2), and he would be welcomed.

Joab Arranges for Absalom's Return

2 SAMUEL 14:1-24

Joab realized how much the king longed to see Absalom. [2]So he sent for a woman from Tekoa who had a reputation for great wisdom. He said to her, "Pretend you are in mourning; wear mourning clothes and don't put on lotions.* Act like a woman who has been mourning for the dead for a long time. [3]Then go to the king and tell him the story I am about to tell you." Then Joab told her what to say.

[4]When the woman from Tekoa approached the king, she bowed with her face to the ground in deep respect and cried out, "O king! Help me!"

[5]"What's the trouble?" the king asked.

"Alas, I am a widow!" she replied. "My husband is dead. [6]My two sons had a fight out in the field. And since no one was there to stop it, one of them was killed. [7]Now the rest of the family is demanding, 'Let us have your son. We will execute him for murdering his brother. He doesn't deserve to inherit his family's property.' They want to extinguish the only coal I have left, and my husband's name and family will disappear from the face of the earth."

[8]"Leave it to me," the king told her. "Go home, and I'll see to it that no one touches him."

[9]"Oh, thank you, my lord the king," the woman from Tekoa replied. "If you are criticized for helping me, let the blame fall on me and on my father's house, and let the king and his throne be innocent."

[10]"If anyone objects," the king said, "bring him to me. I can assure you he will never complain again!"

[11]Then she said, "Please swear to me by the LORD your God that you won't let anyone take vengeance against my son. I want no more bloodshed."

"As surely as the LORD lives," he replied, "not a hair on your son's head will be disturbed!"

[12]"Please allow me to ask one more thing of my lord the king," she said.

"Go ahead and speak," he responded.

[13]She replied, "Why don't you do as much for the people of God as you have promised to do for me? You have convicted yourself in making this decision, because you have refused to bring home your own banished son. [14]All of us must die eventually. Our lives are like water spilled out on the ground, which cannot be gathered up again. But God does not just sweep life away; instead, he devises ways to bring us back when we have been separated from him.

[15]"I have come to plead with my lord the king because people have threatened me. I said to myself, 'Perhaps the king will listen to me [16]and rescue us from those who would cut us off from the inheritance* God has given us. [17]Yes, my lord the king will give us peace of mind again.' I know that you are like an angel of God in discerning good from evil. May the LORD your God be with you."

[18]"I must know one thing," the king replied, "And tell me the truth."

"Yes, my lord the king," she responded.

[19]"Did Joab put you up to this?"

And the woman replied, "My lord the king, how can I deny it? Nobody can hide anything from you. Yes, Joab sent me and told me what to say. [20]He did it to place the matter before you in a different light. But you are as wise as an angel of God, and you understand everything that happens among us!"

[21]So the king sent for Joab and told him, "All right, go and bring back the young man Absalom."

[22]Joab bowed with his face to the ground in deep respect and said, "At last I know that I have gained your approval, my lord the king, for you have granted me this request!"

[23]Then Joab went to Geshur and brought Absalom back to Jerusalem. [24]But the king gave this order: "Absalom may go to his own house, but he must never come into my presence." So Absalom did not see the king.

Absalom Reconciled to David

2 SAMUEL 14:25-33

Now Absalom was praised as the most handsome man in all Israel. He was flawless from head to foot. [26]He cut his hair only once a year, and then only because it was so heavy. When he weighed it out, it came to five pounds!* [27]He had three sons and one daughter.

2 Sm 14:2 Hebrew *don't anoint yourself with oil.* **2 Sm 14:16** Or *the property;* or *the people.* **2 Sm 14:26** Hebrew *200 shekels* [2.3 kilograms] *by the royal standard.*

2 Sam 14:1 Why is so much attention given to Absalom in 2 Samuel 13–19? His revenge against Amnon and rebellion against David were beginning the final decline of David's kingdom that had been prophesied in 2 Samuel 12:10-12. The cycle of lust and murder had begun with David's adultery with Bathsheba. By killing his half brother Amnon, Absalom was getting revenge for the rape of his sister Tamar, as well as getting rid of the firstborn son, the one next in line to be king. Clearly he had his sights set on being Israel's king and he did everything in his power to obtain that goal—killing a half brother and rebelling against his father. Absalom was handsome and popular like his father, but he lacked his father's heart for God.

What can we learn from this terrible story? (1) Even the highest-ranking and best-equipped people are sinners and rebels at heart. We must guard our own hearts against sin and rebellion. (2) David failed to teach his children God's ways. Even if our children are raised in church, we must teach and exemplify character and obedience to God. (3) David was preoccupied with government, wives, and concubines; he failed to act decisively to correct the evil in his family. At times, his guilt over his own sin caused him to decline to discipline his sons caught in similar sins. That proved to be his family's undoing. Whenever possible, we must break cycles of lust, hatred, and rebellion. To do so, we must stay involved in guiding our children's lives while they are still under our care.

2 Sam 14:11 The law provided for a way to avenge murder. Numbers 35:9-21 records how cities of refuge protected people from revenge and how blood avengers were to pursue murderers. This woman was asking for the king's protection from any claim against her.

2 Sam 14:27 By naming his daughter Tamar, Absalom was showing his love and respect for his sister Tamar. This was also a reminder to everyone of the Amnon/Tamar incident.

His daughter's name was Tamar, and she was very
beautiful.
[28]Absalom lived in Jerusalem for two years, but he
never got to see the king. [29]Then Absalom sent for
Joab to ask him to intercede for him, but Joab refused
to come. Absalom sent for him a second time, but
again Joab refused to come. [30]So Absalom said to his
servants, "Go and set fire to Joab's barley field, the field
next to mine." So they set his field on fire, as Absalom
had commanded.
[31]Then Joab came to Absalom at his house and demanded, "Why did your servants set my field on fire?"
[32]And Absalom replied, "Because I wanted you to
ask the king why he brought me back from Geshur if
he didn't intend to see me. I might as well have stayed
there. Let me see the king; if he finds me guilty of
anything, then let him kill me."
[33]So Joab told the king what Absalom had said.
Then at last David summoned Absalom, who came and
bowed low before the king, and the king kissed him.

ABSALOM

A father's mistakes are often reflected in the lives of his children. In Absalom, David saw a bitter replay and amplification of many of his own past sins. God had predicted that David's family would suffer because of his sins against Bathsheba and Uriah. David's heart was broken as he realized that God's predictions were coming true. God forgave David, but he did not cancel the consequences of his sin. David was horrified as he saw his son's strengths run wild without the controls God had built into his own life. • By most casual evaluations, Absalom would have made an excellent king, and the people loved him. But he lacked the inner character and control needed in a good leader. His appearance, skill, and position did not make up for his lack of personal integrity. • David's sins took him away from God, but repentance brought him back. In contrast, Absalom sinned and kept on sinning. Although he relied heavily on the advice of others, he was not wise enough to evaluate the counsel he received. • Can you identify with Absalom? Do you find yourself on a fast track toward self-destruction? Absalom wasn't able to say, "I was wrong. I need forgiveness." God offers forgiveness, but we will not experience that forgiveness until we genuinely admit our sins and confess them to God. Absalom rejected his father's love and ultimately God's love. How often do you miss entering back into God's love through the door of forgiveness?

Strengths and accomplishments	• Was handsome and charismatic like his father, David • Kindly comforted his sister, Tamar, after she had been raped, and allowed her to live with him
Weaknesses and mistakes	• Avenged the rape of his sister, Tamar, by killing his half brother Amnon • Plotted against his father to take away the throne • Consistently listened to the wrong advice
Lessons from his life	• The sins of parents are often repeated and amplified in their children • A smart man gets a lot of advice; a wise man evaluates the advice he gets • Actions against God's plans will fail, sooner or later
Vital statistics	• Where: Hebron • Occupation: Prince • Relatives: Father: David. Mother: Maacah. Half brothers: Amnon, Kileab, Solomon, and others. Sister: Tamar. • Contemporaries: Nathan, Jonadab, Joab, Ahithophel, Hushai
Key verse	"But while he was there, he sent secret messengers to all the tribes of Israel to stir up a rebellion against the king. 'As soon as you hear the ram's horn,' his message read, 'you are to say, "Absalom has been crowned king in Hebron"'" (2 Sam 15:10).

Absalom's story is told in 2 Samuel 3:3; 13–19.

2 Sam 14:30 Already we can see the seeds of rebellion in Absalom. As an independent and scheming young man, he took matters into his own hands and killed his brother (2 Sam 13:22-29). Without his father or anyone else to keep him in check, he probably did whatever he wanted, as evidenced by his setting Joab's field on fire to get his attention (2 Sam 14:30). Undoubtedly his good looks also added to his self-centeredness (2 Sam 14:25). Children need discipline, especially those with natural abilities and beauty. Otherwise, like Absalom, they will grow up thinking they can do whatever they want whenever they want to.

2 Sam 14:33 David only made halfhearted efforts to correct his children. He did not punish Amnon for his sin against Tamar, nor did he deal decisively with Absalom's murder of Amnon. Such indecisiveness became David's undoing. When we ignore sin, we experience greater pain than if we deal with it immediately.

3. NATIONAL REBELLION AGAINST DAVID

David faced two major rebellions: one led by his son Absalom and another by Sheba from the tribe of Benjamin. Absalom's rebellion was so successful that David had to flee from Israel, and Absalom took over the palace. This difficult situation provides the background for two of David's psalms. David relied on God to rescue him from his enemies and restore him to the throne, and God proved faithful to his promise.

Absalom's Rebellion

2 SAMUEL 15:1-12

After this, Absalom bought a chariot and horses, and
he hired fifty bodyguards to run ahead of him. 2He
got up early every morning and went out to the gate
of the city. When people brought a case to the king
for judgment, Absalom would ask where in Israel they
were from, and they would tell him their tribe. 3Then
Absalom would say, "You've really got a strong case
here! It's too bad the king doesn't have anyone to hear
it. 4I wish I were the judge. Then everyone could bring
their cases to me for judgment, and I would give them
justice!"

5When people tried to bow before him, Absalom
wouldn't let them. Instead, he took them by the hand
and kissed them. 6Absalom did this with everyone
who came to the king for judgment, and so he stole
the hearts of all the people of Israel.

7After four years,* Absalom said to the king, "Let
me go to Hebron to offer a sacrifice to the LORD and
fulfill a vow I made to him. 8For while your servant was
at Geshur in Aram, I promised to sacrifice to the LORD
in Hebron* if he would bring me back to Jerusalem."
9"All right," the king told him. "Go and fulfill your
vow."

So Absalom went to Hebron. 10But while he was
there, he sent secret messengers to all the tribes of
Israel to stir up a rebellion against the king. "As soon as
you hear the ram's horn," his message read, "you are to
say, 'Absalom has been crowned king in Hebron.'" 11He
took 200 men from Jerusalem with him as guests, but
they knew nothing of his intentions. 12While Absalom
was offering the sacrifices, he sent for Ahithophel,
one of David's counselors who lived in Giloh. Soon
many others also joined Absalom, and the conspiracy
gained momentum.

David Escapes from Jerusalem

2 SAMUEL 15:13-37

A messenger soon arrived in Jerusalem to tell David,
"All Israel has joined Absalom in a conspiracy against
you!"

14"Then we must flee at once, or it will be too late!"
David urged his men. "Hurry! If we get out of the city
before Absalom arrives, both we and the city of Jerusalem will be spared from disaster."

2 Sm 15:7 As in Greek and Syriac versions; Hebrew reads *forty years*. **2 Sm 15:8** As in some Greek manuscripts; Hebrew lacks *in Hebron*.

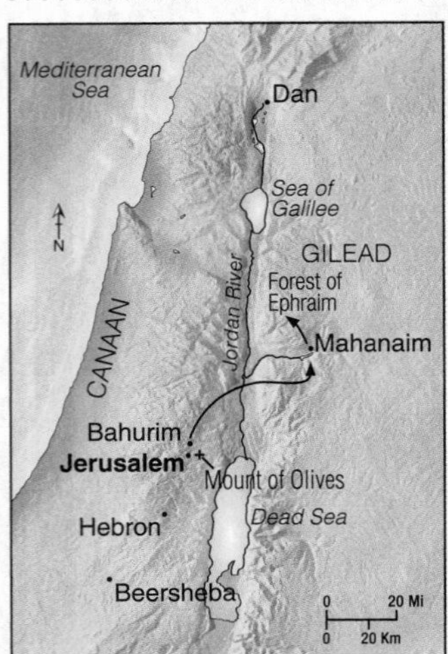

***ABSALOM'S REBELLION** Absalom crowned himself king in Hebron. David and his men fled from Jerusalem, crossed the Jordan, and went to Mahanaim. Absalom and his army followed, only to be defeated in the forest of Ephraim, where Absalom was killed.*

2 Sam 15:2 The city gate was like city hall and a shopping center combined. Because Jerusalem was the nation's capital, both local and national leaders met there daily to transact business and conduct government affairs. The city gate was the perfect spot for this because government and business transactions needed witnesses to be legitimate, and anyone entering or leaving the city had to enter through the gate. Merchants set up their tent-shops near the gate for the same reason. Absalom, therefore, went to the city gate to win the hearts of Israel's leaders as well as those of the common people.

2 Sam 15:5-6 Absalom's political strategy was to steal the hearts of the people with his good looks, grand entrances, apparent concern for justice, and friendly embraces. Many were fooled and switched their allegiance. Later, however, Absalom proved to be an evil ruler.

We need to evaluate our leaders to make sure their charisma is not a mask covering graft, deception, or hunger for power. Make sure that underneath their style and charm, they are able to make good decisions and handle people wisely.

2 Sam 15:9 Absalom went to Hebron because it was his hometown (2 Sam 3:2-3). Hebron was David's first capital as well, and there Absalom could expect to find loyal friends who would be proud of him.

2 Sam 15:14 Had David not escaped from Jerusalem, the ensuing fight might have killed him as well as many innocent inhabitants of the city. Some fights that we think necessary can be costly and destructive to those around us. In such cases, it may be wise to back down and save the fight for another day—even if doing so hurts our pride. It takes courage to stand and fight, but it also takes courage to back down for the sake of others.

2 Sam 15:14 Why couldn't David just crush this rebellion? There were several reasons he chose to flee: (1) The rebellion was widespread (2 Sam 15:10-13) and would not have been easily suppressed; (2) David did not want the city of Jerusalem to be destroyed; (3) David still cared for his son and did not want to hurt him. We know that David expected to return to Jerusalem soon because he left 10 of his concubines to take care of the palace (2 Sam 15:16).

15“We are with you,” his advisers replied. “Do what
you think is best.”
16So the king and all his household set out at once.
He left no one behind except ten of his concubines
to look after the palace. 17The king and all his people
set out on foot, pausing at the last house 18to let all
the king’s men move past to lead the way. There were
600 men from Gath who had come with David, along
with the king’s bodyguard.*
19Then the king turned and said to Ittai, a leader of
the men from Gath, “Why are you coming with us? Go
on back to King Absalom, for you are a guest in Israel,
a foreigner in exile. 20You arrived only recently, and
should I force you today to wander with us? I don’t
even know where we will go. Go on back and take your
kinsmen with you, and may the LORD show you his
unfailing love and faithfulness.*”
21But Ittai said to the king, “I vow by the LORD and
by your own life that I will go wherever my lord the
king goes, no matter what happens—whether it means
life or death.”
22David replied, “All right, come with us.” So Ittai
and all his men and their families went along.
23Everyone cried loudly as the king and his followers passed by. They crossed the Kidron Valley and then
went out toward the wilderness.
24Zadok and all the Levites also came along, carrying
the Ark of the Covenant of God. They set down the Ark
of God, and Abiathar offered sacrifices* until everyone
had passed out of the city.
25Then the king instructed Zadok to take the Ark
of God back into the city. “If the LORD sees fit,” David
said, “he will bring me back to see the Ark and the
Tabernacle* again. 26But if he is through with me, then
let him do what seems best to him.”
27The king also told Zadok the priest, “Look,* here
is my plan. You and Abiathar* should return quietly
to the city with your son Ahimaaz and Abiathar’s son
Jonathan. 28I will stop at the shallows of the Jordan
River* and wait there for a report from you.” 29So Zadok and Abiathar took the Ark of God back to the city
and stayed there.
30David walked up the road to the Mount of Olives,
weeping as he went. His head was covered and his feet
were bare as a sign of mourning. And the people who
were with him covered their heads and wept as they
climbed the hill. 31When someone told David that
his adviser Ahithophel was now backing Absalom,
David prayed, “O LORD, let Ahithophel give Absalom
foolish advice!”
32When David reached the summit of the Mount of
Olives where people worshiped God, Hushai the Arkite
was waiting there for him. Hushai had torn his clothing and put dirt on his head as a sign of mourning.

2 Sm 15:18 Hebrew *the Kerethites and Pelethites.* **2 Sm 15:20** As in Greek version; Hebrew reads *and may unfailing love and faithfulness go with you.* **2 Sm 15:24** Or *Abiathar went up.* **2 Sm 15:25** Hebrew *and his dwelling place.* **2 Sm 15:27a** As in Greek version; Hebrew reads *Are you a seer?* or *Do you see?* **2 Sm 15:27b** Hebrew lacks *and Abiathar;* compare 15:29. **2 Sm 15:28** Hebrew *at the crossing points of the wilderness.*

2 Sam 15:17-18 David had many loyal non-Israelites in his armed forces. The men from the Philistine city of Gath were apparently friends David had acquired while hiding from Saul. “The king’s bodyguard” could also be translated “the Kerethites and Pelethites”; these men were also from Philistine territory. Although Israel was supposed to destroy wicked enemies, the nation was to welcome foreigners who came on friendly terms (Exod 23:9; Deut 10:19) and to try to show them the importance of obeying God.

2 Sam 15:24-25 The priests and Levites were also loyal to David.

2 Sam 15:27-37 David needed spies in Absalom’s court to inform him of Absalom’s decisions. By sending Hushai to Absalom as a supposed traitor to David, Hushai could offer advice contradictory to Ahithophel’s advice. Ahithophel had become Absalom’s adviser (he was also Bathsheba’s grandfather).

Kidron Valley

The Kidron Valley runs below the southeast wall of Jerusalem, separating the city from the Mount of Olives on the east. It then turns southeast from Jerusalem and follows a winding course to the Dead Sea. The Kidron Valley is nearly always dry since the watercourse flows only in the rainy season, partly maintained by two irregular springs, Gihon and En-rogel.

The first reference to the Kidron Valley is in 2 Samuel 15:23, where the people and David crossed over toward the desert. This strategic move would give them a way of escape if the forces of rebellious Absalom decided to attack the city. The people and the king wept bitterly during this move (2 Sam 15:30) because it had such a depressing significance—David was abandoning Zion without a fight. Later, Shimei was forbidden by Solomon to cross the Kidron Valley on pain of death (1 Kgs 2:36-38). Josephus mentions that the wicked queen Athaliah was put to death in the Kidron Valley (*Antiquities* 9.7.3). Jesus crossed the Kidron Valley on the way to the Garden of Gethsemane just prior to his crucifixion (John 18:1). Because of David’s sad crossing and Jesus’ sad crossing, the Kidron Valley has come to symbolize suffering. We may have our own “Kidron Valley” to pass through; stay true to God, and he will stay true to you throughout your sufferings.

▸ **2 SAMUEL 15:13-37** ***(cont.)***
33But David told him, "If you go with me, you will only
be a burden. 34Return to Jerusalem and tell Absalom,
'I will now be your adviser, O king, just as I was your
father's adviser in the past.' Then you can frustrate
and counter Ahithophel's advice. 35Zadok and Abiathar, the priests, will be there. Tell them about the
plans being made in the king's palace, 36and they will
send their sons Ahimaaz and Jonathan to tell me what
is going on."
37So David's friend Hushai returned to Jerusalem,
getting there just as Absalom arrived.

David and Ziba

2 SAMUEL 16:1-4

When David had gone a little beyond the summit of the Mount of Olives, Ziba, the servant of Mephibosheth,* was waiting there for him. He had two donkeys loaded with 200 loaves of bread, 100 clusters of raisins, 100 bunches of summer fruit, and a wineskin full of wine.
2"What are these for?" the king asked Ziba.
Ziba replied, "The donkeys are for the king's people
to ride on, and the bread and summer fruit are for the
young men to eat. The wine is for those who become
exhausted in the wilderness."
3"And where is Mephibosheth, Saul's grandson?"
the king asked him.
"He stayed in Jerusalem," Ziba replied. "He said,
'Today I will get back the kingdom of my grandfather
Saul.'"
4"In that case," the king told Ziba, "I give you everything Mephibosheth owns."
"I bow before you," Ziba replied. "May I always be
pleasing to you, my lord the king."

2 Sm 16:1 *Mephibosheth* is another name for Merib-baal.

Shimei Curses David

2 SAMUEL 16:5-14

As King David came to Bahurim, a man came out of
the village cursing them. It was Shimei son of Gera,
from the same clan as Saul's family. 6He threw stones
at the king and the king's officers and all the mighty

HIGHS AND LOWS OF DAVID'S LIFE

The Bible calls David a man after God's own heart (1 Sam 13:14; Acts 13:22), but that didn't mean his life was free of troubles. David's life was full of highs and lows. Some of David's troubles were a result of his sins; some were a result of the sins of others. We can't always control our ups and downs, but we can trust God every day. We can be certain that he will help us through our trials, just as he helped David. In the end, he will reward us for our consistent faith.

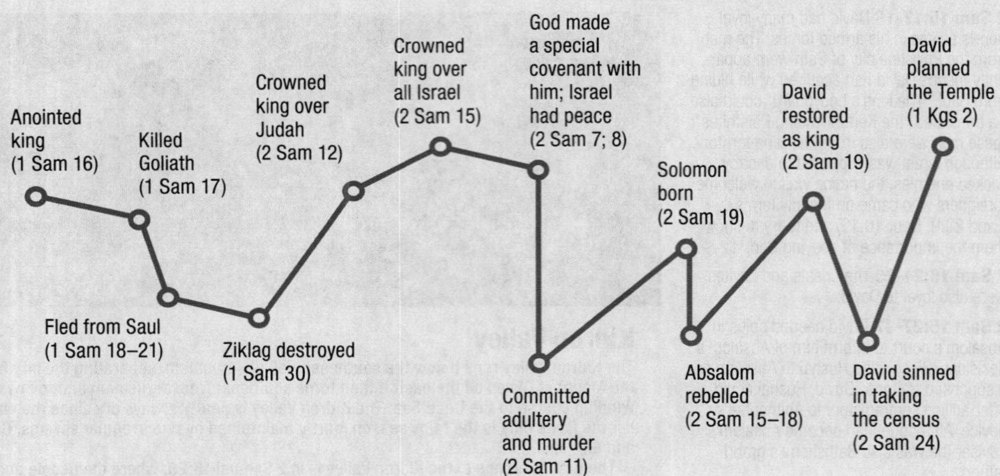

2 Sam 16:3 Saul was Mephibosheth's grandfather. Most likely Ziba was lying, hoping to receive a reward from David. (See 2 Sam 19:24-30 for Mephibosheth's side of the story.) For the story of Mephibosheth, see 2 Samuel 9.

2 Sam 16:4 David believed Ziba's charge against Mephibosheth without checking into it or even being skeptical. Don't be hasty to accept someone's condemnation of another, especially when the accuser may profit from the other's downfall. David should have been skeptical of Ziba's comments until he checked them out for himself.

2 Sam 16:5-14 Shimei kept up a steady tirade against David. Although his curses were unjustified because David had had no part in Saul's death, David and his followers quietly tolerated the abuse. Maintaining your composure in the face of unjustified criticism can be a trying experience and an emotional drain, but if you can't stop criticism, it is best just to ignore it. Remember that God knows what you are enduring, and he will vindicate you if you are in the right.

warriors who surrounded him. 7“Get out of here, you murderer, you scoundrel!” he shouted at David. 8“The LORD is paying you back for all the bloodshed in Saul’s clan. You stole his throne, and now the LORD has given it to your son Absalom. At last you will taste some of your own medicine, for you are a murderer!”

9“Why should this dead dog curse my lord the king?” Abishai son of Zeruiah demanded. “Let me go over and cut off his head!”

10“No!” the king said. “Who asked your opinion, you sons of Zeruiah! If the LORD has told him to curse me, who are you to stop him?”

11Then David said to Abishai and to all his servants, “My own son is trying to kill me. Doesn’t this relative of Saul* have even more reason to do so? Leave him alone and let him curse, for the LORD has told him to do it. 12And perhaps the LORD will see that I am being wronged and will bless me because of these curses today.” 13So David and his men continued down the road, and Shimei kept pace with them on a nearby hillside, cursing as he went and throwing stones at David and tossing dust into the air.

14The king and all who were with him grew weary along the way, so they rested when they reached the Jordan River.*

Ahithophel Advises Absalom

2 SAMUEL 16:15–17:4

Meanwhile, Absalom and all the army of Israel arrived at Jerusalem, accompanied by Ahithophel. 16When David’s friend Hushai the Arkite arrived, he went immediately to see Absalom. “Long live the king!” he exclaimed. “Long live the king!”

17“Is this the way you treat your friend David?” Absalom asked him. “Why aren’t you with him?”

18“I’m here because I belong to the man who is chosen by the LORD and by all the men of Israel,” Hushai replied. 19“And anyway, why shouldn’t I serve you? Just as I was your father’s adviser, now I will be your adviser!”

20Then Absalom turned to Ahithophel and asked him, “What should I do next?”

21Ahithophel told him, “Go and sleep with your father’s concubines, for he has left them here to look after the palace. Then all Israel will know that you have insulted your father beyond hope of reconciliation, and they will throw their support to you.” 22So they set up a tent on the palace roof where everyone could see it, and Absalom went in and had sex with his father’s concubines.

23Absalom followed Ahithophel’s advice, just as David had done. For every word Ahithophel spoke seemed as wise as though it had come directly from the mouth of God.

17:1 Now Ahithophel urged Absalom, “Let me choose 12,000 men to start out after David tonight. 2I will catch up with him while he is weary and discouraged. He and his troops will panic, and everyone will run away. Then I will kill only the king, 3and I will bring all the people back to you as a bride returns to her husband. After all, it is only one man’s life that you seek.* Then you will be at peace with all the people.” 4This plan seemed good to Absalom and to all the elders of Israel.

Hushai Counters Ahithophel’s Advice

2 SAMUEL 17:5-14

But then Absalom said, “Bring in Hushai the Arkite. Let’s see what he thinks about this.” 6When Hushai arrived, Absalom told him what Ahithophel had said. Then he asked, “What is your opinion? Should we follow Ahithophel’s advice? If not, what do you suggest?”

7“Well,” Hushai replied to Absalom, “this time Ahithophel has made a mistake. 8You know your father and his men; they are mighty warriors. Right now they are as enraged as a mother bear who has been robbed of her cubs. And remember that your father is an experienced man of war. He won’t be spending the night among the troops. 9He has probably already hidden in some pit or cave. And when he comes out and attacks and a few of your men fall, there will be panic among your troops, and the word will spread that Absalom’s men are being slaughtered. 10Then even the bravest soldiers, though they have the heart of a lion, will be paralyzed with fear. For all Israel knows what a mighty warrior your father is and how courageous his men are.

11“I recommend that you mobilize the entire army of Israel, bringing them from as far away as Dan in the north and Beersheba in the south. That way you will have an army as numerous as the sand on the seashore. And I advise that you personally lead the troops. 12When we find David, we’ll fall on him like dew that falls on the ground. Then neither he nor any of his men will be left alive. 13And if David were to escape into some town, you will have all Israel there at your command. Then we can take ropes and drag the walls of the town into the nearest valley until every stone is torn down.”

2 Sm 16:11 Hebrew *this Benjaminite.* **2 Sm 16:14** As in Greek version (see also 17:16); Hebrew reads *when they reached their destination.* **2 Sm 17:3** As in Greek version; Hebrew reads *like the return of all is the man whom you seek.*

2 Sam 16:21-22 This incident fulfilled Nathan’s prediction that because of David’s sin, another man would sleep with his wives (2 Sam 12:11-12). (See the note on 2 Sam 3:6-7, p. 483.)

2 Sam 16:23 Ahithophel was an adviser to Absalom. Most rulers had advisers to help them make decisions about governmental and political matters. They probably arranged the king’s marriages as well because these were usually politically motivated unions. But God made Ahithophel’s advice seem foolish, just as David had prayed (2 Sam 15:31).

2 Sam 17:11 Hushai appealed to Absalom through flattery, and Absalom’s vanity became his own trap. Hushai predicted great glory for Absalom if he personally led the entire army against David. “Pride goes before destruction” (Prov 16:18) is an appropriate comment on Absalom’s ambitions.

▶ **2 SAMUEL 17:5-14 *(cont.)***

[14]Then Absalom and all the men of Israel said, "Hushai's advice is better than Ahithophel's." For the LORD had determined to defeat the counsel of Ahithophel, which really was the better plan, so that he could bring disaster on Absalom!

David Escapes through the Wilderness

2 SAMUEL 17:15-29

Hushai told Zadok and Abiathar, the priests, what Ahithophel had said to Absalom and the elders of Israel and what he himself had advised instead.
[16]"Quick!" he told them. "Find David and urge him not to stay at the shallows of the Jordan River* tonight. He must go across at once into the wilderness beyond. Otherwise he will die and his entire army with him."

[17]Jonathan and Ahimaaz had been staying at En-rogel so as not to be seen entering and leaving the city. Arrangements had been made for a servant girl to bring them the message they were to take to King
David. [18]But a boy spotted them at En-rogel, and he told Absalom about it. So they quickly escaped to Bahurim, where a man hid them down inside a well in
his courtyard. [19]The man's wife put a cloth over the top of the well and scattered grain on it to dry in the sun; so no one suspected they were there.

[20]When Absalom's men arrived, they asked her, "Have you seen Ahimaaz and Jonathan?"

The woman replied, "They were here, but they crossed over the brook." Absalom's men looked for them without success and returned to Jerusalem.

[21]Then the two men crawled out of the well and hurried on to King David. "Quick!" they told him, "cross the Jordan tonight!" And they told him how Ahithophel had advised that he be captured and killed. [22]So David and all the people with him went across the Jordan River during the night, and they were all on the other bank before dawn.

[23]When Ahithophel realized that his advice had not been followed, he saddled his donkey, went to his hometown, set his affairs in order, and hanged himself. He died there and was buried in the family tomb.

[24]David soon arrived at Mahanaim. By now, Absalom had mobilized the entire army of Israel and was
leading his troops across the Jordan River. [25]Absalom had appointed Amasa as commander of his army, replacing Joab, who had been commander under David. (Amasa was Joab's cousin. His father was Jether,* an Ishmaelite.* His mother, Abigail daughter of Nahash,
was the sister of Joab's mother, Zeruiah.)[26]Absalom and the Israelite army set up camp in the land of Gilead.

[27]When David arrived at Mahanaim, he was warmly greeted by Shobi son of Nahash, who came from Rabbah of the Ammonites, and by Makir son of Ammiel from Lo-debar, and by Barzillai of Gilead from Rogelim. [28]They brought sleeping mats,

2 Sm 17:16 Hebrew *at the crossing points of the wilderness.* **2 Sm 17:25a** Hebrew *Ithra,* a variant spelling of Jether. **2 Sm 17:25b** As in some Greek manuscripts (see also 1 Chr 2:17); Hebrew reads *an Israelite.*

PSALMS FROM DAVID'S LIFE

Of the more than 70 psalms attributed to David, at least 13 of them are connected with specific events in his life. From them we see an outline of a growing relationship with God. They are listed here, roughly in chronological order.

Event in David's Life	*Reference*	*Psalm*	*What David Learned about God*
When Saul sent men to David's home to kill him	1 Sam 19	**59**	God is my refuge.
While running from Saul	1 Sam 21	**34**	I will praise the Lord at all times.
While hiding in a cave	1 Sam 24	**57**	I will hide in the shadow of God's wings until the danger has passed.
While hiding in the cave of Adullam	1 Sam 22	**142**	God is my refuge.
After learning that Doeg had murdered 85 priests and their families	1 Sam 22	**52**	God will strike down evil people.
When the Ziphites tried to betray him	1 Sam 23	**54**	God is my helper.
While running from Saul	1 Sam 21	**56**	When I am afraid, I put my trust in God.
When Jerusalem was threatened by the Edomites	2 Sam 8	**60**	God will protect his people from their enemies.
After being confronted about his adultery with Bathsheba	2 Sam 12	**51**	The sacrifices God desires are a broken spirit; a broken and repentant heart he will not reject.
During Absalom's rebellion	2 Sam 15	**3**	Victory comes from the Lord.
While hiding in the wilderness of Judah	2 Sam 17	**63**	My soul thirsts for God; his right hand holds me securely.
During Sheba's rebellion	2 Sam 20	**7**	He is a righteous God who searches minds and hearts and can bring to an end the violence of the wicked and make the righteous secure.
When David's battles were over	2 Sam 22	**18**	To the faithful, God shows himself faithful.

cooking pots, serving bowls, wheat and barley, flour and roasted grain, beans, lentils, 29honey, butter, sheep, goats, and cheese for David and those who were with him. For they said, "You must all be very hungry and tired and thirsty after your long march through the wilderness."

Psalm 3

THEME: Confidently trusting God for protection and peace.

AUTHOR: David

A psalm of David, regarding the time David fled from his son Absalom.

1 O LORD, I have so many enemies;
so many are against me.
2 So many are saying,
"God will never rescue him!" *Interlude**
3 But you, O LORD, are a shield around me;
you are my glory, the one who holds my head high.
4 I cried out to the LORD,
and he answered me from his holy mountain. *Interlude*
5 I lay down and slept,
yet I woke up in safety,
for the LORD was watching over me.
6 I am not afraid of ten thousand enemies
who surround me on every side.
7 Arise, O LORD!
Rescue me, my God!
Slap all my enemies in the face!
Shatter the teeth of the wicked!
8 Victory comes from you, O LORD.
May you bless your people. *Interlude*

Psalm 63

THEME: A desire for God's presence, provision, and protection. No matter where we are, our desire should be for God because only he satisfies fully.

AUTHOR: David

A psalm of David, regarding a time when David was in the wilderness of Judah.

1 O God, you are my God;
I earnestly search for you.
My soul thirsts for you;
my whole body longs for you
in this parched and weary land
where there is no water.
2 I have seen you in your sanctuary
and gazed upon your power and glory.
3 Your unfailing love is better than life itself;
how I praise you!
4 I will praise you as long as I live,
lifting up my hands to you in prayer.
5 You satisfy me more than the richest feast.
I will praise you with songs of joy.

Ps 3:2 Hebrew *Selah*. The meaning of this word is uncertain, though it is probably a musical or literary term. It is rendered *Interlude* throughout the Psalms.

2 Sam 17:25 Joab and Amasa were David's nephews and Absalom's cousins. Because Joab had left Jerusalem with David (see 2 Sam 18:5, 10ff), Amasa took his place as commander of Israel's troops.

Ps 3:1-2 David felt like he was in the minority. As many as 10,000 soldiers may have been surrounding him at this time (Ps 3:6). Not only did David's enemies view life differently, but they actively sought to harm him. As king, David could have trusted his army to defeat Absalom. Instead, he depended upon God's mercy (Ps 3:4); therefore, he was at peace with whatever outcome occurred, knowing that God's great purposes would prevail. We can overcome fear by trusting God for his protection in our darkest hour.

Ps 3:1-3 David was not sitting on his throne in a place of power; he was running for his life from his rebellious son, Absalom, and a host of traitors. When circumstances go against us, we may be tempted to think that God also is against us. But David reminds us that the opposite is true. When everything seems to go wrong, God is still for us. If a circumstance has turned against you, don't blame God—seek him!

Ps 3:2 The word *Interlude* is a translation of the Hebrew word *selah* which occurs 71 times in Psalms and three times in Habakkuk (Hab 3:3, 9, 13). Though its precise use is unknown, the word was most likely a musical sign. Three suggestions for its meaning include: (1) It was a musical direction to the singers and orchestra to play *forte* or *crescendo*. (2) It was a signal to lift up the hands or voice in worship, or to the priest to give a benediction. (3) It was a phrase like *Amen* meaning "So be it," or *Hallelujah* meaning "Praise the Lord."

Ps 3:4 God's holy mountain was Mount Moriah in Jerusalem, the place where David's son Solomon would build the Temple (2 Chr 3:1). David knew that God could not be confined to any space, but he wrote poetically, expressing confidence that God would hear him when he prayed. God responds to us when we earnestly pray to him.

Ps 3:5 Sleep does not come easily during a crisis. David could have had sleepless nights when his son Absalom rebelled and gathered an army to kill him. But he slept peacefully, even during the rebellion. What made the difference? David cried out to the Lord, and the Lord heard him. The assurance of answered prayer brings peace. It is easier to sleep well when we have full assurance that God is in control of circumstances. If you are lying awake at night worrying about what you can't change, pour out your heart to God, and thank him that he is in control.

Ps 3:7 David's call for God to act reveals his desire for justice against his persecutors. David himself had been slapped and insulted, and here he simply asks for equal treatment for his enemies. He did this, not out of personal revenge, but for the sake of God's justice. Psalm 3:8 shows the humility behind David's words—he realized that faith in God's timing was the answer to his question about the success the wicked had unfairly achieved.

Ps 63:1ff Psalm 63 was probably written when David was seeking refuge during Absalom's rebellion (2 Sam 15–18). David had already lived a full life. David's quiet confidence as stated in this psalm can be seen in the account in 2 Samuel of the events that shook his life. His actions closely paralleled his beliefs during those turbulent days.

Ps 63:1-5 Hiding from his enemies in the barren wilderness of Judah, David was intensely lonely. He longed for a friend he could trust to ease his loneliness. No wonder he cried out, "O God, . . . My soul thirsts for you . . . in this parched and weary land." If you are lonely or thirsty for something lasting in your life, remember David's prayer. God alone can satisfy our deepest longings!

▸ **PSALM 63** ***(cont.)***

6 I lie awake thinking of you,
meditating on you through the night.
7 Because you are my helper,
I sing for joy in the shadow of your wings.
8 I cling to you;
your strong right hand holds me securely.

9 But those plotting to destroy me will come to ruin.
They will go down into the depths of the earth.
10 They will die by the sword
and become the food of jackals.
11 But the king will rejoice in God.
All who trust in him will praise him,
while liars will be silenced.

Absalom's Defeat and Death

2 SAMUEL 18:1-18

David now mustered the men who were with him and
appointed generals and captains* to lead them. 2He
sent the troops out in three groups, placing one group
under Joab, one under Joab's brother Abishai son of
Zeruiah, and one under Ittai, the man from Gath. The
king told his troops, "I am going out with you."
3But his men objected strongly. "You must not go,"
they urged. "If we have to turn and run—and even if
half of us die—it will make no difference to Absalom's
troops; they will be looking only for you. You are worth
10,000 of us,* and it is better that you stay here in the
town and send help if we need it."
4"If you think that's the best plan, I'll do it," the king
answered. So he stood alongside the gate of the town
as all the troops marched out in groups of hundreds
and of thousands.
5And the king gave this command to Joab, Abishai,
and Ittai: "For my sake, deal gently with young Absalom." And all the troops heard the king give this order
to his commanders.
6So the battle began in the forest of Ephraim, 7and
the Israelite troops were beaten back by David's men.
There was a great slaughter that day, and 20,000 men
laid down their lives. 8The battle raged all across the
countryside, and more men died because of the forest
than were killed by the sword.
9During the battle, Absalom happened to come
upon some of David's men. He tried to escape on his
mule, but as he rode beneath the thick branches of a
great tree, his hair* got caught in the tree. His mule
kept going and left him dangling in the air. 10One of
David's men saw what had happened and told Joab, "I
saw Absalom dangling from a great tree."
11"What?" Joab demanded. "You saw him there and
didn't kill him? I would have rewarded you with ten
pieces of silver* and a hero's belt!"
12"I would not kill the king's son for even a thousand
pieces of silver,*" the man replied to Joab. "We all heard
the king say to you and Abishai and Ittai, 'For my sake,
please spare young Absalom.' 13And if I had betrayed
the king by killing his son—and the king would certainly find out who did it—you yourself would be the
first to abandon me."
14"Enough of this nonsense," Joab said. Then he
took three daggers and plunged them into Absalom's
heart as he dangled, still alive, in the great tree. 15Ten
of Joab's young armor bearers then surrounded Absalom and killed him.
16Then Joab blew the ram's horn, and his men returned from chasing the army of Israel. 17They threw
Absalom's body into a deep pit in the forest and piled
a great heap of stones over it. And all Israel fled to
their homes.
18During his lifetime, Absalom had built a monument to himself in the King's Valley, for he said, "I
have no son to carry on my name." He named the
monument after himself, and it is known as Absalom's Monument to this day.

David Mourns Absalom's Death

2 SAMUEL 18:19-33

Then Zadok's son Ahimaaz said, "Let me run to the
king with the good news that the LORD has rescued
him from his enemies."
20"No," Joab told him, "it wouldn't be good news to
the king that his son is dead. You can be my messenger
another time, but not today."
21Then Joab said to a man from Ethiopia,* "Go tell the
king what you have seen." The man bowed and ran off.
22But Ahimaaz continued to plead with Joab, "Whatever happens, please let me go, too."
"Why should you go, my son?" Joab replied. "There
will be no reward for your news."
23"Yes, but let me go anyway," he begged.
Joab finally said, "All right, go ahead." So Ahimaaz

2 Sm 18:1 Hebrew *appointed commanders of thousands and commanders of hundreds.* **2 Sm 18:3** As in two Hebrew manuscripts and some Greek and Latin manuscripts; most Hebrew manuscripts read *Now there are 10,000 like us.* **2 Sm 18:9** Hebrew *his head.* **2 Sm 18:11** Hebrew *10 shekels of silver,* about 4 ounces or 114 grams in weight. **2 Sm 18:12** Hebrew *1,000 shekels,* about 25 pounds or 11.4 kilograms in weight. **2 Sm 18:21** Hebrew *from Cush;* similarly in 18:23, 31, 32.

Ps 63:6 During sleepless, uncomfortable nights, David thought about God. Instead of counting sheep, he meditated on his Shepherd. He reviewed all the ways God had already helped him, and he greeted the next day with songs of praise. In quiet moments or wakeful nights, make it a point to count examples of God's faithfulness to you. Doing so is far more likely to give you rest than any other items you might count!

2 Sam 18:1 David took command as he had in former days. In recent years, his life had been characterized by indecisiveness and moral paralysis. At this time he began to take charge and do his duty.

2 Sam 18:12-14 This man had caught Joab in his hypocrisy. He knew Joab would have turned on him for killing Absalom if the king had found out about it. Joab could not answer but only dismissed him. Those about to do evil often don't pause to consider what they are about to do. They don't care whether or not it is right or lawful. Don't rush into action without thinking. Consider whether what you are about to do is right or wrong.

2 Sam 18:29 Although he reached the city first, Ahimaaz was afraid to tell the king the truth about the death of his son Absalom.

took the less demanding route by way of the plain and
ran to Mahanaim ahead of the Ethiopian.
[24]While David was sitting between the inner and
outer gates of the town, the watchman climbed to
the roof of the gateway by the wall. As he looked, he
saw a lone man running toward them. [25]He shouted
the news down to David, and the king replied, "If he
is alone, he has news."
As the messenger came closer, [26]the watchman saw
another man running toward them. He shouted down,
"Here comes another one!"
The king replied, "He also will have news."
[27]"The first man runs like Ahimaaz son of Zadok,"
the watchman said.
"He is a good man and comes with good news,"
the king replied.
[28]Then Ahimaaz cried out to the king, "Everything
is all right!" He bowed before the king with his face
to the ground and said, "Praise to the LORD your God,
who has handed over the rebels who dared to stand
against my lord the king."
[29]"What about young Absalom?" the king demanded. "Is he all right?"
Ahimaaz replied, "When Joab told me to come,
there was a lot of commotion. But I didn't know what
was happening."
[30]"Wait here," the king told him. So Ahimaaz
stepped aside.
[31]Then the man from Ethiopia arrived and said, "I
have good news for my lord the king. Today the LORD has
rescued you from all those who rebelled against you."
[32]"What about young Absalom?" the king demanded.
"Is he all right?"
And the Ethiopian replied, "May all of your enemies,

REBELLION

The Bible records numerous rebellions. Many were against God's chosen leaders. They were doomed for failure. Others were begun by wicked men against wicked men. While these were sometimes successful, the rebel's life usually came to a violent end. Still other rebellions were begun by good people against the wicked or unjust actions of others. This kind of rebellion is sometimes good in freeing the common people from oppression and giving them the freedom to turn back to God.

Who Rebelled?	*Whom They Rebelled Against*	*What Happened*	*Reference*
Adam and Eve	God	Expelled from Eden	Gen 3
Israelites	God, Moses	Forced to wander in wilderness for 40 years	Num 14
Korah	Moses	Swallowed by the earth	Num 16
Israelites	God	God took away his special promise of protection.	Judg 2
Absalom (David's son)	David	Killed in battle	2 Sam 15–18
Sheba	David	Killed in battle	2 Sam 20
Adonijah (David's son)	David, Solomon	Killed for treason	1 Kgs 1–2
Joab	David, Solomon	Supported Adonijah's kingship without seeking God's choice. Killed for treason	1 Kgs 1–2
Ten tribes of Israel	Rehoboam	The kingdom was divided. The 10 tribes forgot about God, sinned, and were eventually taken into captivity.	1 Kgs 12:16-20
Baasha, king of Israel	Nadab, king of Israel	Overthrew the throne and became king. God destroyed his descendants.	1 Kgs 15:27–16:7
Zimri, king of Israel	Elah, king of Israel	Overthrew the throne, but killed himself when his rule was not accepted	1 Kgs 16:9-16
Jehu, king of Israel	Joram, king of Israel; Ahaziah, king of Judah	Killed both kings. Later turned from God and his dynasty was wiped out	2 Kgs 9–10
Joash, king of Judah; Jehoiada, a priest	Athaliah, queen of Judah	Athaliah, a wicked queen, was overthrown. This was a "good" rebellion.	2 Kgs 11
Shallum, king of Israel	Zechariah, king of Israel	Overthrew the throne, but then was assassinated	2 Kgs 15:8-15
Menahem, king of Israel	Shallum, king of Israel	Overthrew the throne, but then was invaded by Assyrian army	2 Kgs 15:16-22
Hoshea, king of Israel	Assyria	The city of Samaria was destroyed, the nation of Israel taken into captivity.	2 Kgs 17
Zedekiah, king of Judah	Nebuchadnezzar, king of Babylon	The city of Jerusalem was destroyed, the nation of Judah taken into captivity.	2 Kgs 24–25

▶ **2 SAMUEL 18:19-33 *(cont.)***

my lord the king, both now and in the future, share
the fate of that young man!"
33*The king was overcome with emotion. He went
up to the room over the gateway and burst into tears.
And as he went, he cried, "O my son Absalom! My son,
my son Absalom! If only I had died instead of you!
O Absalom, my son, my son."

Joab Rebukes the King

2 SAMUEL 19:1-14

1*Word soon reached Joab that the king was weeping and mourning for Absalom. 2As all the people
heard of the king's deep grief for his son, the joy of
that day's victory was turned into deep sadness. 3They
crept back into the town that day as though they were
ashamed and had deserted in battle. 4The king covered his face with his hands and kept on crying, "O my
son Absalom! O Absalom, my son, my son!"
5Then Joab went to the king's room and said to him,
"We saved your life today and the lives of your sons,
your daughters, and your wives and concubines. Yet
you act like this, making us feel ashamed of ourselves.
6You seem to love those who hate you and hate those
who love you. You have made it clear today that your
commanders and troops mean nothing to you. It seems
that if Absalom had lived and all of us had died, you
would be pleased. 7Now go out there and congratulate
your troops, for I swear by the LORD that if you don't go
out, not a single one of them will remain here tonight.
Then you will be worse off than ever before."
8So the king went out and took his seat at the town
gate, and as the news spread throughout the town that
he was there, everyone went to him.
Meanwhile, the Israelites who had supported Absalom fled to their homes. 9And throughout all the tribes
of Israel there was much discussion and argument going
on. The people were saying, "The king rescued us from
our enemies and saved us from the Philistines, but Absalom chased him out of the country. 10Now Absalom,

2 Sm 18:33 Verse 18:33 is numbered 19:1 in Hebrew text. **2 Sm 19:1** Verses 19:1-43 are numbered 19:2-44 in Hebrew text.

2 Sam 18:33 Why was David so upset over the death of his rebel son? (1) David realized that he, in part, was responsible for Absalom's death. Nathan the prophet had said that because David had killed Uriah, his own sons would rebel against him. (2) David was angry at Joab and his officers for killing Absalom against his wishes. (3) David truly loved his son even though Absalom did nothing to deserve his love. It would have been kinder and more loving to deal with Absalom and his runaway ego when he was younger.

2 Sam 19:4-7 At times we must reprove those in authority over us. Joab knew he was risking the king's displeasure by confronting him, but he saw what had to be done. Joab told David that there would be dreadful consequences if he didn't commend the troops for their victory. Joab's actions are a helpful example to us when personal confrontation is necessary.

2 Sam 19:8 David sat at the town gate because that was where business was conducted and judgment rendered. His presence there showed that he was over his mourning and back in control.

2 Sam 19:8-10 Just a few days before, most of Israel was supporting the rebel ruler Absalom. Now the people wanted David back as their king. Because crowds are often fickle, there must be a higher moral code to follow than the pleasure of the majority. Following the moral principles given in God's Word will help you avoid being swayed by popular opinion.

JOAB

Joab, the great military leader, had two brothers who were also famous soldiers: Abishai and Asahel. Joab was the greatest leader of the three and was the commander of David's army throughout most of David's reign. There is no record that his troops ever lost a battle. • Joab was a brilliant and ruthless strategist. His plans usually worked, but he did not hesitate to use treachery or murder to achieve his goals. His career is a story of great accomplishments and shameful acts. He conquered Jerusalem and the surrounding nations, defeated Abner, and reconciled Absalom and David. But he also murdered Abner, Amasa, and Absalom, took part in Uriah's murder, and plotted with Adonijah against Solomon. That plot led to his execution. • Joab set his own standards—he lived by them and died because of them. There is little evidence that Joab ever acknowledged God's standards. Joab's self-centeredness eventually destroyed him. He was loyal only to himself, even willing to betray his lifelong relationship with David to preserve his power. • Joab's life illustrates the disastrous results of having no source of direction outside oneself. Brilliance and power are self-destructive without God's guidance. Only God can give the direction we need. For that reason, he has made available his Word, the Bible, and he is personally present in the lives of those who are in a relationahip with him.

Strengths and accomplishments	• Brilliant planner and strategist • Confident leader who would confront even the king • Helped reconcile David and Absalom
Weaknesses and mistakes	• Was repeatedly ruthless, violent, and vengeful • Avenged his brother's murder by murdering Abner • Killed Absalom against David's orders • Plotted with Adonijah against David and Solomon
Lessons from his life	• Those who live by violence often die by violence • Even brilliant leaders need guidance
Vital statistics	• Occupation: Commander in chief of David's army • Relatives: Mother: Zeruiah. Brothers: Abishai, Asahel. Uncle: David. • Contemporaries: Saul, Abner, Absalom
Key verse	"'Do as he said,' the king replied. 'Kill him there beside the altar and bury him. This will remove the guilt of Joab's senseless murders from me and from my father's family'" (1 Kgs 2:31).

Joab's story is told in 2 Samuel 2—1 Kings 2. He is also mentioned in 1 Chronicles 2:16; 11:5-9, 20, 26; 19:8-15; 20:1; 21:2-6; 26:28; the title of Psalm 60.

whom we anointed to rule over us, is dead. Why not ask David to come back and be our king again?"

11Then King David sent Zadok and Abiathar, the priests, to say to the elders of Judah, "Why are you the last ones to welcome back the king into his palace? For I have heard that all Israel is ready. 12You are my relatives, my own tribe, my own flesh and blood! So why are you the last ones to welcome back the king?" 13And David told them to tell Amasa, "Since you are my own flesh and blood, like Joab, may God strike me and even kill me if I do not appoint you as commander of my army in his place."

14Then Amasa* convinced all the men of Judah, and they responded unanimously. They sent word to the king, "Return to us, and bring back all who are with you."

David's Return to Jerusalem

2 SAMUEL 19:15-18a

So the king started back to Jerusalem. And when he arrived at the Jordan River, the people of Judah came to Gilgal to meet him and escort him across the river. 16Shimei son of Gera, the man from Bahurim in Benjamin, hurried across with the men of Judah to welcome King David. 17A thousand other men from the tribe of Benjamin were with him, including Ziba, the chief servant of the house of Saul, and Ziba's fifteen sons and twenty servants. They rushed down to the Jordan to meet the king. 18They crossed the shallows of the Jordan to bring the king's household across the river, helping him in every way they could.

David's Mercy to Shimei

2 SAMUEL 19:18b-23

As the king was about to cross the river, Shimei fell down before him. 19"My lord the king, please forgive me," he pleaded. "Forget the terrible thing your servant did when you left Jerusalem. May the king put it out of his mind. 20I know how much I sinned. That is why I have come here today, the very first person in all Israel* to greet my lord the king."

21Then Abishai son of Zeruiah said, "Shimei should die, for he cursed the LORD's anointed king!"

22"Who asked your opinion, you sons of Zeruiah!" David exclaimed. "Why have you become my adversary* today? This is not a day for execution but for celebration! Today I am once again the king of Israel!" 23Then, turning to Shimei, David vowed, "Your life will be spared."

David's Kindness to Mephibosheth

2 SAMUEL 19:24-30

Now Mephibosheth,* Saul's grandson, came down from Jerusalem to meet the king. He had not cared for his feet, trimmed his beard, or washed his clothes since the day the king left Jerusalem. 25"Why didn't you come with me, Mephibosheth?" the king asked him.

26Mephibosheth replied, "My lord the king, my servant Ziba deceived me. I told him, 'Saddle my donkey* so I can go with the king.' For as you know I am crippled. 27Ziba has slandered me by saying that I refused to come. But I know that my lord the king is like an angel of God, so do what you think is best. 28All my relatives and I could expect only death from you, my lord, but instead you have honored me by allowing me to eat at your own table! What more can I ask?"

29"You've said enough," David replied. "I've decided that you and Ziba will divide your land equally between you."

30"Give him all of it," Mephibosheth said. "I am content just to have you safely back again, my lord the king!"

2 Sm 19:14 Or *David;* Hebrew reads *he.* **2 Sm 19:20** Hebrew *in the house of Joseph.* **2 Sm 19:22** Or *my prosecutor.* **2 Sm 19:24** *Mephibosheth* is another name for Merib-baal. **2 Sm 19:26** As in Greek, Syriac, and Latin versions; Hebrew reads *I will saddle a donkey for myself.*

Now Mephibosheth, Saul's grandson, came down from Jerusalem to meet the king.
2 Samuel 19:24

2 Sam 19:13 David's appointment of Amasa was a shrewd political move. First, Amasa had been commander of Absalom's army; by making Amasa his commander, David would secure the allegiance of the rebel army. Second, by replacing Joab as commander in chief, David punished him for his previous crimes (2 Sam 3:26-29). Third, Amasa had a great deal of influence over the leaders of Judah (2 Sam 19:14). All of these moves would help to unite the kingdom.

2 Sam 19:19-20 By admitting his wrong and asking David's forgiveness, Shimei was trying to save his own life. His plan worked for a while. This was a day of celebration, not execution. But we read in 1 Kings 2:8-9 that David advised Solomon to execute Shimei.

2 Sam 19:21ff David showed tremendous mercy and generosity as he returned to Jerusalem. He spared Shimei, restored Mephibosheth, and rewarded faithful Barzillai.

2 Sam 19:24-30 David could not be certain if Mephibosheth or Ziba was in the right, and Scripture leaves the question unanswered. (For the whole story on Mephibosheth, see also 2 Sam 9:1-13; 16:1-4.)

David's Kindness to Barzillai

2 SAMUEL 19:31-40

Barzillai of Gilead had come down from Rogelim to escort the king across the Jordan. 32He was very old, about eighty, and very wealthy. He was the one who had provided food for the king during his stay in Mahanaim. 33"Come across with me and live in Jerusalem," the king said to Barzillai. "I will take care of you there."

34"No," he replied, "I am far too old to go with the king to Jerusalem. 35I am eighty years old today, and I can no longer enjoy anything. Food and wine are no longer tasty, and I cannot hear the singers as they sing. I would only be a burden to my lord the king. 36Just to go across the Jordan River with the king is all the honor I need! 37Then let me return again to die in my own town, where my father and mother are buried. But here is your servant, my son Kimham. Let him go with my lord the king and receive whatever you want to give him."

38"Good," the king agreed. "Kimham will go with me, and I will help him in any way you would like. And I will do for you anything you want." 39So all the people crossed the Jordan with the king. After David had blessed Barzillai and kissed him, Barzillai returned to his own home.

40The king then crossed over to Gilgal, taking Kimham with him. All the troops of Judah and half the troops of Israel escorted the king on his way.

An Argument over the King

2 SAMUEL 19:41-43

But all the men of Israel complained to the king, "The men of Judah stole the king and didn't give us the honor of helping take you, your household, and all your men across the Jordan."

42The men of Judah replied, "The king is one of our own kinsmen. Why should this make you angry? We haven't eaten any of the king's food or received any special favors!"

43"But there are ten tribes in Israel," the others replied. "So we have ten times as much right to the king as you do. What right do you have to treat us with such contempt? Weren't we the first to speak of bringing him back to be our king again?" The argument continued back and forth, and the men of Judah spoke even more harshly than the men of Israel.

The Revolt of Sheba

2 SAMUEL 20:1-26

There happened to be a troublemaker there named Sheba son of Bicri, a man from the tribe of Benjamin. Sheba blew a ram's horn and began to chant:

"Down with the dynasty of David!
We have no interest in the son of Jesse.
Come on, you men of Israel,
back to your homes!"

2So all the men of Israel deserted David and followed Sheba son of Bicri. But the men of Judah stayed with their king and escorted him from the Jordan River to Jerusalem.

3When David came to his palace in Jerusalem, he took the ten concubines he had left to look after the palace and placed them in seclusion. Their needs were provided for, but he no longer slept with them. So each of them lived like a widow until she died.

4Then the king told Amasa, "Mobilize the army of Judah within three days, and report back at that time." 5So Amasa went out to notify Judah, but it took him longer than the time he had been given.

6Then David said to Abishai, "Sheba son of Bicri is going to hurt us more than Absalom did. Quick, take my troops and chase after him before he gets into a fortified town where we can't reach him."

7So Abishai and Joab,* together with the king's bodyguard* and all the mighty warriors, set out from Jerusalem to go after Sheba. 8As they arrived at the great stone in Gibeon, Amasa met them. Joab was wearing his military tunic with a dagger strapped to his belt. As he stepped forward to greet Amasa, he slipped the dagger from its sheath.*

9"How are you, my cousin?" Joab said and took him by the beard with his right hand as though to kiss him. 10Amasa didn't notice the dagger in his left hand, and Joab stabbed him in the stomach with it so that his insides gushed out onto the ground. Joab did not need to strike again, and Amasa soon died. Joab and his brother Abishai left him lying there and continued after Sheba.

11One of Joab's young men shouted to Amasa's troops, "If you are for Joab and David, come and follow Joab." 12But Amasa lay in his blood in the middle of the road, and Joab's man saw that everyone was stopping to stare at him. So he pulled him off the road into a field and threw a cloak over him. 13With Amasa's body out of the way, everyone went on with Joab to capture Sheba son of Bicri.

14Meanwhile, Sheba traveled through all the tribes of Israel and eventually came to the town of Abel-beth-maacah. All the members of his own clan, the Bicrites,* assembled for battle and followed him into the town. 15When Joab's forces arrived, they attacked Abel-beth-maacah. They built a siege ramp against the

2 Sm 20:7a Hebrew *So Joab's men.* **2 Sm 20:7b** Hebrew *the Kerethites and Pelethites;* also in 20:23. **2 Sm 20:8** Hebrew *As he stepped forward, it fell out.* **2 Sm 20:14** As in Greek and Latin versions; Hebrew reads *All the Berites.*

---

2 Sam 20:1 Although Israel was a united kingdom, it was still made up of 12 separate tribes. These tribes often had difficulty agreeing on the goals of the nation as a whole. Tribal jealousies had originally kept Israel from completely conquering the Promised Land (read the book of Joshua), and now tribal jealousies were threatening the stability of David's reign by giving Sheba an opportunity to rebel (2 Sam 20:1ff).

2 Sam 20:7-10 Once again Joab's murderous act went unpunished, just as it did when he killed Abner (2 Sam 3:26-27). Eventually, however, justice caught up with him (1 Kgs 2:28-35). It may seem that sin and treachery

town's fortifications and began battering down the wall.
16 But a wise woman in the town called out to Joab, "Listen to me, Joab. Come over here so I can talk to you."
17 As he approached, the woman asked, "Are you Joab?"

"I am," he replied.

So she said, "Listen carefully to your servant."

"I'm listening," he said.

18 Then she continued, "There used to be a saying, 'If
you want to settle an argument, ask advice at the town
of Abel.' 19 I am one who is peace loving and faithful
in Israel. But you are destroying an important town in
Israel.* Why do you want to devour what belongs to
the LORD?"

20 And Joab replied, "Believe me, I don't want to devour or destroy your town! 21 That's not my purpose.
All I want is a man named Sheba son of Bicri from the
hill country of Ephraim, who has revolted against King
David. If you hand over this one man to me, I will leave
the town in peace."

"All right," the woman replied, "we will throw his
head over the wall to you." 22 Then the woman went
to all the people with her wise advice, and they cut off
Sheba's head and threw it out to Joab. So he blew the
ram's horn and called his troops back from the attack.
They all returned to their homes, and Joab returned to
the king at Jerusalem.

23 Now Joab was the commander of the army of Israel. Benaiah son of Jehoiada was captain of the king's
bodyguard. 24 Adoniram* was in charge of the labor
force. Jehoshaphat son of Ahilud was the royal historian. 25 Sheva was the court secretary. Zadok and Abiathar were the priests. 26 And Ira, a descendant of Jair,
was David's personal priest.

Psalm 7

THEME: A request for justice against those who make slanderous comments. God is the perfect judge and will punish those who persecute the innocent.

AUTHOR: David

A psalm of David, which he sang to the LORD concerning Cush of the tribe of Benjamin.

1 I come to you for protection, O LORD my God.
Save me from my persecutors—rescue me!
2 If you don't, they will maul me like a lion,
tearing me to pieces with no one to rescue me.
3 O LORD my God, if I have done wrong
or am guilty of injustice,
4 if I have betrayed a friend
or plundered my enemy without cause,
5 then let my enemies capture me.
Let them trample me into the ground
and drag my honor in the dust. *Interlude*

6 Arise, O LORD, in anger!
Stand up against the fury of my enemies!
Wake up, my God, and bring justice!
7 Gather the nations before you.
Rule over them from on high.
8 The LORD judges the nations.
Declare me righteous, O LORD,
for I am innocent, O Most High!
9 End the evil of those who are wicked,
and defend the righteous.
For you look deep within the mind and heart,
O righteous God.

2 Sm 20:19 Hebrew *a town that is a mother in Israel.* **2 Sm 20:24** As in Greek version (see also 1 Kgs 4:6; 5:14); Hebrew reads *Adoram.*

often go unpunished, but God's justice is not limited to this life's rewards. Even if Joab had died of old age, he would still have had to face the day of judgment.

2 Sam 20:16ff Joab's men were attacking the city, and it looked as if it would be destroyed. Though women in that society were usually quiet in public, this woman spoke out. She stopped Joab's attack not with weapons but with wise words and a plan of action. Often the courage to speak a few sensible words can prevent great disaster.

2 Sam 20:23 Benaiah was the captain of David's bodyguard and a famous member of that special group of mighty men called "the Thirty" (2 Sam 23:24). He remained loyal to David during Absalom's rebellion. Later he helped establish Solomon as king (1 Kgs 1:32-40; 2:28-34) and eventually replaced Joab as commander of Israel's army (1 Kgs 2:35).

Ps 7:1-6 Have you ever been falsely accused or so badly hurt that you wanted revenge? Instead of taking matters into his own hands and striking back, David cried out to God for justice. The proper response to slander is prayer, not revenge, because God says, "I will take revenge; I will pay them back" (Rom 12:19; see also Deut 32:35-36; Heb 10:30). Instead of striking back, ask God to take your case, bring justice, and restore your reputation.

Ps 7:9 God looks "deep within the mind and heart." Nothing is hidden from God—this can be either terrifying or comforting. Our thoughts are an open book to him. Because God knows even our motives, we have no place to hide, no way to pretend we can get away with sin. But that very knowledge also gives us great comfort. We don't have to impress God or put up a false front. Instead, we can trust God to help us work through our weaknesses in order to serve him as he has planned. When we truly follow God, he rewards our efforts.

SHEBA'S REBELLION ▶
After defeating Absalom, David returned to Jerusalem from Mahanaim. But Sheba incited a rebellion against David, so David sent Joab, Abishai, and a small army after him. Joab and his troops besieged Abel-beth-maacah, Sheba's hideout, until the people of Abel-beth-maacah killed Sheba themselves.

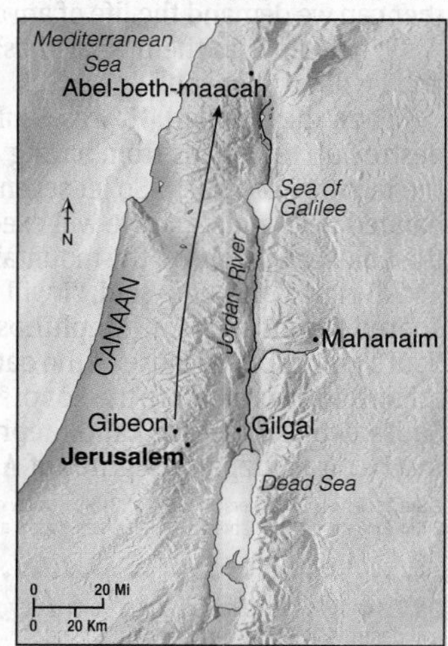

▶ **PSALM 7** ***(cont.)***

10 God is my shield,
saving those whose hearts are true
and right.
11 God is an honest judge.
He is angry with the wicked every day.

12 If a person does not repent,
God* will sharpen his sword;
he will bend and string his bow.
13 He will prepare his deadly weapons
and shoot his flaming arrows.

Ps 7:12 Hebrew *he.*

14 The wicked conceive evil;
they are pregnant with trouble
and give birth to lies.
15 They dig a deep pit to trap others,
then fall into it themselves.
16 The trouble they make for others backfires on
them.
The violence they plan falls on their own heads.
17 I will thank the LORD because he is just;
I will sing praise to the name of the LORD
Most High.

4. THE LATER YEARS OF DAVID'S REIGN

David ruled over Israel many more years after the rebellions of Absalom and Sheba. He finally subdued the Philistines and wrote a song of praise to God for giving the nation rest from all their enemies. Near the end of his reign, he decided to take a census in violation of God's wishes, leading to tragic consequences for the nation.

David Avenges the Gibeonites

2 SAMUEL 21:1-14

There was a famine during David's reign that lasted for three years, so David asked the LORD about it. And the LORD said, "The famine has come because Saul and his family are guilty of murdering the Gibeonites."

2So the king summoned the Gibeonites. They were not part of Israel but were all that was left of the nation of the Amorites. The people of Israel had sworn not to kill them, but Saul, in his zeal for Israel and Judah, had tried to wipe them out.
3David asked them, "What can I do for you? How can I make amends so that you will bless the LORD's people again?"

4"Well, money can't settle this matter between us and the family of Saul," the Gibeonites replied. "Neither can we demand the life of anyone in Israel."

"What can I do then?" David asked. "Just tell me and I will do it for you."

5Then they replied, "It was Saul who planned to destroy us, to keep us from having any place at all in the territory of Israel.
6So let seven of Saul's sons be handed over to us, and we will execute them before the LORD at Gibeon, on the mountain of the LORD.*"

"All right," the king said, "I will do it."
7The king spared Jonathan's son Mephibosheth,* who was Saul's grandson, because of the oath David and Jonathan had sworn before the LORD.
8But he gave them Saul's two sons Armoni and Mephibosheth, whose mother was Rizpah daughter of Aiah. He also gave them the five sons of Saul's daughter Merab,* the wife of Adriel son of Barzillai from Meholah.
9The men of Gibeon executed them on the mountain before the LORD. So all seven of them died together at the beginning of the barley harvest.

10Then Rizpah daughter of Aiah, the mother of two of the men, spread burlap on a rock and stayed there the entire harvest season. She prevented the scavenger birds from tearing at their bodies during the day and stopped wild animals from eating them at night.
11When David learned what Rizpah, Saul's concubine, had done,
12he went to the people of Jabesh-gilead and retrieved the bones of Saul and his son Jonathan. (When the Philistines had killed Saul and Jonathan on Mount Gilboa, the people of Jabesh-gilead stole their bodies from the public square of Beth-shan, where the Philistines had hung them.)
13So David obtained the bones of Saul and Jonathan, as well as the bones of the men the Gibeonites had executed.

14Then the king ordered that they bury the bones in the tomb of Kish, Saul's father, at the town of Zela in the land of Benjamin. After that, God ended the famine in the land.

Battles against Philistine Giants PARALLEL

2 SAMUEL 21:15-22

Once again the Philistines were at war with Israel. And when David and his men were in the thick of battle,

2 Sm 21:6 As in Greek version (see also 21:9); Hebrew reads *at Gibeah of Saul, the chosen of the LORD.* **2 Sm 21:7** *Mephibosheth* is another name for Merib-baal.
2 Sm 21:8 As in a few Hebrew and Greek manuscripts and Syriac version (see also 1 Sam 18:19); most Hebrew manuscripts read *Michal.*

Ps 7:14-16 When allowed to run its course, evil destroys itself. Violent people become victims of violence, and liars become victims of others' deceit (Ps 9:15-16). In the process, however, innocent people are hurt. Sometimes God intervenes and stops evildoers in their tracks in order to protect his followers. At other times, for reasons known only to him, God allows evil to continue even though innocent people are hurt. It is during these times that we must ask God to protect us. Remember that God will execute final justice, although it may not be during our lifetime.

Ps 7:17 During a time of great evil and injustice, David was grateful that God was just and fair (see also Ps 7:11). When we wonder if anyone is honest or fair, we can be assured that God will continue to bring justice and fairness when we involve him in our activities. If you ever feel that you are being

David became weak and exhausted. [16]Ishbi-benob was a descendant of the giants*; his bronze spearhead weighed more than seven pounds,* and he was armed with a new sword. He had cornered David and was about to kill him. [17]But Abishai son of Zeruiah came to David's rescue and killed the Philistine. Then David's men declared, "You are not going out to battle with us again! Why risk snuffing out the light of Israel?"

[18]After this, there was another battle against the Philistines at Gob. As they fought, Sibbecai from Hushah killed Saph, another descendant of the giants.

[19]During another battle at Gob, Elhanan son of Jair* from Bethlehem killed the brother of Goliath of Gath.* The handle of his spear was as thick as a weaver's beam!

[20]In another battle with the Philistines at Gath, they encountered a huge man with six fingers on each hand and six toes on each foot, twenty-four in all, who was also a descendant of the giants. [21]But when he defied and taunted Israel, he was killed by Jonathan, the son of David's brother Shimea.*

[22]These four Philistines were descendants of the giants of Gath, but David and his warriors killed them.

1 CHRONICLES 20:4-8

After this, war broke out with the Philistines at Gezer. As they fought, Sibbecai from Hushah killed Saph,* a descendant of the giants,* and so the Philistines were subdued.

[5]During another battle with the Philistines, Elhanan son of Jair killed Lahmi, the brother of Goliath of Gath. The handle of Lahmi's spear was as thick as a weaver's beam!

[6]In another battle with the Philistines at Gath, they encountered a huge man with six fingers on each hand and six toes on each foot, twenty-four in all, who was

2 Sm 21:16a Or *a descendant of the Rapha;* also in 21:18, 20, 22. **2 Sm 21:16b** Hebrew *300 shekels* [3.4 kilograms]. **2 Sm 21:19a** As in parallel text at 1 Chr 20:5; Hebrew reads *son of Jaare-oregim.* **2 Sm 21:19b** As in parallel text at 1 Chr 20:5; Hebrew reads *killed Goliath of Gath.* **2 Sm 21:21** As in parallel text at 1 Chr 20:7; Hebrew reads *Shimei,* a variant spelling of Shimea. **1 Chr 20:4a** As in parallel text at 2 Sam 21:18; Hebrew reads *Sippai.* **1 Chr 20:4b** Hebrew *descendant of the Rephaites;* also in 20:6, 8.

treated unfairly, ask the one who is always fair and just to be with you. Then thank him for his presence (see Isa 42:1-6).

2 Sam 21:1 Farmers relied heavily on spring and fall rains for their crops. If the rains stopped or came at the wrong time, or if the plants became insect infested, there would be drastic food shortages in the coming year. Agriculture at that time was completely dependent upon natural conditions. There were no irrigation sprinklers, fertilizers, or pesticides. Even moderate variations in rainfall or insect activity could destroy an entire harvest.

2 Sam 21:1-14 Although the Bible does not record Saul's act of vengeance against the Gibeonites, it was apparently a serious crime making him guilty of their blood. Still, why were Saul's sons killed for the murders their father committed? In many Near Eastern cultures, including Israel's, an entire family was held guilty for the crime of the father because the family was considered an indissoluble unit. Saul broke the vow that the Israelites had made to the Gibeonites (Josh 9:16-20). This was a serious offense against God's law (Num 30:1-2). Either David was following the custom of treating the family as a unit, or Saul's sons were guilty of helping Saul kill the Gibeonites.

2 Sam 21:9-10 The barley harvest was in late April and early May. Barley was similar to wheat but less suitable for breadmaking. Rizpah guarded the men's bodies during the entire harvest season, which lasted from April to October.

2 Sam 21:16-18 For more information on giants, see 1 Samuel 17:4-7 and the note on Genesis 6:4, p. 17.

ABISHAI

Most great leaders struggle with a few followers who try too hard. For David, Abishai was that kind of follower. His fierce loyalty to David had to be kept from becoming destructive—he was too willing to leap to his leader's defense. David never put down Abishai's eager loyalty. Instead, he patiently tried to direct its powerful energy. This approach, while not completely successful, saved David's life on at least one occasion. At three other times, however, Abishai would have killed for the king if David had not stopped him. • Abishai was an excellent soldier, but he was better at taking orders than giving them. Abishai was usually under the command of his younger brother Joab. The two brothers helped each other accomplish great military feats as well as shameful acts of violence—Abishai helped Joab murder Abner and Amasa. When he was effective as a leader, he led mostly by example. But all too often he did not think before he acted. • We should be challenged by Abishai's admirable qualities of fearlessness and loyalty, but we should be warned by his tendency to act without thinking. It is not enough to be strong and effective; we must also have the self-control and wisdom that God can give us. We are to follow and obey with our hearts and our minds.

Strengths and accomplishments	• Known as one of the heroes among David's fighting men • A fearless and willing volunteer, fiercely loyal to David • Saved David's life
Weaknesses and mistakes	• Tended to act without thinking • Helped Joab murder Abner and Amasa
Lessons from his life	• Effective followers combine careful thought and action • Blind loyalty can cause great evil
Vital statistics	• Occupation: Soldier • Relatives: Mother: Zeruiah. Brothers: Joab, Asahel. Uncle: David.
Key verses	"Abishai son of Zeruiah, the brother of Joab, was the leader of the Thirty. He once used his spear to kill 300 enemy warriors in a single battle. It was by such feats that he became as famous as the Three. Abishai was the most famous of the Thirty and was their commander, though he was not one of the Three" (2 Sam 23:18-19).

Abishai's story is told in 2 Samuel 2:18–23:19. He is also mentioned in 1 Samuel 26:1-13; 1 Chronicles 2:16; 11:20; 18:12; 19:11, 15.

▶ **1 CHRONICLES 20:4-8 *(cont.)***

also a descendant of the giants. [7]But when he defied
and taunted Israel, he was killed by Jonathan, the son
of David's brother Shimea.

[8]These Philistines were descendants of the giants of
Gath, but David and his warriors killed them.

David's Song of Praise PARALLEL

2 SAMUEL 22:1-51

David sang this song to the LORD on the day the LORD
rescued him from all his enemies and from Saul.
[2]He sang:

"The LORD is my rock, my fortress, and my savior;
3 my God is my rock, in whom I find protection.
He is my shield, the power that saves me,
and my place of safety.
He is my refuge, my savior,
the one who saves me from violence.
4 I called on the LORD, who is worthy of praise,
and he saved me from my enemies.

5 "The waves of death overwhelmed me;
floods of destruction swept over me.
6 The grave* wrapped its ropes around me;
death laid a trap in my path.
7 But in my distress I cried out to the LORD;
yes, I cried to my God for help.
He heard me from his sanctuary;
my cry reached his ears.

8 "Then the earth quaked and trembled.
The foundations of the heavens shook;
they quaked because of his anger.
9 Smoke poured from his nostrils;
fierce flames leaped from his mouth.
Glowing coals blazed forth from him.
10 He opened the heavens and came down;
dark storm clouds were beneath his feet.
11 Mounted on a mighty angelic being,* he flew,
soaring* on the wings of the wind.
12 He shrouded himself in darkness,
veiling his approach with dense rain clouds.
13 A great brightness shone around him,
and burning coals* blazed forth.
14 The LORD thundered from heaven;
the voice of the Most High resounded.
15 He shot arrows and scattered his enemies;
his lightning flashed, and they were confused.
16 Then at the command of the LORD,
at the blast of his breath,
the bottom of the sea could be seen,
and the foundations of the earth were laid bare.

17 "He reached down from heaven and rescued me;
he drew me out of deep waters.
18 He rescued me from my powerful enemies,
from those who hated me and were too strong
for me.
19 They attacked me at a moment when I was
in distress,
but the LORD supported me.
20 He led me to a place of safety;
he rescued me because he delights in me.
21 The LORD rewarded me for doing right;
he restored me because of my innocence.
22 For I have kept the ways of the LORD;
I have not turned from my God to follow evil.
23 I have followed all his regulations;
I have never abandoned his decrees.
24 I am blameless before God;
I have kept myself from sin.
25 The LORD rewarded me for doing right.
He has seen my innocence.

26 "To the faithful you show yourself faithful;
to those with integrity you show integrity.
27 To the pure you show yourself pure,
but to the wicked you show yourself hostile.
28 You rescue the humble,
but your eyes watch the proud and
humiliate them.

2 Sm 22:6 Hebrew *Sheol.* **2 Sm 22:11a** Hebrew *a cherub.* **2 Sm 22:11b** As in some Hebrew manuscripts (see also Ps 18:10); other Hebrew manuscripts read *appearing.* **2 Sm 22:13** Or *and lightning bolts.*

2 Sam 22:1ff David was a skilled musician who played his harp for Saul (1 Sam 16:23), instituted the music programs in the Temple (1 Chr 25), and wrote more of the book of Psalms than anyone else. Writing a song like this was not unusual for David. This royal hymn of thanksgiving is almost identical to Psalm 18. (For other songs in the Bible, see the chart on p. 163.)

2 Sam 22:22-24 David was not denying that he had ever sinned. Psalm 51 shows his tremendous anguish over his sin against Uriah and Bathsheba. But David understood God's faithfulness and was writing this hymn from God's perspective. He knew that God had made him clean again—"whiter than snow" (Ps 51:7), with a "clean heart" (Ps 51:10). Through the death and resurrection of Jesus Christ, we also are made clean and perfect. God replaces our sin with his purity, and he no longer sees our sin.

DAVID REVEALS TRUTHS ABOUT GOD IN HIS SONG OF PRAISE

David says, **"The LORD is my . . ."**	Rock, Fortress, Savior, Protection, Shield, Power that Saves, Place of Safety, Refuge, Lamp
David names these characteristics of God. **He is . . .**	Saving, worthy of praise, hearing, angry (against enemies), rescuing, rewarding, seeing, faithful, showing (revealing) himself, shrewd, powerful, strong, perfect, pure, flawless, shielding (us from enemies), giving, gentle, preserving, living

2 Sam 22:27 "To the wicked you show yourself hostile" means that to those who sin, God is a judge who will punish them for their sins. God destroys those who are evil.

29 O LORD, you are my lamp.
The LORD lights up my darkness.
30 In your strength I can crush an army;
with my God I can scale any wall.

31 "God's way is perfect.
All the LORD's promises prove true.
He is a shield for all who look to him for protection.
32 For who is God except the LORD?
Who but our God is a solid rock?
33 God is my strong fortress,
and he makes my way perfect.
34 He makes me as surefooted as a deer,
enabling me to stand on mountain heights.
35 He trains my hands for battle;
he strengthens my arm to draw a bronze bow.
36 You have given me your shield of victory;
your help* has made me great.
37 You have made a wide path for my feet
to keep them from slipping.

38 "I chased my enemies and destroyed them;
I did not stop until they were conquered.
39 I consumed them;
I struck them down so they did not get up;
they fell beneath my feet.
40 You have armed me with strength for the battle;
you have subdued my enemies under my feet.
41 You placed my foot on their necks.
I have destroyed all who hated me.
42 They looked for help, but no one came to their rescue.
They even cried to the LORD, but he refused to answer.
43 I ground them as fine as the dust of the earth;
I trampled them* in the gutter like dirt.
44 "You gave me victory over my accusers.
You preserved me as the ruler over nations;
people I don't even know now serve me.
45 Foreign nations cringe before me;
as soon as they hear of me, they submit.
46 They all lose their courage
and come trembling* from their strongholds.

47 "The LORD lives! Praise to my Rock!
May God, the Rock of my salvation, be exalted!
48 He is the God who pays back those who harm me;
he brings down the nations under me
49 and delivers me from my enemies.
You hold me safe beyond the reach of my enemies;
you save me from violent opponents.
50 For this, O LORD, I will praise you among the nations;
I will sing praises to your name.
51 You give great victories to your king;
you show unfailing love to your anointed,
to David and all his descendants forever."

PSALM 18:1-50

THEME: Gratitude for deliverance and victory. The only sure way to be delivered from surrounding evil is to call upon God for help and strength.

AUTHOR: David

For the choir director: A psalm of David, the servant of the LORD. He sang this song to the LORD on the day the LORD rescued him from all his enemies and from Saul. He sang:

1 I love you, LORD;
you are my strength.
2 The LORD is my rock, my fortress, and my savior;
my God is my rock, in whom I find protection.

2 Sm 22:36 As in Dead Sea Scrolls (see also Ps 18:35); Masoretic Text reads *your answering.* **2 Sm 22:43** As in Dead Sea Scrolls (see also Ps 18:42); Masoretic Text reads *I crushed and trampled them.* **2 Sm 22:46** As in parallel text at Ps 18:45; Hebrew reads *come girding themselves.*

2 Sam 22:47 David praises God wholeheartedly. Praise is not just a song *about* God; it is a song *to* God. In this song, David uses many word pictures such as rock, light, and shield to portray God's marvelous attributes. Praising God has several aspects to it. We praise God when we: (1) Say thank you to him for each attribute of his divine nature. As you read the Bible, look for other characteristics of God for which to thank him. (2) Focus our hearts on God. Take one attribute of God, such as his mercy, then concentrate on it for an entire week in your meditation and prayer. (3) Thank God for his many gracious gifts to us. Make a list and count your blessings. (4) Thank God for our relationship with him. Through Christ you have been given the gift of salvation. Tell God afresh how much you appreciate it.

Ps 18:1ff This psalm is almost a duplicate of 2 Samuel 22. It was probably written toward the end of David's life when there was peace. God is praised for his glorious works and blessings through the years.

Ps 18:2-3 God's protection of his people is limitless and can take many forms. David characterized God's care with five military symbols. God is like (1) a rock that can't be moved by any who would harm us, (2) a fortress or place of safety where the enemy can't follow, (3) a shield that comes between us and harm, (4) power that saves, a symbol of might that can save us, and (5) a place of safety high above our enemies. If you need protection, look to God.

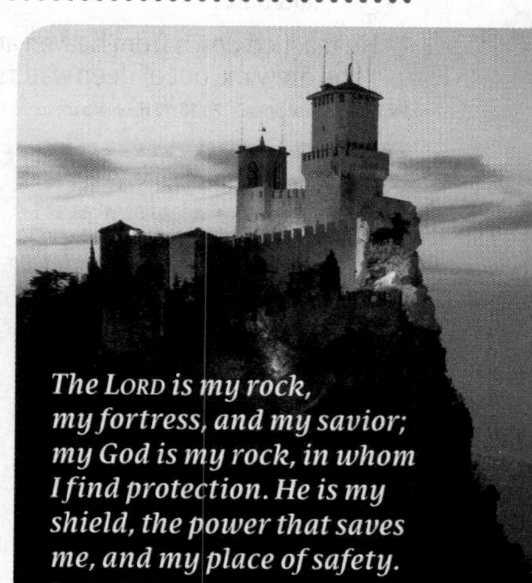
The LORD is my rock, my fortress, and my savior; my God is my rock, in whom I find protection. He is my shield, the power that saves me, and my place of safety.
Psalm 18:2

▸ **PSALM 18:1-50** ***(cont.)***

He is my shield, the power that saves me,
and my place of safety.
3 I called on the LORD, who is worthy of praise,
and he saved me from my enemies.

4 The ropes of death entangled me;
floods of destruction swept over me.
5 The grave* wrapped its ropes around me;
death laid a trap in my path.
6 But in my distress I cried out to the LORD;
yes, I prayed to my God for help.
He heard me from his sanctuary;
my cry to him reached his ears.
7 Then the earth quaked and trembled.
The foundations of the mountains shook;
they quaked because of his anger.
8 Smoke poured from his nostrils;
fierce flames leaped from his mouth.
Glowing coals blazed forth from him.
9 He opened the heavens and came down;
dark storm clouds were beneath his feet.
10 Mounted on a mighty angelic being,* he flew,
soaring on the wings of the wind.
11 He shrouded himself in darkness,
veiling his approach with dark rain clouds.
12 Thick clouds shielded the brightness
around him
and rained down hail and burning coals.*
13 The LORD thundered from heaven;
the voice of the Most High resounded
amid the hail and burning coals.
14 He shot his arrows and scattered his enemies;
his lightning flashed, and they were greatly
confused.
15 Then at your command, O LORD,
at the blast of your breath,
the bottom of the sea could be seen,
and the foundations of the earth were
laid bare.

16 He reached down from heaven and rescued me;
he drew me out of deep waters.
17 He rescued me from my powerful enemies,
from those who hated me and were too
strong for me.
18 They attacked me at a moment when I was
in distress,
but the LORD supported me.
19 He led me to a place of safety;
he rescued me because he delights in me.
20 The LORD rewarded me for doing right;
he restored me because of my innocence.
21 For I have kept the ways of the LORD;
I have not turned from my God to follow evil.
22 I have followed all his regulations;
I have never abandoned his decrees.
23 I am blameless before God;
I have kept myself from sin.
24 The LORD rewarded me for doing right.
He has seen my innocence.

25 To the faithful you show yourself faithful;
to those with integrity you show integrity.
26 To the pure you show yourself pure,
but to the wicked you show yourself hostile.
27 You rescue the humble,
but you humiliate the proud.
28 You light a lamp for me.
The LORD, my God, lights up my darkness.
29 In your strength I can crush an army;
with my God I can scale any wall.

30 God's way is perfect.
All the LORD's promises prove true.
He is a shield for all who look to him for
protection.
31 For who is God except the LORD?
Who but our God is a solid rock?
32 God arms me with strength,
and he makes my way perfect.
33 He makes me as surefooted as a deer,
enabling me to stand on mountain heights.
34 He trains my hands for battle;
he strengthens my arm to draw a
bronze bow.

Ps 18:5 Hebrew *Sheol.* **Ps 18:10** Hebrew *a cherub.* **Ps 18:12** Or *and lightning bolts;* also in 18:13.

Ps 18:10 One of the functions of this "mighty angelic being" was to serve as a guardian. Angels guarded the entrances to both the tree of life (Gen 3:24) and the Most Holy Place (Exod 26:31-33). Two angels of hammered gold were part of the Ark of the Covenant (Exod 25:18-22). The living beings carrying God's throne in Ezekiel 1 may have been these mighty angels.

Ps 18:13 The "Most High" was an important designation for David to make. Pagan idol worship was deeply rooted in the land, and each region had its own deity. But these images of wood and stone were powerless. David was placing the Lord alone in a superior category: He is by far the Most High.

Ps 18:16 Do your troubles, like "deep waters," threaten to drown you? David, helpless and weak, knew that God alone had rescued him from his enemies when he was defenseless. When you wish that God would quickly rescue you from your troubles, remember that he can either deliver you or be your support as you go through them (Ps 18:18). Either way, his protection is best for you. When you feel as though you're drowning in troubles, ask God to help you, hold you steady, and protect you. In his care, you are never helpless.

Ps 18:30 Some people think that belief in God is a crutch for weak people who cannot make it on their own. God is indeed a shield to protect us when we are too weak to face certain trials by ourselves, but he does not want us to remain weak. He strengthens, protects, and guides us in order to send us back into an evil world to fight for him. Then he continues to work with us because the strongest person on earth is infinitely weaker than God and needs his help. David was not a coward; he was a mighty warrior who, even with all his armies and weapons, knew that only God could ultimately protect and save him.

Ps 18:32-34 God doesn't promise to eliminate challenges; instead, he promises to give us strength to meet those challenges. If he gave us no rough roads to walk, no

35 You have given me your shield of victory.
Your right hand supports me;
your help has made me great.
36 You have made a wide path for my feet
to keep them from slipping.

37 I chased my enemies and caught them;
I did not stop until they were conquered.
38 I struck them down so they could not get up;
they fell beneath my feet.
39 You have armed me with strength for the battle;
you have subdued my enemies under my feet.
40 You placed my foot on their necks.
I have destroyed all who hated me.
41 They called for help, but no one came to their rescue.
They even cried to the LORD, but he refused to answer.
42 I ground them as fine as dust in the wind.
I swept them into the gutter like dirt.
43 You gave me victory over my accusers.
You appointed me ruler over nations;
people I don't even know now serve me.
44 As soon as they hear of me, they submit;
foreign nations cringe before me.
45 They all lose their courage
and come trembling from their strongholds.

46 The LORD lives! Praise to my Rock!
May the God of my salvation be exalted!
47 He is the God who pays back those who harm me;
he subdues the nations under me
48 and rescues me from my enemies.
You hold me safe beyond the reach of my enemies;
you save me from violent opponents.
49 For this, O LORD, I will praise you among the nations;
I will sing praises to your name.
50 You give great victories to your king;
you show unfailing love to your anointed,
to David and all his descendants forever.

David Takes a Census PARALLEL

2 SAMUEL 24:1-9

Once again the anger of the LORD burned against Israel, and he caused David to harm them by taking a
census. "Go and count the people of Israel and Judah,"
the LORD told him.
2So the king said to Joab and the commanders* of
the army, "Take a census of all the tribes of Israel—
from Dan in the north to Beersheba in the south—so
I may know how many people there are."
3But Joab replied to the king, "May the LORD your
God let you live to see a hundred times as many people
as there are now! But why, my lord the king, do you
want to do this?"
4But the king insisted that they take the census,
so Joab and the commanders of the army went out
to count the people of Israel. 5First they crossed the
Jordan and camped at Aroer, south of the town in the
valley, in the direction of Gad. Then they went on to
Jazer, 6then to Gilead in the land of Tahtim-hodshi*
and to Dan-jaan and around to Sidon. 7Then they came
to the fortress of Tyre, and all the towns of the Hivites
and Canaanites. Finally, they went south to Judah* as
far as Beersheba.
8Having gone through the entire land for nine
months and twenty days, they returned to Jerusalem.
9Joab reported the number of people to the king.
There were 800,000 capable warriors in Israel who
could handle a sword, and 500,000 in Judah.

2 Sm 24:2 As in Greek version (see also 24:4 and 1 Chr 21:2); Hebrew reads *Joab the commander.* **2 Sm 24:6** Greek version reads *to Gilead and to Kadesh in the land of the Hittites.* **2 Sm 24:7** Or *they went to the Negev of Judah.*

mountains to climb, and no battles to fight, we would not grow. But he does not leave us alone with our challenges. Instead, he stands beside us, teaches us, and strengthens us to face them.

Ps 18:40-42 David was a merciful man. He spared the lives of Saul (1 Sam 24:1-8), Nabal (1 Sam 25:21-35), and Shimei (2 Sam 16:5-12) and showed great kindness to Mephibosheth (2 Sam 9). In asking God to destroy his enemies, David was simply asking him to give the wicked the punishment they deserved.

Ps 18:43-45 David's great power had become legendary. God had given him victory in every battle. The book of 2 Samuel records victories over the Jebusites (2 Sam 5:6-10), the Philistines (2 Sam 5:17-25; 8:1), Hadadezer of Zobah (2 Sam 8:3-4), the Arameans (2 Sam 8:5-6, 10), the Edomites (2 Sam 8:13-14), and the Ammonites (2 Sam 12:26-31). In addition, the king of Tyre had sent supplies and workmen to help David build his palace (2 Sam 5:11). But David did not attribute his victories to himself. He fully realized that the purpose of his position was to bless God's people (1 Chr 14:2).

2 Sam 24:1 Did God cause David to sin? God does not cause people to sin, but he does allow sinners to reveal the sinfulness of their hearts by their actions. God presented the opportunity to David in order to deal with a disastrous national tendency, and he wanted this desire to show itself. According to 1 Chronicles 21:1, Satan incited David to do it. Hebrew writers do not always distinguish between primary and secondary causes. So if God allowed Satan to tempt David, to them it is as if God did it.

2 Sam 24:1-3 What was wrong with taking a census? A census was commanded in Numbers to prepare an army for conquering the Promised Land (Num 1:2; 26:2). A census amounted to a draft or conscription for the army. The land was now at peace, so there was no need to enlist troops. Israel had extended its borders and become a recognized power. David's sin was pride and ambition in counting the people so that he could glory in the size of his army, its power and its defenses. By doing this, he put his faith in the size of his army rather than in God's ability to protect them regardless of their number. Even Joab, not known for his high moral ideals, knew a census was wrong, but David did not heed his advice. We sin in a similar way when we place our security in money, possessions, or the might of our nation. There is a thin line between feeling confident because you are relying on God's power and becoming proud because you have been used by God for great purposes.

1 CHRONICLES 21:1-6

Satan rose up against Israel and caused David to take a census of the people of Israel. 2So David said to Joab and the commanders of the army, "Take a census of all the people of Israel—from Beersheba in the south to Dan in the north—and bring me a report so I may know how many there are."

3But Joab replied, "May the LORD increase the number of his people a hundred times over! But why, my lord the king, do you want to do this? Are they not all your servants? Why must you cause Israel to sin?"

4But the king insisted that they take the census, so Joab traveled throughout all Israel to count the people. Then he returned to Jerusalem 5and reported the number of people to David. There were 1,100,000 warriors in all Israel who could handle a sword, and 470,000 in Judah. 6But Joab did not include the tribes of Levi and Benjamin in the census because he was so distressed at what the king had made him do.

Judgment for David's Sin PARALLEL

2 SAMUEL 24:10-17

But after he had taken the census, David's conscience began to bother him. And he said to the LORD, "I have sinned greatly by taking this census. Please forgive my guilt, LORD, for doing this foolish thing."

11The next morning the word of the LORD came to the prophet Gad, who was David's seer. This was the message: 12"Go and say to David, 'This is what the LORD says: I will give you three choices. Choose one of these punishments, and I will inflict it on you.'"

13So Gad came to David and asked him, "Will you choose three* years of famine throughout your land, three months of fleeing from your enemies, or three days of severe plague throughout your land? Think this over and decide what answer I should give the LORD who sent me."

14"I'm in a desperate situation!" David replied to Gad. "But let us fall into the hands of the LORD, for his mercy is great. Do not let me fall into human hands."

15So the LORD sent a plague upon Israel that morning, and it lasted for three days.* A total of 70,000 people died throughout the nation, from Dan in the north to Beersheba in the south. 16But as the angel was preparing to destroy Jerusalem, the LORD relented and said to the death angel, "Stop! That is enough!" At that moment the angel of the LORD was by the threshing floor of Araunah the Jebusite.

17When David saw the angel, he said to the LORD, "I am the one who has sinned and done wrong! But these people are as innocent as sheep—what have they done? Let your anger fall against me and my family."

1 CHRONICLES 21:7-17

God was very displeased with the census, and he punished Israel for it. 8Then David said to God, "I have sinned greatly by taking this census. Please forgive my guilt for doing this foolish thing."

9Then the LORD spoke to Gad, David's seer. This was the message: 10"Go and say to David, 'This is what the LORD says: I will give you three choices. Choose one of these punishments, and I will inflict it on you.'"

11So Gad came to David and said, "These are the choices the LORD has given you. 12You may choose three years of famine, three months of destruction by the sword of your enemies, or three days of severe plague as the angel of the LORD brings devastation throughout the land of Israel. Decide what answer I should give the LORD who sent me."

13"I'm in a desperate situation!" David replied to Gad. "But let me fall into the hands of the LORD, for his mercy is very great. Do not let me fall into human hands."

14So the LORD sent a plague upon Israel, and 70,000

2 Sm 24:13 As in Greek version (see also 1 Chr 21:12); Hebrew reads *seven.* **2 Sm 24:15** Hebrew *for the designated time.*

---

1 Chr 21:1 The Bible text says Satan "caused David to take a census." Can Satan force people to do wrong? No, Satan only tempted David with the idea, but David decided to act on the temptation. Ever since the Garden of Eden, Satan has been tempting people to sin. David's census was not against God's law, but his reason for the census was wrong—pride in his mighty army. He forgot that his real strength came from God. From David's example we learn that an action that may not be wrong in itself can be sinful if it is motivated by greed, arrogance, or selfishness. Often our motives, not the action itself, contain the sin. We must constantly weigh our motives before we act.

1 Chr 21:1-3 David fell to Satan's temptation. God provided a way out in Joab's counsel, but David's curiosity was spurred on by arrogance. His faith was in his own strength rather than in God's. If we feel self-sufficient and put confidence in ourselves apart from God, we soon fall to Satan's schemes. Self-sufficiency pulls us away from God. When tempted, we should examine our inner desires to understand why the external temptation is so appealing. (See 1 Cor 10:13 for more about escaping temptation.)

2 Sam 24:12-14 Both David and the Israelites were guilty of sin (2 Sam 24:1). David's sin was pride, but the Bible does not say why God was angry with the people of Israel. Perhaps it was due to their support of the rebellions of Absalom (2 Sam 15–18) and Sheba (2 Sam 20), or perhaps they put their security in military and financial prosperity rather than in God, as David did. God dealt with the whole nation through David, who exemplified the national sin of pride.

God gave David three choices. Each was a form of punishment God had told the people they could expect if they disobeyed his laws: plague, famine, war (Deut 28:20-26). David wisely chose the form of punishment that came most directly from God. He knew how brutal and harsh men in war could be, and he also knew God's great mercy. When you sin greatly, turn back to God. To be punished by him is far better than to take your chances without him.

1 Chr 21:8 When David realized his sin, he took full responsibility, admitted he was wrong, and asked God to forgive him. Many people want to add God and the benefits of Christianity to their lives without acknowledging their personal sin and guilt. But confession and repentance must come before receiving forgiveness. Like David, we must take full responsibility for our actions and confess them to God before we can expect him to forgive us and continue his work in us.

1 Chr 21:13-14 Sin has a domino effect; once a sin is committed, a series of consequences follows. God will forgive our sin if we ask him, but the consequences of that

people died as a result. 15 And God sent an angel to destroy Jerusalem. But just as the angel was preparing to destroy it, the LORD relented and said to the death angel, "Stop! That is enough!" At that moment the angel of the LORD was standing by the threshing floor of Araunah* the Jebusite.

16 David looked up and saw the angel of the LORD standing between heaven and earth with his sword drawn, reaching out over Jerusalem. So David and the leaders of Israel put on burlap to show their deep distress and fell face down on the ground. 17 And David said to God, "I am the one who called for the census! I am the one who has sinned and done wrong! But these people are as innocent as sheep—what have they done? O LORD my God, let your anger fall against me and my family, but do not destroy your people."

David Builds an Altar PARALLEL

2 SAMUEL 24:18-25

That day Gad came to David and said to him, "Go up and build an altar to the LORD on the threshing floor of Araunah the Jebusite."

19 So David went up to do what the LORD had commanded him. 20 When Araunah saw the king and his men coming toward him, he came and bowed before the king with his face to the ground. 21 "Why have you come, my lord the king?" Araunah asked.

David replied, "I have come to buy your threshing floor and to build an altar to the LORD there, so that he will stop the plague."

22 "Take it, my lord the king, and use it as you wish," Araunah said to David. "Here are oxen for the burnt offering, and you can use the threshing boards and ox yokes for wood to build a fire on the altar. 23 I will give it all to you, Your Majesty, and may the LORD your God accept your sacrifice."

24 But the king replied to Araunah, "No, I insist on buying it, for I will not present burnt offerings to the LORD my God that have cost me nothing." So David paid him fifty pieces of silver* for the threshing floor and the oxen.

25 David built an altar there to the LORD and sacrificed burnt offerings and peace offerings. And the LORD answered his prayer for the land, and the plague on Israel was stopped.

1 CHRONICLES 21:18–22:1

Then the angel of the LORD told Gad to instruct David to go up and build an altar to the LORD on the threshing floor of Araunah the Jebusite. 19 So David went up to do what the LORD had commanded him through Gad. 20 Araunah, who was busy threshing wheat at the time, turned and saw the angel there. His four sons, who were with him, ran away and hid. 21 When Araunah saw David approaching, he left his threshing floor and bowed before David with his face to the ground.

22 David said to Araunah, "Let me buy this threshing floor from you at its full price. Then I will build an altar to the LORD there, so that he will stop the plague."

23 "Take it, my lord the king, and use it as you wish," Araunah said to David. "I will give the oxen for the

1 Chr 21:15 As in parallel text at 2 Sam 24:16; Hebrew reads *Ornan,* another name for Araunah; also in 21:18-28. **2 Sm 24:24** Hebrew *50 shekels of silver,* about 20 ounces or 570 grams in weight.

---

sin have already been set in motion. David pleaded for mercy, and God responded by stopping the angel before his mission of death was complete. The consequences of David's sin, however, had already caused severe damage. God will always forgive our sins and will often intervene to make their bitter consequences less severe, but the scars will remain. Thinking through the possible consequences before we act can stop us and thus save us much sorrow and suffering.

1 Chr 21:14 Why did 70,000 innocent people die for David's sin? Our society places great emphasis upon the individual. But in ancient times, the family leaders, tribal leaders, and kings represented the people they led, and all expected to share in their successes as well as in their failures and punishments. David deserved punishment for his sin, but his death could have resulted in political chaos and invasion by enemy armies, leaving hundreds of thousands dead. Instead, God graciously spared David's life. He also put a stop to the plague so that most of the people of Jerusalem were spared.

God made us to work together interdependently. Whether we think it is fair or not, the group usually suffers because of the sins of its leaders. Similarly, our actions always affect other people whether we want them to or not. We cannot fully know the mind of God in this severe judgment. We don't know where the prophets, the tribal leaders, and the other advisers were during this incident and whether or not they chose to go along with the king. We do know that putting confidence in military might alone is idolatry. To allow anything to take God's place is sinful, and it may cause disastrous consequences.

2 Sam 24:18 Many believe that this threshing floor where David built the altar is the location where Abraham nearly sacrificed his son Isaac (Gen 22:1-18). After David's death, Solomon built the Temple on this spot. Centuries later, Jesus would teach and preach here.

2 Sam 24:25 The book of 2 Samuel describes David's reign. Since the Israelites first entered the Promised Land under Joshua, they had been struggling to unite the nation and drive out the wicked inhabitants. Now, after more than 400 years, Israel was finally at peace. David had accomplished what no leader before him, judge or king, had done. His administration was run on the principle of dedication to God and to the well-being of the people. Yet David also sinned. Despite his sins, the Bible calls David a man after God's own heart (1 Sam 13:14; Acts 13:22) because when he sinned, he recognized it and confessed his sins to God. David committed his life to God and remained loyal to him throughout his lifetime. David's psalms give an even deeper insight into his love for God.

1 Chr 21:22-24 When David wanted to buy Araunah's land to build an altar, Araunah generously offered it as a gift. But David refused, saying, "I will not take what is yours and give it to the LORD. I will not present burnt offerings that have cost me nothing!" David wanted to present an offering (or sacrifice) to God. An offering should cost the giver in terms of self, time, or money. To give sacrificially requires more than a token effort or gift. God wants us to give voluntarily, but he wants it to mean something. Giving to God what costs you nothing does not demonstrate commitment.

▶ **1 CHRONICLES 21:18–22:1** ***(cont.)***
burnt offerings, and the threshing boards for wood to build a fire on the altar, and the wheat for the grain offering. I will give it all to you."

24But King David replied to Araunah, "No, I insist on buying it for the full price. I will not take what is yours and give it to the LORD. I will not present burnt offerings that have cost me nothing!" 25So David gave Araunah 600 pieces of gold* in payment for the threshing floor.

26David built an altar there to the LORD and sacrificed burnt offerings and peace offerings. And when David prayed, the LORD answered him by sending fire from heaven to burn up the offering on the altar.

27Then the LORD spoke to the angel, who put the sword back into its sheath.

28When David saw that the LORD had answered his prayer, he offered sacrifices there at Araunah's threshing floor. 29At that time the Tabernacle of the LORD and the altar of burnt offering that Moses had made in the wilderness were located at the place of worship in Gibeon. 30But David was not able to go there to inquire of God, because he was terrified by the drawn sword of the angel of the LORD.

22:1 Then David said, "This will be the location for the Temple of the LORD God and the place of the altar for Israel's burnt offerings!"

1 Chr 21:25 Hebrew *600 shekels of gold,* about 15 pounds or 6.8 kilograms in weight.

5. DAVID ARRANGES FOR THE BUILDING OF THE TEMPLE

David wanted to build a Temple for God in Jerusalem, but God had told him that his son would be the one to do that. David still wanted to honor God, and so before his reign ended he took several steps to prepare for the building of the Temple. He gathered gifts from the people of Israel to have ample supplies for building a magnificent Temple, and he laid out the duties of various groups of Levites and priests for service in the Temple. Although David made several major mistakes with tragic consequences, he also demonstrated great care in following God and leading the nation in worshiping God properly.

Preparations for the Temple

1 CHRONICLES 22:2-19
So David gave orders to call together the foreigners living in Israel, and he assigned them the task of preparing finished stone for building the Temple of God.
3David provided large amounts of iron for the nails that would be needed for the doors in the gates and for the clamps, and he gave more bronze than could be weighed. 4He also provided innumerable cedar logs, for the men of Tyre and Sidon had brought vast amounts of cedar to David.

5David said, "My son Solomon is still young and inexperienced. And since the Temple to be built for the LORD must be a magnificent structure, famous and glorious throughout the world, I will begin making preparations for it now." So David collected vast amounts of building materials before his death.

6Then David sent for his son Solomon and instructed him to build a Temple for the LORD, the God of Israel. 7"My son, I wanted to build a Temple to honor the name of the LORD my God," David told him. 8"But the LORD said to me, 'You have killed many men in the battles you have fought. And since you have shed so much blood in my sight, you will not be the one to build a Temple to honor my name.
9But you will have a son who will be a man of peace. I will give him peace with his enemies in all the surrounding lands. His name will be Solomon,* and I will give peace and quiet to Israel during his reign.
10He is the one who will build a Temple to honor my name. He will be my son, and I will be his father. And I will secure the throne of his kingdom over Israel forever.'

11"Now, my son, may the LORD be with you and give

1 Chr 22:9 *Solomon* sounds like and is probably derived from the Hebrew word for "peace."

1 Chr 21:29–22:1 Gibeon was a Benjaminite city about a two-hour journey northwest of Jerusalem. Years before, Saul had moved the Tabernacle there. In this instance, David didn't go there because he was overwhelmed by God's holy wrath, as he had been earlier when one person died moving the Ark toward Jerusalem. Now 70,000 had died as a result of his pride. The fear David felt was the kind of awe that each of us should have when we consider God's character and God's standards. While we may enjoy God's mercy and acceptance, we dare not take for granted that our God is also holy.

1 Chr 22:1 Out of David's tragic mistake came the purchase of a plot of land that would become the site of God's Temple, the symbol of God's presence among his people. Every time the people would go to the Temple they would remember that God was their true King and that everyone, including their human king, was fallible and subject to sin. God can use our sins for good purposes if we are sorry for them and seek his forgiveness. When we confess our sins, the way is opened for God to bring good from a bad situation.

1 Chr 22:7-10 God told David he would not be the one to build the Temple. Instead, the task would be left to his son Solomon. David graciously accepted this no from God. He was not jealous of the fact that his son would have the honor of building God's Temple but instead made preparations for Solomon to carry out his task. Similarly, we should take steps now to prepare the way for our children to find and fulfill God's purpose. Sooner or later our children will have to make their own decisions, but we can help by supplying them with the proper tools: showing them how to pray and study God's Word, teaching the difference between right and wrong, and modeling the importance of church involvement.

1 Chr 22:11-16 David made it a point to explain to Solomon exactly why he would be charged with the privilege of building the Temple. His instructions to Solomon, including God's reasons for using David in a limited way, must have been memorable moments for Solomon. The conversations you success as you follow his directions in building the Temple of the LORD your God. [12]And may the LORD give you wisdom and understanding, that you may obey the Law of the LORD your God as you rule over Israel. [13]For you will be successful if you carefully obey the decrees and regulations that the LORD gave to Israel through Moses. Be strong and courageous; do not be afraid or lose heart!

[14]"I have worked hard to provide materials for building the Temple of the LORD—nearly 4,000 tons of gold, 40,000 tons of silver,* and so much iron and bronze that it cannot be weighed. I have also gathered timber and stone for the walls, though you may need to add more. [15]You have a large number of skilled stonemasons and carpenters and craftsmen of every kind. [16]You have expert goldsmiths and silversmiths and workers of bronze and iron. Now begin the work, and may the LORD be with you!"

[17]Then David ordered all the leaders of Israel to assist Solomon in this project. [18]"The LORD your God is with you," he declared. "He has given you peace with the surrounding nations. He has handed them over to me, and they are now subject to the LORD and his people. [19]Now seek the LORD your God with all your heart and soul. Build the sanctuary of the LORD God so that you can bring the Ark of the LORD's Covenant and the holy vessels of God into the Temple built to honor the LORD's name."

Duties of the Levites

1 CHRONICLES 23:1-6

When David was an old man, he appointed his son Solomon to be king over Israel. [2]David summoned all the leaders of Israel, together with the priests and Levites. [3]All the Levites who were thirty years old or older were counted, and the total came to 38,000. [4]Then David said, "From all the Levites, 24,000 will supervise the work at the Temple of the LORD. Another 6,000 will serve as officials and judges. [5]Another 4,000 will work as gatekeepers, and 4,000 will praise the LORD with the musical instruments I have made." [6]Then David divided the Levites into divisions named after the clans descended from the three sons of Levi—Gershon, Kohath, and Merari.

The Gershonites

1 CHRONICLES 23:7-11

[7]The Gershonite family units were defined by their lines of descent from Libni* and Shimei, the sons of Gershon. [8]Three of the descendants of Libni were Jehiel (the family leader), Zetham, and Joel. [9]These were the leaders of the family of Libni.

1 Chr 22:14 Hebrew *100,000 talents* [3,400 metric tons] *of gold, 1,000,000 talents* [34,000 metric tons] *of silver.* **1 Chr 23:7** Hebrew *Ladan* (also in 23:8, 9), a variant spelling of Libni; compare 6:17.

DUTIES ASSIGNED IN THE TEMPLE

King David charged all these people to do their jobs "to honor the LORD's name" (1 Chr 22:17-19). God needs people of every talent—not just prophets and priests—to obey him.

Administrative Duties	Supervisors	1 Chr 23:4-5
	Officials	1 Chr 23:4-5
	Judges	1 Chr 23:4-5
	Public administrators	1 Chr 26:29-30
Ministerial Duties	Priests	1 Chr 24:1
	Prophets	1 Chr 25:1
	Assistants for sacrifices	1 Chr 23:29-31
	Assistants for purification ceremonies	1 Chr 23:28
Service Duties	Bakers of the sacred bread	1 Chr 23:29
	Those who checked the weights and measures	1 Chr 23:29
	Caretakers	1 Chr 23:28
Financial Duties	Those who cared for the treasuries	1 Chr 26:20
	Those who cared for the dedicated gifts	1 Chr 26:26-28
Artistic Duties	Musicians	1 Chr 25:6
	Singers	1 Chr 25:7
Protective Duties	Gatekeepers	1 Chr 26:12-18
Individual Assignments	Chief of the gatekeepers	1 Chr 9:19-21
	Secretary	1 Chr 24:6
	Seer	1 Chr 25:5
	Prophet under the king	1 Chr 25:2
	Chief officer of the treasuries	1 Chr 26:23-24

we have with our children deserve our attention, honesty, and vision. Times when we tell our children what we pray God will accomplish in their lives can be some of the best gifts we give them.

1 Chr 23:1ff Although David couldn't build the Temple, he could make preparations, and he took that job seriously. He not only gathered funds and materials for God's house but also planned much of the administration and arranged the worship services. The original readers of Chronicles were rebuilding the Temple after it had been destroyed by invading armies, and this information about its procedures was invaluable to them. The next five chapters demonstrate that organization is essential for smooth and effective service.

1 Chr 23:3 Why was this census acceptable when the other was not (1 Chr 21)? This census counted only the Levites—those set apart to serve God—and was used to organize the work in the Temple. The census was not based on pride or self-sufficiency, as was the previous census of fighting men.

▸ **1 CHRONICLES 23:7-11** ***(cont.)***

Three of the descendants of Shimei were Shelomoth,
Haziel, and Haran. [10]Four other descendants of
Shimei were Jahath, Ziza,* Jeush, and Beriah.
[11]Jahath was the family leader, and Ziza was next.
Jeush and Beriah were counted as a single family
because neither had many sons.

The Kohathites

1 CHRONICLES 23:12-20

[12]Four of the descendants of Kohath were Amram,
Izhar, Hebron, and Uzziel.
[13]The sons of Amram were Aaron and Moses.
Aaron and his descendants were set apart to
dedicate the most holy things, to offer sacrifices
in the LORD's presence, to serve the LORD, and to
pronounce blessings in his name forever.
[14]As for Moses, the man of God, his sons
were included with the tribe of Levi. [15]The sons
of Moses were Gershom and Eliezer. [16]The
descendants of Gershom included Shebuel,
the family leader. [17]Eliezer had only one son,
Rehabiah, the family leader. Rehabiah had
numerous descendants.
[18]The descendants of Izhar included Shelomith, the
family leader.
[19]The descendants of Hebron included Jeriah (the
family leader), Amariah (the second), Jahaziel (the
third), and Jekameam (the fourth).
[20]The descendants of Uzziel included Micah (the
family leader) and Isshiah (the second).

The Merarites

1 CHRONICLES 23:21-32

[21]The descendants of Merari included Mahli and
Mushi.
The sons of Mahli were Eleazar and Kish. [22]Eleazar
died with no sons, only daughters. His daughters
married their cousins, the sons of Kish.
[23]Three of the descendants of Mushi were Mahli,
Eder, and Jerimoth.
[24]These were the descendants of Levi by clans,
the leaders of their family groups, registered carefully by name. Each had to be twenty years old or
older to qualify for service in the house of the LORD.
[25]For David said, "The LORD, the God of Israel, has
given us peace, and he will always live in Jerusalem.
[26]Now the Levites will no longer need to carry the
Tabernacle and its furnishings from place to place."
[27]In accordance with David's final instructions, all
the Levites twenty years old or older were registered
for service.
[28]The work of the Levites was to assist the priests,
the descendants of Aaron, as they served at the house
of the LORD. They also took care of the courtyards
and side rooms, helped perform the ceremonies of
purification, and served in many other ways in the
house of God. [29]They were in charge of the sacred
bread that was set out on the table, the choice flour
for the grain offerings, the wafers made without yeast,
the cakes cooked in olive oil, and the other mixed
breads. They were also responsible to check all the
weights and measures. [30]And each morning and
evening they stood before the LORD to sing songs of
thanks and praise to him. [31]They assisted with the
burnt offerings that were presented to the LORD on
Sabbath days, at new moon celebrations, and at all the
appointed festivals. The required number of Levites
served in the LORD's presence at all times, following
all the procedures they had been given.
[32]And so, under the supervision of the priests, the
Levites watched over the Tabernacle and the Temple*
and faithfully carried out their duties of service at the
house of the LORD.

Duties of the Priests

1 CHRONICLES 24:1-19

This is how Aaron's descendants, the priests, were
divided into groups for service. The sons of Aaron
were Nadab, Abihu, Eleazar, and Ithamar. [2]But Nadab
and Abihu died before their father, and they had no
sons. So only Eleazar and Ithamar were left to carry
on as priests.

1 Chr 23:10 As in Greek version and Latin Vulgate (see also 23:11); Hebrew reads *Zina.* **1 Chr 23:32** Hebrew *the Tent of Meeting and the sanctuary.*

1 Chr 23:14 All that is stated here about Moses is that he was "the man of God." What a profound description of a person! A man or woman of God is one whose life reflects God's presence, priorities, and power.

1 Chr 23:28-32 Priests and Levites had different jobs in and around the Temple. Priests were authorized to perform the sacrifices. Levites were set apart to help the priests. They did the work of elders, deacons, custodians, assistants, musicians, moving men, and repairmen. Both priests and Levites came from the tribe of Levi, but priests also had to be descendants of Aaron, Israel's first high priest (Exod 28:1-3). Priests and Levites were supported by Israel's tithes and by revenues from certain cities that had been given to them. Worship in the house of the Lord could not have taken place without the combined efforts of the priests and Levites. Their responsibilities were different, but they were equally important to God's plan. No matter what place of service you have in the church, you are important to the healthy functioning of the congregation.

1 Chr 24:1ff The Temple service was highly structured, but this did not hinder the Spirit of God. Rather, it provided an orderly context for worship. (Compare this passage to 1 Cor 14:40.) Sometimes we feel that planning and structure are unspiritual activities that may hinder spontaneity in worship. But order and structure can free us to respond to God. Order brings glory to God as we experience the joy, freedom, and calm that come when we have wisely planned in advance.

1 Chr 24:3 This Ahimelech was the son of Abiathar and the grandson of another Ahimelech, one of the priests massacred by Saul (1 Sam 22:11-18). Abiathar and Zadok were co–high priests under David: One was at Jerusalem where the Ark of God was kept, and one was at Gibeon serving at the Tabernacle. It appears from this verse and 1 Chronicles 18:16 that Ahimelech began to assume some of Abiathar's duties as his father grew old.

[3]With the help of Zadok, who was a descendant of Eleazar, and of Ahimelech, who was a descendant of Ithamar, David divided Aaron's descendants into groups according to their various duties. [4]Eleazar's descendants were divided into sixteen groups and Ithamar's into eight, for there were more family leaders among the descendants of Eleazar.

[5]All tasks were assigned to the various groups by means of sacred lots so that no preference would be shown, for there were many qualified officials serving God in the sanctuary from among the descendants of both Eleazar and Ithamar. [6]Shemaiah son of Nethanel, a Levite, acted as secretary and wrote down the names and assignments in the presence of the king, the officials, Zadok the priest, Ahimelech son of Abiathar, and the family leaders of the priests and Levites. The descendants of Eleazar and Ithamar took turns casting lots.

7 The first lot fell to Jehoiarib.
The second lot fell to Jedaiah.
8 The third lot fell to Harim.
The fourth lot fell to Seorim.
9 The fifth lot fell to Malkijah.
The sixth lot fell to Mijamin.
10 The seventh lot fell to Hakkoz.
The eighth lot fell to Abijah.
11 The ninth lot fell to Jeshua.
The tenth lot fell to Shecaniah.
12 The eleventh lot fell to Eliashib.
The twelfth lot fell to Jakim.
13 The thirteenth lot fell to Huppah.
The fourteenth lot fell to Jeshebeab.
14 The fifteenth lot fell to Bilgah.
The sixteenth lot fell to Immer.
15 The seventeenth lot fell to Hezir.
The eighteenth lot fell to Happizzez.
16 The nineteenth lot fell to Pethahiah.
The twentieth lot fell to Jehezkel.
17 The twenty-first lot fell to Jakin.
The twenty-second lot fell to Gamul.
18 The twenty-third lot fell to Delaiah.
The twenty-fourth lot fell to Maaziah.

[19]Each group carried out its appointed duties in the house of the Lord according to the procedures established by their ancestor Aaron in obedience to the commands of the Lord, the God of Israel.

Family Leaders among the Levites

1 CHRONICLES 24:20-31

These were the other family leaders descended from Levi:

From the descendants of Amram, the leader was Shebuel.*
From the descendants of Shebuel, the leader was Jehdeiah.
21 From the descendants of Rehabiah, the leader was Isshiah.
22 From the descendants of Izhar, the leader was Shelomith.*
From the descendants of Shelomith, the leader was Jahath.
23 From the descendants of Hebron, Jeriah was the leader,* Amariah was second, Jahaziel was third, and Jekameam was fourth.
24 From the descendants of Uzziel, the leader was Micah.
From the descendants of Micah, the leader was Shamir, [25]along with Isshiah, the brother of Micah.
From the descendants of Isshiah, the leader was Zechariah.
26 From the descendants of Merari, the leaders were Mahli and Mushi.
From the descendants of Jaaziah, the leader was Beno.
27 From the descendants of Merari through Jaaziah, the leaders were Beno, Shoham, Zaccur, and Ibri.
28 From the descendants of Mahli, the leader was Eleazar, though he had no sons.
29 From the descendants of Kish, the leader was Jerahmeel.
30 From the descendants of Mushi, the leaders were Mahli, Eder, and Jerimoth.

These were the descendants of Levi in their various families. [31]Like the descendants of Aaron, they were assigned to their duties by means of sacred lots, without regard to age or rank. Lots were drawn in the presence of King David, Zadok, Ahimelech, and the family leaders of the priests and the Levites.

1 Chr 24:20 Hebrew *Shubael* (also in 24:20b), a variant spelling of Shebuel; compare 23:16 and 26:24. **1 Chr 24:22** Hebrew *Shelomoth* (also in 24:22b), a variant spelling of Shelomith; compare 23:18. **1 Chr 24:23** Hebrew *From the descendants of Jeriah;* compare 23:19.

1 Chr 24:4 Eleazar's descendants were divided into 16 groups (as opposed to Ithamar's 8) for three reasons: (1) Eleazar had received the birthright since his two older brothers, Nadab and Abihu, had been killed (Lev 10). The birthright included a double portion of the father's estate. (2) His descendants were greater in number than Ithamar's. (3) His descendants had greater leadership ability. These 24 groups gave order to the functioning of the house of the Lord.

1 Chr 24:7-18 Each of these 24 groups of priests served a two-week shift each year at the house of the Lord. The rest of the time they served in their hometowns. This system was still in place in Jesus' day (Luke 1:5-9). Zechariah was a member of the Abijah division. During his shift at the Temple, an angel appeared to him and predicted that he would have a son, John.

Duties of the Musicians

1 CHRONICLES 25:1-31

David and the army commanders then appointed men from the families of Asaph, Heman, and Jeduthun to proclaim God's messages to the accompaniment of lyres, harps, and cymbals. Here is a list of their names and their work:

2 From the sons of Asaph, there were Zaccur, Joseph, Nethaniah, and Asarelah. They worked under the direction of their father, Asaph, who proclaimed God's messages by the king's orders.

3 From the sons of Jeduthun, there were Gedaliah, Zeri, Jeshaiah, Shimei,* Hashabiah, and Mattithiah, six in all. They worked under the direction of their father, Jeduthun, who proclaimed God's messages to the accompaniment of the lyre, offering thanks and praise to the LORD.

4 From the sons of Heman, there were Bukkiah, Mattaniah, Uzziel, Shubael,* Jerimoth, Hananiah, Hanani, Eliathah, Giddalti, Romamti-ezer, Joshbekashah, Mallothi, Hothir, and Mahazioth.
5 All these were the sons of Heman, the king's seer, for God had honored him with fourteen sons and three daughters.

6 All these men were under the direction of their fathers as they made music at the house of the LORD. Their responsibilities included the playing of cymbals, harps, and lyres at the house of God. Asaph, Jeduthun, and Heman reported directly to the king.
7 They and their families were all trained in making music before the LORD, and each of them—288 in all—was an accomplished musician.
8 The musicians were appointed to their term of service by means of sacred lots, without regard to whether they were young or old, teacher or student.

9 The first lot fell to Joseph of the Asaph clan and twelve of his sons and relatives.*
The second lot fell to Gedaliah and twelve of his sons and relatives.
10 The third lot fell to Zaccur and twelve of his sons and relatives.

1 Chr 25:3 As in one Hebrew manuscript and some Greek manuscripts (see also 25:17); most Hebrew manuscripts lack *Shimei*. **1 Chr 25:4** Hebrew *Shebuel*, a variant spelling of Shubael; compare 25:20. **1 Chr 25:9** As in Greek version; Hebrew lacks *and twelve of his sons and relatives.*

MUSIC IN BIBLE TIMES

Highlights of Musical Use in Scripture	*Reference*
Jubal was father of all musicians	**Gen 4:21**
Miriam and other women sang and danced to praise God	**Exod 15:1-21**
The priest was to have bells on his robes	**Exod 28:34-35**
Jericho fell to the sound of horns	**Josh 6:4-20**
Saul experienced the soothing effect of music	**1 Sam 16:14-23**
The king's coronation was accompanied by music	**1 Kgs 1:39-40**
The Ark was accompanied by trumpeters	**1 Chr 16:6**
There were musicians for the king's court	**Eccl 2:8**
From David's time on, the use of music in worship was much more organized. Music for the Temple became refined.	**1 Chr 15:16-24** **1 Chr 16:4-7** **2 Chr 5:11-14**
Everything was to be used by everyone to praise the Lord	**Ps 150**

In the New Testament, worship continued in the synagogues until the Christians became unwelcome there, so there was a rich musical heritage already established. The fact that music is mentioned less often in the New Testament does not mean it was less important.

Jesus and the disciples sang a hymn	**Matt 26:30**
Paul and Silas sang in jail	**Acts 16:25**
We are to sing to the Lord as a response to what he has done in our lives	**Eph 5:19-20** **Col 3:16** **Jas 5:13**

Paul clearly states that things are not good or bad in and of themselves (see Rom 14; 1 Cor 14:7-8, 26). The point is, we can use the things of this world, including music, to worship the Lord. Music was created by God and can be returned to him in praise. Does the music you play or listen to have a negative or positive impact upon your relationship with God?

1 Chr 25:1-7 There were many ways to contribute to the worship in the Tabernacle. Some proclaimed God's messages (1 Chr 25:1), some offered thanks and praise (1 Chr 25:3), and others played instruments (1 Chr 25:6-7). God wants all his people to participate in worship. You may not be a master musician, a prophet, or a teacher, but God appreciates whatever you have to offer. Develop your special gifts to offer in service to God (Rom 12:3-8; 1 Cor 12:29-31).

1 Chr 25:9-31 The musicians were divided into 24 groups to match the 24 groups of Levites (1 Chr 24:7-18). This division of labor gave order to the planning of Temple work, promoted excellence by making training easier, gave variety to worship because each group worked a term, and provided opportunities for many to be involved.

1 Chr 26:1 There were 4,000 gatekeepers (1 Chr 23:5). They were all Levites and did many other jobs as well. Some of their duties included (1) checking out the equipment and utensils used each day and making sure they were returned; (2) storing, ordering, and maintaining the food supplies for the priests and sacrifices; (3) caring for the furniture; (4) mixing the incense that was burned daily; and (5) accounting for the gifts brought. (For more on gatekeepers, see the note on 1 Chr 9:17-18, p. 1237.)

1 Chr 26:5 "God had richly blessed Obed-edom." The status of children in society has fluctuated throughout history; sometimes they are highly esteemed, and sometimes they are abused and cheated. But Scripture shows no such vacillation—children are called a gift from the Lord, and God never views them as a burden (Ps 127:3-5; Mark 10:13-15).

11 The fourth lot fell to Zeri* and twelve of his sons and relatives.
12 The fifth lot fell to Nethaniah and twelve of his sons and relatives.
13 The sixth lot fell to Bukkiah and twelve of his sons and relatives.
14 The seventh lot fell to Asarelah* and twelve of his sons and relatives.
15 The eighth lot fell to Jeshaiah and twelve of his sons and relatives.
16 The ninth lot fell to Mattaniah and twelve of his sons and relatives.
17 The tenth lot fell to Shimei and twelve of his sons and relatives.
18 The eleventh lot fell to Uzziel* and twelve of his sons and relatives.
19 The twelfth lot fell to Hashabiah and twelve of his sons and relatives.
20 The thirteenth lot fell to Shubael and twelve of his sons and relatives.
21 The fourteenth lot fell to Mattithiah and twelve of his sons and relatives.
22 The fifteenth lot fell to Jerimoth* and twelve of his sons and relatives.
23 The sixteenth lot fell to Hananiah and twelve of his sons and relatives.
24 The seventeenth lot fell to Joshbekashah* and twelve of his sons and relatives.
25 The eighteenth lot fell to Hanani and twelve of his sons and relatives.
26 The nineteenth lot fell to Mallothi and twelve of his sons and relatives.
27 The twentieth lot fell to Eliathah and twelve of his sons and relatives.
28 The twenty-first lot fell to Hothir and twelve of his sons and relatives.
29 The twenty-second lot fell to Giddalti and twelve of his sons and relatives.
30 The twenty-third lot fell to Mahazioth and twelve of his sons and relatives.
31 The twenty-fourth lot fell to Romamti-ezer and twelve of his sons and relatives.

Duties of the Gatekeepers

1 CHRONICLES 26:1-19

These are the divisions of the gatekeepers:
From the Korahites, there was Meshelemiah son
of Kore, of the family of Abiasaph.* 2The sons of
Meshelemiah were Zechariah (the oldest), Jediael
(the second), Zebadiah (the third), Jathniel (the
fourth), 3Elam (the fifth), Jehohanan (the sixth),
and Eliehoenai (the seventh).
4The sons of Obed-edom, also gatekeepers, were
Shemaiah (the oldest), Jehozabad (the second),
Joah (the third), Sacar (the fourth), Nethanel (the
fifth), 5Ammiel (the sixth), Issachar (the seventh),
and Peullethai (the eighth). God had richly
blessed Obed-edom.

6Obed-edom's son Shemaiah had sons with
great ability who earned positions of great
authority in the clan. 7Their names were Othni,
Rephael, Obed, and Elzabad. Their relatives, Elihu
and Semakiah, were also very capable men.

8All of these descendants of Obed-edom,
including their sons and grandsons—sixty-two
of them in all—were very capable men, well
qualified for their work.
9Meshelemiah's eighteen sons and relatives were
also very capable men.

10Hosah, of the Merari clan, appointed Shimri as
the leader among his sons, though he was not
the oldest. 11His other sons included Hilkiah (the
second), Tebaliah (the third), and Zechariah (the
fourth). Hosah's sons and relatives, who served as
gatekeepers, numbered thirteen in all.

12These divisions of the gatekeepers were named
for their family leaders, and like the other Levites,
they served at the house of the LORD. 13They were assigned by families for guard duty at the various gates,
without regard to age or training, for it was all decided
by means of sacred lots.
14The responsibility for the east gate went to Meshelemiah* and his group. The north gate was assigned to his son Zechariah, a man of unusual wisdom.
15The south gate went to Obed-edom, and his sons
were put in charge of the storehouse. 16Shuppim and
Hosah were assigned the west gate and the gateway
leading up to the Temple.* Guard duties were divided
evenly. 17Six Levites were assigned each day to the east
gate, four to the north gate, four to the south gate, and
two pairs at the storehouse. 18Six were assigned each
day to the west gate, four to the gateway leading up to
the Temple, and two to the courtyard.*
19These were the divisions of the gatekeepers from
the clans of Korah and Merari.

Treasurers and Other Officials

1 CHRONICLES 26:20-32

Other Levites, led by Ahijah, were in charge of the
treasuries of the house of God and the treasuries of
the gifts dedicated to the LORD. 21From the family of
Libni* in the clan of Gershon, Jehiel* was the leader.
22The sons of Jehiel, Zetham and his brother Joel, were
in charge of the treasuries of the house of the LORD.
23These are the leaders that descended from Amram, Izhar, Hebron, and Uzziel:

1 Chr 25:11 Hebrew *Izri*, a variant spelling of Zeri; compare 25:3. **1 Chr 25:14** Hebrew *Jesarelah*, a variant spelling of Asarelah; compare 25:2. **1 Chr 25:18** Hebrew *Azarel*, a variant spelling of Uzziel; compare 25:4. **1 Chr 25:22** Hebrew *Jeremoth*, a variant spelling of Jerimoth; compare 25:4. **1 Chr 25:24** Hebrew *Joshbekasha*, a variant spelling of Joshbekashah; compare 25:4. **1 Chr 26:1** As in Greek version (see also Exod 6:24); Hebrew reads *Asaph*. **1 Chr 26:14** Hebrew *Shelemiah*, a variant spelling of Meshelemiah; compare 26:2. **1 Chr 26:16** Or *the gate of Shalleketh on the upper road* (also in 26:18). The meaning of the Hebrew is uncertain. **1 Chr 26:18** Or *the colonnade*. The meaning of the Hebrew is uncertain. **1 Chr 26:21a** Hebrew *Ladan*, a variant spelling of Libni; compare 6:17. **1 Chr 26:21b** Hebrew *Jehieli* (also in 26:22), a variant spelling of Jehiel; compare 23:8.

▸ **1 CHRONICLES 26:20-32 *(cont.)***

24 From the clan of Amram, Shebuel was a
descendant of Gershom son of Moses. He was
the chief officer of the treasuries. 25 His relatives
through Eliezer were Rehabiah, Jeshaiah, Joram,
Zicri, and Shelomoth.
26 Shelomoth and his relatives were in charge
of the treasuries containing the gifts that King
David, the family leaders, and the generals and
captains* and other officers of the army had
dedicated to the LORD. 27 These men dedicated
some of the plunder they had gained in battle to
maintain the house of the LORD. 28 Shelomoth*
and his relatives also cared for the gifts dedicated
to the LORD by Samuel the seer, Saul son of Kish,
Abner son of Ner, and Joab son of Zeruiah. All the
other dedicated gifts were in their care, too.
29 From the clan of Izhar came Kenaniah. He and his
sons were given administrative responsibilities*
over Israel as officials and judges.
30 From the clan of Hebron came Hashabiah. He and
his relatives—1,700 capable men—were put in
charge of the Israelite lands west of the Jordan
River. They were responsible for all matters
related to the things of the LORD and the service
of the king in that area.
31 Also from the clan of Hebron came Jeriah,*
who was the leader of the Hebronites according
to the genealogical records. (In the fortieth year
of David's reign, a search was made in the records,
and capable men from the clan of Hebron were
found at Jazer in the land of Gilead.) 32 There
were 2,700 capable men among the relatives of
Jeriah. King David sent them to the east side of
the Jordan River and put them in charge of the
tribes of Reuben and Gad and the half-tribe of
Manasseh. They were responsible for all matters
related to God and to the king.

Military Commanders and Divisions

1 CHRONICLES 27:1-15

This is the list of Israelite generals and captains,* and their officers, who served the king by supervising the army divisions that were on duty each month of the year. Each division served for one month and had 24,000 troops.

2 Jashobeam son of Zabdiel was commander of the
first division of 24,000 troops, which was on duty
during the first month. 3 He was a descendant of
Perez and was in charge of all the army officers
for the first month.
4 Dodai, a descendant of Ahoah, was commander of
the second division of 24,000 troops, which was
on duty during the second month. Mikloth was
his chief officer.
5 Benaiah son of Jehoiada the priest was commander
of the third division of 24,000 troops, which was
on duty during the third month. 6 This was the
Benaiah who commanded David's elite military
group known as the Thirty. His son Ammizabad
was his chief officer.
7 Asahel, the brother of Joab, was commander of
the fourth division of 24,000 troops, which was
on duty during the fourth month. Asahel was
succeeded by his son Zebadiah.
8 Shammah* the Izrahite was commander of the
fifth division of 24,000 troops, which was on
duty during the fifth month.
9 Ira son of Ikkesh from Tekoa was commander of
the sixth division of 24,000 troops, which was on
duty during the sixth month.
10 Helez, a descendant of Ephraim from Pelon, was
commander of the seventh division of 24,000
troops, which was on duty during the seventh
month.
11 Sibbecai, a descendant of Zerah from Hushah,
was commander of the eighth division of 24,000
troops, which was on duty during the eighth
month.
12 Abiezer from Anathoth in the territory of
Benjamin was commander of the ninth division
of 24,000 troops, which was on duty during the
ninth month.
13 Maharai, a descendant of Zerah from Netophah,
was commander of the tenth division of 24,000
troops, which was on duty during the tenth
month.
14 Benaiah from Pirathon in Ephraim was commander
of the eleventh division of 24,000 troops, which
was on duty during the eleventh month.
15 Heled,* a descendant of Othniel from Netophah,
was commander of the twelfth division of 24,000
troops, which was on duty during the twelfth
month.

Leaders of the Tribes

1 CHRONICLES 27:16-24

The following were the tribes of Israel and their leaders:

Tribe	*Leader*
Reuben	Eliezer son of Zicri
Simeon	Shephatiah son of Maacah

1 Chr 26:26 Hebrew *the commanders of thousands and of hundreds.* **1 Chr 26:28** Hebrew *Shelomith,* a variant spelling of Shelomoth. **1 Chr 26:29** Or *were given outside work;* or *were given work away from the Temple area.* **1 Chr 26:31** Hebrew *Jerijah,* a variant spelling of Jeriah; compare 23:19. **1 Chr 27:1** Hebrew *commanders of thousands and of hundreds.* **1 Chr 27:8** Hebrew *Shamhuth,* a variant spelling of Shammah; compare 11:27 and 2 Sam 23:25. **1 Chr 27:15** Hebrew *Heldai,* a variant spelling of Heled; compare 11:30 and 2 Sam 23:29.

1 Chr 26:27 War plunder rightfully belonged to the victorious army. These soldiers, however, gave their portion of all the plunder to the house of the Lord to express their dedication to God. Like these commanders, we should think of what we *can* give, rather than what we are obligated to give. Is your giving a matter of rejoicing rather than duty? Give as a response of joy and love for God.

[17] Levi . . . . Hashabiah son of Kemuel
Aaron (the priests) . . . . Zadok
[18] Judah . . . . Elihu (a brother of David)
Issachar . . . . Omri son of Michael
[19] Zebulun . . . . Ishmaiah son of Obadiah
Naphtali . . . . Jeremoth son of Azriel
[20] Ephraim . . . . Hoshea son of Azaziah
Manasseh (west) . . . . Joel son of Pedaiah
[21] Manasseh in Gilead (east) . . Iddo son of Zechariah
Benjamin . . . . Jaasiel son of Abner
[22] Dan . . . . Azarel son of Jeroham

These were the leaders of the tribes of Israel.

[23]When David took his census, he did not count
those who were younger than twenty years of age, because the LORD had promised to make the Israelites as
numerous as the stars in heaven. [24]Joab son of Zeruiah
began the census but never finished it because* the
anger of God fell on Israel. The total number was never
recorded in King David's official records.

Officials of David's Kingdom

1 CHRONICLES 27:25-34

[25]Azmaveth son of Adiel was in charge of the palace treasuries.
Jonathan son of Uzziah was in charge of the regional treasuries throughout the towns, villages, and fortresses of Israel.
[26]Ezri son of Kelub was in charge of the field workers who farmed the king's lands.
[27]Shimei from Ramah was in charge of the king's vineyards.
Zabdi from Shepham was responsible for the grapes and the supplies of wine.
[28]Baal-hanan from Geder was in charge of the king's olive groves and sycamore-fig trees in the foothills of Judah.*
Joash was responsible for the supplies of olive oil.
[29]Shitrai from Sharon was in charge of the cattle on the Sharon Plain.
Shaphat son of Adlai was responsible for the cattle in the valleys.
[30]Obil the Ishmaelite was in charge of the camels.
Jehdeiah from Meronoth was in charge of the donkeys.
[31]Jaziz the Hagrite was in charge of the king's flocks of sheep and goats.
All these officials were overseers of King David's property.

[32]Jonathan, David's uncle, was a wise counselor to
the king, a man of great insight, and a scribe. Jehiel
the Hacmonite was responsible for teaching the king's
sons. [33]Ahithophel was the royal adviser. Hushai the
Arkite was the king's friend. [34]Ahithophel was succeeded by Jehoiada son of Benaiah and by Abiathar.
Joab was commander of the king's army.

David's Instructions to Solomon

1 CHRONICLES 28:1-21

David summoned all the officials of Israel to Jerusalem—the leaders of the tribes, the commanders of the
army divisions, the other generals and captains,* the
overseers of the royal property and livestock, the palace officials, the mighty men, and all the other brave
warriors in the kingdom. [2]David rose to his feet and
said: "My brothers and my people! It was my desire to
build a temple where the Ark of the LORD's Covenant,
God's footstool, could rest permanently. I made the
necessary preparations for building it, [3]but God said
to me, 'You must not build a temple to honor my name,
for you are a warrior and have shed much blood.'

[4]"Yet the LORD, the God of Israel, has chosen me
from among all my father's family to be king over Israel forever. For he has chosen the tribe of Judah to
rule, and from among the families of Judah he chose
my father's family. And from among my father's sons
the LORD was pleased to make me king over all Israel. [5]And from among my sons—for the LORD has
given me many—he chose Solomon to succeed me
on the throne of Israel and to rule over the LORD's
kingdom. [6]He said to me, 'Your son Solomon will build
my Temple and its courtyards, for I have chosen him as
my son, and I will be his father. [7]And if he continues to
obey my commands and regulations as he does now, I
will make his kingdom last forever.'

[8]"So now, with God as our witness, and in the sight
of all Israel—the LORD's assembly—I give you this
charge. Be careful to obey all the commands of the
LORD your God, so that you may continue to possess

1 Chr 27:24 Or *never finished it, and yet.* **1 Chr 27:28** Hebrew *the Shephelah.* **1 Chr 28:1** Hebrew *the commanders of thousands and commanders of hundreds.*

1 Chr 27:24 King David's official records were historical documents kept in the royal archives with other official records. They no longer exist. (See 1 Kgs 14:19.)

1 Chr 27:33-34 When Absalom rebelled against David, Ahithophel betrayed David and joined the rebellion. Hushai pretended loyalty to Absalom, and his advice caused Absalom's downfall (2 Sam 15:31–17:23).

1 Chr 28:1 The last two chapters of 1 Chronicles present the transition from David to Solomon as king of Israel. The writer doesn't mention Adonijah's conspiracy or David's frailty (1 Kgs 1–2). Instead, he focuses on the positive—God's plans for Israel and his promise to David's descendants.

1 Chr 28:5 The kingdom of Israel belonged to the Lord, not to David or anyone else. Israel's king, then, was God's deputy, commissioned to carry out God's will for the nation. Thus, God could choose the person he wanted as king without following customary lines of succession. David was not Saul's heir, and Solomon was not David's oldest son, but this did not matter because God appointed them.

1 Chr 28:8 David told Solomon to be careful to obey every one of God's commands to ensure Israel's prosperity and the continuation of David's descendants upon the throne. It was the king's solemn duty to study and obey God's laws. The teachings of Scripture are the keys to security, happiness, and justice, but we'll never discover them unless we search God's Word. If we ignore God's will and neglect his teaching, anything we attempt to build, even if it has God's name on it, will be headed for collapse. Get to know God's commands through regular Bible study, and find ways to apply them consistently.

▸ 1 CHRONICLES 28:1-21 *(cont.)*

this good land and leave it to your children as a permanent inheritance.

9“And Solomon, my son, learn to know the God of your ancestors intimately. Worship and serve him with your whole heart and a willing mind. For the LORD sees every heart and knows every plan and thought. If you seek him, you will find him. But if you forsake him, he will reject you forever. 10So take this seriously. The LORD has chosen you to build a Temple as his sanctuary. Be strong, and do the work.”

11Then David gave Solomon the plans for the Temple and its surroundings, including the entry room, the storerooms, the upstairs rooms, the inner rooms, and the inner sanctuary—which was the place of atonement. 12David also gave Solomon all the plans he had in mind* for the courtyards of the LORD's Temple, the outside rooms, the treasuries, and the rooms for the gifts dedicated to the LORD. 13The king also gave Solomon the instructions concerning the work of the various divisions of priests and Levites in the Temple of the LORD. And he gave specifications for the items in the Temple that were to be used for worship.

14David gave instructions regarding how much gold and silver should be used to make the items needed for service. 15He told Solomon the amount of gold needed for the gold lampstands and lamps, and the amount of silver for the silver lampstands and lamps, depending on how each would be used. 16He designated the amount of gold for the table on which the Bread of the Presence would be placed and the amount of silver for other tables.

17David also designated the amount of gold for the solid gold meat hooks used to handle the sacrificial meat and for the basins, pitchers, and dishes, as well as the amount of silver for every dish. 18He designated the amount of refined gold for the altar of incense. Finally, he gave him a plan for the LORD's “chariot”—the gold cherubim* whose wings were stretched out over the Ark of the LORD's Covenant. 19“Every part of this plan,” David told Solomon, “was given to me in writing from the hand of the LORD.*”

20Then David continued, “Be strong and courageous, and do the work. Don't be afraid or discouraged, for the LORD God, my God, is with you. He will not fail you or forsake you. He will see to it that all the work related to the Temple of the LORD is finished correctly. 21The various divisions of priests and Levites will serve in the Temple of God. Others with skills of every kind will volunteer, and the officials and the entire nation are at your command.”

Gifts for Building the Temple

1 CHRONICLES 29:1-9

Then King David turned to the entire assembly and said, “My son Solomon, whom God has clearly chosen as the next king of Israel, is still young and inexperienced. The work ahead of him is enormous, for the Temple he will build is not for mere mortals—it is for the LORD God himself! 2Using every resource at my command, I have gathered as much as I could for building the Temple of my God. Now there is enough gold, silver, bronze, iron, and wood, as well as great quantities of onyx, other precious stones, costly jewels, and all kinds of fine stone and marble.

3“And now, because of my devotion to the Temple of my God, I am giving all of my own private treasures of gold and silver to help in the construction. This is in addition to the building materials I have already collected for his holy Temple. 4I am donating more than 112 tons of gold* from Ophir and 262 tons of refined silver* to be used for overlaying the walls of

1 Chr 28:12 Or *the plans of the spirit that was with him.* **1 Chr 28:18** Hebrew *for the gold cherub chariot.* **1 Chr 28:19** Or *was written under the direction of the LORD.* **1 Chr 29:4a** Hebrew *3,000 talents* [102 metric tons] *of gold.* **1 Chr 29:4b** Hebrew *7,000 talents* [238 metric tons] *of silver.*

1 Chr 28:9 “The LORD sees every heart.” Nothing can be hidden from God. He sees and understands everything in our hearts. David found this out the hard way when God sent Nathan to expose David's sins of adultery and murder (2 Sam 12). David told Solomon to be completely open with God and dedicated to him. It makes no sense to try to hide any thoughts or actions from an all-knowing God. This should cause us joy, not fear, because God knows even the worst about us and loves us anyway.

1 Chr 28:13 Some of the instructions about the work of the priests and Levites are in 1 Chronicles 23 and 24.

1 Chr 28:20 David advised Solomon not to be frightened about the size of his task as king and builder of the Temple. Fear can immobilize us. The size of a job, its risks, or the pressure of the situation can cause us to freeze and do nothing. One remedy for fear is found here: Don't focus on the fear; instead, get to work. Getting started is often the most difficult and frightening part of a job.

1 Chr 29:1 Solomon became king in 970 B.C.

1 Chr 29:3-5 David gave from his personal fortune to the Temple. He encouraged others to follow his example, and they willingly did. Both the Tabernacle (Exod 35:5–36:7) and the Temple were built from the voluntary gifts of the people. Like David, we can acknowledge that all we have comes from God (1 Chr 29:14-16). We may not have David's wealth, but we can develop his willingness to give. It is not what we have that counts with God, but our willingness to give it.

PRINCIPLES TO LIVE BY

King David gave his son Solomon principles to guide him through life (see 1 Chr 28:9-10). These same ideas are ones that any Christian parent would want to present to a child:

1. Get to know God personally.
2. Learn God's commands and discover what he wants you to do.
3. Worship God with wholehearted devotion.
4. Serve God with a willing mind.
5. Be faithful.
6. Don't become discouraged.

the buildings 5and for the other gold and silver work to be done by the craftsmen. Now then, who will follow my example and give offerings to the LORD today?"

6Then the family leaders, the leaders of the tribes of Israel, the generals and captains of the army,* and the king's administrative officers all gave willingly. 7For the construction of the Temple of God, they gave about 188 tons of gold,* 10,000 gold coins,* 375 tons of silver,* 675 tons of bronze,* and 3,750 tons of iron.* 8They also contributed numerous precious stones, which were deposited in the treasury of the house of the LORD under the care of Jehiel, a descendant of Gershon. 9The people rejoiced over the offerings, for they had given freely and wholeheartedly to the LORD, and King David was filled with joy.

David's Prayer of Praise

1 CHRONICLES 29:10-20

Then David praised the LORD in the presence of the whole assembly:

> "O LORD, the God of our ancestor Israel,* may you be praised forever and ever! 11Yours, O LORD, is the greatness, the power, the glory, the victory, and the majesty. Everything in the heavens and on earth is yours, O LORD, and this is your kingdom. We adore you as the one who is over all things. 12Wealth and honor come from you alone, for you rule over everything. Power and might are in your hand, and at your discretion people are made great and given strength.
>
> 13"O our God, we thank you and praise your glorious name! 14But who am I, and who are my people, that we could give anything to you? Everything we have has come from you, and we give you only what you first gave us! 15We are here for only a moment, visitors and strangers in the land as our ancestors were before us. Our days on earth are like a passing shadow, gone so soon without a trace.
>
> 16"O LORD our God, even this material we have gathered to build a Temple to honor your holy name comes from you! It all belongs to you! 17I know, my God, that you examine our hearts and rejoice when you find integrity there. You know I have done all this with good motives, and I have watched your people offer their gifts willingly and joyously.
>
> 18"O LORD, the God of our ancestors Abraham, Isaac, and Israel, make your people always want to obey you. See to it that their love for you never changes. 19Give my son Solomon the wholehearted desire to obey all your commands, laws, and decrees, and to do everything necessary to build this Temple, for which I have made these preparations."

20Then David said to the whole assembly, "Give praise to the LORD your God!" And the entire assembly praised the LORD, the God of their ancestors, and they bowed low and knelt before the LORD and the king.

1 Chr 29:6 Hebrew *the commanders of thousands and commanders of hundreds.* **1 Chr 29:7a** Hebrew *5,000 talents* [170 metric tons] *of gold.* **1 Chr 29:7b** Hebrew *10,000 darics* [a Persian coin] *of gold,* about 185 pounds or 84 kilograms in weight. **1 Chr 29:7c** Hebrew *10,000 talents* [340 metric tons] *of silver.* **1 Chr 29:7d** Hebrew *18,000 talents* [612 metric tons] *of bronze.* **1 Chr 29:7e** Hebrew *100,000 talents* [3,400 metric tons] *of iron.* **1 Chr 29:10** *Israel* is the name that God gave to Jacob.

6. DAVID'S FINAL DAYS AND THE TRANSITION TO SOLOMON

David had many sons, and one of the last things David had to do was to establish his son Solomon as the heir to his throne. Another of David's sons, Adonijah, made a claim to the throne as well, but David clearly named Solomon as his successor and gave him instructions on how to lead the nation. David lived a long life and passed on a godly legacy to his son Solomon.

Solomon Named as King

1 CHRONICLES 29:21-22

The next day they brought 1,000 bulls, 1,000 rams, and 1,000 male lambs as burnt offerings to the LORD. They also brought liquid offerings and many other sacrifices on behalf of all Israel. 22They feasted and drank in the LORD's presence with great joy that day.

And again they crowned David's son Solomon as their new king. They anointed him before the LORD as their leader, and they anointed Zadok as priest.

1 Chr 29:6-9 These leaders displayed a right attitude toward their money by giving willingly to God's work. This attitude is described by Paul in 2 Corinthians 9:7: "You must each decide in your heart how much to give. And don't give reluctantly or in response to pressure. 'For God loves a person who gives cheerfully.'" When we are generous because we are thankful, our attitude can inspire others. Give generously to God's work.

1 Chr 29:15 David contrasts God's everlasting nature with the fleeting lives of his people. Nothing lasts unless it is rooted in God's unchanging character. If our most impressive deeds fade to dust before God, where should we place our confidence? Only in a relationship with God can we find anything permanent. His love never fades, and nothing can take it away.

1 Chr 29:19 "Wholehearted desire to obey" means to be entirely dedicated to God. This is what David prayed for Solomon—that he would desire, above all else, to serve God. Do you find it hard to do what God wants, or do you find it harder to *want* to do it? God can give you wholehearted devotion. If you believe in Jesus Christ, this is already happening in you. Paul wrote: "For God is working in you, giving you the desire and the power to do what pleases him" (Phil 2:13). Consider yourself blessed if someone in your life is praying this way for you.

1 Chr 29:21 Liquid offerings of wine were poured out as sacrifices to God to acknowledge his role in providing for his people.

David in His Old Age

1 KINGS 1:1-4

King David was now very old, and no matter how many
blankets covered him, he could not keep warm. 2So his
advisers told him, "Let us find a young virgin to wait
on you and look after you, my lord. She will lie in your
arms and keep you warm."
3So they searched throughout the land of Israel for
a beautiful girl, and they found Abishag from Shunem and brought her to the king. 4The girl was very
beautiful, and she looked after the king and took care
of him. But the king had no sexual relations with her.

Adonijah Claims the Throne

1 KINGS 1:5-27

About that time David's son Adonijah, whose mother
was Haggith, began boasting, "I will make myself king."
So he provided himself with chariots and charioteers
and recruited fifty men to run in front of him. 6Now
his father, King David, had never disciplined him at
any time, even by asking, "Why are you doing that?"
Adonijah had been born next after Absalom, and he
was very handsome.
7Adonijah took Joab son of Zeruiah and Abiathar
the priest into his confidence, and they agreed to help
him become king. 8But Zadok the priest, Benaiah son
of Jehoiada, Nathan the prophet, Shimei, Rei, and David's personal bodyguard refused to support Adonijah.
9Adonijah went to the Stone of Zoheleth* near the
spring of En-rogel, where he sacrificed sheep, cattle,
and fattened calves. He invited all his brothers—the
other sons of King David—and all the royal officials
of Judah. 10But he did not invite Nathan the prophet
or Benaiah or the king's bodyguard or his brother
Solomon.
11Then Nathan went to Bathsheba, Solomon's

1 Kgs 1:9 Or *to the Serpent's Stone;* Greek version supports reading *Zoheleth* as a proper name.

---

1 Kgs 1:1 Israel was near the end of the golden years of David's reign. The book of 1 Kings begins with a unified kingdom, glorious and God-centered; it ends with a divided kingdom, degraded and idolatrous. The reason for Israel's decline appears simple to us—they failed to obey God. But we are vulnerable to the same forces that brought about Israel's decay—greed, jealousy, lust for power, weakening of marriage vows, and superficiality in our devotion to God. As we read about these tragic events in Israel's history, we must see ourselves in the mirror of their experiences.

1 Kgs 1:4 David was about 70 years old. His health had deteriorated from years of hardship. Abishag served as his nurse and to help keep him warm. In times when polygamy was accepted and kings had harems, this action was not considered offensive.

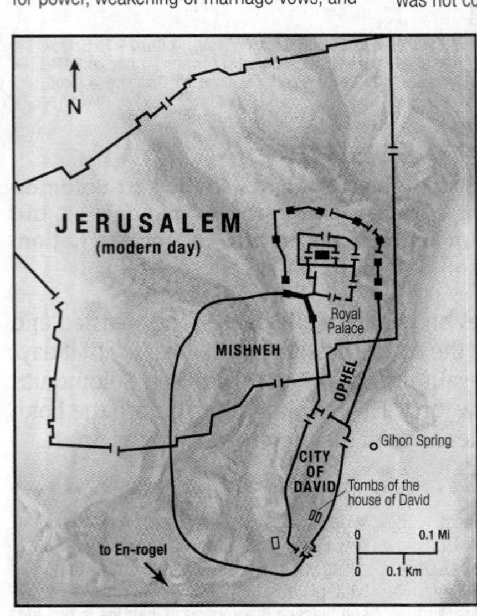

***TWO CORONATIONS** As David lay on his deathbed, his son Adonijah crowned himself king at En-rogel outside Jerusalem. When the news reached David, he declared that Solomon was to be the next ruler. Solomon was anointed at Gihon. It may have been more than coincidence that Gihon was not only within shouting distance of En-rogel but also closer to the royal palace.*

1 Kgs 1:5 Adonijah was David's fourth son and the logical choice to succeed him as king. David's first son, Amnon, had been killed by Absalom for having raped his sister (2 Sam 13:20-33). His second son, Daniel, is mentioned only in the genealogy of 1 Chronicles 3:1 and had probably died by this time. David's third son, Absalom, died in an earlier rebellion (2 Sam 18:1-18). Although many people expected Adonijah to be the next king (1 Kgs 2:13-25), David (and God) had other plans (1 Kgs 1:29-30).

1 Kgs 1:5 Adonijah decided to seize the throne without David's knowledge. He knew that Solomon, not he, was David's first choice to be the next king (1 Kgs 1:17). This was why he did not invite Solomon and David's loyal advisers when he declared himself king (1 Kgs 1:9-10). But his deceptive plans to gain the throne were unsuccessful. Adonijah is a reminder of what Jesus said: "Those who exalt themselves will be humbled" (Luke 18:14).

1 Kgs 1:6 God-fearing people like David and Samuel were used by God to lead nations; nevertheless they had problems in family relationships. God-fearing leaders cannot take for granted the spiritual well-being of their children. They are used to having others follow their orders, but they cannot expect their children to manufacture faith upon request. Moral and spiritual character takes years to build, and it requires constant attention and patient discipline.

David served God well as a king, but as a parent he often failed both God and his children. Don't let your service to God, even in leadership positions, take up so much of your time and energy that you neglect your God-given responsibilities to your family.

1 Kgs 1:6 Because David had never interfered by opposing or even questioning his son, Adonijah did not know how to work within limits. The result was that he always wanted his own way, regardless of how it affected others. Adonijah did whatever he wanted and paid no respect to God's wishes. An undisciplined child may look cute to the parents, but an undisciplined adult spreads havoc and self-destructs. As you set limits for your children, you make it possible for them to develop the self-restraint they will need in order to control themselves later. Discipline your children carefully while they are young, so that they will grow into self-disciplined adults.

1 Kgs 1:7 See Joab's Profile on p. 520 for a more complete picture of his life. For more information on Abiathar, see the note on 1 Samuel 22:20, p. 462.

1 Kgs 1:9 When Saul was anointed king, peace offerings were sacrificed as a reminder of the nation's covenant with God given at Mount Sinai. Adonijah wanted sacrifices offered, perhaps hoping to legitimize his takeover. But Adonijah was not God's

mother, and asked her, "Haven't you heard that Haggith's son, Adonijah, has made himself king, and our lord David doesn't even know about it? [12]If you want to save your own life and the life of your son Solomon, follow my advice. [13]Go at once to King David and say to him, 'My lord the king, didn't you make a vow and say to me, "Your son Solomon will surely be the next king and will sit on my throne"? Why then has Adonijah become king?' [14]And while you are still talking with him, I will come and confirm everything you have said."

[15]So Bathsheba went into the king's bedroom. (He was very old now, and Abishag was taking care of him.) [16]Bathsheba bowed down before the king.

"What can I do for you?" he asked her.

[17]She replied, "My lord, you made a vow before the LORD your God when you said to me, 'Your son Solomon will surely be the next king and will sit on my throne.' [18]But instead, Adonijah has made himself king, and my lord the king does not even know about it. [19]He has sacrificed many cattle, fattened calves, and sheep, and he has invited all the king's sons to attend the celebration. He also invited Abiathar the priest and Joab, the commander of the army. But he did not invite your servant Solomon. [20]And now, my lord the king, all Israel is waiting for you to announce who will become king after you. [21]If you do not act, my son Solomon and I will be treated as criminals as soon as my lord the king has died."

[22]While she was still speaking with the king, Nathan the prophet arrived. [23]The king's officials told him, "Nathan the prophet is here to see you."

Nathan went in and bowed before the king with his face to the ground. [24]Nathan asked, "My lord the king, have you decided that Adonijah will be the next king and that he will sit on your throne? [25]Today he has sacrificed many cattle, fattened calves, and sheep, and he has invited all the king's sons to attend the celebration. He also invited the commanders of the

choice to succeed David. Sealing an action with religious ceremony does not make it God's will.

1 Kgs 1:11 For more on Bathsheba, David's wife, read 2 Samuel 11–12. As wife of the king, Bathsheba was highly influential in the royal palace.

1 Kgs 1:11-14 When Nathan learned of Adonijah's conspiracy, he immediately tried to stop it. He was a man of both faith and action. He knew that Solomon should rightly be king, and he moved quickly when he saw someone else trying to take the throne. We often know what is right but don't act on it. Perhaps we don't want to get involved, or maybe we are fearful or lazy. Don't stop with prayer, good intentions, or angry feelings. Take the action needed to correct the situation.

1 Kgs 1:13 The Bible does not record David's promise that Solomon would be Israel's next king, but it is clear that Solomon was the choice of both David (1 Kgs 1:17, 30) and God (1 Chr 22:9-10).

WHO JOINED ADONIJAH'S CONSPIRACY AND WHO REMAINED LOYAL TO DAVID?

Contrast the fate of those who rebelled and those who remained loyal to David, God's appointed leader. Adonijah, the leader of the conspiracy, met a violent death (1 Kgs 2:25). Those who rebel against God's leaders rebel against God.

Joined Adonijah	*Remained with David*
Joab (1 Kgs 1:7) Brilliant military general and commander of David's army. He continually demonstrated his belief that cold-blooded murder was as acceptable as a fairly fought battle. Solomon later had him executed.	**Zadok (1 Kgs 1:8)** The other high priest under David. His loyalty gave him the privilege of crowning Solomon. He became the sole high priest under King Solomon.
Abiathar (1 Kgs 1:7) One of two high priests under David. He was a son of Ahimelech who had helped David, and David promised to protect him. Abiathar repaid David with treachery. Solomon later had him banished, fulfilling the prophecy that Eli's priestly line would end (1 Sam 2:31).	**Benaiah (1 Kgs 1:8)** Distinguished himself as a great warrior. Commanded a division of David's army—over 24,000 men. One of the Thirty, he was also placed in charge of David's bodyguard. Solomon later made him chief commander of the army.
Jonathan (1 Kgs 1:42) Abiathar's son. He helped David stop Absalom's rebellion (2 Sam 17:17-22) but supported this rebellion by another of David's sons.	**Nathan (1 Kgs 1:8)** God's prominent prophet during David's reign. The Bible says he wrote a history of David and Solomon.
Charioteers (1 Kgs 1:5) Hired by Adonijah, apparently more loyal to money than to their king	**Shimei (1 Kgs 1:8)** This man was probably the Shimei who was rewarded by Solomon and appointed district governor in Benjamin (1 Kgs 4:18). (He was not the same person who cursed David at Bahurim and brought on his own death under Solomon.)
50 Runners (1 Kgs 1:5) Recruited to give Adonijah a "royal" appearance	**Rei (1 Kgs 1:8)** Only mentioned here. Possibly he was an army officer. The word means "and his friends."

▸ **1 KINGS 1:5-27** ***(cont.)***
army and Abiathar the priest. They are feasting and
drinking with him and shouting, 'Long live King Adonijah!' 26But he did not invite me or Zadok the priest or
Benaiah or your servant Solomon. 27Has my lord the
king really done this without letting any of his officials
know who should be the next king?"

David Confirms Solomon as King

1 KINGS 1:28-53
King David responded, "Call Bathsheba!" So she came
back in and stood before the king. 29And the king
repeated his vow: "As surely as the LORD lives, who
has rescued me from every danger, 30your son Solomon will be the next king and will sit on my throne
this very day, just as I vowed to you before the LORD,
the God of Israel."
31Then Bathsheba bowed down with her face to the
ground before the king and exclaimed, "May my lord
King David live forever!"
32Then King David ordered, "Call Zadok the priest,
Nathan the prophet, and Benaiah son of Jehoiada."
When they came into the king's presence, 33the king
said to them, "Take Solomon and my officials down
to Gihon Spring. Solomon is to ride on my own mule.
34There Zadok the priest and Nathan the prophet are

BATHSHEBA

Bathsheba was the unlikely link between Israel's two most famous kings—David and Solomon. She was lover and wife to one, mother to the other. Her adultery with David almost brought an end to David's family line. Out of the ashes of that sin, God brought good. Eventually Jesus Christ, the salvation of mankind, was born to a descendant of David and Bathsheba. • David and Bathsheba's story shows that little but wrong decisions often lead to big mistakes. It is likely that neither was where he or she should have been. Bathsheba may have been rash in bathing where she might be seen; David should have been at war with his army. Each decision contributed to the beginning of a very sad series of events. • Bathsheba must have been devastated by the chain of events—unfaithfulness to her husband, discovery of pregnancy, death of her husband, death of her child. We are told that David comforted her (2 Sam 12:24), and she lived to see another son, Solomon, sit on the throne. • From her life we see that the little, day-to-day choices we make are very important. They prepare us to make the right choices when the big decisions come. The wisdom to make right choices in small and large matters is a gift from God. Understanding this should make us more conscious of the decisions we make and more willing to include God in our decision making. Have you asked for his help with today's decisions?

Strengths and accomplishments	• Became influential in the palace alongside her son, Solomon • Was the mother of Israel's wisest king and an ancestor of Jesus Christ
Weakness and mistake	• Committed adultery
Lessons from her life	• Although we may feel caught up in a chain of events, we are still responsible for the way we participate in those events • A sin may seem like one small seed, but the harvest of consequences is beyond measure • In the worst possible situations, God is still able to bring about good when people truly turn to him • While we must live with the natural consequences of our sins, God's forgiveness of sin is complete
Vital statistics	• Where: Jerusalem • Occupations: Queen and queen mother • Relatives: Father: Elim. Husbands: Uriah, David. Son: Solomon. • Contemporaries: Nathan, Joab, Adonijah
Key verses	"When Uriah's wife heard that her husband was dead, she mourned for him. When the period of mourning was over, David sent for her and brought her to the palace, and she became one of his wives. Then she gave birth to a son. But the LORD was displeased with what David had done" (2 Sam 11:26-27).

Bathsheba's story is told in 2 Samuel 11–12; 1 Kings 1–2. A related passage is Psalm 51.

1 Kgs 1:33 We might expect King David to send a great war horse to bring his son Solomon to the ceremony; instead, Solomon rode David's mule. In David's time, mules were prized animals, ridden by the wealthy and powerful. When Jesus entered Jerusalem, he came in not on a horse, but on a donkey (Zech 9:9; Matt 21:7).

1 Kgs 1:39 The olive oil was used to anoint Israel's kings and high priests, as well as to dedicate certain objects to God. The sacred tent where the oil was kept was probably the tent David set up to shelter the Ark of the Covenant (2 Sam 6:17). It was not the Tabernacle Moses carried in the wilderness; that Tabernacle was still at Gibeon (see the note on 1 Sam 7:1, p. 426). The recipe and uses for the sacred oil are found in Exodus 30:22-33. (For more on anointing, see the notes on 1 Sam 10:1, p. 437, and 1 Sam 16:13, p. 448.)

1 Kgs 1:49-50 Sometimes it takes getting caught before someone is willing to give up his scheme. When Adonijah learned that his plans were doomed to fail, he ran in panic to the altar, the place of God's mercy and forgiveness. He went there, however, after his plans for treason were exposed. If Adonijah had first considered what God wanted, he might have avoided trouble. Don't wait until you have made a mess of your life before you run to God. Seek God's guidance before you act.

1 Kgs 1:49-51 Adonijah thought he would be safe by clutching the horns (or corner posts) of the sacred altar of burnt offering in the Tabernacle court. By doing this, he hoped to place himself under God's protection. Solomon granted Adonijah a reprieve, hoping that this would end Adonijah's conspiracy. Unfortunately, it did not, and he was later executed (1 Kgs 2:25). At the execution of Adonijah, Joab ran and clutched the horns of the altar hoping for safety, but Solomon had Joab killed right at the altar (1 Kgs 2:28-34). This punishment was appropriate justice for a cold-blooded murderer such as Joab (Exod 21:14).

1 Kgs 1:52-53 While Adonijah feared for his life and expected the severest punishment, Solomon simply dismissed his brother

to anoint him king over Israel. Blow the ram's horn and shout, 'Long live King Solomon!' 35Then escort him back here, and he will sit on my throne. He will succeed me as king, for I have appointed him to be ruler over Israel and Judah."

36"Amen!" Benaiah son of Jehoiada replied. "May the LORD, the God of my lord the king, decree that it happen. 37And may the LORD be with Solomon as he has been with you, my lord the king, and may he make Solomon's reign even greater than yours!"

38So Zadok the priest, Nathan the prophet, Benaiah son of Jehoiada, and the king's bodyguard* took Solomon down to Gihon Spring, with Solomon riding on King David's own mule. 39There Zadok the priest took the flask of olive oil from the sacred tent and anointed Solomon with the oil. Then they sounded the ram's horn and all the people shouted, "Long live King Solomon!" 40And all the people followed Solomon into Jerusalem, playing flutes and shouting for joy. The celebration was so joyous and noisy that the earth shook with the sound.

41Adonijah and his guests heard the celebrating and shouting just as they were finishing their banquet. When Joab heard the sound of the ram's horn, he asked, "What's going on? Why is the city in such an uproar?"

42And while he was still speaking, Jonathan son of Abiathar the priest arrived. "Come in," Adonijah said to him, "for you are a good man. You must have good news."

43"Not at all!" Jonathan replied. "Our lord King David has just declared Solomon king! 44The king sent him down to Gihon Spring with Zadok the priest, Nathan the prophet, and Benaiah son of Jehoiada, protected by the king's bodyguard. They had him ride on the king's own mule, 45and Zadok and Nathan have anointed him at Gihon Spring as the new king. They have just returned, and the whole city is celebrating and rejoicing. That's what all the noise is about. 46What's more, Solomon is now sitting on the royal throne as king. 47And all the royal officials have gone to King David and congratulated him, saying, 'May your God make Solomon's fame even greater than your own, and may Solomon's reign be even greater than yours!' Then the king bowed his head in worship as he lay in his bed, 48and he said, 'Praise the LORD, the God of Israel, who today has chosen a successor to sit on my throne while I am still alive to see it.'"

49Then all of Adonijah's guests jumped up in panic from the banquet table and quickly scattered. 50Adonijah was afraid of Solomon, so he rushed to the sacred tent and grabbed on to the horns of the altar. 51Word soon reached Solomon that Adonijah had seized the horns of the altar in fear, and that he was pleading, "Let King Solomon swear today that he will not kill me!"

52Solomon replied, "If he proves himself to be loyal, not a hair on his head will be touched. But if he makes trouble, he will die." 53So King Solomon summoned Adonijah, and they brought him down from the altar. He came and bowed respectfully before King Solomon, who dismissed him, saying, "Go on home."

David's Final Instructions to Solomon

1 KINGS 2:1-12

As the time of King David's death approached, he gave this charge to his son Solomon:

2"I am going where everyone on earth must someday go. Take courage and be a man. 3Observe the requirements of the LORD your God, and follow all his ways. Keep the decrees, commands, regulations, and laws written in the Law of Moses so that you will be successful in all you do and wherever you go. 4If you do this, then the LORD will keep the promise he made to me. He told me, 'If your descendants live as they should and follow me faithfully with all their heart and soul, one of them will always sit on the throne of Israel.'

5"And there is something else. You know what Joab son of Zeruiah did to me when he murdered my two army commanders, Abner son of Ner and Amasa son of Jether. He pretended that it was an act of war, but

970 BC

Solomon becomes king

1 Kgs 1:38 Hebrew *the Kerethites and Pelethites;* also in 1:44.

and sent him home. As a new king, Solomon had the power to kill his rivals, something Adonijah would have done had his conspiracy succeeded. But Solomon acted as if he had nothing to prove, thus demonstrating his authority and power. Sometimes forgiving a personal attack shows more strength than lashing out in revenge. Trying to prove one's power and authority often only proves one's fear and self-doubt. Only after Adonijah made another attempt to secure royal power was Solomon forced to have him executed (1 Kgs 2:13-25).

1 Kgs 2:3-4 David stressed to Solomon the need to make God and his laws the center of personal life and government in order to preserve the kingdom, as God had promised to do (2 Sam 7). This promise from God had two parts. One part was conditional and depended upon the king's actions. The other part was unconditional.

God's conditional promise was that David and his descendants would remain in office as kings only when they honored and obeyed him. When David's descendants failed to do this, they lost the throne (2 Kgs 25). God's unconditional promise was that David's line would go on forever. This was fulfilled in the birth of Jesus Christ, a descendant of David who is also the eternal Son of God (Rom 1:3-4). David, whose life exemplified obedience, gave well-seasoned advice to his son, the next king. It would be up to Solomon to follow it.

1 Kgs 2:5-7 Joab epitomizes those who are ruthless in accomplishing their goals. To Joab, winning was everything. He wanted to get power for himself and protect it. In contrast, Barzillai stands for those who are loyal to God and live by his standards. When offered glory, for example, he unselfishly asked that it be given to his son. Is your leadership self-serving or God-serving?

1 Kgs 2:5-9 David had some harsh advice for Solomon concerning his enemies. This advice was designed to help the young king establish and secure his throne, and it was directed only toward blatant enemies—those who opposed God by opposing God's appointed king. Legally, David was asking Solomon to give his enemies the punishment they deserved. It was against both civil law and God's laws for Shimei to curse a king (Exod 22:28).

▶ **1 KINGS 2:1-12 *(cont.)***

it was done in a time of peace,* staining his belt and sandals with innocent blood.* [6]Do with him what you think best, but don't let him grow old and go to his grave in peace.*

[7]"Be kind to the sons of Barzillai of Gilead. Make them permanent guests at your table, for they took care of me when I fled from your brother Absalom.

[8]"And remember Shimei son of Gera, the man from Bahurim in Benjamin. He cursed me with a terrible curse as I was fleeing to Mahanaim. When he came down to meet me at the Jordan River, I swore by the LORD that I would not kill him. [9]But that oath does not make him innocent. You are a wise man, and you will know how to arrange a bloody death for him.*"

[10]Then David died and was buried with his ancestors in the City of David. [11]David had reigned over Israel for forty years, seven of them in Hebron and thirty-three in Jerusalem. [12]Solomon became king and sat on the throne of David his father, and his kingdom was firmly established.

David's Last Words

2 SAMUEL 23:1-7

These are the last words of David:

"David, the son of Jesse, speaks—
David, the man who was raised up so high,
David, the man anointed by the God of Jacob,
David, the sweet psalmist of Israel.*

2 "The Spirit of the LORD speaks through me;
his words are upon my tongue.
3 The God of Israel spoke.
The Rock of Israel said to me:
'The one who rules righteously,
who rules in the fear of God,
4 is like the light of morning at sunrise,
like a morning without clouds,
like the gleaming of the sun
on new grass after rain.'

5 "Is it not my family God has chosen?
Yes, he has made an everlasting covenant
with me.
His agreement is arranged and guaranteed
in every detail.
He will ensure my safety and success.
6 But the godless are like thorns to be thrown away,
for they tear the hand that touches them.
7 One must use iron tools to chop them down;
they will be totally consumed by fire."

Summary of David's Reign

1 CHRONICLES 29:26-30

So David son of Jesse reigned over all Israel. [27]He reigned over Israel for forty years, seven of them in Hebron and thirty-three in Jerusalem. [28]He died at a ripe old age, having enjoyed long life, wealth, and honor. Then his son Solomon ruled in his place.

[29]All the events of King David's reign, from beginning to end, are written in *The Record of Samuel the Seer*, *The Record of Nathan the Prophet*, and *The Record of Gad the Seer*. [30]These accounts include the mighty deeds of his reign and everything that happened to him and to Israel and to all the surrounding kingdoms.

1 Kgs 2:5a Or *He murdered them during a time of peace as revenge for deaths they had caused in time of war.* **1 Kgs 2:5b** As in some Greek and Old Latin manuscripts; Hebrew reads *with the blood of war.* **1 Kgs 2:6** Hebrew *don't let his white head go down to Sheol in peace.* **1 Kgs 2:9** Hebrew *how to bring his white head down to Sheol in blood.* **2 Sm 23:1** Or *the favorite subject of the songs of Israel;* or *the favorite of the Strong One of Israel.*

---

1 Kgs 2:10 David died at about age 70 (2 Sam 5:4-5). See David's Profile on p. 485 for more on his life.

2 Sam 23:3 In the style of a prophet, David spoke of a righteous ruler. This will be fulfilled in Jesus Christ when he returns to rule in perfect justice and peace. (For similar prophecies, see Isa 11:1-10; Jer 23:5-6; 33:15-18; Zech 9:9-10. For the fulfillment of some of these prophecies, see Matt 4:14-16; Luke 24:25-27, 44-49; John 5:45-47; 8:28-29.)

1 Chr 29:29 A seer was someone who received messages from God for the nation in visions or dreams.

1 Chr 29:30 First Chronicles vividly illustrates the importance of maintaining a relationship with God. The genealogies in chapters 1–9 emphasize the importance of a spiritual heritage. The second part of the book details the life of David. Few men or women in the Bible were as close to God as David was. His daily contact with God increased his capacity to worship and strengthened his desire to build God's Temple. David's life shows us the importance of staying close to God—through studying and obeying his Word and communicating with him daily. Second Chronicles, on the other hand, reveals how quickly our lives can deteriorate (spiritually, mentally, and socially) when we fail to stay well grounded in God.

Ps 4:1ff This psalm may have been written as David was asking his enemies to reconsider their support of Absalom. Others see this psalm as a prayer for relief from a calamity such as a drought (see Ps 4:7).

Ps 4:3 The godly are those who are faithful and devoted to God. David knew that God would hear him when he called and would answer him. We, too, can be confident that God listens to our prayers and answers when we call on him. Sometimes we think that God will not hear us because we have fallen short of his high standards for holy living. But if we have trusted Christ for salvation, God has forgiven us and he will listen to us. When you feel as though your prayers are bouncing off the ceiling, remember that as a believer you have been set apart by God and that he loves you. He hears and answers although his answers may not be what you expect. Look at your problems in the light of God's power instead of looking at God in the shadow of your problems.

Ps 4:5 Worship in David's day included animal sacrifices by the priests in the Tabernacle. The animal's blood covered the sins of the one who offered the animal. Specific rules had been given for offering sacrifices, but more important to God than ceremony was the person's attitude of submission and obedience (1 Sam 15:22-23). Today, a sacrifice offered in the right spirit is still pleasing to God. He wants our obedience and our praise before our gifts (Heb 13:15). Offer God your sacrifice of total obedience and heartfelt praise.

Ps 4:7 Two kinds of joy are contrasted here—inward joy that comes from knowing and trusting God and happiness that comes as a result of pleasant circumstances. Inward joy is steady as long as we trust God; happiness is unpredictable. Inward joy defeats discouragement; happiness covers it up. Inward joy is lasting; happiness is temporary.

E. Psalms from David's Reign

This collection of 74 psalms are attributed to David or one of his associates, but they are not explicitly connected with a specific event in the life of David. Many of these are generic enough that they are difficult to place chronologically, so we have collected them here at the end of David's life. These psalms are the earnest prayers of people who cry out to God in the midst of their real lives. Some of them are filled with effusive praise for the goodness of God, and others reflect a desperate cry for help from God in the face of trials. Use the psalms as a model for your own prayer life; cry out to God in joy or in pain, and rely on him to carry you through.

1. PSALMS ATTRIBUTED TO DAVID

David was a prolific writer. There are 72 psalms that mention David as their author, and 60 of them are gathered here. The other 12 psalms that David wrote are specifically connected to events during his life, and they are placed with them chronologically in this Bible. These 60 could have been written at any time during his reign.

Psalm 4

THEME: Rejoicing in God's protection and peace. We can place our confidence in God because he will listen when we call on him.

AUTHOR: David

For the choir director: A psalm of David, to be accompanied by stringed instruments.

1 Answer me when I call to you,
O God who declares me innocent.
Free me from my troubles.
Have mercy on me and hear my prayer.

2 How long will you people ruin my reputation?
How long will you make groundless accusations?
How long will you continue your lies?
Interlude

3 You can be sure of this:
The LORD set apart the godly for himself.
The LORD will answer when I call to him.

4 Don't sin by letting anger control you.
Think about it overnight and remain silent.
Interlude

5 Offer sacrifices in the right spirit,
and trust the LORD.

6 Many people say, "Who will show us better times?"
Let your face smile on us, LORD.

7 You have given me greater joy
than those who have abundant harvests of grain and new wine.

8 In peace I will lie down and sleep,
for you alone, O LORD, will keep me safe.

Psalm 5

THEME: The lies of enemies. God is able to defend us from lies spoken against us.

AUTHOR: David

For the choir director: A psalm of David, to be accompanied by the flute.

1 O LORD, hear me as I pray;
pay attention to my groaning.

2 Listen to my cry for help, my King and my God,
for I pray to no one but you.

3 Listen to my voice in the morning, LORD.
Each morning I bring my requests to you and wait expectantly.

4 O God, you take no pleasure in wickedness;
you cannot tolerate the sins of the wicked.

5 Therefore, the proud may not stand in your presence,
for you hate all who do evil.

6 You will destroy those who tell lies.
The LORD detests murderers and deceivers.

7 Because of your unfailing love, I can enter your house;
I will worship at your Temple with deepest awe.

8 Lead me in the right path, O LORD,
or my enemies will conquer me.
Make your way plain for me to follow.

9 My enemies cannot speak a truthful word.
Their deepest desire is to destroy others.
Their talk is foul, like the stench from an open grave.
Their tongues are filled with flattery.*

Ps 5:9 Greek version reads *with lies.* Compare Rom 3:13.

Ps 5:1-3 The secret of a close relationship with God is to pray to him earnestly each morning. In the morning, our minds are more free from problems, and then we can commit the whole day to God. Regular communication helps any friendship and is certainly necessary for a strong relationship with God. We need to communicate with him daily. Do you have a regular time to pray and read God's Word?

Ps 5:5 God cannot condone or excuse even the smallest sin; therefore, we cannot excuse ourselves for sinning only a little bit. As we grow spiritually, our sensitivity to sin increases. As God makes us aware of sin, we must be intolerant toward it and be willing to change. All believers should strive to be more tolerant of people but less tolerant of the sin in themselves and others. What is your reaction to sin in your life? Are you insensitive, unconcerned, disappointed, or comfortable?

▶ **PSALM 5** ***(cont.)***

10 O God, declare them guilty.
Let them be caught in their own traps.
Drive them away because of their many sins,
for they have rebelled against you.
11 But let all who take refuge in you rejoice;
let them sing joyful praises forever.
Spread your protection over them,
that all who love your name may be filled with joy.
12 For you bless the godly, O LORD;
you surround them with your shield of love.

Psalm 6

THEME: Deliverance in trouble. God is able to rescue us.

AUTHOR: David

*For the choir director: A psalm of David, to be accompanied by an eight-stringed instrument.**

1 O LORD, don't rebuke me in your anger
or discipline me in your rage.
2 Have compassion on me, LORD, for I am weak.
Heal me, LORD, for my bones are in agony.
3 I am sick at heart.
How long, O LORD, until you restore me?
4 Return, O LORD, and rescue me.
Save me because of your unfailing love.
5 For the dead do not remember you.
Who can praise you from the grave?*
6 I am worn out from sobbing.
All night I flood my bed with weeping,
drenching it with my tears.
7 My vision is blurred by grief;
my eyes are worn out because of all my enemies.
8 Go away, all you who do evil,
for the LORD has heard my weeping.
9 The LORD has heard my plea;
the LORD will answer my prayer.
10 May all my enemies be disgraced and terrified.
May they suddenly turn back in shame.

Psalm 8

THEME: The greatness of God assures the worth of mankind. God, the all-powerful Creator, cares for his most valuable creation—people.

AUTHOR: David

*For the choir director: A psalm of David, to be accompanied by a stringed instrument.**

1 O LORD, our Lord, your majestic name fills the earth!
Your glory is higher than the heavens.
2 You have taught children and infants
to tell of your strength,*
silencing your enemies
and all who oppose you.
3 When I look at the night sky and see the work of your fingers—
the moon and the stars you set in place—
4 what are mere mortals that you should think about them,
human beings that you should care for them?*
5 Yet you made them only a little lower than God*
and crowned them* with glory and honor.
6 You gave them charge of everything you made,
putting all things under their authority—

Ps 6:TITLE Hebrew *with stringed instruments; according to the sheminith.* **Ps 6:5** Hebrew *from Sheol?* **Ps 8:TITLE** Hebrew *according to the gittith.* **Ps 8:2** Greek version reads *to give you praise.* Compare Matt 21:16. **Ps 8:4** Hebrew *what is man that you should think of him, / the son of man that you should care for him?* **Ps 8:5a** Or *Yet you made them only a little lower than the angels;* Hebrew reads *Yet you made him* [i.e., man] *a little lower than Elohim.* **Ps 8:5b** Hebrew *him* [i.e., man]; similarly in 8:6.

Ps 6:1ff This is the first of seven penitential psalms, in which the writer humbly realizes his predicament (usually the result of sin), expresses sorrow over it, and demonstrates a fresh commitment to remain close to God. We don't know the cause of David's pain, but whatever the cause, he sought God for the remedy.

Ps 6:1-3 David accepted God's punishment, but he begged God not to discipline him in anger. Jeremiah also asked God to correct him gently and not in anger (Jer 10:24). David recognized that if God treated him with justice alone and not with mercy, he would be wiped out by God's wrath. Often we want God to show mercy to us and justice to everyone else. God in his kindness forgives us instead of giving us what we deserve.

Ps 6:6 Pouring out his heart with tears, David was completely honest with God. We can be honest with God even when we are filled with anger or despair because God knows us thoroughly and wants the very best for us. Anger may result in rash outward acts or turning inward in depression. But because we trust in our all-powerful God, we don't have to be victims of circumstance or be weighed down by the guilt of sin. Be honest with God, and he will help you turn your attention from yourself to him and his mercy.

Ps 8:1ff Portions of this psalm are quoted in the New Testament and applied to Christ (1 Cor 15:27; Heb 2:6-8). God became human in the person of Jesus, and he will raise all who belong to him when he comes to reign over the new heaven and new earth. Jesus is the only person who perfectly reflects God's image (Gal 2:20; Col 1:15).

Ps 8:2 Children are able to trust and praise God without doubts or reservations. As we get older, many of us find this more and more difficult to do. Ask God to give you childlike faith, removing any barriers to having a closer walk with him.

Ps 8:3-4 To respect God's majesty, we must compare ourselves to his greatness. When we look at creation, we often feel small by comparison. This is a healthy way to get back to reality, but God does not want us to dwell on our smallness. Humility means proper respect for God, not self-depreciation.

Ps 8:3-5 When we look at the vast expanse of creation, we wonder how God could be concerned for people who constantly disappoint him. Yet God created us only a little lower than himself! The next time you question your worth as a person, remember that God considers you highly valuable. We have great worth because we bear the stamp of the Creator. (See Gen 1:26-27 for the extent of worth God places on all people.) Because God has already declared how valuable we are to him, we can be set free from feelings of worthlessness.

Ps 8:6 God gave human beings tremendous authority—to be in charge of the

7 the flocks and the herds
and all the wild animals,
8 the birds in the sky, the fish in the sea,
and everything that swims the ocean currents.

9 O LORD, our Lord, your majestic name fills the earth!

Psalm 9

THEME: God never ignores our cries for help.

AUTHOR: David, possibly written after a victory over the Philistines

For the choir director: A psalm of David, to be sung to the tune "Death of the Son."

1 I will praise you, LORD, with all my heart;
I will tell of all the marvelous things you have done.
2 I will be filled with joy because of you.
I will sing praises to your name, O Most High.

3 My enemies retreated;
they staggered and died when you appeared.
4 For you have judged in my favor;
from your throne you have judged with fairness.
5 You have rebuked the nations and destroyed the wicked;
you have erased their names forever.
6 The enemy is finished, in endless ruins;
the cities you uprooted are now forgotten.

7 But the LORD reigns forever,
executing judgment from his throne.
8 He will judge the world with justice
and rule the nations with fairness.
9 The LORD is a shelter for the oppressed,
a refuge in times of trouble.
10 Those who know your name trust in you,
for you, O LORD, do not abandon those who search for you.

11 Sing praises to the LORD who reigns in Jerusalem.*
Tell the world about his unforgettable deeds.
12 For he who avenges murder cares for the helpless.
He does not ignore the cries of those who suffer.

13 LORD, have mercy on me.
See how my enemies torment me.
Snatch me back from the jaws of death.
14 Save me so I can praise you publicly at Jerusalem's gates,
so I can rejoice that you have rescued me.

15 The nations have fallen into the pit they dug for others.

Ps 9:11 Hebrew *Zion;* also in 9:14.

whole earth. But with great authority comes great responsibility. How do you treat God's creation? Use your resources wisely because God holds you accountable as his steward.

Ps 9:1ff Praise is expressing to God our appreciation and understanding of his worth. It is saying thank you for each aspect of his divine nature. Our inward attitude becomes outward expression. When we praise God, we expand our awareness of who he is. In each psalm you read, look for an attribute or characteristic of God for which you can thank him.

Ps 9:4 God upholds our just cause; he is our vindicator (one who clears us from criticism and justifies us before others). In this life, we may face many injustices: We may be falsely accused and misunderstood by friends and enemies; we may not be truly appreciated by others for the love we show; the true value of our work and service may not be duly rewarded; our ideas may be ignored. But God is to be praised, for he sees and remembers all the good we do, and it is up to him to decide the timing and the appropriateness of our rewards. If we do not trust him to vindicate us, then we will be susceptible to hatred, self-promotion, or self-pity. If we do trust him, we can experience God's peace and be free from the worry of how others perceive us and treat us.

Ps 9:10 God will never abandon those who seek him. God's promise does not mean that if we trust in him we will escape loss or suffering; it means that God himself will never leave us no matter what we face.

Ps 9:11 God does not live only in Jerusalem (or Zion, another name for Mount Moriah, the hill in Jerusalem on which the Temple was built); he is everywhere all the time. The focal point of Israelite worship came to be Jerusalem and its beautiful Temple. God was present in the Tabernacle (Exod 25:8-9) and in the Temple built by Solomon (2 Chr 7:16). From this central place of worship, the Jews were to tell the world about the one true God.

O LORD, our Lord,
your majestic name fills the earth!
Psalm 8:1

▶ **PSALM 9** ***(cont.)***

Their own feet have been caught in the trap
they set.
16 The LORD is known for his justice.
The wicked are trapped by their own deeds.
*Quiet Interlude**
17 The wicked will go down to the grave.*
This is the fate of all the nations who
ignore God.
18 But the needy will not be ignored forever;
the hopes of the poor will not always be
crushed.
19 Arise, O LORD!
Do not let mere mortals defy you!
Judge the nations!
20 Make them tremble in fear, O LORD.
Let the nations know they are merely human.
Interlude

Psalm 11

THEME: God's rule provides stability in the midst of panic. Because we can trust him, we can face our problems.

AUTHOR: David

For the choir director: A psalm of David.

1 I trust in the LORD for protection.
So why do you say to me,
"Fly like a bird to the mountains for safety!
2 The wicked are stringing their bows
and fitting their arrows on the bowstrings.
They shoot from the shadows
at those whose hearts are right.
3 The foundations of law and order have collapsed.
What can the righteous do?"

4 But the LORD is in his holy Temple;
the LORD still rules from heaven.
He watches everyone closely,
examining every person on earth.
5 The LORD examines both the righteous and the
wicked.
He hates those who love violence.
6 He will rain down blazing coals and burning
sulfur on the wicked,
punishing them with scorching winds.
7 For the righteous LORD loves justice.
The virtuous will see his face.

Psalm 12

THEME: The proud and lying words of people versus the true and pure words of God. A call for protection against those who try to manipulate us.

AUTHOR: David

*For the choir director: A psalm of David, to be accompanied by an eight-stringed instrument.**

1 Help, O LORD, for the godly are fast disappearing!
The faithful have vanished from the earth!
2 Neighbors lie to each other,
speaking with flattering lips and deceitful
hearts.
3 May the LORD cut off their flattering lips
and silence their boastful tongues.

Ps 9:16 Hebrew *Higgaion Selah*. The meaning of this phrase is uncertain. **Ps 9:17** Hebrew *to Sheol*. **Ps 12:TITLE** Hebrew *according to the sheminith*.

Ps 9:13-14 All of us want God to help us when we are in trouble, but often for different reasons. Some want God's help so that they will be successful and other people will like them. Others want God's help so that they will be comfortable and feel good about themselves. David, however, wanted help from God so that justice would be restored to Israel and so that he could show others God's power. When you call to God for help, consider your motive. Is it to save yourself pain and embarrassment or to bring God glory and honor?

Ps 9:18 The world may ignore the plight of the needy, crushing any earthly hope they may have. But God, the champion of the weak, promises that this will not be the case forever. Wicked nations, which forget the Lord and refuse to help their people, will be judged by God. He knows our needs, he knows our tendency to despair, and he has promised to care for us (see also Ps 9:9, 12). Even when others forget us, he will remember.

Ps 11:1-4 David was forced to flee for safety several times. Being God's anointed king did not make him immune to injustice and hatred from others. He may have written this psalm when he was being hunted by Saul (1 Sam 18–31) or during the days of Absalom's rebellion (2 Sam 15–18). In both instances, David fled, but not as if all was lost. He knew God was in control. While David wisely avoided trouble, he did not fearfully run away from his troubles.

Ps 11:1-4 David seems to be speaking to those who are advising him to run from his enemies. David's faith contrasts dramatically with the fear of the advisers who tell him to flee. Faith in God keeps us from losing hope and helps us resist fear. David's advisers were afraid because they saw only frightening circumstances and crumbling foundations. David was comforted and optimistic because he knew God was greater than anything his enemies could bring against him (Pss 7:10; 16:1; 31:2-3).

Ps 11:4 When the foundations are shaking and you wish you could hide, remember that God is still in control. His power is not diminished by any turn of events. Nothing happens without his knowledge and permission. When you feel like running away—run to God instead. He will restore justice and goodness on the earth in his good time.

Ps 11:5 God does not shield believers from difficult circumstances, but he examines (or tests) both the righteous and the wicked. For some, God's tests become a refining fire, while for others they become an incinerator for destruction. Don't ignore or defy the tests and challenges that come your way. Use them as opportunities for you to grow.

Ps 12:1 Living for God in a deceitful world can be difficult and lonely. At one time the great prophet Elijah felt so lonely he wanted to die. But God told him that there were 7,000 other faithful servants (1 Kgs 19:4, 14, 18). We are never alone in our battle against evil. When you feel alone, seek out other believers for strength and support.

Ps 12:2-4 We may be tempted to believe that some lies are relatively harmless, even useful at times. But God does not overlook lies, flattery, deception, or boasting. Each of these sins originates from a bad attitude that is eventually expressed in our speech. The tongue can be our greatest enemy because, though small, it can do great damage (Jas 3:5-6). Be careful how you use yours.

4 They say, "We will lie to our hearts' content.
Our lips are our own—who can stop us?"
5 The LORD replies, "I have seen violence done
to the helpless,
and I have heard the groans of the poor.
Now I will rise up to rescue them,
as they have longed for me to do."
6 The LORD's promises are pure,
like silver refined in a furnace,
purified seven times over.
7 Therefore, LORD, we know you will protect the
oppressed,
preserving them forever from this lying
generation,
8 even though the wicked strut about,
and evil is praised throughout the land.

Psalm 13

THEME: Praying for relief from despair. We must continue to trust God even when he doesn't answer us immediately.

AUTHOR: David

For the choir director: A psalm of David.

1 O LORD, how long will you forget me? Forever?
How long will you look the other way?
2 How long must I struggle with anguish in my
soul,
with sorrow in my heart every day?
How long will my enemy have the upper hand?
3 Turn and answer me, O LORD my God!
Restore the sparkle to my eyes, or I will die.
4 Don't let my enemies gloat, saying, "We have
defeated him!"
Don't let them rejoice at my downfall.
5 But I trust in your unfailing love.
I will rejoice because you have rescued me.
6 I will sing to the LORD
because he is good to me.

Psalm 14

THEME: Only the fool denies God. How foolish it must seem to God when people say there is no God.

AUTHOR: David

For the choir director: A psalm of David.

1 Only fools say in their hearts,
"There is no God."
They are corrupt, and their actions are evil;
not one of them does good!

TROUBLES AND COMPLAINTS IN PSALMS

We can relate to the psalms because they express our feelings. We all face troubles, as did the psalm writers thousands of years ago, and we often respond as they did. In Psalm 3, David told God how he felt about the odds against him. But within three verses, the king realized that God's presence and care made the odds meaningless. This experience is repeated in many of the psalms. Usually the hope and confidence in God outweigh the fear and suffering; sometimes they do not. Still, the psalm writers consistently poured out their thoughts and emotions to God. When they felt abandoned by God, they told him so. When they were impatient with how slowly God seemed to be answering their prayers, they also told him so. Because they recognized the difference between themselves and God, they were free to be human and to be honest with their Creator. That is why so many of the dark psalms end in the light. The psalm writers started by expressing their feelings and ended up remembering to whom they were speaking!

Although we have much in common with these writers, we may differ in two ways: We might not tell God what we are really thinking and feeling; therefore, we also might not recognize, even faintly, who is listening to our prayers!

Notice this pattern as you read Psalms, and put the writers' insights to the test. You may well find that your awareness and appreciation of God will grow as you are honest with him. (See Pss 3; 6; 13; 31; 37; 64; 77; 102; 121; 142.)

Ps 12:5 God cares for the helpless and the poor. Here he promises to protect the downtrodden and confront their oppressors. We should identify with God's attitude. His work is not done until we care for the needs of the poor.

Ps 12:6 Sincerity and truth are extremely valuable because they are so rare. Many people are deceivers, liars, flatterers; they think they will get what they want by deception. As a king, David certainly faced his share of such people who hoped to win his favor and gain advancement through flattery. When we feel as though sincerity and truth have nearly gone out of existence, we have one hope—the Word of God. God's Word is as pure and flawless as refined silver. So listen carefully when he speaks to you through his Word.

Ps 13:1 Sometimes all we need to do is talk over a problem with a friend to help put it in perspective. In this psalm, the phrase "how long" occurs four times in the first two verses, indicating the depth of David's distress. David expressed his feelings to God and found strength. By the end of his prayer, he was able to profess hope and trust in God. Through prayer we can express our feelings and talk our problems out with God. He helps us regain the right perspective, and this gives us peace (Hab 3:17-19).

Ps 13:1-5 David frequently claimed that God was slow to act on his behalf. We often feel this same impatience. It seems that evil and suffering go unchecked, and we wonder when God is going to stop them. David affirmed that he would continue to trust God no matter how long he had to wait for God's justice to be realized. When you feel impatient, remember David's steadfast faith in God's unfailing love.

Ps 13:5-6 David was faithful to God and trusted wholeheartedly in him, but he felt the pressure of his problems as much as anyone. But instead of giving up or giving in, David held on to his faith. In times of despair, it is much harder to hold on than to give up. But if you give up on God, you give in to a life of despair.

Ps 14:1-3 The true atheist is either foolish or wicked—foolish because he ignores the evidence that God exists or wicked because he refuses to live by God's truths. We become atheists in practice when we rely more on ourselves than on God. The fools mentioned here are aggressively perverse in their actions. To speak in direct defiance of God is utterly foolish according to the Bible.

▸ **PSALM 14** ***(cont.)***

2 The LORD looks down from heaven
on the entire human race;
he looks to see if anyone is truly wise,
if anyone seeks God.
3 But no, all have turned away;
all have become corrupt.*
No one does good,
not a single one!
4 Will those who do evil never learn?
They eat up my people like bread
and wouldn't think of praying to the LORD.
5 Terror will grip them,
for God is with those who obey him.
6 The wicked frustrate the plans of the oppressed,
but the LORD will protect his people.
7 Who will come from Mount Zion to rescue
Israel?
When the LORD restores his people,
Jacob will shout with joy, and Israel will rejoice.

Psalm 15

THEME: Guidelines for living a blameless life.

AUTHOR: David

A psalm of David.

1 Who may worship in your sanctuary, LORD?
Who may enter your presence on your
holy hill?
2 Those who lead blameless lives and do what
is right,
speaking the truth from sincere hearts.
3 Those who refuse to gossip
or harm their neighbors
or speak evil of their friends.
4 Those who despise flagrant sinners,
and honor the faithful followers of the LORD,
and keep their promises even when it hurts.
5 Those who lend money without charging interest,
and who cannot be bribed to lie about the
innocent.
Such people will stand firm forever.

Psalm 16

THEME: The joys and benefits of a life lived in companionship with God. We enjoy these benefits now and eternally.

AUTHOR: David

A psalm of David.*

1 Keep me safe, O God,
for I have come to you for refuge.
2 I said to the LORD, "You are my Master!
Every good thing I have comes from you."
3 The godly people in the land
are my true heroes!
I take pleasure in them!
4 Troubles multiply for those who chase after
other gods.

Ps 14:3 Greek version reads *have become useless.* Compare Rom 3:12. **Ps 16:TITLE** Hebrew *miktam.* This may be a literary or musical term.

Ps 14:3 No one but God is perfect; all of us stand guilty before him (see Rom 3:23) and need his forgiveness. No matter how well we perform or how much we achieve compared to others, we can't boast of our goodness when compared to God's standard. God not only expects us to obey his laws, but he wants us to love him with all our heart. No one except Jesus Christ has done that perfectly. Because we all fall short, we must turn to Christ to save us (Rom 10:9-11). Have you asked him to save you?

Ps 14:3-4 David applies these observations to his enemies when he says the evildoers "eat up my people like bread" (Ps 14:4). "All have turned away; all have become corrupt. No one does good, not a single one!" (Ps 14:3). By contrast, David said, "You have scrutinized me and found nothing wrong" (Ps 17:3).

There is a clear distinction between those who worship God and those who refuse to worship him. David worshiped God, and under his leadership Israel obeyed God and prospered. Several hundred years later, however, Israel forgot God, and it became difficult to distinguish between God's followers and those who worshiped idols. When Isaiah called Israel to repentance, he, like David, spoke of people who had gone astray (Isa 53:6). But Isaiah was talking about the Israelites themselves. Paul quoted Psalm 14 in Romans 3:10-12. He made the image of straying sheep even more general, referring to all people. The whole human race—Jew and Gentile alike—has turned away from God.

Ps 14:5 If "God is with those who obey him," then those who attack God's followers may be attacking God. To attack God is utterly futile (see Ps 2:4-5, 10-12). Thus, while we may feel we are losing the battle, we can be absolutely sure that our ultimate victory is in God.

Ps 15:1 *Sanctuary* and *holy hill* are interchangeable words describing the focal point of Israelite worship—the dwelling place of God. In Hebrew poetry the repeating pattern is found more in the thought than in the sound or rhythm.

Ps 15:1ff God calls his people to be morally upright, and in this psalm, he gives us 10 standards to determine how we are doing. We live among evil people whose standards and morals are eroding. Our standards for living should not come from our evil society but from God. (For other references where righteous conduct is summarized, see Isa 33:15; 56:1; Mic 6:8; Hab 2:4; Mark 12:29-31.)

Ps 15:2-5 As we grow in our relationship with our Redeemer, we develop a desire to live by his standards. The depth of our eternal relationship with him can often be measured by the way we reflect his standards in our daily activities.

Ps 15:3-4 Words are powerful, and how you use them reflects on your relationship with God. Perhaps nothing so identifies Christians as their ability to control their speech—speaking the truth, refusing to slander, and keeping oaths (promises). Watch what you say. (See Jas 3:1-12 for more on the importance of controlling your tongue.)

Ps 15:5 God was against the Jews' charging interest or making a profit on loans to needy, fellow Jews (see also Exod 22:25; Lev 25:35-37), although charging interest on loans to foreigners was allowed (Deut 23:20). Interest was also permitted for business purposes, as long as it wasn't exorbitant (Prov 28:8).

Ps 15:5 Some people are so obsessed with money that they will change their God-given standards and lifestyle to get it. If money is a controlling force in your life, it must be curbed, or it will harm others and destroy your relationship with God.

I will not take part in their sacrifices
of blood
or even speak the names of their gods.

5 LORD, you alone are my inheritance, my cup
of blessing.
You guard all that is mine.
6 The land you have given me is a pleasant land.
What a wonderful inheritance!

7 I will bless the LORD who guides me;
even at night my heart instructs me.
8 I know the LORD is always with me.
I will not be shaken, for he is right beside me.

9 No wonder my heart is glad, and I rejoice.*
My body rests in safety.
10 For you will not leave my soul among the dead*
or allow your holy one* to rot in the grave.
11 You will show me the way of life,
granting me the joy of your presence
and the pleasures of living with you forever.*

Psalm 17

THEME: A plea for justice in the face of false accusations and persecution. David urges us to realize the true goal of life—to know God—and the true reward of life—to see God one day.

AUTHOR: David, possibly written while he was being persecuted by Saul.

A prayer of David.

1 O LORD, hear my plea for justice.
Listen to my cry for help.
Pay attention to my prayer,
for it comes from honest lips.
2 Declare me innocent,
for you see those who do right.

3 You have tested my thoughts and examined
my heart in the night.
You have scrutinized me and found nothing
wrong.
I am determined not to sin in what I say.
4 I have followed your commands,
which keep me from following cruel and
evil people.
5 My steps have stayed on your path;
I have not wavered from following you.

6 I am praying to you because I know you will
answer, O God.
Bend down and listen as I pray.
7 Show me your unfailing love in wonderful ways.
By your mighty power you rescue
those who seek refuge from their enemies.
8 Guard me as you would guard your own eyes.*
Hide me in the shadow of your wings.
9 Protect me from wicked people who attack me,
from murderous enemies who surround me.
10 They are without pity.
Listen to their boasting!
11 They track me down and surround me,
watching for the chance to throw me to the
ground.
12 They are like hungry lions, eager to tear me
apart—
like young lions hiding in ambush.

Ps 16:9 Greek version reads *and my tongue shouts his praises.* Compare Acts 2:26. **Ps 16:10a** Hebrew *in Sheol.* **Ps 16:10b** Or *your Holy One.* **Ps 16:11** Greek version reads *You have shown me the way of life, / and you will fill me with the joy of your presence.* Compare Acts 2:28. **Ps 17:8** Hebrew *as the pupil of your eye.*

Ps 16:7-8 It is human nature to make our own plans and then ask God to bless them. Instead, we should seek God's will first. By constantly thinking about the Lord and his way of living, we will gain insights that will help us make right decisions and live the way God desires. Communicating with God allows him to counsel us and give us wisdom.

Ps 16:8 By saying that he "will not be shaken," David was talking about the unique sense of security felt by believers. God does not exempt believers from the day-to-day circumstances of life. Believers and unbelievers alike experience pain, trouble, and failure at times (Matt 5:45). Unbelievers have a sense of hopelessness about life and confusion over their true purpose on earth. Those who seek God can move ahead, confident in knowing what is right in God's eyes. They know that God will keep them from straying off his chosen path.

Ps 16:8-11 This psalm is often called a messianic psalm because it is quoted in the New Testament as referring to the resurrection of Jesus Christ. Both Peter and Paul quoted from this psalm when speaking of Christ's bodily resurrection (see Acts 2:25-28, 31; 13:35-37).

Ps 16:9 David's heart was glad—he had found the secret to joy. True joy is far deeper than happiness; we can feel joy in spite of our deepest troubles. Happiness is temporary because it is based on external circumstances, but joy is lasting because it is based on God's presence within us. As we contemplate his daily presence, we will find contentment. As we understand the future he has for us, we will experience joy. Don't base your life on circumstances, but on God.

Ps 16:10 David stated confidently that God would not leave him in the grave. Many people fear death because they can neither control nor understand it. As believers, we can be assured that God will not forget us when we die. He will bring us to life again to live with him forever. This provides real security. (For other passages about resurrection, see Job 19:25-26; Isa 26:19; Dan 12:2, 13; Mark 13:27; 1 Cor 15:12-58; 1 Thes 4:13-18; Rev 20:11–21:4.)

Ps 17:3 Was David saying he was sinless? Far from a proud assumption of purity, David's claim was an understanding of his relationship with God. In Psalms 32 and 51, David freely acknowledged his own sins. Nevertheless his relationship with God was one of close fellowship and constant repentance and forgiveness. His claim to goodness, therefore, was based on his continual seeking after God.

Ps 17:8 Just as we protect our eyes, so God will protect us. But we must not conclude that we have somehow missed God's protection if we experience troubles. God's protection has far greater purposes than helping us avoid pain; it is to make us better servants for him. God also protects us by guiding us through painful circumstances, not only by helping us escape them.

Ps 17:8 The "shadow of your wings" is a figure of speech symbolizing God's protection. He guards us just as a mother bird protects her young by covering them with her wings. Moses used a similar metaphor in Deuteronomy 32:11.

▸ **PSALM 17 *(cont.)***

13 Arise, O LORD!
Stand against them, and bring them to their knees!
Rescue me from the wicked with your sword!
14 By the power of your hand, O LORD,
destroy those who look to this world for their reward.
But satisfy the hunger of your treasured ones.
May their children have plenty,
leaving an inheritance for their descendants.
15 Because I am righteous, I will see you.
When I awake, I will see you face to face and be satisfied.

Psalm 19

THEME: Both God's creation and his word reveal his greatness.
AUTHOR: David

For the choir director: A psalm of David.

1 The heavens proclaim the glory of God.
The skies display his craftsmanship.
2 Day after day they continue to speak;
night after night they make him known.
3 They speak without a sound or word;
their voice is never heard.*
4 Yet their message has gone throughout the earth,
and their words to all the world.

God has made a home in the heavens for the sun.
5 It bursts forth like a radiant bridegroom after his wedding.
It rejoices like a great athlete eager to run the race.
6 The sun rises at one end of the heavens
and follows its course to the other end.
Nothing can hide from its heat.
7 The instructions of the LORD are perfect,
reviving the soul.
The decrees of the LORD are trustworthy,
making wise the simple.
8 The commandments of the LORD are right,
bringing joy to the heart.
The commands of the LORD are clear,
giving insight for living.
9 Reverence for the LORD is pure,
lasting forever.
The laws of the LORD are true;
each one is fair.

Ps 19:3 Or *There is no speech or language where their voice is not heard.*

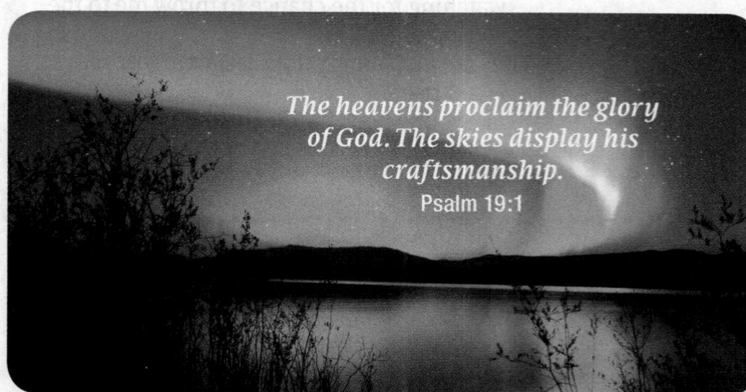
The heavens proclaim the glory of God. The skies display his craftsmanship.
Psalm 19:1

Ps 17:13-15 We deceive ourselves when we measure our happiness or contentment in life by the amount of wealth we possess. When we put riches at the top of our value system, we let power, pleasure, and financial security overshadow the eternal value of our relationship with God. We think we will be happy or content when we get riches, only to discover that they don't really satisfy, and the pleasures fade away. The true measurement of happiness or contentment is found in God's love and in doing his will. You will find true happiness if you put your relationship with God above earthly riches.

Ps 17:15 The word *awake* shows that David believed in life after death. Although belief in resurrection was not widespread in Old Testament times, several verses show that it was partially understood. Some of these are Job 19:25-27; Psalms 16:10; 49:15; 139:17-18; Isaiah 26:19; Daniel 12:2, 13.

Ps 19:1ff In this psalm, David meditates on God's creation, God's Word, his own sinfulness, and God's forgiveness. As God reveals himself through nature (Ps 19:1-6), we learn about his power and our finiteness. As God reveals himself through Scripture (Ps 19:7-11), we learn about his holiness and our sinfulness. As God reveals himself through daily experiences (Ps 19:12-14), we learn about his gracious forgiveness that frees us from guilt.

Ps 19:1-6 We are surrounded by fantastic displays of God's craftsmanship—the heavens give dramatic evidence of his existence, his power, his love, his care. To say that the universe happened by chance is absurd. Its design, intricacy, and orderliness point to a personally involved Creator. As you look at God's handiwork in nature and the heavens, thank him for such magnificent beauty and the truth it reveals about the Creator.

Ps 19:3-4 The apostle Paul referred to this psalm when he explained that everyone knows about God because nature proclaims God's existence and power (Rom 1:19-20). This does not cancel the need for missions because the message of God's salvation found in his Word, the Bible, must still be told to the ends of the earth. While nature points to the existence of God, the Bible tells us about God's plan of salvation. God's people must explain to others how they can have a relationship with God. Although most people believe in a Creator because of the evidence of nature around them, they need to know about his love, mercy, and grace. What are you doing to take God's message to the world?

Ps 19:7-11 When we think of instructions, decrees, and commandments, we often think of rules that keep us from having fun. But here we see the opposite: God's laws revive us, make us wise, bring joy to the heart, give insight, warn us, and reward us. God's laws are guidelines and lights for our path, rather than chains on our hands and feet. They point at danger to warn us, and then point at success to guide us.

Ps 19:12-13 Many Christians are plagued by guilt. They worry that they may have committed a sin unknowingly, done something good with selfish intentions, failed to put their

10 They are more desirable than gold,
even the finest gold.
They are sweeter than honey,
even honey dripping from the comb.
11 They are a warning to your servant,
a great reward for those who obey them.

12 How can I know all the sins lurking in my heart?
Cleanse me from these hidden faults.
13 Keep your servant from deliberate sins!
Don't let them control me.
Then I will be free of guilt
and innocent of great sin.

14 May the words of my mouth
and the meditation of my heart
be pleasing to you,
O LORD, my rock and my redeemer.

Psalm 20

THEME: A prayer for victory in battle. Such a prayer can help us prepare for any great challenge. David knew that trust should be placed in the Lord more than in human power.

AUTHOR: David. The events in 2 Samuel 10 (p. 500) may have prompted this prayer.

For the choir director: A psalm of David.

1 In times of trouble, may the LORD answer your cry.
May the name of the God of Jacob keep you
safe from all harm.
2 May he send you help from his sanctuary
and strengthen you from Jerusalem.*
3 May he remember all your gifts
and look favorably on your burnt offerings.
Interlude

4 May he grant your heart's desires
and make all your plans succeed.
5 May we shout for joy when we hear of your victory
and raise a victory banner in the name
of our God.
May the LORD answer all your prayers.
6 Now I know that the LORD rescues his anointed
king.
He will answer him from his holy heaven
and rescue him by his great power.
7 Some nations boast of their chariots and horses,
but we boast in the name of the LORD our God.
8 Those nations will fall down and collapse,
but we will rise up and stand firm.

9 Give victory to our king, O LORD!
Answer our cry for help.

Ps 20:2 Hebrew *Zion.*

Psalm 21

THEME: Praising God after victory in battle. When God answers our prayers for victory, we must quickly and openly thank him for his help.

AUTHOR: David

For the choir director: A psalm of David.

1 How the king rejoices in your strength, O LORD!
He shouts with joy because you give him
victory.
2 For you have given him his heart's desire;
you have withheld nothing he requested.
Interlude

3 You welcomed him back with success and
prosperity.
You placed a crown of finest gold on his head.
4 He asked you to preserve his life,
and you granted his request.
The days of his life stretch on forever.
5 Your victory brings him great honor,
and you have clothed him with splendor and
majesty.
6 You have endowed him with eternal blessings
and given him the joy of your presence.
7 For the king trusts in the LORD.
The unfailing love of the Most High will keep
him from stumbling.

---

whole heart into a task, or neglected what they should have done. Guilt can play an important role in bringing us to Christ and in keeping us behaving properly, but it should not cripple us or make us fearful. God fully and completely forgives us—even for those sins we do unknowingly.

Ps 19:14 Would you change the way you live if you knew that every word and thought would be examined by God first? David asks that God approve his words and reflections as though they were offerings brought to the altar. As you begin each day, determine that God's love will guide what you say and how you think.

Ps 20:6-8 As long as there have been armies and weapons, nations have boasted of their power; but such power does not last. Throughout history, empires and kingdoms have risen to great power only to vanish in the dust. David, however, knew that the true might of his nation was not in weaponry but in worship, not in firepower but in God's power. Because God alone can preserve a nation or an individual, be sure your confidence is in God, who gives eternal victory. Whom do you trust?

Ps 21:1-6 David described all that he had as gifts from God: his heart's desire, success and prosperity, a crown of finest gold, long life, splendor and majesty, eternal blessings, joy. We, too, should look upon all we have—position, family, wealth, talent—as gifts from God. Only then will we use them to give glory back to him.

Ps 21:7 A good leader trusts the Lord and depends upon his unfailing love. Too often leaders trust in their own cleverness, popular support, or military power. But God is above all these "gods." If you aspire to leadership, keep the Lord God at the center of your life and depend on him. His love will keep you from stumbling.

Ps 21:7 Because David trusted in God, God would not let him stumble (be removed from the throne). When we trust in God, we have permanence and stability. We may lose a great deal—families, jobs, material possessions—but we cannot be shaken from God's favor. He will be our foundation of solid rock. He will never leave or desert us.

▸ **PSALM 21 *(cont.)***

8 You will capture all your enemies.
Your strong right hand will seize all who hate you.
9 You will throw them in a flaming furnace when you appear.
The LORD will consume them in his anger;
fire will devour them.
10 You will wipe their children from the face of the earth;
they will never have descendants.
11 Although they plot against you,
their evil schemes will never succeed.
12 For they will turn and run
when they see your arrows aimed at them.
13 Rise up, O LORD, in all your power.
With music and singing we celebrate your mighty acts.

Psalm 22

THEME: A prayer that carries us from great suffering to great joy. Despite apparent rejection by his friends and God, David believed that God would lead him out of despair. He looked forward to that future day when God would rule over the entire earth.

AUTHOR: David

For the choir director: A psalm of David, to be sung to the tune "Doe of the Dawn."

1 My God, my God, why have you abandoned me?
Why are you so far away when I groan for help?
2 Every day I call to you, my God, but you do not answer.
Every night you hear my voice, but I find no relief.

3 Yet you are holy,
enthroned on the praises of Israel.
4 Our ancestors trusted in you,
and you rescued them.
5 They cried out to you and were saved.
They trusted in you and were never disgraced.

6 But I am a worm and not a man.
I am scorned and despised by all!
7 Everyone who sees me mocks me.
They sneer and shake their heads, saying,
8 "Is this the one who relies on the LORD?
Then let the LORD save him!
If the LORD loves him so much,
let the LORD rescue him!"

9 Yet you brought me safely from my mother's womb
and led me to trust you at my mother's breast.
10 I was thrust into your arms at my birth.
You have been my God from the moment I was born.

11 Do not stay so far from me,
for trouble is near,
and no one else can help me.
12 My enemies surround me like a herd of bulls;
fierce bulls of Bashan have hemmed me in!
13 Like lions they open their jaws against me,
roaring and tearing into their prey.
14 My life is poured out like water,
and all my bones are out of joint.
My heart is like wax,
melting within me.
15 My strength has dried up like sunbaked clay.
My tongue sticks to the roof of my mouth.
You have laid me in the dust and left me for dead.
16 My enemies surround me like a pack of dogs;
an evil gang closes in on me.
They have pierced my hands and feet.
17 I can count all my bones.
My enemies stare at me and gloat.
18 They divide my garments among themselves
and throw dice* for my clothing.

19 O LORD, do not stay far away!
You are my strength; come quickly to my aid!
20 Save me from the sword;
spare my precious life from these dogs.
21 Snatch me from the lion's jaws
and from the horns of these wild oxen.

Ps 22:18 Hebrew *cast lots.*

Ps 21:11 When you see evil schemes unfold, remember that they will not succeed forever. The power of evildoers is only temporary, and God's very presence can send them scattering in a moment. God, according to his plan and purpose, will intervene for his people and give the wicked the judgment they deserve. We should not be dismayed when we see the temporary advantage God's enemies seem to have.

Ps 22:1 David gave an amazingly accurate description of the suffering the Messiah would endure hundreds of years later. David was obviously enduring some great trial, but through his suffering, he, like the Messiah to come, gained victory. Jesus, the Messiah, quoted this verse while hanging on the cross carrying our burden of sin (Matt 27:46). It was not a cry of doubt, but an urgent appeal to God.

Ps 22:6 When others despise us and heap scorn upon us, they treat us as less than human. After much degradation, we, like David, may begin to feel like worms. When we feel the sting of rejection, we must keep in mind the hope and victory that God promises us (Ps 22:22ff).

Ps 22:9-11 God's loving concern does not begin on the day we are born and conclude on the day we die. It reaches back to those days before we were born and reaches ahead along the unending path of eternity. Our only sure help comes from a God whose concern for us reaches beyond our earthly existence. How can anyone reject such love?

Ps 22:12 The land of Bashan, located east of the Sea of Galilee, was known for its strong, well-fed cattle (Amos 4:1). Because of its grain fields, it was often called the breadbasket of Palestine.

22 I will proclaim your name to my brothers
and sisters.*
I will praise you among your assembled
people.
23 Praise the LORD, all you who fear him!
Honor him, all you descendants of Jacob!
Show him reverence, all you descendants
of Israel!
24 For he has not ignored or belittled the suffering
of the needy.
He has not turned his back on them,
but has listened to their cries for help.
25 I will praise you in the great assembly.
I will fulfill my vows in the presence of those
who worship you.
26 The poor will eat and be satisfied.
All who seek the LORD will praise him.
Their hearts will rejoice with
everlasting joy.
27 The whole earth will acknowledge the LORD
and return to him.
All the families of the nations will bow down
before him.
28 For royal power belongs to the LORD.
He rules all the nations.
29 Let the rich of the earth feast and worship.
Bow before him, all who are mortal,
all whose lives will end as dust.
30 Our children will also serve him.
Future generations will hear about the
wonders of the Lord.
31 His righteous acts will be told to those not
yet born.
They will hear about everything he has done.

Ps 22:22 Hebrew *my brothers.*

CHRIST IN THE PSALMS

Both the Jewish and Christian faiths have long believed that many psalms referred as much to the promised Messiah as they did to events at the time. Because the Messiah was to be a descendant of David, it was expected that many of the royal psalms would apply to him. Christians noted how many of the passages seemed to describe in detail events from Christ's life and death. Jesus himself frequently quoted from Psalms. Almost everything that happened at the Crucifixion and most of Jesus' words during his final hours were prophesied in Psalms.

The following is a list of the main references in Psalms pertaining to Christ.

Reference in Psalms	*Reference to Christ*	*Fulfillment in the New Testament*
Ps 2:7	The Messiah will be God's Son	Heb 1:5-6
Ps 16:8-10	He will rise from the dead	Luke 24:5-7
Ps 22:1-21	He will experience agony on the cross	Matt 26–27
Ps 22:15	He will thirst while on the cross	John 19:28
Ps 22:18	Evil men will throw dice for his clothing	Matt 27:35; John 19:23-24
Ps 22:22	He will declare God's name	Heb 2:12
Ps 34:20	His bones will not be broken	John 19:36-37
Ps 40:6-8	He will come to do God's will	Heb 10:5-7
Ps 41:9	His close friend will betray him	Luke 22:48
Ps 45:6-7	His throne will last forever	Heb 1:8-9
Ps 68:18	He will ascend into heaven	Eph 4:8-10
Ps 69:9	He will be zealous for God	John 2:17
Ps 69:21	He will be offered vinegar for his thirst on the cross	Matt 27:48
Ps 89:3-4, 35-36	He will be a descendant of David	Luke 1:31-33
Ps 96:13	He will return to judge the world	1 Thes 1:10
Ps 110:1	He is David's son and David's Lord	Matt 22:44
Ps 110:4	He is the eternal priest-king	Heb 6:20
Ps 118:22	He is rejected by many but accepted by God	1 Pet 2:7-8

Ps 22:22 David would praise God among the people because his private deliverance deserved a public testimony. God may wonderfully deliver us in the quiet moments when we are hurting; if so, we must be prepared to offer public praise for his care.

Ps 22:30-31 Unborn generations are depending on our faithfulness today. As we teach our children about the Lord, so they will teach their children and their children's children. If we fail to tell our children about the Lord, we may well be breaking the chain of God's influence on generations to come. We must view our children and all the young people we meet as God's future leaders. If we are faithful in opportunities today, we may well be affecting the future.

Ps 22:30-31 If we want our children to serve the Lord, they must hear about him from us. It is not enough to rely on the church or those with more knowledge to provide all their Christian education. We must reinforce the lessons of the Bible in our homes.

Psalm 23

THEME: God is seen as a caring shepherd and a dependable guide. We must follow God and obey his commands. He is our only hope for eternal life and security.

AUTHOR: David

A psalm of David.

1 The LORD is my shepherd;
I have all that I need.
2 He lets me rest in green meadows;
he leads me beside peaceful streams.
3 He renews my strength.
He guides me along right paths,
bringing honor to his name.
4 Even when I walk
through the darkest valley,*
I will not be afraid,
for you are close beside me.
Your rod and your staff
protect and comfort me.
5 You prepare a feast for me
in the presence of my enemies.
You honor me by anointing my head
with oil.
My cup overflows with blessings.
6 Surely your goodness and unfailing love will
pursue me
all the days of my life,
and I will live in the house of the LORD
forever.

Psalm 24

THEME: Everything belongs to God—the glorious eternal King. Let us worship him and welcome his glorious reign.

AUTHOR: David

A psalm of David.

1 The earth is the LORD's, and everything in it.
The world and all its people belong to him.
2 For he laid the earth's foundation on the seas
and built it on the ocean depths.

3 Who may climb the mountain of the LORD?
Who may stand in his holy place?
4 Only those whose hands and hearts
are pure,

Ps 23:4 Or *the dark valley of death.*

Ps 23:1 In describing the Lord as a shepherd, David wrote out of his own experience because he had spent his early years caring for sheep (1 Sam 16:10-11). Sheep are completely dependent on the shepherd for provision, guidance, and protection. The New Testament calls Jesus the good shepherd (John 10:11), the great Shepherd (Heb 13:20), and the Great Shepherd (1 Pet 5:4). As the Lord is the good shepherd, so we are his sheep—not frightened, passive animals, but obedient followers, wise enough to follow one who will lead us in the right places and in right ways. This psalm does not focus on the animal-like qualities of sheep but on the discipleship qualities of those who follow. When you recognize the good shepherd, follow him!

Ps 23:2-3 When we allow God, our shepherd, to guide us, we have contentment. When we choose to sin and go our own way, however, we cannot blame God for the environment we create for ourselves. Our shepherd knows the "green meadows" and "peaceful streams" that will restore us. We will reach these places only by following him obediently. Rebelling against the shepherd's leading is actually rebelling against our own best interests. We must remember this the next time we are tempted to go our own way rather than the shepherd's way.

Ps 23:4 Death casts a frightening shadow over us because we are entirely helpless in its presence. We can struggle with other enemies—pain, suffering, disease, injury—but strength and courage cannot overcome death. It has the final word. Only one person can walk with us through death's dark valley and bring us safely to the other side—the God of life, our shepherd. Because life is uncertain, we should follow this shepherd who offers us eternal comfort.

Ps 23:5-6 In ancient Near Eastern culture, it was customary at a feast to anoint a person with fragrant oil. Hosts were also expected to protect their guests at all costs. God offers the protection of a host even when enemies surround us. In the final scene of this psalm, we see that believers will dwell with the Lord. God, the perfect shepherd and host, promises to guide and protect us throughout our life and to bring us into his house forever.

PSALMS TO LEARN AND LOVE

Almost everyone, whether religious or not, has heard Psalm 23 because it is quoted so frequently. Many other psalms are also familiar because they are quoted in music, in literature, or in the words of our worship services.

The psalms we know and love are the ones that come into our minds when we need them. They inspire us, comfort us, or correct us just when we need a word from the Lord. If you want to begin memorizing psalms, start with some of these favorites. Memorize the whole psalm or just the verses that speak most directly to you. Or read the psalm aloud several times a day until it is part of you.

Psalms to bring us into God's presence	29; 95:1-7a; 96; 100
Psalms about goodness	1; 19; 24; 133; 136; 139
Psalms of praise	8; 97; 103; 107; 113; 145; 150
Psalms of repentance and forgiveness	32:1-5; 51; 103
Psalms for times of trouble	3; 14; 22; 37:1-11; 42; 46; 53; 116:1-7
Psalms of confidence and trust	23; 40:1-4; 91; 119:11; 121; 127

Ps 24:1 Because "the earth is the LORD's," all of us are stewards, or caretakers. We should be committed to the proper management of this world and its resources. But we are not to become devoted to anything created or act as sole proprietors because this world will pass away (1 Jn 2:17).

Ps 24:1ff This psalm may have been written to celebrate moving the Ark of the Covenant from Obed-edom's house to Jerusalem (2 Sam 6:10-12). Tradition says that this psalm was sung on the first day of each week in the Temple services. Psalm 24:1-6

who do not worship idols
and never tell lies.
5 They will receive the LORD's blessing
and have a right relationship with
God their savior.
6 Such people may seek you
and worship in your presence,
O God of Jacob. *Interlude*

7 Open up, ancient gates!
Open up, ancient doors,
and let the King of glory enter.
8 Who is the King of glory?
The LORD, strong and mighty;
the LORD, invincible in battle.
9 Open up, ancient gates!
Open up, ancient doors,
and let the King of glory enter.
10 Who is the King of glory?
The LORD of Heaven's Armies—
he is the King of glory. *Interlude*

*Psalm 25**

THEME: A prayer for defense, guidance, and pardon. As we trust in God, he grants these same requests for us.

AUTHOR: David

A psalm of David.

1 O LORD, I give my life to you.
2 I trust in you, my God!
Do not let me be disgraced,
or let my enemies rejoice in my defeat.
3 No one who trusts in you will ever be
disgraced,
but disgrace comes to those who try
to deceive others.

4 Show me the right path, O LORD;
point out the road for me to follow.
5 Lead me by your truth and teach me,
for you are the God who saves me.
All day long I put my hope in you.

Ps 25 This psalm is a Hebrew acrostic poem; each verse begins with a successive letter of the Hebrew alphabet.

tells who is worthy to join in such a celebration of worship.

Ps 24:4 This refers to all lies, especially those told under oath. How greatly God values honesty! Dishonesty comes easily, especially when complete truthfulness could cost us something, make us uncomfortable, or put us in an unfavorable light. Dishonest communication hinders relationships. Without honesty, a relationship with God is impossible. If we lie to others, we will begin to deceive ourselves. God cannot hear us or speak to us if we are building a wall of self-deception.

Ps 24:7-10 Who is this King of glory? The King of glory, identified here also as the Lord of Heaven's Armies, is the Messiah himself—eternal, holy, and mighty. This psalm is not only a battle cry for the church, but it also looks forward to Christ's future entry into the new Jerusalem to reign forever (Rev 19:11-21).

Ps 24:7-10 This psalm, often set to music, was probably used in corporate worship. It may have been reenacted many times at the Temple. The people outside would call out to the Temple gates to open up and let the King of glory in. From inside, the priests or another group would ask, "Who is the King of glory?" Outside, the people would respond in unison, "The LORD, strong and mighty, the LORD, invincible in battle," proclaiming his great power and strength. The exchange then would be repeated (Ps 24:9-10), and the Temple gates would swing open, symbolizing the people's desire to have God's presence among them. This would have been an important lesson for children who were participating.

Ps 25:2 Almost half of the psalms—72 of them—speak about enemies. Enemies are those who oppose not only us but also God's way of living. We can view temptations—money, success, prestige, lust—as our enemies. And our greatest enemy is Satan. David asked God to keep his enemies from overcoming him because they opposed what God stood for. If his enemies succeeded, David feared that many would think that living for God was futile. David did not question his own faith—he knew that God would triumph. But he didn't want his enemies' success to be an obstacle to the faith of others.

Ps 25:4 David expressed his desire for guidance. How do we receive God's guidance? The first step is to want to be guided and to realize that God's primary guidance system is in his Word, the Bible. Psalm 119 tells of the endless knowledge found in God's Word. By reading the Bible and constantly learning from it, we will gain the wisdom to perceive God's direction for our lives. We may be tempted to demand answers from God, but David asked for direction. When we are willing to seek God, learn from his Word, and obey his commands, then we will receive his specific guidance.

The LORD is my shepherd; I have all that I need.
He lets me rest in green meadows;
he leads me beside peaceful streams.
Psalm 23:1-2

▸ **PSALM 25** ***(cont.)***

6 Remember, O LORD, your compassion and unfailing love,
which you have shown from long ages past.
7 Do not remember the rebellious sins of my youth.
Remember me in the light of your unfailing love,
for you are merciful, O LORD.

8 The LORD is good and does what is right;
he shows the proper path to those who go astray.
9 He leads the humble in doing right,
teaching them his way.
10 The LORD leads with unfailing love and faithfulness
all who keep his covenant and obey his demands.

11 For the honor of your name, O LORD,
forgive my many, many sins.
12 Who are those who fear the LORD?
He will show them the path they should choose.
13 They will live in prosperity,
and their children will inherit the land.
14 The LORD is a friend to those who fear him.
He teaches them his covenant.
15 My eyes are always on the LORD,
for he rescues me from the traps of my enemies.

16 Turn to me and have mercy,
for I am alone and in deep distress.
17 My problems go from bad to worse.
Oh, save me from them all!
18 Feel my pain and see my trouble.
Forgive all my sins.
19 See how many enemies I have
and how viciously they hate me!
20 Protect me! Rescue my life from them!
Do not let me be disgraced, for in you I take refuge.
21 May integrity and honesty protect me,
for I put my hope in you.

22 O God, ransom Israel
from all its troubles.

Psalm 26

THEME: Declaring loyalty to God. If we are genuinely committed to God, we can stand up to opposition and examination.

AUTHOR: David, possibly written during the days of Absalom's rebellion

A psalm of David.

1 Declare me innocent, O LORD,
for I have acted with integrity;
I have trusted in the LORD without wavering.
2 Put me on trial, LORD, and cross-examine me.
Test my motives and my heart.
3 For I am always aware of your unfailing love,
and I have lived according to your truth.
4 I do not spend time with liars
or go along with hypocrites.
5 I hate the gatherings of those who do evil,
and I refuse to join in with the wicked.
6 I wash my hands to declare my innocence.
I come to your altar, O LORD,
7 singing a song of thanksgiving
and telling of all your wonders.
8 I love your sanctuary, LORD,
the place where your glorious presence dwells.
9 Don't let me suffer the fate of sinners.
Don't condemn me along with murderers.
10 Their hands are dirty with evil schemes,
and they constantly take bribes.

Ps 25:12 To "fear the LORD" is to recognize God's attributes: He is holy, almighty, righteous, pure, all-knowing, all-powerful, and all-wise. When we regard God correctly, we gain a clearer picture of ourselves: sinful, weak, frail, and needy. When we recognize who God is and who we are, we will fall at his feet in humble respect. Only then will he show us how to choose his way.

Ps 25:14 "The LORD is a friend to those who fear him." God offers intimate and lasting friendship to those who revere him, who hold him in highest honor. What relationship could ever compare with having the Lord of all creation for a friend? Your everlasting friendship with God will grow as you respect and honor him.

Ps 25:16-17 Do life's problems always seem to go from bad to worse? God is the only one who can reverse this downward spiral. He can take our problems and turn them into glorious victories. The first and most important step is that we, like David, must cry out, "Turn to me and have mercy." When we are willing to do that, God will do his work in us and in our situation. The next step is yours—God has already made his offer.

Ps 25:21 We need integrity and honesty to preserve us along life's way. The psalm writer asks for these to protect him step by step. Honesty says, "This is the Shepherd's way," and integrity says, "I will walk consistently in it."

Ps 26:1-3 In asking God to declare him "innocent," David was not claiming to be sinless—that is impossible for any human being to achieve. Instead, he was pleading with God to clear his name of the false charges made against him by his enemies. We also can ask God to examine us, trusting him to forgive our sins and clear our record according to his mercy.

Ps 26:4-5 Should we stay away from unbelievers? No. Although Christians should avoid some places, Jesus demonstrated that we must go among unbelievers to help them. There is a difference, however, between being *with* unbelievers and being *one of* them. Acting like unbelievers harms our witness for God. Ask yourself about the people you enjoy: If you are with them often, will you become less obedient to God in outlook or action? If the answer is yes, carefully monitor how you spend your time with these people and their effect on you.

Ps 26:8 God's sanctuary in this verse refers to either the Tabernacle in Gibeon (the one constructed in the days of Moses; see Exod 40:35) or the temporary dwelling David built to house the Ark of the Covenant (2 Sam 6:17). David exclaimed how he loved to worship God at this place. Do you love to worship?

11 But I am not like that; I live with integrity.
So redeem me and show me mercy.
12 Now I stand on solid ground,
and I will publicly praise the LORD.

Psalm 27

THEME: God offers help for today and hope for the future. Unwavering confidence in God is our antidote for fear and loneliness.

AUTHOR: David

A psalm of David.

1 The LORD is my light and my salvation—
so why should I be afraid?
The LORD is my fortress, protecting me
from danger,
so why should I tremble?
2 When evil people come to devour me,
when my enemies and foes attack me,
they will stumble and fall.
3 Though a mighty army surrounds me,
my heart will not be afraid.
Even if I am attacked,
I will remain confident.

4 The one thing I ask of the LORD—
the thing I seek most—
is to live in the house of the LORD all the days
of my life,
delighting in the LORD's perfections
and meditating in his Temple.
5 For he will conceal me there when troubles come;
he will hide me in his sanctuary.
He will place me out of reach on a high rock.
6 Then I will hold my head high
above my enemies who surround me.
At his sanctuary I will offer sacrifices with
shouts of joy,
singing and praising the LORD with music.

7 Hear me as I pray, O LORD.
Be merciful and answer me!
8 My heart has heard you say, "Come and talk
with me."
And my heart responds, "LORD, I am coming."
9 Do not turn your back on me.
Do not reject your servant in anger.
You have always been my helper.
Don't leave me now; don't abandon me,
O God of my salvation!
10 Even if my father and mother abandon me,
the LORD will hold me close.

11 Teach me how to live, O LORD.
Lead me along the right path,
for my enemies are waiting for me.
12 Do not let me fall into their hands.
For they accuse me of things I've never done;
with every breath they threaten me with
violence.
13 Yet I am confident I will see the LORD's
goodness
while I am here in the land of the living.

14 Wait patiently for the LORD.
Be brave and courageous.
Yes, wait patiently for the LORD.

Ps 26:12 Too often we complain about our problems to anyone who will listen and we praise God only in private. Instead, we ought to complain privately and praise God publicly.

Ps 27:1 Fear is a dark shadow that envelops us and ultimately imprisons us within ourselves. Everyone has been a prisoner of fear at one time or another—fear of rejection, misunderstanding, uncertainty, sickness, or even death. But we can conquer fear by trusting in the Lord, who brings salvation. If we want to dispel the darkness of fear, let us remember with the psalm writer that "the LORD is my light and my salvation."

Ps 27:4 By the "house of the LORD" and "his Temple," David could be referring to the Tabernacle in Gibeon, to the sanctuary he had built to house the Ark of the Covenant, or to the Temple that his son Solomon was to build. David probably had the Temple in mind because he made many of the plans for it (1 Chr 22). David may also have used the word Temple to refer to the presence of the Lord. David's greatest desire was to live in God's presence each day of his life. Sadly, this is not the greatest desire of many who claim to be believers. What do you most desire? Do you look forward to being in the presence of the Lord?

Ps 27:7 We often run to God when we experience difficulties. But David sought God's guiding presence every day. When troubles came his way, he was already in God's presence and prepared to handle any test. Believers can call to God for help at any time, but how shortsighted to call on God only when troubles come. Many of our problems could be avoided or handled far more easily by seeking God's help and direction beforehand.

Ps 27:10 Many have had the sad experience of being abandoned by father or mother. Broken homes, differences of belief, addiction to drugs or alcohol, even psychological isolation can leave children crippled by this loss. Even as adults, the pain may linger. God can take that place in our life, fill that void, and heal that hurt. He can direct us to those who may take the role of father or mother for us. His love is sufficient for all our needs.

Ps 27:13 The "land of the living" simply means "this life" or "while I am living." David was obviously going through a trial, but he was confident that in this present life, God would see him through it.

Ps 27:14 David knew from experience what it meant to wait for the Lord. He had been anointed king at age 16 but didn't become king until he was 30. During the interim, he had been chased through the wilderness by jealous King Saul. David had to wait on God for the fulfillment of his promise to reign. Later, after becoming king, he was chased by his rebellious son, Absalom.

Waiting for God is not easy. Often it seems that he isn't answering our prayers or doesn't understand the urgency of our situation. That kind of thinking implies that God is not in control or is not fair. But God is worth waiting for. Lamentations 3:24-26 calls us to hope in and wait for the Lord because often God uses times of waiting to refresh, renew, and teach us. Make good use of your waiting times by discovering what God may be trying to teach you in them.

Psalm 28

THEME: Prayer when surrounded by trouble or wickedness. God is our only real source of safety. Prayer is our best help when trials come our way because it keeps us in communion with God.

AUTHOR: David

A psalm of David.

1 I pray to you, O LORD, my rock.
Do not turn a deaf ear to me.
For if you are silent,
I might as well give up and die.
2 Listen to my prayer for mercy
as I cry out to you for help,
as I lift my hands toward your holy sanctuary.

3 Do not drag me away with the wicked—
with those who do evil—
those who speak friendly words to their neighbors
while planning evil in their hearts.
4 Give them the punishment they so richly deserve!
Measure it out in proportion to their wickedness.
Pay them back for all their evil deeds!
Give them a taste of what they have done to others.
5 They care nothing for what the LORD has done
or for what his hands have made.
So he will tear them down,
and they will never be rebuilt!

6 Praise the LORD!
For he has heard my cry for mercy.
7 The LORD is my strength and shield.
I trust him with all my heart.
He helps me, and my heart is filled with joy.
I burst out in songs of thanksgiving.

8 The LORD gives his people strength.
He is a safe fortress for his anointed king.
9 Save your people!
Bless Israel, your special possession.*
Lead them like a shepherd,
and carry them in your arms forever.

Psalm 29

THEME: God reveals his great power in nature. We can trust God to give us both the peace and the strength to weather the storms of life.

AUTHOR: David

A psalm of David.

1 Honor the LORD, you heavenly beings*;
honor the LORD for his glory and strength.
2 Honor the LORD for the glory of his name.
Worship the LORD in the splendor of his holiness.

3 The voice of the LORD echoes above the sea.
The God of glory thunders.
The LORD thunders over the mighty sea.
4 The voice of the LORD is powerful;
the voice of the LORD is majestic.
5 The voice of the LORD splits the mighty cedars;
the LORD shatters the cedars of Lebanon.
6 He makes Lebanon's mountains skip like a calf;
he makes Mount Hermon* leap like a young wild ox.
7 The voice of the LORD strikes
with bolts of lightning.
8 The voice of the LORD makes the barren wilderness quake;
the LORD shakes the wilderness of Kadesh.
9 The voice of the LORD twists mighty oaks*
and strips the forests bare.
In his Temple everyone shouts, "Glory!"

10 The LORD rules over the floodwaters.
The LORD reigns as king forever.
11 The LORD gives his people strength.
The LORD blesses them with peace.

Psalm 30

THEME: A celebration of God's deliverance. Earthly security is uncertain, but God is always faithful.

AUTHOR: David

A psalm of David. A song for the dedication of the Temple.

1 I will exalt you, LORD, for you rescued me.
You refused to let my enemies triumph over me.

Ps 28:9 Hebrew *Bless your inheritance.* **Ps 29:1** Hebrew *you sons of God.* **Ps 29:6** Hebrew *Sirion,* another name for Mount Hermon. **Ps 29:9** Or *causes the deer to writhe in labor.*

Ps 28:3-5 It's easy to pretend friendship. Wicked people often put on a show of kindness or friendship in order to gain their own ends. David, in his royal position, may have met many who pretended friendship only to meet their own needs. David knew that God would punish these people eventually, but he prayed that their punishment would come swiftly. True believers should be straightforward and sincere in all their relationships.

Ps 29:5-6 The cedars of Lebanon were giant trees that could grow to 120 feet in height and 30 feet in circumference. A voice that could split the cedars of Lebanon would be a truly powerful voice—the voice of God. *All* that was impressive to people was under God's complete control.

Ps 29:10-11 Throughout history, God has revealed his power through mighty miracles over nature, such as the great Flood (Gen 6–9). He promises to continue to reveal his power. Paul urged us to understand how great God's power is (Eph 1:18-23). The same power that raised Christ from the dead is available to help us with our daily problems. When you feel weak and limited, don't despair. Remember that God can give you strength. The same power that controls creation and raises the dead is available to you.

2 O LORD my God, I cried to you for help,
and you restored my health.
3 You brought me up from the grave,* O LORD.
You kept me from falling into the pit of death.
4 Sing to the LORD, all you godly ones!
Praise his holy name.
5 For his anger lasts only a moment,
but his favor lasts a lifetime!
Weeping may last through the night,
but joy comes with the morning.
6 When I was prosperous, I said,
"Nothing can stop me now!"
7 Your favor, O LORD, made me as secure as a
mountain.
Then you turned away from me, and I was
shattered.
8 I cried out to you, O LORD.
I begged the Lord for mercy, saying,
9 "What will you gain if I die,
if I sink into the grave?
Can my dust praise you?
Can it tell of your faithfulness?
10 Hear me, LORD, and have mercy on me.
Help me, O LORD."
11 You have turned my mourning into joyful
dancing.
You have taken away my clothes of mourning
and clothed me with joy,
12 that I might sing praises to you and not
be silent.
O LORD my God, I will give you thanks
forever!

Ps 30:3 Hebrew *from Sheol.*

Psalm 31

THEME: In times of stress, depending upon God requires complete commitment.

AUTHOR: David, although some say Jeremiah

For the choir director: A psalm of David.

1 O LORD, I have come to you for protection;
don't let me be disgraced.
Save me, for you do what is right.
2 Turn your ear to listen to me;
rescue me quickly.
Be my rock of protection,
a fortress where I will be safe.
3 You are my rock and my fortress.
For the honor of your name, lead me out
of this danger.
4 Pull me from the trap my enemies set for me,
for I find protection in you alone.
5 I entrust my spirit into your hand.
Rescue me, LORD, for you are a faithful God.

CONFESSION, REPENTANCE, AND FORGIVENESS IN THE PSALMS

Over the centuries, many believers, overcome by an awareness of their own sins, have found a ray of hope in the words of the penitential (repentance) psalms. The psalm writers shared with God the depth of their sorrow and repentance, as well as the height of joy at being forgiven. They rejoiced in the knowledge that God would respond to confession and repentance with complete forgiveness. We who live on the other side of the cross of Christ can rejoice even more because we understand more. God has shown us that he is willing to forgive because his judgment on sin was satisfied by Christ's death on the cross.

As you read these psalms, note the pattern followed by the psalm writers in responding to God: (1) They recognized their sinfulness and tendency to do wrong; (2) they realized that sin was rebellion against God himself; (3) they admitted their sins to God; (4) they trusted in God's willingness to forgive; and (5) they accepted his forgiveness. Use these psalms as a reminder of how easy it is to drift away from God and fall into sin, and what is needed to reestablish that fellowship.

Selected psalms that emphasize these themes are 6; 14; 31; 32; 38; 41; 51; 102; 130; 143.

Ps 30:1ff David may have written this psalm when he dedicated Araunah's threshing floor (which became the future site of the Temple), after God stopped the great plague he had used to discipline David (1 Chr 21:1–22:6). The serious illness mentioned in Psalm 30:2-3 may refer to an illness David experienced or to the plague itself.

Ps 30:5 Like a shot given by a doctor, the discomfort of God's anger lasts only a moment, but the good effects go on for a long time. Let God's anger be a sharp pain that warns you to turn from sin.

Ps 30:6-7 Security had made David feel invincible. Although he knew that his riches and power had come from God, they had gone to his head, making him proud. Wealth, power, and fame can be intoxicating, making us feel self-reliant, self-secure, and independent of God. But this false security can be easily shattered. Don't be trapped by the false security of prosperity. Depend on God for your security, and you won't be shaken when worldly possessions disappear.

Ps 31:1 David called on the Lord to deliver him. He wanted God to stop those who were unjustly causing trouble. Therefore, David made his request based upon what he knew of God's name, or character. Because God is righteous and loving, he desires to deliver his people.

Ps 31:1-6 We say we have faith in God, but do we really trust him? David's words, "I entrust my spirit into your hand," convey his complete trust in God. Jesus used this phrase as he was dying on the cross—showing his absolute dependence on God the Father (Luke 23:46). Stephen repeated these words as he was being stoned to death (Acts 7:59), confident that in death he was simply passing from God's earthly care to God's eternal care. We should commit our possessions, our families, and our vocations to God. But first and foremost, we should commit ourselves completely to him.

▶ **PSALM 31 *(cont.)***

6 I hate those who worship worthless idols.
I trust in the LORD.
7 I will be glad and rejoice in your unfailing love,
for you have seen my troubles,
and you care about the anguish of my soul.
8 You have not handed me over to my enemies
but have set me in a safe place.

9 Have mercy on me, LORD, for I am in distress.
Tears blur my eyes.
My body and soul are withering away.
10 I am dying from grief;
my years are shortened by sadness.
Sin has drained my strength;
I am wasting away from within.
11 I am scorned by all my enemies
and despised by my neighbors—
even my friends are afraid to come near me.
When they see me on the street,
they run the other way.
12 I am ignored as if I were dead,
as if I were a broken pot.
13 I have heard the many rumors about me,
and I am surrounded by terror.
My enemies conspire against me,
plotting to take my life.

14 But I am trusting you, O LORD,
saying, "You are my God!"
15 My future is in your hands.
Rescue me from those who hunt me down
relentlessly.
16 Let your favor shine on your servant.
In your unfailing love, rescue me.
17 Don't let me be disgraced, O LORD,
for I call out to you for help.
Let the wicked be disgraced;
let them lie silent in the grave.*
18 Silence their lying lips—
those proud and arrogant lips that accuse
the godly.

19 How great is the goodness
you have stored up for those who fear you.
You lavish it on those who come to you for
protection,
blessing them before the watching world.
20 You hide them in the shelter of your presence,
safe from those who conspire against them.
You shelter them in your presence,
far from accusing tongues.

21 Praise the LORD,
for he has shown me the wonders of his
unfailing love.
He kept me safe when my city was under attack.
22 In panic I cried out,
"I am cut off from the LORD!"
But you heard my cry for mercy
and answered my call for help.

23 Love the LORD, all you godly ones!
For the LORD protects those who are loyal
to him,
but he harshly punishes the arrogant.
24 So be strong and courageous,
all you who put your hope in the LORD!

Psalm 32

THEME: Forgiveness brings true joy. Only when we ask God to forgive our sins will he give us real happiness and relief from guilt.

AUTHOR: David

A psalm of David.*

1 Oh, what joy for those
whose disobedience is forgiven,
whose sin is put out of sight!
2 Yes, what joy for those
whose record the LORD has cleared of guilt,*
whose lives are lived in complete honesty!

3 When I refused to confess my sin,
my body wasted away,
and I groaned all day long.
4 Day and night your hand of discipline was heavy
on me.
My strength evaporated like water in the
summer heat. *Interlude*

Ps 31:17 Hebrew *in Sheol.* **Ps 32:TITLE** Hebrew *maskil.* This may be a literary or musical term. **Ps 32:2** Greek version reads *of sin.* Compare Rom 4:7.

Ps 31:6 Why did David suddenly bring up the subject of idol worship? He wanted to contrast his total devotion to God with the diluted worship offered by many Israelites. Pagan religious rituals were never completely banished from Israel and Judah, despite the efforts of David and a few other kings. Obviously a person who clung to idols could not commit his spirit into God's hands. When we put today's idols (wealth, material possessions, success) first in our lives, we cannot expect God's Spirit to guide us. God is our highest authority and requires our first allegiance.

Ps 31:9-13 In describing his feelings, David wrote of the helplessness and hopelessness everyone feels when hated or rejected. But adversity is easier to accept when we recognize our true relationship with the sovereign God (Ps 31:14-18). Although our enemies may seem to have the upper hand, they are ultimately the helpless and hopeless ones. Those who know God will be victorious in the end (Ps 31:23). We can have courage today because God will preserve us.

Ps 31:14-15 In saying, "My future is in your hands," David was expressing his belief that all of life's circumstances are under God's control. Knowing that God loves and cares for us enables us to keep steady in our faith regardless of our circumstances. It keeps us from sinning foolishly by taking matters into our own hands or resenting God's timetable.

Ps 32:1ff This is another of the penitential (repentance) psalms where the writer confesses his sin to God. Read this psalm in conjunction with Psalm 51—both are penitential psalms. Here David expressed the joy of forgiveness. God had forgiven him for the sins he had committed against Bathsheba and Uriah (2 Sam 11–12).

Ps 32:1-2 God wants to forgive sinners. Forgiveness has always been part of his loving nature. He announced this to Moses (Exod 34:6-7); he revealed it to David; he

5 Finally, I confessed all my sins to you
and stopped trying to hide my guilt.
I said to myself, "I will confess my rebellion
to the LORD."
And you forgave me! All my guilt is gone.
Interlude

6 Therefore, let all the godly pray to you while
there is still time,
that they may not drown in the floodwaters
of judgment.
7 For you are my hiding place;
you protect me from trouble.
You surround me with songs of victory.
Interlude

8 The LORD says, "I will guide you along the best
pathway for your life.
I will advise you and watch over you.
9 Do not be like a senseless horse or mule
that needs a bit and bridle to keep it under
control."

10 Many sorrows come to the wicked,
but unfailing love surrounds those who trust
the LORD.
11 So rejoice in the LORD and be glad, all you who
obey him!
Shout for joy, all you whose hearts are pure!

Psalm 35

THEME: A prayer to God for help against those who try to inflict injury for no reason. When our enemies are unjust and lie about us, even when we do good to them, we can appeal to God who is always just.

AUTHOR: David, possibly written when he was being hunted by Saul (1 Samuel 24, p. 464)

A psalm of David.

1 O LORD, oppose those who oppose me.
Fight those who fight against me.
2 Put on your armor, and take up your shield.
Prepare for battle, and come to my aid.
3 Lift up your spear and javelin
against those who pursue me.
Let me hear you say,
"I will give you victory!"

4 Bring shame and disgrace on those trying
to kill me;
turn them back and humiliate those who want
to harm me.
5 Blow them away like chaff in the wind—
a wind sent by the angel of the LORD.
6 Make their path dark and slippery,
with the angel of the LORD pursuing them.
7 I did them no wrong, but they laid a trap for me.
I did them no wrong, but they dug a pit to
catch me.
8 So let sudden ruin come upon them!
Let them be caught in the trap they set for me!
Let them be destroyed in the pit they dug
for me.

9 Then I will rejoice in the LORD.
I will be glad because he rescues me.
10 With every bone in my body I will praise him:
"LORD, who can compare with you?
Who else rescues the helpless from the strong?
Who else protects the helpless and poor from
those who rob them?"

11 Malicious witnesses testify against me.
They accuse me of crimes I know nothing
about.
12 They repay me evil for good.
I am sick with despair.
13 Yet when they were ill, I grieved for them.
I denied myself by fasting for them,
but my prayers returned unanswered.
14 I was sad, as though they were my friends
or family,
as if I were grieving for my own mother.

---

dramatically showed it to the world through Jesus Christ. These verses convey several aspects of God's forgiveness: He forgives disobedience, puts sin out of sight, and clears our record of guilt. Paul quoted these verses in Romans 4:7-8 and then explained that we can have this joyous experience of forgiveness through faith in Christ.

Ps 32:5 What is confession? To confess our sin is to agree with God, acknowledging that he is right to declare what we have done as sinful and that we are wrong to desire or to do it. It means affirming our intention of forsaking that sin in order to follow God more faithfully.

Ps 32:8-9 God describes some people as being like horses or mules that have to be controlled by bits and bridles. Rather than letting God guide them step by step, they stubbornly leave God only one option. If God wants to keep them useful for him, he must use discipline and punishment. God longs to guide us with love and wisdom rather than punishment. He offers to teach us the best way to go. Accept the advice written in God's Word and don't let your stubbornness keep you from obeying God.

Ps 35:1ff This is one of the imprecatory (cursing) psalms that call upon God to deal with enemies. These psalms sound extremely harsh, but we must remember the following: (1) David could not understand why he was forced to flee from men who were unjustly seeking to kill him. He was God's anointed king over a nation called to annihilate the evil people of the land. (2) David's call for justice was sincere; it was not a cover for his own personal vengeance. He truly wanted God's perfect ideal for his nation. (3) David did not say that he would take revenge, but he gave the matter to God. These are merely his suggestions. (4) These psalms use hyperbole (or overstatement). They were meant to motivate others to take a strong stand against sin and evil.

Cruelty may be far removed from some people's experience, but it is a daily reality to others. God promises to help the persecuted and to bring judgment on unrepentant sinners. When we pray for justice to be done, we are praying as David did. When Christ returns, the wicked will be punished.

Ps 35:13 David was sad when his prayers seemed unanswered. When our deliverance is delayed, we may assume that God hasn't answered our prayers. God hears every prayer, but he answers according to his wisdom. Don't let the absence of an immediate answer cause you to doubt or resent God. Instead, let it be an occasion to deepen your faith.

▸ **PSALM 35 *(cont.)***

15 But they are glad now that I am in trouble;
they gleefully join together against me.
I am attacked by people I don't even know;
they slander me constantly.
16 They mock me and call me names;
they snarl at me.

17 How long, O Lord, will you look on and do nothing?
Rescue me from their fierce attacks.
Protect my life from these lions!
18 Then I will thank you in front of the great assembly.
I will praise you before all the people.
19 Don't let my treacherous enemies rejoice over my defeat.
Don't let those who hate me without cause gloat over my sorrow.
20 They don't talk of peace;
they plot against innocent people who mind their own business.
21 They shout, "Aha! Aha!
With our own eyes we saw him do it!"
22 O LORD, you know all about this.
Do not stay silent.
Do not abandon me now, O Lord.
23 Wake up! Rise to my defense!
Take up my case, my God and my Lord.
24 Declare me not guilty, O LORD my God, for you give justice.
Don't let my enemies laugh about me in my troubles.
25 Don't let them say, "Look, we got what we wanted!
Now we will eat him alive!"

26 May those who rejoice at my troubles
be humiliated and disgraced.
May those who triumph over me
be covered with shame and dishonor.
27 But give great joy to those who came to my defense.
Let them continually say, "Great is the LORD,
who delights in blessing his servant with peace!"
28 Then I will proclaim your justice,
and I will praise you all day long.

Psalm 36

THEME: God's faithfulness, justice, and love are contrasted with the sinful hearts of men and women. In spite of our fallen condition, God pours out his love on those who know him.

AUTHOR: David

For the choir director: A psalm of David, the servant of the LORD.

1 Sin whispers to the wicked, deep within their hearts.
They have no fear of God at all.
2 In their blind conceit,
they cannot see how wicked they really are.
3 Everything they say is crooked and deceitful.
They refuse to act wisely or do good.
4 They lie awake at night, hatching sinful plots.
Their actions are never good.
They make no attempt to turn from evil.

5 Your unfailing love, O LORD, is as vast as the heavens;
your faithfulness reaches beyond the clouds.
6 Your righteousness is like the mighty mountains,
your justice like the ocean depths.
You care for people and animals alike, O LORD.
7 How precious is your unfailing love, O God!
All humanity finds shelter
in the shadow of your wings.
8 You feed them from the abundance of your own house,
letting them drink from your river of delights.
9 For you are the fountain of life,
the light by which we see.

10 Pour out your unfailing love on those who love you;
give justice to those with honest hearts.
11 Don't let the proud trample me
or the wicked push me around.
12 Look! Those who do evil have fallen!
They are thrown down, never to rise again.

Ps 35:21-23 David cried out to God to defend him when people wrongly accused him. If you are unjustly accused, your natural reaction may be to lash out in revenge or to give a detailed defense of your every move. Instead, ask God to fight the battle for you. He will clear your name in the eyes of those who really matter.

Ps 36:1 Because the wicked have no fear of God, nothing restrains them from sinning. They plunge ahead as if nothing will happen to them. But God is just and is only delaying their punishment. This knowledge should hold us back from sinning. Let the fear of God do its work in you to keep you from sin. In your gratitude for God's love and mercy, don't ignore his justice.

Ps 36:5-8 In contrast to evil people and their wicked plots that end in failure, God will triumph. He is faithful, righteous, and just. His love is as vast as the heavens; his faithfulness reaches beyond the clouds; his righteousness is as solid as mighty mountains; his judgments are as full of wisdom as the oceans are with water. We need not fear evil people because we know God loves us, judges evil, and will care for us throughout eternity.

Ps 36:9 "Fountain of life" is a vivid image of fresh, cleansing water that gives life to the spiritually thirsty. This same picture is used in Jeremiah 2:13, where God is called the "fountain of living water." Jesus spoke of himself as living water that could quench thirst forever and give eternal life (John 4:14).

*Psalm 37**

THEME: **Trust in the Lord and wait patiently for him to act. This psalm vividly contrasts the wicked person with the righteous.**

AUTHOR: David

A psalm of David.

1 Don't worry about the wicked
or envy those who do wrong.
2 For like grass, they soon fade away.
Like spring flowers, they soon wither.

3 Trust in the LORD and do good.
Then you will live safely in the land and prosper.
4 Take delight in the LORD,
and he will give you your heart's desires.

5 Commit everything you do to the LORD.
Trust him, and he will help you.
6 He will make your innocence radiate like the dawn,
and the justice of your cause will shine like the noonday sun.

7 Be still in the presence of the LORD,
and wait patiently for him to act.
Don't worry about evil people who prosper
or fret about their wicked schemes.

8 Stop being angry!
Turn from your rage!
Do not lose your temper—
it only leads to harm.
9 For the wicked will be destroyed,
but those who trust in the LORD will possess the land.

10 Soon the wicked will disappear.
Though you look for them, they will be gone.
11 The lowly will possess the land
and will live in peace and prosperity.

12 The wicked plot against the godly;
they snarl at them in defiance.
13 But the Lord just laughs,
for he sees their day of judgment coming.

14 The wicked draw their swords
and string their bows
to kill the poor and the oppressed,
to slaughter those who do right.
15 But their swords will stab their own hearts,
and their bows will be broken.

16 It is better to be godly and have little
than to be evil and rich.
17 For the strength of the wicked will be shattered,
but the LORD takes care of the godly.

18 Day by day the LORD takes care of the innocent,
and they will receive an inheritance that lasts forever.
19 They will not be disgraced in hard times;
even in famine they will have more than enough.

20 But the wicked will die.
The LORD's enemies are like flowers in a field—
they will disappear like smoke.

21 The wicked borrow and never repay,
but the godly are generous givers.
22 Those the LORD blesses will possess the land,
but those he curses will die.

23 The LORD directs the steps of the godly.
He delights in every detail of their lives.
24 Though they stumble, they will never fall,
for the LORD holds them by the hand.

Ps 37 This psalm is a Hebrew acrostic poem; each stanza begins with a successive letter of the Hebrew alphabet.

Ps 37:1 We should never envy evil people, even though some may be extremely popular or excessively rich. No matter how much they have, it will fade and vanish like grass that withers and dies. Those who follow God live differently from the wicked and, in the end, will have treasures in heaven. What an unbeliever gets on earth may last a lifetime, but what you get from following God lasts forever.

Ps 37:4-5 David calls us to take delight in the Lord and to commit everything we have and do to him. But how do we do this? To *delight* in someone means to experience great pleasure and joy being with that person. This happens only when we know that person well. Thus, to delight in the Lord, we must know him better. Knowledge of God's great love for us will indeed give us delight.

To *commit* ourselves to the Lord means entrusting everything—our lives, families, jobs, possessions—to his control and guidance. To commit ourselves to the Lord means to trust in him (Ps 37:5), believing that he can care for us better than we can ourselves. We should be willing to wait patiently (Ps 37:7) for him to work out what is best for us.

Ps 37:8-9 Anger, rage, and losing our temper are very destructive emotions. They reveal a lack of faith that God loves us and is in control. We should not worry; instead, we should trust in God, giving ourselves to him for his use and safekeeping. When you dwell on your problems, you will become anxious and angry. But if you concentrate on God and his goodness, you will find peace. Where do you focus your attention?

Ps 37:11 Being lowly hardly seems the proper demeanor to deal with enemies. God's warfare, however, must be carried out with calm faith, humility before God, and hope in his deliverance. Jesus also promises a sure reward for those with humble attitudes (Matt 5:5).

Ps 37:21 You can tell a lot about people's character by the way they handle money. The wicked person steals under the guise of borrowing. The righteous person gives generously to the needy. Wicked people, therefore, focus on themselves, while righteous people look to the welfare of others.

Ps 37:23-24 The person in whom God delights is one who follows God, trusts him, and tries to do his will. God watches over and makes firm every step that person takes. If you would like to have God direct your way, then seek his advice before you step out.

▸ **PSALM 37 *(cont.)***

25 Once I was young, and now I am old.
Yet I have never seen the godly abandoned
or their children begging for bread.
26 The godly always give generous loans
to others,
and their children are a blessing.

27 Turn from evil and do good,
and you will live in the land forever.
28 For the LORD loves justice,
and he will never abandon the godly.

He will keep them safe forever,
but the children of the wicked will die.
29 The godly will possess the land
and will live there forever.
30 The godly offer good counsel;
they teach right from wrong.
31 They have made God's law their own,
so they will never slip from his path.

32 The wicked wait in ambush for the godly,
looking for an excuse to kill them.
33 But the LORD will not let the wicked succeed
or let the godly be condemned when
they are put on trial.

34 Put your hope in the LORD.
Travel steadily along his path.
He will honor you by giving you the land.
You will see the wicked destroyed.

35 I have seen wicked and ruthless people
flourishing like a tree in its native soil.
36 But when I looked again, they were gone!
Though I searched for them, I could not
find them!

37 Look at those who are honest and good,
for a wonderful future awaits those who
love peace.
38 But the rebellious will be destroyed;
they have no future.

39 The LORD rescues the godly;
he is their fortress in times of trouble.
40 The LORD helps them,
rescuing them from the wicked.
He saves them,
and they find shelter in him.

Psalm 38

THEME: Sorrow for sin brings hope. God alone is the true source of healing and protection for those who confess their sins to him.

AUTHOR: David

A psalm of David, asking God to remember him.

1 O LORD, don't rebuke me in your anger
or discipline me in your rage!
2 Your arrows have struck deep,
and your blows are crushing me.
3 Because of your anger, my whole body
is sick;
my health is broken because of my sins.
4 My guilt overwhelms me—
it is a burden too heavy to bear.
5 My wounds fester and stink
because of my foolish sins.
6 I am bent over and racked with pain.
All day long I walk around filled with grief.
7 A raging fever burns within me,
and my health is broken.
8 I am exhausted and completely crushed.
My groans come from an anguished
heart.

9 You know what I long for, Lord;
you hear my every sigh.
10 My heart beats wildly, my strength fails,
and I am going blind.
11 My loved ones and friends stay away, fearing
my disease.
Even my own family stands at a distance.
12 Meanwhile, my enemies lay traps to kill me.

Ps 37:25 Because children starve today, as they did in David's time, what did David mean by these words? The children of the righteous need not go hungry because other believers should help them in their time of need. In David's day, Israel obeyed God's laws, which ensured that the poor were treated fairly and mercifully. As long as Israel was obedient, food would be available for everyone. When Israel forgot God, the rich took care of themselves only, and the poor suffered (Amos 2:6-7).

When we see a Christian brother or sister suffering today, we can respond in one of three ways: (1) We can say, as Job's friends did, that the afflicted person brought this on himself. (2) We can say that this is a test to help the person develop more patience and trust in God. (3) We can help the person in need. David would approve of only the last option. Although many governments today have their own programs for helping those in need, this is no excuse for ignoring the poor and needy within our reach.

Ps 38:1 As a child might cry to his father, so David cried to God. David was not saying, "Don't punish me," but, "Don't punish me while you are angry." He acknowledged that he deserved to be punished, but he asked that God temper his discipline with mercy. Like children, we are free to ask for mercy, but we should not deny that we deserve punishment.

Ps 38:1ff This is called a penitential psalm because David expressed sorrow for his sin (Ps 38:18). He stated that his sin led to health problems (Ps 38:1-8) and separated him from God and others, causing extreme loneliness (Ps 38:9-14). He then confessed his sin and repented (Ps 38:15-22).

Ps 38:2-4 David saw his anguish as judgment from God for his sins. Although God does not always send physical illness to punish us for sin, this verse and others in Scripture (Acts 12:21-23; 1 Cor 11:30-32) indicate that he does in certain circumstances. Our sin can have physical or mental side effects that can cause great suffering. Sometimes God has to punish his children in order to bring them back to himself (Heb 12:5-11). When we repent of our sin, God promises to forgive us. He delivers us from sin's eternal consequences, although he does not promise to undo all of sin's earthly consequences.

Those who wish me harm make plans
to ruin me.
All day long they plan their treachery.
13 But I am deaf to all their threats.
I am silent before them as one who cannot
speak.
14 I choose to hear nothing,
and I make no reply.
15 For I am waiting for you, O LORD.
You must answer for me, O Lord my God.
16 I prayed, "Don't let my enemies gloat over me
or rejoice at my downfall."
17 I am on the verge of collapse,
facing constant pain.
18 But I confess my sins;
I am deeply sorry for what I have done.
19 I have many aggressive enemies;
they hate me without reason.
20 They repay me evil for good
and oppose me for pursuing good.
21 Do not abandon me, O LORD.
Do not stand at a distance, my God.
22 Come quickly to help me,
O Lord my savior.

Psalm 39

THEME: Apart from God, life is fleeting and empty. This is an appeal for God's mercy because life is so brief.

AUTHOR: David

For Jeduthun, the choir director: A psalm of David.

1 I said to myself, "I will watch what I do
and not sin in what I say.
I will hold my tongue
when the ungodly are around me."
2 But as I stood there in silence—
not even speaking of good things—
the turmoil within me grew worse.
3 The more I thought about it,
the hotter I got,
igniting a fire of words:
4 "LORD, remind me how brief my time on earth
will be.
Remind me that my days are numbered—
how fleeting my life is.
5 You have made my life no longer than the width
of my hand.
My entire lifetime is just a moment to you;
at best, each of us is but a breath." *Interlude*
6 We are merely moving shadows,
and all our busy rushing ends in nothing.
We heap up wealth,
not knowing who will spend it.
7 And so, Lord, where do I put my hope?
My only hope is in you.
8 Rescue me from my rebellion.
Do not let fools mock me.
9 I am silent before you; I won't say a word,
for my punishment is from you.
10 But please stop striking me!
I am exhausted by the blows from your hand.
11 When you discipline us for our sins,
you consume like a moth what is precious
to us.
Each of us is but a breath. *Interlude*
12 Hear my prayer, O LORD!
Listen to my cries for help!

Ps 38:13-14 Being silent can be extremely difficult when others tear us down; we want to protect our reputation. We find it difficult to do nothing while they assault something so precious to us. But we don't need to lash out in revenge or justify our position; we can trust God to protect our reputation. Jesus was silent before his accusers (Luke 23:9-10); he left his case in God's hands (1 Pet 2:21-24). That is a good place to leave our case too!

Ps 39:1-3 David resolved to keep his tongue from sin; that is, he decided not to complain to other people about God's treatment of him. David certainly had reason to complain. He was the anointed king of Israel, but he had to wait many years before taking the throne. Then one of his sons tried to kill him and become king instead. But when David could not keep still any longer, he took his complaints directly to God. We all have complaints about our job, money, or situation, but complaining to others may make them think that God cannot take care of us. It may also look as if we blame God for our troubles. Instead, like David, we should take our complaints directly to God. He can take it.

Ps 39:4 Life is short no matter how long we live. If we have something important we want to do, we must not put it off for a better day. Ask yourself, If I had only six months to live, what would I do? Tell someone that you love him or her? Deal with an undisciplined area in your life? Tell someone about Jesus? Because life is short, don't neglect what is truly important.

Ps 39:5-6 The brevity of life is a theme throughout the books of Psalms, Proverbs, and Ecclesiastes. Jesus also spoke about it (Luke 12:20). Ironically, people spend so much time securing their lives on earth but take little or no thought about where they will spend eternity. David realized that amassing riches and busily accomplishing worldly tasks would make no difference in eternity. Few people understand that their only hope is in the Lord. (For other verses on the brevity of life, see Eccl 2:18; Jas 4:14.)

Ps 39:10 What did David mean when he asked God to stop punishing him with "blows" from his hand? It may be a picture of the difficulties David was facing that caused him to feel as if he were being struck. Evidently David thought God was disciplining him, punishing him for his sins. David was expressing his feelings to God, yet David also submitted himself to his powerful and loving heavenly Father.

We are merely moving shadows, and all our busy rushing ends in nothing. We heap up wealth, not knowing who will spend it.
Psalm 39:6

▸ **PSALM 39 *(cont.)***

Don't ignore my tears.
For I am your guest—
a traveler passing through,
as my ancestors were before me.
13 Leave me alone so I can smile again
before I am gone and exist no more.

Psalm 40

THEME: Doing God's will sometimes means waiting patiently. While we wait, we can love God, serve others, and tell others about him.
AUTHOR: David

For the choir director: A psalm of David.

1 I waited patiently for the LORD to help me,
and he turned to me and heard my cry.
2 He lifted me out of the pit of despair,
out of the mud and the mire.
He set my feet on solid ground
and steadied me as I walked along.
3 He has given me a new song to sing,
a hymn of praise to our God.
Many will see what he has done and be amazed.
They will put their trust in the LORD.

4 Oh, the joys of those who trust the LORD,
who have no confidence in the proud
or in those who worship idols.
5 O LORD my God, you have performed many
wonders for us.
Your plans for us are too numerous to list.
You have no equal.
If I tried to recite all your wonderful deeds,
I would never come to the end of them.

6 You take no delight in sacrifices or offerings.
Now that you have made me listen, I finally
understand*—
you don't require burnt offerings or sin
offerings.
7 Then I said, "Look, I have come.
As is written about me in the Scriptures:
8 I take joy in doing your will, my God,
for your instructions are written on my heart."
9 I have told all your people about your justice.
I have not been afraid to speak out,
as you, O LORD, well know.
10 I have not kept the good news of your justice
hidden in my heart;
I have talked about your faithfulness and
saving power.
I have told everyone in the great assembly
of your unfailing love and faithfulness.

11 LORD, don't hold back your tender mercies
from me.
Let your unfailing love and faithfulness always
protect me.
12 For troubles surround me—
too many to count!
My sins pile up so high
I can't see my way out.
They outnumber the hairs on my head.
I have lost all courage.
13 Please, LORD, rescue me!
Come quickly, LORD, and help me.
14 May those who try to destroy me
be humiliated and put to shame.
May those who take delight in my trouble
be turned back in disgrace.
15 Let them be horrified by their shame,
for they said, "Aha! We've got him now!"
16 But may all who search for you
be filled with joy and gladness in you.
May those who love your salvation
repeatedly shout, "The LORD is great!"
17 As for me, since I am poor and needy,
let the Lord keep me in his thoughts.
You are my helper and my savior.
O my God, do not delay.

Ps 40:6 Greek text reads *You have given me a body.* Compare Heb 10:5.

Ps 40:1-3 Waiting for God to help us is not easy, but David received four benefits from waiting: (1) God lifted him out of his despair, (2) God set his feet on solid ground, (3) God steadied him as he walked, and (4) God put a new song of praise in his mouth. Often blessings cannot be received unless we go through the trial of waiting.

Ps 40:6 The religious ritual of David's day involved sacrificing animals in the Tabernacle. David said these acts were meaningless unless done for the right reasons. Today we often make rituals of going to church, taking Communion, or paying tithes. These activities are also empty if our reasons for doing them are selfish. God doesn't want these sacrifices and offerings without an attitude of devotion to him. The prophet Samuel told Saul, "Obedience is better than sacrifice" (1 Sam 15:22). Make sure that you give God the obedience and lifelong service he desires from you.

Ps 40:7-8 "I take joy in doing your will, my God." Jesus portrayed this attitude of obeying and serving God (John 4:34; 5:30). He came as the prophets foretold, proclaiming the Good News of God's righteousness and forgiveness of sins. In Hebrews 10:5-10, verses 6-8 are applied to Jesus.

Ps 40:9-10 David said he would speak of God's faithfulness and salvation to those around him. When we realize the impact of God's righteousness on our lives, we cannot keep it hidden. We want to tell other people what God has done for us. If God's faithfulness has changed your life, don't be timid. It is natural to share a good bargain with others or recommend a skillful doctor, so it should also be natural to share what God has done for us.

Ps 40:10 When we think of faithfulness, a friend or a spouse may come to mind. Friends who are faithful accept and love us, even when we are unlovable. Faithful people keep their promises. God's faithfulness is like human faithfulness, only perfect. His love is absolute, and his promises are irrevocable. He loves us in spite of our constant bent toward sin, and he keeps all the promises he has made to us, even when we break our promises to him.

Psalm 41

THEME: A prayer for God's mercy when feeling sick or abandoned. When we're sick or when everyone deserts us, God remains at our side.

AUTHOR: David

For the choir director: A psalm of David.

1 Oh, the joys of those who are kind to the poor!
The LORD rescues them when they are in trouble.
2 The LORD protects them
and keeps them alive.
He gives them prosperity in the land
and rescues them from their enemies.
3 The LORD nurses them when they are sick
and restores them to health.

4 "O LORD," I prayed, "have mercy on me.
Heal me, for I have sinned against you."
5 But my enemies say nothing but evil about me.
"How soon will he die and be forgotten?" they ask.
6 They visit me as if they were my friends,
but all the while they gather gossip,
and when they leave, they spread it everywhere.
7 All who hate me whisper about me,
imagining the worst.
8 "He has some fatal disease," they say.
"He will never get out of that bed!"
9 Even my best friend, the one I trusted completely,
the one who shared my food, has turned against me.

10 LORD, have mercy on me.
Make me well again, so I can pay them back!
11 I know you are pleased with me,
for you have not let my enemies triumph over me.
12 You have preserved my life because I am innocent;
you have brought me into your presence forever.

13 Praise the LORD, the God of Israel,
who lives from everlasting to everlasting.
Amen and amen!

Psalm 53

THEME: All have sinned. Because of sin, no person can find God on his own. Only God can save us.

AUTHOR: David

For the choir director: A meditation; a psalm of David.*

1 Only fools say in their hearts,
"There is no God."
They are corrupt, and their actions are evil;
not one of them does good!

2 God looks down from heaven
on the entire human race;
he looks to see if anyone is truly wise,
if anyone seeks God.
3 But no, all have turned away;
all have become corrupt.*
No one does good,
not a single one!

4 Will those who do evil never learn?
They eat up my people like bread
and wouldn't think of praying to God.
5 Terror will grip them,
terror like they have never known before.
God will scatter the bones of your enemies.
You will put them to shame, for God has rejected them.

6 Who will come from Mount Zion to rescue Israel?
When God restores his people,
Jacob will shout with joy, and Israel will rejoice.

Ps 53:TITLE Hebrew *According to mahalath; a maskil.* These may be literary or musical terms. **Ps 53:3** Greek version reads *have become useless.* Compare Rom 3:12.

Ps 41:1 The Bible often speaks of God's care for the weak, poor, and needy and of his blessing those who share this concern. God wants our generosity to reflect his own free giving. As he has blessed us, we should bless others.

Ps 41:9 This verse, a prophecy of Christ's betrayal, is referred to in John 13:18. Judas, one of Jesus' 12 disciples, had spent 3 years learning from Jesus, traveling and eating with him (Mark 3:14-19), and handling the finances for the group. Eventually this "best friend" betrayed Jesus (Matt 26:14-16, 20-25).

Ps 41:13 Psalms is divided into five books, and each one ends with a doxology, an expression of praise to God. The first book of the psalms, Psalms 1–41, takes us on a journey through suffering, sorrow, and great joy. It teaches us about God's eternal love and care for us and how we should trust him even in the day-to-day experiences of life.

Ps 53:1 Echoing the message of Psalm 14, this psalm proclaims the foolishness of atheism (see also Rom 3:10). People may say there is no God in order to cover up their sin, to have an excuse to continue in sin, and/or to ignore the Judge in order to avoid the judgment. "Fools" do not necessarily lack intelligence; many atheists and unbelievers are highly educated. Fools are people who reject God, the only one who can save them.

Ps 53:4-5 While God is not affected by what we think of him, we are definitely and eternally affected by what God thinks of us. This psalm begins with the bold claim that there is no God, but by this verse, the true reason for rejecting God has become clear. The reason people reject God has nothing to do with God's existence and everything to do with people's sinfulness. In our desire to do wrong, we treat God as if he doesn't exist. When God passes judgment, it will be too late to apologize and admit we were wrong. Rejection of God will turn into terror of God.

Psalm 55

THEME: Expressing deep dismay over the treachery of a close friend. When friends hurt us, the burden is too difficult to carry alone.

AUTHOR: David

For the choir director: A psalm of David, to be accompanied by stringed instruments.*

1 Listen to my prayer, O God.
Do not ignore my cry for help!
2 Please listen and answer me,
for I am overwhelmed by my troubles.
3 My enemies shout at me,
making loud and wicked threats.
They bring trouble on me
and angrily hunt me down.

4 My heart pounds in my chest.
The terror of death assaults me.
5 Fear and trembling overwhelm me,
and I can't stop shaking.
6 Oh, that I had wings like a dove;
then I would fly away and rest!
7 I would fly far away
to the quiet of the wilderness. *Interlude*
8 How quickly I would escape—
far from this wild storm of hatred.

9 Confuse them, Lord, and frustrate their plans,
for I see violence and conflict in the city.
10 Its walls are patrolled day and night against invaders,
but the real danger is wickedness within the city.
11 Everything is falling apart;
threats and cheating are rampant in the streets.

12 It is not an enemy who taunts me—
I could bear that.
It is not my foes who so arrogantly insult me—
I could have hidden from them.
13 Instead, it is you—my equal,
my companion and close friend.
14 What good fellowship we once enjoyed
as we walked together to the house of God.

15 Let death stalk my enemies;
let the grave* swallow them alive,
for evil makes its home within them.

16 But I will call on God,
and the LORD will rescue me.
17 Morning, noon, and night
I cry out in my distress,
and the LORD hears my voice.
18 He ransoms me and keeps me safe
from the battle waged against me,
though many still oppose me.
19 God, who has ruled forever,
will hear me and humble them. *Interlude*
For my enemies refuse to change their ways;
they do not fear God.

20 As for my companion, he betrayed his friends;
he broke his promises.

Ps 55:TITLE Hebrew *maskil.* This may be a literary or musical term. **Ps 55:15** Hebrew *let Sheol.*

Confuse them, Lord, and frustrate their plans, for I see violence and conflict in the city.
Psalm 55:9

Ps 55:1ff This psalm was most likely written during the time of Absalom's rebellion and Ahithophel's betrayal (2 Sam 15–17). Some say Psalm 55:12-14 is messianic because it also describes Judas's betrayal of Christ (Matt 26:14-16, 20-25).

Ps 55:6-8 Even those who are especially close to God, as David was, have moments when they want to escape from their problems and pressures.

Ps 55:9-11 The city that was supposed to be holy was plagued by internal problems: violence, conflict, wickedness, threats, and cheating. External enemies, though a constant threat, were not nearly as dangerous as the corruption inside. Even today, churches often look to defend themselves against troubles from the sinful world while failing to see that their own sins are causing their troubles.

Ps 55:12-14 Nothing hurts more than a wound from a friend. At times friends may need to lovingly confront you in order to help you, but betrayal truly hurts. Betrayal by a friend had caused David great anguish. Real friends stick by you in times of trouble and bring healing, love, acceptance, and understanding. What kind of friend are you? Don't betray those you love.

Ps 55:17 Praying morning, noon, and night is certainly an excellent way to maintain correct priorities throughout every day. Daniel followed this pattern (Dan 6:10), as did Peter (Acts 10:9-10). The prayers of God's people are effective against the overwhelming evil in the world.

Ps 55:22 God wants us to give our burdens to him, but often we continue to bear them ourselves even when we say we are trusting in him. Trust the same strength that sustains you to carry your cares also.

21 His words are as smooth as butter,
but in his heart is war.
His words are as soothing as lotion,
but underneath are daggers!

22 Give your burdens to the LORD,
and he will take care of you.
He will not permit the godly to slip and fall.

23 But you, O God, will send the wicked
down to the pit of destruction.
Murderers and liars will die young,
but I am trusting you to save me.

Psalm 58

THEME: A prayer for God's justice. When no justice can be found, rejoice in knowing that justice will triumph because there is a God who will judge with complete fairness.

AUTHOR: David, at a time when men in authority were twisting justice

For the choir director: A psalm of David, to be sung to the tune "Do Not Destroy!"*

1 Justice—do you rulers* know the meaning
of the word?
Do you judge the people fairly?
2 No! You plot injustice in your hearts.
You spread violence throughout the land.
3 These wicked people are born sinners;
even from birth they have lied and gone
their own way.
4 They spit venom like deadly snakes;
they are like cobras that refuse to listen,
5 ignoring the tunes of the snake charmers,
no matter how skillfully they play.

6 Break off their fangs, O God!
Smash the jaws of these lions, O LORD!
7 May they disappear like water into thirsty
ground.
Make their weapons useless in their hands.*
8 May they be like snails that dissolve into slime,
like a stillborn child who will never see the sun.
9 God will sweep them away, both young and old,
faster than a pot heats over burning thorns.

10 The godly will rejoice when they see injustice
avenged.
They will wash their feet in the blood of the
wicked.
11 Then at last everyone will say,
"There truly is a reward for those who live
for God;
surely there is a God who judges justly here
on earth."

Psalm 61

THEME: Prayer for security and assurance. Wherever we are, we can trust that God will be there to answer our cries for help.

AUTHOR: David, possibly written when he was forced to escape during the days of Absalom's rebellion (2 Samuel 15–18, pp. 512-520), or after he had narrowly escaped one of Saul's efforts to kill him while hiding in the wilderness

For the choir director: A psalm of David, to be accompanied by stringed instruments.

1 O God, listen to my cry!
Hear my prayer!
2 From the ends of the earth,
I cry to you for help
when my heart is overwhelmed.
Lead me to the towering rock of safety,
3 for you are my safe refuge,
a fortress where my enemies cannot reach me.
4 Let me live forever in your sanctuary,
safe beneath the shelter of your wings!
Interlude

5 For you have heard my vows, O God.
You have given me an inheritance reserved
for those who fear your name.

Ps 58:TITLE Hebrew *miktam.* This may be a literary or musical term. **Ps 58:1** Or *you gods.* **Ps 58:7** Or *Let them be trodden down and wither like grass.* The meaning of the Hebrew is uncertain.

Ps 58:1ff This is called an imprecatory psalm (see the note on Ps 35:1ff, p. 565). It is a cry for justice so intense that it seems, at first glance, to be a call for revenge.

Ps 58:1ff The Old Testament is filled with references to justice—it is a key topic in the psalms. Unfortunately, many judges and rulers in ancient times took justice into their own hands. They had complete authority with no accountability and the power to make their own laws. When earth's judges are corrupt, there is little hope of justice in this life. But God loves justice, and those who obey him will experience perfect justice in eternity.

Ps 58:6-10 Shifting from prayer to prediction, David fervently calls for justice that veers into grisly judgment. Broken fangs and smashed jaws give way to the godly wading in the blood of the wicked. The words convey ugly pictures of the gruesome results of sin. Even uglier pictures are often revealed by our own demands for justice and more. This is certainly not the only time David's forceful sense of justice turned back on him (see 2 Sam 12:1-15). Ironically, David himself would eventually occupy the throne and be subject to the very imprecation he called down on others. We can be grateful that God hears our prayers, but we can also be grateful that God doesn't have to abide by our requests.

Ps 58:11 Of all people, our national leaders should be just and fair. When they are unjust and unfair, people suffer as politicians wrest power from the people, national morality deteriorates, and God is ignored. When right triumphs at last, "the godly will rejoice" (Ps 58:10). Be assured that there will be a day of accountability and that God judges fairly. Be careful never to side with injustice lest you find yourself standing before an angry Judge.

Ps 61:1-2 David must have been far from home when he wrote this psalm. Fortunately, God is not limited to any geographic location. Even when we are among strange people and surroundings, God never abandons us. His all-surpassing strength is always with us.

▸ **PSALM 61** ***(cont.)***

6 Add many years to the life of the king!
May his years span the generations!
7 May he reign under God's protection forever.
May your unfailing love and faithfulness watch over him.
8 Then I will sing praises to your name forever
as I fulfill my vows each day.

Psalm 62

THEME: Placing all hope in God. Knowing that God is in control allows us to wait patiently for him to rescue us. True relief does not come when the problem is resolved because more problems are on the way! True relief comes from an enduring hope in God's ultimate salvation. Only then will all trials be resolved.

AUTHOR: David, possibly written during the days of Absalom's rebellion (2 Samuel 15–18, pp. 512-520)

For Jeduthun, the choir director: A psalm of David.

1 I wait quietly before God,
for my victory comes from him.
2 He alone is my rock and my salvation,
my fortress where I will never be shaken.

3 So many enemies against one man—
all of them trying to kill me.
To them I'm just a broken-down wall
or a tottering fence.
4 They plan to topple me from my high position.
They delight in telling lies about me.
They praise me to my face
but curse me in their hearts. *Interlude*

5 Let all that I am wait quietly before God,
for my hope is in him.
6 He alone is my rock and my salvation,
my fortress where I will not be shaken.
7 My victory and honor come from God alone.
He is my refuge, a rock where no enemy can reach me.
8 O my people, trust in him at all times.
Pour out your heart to him,
for God is our refuge. *Interlude*

9 Common people are as worthless as a puff of wind,
and the powerful are not what they appear to be.
If you weigh them on the scales,
together they are lighter than a breath of air.

10 Don't make your living by extortion
or put your hope in stealing.
And if your wealth increases,
don't make it the center of your life.

11 God has spoken plainly,
and I have heard it many times:
Power, O God, belongs to you;
12 unfailing love, O Lord, is yours.
Surely you repay all people
according to what they have done.

Psalm 64

THEME: A complaint against conspiracy. When others conspire against us, we can ask God for protection because he knows everything.

AUTHOR: David

For the choir director: A psalm of David.

1 O God, listen to my complaint.
Protect my life from my enemies' threats.
2 Hide me from the plots of this evil mob,
from this gang of wrongdoers.
3 They sharpen their tongues like swords
and aim their bitter words like arrows.
4 They shoot from ambush at the innocent,
attacking suddenly and fearlessly.
5 They encourage each other to do evil
and plan how to set their traps in secret.
"Who will ever notice?" they ask.
6 As they plot their crimes, they say,
"We have devised the perfect plan!"
Yes, the human heart and mind are cunning.

Ps 61:8 David made a vow to praise God each day. David continually praised God through both the good and difficult times of his life. Do you find something to praise God for each day? As you do, you will find your heart elevated from daily distractions to lasting confidence.

Ps 62:3-6 David expressed his feelings to God and then reaffirmed his faith. Prayer can release our tensions in times of emotional stress. Trusting God to be our rock, salvation, and fortress (Ps 62:2) will change our entire outlook on life. No longer must we be held captive by resentment toward others when they hurt us. When we are resting in God's strength, nothing can shake us.

Ps 62:9-12 It is tempting to use honor, power, wealth, or prestige to measure people. We may even think that such people are really getting ahead in life. But on God's scales, these people are "lighter than a breath of air." What, then, can tilt the scales when God weighs us? Trusting God and working for him (Ps 62:12). Wealth, honor, power, or prestige add nothing to our value in God's eyes; only the faithful work we do for him has eternal value.

Ps 64:1ff Evil can come in the form of a conspiracy or an ambush because Satan wants to catch us unprepared. He tempts us in our weakest areas when we least expect it. But God himself will strike down our enemies (Ps 64:7), whether they are physical or spiritual. Wickedness is widespread and affects us in many ways, but the final victory already belongs to God and to those who trust and believe in him.

Ps 64:1-2 We may believe that God hears only certain requests from us. While it is true that we should offer praise, confession, and respectful petitions, it is true also that God is willing to listen to anything we want to tell him. David expressed himself honestly knowing that God would hear his voice. God will always listen to us, and he fully understands us.

Ps 64:3-10 Words spoken against us are among the most painful attacks we may have to face. If we trust in God, however, these attacks need not cause any lasting damage.

7 But God himself will shoot them with his arrows,
suddenly striking them down.
8 Their own tongues will ruin them,
and all who see them will shake their heads
in scorn.
9 Then everyone will be afraid;
they will proclaim the mighty acts of God
and realize all the amazing things he does.
10 The godly will rejoice in the LORD
and find shelter in him.
And those who do what is right
will praise him.

Psalm 65

THEME: God provides abundantly. We can be thankful to God for his many blessings.
AUTHOR: David

For the choir director: A song. A psalm of David.

1 What mighty praise, O God,
belongs to you in Zion.
We will fulfill our vows to you,
2 for you answer our prayers.
All of us must come to you.
3 Though we are overwhelmed by our sins,
you forgive them all.
4 What joy for those you choose to bring near,
those who live in your holy courts.
What festivities await us
inside your holy Temple.

5 You faithfully answer our prayers with
awesome deeds,
O God our savior.
You are the hope of everyone on earth,
even those who sail on distant seas.
6 You formed the mountains by your power
and armed yourself with mighty strength.
7 You quieted the raging oceans
with their pounding waves
and silenced the shouting of the nations.
8 Those who live at the ends of the earth
stand in awe of your wonders.
From where the sun rises to where it sets,
you inspire shouts of joy.

9 You take care of the earth and water it,
making it rich and fertile.
The river of God has plenty of water;
it provides a bountiful harvest of grain,
for you have ordered it so.
10 You drench the plowed ground with rain,
melting the clods and leveling the ridges.
You soften the earth with showers
and bless its abundant crops.
11 You crown the year with a bountiful harvest;
even the hard pathways overflow with
abundance.
12 The grasslands of the wilderness become a lush
pasture,
and the hillsides blossom with joy.
13 The meadows are clothed with flocks of sheep,
and the valleys are carpeted with grain.
They all shout and sing for joy!

Psalm 68

THEME: Remembering God's glory and power. Times and cultures change, but God is always majestically present as defender and provider.
AUTHOR: David

For the choir director: A song. A psalm of David.

1 Rise up, O God, and scatter your enemies.
Let those who hate God run for their lives.
2 Blow them away like smoke.
Melt them like wax in a fire.
Let the wicked perish in the presence of God.
3 But let the godly rejoice.
Let them be glad in God's presence.
Let them be filled with joy.

Ps 65:1-2 In Old Testament times, vows were taken seriously and fulfilled completely. No one had to make a vow, but once made, it was binding (Deut 23:21-23). The vows mentioned here involved promises to praise God for his answers to prayer.

Ps 65:3 Although we may feel overwhelmed by the multitude of our sins, God will forgive them all if we ask sincerely. Do you feel as though God could never forgive you, that your sins are too many, or that some of them are too great? The good news is that God can and will forgive them all. Nobody is beyond redemption, and nobody is so full of sin that he or she cannot be forgiven.

Ps 65:4 Access to God—the joy of living in the Temple courts—was a great honor. God had chosen a special group of Israelites from the tribe of Levi to serve as priests in the Tabernacle (Num 3:5-51). They were the only ones who could enter the sacred rooms where God's presence resided. Because of Jesus' death on the cross, believers today have access to God's presence in every place and at any time.

Ps 65:6-13 This harvest psalm glorifies God the Creator as reflected in the beauty of nature. Nature helps us understand something of God's character. The Jews believed that God's care of nature was a sign of his love and provision for them. Nature shows God's generosity—giving us more than we need or deserve. God's abundant generosity should make us grateful to him and generous to others.

Ps 68:1ff This psalm begins just like Moses' cry in Numbers 10:35 as the Israelites followed the Ark of the Covenant. It undoubtedly brought to mind the time when David led a joyous procession and brought the Ark from the house of Obed-edom to Jerusalem (2 Sam 6:11-15). David probably wrote this sometime later, reflecting on that joyous event.

Ps 68:3-6 With shouts of praise and the sound of trumpets, David and his people took the holy Ark toward Mount Zion (2 Sam 6:15). It was a time to sing praises to the Lord, whose presence brings great joy. Only in God is there hope for orphans, widows, prisoners, and all other lonely people. If you are lonely or disadvantaged, join David in praise, and discover great joy from loving and praising God.

▸ **PSALM 68 *(cont.)***

4 Sing praises to God and to his name!
Sing loud praises to him who rides the clouds.
His name is the LORD—
rejoice in his presence!

5 Father to the fatherless, defender of widows—
this is God, whose dwelling is holy.
6 God places the lonely in families;
he sets the prisoners free and gives them joy.
But he makes the rebellious live in a sun-scorched land.

7 O God, when you led your people out from Egypt,
when you marched through the dry wasteland, *Interlude*
8 the earth trembled, and the heavens poured down rain
before you, the God of Sinai,
before God, the God of Israel.
9 You sent abundant rain, O God,
to refresh the weary land.
10 There your people finally settled,
and with a bountiful harvest, O God,
you provided for your needy people.

11 The Lord gives the word,
and a great army* brings the good news.
12 Enemy kings and their armies flee,
while the women of Israel divide the plunder.
13 Even those who lived among the sheepfolds found treasures—
doves with wings of silver
and feathers of gold.
14 The Almighty scattered the enemy kings
like a blowing snowstorm on Mount Zalmon.

15 The mountains of Bashan are majestic,
with many peaks stretching high into the sky.
16 Why do you look with envy, O rugged mountains,
at Mount Zion, where God has chosen to live,
where the LORD himself will live forever?
17 Surrounded by unnumbered thousands of chariots,
the Lord came from Mount Sinai into his sanctuary.
18 When you ascended to the heights,
you led a crowd of captives.
You received gifts from the people,
even from those who rebelled against you.
Now the LORD God will live among us there.

19 Praise the Lord; praise God our savior!
For each day he carries us in his arms. *Interlude*
20 Our God is a God who saves!
The Sovereign LORD rescues us from death.
21 But God will smash the heads of his enemies,
crushing the skulls of those who love their guilty ways.
22 The Lord says, "I will bring my enemies down from Bashan;
I will bring them up from the depths of the sea.
23 You, my people, will wash your feet in their blood,
and even your dogs will get their share!"

Ps 68:11 Or *a host of women.*

Father to the fatherless, defender of widows— this is God, whose dwelling is holy.
Psalm 68:5

Ps 68:4-6 David praised God for his protection and provision. When we see God's true majesty, our response should be to praise him. This was a song of faith because many of these benefits had not yet come true in David's time. It should be our song of faith also. We must continue to trust God because, in time, he will fulfill all his promises.

Ps 68:8 Mount Sinai had a prominent role in Israelite history. It was at Mount Sinai that God met Moses and commissioned him to lead Israel out of Egypt (Exod 3:1-10). It was to Mount Sinai that the nation of Israel returned to receive God's laws (Exod 19:1-3), and God's presence made the entire mountain tremble (Exod 19:18). This sacred mountain was a constant reminder of God's words and promises.

Ps 68:13 The dove is a symbol of God's beloved Israel, who is so protected and blessed that it has taken silver and gold from its enemies, even though it stayed in camp.

Ps 68:15-16 Bashan, the land northeast of Israel, was the home of mighty mountains, including Mount Hermon, the tallest and most awesome mountain in the region. God's choice of Mount Zion, a foothill by comparison, for the site of the Temple led the psalm writer to poetically describe the envy of the mountains of Bashan.

Ps 68:17 This psalm celebrates the final stages of a journey that began at Mount Sinai with the construction of the Ark of the Covenant and finally ended at Mount Zion (site of the sanctuary), the chosen dwelling place of God among his people. It may describe the moving of the Ark of the Covenant into Jerusalem.

Ps 68:18 This verse, quoted in Ephesians 4:8, is applied to the ministry of the ascended Christ. It celebrates his victory over evil. It assures all of us who believe in Christ that by trusting him, we can overcome evil.

Ps 68:19-21 God sets his people free and crushes his enemies. Salvation is freedom from sin and death. Those who refuse to turn to God will be crushed by sin and death. They will be trapped by the sin they loved and destroyed by the death they feared. How much better it will be for those who love God and fear the consequences of sin.

24 Your procession has come into view, O God—
the procession of my God and King as
he goes into the sanctuary.
25 Singers are in front, musicians behind;
between them are young women playing
tambourines.
26 Praise God, all you people of Israel;
praise the LORD, the source of
Israel's life.
27 Look, the little tribe of Benjamin leads
the way.
Then comes a great throng of rulers from
Judah
and all the rulers of Zebulun and Naphtali.
28 Summon your might, O God.
Display your power, O God, as you have
in the past.
29 The kings of the earth are bringing tribute
to your Temple in Jerusalem.
30 Rebuke these enemy nations—
these wild animals lurking in the reeds,
this herd of bulls among the weaker
calves.
Make them bring bars of silver in humble
tribute.
Scatter the nations that delight in war.
31 Let Egypt come with gifts of precious
metals*;
let Ethiopia* bow in submission to God.
32 Sing to God, you kingdoms of the earth.
Sing praises to the Lord. *Interlude*
33 Sing to the one who rides across the ancient
heavens,
his mighty voice thundering from the sky.
34 Tell everyone about God's power.
His majesty shines down on Israel;
his strength is mighty in the heavens.
35 God is awesome in his sanctuary.
The God of Israel gives power and strength
to his people.

Praise be to God!

Ps 68:31a Or *of rich cloth.* **Ps 68:31b** Hebrew *Cush.*

Psalm 69

THEME: A cry of distress in a sea of trouble. We may have to suffer severely for our devotion to God, but that should cause us to look forward with joy to the day when evil and injustice will be gone forever.

AUTHOR: David

For the choir director: A psalm of David, to be sung to the tune "Lilies."

1 Save me, O God,
for the floodwaters are up to my neck.
2 Deeper and deeper I sink into the mire;
I can't find a foothold.
I am in deep water,
and the floods overwhelm me.
3 I am exhausted from crying for help;
my throat is parched.
My eyes are swollen with weeping,
waiting for my God to help me.
4 Those who hate me without cause
outnumber the hairs on my head.
Many enemies try to destroy me with lies,
demanding that I give back what I didn't steal.
5 O God, you know how foolish I am;
my sins cannot be hidden from you.
6 Don't let those who trust in you be ashamed
because of me,
O Sovereign LORD of Heaven's Armies.
Don't let me cause them to be humiliated,
O God of Israel.
7 For I endure insults for your sake;
humiliation is written all over my face.
8 Even my own brothers pretend they don't
know me;
they treat me like a stranger.
9 Passion for your house has consumed me,
and the insults of those who insult you have
fallen on me.
10 When I weep and fast,
they scoff at me.

Ps 68:34-35 When we consider all God has done for us, we should feel an overwhelming sense of awe as we kneel before the Lord in his sanctuary. Nature surrounds us with countless signs of God's wonderful power. His unlimited power and unspeakable majesty leave us breathless in his presence. How fortunate we are that God cares for us.

Ps 69:1ff This is one of the most quoted psalms in the New Testament, and it is often applied to the ministry and suffering of Jesus. Like John 15:25, Psalm 69:4 speaks of Jesus' many enemies. The experience of being scorned by his brothers (Ps 69:8) is expressed in John 7:5. Psalm 69:9 portrays David's zeal for God; Christ showed great zeal when he threw the money changers out of the Temple (John 2:14-17). Paul quoted part of Psalm 69:9 in Romans 15:3. Christ's great suffering is portrayed in Psalm 69:20-21 (Matt 27:48; Mark 15:23; Luke 23:36; John 19:28-30). Psalm 69:22-28 is quoted in Romans 11:9-10; and Peter applied Psalm 69:25 to Judas (Acts 1:20).

Ps 69:3 David cried out until he was physically exhausted, with a parched throat and eyes swollen from weeping. Yet he still trusted God to save him. When devastated by death or tragedy, we need not collapse or despair, because we can turn to God and ask him to save us and help us. The tears will still come, but we will not be crying in vain.

▸ **PSALM 69** ***(cont.)***

11 When I dress in burlap to show sorrow,
they make fun of me.
12 I am the favorite topic of town gossip,
and all the drunks sing about me.

13 But I keep praying to you, LORD,
hoping this time you will show me favor.
In your unfailing love, O God,
answer my prayer with your sure salvation.
14 Rescue me from the mud;
don't let me sink any deeper!
Save me from those who hate me,
and pull me from these deep waters.
15 Don't let the floods overwhelm me,
or the deep waters swallow me,
or the pit of death devour me.

16 Answer my prayers, O LORD,
for your unfailing love is wonderful.
Take care of me,
for your mercy is so plentiful.
17 Don't hide from your servant;
answer me quickly, for I am in deep trouble!
18 Come and redeem me;
free me from my enemies.

19 You know of my shame, scorn, and disgrace.
You see all that my enemies are doing.
20 Their insults have broken my heart,
and I am in despair.
If only one person would show some pity;
if only one would turn and comfort me.
21 But instead, they give me poison* for food;
they offer me sour wine for my thirst.

22 Let the bountiful table set before them
become a snare
and their prosperity become a trap.*
23 Let their eyes go blind so they cannot see,
and make their bodies shake continually.*
24 Pour out your fury on them;
consume them with your burning anger.
25 Let their homes become desolate
and their tents be deserted.
26 To the one you have punished, they add insult
to injury;
they add to the pain of those you have hurt.
27 Pile their sins up high,
and don't let them go free.
28 Erase their names from the Book of Life;
don't let them be counted among the
righteous.

29 I am suffering and in pain.
Rescue me, O God, by your saving power.

30 Then I will praise God's name with singing,
and I will honor him with thanksgiving.
31 For this will please the LORD more than
sacrificing cattle,
more than presenting a bull with its horns
and hooves.
32 The humble will see their God at work and
be glad.
Let all who seek God's help be encouraged.
33 For the LORD hears the cries of the needy;
he does not despise his imprisoned people.

34 Praise him, O heaven and earth,
the seas and all that move in them.
35 For God will save Jerusalem*
and rebuild the towns of Judah.
His people will live there
and settle in their own land.
36 The descendants of those who obey him will
inherit the land,
and those who love him will live there in safety.

Psalm 70

THEME: An urgent prayer for help. It can be your prayer when you're short on time and long on need.

AUTHOR: David

For the choir director: A psalm of David, asking God to remember him.

1 Please, God, rescue me!
Come quickly, LORD, and help me.
2 May those who try to kill me
be humiliated and put to shame.
May those who take delight in my trouble
be turned back in disgrace.
3 Let them be horrified by their shame,
for they said, "Aha! We've got him now!"

Ps 69:21 Or *gall.* **Ps 69:22** Greek version reads *Let their bountiful table set before them become a snare, / a trap that makes them think all is well. / Let their blessings cause them to stumble, / and let them get what they deserve.* Compare Rom 11:9. **Ps 69:23** Greek version reads *and let their backs be bent forever.* Compare Rom 11:10. **Ps 69:35** Hebrew *Zion.*

Ps 69:13 What problems David faced! He was scoffed at, mocked, insulted, humiliated, and made the object of citywide gossip. But still he prayed. When we are completely beaten down, we are tempted to turn from God, give up, and quit trusting him. When your situation seems hopeless, determine that no matter how bad things become you will continue to pray. God will hear your prayer, and he will rescue you. When others reject us, we need God most. Don't turn from your most faithful friend.

Ps 69:28 The "Book of Life" is God's list of those who are in right relationship to him and who remain faithful (Pss 1:3; 7:9; 11:7; 34:12; 37:17, 29; 55:22; 75:10; 92:12-14; 140:13). This term in the New Testament refers to those who will receive eternal life (see Phil 4:3; Rev 3:5; 13:8; 20:15).

Ps 70:1-5 When others disappoint and threaten us, we feel empty, as though a vital part of ourselves has been stolen. When others break the trust we have placed in them, they also break our spirits. At those empty, broken moments, we must join the writer in begging God to rush to our aid. He alone can fill our lives with his joy (Ps 70:4). With the psalm writer we should cry out, "O LORD, do not delay."

4 But may all who search for you
be filled with joy and gladness in you.
May those who love your salvation
repeatedly shout, "God is great!"
5 But as for me, I am poor and needy;
please hurry to my aid, O God.
You are my helper and my savior;
O LORD, do not delay.

Psalm 86

THEME: Devoted trust in times of deep trouble.

AUTHOR: David

A prayer of David.

1 Bend down, O LORD, and hear my prayer;
answer me, for I need your help.
2 Protect me, for I am devoted to you.
Save me, for I serve you and trust you.
You are my God.
3 Be merciful to me, O Lord,
for I am calling on you constantly.
4 Give me happiness, O Lord,
for I give myself to you.
5 O Lord, you are so good, so ready to forgive,
so full of unfailing love for all who ask for
your help.
6 Listen closely to my prayer, O LORD;
hear my urgent cry.
7 I will call to you whenever I'm in trouble,
and you will answer me.
8 No pagan god is like you, O Lord.
None can do what you do!
9 All the nations you made
will come and bow before you, Lord;
they will praise your holy name.
10 For you are great and perform wonderful deeds.
You alone are God.
11 Teach me your ways, O LORD,
that I may live according to your truth!
Grant me purity of heart,
so that I may honor you.
12 With all my heart I will praise you, O Lord
my God.
I will give glory to your name forever,
13 for your love for me is very great.
You have rescued me from the depths
of death.*
14 O God, insolent people rise up against me;
a violent gang is trying to kill me.
You mean nothing to them.
15 But you, O Lord,
are a God of compassion and mercy,
slow to get angry
and filled with unfailing love and faithfulness.
16 Look down and have mercy on me.
Give your strength to your servant;
save me, the son of your servant.
17 Send me a sign of your favor.
Then those who hate me will be put to shame,
for you, O LORD, help and comfort me.

Psalm 101

THEME: A prayer for help to walk a blameless path. To live with integrity, both our efforts and God's help are necessary.

AUTHOR: David

A psalm of David.

1 I will sing of your love and justice, LORD.
I will praise you with songs.
2 I will be careful to live a blameless life—
when will you come to help me?
I will lead a life of integrity
in my own home.

Ps 86:13 Hebrew *of Sheol.*

Ps 70:4 This short psalm (similar in content to Ps 40:13-17) was David's plea for God to come quickly with his help. Yet even in his moment of panic, he did not forget praise. Praise is important because it helps us remember who God is. Often our prayers are filled with requests for ourselves and others, and we forget to thank God for what he has done and to worship him for who he is. Don't take God for granted and treat him as a vending machine. Even when David was afraid, he praised God.

Ps 86:7 Sometimes our trouble or pain is so great that all we can do is cry out to God for protection (Ps 86:2). And often, when there is no relief in sight, all we can do is acknowledge the greatness of God and wait for better days ahead. The conviction that God answers prayer will sustain us in such difficult times.

Ps 86:8-10 "No pagan god is like you." The God of the Bible is unique! He is alive and able to do mighty deeds for those who love him. All human-created deities are powerless because they are merely inventions of the mind, not living beings. The Lord alone is "worthy . . . to receive glory and honor and power" (Rev 4:11). Although people believe in many gods, you need never fear that God is only one among many or that you may be worshiping the wrong God. The Lord alone is God.

Ps 86:11-14 This prayer within a prayer captures a glimpse of vibrant spiritual vitality. Two requests are made: "teach me your ways" and "grant me purity of heart." Each request has a God-centered purpose: that the person praying would "live according to your truth" and "honor you." No matter how well we know and follow God, we can always ask him to increase our awareness and improve our obedience. Jesus echoed one of these requests in the sixth beatitude: "God blesses those whose hearts are pure, for they will see God" (Matt 5:8). Commit this prayer to memory and use it often.

Ps 86:17 It is right to pray for a sign of God's favor. As David found, it may be just what we need. But let us not overlook the signs he has already given: the support of family and friends, the fellowship of other Christians, the light of each new day. We can be confident that he knows our situation no matter how desperate it becomes, and he cares.

Ps 101:1ff David may have written this psalm early in his reign as king as he set down the standards he wanted to follow. David knew that to lead a blameless life he would need God's help (Ps 101:2). We can lead blameless lives if we avoid looking at wickedness (Ps 101:3), evil thoughts (Ps 101:4), slander (Ps 101:5), and pride (Ps 101:5). While avoiding these wrongs, we must also let God's Word show us the standards by which to live.

▸ **PSALM 101** ***(cont.)***

3 I will refuse to look at
anything vile and vulgar.
I hate all who deal crookedly;
I will have nothing to do with them.
4 I will reject perverse ideas
and stay away from every evil.
5 I will not tolerate people who slander their
neighbors.
I will not endure conceit and pride.

6 I will search for faithful people
to be my companions.
Only those who are above reproach
will be allowed to serve me.
7 I will not allow deceivers to serve in my house,
and liars will not stay in my presence.
8 My daily task will be to ferret out the wicked
and free the city of the LORD from their grip.

Psalm 103

THEME: God's great love for us. What God does for us tells us what he is really like.

AUTHOR: David

A psalm of David.

1 Let all that I am praise the LORD;
with my whole heart, I will praise his holy
name.
2 Let all that I am praise the LORD;
may I never forget the good things he does
for me.
3 He forgives all my sins
and heals all my diseases.
4 He redeems me from death
and crowns me with love and tender mercies.
5 He fills my life with good things.
My youth is renewed like the eagle's!
6 The LORD gives righteousness
and justice to all who are treated unfairly.

7 He revealed his character to Moses
and his deeds to the people of Israel.
8 The LORD is compassionate and merciful,
slow to get angry and filled with unfailing love.
9 He will not constantly accuse us,
nor remain angry forever.
10 He does not punish us for all our sins;
he does not deal harshly with us, as we deserve.
11 For his unfailing love toward those who fear him
is as great as the height of the heavens above
the earth.
12 He has removed our sins as far from us
as the east is from the west.
13 The LORD is like a father to his children,
tender and compassionate to those who
fear him.
14 For he knows how weak we are;
he remembers we are only dust.
15 Our days on earth are like grass;
like wildflowers, we bloom and die.
16 The wind blows, and we are gone—
as though we had never been here.
17 But the love of the LORD remains forever
with those who fear him.
His salvation extends to the children's children
18 of those who are faithful to his covenant,
of those who obey his commandments!

19 The LORD has made the heavens his throne;
from there he rules over everything.

20 Praise the LORD, you angels,
you mighty ones who carry out his plans,
listening for each of his commands.
21 Yes, praise the LORD, you armies of angels
who serve him and do his will!

Ps 101:6 David said that he would "search for faithful people" to be his companions. He would choose as models and as friends those who were godly and truthful. Our friends and associates can have a profound influence on us. Make sure to choose as your closest companions those who are faithful to God and his Word.

Ps 103:1ff David's praise focused on the good things God was doing for him. It is easy to complain about life, but David's list gives us plenty for which to praise God: He forgives our sins, heals our diseases, redeems us from death, crowns us with love and compassion, satisfies our desires, and gives righteousness and justice. We receive all of these without deserving any of them. No matter how difficult your life's journey, you can always count your blessings—past, present, and future. When you feel as though you have nothing for which to praise God, read David's list.

Ps 103:7 God's law was given first to Moses and the people of Israel. God's law presents a clear picture of God's character and his will for his people. It was God's training manual to prepare his people to serve him and to follow his ways. Review the Ten Commandments (Exod 20) and the history of how they were given, asking God to show you his will and his ways through them.

Ps 103:12 East and west can never meet. This is a symbolic portrait of God's forgiveness: When he forgives our sin, he separates it from us completely. We need never wallow in the past, for God forgives. We tend to dredge up the ugly past, but God has wiped our record clean. If we are to follow God, we must model his forgiveness in our dealings with one another. Otherwise we have not truly forgiven.

Ps 103:13 God is like a father—tender and compassionate. But not every child has a tender and compassionate father. Too often, the cycles of abuse and dysfunction rob children of loving fathers. If that is your situation, God offers himself to you to be the Father you never had or perhaps felt you never needed. Of course, you can't go fishing with God or be held physically by him, but you can receive his love in your heart by means of his Holy Spirit (Rom 5:5). God can tenderly heal your deep loss.

Ps 103:13-14 We are fragile, but God's care is eternal. Too often we focus on God as judge and lawgiver, ignoring his compassion and concern for us. When God examines our lives, he remembers our human condition. Our weakness should never be used as a justification for sin. His mercy takes everything into account. God will deal with you compassionately. Trust him.

Ps 103:20-22 Everything everywhere is to praise the Lord: all his angels and all his works! Praising God means remembering all he has done for us (Ps 103:2), fearing him and obeying his commands (Ps 103:17-18),

22 Praise the LORD, everything he has created,
everything in all his kingdom.

Let all that I am praise the LORD.

Psalm 108

THEME: Victory in God's strength. With God's help, we can do more than we think.

AUTHOR: David

A song. A psalm of David.

1 My heart is confident in you, O God;
no wonder I can sing your praises with all my heart!
2 Wake up, lyre and harp!
I will wake the dawn with my song.
3 I will thank you, LORD, among all the people.
I will sing your praises among the nations.
4 For your unfailing love is higher than the heavens.
Your faithfulness reaches to the clouds.
5 Be exalted, O God, above the highest heavens.
May your glory shine over all the earth.

6 Now rescue your beloved people.
Answer and save us by your power.
7 God has promised this by his holiness*:
"I will divide up Shechem with joy.
I will measure out the valley of Succoth.
8 Gilead is mine,
and Manasseh, too.
Ephraim, my helmet, will produce my warriors,
and Judah, my scepter, will produce my kings.
9 But Moab, my washbasin, will become my servant,
and I will wipe my feet on Edom
and shout in triumph over Philistia."
10 Who will bring me into the fortified city?
Who will bring me victory over Edom?
11 Have you rejected us, O God?
Will you no longer march with our armies?
12 Oh, please help us against our enemies,
for all human help is useless.
13 With God's help we will do mighty things,
for he will trample down our foes.

Psalm 109

THEME: Righteous indignation against liars and slanderers. We can tell God our true feelings and desires.

AUTHOR: David

For the choir director: A psalm of David.

1 O God, whom I praise,
don't stand silent and aloof
2 while the wicked slander me
and tell lies about me.
3 They surround me with hateful words
and fight against me for no reason.
4 I love them, but they try to destroy me with accusations
even as I am praying for them!
5 They repay evil for good,
and hatred for my love.

6 They say,* "Get an evil person to turn against him.
Send an accuser to bring him to trial.
7 When his case comes up for judgment,
let him be pronounced guilty.
Count his prayers as sins.
8 Let his years be few;
let someone else take his position.
9 May his children become fatherless,
and his wife a widow.
10 May his children wander as beggars
and be driven from their ruined homes.
11 May creditors seize his entire estate,
and strangers take all he has earned.
12 Let no one be kind to him;
let no one pity his fatherless children.
13 May all his offspring die.
May his family name be blotted out in a single generation.
14 May the LORD never forget the sins of his fathers;
may his mother's sins never be erased from the record.
15 May the LORD always remember these sins,
and may his name disappear from human memory.

Ps 108:7 Or *in his sanctuary.* **Ps 109:6** Hebrew lacks *They say.*

---

and doing his will (Ps 103:21). Does your life praise the Lord?

Ps 108:1ff This psalm is closely related to two other psalms. The first five verses are identical to Psalm 57:7-11, and the next eight verses (Ps 108:6-13) are also seen in Psalm 60:5-12.

Ps 108:9 Moab, Edom, and Philistia were Israel's enemies to the east, south, and west, respectively. They despised the Israelites and Israel's God.

Ps 108:13 Do our prayers end with requests for help to make it through stressful situations? David prayed not merely for rescue, but for victory. With God's help we can claim more than mere survival, we can claim victory! Look for ways God can use your distress as an opportunity to show his mighty power.

Ps 109:1ff David endured many false accusations (1 Sam 22:7-13; 2 Sam 15:3-4), as did Christ centuries later (Matt 26:59-61; 27:39-44). Psalm 109:8 is quoted in Acts 1:20 as being fulfilled in Judas's death.

Ps 109:4 David was angry at being attacked by evil people who slandered him and lied. Yet David remained a friend and a man of prayer. While we must hate evil and work to overcome it, we must love everyone, including those who do evil, because God loves them. We are called to hate the sin, but love the person. Only through God's strength will we be able to follow David's example.

Ps 109:6-20 This is another of the imprecatory psalms, a call for God to judge the wicked. (For an explanation of imprecatory psalms, see the note on Ps 35:1ff, p. 565.) David was not taking vengeance into his own hands; he was asking that God be swift in his promised judgment of evil people. David's words depict the eventual doom of all God's enemies.

▸ **PSALM 109 *(cont.)***

16 For he refused all kindness to others;
he persecuted the poor and needy,
and he hounded the brokenhearted to death.
17 He loved to curse others;
now you curse him.
He never blessed others;
now don't you bless him.
18 Cursing is as natural to him as his clothing,
or the water he drinks,
or the rich food he eats.
19 Now may his curses return and cling to him
like clothing;
may they be tied around him like a belt."

20 May those curses become the LORD's punishment
for my accusers who speak evil of me.
21 But deal well with me, O Sovereign LORD,
for the sake of your own reputation!
Rescue me
because you are so faithful and good.
22 For I am poor and needy,
and my heart is full of pain.
23 I am fading like a shadow at dusk;
I am brushed off like a locust.
24 My knees are weak from fasting,
and I am skin and bones.
25 I am a joke to people everywhere;
when they see me, they shake their heads
in scorn.

26 Help me, O LORD my God!
Save me because of your unfailing love.
27 Let them see that this is your doing,
that you yourself have done it, LORD.
28 Then let them curse me if they like,
but you will bless me!
When they attack me, they will be disgraced!
But I, your servant, will go right on rejoicing!
29 May my accusers be clothed with disgrace;
may their humiliation cover them like a cloak.
30 But I will give repeated thanks to the LORD,
praising him to everyone.
31 For he stands beside the needy,
ready to save them from those who condemn
them.

Psalm 110

THEME: The credentials for the Messiah. Jesus is the Messiah.

AUTHOR: David

A psalm of David.

1 The LORD said to my Lord,
"Sit in the place of honor at my right hand
until I humble your enemies,
making them a footstool under your feet."

2 The LORD will extend your powerful kingdom
from Jerusalem*;
you will rule over your enemies.
3 When you go to war,
your people will serve you willingly.
You are arrayed in holy garments,
and your strength will be renewed each day
like the morning dew.

4 The LORD has taken an oath and will not break
his vow:
"You are a priest forever in the order
of Melchizedek."

5 The Lord stands at your right hand to
protect you.
He will strike down many kings when his
anger erupts.
6 He will punish the nations
and fill their lands with corpses;
he will shatter heads over the whole earth.
7 But he himself will be refreshed from brooks
along the way.
He will be victorious.

Ps 110:2 Hebrew *Zion.*

Ps 110:1ff This is one of the most-quoted psalms in the New Testament because of its clear references to the Messiah. In Matthew 22:41-45, Jesus quoted Psalm 110:1 and applied it to himself. There are several other references to the Messiah in this psalm: Christ's final and total destruction of the wicked (Ps 110:1, 6; see Rev 6–9); Christ's reign on the earth (Ps 110:2; see Rev 20:1-7); Christ's priestly work for his people (Ps 110:3-4; see Heb 5–8); and the final battle on earth when Christ will overcome the forces of evil (Ps 110:5-6; see Rev 19:11-21).

Ps 110:1-7 Many people have a vague belief in God but refuse to accept Jesus as anything more than a great human teacher. But the Bible does not allow that option. Both the Old and New Testaments proclaim the deity of the one who came to save and to reign. Jesus explained that this psalm spoke of the Messiah as greater than David, Israel's greatest king (Mark 12:35-37). Peter used this psalm to show that Jesus, the Messiah, sits at God's right hand and is Lord over all (Acts 2:32-35). You can't straddle the fence, calling Jesus "just a good teacher," because the Bible clearly calls him Lord.

Ps 110:4 For more about Melchizedek, see his Profile on p. 35. As a priest like Melchizedek, Christ will never abuse his divine position, and his reign will be forever. Jesus is more fully described as our High Priest in Hebrews 5.

Jerusalem ▸

Jerusalem is a city set on hills. Psalms 120–134 is a collection of psalms that are labeled as "songs for pilgrims ascending to Jerusalem," often called the Psalms of Ascent. These short, appealing psalms were sung during pilgrims' journeys to Jerusalem for the national festivals three times each year.

This illustration shows what Jerusalem would have looked like during the days of David's reign, when some of these psalms (122, 124, 131, and 133) would have been written.

Jerusalem in the Time of David

Formerly Salem (Gen 14:18) and Jebus (1 Chr 11:4)

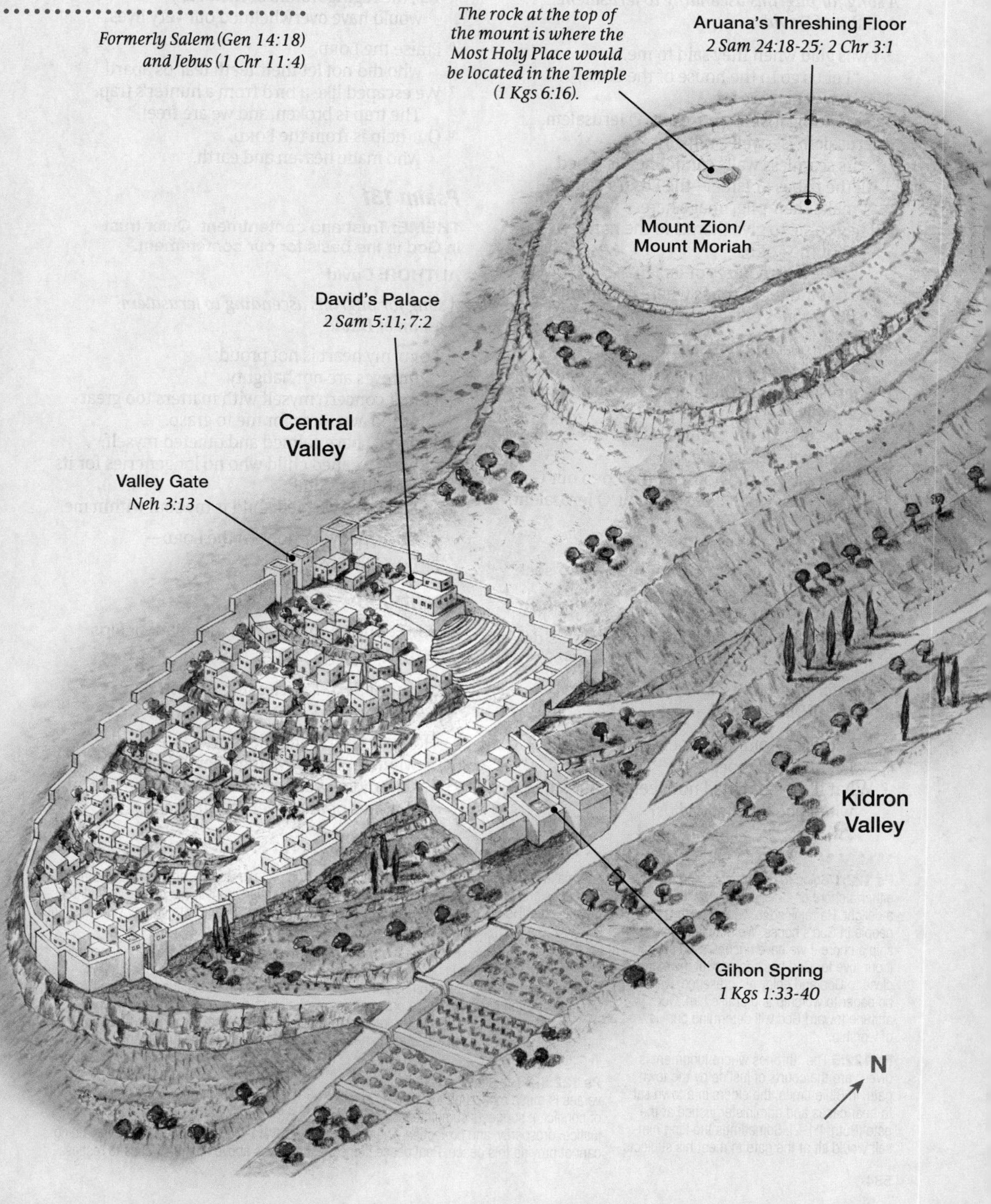

The rock at the top of the mount is where the Most Holy Place would be located in the Temple (1 Kgs 6:16).

Aruana's Threshing Floor
2 Sam 24:18-25; 2 Chr 3:1

Mount Zion/
Mount Moriah

David's Palace
2 Sam 5:11; 7:2

Central
Valley

Valley Gate
Neh 3:13

Kidron
Valley

Gihon Spring
1 Kgs 1:33-40

N

Psalm 122

THEME: Stepping into the presence of God.

AUTHOR: David

A song for pilgrims ascending to Jerusalem. A psalm of David.

1 I was glad when they said to me,
"Let us go to the house of the LORD."
2 And now here we are,
standing inside your gates, O Jerusalem.
3 Jerusalem is a well-built city;
its seamless walls cannot be breached.
4 All the tribes of Israel—the LORD's people—
make their pilgrimage here.
They come to give thanks to the name
of the LORD,
as the law requires of Israel.
5 Here stand the thrones where judgment is given,
the thrones of the dynasty of David.

6 Pray for peace in Jerusalem.
May all who love this city prosper.
7 O Jerusalem, may there be peace within your walls
and prosperity in your palaces.
8 For the sake of my family and friends, I will say,
"May you have peace."
9 For the sake of the house of the LORD our God,
I will seek what is best for you, O Jerusalem.

Psalm 124

THEME: God delivers us from those who seek to destroy us. God is on the side of those who seek him.

AUTHOR: David, possibly written after his defeat of the Philistines (2 Samuel 5:17-25, p. 489)

A song for pilgrims ascending to Jerusalem. A psalm of David.

1 What if the LORD had not been on our side?
Let all Israel repeat:
2 What if the LORD had not been on our side
when people attacked us?
3 They would have swallowed us alive
in their burning anger.
4 The waters would have engulfed us;
a torrent would have overwhelmed us.
5 Yes, the raging waters of their fury
would have overwhelmed our very lives.

6 Praise the LORD,
who did not let their teeth tear us apart!
7 We escaped like a bird from a hunter's trap.
The trap is broken, and we are free!
8 Our help is from the LORD,
who made heaven and earth.

Psalm 131

THEME: Trust and contentment. Quiet trust in God is the basis for our contentment.

AUTHOR: David

A song for pilgrims ascending to Jerusalem. A psalm of David.

1 LORD, my heart is not proud;
my eyes are not haughty.
I don't concern myself with matters too great
or too awesome for me to grasp.
2 Instead, I have calmed and quieted myself,
like a weaned child who no longer cries for its
mother's milk.
Yes, like a weaned child is my soul within me.

3 O Israel, put your hope in the LORD—
now and always.

Psalm 133

THEME: The joy of harmonious relationships.

AUTHOR: David

A song for pilgrims ascending to Jerusalem. A psalm of David.

1 How wonderful and pleasant it is
when brothers live together in harmony!
2 For harmony is as precious as the anointing oil
that was poured over Aaron's head,

Ps 122:1 Going to God's house can be either a chore or a delight. For David, it was a delight. He rejoiced to worship with God's people in God's house. We may find worship a chore if we have unconfessed sin or if our love for God has cooled. But if we are close to God and enjoy his presence, we will be eager to worship and praise him. Our attitude toward God will determine our view of worship.

Ps 122:5 The "thrones where judgment is given" are the courts of justice by the town gate. In Bible times, the elders in a town sat to hear cases and administer justice at the gate (Ruth 4:1-2). Sometimes the king himself would sit at the gate to meet his subjects and make legal decisions (2 Sam 19:8). Speeches and prophecies were also made at the city gate (Neh 8:1; Jer 17:19-20).

Ps 122:6-9 The writer was not praying for his own peace and prosperity but for that of his family and friends in Jerusalem. This is intercessory prayer, prayer on behalf of others. Too often we are quick to pray for our own needs and desires but neglect interceding for others. Will you intercede for someone in need today?

Ps 122:6-9 The peace sought in these verses is much more than the mere absence of conflict. It suggests completeness, health, justice, prosperity, and protection. The world cannot provide this peace. Real peace comes from faith in God because he alone embodies all the characteristics of peace. To find peace of mind and peace with others, you must find peace with God.

Ps 124:7-8 Do you ever feel trapped by overwhelming odds? With God, there is always a way out because he is the Creator of all that exists. No problem is beyond his ability to solve; no circumstance is too difficult for him. We can turn to the Creator for help in our time of need, for he is on our side. God will provide a way out; we need only trust him and look for it. David compared this to a bird escaping the hunter's trap.

Ps 131:1-2 Pride results from overvaluing ourselves above others. It leads to restless-

that ran down his beard
and onto the border of his robe.
3 Harmony is as refreshing as the dew from Mount Hermon
that falls on the mountains of Zion.
And there the LORD has pronounced his blessing,
even life everlasting.

Psalm 138

THEME: Thanksgiving for answered prayer. God works out his plans for our lives and will bring us through the difficulties we face.

AUTHOR: David

A psalm of David.

1 I give you thanks, O LORD, with all my heart;
I will sing your praises before the gods.
2 I bow before your holy Temple as I worship.
I praise your name for your unfailing love and faithfulness;
for your promises are backed
by all the honor of your name.
3 As soon as I pray, you answer me;
you encourage me by giving me strength.

4 Every king in all the earth will thank you, LORD,
for all of them will hear your words.
5 Yes, they will sing about the LORD's ways,
for the glory of the LORD is very great.
6 Though the LORD is great, he cares for the humble,
but he keeps his distance from the proud.
7 Though I am surrounded by troubles,
you will protect me from the anger of my enemies.
You reach out your hand,
and the power of your right hand saves me.
8 The LORD will work out his plans for my life—
for your faithful love, O LORD, endures forever.
Don't abandon me, for you made me.

---

ness because it makes us dissatisfied with what we have and concerned about what everyone else is doing. It keeps us always hungering for more attention and adoration. By contrast, humility puts others first and allows us to be content with God's leading in our lives. Such contentment gives us security so that we no longer have to prove ourselves to others. Let humility and trust affect your perspective and give you the strength and freedom to serve God and others.

Ps 133:1-3 David stated that harmony is pleasant and precious. Unfortunately, harmony is not always found in the church, as it should be. People disagree and cause division over unimportant issues. Some delight in causing tension by discrediting others. Harmony is important because it makes the church a positive example to the world and helps draw others to the Lord; it helps us cooperate as a body of believers as God meant us to, giving us a foretaste of heaven; and it renews and revitalizes ministry because there is less tension to sap our energy.

Living in harmony does not mean that we will agree on everything; there will be many opinions just as there are many notes in a musical chord. But we must agree on our purpose in life—to work together for God. Our outward expression of harmony will reflect our inward harmony of purpose.

Ps 133:2 Moses used costly oil to anoint Aaron as the first high priest of Israel (Exod 29:7) and to dedicate all the priests to God's service. Brotherly harmony, like the anointing oil, shows that we are dedicated to serving God wholeheartedly.

Ps 133:3 Mount Hermon is the tallest mountain in the entire area, located northeast of the Sea of Galilee.

Ps 138:1 "Before the gods" may mean in the presence of subordinate heavenly beings (angels), or, more likely, it may be a statement ridiculing the kings or gods of the pagan nations. God is supreme in the whole earth.

Ps 138:1-3 Thanksgiving should be an integral part of our praise to God. This theme is woven throughout the Psalms. As we praise and thank God for material and spiritual blessings, we should also thank him for answered prayer. Remember when you asked God for protection, strength, comfort, patience, love, or other special needs, and he supplied them. Beware of taking God's provision and answered prayer for granted.

Ps 138:8 We all dream and make plans for the future; then we usually work hard to see those dreams and plans come true. But to make the most of life, we must include God's plan in our plans. He alone knows what is best for us; he alone can fulfill his purpose for us. As you make plans and dream dreams, talk with God about them.

*How wonderful and pleasant
it is when brothers live
together in harmony!*
Psalm 133:1

Psalm 139

THEME: God is all-seeing, all-knowing, all-powerful, and everywhere present. God knows us, God is with us, and his greatest gift is to allow us to know him.

AUTHOR: David

For the choir director: A psalm of David.

1 O LORD, you have examined my heart
and know everything about me.
2 You know when I sit down or stand up.
You know my thoughts even when I'm far away.
3 You see me when I travel
and when I rest at home.
You know everything I do.
4 You know what I am going to say
even before I say it, LORD.
5 You go before me and follow me.
You place your hand of blessing on my head.
6 Such knowledge is too wonderful for me,
too great for me to understand!

7 I can never escape from your Spirit!
I can never get away from your presence!
8 If I go up to heaven, you are there;
if I go down to the grave,* you are there.
9 If I ride the wings of the morning,
if I dwell by the farthest oceans,
10 even there your hand will guide me,
and your strength will support me.
11 I could ask the darkness to hide me
and the light around me to become night—
12 but even in darkness I cannot hide from you.
To you the night shines as bright as day.
Darkness and light are the same to you.

13 You made all the delicate, inner parts of my body
and knit me together in my mother's womb.
14 Thank you for making me so wonderfully complex!
Your workmanship is marvelous—how well I know it.
15 You watched me as I was being formed in utter seclusion,
as I was woven together in the dark of the womb.
16 You saw me before I was born.
Every day of my life was recorded in your book.
Every moment was laid out
before a single day had passed.

17 How precious are your thoughts about me,* O God.
They cannot be numbered!
18 I can't even count them;
they outnumber the grains of sand!
And when I wake up,
you are still with me!

19 O God, if only you would destroy the wicked!
Get out of my life, you murderers!
20 They blaspheme you;
your enemies misuse your name.
21 O LORD, shouldn't I hate those who hate you?
Shouldn't I despise those who oppose you?
22 Yes, I hate them with total hatred,
for your enemies are my enemies.
23 Search me, O God, and know my heart;
test me and know my anxious thoughts.
24 Point out anything in me that offends you,
and lead me along the path of everlasting life.

Ps 139:8 Hebrew *to Sheol.* **Ps 139:17** Or *How precious to me are your thoughts.*

You made all the delicate, inner parts of my body and knit me together in my mother's womb.
Psalm 139:13

Ps 139:1-5 Sometimes we don't let people get to know us completely because we are afraid they will discover something about us that they won't like. But God already knows everything about us, even to the number of hairs on our heads (Matt 10:30), and still he accepts and loves us. God is with us through every situation, in every trial—protecting, loving, guiding. He knows and loves us completely.

Ps 139:7 God is omnipresent—he is present everywhere. Because this is so, you can never escape from his Spirit. This is good news to those who know and love God, because no matter what we do or where we go, we can never be far from God's comforting presence (see Rom 8:35-39).

Ps 139:13-15 God's character goes into the creation of every person. When you feel worthless or even begin to hate yourself, remember that God's Spirit is ready and willing to work within you. We should have as much respect for ourselves as our Maker has for us.

Ps 139:21-24 David's hatred for his enemies came from his zeal for God. David regarded his enemies as God's enemies, so his hatred was a desire for God's righteous justice and not for personal vengeance. Is it all right to be angry at people who hate God? Yes, but we must remember that it is God who will deal with them, not us. If we truly love God, then we will be deeply hurt if someone hates him. David asked God to search his heart and mind and point out any wrong motives that may have been behind his strong words. But while we seek justice against evil, we must also pray that God's enemies will turn to him before he judges them (see Matt 5:44).

Ps 139:23-24 David asked God to search for sin and point it out, even to the level of testing his thoughts. This is exploratory surgery for sin. How are we to recognize sin unless God points it out? Then, when God shows us, we can repent and be forgiven. Make this verse your prayer. If you ask the Lord to search your heart and your thoughts

Psalm 140

THEME: Prayer for protection against those who slander or threaten you. Deliverance begins with concentrating on our future life with God.

AUTHOR: David

For the choir director: A psalm of David.

1 O LORD, rescue me from evil people.
Protect me from those who are violent,
2 those who plot evil in their hearts
and stir up trouble all day long.
3 Their tongues sting like a snake;
the venom of a viper drips from their lips. *Interlude*

4 O LORD, keep me out of the hands of the wicked.
Protect me from those who are violent,
for they are plotting against me.
5 The proud have set a trap to catch me;
they have stretched out a net;
they have placed traps all along the way. *Interlude*

6 I said to the LORD, "You are my God!"
Listen, O LORD, to my cries for mercy!
7 O Sovereign LORD, the strong one who rescued me,
you protected me on the day of battle.
8 LORD, do not let evil people have their way.
Do not let their evil schemes succeed,
or they will become proud. *Interlude*

9 Let my enemies be destroyed
by the very evil they have planned for me.
10 Let burning coals fall down on their heads.
Let them be thrown into the fire
or into watery pits from which they can't escape.
11 Don't let liars prosper here in our land.
Cause great disasters to fall on the violent.
12 But I know the LORD will help those they persecute;
he will give justice to the poor.
13 Surely righteous people are praising your name;
the godly will live in your presence.

ANGER AND VENGEANCE IN THE BOOK OF PSALMS

Several psalms shock those familiar with New Testament teachings. The psalmists didn't hesitate to demand God's justice and make vivid suggestions on how he might carry it out. Apparently, no subject was unsuitable for discussion with God, but our tendency is to avoid the subjects of anger and vengeance in the book of Psalms.

To understand the words of anger and vengeance, we need to understand several things:

(1) The judgments asked for are to be carried out by God and are written out of intense personal and national suffering. The people are unable or unwilling to take revenge themselves and are asking God to intervene. Because few of us have suffered intense cruelty on a personal or national level, we find it difficult to grasp these outbursts.

(2) These writers were intimately aware of God's justice. Some of their words are efforts to vividly imagine what God might allow to happen to those who had harmed his people.

(3) If we dared to write down our thoughts while being unjustly attacked or suffering cruelty, we might be shocked at our own bold desire for vengeance. We would be surprised at how much we have in common with these men of old. The psalmists did not have Jesus' command to pray for one's enemies, but they did point to the right place to start. We are challenged to pay back good for evil, but until we respond to this challenge, we will not know how much we need God's help in order to forgive others.

(4) There is a helpful parallel between the psalms of anger and the psalms of vengeance. The "angry" psalms are intense and graphic, but they are directed at God. He is boldly told how disappointing it is when he turns his back on his people or acts too slowly. But while these thoughts and feelings are sincerely expressed, we know from the psalms themselves that these passing feelings are followed by renewed confidence in God's faithfulness. It is reasonable to expect the same of the "vengeance" psalms. We read, for example, David's angry outburst against Saul's pursuit in Psalm 59, yet we know that David never took personal revenge on Saul. The psalmists freely spoke their minds to God, having confidence that he could sort out what was meant and what was felt. Pray with that same confidence—God can be trusted with your heart.

Selected psalms that emphasize these themes are 10; 23; 28; 35; 59; 69; 109; 137; 139; 140.

and to reveal your sin, you will be continuing on "the path of everlasting life."

Ps 140:12 To whom can the poor turn when they are persecuted? They lack the money to get professional help and so are usually unable to defend themselves. But there is always someone on their side—the Lord will stand by them and ultimately bring about justice. This should be a comfort for us all. No matter what our situation may be, the Lord is with us. But this truth should also call us to live responsibly with others. As God's people, we are required to defend the rights of the powerless.

Psalm 141

THEME: A prayer for help when facing temptation. David asks God to protect him and to give him wisdom in accepting criticism. Be open to honest criticism—God may be speaking to you through others.

AUTHOR: David

A psalm of David.

1 O LORD, I am calling to you. Please hurry!
Listen when I cry to you for help!
2 Accept my prayer as incense offered to you,
and my upraised hands as an evening offering.

3 Take control of what I say, O LORD,
and guard my lips.
4 Don't let me drift toward evil
or take part in acts of wickedness.
Don't let me share in the delicacies
of those who do wrong.

5 Let the godly strike me!
It will be a kindness!
If they correct me, it is soothing medicine.
Don't let me refuse it.

But I pray constantly
against the wicked and their deeds.
6 When their leaders are thrown down from a cliff,
the wicked will listen to my words and find them true.
7 Like rocks brought up by a plow,
the bones of the wicked will lie scattered without burial.*

8 I look to you for help, O Sovereign LORD.
You are my refuge; don't let them kill me.
9 Keep me from the traps they have set for me,
from the snares of those who do wrong.
10 Let the wicked fall into their own nets,
but let me escape.

Ps 141:7 Hebrew *scattered at the mouth of Sheol.*

Psalm 143

THEME: A prayer in the midst of hopelessness and depression. Our prayers should fit into what we know is consistent with God's character and plans.

AUTHOR: David

A psalm of David.

1 Hear my prayer, O LORD;
listen to my plea!
Answer me because you are faithful and righteous.
2 Don't put your servant on trial,
for no one is innocent before you.
3 My enemy has chased me.
He has knocked me to the ground
and forces me to live in darkness like those in the grave.
4 I am losing all hope;
I am paralyzed with fear.
5 I remember the days of old.
I ponder all your great works
and think about what you have done.
6 I lift my hands to you in prayer.
I thirst for you as parched land thirsts for rain. *Interlude*

7 Come quickly, LORD, and answer me,
for my depression deepens.
Don't turn away from me,
or I will die.
8 Let me hear of your unfailing love each morning,
for I am trusting you.
Show me where to walk,
for I give myself to you.
9 Rescue me from my enemies, LORD;
I run to you to hide me.
10 Teach me to do your will,
for you are my God.
May your gracious Spirit lead me forward
on a firm footing.

Ps 141:3 James wrote that "the tongue is a flame of fire. It is a whole world of wickedness, corrupting your entire body" (Jas 3:6). On the average, a person opens the mouth to speak approximately 700 times a day. David wisely asked God to keep him from speaking evil—even as he underwent persecution. Jesus himself was silent before his accusers (Matt 26:63). Knowing the power of the tongue, we would do well to ask God to guard what we say so that our words will bring honor to his name.

Ps 141:4 Evil acts begin with evil desires. It isn't enough to ask God to keep you away from temptation, make you stronger, or change your circumstances. You must ask him to change you on the inside—at the level of your desires.

Ps 141:5 David says that being rebuked by a godly person is a kindness. Nobody really likes criticism, but everybody can benefit from it when it is given wisely and taken humbly. David suggested how to accept criticism: (1) Don't refuse it, (2) consider it a kindness, and (3) keep quiet (don't fight back). Putting these suggestions into practice will help you control how you react to criticism, making it productive rather than destructive, no matter how it was originally intended.

Ps 143:7 David was losing hope, caught in paralyzing fear and deep depression. At times we feel caught in deepening depression, and we are unable to pull ourselves out. At those times we can come to the Lord and, like David, express our true feelings. Then we will find help as we remember his works (Ps 143:5), reach out to him in prayer (Ps 143:6), trust him (Ps 143:8), and seek to do his will (Ps 143:10).

Ps 143:10 David's prayer was that he be taught to do God's will, not his own. A prayer for guidance is self-centered if it doesn't recognize God's power to redirect our lives. Asking God to restructure our priorities awakens our minds and stirs our will.

[11] For the glory of your name, O LORD, preserve
my life.
Because of your faithfulness, bring me out
of this distress.
[12] In your unfailing love, silence all my enemies
and destroy all my foes,
for I am your servant.

Psalm 144

THEME: Rejoicing in God's care. Whether in times of prosperity or adversity, blessed are those whose God is the Lord.
AUTHOR: David

A psalm of David.

[1] Praise the LORD, who is my rock.
He trains my hands for war
and gives my fingers skill for battle.
[2] He is my loving ally and my fortress,
my tower of safety, my rescuer.
He is my shield, and I take refuge in him.
He makes the nations* submit to me.

[3] O LORD, what are human beings that you
should notice them,
mere mortals that you should think
about them?
[4] For they are like a breath of air;
their days are like a passing shadow.

[5] Open the heavens, LORD, and come down.
Touch the mountains so they billow smoke.
[6] Hurl your lightning bolts and scatter your
enemies!
Shoot your arrows and confuse them!
[7] Reach down from heaven and rescue me;
rescue me from deep waters,
from the power of my enemies.
[8] Their mouths are full of lies;
they swear to tell the truth, but they lie instead.

[9] I will sing a new song to you, O God!
I will sing your praises with a ten-stringed harp.
[10] For you grant victory to kings!
You rescued your servant David from the
fatal sword.
[11] Save me!
Rescue me from the power of my enemies.
Their mouths are full of lies;
they swear to tell the truth, but they lie instead.

[12] May our sons flourish in their youth
like well-nurtured plants.
May our daughters be like graceful pillars,
carved to beautify a palace.
[13] May our barns be filled
with crops of every kind.
May the flocks in our fields multiply by the
thousands,
even tens of thousands,
[14] and may our oxen be loaded down with
produce.
May there be no enemy breaking through
our walls,
no going into captivity,
no cries of alarm in our town squares.
[15] Yes, joyful are those who live like this!
Joyful indeed are those whose God is the LORD.

Psalm 145*

THEME: A time will come when all people will join together in recognizing and worshiping God. Because God is full of love, he satisfies all who trust in him.
AUTHOR: David

A psalm of praise of David.

[1] I will exalt you, my God and King,
and praise your name forever and ever.
[2] I will praise you every day;
yes, I will praise you forever.
[3] Great is the LORD! He is most worthy of praise!
No one can measure his greatness.

[4] Let each generation tell its children of your
mighty acts;
let them proclaim your power.
[5] I will meditate* on your majestic, glorious
splendor
and your wonderful miracles.
[6] Your awe-inspiring deeds will be on every tongue;
I will proclaim your greatness.
[7] Everyone will share the story of your wonderful
goodness;
they will sing with joy about your
righteousness.

[8] The LORD is merciful and compassionate,
slow to get angry and filled with unfailing love.
[9] The LORD is good to everyone.
He showers compassion on all his creation.
[10] All of your works will thank you, LORD,
and your faithful followers will praise you.
[11] They will speak of the glory of your kingdom;
they will give examples of your power.

Ps 144:2 Some manuscripts read *my people.* **Ps 145** This psalm is a Hebrew acrostic poem; each verse (including 13b) begins with a successive letter of the Hebrew alphabet. **Ps 145:5** Some manuscripts read *They will speak.*

Ps 144:3-4 Life is short. David reminds us that it is "like a breath" and that our "days are like a passing shadow." James says that our life is "like the morning fog—it's here a little while, then it's gone" (Jas 4:14). Because life is short, live for God while you have the time. Don't waste your life by selecting an inferior purpose that has no lasting value. Only God can make your life worthwhile, purposeful, and meaningful.

▸ **PSALM 145 *(cont.)***

12 They will tell about your mighty deeds
and about the majesty and glory of your reign.
13 For your kingdom is an everlasting kingdom.
You rule throughout all generations.

The LORD always keeps his promises;
he is gracious in all he does.*
14 The LORD helps the fallen
and lifts those bent beneath their loads.
15 The eyes of all look to you in hope;
you give them their food as they need it.
16 When you open your hand,
you satisfy the hunger and thirst of every living thing.
17 The LORD is righteous in everything he does;
he is filled with kindness.
18 The LORD is close to all who call on him,
yes, to all who call on him in truth.
19 He grants the desires of those who fear him;
he hears their cries for help and rescues them.
20 The LORD protects all those who love him,
but he destroys the wicked.

21 I will praise the LORD,
and may everyone on earth bless his holy name forever and ever.

Ps 145:13 The last two lines of 145:13 are not found in many of the ancient manuscripts.

2. PSALMS ATTRIBUTED TO DAVID'S MUSIC LEADERS

These 14 psalms are attributed to people that served under David during his reign. Heman, Ethan, and Asaph were Levites that served as musicians in the worship of the Lord. Some of these psalms might have been written later, by descendants of these prominent Temple servants, but they are placed here chronologically because the psalms name these men as their authors.

Psalm 88

THEME: When there is no relief in sight. God understands even our deepest misery.

AUTHOR: Heman, one of the sons of Korah (possibly the same man mentioned in 1 Chronicles 15:19; 16:41; 25:4-5 as a musician and the king's seer)

For the choir director: A psalm of the descendants of Korah. A song to be sung to the tune "The Suffering of Affliction." A psalm of Heman the Ezrahite.*

1 O LORD, God of my salvation,
I cry out to you by day.
I come to you at night.
2 Now hear my prayer;
listen to my cry.
3 For my life is full of troubles,
and death* draws near.
4 I am as good as dead,
like a strong man with no strength left.
5 They have left me among the dead,
and I lie like a corpse in a grave.
I am forgotten,
cut off from your care.
6 You have thrown me into the lowest pit,
into the darkest depths.
7 Your anger weighs me down;
with wave after wave you have engulfed me. *Interlude*
8 You have driven my friends away
by making me repulsive to them.
I am in a trap with no way of escape.
9 My eyes are blinded by my tears.
Each day I beg for your help, O LORD;
I lift my hands to you for mercy.
10 Are your wonderful deeds of any use
to the dead?
Do the dead rise up and praise you? *Interlude*

Ps 88:TITLE Hebrew *maskil.* This may be a literary or musical term. **Ps 88:3** Hebrew *Sheol.*

Ps 145:14 Sometimes our burdens seem more than we can bear, and we wonder how we can go on. David stands at this bleak intersection of life's road and meditates on the Lord, the great burden bearer. God is able to lift us up because (1) his greatness is beyond discovery (Ps 145:3); (2) he does mighty acts for each generation (Ps 145:4); (3) he is magnificent (Ps 145:5); (4) he does breathtaking deeds (Ps 145:5-6); (5) he is righteous (Ps 145:7); (6) he is kind, merciful, patient, loving, and compassionate (Ps 145:8-9); (7) he rules over a never-ending kingdom (Ps 145:13); (8) he is the source for all our daily needs (Ps 145:15-16); (9) he is righteous and kind in all his dealings (Ps 145:17); (10) he remains near to those who call on him (Ps 145:18); (11) he hears our cries and rescues us (Ps 145:19-20). If you are bending under a burden and feel that you are about to fall, turn to God for help. He is ready to lift you up and bear your burden.

Ps 88:1ff Have you ever felt as though you have hit bottom? The writer is so low that he even despairs of life itself. Although everything is bad and getting worse, he is able to tell it all to God. This is one of the few psalms that gives no answer or expression of hope. Don't think that you must always be cheerful and positive. Grief and depression take time to heal. No matter how low we feel, we can always take our problems to God and express our anguish to him.

Ps 88:5 Our feelings may be as obvious and painful as those expressed by the psalm writer, but they are never the complete picture. In fact, our feelings are usually very unstable. When we bring our unedited feelings to God, we allow him to point out where they are incomplete. We are in trouble whenever we give our feelings divine authority or assume that God can't handle what we feel. Praying the psalms teaches us to bring God everything about us and trains us to experience his presence even when our feelings tell us otherwise.

11 Can those in the grave declare your unfailing
love?
Can they proclaim your faithfulness in the
place of destruction?*
12 Can the darkness speak of your wonderful deeds?
Can anyone in the land of forgetfulness talk
about your righteousness?
13 O LORD, I cry out to you.
I will keep on pleading day by day.
14 O LORD, why do you reject me?
Why do you turn your face from me?
15 I have been sick and close to death since
my youth.
I stand helpless and desperate before your
terrors.
16 Your fierce anger has overwhelmed me.
Your terrors have paralyzed me.
17 They swirl around me like floodwaters all
day long.
They have engulfed me completely.
18 You have taken away my companions and
loved ones.
Darkness is my closest friend.

Psalm 89

THEME: God's promise to preserve David's descendants. God's promise is fulfilled in Jesus Christ, who will reign for eternity. The love and kindness promised to David is ours in Christ.

AUTHOR: Ethan (a Levite leader and possibly one of the head musicians in the Temple, 1 Chronicles 15:17, 19), or one of his descendants

A psalm of Ethan the Ezrahite.*

1 I will sing of the LORD's unfailing love forever!
Young and old will hear of your faithfulness.
2 Your unfailing love will last forever.
Your faithfulness is as enduring as the heavens.

3 The LORD said, "I have made a covenant with
David, my chosen servant.
I have sworn this oath to him:
4 'I will establish your descendants as kings forever;
they will sit on your throne from now until
eternity.'" *Interlude*
5 All heaven will praise your great wonders, LORD;
myriads of angels will praise you for your
faithfulness.
6 For who in all of heaven can compare with the
LORD?
What mightiest angel is anything like the LORD?
7 The highest angelic powers stand in awe of God.
He is far more awesome than all who surround
his throne.
8 O LORD God of Heaven's Armies!
Where is there anyone as mighty as you, O LORD?
You are entirely faithful.
9 You rule the oceans.
You subdue their storm-tossed waves.
10 You crushed the great sea monster.*
You scattered your enemies with your
mighty arm.
11 The heavens are yours, and the earth is yours;
everything in the world is yours—you created
it all.
12 You created north and south.
Mount Tabor and Mount Hermon praise
your name.
13 Powerful is your arm!
Strong is your hand!
Your right hand is lifted high in glorious
strength.
14 Righteousness and justice are the foundation
of your throne.
Unfailing love and truth walk before you as
attendants.
15 Happy are those who hear the joyful call to
worship,
for they will walk in the light of your presence,
LORD.
16 They rejoice all day long in your wonderful
reputation.
They exult in your righteousness.

Ps 88:11 Hebrew *in Abaddon?* **Ps 89:TITLE** Hebrew *maskil.* This may be a literary or musical term. **Ps 89:10** Hebrew *Rahab,* the name of a mythical sea monster that represents chaos in ancient literature.

Ps 88:13-14 The writer of this psalm was close to death, perhaps debilitated by disease, and forsaken by friends; but he could still pray. You might not be so afflicted, but you probably know someone who is. Consider being a prayer companion for that person; this psalm can be a prayer you can lift to God.

Ps 89:1ff This psalm was written to describe the glorious reign of David. God had promised to make David the mightiest king on earth and to keep his descendants on the throne forever (2 Sam 7:8-16). But Jerusalem was destroyed, and kings no longer reign there. So these verses can only look forward, prophetically, to the future reign of Jesus Christ, David's descendant. Psalm 89:27 is a prophecy concerning David's never-ending dynasty, which will reach its fulfillment and highest expression in Christ's future reign over the world (see Rev 22:5).

Ps 89:5-7 In the courts of heaven, a host of angels praise the Lord. This scene is one of majesty and grandeur; God is beyond compare. His power and purity place him high above nature and angels. (For more about angels, see Deut 33:2; Luke 2:13; Heb 12:22.)

Ps 89:12 Mount Tabor, though low in elevation (1,900 feet), was the scene of Deborah's victory in Judges 4. Mount Hermon (9,000 feet) was tall and majestic.

Ps 89:14-15 Righteousness, justice, love, and truth are the foundation of God's throne; they are central characteristics of the way God rules. They summarize his character. As God's ambassadors, we should exhibit the same traits when we deal with people. Make sure your actions flow out of righteousness, justice, love, and faithfulness, because any unfair, unloving, or dishonest action cannot come from God.

▸ **PSALM 89 *(cont.)***

17 You are their glorious strength.
It pleases you to make us strong.
18 Yes, our protection comes from the LORD,
and he, the Holy One of Israel, has given
us our king.

19 Long ago you spoke in a vision to your faithful
people.
You said, "I have raised up a warrior.
I have selected him from the common people
to be king.
20 I have found my servant David.
I have anointed him with my holy oil.
21 I will steady him with my hand;
with my powerful arm I will make him strong.
22 His enemies will not defeat him,
nor will the wicked overpower him.
23 I will beat down his adversaries before him
and destroy those who hate him.
24 My faithfulness and unfailing love will be
with him,
and by my authority he will grow in power.
25 I will extend his rule over the sea,
his dominion over the rivers.
26 And he will call out to me, 'You are my Father,
my God, and the Rock of my salvation.'
27 I will make him my firstborn son,
the mightiest king on earth.
28 I will love him and be kind to him forever;
my covenant with him will never end.
29 I will preserve an heir for him;
his throne will be as endless as the days
of heaven.
30 But if his descendants forsake my instructions
and fail to obey my regulations,
31 if they do not obey my decrees
and fail to keep my commands,
32 then I will punish their sin with the rod,
and their disobedience with beating.
33 But I will never stop loving him
nor fail to keep my promise to him.
34 No, I will not break my covenant;
I will not take back a single word I said.
35 I have sworn an oath to David,
and in my holiness I cannot lie:
36 His dynasty will go on forever;
his kingdom will endure as the sun.
37 It will be as eternal as the moon,
my faithful witness in the sky!" *Interlude*

38 But now you have rejected him and cast him off.
You are angry with your anointed king.
39 You have renounced your covenant with him;
you have thrown his crown in the dust.
40 You have broken down the walls protecting him
and ruined every fort defending him.
41 Everyone who comes along has robbed him,
and he has become a joke to his neighbors.
42 You have strengthened his enemies
and made them all rejoice.
43 You have made his sword useless
and refused to help him in battle.
44 You have ended his splendor
and overturned his throne.
45 You have made him old before his time
and publicly disgraced him. *Interlude*

46 O LORD, how long will this go on?
Will you hide yourself forever?
How long will your anger burn like fire?
47 Remember how short my life is,
how empty and futile this human existence!
48 No one can live forever; all will die.
No one can escape the power of the grave.*
Interlude

49 Lord, where is your unfailing love?
You promised it to David with a faithful
pledge.
50 Consider, Lord, how your servants are disgraced!
I carry in my heart the insults of so many
people.
51 Your enemies have mocked me, O LORD;
they mock your anointed king wherever he
goes.

52 Praise the LORD forever!
Amen and amen!

Ps 89:48 Hebrew *of Sheol.*

Ps 89:17, 24 David is promised to have God's power to accomplish God's will. Without God's help, we are weak and powerless, inadequate for even the simplest spiritual tasks. But when we are filled with God's Spirit, his power flows through us and our accomplishments will exceed our expectations.

Ps 89:34-37 In light of Israel's continual disobedience throughout history, this is an amazing promise. God promised that David's descendants would always sit on the throne (Ps 89:29), but that if the people disobeyed, they would be punished (Ps 89:30-32). Yet, even through their disobedience and punishment, God would never break faith with them (Ps 89:33). Israel did disobey, evil ran rampant, the nation was divided, exile came—but through it all, a remnant of God's people remained faithful. Centuries later, the Messiah arrived, the eternal King from David's line, just as God had promised. All that God promises, he fulfills. He will not take back even one word of what he says. God can also be trusted to save us as he promised he would (Heb 6:13-18). God is completely reliable.

Ps 50:1ff God judges people for treating him lightly. First, he speaks to the superficially religious people who bring their sacrifices but are only going through the motions (Ps 50:1-15). They do not honor God with true praise and thankfulness. Second, he chides wicked, hard-hearted people for their evil words and immoral lives (Ps 50:16-22). He asks the superficially religious for genuine thanksgiving and trust, and he warns the evil people to consider their deeds, lest he destroy them in his anger.

Ps 50:1-4 Asaph begins his psalm by describing God's final judgment of people on earth. Surprisingly, we read that God's great fury is leveled against his own people (or at

Psalm 50

THEME: The contrast between true and false faith. God desires sincere thanks, trust, and praise.

AUTHOR: Asaph, one of David's chief musicians

A psalm of Asaph.

1 The LORD, the Mighty One, is God,
and he has spoken;
he has summoned all humanity
from where the sun rises to where it sets.
2 From Mount Zion, the perfection of beauty,
God shines in glorious radiance.
3 Our God approaches,
and he is not silent.
Fire devours everything in his way,
and a great storm rages around him.
4 He calls on the heavens above and earth below
to witness the judgment of his people.
5 "Bring my faithful people to me—
those who made a covenant with me by giving sacrifices."
6 Then let the heavens proclaim his justice,
for God himself will be the judge. *Interlude*
7 "O my people, listen as I speak.
Here are my charges against you, O Israel:
I am God, your God!
8 I have no complaint about your sacrifices
or the burnt offerings you constantly offer.
9 But I do not need the bulls from your barns
or the goats from your pens.
10 For all the animals of the forest are mine,
and I own the cattle on a thousand hills.
11 I know every bird on the mountains,
and all the animals of the field are mine.
12 If I were hungry, I would not tell you,
for all the world is mine and everything in it.
13 Do I eat the meat of bulls?
Do I drink the blood of goats?
14 Make thankfulness your sacrifice to God,
and keep the vows you made to the Most High.
15 Then call on me when you are in trouble,
and I will rescue you,
and you will give me glory."
16 But God says to the wicked:
"Why bother reciting my decrees
and pretending to obey my covenant?
17 For you refuse my discipline
and treat my words like trash.
18 When you see thieves, you approve of them,
and you spend your time with adulterers.
19 Your mouth is filled with wickedness,
and your tongue is full of lies.
20 You sit around and slander your brother—
your own mother's son.
21 While you did all this, I remained silent,
and you thought I didn't care.
But now I will rebuke you,
listing all my charges against you.
22 Repent, all of you who forget me,
or I will tear you apart,
and no one will help you.
23 But giving thanks is a sacrifice that truly honors me.
If you keep to my path,
I will reveal to you the salvation of God."

Psalm 73

THEME: The temporary prosperity of the wicked and the lasting rewards of the righteous. We should live holy lives and trust God for our future rewards.

AUTHOR: Asaph, a leader of one of the Temple choirs (see 1 Chronicles 25:1, p. 536)

A psalm of Asaph.

1 Truly God is good to Israel,
to those whose hearts are pure.

---

least those who claim to be his). God's judgment must first begin with his own children (1 Pet 4:17).

Ps 50:5-9 God's perfect moral nature demands that the penalty for sin be death; however, people could offer an animal to God as a substitute for their own lives, symbolizing their faith in the merciful, forgiving God. But the people were offering sacrifices and forgetting their significance! The very act of sacrifice showed that they had once agreed to follow God wholeheartedly. But at this time their hearts were not in it. We may fall into the same pattern when we participate in religious activities, tithe, or attend church out of habit or conformity rather than out of heartfelt love and obedience. God wants righteousness, not empty ritual. (See the note on Ps 40:6, p. 570.)

Ps 50:16-22 Some people glibly recite God's laws but are filled with deceit and evil. They claim his promises but refuse to obey him. This is sin, and God will judge people for it. We, too, are hypocrites when we are not what we claim to be. To let this inconsistency remain shows that we are not true followers of God.

Ps 50:21 Just because God is silent does not mean he is condoning sin or is indifferent to it. Instead, he is withholding deserved punishment, giving time for people to repent (2 Pet 3:9). God takes no pleasure in the death of the wicked and wants them to turn from evil (Ezek 33:11). But his silence does not last forever—a time of punishment will surely come.

Ps 73:1ff Asaph was the leader of one of David's levitical choirs. He collected Psalms 73–83 but may not have written all of them. In this psalm, Asaph explains that until he entered God's sanctuary he could not understand the justice in allowing the wicked to thrive while the righteous endured hardship. But when he saw that one day justice would be done, he acknowledged God's wisdom.

Ps 73:1-20 Two strong themes wind their way through these verses: (1) The wicked prosper, leaving godly people wondering why they bother to be good, and (2) the wealth of the wicked looks so inviting that faithful people may wish they could trade places. But these two themes come to unexpected ends, for the wealth of the wicked suddenly loses its power at death, and the rewards for the godly suddenly take on eternal value. What seemed like wealth is now waste, and what seemed worthless now lasts forever. Don't wish you could trade places with evil people to get their wealth. One day they will wish they could trade places with you and have your eternal life.

▸ **PSALM 73** ***(cont.)***

2 But as for me, I almost lost my footing.
My feet were slipping, and I was almost gone.
3 For I envied the proud
when I saw them prosper despite their wickedness.
4 They seem to live such painless lives;
their bodies are so healthy and strong.
5 They don't have troubles like other people;
they're not plagued with problems like everyone else.
6 They wear pride like a jeweled necklace
and clothe themselves with cruelty.
7 These fat cats have everything
their hearts could ever wish for!
8 They scoff and speak only evil;
in their pride they seek to crush others.
9 They boast against the very heavens,
and their words strut throughout the earth.
10 And so the people are dismayed and confused,
drinking in all their words.
11 "What does God know?" they ask.
"Does the Most High even know what's happening?"
12 Look at these wicked people—
enjoying a life of ease while their riches multiply.
13 Did I keep my heart pure for nothing?
Did I keep myself innocent for no reason?
14 I get nothing but trouble all day long;
every morning brings me pain.

15 If I had really spoken this way to others,
I would have been a traitor to your people.
16 So I tried to understand why the wicked prosper.
But what a difficult task it is!
17 Then I went into your sanctuary, O God,
and I finally understood the destiny of the wicked.
18 Truly, you put them on a slippery path
and send them sliding over the cliff to destruction.
19 In an instant they are destroyed,
completely swept away by terrors.
20 When you arise, O Lord,
you will laugh at their silly ideas
as a person laughs at dreams in the morning.

21 Then I realized that my heart was bitter,
and I was all torn up inside.
22 I was so foolish and ignorant—
I must have seemed like a senseless animal to you.
23 Yet I still belong to you;
you hold my right hand.
24 You guide me with your counsel,
leading me to a glorious destiny.
25 Whom have I in heaven but you?
I desire you more than anything on earth.
26 My health may fail, and my spirit may grow weak,
but God remains the strength of my heart;
he is mine forever.

27 Those who desert him will perish,
for you destroy those who abandon you.
28 But as for me, how good it is to be near God!
I have made the Sovereign LORD my shelter,
and I will tell everyone about the wonderful things you do.

These fat cats have everything their hearts could ever wish for!
Psalm 73:7

Ps 73:20 Asaph realizes that the rich who put their hope, joy, and confidence in their wealth live in a dream world. A dream exists only in the mind of the dreamer. Don't let your life's goals be so unreal that you awaken too late and miss the reality of God's truth. Happiness and hope can be a reality, but only when they are based on God, not on riches. Because reality is in God, we should get as close to him as we can in order to be realistic about life.

Ps 73:23-24 Asaph declares his confidence in God's presence and guidance. From birth to death, we are continually in God's grip. But far more, we have the hope of the resurrection of the dead. Though our courage and strength may fail, we know that one day we will be raised to life to serve him forever. He is our security, and we must cling to him.

Psalm 74

THEME: A plea for God to help his people defend his cause and remember his promises. When we feel devastated or forgotten, we can ask God for help, knowing that he hears.

AUTHOR: Asaph (or one of his descendants, since many believe this to have been written after Jerusalem's fall in 586 B.C.)

A psalm of Asaph.*

1 O God, why have you rejected us so long?
Why is your anger so intense against the sheep
of your own pasture?
2 Remember that we are the people you chose
long ago,
the tribe you redeemed as your own special
possession!
And remember Jerusalem,* your home here
on earth.
3 Walk through the awful ruins of the city;
see how the enemy has destroyed your
sanctuary.

4 There your enemies shouted their victorious
battle cries;
there they set up their battle standards.
5 They swung their axes
like woodcutters in a forest.
6 With axes and picks,
they smashed the carved paneling.
7 They burned your sanctuary to the ground.
They defiled the place that bears your name.
8 Then they thought, "Let's destroy everything!"
So they burned down all the places where God
was worshiped.

9 We no longer see your miraculous signs.
All the prophets are gone,
and no one can tell us when it will end.
10 How long, O God, will you allow our enemies
to insult you?
Will you let them dishonor your name forever?
11 Why do you hold back your strong right hand?
Unleash your powerful fist and destroy them.

12 You, O God, are my king from ages past,
bringing salvation to the earth.
13 You split the sea by your strength
and smashed the heads of the sea monsters.
14 You crushed the heads of Leviathan*
and let the desert animals eat him.
15 You caused the springs and streams to gush forth,
and you dried up rivers that never run dry.
16 Both day and night belong to you;
you made the starlight* and the sun.
17 You set the boundaries of the earth,
and you made both summer and winter.

18 See how these enemies insult you, LORD.
A foolish nation has dishonored your name.
19 Don't let these wild beasts destroy your
turtledoves.
Don't forget your suffering people forever.

20 Remember your covenant promises,
for the land is full of darkness and violence!
21 Don't let the downtrodden be humiliated again.
Instead, let the poor and needy praise
your name.

22 Arise, O God, and defend your cause.
Remember how these fools insult you
all day long.
23 Don't overlook what your enemies have said
or their growing uproar.

Psalm 75

THEME: Because God is the final judge, the tables will be turned upon the wicked. When arrogant people threaten our security, we can be confident that God will ultimately overrule and destroy them.

AUTHOR: Asaph

For the choir director: A psalm of Asaph. A song to be sung to the tune "Do Not Destroy!"

1 We thank you, O God!
We give thanks because you are near.
People everywhere tell of your wonderful
deeds.

Ps 74:TITLE Hebrew *maskil.* This may be a literary or musical term. **Ps 74:2** Hebrew *Mount Zion.* **Ps 74:14** The identification of Leviathan is disputed, ranging from an earthly creature to a mythical sea monster in ancient literature. **Ps 74:16** Or *moon;* Hebrew reads *light.*

Ps 74:1-2 God's anger against Israel had grown hot during the many years of their sin and idolatry. His patience endured for generations, but at last it was set aside for judgment. If you fall into sin but quickly seek God's forgiveness, his mercy may come quickly and his anger may leave quickly. If you persist in sinning against him, don't be surprised when his patience runs out.

Ps 74:8 When enemy armies defeated Israel, they sacked and burned Jerusalem, trying to wipe out every trace of God. This has often been the response of people who hate God. Today many are trying to eliminate God from our public life entirely. Do what you can to maintain a Christian influence, but don't become discouraged when others appear to make great strides in removing all traces of God. They cannot eliminate his presence among believers.

Ps 74:10-18 From our perspective, God sometimes seems slow to intervene on our behalf. But what might appear slow to us is good timing from God's perspective. It's easy to become impatient while waiting for God to act, but we must never give up on him. When God is silent and you are in deep anguish, follow the method in this psalm. Review the great acts of God throughout biblical history; then review what he has done for you. This will remind you that God is at work, not only in history but also in your life today.

Ps 74:13-14 "The sea monsters" recalls the Lord's words to Egypt (Ezek 32:2ff). "Leviathan" refers to the Canaanite seven-headed serpent, Lotan. In their legends, Baal defeated these creatures. This psalm praises God for doing in reality what the Canaanite gods could only do in legends.

▸ **PSALM 75 *(cont.)***

2 God says, "At the time I have planned,
I will bring justice against the wicked.
3 When the earth quakes and its people live in turmoil,
I am the one who keeps its foundations firm. *Interlude*

4 "I warned the proud, 'Stop your boasting!'
I told the wicked, 'Don't raise your fists!
5 Don't raise your fists in defiance at the heavens
or speak with such arrogance.'"
6 For no one on earth—from east or west,
or even from the wilderness—
should raise a defiant fist.*
7 It is God alone who judges;
he decides who will rise and who will fall.
8 For the LORD holds a cup in his hand
that is full of foaming wine mixed with spices.
He pours out the wine in judgment,
and all the wicked must drink it,
draining it to the dregs.

9 But as for me, I will always proclaim what God has done;
I will sing praises to the God of Jacob.
10 For God says, "I will break the strength of the wicked,
but I will increase the power of the godly."

Psalm 76

THEME: A call for God to punish evildoers. Even people's angry revolts will be used by God to bring glory to himself.

AUTHOR: Asaph

For the choir director: A psalm of Asaph. A song to be accompanied by stringed instruments.

1 God is honored in Judah;
his name is great in Israel.
2 Jerusalem* is where he lives;
Mount Zion is his home.
3 There he has broken the fiery arrows of the enemy,
the shields and swords and weapons of war. *Interlude*

4 You are glorious and more majestic
than the everlasting mountains.*
5 Our boldest enemies have been plundered.
They lie before us in the sleep of death.
No warrior could lift a hand against us.
6 At the blast of your breath, O God of Jacob,
their horses and chariots lay still.

7 No wonder you are greatly feared!
Who can stand before you when your anger explodes?
8 From heaven you sentenced your enemies;
the earth trembled and stood silent before you.

Ps 75:6 Hebrew *should lift.* **Ps 76:2** Hebrew *Salem,* another name for Jerusalem. **Ps 76:4** As in Greek version; Hebrew reads *than mountains filled with beasts of prey.*

Horses

Horses were used in war not only for riding but also for pulling the heavy, springless war chariots. Two kinds of horses were needed for these different purposes, and the Hebrews distinguished between chariot horses and cavalry horses. The Lord warned the early Israelites against amassing military strength in the form of horses, but the demands of war caused both David and Solomon to import horses from Egypt into their kingdoms and to breed them in violation of God's command. In early Israel, using horses was opposed because it symbolized dependence on physical power for defense. Psalm 20:7 is indicative of this: "Some nations boast of their chariots and horses, but we boast in the name of the LORD our God." Psalm 76:6 reinforces this idea, proclaiming the power of the Lord over the military strength of other nations. Whose power are you depending on?

Ps 75:2 God will act when he is ready. Children have difficulty grasping the concept of time. "It's not time yet" is not a reason they easily understand because they only comprehend the present. As limited human beings, we can't understand God's perspective about time. We want everything now, unaware that God's timing is better. When God is ready, he will do what needs to be done, not what we would like him to do. We may be as impatient as children, but we must not doubt the wisdom of God's timing. Wait for God to reveal his plan. Don't take matters into your own hands.

Ps 75:8 The cup of wine represents God's judgment that is coming against the wicked. God will pour out his fury on his enemies, and they will be forced to drink it. Drinking the cup of God's judgment is a picture used frequently in Scripture (Isa 51:17, 22; Jer 25:15; 49:12; Hab 2:16; Rev 14:10; 16:19; 18:6). It gives the impression of taking a dose of one's own medicine. To drink it down "to the dregs" means to be punished completely.

Ps 75:10 God will have the last word. He will decide the final outcome, settling all matters that concern both the wicked and the godly. The former will eventually experience his judgment; the latter will experience his faithful love. No matter how dark the days you face, make it your continual practice to acknowledge God's sovereignty over your world. Tell him regularly how grateful you are that he has the final word.

9 You stand up to judge those who do evil, O God,
and to rescue the oppressed of the earth.
Interlude
10 Human defiance only enhances your glory,
for you use it as a weapon.*
11 Make vows to the LORD your God, and
keep them.
Let everyone bring tribute to the
Awesome One.
12 For he breaks the pride of princes,
and the kings of the earth fear him.

Psalm 77

THEME: We are comforted through the hard times by remembering God's help in the past. Recalling God's miracles and previous works can give us courage to continue.

AUTHOR: Asaph

For Jeduthun, the choir director: A psalm of Asaph.

1 I cry out to God; yes, I shout.
Oh, that God would listen to me!
2 When I was in deep trouble,
I searched for the Lord.
All night long I prayed, with hands lifted toward
heaven,
but my soul was not comforted.
3 I think of God, and I moan,
overwhelmed with longing for his help.
Interlude
4 You don't let me sleep.
I am too distressed even to pray!
5 I think of the good old days,
long since ended,
6 when my nights were filled with joyful songs.
I search my soul and ponder the
difference now.
7 Has the Lord rejected me forever?
Will he never again be kind to me?
8 Is his unfailing love gone forever?
Have his promises permanently failed?
9 Has God forgotten to be gracious?
Has he slammed the door on his
compassion? *Interlude*
10 And I said, "This is my fate;
the Most High has turned his hand
against me."
11 But then I recall all you have done, O LORD;
I remember your wonderful deeds of
long ago.
12 They are constantly in my thoughts.
I cannot stop thinking about your mighty
works.
13 O God, your ways are holy.
Is there any god as mighty as you?
14 You are the God of great wonders!
You demonstrate your awesome power
among the nations.
15 By your strong arm, you redeemed your
people,
the descendants of Jacob and Joseph.
Interlude
16 When the Red Sea* saw you, O God,
its waters looked and trembled!
The sea quaked to its very depths.
17 The clouds poured down rain;
the thunder rumbled in the sky.
Your arrows of lightning flashed.
18 Your thunder roared from the whirlwind;
the lightning lit up the world!
The earth trembled and shook.
19 Your road led through the sea,
your pathway through the mighty waters—
a pathway no one knew was there!
20 You led your people along that road like a flock
of sheep,
with Moses and Aaron as their shepherds.

Ps 76:10 The meaning of the Hebrew is uncertain. **Ps 77:16** Hebrew *the waters.*

Ps 76:10 How can defiance bring glory to God? Hostility to God and his people gives God the opportunity to do great deeds. For example, the pharaoh of Egypt refused to free the Hebrew slaves (Exod 5:1-2) and thus allowed God to work mighty miracles for his people (Exod 11:9). God turns the tables on evildoers and brings glory to himself from the foolishness of those who deny him or revolt against him. God's wrath expressed in judgment brings praise from those who have been delivered.

Ps 76:11-12 This psalm closes with an invitation to the reader or listener. Having stated the futility of resisting God, the writer shifts to the alternatives. These verses speak of more than surrender to God; they encourage us to actively move toward God, making commitments (vows) to him and carrying them out. What was the last promise you made to God? How much progress have you made in fulfilling it?

Ps 77:1ff Asaph cried out to God for courage during a time of deep distress. The source of his distress (Ps 77:4) was his doubt (Ps 77:7-9). But Asaph's perspective changed (Ps 77:11) and in a few moments (Ps 77:13-20), the "I" was gone. As Asaph expressed his requests to God, his focus changed from thinking of himself to worshiping God: "You are the God of great wonders!" (Ps 77:14). Only after he put aside his doubts about God's holiness and care for him (Ps 77:13-14) did he eliminate his distress (Ps 77:20). As we pray to God, he shifts our focus from ourselves to him.

Ps 77:11-12 Memories of God's miracles and faithfulness sustained Israel through their difficulties. They knew that God was capable and trustworthy. When you meet new trials, review how good God has been to you, and this will strengthen your faith.

Ps 77:16-20 These verses refer to the miraculous parting of the Red Sea. This great event is mentioned many times in the Old Testament (Exod 14:21-22; Josh 24:6; Neh 9:9; Pss 74:13; 106:9; 136:13-15). The story of this incredible miracle was handed down from generation to generation, continually reminding the Israelites of God's power, protection, and love.

Psalm 78

THEME: Lessons from history. Asaph retells the history of the Jewish nation from the time of slavery in Egypt to David's reign. It was told over and over to each generation so they would not forget God and make the same mistakes as their ancestors.

AUTHOR: Asaph

A psalm of Asaph.*

1 O my people, listen to my instructions.
Open your ears to what I am saying,
2 for I will speak to you in a parable.
I will teach you hidden lessons from our past—
3 stories we have heard and known,
stories our ancestors handed down to us.
4 We will not hide these truths from our children;
we will tell the next generation
about the glorious deeds of the LORD,
about his power and his mighty wonders.
5 For he issued his laws to Jacob;
he gave his instructions to Israel.
He commanded our ancestors
to teach them to their children,
6 so the next generation might know them—
even the children not yet born—
and they in turn will teach their own children.
7 So each generation should set its hope anew
on God,
not forgetting his glorious miracles
and obeying his commands.
8 Then they will not be like their ancestors—
stubborn, rebellious, and unfaithful,
refusing to give their hearts to God.

9 The warriors of Ephraim, though armed
with bows,
turned their backs and fled on the day of battle.
10 They did not keep God's covenant
and refused to live by his instructions.
11 They forgot what he had done—
the great wonders he had shown them,
12 the miracles he did for their ancestors
on the plain of Zoan in the land of Egypt.
13 For he divided the sea and led them through,
making the water stand up like walls!
14 In the daytime he led them by a cloud,
and all night by a pillar of fire.
15 He split open the rocks in the wilderness
to give them water, as from a gushing spring.
16 He made streams pour from the rock,
making the waters flow down like a river!

17 Yet they kept on sinning against him,
rebelling against the Most High in the desert.
18 They stubbornly tested God in their hearts,
demanding the foods they craved.
19 They even spoke against God himself, saying,
"God can't give us food in the wilderness.
20 Yes, he can strike a rock so water gushes out,
but he can't give his people bread and meat."
21 When the LORD heard them, he was furious.
The fire of his wrath burned against Jacob.
Yes, his anger rose against Israel,
22 for they did not believe God
or trust him to care for them.
23 But he commanded the skies to open;
he opened the doors of heaven.
24 He rained down manna for them to eat;
he gave them bread from heaven.
25 They ate the food of angels!
God gave them all they could hold.
26 He released the east wind in the heavens
and guided the south wind by his mighty
power.
27 He rained down meat as thick as dust—
birds as plentiful as the sand on the
seashore!
28 He caused the birds to fall within their camp
and all around their tents.
29 The people ate their fill.
He gave them what they craved.
30 But before they satisfied their craving,
while the meat was yet in their mouths,
31 the anger of God rose against them,
and he killed their strongest men.
He struck down the finest of Israel's
young men.

Ps 78:TITLE Hebrew *maskil.* This may be a literary or musical term.

Ps 78:1ff The people of Israel rebelled and were not faithful to God (Ps 78:8). They forgot about the miracles God had done (Ps 78:11-12) and put God to the test by making demands of him (Ps 78:18). They lied to him, tried to flatter him (Ps 78:36), and continued to turn away from him even after he did great works on their behalf (Ps 78:42-56). God recorded these painful and shameful truths in his Word so that we can avoid the same errors. In 1 Corinthians 10:5-12, Paul used this classic story of Israel's unfaithfulness to warn the early Christians to be faithful.

Ps 78:5 God commanded that the stories of his mighty acts in Israel's history and his laws be passed on from parents to children. This shows the purpose and importance of religious education: to help each generation obey God and set its hope on him. It is important to keep children from repeating the same mistakes as their ancestors. What are you doing to pass on the history of God's work to the next generation?

Ps 78:9-10 Ephraim was the most prominent tribe of Israel from the days of Moses to Saul's time. The Tabernacle was set up in its territory. There is no biblical record of Ephraim's soldiers turning back from battle, so this is probably a metaphor referring to Ephraim's failure to provide strong leadership during those years. When David became king, the tribe of Judah gained prominence. Because of David's faith and obedience, God chose Jerusalem in Judah to be the place for the new Temple and rejected Ephraim (Ps 78:67). This caused tension between the two tribes. This psalm may have been written because of that tension in order to demonstrate once again why God chose Judah. God works through those who are faithful to him.

32 But in spite of this, the people kept sinning.
Despite his wonders, they refused to trust him.
33 So he ended their lives in failure,
their years in terror.
34 When God began killing them,
they finally sought him.
They repented and took God seriously.
35 Then they remembered that God was their rock,
that God Most High* was their redeemer.
36 But all they gave him was lip service;
they lied to him with their tongues.
37 Their hearts were not loyal to him.
They did not keep his covenant.
38 Yet he was merciful and forgave their sins
and did not destroy them all.
Many times he held back his anger
and did not unleash his fury!
39 For he remembered that they were merely
mortal,
gone like a breath of wind that never returns.
40 Oh, how often they rebelled against him in the
wilderness
and grieved his heart in that dry wasteland.
41 Again and again they tested God's patience
and provoked the Holy One of Israel.
42 They did not remember his power
and how he rescued them from their
enemies.
43 They did not remember his miraculous signs
in Egypt,
his wonders on the plain of Zoan.
44 For he turned their rivers into blood,
so no one could drink from the streams.
45 He sent vast swarms of flies to consume them
and hordes of frogs to ruin them.
46 He gave their crops to caterpillars;
their harvest was consumed by locusts.
47 He destroyed their grapevines with hail
and shattered their sycamore-figs with sleet.
48 He abandoned their cattle to the hail,
their livestock to bolts of lightning.
49 He loosed on them his fierce anger—
all his fury, rage, and hostility.
He dispatched against them
a band of destroying angels.
50 He turned his anger against them;
he did not spare the Egyptians' lives
but ravaged them with the plague.
51 He killed the oldest son in each Egyptian
family,
the flower of youth throughout the land
of Egypt.*
52 But he led his own people like a flock of sheep,
guiding them safely through the wilderness.
53 He kept them safe so they were not afraid;
but the sea covered their enemies.
54 He brought them to the border of his holy land,
to this land of hills he had won for them.
55 He drove out the nations before them;
he gave them their inheritance by lot.
He settled the tribes of Israel into their homes.
56 But they kept testing and rebelling against God
Most High.
They did not obey his laws.
57 They turned back and were as faithless as their
parents.
They were as undependable as a crooked bow.
58 They angered God by building shrines to
other gods;
they made him jealous with their idols.
59 When God heard them, he was very angry,
and he completely rejected Israel.
60 Then he abandoned his dwelling at Shiloh,
the Tabernacle where he had lived among
the people.
61 He allowed the Ark of his might to be captured;
he surrendered his glory into enemy hands.
62 He gave his people over to be butchered by
the sword,
because he was so angry with his own people—
his special possession.
63 Their young men were killed by fire;
their young women died before singing their
wedding songs.
64 Their priests were slaughtered,
and their widows could not mourn their deaths.
65 Then the Lord rose up as though waking
from sleep,
like a warrior aroused from a drunken stupor.
66 He routed his enemies
and sent them to eternal shame.
67 But he rejected Joseph's descendants;
he did not choose the tribe of Ephraim.
68 He chose instead the tribe of Judah,
and Mount Zion, which he loved.

Ps 78:35 Hebrew *El-Elyon.* **Ps 78:51** Hebrew *in the tents of Ham.*

Ps 78:36-37 Over and over the children of Israel claimed that they would follow God, but then they turned away from him. The problem was that they made commitments to God with their mouths and not with their hearts; thus, their repentance was empty. Talk is cheap. God wants our conduct to back up our spiritual claims and promises.

Ps 78:58 Can God be jealous? According to Scripture, yes (see Deut 4:24; 5:9; Nah 1:2). Like everything else about God, his jealousy is perfect. In this case, the offense caused by the ungratefulness and unfaithfulness of his people provoked a just and holy response from God. The shock conveyed in these verses comes not from God's jealousy but from the fact that God, though justified in passing absolute judgment, persistently seasons his responses with grace and patience. God's jealousy over you represents an honor worthy of your deepest gratitude.

▸ **PSALM 78 *(cont.)***

69 There he built his sanctuary as high as the
heavens,
as solid and enduring as the earth.
70 He chose his servant David,
calling him from the sheep pens.
71 He took David from tending the ewes and lambs
and made him the shepherd of Jacob's
descendants—
God's own people, Israel.
72 He cared for them with a true heart
and led them with skillful hands.

Psalm 79

THEME: When outraged by injustice, cry out to God, not against him. In times of disaster, our mood may be anger, but our trust must remain in God.

AUTHOR: Asaph (or one of his descendants), possibly written after the Babylonians had leveled Jerusalem (see 2 Kings 25, p. 1072)

A psalm of Asaph.

1 O God, pagan nations have conquered your land,
your special possession.
They have defiled your holy Temple
and made Jerusalem a heap of ruins.
2 They have left the bodies of your servants
as food for the birds of heaven.
The flesh of your godly ones
has become food for the wild animals.
3 Blood has flowed like water all around
Jerusalem;
no one is left to bury the dead.
4 We are mocked by our neighbors,
an object of scorn and derision to those
around us.
5 O LORD, how long will you be angry with us?
Forever?
How long will your jealousy burn like fire?
6 Pour out your wrath on the nations that refuse
to acknowledge you—
on kingdoms that do not call upon your name.
7 For they have devoured your people Israel,*
making the land a desolate wilderness.
8 Do not hold us guilty for the sins of our ancestors!
Let your compassion quickly meet our needs,
for we are on the brink of despair.

9 Help us, O God of our salvation!
Help us for the glory of your name.
Save us and forgive our sins
for the honor of your name.
10 Why should pagan nations be allowed to scoff,
asking, "Where is their God?"
Show us your vengeance against the nations,
for they have spilled the blood of your servants.
11 Listen to the moaning of the prisoners.
Demonstrate your great power by saving those
condemned to die.

12 O Lord, pay back our neighbors seven times
for the scorn they have hurled at you.
13 Then we your people, the sheep of your pasture,
will thank you forever and ever,
praising your greatness from generation
to generation.

Psalm 80

THEME: A prayer for revival and restoration after experiencing destruction. God is our only hope for salvation.

AUTHOR: Asaph (or one of his descendants), possibly written after the northern kingdom of Israel was defeated and its people deported to Assyria.

For the choir director: A psalm of Asaph, to be sung to the tune "Lilies of the Covenant."

1 Please listen, O Shepherd of Israel,
you who lead Joseph's descendants like
a flock.
O God, enthroned above the cherubim,
display your radiant glory
2 to Ephraim, Benjamin, and Manasseh.
Show us your mighty power.
Come to rescue us!

Ps 79:7 Hebrew *devoured Jacob.* See note on 44:4.

Ps 78:71-72 Although David was occupying the throne of Israel when this psalm was written, he is called a shepherd and not a king. Shepherding, a common profession in biblical times, was a highly responsible job. The flocks were completely dependent upon shepherds for guidance, provision, and protection. David had spent his early years as a shepherd (1 Sam 16:10-11). This was a training ground for the future responsibilities God had in store for him. When he was ready, God took him from caring for sheep to caring for Israel, God's people. Don't treat your present situation lightly or irresponsibly; it may be God's training ground for your future.

Ps 79:6 According to the Old Testament, God's wrath and judgment often fell on entire nations because of the sins of people within those nations. Here Asaph pleaded for judgment on kingdoms that refused to acknowledge God's authority. Ironically, Asaph's own nation of Judah would be judged by God for refusing to do this very thing (2 Chr 36:14-20). These were people who had sworn allegiance to God but rejected him. This made their judgment even worse.

Ps 79:10 In the end, God's glory will be evident to all people; but in the meantime, we must endure suffering with patience and allow God to strengthen our character through it. For reasons that we do not know, God sometimes allows pagan people to scoff at believers. We should be prepared for criticism, jokes, and unkind remarks because God does not place us beyond the attacks of scoffers.

Ps 80:1 Cherubim are mighty angels. That God is "enthroned above the cherubim" is a reminder of his presence on the Ark of the Covenant (Exod 25:17-22).

3 Turn us again to yourself, O God.
Make your face shine down upon us.
Only then will we be saved.
4 O LORD God of Heaven's Armies,
how long will you be angry with our prayers?
5 You have fed us with sorrow
and made us drink tears by the bucketful.
6 You have made us the scorn* of neighboring nations.
Our enemies treat us as a joke.

7 Turn us again to yourself, O God of Heaven's Armies.
Make your face shine down upon us.
Only then will we be saved.
8 You brought us from Egypt like a grapevine;
you drove away the pagan nations and transplanted us into your land.
9 You cleared the ground for us,
and we took root and filled the land.
10 Our shade covered the mountains;
our branches covered the mighty cedars.
11 We spread our branches west to the Mediterranean Sea;
our shoots spread east to the Euphrates River.*
12 But now, why have you broken down our walls
so that all who pass by may steal our fruit?
13 The wild boar from the forest devours it,
and the wild animals feed on it.

14 Come back, we beg you, O God of Heaven's Armies.
Look down from heaven and see our plight.
Take care of this grapevine
15 that you yourself have planted,
this son you have raised for yourself.
16 For we are chopped up and burned by our enemies.
May they perish at the sight of your frown.
17 Strengthen the man you love,
the son of your choice.
18 Then we will never abandon you again.
Revive us so we can call on your name once more.

19 Turn us again to yourself, O LORD God of Heaven's Armies.
Make your face shine down upon us.
Only then will we be saved.

Ps 80:6 As in Syriac version; Hebrew reads *the strife.* **Ps 80:11** Hebrew *west to the sea, . . . east to the river.*

PRAYER IN THE BOOK OF PSALMS

Prayer is human communication with God. Psalms could be described as a collection of song-prayers. Probably the most striking feature of these prayers is their unedited honesty. The words often express our own feelings—feelings that we would prefer no one, much less God, ever knew. Making these psalms our prayers can teach us a great deal about how God wants us to communicate with him. Too often we give God a watered-down version of our feelings, hoping we won't offend him or make him curious about our motives. As we use the psalms to express our feelings, we learn that honesty, openness, and sincerity are valuable to God.

Following are several types of prayers with examples from Psalms. Note that the psalm writers communicated with God in a variety of ways for a variety of reasons. Each of us is invited to communicate with God. Using the psalms will enrich your personal prayer life.

Prayers of:	*Psalms:*
Praise to God	100; 113; 117
Thanksgiving by a community	67; 75; 136
Thanksgiving by an individual	18; 30; 32
Request by the community	79; 80; 123
Request by an individual	3; 55; 86
Sorrow by the community	44; 74; 137
Sorrow by an individual	5; 6; 120
Anger	35; 109; 140
Confession	6; 32; 51
Faith	11; 16; 23

Ps 80:3, 7 Twice the writer calls on God to "turn us again to yourself." Repentance involves humbling ourselves and turning to God to receive his forgiveness. As we turn to God, he helps us see ourselves, including our sin, more clearly, and we see our need to repent and be forgiven. This is how we can be continually restored to and maintain fellowship with God.

Ps 80:17 "The son of your choice" is probably not the Messiah but Israel, whom God calls elsewhere his "firstborn son" (Exod 4:22). The psalm writer is making a plea that God would restore his mercy to Israel, the people he chose to bring his message into the world.

Psalm 81

THEME: A holiday hymn. This hymn celebrates the Exodus from Egypt—God's goodness versus Israel's waywardness. God is our deliverer in spite of our wanderings.

AUTHOR: Asaph, probably written to be used during the Festival of Shelters

*For the choir director: A psalm of Asaph, to be accompanied by a stringed instrument.**

1 Sing praises to God, our strength.
Sing to the God of Jacob.
2 Sing! Beat the tambourine.
Play the sweet lyre and the harp.
3 Blow the ram's horn at new moon,
and again at full moon to call a festival!
4 For this is required by the decrees of
Israel;
it is a regulation of the God of Jacob.
5 He made it a law for Israel*
when he attacked Egypt to set us free.

I heard an unknown voice say,
6 "Now I will take the load from your shoulders;
I will free your hands from their
heavy tasks.
7 You cried to me in trouble, and I saved you;
I answered out of the thundercloud
and tested your faith when there was
no water at Meribah. *Interlude*

8 "Listen to me, O my people, while I give you
stern warnings.
O Israel, if you would only listen to me!
9 You must never have a foreign god;
you must not bow down before a false god.
10 For it was I, the LORD your God,
who rescued you from the land of Egypt.
Open your mouth wide, and I will fill it with
good things.

11 "But no, my people wouldn't listen.
Israel did not want me around.
12 So I let them follow their own stubborn desires,
living according to their own ideas.
13 Oh, that my people would listen to me!
Oh, that Israel would follow me, walking
in my paths!
14 How quickly I would then subdue their
enemies!
How soon my hands would be upon
their foes!
15 Those who hate the LORD would cringe
before him;
they would be doomed forever.
16 But I would feed you with the finest wheat.
I would satisfy you with wild honey from
the rock."

Psalm 82

THEME: A fair judge. God will judge the wicked who have unfairly treated others.

AUTHOR: Asaph

A psalm of Asaph.

1 God presides over heaven's court;
he pronounces judgment on the heavenly
beings:
2 "How long will you hand down unjust decisions
by favoring the wicked? *Interlude*

3 "Give justice to the poor and the orphan;
uphold the rights of the oppressed and the
destitute.
4 Rescue the poor and helpless;
deliver them from the grasp of evil people.
5 But these oppressors know nothing;
they are so ignorant!
They wander about in darkness,
while the whole world is shaken to the core.

Ps 81:TITLE Hebrew *according to the gittith.* **Ps 81:5** Hebrew *for Joseph.*

Ps 81:1-5 Israel's holidays reminded the nation of God's great miracles. They were times of rejoicing and times to renew one's strength for life's daily struggles. At Christmas, do your thoughts revolve mostly around presents? Is Easter only a warm anticipation of spring? Remember the spiritual origins of these special days, and use them as opportunities to worship God for his goodness to you, your family, and your Christian brothers and sisters.

Ps 81:2-4 David instituted music for the Temple worship services (1 Chr 25). Music and worship go hand in hand. Worship involves the whole person, and music helps lift a person's thoughts and emotions to God. Through music we can reflect upon our needs and shortcomings as well as celebrate God's greatness.

Ps 81:11-12 God let the Israelites go on blindly, stubbornly, and selfishly, when they should have been obeying and following God's desires. God sometimes lets us continue in our stubbornness to bring us to our senses. He does not keep us from rebelling because he wants us to learn the consequences of sin. He uses these experiences to turn people away from greater sin to faith in him.

Ps 81:13-16 In his covenant God had promised that he would restore his people if they would listen to him and return to him (Exod 23:22-27; Lev 26:3-13; Deut 7:12-26; 28:1-14). God remains faithful in our relationship with him (2 Tim 2:11-13), patiently waiting for our response so he can pour out his blessings. Conduct an inventory of your spiritual life right now. In what ways are you allowing God to affect your daily decisions?

Ps 82:1ff God judges human judges. The integrity of the justice system in a nation provides a clear indication of the health of that society. As is the case with all leadership, judges derive their authority ultimately from God and will give an account to God for their verdicts. Believers are commanded to pray for "kings and all who are in authority so we can live peaceful and quiet lives marked by godliness and dignity" (1 Tim 2:2). This psalm reminds us to include judges of every kind in our prayers because we directly benefit from their integrity.

6 I say, 'You are gods;
you are all children of the Most High.
7 But you will die like mere mortals
and fall like every other ruler.'"
8 Rise up, O God, and judge the earth,
for all the nations belong to you.

Psalm 83

THEME: Combating God's enemies. This psalm is a prayer for God to do whatever it takes to convince the world that he is indeed God. Someday all will recognize and admit that God is in charge.

AUTHOR: Asaph (or one of his descendants)

A song. A psalm of Asaph.

1 O God, do not be silent!
Do not be deaf.
Do not be quiet, O God.
2 Don't you hear the uproar of your enemies?
Don't you see that your arrogant enemies
are rising up?
3 They devise crafty schemes against your
people;
they conspire against your precious ones.
4 "Come," they say, "let us wipe out Israel as
a nation.
We will destroy the very memory of its
existence."
5 Yes, this was their unanimous decision.
They signed a treaty as allies
against you—
6 these Edomites and Ishmaelites;
Moabites and Hagrites;
7 Gebalites, Ammonites, and Amalekites;
and people from Philistia and Tyre.
8 Assyria has joined them, too,
and is allied with the descendants of Lot.
Interlude

9 Do to them as you did to the Midianites
and as you did to Sisera and Jabin at the
Kishon River.
10 They were destroyed at Endor,
and their decaying corpses fertilized the soil.
11 Let their mighty nobles die as Oreb and
Zeeb did.
Let all their princes die like Zebah and
Zalmunna,
12 for they said, "Let us seize for our own use
these pasturelands of God!"
13 O my God, scatter them like tumbleweed,
like chaff before the wind!
14 As a fire burns a forest
and as a flame sets mountains ablaze,
15 chase them with your fierce storm;
terrify them with your tempest.
16 Utterly disgrace them
until they submit to your name, O LORD.
17 Let them be ashamed and terrified forever.
Let them die in disgrace.
18 Then they will learn that you alone are called
the LORD,
that you alone are the Most High,
supreme over all the earth.

Ps 82:6 This psalm calls the rulers and judges of Israel "gods" and "children of the Most High." They were called gods because they represented God in executing judgment. John 10:34-36 records Jesus using this passage to defend his claims to be God. His argument was as follows: If God would call mere people "gods," why was it blasphemous for him, the true Son of God, to declare himself equal with God?

Ps 83:5-8 This alliance against God may refer to the gathering of certain kings to fight against Jehoshaphat and the people of Judah (2 Chr 20). The psalm's author is called Asaph, but it could be Asaph or one of his descendants. A descendant of Asaph named Jahaziel prophesied victory for Judah in the battle against Jehoshaphat (2 Chr 20:13-17) and exclaimed, "The battle is not yours, but God's" (2 Chr 20:15). The enemies of Israel were considered God's enemies.

Ps 83:6 The Hagrites may have been the descendants of Hagar (Gen 21:8-21).

Ps 83:8-11 The "descendants of Lot" refers to the Moabites and Ammonites (Gen 19:36-38). Sisera was the commander of the army of the oppressive Canaanite king Jabin. He was killed by a woman (see Judg 4 for the complete story). (For the story of Oreb and Zeeb, see Judg 7:25; for Zebah and Zalmunna, see Judg 8:21.)

Ps 83:13-18 Surrounding Judah were pagan nations that sought Judah's downfall. The writer prayed that God would blow these nations away like tumbleweed until they recognized that the Lord is supreme over all rulers of the earth. Sometimes we must be humbled by adversity before we will look up and see the Lord; we must be defeated before we can have the ultimate victory. Wouldn't it be better to seek the Lord in times of prosperity than to wait until his judgment is upon us?

Sing praises to God, our strength. Sing to the God of Jacob. Sing! Beat the tambourine. Play the sweet lyre and the harp.
Psalms 81:1-2

F. Solomon's Reign

Solomon established himself on the throne and then proceeded to fulfill the mission David had given him. He built the Temple, established a strong army, and became the richest and wisest king in the history of Israel. But his pagan wives led him into idolatry, and as a result, he led the nation into spiritual decline. No matter what position in life we attain, we are always vulnerable and must never let our guard down against sin and temptation.

1. SOLOMON BECOMES KING

When Solomon was anointed king, he eliminated all opposition to the throne. He wanted to ensure that no one would challenge his rule, as Absalom and Sheba had done to his father, David. Solomon's ruthless stance against potential challengers to his throne stands in stark contrast to David's practice of trusting God to vindicate him.

Solomon Takes the Throne PARALLEL

1 CHRONICLES 29:23-25

So Solomon took the throne of the LORD in place of his father, David, and he succeeded in everything, and all Israel obeyed him. [24]All the officials, the warriors, and the sons of King David pledged their loyalty to King Solomon. [25]And the LORD exalted Solomon in the sight of all Israel, and he gave Solomon greater royal splendor than any king in Israel before him.

2 CHRONICLES 1:1

Solomon son of David took firm control of his kingdom, for the LORD his God was with him and made him very powerful.

Solomon Establishes His Rule

1 KINGS 2:13-46

One day Adonijah, whose mother was Haggith, came to see Bathsheba, Solomon's mother. "Have you come with peaceful intentions?" she asked him.

"Yes," he said, "I come in peace. [14]In fact, I have a favor to ask of you."

"What is it?" she asked.

[15]He replied, "As you know, the kingdom was rightfully mine; all Israel wanted me to be the next king. But the tables were turned, and the kingdom went to my brother instead; for that is the way the LORD wanted it. [16]So now I have just one favor to ask of you. Please don't turn me down."

"What is it?" she asked.

[17]He replied, "Speak to King Solomon on my behalf, for I know he will do anything you request. Ask him to let me marry Abishag, the girl from Shunem."

[18]"All right," Bathsheba replied. "I will speak to the king for you."

[19]So Bathsheba went to King Solomon to speak on Adonijah's behalf. The king rose from his throne to meet her, and he bowed down before her. When he sat down on his throne again, the king ordered that a throne be brought for his mother, and she sat at his right hand.

[20]"I have one small request to make of you," she said. "I hope you won't turn me down."

"What is it, my mother?" he asked. "You know I won't refuse you."

[21]"Then let your brother Adonijah marry Abishag, the girl from Shunem," she replied.

[22]"How can you possibly ask me to give Abishag to Adonijah?" King Solomon demanded. "You might as well ask me to give him the kingdom! You know that he is my older brother, and that he has Abiathar the priest and Joab son of Zeruiah on his side."

[23]Then King Solomon made a vow before the LORD: "May God strike me and even kill me if Adonijah has not sealed his fate with this request. [24]The LORD has confirmed me and placed me on the throne of my father, David; he has established my dynasty as he promised. So as surely as the LORD lives, Adonijah will die this very day!" [25]So King Solomon ordered Benaiah son of Jehoiada to execute him, and Adonijah was put to death.

[26]Then the king said to Abiathar the priest, "Go back to your home in Anathoth. You deserve to die, but I will not kill you now, because you carried the Ark of the Sovereign LORD for David my father and you shared all

1 Chr 29:25 Solomon surpassed his father's wealth and splendor. David's legacy resulted from his vital relationship with the Lord, and he passed his spiritual values on to Solomon. Any money or power we leave to our children is far less valuable than the spiritual legacy we pass on. What spiritual inheritance will your children receive? In what specific ways are you passing on that legacy today?

2 Chr 1:1 While the book of 1 Chronicles focuses mainly on David's life, 2 Chronicles focuses on the lives of the rest of the kings of Judah, the southern kingdom. Very little is mentioned about Israel, the northern kingdom, because (1) Chronicles was written for Judeans who had returned from captivity in Babylon, and (2) Judah represented David's family, from which the Messiah would come. Israel was in a state of constant turmoil, anarchy, and rebellion against God, but Judah, at least, made sporadic efforts to follow God.

1 Kgs 2:15-22 This was not a case of thwarted love; Adonijah had more in mind than his supposed love for Abishag. Although she was still a virgin, Abishag was considered part of David's harem. Adonijah wanted Abishag because possessing the king's harem was equivalent to claiming the throne. Absalom had done the same thing in his rebellion against David (2 Sam 16:20-23). Solomon well understood what Adonijah was trying to do.

1 Kgs 2:26-27 As a young man, Abiathar had been the only one to escape when King Saul massacred all the priests in the

his hardships." 27So Solomon deposed Abiathar from his position as priest of the LORD, thereby fulfilling the prophecy the LORD had given at Shiloh concerning the descendants of Eli.

28Joab had not joined Absalom's earlier rebellion, but he had joined Adonijah's rebellion. So when Joab heard about Adonijah's death, he ran to the sacred tent of the LORD and grabbed on to the horns of the altar. 29When this was reported to King Solomon, he sent Benaiah son of Jehoiada to execute him.

30Benaiah went to the sacred tent of the LORD and said to Joab, "The king orders you to come out!"

But Joab answered, "No, I will die here."

So Benaiah returned to the king and told him what Joab had said.

31"Do as he said," the king replied. "Kill him there beside the altar and bury him. This will remove the guilt of Joab's senseless murders from me and from my father's family. 32The LORD will repay him* for the murders of two men who were more righteous and better than he. For my father knew nothing about the deaths of Abner son of Ner, commander of the army of Israel, and of Amasa son of Jether, commander of the army of Judah. 33May their blood be on Joab and his descendants forever, and may the LORD grant peace forever to David, his descendants, his dynasty, and his throne."

34So Benaiah son of Jehoiada returned to the sacred tent and killed Joab, and he was buried at his home in the wilderness. 35Then the king appointed Benaiah to command the army in place of Joab, and he installed Zadok the priest to take the place of Abiathar.

36The king then sent for Shimei and told him, "Build a house here in Jerusalem and live there. But don't step outside the city to go anywhere else. 37On the day you so much as cross the Kidron Valley, you will surely die; and your blood will be on your own head."

38Shimei replied, "Your sentence is fair; I will do whatever my lord the king commands." So Shimei lived in Jerusalem for a long time.

1 Kgs 2:32 Hebrew *will return his blood on his own head.*

ABISHAG

Chosen for her youth and beauty, Abishag was selected to be the live-in nurse of the great but elderly King David. Her job was to keep the ailing king warm. Within months her patient died. We know little about their relationship (although the writer makes it clear that they never had sexual intercourse). • Almost immediately after David's death, Abishag became the bargaining chip in a power struggle between his sons Solomon and Adonijah. Solomon had been chosen for the throne; Adonijah had tried to usurp it. Solomon could have killed his rival, but instead said that if Adonijah proved to be loyal, he would not be harmed (1 Kgs 1:52). • Loyalty, however, was not in Adonijah's vocabulary. When he went to Bathsheba asking for Abishag's hand in marriage, he had strong ulterior motives. For Adonijah, Abishag was probably little more than a possible angle to renew his claim to the throne of David. Solomon saw through the ruse and understood that Adonijah was planning to use Abishag (who had technically been a part of King David's harem) to gain leverage in his fight for the throne. Adonijah paid for this request with his life, for he had proven that he would not be loyal to Solomon. These maneuvers revealed one clear fact: No one cared what Abishag thought. She might as well have been listed with the furniture. • Home and work are both settings in which persons are sometimes treated as objects. You may be hurt today by such treatment. Family members may withhold appreciation. Fellow workers may treat you like just another office machine. Resist these invitations to hopelessness by remembering that God knows you intimately and will always treat you as a person.

Strengths and accomplishments	• Served an apparently thankless role as a king's personal servant with grace and silence
Lessons from her life	• We may go unnoticed and be devalued by others, but God never loses track of us • We frequently know only a small part of the significance of events in our lives as they relate to God's larger plan for the world
Vital statistics	• Where: Shunem, Jerusalem • Occupation: King David's nurse and companion • Contemporaries: Nathan, Bathsheba, Solomon, Adonijah
Key verse	"The girl was very beautiful, and she looked after the king and took care of him. But the king had no sexual relations with her" (1 Kgs 1:4).

Abishag's story is told in 1 Kings 1:1-4; 2:13-24.

city of Nob (1 Sam 22:11-23). Abiathar then became the high priest under David and remained loyal to David throughout his reign. When Abiathar supported Adonijah's wrongful claim to the throne after David's death (1 Kgs 1:7), Solomon forced him to give up the priesthood, fulfilling the prophecy of 1 Samuel 2:27-36 that Eli's descendants would not continue to serve as priests.

1 Kgs 2:31 Joab had spent his life trying to defend his position as David's commander. Twice David tried to replace him, and both times Joab treacherously killed his rivals before they could assume command (2 Sam 3:17-30; 19:13; 20:4-10). Because Joab was in his service, David was ultimately responsible for these senseless deaths. But for political and military reasons (see the note on 2 Sam 3:39, p. 484), David decided not to publicly punish Joab. Instead, he put a curse on Joab and his family (2 Sam 3:29). Solomon, in punishing Joab, was publicly declaring that David was not part of Joab's crimes, thus removing the guilt from David and placing it on Joab where it belonged.

1 Kgs 2:35 Abiathar the high priest and Joab the army commander were key men in David's kingdom. But when they conspired against Solomon, they were replaced with Zadok and Benaiah. Zadok, a descendant of Aaron, had been a prominent priest during David's reign, and he was also loyal to Solomon after David's death. He was put in charge of the Ark of the Covenant (2 Sam 15:24ff). His descendants were in charge of the Temple until its destruction. Benaiah was one of David's mighty men (2 Sam 23:20-23) and the captain of David's bodyguard.

▸ **1 KINGS 2:13-46 *(cont.)***
39But three years later two of Shimei's slaves ran
away to King Achish son of Maacah of Gath. When
Shimei learned where they were, 40he saddled his
donkey and went to Gath to search for them. When
he found them, he brought them back to Jerusalem.
41Solomon heard that Shimei had left Jerusalem
and had gone to Gath and returned. 42So the king sent
for Shimei and demanded, "Didn't I make you swear
by the LORD and warn you not to go anywhere else or
you would surely die? And you replied, 'The sentence
is fair; I will do as you say.' 43Then why haven't you kept
your oath to the LORD and obeyed my command?"
44The king also said to Shimei, "You certainly remember all the wicked things you did to my father,
David. May the LORD now bring that evil on your own
head. 45But may I, King Solomon, receive the LORD's
blessings, and may one of David's descendants always
sit on this throne in the presence of the LORD." 46Then,
at the king's command, Benaiah son of Jehoiada took
Shimei outside and killed him.

So the kingdom was now firmly in Solomon's grip.

2. SOLOMON'S WISDOM

When God gave Solomon the opportunity to ask for anything he wanted, Solomon asked for wisdom to be a good king. In response to Solomon's request, God gave to Solomon great wisdom. God assures us that any time we ask him for wisdom, he will give it to us generously (Jas 1:5).

Solomon Asks for Wisdom PARALLEL

1 KINGS 3:1-15
Solomon made an alliance with Pharaoh, the king of
Egypt, and married one of his daughters. He brought
her to live in the City of David until he could finish
building his palace and the Temple of the LORD and
the wall around the city. 2At that time the people of
Israel sacrificed their offerings at local places of worship, for a temple honoring the name of the LORD had
not yet been built.
3Solomon loved the LORD and followed all the decrees of his father, David, except that Solomon, too, offered sacrifices and burned incense at the local places
of worship. 4The most important of these places of
worship was at Gibeon, so the king went there and
sacrificed 1,000 burnt offerings. 5That night the LORD
appeared to Solomon in a dream, and God said, "What
do you want? Ask, and I will give it to you!"
6Solomon replied, "You showed faithful love to your
servant my father, David, because he was honest and
true and faithful to you. And you have continued your
faithful love to him today by giving him a son to sit
on his throne.
7"Now, O LORD my God, you have made me king
instead of my father, David, but I am like a little child
who doesn't know his way around. 8And here I am
in the midst of your own chosen people, a nation so
great and numerous they cannot be counted! 9Give
me an understanding heart so that I can govern your
people well and know the difference between right
and wrong. For who by himself is able to govern this
great people of yours?"
10The Lord was pleased that Solomon had asked for
wisdom. 11So God replied, "Because you have asked
for wisdom in governing my people with justice and
have not asked for a long life or wealth or the death of
your enemies—12I will give you what you asked for! I
will give you a wise and understanding heart such as

1 Kgs 2:46 Solomon ordered the executions of Adonijah, Joab, and Shimei; forced Abiathar out as priest; and then appointed new men to take their places. He took these actions swiftly, securing his grip on the kingdom. By executing justice and tying up loose ends that could affect the future stability of his kingdom, Solomon was promoting peace, not bloodshed. He was a man of peace in two ways: He did not go to war, and he put an end to internal rebellion.

1 Kgs 3:1 Marriage between royal families was a common practice in the ancient Near East because it secured peace. Although Solomon's marital alliances built friendships with surrounding nations, they were also the beginning of his downfall. These relationships became inroads for pagan ideas and practices. Solomon's foreign wives brought their gods to Jerusalem and eventually lured him into idolatry (1 Kgs 11:1-6).

It is easy to minimize religious differences in order to encourage the development of a friendship. When you're young and in love, you may be idealistic, minimizing religious differences as something you can "work out." What can seem small in a friendship will have an enormous impact upon a marriage. The reality is that God gives us standards to follow for all our relationships—including marriage—for our own good. If we follow God's will, we will not be lured away from our true focus.

1 Kgs 3:2-3 God's laws said that the Israelites could make sacrifices only in specified places (Deut 12:13-14). This was to prevent the people from instituting their own methods of worship and allowing pagan practices to creep into their worship. But many Israelites, including Solomon, made sacrifices in the surrounding hills. Solomon loved God, but this act was sin. It took the offerings out of the watchful care of priests and ministers loyal to God and opened the way for false teaching to be tied to these sacrifices. God appeared to Solomon to grant him wisdom, not during the sacrifice, but at night. God honored his prayer but did not condone the sacrifice.

1 Kgs 3:6-9 When given a chance to have anything in the world, Solomon asked for wisdom—"an understanding heart"—in order to lead well and to make right decisions. We can ask God for this same wisdom (Jas 1:5). Notice that Solomon asked for understanding to carry out his job; he did not ask God to do the job for him. We should not ask God to do *for* us what he wants to do *through* us. Instead, we should ask God to give us the wisdom to know what to do and the courage to follow through on it.

1 Kgs 3:11-14 Solomon asked for wisdom, not wealth, but God gave him riches and long life as well. While God does not promise riches to those who follow him, he gives us what we need if we put his kingdom, his interests, and his principles first (Matt 6:31-33). Setting your sights on riches will only leave you dissatisfied because even if you get the riches you crave, you will still want something more. But if you put God and his work first, he will satisfy your deepest needs.

no one else has had or ever will have! 13And I will also give you what you did not ask for—riches and fame! No other king in all the world will be compared to you for the rest of your life! 14And if you follow me and obey my decrees and my commands as your father, David, did, I will give you a long life."

15Then Solomon woke up and realized it had been a dream. He returned to Jerusalem and stood before the Ark of the Lord's Covenant, where he sacrificed burnt offerings and peace offerings. Then he invited all his officials to a great banquet.

2 CHRONICLES 1:2-13

Solomon called together all the leaders of Israel—the generals and captains of the army,* the judges, and all the political and clan leaders. 3Then he led the entire assembly to the place of worship in Gibeon, for God's Tabernacle* was located there. (This was the Tabernacle that Moses, the LORD's servant, had made in the wilderness.)

4David had already moved the Ark of God from Kiriath-jearim to the tent he had prepared for it in Jerusalem. 5But the bronze altar made by Bezalel son of Uri and grandson of Hur was there* at Gibeon in front of the Tabernacle of the LORD. So Solomon and the people gathered in front of it to consult the LORD.* 6There in front of the Tabernacle, Solomon went up to the bronze altar in the LORD's presence and sacrificed 1,000 burnt offerings on it.

2 Chr 1:2 Hebrew *the commanders of thousands and of hundreds.* **2 Chr 1:3** Hebrew *Tent of Meeting;* also in 1:6, 13. **2 Chr 1:5a** As in Greek version and Latin Vulgate, and some Hebrew manuscripts. Masoretic Text reads *he placed.* **2 Chr 1:5b** Hebrew *to consult him.*

SOLOMON

Wisdom is only effective when it is put into action. Early in his life, Solomon had the sense to recognize his need for wisdom. But by the time Solomon asked for wisdom to rule his kingdom, he had already started a habit that would make his wisdom ineffective for his own life—he sealed a pact with Egypt by marrying Pharaoh's daughter. She was the first of hundreds of wives married for political reasons. In doing this, Solomon went against not only his father's last words but also against God's direct commands. His action reminds us how easy it is to know what is right and yet not do it. • It is clear that God's gift of wisdom to Solomon did not mean that he couldn't make mistakes. He had been given great possibilities as the king of God's chosen people, but with them came great responsibilities; unfortunately, he tended to pursue the former and neglect the latter. While becoming famous as the builder of the Temple and the palace, he became infamous as a leader who excessively taxed and overworked his people. Visitors from distant lands came to admire this wise king, while his own people were gradually alienated from him. • Little is mentioned in the Bible about the last decade of Solomon's reign. Ecclesiastes probably records his last reflections on life. In that book we find a man proving through bitter experience that finding meaning in life apart from God is a vain pursuit. Security and contentment are found only in a personal relationship with God. The contentment we find in the opportunities and successes of this life is temporary. The more we expect our successes to be permanent, the more quickly they are gone. Be sure to balance your pursuit of life's possibilities with reliable fulfillment of your responsibilities.

Strengths and accomplishments	• Third king of Israel, David's chosen heir • Author of Ecclesiastes and Song of Songs, as well as many of the proverbs and a couple of the psalms • Built God's Temple in Jerusalem
Weaknesses and mistakes	• Sealed many foreign agreements by marrying pagan women • Allowed his wives to affect his loyalty to God • Excessively taxed his people and drafted them into labor and military forces
Lessons from his life	• Effective leadership can be nullified by an ineffective personal life • Solomon failed to obey God, but did not learn the lesson of repentance until late in life • Knowing what actions are required of us means little without the will to do those actions
Vital statistics	• Where: Jerusalem • Occupation: King of Israel • Relatives: Father: David. Mother: Bathsheba. Brothers: Absalom, Adonijah. Sister: Tamar. Son: Rehoboam.
Key verse	"'Wasn't this exactly what led King Solomon of Israel into sin?' I demanded. 'There was no king from any nation who could compare to him, and God loved him and made him king over all Israel. But even he was led into sin by his foreign wives'" (Neh 13:26).

Solomon's story is told in 2 Samuel 12:24—1 Kings 11:43. He is also mentioned in 1 Chronicles 28–29; 2 Chronicles 1–10; Nehemiah 13:26; Psalm 72; Matthew 6:29; 12:42.

1 Kgs 3:12 Solomon received "a wise and understanding heart" from God, but it was up to Solomon to apply that wisdom to all areas of his life. Solomon was obviously wise in governing the nation, but he was foolish in running his household. Wisdom is both the ability to discern what is best and the strength of character to act upon that knowledge. While Solomon remained wise all his life, he did not always act upon his wisdom (1 Kgs 11:6).

2 Chr 1:2-5 The Tabernacle that Moses had built centuries earlier (Exod 35–40) was still in operation although it had been moved several times. When Solomon became king, the Tabernacle was located at Gibeon, a town about six miles northwest of Jerusalem. All the Tabernacle furniture was kept at Gibeon except the Ark of God, which David had moved to Jerusalem (1 Chr 13; 15–16). David wanted the Ark, the symbol of God's presence, to reside in the city where he ruled the people. The Tabernacle at Gibeon was still considered Israel's main religious center until Solomon built the Temple in Jerusalem.

▶ **2 CHRONICLES 1:2-13** ***(cont.)***

7That night God appeared to Solomon and said,
"What do you want? Ask, and I will give it to you!"
8Solomon replied to God, "You showed faithful love
to David, my father, and now you have made me king
in his place. 9O LORD God, please continue to keep
your promise to David my father, for you have made
me king over a people as numerous as the dust of the
earth! 10Give me the wisdom and knowledge to lead
them properly,* for who could possibly govern this
great people of yours?"
11God said to Solomon, "Because your greatest desire
is to help your people, and you did not ask for wealth,
riches, fame, or even the death of your enemies or a long
life, but rather you asked for wisdom and knowledge to
properly govern my people—12I will certainly give you
the wisdom and knowledge you requested. But I will
also give you wealth, riches, and fame such as no other
king has had before you or will ever have in the future!"
13Then Solomon returned to Jerusalem from the
Tabernacle at the place of worship in Gibeon, and he
reigned over Israel.

Solomon Judges Wisely

1 KINGS 3:16-28

Some time later two prostitutes came to the king to
have an argument settled. 17"Please, my lord," one of
them began, "this woman and I live in the same house.
I gave birth to a baby while she was with me in the
house. 18Three days later this woman also had a baby.
We were alone; there were only two of us in the house.
19"But her baby died during the night when she
rolled over on it. 20Then she got up in the night and
took my son from beside me while I was asleep. She
laid her dead child in my arms and took mine to
sleep beside her. 21And in the morning when I tried
to nurse my son, he was dead! But when I looked
more closely in the morning light, I saw that it wasn't
my son at all."
22Then the other woman interrupted, "It certainly
was your son, and the living child is mine."
"No," the first woman said, "the living child is mine,
and the dead one is yours." And so they argued back
and forth before the king.
23Then the king said, "Let's get the facts straight.
Both of you claim the living child is yours, and each
says that the dead one belongs to the other. 24All right,
bring me a sword." So a sword was brought to the king.
25Then he said, "Cut the living child in two, and give
half to one woman and half to the other!"
26Then the woman who was the real mother of the
living child, and who loved him very much, cried out,
"Oh no, my lord! Give her the child—please do not
kill him!"
But the other woman said, "All right, he will be neither yours nor mine; divide him between us!"
27Then the king said, "Do not kill the child, but give
him to the woman who wants him to live, for she is
his mother!"
28When all Israel heard the king's decision, the
people were in awe of the king, for they saw the wisdom God had given him for rendering justice.

2 Chr 1:10 Hebrew *to go out and come in before this people.*

---

2 Chr 1:10 Wisdom is the ability to make good decisions based on proper discernment and judgment. Knowledge, in this verse, refers to the practical know-how necessary for handling everyday matters. Wisdom applies knowledge. Solomon used his wisdom and knowledge not only to build the Temple from his father's plans but also to put the nation on firm economic footing.

2 Chr 1:10 God's offer to Solomon stretches the imagination: "Ask, and I will give it to you!" (2 Chr 1:7). But Solomon put the needs of his people first and asked for wisdom rather than riches. He realized that wisdom would be the most valuable asset he could have as king. Later he wrote, "Wisdom is more precious than rubies; nothing you desire can compare with her" (Prov 3:15). The same wisdom that was given to Solomon is available to us; the same God offers it. How can we acquire wisdom? First, we must ask God, who "will not rebuke you for asking" (Jas 1:5). Second, we must devote ourselves wholeheartedly to studying and applying God's Word, the source of divine wisdom, to our lives. (For more on Solomon's wisdom, read the notes on 1 Kgs 3:6-9, p. 606, and 1 Kgs 3:12, p. 607.)

2 Chr 1:11-12 Solomon could have had anything, but he asked for wisdom to rule the nation. Because God approved of the way Solomon ordered his priorities, he gave Solomon wealth, riches, and honor as well. Jesus also spoke about priorities. He said that when we put God first, everything we really need will be given to us as well (Matt 6:33). This does not guarantee that we will be wealthy and famous like Solomon, but it means that when we put God first, the wisdom he gives will enable us to have richly rewarding lives. When we have a purpose for living and learn to be content with what we have, we have greater wealth than we could ever imagine.

SHIPPING RESOURCES FOR THE TEMPLE ▶
Solomon asked King Hiram of Tyre to provide supplies and skilled workmen to help build God's Temple in Jerusalem. The plan was to cut the cedar logs in the mountains of Lebanon, float them by sea to Joppa, then bring them inland to Jerusalem by the shortest and easiest route.

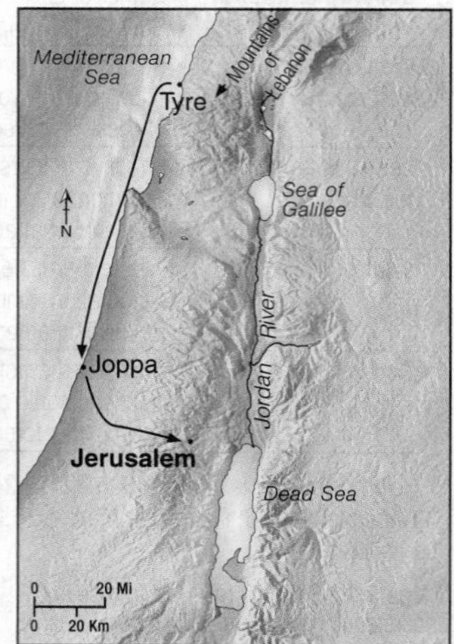

1 Kgs 3:16-28 Solomon's settlement of this dispute was a classic example of his wisdom. This wise ruling was verification that God had answered Solomon's prayer and given him an understanding heart. We have God's wisdom available to us as we pray and request it. But, like Solomon, we must put it into action. Applying wisdom to life demonstrates our understanding.

3. SOLOMON'S BUILDING PROJECTS

Solomon launched great building programs, including the Temple, his greatest achievement. In the midst of the celebration dedicating the Temple, fire flashed down from heaven, and God's glory filled the Temple. God wants to live among his people and to be central in their lives. Today, the people of the church are God's temple, the place where God, through his Holy Spirit, lives and reigns.

Preparations for Building the Temple PARALLEL

1 KINGS 5:1-18

1*King Hiram of Tyre had always been a loyal friend of David. When Hiram learned that David's son Solomon was the new king of Israel, he sent ambassadors to congratulate him.

2Then Solomon sent this message back to Hiram:

> 3"You know that my father, David, was not able to build a Temple to honor the name of the LORD his God because of the many wars waged against him by surrounding nations. He could not build until the LORD gave him victory over all his enemies. 4But now the LORD my God has given me peace on every side; I have no enemies, and all is well. 5So I am planning to build a Temple to honor the name of the LORD my God, just as he had instructed my father, David. For the LORD told him, 'Your son, whom I will place on your throne, will build the Temple to honor my name.'
>
> 6"Therefore, please command that cedars from Lebanon be cut for me. Let my men work alongside yours, and I will pay your men whatever wages you ask. As you know, there is no one among us who can cut timber like you Sidonians!"

7When Hiram received Solomon's message, he was very pleased and said, "Praise the LORD today for giving David a wise son to be king of the great nation of Israel." 8Then he sent this reply to Solomon:

> "I have received your message, and I will supply all the cedar and cypress timber you need. 9My servants will bring the logs from the Lebanon mountains to the Mediterranean Sea* and make them into rafts and float them along the coast to whatever place you choose. Then we will break the rafts apart so you can carry the logs away. You can pay me by supplying me with food for my household."

10So Hiram supplied as much cedar and cypress timber as Solomon desired. 11In return, Solomon sent him an annual payment of 100,000 bushels* of wheat for his household and 110,000 gallons* of pure olive oil. 12So the LORD gave wisdom to Solomon, just as he had promised. And Hiram and Solomon made a formal alliance of peace.

13Then King Solomon conscripted a labor force of 30,000 men from all Israel. 14He sent them to Lebanon in shifts, 10,000 every month, so that each man would be one month in Lebanon and two months at home. Adoniram was in charge of this labor force. 15Solomon also had 70,000 common laborers, 80,000 quarry workers in the hill country, 16and 3,600* foremen to supervise the work. 17At the king's command, they quarried large blocks of high-quality stone and shaped them to make the foundation of the Temple. 18Men from the city of Gebal helped Solomon's and Hiram's builders prepare the timber and stone for the Temple.

2 CHRONICLES 2:1-18

1*Solomon decided to build a Temple to honor the name of the LORD, and also a royal palace for himself. 2*He enlisted a force of 70,000 laborers, 80,000 men to quarry stone in the hill country, and 3,600 foremen.

3Solomon also sent this message to King Hiram* at Tyre:

1 Kgs 5:1 Verses 5:1-18 are numbered 5:15-32 in Hebrew text. **1 Kgs 5:9** Hebrew *the sea.* **1 Kgs 5:11a** Hebrew *20,000 cors* [3,640 kiloliters]. **1 Kgs 5:11b** As in Greek version, which reads *20,000 baths* [420 kiloliters] (see also 2 Chr 2:10); Hebrew reads *20 cors,* about 800 gallons or 3.6 kiloliters in volume. **1 Kgs 5:16** As in some Greek manuscripts (see also 2 Chr 2:2, 18); Hebrew reads *3,300.* **2 Chr 2:1** Verse 2:1 is numbered 1:18 in Hebrew text. **2 Chr 2:2** Verses 2:2-18 are numbered 2:1-17 in Hebrew text. **2 Chr 2:3** Hebrew *Huram,* a variant spelling of Hiram; also in 2:11.

967 BC

Solomon begins building the Temple

---

1 Kgs 5:2-3 When David offered to build a Temple, God said no through the prophet Nathan (2 Sam 7:1-17). God wanted a peacemaker, not a warrior, to build his house of prayer (1 Chr 28:2-3).

1 Kgs 5:13-14 Solomon drafted three times the number of workers needed for the Temple project and then arranged their schedules so they didn't have to be away from home for long periods of time. This showed his concern for the welfare of his workers and the importance he placed on family life. The strength of a nation is in direct proportion to the strength of its families. Solomon wisely recognized that family should always be a top priority. As you structure your own work or arrange the schedules of others, watch for the impact of your plans on families.

1 Kgs 5:18 Gebal, also called Byblos, was located north of what is now Beirut, near the cedar forest. These men were Phoenicians, probably skilled as shipbuilders, but employed for this project.

2 Chr 2:1 David had wanted to build a Temple for God (2 Sam 7). God denied his request because David had been a warrior, but God said that David's son Solomon would build the Temple. God allowed David to make the plans and preparations (1 Chr 23–26; 28:11-19). David bought the land (2 Sam 24:18-25; 1 Chr 22:1), gathered most of the construction materials (1 Chr 22:14-16), and received the plans from God (1 Chr 28:11-12, 19). It was Solomon's responsibility to make the plans a reality. His job was made easier by his father's exhaustive preparations. God's work can be moved forward when the older generation paves the way for the younger.

2 Chr 2:3-12 Although Hiram was one of David's and Solomon's friendly allies, he was the ruler of a nation that worshiped many different gods. Hiram was happy to send materials for the Temple, and both David and Solomon used this occasion to testify about the one true God.

▸ **2 CHRONICLES 2:1-18** ***(cont.)***

"Send me cedar logs as you did for my father,
David, when he was building his palace. 4I am
about to build a Temple to honor the name of the
LORD my God. It will be a place set apart to burn
fragrant incense before him, to display the special
sacrificial bread, and to sacrifice burnt offerings
each morning and evening, on the Sabbaths,
at new moon celebrations, and at the other
appointed festivals of the LORD our God. He has
commanded Israel to do these things forever.

5"This must be a magnificent Temple because
our God is greater than all other gods. 6But who
can really build him a worthy home? Not even the
highest heavens can contain him! So who am I to
consider building a Temple for him, except as a
place to burn sacrifices to him?

7"So send me a master craftsman who can
work with gold, silver, bronze, and iron, as well as
with purple, scarlet, and blue cloth. He must be a
skilled engraver who can work with the craftsmen
of Judah and Jerusalem who were selected by my
father, David.

8"Also send me cedar, cypress, and red
sandalwood* logs from Lebanon, for I know
that your men are without equal at cutting
timber in Lebanon. I will send my men to help
them. 9An immense amount of timber will be
needed, for the Temple I am going to build will
be very large and magnificent. 10In payment for
your woodcutters, I will send 100,000 bushels
of crushed wheat, 100,000 bushels of barley,*
110,000 gallons of wine, and 110,000 gallons of
olive oil.*"

11King Hiram sent this letter of reply to Solomon:

"It is because the LORD loves his people that he
has made you their king! 12Praise the LORD, the
God of Israel, who made the heavens and the
earth! He has given King David a wise son, gifted
with skill and understanding, who will build
a Temple for the LORD and a royal palace for
himself.

13"I am sending you a master craftsman named
Huram-abi, who is extremely talented. 14His
mother is from the tribe of Dan in Israel, and his
father is from Tyre. He is skillful at making things
from gold, silver, bronze, and iron, and he also
works with stone and wood. He can work with
purple, blue, and scarlet cloth and fine linen. He
is also an engraver and can follow any design
given to him. He will work with your craftsmen

2 Chr 2:8 Or *juniper;* Hebrew reads *algum,* perhaps a variant spelling of *almug;* compare 9:10-11 and parallel text at 1 Kgs 10:11-12. **2 Chr 2:10a** Hebrew *20,000 cors* [3,640 kiloliters] *of crushed wheat, 20,000 cors of barley.* **2 Chr 2:10b** Hebrew *20,000 baths* [420 kiloliters] *of wine, and 20,000 baths of olive oil.*

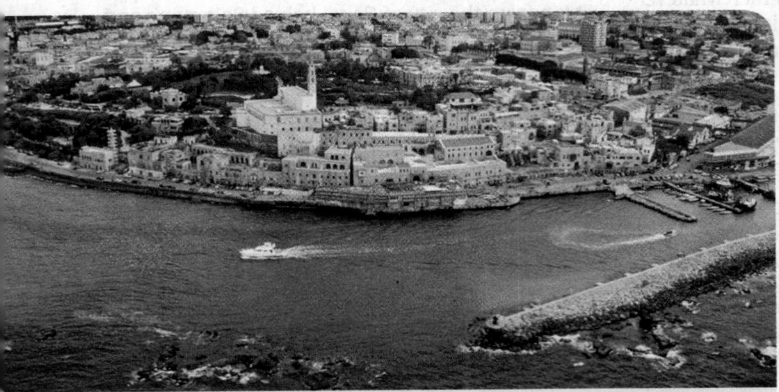

Joppa

Joppa (present-day Jaffa) was a city about 35 miles northwest of Jerusalem; it served as Jerusalem's seaport. Joppa was built on a rocky hill about 115 feet high, with a cape projecting beyond the coastline into the sea; it was the only natural harbor on the Mediterranean coast between Egypt and Acco. A series of reefs formed a breakwater some 300 to 400 feet offshore, protecting the harbor from waves. It is possible that the harbor was larger and better protected in biblical times than it is today. The biblical city was well supplied with water, and the land surrounding it was quite fertile. During Solomon's reign, it became a major port serving Jerusalem. Cedar logs were floated from Lebanon to Joppa and then transported to Jerusalem for use in building the Temple (2 Chr 2:16). Joppa was the seaport to which Jonah fled in an attempt to avoid preaching to Nineveh (Jon 1:3); there, hoping to escape his responsibility, he boarded a ship bound for Tarshish. We may laugh at Jonah for trying to escape God, but many of us have also tried to shirk what God wants us to do. Let's be faithful to God, facing the tasks he gives us head-on and trusting that he will care for us as we obey him.

2 Chr 2:5-6 We should try our best to build beautiful, accessible, and welcoming places of worship to be a testimony and credit to God. In so doing, however, we must remember that God cannot be contained in our building or lovely setting. He is far greater than any structure, so we must focus our praise on him and not on the place of worship.

2 Chr 2:7 Why use foreign craftsmen? The Israelites had great knowledge of agriculture but knew little about metalworking. So they found people who were experts in this area. It is not a sin to obtain secular expertise as we go about God's work. He distributes talents as he chooses, giving skill to Christians and non-Christians alike. When we hire secular contractors to build or repair our church buildings, we are recognizing that God gives gifts liberally. We may also be gaining an opportunity to tell the them about God.

2 Chr 2:8-9 Israel did not have much wood, but Lebanon, a small nation on the seacoast, had some of the finest cedar forests in the ancient Near East. Lebanon also imported a great deal of food from Israel. Thus, the two kings made a trade agreement that was beneficial to both nations.

2 Chr 2:17-18 Why would Solomon force foreigners living in Israel to do the work of slaves? These foreigners were descendants of the pagan nations that had not been driven out of the land in Joshua's day (Josh

and those appointed by my lord David, your father.

15"Send along the wheat, barley, olive oil, and wine that my lord has mentioned. 16We will cut whatever timber you need from the Lebanon mountains and will float the logs in rafts down the coast of the Mediterranean Sea* to Joppa. From there you can transport the logs up to Jerusalem."

17Solomon took a census of all foreigners in the land of Israel, like the census his father had taken, and he counted 153,600. 18He assigned 70,000 of them as common laborers, 80,000 as quarry workers in the hill country, and 3,600 as foremen.

Solomon Builds the Temple PARALLEL

1 KINGS 6:1-13

It was in midspring, in the month of Ziv,* during the fourth year of Solomon's reign, that he began to construct the Temple of the LORD. This was 480 years after the people of Israel were rescued from their slavery in the land of Egypt.

2The Temple that King Solomon built for the LORD was 90 feet long, 30 feet wide, and 45 feet high.* 3The entry room at the front of the Temple was 30 feet* wide, running across the entire width of the Temple. It projected outward 15 feet* from the front of the Temple. 4Solomon also made narrow recessed windows throughout the Temple.

5He built a complex of rooms against the outer walls of the Temple, all the way around the sides and rear of the building. 6The complex was three stories high, the bottom floor being 7½ feet wide, the second floor 9 feet wide, and the top floor 10½ feet wide.* The rooms were connected to the walls of the Temple by beams resting on ledges built out from the wall. So the beams were not inserted into the walls themselves.

7The stones used in the construction of the Temple were finished at the quarry, so there was no sound of hammer, ax, or any other iron tool at the building site.

8The entrance to the bottom floor* was on the south side of the Temple. There were winding stairs going up to the second floor, and another flight of stairs between the second and third floors. 9After completing the Temple structure, Solomon put in a ceiling made of cedar beams and planks. 10As already stated, he built a complex of rooms on three sides of the building, attached to the Temple walls by cedar timbers. Each story of the complex was 7½ feet* high.

11Then the LORD gave this message to Solomon: 12"Concerning this Temple you are building, if you keep all my decrees and regulations and obey all my commands, I will fulfill through you the promise I made to your father, David. 13I will live among the Israelites and will never abandon my people Israel."

2 CHRONICLES 3:1-14

So Solomon began to build the Temple of the LORD in Jerusalem on Mount Moriah, where the LORD had appeared to David, his father. The Temple was built on the threshing floor of Araunah* the Jebusite, the site that David had selected. 2The construction began in midspring,* during the fourth year of Solomon's reign.

3These are the dimensions Solomon used for the foundation of the Temple of God (using the old

2 Chr 2:16 Hebrew *the sea.* **1 Kgs 6:1** Hebrew *It was in the month of Ziv, which is the second month.* This month of the ancient Hebrew lunar calendar usually occurs within the months of April and May. **1 Kgs 6:2** Hebrew *60 cubits* [27.6 meters] *long, 20 cubits* [9.2 meters] *wide, and 30 cubits* [13.8 meters] *high.* **1 Kgs 6:3a** Hebrew *20 cubits* [9.2 meters]; also in 6:16, 20. **1 Kgs 6:3b** Hebrew *10 cubits* [4.6 meters]. **1 Kgs 6:6** Hebrew *the bottom floor being 5 cubits* [2.3 meters] *wide, the second floor 6 cubits* [2.8 meters] *wide, and the top floor 7 cubits* [3.2 meters] *wide.* **1 Kgs 6:8** As in Greek version; Hebrew reads *middle floor.* **1 Kgs 6:10** Hebrew *5 cubits* [2.3 meters]. **2 Chr 3:1** Hebrew reads *Ornan,* a variant spelling of Araunah; compare 2 Sam 24:16. **2 Chr 3:2** Hebrew *on the second day of the second month.* This day of the ancient Hebrew lunar calendar occurred in April or May.

9:23-27; Judg 1:21-33; 1 Kgs 9:20-21). Scripture has specific laws about treating slaves fairly (Lev 25:39-55), so Solomon would not have treated them harshly as other nations might. Solomon's action was probably only in force during the construction of the Temple.

1 Kgs 6:1ff For more information on the purpose of the Temple, see the note on 2 Chronicles 5:1ff, p. 617.

1 Kgs 6:3 The entry room was like a large porch.

1 Kgs 6:4 These narrow, recessed windows were near the tops of the walls to help light the center of the Temple.

1 Kgs 6:7 In honor of God, the Temple in Jerusalem was built without the sound of a hammer or any other tool at the building site. This meant that the stone had to be prefinished (cut and shaped) miles away at the quarry. The people's honor and respect for God extended to every aspect of constructing this house of worship. This detail is recorded not to teach us how to build a church but to show us the importance of demonstrating care, concern, honor, and respect for God and his sanctuary.

1 Kgs 6:13 This verse summarizes the Temple's main purpose. God promised that his eternal presence would never leave the Temple as long as one condition was met: The Israelites had to obey God's law. Knowing how many laws they had to follow, we may think this condition was difficult. But the Israelites' situation was much like ours today: They were not cut off from God for failing to keep some small part of a law. Forgiveness was amply provided for all their sins, no matter how large or small. As you read the history of the kings, you will see that lawbreaking was the result, not the cause, of estrangement from God. The kings abandoned God in their hearts first and then failed to keep his laws. When we close our hearts to God, we soon lose his power and presence.

2 Chr 3:1 Solomon built a permanent Temple on Mount Moriah to replace the movable Tabernacle (now at Gibeon) that had accompanied Israel in the wilderness. Mount Moriah was also the place where God had stopped Abraham from sacrificing Isaac (Gen 22:1-18). David purchased the land when it was a threshing floor (see 2 Sam 24:15-25 and the note on 1 Chr 21:22-24, p. 531).

2 Chr 3:1ff Why was the Temple decorated so ornately? Although no one can build God a worthy home (2 Chr 2:6), this Temple was going to be the best that humans could do. The care and craftsmanship were acts of worship in themselves. Although a simple chapel is an adequate place to pray and meet God, it is not wrong to want to make a beautiful place of worship.

▶ **2 CHRONICLES 3:1-14** ***(cont.)***

standard of measurement).* It was 90 feet long and 30 feet wide.* [4]The entry room at the front of the Temple was 30 feet* wide, running across the entire width of the Temple, and 30 feet* high. He overlaid the inside with pure gold.

[5]He paneled the main room of the Temple with cypress wood, overlaid it with fine gold, and decorated it with carvings of palm trees and chains. [6]He decorated the walls of the Temple with beautiful jewels and with gold from the land of Parvaim. [7]He overlaid the beams, thresholds, walls, and doors throughout the Temple with gold, and he carved figures of cherubim on the walls.

[8]He made the Most Holy Place 30 feet wide, corresponding to the width of the Temple, and 30 feet deep. He overlaid its interior with 23 tons* of fine gold. [9]The gold nails that were used weighed 20 ounces* each. He also overlaid the walls of the upper rooms with gold.

[10]He made two figures shaped like cherubim, overlaid them with gold, and placed them in the Most Holy Place. [11]The total wingspan of the two cherubim standing side by side was 30 feet. One wing of the first figure was 7½ feet* long, and it touched the Temple wall. The other wing, also 7½ feet long, touched one of the wings of the second figure. [12]In the same way, the second figure had one wing 7½ feet long that touched the opposite wall. The other wing, also 7½ feet long, touched the wing of the first figure. [13]So the wingspan of the two cherubim side by side was 30 feet. They stood on their feet and faced out toward the main room of the Temple.

[14]Across the entrance of the Most Holy Place he hung a curtain made of fine linen, decorated with blue, purple, and scarlet thread and embroidered with figures of cherubim.

The Temple's Interior

1 KINGS 6:14-38

So Solomon finished building the Temple. [15]The entire inside, from floor to ceiling, was paneled with wood. He paneled the walls and ceilings with cedar, and he used planks of cypress for the floors. [16]He partitioned off an inner sanctuary—the Most Holy Place—at the far end of the Temple. It was 30 feet deep and was paneled with cedar from floor to ceiling. [17]The main room of the Temple, outside the Most Holy Place, was 60 feet* long. [18]Cedar paneling completely covered the stone walls throughout the Temple, and the paneling was decorated with carvings of gourds and open flowers.

[19]He prepared the inner sanctuary at the far end of the Temple, where the Ark of the LORD's Covenant would be placed. [20]This inner sanctuary was 30 feet long, 30 feet wide, and 30 feet high. He overlaid the inside with solid gold. He also overlaid the altar made of cedar.* [21]Then Solomon overlaid the rest of the Temple's interior with solid gold, and he made gold chains to protect the entrance* to the Most Holy Place. [22]So he finished overlaying the entire Temple with gold, including the altar that belonged to the Most Holy Place.

[23]He made two cherubim of wild olive* wood, each 15 feet* tall, and placed them in the inner sanctuary. [24]The wingspan of each of the cherubim was 15 feet, each wing being 7½ feet* long. [25]The two cherubim were identical in shape and size; [26]each was 15 feet tall. [27]He placed them side by side in the inner sanctuary of the Temple. Their outspread wings reached from wall to wall, while their inner wings touched at the center of the room. [28]He overlaid the two cherubim with gold.

[29]He decorated all the walls of the inner sanctuary and the main room with carvings of cherubim, palm trees, and open flowers. [30]He overlaid the floor in both rooms with gold.

[31]For the entrance to the inner sanctuary, he made double doors of wild olive wood with five-sided doorposts.* [32]These double doors were decorated with carvings of cherubim, palm trees, and open flowers. The doors, including the decorations of cherubim and palm trees, were overlaid with gold.

[33]Then he made four-sided doorposts of wild olive wood for the entrance to the Temple. [34]There were two folding doors of cypress wood, and each door was hinged to fold back upon itself. [35]These doors were decorated with carvings of cherubim, palm trees, and open flowers—all overlaid evenly with gold.

[36]The walls of the inner courtyard were built so that there was one layer of cedar beams between every three layers of finished stone.

[37]The foundation of the LORD's Temple was laid in midspring, in the month of Ziv,* during the fourth year of Solomon's reign. [38]The entire building was completed in every detail by midautumn, in the month of Bul,* during the eleventh year of his reign. So it took seven years to build the Temple.

2 Chr 3:3a The "old standard of measurement" was a cubit equal to 18 inches [46 centimeters]. The new standard was a cubit of approximately 21 inches [53 centimeters]. **2 Chr 3:3b** Hebrew *60 cubits* [27.6 meters] *long and 20 cubits* [9.2 meters] *wide.* **2 Chr 3:4a** Hebrew *20 cubits* [9.2 meters]; also in 3:8, 11, 13. **2 Chr 3:4b** As in some Greek and Syriac manuscripts, which read *20 cubits* [9.2 meters]; Hebrew reads *120 [cubits]*, which is 180 feet or 55 meters. **2 Chr 3:8** Hebrew *600 talents* [20.4 metric tons]. **2 Chr 3:9** Hebrew *50 shekels* [570 grams]. **2 Chr 3:11** Hebrew *5 cubits* [2.3 meters]; also in 3:11b, 12, 15. **1 Kgs 6:17** Hebrew *40 cubits* [18.4 meters]. **1 Kgs 6:20** Or *overlaid the altar with cedar.* The meaning of the Hebrew is uncertain. **1 Kgs 6:21** Or *to draw curtains across.* The meaning of the Hebrew is uncertain. **1 Kgs 6:23a** Or *pine;* Hebrew reads *oil tree;* also in 6:31, 33. **1 Kgs 6:23b** Hebrew *10 cubits* [4.6 meters]; also in 6:24, 25. **1 Kgs 6:24** Hebrew *5 cubits* [2.3 meters]. **1 Kgs 6:31** The meaning of the Hebrew is uncertain. **1 Kgs 6:37** Hebrew *was laid in the month of Ziv.* This month of the ancient Hebrew lunar calendar usually occurs within the months of April and May. **1 Kgs 6:38** Hebrew *by the month of Bul, which is the eighth month.* This month of the ancient Hebrew lunar calendar usually occurs within the months of October and November.

2 Chr 3:10 Cherubim are angels.

1 Kgs 6:14 The concept of Solomon's Temple was more like a palace for God than a place of worship. As a dwelling place for God, it was fitting for it to be ornate and beautiful. It had small inside dimensions because most worshipers would gather outside.

Solomon Builds His Palace

1 KINGS 7:1-12

Solomon also built a palace for himself, and it took him thirteen years to complete the construction.

[2]One of Solomon's buildings was called the Palace of the Forest of Lebanon. It was 150 feet long, 75 feet wide, and 45 feet high.* There were four rows of cedar pillars, and great cedar beams rested on the pillars. [3]The hall had a cedar roof. Above the beams on the pillars were forty-five side rooms,* arranged in three tiers of fifteen each. [4]On each end of the long hall were three rows of windows facing each other. [5]All the doorways and doorposts* had rectangular frames and were arranged in sets of three, facing each other.

[6]Solomon also built the Hall of Pillars, which was 75 feet long and 45 feet wide.* There was a porch in front, along with a canopy supported by pillars.

[7]Solomon also built the throne room, known as the Hall of Justice, where he sat to hear legal matters. It was paneled with cedar from floor to ceiling.* [8]Solomon's living quarters surrounded a courtyard behind this hall, and they were constructed the same way. He also built similar living quarters for Pharaoh's daughter, whom he had married.

[9]From foundation to eaves, all these buildings were built from huge blocks of high-quality stone, cut with saws and trimmed to exact measure on all sides. [10]Some of the huge foundation stones were 15 feet long, and some were 12 feet* long. [11]The blocks of high-quality stone used in the walls were also cut to measure, and cedar beams were also used. [12]The walls of the great courtyard were built so that there was one layer of cedar beams between every three layers of finished stone, just like the walls of the inner courtyard of the LORD's Temple with its entry room.

Furnishings for the Temple PARALLEL

1 KINGS 7:13-51

King Solomon then asked for a man named Huram* to come from Tyre. [14]He was half Israelite, since his mother was a widow from the tribe of Naphtali, and his father had been a craftsman in bronze from Tyre. Huram was extremely skillful and talented in any work in bronze, and he came to do all the metal work for King Solomon.

[15]Huram cast two bronze pillars, each 27 feet tall and 18 feet in circumference.* [16]For the tops of the pillars he cast bronze capitals, each 7½ feet* tall. [17]Each capital was decorated with seven sets of latticework and interwoven chains. [18]He also encircled the latticework with two rows of pomegranates to decorate the capitals over the pillars. [19]The capitals on the columns inside the entry room were shaped like water lilies, and they were six feet* tall. [20]The capitals on the two pillars had 200 pomegranates in two rows around them, beside the rounded surface next to the latticework. [21]Huram set the pillars at the entrance of the Temple, one toward the south and one toward the north. He named the one on the south Jakin, and the one on the north Boaz.* [22]The capitals on the pillars were shaped like water lilies. And so the work on the pillars was finished.

[23]Then Huram cast a great round basin, 15 feet across from rim to rim, called the Sea. It was 7½ feet deep and about 45 feet in circumference.* [24]It was encircled just below its rim by two rows of decorative gourds. There were about six gourds per foot* all the way around, and they were cast as part of the basin.

[25]The Sea was placed on a base of twelve bronze oxen,* all facing outward. Three faced north, three faced west, three faced south, and three faced east, and the Sea rested on them. [26]The walls of the Sea were about three inches* thick, and its rim flared out like a cup and resembled a water lily blossom. It could hold about 11,000 gallons* of water.

[27]Huram also made ten bronze water carts, each 6 feet long, 6 feet wide, and 4½ feet tall.* [28]They were constructed with side panels braced with crossbars. [29]Both the panels and the crossbars were decorated with carved lions, oxen, and cherubim. Above and below the lions and oxen were wreath decorations. [30]Each of these carts had four bronze wheels and bronze axles. There were supporting posts for the bronze basins at the corners of the carts; these supports were decorated on each side with carvings of wreaths. [31]The top of each cart had a rounded frame for the basin. It projected 1½ feet* above the cart's top

1 Kgs 7:2 Hebrew *100 cubits* [46 meters] *long, 50 cubits* [23 meters] *wide, and 30 cubits* [13.5 meters] *high.* **1 Kgs 7:3** Or *45 rafters*, or *45 beams*, or *45 pillars.* The architectural details in 7:2-6 can be interpreted in many different ways. **1 Kgs 7:5** Greek version reads *windows.* **1 Kgs 7:6** Hebrew *50 cubits* [23 meters] *long and 30 cubits* [13.8 meters] *wide.* **1 Kgs 7:7** As in Syriac version and Latin Vulgate; Hebrew reads *from floor to floor.* **1 Kgs 7:10** Hebrew *10 cubits* [4.6 meters] . . . *8 cubits* [3.7 meters]. **1 Kgs 7:13** Hebrew *Hiram* (also in 7:40, 45); compare 2 Chr 2:13. This is not the same person mentioned in 5:1. **1 Kgs 7:15** Hebrew *18 cubits* [8.3 meters] *tall and 12 cubits* [5.5 meters] *in circumference.* **1 Kgs 7:16** Hebrew *5 cubits* [2.3 meters]. **1 Kgs 7:19** Hebrew *4 cubits* [1.8 meters]; also in 7:38. **1 Kgs 7:21** *Jakin* probably means "he establishes"; *Boaz* probably means "in him is strength." **1 Kgs 7:23** Hebrew *10 cubits* [4.6 meters] *across. . . . 5 cubits* [2.3 meters] *deep and 30 cubits* [13.8 meters] *in circumference.* **1 Kgs 7:24** Or *20 gourds per meter;* Hebrew reads *10 per cubit.* **1 Kgs 7:25** Hebrew *12 oxen;* compare 2 Kgs 16:17, which specifies *bronze oxen.* **1 Kgs 7:26a** Hebrew *a handbreadth* [8 centimeters]. **1 Kgs 7:26b** Hebrew *2,000 baths* [42 kiloliters]. **1 Kgs 7:27** Hebrew *4 cubits* [1.8 meters] *long, 4 cubits wide, and 3 cubits* [1.4 meters] *high.* **1 Kgs 7:31a** Hebrew *a cubit* [46 centimeters].

1 Kgs 7:1 That Solomon took longer to build his palace than to build the Temple (13 years as opposed to 7) gives us an early glimpse at his weakening value system. Solomon appeared to be just as concerned with building his own wealth and reputation as he was with the glory of God's name.

1 Kgs 7:14 Huram was an expert craftsman. Solomon chose only the best.

1 Kgs 7:23 The "Sea" was an enormous tank. Designed and used for the priests' ceremonial washings, it stood in the Temple court near the altar of burnt offering. There the priests washed themselves before offering sacrifices or entering the Temple (Exod 30:17-21).

1 Kgs 7:27-39 These 10 "water carts" held basins of water. The basins were used for washing the various parts of the animal sacrifices. The basins were movable so they could be used where needed.

▶ 1 KINGS 7:13-51 *(cont.)*

like a round pedestal, and its opening was 2¼ feet*
across; it was decorated on the outside with carvings
of wreaths. The panels of the carts were square, not
round. 32Under the panels were four wheels that were
connected to axles that had been cast as one unit with
the cart. The wheels were 2¼ feet in diameter 33and
were similar to chariot wheels. The axles, spokes, rims,
and hubs were all cast from molten bronze.

34There were handles at each of the four corners
of the carts, and these, too, were cast as one unit with
the cart. 35Around the top of each cart was a rim nine
inches wide.* The corner supports and side panels
were cast as one unit with the cart. 36Carvings of cherubim, lions, and palm trees decorated the panels and
corner supports wherever there was room, and there
were wreaths all around. 37All ten water carts were
the same size and were made alike, for each was cast
from the same mold.

38Huram also made ten smaller bronze basins, one
for each cart. Each basin was six feet across and could
hold 220 gallons* of water. 39He set five water carts
on the south side of the Temple and five on the north
side. The great bronze basin called the Sea was placed
near the southeast corner of the Temple. 40He also
made the necessary washbasins, shovels, and bowls.

So at last Huram completed everything King Solomon had assigned him to make for the Temple of
the LORD:

41 the two pillars;
the two bowl-shaped capitals on top of the pillars;
the two networks of interwoven chains that
decorated the capitals;
42 the 400 pomegranates that hung from the chains
on the capitals (two rows of pomegranates for
each of the chain networks that decorated the
capitals on top of the pillars);
43 the ten water carts holding the ten basins;
44 the Sea and the twelve oxen under it;
45 the ash buckets, the shovels, and the bowls.

Huram made all these things of burnished bronze
for the Temple of the LORD, just as King Solomon had
directed. 46The king had them cast in clay molds in
the Jordan Valley between Succoth and Zarethan.
47Solomon did not weigh all these things because
there were so many; the weight of the bronze could
not be measured.

48Solomon also made all the furnishings of the
Temple of the LORD:

the gold altar;
the gold table for the Bread of the Presence;
49 the lampstands of solid gold, five on the south
and five on the north, in front of the Most
Holy Place;
the flower decorations, lamps, and tongs—all
of gold;
50 the small bowls, lamp snuffers, bowls, dishes,
and incense burners—all of solid gold;
the doors for the entrances to the Most Holy
Place and the main room of the Temple, with
their fronts overlaid with gold.

51So King Solomon finished all his work on the
Temple of the LORD. Then he brought all the gifts his
father, David, had dedicated—the silver, the gold, and
the various articles—and he stored them in the treasuries of the LORD's Temple.

2 CHRONICLES 3:15–4:22

For the front of the Temple, he made two pillars that
were 27 feet* tall, each topped by a capital extending upward another 7½ feet. 16He made a network
of interwoven chains and used them to decorate
the tops of the pillars. He also made 100 decorative pomegranates and attached them to the chains.
17Then he set up the two pillars at the entrance of
the Temple, one to the south of the entrance and the
other to the north. He named the one on the south
Jakin, and the one on the north Boaz.*

4:1 Solomon* also made a bronze altar 30 feet long,
30 feet wide, and 15 feet high.* 2Then he cast a great
round basin, 15 feet across from rim to rim, called
the Sea. It was 7½ feet deep and about 45 feet in circumference.* 3It was encircled just below its rim by
two rows of figures that resembled oxen. There were
about six oxen per foot* all the way around, and they
were cast as part of the basin.

1 Kgs 7:31b Hebrew *1½ cubits* [69 centimeters]; also in 7:32. **1 Kgs 7:35** Hebrew *half a cubit wide* [23 centimeters]. **1 Kgs 7:38** Hebrew *40 baths* [840 liters]. **2 Chr 3:15** As in Syriac version (see also 1 Kgs 7:15; 2 Kgs 25:17; Jer 52:21), which reads *18 cubits* [8.3 meters]; Hebrew reads *35 cubits,* which is 52.5 feet or 16.5 meters. **2 Chr 3:17** *Jakin* probably means "he establishes"; *Boaz* probably means "in him is strength." **2 Chr 4:1a** Or *Huram-abi;* Hebrew reads *He.* **2 Chr 4:1b** Hebrew *20 cubits* [9.2 meters] *long, 20 cubits wide, and 10 cubits* [4.6 meters] *high.* **2 Chr 4:2** Hebrew *10 cubits* [4.6 meters] *across . . . 5 cubits* [2.3 meters] *deep and 30 cubits* [13.8 meters] *in circumference.* **2 Chr 4:3** Or *20 oxen per meter;* Hebrew reads *10 per cubit.*

1 Kgs 7:40-47 Huram's items of bronze would look strange in today's churches, but we use other articles to enhance worship (stained-glass windows, crosses, pulpits, hymnbooks, banners, communion tables, projection screens, sound systems, etc.). While the instruments of worship may change, the purpose of worship should never change—to give honor and praise to God.

Solomon's Temple ▶

It took Solomon seven years to build the Temple in Jerusalem, beginning in the fourth year of his reign (967 B.C.). This Temple, laid out like the Tabernacle before it, stood until Jerusalem was destroyed in 586 B.C. This is one rendition of how Solomon's Temple might have been designed.

Solomon's Temple

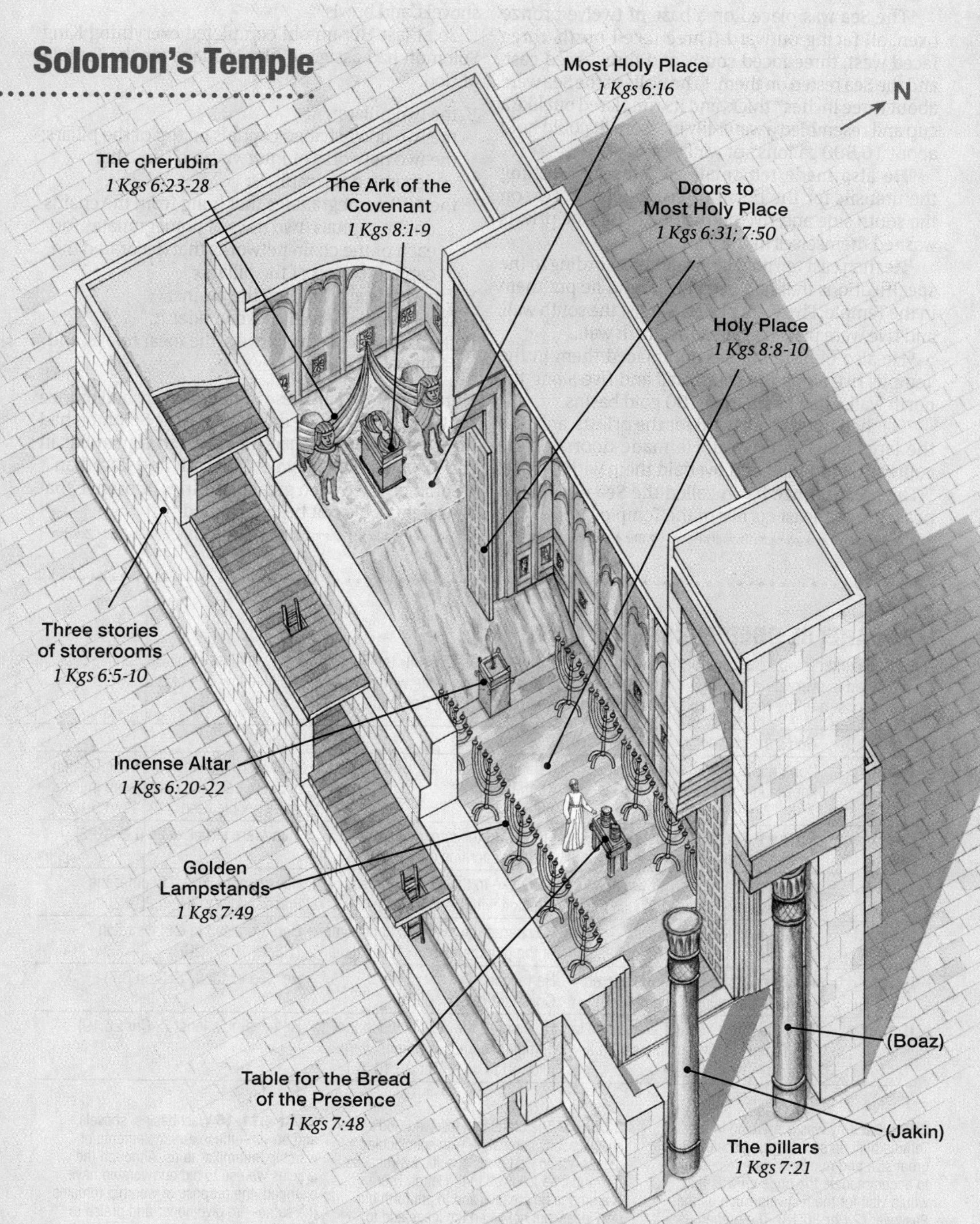
Most Holy Place
1 Kgs 6:16
N
The cherubim
1 Kgs 6:23-28
The Ark of the Covenant
1 Kgs 8:1-9
Doors to Most Holy Place
1 Kgs 6:31; 7:50
Holy Place
1 Kgs 8:8-10
Three stories of storerooms
1 Kgs 6:5-10
Incense Altar
1 Kgs 6:20-22
Golden Lampstands
1 Kgs 7:49
Table for the Bread of the Presence
1 Kgs 7:48
(Boaz)
(Jakin)
The pillars
1 Kgs 7:21
The washbasin and altar of burnt offering were in the courtyard
1 Kgs 7:23; 8:54

▶ **2 CHRONICLES 3:15–4:22** ***(cont.)***

[4]The Sea was placed on a base of twelve bronze
oxen, all facing outward. Three faced north, three
faced west, three faced south, and three faced east,
and the Sea rested on them. [5]The walls of the Sea were
about three inches* thick, and its rim flared out like a
cup and resembled a water lily blossom. It could hold
about 16,500 gallons* of water.
[6]He also made ten smaller basins for washing
the utensils for the burnt offerings. He set five on
the south side and five on the north. But the priests
washed themselves in the Sea.
[7]He then cast ten gold lampstands according to the
specifications that had been given, and he put them
in the Temple. Five were placed against the south wall,
and five were placed against the north wall.
[8]He also built ten tables and placed them in the
Temple, five along the south wall and five along the
north wall. Then he molded 100 gold basins.
[9]He then built a courtyard for the priests, and also
the large outer courtyard. He made doors for the
courtyard entrances and overlaid them with bronze.
[10]The great bronze basin called the Sea was placed
near the southeast corner of the Temple.
[11]Huram-abi also made the necessary washbasins,
shovels, and bowls.

So at last Huram-abi completed everything King Solomon had assigned him to make for the Temple of God:

12 the two pillars;
the two bowl-shaped capitals on top of the pillars;
the two networks of interwoven chains that decorated the capitals;
13 the 400 pomegranates that hung from the chains on the capitals (two rows of pomegranates for each of the chain networks that decorated the capitals on top of the pillars);
14 the water carts holding the basins;
15 the Sea and the twelve oxen under it;
16 the ash buckets, the shovels, the meat hooks, and all the related articles.

Huram-abi made all these things of burnished bronze
for the Temple of the LORD, just as King Solomon had
directed. [17]The king had them cast in clay molds in
the Jordan Valley between Succoth and Zarethan.*
[18]Solomon used such great quantities of bronze that
its weight could not be determined.

2 Chr 4:5a Hebrew *a handbreadth* [8 centimeters]. **2 Chr 4:5b** Hebrew *3,000 baths* [63 kiloliters]. **2 Chr 4:17** As in parallel text at 1 Kgs 7:46; Hebrew reads *Zeredah*.

CAREFUL OBEDIENCE

Solomon and his workers carefully followed God's instructions. As a result, the Temple work was blessed by God and completed in every detail. Here are a few examples of people in the Bible who did *not* carefully follow one of God's instructions, and the resulting consequences. It is not enough to obey God halfheartedly.

Who?	*God's Instruction*	*Disobedience*	*Result*
Adam and Eve	Don't eat fruit from the tree of the knowledge of good and evil (Gen 2:16-17)	Satan tempted them, and they ate (Gen 3:1-6)	They were banished from the Garden of Eden, pain and death were inflicted on all people (Gen 3:24; Rom 5:12)
Nadab and Abihu	Fire for the sacrifice must come from the proper source (Lev 6:12-13)	They used the wrong kind of fire for their sacrifice (Lev 10:1)	They were struck dead (Lev 10:2)
Moses	"Speak to the rock . . . it will pour out its water" (Num 20:8)	He spoke to the rock, but also struck it with his staff (Num 20:11)	He was not allowed to enter the Promised Land (Num 20:12)
Saul	Completely destroy the evil Amalekites (1 Sam 15:3)	He spared the king and kept some of the plunder (1 Sam 15:8-9)	God promised to end his reign (1 Sam 15:16-26)
Uzzah	Only a priest can touch the sacred utensils and objects (Num 4:15)	He touched the Ark of the Covenant (2 Sam 6:6)	He died instantly (2 Sam 6:7)
Uzziah	Only the priests can offer incense in the Temple or Tabernacle sanctuary (Num 16:39-40; 18:7)	He entered the Holy Place in the Temple where only priests were allowed to go (2 Chr 26:16-18)	He became a leper (2 Chr 26:19)

2 Chr 4:6 Why was everything in the Temple built on such a grand scale? The great size and numbers were necessary to accommodate the huge crowds that would visit for the festivals, such as the Passover (2 Chr 30:13). The numerous daily sacrifices required many priests and much equipment.

2 Chr 4:7 The craftsmen followed God's specifications carefully—with spectacular results. When God gives specific instructions, they must be followed to the letter. There is a time to be creative and to put forth our own ideas, but not when the ideas add to, alter, or contradict any specific directions God has already given to us in the Bible. For best results in your spiritual life, carefully seek and follow God's instructions.

2 Chr 4:11-16 Washbasins, shovels, and bowls—these are implements of worship unfamiliar to us. Although the articles we use to aid our worship have changed, the purpose of worship remains the same—to give honor and praise to God. We must never let our worship of God be overshadowed by things we use to help us worship him.

19Solomon also made all the furnishings for the
Temple of God:

the gold altar;
the tables for the Bread of the Presence;
20 the lampstands and their lamps of solid gold,
to burn in front of the Most Holy Place as
prescribed;
21 the flower decorations, lamps, and tongs—
all of the purest gold;
22 the lamp snuffers, bowls, dishes, and incense
burners—all of solid gold;
the doors for the entrances to the Most Holy
Place and the main room of the Temple,
overlaid with gold.

The Ark Brought to the Temple PARALLEL

1 KINGS 8:1-11
Solomon then summoned to Jerusalem the elders of
Israel and all the heads of the tribes—the leaders of the
ancestral families of the Israelites. They were to bring
the Ark of the LORD's Covenant to the Temple from its
location in the City of David, also known as Zion. 2So
all the men of Israel assembled before King Solomon
at the annual Festival of Shelters, which is held in early
autumn in the month of Ethanim.*
3When all the elders of Israel arrived, the priests
picked up the Ark. 4The priests and Levites brought
up the Ark of the LORD along with the special tent* and
all the sacred items that had been in it. 5There, before
the Ark, King Solomon and the entire community of
Israel sacrificed so many sheep, goats, and cattle that
no one could keep count!
6Then the priests carried the Ark of the LORD's Covenant into the inner sanctuary of the Temple—the
Most Holy Place—and placed it beneath the wings of
the cherubim. 7The cherubim spread their wings over
the Ark, forming a canopy over the Ark and its carrying poles. 8These poles were so long that their ends
could be seen from the Temple's main room—the Holy
Place—but not from the outside. They are still there to
this day. 9Nothing was in the Ark except the two stone
tablets that Moses had placed in it at Mount Sinai,*
where the LORD made a covenant with the people of
Israel when they left the land of Egypt.
10When the priests came out of the Holy Place,
a thick cloud filled the Temple of the LORD. 11The
priests could not continue their service because of
the cloud, for the glorious presence of the LORD filled
the Temple.

2 CHRONICLES 5:1-14
So Solomon finished all his work on the Temple of the
LORD. Then he brought all the gifts his father, David,
had dedicated—the silver, the gold, and the various
articles—and he stored them in the treasuries of the
Temple of God.
2Solomon then summoned to Jerusalem the elders
of Israel and all the heads of tribes—the leaders of the
ancestral families of Israel. They were to bring the Ark
of the LORD's Covenant to the Temple from its location
in the City of David, also known as Zion. 3So all the

The Temple is completed

1 Kgs 8:2 Hebrew *at the festival in the month Ethanim, which is the seventh month.* The Festival of Shelters began on the fifteenth day of the seventh month of the ancient Hebrew lunar calendar. This day occurred in late September, October, or early November. **1 Kgs 8:4** Hebrew *the Tent of Meeting;* i.e., the tent mentioned in 2 Sam 6:17 and 1 Chr 16:1. **1 Kgs 8:9** Hebrew *at Horeb,* another name for Sinai.

2 Chr 4:22 All these details about the Temple demonstrated the care Israel gave to acts of worship (see the note on 2 Chr 3:1ff, p. 611). The instructions also served as a manual to the original readers of 2 Chronicles, those who would rebuild a new Temple on its original site (Ezra 3:8–6:15) after Solomon's Temple was destroyed by the Babylonians (2 Kgs 25).

1 Kgs 8:1ff Solomon gathered the people not just to dedicate the Temple, but to rededicate themselves to God's service. Solomon could well be speaking these words to us today: "And may you be completely faithful to the LORD our God. May you always obey his decrees and commands, just as you are doing today" (1 Kgs 8:61).

1 Kgs 8:1ff What was the difference between the Tabernacle and the Temple, and why did the Israelites change from one to the other? As a tent, the Tabernacle was a portable place of worship designed for the people as they were traveling toward the Promised Land. The Temple was a permanent place to worship God after the Israelites were at peace in their land. To bring the Ark of the Lord's Covenant to the Temple signified God's actual presence there.

2 Chr 5:1ff Why is there so much emphasis on the Temple in the Old Testament?

(1) *It was a symbol of religious authority.* The Temple was God's way of centralizing worship at Jerusalem in order to ensure that correct belief would be kept intact through many generations.

(2) *It was a symbol of God's holiness.* The Temple's beautiful atmosphere inspired respect and awe for God; it was the setting for many of the great visions of the prophets.

(3) *It was a symbol of God's covenant with Israel.* The Temple kept the people focused upon God's law (the tablets of the Ten Commandments were kept in the Temple) rather than on the kings' exploits. It was a place where God was especially present with his people.

(4) *It was a symbol of forgiveness.* The Temple's design, furniture, and customs were great object lessons for all the people, reminding them of the seriousness of sin, the penalty that sin incurred, and their need of forgiveness.

(5) *It prepared the people for the Messiah.* In the New Testament, Christ said he came to fulfill the law, not destroy it. Hebrews 8:1-2; 9:11-12 use Temple customs to explain what Christ did when he died for us.

(6) *It was a testimony to human effort and creativity.* Inspired by the beauty of God's character, people devoted themselves to high achievements in engineering, science, and art in order to praise him.

(7) *It was a place of prayer.* In the Temple, people could spend time in prayer to God.

2 Chr 5:1-3 The Temple took seven years to build. It was completed in the eighth month (November) of Solomon's eleventh year as king, 959 B.C. (1 Kgs 6:38). Because the dedication ceremonies were held in early autumn, they must have occurred either one month before or eleven months after the Temple's completion.

2 Chr 5:3 The Festival of Shelters celebrated God's protection of Israel as they wandered in the wilderness before entering the Promised Land. The purpose of this annual festival was to renew Israel's commitment to God and their trust in his guidance and protection. The festival beautifully coincided with the dedication of the Temple. As the people remembered the wanderings in the wilderness when their ancestors had lived in tents, they were even more thankful for the permanence of this glorious Temple.

▶ **2 CHRONICLES 5:1-14** ***(cont.)***
men of Israel assembled before the king at the annual
Festival of Shelters, which is held in early autumn.*
[4]When all the elders of Israel arrived, the Levites
picked up the Ark. [5]The priests and Levites brought
up the Ark along with the special tent* and all the sacred items that had been in it. [6]There, before the Ark,
King Solomon and the entire community of Israel
sacrificed so many sheep, goats, and cattle that no
one could keep count!
[7]Then the priests carried the Ark of the LORD's Covenant into the inner sanctuary of the Temple—the
Most Holy Place—and placed it beneath the wings
of the cherubim. [8]The cherubim spread their wings
over the Ark, forming a canopy over the Ark and its
carrying poles. [9]These poles were so long that their
ends could be seen from the Temple's main room—
the Holy Place*—but not from the outside. They are
still there to this day. [10]Nothing was in the Ark except
the two stone tablets that Moses had placed in it at
Mount Sinai,* where the LORD made a covenant with
the people of Israel when they left Egypt.
[11]Then the priests left the Holy Place. All the priests
who were present had purified themselves, whether
or not they were on duty that day. [12]And the Levites
who were musicians—Asaph, Heman, Jeduthun, and
all their sons and brothers—were dressed in fine
linen robes and stood at the east side of the altar playing cymbals, lyres, and harps. They were joined by
120 priests who were playing trumpets. [13]The trumpeters and singers performed together in unison to
praise and give thanks to the LORD. Accompanied by
trumpets, cymbals, and other instruments, they raised
their voices and praised the LORD with these words:

"He is good!
His faithful love endures forever!"

At that moment a thick cloud filled the Temple of
the LORD. [14]The priests could not continue their service because of the cloud, for the glorious presence
of the LORD filled the Temple of God.

Solomon Praises the LORD PARALLEL

1 KINGS 8:12-21
Then Solomon prayed, "O LORD, you have said that
you would live in a thick cloud of darkness. [13]Now

2 Chr 5:3 Hebrew *at the festival that is in the seventh month.* The Festival of Shelters began on the fifteenth day of the seventh month of the ancient Hebrew lunar calendar. This day occurred in late September, October, or early November. **2 Chr 5:5** Hebrew *the Tent of Meeting;* i.e., the tent mentioned in 2 Sam 6:17 and 1 Chr 16:1. **2 Chr 5:9** As in some Hebrew manuscripts and Greek version (see also 1 Kgs 8:8); Masoretic Text reads *from the Ark in front of the Most Holy Place.* **2 Chr 5:10** Hebrew *Horeb,* another name for Sinai.

Zion

Zion was the Jebusite fortress in Jerusalem conquered by David. Thereafter, Zion was used by biblical writers to identify other areas of Jerusalem and was eventually used as a designation of the entire city. The transfer of the Ark from "the City of David, also known as Zion" (2 Chr 5:2) to the Temple hill brought both an extension and a reduction of the territory embraced by the term "Zion." The whole city could still be called Zion, but from this point on, there would be a close identification between Zion and the Temple hill. The Temple precincts became the primary Zion; references to Zion in the poetic books and in the prophets are primarily to the Temple area as the dwelling place of God. Zion was also used to describe, spiritually speaking, the eternal city of God, where all God's people will dwell (Ps 146:10). We can hold on to this precious promise!

2 Chr 5:7-12 The priests came out of the Holy Place after having placed the Ark in the Most Holy Place of the Temple. The Holy Place is the outer room, where the Bread of the Presence, the altar of incense, and the lampstand were kept. Ordinarily the Most Holy Place could be entered only once a year by the high priest on the Day of Atonement. On this unique occasion, however, several priests had to enter the Most Holy Place to carry the Ark to its new resting place. The Levites praised God when these priests emerged from the Holy Place because they then knew God had accepted this new home for the Ark (2 Chr 5:13).

2 Chr 5:9 Under God's inspiration, some books of the Bible were compiled and edited from other sources. Because 1 and 2 Chronicles cover many centuries, they were compiled from several sources. The phrase "they are still there to this day" (see also 1 Kgs 8:8) was likely taken from material written before Judah's exile in 586 B.C. Although 1 and 2 Chronicles were compiled after the Exile and after Solomon's Temple was destroyed, the writer thought it best to leave this phrase in the narrative.

2 Chr 5:13 The first service at the Temple began with honoring God and acknowledging his presence and goodness. In the same way, our worship should begin by acknowledging God's love. Praise God first; then you will be prepared to present your needs to him. Recalling God's love and mercy will inspire you to worship him daily. Psalm 107 is an example of how David recalled God's enduring love.

1 Kgs 8:15-21 For 480 years after Israel's escape from Egypt, God did not ask his people to build a temple for him. Instead, he emphasized the importance of his presence among them and their need for spiritual leaders. It is easy to think of a building as the focus of God's presence and power, but

I have built a glorious Temple for you, a place where you can live forever!*"

14Then the king turned around to the entire community of Israel standing before him and gave this blessing: 15"Praise the LORD, the God of Israel, who has kept the promise he made to my father, David. For he told my father, 16'From the day I brought my people Israel out of Egypt, I have never chosen a city among any of the tribes of Israel as the place where a Temple should be built to honor my name. But I have chosen David to be king over my people Israel.'"

17Then Solomon said, "My father, David, wanted to build this Temple to honor the name of the LORD, the God of Israel. 18But the LORD told him, 'You wanted to build the Temple to honor my name. Your intention is good, 19but you are not the one to do it. One of your own sons will build the Temple to honor me.'

20"And now the LORD has fulfilled the promise he made, for I have become king in my father's place, and I now sit on the throne of Israel, just as the LORD promised. I have built this Temple to honor the name of the LORD, the God of Israel. 21And I have prepared a place there for the Ark, which contains the covenant that the LORD made with our ancestors when he brought them out of Egypt."

2 CHRONICLES 6:1-11

Then Solomon prayed, "O LORD, you have said that you would live in a thick cloud of darkness. 2Now I have built a glorious Temple for you, a place where you can live forever!"

3Then the king turned around to the entire community of Israel standing before him and gave this blessing: 4"Praise the LORD, the God of Israel, who has kept the promise he made to my father, David. For he told my father, 5'From the day I brought my people out of the land of Egypt, I have never chosen a city among any of the tribes of Israel as the place where a Temple should be built to honor my name. Nor have I chosen a king to lead my people Israel. 6But now I have chosen Jerusalem as the place for my name to be honored, and I have chosen David to be king over my people Israel.'"

7Then Solomon said, "My father, David, wanted to build this Temple to honor the name of the LORD, the God of Israel. 8But the LORD told him, 'You wanted to build the Temple to honor my name. Your intention is good, 9but you are not the one to do it. One of your own sons will build the Temple to honor me.'

10"And now the LORD has fulfilled the promise he made, for I have become king in my father's place, and now I sit on the throne of Israel, just as the LORD promised. I have built this Temple to honor the name of the LORD, the God of Israel. 11There I have placed the Ark, which contains the covenant that the LORD made with the people of Israel."

Solomon's Prayer of Dedication PARALLEL

1 KINGS 8:22-53

Then Solomon stood before the altar of the LORD in front of the entire community of Israel. He lifted his hands toward heaven, 23and he prayed,

"O LORD, God of Israel, there is no God like you in all of heaven above or on the earth below. You keep your covenant and show unfailing love to all who walk before you in wholehearted devotion. 24You have kept your promise to your servant David, my father. You made that promise with your own mouth, and with your own hands you have fulfilled it today.

25"And now, O LORD, God of Israel, carry out the additional promise you made to your servant David, my father. For you said to him, 'If your descendants guard their behavior and faithfully follow me as you have done, one of them will always sit on the throne of Israel.' 26Now, O God of Israel, fulfill this promise to your servant David, my father.

27"But will God really live on earth? Why, even the highest heavens cannot contain you. How much less this Temple I have built! 28Nevertheless, listen to my prayer and my plea, O LORD my God. Hear the cry and the prayer that your servant is making to you today. 29May you watch over this Temple night and day, this place where you have said, 'My name will be there.' May you always hear the prayers I make toward this place. 30May you hear the humble and earnest requests from me and your people Israel when we pray toward this place. Yes, hear us from heaven where you live, and when you hear, forgive.

31"If someone wrongs another person and is required to take an oath of innocence in front of your altar in this Temple, 32then hear from heaven and judge between your servants—the accuser and the accused. Punish the guilty as

1 Kgs 8:13 Some Greek texts add the line *Is this not written in the Book of Jashar?*

God chooses and uses *people* to do his work. Building or enlarging our place of worship may be necessary, but it should never take priority over developing spiritual leaders.

2 Chr 6:3 As the people received Solomon's blessing, they stood; as Solomon prayed, he knelt (2 Chr 6:13). Both standing and kneeling are acts of reverence. Acts of reverence make us feel more worshipful, and they let others see that we are honoring God. When you stand or kneel in church or at prayer, make these actions more than mere forms prescribed by tradition. Let them indicate your love for God.

1 Kgs 8:24 Solomon was referring to the promise God had made to David in 2 Samuel 7:12-15 that one of David's sons would build the Temple.

1 Kgs 8:27 In his prayer of dedication, Solomon declared that even the highest heavens cannot contain God. Isn't it amazing that, though the heavens can't contain God, he is willing to live in the hearts of those who love him? The God of the universe takes up residence in his people.

▶ **1 KINGS 8:22-53 *(cont.)***
they deserve. Acquit the innocent because of
their innocence.
33"If your people Israel are defeated by their
enemies because they have sinned against you,
and if they turn to you and acknowledge your
name and pray to you here in this Temple, 34then
hear from heaven and forgive the sin of your
people Israel and return them to this land you
gave their ancestors.
35"If the skies are shut up and there is no rain
because your people have sinned against you, and
if they pray toward this Temple and acknowledge
your name and turn from their sins because you
have punished them, 36then hear from heaven
and forgive the sins of your servants, your people
Israel. Teach them to follow the right path, and
send rain on your land that you have given to your
people as their special possession.
37"If there is a famine in the land or a plague or
crop disease or attacks of locusts or caterpillars,
or if your people's enemies are in the land
besieging their towns—whatever disaster or
disease there is—38and if your people Israel pray
about their troubles, raising their hands toward
this Temple, 39then hear from heaven where you
live, and forgive. Give your people what their
actions deserve, for you alone know each human
heart. 40Then they will fear you as long as they
live in the land you gave to our ancestors.
41"In the future, foreigners who do not belong
to your people Israel will hear of you. They will
come from distant lands because of your name,
42for they will hear of your great name and your
strong hand and your powerful arm. And when
they pray toward this Temple, 43then hear from
heaven where you live, and grant what they ask
of you. In this way, all the people of the earth
will come to know and fear you, just as your own
people Israel do. They, too, will know that this
Temple I have built honors your name.
44"If your people go out where you send them
to fight their enemies, and if they pray to the
LORD by turning toward this city you have chosen
and toward this Temple I have built to honor your
name, 45then hear their prayers from heaven and
uphold their cause.
46"If they sin against you—and who has never
sinned?—you might become angry with them
and let their enemies conquer them and take
them captive to their land far away or near.
47But in that land of exile, they might turn to
you in repentance and pray, 'We have sinned,
done evil, and acted wickedly.' 48If they turn to
you with their whole heart and soul in the land
of their enemies and pray toward the land you
gave to their ancestors—toward this city you
have chosen, and toward this Temple I have built
to honor your name—49then hear their prayers
and their petition from heaven where you live,
and uphold their cause. 50Forgive your people
who have sinned against you. Forgive all the
offenses they have committed against you. Make
their captors merciful to them, 51for they are
your people—your special possession—whom
you brought out of the iron-smelting furnace of
Egypt.
52"May your eyes be open to my requests and
to the requests of your people Israel. May you
hear and answer them whenever they cry out
to you. 53For when you brought our ancestors
out of Egypt, O Sovereign LORD, you told your
servant Moses that you had set Israel apart from
all the nations of the earth to be your own special
possession."

2 CHRONICLES 6:12-42
Then Solomon stood before the altar of the LORD
in front of the entire community of Israel, and he
lifted his hands in prayer. 13Now Solomon had made
a bronze platform 7½ feet long, 7½ feet wide, and
4½ feet high* and had placed it at the center of the
Temple's outer courtyard. He stood on the platform,
and then he knelt in front of the entire community of
Israel and lifted his hands toward heaven. 14He prayed,

2 Chr 6:13 Hebrew *5 cubits* [2.3 meters] *long, 5 cubits wide, and 3 cubits* [1.4 meters] *high.*

---

1 Kgs 8:33-34 After Solomon's reign, the people continually turned away from God. The rest of the kingdom era is a vivid fulfillment of Solomon's description in these verses. As a result of the people's sin, God let them be overrun by enemies several times. Then, in desperation, they cried out to God for forgiveness, and God restored them.

1 Kgs 8:41-43 God chose Israel to be a blessing to the whole world (Gen 12:1-3). This blessing found its fulfillment in Jesus—a descendant of Abraham and David (Gal 3:8-9)—who became the Messiah for all people, Jews and non-Jews. When the Israelites first entered the Promised Land, they were ordered to clear out several wicked nations; thus, the Old Testament records many wars. But we should not conclude that war was Israel's first duty. After subduing the evil people, Israel was to become a light to the surrounding nations. Sadly, Israel's own sin and spiritual blindness prevented them from reaching out to the rest of the world with God's love. Reaching out to the world is still the commission of God's people today. Christians need to take every opportunity to spread God's love to the world.

1 Kgs 8:46-53 Solomon, who seemed to have prophetic insight into the future captivities of his people (2 Kgs 17; 25), asked God to be merciful to them when they cried out to him, to forgive them, and to return them to their homeland. Ezra 1–2; Nehemiah 1–2 reference their return.

2 Chr 6:12-13 It was unusual for a king to kneel before someone else in front of his own people, because kneeling meant submitting to a higher authority. Solomon demonstrated his great love and respect for God by kneeling before him. His action showed that he acknowledged God as the ultimate king and authority, and it encouraged the people to do the same.

"O LORD, God of Israel, there is no God like you in
all of heaven and earth. You keep your covenant
and show unfailing love to all who walk before
you in wholehearted devotion. 15You have kept
your promise to your servant David, my father. You
made that promise with your own mouth, and with
your own hands you have fulfilled it today.
16"And now, O LORD, God of Israel, carry out
the additional promise you made to your servant
David, my father. For you said to him, 'If your
descendants guard their behavior and faithfully
follow my Law as you have done, one of them will
always sit on the throne of Israel.' 17Now, O LORD,
God of Israel, fulfill this promise to your servant
David.
18"But will God really live on earth among
people? Why, even the highest heavens cannot
contain you. How much less this Temple I have
built! 19Nevertheless, listen to my prayer and
my plea, O LORD my God. Hear the cry and the
prayer that your servant is making to you. 20May
you watch over this Temple day and night, this
place where you have said you would put your
name. May you always hear the prayers I make
toward this place. 21May you hear the humble
and earnest requests from me and your people
Israel when we pray toward this place. Yes, hear
us from heaven where you live, and when you
hear, forgive.
22"If someone wrongs another person and is
required to take an oath of innocence in front of
your altar at this Temple, 23then hear from heaven
and judge between your servants—the accuser
and the accused. Pay back the guilty as they
deserve. Acquit the innocent because of their
innocence.
24"If your people Israel are defeated by their
enemies because they have sinned against you,
and if they turn back and acknowledge your
name and pray to you here in this Temple, 25then
hear from heaven and forgive the sin of your
people Israel and return them to this land you
gave to them and to their ancestors.
26"If the skies are shut up and there is no rain
because your people have sinned against you, and
if they pray toward this Temple and acknowledge
your name and turn from their sins because you
have punished them, 27then hear from heaven
and forgive the sins of your servants, your people
Israel. Teach them to follow the right path, and
send rain on your land that you have given to your
people as their special possession.
28"If there is a famine in the land or a plague or
crop disease or attacks of locusts or caterpillars, or
if your people's enemies are in the land besieging
their towns—whatever disaster or disease there is—
29and if your people Israel pray about their troubles
or sorrow, raising their hands toward this Temple,
30then hear from heaven where you live, and forgive.
Give your people what their actions deserve, for you
alone know each human heart. 31Then they will fear
you and walk in your ways as long as they live in the
land you gave to our ancestors.
32"In the future, foreigners who do not belong to
your people Israel will hear of you. They will come
from distant lands when they hear of your great
name and your strong hand and your powerful
arm. And when they pray toward this Temple,
33then hear from heaven where you live, and grant
what they ask of you. In this way, all the people of
the earth will come to know and fear you, just as
your own people Israel do. They, too, will know that
this Temple I have built honors your name.
34"If your people go out where you send them
to fight their enemies, and if they pray to you by
turning toward this city you have chosen and
toward this Temple I have built to honor your
name, 35then hear their prayers from heaven and
uphold their cause.
36"If they sin against you—and who has never
sinned?—you might become angry with them
and let their enemies conquer them and take

2 Chr 6:18 Solomon marveled that God would be willing to live on earth among sinful people. We marvel that God, through his Son, Jesus, lived among us in human form to reveal his eternal purposes to us. In doing so, God was reaching out to us in love. God wants us to reach out to him in return in order to know him and to love him with all our hearts. Don't simply marvel at his power; take time to get to know him.

2 Chr 6:19-42 As Solomon led the people in prayer, he asked God to hear their prayers concerning a variety of situations: (1) crime (2 Chr 6:22-23); (2) enemy attacks (2 Chr 6:24-25); (3) drought (2 Chr 6:26-27); (4) famine (2 Chr 6:28-31); (5) the influx of foreigners (2 Chr 6:32-33); (6) war (2 Chr 6:34-35); and (7) sin (2 Chr 6:36-39). God is concerned with whatever we face, even the difficult consequences we bring upon ourselves. He wants us to turn to him in prayer. When you pray, remember that God hears you. Don't let the extremity of your situation cause you to doubt his care for you.

2 Chr 6:26 Why would Solomon assume that drought would come as a result of sin? Sin is not necessarily the direct cause of natural disasters today, but this was a special case. God had made a specific covenant with the Israelites that drought could be a consequence of their sins (Deut 28:20-24).

2 Chr 6:30 Have you ever felt far from God, separated by feelings of failure and personal problems? In his prayer, Solomon underscored the fact that God stands ready to hear his people, to forgive their sins, and to restore their relationship with him. God is waiting and listening for our confessions of guilt and our recommitment to obey him. He hears us when we pour out our needs and problems to him and is ready to forgive us and restore us to fellowship with him. Don't wait to experience his loving forgiveness.

2 Chr 6:36 "Who has never sinned?" The Bible makes it clear that no one is exempt from sin, not even God's appointed kings. Sin is a condition we all share, and we all should acknowledge it as Solomon did. When we realize we have sinned, we should quickly ask God for forgiveness and restoration. Knowing we have a tendency to sin should keep us close to God, seeking his guidance and strength. This truth is also mentioned in Psalm 14:3; Ecclesiastes 7:20; and Romans 3:23.

▶ 2 CHRONICLES 6:12-42 *(cont.)*

them captive to a foreign land far away or near.
37But in that land of exile, they might turn to you
in repentance and pray, 'We have sinned, done
evil, and acted wickedly.' 38If they turn to you with
their whole heart and soul in the land of their
captivity and pray toward the land you gave to
their ancestors—toward this city you have chosen,
and toward this Temple I have built to honor
your name—39then hear their prayers and their
petitions from heaven where you live, and uphold
their cause. Forgive your people who have sinned
against you.
40"O my God, may your eyes be open and your
ears attentive to all the prayers made to you in
this place.

41 "And now arise, O LORD God, and enter your
resting place,
along with the Ark, the symbol of your power.
May your priests, O LORD God, be clothed with
salvation;
may your loyal servants rejoice in your
goodness.
42 O LORD God, do not reject the king you have
anointed.
Remember your unfailing love for your
servant David."

The Dedication of the Temple PARALLEL

1 KINGS 8:54-66

When Solomon finished making these prayers and petitions to the LORD, he stood up in front of the altar of
the LORD, where he had been kneeling with his hands
raised toward heaven. 55He stood and in a loud voice
blessed the entire congregation of Israel:
56"Praise the LORD who has given rest to his people
Israel, just as he promised. Not one word has failed
of all the wonderful promises he gave through his
servant Moses. 57May the LORD our God be with us as
he was with our ancestors; may he never leave us or
abandon us. 58May he give us the desire to do his will
in everything and to obey all the commands, decrees,
and regulations that he gave our ancestors. 59And may
these words that I have prayed in the presence of the
LORD be before him constantly, day and night, so that
the LORD our God may give justice to me and to his
people Israel, according to each day's needs. 60Then
people all over the earth will know that the LORD alone
is God and there is no other. 61And may you be completely faithful to the LORD our God. May you always
obey his decrees and commands, just as you are doing
today."
62Then the king and all Israel with him offered sacrifices to the LORD. 63Solomon offered to the LORD a
peace offering of 22,000 cattle and 120,000 sheep
and goats. And so the king and all the people of Israel
dedicated the Temple of the LORD.
64That same day the king consecrated the central
area of the courtyard in front of the LORD's Temple.
He offered burnt offerings, grain offerings, and the
fat of peace offerings there, because the bronze altar
in the LORD's presence was too small to hold all the
burnt offerings, grain offerings, and the fat of the
peace offerings.
65Then Solomon and all Israel celebrated the Festival of Shelters* in the presence of the LORD our God.
A large congregation had gathered from as far away as
Lebo-hamath in the north and the Brook of Egypt in
the south. The celebration went on for fourteen days
in all—seven days for the dedication of the altar and
seven days for the Festival of Shelters.* 66After the
festival was over,* Solomon sent the people home.
They blessed the king and went to their homes joyful and glad because the LORD had been good to his
servant David and to his people Israel.

2 CHRONICLES 7:1-10

When Solomon finished praying, fire flashed down
from heaven and burned up the burnt offerings and
sacrifices, and the glorious presence of the LORD filled
the Temple. 2The priests could not enter the Temple of
the LORD because the glorious presence of the LORD
filled it. 3When all the people of Israel saw the fire
coming down and the glorious presence of the LORD
filling the Temple, they fell face down on the ground
and worshiped and praised the LORD, saying,

"He is good!
His faithful love endures forever!"

4Then the king and all the people offered sacrifices to the LORD. 5King Solomon offered a sacrifice
of 22,000 cattle and 120,000 sheep and goats. And
so the king and all the people dedicated the Temple

1 Kgs 8:65a Hebrew *the festival;* see note on 8:2. **1 Kgs 8:65b** Hebrew *seven days and seven days, fourteen days;* compare parallel text at 2 Chr 7:8-10.
1 Kgs 8:66 Hebrew *On the eighth day,* probably referring to the day following the seven-day Festival of Shelters; compare parallel text at 2 Chr 7:9-10.

1 Kgs 8:56-60 Solomon praised the Lord and prayed for the people. His prayer can be a pattern for our prayers. He had five basic requests: (1) for God's presence (1 Kgs 8:57); (2) for the desire to do God's will in everything (1 Kgs 8:58); (3) for the desire and ability to obey God's decrees and commands (1 Kgs 8:58); (4) for help with each day's needs (1 Kgs 8:59); and (5) for the spread of God's Kingdom to the entire world (1 Kgs 8:60). These needs are just as important today. When you pray for your church or family, you can make these same requests to God.

2 Chr 7:1-2 God sent fire from heaven to consume the offering and to begin the fire that was to burn continuously under the altar of burnt offering (see Lev 6:8-13). This perpetual fire symbolized God's presence. God also sent fire when inaugurating the Tabernacle (Lev 9:22-24). This was the real dedication of the Temple because only God's purifying power can make something holy.

2 Chr 7:4-5 The Temple was dedicated to God, and Solomon and the people prepared to worship him. *Dedication* means setting apart a place, an object, or a person for an exclusive purpose. The purpose of this dedication was to set apart the Temple as a place to worship God. Today, our bodies are God's

of God. 6The priests took their assigned positions, and
so did the Levites who were singing, "His faithful love
endures forever!" They accompanied the singing with
music from the instruments King David had made for
praising the LORD. Across from the Levites, the priests
blew the trumpets, while all Israel stood.
7Solomon then consecrated the central area of the
courtyard in front of the LORD's Temple. He offered
burnt offerings and the fat of peace offerings there,
because the bronze altar he had built could not hold all
the burnt offerings, grain offerings, and sacrificial fat.
8For the next seven days Solomon and all Israel celebrated the Festival of Shelters.* A large congregation
had gathered from as far away as Lebo-hamath in the
north and the Brook of Egypt in the south. 9On the
eighth day they had a closing ceremony, for they had
celebrated the dedication of the altar for seven days
and the Festival of Shelters for seven days. 10Then at
the end of the celebration,* Solomon sent the people
home. They were all joyful and glad because the LORD
had been so good to David and to Solomon and to his
people Israel.

2 Chr 7:8 Hebrew *the festival* (also in 7:9); see note on 5:3. **2 Chr 7:10** Hebrew *Then on the twenty-third day of the seventh month.* This day of the ancient Hebrew lunar calendar occurred in October or early November.

4. SOLOMON'S GREATNESS

The nation of Israel flourished under Solomon's leadership. In addition to completing the Temple and a magnificent palace complex, Solomon built up great wealth and expanded the borders of Israel to its largest territory ever. Solomon's wealth and wisdom were so legendary that leaders of other nations came to see if the reports were exaggerated.

The LORD's Response to Solomon PARALLEL

1 KINGS 9:1-9

So Solomon finished building the Temple of the LORD,
as well as the royal palace. He completed everything he
had planned to do. 2Then the LORD appeared to Solomon a second time, as he had done before at Gibeon.
3The LORD said to him,

"I have heard your prayer and your petition. I
have set this Temple apart to be holy—this place
you have built where my name will be honored
forever. I will always watch over it, for it is dear
to my heart.
4"As for you, if you will follow me with integrity
and godliness, as David your father did, obeying
all my commands, decrees, and regulations,
5then I will establish the throne of your dynasty
over Israel forever. For I made this promise to
your father, David: 'One of your descendants will
always sit on the throne of Israel.'
6"But if you or your descendants abandon me
and disobey the commands and decrees I have
given you, and if you serve and worship other
gods, 7then I will uproot Israel from this land
that I have given them. I will reject this Temple
that I have made holy to honor my name. I will
make Israel an object of mockery and ridicule
among the nations. 8And though this Temple is
impressive now, all who pass by will be appalled
and will shake their heads in amazement. They
will ask, 'Why did the LORD do such terrible things
to this land and to this Temple?'
9"And the answer will be, 'Because his people
abandoned the LORD their God, who brought
their ancestors out of Egypt, and they worshiped
other gods instead and bowed down to them.
That is why the LORD has brought all these
disasters on them.'"

2 CHRONICLES 7:11-22

So Solomon finished the Temple of the LORD, as well
as the royal palace. He completed everything he had
planned to do in the construction of the Temple and
the palace. 12Then one night the LORD appeared to
Solomon and said,

"I have heard your prayer and have chosen this
Temple as the place for making sacrifices. 13At
times I might shut up the heavens so that no rain
falls, or command grasshoppers to devour your
crops, or send plagues among you. 14Then if my
people who are called by my name will humble
themselves and pray and seek my face and turn
from their wicked ways, I will hear from heaven

temple (2 Cor 6:16). Solomon's dedication of the Temple shows us that we should dedicate ourselves to carry out God's special purpose (Eph 1:11-12).

1 Kgs 9:4-9 God appeared to Solomon a second time; the first had been at Gibeon (1 Kgs 3:4-15). For more on the conditions of God's great promise to David and his descendants, see the note on 1 Kings 2:3-4, p. 545.

2 Chr 7:12 Months, maybe years, had passed since Solomon's prayer of dedication (2 Chr 6). Several other building projects had been completed after the Temple (2 Chr 7:11; 8:1). Then after all this time, God told Solomon that he had heard Solomon's prayer. How often do we look for immediate answers to our prayers and, when nothing happens, wonder if God has heard us? God does hear, and he will provide for us. We must trust that God will answer at the proper time.

2 Chr 7:14 In 2 Chronicles 6:37-39, Solomon asked God to make provision for the people when they sinned. God answered with four conditions for forgiveness: (1) Humble yourself by admitting your sins, (2) pray to God, asking for forgiveness, (3) seek God continually, and (4) turn from sinful behavior. True repentance is more than talk—it is changed behavior. Whether we sin individually, as a group, or as a nation, following these steps will lead to forgiveness. God will answer our earnest prayers.

▸ 2 CHRONICLES 7:11-22 ***(cont.)***

and will forgive their sins and restore their land.
15My eyes will be open and my ears attentive
to every prayer made in this place. 16For I have
chosen this Temple and set it apart to be holy—a
place where my name will be honored forever. I
will always watch over it, for it is dear to my heart.
17"As for you, if you faithfully follow me as
David your father did, obeying all my commands,
decrees, and regulations, 18then I will establish
the throne of your dynasty. For I made this
covenant with your father, David, when I said,
'One of your descendants will always rule over
Israel.'
19"But if you or your descendants abandon
me and disobey the decrees and commands I
have given you, and if you serve and worship
other gods, 20then I will uproot the people from
this land that I have given them. I will reject this
Temple that I have made holy to honor my name.
I will make it an object of mockery and ridicule
among the nations. 21And though this Temple is
impressive now, all who pass by will be appalled.
They will ask, 'Why did the LORD do such terrible
things to this land and to this Temple?'
22"And the answer will be, 'Because his people
abandoned the LORD, the God of their ancestors,
who brought them out of Egypt, and they
worshiped other gods instead and bowed down
to them. That is why he has brought all these
disasters on them.'"

Solomon's Agreement with Hiram

1 KINGS 9:10-14

It took Solomon twenty years to build the LORD's
Temple and his own royal palace. At the end of that
time, 11he gave twenty towns in the land of Galilee to
King Hiram of Tyre. (Hiram had previously provided
all the cedar and cypress timber and gold that Solomon had requested.) 12But when Hiram came from
Tyre to see the towns Solomon had given him, he was
not at all pleased with them. 13"What kind of towns
are these, my brother?" he asked. So Hiram called
that area Cabul (which means "worthless"), as it is still
known today. 14Nevertheless, Hiram paid* Solomon
9,000 pounds* of gold.

Solomon's Many Achievements PARALLEL

1 KINGS 9:15-28

This is the account of the forced labor that King Solomon conscripted to build the LORD's Temple, the
royal palace, the supporting terraces,* the wall of Jerusalem, and the cities of Hazor, Megiddo, and Gezer.
16(Pharaoh, the king of Egypt, had attacked and captured Gezer, killing the Canaanite population and
burning it down. He gave the city to his daughter as
a wedding gift when she married Solomon. 17So Solomon rebuilt the city of Gezer.) He also built up the
towns of Lower Beth-horon, 18Baalath, and Tamar*
in the wilderness within his land. 19He built towns
as supply centers and constructed towns where his
chariots and horses* could be stationed. He built

1 Kgs 9:14a Or *For Hiram had paid.* **1 Kgs 9:14b** Hebrew *120 talents* [4,000 kilograms]. **1 Kgs 9:15** Hebrew *the millo;* also in 9:24. The meaning of the Hebrew is uncertain. **1 Kgs 9:18** An alternate reading in the Masoretic Text reads *Tadmor.* **1 Kgs 9:19** Or *and charioteers.*

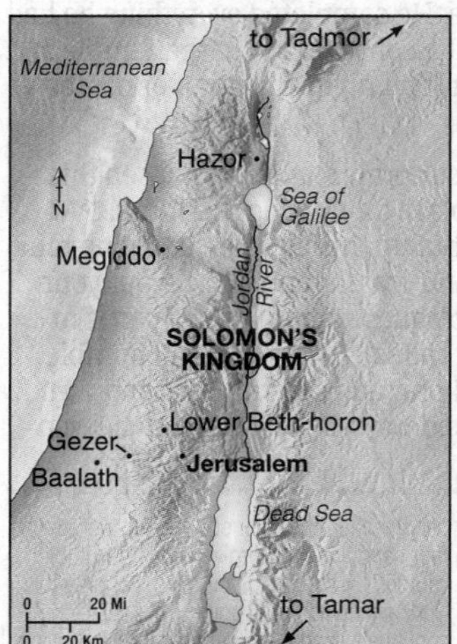

◀ ***SOLOMON'S BUILDING PROJECTS*** *Solomon became known as one of the greatest builders in Israel's history. He built Hazor, Megiddo, and Gezer as fortress cities at key points during his reign. He also rebuilt the cities of lower Beth-horon, Baalath, and Tamar.*

2 Chr 7:17-22 God plainly set forth certain conditions for Solomon to meet if he wanted the kingdom to continue. If Solomon followed God, he and his descendants would prosper; if Solomon did not, he and the nation would be destroyed. In Deuteronomy 27 and 28, these conditions were outlined before all the people.

Sin is deceptively attractive, and Solomon eventually turned from God. As a result, his son and heir lost most of the kingdom. Following God brings benefits and rewards (not necessarily material). Turning away from God brings suffering, punishment, and ultimately destruction. Today, God's conditions are just as clear as they were in Solomon's day. Choose to obey God no matter what happens, knowing that God will eventually bless your efforts.

2 Chr 7:21-22 Soon after Solomon's reign, the Temple was ransacked (2 Chr 12:9). It is difficult for us to imagine that such a great and wise king could become corrupted by idols—symbols of power, prosperity, and sexuality. But even today these idols lure us into their traps. When we allow any desire to rival God's proper place, we have taken the first step toward moral and spiritual decay.

1 Kgs 9:11-14 Was Solomon being unfair to Hiram? It is not clear from these verses whether Solomon gave these towns to Hiram, or they were collateral until he could repay Hiram for the gold he had borrowed. Second Chronicles 8:1-2 implies that the towns were returned to Solomon. In either case, Hiram probably preferred a piece of land on the coast as more suitable for trade (the name he gave these cities, Cabul, sounds like the Hebrew word for "worthless"). In the end, Hiram was repaid many times over through his trade partnerships with Solomon (2 Chr 9:10, 21). Because Phoenicia was on friendly terms with Israel and dependent on it for grain and oil, Hiram's relationship with Solomon was more important than a feud over some cities.

1 Kgs 9:16 At this time Israel and Egypt were the major powers in the Near East. For many years Egypt had retained control of Gezer, even though it was in Israelite territory. In Solomon's time the Pharaoh gave the city to his daughter, whom Solomon married, putting Gezer under Israelite control. Intermarriage among royal families was common, but God did not endorse it (Deut 17:17).

everything he desired in Jerusalem and Lebanon and throughout his entire realm.

[20]There were still some people living in the land who were not Israelites, including Amorites, Hittites, Perizzites, Hivites, and Jebusites. [21]These were descendants of the nations whom the people of Israel had not completely destroyed.* So Solomon conscripted them for his labor force, and they serve in the labor force to this day. [22]But Solomon did not conscript any of the Israelites for forced labor. Instead, he assigned them to serve as fighting men, government officials, officers and captains in his army, commanders of his chariots, and charioteers. [23]Solomon appointed 550 of them to supervise the people working on his various projects.

[24]Solomon moved his wife, Pharaoh's daughter, from the City of David to the new palace he had built for her. Then he constructed the supporting terraces.

[25]Three times each year Solomon presented burnt offerings and peace offerings on the altar he had built for the LORD. He also burned incense to the LORD. And so he finished the work of building the Temple.

[26]King Solomon also built a fleet of ships at Ezion-geber, a port near Elath* in the land of Edom, along the shore of the Red Sea.* [27]Hiram sent experienced crews of sailors to sail the ships with Solomon's men. [28]They sailed to Ophir and brought back to Solomon some sixteen tons* of gold.

2 CHRONICLES 8:1-18

It took Solomon twenty years to build the LORD's Temple and his own royal palace. At the end of that time, [2]Solomon turned his attention to rebuilding the towns that King Hiram* had given him, and he settled Israelites in them.

[3]Solomon also fought against the town of Hamath-zobah and conquered it. [4]He rebuilt Tadmor in the wilderness and built towns in the region of Hamath as supply centers. [5]He fortified the towns of Upper Beth-horon and Lower Beth-horon, rebuilding their walls and installing barred gates. [6]He also rebuilt Baalath and other supply centers and constructed towns where his chariots and horses* could be stationed. He built everything he desired in Jerusalem and Lebanon and throughout his entire realm.

[7]There were still some people living in the land who were not Israelites, including the Hittites, Amorites, Perizzites, Hivites, and Jebusites. [8]These were descendants of the nations whom the people of Israel had not destroyed. So Solomon conscripted them for his labor force, and they serve in the labor force to this day. [9]But Solomon did not conscript any of the Israelites for his labor force. Instead, he assigned them to serve as fighting men, officers in his army, commanders of his chariots, and charioteers. [10]King Solomon appointed 250 of them to supervise the people.

[11]Solomon moved his wife, Pharaoh's daughter, from the City of David to the new palace he had built for her. He said, "My wife must not live in King David's palace, for the Ark of the LORD has been there, and it is holy ground."

[12]Then Solomon presented burnt offerings to the LORD on the altar he had built for him in front of the entry room of the Temple. [13]He offered the sacrifices for the Sabbaths, the new moon festivals, and the three annual festivals—the Passover celebration, the Festival of Harvest,* and the Festival of Shelters—as Moses had commanded.

[14]In assigning the priests to their duties, Solomon followed the regulations of his father, David. He also assigned the Levites to lead the people in praise and to assist the priests in their daily duties. And he assigned the gatekeepers to their gates by their divisions, following the commands of David, the man of God. [15]Solomon did not deviate in any way from David's commands concerning the priests and Levites and the treasuries.

[16]So Solomon made sure that all the work related to building the Temple of the LORD was carried out, from the day its foundation was laid to the day of its completion.

[17]Later Solomon went to Ezion-geber and Elath,* ports along the shore of the Red Sea* in the land of Edom. [18]Hiram sent him ships commanded by his own officers and manned by experienced crews of sailors. These ships sailed to Ophir with Solomon's men and brought back to Solomon almost seventeen tons* of gold.

1 Kgs 9:21 The Hebrew term used here refers to the complete consecration of things or people to the LORD, either by destroying them or by giving them as an offering. **1 Kgs 9:26a** As in Greek version (see also 2 Kgs 14:22; 16:6); Hebrew reads *Eloth,* a variant spelling of Elath. **1 Kgs 9:26b** Hebrew *sea of reeds.* **1 Kgs 9:28** Hebrew *420 talents* [14 metric tons]. **2 Chr 8:2** Hebrew *Huram,* a variant spelling of Hiram; also in 8:18. **2 Chr 8:6** Or *and charioteers.* **2 Chr 8:13** Or *Festival of Weeks.* **2 Chr 8:17a** As in Greek version (see also 2 Kgs 14:22; 16:6); Hebrew reads *Eloth,* a variant spelling of Elath. **2 Chr 8:17b** As in parallel text at 1 Kgs 9:26; Hebrew reads *the sea.* **2 Chr 8:18** Hebrew *450 talents* [15.3 metric tons].

2 Chr 8:11 Solomon married Pharaoh's daughter to secure a military alliance with Egypt. He did not let the woman live in David's palace, however, where the Ark of God had once been kept. This implies that Solomon knew his pagan marriage would not please God. Solomon married many other foreign women, and this was contrary to God's law (Deut 7:3-4). These women worshiped false gods and were certain to contaminate Israel with their beliefs and practices. Eventually Solomon's pagan wives caused his downfall (1 Kgs 11:1-11).

2 Chr 8:15 Although Solomon carefully followed God's instructions for building the Temple and offering sacrifices (2 Chr 8:13), he paid no attention to what God said about marrying pagan women. His sin in marrying a foreign wife (2 Chr 8:11) confirmed his slide away from God. No matter how good or spiritual we are in most areas of life, one unsurrendered area can begin a downfall. Guard carefully every area of your life, especially your relationships. Don't give sin any foothold.

Visit of the Queen of Sheba PARALLEL

1 KINGS 10:1-13

When the queen of Sheba heard of Solomon's fame, which brought honor to the name of the LORD,* she came to test him with hard questions. 2She arrived in Jerusalem with a large group of attendants and a great caravan of camels loaded with spices, large quantities of gold, and precious jewels. When she met with Solomon, she talked with him about everything she had on her mind. 3Solomon had answers for all her questions; nothing was too hard for the king to explain to her. 4When the queen of Sheba realized how very wise Solomon was, and when she saw the palace he had built, 5she was overwhelmed. She was also amazed at the food on his tables, the organization of his officials and their splendid clothing, the cup-bearers, and the burnt offerings Solomon made at the Temple of the LORD.

6She exclaimed to the king, "Everything I heard in my country about your achievements* and wisdom is true! 7I didn't believe what was said until I arrived here and saw it with my own eyes. In fact, I had not heard the half of it! Your wisdom and prosperity are far beyond what I was told. 8How happy your people* must be! What a privilege for your officials to stand here day after day, listening to your wisdom! 9Praise the LORD your God, who delights in you and has placed you on the throne of Israel. Because of the LORD's eternal love for Israel, he has made you king so you can rule with justice and righteousness."

950 BC

Gold vessels and jewelry popular in Northern Europe

10Then she gave the king a gift of 9,000 pounds* of gold, great quantities of spices, and precious jewels. Never again were so many spices brought in as those the queen of Sheba gave to King Solomon.

11(In addition, Hiram's ships brought gold from Ophir, and they also brought rich cargoes of red sandalwood* and precious jewels. 12The king used the sandalwood to make railings for the Temple of the LORD and the royal palace, and to construct lyres and harps for the musicians. Never before or since has there been such a supply of sandalwood.)

13King Solomon gave the queen of Sheba whatever she asked for, besides all the customary gifts he had so generously given. Then she and all her attendants returned to their own land.

2 CHRONICLES 9:1-12

When the queen of Sheba heard of Solomon's fame, she came to Jerusalem to test him with hard questions. She arrived with a large group of attendants and a great caravan of camels loaded with spices, large quantities of gold, and precious jewels. When she met with Solomon, she talked with him about everything she had on her mind. 2Solomon had answers for all her questions; nothing was too hard for him to explain to her. 3When the queen of Sheba realized how wise Solomon was, and when she saw the palace he had built, 4she was overwhelmed. She was also amazed at the food on his tables, the organization of his officials and their splendid clothing, the cup-bearers and their robes, and the burnt offerings Solomon made at the Temple of the LORD.

5She exclaimed to the king, "Everything I heard in my country about your achievements* and wisdom is true! 6I didn't believe what was said until I arrived here and saw it with my own eyes. In fact, I had not heard the half of your great wisdom! It is far beyond what I was told. 7How happy your people must be! What a privilege for your officials to stand here day after day, listening to your wisdom! 8Praise the LORD your God, who delights in you and has placed you on the throne as king to rule for him. Because God loves Israel and desires this kingdom to last forever, he has made you king over them so you can rule with justice and righteousness."

9Then she gave the king a gift of 9,000 pounds* of gold, great quantities of spices, and precious jewels. Never before had there been spices as fine as those the queen of Sheba gave to King Solomon.

10(In addition, the crews of Hiram and Solomon brought gold from Ophir, and they also brought red sandalwood* and precious jewels. 11The king used the sandalwood to make steps* for the Temple of the LORD and the royal palace, and to construct lyres and harps for the musicians. Never before had such beautiful things been seen in Judah.)

1 Kgs 10:1 Or *which was due to the name of the LORD.* The meaning of the Hebrew is uncertain. **1 Kgs 10:6** Hebrew *your words.* **1 Kgs 10:8** Greek and Syriac versions and Latin Vulgate read *your wives.* **1 Kgs 10:10** Hebrew *120 talents* [4,000 kilograms]. **1 Kgs 10:11** Hebrew *almug wood;* also in 10:12. **2 Chr 9:5** Hebrew *your words.* **2 Chr 9:9** Hebrew *120 talents* [4,000 kilograms]. **2 Chr 9:10** Hebrew *algum wood* (also in 9:11); perhaps a variant spelling of *almug.* Compare parallel text at 1 Kgs 10:11-12. **2 Chr 9:11** Or *gateways.* The meaning of the Hebrew is uncertain.

1 Kgs 10:1-5 The queen of Sheba came to see for herself if everything she had heard about Solomon was true. Contests using riddles or proverbs were often used to test wisdom. The queen may have used some of these as she questioned Solomon (1 Kgs 10:1, 3). When she realized the extent of his riches and wisdom, she was overwhelmed and no longer questioned his power or wisdom. No longer a competitor, she became an admirer. Her experience was repeated by many kings and foreign dignitaries who paid honor to Solomon (1 Kgs 4:34).

2 Chr 9:1-8 The queen of Sheba had heard about Solomon's wisdom, but she was overwhelmed when she saw for herself the fruits of that wisdom. Although Solomon had married Pharaoh's daughter, he still sincerely tried to follow God at this stage in his life. When people get to know you and ask hard questions, will your responses reflect God? Your life can be a powerful witness; let others see God at work in you.

2 Chr 9:8 The queen of Sheba marveled at Solomon, claiming that God must love his people greatly to give them such a king. Israel greatly prospered during Solomon's reign, witnessing to God's power and love for his people. The good times show God's love and faithfulness, but hard times come to believers too. Our perseverance and steadfast hope during those times will demonstrate our love and faithfulness to God.

2 Chr 9:11 Sandalwood is a smooth, red-colored wood that accepts a high polish. This beautiful wood was extremely expensive.

[12]King Solomon gave the queen of Sheba whatever she asked for—gifts of greater value than the gifts she had given him. Then she and all her attendants returned to their own land.

Solomon's Wealth and Splendor PARALLEL

1 KINGS 10:14-29
Each year Solomon received about 25 tons* of gold.
[15]This did not include the additional revenue he received from merchants and traders, all the kings of Arabia, and the governors of the land.

[16]King Solomon made 200 large shields of hammered gold, each weighing more than fifteen pounds.* [17]He also made 300 smaller shields of hammered gold, each weighing nearly four pounds.* The king placed these shields in the Palace of the Forest of Lebanon.

[18]Then the king made a huge throne, decorated with ivory and overlaid with fine gold. [19]The throne had six steps and a rounded back. There were armrests on both sides of the seat, and the figure of a lion stood on each side of the throne. [20]There were also twelve other lions, one standing on each end of the six steps. No other throne in all the world could be compared with it!

[21]All of King Solomon's drinking cups were solid gold, as were all the utensils in the Palace of the Forest of Lebanon. They were not made of silver, for silver was considered worthless in Solomon's day!

[22]The king had a fleet of trading ships* that sailed with Hiram's fleet. Once every three years the ships returned, loaded with gold, silver, ivory, apes, and peacocks.*

[23]So King Solomon became richer and wiser than any other king on earth. [24]People from every nation came to consult him and to hear the wisdom God had given him. [25]Year after year everyone who visited brought him gifts of silver and gold, clothing, weapons, spices, horses, and mules.

1 Kgs 10:14 Hebrew *666 talents* [23 metric tons]. **1 Kgs 10:16** Hebrew *600 [shekels] of gold* [6.8 kilograms]. **1 Kgs 10:17** Hebrew *3 minas* [1.8 kilograms]. **1 Kgs 10:22a** Hebrew *fleet of ships of Tarshish.* **1 Kgs 10:22b** Or *and baboons.*

SOLOMON'S KINGDOM ▶ *Solomon's kingdom spread from the Euphrates River in the north to the borders of Egypt. The entire land was at peace under his rule.*

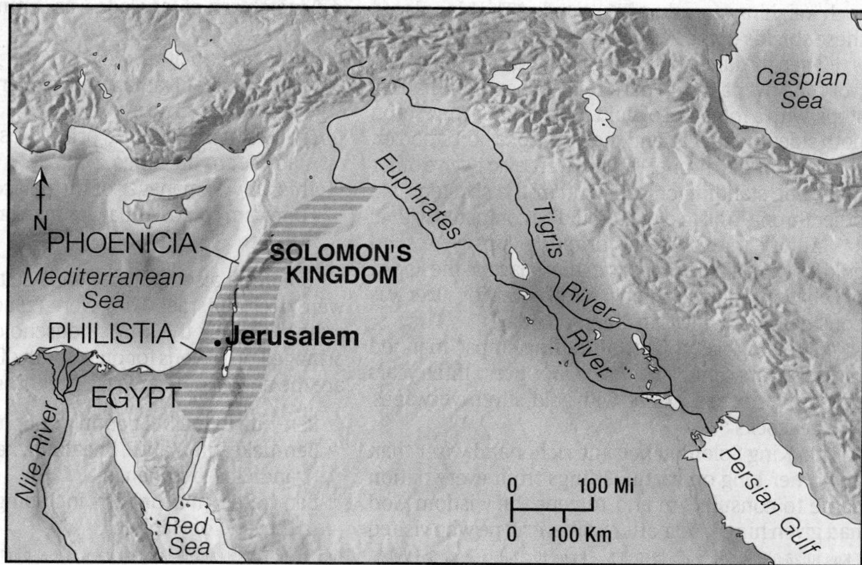

1 Kgs 10:14ff When Solomon asked for wisdom, God promised him riches and honor as well (1 Kgs 3:13). These verses show just how extensive his wealth became. No longer a second-rate nation, Israel was at the height of its power and wealth. Solomon's riches became legendary. Great leaders came from many nations to listen to Israel's powerful king. Jesus would later refer to "Solomon in all his glory" (Matt 6:29).

1 Kgs 10:23 Why does the Bible place so much emphasis on Solomon's material possessions? In the Old Testament, riches were considered tangible evidence of God's blessing. Prosperity was seen as a proof of right living. In the books of Ecclesiastes and Job this concept is placed in a broader perspective. In ideal conditions, people prosper when God runs their lives, but prosperity is not guaranteed. Wealth does not prove that a person is living right before God, and poverty does not indicate sin.

In fact, a greater evidence that a person is living for God is the presence of suffering and persecution (Mark 10:29-31; 13:13). The most important "treasure" is not earthly but heavenly (Matt 6:19-21; 19:21; 1 Tim 6:17-19). The gift of greatest worth has no price tag—it is the gift of salvation freely offered by God.

▸ **1 KINGS 10:14-29 *(cont.)***

26Solomon built up a huge force of chariots and
horses.* He had 1,400 chariots and 12,000 horses.
He stationed some of them in the chariot cities and
some near him in Jerusalem. 27The king made silver
as plentiful in Jerusalem as stone. And valuable cedar
timber was as common as the sycamore-fig trees that
grow in the foothills of Judah.* 28Solomon's horses
were imported from Egypt* and from Cilicia*; the
king's traders acquired them from Cilicia at the standard price. 29At that time chariots from Egypt could
be purchased for 600 pieces of silver,* and horses for
150 pieces of silver.* They were then exported to the
kings of the Hittites and the kings of Aram.

2 CHRONICLES 9:13-28

Each year Solomon received about 25 tons* of gold.
14This did not include the additional revenue he received from merchants and traders. All the kings of
Arabia and the governors of the provinces also brought
gold and silver to Solomon.

15King Solomon made 200 large shields of hammered gold, each weighing more than 15 pounds.*
16He also made 300 smaller shields of hammered gold,
each weighing more than 7½ pounds.* The king placed
these shields in the Palace of the Forest of Lebanon.

17Then the king made a huge throne, decorated with
ivory and overlaid with pure gold. 18The throne had six
steps, with a footstool of gold. There were armrests on
both sides of the seat, and the figure of a lion stood on
each side of the throne. 19There were also twelve other
lions, one standing on each end of the six steps. No
other throne in all the world could be compared with it!

20All of King Solomon's drinking cups were solid
gold, as were all the utensils in the Palace of the Forest
of Lebanon. They were not made of silver, for silver was
considered worthless in Solomon's day!

21The king had a fleet of trading ships* manned
by the sailors sent by Hiram.* Once every three years
the ships returned, loaded with gold, silver, ivory, apes,
and peacocks.*

22So King Solomon became richer and wiser than
any other king on earth. 23Kings from every nation
came to consult him and to hear the wisdom God
had given him. 24Year after year everyone who visited
brought him gifts of silver and gold, clothing, weapons, spices, horses, and mules.

25Solomon had 4,000 stalls for his horses and
chariots, and he had 12,000 horses.* He stationed
some of them in the chariot cities, and some near
him in Jerusalem. 26He ruled over all the kings from
the Euphrates River* in the north to the land of the
Philistines and the border of Egypt in the south. 27The
king made silver as plentiful in Jerusalem as stone.
And valuable cedar timber was as common as the
sycamore-fig trees that grow in the foothills of Judah.* 28Solomon's horses were imported from Egypt*
and many other countries.

Solomon's Officials and Governors

1 KINGS 4:1-19

King Solomon now ruled over all Israel, 2and these
were his high officials:

Azariah son of Zadok was the priest.
3 Elihoreph and Ahijah, the sons of Shisha, were court secretaries.
Jehoshaphat son of Ahilud was the royal historian.
4 Benaiah son of Jehoiada was commander of the army.
Zadok and Abiathar were priests.
5 Azariah son of Nathan was in charge of the district governors.
Zabud son of Nathan, a priest, was a trusted adviser to the king.
6 Ahishar was manager of the palace property.
Adoniram son of Abda was in charge of the labor force.

7Solomon also had twelve district governors who
were over all Israel. They were responsible for providing food for the king's household. Each of them
arranged provisions for one month of the year. 8These
are the names of the twelve governors:

Ben-hur, in the hill country of Ephraim.
9 Ben-deker, in Makaz, Shaalbim, Beth-shemesh, and Elon-bethhanan.
10 Ben-hesed, in Arubboth, including Socoh and all the land of Hepher.

1 Kgs 10:26 Or *charioteers;* also in 10:26b. **1 Kgs 10:27** Hebrew *the Shephelah.* **1 Kgs 10:28a** Possibly *Muzur,* a district near Cilicia; also in 10:29. **1 Kgs 10:28b** Hebrew *Kue,* probably another name for Cilicia. **1 Kgs 10:29a** Hebrew *600 [shekels] of silver,* about 15 pounds or 6.8 kilograms in weight. **1 Kgs 10:29b** Hebrew *150 [shekels],* about 3.8 pounds or 1.7 kilograms in weight. **2 Chr 9:13** Hebrew *666 talents* [23 metric tons]. **2 Chr 9:15** Hebrew *600 [shekels] of hammered gold* [6.8 kilograms]. **2 Chr 9:16** Hebrew *300 [shekels] of gold* [3.4 kilograms]. **2 Chr 9:21a** Hebrew *fleet of ships that could sail to Tarshish.* **2 Chr 9:21b** Hebrew *Huram,* a variant spelling of Hiram. **2 Chr 9:21c** Or *and baboons.* **2 Chr 9:25** Or *12,000 charioteers.* **2 Chr 9:26** Hebrew *the river.* **2 Chr 9:27** Hebrew *the Shephelah.* **2 Chr 9:28** Possibly *Muzur,* a district near Cilicia.

1 Kgs 10:26-29 In accumulating chariots and horses, a huge harem (1 Kgs 11:1-3), and incredible wealth, Solomon was violating God's commands for a king (Deut 17:14-20). God prohibited these actions because he knew how they would hurt the nation both politically and spiritually (1 Sam 8:11-18). The more luxurious Solomon's court became, the more the people were taxed. Excessive taxation created unrest, and soon conditions became ripe for a revolution. Having everything he wanted, Solomon forgot God and allowed pagan influences to enter his court through his pagan wives, thus accelerating the spiritual corruption of the nation.

1 Kgs 4:1ff Solomon was well organized, with 11 high officials who had specific responsibilities, 12 district governors, and a governor in charge of the district governors. Each person had a specific responsibility or territory to manage. This organization was essential to maintain the government's effectiveness: It was a wise move by a wise man. It is good stewardship to be well organized. Good organization helps people work together in harmony and ensures that the desired goal will be reached.

11 Ben-abinadab, in all of Naphoth-dor.* (He was married to Taphath, one of Solomon's daughters.)
12 Baana son of Ahilud, in Taanach and Megiddo, all of Beth-shan* near Zarethan below Jezreel, and all the territory from Beth-shan to Abel-meholah and over to Jokmeam.
13 Ben-geber, in Ramoth-gilead, including the Towns of Jair (named for Jair of the tribe of Manasseh*) in Gilead, and in the Argob region of Bashan, including sixty large fortified towns with bronze bars on their gates.
14 Ahinadab son of Iddo, in Mahanaim.
15 Ahimaaz, in Naphtali. (He was married to Basemath, another of Solomon's daughters.)
16 Baana son of Hushai, in Asher and in Aloth.
17 Jehoshaphat son of Paruah, in Issachar.
18 Shimei son of Ela, in Benjamin.
19 Geber son of Uri, in the land of Gilead,* including the territories of King Sihon of the Amorites and King Og of Bashan.

There was also one governor over the land of Judah.*

Solomon's Prosperity and Wisdom PARALLEL

1 KINGS 4:20-34

The people of Judah and Israel were as numerous as
the sand on the seashore. They were very contented,
with plenty to eat and drink. 21 *Solomon ruled over
all the kingdoms from the Euphrates River* in the
north to the land of the Philistines and the border of
Egypt in the south. The conquered peoples of those
lands sent tribute money to Solomon and continued
to serve him throughout his lifetime.
22 The daily food requirements for Solomon's palace
were 150 bushels of choice flour and 300 bushels
of meal*; 23 also 10 oxen from the fattening pens,
20 pasture-fed cattle, 100 sheep or goats, as well as
deer, gazelles, roe deer, and choice poultry.*
24 Solomon's dominion extended over all the kingdoms west of the Euphrates River, from Tiphsah to
Gaza. And there was peace on all his borders. 25 During the lifetime of Solomon, all of Judah and Israel
lived in peace and safety. And from Dan in the north
to Beersheba in the south, each family had its own
home and garden.*
26 Solomon had 4,000* stalls for his chariot horses,
and he had 12,000 horses.*
27 The district governors faithfully provided food for
King Solomon and his court; each made sure nothing
was lacking during the month assigned to him. 28 They
also brought the necessary barley and straw for the
royal horses in the stables.
29 God gave Solomon very great wisdom and understanding, and knowledge as vast as the sands of the
seashore. 30 In fact, his wisdom exceeded that of all
the wise men of the East and the wise men of Egypt.
31 He was wiser than anyone else, including Ethan the
Ezrahite and the sons of Mahol—Heman, Calcol, and
Darda. His fame spread throughout all the surrounding nations. 32 He composed some 3,000 proverbs and
wrote 1,005 songs. 33 He could speak with authority
about all kinds of plants, from the great cedar of Lebanon to the tiny hyssop that grows from cracks in a
wall. He could also speak about animals, birds, small
creatures, and fish. 34 And kings from every nation
sent their ambassadors to listen to the wisdom of
Solomon.

2 CHRONICLES 1:14-17

Solomon built up a huge force of chariots and horses.*
He had 1,400 chariots and 12,000 horses. He stationed some of them in the chariot cities and some
near him in Jerusalem. 15 The king made silver and gold
as plentiful in Jerusalem as stone. And valuable cedar
timber was as common as the sycamore-fig trees that
grow in the foothills of Judah.* 16 Solomon's horses
were imported from Egypt* and from Cilicia*; the
king's traders acquired them from Cilicia at the standard price. 17 At that time chariots from Egypt could
be purchased for 600 pieces of silver,* and horses for
150 pieces of silver.* They were then exported to the
kings of the Hittites and the kings of Aram.

1 Kgs 4:11 Hebrew *Naphath-dor,* a variant spelling of Naphoth-dor. **1 Kgs 4:12** Hebrew *Beth-shean,* a variant spelling of Beth-shan; also in 4:12b. **1 Kgs 4:13** Hebrew *Jair son of Manasseh;* compare 1 Chr 2:22. **1 Kgs 4:19a** Greek version reads *of Gad;* compare 4:13. **1 Kgs 4:19b** As in some Greek manuscripts; Hebrew lacks *of Judah.* The meaning of the Hebrew is uncertain. **1 Kgs 4:21a** Verses 4:21-34 are numbered 5:1-14 in Hebrew text. **1 Kgs 4:21b** Hebrew *the river;* also in 4:24. **1 Kgs 4:22** Hebrew *30 cors* [5.5 kiloliters] *of choice flour and 60 cors* [11 kiloliters] *of meal.* **1 Kgs 4:23** Or *and fattened geese.* **1 Kgs 4:25** Hebrew *each family lived under its own grapevine and under its own fig tree.* **1 Kgs 4:26a** As in some Greek manuscripts (see also 2 Chr 9:25); Hebrew reads *40,000.* **1 Kgs 4:26b** Or *12,000 charioteers.* **2 Chr 1:14** Or *charioteers;* also in 1:14b. **2 Chr 1:15** Hebrew *the Shephelah.* **2 Chr 1:16a** Possibly *Muzur,* a district near Cilicia; also in 1:17. **2 Chr 1:16b** Hebrew *Kue,* probably another name for Cilicia. **2 Chr 1:17a** Hebrew *600 [shekels] of silver,* about 15 pounds or 6.8 kilograms in weight. **2 Chr 1:17b** Hebrew *150 [shekels],* about 3.8 pounds or 1.7 kilograms in weight.

---

1 Kgs 4:20-25 Throughout most of his reign, Solomon applied his wisdom well because he sought God. The fruits of this wisdom were peace, security, and prosperity for the nation. Solomon's era is often looked upon as the ideal of what any nation can become when united in its trust in and obedience to God.

1 Kgs 4:32 The book of Proverbs records many of these 3,000 wise proverbs. Other biblical writings of Solomon include Psalms 72 and 127 and the books of Ecclesiastes and Song of Songs. Solomon's wisdom was known throughout the world.

G. Solomon's Poetry

Like his father before him, Solomon was a prolific writer. Two psalms are attributed to Solomon, along with much of Proverbs and the Song of Songs. We are placing these writings during the height of Solomon's prosperity. They reflect the wisdom and joy that characterized the beginning of his reign. Solomon also wrote Ecclesiastes much later in life.

1. SOLOMON'S PSALMS

These two psalms are attributed to Solomon. They reflect the wisdom and attention to God that marked the early years of Solomon's reign as king of Israel.

Psalm 72

THEME: The perfect king. In this psalm, a king asks God to help his son rule the nation justly and wisely. It looks forward to the endless reign of the Messiah, who alone can rule with perfect justice and whose citizens will enjoy perfect peace.

AUTHOR: Solomon

A psalm of Solomon.

1 Give your love of justice to the king, O God,
and righteousness to the king's son.
2 Help him judge your people in the right way;
let the poor always be treated fairly.
3 May the mountains yield prosperity for all,
and may the hills be fruitful.
4 Help him to defend the poor,
to rescue the children of the needy,
and to crush their oppressors.
5 May they fear you* as long as the sun shines,
as long as the moon remains in the sky.
Yes, forever!
6 May the king's rule be refreshing like spring
rain on freshly cut grass,
like the showers that water the earth.
7 May all the godly flourish during his reign.
May there be abundant prosperity until the
moon is no more.
8 May he reign from sea to sea,
and from the Euphrates River* to the ends
of the earth.
9 Desert nomads will bow before him;
his enemies will fall before him in the dust.
10 The western kings of Tarshish and other distant
lands
will bring him tribute.
The eastern kings of Sheba and Seba
will bring him gifts.
11 All kings will bow before him,
and all nations will serve him.
12 He will rescue the poor when they cry to him;
he will help the oppressed, who have no one
to defend them.
13 He feels pity for the weak and the needy,
and he will rescue them.
14 He will redeem them from oppression and
violence,
for their lives are precious to him.
15 Long live the king!
May the gold of Sheba be given to him.
May the people always pray for him
and bless him all day long.
16 May there be abundant grain throughout the
land,
flourishing even on the hilltops.
May the fruit trees flourish like the trees
of Lebanon,
and may the people thrive like grass
in a field.
17 May the king's name endure forever;
may it continue as long as the sun shines.
May all nations be blessed through him
and bring him praise.
18 Praise the LORD God, the God of Israel,
who alone does such wonderful things.
19 Praise his glorious name forever!
Let the whole earth be filled with his glory.
Amen and amen!
20 (This ends the prayers of David son of Jesse.)

Ps 72:5 Greek version reads *May they endure.* **Ps 72:8** Hebrew *the river.*

Ps 72:1-2 What qualities do we want most in our leaders? God desires all who rule under him to be just and righteous. Think how the world would change if world leaders would commit themselves to these two qualities. Pray for leaders as you hear about them in the news. Ask God to help them see their need for him; ask God to help them lead with justice and righteousness (see 1 Tim 2:1-2).

Ps 72:12-14 God cares for the poor, oppressed, weak, and needy because they are precious to him. If God feels so strongly about these needy ones and loves them so deeply, how can we ignore their plight? Examine what you are doing to reach out with God's love. Are you ignoring their plight or are you helping to meet their needs?

Ps 72:17 Solomon, David's son, reigned in Israel's golden age. He built the magnificent Temple, and the land rested in peace. This psalm, though written by Solomon, looks beyond Solomon's reign to that of Jesus the Messiah, whose kingdom extends "to the ends of the earth" (Ps 72:8) and is greater than any human empire. This will be fulfilled when Christ returns to reign forever (Rev 11:15). When we anticipate his worldwide rule, it fills our hearts with hope.

Psalm 127

THEME: Life without God is senseless. All of life's work—building a home, establishing a career, and raising a family—must have God as the foundation.

AUTHOR: Solomon

A song for pilgrims ascending to Jerusalem. A psalm of Solomon.

1 Unless the LORD builds a house,
the work of the builders is wasted.
Unless the LORD protects a city,
guarding it with sentries will do no good.
2 It is useless for you to work so hard
from early morning until late at night,
anxiously working for food to eat;
for God gives rest to his loved ones.

3 Children are a gift from the LORD;
they are a reward from him.
4 Children born to a young man
are like arrows in a warrior's hands.
5 How joyful is the man whose quiver is full
of them!
He will not be put to shame when he confronts
his accusers at the city gates.

2. SOLOMON'S PROVERBS

Solomon wrote most of the book of Proverbs. The first few chapters are Solomon's fatherly advice to young people. Although most of the material in this section is directed toward young people, all who seek wisdom will greatly benefit from these wise words. This is where we can discover the source of wisdom, the value of wisdom, and the benefits of wisdom. In chapters 10–24, Solomon offers a collection of the short couplets that are commonly recognized as proverbs. They cover a wide range of topics. These sayings give people practical wisdom for godly living at every stage of life.

The Purpose of Proverbs

PROVERBS 1:1-7

These are the proverbs of Solomon, David's son, king of Israel.

2 Their purpose is to teach people wisdom
and discipline,
to help them understand the insights
of the wise.
3 Their purpose is to teach people to live
disciplined and successful lives,
to help them do what is right, just, and fair.
4 These proverbs will give insight to the simple,
knowledge and discernment to the young.

5 Let the wise listen to these proverbs and become
even wiser.
Let those with understanding receive
guidance
6 by exploring the meaning in these proverbs
and parables,
the words of the wise and their riddles.

Ps 72:19-20 Psalms is traditionally broken up into five "books." Book Two ends with "Amen and amen," as did Psalm 41, which closed Book One. This last verse does not mean that David wrote this psalm but that he wrote most of the psalms in Book Two.

Ps 127:1 Families establish homes and sentries guard cities, but both these activities are futile unless God is in them. A family without God can never experience the spiritual bond God brings to relationships. A city without God will crumble from evil and corruption on the inside. Don't make the mistake of leaving God out of your life. If you do, all your accomplishments will be futile. Make God your highest priority, and let him do the building.

Ps 127:2 God is not against human effort. Hard work honors God (Prov 31:10-29). But working to the exclusion of rest or to the neglect of family may be a cover-up for an inability to trust God to provide for our needs. We all need adequate rest and times of spiritual refreshment. On the other hand, this verse is not an excuse to be lazy (Prov 18:9). Be careful to maintain a balance: Work while trusting God, and also rest while trusting him.

Ps 127:3-5 Too often children are seen as liabilities rather than assets. But the Bible calls children "a gift from the LORD," a reward. We can learn valuable lessons from their inquisitive minds and trusting spirits. Those who view children as a distraction or nuisance should instead see them as an opportunity to shape the future. We dare not treat children as an inconvenience when God values them so highly.

Prov 1:1 What the book of Psalms is to prayer and devotional life, the book of Proverbs is to everyday life. Proverbs gives practical suggestions for effective living. This book is not just a collection of interesting tidbits; it contains deep spiritual insights drawn from experience. A proverb is a short, wise, easy-to-remember saying that calls a person to action. It doesn't argue about basic spiritual and moral beliefs; it assumes we already hold them. The book of Proverbs focuses on God—his character, works, and blessings—and it tells how we can live in close relationship to him.

Prov 1:1 Solomon, the third king of Israel, son of the great king David, reigned during Israel's golden age. When God said he would give him whatever he wanted, Solomon asked for an understanding mind (1 Kgs 3:5-14). God was pleased with this request. He not only made Solomon wise but also gave him great riches and power and an era of peace. Solomon built the glorious Temple in Jerusalem (1 Kgs 6) and wrote most of the book of Proverbs. See his Profile on p. 607.

Prov 1:6 Riddles were thought-provoking questions.

▸ **PROVERBS 1:1-7 *(cont.)***

7 Fear of the LORD is the foundation of true
knowledge,
but fools despise wisdom and discipline.

A Father's Exhortation: Acquire Wisdom

PROVERBS 1:8-19

8 My child,* listen when your father corrects you.
Don't neglect your mother's instruction.
9 What you learn from them will crown you
with grace
and be a chain of honor around your neck.

10 My child, if sinners entice you,
turn your back on them!
11 They may say, "Come and join us.
Let's hide and kill someone!
Just for fun, let's ambush the innocent!
12 Let's swallow them alive, like the grave*;
let's swallow them whole, like those who
go down to the pit of death.
13 Think of the great things we'll get!
We'll fill our houses with all the stuff
we take.
14 Come, throw in your lot with us;
we'll all share the loot."

15 My child, don't go along with them!
Stay far away from their paths.
16 They rush to commit evil deeds.
They hurry to commit murder.
17 If a bird sees a trap being set,
it knows to stay away.
18 But these people set an ambush for themselves;
they are trying to get themselves killed.
19 Such is the fate of all who are greedy for money;
it robs them of life.

Prv 1:8 Hebrew *My son;* also in 1:10, 15. **Prv 1:12** Hebrew *like Sheol.*

Wisdom Shouts in the Streets

PROVERBS 1:20-33

20 Wisdom shouts in the streets.
She cries out in the public square.
21 She calls to the crowds along the main street,
to those gathered in front of the city gate:
22 "How long, you simpletons,
will you insist on being simpleminded?
How long will you mockers relish your mocking?
How long will you fools hate knowledge?
23 Come and listen to my counsel.
I'll share my heart with you
and make you wise.

24 "I called you so often, but you wouldn't come.
I reached out to you, but you paid no attention.
25 You ignored my advice
and rejected the correction I offered.
26 So I will laugh when you are in trouble!
I will mock you when disaster overtakes you—
27 when calamity overtakes you like a storm,
when disaster engulfs you like a cyclone,
and anguish and distress overwhelm you.

28 "When they cry for help, I will not answer.
Though they anxiously search for me, they will
not find me.
29 For they hated knowledge
and chose not to fear the LORD.

Prov 1:7 One of the most annoying types of people is a know-it-all—a person who has a dogmatic opinion about everything, is closed to anything new, resents discipline, and refuses to learn. Solomon calls this kind of person a fool. Don't be a know-it-all. Instead, be open to the advice of others, especially those who know you well and can give valuable insight and counsel. Learn how to learn from others. Remember, only God knows it all.

Prov 1:7-9 In this age of information, knowledge is plentiful, but wisdom is scarce. Wisdom means far more than simply knowing a lot. It is a basic attitude that affects every aspect of life. The foundation of knowledge is to fear the Lord—to honor and respect God, to live in awe of his power, and to obey his Word. Faith in God should be the controlling principle for your understanding of the world, your attitudes, and your actions. Trust in God—he will make you truly wise.

Prov 1:8 Our actions speak louder than our words. This is especially true in the home. Children learn values, morals, and priorities by observing how their parents act and react every day. If parents exhibit a deep reverence for and dependence on God, the children will catch these attitudes. Let them see your reverence for God. Teach them right living by giving worship an important place in your family life and by reading the Bible together.

Prov 1:10-19 Sin is enticing because it offers a quick route to prosperity or pleasure and makes us feel like one of the crowd. But when we go along with others and refuse to listen to the truth, our own appetites become our masters, and we'll do anything to satisfy them. Sin, even when attractive, is deadly. We must learn to make choices not on the basis of flashy appeal or short-range pleasure but in view of the long-range effects. Sometimes this means steering clear of people who want to entice us into activities that we know are wrong. We can't be friendly with sin and expect our lives to remain unaffected.

Prov 1:19 Being "greedy for money" is one of Satan's surest traps. It begins when he plants the suggestion that we can't live without some possession or more money. Then that desire fans its own fire until it becomes an all-consuming obsession. Ask God for wisdom to recognize any greedy desire before it destroys you. God will help you overcome it.

Prov 1:20 The picture of Wisdom shouting in the streets is a personification—a literary device to make wisdom come alive for us. Wisdom is not a living being; it is the mind of God revealed. By reading about Jesus Christ's earthly ministry, we can see Wisdom in action. In order to understand how to become wise, we need to heed Wisdom calling and instructing us in the book of Proverbs. For a New Testament call to wisdom, see James 1:5. Make sure you don't reject God's offer of wisdom to you.

Prov 1:22 In the book of Proverbs, a "simpleton" or a fool is not someone with a *mental* deficiency but someone with a *character* deficiency (such as rebellion, laziness, or anger). The fool is not stupid but rather unable to tell right from wrong or good from bad.

Prov 1:23-28 God is more than willing to pour out his heart and make his thoughts known to us. To receive his advice, we must be willing to listen, refusing to let pride stand in our way. Pride is thinking more highly of our own wisdom and desires than of God's. If we think we know better than God or feel we have no need of God's direction, we have fallen into foolish and disastrous pride.

30 They rejected my advice
and paid no attention when I corrected them.
31 Therefore, they must eat the bitter fruit of living
their own way,
choking on their own schemes.
32 For simpletons turn away from me—to death.
Fools are destroyed by their own complacency.
33 But all who listen to me will live in peace,
untroubled by fear of harm."

The Benefits of Wisdom

PROVERBS 2:1-22

1 My child,* listen to what I say,
and treasure my commands.
2 Tune your ears to wisdom,
and concentrate on understanding.
3 Cry out for insight,
and ask for understanding.
4 Search for them as you would for silver;
seek them like hidden treasures.
5 Then you will understand what it means to fear
the LORD,
and you will gain knowledge of God.
6 For the LORD grants wisdom!
From his mouth come knowledge and
understanding.
7 He grants a treasure of common sense to the
honest.
He is a shield to those who walk with
integrity.
8 He guards the paths of the just
and protects those who are faithful to him.

Prv 2:1 Hebrew *My son.*

PEOPLE CALLED "WISE" IN THE BIBLE

The special description "wise" is used for 12 significant people in the Bible. They can be helpful models in our own pursuit of wisdom.

The Person	*Their Role*	*Reference*	*How They Practiced Wisdom*
Joseph	Wise leader	Acts 7:10	Prepared for a major famine; helped rule Egypt
Moses	Wise leader	Acts 7:20-22	Learned all the Egyptian wisdom, then graduated to God's lessons in wisdom to lead Israel out of Egypt
Bezalel	Wise artist	Exod 31:1-5	Designed and supervised the construction of the Tabernacle and its utensils in the wilderness
Joshua	Wise leader	Deut 34:9	Learned by observing Moses, obeyed God, led the people into the Promised Land
David	Wise leader	2 Sam 14:20	Never let his failures keep him from the source of wisdom—reverence for God
Abigail	Wise wife	1 Sam 25:3	Managed her household sensibly in spite of a mean and dishonest husband
Solomon	Wise leader	1 Kgs 3:5-14; 4:29-34	Knew what to do even though he often failed to put his own wisdom into action
Daniel	Wise counselor	Dan 5:11-12	Known as a man in touch with God; a solver of complex problems with God's help
Astrologers	Wise learners	Matt 2:1-12	Not only received special knowledge of God's visit to earth but checked it out personally
Stephen	Wise leader	Acts 6:8-10	Organized the distribution of food to the Grecian widows; preached the gospel to the Jews
Paul	Wise messenger	2 Pet 3:15-16	Spent his life communicating God's love to all who would listen
Christ	Wise youth Wise Savior Wisdom of God	Luke 2:40, 52; 1 Cor 1:20-25	Not only lived a perfect life but died on the cross to save us and make God's wise plan of eternal life available to us

Prov 1:31-32 Many proverbs point out that the "bitter fruit of living their own way" will be the consequence people will experience in this life. Faced with either choosing God's wisdom or persisting in rebellious independence, many decide to go it alone. The problems such people create for themselves will destroy them. Don't ignore God's advice even if it is painful for the present. It will keep you from greater pain in the future.

Prov 2:3-6 Wisdom comes in two ways: It is a God-given gift and also the result of an energetic search. Wisdom's starting point is God and his revealed Word, the source of "knowledge and understanding" (Prov 2:6). In that sense, wisdom is God's gift to us. But he gives it only to those who earnestly seek it. But because God's wisdom is hidden from the rebellious and foolish, it takes effort to find it and use it. The pathway to wisdom is strenuous. When we are on the path, we discover that true wisdom is God's and that he will guide us and reward our sincere and persistent search.

Prov 2:6-7 God gives wisdom and victory to the godly but not to those drifting through life or acting irresponsibly with his gifts and resources. If we are faithful to him and keep our purpose in life clearly in mind, he will keep us from pride and greed.

▶ **PROVERBS 2:1-22 *(cont.)***

9 Then you will understand what is right, just, and fair,
and you will find the right way to go.
10 For wisdom will enter your heart,
and knowledge will fill you with joy.
11 Wise choices will watch over you.
Understanding will keep you safe.

12 Wisdom will save you from evil people,
from those whose words are twisted.
13 These men turn from the right way
to walk down dark paths.
14 They take pleasure in doing wrong,
and they enjoy the twisted ways of evil.
15 Their actions are crooked,
and their ways are wrong.

16 Wisdom will save you from the immoral woman,
from the seductive words of the promiscuous woman.
17 She has abandoned her husband
and ignores the covenant she made before God.
18 Entering her house leads to death;
it is the road to the grave.*
19 The man who visits her is doomed.
He will never reach the paths of life.
20 Follow the steps of good men instead,
and stay on the paths of the righteous.
21 For only the godly will live in the land,
and those with integrity will remain in it.
22 But the wicked will be removed from the land,
and the treacherous will be uprooted.

Trusting in the Lord

PROVERBS 3:1-35

1 My child,* never forget the things I have taught you.
Store my commands in your heart.
2 If you do this, you will live many years,
and your life will be satisfying.
3 Never let loyalty and kindness leave you!
Tie them around your neck as a reminder.
Write them deep within your heart.
4 Then you will find favor with both God and people,
and you will earn a good reputation.

5 Trust in the Lord with all your heart;
do not depend on your own understanding.
6 Seek his will in all you do,
and he will show you which path to take.

7 Don't be impressed with your own wisdom.
Instead, fear the Lord and turn away from evil.

Prv 2:18 Hebrew *to the spirits of the dead.* **Prv 3:1** Hebrew *My son;* also in 3:11, 21.

Prov 2:9-10 We gain wisdom through a constant process of growing. First, we must trust and honor God. Second, we must realize that the Bible reveals God's wisdom to us. Third, we must make a lifelong series of right choices and avoid moral pitfalls. Fourth, when we make sinful choices or mistakes, we must learn from our errors and recover. People don't develop all aspects of wisdom at once. For example, some people have more insight than discretion; others have more knowledge than common sense. But we can pray for all aspects of wisdom and take the steps to develop them.

Prov 2:16-17 An immoral or promiscuous woman is seductive. Two of the most difficult sins to resist are pride and sexual immorality. Both are seductive. Pride says, "I deserve it"; sexual desire says, "I need it." In combination, their appeal is deadly. In fact, says Solomon, only by relying on God's strength can we overcome them. Pride appeals to the empty head; sexual enticement to the empty heart. By looking to God, we can fill our heads with his wisdom and our hearts with his love. Don't be fooled—remember what God says about who you are and what you were meant to be. Ask him for strength to resist these temptations.

WISDOM: APPLIED TRUTH

The book of Proverbs tells us about people who have wisdom and enjoy its benefits.

Reference	*The Person Who Has Wisdom*	*Benefits of Wisdom*
Prov 3–4 A father's instructions	Is kind Is loyal Trusts in the Lord Puts God first Turns away from evil Knows right from wrong Listens and learns Does what is right	Long, satisfying life Favor with God and people Reputation for good judgment Success Health, vitality Riches, honor, pleasure, peace Protection
Prov 8–9 Wisdom speaks	Discovers knowledge and discernment Hates pride, arrogance, and corruption Respects and fears God Gives good advice and has common sense Loves correction and is teachable Knows God	Riches, honor Justice Righteousness Life God's approval Constant learning Understanding

Prov 3:3 Loyalty and kindness are important character qualities. Both involve actions as well as attitudes. A loyal person acts responsibly. A kind person works for justice for others. Thoughts and words are not enough—our life reveals whether we are truly loyal and kind. Do your actions measure up to your attitudes?

Prov 3:5-6 When we have an important decision to make, we sometimes feel that we can't trust anyone—not even God. But God knows what is best for us. He is a better judge of what we want than we are! We must trust him completely in every choice we make. We should not omit careful thinking or belittle our God-given ability to reason; but we should not trust our own ideas to the exclusion of all others. We must not be wise in our own eyes but be willing to listen to and be corrected by God's Word and wise counselors. Bring your decisions to God in prayer; use the Bible as your guide; and then follow God's leading.

8 Then you will have healing for your body
and strength for your bones.
9 Honor the LORD with your wealth
and with the best part of everything you
produce.
10 Then he will fill your barns with grain,
and your vats will overflow with good wine.

11 My child, don't reject the LORD's discipline,
and don't be upset when he corrects you.
12 For the LORD corrects those he loves,
just as a father corrects a child in whom he
delights.*

13 Joyful is the person who finds wisdom,
the one who gains understanding.
14 For wisdom is more profitable than silver,
and her wages are better than gold.
15 Wisdom is more precious than rubies;
nothing you desire can compare with her.
16 She offers you long life in her right hand,
and riches and honor in her left.
17 She will guide you down delightful paths;
all her ways are satisfying.
18 Wisdom is a tree of life to those who embrace her;
happy are those who hold her tightly.

19 By wisdom the LORD founded the earth;
by understanding he created the heavens.
20 By his knowledge the deep fountains of the earth
burst forth,
and the dew settles beneath the night sky.

21 My child, don't lose sight of common sense and
discernment.
Hang on to them,
22 for they will refresh your soul.
They are like jewels on a necklace.
23 They keep you safe on your way,
and your feet will not stumble.
24 You can go to bed without fear;
you will lie down and sleep soundly.
25 You need not be afraid of sudden disaster
or the destruction that comes upon the
wicked,
26 for the LORD is your security.
He will keep your foot from being caught
in a trap.

27 Do not withhold good from those who
deserve it
when it's in your power to help them.
28 If you can help your neighbor now, don't say,
"Come back tomorrow, and then I'll help you."

29 Don't plot harm against your neighbor,
for those who live nearby trust you.
30 Don't pick a fight without reason,
when no one has done you harm.

31 Don't envy violent people
or copy their ways.
32 Such wicked people are detestable to the LORD,
but he offers his friendship to the godly.
33 The LORD curses the house of the wicked,
but he blesses the home of the upright.
34 The LORD mocks the mockers
but is gracious to the humble.*
35 The wise inherit honor,
but fools are put to shame!

Prv 3:12 Greek version reads *And he punishes those he accepts as his children.* Compare Heb 12:6. **Prv 3:34** Greek version reads *The LORD opposes the proud / but favors the humble.* Compare Jas 4:6; 1 Pet 5:5.

He will direct your paths by both guiding and protecting you.

Prov 3:6 To receive God's guidance, said Solomon, we must seek God's will in all we do. This means turning every area of life over to him. About a thousand years later, Jesus emphasized this same truth (Matt 6:33). Examine your values and priorities. What is important to you? In what areas have you not acknowledged him? You may already acknowledge God in many areas of your life, but the areas where you attempt to restrict or ignore him will cause you grief. Make him a vital part of everything you do; then he will guide you because you will be working to accomplish his purposes.

Prov 3:9-10 This refers to the practice of giving to God the first and best portion of the harvest (Deut 26:9-11). Many people give God their leftovers. If they can afford to donate anything after the bills are paid, they do so. These people may be sincere and contribute willingly, but they are not obeying what God says. God wants the first part of our income. This demonstrates that God, not possessions, has first place in our life and that our resources belong to him (we are only managers). Giving to God helps us conquer greed, helps us properly manage God's resources, and opens us up to receive God's special blessings.

Prov 3:11-12 *Discipline* means "to teach and to train." Discipline sounds negative to many people because some disciplinarians are not loving. But God is the source of all love. He doesn't punish us because he enjoys inflicting pain but because he is deeply concerned about our development. He knows that in order to become morally strong and good, we must learn the difference between right and wrong. His loving discipline enables us to do that.

Prov 3:11-12 It's sometimes difficult to know when God has been disciplining us until we look back on the situation. Not every calamity comes directly from God, of course. But if we rebel against God and refuse to repent when God has identified some sin in our lives, he may use guilt, crises, or bad experiences to bring us back to him. Sometimes difficult times come even when we have no flagrant sin. Then our response should be patience, integrity, and confidence that God will show us what to do.

Prov 3:16-17 The book of Proverbs contains many strong statements about the benefits of wisdom, including long life, wealth, honor, and peace. If you aren't experiencing them, does this mean you are short on wisdom? Not necessarily. Instead of guarantees, these statements are general principles. In a perfect world, wise behavior would always lead to these benefits. Even in our troubled world, living wisely usually results in obvious blessings—but not always. Sometimes sin intervenes, and some blessings must be delayed until Jesus returns to establish his eternal Kingdom. That is why we must "live by believing and not by seeing" (2 Cor 5:7). We can be sure that wisdom ultimately leads to blessing.

Prov 3:27-28 Withholding good is inconsiderate and unfair, whether it is repaying a loan, returning a tool, or fulfilling a promise. Withholding destroys trust and creates a great inconvenience for the other person. Be as eager to do good as you are to have good done to you.

A Father's Wise Advice

PROVERBS 4:1-27

1 My children,* listen when your father
corrects you.
Pay attention and learn good judgment,
2 for I am giving you good guidance.
Don't turn away from my instructions.
3 For I, too, was once my father's son,
tenderly loved as my mother's only child.

4 My father taught me,
"Take my words to heart.
Follow my commands, and you will live.
5 Get wisdom; develop good judgment.
Don't forget my words or turn away
from them.
6 Don't turn your back on wisdom, for she will
protect you.
Love her, and she will guard you.
7 Getting wisdom is the wisest thing you can do!
And whatever else you do, develop good
judgment.
8 If you prize wisdom, she will make you great.
Embrace her, and she will honor you.
9 She will place a lovely wreath on your head;
she will present you with a beautiful crown."

10 My child,* listen to me and do as I say,
and you will have a long, good life.
11 I will teach you wisdom's ways
and lead you in straight paths.
12 When you walk, you won't be held back;
when you run, you won't stumble.
13 Take hold of my instructions; don't let them go.
Guard them, for they are the key to life.

14 Don't do as the wicked do,
and don't follow the path of evildoers.
15 Don't even think about it; don't go that way.
Turn away and keep moving.
16 For evil people can't sleep until they've done their
evil deed for the day.
They can't rest until they've caused someone
to stumble.
17 They eat the food of wickedness
and drink the wine of violence!

18 The way of the righteous is like the first gleam
of dawn,
which shines ever brighter until the full light
of day.
19 But the way of the wicked is like total darkness.
They have no idea what they are stumbling over.

20 My child, pay attention to what I say.
Listen carefully to my words.
21 Don't lose sight of them.
Let them penetrate deep into your heart,
22 for they bring life to those who find them,
and healing to their whole body.

23 Guard your heart above all else,
for it determines the course of your life.

Prv 4:1 Hebrew *My sons.* **Prv 4:10** Hebrew *My son;* also in 4:20.

Prov 4:3-4 One of the greatest responsibilities of parents is to encourage their children to become wise. Here Solomon tells how his father, David, encouraged him to seek wisdom when he was young (see 1 Kgs 2:1-9; 1 Chr 28–29 for David's charge to his son). This encouragement may have prompted Solomon to ask God for an understanding mind above everything else (1 Kgs 3:9). Wisdom can be passed on from parents to children, from generation to generation. Ultimately, of course, all wisdom comes from God; parents can only urge their children to turn to him. If your parents never taught you in this way, you can learn from the Scriptures and then create a legacy of wisdom as you teach your own children.

Prov 4:5-7 If you want wisdom, you must decide to go after it. This will take resolve—a determination not to abandon the search once you begin, no matter how difficult the road may become. This is not a once-in-a-lifetime step but a daily process of choosing between two paths—the way of the wicked (Prov 4:14-17, 19) and that of the righteous (Prov 4:18). Nothing is more important or more valuable.

Prov 4:7 David taught Solomon as a young boy that seeking God's wisdom was the most important choice he could make. Solomon learned the lesson well. When God appeared to Solomon to fulfill any request, the new king chose wisdom above all else. We should also make God's wisdom our first choice. We don't have to wait for God to appear to us. We can boldly ask him for wisdom today through prayer. James 1:5 assures us that God will grant our request.

Prov 4:13-17 Even friends can make you fall. It is difficult for people to accept the fact that friends and acquaintances may lure them to do wrong. Young people who want to be accepted would never confront or criticize a friend for wrong plans or actions. Many other people can't see how their friends' actions could lead to trouble. While we should be accepting of others, we need a healthy skepticism about human behavior. When you feel yourself being heavily influenced, proceed with caution. Don't let your friends cause you to fall into sin.

Prov 4:23-27 Our hearts—our feelings of love and desire—dictate to a great extent how we live because we always find time to do what we enjoy. Solomon tells us to guard our hearts above all else, making sure we concentrate on those desires that will keep us on the right path. Make sure your affections lead you in the right direction. Put boundaries on your desires: Don't go after everything you see. Look straight ahead, keep your eyes fixed on your goal,

STRATEGY FOR EFFECTIVE LIVING

Begins with	**God's wisdom**	Respecting and appreciating who God is; reverence and awe toward God
Requires	**Moral application**	Trusting in God and his Word; allowing his Word to speak to us personally; being willing to obey
Requires	**Practical application**	Acting on God's direction daily
Results in	**Effective living**	Experiencing what God does with our obedience

24 Avoid all perverse talk;
stay away from corrupt speech.
25 Look straight ahead,
and fix your eyes on what lies before you.
26 Mark out a straight path for your feet;
stay on the safe path.
27 Don't get sidetracked;
keep your feet from following evil.

Avoid Immoral Women

PROVERBS 5:1-23

1 My son, pay attention to my wisdom;
listen carefully to my wise counsel.
2 Then you will show discernment,
and your lips will express what you've learned.
3 For the lips of an immoral woman are as sweet as honey,
and her mouth is smoother than oil.
4 But in the end she is as bitter as poison,
as dangerous as a double-edged sword.
5 Her feet go down to death;
her steps lead straight to the grave.*
6 For she cares nothing about the path to life.
She staggers down a crooked trail and doesn't realize it.

7 So now, my sons, listen to me.
Never stray from what I am about to say:
8 Stay away from her!
Don't go near the door of her house!
9 If you do, you will lose your honor
and will lose to merciless people all you have achieved.
10 Strangers will consume your wealth,
and someone else will enjoy the fruit of your labor.
11 In the end you will groan in anguish
when disease consumes your body.
12 You will say, "How I hated discipline!
If only I had not ignored all the warnings!
13 Oh, why didn't I listen to my teachers?
Why didn't I pay attention to my instructors?
14 I have come to the brink of utter ruin,
and now I must face public disgrace."

15 Drink water from your own well—
share your love only with your wife.*
16 Why spill the water of your springs in the streets,
having sex with just anyone?*
17 You should reserve it for yourselves.
Never share it with strangers.

18 Let your wife be a fountain of blessing for you.
Rejoice in the wife of your youth.
19 She is a loving deer, a graceful doe.
Let her breasts satisfy you always.
May you always be captivated by her love.
20 Why be captivated, my son, by an immoral woman,
or fondle the breasts of a promiscuous woman?
21 For the LORD sees clearly what a man does,
examining every path he takes.
22 An evil man is held captive by his own sins;
they are ropes that catch and hold him.
23 He will die for lack of self-control;
he will be lost because of his great foolishness.

Prv 5:5 Hebrew *to Sheol.* **Prv 5:15** Hebrew *Drink water from your own cistern, / flowing water from your own well.* **Prv 5:16** Hebrew *Why spill your springs in the streets, / your streams in the city squares?*

and don't get sidetracked on detours that lead to sin.

Prov 5:3 This "immoral woman" is a prostitute. Proverbs includes many warnings against illicit sex for several reasons. First, a prostitute's charm is used as an example of any temptation to do wrong or to leave the pursuit of wisdom. Second, sexual immorality of any kind was and still is extremely dangerous because it destroys family life, erodes a person's ability to love, degrades human beings and turns them into objects, can lead to disease, and can result in unplanned children. Third, sexual immorality is against God's law.

Prov 5:3-8 We should be on guard against those who use flattery and smooth talk (lips that "are as sweet as honey") that could lead us into sin. The best advice is to take a detour and even avoid conversation with such people.

Prov 5:11-13 At the end of your life, it will be too late to ask for advice. When desire is fully activated, people don't want advice—they want satisfaction. The best time to learn the dangers and foolishness of going after forbidden sex (or anything else that is harmful) is long before the temptation comes. Resistance is easier if the decision has already been made. Don't wait to see what happens. Prepare for temptation by deciding now how you will act when you face it.

Prov 5:15 "Drink water from your own well" is a picture of faithfulness in marriage. It means to enjoy the spouse God has given you. In desert lands, water is precious, and a well is a family's most important possession. In Old Testament times, it was considered a crime to steal water from someone else's well, just as it was a crime to have intercourse with another person's spouse. In both cases, the offender endangers the health and security of the family.

Prov 5:15-21 In contrast to much of what we read, see, and hear today, this passage urges couples to look to each other for lifelong satisfaction and companionship. Many temptations entice husbands and wives to leave when marriage becomes dull in order to find excitement and pleasures elsewhere. But God designed marriage and sanctified it, and only within this covenant relationship can we find real love and fulfillment. Don't let God's best for you be wasted on the illusion of greener pastures somewhere else. Instead, rejoice with your spouse as you give yourselves to God and to each other.

Prov 5:18-20 God never intended marriage to become boring, lifeless, and dull. Sex is a gift God gives to married people for their mutual enjoyment. Real happiness comes when we decide to find pleasure in the spouse God has given us and to commit ourselves to meeting that person's needs. The real danger is in doubting that God knows and cares for us. We then may resent his timing and carelessly pursue sexual pleasure without his blessing.

Prov 5:19 See Song of Songs (especially Song 4), for parallels to this frank expression of the joys of sexual pleasure in marriage.

Lessons for Daily Life

PROVERBS 6:1-35

1 My child,* if you have put up security for a
friend's debt
or agreed to guarantee the debt of a stranger—
2 if you have trapped yourself by your agreement
and are caught by what you said—
3 follow my advice and save yourself,
for you have placed yourself at your friend's
mercy.
Now swallow your pride;
go and beg to have your name erased.
4 Don't put it off; do it now!
Don't rest until you do.
5 Save yourself like a gazelle escaping from
a hunter,
like a bird fleeing from a net.

6 Take a lesson from the ants, you lazybones.
Learn from their ways and become wise!
7 Though they have no prince
or governor or ruler to make them work,
8 they labor hard all summer,
gathering food for the winter.
9 But you, lazybones, how long will you sleep?
When will you wake up?
10 A little extra sleep, a little more slumber,
a little folding of the hands to rest—
11 then poverty will pounce on you like a bandit;
scarcity will attack you like an armed robber.

12 What are worthless and wicked people like?
They are constant liars,
13 signaling their deceit with a wink of the eye,
a nudge of the foot, or the wiggle of fingers.
14 Their perverted hearts plot evil,
and they constantly stir up trouble.
15 But they will be destroyed suddenly,
broken in an instant beyond all hope of healing.

16 There are six things the LORD hates—
no, seven things he detests:
17 haughty eyes,
a lying tongue,
hands that kill the innocent,
18 a heart that plots evil,
feet that race to do wrong,
19 a false witness who pours out lies,
a person who sows discord in a family.

20 My son, obey your father's commands,
and don't neglect your mother's instruction.
21 Keep their words always in your heart.
Tie them around your neck.
22 When you walk, their counsel will lead you.
When you sleep, they will protect you.
When you wake up, they will advise you.
23 For their command is a lamp
and their instruction a light;
their corrective discipline
is the way to life.
24 It will keep you from the immoral woman,
from the smooth tongue of a promiscuous
woman.
25 Don't lust for her beauty.
Don't let her coy glances seduce you.

Prv 6:1 Hebrew *My son.*

Prov 6:1-5 These verses are not a plea against generosity but against overextending one's financial resources and acting in irresponsible ways that could lead to poverty. It is important to maintain a balance between generosity and good stewardship. God wants us to help our friends and the needy, but he does not promise to cover the costs of every unwise commitment we make. We should also act responsibly so that our families do not suffer.

Prov 6:6-11 Those last few moments of sleep are delicious; we savor them as we resist beginning another workday. But Proverbs warns against giving in to the temptation of laziness, of sleeping instead of working. This does not mean we should never rest: God gave the Jews the Sabbath, a weekly day of rest and restoration. But we should not rest when we should be working. The ant is used as an example because it utilizes its energy and resources economically. If laziness turns us from our responsibilities, poverty may soon bar us from the legitimate rest we should enjoy.

Prov 6:20-23 It is natural and good for children, as they grow toward adulthood, to become increasingly independent of their parents. Young adults, however, should take care not to turn a deaf ear to their parents—to reject their advice just when it is needed most. If you are struggling with a decision or looking for insight, check with your parents or other older adults who know you well. Their years of experience may have given them the wisdom you seek.

THINGS GOD HATES

The book of Proverbs notes 14 types of people and actions that God hates. Let these be guidelines of what we are *not* to be and do!

Violent people	**Prov 3:31-32**
Haughtiness, lying, murdering, scheming, eagerness to do wrong, a false witness, stirring up discord	**Prov 6:16-19**
Those who are untruthful	**Prov 12:22**
The sacrifice of the wicked	**Prov 15:8**
The way of the wicked	**Prov 15:9**
Evil plans	**Prov 15:26**
Those who are proud	**Prov 16:5**
Those who judge unjustly	**Prov 17:15**

Prov 6:25 Regard lust as a warning sign of danger ahead. When you notice that you are attracted to a person of the opposite sex or preoccupied with lustful thoughts, your desires may lead you to sin. Ask God to help you change your desires before you are drawn into sin.

26 For a prostitute will bring you to poverty,*
but sleeping with another man's wife will cost
you your life.
27 Can a man scoop a flame into his lap
and not have his clothes catch on fire?
28 Can he walk on hot coals
and not blister his feet?
29 So it is with the man who sleeps with another
man's wife.
He who embraces her will not go unpunished.
30 Excuses might be found for a thief
who steals because he is starving.
31 But if he is caught, he must pay back seven times
what he stole,
even if he has to sell everything in his house.
32 But the man who commits adultery is an
utter fool,
for he destroys himself.
33 He will be wounded and disgraced.
His shame will never be erased.
34 For the woman's jealous husband will be
furious,
and he will show no mercy when he takes
revenge.
35 He will accept no compensation,
nor be satisfied with a payoff of any size.

Another Warning about Immoral Women

PROVERBS 7:1-27

1 Follow my advice, my son;
always treasure my commands.
2 Obey my commands and live!
Guard my instructions as you guard your
own eyes.*
3 Tie them on your fingers as a reminder.
Write them deep within your heart.
4 Love wisdom like a sister;
make insight a beloved member of your family.
5 Let them protect you from an affair with an
immoral woman,
from listening to the flattery of a promiscuous
woman.

6 While I was at the window of my house,
looking through the curtain,
7 I saw some naive young men,
and one in particular who lacked common
sense.
8 He was crossing the street near the house
of an immoral woman,
strolling down the path by her house.
9 It was at twilight, in the evening,
as deep darkness fell.
10 The woman approached him,
seductively dressed and sly of heart.
11 She was the brash, rebellious type,
never content to stay at home.
12 She is often in the streets and markets,
soliciting at every corner.
13 She threw her arms around him and kissed him,
and with a brazen look she said,
14 "I've just made my peace offerings
and fulfilled my vows.
15 You're the one I was looking for!
I came out to find you, and here you are!
16 My bed is spread with beautiful blankets,
with colored sheets of Egyptian linen.
17 I've perfumed my bed
with myrrh, aloes, and cinnamon.
18 Come, let's drink our fill of love until morning.
Let's enjoy each other's caresses,
19 for my husband is not home.
He's away on a long trip.

Prv 6:26 Hebrew *to a loaf of bread.* **Prv 7:2** Hebrew *as the pupil of your eye.*

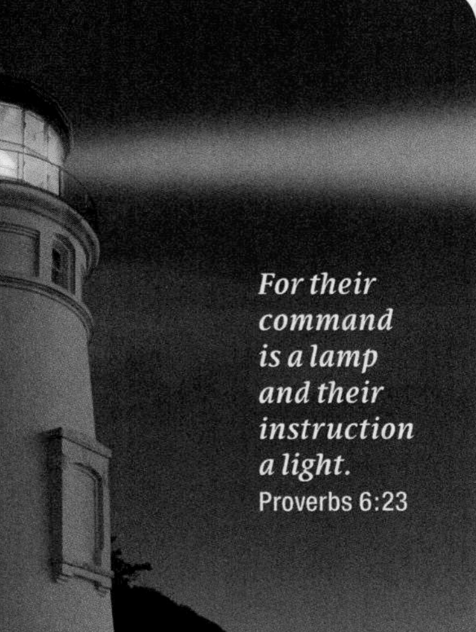

For their command is a lamp and their instruction a light.
Proverbs 6:23

Prov 6:25-35 Some people argue that it is all right to break God's law against sexual sin if nobody gets hurt. In truth, somebody always gets hurt. In the case of adultery, spouses are devastated and children are scarred. Even if the partners escape disease and unwanted pregnancy, they may lose their ability to fulfill commitments, to feel sexual desire, to trust, and to be entirely open with another person. God's laws are not arbitrary. They do not forbid good, clean fun; rather, they warn us against destroying ourselves through unwise actions or running ahead of God's timetable.

Prov 7:6-23 Although this advice is directed toward young men, young women should heed it as well. The person who has no purpose in life is naive (Prov 7:7). Without aim or direction, an empty life is unstable, vulnerable to many temptations. Even though the young man in this passage doesn't know where he is going, the immoral woman knows where she wants him. Notice her strategies: She is dressed to allure men (Prov 7:10); her approach is bold (Prov 7:13); she invites him over to her place (Prov 7:16-18); she cunningly answers his every objection (Prov 7:19-20); she persuades him with smooth talk (Prov 7:21); she traps him (Prov 7:23). To combat temptation, make sure your life is full of God's Word and wisdom (Prov 7:4). Recognize the strategies of temptation, and run away from them—fast.

▸ **PROVERBS 7:1-27 *(cont.)***

20 He has taken a wallet full of money with him
and won't return until later this month.*"

21 So she seduced him with her pretty speech
and enticed him with her flattery.
22 He followed her at once,
like an ox going to the slaughter.
He was like a stag caught in a trap,
23 awaiting the arrow that would pierce its heart.
He was like a bird flying into a snare,
little knowing it would cost him his life.

24 So listen to me, my sons,
and pay attention to my words.
25 Don't let your hearts stray away toward her.
Don't wander down her wayward path.
26 For she has been the ruin of many;
many men have been her victims.
27 Her house is the road to the grave.*
Her bedroom is the den of death.

Wisdom Calls for a Hearing

PROVERBS 8:1–9:12

1 Listen as Wisdom calls out!
Hear as understanding raises her voice!
2 On the hilltop along the road,
she takes her stand at the crossroads.
3 By the gates at the entrance to the town,
on the road leading in, she cries aloud,
4 "I call to you, to all of you!
I raise my voice to all people.
5 You simple people, use good judgment.
You foolish people, show some understanding.
6 Listen to me! For I have important things to tell you.
Everything I say is right,
7 for I speak the truth
and detest every kind of deception.
8 My advice is wholesome.
There is nothing devious or crooked in it.
9 My words are plain to anyone with understanding,
clear to those with knowledge.
10 Choose my instruction rather than silver,
and knowledge rather than pure gold.
11 For wisdom is far more valuable than rubies.
Nothing you desire can compare with it.

12 "I, Wisdom, live together with good judgment.
I know where to discover knowledge and discernment.
13 All who fear the LORD will hate evil.
Therefore, I hate pride and arrogance,
corruption and perverse speech.
14 Common sense and success belong to me.
Insight and strength are mine.
15 Because of me, kings reign,
and rulers make just decrees.
16 Rulers lead with my help,
and nobles make righteous judgments.*

17 "I love all who love me.
Those who search will surely find me.
18 I have riches and honor,
as well as enduring wealth and justice.
19 My gifts are better than gold, even the purest gold,
my wages better than sterling silver!
20 I walk in righteousness,
in paths of justice.
21 Those who love me inherit wealth.
I will fill their treasuries.

22 "The LORD formed me from the beginning,
before he created anything else.
23 I was appointed in ages past,
at the very first, before the earth began.
24 I was born before the oceans were created,
before the springs bubbled forth their waters.
25 Before the mountains were formed,
before the hills, I was born—
26 before he had made the earth and fields
and the first handfuls of soil.
27 I was there when he established the heavens,
when he drew the horizon on the oceans.
28 I was there when he set the clouds above,
when he established springs deep in the earth.
29 I was there when he set the limits of the seas,
so they would not spread beyond their boundaries.

Prv 7:20 Hebrew *until the moon is full.* **Prv 7:27** Hebrew *to Sheol.* **Prv 8:16** Some Hebrew manuscripts and Greek version read *and nobles are judges over the earth.*

Prov 7:25-27 You can take definite steps to avoid sexual sins. First, guard your mind. Don't read books, look at pictures, or encourage fantasies that stimulate the wrong desires. Second, keep away from settings and friends that tempt you to sin. Third, don't think only of the moment—focus on the future. Today's thrill may lead to tomorrow's ruin.

Prov 8:1ff Wisdom's call is contrasted to the call of the immoral woman (in Prov 7). Wisdom is portrayed as a woman who guides us (Prov 8:1-13) and makes us succeed (Prov 8:14-21). Wisdom was present at the Creation and works with the Creator (Prov 8:22-31). God approves of those who listen to Wisdom's counsel (Prov 8:32-35). Those who hate wisdom love death (Prov 8:36). Wisdom should affect every aspect of one's life, from beginning to end. Be sure to open all corners of your life to God's direction and guidance.

Prov 8:13 The more you fear and respect God, the more you will hate evil. Love for God and love for sin cannot coexist. Harboring secret sins means that you are tolerating evil within yourself. Make a clean break with sin and commit yourself completely to God.

Prov 8:22-31 God says that wisdom is primary and fundamental. It is the foundation on which all life is built. Paul and John may have alluded to some of Solomon's statements about wisdom to describe Christ's presence at the creation of the world (Col 1:15-17; 2:2-3; Rev 3:14).

And when he marked off the earth's foundations,
30 I was the architect at his side.
I was his constant delight,
rejoicing always in his presence.
31 And how happy I was with the world he created;
how I rejoiced with the human family!

32 "And so, my children,* listen to me,
for all who follow my ways are joyful.
33 Listen to my instruction and be wise.
Don't ignore it.
34 Joyful are those who listen to me,
watching for me daily at my gates,
waiting for me outside my home!
35 For whoever finds me finds life
and receives favor from the LORD.
36 But those who miss me injure themselves.
All who hate me love death."

9:1 Wisdom has built her house;
she has carved its seven columns.
2 She has prepared a great banquet,
mixed the wines, and set the table.
3 She has sent her servants to invite everyone
to come.
She calls out from the heights overlooking
the city.
4 "Come in with me," she urges the simple.
To those who lack good judgment, she says,
5 "Come, eat my food,
and drink the wine I have mixed.
6 Leave your simple ways behind, and begin to live;
learn to use good judgment."

7 Anyone who rebukes a mocker will get an insult
in return.
Anyone who corrects the wicked will get hurt.
8 So don't bother correcting mockers;
they will only hate you.
But correct the wise,
and they will love you.
9 Instruct the wise,
and they will be even wiser.
Teach the righteous,
and they will learn even more.

10 Fear of the LORD is the foundation of wisdom.
Knowledge of the Holy One results in good
judgment.

11 Wisdom will multiply your days
and add years to your life.
12 If you become wise, you will be the one
to benefit.
If you scorn wisdom, you will be the one
to suffer.

Folly Calls for a Hearing

PROVERBS 9:13-18

13 The woman named Folly is brash.
She is ignorant and doesn't know it.
14 She sits in her doorway
on the heights overlooking the city.
15 She calls out to men going by
who are minding their own business.
16 "Come in with me," she urges the simple.
To those who lack good judgment, she says,
17 "Stolen water is refreshing;
food eaten in secret tastes the best!"
18 But little do they know that the dead
are there.
Her guests are in the depths of the grave.*

The Proverbs of Solomon

PROVERBS 10:1–22:16

The proverbs of Solomon:

A wise child* brings joy to a father;
a foolish child brings grief to a mother.

2 Tainted wealth has no lasting value,
but right living can save your life.

Prv 8:32 Hebrew *my sons.* **Prv 9:18** Hebrew *in Sheol.* **Prv 10:1** Hebrew *son;* also in 10:1b.

Prov 9:1 The seven columns are figurative; they do not represent seven principles of wisdom. In the Bible, the number seven represents completeness and perfection. This verse poetically states that wisdom lacks nothing—it is complete and perfect.

Prov 9:1ff Wisdom and Folly (foolishness) are portrayed in this chapter as rival young women, each preparing a feast and inviting people to it. But Wisdom is a responsible woman of character, while Folly is a prostitute serving stolen food. Wisdom appeals to the mind; Folly to the senses. It is easier to excite the senses, but the pleasures of Folly are temporary. By contrast, the satisfaction that Wisdom brings lasts forever.

Prov 9:1-5 The banquet described in this chapter has some interesting parallels to the banquet Jesus described in one of his parables (Luke 14:15-24). Many may intend to go, but they never make it because they get sidetracked by other activities that seem more important at the time. Don't let anything become more important than your search for God's wisdom.

Prov 9:7-10 Are you a mocker or a wise person? You can tell by the way you respond to criticism. Instead of replying with a quick put-down or clever retort when rebuked, listen to what is being said. Learn from your critics; this is the path to wisdom. Wisdom begins with knowing God. He gives insight into living because he created life. To know God you must not just know the facts about him; you must have a personal relationship with him. Do you really want to be wise? Get to know God better and better. (See Jas 1:5; 2 Pet 1:2-4 for more on how to become wise.)

Prov 9:14-17 There is something hypnotic and intoxicating about wickedness. One sin leads to another; sinful behavior seems more exciting than the Christian life. That is why many people put aside all thought of Wisdom's sumptuous banquet (Prov 9:1-5) in order to eat the stolen food of Folly. Don't be deceived—sin is dangerous. Before reaching for forbidden fruit, take a long look at what happens to those who eat it.

Prov 10:2 Some people bring unhappiness on themselves by choosing tainted wealth, ill-gotten gain. Craving satisfaction, they may do something that destroys their chances of ever achieving happiness. God's principles for right living bring lasting happiness because they guide us into long-term right behavior in spite of our ever-changing feelings.

▶ **PROVERBS 10:1–22:16 *(cont.)***

3 The LORD will not let the godly go hungry,
but he refuses to satisfy the craving
of the wicked.

4 Lazy people are soon poor;
hard workers get rich.

5 A wise youth harvests in the summer,
but one who sleeps during harvest
is a disgrace.

6 The godly are showered with blessings;
the words of the wicked conceal violent
intentions.

7 We have happy memories of the godly,
but the name of a wicked person rots away.

8 The wise are glad to be instructed,
but babbling fools fall flat on their faces.

9 People with integrity walk safely,
but those who follow crooked paths will slip
and fall.

10 People who wink at wrong cause trouble,
but a bold reproof promotes peace.*

11 The words of the godly are a life-giving
fountain;
the words of the wicked conceal violent
intentions.

12 Hatred stirs up quarrels,
but love makes up for all offenses.

13 Wise words come from the lips of people with
understanding,
but those lacking sense will be beaten
with a rod.

14 Wise people treasure knowledge,
but the babbling of a fool invites disaster.

15 The wealth of the rich is their fortress;
the poverty of the poor is their destruction.

16 The earnings of the godly enhance their lives,
but evil people squander their money on sin.

17 People who accept discipline are on the
pathway to life,
but those who ignore correction will go astray.

18 Hiding hatred makes you a liar;
slandering others makes you a fool.

19 Too much talk leads to sin.
Be sensible and keep your mouth shut.

20 The words of the godly are like sterling silver;
the heart of a fool is worthless.

21 The words of the godly encourage many,
but fools are destroyed by their lack of
common sense.

Prv 10:10 As in Greek version; Hebrew reads *but babbling fools fall flat on their faces.*

Prov 10:3 Proverbs is filled with verses that contrast the godly (righteous) person with the wicked. These statements are not intended to apply universally to all people in every situation. For example, some good people do go hungry. Rather, they are intended to communicate the general truth that the life of the person who seeks God is better in the long run than the life of the wicked person—a life that leads to ruin. These statements are not ironclad promises but general truths. In addition, a proverb like this assumes a just government that cares for the poor and needy—the kind of government Israel was intended to have (see Deut 24:17-22). A corrupt government often thwarts the plans of godly men and women.

Prov 10:3 Proverbs often describes God's care for "the godly." Being "godly" does not mean being "like God" in the sense of being perfect. Obviously that is impossible for human beings. Godly people are those who love the Lord and are seeking to follow him (Ps 4:3). As Christians, we have been given the power of the Holy Spirit to help us live godly lives (2 Pet 1:3).

Prov 10:4-5 Every day has 24 hours filled with opportunities to grow, serve, and be productive. Yet it is so easy to waste time, letting life slip from our grasp. Refuse to be a lazy person, sleeping or frittering away the hours meant for productive work. See time as God's gift, and seize your opportunities to live diligently for him.

UNDERSTANDING PROVERBS

Most often, proverbs are written in the form of couplets. These are constructed in three ways:

Type	*Description*	*Key Word(s)*	*Examples*
Contrasting	Meaning and application come from the differences or contrast between the two statements of the proverb.	"but"	Prov 10:3; 14:11, 18
Comparing	Meaning and application come from the similarities or comparison between the two statements of the proverb.	"as/so" "better/than" "like"	Prov 15:16-17; 22:7; 25:25
Complementing	Meaning and application come from the way the second statement complements the first.	"and"	Prov 14:10, 17; 23:22

Prov 10:18 By hating another person you may become a liar or a fool. If you try to conceal your hatred, you end up lying. If you slander the other person and are proven wrong, you are a fool. The only way out is to admit your hateful feelings to God. Ask him to change your heart, to help you love instead of hate.

Prov 10:20 Words from a good person are valuable ("sterling silver"). A lot of poor advice is worth less than a little good advice. It is easy to get opinions from people who will tell us only what they think will please us, but such advice is not helpful. Instead, we should look for those who will speak the truth, even when it hurts. Think about the people to whom you go for advice. What do you expect to hear from them?

22 The blessing of the LORD makes a person rich,
and he adds no sorrow with it.

23 Doing wrong is fun for a fool,
but living wisely brings pleasure to the sensible.

24 The fears of the wicked will be fulfilled;
the hopes of the godly will be granted.

25 When the storms of life come, the wicked are whirled away,
but the godly have a lasting foundation.

26 Lazy people irritate their employers,
like vinegar to the teeth or smoke in the eyes.

27 Fear of the LORD lengthens one's life,
but the years of the wicked are cut short.

28 The hopes of the godly result in happiness,
but the expectations of the wicked come to nothing.

29 The way of the LORD is a stronghold to those with integrity,
but it destroys the wicked.

30 The godly will never be disturbed,
but the wicked will be removed from the land.

31 The mouth of the godly person gives wise advice,
but the tongue that deceives will be cut off.

32 The lips of the godly speak helpful words,
but the mouth of the wicked speaks perverse words.

11:1 The LORD detests the use of dishonest scales,
but he delights in accurate weights.

2 Pride leads to disgrace,
but with humility comes wisdom.

3 Honesty guides good people;
dishonesty destroys treacherous people.

4 Riches won't help on the day of judgment,
but right living can save you from death.

5 The godly are directed by honesty;
the wicked fall beneath their load of sin.

6 The godliness of good people rescues them;
the ambition of treacherous people traps them.

7 When the wicked die, their hopes die with them,
for they rely on their own feeble strength.

8 The godly are rescued from trouble,
and it falls on the wicked instead.

9 With their words, the godless destroy their friends,
but knowledge will rescue the righteous.

10 The whole city celebrates when the godly succeed;
they shout for joy when the wicked die.

11 Upright citizens are good for a city and make it prosper,
but the talk of the wicked tears it apart.

12 It is foolish to belittle one's neighbor;
a sensible person keeps quiet.

13 A gossip goes around telling secrets,
but those who are trustworthy can keep a confidence.

14 Without wise leadership, a nation falls;
there is safety in having many advisers.

15 There's danger in putting up security for a stranger's debt;
it's safer not to guarantee another person's debt.

16 A gracious woman gains respect,
but ruthless men gain only wealth.

17 Your kindness will reward you,
but your cruelty will destroy you.

Prov 10:22 God supplies most people with the personal and financial abilities to respond to the needs of others. If we all realized how God has blessed us, and if we all used our resources to do God's will, hunger and poverty would be wiped out. Wealth is a blessing only if we use it in the way God intended.

Prov 10:24 The wicked person dreads death. Those who do not believe in God usually fear death, and with good reason. By contrast, believers desire eternal life and God's salvation, and their hopes will be rewarded. This verse offers a choice: You can have either your fears or your hopes come true. You make that choice by rejecting God and living your own way or by accepting God and following him.

Prov 11:4 "The day of judgment" refers to when we die or to the time when God settles accounts with all people. On judgment day, each person will stand alone, accountable for all deeds done while on earth. At that time, no amount of riches will buy reconciliation with God. Only our love for God and obedience to him will count.

Prov 11:7-8 These verses (like Prov 10:3) contrast two paths in life but are not intended to apply universally to all people in all circumstances. God's people are not excluded from problems or struggles. A person who follows God's wisdom can be rescued from trouble. But a wicked person will fall into self-made traps. Even if godly people suffer, they can be sure they will ultimately be rescued from eternal death.

Prov 11:9 The mouth can be used as either a weapon or a tool, hurting relationships or building them up. Sadly, it is often easier to destroy than to build, and most people have received more destructive comments than those that build up. Every person you meet today is either a demolition site or a construction opportunity. Your words will make a difference. Will they be weapons for destruction or tools for construction?

Prov 11:14 A good leader needs and uses wise advisers. One person's perspective and understanding can be severely limited—such as not having all the facts or being blinded by bias, emotions, or wrong impressions. To be a wise leader at home, at church, or at work, seek the counsel of others and be open to their advice. Then, after considering all the facts, make your decision.

▶ **PROVERBS 10:1–22:16 *(cont.)***

18 Evil people get rich for the moment,
but the reward of the godly will last.

19 Godly people find life;
evil people find death.

20 The LORD detests people with crooked hearts,
but he delights in those with integrity.

21 Evil people will surely be punished,
but the children of the godly will go free.

22 A beautiful woman who lacks discretion
is like a gold ring in a pig's snout.

23 The godly can look forward to a reward,
while the wicked can expect only judgment.

24 Give freely and become more wealthy;
be stingy and lose everything.

25 The generous will prosper;
those who refresh others will themselves
be refreshed.

26 People curse those who hoard their grain,
but they bless the one who sells in time of need.

27 If you search for good, you will find favor;
but if you search for evil, it will find you!

28 Trust in your money and down you go!
But the godly flourish like leaves in spring.

29 Those who bring trouble on their families inherit
the wind.
The fool will be a servant to the wise.

30 The seeds of good deeds become a tree of life;
a wise person wins friends.*

31 If the righteous are rewarded here on earth,
what will happen to wicked sinners?*

12:1 To learn, you must love discipline;
it is stupid to hate correction.

2 The LORD approves of those who are good,
but he condemns those who plan wickedness.

3 Wickedness never brings stability,
but the godly have deep roots.

4 A worthy wife is a crown for her husband,
but a disgraceful woman is like cancer in his
bones.

Prv 11:30 Or *and those who win souls are wise.* **Prv 11:31** Greek version reads *If the righteous are barely saved, / what will happen to godless sinners?* Compare 1 Pet 4:18.

Prov 11:19 "Godly people find life" because they live life more fully each day. In addition, they need not fear death because eternal life is God's gift to them (John 11:25). By contrast, evil people not only find eternal death but also miss out on real life on earth.

Prov 11:22 Physical attractiveness without discretion is soon discovered to be quite ugly indeed. We are to seek those character strengths that help us make wise decisions, not just those that make us look good. Not everyone who looks good is pleasant to live or work with. While taking good care of our body and appearance is not wrong, we also need to develop our ability to think and make wise decisions.

Prov 11:24-25 These two verses present a paradox: We become richer by being generous. The world says to hold on to as much as possible, but God blesses those who give freely of their possessions, time, and energy. When we give, God supplies us with more so that we can give more. In addition, giving helps us gain a right perspective on our possessions. We realize they were never really ours to begin with; they were given by God to be used to help others. What then do we gain by giving? Freedom from enslavement to our possessions, the joy of helping others, and God's approval.

Prov 11:29 One of the greatest resources God gives us is the family. Families provide acceptance, encouragement, guidance, and counsel. Bringing trouble on your family—whether through anger or through an exaggerated desire for independence—is foolish because you cut yourself off from all they provide. In your family, strive for healing, communication, and understanding.

Prov 11:30 A wise person is a model of a meaningful life. Like a tree attracts people to its shade, a wise person's sense of purpose attracts others who want to know how they, too, can find meaning. Gaining wisdom yourself can be the first step in leading people to God.

Prov 11:31 Contrary to popular opinion, no one sins and gets away with it. The righteous are rewarded for their faith; the wicked are punished for their sins. Don't think for a moment that "it won't matter" or "nobody will know" or "I won't get caught" (see also 1 Pet 4:18).

Prov 12:1 If you don't want to learn, years of schooling will teach you very little. But if you want to be taught, there is no end to what you can learn. This includes being willing to accept discipline and correction and to learn from the wisdom of others. A person who refuses constructive criticism has a problem with pride. Such a person is unlikely to learn very much.

Prov 12:3 To have deep roots and to be stable means to be successful. Real stability and success come only to those who do what is right. Their efforts stand the test of time. Yet sometimes it seems that wickedness does indeed bring success. We may know people who cheated to pass a class or to get a larger tax refund. And what about the person who ignores his family commitments and mistreats his workers but gets ahead in business? These apparent suc-

GOD'S ADVICE ABOUT MONEY

Proverbs gives some practical instruction on the use of money, although sometimes it is advice we would rather not hear. It's more comfortable to continue in our habits than to learn how to use money more wisely. The advice includes:

Be generous in giving	Prov 11:24-25; 22:9
Place people's needs ahead of profit	Prov 11:26
Be cautious of countersigning for another	Prov 17:18; 22:26-27
Don't accept bribes	Prov 17:23
Help the poor	Prov 19:17; 21:13
Store up for the future	Prov 21:20
Be careful about borrowing	Prov 22:7

Other verses to study include Proverbs 11:15; 20:16; 25:14; 27:13.

5 The plans of the godly are just;
the advice of the wicked is treacherous.
6 The words of the wicked are like a murderous ambush,
but the words of the godly save lives.
7 The wicked die and disappear,
but the family of the godly stands firm.
8 A sensible person wins admiration,
but a warped mind is despised.
9 Better to be an ordinary person with a servant
than to be self-important but have no food.
10 The godly care for their animals,
but the wicked are always cruel.
11 A hard worker has plenty of food,
but a person who chases fantasies has no sense.
12 Thieves are jealous of each other's loot,
but the godly are well rooted and bear their own fruit.
13 The wicked are trapped by their own words,
but the godly escape such trouble.
14 Wise words bring many benefits,
and hard work brings rewards.
15 Fools think their own way is right,
but the wise listen to others.
16 A fool is quick-tempered,
but a wise person stays calm when insulted.
17 An honest witness tells the truth;
a false witness tells lies.
18 Some people make cutting remarks,
but the words of the wise bring healing.
19 Truthful words stand the test of time,
but lies are soon exposed.
20 Deceit fills hearts that are plotting evil;
joy fills hearts that are planning peace!
21 No harm comes to the godly,
but the wicked have their fill of trouble.
22 The LORD detests lying lips,
but he delights in those who tell the truth.
23 The wise don't make a show of their knowledge,
but fools broadcast their foolishness.
24 Work hard and become a leader;
be lazy and become a slave.
25 Worry weighs a person down;
an encouraging word cheers a person up.

TEACHING AND LEARNING

Good teaching comes from good learning—and Proverbs has more to say to students than to teachers. Proverbs is concerned with the learning of wisdom. The book makes it clear that there are no good alternatives to learning wisdom. We are either becoming wise learners or refusing to learn and becoming foolish failures. Proverbs encourages us to make the right choice.

Wise Learners	*Proverb(s)*	*Foolish Failures*
Gladly accept instruction	**Prov 10:8; 23:12**	Ignore instruction
Love discipline	**Prov 12:1**	Hate correction
Listen to advice	**Prov 12:15; 21:11; 24:6**	Think they need no advice
Accept parents' discipline	**Prov 13:1**	Mock parents
Are on the pathway to life	**Prov 10:17**	Will go astray
Will be honored	**Prov 13:18**	End in poverty and disgrace
Profit from constructive criticism	**Prov 15:31-32; 29:1**	Harm themselves by refusing criticism

Advice to Teachers: Help people avoid traps (Prov 13:14), use pleasant words (Prov 16:21), and speak wise words at the right time (Prov 15:23; 18:20).

cesses are only temporary. They are bought at the expense of character. Cheaters grow more dishonest, and those who hurt others become callous and cruel. In the long run, evil behavior does not lead to success; it leads to more evil. Real success maintains personal integrity. If you are not a success by God's standards, you have not achieved true success.

Prov 12:13 Evil people twist the facts to support their claims. Those who do this will eventually be trapped by their own lies. But for those who always tell the truth, the facts—plain and unvarnished—give an unshakable defense. If you find that you always have to defend yourself to others, maybe you are not being honest.

Prov 12:16 When someone annoys or insults you, it is natural to retaliate. But this solves nothing and only encourages trouble. Instead, stay calm and answer slowly and quietly. Your positive response will achieve positive results. Proverbs 15:1 says, "A gentle answer deflects anger."

Prov 12:19 Truth is always timely; it applies today and in the future. Because it is connected with God's changeless character, it is also changeless. Think for a moment about the centuries that have passed since these proverbs were written. Consider the countless hours that have been spent carefully studying every sentence of Scripture. The Bible has withstood the test of time. Because God is truth, you can trust his Word to guide you.

Prov 12:21 This is a general, but not universal, truth. Although harm does befall the godly, they are able to see opportunities in their problems and move ahead. The wicked, without God's wisdom, are ill-equipped to handle their problems. (See the notes on Prov 3:16-17, p. 635; Prov 10:3, p. 642; Prov 11:7-8, p. 643 for more about general truths that are not intended as universal statements.)

Prov 12:23 Wise people have a quiet confidence. Unstable people (fools) feel the need to prove themselves, but wise people don't have to prove anything. They know they are capable, so they can get on with their work. Beware of showing off. If you are modest, people may not notice you at first, but they will respect you later.

▶ **PROVERBS 10:1–22:16** ***(cont.)***

26 The godly give good advice to their friends;*
the wicked lead them astray.

27 Lazy people don't even cook the game they catch,
but the diligent make use of everything they find.

28 The way of the godly leads to life;
that path does not lead to death.

13:1 A wise child accepts a parent's discipline;*
a mocker refuses to listen to correction.

2 Wise words will win you a good meal,
but treacherous people have an appetite for violence.

3 Those who control their tongue will have a long life;
opening your mouth can ruin everything.

4 Lazy people want much but get little,
but those who work hard will prosper.

5 The godly hate lies;
the wicked cause shame and disgrace.

6 Godliness guards the path of the blameless,
but the evil are misled by sin.

7 Some who are poor pretend to be rich;
others who are rich pretend to be poor.

8 The rich can pay a ransom for their lives,
but the poor won't even get threatened.

9 The life of the godly is full of light and joy,
but the light of the wicked will be snuffed out.

10 Pride leads to conflict;
those who take advice are wise.

11 Wealth from get-rich-quick schemes quickly disappears;
wealth from hard work grows over time.

12 Hope deferred makes the heart sick,
but a dream fulfilled is a tree of life.

13 People who despise advice are asking for trouble;
those who respect a command will succeed.

14 The instruction of the wise is like a life-giving fountain;
those who accept it avoid the snares of death.

15 A person with good sense is respected;
a treacherous person is headed for destruction.*

16 Wise people think before they act;
fools don't—and even brag about their foolishness.

17 An unreliable messenger stumbles into trouble,
but a reliable messenger brings healing.

18 If you ignore criticism, you will end in poverty and disgrace;
if you accept correction, you will be honored.

19 It is pleasant to see dreams come true,
but fools refuse to turn from evil to attain them.

20 Walk with the wise and become wise;
associate with fools and get in trouble.

Prv 12:26 Or *The godly are cautious in friendship;* or *The godly are freed from evil.* The meaning of the Hebrew is uncertain. **Prv 13:1** Hebrew *A wise son accepts his father's discipline.* **Prv 13:15** As in Greek version; Hebrew reads *the way of the treacherous is lasting.*

Prov 12:27 The diligent make wise use of their possessions and resources; the lazy waste them. Waste has become a way of life for many who live in a land of plenty. Waste is poor stewardship. Make good use of everything God has given you, and prize it.

Prov 12:28 For many, death is a darkened door at the end of life, a passageway to an unknown and feared destiny. But for God's people, death is a bright pathway to a new and better life. So why do we fear death? Is it fear of the pain we expect, the separation from loved ones, or the unknown? God can help us deal with those fears. He has shown us that death is not final but just another step in the eternal life we received when we followed him.

Prov 13:3 You have not mastered self-control if you do not control what you say. Words can cut and destroy. James recognized this truth when he stated, "The tongue is a flame of fire. It is a whole world of wickedness" (Jas 3:6). If you want to be self-controlled, begin with your tongue. Stop and think before you react or speak. If you can control this small but powerful member, you can control the rest of your body.

Prov 13:6 Blameless living safeguards your life. Every choice for good sets into motion other opportunities for good. Evil choices follow the same pattern, but in the opposite direction. Each decision you make to obey God's Word will bring a greater sense of order to your life, while each decision to disobey will bring confusion and destruction. The right choices you make reflect your integrity. Obedience brings the greatest safeguard and security.

Prov 13:10 "I was wrong" or "I need advice" are difficult phrases to utter because they require humility. Pride is an ingredient in every quarrel. It stirs up conflict and divides people. Humility, by contrast, heals. Guard against pride. If you find yourself constantly arguing, examine your life for pride. Be open to the advice of others, ask for help when you need it, and be willing to admit your mistakes.

Prov 13:13 God created us, knows us, and loves us. It only makes sense, then, to listen to his instructions and do what he says. The Bible is his unfailing word to us. If you obey God's instructions, you will find his kind of power to live. If you ignore them, you will have problems, difficulties, and failures.

Prov 13:17 In Solomon's day, a king had to rely on messengers for information about his country. These messengers had to be trustworthy. Inaccurate information could lead to bloodshed. Reliable communication is still vital. If the message received is different from the message sent, marriages, businesses, and diplomatic relations can all break down. It is important to choose your words well and to avoid reacting until you clearly understand what the other person means.

Prov 13:19 Whether a "dream come true" is good or bad depends on the nature of the dream or desire. It is pleasant to achieve worthwhile goals, but not all goals are worth pursuing. When you set your heart on something, you may lose your ability to assess it objectively. With your desire blinding your judgment, you may proceed with an unwise relationship, a wasteful purchase, or a poorly

21 Trouble chases sinners,
while blessings reward the righteous.

22 Good people leave an inheritance to their grandchildren,
but the sinner's wealth passes to the godly.

23 A poor person's farm may produce much food,
but injustice sweeps it all away.

24 Those who spare the rod of discipline hate their children.
Those who love their children care enough to discipline them.

25 The godly eat to their hearts' content,
but the belly of the wicked goes hungry.

14:1 A wise woman builds her home,
but a foolish woman tears it down with her own hands.

2 Those who follow the right path fear the LORD;
those who take the wrong path despise him.

3 A fool's proud talk becomes a rod that beats him,
but the words of the wise keep them safe.

4 Without oxen a stable stays clean,
but you need a strong ox for a large harvest.

5 An honest witness does not lie;
a false witness breathes lies.

6 A mocker seeks wisdom and never finds it,
but knowledge comes easily to those with understanding.

7 Stay away from fools,
for you won't find knowledge on their lips.

8 The prudent understand where they are going,
but fools deceive themselves.

9 Fools make fun of guilt,
but the godly acknowledge it and seek reconciliation.

10 Each heart knows its own bitterness,
and no one else can fully share its joy.

11 The house of the wicked will be destroyed,
but the tent of the godly will flourish.

12 There is a path before each person that seems right,
but it ends in death.

13 Laughter can conceal a heavy heart,
but when the laughter ends, the grief remains.

14 Backsliders get what they deserve;
good people receive their reward.

15 Only simpletons believe everything they're told!
The prudent carefully consider their steps.

---

conceived plan. Faithfulness is a virtue, but stubbornness is not.

Prov 13:20 The old saying "A rotten apple spoils the barrel" is often applied to friendships, and with good reason. Our friends and associates affect us, sometimes profoundly. Be careful whom you choose as your closest friends. Spend time with people you want to be like because you and your friends will surely grow to resemble each other.

Prov 13:20 When most people need advice, they go to their friends first because friends accept them and usually agree with them. But that is why they may not be able to help them with difficult problems. Our friends are so much like us that they may not have any answers we haven't already heard. Instead, we should seek out older and wiser people to advise us. Wise people have experienced a lot in life—and have succeeded. They are not afraid to tell the truth. Who are the wise, godly people who can warn you of the pitfalls ahead?

Prov 13:23 The poor are often victims of an unjust society. A poor man's soil may be good, but unjust laws may rob him of his own produce. This proverb does not take poverty lightly or wink at injustice; it simply describes what often occurs. We should do what we can to fight injustice of every sort. Our efforts may seem inadequate, but it is comforting to know that in the end God's justice will prevail.

Prov 13:24 It is not easy for a loving parent to discipline a child, but it is necessary. The greatest responsibility that God gives parents is the nurture and guidance of their children. Lack of discipline puts parents' love in question because it shows a lack of concern for the character development of their children. Disciplining children averts long-range disaster. Without correction, children grow up with no clear understanding of right and wrong and with little direction to their lives. Don't be afraid to discipline your children. It is an act of love. Remember, though, that *your* efforts cannot make your *children* wise; they can only encourage your children to seek God's wisdom above all else!

Prov 14:4 When a farmer has no oxen, the stable will be clean but he will be unable to make a living. The only way to keep your life free of people problems is to keep it free of people. But if your life is empty of people, it is useless; and if you live only for yourself, your life loses its meaning. Instead of avoiding people, our lives should be characterized by serving others, sharing our faith, and working for justice. Is your life clean but empty? Or does it give evidence of your serving God wholeheartedly?

Prov 14:6 We all know mockers, people who scoff at every word of instruction or advice. They never find wisdom because they don't seek it seriously. Wisdom comes to those who apply God's Word to their lives and

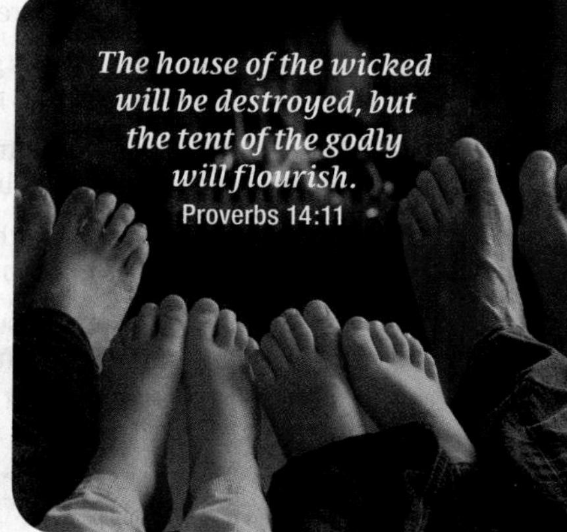
The house of the wicked will be destroyed, but the tent of the godly will flourish.
Proverbs 14:11

seek out godly counselors. If the wisdom you need does not come easily to you, perhaps your attitude is the barrier.

Prov 14:12 The "path . . . that seems right" may offer many options and require few sacrifices. Easy choices should make us take a second look. Is this solution attractive because it allows me to be lazy? because it doesn't ask me to change my lifestyle? because it requires no moral restraints? The right choice often requires hard work and self-sacrifice. Don't be enticed by apparent shortcuts that seem right but end in death.

▸ **PROVERBS 10:1–22:16 *(cont.)***

16 The wise are cautious* and avoid danger;
fools plunge ahead with reckless confidence.

17 Short-tempered people do foolish things,
and schemers are hated.

18 Simpletons are clothed with foolishness,*
but the prudent are crowned with knowledge.

19 Evil people will bow before good people;
the wicked will bow at the gates of the godly.

20 The poor are despised even by their neighbors,
while the rich have many "friends."

21 It is a sin to belittle one's neighbor;
blessed are those who help the poor.

22 If you plan to do evil, you will be lost;
if you plan to do good, you will receive
unfailing love and faithfulness.

23 Work brings profit,
but mere talk leads to poverty!

24 Wealth is a crown for the wise;
the effort of fools yields only foolishness.

25 A truthful witness saves lives,
but a false witness is a traitor.

26 Those who fear the LORD are secure;
he will be a refuge for their children.

27 Fear of the LORD is a life-giving fountain;
it offers escape from the snares of death.

28 A growing population is a king's glory;
a prince without subjects has nothing.

29 People with understanding control their anger;
a hot temper shows great foolishness.

30 A peaceful heart leads to a healthy body;
jealousy is like cancer in the bones.

31 Those who oppress the poor insult their Maker,
but helping the poor honors him.

32 The wicked are crushed by disaster,
but the godly have a refuge when they die.

33 Wisdom is enshrined in an understanding heart;
wisdom is not* found among fools.

34 Godliness makes a nation great,
but sin is a disgrace to any people.

35 A king rejoices in wise servants
but is angry with those who disgrace him.

15:1 A gentle answer deflects anger,
but harsh words make tempers flare.

2 The tongue of the wise makes knowledge
appealing,
but the mouth of a fool belches out
foolishness.

3 The LORD is watching everywhere,
keeping his eye on both the evil and the good.

4 Gentle words are a tree of life;
a deceitful tongue crushes the spirit.

5 Only a fool despises a parent's* discipline;
whoever learns from correction is wise.

6 There is treasure in the house of the godly,
but the earnings of the wicked bring trouble.

7 The lips of the wise give good advice;
the heart of a fool has none to give.

8 The LORD detests the sacrifice of the wicked,
but he delights in the prayers of the upright.

9 The LORD detests the way of the wicked,
but he loves those who pursue godliness.

10 Whoever abandons the right path will be severely
disciplined;
whoever hates correction will die.

11 Even Death and Destruction* hold no secrets
from the LORD.
How much more does he know the human
heart!

Prv 14:16 Hebrew *The wise fear.* **Prv 14:18** Or *inherit foolishness.* **Prv 14:33** As in Greek and Syriac versions; Hebrew lacks *not.* **Prv 15:5** Hebrew *father's.* **Prv 15:11** Hebrew *Sheol and Abaddon.*

Prov 14:29 A nasty and quick temper can be like a fire out of control, burning us and everyone in its path. Anger divides people. It pushes us into hasty decisions that only cause bitterness and guilt. Yet anger, in itself, is not wrong. Anger can be a legitimate reaction to injustice and sin. When you feel yourself getting angry, look for the cause. Are you reacting to an evil situation that you are going to set right? Or are you responding selfishly to a personal insult? Pray that God will help you control a quick temper, channeling your feelings into effective action and conquering selfish anger through humility and repentance.

Prov 14:31 God has a special concern for the poor. He insists that people who have material goods should be generous with those who are needy. Providing for the poor is not just a suggestion in the Bible; it is a command that may require a change of attitude (see Lev 23:22; Deut 15:7-8; Pss 113:5-9; 146:5-9; Isa 58:7; 2 Cor 9:9; Jas 2:1-9).

Prov 15:1 Have you ever tried to argue in a whisper? It is equally hard to argue with someone who insists on answering gently. On the other hand, a raised voice and harsh words almost always trigger an angry response. To turn away wrath and seek peace, choose gentle words.

Prov 15:3 At times it seems that God has let evil run rampant in the world and we wonder if he even notices it. But God sees everything clearly—both the evil actions and the evil intentions behind them (Prov 15:11). He is not an indifferent observer. He cares and is active in our world. Right now, his work may be unseen and unfelt, but don't give up. One day he will wipe out evil and punish the evildoers, just as he will establish the good and reward those who do his will.

Prov 15:14 What we feed our minds is just as important as what we feed our bodies. The kinds of books we read, the people we talk with, the music we listen to, and the films

12 Mockers hate to be corrected,
so they stay away from the wise.
13 A glad heart makes a happy face;
a broken heart crushes the spirit.
14 A wise person is hungry for knowledge,
while the fool feeds on trash.
15 For the despondent, every day brings trouble;
for the happy heart, life is a continual feast.
16 Better to have little, with fear for the LORD,
than to have great treasure and inner turmoil.
17 A bowl of vegetables with someone you love
is better than steak with someone you hate.

WISDOM AND FOOLISHNESS

The wise and the foolish are often contrasted in Proverbs. The characteristics, reputation, and results of each are worth knowing if wisdom is our goal.

	The Wise	*The Foolish*	
Characteristics	Give encouragement	Lack common sense	Prov 10:21
	Enjoy living wisely	Enjoy foolishness	Prov 10:23
	Consider their steps	Gullible	Prov 14:15
		Avoid the wise	Prov 15:12
	Hunger for knowledge	Feed on the trash of foolishness	Prov 15:14
	Value wisdom above riches		Prov 16:16
	Respond to correction	Do not respond to punishment	Prov 17:10
	Pursue wisdom	Pursue illusive dreams	Prov 17:24
		Blame failure on God	Prov 19:3
	Profit from correction	An example to others	Prov 19:25
		Proud and arrogant	Prov 21:24
		Despise wise advice	Prov 23:9
		Make truth useless	Prov 26:7
		Repeat their folly	Prov 26:11
	Trust in wisdom	Trust in themselves	Prov 28:26
	Control their anger	Unleash their anger	Prov 29:11
Reputation	Crowned with knowledge	Clothed with foolishness	Prov 14:18
		Cause quarrels	Prov 22:10
		Receive no honor	Prov 26:1
	Calm anger	Stir up anger	Prov 29:8
Results	Stay on right paths	Enjoy the wrong paths	Prov 15:21
		Lash out when discovered in folly	Prov 17:12
		Endangered by their words	Prov 18:6-7
	Their wisdom conquers others' strength		Prov 21:22
	Avoid wicked paths	Walk a treacherous road	Prov 22:5
	Grow stronger		Prov 24:5
		Will never be chosen as leaders	Prov 24:7
		Must be guided by hardship	Prov 26:3
		Persist in foolishness	Prov 27:22

we watch are all part of our mental diet. Be discerning because what you feed your mind influences your total health and well-being. Thus, a strong desire to discover knowledge is a mark of wisdom.

Prov 15:15 Our attitudes color our whole personality. We cannot always choose what happens to us, but we can choose our attitude toward each situation. The secret to a happy heart is filling our mind with thoughts that are true, pure, and lovely—thoughts that dwell on the good things in life (Phil 4:8). This was Paul's secret as he faced imprisonment, and it can be ours as we face the struggles of daily living. Look at your attitudes and then examine what you allow to enter your mind and what you choose to dwell on. You may need to make some changes.

Prov 15:17-19 The "path of the upright" doesn't always seem easy, but look at the alternatives. Hatred, dissension, and laziness cause problems that the upright person does not have to face. By comparison, a life built on a solid foundation of love for God is like a smooth, level road.

▸ **PROVERBS 10:1–22:16** ***(cont.)***

18 A hot-tempered person starts fights;
a cool-tempered person stops them.

19 A lazy person's way is blocked with briers,
but the path of the upright is an open highway.

20 Sensible children bring joy to their father;
foolish children despise their mother.

21 Foolishness brings joy to those with no sense;
a sensible person stays on the right path.

22 Plans go wrong for lack of advice;
many advisers bring success.

23 Everyone enjoys a fitting reply;
it is wonderful to say the right thing at the right time!

24 The path of life leads upward for the wise;
they leave the grave* behind.

25 The LORD tears down the house of the proud,
but he protects the property of widows.

26 The LORD detests evil plans,
but he delights in pure words.

27 Greed brings grief to the whole family,
but those who hate bribes will live.

28 The heart of the godly thinks carefully before speaking;
the mouth of the wicked overflows with evil words.

29 The LORD is far from the wicked,
but he hears the prayers of the righteous.

30 A cheerful look brings joy to the heart;
good news makes for good health.

31 If you listen to constructive criticism,
you will be at home among the wise.

32 If you reject discipline, you only harm yourself;
but if you listen to correction, you grow in understanding.

33 Fear of the LORD teaches wisdom;
humility precedes honor.

16:1 We can make our own plans,
but the LORD gives the right answer.

2 People may be pure in their own eyes,
but the LORD examines their motives.

3 Commit your actions to the LORD,
and your plans will succeed.

Prv 15:24 Hebrew *Sheol.*

Prov 15:22 People with tunnel vision—those who are locked into one way of thinking—are likely to miss the right road because they have closed their minds to any new options. We need the help of those who can enlarge our vision and broaden our perspective. Seek out the advice of those who know you and have a wealth of experience. Build a network of advisers. Then be open to new ideas, and be willing to weigh their suggestions carefully. Your plans will be stronger and more likely to succeed.

Prov 15:28 The godly weigh their answers; the wicked don't think before speaking because they don't care about the effects of their words. It is important to have something to say, but it is equally important to think about it first. Do you carefully plan your words, or do you pour out your thoughts without concern for their impact?

Prov 16:1 This verse can be understood to mean that the final outcome of the plans we make is in God's hands. If this is so, why make plans? In doing God's will, there must be partnership between our efforts and God's control. He wants us to use our minds, to seek the advice of others, and to plan. Nevertheless, the results are up to him. Planning, then, helps us act God's way. As you live for him, ask for guidance as you plan, and then act on your plan as you trust in him.

Prov 16:2 People can rationalize anything if they have no standards for judging right and wrong. We can always "prove" that we are right. Before putting any plan into action, ask yourself these three questions: (1) Is this plan in harmony with God's truth? (2) Will it work under real-life conditions? (3) Is my attitude pleasing to God?

Prov 16:3 There are different ways to fail to commit whatever we do to the Lord. Some

HOW GOD IS DESCRIBED IN PROVERBS

God . . .	is aware of all that happens (Prov 15:3)
	knows the hearts of all people (Prov 15:11; 16:2; 21:2)
	controls all things (Prov 16:33; 21:30)
	is a place of safety (Prov 18:10)
	rescues good people from danger (Prov 11:8, 21)
	condemns the wicked (Prov 11:31)
	hears and delights in our prayers (Prov 15:8, 29)
	loves those who obey him (Prov 15:9)
	cares for the poor and needy (Prov 15:25; 22:22-23)
	tests and purifies hearts (Prov 17:3)
	detests evil (Prov 21:27; 28:9)
Our response should be . . .	to fear and revere God (Prov 10:27; 14:26-27; 15:16; 16:6; 19:23; 28:14)
	to obey God's Word (Prov 13:13; 19:16)
	to please God by doing what is right and just (Prov 21:3)
	to trust in God (Prov 22:17-19; 29:25)

Proverbs is a book about wise living. It often focuses on a person's response and attitude toward God, who is the source of wisdom. And a number of proverbs point out aspects of God's character. Knowing God helps us on the way to wisdom.

4 The LORD has made everything for his own
purposes,
even the wicked for a day of disaster.

5 The LORD detests the proud;
they will surely be punished.

6 Unfailing love and faithfulness make atonement
for sin.
By fearing the LORD, people avoid evil.

7 When people's lives please the LORD,
even their enemies are at peace with them.

8 Better to have little, with godliness,
than to be rich and dishonest.

9 We can make our plans,
but the LORD determines our steps.

10 The king speaks with divine wisdom;
he must never judge unfairly.

11 The LORD demands accurate scales and balances;
he sets the standards for fairness.

12 A king detests wrongdoing,
for his rule is built on justice.

13 The king is pleased with words from
righteous lips;
he loves those who speak honestly.

14 The anger of the king is a deadly threat;
the wise will try to appease it.

15 When the king smiles, there is life;
his favor refreshes like a spring rain.

16 How much better to get wisdom than gold,
and good judgment than silver!

17 The path of the virtuous leads away
from evil;
whoever follows that path is safe.

18 Pride goes before destruction,
and haughtiness before a fall.

19 Better to live humbly with the poor
than to share plunder with the proud.

20 Those who listen to instruction will prosper;
those who trust the LORD will be joyful.

21 The wise are known for their understanding,
and pleasant words are persuasive.

22 Discretion is a life-giving fountain to those
who possess it,
but discipline is wasted on fools.

23 From a wise mind comes wise speech;
the words of the wise are persuasive.

24 Kind words are like honey—
sweet to the soul and healthy for the body.

25 There is a path before each person that seems
right,
but it ends in death.

26 It is good for workers to have an appetite;
an empty stomach drives them on.

27 Scoundrels create trouble;
their words are a destructive blaze.

people commit their work only superficially. They say the project is being done for the Lord, but in reality they are doing it for themselves. Others give God temporary control of their interests, only to take control back the moment things stop going the way they expect. Still others commit a task fully to the Lord but put forth no effort themselves, and then they wonder why they do not succeed. We must maintain a delicate balance: trusting God as if everything depended on him, while working as if everything depended on us. Think of a specific effort in which you are involved right now. Have you committed it to the Lord?

Prov 16:4 This verse doesn't mean that God created some people to be wicked, but rather that God uses even the activities of wicked people for his good purposes (see Gen 50:20). God is infinite and we are finite. No matter how great our intellects, we will never be able to understand him completely. But we can accept by faith that he is all-powerful, all-loving, and perfectly good. We can believe that he is not the cause of evil (Jas 1:13, 17); and we can trust that there are no loose ends in his system of judgment. Evil is a temporary condition in the universe. One day God will destroy it.

Prov 16:5 Pride is the inner voice that whispers, "My way is best." It is resisting God's leadership and believing that we are able to live without his help. Whenever you find yourself wanting to do it your way or looking down on other people, you are being controlled by pride. Only when you eliminate pride can God help you become all he meant you to be.

Prov 16:7 We want other people to like us, and sometimes we will do almost anything to win their approval. But God tells us to put our energy into pleasing him instead. Our effort to be peacemakers will usually make us more attractive to those around us, even our enemies. But even if it doesn't, we haven't lost anything. We are still pleasing God, the only one who truly matters.

Prov 16:11 Whether we buy or sell, make a product or offer a service, we know what is fair and honest and what is unfair and dishonest. Sometimes we feel pressure to be dishonest in order to advance ourselves or gain more profit. But if we want to obey God, there is no middle ground: God demands honesty in every business transaction. No amount of rationalizing can justify a dishonest business practice. Honesty and fairness are not always easy, but they are what God demands. Ask him for discernment and courage to be consistently honest and fair.

Prov 16:18 Proud people take little account of their weaknesses and do not anticipate stumbling blocks. They think they are above the frailties of common people. In this state of mind they are easily tripped up. Ironically, proud people seldom realize that pride is their problem, although everyone around them is well aware of it. Ask someone you trust whether self-satisfaction has blinded you to warning signs. That person may help you avoid a fall.

Prov 16:22 For centuries people sought a fountain of youth, a spring that promised to give eternal life and vitality. It was never found. But God's wisdom gives us discretion that proves to be a life-giving fountain that can make us happy, healthy, and alive forever. How? When we live by God's Word, he washes away the deadly effects of sin (see Titus 3:4-8), and the hope of eternal life with him gives us a joyful perspective on our present life. The fountain of youth was only a dream, but the life-giving fountain is a reality. The choice is yours. You can be enlightened by God's wisdom, or you can be dragged down by the weight of your own foolishness.

▶ **PROVERBS 10:1–22:16 *(cont.)***

28 A troublemaker plants seeds of strife;
gossip separates the best of friends.

29 Violent people mislead their companions,
leading them down a harmful path.

30 With narrowed eyes, people plot evil;
with a smirk, they plan their mischief.

31 Gray hair is a crown of glory;
it is gained by living a godly life.

32 Better to be patient than powerful;
better to have self-control than to conquer a city.

33 We may throw the dice,*
but the LORD determines how they fall.

17:1 Better a dry crust eaten in peace
than a house filled with feasting—and conflict.

2 A wise servant will rule over the master's disgraceful son
and will share the inheritance of the master's children.

3 Fire tests the purity of silver and gold,
but the LORD tests the heart.

4 Wrongdoers eagerly listen to gossip;
liars pay close attention to slander.

5 Those who mock the poor insult their Maker;
those who rejoice at the misfortune of others will be punished.

6 Grandchildren are the crowning glory of the aged;
parents* are the pride of their children.

7 Eloquent words are not fitting for a fool;
even less are lies fitting for a ruler.

8 A bribe is like a lucky charm;
whoever gives one will prosper!

9 Love prospers when a fault is forgiven,
but dwelling on it separates close friends.

10 A single rebuke does more for a person of understanding
than a hundred lashes on the back of a fool.

11 Evil people are eager for rebellion,
but they will be severely punished.

12 It is safer to meet a bear robbed of her cubs
than to confront a fool caught in foolishness.

13 If you repay good with evil,
evil will never leave your house.

14 Starting a quarrel is like opening a floodgate,
so stop before a dispute breaks out.

15 Acquitting the guilty and condemning the innocent—
both are detestable to the LORD.

16 It is senseless to pay tuition to educate a fool,
since he has no heart for learning.

17 A friend is always loyal,
and a brother is born to help in time of need.

18 It's poor judgment to guarantee another person's debt
or put up security for a friend.

Prv 16:33 Hebrew *We may cast lots.* **Prv 17:6** Hebrew *fathers.*

Prov 16:31 The Hebrews believed that a long life was a sign of God's blessing; therefore, gray hair and old age were good. While young people glory in their strength, old people can rejoice in their years of experience and practical wisdom. Gray hair is not a sign of disgrace to be covered over; it is a crown of splendor. As you deal with older people, treat them with respect.

Prov 16:32 Self-control is superior to conquest. Success in business, school, or home life can be ruined by those who lose control of their tempers. So it is a great personal victory to control your temper. When you feel yourself ready to explode, remember that losing control may cause you to forfeit what you want the most.

Prov 17:3 It takes intense heat to purify gold and silver. Similarly, it often takes the heat of trials for the Christian to be purified. Through trials, God shows us what is in us and clears out anything that gets in the way of complete trust in him. Peter says, "These trials will show that your faith is genuine. It is being tested as fire tests and purifies gold—though your faith is far more precious than mere gold" (1 Pet 1:7). So when tough times come your way, realize that God wants to use them to refine your faith and purify your heart.

Prov 17:5 Few acts are as cruel as making fun of the less fortunate, but many people do this because it makes them feel good to be better off or more successful than someone else. Mocking the poor is mocking the God who made them. We also ridicule God when we mock the weak, those who are different, or anyone else. When you catch yourself putting others down just for fun, stop and think about who created them.

Prov 17:8 Solomon is not condoning bribery (see Prov 17:15, 23), but he is making an observation about the way the world operates. Bribes may get people what they want, but the Bible clearly condemns using them (Exod 23:8; Matt 28:11-15).

Prov 17:9 This proverb is saying that we should be willing to disregard the faults of others. Forgiving faults is necessary in any relationship. It is tempting, especially in an argument, to bring up all the mistakes the other person has ever made. But love keeps its mouth shut—difficult though that may be. Try never to bring anything into an argument that is unrelated to the topic being discussed. As we grow to be like Christ, we will acquire God's ability to forget the confessed sins of the past.

Prov 17:17 What kind of friend are you? There is a vast difference between knowing someone well and being a true friend. The greatest evidence of genuine friendship is loyalty (see 1 Cor 13:7)—being available to help in times of distress or personal struggle. Too many people are fair-weather friends. They stick around when the friendship helps them and leave when they're not getting anything out of the relationship. Think of your friends and assess your loyalty to them. Be the kind of true friend the Bible encourages.

19 Anyone who loves to quarrel loves sin;
anyone who trusts in high walls invites disaster.

20 The crooked heart will not prosper;
the lying tongue tumbles into trouble.

21 It is painful to be the parent of a fool;
there is no joy for the father of a rebel.

22 A cheerful heart is good medicine,
but a broken spirit saps a person's strength.

23 The wicked take secret bribes
to pervert the course of justice.

24 Sensible people keep their eyes glued on wisdom,
but a fool's eyes wander to the ends of the earth.

25 Foolish children* bring grief to their father
and bitterness to the one who gave them birth.

26 It is wrong to punish the godly for being good
or to flog leaders for being honest.

27 A truly wise person uses few words;
a person with understanding is even-tempered.

28 Even fools are thought wise when they keep silent;
with their mouths shut, they seem intelligent.

18:1 Unfriendly people care only about themselves;
they lash out at common sense.

2 Fools have no interest in understanding;
they only want to air their own opinions.

3 Doing wrong leads to disgrace,
and scandalous behavior brings contempt.

4 Wise words are like deep waters;
wisdom flows from the wise like a bubbling brook.

5 It is not right to acquit the guilty
or deny justice to the innocent.

6 Fools' words get them into constant quarrels;
they are asking for a beating.

7 The mouths of fools are their ruin;
they trap themselves with their lips.

8 Rumors are dainty morsels
that sink deep into one's heart.

9 A lazy person is as bad as
someone who destroys things.

10 The name of the LORD is a strong fortress;
the godly run to him and are safe.

11 The rich think of their wealth as a strong defense;
they imagine it to be a high wall of safety.

12 Haughtiness goes before destruction;
humility precedes honor.

Prv 17:25 Hebrew *A foolish son.*

HUMILITY AND PRIDE

Results of . . .	*Humility*	*Pride*	
	Leads to wisdom	Leads to disgrace	**Prov 11:2**
	Takes advice	Leads to conflict	**Prov 13:10**
	Leads to honor		**Prov 15:33**
		Leads to punishment	**Prov 16:5**
		Leads to destruction	**Prov 16:18**
	Ends in honor	Ends in downfall	**Prov 18:12**
	Brings honor	Brings humiliation	**Prov 29:23**

Proverbs is direct and forceful in rejecting pride. The proud attitude heads the list of seven things God hates (Prov 6:16-17). The harmful results of pride are constantly contrasted with humility and its benefits.

Prov 17:22 To be cheerful is to be ready to greet others with a welcome or a word of encouragement, to have enthusiasm for the task at hand and a positive outlook on the future. Such people are as welcome as pain-relieving medicine.

Prov 17:24 While there is something to be said for having big dreams, this proverb points out the folly of chasing fantasies (having eyes that "wander to the ends of the earth"; see also Prov 12:11). How much better to align your goals with God's, being the kind of person he wants you to be! Such goals (wisdom, honesty, patience, love) may not seem exciting, but they will determine your eternal future. Take time to think about your dreams and goals, and make sure they cover the really important areas of life.

Prov 17:27-28 This proverb highlights several benefits of keeping quiet: (1) It is the best policy if you have nothing worthwhile to say; (2) it allows you the opportunity to listen and learn; (3) it gives you something in common with those who are wiser. Make sure you pause to think and to listen so that when you do speak, you will have something important to say.

Prov 18:8 It is as hard to refuse to listen to rumors and gossip as it is to turn down a delicious dessert. Taking just one morsel of either one creates a taste for more. You can resist rumors the same way a determined dieter resists candy—never even open the box. If you don't nibble on the first bite of gossip, you can't take the second and the third.

Prov 18:11 In imagining that their wealth is their strongest defense, rich people are sadly mistaken. Money cannot provide safety—there are too many ways for it to lose its power. The government may cease to back it; thieves may steal it; inflation may rob it of all value. But God never loses his power. He is always dependable. Where do you look for security and safety—uncertain wealth or God who is always faithful?

▶ **PROVERBS 10:1–22:16 *(cont.)***

13 Spouting off before listening to the facts
is both shameful and foolish.

14 The human spirit can endure a sick body,
but who can bear a crushed spirit?

15 Intelligent people are always ready to learn.
Their ears are open for knowledge.

16 Giving a gift can open doors;
it gives access to important people!

17 The first to speak in court sounds right—
until the cross-examination begins.

18 Flipping a coin* can end arguments;
it settles disputes between powerful opponents.

19 An offended friend is harder to win back
than a fortified city.
Arguments separate friends like a gate
locked with bars.

20 Wise words satisfy like a good meal;
the right words bring satisfaction.

21 The tongue can bring death or life;
those who love to talk will reap the consequences.

22 The man who finds a wife finds a treasure,
and he receives favor from the LORD.

23 The poor plead for mercy;
the rich answer with insults.

24 There are "friends" who destroy each other,
but a real friend sticks closer than a brother.

19:1 Better to be poor and honest
than to be dishonest and a fool.

2 Enthusiasm without knowledge is no good;
haste makes mistakes.

3 People ruin their lives by their own foolishness
and then are angry at the LORD.

4 Wealth makes many "friends";
poverty drives them all away.

5 A false witness will not go unpunished,
nor will a liar escape.

6 Many seek favors from a ruler;
everyone is the friend of a person who gives gifts!

7 The relatives of the poor despise them;
how much more will their friends avoid them!
Though the poor plead with them,
their friends are gone.

8 To acquire wisdom is to love oneself;
people who cherish understanding will prosper.

9 A false witness will not go unpunished,
and a liar will be destroyed.

10 It isn't right for a fool to live in luxury
or for a slave to rule over princes!

11 Sensible people control their temper;
they earn respect by overlooking wrongs.

12 The king's anger is like a lion's roar,
but his favor is like dew on the grass.

Prv 18:18 Hebrew *Casting lots.*

Prov 18:13, 15, 17 These concise statements give three basic principles for making sound decisions: (1) Get the facts before answering; (2) be open to new ideas; (3) make sure you hear both sides of a story before judging. All three principles center around seeking additional information. This is difficult work, but the only alternative is prejudice—judging before getting the facts.

Prov 18:22 This verse is stating that marriage should be enjoyed and viewed as a great gift from God. God created marriage for our enjoyment, and he pronounced it good. Married people need to see their marriages as great treasures—guarding and protecting them as such. This is one of many passages in the Bible that show marriage as a joyful and good creation of God (Gen 2:21-25; Prov 5:15-19; John 2:1-11).

Prov 18:23 This verse does not condone insulting the poor; it is simply recording an unfortunate fact of life. It is wrong for rich people to treat the less fortunate with contempt and arrogance, and God will judge such actions severely (see Prov 14:31).

Prov 18:24 Loneliness is everywhere—many people feel cut off and alienated from others. Being in a crowd just makes people more aware of their isolation. We all need friends who will stick close, listen, care, and offer help when it is needed—in good times and bad. It is better to have one such friend than dozens of superficial acquaintances. Instead of wishing you could find a true friend, seek to become one. If you look around, you'll find people who need your friendship. Ask God to reveal them to you, and then take on the challenge of being a true friend.

Prov 19:1 A blameless life is far more valuable than wealth, but most people don't act as if they believe this. Afraid of not getting everything they want, they will pay any price to increase their wealth—cheating on their taxes, stealing from stores or employers, withholding tithes, refusing to give. But when we know and love God, we realize that a lower standard of living—or even poverty—is a small price to pay for personal integrity. Do your actions show that you sacrifice your integrity to increase your wealth? What changes do you need to make in order to get your priorities straight?

Prov 19:2 We often move hastily through life, rushing headlong into the unknown. Some people marry without really getting to know the other person. Others try illicit sex or drugs without considering the consequences. Some plunge into jobs without evaluating whether or not they are suitable to that line of work. Enthusiasm is no good without knowledge, and it will not make a bad situation better. Don't rush into the unknown. Be sure you understand what you're getting into and where you want to go before you take the first step. Obviously you cannot tell all that the future will hold, but do your homework, ask the right questions, and be sure you are following God.

Prov 19:8 Is it good to love yourself? Yes, when your soul is at stake! This proverb does not condone self-centered people who love and protect their selfish interests and will do anything to serve them. Instead, it encourages those who really care about themselves to seek wisdom.

13 A foolish child* is a calamity to a father;
a quarrelsome wife is as annoying as constant dripping.

14 Fathers can give their sons an inheritance of houses and wealth,
but only the LORD can give an understanding wife.

15 Lazy people sleep soundly,
but idleness leaves them hungry.

16 Keep the commandments and keep your life;
despising them leads to death.

17 If you help the poor, you are lending to the LORD—
and he will repay you!

18 Discipline your children while there is hope.
Otherwise you will ruin their lives.

19 Hot-tempered people must pay the penalty.
If you rescue them once, you will have to do it again.

20 Get all the advice and instruction you can,
so you will be wise the rest of your life.

21 You can make many plans,
but the LORD's purpose will prevail.

22 Loyalty makes a person attractive.
It is better to be poor than dishonest.

23 Fear of the LORD leads to life,
bringing security and protection from harm.

24 Lazy people take food in their hand
but don't even lift it to their mouth.

25 If you punish a mocker, the simpleminded will learn a lesson;
if you correct the wise, they will be all the wiser.

26 Children who mistreat their father or chase away their mother
are an embarrassment and a public disgrace.

27 If you stop listening to instruction, my child,
you will turn your back on knowledge.

28 A corrupt witness makes a mockery of justice;
the mouth of the wicked gulps down evil.

29 Punishment is made for mockers,
and the backs of fools are made to be beaten.

20:1 Wine produces mockers; alcohol leads to brawls.
Those led astray by drink cannot be wise.

2 The king's fury is like a lion's roar;
to rouse his anger is to risk your life.

Prv 19:13 Hebrew *son;* also in 19:27.

HOW TO SUCCEED IN GOD'S EYES

Proverbs notes two significant by-products of wise living: success and a good reputation. Several verses also point out what causes failure and a poor reputation.

Qualities that promote success and a good reputation	
Godliness (righteousness)	**Prov 10:7; 12:3; 28:12**
Hating what is false	**Prov 13:5**
Committing all work to the Lord	**Prov 16:3**
Using words with restraint; being even-tempered	**Prov 17:27-28**
Acquiring wisdom and cherishing understanding	**Prov 19:8**
Humility and fear of the Lord	**Prov 22:4**
Willingness to confess and forsake sin	**Prov 28:13**

Qualities that prevent success and cause a bad reputation	
Wickedness	**Prov 10:7; 12:3; 28:12**
Seeking honors	**Prov 25:27**
Hatred, especially when masked as kindness	**Prov 26:24-26**
Praising oneself	**Prov 27:2**
Concealing sin	**Prov 28:13**

Other verses dealing with one's reputation are Proverbs 11:10, 16; 14:3; 19:10; 22:1; 23:17-18; 24:13-14.

Prov 19:16 The commandments we are told to obey are those found in God's Word, such as the Ten Commandments (Exod 20) and other passages of instruction. To obey what God teaches in the Bible is self-preserving. To disobey is self-destructive.

Prov 19:17 Here God identifies with the poor as Jesus does in Matthew 25:31-46. As our Creator, God values all of us, whether we are poor or rich. When we help the poor, we honor both the Creator and his creation. God accepts our help as if we had offered it directly to him.

Prov 19:23 Those who fear the Lord receive "protection from harm" because of their healthy habits, their beneficial lifestyle, and sometimes through God's direct intervention. Nevertheless, the fear of the Lord does not always protect us from trouble in this life: Evil things still happen to people who love God. This verse is not a universal promise but a general guideline. It describes what would happen if this world were sinless and what will happen in the new earth when faithful believers will be under God's protection forever. (See the note on Prov 3:16-17, p. 635.)

Prov 19:25 A great difference exists between the person who learns from criticism and the person who refuses to accept correction. How we respond to criticism determines whether or not we grow in wisdom. The next time someone criticizes you, listen carefully to all that is said. You might learn something.

▸ **PROVERBS 10:1–22:16** ***(cont.)***

3 Avoiding a fight is a mark of honor;
only fools insist on quarreling.

4 Those too lazy to plow in the right season
will have no food at the harvest.

5 Though good advice lies deep within the heart,
a person with understanding will draw it out.

6 Many will say they are loyal friends,
but who can find one who is truly reliable?

7 The godly walk with integrity;
blessed are their children who follow them.

8 When a king sits in judgment, he weighs all the evidence,
distinguishing the bad from the good.

9 Who can say, "I have cleansed my heart;
I am pure and free from sin"?

10 False weights and unequal measures*—
the LORD detests double standards of every kind.

11 Even children are known by the way they act,
whether their conduct is pure, and whether it is right.

12 Ears to hear and eyes to see—
both are gifts from the LORD.

13 If you love sleep, you will end in poverty.
Keep your eyes open, and there will be plenty to eat!

14 The buyer haggles over the price, saying, "It's worthless,"
then brags about getting a bargain!

15 Wise words are more valuable
than much gold and many rubies.

Prv 20:10 Hebrew *A stone and a stone, an ephah and an ephah.*

HONESTY AND DISHONESTY

Proverbs tells us plainly that God despises all forms of dishonesty. Not only does God hate dishonesty, but we are told that it works against us—others no longer trust us, and we cannot even enjoy our dishonest gains. It is wiser to be honest because "the godly escape such trouble" (Prov 12:13).

Others' Opinions	
Leaders value those who speak honestly	**Prov 16:13**
In the end most people will appreciate truth more than flattery	**Prov 28:23**
Quality of Life	
The godly person's plans are just	**Prov 12:5**
Honest witnesses do not lie; false witnesses breathe lies	**Prov 14:5**
Truthful witnesses save lives; false witnesses are traitors	**Prov 14:25**
The children of the righteous are blessed	**Prov 20:7**
Short-Term Results	
Tainted wealth has no lasting value	**Prov 10:2**
The godly are rescued from trouble	**Prov 11:8**
The wicked are trapped by their own words	**Prov 12:13**
Fraudulent gain is sweet only for a short while	**Prov 20:17**
Long-Term Results	
Good people are guided by their honesty	**Prov 11:3**
Truth endures	**Prov 12:19**
Riches gained quickly don't last	**Prov 20:21**
Riches gained dishonestly don't last	**Prov 21:6**
The blameless are rescued from harm	**Prov 28:18**
God's Opinion	
God delights in honesty	**Prov 11:1**
God delights in those who are truthful	**Prov 12:22**
God despises double standards	**Prov 20:10**
God is pleased when we do what is right and just	**Prov 21:3**

Prov 20:3 A person who is truly confident of his or her strength does not need to parade it. A truly brave person does not look for chances to prove it. A resourceful person can find a way out of a fight and avoid retaliating. Foolish people find it impossible to avoid strife. Men and women of character can. What kind of person are you?

Prov 20:4 You've heard similar warnings: If you don't study, you'll fail the test; if you don't save, you won't have money when you need it. God wants us to anticipate future needs and prepare for them. We can't expect him to come to our rescue when we cause our own problems through lack of planning and action. He provides for us, but he also expects us to be responsible.

Prov 20:9 No one is without sin. As soon as we confess our sin and repent, sinful thoughts and actions begin to creep back into our minds and hearts. We all need ongoing cleansing, moment by moment. Thank God he provides forgiveness by his mercy when we ask for it. Make confession and repentance a regular part of your talks with God. Rely on him moment by moment for the cleansing you need.

Prov 20:23 "Dishonest scales" refers to the loaded scales a merchant might use in order to cheat customers. Dishonesty is a difficult sin to avoid. It is easy to cheat if we think no one is looking. But dishonesty affects the very core of a person. It makes him untrustworthy and untrusting. It eventually makes him unable to know himself or relate to others. Don't take dishonesty lightly. Even the smallest portion of dishonesty contains enough of the poison of deceit to kill your spiritual life. If there is any dishonesty in your life, tell God about it now.

Prov 20:24 We are often confused by the events around us. Some things we will never

16 Get security from someone who guarantees
a stranger's debt.
Get a deposit if he does it for foreigners.*

17 Stolen bread tastes sweet,
but it turns to gravel in the mouth.

18 Plans succeed through good counsel;
don't go to war without wise advice.

19 A gossip goes around telling secrets,
so don't hang around with chatterers.

20 If you insult your father or mother,
your light will be snuffed out in total darkness.

21 An inheritance obtained too early in life
is not a blessing in the end.

22 Don't say, "I will get even for this wrong."
Wait for the LORD to handle the matter.

23 The LORD detests double standards;
he is not pleased by dishonest scales.

24 The LORD directs our steps,
so why try to understand everything along
the way?

25 Don't trap yourself by making a rash promise
to God
and only later counting the cost.

26 A wise king scatters the wicked like wheat,
then runs his threshing wheel over them.

27 The LORD's light penetrates the human spirit,*
exposing every hidden motive.

28 Unfailing love and faithfulness protect the king;
his throne is made secure through love.

29 The glory of the young is their strength;
the gray hair of experience is the splendor
of the old.

30 Physical punishment cleanses away evil;*
such discipline purifies the heart.

21:1 The king's heart is like a stream of water
directed by the LORD;
he guides it wherever he pleases.

2 People may be right in their own eyes,
but the LORD examines their heart.

3 The LORD is more pleased when we do what
is right and just
than when we offer him sacrifices.

4 Haughty eyes, a proud heart,
and evil actions are all sin.

5 Good planning and hard work lead to prosperity,
but hasty shortcuts lead to poverty.

6 Wealth created by a lying tongue
is a vanishing mist and a deadly trap.*

7 The violence of the wicked sweeps them away,
because they refuse to do what is just.

8 The guilty walk a crooked path;
the innocent travel a straight road.

9 It's better to live alone in the corner of an attic
than with a quarrelsome wife in a lovely home.

10 Evil people desire evil;
their neighbors get no mercy from them.

11 If you punish a mocker, the simpleminded
become wise;

Prv 20:16 An alternate reading in the Masoretic Text is *for a promiscuous woman.* **Prv 20:27** Or *The human spirit is the LORD's light.* **Prv 20:30** The meaning of the Hebrew is uncertain. **Prv 21:6** As in Greek version; Hebrew reads *mist for those who seek death.*

understand until years later when we look back and see how God was working. This proverb counsels us to not worry if we don't understand everything as it happens. Instead, we should trust that God knows what he's doing, even if his timing or design is not clear to us. (See Ps 37:23 for a reassuring promise of God's direction in your life.)

Prov 20:25 This proverb points out the danger of making a promise rashly and then reconsidering it. God takes promises seriously and requires that they be carried out (Deut 23:21-23). We often have good intentions when making a promise because we want to show God that we are determined to please him. Jesus, however, says it is better not to make promises to God because he knows how difficult they are to keep (Matt 5:33-37). If you still feel it is important to make a promise, make sure that you weigh the consequences of breaking it. (In Judg 11, Jephthah made a rash promise to sacrifice the first thing he saw on his return home. As it happened, he saw his daughter first.) It is better not to make promises than to make them and then later not keep them. It is best to count the cost beforehand and then to fulfill them. (For a list of other Bible people who made rash promises, see the chart on p. 394.)

Prov 21:1 In Solomon's day, kings possessed absolute authority and were often considered to be like gods. This proverb shows that God has ultimate authority over world rulers. Although they may not have realized it, the earth's most powerful kings have always been under God's control. (See Isa 10:5-8 for an example of a pagan king who was used for God's purposes.)

Prov 21:2 People may mistakenly think they are doing right, but God sees the motives of their hearts. We often have to make choices in areas where the right action is difficult to discern. We can help ourselves make such decisions by trying to identify our motives first and then asking, "Would God be pleased with my real reasons for doing this?" God is not pleased when we do good deeds only to receive something in return.

Prov 21:3 Sacrifices are not bribes to make God overlook our character faults. We can't exchange good behavior in one area for bad behavior in another. If our personal and business dealings are not characterized by justice, no amount of generosity when the offering plate is passed will make up for it.

Prov 21:5 Faithful completion of one's work is a great accomplishment. Being a diligent worker does not come naturally to some people; it is a result of strong character. Don't look for shortcuts that result in inefficiency. Work hard as if in the service of God.

Prov 21:11-12 It is usually better to learn from the mistakes of others than from our own. We can do this by observing other people's lives and listening to their advice. Take counsel from others instead of plunging ahead and learning the hard way.

▶ **PROVERBS 10:1–22:16 *(cont.)***

if you instruct the wise, they will be all
the wiser.

12 The Righteous One* knows what is going
on in the homes of the wicked;
he will bring disaster on them.

13 Those who shut their ears to the cries of the poor
will be ignored in their own time of need.

14 A secret gift calms anger;
a bribe under the table pacifies fury.

15 Justice is a joy to the godly,
but it terrifies evildoers.

16 The person who strays from common sense
will end up in the company of the dead.

17 Those who love pleasure become poor;
those who love wine and luxury will never
be rich.

18 The wicked are punished in place of the godly,
and traitors in place of the honest.

19 It's better to live alone in the desert
than with a quarrelsome, complaining wife.

20 The wise have wealth and luxury,
but fools spend whatever they get.

21 Whoever pursues righteousness and
unfailing love
will find life, righteousness, and honor.

22 The wise conquer the city of the strong
and level the fortress in which they trust.

23 Watch your tongue and keep your mouth shut,
and you will stay out of trouble.

24 Mockers are proud and haughty;
they act with boundless arrogance.

25 Despite their desires, the lazy will come to ruin,
for their hands refuse to work.

26 Some people are always greedy for more,
but the godly love to give!

27 The sacrifice of an evil person is detestable,
especially when it is offered with wrong
motives.

28 A false witness will be cut off,
but a credible witness will be allowed to speak.

29 The wicked bluff their way through,
but the virtuous think before they act.

30 No human wisdom or understanding or plan
can stand against the LORD.

31 The horse is prepared for the day of battle,
but the victory belongs to the LORD.

22:1 Choose a good reputation over great riches;
being held in high esteem is better than silver
or gold.

2 The rich and poor have this in common:
The LORD made them both.

Prv 21:12 Or *The righteous man.*

Prov 21:13 We should work to meet the needs of the poor and protect their rights, for it is always possible that someday we may find ourselves in their place.

Prov 21:20 This proverb is about saving for the future. Easy credit has many people living on the edge of bankruptcy. The desire to keep up appearances and to accumulate more drives them to spend every penny they earn, and they stretch their credit to the limit. But anyone who spends all he has is spending more than he can afford. A wise person puts money aside for hard times. God approves of foresight and restraint. God's people need to examine their lifestyles to see whether their spending is God-pleasing or merely self-pleasing.

Prov 21:27 The kind of worship ("sacrifice") described in this proverb is no better than a bribe. How do people try to bribe God? They may go to church, tithe, or volunteer, not because of their love and devotion to God, but because they hope God will bless them in return. But God has made it very clear that he desires obedience and love more than religious ritual (see Prov 21:3; 1 Sam 15:22). God does not want our sacrifices of time, energy, and money alone; he wants our hearts—our complete love and devotion. We may be able to bribe people (Prov 21:14), but we cannot bribe God.

Prov 21:31 This proverb refers to preparing for battle. All our preparation for any task is useless without God. But even with God's help we still must do our part and prepare. His control of the outcome does not negate our responsibilities. God might want you to produce a great book, but you must learn to write. God might want to use you in foreign missions, but you must learn the language. God will accomplish his purposes, and he will be able to use you if you have done your part by being well prepared.

Prov 22:4 The general observation that fear of the Lord leads to riches, honor, and long life would have been especially applicable to an obedient Israelite living in Solomon's God-fearing kingdom. Nevertheless some have been martyrs at a young age, and some have given away all their wealth for the sake of God's Kingdom. The book of Proverbs describes life the way it should be. It does not dwell on the exceptions. (For more on this concept, see the note on Prov 3:16-17, p. 635.)

Prov 22:6 In the process of helping our children choose the right path, we must discern differing paths for each child. It is natural to want to bring up all our children alike or train them the same way. This verse implies that parents should discern the individuality and special strengths that God has given each one. While we should not condone or excuse self-will, each child has natural inclinations that parents can develop. By talking to teachers, other parents, and grandparents, we can better discern and develop the individual capabilities of each child.

Prov 22:6 Many parents want to make all the choices for their children, but this hurts them in the long run. When parents teach their children how to make decisions, they don't have to watch every step they take. They know their children will remain on the right path because they have made the choice themselves. Train your children to choose the right way.

Prov 22:7 Does this mean we should never borrow? No, but it warns us never to take on a loan without carefully examining our ability to repay it. A loan we can handle is enabling; a loan we can't handle is enslaving. The borrower must realize that until the loan is repaid, he is a servant to the individual or institution that made it.

3 A prudent person foresees danger and takes
precautions.
The simpleton goes blindly on and suffers the
consequences.

4 True humility and fear of the LORD
lead to riches, honor, and long life.

5 Corrupt people walk a thorny, treacherous road;
whoever values life will avoid it.

6 Direct your children onto the right path,
and when they are older, they will not
leave it.

7 Just as the rich rule the poor,
so the borrower is servant to the lender.

8 Those who plant injustice will harvest disaster,
and their reign of terror will come
to an end.*

Prv 22:8 The Greek version includes an additional proverb: *God blesses a man who gives cheerfully, / but his worthless deeds will come to an end.* Compare 2 Cor 9:7.

RIGHTEOUSNESS AND WICKEDNESS

Proverbs often compares the lifestyles of the wicked and the righteous, and makes a strong case for living by God's pattern. The advantages of righteous living and the disadvantages of wicked living are pointed out. The kind of person we decide to be will affect every area of our lives.

	Righteous	*Wicked*	*Reference*
Outlook on life	Hopeful	Fearful	Prov 10:24
	Concerned about the welfare of God's creation	Even their kindness is cruel	Prov 12:10
	Understand justice	Don't understand justice	Prov 28:5
Response to life	Showered with blessings	Covered with violence	Prov 10:6
		Plot evil	Prov 16:30
	Proceed with care	Put up a bold front	Prov 21:29
	Persevere against evil	Brought down by calamity	Prov 24:15-16
	Seek out the honest	Hate the honest	Prov 29:10
How they are seen by others	Are respected	Headed for destruction	Prov 13:15
		Lead others into sin	Prov 16:29
	Walk a straight road	Walk a crooked road	Prov 21:8
	Are not to desire the company of godless people	Plot violence	Prov 24:1-2
	Others are glad when they succeed	Others hide when they rise to power	Prov 28:12
	Care for the poor	Unconcerned about the poor	Prov 29:7
	Despise the unjust	Despise the godly	Prov 29:27
Quality of life	Stand firm	Swept away	Prov 10:25
	Rescued by godliness	Trapped by evil ambitions	Prov 11:6
	No real harm befalls them	Constant trouble befalls them	Prov 12:21
	Income results in treasure	Income results in trouble	Prov 15:6
	Avoid evil		Prov 16:17
		Will not prosper	Prov 17:20
	Are bold as lions	Are constantly fearful	Prov 28:1
	Will be rescued	Will be suddenly destroyed	Prov 28:18
Short-term results	Walk safely	Will slip and fall	Prov 10:9
	Chased by blessings	Chased by trouble	Prov 13:21
Long-term results	God protects them	God destroys them	Prov 10:29
	Evil people will bow to them	Will bow to the righteous	Prov 14:19
		Will be punished for rebellion	Prov 17:11
Eternal expectations	Never disturbed	Removed from the land	Prov 10:30
	Reward will last	Reward will not last	Prov 11:18
	Find life	Find death	Prov 11:19
	Look forward to reward	Look forward to judgment	Prov 11:23
	Will stand firm	Will die and disappear	Prov 12:7
	Have a refuge when they die	Crushed by their sins	Prov 14:32
God's opinion of them	Delights in those with integrity	Detests those with crooked hearts	Prov 11:20

▶ **PROVERBS 10:1–22:16 *(cont.)***

9 Blessed are those who are generous,
because they feed the poor.

10 Throw out the mocker, and fighting goes, too.
Quarrels and insults will disappear.

11 Whoever loves a pure heart and gracious speech
will have the king as a friend.

12 The LORD preserves those with knowledge,
but he ruins the plans of the treacherous.

13 The lazy person claims, "There's a lion out there!
If I go outside, I might be killed!"

14 The mouth of an immoral woman is a
dangerous trap;
those who make the LORD angry will fall into it.

15 A youngster's heart is filled with foolishness,
but physical discipline will drive it far away.

16 A person who gets ahead by oppressing the poor
or by showering gifts on the rich will end
in poverty.

Sayings of the Wise

PROVERBS 22:17–24:22

17 Listen to the words of the wise;
apply your heart to my instruction.
18 For it is good to keep these sayings in your heart
and always ready on your lips.
19 I am teaching you today—yes, you—
so you will trust in the LORD.
20 I have written thirty sayings* for you,
filled with advice and knowledge.
21 In this way, you may know the truth
and take an accurate report to those who
sent you.

22 Don't rob the poor just because you can,
or exploit the needy in court.
23 For the LORD is their defender.
He will ruin anyone who ruins them.

24 Don't befriend angry people
or associate with hot-tempered people,
25 or you will learn to be like them
and endanger your soul.

26 Don't agree to guarantee another person's debt
or put up security for someone else.
27 If you can't pay it,
even your bed will be snatched from under
you.

28 Don't cheat your neighbor by moving the ancient
boundary markers
set up by previous generations.

29 Do you see any truly competent workers?
They will serve kings
rather than working for ordinary people.

Prv 22:20 Or *excellent sayings;* the meaning of the Hebrew is uncertain.

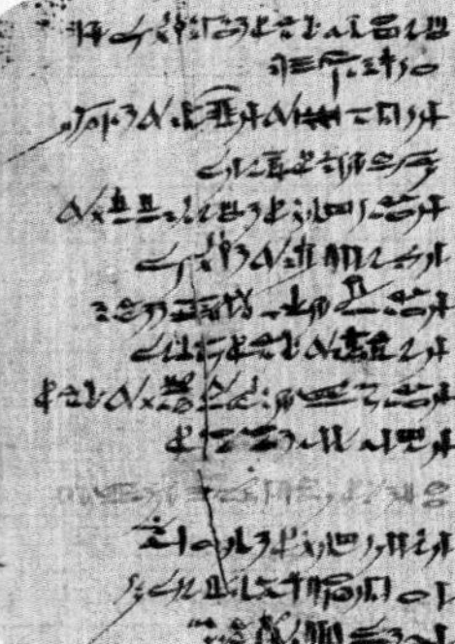

Wisdom of Amenemope

This section of Proverbs (Prov 22:17–24:34), titled "Sayings of the Wise" (see also Prov 24:23) has quite a different style from the rest of Proverbs. It replaces the simple, one-verse proverb with an approach that deals with a subject over several verses. This strongly suggests that the section is a unit and was likely written independently of the earlier proverbs. Of major interest is the remarkably close parallel between Proverbs 22:17–23:11 and the Egyptian book of Amenemope, which has been dated variously between the 13th and 7th centuries B.C. Scholars have detected as many as 30 connections between them. Some think that this section in Proverbs is an adaptation of an Egyptian original (with the biblical author doing such selection and modification under divine inspiration). However, a minority of scholars, including several prominent Egyptologists, argue persuasively on the basis of grammatical structure that Amenemope is derived from a Hebrew original. Either way, we can trust the antiquity of the Proverbs passage and appreciate its inspired worth.

Prov 22:12 "Knowledge" refers to those who have knowledge, those who live right and speak the truth. It takes discipline, determination, and hard work to live God's way, but God protects and rewards those who make the commitment to follow him. The unfaithful may seem to have an easier time of it, but in the long run their plans fail and their lives amount to nothing. Don't resist God and expect lasting success.

Prov 22:13 This proverb refers to an excuse a lazy person might use to avoid going to work. The excuse sounds silly to us, but that's often how our excuses sound to others. Don't rationalize laziness. Take your responsibilities seriously and get to work.

Prov 22:15 Young children often do foolish and dangerous things simply because they don't understand the consequences. Wisdom and common sense are not transferred by a parent's good example alone. Just as God trains and corrects us to make us better, so parents must discipline their children to help them learn the difference between right and wrong. To see how God corrects us, read Proverbs 3:11-12.

Prov 22:22-23 This proverb is a message of hope to people who must live and work under unjust authoritarian leaders. It is also a warning to those who enjoy ruling with an iron hand. Sometimes God intervenes and directly destroys tyrants. More often, he uses other rulers to overthrow them or their own oppressed people to rebel against them. If you are in a position of authority at church, work, or home, remember what happens to tyrants. Leadership through kindness is more effective and longer lasting than leadership by force.

Prov 22:24-25 People tend to become like those with whom they spend a lot of time. Even negative characteristics and habits can

23:1 While dining with a ruler,
pay attention to what is put before you.
2 If you are a big eater,
put a knife to your throat;
3 don't desire all the delicacies,
for he might be trying to trick you.

4 Don't wear yourself out trying to get rich.
Be wise enough to know when to quit.
5 In the blink of an eye wealth disappears,
for it will sprout wings
and fly away like an eagle.

6 Don't eat with people who are stingy;
don't desire their delicacies.
7 They are always thinking about how much
it costs.*
"Eat and drink," they say, but they don't
mean it.
8 You will throw up what little you've eaten,
and your compliments will be wasted.

9 Don't waste your breath on fools,
for they will despise the wisest advice.

10 Don't cheat your neighbor by moving the ancient
boundary markers;
don't take the land of defenseless orphans.
11 For their Redeemer* is strong;
he himself will bring their charges
against you.

12 Commit yourself to instruction;
listen carefully to words of knowledge.

13 Don't fail to discipline your children.
They won't die if you spank them.
14 Physical discipline
may well save them from death.*

15 My child,* if your heart is wise,
my own heart will rejoice!
16 Everything in me will celebrate
when you speak what is right.

17 Don't envy sinners,
but always continue to fear the LORD.
18 You will be rewarded for this;
your hope will not be disappointed.

19 My child, listen and be wise:
Keep your heart on the right course.
20 Do not carouse with drunkards
or feast with gluttons,
21 for they are on their way to poverty,
and too much sleep clothes them in rags.

22 Listen to your father, who gave you life,
and don't despise your mother when she is old.
23 Get the truth and never sell it;
also get wisdom, discipline, and good
judgment.
24 The father of godly children has cause for joy.
What a pleasure to have children who are wise.*
25 So give your father and mother joy!
May she who gave you birth be happy.

26 O my son, give me your heart.
May your eyes take delight in following my
ways.
27 A prostitute is a dangerous trap;
a promiscuous woman is as dangerous as
falling into a narrow well.

Prv 23:7 The meaning of the Hebrew is uncertain. **Prv 23:11** Or *redeemer.* **Prv 23:14** Hebrew *from Sheol.* **Prv 23:15** Hebrew *My son;* also in 23:19. **Prv 23:24** Hebrew *to have a wise son.*

rub off. The Bible exhorts us to be cautious in our choice of companions. Choose people with qualities you would like to develop in your own life.

Prov 22:28 In Joshua 13–21, the land was divided, and the boundaries were marked out for each tribe. Moses had already warned the people that when they reached the Promised Land they shouldn't cheat their neighbors by moving any of the boundary markers to give themselves more land and their neighbors less (Deut 19:14; 27:17).

Prov 23:1-3 The point of this proverb is to be careful when eating with an important or influential person because that individual may be trying to influence or bribe you. Unwary meetings over meals can lead to undermined convictions. No good will come from such meals.

Prov 23:4-5 We have all heard of people who have won millions of dollars and then lost everything. Even the average person can spend an inheritance—or a paycheck—with lightning speed and have little to show for it. Don't spend your time chasing fleeting earthly treasures. Instead, store up treasures in heaven, for such treasures will never be lost. (See Luke 12:33-34 for Jesus' teaching on this subject.)

Prov 23:6-8 In graphic language, the writer warns us not to envy the lifestyles of those who have become rich by being stingy and miserly, and not try to gain their favor by fawning over them. Their "friendship" is phony—they will just use you for their own gain.

Prov 23:10-11 The word *redeemer* referred to someone who bought back a family member who had fallen into slavery or who accepted the obligation to marry the widow of a family member (Ruth 4:3-10). God is also called a Redeemer (Exod 6:6; Job 19:25). (For an explanation of ancient boundary markers, see the note on Prov 22:28, above.)

Prov 23:12 The people most likely to gain knowledge are those who are willing to listen. It is a sign of strength, not weakness, to pay attention to what others have to say. People who are eager to listen continue to learn and grow throughout their lives. If we refuse to become set in our ways, we can always expand the limits of our knowledge.

Prov 23:13-14 The stern tone of discipline here is offset by the affection expressed in Proverbs 23:15. However, many parents are reluctant to discipline their children at all. Some fear that they will forfeit their relationship, their children will resent them, or they will stifle their children's development. But correction won't kill children, and it may prevent them from foolish moves that will.

Prov 23:17-18 How easy it is to envy those who get ahead unhampered by responsibility to God's laws. For a time they do seem to prosper without paying any attention to what God wants, but they have no future. To those who follow him, God promises a hope and a wonderful future, even if they don't achieve it in this life.

▸ PROVERBS 22:17–24:22 *(cont.)*

28 She hides and waits like a robber,
eager to make more men unfaithful.

29 Who has anguish? Who has sorrow?
Who is always fighting? Who is always complaining?
Who has unnecessary bruises? Who has bloodshot eyes?
30 It is the one who spends long hours in the taverns,
trying out new drinks.
31 Don't gaze at the wine, seeing how red it is,
how it sparkles in the cup, how smoothly it goes down.
32 For in the end it bites like a poisonous snake;
it stings like a viper.
33 You will see hallucinations,
and you will say crazy things.
34 You will stagger like a sailor tossed at sea,
clinging to a swaying mast.
35 And you will say, "They hit me, but I didn't feel it.
I didn't even know it when they beat me up.
When will I wake up
so I can look for another drink?"

24:1 Don't envy evil people
or desire their company.
2 For their hearts plot violence,
and their words always stir up trouble.

3 A house is built by wisdom
and becomes strong through good sense.
4 Through knowledge its rooms are filled
with all sorts of precious riches and valuables.

5 The wise are mightier than the strong,*
and those with knowledge grow stronger and stronger.
6 So don't go to war without wise guidance;
victory depends on having many advisers.

7 Wisdom is too lofty for fools.
Among leaders at the city gate, they have nothing to say.

8 A person who plans evil
will get a reputation as a troublemaker.
9 The schemes of a fool are sinful;
everyone detests a mocker.

10 If you fail under pressure,
your strength is too small.

11 Rescue those who are unjustly sentenced to die;
save them as they stagger to their death.
12 Don't excuse yourself by saying, "Look, we didn't know."
For God understands all hearts, and he sees you.
He who guards your soul knows you knew.
He will repay all people as their actions deserve.

13 My child,* eat honey, for it is good,
and the honeycomb is sweet to the taste.
14 In the same way, wisdom is sweet to your soul.
If you find it, you will have a bright future,
and your hopes will not be cut short.

15 Don't wait in ambush at the home of the godly,
and don't raid the house where the godly live.
16 The godly may trip seven times, but they will get up again.
But one disaster is enough to overthrow the wicked.

17 Don't rejoice when your enemies fall;
don't be happy when they stumble.
18 For the LORD will be displeased with you
and will turn his anger away from them.

Prv 24:5 As in Greek version; Hebrew reads *A wise man is strength.* **Prv 24:13** Hebrew *My son;* also in 24:21.

Prov 23:29-30 The soothing comfort of alcohol is only temporary. Real relief comes from dealing with the cause of the anguish and sorrow and turning to God for peace. Don't lose yourself in alcohol; find yourself in God.

Prov 23:29-35 Israel was a wine-producing country. In the Old Testament, winepresses bursting with new wine were considered a sign of blessing (Prov 3:10). Wisdom is even said to have set her table with wine (Prov 9:2, 5). But the Old Testament writers were alert to the dangers of wine. It dulls the senses; it limits clear judgment (Prov 31:1-9); it lowers the capacity for control (Prov 4:17); it destroys a person's efficiency (Prov 21:17). To make wine an end in itself, a means of self-indulgence, or as an escape from life is to misuse it and invite the consequences of the drunkard.

Prov 24:5 The athlete who has wisdom—who assesses the situation and plans strategies—has an advantage over a physically stronger but unwise opponent. We exercise regularly and eat well to build our strength, but do we take equal pains to develop wisdom and knowledge? Because wisdom is a vital part of strength, it pays to attain it.

Prov 24:6 In any major decision we make concerning college, marriage, career, children, etc., it is not a sign of weakness to ask for advice. Instead, it is foolish not to ask for it. Find good advisers before making any big decision. They can help you expand your alternatives and evaluate your choices.

Prov 24:8 Planning to do evil can be as wrong as doing it because what you think determines what you will do. Left unchecked, wrong desires will lead us to sin. God wants pure hearts, free from sin, and planning evil brings sinful thoughts into our mind. Should you say, "Then I might as well go ahead and do it because I've already planned it"? No. You have sinned in your attitude, but you have not yet harmed other people. Stop in your tracks and ask God to forgive you and put you on a different path.

Prov 24:10 Times of trouble can be useful. They can show you who you really are—what kind of character you have developed. In addition, they can help you grow stronger. When Jeremiah questioned God because of the trouble he faced, God asked how he ever expected to face big challenges if the little ones tired him out (Jer 12:5). Don't complain about your problems. The trouble you face today is training you to be strong for the more difficult situations you will face in the future.

Prov 24:17-18 David, Solomon's father, refused to gloat over the death of his lifelong enemy, Saul (see 2 Sam 1). On the other hand, the nation of Edom rejoiced over Israel's defeat and was punished by God for their attitude (Obad 1:12). To gloat over others' misfortune is to make yourself the avenger and to put yourself in the place of God, who alone is the real Judge of all the earth (see Deut 32:35).

19 Don't fret because of evildoers;
don't envy the wicked.
20 For evil people have no future;
the light of the wicked will be snuffed out.

21 My child, fear the LORD and the king.
Don't associate with rebels,
22 for disaster will hit them suddenly.
Who knows what punishment will come
from the LORD and the king?

More Sayings of the Wise

PROVERBS 24:23-34

Here are some further sayings of the wise:

It is wrong to show favoritism when passing
judgment.
24 A judge who says to the wicked, "You are
innocent,"
will be cursed by many people and denounced
by the nations.
25 But it will go well for those who convict the guilty;
rich blessings will be showered on them.

26 An honest answer
is like a kiss of friendship.

27 Do your planning and prepare your fields
before building your house.

28 Don't testify against your neighbors without
cause;
don't lie about them.
29 And don't say, "Now I can pay them back
for what they've done to me!
I'll get even with them!"

30 I walked by the field of a lazy person,
the vineyard of one with no common sense.
31 I saw that it was overgrown with nettles.
It was covered with weeds,
and its walls were broken down.
32 Then, as I looked and thought about it,
I learned this lesson:
33 A little extra sleep, a little more slumber,
a little folding of the hands to rest—
34 then poverty will pounce on you like a bandit;
scarcity will attack you like an armed robber.

3. SOLOMON'S MOST WONDERFUL SONG

Song of Songs is a wedding song honoring marriage. The most explicit statements on sex in the Bible are found in this book. It has often been criticized because of its sensuous language, but the purity and sacredness of love presented here are greatly needed in our day in which distorted attitudes about love and marriage are commonplace. God created sex and intimacy, and they are holy and good when enjoyed in marriage. A husband and wife honor God when they love and enjoy each other.

The Wedding Day

SONG 1:1–2:7

This is Solomon's song of songs, more wonderful than any other.

*Young Woman**

2 Kiss me and kiss me again,
for your love is sweeter than wine.
3 How fragrant your cologne;
your name is like its spreading
fragrance.
No wonder all the young women
love you!
4 Take me with you; come, let's run!
The king has brought me into his bedroom.

Sg 1:1 The headings identifying the speakers are not in the original text, though the Hebrew usually gives clues by means of the gender of the person speaking.

Prov 24:26 People often think that they should bend the truth to avoid hurting a friend. But one who gives an honest, straightforward answer is a true friend. To be entrusted with the truth even at the risk of offense, says this proverb, represents a gesture of high honor.

Prov 24:27 We should carry out our work in its proper order. If a farmer builds his house in the spring, he will miss the planting season and go a year without food. If a businessman invests his money in a house while his business is struggling to grow, he may lose both. It is possible to work hard and still lose everything if the timing is wrong or the resources to carry it out are not in place.

Prov 24:29 Here is a reverse version of the Golden Rule (see Luke 6:31). Revenge is the way the world operates, but it is not God's way.

Song 1:1 Solomon, a son of King David, became king and was chosen by God to build the Temple in Jerusalem. God gave him extraordinary wisdom. Much of Solomon's reign was characterized by wisdom and reverence for God although, toward the end of his life, he became proud and turned from God. Solomon wrote and collected more than 3,000 proverbs (see the book of Proverbs) and over 1,000 songs, one of which is this book, Song of Songs. See his Profile on p. 607.

Song 1:1ff Solomon frequently visited the various parts of his kingdom. One day, as he was visiting some royal vineyards in the north, his royal entourage came by surprise upon a beautiful peasant woman tending the vines. Embarrassed, she ran from them. But Solomon could not forget her. Later, disguised as a shepherd, he returned to the vineyards and won her love. Then he revealed his true identity and asked her to return to Jerusalem with him. Solomon and his beloved are being married in the palace as this book begins.

The Song of Songs is a series of seven poems, not necessarily in chronological order, describing the first meeting of Solomon and the peasant woman, their engagement, their wedding, their wedding night, and the growth of their marriage after the wedding.

Song 1:1ff This book features three characters or groups of characters: the girl (the "young woman"), Solomon (the "young man"), and "young women of Jerusalem." The girl who caught Solomon's attention may have been from Shunem, a farming community about 60 miles north of Jerusalem. Her tanned skin indicates that she probably worked outside in the vineyards (Song 1:6); thus, she may not have been from the upper class. The young women of Jerusalem

▸ **SONG 1:1–2:7 *(cont.)***

Young Women of Jerusalem

How happy we are for you, O king.
We praise your love even more than wine.

Young Woman

How right they are to adore you.

5 I am dark but beautiful,
O women of Jerusalem—
dark as the tents of Kedar,
dark as the curtains of Solomon's tents.
6 Don't stare at me because I am dark—
the sun has darkened my skin.
My brothers were angry with me;
they forced me to care for their vineyards,
so I couldn't care for myself—my own vineyard.
7 Tell me, my love, where are you leading your flock today?
Where will you rest your sheep at noon?
For why should I wander like a prostitute*
among your friends and their flocks?

Young Man

8 If you don't know, O most beautiful woman,
follow the trail of my flock,
and graze your young goats by the shepherds' tents.
9 You are as exciting, my darling,
as a mare among Pharaoh's stallions.
10 How lovely are your cheeks;
your earrings set them afire!
How lovely is your neck,
enhanced by a string of jewels.
11 We will make for you earrings of gold
and beads of silver.

Young Woman

12 The king is lying on his couch,
enchanted by the fragrance of my perfume.
13 My lover is like a sachet of myrrh
lying between my breasts.
14 He is like a bouquet of sweet henna blossoms
from the vineyards of En-gedi.

Young Man

15 How beautiful you are, my darling,
how beautiful!
Your eyes are like doves.

Young Woman

16 You are so handsome, my love,
pleasing beyond words!
The soft grass is our bed;
17 fragrant cedar branches are the beams of our house,
and pleasant smelling firs are the rafters.

Young Woman

2:1 I am the spring crocus blooming on the Sharon Plain,*
the lily of the valley.

Young Man

2 Like a lily among thistles
is my darling among young women.

Young Woman

3 Like the finest apple tree in the orchard
is my lover among other young men.
I sit in his delightful shade
and taste his delicious fruit.
4 He escorts me to the banquet hall;
it's obvious how much he loves me.
5 Strengthen me with raisin cakes,
refresh me with apples,
for I am weak with love.
6 His left arm is under my head,
and his right arm embraces me.
7 Promise me, O women of Jerusalem,
by the gazelles and wild deer,
not to awaken love until the time is right.*

Sg 1:7 Hebrew *like a veiled woman.* **Sg 2:1** Traditionally rendered *I am the rose of Sharon.* Sharon Plain is a region in the coastal plain of Palestine. **Sg 2:7** Or *not to awaken love until it is ready.*

include either members of Solomon's harem or workers in the palace.

Song 1:1-4 This vivid description of a love relationship begins with a picture of love itself. Love is "sweeter than wine"; it makes the lovers rejoice. Acts 10:9-16 teaches that what God has created and cleansed we should not misuse or call common. We can enjoy love. God created it as a gift to us and a delight for all our senses.

Song 1:5 Kedar was a nomadic community in northern Arabia. It was known for its tents that were woven from black goats' hair.

Song 1:6 The vineyard mentioned here was apparently owned by Solomon (because he came to visit it) and leased to the girl's brothers, who made her take care of the vineyards in the hot sun. Thus, she could not take care of her own skin. When she was brought to Jerusalem, the young girl was embarrassed about her tanned complexion because the girls in the city had fair, delicate skin that was considered much more beautiful. But Solomon loved her dark skin.

Song 1:7 The girl felt insecure at being different from the women of Jerusalem (Song 1:6) and at being alone while her lover was away (Song 1:7). She longed for the security of his presence. The basis of true love is commitment; so in a relationship built on genuine love, there is never any fear of deceit, manipulation, or exploitation.

Song 1:14 En-gedi was an oasis hidden at the base of rugged limestone cliffs west of the Dead Sea. It was known for its fruitful palm trees and fragrant balsam oil. The terrain surrounding En-gedi was some of the most desolate in Palestine and had an extremely hot desert climate. The henna blossoms in En-gedi would have appeared all the more beautiful because of their stark surroundings; thus, the girl was complimenting Solomon's looks, saying that he stood out among all the men.

Song 1:16-17 The lover and his beloved describe their woodland surroundings as a wedding bedroom.

Song 2:1 The rose of Sharon and lily of the valley were flowers commonly found in Israel. Perhaps the girl was saying, "I'm not so special; I'm just an ordinary flower," to which Solomon replied, "Oh no, you are extraordinary—a lily among thorns."

Memories of Courtship

SONG 2:8–3:5

8 Ah, I hear my lover coming!
He is leaping over the mountains,
bounding over the hills.
9 My lover is like a swift gazelle
or a young stag.
Look, there he is behind the wall,
looking through the window,
peering into the room.
10 My lover said to me,
"Rise up, my darling!
Come away with me, my fair one!
11 Look, the winter is past,
and the rains are over and gone.
12 The flowers are springing up,
the season of singing birds* has come,
and the cooing of turtledoves fills the air.
13 The fig trees are forming young fruit,
and the fragrant grapevines are
blossoming.
Rise up, my darling!
Come away with me, my fair one!"

Young Man

14 My dove is hiding behind the rocks,
behind an outcrop on the cliff.
Let me see your face;
let me hear your voice.
For your voice is pleasant,
and your face is lovely.

Young Women of Jerusalem

15 Catch all the foxes,
those little foxes,
before they ruin the vineyard of love,
for the grapevines are blossoming!

Young Woman

16 My lover is mine, and I am his.
He browses among the lilies.
17 Before the dawn breezes blow
and the night shadows flee,
return to me, my love, like a gazelle
or a young stag on the rugged mountains.*

Young Woman

3:1 One night as I lay in bed, I yearned for
my lover.
I yearned for him, but he did not come.
2 So I said to myself, "I will get up and roam
the city,
searching in all its streets and squares.
I will search for the one I love."
So I searched everywhere but did not
find him.
3 The watchmen stopped me as they made their
rounds,
and I asked, "Have you seen the one
I love?"
4 Then scarcely had I left them
when I found my love!
I caught and held him tightly,
then I brought him to my mother's house,
into my mother's bed, where I had been
conceived.

5 Promise me, O women of Jerusalem,
by the gazelles and wild deer,
not to awaken love until the time
is right.*

Sg 2:12 Or *the season of pruning vines.* **Sg 2:17** Or *on the hills of Bether.* **Sg 3:5** Or *not to awaken love until it is ready.*

Solomon used the language of love. Nothing is more vital than encouraging and appreciating the person you love. Be sure to tell your spouse, "I love you" every day, and show that love by your actions.

Song 2:7 Feelings of love can create emotions that overpower reason. Young people are too often in a hurry to develop an intimate relationship based on their strong feelings. But feelings aren't enough to support a lasting relationship. This verse encourages us not to force romance lest the feelings of love grow faster than the commitment needed to make love last. Patiently wait for feelings of love and commitment to develop together.

Song 2:8–3:5 In this section Solomon's beloved reflects on her courtship with Solomon, remembering the first day they met and recalling one of her dreams about their being together.

Song 2:12-13 The lovers celebrated their joy in the creation and in their love. God created the world, the beauty of nature, and the gift of love and sex, and he gave us senses to enjoy them. Never let problems, conflicts, or the ravages of time ruin your ability to enjoy God's gifts. Take time to enjoy the world God has created.

Song 2:15 The "little foxes" are an example of the kinds of problems that can disturb or destroy a relationship. The lovers wanted anything that could potentially cause problems between them to be removed. Often the "little foxes" cause the biggest problems in marriage. These irritations must not be minimized or ignored but identified so that, together, the couple can deal with them.

Song 3:1-4 Many scholars agree that in these verses the girl is recalling a dream that caused her to become so concerned about her lover's whereabouts that she arose in the middle of the night to search for him. When you love someone, you will do all you can to ensure the safety of that person and care for his or her needs, even at a cost to your personal comfort. This is demonstrated most often in small actions—getting your spouse a glass of water, leaving work early to attend some function your child is involved in, or sacrificing your personal comfort to tend to the needs of a friend.

The flowers are springing up, the season of singing birds has come, and the cooing of turtledoves fills the air.
Song of Songs 2:12

Memories of Engagement

SONG 3:6–5:1

Young Women of Jerusalem

6 Who is this sweeping in from the wilderness
like a cloud of smoke?
Who is it, fragrant with myrrh and frankincense
and every kind of spice?
7 Look, it is Solomon's carriage,
surrounded by sixty heroic men,
the best of Israel's soldiers.
8 They are all skilled swordsmen,
experienced warriors.
Each wears a sword on his thigh,
ready to defend the king against an attack
in the night.
9 King Solomon's carriage is built
of wood imported from Lebanon.
10 Its posts are silver,
its canopy gold;
its cushions are purple.
It was decorated with love
by the young women of Jerusalem.

Young Woman

11 Come out to see King Solomon,
young women of Jerusalem.*
He wears the crown his mother gave him on his
wedding day,
his most joyous day.

Young Man

4:1 You are beautiful, my darling,
beautiful beyond words.
Your eyes are like doves
behind your veil.
Your hair falls in waves,
like a flock of goats winding down the slopes
of Gilead.
2 Your teeth are as white as sheep,
recently shorn and freshly washed.
Your smile is flawless,
each tooth matched with its twin.*
3 Your lips are like scarlet ribbon;
your mouth is inviting.
Your cheeks are like rosy pomegranates
behind your veil.
4 Your neck is as beautiful as the tower of David,
jeweled with the shields of a thousand heroes.
5 Your breasts are like two fawns,
twin fawns of a gazelle grazing among the lilies.
6 Before the dawn breezes blow
and the night shadows flee,
I will hurry to the mountain of myrrh
and to the hill of frankincense.
7 You are altogether beautiful, my darling,
beautiful in every way.

8 Come with me from Lebanon, my bride,
come with me from Lebanon.
Come down* from Mount Amana,
from the peaks of Senir and Hermon,
where the lions have their dens
and leopards live among the hills.

9 You have captured my heart,
my treasure,* my bride.
You hold it hostage with one glance of your eyes,
with a single jewel of your necklace.
10 Your love delights me,
my treasure, my bride.
Your love is better than wine,
your perfume more fragrant than spices.
11 Your lips are as sweet as nectar, my bride.
Honey and milk are under your tongue.
Your clothes are scented
like the cedars of Lebanon.

12 You are my private garden, my treasure, my bride,
a secluded spring, a hidden fountain.
13 Your thighs shelter a paradise of pomegranates
with rare spices—
henna with nard,
14 nard and saffron,
fragrant calamus and cinnamon,
with all the trees of frankincense, myrrh, and aloes,
and every other lovely spice.
15 You are a garden fountain,
a well of fresh water
streaming down from Lebanon's mountains.

Sg 3:11 Hebrew *of Zion.* **Sg 4:2** Hebrew *Not one is missing; each has a twin.* **Sg 4:8** Or *Look down.* **Sg 4:9** Hebrew *my sister;* also in 4:10, 12.

Song 3:6–5:1 Here the scene changes. Some believe that the wedding procession is described in 3:6-11, the wedding night in 4:1–5:1, and the consummation of the marriage in 4:16–5:1. Another possible explanation is that the period of Solomon's engagement to the girl is being remembered. In the previous section (Song 2:8–3:5), Solomon and the girl fell in love. In this section, Solomon returns to the girl in all his royal splendor (Song 3:6-11), expresses his great love for her (Song 4:1-5), and then proposes (Song 4:7-15). The girl accepts (Song 4:16), and Solomon responds to her acceptance (Song 5:1).

Song 3:7, 9 Solomon's carriage was probably a covered and curtained couch for a single passenger that was carried on the shoulders of men.

Song 4:1-7 We feel like awkward onlookers when we read this intensely private and intimate exchange. In the ecstasy of their love, the lovers praise each other using beautiful imagery. Their words may seem strange to readers from a different culture, but their intense feelings of love and admiration are universal. Communicating love and expressing admiration in both words and actions can enhance every marriage.

Song 4:12 In comparing his bride to a private garden, Solomon is praising her virginity. Virginity, considered old-fashioned by many in today's culture, has always been God's plan for unmarried people—and with good reason. Sex without marriage is cheap. It cannot compare with the joy of giving yourself completely to the one who is totally committed to you in marriage.

Song 4:15 Solomon's bride was as refreshing to him as a garden spring. Could your spouse say the same about you? Sometimes

Young Woman
16 Awake, north wind!
Rise up, south wind!
Blow on my garden
and spread its fragrance all around.
Come into your garden, my love;
taste its finest fruits.

Young Man
5:1 I have entered my garden, my treasure,*
my bride!
I gather myrrh with my spices
and eat honeycomb with my honey.
I drink wine with my milk.

Young Women of Jerusalem
Oh, lover and beloved, eat and drink!
Yes, drink deeply of your love!

A Troubling Dream

SONG 5:2–6:3

Young Woman
2 I slept, but my heart was awake,
when I heard my lover knocking and calling:
"Open to me, my treasure, my darling,
my dove, my perfect one.
My head is drenched with dew,
my hair with the dampness of the night."
3 But I responded,
"I have taken off my robe.
Should I get dressed again?
I have washed my feet.
Should I get them soiled?"
4 My lover tried to unlatch the door,
and my heart thrilled within me.
5 I jumped up to open the door for my love,
and my hands dripped with perfume.
My fingers dripped with lovely myrrh
as I pulled back the bolt.
6 I opened to my lover,
but he was gone!
My heart sank.
I searched for him
but could not find him anywhere.
I called to him,
but there was no reply.
7 The night watchmen found me
as they made their rounds.
They beat and bruised me
and stripped off my veil,
those watchmen on the walls.
8 Make this promise, O women of Jerusalem—
If you find my lover,
tell him I am weak with love.

Young Women of Jerusalem
9 Why is your lover better than all others,
O woman of rare beauty?
What makes your lover so special
that we must promise this?

Young Woman
10 My lover is dark and dazzling,
better than ten thousand others!
11 His head is finest gold,
his wavy hair is black as a raven.
12 His eyes sparkle like doves
beside springs of water;
they are set like jewels
washed in milk.
13 His cheeks are like gardens of spices
giving off fragrance.
His lips are like lilies,
perfumed with myrrh.
14 His arms are like rounded bars of gold,
set with beryl.
His body is like bright ivory,
glowing with lapis lazuli.

Sg 5:1 Hebrew *my sister;* also in 5:2.

the familiarity that comes with marriage causes us to forget the overwhelming feelings of love and bliss we shared at the beginning. Many marriages could use a course in "refreshing." Do you refresh your spouse, or are you a burden of complaints, sorrows, and problems? Partners in marriage should continually work at refreshing each other by an encouraging word, an unexpected gift, a change of pace, a surprise call or note, or even the withholding of a discussion of some problem until the proper time. Your spouse needs you to be a haven of refreshment because the rest of the world usually isn't.

Song 5:2ff This new section tells how the couple's marriage grew and matured in spite of problems. Some time had passed since the wedding, and the girl felt as though some indifference had developed in their relationship. She had become cool to her husband's advances, and by the time she changed her mind and responded to him, he had left. Her self-centeredness and impatience, though brief, caused separation. But she quickly moved to correct the problem by searching for her husband (Song 5:6-8).

Song 5:2-8 Inevitably, with the passing of time and the growth of familiarity, a marriage will start to lose its initial sparkle. Glances and touches no longer produce the same emotional response. Conflicts and pressures may creep in, causing you to lose your tenderness toward your spouse. The world is not a haven for lovers; in fact, external stress often works against the marriage relationship. But you and your spouse can learn to be a haven for each other. If intimacy and passion decline, remember that they can be renewed and regenerated. Take time to remember the commitment you made, those first thrills, the excitement of sex, and your spouse's strengths. When you focus on the positives, reconciliation and renewal can result.

Song 5:7 The girl was alone outside during the night. In Old Testament times, she would have been looked upon as a criminal or a prostitute and treated as such. This image symbolizes the pain she felt at being separated from her lover.

Song 5:16 The girl calls Solomon her "friend." In a healthy marriage, lovers are also good friends. Too often people are driven into marriage by the exciting feelings of love and passion before they take the time to develop a deep friendship. This involves listening, sharing, and showing understanding for the other's likes and dislikes. Friendship takes time, but it makes a love relationship much deeper and far more satisfying.

▸ **SONG 5:2–6:3 *(cont.)***

15 His legs are like marble pillars
set in sockets of finest gold.
His posture is stately,
like the noble cedars of Lebanon.
16 His mouth is sweetness itself;
he is desirable in every way.
Such, O women of Jerusalem,
is my lover, my friend.

Young Women of Jerusalem

6:1 Where has your lover gone,
O woman of rare beauty?
Which way did he turn
so we can help you find him?

Young Woman

2 My lover has gone down to his garden,
to his spice beds,
to browse in the gardens
and gather the lilies.
3 I am my lover's, and my lover is mine.
He browses among the lilies.

Praising the Bride's Beauty

SONG 6:4–7:9

Young Man

4 You are beautiful, my darling,
like the lovely city of Tirzah.
Yes, as beautiful as Jerusalem,
as majestic as an army with billowing
banners.
5 Turn your eyes away,
for they overpower me.
Your hair falls in waves,
like a flock of goats winding down the slopes
of Gilead.
6 Your teeth are as white as sheep
that are freshly washed.
Your smile is flawless,
each tooth matched with its twin.*
7 Your cheeks are like rosy pomegranates
behind your veil.
8 Even among sixty queens
and eighty concubines
and countless young women,
9 I would still choose my dove, my perfect one—
the favorite of her mother,
dearly loved by the one who bore her.
The young women see her and praise her;
even queens and royal concubines sing her
praises:
10 "Who is this, arising like the dawn,
as fair as the moon,
as bright as the sun,
as majestic as an army with billowing
banners?"

Young Woman

11 I went down to the grove of walnut trees
and out to the valley to see the new spring
growth,
to see whether the grapevines had budded
or the pomegranates were in bloom.
12 Before I realized it,
my strong desires had taken me to the chariot
of a noble man.*

Young Women of Jerusalem

13 *Return, return to us, O maid of Shulam.
Come back, come back, that we may see you
again.

Young Man

Why do you stare at this young woman of Shulam,
as she moves so gracefully between two lines
of dancers?*

7:1*How beautiful are your sandaled feet,
O queenly maiden.
Your rounded thighs are like jewels,
the work of a skilled craftsman.
2 Your navel is perfectly formed
like a goblet filled with mixed wine.
Between your thighs lies a mound of wheat
bordered with lilies.
3 Your breasts are like two fawns,
twin fawns of a gazelle.
4 Your neck is as beautiful as an ivory tower.
Your eyes are like the sparkling pools in Heshbon
by the gate of Bath-rabbim.
Your nose is as fine as the tower of Lebanon
overlooking Damascus.

Sg 6:6 Hebrew *Not one is missing; each has a twin.* **Sg 6:12** Or *to the royal chariots of my people,* or *to the chariots of Amminadab.* The meaning of the Hebrew is uncertain. **Sg 6:13a** Verse 6:13 is numbered 7:1 in Hebrew text. **Sg 6:13b** Or *as you would at the movements of two armies?* or *as you would at the dance of Mahanaim?* The meaning of the Hebrew is uncertain. **Sg 7:1** Verses 7:1-13 are numbered 7:2-14 in Hebrew text.

Song 6:3 The girl said that she and her lover belonged to each other—they had given themselves to each other unreservedly. No matter how close we may be to our parents or our best friends, only in marriage can we realize complete union of mind, heart, and body.

Song 6:4 Tirzah was a city about 35 miles northeast of Jerusalem. Its name means "pleasure" or "beauty." Jeroboam made Tirzah the first capital of the divided northern kingdom (1 Kgs 14:17). "Majestic as an army with billowing banners" means that his beloved must have had awe-inspiring beauty, like a mighty army readying for battle.

Song 6:8-9 Solomon did indeed have many queens (wives) and concubines (1 Kgs 11:3). Polygamy, though not condoned by God, was common in Old Testament days. Solomon said that his love for this woman had not diminished since their wedding night, even though many other women were available to him.

Song 7:4-5 Heshbon was the ancient capital of the Amorites. Bath-rabbim may have been a gate of Heshbon. The "tower of Lebanon" may have been a watchtower (evidently a prominent one and seen as very beautiful). Some suggest that this refers to the Lebanon mountain range. Mount Carmel overlooks the Mediterranean Sea and Palestine.

5 Your head is as majestic as Mount Carmel,
and the sheen of your hair radiates royalty.
The king is held captive by its tresses.
6 Oh, how beautiful you are!
How pleasing, my love, how full of delights!
7 You are slender like a palm tree,
and your breasts are like its clusters of fruit.
8 I said, "I will climb the palm tree
and take hold of its fruit."
May your breasts be like grape clusters,
and the fragrance of your breath like apples.
9 May your kisses be as exciting as the best wine,
flowing gently over lips and teeth.*

The Bride's Tender Appeal

SONG 7:10–8:4

Young Woman

10 I am my lover's,
and he claims me as his own.
11 Come, my love, let us go out to the fields
and spend the night among the wildflowers.*
12 Let us get up early and go to the vineyards
to see if the grapevines have budded,
if the blossoms have opened,
and if the pomegranates have bloomed.
There I will give you my love.
13 There the mandrakes give off their fragrance,
and the finest fruits are at our door,
new delights as well as old,
which I have saved for you, my lover.

Young Woman

8:1 Oh, I wish you were my brother,
who nursed at my mother's breasts.
Then I could kiss you no matter who was watching,
and no one would criticize me.
2 I would bring you to my childhood home,
and there you would teach me.*
I would give you spiced wine to drink,
my sweet pomegranate wine.
3 Your left arm would be under my head,
and your right arm would embrace me.
4 Promise me, O women of Jerusalem,
not to awaken love until the time is right.*

The Power of Love

SONG 8:5-14

Young Women of Jerusalem

5 Who is this sweeping in from the desert,
leaning on her lover?

Young Woman

I aroused you under the apple tree,
where your mother gave you birth,
where in great pain she delivered you.
6 Place me like a seal over your heart,
like a seal on your arm.
For love is as strong as death,
its jealousy* as enduring as the grave.*
Love flashes like fire,
the brightest kind of flame.

Sg 7:9 As in Greek and Syriac versions and Latin Vulgate; Hebrew reads *over lips of sleepers.* **Sg 7:11** Or *in the villages.* **Sg 8:2** Or *there she will teach me;* or *there she bore me.* **Sg 8:4** Or *not to awaken love until it is ready.* **Sg 8:6a** Or *its passion.* **Sg 8:6b** Hebrew *as Sheol.*

Song 7:10-13 As a marriage matures, love and freedom between marriage partners should increase. Here the girl takes the initiative in lovemaking. Many cultures have stereotypes of the roles men and women play in lovemaking, but the security of true love gives both marriage partners the freedom to initiate acts of love and express their true feelings.

Song 7:13 Mandrakes were a somewhat rare plant often thought to increase fertility. Mandrakes are also mentioned in Genesis 30:14-17.

Song 8:1 In the ancient Near East, it was improper to show public affection except between family members. The girl is wishing that she could freely show affection to her lover, even in public.

Song 8:6-7 In this final description of their love, the girl includes some of its significant characteristics (see also 1 Cor 13). Love is as strong as death; it cannot be killed by time or disaster and cannot be bought for any price because it is freely given. Love is priceless, and even the richest king cannot buy it. Love must be accepted as a gift from God and then shared within the guidelines God provides. Accept the love of your spouse as God's gift, and strive to make your love a reflection of the perfect love that comes from God himself.

Seals

Seals were produced in many shapes and sizes, the earliest being the stamp seal: a flat, engraved gem or bead that produced a copy of itself when pressed against soft clay. It was superseded in about 3000 B.C. in Mesopotamia by the cylinder seal. Since their first creation as amulets, seals served as guarantees of protection. An unbroken seal proved that the contents had not been tampered with, whether on a document, a granary door, or a wine jar. The seal also served as a mark of ownership or as a trademark. It was also used to validate documents (letters, bills of sale, government documents). The seal was suspended by a cord about the neck or the wrist or attached to some part of the owner's clothing (Song 8:6). In the New Testament, believers are "sealed" with the Holy Spirit as a mark of God's personal ownership of them (2 Cor 1:22; Eph 1:13; 4:30). How good it is to be "stamped" as God's personal possession.

▶ **SONG 8:5-14 *(cont.)***

7 Many waters cannot quench love,
nor can rivers drown it.
If a man tried to buy love
with all his wealth,
his offer would be utterly scorned.

The Young Woman's Brothers

8 We have a little sister
too young to have breasts.
What will we do for our sister
if someone asks to marry her?
9 If she is a virgin, like a wall,
we will protect her with a silver tower.
But if she is promiscuous, like a
swinging door,
we will block her door with a cedar bar.

Young Woman

10 I was a virgin, like a wall;
now my breasts are like towers.
When my lover looks at me,
he is delighted with what he sees.

11 Solomon has a vineyard at Baal-hamon,
which he leases out to tenant farmers.
Each of them pays a thousand pieces of silver*
for harvesting its fruit.
12 But my vineyard is mine to give,
and Solomon need not pay a thousand pieces
of silver.
But I will give two hundred pieces
to those who care for its vines.

Young Man

13 O my darling, lingering in the gardens,
your companions are fortunate to hear your
voice.
Let me hear it, too!

Young Woman

14 Come away, my love! Be like a gazelle
or a young stag on the mountains of spices.

Sg 8:11 Hebrew *1,000 shekels of silver.*

FRIENDS AND ENEMIES ▶ ***Solomon's reputation brought acclaim and riches from many nations, but he disobeyed God, marrying pagan women and worshiping their gods. So God raised up enemies like Hadad from Edom and Rezon from Zobah (modern-day Syria). Jeroboam from Zeredah was another enemy who would eventually divide this mighty kingdom.***

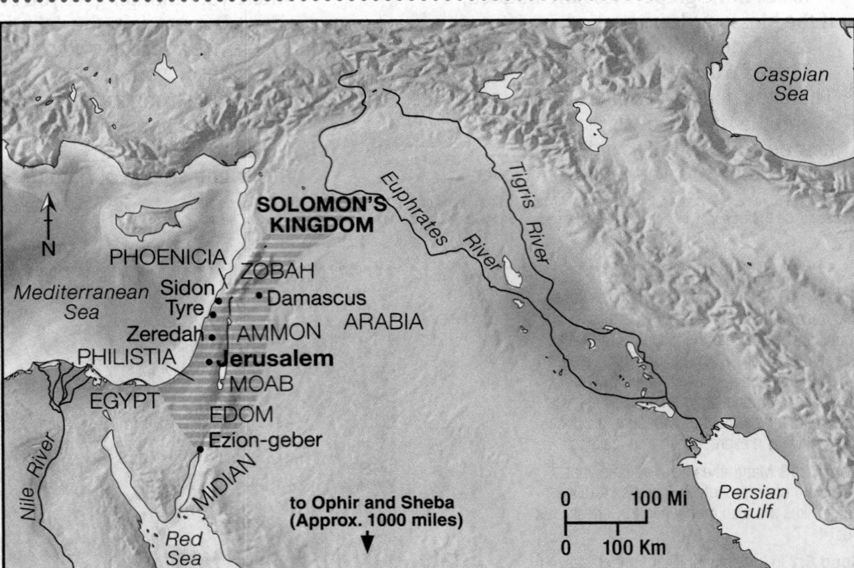

Song 8:8-9 The girl is reflecting on the days when she was younger and under the care of her brothers, who wondered how to help her prepare for marriage. They decided that if she remained a virgin before marriage, standing firm like a wall against sexual temptation, they would praise her. But if she was promiscuous and given over to immorality, they would take steps to guard her from doing something foolish. In Song of Songs 8:10, she testifies that she has been persistent in her morality and thus has found favor in Solomon's eyes.

Song 8:11-12 Solomon could demand rent from the tenants for his vineyard, but the girl had her own vineyard, and it was her right to assign it. But she willingly gave Solomon its fruit. In a good marriage, there is no private property, for everything is shared between the partners. This is the only time Baal-hamon is mentioned in the Bible, and its location is unknown.

Song 8:14 The love between Solomon and his bride did not diminish in intensity after their wedding night. The lovers relied on each other and kept no secrets from each other. Devotion and commitment were the keys to their relationship, just as they are in our relationships to our spouses and to God. The faithfulness of our marital love should reflect God's perfect faithfulness to us.

Paul shows how marriage represents Christ's relationship to his church (Eph 5:22-33), and John pictures the Second Coming as a great marriage feast for Christ and his bride, his faithful followers (Rev 19:7-8; 21:1-2). Many people have thought that Song of Songs is an allegory showing Christ's love for his church. It might be even better to say that it is a love poem about a real human love relationship, and that all loving, committed marriages are reflections of God's love.

H. Solomon's Downfall

Solomon enjoyed God's blessing throughout his reign, but his heart was not fully devoted to God. He never completely abandoned following the Lord, but he also observed the practices of following other gods from the surrounding nations. His halfhearted devotion to God led Israel astray and eventually led to the division of the nation into two separate kingdoms after his death. We must follow God with our entire lives and set an example of godliness for the generations that will follow us.

1. SOLOMON STRAYS FROM THE LORD

Solomon made a practice of marrying foreign women to solidify political alliances, in spite of God's clear instructions that the king of Israel should not do this. As a result, Solomon began to add the religious practices of these foreign wives to his worship of the Lord. Solomon introduced these detestable religious practices to the nation of Israel, leading to their quick decline from the spiritual high-point of the dedication of the Temple.

Solomon's Many Wives

1 KINGS 11:1-13

Now King Solomon loved many foreign women. Besides Pharaoh's daughter, he married women from
Moab, Ammon, Edom, Sidon, and from among the
Hittites. 2The LORD had clearly instructed the people
of Israel, "You must not marry them, because they will
turn your hearts to their gods." Yet Solomon insisted
on loving them anyway. 3He had 700 wives of royal
birth and 300 concubines. And in fact, they did turn
his heart away from the LORD.
4In Solomon's old age, they turned his heart to worship other gods instead of being completely faithful
to the LORD his God, as his father, David, had been.
5Solomon worshiped Ashtoreth, the goddess of the
Sidonians, and Molech,* the detestable god of the
Ammonites. 6In this way, Solomon did what was evil
in the LORD's sight; he refused to follow the LORD completely, as his father, David, had done.
7On the Mount of Olives, east of Jerusalem,* he even
built a pagan shrine for Chemosh, the detestable god
of Moab, and another for Molech, the detestable god
of the Ammonites. 8Solomon built such shrines for
all his foreign wives to use for burning incense and
sacrificing to their gods.
9The LORD was very angry with Solomon, for his
heart had turned away from the LORD, the God of Israel, who had appeared to him twice. 10He had warned
Solomon specifically about worshiping other gods,
but Solomon did not listen to the LORD's command.
11So now the LORD said to him, "Since you have not
kept my covenant and have disobeyed my decrees, I

1 Kgs 11:5 Hebrew *Milcom,* a variant spelling of Molech; also in 11:33. **1 Kgs 11:7** Hebrew *On the mountain east of Jerusalem.*

1 Kgs 11:2 Although Solomon had clear instructions from God not to marry women from foreign nations, he chose to disregard God's commands. He married not one, but many foreign women, who subsequently led him away from God. God knows our strengths and weaknesses, and his commands are always for our good. When people ignore God's commands, negative consequences inevitably result. It is not enough to know God's Word or even to believe it; we must follow it and apply it to our daily activities and decisions. Take God's commands seriously. Like Solomon, the wisest man who ever lived, we are not as strong as we may think.

1 Kgs 11:3 For all his wisdom, Solomon had some weak spots. He could not say no to compromise or to lustful desires. Whether he married to strengthen political alliances or to gain personal pleasure, these foreign wives led him into idolatry. You may have strong faith, but you also have areas of weakness—and that is where temptation usually strikes. Strengthen and protect yourself where you are weak because a chain is only as strong as its weakest link. If Solomon, the wisest man, could fall, so can you.

1 Kgs 11:4 Solomon handled great pressures in running the government, but he could not handle the pressure from his wives who wanted him to worship their gods. In marriage and close friendships, it is difficult to resist pressure to compromise. Our love leads us to identify with the desires of those we care about.

Faced with such pressure, Solomon at first resisted it, maintaining pure faith. Then he tolerated a more widespread practice of idolatry. Finally, he became involved in idolatrous worship, rationalizing away the potential danger to himself and to the kingdom. Because of the tendency to please and identify with loved ones, God asks us not to marry those who do not share our commitment to him.

1 Kgs 11:5-8 Ashtoreth was a goddess that symbolized reproductive power—a mistress of the god Baal. Molech was the national god of the Ammonites and was called "detestable" because its worship rites included child sacrifice. Chemosh was the Moabites' national god. The Israelites were warned against worshiping all other gods in general and Molech in particular (Exod 20:1-6; Lev 18:21; 20:1-5).

1 Kgs 11:9-10 Solomon didn't turn away from God all at once or in a brief moment. His spiritual coldness started with a seemingly minor departure from God's laws (1 Kgs 3:1). Over the years, that little sin grew until it resulted in Solomon's downfall. A little sin can be the first step in turning away from God. It is not the sins we don't know about but the sins we excuse that cause us the greatest trouble. We must never let any sin go unchallenged. In your life, is an unchallenged sin spreading like a deadly cancer? Don't excuse it. Confess this sin to God and ask him for strength to resist temptation.

1 Kgs 11:11-13 Solomon's powerful and glorious kingdom could have been blessed for all time; instead, it was approaching its end. Solomon had God's promises, guidance, and answers to prayer, yet he allowed sin to remain all around him. Eventually it corrupted him so much that he was no longer interested in God. Psalm 127:1, written by Solomon, says, "Unless the LORD builds a house, the work of the builders is wasted." Solomon had begun by laying the foundation with God, but he did not follow through in his later years. As a result, he lost everything. It is not enough to get off to a right start in building our marriage, career, or church on God's principles; we must remain faithful to God to the end (Mark 13:13). God must be in control of our lives from start to finish.

▸ 1 KINGS 11:1-13 *(cont.)*
will surely tear the kingdom away from you and give
it to one of your servants. 12But for the sake of your
father, David, I will not do this while you are still alive. I
will take the kingdom away from your son. 13And even
so, I will not take away the entire kingdom; I will let
him be king of one tribe, for the sake of my servant
David and for the sake of Jerusalem, my chosen city."

Solomon's Enemies

1 KINGS 11:14-25
Then the LORD raised up Hadad the Edomite, a member of Edom's royal family, to be Solomon's adversary.
15Years before, David had defeated Edom. Joab, his
army commander, had stayed to bury some of the
Israelite soldiers who had died in battle. While there,
they killed every male in Edom. 16Joab and the army
of Israel had stayed there for six months, killing them.
17But Hadad and a few of his father's royal officials
escaped and headed for Egypt. (Hadad was just a boy
at the time.) 18They set out from Midian and went to
Paran, where others joined them. Then they traveled
to Egypt and went to Pharaoh, who gave them a home,
food, and some land. 19Pharaoh grew very fond of Hadad, and he gave him his wife's sister in marriage—the
sister of Queen Tahpenes. 20She bore him a son named
Genubath. Tahpenes raised him* in Pharaoh's palace
among Pharaoh's own sons.
21When the news reached Hadad in Egypt that David and his commander Joab were both dead, he said
to Pharaoh, "Let me return to my own country."
22"Why?" Pharaoh asked him. "What do you lack
here that makes you want to go home?"

"Nothing," he replied. "But even so, please let me
return home."
23God also raised up Rezon son of Eliada as Solomon's adversary. Rezon had fled from his master,
King Hadadezer of Zobah, 24and had become the
leader of a gang of rebels. After David conquered Hadadezer, Rezon and his men fled to Damascus, where
he became king. 25Rezon was Israel's bitter adversary
for the rest of Solomon's reign, and he made trouble,
just as Hadad did. Rezon hated Israel intensely and
continued to reign in Aram.

Jeroboam Rebels against Solomon

1 KINGS 11:26-40
Another rebel leader was Jeroboam son of Nebat, one
of Solomon's own officials. He came from the town
of Zeredah in Ephraim, and his mother was Zeruah,
a widow.
27This is the story behind his rebellion. Solomon
was rebuilding the supporting terraces* and repairing
the walls of the city of his father, David. 28Jeroboam
was a very capable young man, and when Solomon saw
how industrious he was, he put him in charge of the
labor force from the tribes of Ephraim and Manasseh,
the descendants of Joseph.
29One day as Jeroboam was leaving Jerusalem, the
prophet Ahijah from Shiloh met him along the way.
Ahijah was wearing a new cloak. The two of them were
alone in a field, 30and Ahijah took hold of the new
cloak he was wearing and tore it into twelve pieces.
31Then he said to Jeroboam, "Take ten of these pieces,
for this is what the LORD, the God of Israel, says: 'I
am about to tear the kingdom from the hand of Solomon, and I will give ten of the tribes to you! 32But
I will leave him one tribe for the sake of my servant
David and for the sake of Jerusalem, which I have
chosen out of all the tribes of Israel. 33For Solomon
has* abandoned me and worshiped Ashtoreth, the
goddess of the Sidonians; Chemosh, the god of Moab;
and Molech, the god of the Ammonites. He has not
followed my ways and done what is pleasing in my
sight. He has not obeyed my decrees and regulations
as David his father did.
34"'But I will not take the entire kingdom from Solomon at this time. For the sake of my servant David,
the one whom I chose and who obeyed my commands
and decrees, I will keep Solomon as leader for the rest
of his life. 35But I will take the kingdom away from his
son and give ten of the tribes to you. 36His son will
have one tribe so that the descendants of David my
servant will continue to reign, shining like a lamp in
Jerusalem, the city I have chosen to be the place for
my name. 37And I will place you on the throne of Israel,
and you will rule over all that your heart desires. 38If
you listen to what I tell you and follow my ways and
do whatever I consider to be right, and if you obey my
decrees and commands, as my servant David did, then
I will always be with you. I will establish an enduring
dynasty for you as I did for David, and I will give Israel
to you. 39Because of Solomon's sin I will punish the
descendants of David—though not forever.'"
40Solomon tried to kill Jeroboam, but he fled to
King Shishak of Egypt and stayed there until Solomon
died.

1 Kgs 11:20 As in Greek version; Hebrew reads *weaned him.* **1 Kgs 11:27** Hebrew *the millo.* The meaning of the Hebrew is uncertain. **1 Kgs 11:33** As in Greek, Syriac, and Latin Vulgate; Hebrew reads *For they have.*

1 Kgs 11:14-22 Edom was the kingdom southeast of the Dead Sea. David had added this nation to his empire (2 Sam 8:13-14). It was of strategic importance because it controlled the route to the Red Sea. Edom's revolt was disturbing the peace of Solomon's kingdom.

1 Kgs 11:29-39 The prophet Ahijah predicted the division of the kingdom of Israel. After Solomon's death, 10 of Israel's 12 tribes would follow Jeroboam. The other two tribes, Judah and the area of Benjamin around Jerusalem, would remain loyal to the house of David. Judah, the largest tribe, and Benjamin, the smallest, were often mentioned as one tribe because they shared the same border. Both Jeroboam and Ahijah were from Ephraim, the most prominent of the 10 rebel tribes. (For more on the divided kingdom, see the note on 1 Kgs 12:20, p. 697.)

Summary of Solomon's Reign PARALLEL

1 KINGS 11:41-43

The rest of the events in Solomon's reign, including all his deeds and his wisdom, are recorded in *The Book of the Acts of Solomon.* 42 Solomon ruled in Jerusalem over all Israel for forty years. 43 When he died, he was buried in the City of David, named for his father. Then his son Rehoboam became the next king.

2 CHRONICLES 9:29-31

The rest of the events of Solomon's reign, from beginning to end, are recorded in *The Record of Nathan the Prophet,* and *The Prophecy of Ahijah from Shiloh,* and also in *The Visions of Iddo the Seer,* concerning Jeroboam son of Nebat. 30 Solomon ruled in Jerusalem over all Israel for forty years. 31 When he died, he was buried in the City of David, named for his father. Then his son Rehoboam became the next king.

2. THE WISDOM OF THE TEACHER

Solomon likely wrote Ecclesiastes near the end of his reign, reflecting on the entire course of his life. It shows that certain paths in life lead to emptiness. This profound book also helps us discover true purpose in life. Such wisdom can spare us from the emptiness that results from a life apart from God. Solomon teaches that people will not find meaning through knowledge, money, pleasure, work, or popularity. True satisfaction comes from knowing that what we are doing is part of God's purpose for our life. Everything temporal must be seen in light of the eternal.

Everything is Meaningless

ECCLESIASTES 1:1-11

These are the words of the Teacher,* King David's son, who ruled in Jerusalem.

2 "Everything is meaningless," says the Teacher, "completely meaningless!"

3 What do people get for all their hard work under the sun? 4 Generations come and generations go, but the earth never changes. 5 The sun rises and the sun sets, then hurries around to rise again. 6 The wind blows south, and then turns north. Around and around it goes, blowing in circles. 7 Rivers run into the sea, but the sea is never full. Then the water returns again to the rivers and flows out again to the sea. 8 Everything is wearisome beyond description. No matter how much we see, we are never satisfied. No matter how much we hear, we are not content.

9 History merely repeats itself. It has all been done before. Nothing under the sun is truly new. 10 Sometimes people say, "Here is something new!" But actually it is old; nothing is ever truly new. 11 We don't remember what happened in the past, and in future generations, no one will remember what we are doing now.

Eccl 1:1 Hebrew *Qoheleth;* this term is rendered "the Teacher" throughout this book.

The Teacher Speaks: The Futility of Wisdom

ECCLESIASTES 1:12-18

I, the Teacher, was king of Israel, and I lived in Jerusalem. 13 I devoted myself to search for understanding

---

1 Kgs 11:41 Nothing is known of *The Book of the Acts of Solomon.* (See also the note on 1 Kgs 14:19, p. 706.)

2 Chr 9:29 In his later years, Solomon turned away from God and led the nation into worshiping idols.

Eccl 1:1 The author, possibly Solomon (the "king of Israel," see Eccl 1:12), referred to himself as the Teacher, or leader of the assembly. He was both assembling people to hear a message and gathering wise sayings (proverbs). Solomon, one person in the Bible who had everything (wisdom, power, riches, honor, reputation, God's favor), is the one who discussed the ultimate emptiness of all that this world has to offer. His purpose in this book is to make people realize that their confidence in their own efforts, abilities, and righteousness was meaningless. Instead, their commitment to God is the only reason for living.

Eccl 1:1-11 Solomon had a purpose for writing skeptically and pessimistically. Near the end of his life, looking back on everything he had done, he saw that most of it seemed meaningless. A common belief was that good people prospered and the wicked suffered, but that hadn't proven true in Solomon's experience. Solomon wrote this book after he had tried everything and achieved much, only to find that nothing apart from God made him happy. He wanted his readers to avoid these same senseless pursuits. If we try to find meaning in our accomplishments rather than in God, we will never be satisfied, and everything we pursue will become meaningless.

Eccl 1:2 Solomon's kingdom, Israel, was in its golden age, but Solomon wanted the people to understand that success and prosperity don't last long (Ps 103:14-16; Isa 40:6-8; Jas 4:14). All human accomplishments will one day disappear; we must keep this in mind in order to live wisely. If we don't, we will become either proud and self-sufficient when we succeed or sorely disappointed when we fail. Solomon's goal was to show that earthly possessions and accomplishments are ultimately meaningless. Only the pursuit of God brings real satisfaction. We should honor God in all we say, think, and do.

Eccl 1:8-11 Many people feel restless and dissatisfied. They wonder: If I am in God's will, why am I so tired and unfulfilled? What is the meaning of life? When I look back on it all, will I be happy with my accomplishments? Why do I feel burned out, disillusioned, dry? What is to become of me? Solomon tests our faith, challenging us to find true and lasting meaning in God alone. As you take a hard look at your life, as Solomon did his, you will see how important serving God is over all other options. Perhaps God is asking you to rethink your purpose and direction in life, just as Solomon did in Ecclesiastes.

Eccl 1:12-15 "What is wrong cannot be made right. What is missing cannot be recovered." This refers to the ultimate perplexity and confusion that come to us because of all the unanswered questions in life. Solomon, writing about his own life, discovered that neither his accomplishments nor his wisdom could make him truly happy. True wisdom is found in God, and true happiness comes from pleasing him.

▸ **ECCLESIASTES 1:12-18 *(cont.)***

and to explore by wisdom everything being done under heaven. I soon discovered that God has dealt a tragic existence to the human race. [14]I observed everything going on under the sun, and really, it is all meaningless—like chasing the wind.

15 What is wrong cannot be made right.
What is missing cannot be recovered.

[16]I said to myself, "Look, I am wiser than any of the kings who ruled in Jerusalem before me. I have greater wisdom and knowledge than any of them." [17]So I set out to learn everything from wisdom to madness and folly. But I learned firsthand that pursuing all this is like chasing the wind.

18 The greater my wisdom, the greater my grief.
To increase knowledge only increases sorrow.

The Futility of Pleasure

ECCLESIASTES 2:1-11

I said to myself, "Come on, let's try pleasure. Let's look for the 'good things' in life." But I found that this, too, was meaningless. [2]So I said, "Laughter is silly. What good does it do to seek pleasure?" [3]After much thought, I decided to cheer myself with wine. And while still seeking wisdom, I clutched at foolishness. In this way, I tried to experience the only happiness most people find during their brief life in this world.

[4]I also tried to find meaning by building huge homes for myself and by planting beautiful vineyards. [5]I made gardens and parks, filling them with all kinds of fruit trees. [6]I built reservoirs to collect the water to irrigate my many flourishing groves. [7]I bought slaves, both men and women, and others were born into my household. I also owned large herds and flocks, more than any of the kings who had lived in Jerusalem before me. [8]I collected great sums of silver and gold, the treasure of many kings and provinces. I hired wonderful singers, both men and women, and had many beautiful concubines. I had everything a man could desire!

[9]So I became greater than all who had lived in Jerusalem before me, and my wisdom never failed me. [10]Anything I wanted, I would take. I denied myself no pleasure. I even found great pleasure in hard work, a reward for all my labors. [11]But as I looked at everything I had worked so hard to accomplish, it was all so meaningless—like chasing the wind. There was nothing really worthwhile anywhere.

The Wise and the Foolish

ECCLESIASTES 2:12-17

So I decided to compare wisdom with foolishness and madness (for who can do this better than I, the king?*). [13]I thought, "Wisdom is better than foolishness, just as light is better than darkness. [14]For the wise can see where they are going, but fools walk in the dark." Yet I saw that the wise and the foolish share the same fate. [15]Both will die. So I said to myself, "Since I will end up the same as the fool, what's the value of all my wisdom? This is all so meaningless!" [16]For the wise and the foolish both die. The wise will not be remembered any longer than the fool. In the days to come, both will be forgotten.

Eccl 2:12 The meaning of the Hebrew is uncertain.

Eccl 1:16-18 The more you understand, the greater your pain and difficulty. For example, the more you know, the more imperfection you see around you; and the more you observe, the more evil becomes evident. As you set out with Solomon to find the meaning of life, you must be ready to feel more, think more, question more, hurt more, and do more. Are you ready to pay the price for wisdom?

Eccl 1:16-18 Solomon highlights two kinds of wisdom in the book of Ecclesiastes: (1) human knowledge, reasoning, or philosophy, and (2) the wisdom that comes from God. In these verses Solomon is talking about human knowledge. When human knowledge ignores God, it only highlights our problems because it can't provide answers without God's eternal perspective and solution.

Eccl 2:1ff Solomon conducted his search for life's meaning as an experiment. He first tried pursuing pleasure. He undertook great projects, bought slaves and herds and flocks, amassed wealth, acquired singers, added many concubines to his harem, and became the greatest person in Jerusalem. But none of these gave him satisfaction: "But as I looked at everything I had worked so hard to accomplish, it was all so meaningless—like chasing the wind. There was nothing really worthwhile anywhere" (Eccl 2:11). Some of the pleasures Solomon sought were wrong, and some were worthy; but even the worthy pursuits were futile when he pursued them as an end in themselves. We must look beyond our activities to the reasons we do them and the purpose they fulfill. Is your goal in life to search for meaning or to pursue God, who gives meaning?

Eccl 2:4-6 Solomon had built houses, the Temple, a kingdom, and a family (see 1 Kgs 3–11). In the course of history, they all would be ruined. In Psalm 127:1, Solomon wrote, "Unless the LORD builds a house, the work of the builders is wasted. Unless the LORD protects a city, guarding it with sentries will do no good." This book is part of Solomon's testimony as to what happens to a kingdom or family that forgets God. As you examine your projects or goals, what is your starting point, your motivation? Without God as your foundation, all you are living for is meaningless.

Eccl 2:11 Solomon summarized his many attempts at finding life's meaning as "chasing the wind." We feel the wind as it passes, but we can't catch hold of it or keep it. In all our accomplishments, even the big ones, our good feelings are only temporary. Security and self-worth are not found in these accomplishments but far beyond them in the love of God. Think about what you consider worthwhile—where you place your time, energy, and money. Will you one day look back and decide that you, too, were "chasing the wind"?

Eccl 2:16 Solomon realized that wisdom alone cannot guarantee eternal life. Wisdom, riches, and personal achievement matter very little after death—and everyone must die. We must not build our life on perishable pursuits, but on the solid foundation of God. Then even if everything we have is taken away, we still will have God, who is all we really need anyway. This is the point of the book of Job. (For more about Job, see his Profile on p. 97.)

Eccl 2:16 Is death the ultimate equalizer of all people, no matter what they attained in life? While this appears to be true from an earthly perspective, God makes it clear (as Solomon later points out in Eccl 12:14) that what we do here has a great impact upon our eternal reward.

17 So I came to hate life because everything done here under the sun is so troubling. Everything is meaningless—like chasing the wind.

The Futility of Work

ECCLESIASTES 2:18-26

I came to hate all my hard work here on earth, for I must leave to others everything I have earned. 19 And who can tell whether my successors will be wise or foolish? Yet they will control everything I have gained by my skill and hard work under the sun. How meaningless! 20 So I gave up in despair, questioning the value of all my hard work in this world.

21 Some people work wisely with knowledge and skill, then must leave the fruit of their efforts to someone who hasn't worked for it. This, too, is meaningless, a great tragedy. 22 So what do people get in this life for all their hard work and anxiety? 23 Their days of labor are filled with pain and grief; even at night their minds cannot rest. It is all meaningless.

24 So I decided there is nothing better than to enjoy food and drink and to find satisfaction in work. Then I realized that these pleasures are from the hand of God. 25 For who can eat or enjoy anything apart from him?* 26 God gives wisdom, knowledge, and joy to those who please him. But if a sinner becomes wealthy, God takes the wealth away and gives it to those who please him. This, too, is meaningless—like chasing the wind.

A Time for Everything

ECCLESIASTES 3:1-15

1 For everything there is a season,
a time for every activity under heaven.
2 A time to be born and a time to die.
A time to plant and a time to harvest.
3 A time to kill and a time to heal.
A time to tear down and a time to build up.
4 A time to cry and a time to laugh.
A time to grieve and a time to dance.
5 A time to scatter stones and a time to gather stones.
A time to embrace and a time to turn away.
6 A time to search and a time to quit searching.
A time to keep and a time to throw away.
7 A time to tear and a time to mend.
A time to be quiet and a time to speak.
8 A time to love and a time to hate.
A time for war and a time for peace.

9 What do people really get for all their hard work?
10 I have seen the burden God has placed on us all.
11 Yet God has made everything beautiful for its own
time. He has planted eternity in the human heart, but
even so, people cannot see the whole scope of God's

Eccl 2:25 As in Greek and Syriac versions; Hebrew reads *apart from me?*

Eccl 2:17 As king, Solomon had everything a person could want, but here he says that he "came to hate life." What happened? His marvelous accomplishments left him sour because he pursued them as a means to personal satisfaction. Personal satisfaction, by itself, is empty because we are alone in the enjoyment we receive. What is your attitude about what you do? If your goals are to satisfy only yourself, you will find yourself empty, seeking one thing after another, as Solomon did. If your goal is to serve God and others, then you will experience a full life, one that won't leave you sour.

Eccl 2:18-23 Solomon continued to show that hard work bears no lasting fruit for those who work solely to earn money and gain possessions. Not only will everything be left behind at death, but it may be left to those who have done nothing to earn it. In addition, it may not be well cared for, and all that was gained may be lost. In fact, Solomon's son, who inherited his throne, immediately made a foolish decision which split the kingdom (see 1 Kgs 12). Hard work done with proper motives (caring for your family, serving God) is not wrong. We must work to survive, and more important, we are responsible for the physical and spiritual well-being of those under our care. But the fruit of hard work done to glorify only ourselves will be passed on to those who may later lose or spoil it all. Such toil often leads to grief, while serving God leads to everlasting joy. Do you know the real reason you are working so hard?

Eccl 2:24-26 Is Solomon recommending we make life a big, irresponsible party? No, he is encouraging us to take pleasure in what we're doing now and to enjoy life because it comes from God's hand. True enjoyment in life comes only as we follow God's guidelines for living. Without him, searching for satisfaction is in vain. Those who really know how to enjoy life are the ones who take life each day as a gift from God, thanking him for it and serving him in it. Those without God will have no relief from toil and no direction to guide them through life's complications.

Eccl 3:1–5:20 Solomon's point in this section is that God has a plan for all people. Thus, he provides cycles of life, each with its work for us to do. Although we may face many problems that seem to contradict God's plan, these should not be barriers to believing in him but rather opportunities to discover that, without God, life's problems have no lasting solutions!

Eccl 3:1-8 Timing is important. All the experiences listed in these verses are appropriate at certain times. The secret to peace with God is to discover, accept, and appreciate God's perfect timing. The danger is to doubt or resent God's timing. This can lead to despair, rebellion, or moving ahead without his advice.

Eccl 3:8 When is the time for hating? We shouldn't hate evil people, but we should hate what they do. We should also hate it when people are mistreated, when children are starving, and when God is being dishonored. In addition, we must hate the sin in our own lives—this is God's attitude (see Ps 5:5).

Eccl 3:9-13 Your ability to find satisfaction in your work depends to a large extent upon your attitude. You will become dissatisfied if you lose the sense of purpose God intended for your work. We can enjoy our work if we remember that God has given us work to do (Eccl 3:10) and realize that the fruit of our labor is a gift from him (Eccl 3:13). See your work as a way to serve God.

Eccl 3:11 God has "planted eternity in the human heart." This means that we can never be completely satisfied with earthly pleasures and pursuits. Because we are created in God's image, we have a spiritual thirst, we have eternal value, and nothing but the eternal God can truly satisfy us. God has built in us a restless yearning for the kind of perfect world that can only be found in his perfect rule. He has given us a glimpse of the perfection of his creation. But it is only a glimpse; we cannot see into the future or comprehend everything. So we must trust God now and do his work on earth.

▸ **ECCLESIASTES 3:1-15 *(cont.)***

work from beginning to end. [12]So I concluded there is nothing better than to be happy and enjoy ourselves as long as we can. [13]And people should eat and drink and enjoy the fruits of their labor, for these are gifts from God.

[14]And I know that whatever God does is final. Nothing can be added to it or taken from it. God's purpose is that people should fear him. [15]What is happening now has happened before, and what will happen in the future has happened before, because God makes the same things happen over and over again.

The Injustices of Life

ECCLESIASTES 3:16–4:6

I also noticed that under the sun there is evil in the courtroom. Yes, even the courts of law are corrupt! [17]I said to myself, "In due season God will judge everyone, both good and bad, for all their deeds."

[18]I also thought about the human condition—how God proves to people that they are like animals. [19]For people and animals share the same fate—both breathe* and both must die. So people have no real advantage over the animals. How meaningless! [20]Both go to the same place—they came from dust and they return to dust. [21]For who can prove that the human spirit goes up and the spirit of animals goes down into the earth? [22]So I saw that there is nothing better for people than to be happy in their work. That is why we are here! No one will bring us back from death to enjoy life after we die.

[4:1]Again, I observed all the oppression that takes place under the sun. I saw the tears of the oppressed, with no one to comfort them. The oppressors have great power, and their victims are helpless. [2]So I concluded that the dead are better off than the living. [3]But most fortunate of all are those who are not yet born. For they have not seen all the evil that is done under the sun.

[4]Then I observed that most people are motivated to success because they envy their neighbors. But this, too, is meaningless—like chasing the wind.

[5] "Fools fold their idle hands,
leading them to ruin."

[6]And yet,

"Better to have one handful with quietness
than two handfuls with hard work
and chasing the wind."

The Advantages of Companionship

ECCLESIASTES 4:7-12

I observed yet another example of something meaningless under the sun. [8]This is the case of a man who is all alone, without a child or a brother, yet who works hard to gain as much wealth as he can. But then he asks himself, "Who am I working for? Why am I giving up so much pleasure now?" It is all so meaningless and depressing.

[9]Two people are better off than one, for they can help each other succeed. [10]If one person falls, the other can reach out and help. But someone who falls alone is in real trouble. [11]Likewise, two people lying close together can keep each other warm. But how can one be warm alone? [12]A person standing alone can be attacked and defeated, but two can stand back-to-back

Eccl 3:19 Or *both have the same spirit.*

Eccl 3:12 To be happy and do good are worthy goals for life, but we can pursue them in the wrong way. God wants us to enjoy life. When we have the proper view of God, we discover that real pleasure is found in enjoying whatever we have as gifts from God, not in what we accumulate.

Eccl 3:14 What is the purpose of life? It is that we should fear the all-powerful God. To fear God means to respect and stand in awe of him because of who he is. Purpose in life starts with whom we know, not what we know or how good we are. It is impossible to fulfill your God-given purpose unless you revere God and give him first place in your life.

Eccl 3:16 Evil and corruption sit in the place where justice should be, thus affecting the legal system. Solomon asked how God's plan can be perfect when so much injustice and oppression exist in the world (Eccl 4:1). He concluded that God does not ignore injustice but will bring it to an end at his appointed time (Eccl 12:13-14).

Eccl 3:16ff Solomon reflects on several apparent contradictions in God's control of the world: (1) There is evil and corruption where there should be justice (Eccl 3:16-17); (2) people created in God's image die just like the animals (Eccl 3:18-21); (3) no one comforts the oppressed (Eccl 4:1-3); (4) many people are motivated by envy (Eccl 4:4-6); (5) people are lonely (Eccl 4:7-12); and (6) recognition for accomplishments is temporary (Eccl 4:13-16). It is easy to use such contradictions as excuses to not believe in God. But Solomon used them to show how we can honestly look at life's problems and still keep our faith. This life is not all there is, yet even in this life we should not pass judgment on God because we don't know everything. God's plan is for us to live forever with him. So live with eternal values in view, realizing that all contradictions will one day be cleared up by the Creator himself (Eccl 12:14).

Eccl 3:19-22 Our bodies can't live forever in their present state. In that sense, humans and animals are alike. But Solomon acknowledged that God has given people the hope of eternity (see the note on Eccl 3:11, p. 675), and that we will undergo judgment in the next life (Eccl 3:17; 12:7, 14)—making us different from animals. Because we have eternity planted in our hearts, we have a unique purpose in God's overall plan. Yet we cannot discover God's purpose for our lives by our own efforts—only through building a relationship with him and seeking his guidance. Are you now living as God wants? Do you see life as a gift from him?

Eccl 4:4-6 Some people are lazy while others are workaholics. Lazy people, seeing the futility of dashing about for success, idle away their time and hurt both themselves and those who depend on them. Workaholics are often driven by envy, greed, and a constant desire to stay ahead of everyone else. Both extremes are foolish and irresponsible. The answer is to work hard but with moderation. Take time to enjoy the other gifts God has given, and realize that it is God who gives out the assignments and the rewards, not us.

Eccl 4:9-12 Cooperating with others has advantages. Life is designed for companionship, not isolation; for intimacy, not loneliness. Some people prefer isolation, thinking they cannot trust anyone. We are not here

and conquer. Three are even better, for a triple-braided cord is not easily broken.

The Futility of Political Power

ECCLESIASTES 4:13-16

It is better to be a poor but wise youth than an old and foolish king who refuses all advice. 14Such a youth could rise from poverty and succeed. He might even become king, though he has been in prison. 15But then everyone rushes to the side of yet another youth* who replaces him. 16Endless crowds stand around him,* but then another generation grows up and rejects him, too. So it is all meaningless—like chasing the wind.

The Importance of Fearing God

ECCLESIASTES 5:1-7

1*As you enter the house of God, keep your ears open and your mouth shut. It is evil to make mindless offerings to God. 2*Don't make rash promises, and don't be hasty in bringing matters before God. After all, God is in heaven, and you are here on earth. So let your words be few.

3Too much activity gives you restless dreams; too many words make you a fool.

4When you make a promise to God, don't delay in following through, for God takes no pleasure in fools. Keep all the promises you make to him. 5It is better to say nothing than to make a promise and not keep it. 6Don't let your mouth make you sin. And don't defend yourself by telling the Temple messenger that the promise you made was a mistake. That would make God angry, and he might wipe out everything you have achieved.

7Talk is cheap, like daydreams and other useless activities. Fear God instead.

The Futility of Wealth

ECCLESIASTES 5:8–6:9

Don't be surprised if you see a poor person being oppressed by the powerful and if justice is being miscarried throughout the land. For every official is under orders from higher up, and matters of justice get lost in red tape and bureaucracy. 9Even the king milks the land for his own profit!*

10Those who love money will never have enough. How meaningless to think that wealth brings true happiness! 11The more you have, the more people come to help you spend it. So what good is wealth—except perhaps to watch it slip through your fingers!

12People who work hard sleep well, whether they eat little or much. But the rich seldom get a good night's sleep.

13There is another serious problem I have seen under the sun. Hoarding riches harms the saver. 14Money is put into risky investments that turn sour, and everything is lost. In the end, there is nothing left to pass on to one's children. 15We all come to the end of our lives as naked and empty-handed as on the day we were born. We can't take our riches with us.

16And this, too, is a very serious problem. People leave this world no better off than when they came. All their hard work is for nothing—like working for the wind. 17Throughout their lives, they live under a cloud—frustrated, discouraged, and angry.

18Even so, I have noticed one thing, at least, that is good. It is good for people to eat, drink, and enjoy their work under the sun during the short life God has given them, and to accept their lot in life. 19And it is a good thing to receive wealth from God and the good health to enjoy it. To enjoy your work and accept your lot in

Eccl 4:15 Hebrew *the second youth.* **Eccl 4:16** Hebrew *There is no end to all the people, to all those who are before them.* **Eccl 5:1** Verse 5:1 is numbered 4:17 in Hebrew text. **Eccl 5:2** Verses 5:2-20 are numbered 5:1-19 in Hebrew text. **Eccl 5:9** The meaning of the Hebrew in verses 8 and 9 is uncertain.

on earth to serve ourselves, but to serve God and others. Don't isolate yourself and try to go it alone. Seek companions; be a team member.

Eccl 4:13-16 Advancement or getting to the top is meaningless. Position, popularity, and prestige are poor goals for a life's work. Although many pursue them, they are shadows without substance. Many people seek recognition for their accomplishments; but people are fickle, changing quickly and easily. How much better to seek God's approval. His love never changes.

Eccl 5:1 When we enter the house of God, we should have the attitude of being open and ready to listen to God and not dictate to him what we think he should do.

Eccl 5:4-5 Solomon warns his readers about making foolish promises to God. In Israelite culture, making vows was a serious matter. Vows were voluntary, but once made, they were unbreakable (Deut 23:21-23). It is foolish to make a vow you cannot keep or to play games with God by only partially fulfilling your vow (Prov 20:25). It's better not to vow than to make a vow to God and break it. If you make a vow, keep it. (See the note on Matt 5:33ff, p. 1329.)

Eccl 5:10-11 We always want more than we have. Solomon observed that those who spend their lives obsessively seeking after money never find the happiness it promises. Wealth attracts freeloaders and thieves, causes sleeplessness and fear, and ultimately ends in loss because it must be left behind (Mark 10:23-25; Luke 12:16-21). No matter how much you earn, if you try to create happiness by accumulating wealth, you will never have enough. Money in itself is not wrong, but loving money leads to all sorts of sin. Whatever your financial situation, don't depend on money to make you happy. Instead, use what you have for the Lord.

Eccl 5:19-20 God wants us to view what we have (whether it is much or little) with the right perspective—our possessions are a gift from God. Although they are not the source of joy, they are a reason to rejoice, because every good thing comes from God. We should focus more on the Giver than the gift. We can be content with what we have when we realize that in God we have everything we need.

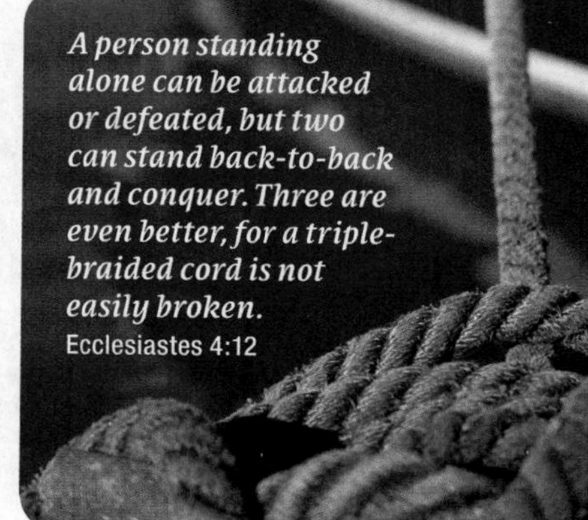
A person standing alone can be attacked or defeated, but two can stand back-to-back and conquer. Three are even better, for a triple-braided cord is not easily broken.
Ecclesiastes 4:12

▸ **ECCLESIASTES 5:8–6:9 *(cont.)***

life—this is indeed a gift from God. [20]God keeps such people so busy enjoying life that they take no time to brood over the past.

6:1 There is another serious tragedy I have seen under the sun, and it weighs heavily on humanity. [2]God gives some people great wealth and honor and everything they could ever want, but then he doesn't give them the chance to enjoy these things. They die, and someone else, even a stranger, ends up enjoying their wealth! This is meaningless—a sickening tragedy.

[3]A man might have a hundred children and live to be very old. But if he finds no satisfaction in life and doesn't even get a decent burial, it would have been better for him to be born dead. [4]His birth would have been meaningless, and he would have ended in darkness. He wouldn't even have had a name, [5]and he would never have seen the sun or known of its existence. Yet he would have had more peace than in growing up to be an unhappy man. [6]He might live a thousand years twice over but still not find contentment. And since he must die like everyone else—well, what's the use?

[7]All people spend their lives scratching for food, but they never seem to have enough. [8]So are wise people really better off than fools? Do poor people gain anything by being wise and knowing how to act in front of others?

[9]Enjoy what you have rather than desiring what you don't have. Just dreaming about nice things is meaningless—like chasing the wind.

The Future—Determined and Unknown

ECCLESIASTES 6:10-12

Everything has already been decided. It was known long ago what each person would be. So there's no use arguing with God about your destiny.

[11]The more words you speak, the less they mean. So what good are they?

[12]In the few days of our meaningless lives, who knows how our days can best be spent? Our lives are like a shadow. Who can tell what will happen on this earth after we are gone?

Wisdom for Life

ECCLESIASTES 7:1-14

1 A good reputation is more valuable than
costly perfume.
And the day you die is better than the day
you are born.

2 Better to spend your time at funerals than
at parties.
After all, everyone dies—
so the living should take this to heart.

3 Sorrow is better than laughter,
for sadness has a refining influence
on us.

4 A wise person thinks a lot about death,
while a fool thinks only about having
a good time.

5 Better to be criticized by a wise person
than to be praised by a fool.

6 A fool's laughter is quickly gone,
like thorns crackling in a fire.
This also is meaningless.

7 Extortion turns wise people into fools,
and bribes corrupt the heart.

8 Finishing is better than starting.
Patience is better than pride.

9 Control your temper,
for anger labels you a fool.

Eccl 6:1–8:15 In this section, Solomon shows that having the right attitude about God can help us deal with present injustices. Prosperity is not always good, and adversity is not always bad. But God is always good; if we live as he wants us to, we will be content.

Eccl 6:1-6 This person has died without being able to enjoy his wealth and honor. Everyone dies, and both rich and poor end up in the grave. Many people work hard to prolong life and improve their physical condition. Yet people spend little time or effort on their spiritual health. How shortsighted it is to work hard to extend this life and not take the time to prepare for eternity.

Eccl 6:10 God knows and directs everything that happens, and he is in complete control over our lives even though at times it may not seem that way. How foolish it is for us to contend with our Creator, who knows us completely and can see the future. (See also Jer 18:6; Rom 9:19-24.)

Eccl 6:12 Solomon is stating the profound truth that we cannot predict what the future holds. The only one who knows what will happen after we're gone is God. No human knows the future, so each day must be lived for its own value. Solomon is arguing against the notion that human beings can take charge of their own destiny. In all our plans we should look up to God, not just ahead to the future.

Eccl 7:1-4 This seems to contradict Solomon's previous advice to eat, drink, and find satisfaction in one's work—to enjoy what God has given. We are to enjoy what we have while we can but realize that adversity also strikes. Adversity reminds us that life is short, teaches us to live wisely, and refines our character. Christianity and Judaism see value in suffering and sorrow. The Greeks and Romans despised it; Eastern religions seek to live above it; but Christians and Jews see it as a refining fire. Most would agree that we learn more about God from difficult times than from happy times. Do you try to avoid sorrow and suffering at all cost? See your struggles as great opportunities to learn from God.

Eccl 7:2, 4 Many people avoid thinking about death, refuse to face it, and are reluctant to attend funerals. Solomon is not encouraging us to think morbidly, but he knows that it is helpful to think clearly about death. It reminds us that we still have time to change, time to examine the direction of our lives, and time to confess our sins and find forgiveness from God. Because everyone will eventually die, it makes sense to plan ahead to experience God's mercy rather than his justice.

Eccl 7:7 Money talks, and it can confuse those who would otherwise judge fairly. We hear about bribes given to judges, police officers, and witnesses. Bribes are given to hurt those who tell the truth and help those who oppose it. People who are involved in extortion or take bribes are indeed fools, no matter how wise they thought they were beforehand. It is said that everyone has a price, but those who are truly wise cannot be bought at any price.

Eccl 7:8 To finish what we start takes hard work, wisdom, self-discipline, and patience.

10 Don't long for "the good old days."
This is not wise.
11 Wisdom is even better when you have money.
Both are a benefit as you go through life.
12 Wisdom and money can get you almost anything,
but only wisdom can save your life.

13 Accept the way God does things,
for who can straighten what he has made
crooked?
14 Enjoy prosperity while you can,
but when hard times strike, realize that both
come from God.
Remember that nothing is certain in this life.

The Limits of Human Wisdom

ECCLESIASTES 7:15–8:1

I have seen everything in this meaningless life, including the death of good young people and the long life
of wicked people. 16 So don't be too good or too wise!
Why destroy yourself? 17 On the other hand, don't be
too wicked either. Don't be a fool! Why die before your
time? 18 Pay attention to these instructions, for anyone
who fears God will avoid both extremes.*
19 One wise person is stronger than ten leading citizens of a town!
20 Not a single person on earth is always good and
never sins.
21 Don't eavesdrop on others—you may hear your
servant curse you. 22 For you know how often you yourself have cursed others.
23 I have always tried my best to let wisdom guide my
thoughts and actions. I said to myself, "I am determined
to be wise." But it didn't work. 24 Wisdom is always distant and difficult to find. 25 I searched everywhere, determined to find wisdom and to understand the reason
for things. I was determined to prove to myself that
wickedness is stupid and that foolishness is madness.
26 I discovered that a seductive woman* is a trap
more bitter than death. Her passion is a snare, and her
soft hands are chains. Those who are pleasing to God
will escape her, but sinners will be caught in her snare.
27 "This is my conclusion," says the Teacher. "I discovered this after looking at the matter from every
possible angle. 28 Though I have searched repeatedly,
I have not found what I was looking for. Only one out
of a thousand men is virtuous, but not one woman!
29 But I did find this: God created people to be virtuous, but they have each turned to follow their own
downward path."

8:1 How wonderful to be wise,
to analyze and interpret things.
Wisdom lights up a person's face,
softening its harshness.

Obedience to the King

ECCLESIASTES 8:2-8

Obey the king since you vowed to God that you would.
3 Don't try to avoid doing your duty, and don't stand
with those who plot evil, for the king can do whatever
he wants. 4 His command is backed by great power. No
one can resist or question it. 5 Those who obey him will
not be punished. Those who are wise will find a time
and a way to do what is right, 6 for there is a time and
a way for everything, even when a person is in trouble.
7 Indeed, how can people avoid what they don't
know is going to happen? 8 None of us can hold back
our spirit from departing. None of us has the power
to prevent the day of our death. There is no escaping
that obligation, that dark battle. And in the face of
death, wickedness will certainly not rescue the wicked.

Eccl 7:18 Or *will follow them both.* **Eccl 7:26** Hebrew *a woman.*

Anyone with vision can start a big project. But vision without wisdom will result in unfinished projects and goals.

Eccl 7:14 God allows both good times and bad times to come to everyone. He blends them into our lives in such a way that we can't predict the future or count on human wisdom and power. We usually give ourselves the credit for the good times. Then in bad times, we tend to blame God without thanking him for the good that comes out of it. When life appears certain and controllable, don't let self-satisfaction or complacency make you too comfortable, or God may allow bad times to drive you back to him. When life seems uncertain and uncontrollable, don't despair—God is in control and will bring good results out of your struggles.

Eccl 7:16-18 How can a person be too good or too wise? This is a warning against pride—legalism or false righteousness. Solomon was saying that some people become so good or wise in their own eyes that they become deluded by their own religious acts. They are so rigid or narrow in their views that they lose their sensitivity to the true reason for being good—to honor God. Balance is important. God created us to be whole people who seek his righteousness and goodness. Thus, we should avoid both extremes of legalism and immorality.

Eccl 7:23-25 Solomon, the wisest man in the world, confesses how difficult it has been to act and think wisely. He emphasizes that no matter how much we know, some mysteries we will never understand. So thinking you have wisdom is a sure sign that you don't.

Eccl 7:27-28 Did Solomon think women were not capable of being virtuous (wise and good)? No, because in the book of Proverbs he personified wisdom as a responsible woman. The point of Solomon's statement is not that women are unwise, but that hardly anyone, man or woman, is upright before God. In his search, Solomon found that goodness and wisdom were almost as scarce among men as among women, even though men were given a religious education program in his culture and women were not. In effect, the verse is saying, "I have found only one in a thousand people who is wise in God's eyes. No, I have found even fewer than that!"

Eccl 8:1 Wisdom is the ability to see life from God's perspective and then to know the best course of action to take. Most people would agree that wisdom is a valuable asset, but how can we acquire it? Proverbs 9:10 teaches that the fear of the Lord (respect and honor) is the beginning of wisdom. Wisdom comes from knowing and trusting God; it is not merely the way to find God. Knowing God will lead to understanding and then to sharing this knowledge with others.

The Wicked and the Righteous

ECCLESIASTES 8:9-17

I have thought deeply about all that goes on here
under the sun, where people have the power to
hurt each other. 10I have seen wicked people buried with honor. Yet they were the very ones who
frequented the Temple and are now praised* in the
same city where they committed their crimes! This,
too, is meaningless. 11When a crime is not punished
quickly, people feel it is safe to do wrong. 12But even
though a person sins a hundred times and still lives
a long time, I know that those who fear God will be
better off. 13The wicked will not prosper, for they do
not fear God. Their days will never grow long like the
evening shadows.

14And this is not all that is meaningless in our world.
In this life, good people are often treated as though
they were wicked, and wicked people are often treated
as though they were good. This is so meaningless!

15So I recommend having fun, because there is
nothing better for people in this world than to eat,
drink, and enjoy life. That way they will experience
some happiness along with all the hard work God gives
them under the sun.

16In my search for wisdom and in my observation of
people's burdens here on earth, I discovered that there
is ceaseless activity, day and night. 17I realized that no
one can discover everything God is doing under the
sun. Not even the wisest people discover everything,
no matter what they claim.

Death Comes to All

ECCLESIASTES 9:1-12

This, too, I carefully explored: Even though the actions
of godly and wise people are in God's hands, no one
knows whether God will show them favor. 2The same
destiny ultimately awaits everyone, whether righteous
or wicked, good or bad,* ceremonially clean or unclean, religious or irreligious. Good people receive
the same treatment as sinners, and people who make
promises to God are treated like people who don't.

3It seems so tragic that everyone under the sun suffers the same fate. That is why people are not more
careful to be good. Instead, they choose their own mad
course, for they have no hope. There is nothing ahead
but death anyway. 4There is hope only for the living. As
they say, "It's better to be a live dog than a dead lion!"

5The living at least know they will die, but the dead
know nothing. They have no further reward, nor are
they remembered. 6Whatever they did in their lifetime—loving, hating, envying—is all long gone. They
no longer play a part in anything here on earth. 7So
go ahead. Eat your food with joy, and drink your wine
with a happy heart, for God approves of this! 8Wear
fine clothes, with a splash of cologne!

9Live happily with the woman you love through all
the meaningless days of life that God has given you
under the sun. The wife God gives you is your reward
for all your earthly toil. 10Whatever you do, do well.
For when you go to the grave,* there will be no work
or planning or knowledge or wisdom.

Eccl 8:10 As in some Hebrew manuscripts and Greek version; many Hebrew manuscripts read *and are forgotten.* **Eccl 9:2** As in Greek and Syriac versions and Latin Vulgate; Hebrew lacks *or bad.* **Eccl 9:10** Hebrew *to Sheol.*

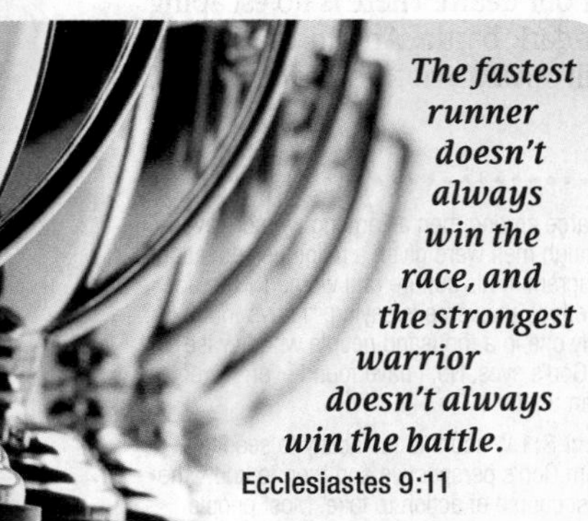

The fastest runner doesn't always win the race, and the strongest warrior doesn't always win the battle.
Ecclesiastes 9:11

Eccl 8:10 This verse probably refers to how we quickly forget the evil done by some people after they have died. Returning from the cemetery, we praise them in the very city where they did their evil deeds.

Eccl 8:11 If God doesn't punish us immediately for sin, we must not assume that he doesn't care or that sin has no consequences. When a young child does something wrong and is not punished, that child will be much more likely to repeat the act. Remember, God knows every wrong we commit, and one day we will have to answer for all that we have done (Eccl 12:14).

Eccl 8:15 Solomon recommends the remedy for life's unanswered questions: joy and contentment. We must accept each day with its measure of work, food, and pleasure. Let us learn to enjoy what God has given to refresh and strengthen us so we may continue his work.

Eccl 8:16-17 Even if he had access to all the world's wisdom, the wisest man would know very little. No one can fully comprehend God and all that he has done, and there are always more questions than answers. But the unknown should not cast a shadow over our joy, faith, or work because we know that someone greater is in control and that we can put our trust in him. Don't let what you don't know about the future destroy the joy God wants to give you today.

Eccl 9:2 "The same destiny ultimately awaits everyone" means that all will eventually die.

Eccl 9:5, 10 When Solomon says the dead know nothing and that there is no work, planning, knowledge, or wisdom after death, he is not contrasting life with afterlife, but life with death. After you die, you can't change what you have done. Resurrection to a new life after death was a vague concept for Old Testament believers. It was only made clear after Jesus rose from the dead.

Eccl 9:7-10 Considering the uncertainties of the future and the certainty of death, Solomon recommends enjoying life as God's gift. He may have been criticizing those who put off all present pleasures in order to accumulate wealth, much like those who get caught up in today's rat race. Solomon asks, "What is your wealth really worth, anyway?" Because the future is so uncertain, we should enjoy God's gifts while we are able.

Eccl 9:9 Solomon also wrote a proverb about marriage. "The man who finds a wife finds a treasure, and he receives favor from the LORD" (Prov 18:22). How sad it would be to be married and not appreciate or enjoy the companion God has given you.

Eccl 9:10-11 It isn't difficult to think of cases where the fastest and the strongest don't win, the wise are poor, and the skillful are unrewarded with wealth or honor. Some people see such examples and call life unfair, and they are right. The world is finite, and sin has twisted life, making it what God did not intend. Solomon is trying to reduce our expectations. The book of Proverbs emphasizes how life would go if everyone acted

11 I have observed something else under the sun.
The fastest runner doesn't always win the race,
and the strongest warrior doesn't always win the
battle. The wise sometimes go hungry, and the skillful are not necessarily wealthy. And those who are
educated don't always lead successful lives. It is
all decided by chance, by being in the right place
at the right time.
12 People can never predict when hard times might
come. Like fish in a net or birds in a trap, people are
caught by sudden tragedy.

Thoughts on Wisdom and Folly

ECCLESIASTES 9:13–10:4

Here is another bit of wisdom that has impressed me
as I have watched the way our world works. 14 There
was a small town with only a few people, and a great
king came with his army and besieged it. 15 A poor,
wise man knew how to save the town, and so it was
rescued. But afterward no one thought to thank him.
16 So even though wisdom is better than strength, those
who are wise will be despised if they are poor. What
they say will not be appreciated for long.

17 Better to hear the quiet words of a wise person
  than the shouts of a foolish king.
18 Better to have wisdom than weapons of war,
  but one sinner can destroy much that
   is good.

10:1 As dead flies cause even a bottle of perfume
   to stink,
  so a little foolishness spoils great wisdom
   and honor.

2 A wise person chooses the right road;
  a fool takes the wrong one.

3 You can identify fools
  just by the way they walk down the street!

4 If your boss is angry at you, don't quit!
  A quiet spirit can overcome even great
   mistakes.

The Ironies of Life

ECCLESIASTES 10:5-20

There is another evil I have seen under the sun. Kings
and rulers make a grave mistake 6 when they give great
authority to foolish people and low positions to people
of proven worth. 7 I have even seen servants riding
horseback like princes—and princes walking like
servants!

8 When you dig a well,
  you might fall in.
 When you demolish an old wall,
  you could be bitten by a snake.
9 When you work in a quarry,
  stones might fall and crush you.
 When you chop wood,
  there is danger with each stroke of your ax.

10 Using a dull ax requires great strength,
  so sharpen the blade.
 That's the value of wisdom;
  it helps you succeed.

11 If a snake bites before you charm it,
  what's the use of being a snake charmer?

12 Wise words bring approval,
  but fools are destroyed by their own words.

13 Fools base their thoughts on foolish assumptions,
  so their conclusions will be wicked madness;
14 they chatter on and on.
 No one really knows what is going to happen;
  no one can predict the future.

15 Fools are so exhausted by a little work
  that they can't even find their way home.

16 What sorrow for the land ruled by a servant,*
  the land whose leaders feast in the morning.
17 Happy is the land whose king is a noble leader
  and whose leaders feast at the proper time
  to gain strength for their work, not to get
   drunk.

Eccl 10:16 *Or a child.*

fairly; Ecclesiastes explains what usually happens in our sinful and imperfect world. We must keep our perspective. Don't let the inequities of life keep you from earnest, dedicated work. We serve God, not people (see Col 3:23).

Eccl 9:13-18 Our society honors wealth, attractiveness, and success above wisdom. Yet wisdom is a greater asset than strength, although it is often overlooked. Even though it is more effective, wisdom from people who are poor often goes unheeded. From this parable we can learn to appreciate wisdom, no matter whom it comes from.

Eccl 10:4 This proverb has implications for employer/employee relationships. Employees should ride out the temper tantrums of their employer. If we quietly do our work and don't get upset, the employer will probably get over the anger and calm down.

Eccl 10:5-7 By describing these circumstances that aren't fair or don't make sense, Solomon is saying that wealth alone can't bring justice. He continues to build to his conclusion that everything we have (from wisdom to riches) is nothing without God. But when God uses what little we have, it becomes all we could ever want or need.

Eccl 10:10 Trying to do anything without the necessary skills or tools is like chopping wood with a dull ax. If your tool is dull, you should sharpen it to do a better job. Similarly, if you lack skills, you should sharpen them through training and practice. "Sharpen the blade" means to recognize where a problem exists, acquire or hone the skills (or tools) to do the job better, and then go out and do it. Find the areas of your life where your "ax" is dull, and sharpen your skills so you can be more effective for God's work.

Eccl 10:16-18 When the Israelites had immature and irresponsible leaders, their nation fell. The books of 1 and 2 Kings describe the decline of the kingdoms when the leaders were concerned only about themselves. These verses pinpoint the basic problems of these leaders—selfishness and laziness.

▸ **ECCLESIASTES 10:5-20 *(cont.)***

18 Laziness leads to a sagging roof;
idleness leads to a leaky house.
19 A party gives laughter,
wine gives happiness,
and money gives everything!
20 Never make light of the king, even in your
thoughts.
And don't make fun of the powerful,
even in your own bedroom.
For a little bird might deliver your message
and tell them what you said.

The Uncertainties of Life

ECCLESIASTES 11:1-6

1 Send your grain across the seas,
and in time, profits will flow back to you.*
2 But divide your investments among many
places,*
for you do not know what risks might lie ahead.

3 When clouds are heavy, the rains come down.
Whether a tree falls north or south, it stays
where it falls.

4 Farmers who wait for perfect weather never plant.
If they watch every cloud, they never harvest.

5Just as you cannot understand the path of the wind
or the mystery of a tiny baby growing in its mother's
womb,* so you cannot understand the activity of God,
who does all things.
6Plant your seed in the morning and keep busy all
afternoon, for you don't know if profit will come from
one activity or another—or maybe both.

Advice for Young and Old

ECCLESIASTES 11:7–12:7

Light is sweet; how pleasant to see a new day dawning.
8When people live to be very old, let them rejoice
in every day of life. But let them also remember there
will be many dark days. Everything still to come is
meaningless.
9Young people,* it's wonderful to be young! Enjoy
every minute of it. Do everything you want to do; take
it all in. But remember that you must give an account
to God for everything you do. 10So refuse to worry, and
keep your body healthy. But remember that youth,
with a whole life before you, is meaningless.

12:1 Don't let the excitement of youth cause you to
forget your Creator. Honor him in your youth before
you grow old and say, "Life is not pleasant anymore."
2Remember him before the light of the sun, moon,
and stars is dim to your old eyes, and rain clouds continually darken your sky. 3Remember him before your
legs—the guards of your house—start to tremble; and
before your shoulders—the strong men—stoop. Remember him before your teeth—your few remaining
servants—stop grinding; and before your eyes—the
women looking through the windows—see dimly.
4Remember him before the door to life's opportunities is closed and the sound of work fades. Now you
rise at the first chirping of the birds, but then all their
sounds will grow faint.
5Remember him before you become fearful of falling and worry about danger in the streets; before your
hair turns white like an almond tree in bloom, and you
drag along without energy like a dying grasshopper,
and the caperberry no longer inspires sexual desire.

Eccl 11:1 Or *Give generously, / for your gifts will return to you later.* Hebrew reads *Throw your bread on the waters, / for after many days you will find it again.* **Eccl 11:2** Hebrew *among seven or even eight.* **Eccl 11:5** Some manuscripts read *Just as you cannot understand how breath comes to a tiny baby in its mother's womb.* **Eccl 11:9** Hebrew *Young man.*

Eccl 10:19 Government leaders, businesses, families, even churches get trapped into thinking money can meet all their needs. We throw money at our problems. But just as the thrill of wine is only temporary, the soothing effect of the last purchase soon wears off, and we have to buy more. Scripture recognizes that money is necessary for survival, but it warns against the love of money (see Matt 6:24; 1 Tim 6:10; Heb 13:5). Money is dangerous because it deceives us into thinking that wealth is the easiest way to get everything we want. The love of money is sinful because we trust money rather than God to solve our problems. Those who pursue its empty promises will one day discover that they have nothing because they are spiritually bankrupt.

Eccl 11:1-5 In these verses Solomon summarizes that life involves both risk and opportunity. Because life has no guarantees, we must be prepared. Solomon does not support a stingy, despairing attitude. Just because life is uncertain does not mean we should do nothing. We need a spirit of trust and adventure, facing life's risks and opportunities with God-directed enthusiasm and faith.

Eccl 11:4 Waiting for perfect conditions will mean inactivity. This practical insight is especially applicable to our spiritual lives. If we wait for the perfect time and place for personal Bible reading, we will never begin. If we wait for a perfect church, we will never join. If we wait for the perfect ministry, we will never serve. Take steps now to grow spiritually. Don't wait for conditions that may never exist.

Eccl 11:7-8 Solomon is no dreary pessimist in Ecclesiastes 11:7–12:14. He encourages us to rejoice in every day but to remember that eternity is far longer than a person's life span. Psalm 90:12 says, "Teach us to realize the brevity of life, so that we may grow in wisdom." The wise person does not just think about the moment and its impact but takes the long-range view toward eternity. Approach your decisions with God's perspective—consider their impact 10 years from now and into eternity. Live with the attitude that although our life is short, we will live with God forever.

Eccl 11:9-10 People often say, "It doesn't matter." But many of a person's choices will be irreversible—they will affect that person for a lifetime. What you do when you're young *does* matter. Enjoy life now, but don't do anything physically, morally, or spiritually that will prevent you from enjoying life when you are old.

Eccl 12:1 A life without God can produce bitterness, loneliness, and hopelessness in old age. When faced with disabilities, sickness, or handicaps, a life centered around God is still fulfilling and can be rich and bearable even in old age. Being young is exciting. But the excitement of youth can become a barrier to closeness with God if it makes young people focus on passing pleasures instead of eternal values. Make your strength available to God while it is still yours—during your youthful years. Don't waste it on evil or meaningless activities that become bad habits and make you callous. Seek God now.

Remember him before you near the grave, your everlasting home, when the mourners will weep at your funeral.
6Yes, remember your Creator now while you are young, before the silver cord of life snaps and the golden bowl is broken. Don't wait until the water jar is smashed at the spring and the pulley is broken at
the well. 7For then the dust will return to the earth, and the spirit will return to God who gave it.

Concluding Thoughts about the Teacher

ECCLESIASTES 12:8-14

"Everything is meaningless," says the Teacher, "completely meaningless."
9Keep this in mind: The Teacher was considered wise, and he taught the people everything he knew. He listened carefully to many proverbs, studying and
classifying them. 10The Teacher sought to find just the right words to express truths clearly.*
11The words of the wise are like cattle prods—painful but helpful. Their collected sayings are like a nail-studded stick with which a shepherd* drives the sheep.
12But, my child,* let me give you some further advice: Be careful, for writing books is endless, and much study wears you out.
13That's the whole story. Here now is my final conclusion: Fear God and obey his commands, for this is
everyone's duty. 14God will judge us for everything we do, including every secret thing, whether good or bad.

Eccl 12:10 Or *sought to write what was upright and true.* **Eccl 12:11** Or *one shepherd.* **Eccl 12:12** Hebrew *my son.*

Eccl 12:6-8 The silver cord, golden bowl, water jar, and pulley symbolize life's fragility. How easily death comes to us; how swiftly and unexpectedly we may return to the dust from which we came. Therefore, we should recognize life as a precious resource to be used wisely and not squandered frivolously.

Eccl 12:7-8 Stripped of the life-giving spirit breathed into us by God, our bodies return to dust. Stripped of God's purpose, our work is in vain. Stripped of God's love, our service is futile. We must put God first over all we do and in all we do because without him we have nothing. Knowing that life is futile without God motivates the wise person to seek God first.

Eccl 12:12 Opinions about life and philosophies about how we should live could be read and studied forever. It is not wrong to study these opinions, but because our life on earth is so short, we should make the best use of time by learning the important truths in God's Word. They affect this life and eternity. Wise students of the Bible will understand and do what it says.

Eccl 12:13-14 In his conclusion, Solomon presents his antidotes for the two main ailments presented in this book. Those who lack purpose and direction in life should fear God and obey his commands. Those who think life is unfair should remember that God will review every person's life to determine how that individual has responded to him, and he will bring every deed into judgment. Have you committed your life to God? Does your life measure up to his standards?

Eccl 12:13-14 The book of Ecclesiastes cannot be interpreted correctly without reading these final verses. No matter what the mysteries and apparent contradictions of life are, we must work toward the single purpose of knowing God.

In Ecclesiastes, Solomon shows us that we should enjoy life, but this does not exempt us from obeying God's commands. We should search for purpose and meaning in life, but these cannot be found in human endeavors. We should acknowledge the evil, foolishness, and injustice in life yet maintain a positive attitude and strong faith in God.

All people will have to stand before God and be judged for what they have done in this life. We will not be able to use the inequities of life as an excuse for failing to live properly. We need to: recognize that human effort apart from God is futile, put God first—now, receive everything good as a gift from God, and realize that God will judge every person's life, whether good or evil. How strange that people spend their lives striving for the joy that God gives freely.

But, my child, let me give you some further advice: Be careful, for writing books is endless, and much study wears you out.
Ecclesiastes 12:12

Splintered Nation

THE PEOPLE OF GOD seemed to be headed in the right direction. They had seen great military victories under David's leadership, and God had given them rest from their enemies on every side. Solomon had built a magnificent Temple for worshiping the Lord in Jerusalem and had made the nation unbelievably prosperous—their borders were expanding. But the people and their leaders were moving farther and farther from God and were making compromises in their worship and allegiances. Small cracks had formed in the beautiful picture they had created.

After Solomon's death, things fell apart rather quickly. His son Rehoboam continued imposing heavy taxes and labor on the people, and they revolted against him. Ten of the twelve tribes united under Jeroboam and formed a new nation—the northern kingdom of Israel. This left just two tribes under Rehoboam's leadership—the southern kingdom of Judah. God's people, once a mighty unified nation, were now splintered into two nations at odds with one another.

The two nations were often at war with each other, and rarely was either of them focused on worshiping God and displaying him to the world, as they were intended to do. God sent prophets to speak to the people and their leaders, but often they were ignored or even persecuted. Leaders preferred to surround themselves with people who told them what they wanted to hear rather than those who called them to repent and return to God.

The northern kingdom of Israel consistently rejected God and followed their own way, both through the idol shrines that Jeroboam set up in Bethel and Dan and through worshiping Baal and the other deities of the nations around them. Although they saw the great power of the true God through the ministry of Elijah and heard about his great love for them from prophets like Jonah and especially Hosea, they never returned to God while they were in the land. So God raised up the Assyrians to conquer Israel, scatter the Israelites throughout the world, and repopulate the land with exiles from other conquered nations.

Judah saw the fate of their northern neighbor, but they didn't heed the warning. God spared them from Assyria, using the prophets Isaiah and Micah along with the good king

BOOKS

- 1 KINGS
- 2 KINGS
- 2 CHRON
- PSALMS
- PROV
- ISAIAH
- JER
- EZEKIEL
- DANIEL
- HOSEA
- AMOS
- JONAH
- MICAH
- NAHUM
- HAB
- ZEPH

DATES

FROM:
930 BC
TO:
586 BC

THEMES

- Division
- Disobedience
- Judgment
- Repentance
- Faithfulness

Hezekiah to lead the nation back to God temporarily, but the reforms wouldn't last. Judah always went back to worshiping idols, rejecting God and his prophets, and neglecting their role as witnesses to God's power and love to the nations. Instead, they continued to try to be like the nations around them, and so God brought the powerful Babylonian Empire against them in judgment.

The once-unified people of God were splintered into two rebellious nations, and ultimately they were splintered even further when they were cast out of the land, exiled to Assyria, then Babylon, and beyond. In the last decades of Judah's decline, we get a glimpse of God still active among his people even in exile: Daniel and Ezekiel began their ministries during this period. They were a shining light pointing the way forward for the people of God in this bleak and dark time.

Jeroboam Sacrificing to the Idols, by Jean-Honore Fagonard

PEOPLE & CULTURE

■ **Jeroboam and Rehoboam.** These two kings set many things in motion that had a profound impact on both nations for their entire history. Rehoboam's attempt to strengthen his position over the people led to a revolt and the split of the nations, and his disregard for God and the Temple led the people away from following God wholeheartedly. He built pagan shrines and encouraged the people to imitate the practices of their neighbors rather than shining the light of the Lord's presence to the world, as they were intended to do. Jeroboam, on the other hand, understood the importance of the Temple in the life of the nation of Israel; however, he was more concerned about establishing his power over the new nation in the north than he was about proper worship of God. So he set up his own centers for worship with idols that were supposed to represent the gods who led Israel out of Egypt—cheap imitations that were highly offensive to the true God. This idol religion was a constant snare for the northern kingdom, and they were destroyed and scattered because of their idolatry.

■ Elijah and Elisha. Israel and Judah were largely led by kings that ignored and defied God, but they were not the only influential people in these nations. God sent powerful prophets to demonstrate his sovereignty over the world in spite of such evil political leadership. Elijah confronted the prophets of Baal that were being supported by Israel's government and showed dramatically that God is the only true deity. Along with Elisha, his successor, he showed God's power over nature, foreign armies, and even life itself. They also showed that God is concerned about even the daily necessities for the poorest Israelites, miraculously providing food and healing for those who were suffering. Although it sometimes seemed like nobody in all of Israel and Judah was following God, Elijah and Elisha remind us that there were faithful people—more than we even know about.

■ Hezekiah and Josiah. Although the great majority of the kings of Israel and Judah were evil, there were a few who followed in the footsteps of David as a godly leader and who brought the people back to worshiping God. Hezekiah and Josiah were not the only good kings in Judah, but they are good representatives of reform and return to the Lord. Hezekiah had the altars, pagan shrines, and Asherah poles torn down throughout Judah. He listened to the advice of Isaiah, God's prophet, and modeled a life of prayer and dependence on God in difficult circumstances. Josiah went even further than Hezekiah in his zeal to renew proper worship of God. After finding a lost scroll containing God's laws, he led a complete purge of pagan religious traditions from the land, even traveling north to destroy and defile the altars in Dan and Bethel that Jeroboam had built for the northern kingdom centuries earlier. This godly leadership was the exception rather than the rule, and it wasn't enough to prevent God's judgment of exile for Judah's many sins.

■ Prophets. While Elijah and Elisha performed powerful signs that demonstrated God's sovereignty early in the history of the splintered nations, God also sent many other prophets with powerful words declaring his reign and calling his people back to himself. Many of them wrote their prophecies down for us. These prophets were sent to speak to kings, officials, religious leaders, and even foreign nations, but their words are also for us. We need to constantly listen to the voices of the prophets to ensure that we are truly following God with all of our hearts, and heed their call to return to him if we have strayed. Israel and Judah didn't listen to the messages of the prophets. Will you?

■ Empires and Alliances. This was a period in history when great empires dominated the world landscape and executed great campaigns to conquer and subdue as much of the known world as they could manage. Assyria, Egypt, and ultimately Babylon were the major powers who vied with one another to dominate, and all of them harassed and subjugated Israel and Judah at least once. At various points in their history, Israel and Judah attempted to forge alliances with one of these world powers to protect them from other enemies, forgetting that God was their strength and protection. Ultimately, God was the one who gave these empires their power, and he used them as his hand of judgment against his rebellious people. The prophets remind us that it was God's power, not the power of these nations, that was behind the Exile. And God would restore his people by his own power as well.

Landscape with the Prophet Elijah in the Desert, by Abraham Bloemaert

■ **Temple Worship.** A central theme in the history of Israel and Judah is the proper worship of God in his Temple. Right after the nations split, the northern kingdom formally rejected the Temple by constructing their own shrines and idols to avoid having to go down to Judah to worship. This rejection is consistently mentioned throughout the history of the northern kingdom, as each king continued to follow "the example of Jeroboam son of Nebat, who had led Israel to sin" (see, e.g., 1 Kgs 22:52). Judah also neglected and profaned the Temple, occasionally renovating and renewing it, but never being fully committed to the true worship of God as he required. When Ezekiel was in exile, he saw the glory of the Lord departing the Temple, and the final image of this long, sad period in the history of God's people is the Temple being completely destroyed by the conquering armies of Babylon. God's judgment was severe, but he hadn't forgotten his people.

BOOKS IN THIS SECTION

1 KINGS

AUTHOR: Unknown

AUDIENCE: The people of Israel

PURPOSE: To contrast the lives of those who live for God and those who refuse to do so through the history of the kings of Israel and Judah

SETTING: The once great nation of Israel turned into a land divided, not only physically, but also spiritually

SPECIAL FEATURE: The books of 1 and 2 Kings were originally one book.

2 KINGS

AUTHOR: Unknown

AUDIENCE: The people of Israel

PURPOSE: To demonstrate the fate that awaits all who refuse to make God their true leader

SETTING: The once-united nation of Israel has been divided into two kingdoms for over a century.

2 CHRONICLES

AUTHOR: Ezra, according to Jewish tradition

AUDIENCE: The exiles who returned from captivity

DATE WRITTEN: c. 430 B.C., recording events that had occurred much earlier

PURPOSE: To unify the nation around the worship of God by showing his true standard for judging kings. The righteous kings of Judah and the religious festivals under their rule are highlighted, and the sins of the evil kings are exposed.

SPECIAL FEATURES: Parallels 1 and 2 Kings and serves as their commentary. Written after the Exile from a priestly point of view, 2 Chronicles highlights the importance of the Temple and the religious festivals in Judah.

ISAIAH

AUTHOR: The prophet Isaiah son of Amoz

PURPOSE: To call the nation of Judah back to God and to tell of God's salvation through the Messiah

SETTING: Isaiah is speaking and writing mainly from Jerusalem

SPECIAL FEATURES: Many of the prophecies in Isaiah contain predictions that foretell a soon-to-occur event and a distant future event at the same time.

JEREMIAH

AUTHOR: Jeremiah

AUDIENCE: Judah and its capital city, Jerusalem

PURPOSE: To urge God's people to turn from their sins and back to God

SETTING: Jeremiah ministered under Judah's last five kings. The nation was sliding quickly toward destruction and was eventually conquered by Babylon in 586 B.C.

SPECIAL FEATURES: The book is a combination of history, poetry, and biography. Jeremiah often used symbolism to communicate his message.

EZEKIEL

AUTHOR: Ezekiel son of Buzi, a Zadokite priest

AUDIENCE: The Jews in captivity in Babylonia

PURPOSE: To announce God's judgment on Israel and other nations and to foretell the eventual salvation of God's people

SETTING: Ezekiel was a younger contemporary of Jeremiah, but he was already exiled to Babylon in 597 B.C., and he prophesied from there.

HOSEA

AUTHOR: Hosea son of Beeri ("Hosea" means "salvation")

AUDIENCE: The people of Israel (the northern kingdom)

PURPOSE: To illustrate God's love for his sinful people

SPECIAL FEATURES: Hosea employs many images from daily life: God is depicted as a husband, lion, leopard, bear, dew, rain, moth, and others; Israel is pictured as a wife, sick person, vine, grapes, early fruit, olive tree, woman in childbirth, oven, morning mist, chaff, and smoke, to name a few.

AMOS

AUTHOR: Amos

AUDIENCE: The people of Israel (the northern kingdom)

PURPOSE: To pronounce God's judgment upon Israel, the northern kingdom, for its complacency, idolatry, and oppression of the poor

SETTING: The wealthy people of Israel were enjoying peace and prosperity. They were quite complacent and were oppressing the poor, even selling them into slavery. Soon, however, Israel would be conquered by Assyria, and the rich would themselves become slaves.

JONAH

AUTHOR: Jonah son of Amittai

AUDIENCE: All the people of Israel

PURPOSE: To show the extent of God's grace—the message of salvation is for all people

SPECIAL FEATURE: This book is different from the other prophetic books because it tells the story of the prophet and does not center on his prophecies. In fact, only one verse summarizes his message to the people of Nineveh (Jon 3:4).

For book information on **PSALMS** and **PROVERBS**, see the introduction to United Monarchy, pp. 430-431.

For book information on **DANIEL**, see the introduction to Exile, p. 1092.

MICAH

AUTHOR: Micah, a native of Moresheth, near Gath, about 20 miles southwest of Jerusalem

AUDIENCE: The people of Israel (the northern kingdom) and of Judah (the southern kingdom)

PURPOSE: To warn God's people that judgment is coming and to offer pardon to all who repent

SPECIAL FEATURE: This is a beautiful example of classical Hebrew poetry. There are three parts, each beginning with "Attention!" or "Listen" (Mic 1:2; 3:1; 6:1) and closing with a promise.

NAHUM

AUTHOR: Nahum

AUDIENCE: The people of Nineveh and of Judah (the southern kingdom)

PURPOSE: To pronounce God's judgment on Assyria and to comfort Judah with this truth

SETTING: This particular prophecy took place after the fall of Thebes in 663 B.C. (see Nah 3:8-10).

HABAKKUK

AUTHOR: Habakkuk

AUDIENCE: The people of Judah (the southern kingdom)

PURPOSE: To show that God is still in control of the world despite the apparent triumph of evil

SETTING: Babylon was becoming the dominant world power and Judah would soon feel Babylon's destructive force.

ZEPHANIAH

AUTHOR: Zephaniah

AUDIENCE: The people of Judah (the southern kingdom)

PURPOSE: To shake the people of Judah out of their complacency and urge them to return to God

SETTING: King Josiah of Judah was attempting to reverse the evil trends set by the two previous kings of Judah—Manasseh and Amon. Josiah was able to extend his influence because no strong superpower was dominating the world at that time (Assyria was declining rapidly). Zephaniah's prophecy may have been the motivating factor in Josiah's reform. Zephaniah was a contemporary of Jeremiah.

MEGATHEMES

■ **Evil Kings/Good Kings.** All the kings of Israel and Judah were told to obey God and to govern according to his laws. But their tendency to abandon God's commands and to worship other gods led them to change the religion and government to meet their personal desires. This neglect of God's law led to their downfall. Only a handful of kings in Judah broke this pattern, and they spent most of their time trying to undo the great evil that had been done by their predecessors. Although the evil kings were the ones who led the people into sin, the priests, princes, heads of families, and military leaders all had to cooperate with the evil plans and practices in order for them to be carried out. We cannot discharge our responsibility to obey God by blaming our leaders. We are responsible to know God's Word and obey it.

■ **Other Gods.** Although the Israelites had God's law and experienced his presence among them, they became attracted to other gods. When this happened, their hearts became cold to God's law, resulting in the ruin of families and government, and eventually leading to the destruction of the nation. Through the years, the people took on the false qualities of the false gods they worshiped. They became cruel, power-hungry, and sexually perverse. We tend to become what we worship. Unless we serve the true God, we will become slaves to whatever takes his rightful place.

■ **The Prophet's Message.** The prophet's responsibility was to confront and correct any deviation from God's law. Elijah was a bolt of judgment against Israel. His messages and miracles were a warning to the evil and rebellious kings and people. And many prophets followed after him, all with the message that the people and the king needed to turn away from their evil ways and return to loving and serving the true God alone. Today we have the Bible, teaching from our pastors, and wise counsel from fellow believers as prophetic warnings to us. Anyone who points out how we are deviating from God's Word is a blessing to us. Changing our lives in order to obey God and get back on track often takes painful discipline and hard work, but it is better than the alternative.

■ **Sin and Repentance.** Each king had God' commands, a priest or prophet, and the lessons of the past to draw him back to God. All the people had the same resources. Whenever they repented and returned to God, God heard their prayers and forgave them, no matter how far away from him they had strayed. God hears and forgives us when we pray—if we are willing to trust him and turn from sin. Our desire to forsake our sin must be heartfelt and sincere. Then he will give us a fresh start and a desire to continue living for him.

■ **Superficial Religion.** Although many people had abandoned real faith in God, they still pretended to be religious. They were carrying on superficial religious exercises instead of having spiritual integrity and obedience toward God. Merely participating in ceremony or ritual falls short of true religion. Don't settle for impressing others with external rituals when God wants heartfelt obedience and commitment.

■ **Reform.** Although idolatry and injustice were common, some kings turned to God and led the people in spiritual revival—renewing their commitment to God and reforming their society. Revival included the destruction of idols, obedience to the law, and the restoration of the Temple. We must constantly commit ourselves to obeying God. We are never secure in what others have done for us. Believers in each generation must dedicate themselves to the task of carrying out God's will in their own lives.

■ **God's Patience.** God told his people that if they obeyed him, they would live successfully; if they disobeyed, they would be judged and destroyed. God had been patient with the people for hundreds of years. He sent many prophets to guide them. And he gave ample warning of coming destruction. But even God's patience has limits. God is also patient with us. He gives us many chances to hear his message, turn from sin, and believe in him. His patience does not mean he is indifferent to how we live, nor does it mean we can ignore his warnings. His patience should make us want to come to him now.

■ **Judgment.** After the nation split, the northern kingdom lasted 209 years before the Assyrians destroyed it; Judah lasted 345 years before the Babylonians took Jerusalem. After repeated warnings to his people, God used these evil nations as instruments of his justice. The consequences of rejecting God's commands and purpose for our lives are severe. He will not ignore unbelief or rebellion. We must believe in him and accept Christ's sacrificial death on our behalf, or we will be judged also.

■ **Salvation.** Because God's judgment on sin is sure, we need a savior. No person or nation can be saved without God's help. The prophets often spoke about God's coming salvation for his people, especially through the coming Messiah. All who trust God can be freed from their sin and restored to him through the perfect sacrifice of Christ. He died to save us from our sin; we cannot save ourselves. He is willing to save all who turn from their sin and come to him, but salvation is from God alone. No amount of good works, however sincere, can earn it.

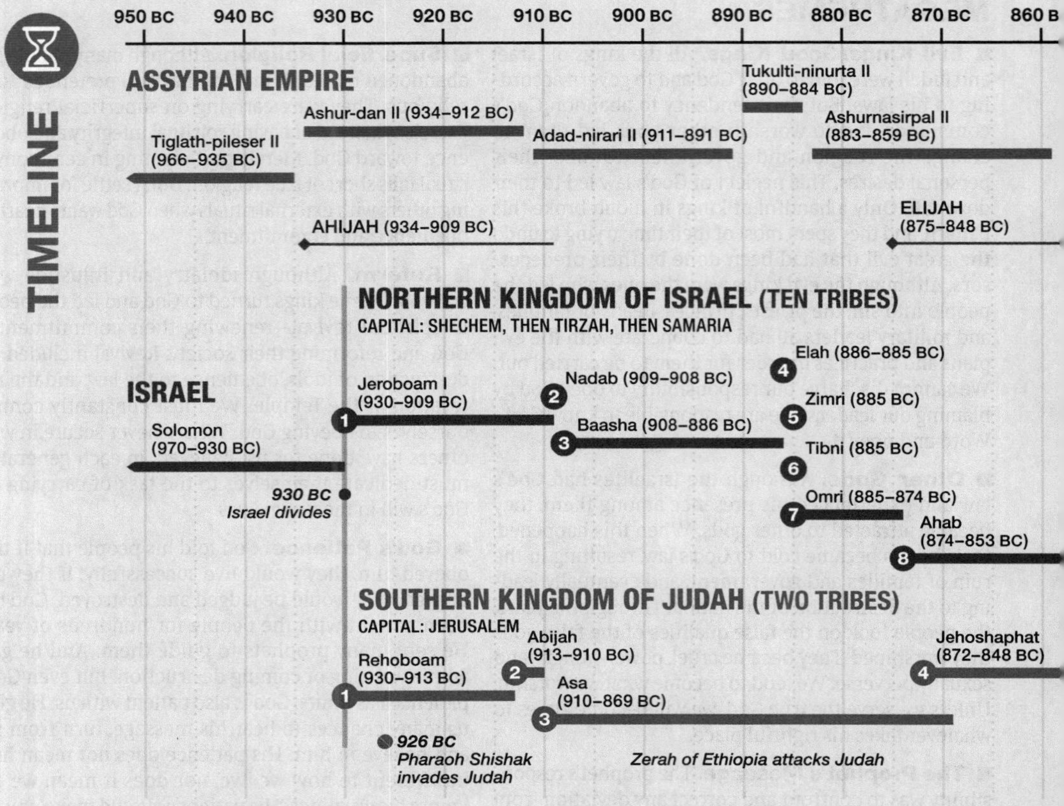

TIMELINE

1 Jeroboam I (22 years) Fortified a capital city (Shechem), set up two gold calf-idols, led the nation into sin, allowed anyone to be a priest (*1 Kgs 11:26–14:31; 2 Chr 10:12–13:20*).

2 Nadab (2 years) (*1 Kgs 15:25-28*)

3 Baasha (24 years) Led people into idol worship (*1 Kgs 15:27–16:7; 2 Chr 16:1-6*).

4 Elah (2 years) Continued idol worship (*1 Kgs 16:6-14*).

5 Zimri (7 days) (*1 Kgs 16:9-20*)

6 Tibni (4 years) (*1 Kgs 16:21-22*)

7 Omri (12 years) Built the capital city of Samaria, had great military power, but continued to lead Israel into idolatry (*1 Kgs 16:16-28*).

8 Ahab (22 years) Married Jezebel (a non-Jew and extremely wicked woman), worshiped Baal, and suffered three years of famine caused by his consistent disobedience to God (*1 Kgs 16:28–22:40; 2 Chr 18:1-34*).

NOTE: The total years of reign sometimes include years of co-regency.

1 Rehoboam (17 years) Built many fortified cities, strengthened the economy (despite the tribute paid to Egypt), followed God for three years, but then set up idols and shrines to foreign gods (*1 Kgs 11:43–14:31; 2 Chr 9:31–12:16*).

2 Abijah (3 years) Despite his wickedness, he called for God's help to win the battle against Israel (*1 Kgs 11:31–15:8; 2 Chr 13:1–14:1*).

3 Asa (41 years) Destroyed pagan altars and rebuilt altar of God, built fortified cities, gained much wealth from plunder of foreign conquest, removed the queen mother for worshiping Asherah, led the people to worship God with their hearts, provided peace on home soil, was greatly loved and given a beautiful funeral (*1 Kgs 15:8-24; 2 Chr 14:1–16:14*).

4 Jehoshaphat (25 years) Arranged for the marriage of his son to a daughter of Ahab (who made trouble later on), had a strong military (kept troops in cities of Israel his father had conquered), collected tribute from the Philistines, worshiped the Lord and destroyed idols, established education, and appointed judges and courts (*1 Kgs 15:24; 22:4-50; 2 Chr 17:1–21:1*).

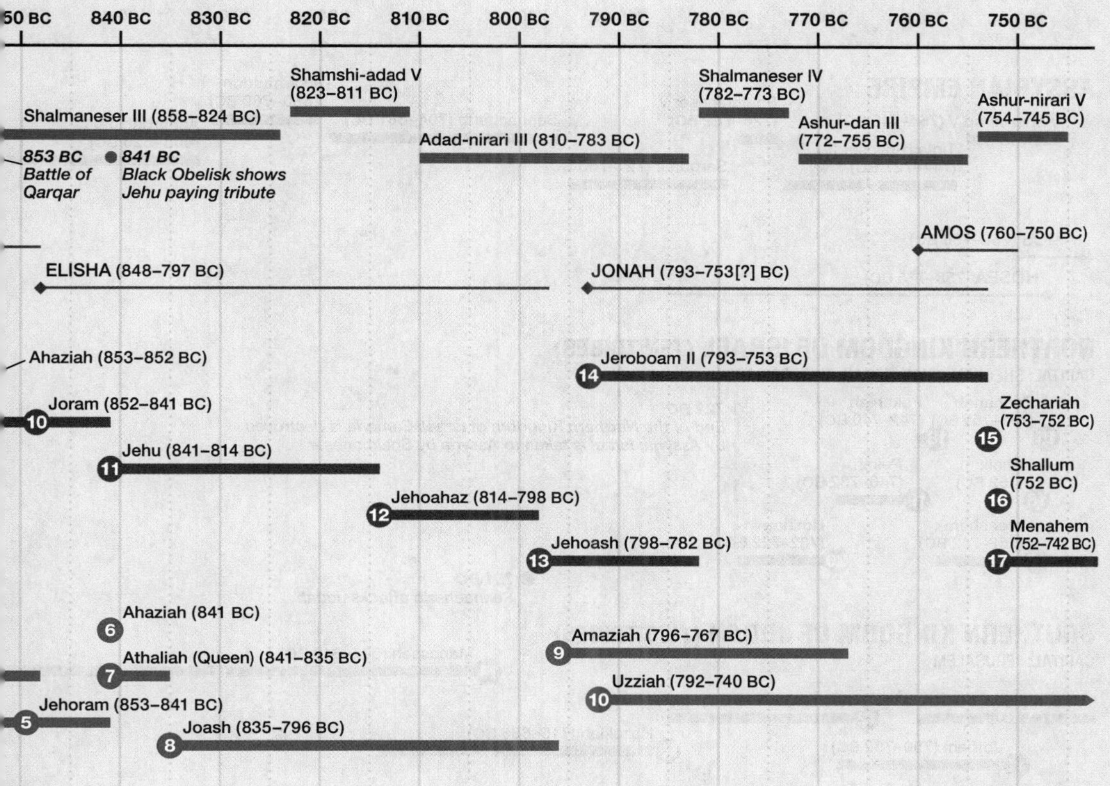

❾ **Ahaziah** (2 years) Proposed a joint trade venture with Judah (*1 Kgs 22:40—2 Kgs 1:18; 2 Chr 20:35-37*).

❿ **Joram** (12 years) Suffered famine and war during most of his reign (*2 Kgs 3:1–9:24; 2 Chr 22:5-7*).

⓫ **Jehu** (28 years) Was responsible for the deaths of Joram (king of Israel), Ahaziah (king of Judah), and Jezebel (wicked mother of Joram); destroyed the priests and temples of Baal but did not consistently follow God (*2 Kgs 9:1–10:36; 2 Chr 22:7-9*).

⓬ **Jehoahaz** (17 years) Evil reign included worship of Asherah, usually called "detestable" (*2 Kgs 13:1-9*).

⓭ **Jehoash** (16 years) Even though he was evil, he recognized the authority of Elisha as a prophet of God (*2 Kgs 13:10–14:16; 2 Chr 25:17-24*).

⓮ **Jeroboam II** (41 years) Very evil but politically powerful; his nation enjoyed economic prosperity and military peace (*2 Kgs 14:16-29*).

⓯ **Zechariah** (6 months) Encouraged idol worship (*2 Kgs 14:29–15:11*).

⓰ **Shallum** (1 month) (*2 Kgs 15:10-15*)

⓱ **Menahem** (10 years) Imposed heavy taxes and oppressed his people (*2 Kgs 15:14-22*).

❺ **Jehoram** (8 years) Married a wicked daughter of Ahab, compelled the people to worship idols, and killed all his brothers (*2 Kgs 8:16-24; 2 Chr 21:1-20*).

❻ **Ahaziah** (1 year) Friend of Joram of Israel (*2 Kgs 8:24–9:29; 2 Chr 22:1-10*).

❼ **Athaliah (Queen)** (6 years) Killed her grandchildren except Joash, who was hidden by his nurse for six years; ravaged the Temple to furnish Baal's temple (*2 Kgs 11:1-20; 2 Chr 22:10–23:21*).

❽ **Joash** (40 years) Was crowned king at the age of seven by Jehoiada (the high priest), promoted peace and prosperity, repaired the Temple, and smashed the altars to Baal; abandoned God after Jehoiada died, and even had Jehoiada's son killed (*2 Kgs 11:2–12:21; 2 Chr 22:11–24:27*).

❾ **Amaziah** (29 years) Was basically good but did not completely wipe out idol worship; organized and mustered the army (*2 Kgs 14:1-20; 2 Chr 25:1-28*).

❿ **Uzziah** (52 years) Rebuilt a city named Elath, owned many farms and vineyards, constructed water reservoirs and fortified towers, reorganized the army (so powerful that his fame spread to Egypt), but violated God's laws for priestly function—so God struck him with leprosy (*2 Kgs 15:1-7; 2 Chr 26:1-23*).

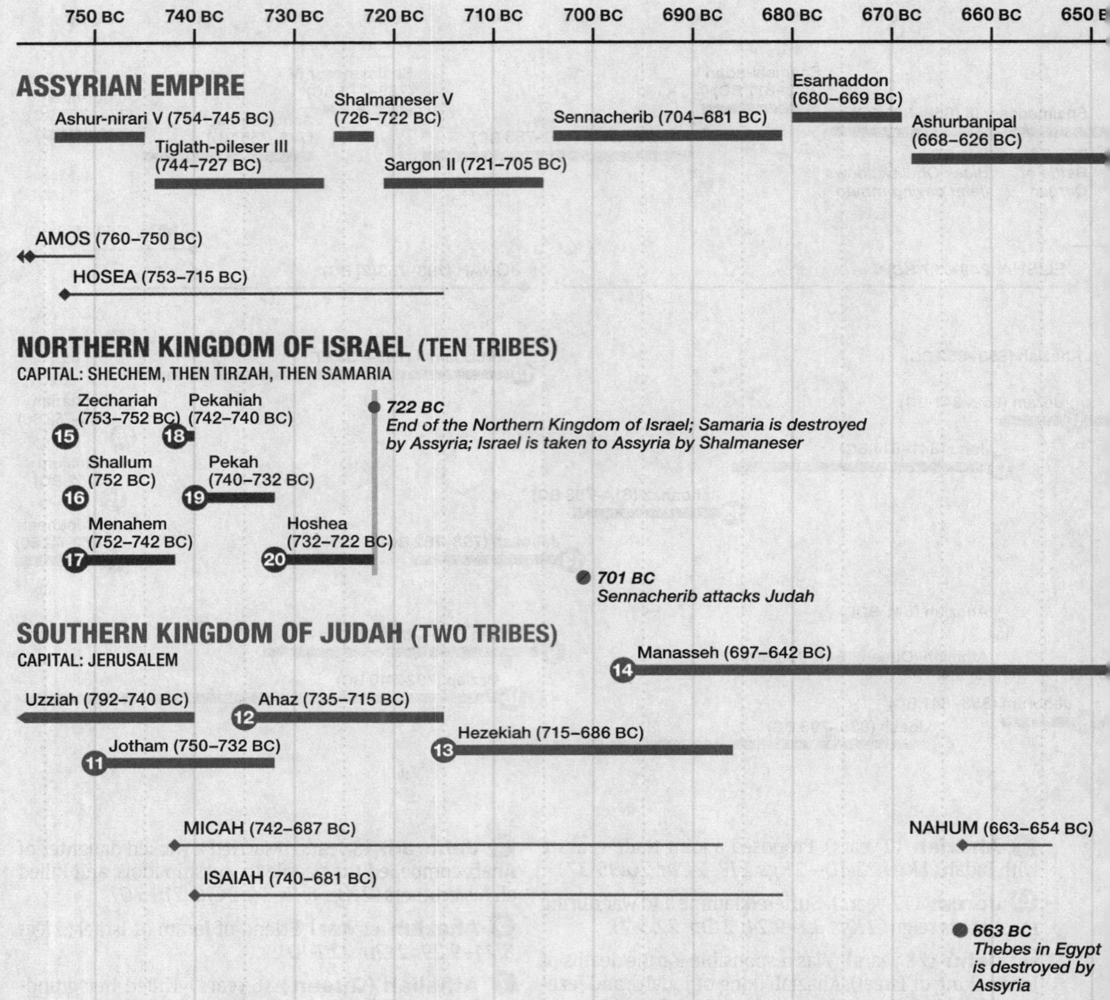

15 Zechariah (6 months) Encouraged idol worship (*2 Kgs 14:29–15:11*).

16 Shallum (1 month) (*2 Kgs 15:10-15*)

17 Menahem (10 years) Imposed heavy taxes and oppressed his people (*2 Kgs 15:14-22*).

18 Pekahiah (2 years) Continued idol worship (*2 Kgs 15:22-26*).

19 Pekah (8 years) During his reign many of the people were taken captive to Assyria (*2 Kgs 15:25-31; 2 Chr 28:5-8*).

20 Hoshea (9 years) Suffered heavy taxation by Assyria and eventual conquest—bringing about Israelite captivity and resettlement of foreigners in Israel (*2 Kgs 15:30; 17:1-6*).

11 Jotham (16 years) Rebuilt the upper gate of the Temple, rebuilt walls and cities, but still permitted idol worship (*2 Kgs 15:32-38; 2 Chr 27:1-9*).

12 Ahaz (16 years) Sacrificed his own son to pagan gods, nailed the Temple doors shut (*2 Kgs 16:1-20; 2 Chr 28:1-27*).

13 Hezekiah (29 years) Was a devoted follower of God, reopened the Temple doors, purified the Temple, reinstated priests and their duties, organized an orchestra to aid worship, destroyed idols (including the bronze serpent of Moses because people had begun to worship it), celebrated the Passover and even invited people who were living in the north to participate, constructed large public waterworks, was given 15 extra years of life, foolishly showed Babylonian messengers the wealth in the Temple (*2 Kgs 16:20; 18:1–20:21; 2 Chr 29:1–32:33*).

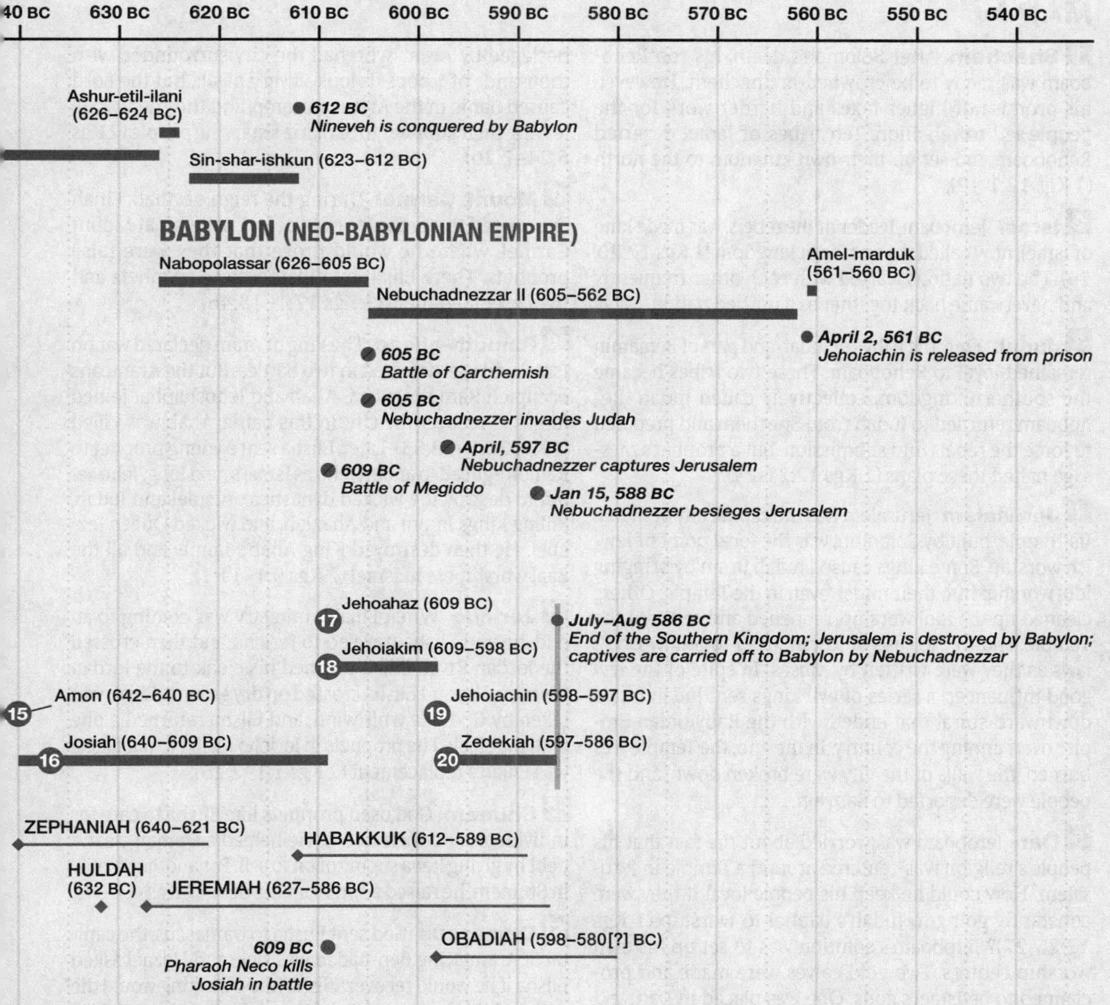

14 Manasseh (55 years) Rebuilt all the pagan shrines, sacrificed one of his own sons, practiced sorcery, set up an idol right in the Temple, murdered many of his own people, but repented during his Assyrian captivity (*2 Kgs 21:1-18; 2 Chr 33:1-20*).

15 Amon (2 years) (*2 Kgs 21:18-26; 2 Chr 33:20-25*)

16 Josiah (31 years) Loved God with all his heart, repaired the Temple, found a lost scroll of the law (he promised to obey it, thus God delayed destruction for Judah until after his death), personally oversaw the major project of destroying idol shrines, reinstated the priests of God, celebrated the Passover with greater zeal than had been since Samuel's day, was greatly loved by his people (*2 Kgs 21:26–23:30; 2 Chr 33:25–35:27*).

17 Jehoahaz (3 months) Jailed and taken to Egypt, where he died (*2 Kgs 23:30-34; 2 Chr 36:1-4*).

18 Jehoiakim (11 years) Burned part of God's word given to Jeremiah, was a puppet king for Egypt and then Babylon, watched gold and articles taken from the Temple to Babylon, saw first exile (in which Daniel was taken) (*2 Kgs 23:34–24:6; 2 Chr 36:4-8*).

19 Jehoiachin (3 months) Saw next exile to Babylon (*2 Kgs 24:6-15; 25:27-30; 2 Chr 36:8-10*).

20 Zedekiah (11 years) Saw the Temple burned and Jerusalem destroyed, was tortured and carried away in the final exile to Babylon (*2 Kgs 24:17–25:21; 2 Chr 36:10-21*).

MAP ▶

1 Shechem After Solomon's death, his son Rehoboam was ready to be crowned in Shechem. However, his promise of higher taxes and harder work for the people led to rebellion. Ten tribes of Israel deserted Rehoboam and set up their own kingdom to the north (1 Kgs 12:1-19).

2 Israel Jeroboam, leader of the rebels, was made king of Israel, now called the northern kingdom (1 Kgs 12:20, 25). The two nations warred with each other frequently and never came back together as a unified nation.

3 Judah Only the tribes of Judah and part of Benjamin remained loyal to Rehoboam. These two tribes became the southern kingdom, collectively called Judah. Rehoboam returned to Judah from Shechem and prepared to force the rebels into submission, but a prophet's message halted these plans (1 Kgs 12:21-24).

4 Jerusalem Jerusalem was the capital city of Judah. Its Temple, built by Solomon, was the focal point of Jewish worship. Some kings caused Judah to sin by bringing idol worship into their midst, even in the Temple. Others cleaned up the idol worship, reopened and restored the Temple, and in the case of Josiah, tried to follow God's laws as they were written by Moses. In spite of the few good influences, a series of evil kings sent Judah into a downward spiral that ended with the Babylonian Empire overrunning the country. In the end, the Temple was burned, the walls of the city were broken down, and the people were deported to Babylon.

5 Dan Jeroboam was worried about the fact that his people's religion was centered around a Temple in Jerusalem. How could he keep his people loyal if they were constantly going to Judah's capital to worship (1 Kgs 12:26-27)? Jeroboam's solution was to set up his own worship centers. Two gold calves were made and proclaimed to be Israel's gods. One was placed in Dan, and the people were told that they could go there instead of to Jerusalem to worship (1 Kgs 12:28-29).

6 Bethel The other gold calf was placed in Bethel. The people of the northern kingdom had two convenient locations for worship in their own country, but their sin displeased God. Jeroboam's plan might have been politically savvy, but it was an insidious sin that led to Israel's eventual exile as judgment from God.

7 Tirzah Jeroboam moved the capital city of the northern kingdom to Tirzah (1 Kgs 14:17), where it remained until his grandson Baasha was overthrown by his general Omri.

8 Samaria When Omri became king, he bought a hill on which he built a new capital city, Samaria. Omri's son, Ahab, became the most wicked king of Israel. His wife, Jezebel, worshiped Baal. Ahab erected a temple to Baal in Samaria (1 Kgs 16:23-34). Later, Samaria was besieged by Aram, who had the city surrounded with thousands of troops. It looked very bleak, but the Lord caused panic in the Aramean camp, and the enemy ran, leaving their supplies to Samaria's starving people (2 Kgs 6:24–7:20).

9 Mount Carmel During the reign of Ahab, Elijah challenged the prophets of Baal and Asherah at Mount Carmel, where he would prove that they were false prophets. There Elijah humiliated these prophets and then executed them (1 Kgs 17:1–18:46).

10 Ramoth-gilead The king of Aram declared war on Israel and was defeated in two battles. But the Arameans occupied Ramoth-gilead. Ahab and Jehoshaphat joined forces to recover the city. In this battle, Ahab was killed (1 Kgs 20:1–22:53). Later, Elisha sent a young prophet to Ramoth-gilead to anoint Jehu as Israel's next king. Jehu set out to destroy the wicked dynasties of Israel and Judah, killing kings Joram and Ahaziah, and wicked Queen Jezebel. He then destroyed King Ahab's family and all the Baal worshipers in Israel (2 Kgs 9:1–11:1).

11 Jericho When Elijah's ministry was coming to an end, he and Elisha traveled to Jericho and then crossed the Jordan River. Elijah touched his cloak to the Jordan River, and he and Elisha crossed on dry ground. Elijah was taken by God in a whirlwind, and Elisha returned alone with the cloak. The prophets in Jericho realized that Elisha was Elijah's replacement (2 Kgs 1:1–2:25).

12 Shunem God used prophets like Elisha to care for individuals and their needs. He helped a woman clear a debt by giving her a supply of oil to sell. For another family in Shunem, he raised a son from the dead (2 Kgs 4:1-37).

13 Damascus God sent Elisha to Damascus, the capital of Aram. King Ben-hadad was sick, and Hazael asked Elisha if he would recover. Elisha knew the king would die and told this to Hazael. But Hazael then murdered Ben-hadad, making himself king. Later, Israel and Judah joined forces to fight this new Aramean threat (2 Kgs 8:1-29).

14 Assyria God's patience with the northern kingdom of Israel had worn out, and his chosen instrument of judgment was the powerful Assyrian Empire. Assyria had been the dominant world power for most of the time since Israel and Judah split into two nations, but within a few generations after they conquered Israel and severely threatened Judah, their power began to fade and they were replaced with a new world power.

15 Babylon Babylon quickly rose to prominence on the world scene, crushing the previously dominant Assyrian Empire and expanding their own new empire rapidly. The Babylonians brought their armies and threatened Jerusalem several times, carrying off captives twice, before ultimately destroying Jerusalem and the Temple, sending Judah into exile, in 586 B.C.

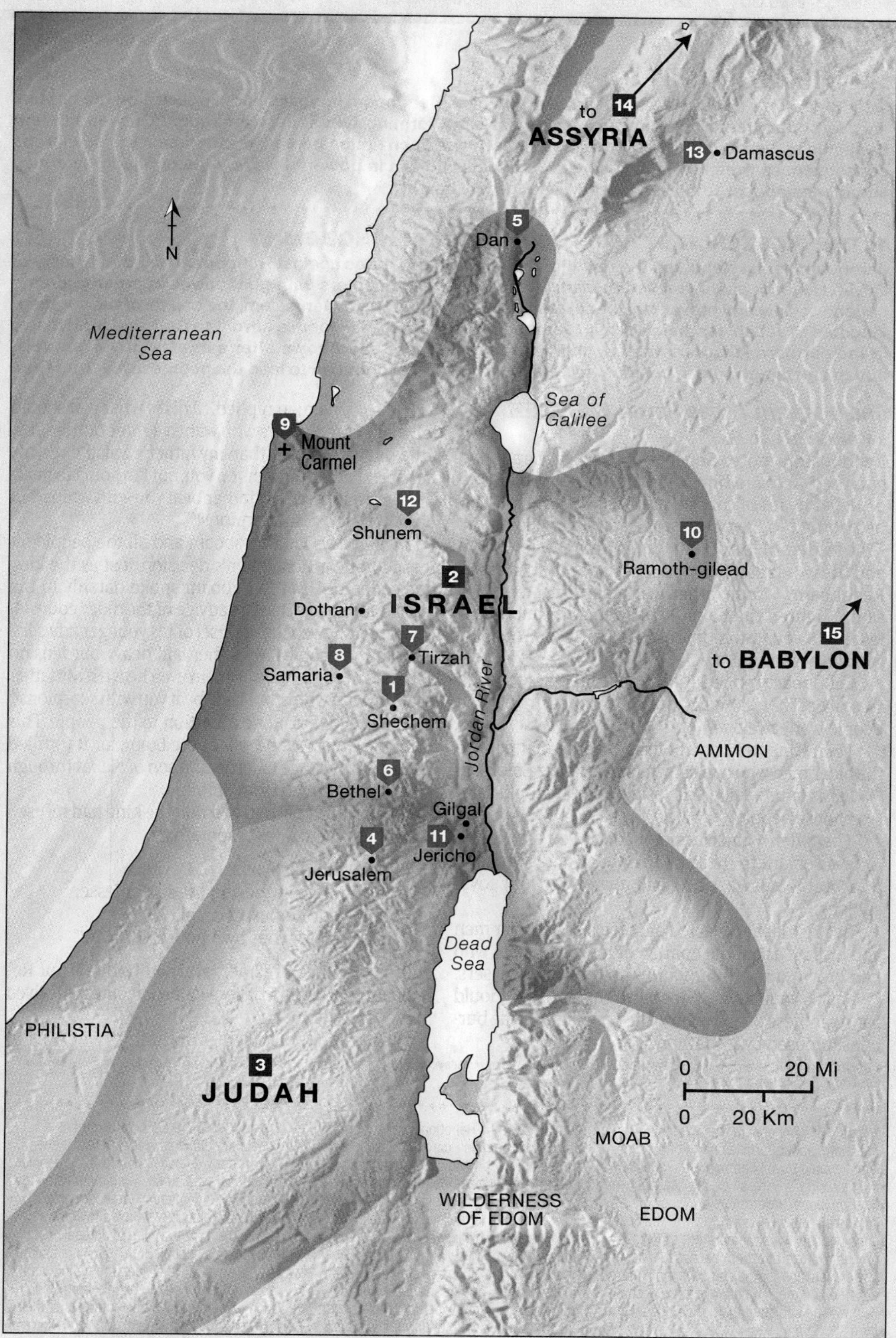
to
14
ASSYRIA
13
Damascus
N
5
Dan
Mediterranean
Sea
Sea of
Galilee
9
Mount
Carmel
12
Shunem
10
Ramoth-gilead
2
ISRAEL
Dothan
7
Tirzah
8
Samaria
15
to BABYLON
1
Shechem
Jordan River
AMMON
6
Bethel
Gilgal
11
Jericho
4
Jerusalem
Dead
Sea
PHILISTIA
3
JUDAH
0
20 Mi
0
20 Km
MOAB
WILDERNESS
OF EDOM
EDOM

A. The Kingdom Divides

After Solomon's death, the nation's unity crumbles. Rehoboam imposes harsh policies on the people, and Jeroboam leads the northern tribes in revolt, forming two separate nations. Only Judah and Benjamin stayed loyal to Solomon's heir Rehoboam. Each nation begins to experience the disastrous consequences from having evil kings. God deals with sin in powerful ways. Although judgment may sometimes appear to be slow, God will judge evil harshly.

1. THE FIRST DYNASTY OF THE NORTHERN KINGDOM

Jeroboam son of Nebat led the revolt of the ten northern tribes against Rehoboam and the dynasty of David. He immediately moved to create his own worship centers with gold calves in order to create national loyalty and prevent the people of Israel from returning to Jerusalem, the capital of the southern kingdom of Judah, for their worship. Jeroboam was condemned for this affront to God, and his dynasty in the northern kingdom was cut short; his son would be overthrown after a brief reign. Meanwhile, Judah and Israel were in conflict, and the kings in Judah continued to lead the people away from God.

The Northern Tribes Revolt PARALLEL

1 KINGS 12:1-20

930 BC

Israel divides into two nations

Rehoboam went to Shechem, where all Israel had gathered to make him king. 2When Jeroboam son of Nebat heard of this, he returned from Egypt,* for he had fled to Egypt to escape from King Solomon. 3The leaders of Israel summoned him, and Jeroboam and the whole assembly of Israel went to speak with Rehoboam. 4"Your father was a hard master," they said. "Lighten the harsh labor demands and heavy taxes that your father imposed on us. Then we will be your loyal subjects."

5Rehoboam replied, "Give me three days to think this over. Then come back for my answer." So the people went away.

6Then King Rehoboam discussed the matter with the older men who had counseled his father, Solomon. "What is your advice?" he asked. "How should I answer these people?"

7The older counselors replied, "If you are willing to be a servant to these people today and give them a favorable answer, they will always be your loyal subjects."

8But Rehoboam rejected the advice of the older men and instead asked the opinion of the young men who had grown up with him and were now his advisers. 9"What is your advice?" he asked them. "How should I answer these people who want me to lighten the burdens imposed by my father?"

10The young men replied, "This is what you should tell those complainers who want a lighter burden: 'My little finger is thicker than my father's waist! 11Yes, my father laid heavy burdens on you, but I'm going to make them even heavier! My father beat you with whips, but I will beat you with scorpions!'"

12Three days later Jeroboam and all the people returned to hear Rehoboam's decision, just as the king had ordered. 13But Rehoboam spoke harshly to the people, for he rejected the advice of the older counselors 14and followed the counsel of his younger advisers. He told the people, "My father laid heavy burdens on you, but I'm going to make them even heavier! My father beat you with whips, but I will beat you with scorpions!"

15So the king paid no attention to the people. This turn of events was the will of the LORD, for it fulfilled the LORD's message to Jeroboam son of Nebat through the prophet Ahijah from Shiloh.

16When all Israel realized that the king had refused to listen to them, they responded,

"Down with the dynasty of David!
  We have no interest in the son of Jesse.
Back to your homes, O Israel!
  Look out for your own house, O David!"

So the people of Israel returned home. 17But Rehoboam continued to rule over the Israelites who lived in the towns of Judah.

18King Rehoboam sent Adoniram,* who was in

1 Kgs 12:2 As in Greek version and Latin Vulgate (see also 2 Chr 10:2); Hebrew reads *he lived in Egypt.* **1 Kgs 12:18** As in some Greek manuscripts and Syriac version (see also 4:6; 5:14); Hebrew reads *Adoram.*

1 Kgs 12:1 Rehoboam was made king at Shechem, about 35 miles north of Jerusalem. It would have been normal to anoint the new king in Jerusalem, the capital city, but Rehoboam saw trouble brewing with Jeroboam and went north to try to maintain good relations with the northern tribes. He probably chose Shechem because it was an ancient location for making covenants (Josh 24:1). When the kingdom divided, Shechem became the capital of the northern kingdom for a short time (1 Kgs 12:25).

1 Kgs 12:6-14 Rehoboam asked for advice, but he didn't carefully assess what he was told. If he had, he would have realized that the advice offered by the elders was wiser than that of his peers. To evaluate advice, ask if it is realistic, workable, and consistent with biblical principles. Determine if the results of following the advice will give a positive solution or direction, make improvements, and be fair. Seek counsel from those who are wiser and more experienced. Advice is helpful only if it is consistent with God's standards.

1 Kgs 12:15-19 Both Jeroboam and Rehoboam did what was good for themselves, not what was good for their people. Rehoboam was harsh and did not listen to the people's demands; Jeroboam established new places of worship to keep his people from traveling to Jerusalem, Rehoboam's capital. Both actions backfired. Rehoboam's move divided the nation, and Jeroboam's turned the people from God. Good leaders put the best interests of their followers above their own. Making decisions only for yourself will backfire and cause you

charge of the labor force, to restore order, but the people of Israel stoned him to death. When this news reached King Rehoboam, he quickly jumped into his chariot and fled to Jerusalem.
[19]And to this day the northern tribes of Israel have refused to be ruled by a descendant of David.

[20]When the people of Israel learned of Jeroboam's return from Egypt, they called an assembly and made him king over all Israel. So only the tribe of Judah remained loyal to the family of David.

2 CHRONICLES 10:1-19

Rehoboam went to Shechem, where all Israel had gathered to make him king.
[2]When Jeroboam son of Nebat heard of this, he returned from Egypt, for he had fled to Egypt to escape from King Solomon.
[3]The leaders of Israel summoned him, and Jeroboam and all Israel went to speak with Rehoboam.
[4]"Your father was a hard master," they said. "Lighten the harsh labor demands and heavy taxes that your father imposed on us. Then we will be your loyal subjects."

[5]Rehoboam replied, "Come back in three days for my answer." So the people went away.

[6]Then King Rehoboam discussed the matter with the older men who had counseled his father, Solomon. "What is your advice?" he asked. "How should I answer these people?"

REHOBOAM

Settling for cheap imitations in exchange for the real thing is a poor way to live. In every area of his life, Rehoboam consistently traded away what was real for what was counterfeit. Given wise and unwise counsel by his advisers at his coronation, he chose to grab for power and control rather than take the counsel of those older and wiser to treat his people with kindness. These unwise decisions made him weaker rather than stronger. When Egypt attacked Judah and ransacked the Temple, he replaced the valuable gold shields with cheap bronze imitations. Although his position came from God, he chose to abandon God. • Throughout the early part of his reign, Rehoboam fluctuated between obeying God and going his own way. Outward appearances were kept up, but his inward attitudes were evil. Following in the tradition of David gave Rehoboam many opportunities for real greatness. Instead, he ended up with a divided and broken kingdom. • How much of real living have we traded away for the things that do not last? We trade healthy bodies for momentary excitement, personal integrity for fast-fading wealth, honesty for lies, God's wise guidance for our selfish ways. We sin when we willingly give little value to "the real thing" God has already given us. • Our counterfeit lives may fool some people, but they never fool God. Yet in spite of what he sees in us, God offers mercy. Are you a self-managed enterprise, counterfeit at best? Or have you placed yourself in God's care? Do the decisions you must make today need a second consideration in light of Rehoboam's example?

Strengths and accomplishments	• Fourth and last king of the united nation of Israel, but only for a short time • Fortified his kingdom and achieved a measure of popularity
Weaknesses and mistakes	• Followed unwise advice and divided his kingdom • Married foreign women, as his father, Solomon, had done • Abandoned the worship of God and allowed idolatry to flourish
Lessons from his life	• Thoughtless decisions often lead to exchanging what is most valuable for something of far less value • Every choice we make has real and long-lasting consequences
Vital statistics	• Where: Jerusalem • Occupation: King of the united kingdom of Israel and later of the southern kingdom of Judah • Relatives: Father: Solomon. Mother: Naamah. Wife: Maacah. Son: Abijah. • Contemporaries: Jeroboam, Shishak, Shemaiah
Key verse	"But when Rehoboam was firmly established and strong, he abandoned the Law of the LORD, and all Israel followed him in this sin" (2 Chr 12:1).

Rehoboam's story is told in 1 Kings 11:43–14:31 and 2 Chronicles 9:31–13:7. He is also mentioned in Matthew 1:7.

to lose more than if you had kept the welfare of others in mind.

1 Kgs 12:20 This marks the beginning of the division of the kingdom that lasted for centuries. Of Israel's 12 tribes, 10 followed Jeroboam and called their new nation Israel (the northern kingdom). Only the tribes of Judah and Benjamin remained loyal to Rehoboam and called their nation Judah (the southern kingdom). The kingdom did not split overnight. It was already dividing as early as the days of the judges because of tribal jealousies, especially between Ephraim, the most influential tribe of the north, and Judah, the chief tribe of the south.

Before the days of Saul and David, the religious center of Israel was located, for the most part, in the territory of Ephraim. When Solomon built the Temple, Jerusalem became the religious center of Israel. This eventually brought tribal rivalries to the breaking point. (For more information on tribal jealousies and how they affected Israel, see Judg 12:1ff; 2 Sam 2:4ff; 19:41-43.)

2 Chr 10:1-15 Following bad advice can cause disaster. Rehoboam lost the chance to rule a peaceful, united kingdom because he rejected the advice of Solomon's older counselors, preferring the counsel of his peers. Rehoboam made two errors in seeking advice: (1) He did not give extra consideration to the suggestions of those who knew the situation better than he, and (2) he did not ask God for wisdom to discern which was the better option.

It is easy to follow the advice of our peers because they often feel as we do. But their view may be limited. It is important to listen carefully to those who have more experience than we do—they can see the bigger picture.

2 Chr 10:2-3 Why was Jeroboam in Egypt? Ahijah the prophet had predicted that Israel would split in two and that Jeroboam would become king of the northern section. When Solomon learned of this prophecy, he tried to kill Jeroboam, and Jeroboam was forced to flee to Egypt (1 Kgs 11:26-40).

▸ 2 CHRONICLES 10:1-19 *(cont.)*

[7]The older counselors replied, "If you are good to
these people and do your best to please them and
give them a favorable answer, they will always be your
loyal subjects."
[8]But Rehoboam rejected the advice of the older
men and instead asked the opinion of the young men
who had grown up with him and were now his advisers. [9]"What is your advice?" he asked them. "How
should I answer these people who want me to lighten
the burdens imposed by my father?"
[10]The young men replied, "This is what you should
tell those complainers who want a lighter burden: 'My
little finger is thicker than my father's waist! [11]Yes,
my father laid heavy burdens on you, but I'm going
to make them even heavier! My father beat you with
whips, but I will beat you with scorpions!'"
[12]Three days later Jeroboam and all the people returned to hear Rehoboam's decision, just as the king
had ordered. [13]But Rehoboam spoke harshly to them,
for he rejected the advice of the older counselors [14]and
followed the counsel of his younger advisers. He told
the people, "My father laid* heavy burdens on you, but
I'm going to make them even heavier! My father beat
you with whips, but I will beat you with scorpions!"
[15]So the king paid no attention to the people. This
turn of events was the will of God, for it fulfilled the
LORD's message to Jeroboam son of Nebat through the
prophet Ahijah from Shiloh.
[16]When all Israel realized* that the king had refused to listen to them, they responded,

"Down with the dynasty of David!
We have no interest in the son of Jesse.
Back to your homes, O Israel!
Look out for your own house, O David!"

So all the people of Israel returned home. [17]But
Rehoboam continued to rule over the Israelites who
lived in the towns of Judah.
[18]King Rehoboam sent Adoniram,* who was in
charge of the labor force, to restore order, but the
people of Israel stoned him to death. When this news
reached King Rehoboam, he quickly jumped into his
chariot and fled to Jerusalem. [19]And to this day the
northern tribes of Israel have refused to be ruled by
a descendant of David.

Shemaiah's Prophecy PARALLEL ●●

1 KINGS 12:21-24 ●●

When Rehoboam arrived at Jerusalem, he mobilized
the men of Judah and the tribe of Benjamin—180,000
select troops—to fight against the men of Israel and
to restore the kingdom to himself.
[22]But God said to Shemaiah, the man of God, [23]"Say
to Rehoboam son of Solomon, king of Judah, and to all
the people of Judah and Benjamin, and to the rest of
the people, [24]'This is what the LORD says: Do not fight
against your relatives, the Israelites. Go back home,
for what has happened is my doing!'" So they obeyed
the message of the LORD and went home, as the LORD
had commanded.

2 CHRONICLES 11:1-4 ●●

When Rehoboam arrived at Jerusalem, he mobilized
the men of Judah and Benjamin—180,000 select
troops—to fight against Israel and to restore the kingdom to himself.
[2]But the LORD said to Shemaiah, the man of God,
[3]"Say to Rehoboam son of Solomon, king of Judah, and
to all the Israelites in Judah and Benjamin: [4]'This is
what the LORD says: Do not fight against your relatives.
Go back home, for what has happened is my doing!'"

2 Chr 10:14 As in Greek version and many Hebrew manuscripts (see also 1 Kgs 12:14); Masoretic Text reads *I will lay.* **2 Chr 10:16** As in Syriac version, Latin Vulgate, and many Hebrew manuscripts (see also 1 Kgs 12:16); Masoretic Text lacks *realized.* **2 Chr 10:18** Hebrew *Hadoram,* a variant spelling of Adoniram; compare 1 Kgs 4:6; 5:14; 12:18.

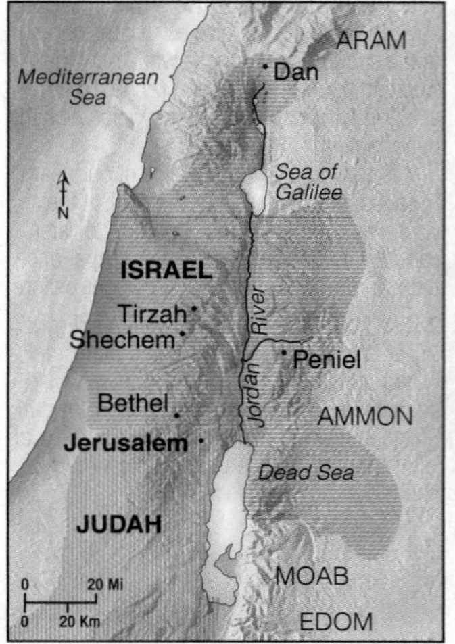

2 Chr 10:14 Rehoboam must have gotten an unbalanced picture of leadership from his father, Solomon. Apparently Rehoboam saw only the difficulty of leading the nation, not the opportunities. He mentioned only the harsher aspects of Solomon's rule, and he himself decided to be very harsh toward the people. As you discuss your responsibilities with your children, be sure that you temper words of complaint with words of joy. Otherwise you may sour their attitudes toward the work you do and those you serve.

◀ *THE KINGDOM DIVIDES*
Rehoboam's threat of heavier burdens caused a rebellion and divided the nation. Rehoboam ruled the southern kingdom; Jeroboam ruled the northern kingdom. Jeroboam set up idols in Dan and Bethel to discourage worship in Jerusalem. At the same time, Aram, Ammon, Moab, and Edom claimed independence from the divided nation.

2 Chr 10:16-19 In trying to have it all, Rehoboam lost almost everything. Motivated by greed and power, he pressed too hard and divided his kingdom. He didn't need more money or power because he had inherited the richest kingdom in the world. He didn't need more control because he was the king. His demands were based on selfishness rather than reason or spiritual discernment. Those who insist on having it all often wind up with little or nothing.

2 Chr 11:1 Rehoboam's foolishness divided his kingdom, and he tried to reunite it by force. True unity, however, cannot be forced—it must be the free response of willing hearts. If you want the loyalty of employees, children, or anyone else in your charge, win their respect through love instead of trying to gain their submission through force.

2 Chr 11:4 Why would God support this rebellion? It was part of the nation's punishment for turning away from God (1 Kgs

So they obeyed the message of the LORD and did not fight against Jeroboam.

Jeroboam Makes Gold Calves

1 KINGS 12:25-33

Jeroboam then built up the city of Shechem in the hill country of Ephraim, and it became his capital. Later he went and built up the town of Peniel.*

[26]Jeroboam thought to himself, "Unless I am careful, the kingdom will return to the dynasty of David.
[27]When these people go to Jerusalem to offer sacri-
fices at the Temple of the LORD, they will again give their allegiance to King Rehoboam of Judah. They will kill me and make him their king instead."

[28]So on the advice of his counselors, the king made two gold calves. He said to the people,* "It is too much trouble for you to worship in Jerusalem. Look, Israel, these are the gods who brought you out of Egypt!"

[29]He placed these calf idols in Bethel and in Dan—at
either end of his kingdom. [30]But this became a great
sin, for the people worshiped the idols, traveling as far north as Dan to worship the one there.

[31]Jeroboam also erected buildings at the pagan shrines and ordained priests from the common people—those who were not from the priestly tribe of
Levi. [32]And Jeroboam instituted a religious festival in
Bethel, held on the fifteenth day of the eighth month,* in imitation of the annual Festival of Shelters in Judah. There at Bethel he himself offered sacrifices to the calves he had made, and he appointed priests for
the pagan shrines he had made. [33]So on the fifteenth
day of the eighth month, a day that he himself had designated, Jeroboam offered sacrifices on the altar at Bethel. He instituted a religious festival for Israel, and he went up to the altar to burn incense.

Rehoboam Fortifies Judah

2 CHRONICLES 11:5-17

Rehoboam remained in Jerusalem and fortified various towns for the defense of Judah. [6]He built up Bethlehem, Etam, Tekoa, [7]Beth-zur, Soco, Adullam, [8]Gath,
Mareshah, Ziph, [9]Adoraim, Lachish, Azekah, [10]Zorah,
Aijalon, and Hebron. These became the fortified towns
of Judah and Benjamin. [11]Rehoboam strengthened

1 Kgs 12:25 Hebrew *Penuel,* a variant spelling of Peniel. **1 Kgs 12:28** Hebrew *to them.* **1 Kgs 12:32** This day of the ancient Hebrew lunar calendar occurred in late October or early November, exactly one month after the annual Festival of Shelters in Judah (see Lev 23:34).

TRIBAL JEALOUSIES

Although the kingdom of Israel was "united" under David and Solomon, the tensions between north and south were never resolved. The jealousy and animosity behind this civil war didn't begin with Rehoboam and Jeroboam but had its roots in the days of the judges, when the people were more interested in tribal loyalty than in national unity. Note how easily tension arose between Ephraim, the most prominent tribe in the north, and Judah, the prominent tribe of the south.

- Ephraim claimed the promises in Gen 48:17-22; 49:22-26 for its leadership role.
- Joshua, who conquered the Promised Land, was an Ephraimite (Num 13:8).
- Samuel, Israel's greatest judge, was from Ephraim (1 Sam 1:1ff).
- Ephraim allied with Ishbosheth in revolt against David, who was from the tribe of Judah (2 Sam 2:8-11).
- David, a shepherd from the tribe of Judah, became king over all Israel, including Ephraim, which no longer had a claim to leadership.
- Although David helped to smooth over the bad feelings, the heavy yoke under Solomon and Rehoboam led the northern tribes to the breaking point.

Such tension developed because Ephraim was the key tribe in the north. They resented Judah's role in leadership under David and resented that the nation's capital and center of worship were located in Jerusalem.

11:11). It may also have been God's way of saving Rehoboam's smaller kingdom from defeat. In doing so, God preserved David's line and kept intact his plan for the Messiah to be a descendant of David (see 2 Sam 7:16). When we see division, especially in a church that splits, we wonder what God would have us do. God desires unity, but while we should always work toward reconciliation, we must recognize that only God knows the future. He may allow a division in order to fulfill his greater purposes.

1 Kgs 12:28 All Jewish men were required to travel to the Temple three times each year (Deut 16:16), but Jeroboam set up his own worship centers and told his people it was too much trouble to travel all the way to Jerusalem. Those who obeyed Jeroboam were disobeying God. Some ideas, though practical, may include suggestions that lead you away from God. Don't let anyone talk you out of doing what is right by telling you that moral actions are not worth the effort. Do what God wants, no matter what the cost in time, energy, reputation, or resources.

1 Kgs 12:28-29 Calves were used as idols to symbolize fertility and strength. Pagan gods of the Canaanites were often depicted as standing on calves or bulls. Jeroboam shrewdly placed the gold calves in Bethel and Dan, strategic locations. Bethel was just 10 miles north of Jerusalem on the main road, enticing the citizens from the north to stop there instead of traveling the rest of the way to Jerusalem. Dan was the northernmost city in Israel, so people living in the north far from Jerusalem were attracted to its convenient location. As leader of the northern kingdom, Jeroboam wanted to establish his own worship centers; otherwise his people would make regular trips to Jerusalem, and his authority would be undermined. Soon this substitute religion had little in common with true faith in God.

1 Kgs 12:30 Jeroboam and his advisers did not learn from Israel's previous disaster with a gold calf (Exod 32). Perhaps they were ignorant, or maybe they knew about the event and decided to ignore it. Study the Bible to become aware of God's acts in history, and then apply the important lessons to your life. If you learn from the past, you will not face disaster as a result of repeating others' mistakes (Isa 42:23; 1 Cor 10:11).

1 Kgs 12:32-33 Early in Israel's history, the city of Bethel was a symbol of commitment to God because there Jacob had rededicated himself to God (Gen 28:16-22). But Jeroboam turned the city into Israel's chief religious center, intending it to compete with Jerusalem. Bethel's religion, however, centered on an idol, and this led to Israel's eventual downfall. Bethel developed a reputation as a wicked and idolatrous city because of the presence of this calf idol. The prophets Hosea and Amos recognized the sins of Bethel and condemned the city for its godless ways (Hos 4:15-17; 10:8; Amos 5:4-6).

▸ **2 CHRONICLES 11:5-17 *(cont.)***
their defenses and stationed commanders in them,
and he stored supplies of food, olive oil, and wine.
12 He also put shields and spears in these towns as a
further safety measure. So only Judah and Benjamin
remained under his control.
13 But all the priests and Levites living among the
northern tribes of Israel sided with Rehoboam. 14 The
Levites even abandoned their pasturelands and property and moved to Judah and Jerusalem, because Jeroboam and his sons would not allow them to serve the
LORD as priests. 15 Jeroboam appointed his own priests
to serve at the pagan shrines, where they worshiped the
goat and calf idols he had made. 16 From all the tribes of
Israel, those who sincerely wanted to worship the LORD,
the God of Israel, followed the Levites to Jerusalem,
where they could offer sacrifices to the LORD, the God
of their ancestors. 17 This strengthened the kingdom of
Judah, and for three years they supported Rehoboam
son of Solomon, for during those years they faithfully
followed in the footsteps of David and Solomon.

A Prophet Denounces Jeroboam

1 KINGS 13:1-34

At the LORD's command, a man of God from Judah
went to Bethel, arriving there just as Jeroboam was

2 Chr 11:13-14 Before the nation split, the center of worship was in Jerusalem, and people flocked there for the three great annual religious festivals. During the rest of the year, other worship services and rituals were conducted in the tribal territories by priests and Levites who lived throughout the land. They offered sacrifices, taught God's laws, and encouraged the people to continue to follow God and avoid pagan influences.

After the nation split, Jeroboam, the new king of Israel, saw these priests and Levites as threats to his new government because they retained loyalty to Jerusalem, now the capital of Judah. So he appointed his own priests, effectively banning the Levites from their duties and forcing them to move to the southern kingdom. Jeroboam's pagan priests encouraged idol worship. With the absence of spiritual leaders, the new northern kingdom was in danger of abandoning God.

2 Chr 11:16 These people obeyed God rather than Jeroboam. By their actions, they preserved their integrity and strengthened the southern kingdom. In the future, most of the people in the northern kingdom would go along with the evil designs of the kings, hoping to benefit by cooperating. Don't follow their example and rationalize away God's teachings in order to gain earthly reward.

JEROBOAM

Even clear warnings are hard to obey. The Bible is filled with stories of people who had direction from God and yet chose their own way out of stubborn selfishness. Jeroboam was a consistent example of this all-too-human trait. • During his construction activities, Solomon noticed young Jeroboam's natural leadership skills and made him a special project foreman. Shortly after this, God contacted Jeroboam through the prophet Ahijah. He told Jeroboam that God would punish David's dynasty by tearing the kingdom from Solomon's son and that Jeroboam would rule the 10 northern tribes. And God made it clear that the same fate would destroy Jeroboam's family if they refused to obey God. • When Rehoboam, Solomon's heir, took the throne, Jeroboam represented the people in demanding that the new king be more lenient than his father. Rehoboam's unwise choice to reject his people's request led to their rejecting him as king. Only Judah and Benjamin remained loyal to David's dynasty. The other 10 tribes made Jeroboam king. • Rather than seeing this fulfillment of God's promise as motivation to obey God, Jeroboam decided to do whatever he could to secure his position. He led his kingdom away from the God who had allowed him to reign by establishing an idol religion as an alternative to the true worship of God in the Temple. God had already warned him of the consequences of this action—his family was eventually wiped out. And Jeroboam set into motion events that would lead to the destruction of the northern kingdom. • Sin's consequences are guaranteed in God's Word, but the timing of those consequences is hard to predict. When we do something directly opposed to God's commands and there isn't immediate disaster, we are often fooled into believing we got away with disobedience. But Jeroboam's life should make us recognize our frequent need to admit our disobedience, repent, and ask God to forgive us.

Strengths and accomplishments	• An effective leader and organizer • First king of the 10 tribes of Israel in the divided kingdom
Weaknesses and mistakes	• Erected idols in Israel to keep people away from Jerusalem • Appointed priests from outside the tribe of Levi • Depended more on his own cunning than on God's promises
Lessons from his life	• Great opportunities are often destroyed by bad decisions
Vital statistics	• Where: The northern kingdom of Israel • Occupations: Project foreman, king of Israel • Relatives: Father: Nebat. Mother: Zeruah. Sons: Abijah, Nadab. • Contemporaries: Solomon, Nathan, Ahijah, Rehoboam
Key verses	"But even after this, Jeroboam did not turn from his evil ways. He continued to choose priests from the common people. He appointed anyone who wanted to become a priest for the pagan shrines. This became a great sin and resulted in the utter destruction of Jeroboam's dynasty from the face of the earth" (1 Kgs 13:33-34).

Jeroboam's story is told in 1 Kings 11:26–14:20.

approaching the altar to burn incense. 2Then at the
LORD's command, he shouted, "O altar, altar! This is
what the LORD says: A child named Josiah will be born
into the dynasty of David. On you he will sacrifice the
priests from the pagan shrines who come here to burn
incense, and human bones will be burned on you."
3That same day the man of God gave a sign to prove
his message. He said, "The LORD has promised to give
this sign: This altar will split apart, and its ashes will
be poured out on the ground."
4When King Jeroboam heard the man of God speaking against the altar at Bethel, he pointed at him and
shouted, "Seize that man!" But instantly the king's hand
became paralyzed in that position, and he couldn't pull
it back. 5At the same time a wide crack appeared in the
altar, and the ashes poured out, just as the man of God
had predicted in his message from the LORD.
6The king cried out to the man of God, "Please ask
the LORD your God to restore my hand again!" So the
man of God prayed to the LORD, and the king's hand
was restored and he could move it again.
7Then the king said to the man of God, "Come to
the palace with me and have something to eat, and I
will give you a gift."
8But the man of God said to the king, "Even if you
gave me half of everything you own, I would not go
with you. I would not eat or drink anything in this
place. 9For the LORD gave me this command: 'You must
not eat or drink anything while you are there, and do
not return to Judah by the same way you came.'" 10So
he left Bethel and went home another way.
11As it happened, there was an old prophet living in
Bethel, and his sons* came home and told him what
the man of God had done in Bethel that day. They also
told their father what the man had said to the king.
12The old prophet asked them, "Which way did he go?"
So they showed their father* which road the man of
God had taken. 13"Quick, saddle the donkey," the old
man said. So they saddled the donkey for him, and
he mounted it.
14Then he rode after the man of God and found
him sitting under a great tree. The old prophet asked
him, "Are you the man of God who came from Judah?"
"Yes, I am," he replied.
15Then he said to the man of God, "Come home with
me and eat some food."
16"No, I cannot," he replied. "I am not allowed to eat
or drink anything here in this place. 17For the LORD
gave me this command: 'You must not eat or drink
anything while you are there, and do not return to
Judah by the same way you came.'"
18But the old prophet answered, "I am a prophet, too,
just as you are. And an angel gave me this command
from the LORD: 'Bring him home with you so he can
have something to eat and drink.'" But the old man
was lying to him. 19So they went back together, and
the man of God ate and drank at the prophet's home.
20Then while they were sitting at the table, a command from the LORD came to the old prophet. 21He
cried out to the man of God from Judah, "This is what
the LORD says: You have defied the word of the LORD
and have disobeyed the command the LORD your God
gave you. 22You came back to this place and ate and
drank where he told you not to eat or drink. Because
of this, your body will not be buried in the grave of
your ancestors."
23After the man of God had finished eating and
drinking, the old prophet saddled his own donkey
for him, 24and the man of God started off again. But
as he was traveling along, a lion came out and killed
him. His body lay there on the road, with the donkey
and the lion standing beside it. 25People who passed
by saw the body lying in the road and the lion standing beside it, and they went and reported it in Bethel,
where the old prophet lived.
26When the prophet heard the report, he said, "It is
the man of God who disobeyed the LORD's command.
The LORD has fulfilled his word by causing the lion to
attack and kill him."
27Then the prophet said to his sons, "Saddle a donkey for me." So they saddled a donkey, 28and he went
out and found the body lying in the road. The donkey
and lion were still standing there beside it, for the lion
had not eaten the body nor attacked the donkey. 29So
the prophet laid the body of the man of God on the
donkey and took it back to the town to mourn over
him and bury him. 30He laid the body in his own grave,
crying out in grief, "Oh, my brother!"
31Afterward the prophet said to his sons, "When
I die, bury me in the grave where the man of God is
buried. Lay my bones beside his bones. 32For the message the LORD told him to proclaim against the altar
in Bethel and against the pagan shrines in the towns
of Samaria will certainly come true."

1 Kgs 13:11 As in Greek version; Hebrew reads *son.* **1 Kgs 13:12** As in Greek version; Hebrew reads *They had seen.*

1 Kgs 13:2 This prophecy was fulfilled in every detail 300 years later when Josiah killed the pagan priests at their own altars. This story is found in 2 Kings 23:1-20.

1 Kgs 13:7-32 This prophet had been given strict orders from God not to eat or drink anything while on his mission (1 Kgs 13:9). He died because he listened to a man who claimed to have a message from God. This prophet should have followed God's word instead of hearsay. Trust what God's Word says rather than what someone claims is true. And disregard what others claim are messages from God if their words contradict the Bible.

1 Kgs 13:24-25 Lions are mentioned frequently in the Old Testament. They were common enough to be a threat both to people and to their flocks. Samson (Judg 14:5-6), David (1 Sam 17:34-37), and Benaiah (2 Sam 23:20) all faced lions. The fact that the lion and the donkey were standing by the prophet's body showed that this was a divine judgment. Normally, the lion would have attacked the donkey or devoured the man.

▸ 1 KINGS 13:1-34 *(cont.)*

[33]But even after this, Jeroboam did not turn from
his evil ways. He continued to choose priests from the
common people. He appointed anyone who wanted to
become a priest for the pagan shrines. [34]This became
a great sin and resulted in the utter destruction of Jeroboam's dynasty from the face of the earth.

Ahijah's Prophecy against Jeroboam

1 KINGS 14:1-18

At that time Jeroboam's son Abijah became very sick.
[2]So Jeroboam told his wife, "Disguise yourself so that
no one will recognize you as my wife. Then go to the
prophet Ahijah at Shiloh—the man who told me I
would become king. [3]Take him a gift of ten loaves
of bread, some cakes, and a jar of honey, and ask him
what will happen to the boy."

[4]So Jeroboam's wife went to Ahijah's home at Shiloh. He was an old man now and could no longer see.
[5]But the LORD had told Ahijah, "Jeroboam's wife will
come here, pretending to be someone else. She will
ask you about her son, for he is very sick. Give her the
answer I give you."

[6]So when Ahijah heard her footsteps at the door, he
called out, "Come in, wife of Jeroboam! Why are you
pretending to be someone else?" Then he told her, "I
have bad news for you. [7]Give your husband, Jeroboam,
this message from the LORD, the God of Israel: 'I promoted you from the ranks of the common people and
made you ruler over my people Israel. [8]I ripped the
kingdom away from the family of David and gave it to
you. But you have not been like my servant David, who
obeyed my commands and followed me with all his
heart and always did whatever I wanted. [9]You have done
more evil than all who lived before you. You have made
other gods for yourself and have made me furious with
your gold calves. And since you have turned your back
on me, [10]I will bring disaster on your dynasty and will
destroy every one of your male descendants, slave and
free alike, anywhere in Israel. I will burn up your royal
dynasty as one burns up trash until it is all gone. [11]The
members of Jeroboam's family who die in the city will
be eaten by dogs, and those who die in the field will be
eaten by vultures. I, the LORD, have spoken.'"

[12]Then Ahijah said to Jeroboam's wife, "Go on home,
and when you enter the city, the child will die. [13]All
Israel will mourn for him and bury him. He is the only
member of your family who will have a proper burial,
for this child is the only good thing that the LORD, the
God of Israel, sees in the entire family of Jeroboam.

[14]"In addition, the LORD will raise up a king over Israel who will destroy the family of Jeroboam. This will
happen today, even now! [15]Then the LORD will shake
Israel like a reed whipped about in a stream. He will
uproot the people of Israel from this good land that
he gave their ancestors and will scatter them beyond
the Euphrates River,* for they have angered the LORD
with the Asherah poles they have set up for worship.
[16]He will abandon Israel because Jeroboam sinned
and made Israel sin along with him."

[17]So Jeroboam's wife returned to Tirzah, and the
child died just as she walked through the door of her
home. [18]And all Israel buried him and mourned for
him, as the LORD had promised through the prophet
Ahijah.

Rehoboam Rules in Judah PARALLEL

1 KINGS 14:21-24

Meanwhile, Rehoboam son of Solomon was king in
Judah. He was forty-one years old when he became
king, and he reigned seventeen years in Jerusalem, the
city the LORD had chosen from among all the tribes
of Israel as the place to honor his name. Rehoboam's
mother was Naamah, an Ammonite woman.

[22]During Rehoboam's reign, the people of Judah
did what was evil in the LORD's sight, provoking his
anger with their sin, for it was even worse than that
of their ancestors. [23]For they also built for themselves
pagan shrines and set up sacred pillars and Asherah
poles on every high hill and under every green tree.
[24]There were even male and female shrine prostitutes
throughout the land. The people imitated the detestable practices of the pagan nations the LORD had
driven from the land ahead of the Israelites.

2 CHRONICLES 12:13-14

King Rehoboam firmly established himself in Jerusalem and continued to rule. He was forty-one years
old when he became king, and he reigned seventeen

1 Kgs 14:15 Hebrew *the river.*

1 Kgs 13:33-34 Under penalty of death, God had forbidden anyone to be a priest who was not from the tribe of Levi (Num 3:10). Levitical priests were assured of lifetime support from the tithe, so they did not have to spend time farming, worrying about tribal interests, or fearing for their financial future. Jeroboam's new priests were financed by the king and his fees. They had to mix priestly and secular duties, and they quickly fell into party politics. Because they didn't have job security, these priests were easily corrupted by bribes. Jeroboam's disobedience was the downfall of true religion in the northern kingdom.

1 Kgs 14:10-11 These disasters were practical applications to Israel of the specific teachings of Deuteronomy (see Deut 28:15-19, 36-68; 30:15-20). Ahijah was prophesying the downfall of Israel for its flagrant violation of God's commands.

1 Kgs 14:14 Who was this king who would "destroy the family of Jeroboam"? His name was Baasha, and he would kill all of Jeroboam's descendants (1 Kgs 15:27-30).

1 Kgs 14:15 "Asherah poles" refers to idol worship. Wooden images were used in the worship of Asherah, a Canaanite mother-goddess.

1 Kgs 14:23 "Sacred pillars" were pillars of stone placed next to pagan altars. These pillars were supposed to represent deity.

2 Chr 12:14 Rehoboam's story is tragic because he "did not seek the LORD with all his heart." How tragic a description of the grandson of David, who had been called a man after God's own heart (1 Sam 13:14).

years in Jerusalem, the city the LORD had chosen from among all the tribes of Israel as the place to honor his name. Rehoboam's mother was Naamah, a woman from Ammon. 14But he was an evil king, for he did not seek the LORD with all his heart.

Rehoboam's Family

2 CHRONICLES 11:18-23

Rehoboam married his cousin Mahalath, the daughter of David's son Jerimoth and of Abihail, the daughter of Eliab son of Jesse. 19Mahalath had three sons—Jeush, Shemariah, and Zaham.

20Later Rehoboam married another cousin, Maacah, the daughter of Absalom. Maacah gave birth to Abijah, Attai, Ziza, and Shelomith. 21Rehoboam loved Maacah more than any of his other wives and concubines. In all, he had eighteen wives and sixty concubines, and they gave birth to twenty-eight sons and sixty daughters.

22Rehoboam appointed Maacah's son Abijah as leader among the princes, making it clear that he would be the next king. 23Rehoboam also wisely gave responsibilities to his other sons and stationed some of them in the fortified towns throughout the land of Judah and Benjamin. He provided them with generous provisions, and he found many wives for them.

Egypt Invades Judah PARALLEL

1 KINGS 14:25-28

In the fifth year of King Rehoboam's reign, King Shishak of Egypt came up and attacked Jerusalem. 26He ransacked the treasuries of the LORD's Temple and the royal palace; he stole everything, including all the gold shields Solomon had made. 27King Rehoboam later replaced them with bronze shields as substitutes, and he entrusted them to the care of the commanders of the guard who protected the entrance to the royal palace. 28Whenever the king went to the Temple of the LORD, the guards would also take the shields and then return them to the guardroom.

2 CHRONICLES 12:1-12

But when Rehoboam was firmly established and strong, he abandoned the Law of the LORD, and all Israel followed him in this sin. 2Because they were unfaithful to the LORD, King Shishak of Egypt came up and attacked Jerusalem in the fifth year of King Rehoboam's reign. 3He came with 1,200 chariots, 60,000 horses,* and

2 Chr 12:3a Or *charioteers*, or *horsemen*.

It is dangerous to put off responding to God. God asks us for a firm commitment, and unless we respond by trusting him completely, we will find ourselves alienated from him.

1 Kgs 14:25 When Rehoboam came to power, he inherited a mighty kingdom. Everything he could ever want was given to him. But apparently he did not recognize why he had so much or how it had been obtained. To teach Rehoboam a lesson, God allowed Shishak of Egypt to invade Judah and Israel. Egypt was no longer the world power it had once been, and Shishak, possibly resenting Solomon's enormous success, was determined to change that. Shishak's army was not strong enough to destroy Judah and Israel, but he weakened them so much that they were never the same again.

1 Kgs 14:25-26 Just five years after Solomon died, the Temple and palace were ransacked by foreign invaders. How quickly the glory, power, and money disappeared! When the people became spiritually corrupt and immoral (1 Kgs 14:24), it was just a short time until they lost everything. Wealth, idol worship, and immorality had become more important to them than God. When God is gone from our lives, everything else becomes useless, no matter how valuable it seems.

2 Chr 12:1-2 Here "Israel" refers to Judah, the southern kingdom. During his first three years on the throne, Rehoboam made an attempt to obey God, and as a result, Judah prospered. But then, at his peak of popularity and power, he abandoned God. The result was destruction because God allowed Judah to be conquered by Egypt. How could this happen? Often it is more difficult to be a believer in good times than in bad. Tough times push us toward God; but easy times can make us feel self-sufficient and self-satisfied. When everything is going right, guard your faith closely.

2 Chr 12:2 A record of this invasion has been found on an Egyptian stone that says Shishak's army penetrated as far north as the Sea of Galilee, in the northern kingdom. Egypt was not the world power it had once been, and Shishak wanted to restore his nation to its former greatness. He was not strong enough to conquer both Israel and Judah, but he managed to destroy key cities in Judah in an effort to regain control of the trade routes and strike terror among the people.

Shishak

King Shishak of Egypt memorialized his military campaign into Israel in a large relief at the temple in Karnack (ancient Thebes). This inscription is of great importance for biblical history and helps confirm the historicity of the Bible. It contains the names of many towns Shishak claims to have captured on his raids into the region. Some of these names, in Egyptian script, correspond to names that originated in the Hebrew language. Two dozen can be identified with certainty, affording valuable outside confirmation of biblical geography and history. Pictured are two golden bracelets that belonged to Shishak. Additional evidence of Shishak's raid into Palestine (1 Kgs 14:25) was found at Megiddo, where a fragment of a triumphal stele erected by the pharaoh has been located.

▸ 2 CHRONICLES 12:1-12 ***(cont.)***

a countless army of foot soldiers, including Libyans, Sukkites, and Ethiopians.* [4]Shishak conquered Judah's fortified towns and then advanced to attack Jerusalem.

[5]The prophet Shemaiah then met with Rehoboam and Judah's leaders, who had all fled to Jerusalem because of Shishak. Shemaiah told them, "This is what the LORD says: You have abandoned me, so I am abandoning you to Shishak."

[6]Then the leaders of Israel and the king humbled themselves and said, "The LORD is right in doing this to us!"

[7]When the LORD saw their change of heart, he gave this message to Shemaiah: "Since the people have humbled themselves, I will not completely destroy them and will soon give them some relief. I will not use Shishak to pour out my anger on Jerusalem. [8]But they will become his subjects, so they will know the difference between serving me and serving earthly rulers."

[9]So King Shishak of Egypt came up and attacked Jerusalem. He ransacked the treasuries of the LORD's Temple and the royal palace; he stole everything, including all the gold shields Solomon had made. [10]King Rehoboam later replaced them with bronze shields as substitutes, and he entrusted them to the care of the commanders of the guard who protected the entrance to the royal palace. [11]Whenever the king went to the Temple of the LORD, the guards would also take the shields and then return them to the guardroom. [12]Because Rehoboam humbled himself, the LORD's anger was turned away, and he did not destroy him completely. There were still some good things in the land of Judah.

Summary of Rehoboam's Reign PARALLEL

1 KINGS 14:29-31

The rest of the events in Rehoboam's reign and everything he did are recorded in *The Book of the History of the Kings of Judah.* [30]There was constant war between Rehoboam and Jeroboam. [31]When Rehoboam died, he was buried among his ancestors in the City of David. His mother was Naamah, an Ammonite woman. Then his son Abijam* became the next king.

2 CHRONICLES 12:15-16

The rest of the events of Rehoboam's reign, from beginning to end, are recorded in *The Record of Shemaiah the Prophet* and *The Record of Iddo the Seer,* which are part of the genealogical record. Rehoboam and Jeroboam were continually at war with each other. [16]When Rehoboam died, he was buried in the City of David. Then his son Abijah became the next king.

Abijam Rules in Judah PARALLEL

1 KINGS 15:1-8

Abijam* began to rule over Judah in the eighteenth year of Jeroboam's reign in Israel. [2]He reigned in Jerusalem three years. His mother was Maacah, the daughter of Absalom.*

[3]He committed the same sins as his father before him, and he was not faithful to the LORD his God, as his ancestor David had been. [4]But for David's sake, the LORD his God allowed his descendants to continue ruling, shining like a lamp, and he gave Abijam a son to rule after him in Jerusalem. [5]For David had done what was pleasing in the LORD's sight and had obeyed the LORD's commands throughout his life, except in the affair concerning Uriah the Hittite.

[6]There was war between Abijam and Jeroboam* throughout Abijam's reign. [7]The rest of the events in Abijam's reign and everything he did are recorded in *The Book of the History of the Kings of Judah.* There was constant war between Abijam and Jeroboam. [8]When Abijam died, he was buried in the City of David. Then his son Asa became the next king.

2 CHRONICLES 13:1-22

Abijah began to rule over Judah in the eighteenth year of Jeroboam's reign in Israel. [2]He reigned in Jerusalem three years. His mother was Maacah,* the daughter of Uriel from Gibeah.

Then war broke out between Abijah and Jeroboam. [3]Judah, led by King Abijah, fielded 400,000 select

2 Chr 12:3b Hebrew *and Cushites.* **1 Kgs 14:31** Also known as *Abijah.* **1 Kgs 15:1** Also known as *Abijah.* **1 Kgs 15:2** Hebrew *Abishalom* (also in 15:10), a variant spelling of Absalom; compare 2 Chr 11:20. **1 Kgs 15:6** As in a few Hebrew and Greek manuscripts; most Hebrew manuscripts read *between Rehoboam and Jeroboam.* **2 Chr 13:2** As in most Greek manuscripts and Syriac version (see also 2 Chr 11:20-21; 1 Kgs 15:2); Hebrew reads *Micaiah,* a variant spelling of Maacah.

2 Chr 12:6-8 God lessened his judgment when Israel's leaders confessed their sins, humbled themselves, and recognized God's justice in punishing them. It's never too late to repent, even in the midst of punishment. Regardless of what we have done, God is willing to receive us back into fellowship. Are you struggling and alone because sin has broken your fellowship with God? Confession and humility will open the door to receiving God's mercy.

2 Chr 12:8 Subjection to other kings was the price Judah had to pay for disobeying God. The nation's leaders thought they could succeed in their own strength, but they were wrong. When we rebel against God, we always pay for it. When we leave God out of our lives, we lose more spiritually than we ever gain financially.

2 Chr 12:10-11 How ironic that the treasures in Solomon's Temple were removed and the missing royal shields were replaced by cheaper bronze. Rehoboam tried to maintain the trappings and appearance of former glory, but he couldn't measure up. When God is no longer central in our lives, we might find ourselves maintaining the appearance of a Christian life. Outer beauty must come from inner strength; otherwise it is superficial.

1 Kgs 15:5 See 2 Samuel 11 for the story of David and Uriah the Hittite.

2 Chr 13:1ff According to 1 Kings 15:3, Abijah committed many sins, but the Chronicles account has only positive comments about him. For the most part, Abijah was a wicked king. The writer of Chronicles chose to highlight the little good he did in order to show that he was still under God's covenant promise to David. Because of Abijah's fiery speech to Jeroboam (2 Chr 13:4-12), he was spared the immediate consequences of his sin.

warriors, while Jeroboam mustered 800,000 select
troops from Israel.
4When the army of Judah arrived in the hill country
of Ephraim, Abijah stood on Mount Zemaraim and
shouted to Jeroboam and all Israel: "Listen to me!
5Don't you realize that the LORD, the God of Israel,
made a lasting covenant* with David, giving him and
his descendants the throne of Israel forever? 6Yet Jeroboam son of Nebat, a mere servant of David's son
Solomon, rebelled against his master. 7Then a whole
gang of scoundrels joined him, defying Solomon's son
Rehoboam when he was young and inexperienced and
could not stand up to them.
8"Do you really think you can stand against the
kingdom of the LORD that is led by the descendants
of David? You may have a vast army, and you have
those gold calves that Jeroboam made as your gods.
9But you have chased away the priests of the LORD
(the descendants of Aaron) and the Levites, and you
have appointed your own priests, just like the pagan
nations. You let anyone become a priest these days!
Whoever comes to be dedicated with a young bull
and seven rams can become a priest of these so-called
gods of yours!
10"But as for us, the LORD is our God, and we have
not abandoned him. Only the descendants of Aaron
serve the LORD as priests, and the Levites alone may
help them in their work. 11They present burnt offerings and fragrant incense to the LORD every morning
and evening. They place the Bread of the Presence on
the holy table, and they light the gold lampstand every
evening. We are following the instructions of the LORD
our God, but you have abandoned him. 12So you see,
God is with us. He is our leader. His priests blow their
trumpets and lead us into battle against you. O people
of Israel, do not fight against the LORD, the God of your
ancestors, for you will not succeed!"
13Meanwhile, Jeroboam had secretly sent part of
his army around behind the men of Judah to ambush
them. 14When Judah realized that they were being
attacked from the front and the rear, they cried out to
the LORD for help. Then the priests blew the trumpets,
15and the men of Judah began to shout. At the sound of
their battle cry, God defeated Jeroboam and all Israel
and routed them before Abijah and the army of Judah.
16The Israelite army fled from Judah, and God
handed them over to Judah in defeat. 17Abijah and
his army inflicted heavy losses on them; 500,000 of
Israel's select troops were killed that day. 18So Judah
defeated Israel on that occasion because they trusted
in the LORD, the God of their ancestors. 19Abijah and
his army pursued Jeroboam's troops and captured
some of his towns, including Bethel, Jeshanah, and
Ephron, along with their surrounding villages.
20So Jeroboam of Israel never regained his power
during Abijah's lifetime, and finally the LORD struck
him down and he died. 21Meanwhile, Abijah of Judah
grew more and more powerful. He married fourteen
wives and had twenty-two sons and sixteen daughters.
22The rest of the events of Abijah's reign, including
his words and deeds, are recorded in *The Commentary
of Iddo the Prophet*.

Asa Rules in Judah PARALLEL

1 KINGS 15:9-15

Asa began to rule over Judah in the twentieth year of
Jeroboam's reign in Israel. 10He reigned in Jerusalem
forty-one years. His grandmother* was Maacah, the
daughter of Absalom.
11Asa did what was pleasing in the LORD's sight,
as his ancestor David had done. 12He banished the
male and female shrine prostitutes from the land
and got rid of all the idols* his ancestors had made.
13He even deposed his grandmother Maacah from
her position as queen mother because she had made
an obscene Asherah pole. He cut down her obscene
pole and burned it in the Kidron Valley. 14Although the
pagan shrines were not removed, Asa's heart remained
completely faithful to the LORD throughout his life.
15He brought into the Temple of the LORD the silver
and gold and the various items that he and his father
had dedicated.

910 BC

Asa begins to rule in Judah

2 Chr 13:5 Hebrew *a covenant of salt.* **1 Kgs 15:10** Or *The queen mother;* Hebrew reads *His mother* (also in 15:13); compare 15:2. **1 Kgs 15:12** The Hebrew term (literally *round things*) probably alludes to dung.

2 Chr 13:8 Jeroboam's army was cursed because of the gold calves they carried with them. It was as though they had put sin into a physical form so they could haul it around. Consider carefully the things you cherish. If you value anything more than God, it will one day drag you down. Let go of anything that interferes with your relationship with God.

2 Chr 13:9 Abijah criticized Jeroboam's low standards in appointing priests. Anyone is qualified to represent a god that is worthless. To represent the Lord God Almighty, however, a person must live by God's standards. Those appointed to positions of responsibility in your church should not be selected merely because they volunteer, are influential, or are highly educated. Instead, they should demonstrate sound doctrine, dedication to God, and strong spiritual character (see 1 Tim 3).

2 Chr 13:18-19 Although outnumbered by Israel, Judah won this conflict by depending on God's help. Some kings in Judah's history focused on God, but not one Israelite king consistently followed God—all followed Jeroboam's idolatry or served Baal. As a result, Israel experienced God's punishment many years before Judah did.

Judah had an advantage: The Temple, with its sacrifices and the loyal priests and prophets, was in the southern kingdom. Many of Judah's kings were good, at least for parts of their reigns. Whenever an idolatrous king reigned, his rule was later followed by that of a God-honoring king who reformed religious life. Also, the idolatrous kings usually served for a much shorter time than the good ones. The result was that true faith in God ran stronger and deeper in Judah than in Israel, but it was still not up to God's standards.

1 Kgs 15:15 These gifts for the Temple were articles dedicated to God as sacred offerings that Abijah had taken in his war with Jeroboam (2 Chr 13:16-17) and that Asa had taken when he defeated the Ethiopians (2 Chr 14:12-13).

2 CHRONICLES 14:1-8

*When Abijah died, he was buried in the City of David. Then his son Asa became the next king. There was peace in the land for ten years. [2]*Asa did what was pleasing and good in the sight of the LORD his God. [3]He removed the foreign altars and the pagan shrines. He smashed the sacred pillars and cut down the Asherah poles. [4]He commanded the people of Judah to seek the LORD, the God of their ancestors, and to obey his law and his commands. [5]Asa also removed the pagan shrines, as well as the incense altars from every one of Judah's towns. So Asa's kingdom enjoyed a period of peace. [6]During those peaceful years, he was able to build up the fortified towns throughout Judah. No one tried to make war against him at this time, for the LORD was giving him rest from his enemies.

[7]Asa told the people of Judah, "Let us build towns and fortify them with walls, towers, gates, and bars. The land is still ours because we sought the LORD our God, and he has given us peace on every side." So they went ahead with these projects and brought them to completion. [8]King Asa had an army of 300,000 warriors from the tribe of Judah, armed with large shields and spears. He also had an army of 280,000 warriors from the tribe of Benjamin, armed with small shields and bows. Both armies were composed of well-trained fighting men.

The End of Jeroboam's Reign in Israel

1 KINGS 14:19-20

The rest of the events in Jeroboam's reign, including all his wars and how he ruled, are recorded in *The Book of the History of the Kings of Israel.* [20]Jeroboam reigned in Israel twenty-two years. When Jeroboam died, his son Nadab became the next king.

Nadab Rules in Israel

1 KINGS 15:25-26

Nadab son of Jeroboam began to rule over Israel in the second year of King Asa's reign in Judah. He reigned in Israel two years. [26]But he did what was evil in the LORD's sight and followed the example of his father, continuing the sins that Jeroboam had led Israel to commit.

2 Chr 14:1 Verse 14:1 is numbered 13:23 in Hebrew text. **2 Chr 14:2** Verses 14:2-15 are numbered 14:1-14 in Hebrew text.

B. The Era of Baasha's Dynasty in the Northern Kingdom

The second dynasty of the northern kingdom began when Baasha assassinated Nadab and took control. This was another brief and tumultuous dynasty in the northern kingdom of Israel, constantly at war with King Asa of Judah and eventually Syria. Baasha's son Elah was murdered by one of his military commanders, Zimri, putting an end to Baasha's dynasty. During this time, Judah was ruled by Asa, a good king who instituted religious reforms to tear down pagan shrines and restore worship of the Lord in Jerusalem.

Baasha Rules in Israel

1 KINGS 15:27-34

Then Baasha son of Ahijah, from the tribe of Issachar, plotted against Nadab and assassinated him while he and the Israelite army were laying siege to the Philistine town of Gibbethon. [28]Baasha killed Nadab in the third year of King Asa's reign in Judah, and he became the next king of Israel.

[29]He immediately slaughtered all the descendants of King Jeroboam, so that not one of the royal family was left, just as the LORD had promised concerning Jeroboam by the prophet Ahijah from Shiloh.

2 Chr 14:1-6 Asa's reign was marked by peace because he "did what was pleasing and good in the sight of the LORD his God." This refrain is often repeated in Chronicles—obedience to God leads to peace with God and others. In the case of Judah's kings, obedience to God led to national peace, just as God had promised centuries earlier. In our case, obedience may not always bring peace with our enemies, but it will bring peace with God and complete peace in his future Kingdom. Obeying God is the first step on the path to peace.

2 Chr 14:3-5 Simply attending worship services is not enough to secure God's peace. Like Asa, we must also actively remove anything that is offensive to God. Becoming more active in church attendance or doing good deeds will still leave us in turmoil if we have failed to eliminate sinful practices from our lives. We should continually ask God to help us remove any source of temptation from our lives.

2 Chr 14:7 Judah had peace with all her neighbors. Times of peace are not just for resting. They allow us to prepare for times of trouble. King Asa recognized the period of peace as the right time to build his defenses—the moment of attack would be too late. It is also difficult to withstand spiritual attack unless defenses are prepared beforehand. Decisions about how to face temptation must be made with cool heads long before we feel the heat of temptation. Build your defenses now before temptation strikes.

1 Kgs 14:19 Three non-biblical books are mentioned in 1 and 2 Kings—*The Book of the History of the Kings of Israel* (1 Kgs 14:19), *The Book of the History of the Kings of Judah* (1 Kgs 14:29), and *The Book of the Acts of Solomon* (1 Kgs 11:41). These historical records of Israel and Judah were the main sources of material God directed the author to use to write 1 and 2 Kings. No copies of these books have been found.

1 Kgs 15:29 See 1 Kings 14:12-14 for Ahijah's prediction of this event.

Jerusalem from Solomon to Hezekiah ▶

Solomon engaged in considerable building and expansion of the city in addition to building the magnificent Temple. He also constructed a royal compound and expanded the border of the city considerably. The city remained essentially unchanged until the time of Hezekiah, when a further expansion was undertaken.

Jerusalem from Solomon to Hezekiah

see also Jerusalem in the Time of David, p. 583

▸ 1 KINGS 15:27-34 ***(cont.)***

30This was done because Jeroboam had provoked the anger of the LORD, the God of Israel, by the sins he had committed and the sins he had led Israel to commit.

31The rest of the events in Nadab's reign and everything he did are recorded in *The Book of the History of the Kings of Israel.*

32There was constant war between King Asa of Judah and King Baasha of Israel. 33Baasha son of Ahijah began to rule over all Israel in the third year of King Asa's reign in Judah. Baasha reigned in Tirzah twenty-four years. 34But he did what was evil in the LORD's sight and followed the example of Jeroboam, continuing the sins that Jeroboam had led Israel to commit.

Judah Battles the Ethiopians

2 CHRONICLES 14:9-15

Once an Ethiopian* named Zerah attacked Judah with an army of 1,000,000 men* and 300 chariots. They advanced to the town of Mareshah, 10so Asa deployed his armies for battle in the valley north of Mareshah.* 11Then Asa cried out to the LORD his God, "O LORD, no one but you can help the powerless against the mighty! Help us, O LORD our God, for we trust in you alone. It is in your name that we have come against this vast horde. O LORD, you are our God; do not let mere men prevail against you!"

12So the LORD defeated the Ethiopians* in the presence of Asa and the army of Judah, and the enemy fled. 13Asa and his army pursued them as far as Gerar, and so many Ethiopians fell that they were unable to rally. They were destroyed by the LORD and his army, and the army of Judah carried off a vast amount of plunder.

14While they were at Gerar, they attacked all the towns in that area, and terror from the LORD came upon the people there. As a result, a vast amount of plunder was taken from these towns, too. 15They also attacked the camps of herdsmen and captured many sheep, goats, and camels before finally returning to Jerusalem.

Asa's Religious Reforms

2 CHRONICLES 15:1-19

Then the Spirit of God came upon Azariah son of Oded, 2and he went out to meet King Asa as he was returning from the battle. "Listen to me, Asa!" he shouted. "Listen, all you people of Judah and Benjamin! The LORD will stay with you as long as you stay with him! Whenever you seek him, you will find him. But if you abandon him, he will abandon you. 3For a long time Israel was without the true God, without a priest to teach them, and without the Law to instruct them. 4But whenever they were in trouble and turned to the LORD, the God of Israel, and sought him out, they found him.

5"During those dark times, it was not safe to travel. Problems troubled the people of every land. 6Nation fought against nation, and city against city, for God was troubling them with every kind of problem. 7But as for you, be strong and courageous, for your work will be rewarded."

8When Asa heard this message from Azariah the

2 Chr 14:9a Hebrew *a Cushite.* **2 Chr 14:9b** *Or an army of thousands and thousands;* Hebrew reads *an army of a thousand thousands.* **2 Chr 14:10** *Or in the Zephathah Valley near Mareshah.* **2 Chr 14:12** Hebrew *Cushites;* also in 14:13.

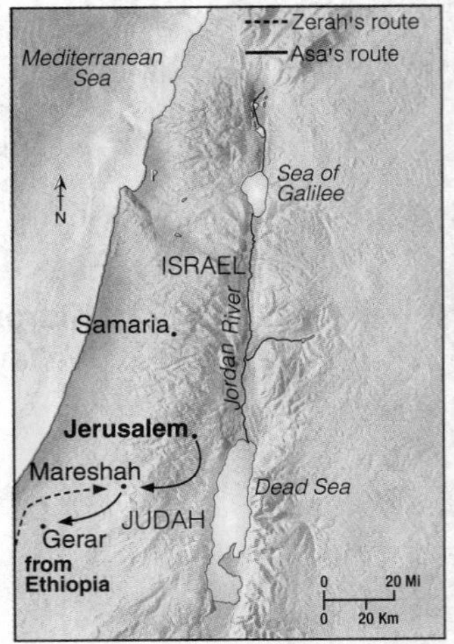

ASA'S BATTLES *A huge army from Ethiopia under Zerah advanced toward Mareshah, greatly outnumbering King Asa's army. Asa sent his troops to meet them, and the battle took place in the valley north of Mareshah. Asa prayed to God, and the Ethiopians were defeated and chased as far as Gerar.*

1 Kgs 15:30 All the descendants of Jeroboam were killed because Jeroboam had led Israel into sin. Sin is always judged harshly, but the worst sinners are those who lead others into doing wrong. Jesus said it would be better if such people had millstones tied around their necks and were thrown into the sea (Mark 9:42). If you have taken the responsibility for leading others, remember the consequences of leading them astray. Teaching the truth is a responsibility that goes with the privilege of leadership.

2 Chr 14:11 If you are facing battles you feel you can't possibly win, don't give up. In the face of a vast horde of enemy soldiers, Asa prayed for God's help, recognizing his powerlessness against such a mighty army. The secret of victory is first to admit the futility of unaided human effort and then to trust God to save. His power works best through those who recognize their limitations (2 Cor 12:9). It is those who think they can do it all on their own who are in the greatest danger.

2 Chr 15:1-2 Asa wisely welcomed people who had a close relationship with God, and he listened to their messages. Azariah gave the armies an important warning and encouraged them to stay close to God. Keep in contact with people who are filled with God's Spirit, and you will learn God's counsel. Spend regular time in discussion and prayer with those who can help explain and apply God's message.

2 Chr 15:3 Azariah said that Israel, the northern kingdom, was "without the true God." Eight kings reigned in Israel during the 41-year rule of Asa in Judah, and all eight were evil. Jeroboam, the first ruler of Israel, began this wicked trend by setting up idols and expelling God's priests (2 Chr 11:13-15). Azariah used Israel's problems as an example of the evil that would come to the people of Judah if they turned away from God as their northern brothers and sisters had.

2 Chr 15:7 Azariah encouraged the men of Judah to keep up the good work, "for your work will be rewarded." This is an inspiration for us, too. Recognition and reward are great motivators that have two dimensions: (1) *The temporal dimension.* Living by God's standards may result in acclaim here on earth. (2) *The eternal dimension.* Permanent recognition and reward will be given in the next life. Don't be discouraged if you feel your faith in God is going unrewarded here on earth. The best rewards are not in this life but in the life to come.

prophet,* he took courage and removed all the detestable idols from the land of Judah and Benjamin and
in the towns he had captured in the hill country of
Ephraim. And he repaired the altar of the LORD, which
stood in front of the entry room of the LORD's Temple.
9Then Asa called together all the people of Judah
and Benjamin, along with the people of Ephraim, Manasseh, and Simeon who had settled among them.
For many from Israel had moved to Judah during
Asa's reign when they saw that the LORD his God was
with him. 10The people gathered at Jerusalem in late
spring,* during the fifteenth year of Asa's reign.
11On that day they sacrificed to the LORD 700 cattle
and 7,000 sheep and goats from the plunder they had
taken in the battle. 12Then they entered into a covenant to seek the LORD, the God of their ancestors,
with all their heart and soul. 13They agreed that anyone who refused to seek the LORD, the God of Israel,
would be put to death—whether young or old, man
or woman. 14They shouted out their oath of loyalty
to the LORD with trumpets blaring and rams' horns
sounding. 15All in Judah were happy about this covenant, for they had entered into it with all their heart.
They earnestly sought after God, and they found him.
And the LORD gave them rest from their enemies on
every side.
16King Asa even deposed his grandmother* Maacah from her position as queen mother because she
had made an obscene Asherah pole. He cut down her
obscene pole, broke it up, and burned it in the Kidron
Valley. 17Although the pagan shrines were not removed
from Israel, Asa's heart remained completely faithful
throughout his life. 18He brought into the Temple of
God the silver and gold and the various items that he
and his father had dedicated.
19So there was no more war until the thirty-fifth
year of Asa's reign.

War between Baasha and Asa PARALLEL

1 KINGS 15:16-22

There was constant war between King Asa of Judah
and King Baasha of Israel. 17King Baasha of Israel invaded Judah and fortified Ramah in order to prevent
anyone from entering or leaving King Asa's territory
in Judah.
18Asa responded by removing all the silver and gold
that was left in the treasuries of the Temple of the
LORD and the royal palace. He sent it with some of
his officials to Ben-hadad son of Tabrimmon, son of
Hezion, the king of Aram, who was ruling in Damascus,
along with this message:

> 19"Let there be a treaty* between you and me like
> the one between your father and my father. See,
> I am sending you a gift of silver and gold. Break
> your treaty with King Baasha of Israel so that he
> will leave me alone."

20Ben-hadad agreed to King Asa's request and sent
the commanders of his army to attack the towns of
Israel. They conquered the towns of Ijon, Dan, Abel-
beth-maacah, and all Kinnereth, and all the land of
Naphtali. 21As soon as Baasha of Israel heard what was

900 BC
Celts invade Britain

2 Chr 15:8 As in Syriac version and Latin Vulgate (see also 15:1); Hebrew reads *from Oded the prophet.* **2 Chr 15:10** Hebrew *in the third month.* This month of the ancient Hebrew lunar calendar usually occurs within the months of May and June. **2 Chr 15:16** Hebrew *his mother.* **1 Kgs 15:19** As in Greek version; Hebrew reads *There is a treaty.*

Mareshah

Mareshah was a city on the road from the coastal plain of Judah toward Hebron and Jerusalem. Remains of Jewish pottery indicate that people lived there from at least 800 B.C.

During Israel's occupation of Canaan, Joshua allotted Mareshah to Judah (Josh 15:44). Later, at the division of the kingdom, Rehoboam fortified it as a protective outpost covering Jerusalem from the southwest, from which many invaders were to approach (2 Chr 11:8-12). Zerah the Ethiopian, with a million men and 300 chariots, penetrated as far as Mareshah and was defeated there by Asa, who cried out to God for help (2 Chr 14:9-13). When foes come against us, we need to seek God's rescue. He is faithful.

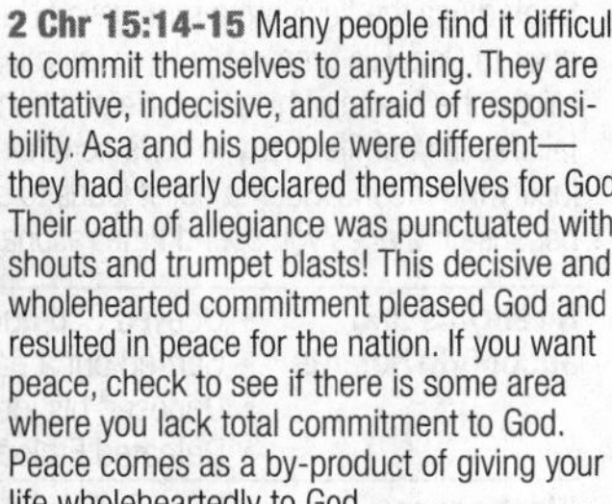

2 Chr 15:14-15 Many people find it difficult to commit themselves to anything. They are tentative, indecisive, and afraid of responsibility. Asa and his people were different—they had clearly declared themselves for God. Their oath of allegiance was punctuated with shouts and trumpet blasts! This decisive and wholehearted commitment pleased God and resulted in peace for the nation. If you want peace, check to see if there is some area where you lack total commitment to God. Peace comes as a by-product of giving your life wholeheartedly to God.

2 Chr 15:16 The Ten Commandments tell us to honor our fathers and mothers, and yet Asa removed his grandmother from the throne. While honoring parents is God's command, maintaining loyalty to God is an even higher priority. Jesus warned that respect for parents should never keep us from following him (Luke 14:26). If you have unbelieving parents, you must respect and honor them, but you must make devotion to God an even higher priority.

1 Kgs 15:16 Baasha seized the throne from Nadab (1 Kgs 15:27-28), who had replaced his father, Jeroboam, as king.

▸ 1 KINGS 15:16-22 *(cont.)*

happening, he abandoned his project of fortifying Ramah and withdrew to Tirzah. [22]Then King Asa sent an order throughout Judah, requiring that everyone, without exception, help to carry away the building stones and timbers that Baasha had been using to fortify Ramah. Asa used these materials to fortify the town of Geba in Benjamin and the town of Mizpah.

2 CHRONICLES 16:1-10

In the thirty-sixth year of Asa's reign, King Baasha of Israel invaded Judah and fortified Ramah in order to prevent anyone from entering or leaving King Asa's territory in Judah.

[2]Asa responded by removing the silver and gold from the treasuries of the Temple of the LORD and the royal palace. He sent it to King Ben-hadad of Aram, who was ruling in Damascus, along with this message:

> [3]"Let there be a treaty* between you and me like the one between your father and my father. See, I am sending you silver and gold. Break your treaty with King Baasha of Israel so that he will leave me alone."

[4]Ben-hadad agreed to King Asa's request and sent the commanders of his army to attack the towns of Israel. They conquered the towns of Ijon, Dan, Abel-beth-maacah,* and all the store cities in Naphtali. [5]As soon as Baasha of Israel heard what was happening, he abandoned his project of fortifying Ramah and stopped all work on it. [6]Then King Asa called out all the men of Judah to carry away the building stones and timbers that Baasha had been using to fortify Ramah. Asa used these materials to fortify the towns of Geba and Mizpah.

[7]At that time Hanani the seer came to King Asa and told him, "Because you have put your trust in the king of Aram instead of in the LORD your God, you missed your chance to destroy the army of the king of Aram. [8]Don't you remember what happened to the Ethiopians* and Libyans and their vast army, with all of their chariots and charioteers?* At that time you relied on the LORD, and he handed them over to you.

2 Chr 16:3 As in Greek version; Hebrew reads *There is a treaty.* **2 Chr 16:4** As in parallel text at 1 Kgs 15:20; Hebrew reads *Abel-maim,* another name for Abel-beth-maacah. **2 Chr 16:8a** Hebrew *Cushites.* **2 Chr 16:8b** Or *and horsemen?*

ASA

God does not condone the idea that "the end justifies the means." He is just and perfect in all his ways. People, on the other hand, are far from perfect. That a bond can exist between a loving and merciful Creator and his rebellious creation is as great a miracle as creation itself! As a king, Asa came very close to being good. He traveled a long way with God before getting off track. His sin was not so much deliberate disobedience as choosing the easy way rather than the right way. • When the odds seemed impossible in the battle with the Ethiopians, Asa recognized his need to depend on God. Following that victory, God's promise of peace based on obedience spurred the king and people to many years of right living. But Asa was to face a tougher test. • Years of animosity between Asa and Israel's king Baasha took an ugly turn. Baasha, king of the rival northern kingdom, was building a fort that threatened both the peace and the economy of Judah. Asa thought he saw a way out—he bribed King Ben-hadad of Aram to break his alliance with King Baasha. The plan worked brilliantly, but it wasn't God's way. When God's prophet Hanani confronted Asa, he flew into a rage, jailed Hanani, and took out his anger on his people. Asa rejected correction and refused to admit his error to God. His greatest failure was missing what God could have done with his life if he had been willing to be humble. His pride ruined the health of his reign. He stubbornly held on to his failure until his death. • Does this attitude sound familiar? Can you identify failures in your life that you have continued to rationalize rather than admit to God and accept his forgiveness? The end does not justify the means. Such a belief leads to sin and failure. The stubborn refusal to admit a failure due to sin can become a big problem because it makes you spend time rationalizing rather than learning from your mistakes and moving on.

Strengths and accomplishments	• Obeyed God during the first 10 years of his reign • Carried out a partially successful effort to abolish idolatry • Deposed his idolatrous grandmother, Maacah • Defeated Ethiopia's mighty army
Weaknesses and mistakes	• Responded with rage when confronted about his sin • Made alliances with foreign nations and evil people
Lessons from his life	• God not only reinforces good, he confronts evil • Efforts to follow God's plans and rules yield positive results • How well a plan works is no measure of its rightness or approval by God
Vital statistics	• Where: Jerusalem • Occupation: King of Judah • Relatives: Grandmother: Maacah. Father: Abijah. Son: Jehoshaphat. • Contemporaries: Hanani, Ben-hadad, Zerah, Azariah, Baasha
Key verse	"The eyes of the LORD search the whole earth in order to strengthen those whose hearts are fully committed to him. What a fool you have been! From now on you will be at war" (2 Chr 16:9).

Asa's story is told in 1 Kings 15:8-24; 2 Chronicles 14–16. He is also mentioned in Jeremiah 41:9; Matthew 1:7.

9The eyes of the LORD search the whole earth in order
to strengthen those whose hearts are fully committed
to him. What a fool you have been! From now on you
will be at war."
10Asa became so angry with Hanani for saying this
that he threw him into prison and put him in stocks. At
that time Asa also began to oppress some of his people.

Summary of Baasha's Reign

1 KINGS 16:1-7

This message from the LORD was delivered to King Baasha by the prophet Jehu son of Hanani: 2"I lifted you
out of the dust to make you ruler of my people Israel,
but you have followed the evil example of Jeroboam.
You have provoked my anger by causing my people
Israel to sin. 3So now I will destroy you and your family,
just as I destroyed the descendants of Jeroboam son
of Nebat. 4The members of Baasha's family who die
in the city will be eaten by dogs, and those who die in
the field will be eaten by vultures."
5The rest of the events in Baasha's reign and the
extent of his power are recorded in *The Book of the
History of the Kings of Israel.* 6When Baasha died,
he was buried in Tirzah. Then his son Elah became
the next king.
7The message from the LORD against Baasha and his
family came through the prophet Jehu son of Hanani.
It was delivered because Baasha had done what was
evil in the LORD's sight (just as the family of Jeroboam
had done), and also because Baasha had destroyed the
family of Jeroboam. The LORD's anger was provoked
by Baasha's sins.

Elah Rules in Israel

1 KINGS 16:8-14

Elah son of Baasha began to rule over Israel in the
twenty-sixth year of King Asa's reign in Judah. He
reigned in the city of Tirzah for two years.
9Then Zimri, who commanded half of the royal
chariots, made plans to kill him. One day in Tirzah,
Elah was getting drunk at the home of Arza, the supervisor of the palace. 10Zimri walked in and struck him
down and killed him. This happened in the twenty-
seventh year of King Asa's reign in Judah. Then Zimri
became the next king.
11Zimri immediately killed the entire royal family
of Baasha, leaving him not even a single male child.
He even destroyed distant relatives and friends. 12So
Zimri destroyed the dynasty of Baasha as the LORD had
promised through the prophet Jehu. 13This happened
because of all the sins Baasha and his son Elah had
committed, and because of the sins they led Israel

2 Chr 16:7-10 Both Judah and Israel suffered from faithless forgetfulness! Although God had delivered them even when they were outnumbered (2 Chr 13:3ff; 14:9ff), they repeatedly sought help from pagan nations rather than from God. That Asa sought help from Aram was evidence of national spiritual decline. With help from God alone, Asa had defeated the Ethiopians in open battle. But his confidence in God had slipped, and now he sought only a human solution to his problem. When confronted by the prophet Hanani, Asa threw him in prison, revealing the true condition of his heart. It is not sin to use human means to solve our problems, but it is sin to trust them more than God, to think they are better than God's ways, or to leave God completely out of the problem-solving process.

1 Kgs 16:1-7 God had destroyed Jeroboam's descendants for their flagrant sins, and yet Baasha repeated the same mistakes. He did not learn from the example of those who had gone before him; he did not stop to think that his sin would be punished. Make sure you learn from your past, the experiences of others, and the lives of those whose stories are told in the Bible. Don't repeat mistakes.

THE APPEAL OF IDOLS

On the surface, the lives of the kings don't make sense. How could they run to idolatry so fast when they had God's Word (at least some of it), prophets, and the example of David? Here are some of the reasons for the enticement of idols:

	The Appeal of Idols	*Modern Parallel*
Power	The people wanted freedom from the authority of both God and the priests. They wanted their religion to fit their lifestyle, not their lifestyle to fit their religion.	People do not want to answer to a greater authority. Instead of having power over others, God wants us to have the Holy Spirit's power to help others.
Pleasure	Idol worship exalted sensuality without responsibility or guilt. People acted out the vicious and sensuous personalities of the gods they worshiped, thus gaining approval for their degraded lives.	People deify pleasure, seeking it at the expense of everything else. Instead of seeking pleasure that leads to long-range disaster, God calls us to seek the kind of pleasure that leads to long-range rewards.
Passion	Humanity was reduced to little more than animals. The people did not have to be viewed as unique individuals but could be exploited sexually, politically, and economically.	Like animals, people let physical drives and passion rule them. Instead of expressing passions that exploit others, God calls us to redirect our passions to areas that build others up.
Praise and Popularity	The high and holy nature of God was replaced by gods who were more a reflection of human nature, thus more culturally suitable to the people. These gods no longer required sacrifice, just a token of appeasement.	Sacrifice is seen as self-inflicted punishment, making no sense. Success is to be sought at all costs. Instead of seeking praise for ourselves, God calls us to praise him and those who honor him.

▸ **1 KINGS 16:8-14** ***(cont.)***

to commit. They provoked the anger of the LORD, the God of Israel, with their worthless idols.

14The rest of the events in Elah's reign and everything he did are recorded in *The Book of the History of the Kings of Israel.*

Zimri Rules in Israel

1 KINGS 16:15-20

Zimri began to rule over Israel in the twenty-seventh year of King Asa's reign in Judah, but his reign in Tirzah lasted only seven days. The army of Israel was then attacking the Philistine town of Gibbethon. 16When they heard that Zimri had committed treason and had assassinated the king, that very day they chose Omri, commander of the army, as the new king of Israel. 17So Omri led the entire army of Israel up from Gibbethon to attack Tirzah, Israel's capital. 18When Zimri saw that the city had been taken, he went into the citadel of the palace and burned it down over himself and died in the flames. 19For he, too, had done what was evil in the LORD's sight. He followed the example of Jeroboam in all the sins he had committed and led Israel to commit.

20The rest of the events in Zimri's reign and his conspiracy are recorded in *The Book of the History of the Kings of Israel.*

C. The Era of Omri's Dynasty in the Northern Kingdom

Omri and his son Ahab were very evil kings in God's sight, and less than fifty years after Omri came to power, another would seize control of Israel's throne. During this time, the famous prophets Elijah and Elisha confronted the evil they saw in both the northern and southern kingdoms, and Judah had a pair of good kings (Asa and Jehoshaphat), followed by a pair of evil kings influenced by their intermarriage with Omri's line.

1. OMRI SEIZES CONTROL

885 BC

Omri begins to rule in Israel

After Zimri's extremely brief reign over the northern kingdom of Israel, the army commander Omri seized control of the nation by defeating his rival Tibni. Omri moved the capital of Israel to Samaria, where it would remain for the rest of its history, and gave the nation their first taste of peace. But Omri ignored God and continued to follow the religion set up by Jeroboam, and so his dynasty did not last long. Peace and prosperity are not always a sign of God's approval; his judgment on wickedness is sure.

Omri Rules in Israel

1 KINGS 16:21-28

But now the people of Israel were split into two factions. Half the people tried to make Tibni son of Ginath their king, while the other half supported Omri. 22But Omri's supporters defeated the supporters of Tibni. So Tibni was killed, and Omri became the next king.

23Omri began to rule over Israel in the thirty-first year of King Asa's reign in Judah. He reigned twelve years in all, six of them in Tirzah. 24Then Omri bought the hill now known as Samaria from its owner, Shemer, for 150 pounds of silver.* He built a city on it and called the city Samaria in honor of Shemer.

25But Omri did what was evil in the LORD's sight, even more than any of the kings before him. 26He followed the example of Jeroboam son of Nebat in all the sins he had committed and led Israel to commit. The people provoked the anger of the LORD, the God of Israel, with their worthless idols.

27The rest of the events in Omri's reign, the extent of his power, and everything he did are recorded in *The Book of the History of the Kings of Israel.* 28When Omri died, he was buried in Samaria. Then his son Ahab became the next king.

Ahab Begins His Reign in Israel

1 KINGS 16:29-34

Ahab son of Omri began to rule over Israel in the thirty-eighth year of King Asa's reign in Judah. He reigned in Samaria twenty-two years. 30But Ahab son of Omri did what was evil in the LORD's sight, even more than any of the kings before him. 31And as though it were not enough to follow the example of Jeroboam, he married Jezebel, the daughter of King Ethbaal of the Sidonians, and he began to bow down in worship of Baal. 32First

1 Kgs 16:24 Hebrew *for 2 talents* [68 kilograms] *of silver.*

1 Kgs 16:21-22 Omri began his reign as political dissension brewed in Israel. After Zimri killed himself, the Israelite army chose Omri, their commander, as the next ruler. Tibni, Omri's chief rival to the throne, died, and Omri then began his evil reign. During his 12-year rule over Israel, he was a shrewd and capable leader. He organized the building of his new capital city, Samaria, while strengthening the nation politically and militarily. But he did not care about the nation's spiritual condition (Mic 6:16), and he purposely led Israel farther from God in order to put more power in his own hands.

1 Kgs 16:24 Omri's new capital, Samaria, offered some political advantages. The city was his personal property, so he had total control over it. Samaria also commanded a hilltop position, which made it easy to defend. Omri died before completing the city. So his son Ahab completed it, building not only the beautiful ivory palace (1 Kgs 22:39; Amos 3:13-15), but also a temple to the god Baal. Samaria served as the capital city for the rest of Israel's dynasties until it fell to the Assyrians in 722 B.C. (2 Kgs 17:5).

Ahab built a temple and an altar for Baal in Samaria.
[33]Then he set up an Asherah pole. He did more to provoke the anger of the LORD, the God of Israel, than any of the other kings of Israel before him.

[34]It was during his reign that Hiel, a man from Bethel, rebuilt Jericho. When he laid its foundations, it cost him the life of his oldest son, Abiram. And when he completed it and set up its gates, it cost him the life of his youngest son, Segub.* This all happened according to the message from the LORD concerning Jericho spoken by Joshua son of Nun.

Summary of Asa's Reign PARALLEL

1 KINGS 15:23-24

The rest of the events in Asa's reign—the extent of his power, everything he did, and the names of the cities he built—are recorded in *The Book of the History of the Kings of Judah.* In his old age his feet became diseased.
[24]When Asa died, he was buried with his ancestors in the City of David.

Then Jehoshaphat, Asa's son, became the next king.

2 CHRONICLES 16:11-14

The rest of the events of Asa's reign, from beginning to end, are recorded in *The Book of the Kings of Judah and Israel.*
[12]In the thirty-ninth year of his reign, Asa developed a serious foot disease. Yet even with the severity of his disease, he did not seek the LORD's help but turned only to his physicians.
[13]So he died in the forty-first year of his reign.
[14]He was buried in the tomb he had carved out for himself in the City of David. He was laid on a bed perfumed with sweet spices and fragrant ointments, and the people built a huge funeral fire in his honor.

1 Kgs 16:34 An ancient Hebrew scribal tradition reads *He killed his oldest son when he laid its foundations, and he killed his youngest son when he set up its gates.*

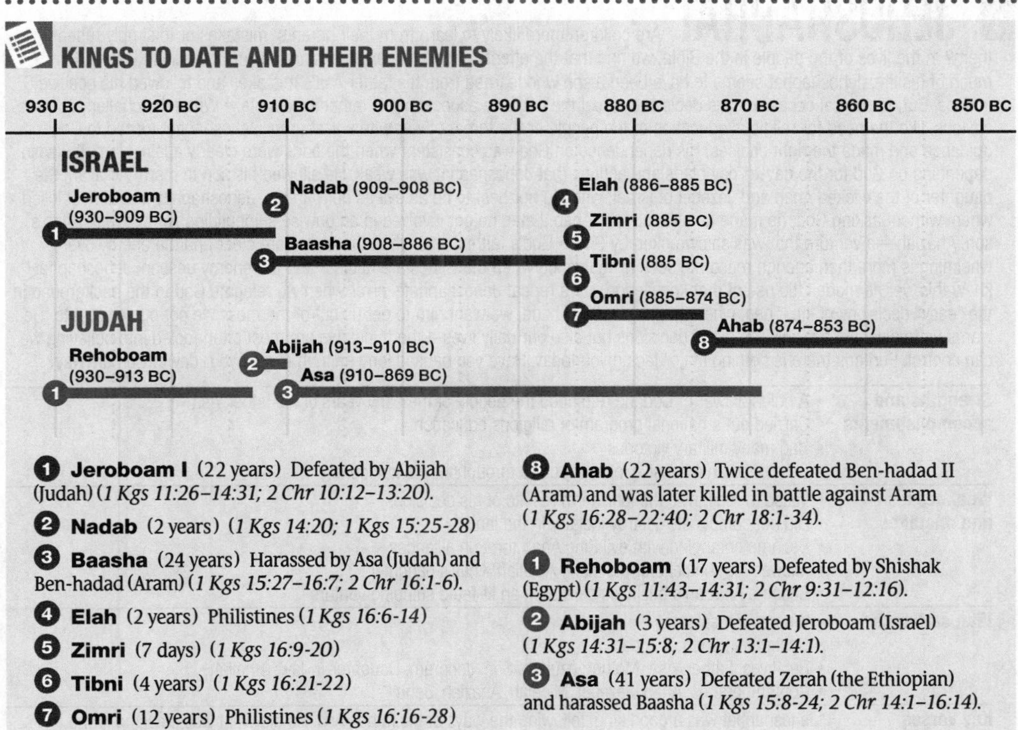

1 **Jeroboam I** (22 years) Defeated by Abijah (Judah) (*1 Kgs 11:26–14:31; 2 Chr 10:12–13:20*).

2 **Nadab** (2 years) (*1 Kgs 14:20; 1 Kgs 15:25-28*)

3 **Baasha** (24 years) Harassed by Asa (Judah) and Ben-hadad (Aram) (*1 Kgs 15:27–16:7; 2 Chr 16:1-6*).

4 **Elah** (2 years) Philistines (*1 Kgs 16:6-14*)

5 **Zimri** (7 days) (*1 Kgs 16:9-20*)

6 **Tibni** (4 years) (*1 Kgs 16:21-22*)

7 **Omri** (12 years) Philistines (*1 Kgs 16:16-28*)

8 **Ahab** (22 years) Twice defeated Ben-hadad II (Aram) and was later killed in battle against Aram (*1 Kgs 16:28–22:40; 2 Chr 18:1-34*).

1 **Rehoboam** (17 years) Defeated by Shishak (Egypt) (*1 Kgs 11:43–14:31; 2 Chr 9:31–12:16*).

2 **Abijah** (3 years) Defeated Jeroboam (Israel) (*1 Kgs 14:31–15:8; 2 Chr 13:1–14:1*).

3 **Asa** (41 years) Defeated Zerah (the Ethiopian) and harassed Baasha (*1 Kgs 15:8-24; 2 Chr 14:1–16:14*).

1 Kgs 16:31 Ahab's evil wife, Jezebel, came from the Phoenician city of Tyre where her father had been a high priest and eventually king. Jezebel worshiped the god Baal. In order to please her, Ahab built a temple and an altar for Baal (1 Kgs 16:32), thus promoting idolatry and leading the entire nation into sin. (For more about Baal, see the note on 1 Kgs 18:18, p. 716.)

2 Chr 16:12 The criticism of Asa's visit to the physicians was not a general indictment of medicine. Asa's problem was that he completely ignored God's help. The medicine practiced at this time was a mixture of superstition and folk remedies. We should certainly avoid any medicinal treatments derived from occult sources. Asa's experience should encourage us to follow the New Testament practice of receiving prayer for our sickness (Jas 5:14) as we seek responsible medical help.

Jehoshaphat Begins His Reign in Judah

2 CHRONICLES 17:1-19

Then Jehoshaphat, Asa's son, became the next king.
He strengthened Judah to stand against any attack
from Israel. 2He stationed troops in all the fortified
towns of Judah, and he assigned additional garrisons
to the land of Judah and to the towns of Ephraim that
his father, Asa, had captured.
3The LORD was with Jehoshaphat because he followed the example of his father's early years* and
did not worship the images of Baal. 4He sought his
father's God and obeyed his commands instead of
following the evil practices of the kingdom of Israel.
5So the LORD established Jehoshaphat's control over
the kingdom of Judah. All the people of Judah brought
gifts to Jehoshaphat, so he became very wealthy and
highly esteemed. 6He was deeply committed to* the
ways of the LORD. He removed the pagan shrines and
Asherah poles from Judah.
7In the third year of his reign Jehoshaphat sent
his officials to teach in all the towns of Judah. These
officials included Ben-hail, Obadiah, Zechariah, Nethanel, and Micaiah. 8He sent Levites along with them,
including Shemaiah, Nethaniah, Zebadiah, Asahel,
Shemiramoth, Jehonathan, Adonijah, Tobijah, and
Tob-adonijah. He also sent out the priests Elishama
and Jehoram. 9They took copies of the Book of the
Law of the LORD and traveled around through all the
towns of Judah, teaching the people.
10Then the fear of the LORD fell over all the surrounding kingdoms so that none of them wanted to
declare war on Jehoshaphat. 11Some of the Philistines

2 Chr 17:3 Some Hebrew manuscripts read *the example of his father, David.* **2 Chr 17:6** Hebrew *His heart was courageous in.*

JEHOSHAPHAT

Are children more likely to learn from their parents' mistakes or to simply repeat them? In the lives of the people in the Bible, we find that the effects of parental examples are powerful and long lasting. For much of his life, Jehoshaphat seems to have been a son who learned from his father Asa's mistakes and followed his positive actions. But on several occasions, his decisions reveal the negative aspects of his father's example. • When the challenges were obvious, like the need for religious education of the people or the threat of war with a vast army, Jehoshaphat turned to God for guidance and made the right choices. His dependence on God was consistent when the odds were clearly against him. It was in depending on God for the day-to-day plans and actions that Jehoshaphat was weak. He allowed his son to marry Athaliah, the daughter of the wicked Ahab and Jezebel of Israel, who did her best to be as evil as her parents. Jehoshaphat was almost killed when, without asking God, he made an alliance with Ahab. Later, he got involved in an unwise shipbuilding venture with Ahab's son, Ahaziah—a venture that was shipwrecked by God. • God's faithfulness when the issues are clear and the enemy overwhelming is more than enough reason to seek his guidance when the issues are unclear and the enemy unseen. Jehoshaphat knew this, yet he made little use of that knowledge. • We repeat Jehoshaphat's error when we relegate God to the background in the "easy" decisions of life. Then, when things get out of hand, we want him to get us out of the mess we got ourselves into. God wants us to give him not only the major decisions but also our daily lives—the things we are most often fooled into believing we can control. Perhaps there is nothing major facing you today. Have you paused long enough to give your day to God anyway?

Strengths and accomplishments	• A bold follower of God, he reminded the people of the early years of his father, Asa • Carried out a national program of religious education • Had many military victories • Developed an extensive legal structure throughout the kingdom
Weaknesses and mistakes	• Failed to recognize the long-term results of his decisions • Did not completely destroy idolatry in the land • Became entangled with evil King Ahab through alliances • Allowed his son Jehoram to marry Athaliah, Ahab's daughter • Became Ahaziah's business partner in an ill-fated shipping venture
Vital statistics	• Where: Jerusalem • Occupation: King of Judah • Relatives: Father: Asa. Mother: Azubah. Son: Jehoram. Daughter-in-law: Athaliah. • Contemporaries: Ahab, Jezebel, Micaiah, Ahaziah, Jehu
Key verses	"Jehoshaphat was a good king, following the ways of his father, Asa. He did what was pleasing in the LORD's sight. During his reign, however, he failed to remove all the pagan shrines, and the people never fully committed themselves to follow the God of their ancestors" (2 Chr 20:32-33).

Jehoshaphat's story is told in 1 Kings 15:24–22:50; 2 Chronicles 17:1–21:1. He is also mentioned in 2 Kings 3:1-14; Joel 3:2, 12.

2 Chr 17:7-9 The people of Judah were biblically illiterate. They had never taken time to listen to and discuss God's law and understand how it could change them. Jehoshaphat realized that knowing God's commands was the first step to getting people to live as they should, so he initiated a nationwide religious education program. He reversed the religious decline that had occurred at the end of Asa's reign by putting God first in the people's minds and instilling in them a sense of commitment and mission. Because of this action, the nation began to follow God. Churches today need solid Christian education programs. Exposure to good Bible teaching is essential for living as God intended.

brought him gifts and silver as tribute, and the Arabs
brought 7,700 rams and 7,700 male goats.
12 So Jehoshaphat became more and more powerful
and built fortresses and storage cities throughout Judah. 13 He stored numerous supplies in Judah's towns
and stationed an army of seasoned troops at Jerusalem.
14 His army was enrolled according to ancestral clans.

From Judah there were 300,000 troops organized
in units of 1,000, under the command of
Adnah. 15 Next in command was Jehohanan,
who commanded 280,000 troops. 16 Next was
Amasiah son of Zicri, who volunteered for the
LORD's service, with 200,000 troops under his
command.
17 From Benjamin there were 200,000 troops
equipped with bows and shields. They were
under the command of Eliada, a veteran soldier.
18 Next in command was Jehozabad, who
commanded 180,000 armed men.

19 These were the troops stationed in Jerusalem to
serve the king, besides those Jehoshaphat stationed
in the fortified towns throughout Judah.

2. ELIJAH'S MINISTRY

God sent the prophet Elijah to confront the northern kingdom of Israel about their idolatry. Elijah performed many miracles in God's name, demonstrating God's power over nature, other gods, and even life itself. Elijah was a complex person, noted both for his bold dependence on God in the confrontation at Mount Carmel as well as for his bouts with despair in thinking he was the only one who served God. He was a bright light for God in a dark time.

Elijah Fed by Ravens

1 KINGS 17:1-7

Now Elijah, who was from Tishbe in Gilead, told King
Ahab, "As surely as the LORD, the God of Israel, lives—
the God I serve—there will be no dew or rain during
the next few years until I give the word!"
2 Then the LORD said to Elijah, 3 "Go to the east and
hide by Kerith Brook, near where it enters the Jordan
River. 4 Drink from the brook and eat what the ravens
bring you, for I have commanded them to bring you
food."
5 So Elijah did as the LORD told him and camped
beside Kerith Brook, east of the Jordan. 6 The ravens
brought him bread and meat each morning and evening, and he drank from the brook. 7 But after a while
the brook dried up, for there was no rainfall anywhere
in the land.

The Widow at Zarephath

1 KINGS 17:8-24

Then the LORD said to Elijah, 9 "Go and live in the village
of Zarephath, near the city of Sidon. I have instructed
a widow there to feed you."
10 So he went to Zarephath. As he arrived at the gates
of the village, he saw a widow gathering sticks, and he
asked her, "Would you please bring me a little water
in a cup?" 11 As she was going to get it, he called to her,
"Bring me a bite of bread, too."
12 But she said, "I swear by the LORD your God that I
don't have a single piece of bread in the house. And I
have only a handful of flour left in the jar and a little
cooking oil in the bottom of the jug. I was just gathering a few sticks to cook this last meal, and then my
son and I will die."
13 But Elijah said to her, "Don't be afraid! Go ahead

---

1 Kgs 17:1 Elijah was the first in a long line of important prophets God sent to Israel and Judah. Israel, the northern kingdom, had no faithful kings throughout its history. Each king was wicked, actually leading the people in worshiping pagan gods. Few priests were left from the tribe of Levi (most had gone to Judah), and the priests appointed by Israel's kings were corrupt and ineffective. With no king or priests to bring God's word to the people, God called prophets to try to rescue Israel from its moral and spiritual decline. For the next 300 years these men and women would play vital roles in both nations, encouraging the people and leaders to turn back to God.

1 Kgs 17:1 Those who worshiped Baal believed he was the god who brought the rains and bountiful harvests. So when Elijah walked into the presence of this Baal-worshiping king and told him there would be no rain for several years, Ahab was shocked. Ahab had built a strong military defense, but it would be no help against drought. He had many priests of Baal, but they could not bring rain. Elijah bravely confronted the man who led his people into evil, and he told of a power far greater than any pagan god—the Lord God of Israel. When rebellion and heresy were at an all-time high in Israel, God responded not only with words but with action.

1 Kgs 17:10ff In a nation that was required by law to care for its prophets, it is ironic that God turned to ravens (unclean birds) and a widow (a foreigner from Jezebel's home territory) to care for Elijah. God has help where we least expect it. He provides for us in ways that go beyond our narrow definitions or expectations. No matter how bitter our trials or how seemingly hopeless our situation, we should look for God's caring touch. We may find his providence in some strange places!

1 Kgs 17:13-16 When the widow of Zarephath met Elijah, she thought she was preparing her last meal. But a simple act of faith produced a miracle. She trusted Elijah and gave him all she had to eat. Faith is the step between promise and assurance. Miracles seem so out of reach for our feeble faith. But every miracle, large or small, begins with an act of obedience. We may not see the solution until we take the first step of faith.

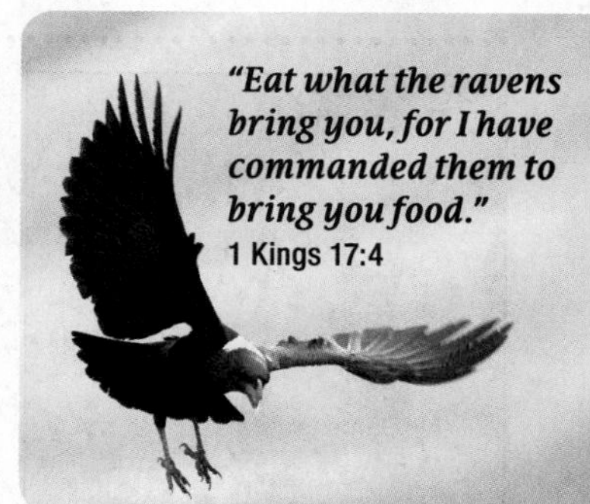
"Eat what the ravens bring you, for I have commanded them to bring you food."
1 Kings 17:4

▶ **1 KINGS 17:8-24** ***(cont.)***

and do just what you've said, but make a little bread for me first. Then use what's left to prepare a meal for yourself and your son. 14For this is what the LORD, the God of Israel, says: There will always be flour and olive oil left in your containers until the time when the LORD sends rain and the crops grow again!"

15So she did as Elijah said, and she and Elijah and her family continued to eat for many days. 16There was always enough flour and olive oil left in the containers, just as the LORD had promised through Elijah.

17Some time later the woman's son became sick. He grew worse and worse, and finally he died. 18Then she said to Elijah, "O man of God, what have you done to me? Have you come here to point out my sins and kill my son?"

19But Elijah replied, "Give me your son." And he took the child's body from her arms, carried him up the stairs to the room where he was staying, and laid the body on his bed. 20Then Elijah cried out to the LORD, "O LORD my God, why have you brought tragedy to this widow who has opened her home to me, causing her son to die?"

21And he stretched himself out over the child three times and cried out to the LORD, "O LORD my God, please let this child's life return to him." 22The LORD heard Elijah's prayer, and the life of the child returned, and he revived! 23Then Elijah brought him down from the upper room and gave him to his mother. "Look!" he said. "Your son is alive!"

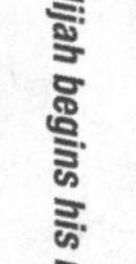

Elijah begins his ministry

24Then the woman told Elijah, "Now I know for sure that you are a man of God, and that the LORD truly speaks through you."

The Contest on Mount Carmel

1 KINGS 18:1-40

Later on, in the third year of the drought, the LORD said to Elijah, "Go and present yourself to King Ahab. Tell him that I will soon send rain!" 2So Elijah went to appear before Ahab.

Meanwhile, the famine had become very severe in Samaria. 3So Ahab summoned Obadiah, who was in charge of the palace. (Obadiah was a devoted follower of the LORD. 4Once when Jezebel had tried to kill all the LORD's prophets, Obadiah had hidden 100 of them in two caves. He put fifty prophets in each cave and supplied them with food and water.) 5Ahab said to Obadiah, "We must check every spring and valley in the land to see if we can find enough grass to save at least some of my horses and mules." 6So they divided the land between them. Ahab went one way by himself, and Obadiah went another way by himself.

7As Obadiah was walking along, he suddenly saw Elijah coming toward him. Obadiah recognized him at once and bowed low to the ground before him. "Is it really you, my lord Elijah?" he asked.

8"Yes, it is," Elijah replied. "Now go and tell your master, 'Elijah is here.'"

9"Oh, sir," Obadiah protested, "what harm have I done to you that you are sending me to my death at the hands of Ahab? 10For I swear by the LORD your God that the king has searched every nation and kingdom on earth from end to end to find you. And each time he was told, 'Elijah isn't here,' King Ahab forced the king of that nation to swear to the truth of his claim. 11And now you say, 'Go and tell your master, "Elijah is here."' 12But as soon as I leave you, the Spirit of the LORD will carry you away to who knows where. When Ahab comes and cannot find you, he will kill me. Yet I have been a true servant of the LORD all my life. 13Has no one told you, my lord, about the time when Jezebel was trying to kill the LORD's prophets? I hid 100 of them in two caves and supplied them with food and water. 14And now you say, 'Go and tell your master, "Elijah is here."' Sir, if I do that, Ahab will certainly kill me."

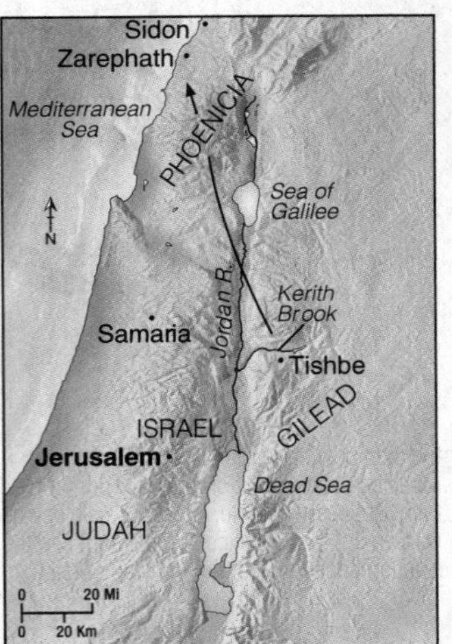

◀ ***ELIJAH HIDES FROM AHAB***
Elijah prophesied a drought and then hid from King Ahab by the Kerith Brook, where he was fed by ravens. When the brook dried up, God sent him to Zarephath in Phoenicia, where a widow and her son fed him and gave him lodging.

1 Kgs 17:17 Even when God has done a miracle in our lives, our troubles may not be over. The famine was a terrible experience, but the worst was yet to come. God's provision is never given in order to let us rest upon it. We need to depend on him as we face each new trial.

1 Kgs 18:3-4 Although Elijah was alone in his confrontation with Ahab and Jezebel, he was not the only one in Israel who believed in God. Obadiah had been faithful in hiding 100 prophets still true to the Lord.

1 Kgs 18:18 Instead of worshiping the true God, Ahab and his wife, Jezebel, worshiped Baal, the most popular Canaanite god. Baal idols were often made in the shape of a bull, representing strength and fertility and reflecting lust for power and sexual pleasure.

1 Kgs 18:19 Ahab brought 850 pagan prophets to Mount Carmel to match wits and power with Elijah. Evil kings hated God's prophets because they spoke against sin and

15But Elijah said, "I swear by the LORD Almighty, in
whose presence I stand, that I will present myself to
Ahab this very day."
16So Obadiah went to tell Ahab that Elijah had come,
and Ahab went out to meet Elijah. 17When Ahab saw
him, he exclaimed, "So, is it really you, you troublemaker of Israel?"
18"I have made no trouble for Israel," Elijah replied.
"You and your family are the troublemakers, for you
have refused to obey the commands of the LORD and
have worshiped the images of Baal instead. 19Now
summon all Israel to join me at Mount Carmel, along
with the 450 prophets of Baal and the 400 prophets
of Asherah who are supported by Jezebel.*"
20So Ahab summoned all the people of Israel and
the prophets to Mount Carmel. 21Then Elijah stood
in front of them and said, "How much longer will you
waver, hobbling between two opinions? If the LORD is
God, follow him! But if Baal is God, then follow him!"
But the people were completely silent.
22Then Elijah said to them, "I am the only prophet
of the LORD who is left, but Baal has 450 prophets.
23Now bring two bulls. The prophets of Baal may
choose whichever one they wish and cut it into
pieces and lay it on the wood of their altar, but without setting fire to it. I will prepare the other bull and
lay it on the wood on the altar, but not set fire to it.
24Then call on the name of your god, and I will call
on the name of the LORD. The god who answers by
setting fire to the wood is the true God!" And all the
people agreed.
25Then Elijah said to the prophets of Baal, "You go
first, for there are many of you. Choose one of the
bulls, and prepare it and call on the name of your god.
But do not set fire to the wood."
26So they prepared one of the bulls and placed it on
the altar. Then they called on the name of Baal from
morning until noontime, shouting, "O Baal, answer
us!" But there was no reply of any kind. Then they
danced, hobbling around the altar they had made.
27About noontime Elijah began mocking them.
"You'll have to shout louder," he scoffed, "for surely
he is a god! Perhaps he is daydreaming, or is relieving
himself.* Or maybe he is away on a trip, or is asleep
and needs to be wakened!"
28So they shouted louder, and following their normal custom, they cut themselves with knives and
swords until the blood gushed out. 29They raved all
afternoon until the time of the evening sacrifice, but
still there was no sound, no reply, no response.
30Then Elijah called to the people, "Come over here!"
They all crowded around him as he repaired the altar

1 Kgs 18:19 Hebrew *who eat at Jezebel's table.* **1 Kgs 18:27** Or *is busy somewhere else,* or *is engaged in business.*

PROPHETS—FALSE AND TRUE

The false prophets were an obstacle to bringing God's word to the people. They would bring messages that contradicted the words of the true prophets. They gave "messages" that appealed to the people's sinful nature and comforted their fears. False prophets told people what they wanted to hear. True prophets told God's truth.

False Prophets	True Prophets
Worked for political purposes to benefit themselves	Worked for spiritual purposes to serve God and the people
Held positions of great wealth	Owned little or nothing
Gave false messages	Spoke only true messages
Spoke only what the people wanted to hear	Spoke only what God told them to say—no matter how unpopular

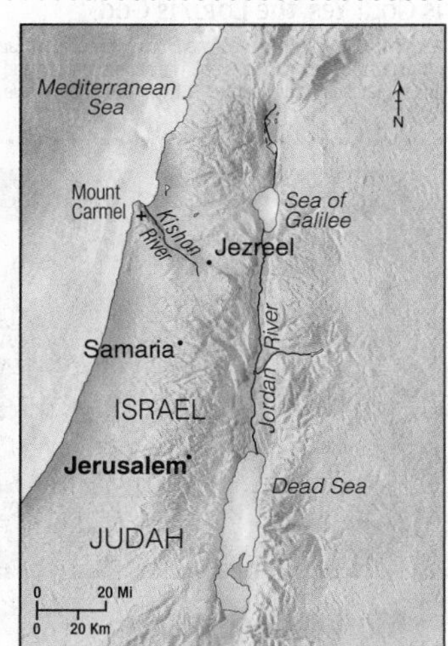

***THE SHOWDOWN AT CARMEL** In a showdown with the false prophets of Baal at Mount Carmel, Elijah set out to prove to evil Ahab that only the Lord is God. Elijah then killed the false prophets by the Kishon Valley and ran back to Jezreel.*

idolatry and undermined their control over the people. With the wicked kings' backing, many pagan prophets sprang up to counter the words of God's prophets. But Elijah showed the people that speaking a prophecy wasn't enough. One needed the power of the living God to fulfill it.

1 Kgs 18:21 Elijah challenged the people to take a stand—to follow whoever was the true God. Why did so many people waver between the two choices? Perhaps some were not sure. Many knew that the Lord was God, but they enjoyed the sinful pleasures and other benefits that came with following Ahab in his idolatrous worship. It is important to take a stand for the Lord. If we just drift along with whatever is pleasant and easy, we will someday discover that we have been worshiping a false god—ourselves.

1 Kgs 18:29 Although the prophets of Baal "raved all afternoon," no one answered them. Their god was silent because it was not real. The gods we may be tempted to follow are not idols of wood or stone, but they are just as false and dangerous because they cause us to depend on something other than God. Power, status, appearance, or material possessions can become our gods if we devote our lives to them. But when we reach times of crisis and desperately call out to these gods, there will only be silence. They can offer no true answers, no guidance, and no wisdom.

▶ **1 KINGS 18:1-40** ***(cont.)***
of the LORD that had been torn down. 31He took twelve
stones, one to represent each of the tribes of Israel,*
32and he used the stones to rebuild the altar in the
name of the LORD. Then he dug a trench around the
altar large enough to hold about three gallons.* 33He
piled wood on the altar, cut the bull into pieces, and
laid the pieces on the wood.

Then he said, "Fill four large jars with water, and pour the water over the offering and the wood."

34After they had done this, he said, "Do the same
thing again!" And when they were finished, he said,
"Now do it a third time!" So they did as he said, 35and
the water ran around the altar and even filled the
trench.

36At the usual time for offering the evening sacrifice, Elijah the prophet walked up to the altar and prayed, "O LORD, God of Abraham, Isaac, and Jacob,* prove today that you are God in Israel and that I am your servant. Prove that I have done all this at your
command. 37O LORD, answer me! Answer me so these
people will know that you, O LORD, are God and that
you have brought them back to yourself."

38Immediately the fire of the LORD flashed down from heaven and burned up the young bull, the wood, the stones, and the dust. It even licked up all the water
in the trench! 39And when all the people saw it, they fell
face down on the ground and cried out, "The LORD—he is God! Yes, the LORD is God!"

40Then Elijah commanded, "Seize all the prophets of Baal. Don't let a single one escape!" So the people seized them all, and Elijah took them down to the Kishon Valley and killed them there.

Elijah Prays for Rain

1 KINGS 18:41-46
Then Elijah said to Ahab, "Go get something to eat and drink, for I hear a mighty rainstorm coming!"

42So Ahab went to eat and drink. But Elijah climbed to the top of Mount Carmel and bowed low to the ground and prayed with his face between his knees.

43Then he said to his servant, "Go and look out toward the sea."

The servant went and looked, then returned to Elijah and said, "I didn't see anything."

Seven times Elijah told him to go and look. 44Fi-
nally the seventh time, his servant told him, "I saw a little cloud about the size of a man's hand rising from the sea."

Then Elijah shouted, "Hurry to Ahab and tell him, 'Climb into your chariot and go back home. If you don't hurry, the rain will stop you!'"

45And soon the sky was black with clouds. A
heavy wind brought a terrific rainstorm, and Ahab
left quickly for Jezreel. 46Then the LORD gave special
strength to Elijah. He tucked his cloak into his belt*
and ran ahead of Ahab's chariot all the way to the entrance of Jezreel.

1 Kgs 18:31 Hebrew *each of the tribes of the sons of Jacob to whom the LORD had said, "Your name will be Israel."* **1 Kgs 18:32** Hebrew *2 seahs* [12 liters] *of seed.* **1 Kgs 18:36** Hebrew *and Israel.* The names "Jacob" and "Israel" are often interchanged throughout the Old Testament, referring sometimes to the individual patriarch and sometimes to the nation. **1 Kgs 18:46** Hebrew *He bound up his loins.*

Mount Carmel

Mount Carmel is more of a ridge than a mountain. It extends about 20 miles along the Mediterranean Sea and juts southeastward into the Jezreel Valley. Its greatest width at the southeast is 13 miles; its highest point, 1,742 feet. It was here that the contest between Elijah and the prophets of Baal took place (1 Kgs 18). The site was fitting because Carmel was disputed territory between Israel and the Phoenicians, and thus between the Phoenician god Baal and Israel's God. Baal did not respond to the prophets of Baal because he was a false god, a "dead" god. The God of Elijah responded because he is the true God, the living God.

Elijah was not the first to build a Hebrew altar on the mountain; the narrative describes him as repairing a ruined "altar of the LORD" before offering his sacrifice (1 Kgs 18:30). The traditional location of that contest is Qeren ha-Carmel at 1,581 feet, overlooking the Jezreel Valley. The Kishon River (1 Kgs 18:40) flows through that valley and around to the north of Carmel.

1 Kgs 18:31 Using 12 stones to build the altar took courage. This would have angered some of the people because it was a silent reminder of the split between the tribes. While the 10 tribes of the north called themselves Israel, this name originally was given to all 12 of the tribes together.

1 Kgs 18:36-38 God flashed fire from heaven for Elijah. He will also help us accomplish what he commands us to do. The proof may not be as dramatic in our lives as in Elijah's, but God will make resources available to us in creative ways to accomplish his purposes. He will give us the wisdom to raise a family, the courage to take a stand for truth, or the means to provide help for someone in need. Like Elijah, we can have faith that whatever God commands us to do, he will provide what we need to carry it through.

1 Kgs 18:46 Elijah ran the six miles back to the city in order to give Ahab a last chance to turn from his sin before joining Jezebel in Jezreel. His run also ensured that the correct story of what happened would reach Jezreel.

Elijah Flees to Sinai

1 KINGS 19:1-9a

When Ahab got home, he told Jezebel everything
Elijah had done, including the way he had killed all
the prophets of Baal. 2So Jezebel sent this message
to Elijah: "May the gods strike me and even kill me
if by this time tomorrow I have not killed you just as
you killed them."
3Elijah was afraid and fled for his life. He went to
Beersheba, a town in Judah, and he left his servant
there. 4Then he went on alone into the wilderness,
traveling all day. He sat down under a solitary broom
tree and prayed that he might die. "I have had enough,
LORD," he said. "Take my life, for I am no better than
my ancestors who have already died."
5Then he lay down and slept under the broom tree.
But as he was sleeping, an angel touched him and
told him, "Get up and eat!" 6He looked around and

ELIJAH

Elijah's single-minded commitment to God shocks and challenges us. He was sent to confront—not comfort. And Elijah spoke God's words to a king who often rejected the message just because he brought it. Elijah chose to carry out his ministry for God alone and paid for that decision by experiencing isolation from others who were also faithful to God. • It is interesting to think about the amazing miracles God accomplished through Elijah, but we would do well to focus on the relationship they shared. All that happened in Elijah's life began with the same miracle that is available to us—he responded to the miracle of being able to know God. • For example, after God worked an overwhelming miracle through Elijah in defeating the prophets of Baal, Queen Jezebel retaliated by threatening Elijah's life. And Elijah ran. He felt afraid, depressed, and abandoned. Despite God's provision of food and shelter in the wilderness, Elijah wanted to die. So God presented Elijah with a message he needed to hear. Elijah witnessed a windstorm, an earthquake, and a fire. But the Lord was not in any of those powerful things. Instead, God displayed his presence in a gentle whisper. • Elijah, like us, struggled with his feelings even after this comforting message from God. So God confronted Elijah's emotions and commanded action. He told Elijah what to do next and informed him that part of his loneliness was based on ignorance: Seven thousand others in Israel were still faithful to God. • Even today, God often speaks through the gentle and obvious rather than the spectacular and unusual. God has work for us to do even when we experience fear and failure. And God always has more resources and people than we know about. Although we might wish to do amazing miracles for God, we should instead focus on developing a relationship with him. The real miracle of Elijah's life was his very personal relationship with God. And that miracle is available to us.

Strengths and accomplishments	• Was the most famous and dramatic of Israel's prophets • Predicted the beginning and end of a three-year drought • Was used by God to restore a dead child to his mother • Represented God in a showdown with priests of Baal and Asherah • Appeared with Moses and Jesus in the New Testament Transfiguration scene
Weaknesses and mistakes	• Gave in to his feelings of isolation and loneliness • Fled in fear from Jezebel when she threatened his life
Lessons from his life	• We are never closer to defeat than in our moments of greatest victory • We are never as alone as we may feel; God is always there • God speaks more frequently in persistent whispers than in shouts
Vital statistics	• Where: Gilead • Occupation: Prophet • Contemporaries: Ahab, Jezebel, Ahaziah, Obadiah, Jehu, Hazael
Key verses	"At the usual time for offering the evening sacrifice, Elijah the prophet walked up to the altar and prayed, 'O LORD, God of Abraham, Isaac, and Jacob, prove today that you are God in Israel and that I am your servant. Prove that I have done all this at your command. O LORD, answer me! Answer me so these people will know that you, O LORD, are God and that you have brought them back to yourself.' "Immediately the fire of the LORD flashed down from heaven and burned up the young bull, the wood, the stones, and the dust. It even licked up all the water in the trench!" (1 Kgs 18:36-38).

Elijah's story is told in 1 Kings 17:1—2 Kings 2:11. He is also mentioned in 2 Chronicles 21:12-15; Malachi 4:5-6; Matthew 11:14; 16:14; 17:3-13; 27:47-49; Luke 1:17; 4:25-26; John 1:19-25; Romans 11:2-4; James 5:17-18.

1 Kgs 19:2 Jezebel was enraged about the death of her prophets because they had told her everything she wanted to hear, prophesying her future power and glory. Their job was to deify the king and queen and help perpetuate their kingdom. Jezebel was also angry because her supporters had been eliminated and her pride and authority damaged. The money she had invested in these prophets was now lost.

Elijah, who caused the prophets' deaths, was a constant thorn in Jezebel's side because he was always predicting gloom and doom. Since she could not control his actions, Jezebel vowed to kill him. As long as God's prophet was around, she could not carry out all the evil she wanted.

1 Kgs 19:3ff Elijah experienced the depths of fatigue and discouragement just after his two great spiritual victories: the defeat of the prophets of Baal and the answered prayer for rain. Often discouragement sets in after great spiritual experiences, especially those requiring physical effort or involving great emotion. To lead him out of depression, God first let Elijah rest and eat. Then God confronted him with the need to return to his mission—to speak God's words in Israel. Elijah's battles were not over; he still had work to do. When you feel let down after a great spiritual experience, remember that God's purpose for your life is not yet over.

▸ **1 KINGS 19:1-9a** ***(cont.)***

there beside his head was some bread baked on hot stones and a jar of water! So he ate and drank and lay down again.

7 Then the angel of the LORD came again and touched him and said, "Get up and eat some more, or the journey ahead will be too much for you."

8 So he got up and ate and drank, and the food gave him enough strength to travel forty days and forty nights to Mount Sinai,* the mountain of God. 9 There he came to a cave, where he spent the night.

The LORD Speaks to Elijah

1 KINGS 19:9b-18

But the LORD said to him, "What are you doing here, Elijah?"

10 Elijah replied, "I have zealously served the LORD God Almighty. But the people of Israel have broken their covenant with you, torn down your altars, and killed every one of your prophets. I am the only one left, and now they are trying to kill me, too."

11 "Go out and stand before me on the mountain," the LORD told him. And as Elijah stood there, the LORD passed by, and a mighty windstorm hit the mountain. It was such a terrible blast that the rocks were torn loose, but the LORD was not in the wind. After the wind there was an earthquake, but the LORD was not in the earthquake. 12 And after the earthquake there was a fire, but the LORD was not in the fire. And after the fire there was the sound of a gentle whisper. 13 When Elijah heard it, he wrapped his face in his cloak and went out and stood at the entrance of the cave.

And a voice said, "What are you doing here, Elijah?"

14 He replied again, "I have zealously served the LORD God Almighty. But the people of Israel have broken their covenant with you, torn down your altars, and killed every one of your prophets. I am the only one left, and now they are trying to kill me, too."

15 Then the LORD told him, "Go back the same way you came, and travel to the wilderness of Damascus. When you arrive there, anoint Hazael to be king of Aram. 16 Then anoint Jehu grandson of Nimshi* to be king of Israel, and anoint Elisha son of Shaphat from the town of Abel-meholah to replace you as my prophet. 17 Anyone who escapes from Hazael will be killed by Jehu, and those who escape Jehu will be killed by Elisha! 18 Yet I will preserve 7,000 others in Israel who have never bowed down to Baal or kissed him!"

The Call of Elisha

1 KINGS 19:19-21

So Elijah went and found Elisha son of Shaphat plowing a field. There were twelve teams of oxen in the field, and Elisha was plowing with the twelfth team. Elijah went over to him and threw his cloak across his shoulders and then walked away. 20 Elisha left the oxen standing there, ran after Elijah, and said to him, "First

1 Kgs 19:8 Hebrew *to Horeb,* another name for Sinai. **1 Kgs 19:16** Hebrew *descendant of Nimshi;* compare 2 Kgs 9:2, 14.

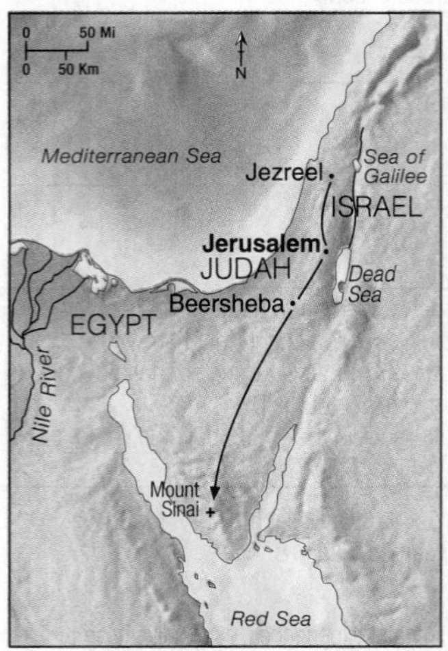

ELIJAH FLEES FROM JEZEBEL *After killing Baal's prophets, Elijah ran from the furious Queen Jezebel. He fled to Beersheba, then into the wilderness, and finally to Mount Sinai. There, like Moses centuries earlier, he talked with God.*

1 Kgs 19:8 When Elijah fled to Mount Sinai, he was returning to the sacred place where God had met Moses and had given his laws to the people. Obviously, God gave Elijah special strength to travel this great distance—over 200 miles—without additional food. Like Moses before him and Jesus after him, Elijah fasted for 40 days and 40 nights (Deut 9:9; Matt 4:1-2). Centuries later, Moses, Elijah, and Jesus would meet together on a mountaintop (Luke 9:28-36).

1 Kgs 19:10 Elijah thought he was the only person left who was still true to God. He had seen both the king's court and the priesthood become corrupt. After experiencing great victory at Mount Carmel, he had to run for his life. Lonely and discouraged, he forgot that others had remained faithful during the nation's wickedness. When you are tempted to think that you are the only one remaining faithful to a task, don't stop to feel sorry for yourself. Self-pity will dilute the good you are doing. Be assured that even if you don't know who they are, others are faithfully obeying God and fulfilling their duties.

1 Kgs 19:11-13 Elijah knew that the sound of a gentle whisper was God's voice. He realized that God doesn't reveal himself only in powerful, miraculous ways. To look for God only in something big (rallies, megachurches, conferences, highly visible leaders) may be to miss him because he is often found gently whispering in the quietness of a humbled heart. Are you listening for God? Step back from the noise and activity of your busy life and listen humbly and quietly for his guidance. It may come when you least expect it.

1 Kgs 19:15-16 God told Elijah to anoint three different people: (1) Hazael, as king of Aram. God was going to use Aram as his external instrument to punish Israel for its sin. (2) Jehu, as king of Israel. Jehu would destroy those who worshiped the false god Baal (2 Kgs 9–10). (3) Elisha, the prophet who would succeed him. Elisha's job was to work in Israel, the northern kingdom, to help point the people back to God. At this time, the southern kingdom was ruled by Jehoshaphat, a king devoted to God.

1 Kgs 19:18 Kissing Baal meant kissing some object representing him to show loyalty to him.

1 Kgs 19:19 The cloak was the most important article of clothing a person could own. It was used as protection against the weather, as bedding, as a place to sit, and as luggage. It could be given as a pledge for a debt or torn into pieces to show grief. Elijah put his cloak on Elisha's shoulders to show that he would become Elijah's successor. Later, when the transfer of authority was complete, Elijah left his cloak for Elisha (2 Kgs 2:11-14).

let me go and kiss my father and mother good-bye, and then I will go with you!"

Elijah replied, "Go on back, but think about what I have done to you."

21So Elisha returned to his oxen and slaughtered them. He used the wood from the plow to build a fire to roast their flesh. He passed around the meat to the townspeople, and they all ate. Then he went with Elijah as his assistant.

Ben-Hadad Attacks Samaria

1 KINGS 20:1-12

About that time King Ben-hadad of Aram mobilized his army, supported by the chariots and horses of thirty-two allied kings. They went to besiege Samaria, the capital of Israel, and launched attacks against it. 2Ben-hadad sent messengers into the city to relay this message to King Ahab of Israel: "This is what Ben-hadad says: 3'Your silver and gold are mine, and so are your wives and the best of your children!'"

4"All right, my lord the king," Israel's king replied. "All that I have is yours!"

5Soon Ben-hadad's messengers returned again and said, "This is what Ben-hadad says: 'I have already demanded that you give me your silver, gold, wives, and children. 6But about this time tomorrow I will send my officials to search your palace and the homes of your

AHAB

The kings of Israel and Judah, both good and evil, had prophets sent by God to advise, confront, and aid them. King David had a faithful friend in God's prophet Nathan; Ahab could have had an equally faithful friend in Elijah. But while David listened to Nathan and was willing to repent of his sins, Ahab saw Elijah as his enemy. Why? Because Elijah always brought bad news to Ahab, and Ahab refused to acknowledge that it was his own constant disobedience to God and persistent idol worship, not Elijah's prophecies, that brought the evil on his nation. He blamed Elijah for bringing the prophecies of judgment, rather than taking his advice and changing his own evil ways. • Ahab was trapped by his own choices, and he was unwilling to take the right action. As king, he was responsible to God and his prophet Elijah, but he was married to an evil woman who drew him into idol worship. He was a childish man who brooded for days if unable to get his own way. He took his evil wife's advice, listened only to the "prophets" who gave good news, and surrounded himself with people who encouraged him to do whatever he wanted. But the value of advice cannot be judged by the number of people for or against it. Ahab consistently chose to follow the majority opinion of those who surrounded him, and that led to his death. • It may seem nice to have someone encourage us to do whatever we want because advice that goes against our wishes is difficult to accept. However, our decisions must be based on the quality of the advice, not on its attractiveness or the majority opinion of our peers. God encourages us to get advice from wise counselors, but how can we test the advice we receive? Advice that agrees with the principles in God's Word is reliable. We must always separate advice from our own desires, the majority opinion, or whatever seems best in our limited perspective, and weigh it against God's commands. He will never lead us to do what he has forbidden in his Word—even in principle. Unlike Ahab, we should trust godly counselors and have the courage to stand against those who would have us do otherwise.

Strengths and accomplishments	• Eighth king of Israel • Capable leader and military strategist
Weaknesses and mistakes	• Was the most evil king of Israel • Married Jezebel, a pagan woman, and allowed her to promote Baal worship • Brooded about not being able to get a piece of land, which prompted his wife to have its owner, Naboth, killed
Lessons from his life	• The choice of a spouse will have a significant effect on life—physically, spiritually, and emotionally • Selfishness, left unchecked, can lead to great evil
Vital statistics	• Where: Northern kingdom of Israel • Occupation: King • Relatives: Wife: Jezebel. Father: Omri. Sons: Ahaziah, Joram. • Contemporaries: Elijah, Naboth, Jehu, Ben-hadad, Jehoshaphat
Key verses	"But Ahab son of Omri did what was evil in the LORD's sight, even more than any of the kings before him. And as though it were not enough to follow the example of Jeroboam, he married Jezebel, the daughter of King Ethbaal of the Sidonians, and he began to bow down in worship of Baal. First Ahab built a temple and an altar for Baal in Samaria. Then he set up an Asherah pole. He did more to provoke the anger of the LORD, the God of Israel, than any of the other kings of Israel before him" (1 Kgs 16:30-33).

Ahab's story is told in 1 Kings 16:28–22:40. He is also mentioned in 2 Chronicles 18–22; Micah 6:16.

1 Kgs 19:21 By killing his oxen, Elisha made a strong commitment to follow Elijah. Without them, he could not return to his life as a wealthy farmer. This meal was more than a feast among farmers. It was an offering of thanks to the Lord who chose Elisha to be his prophet.

1 Kgs 20:1ff With two evil and two good kings up to this point, the southern kingdom, Judah, wavered between godly and ungodly living. But the northern kingdom, Israel, had eight evil kings in succession. To punish both kingdoms for living their own way instead of following God, God allowed other nations to gain strength and become their enemies. Three main enemies threatened Israel and Judah during the next two centuries—Aram, Assyria, and Babylon. Aram, the first to rise to power, presented an immediate threat to Ahab and Israel.

▸ 1 KINGS 20:1-12 ***(cont.)***

people. They will take away everything you consider valuable!'"

[7]Then Ahab summoned all the elders of the land and said to them, "Look how this man is stirring up trouble! I already agreed with his demand that I give him my wives and children and silver and gold."

[8]"Don't give in to any more demands," all the elders and the people advised.

[9]So Ahab told the messengers from Ben-hadad, "Say this to my lord the king: 'I will give you everything you asked for the first time, but I cannot accept this last demand of yours.'" So the messengers returned to Ben-hadad with that response.

[10]Then Ben-hadad sent this message to Ahab: "May the gods strike me and even kill me if there remains enough dust from Samaria to provide even a handful for each of my soldiers."

[11]The king of Israel sent back this answer: "A warrior putting on his sword for battle should not boast like a warrior who has already won."

[12]Ahab's reply reached Ben-hadad and the other kings as they were drinking in their tents.* "Prepare to attack!" Ben-hadad commanded his officers. So they prepared to attack the city.

Ahab's Victory over Ben-Hadad

1 KINGS 20:13-22

Then a certain prophet came to see King Ahab of Israel and told him, "This is what the LORD says: Do you see all these enemy forces? Today I will hand them all over to you. Then you will know that I am the LORD."

[14]Ahab asked, "How will he do it?"

And the prophet replied, "This is what the LORD says: The troops of the provincial commanders will do it."

"Should we attack first?" Ahab asked.

"Yes," the prophet answered.

[15]So Ahab mustered the troops of the 232 provincial commanders. Then he called out the rest of the army of Israel, some 7,000 men. [16]About noontime, as Ben-hadad and the thirty-two allied kings were still in their tents drinking themselves into a stupor, [17]the troops of the provincial commanders marched out of the city as the first contingent.

As they approached, Ben-hadad's scouts reported to him, "Some troops are coming from Samaria."

[18]"Take them alive," Ben-hadad commanded, "whether they have come for peace or for war."

[19]But Ahab's provincial commanders and the entire army had now come out to fight. [20]Each Israelite soldier killed his Aramean opponent, and suddenly the entire Aramean army panicked and fled. The Israelites chased them, but King Ben-hadad and a few of his charioteers escaped on horses. [21]However, the king of Israel destroyed the other horses and chariots and slaughtered the Arameans.

[22]Afterward the prophet said to King Ahab, "Get ready for another attack. Begin making plans now, for the king of Aram will come back next spring.*"

Ben-Hadad's Second Attack

1 KINGS 20:23-34

After their defeat, Ben-hadad's officers said to him, "The Israelite gods are gods of the hills; that is why they won. But we can beat them easily on the plains. [24]Only this time replace the kings with field commanders! [25]Recruit another army like the one you lost. Give us the same number of horses, chariots, and men, and we will fight against them on the plains. There's no doubt that we will beat them." So King Ben-hadad did as they suggested.

1 Kgs 20:12 Or *in Succoth;* also in 20:16. **1 Kgs 20:22** Hebrew *at the turn of the year;* similarly in 20:26. The first day of the year in the ancient Hebrew lunar calendar occurred in March or April.

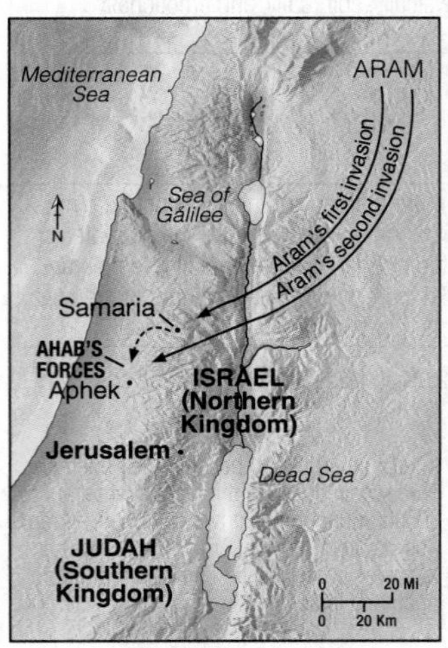

◀ ***GOD DELIVERS AHAB***
Despite Ahab's wickedness, God approached him in love. When Aramean forces surrounded Samaria, God miraculously delivered the city. But Ahab refused to give God credit. A year later, the Arameans attacked near Aphek. Again God gave Ahab victory, but again the king refused to acknowledge God's help.

1 Kgs 20:13 God defeated the Aramean army for Ahab so that Ahab would know that God alone is the Lord. Despite this great victory and the one to follow on the plains (1 Kgs 20:28-29), Ahab continued to live without God. Evidence of God's greatness surrounds us, but, like Ahab, we can choose to ignore it and go our own way. But when we do, as with this evil king of Israel, disaster will strike. Open your eyes to the evidence—the victories that God is winning for you. Then rededicate yourself to him.

1 Kgs 20:23 Since the days of Joshua, Israel's soldiers had the reputation of being superior fighters in the hills but ineffective in the open plains and valleys because they did not use chariots in battle. Horse-drawn chariots, useless in hilly terrain and dense forests, could easily run down great numbers of foot soldiers on the plains. What Ben-hadad's officers did not understand was that God, not chariots, made the difference in battle.

26 The following spring he called up the Aramean army and marched out against Israel, this time at Aphek. 27 Israel then mustered its army, set up supply lines, and marched out for battle. But the Israelite army looked like two little flocks of goats in comparison to the vast Aramean forces that filled the countryside!

28 Then the man of God went to the king of Israel and said, "This is what the LORD says: The Arameans have said, 'The LORD is a god of the hills and not of the plains.' So I will defeat this vast army for you. Then you will know that I am the LORD."

29 The two armies camped opposite each other for seven days, and on the seventh day the battle began. The Israelites killed 100,000 Aramean foot soldiers in one day. 30 The rest fled into the town of Aphek, but the wall fell on them and killed another 27,000. Ben-hadad fled into the town and hid in a secret room.

31 Ben-hadad's officers said to him, "Sir, we have heard that the kings of Israel are merciful. So let's humble ourselves by wearing burlap around our waists and putting ropes on our heads, and surrender to the king of Israel. Then perhaps he will let you live."

32 So they put on burlap and ropes, and they went to the king of Israel and begged, "Your servant Ben-hadad says, 'Please let me live!'"

The king of Israel responded, "Is he still alive? He is my brother!"

33 The men took this as a good sign and quickly picked up on his words. "Yes," they said, "your brother Ben-hadad!"

"Go and get him," the king of Israel told them. And when Ben-hadad arrived, Ahab invited him up into his chariot.

34 Ben-hadad told him, "I will give back the towns my father took from your father, and you may establish places of trade in Damascus, as my father did in Samaria."

Then Ahab said, "I will release you under these conditions." So they made a new treaty, and Ben-hadad was set free.

A Prophet Condemns Ahab

1 KINGS 20:35-43

Meanwhile, the LORD instructed one of the group of prophets to say to another man, "Hit me!" But the man refused to hit the prophet. 36 Then the prophet told him, "Because you have not obeyed the voice of the LORD, a lion will kill you as soon as you leave me." And when he had gone, a lion did attack and kill him.

37 Then the prophet turned to another man and said, "Hit me!" So he struck the prophet and wounded him.

38 The prophet placed a bandage over his eyes to disguise himself and then waited beside the road for the king. 39 As the king passed by, the prophet called out to him, "Sir, I was in the thick of battle, and suddenly a man brought me a prisoner. He said, 'Guard this man; if for any reason he gets away, you will either die or pay a fine of seventy-five pounds* of silver!' 40 But while I was busy doing something else, the prisoner disappeared!"

"Well, it's your own fault," the king replied. "You have brought the judgment on yourself."

41 Then the prophet quickly pulled the bandage from his eyes, and the king of Israel recognized him as one of the prophets. 42 The prophet said to him, "This is what the LORD says: Because you have spared the man I said must be destroyed,* now you must die in his place, and your people will die instead of his people." 43 So the king of Israel went home to Samaria angry and sullen.

Naboth's Vineyard

1 KINGS 21:1-29

Now there was a man named Naboth, from Jezreel, who owned a vineyard in Jezreel beside the palace of King Ahab of Samaria. 2 One day Ahab said to Naboth, "Since your vineyard is so convenient to my palace, I would like to buy it to use as a vegetable garden. I will give you a better vineyard in exchange, or if you prefer, I will pay you for it."

3 But Naboth replied, "The LORD forbid that I should give you the inheritance that was passed down by my ancestors."

4 So Ahab went home angry and sullen because of

1 Kgs 20:39 Hebrew *1 talent* [34 kilograms]. **1 Kgs 20:42** The Hebrew term used here refers to the complete consecration of things or people to the LORD, either by destroying them or by giving them as an offering.

1 Kgs 20:31 Burlap was coarse cloth usually made of goats' hair and was worn as a symbol of mourning for the dead or because of a natural disaster. Wearing ropes around the head may have been a symbol of putting oneself at another's disposal. In other words, Ahab could have hung them if he wished. Wearing ropes around the head, therefore, showed submission.

1 Kgs 20:35-36 The prophet needed a wound so he would look like an injured soldier and could effectively deliver his prophecy to Ahab. The first man was killed by a lion because he refused to obey the Lord's instructions through the prophet.

1 Kgs 20:41-42 It is difficult to explain why Ahab let Ben-hadad go, especially after all the trouble the Arameans had caused him. God helped Ahab destroy the Aramean army to prove to Ahab and to Aram that he alone was God. But Ahab failed to destroy the king, his greatest enemy. Ben-hadad was under God's judgment to die, and Ahab had no authority to let him live. For this, God told Ahab that *he* must now die instead. This prophet's message soon came true when Ahab was killed on the battlefield (1 Kgs 22:35).

1 Kgs 21:4 After hearing God's judgment (1 Kgs 20:42), Ahab went home to pout. Driven by anger and rebellion against God, he had a fit of rage when Naboth refused to sell his vineyard. The same feelings that led him to a career of power grabbing drove him to resent Naboth. Rage turned to hatred and led to murder. Naboth wanted to uphold God's laws: It was considered a duty to keep ancestral land in the family. This incident shows the cruel interplay between Ahab and Jezebel, two of the most wicked leaders in Israel's history.

▸ **1 KINGS 21:1-29** ***(cont.)***

Naboth's answer. The king went to bed with his face
to the wall and refused to eat!
5"What's the matter?" his wife Jezebel asked him.
"What's made you so upset that you're not eating?"
6"I asked Naboth to sell me his vineyard or trade it,
but he refused!" Ahab told her.
7"Are you the king of Israel or not?" Jezebel demanded. "Get up and eat something, and don't worry
about it. I'll get you Naboth's vineyard!"
8So she wrote letters in Ahab's name, sealed them
with his seal, and sent them to the elders and other
leaders of the town where Naboth lived. 9In her letters
she commanded: "Call the citizens together for fasting
and prayer, and give Naboth a place of honor. 10And
then seat two scoundrels across from him who will
accuse him of cursing God and the king. Then take
him out and stone him to death."
11So the elders and other town leaders followed the
instructions Jezebel had written in the letters. 12They
called for a fast and put Naboth at a prominent place
before the people. 13Then the two scoundrels came
and sat down across from him. And they accused Naboth before all the people, saying, "He cursed God and
the king." So he was dragged outside the town and
stoned to death. 14The town leaders then sent word to
Jezebel, "Naboth has been stoned to death."
15When Jezebel heard the news, she said to Ahab,
"You know the vineyard Naboth wouldn't sell you?
Well, you can have it now! He's dead!" 16So Ahab immediately went down to the vineyard of Naboth to
claim it.
17But the LORD said to Elijah,* 18"Go down to meet
King Ahab of Israel, who rules in Samaria. He will be
at Naboth's vineyard in Jezreel, claiming it for himself.
19Give him this message: 'This is what the LORD says:
Wasn't it enough that you killed Naboth? Must you
rob him, too? Because you have done this, dogs will

1 Kgs 21:17 Hebrew *Elijah the Tishbite;* also in 21:28.

JEZEBEL

The Bible is as honest about the lives of its heroes as it is about those who rejected God. Some Bible characters found out what God can do with failures when they turned to him. But many neither admitted their failures nor turned to God. • Jezebel ranks as the most evil woman in the Bible. The Bible even uses her name as an example of people who completely reject God (Rev 2:20-21). Many pagan women married into Israel without acknowledging the God their husbands worshiped. They brought their religions with them. But no one was as determined as Jezebel to make all Israel worship her gods. To the prophet Elijah, she seemed to have succeeded. He felt he was the only one still faithful to God until God told him there were still 7,000 who had not turned from the faith. Jezebel's one outstanding "success" was in contributing to the cause of the eventual downfall of the northern kingdom—idolatry. God punished the northern tribes for their idolatry by having them carried off into captivity. • Jezebel held great power. She not only managed her husband, Ahab, but she also had 850 assorted pagan priests under her control. She was committed to her gods and to getting what she wanted. And she believed that the king had the right to possess anything *he* wanted. When Naboth refused to sell Ahab his vineyard, Jezebel ruthlessly had Naboth killed and took ownership of the land. Jezebel's plan to wipe out worship of God in Israel led to painful consequences. Before she died, Jezebel suffered the loss of her husband in combat and her son at the hand of Jehu, who took the throne by force. She died in the defiant and scornful way she had lived. • When comparing Jezebel and Elijah, we have to admire each one's strength of commitment. The big difference was to whom they were committed. Jezebel was committed to herself and her false gods; Elijah was totally committed to the one true God. In the end, God proved Elijah right. To what or to whom are you most committed? How would God evaluate your commitment?

Weaknesses and mistakes	• Systematically eliminated the representatives of God in Israel • Promoted and funded Baal worship • Threatened to have Elijah killed • Believed kings and queens could rightfully do or have anything they wanted
Lessons from her life	• It is not enough to be committed or sincere; where our commitment lies makes a great difference • Rejecting God always leads to disaster
Vital statistics	• Where: Sidon, Samaria • Occupation: Queen of Israel • Relatives: Husband: Ahab. Father: Ethbaal. Sons: Joram, Ahaziah. • Contemporaries: Elijah, Jehu
Key verse	"No one else so completely sold himself to what was evil in the LORD's sight as Ahab did under the influence of his wife Jezebel" (1 Kgs 21:25).

Jezebel's story is told in 1 Kings 16:31—2 Kings 9:37. Her name is used as a synonym for great evil in Revelation 2:20.

1 Kgs 21:13 To get the land for her husband, Jezebel devised a scheme that appeared legal. Two witnesses were required to establish guilt, and the punishment for blasphemy was death by stoning. Today, those who twist the law and legal procedures to get what they want may be more sophisticated in how they go about it, but they are guilty of the same sin.

1 Kgs 21:19, 23 For the fulfillment of these verses, see 1 Kings 22:38 where dogs licked Ahab's blood, and 2 Kings 9:30–10:28 where Jezebel and the rest of Ahab's family were destroyed.

1 Kgs 21:20 Ahab still refused to admit his sin against God. Instead, he accused Elijah of being his enemy. When we are blinded by

lick your blood at the very place where they licked the blood of Naboth!'"

20"So, my enemy, you have found me!" Ahab exclaimed to Elijah.

"Yes," Elijah answered, "I have come because you have sold yourself to what is evil in the LORD's sight. 21So now the LORD says, 'I will bring disaster on you and consume you. I will destroy every one of your male descendants, slave and free alike, anywhere in Israel! 22I am going to destroy your family as I did the family of Jeroboam son of Nebat and the family of Baasha son of Ahijah, for you have made me very angry and have led Israel into sin.'

23"And regarding Jezebel, the LORD says, 'Dogs will eat Jezebel's body at the plot of land in Jezreel.*'

24"The members of Ahab's family who die in the city will be eaten by dogs, and those who die in the field will be eaten by vultures."

25(No one else so completely sold himself to what was evil in the LORD's sight as Ahab did under the influence of his wife Jezebel. 26His worst outrage was worshiping idols* just as the Amorites had done—the people whom the LORD had driven out from the land ahead of the Israelites.)

27But when Ahab heard this message, he tore his clothing, dressed in burlap, and fasted. He even slept in burlap and went about in deep mourning.

28Then another message from the LORD came to Elijah: 29"Do you see how Ahab has humbled himself before me? Because he has done this, I will not do what I promised during his lifetime. It will happen to his sons; I will destroy his dynasty."

1 Kgs 21:23 As in several Hebrew manuscripts, Syriac, and Latin Vulgate (see also 2 Kgs 9:26, 36); most Hebrew manuscripts read *at the city wall.* **1 Kgs 21:26** The Hebrew term (literally *round things*) probably alludes to dung.

3. AHAB AND JEHOSHAPHAT

The splintered nations of Israel and Judah formed an alliance under the rule of Ahab in the north and Jehoshaphat in the south. This alliance was more than simply for a single battle, as Jehoshaphat married his royal heir to one of Ahab's daughters, Athaliah. This alliance between the two kingdoms was condemned by God's prophets, and it led to great suffering and idolatry in the southern kingdom of Judah. God wants our wholehearted devotion to him, and he doesn't want us to allow anything or anyone to draw us away from serving him wholeheartedly.

Jehoshaphat and Ahab PARALLEL

1 KINGS 22:1-9

For three years there was no war between Aram and Israel. 2Then during the third year, King Jehoshaphat of Judah went to visit King Ahab of Israel. 3During the visit, the king of Israel said to his officials, "Do you realize that the town of Ramoth-gilead belongs to us? And yet we've done nothing to recapture it from the king of Aram!"

4Then he turned to Jehoshaphat and asked, "Will you join me in battle to recover Ramoth-gilead?"

Jehoshaphat replied to the king of Israel, "Why, of course! You and I are as one. My troops are your troops, and my horses are your horses." 5Then Jehoshaphat added, "But first let's find out what the LORD says."

6So the king of Israel summoned the prophets, about 400 of them, and asked them, "Should I go to war against Ramoth-gilead, or should I hold back?"

They all replied, "Yes, go right ahead! The Lord will give the king victory."

7But Jehoshaphat asked, "Is there not also a prophet of the LORD here? We should ask him the same question."

8The king of Israel replied to Jehoshaphat, "There is one more man who could consult the LORD for us, but I hate him. He never prophesies anything but trouble for me! His name is Micaiah son of Imlah."

Jehoshaphat replied, "That's not the way a king should talk! Let's hear what he has to say."

9So the king of Israel called one of his officials and said, "Quick! Bring Micaiah son of Imlah."

2 CHRONICLES 18:1-8

Jehoshaphat enjoyed great riches and high esteem, and he made an alliance with Ahab of Israel by having

envy and hatred, we find it almost impossible to see our own sin.

1 Kgs 21:29 Ahab was more wicked than any other king of Israel (1 Kgs 16:30; 21:25), but when he repented in deep humility, God took notice and reduced his punishment. The same Lord who was merciful to Ahab wants to be merciful to you. No matter how evil you have been, it is never too late to humble yourself, turn to God, and ask for forgiveness.

1 Kgs 22:6 These 400 prophets may have been the 400 Asherah priests left alive by Elijah at Carmel, because the 450 prophets of Baal were killed (see 1 Kgs 18:19-40).

1 Kgs 22:7 Jehoshaphat knew the difference between these pagan prophets and a "prophet of the LORD," so he asked if God's prophet was available. Evidently Jehoshaphat wanted to do what was right, although Ahab didn't. Both kings disregarded God's message, however, and listened only to the pagan prophets.

2 Chr 18:1ff Although Jehoshaphat was deeply committed to God, he arranged for his son to marry Athaliah, the daughter of wicked King Ahab of Israel, and then made a military alliance with him. Jehoshaphat's popularity and power made him attractive to the cunning and opportunistic Ahab. This alliance had three devastating consequences: (1) Jehoshaphat incurred God's anger (2 Chr 19:2); (2) when Jehoshaphat's grandson died, Athaliah seized the throne and almost destroyed all of David's descendants (2 Chr 22:10-12); (3) Athaliah brought the evil practices of Israel into Judah, which eventually led to the nation's downfall.

When believers in leadership positions become allied with unbelievers, values can be compromised and spiritual awareness dulled. The Bible often warns against teaming up with unbelievers (2 Cor 6:14). (See the note on 2 Chr 20:37, p. 737, for more on alliances.)

▸ **2 CHRONICLES 18:1-8** ***(cont.)***
his son marry Ahab's daughter. 2A few years later he
went to Samaria to visit Ahab, who prepared a great
banquet for him and his officials. They butchered
great numbers of sheep, goats, and cattle for the feast.
Then Ahab enticed Jehoshaphat to join forces with
him to recover Ramoth-gilead.

3"Will you go with me to Ramoth-gilead?" King
Ahab of Israel asked King Jehoshaphat of Judah.

Jehoshaphat replied, "Why, of course! You and I
are as one, and my troops are your troops. We will
certainly join you in battle." 4Then Jehoshaphat added,
"But first let's find out what the LORD says."

5So the king of Israel summoned the prophets,
400 of them, and asked them, "Should we go to war
against Ramoth-gilead, or should I hold back?"

They all replied, "Yes, go right ahead! God will give
the king victory."

6But Jehoshaphat asked, "Is there not also a prophet
of the LORD here? We should ask him the same question."

7The king of Israel replied to Jehoshaphat, "There is
one more man who could consult the LORD for us, but
I hate him. He never prophesies anything but trouble
for me! His name is Micaiah son of Imlah."

Jehoshaphat replied, "That's not the way a king
should talk! Let's hear what he has to say."

8So the king of Israel called one of his officials and
said, "Quick! Bring Micaiah son of Imlah."

Micaiah Prophesies against Ahab PARALLEL

1 KINGS 22:10-28
King Ahab of Israel and King Jehoshaphat of Judah,
dressed in their royal robes, were sitting on thrones
at the threshing floor near the gate of Samaria. All
of Ahab's prophets were prophesying there in front
of them. 11One of them, Zedekiah son of Kenaanah,

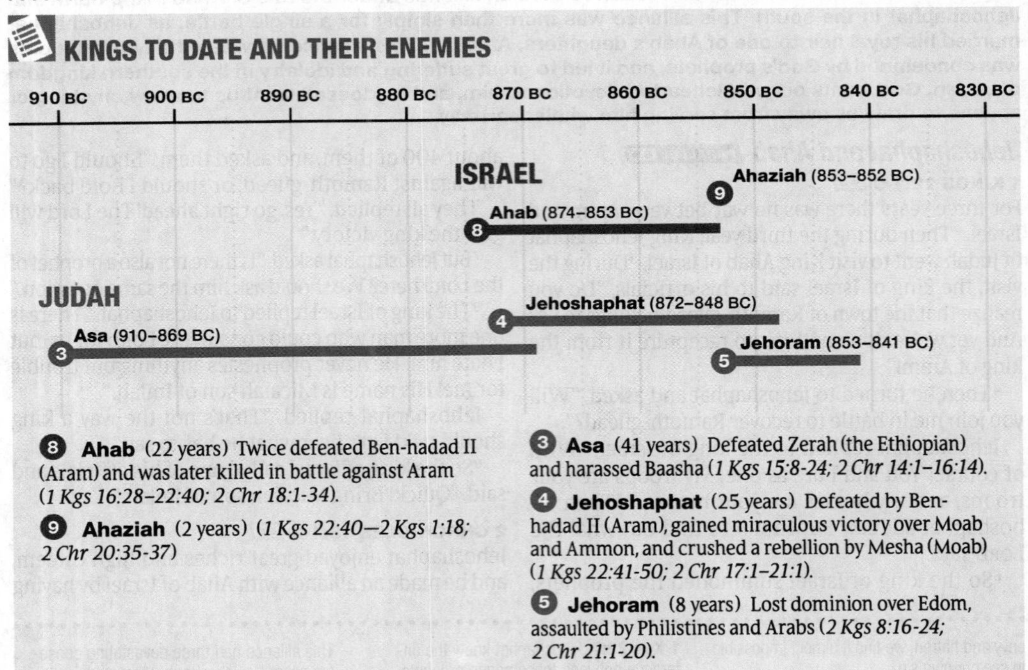

8 Ahab (22 years) Twice defeated Ben-hadad II (Aram) and was later killed in battle against Aram (*1 Kgs 16:28–22:40; 2 Chr 18:1-34*).

9 Ahaziah (2 years) (*1 Kgs 22:40—2 Kgs 1:18; 2 Chr 20:35-37*)

3 Asa (41 years) Defeated Zerah (the Ethiopian) and harassed Baasha (*1 Kgs 15:8-24; 2 Chr 14:1–16:14*).

4 Jehoshaphat (25 years) Defeated by Ben-hadad II (Aram), gained miraculous victory over Moab and Ammon, and crushed a rebellion by Mesha (Moab) (*1 Kgs 22:41-50; 2 Chr 17:1–21:1*).

5 Jehoram (8 years) Lost dominion over Edom, assaulted by Philistines and Arabs (*2 Kgs 8:16-24; 2 Chr 21:1-20*).

2 Chr 18:3-8 Evil kings did not like God's prophets bringing messages of doom (2 Chr 18:17; Jer 5:13). So many hired prophets who told them only what they wanted to hear (Isa 30:10-11; Jer 14:13-16; 23:16, 21, 30-36). These men were false prophets because they extolled the greatness of the king and predicted victory regardless of the real situation.

2 Chr 18:3-8 Wicked Ahab asked Jehoshaphat to join forces with him in battle (2 Chr 18:2-3). Before making that commitment, Jehoshaphat rightly sought God's advice. However, when God gave his answer through the prophet Micaiah (2 Chr 18:16), Jehoshaphat ignored it (2 Chr 18:28). It does us no good to seek God's advice if we ignore it when it is given. Real love for God is shown, not by merely asking for direction, but by following that direction once it is given.

1 Kgs 22:10 Threshing floors were placed in elevated areas to allow the wind to blow away the discarded hulls of grain.

made some iron horns and proclaimed, "This is what
the LORD says: With these horns you will gore the
Arameans to death!"
12 All the other prophets agreed. "Yes," they said, "go
up to Ramoth-gilead and be victorious, for the LORD
will give the king victory!"
13 Meanwhile, the messenger who went to get Micaiah said to him, "Look, all the prophets are promising
victory for the king. Be sure that you agree with them
and promise success."
14 But Micaiah replied, "As surely as the LORD lives, I
will say only what the LORD tells me to say."
15 When Micaiah arrived before the king, Ahab
asked him, "Micaiah, should we go to war against
Ramoth-gilead, or should we hold back?"
Micaiah replied sarcastically, "Yes, go up and be
victorious, for the LORD will give the king victory!"
16 But the king replied sharply, "How many times
must I demand that you speak only the truth to me
when you speak for the LORD?"
17 Then Micaiah told him, "In a vision I saw all Israel scattered on the mountains, like sheep without a
shepherd. And the LORD said, 'Their master has been
killed.* Send them home in peace.'"
18 "Didn't I tell you?" the king of Israel exclaimed
to Jehoshaphat. "He never prophesies anything but
trouble for me."
19 Then Micaiah continued, "Listen to what the LORD
says! I saw the LORD sitting on his throne with all the
armies of heaven around him, on his right and on his
left. 20 And the LORD said, 'Who can entice Ahab to go
into battle against Ramoth-gilead so he can be killed?'
"There were many suggestions, 21 and finally a spirit
approached the LORD and said, 'I can do it!'
22 "'How will you do this?' the LORD asked.
"And the spirit replied, 'I will go out and inspire all
of Ahab's prophets to speak lies.'
"'You will succeed,' said the LORD. 'Go ahead and
do it.'
23 "So you see, the LORD has put a lying spirit in the
mouths of all your prophets. For the LORD has pronounced your doom."
24 Then Zedekiah son of Kenaanah walked up to
Micaiah and slapped him across the face. "Since when
did the Spirit of the LORD leave me to speak to you?"
he demanded.
25 And Micaiah replied, "You will find out soon
enough when you are trying to hide in some secret
room!"
26 "Arrest him!" the king of Israel ordered. "Take him
back to Amon, the governor of the city, and to my son
Joash. 27 Give them this order from the king: 'Put this
man in prison, and feed him nothing but bread and
water until I return safely from the battle!'"
28 But Micaiah replied, "If you return safely, it will
mean that the LORD has not spoken through me!" Then
he added to those standing around, "Everyone mark
my words!"

1 Kgs 22:17 Hebrew *These people have no master.*

1 Kgs 22:15-16 Why did Micaiah tell Ahab to attack when he had previously vowed to speak only what God had told him? Perhaps he was speaking sarcastically, making fun of the messages from the pagan prophets by showing that they were telling the king only what he wanted to hear. Somehow, Micaiah's tone of voice let everyone know he was mocking the pagan prophets. When confronted, he predicted that the king would die and the battle would be lost. Although Ahab repented temporarily (1 Kgs 21:27), he still maintained the system of false prophets. These false prophets would be instrumental in leading him to his own ruin.

1 Kgs 22:19-22 The vision Micaiah saw was either a picture of a real incident in heaven or a parable of what was happening on earth, illustrating that the seductive influence of the false prophets would be part of God's judgment upon Ahab (1 Kgs 22:23). Whether or not God sent an angel in disguise, he used the system of false prophets to snare Ahab in his sin. The lying spirit (1 Kgs 22:22) symbolized the way of life for these prophets, who told the king only what he wanted to hear.

1 Kgs 22:20-22 Does God allow angels to entice people to do evil? To understand evil, we must first understand God. (1) God himself is good (Ps 11:7). (2) God created a good world that fell because of sin (Rom 5:12). (3) Someday God will recreate the world, and it will be good again (Rev 21:1). (4) God is stronger than evil (Matt 13:41-43; Rev 19:11-21). (5) God allows evil, and thus he has control over it. God did not create evil, and he offers help to those who wish to overcome it (Matt 11:28-30). (6) God uses everything—both good and evil—for his good purposes (Gen 50:20; Rom 8:28).

The Bible shows us a God who hates all evil and will one day do away with it completely and forever (Rev 20:10-15). God does not entice anyone to become evil. Those committed to evil, however, may be used by God to sin even more in order to hurry their deserved judgment (Exod 11:10). We don't need to understand every detail of how God works in order to have perfect confidence in his absolute power over evil and his total goodness toward us.

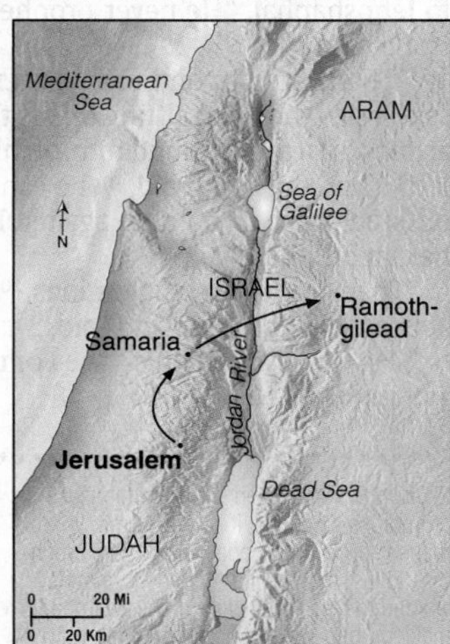

***BATTLE WITH ARAM** King Jehoshaphat of Judah made an alliance with evil King Ahab of Israel. Together they decided to attack Ramoth-gilead and rout the Arameans who had occupied the city. But Jehoshaphat first wanted to seek the advice of a prophet. Ahab's prophets predicted victory, but Micaiah predicted defeat. The two kings were defeated, and Ahab was killed.*

853 BC

Ahab dies in battle

2 CHRONICLES 18:9-27

King Ahab of Israel and King Jehoshaphat of Judah, dressed in their royal robes, were sitting on thrones at the threshing floor near the gate of Samaria. All of Ahab's prophets were prophesying there in front of them. 10 One of them, Zedekiah son of Kenaanah, made some iron horns and proclaimed, "This is what the LORD says: With these horns you will gore the Arameans to death!"

11 All the other prophets agreed. "Yes," they said, "go up to Ramoth-gilead and be victorious, for the LORD will give the king victory!"

12 Meanwhile, the messenger who went to get Micaiah said to him, "Look, all the prophets are promising victory for the king. Be sure that you agree with them and promise success."

13 But Micaiah replied, "As surely as the LORD lives, I will say only what my God says."

14 When Micaiah arrived before the king, Ahab asked him, "Micaiah, should we go to war against Ramoth-gilead, or should I hold back?"

Micaiah replied sarcastically, "Yes, go up and be victorious, for you will have victory over them!"

15 But the king replied sharply, "How many times must I demand that you speak only the truth to me when you speak for the LORD?"

16 Then Micaiah told him, "In a vision I saw all Israel scattered on the mountains, like sheep without a shepherd. And the LORD said, 'Their master has been killed.* Send them home in peace.'"

17 "Didn't I tell you?" the king of Israel exclaimed to Jehoshaphat. "He never prophesies anything but trouble for me."

18 Then Micaiah continued, "Listen to what the LORD says! I saw the LORD sitting on his throne with all the armies of heaven around him, on his right and on his left. 19 And the LORD said, 'Who can entice King Ahab of Israel to go into battle against Ramoth-gilead so he can be killed?'

"There were many suggestions, 20 and finally a spirit approached the LORD and said, 'I can do it!'

"'How will you do this?' the LORD asked.

21 "And the spirit replied, 'I will go out and inspire all of Ahab's prophets to speak lies.'

"'You will succeed,' said the LORD. 'Go ahead and do it.'

22 "So you see, the LORD has put a lying spirit in the mouths of your prophets. For the LORD has pronounced your doom."

23 Then Zedekiah son of Kenaanah walked up to Micaiah and slapped him across the face. "Since when did the Spirit of the LORD leave me to speak to you?" he demanded.

24 And Micaiah replied, "You will find out soon enough when you are trying to hide in some secret room!"

25 "Arrest him!" the king of Israel ordered. "Take him back to Amon, the governor of the city, and to my son Joash. 26 Give them this order from the king: 'Put this man in prison, and feed him nothing but bread and water until I return safely from the battle!'"

27 But Micaiah replied, "If you return safely, it will mean that the LORD has not spoken through me!" Then he added to those standing around, "Everyone mark my words!"

The Death of Ahab PARALLEL

1 KINGS 22:29-40

So King Ahab of Israel and King Jehoshaphat of Judah led their armies against Ramoth-gilead. 30 The king of Israel said to Jehoshaphat, "As we go into battle, I will disguise myself so no one will recognize me, but you wear your royal robes." So the king of Israel disguised himself, and they went into battle.

31 Meanwhile, the king of Aram had issued these orders to his thirty-two chariot commanders: "Attack only the king of Israel. Don't bother with anyone else!" 32 So when the Aramean chariot commanders saw Jehoshaphat in his royal robes, they went after him. "There is the king of Israel!" they shouted. But when Jehoshaphat called out, 33 the chariot commanders realized he was not the king of Israel, and they stopped chasing him.

34 An Aramean soldier, however, randomly shot an arrow at the Israelite troops and hit the king of Israel

2 Chr 18:16 Hebrew *These people have no master.*

2 Chr 18:5-16 When you want to please or impress someone, it is tempting to lie to make yourself look good. Ahab's 400 prophets did just that, telling Ahab only what he wanted to hear. They were then rewarded for making Ahab happy. Micaiah told the truth and got arrested (2 Chr 18:25-26). Obeying God doesn't always protect us from evil consequences. Obedience may, in fact, provoke them. But it is better to suffer from people's displeasure than from God's wrath (Matt 10:28). If you are ridiculed for being honest, remember that this can be a sign that you are indeed doing what is right in God's eyes (Matt 5:10-12; Rom 8:17, 35-39).

2 Chr 18:22 God used the seductive influence of false prophets to judge Ahab. They were determined to tell Ahab what he wanted to hear. God confirmed their plans to lie as a means to remove Ahab from the throne. These prophets, supported by Ahab, snared him in his sin. Because he listened to them instead of God, he was killed in battle. The lying spirit is a picture of the prophets' entire way of life—telling the king only what he wanted to hear, not what he needed to hear. Leaders will only find trouble if they surround themselves with advisers whose only thought is to please them.

1 Kgs 22:30-34 Ahab could not escape God's judgment. The king of Aram sent 32 of his best chariot commanders with the sole purpose of killing Ahab. Thinking he could escape, Ahab tried a disguise, but a random arrow struck him while the chariots chased the wrong king—Jehoshaphat. It was foolish for Ahab to think he could escape by wearing a disguise. Sometimes people try to escape reality by disguising themselves—changing jobs, moving to a new town, even changing spouses. But God sees and evaluates the motives of each person. Any attempted disguise is futile.

between the joints of his armor. "Turn the horses* and
get me out of here!" Ahab groaned to the driver of his
chariot. "I'm badly wounded!"
35The battle raged all that day, and the king remained
propped up in his chariot facing the Arameans. The
blood from his wound ran down to the floor of his
chariot, and as evening arrived he died. 36Just as the
sun was setting, the cry ran through his troops: "We're
done for! Run for your lives!"
37So the king died, and his body was taken to Samaria and buried there. 38Then his chariot was washed
beside the pool of Samaria, and dogs came and licked
his blood at the place where the prostitutes bathed,*
just as the LORD had promised.
39The rest of the events in Ahab's reign and everything he did, including the story of the ivory palace
and the towns he built, are recorded in *The Book of
the History of the Kings of Israel.* 40So Ahab died, and
his son Ahaziah became the next king.

2 CHRONICLES 18:28-34

So King Ahab of Israel and King Jehoshaphat of Judah
led their armies against Ramoth-gilead. 29The king of
Israel said to Jehoshaphat, "As we go into battle, I will
disguise myself so no one will recognize me, but you
wear your royal robes." So the king of Israel disguised
himself, and they went into battle.
30Meanwhile, the king of Aram had issued these
orders to his chariot commanders: "Attack only the
king of Israel! Don't bother with anyone else." 31So
when the Aramean chariot commanders saw Jehoshaphat in his royal robes, they went after him. "There
is the king of Israel!" they shouted. But Jehoshaphat
called out, and the LORD saved him. God helped him
by turning the attackers away from him. 32As soon as
the chariot commanders realized he was not the king
of Israel, they stopped chasing him.
33An Aramean soldier, however, randomly shot an
arrow at the Israelite troops and hit the king of Israel
between the joints of his armor. "Turn the horses* and
get me out of here!" Ahab groaned to the driver of the
chariot. "I'm badly wounded!"
34The battle raged all that day, and the king of
Israel propped himself up in his chariot facing the
Arameans. In the evening, just as the sun was setting,
he died.

Ahaziah Begins His Reign in Israel

1 KINGS 22:51-53

Ahaziah son of Ahab began to rule over Israel in the
seventeenth year of King Jehoshaphat's reign in Judah. He reigned in Samaria two years. 52But he did
what was evil in the LORD's sight, following the example of his father and mother and the example of Jeroboam son of Nebat, who had led Israel to sin. 53He
served Baal and worshiped him, provoking the anger of the LORD, the God of Israel, just as his father
had done.

Jehoshaphat Appoints Judges in Judah

2 CHRONICLES 19:1-11

When King Jehoshaphat of Judah arrived safely
home in Jerusalem, 2Jehu son of Hanani the seer
went out to meet him. "Why should you help the
wicked and love those who hate the LORD?" he
asked the king. "Because of what you have done,
the LORD is very angry with you. 3Even so, there is
some good in you, for you have removed the Asherah
poles throughout the land, and you have committed
yourself to seeking God."
4Jehoshaphat lived in Jerusalem, but he went out
among the people, traveling from Beersheba to the hill
country of Ephraim, encouraging the people to return
to the LORD, the God of their ancestors. 5He appointed
judges throughout the nation in all the fortified towns,
6and he said to them, "Always think carefully before
pronouncing judgment. Remember that you do not

1 Kgs 22:34 Hebrew *Turn your hand.* **1 Kgs 22:38** Or *his blood, and the prostitutes bathed [in it];* or *his blood, and they washed his armor.* **2 Chr 18:33** Hebrew *Turn your hand.*

---

1 Kgs 22:35 Just as the prophet had predicted (1 Kgs 20:42), Ahab was killed. See Ahab's Profile on p. 721 for more of his tragic story.

2 Chr 18:31 Jehoshaphat's troubles began when he joined forces with evil King Ahab. Almost at once he found himself the target for soldiers who mistakenly identified him as Ahab. He could have accepted this fate because he deserved it, but instead he cried out to God, who miraculously saved him. When we sin and the inevitable consequences follow, we may be tempted to give up, thinking, *I chose to sin. It's my fault, and I must accept the consequences.* While we may deserve what comes to us, that is no reason to avoid calling on God for urgent help. Had Jehoshaphat given up, he might have died. No matter how greatly you have sinned, you can still call upon God.

2 Chr 18:33 Micaiah had prophesied death for Ahab (2 Chr 18:16, 27), so Ahab disguised himself to fool the enemy. But Ahab's disguise didn't change the prophecy. A random arrow found a crack in his armor and killed him. God fulfills his will despite the defenses people try to erect. God can use anything, even an error, to bring his will to pass. This is good news for God's followers because we can trust him to work out his plans and keep his promises no matter how desperate our circumstances are.

1 Kgs 22:52-53 The book of 1 Kings begins with a nation united under David, the most devout king in Israel's history. The book ends with a divided kingdom and the death of Ahab, the most wicked king of all. What happened? The people forgot to acknowledge God as their ultimate leader; they appointed human leaders who ignored God; then they conformed to the lifestyles of these evil leaders. Occasional wrongdoing gradually turned into a way of life. Their blatant wickedness could be met only with judgment from God, who allowed enemy nations to arise and defeat Israel and Judah in battle as punishment for their sins. Failing to acknowledge God as our ultimate leader is the first step toward ruin.

2 Chr 19:5-10 Jehoshaphat delegated some of the responsibilities for ruling and judging the people, but he warned his appointees that they were accountable to God for the standards they used to judge others. Jehoshaphat's advice is helpful for all leaders: (1) Realize that you are judging for God (2 Chr 19:6); (2) be impartial and honest (2 Chr 19:7); (3) be faithful (2 Chr 19:9); (4) act only out of fear of God, not people (2 Chr 19:9). God holds us accountable for the authority we exercise.

▸ 2 CHRONICLES 19:1-11 ***(cont.)***

judge to please people but to please the LORD. He will
be with you when you render the verdict in each case.
7Fear the LORD and judge with integrity, for the LORD
our God does not tolerate perverted justice, partiality,
or the taking of bribes."
8In Jerusalem, Jehoshaphat appointed some of the
Levites and priests and clan leaders in Israel to serve
as judges for cases involving the LORD's regulations
and for civil disputes. 9These were his instructions
to them: "You must always act in the fear of the LORD,
with faithfulness and an undivided heart. 10Whenever
a case comes to you from fellow citizens in an outlying
town, whether a murder case or some other violation
of God's laws, commands, decrees, or regulations, you
must warn them not to sin against the LORD, so that
he will not be angry with you and them. Do this and
you will not be guilty.

BIBLE PERSECUTIONS

Micaiah, like thousands of believers before and after him, was persecuted for his faith. The chart shows that persecution comes from a variety of people and is given in a variety of ways. Sometimes God protects us from it; sometimes he doesn't. But as long as we remain faithful to God alone, we must expect persecution (see also Luke 6:22; 2 Cor 6:4-10; 2 Tim 2:9-12; Rev 2:10). God also seems to have a special reward for those who endure such persecution (Rev 6:9-11; 20:4).

The Persecuted	*The Persecutors*	*Why the Persecution*	*Result*	*Reference*
Isaac	The Philistines	God was blessing Isaac, and they envied him	The Philistines could not subdue Isaac, so they made peace with him	Gen 26:12-33
Moses	Israelites	The Israelites wanted water	God provided water, in answer to Moses' prayer	Exod 17:1-7
David	Saul and others	David was becoming a powerful leader, threatening Saul's position as king	David endured the persecution and became king	1 Sam 19–27; Pss 31:13; 59:1-4
Priests of Nob	Saul and Doeg	Saul and Doeg thought the priests helped David escape	85 priests were killed	1 Sam 22
Prophets	Jezebel	Jezebel didn't like to have her evil ways pointed out	Many prophets were killed	1 Kgs 18:3-4
Elijah	Ahab and Jezebel	Elijah confronted their sins	Elijah had to flee for his life	1 Kgs 18:10–19:2
Micaiah	Ahab	Ahab thought Micaiah was stirring up trouble rather than prophesying from God	Micaiah was thrown into prison	2 Chr 18:12-26
Elisha	A king of Israel (Probably Joram)	The king thought Elisha had caused the famine	Elisha ignored the threatened persecution and prophesied the famine's end	2 Kgs 6:31
Hanani	Asa	Hanani criticized Asa for trusting in Aram's help more than in God's help	Hanani was thrown into prison	2 Chr 16:7-10
Zechariah	Joash	Zechariah confronted the people of Judah for disregarding God's commands	Zechariah was executed	2 Chr 24:20-22
Uriah	Jehoiakim	Uriah confronted Jehoiakim about his evil ways	Uriah was killed with a sword	Jer 26:20-23

2 Chr 19:8 Jehoshaphat appointed priests and Levites to help in administering civil laws. Many years earlier, Moses had chosen men who were capable, faithful, and honest to help him judge disputes among the people (Exod 18:21-22). Obviously the best kind of leader is one who always acts with reverence for God. Effective leaders get the job done; faithful leaders make sure the job is done in God's way and in God's time. They are careful to instill God's wisdom in future leaders and God's values in the entire community.

[11]"Amariah the high priest will have final say in all cases involving the LORD. Zebadiah son of Ishmael, a leader from the tribe of Judah, will have final say in all civil cases. The Levites will assist you in making sure that justice is served. Take courage as you fulfill your duties, and may the LORD be with those who do what is right."

Judah's War with Moab, Ammon, and Edom

2 CHRONICLES 20:1-30

After this, the armies of the Moabites, Ammonites, and some of the Meunites* declared war on Jehoshaphat. [2]Messengers came and told Jehoshaphat, "A vast army from Edom* is marching against you from beyond the

2 Chr 20:1 As in some Greek manuscripts (see also 26:7); Hebrew repeats *Ammonites.* **2 Chr 20:2a** As in one Hebrew manuscript; most Hebrew manuscripts and ancient versions read *Aram.*

The Persecuted	*The Persecutors*	*Why the Persecution*	*Result*	*Reference*
Jeremiah	Zedekiah	Zedekiah thought Jeremiah was a traitor for prophesying Jerusalem's fall	Jeremiah was thrown into prison, then into a muddy cistern	Jer 37:1–38:13
Shadrach, Meshach, Abednego	Nebuchadnezzar	The three men refused to bow down to anyone but God	They were thrown into a blazing furnace, but God miraculously saved them	Dan 3
Daniel	National leaders	Daniel was praying	Daniel was thrown into a den of lions, but God miraculously saved him	Dan 6
Job	Satan	Satan wanted to prove that pain and suffering would make a person abandon God	Job remained faithful to God and was restored	Job 1:8-12; 2:3-7
John the Baptist	Herod and Herodias	John confronted King Herod's adultery	John was beheaded	Matt 14:3-12
Jesus	Religious leaders	Jesus exposed their sinful motives	Jesus was crucified, but rose again from the dead to show his authority over all evil	Mark 7:1-16; Luke 2:63–24:7
Peter and John	Religious leaders	Peter and John preached that Jesus was God's Son and the only way to salvation	They were thrown into prison, but later released	Acts 4:1-31
Stephen	Religious leaders	Stephen exposed their guilt in crucifying Jesus	Stephen was stoned to death	Acts 6–7
The church	Paul and others	The Christians preached Jesus as the Messiah	Believers faced death, prison, torture, exile	Acts 8:1-3; 9:1-3
James	Herod Agrippa I	To please the Jewish leaders	James was executed	Acts 12:1-2
Peter	Herod Agrippa I	To please the Jewish leaders	Peter was thrown into prison	Acts 12:3-17
Paul	Jews, city officials	Paul preached about Jesus and confronted those who made money by manipulating others	Paul was stoned; thrown into prison	Acts 14:19; 16:16-24
Timothy	Unknown	Unknown	Timothy was thrown into prison	Heb 13:23
John	Probably the Romans	John told others about Jesus	John was sent into exile on a remote island	Rev 1:9

2 Chr 20:3 When the nation was faced with disaster, Jehoshaphat called upon the people to get serious with God by going without food (fasting) for a designated time. By separating themselves from the daily routine of food preparation and eating, they could devote that extra time to considering their sin and praying to God for help. Hunger pangs would reinforce their penitence and remind them of their weakness and their dependence upon God. Fasting is still helpful today as we seek God.

▸ **2 CHRONICLES 20:1-30** ***(cont.)***
Dead Sea.* They are already at Hazazon-tamar." (This
was another name for En-gedi.)
[3]Jehoshaphat was terrified by this news and begged
the LORD for guidance. He also ordered everyone in
Judah to begin fasting. [4]So people from all the towns
of Judah came to Jerusalem to seek the LORD's help.
[5]Jehoshaphat stood before the community of Judah
and Jerusalem in front of the new courtyard at the
Temple of the LORD. [6]He prayed, "O LORD, God of our
ancestors, you alone are the God who is in heaven. You
are ruler of all the kingdoms of the earth. You are powerful and mighty; no one can stand against you! [7]O our
God, did you not drive out those who lived in this land
when your people Israel arrived? And did you not give
this land forever to the descendants of your friend
Abraham? [8]Your people settled here and built this
Temple to honor your name. [9]They said, 'Whenever
we are faced with any calamity such as war,* plague,
or famine, we can come to stand in your presence
before this Temple where your name is honored. We
can cry out to you to save us, and you will hear us and
rescue us.'
[10]"And now see what the armies of Ammon, Moab,
and Mount Seir are doing. You would not let our ancestors invade those nations when Israel left Egypt,
so they went around them and did not destroy them.
[11]Now see how they reward us! For they have come
to throw us out of your land, which you gave us as an
inheritance. [12]O our God, won't you stop them? We
are powerless against this mighty army that is about
to attack us. We do not know what to do, but we are
looking to you for help."
[13]As all the men of Judah stood before the LORD
with their little ones, wives, and children, [14]the Spirit
of the LORD came upon one of the men standing there.
His name was Jahaziel son of Zechariah, son of Benaiah, son of Jeiel, son of Mattaniah, a Levite who was a
descendant of Asaph.
[15]He said, "Listen, all you people of Judah and Jerusalem! Listen, King Jehoshaphat! This is what the
LORD says: Do not be afraid! Don't be discouraged by
this mighty army, for the battle is not yours, but God's.
[16]Tomorrow, march out against them. You will find
them coming up through the ascent of Ziz at the end
of the valley that opens into the wilderness of Jeruel.
[17]But you will not even need to fight. Take your positions; then stand still and watch the LORD's victory.
He is with you, O people of Judah and Jerusalem. Do
not be afraid or discouraged. Go out against them
tomorrow, for the LORD is with you!"
[18]Then King Jehoshaphat bowed low with his face
to the ground. And all the people of Judah and Jerusalem did the same, worshiping the LORD. [19]Then the
Levites from the clans of Kohath and Korah stood to
praise the LORD, the God of Israel, with a very loud
shout.
[20]Early the next morning the army of Judah went
out into the wilderness of Tekoa. On the way Jehoshaphat stopped and said, "Listen to me, all you people
of Judah and Jerusalem! Believe in the LORD your God,
and you will be able to stand firm. Believe in his prophets, and you will succeed."
[21]After consulting the people, the king appointed
singers to walk ahead of the army, singing to the LORD
and praising him for his holy splendor. This is what
they sang:

"Give thanks to the LORD;
his faithful love endures forever!"

[22]At the very moment they began to sing and give
praise, the LORD caused the armies of Ammon, Moab,
and Mount Seir to start fighting among themselves.
[23]The armies of Moab and Ammon turned against
their allies from Mount Seir and killed every one of
them. After they had destroyed the army of Seir, they
began attacking each other. [24]So when the army of
Judah arrived at the lookout point in the wilderness,
all they saw were dead bodies lying on the ground as
far as they could see. Not a single one of the enemy
had escaped.
[25]King Jehoshaphat and his men went out to gather
the plunder. They found vast amounts of equipment,
clothing,* and other valuables—more than they could
carry. There was so much plunder that it took them
three days just to collect it all! [26]On the fourth day they
gathered in the Valley of Blessing,* which got its name
that day because the people praised and thanked the
LORD there. It is still called the Valley of Blessing today.
[27]Then all the men returned to Jerusalem, with

2 Chr 20:2b Hebrew *the sea.* **2 Chr 20:9** Or *sword of judgment;* or *sword, judgment.* **2 Chr 20:25** As in some Hebrew manuscripts and Latin Vulgate; most Hebrew manuscripts read *corpses.* **2 Chr 20:26** Hebrew *valley of Beracah.*

2 Chr 20:6ff Jehoshaphat's prayer had several essential ingredients. (1) He committed the situation to God, acknowledging that only God could save the nation. (2) He sought God's favor because his people were God's people. (3) He acknowledged God's sovereignty over the current situation. (4) He praised God's glory and took comfort in his promises. (5) He professed complete dependence on God, not himself, for deliverance. To be God's kind of leader today, follow Jehoshaphat's example: Focus entirely on God's power rather than your own.

2 Chr 20:15 As the enemy bore down on Judah, God spoke through Jahaziel: "Do not be afraid! . . . for the battle is not yours, but God's." We may not fight an enemy army, but every day we battle temptation, pressure, and "evil rulers . . . of the unseen world" (Eph 6:12) who want us to rebel against God. Remember: As believers, we have God's Spirit in us. If we ask for God's help when we face struggles, God will fight for us. And God always triumphs.

How do we let God fight for us? (1) Realize that the battle is not ours, but God's. (2) Recognize human limitations and allow God's strength to work through our fears and weaknesses. (3) Make sure we are pursuing God's interests and not just our own selfish desires. (4) Ask God for help in our daily battles.

Jehoshaphat leading them, overjoyed that the LORD
had given them victory over their enemies. 28They
marched into Jerusalem to the music of harps, lyres,
and trumpets, and they proceeded to the Temple of
the LORD.
29When all the surrounding kingdoms heard that
the LORD himself had fought against the enemies of
Israel, the fear of God came over them. 30So Jehoshaphat's kingdom was at peace, for his God had given
him rest on every side.

Elijah Confronts King Ahaziah of Israel

2 KINGS 1:1-18

After King Ahab's death, the land of Moab rebelled
against Israel.
2One day Israel's new king, Ahaziah, fell through the
latticework of an upper room at his palace in Samaria
and was seriously injured. So he sent messengers to
the temple of Baal-zebub, the god of Ekron, to ask
whether he would recover.
3But the angel of the LORD told Elijah, who was from
Tishbe, "Go and confront the messengers of the king
of Samaria and ask them, 'Is there no God in Israel?
Why are you going to Baal-zebub, the god of Ekron,
to ask whether the king will recover? 4Now, therefore,
this is what the LORD says: You will never leave the bed
you are lying on; you will surely die.'" So Elijah went
to deliver the message.
5When the messengers returned to the king, he
asked them, "Why have you returned so soon?"
6They replied, "A man came up to us and told us to
go back to the king and give him this message. 'This
is what the LORD says: Is there no God in Israel? Why
are you sending men to Baal-zebub, the god of Ekron,
to ask whether you will recover? Therefore, because
you have done this, you will never leave the bed you
are lying on; you will surely die.'"
7"What sort of man was he?" the king demanded.
"What did he look like?"
8They replied, "He was a hairy man,* and he wore
a leather belt around his waist."
"Elijah from Tishbe!" the king exclaimed.
9Then he sent an army captain with fifty soldiers
to arrest him. They found him sitting on top of a hill.
The captain said to him, "Man of God, the king has
commanded you to come down with us."
10But Elijah replied to the captain, "If I am a man
of God, let fire come down from heaven and destroy
you and your fifty men!" Then fire fell from heaven
and killed them all.

2 Kgs 1:8 Or *He was wearing clothing made of hair.*

2 Kgs 1:1 Because 1 and 2 Kings were originally one book, 2 Kings continues where 1 Kings ends. The once great nation of Israel was split in two because the people forgot God. The book begins with Elijah, a prophet of God, being carried away into heaven. It ends with the people of Israel and Judah being taken into captivity. In 1 Kings, the beautiful Temple of God was built. In 2 Kings, it is desecrated and destroyed.

Our chaotic and corrupt world is strikingly similar to the world described in 2 Kings. Countries are tormented by war. Many people follow the false gods of technology, materialism, and war. True worship of God is rare on the earth.

We can turn to examples such as David, Elijah, and Elisha, who were devoted to God's high honor and moral law and who brought about renewal and change in their society. More important, we can look to Jesus Christ, the perfect example. For nations to do God's will, they need individuals who will do God's work. If your heart is committed to God, he can work through you to accomplish the work he has called you to do.

2 Kgs 1:2 Baal-zebub was not the same god as Baal, the Canaanite god worshiped by Ahab and Jezebel (1 Kgs 16:31-33). Baal-zebub was another popular god whose temple was located in the city of Ekron. Because this god was thought to have the power of prophecy, King Ahaziah sent messengers to Ekron to learn of his fate. Supernatural power and mystery were associated with Baal-zebub. Ahaziah's action showed the king's disrespect for God.

2 Kgs 1:8 For more information on Elijah, see his Profile on p. 719.

. . . all the men of Judah stood before the LORD with their little ones, wives, and children . . .
2 Chronicles 20:13

▸ **2 KINGS 1:1-18** ***(cont.)***

11So the king sent another captain with fifty men.
The captain said to him, "Man of God, the king demands that you come down at once."
12Elijah replied, "If I am a man of God, let fire come
down from heaven and destroy you and your fifty
men!" And again the fire of God fell from heaven and
killed them all.
13Once more the king sent a third captain with fifty
men. But this time the captain went up the hill and
fell to his knees before Elijah. He pleaded with him,
"O man of God, please spare my life and the lives of
these, your fifty servants. 14See how the fire from
heaven came down and destroyed the first two groups.
But now please spare my life!"
15Then the angel of the LORD said to Elijah, "Go
down with him, and don't be afraid of him." So Elijah
got up and went with him to the king.
16And Elijah said to the king, "This is what the LORD
says: Why did you send messengers to Baal-zebub, the
god of Ekron, to ask whether you will recover? Is there
no God in Israel to answer your question? Therefore,
because you have done this, you will never leave the
bed you are lying on; you will surely die."
17So Ahaziah died, just as the LORD had promised
through Elijah. Since Ahaziah did not have a son to
succeed him, his brother Joram* became the next
king. This took place in the second year of the reign
of Jehoram son of Jehoshaphat, king of Judah.
18The rest of the events in Ahaziah's reign are recorded in *The Book of the History of the Kings of Israel.*

Joram Begins His Reign in Israel

2 KINGS 3:1-3

Ahab's son Joram* began to rule over Israel in the
eighteenth year of King Jehoshaphat's reign in Judah.

2 Kgs 1:17 Hebrew *Jehoram,* a variant spelling of Joram. **2 Kgs 3:1** Hebrew *Jehoram,* a variant spelling of Joram; also in 3:6.

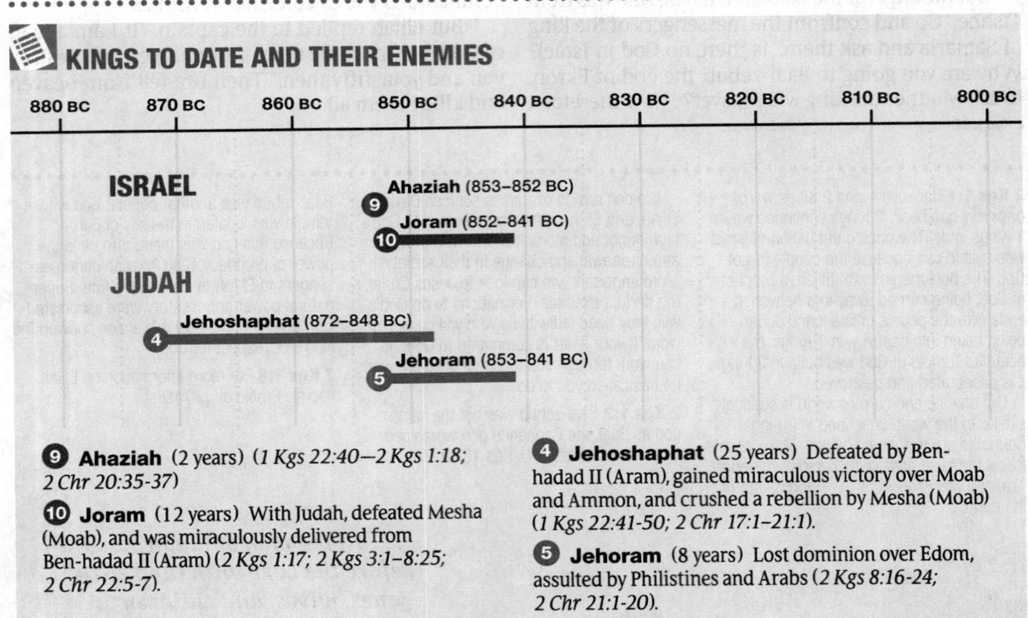

9 Ahaziah (2 years) (*1 Kgs 22:40–2 Kgs 1:18; 2 Chr 20:35-37*)

10 Joram (12 years) With Judah, defeated Mesha (Moab), and was miraculously delivered from Ben-hadad II (Aram) (*2 Kgs 1:17; 2 Kgs 3:1–8:25; 2 Chr 22:5-7*).

4 Jehoshaphat (25 years) Defeated by Ben-hadad II (Aram), gained miraculous victory over Moab and Ammon, and crushed a rebellion by Mesha (Moab) (*1 Kgs 22:41-50; 2 Chr 17:1–21:1*).

5 Jehoram (8 years) Lost dominion over Edom, assulted by Philistines and Arabs (*2 Kgs 8:16-24; 2 Chr 21:1-20*).

2 Kgs 1:13-15 Notice how the third captain went to Elijah. Although the first two captains called Elijah "man of God," they were not being genuine—God was not in their hearts. The third captain also called him "man of God," but he humbly begged for mercy. His attitude showed respect for God, and God spared the lives of his men. Effective living begins with a right attitude toward God. Before religious words come out of your mouth, make sure they are from your heart. Let respect, humility, and servanthood characterize your attitude toward God and others.

2 Kgs 1:18 *The Book of the History of the Kings of Israel* and *The Book of the History of the Kings of Judah* (2 Kgs 8:23) were history books. The inspired writer of 2 Kings selected facts from these books to retell the story of Israel and Judah from God's perspective. God directed the writer's thoughts and selection process to make sure that the truth, God's Word, would be written.

2 Kgs 3:1 Although 2 Kings 1:17 says that Jehoram was king of Judah, here it says that Jehoshaphat was Judah's king. As a king grew older, often his son would rule beside him. Jehoshaphat, nearing the end of his reign, appointed his son Jehoram to rule with him. Jehoram served as co-ruler with Jehoshaphat for five years (853–848 B.C.; he is mentioned again in 2 Kgs 8:16-24). Joram, king of Israel, was Ahab's son and Ahaziah's brother (2 Kgs 1:17). Both Ahab (1 Kgs 16:29–22:40) and Ahaziah (2 Kgs 1:2-18) served as kings of Israel before Joram.

He reigned in Samaria twelve years. 2He did what was
evil in the LORD's sight, but not to the same extent as
his father and mother. He at least tore down the sacred pillar of Baal that his father had set up. 3Never-
theless, he continued in the sins that Jeroboam son
of Nebat had committed and led the people of Israel to commit.

War between Israel and Moab

2 KINGS 3:4-27

King Mesha of Moab was a sheep breeder. He used to
pay the king of Israel an annual tribute of 100,000
lambs and the wool of 100,000 rams. 5But after Ahab's
death, the king of Moab rebelled against the king of
Israel. 6So King Joram promptly mustered the army
of Israel and marched from Samaria. 7On the way, he
sent this message to King Jehoshaphat of Judah: "The
king of Moab has rebelled against me. Will you join
me in battle against him?"

And Jehoshaphat replied, "Why, of course! You and
I are as one. My troops are your troops, and my horses
are your horses." 8Then Jehoshaphat asked, "What
route will we take?"

"We will attack from the wilderness of Edom," Joram replied.

9The king of Edom and his troops joined them, and
all three armies traveled along a roundabout route
through the wilderness for seven days. But there was
no water for the men or their animals.

10"What should we do?" the king of Israel cried out.
"The LORD has brought the three of us here to let the
king of Moab defeat us."

11But King Jehoshaphat of Judah asked, "Is there no
prophet of the LORD with us? If there is, we can ask
the LORD what to do through him."

One of King Joram's officers replied, "Elisha son
of Shaphat is here. He used to be Elijah's personal
assistant.*"

12Jehoshaphat said, "Yes, the LORD speaks through
him." So the kings of Israel, Judah, and Edom went to
consult with Elisha.

13"Why are you coming to me?"* Elisha asked the
king of Israel. "Go to the pagan prophets of your father
and mother!"

But King Joram of Israel said, "No! For it was the
LORD who called us three kings here—only to be defeated by the king of Moab!"

14Elisha replied, "As surely as the LORD Almighty
lives, whom I serve, I wouldn't even bother with you
except for my respect for King Jehoshaphat of Judah.
15Now bring me someone who can play the harp."

While the harp was being played, the power* of the
LORD came upon Elisha, 16and he said, "This is what
the LORD says: This dry valley will be filled with pools
of water! 17You will see neither wind nor rain, says the
LORD, but this valley will be filled with water. You will
have plenty for yourselves and your cattle and other
animals. 18But this is only a simple thing for the LORD,
for he will make you victorious over the army of Moab!
19You will conquer the best of their towns, even the

2 Kgs 3:11 Hebrew *He used to pour water on the hands of Elijah.* **2 Kgs 3:13** Hebrew *What is there in common between you and me?* **2 Kgs 3:15** Hebrew *the hand.*

Evidence of highly developed metal and stone sculptures in Africa

2 Kgs 3:3 The sins of Israel's kings are often compared to the sins of Jeroboam, the first ruler of the northern kingdom of Israel. His great sin was to institute idol worship throughout his kingdom, causing people to turn away from God (1 Kgs 12:25-33). By ignoring God and allowing idol worship, Joram clung to Jeroboam's sins.

2 Kgs 3:4-5 Israel and Judah held some of the most fertile land and strategic positions in the ancient Near East. It is no wonder that neighboring nations like Moab envied them and constantly attempted to seize the land. Moab lay just southeast of Israel. The country had been under Israel's control for some time due to Ahab's strong military leadership. When Ahab died, Mesha, the Moabite king, took the opportunity to rebel. While Israel's next king, Ahaziah, did nothing about the revolt, his successor, Joram, decided to take action. He joined forces with Jehoshaphat, king of Judah, and went to fight the Moabites. Together, Israel and Judah brought the Moabites to the brink of surrender. But when they saw the Moabite king sacrifice his own son and successor (2 Kgs 3:27), they withdrew even though they had won the battle. Moab fought many other battles with both Israel and Judah. Some of them, in fact, were recorded by Mesha (c. 840 B.C.), who carved his exploits on a plaque called the Moabite Stone (discovered in A.D. 1868).

2 Kgs 3:9-10 Edom was under Judah's control; thus, they marched with them, making three kings.

2 Kgs 3:11-20 Jehoshaphat's request for a "prophet of the LORD" shows how true worship and religious experience in both Israel and Judah had declined. In David's day, both the high priest and the prophets gave the king advice. But most of the priests had left Israel (see the first note on 1 Kgs 17:1, p. 715), and God's prophets were seen as messengers of doom (1 Kgs 22:18). This miracle predicted by Elisha affirmed God's power and authority and validated Elisha's ministry. In 2 Chronicles 18, King Jehoshaphat of Judah and King Ahab of Israel gave the prophet Micaiah a similar request. But they ignored God's advice—with disastrous results.

2 Kgs 3:15 In Old Testament times music often accompanied prophecy (1 Chr 25:1).

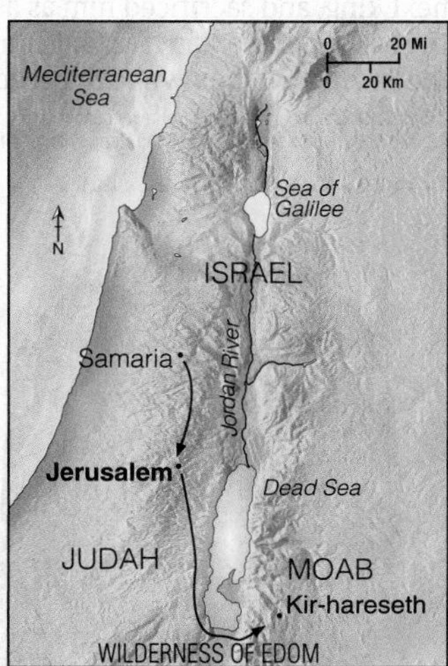

***WAR AGAINST MOAB** Moab's king rebelled against Israel. So Joram, Israel's king, and Jehoshaphat, Judah's king, attacked Moab. In the parched and rugged wilderness of Edom, the armies ran out of water, but Elisha promised that both water and victory would soon come.*

▸ **2 KINGS 3:4-27** ***(cont.)***
fortified ones. You will cut down all their good trees,
stop up all their springs, and ruin all their good land
with stones."
20The next day at about the time when the morning
sacrifice was offered, water suddenly appeared! It was
flowing from the direction of Edom, and soon there
was water everywhere.
21Meanwhile, when the people of Moab heard about
the three armies marching against them, they mobilized every man who was old enough to strap on
a sword, and they stationed themselves along their
border. 22But when they got up the next morning, the
sun was shining across the water, making it appear
red to the Moabites—like blood. 23"It's blood!" the
Moabites exclaimed. "The three armies must have
attacked and killed each other! Let's go, men of Moab,
and collect the plunder!"
24But when the Moabites arrived at the Israelite
camp, the army of Israel rushed out and attacked them
until they turned and ran. The army of Israel chased
them into the land of Moab, destroying everything as
they went.* 25They destroyed the towns, covered their
good land with stones, stopped up all the springs, and
cut down all the good trees. Finally, only Kir-hareseth
and its stone walls were left, but men with slings surrounded and attacked it.
26When the king of Moab saw that he was losing
the battle, he led 700 of his swordsmen in a desperate attempt to break through the enemy lines near
the king of Edom, but they failed. 27Then the king of
Moab took his oldest son, who would have been the
next king, and sacrificed him as a burnt offering on
the wall. So there was great anger against Israel,* and
the Israelites withdrew and returned to their own land.

Summary of Jehoshaphat's Reign PARALLEL

1 KINGS 22:41-49
Jehoshaphat son of Asa began to rule over Judah
in the fourth year of King Ahab's reign in Israel.
42Jehoshaphat was thirty-five years old when he became king, and he reigned in Jerusalem twenty-five
years. His mother was Azubah, the daughter of Shilhi.
43Jehoshaphat was a good king, following the
example of his father, Asa. He did what was pleasing in the LORD's sight. *During his reign, however,
he failed to remove all the pagan shrines, and the
people still offered sacrifices and burned incense
there. 44Jehoshaphat also made peace with the king
of Israel.
45The rest of the events in Jehoshaphat's reign,
the extent of his power, and the wars he waged are
recorded in *The Book of the History of the Kings of
Judah*. 46He banished from the land the rest of the
male and female shrine prostitutes, who still continued their practices from the days of his father, Asa.
47(There was no king in Edom at that time, only a
deputy.)
48Jehoshaphat also built a fleet of trading ships* to
sail to Ophir for gold. But the ships never set sail, for
they met with disaster in their home port of Ezion-
geber. 49At one time Ahaziah son of Ahab had proposed to Jehoshaphat, "Let my men sail with your men
in the ships." But Jehoshaphat refused the request.

2 CHRONICLES 20:31-37
So Jehoshaphat ruled over the land of Judah. He was
thirty-five years old when he became king, and he
reigned in Jerusalem twenty-five years. His mother
was Azubah, the daughter of Shilhi.

2 Kgs 3:24 The meaning of the Hebrew is uncertain. **2 Kgs 3:27** Or *So Israel's anger was great.* The meaning of the Hebrew is uncertain. **1 Kgs 22:43** Verses 22:43b-53 are numbered 22:44-54 in Hebrew text. **1 Kgs 22:48** Hebrew *fleet of ships of Tarshish.*

The Moabite Stone

This stone was discovered in the 1860s and has a fairly complete narrative of the reign of Mesha, the Moabite king from this time period. A short sketch of Mesha's account of his dealings with Israel and Judah can be correlated with the Old Testament narrative. According to Mesha, "Omri, king of Israel," had oppressed Moab for many days because the Moabite god Chemosh was angry with Moab. Omri's son "succeeded him and he too said, 'I will oppress Moab.' In my [Mesha's] time he said [this] but I triumphed over him and over his house, while Israel has perished forever." The 40-year domination of Israel over Moab involved the reigns of Omri (885–874 B.C.; 1 Kgs 16), his son Ahab (874–853 B.C.), Ahaziah (853–852 B.C.), and the first half of Jehoram's reign (852–841 B.C.). Thus, the son mentioned by Mesha was actually Omri's grandson Jehoram, who tried to destroy the Moabite rebels (2 Kgs 3:4-27). Mesha's boast that Israel perished forever was a premature exaggeration. In the end, Israel's God, Yahweh, triumphs over false gods such as Chemosh because Yahweh is real and living.

2 Kgs 3:20 The morning sacrifice was one of two sacrifices that the priests were required to offer each day.

1 Kgs 22:43 Just like his ancestors Solomon and Asa, Jehoshaphat followed God, but he didn't remove the pagan shrines in the hills (2 Chr 20:33). It was against God's laws to worship idols in the shrines (Num 33:52), and at first Jehoshaphat attempted to remove them (2 Chr 17:6). They were so popular that this proved difficult. In spite of Jehoshaphat's many contributions to the spiritual, moral, and material health of his country, he did not succeed in eradicating the hill shrines.

32Jehoshaphat was a good king, following the ways of his father, Asa. He did what was pleasing in the LORD's sight. 33During his reign, however, he failed to remove all the pagan shrines, and the people never fully committed themselves to follow the God of their ancestors.

34The rest of the events of Jehoshaphat's reign, from beginning to end, are recorded in *The Record of Jehu Son of Hanani,* which is included in *The Book of the Kings of Israel.*

35Some time later King Jehoshaphat of Judah made an alliance with King Ahaziah of Israel, who was very wicked.* 36Together they built a fleet of trading ships* at the port of Ezion-geber. 37Then Eliezer son of Dodavahu from Mareshah prophesied against Jehoshaphat. He said, "Because you have allied yourself with King Ahaziah, the LORD will destroy your work." So the ships met with disaster and never put out to sea.*

Jehoshaphat Dies PARALLEL

1 KINGS 22:50
When Jehoshaphat died, he was buried with his ancestors in the City of David. Then his son Jehoram became the next king.

2 CHRONICLES 21:1-4
When Jehoshaphat died, he was buried with his ancestors in the City of David. Then his son Jehoram became the next king.

2Jehoram's brothers—the other sons of Jehoshaphat—were Azariah, Jehiel, Zechariah, Azariahu, Michael, and Shephatiah; all these were the sons of Jehoshaphat king of Judah.* 3Their father had given each of them valuable gifts of silver, gold, and costly items, and also some of Judah's fortified towns. However, he designated Jehoram as the next king because he was the oldest. 4But when Jehoram had become solidly established as king, he killed all his brothers and some of the other leaders of Judah.

Jehoram Begins His Reign in Judah PARALLEL

2 KINGS 8:16-22
Jehoram son of King Jehoshaphat of Judah began to rule over Judah in the fifth year of the reign of Joram son of Ahab, king of Israel. 17Jehoram was thirty-two years old when he became king, and he reigned in Jerusalem eight years. 18But Jehoram followed the example of the kings of Israel and was as wicked as King Ahab, for he had married one of Ahab's daughters. So Jehoram did what was evil in the LORD's sight. 19But the LORD did not want to destroy Judah, for he had made a covenant with David and promised that his descendants would continue to rule, shining like a lamp forever.

20During Jehoram's reign, the Edomites revolted against Judah and crowned their own king. 21So Jehoram* went with all his chariots to attack the town of Zair.* The Edomites surrounded him and his chariot commanders, but he went out at night and attacked them* under cover of darkness. But Jehoram's army deserted him and fled to their homes. 22So Edom has been independent from Judah to this day. The town of Libnah also revolted about that same time.

2 CHRONICLES 21:5-17
Jehoram was thirty-two years old when he became king, and he reigned in Jerusalem eight years. 6But Jehoram followed the example of the kings of Israel and was as wicked as King Ahab, for he had married one of Ahab's daughters. So Jehoram did what was

2 Chr 20:35 Or *who made him do what was wicked.* **2 Chr 20:36** Hebrew *fleet of ships that could go to Tarshish.* **2 Chr 20:37** Hebrew *never set sail for Tarshish.* **2 Chr 21:2** Masoretic Text reads *of Israel;* also in 21:4. The author of Chronicles sees Judah as representative of the true Israel. (Some Hebrew manuscripts, Greek and Syriac versions, and Latin Vulgate read *of Judah.*) **2 Kgs 8:21a** Hebrew *Joram,* a variant spelling of Jehoram; also in 8:23, 24. **2 Kgs 8:21b** Greek version reads *Seir.* **2 Kgs 8:21c** Or *he went out and escaped.* The meaning of the Hebrew is uncertain.

2 Chr 20:33 This summary says that Jehoshaphat did not remove the pagan shrines, while 2 Chronicles 17:6; 19:3 say he did remove them. Jehoshaphat destroyed most of the Baal and Asherah idols, but since he did not succeed in wiping out the corrupt religions practiced at the shrines, they were probably rebuilt each time he had them removed.

2 Chr 20:37 Jehoshaphat met disaster when he joined forces with wicked King Ahaziah. He did not learn from his disastrous alliance with Ahab (2 Chr 18:28-34) or from his father's alliance with Aram (2 Chr 16:2-9). The partnership stood on unequal footing because one man served the Lord and the other worshiped idols. We court disaster when we enter into partnership with unbelievers because our very foundations differ (2 Cor 6:14-18). While one serves the Lord, the other does not recognize God's authority. Inevitably, the one who serves God is faced with the temptation to compromise values. When that happens, spiritual disaster results.

Before entering into partnerships, ask: (1) What are my motives? (2) What problems am I avoiding by seeking this partnership? (3) Is this partnership the best solution, or is it only a quick solution to my problem? (4) Have I prayed or asked others to pray for guidance? (5) Are my partner and I really working toward the same goals? (6) Am I willing to settle for less financial gain in order to do what God wants?

2 Kgs 8:18 King Jehoshaphat arranged the marriage between Jehoram, his son, and Athaliah, the daughter of wicked Ahab and Jezebel. Athaliah followed the idolatrous ways of the northern kingdom, bringing Baal worship into Judah and starting the southern kingdom's decline. When Jehoram died, his son Ahaziah became king. Then, when Ahaziah was killed in battle, Athaliah murdered all her grandsons except Joash and made herself queen (2 Kgs 11:1-3). Jehoram's marriage may have been politically advantageous, but spiritually it was deadly.

2 Kgs 8:20-22 Although Judah and Edom shared a common border and a common ancestor (Isaac), the two nations fought continually. Edom had been a vassal state of the united kingdom of Israel and then the southern kingdom of Judah since the days of David (2 Sam 8:13-14). Here Edom rebelled against Jehoram and declared independence. Immediately Jehoram marched out to attack Edom, but his ambush failed. Thus, Jehoram lost some of his borderlands as punishment for his failure to honor God.

▶ **2 CHRONICLES 21:5-17** ***(cont.)***

evil in the LORD's sight. 7But the LORD did not want to destroy David's dynasty, for he had made a covenant with David and promised that his descendants would continue to rule, shining like a lamp forever.

8During Jehoram's reign, the Edomites revolted against Judah and crowned their own king. 9So Jehoram went out with his full army and all his chariots. The Edomites surrounded him and his chariot commanders, but he went out at night and attacked them* under cover of darkness. 10Even so, Edom has been independent from Judah to this day. The town of Libnah also revolted about that same time. All this happened because Jehoram had abandoned the LORD, the God of his ancestors. 11He had built pagan shrines in the hill country of Judah and had led the people of Jerusalem and Judah to give themselves to pagan gods and to go astray.

12Then Elijah the prophet wrote Jehoram this letter:

"This is what the LORD, the God of your ancestor David, says: You have not followed the good example of your father, Jehoshaphat, or your grandfather King Asa of Judah. 13Instead, you have been as evil as the kings of Israel. You have led the people of Jerusalem and Judah to worship idols, just as King Ahab did in Israel. And you have even killed your own brothers, men who were better than you. 14So now the LORD is about to strike you, your people, your children, your wives, and all that is yours with a heavy blow. 15You yourself will suffer with a severe intestinal disease that will get worse each day until your bowels come out."

16Then the LORD stirred up the Philistines and the Arabs, who lived near the Ethiopians,* to attack Jehoram. 17They marched against Judah, broke down its defenses, and carried away everything of value in the royal palace, including the king's sons and his wives. Only his youngest son, Ahaziah,* was spared.

2 Chr 21:9 Or *he went out and escaped.* The meaning of the Hebrew is uncertain. **2 Chr 21:16** Hebrew *the Cushites.* **2 Chr 21:17** Hebrew *Jehoahaz,* a variant spelling of Ahaziah; compare 22:1.

4. ELISHA'S MINISTRY

Elisha begins his ministry to the northern kingdom after Elijah is taken away by a whirlwind. We can see many parallels between the ministry of Elijah and that of his successor, Elisha. Elisha performs many miracles and calls Israel to return to God, but they persist in their wickedness.

Elisha's ministry begins

Elijah Taken into Heaven

2 KINGS 2:1-18

When the LORD was about to take Elijah up to heaven in a whirlwind, Elijah and Elisha were traveling from Gilgal. 2And Elijah said to Elisha, "Stay here, for the LORD has told me to go to Bethel."

But Elisha replied, "As surely as the LORD lives and you yourself live, I will never leave you!" So they went down together to Bethel.

3The group of prophets from Bethel came to Elisha and asked him, "Did you know that the LORD is going to take your master away from you today?"

"Of course I know," Elisha answered. "But be quiet about it."

4Then Elijah said to Elisha, "Stay here, for the LORD has told me to go to Jericho."

But Elisha replied again, "As surely as the LORD lives and you yourself live, I will never leave you." So they went on together to Jericho.

5Then the group of prophets from Jericho came to Elisha and asked him, "Did you know that the LORD is going to take your master away from you today?"

"Of course I know," Elisha answered. "But be quiet about it."

6Then Elijah said to Elisha, "Stay here, for the LORD has told me to go to the Jordan River."

But again Elisha replied, "As surely as the LORD lives and you yourself live, I will never leave you." So they went on together.

7Fifty men from the group of prophets also went and watched from a distance as Elijah and Elisha stopped beside the Jordan River. 8Then Elijah folded

2 Chr 21:7 God promised that a descendant of David would always sit on the throne (2 Sam 7:8-16). What happened to this promise when the nation was destroyed and carried away? There were two parts to God's promise. (1) In the physical sense, as long as there was an actual throne in Judah, a descendant of David would sit upon it. But this part of the promise depended on the obedience of these kings. When they disobeyed, God was not bound to continue David's temporal line. (2) In the spiritual sense, this promise was completely fulfilled in the coming of Jesus the Messiah, a descendant of David, who would sit on the throne of David forever.

2 Chr 21:8-11 Jehoram's reign was marked by sin and cruelty. He married a woman who worshiped idols; he killed his six brothers; he allowed and even promoted idol worship. Yet he was not killed in battle or by treachery—he died by a lingering and painful disease (2 Chr 21:18-19). Punishment for sin is not always immediate or dramatic. But if we ignore God's laws, we will eventually suffer the consequences of our sin.

2 Chr 21:12 Chronicles mentions Elijah only here. Much more about this great prophet can be found in the parallel narratives in 1 Kings and 2 Kings. Elijah's Profile is found on p. 719.

2 Kgs 2:3 A "group of prophets from Bethel" was similar to a school, a gathering of disciples around a recognized prophet, such as Elijah or Elisha. These groups of prophets, located throughout the country, helped stem the tide of spiritual and moral decline in the nation begun under Jeroboam. The students at Bethel were eyewitnesses to the succession of the prophetic ministry from Elijah to Elisha.

2 Kgs 2:8 Elijah's cloak was a symbol of his authority as a prophet.

his cloak together and struck the water with it. The
river divided, and the two of them went across on
dry ground!
9When they came to the other side, Elijah said to
Elisha, "Tell me what I can do for you before I am taken
away."

And Elisha replied, "Please let me inherit a double
share of your spirit and become your successor."
10"You have asked a difficult thing," Elijah replied.
"If you see me when I am taken from you, then you will
get your request. But if not, then you won't."
11As they were walking along and talking, suddenly
a chariot of fire appeared, drawn by horses of fire. It
drove between the two men, separating them, and
Elijah was carried by a whirlwind into heaven. 12Elisha
saw it and cried out, "My father! My father! I see the
chariots and charioteers of Israel!" And as they disappeared from sight, Elisha tore his clothes in distress.
13Elisha picked up Elijah's cloak, which had fallen
when he was taken up. Then Elisha returned to the bank
of the Jordan River. 14He struck the water with Elijah's
cloak and cried out, "Where is the LORD, the God of
Elijah?" Then the river divided, and Elisha went across.
15When the group of prophets from Jericho saw
from a distance what happened, they exclaimed, "Elijah's spirit rests upon Elisha!" And they went to meet
him and bowed to the ground before him. 16"Sir," they
said, "just say the word and fifty of our strongest men
will search the wilderness for your master. Perhaps the
Spirit of the LORD has left him on some mountain or
in some valley."

"No," Elisha said, "don't send them." 17But they kept
urging him until they shamed him into agreeing, and
he finally said, "All right, send them." So fifty men
searched for three days but did not find Elijah. 18Elisha
was still at Jericho when they returned. "Didn't I tell
you not to go?" he asked.

Elisha's First Miracles

2 KINGS 2:19-25

One day the leaders of the town of Jericho visited Elisha. "We have a problem, my lord," they told him. "This
town is located in pleasant surroundings, as you can
see. But the water is bad, and the land is unproductive."
20Elisha said, "Bring me a new bowl with salt in it."
So they brought it to him. 21Then he went out to the

2 Kgs 2:9 Elisha asked to be Elijah's "successor," or heir, the one who would continue Elijah's work as leader of the prophets. That is why he asked for a double share of Elijah's spirit. Deuteronomy 21:17 helps explain Elisha's request. According to custom, the firstborn son would receive a double portion of the father's inheritance (see the note on Gen 25:31, p. 51). But the decision to grant this request was up to God. Elijah only told Elisha how he would know if his request had been granted.

2 Kgs 2:9 God granted Elisha's request because Elisha's motives were pure. His main goal was not to be better or more powerful than Elijah but to accomplish more for God. If our motives are pure, we don't have to be afraid to ask great things from God, but we must be willing to ask. And when we ask God for great power or ability, we need to examine our desires and get rid of any selfishness we find.

2 Kgs 2:11 Elijah was taken to heaven without dying. He is the second person mentioned in Scripture to have this honor. Enoch was the first (Gen 5:21-24). The other prophets may not have seen God take Elijah, or they may have had a difficult time believing what they had seen. In either case, they wanted to search for Elijah (2 Kgs 2:16-18). Finding no physical trace of him would confirm what had happened and strengthen their faith. The only other person taken to heaven in bodily form was Jesus after his resurrection from the dead (Acts 1:9).

2 Kgs 2:13-25 These three incidents were testimonies to Elisha's commission as a prophet of God. They are recorded to demonstrate Elisha's new power and authority as Israel's chief prophet under God's ultimate power and authority.

2 Kgs 2:14 Elisha did not strike the water out of disrespect for God or Elijah. He was pleading with God to confirm his appointment as Elijah's successor.

As they were walking along and talking, suddenly a chariot of fire appeared, drawn by horses of fire. It drove between the two men, separating them, and Elijah was carried by a whirlwind into heaven.
2 Kings 2:11

▸ **2 KINGS 2:19-25 *(cont.)***

spring that supplied the town with water and threw the salt into it. And he said, "This is what the LORD says: I have purified this water. It will no longer cause death or infertility.*" 22And the water has remained pure ever since, just as Elisha said.

23Elisha left Jericho and went up to Bethel. As he was walking along the road, a group of boys from the town began mocking and making fun of him. "Go away, baldy!" they chanted. "Go away, baldy!" 24Elisha turned around and looked at them, and he cursed them in the name of the LORD. Then two bears came out of the woods and mauled forty-two of them. 25From there Elisha went to Mount Carmel and finally returned to Samaria.

Elisha Helps a Poor Widow

2 KINGS 4:1-7

One day the widow of a member of the group of prophets came to Elisha and cried out, "My husband who served you is dead, and you know how he feared the LORD. But now a creditor has come, threatening to take my two sons as slaves."

2"What can I do to help you?" Elisha asked. "Tell me, what do you have in the house?"

"Nothing at all, except a flask of olive oil," she replied.

3And Elisha said, "Borrow as many empty jars as you can from your friends and neighbors. 4Then go into your house with your sons and shut the door behind you. Pour olive oil from your flask into the jars, setting each one aside when it is filled."

5So she did as she was told. Her sons kept bringing jars to her, and she filled one after another. 6Soon every container was full to the brim!

"Bring me another jar," she said to one of her sons.

"There aren't any more!" he told her. And then the olive oil stopped flowing.

7When she told the man of God what had happened, he said to her, "Now sell the olive oil and pay

2 Kgs 2:21 Or *or make the land unproductive;* Hebrew reads *or barrenness.*

2 Kgs 2:23-24 This group of boys was from Bethel, the religious center of idolatry in the northern kingdom, and they probably were warning Elisha not to speak against their immorality as Elijah had done. They were not merely teasing Elisha about his baldness, but showing severe disrespect for Elisha's message and God's power. They may also have jeered because of their disbelief in the chariot of fire that had taken Elijah. When Elisha cursed them, he did not call out the bears himself. God sent them as a judgment for their callous unbelief.

2 Kgs 2:23-24 These young men mocked God's messenger and paid for it with their lives. Making fun of religious leaders has been a popular sport through the ages. To take a stand for God is to be different from the world and vulnerable to verbal abuse. When we are cynical and sarcastic toward religious leaders, we are in danger of mocking not just the person but also the spiritual message. While we are not to condone the sin that some leaders commit, we need to pray for them, not laugh at them. True leaders, those who follow God, need to be heard with respect and encouraged in their ministry.

2 Kgs 4:1 Poor people and debtors were allowed to pay their debts by selling themselves or their children as slaves. God ordered rich people and creditors not to take advantage of these people during their time of extreme need (see Deut 15:1-18 for an explanation of these practices). This woman's creditor was not acting in the spirit of God's law. Elisha's kind deed demonstrates that God wants us to go beyond simply keeping the law. We must also show compassion.

2 Kgs 4:1ff This chapter records four of God's miracles through Elisha: providing money for a poverty-stricken widow (2 Kgs 4:1-7); raising a dead boy to life (2 Kgs 4:32-37); purifying poisonous food (2 Kgs 4:38-41); and providing food for 100 men (2 Kgs 4:42-44). These miracles show God's tenderness and care for those who are faithful to him.

When reading the Old Testament, it is easy to focus on God's harsh judgment of the rebellious and to minimize his tender care for those who love and serve him. Seeing God at work providing for his followers helps us keep his severe justice toward the unrepentant in proper perspective.

MIRACLES OF ELIJAH & ELISHA

Baal, the false god worshiped by many Israelites, was the god of rain, fire, and farm crops. He also demanded child sacrifice. Elijah's and Elisha's miracles repeatedly show the power of the true God over the purported realm of Baal, as well as the value God places on the life of a child.

Miracle	*Reference*	*Factors*
ELIJAH		
1. Food brought by ravens	1 Kgs 17:5-6	Food
2. Widow's food multiplied	1 Kgs 17:12-16	Flour and oil
3. Widow's son raised to life	1 Kgs 17:17-24	Life of a child
4. Altar and sacrifice consumed	1 Kgs 18:16-40	Fire and water
5. Ahaziah's soldiers consumed	2 Kgs 1:9-14	Fire
6. Jordan River parted	2 Kgs 2:6-8	Water
7. Transported to heaven	2 Kgs 2:11-12	Fire and wind
ELISHA		
1. Jordan River parted	2 Kgs 2:13-14	Water
2. Spring purified at Jericho	2 Kgs 2:19-22	Water
3. Widow's oil multiplied	2 Kgs 4:1-7	Oil
4. Dead boy raised to life	2 Kgs 4:18-37	Life of a child
5. Poison in stew purified	2 Kgs 4:38-41	Flour
6. Prophets' food multiplied	2 Kgs 4:42-44	Bread and grain
7. Naaman healed of leprosy	2 Kgs 5:1-14	Water
8. Gehazi became leprous	2 Kgs 5:15-27	Words alone
9. Ax head floated	2 Kgs 6:1-7	Water
10. Aramean army blinded	2 Kgs 6:8-23	Elisha's prayer

your debts, and you and your sons can live on what
is left over."

Elisha and the Woman from Shunem

2 KINGS 4:8-37

One day Elisha went to the town of Shunem. A wealthy
woman lived there, and she urged him to come to her
home for a meal. After that, whenever he passed that
way, he would stop there for something to eat.
9She said to her husband, "I am sure this man who
stops in from time to time is a holy man of God. 10Let's
build a small room for him on the roof and furnish it
with a bed, a table, a chair, and a lamp. Then he will
have a place to stay whenever he comes by."
11One day Elisha returned to Shunem, and he went
up to this upper room to rest. 12He said to his servant
Gehazi, "Tell the woman from Shunem I want to speak
to her." When she appeared, 13Elisha said to Gehazi,
"Tell her, 'We appreciate the kind concern you have
shown us. What can we do for you? Can we put in a
good word for you to the king or to the commander
of the army?'"
"No," she replied, "my family takes good care of me."
14Later Elisha asked Gehazi, "What can we do for
her?"
Gehazi replied, "She doesn't have a son, and her
husband is an old man."
15"Call her back again," Elisha told him. When the
woman returned, Elisha said to her as she stood in the
doorway, 16"Next year at this time you will be holding
a son in your arms!"
"No, my lord!" she cried. "O man of God, don't deceive me and get my hopes up like that."
17But sure enough, the woman soon became pregnant. And at that time the following year she had a
son, just as Elisha had said.
18One day when her child was older, he went out to
help his father, who was working with the harvesters.
19Suddenly he cried out, "My head hurts! My head
hurts!"
His father said to one of the servants, "Carry him
home to his mother."
20So the servant took him home, and his mother
held him on her lap. But around noontime he died.
21She carried him up and laid him on the bed of the
man of God, then shut the door and left him there.
22She sent a message to her husband: "Send one of
the servants and a donkey so that I can hurry to the
man of God and come right back."
23"Why go today?" he asked. "It is neither a new
moon festival nor a Sabbath."
But she said, "It will be all right."
24So she saddled the donkey and said to the servant,
"Hurry! Don't slow down unless I tell you to."
25As she approached the man of God at Mount Carmel, Elisha saw her in the distance. He said to Gehazi,
"Look, the woman from Shunem is coming. 26Run out
to meet her and ask her, 'Is everything all right with
you, your husband, and your child?'"
"Yes," the woman told Gehazi, "everything is fine."
27But when she came to the man of God at the mountain, she fell to the ground before him and caught hold
of his feet. Gehazi began to push her away, but the man
of God said, "Leave her alone. She is deeply troubled,
but the LORD has not told me what it is."
28Then she said, "Did I ask you for a son, my lord?
And didn't I say, 'Don't deceive me and get my hopes
up'?"
29Then Elisha said to Gehazi, "Get ready to travel*;
take my staff and go! Don't talk to anyone along the
way. Go quickly and lay the staff on the child's face."
30But the boy's mother said, "As surely as the LORD

2 Kgs 4:29 Hebrew *Bind up your loins.*

2 Kgs 4:6 The woman and her sons collected jars from their neighbors, pouring olive oil into them from their one flask. The olive oil was used for cooking, for lamps, and for fuel. The oil stopped flowing only when they ran out of containers. The number of jars they gathered was an indication of their faith. God's provision was as large as their faith and willingness to obey. Beware of limiting God's blessings by a lack of faith and obedience. God is able to do immeasurably more than all we ask or imagine (Eph 3:20).

2 Kgs 4:9 The woman from Shunem realized that Elisha was a man of God, and so she prepared a room for him to use whenever he was in town. She did this out of kindness and because she sensed a need, not for any selfish motives. Soon her kindness would be rewarded far beyond her wildest dreams. How sensitive are you to those who pass by your home and flow through your life—especially those who teach and preach God's Word? What special needs do they have that you could meet? Look for ways to serve and help.

THE FAMILY IN SHUNEM ▶
Elisha often stayed with a kind family in Shunem. When the son suddenly died, his mother traveled to Mount Carmel to find Elisha. He returned with her and raised the boy from the dead. Elisha then went to his home in Gilgal.

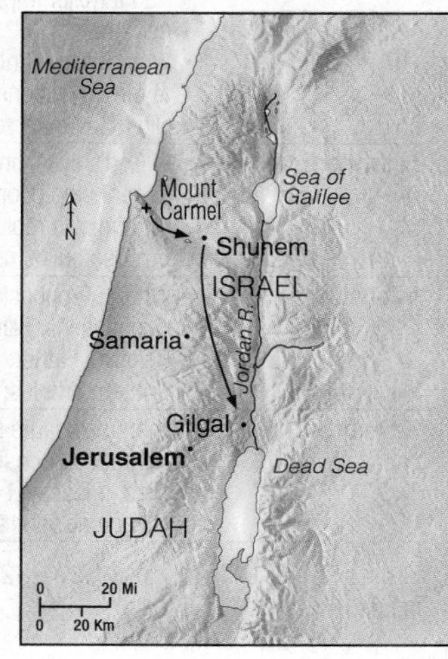

▸ **2 KINGS 4:8-37** ***(cont.)***
lives and you yourself live, I won't go home unless you
go with me." So Elisha returned with her.
31 Gehazi hurried on ahead and laid the staff on the
child's face, but nothing happened. There was no sign
of life. He returned to meet Elisha and told him, "The
child is still dead."
32 When Elisha arrived, the child was indeed dead,
lying there on the prophet's bed. 33 He went in alone
and shut the door behind him and prayed to the LORD.
34 Then he lay down on the child's body, placing his
mouth on the child's mouth, his eyes on the child's
eyes, and his hands on the child's hands. And as he
stretched out on him, the child's body began to grow
warm again! 35 Elisha got up, walked back and forth
across the room once, and then stretched himself out
again on the child. This time the boy sneezed seven
times and opened his eyes!
36 Then Elisha summoned Gehazi. "Call the child's
mother!" he said. And when she came in, Elisha said,
"Here, take your son!" 37 She fell at his feet and bowed
before him, overwhelmed with gratitude. Then she
took her son in her arms and carried him downstairs.

Miracles during a Famine

2 KINGS 4:38-44

Elisha now returned to Gilgal, and there was a famine
in the land. One day as the group of prophets was

ELISHA

Few "replacements" in Scripture were as effective as Elisha, who was Elijah's replacement as God's prophet to Israel. But Elisha had a great example to follow in the prophet Elijah. He remained with Elijah until the last moments of his teacher's life on earth. He was willing to follow and learn in order to gain power to do the work to which God had called him. • Both Elijah and Elisha concentrated their efforts on the particular needs of the people around them. The fiery Elijah confronted and exposed idolatry, helping to create an atmosphere where people could freely and publicly worship God. Elisha then moved in to demonstrate God's powerful, yet caring, nature to all who came to him for help. He spent less time in conflict with evil and more in compassionate care of people. The Bible records 18 encounters between Elisha and needy people. • Elisha saw more in life than most people because he recognized that with God there was more to life. He knew that all we are and have comes to us from God. The miracles that occurred during Elisha's ministry put people in touch with the personal and all-powerful God. Elijah would have been proud of his replacement's work. • We, too, have great examples to follow—people we learn about in Scripture and in church history and those people in our lives who have positively influenced us. We must resist the tendency to think about the limitations that our family background or environment create for us. Instead, we should ask God to use us for his purposes—perhaps, like Elijah, to take a stand against great wrongs or, like Elisha, to show compassion for the daily needs of those around us. Ask him to use you as only he can.

Strengths and accomplishments	• Was Elijah's successor as a prophet of God • Had a ministry that lasted over 50 years • Had a major impact on four nations: Israel, Judah, Moab, and Aram • Was a man of integrity who did not try to enrich himself at others' expense • Did many miracles to help those in need
Lessons from his life	• In God's eyes, one measure of greatness is the willingness to serve the poor as well as the powerful • An effective replacement not only learns from his master but also builds upon his master's achievements
Vital statistics	• Where: Prophesied to the northern kingdom • Occupations: Farmer, prophet • Relative: Father: Shaphat • Contemporaries: Elijah, Ahab, Jezebel, Jehu
Key verse	"When they came to the other side, Elijah said to Elisha, 'Tell me what I can do for you before I am taken away.' And Elisha replied, 'Please let me inherit a double share of your spirit and become your successor'" (2 Kgs 2:9).

Elisha's story is told in 1 Kings 19:16—2 Kings 13:20. He is also mentioned in Luke 4:27.

2 Kgs 4:32-36 Elisha's prayer and method of raising the dead boy show God's personal care for hurting people. We must express genuine concern for others as we carry God's message to them. Only then will we faithfully represent our compassionate Father in heaven.

2 Kgs 5:1 Leprosy, much like AIDS today, was one of the most feared diseases of the time. Some forms were extremely contagious and, in many cases, incurable. In its worst forms, leprosy led to death. Many lepers were forced out of the cities into quarantined camps. Because Naaman still held his post, he probably had a mild form of the disease, or perhaps it was still in the early stages. In either case, his life would have been tragically shortened by his disease. (For more about leprosy in Bible times, see the note on Lev 13:1ff, p. 216.)

2 Kgs 5:2 Aram was Israel's neighbor to the northeast, but the two nations were rarely on friendly terms. Under David, Aram paid tribute to Israel. In Elisha's day, Aram was growing in power and frequently conducted raids on Israel, trying to frustrate the people and bring about political confusion. Israelite captives often would be taken back to Aram after successful raids. Naaman's servant girl was an Israelite, kidnapped from her home and family. Ironically, Naaman's only hope of being cured came from Israel.

2 Kgs 5:3-4 The little girl's faith and Naaman's quest contrast with the stubbornness of Israel's king (2 Kgs 5:7). A leader in mighty Aram sought the God of Israel; Israel's own king would not. We don't know the little girl's name or much about her, but her brief word to her mistress brought healing and faith in God to a powerful Aramean captain. God had placed her for a purpose, and she was faithful. Where has God put you? No matter how humble or small your position, God can use you to spread his Word. Look for opportunities to tell others what God can do. There's no telling who will hear your message!

2 Kgs 5:5 The name of Israel's king is not mentioned in this story. The events of 2 Kings 1–8 are mainly about Elisha's ministry and are not intended to be chronological. The king was most likely Jehoram (2 Kgs 3:1), but we cannot know for sure.

seated before him, he said to his servant, "Put a large pot on the fire, and make some stew for the rest of the group."
39One of the young men went out into the field to gather herbs and came back with a pocketful of wild gourds. He shredded them and put them into the pot without realizing they were poisonous. 40Some of the stew was served to the men. But after they had eaten a bite or two they cried out, "Man of God, there's poison in this stew!" So they would not eat it.
41Elisha said, "Bring me some flour." Then he threw it into the pot and said, "Now it's all right; go ahead and eat." And then it did not harm them.
42One day a man from Baal-shalishah brought the man of God a sack of fresh grain and twenty loaves of barley bread made from the first grain of his harvest. Elisha said, "Give it to the people so they can eat."
43"What?" his servant exclaimed. "Feed a hundred people with only this?"

But Elisha repeated, "Give it to the people so they can eat, for this is what the LORD says: Everyone will eat, and there will even be some left over!" 44And when they gave it to the people, there was plenty for all and some left over, just as the LORD had promised.

The Healing of Naaman

2 KINGS 5:1-19

The king of Aram had great admiration for Naaman, the commander of his army, because through him the LORD had given Aram great victories. But though Naaman was a mighty warrior, he suffered from leprosy.*
2At this time Aramean raiders had invaded the land of Israel, and among their captives was a young girl who had been given to Naaman's wife as a maid. 3One day the girl said to her mistress, "I wish my master would go to see the prophet in Samaria. He would heal him of his leprosy."
4So Naaman told the king what the young girl from Israel had said. 5"Go and visit the prophet," the king of Aram told him. "I will send a letter of introduction for you to take to the king of Israel." So Naaman started out, carrying as gifts 750 pounds of silver, 150 pounds of gold,* and ten sets of clothing. 6The letter to the king of Israel said: "With this letter I present my servant Naaman. I want you to heal him of his leprosy."
7When the king of Israel read the letter, he tore his clothes in dismay and said, "This man sends me a leper to heal! Am I God, that I can give life and take it away? I can see that he's just trying to pick a fight with me."
8But when Elisha, the man of God, heard that the king of Israel had torn his clothes in dismay, he sent this message to him: "Why are you so upset? Send Naaman to me, and he will learn that there is a true prophet here in Israel."
9So Naaman went with his horses and chariots and waited at the door of Elisha's house. 10But Elisha sent a messenger out to him with this message: "Go and wash yourself seven times in the Jordan River. Then

2 Kgs 5:1 Or *from a contagious skin disease.* The Hebrew word used here and throughout this passage can describe various skin diseases. **2 Kgs 5:5** Hebrew *10 talents* [340 kilograms] *of silver, 6,000 shekels* [68 kilograms] *of gold.*

2 Kgs 5:9-15 Naaman, a great hero, was used to getting respect, so he was outraged when Elisha treated him like an ordinary person. A proud man, he expected royal treatment. To wash in a great river would be one thing, but the Jordan was small and dirty. To wash in the Jordan, Naaman thought, was beneath a man of his position. But Naaman had to humble himself and obey Elisha's commands in order to be healed.

Obedience to God begins with humility. We must believe that his way is better than our own. We may not always understand his ways of working, but by humbly obeying, we will receive his blessings. We must remember that (1) God's ways are best; (2) God wants our obedience more than anything else; (3) God can use anything to accomplish his purposes.

So Naaman went down to the Jordan River and dipped himself seven times, as the man of God had instructed him. And his skin became as healthy as the skin of a young child's, and he was healed!
2 Kings 5:14

▸ 2 KINGS 5:1-19 *(cont.)*

your skin will be restored, and you will be healed of
your leprosy."
11 But Naaman became angry and stalked away. "I
thought he would certainly come out to meet me!" he
said. "I expected him to wave his hand over the leprosy
and call on the name of the LORD his God and heal me!
12 Aren't the rivers of Damascus, the Abana and the
Pharpar, better than any of the rivers of Israel? Why
shouldn't I wash in them and be healed?" So Naaman
turned and went away in a rage.
13 But his officers tried to reason with him and said,
"Sir,* if the prophet had told you to do something very
difficult, wouldn't you have done it? So you should certainly obey him when he says simply, 'Go and wash and
be cured!'" 14 So Naaman went down to the Jordan River
and dipped himself seven times, as the man of God had
instructed him. And his skin became as healthy as the
skin of a young child's, and he was healed!
15 Then Naaman and his entire party went back to
find the man of God. They stood before him, and Naaman said, "Now I know that there is no God in all the
world except in Israel. So please accept a gift from
your servant."
16 But Elisha replied, "As surely as the LORD lives,
whom I serve, I will not accept any gifts." And though
Naaman urged him to take the gift, Elisha refused.
17 Then Naaman said, "All right, but please allow me
to load two of my mules with earth from this place,
and I will take it back home with me. From now on I
will never again offer burnt offerings or sacrifices to
any other god except the LORD. 18 However, may the
LORD pardon me in this one thing: When my master
the king goes into the temple of the god Rimmon to
worship there and leans on my arm, may the LORD
pardon me when I bow, too."
19 "Go in peace," Elisha said. So Naaman started
home again.

The Greed of Gehazi

2 KINGS 5:20-27

But Gehazi, the servant of Elisha, the man of God, said
to himself, "My master should not have let this Aramean
get away without accepting any of his gifts. As surely as
the LORD lives, I will chase after him and get something
from him." 21 So Gehazi set off after Naaman.
When Naaman saw Gehazi running after him, he
climbed down from his chariot and went to meet him.
"Is everything all right?" Naaman asked.
22 "Yes," Gehazi said, "but my master has sent me to
tell you that two young prophets from the hill country
of Ephraim have just arrived. He would like 75 pounds*
of silver and two sets of clothing to give to them."
23 "By all means, take twice as much* silver," Naaman insisted. He gave him two sets of clothing, tied up
the money in two bags, and sent two of his servants to
carry the gifts for Gehazi. 24 But when they arrived at
the citadel,* Gehazi took the gifts from the servants
and sent the men back. Then he went and hid the gifts
inside the house.
25 When he went in to his master, Elisha asked him,
"Where have you been, Gehazi?"
"I haven't been anywhere," he replied.
26 But Elisha asked him, "Don't you realize that I was
there in spirit when Naaman stepped down from his
chariot to meet you? Is this the time to receive money
and clothing, olive groves and vineyards, sheep and
cattle, and male and female servants? 27 Because you
have done this, you and your descendants will suffer
from Naaman's leprosy forever." When Gehazi left
the room, he was covered with leprosy; his skin was
white as snow.

The Floating Ax Head

2 KINGS 6:1-7

One day the group of prophets came to Elisha and told
him, "As you can see, this place where we meet with

2 Kgs 5:13 Hebrew *My father.* **2 Kgs 5:22** Hebrew *1 talent* [34 kilograms]. **2 Kgs 5:23** Hebrew *take 2 talents* [68 kilograms]. **2 Kgs 5:24** Hebrew *the Ophel.*

2 Kgs 5:12 Naaman left in a rage because the cure for his disease seemed too simple. He was a hero, and he expected a heroic cure. Full of pride and self-will, Naaman could not accept the simple cure of faith. Sometimes people react to God's offer of forgiveness in the same way. Just to believe in Jesus Christ somehow doesn't seem significant enough to bring eternal life. To obey God's commands doesn't seem heroic. What Naaman had to do to have his leprosy washed away is similar to what we must do to have our sin washed away—humbly accept God's mercy. Don't let your reaction to the way of faith keep you from the cure you need the most.

2 Kgs 5:16 Elisha refused Naaman's money to show that God's favor cannot be purchased. Our money, like Naaman's, is useless when we face death. No matter how much wealth we accumulate in this life, it will evaporate when we stand before God, our Creator. It is not our bank accounts but our faith in Jesus Christ that will save us.

2 Kgs 5:18-19 How could Naaman be forgiven for bowing to a pagan idol? Naaman was not asking for permission to worship the god Rimmon (the god of Damascus) but to do his civil duty, helping the king get down and up as he bowed. Also known as Hadad, Rimmon was believed to be a god of rain and thunder. Unlike most of his contemporaries, Naaman showed a keen awareness of God's power. Instead of adding God to his nation's collection of idols, he acknowledged that there was only one true God. He did not intend to worship other gods. His asking for pardon in this one area shows the marked contrast between Naaman and the Israelites, who were continually worshiping many idols.

2 Kgs 5:20-27 Gehazi saw a perfect opportunity to get rich by selfishly asking for the reward Elisha had refused. Unfortunately, his plan had three problems: (1) He willingly accepted money that had been offered to someone else; (2) he wrongly implied that money could be exchanged for God's free gift of healing and mercy; (3) he lied and tried to cover up his motives for accepting the money. Although Gehazi had been a helpful servant, personal gain had become more important to him than serving God.

This passage is not teaching that money is evil or that ministers should not get paid; instead, it is warning against greed and deceit. True service is motivated by love and devotion to God and seeks no personal gain. As you serve God, check your motives—you can't serve both God and money (Matt 6:24).

you is too small. 2Let's go down to the Jordan River, where there are plenty of logs. There we can build a new place for us to meet."

"All right," he told them, "go ahead."

3"Please come with us," someone suggested.

"I will," he said. 4So he went with them.

When they arrived at the Jordan, they began cutting
down trees. 5But as one of them was cutting a tree, his
ax head fell into the river. "Oh, sir!" he cried. "It was a borrowed ax!"

6"Where did it fall?" the man of God asked. When he showed him the place, Elisha cut a stick and threw it into the water at that spot. Then the ax head floated
to the surface. 7"Grab it," Elisha said. And the man reached out and grabbed it.

Elisha Traps the Arameans

2 KINGS 6:8-23

When the king of Aram was at war with Israel, he would confer with his officers and say, "We will mobilize our forces at such and such a place."

9But immediately Elisha, the man of God, would warn the king of Israel, "Do not go near that place, for the Arameans are planning to mobilize their troops there."
10So the king of Israel would send word to the place indicated by the man of God. Time and again Elisha warned the king, so that he would be on the alert there.

11The king of Aram became very upset over this. He called his officers together and demanded, "Which of you is the traitor? Who has been informing the king of Israel of my plans?"

12"It's not us, my lord the king," one of the officers replied. "Elisha, the prophet in Israel, tells the king of Israel even the words you speak in the privacy of your bedroom!"

13"Go and find out where he is," the king commanded, "so I can send troops to seize him."

And the report came back: "Elisha is at Dothan."
14So one night the king of Aram sent a great army with many chariots and horses to surround the city.

15When the servant of the man of God got up early the next morning and went outside, there were troops, horses, and chariots everywhere. "Oh, sir, what will we do now?" the young man cried to Elisha.

16"Don't be afraid!" Elisha told him. "For there are
more on our side than on theirs!" 17Then Elisha prayed,
"O LORD, open his eyes and let him see!" The LORD opened the young man's eyes, and when he looked up, he saw that the hillside around Elisha was filled with horses and chariots of fire.

18As the Aramean army advanced toward him, Elisha prayed, "O LORD, please make them blind." So the LORD struck them with blindness as Elisha had asked.

19Then Elisha went out and told them, "You have come the wrong way! This isn't the right city! Follow me, and I will take you to the man you are looking for." And he led them to the city of Samaria.

20As soon as they had entered Samaria, Elisha prayed, "O LORD, now open their eyes and let them see." So the LORD opened their eyes, and they discovered that they were in the middle of Samaria.

21When the king of Israel saw them, he shouted to Elisha, "My father, should I kill them? Should I kill them?"

22"Of course not!" Elisha replied. "Do we kill prisoners of war? Give them food and drink and send them home again to their master."

23So the king made a great feast for them and then sent them home to their master. After that, the Aramean raiders stayed away from the land of Israel.

2 Kgs 6:1-7 The incident of the floating ax head is recorded to show God's care and provision for those who trust him, even in the insignificant events of everyday life. God is always present. Placed in the Bible between the healing of an Aramean general and the deliverance of Israel's army, this miracle also shows Elisha's personal contact with the students in the groups of the prophets. Although he had the respect of kings, Elisha never forgot to care for the faithful. Don't let the importance of your work crowd out your concern for human need.

2 Kgs 6:16-17 Elisha's servant was no longer afraid when he saw God's mighty heavenly army. Faith reveals that God is doing more for his people than we can ever realize through sight alone. When you face difficulties that seem insurmountable, remember that spiritual resources are there even if you can't see them. Look with the eyes of faith, and let God show you his resources. If you don't see God working in your life, the problem may be your spiritual eyesight, not God's power.

***ELISHA AND THE ARAMEANS* ▶**
Elisha knew Aram's battle plans and kept Israel's king informed. The Aramean king tracked down Elisha at Dothan, but Elisha prayed that the Aramean army would be blinded. He then led the blind army into Samaria, Israel's capital city!

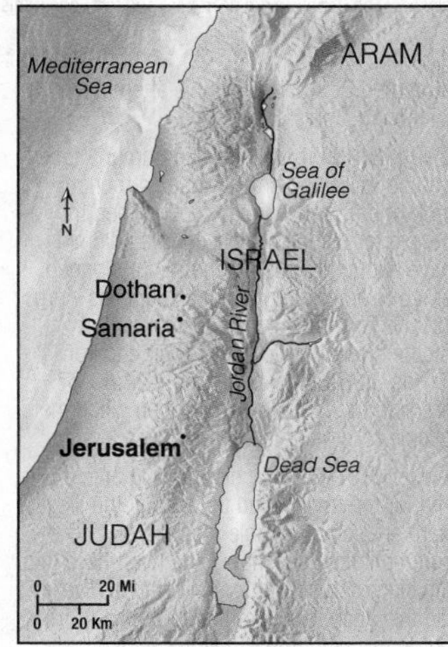

2 Kgs 6:21-22 Elisha told the king not to kill the Arameans. The king was not to take credit for what God alone had done. In setting food and water before them, he was heaping "burning coals" on their heads (Prov 25:21-22).

2 Kgs 6:23 How long the Arameans stayed away from Israel is not known, but a number of years probably passed before the invasion recorded in 2 Kings 6:24 occurred. The Arameans must have forgotten the time their army had been supernaturally blinded and sent home.

2 Kgs 6:24 This was probably Ben-hadad II, whose father had ruled Aram in the days of Baasha (1 Kgs 15:18). Elisha constantly

Ben-Hadad Besieges Samaria

2 KINGS 6:24-7:2

Some time later, however, King Ben-hadad of Aram
mustered his entire army and besieged Samaria. 25As
a result, there was a great famine in the city. The siege
lasted so long that a donkey's head sold for eighty
pieces of silver, and a cup of dove's dung sold for five
pieces* of silver.

26One day as the king of Israel was walking along
the wall of the city, a woman called to him, "Please
help me, my lord the king!"

27He answered, "If the LORD doesn't help you, what
can I do? I have neither food from the threshing floor
nor wine from the press to give you." 28But then the
king asked, "What is the matter?"

She replied, "This woman said to me: 'Come on, let's
eat your son today, then we will eat my son tomorrow.'
29So we cooked my son and ate him. Then the next day
I said to her, 'Kill your son so we can eat him,' but she
has hidden her son."

30When the king heard this, he tore his clothes in
despair. And as the king walked along the wall, the
people could see that he was wearing burlap under
his robe next to his skin. 31"May God strike me and
even kill me if I don't separate Elisha's head from his
shoulders this very day," the king vowed.

32Elisha was sitting in his house with the elders of
Israel when the king sent a messenger to summon
him. But before the messenger arrived, Elisha said to
the elders, "A murderer has sent a man to cut off my
head. When he arrives, shut the door and keep him out.
We will soon hear his master's steps following him."

33While Elisha was still saying this, the messenger
arrived. And the king* said, "All this misery is from
the LORD! Why should I wait for the LORD any longer?"

7:1Elisha replied, "Listen to this message from the
LORD! This is what the LORD says: By this time tomorrow in the markets of Samaria, five quarts of choice
flour will cost only one piece of silver,* and ten quarts
of barley grain will cost only one piece of silver.*"

2The officer assisting the king said to the man of
God, "That couldn't happen even if the LORD opened
the windows of heaven!"

But Elisha replied, "You will see it happen with your
own eyes, but you won't be able to eat any of it!"

Lepers Visit the Enemy Camp

2 KINGS 7:3-11

Now there were four men with leprosy* sitting at the
entrance of the city gates. "Why should we sit here
waiting to die?" they asked each other. 4"We will starve
if we stay here, but with the famine in the city, we will
starve if we go back there. So we might as well go out
and surrender to the Aramean army. If they let us live,
so much the better. But if they kill us, we would have
died anyway."

5So at twilight they set out for the camp of the
Arameans. But when they came to the edge of the
camp, no one was there! 6For the Lord had caused
the Aramean army to hear the clatter of speeding
chariots and the galloping of horses and the sounds
of a great army approaching. "The king of Israel has
hired the Hittites and Egyptians* to attack us!" they
cried to one another. 7So they panicked and ran into
the night, abandoning their tents, horses, donkeys,
and everything else, as they fled for their lives.

8When the lepers arrived at the edge of the camp,
they went into one tent after another, eating and
drinking wine; and they carried off silver and gold and
clothing and hid it. 9Finally, they said to each other,

2 Kgs 6:25 Hebrew *sold for 80 shekels* [2 pounds, or 0.9 kilograms] *of silver, and ¼ of a cab* [0.3 liters] *of dove's dung sold for 5 shekels* [2 ounces, or 57 grams]. *Dove's dung* may be a variety of wild vegetable. **2 Kgs 6:33** Hebrew *he.* **2 Kgs 7:1a** Hebrew *1 seah* [6 liters] *of choice flour will cost 1 shekel* [0.4 ounces, or 11 grams]; also in 7:16, 18. **2 Kgs 7:1b** Hebrew *2 seahs* [12 liters] *of barley grain will cost 1 shekel* [0.4 ounces, or 11 grams]; also in 7:16, 18. **2 Kgs 7:3** Or *with a contagious skin disease.* The Hebrew word used here and throughout this passage can describe various skin diseases. **2 Kgs 7:6** Possibly *and the people of Muzur,* a district near Cilicia.

frustrated Ben-hadad II in his attempts to take control of Israel.

2 Kgs 6:25 When a city like Samaria faced famine, it was no small matter. Although its farmers grew enough food to feed the people for a specific season, they did not have enough to sustain them in prolonged times of emergency when all supplies were cut off. This famine was so severe that mothers resorted to eating their children (2 Kgs 6:26-30). Deuteronomy 28:49-57 predicted that this would happen when the people of Israel rejected God's leadership.

2 Kgs 6:31-33 Why did the king blame Elisha for the famine and troubles of the siege? Here are some possible reasons: (1) Some commentators say that Elisha must have told the king to trust God for deliverance. The king did this and even wore burlap (2 Kgs 6:30), but at this point the situation seemed hopeless. Apparently the king thought Elisha had given him bad advice and not even God could help them. (2) For years the kings of Israel and the prophets of God had been in conflict. The prophets often predicted doom because of the kings' evil, so the kings saw them as troublemakers. Thus, Israel's king was striking out in frustration at Elisha. (3) The king may have remembered when Elijah helped bring an end to a famine (1 Kgs 18:41-46). Knowing Elisha was a man of God, perhaps the king thought he could do any miracle he wanted and was angry that he had not come to Israel's rescue.

2 Kgs 7:1-2 When Elisha prophesied God's deliverance, the king's officer said it couldn't happen. The officer's faith and hope were gone, but God's words came true anyway (2 Kgs 7:14-16)! Sometimes we become preoccupied with problems when we should be looking for opportunities. Instead of focusing on the negatives, we should develop an attitude of expectancy. To say that God cannot rescue someone or that a situation is impossible demonstrates a lack of faith.

2 Kgs 7:3 According to the law, lepers were not allowed in the city but were to depend on charity outside the gate (Lev 13:45-46; Num 5:1-4). Because of the famine and the presence of the Aramean army, their situation was desperate.

2 Kgs 7:3-10 The lepers discovered the deserted camp and realized that their lives had been spared. At first they kept the good news to themselves, forgetting their fellow citizens who were starving in the city. The Good News about Jesus Christ must be shared, too, for no news is more important. We must not forget those who are dying without it. We must not become so preoccupied with our own faith that we neglect sharing it with those around us. Our "good news," like that of the lepers, will not "wait until morning."

2 Kgs 7:19-20 God, not worthless idols, provides our daily food. Although our faith may be weak or very small, we must avoid

"This is not right. This is a day of good news, and we aren't sharing it with anyone! If we wait until morning, some calamity will certainly fall upon us. Come on, let's go back and tell the people at the palace."
10So they went back to the city and told the gatekeepers what had happened. "We went out to the Aramean camp," they said, "and no one was there! The horses and donkeys were tethered and the tents were all in order, but there wasn't a single person around!" 11Then the gatekeepers shouted the news to the people in the palace.

Israel Plunders the Camp

2 KINGS 7:12-20

The king got out of bed in the middle of the night and told his officers, "I know what has happened. The Arameans know we are starving, so they have left their camp and have hidden in the fields. They are expecting us to leave the city, and then they will take us alive and capture the city."
13One of his officers replied, "We had better send out scouts to check into this. Let them take five of the remaining horses. If something happens to them, it will be no worse than if they stay here and die with the rest of us."
14So two chariots with horses were prepared, and the king sent scouts to see what had happened to the Aramean army. 15They went all the way to the Jordan River, following a trail of clothing and equipment that the Arameans had thrown away in their mad rush to escape. The scouts returned and told the king about it. 16Then the people of Samaria rushed out and plundered the Aramean camp. So it was true that five quarts of choice flour were sold that day for one piece of silver, and ten quarts of barley grain were sold for one piece of silver, just as the LORD had promised.
17The king appointed his officer to control the traffic at the gate, but he was knocked down and trampled to death as the people rushed out.
So everything happened exactly as the man of God had predicted when the king came to his house. 18The man of God had said to the king, "By this time tomorrow in the markets of Samaria, five quarts of choice flour will cost one piece of silver, and ten quarts of barley grain will cost one piece of silver."
19The king's officer had replied, "That couldn't happen even if the LORD opened the windows of heaven!" And the man of God had said, "You will see it happen with your own eyes, but you won't be able to eat any of it!" 20And so it was, for the people trampled him to death at the gate!

The Woman from Shunem Returns Home

2 KINGS 8:1-6

Elisha had told the woman whose son he had brought back to life, "Take your family and move to some other place, for the LORD has called for a famine on Israel that will last for seven years." 2So the woman did as the man of God instructed. She took her family and settled in the land of the Philistines for seven years.
3After the famine ended she returned from the land of the Philistines, and she went to see the king about getting back her house and land. 4As she came in, the king was talking with Gehazi, the servant of the man of God. The king had just said, "Tell me some stories about the great things Elisha has done." 5And Gehazi was telling the king about the time Elisha had brought a boy back to life. At that very moment, the mother of the boy walked in to make her appeal to the king about her house and land.
"Look, my lord the king!" Gehazi exclaimed. "Here is the woman now, and this is her son—the very one Elisha brought back to life!"
6"Is this true?" the king asked her. And she told him the story. So he directed one of his officials to see that everything she had lost was restored to her, including the value of any crops that had been harvested during her absence.

Hazael Murders Ben-Hadad

2 KINGS 8:7-15

Elisha went to Damascus, the capital of Aram, where King Ben-hadad lay sick. When someone told the king that the man of God had come, 8the king said to Hazael, "Take a gift to the man of God. Then tell him to ask the LORD, 'Will I recover from this illness?'"

PEOPLE RAISED FROM THE DEAD

God is all-powerful. Nothing in life is beyond his control, not even death.

Elijah raised a boy from the dead	**1 Kgs 17:22**
Elisha raised a boy from the dead	**2 Kgs 4:34-35**
Elisha's bones raised a man from the dead	**2 Kgs 13:20-21**
Jesus raised a boy from the dead	**Luke 7:14-15**
Jesus raised a girl from the dead	**Luke 8:52-56**
Jesus raised Lazarus from the dead	**John 11:38-44**
Peter raised a woman from the dead	**Acts 9:40-41**
Paul raised a man from the dead	**Acts 20:9-12**

becoming skeptical of God's provision. When our resources are low and our doubts are the strongest, remember that God can open the floodgates of heaven.

2 Kgs 8:1-6 This story shows Elisha's long-term concern for this widow and contrasts his miraculous public ministry with his private ministry to this family. Elisha exemplifies the kind of concern we should have for others.

2 Kgs 8:12-13 When Elisha told Hazael he would sin greatly, Hazael protested that he would never do that sort of thing. He did not

▸ **2 KINGS 8:7-15** ***(cont.)***

9So Hazael loaded down forty camels with the finest products of Damascus as a gift for Elisha. He went to him and said, "Your servant Ben-hadad, the king of Aram, has sent me to ask, 'Will I recover from this illness?'"

10And Elisha replied, "Go and tell him, 'You will surely recover.' But actually the LORD has shown me that he will surely die!" 11Elisha stared at Hazael* with a fixed gaze until Hazael became uneasy.* Then the man of God started weeping.

12"What's the matter, my lord?" Hazael asked him.

Elisha replied, "I know the terrible things you will do to the people of Israel. You will burn their fortified cities, kill their young men with the sword, dash their little children to the ground, and rip open their pregnant women!"

13Hazael responded, "How could a nobody like me* ever accomplish such great things?"

Elisha answered, "The LORD has shown me that you are going to be the king of Aram."

14When Hazael left Elisha and went back, the king asked him, "What did Elisha tell you?"

And Hazael replied, "He told me that you will surely recover."

15But the next day Hazael took a blanket, soaked it in water, and held it over the king's face until he died. Then Hazael became the next king of Aram.

Jehoram Dies PARALLEL

2 KINGS 8:23-24

The rest of the events in Jehoram's reign and everything he did are recorded in *The Book of the History of the Kings of Judah.* 24When Jehoram died, he was buried with his ancestors in the City of David. Then his son Ahaziah became the next king.

2 CHRONICLES 21:18-20

After all this, the LORD struck Jehoram with the severe intestinal disease. 19The disease grew worse and worse, and at the end of two years it caused his bowels to come out, and he died in agony. His people did not build a great funeral fire to honor him as they had done for his ancestors.

20Jehoram was thirty-two years old when he became king, and he reigned in Jerusalem eight years. No one was sorry when he died. They buried him in the City of David, but not in the royal cemetery.

Ahaziah Rules in Judah PARALLEL

2 KINGS 8:25-29

Ahaziah son of Jehoram began to rule over Judah in the twelfth year of the reign of Joram son of Ahab, king of Israel.

26Ahaziah was twenty-two years old when he became king, and he reigned in Jerusalem one year. His mother was Athaliah, a granddaughter of King Omri of Israel. 27Ahaziah followed the evil example of King Ahab's family. He did what was evil in the LORD's sight, just as Ahab's family had done, for he was related by marriage to the family of Ahab.

28Ahaziah joined Joram son of Ahab, the king of Israel, in his war against King Hazael of Aram at Ramoth-gilead. When the Arameans wounded King Joram in the battle, 29he returned to Jezreel to recover from the wounds he had received at Ramoth.* Because Joram was wounded, King Ahaziah of Judah went to Jezreel to visit him.

2 CHRONICLES 22:1-7

Then the people of Jerusalem made Ahaziah, Jehoram's youngest son, their next king, since the marauding bands who came with the Arabs* had killed all the older sons. So Ahaziah son of Jehoram reigned as king of Judah.

2Ahaziah was twenty-two* years old when he became king, and he reigned in Jerusalem one year. His mother was Athaliah, a granddaughter of King Omri. 3Ahaziah also followed the evil example of King Ahab's family, for his mother encouraged him in doing wrong. 4He did what was evil in the LORD's sight, just as Ahab's family had done. They even became his advisers after the death of his father, and they led him to ruin.

2 Kgs 8:11a Hebrew *He stared at him.* **2 Kgs 8:11b** The meaning of the Hebrew is uncertain. **2 Kgs 8:13** Hebrew *a dog.* **2 Kgs 8:29** Hebrew *Ramah,* a variant spelling of Ramoth. **2 Chr 22:1** Or *marauding bands of Arabs.* **2 Chr 22:2** As in some Greek manuscripts and Syriac version (see also 2 Kgs 8:26); Hebrew reads *forty-two.*

acknowledge his personal potential for evil. In our enlightened society, we might think that we are above gross sin and can control our actions. We think that we would never sink so low. Instead, we should take a more biblical and realistic look at ourselves and admit our sinful potential. Then we will ask for God's strength to resist such evil.

2 Kgs 8:12-15 Elisha's words about Hazael's treatment of Israel were partially fulfilled in 2 Kings 10:32-33. Apparently Hazael had known he would be king because Elijah had anointed him (1 Kgs 19:15). But he was impatient and, instead of waiting for God's timing, took matters into his own hands, killing Ben-hadad. God used Hazael as an instrument of judgment against the disobedient Israelites.

2 Kgs 8:26 Ahaziah was the only remaining son of Jehoram of Judah. Although he was the youngest son, he took the throne because the rest of his brothers had been taken captive in a raid by the Philistines and Arabs (2 Chr 21:16-17).

2 Kgs 8:26-27 Ahaziah's mother was Athaliah, daughter of Ahab and Jezebel, former king and queen of Israel, and granddaughter of Omri, Ahab's father and predecessor. The evil of Ahab and Jezebel spread to Judah through Athaliah.

2 Kgs 8:29 Jezreel was the location of the summer palace of the kings of Israel.

2 Chr 22:4-5 Although it is wise to seek advice, we must also carefully weigh the advice we receive. Ahaziah had advisers, but they were wicked and led him to ruin. When you seek advice, listen carefully and use God's Word to "test everything. . . . Hold on to what is good" (1 Thes 5:21).

2 Kgs 9:3 Elijah had prophesied that many

[5]Following their evil advice, Ahaziah joined King Joram,* the son of King Ahab of Israel, in his war against King Hazael of Aram at Ramoth-gilead. When the Arameans wounded Joram in the battle, [6]he returned to Jezreel to recover from the wounds he had received at Ramoth.* Because Joram was wounded, King Ahaziah* of Judah went to Jezreel to visit him.

[7]But God had decided that this visit would be Ahaziah's downfall. While he was there, Ahaziah went out with Joram to meet Jehu grandson of Nimshi,* whom the LORD had appointed to destroy the dynasty of Ahab.

2 Chr 22:5 Hebrew *Jehoram,* a variant spelling of Joram; also in 22:6, 7. **2 Chr 22:6a** Hebrew *Ramah,* a variant spelling of Ramoth. **2 Chr 22:6b** As in some Hebrew manuscripts, Greek and Syriac versions, and Latin Vulgate (see also 2 Kgs 8:29); most Hebrew manuscripts read *Azariah.* **2 Chr 22:7** Hebrew *descendant of Nimshi;* compare 2 Kgs 9:2, 14.

D. The Era of Jehu's Dynasty in the Northern Kingdom

Jehu was God's instrument to punish the house of Ahab. An associate of the prophet Elisha was sent to anoint Jehu as king while Ahab's son still sat on the throne of Israel, and Jehu seized power in a bloody coup. His dynasty was the longest in the history of the northern kingdom, spanning nearly 100 years and five generations, but it continued to be marked by the detestable practices of idol worship set up by Jeroboam, the first king of Israel. During this time, Judah had a series of mostly good rulers after the remnants of Ahab's influence through his daughter Athaliah were removed by Jehoiada the priest early in Joash's reign.

Jehu Anointed King of Israel

2 KINGS 9:1-13

Meanwhile, Elisha the prophet had summoned a member of the group of prophets. "Get ready to travel,"* he told him, "and take this flask of olive oil with you. Go to Ramoth-gilead, [2]and find Jehu son of Jehoshaphat, son of Nimshi. Call him into a private room away from his friends, [3]and pour the oil over his head. Say to him, 'This is what the LORD says: I anoint you to be the king over Israel.' Then open the door and run for your life!"

[4]So the young prophet did as he was told and went to Ramoth-gilead. [5]When he arrived there, he found Jehu sitting around with the other army officers. "I have a message for you, Commander," he said.

"For which one of us?" Jehu asked.

"For you, Commander," he replied.

[6]So Jehu left the others and went into the house. Then the young prophet poured the oil over Jehu's head and said, "This is what the LORD, the God of Israel, says: I anoint you king over the LORD's people, Israel. [7]You are to destroy the family of Ahab, your master. In this way, I will avenge the murder of my prophets and all the LORD's servants who were killed by Jezebel. [8]The entire family of Ahab must be wiped out. I will destroy every one of his male descendants, slave and free alike, anywhere in Israel. [9]I will destroy the family of Ahab as I destroyed the families of Jeroboam son of Nebat and of Baasha son of Ahijah. [10]Dogs will eat Ahab's wife Jezebel at the plot of land in Jezreel, and no one will bury her." Then the young prophet opened the door and ran.

2 Kgs 9:1 Hebrew *Bind up your loins.*

people would be killed when Jehu became king (1 Kgs 19:16-17). Thus Elisha advised the young prophet to get out of the area as soon as he delivered his message, before the slaughter began. Jehu's actions seem harsh, as he hunted down relatives and friends of Ahab (2 Chr 22:8-9), but unchecked Baal worship was destroying the nation. If Israel was to survive, the followers of Baal had to be eliminated. Jehu fulfilled the need of the hour—justice.

2 Kgs 9:7 Elisha's statement fulfilled Elijah's prophecy made 20 years earlier that all of Ahab's family would be killed (1 Kgs 21:17-24). Jezebel's death, predicted by Elijah, is described in 2 Kings 9:30-37.

2 Kgs 9:9 Ahab's dynasty would end as had those of Jeroboam and Baasha. Ahijah had prophesied the end of Jeroboam's dynasty (1 Kgs 14:1-11), and this was fulfilled by Baasha (1 Kgs 15:29). The prophet Jehu—not King Jehu—then foretold the end of Baasha's family (1 Kgs 16:1-7), and this, too, was fulfilled (1 Kgs 16:11-12). The end of Ahab's family, therefore, was certain—Elijah had predicted it (1 Kgs 21:17-24), and God brought it to pass.

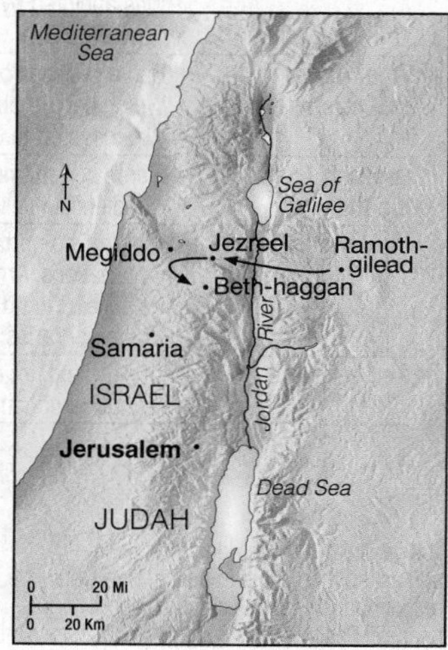

JEHU TAKES OVER ISRAEL ▶
Elisha sent a prophet to Ramoth-gilead to anoint Jehu as Israel's new king. Jehu immediately rode to Jezreel to find and kill King Joram of Israel and King Ahaziah of Judah. Jehu killed Joram; Ahaziah fled toward Beth-haggan, where he was wounded. He later died at Megiddo. Back in Jezreel, Jehu had Jezebel killed.

▸ 2 KINGS 9:1-13 *(cont.)*

11 Jehu went back to his fellow officers, and one of them asked him, "What did that madman want? Is everything all right?"

"You know how a man like that babbles on," Jehu replied.

12 "You're hiding something," they said. "Tell us."

So Jehu told them, "He said to me, 'This is what the LORD says: I have anointed you to be king over Israel.'"

13 Then they quickly spread out their cloaks on the bare steps and blew the ram's horn, shouting, "Jehu is king!"

Jehu Kills Joram and Ahaziah

2 KINGS 9:14-29

So Jehu son of Jehoshaphat, son of Nimshi, led a conspiracy against King Joram. (Now Joram had been with
the army at Ramoth-gilead, defending Israel against
the forces of King Hazael of Aram. 15 But King Joram*
was wounded in the fighting and returned to Jezreel to
recover from his wounds.) So Jehu told the men with
him, "If you want me to be king, don't let anyone leave
town and go to Jezreel to report what we have done."
16 Then Jehu got into a chariot and rode to Jezreel to
find King Joram, who was lying there wounded. King
Ahaziah of Judah was there, too, for he had gone to
visit him. 17 The watchman on the tower of Jezreel saw
Jehu and his company approaching, so he shouted to
Joram, "I see a company of troops coming!"
"Send out a rider to ask if they are coming in peace,"
King Joram ordered.
18 So a horseman went out to meet Jehu and said,
"The king wants to know if you are coming in peace."
Jehu replied, "What do you know about peace? Fall
in behind me!"
The watchman called out to the king, "The mes-
senger has met them, but he's not returning."
19 So the king sent out a second horseman. He rode
up to them and said, "The king wants to know if you
come in peace."
Again Jehu answered, "What do you know about
peace? Fall in behind me!"

2 Kgs 9:15 Hebrew *Jehoram,* a variant spelling of Joram; also in 9:17, 21, 22, 23, 24.

JEHU

Jehu had the basic qualities that could have made him a great success. From a human perspective, in fact, he was a successful king. His family ruled the northern kingdom longer than any other. God used him as an instrument of punishment to Ahab's evil dynasty, and he fiercely attacked Baal worship. He came close to being God's kind of king, but he recklessly went beyond God's commands and failed to follow through on the obedient actions that began his reign. Within sight of victory, he settled for mediocrity. • Jehu was a man of immediate action but without ultimate purpose. His kingdom moved, but its destination was unclear. He eliminated one form of idolatry, Baal worship, only to uphold another by continuing to worship the gold calves Jeroboam had set up. He could have accomplished much for God if he had been obedient to the one who made him king. Even when he was carrying out God's directions, Jehu's style showed he was not fully aware of who was directing him. • As he did with Jehu, God gives each person strengths and abilities that will find their greatest usefulness only under his control. Outside that control, they don't accomplish what they could and often become tools for evil. One way to make sure this does not happen is to tell God of your willingness to be under his control. With his presence in your life, your natural strengths and abilities will be used to their greatest potential for the greatest good.

Strengths and accomplishments	• Took the throne from Ahab's family and destroyed his evil influence • Founded the longest-lived dynasty of the northern kingdom • Was anointed by Elijah and confirmed by Elisha • Destroyed Baal worship
Weaknesses and mistakes	• Had a reckless outlook on life that made him bold and prone to error • Worshiped Jeroboam's gold calves • Was devoted to God only to the point that obedience served his own interests
Lessons from his life	• Fierce commitment needs control because it can result in recklessness • Obedience involves both action and direction
Vital statistics	• Where: The northern kingdom of Israel • Occupations: Army commander, king of Israel • Relatives: Grandfather: Nimshi. Father: Jehoshaphat. Son: Jehoahaz. • Contemporaries: Elijah, Elisha, Ahab, Jezebel, Joram, Ahaziah
Key verse	"But Jehu did not obey the Law of the LORD, the God of Israel, with all his heart. He refused to turn from the sins that Jeroboam had led Israel to commit" (2 Kgs 10:31).

Jehu's story is told in 1 Kings 19:16—2 Kings 10:36. He is also mentioned in 2 Kings 15:12; 2 Chronicles 22:7-9; Hosea 1:4-5.

2 Kgs 9:18-19 The riders met Jehu and asked if he came in peace. But Jehu responded, "What do you know about peace?" Peace, properly understood, comes from God. It is not genuine except when rooted in belief in God and love for him. Jehu knew the men represented a disobedient, wicked king. Don't seek peace and friendship with those who are enemies of the good and the true. Lasting peace can come only from knowing God who gives it to us.

20 The watchman exclaimed, "The messenger has met them, but he isn't returning either! It must be Jehu son of Nimshi, for he's driving like a madman."

21 "Quick! Get my chariot ready!" King Joram commanded.

Then King Joram of Israel and King Ahaziah of Judah rode out in their chariots to meet Jehu. They met him at the plot of land that had belonged to Naboth of Jezreel. 22 King Joram demanded, "Do you come in peace, Jehu?"

Jehu replied, "How can there be peace as long as the idolatry and witchcraft of your mother, Jezebel, are all around us?"

23 Then King Joram turned the horses around* and fled, shouting to King Ahaziah, "Treason, Ahaziah!" 24 But Jehu drew his bow and shot Joram between the shoulders. The arrow pierced his heart, and he sank down dead in his chariot.

25 Jehu said to Bidkar, his officer, "Throw him into the plot of land that belonged to Naboth of Jezreel. Do you remember when you and I were riding along behind his father, Ahab? The LORD pronounced this message against him: 26 'I solemnly swear that I will repay him here on this plot of land, says the LORD, for the murder of Naboth and his sons that I saw yesterday.' So throw him out on Naboth's property, just as the LORD said."

27 When King Ahaziah of Judah saw what was happening, he fled along the road to Beth-haggan. Jehu rode after him, shouting, "Shoot him, too!" So they shot Ahaziah in his chariot at the Ascent of Gur, near Ibleam. He was able to go on as far as Megiddo, but he died there. 28 His servants took him by chariot to Jerusalem, where they buried him with his ancestors in the City of David. 29 Ahaziah had become king over Judah in the eleventh year of the reign of Joram son of Ahab.

The Death of Jezebel

2 KINGS 9:30-37

When Jezebel, the queen mother, heard that Jehu had come to Jezreel, she painted her eyelids and fixed her hair and sat at a window. 31 When Jehu entered the gate of the palace, she shouted at him, "Have you come in peace, you murderer? You're just like Zimri, who murdered his master!"*

32 Jehu looked up and saw her at the window and shouted, "Who is on my side?" And two or three eunuchs looked out at him. 33 "Throw her down!" Jehu yelled. So they threw her out the window, and her blood spattered against the wall and on the horses. And Jehu trampled her body under his horses' hooves.

34 Then Jehu went into the palace and ate and drank. Afterward he said, "Someone go and bury this cursed woman, for she is the daughter of a king." 35 But when they went out to bury her, they found only her skull, her feet, and her hands.

36 When they returned and told Jehu, he stated, "This fulfills the message from the LORD, which he spoke through his servant Elijah from Tishbe: 'At the plot of land in Jezreel, dogs will eat Jezebel's body. 37 Her remains will be scattered like dung on the plot of land in Jezreel, so that no one will be able to recognize her.'"

Jehu Kills Ahab's Family PARALLEL

2 KINGS 10:1-17

Ahab had seventy sons living in the city of Samaria. So Jehu wrote letters and sent them to Samaria, to the elders and officials of the city,* and to the guardians of King Ahab's sons. He said, 2 "The king's sons are with you, and you have at your disposal chariots, horses, a fortified city, and weapons. As soon as you receive this letter, 3 select the best qualified of your master's sons to be your king, and prepare to fight for Ahab's dynasty."

841 BC

Jehu's bloody coup

4 But they were paralyzed with fear and said, "We've seen that two kings couldn't stand against this man! What can we do?"

5 So the palace and city administrators, together with the elders and the guardians of the king's sons, sent this message to Jehu: "We are your servants and will do anything you tell us. We will not make anyone king; do whatever you think is best."

6 Jehu responded with a second letter: "If you are on my side and are going to obey me, bring the heads of your master's sons to me at Jezreel by this time tomorrow." Now the seventy sons of the king were being cared for by the leaders of Samaria, where they had been raised since childhood. 7 When the letter arrived, the leaders killed all seventy of the king's sons. They placed their heads in baskets and presented them to Jehu at Jezreel.

2 Kgs 9:23 Hebrew *turned his hands.* **2 Kgs 9:31** See 1 Kgs 16:9-10, where Zimri killed his master, King Elah. **2 Kgs 10:1** As in some Greek manuscripts and Latin Vulgate (see also 10:6); Hebrew reads *of Jezreel.*

2 Kgs 9:26 Joram of Israel was wicked like his father and mother, Ahab and Jezebel; therefore, his body was thrown into the field that his parents had unlawfully taken. Jezebel had arranged the murder of Naboth, the previous owner, because he would not sell his vineyard—which Ahab wanted for a garden (1 Kgs 21:1-24). Little did Ahab know that it would become a burial plot for his evil son.

2 Kgs 9:31 Why did Jezebel refer to Zimri? Zimri was an army commander who, some 40 years earlier, had killed Elah and then had declared himself king of Israel (1 Kgs 16:8-10). Jezebel was accusing Jehu of trying the same treachery.

2 Kgs 9:35 Jezebel's skull, feet, and hands were all that remained of her evil life—no power, no money, no prestige, no royal finery, no family, no spiritual heritage. In the end, her life of luxury and treachery amounted to nothing. Power, health, and wealth may make you feel as if you can live forever. But death strips everyone of all external security. The time to set your life's course is now, while you still have time and before your heart becomes hardened. The end will come soon enough.

2 Kgs 10:7 This fulfilled Elijah's prophecy that not one of Ahab's male descendants would survive (1 Kgs 21:17-24).

▸ 2 KINGS 10:1-17 *(cont.)*

8A messenger went to Jehu and said, "They have brought the heads of the king's sons."

So Jehu ordered, "Pile them in two heaps at the entrance of the city gate, and leave them there until morning."

9In the morning he went out and spoke to the crowd that had gathered around them. "You are not to blame," he told them. "I am the one who conspired against my master and killed him. But who killed all these? 10You can be sure that the message of the LORD that was spoken concerning Ahab's family will not fail. The LORD declared through his servant Elijah that this would happen." 11Then Jehu killed all who were left of Ahab's relatives living in Jezreel and all his important officials, his personal friends, and his priests. So Ahab was left without a single survivor.

12Then Jehu set out for Samaria. Along the way, while he was at Beth-eked of the Shepherds, 13he met some relatives of King Ahaziah of Judah. "Who are you?" he asked them.

And they replied, "We are relatives of King Ahaziah. We are going to visit the sons of King Ahab and the sons of the queen mother."

14"Take them alive!" Jehu shouted to his men. And they captured all forty-two of them and killed them at the well of Beth-eked. None of them escaped.

15When Jehu left there, he met Jehonadab son of Recab, who was coming to meet him. After they had greeted each other, Jehu said to him, "Are you as loyal to me as I am to you?"

"Yes, I am," Jehonadab replied.

"If you are," Jehu said, "then give me your hand." So Jehonadab put out his hand, and Jehu helped him into the chariot. 16Then Jehu said, "Now come with me, and see how devoted I am to the LORD." So Jehonadab rode along with him.

17When Jehu arrived in Samaria, he killed everyone who was left there from Ahab's family, just as the LORD had promised through Elijah.

2 CHRONICLES 22:8-9

While Jehu was executing judgment against the family of Ahab, he happened to meet some of Judah's officials and Ahaziah's relatives* who were traveling with Ahaziah. So Jehu killed them all. 9Then Jehu's men searched for Ahaziah, and they found him hiding in the city of Samaria. They brought him to Jehu, who killed him. Ahaziah was given a decent burial because the people said, "He was the grandson of Jehoshaphat—a man who sought the LORD with all his heart." But none of the surviving members of Ahaziah's family was capable of ruling the kingdom.

Jehu Kills the Priests of Baal

2 KINGS 10:18-31

Then Jehu called a meeting of all the people of the city and said to them, "Ahab's worship of Baal was nothing compared to the way I will worship him! 19Therefore, summon all the prophets and worshipers of Baal, and call together all his priests. See to it that every one of them comes, for I am going to offer a great sacrifice to Baal. Anyone who fails to come will be put to death." But Jehu's cunning plan was to destroy all the worshipers of Baal.

20Then Jehu ordered, "Prepare a solemn assembly to worship Baal!" So they did. 21He sent messengers throughout all Israel summoning those who worshiped Baal. They all came—not a single one remained behind—and they filled the temple of Baal from one end to the other. 22And Jehu instructed the keeper of the wardrobe, "Be sure that every worshiper of Baal wears one of these robes." So robes were given to them.

23Then Jehu went into the temple of Baal with Jehonadab son of Recab. Jehu said to the worshipers of Baal, "Make sure no one who worships the LORD is here—only those who worship Baal." 24So they were all inside the temple to offer sacrifices and burnt offerings. Now Jehu had stationed eighty of his men outside the building and had warned them, "If you let anyone escape, you will pay for it with your own life."

25As soon as Jehu had finished sacrificing the burnt offering, he commanded his guards and officers, "Go in and kill all of them. Don't let a single one escape!" So they killed them all with their swords, and the guards and officers dragged their bodies outside.* Then Jehu's men went into the innermost fortress* of the temple of Baal. 26They dragged out the sacred pillar* used in the

2 Chr 22:8 As in Greek version (see also 2 Kgs 10:13); Hebrew reads *and sons of the brothers of Ahaziah.* **2 Kgs 10:25a** Or *they left their bodies lying there;* or *they threw them out into the outermost court.* **2 Kgs 10:25b** Hebrew *city.* **2 Kgs 10:26** As in Greek and Syriac versions and Latin Vulgate; Hebrew reads *sacred pillars.*

2 Kgs 10:11 In his zeal, Jehu went far beyond the Lord's command with this bloodbath. The prophet Hosea later announced punishment upon Jehu's dynasty for this senseless slaughter (Hos 1:4-5). Many times in history, "religious" people have mixed faith with personal ambition, power, or cruelty, without God's consent or blessing. To use God or the Bible to condone oppression is wrong. When people attack Christianity because of atrocities that "Christians" carried out, help them to see that these men and women were using faith for their own political ends and not following Christ.

2 Kgs 10:15 Jehonadab was a man who, like Jehu, was zealous in following God. But Jehonadab demonstrated his zeal by separating himself and his family from the materialistic, idol-worshiping culture. He founded a group called the Recabites (named after his father Recab), who strove to keep their lives pure by living apart from society's pressures and temptations. Jeremiah 35 gives us an example of their dedication to God. Because of their dedication, God promised that they would always have descendants who would worship him.

2 Kgs 10:24 Israel was supposed to be intolerant of any religion that did not worship the true God. The religions of surrounding nations were evil and corrupt. They were designed to destroy life, not uphold it. Israel was God's special nation, chosen to be an example of what was right. But Israel's kings, priests, and elders first tolerated, then incorporated surrounding pagan beliefs and thus became apathetic to God's way. We are to be completely intolerant of sin and

worship of Baal and burned it. 27They smashed the sacred pillar and wrecked the temple of Baal, converting it into a public toilet, as it remains to this day.

28In this way, Jehu destroyed every trace of Baal worship from Israel. 29He did not, however, destroy the gold calves at Bethel and Dan, with which Jeroboam son of Nebat had caused Israel to sin.

30Nonetheless the LORD said to Jehu, "You have done well in following my instructions to destroy the family of Ahab. Therefore, your descendants will be kings of Israel down to the fourth generation." 31But Jehu did not obey the Law of the LORD, the God of Israel, with all his heart. He refused to turn from the sins that Jeroboam had led Israel to commit.

Queen Athaliah Rules in Judah PARALLEL

2 KINGS 11:1-3

When Athaliah, the mother of King Ahaziah of Judah, learned that her son was dead, she began to destroy the rest of the royal family. 2But Ahaziah's sister Jehosheba, the daughter of King Jehoram,* took Ahaziah's infant son, Joash, and stole him away from among the rest of the king's children, who were about to be killed. She put Joash and his nurse in a bedroom to hide him from Athaliah, so the child was not murdered. 3Joash remained hidden in the Temple of the LORD for six years while Athaliah ruled over the land.

2 CHRONICLES 22:10-12

When Athaliah, the mother of King Ahaziah of Judah, learned that her son was dead, she began to destroy the rest of Judah's royal family. 11But Ahaziah's sister Jehosheba,* the daughter of King Jehoram, took Ahaziah's infant son, Joash, and stole him away from among the rest of the king's children, who were about to be killed. She put Joash and his nurse in a bedroom. In this way, Jehosheba, wife of Jehoiada the priest and sister of Ahaziah, hid the child so that Athaliah could not murder him. 12Joash remained hidden in the Temple of God for six years while Athaliah ruled over the land.

Revolt against Athaliah PARALLEL

2 KINGS 11:4-12

In the seventh year of Athaliah's reign, Jehoiada the priest summoned the commanders, the Carite mercenaries, and the palace guards to come to the Temple of the LORD. He made a solemn pact with them and

2 Kgs 11:2 Hebrew *Joram,* a variant spelling of Jehoram. **2 Chr 22:11** As in parallel text at 2 Kgs 11:2; Hebrew lacks *Ahaziah's sister* and reads *Jehoshabeath* [a variant spelling of Jehosheba].

remove it from our lives. We should be tolerant of people who hold differing views, but we should not condone beliefs or practices that lead people away from God's standards of living.

2 Kgs 10:28-29 Why did Jehu destroy the idols of Baal but not the gold calves in Bethel and Dan? Jehu's motives may have been more political than spiritual. (1) If Jehu had destroyed the gold calves, his people would have traveled to the Temple in Jerusalem, in the rival southern kingdom, and worshiped there (which is why Jeroboam had set them up in the first place; see 1 Kgs 12:25-33). (2) Baal worship was associated with the dynasty of Ahab, so it was politically advantageous to destroy Baal. The gold calves, on the other hand, had a longer history in the northern kingdom and were valued by all political factions. (3) Baal worship was anti-God, but the gold calves were thought by many to be visible representations of God himself, even though God's law stated clearly that such worship was idolatrous (Exod 20:3-6). Like Jehu, it is easy for us to denounce the sins of others while excusing sin in our own lives.

2 Kgs 10:30-31 Jehu did much of what the Lord told him to, but he did not obey him with all his heart. He had become God's instrument for carrying out justice, but he had not become God's servant. As a result, he gave only lip service to God while permitting the worship of the gold calves. Check the condition of your heart toward God. We can be very active in our work for God and still not give the heartfelt obedience he desires.

Black Obelisk of Shalmaneser III

This shaft of black limestone describes the military successes of Shalmaneser III of Syria (858–824 B.C.) during the first 31 years of his reign. Six and one-half feet high, there are five rows of reliefs with inscriptions between them written in cuneiform. The pictures show payment of tribute from five parts of Shalmaneser's empire.

Of special interest to Bible students is the second row of reliefs, which portrays King Jehu of the northern kingdom of Israel (2 Kgs 9–10), accompanied by 13 Israelites bearing tribute, bowing before Shalmaneser. The inscription identifies him as Jehu and lists the tribute brought as including silver and gold bowls and vases, tin, and a royal staff. The relief is the only contemporary representation of any Israelite king. Jehu is shown in a long fringed cloak, a pointed soft cap, and a short, rounded beard.

2 Kgs 11:1 This story is continued from 2 Kings 9:27, where Ahaziah, Athaliah's son, had been killed by Jehu. Athaliah's attempt to kill all of Ahaziah's sons was futile because God had promised that the Messiah would be born through David's descendants (2 Sam 7).

2 Kgs 11:2-3 Jehosheba was the wife of Jehoiada, the high priest, so the Temple was a practical and natural place to hide baby Joash. Athaliah, who loved idolatry, would have had no interest in the Temple.

2 Kgs 11:4 The Carites were mercenary troops possibly associated with the Philistines. Some scholars believe they settled in southern Palestine from Crete.

▸ **2 KINGS 11:4-12** ***(cont.)***
made them swear an oath of loyalty there in the LORD's
Temple; then he showed them the king's son.
5Jehoiada told them, "This is what you must do. A
third of you who are on duty on the Sabbath are to
guard the royal palace itself. 6Another third of you are
to stand guard at the Sur Gate. And the final third must
stand guard behind the palace guard. These three
groups will all guard the palace. 7The other two units
who are off duty on the Sabbath must stand guard
for the king at the LORD's Temple. 8Form a bodyguard
around the king and keep your weapons in hand. Kill
anyone who tries to break through. Stay with the king
wherever he goes."
9So the commanders did everything as Jehoiada the
priest ordered. The commanders took charge of the
men reporting for duty that Sabbath, as well as those
who were going off duty. They brought them all to
Jehoiada the priest, 10and he supplied them with the
spears and small shields that had once belonged to
King David and were stored in the Temple of the LORD.
11The palace guards stationed themselves around the
king, with their weapons ready. They formed a line
from the south side of the Temple around to the north
side and all around the altar.
12Then Jehoiada brought out Joash, the king's son,
placed the crown on his head, and presented him with
a copy of God's laws.* They anointed him and proclaimed him king, and everyone clapped their hands
and shouted, "Long live the king!"

2 CHRONICLES 23:1-11
In the seventh year of Athaliah's reign, Jehoiada the
priest decided to act. He summoned his courage and
made a pact with five army commanders: Azariah son
of Jeroham, Ishmael son of Jehohanan, Azariah son of
Obed, Maaseiah son of Adaiah, and Elishaphat son of
Zicri. 2These men traveled secretly throughout Judah
and summoned the Levites and clan leaders in all the
towns to come to Jerusalem. 3They all gathered at the
Temple of God, where they made a solemn pact with
Joash, the young king.
Jehoiada said to them, "Here is the king's son! The
time has come for him to reign! The LORD has promised that a descendant of David will be our king. 4This
is what you must do. When you priests and Levites
come on duty on the Sabbath, a third of you will serve
as gatekeepers. 5Another third will go over to the royal
palace, and the final third will be at the Foundation
Gate. Everyone else should stay in the courtyards of
the LORD's Temple. 6Remember, only the priests and
Levites on duty may enter the Temple of the LORD, for
they are set apart as holy. The rest of the people must
obey the LORD's instructions and stay outside. 7You
Levites, form a bodyguard around the king and keep
your weapons in hand. Kill anyone who tries to enter
the Temple. Stay with the king wherever he goes."
8So the Levites and all the people of Judah did everything as Jehoiada the priest ordered. The commanders
took charge of the men reporting for duty that Sabbath, as well as those who were going off duty. Jehoiada
the priest did not let anyone go home after their shift
ended. 9Then Jehoiada supplied the commanders with
the spears and the large and small shields that had
once belonged to King David and were stored in the
Temple of God. 10He stationed all the people around
the king, with their weapons ready. They formed a line
from the south side of the Temple around to the north
side and all around the altar.
11Then Jehoiada and his sons brought out Joash,
the king's son, placed the crown on his head, and
presented him with a copy of God's laws.* They
anointed him and proclaimed him king, and everyone shouted, "Long live the king!"

The Death of Athaliah PARALLEL

2 KINGS 11:13-16
When Athaliah heard all the noise made by the palace guards and the people, she hurried to the LORD's
Temple to see what was happening. 14When she arrived, she saw the newly crowned king standing in his
place of authority by the pillar, as was the custom at
times of coronation. The commanders and trumpeters were surrounding him, and people from all over
the land were rejoicing and blowing trumpets. When
Athaliah saw all this, she tore her clothes in despair
and shouted, "Treason! Treason!"
15Then Jehoiada the priest ordered the commanders who were in charge of the troops, "Take her to the
soldiers in front of the Temple,* and kill anyone who
tries to rescue her." For the priest had said, "She must
not be killed in the Temple of the LORD." 16So they
seized her and led her out to the gate where horses
enter the palace grounds, and she was killed there.

2 CHRONICLES 23:12-15
When Athaliah heard the noise of the people running
and the shouts of praise to the king, she hurried to the
LORD's Temple to see what was happening. 13When
she arrived, she saw the newly crowned king standing

2 Kgs 11:12 Or *a copy of the covenant.* **2 Chr 23:11** Or *a copy of the covenant.* **2 Kgs 11:15** Or *Bring her out from between the ranks;* or *Take her out of the Temple precincts.* The meaning of the Hebrew is uncertain.

2 Chr 23:1 After seven years of rule by Athaliah, the queen mother, Jehoiada the priest finally got up his courage and took action to get rid of the idolatrous ruler. To confront the king (or queen) with the demands of God's law was supposed to be the role of every priest in every generation. Tragically, many priests shied away from this duty, and thus only a few made a difference in the nation.

2 Chr 23:1 Although it could have cost him his life, this priest did what was right, restoring the Temple worship and anointing the new king. There are times when we must correct a wrong or speak out for what is right. When such a situation arises, gather up your courage and act.

in his place of authority by the pillar at the Temple entrance. The commanders and trumpeters were surrounding him, and people from all over the land were rejoicing and blowing trumpets. Singers with musical instruments were leading the people in a great celebration. When Athaliah saw all this, she tore her clothes in despair and shouted, "Treason! Treason!"

[14]Then Jehoiada the priest ordered the commanders who were in charge of the troops, "Take her to the soldiers in front of the Temple,* and kill anyone who tries to rescue her." For the priest had said, "She must not be killed in the Temple of the LORD." [15]So they seized her and led her out to the entrance of the Horse Gate on the palace grounds, and they killed her there.

Jehoiada's Religious Reforms in Judah PARALLEL

2 KINGS 11:17-21

Then Jehoiada made a covenant between the LORD and the king and the people that they would be the LORD's people. He also made a covenant between the king and the people. [18]And all the people of the land went over to the temple of Baal and tore it down. They demolished the altars and smashed the idols to pieces, and they killed Mattan the priest of Baal in front of the altars.

Jehoiada the priest stationed guards at the Temple of the LORD. [19]Then the commanders, the Carite mercenaries, the palace guards, and all the people of the land escorted the king from the Temple of the LORD. They went through the gate of the guards and into the palace, and the king took his seat on the royal throne. [20]So all the people of the land rejoiced, and the city was peaceful because Athaliah had been killed at the king's palace.

[21]*Joash* was seven years old when he became king.

2 CHRONICLES 23:16-21

Then Jehoiada made a covenant between himself and the king and the people that they would be the LORD's people. [17]And all the people went over to the temple of Baal and tore it down. They demolished the altars and smashed the idols, and they killed Mattan the priest of Baal in front of the altars.

[18]Jehoiada now put the priests and Levites in charge of the Temple of the LORD, following all the directions given by David. He also commanded them to present burnt offerings to the LORD, as prescribed by the Law of Moses, and to sing and rejoice as David had instructed. [19]He also stationed gatekeepers at the gates of the LORD's Temple to keep out those who for any reason were ceremonially unclean.

[20]Then the commanders, nobles, rulers, and all the people of the land escorted the king from the Temple of the LORD. They went through the upper gate and into the palace, and they seated the king on the royal throne. [21]So all the people of the land rejoiced, and the city was peaceful because Athaliah had been killed.

Joash Repairs the Temple PARALLEL

2 KINGS 12:1-16

Joash began to rule over Judah in the seventh year of King Jehu's reign in Israel. He reigned in Jerusalem forty years. His mother was Zibiah from Beersheba. [2]All his life Joash did what was pleasing in the LORD's sight because Jehoiada the priest instructed him. [3]Yet even so, he did not destroy the pagan shrines, and the people still offered sacrifices and burned incense there.

835 BC

Joash begins to rule in Judah

2 Chr 23:14 Or *Bring her out from between the ranks;* or *Take her out of the Temple precincts.* The meaning of the Hebrew is uncertain. **2 Kgs 11:21a** Verse 11:21 is numbered 12:1 in Hebrew text. **2 Kgs 11:21b** Hebrew *Jehoash,* a variant spelling of Joash. **2 Kgs 12:1a** Verses 12:1-21 are numbered 12:2-22 in Hebrew text. **2 Kgs 12:1b** Hebrew *Jehoash,* a variant spelling of Joash; also in 12:2, 4, 6, 7, 18.

2 Chr 23:12-15 Athaliah thought she had it made. After assuming the throne, she killed all potential heirs to it—or so she thought. But even the best plans for evil go sour. When the truth was revealed, she was overthrown immediately. It is much safer to live according to the truth, even if it means not obtaining everything you want.

2 Kgs 11:17 This covenant was, in fact, a recommitment to a very old covenant—the one set up in the book of Deuteronomy for the righteous rule of the nation. It was meant to function as a constitution for the people. This covenant had been virtually ignored for over 100 years. Unfortunately, after Jehoiada's death, the reforms were discontinued.

2 Kgs 11:21 If Joash became king at only seven years of age, who really ran the country? Although the answer is not spelled out in the Bible, Judah was probably run during the first seven years of Joash's reign by the king's mother, the high priest Jehoiada, and other advisers.

2 Chr 23:15-17 Athaliah's life ended as her mother Jezebel's had—by execution. Her life of idolatry and treachery was cut short by God's judgment of her sin. By this time Judah had slipped so far away from God that Baal was worshiped in Jerusalem.

2 Chr 23:18 Jehoiada restored the Temple procedures and its worship services according to David's original plans, recorded in 1 Chronicles 24–25.

2 Kgs 12:2ff Joash didn't go far enough in removing sin from the nation, but he did much that was good and right. When we aren't sure if we've gone far enough in correcting our actions, we can ask: (1) Does the Bible expressly prohibit this action? (2) Does this action take me away from loving, worshiping, or serving God? (3) Does it make me its slave? (4) Is it bringing out the best in me, consistent with God's purpose? (5) Does it benefit other believers?

2 Kgs 12:3 The Israelites were supposed to offer sacrifices to God only in designated areas under supervision of the priests, not just anywhere (Deut 12:13-14). Making sacrifices in the shrines copied pagan customs and encouraged other pagan practices to enter into their worship. By blending in these beliefs, people were custom-making their religion, and it led them far away from God. (For more information on these pagan shrines, see the note on 1 Kgs 22:43, p. 736.)

▸ 2 KINGS 12:1-16 *(cont.)*

[4]One day King Joash said to the priests, "Collect all the money brought as a sacred offering to the LORD's Temple, whether it is a regular assessment, a payment of vows, or a voluntary gift. [5]Let the priests take some of that money to pay for whatever repairs are needed at the Temple."

[6]But by the twenty-third year of Joash's reign, the priests still had not repaired the Temple. [7]So King Joash called for Jehoiada and the other priests and asked them, "Why haven't you repaired the Temple? Don't use any more money for your own needs. From now on, it must all be spent on Temple repairs." [8]So the priests agreed not to accept any more money from the people, and they also agreed to let others take responsibility for repairing the Temple.

[9]Then Jehoiada the priest bored a hole in the lid of a large chest and set it on the right-hand side of the altar at the entrance of the Temple of the LORD. The priests guarding the entrance put all of the people's contributions into the chest. [10]Whenever the chest became full, the court secretary and the high priest counted the money that had been brought to the LORD's Temple and put it into bags. [11]Then they gave the money to the construction supervisors, who used it to pay the people working on the LORD's Temple—the carpenters, the builders, [12]the masons, and the stonecutters. They also used the money to buy the timber

JOASH

All parents want their children to make the right decisions. But to do this, children must first learn to make their own decisions. Making bad ones helps them learn to make good ones. If parents make all the decisions for their children, they leave their children without the skills for wise decision making when they are on their own. This problem seriously affected Joash. He had great advice, but he never grew up. He became so dependent on what he was told that his effectiveness was limited to the quality of his advisers. • When Joash was one year old, his grandmother Athaliah decided to slaughter all her descendants in a desperate bid for power. Joash, the only survivor, was rescued and hidden by his aunt and uncle, Jehosheba and Jehoiada. Jehoiada's work as a priest made it possible to keep Joash hidden in the Temple for six years. At that point, Jehoiada arranged for the overthrow of Athaliah and the crowning of Joash. For many years following, Jehoiada made most of the kingdom's decisions for Joash. When the old priest died, he was buried in the royal cemetery as a tribute to his role. • But after Jehoiada's death, Joash didn't know what to do. He listened to counsel that led him into evil. Within a short time he even ordered the death of Jehoiada's son Zechariah. After a few months, Joash's army was soundly defeated by the Arameans. Jerusalem was saved only because Joash stripped the Temple of its treasures as a bribe. Finally, the king's own officials assassinated him. In contrast to Jehoiada, Joash was not buried among the kings; he is not even listed in Jesus' genealogy in the New Testament. • As dependent as Joash was on Jehoiada, there is little evidence that he ever established a real dependence on the God Jehoiada obeyed. Like many children, Joash's knowledge of God was secondhand. It was a start, but the king needed his own relationship with God that would outlast and overrule any bad advice he received. • It would be easy to criticize Joash's failure were it not for the fact that we often fall into the same traps. How often have we acted on poor advice without considering God's Word?

Strengths and accomplishments	• Carried out extensive repairs on the Temple • Was faithful to God as long as Jehoiada lived
Weaknesses and mistakes	• Allowed idolatry to continue among his people • Used the Temple treasures to bribe King Hazael of Aram • Killed Jehoiada's son Zechariah • Allowed his advisers to lead the people away from God
Lessons from his life	• A good and hopeful start can be ruined by an evil end • Even the best counsel is ineffective if it does not help us make wise decisions • As helpful or hurtful as others may be, we are individually responsible for what we do
Vital statistics	• Where: Jerusalem • Occupation: King of Judah • Relatives: Father: Ahaziah. Mother: Zibiah. Grandmother: Athaliah. Uncle: Jehoiada. Son: Amaziah. Cousin: Zechariah. • Contemporaries: Jehu, Hazael
Key verses	"But after Jehoiada's death, the leaders of Judah came and bowed before King Joash and persuaded him to listen to their advice. They decided to abandon the Temple of the LORD, the God of their ancestors, and they worshiped Asherah poles and idols instead! Because of this sin, divine anger fell on Judah and Jerusalem" (2 Chr 24:17-18).

Joash's story is told in 2 Kings 11:1–12:21; 2 Chronicles 22:11–24:27.

2 Kgs 12:4-5 The Temple needed repair because it had been damaged and neglected by previous evil leaders, especially Athaliah (2 Chr 24:7). The Temple was to be a holy place, set apart for worship of God. Thanks to Joash's fund-raising program, it could be restored. The dirt and filth that had collected inside over the years were cleaned out; joints were remortared; pagan idols and other traces of idol worship were removed; and the gold and bronze were polished. The neglected condition of the Temple reveals how far the people had strayed from God.

and the finished stone needed for repairing the LORD's Temple, and they paid any other expenses related to the Temple's restoration.
[13]The money brought to the Temple was not used for making silver bowls, lamp snuffers, basins, trumpets, or other articles of gold or silver for the Temple of
the LORD. [14]It was paid to the workmen, who used it for
the Temple repairs. [15]No accounting of this money was required from the construction supervisors, because
they were honest and trustworthy men. [16]However, the money that was contributed for guilt offerings and sin offerings was not brought into the LORD's Temple. It was given to the priests for their own use.

2 CHRONICLES 24:1-16

Joash was seven years old when he became king, and he reigned in Jerusalem forty years. His mother was
Zibiah from Beersheba. [2]Joash did what was pleasing in the LORD's sight throughout the lifetime of Jehoiada
the priest. [3]Jehoiada chose two wives for Joash, and he had sons and daughters.
[4]At one point Joash decided to repair and restore
the Temple of the LORD. [5]He summoned the priests and Levites and gave them these instructions: "Go to all the towns of Judah and collect the required annual offerings, so that we can repair the Temple of your God. Do not delay!" But the Levites did not act immediately.
[6]So the king called for Jehoiada the high priest and asked him, "Why haven't you demanded that the Levites go out and collect the Temple taxes from the towns of Judah and from Jerusalem? Moses, the servant of the LORD, levied this tax on the community of Israel in order to maintain the Tabernacle of the Covenant.*"
[7]Over the years the followers of wicked Athaliah had broken into the Temple of God, and they had used all the dedicated things from the Temple of the LORD to worship the images of Baal.
[8]So now the king ordered a chest to be made and set outside the gate leading to the Temple of the LORD.
[9]Then a proclamation was sent throughout Judah and Jerusalem, telling the people to bring to the LORD the tax that Moses, the servant of God, had required of
the Israelites in the wilderness. [10]This pleased all the leaders and the people, and they gladly brought their money and filled the chest with it.
[11]Whenever the chest became full, the Levites would carry it to the king's officials. Then the court secretary and an officer of the high priest would come and empty the chest and take it back to the Temple again. This went on day after day, and a large amount
of money was collected. [12]The king and Jehoiada gave the money to the construction supervisors, who hired masons and carpenters to restore the Temple of the LORD. They also hired metalworkers, who made articles of iron and bronze for the LORD's Temple.
[13]The men in charge of the renovation worked hard and made steady progress. They restored the Temple of God according to its original design and
strengthened it. [14]When all the repairs were finished, they brought the remaining money to the king and Jehoiada. It was used to make various articles for the Temple of the LORD—articles for worship services and for burnt offerings, including ladles and other articles made of gold and silver. And the burnt offerings were sacrificed continually in the Temple of the LORD during the lifetime of Jehoiada the priest.
[15]Jehoiada lived to a very old age, finally dying at
130. [16]He was buried among the kings in the City of David, because he had done so much good in Israel for God and his Temple.

Jehoiada's Reforms Reversed

2 CHRONICLES 24:17-22

But after Jehoiada's death, the leaders of Judah came and bowed before King Joash and persuaded him

2 Chr 24:6 Hebrew *Tent of the Testimony.*

2 Kgs 12:15 What a contrast between the construction supervisors, who needed no accounting of their use of the money, and the priests, who couldn't be trusted to handle their funds well enough to set some aside for the Temple (2 Kgs 12:7-8). As trained men of God, the Levites should have been responsible and concerned. After all, the Temple was their life's vocation. Though the priests were not dishonest, they did not have the commitment or energy needed to finish the work. Sometimes God's tasks are better accomplished by devoted laypeople. Don't let your lack of training or position stop you from contributing to God's Kingdom. Everyone's energy is needed to carry out God's work.

2 Kgs 12:16 To read more about guilt and sin offerings, see Leviticus 4–5; 6:24–7:10.

2 Chr 24:5 The Levites took their time carrying out the king's order, even though he told them not to delay. Offerings for keeping the Temple in order were not just the king's wish, but God's command (Exod 30:11-16). The Levites, therefore, were not only disregarding the king but disregarding God. When it comes to following God's commands, a slow response may be little better than disobedience. Obey God willingly and immediately.

2 Chr 24:10 Evidently the Levites weren't convinced that the people would want to contribute to the rebuilding of the Temple (2 Chr 24:5), but the people were glad to give of what they had for this project. Don't underestimate people's desire to be faithful to God. When challenged to do God's work, they will often respond willingly and generously.

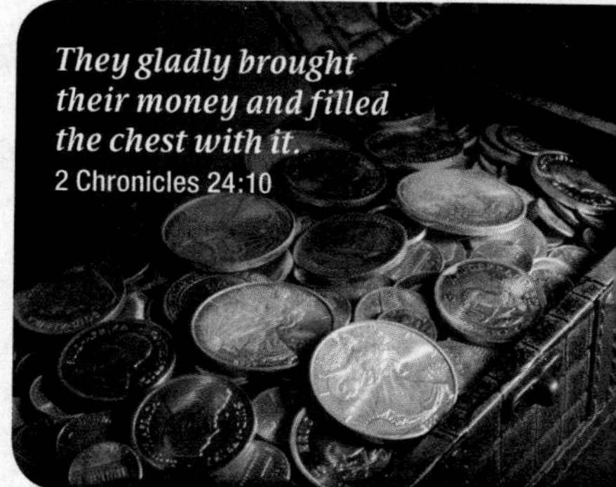
They gladly brought their money and filled the chest with it.
2 Chronicles 24:10

▸ **2 CHRONICLES 24:17-22** ***(cont.)***
to listen to their advice. 18They decided to abandon
the Temple of the LORD, the God of their ancestors,
and they worshiped Asherah poles and idols instead!
Because of this sin, divine anger fell on Judah and Jerusalem. 19Yet the LORD sent prophets to bring them
back to him. The prophets warned them, but still the
people would not listen.
20Then the Spirit of God came upon Zechariah son
of Jehoiada the priest. He stood before the people and
said, "This is what God says: Why do you disobey the
LORD's commands and keep yourselves from prospering? You have abandoned the LORD, and now he has
abandoned you!"
21Then the leaders plotted to kill Zechariah, and
King Joash ordered that they stone him to death in the
courtyard of the LORD's Temple. 22That was how King
Joash repaid Jehoiada for his loyalty—by killing his
son. Zechariah's last words as he died were, "May the
LORD see what they are doing and avenge my death!"

The Death of Jehu

2 KINGS 10:32-36
At about that time the LORD began to cut down the
size of Israel's territory. King Hazael conquered several sections of the country 33east of the Jordan River,
including all of Gilead, Gad, Reuben, and Manasseh.
He conquered the area from the town of Aroer by the
Arnon Gorge to as far north as Gilead and Bashan.
34The rest of the events in Jehu's reign—everything
he did and all his achievements—are recorded in *The
Book of the History of the Kings of Israel.*
35When Jehu died, he was buried in Samaria. Then
his son Jehoahaz became the next king. 36In all, Jehu
reigned over Israel from Samaria for twenty-eight
years.

Jehoahaz Rules in Israel

2 KINGS 13:1-9
Jehoahaz son of Jehu began to rule over Israel in the
twenty-third year of King Joash's reign in Judah. He
reigned in Samaria seventeen years. 2But he did what
was evil in the LORD's sight. He followed the example
of Jeroboam son of Nebat, continuing the sins that Jeroboam had led Israel to commit. 3So the LORD was very
angry with Israel, and he allowed King Hazael of Aram
and his son Ben-hadad to defeat them repeatedly.
4Then Jehoahaz prayed for the LORD's help, and the
LORD heard his prayer, for he could see how severely
the king of Aram was oppressing Israel. 5So the LORD
provided someone to rescue the Israelites from the
tyranny of the Arameans. Then Israel lived in safety
again as they had in former days.
6But they continued to sin, following the evil ex-

814 BC *Founding of Carthage*

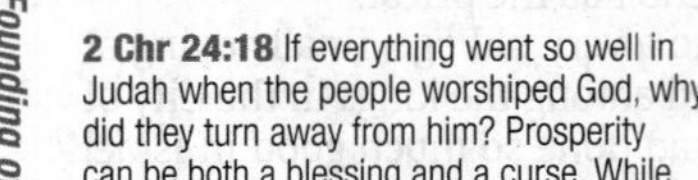

GOD OR IDOLS

Why did people continually turn to idols instead of to God?

Idols were:	Worshiping idols involved:	God is:	Worshiping God involves:
Tangible	Materialism	Intangible—no physical form	Sacrifice
Morally similar—had human characteristics	Sexual immorality	Morally dissimilar—has divine characteristics	Purity and commitment
Comprehensible	Doing whatever a person wants	Incomprehensible	Doing what God wants
Able to be manipulated	Focusing on self	Not able to be manipulated	Focusing on others

2 Chr 24:18 If everything went so well in Judah when the people worshiped God, why did they turn away from him? Prosperity can be both a blessing and a curse. While it can be a sign of God's blessing to those who follow him, it carries with it the potential for moral and spiritual decline. Prosperous people are tempted to become self-sufficient and proud—to take God for granted. In our prosperity, we must not forget that God is the source of our blessings. (See Deut 6:10-12; 8:11-14.)

2 Chr 24:18-20 When King Joash and the nation of Judah abandoned God, God sent Zechariah to call them to repentance. Before dispensing judgment and punishment, God gave them another chance. In the same way, God does not abandon us or lash out in revenge when we sin. Instead, he aggressively pursues us through his Word, his Spirit in us, the words of others, and sometimes discipline. He does not intend to destroy us but to urge us to return to him. When you are moving away from God, remember that he is pursuing you. Stop and listen. Allow him to point out your sin so you can repent and follow him again.

2 Chr 24:19 God sent many prophets to Joash and the people to warn them that they were headed for destruction. Some scholars believe that Joel may have been one of these prophets, though many believe Joel prophesied much later in Israel's history (this Bible follows the later chronology). There were also many prophets who did not write books of the Bible, but God used them to warn and direct his people.

2 Chr 24:22 Zechariah asked God to call the people to account for their sins. He was not seeking revenge but pleading for justice. When we feel like despairing over the wickedness around us, we can rest assured that in the end, God will bring complete justice to the earth.

2 Kgs 13:4-6 The Lord heard Jehoahaz's prayer for help. God delayed his judgment on Israel when they turned to him, but they did not sustain their dependence on God for long. Although Israel had periodic breaks in their idol worship, they rarely showed genuine faith. It is not enough to say no to sin; we must also say yes to a life of commitment to God. An occasional call for help is not a substitute for a daily life of trust in God.

2 Kgs 13:5 Aram, which lay to the north of Israel, was always Israel's enemy. This was partly because Israel blocked most of Aram's trade from the south, and Aram cut off most of Israel's from the north. If one nation could conquer the other, all its trade routes would be open, and its economy would flourish. Israel and Aram were so busy fighting each other that they didn't notice the rapidly growing strength of the Assyrians to the far north. Soon both nations would be surprised (2 Kgs 16:9; 17:6).

ample of Jeroboam. They also allowed the Asherah pole in Samaria to remain standing. [7]Finally, Jehoahaz's army was reduced to 50 charioteers, 10 chariots, and 10,000 foot soldiers. The king of Aram had killed the others, trampling them like dust under his feet.

[8]The rest of the events in Jehoahaz's reign—everything he did and the extent of his power—are recorded in *The Book of the History of the Kings of Israel.* [9]When Jehoahaz died, he was buried in Samaria. Then his son Jehoash* became the next king.

Jehoash Begins His Reign in Israel

2 KINGS 13:10-11

Jehoash son of Jehoahaz began to rule over Israel in the thirty-seventh year of King Joash's reign in Judah. He reigned in Samaria sixteen years. [11]But he did what was evil in the LORD's sight. He refused to turn from the sins that Jeroboam son of Nebat had led Israel to commit.

The End of Joash's Reign in Judah PARALLEL

2 KINGS 12:17-21

About this time King Hazael of Aram went to war against Gath and captured it. Then he turned to attack Jerusalem. [18]King Joash collected all the sacred objects that Jehoshaphat, Jehoram, and Ahaziah, the previous kings of Judah, had dedicated, along with what he himself had dedicated. He sent them all to Hazael, along with all the gold in the treasuries of the LORD's Temple and the royal palace. So Hazael called off his attack on Jerusalem.

[19]The rest of the events in Joash's reign and everything he did are recorded in *The Book of the History of the Kings of Judah.*

[20]Joash's officers plotted against him and assassinated him at Beth-millo on the road to Silla. [21]The assassins were Jozacar* son of Shimeath and Jehozabad son of Shomer—both trusted advisers. Joash was buried with his ancestors in the City of David. Then his son Amaziah became the next king.

2 CHRONICLES 24:23-27

In the spring of the year* the Aramean army marched against Joash. They invaded Judah and Jerusalem and killed all the leaders of the nation. Then they sent all the plunder back to their king in Damascus. [24]Although the Arameans attacked with only a small army, the LORD helped them conquer the much larger army of Judah. The people of Judah had abandoned the LORD, the God of their ancestors, so judgment was carried out against Joash.

[25]The Arameans withdrew, leaving Joash severely wounded. But his own officials plotted to kill him for murdering the son* of Jehoiada the priest. They assassinated him as he lay in bed. Then he was buried in the City of David, but not in the royal cemetery. [26]The assassins were Jozacar,* the son of an Ammonite woman named Shimeath, and Jehozabad, the son of a Moabite woman named Shomer.*

[27]The account of the sons of Joash, the prophecies about him, and the record of his restoration of the Temple of God are written in *The Commentary on the Book of the Kings.* His son Amaziah became the next king.

Elisha's Final Prophecy

2 KINGS 13:14-25

When Elisha was in his last illness, King Jehoash of Israel visited him and wept over him. "My father! My father! I see the chariots and charioteers of Israel!" he cried.

[15]Elisha told him, "Get a bow and some arrows." And the king did as he was told. [16]Elisha told him, "Put your hand on the bow," and Elisha laid his own hands on the king's hands.

[17]Then he commanded, "Open that eastern window," and he opened it. Then he said, "Shoot!" So he shot an arrow. Elisha proclaimed, "This is the LORD's arrow, an arrow of victory over Aram, for you will completely conquer the Arameans at Aphek."

[18]Then he said, "Now pick up the other arrows and strike them against the ground." So the king picked

800 BC

Homer's Iliad and Odyssey written down

2 Kgs 13:9 Hebrew *Joash,* a variant spelling of Jehoash; also in 13:10, 12, 13, 14, 25. **2 Kgs 12:21** As in Greek and Syriac versions; Hebrew reads *Jozabad.* **2 Chr 24:23** Hebrew *At the turn of the year.* The first day of the year in the ancient Hebrew lunar calendar occurred in March or April. **2 Chr 24:25** As in Greek version and Latin Vulgate; Hebrew reads *sons.* **2 Chr 24:26a** As in parallel text at 2 Kgs 12:21; Hebrew reads *Zabad.* **2 Chr 24:26b** As in parallel text at 2 Kgs 12:21; Hebrew reads *Shimrith,* a variant spelling of Shomer.

2 Kgs 13:9-10 Jehoash assumed the throne of Israel in 798 B.C. At that time the king of Judah, Joash, was nearing the end of his reign. In Hebrew, Jehoash and Joash are two forms of the same name. Thus, two kings with the same name, one in the south and one in the north, reigned at approximately the same time. While Joash of Judah began as a good king, Jehoash of Israel was evil.

2 Kgs 12:20 The reasons for the officers' plot against Joash are listed in 2 Chronicles 24:17-26. Joash had begun to worship idols, had killed the prophet Zechariah, and had been conquered by the Arameans. When Joash turned away from God, his life began to unravel. The officers didn't kill Joash because he turned from God; they killed him because his kingdom was out of control. In the end he became an evil man and was killed by evil people.

2 Kgs 13:14 Elisha was highly regarded for his prophetic powers and miracles on Israel's behalf. Jehoash called him "The chariots and charioteers of Israel!" This recalls the title Elisha had given to Elijah (2 Kgs 2:12). Jehoash feared Elisha's death because he ascribed the nation's well-being to Elisha rather than to God. Jehoash's fear revealed his lack of spiritual understanding. At least 43 years had passed since Elisha was last mentioned in Scripture (2 Kgs 9:1), when he anointed Jehu king (841 B.C.). Jehoash's reign began in 798 B.C.

2 Kgs 13:15-19 When Jehoash was told to strike the ground with the arrows, he did it only halfheartedly. As a result, Elisha told the king that his victory over Aram would not be complete. Receiving the full benefits of God's plan for our lives requires us to receive and obey God's commands fully. If we don't follow God's complete instructions, we should not be surprised that we don't receive his full benefits and blessings.

▸ **2 KINGS 13:14-25** ***(cont.)***
them up and struck the ground three times. 19But the
man of God was angry with him. "You should have
struck the ground five or six times!" he exclaimed.
"Then you would have beaten Aram until it was entirely
destroyed. Now you will be victorious only three times."
20Then Elisha died and was buried.

Groups of Moabite raiders used to invade the land
each spring. 21Once when some Israelites were burying a man, they spied a band of these raiders. So they
hastily threw the corpse into the tomb of Elisha and
fled. But as soon as the body touched Elisha's bones,
the dead man revived and jumped to his feet!
22King Hazael of Aram had oppressed Israel during
the entire reign of King Jehoahaz. 23But the LORD was
gracious and merciful to the people of Israel, and they
were not totally destroyed. He pitied them because of
his covenant with Abraham, Isaac, and Jacob. And to
this day he still has not completely destroyed them or
banished them from his presence.
24King Hazael of Aram died, and his son Ben-hadad
became the next king. 25Then Jehoash son of Jehoahaz
recaptured from Ben-hadad son of Hazael the towns
that had been taken from Jehoash's father, Jehoahaz.
Jehoash defeated Ben-hadad on three occasions, and
he recovered the Israelite towns.

Amaziah Rules in Judah PARALLEL

2 KINGS 14:1-14
Amaziah son of Joash began to rule over Judah in the
second year of the reign of King Jehoash* of Israel.
2Amaziah was twenty-five years old when he became
king, and he reigned in Jerusalem twenty-nine years.
His mother was Jehoaddin from Jerusalem. 3Amaziah
did what was pleasing in the LORD's sight, but not like
his ancestor David. Instead, he followed the example
of his father, Joash. 4Amaziah did not destroy the pagan shrines, and the people still offered sacrifices and
burned incense there.
5When Amaziah was well established as king, he
executed the officials who had assassinated his father.
6However, he did not kill the children of the assassins,
for he obeyed the command of the LORD as written by
Moses in the Book of the Law: "Parents must not be put
to death for the sins of their children, nor children for
the sins of their parents. Those deserving to die must
be put to death for their own crimes."*
7Amaziah also killed 10,000 Edomites in the Valley

2 Kgs 14:1 Hebrew *Joash,* a variant spelling of Jehoash; also in 14:13, 23, 27. **2 Kgs 14:6** Deut 24:16.

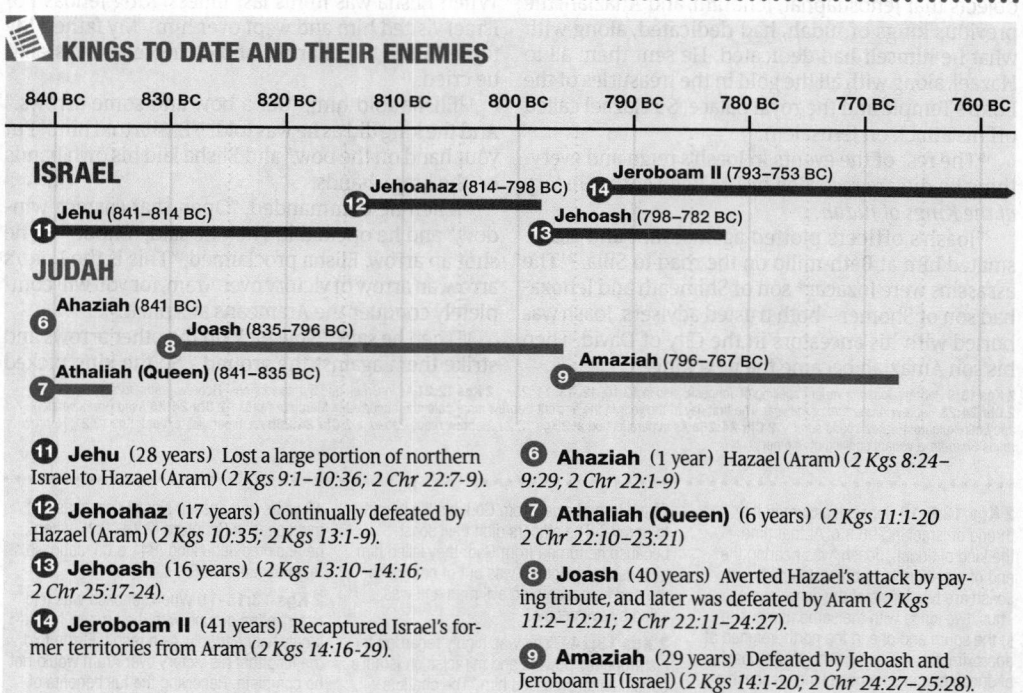

KINGS TO DATE AND THEIR ENEMIES

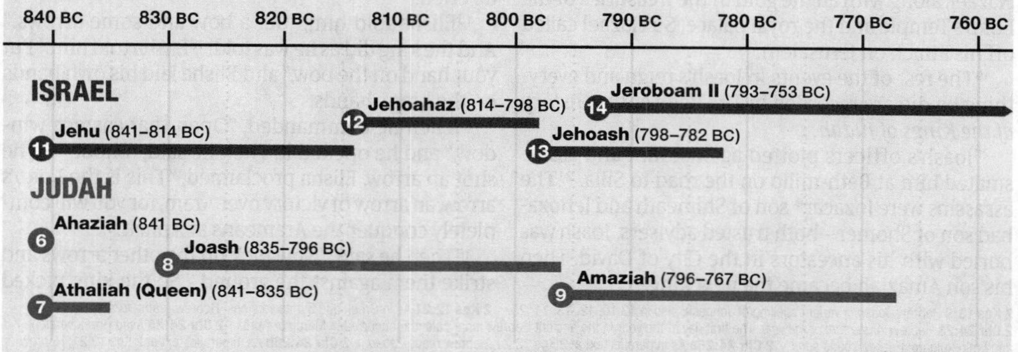

840 BC | 830 BC | 820 BC | 810 BC | 800 BC | 790 BC | 780 BC | 770 BC | 760 BC

ISRAEL

11 Jehu (841–814 BC)
12 Jehoahaz (814–798 BC)
13 Jehoash (798–782 BC)
14 Jeroboam II (793–753 BC)

JUDAH

6 Ahaziah (841 BC)
7 Athaliah (Queen) (841–835 BC)
8 Joash (835–796 BC)
9 Amaziah (796–767 BC)

11 **Jehu** (28 years) Lost a large portion of northern Israel to Hazael (Aram) (*2 Kgs 9:1–10:36; 2 Chr 22:7-9*).

12 **Jehoahaz** (17 years) Continually defeated by Hazael (Aram) (*2 Kgs 10:35; 2 Kgs 13:1-9*).

13 **Jehoash** (16 years) (*2 Kgs 13:10–14:16; 2 Chr 25:17-24*).

14 **Jeroboam II** (41 years) Recaptured Israel's former territories from Aram (*2 Kgs 14:16-29*).

6 **Ahaziah** (1 year) Hazael (Aram) (*2 Kgs 8:24–9:29; 2 Chr 22:1-9*)

7 **Athaliah (Queen)** (6 years) (*2 Kgs 11:1-20 2 Chr 22:10–23:21*)

8 **Joash** (40 years) Averted Hazael's attack by paying tribute, and later was defeated by Aram (*2 Kgs 11:2–12:21; 2 Chr 22:11–24:27*).

9 **Amaziah** (29 years) Defeated by Jehoash and Jeroboam II (Israel) (*2 Kgs 14:1-20; 2 Chr 24:27–25:28*).

2 Kgs 13:20-21 Elisha was dead, but his good influence remained, even causing miracles. This demonstrated that Elisha was indeed a prophet of God. It also attested to God's power—no pagan idol had ever raised anyone from the dead. This miracle served as one more reminder to Israel that it had rejected God's word as given through Elisha.

2 Kgs 14:7 Sela was the ancient stronghold of Petra, a city carved into a rock cliff. It was not only a stronghold for Edom but also a wealthy outpost for trade with India.

of Salt. He also conquered Sela and changed its name to Joktheel, as it is called to this day.

8One day Amaziah sent messengers with this challenge to Israel's king Jehoash, the son of Jehoahaz and grandson of Jehu: "Come and meet me in battle!"*

9But King Jehoash of Israel replied to King Amaziah of Judah with this story: "Out in the Lebanon mountains, a thistle sent a message to a mighty cedar tree: 'Give your daughter in marriage to my son.' But just then a wild animal of Lebanon came by and stepped on the thistle, crushing it!

10"You have indeed defeated Edom, and you are very proud of it. But be content with your victory and stay at home! Why stir up trouble that will only bring disaster on you and the people of Judah?"

11But Amaziah refused to listen, so King Jehoash of Israel mobilized his army against King Amaziah of Judah. The two armies drew up their battle lines at Beth-shemesh in Judah. 12Judah was routed by the army of Israel, and its army scattered and fled for home. 13King Jehoash of Israel captured Judah's king, Amaziah son of Joash and grandson of Ahaziah, at Beth-shemesh. Then he marched to Jerusalem, where he demolished 600 feet* of Jerusalem's wall, from the Ephraim Gate to the Corner Gate. 14He carried off all the gold and silver and all the articles from the Temple of the LORD. He also seized the treasures from the royal palace, along with hostages, and then returned to Samaria.

2 CHRONICLES 25:1-24

Amaziah was twenty-five years old when he became king, and he reigned in Jerusalem twenty-nine years. His mother was Jehoaddin* from Jerusalem. 2Amaziah did what was pleasing in the LORD's sight, but not wholeheartedly.

3When Amaziah was well established as king, he executed the officials who had assassinated his father. 4However, he did not kill the children of the assassins, for he obeyed the command of the LORD as written by Moses in the Book of the Law: "Parents must not be put to death for the sins of their children, nor children for the sins of their parents. Those deserving to die must be put to death for their own crimes."*

5Then Amaziah organized the army, assigning generals and captains* for all Judah and Benjamin. He took a census and found that he had an army of 300,000 select troops, twenty years old and older, all trained in the use of spear and shield. 6He also paid about 7,500 pounds* of silver to hire 100,000 experienced fighting men from Israel.

7But a man of God came to him and said, "Your Majesty, do not hire troops from Israel, for the LORD is not with Israel. He will not help those people of Ephraim! 8If you let them go with your troops into battle, you will be defeated by the enemy no matter how well you fight. God will overthrow you, for he has the power to help you or to trip you up."

9Amaziah asked the man of God, "But what about all that silver I paid to hire the army of Israel?"

The man of God replied, "The LORD is able to give you much more than this!" 10So Amaziah discharged the hired troops and sent them back to Ephraim. This made them very angry with Judah, and they returned home in a great rage.

11Then Amaziah summoned his courage and led his army to the Valley of Salt, where they killed 10,000 Edomite troops from Seir. 12They captured another 10,000 and took them to the top of a cliff and threw them off, dashing them to pieces on the rocks below.

13Meanwhile, the hired troops that Amaziah had sent home raided several of the towns of Judah between Samaria and Beth-horon. They killed 3,000 people and carried off great quantities of plunder.

14When King Amaziah returned from slaughtering the Edomites, he brought with him idols taken from the people of Seir. He set them up as his own gods, bowed down in front of them, and offered sacrifices to them! 15This made the LORD very angry, and he sent

2 Kgs 14:8 Hebrew *Come, let us look one another in the face.* **2 Kgs 14:13** Hebrew *400 cubits* [180 meters]. **2 Chr 25:1** As in parallel text at 2 Kgs 14:2; Hebrew reads *Jehoaddan,* a variant spelling of Jehoaddin. **2 Chr 25:4** Deut 24:16. **2 Chr 25:5** Hebrew *commanders of thousands and commanders of hundreds.* **2 Chr 25:6** Hebrew *100 talents* [3,400 kilograms].

2 Kgs 14:9-10 This parable compares Judah to a small thistle. King Amaziah of Judah had become proud after defeating the Edomites. Here he was trying to pick a fight with Israel because he was sure his army was stronger. Jehoash tried to warn Amaziah not to attack by comparing his army to a thistle and Israel's army to a cedar tree. Amaziah had overrated his strength; his ambition was greater than his ability. He didn't listen to Jehoash and was soundly defeated.

2 Kgs 14:13 A broken-down city wall disgraced the citizens and left them defenseless against future invasions.

2 Chr 25:2 Amaziah did what was right on the outside, but inside he often resented what he had to do. His obedience was at best halfhearted. When the prophet promised God's deliverance, Amaziah first complained about the money that had been lost (2 Chr 25:9). And he valued military success more than God's will. We must search our own hearts and root out any resistance to obeying God. Grudging compliance is not true obedience.

2 Chr 25:9-10 Amaziah made a financial agreement with Israelite soldiers, offering to pay them to fight for him (2 Chr 25:6). But before they could go to battle, Amaziah sent them home with their pay because of the prophet's warning. Although it cost him plenty, he wisely realized that the money was not worth the ruin the alliance could cause. How would you have reacted? Money must never stand in the way of making right decisions. The Lord's favor is priceless, worth more than any amount of money.

2 Chr 25:14 After the victory, Amaziah returned and sacrificed to idols. We are very susceptible to sin after great victories. It is then that we feel confident, relaxed, and ready to celebrate. If, in that excitement, we let our defenses down, Satan can attack with all sorts of temptations. When you win, watch out. After the mountain peaks come the valleys.

2 Chr 25:15 Amaziah made a foolish mistake by worshiping the gods of the nation he had just conquered. Impressed by the accomplishments of the Edomites, Amaziah worshiped their idols! How foolish to serve the gods of a defeated enemy. We make the same mistake as Amaziah when we run after money, power, or recognition. By recognizing the emptiness of these worldly pursuits, we can free ourselves from the desire to follow them.

▶ **2 CHRONICLES 25:1-24 *(cont.)***

a prophet to ask, "Why do you turn to gods who could not even save their own people from you?"

16But the king interrupted him and said, "Since when have I made you the king's counselor? Be quiet now before I have you killed!"

So the prophet stopped with this warning: "I know that God has determined to destroy you because you have done this and have refused to accept my counsel."

17After consulting with his advisers, King Amaziah of Judah sent this challenge to Israel's king Jehoash,* the son of Jehoahaz and grandson of Jehu: "Come and meet me in battle!"*

18But King Jehoash of Israel replied to King Amaziah of Judah with this story: "Out in the Lebanon mountains, a thistle sent a message to a mighty cedar tree: 'Give your daughter in marriage to my son.' But just then a wild animal of Lebanon came by and stepped on the thistle, crushing it!

19"You are saying, 'I have defeated Edom,' and you are very proud of it. But my advice is to stay at home. Why stir up trouble that will only bring disaster on you and the people of Judah?"

20But Amaziah refused to listen, for God was determined to destroy him for turning to the gods of Edom. 21So King Jehoash of Israel mobilized his army against King Amaziah of Judah. The two armies drew up their battle lines at Beth-shemesh in Judah. 22Judah was routed by the army of Israel, and its army scattered and fled for home. 23King Jehoash of Israel captured Judah's king, Amaziah son of Joash and grandson of Ahaziah, at Beth-shemesh. Then he brought him to Jerusalem, where he demolished 600 feet* of Jerusalem's wall, from the Ephraim Gate to the Corner Gate. 24He carried off all the gold and silver and all the articles from the Temple of God that had been in the care of Obed-edom. He also seized the treasures of the royal palace, along with hostages, and then returned to Samaria.

The End of Jehoash's Reign in Israel PARALLEL

2 KINGS 13:12-13

The rest of the events in Jehoash's reign and everything he did, including the extent of his power and his war with King Amaziah of Judah, are recorded in *The Book of the History of the Kings of Israel.* 13When Jehoash died, he was buried in Samaria with the kings of Israel. Then his son Jeroboam II became the next king.

2 KINGS 14:15-16

The rest of the events in Jehoash's reign and everything he did, including the extent of his power and his war with King Amaziah of Judah, are recorded in *The Book of the History of the Kings of Israel.* 16When Jehoash died, he was buried in Samaria with the kings of Israel. And his son Jeroboam II became the next king.

Jeroboam II Begins His Reign in Israel

2 KINGS 14:23-27

Jeroboam II, the son of Jehoash, began to rule over Israel in the fifteenth year of King Amaziah's reign in Judah. Jeroboam reigned in Samaria forty-one years. 24He did what was evil in the LORD's sight. He refused to turn from the sins that Jeroboam son of Nebat had led Israel to commit. 25Jeroboam II recovered the territories of Israel between Lebo-hamath and the Dead Sea,* just as the LORD, the God of Israel, had promised through Jonah son of Amittai, the prophet from Gath-hepher.

26For the LORD saw the bitter suffering of everyone in Israel, and that there was no one in Israel, slave or free, to help them. 27And because the LORD had not said he would blot out the name of Israel completely, he used Jeroboam II, the son of Jehoash, to save them.

The End of Amaziah's Reign in Judah PARALLEL

2 KINGS 14:17-22

King Amaziah of Judah lived for fifteen years after the death of King Jehoash of Israel. 18The rest of the events in Amaziah's reign are recorded in *The Book of the History of the Kings of Judah.*

19There was a conspiracy against Amaziah's life in Jerusalem, and he fled to Lachish. But his enemies sent assassins after him, and they killed him there. 20They brought his body back to Jerusalem on a horse, and he was buried with his ancestors in the City of David.

21All the people of Judah had crowned Amaziah's sixteen-year-old son, Uzziah,* as king in place of his father, Amaziah. 22After his father's death, Uzziah rebuilt the town of Elath and restored it to Judah.

2 Chr 25:17a Hebrew *Joash,* a variant spelling of Jehoash; also in 25:18, 21, 23, 25. **2 Chr 25:17b** Hebrew *Come, let us look one another in the face.* **2 Chr 25:23** Hebrew *400 cubits* [180 meters]. **2 Kgs 14:25** Hebrew *the sea of the Arabah.* **2 Kgs 14:21** Hebrew *Azariah,* a variant spelling of Uzziah.

2 Chr 25:18 In this parable, Judah is the thistle and Israel's army is the cedar. Amaziah was proud after defeating Edom. He wanted to defeat Israel, but Jehoash warned him not to attack. Amaziah had more ambition than ability, and he paid for it when he was soundly defeated. Don't let ambition and pride into your life, for they will cause you to forget God.

2 Kgs 14:25 During this period of history, many prophets—such as Hosea, Amos, Jonah, Micah, and Isaiah—began collecting their prophecies and writing them under God's direction. They continued to preach about the worldwide significance of God's work as they looked forward to the future spiritual Kingdom. God would use Israel's moral and spiritual decline to prepare the way for the Messiah's coming. Because the kingdom and military power of Israel would be stripped away, many people would be ready to turn to the Good News that Jesus would bring.

2 Kgs 14:25 For more information about the prophet Jonah, see the book of Jonah.

2 CHRONICLES 25:25-28
King Amaziah of Judah lived on for fifteen years after the death of King Jehoash of Israel. [26]The rest of the events in Amaziah's reign, from beginning to end, are recorded in *The Book of the Kings of Judah and Israel.*

[27]After Amaziah turned away from the LORD, there was a conspiracy against his life in Jerusalem, and he fled to Lachish. But his enemies sent assassins after him, and they killed him there. [28]They brought his body back on a horse, and he was buried with his ancestors in the City of David.*

Uzziah Begins His Reign in Judah PARALLEL

2 KINGS 15:1-4
Uzziah* son of Amaziah began to rule over Judah in the twenty-seventh year of the reign of King Jeroboam II of Israel. [2]He was sixteen years old when he became king, and he reigned in Jerusalem fifty-two years. His mother was Jecoliah from Jerusalem.

[3]He did what was pleasing in the LORD's sight, just as his father, Amaziah, had done. [4]But he did not destroy the pagan shrines, and the people still offered sacrifices and burned incense there.

2 Chr 25:28 As in some Hebrew manuscripts and other ancient versions (see also 2 Kgs 14:20); most Hebrew manuscripts read *the city of Judah.* **2 Kgs 15:1** Hebrew *Azariah,* a variant spelling of Uzziah; also in 15:6, 7, 8, 17, 23, 27.

UZZIAH

We are never closer to failure than during our greatest successes. If we fail to recognize God's part in our achievements, they are no better than failures. Uzziah was a remarkably successful king. His achievements brought him fame. He was successful in war and peace, in planning and execution, in building and planting. • Uzziah overestimated his own importance in bringing about the great achievements he experienced. He did so many things well that a consuming pride gradually invaded his life like the leprous disease that finally destroyed his body. In trying to act like a priest, he took on a role that God did not mean for him to have. He had forgotten not only how much God had given him but also that God had certain roles for others that he needed to respect. • Uzziah's pride was rooted in his lack of thankfulness. We have no accounts of this king's ever showing appreciation to God for the marvelous gifts he received. Our accomplishments may not compare with Uzziah's, but we still owe a debt of thanksgiving to God for our very lives. If God is not getting the credit for your successes, shouldn't you start looking at your life differently?

Strengths and accomplishments	• Pleased God during his early years as king • Successful warrior and city builder • Skillful in organizing and delegating • Reigned for 52 years
Weaknesses and mistakes	• Developed a prideful attitude due to his great success • Tried to perform the priests' duties, in direct disobedience to God • Failed to remove many of the symbols of idolatry in the land
Lessons from his life	• Lack of thankfulness to God can lead to pride • Even successful people must acknowledge the role God has for others in their lives
Vital statistics	• Where: Jerusalem • Occupation: King of Judah • Relatives: Father: Amaziah. Mother: Jecoliah. Son: Jotham. • Contemporaries: Isaiah, Amos, Hosea, Jeroboam, Zechariah, Azariah
Key verses	"And he built structures on the walls of Jerusalem, designed by experts to protect those who shot arrows and hurled large stones from the towers and the corners of the wall. His fame spread far and wide, for the LORD gave him marvelous help, and he became very powerful. But when he had become powerful, he also became proud, which led to his downfall. He sinned against the LORD his God by entering the sanctuary of the LORD's Temple and personally burning incense on the incense altar" (2 Chr 26:15-16).

Uzziah's story is told in 2 Kings 15:1-7; 2 Chronicles 26:1-23. He is also mentioned in Isaiah 1:1; 6:1; 7:1; Hosea 1:1; Amos 1:1; Zechariah 14:5.

2 Kgs 15:1 Uzziah was also known as Azariah. His story is given in greater detail in 2 Chronicles 26. He is mentioned in Isaiah 1:1; 6:1. Before the beginning of Uzziah's reign, Israel broke down 600 feet of Jerusalem's walls after defeating Judah and carrying off their king, Amaziah (2 Kgs 14:13; 2 Chr 25:23-24). But during Uzziah's 52-year reign, Judah rebuilt the wall, refortified the city with anti-siege weapons, and gained independence from Israel. Uzziah's devotion to God helped Judah enjoy peace and prosperity such as it had not experienced since the days of Solomon.

2 Kgs 15:4 Although Uzziah accomplished a great deal, he failed to destroy the pagan shrines in Judah just as his father, Amaziah, and grandfather Joash had failed to do. Uzziah imitated the kings he had heard stories about and had watched while growing up. Although Uzziah's father and grandfather were basically good kings, they were poor models in some important areas. To rise above the influence of poor models, we must seek better ones. Christ provides a perfect model. No matter how you were raised or who has influenced your life, you can move beyond those limitations by taking Christ as your example and consciously trying to live as he did.

2 CHRONICLES 26:1-15

All the people of Judah had crowned Amaziah's sixteen-year-old son, Uzziah, as king in place of his father. 2After his father's death, Uzziah rebuilt the town of Elath* and restored it to Judah.

3Uzziah was sixteen years old when he became king, and he reigned in Jerusalem fifty-two years. His mother was Jecoliah from Jerusalem. 4He did what was pleasing in the LORD's sight, just as his father, Amaziah, had done. 5Uzziah sought God during the days of Zechariah, who taught him to fear God.* And as long as the king sought guidance from the LORD, God gave him success.

6Uzziah declared war on the Philistines and broke down the walls of Gath, Jabneh, and Ashdod. Then he built new towns in the Ashdod area and in other parts of Philistia. 7God helped him in his wars against the Philistines, his battles with the Arabs of Gur,* and his wars with the Meunites. 8The Meunites* paid annual tribute to him, and his fame spread even to Egypt, for he had become very powerful.

9Uzziah built fortified towers in Jerusalem at the Corner Gate, at the Valley Gate, and at the angle in the wall. 10He also constructed forts in the wilderness and dug many water cisterns, because he kept great herds of livestock in the foothills of Judah* and on the plains. He was also a man who loved the soil. He had many workers who cared for his farms and vineyards, both on the hillsides and in the fertile valleys.

11Uzziah had an army of well-trained warriors, ready to march into battle, unit by unit. This army had been mustered and organized by Jeiel, the secretary of the army, and his assistant, Maaseiah. They were under the direction of Hananiah, one of the king's officials. 12These regiments of mighty warriors were commanded by 2,600 clan leaders. 13The army consisted of 307,500 men, all elite troops. They were prepared to assist the king against any enemy.

14Uzziah provided the entire army with shields, spears, helmets, coats of mail, bows, and sling stones. 15And he built structures on the walls of Jerusalem, designed by experts to protect those who shot arrows and hurled large stones* from the towers and the corners of the wall. His fame spread far and wide, for the LORD gave him marvelous help, and he became very powerful.

Uzziah's Sin and Punishment PARALLEL

2 KINGS 15:5

The LORD struck the king with leprosy,* which lasted until the day he died. He lived in isolation in a separate house. The king's son Jotham was put in charge of the royal palace, and he governed the people of the land.

2 CHRONICLES 26:16-21

But when he had become powerful, he also became proud, which led to his downfall. He sinned against the LORD his God by entering the sanctuary of the LORD's Temple and personally burning incense on the incense altar. 17Azariah the high priest went in after him with eighty other priests of the LORD, all brave men. 18They confronted King Uzziah and said, "It is not for you, Uzziah, to burn incense to the LORD. That is the work of the priests alone, the descendants of Aaron who are set apart for this work. Get out of the sanctuary, for you have sinned. The LORD God will not honor you for this!"

19Uzziah, who was holding an incense burner, became furious. But as he was standing there raging at the priests before the incense altar in the LORD's Temple, leprosy* suddenly broke out on his forehead. 20When Azariah the high priest and all the other priests saw the leprosy, they rushed him out. And the king himself was eager to get out because the LORD had struck him. 21So King Uzziah had leprosy until the day he died. He lived in isolation in a separate house, for he was excluded from the Temple of the LORD. His son Jotham was put in charge of the royal palace, and he governed the people of the land.

2 Chr 26:2 As in Greek version (see also 2 Kgs 14:22; 16:6); Hebrew reads *Eloth,* a variant spelling of Elath. **2 Chr 26:5** As in Syriac and Greek versions; Hebrew reads *who instructed him in divine visions.* **2 Chr 26:7** As in Greek version; Hebrew reads *Gur-baal.* **2 Chr 26:8** As in Greek version; Hebrew reads *Ammonites.* Compare 26:7. **2 Chr 26:10** Hebrew *the Shephelah.* **2 Chr 26:15** Or *to shoot arrows and hurl large stones.* **2 Kgs 15:5** Or *with a contagious skin disease.* The Hebrew word used here and throughout this passage can describe various skin diseases. **2 Chr 26:19** Or *a contagious skin disease.* The Hebrew word used here and throughout this passage can describe various skin diseases.

---

2 Chr 26:15 These machines were similar to the catapults later used by the Romans and were capable of slinging stones or arrows a great distance.

2 Kgs 15:5 For 10 years Jotham was the co-ruler with his father, Uzziah. A father and son would rule together for any of the following reasons: (1) The father was very old and needed help; (2) the father wanted to train his son in leading the nation; (3) the father was sick or exiled. Many co-regents ruled during the period of the kings—Asa/Jehoshaphat; Jehoshaphat/Jehoram; Azariah/Jotham; Jehoash/Jeroboam II; Hezekiah/Manasseh.

2 Chr 26:16 After God gave Uzziah great prosperity and power, he became proud and corrupt. It is true that "pride goes before destruction" (Prov 16:18). If God has given you wealth, influence, popularity, and power, be thankful, but be careful. God hates pride. While it is normal to feel elation when we accomplish something, it is wrong to be disdainful of God or to look down on others. Check your attitudes and remember to give God the credit for what you have. Use your gifts in ways that please him.

2 Chr 26:17-21 When people have power, they often think they can live above the law. But even rulers are subject to God, as Uzziah discovered. No matter what your position in society, God expects you to honor, worship, and obey him.

2 Chr 26:21 For much of his life, Uzziah "did what was pleasing in the LORD's sight" (2 Chr 26:4). But Uzziah turned away from God, and he was struck with leprosy and remained leprous until his death. He is remembered more for his arrogant act and subsequent punishment than for his great reforms. God requires lifelong obedience. Spurts of obedience are not enough. Only "the one who endures to the end" will be rewarded (Mark 13:13). Practice being consistent in your faith every day; that way you will build a lifetime of obedience. Otherwise you, too, may become more famous for your downfall than for your success.

E. The Ministry of the Prophet Jonah

The prophet Jonah is the earliest of the writing prophets to appear in the biblical narrative. He served during the reigns of Jeroboam II in the northern kingdom and Uzziah in the southern kingdom. Although he was active in prophesying to the northern kingdom of Israel (see 2 Kgs 14:25), his book deals exclusively with his assignment from God to preach to a foreign nation that he despised: Assyria.

1. JONAH FORSAKES HIS MISSION

Jonah was a reluctant prophet given a mission he found distasteful. He chose to run away from God rather than obey him. Like Jonah, we may have to do things in life that we don't want to do. Sometimes we find ourselves wanting to turn and run. But it is better to obey God than to defy him and run away. Often, in spite of our defiance, God in his mercy will give us another chance to serve him.

Jonah Runs from the Lord

JONAH 1:1-17

The Lord gave this message to Jonah son of Amittai: 2"Get up and go to the great city of Nineveh. Announce my judgment against it because I have seen
how wicked its people are."
3But Jonah got up and went in the opposite direction to get away from the Lord. He went down to
the port of Joppa, where he found a ship leaving for
Tarshish. He bought a ticket and went on board, hoping to escape from the Lord by sailing to Tarshish.
4But the Lord hurled a powerful wind over the sea,
causing a violent storm that threatened to break the
ship apart. 5Fearing for their lives, the desperate sailors shouted to their gods for help and threw the cargo
overboard to lighten the ship.
But all this time Jonah was sound asleep down in
the hold. 6So the captain went down after him. "How

Jon 1:1-2 Jonah prophesied during the reign of Jeroboam II, the king of Israel from 793 to 753 B.C. He may have been a member of the company of prophets mentioned in connection with Elisha's ministry (2 Kgs 2:3).

God told Jonah to preach to Nineveh, the most important city in Assyria, the rising world power of Jonah's day. Within 50 years, Nineveh would become the capital of the vast Assyrian Empire. Jonah doesn't say much about Nineveh's wickedness, but the prophet Nahum gives us more insight. Nahum says that Nineveh was guilty of (1) evil plots against God (Nah 1:9); (2) exploitation of the helpless (Nah 2:12); (3) cruelty in war (Nah 2:12-13); (4) idolatry, prostitution, and witchcraft (Nah 3:4). God told Jonah to go to Nineveh, about 500 miles northeast of Israel, to warn of judgment and to declare that the people could receive mercy and forgiveness if they repented.

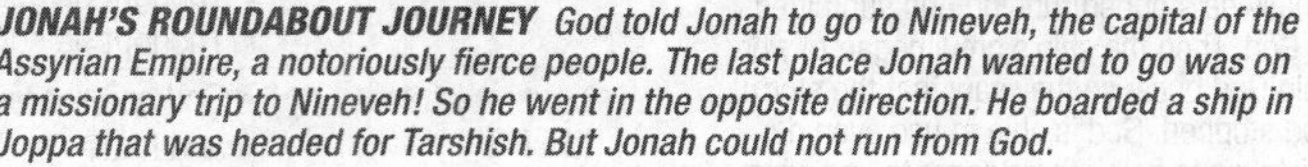
***JONAH'S ROUNDABOUT JOURNEY** God told Jonah to go to Nineveh, the capital of the Assyrian Empire, a notoriously fierce people. The last place Jonah wanted to go was on a missionary trip to Nineveh! So he went in the opposite direction. He boarded a ship in Joppa that was headed for Tarshish. But Jonah could not run from God.*

Jon 1:3 Nineveh was a powerful and wicked city. Jonah had grown up hating the Assyrians and fearing their atrocities. His hatred was so strong that he didn't want them to receive God's mercy. Jonah was actually afraid the people would repent (Jon 4:2-3). Jonah's attitude is representative of Israel's reluctance to share God's love and mercy with others, even though this was their God-given mission (Gen 12:3). They, like Jonah, did not want non-Jews (Gentiles) to obtain God's favor.

Jon 1:3 Jonah knew that God had a specific job for him, but he didn't want to do it. Tarshish could be one of any number of Phoenicia's western ports. Nineveh was toward the east. Jonah decided to go as far west as he could. When God gives us directions through his Word, sometimes we run in fear or in stubbornness, claiming that God is asking too much. It may have been fear or anger at the wideness of God's mercy that made Jonah run. But running got him into worse trouble. In the end, Jonah understood that it is best to do what God asks in the first place. But by then he had paid a costly price for running. It is far better to obey from the start.

Jon 1:4 Before settling in the Promised Land, the Israelites had been nomads, wandering from place to place, seeking good pastureland for their flocks. Although they were not a seafaring people, their location along the Mediterranean Sea and near the neighboring maritime powers of Phoenicia and Philistia allowed much contact with ships and sailors. The ship Jonah sailed on was probably a large trading vessel with a deck.

Jon 1:4 Jonah's disobedience to God endangered the lives of the ship's crew. We have a great responsibility to obey God's Word because our sin and disobedience can hurt others around us.

Jon 1:4-5 While the storm raged, Jonah was sound asleep below deck. Even as he ran from God, Jonah's actions apparently didn't bother his conscience. But the absence of guilt isn't always a barometer of whether we are doing right. Because we can deny reality, we cannot measure obedience by our feelings. Instead, we must compare what we do with God's standards for living.

▸ **JONAH 1:1-17** ***(cont.)***

can you sleep at a time like this?" he shouted. "Get up
and pray to your god! Maybe he will pay attention to
us and spare our lives."
7 Then the crew cast lots to see which of them had
offended the gods and caused the terrible storm. When
they did this, the lots identified Jonah as the culprit.
8 "Why has this awful storm come down on us?" they
demanded. "Who are you? What is your line of work?
What country are you from? What is your nationality?"
9 Jonah answered, "I am a Hebrew, and I worship
the LORD, the God of heaven, who made the sea and
the land."
10 The sailors were terrified when they heard this,
for he had already told them he was running away
from the LORD. "Oh, why did you do it?" they groaned.
11 And since the storm was getting worse all the time,
they asked him, "What should we do to you to stop
this storm?"
12 "Throw me into the sea," Jonah said, "and it will
become calm again. I know that this terrible storm
is all my fault."

Jon 1:7 The crew cast lots to find the guilty person, relying on their superstition to give them the answer. Their system worked, but only because God intervened to let Jonah know that he couldn't run away.

Jon 1:9-12 You cannot seek God's love and run from him at the same time. Jonah soon realized that no matter where he went, he couldn't get away from God. But before Jonah could return to God, he first had to stop going in the opposite direction. What has God told you to do? If you want more of God's love and power, you must be willing to carry out the responsibilities he gives you. You cannot say that you truly believe in God if you don't do what he says (1 Jn 2:3-6).

Jon 1:12 Jonah knew that he had disobeyed and that the storm was his fault, but he didn't say anything until the crew cast lots and he lost the toss (Jon 1:7). Then Jonah was willing to give his life to save the sailors, although he had refused to even speak to the people of Nineveh. Jonah's hatred for the Assyrians had affected his perspective.

Jon 1:13 By trying to save Jonah's life, the pagan sailors showed more compassion than Jonah, because Jonah did not want to warn the Ninevites of the coming judgment of God. Believers should be ashamed when unbelievers show more concern and compassion than they do. God wants us to be concerned for all of his people, lost and saved.

Jon 1:14-16 Jonah had disobeyed God. Finally he stopped running and submitted to God. Then the ship's crew began to worship God because they saw that the storm had stopped. God is able to use even our mistakes to help others come to know him. It may be painful, but admitting our sins can be a powerful example to those who don't know God. Ironically, the pagan sailors did what the entire nation of Israel would not do—prayed to God and vowed to serve him.

Jon 1:17 Many have tried to dismiss this miraculous event as fiction, but the Bible does not describe it as a dream or a legend. We should not explain away this miracle as if we can pick and choose which of the miracles in the Bible to believe. That kind of attitude would allow us to question any part of the Bible and cause us to lose our trust in the Bible as God's true and reliable Word. Jonah's experience was used by Christ himself as an illustration of his death and resurrection (Matt 12:39-40).

JONAH

Few Old Testament personalities can compare in transparency with the prophet Jonah. We can see right through him. And most of what we see we don't like. He reminds us too much of ourselves: fearful, selfish, spiteful, and proud. • Even when Jonah wasn't physically running away from God, he was still resisting on the inside. He was quite capable of putting on a show of obedience to cover a seething internal mutiny. When he finally arrived in Nineveh with God's message, he delivered it as a summary judgment. He offered no way of escape. Jonah flatly declared the city's destruction. • Jonah knew (as he admitted later) that God was "a merciful and compassionate God, slow to get angry and filled with unfailing love . . . eager to turn back from destroying people" (Jon 4:2). He hoped the Ninevites wouldn't listen and was offended and resentful when they did. Jonah suffered under the painful mistake of assuming that he was the center of the universe. • Some people don't even think about God until they become angry. Discouragement, disappointment, and disgust seem to clear away the haziness around God, and we're all too eager to blame him for our troubles. God bluntly confronted Jonah with the reality of his disobedience, the pettiness of his demand for comfort, and the sinfulness of his blatant disregard for others. What Jonah wanted to withhold from the Ninevites—God's mercy and compassion—was what he himself had been taking for granted. • Fortunately, God will be just as blunt with us. He will shatter our comfort if that will place us in the best place to meet him. As long as we are surrounded by our sense of control and importance, we will not know God as God. What has God done lately in your life to open your eyes a little wider?

Strengths and accomplishments	• Was sent (and finally went) to an enemy nation with God's message • Was instrumental in the repentance of the population of a huge city, keeping it from destruction
Weaknesses and mistakes	• Thought he could avoid God's call in his life by running away • Thought he could avoid God's call by sacrificing himself • Thought he could avoid God's call by belligerent obedience • Thought he could nullify God's call by sulking
Lessons from his life	• God cares deeply for us as well as for people we resent and hate • God will accomplish his purposes, even through reluctant and unwilling servants • God is patient with sinners and patient with his servants
Vital statistics	• Where: Gath-hepher • Occupation: Prophet • Relatives: Father: Amittai
Key verse	"But Jonah got up and went in the opposite direction to get away from the LORD. He went down to the port of Joppa, where he found a ship leaving for Tarshish. He bought a ticket and went on board, hoping to escape from the LORD by sailing to Tarshish" (Jon 1:3).

Jonah's story is told in the book of Jonah. He is also mentioned in 2 Kings 14:25; Matthew 12:39-41; 16:4; Luke 11:29, 32.

13Instead, the sailors rowed even harder to get the
ship to the land. But the stormy sea was too violent
for them, and they couldn't make it. 14Then they cried
out to the LORD, Jonah's God. "O LORD," they pleaded,
"don't make us die for this man's sin. And don't hold
us responsible for his death. O LORD, you have sent this
storm upon him for your own good reasons."
15Then the sailors picked Jonah up and threw him
into the raging sea, and the storm stopped at once! 16The
sailors were awestruck by the LORD's great power, and
they offered him a sacrifice and vowed to serve him.
17*Now the LORD had arranged for a great fish to
swallow Jonah. And Jonah was inside the fish for three
days and three nights.

Jonah's Prayer

JONAH 2:1-10

1*Then Jonah prayed to the LORD his God from inside
the fish. 2He said,

"I cried out to the LORD in my great trouble,
and he answered me.
I called to you from the land of the dead,*
and LORD, you heard me!
3 You threw me into the ocean depths,
and I sank down to the heart of the sea.
The mighty waters engulfed me;
I was buried beneath your wild and stormy waves.
4 Then I said, 'O LORD, you have driven me from
your presence.
Yet I will look once more toward your holy
Temple.'
5 "I sank beneath the waves,
and the waters closed over me.
Seaweed wrapped itself around my head.
6 I sank down to the very roots of the mountains.
I was imprisoned in the earth,
whose gates lock shut forever.
But you, O LORD my God,
snatched me from the jaws of death!
7 As my life was slipping away,
I remembered the LORD.
And my earnest prayer went out to you
in your holy Temple.
8 Those who worship false gods
turn their backs on all God's mercies.

Jon 1:17 Verse 1:17 is numbered 2:1 in Hebrew text. **Jon 2:1** Verses 2:1-10 are numbered 2:2-11 in Hebrew text. **Jon 2:2** Hebrew *from Sheol.*

MIRACLES IN THE BOOK OF JONAH

God sent a violent storm	**Jon 1:4**
God ended the storm instantly	**Jon 1:15**
God provided a great fish to swallow Jonah	**Jon 1:17**
God ordered the fish to spit up Jonah	**Jon 2:10**
God made a leafy plant to shade Jonah	**Jon 4:6**
God arranged for a worm to eat the plant	**Jon 4:7**
God arranged for a scorching wind to blow on Jonah	**Jon 4:8**

Jon 1:17 God sent Jonah to the Assyrians, but he ran from the task and was swallowed by a great fish. The Bible tells us that he "was inside the fish for three days and three nights." Then he was delivered and went to Nineveh where the people responded with repentance. Jesus cited these events in Jonah's life. When the religious leaders demanded that Jesus give them a sign to prove his authority, Jesus said the only sign they would receive was the sign of Jonah: They would see Jesus swallowed by death and delivered after three days (Matt 12:39-41; 16:4).

Jesus was making it very clear to the religious leaders of the day that their stubbornness to believe in him would be judged. The people of Nineveh responded to God's word spoken by Jonah, but the religious leaders refused to believe God's word spoken by his very own Son. Often people of our generation demand a sign from God, but the only sign they will receive is the sign of Jonah—the death and resurrection of Christ.

Jon 2:1ff This is a prayer of thanksgiving, not a prayer for deliverance. Jonah was simply thankful that he had not drowned. He was delivered in a most spectacular way and was overwhelmed that he had escaped certain death. Even from inside the fish, Jonah's prayer was heard by God. We can pray anywhere and at any time, and God will hear us. Your sin is never too great, your predicament never too difficult, for God.

Jon 2:1-7 Jonah said, "As my life was slipping away, I remembered the LORD" (Jon 2:7). Often we act the same way. When life is going well, we tend to take God for granted; but when we lose hope, we cry out to him. This kind of relationship with God can result only in an inconsistent, up-and-down spiritual life. A consistent, daily commitment to God promotes a solid relationship with him. Look to God during both the good and bad times, and you will have a stronger spiritual life.

Jon 2:2 Jonah pictured his predicament inside the fish as though he had been buried alive.

Jon 2:8 Those who worship worthless idols (false gods) forfeit God's grace and abandon any hope for mercy from the Lord. Any object of our devotion that replaces God is a lying vanity. We deceive ourselves with something that is ultimately empty and foolish. Make sure that nothing takes God's rightful place in your life.

Ancient Ship

When Jonah boarded a ship bound for Tarshish, he was most likely using a Phoenician or a Philistine ship. Coastal traffic in Old Testament times was in the hands of Phoenicians and Philistines. There were several ports along the Mediterranean Sea, such as Gaza, Joppa, Dor, and Acco, but none were very good. There were also sea lanes linking the Mediterranean coast with Egypt and distant Tarshish (probably Spain).

▸ **JONAH 2:1-10** ***(cont.)***

9 But I will offer sacrifices to you with songs
of praise,
and I will fulfill all my vows.
For my salvation comes from the LORD
alone."

10Then the LORD ordered the fish to spit Jonah out
onto the beach.

2. JONAH FULFILLS HIS MISSION

God gave Jonah a second chance to go to Nineveh, and this time Jonah didn't run. He went to Nineveh, and when the people responded to his announcement of God's judgment by repenting, Jonah became angry that God did not destroy the city as he had threatened. Jonah was a prophet who didn't want to see the people respond; he simply wanted God to destroy people he considered to be enemies. Do you ever find yourself upset at the mercy God shows to others? Consider God's response to Jonah and rethink your anger.

Jonah Goes to Nineveh

JONAH 3:1-10

Then the LORD spoke to Jonah a second time: 2"Get
up and go to the great city of Nineveh, and deliver the
message I have given you."
3This time Jonah obeyed the LORD's command and
went to Nineveh, a city so large that it took three days
to see it all.* 4On the day Jonah entered the city, he
shouted to the crowds: "Forty days from now Nineveh
will be destroyed!" 5The people of Nineveh believed
God's message, and from the greatest to the least, they
declared a fast and put on burlap to show their sorrow.
6When the king of Nineveh heard what Jonah was
saying, he stepped down from his throne and took
off his royal robes. He dressed himself in burlap and
sat on a heap of ashes. 7Then the king and his nobles
sent this decree throughout the city:

"No one, not even the animals from your herds
and flocks, may eat or drink anything at all.
8People and animals alike must wear garments
of mourning, and everyone must pray earnestly
to God. They must turn from their evil ways and
stop all their violence. 9Who can tell? Perhaps
even yet God will change his mind and hold back
his fierce anger from destroying us."

10When God saw what they had done and how
they had put a stop to their evil ways, he changed his

Jon 3:3 Hebrew *a great city to God, of three days' journey.*

776 BC *First known Olympics occurs*

Jon 2:9 Obviously Jonah was not in a position to bargain with God. Instead, he simply thanked God for saving his life. Our troubles should cause us to cling tightly to God, not attempt to bargain our way out of the pain. We can thank and praise God for what he has already done for us, and for his love and mercy.

Jon 2:9 It took a miracle of deliverance to get Jonah to do as God had commanded. As a prophet, Jonah was obligated to obey God's word, but he had tried to escape his responsibilities. At this time, he pledged to fulfill his vows. Jonah's story began with a tragedy, but a greater tragedy would have happened if God had allowed him to keep running. When you know God wants you to do something, don't run. God may not stop you as he did Jonah.

Jon 3:1-2 Jonah had run away from God but was given a second chance to participate in God's work. You may feel as though you are disqualified from serving God because of past mistakes. But serving God is not an earned position. No one qualifies for God's service, but God still asks us to carry out his work. You may yet have another chance.

Jon 3:1-2 Jonah was to preach only what God told him—a message of doom to one of the most powerful cities in the world. This was not the most desirable assignment, but those who bring God's word to others should not let social pressures or fear of people dictate their words. They are called to preach God's message and his truth, no matter how unpopular it may be.

Jon 3:3 Nineveh was a huge city. The Hebrew text makes no distinction between the city proper (the walls of which were only about eight miles in circumference, accommodating a population of about 175,000 persons) and the administrative district of Nineveh that was about 30 to 60 miles across.

Jon 3:4-9 God's word is for everyone. Despite the wickedness of the Ninevite people, they were open to God's message and repented immediately. If we simply proclaim God's message of salvation, we may be surprised at how many people will listen.

Jon 3:10 The pagan people of Nineveh believed Jonah's message and repented. What a miraculous effect God's words had on those evil people! Their repentance stood in stark contrast to Israel's stubbornness. The people of Israel had heard many messages from the prophets, but they had refused to repent. The people of Nineveh only needed

JONAH

Jonah served as a prophet to Israel and Assyria from 793–753 B.C.

Climate of the times	Nineveh was the most important city in Assyria and would soon become the capital of the huge Assyrian Empire. But Nineveh was also a very wicked city.
Main message	Jonah, who hated the powerful and wicked Assyrians, was called by God to warn the Assyrians that they would receive judgment if they did not repent.
Importance of message	Jonah didn't want to go to Nineveh, so he tried to run from God. But God has ways of teaching us to obey and follow him. When Jonah preached, the city repented and God withheld his judgment. Even the most wicked will be saved if they truly repent of their sins and turn to God.
Contemporary prophet	Amos (760–750 B.C.)

mind and did not carry out the destruction he had threatened.

Jonah's Anger at the LORD's Mercy

JONAH 4:1-11

This change of plans greatly upset Jonah, and he became very angry. 2So he complained to the LORD about
it: "Didn't I say before I left home that you would do
this, LORD? That is why I ran away to Tarshish! I knew
that you are a merciful and compassionate God, slow
to get angry and filled with unfailing love. You are
eager to turn back from destroying people. 3Just kill
me now, LORD! I'd rather be dead than alive if what I
predicted will not happen."

4The LORD replied, "Is it right for you to be angry
about this?"

5Then Jonah went out to the east side of the city and
made a shelter to sit under as he waited to see what
would happen to the city. 6And the LORD God arranged
for a leafy plant to grow there, and soon it spread its
broad leaves over Jonah's head, shading him from the
sun. This eased his discomfort, and Jonah was very
grateful for the plant.

7But God also arranged for a worm! The next morning at dawn the worm ate through the stem of the
plant so that it withered away. 8And as the sun grew
hot, God arranged for a scorching east wind to blow
on Jonah. The sun beat down on his head until he grew
faint and wished to die. "Death is certainly better than
living like this!" he exclaimed.

9Then God said to Jonah, "Is it right for you to be
angry because the plant died?"

"Yes," Jonah retorted, "even angry enough to die!"

10Then the LORD said, "You feel sorry about the
plant, though you did nothing to put it there. It came
quickly and died quickly. 11But Nineveh has more than
120,000 people living in spiritual darkness,* not to
mention all the animals. Shouldn't I feel sorry for such
a great city?"

Jon 4:11 Hebrew *people who don't know their right hand from their left.*

to hear God's message once. Jesus said that at the judgment, the people of Nineveh will stand up to condemn the Israelites for their failure to repent (Matt 12:39-41). It is not our hearing God's Word that pleases him, but our responding obediently to it.

Jon 3:10 God responded in mercy by canceling his threatened destruction. God had said that any nation on which he had pronounced judgment would be saved if it repented (Jer 18:7-8). God forgave Nineveh, just as he had forgiven Jonah. The purpose of God's judgment is correction, not revenge. He is always ready to show compassion to anyone willing to seek him.

Jon 4:1 Why did Jonah become angry when God spared Nineveh? The Jews did not want to share God's message with Gentile nations in Jonah's day, just as they resisted that role in Paul's day (1 Thes 2:14-16). They had forgotten their original purpose as a nation—to be a blessing to the rest of the world by sharing God's message with other nations (Gen 22:18). Jonah thought that God should not freely give his salvation to a wicked pagan nation. Yet this is exactly what God does for all who come to him today in faith.

Jon 4:1-2 Jonah revealed the reason for his reluctance to go to Nineveh (Jon 1:3). He didn't want the Ninevites forgiven; he wanted them destroyed. Jonah did not understand that the God of Israel was also the God of the whole world. Are you surprised when some unlikely person turns to God? Is it possible that your view is as narrow as Jonah's? We must not forget that, in reality, we do not deserve to be forgiven by God.

Jon 4:3 Jonah had run from the job of delivering God's message of destruction to Nineveh (Jon 1:2-3); then he wanted to die because the destruction wouldn't happen. How quickly Jonah had forgotten God's mercy for him when he was inside the fish (Jon 2:9-10). Jonah was happy when God saved him, but he was angry when Nineveh was saved. Jonah was learning a valuable lesson about God's mercy and forgiveness. God's forgiveness was not only for Jonah or for Israel alone; it extends to all who repent and believe.

Jon 4:3 Jonah may have been more concerned about his own reputation than God's. He knew that if the people repented, none of his warnings to Nineveh would come true. This would embarrass him, although it would give glory to God. Are you more interested in getting glory for God or for yourself?

Jon 4:5-11 God ministered tenderly to Jonah just as he had done to Nineveh and to Israel—and just as he does to us. God could have destroyed Jonah for his defiant anger, but instead he gently taught him a lesson. If we will obey God, he will lead us. His harsh judgment is reserved for those who persist in rebellion.

Jon 4:9 Jonah was angry at the withering of the plant, but not over what could have happened to Nineveh. Most of us have cried at the death of a pet or when an object with sentimental value is broken, but have we cried over the fact that a friend does not know God? How easy it is to be more sensitive to our own interests than to the spiritual needs of people around us.

Jon 4:10-11 Sometimes people wish that judgment and destruction would come upon sinful people whose wickedness seems to demand immediate punishment. But God is more merciful than we can imagine. God feels compassion for the sinners we want judged, and he devises plans to bring them to himself. What is your attitude toward those who are especially wicked? Do you want them destroyed? Or do you wish that they could experience God's mercy and forgiveness?

Jon 4:11 God spared the sailors when they pleaded for mercy. God saved Jonah when he prayed from inside the fish. God saved the people of Nineveh when they responded to Jonah's preaching. God answers the prayers of those who call upon him. God will always work his will, and he desires that all come to him, trust in him, and be saved. We can be saved if we heed God's warnings to us through his Word. If we respond in obedience, God will be gracious, and we will receive his mercy, not his punishment.

"Nineveh has more than 120,000 people living in spiritual darkness, not to mention all the animals. Shouldn't I feel sorry for such a great city?"

Jonah 4:11

F. The Ministry of the Prophet Amos

Amos speaks with brutal frankness in denouncing sin. He collided with the false religious leaders of his day and was not intimidated by priest or king. He continued to speak his message boldly. Many of the conditions in Israel during Amos's time are evident in today's society. We need Amos's courage to ignore danger and stand against sin.

1. ANNOUNCEMENT OF JUDGMENT

Amos announces judgments from God against eight nations. He begins by announcing God's judgment on six foreign nations around Judah and Israel, which would have had the people nodding their heads in agreement about the wickedness of those around them and the need for punishment. But then Amos turns to Judah and Israel themselves, who also faced the harsh reality of judgment.

The Prophecy of Amos

AMOS 1:1-2

This message was given to Amos, a shepherd from the
town of Tekoa in Judah. He received this message in
visions two years before the earthquake, when Uzziah
was king of Judah and Jeroboam II, the son of Jehoash,* was king of Israel.
²This is what he saw and heard:

"The LORD's voice will roar from Zion
and thunder from Jerusalem!
The lush pastures of the shepherds will dry up;
the grass on Mount Carmel will wither and die."

760 BC

God's Judgment on Israel's Neighbors

AMOS 1:3–2:3

This is what the LORD says:

"The people of Damascus have sinned again
and again,*
and I will not let them go unpunished!
They beat down my people in Gilead
as grain is threshed with iron sledges.
⁴ So I will send down fire on King Hazael's palace,
and the fortresses of King Ben-hadad will be
destroyed.
⁵ I will break down the gates of Damascus
and slaughter the people in the valley of Aven.
I will destroy the ruler in Beth-eden,
and the people of Aram will go as captives to Kir,"
says the LORD.

⁶This is what the LORD says:

"The people of Gaza have sinned again and again,
and I will not let them go unpunished!
They sent whole villages into exile,
selling them as slaves to Edom.
⁷ So I will send down fire on the walls of Gaza,
and all its fortresses will be destroyed.
⁸ I will slaughter the people of Ashdod
and destroy the king of Ashkelon.

Am 1:1 Hebrew *Joash,* a variant spelling of Jehoash. **Am 1:3** Hebrew *have committed three sins, even four;* also in 1:6, 9, 11, 13.

Amos begins his ministry

Amos 1:1 Amos was a shepherd and fig grower from the southern kingdom (Judah), but he prophesied to the northern kingdom (Israel). Israel was politically at the height of its power with a prosperous economy, but the nation was spiritually corrupt. Idols were worshiped throughout the land and especially at Bethel, which was supposed to be the nation's religious center. Like Hosea, Amos was sent by God to denounce this social and religious corruption. About 30 or 40 years after Amos prophesied, Assyria destroyed the capital city, Samaria, and conquered Israel (722 B.C.). Uzziah reigned in Judah from 792–740 B.C.; Jeroboam II reigned in Israel from 793–753 B.C.

Amos 1:1 Tekoa, Amos's hometown, was located in the rugged sheep country of Judah, about 10 miles south of Jerusalem. Long before Amos was born, a woman of Tekoa had helped reconcile David and his rebellious son Absalom (2 Sam 14:1-23).

Amos 1:1 Amos raised sheep—not a particularly "spiritual" job; yet he became a channel of God's message to others. Your job may not cause you to feel spiritual or successful, but it is vital work if you are in the place God wants you to be. God can work through you to do extraordinary things, no matter how ordinary your occupation.

Amos 1:1 Other historical records from this period mention an earthquake that occurred at this time, and it is mentioned later by the prophet Zechariah (Zech 14:5).

Amos 1:2 In the Bible, God is often pictured as a shepherd and his people as sheep. As a shepherd, God leads and protects his flock. But here God is depicted as a ferocious lion ready to devour those who are evil or unfaithful (see also Hos 11:10).

Amos 1:2 *Carmel* means "fertile field." It was a very fertile area. A drought capable of drying up this area would have to be quite severe.

Amos 1:3 Damascus was the capital of Aram. In the past, Aram had been one of Israel's most formidable enemies. After Assyria defeated Aram in 732 B.C. (2 Kgs 16:9), Damascus was no longer a real threat.

Amos 1:3–2:6 Amos pronounced God's judgment on nation after nation around Israel's borders—even Judah. Perhaps the people of Israel cheered when they heard the rebukes leveled against those nations. But then Amos proclaimed God's judgment on the people of Israel. They could not excuse their own sin just because the sins of their neighbors seemed worse. God judges all people fairly and impartially.

Amos 1:3–2:6 The accusation "The people . . . have sinned again and again, and I will not let them go unpunished" echoes through these verses as God evaluates nation after nation. Each nation had persistently refused to follow God's commands. A sinful practice can become a way of life. Ignoring or denying the problem will not help us. We must begin the process of correction by confessing our sins to God and asking him to forgive us. Otherwise we have no hope but to continue our pattern of sin.

Amos 1:4 King Hazael was king of Aram. Ben-hadad was Hazael's son (2 Kgs 13:24).

Amos 1:5 The Arameans had been slaves in Kir, but here they were free (Amos 9:7). Decreeing that the Arameans should go back to Kir was like saying the Israelites should go back to Egypt as slaves (Exod 1).

Then I will turn to attack Ekron,
and the few Philistines still left will be killed,"
says the Sovereign LORD.

9 This is what the LORD says:

"The people of Tyre have sinned again and again,
and I will not let them go unpunished!
They broke their treaty of brotherhood with Israel,
selling whole villages as slaves to Edom.
10 So I will send down fire on the walls of Tyre,
and all its fortresses will be destroyed."

11 This is what the LORD says:

"The people of Edom have sinned again and again,
and I will not let them go unpunished!
They chased down their relatives, the Israelites, with swords,
showing them no mercy.
In their rage, they slashed them continually
and were unrelenting in their anger.
12 So I will send down fire on Teman,
and the fortresses of Bozrah will be destroyed."

13 This is what the LORD says:

"The people of Ammon have sinned again and again,
and I will not let them go unpunished!
When they attacked Gilead to extend their borders,
they ripped open pregnant women with their swords.
14 So I will send down fire on the walls of Rabbah,
and all its fortresses will be destroyed.
The battle will come upon them with shouts,
like a whirlwind in a mighty storm.
15 And their king* and his princes will go into exile together,"
says the LORD.

2:1 This is what the LORD says:

"The people of Moab have sinned again and again,*
and I will not let them go unpunished!
They desecrated the bones of Edom's king,
burning them to ashes.
2 So I will send down fire on the land of Moab,
and all the fortresses in Kerioth will be destroyed.
The people will fall in the noise of battle,
as the warriors shout and the ram's horn sounds.
3 And I will destroy their king
and slaughter all their princes,"
says the LORD.

Am 1:15 Hebrew *malcam,* possibly referring to their god Molech. **Am 2:1** Hebrew *have committed three sins, even four;* also in 2:4, 6.

AMOS

Amos served as a prophet to Israel (the northern kingdom) from 760–750 B.C.

Climate of the times	Israel was enjoying peace and economic prosperity. But this blessing had caused her to become a selfish, materialistic society. Those who were well-off ignored the needs of those less fortunate. The people were self-centered and indifferent toward God.
Main message	Amos spoke against those who exploited or ignored the needy.
Importance of message	Believing in God is more than a matter of individual faith. God calls all believers to work against injustices in society and to aid those less fortunate.
Contemporary prophets	Jonah (793–753 B.C.), Hosea (753–715 B.C.)

Amos 1:7-8 Gaza, Ashdod, Ashkelon, and Ekron were four of the five major cities of Philistia, an enemy who often threatened Israel. The fifth city, Gath, had probably already been destroyed. Therefore, Amos was saying that the entire nation of Philistia would be destroyed for its sins.

Amos 1:9 Tyre was one of two major cities in Phoenicia. Several treaties had been made with this city, which supplied the cedar used to build David's palace and God's Temple (2 Sam 5:11; 1 Kgs 5).

Amos 1:11-12 Both Edom and Israel had descended from Isaac: Edom from Isaac's son Esau, and Israel from Esau's twin brother, Jacob (Gen 25:19-28; 27). But these two nations, like the two brothers, were always fighting. Edom had rejoiced at Israel's misfortunes. As a result, God promised to destroy Edom completely, from Teman in the south to Bozrah in the north.

Amos 1:13-15 The Ammonites had descended from an incestuous relationship between Lot and his younger daughter (Gen 19:30-38). The Ammonites were hostile to Israel; and although Israel began to worship their idols, the Ammonites still attacked (Judg 10:6-8). After Saul had been anointed Israel's king, his first victory in battle was against the Ammonites (1 Sam 11). Rabbah was Ammon's capital city. Amos's prophecy of Ammon's destruction was fulfilled through the Assyrian invasion.

Amos 2:1-3 The Moabites had descended from an incestuous relationship between Lot and his older daughter (Gen 19:30-37). Balak, king of Moab, had tried to hire the prophet Balaam to curse the Israelites so they could be defeated (Num 22–24). Balaam spoke the Lord's word of blessing instead, but some of the Moabites had succeeded in getting Israel to worship Baal (Num 25:1-3). The Moabites were known for their atrocities (2 Kgs 3:26-27). An archaeological artifact, the Moabite Stone, reveals that Moab was always ready to profit from the downfall of others.

God's Judgment on Judah and Israel

AMOS 2:4-16

This is what the LORD says:

"The people of Judah have sinned again
and again,
and I will not let them go unpunished!
They have rejected the instruction of the LORD,
refusing to obey his decrees.
They have been led astray by the same lies
that deceived their ancestors.
5 So I will send down fire on Judah,
and all the fortresses of Jerusalem will be
destroyed."

6This is what the LORD says:

"The people of Israel have sinned again
and again,
and I will not let them go unpunished!
They sell honorable people for silver
and poor people for a pair of sandals.
7 They trample helpless people in the dust
and shove the oppressed out of the way.
Both father and son sleep with the same woman,
corrupting my holy name.
8 At their religious festivals,
they lounge in clothing their debtors put up
as security.
In the house of their gods,*
they drink wine bought with unjust fines.

9 "But as my people watched,
I destroyed the Amorites,
though they were as tall as cedars
and as strong as oaks.
I destroyed the fruit on their branches
and dug out their roots.
10 It was I who rescued you from Egypt
and led you through the desert for
forty years,
so you could possess the land of the
Amorites.
11 I chose some of your sons to be prophets
and others to be Nazirites.
Can you deny this, my people of Israel?"
asks the LORD.
12 "But you caused the Nazirites to sin by making
them drink wine,
and you commanded the prophets, 'Shut up!'

13 "So I will make you groan
like a wagon loaded down with sheaves
of grain.
14 Your fastest runners will not get away.
The strongest among you will become weak.
Even mighty warriors will be unable to save
themselves.
15 The archers will not stand their ground.
The swiftest runners won't be fast enough
to escape.
Even those riding horses won't be able to save
themselves.
16 On that day the most courageous of your
fighting men
will drop their weapons and run for their lives,"
says the LORD.

Am 2:8 Or *their God.*

Amos 2:4-6 After Solomon died, the kingdom divided, and the tribes of Judah and Benjamin became the southern kingdom (Judah) under Solomon's son Rehoboam. The other 10 tribes became the northern kingdom (Israel) and followed Jeroboam, who had rebelled against Rehoboam.

God had punished other nations harshly for their evil actions and atrocities. But God also promised to judge both Israel and Judah because they ignored the revealed law of God. The other nations were ignorant, but Judah and Israel, God's people, knew what God wanted. Still they ignored him and joined pagan nations in worshiping idols. If we know God's Word and refuse to obey it, like Israel, our guilt is greater than those who are ignorant of it.

Amos 2:4-6 Amos must have won over his audience as he proclaimed God's judgment against the evil nations surrounding Israel. But then he even spoke against his own nation, Judah.

Amos 2:6ff Now the focus turned to the northern kingdom. God condemned Israel for five specific sins: (1) selling the poor as slaves (see Deut 15:7-11; Amos 8:6), (2) exploiting the poor (see Exod 23:6; Deut 16:19), (3) engaging in perverse sexual sins (see Lev 20:11-12), (4) taking illegal collateral for loans (see Exod 22:26-27; Deut 24:6, 12-13), and (5) worshiping false gods (see Exod 20:3-5).

Amos 2:6-7 Amos was speaking to the upper class. There was no middle class in the country—only the very rich and the very poor. The rich observed religious rituals. They gave extra tithes, went to places of worship, and offered sacrifices. But they were greedy and unjust, and they took advantage of the helpless. Be sure that you do not neglect the needs of the poor while you faithfully attend church and fulfill your religious obligations. God expects us to live out our faith—this means responding to those in need.

Amos 2:9-11 The prophets were constantly challenging people to remember what God had done! When we read a list like this one, we are amazed at Israel's forgetfulness. But what would the prophets say about us? God's past faithfulness should have reminded the Israelites to obey him; likewise, what he has done for us should remind us to live for him.

Amos 2:11 The Nazirites took a vow of service to God. The vow included abstaining from wine and never cutting their hair. But instead of being respected for their disciplined and temperate lives, they were being urged to break their vows. If the Nazirites were corrupted, there would remain little influence for good among the Israelites.

Amos 2:16 "That day" refers to the time when Assyria would attack Israel, destroy Samaria, and take the people captive (722 B.C.). This military defeat came only a few decades after this pronouncement.

Amos 2:16 Television and movies are filled with images of people who seem to have no fear. Many today have modeled their lives after these images—they want to be tough. But God is not impressed with bravado. He says that even the toughest people will run in fear when God's judgment comes. Do you know people who think they can make it through life without God? Don't be swayed by their self-assured rhetoric. Recognize that God fears no one, and one day all people will fear him.

2. REASONS FOR JUDGMENT

Amos explains to Israel and Judah that they deserve judgment because they had a false understanding of what their status as God's chosen people meant. They weren't exempt from God's judgment; in fact, they would be held to an even higher standard than the surrounding nations.

Witnesses against Guilty Israel

AMOS 3:1-15

Listen to this message that the LORD has spoken
against you, O people of Israel and Judah—against
the entire family I rescued from Egypt:

2 "From among all the families on the earth,
I have been intimate with you alone.
That is why I must punish you
for all your sins."

3 Can two people walk together
without agreeing on the direction?
4 Does a lion ever roar in a thicket
without first finding a victim?
Does a young lion growl in its den
without first catching its prey?
5 Does a bird ever get caught in a trap
that has no bait?
Does a trap spring shut
when there's nothing to catch?
6 When the ram's horn blows a warning,
shouldn't the people be alarmed?
Does disaster come to a city
unless the LORD has planned it?

7 Indeed, the Sovereign LORD never does anything
until he reveals his plans to his servants the
prophets.

8 The lion has roared—
so who isn't frightened?
The Sovereign LORD has spoken—
so who can refuse to proclaim his message?

9 Announce this to the leaders of Philistia*
and to the great ones of Egypt:
"Take your seats now on the hills around Samaria,
and witness the chaos and oppression in
Israel."

10 "My people have forgotten how to do right,"
says the LORD.
"Their fortresses are filled with wealth
taken by theft and violence.
11 Therefore," says the Sovereign LORD,
"an enemy is coming!
He will surround them and shatter their
defenses.
Then he will plunder all their fortresses."

12 This is what the LORD says:

"A shepherd who tries to rescue a sheep from
a lion's mouth
will recover only two legs or a piece of an ear.
So it will be for the Israelites in Samaria lying
on luxurious beds,
and for the people of Damascus reclining
on couches.*

13 "Now listen to this, and announce it throughout
all Israel,*" says the Lord, the LORD God of Heaven's
Armies.

14 "On the very day I punish Israel for its sins,
I will destroy the pagan altars at Bethel.
The horns of the altar will be cut off
and fall to the ground.

Am 3:9 Hebrew *Ashdod.* **Am 3:12** The meaning of the Hebrew in this sentence is uncertain. **Am 3:13** Hebrew *the house of Jacob.* The names "Jacob" and "Israel" are often interchanged throughout the Old Testament, referring sometimes to the individual patriarch and sometimes to the nation.

Amos 3:2 God chose Israel to be the people through whom all other nations of the world could know him. He made this promise to Abraham, father of the Israelites (Gen 12:1-3). Israel didn't have to do anything to be chosen; God had given them this special privilege because he wanted to, not because they deserved special treatment (Deut 9:4-6). Pride in their privileged position ruined Israel's sensitivity to the will of God and to the plight of others.

Amos 3:3-6 With a series of seven rhetorical questions, Amos shows how two events can be linked together. Once one event takes place, the second will surely follow. Amos was showing that God's revelation to him was the sure sign that judgment would follow.

Amos 3:6 This verse means that God himself would be sending disaster to Israel.

Amos 3:7 Even in anger, God is merciful: He always warned his people through prophets before punishing them so they could not rationalize or complain when judgment came. Warnings about sin and judgment apply to people today just as they did to Israel. Because we have been warned about our sin, we have no excuse when punishment comes. Do not take lightly the warnings in God's Word about judgment. His warnings are a way of showing mercy to you.

Amos 3:9 Amos pictured Philistia and Egypt summoned to witness Israel's great sins. Even Israel's most wicked and idolatrous neighbors would see God judge Israel.

Amos 3:10 The people of Israel no longer knew how to do what was right. The more they sinned, the harder it was to remember what God wanted. The same is true for us. The longer we wait to deal with sin, the greater the hold it has on us. Finally, we forget what it means to do right. Are you on the verge of forgetting?

Amos 3:11-12 The enemy mentioned here was Assyria, which conquered Israel and did just as Amos predicted. The people were scattered to foreign lands, and foreigners were placed in the land to keep the peace. Israel's leaders had robbed their defenseless countrymen, and here they would be rendered defenseless by the Assyrians. Amos added that even if the Israelites tried to repent, it would be too late. The destruction would be so complete that nothing of value would be left.

Amos 3:14 God's judgment against Israel's altars shows that he was rejecting Israel's entire religious system because it was so polluted. The horns of the altar stood for protection (1 Kgs 1:49-53), and the false altars would soon be gone. Then the people would have no sanctuary or protection (see Amos 4:4) when judgment came.

▸ **AMOS 3:1-15** ***(cont.)***

15 And I will destroy the beautiful homes of the
wealthy—
their winter mansions and their summer
houses, too—
all their palaces filled with ivory,"
says the LORD.

Israel's Failure to Learn

AMOS 4:1-13

1 Listen to me, you fat cows*
living in Samaria,
you women who oppress the poor
and crush the needy,
and who are always calling to your husbands,
"Bring us another drink!"
2 The Sovereign LORD has sworn this by his
holiness:
"The time will come when you will be led away
with hooks in your noses.
Every last one of you will be dragged away
like a fish on a hook!
3 You will be led out through the ruins
of the wall;
you will be thrown from your fortresses,*"
says the LORD.

4 "Go ahead and offer sacrifices to the idols
at Bethel.
Keep on disobeying at Gilgal.
Offer sacrifices each morning,
and bring your tithes every three days.
5 Present your bread made with yeast
as an offering of thanksgiving.
Then give your extra voluntary offerings
so you can brag about it everywhere!
This is the kind of thing you Israelites love
to do,"
says the Sovereign LORD.

6 "I brought hunger to every city
and famine to every town.
But still you would not return to me,"
says the LORD.

7 "I kept the rain from falling
when your crops needed it the most.
I sent rain on one town
but withheld it from another.
Rain fell on one field,
while another field withered away.
8 People staggered from town to town looking
for water,
but there was never enough.
But still you would not return to me,"
says the LORD.

9 "I struck your farms and vineyards with blight
and mildew.
Locusts devoured all your fig and olive trees.
But still you would not return to me,"
says the LORD.

10 "I sent plagues on you
like the plagues I sent on Egypt long ago.
I killed your young men in war
and led all your horses away.*
The stench of death filled the air!
But still you would not return to me,"
says the LORD.

11 "I destroyed some of your cities,
as I destroyed* Sodom and Gomorrah.
Those of you who survived
were like charred sticks pulled from a fire.
But still you would not return to me,"
says the LORD.

12 "Therefore, I will bring upon you all the disasters
I have announced.
Prepare to meet your God in judgment,
you people of Israel!"

13 For the LORD is the one who shaped the
mountains,
stirs up the winds, and reveals his thoughts
to mankind.
He turns the light of dawn into darkness
and treads on the heights of the earth.
The LORD God of Heaven's Armies is
his name!

Am 4:1 Hebrew *you cows of Bashan.* **Am 4:3** Or *thrown out toward Harmon,* possibly a reference to Mount Hermon. **Am 4:10** Or *and slaughtered your captured horses.* **Am 4:11** Hebrew *as when God destroyed.*

Amos 4:1 Israel's wealthy women were called "fat cows"—pampered, sleek, and well fed (see Ps 22:12). These women selfishly pushed their husbands to oppress the helpless in order to support their lavish lifestyles. Be careful not to desire material possessions so much that you are willing to oppress others and displease God to get them.

Amos 4:4 Amos sarcastically invited the people to sin in Bethel and Gilgal, where they worshiped idols instead of God. Bethel was where God had renewed his covenant to Abraham with Jacob (Gen 28:10-22). At this time, Bethel was the religious center of the northern kingdom, and Jeroboam had placed an idol there to discourage the people from traveling to Jerusalem in the southern kingdom to worship (1 Kgs 12:26-29). Gilgal was Israel's first campground after entering the Promised Land (Josh 4:19). Here Joshua had renewed the covenant and the rite of circumcision, and the people had celebrated the Passover (Josh 5:2-11). Saul was crowned Israel's first king in Gilgal (1 Sam 11:15).

Amos 4:6-13 No matter how God warned the people—through famine, drought, blight, locusts, plagues, or war—they still ignored him. Because the Israelites didn't get the message, they would have to meet God face to face in judgment. No longer could they ignore God; they would have to face the one they had rejected, the one they had refused to obey when he commanded them to care for the poor. One day each of us will meet God face to face to give account for what we have done or refused to do. Are you prepared to meet him?

A Call to Repentance

AMOS 5:1-17

Listen, you people of Israel! Listen to this funeral song I am singing:

2 "The virgin Israel has fallen,
never to rise again!
She lies abandoned on the ground,
with no one to help her up."

3 The Sovereign LORD says:

"When a city sends a thousand men to battle,
only a hundred will return.
When a town sends a hundred,
only ten will come back alive."

4 Now this is what the LORD says to the family of Israel:

"Come back to me and live!
5 Don't worship at the pagan altars at Bethel;
don't go to the shrines at Gilgal or Beersheba.
For the people of Gilgal will be dragged off into exile,
and the people of Bethel will be reduced to nothing."
6 Come back to the LORD and live!
Otherwise, he will roar through Israel* like a fire,
devouring you completely.
Your gods in Bethel
won't be able to quench the flames.
7 You twist justice, making it a bitter pill for the oppressed.
You treat the righteous like dirt.

8 It is the LORD who created the stars,
the Pleiades and Orion.
He turns darkness into morning
and day into night.
He draws up water from the oceans
and pours it down as rain on the land.
The LORD is his name!
9 With blinding speed and power he destroys the strong,
crushing all their defenses.

10 How you hate honest judges!
How you despise people who tell the truth!
11 You trample the poor,
stealing their grain through taxes and unfair rent.
Therefore, though you build beautiful stone houses,
you will never live in them.
Though you plant lush vineyards,
you will never drink wine from them.
12 For I know the vast number of your sins
and the depth of your rebellions.
You oppress good people by taking bribes
and deprive the poor of justice in the courts.
13 So those who are smart keep their mouths shut,
for it is an evil time.

14 Do what is good and run from evil
so that you may live!
Then the LORD God of Heaven's Armies will be your helper,
just as you have claimed.
15 Hate evil and love what is good;
turn your courts into true halls of justice.
Perhaps even yet the LORD God of Heaven's Armies
will have mercy on the remnant of his people.*

Am 5:6 Hebrew *the house of Joseph.* **Am 5:15** Hebrew *the remnant of Joseph.*

Amos 5:1 Amos shocked his listeners by singing a funeral song for them as though they had already been destroyed. The Israelites believed that their wealth and following religious rituals made them secure, but Amos lamented their sure destruction.

Amos 5:6 There is one sure remedy for a world that is sick and dying in sin: "Come back to the LORD and live!" Sin seeks to destroy, but hope is found in seeking God. In times of difficulty, seek God. In personal discomfort and struggle, seek God. When others are struggling, encourage them to seek God too.

Amos 5:7 The courts should have been places of justice where the poor and oppressed could find relief. Instead, they had become places of greed and injustice.

Amos 5:8 Pleiades and Orion are star constellations. For thousands of years, navigators have staked lives and fortunes on the reliability of the stars. The constancy and orderliness of the heavens challenge us to look beyond them to their Creator.

Amos 5:10-12 A society is in trouble when those who try to do right are hated for their commitment to justice. Any society that exploits the poor and defenseless or hates the truth is bent on destroying itself.

Amos 5:12 Why does God put so much emphasis on the way we treat the poor and needy? Because how we treat the poor reflects our true character. We know we can expect nothing in return. Do we, like Christ, give without thought of gain? We should treat the poor as we would like God to treat us.

Amos 5:12 Here are eight common excuses for not helping the poor and needy: (1) They don't deserve help. They got themselves into poverty; let them get themselves out. (2) God's call to help the poor applies to another time. (3) We don't know any people like this. (4) I have my own needs. (5) Any money I give will be wasted, stolen, or spent. The poor will never see it. (6) I may become a victim myself. (7) I don't know where to start, and I don't have time. (8) My little bit won't make any difference.

Instead of making lame excuses, ask what can be done to help. Does your church have programs to help the needy? Could you volunteer to work with a community group that fights poverty? As one individual, you may not be able to accomplish much, but join with similarly motivated people and watch mountains begin to move.

Amos 5:15 If Israel were to sweep away the corrupt system of false accusations, bribery, and corruption, and were to insist that only just decisions be given, this would show their change of heart. We dare not read this passage lightly or write it off simply as an encouragement to be good. It is a command to reform our own legal and social system.

▸ **AMOS 5:1-17** ***(cont.)***

16 Therefore, this is what the Lord, the LORD God of
Heaven's Armies, says:

"There will be crying in all the public squares
and mourning in every street.
Call for the farmers to weep with you,
and summon professional mourners to wail.
17 There will be wailing in every vineyard,
for I will destroy them all,"
says the LORD.

Warning of Coming Judgment

AMOS 5:18–6:14

18 What sorrow awaits you who say,
"If only the day of the LORD were here!"
You have no idea what you are wishing for.
That day will bring darkness, not light.
19 In that day you will be like a man who runs from a lion—
only to meet a bear.
Escaping from the bear, he leans his hand against a wall in his house—
and he's bitten by a snake.
20 Yes, the day of the LORD will be dark and hopeless,
without a ray of joy or hope.

21 "I hate all your show and pretense—
the hypocrisy of your religious festivals and solemn assemblies.
22 I will not accept your burnt offerings and grain offerings.
I won't even notice all your choice peace offerings.
23 Away with your noisy hymns of praise!
I will not listen to the music of your harps.
24 Instead, I want to see a mighty flood of justice,
an endless river of righteous living.

25 "Was it to me you were bringing sacrifices and
offerings during the forty years in the wilderness, Israel? 26 No, you served your pagan gods—Sakkuth your
king god and Kaiwan your star god—the images you
made for yourselves. 27 So I will send you into exile, to
a land east of Damascus,*" says the LORD, whose name
is the God of Heaven's Armies.

6:1 What sorrow awaits you who lounge in luxury in Jerusalem,*
and you who feel secure in Samaria!
You are famous and popular in Israel,
and people go to you for help.
2 But go over to Calneh
and see what happened there.
Then go to the great city of Hamath
and down to the Philistine city of Gath.
You are no better than they were,
and look at how they were destroyed.
3 You push away every thought of coming disaster,
but your actions only bring the day of judgment closer.
4 How terrible for you who sprawl on ivory beds
and lounge on your couches,
eating the meat of tender lambs from the flock
and of choice calves fattened in the stall.
5 You sing trivial songs to the sound of the harp
and fancy yourselves to be great musicians like David.

Am 5:26-27 Greek version reads *No, you carried your pagan gods—the shrine of Molech, the star of your god Rephan, and the images you made for yourselves. So I will send you into exile, to a land east of Damascus.* Compare Acts 7:43. **Am 6:1** Hebrew *in Zion.*

Amos 5:16 Failure to honor the dead was considered horrible in Israel, so loud weeping was common at funerals. Paid mourners, usually women, cried and mourned loudly with dirges and eulogies. Amos said there would be so many funerals that there would be a shortage of professional mourners, so farmers would be called from the fields to help (see also Jer 9:17-20).

Amos 5:18 Here "the day of the LORD" means the imminent destruction by the Assyrian army as well as the future day of God's judgment. For the faithful, "the day of the LORD" will be glorious, but for the unfaithful it will be a day of darkness and doom. (See Joel 1:15 for more discussion of the Day of the Lord.)

Amos 5:18-24 These people were calling for the Day of the Lord, thinking it would bring an end to their troubles. But God said, "You have no idea what you are wishing for." This "day of the LORD" would bring justice, and justice would bring the punishment the people deserved for their sins.

Amos 5:21-23 God hates worship by people who go through the motions only for show. If we are living sinful lives and using religious rituals and traditions to make ourselves look good, God will despise our worship and not accept what we offer. He wants sincere hearts, not praise from hypocrites. When you worship at church, are you more concerned about your image or your attitude toward God?

Amos 5:26 In days past, Israel had turned to worshiping stars and planets, preferring nature over nature's God (2 Kgs 23:4-5). Pagan religion allowed them to indulge in sexual immorality and to become wealthy through any means possible. Because they refused to worship and obey the one true God, they would cause their own destruction.

Amos 5:27 Israel's captivity was indeed to a land east of Damascus—the people were taken to Assyria. God's punishment was more than defeat; it was complete exile from their homeland.

Amos 6:1-6 Amos leveled his attack at those living in complacency and luxury in both Israel and Judah. Great wealth and comfortable lifestyles may make people think they are secure, but God is not pleased if we isolate ourselves from others' needs. God wants us to care for others as he cares for us. His Kingdom has no place for selfishness or indifference. We must learn to put the needs of others before our wants. Using our wealth to help others is one way to guard against pride and complacency.

Amos 6:2 Great cities to the east, north, and west had been destroyed because of their pride. What happened to them would happen to Israel because Israel's sin was just as great as theirs.

Amos 6:4 Ivory was an imported luxury, rare and extremely expensive. Even a small amount of ivory symbolized wealth. Something as extravagant as a bed inlaid with ivory shows the gross waste of resources that should have been used to help the poor.

6 You drink wine by the bowlful
and perfume yourselves with fragrant lotions.
You care nothing about the ruin of your nation.*
7 Therefore, you will be the first to be led away as captives.
Suddenly, all your parties will end.

8 The Sovereign LORD has sworn by his own name,
and this is what he, the LORD God of Heaven's Armies, says:

"I despise the arrogance of Israel,*
and I hate their fortresses.
I will give this city
and everything in it to their enemies."

9 (If there are ten men left in one house, they will all die.
10 And when a relative who is responsible to dispose of
the dead* goes into the house to carry out the bodies,
he will ask the last survivor, "Is anyone else with you?"
When the person begins to swear, "No, by . . . ," he will
interrupt and say, "Stop! Don't even mention the name
of the LORD.")

11 When the LORD gives the command,
homes both great and small will be smashed to pieces.

12 Can horses gallop over boulders?
Can oxen be used to plow them?
But that's how foolish you are when you turn justice into poison
and the sweet fruit of righteousness into bitterness.
13 And you brag about your conquest of Lo-debar.*
You boast, "Didn't we take Karnaim* by our own strength?"

14 "O people of Israel, I am about to bring an enemy nation against you,"
says the LORD God of Heaven's Armies.
"They will oppress you throughout your land—
from Lebo-hamath in the north
to the Arabah Valley in the south."

Am 6:6 Hebrew *of Joseph.* **Am 6:8** Hebrew *Jacob.* See note on 3:13. **Am 6:10** Or *to burn the dead.* The meaning of the Hebrew is uncertain. **Am 6:13a** *Lo-debar* means "nothing." **Am 6:13b** *Karnaim* means "horns," a term that symbolizes strength.

Amos 6:8-11 The people had built luxurious homes to flaunt their achievements. While it is not wrong to live in comfortable houses, we must not let them become sources of inflated pride and self-glorification. God gave our homes to us, and they are to be used for service, not just for show.

Amos 6:10 Amos gives us a picture of God's fearful judgment: The people hesitated to speak God's name, even during a time of grief, for fear that they would attract his attention and be judged also.

Amos 6:13-14 Karnaim was a city north-east of Israel, an insignificant border town compared to the nation they were about to face, Assyria. Lebo-hamath was to the north, and the Arabah Valley to the south. The entire nation would be destroyed by Assyria (2 Kgs 17).

"I want to see a mighty flood of justice, an endless river of righteous living."
Amos 5:24

3. VISIONS OF JUDGMENT

Amos gives five different visions pertaining to the judgment of God against his people, but he ends with a note of hope for restoration. God's judgment ultimately aims at bringing about repentance and renewal in relationship with him.

A Vision of Locusts

AMOS 7:1-3

The Sovereign LORD showed me a vision. I saw him
preparing to send a vast swarm of locusts over the
land. This was after the king's share had been harvested from the fields and as the main crop was coming up. 2In my vision the locusts ate every green plant
in sight. Then I said, "O Sovereign LORD, please forgive
us or we will not survive, for Israel* is so small."
3So the LORD relented from this plan. "I will not
do it," he said.

A Vision of Fire

AMOS 7:4-6

Then the Sovereign LORD showed me another vision.
I saw him preparing to punish his people with a great
fire. The fire had burned up the depths of the sea and
was devouring the entire land. 5Then I said, "O Sovereign LORD, please stop or we will not survive, for
Israel is so small."
6Then the LORD relented from this plan, too. "I will
not do that either," said the Sovereign LORD.

A Vision of a Plumb Line

AMOS 7:7-9

Then he showed me another vision. I saw the Lord
standing beside a wall that had been built using a
plumb line. He was using a plumb line to see if it was
still straight. 8And the LORD said to me, "Amos, what
do you see?"
I answered, "A plumb line."
And the Lord replied, "I will test my people with this
plumb line. I will no longer ignore all their sins. 9The
pagan shrines of your ancestors* will be ruined, and
the temples of Israel will be destroyed; I will bring the
dynasty of King Jeroboam to a sudden end."

Amos and Amaziah

AMOS 7:10-17

Then Amaziah, the priest of Bethel, sent a message
to Jeroboam, king of Israel: "Amos is hatching a plot
against you right here on your very doorstep! What he
is saying is intolerable. 11He is saying, 'Jeroboam will
soon be killed, and the people of Israel will be sent
away into exile.'"
12Then Amaziah sent orders to Amos: "Get out of
here, you prophet! Go on back to the land of Judah, and
earn your living by prophesying there! 13Don't bother
us with your prophecies here in Bethel. This is the
king's sanctuary and the national place of worship!"
14But Amos replied, "I'm not a professional prophet,
and I was never trained to be one.* I'm just a shepherd,
and I take care of sycamore-fig trees. 15But the LORD
called me away from my flock and told me, 'Go and

Am 7:2 Hebrew *Jacob;* also in 7:5. See note on 3:13. **Am 7:9** Hebrew *of Isaac.* **Am 7:14** Or *I'm not a prophet nor the son of a prophet.*

Amos 7:1ff The following series of visions conveyed God's message to the people, using images that were familiar to them—locusts, fire, and a plumb line.

Amos 7:1-6 Twice Amos was shown a vision of Israel's impending punishment, and his immediate response was to pray that God would spare Israel. Prayer is a powerful privilege. Amos's prayers should remind us to pray for our nation.

Amos 7:7-9 A plumb line is a device used to ensure the straightness of a wall. A wall that is not straight will eventually collapse. God wants people to be right with him; he wants the sin that makes us crooked removed immediately. God's Word is the plumb line that helps us be aware of our sin. How do you measure up to God's plumb line?

Amos 7:10 Prophets like Amos were often seen as traitors and conspirators because they spoke out against the king and his advisers, questioning their authority and exposing their sin. The kings often saw the prophets as enemies rather than as God's spokesmen who were really trying to help them and the nation.

Amos 7:10ff Amaziah was the chief priest in Bethel, representing Israel's official religion. He was not concerned about hearing God's message; he was only worried about his own position, and maintaining it was more important than listening to the truth. Don't let your desire for prestige, authority, or money keep you tied to a job or position you should leave. Don't let anything come between you and obeying God.

Amos 7:14-15 Without any special preparation, education, or upbringing, Amos obeyed God's call to "go and prophesy to my people in Israel." Obedience is the test of a

AMOS'S VISIONS

Amos had a series of visions concerning God's judgment on Israel. God was planning to judge Israel by sending a swarm of locusts or by sending fire. In spite of Amos's intercession on Israel's behalf, God would still carry out his judgment because Israel persisted in disobedience.

Vision/Reference	*Significance*
Swarm of locusts Amos 7:1-3	God was preparing punishment, which he delayed only because of Amos's intervention.
Fire Amos 7:4-6	God was preparing to devour the land, but Amos intervened on behalf of the people.
Wall and plumb line Amos 7:7-9	God would see if the people were crooked, and if they were, he would punish them.
Basket of ripe fruit Amos 8:1ff	The people were ripe for punishment; though once beautiful, they were now rotten.
God standing by the altar Amos 9:1ff	Punishment was executed.

prophesy to my people in Israel.' 16Now then, listen to
this message from the LORD:

"You say,
'Don't prophesy against Israel.
Stop preaching against my people.*'
17 But this is what the LORD says:
'Your wife will become a prostitute in this city,
and your sons and daughters will be killed.
Your land will be divided up,
and you yourself will die in a foreign land.
And the people of Israel will certainly become
captives in exile,
far from their homeland.'"

A Vision of Ripe Fruit

AMOS 8:1-14

Then the Sovereign LORD showed me another vision.
In it I saw a basket filled with ripe fruit. 2"What do
you see, Amos?" he asked.

I replied, "A basket full of ripe fruit."

Then the LORD said, "Like this fruit, Israel is ripe
for punishment! I will not delay their punishment
again. 3In that day the singing in the Temple will turn
to wailing. Dead bodies will be scattered everywhere.
They will be carried out of the city in silence. I, the
Sovereign LORD, have spoken!"

4 Listen to this, you who rob the poor
and trample down the needy!
5 You can't wait for the Sabbath day to be over
and the religious festivals to end
so you can get back to cheating the helpless.
You measure out grain with dishonest
measures
and cheat the buyer with dishonest scales.*
6 And you mix the grain you sell
with chaff swept from the floor.
Then you enslave poor people
for one piece of silver or a pair of sandals.

7 Now the LORD has sworn this oath
by his own name, the Pride of Israel*:
"I will never forget
the wicked things you have done!
8 The earth will tremble for your deeds,
and everyone will mourn.
The ground will rise like the Nile River
at floodtime;
it will heave up, then sink again.

9 "In that day," says the Sovereign LORD,
"I will make the sun go down at noon
and darken the earth while it is still day.
10 I will turn your celebrations into times of
mourning
and your singing into weeping.
You will wear funeral clothes
and shave your heads to show your
sorrow—
as if your only son had died.
How very bitter that day will be!

11 "The time is surely coming," says the Sovereign
LORD,
"when I will send a famine on the land—
not a famine of bread or water
but of hearing the words of the LORD.
12 People will stagger from sea to sea
and wander from border to border*
searching for the word of the LORD,
but they will not find it.
13 Beautiful girls and strong young men
will grow faint in that day,
thirsting for the LORD's word.
14 And those who swear by the shameful idols
of Samaria—
who take oaths in the name of the god of Dan
and make vows in the name of the god of
Beersheba*—
they will all fall down,
never to rise again."

A Vision of God at the Altar

AMOS 9:1-10

Then I saw a vision of the Lord standing beside the
altar. He said,

"Strike the tops of the Temple columns,
so that the foundation will shake.

Am 7:16 Hebrew *against the house of Isaac.* **Am 8:5** Hebrew *You make the ephah* [a unit for measuring grain] *small and the shekel* [a unit of weight] *great, and you deal falsely by using deceitful balances.* **Am 8:7** Hebrew *the pride of Jacob.* See note on 3:13. **Am 8:12** Hebrew *from north to east.* **Am 8:14** Hebrew *the way of Beersheba.*

faithful servant of God. Are you obeying God's call to you?

Amos 8:5-6 These merchants were keeping the religious festivals, but not with a right spirit. They couldn't wait for the holy days and Sabbaths to be over so they could go back to making money. Their real interest was in enriching themselves, even if that meant cheating (shortchanging the quantity while boosting the price, or even selling chaff as wheat). Do you take a day to rest and worship God at least once a week, or is making money more important to you than anything else? When you give time to God, is your heart in your worship? Or is your religion only a front for unethical practices?

Amos 8:11-13 The people had no appetite for God's word when prophets like Amos brought it. Because of their apathy, God said he would take away even the opportunity to hear his word. We have God's Word, the Bible. But many still look everywhere except in Scripture for answers to life's problems. You can help them by directing them to the Bible, showing them the parts that speak to their special needs and questions. God's Word is available to us. Let us help people know it before a time comes when they cannot find it.

Amos 9:1 Judgment would begin at the altar, the center of the nation's life, the place where the people expected protection and blessing. This judgment would cover all 12 tribes. Commentators disagree concerning this altar. Some think it was the altar at Bethel; more likely it was the altar in the Temple in Jerusalem. God would destroy their base of security in order to bring them to himself. But he also promises to restore his renewed people and their broken world (Amos 9:11).

▸ **AMOS 9:1-10** ***(cont.)***

Bring down the roof
on the heads of the people below.
I will kill with the sword those who survive.
No one will escape!

2 "Even if they dig down to the place of the dead,*
I will reach down and pull them up.
Even if they climb up into the heavens,
I will bring them down.
3 Even if they hide at the very top of Mount Carmel,
I will search them out and capture them.
Even if they hide at the bottom of the ocean,
I will send the sea serpent after them to bite them.
4 Even if their enemies drive them into exile,
I will command the sword to kill them there.
I am determined to bring disaster upon them
and not to help them."

5 The Lord, the LORD of Heaven's Armies,
touches the land and it melts,
and all its people mourn.
The ground rises like the Nile River at floodtime,
and then it sinks again.
6 The LORD's home reaches up to the heavens,
while its foundation is on the earth.
He draws up water from the oceans
and pours it down as rain on the land.
The LORD is his name!

7 "Are you Israelites more important to me
than the Ethiopians?*" asks the LORD.
"I brought Israel out of Egypt,
but I also brought the Philistines from Crete*
and led the Arameans out of Kir.

8 "I, the Sovereign LORD,
am watching this sinful nation of Israel.
I will destroy it
from the face of the earth.
But I will never completely destroy the family of Israel,*"
says the LORD.
9 "For I will give the command
and will shake Israel along with the other nations
as grain is shaken in a sieve,
yet not one true kernel will be lost.
10 But all the sinners will die by the sword—
all those who say, 'Nothing bad will happen to us.'

A Promise of Restoration

AMOS 9:11-15

11 "In that day I will restore the fallen house*
of David.
I will repair its damaged walls.
From the ruins I will rebuild it
and restore its former glory.
12 And Israel will possess what is left of Edom
and all the nations I have called to be mine.*"
The LORD has spoken,
and he will do these things.

Am 9:2 Hebrew *to Sheol.* **Am 9:7a** Hebrew *the Cushites?* **Am 9:7b** Hebrew *Caphtor.* **Am 9:8** Hebrew *the house of Jacob.* See note on 3:13. **Am 9:11a** Or *kingdom;* Hebrew reads *tent.* **Am 9:11b-12** Greek version reads *and restore its former glory, / so that the rest of humanity, including the Gentiles— / all those I have called to be mine—might seek me.* Compare Acts 15:16-17.

753 BC Legendary date for founding of Rome

Amos 9:2-4 The "place of the dead" was the grave. The grave and Mount Carmel were symbols of inaccessibility. No one can escape God's judgment. This was good news for the faithful but bad news for the unfaithful. Whether we go to the mountaintops or the bottom of the sea, God will find us and judge us for our deeds. Amos pictured the judgment of the wicked as a sea serpent, relentlessly pursuing the condemned. For God's faithful followers, the judgment brings a new earth of peace and prosperity. Does God's judgment sound like good news or bad news to you?

Amos 9:7 Ethiopia, south of Egypt, was a remote and exotic land to the Israelites. Crete was where the Philistines lived as they migrated to Palestine. God would judge Israel no differently than he judges foreign nations. He is not the God of Israel only; he is God of the universe, and he controls all nations.

Amos 9:8 Amos assured the Israelites that God would "never completely destroy" Israel—in other words, the punishment would not be permanent or total. God wants to redeem, not punish. But when punishment is necessary, he doesn't withhold it. Like a loving father, God disciplines those he loves in order to correct them. If God disciplines you, accept it as a sign of his love.

Amos 9:8-9 Although Assyria would destroy Israel and take the people into exile, some would be preserved. This exile had been predicted hundreds of years earlier (Deut 28:63-68). Although the nation would be purified through this invasion and captivity, not one true believer would be eternally lost. Our system of justice is not perfect, but God's is. Sinners will not get away, and the faithful will not be forgotten. True believers will not be lost.

Amos 9:11-12 In the punishment, the house of David was reduced to a "fallen house." God's covenant with David stated that one of David's descendants would always sit on his throne (2 Sam 7:12-16). The Exile made this promise seem impossible. But "in that day" God would raise up and restore the kingdom to its promised glory. This was a promise to both Israel and Judah; it would not be fulfilled by an earthly, political ruler but by the Messiah, who would renew the spiritual Kingdom and rule forever.

James quoted these verses (Acts 15:16-17), finding the promise fulfilled in Christ's resurrection and in the presence of both Jews and Gentiles in the church. "Possess what is left of Edom" envisions the messianic Kingdom, which will be universal and include Gentiles. When God brings in the Gentiles, he is restoring the ruins. After the Gentiles are called together, God will renew and restore the fortunes of the new Israel. All the land that was once under David's rule will again be part of God's nation.

Amos 9:13 This verse describes a time of such an abundance of crops that the people won't be able to harvest them all.

Amos 9:13-15 The Jews of Amos's day had lost sight of God's love for them and his purpose for calling them. The rich were carefree and comfortable, refusing to help others in need. They observed their religious rituals in hopes of appeasing God, but they did not truly love him. Amos announced God's warnings of destruction for their evil ways.

We must not assume that going to church and being good are enough. God expects our belief in him to affect all areas of our conduct and to extend to all people and circumstances. We should let Amos's words inspire us to live faithfully according to God's desires.

13 "The time will come," says the LORD,
"when the grain and grapes will grow faster
than they can be harvested.
Then the terraced vineyards on the hills of Israel
will drip with sweet wine!
14 I will bring my exiled people of Israel
back from distant lands,
and they will rebuild their ruined cities
and live in them again.
They will plant vineyards and gardens;
they will eat their crops and drink their wine.
15 I will firmly plant them there
in their own land.
They will never again be uprooted
from the land I have given them,"
says the LORD your God.

G. The Era of the Northern Kingdom's Collapse

The northern kingdom of Israel, coming to the end of the most peaceful and stable dynasty in its history, begins to show the early signs of collapse. The promises of God's judgment from prophets like Amos begin to come into focus during this era, while the great prophets Isaiah and Micah begin their ministries in the southern kingdom of Judah.

1. STRUGGLE FOR POWER IN THE NORTHERN KINGDOM

The long and prosperous dynasty of Jehu in the northern kingdom of Israel unravels. The final king in Jehu's line, Zechariah, is assassinated by Shallum. Shallum is just the first challenger to the throne. Shortly after he took power, Menahem killed him and seized control of the kingdom. Twelve years later, Pekah murdered Menahem's son Pekahiah to ascend to the throne. Israel was crumbling from within, as they were being threatened from outside by other nations and the imminent threat of God's judgment.

The End of Jeroboam II's Reign in Israel

2 KINGS 14:28-29

The rest of the events in the reign of Jeroboam II and
everything he did—including the extent of his power,
his wars, and how he recovered for Israel both Damascus
and Hamath, which had belonged to Judah*—are
recorded in *The Book of the History of the Kings of
Israel.* 29When Jeroboam II died, he was buried in Samaria*
with the kings of Israel. Then his son Zechariah
became the next king.

Zechariah Rules in Israel

2 KINGS 15:8-12

Zechariah son of Jeroboam II began to rule over Israel
in the thirty-eighth year of King Uzziah's reign in
Judah. He reigned in Samaria six months. 9Zechariah
did what was evil in the LORD's sight, as his ancestors
had done. He refused to turn from the sins
that Jeroboam son of Nebat had led Israel to commit.
10Then Shallum son of Jabesh conspired against
Zechariah, assassinated him in public,* and became
the next king.

11The rest of the events in Zechariah's reign are
recorded in *The Book of the History of the Kings of Israel.*
12So the LORD's message to Jehu came true: "Your
descendants will be kings of Israel down to the fourth
generation."

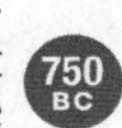

Earliest musical notation in Greece

Shallum Rules in Israel

2 KINGS 15:13-15

Shallum son of Jabesh began to rule over Israel in
the thirty-ninth year of King Uzziah's reign in Judah.
Shallum reigned in Samaria only one month.
14Then Menahem son of Gadi went to Samaria from
Tirzah and assassinated him, and he became the
next king.

2 Kgs 14:28 Or *to Yaudi.* The meaning of the Hebrew is uncertain. **2 Kgs 14:29** As in some Greek manuscripts; Hebrew lacks *he was buried in Samaria.* **2 Kgs 15:10** Or *at Ibleam.*

2 Kgs 14:28 Jeroboam II had no devotion to God, yet under his warlike policies and skillful administration, Israel enjoyed more national power and material prosperity than at any time since the days of Solomon. The prophets Amos and Hosea, however, tell us what was really happening within the kingdom (Hos 13:4-8; Amos 6:11-14). Jeroboam's administration ignored policies of justice and fairness. As a result, the rich became richer, and the poor, poorer. The people became self-centered, relying more on their power, security, and possessions than on God. The poor were so oppressed that it was hard for them to believe God noticed their plight. Material prosperity is not always an indication of God's blessing. It can also be a result of self-centeredness. If you are experiencing prosperity, remember that God holds us accountable for how we attain success and how we use our wealth. Everything we have really belongs to him. We must use God's gifts with his interests in mind.

2 Kgs 15:8 Zechariah was an evil king because he encouraged Israel to sin by worshiping idols. Sin in our lives is serious. But it is even more serious to encourage others to disobey God. We are responsible for the way we influence others. Beware of double sins: ones that not only hurt us but also hurt others by encouraging them to sin.

2 Kgs 15:10 The prophet Amos warned Zechariah of his impending death and the subsequent end of Jeroboam's dynasty (Amos 7:9).

2 Kgs 15:14 Ancient historical documents say that Menahem was the commander in chief of Jeroboam's army (see 2 Kgs 14:23-29 for an account of Jeroboam II's reign). After Jeroboam's son Zechariah was assassinated (2 Kgs 15:8-10), Menahem probably saw himself, not Shallum, as the rightful successor to Israel's throne.

▸ 2 KINGS 15:13-15 *(cont.)*

15The rest of the events in Shallum's reign, including his conspiracy, are recorded in *The Book of the History of the Kings of Israel.*

Menahem Rules in Israel

2 KINGS 15:16-22

At that time Menahem destroyed the town of Tappuah* and all the surrounding countryside as far as Tirzah, because its citizens refused to surrender the town. He killed the entire population and ripped open the pregnant women.

17Menahem son of Gadi began to rule over Israel in
the thirty-ninth year of King Uzziah's reign in Judah.
He reigned in Samaria ten years. 18But Menahem did
what was evil in the LORD's sight. During his entire reign, he refused to turn from the sins that Jeroboam son of Nebat had led Israel to commit.

19Then King Tiglath-pileser* of Assyria invaded
the land. But Menahem paid him thirty-seven tons* of silver to gain his support in tightening his grip on
royal power. 20Menahem extorted the money from
the rich of Israel, demanding that each of them pay fifty pieces* of silver to the king of Assyria. So the king of Assyria turned from attacking Israel and did not stay in the land.

21The rest of the events in Menahem's reign and everything he did are recorded in *The Book of the History of the Kings of Israel.*
22When Menahem died, his
son Pekahiah became the next king.

Pekahiah Rules in Israel

2 KINGS 15:23-26

Pekahiah son of Menahem began to rule over Israel in the fiftieth year of King Uzziah's reign in Judah. He
reigned in Samaria two years. 24But Pekahiah did what
was evil in the LORD's sight. He refused to turn from the sins that Jeroboam son of Nebat had led Israel to commit.

25Then Pekah son of Remaliah, the commander of Pekahiah's army, conspired against him. With fifty men from Gilead, Pekah assassinated the king, along with Argob and Arieh, in the citadel of the palace at Samaria. And Pekah reigned in his place.

26The rest of the events in Pekahiah's reign and everything he did are recorded in *The Book of the History of the Kings of Israel.*

Pekah Rules in Israel

2 KINGS 15:27-29

Pekah son of Remaliah began to rule over Israel in the fifty-second year of King Uzziah's reign in Judah. He
reigned in Samaria twenty years. 28But Pekah did what
was evil in the LORD's sight. He refused to turn from the sins that Jeroboam son of Nebat had led Israel to commit.

29During Pekah's reign, King Tiglath-pileser of Assyria attacked Israel again, and he captured the towns of Ijon, Abel-beth-maacah, Janoah, Kedesh, and Hazor. He also conquered the regions of Gilead, Galilee, and all of Naphtali, and he took the people to Assyria as captives.

2 Kgs 15:16 As in some Greek manuscripts; other Greek manuscripts read *at Ibleam.* Hebrew reads *Tiphsah.* **2 Kgs 15:19a** Hebrew *Pul,* another name for Tiglath-pileser. **2 Kgs 15:19b** Hebrew *1,000 talents* [34 metric tons]. **2 Kgs 15:20** Hebrew *50 shekels* [20 ounces, or 570 grams].

2. THE MINISTRIES OF ISAIAH AND MICAH BEGIN

Micah and Isaiah began their long prophetic ministries during the turbulent era of the collapse of the northern kingdom of Israel. Both of them spent most of their prophetic energies in the southern kingdom of Judah, but the spiritual condition of both kingdoms was important to both prophets. God used these two men to speak to his people in their time, but they also left us records of their prophecies that are meant to encourage and challenge us today as well.

The End of Uzziah's Reign in Judah PARALLEL

2 KINGS 15:6-7

The rest of the events in Uzziah's reign and everything he did are recorded in *The Book of the History of the Kings of Judah.*
7When Uzziah died, he was buried with his ancestors in the City of David. And his son Jotham became the next king.

2 CHRONICLES 26:22-23

The rest of the events of Uzziah's reign, from beginning to end, are recorded by the prophet Isaiah
son of Amoz. 23When Uzziah died, he was buried

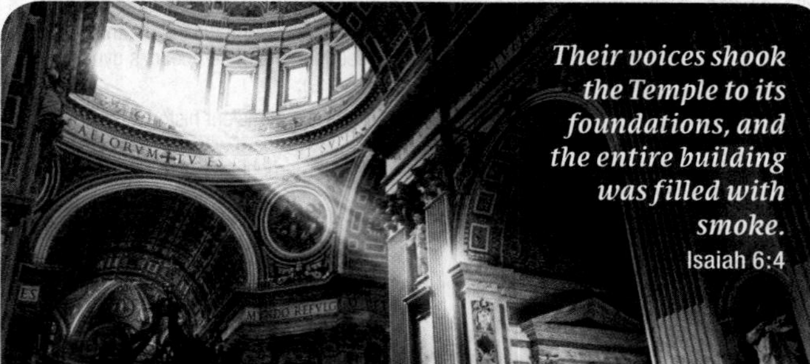

Their voices shook the Temple to its foundations, and the entire building was filled with smoke.
Isaiah 6:4

2 Kgs 15:18 Menahem, like the kings before him, led his people into sin: He "did what was evil in the LORD's sight." What a horrible epitaph for a leader! Leaders profoundly affect the people they serve. They can either encourage or discourage devotion to God both by their example and by the structure they give their organization. Good leaders do not put up obstacles to faith in God or to right living.

2 Kgs 15:19-20 When King Tiglath-pileser took the throne of Assyria, the Assyrian Empire

with his ancestors; his grave was in a nearby burial field belonging to the kings, for the people said, "He had leprosy." And his son Jotham became the next king.

Isaiah's Cleansing and Call

ISAIAH 6:1-13

It was in the year King Uzziah died* that I saw the Lord. He was sitting on a lofty throne, and the train of his robe filled the Temple. 2Attending him were mighty seraphim, each having six wings. With two wings they covered their faces, with two they covered their feet, and with two they flew. 3They were calling out to each other,

"Holy, holy, holy is the LORD of Heaven's Armies!
The whole earth is filled with his glory!"

4Their voices shook the Temple to its foundations, and the entire building was filled with smoke.

Is 6:1 King Uzziah died in 740 B.C.

ISAIAH

Trees and prophets share at least one important characteristic—both are planted for the future. Yet seedlings are often overlooked and prophets often ignored. Isaiah is one of the best examples of this. The people of his time could have been rescued by his words. Instead, they refused to believe him. With the passing of centuries, however, Isaiah's words have cast a shadow on all of history. • Isaiah was active as a prophet during the reigns of five kings, but he did not set out to be a prophet. By the time King Uzziah died, Isaiah may have been established as a scribe in the royal palace in Jerusalem. It was a respectable career, but God had other plans for his servant. Isaiah's account of God's call leaves little doubt about what motivated the prophet for the next half century. His vision of God was unforgettable. • His encounter with God permanently affected Isaiah's character. He reflected the God he represented. Isaiah's messages—some comforting, some confronting—are so dissimilar that some have guessed they came from different authors. Isaiah's testimony is that the messages came from the only one capable of being perfect in justice as well as in mercy—God himself. • When he called Isaiah as a prophet, God did not encourage him with predictions of great success. God told Isaiah that the people would not listen. But he was to speak and write his messages anyway because eventually some *would* listen. God compared his people to a tree that would have to be cut down so that a new tree could grow from the old stump (Isa 6:13). • We who are part of that future can see that many of the promises God gave through Isaiah have been fulfilled in Jesus Christ. We also gain the hope of knowing that God is active in all of history, including our own.

Strengths and accomplishments	• Considered the greatest Old Testament prophet • Quoted at least 50 times in the New Testament • Brought powerful messages of both judgment and hope • Carried out a consistent ministry even though there was little positive response from his listeners • His ministry spanned the reigns of five kings of Judah
Lessons from his life	• God's help is needed in order to comfort people while effectively confronting sin • One result of experiencing forgiveness is the desire to share that forgiveness with others • God is purely and perfectly holy, just, and loving
Vital statistics	• Where: Jerusalem • Occupations: Scribe, prophet • Relatives: Father: Amoz. Sons: Shear-jashub, Maher-shalal-hash-baz. • Contemporaries: Uzziah, Jotham, Ahaz, Hezekiah, Manasseh, Micah
Key verse	"Then I heard the Lord asking, 'Whom should I send as a messenger to this people? Who will go for us?' I said, 'Here I am. Send me'" (Isa 6:8).

Isaiah's story is told in 2 Kings 19:2–20:19. He is also mentioned in 2 Chronicles 26:22; 32:20, 32; Matthew 3:3; 8:17; 12:17-21; John 12:38-41; Romans 10:16, 20-21.

was becoming a world power, and the nations of Aram, Israel, and Judah were in decline. This is the first mention of Assyria in 2 Kings. Tiglath-pileser's invasion occurred in 743 B.C. Assyria made Israel a vassal state, and Menahem was forced to pay tribute to Assyria. This was the first of three Assyrian invasions (2 Kgs 15:29; 17:6 tell of the others).

Isa 6:1 The year that King Uzziah died was approximately 740 B.C. He remained leprous until he died because he tried to take over the high priest's duties (2 Chr 26:18-21). Although Uzziah was generally a good king with a long and prosperous reign, many of his people turned away from God.

Isa 6:1ff Isaiah's vision was his commission to be God's messenger to his people. Isaiah was given a difficult mission. He had to tell people who believed they were blessed by God that God was going to destroy them because of their disobedience.

Isaiah begins his ministry

Isa 6:1ff Isaiah's lofty view of God in Isaiah 6:1-4 gives us a sense of God's greatness, mystery, and power. Isaiah's example of recognizing his sinfulness before God encourages us to confess our sin. His picture of forgiveness reminds us that we, too, are forgiven. When we recognize how great our God is, how sinful we are, and the extent of God's forgiveness, we receive power to do his work. How does your concept of the greatness of God measure up to Isaiah's?

Isa 6:1-3 The throne, the attending seraphim (angels), and the threefold *holy* all stressed God's holiness. Seraphim were a type of angel whose name is derived from the word for "burn," perhaps indicating their purity as God's ministers. In a time when moral and spiritual decay had peaked, it was important for Isaiah to see God in his holiness. *Holiness* means "morally perfect, pure, and set apart from all sin." We also need to discover God's holiness. Our daily frustrations, society's pressures, and our shortcomings narrow our view of God. We need the Bible's view of God as high and lifted up to empower us to deal with our problems and concerns. God's moral perfection, properly seen, will purify us from sin, cleanse our mind of our problems and put them into perspective, and enable us to worship and to serve him.

▸ ISAIAH 6:1-13 ***(cont.)***

5Then I said, "It's all over! I am doomed, for I am a sinful man. I have filthy lips, and I live among a people with filthy lips. Yet I have seen the King, the LORD of Heaven's Armies."

6Then one of the seraphim flew to me with a burning coal he had taken from the altar with a pair of tongs. 7He touched my lips with it and said, "See, this coal has touched your lips. Now your guilt is removed, and your sins are forgiven."

Isa 6:5-8 Seeing the Lord and listening to the praise of the angels, Isaiah realized that he was sinful before God, with no hope of measuring up to God's standard of holiness. When Isaiah's lips were touched with a live burning coal, he was told that his sins were forgiven. It wasn't the coal that cleansed him, but God. In response, Isaiah submitted himself entirely to God's service. No matter how difficult his task would be, he said, "Here I am. Send me." The painful cleansing process was necessary before Isaiah could fulfill the task to which God was calling him. Before we accept God's call to speak for him to those around us, we must be cleansed as Isaiah was, confessing our sins and submitting to God's control. Letting God purify us may be painful, but we must be purified so that we can truly represent God, who is pure and holy.

Isa 6:8 The more clearly Isaiah saw God (Isa 6:5), the more aware Isaiah became of his own powerlessness and inadequacy to do anything of lasting value without God. But

WHO WERE THESE PROPHETS?

"Again and again the LORD had sent his prophets and seers to warn both Israel and Judah: 'Turn from all your evil ways. Obey my commands and decrees . . .'" (2 Kgs 17:13). Who were these prophets? Here are some of those who tried to turn people back to God. Predicting the future as revealed by God was just one part of a prophet's job; his main role was to preach God's word to the people—warning, instructing, and encouraging them to live as they ought.

Who?	*When? (B.C.)*	*Ministered During the Reign of these Kings*	*Main message*	*Significance*
AHIJAH	934–909	Jeroboam I of Israel (1 Kgs 11:29-39)	Israel would split in two, and God had chosen Jeroboam to lead the 10 tribes. Warned him to remain obedient to God.	We should not take lightly our God-given responsibilities. Jeroboam did and lost his kingdom.
ELIJAH	875–848	Ahab of Israel (1 Kgs 17:1—2 Kings 2:11)	In fiery style, urged wicked Ahab to turn back to God. Proved on Mount Carmel who the one true God is (1 Kgs 18).	Even giants of faith can't force sinners to change. But those who remain faithful to God have a great impact for him.
MICAIAH	865–853	Ahab of Israel, Jehoshaphat of Judah (1 Kgs 22:8; 2 Chr 18:28)	Ahab would be unsuccessful in fighting the Arameans.	It is foolish to move ahead with plans that are contrary to God's Word.
JEHU	853	Jehoshaphat of Judah (2 Chr 19:1-3)	Jehoshaphat should never have allied himself with wicked Ahab.	Partnerships with immoral people can lead us into trouble.
ELISHA	848–797	Joram, Jehu, Jehoahaz, and Jehoash, all of Israel (2 Kgs 2:1–9:1; 13:10-21)	Expressed by his actions the importance of helping ordinary people in need.	God is concerned about the everyday needs of his people.
JONAH	793–753	Jeroboam II of Israel (2 Kgs 14:25; the book of Jonah)	Warned Nineveh, the capital of Assyria, to repent of its sins.	God wants all nations to turn to him. His love reaches out to all peoples.
AMOS	760–750	Jeroboam II of Israel (the book of Amos)	Warned those who exploited or ignored the needy. (In Amos's day, Israel was an affluent and materialistic society.)	Believing in God is more than a personal matter. God calls all believers to work against injustices in society and to aid those less fortunate.
HOSEA	753–715	The last seven kings of Israel; Uzziah, Jotham, Ahaz, and Hezekiah of Judah (the book of Hosea)	Condemned the people of Israel because they had sinned against God as an adulterous woman sins against her husband.	When we sin, we sever our relationship with God, breaking our commitment to him. While all must answer to God for their sins, those who seek God's forgiveness are spared from eternal judgment.
MICAH	742–687	Jotham, Ahaz, and Hezekiah of Judah (the book of Micah)	Predicted the fall of both the northern and southern kingdoms. This was God's discipline on the people, actually showing how much he cared for them.	Choosing to live a life apart from God is making a commitment to sin. Sin leads to judgment and death. God alone shows us the way to eternal peace. His discipline often keeps us on the right path.

8 Then I heard the Lord asking, "Whom should I send
as a messenger to this people? Who will go for us?"
I said, "Here I am. Send me."
9 And he said, "Yes, go, and say to this people,

'Listen carefully, but do not understand.
Watch closely, but learn nothing.'
10 Harden the hearts of these people.
Plug their ears and shut their eyes.
That way, they will not see with their eyes,
nor hear with their ears,
nor understand with their hearts
and turn to me for healing."*

Is 6:9-10 Greek version reads *And he said, "Go and say to this people, / 'When you hear what I say, you will not understand. / When you see what I do, you will not comprehend.' / For the hearts of these people are hardened, / and their ears cannot hear, and they have closed their eyes— / so their eyes cannot see, / and their ears cannot hear, / and their hearts cannot understand, / and they cannot turn to me and let me heal them."* Compare Matt 13:14-15; Mark 4:12; Luke 8:10; Acts 28:26-27.

he was willing to be God's spokesman. When God calls, will you also say, "Send me"?

Isa 6:9-13 God told Isaiah that the people would listen but not learn from his message because their hearts had become hardened beyond repentance. God's patience with their chronic rebellion was finally exhausted. His judgment was to abandon them to their rebellion and hardness of heart. Why did God send Isaiah if he knew the people wouldn't listen? Although the nation itself would not repent and would reap judgment, some individuals

Who?	*When? (B.C.)*	*Ministered During the Reign of these Kings*	*Main message*	*Significance*
ISAIAH	740–681	Uzziah, Jotham, Ahaz, Hezekiah, and Manasseh of Judah (the book of Isaiah)	Called the people back to a special relationship with God—although judgment through other nations was inevitable.	Sometimes we must suffer judgment and discipline before we are restored to God.
NAHUM	663–654	Manasseh of Judah (the book of Nahum)	The mighty empire of Assyria that oppressed God's people would soon tumble.	Those who do evil and oppress others will one day meet a bitter end.
ZEPHANIAH	640–621	Josiah of Judah (the book of Zephaniah)	A day would come when God, as Judge, would severely punish all nations; but afterward he would show mercy to his people.	We will all be judged for our disobedience to God, but if we remain faithful to him, he will show us mercy.
JEREMIAH	627–586	Josiah, Jehoahaz, Jehoiakim, Jehoiachin, Zedekiah of Judah (the book of Jeremiah)	Repentance would postpone Judah's coming judgment at the hands of Babylon.	Repentance is one of the greatest needs in our world of immorality. God's promises to the faithful shine brightly.
HABAKKUK	612–589	Josiah, Jehoahaz, Jehoiakim, Jehoiachin, Zedekiah of Judah (the book of Habakkuk)	Couldn't understand why God seemed to do nothing about the wickedness in society. Then realized that faith in God alone would one day supply the answer.	Instead of questioning the ways of God, we should realize that he is completely just, and we should have faith that he is in control and that one day evil will be utterly destroyed.
DANIEL	605–536	Prophesied as an exile in Babylon during the reigns of Nebuchadnezzar, Darius the Mede, and Cyrus of Persia (the book of Daniel)	Described both near and distant future events. Through it all, God is sovereign and triumphant.	We should spend less time wondering when the events will happen and more time learning how we should live now so we won't be victims of those events.
EZEKIEL	593–571	Prophesied as an exile in Babylon during the reign of Nebuchadnezzar (the book of Ezekiel)	Sent messages back to Jerusalem urging the people to turn back to God before they were all forced to join him in exile. After Jerusalem fell, he urged his fellow exiles to turn back to God so they could eventually return to their homeland.	God disciplines his people to draw them closer to him.

▸ **ISAIAH 6:1-13 *(cont.)***

[11]Then I said, "Lord, how long will this go on?"
And he replied,

"Until their towns are empty,
their houses are deserted,
and the whole country is a wasteland;
12 until the LORD has sent everyone away,
and the entire land of Israel lies deserted.
13 If even a tenth—a remnant—survive,
it will be invaded again and burned.
But as a terebinth or oak tree leaves a stump
when it is cut down,
so Israel's stump will be a holy seed."

Jotham Rules in Judah PARALLEL

2 KINGS 15:32-38

Jotham son of Uzziah began to rule over Judah in the
second year of King Pekah's reign in Israel. [33]He was
twenty-five years old when he became king, and he
reigned in Jerusalem sixteen years. His mother was
Jerusha, the daughter of Zadok.

[34]Jotham did what was pleasing in the LORD's sight.
He did everything his father, Uzziah, had done. [35]But
he did not destroy the pagan shrines, and the people
still offered sacrifices and burned incense there. He
rebuilt the upper gate of the Temple of the LORD.

[36]The rest of the events in Jotham's reign and everything he did are recorded in *The Book of the History
of the Kings of Judah*. [37]In those days the LORD began
to send King Rezin of Aram and King Pekah of Israel
to attack Judah. [38]When Jotham died, he was buried
with his ancestors in the City of David. And his son
Ahaz became the next king.

2 CHRONICLES 27:1-9

Jotham was twenty-five years old when he became
king, and he reigned in Jerusalem sixteen years. His
mother was Jerusha, the daughter of Zadok.

[2]Jotham did what was pleasing in the LORD's sight.
He did everything his father, Uzziah, had done, except
that Jotham did not sin by entering the Temple of the
LORD. But the people continued in their corrupt ways.

[3]Jotham rebuilt the upper gate of the Temple of
the LORD. He also did extensive rebuilding on the
wall at the hill of Ophel. [4]He built towns in the hill
country of Judah and constructed fortresses and towers in the wooded areas. [5]Jotham went to war against
the Ammonites and conquered them. Over the next
three years he received from them an annual tribute
of 7,500 pounds* of silver, 50,000 bushels of wheat,
and 50,000 bushels of barley.*

[6]King Jotham became powerful because he was
careful to live in obedience to the LORD his God.

[7]The rest of the events of Jotham's reign, including
all his wars and other activities, are recorded in *The
Book of the Kings of Israel and Judah*. [8]He was twenty-
five years old when he became king, and he reigned in
Jerusalem sixteen years. [9]When Jotham died, he was
buried in the City of David. And his son Ahaz became
the next king.

Micah's Grief over Samaria and Jerusalem

MICAH 1:1-16

The LORD gave this message to Micah of Moresheth
during the years when Jotham, Ahaz, and Hezekiah
were kings of Judah. The visions he saw concerned
both Samaria and Jerusalem.

2 Attention! Let all the people of the world listen!
Let the earth and everything in it hear.
The Sovereign LORD is making accusations
against you;
the Lord speaks from his holy Temple.
3 Look! The LORD is coming!
He leaves his throne in heaven
and tramples the heights of the earth.
4 The mountains melt beneath his feet
and flow into the valleys
like wax in a fire,
like water pouring down a hill.

2 Chr 27:5a Hebrew *100 talents* [3,400 kilograms]. **2 Chr 27:5b** Hebrew *10,000 cors* [1,820 kiloliters] *of wheat, and 10,000 cors of barley.*

would listen. In Isaiah 6:13 God explains his plan for a remnant (holy seed) of faithful followers. God is merciful even when he judges. We can gain encouragement from God's promise to preserve his people. If we are faithful to him, we can be sure of his mercy.

Isa 6:11-13 When would the people listen? Only after they had come to the end and had nowhere to turn but to God. This would happen when the land was destroyed by invading armies and the people taken into captivity. The "tenth" refers either to those who remained in the land after the captivity or to those who returned from Babylon to rebuild the land. Each group was about a tenth of the total population. When will we listen to God? Must we, like Judah, go through calamities before we will listen to God's words? Consider what God may be telling you, and obey him before time runs out.

2 Kgs 15:34-35 Much good can be said of Jotham and his reign as king of Judah, but he failed in a most important area: He didn't destroy the pagan shrines, although leaving them clearly violated the first commandment (Exod 20:3). Like Jotham, we may live basically good lives and yet miss doing what is most important. A lifetime of doing good is not enough if we make the crucial mistake of not following God with all our hearts. A true follower of God puts him first in all areas of life.

2 Chr 27:2 Although Jotham was generally a good king (2 Chr 27:6), his people remained as corrupt as they had been during his father Uzziah's reign. Those you lead will not always follow your example, but that should not affect the way you live for God.

Mic 1:1 Micah and Isaiah lived at the same time, about 750–680 B.C., and undoubtedly knew of each other. Micah directed his message mainly to Judah, the southern kingdom, but he also had some words for Israel, the northern kingdom. Judah was enjoying great prosperity at this time. Of the three kings mentioned in the book of Micah, Jotham (750–732) and Hezekiah (715–686) had tried to follow God (2 Kgs 15:32-38; 18–20), but Ahaz (735–715) was one of the most evil kings ever to reign in Judah (2 Kgs 16). Moresheth was a Judean village near Gath, on the border with Philistia.

Mic 1:3 "The heights of the earth" could simply mean "mountaintops" or may refer

5 And why is this happening?
Because of the rebellion of Israel*—
yes, the sins of the whole nation.
Who is to blame for Israel's rebellion?
Samaria, its capital city!
Where is the center of idolatry in Judah?
In Jerusalem, its capital!

6 "So I, the LORD, will make the city of Samaria
a heap of ruins.
Her streets will be plowed up
for planting vineyards.
I will roll the stones of her walls into the valley
below,
exposing her foundations.
7 All her carved images will be smashed.
All her sacred treasures will be burned.
These things were bought with the money
earned by her prostitution,
and they will now be carried away
to pay prostitutes elsewhere."

8 Therefore, I will mourn and lament.
I will walk around barefoot and naked.
I will howl like a jackal
and moan like an owl.
9 For my people's wound
is too deep to heal.
It has reached into Judah,
even to the gates of Jerusalem.

10 Don't tell our enemies in Gath*;
don't weep at all.
You people in Beth-leaphrah,*
roll in the dust to show your despair.
11 You people in Shaphir,*
go as captives into exile—naked and
ashamed.
The people of Zaanan*
dare not come outside their walls.
The people of Beth-ezel* mourn,
for their house has no support.
12 The people of Maroth* anxiously wait for relief,
but only bitterness awaits them
as the LORD's judgment reaches
even to the gates of Jerusalem.

13 Harness your chariot horses and flee,
you people of Lachish.*
You were the first city in Judah
to follow Israel in her rebellion,
and you led Jerusalem* into sin.

Mi 1:5 Hebrew *Jacob;* also in 1:5b. The names "Jacob" and "Israel" are often interchanged throughout the Old Testament, referring sometimes to the individual patriarch and sometimes to the nation. **Mi 1:10a** *Gath* sounds like the Hebrew term for "tell." **Mi 1:10b** *Beth-leaphrah* means "house of dust." **Mi 1:11a** *Shaphir* means "pleasant." **Mi 1:11b** *Zaanan* sounds like the Hebrew term for "come out." **Mi 1:11c** *Beth-ezel* means "adjoining house." **Mi 1:12** *Maroth* sounds like the Hebrew term for "bitter." **Mi 1:13a** *Lachish* sounds like the Hebrew term for "team of horses." **Mi 1:13b** Hebrew *the daughter of Zion.*

MICAH

Micah served as a prophet to Judah from 742–687 B.C.

Climate of the times	King Ahaz set up pagan idols in the Temple and finally nailed the Temple doors shut. Four different nations harassed Judah. When Hezekiah became king, the nation began a slow road to recovery and economic strength. Hezekiah probably heeded much of Micah's advice.
Main message	Prediction of the fall of both the northern kingdom of Israel and the southern kingdom of Judah. This was God's discipline upon the people, actually showing how much he cared for them. Hezekiah's good reign helped postpone Judah's punishment.
Importance of message	Choosing to live a life apart from God is making a commitment to sin. Sin leads to judgment and death. God alone shows us the way to eternal peace. His discipline often keeps us on the right path.
Contemporary prophets	Hosea (753–715 B.C.), Isaiah (740–681 B.C.)

to the altars dedicated to various idols, usually placed in elevated areas (see also Mic 1:5).

Mic 1:3-7 Although the 12 tribes of Israel had been united under David and Solomon, after Solomon's death, the kingdom had divided into two parts. Two of the tribes, Judah and Benjamin, stayed loyal to David's line and accepted Solomon's son as their king. They became the southern kingdom, also called Judah, with Jerusalem as their capital city. The other 10 tribes became the northern kingdom, also called Israel, with Samaria as their capital city. The destruction of Samaria was literally fulfilled during Micah's lifetime, in 722 B.C. (2 Kgs 17:1-18), just as he had predicted.

Mic 1:5 Two sins are identified in Micah's message: the perversion of worship (Mic 1:7; 3:5-7, 11; 5:12-13) and injustice toward others (Mic 2:1-2, 8-9; 3:2-3, 9-11; 7:2-6). Rampant in the capital cities, these sins infiltrated and infected the entire country.

Mic 1:9 Samaria's sins were incurable, and God's judgment on the city had already begun. This sin was not like a gash in the skin but more like a stab wound in a vital organ, causing an injury that would soon prove fatal (Samaria was, in fact, destroyed early in Micah's ministry). Tragically, Samaria's sin had influenced Jerusalem, and judgment would come to its very gates. This probably refers to Sennacherib's siege in 701 B.C. (see 2 Kgs 18–19).

Mic 1:10-16 Micah declared God's judgment on city after city because of the people's sins. The Hebrew of Micah 1:10-13 includes a clever wordplay (see the textual notes). Micah bitterly denounced each town by using puns. *Shaphir* sounds like the Hebrew word for "pleasant"; *Zaanan* sounds like the verb meaning "come out"; *Maroth* sounds like a word for "bitter." Read Micah 1:11-12 aloud, substituting the meaning for each city's name, and you will realize the effect of Micah's word choice. Not all these cities can be identified now, but Lachish was on the border with Philistia and took the brunt of the Assyrian invasion.

Mic 1:13 The people of Lachish had influenced many to follow their evil example. They "led Jerusalem into sin." We often do the same when we sin. Regardless of whether you consider yourself a leader, your actions and words are observed by others who may choose to follow your example, whether you know it or not.

▸ **MICAH 1:1-16** ***(cont.)***

14 Send farewell gifts to Moresheth-gath*;
there is no hope of saving it.
The town of Aczib*
has deceived the kings of Israel.
15 O people of Mareshah,*
I will bring a conqueror to capture
your town.
And the leaders* of Israel
will go to Adullam.
16 Oh, people of Judah, shave your heads in sorrow,
for the children you love will be
snatched away.
Make yourselves as bald as a vulture,
for your little ones will be exiled to distant
lands.

Ahaz Begins His Reign in Judah PARALLEL

2 KINGS 16:1-9

Ahaz son of Jotham began to rule over Judah in the
seventeenth year of King Pekah's reign in Israel. 2 Ahaz
was twenty years old when he became king, and he
reigned in Jerusalem sixteen years. He did not do what
was pleasing in the sight of the LORD his God, as his
ancestor David had done. 3 Instead, he followed the
example of the kings of Israel, even sacrificing his own
son in the fire.* In this way, he followed the detestable
practices of the pagan nations the LORD had driven
from the land ahead of the Israelites. 4 He offered sacrifices and burned incense at the pagan shrines and
on the hills and under every green tree.
5 Then King Rezin of Aram and King Pekah of Israel
came up to attack Jerusalem. They besieged Ahaz

Mi 1:14a *Moresheth* sounds like the Hebrew term for "gift" or "dowry." **Mi 1:14b** *Aczib* means "deception." **Mi 1:15a** *Mareshah* sounds like the Hebrew term for "conqueror." **Mi 1:15b** Hebrew *the glory.* **2 Kgs 16:3** Or *even making his son pass through the fire.*

Mic 1:14 Moresheth-gath was Micah's hometown (Mic 1:1).

Mic 1:15 The terrain surrounding Adullam had numerous caves. Micah was warning that when the enemy approached, Judah's proud leaders would be forced to flee and hide in these caves.

Mic 1:16 Micah pictured the devastating sorrow of parents seeing their children taken away to be slaves in a distant land. This happened frequently in both Israel and Judah, most horribly when each nation was completely conquered—Israel in 722 B.C. and Judah in 586 B.C.

2 Kgs 16:3 Ahaz was so depraved that he sacrificed his own son to the pagan gods. This was a practice of the Canaanites, whom the Israelites were supposed to have driven out of the land in the time of Joshua.

2 Kgs 16:5 Israel and Aram were both under Assyria's control. They joined forces against Judah, hoping to force the southern kingdom to join their revolt against Assyria and strengthen their western alliance. But the plan backfired when King Ahaz of Judah unexpectedly asked Assyria to come to his aid (2 Kgs 16:8-9).

AHAZ

Our heritage influences, but doesn't necessarily determine, our life decisions. King Ahaz of Judah illustrates this truth. He turned away from the good examples of his father Jotham and his grandfather Uzziah, but his poor example seems to have had little effect on his own son Hezekiah, who proved to be a great and godly king. • The circumstances in the life of King Ahaz fall into the general categories of bad and worse. When Judah suffered a debilitating attack from rivals Israel and Aram, the king ignored an opportunity to seek God's help and turned instead to Assyria for assistance. Ahaz's cowardly leadership forced Judah into virtual slavery to the Assyrians. • Soon every evidence that Judah had once been a God-fearing nation was smashed, defaced, or tucked out of sight. Ahaz imported idolatry. He even presented some of his children as offerings to the gods he hoped would rescue him and his nation from their disastrous situation. • We share Ahaz's sin when, from beneath a load of failures and trials, we turn away from good examples and from God. Instead of repenting of any known sin and calling upon God for relief, we, like Ahaz, may appeal to every other source of aid but God—our own abilities, money, or harmful habits. The results only serve to increase our tragic circumstances. • Difficulties and mistakes will either devastate our faith or they will stimulate growth and maturity. The positive differences come when we humbly seek God's help, whatever the situation. Trials that tempt us to turn away from God should, instead, spur us to turn toward God.

Weaknesses and mistakes	• Failed to trust God • Asked Assyria for help and submitted Judah to crushing domination • Adopted Assyrian religious practices that undermined his people's faith • Sacrificed some of his own children in pagan worship
Lessons from his life	• Fear is never a good excuse for failing to trust God • Some people or things that seem like obvious sources of help or relief may turn out to be controlling and enslaving instead • Good examples in our lives can't prevent us from making the wrong choices
Vital statistics	• Where: Jerusalem • Occupation: King of Judah • Relatives: Father: Jotham. Son: Hezekiah.
Key verse	"Even during this time of trouble, King Ahaz continued to reject the LORD" (2 Chr 28:22).

Ahaz's story is told in 2 Kings 16; 2 Chronicles 28. Isaiah 7–10 records several amazing prophecies given during his reign.

but could not conquer him. [6]At that time the king of Edom* recovered the town of Elath for Edom.* He drove out the people of Judah and sent Edomites* to live there, as they do to this day.

[7]King Ahaz sent messengers to King Tiglath-pileser of Assyria with this message: "I am your servant and your vassal.* Come up and rescue me from the attacking armies of Aram and Israel." [8]Then Ahaz took the silver and gold from the Temple of the LORD and the palace treasury and sent it as a payment to the Assyrian king. [9]So the king of Assyria attacked the Aramean capital of Damascus and led its population away as captives, resettling them in Kir. He also killed King Rezin.

2 CHRONICLES 28:1-15

Ahaz was twenty years old when he became king, and he reigned in Jerusalem sixteen years. He did not do what was pleasing in the sight of the LORD, as his ancestor David had done. [2]Instead, he followed the example of the kings of Israel. He cast metal images for the worship of Baal. [3]He offered sacrifices in the valley of Ben-Hinnom, even sacrificing his own sons in the fire.* In this way, he followed the detestable practices of the pagan nations the LORD had driven from the land ahead of the Israelites. [4]He offered sacrifices and burned incense at the pagan shrines and on the hills and under every green tree.

[5]Because of all this, the LORD his God allowed the king of Aram to defeat Ahaz and to exile large numbers of his people to Damascus. The armies of the king of Israel also defeated Ahaz and inflicted many casualties on his army. [6]In a single day Pekah son of Remaliah, Israel's king, killed 120,000 of Judah's troops, all of them experienced warriors, because they had abandoned the LORD, the God of their ancestors. [7]Then Zicri, a warrior from Ephraim, killed Maaseiah, the king's son; Azrikam, the king's palace commander; and Elkanah, the king's second-in-command. [8]The armies of Israel captured 200,000 women and children from Judah and seized tremendous amounts of plunder, which they took back to Samaria.

[9]But a prophet of the LORD named Oded was there in Samaria when the army of Israel returned home. He went out to meet them and said, "The LORD, the God of your ancestors, was angry with Judah and let you defeat them. But you have gone too far, killing them without mercy, and all heaven is disturbed. [10]And now you are planning to make slaves of these people from Judah and Jerusalem. What about your own sins against the LORD your God? [11]Listen to me and return these prisoners you have taken, for they are your own relatives. Watch out, because now the LORD's fierce anger has been turned against you!"

[12]Then some of the leaders of Israel*—Azariah son of Jehohanan, Berekiah son of Meshillemoth, Jehizkiah son of Shallum, and Amasa son of Hadlai—agreed with this and confronted the men returning from battle. [13]"You must not bring the prisoners here!" they declared. "We cannot afford to add to our sins and guilt. Our guilt is already great, and the LORD's fierce anger is already turned against Israel."

[14]So the warriors released the prisoners and handed over the plunder in the sight of the leaders and all the people. [15]Then the four men just mentioned by name came forward and distributed clothes from the plunder to the prisoners who were naked. They provided clothing and sandals to wear, gave them enough food and drink, and dressed their wounds with olive oil. They put those who were weak on donkeys and took all the prisoners back to their own people in Jericho, the city of palms. Then they returned to Samaria.

2 Kgs 16:6a As in Latin Vulgate; Hebrew reads *Rezin king of Aram.* **2 Kgs 16:6b** As in Latin Vulgate; Hebrew reads *Aram.* **2 Kgs 16:6c** As in Greek version, Latin Vulgate, and an alternate reading of the Masoretic Text; the other alternate reads *Arameans.* **2 Kgs 16:7** Hebrew *your son.* **2 Chr 28:3** Or *even making his sons pass through the fire.* **2 Chr 28:12** Hebrew *Ephraim,* referring to the northern kingdom of Israel.

2 Chr 28:3 Imagine the monstrous evil of a religion that offers young children as sacrifices. God allowed the nation to be conquered in response to Ahaz's evil practices. Even today the practice hasn't abated. The sacrifice of children to the harsh gods of convenience, economy, and whim continues in sterile medical facilities in numbers that would astound the wicked Ahaz. If we are to allow children to come to Christ (Matt 19:14), we must first allow them to come into the world.

Ahaz Pays Tribute to Assyria

"Jehoahaz of Judah" is named on this cuneiform inscription as paying tribute to Tiglath-pileser III of Assyria. This is the full form of the abbreviated name Ahaz, 13th king of Judah, who sent gifts to the Assyrian king (2 Kgs 16:7-8). The three main accounts of Ahaz (2 Kgs 16; 2 Chr 28; Isa 7) treat him as one of the most evil rulers of the southern kingdom of Judah. Ahaz's lack of trust in God seems to have stemmed from his complete rejection of the traditional Jewish faith rather than from the dangerous political situation.

Isaiah's Message for Ahaz

ISAIAH 7:1-9

When Ahaz, son of Jotham and grandson of Uzziah,
was king of Judah, King Rezin of Syria* and Pekah son
of Remaliah, the king of Israel, set out to attack Jerusalem. However, they were unable to carry out their plan.
2The news had come to the royal court of Judah:
"Syria is allied with Israel* against us!" So the hearts of
the king and his people trembled with fear, like trees
shaking in a storm.
3Then the LORD said to Isaiah, "Take your son Shear-
jashub* and go out to meet King Ahaz. You will find
him at the end of the aqueduct that feeds water into
the upper pool, near the road leading to the field
where cloth is washed.* 4Tell him to stop worrying.
Tell him he doesn't need to fear the fierce anger of
those two burned-out embers, King Rezin of Syria
and Pekah son of Remaliah. 5Yes, the kings of Syria
and Israel are plotting against him, saying, 6'We will
attack Judah and capture it for ourselves. Then we will
install the son of Tabeel as Judah's king.' 7But this is
what the Sovereign LORD says:

"This invasion will never happen;
it will never take place;
8 for Syria is no stronger than its capital, Damascus,
and Damascus is no stronger than its king,
Rezin.
As for Israel, within sixty-five years
it will be crushed and completely destroyed.
9 Israel is no stronger than its capital, Samaria,
and Samaria is no stronger than its king,
Pekah son of Remaliah.
Unless your faith is firm,
I cannot make you stand firm."

The Sign of Immanuel

ISAIAH 7:10-25

Later, the LORD sent this message to King Ahaz: 11"Ask
the LORD your God for a sign of confirmation, Ahaz.
Make it as difficult as you want—as high as heaven or
as deep as the place of the dead.*"
12But the king refused. "No," he said, "I will not test
the LORD like that."
13Then Isaiah said, "Listen well, you royal family
of David! Isn't it enough to exhaust human patience?
Must you exhaust the patience of my God as well?
14All right then, the Lord himself will give you the
sign. Look! The virgin* will conceive a child! She
will give birth to a son and will call him Immanuel
(which means 'God is with us'). 15By the time this child
is old enough to choose what is right and reject what
is wrong, he will be eating yogurt* and honey. 16For
before the child is that old, the lands of the two kings
you fear so much will both be deserted.
17"Then the LORD will bring things on you, your
nation, and your family unlike anything since Israel
broke away from Judah. He will bring the king of Assyria upon you!"
18In that day the LORD will whistle for the army of

Is 7:1 Hebrew *Aram;* also in 7:2, 4, 5, 8. **Is 7:2** Hebrew *Ephraim,* referring to the northern kingdom of Israel; also in 7:5, 8, 9, 17. **Is 7:3a** *Shear-jashub* means "A remnant will return." **Is 7:3b** Or *bleached.* **Is 7:11** Hebrew *as deep as Sheol.* **Is 7:14** Or *young woman.* **Is 7:15** Or *curds;* also in 7:22.

Isa 7:1 The year was 734 B.C. Ahaz, king of Judah in Jerusalem, was about to be attacked by an alliance of the northern kingdom of Israel and Aram. He was frightened by the prospect of the possible end of his reign and by the invading armies that killed many people or took them as captives (2 Chr 28:5-21). But, as Isaiah predicted, the kingdom of Judah did not come to an end at this time. The sign of Immanuel would be a sign of deliverance.

Isa 7:3 *Shear-jashub* means "a remnant will return." God told Isaiah to give his son this name as a reminder of his plan for mercy. From the beginning of God's judgment he planned to restore a remnant of his people. Shear-jashub was a reminder to the people of God's faithfulness to them.

Isa 7:3 The "aqueduct" may have been the site of the Gihon Spring, located east of Jerusalem. The Gihon Spring was the main source of water for the holy city and was also the spring that emptied into Hezekiah's famous water tunnel (2 Chr 32:30). The field where the cloth is washed was a well-known place where clothing or newly woven cloth was laid in the sun to dry and whiten (see Isa 36:2).

Isa 7:4–8:15 Isaiah predicted the breakup of Israel's alliance with Aram (Isa 7:4-9). Because of this alliance, Israel would be destroyed; Assyria would be the instrument God would use to destroy them (Isa 7:8-25) and to punish Judah. But God would not let Assyria destroy Judah, only punish them (Isa 8:1-15). They would be spared because God's gracious plans cannot be thwarted.

Isa 7:8 Ahaz, one of Judah's worst kings, refused God's help, and instead, he tried to buy aid from the Assyrians with silver and gold from the Temple (2 Kings 16:8). When the Assyrians came, they brought further trouble instead of help. In 722 B.C., Samaria, the capital of Israel, the northern kingdom, fell to the Assyrian armies, thus ending the northern kingdom.

Isa 7:12 Ahaz appeared righteous by saying he would not test God with a sign ("I will not test the LORD like that"). In fact, God had told him to ask, but Ahaz didn't really want to know what God would say. Often we use some excuse—such as not wanting to bother God or blaming some theological question that concerns us—to keep us from communicating with him. Don't let anything keep you from hearing and obeying God.

Isa 7:14-16 "Virgin" is translated from a Hebrew word used for an unmarried woman who is old enough to be married, one who is sexually mature (see Gen 24:43; Exod 2:8; Ps 68:25; Prov 30:19; Song 1:3; 6:8). Some have compared this young woman to Isaiah's young wife and newborn son (Isa 8:1-4). This is not likely because she already had a child, Shear-jashub, and her second child was not named Immanuel. Some believe that Isaiah's first wife may have died, and so this is his second wife. It is more likely that this prophecy had a double fulfillment: (1) A young woman from the house of Ahaz who was not married would marry and have a son. Before three years passed (one year for pregnancy and two for the child to be old enough to talk), the two invading kings would be destroyed. (2) Matthew 1:23 quotes Isaiah 7:14 to show a further fulfillment of this prophecy in that a virgin named Mary conceived and bore a son, Immanuel, the Christ.

Isa 7:18 Flies and bees are symbols of God's judgment (see Exod 23:28). Egypt and Assyria did not at this time devastate Judah. Hezekiah followed Ahaz as king, and he honored God; therefore, God held back his hand of judgment. Two more evil kings reigned before Josiah, of whom it was said that no other king turned so completely to the Lord (2 Kgs

southern Egypt and for the army of Assyria. They will
swarm around you like flies and bees. [19]They will come
in vast hordes and settle in the fertile areas and also in
the desolate valleys, caves, and thorny places. [20]In that
day the Lord will hire a "razor" from beyond the Euphrates River*—the king of Assyria—and use it to shave off
everything: your land, your crops, and your people.*
[21]In that day a farmer will be fortunate to have a cow
and two sheep or goats left. [22]Nevertheless, there will
be enough milk for everyone because so few people
will be left in the land. They will eat their fill of yogurt and honey. [23]In that day the lush vineyards, now
worth 1,000 pieces of silver,* will become patches
of briers and thorns. [24]The entire land will become a
vast expanse of briers and thorns, a hunting ground
overrun by wildlife. [25]No one will go to the fertile
hillsides where the gardens once grew, for briers and
thorns will cover them. Cattle, sheep, and goats will
graze there.

The Coming Assyrian Invasion

ISAIAH 8:1-10

Then the LORD said to me, "Make a large signboard
and clearly write this name on it: Maher-shalal-hash-
baz.*" [2]I asked Uriah the priest and Zechariah son
of Jeberekiah, both known as honest men, to witness
my doing this.
[3]Then I slept with my wife, and she became pregnant and gave birth to a son. And the LORD said, "Call
him Maher-shalal-hash-baz. [4]For before this child is
old enough to say 'Papa' or 'Mama,' the king of Assyria
will carry away both the abundance of Damascus and
the riches of Samaria."
[5]Then the LORD spoke to me again and said, [6]"My
care for the people of Judah is like the gently flowing
waters of Shiloah, but they have rejected it. They are
rejoicing over what will happen to* King Rezin and
King Pekah.* [7]Therefore, the Lord will overwhelm
them with a mighty flood from the Euphrates River*—
the king of Assyria and all his glory. This flood will
overflow all its channels [8]and sweep into Judah until
it is chin deep. It will spread its wings, submerging
your land from one end to the other, O Immanuel.

9 "Huddle together, you nations, and be terrified.
Listen, all you distant lands.
Prepare for battle, but you will be crushed!
Yes, prepare for battle, but you will be crushed!
10 Call your councils of war, but they will be
worthless.
Develop your strategies, but they will not
succeed.
For God is with us!*"

A Call to Trust the LORD

ISAIAH 8:11-22

The LORD has given me a strong warning not to think
like everyone else does. He said,

12 "Don't call everything a conspiracy, like they do,
and don't live in dread of what frightens them.
13 Make the LORD of Heaven's Armies holy in
your life.
He is the one you should fear.
He is the one who should make you tremble.
14 He will keep you safe.
But to Israel and Judah
he will be a stone that makes people stumble,
a rock that makes them fall.

Is 7:20a Hebrew *the river.* **Is 7:20b** Hebrew *shave off the head, the hair of the legs, and the beard.* **Is 7:23** Hebrew *1,000 shekels of silver,* about 25 pounds or 11.4 kilograms in weight. **Is 8:1** *Maher-shalal-hash-baz* means "Swift to plunder and quick to carry away." **Is 8:6a** Or *They are rejoicing because of.* **Is 8:6b** Hebrew *and the son of Remaliah.* **Is 8:7** Hebrew *the river.* **Is 8:10** Hebrew *Immanuel!*

23:25). However, Judah's doom had been sealed by the extreme evil of Josiah's father, Amon. During Josiah's reign, Egypt marched against the Assyrians. Josiah then declared war on Egypt, although God told him not to. After Josiah was killed (2 Chr 35:20-27), only weak kings reigned in Judah. The Egyptians carried off Josiah's son, Jehoahaz, after three months. The next king, Jehoiakim, was taken by Nebuchadnezzar to Babylon. Egypt, Assyria, and Assyria's conqueror, Babylon: each in turn would deal death blows to Judah.

Isa 7:20 Hiring Assyria to save them would be Judah's downfall (2 Kgs 16:7-8). To "shave" Judah's hair was symbolic of total humiliation. Numbers 6:9 explains that after being defiled, a person who had been set apart for the Lord had to shave his head as part of the cleansing process. Shaving bodily hair was an embarrassment—an exposure of nakedness. For a Hebrew man to have his beard shaved was humiliating (2 Sam 10:4-5).

Isa 7:21-25 Judah's rich farmland would be trampled until it became pastureland, fit only for grazing. No longer would it be a place of agricultural abundance, "a land flowing with milk and honey" (Exod 3:8), but a land with only briers and thorns.

Isa 8:1-4 These verses predict the fall of Israel and Aram. Aram fell to Assyria in 732 B.C., and Israel followed in 722 B.C. Isaiah put his message on a large scroll in a public place. God was warning all his people. The name of the child means "swift to plunder and quick to spoil."

Isa 8:6-8 Because the people of Judah rejected God's kindness, choosing instead to seek help from other nations, God would punish them. We see two distinct attributes of God—his love and his wrath. To ignore his love and guidance results in sin and invites his wrath. We must recognize the consequences of our choices. God wants to protect us from bad choices, but he still gives us the freedom to make them.

Isa 8:7-8 The heart of the Assyrian Empire was located between the Tigris and Euphrates Rivers. This flood is a poetic way of describing the overwhelming force of the Assyrian army.

Isa 8:9 To "be crushed" means to lose courage by the pressure of sudden fear.

Isa 8:11 Isaiah, along with most of the prophets, was viewed as a traitor because he did not support Judah's national policies. He called the people to commit themselves first to God and then to the king. He even predicted the overthrow of the government.

Isa 8:11-15 For the people of Judah, fear of invasion was a constant threat. They had powerful enemies on their doorstep. Yet Isaiah said, "The LORD of Heaven's Armies . . . is the one you should fear . . . He will keep you safe." Fear is a powerful enemy of our faith and a strong deterrent to the believer's peace of mind. Fear of war, terrorist attacks, disease, and pollution can rob us of our trust in God. God is our shelter and hiding place (Isa 4:6). Ask him to drive inappropriate fear from your heart and to help you fear only him.

▶ **ISAIAH 8:11-22** ***(cont.)***

And for the people of Jerusalem
he will be a trap and a snare.
15 Many will stumble and fall,
never to rise again.
They will be snared and captured."
16 Preserve the teaching of God;
entrust his instructions to those who
follow me.
17 I will wait for the LORD,
who has turned away from the descendants
of Jacob.
I will put my hope in him.

18I and the children the LORD has given me serve as
signs and warnings to Israel from the LORD of Heaven's
Armies who dwells in his Temple on Mount Zion.
19Someone may say to you, "Let's ask the mediums and those who consult the spirits of the dead.
With their whisperings and mutterings, they will
tell us what to do." But shouldn't people ask God
for guidance? Should the living seek guidance from
the dead?
20Look to God's instructions and teachings! People
who contradict his word are completely in the dark.
21They will go from one place to another, weary and
hungry. And because they are hungry, they will rage
and curse their king and their God. They will look
up to heaven 22and down at the earth, but wherever
they look, there will be trouble and anguish and dark
despair. They will be thrown out into the darkness.

Hope in the Messiah

ISAIAH 9:1-7

1*Nevertheless, that time of darkness and despair will
not go on forever. The land of Zebulun and Naphtali
will be humbled, but there will be a time in the future
when Galilee of the Gentiles, which lies along the road
that runs between the Jordan and the sea, will be filled
with glory.

2 * The people who walk in darkness
will see a great light.
For those who live in a land of deep darkness,*
a light will shine.
3 You will enlarge the nation of Israel,
and its people will rejoice.
They will rejoice before you
as people rejoice at the harvest
and like warriors dividing the plunder.
4 For you will break the yoke of their slavery
and lift the heavy burden from their shoulders.
You will break the oppressor's rod,
just as you did when you destroyed the army
of Midian.
5 The boots of the warrior
and the uniforms bloodstained by war
will all be burned.
They will be fuel for the fire.

Is 9:1 Verse 9:1 is numbered 8:23 in Hebrew text. **Is 9:2a** Verses 9:2-21 are numbered 9:1-20 in Hebrew text. **Is 9:2b** Greek version reads *a land where death casts its shadow.* Compare Matt 4:16.

Isa 8:16 Because some people faithfully preserved the teaching of God and passed on these words from generation to generation, we have the book of Isaiah today. Each of us needs to accept the responsibility to pass on God's Word to our children and grandchildren, encouraging them to love the Bible, read it, and learn from it. Then they will faithfully pass it on to their children and grandchildren.

Isa 8:17 Isaiah decided to wait for the Lord, though God had "turned away from" the people of Israel. For some believers, patient waiting becomes the most difficult testing they must face: waiting for illness to pass, for a child to return to God and the church, or for God to make matters right in a particular situation. Many of the prophecies God gave through the prophets would not come true for 700 years; others still haven't been fulfilled in our lifetime. Are you willing to accept the Lord's timing, not yours?

Isa 8:19 The people would consult mediums and psychics, seeking answers from dead people instead of consulting the living God. God alone knows the future, and only he is eternal. We can trust God to guide us.

Isa 8:21 After rejecting God's plan for them, the people of Judah would blame God for their trials. People continually blame God for their self-induced problems.

NAMES FOR MESSIAH

Isaiah uses four names to describe the Messiah (Isa 9:6). These names have special meaning to us.

Wonderful Counselor	He is exceptional, distinguished, and without peer, the one who gives the right advice.
Mighty God	He is God himself.
Everlasting Father	He is timeless; he is God our Father.
Prince of Peace	His government is one of justice and peace.

How do you respond to the unpleasant results of your own choices? Where do you fix the blame? Instead of blaming God, look for ways to grow through your bad choices and failures.

Isa 9:1 In our gloom and despair, we fear that our sorrows and troubles will never end. But we can take comfort in this certainty: Although the Lord may not always spare us from troubles, he will lead us safely through them if we follow him wholeheartedly.

Isa 9:1-7 This child, who would become their deliverer, is the Messiah, Jesus. Matthew quotes these verses in describing Christ's ministry (Matt 4:15-16). The territories of Zebulun and Naphtali represent the northern kingdom as a whole. These were also the territories where Jesus grew up and often ministered; this is why they would see "a great light."

Isa 9:2 The apostle John also referred to Jesus as the "true light" (John 1:9). Jesus referred to himself as "the light of the world" (John 8:12). Whenever we see the lights of Christmas, let them remind us that they recall Christ, our true Light.

Isa 9:2-6 In a time of great darkness, God promised to send a light who would shine on everyone living in the shadow of death. He is both "Wonderful Counselor" and "Mighty God." This message of hope was fulfilled in the birth of Christ and the establishment of

6 For a child is born to us,
a son is given to us.
The government will rest on his shoulders.
And he will be called:
Wonderful Counselor,* Mighty God,
Everlasting Father, Prince of Peace.
7 His government and its peace
will never end.
He will rule with fairness and justice from the throne of his ancestor David
for all eternity.
The passionate commitment of the LORD of Heaven's Armies
will make this happen!

The LORD's Anger against Israel

ISAIAH 9:8–10:4

8 The Lord has spoken out against Jacob;
his judgment has fallen upon Israel.
9 And the people of Israel* and Samaria,
who spoke with such pride and arrogance,
will soon know it.
10 They said, "We will replace the broken bricks of our ruins with finished stone,
and replant the felled sycamore-fig trees with cedars."

11 But the LORD will bring Rezin's enemies against Israel
and stir up all their foes.
12 The Syrians* from the east and the Philistines from the west
will bare their fangs and devour Israel.
But even then the LORD's anger will not be satisfied.
His fist is still poised to strike.

13 For after all this punishment, the people will still not repent.
They will not seek the LORD of Heaven's Armies.
14 Therefore, in a single day the LORD will destroy
both the head and the tail,
the noble palm branch and the lowly reed.
15 The leaders of Israel are the head,
and the lying prophets are the tail.
16 For the leaders of the people have misled them.
They have led them down the path of destruction.
17 That is why the Lord takes no pleasure in the young men
and shows no mercy even to the widows and orphans.
For they are all wicked hypocrites,
and they all speak foolishness.
But even then the LORD's anger will not be satisfied.
His fist is still poised to strike.

18 This wickedness is like a brushfire.
It burns not only briers and thorns
but also sets the forests ablaze.
Its burning sends up clouds of smoke.
19 The land will be blackened
by the fury of the LORD of Heaven's Armies.
The people will be fuel for the fire,
and no one will spare even his own brother.
20 They will attack their neighbor on the right
but will still be hungry.
They will devour their neighbor on the left
but will not be satisfied.
In the end they will even eat their own children.*
21 Manasseh will feed on Ephraim,
Ephraim will feed on Manasseh,
and both will devour Judah.
But even then the LORD's anger will not be satisfied.
His fist is still poised to strike.

Is 9:6 Or *Wonderful, Counselor.* **Is 9:9** Hebrew *of Ephraim,* referring to the northern kingdom of Israel. **Is 9:12** Hebrew *Arameans.* **Is 9:20** Or *eat their own arms.*

his eternal Kingdom. He came to deliver all people from their slavery to sin.

Isa 9:8-10 Pride made Israel think it would recover and rebuild in its own strength. Even though God made the people of Israel a nation and gave them the land they occupied, they put their trust in themselves rather than in him. Too often we take pride in our accomplishments, forgetting that it is God who has given us our resources and abilities. We may even become proud of our unique status as Christians. God is not pleased with any pride or trust in ourselves because it cuts off our contact with him.

Isa 9:21 Ephraim and Manasseh were tribes in the northern kingdom descended from Joseph's two sons. They fought a civil war because of their selfishness and wickedness (see Judg 12:4).

The people who walk in darkness will see a great light. For those who live in a land of deep darkness, a light will shine.
Isaiah 9:2

▸ **ISAIAH 9:8–10:4** ***(cont.)***

10:1 What sorrow awaits the unjust judges
and those who issue unfair laws.
2 They deprive the poor of justice
and deny the rights of the needy among
my people.
They prey on widows
and take advantage of orphans.
3 What will you do when I punish you,
when I send disaster upon you from
a distant land?
To whom will you turn for help?
Where will your treasures be safe?
4 You will stumble along as prisoners
or lie among the dead.
But even then the LORD's anger will not
be satisfied.
His fist is still poised to strike.

Judgment against Assyria

ISAIAH 10:5-19

5 "What sorrow awaits Assyria, the rod
of my anger.
I use it as a club to express my anger.
6 I am sending Assyria against a godless nation,
against a people with whom I am angry.
Assyria will plunder them,
trampling them like dirt beneath its feet.
7 But the king of Assyria will not understand that
he is my tool;
his mind does not work that way.
His plan is simply to destroy,
to cut down nation after nation.
8 He will say,
'Each of my princes will soon be a king.
9 We destroyed Calno just as we did Carchemish.
Hamath fell before us as Arpad did.
And we destroyed Samaria just as we did
Damascus.
10 Yes, we have finished off many a kingdom
whose gods were greater than those in
Jerusalem and Samaria.
11 So we will defeat Jerusalem and her gods,
just as we destroyed Samaria with hers.'"

12 After the Lord has used the king of Assyria to
accomplish his purposes on Mount Zion and in Jerusalem, he will turn against the king of Assyria and
punish him—for he is proud and arrogant. 13 He boasts,

"By my own powerful arm I have done this.
With my own shrewd wisdom I planned it.
I have broken down the defenses of nations
and carried off their treasures.
I have knocked down their kings like a bull.
14 I have robbed their nests of riches
and gathered up kingdoms as a farmer
gathers eggs.
No one can even flap a wing against me
or utter a peep of protest."
15 But can the ax boast greater power than the
person who uses it?
Is the saw greater than the person who saws?

Isa 10:1 God will judge unjust judges and those who make unfair laws. Those who oppress others will be oppressed themselves. It is not enough to live in a land founded on justice; each individual must deal justly with the poor and the powerless. Don't pass your responsibility off onto your nation or even your church. You are accountable to God for what you do for the poor.

Isa 10:7 Although Assyria did not know it was part of God's plan, God used this nation to judge his people. God accomplishes his plans in history despite people or nations who reject him. He did not merely set the world in motion and let it go! Because our all-powerful, sovereign God is still in control today, we have security even in a rapidly changing world.

Isa 10:9 Calno, Carchemish, Hamath, Arpad, Samaria, and Damascus were cities conquered by Assyria. Assured of great victories that would enlarge their empire, the king of Assyria gave an arrogant speech. Already Assyria had conquered several cities and thought Judah would be defeated along with the others. Little did he know that they were under the mightier hand of God.

Isa 10:10 Samaria and Jerusalem were filled with idols that were powerless against the Assyrian military machine. Only the God of the universe could and would overthrow Assyria, but not until he had used the Assyrians for his purposes.

Isa 10:12 The predicted punishment of the Assyrians took place in 701 B.C., when 185,000 Assyrian soldiers were slain by the angel of the Lord (Isa 37:36-37). Later, the Assyrian Empire fell to Babylon, never to rise again as a world power.

Isa 10:12 The Assyrians were arrogant. Proud of the victories God permitted, they thought they had accomplished everything in their own power. Our perspective can also become distorted by pride in our accomplishments. If we do not acknowledge God to be in control of our lives, working out his purposes, we are bound to fail.

Isa 10:15 No instrument or tool accomplishes its purposes without a greater power. The Assyrians were a tool in God's hands, but they failed to recognize it. When a tool boasts of greater power than the one who uses it, it is in danger of being discarded. We are useful only to the extent that we allow God to use us. If God has given us resources and special talents, we must not regard them as our own creation or special privilege.

Assyrian Art

Many examples of Assyrian art—wall paintings, sculpted reliefs, statues, cylinder seals, ivory carvings, as well as bronze and metal work—have been preserved following excavation of Assyria. Some of this artwork is of particular interest in that it mentions Israel. Sennacherib, on his palace sculptures at Nineveh, depicts the siege of Lachish and the use of Judean captives to work on his building projects. This picture shows a winged human-headed bull, pairs of which guarded the entrance of the Assyrian palace at Calah (c. 870 B.C.).

Can a rod strike unless a hand moves it?
Can a wooden cane walk by itself?
16 Therefore, the Lord, the LORD of Heaven's Armies,
will send a plague among Assyria's proud troops,
and a flaming fire will consume its glory.
17 The LORD, the Light of Israel, will be a fire;
the Holy One will be a flame.
He will devour the thorns and briers with fire,
burning up the enemy in a single night.
18 The LORD will consume Assyria's glory
like a fire consumes a forest in a fruitful land;
it will waste away like sick people in a plague.
19 Of all that glorious forest, only a few trees will survive—
so few that a child could count them!

Hope for the LORD's People

ISAIAH 10:20-34

20 In that day the remnant left in Israel,
the survivors in the house of Jacob,
will no longer depend on allies
who seek to destroy them.
But they will faithfully trust the LORD,
the Holy One of Israel.
21 A remnant will return;*
yes, the remnant of Jacob will return to the Mighty God.
22 But though the people of Israel are as numerous
as the sand of the seashore,
only a remnant of them will return.
The LORD has rightly decided to destroy his people.
23 Yes, the Lord, the LORD of Heaven's Armies,
has already decided to destroy the entire land.*

24So this is what the Lord, the LORD of Heaven's
Armies, says: "O my people in Zion, do not be afraid
of the Assyrians when they oppress you with rod and
club as the Egyptians did long ago. 25In a little while
my anger against you will end, and then my anger will
rise up to destroy them." 26The LORD of Heaven's Armies will lash them with his whip, as he did when
Gideon triumphed over the Midianites at the rock of
Oreb, or when the LORD's staff was raised to drown
the Egyptian army in the sea.

27 In that day the LORD will end the bondage of his people.
He will break the yoke of slavery
and lift it from their shoulders.*
28 Look, the Assyrians are now at Aiath.
They are passing through Migron
and are storing their equipment at Micmash.
29 They are crossing the pass
and are camping at Geba.
Fear strikes the town of Ramah.
All the people of Gibeah, the hometown of Saul,
are running for their lives.
30 Scream in terror,
you people of Gallim!
Shout out a warning to Laishah.
Oh, poor Anathoth!
31 There go the people of Madmenah, all fleeing.
The citizens of Gebim are trying to hide.
32 The enemy stops at Nob for the rest of that day.
He shakes his fist at beautiful Mount Zion, the mountain of Jerusalem.
33 But look! The Lord, the LORD of Heaven's Armies,
will chop down the mighty tree of Assyria with great power!
He will cut down the proud.
That lofty tree will be brought down.
34 He will cut down the forest trees with an ax.
Lebanon will fall to the Mighty One.*

A Branch from David's Line

ISAIAH 11:1-16

1 Out of the stump of David's family* will grow a shoot—
yes, a new Branch bearing fruit from the old root.
2 And the Spirit of the LORD will rest on him—
the Spirit of wisdom and understanding,

Is 10:21 Hebrew *Shear-jashub;* see 7:3; 8:18. **Is 10:22-23** Greek version reads *only a remnant of them will be saved. / For he will carry out his sentence quickly and with finality and righteousness; / for God will carry out his sentence upon all the world with finality.* Compare Rom 9:27-28. **Is 10:27** As in Greek version; Hebrew reads *The yoke will be broken, / for you have grown so fat.* **Is 10:34** Or *with an ax / as even the mighty trees of Lebanon fall.* **Is 11:1** Hebrew *the stump of the line of Jesse.* Jesse was King David's father.

Isa 10:17 Assyria's downfall came in 612 B.C. when Nineveh, the capital city, was destroyed. Assyria had been God's instrument of judgment against Israel, but it, too, would be judged for its wickedness. No one escapes God's judgment against sin, not even the most powerful of nations (Ps 2).

Isa 10:20-21 Once Assyria's army was destroyed, a small group of God's people would stop relying on Assyria and start trusting God. This remnant would be but a fraction of the nation's former population. See Ezra 2:64-65 for the small number who returned to Judah (see also Isa 11:10-16).

Isa 10:20-21 Those who remained faithful to God despite the horrors of the invasion were called the remnant. The key to being a part of the remnant was faith. Being a descendant of Abraham, living in the Promised Land, having trusted God at one time—none of these were good enough. Are you relying on your Christian heritage, your participation in church, or a past experience to qualify you for belonging to God's family? The key to being a true Christian is faith in the mighty God.

Isa 10:28-34 The way these cities are listed approximates the route the Assyrians would take in their invasion of Judah in 701 B.C. They would go from Aiath (probably Ai) at the northern border to Nob (only two miles from Jerusalem).

Isa 11:1-9 Assyria would be like a tree cut down at the height of its power (Isa 10:33-34), never to rise again. Judah (the royal line of David) would be like a tree chopped down to a stump. But from that stump a new shoot would grow—the Messiah. He would be greater than the original tree and would bear much fruit. The Messiah is the fulfillment of God's promise that a descendant of David would rule forever (2 Sam 7:16).

▶ **ISAIAH 11:1-16** ***(cont.)***

the Spirit of counsel and might,
the Spirit of knowledge and the fear
of the LORD.
3 He will delight in obeying the LORD.
He will not judge by appearance
nor make a decision based on hearsay.
4 He will give justice to the poor
and make fair decisions for the exploited.
The earth will shake at the force of his word,
and one breath from his mouth will destroy
the wicked.
5 He will wear righteousness like a belt
and truth like an undergarment.
6 In that day the wolf and the lamb will live
together;
the leopard will lie down with the baby goat.
The calf and the yearling will be safe with
the lion,
and a little child will lead them all.
7 The cow will graze near the bear.
The cub and the calf will lie down together.
The lion will eat hay like a cow.
8 The baby will play safely near the hole
of a cobra.
Yes, a little child will put its hand in a nest
of deadly snakes without harm.
9 Nothing will hurt or destroy in all my holy
mountain,
for as the waters fill the sea,
so the earth will be filled with people who
know the LORD.

10 In that day the heir to David's throne*
will be a banner of salvation to all the world.
The nations will rally to him,
and the land where he lives will be a glorious
place.*

11 In that day the Lord will reach out his hand
a second time
to bring back the remnant of his people—
those who remain in Assyria and northern Egypt;
in southern Egypt, Ethiopia,* and Elam;
in Babylonia,* Hamath, and all the distant
coastlands.
12 He will raise a flag among the nations
and assemble the exiles of Israel.
He will gather the scattered people of Judah
from the ends of the earth.
13 Then at last the jealousy between Israel* and
Judah will end.
They will not be rivals anymore.
14 They will join forces to swoop down on Philistia
to the west.
Together they will attack and plunder the
nations to the east.
They will occupy the lands of Edom and Moab,
and Ammon will obey them.
15 The LORD will make a dry path through the gulf
of the Red Sea.*
He will wave his hand over the Euphrates River,*
sending a mighty wind to divide it into seven
streams
so it can easily be crossed on foot.
16 He will make a highway for the remnant of his
people,
the remnant coming from Assyria,
just as he did for Israel long ago
when they returned from Egypt.

Songs of Praise for Salvation

ISAIAH 12:1-6

1 In that day you will sing:
"I will praise you, O LORD!
You were angry with me, but not any more.
Now you comfort me.

Is 11:10a Hebrew *the root of Jesse.* **Is 11:10b** Greek version reads *In that day the heir to David's throne* [literally *the root of Jesse*] *will come, / and he will rule over the Gentiles. / They will place their hopes on him.* Compare Rom 15:12. **Is 11:11a** Hebrew *in Pathros, Cush.* **Is 11:11b** Hebrew *in Shinar.* **Is 11:13** Hebrew *Ephraim,* referring to the northern kingdom of Israel. **Is 11:15a** Hebrew *will destroy the tongue of the sea of Egypt.* **Is 11:15b** Hebrew *the river.*

Isa 11:3-5 God will judge with righteousness. We long for fair treatment from others, but do we give it? We hate those who base their judgments on appearance, false evidence, or hearsay, but are we quick to judge others using those standards? Only Christ can be the perfectly fair judge. Only as he governs our hearts can we learn to be as fair in our treatment of others as we expect others to be toward us.

Isa 11:4-5 Judah had become corrupt and was surrounded by hostile, foreign powers. The nation desperately needed a revival of righteousness, justice, and faithfulness. They needed to turn from selfishness and give justice to the poor and the oppressed. The righteousness that God values is more than refraining from sin. It is actively turning toward others and offering them the help they need.

Isa 11:6-10 A golden age is yet to come, a time of peace when children will play safely with formerly dangerous animals. Not all of this was fulfilled at Christ's first coming. For example, nature has not returned to its intended balance and harmony (see Rom 8:9-22). Such perfect tranquility will be possible only when Christ reigns over the earth.

Isa 11:11 When will this remnant of God's people be returned to their land? Old Testament prophecy is often applied both to the near future and the distant future. Judah would soon be exiled to Babylon, and a remnant would return to Jerusalem in 538 B.C. at Cyrus's decree. In the ages to come, God's people would be dispersed throughout the world. These locations represent the four corners of the known world—Hamath in the north, Egypt in the south, Assyria and Babylonia in the east, the distant coastlands in the west. Ultimately God's people will be regathered when Christ comes to reign over the earth.

Isa 11:14 Edom, Moab, and Ammon were three countries bordering Judah (along with Philistia). They were the nations who, when Judah was defeated, rejoiced and took their land.

Isa 11:15-16 Isaiah is talking about a new or second Exodus when God will bring his scattered people back to himself, and the Messiah will come. The Lord dried up the Red Sea so the Israelites could walk through it on their way to the Promised Land (Exod 14). He dried up the Jordan River so the nation could cross into the land (Josh 3). God will again provide the way of return for his people.

Isa 12:1ff This chapter is a hymn of praise—another graphic description of the people's joy

2 See, God has come to save me.
I will trust in him and not be afraid.
The LORD GOD is my strength and my song;
he has given me victory."
3 With joy you will drink deeply
from the fountain of salvation!
4 In that wonderful day you will sing:
"Thank the LORD! Praise his name!
Tell the nations what he has done.
Let them know how mighty he is!
5 Sing to the LORD, for he has done wonderful things.
Make known his praise around the world.
6 Let all the people of Jerusalem* shout his praise with joy!
For great is the Holy One of Israel who lives among you."

A Message about Damascus and Israel

ISAIAH 17:1-14

This message came to me concerning Damascus:
"Look, the city of Damascus will disappear!
It will become a heap of ruins.
2 The towns of Aroer will be deserted.
Flocks will graze in the streets and lie down undisturbed,
with no one to chase them away.
3 The fortified towns of Israel* will also be destroyed,
and the royal power of Damascus will end.
All that remains of Syria*
will share the fate of Israel's departed glory,"
declares the LORD of Heaven's Armies.

4 "In that day Israel's* glory will grow dim;
its robust body will waste away.
5 The whole land will look like a grainfield
after the harvesters have gathered the grain.
It will be desolate,
like the fields in the valley of Rephaim
after the harvest.
6 Only a few of its people will be left,
like stray olives left on a tree after the harvest.
Only two or three remain in the highest branches,
four or five scattered here and there on the limbs,"
declares the LORD, the God of Israel.

7 Then at last the people will look to their Creator
and turn their eyes to the Holy One of Israel.
8 They will no longer look to their idols for help
or worship what their own hands have made.
They will never again bow down to their Asherah poles
or worship at the pagan shrines they have built.
9 Their largest cities will be like a deserted forest,
like the land the Hivites and Amorites abandoned*
when the Israelites came here so long ago.
It will be utterly desolate.
10 Why? Because you have turned from the God who can save you.
You have forgotten the Rock who can hide you.
So you may plant the finest grapevines
and import the most expensive seedlings.
11 They may sprout on the day you set them out;
yes, they may blossom on the very morning you plant them,
but you will never pick any grapes from them.
Your only harvest will be a load of grief and unrelieved pain.

12 Listen! The armies of many nations
roar like the roaring of the sea.
Hear the thunder of the mighty forces
as they rush forward like thundering waves.
13 But though they thunder like breakers on a beach,
God will silence them, and they will run away.
They will flee like chaff scattered by the wind,
like a tumbleweed whirling before a storm.
14 In the evening Israel waits in terror,
but by dawn its enemies are dead.
This is the just reward of those who plunder us,
a fitting end for those who destroy us.

Is 12:6 Hebrew *Zion.* **Is 17:3a** Hebrew *of Ephraim,* referring to the northern kingdom of Israel. **Is 17:3b** Hebrew *Aram.* **Is 17:4** Hebrew *Jacob's.* See note on 14:1. **Is 17:9** As in Greek version; Hebrew reads *like places of the wood and the highest bough.*

when Jesus Christ comes to reign over the earth. Even now we need to express the depth of our gratitude to God by thanking him, praising him, and telling others about him.

Isa 17:1ff The northern kingdom and Aram made an alliance to fight against Assyria. But Tiglath-pileser III captured Damascus, the capital of Aram, in 732 B.C. and annexed the northern kingdom to the Assyrian Empire. Ahaz, king of Judah, paid tribute to Tiglath-pileser III (2 Kgs 16:1-14).

Isa 17:7-11 God's message to Damascus was that it would be completely destroyed. The Arameans had turned from the God who could save them, depending instead on their idols and their own strength. No matter how successful they were, God's judgment was sure. Often we depend on the trappings of success (expensive cars, pastimes, clothes, homes) to give us fulfillment. But God says we will reap grief and pain if we have depended on temporal things to give us eternal security. If we don't want the same treatment Damascus received, we must turn from these false allurements and trust in God.

Isa 17:8 The Asherah poles were images of Asherah, a Canaanite goddess who was the female consort of Baal. Queen Jezebel may have brought the worship of Asherah into the northern kingdom. The cult encouraged immoral sexual practices and attracted many people. The Bible warns against worshiping Asherah poles (Deut 12:3; 16:21), and Manasseh was condemned for putting up an Asherah pole in the Temple (2 Kgs 21:7).

Asherah poles are no problem in our world, but a religion based on sexuality is. Pornography has become an addiction for many people. Media and entertainment industries feed our society's obsession with sex. The runaway desire for stimulation and gratification often comes from inadequate perspectives on love and happiness. God offers real joy and lasting love. Be on the alert for how sexual images divert us from God.

Ahaz Closes the Temple PARALLEL

2 KINGS 16:10-18

King Ahaz then went to Damascus to meet with King
Tiglath-pileser of Assyria. While he was there, he took
special note of the altar. Then he sent a model of the
altar to Uriah the priest, along with its design in full
detail. [11]Uriah followed the king's instructions and
built an altar just like it, and it was ready before the
king returned from Damascus. [12]When the king returned, he inspected the altar and made offerings on
it. [13]He presented a burnt offering and a grain offering, he poured out a liquid offering, and he sprinkled
the blood of peace offerings on the altar.
[14]Then King Ahaz removed the old bronze altar
from its place in front of the LORD's Temple, between the entrance and the new altar, and placed it
on the north side of the new altar. [15]He told Uriah
the priest, "Use the new altar* for the morning sacrifices of burnt offering, the evening grain offering,
the king's burnt offering and grain offering, and the
burnt offerings of all the people, as well as their grain
offerings and liquid offerings. Sprinkle the blood
from all the burnt offerings and sacrifices on the
new altar. The bronze altar will be for my personal
use only." [16]Uriah the priest did just as King Ahaz
commanded him.
[17]Then the king removed the side panels and basins from the portable water carts. He also removed
the great bronze basin called the Sea from the backs
of the bronze oxen and placed it on the stone pavement. [18]In deference to the king of Assyria, he also
removed the canopy that had been constructed inside the palace for use on the Sabbath day,* as well as
the king's outer entrance to the Temple of the LORD.

2 CHRONICLES 28:16-25

At that time King Ahaz of Judah asked the king of
Assyria for help. [17]The armies of Edom had again invaded Judah and taken captives. [18]And the Philistines
had raided towns located in the foothills of Judah*
and in the Negev of Judah. They had already captured
and occupied Beth-shemesh, Aijalon, Gederoth, Soco
with its villages, Timnah with its villages, and Gimzo
with its villages. [19]The LORD was humbling Judah because of King Ahaz of Judah,* for he had encouraged
his people to sin and had been utterly unfaithful to
the LORD.
[20]So when King Tiglath-pileser* of Assyria arrived,
he attacked Ahaz instead of helping him. [21]Ahaz took
valuable items from the LORD's Temple, the royal palace, and from the homes of his officials and gave
them to the king of Assyria as tribute. But this did
not help him.
[22]Even during this time of trouble, King Ahaz continued to reject the LORD. [23]He offered sacrifices to the
gods of Damascus who had defeated him, for he said,

2 Kgs 16:15 Hebrew *the great altar.* **2 Kgs 16:18** The meaning of the Hebrew is uncertain. **2 Chr 28:18** Hebrew *the Shephelah.* **2 Chr 28:19** Masoretic Text reads *of Israel;* also in 28:23, 27. The author of Chronicles sees Judah as representative of the true Israel. (Some Hebrew manuscripts and Greek version read *of Judah.*) **2 Chr 28:20** Hebrew *Tilgath-pilneser,* a variant spelling of Tiglath-pileser.

Tiglath-pileser III

Tiglath-pileser III (745–727 B.C.) was a strong and resourceful king whose reign is remarkable for the rapid extension of Assyrian boundaries and for the peaceful administration of newly acquired territories. He assisted Babylon by defeating the Arameans, and diplomatically retained Babylonian support while he concentrated his military efforts elsewhere. The illustration shows an image of Tiglath-pileser III from the walls of his palace.

Instead of trusting in the Lord, King Ahaz had tried to pay off Tiglath-pileser with treasures from the Temple and royal palace. This didn't work (2 Chr 28:20-21). Trust in the Lord should be foremost in our lives.

2 Kgs 16:10 The Assyrians had captured Damascus, the capital of Aram (732 B.C.). Ahaz went there to express gratitude to Tiglath-pileser for coming to his aid (2 Kgs 16:7-9). Ahaz also wanted to show loyalty because he was afraid of an Assyrian southern sweep. But he was relying more on money than on God to keep the powerful king out of his land, and his plan failed. Although Tiglath-pileser did not conquer Judah, he caused much trouble, and Ahaz regretted asking for his help (2 Chr 28:20-21).

2 Kgs 16:10-16 Evil King Ahaz copied pagan religious customs, changed the Temple services, and used the Temple altar for his personal benefit. In so doing, he demonstrated a callous disregard for God's commands. We condemn Ahaz for his action, but we act the same way if we try to mold God's message to fit our personal preferences. We must worship God for who he is, not what we would selfishly like him to be.

2 Kgs 16:14-18 Ahaz replaced the bronze altar (the altar of burnt offering) with a replica of the pagan altar he had seen in Damascus. (The bronze altar was not thrown out, but was kept for use in divination. The basins were intended for washing the sacrifices, and the Sea was a huge reservoir of water for Temple use.) These changes were extremely serious because God had given specific directions on how the altar should look and be used (Exod 27:1-8). Building this new altar was like installing an idol. But because Judah was Assyria's vassal state, Ahaz was eager to please the Assyrian king. Sadly, Ahaz allowed the king of Assyria to replace God as Judah's leader. No one, no matter how attractive or powerful, should replace God's leadership in our lives.

2 Kgs 16:18 Ahaz had become a weak king with a weak and compromising high priest. Judah's religious system was in shambles. It now included pagan customs, and its chief aim was only to please those in power. If we copy others in order to please them, we risk making them more important than God in our lives.

2 Chr 28:22 Difficulties and struggles can devastate people, or they can stimulate growth and maturity. For Ahaz, deep troubles

"Since these gods helped the kings of Aram, they will
help me, too, if I sacrifice to them." But instead, they
led to his ruin and the ruin of all Judah.
24The king took the various articles from the Temple of God and broke them into pieces. He shut the
doors of the LORD's Temple so that no one could worship there, and he set up altars to pagan gods in every
corner of Jerusalem. 25He made pagan shrines in all
the towns of Judah for offering sacrifices to other
gods. In this way, he aroused the anger of the LORD,
the God of his ancestors.

Hezekiah Begins His Reign in Judah PARALLEL

2 KINGS 18:1-8

Hezekiah son of Ahaz began to rule over Judah in the
third year of King Hoshea's reign in Israel. 2He was
twenty-five years old when he became king, and he
reigned in Jerusalem twenty-nine years. His mother
was Abijah,* the daughter of Zechariah. 3He did what
was pleasing in the LORD's sight, just as his ancestor
David had done. 4He removed the pagan shrines,
smashed the sacred pillars, and cut down the Asherah

2 Kgs 18:2 As in parallel text at 2 Chr 29:1; Hebrew reads *Abi,* a variant spelling of Abijah.

HEZEKIAH

The past is an important part of today's actions and tomorrow's plans. The people and kings of Judah had a rich past, filled with God's action, guidance, and commands. But with each passing generation, they also had a growing list of tragedies that occurred when the people forgot that their God, who had cared for them in the past, also cared about the present and the future—and demanded their continued obedience. Hezekiah was one of the few kings of Judah who was constantly aware of God's acts in the past and his interest in the events of every day. The Bible describes him as a king who had a close relationship with God. • As a reformer, Hezekiah was most concerned with present obedience. Judah was filled with visual reminders of the people's lack of trust in God, and Hezekiah boldly cleaned house. Altars, idols, and pagan temples were destroyed. Even the bronze serpent Moses had made in the wilderness was not spared because it had ceased to point the people to God and had also become an idol. The Temple in Jerusalem, whose doors had been nailed shut by Hezekiah's own father, was cleaned out and reopened. The Passover was reinstituted as a national holiday, and there was revival in Judah. • Although he had a natural inclination to respond to present problems, Hezekiah's life shows little evidence of concern about the future. He took few actions to preserve the effects of his sweeping reforms. His successful efforts made him proud. His unwise display of wealth to the Babylonian delegation got Judah included on Babylon's "Nations to Conquer" list. When Isaiah informed Hezekiah of the foolishness of his act, the king's answer displayed his persistent lack of foresight—he was thankful that any evil consequences would be delayed until after he died. And the lives of three kings who followed him—Manasseh, Amon, and Josiah—were deeply affected by both Hezekiah's accomplishments and his weaknesses. • The past affects your decisions and actions today, and these, in turn, affect the future. There are lessons to learn and errors to avoid repeating. Remember that part of the success of your past will be measured by what you do with it now and how well you use it to prepare for the future.

Strengths and accomplishments	• Instigated civil and religious reforms in Judah • Had a personal, growing relationship with God • Developed a powerful prayer life • Patron of several chapters in the book of Proverbs (Prov 25:1)
Weaknesses and mistakes	• Showed little interest or wisdom in planning for the future and protecting for others the spiritual heritage he enjoyed • Rashly showed all his wealth to messengers from Babylon
Lessons from his life	• Sweeping reforms are short-lived when little action is taken to preserve them for the future • Past obedience to God does not remove the possibility of present disobedience • Complete dependence on God yields amazing results
Vital statistics	• Where: Jerusalem • Occupation: 13th king of Judah, the southern kingdom • Relatives: Father: Ahaz. Mother: Abijah. Son: Manasseh. • Contemporaries: Isaiah, Hoshea, Micah, Sennacherib
Key verses	"Hezekiah trusted in the LORD, the God of Israel. There was no one like him among all the kings of Judah, either before or after his time. He remained faithful to the LORD in everything, and he carefully obeyed all the commands the LORD had given Moses" (2 Kgs 18:5-6).

Hezekiah's story is told in 2 Kings 16:20–20:21; 2 Chronicles 28:27–32:33; Isaiah 36:1–39:8. He is also mentioned in Proverbs 25:1; Isaiah 1:1; Jeremiah 15:4; 26:18-19; Hosea 1:1; Micah 1:1.

led to spiritual collapse. We do not need to respond like Ahaz. When facing problems or tragedy, we must remember that rough times give us a chance to grow (Jas 1:2-4). When you are facing trials, don't turn away from God; turn *to* him. See these times as opportunities for you to claim God's help.

2 Kgs 18:4 The bronze serpent had been made to cure the Israelites of the bite of poisonous snakes (Num 21:4-9). It had demonstrated God's presence and power and had reminded the people of his mercy and forgiveness. But it had become an object of worship instead of a reminder of whom to worship, so Hezekiah was forced to destroy it. We must be careful that aids to our worship don't become objects of worship themselves. Most objects are not made to be idols, but they become idols by the way people use them.

▸ 2 KINGS 18:1-8 ***(cont.)***

poles. He broke up the bronze serpent that Moses
had made, because the people of Israel had been offering sacrifices to it. The bronze serpent was called
Nehushtan.*
5Hezekiah trusted in the LORD, the God of Israel.
There was no one like him among all the kings of Judah,
either before or after his time. 6He remained faithful to
the LORD in everything, and he carefully obeyed all the
commands the LORD had given Moses. 7So the LORD was
with him, and Hezekiah was successful in everything he
did. He revolted against the king of Assyria and refused
to pay him tribute. 8He also conquered the Philistines as
far distant as Gaza and its territory, from their smallest
outpost to their largest walled city.

2 CHRONICLES 29:1-2

Hezekiah was twenty-five years old when he became
the king of Judah, and he reigned in Jerusalem twenty-
nine years. His mother was Abijah, the daughter of
Zechariah. 2He did what was pleasing in the LORD's
sight, just as his ancestor David had done.

2 Kgs 18:4 *Nehushtan* sounds like the Hebrew terms that mean "snake," "bronze," and "unclean thing."

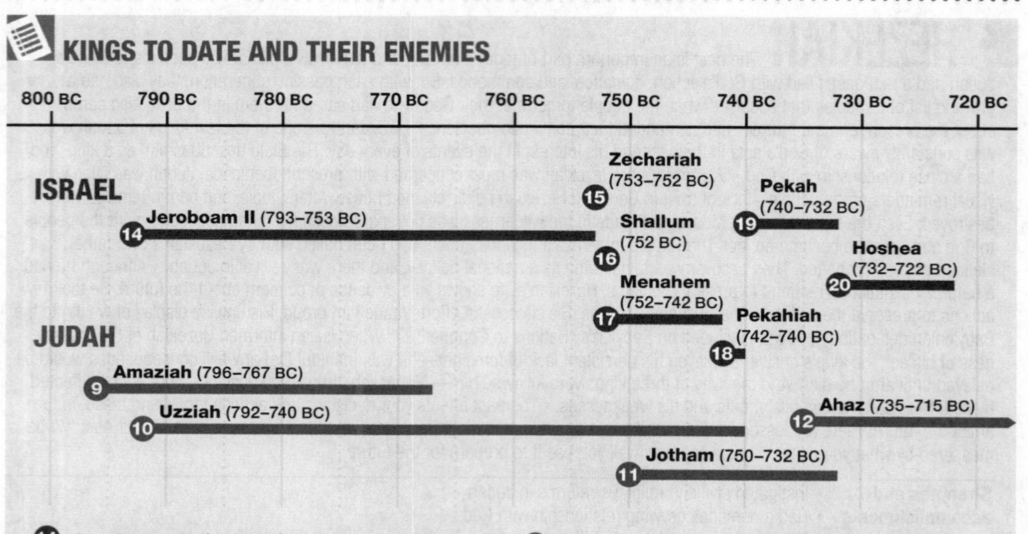

⓮ **Jeroboam II** (41 years) Recaptured Israel's former territories from Aram (*2 Kgs 14:16-29*).

⓯ **Zechariah** (6 months) (*2 Kgs 14:29–15:12*)

⓰ **Shallum** (1 month) (*2 Kgs 15:10-15*)

⓱ **Menahem** (10 years) Paid tribute to Tiglath-pileser (Assyria) (*2 Kgs 15:14-22*).

⓲ **Pekahiah** (2 years) (*2 Kgs 15:22-26*)

⓳ **Pekah** (8 years) Suffered first conquest by Assyria (*2 Kgs 15:25-31; 2 Chr 28:5-8*).

⓴ **Hoshea** (9 years) Suffered complete conquest by Shalmaneser (Assyria) (*2 Kgs 15:30; 17:1-6*).

❾ **Amaziah** (29 years) Won battles against Edom and Selah, defeated by Jehoash and Jeroboam II (Israel) (*2 Kgs 14:1-20; 2 Chr 24:27–25:28*).

❿ **Uzziah** (52 years) Conquered Gath in Philistia (*2 Kgs 15:1-7; 2 Chr 26:1-23*).

⓫ **Jotham** (16 years) Won battles against Ammonites and Arabs, harassed by Pekah (Israel) and Rezin (Aram) (*2 Kgs 15:32-38; 2 Chr 26:23–27:9*).

⓬ **Ahaz** (16 years) Harassed by Pekah (Israel), paid Assyria for protection against Rezin (Aram), also harassed by Edom and Philistia (*2 Kgs 15:38–16:20; 2 Chr 27:9–28:27*).

2 Kgs 18:5 "There was no one like him among all the kings of Judah." In dramatic contrast with his father, Ahaz, Hezekiah followed God more closely and sincerely than any other king of Judah or Israel. This statement refers to the kings after the division of the kingdom and so does not include David, considered the king most devoted to God.

2 Kgs 18:7 Judah was sandwiched between two world powers, Egypt and Assyria. Both wanted to control Judah and Israel because they lay at the vital crossroads of all ancient Near East trade. The nation that controlled Judah would have a military and economic advantage over its rivals. When Hezekiah became king, Assyria controlled Judah. Acting with great courage, Hezekiah rebelled against this mighty empire to whom his father had submitted. He placed his faith in God's strength rather than his own, and he obeyed God's commands in spite of the obstacles and dangers that, from a purely human standpoint, looked overwhelming.

The End of Pekah's Reign in Israel

2 KINGS 15:30-31

Then Hoshea son of Elah conspired against Pekah and assassinated him. He began to rule over Israel in the twentieth year of Jotham son of Uzziah.

[31]The rest of the events in Pekah's reign and everything he did are recorded in *The Book of the History of the Kings of Israel.*

Hoshea Begins His Reign in Israel

2 KINGS 17:1-4

Hoshea son of Elah began to rule over Israel in the twelfth year of King Ahaz's reign in Judah. He reigned in Samaria nine years. [2]He did what was evil in the LORD's sight, but not to the same extent as the kings of Israel who ruled before him.

[3]King Shalmaneser of Assyria attacked King Hoshea, so Hoshea was forced to pay heavy tribute to Assyria. [4]But Hoshea stopped paying the annual tribute and conspired against the king of Assyria by asking King So of Egypt* to help him shake free of Assyria's power. When the king of Assyria discovered this treachery, he seized Hoshea and put him in prison.

2 Kgs 17:4 Or *by asking the king of Egypt at Sais.*

H. The Ministry of the Prophet Hosea

Hosea was the last great prophet that God sent to the northern kingdom of Israel before they were destroyed and exiled by Assyria. He presents a powerful message of God's love for his people, even while they are sinning against him.

1. HOSEA'S WAYWARD WIFE

Hosea highlights the parallels between his relationship with Gomer and God's relationship with the nation of Israel. Although the people made a covenant with the one true God, they went after false gods. In the same way, Hosea married Gomer, knowing ahead of time that she would leave him. Hosea tenderly dealt with his wife in spite of her sin. And God was merciful toward the people of Israel despite their sins. God has not changed; he is still merciful and forgiving.

730 BC

Hosea's prophetic ministry

Hosea's Prophecy

HOSEA 1:1

The LORD gave this message to Hosea son of Beeri during the years when Uzziah, Jotham, Ahaz, and Hezekiah were kings of Judah, and Jeroboam son of Jehoash* was king of Israel.

Hosea's Wife and Children

HOSEA 1:2–2:1

When the LORD first began speaking to Israel through Hosea, he said to him, "Go and marry a prostitute,* so that some of her children will be conceived in prostitution. This will illustrate how Israel has acted like a

Hos 1:1 Hebrew *Joash,* a variant spelling of Jehoash. **Hos 1:2** Or *a promiscuous woman.*

2 Kgs 15:30 Hoshea was Israel's last king.

2 Kgs 17:3 This was probably Shalmaneser V, who had become king of Assyria after Tiglath-pileser (727–722 B.C.). He continued to demand heavy tribute from Israel. Israel's king Hoshea decided to rebel against Assyria and join forces with King So of Egypt (2 Kgs 17:4). This was not only foolish but also against God's commands. To destroy this alliance, Shalmaneser attacked and besieged Samaria for three years. But just before Samaria fell, Shalmaneser died. His successor, Sargon II, took credit for capturing the city, destroying the nation of Israel, and carrying away its people.

Hos 1:1 Hosea was a prophet to the northern kingdom of Israel from 753 to 715 B.C. Under the reign of Jeroboam II, the northern kingdom had prospered materially but had decayed spiritually. The people were greedy and had adopted the moral behavior and idolatrous religion of the surrounding Canaanites. This spiritual and moral decay continued through the end of the northern kingdom in 722 B.C., and Hosea's messages reflect this sad situation.

Hosea's role was to show how the people of the northern kingdom had been unfaithful to God, their "husband" and provider, and had married themselves to Baal and the gods of Canaan. He warned that unless they repented of their sin and turned back to God, they were headed for destruction. Hosea spoke of God's characteristics—his powerful love and justice—and how their practical experience of these should affect their lives and make them return to God. Unfortunately, the people had broken their covenant with God, and they would receive the punishments God had promised (Deut 27–28).

Hos 1:2-3 Did God really order his prophet to marry a woman who was a prostitute? Some who find it difficult to believe God could make such a request view this story as an illustration, not a historical event. Many think the story is historical and give one of these explanations: (1) According to God's law, a priest could not marry a prostitute or a divorced woman (Lev 21:7). But Hosea was not a priest. (2) It is possible that Gomer was not a prostitute when Hosea married her and that God was letting Hosea know that Gomer would later turn to adultery and prostitution. In any case, Hosea knew ahead of time that his wife would be unfaithful and that their married life would become a living object lesson to the adulterous northern kingdom. Hosea's marriage to an unfaithful woman would illustrate God's relationship to the unfaithful nation of Israel.

Hos 1:2-3 It is difficult to imagine Hosea's feelings when God told him to marry a woman who would be unfaithful to him. He may not have wanted to do it, but he obeyed. God often required extraordinary obedience from his prophets who were facing extraordinary times. God may ask you to do something difficult and extraordinary, too. If he does, how will you respond? Will you obey him, trusting that he who knows everything has a special purpose for his request? Will you be able to accept the fact that the pain involved in obedience may benefit those you serve and not you personally?

▸ **HOSEA 1:2–2:1** *(cont.)*
prostitute by turning against the LORD and worshiping other gods."

3So Hosea married Gomer, the daughter of Diblaim,
and she became pregnant and gave Hosea a son. 4And
the LORD said, "Name the child Jezreel, for I am about to punish King Jehu's dynasty to avenge the murders he committed at Jezreel. In fact, I will bring an end to
Israel's independence. 5I will break its military power
in the Jezreel Valley."

6Soon Gomer became pregnant again and gave birth to a daughter. And the LORD said to Hosea, "Name your daughter Lo-ruhamah—'Not loved'—for I will no longer show love to the people of Israel or forgive
them. 7But I will show love to the people of Judah. I will free them from their enemies—not with weapons and armies or horses and charioteers, but by my power as the LORD their God."

8After Gomer had weaned Lo-ruhamah, she again became pregnant and gave birth to a second son.
9And the LORD said, "Name him Lo-ammi—'Not my people'—for Israel is not my people, and I am not their God.

10*"Yet the time will come when Israel's people will be like the sands of the seashore—too many to count! Then, at the place where they were told, 'You are not my people,' it will be said, 'You are children of
the living God.' 11Then the people of Judah and Israel will unite together. They will choose one leader for themselves, and they will return from exile together. What a day that will be—the day of Jezreel*—when God will again plant his people in his land.

2:1*"In that day you will call your brothers Ammi—'My people.' And you will call your sisters Ruhamah—'The ones I love.'

Hos 1:10 Verses 1:10-11 are numbered 2:1-2 in Hebrew text. **Hos 1:11** *Jezreel* means "God plants." **Hos 2:1** Verses 2:1-23 are numbered 2:3-25 in Hebrew text.

Hos 1:4-5 Elijah had predicted that the family of Israel's King Ahab would be destroyed because of their wickedness (1 Kgs 21:20-22), but Jehu went too far in carrying out God's command (2 Kgs 10:1-11). Therefore, Jehu's dynasty would also be punished—in the Jezreel Valley, the very place where he carried out the massacre of Ahab's family. God's promise to put an end to Israel as an independent kingdom came true 25 years later when the Assyrians conquered the northern kingdom and carried the people into captivity.

Hos 1:6, 8 In Hosea 1:3, we read that Gomer gave Hosea a son. In Hosea 1:6, Gomer gave birth to a daughter, and God called the child "your daughter" (referring to Hosea). However, in Hosea 1:8, we learn that Gomer gave birth to a second son, but there is no indication that Hosea was his natural father. The key to this part of the story is found in the names God chose for the children, showing his reaction to Israel's unfaithfulness. God's reaction to unfaithfulness is no different today. He wants our complete devotion.

Hos 1:7 Israel and Judah had been a united kingdom under David and Solomon. After Solomon's death a civil dispute had arisen, and the land was divided into a northern kingdom (Israel, whose capital was Samaria) and a southern kingdom (Judah, whose capital was Jerusalem). Although Hosea spoke mainly to the northern kingdom, his concern, like God's, was for the entire nation of Israelites including those from the kingdom of Judah. Just as Hosea prophesied, God helped Judah because Judah had a few kings who honored him. Shortly after defeating Israel, the Assyrian emperor Sennacherib invaded Judah and besieged Jerusalem. He was driven off by an angel's powerful and dramatic intervention (Isa 36–37).

Hos 1:7 God said he would personally rescue the people of Judah from their enemies with no help from their weapons or armies.

HOSEA

Hosea served as a prophet to Israel (the northern kingdom) from 753–715 B.C.

Climate of the times	Israel's last six kings were especially wicked; they promoted heavy taxes, oppression of the poor, idol worship, and total disregard for God. Israel was subjected to Assyria and was forced to pay tribute, which depleted its few remaining resources.
Main message	The people of Israel had sinned against God as an adulterous woman sins against her husband. Judgment was sure to come for living in total disregard for God and fellow humans. Israel fell to Assyria in 722 B.C.
Importance of message	When we sin, we sever our relationship with God, breaking our commitment to him. While all must answer to God for their sins, those who seek God's forgiveness are spared eternal judgment.
Contemporary prophets	Jonah (793–753 B.C.), Amos (760–750 B.C.), Micah (742–687 B.C.), Isaiah (740–681 B.C.)

Although God asks us to do our part, we should remember that he is not limited to human effort. God often chooses to work through people, but only because it is good for *them*. He can accomplish all his purposes without any help from us if he so chooses. You are very important to God, but on your own you have neither the ability to fulfill nor the power to disrupt God's plans.

Hos 1:9 Here God was in essence dissolving the covenant (Jer 7:23). The name of the third child conveys the finality of God's judgment. God's warnings recorded in Deuteronomy 28:15-68 were beginning to come true: Israel was abandoning God, and in turn, he was leaving them alone and without his blessings.

Hos 1:10 The Old Testament prophetic books sometimes use the word Israel to refer to the people of the united kingdom (north and south) and sometimes just to the northern kingdom. In talking about past events, Hosea usually thought of Israel as the northern kingdom with its capital in Samaria. But when Hosea spoke about future events relating to God's promises of restoration, it is difficult to understand his words as applying only to the northern kingdom because the exiled northerners would become hopelessly intermingled with their conquerors. Thus, most scholars see the promises of return as either: (1) conditional—the Israelites chose not to return to God, and therefore they were not entitled to the blessings included in the promises of restoration, or (2) unconditional—God's promises of restoration have been fulfilled in Jesus Christ, and therefore the church (the new Israel) receives his blessings (Rom 9:25-26; 1 Pet 2:10).

Hos 1:10-11 Although Israel was unfaithful, God's commitment remained unchanged. This promise of a future reuniting confirmed the covenant made with Moses (Deut 30:1-10) and foreshadowed the prophecies of Jeremiah (Jer 29:11-14; 31:31-40) and Ezekiel (Ezek 11:16-21). It was a prediction of the day when all the people of God would be united under Christ. Today all believers every-

Charges against an Unfaithful Wife

HOSEA 2:2-13

2 "But now bring charges against Israel—your
mother—
for she is no longer my wife,
and I am no longer her husband.
Tell her to remove the prostitute's makeup
from her face
and the clothing that exposes her breasts.
3 Otherwise, I will strip her as naked
as she was on the day she was born.
I will leave her to die of thirst,
as in a dry and barren wilderness.
4 And I will not love her children,
for they were conceived in prostitution.
5 Their mother is a shameless prostitute
and became pregnant in a shameful way.
She said, 'I'll run after other lovers
and sell myself to them for food and water,
for clothing of wool and linen,
and for olive oil and drinks.'

6 "For this reason I will fence her in with
thornbushes.
I will block her path with a wall
to make her lose her way.
7 When she runs after her lovers,
she won't be able to catch them.
She will search for them
but not find them.
Then she will think,
'I might as well return to my husband,
for I was better off with him than
I am now.'
8 She doesn't realize it was I who gave her
everything she has—
the grain, the new wine, the olive oil;
I even gave her silver and gold.
But she gave all my gifts to Baal.

9 "But now I will take back the ripened grain and
new wine
I generously provided each harvest season.
I will take away the wool and linen clothing
I gave her to cover her nakedness.
10 I will strip her naked in public,
while all her lovers look on.
No one will be able
to rescue her from my hands.
11 I will put an end to her annual festivals,
her new moon celebrations, and her
Sabbath days—
all her appointed festivals.
12 I will destroy her grapevines and fig trees,
things she claims her lovers gave her.
I will let them grow into tangled thickets,
where only wild animals will eat the fruit.
13 I will punish her for all those times
when she burned incense to her images
of Baal,
when she put on her earrings and jewels
and went out to look for her lovers
but forgot all about me,"
says the LORD.

---

where are God's chosen people, "royal priests, a holy nation, God's very own possession" (see 1 Pet 2:9).

Hos 1:11 Just as the other children's names carried significance, so did Jezreel's. In verse 4, the name depicts divine judgment; here it represents planting. The name means "God plants." This was a sign of a new day and a new relationship between God and Israel.

Hos 2:2ff Israel's punishment and restoration are the themes of this chapter. As in a court case, the prostitute is brought to trial and found guilty. But after her punishment, she is joyfully and tenderly restored to God.

Hos 2:5-7 The Israelites were thanking false gods (specifically Baal, the god whom they believed controlled weather and thus farming) for their food, shelter, and clothing, instead of the true God, who gave those blessings. Therefore, God would fence Israel in "with thornbushes" and "block her path" by making the rewards of idol worship so disappointing that the people would be persuaded to turn back to God. Despite Israel's unfaithfulness, God was still faithful and merciful. He would continue to hold his arms out to his people, even to the point of placing obstacles in their wayward path to turn them back to him.

Hos 2:7 Just as Gomer would return to her husband if she thought she would be better off with him, so people often return to God when they find life's struggle too difficult to handle. Returning to God out of desperation is better than rebelling against him, but it is better yet to turn to God out of gratitude for his care.

Hos 2:8 Material possessions are success symbols in most societies. Israel was a wealthy nation at this time, and Gomer may have accumulated silver and gold. But Gomer didn't realize that Hosea had given her all she owned, just as Israel did not recognize God as the giver of blessings. Both Gomer and Israel used their possessions irresponsibly as they ran after other lovers and other gods. How do you use your possessions? Use what God has given you to honor him.

Hos 2:12 The Israelites were so immersed in idolatry that they actually believed pagan gods gave them their vineyards and orchards. They had forgotten that the entire land was a gift from God (Deut 32:49). Today many people give credit to everything and everyone but God for their prosperity—luck, hard work, quick thinking, the right contacts. When *you* succeed, who gets the credit?

Hos 2:13 Baal was the most important of the Canaanite gods, and his name came to be used to describe all the local deities worshiped throughout the land occupied by Israel. Unfortunately, the Israelites did not get rid of the idols and pagan worship centers as they had been commanded. Instead, they tolerated and frequently joined Baal worshipers, often through the influence of corrupt kings. One Israelite king especially noted for his Baal worship was Ahab. The prophet Elijah, in a dramatic showdown with Ahab's hired prophets, proved God's power far superior to Baal's (1 Kgs 18).

The LORD's Love for Unfaithful Israel

HOSEA 2:14-23

14 "But then I will win her back once again.
I will lead her into the desert
and speak tenderly to her there.
15 I will return her vineyards to her
and transform the Valley of Trouble* into
a gateway of hope.
She will give herself to me there,
as she did long ago when she was young,
when I freed her from her captivity in Egypt.
16 When that day comes," says the LORD,
"you will call me 'my husband'
instead of 'my master.'*
17 O Israel, I will wipe the many names of Baal
from your lips,
and you will never mention them again.
18 On that day I will make a covenant
with all the wild animals and the birds
of the sky
and the animals that scurry along the ground
so they will not harm you.
I will remove all weapons of war from the land,
all swords and bows,
so you can live unafraid
in peace and safety.
19 I will make you my wife forever,
showing you righteousness and justice,
unfailing love and compassion.
20 I will be faithful to you and make you mine,
and you will finally know me as the LORD.
21 "In that day, I will answer,"
says the LORD.
"I will answer the sky as it pleads for clouds.
And the sky will answer the earth with rain.
22 Then the earth will answer the thirsty cries
of the grain, the grapevines, and the olive trees.
And they in turn will answer,
'Jezreel'—'God plants!'
23 At that time I will plant a crop of Israelites
and raise them for myself.
I will show love
to those I called 'Not loved.'*
And to those I called 'Not my people,'*
I will say, 'Now you are my people.'
And they will reply, 'You are our God!'"

Hosea's Wife Is Redeemed

HOSEA 3:1-5

Then the LORD said to me, "Go and love your wife
again, even though she* commits adultery with another lover. This will illustrate that the LORD still loves
Israel, even though the people have turned to other
gods and love to worship them.*"
2So I bought her back for fifteen pieces of silver*
and five bushels of barley and a measure of wine.*
3Then I said to her, "You must live in my house for

Hos 2:15 Hebrew *valley of Achor.* **Hos 2:16** Hebrew *'my baal.'* **Hos 2:23a** Hebrew *Lo-ruhamah;* see 1:6. **Hos 2:23b** Hebrew *Lo-ammi;* see 1:9. **Hos 3:1a** Or *Go and love a woman who.* **Hos 3:1b** Hebrew *love their raisin cakes.* **Hos 3:2a** Hebrew *15 shekels of silver,* about 6 ounces or 171 grams in weight. **Hos 3:2b** As in Greek version, which reads *a homer of barley and a wineskin full of wine;* Hebrew reads *a homer* [5 bushels or 182 liters] *of barley and a lethech* [2.5 bushels or 91 liters] *of barley.*

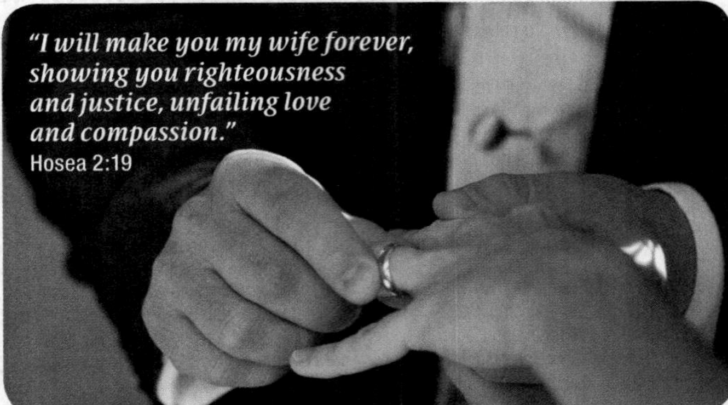
"I will make you my wife forever, showing you righteousness and justice, unfailing love and compassion."
Hosea 2:19

Hos 2:14-15 God was promising (1) to bring the people to the desert, a place free from distractions, so he could clearly communicate with them, and (2) to change what had been a time of trouble into a day of hope. The Valley of Trouble is the site where Achan had sinned by keeping forbidden war plunder (see Josh 7). He had brought great disaster to Joshua's troops when they were attempting to conquer the land. God uses even our negative experiences to create opportunities to turn back to him. As you face problems and trials, remember that God speaks to you in the "desert" and not just in times of prosperity.

Hos 2:16 Not until Judah's exile would the entire nation begin to come to its senses, give up its idols, and turn back to God; and not until that day when God rules through Jesus the Messiah will the relationship between God and his people be restored. In that day, God will no longer be like a master to them; he will be like a husband (Isa 54:4-8). The relationship will be deep and personal, the kind of relationship we can know, though imperfectly, in marriage.

Hos 2:19-20 The time will come when unfaithfulness will be impossible. God will bind us to himself in his perfect righteousness, justice, love, compassion, and faithfulness. God was promising a fresh new beginning, not just a temporary rewriting of a tired old covenant (see Jer 31:31-34).

Hos 2:19-20 God's wedding gift to his people, both in Hosea's day and in our own, is his compassion. Through no merit of our own, God forgives us and makes us right with him. There is no way for us by our own efforts to reach God's high standards, but he graciously accepts us, forgives us, and draws us into a relationship with himself. In that relationship we have personal and intimate communion with him.

Hos 3:1ff This short chapter pictures the nation's exile and return. Israel would experience a time of purification in a foreign land, but God would still love the people and would be willing to accept them back. God commanded Hosea to show the same forgiving spirit to Gomer. Although Hosea had good reason to divorce Gomer, he was told to buy her back and love her.

many days and stop your prostitution. During this
time, you will not have sexual relations with anyone,
not even with me.*"
4 This shows that Israel will go a long time without
a king or prince, and without sacrifices, sacred pillars,
priests,* or even idols! 5 But afterward the people will
return and devote themselves to the LORD their God
and to David's descendant, their king.* In the last
days, they will tremble in awe of the LORD and of his
goodness.

Hos 3:3 Or *and I will live with you.* **Hos 3:4** Hebrew *ephod,* the vest worn by the priest. **Hos 3:5** Hebrew *to David their king.*

Hos 3:1 God asked Hosea to do something almost unthinkable—to buy back his adulterous, unrepentant wife and to continue to love her! When those who knew about Gomer's adultery heard Hosea say that God loved idolatrous Israel as much as Hosea loved Gomer, they must have been amazed. The people had heard God's words many times, but they felt the impact of those words when they saw them acted out in Hosea's merciful love for his wife.

Hos 3:2 Apparently Gomer was on her own for a while. Needing to support herself, she must have either sold herself into slavery or become the mistress of another man. In either case, Hosea had to pay to get her back—although the required amount was pitifully small. Gomer was no longer worth much to anyone except Hosea, but he loved her just as God loved Israel. No matter how low we sink, God is willing to buy us back—to redeem us—and to lift us up again.

Hos 3:3 After this, Gomer is no longer mentioned by Hosea. This is explained in Hosea 3:4. Gomer's isolation showed how God would deal with the northern kingdom (Hos 5:6, 15). It is dangerous to rebel against God. If he were ever to withdraw his love and mercy, we would be without hope.

Hos 3:4 God would separate the Israelites from their treasured idolatrous practices. The sacrifices, pillars, and priests mentioned were those used for idol worship. The priests served the idols; the idols were household gods, which were strictly forbidden for God's people.

Hos 3:4-5 The northern kingdom had rebelled against David's dynasty and had taken Jeroboam as their king (1 Kgs 12–13). Their rebellion was both political and religious. At that time, they reverted back to the worship of gold idols. "David's descendant, their king" refers to the time of Messiah's rule when all people will bow before him in humility and submission. Those who won't accept Christ's blessings now will face his power and judgment later. How much better it is to love and follow Christ now than face his angry judgment later.

GOMER

Gomer was a girl with a reputation. We don't know if she was already a working prostitute or was simply a promiscuous young woman by the time she met Hosea. But she was clearly a high risk for a lasting relationship. She must have been surprised and confused when, instead of propositioning her, Hosea arranged to marry her. By common cultural rule, the decisions were made by Hosea and Diblaim. Gomer may not even have been consulted. Her father was probably eager to remove an embarrassment from his life. • Hosea loved Gomer. Gomer seemed ambivalent toward her husband. Apparently, marriage simply changed the label on Gomer's behavior from promiscuity to adultery. She got pregnant three times, giving birth to two sons and a daughter. Hosea couldn't be sure if the children were his or had been fathered by other men, but he claimed them and named them as God instructed. • God's declarations about Israel overlap Hosea's struggle over Gomer's unfaithfulness. Sometime after the birth of their third child, Gomer became enslaved in prostitution. Hosea had to buy her freedom. He then insisted on her faithfulness. • What did Gomer think and feel during all this? How much did Hosea reveal to her about God's prediction that she would be unfaithful? How did she respond to Hosea's sacrificial faithfulness? We aren't told. After Hosea redeemed her, she isn't mentioned again. Her final appearance in the book leads to hopeful silence. If she responded to Hosea's love, they built a life together. • Probably the closest we come to feeling what Gomer felt are those times when we act unfaithfully toward God yet he continues to faithfully lavish his love on us. Gomer's shameful story turns out to be a thinly veiled version of our story. We know Gomer better than we might think at first, for she was what we are—sinners offered overwhelming grace!

Weaknesses and mistakes	• Developed a persistent promiscuous lifestyle • Sold herself into sexual slavery
Lessons from her life	• Unfaithfulness damages our integrity but does not prevent someone else from loving us in spite of our failure • God is committed to loving us even though he knows our waywardness and bent toward sin
Vital statistics	• Where: Israel • Occupation: Wife, prostitute • Relatives: Husband: Hosea. Father: Diblaim. Sons: Jezreel (God plants), Lo-ammi (Not my people). Daughter: Lo-ruhamah (Not loved).
Key verse	"When the LORD first began speaking to Israel through Hosea, he said to him, 'Go and marry a prostitute, so that some of her children will be conceived in prostitution. This will illustrate how Israel has acted like a prostitute by turning against the LORD and worshiping other gods'" (Hos 1:2).

Gomer's story is told in Hosea 1:1–3:5.

2. GOD'S WAYWARD PEOPLE

The rest of Hosea's prophecy deals with Israel's sin and her impending judgment. Hosea points out the moral and spiritual decay of the nation. He describes the punishment awaiting the people and pleads with them to return to God. Although judgment and condemnation of sin are prevalent in the book, a strand of love and restoration runs throughout. Even in the midst of judgment, God is merciful and will restore those who repent and turn to him.

The Lord's Case against Israel

HOSEA 4:1-19

1 Hear the word of the LORD, O people of Israel!
The LORD has brought charges against you,
saying:
"There is no faithfulness, no kindness,
no knowledge of God in your land.
2 You make vows and break them;
you kill and steal and commit adultery.
There is violence everywhere—
one murder after another.
3 That is why your land is in mourning,
and everyone is wasting away.
Even the wild animals, the birds of the sky,
and the fish of the sea are disappearing.

4 "Don't point your finger at someone else
and try to pass the blame!
My complaint, you priests,
is with you.*
5 So you will stumble in broad daylight,
and your false prophets will fall with you
in the night.
And I will destroy Israel, your mother.
6 My people are being destroyed
because they don't know me.
Since you priests refuse to know me,
I refuse to recognize you as my priests.
Since you have forgotten the laws of your God,
I will forget to bless your children.
7 The more priests there are,
the more they sin against me.
They have exchanged the glory of God
for the shame of idols.*

8 "When the people bring their sin offerings,
the priests get fed.
So the priests are glad when the people sin!
9 'And what the priests do, the people also do.'
So now I will punish both priests and people
for their wicked deeds.
10 They will eat and still be hungry.
They will play the prostitute and gain nothing
from it,
for they have deserted the LORD
11 to worship other gods.

"Wine has robbed my people
of their understanding.

Hos 4:4 Hebrew *Your people are like those with a complaint against the priests.* **Hos 4:7** As in Syriac version and an ancient Hebrew tradition; Masoretic Text reads *I will turn their glory into shame.*

Hos 4:1ff In this chapter, God brings a charge of disobedience against Israel. The religious leaders had failed to turn the people to God, and ritual prostitution had replaced right worship. The nation had declined spiritually and morally, breaking the laws that God had given them. The people found it easy to condemn Hosea's wife for her adultery. They were not so quick to see that *they* had been unfaithful to God.

Hos 4:1-3 God explained the reasons for Israel's suffering. Their lawless behavior had brought the twin judgments of increased violence and ecological crisis. There is not always a direct cause-and-effect relationship between our actions and the problems we face. Nevertheless, when we are facing difficulties, we should seriously ask, "Have I done anything sinful or irresponsible that has caused my suffering?" If we discover that we are at fault, even partially, we must change our ways before God will help us.

Hos 4:2 This verse may allude to the assassinations of kings during Hosea's lifetime. Shallum killed Zechariah (the king, not the prophet) and took the throne. Then Menahem killed Shallum and destroyed an entire city because it refused to accept him as king (2 Kgs 15:8-16). God pointed out that even murder was being taken casually in Israel.

Hos 4:4 We often blame others if we fear punishment for wrongdoing. Hosea warned the priests not to blame anyone else; the nation's sins were largely their fault. Israel's priests pointed out the people's sins, but God would not allow them to overlook their own irresponsible actions. Instead of instructing the nation in religion and morality, they had led the way toward idolatry and immorality. Their failure to lead the people in God's ways placed most of the blame for Israel's destruction on them. Knowing that God will not allow us to blame others for our sinfulness should cause us to admit our own sins. We are responsible for our own sinful actions. Beware of the tendency to blame others because it can keep you from feeling the need to repent.

Hos 4:4-9 Hosea leveled his charges against the religious leaders. Who were these religious leaders? When Jeroboam I rebelled against Solomon's son Rehoboam and set up a rival kingdom in the north, he also set up his own religious system (see 1 Kgs 12:25-33). In violation of God's law, he made two gold calves and told the people to worship them. He also appointed his own priests, who were not descendants of Aaron. At first the residents of the northern kingdom continued to worship God, even though they were doing it in the wrong way; but very soon they also began to worship Canaanite gods. Before long they had substituted Baal for God and no longer worshiped God at all. It is not surprising that Jeroboam's false priests were unable to preserve the true worship of God.

Hos 4:6-9 God accused the religious leaders of keeping the people from knowing him. They were supposed to be spiritual leaders, but they had become leaders in wrongdoing. The people may have said to one another, "It must be okay if the priests do it." Spiritual leadership is a heavy responsibility. Whether you teach a church school class, hold a church office, or lead a Bible study, don't take your leadership responsibilities lightly. Be a leader who leads others to God.

Hos 4:8 The priests were glad when the people sinned. Every time a person brought a sin offering, the priest received a portion of it. The more the people sinned, the more the priests received. Because they couldn't eat all of the offerings themselves, they sold some and gave some to their relatives. The priests profited from the continuation of sin; it gave them power and position in the community. So instead of trying to lead the people out

12 They ask a piece of wood for advice!
They think a stick can tell them the future!
Longing after idols
has made them foolish.
They have played the prostitute,
serving other gods and deserting their God.
13 They offer sacrifices to idols on the
mountaintops.
They go up into the hills to burn incense
in the pleasant shade of oaks, poplars, and
terebinth trees.

"That is why your daughters turn to prostitution,
and your daughters-in-law commit adultery.
14 But why should I punish them
for their prostitution and adultery?
For your men are doing the same thing,
sinning with whores and shrine prostitutes.
O foolish people! You refuse to understand,
so you will be destroyed.

15 "Though you, Israel, are a prostitute,
may Judah avoid such guilt.
Do not join the false worship at Gilgal
or Beth-aven,*
even though they take oaths there in the LORD's
name.
16 Israel is stubborn,
like a stubborn heifer.
So should the LORD feed her
like a lamb in a lush pasture?
17 Leave Israel* alone,
because she is married to idolatry.
18 When the rulers of Israel finish their drinking,
off they go to find some prostitutes.
They love shame more than honor.*
19 So a mighty wind will sweep them away.
Their sacrifices to idols will bring them
shame.

The Failure of Israel's Leaders

HOSEA 5:1-15

1 "Hear this, you priests.
Pay attention, you leaders of Israel.
Listen, you members of the royal family.
Judgment has been handed down
against you.
For you have led the people into a snare
by worshiping the idols at Mizpah and Tabor.

Hos 4:15 *Beth-aven* means "house of wickedness"; it is being used as another name for Bethel, which means "house of God." **Hos 4:17** Hebrew *Ephraim,* referring to the northern kingdom of Israel. **Hos 4:18** As in Greek version; the meaning of the Hebrew is uncertain.

SPIRITUAL UNFAITHFULNESS

Spiritual adultery and physical adultery are alike in many ways, and both are dangerous. God was disappointed with his people because they had committed spiritual adultery against him—as Gomer had committed physical adultery against Hosea.

Parallels	The Danger
Both spiritual and physical adultery are against God's law.	When we break God's law in full awareness of what we're doing, our hearts become hardened to the sin, and our relationship with God is broken.
Both spiritual and physical adultery begin with disappointment and dissatisfaction—either real or imagined—with an already existing relationship.	The feeling that God disappoints can lead you away from him. Feelings of disappointment and dissatisfaction are normal and, when endured, will pass.
Both spiritual and physical adultery begin with diverting affection from one object of devotion to another.	The diverting of our affection is the first step in the blinding process that leads into sin.
Both spiritual and physical adultery involve a process of deterioration; it is not usually an impulsive decision.	The process is dangerous because you don't always realize it is happening until it is too late.
Both spiritual and physical adultery involve the creation of a fantasy about what a new object of love can do for you.	Such fantasy creates unrealistic expectations of what a new relationship can do and only leads to disappointment in all existing and future relationships.

of sin, they encouraged sin to increase their profits.

Hos 4:10-12 The chief Canaanite gods, Baal and Asherah, represented the power of fertility and sexual reproduction. Not surprisingly, their worship included rituals with vile sexual practices. Male worshipers had sex with female temple prostitutes or female priests, and young women wishing to bear children had sex with male priests. But God said their efforts to increase fertility would not succeed.

Hos 4:12 The "stick," or divining rod, was a way of attempting to tell the future. By divorcing themselves from God's authoritative religion centered in Jerusalem, inhabitants of the northern kingdom had effectively cut themselves off from God's word and from his way of forgiveness. The drive to be free from all restrictions can move us completely out of God's will.

Hos 4:15 God sent a warning to the southern kingdom of Judah that its priests should not become like those in Israel. (The southern kingdom was called Judah after its most powerful tribe.) Israel's priests who remained in the north had forgotten their spiritual heritage and had sold out to Baal. They were promoting idol worship and ritual prostitution. Israel would not escape punishment, but Judah could if it refused to follow Israel's example.

Hos 4:19 The mighty wind that would sweep Israel away refers to the Assyrian invasion that would destroy the nation.

Hos 5:1-2 Mizpah and Tabor may have been sites prominent in the false worship of Baal. The leaders likely even encouraged the people to sin at these places. With both their civil and religious leaders hopelessly corrupt, the people of Israel did not have much of a chance. They looked to their leaders for guidance, and they should have found it. Today we can often choose our own leaders, but we still need to be aware of whether they are taking us toward or away from God. God held the people responsible for what they did. Similarly, God holds us responsible for our actions and choices.

▶ **HOSEA 5:1-15** ***(cont.)***

2 You have dug a deep pit to trap them at
Acacia Grove.*
But I will settle with you for what you
have done.
3 I know what you are like, O Ephraim.
You cannot hide yourself from me, O Israel.
You have left me as a prostitute leaves her
husband;
you are utterly defiled.
4 Your deeds won't let you return to your God.
You are a prostitute through and through,
and you do not know the LORD.

5 "The arrogance of Israel testifies against her;
Israel and Ephraim will stumble under their
load of guilt.
Judah, too, will fall with them.
6 When they come with their flocks and herds
to offer sacrifices to the LORD,
they will not find him,
because he has withdrawn from them.
7 They have betrayed the honor of the LORD,
bearing children that are not his.
Now their false religion will devour them
along with their wealth.*

8 "Sound the alarm in Gibeah!
Blow the trumpet in Ramah!
Raise the battle cry in Beth-aven*!
Lead on into battle, O warriors of Benjamin!
9 One thing is certain, Israel*:
On your day of punishment,
you will become a heap of rubble.
10 "The leaders of Judah have become like thieves.*
So I will pour my anger on them like a
waterfall.
11 The people of Israel will be crushed and broken
by my judgment
because they are determined to worship idols.*
12 I will destroy Israel as a moth consumes wool.
I will make Judah as weak as rotten wood.

13 "When Israel and Judah saw how sick they
were,
Israel turned to Assyria—
to the great king there—
but he could neither help nor cure them.
14 I will be like a lion to Israel,
like a strong young lion to Judah.
I will tear them to pieces!
I will carry them off,
and no one will be left to rescue them.
15 Then I will return to my place
until they admit their guilt and turn to me.
For as soon as trouble comes,
they will earnestly search for me."

A Call to Repentance

HOSEA 6:1-11

1 "Come, let us return to the LORD.
He has torn us to pieces;
now he will heal us.
He has injured us;
now he will bandage our wounds.
2 In just a short time he will restore us,
so that we may live in his presence.
3 Oh, that we might know the LORD!
Let us press on to know him.
He will respond to us as surely as the arrival
of dawn
or the coming of rains in early spring."

4 "O Israel* and Judah,
what should I do with you?" asks the LORD.
"For your love vanishes like the morning mist
and disappears like dew in the sunlight.
5 I sent my prophets to cut you to pieces—
to slaughter you with my words,
with judgments as inescapable as light.

Hos 5:2 Hebrew *at Shittim.* The meaning of the Hebrew for this sentence is uncertain. **Hos 5:7** The meaning of the Hebrew is uncertain. **Hos 5:8** *Beth-aven* means "house of wickedness"; it is being used as another name for Bethel, which means "house of God." **Hos 5:9** Hebrew *Ephraim,* referring to the northern kingdom of Israel; also in 5:11, 12, 13, 14. **Hos 5:10** Hebrew *like those who move a boundary marker.* **Hos 5:11** Or *determined to follow human commands.* The meaning of the Hebrew is uncertain. **Hos 6:4** Hebrew *Ephraim,* referring to the northern kingdom of Israel.

Hos 5:3 Ephraim is another name for Israel, the northern kingdom, because Ephraim was the most powerful of the ten tribes in the north. In the same way, the southern kingdom was called Judah after its most powerful tribe.

Hos 5:4 Persistent sin hardens a person's heart, making it difficult to repent. Deliberately choosing to disobey God can sear the conscience; each sin makes the next one easier to commit. Don't allow sin to groove a hard path deep within you. Steer as far away from sinful practices as possible.

Hos 5:8 Gibeah and Ramah were Israelite cities near Jerusalem. Hosea prophesied that these cities would sound the alarm of the coming judgment.

Hos 5:13 During the reigns of Menahem and Hoshea, Israel turned to Assyria for help (2 Kgs 15:19-20; 17:3-4). But even the great world powers of that time could not help Israel, for God himself had determined to judge the nation. If we neglect God's call to repentance, how can we escape? (See Heb 2:3.)

Hos 6:1-3 This is presumption, not genuine repentance. The people did not understand the depth of their sins. They did not turn from idols, repent of their sins, or pledge to make changes. They thought that God's wrath would last only a few days; little did they know that their nation would soon be taken into exile. Israel was interested in God only for the material benefits he provided; they did not value the eternal benefits that come from worshiping him. But before judging Israel, consider your attitude. What do you hope to gain from your religion? Do you "repent" easily, without seriously considering what changes need to take place in your life?

Hos 6:4 God answered his people, pointing out that their profession of loyalty, like mist and dew, evaporated easily and had no substance. Many find it easy and comfortable to maintain the appearance of being committed without deep and sincere loyalty. If you profess loyalty to God, back it up with your actions.

Hos 6:6 Religious rituals can help people understand God and nourish their relation-

6 I want you to show love,*
not offer sacrifices.
I want you to know me*
more than I want burnt offerings.
7 But like Adam,* you broke my covenant
and betrayed my trust.

8 "Gilead is a city of sinners,
tracked with footprints of blood.
9 Priests form bands of robbers,
waiting in ambush for their victims.
They murder travelers along the road
to Shechem
and practice every kind of sin.
10 Yes, I have seen something horrible in Ephraim
and Israel:
My people are defiled by prostituting
themselves with other gods!

11 "O Judah, a harvest of punishment is also waiting
for you,
though I wanted to restore the fortunes
of my people.

Israel's Love for Wickedness

HOSEA 7:1-16

1 "I want to heal Israel,* but its sins are too great.
Samaria is filled with liars.
Thieves are on the inside
and bandits on the outside!
2 Its people don't realize
that I am watching them.
Their sinful deeds are all around them,
and I see them all.

3 "The people entertain the king with their
wickedness,
and the princes laugh at their lies.
4 They are all adulterers,
always aflame with lust.
They are like an oven that is kept hot
while the baker is kneading the dough.
5 On royal holidays, the princes get drunk with wine,
carousing with those who mock them.
6 Their hearts are like an oven
blazing with intrigue.

Hos 6:6a Greek version translates this Hebrew term as *to show mercy.* Compare Matt 9:13; 12:7. **Hos 6:6b** Hebrew *to know God.* **Hos 6:7** Or *But at Adam.* **Hos 7:1** Hebrew *Ephraim,* referring to the northern kingdom of Israel; also in 7:8, 11.

OBEDIENCE VERSUS SACRIFICES

God says many times that he doesn't want our gifts and sacrifices when we give them out of ritual or hypocrisy. God wants us first to love and obey him.

1 Sam 15:22-23	Obedience is better than sacrifice.
Ps 40:6-8	God doesn't want sacrifices or offerings; he wants us to take joy in doing his will.
Ps 51:16-19	God isn't interested in sacrifice; he wants a broken and repentant heart.
Jer 7:21-23	It isn't sacrifices God wants; he desires our obedience, and he promises that he will be our God and we will be his people.
Hos 6:6	God doesn't want sacrifices; he wants us to show love. He doesn't want offerings; he wants us to know him.
Amos 5:21-24	God hates pretense and hypocrisy; he wants to see justice roll on like a river.
Mic 6:6-8	God is not satisfied with offerings; he wants us to do what is right, love mercy, and walk humbly with him.
Matt 9:13	God doesn't want sacrifices; he wants us to be merciful.

ship with him. That is why God instituted circumcision and the sacrificial system in the Old Testament and baptism and the Lord's Supper in the New Testament. But a religious ritual is helpful only if it is carried out with an attitude of love for and obedience to God. If a person's heart is far from God, ritual will become empty mockery. God didn't want the Israelites' rituals; he wanted their hearts. Why do you worship? What is the motive behind your "sacrifices" and "offerings"?

Hos 6:7 One of Hosea's key themes is that Israel had broken the covenant God had made with them at Mount Sinai (Exod 19–20). God wanted to make Israel a blessing and a light to all the nations (Gen 12:2-3; Isa 49:6); and if God's chosen people obeyed him and proclaimed him to the world, he would give them special blessings. If they broke the covenant, however, they would suffer severe penalties, as they should have known (see Deut 28:15-68). Sadly, the people broke the covenant and proved themselves unfaithful to God. How about you? Have you also broken faith with God? What about your forgotten promises to serve him?

Hos 6:8-9 Gilead was once a sacred place, but here it was corrupt. Shechem was once a city of refuge designated by Joshua (Josh 20:1-2, 7-8); Gilead was a region that included Ramoth, also a city of refuge. At this time these areas were associated with murder and crime, with bands of evil priests lying in wait to murder travelers passing through the territory.

Hos 6:11 So that the people of Judah would not become proud as they saw the northern kingdom's destruction, Hosea interjected a solemn warning about God's "harvest." God's Temple was in Judah (Jerusalem), and the people thought that what happened in Israel could never happen to them. But when they had become utterly corrupt, they, too, were led off into captivity (see 2 Kgs 25).

Hos 7:1-2 God sees and knows everything. We, like Israel, often forget this. Thoughts like "No one will ever know," or "No one is watching" may tempt us to try to get away with sin. If you are facing difficult temptations, you will be less likely to give in if you remind yourself that God is watching. When faced with the opportunity to sin, remember that God sees everything.

Hos 7:6 "Their hearts are like an oven blazing with intrigue" refers to the lust for power and intrigue that was burning in these leaders' hearts. Three Israelite kings were assassinated during Hosea's lifetime—Zechariah, Shallum, and Pekahiah (2 Kgs 15:8-26). The kings' foreign relations and domestic lives were ruined because they ignored God and his word.

▸ **HOSEA 7:1-16** ***(cont.)***

Their plot smolders* through the night,
and in the morning it breaks out like a raging fire.
7 Burning like an oven,
they consume their leaders.
They kill their kings one after another,
and no one cries to me for help.

8 "The people of Israel mingle with godless foreigners,
making themselves as worthless as a half-baked cake!
9 Worshiping foreign gods has sapped their strength,
but they don't even know it.
Their hair is gray,
but they don't realize they're old and weak.
10 Their arrogance testifies against them,
yet they don't return to the LORD their God
or even try to find him.

11 "The people of Israel have become like silly, witless doves,
first calling to Egypt, then flying to Assyria for help.
12 But as they fly about,
I will throw my net over them
and bring them down like a bird from the sky.
I will punish them for all the evil they do.*
13 "What sorrow awaits those who have deserted me!
Let them die, for they have rebelled against me.
I wanted to redeem them,
but they have told lies about me.
14 They do not cry out to me with sincere hearts.
Instead, they sit on their couches and wail.
They cut themselves,* begging foreign gods for grain and new wine,
and they turn away from me.
15 I trained them and made them strong,
yet now they plot evil against me.
16 They look everywhere except to the Most High.
They are as useless as a crooked bow.
Their leaders will be killed by their enemies
because of their insolence toward me.
Then the people of Egypt
will laugh at them.

Israel Harvests the Whirlwind

HOSEA 8:1-14

1 "Sound the alarm!
The enemy descends like an eagle on the people of the LORD,

Hos 7:6 Hebrew *Their baker sleeps.* **Hos 7:12** Hebrew *I will punish them because of what was reported against them in the assembly.* **Hos 7:14** As in Greek version; Hebrew reads *They gather together.*

Trumpet

The trumpet is frequently mentioned in the Bible. There are two kinds of trumpets in the Hebrew Bible: *shofar* and *hashoshera*. The shofar, a long horn with a turned-up end, was the national trumpet of the Israelites. It was used on military and religious occasions to summon the people. The hashoshera was a trumpet made of beaten silver. God commanded Moses to make two of them for summoning the congregation and for breaking camp. Numbers 10:1-10 contains God's instructions regarding the occasions for the blowing of the trumpets. They were principally sacred, not military, instruments. The shofar is still used in Jewish synagogues today.

Hos 7:8 The people of Israel had intermarried with foreign people and had picked up their evil ways. When we spend a lot of time with unbelievers, either professionally or socially, we can easily pick up their attitudes and begin to imitate their actions. Beware of the influence they may have on you. Instead of drifting into bad habits, see if you can have a positive influence and point these people to God.

Hos 7:10 Arrogance (pride) keeps a person from turning to God because arrogance claims no need of help from anyone, human or divine. Pride intensifies all our other sins because we cannot repent of any of them without first giving up our pride.

Hos 7:11 Israel's King Menahem had paid Assyria to support him in power (2 Kgs 15:19-20); King Hoshea turned against Assyria and went to Egypt for help (2 Kgs 17:4). Israel's kings went back and forth, allying themselves with different nations when they should have allied themselves with God.

Hos 7:16 A crooked bow is unreliable. Its arrows miss the target, and its owner would be quite vulnerable in battle. Life without God is as unreliable as a crooked bow. Without God's direction, our thoughts are filled with lust, cheating, selfishness, and deceit. As long as we are warped by sin, we will never reach our true potential.

Hos 7:16 People look everywhere except to God for happiness and fulfillment, pursuing possessions, recreation, and relationships. In reality, only God can truly satisfy the deep longings of the soul. Look first to heaven, to the Most High God. He will meet your spiritual needs, not all your materialistic wants.

Hos 8:1-4 "The enemy descends like an eagle on the people of the LORD" refers to Assyria coming to attack Israel and take the people into captivity (2 Kgs 15:28-29). The people would call to God, but it would be too late because they had stubbornly refused to give up their idols. We, like Israel, often call on God to ease our pain without wanting him to change our behavior. And we, like Israel, may repent after it is too late to avoid the painful consequences of sin.

for they have broken my covenant
and revolted against my law.
2 Now Israel pleads with me,
'Help us, for you are our God!'
3 But it is too late.
The people of Israel have rejected what is good,
and now their enemies will chase after them.
4 The people have appointed kings without my consent,
and princes without my knowledge.
By making idols for themselves from their silver and gold,
they have brought about their own destruction.

5 "O Samaria, I reject this calf—
this idol you have made.
My fury burns against you.
How long will you be incapable of innocence?
6 This calf you worship, O Israel,
was crafted by your own hands!
It is not God!
Therefore, it must be smashed to bits.

7 "They have planted the wind
and will harvest the whirlwind.
The stalks of grain wither
and produce nothing to eat.
And even if there is any grain,
foreigners will eat it.
8 The people of Israel have been swallowed up;
they lie among the nations like an old discarded pot.
9 Like a wild donkey looking for a mate,
they have gone up to Assyria.
The people of Israel* have sold themselves—
sold themselves to many lovers.
10 But though they have sold themselves to many allies,
I will now gather them together for judgment.
Then they will writhe
under the burden of the great king.

11 "Israel has built many altars to take away sin,
but these very altars became places for sinning!
12 Even though I gave them all my laws,
they act as if those laws don't apply to them.
13 The people of Israel love their rituals of sacrifice,
but to me their sacrifices are all meaningless.
I will hold my people accountable for their sins,
and I will punish them.
They will return to Egypt.
14 Israel has forgotten its Maker and built great palaces,
and Judah has fortified its cities.
Therefore, I will send down fire on their cities
and will burn up their fortresses."

Hosea Announces Israel's Punishment

HOSEA 9:1-17

1 O people of Israel,
do not rejoice as other nations do.
For you have been unfaithful to your God,
hiring yourselves out like prostitutes,
worshiping other gods on every threshing floor.

Hos 8:9 Hebrew *Ephraim,* referring to the northern kingdom of Israel; also in 8:11.

Hos 8:5 Samaria was the capital of the northern kingdom, and sometimes it stands for the whole kingdom of Israel. Jeroboam I had set up worship of calf idols at Bethel and Dan and had encouraged the people to worship them (1 Kgs 12:25-33). Thus, the people were worshiping the image of a created animal rather than the Creator.

Hos 8:7 Crop yield is the result of good seed planted in good soil and given the proper proportions of sunlight, moisture, and fertilizer. A single seed can produce multiple fruit in good conditions. Israel, however, had sown its spiritual seed to the wind—it had invested itself in activities without substance. Like the wind that comes and goes, its idolatry and foreign alliances offered no protection. In seeking self-preservation apart from God, it had brought about its own destruction. Like a forceful whirlwind, God's judgment would come upon Israel by means of the Assyrians. When we seek security in anything except God, we expose ourselves to great danger. Without God there is no lasting security.

Hos 8:11 The altars that were supposed to remove sin were actually increasing sin through their misuse in worshiping Baal.

Hos 8:12 Though the laws were written for them, the people of Israel acted as if those laws didn't apply to them. It is easy to listen to a sermon and think of all the people we know who should be listening, or to read the Bible and think of those who should do what the passage teaches. The Israelites did this constantly, applying God's laws to others but not to themselves to avoid making needed changes. As you think of others who need to apply what you are hearing or reading, check to see if the same application could fit you. Apply the lessons to your own life first because often our own faults are the very first ones we see in others.

Hos 8:13 The people's sacrifices had become mere ritual, and God refused to accept them. We have rituals, too: attending church, observing a regular quiet time, celebrating Christian holidays, praying before meals. Rituals give us security in a changing world. Because they are repeated often, they can drive God's lessons deep within us. But rituals can be abused. Beware if you find yourself observing a religious ritual for any of the following reasons: (1) to gain community approval, (2) to avoid the risks of doing something different, (3) to make thought unnecessary, (4) to substitute for personal relationships, (5) to make up for bad behavior, (6) to earn God's favor. We should not reject the rituals of our worship, but we must be careful to think about why we do them. Focus on God, and perform every act with sincere devotion.

Hos 8:13 In Egypt, the Israelites had been slaves (Exod 1:11). The people would not literally return to Egypt, but they would return to slavery—this time scattered throughout the Assyrian Empire.

Hos 8:14 Israel had placed its confidence in military strength, strong defenses, and economic stability, just as nations do today. But because of the people's inner moral decay, their apparent sources of strength were inadequate.

Hos 9:1 A threshing floor was a flat area, often built on a hilltop, where harvesters beat the wheat and separated it from the chaff. Often men would stay overnight at the threshing floor to protect their grain, so prostitutes would visit there. Because of the location of threshing floors in the hilltops, they began to be used as places to sacrifice to false gods.

▸ **HOSEA 9:1-17 *(cont.)***

2 So now your harvests will be too small
to feed you.
There will be no grapes for making new wine.
3 You may no longer stay here in the LORD's land.
Instead, you will return to Egypt,
and in Assyria you will eat food
that is ceremonially unclean.
4 There you will make no offerings of wine
to the LORD.
None of your sacrifices there will please him.
They will be unclean, like food touched by a
person in mourning.
All who present such sacrifices will be defiled.
They may eat this food themselves,
but they may not offer it to the LORD.
5 What then will you do on festival days?
How will you observe the LORD's festivals?
6 Even if you escape destruction from Assyria,
Egypt will conquer you, and Memphis* will
bury you.
Nettles will take over your treasures of silver;
thistles will invade your ruined homes.

7 The time of Israel's punishment has come;
the day of payment is here.
Soon Israel will know this all too well.
Because of your great sin and hostility,
you say, "The prophets are crazy
and the inspired men are fools!"
8 The prophet is a watchman over Israel*
for my God,
yet traps are laid for him wherever he goes.
He faces hostility even in the house of God.
9 The things my people do are as depraved
as what they did in Gibeah long ago.
God will not forget.
He will surely punish them for their sins.

10 The LORD says, "O Israel, when I first found you,
it was like finding fresh grapes in the desert.
When I saw your ancestors,
it was like seeing the first ripe figs of the season.
But then they deserted me for Baal-peor,
giving themselves to that shameful idol.
Soon they became vile,
as vile as the god they worshiped.
11 The glory of Israel will fly away like a bird,
for your children will not be born
or grow in the womb
or even be conceived.
12 Even if you do have children who grow up,
I will take them from you.
It will be a terrible day when I turn away
and leave you alone.
13 I have watched Israel become as beautiful as Tyre.
But now Israel will bring out her children for
slaughter."

14 O LORD, what should I request for your people?
I will ask for wombs that don't give birth
and breasts that give no milk.

15 The LORD says, "All their wickedness began
at Gilgal;
there I began to hate them.
I will drive them from my land
because of their evil actions.
I will love them no more
because all their leaders are rebels.
16 The people of Israel are struck down.
Their roots are dried up,
and they will bear no more fruit.

Hos 9:6 Memphis was the capital of northern Egypt. **Hos 9:8** Hebrew *Ephraim,* referring to the northern kingdom of Israel; also in 9:11, 13, 16.

Hos 9:6 Israel's leaders vacillated between alliances with Egypt and alliances with Assyria. Hosea was saying that both were wrong. Breaking an alliance with untrustworthy Assyria and fleeing for help to the equally untrustworthy Egypt would not forestall Israel's destruction. Its only hope was to return to God.

Hos 9:7 By the time Israel began to experience the consequences of its sins, it was no longer listening to God's messengers. Refusing to hear the truth from prophets who spoke out so clearly about its sins, the nation did not hear God's warnings about what was soon to happen. We all listen and read selectively, focusing on what seems to support our present lifestyle and ignoring a radical reordering of our priorities. In doing this, we are likely to miss the warning signs. Listen to people who think your approach is all wrong. Read articles that present viewpoints you would be unlikely to take. Ask yourself, Is God speaking to me through these speakers and writers? Is there something I need to change?

Hos 9:9 A couple had stopped to stay overnight in Gibeah when some wicked men gathered around the house and demanded that the man come out so they could have sex with him. Instead, the traveler gave them his concubine. They raped and abused her all night and then left her dead on the doorstep (Judg 19:14-30). That horrible act revealed the depths to which the people had sunk. Gibeah was destroyed for its evil (Judg 20:8-48), but Hosea said that the whole nation was now as evil as that city. Just as the city didn't escape punishment, neither would the nation.

Hos 9:10 Baal-peor was the god of Peor, a mountain in Moab. In Numbers 22, Balaam, a prophet, was hired by King Balak of Moab to curse the Israelites as they were coming through his land. The Moabites enticed the Israelites into sexual sin and Baal worship. Before long, the Israelites became as corrupt as the gods they worshiped. People soon begin to copy the characteristics and lifestyles of those around them. What do you worship? Are you becoming more like God, or are you becoming more like the world?

Hos 9:14 Hosea prayed this prayer when he foresaw the destruction that Israel's sins would bring (2 Kgs 17:7-23). This vision of Israel's terrible fate moved him to pray that women would not get pregnant and that children would die as infants so they would not have to experience the tremendous suffering and pain that lay ahead.

Hos 9:15 At Gilgal, both the political and the religious failure of the nation began. Here idols and kings were substituted for God. Saul, the united nation's first king, was crowned at Gilgal (1 Sam 11:15), but by Hosea's time, Baal worship flourished there (Hos 4:15; 12:11).

And if they give birth,
I will slaughter their beloved children."

17 My God will reject the people of Israel
because they will not listen or obey.
They will be wanderers,
homeless among the nations.

The LORD's Judgment against Israel

HOSEA 10:1-15

1 How prosperous Israel is—
a luxuriant vine loaded with fruit.
But the richer the people get,
the more pagan altars they build.
The more bountiful their harvests,
the more beautiful their sacred pillars.
2 The hearts of the people are fickle;
they are guilty and must be punished.
The LORD will break down their altars
and smash their sacred pillars.
3 Then they will say, "We have no king
because we didn't fear the LORD.
But even if we had a king,
what could he do for us anyway?"
4 They spout empty words
and make covenants they don't intend
to keep.
So injustice springs up among them
like poisonous weeds in a farmer's field.

5 The people of Samaria tremble in fear
for what might happen to their calf idol
at Beth-aven.*
The people mourn and the priests wail,
because its glory will be stripped away.*
6 This idol will be carted away to Assyria,
a gift to the great king there.
Ephraim will be ridiculed and Israel will be
shamed,
because its people have trusted in this idol.
7 Samaria and its king will be cut off;
they will float away like driftwood on an
ocean wave.
8 And the pagan shrines of Aven,* the place
of Israel's sin, will crumble.
Thorns and thistles will grow up around
their altars.
They will beg the mountains, "Bury us!"
and plead with the hills, "Fall on us!"

9 The LORD says, "O Israel, ever since Gibeah,
there has been only sin and more sin!
You have made no progress whatsoever.
Was it not right that the wicked men of Gibeah
were attacked?
10 Now whenever it fits my plan,
I will attack you, too.
I will call out the armies of the nations
to punish you for your multiplied sins.

11 "Israel* is like a trained heifer treading out the
grain—
an easy job she loves.
But I will put a heavy yoke on her tender neck.
I will force Judah to pull the plow
and Israel* to break up the hard ground.
12 I said, 'Plant the good seeds of righteousness,
and you will harvest a crop of love.
Plow up the hard ground of your hearts,
for now is the time to seek the LORD,
that he may come
and shower righteousness upon you.'

13 "But you have cultivated wickedness
and harvested a thriving crop of sins.

Hos 10:5a *Beth-aven* means "house of wickedness"; it is being used as another name for Bethel, which means "house of God." **Hos 10:5b** Or *will be taken away into exile.* **Hos 10:8** *Aven* is a reference to Beth-aven; see 10:5a and the note there. **Hos 10:11a** Hebrew *Ephraim,* referring to the northern kingdom of Israel. **Hos 10:11b** Hebrew *Jacob.* The names "Jacob" and "Israel" are often interchanged throughout the Old Testament, referring sometimes to the individual patriarch and sometimes to the nation.

Hos 10:1 Israel prospered under Jeroboam II, gaining military and economic strength. But the more prosperous the nation became, the more love it lavished on idols. It seems as though the more God gives, the more we spend. We want bigger houses, better cars, and finer clothes. But the finest things the world offers line the pathway to destruction. As you prosper, consider where your money is going. Is it being used for God's purposes, or are you consuming it all on yourself?

Hos 10:4 God was angry with the people of Israel for their insincere promises. Because the people did not keep their word, there were many lawsuits. People break their promises, but God always keeps his. Are you remaining true to your promises, both to other people and to God? If not, ask God for forgiveness and help to get back on track. Then be careful about the promises you make. Never make a promise unless you are sure you can keep it.

Hos 10:5 *Beth-aven* means "house of wickedness," and it refers to Bethel ("house of God"), where false worship took place. If the Israelites' idols were really gods, they should have been able to protect them. How ironic that the people were fearing for their gods' safety! (For more information on this calf idol, see the notes on Hos 3:4-5, p. 805, and Hos 8:5, p. 811.)

Hos 10:9-10 For information on what happened in Gibeah, see the note on Hosea 9:9, p. 812, or read Judges 19–20. Gibeah stands for cruelty and sensuality, as in Judges, and for rebellion as in Saul's day (Gibeah was Saul's hometown; see 1 Sam 10:5; 11:4).

Hos 10:12 Hosea repeatedly uses illustrations about fields and crops. Here he envisions a plowed field. It is no longer stony and hard; it has been carefully prepared, and it is ready for planting. Is your life ready for God to work in it? You can break up the unplowed ground of your heart by acknowledging your sins and receiving God's forgiveness and guidance.

Hos 10:13 The Israelites were taken in by the lie that military power could keep them safe. Believers today sometimes fall for lies. Those who lead others astray often follow these rules: Make it big; keep it simple; repeat it often. Believers can avoid falling for lies by asking: (1) Am I believing this because there is personal gain in it for me? (2) Am I discounting important facts? (3) Does this conflict with a direct command of Scripture? (4) Are there any biblical parallels to the situation I'm facing that would help me know what to believe?

▸ **HOSEA 10:1-15** ***(cont.)***

You have eaten the fruit of lies—
trusting in your military might,
believing that great armies
could make your nation safe.
14 Now the terrors of war
will rise among your people.
All your fortifications will fall,
just as when Shalman destroyed Beth-arbel.
Even mothers and children
were dashed to death there.
15 You will share that fate, Bethel,
because of your great wickedness.
When the day of judgment dawns,
the king of Israel will be completely
destroyed.

God's Love for Israel

HOSEA 11:1-11

1 "When Israel was a child, I loved him,
and I called my son out of Egypt.
2 But the more I* called to him,
the farther he moved from me,
offering sacrifices to the images of Baal
and burning incense to idols.
3 I myself taught Israel* how to walk,
leading him along by the hand.
But he doesn't know or even care
that it was I who took care of him.
4 I led Israel along
with my ropes of kindness and love.
I lifted the yoke from his neck,
and I myself stooped to feed him.
5 "But since my people refuse to return to me,
they will return to Egypt
and will be forced to serve Assyria.
6 War will swirl through their cities;
their enemies will crash through their gates.
They will destroy them,
trapping them in their own evil plans.
7 For my people are determined to desert me.
They call me the Most High,
but they don't truly honor me.
8 "Oh, how can I give you up, Israel?
How can I let you go?
How can I destroy you like Admah
or demolish you like Zeboiim?
My heart is torn within me,
and my compassion overflows.
9 No, I will not unleash my fierce anger.
I will not completely destroy Israel,
for I am God and not a mere mortal.
I am the Holy One living among you,
and I will not come to destroy.
10 For someday the people will follow me.
I, the LORD, will roar like a lion.
And when I roar,
my people will return trembling from
the west.
11 Like a flock of birds, they will come from
Egypt.

Hos 11:2 As in Greek version; Hebrew reads *they.* **Hos 11:3** Hebrew *Ephraim,* referring to the northern kingdom of Israel; also in 11:8, 9, 12.

Hos 10:14 Some say Shalman was Shalmaneser, king of Assyria; others say Shalman was Salmanu, a Moabite king mentioned in the inscriptions of Tiglath-pileser. Shalman had invaded Gilead around 740 B.C. and destroyed the city of Beth-arbel, killing many people, including women and children. This kind of cruelty was not uncommon in ancient warfare. Hosea was saying such would be Israel's fate.

Hos 10:15 Because Israel had put its confidence in military might rather than in God, it would be destroyed by military power. Israel's king, who had led the people into idol worship, would be the first to fall. Divine judgment is *sometimes* swift, but it is *always* sure.

Hos 11:1ff In the final four chapters, Hosea shifts to the theme of God's intense love for Israel. God had always loved Israel as a parent loves a stubborn child, and that is why he would not release Israel from the consequences of its behavior. The Israelites were sinful, and they would be punished like a rebellious son brought by his parents before the elders (Deut 21:18-21). All through Israel's sad history, God repeatedly offered to restore the nation if it would only turn to him. By stubbornly refusing God's invitation, the northern kingdom had sealed its doom. It would be destroyed, never to rise again. Even so, Israel as a nation was not finished. A remnant of faithful Israelites would return to Jerusalem, where one day the Messiah would come, offering pardon and reconciliation to all who would faithfully follow him.

Hos 11:3 God had consistently provided for his people, but they refused to see what he had done, and they showed no interest in thanking him. Ungratefulness is a common human fault. For example, when was the last time you thanked your parents for caring for you? your pastor for the service given to your church? your child's teacher for the care taken with each day's activities? your heavenly Father for his guidance? Many of the benefits and privileges we enjoy are the result of loving actions done long ago. Look for hidden acts of nurturing, and thank those who make the world better through their love. But begin by thanking God for all his blessings.

Hos 11:4 God's discipline requires times of leading and times of feeding. Sometimes the rope is taut; sometimes it is slack. God's discipline is always loving, and its object is always the well-being of the beloved. When you are called to discipline others—children, students, employees, or church members—do not be rigid. Vary your approach according to the goals you are seeking to accomplish. In each case, ask yourself, Does this person need guidance, or do they need to be nurtured?

Hos 11:5 The northern kingdom survived for only two centuries after its break with Jerusalem. Its spiritual and political leaders did not help the people learn the way to God, so as a nation they would never repent. Hosea prophesied its downfall, which happened when Shalmaneser of Assyria conquered Israel in 722 B.C. Judah also would go into captivity, but a remnant would return to their homeland.

Hos 11:8 Admah and Zeboiim were cities of the plain that had perished with Sodom and Gomorrah (Gen 14:8; Deut 29:23).

Hos 11:9 "I am God and not a mere mortal." It is easy for us to define God in terms of our own expectations and behavior. In so doing, we make him just slightly larger than ourselves. In reality, God is infinitely greater than we are. We should seek to become like him rather than attempt to remake him in our image.

Trembling like doves, they will return from
Assyria.
And I will bring them home again,"
says the LORD.

Charges against Israel and Judah

HOSEA 11:12–12:14

12*Israel surrounds me with lies
and deceit,
but Judah still obeys God
and is faithful to the Holy One.*

12:1* The people of Israel* feed on the wind;
they chase after the east wind all day long.
They pile up lies and violence;
they are making an alliance with Assyria
while sending olive oil to buy support
from Egypt.

2 Now the LORD is bringing charges against Judah.
He is about to punish Jacob* for all his
deceitful ways,
and pay him back for all he has done.

3 Even in the womb,
Jacob struggled with his brother;
when he became a man,
he even fought with God.

4 Yes, he wrestled with the angel and won.
He wept and pleaded for a blessing from him.
There at Bethel he met God face to face,
and God spoke to him*—

5 the LORD God of Heaven's Armies,
the LORD is his name!

6 So now, come back to your God.
Act with love and justice,
and always depend on him.

7 But no, the people are like crafty merchants
selling from dishonest scales—
they love to cheat.

8 Israel boasts, "I am rich!
I've made a fortune all by myself!
No one has caught me cheating!
My record is spotless!"

9 "But I am the LORD your God,
who rescued you from slavery in Egypt.
And I will make you live in tents again,
as you do each year at the Festival
of Shelters.*

10 I sent my prophets to warn you
with many visions and parables."

11 But the people of Gilead are worthless
because of their idol worship.
And in Gilgal, too, they sacrifice bulls;
their altars are lined up like the heaps
of stone
along the edges of a plowed field.

12 Jacob fled to the land of Aram,
and there he* earned a wife by tending
sheep.

Hos 11:12a Verse 11:12 is numbered 12:1 in Hebrew text. **Hos 11:12b** Or *and Judah is unruly against God, the faithful Holy One.* The meaning of the Hebrew is uncertain. **Hos 12:1a** Verses 12:1-14 are numbered 12:2-15 in Hebrew text. **Hos 12:1b** Hebrew *Ephraim,* referring to the northern kingdom of Israel; also in 12:8, 14. **Hos 12:2** *Jacob* sounds like the Hebrew word for "deceiver." **Hos 12:4** As in Greek and Syriac versions; Hebrew reads *to us.* **Hos 12:9** Hebrew *as in the days of your appointed feast.* **Hos 12:12** Hebrew *Israel.* See note on 10:11b.

Hos 11:12 Unlike Israel, Judah had some fairly good kings—Asa, Jehoshaphat, Joash, Amaziah, Uzziah, Jotham, and especially Hezekiah and Josiah. Under some of these kings, God's law was dusted off and taught to the people. The priests continued to serve in God's appointed Temple in Jerusalem, and the festivals were celebrated at least some of the time. Unfortunately, the political or religious leaders were unable to completely wipe out idol worship and pagan rites (although Hezekiah and Josiah came close), which continued to fester until they eventually erupted and infected the whole country. Still, the influence of the good kings enabled Judah to survive more than 150 years longer than Israel, and that memory of their positive influence fortified a small group—a remnant—of faithful people who would one day return and restore their land and Temple.

Hos 12:2-5 Jacob, whose name was later changed to Israel, was the common ancestor of all 12 tribes of Israel (both northern and southern kingdoms). Like the nations that descended from him, Jacob practiced deceit. Unlike Israel and Judah, he constantly searched for God. Jacob wrestled with the angel in order to be blessed, but his descendants thought their blessings came from their own successes. Jacob purged his house of idols (Gen 35:2), but his descendants could not quit their idol worship.

Hos 12:6 The two principles that Hosea called his nation to live by—love and justice—are at the very foundation of God's character. They are essential to his followers, but they are not easy to keep in balance. Some people are loving to the point that they excuse wrongdoing. Others are just to the extent that they forget love. Love without justice leaves people in their sins because it is not aiming at a higher standard. Justice without love drives people away from God because it has no heart. To specialize in one at the expense of the other is to distort our witness. Today's church, just like Hosea's nation, must live by both principles.

Hos 12:7-8 In Israel, dishonesty had become an accepted means of attaining wealth. Israelites who were financially successful could not imagine that God would consider them sinful. They thought that their wealth was a sign of God's approval, and they didn't bother to consider how they had gotten it. But God said that Israel's riches would not make up for its sin. Remember that God's measure of success is different from ours. He calls us to faithfulness, not to affluence. Character is more important to him than our purses.

Hos 12:8 Rich people and nations often claim that their material success is due to their own hard work, initiative, and intelligence. Because they can buy whatever they want, they don't feel the need for God. They believe that their riches are their own and that they have the right to use them any way they please. If you find yourself feeling proud of your accomplishments, remember that all your opportunities, abilities, and resources come from God and that you hold them in sacred trust for him.

Hos 12:9 Once a year the Israelites spent a week living in tents during the Festival of Shelters, which commemorated God's protection as they wandered in the wilderness for 40 years (see Deut 1:19–2:1). Here, because of their sin, God would cause them to live in tents again—this time not as part of a festival but in actual bondage.

Hos 12:12 Hosea was using this reference to Jacob to say, "Don't forget your humble beginnings. What you have is not a result of your own efforts, but it is yours because God has been gracious to you."

▶ **HOSEA 11:12–12:14** ***(cont.)***

13 Then by a prophet
the LORD brought Jacob's descendants*
out of Egypt;
and by that prophet
they were protected.
14 But the people of Israel
have bitterly provoked the LORD,
so their Lord will now sentence them
to death
in payment for their sins.

The LORD's Anger against Israel

HOSEA 13:1-16

1 When the tribe of Ephraim spoke,
the people shook with fear,
for that tribe was important
in Israel.
But the people of Ephraim sinned by
worshiping Baal
and thus sealed their destruction.
2 Now they continue to sin by making
silver idols,
images shaped skillfully with human
hands.
"Sacrifice to these," they cry,
"and kiss the calf idols!"
3 Therefore, they will disappear like the
morning mist,
like dew in the morning sun,
like chaff blown by the wind,
like smoke from a chimney.

4 "I have been the LORD your God
ever since I brought you out of Egypt.
You must acknowledge no God but me,
for there is no other savior.
5 I took care of you in the wilderness,
in that dry and thirsty land.
6 But when you had eaten and were satisfied,
you became proud and forgot me.
7 So now I will attack you like a lion,
like a leopard that lurks along the road.
8 Like a bear whose cubs have been taken away,
I will tear out your heart.
I will devour you like a hungry lioness
and mangle you like a wild animal.

9 "You are about to be destroyed, O Israel—
yes, by me, your only helper.
10 Now where is* your king?
Let him save you!
Where are all the leaders of the land,
the king and the officials you demanded
of me?
11 In my anger I gave you kings,
and in my fury I took them away.

12 "Ephraim's guilt has been collected,
and his sin has been stored up for
punishment.
13 Pain has come to the people
like the pain of childbirth,
but they are like a child
who resists being born.
The moment of birth has arrived,
but they stay in the womb!

14 "Should I ransom them from the grave*?
Should I redeem them from death?
O death, bring on your terrors!
O grave, bring on your plagues!*
For I will not take pity on them.
15 Ephraim was the most fruitful of all his brothers,
but the east wind—a blast from the LORD—
will arise in the desert.
All their flowing springs will run dry,
and all their wells will disappear.
Every precious thing they own
will be plundered and carried away.
16* The people of Samaria
must bear the consequences of their guilt
because they rebelled against their God.

Hos 12:13 Hebrew *brought Israel.* See note on 10:11b. **Hos 13:10** As in Greek and Syriac versions and Latin Vulgate; Hebrew reads *I will be.* **Hos 13:14a** Hebrew *Sheol;* also in 13:14b. **Hos 13:14b** Greek version reads *O death, where is your punishment? / O grave* [Hades], *where is your sting?* Compare 1 Cor 15:55. **Hos 13:16** Verse 16 is numbered 14:1 in Hebrew text.

Hos 12:13 The prophet who brought Israel out of Egypt was Moses (Exod 13:17-19).

Hos 13:1 Israel, represented here by the northern tribe of Ephraim, had been great, but by Hosea's time the people had rebelled against God and had lost their authority among the nations. Greatness in the past is no guarantee of greatness in the future. It is good to remember what God has done for you and through you, but it is equally important to keep your relationship with him vital and up to date. Commit yourself to God moment by moment.

Hos 13:4-6 When abundant possessions made Israel feel self-sufficient, it turned its back on God and forgot him. Self-sufficiency is as destructive today as it was in Hosea's time. Do you see your constant need of God's presence and help? Learn to rely on God, both in good times and bad. If you are traveling along a smooth and easy path right now, beware of forgetting who gave you your good fortune. Don't depend on your gifts; depend on the Giver. (See Deut 6:10-12; 8:7-20 for God's warning.)

Hos 13:11 God had warned the people of Israel that kings would cause more problems than they would solve, and he reluctantly gave them Saul as their first king (1 Sam 8:4-22). The second king, David, was a good king, and Solomon, David's son, had his strengths. But after the nation divided in two, the northern kingdom never had another good ruler. Evil kings led the nation deeper into idolatry and unwise political alliances. Eventually the evil kings destroyed the nation; with Hoshea, the northern kingdom's kings were cut off (2 Kgs 17:1-6).

Hos 13:12 Ephraim's (Israel's) sins were recorded for later punishment. All our sins are known and will be revealed at the day of judgment (2 Cor 5:10; Rev 20:11-15). How will you live differently today knowing that everything you do will be revealed at the day of judgment?

Hos 13:14 The apostle Paul used this passage to teach the resurrection of our bodies from death (1 Cor 15:55). For those who

They will be killed by an invading army,
their little ones dashed to death against
the ground,
their pregnant women ripped open
by swords."

Healing for the Repentant

HOSEA 14:1-9

1*Return, O Israel, to the LORD your God,
for your sins have brought you down.
2 Bring your confessions, and return to the LORD.
Say to him,
"Forgive all our sins and graciously receive us,
so that we may offer you our praises.*
3 Assyria cannot save us,
nor can our warhorses.
Never again will we say to the idols we
have made,
'You are our gods.'
No, in you alone
do the orphans find mercy."

4 The LORD says,
"Then I will heal you of your faithlessness;
my love will know no bounds,
for my anger will be gone forever.
5 I will be to Israel
like a refreshing dew from heaven.
Israel will blossom like the lily;
it will send roots deep into the soil
like the cedars in Lebanon.
6 Its branches will spread out like beautiful
olive trees,
as fragrant as the cedars of Lebanon.
7 My people will again live under my shade.
They will flourish like grain and blossom
like grapevines.
They will be as fragrant as the wines of
Lebanon.

8 "O Israel,* stay away from idols!
I am the one who answers your prayers and
cares for you.
I am like a tree that is always green;
all your fruit comes from me."

9 Let those who are wise understand these
things.
Let those with discernment listen carefully.
The paths of the LORD are true and right,
and righteous people live by walking
in them.
But in those paths sinners stumble and fall.

Hos 14:1 Verses 14:1-9 are numbered 14:2-10 in Hebrew text. **Hos 14:2** As in Greek and Syriac versions, which read *may repay the fruit of our lips;* Hebrew reads *may repay the bulls of our lips.* **Hos 14:8** Hebrew *Ephraim,* referring to the northern kingdom of Israel.

CYCLES OF JUDGMENT/SALVATION IN HOSEA

God promises to judge, but he also promises mercy. Here you can see the cycles of judgment and salvation in Hosea. Prophecies of judgment are consistently followed by prophecies of forgiveness.

Judgment	Salvation
Hos 1:2-9	Hos 1:10–2:1
Hos 2:2-13	Hos 2:14–3:5
Hos 4:1–5:14	Hos 5:15–6:3
Hos 6:4–11:7	Hos 11:8-11
Hos 11:12–13:16	Hos 14:1-9

have trusted in Christ for deliverance from sin, death holds no threat of annihilation.

Hos 14:1ff Hosea 14:1-3 are Hosea's call to repent. Hosea 14:4-8 are God's promise of restoration. God had to punish Israel for its gross and repeated violations of his law, but he would do so with a heavy heart. What God really wanted to do was restore the nation and make it prosper.

Hos 14:1-2 The people could return to God by asking him to forgive their sins. The same is true for us: We can pray Hosea's prayer and know our sins are forgiven because Christ died for them on the cross (John 3:16).

Forgiveness begins when we see the destructiveness of sin and the futility of life without God. Then we must admit we cannot save ourselves; our only hope is in God's mercy. When we seek forgiveness, we must recognize that we do not deserve it and therefore cannot demand it. Our appeal must be for God's love and mercy, not for his justice. Although we cannot demand forgiveness, we can be confident that we have received it because God is gracious and loving and wants to restore us to himself, just as he wanted to restore Israel.

Hos 14:3-8 When our will is weak, when our thinking is confused, and when our conscience is burdened with a load of guilt, we must remember that God cares for us continually; his love knows no bounds. When friends and family desert us, when coworkers don't understand us, and when we are tired of being good, God's love knows no bounds. When we can't see the way or seem to hear God's voice, and when we lack courage to go on, God's love knows no bounds. When our shortcomings and our awareness of our sins overcome us, God's love knows no bounds.

Hos 14:9 Hosea closes with an appeal to listen, learn, and benefit from God's word. To those receiving the Lord's message through Hosea, this meant the difference between life and death. For you, the reader of the book of Hosea, the choice is similar: You can either listen to the book's message and follow God's ways or refuse to walk along the Lord's path. But people who insist on following their own direction without God's guidance are in "total darkness" and "have no idea what they are stumbling over" (Prov 4:19). If you are lost, you can find the way by turning from your sin and following God.

Hos 14:9 God's concern for justice that requires faithfulness and for love that offers forgiveness can be seen in his dealings with Hosea. We can err by forgetting God's love, feeling that our sins are hopeless; but we can also err by forgetting God's wrath against our sins, thinking he will continue to accept us no matter how we act. Forgiveness is a key word: When God forgives us, he judges the sin but shows mercy to the sinner. We should never be afraid to come to God for a clean slate and a renewed life.

I. The End of the Northern Kingdom

The kingdom of Israel never recovered from a beginning that included creating a rival religion—worshiping two calf idols at shrines in Dan and Bethel instead of following God and worshiping him at his Temple in Jerusalem. Ultimately, their judgment came on them in the form of Assyria's armies conquering the land and scattering the people throughout their vast empire. After over 200 years of disobedience, Israel suffered the consequences of their sins.

722 BC

Assyria destroys Samaria

Assyria Besieges Samaria PARALLEL

2 KINGS 17:5

Then the king of Assyria invaded the entire land, and for three years he besieged the city of Samaria.

2 KINGS 18:9

During the fourth year of Hezekiah's reign, which was the seventh year of King Hoshea's reign in Israel, King Shalmaneser of Assyria attacked the city of Samaria and began a siege against it.

Isaiah's Message about Samaria

ISAIAH 28:1-29

1 What sorrow awaits the proud city of Samaria—
the glorious crown of the drunks of Israel.*
It sits at the head of a fertile valley,
but its glorious beauty will fade like a flower.
It is the pride of a people
brought down by wine.
2 For the Lord will send a mighty army against it.
Like a mighty hailstorm and a torrential rain,
they will burst upon it like a surging flood
and smash it to the ground.
3 The proud city of Samaria—
the glorious crown of the drunks of Israel*—
will be trampled beneath its enemies' feet.
4 It sits at the head of a fertile valley,
but its glorious beauty will fade like a flower.
Whoever sees it will snatch it up,
as an early fig is quickly picked and eaten.

5 Then at last the LORD of Heaven's Armies
will himself be Israel's glorious crown.
He will be the pride and joy
of the remnant of his people.
6 He will give a longing for justice
to their judges.
He will give great courage
to their warriors who stand at the gates.

7 Now, however, Israel is led by drunks
who reel with wine and stagger with alcohol.
The priests and prophets stagger with alcohol
and lose themselves in wine.
They reel when they see visions
and stagger as they render decisions.
8 Their tables are covered with vomit;
filth is everywhere.
9 "Who does the LORD think we are?" they ask.
"Why does he speak to us like this?
Are we little children,
just recently weaned?
10 He tells us everything over and over—
one line at a time,
one line at a time,
a little here,
and a little there!"

11 So now God will have to speak to his people
through foreign oppressors who speak
a strange language!
12 God has told his people,
"Here is a place of rest;
let the weary rest here.
This is a place of quiet rest."
But they would not listen.
13 So the LORD will spell out his message for
them again,
one line at a time,
one line at a time,

Is 28:1 Hebrew *What sorrow awaits the crowning glory of the drunks of Ephraim,* referring to Samaria, capital of the northern kingdom of Israel. **Is 28:3** Hebrew *The crowning glory of the drunks of Ephraim;* see note on 28:1.

2 Kgs 17:5 This was Assyria's third and final invasion of Israel. (The first two invasions are recorded in 2 Kgs 15:19, 29.) The first wave had been merely a warning to Israel—to avoid further attack, they had to pay Assyria money and not rebel. The people should have learned their lesson and returned to God. When they didn't, God had allowed Assyria to invade again, this time carrying off some captives from the northern border. But the people still did not realize that they had caused their own troubles. Thus, Assyria invaded for the third and final time, destroying Israel completely, carrying away most of the people, and resettling the land with foreigners.

God was doing what he had said he would do (Deut 28). He had given Israel ample warning; they knew what would come, but they still ignored God. Israel was now no better than the pagan nations it had destroyed in the days of Joshua. The nation had turned sour and rejected its original purpose—to honor God and be a light to the world.

Isa 28:1 Samaria, the capital city of the northern kingdom of Israel, represents the entire kingdom, ruled by a line of evil kings. When Israel split into two kingdoms after Solomon's reign, Jerusalem ended up in the southern kingdom. Leaders in the northern kingdom, wishing to stay entirely separate from their relatives to the south, set up idols to keep the people from going to the Temple in Jerusalem to worship (see 1 Kgs 12). Thus, the people in the northern kingdom were led into idolatry. Isaiah gave this message to Israel to warn them that destruction was certain. It was also meant to encourage Judah to repent before being punished, as the northern kingdom was already experiencing.

Isa 28:9-14 These verses characterize the people's reaction to Isaiah. In effect, they were saying, "He's speaking to us like a schoolteacher speaks to small children. We don't need to be taught. We'll make up our own minds." For this attitude, Isaiah prophesied that the Assyrians would teach them in a way they would like even less.

a little here,
and a little there,
so that they will stumble and fall.
They will be injured, trapped, and captured.
14 Therefore, listen to this message from the LORD,
you scoffing rulers in Jerusalem.
15 You boast, "We have struck a bargain to cheat death
and have made a deal to dodge the grave.*
The coming destruction can never touch us,
for we have built a strong refuge made of lies
and deception."
16 Therefore, this is what the Sovereign LORD says:
"Look! I am placing a foundation stone in Jerusalem,*
a firm and tested stone.
It is a precious cornerstone that is safe to build on.
Whoever believes need never be shaken.*
17 I will test you with the measuring line of justice
and the plumb line of righteousness.
Since your refuge is made of lies,
a hailstorm will knock it down.
Since it is made of deception,
a flood will sweep it away.
18 I will cancel the bargain you made to cheat death,
and I will overturn your deal to dodge the grave.
When the terrible enemy sweeps through,
you will be trampled into the ground.
19 Again and again that flood will come,
morning after morning,
day and night,
until you are carried away."
This message will bring terror to your people.
20 The bed you have made is too short to lie on.
The blankets are too narrow to cover you.
21 The LORD will come as he did against the Philistines at Mount Perazim
and against the Amorites at Gibeon.
He will come to do a strange thing;
he will come to do an unusual deed:
22 For the Lord, the LORD of Heaven's Armies,
has plainly said that he is determined to crush the whole land.
So scoff no more,
or your punishment will be even greater.
23 Listen to me;
listen, and pay close attention.
24 Does a farmer always plow and never sow?
Is he forever cultivating the soil and never planting?
25 Does he not finally plant his seeds—
black cumin, cumin, wheat, barley, and emmer wheat—
each in its proper way,
and each in its proper place?
26 The farmer knows just what to do,
for God has given him understanding.
27 A heavy sledge is never used to thresh black cumin;
rather, it is beaten with a light stick.

Is 28:15 Hebrew *Sheol;* also in 28:18. **Is 28:16a** Hebrew *in Zion.* **Is 28:16b** Greek version reads *Look! I am placing a stone in the foundation of Jerusalem* [literally *Zion*], */ a precious cornerstone for its foundation, chosen for great honor. / Anyone who trusts in him will never be disgraced.* Compare Rom 9:33; 1 Pet 2:6.

Isa 28:15 Judah was afraid of the Assyrians. Instead of trusting God, the Judeans turned to other sources for security. God accused them of making a deal with the grave, referring to the state of being dead. This passage may refer to Hezekiah's alliance with Pharaoh Tirhakah against Assyria (2 Kgs 19:9; Isa 37:9). God would cancel this agreement—Egypt would be of no help when Assyria attacked. Is it worth selling out what you believe in for temporary protection against an enemy? If you want lasting protection, turn to the only one able to deliver you from *eternal* death—God.

Isa 28:16 If you're building anything, you need a firm base. Isaiah speaks of a foundation stone, a precious cornerstone, that will be laid in Zion. This cornerstone is the Messiah, the foundation on whom we build our lives. Is your life built on the flimsy base of your own successes or dreams? Or is it set on a firm foundation (see Ps 118:22; 1 Pet 2:8)?

Isa 28:21 God fought on Joshua's side at the battle of Gibeon (Josh 10:1-14) and on David's side at Mount Perazim (2 Sam 5:20). But here he would fight against Israel, his own people, in these same places.

Threshing Grain

Most grain in biblical times was threshed on a floor placed on high ground so that the wind would carry off the chaff. The method was to scatter the loosened bundles of straw on the floor and to drive oxen over them to dislodge the grains. Sometimes heavy implements (like the sledge pictured here), weighted by stones, and ridden by the driver, were drawn over the straw (Isa 28:27; 41:15). The resulting bits of straw, or chaff, were separated from the grain by a tedious winnowing process that involved throwing the material into the air with a fork or shovel (Isa 30:24; Jer 15:7). The lighter straw would be blown to the edge of the floor, and the grain would collect at the feet of the worker. The chaff was burned or used as fodder. Grain was sifted (Amos 9:9), shoveled into a heap, and later stored in covered pits in the field (Jer 41:8). Sometimes storehouses or granaries were used (Deut 28:8).

John the Baptist referred to this whole process when he was announcing what the Messiah would do: "He is ready to separate the chaff from the wheat with his winnowing fork. Then he will clean up the threshing area, gathering the wheat into his barn but burning the chaff with never-ending fire" (Matt 3:12).

Isa 28:23-29 The farmer uses special tools to plant and harvest tender herbs so he will not destroy them. He takes into account how fragile they are. In the same way God takes all our individual circumstances and weaknesses into account. He deals with each of us sensitively. We should follow his example when we deal with others. Different people require different treatment. Be sensitive to the needs of those around you and the special treatment they may need.

▸ **ISAIAH 28:1-29** *(cont.)*

A threshing wheel is never rolled on cumin;
instead, it is beaten lightly with a flail.
28 Grain for bread is easily crushed,
so he doesn't keep on pounding it.
He threshes it under the wheels of a cart,
but he doesn't pulverize it.
29 The LORD of Heaven's Armies is a wonderful teacher,
and he gives the farmer great wisdom.

Samaria Falls to Assyria PARALLEL

2 KINGS 17:6-23

Finally, in the ninth year of King Hoshea's reign, Samaria fell, and the people of Israel were exiled to Assyria. They were settled in colonies in Halah, along the banks of the Habor River in Gozan, and in the cities of the Medes.

7This disaster came upon the people of Israel because they worshiped other gods. They sinned against
the LORD their God, who had brought them safely out
of Egypt and had rescued them from the power of
Pharaoh, the king of Egypt. 8They had followed the
practices of the pagan nations the LORD had driven
from the land ahead of them, as well as the practices
the kings of Israel had introduced. 9The people of
Israel had also secretly done many things that were
not pleasing to the LORD their God. They built pagan
shrines for themselves in all their towns, from the
smallest outpost to the largest walled city. 10They
set up sacred pillars and Asherah poles at the top of
every hill and under every green tree. 11They offered
sacrifices on all the hilltops, just like the nations the
LORD had driven from the land ahead of them. So the
people of Israel had done many evil things, arousing
the LORD's anger. 12Yes, they worshiped idols,* despite
the LORD's specific and repeated warnings.

13Again and again the LORD had sent his prophets
and seers to warn both Israel and Judah: "Turn from all
your evil ways. Obey my commands and decrees—the
entire law that I commanded your ancestors to obey,
and that I gave you through my servants the prophets."

14But the Israelites would not listen. They were
as stubborn as their ancestors who had refused to
believe in the LORD their God. 15They rejected his
decrees and the covenant he had made with their
ancestors, and they despised all his warnings. They
worshiped worthless idols, so they became worthless
themselves. They followed the example of the nations
around them, disobeying the LORD's command not
to imitate them.

16They rejected all the commands of the LORD their
God and made two calves from metal. They set up an
Asherah pole and worshiped Baal and all the forces
of heaven. 17They even sacrificed their own sons and
daughters in the fire.* They consulted fortune-tellers

2 Kgs 17:12 The Hebrew term (literally *round things*) probably alludes to dung. **2 Kgs 17:17** Or *They even made their sons and daughters pass through the fire.*

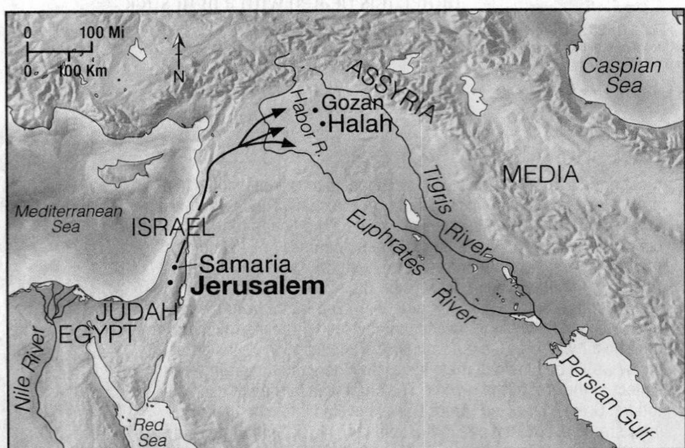

***ISRAEL TAKEN CAPTIVE** Finally the sins of Israel's people caught up with them. God allowed Assyria to defeat and disperse the people. They were led into captivity, swallowed up by the mighty, evil Assyrian Empire. Sin always brings discipline, and the consequences of that sin are sometimes irreversible.*

2 Kgs 17:7-17 The Lord judged the people of Israel because they had copied the evil customs of the surrounding nations, worshiping false gods, accommodating pagan customs, and following their own desires. Those who create their own religion tend to live selfishly. And to live for oneself, as Israel learned, brings serious consequences from God. Sometimes following God is difficult and painful, but consider the alternative. You can live for God or die for yourself. Determine to be God's person and do what he says regardless of the cost. What God thinks of you is infinitely more important than what those around you think. (See Rom 12:1-2; 1 Jn 2:15-17.)

2 Kgs 17:9 Ruin came upon Israel for both their public sins and their secret sins. Not only did they condone wickedness and idolatry in public, but they committed even worse sins in private. Secret sins are the ones we don't want others to know about because they are embarrassing or incriminating. Sins done in private are not secret to God, and secret defiance of him is just as damaging as open rebellion.

2 Kgs 17:13-15 The people took on the characteristics of the idols and imitated the godless nations around them. Israel had forgotten the importance and benefits of obeying God's word. The king and the people had become mired in wickedness. Time and again God had sent prophets to warn them about how far they had turned away from him and to call them to turn back.

God's patience and mercy are beyond our ability to understand. He will pursue us until we either respond to him or, by our own choice and hardness of heart, make ourselves unreachable. Then God's judgment is swift and sure. The only safe course is to turn to God before our stubbornness puts us out of his reach.

2 Kgs 17:16 The "forces of heaven" refers to the Canaanite practice of worshiping the sun, moon, and constellations. These were Assyrian gods that were being added to their religion. (See also 2 Kgs 21:1-6; 23:4-5.)

and practiced sorcery and sold themselves to evil, arousing the LORD's anger.
[18]Because the LORD was very angry with Israel, he swept them away from his presence. Only the tribe of Judah remained in the land. [19]But even the people of Judah refused to obey the commands of the LORD their God, for they followed the evil practices that Israel had introduced. [20]The LORD rejected all the descendants of Israel. He punished them by handing them over to their attackers until he had banished Israel from his presence.
[21]For when the LORD* tore Israel away from the kingdom of David, they chose Jeroboam son of Nebat as their king. But Jeroboam drew Israel away from following the LORD and made them commit a great sin. [22]And the people of Israel persisted in all the evil ways of Jeroboam. They did not turn from these sins [23]until the LORD finally swept them away from his presence, just as all his prophets had warned. So Israel was exiled from their land to Assyria, where they remain to this day.

2 Kgs 17:21 Hebrew *he;* compare 1 Kgs 11:31-32.

2 KINGS 18:10-12

Three years later, during the sixth year of King Hezekiah's reign and the ninth year of King Hoshea's reign in Israel, Samaria fell. [11]At that time the king of Assyria exiled the Israelites to Assyria and placed them in colonies in Halah, along the banks of the Habor River in Gozan, and in the cities of the Medes. [12]For they refused to listen to the LORD their God and obey him. Instead, they violated his covenant—all the laws that Moses the LORD's servant had commanded them to obey.

Foreigners Settle in Israel

2 KINGS 17:24-41

The king of Assyria transported groups of people from Babylon, Cuthah, Avva, Hamath, and Sepharvaim and resettled them in the towns of Samaria, replacing

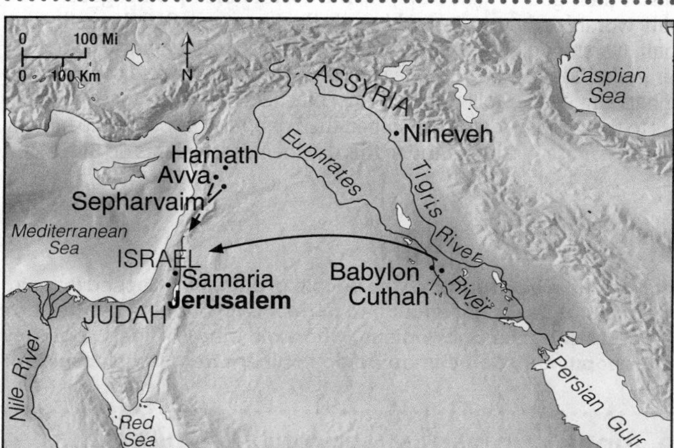

***ISRAEL RESETTLED BY FOREIGNERS** After the Israelites were deported, foreigners from the Assyrian Empire were sent to resettle the land. This policy helped Assyria keep peace in conquered territories.*

2 Kgs 17:17 Forms of witchcraft, fortune-telling, and black magic were forbidden by God (Deut 18:9-14). They were wrong because they sought power and guidance totally apart from God, his law, and his word. Isaiah echoed this law and prophesied of the complete destruction these occult practices would bring to those who participated in them (Isa 8:19-22).

2 Kgs 17:23 Israel was taken into exile, just as God's prophets had warned. Whatever God predicts will come to pass. This, of course, is good news to those who trust and obey him—they can be confident of his promises; but it is bad news to those who ignore or disobey him. Both the promises and warnings God has given in his Word will surely come true.

2 Kgs 18:10-12 These verses flash back to the days just before Israel's destruction. Hezekiah reigned with his father, Ahaz, for 14 years (729–715 B.C.), by himself for 18 years (715–697 B.C.), and with his son Manasseh for 11 years (697–686 B.C.), a total of 43 years. The 29 years listed in 2 Kings 18:2 indicate only those years in which Hezekiah had complete control of the kingdom. While Hezekiah was on the throne, the nation of Israel to the north was destroyed (722 B.C.). Seeing Israel's destruction probably caused Hezekiah to reform his own nation. (For more on Hezekiah, see 2 Chr 29–32; Isa 36–39.)

2 Kgs 17:24 Moving the Israelites out and moving foreigners in was Assyria's resettlement policy to prevent revolt. Spreading the captives across Assyria prevented their uniting, and repopulating Israel with foreign captives made it difficult for the remaining Israelites to unite as well. This mixture of peoples resettled in Israel came to be known as Samaritans. They were despised by the Jews, even through the time of Christ (John 4:9).

Assyrian Captives

From the year 743 B.C., Tiglath-pileser III waged a number of campaigns in Syria and Palestine. King Menahem of Israel (752–742 B.C.) paid him tribute (2 Kgs 15:19-20), as did the rulers in Tyre, Byblos, and Damascus. Responding to an appeal from King Ahaz of Judah (735–715 B.C.) to help resist the pressures of a proposed anti-Assyrian coalition, Tiglath-pileser conquered Damascus in 732 B.C. and Samaria, capital of the northern kingdom of Israel, a decade later. The fall of Samaria in 722 B.C. marked the end of the kingdom of Israel. On both occasions deportations of people to Assyria took place. This relief shows prisoners handcuffed together, escorted by Assyrian guards, while another is executed. This was the heavy price paid for disobedience to God.

▸ **2 KINGS 17:24-41 *(cont.)***
the people of Israel. They took possession of Samaria
and lived in its towns. [25]But since these foreign settlers did not worship the LORD when they first arrived, the LORD sent lions among them, which killed
some of them.
[26]So a message was sent to the king of Assyria: "The
people you have sent to live in the towns of Samaria
do not know the religious customs of the God of the
land. He has sent lions among them to destroy them
because they have not worshiped him correctly."
[27]The king of Assyria then commanded, "Send one
of the exiled priests back to Samaria. Let him live there
and teach the new residents the religious customs
of the God of the land." [28]So one of the priests who
had been exiled from Samaria returned to Bethel and
taught the new residents how to worship the LORD.
[29]But these various groups of foreigners also
continued to worship their own gods. In town after
town where they lived, they placed their idols at the
pagan shrines that the people of Samaria had built.
[30]Those from Babylon worshiped idols of their god
Succoth-benoth. Those from Cuthah worshiped
their god Nergal. And those from Hamath worshiped
Ashima. [31]The Avvites worshiped their gods Nibhaz
and Tartak. And the people from Sepharvaim even
burned their own children as sacrifices to their gods
Adrammelech and Anammelech.
[32]These new residents worshiped the LORD, but
they also appointed from among themselves all sorts
of people as priests to offer sacrifices at their places
of worship. [33]And though they worshiped the LORD,
they continued to follow their own gods according to
the religious customs of the nations from which they
came. [34]And this is still going on today. They continue
to follow their former practices instead of truly worshiping the LORD and obeying the decrees, regulations,
instructions, and commands he gave the descendants
of Jacob, whose name he changed to Israel.
[35]For the LORD had made a covenant with the descendants of Jacob and commanded them: "Do not
worship any other gods or bow before them or serve
them or offer sacrifices to them. [36]But worship only
the LORD, who brought you out of Egypt with great
strength and a powerful arm. Bow down to him alone,
and offer sacrifices only to him. [37]Be careful at all
times to obey the decrees, regulations, instructions,
and commands that he wrote for you. You must not
worship other gods. [38]Do not forget the covenant I
made with you, and do not worship other gods. [39]You
must worship only the LORD your God. He is the one
who will rescue you from all your enemies."
[40]But the people would not listen and continued to
follow their former practices. [41]So while these new residents worshiped the LORD, they also worshiped their
idols. And to this day their descendants do the same.

J. The Era of Judah Alone

After seeing their brothers and sisters carried away into exile, the people of Judah still lapsed into sin. Hezekiah and Josiah begin many reforms, but this is not enough to permanently turn the nation back to God. Ultimately, Judah would be defeated by the Babylonians, who exile many of them, but they are not scattered, and the land is not repopulated. Sometimes we do not learn from the examples of sin and foolishness around us.

1. ISAIAH'S MESSAGES FOR JUDAH AND PAGAN NATIONS

Isaiah begins by bringing a message of divine judgment for both Israel and Judah. Although the advance of the Assyrians poses a problem for Judah, God foretells the destruction of Assyria and other evil surrounding nations through the prophet Isaiah. The section ends with the Assyrian invasion being held off, demonstrating the clear unfolding of God's plan and promises for the nation at this time.

A Message for Rebellious Judah

ISAIAH 1:1-20

These are the visions that Isaiah son of Amoz saw concerning Judah and Jerusalem. He saw these visions during the years when Uzziah, Jotham, Ahaz, and Hezekiah were kings of Judah.*

2 Listen, O heavens! Pay attention, earth!
This is what the LORD says:

Is 1:1 These kings reigned from 792 to 686 B.C.

2 Kgs 17:27-29 The new settlers in Israel worshiped God without giving up their pagan customs. They worshiped God to appease him rather than to please him, treating him as a good luck charm or just another idol to add to their collection. A similar attitude is common today. Many people claim to believe in God while refusing to give up attitudes and actions that God denounces. God cannot be added to the values we already have. He must come first, and his Word must shape all our actions and attitudes.

2 Kgs 17:29-31 Israel was conquered because it had lost sight of the only true God and the importance of following him. When conquering the land, the Israelites were told to destroy the pagan influences that could lead them away from God. Their failure to do so brought about their ruin. Here they faced an even greater influx of gods from the many pagan peoples moving into the land.

Isa 1:1 Isaiah was a prophet during the time when the original nation of Israel had been divided into two kingdoms—Israel in the north

"The children I raised and cared for
have rebelled against me.
3 Even an ox knows its owner,
and a donkey recognizes its master's care—
but Israel doesn't know its master.
My people don't recognize my care for them."
4 Oh, what a sinful nation they are—
loaded down with a burden of guilt.
They are evil people,
corrupt children who have rejected the LORD.
They have despised the Holy One of Israel
and turned their backs on him.

5 Why do you continue to invite punishment?
Must you rebel forever?
Your head is injured,
and your heart is sick.
6 You are battered from head to foot—
covered with bruises, welts, and infected
wounds—
without any soothing ointments
or bandages.
7 Your country lies in ruins,
and your towns are burned.
Foreigners plunder your fields before your eyes
and destroy everything they see.
8 Beautiful Jerusalem* stands abandoned
like a watchman's shelter in a vineyard,
like a lean-to in a cucumber field after the harvest,
like a helpless city under siege.
9 If the LORD of Heaven's Armies
had not spared a few of us,*
we would have been wiped out like Sodom,
destroyed like Gomorrah.

10 Listen to the LORD, you leaders of "Sodom."
Listen to the law of our God, people of
"Gomorrah."
11 "What makes you think I want all your
sacrifices?"
says the LORD.
"I am sick of your burnt offerings of rams
and the fat of fattened cattle.
I get no pleasure from the blood
of bulls and lambs and goats.
12 When you come to worship me,
who asked you to parade through my courts
with all your ceremony?

Is 1:8 Hebrew *The daughter of Zion.* **Is 1:9** Greek version reads *a few of our children.* Compare Rom 9:29.

ISAIAH

Isaiah served as a prophet to Judah from 740–681 B.C.

Climate of the times	Society was in a great upheaval. Under King Ahaz and King Manasseh, the people reverted to idolatry, and there was even child sacrifice.
Main message	Although judgment from other nations was inevitable, the people could still have a special relationship with God.
Importance of message	Sometimes we must suffer judgment and discipline before we are restored to God.
Contemporary prophets	Hosea (753–715 B.C.), Micah (742–687 B.C.)

and Judah in the south. The northern kingdom had sinned greatly against God, and the southern kingdom was headed in the same direction—perverting justice, oppressing the poor, turning from God to idols, and looking for military aid from pagan nations rather than help from God. Isaiah was primarily a prophet to Judah, but his message was also for the northern kingdom. Sometimes "Israel" refers to both kingdoms. Isaiah lived to see the destruction and captivity of the northern kingdom in 722 B.C. Thus, his ministry began with warning the northern kingdom.

Isa 1:2-4 Here "Israel" means the southern kingdom, Judah. God used Isaiah to bring charges against the people of Judah because they were sinning greatly and had turned against God. By these acts, they had broken their moral and spiritual covenant with God (see Deut 28). By breaking their agreement, they were bringing God's punishment upon themselves. First God gave them prosperity, but they didn't serve him. Then God sent them warnings, but they refused to listen. Finally, he would bring the fire of his judgment (see Isa 1:7).

Isa 1:4-9 As long as the people of Judah continued to sin, they cut themselves off from God's help and isolated themselves. When you feel lonely and separated from God, remember that God does not abandon you. Our sins cut us off from him. The only sure cure for this kind of loneliness is to restore a meaningful relationship with God by confessing your sins, obeying his instructions, and communicating regularly with him (see Ps 140:13; Isa 1:16-19; 1 Jn 1:9).

Isa 1:7 Was this destruction taking place at that time? Judah was attacked many times during Isaiah's lifetime. To be plundered by foreigners was the worst kind of judgment. This verse could be a picture of the results of these invasions or a prediction of the coming invasion of Israel by Assyria. But most likely it pointed to Babylon's future invasion of Judah and the fall of Jerusalem in 586 B.C as well.

Isa 1:9 Sodom and Gomorrah were two cities that God completely destroyed for their great wickedness (Gen 19:1-25). They are mentioned elsewhere in the Bible as examples of God's judgment against sin (Jer 50:40; Ezek 16:46-63; Matt 11:23-24; Jude 1:7). Some survivors from Judah would be spared by God because they were faithful.

Isa 1:10 Isaiah compared the rulers and people of Judah to the rulers and people of Sodom and Gomorrah. To hear what God wanted to say, the people had to listen and be willing to obey. When we can't hear God's message, perhaps we are not listening carefully, or we are not truly willing to do what he says.

Isa 1:10-14 God was unhappy with their sacrifices, but he was not revoking the system of sacrifices he had initiated with Moses. Instead, God was calling for sincere faith and devotion. The leaders were carefully making the traditional sacrifices and offerings at holy celebrations, but they were still unfaithful to God in their hearts. Sacrifices were to be an outward sign of their faith in God, but the outward signs became empty because no faith existed. Why, then, did they continue to offer sacrifices? Like many people today, they had come to place more faith in the rituals of their religion than in the God they worshiped. Examine your own worship experience: Is it just entertainment as you enjoy the music and go along with what others do? Or is it genuine heartfelt praise to God? God does not take pleasure in our outward expressions if our inward faith is missing (see Deut 10:12-16; 1 Sam 15:22-23; Ps 51:16-19; Hos 6:6).

▸ ISAIAH 1:1-20 *(cont.)*

13 Stop bringing me your meaningless gifts;
the incense of your offerings disgusts me!
As for your celebrations of the new moon and the Sabbath
and your special days for fasting—
they are all sinful and false.
I want no more of your pious meetings.
14 I hate your new moon celebrations and your annual festivals.
They are a burden to me. I cannot stand them!
15 When you lift up your hands in prayer, I will not look.
Though you offer many prayers, I will not listen,
for your hands are covered with the blood of innocent victims.
16 Wash yourselves and be clean!
Get your sins out of my sight.
Give up your evil ways.
17 Learn to do good.
Seek justice.
Help the oppressed.
Defend the cause of orphans.
Fight for the rights of widows.

18 "Come now, let's settle this,"
says the LORD.
"Though your sins are like scarlet,
I will make them as white as snow.
Though they are red like crimson,
I will make them as white as wool.
19 If you will only obey me,
you will have plenty to eat.
20 But if you turn away and refuse to listen,
you will be devoured by the sword of your enemies.
I, the LORD, have spoken!"

Unfaithful Jerusalem

ISAIAH 1:21-31

21 See how Jerusalem, once so faithful,
has become a prostitute.
Once the home of justice and righteousness,
she is now filled with murderers.
22 Once like pure silver,
you have become like worthless slag.
Once so pure,
you are now like watered-down wine.
23 Your leaders are rebels,
the companions of thieves.
All of them love bribes
and demand payoffs,
but they refuse to defend the cause of orphans
or fight for the rights of widows.

24 Therefore, the Lord, the LORD of Heaven's Armies,
the Mighty One of Israel, says,
"I will take revenge on my enemies
and pay back my foes!
25 I will raise my fist against you.
I will melt you down and skim off your slag.
I will remove all your impurities.
26 Then I will give you good judges again
and wise counselors like you used to have.
Then Jerusalem will again be called the Home of Justice
and the Faithful City."

27 Zion will be restored by justice;
those who repent will be revived by righteousness.
28 But rebels and sinners will be completely destroyed,
and those who desert the LORD will be consumed.

29 You will be ashamed of your idol worship
in groves of sacred oaks.

Isa 1:13 New moon celebrations and Sabbaths refer to monthly offerings (Num 28:11-14) and weekly and special annual Sabbaths on the Day of Atonement and Festival of Shelters (Lev 16:23-34). (For all the festivals, see the chart on p. 233.) Although the people did not feel sorry for their sins, they continued to offer sacrifices for forgiveness. Gifts and sacrifices mean nothing to God when they come from someone with a corrupt heart. God wants us to love him, trust him, and turn from our sin; after that, he will be pleased with our "sacrifices" of time, money, or service.

Isa 1:18 Crimson was the color of a deep-red permanent dye, and its stain was virtually impossible to remove from clothing. The bloodstained hands of the murderers are probably in view here (see Isa 1:15, 21). The stain of sin seems equally permanent, but God can remove sin's stain from our life as he promised to do for the Israelites. We don't have to go through life permanently soiled. God's Word assures us that if we are willing and obedient, Christ will forgive and remove our most indelible stains (Ps 51:1-7). Will you ask him to make you clean?

Isa 1:21-22 Jerusalem here represents all of Judah. God compares the actions of his people to a prostitute. The people had turned from the worship of the true God to worshiping idols. Their faith was worthless, impure, and diluted. Idolatry, outward or inward, is spiritual adultery, breaking our commitment to God in order to love something else. Jesus described the people of his day as adulterous, even though they were religiously strict. As the church, we are the "bride" of Christ (Rev 19:7), and by faith we can be clothed in his righteousness. Has your faith become impure or watered down? Ask God to restore you. Keep your devotion to him strong and pure.

Isa 1:25 God promised to refine his people similar to the way that metal is purged with lye in a smelting pot. This process involves melting the metal and skimming off the impure slag until the worker can see his own image in the liquid metal. We must be willing to submit to God, allowing him to remove our sin so that we might reflect his image.

Isa 1:26 Isaiah often speaks with both the near present and far future in mind. His prophecies do not necessarily apply to one event, but may apply to a series of present and future events.

Isa 1:29-30 Throughout history, the oak tree has been a symbol of strength, but the people were worshiping "sacred oaks." Ezekiel mentions that oak trees were used as places for idol worship (Ezek 6:13). Are you devoted to symbols of strength and power that rival God's place in your life? Does your commitment to any of your interests border

You will blush because you worshiped
in gardens dedicated to idols.
30 You will be like a great tree with withered leaves,
like a garden without water.
31 The strongest among you will disappear like
straw;
their evil deeds will be the spark that sets
it on fire.
They and their evil works will burn up together,
and no one will be able to put out the fire.

The LORD's Future Reign

ISAIAH 2:1-4

This is a vision that Isaiah son of Amoz saw concerning Judah and Jerusalem:

2 In the last days, the mountain of the LORD's
house
will be the highest of all—
the most important place on earth.
It will be raised above the other hills,
and people from all over the world will stream
there to worship.
3 People from many nations will come and say,
"Come, let us go up to the mountain of the LORD,
to the house of Jacob's God.
There he will teach us his ways,
and we will walk in his paths."
For the LORD's teaching will go out
from Zion;
his word will go out from Jerusalem.
4 The LORD will mediate between nations
and will settle international disputes.
They will hammer their swords into
plowshares
and their spears into pruning hooks.
Nation will no longer fight against nation,
nor train for war anymore.

A Warning of Judgment

ISAIAH 2:5-22

5 Come, descendants of Jacob,
let us walk in the light of the LORD!
6 For the LORD has rejected his people,
the descendants of Jacob,

on worship? Make God your first loyalty; everything else will fade in time and burn away under his scrutiny.

Isa 1:31 A spark set to tinder ignites a quick, devouring fire. God compares the evil deeds of powerful people to a roaring fire that will devour them. Our life can be destroyed quickly by a small but deadly spark of evil. What potential "fire hazards" do you need to remove?

Isa 2:2 The Temple was built on the mountain of the Lord, Mount Moriah, highly visible to all the people of Jerusalem. (For more on the significance of the Temple, see the note on 2 Chr 5:1ff, p. 617.) In the last days the Temple will attract the nations, not because of its architecture and prominence, but because of God's presence and influence.

Isa 2:2-4 God gave Isaiah the gift of seeing into the future. At this time, God showed Isaiah what would eventually happen to Jerusalem. Revelation 21 depicts the glorious fulfillment of this prophecy in the new Jerusalem, where only those whose names are written in the Lamb's Book of Life will be allowed to enter. God made a covenant (promise) with his people and will never break it. God's faithfulness gives us hope for the future. Ask God to help you spread his word.

Isa 2:4-5 This describes a wonderful future of peace when instruments of war will be converted to instruments of farming, and we will be taught God's laws and obey them. Although we know that eventually God will remove all sin, which leads to conflicts, wars, and other problems, we should not wait for him to act before we begin to obey him. We should walk in his light now, just as Judah was told to do. Though our eternal reward awaits us, we can enjoy many benefits of obedience *now* as we apply God's Word to our life.

Isa 2:6 The people were following practices of the Assyrian Empire. Filling their land with magicians and sorcerers meant that they were claiming to know and control the future by the power of demons or by interpreting omens. God forbade these practices (see Lev 19:26; Deut 18:10, 14). The Philistines worshiped Dagon, Ashtoreth, and Baal-zebub. During the more sinful periods of their history, the people of Israel worshiped these pagan gods along with Yahweh and even gave them Hebrew names.

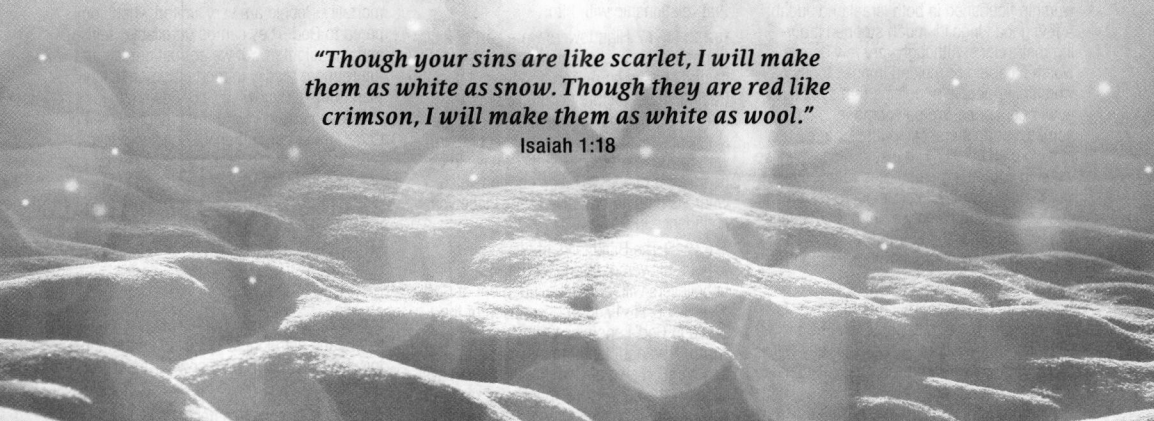

"Though your sins are like scarlet, I will make them as white as snow. Though they are red like crimson, I will make them as white as wool."
Isaiah 1:18

▸ **ISAIAH 2:5-22** ***(cont.)***

because they have filled their land with practices
from the East
and with sorcerers, as the Philistines do.
They have made alliances with pagans.
7 Israel is full of silver and gold;
there is no end to its treasures.
Their land is full of warhorses;
there is no end to its chariots.
8 Their land is full of idols;
the people worship things they have made
with their own hands.
9 So now they will be humbled,
and all will be brought low—
do not forgive them.
10 Crawl into caves in the rocks.
Hide in the dust
from the terror of the LORD
and the glory of his majesty.
11 Human pride will be brought down,
and human arrogance will be humbled.
Only the LORD will be exalted
on that day of judgment.
12 For the LORD of Heaven's Armies
has a day of reckoning.
He will punish the proud and mighty
and bring down everything that is exalted.
13 He will cut down the tall cedars of Lebanon
and all the mighty oaks of Bashan.
14 He will level all the high mountains
and all the lofty hills.
15 He will break down every high tower
and every fortified wall.
16 He will destroy all the great trading ships*
and every magnificent vessel.
17 Human pride will be humbled,
and human arrogance will be brought down.
Only the LORD will be exalted
on that day of judgment.
18 Idols will completely disappear.
19 When the LORD rises to shake the earth,
his enemies will crawl into holes in the
ground.
They will hide in caves in the rocks
from the terror of the LORD
and the glory of his majesty.
20 On that day of judgment they will abandon the
gold and silver idols
they made for themselves to worship.
They will leave their gods to the rodents and bats,
21 while they crawl away into caverns
and hide among the jagged rocks in the cliffs.
They will try to escape the terror of the LORD
and the glory of his majesty
as he rises to shake the earth.
22 Don't put your trust in mere humans.
They are as frail as breath.
What good are they?

Judgment against Judah

ISAIAH 3:1-15

1 The Lord, the LORD of Heaven's Armies,
will take away from Jerusalem and Judah
everything they depend on:
every bit of bread
and every drop of water,
2 all their heroes and soldiers,
judges and prophets,
fortune-tellers and elders,
3 army officers and high officials,
advisers, skilled craftsmen, and astrologers.
4 I will make boys their leaders,
and toddlers their rulers.

Is 2:16 Hebrew *every ship of Tarshish.*

Isa 2:8-9 Under the reign of evil kings, idol worship flourished in both Israel and Judah. A few good kings in Judah stopped it during their reigns. Although very few people worship carved or molded images today, worshiping people or objects that symbolize power continues. We pay homage to cars, homes, sports stars, celebrities, money, etc. Idol worship is evil: (1) It insults God when we worship something he created rather than worshiping him; (2) it keeps us from knowing and serving God when we put our confidence in anything other than him; (3) it causes us to rely on our own efforts rather than on God. (See also Deut 27:15.)

Isa 2:12 The Lord's "day of reckoning" is the day of judgment, the time when God will judge both evil and good. That day will come, and we will want a proper relationship with God when it does. Pride, however, will cripple us. God alone must be exalted (Isa 2:11, 17) as the first step toward developing that relationship with him.

Isa 2:15-17 High towers were part of a city or nation's defenses. This phrase refers to security based on military fortresses. "Great trading ships" picture economic prosperity; and "every magnificent vessel" reveals pleasure and enjoyment. Nothing can compare with or rival the place God must have in our hearts and minds. To place our hope elsewhere is nothing but false pride. Place your confidence in God alone.

Isa 2:19 The Bible talks of two kinds of fear. In this verse, fear is the panic and peril unbelievers will feel at the judgment of God. (See Rev 6:15-17 for a description of the dread in God's enemies on the day of his wrath.) The right kind of fear means to revere and stand in awe of God. Proverbs 1:7 says, "Fear of the LORD is the foundation of true knowledge." Those who honor and respect God need not fear God's wrath.

Isa 2:22 "As frail as breath" refers to our mortality. People are very limited when compared to God. They can be unreliable, selfish, and shortsighted. Yet we entrust our life and future more readily to mortal human beings than to the all-knowing God. Beware of people who want you to trust them instead of God. Remember that only God is completely reliable. He is perfect, and we can rely on his unfailing love (Ps 100:5).

Isa 3:1-3 Jerusalem besieged, her leaders destroyed—this unhappy picture would soon become a reality. Disobedience would bring serious affliction and great destruction, as God had warned (Deut 28).

Isa 3:2 Isaiah was not condoning fortune-tellers and astrologers by including them in this list. He was showing how far the nation had sunk. (See the note on Isa 2:6, p. 825.)

Isa 3:4-9 This section describes what happens when a nation loses its leadership.

5 People will oppress each other—
man against man,
neighbor against neighbor.
Young people will insult their elders,
and vulgar people will sneer at the honorable.

6 In those days a man will say to his brother,
"Since you have a coat, you be our leader!
Take charge of this heap of ruins!"
7 But he will reply,
"No! I can't help.
I don't have any extra food or clothes.
Don't put me in charge!"

8 For Jerusalem will stumble,
and Judah will fall,
because they speak out against the LORD and
refuse to obey him.
They provoke him to his face.
9 The very look on their faces gives them away.
They display their sin like the people of Sodom
and don't even try to hide it.
They are doomed!
They have brought destruction upon
themselves.

10 Tell the godly that all will be well for them.
They will enjoy the rich reward they have
earned!
11 But the wicked are doomed,
for they will get exactly what they deserve.

12 Childish leaders oppress my people,
and women rule over them.
O my people, your leaders mislead you;
they send you down the wrong road.

13 The LORD takes his place in court
and presents his case against his people!
14 The LORD comes forward to pronounce
judgment
on the elders and rulers of his people:
"You have ruined Israel, my vineyard.
Your houses are filled with things stolen
from the poor.
15 How dare you crush my people,
grinding the faces of the poor into the dust?"
demands the Lord, the LORD of Heaven's
Armies.

A Warning to Jerusalem

ISAIAH 3:16–4:1

16 The LORD says, "Beautiful Zion* is haughty:
craning her elegant neck,
flirting with her eyes,
walking with dainty steps,
tinkling her ankle bracelets.
17 So the Lord will send scabs on her head;
the LORD will make beautiful Zion bald."

18 On that day of judgment
the Lord will strip away everything that makes
her beautiful:
ornaments, headbands, crescent necklaces,
19 earrings, bracelets, and veils;
20 scarves, ankle bracelets, sashes,
perfumes, and charms;
21 rings, jewels,
22 party clothes, gowns, capes, and purses;
23 mirrors, fine linen garments,
head ornaments, and shawls.

24 Instead of smelling of sweet perfume,
she will stink.
She will wear a rope for a sash,
and her elegant hair will fall out.

Is 3:16 Or *The women of Zion* (with corresponding changes to plural forms through verse 24); Hebrew reads *The daughters of Zion;* also in 3:17.

Isa 3:9-11 The people would be proud of their sins, parading them out in the open. But sin is self-destructive. In today's world, sinful living often appears glamorous, exciting, and clever. But sin is wrong, regardless of how society perceives it, and in the long run, sin will make us miserable and destroy us. God tries to protect us by warning us about the harm we will cause ourselves by sinning. Those who are proud of their sins will receive the punishment from God they deserve. Having rejected God's path to life (see Ps 1), they had only one alternative—the path to destruction.

Isa 3:10-11 In the middle of this gloomy message, God gives hope: Eventually the righteous will receive God's reward, and the wicked will receive their punishment. It is disheartening to see the wicked prosper while we struggle to obey God and follow his plan. But let us keep holding on to God's truth and take heart! God will bring about justice in the end, and he will reward those who have been faithful.

Isa 3:14 The elders and rulers were responsible to help people, but instead they stole from the poor. Because they were unjust, Isaiah said the leaders would be the first to receive God's judgment. Leaders will be held accountable for how they lead. If you are in a position of leadership, you must lead according to God's just commands. Put the needs of others before your own. Fulfill the purpose God intended for you as a leader. Don't seek your own advantage. Corruption will bring God's wrath, especially if others follow your example.

Isa 3:14 Why is justice so important in the Bible? (1) Justice is part of God's nature; it is the way he runs the universe. (2) It is a natural desire in every person. Even as sinners, we all want justice for ourselves. (3) When government and church leaders are unjust, the poor and powerless suffer. Thus, they are hindered from worshiping God. (4) God holds the poor in high regard. They are the ones most likely to turn to him for help and comfort. Injustice, then, attacks God's children. (5) When *we* do nothing to help the oppressed, we are, in fact, joining with the oppressor. Because we follow a just God, we must uphold justice.

Isa 3:16-26 The women of Judah had placed their emphasis on clothing and jewelry rather than on God. They dressed to be noticed, to gain approval, and to be fashionable. Yet they ignored the real purpose for their lives. Instead of being concerned about the oppression around them (Isa 3:14-15), they were self-serving and self-centered. People who abuse their possessions will end up with nothing. These verses are not an indictment against clothing and jewelry, but a judgment on those who use them lavishly while remaining blind to the needs of others. When God blesses you with money or position, don't flaunt it. Use what you have to help others, not impress them.

▶ **ISAIAH 3:16–4:1** ***(cont.)***

She will wear rough burlap instead of rich robes.
Shame will replace her beauty.*
25 The men of the city will be killed with the sword,
and her warriors will die in battle.
26 The gates of Zion will weep and mourn.
The city will be like a ravaged woman,
huddled on the ground.

4:1 In that day so few men will be left that seven women
will fight for each man, saying, "Let us all marry you!
We will provide our own food and clothing. Only let us
take your name so we won't be mocked as old maids."

A Promise of Restoration

ISAIAH 4:2-6

2 But in that day, the branch* of the LORD
will be beautiful and glorious;
the fruit of the land will be the pride and glory
of all who survive in Israel.
3 All who remain in Zion
will be a holy people—
those who survive the destruction of Jerusalem
and are recorded among the living.
4 The Lord will wash the filth from beautiful Zion*
and cleanse Jerusalem of its bloodstains
with the hot breath of fiery judgment.
5 Then the LORD will provide shade for Mount Zion
and all who assemble there.
He will provide a canopy of cloud during the day
and smoke and flaming fire at night,
covering the glorious land.
6 It will be a shelter from daytime heat
and a hiding place from storms and rain.

A Song about the LORD's Vineyard

ISAIAH 5:1-7

1 Now I will sing for the one I love
a song about his vineyard:
My beloved had a vineyard
on a rich and fertile hill.
2 He plowed the land, cleared its stones,
and planted it with the best vines.
In the middle he built a watchtower
and carved a winepress in the nearby rocks.
Then he waited for a harvest of sweet grapes,
but the grapes that grew were bitter.
3 Now, you people of Jerusalem and Judah,
you judge between me and my vineyard.
4 What more could I have done for my
vineyard
that I have not already done?
When I expected sweet grapes,
why did my vineyard give me bitter grapes?
5 Now let me tell you
what I will do to my vineyard:
I will tear down its hedges
and let it be destroyed.
I will break down its walls
and let the animals trample it.
6 I will make it a wild place
where the vines are not pruned and the
ground is not hoed,
a place overgrown with briers and thorns.
I will command the clouds
to drop no rain on it.
7 The nation of Israel is the vineyard of the LORD
of Heaven's Armies.
The people of Judah are his pleasant garden.
He expected a crop of justice,
but instead he found oppression.
He expected to find righteousness,
but instead he heard cries of violence.

Judah's Guilt and Judgment

ISAIAH 5:8-30

8 What sorrow for you who buy up house after
house and field after field,
until everyone is evicted and you live alone
in the land.
9 But I have heard the LORD of Heaven's Armies
swear a solemn oath:
"Many houses will stand deserted;
even beautiful mansions will be empty.
10 Ten acres* of vineyard will not produce even six
gallons* of wine.
Ten baskets of seed will yield only one basket*
of grain."

Is 3:24 As in Dead Sea Scrolls; Masoretic Text reads *robes / because instead of beauty.* **Is 4:2** Or *the Branch.* **Is 4:4** Or *from the women of Zion;* Hebrew reads *from the daughters of Zion.* **Is 5:10a** Hebrew *A ten yoke,* that is, the area of land plowed by ten teams of oxen in one day. **Is 5:10b** Hebrew *a bath* [21 liters]. **Is 5:10c** Hebrew *A homer* [5 bushels or 182 liters] *of seed will yield only an ephah* [20 quarts or 22 liters].

Isa 4:2-4 The "branch of the LORD" probably refers to the Messiah, although some believe it refers to Judah. The point is that during the distress predicted by Isaiah, some people will be protected by God's loving grace. Those protected will be set apart to serve God when the Messiah rules the earth (Jer 23:5-6; Zech 6:12-13). Their distinctive mark will be their holiness, not wealth or prestige. This holiness comes from a sincere desire to obey God's moral standards and from their wholehearted devotion to him. Evil will not always continue as it does now. The time will come when God will put an end to all evil, and his faithful followers will share in his glorious reign.

Isa 5:1-7 The lesson of the song of the vineyard shows that God's chosen nation was to bear fruit—to carry out his work, to uphold justice. It did bear fruit, but the fruit was bad. Jesus said, "Just as you can identify a tree by its fruit, so you can identify people by their actions" (Matt 7:20). Have you examined your own "fruit" lately? Is it good or bad—useful or wild?

Isa 5:8-25 In this section, God condemns six sins: (1) exploiting others (Isa 5:8-10); (2) drunkenness (Isa 5:11-12); (3) taking pride in sin (Isa 5:18-19); (4) confusing moral standards (Isa 5:20); (5) being conceited (Isa 5:21); (6) perverting justice (Isa 5:22-24). Because of these sins, God punished Israel with destruction by Assyria

11 What sorrow for those who get up early in the morning
looking for a drink of alcohol
and spend long evenings drinking wine
to make themselves flaming drunk.
12 They furnish wine and lovely music at their grand parties—
lyre and harp, tambourine and flute—
but they never think about the LORD
or notice what he is doing.
13 So my people will go into exile far away
because they do not know me.
Those who are great and honored will starve,
and the common people will die of thirst.
14 The grave* is licking its lips in anticipation,
opening its mouth wide.
The great and the lowly
and all the drunken mob will be swallowed up.
15 Humanity will be destroyed, and people brought down;
even the arrogant will lower their eyes in humiliation.
16 But the LORD of Heaven's Armies will be exalted by his justice.
The holiness of God will be displayed by his righteousness.
17 In that day lambs will find good pastures,
and fattened sheep and young goats* will feed among the ruins.
18 What sorrow for those who drag their sins behind them
with ropes made of lies,
who drag wickedness behind them like a cart!
19 They even mock God and say,
"Hurry up and do something!
We want to see what you can do.
Let the Holy One of Israel carry out his plan,
for we want to know what it is."
20 What sorrow for those who say
that evil is good and good is evil,
that dark is light and light is dark,
that bitter is sweet and sweet is bitter.
21 What sorrow for those who are wise in their own eyes
and think themselves so clever.
22 What sorrow for those who are heroes at drinking wine
and boast about all the alcohol they can hold.

Is 5:14 Hebrew *Sheol.* **Is 5:17** As in Greek version; Hebrew reads *and strangers.*

(Isa 5:25-30). A similar fate was awaiting Judah if they didn't turn from these sins.

Isa 5:11-13 These people spent many hours drinking and partying, but Isaiah predicted that eventually many would die of hunger and thirst. Ironically, our pleasures—if they do not have God's blessing—may destroy us. Leaving God out of our lives allows sin to come in. Pursuing our own pleasure while ignoring or exploiting the needs of others leaves us empty and under God's anger. God wants us to enjoy life (1 Tim 6:17) but to avoid those activities that could lead us away from him.

Isa 5:13 The nation's heroes—the "great and honored"—would suffer the same humiliation as the common people. Why? Because they lived by their own values rather than God's. Many of today's media, business, and sports heroes are idolized because of their ability to live as they please. Are your heroes those who defy God or those who defy the world in order to serve God?

Isa 5:18-19 Some people drag their sins around with them. Some do so arrogantly, but for others, their sins have become a burden that wears them out. Are you dragging around a cartload of sins that you refuse to give up? Before you find yourself worn out and useless, turn to the one who promises to take away your burden of sin and replace it with a purpose for living that is a joy to fulfill (see Matt 11:28-30).

Isa 5:20 When people see no distinction between good and evil, destruction soon follows. It is easy for people to say, "No one can decide for anyone else what is really right or wrong." They may think getting drunk can't hurt them, extramarital sex isn't really wrong, or money doesn't control them. But when they make excuses for their actions, they break down the distinction between right and wrong. If people do not take God's Word, the Bible, as their standard, soon all moral choices become fuzzy. Without God, they are headed for a breakdown and much suffering.

Grapevine

The common grapevine is a slender plant which trails on the ground or climbs supports by means of tendrils. It is mentioned throughout Scripture, frequently in a symbolic sense. The vine was the emblem of prosperity and peace among the ancient Hebrews. More particularly it symbolized the chosen people. They were the vine that God had taken out of Egypt and planted in a particularly choice land (Ps 80:8-15; Isa 5:1-7). They had been given all the attention necessary for the production of outstanding fruit, but instead yielded only wild grapes. For this they were to be abandoned to their enemies. The believers in Christ have become branches in a new vine, Jesus himself. By staying connected to him, they will bear fruit. Otherwise, they will become fruitless and thrown into the fire as dead branches (John 15:1-8).

▸ **ISAIAH 5:8-30** ***(cont.)***

23 They take bribes to let the wicked go free,
and they punish the innocent.
24 Therefore, just as fire licks up stubble
and dry grass shrivels in the flame,
so their roots will rot
and their flowers wither.
For they have rejected the law of the LORD
of Heaven's Armies;
they have despised the word of the Holy One
of Israel.
25 That is why the LORD's anger burns against
his people,
and why he has raised his fist to crush them.
The mountains tremble,
and the corpses of his people litter the streets
like garbage.
But even then the LORD's anger is not satisfied.
His fist is still poised to strike!

26 He will send a signal to distant nations
far away
and whistle to those at the ends of
the earth.
They will come racing toward Jerusalem.
27 They will not get tired or stumble.
They will not stop for rest or sleep.
Not a belt will be loose,
not a sandal strap broken.
28 Their arrows will be sharp
and their bows ready for battle.
Sparks will fly from their horses' hooves,
and the wheels of their chariots will spin
like a whirlwind.
29 They will roar like lions,
like the strongest of lions.
Growling, they will pounce on their victims
and carry them off,
and no one will be there to rescue them.
30 They will roar over their victims on that day
of destruction
like the roaring of the sea.
If someone looks across the land,
only darkness and distress will be seen;
even the light will be darkened by clouds.

The End of Ahaz's Reign in Judah PARALLEL

2 KINGS 16:19-20

The rest of the events in Ahaz's reign and everything
he did are recorded in *The Book of the History of the*
Kings of Judah. 20When Ahaz died, he was buried with
his ancestors in the City of David. Then his son Hezekiah became the next king.

2 CHRONICLES 28:26-27

The rest of the events of Ahaz's reign and everything
he did, from beginning to end, are recorded in *The*
Book of the Kings of Judah and Israel. 27When Ahaz
died, he was buried in Jerusalem but not in the royal
cemetery of the kings of Judah. Then his son Hezekiah
became the next king.

A Message about Babylon

ISAIAH 13:1-22

Isaiah son of Amoz received this message concerning
the destruction of Babylon:

2 "Raise a signal flag on a bare hilltop.
Call up an army against Babylon.
Wave your hand to encourage them
as they march into the palaces of the high
and mighty.
3 I, the LORD, have dedicated these soldiers for
this task.
Yes, I have called mighty warriors to express
my anger,
and they will rejoice when I am exalted."

4 Hear the noise on the mountains!
Listen, as the vast armies march!
It is the noise and shouting of many nations.
The LORD of Heaven's Armies has called
this army together.
5 They come from distant countries,
from beyond the farthest horizons.
They are the LORD's weapons to carry out
his anger.
With them he will destroy the whole land.

6 Scream in terror, for the day of the LORD has
arrived—
the time for the Almighty to destroy.

Isa 5:24 The people suffered because they rejected God's law. It is sad to see so many people today searching for meaning in life while spurning God's Word. We can avoid the error of Israel and Judah by making not only reading the Bible but also understanding and obeying it a high priority in our lives.

Isa 5:26-30 This passage describes what God would do if the people disobeyed him (Deut 28). Assyria began to torment Israel during the reign of Ahaz, king of Judah (735–715 B.C.). This powerful aggressor then finally destroyed the northern kingdom in 722 B.C. and scattered the people throughout its own empire. Sin has consequences. Israel's punishment was progressive, not immediate; prophet after prophet warned the people. But eventually Israel was judged.

Isa 13:1ff Isaiah has already spoken of judgment against the southern kingdom and, to a lesser extent, against the northern kingdom. Now he turns to messages of judgment on other nations. Isaiah 13 is an oracle or message from God concerning Babylon. Long before Babylon became a world power and threatened Judah, Isaiah spoke of its destruction. Babylon had been the rallying point of rebellion against God after the Flood (Gen 11). Revelation 17 and 18 use Babylon as a symbol of God's enemies. At the time of this oracle, Babylon was still part of the Assyrian Empire. Isaiah communicated a message of challenge and hope to God's people, telling them not to rely on other nations but to rely on God alone. And he let them know that their greatest enemies would receive from God the punishment they deserved.

7 Every arm is paralyzed with fear.
Every heart melts,
8 and people are terrified.
Pangs of anguish grip them,
like those of a woman in labor.
They look helplessly at one another,
their faces aflame with fear.

9 For see, the day of the LORD is coming—
the terrible day of his fury and fierce anger.
The land will be made desolate,
and all the sinners destroyed with it.
10 The heavens will be black above them;
the stars will give no light.
The sun will be dark when it rises,
and the moon will provide no light.
11 "I, the LORD, will punish the world for its evil
and the wicked for their sin.
I will crush the arrogance of the proud
and humble the pride of the mighty.
12 I will make people scarcer than gold—
more rare than the fine gold of Ophir.
13 For I will shake the heavens.
The earth will move from its place
when the LORD of Heaven's Armies displays his wrath
in the day of his fierce anger."

14 Everyone in Babylon will run about like a hunted gazelle,
like sheep without a shepherd.
They will try to find their own people
and flee to their own land.
15 Anyone who is captured will be cut down—
run through with a sword.
16 Their little children will be dashed to death
before their eyes.
Their homes will be sacked, and their wives
will be raped.

17 "Look, I will stir up the Medes against Babylon.
They cannot be tempted by silver
or bribed with gold.
18 The attacking armies will shoot down the young
men with arrows.
They will have no mercy on helpless babies
and will show no compassion for children."

19 Babylon, the most glorious of kingdoms,
the flower of Chaldean pride,
will be devastated like Sodom and Gomorrah
when God destroyed them.
20 Babylon will never be inhabited again.
It will remain empty for generation after generation.
Nomads will refuse to camp there,
and shepherds will not bed down their sheep.
21 Desert animals will move into the ruined city,
and the houses will be haunted by howling creatures.
Owls will live among the ruins,
and wild goats will go there to dance.
22 Hyenas will howl in its fortresses,
and jackals will make dens in its luxurious palaces.
Babylon's days are numbered;
its time of destruction will soon arrive.

A Taunt for Babylon's King

ISAIAH 14:1-23

But the LORD will have mercy on the descendants of
Jacob. He will choose Israel as his special people once
again. He will bring them back to settle once again in
their own land. And people from many different nations will come and join them there and unite with the
people of Israel.* 2The nations of the world will help
the LORD's people to return, and those who come to
live in their land will serve them. Those who captured
Israel will themselves be captured, and Israel will rule
over its enemies.

3In that wonderful day when the LORD gives his
people rest from sorrow and fear, from slavery and
chains, 4you will taunt the king of Babylon. You will
say,

"The mighty man has been destroyed.
Yes, your insolence* is ended.
5 For the LORD has crushed your wicked power
and broken your evil rule.

Is 14:1 Hebrew *the house of Jacob.* The names "Jacob" and "Israel" are often interchanged throughout the Old Testament, referring sometimes to the individual patriarch and sometimes to the nation. **Is 14:4** As in Dead Sea Scrolls; the meaning of the Masoretic Text is uncertain.

Isa 13:12 Ophir was known for its rare and valuable gold. It is thought to have been located on the southwestern coast of Arabia.

Isa 13:20 Even before Babylon became a world power, Isaiah prophesied that, though it would shine for a while, Babylon's destruction would be so complete that the land would never again be inhabited. Babylon, in present-day Iraq, still lies in utter ruin, buried under mounds of dirt and sand.

Isa 14:1 A prominent theme in Isaiah is that non-Israelites would join the returning Israelites (Isa 56:6-7; 60:10; 61:5). God's intention was that through his faithful people all the world would be blessed (Gen 12:3). Through the family of David, the whole world could be saved by Christ. God's Word must be available to all people groups in their own languages. We must not limit God's love to our own people. God loves the whole world. We must support and help those missions that are reaching out to people who haven't heard the Good News of salvation.

Isa 14:4-11 These verses could have both present and future significance in reference to Babylon. The historical city and empire would be permanently destroyed. Babylon has also been used as a picture of all those who oppose God. Thus, in the end times, all who oppose God will be destroyed, and all evil will be removed from the earth forever.

Isa 14:5-6 Power fades quickly. God permitted Babylon to have temporary power for a purpose—to punish his wayward people. When the purpose ended, so did the power. Beware of placing confidence in human power because one day it will fade, no matter how strong it appears now.

▸ **ISAIAH 14:1-23 *(cont.)***

6 You struck the people with endless blows
of rage
and held the nations in your angry grip
with unrelenting tyranny.
7 But finally the earth is at rest and quiet.
Now it can sing again!
8 Even the trees of the forest—
the cypress trees and the cedars of Lebanon—
sing out this joyous song:
'Since you have been cut down,
no one will come now to cut us down!'

9 "In the place of the dead* there is excitement
over your arrival.
The spirits of world leaders and mighty kings
long dead
stand up to see you.
10 With one voice they all cry out,
'Now you are as weak as we are!
11 Your might and power were buried with you.*
The sound of the harp in your palace has
ceased.
Now maggots are your sheet,
and worms your blanket.'

12 "How you are fallen from heaven,
O shining star, son of the morning!
You have been thrown down to the earth,
you who destroyed the nations of the world.
13 For you said to yourself,
'I will ascend to heaven and set my throne
above God's stars.
I will preside on the mountain of the gods
far away in the north.*
14 I will climb to the highest heavens
and be like the Most High.'
15 Instead, you will be brought down to the place
of the dead,
down to its lowest depths.
16 Everyone there will stare at you and ask,
'Can this be the one who shook the earth
and made the kingdoms of the world tremble?
17 Is this the one who destroyed the world
and made it into a wasteland?
Is this the king who demolished the world's
greatest cities
and had no mercy on his prisoners?'

18 "The kings of the nations lie in stately glory,
each in his own tomb,
19 but you will be thrown out of your grave
like a worthless branch.
Like a corpse trampled underfoot,
you will be dumped into a mass grave
with those killed in battle.
You will descend to the pit.
20 You will not be given a proper burial,
for you have destroyed your nation
and slaughtered your people.
The descendants of such an evil person
will never again receive honor.
21 Kill this man's children!
Let them die because of their father's sins!
They must not rise and conquer the earth,
filling the world with their cities."

22 This is what the LORD of Heaven's
Armies says:
"I, myself, have risen against Babylon!
I will destroy its children and its children's
children,"
says the LORD.
23 "I will make Babylon a desolate place of owls,
filled with swamps and marshes.
I will sweep the land with the broom of
destruction.
I, the LORD of Heaven's Armies, have
spoken!"

A Message about Assyria

ISAIAH 14:24-27

24 The LORD of Heaven's Armies has sworn this oath:

"It will all happen as I have planned.
It will be as I have decided.
25 I will break the Assyrians when they are
in Israel;
I will trample them on my mountains.
My people will no longer be their slaves
nor bow down under their heavy loads.
26 I have a plan for the whole earth,
a hand of judgment upon all the nations.
27 The LORD of Heaven's Armies has spoken—
who can change his plans?
When his hand is raised,
who can stop him?"

Is 14:9 Hebrew *Sheol;* also in 14:15. **Is 14:11** Hebrew *were brought down to Sheol.* **Is 14:13** Or *on the heights of Zaphon.*

Isa 14:12 "Shining star, son of the morning" could be names used to worship the kings of Assyria and Babylon. More likely, it means that they will fade like the morning star when the sun rises.

Isa 14:12-14 There are several interpretations for the fallen one in these verses. (1) He is Satan, because the person here is too powerful to be any human king. Although Satan may fit verses 12-14, he does not fit well with the rest of the chapter. (2) This could be Sennacherib or Nebuchadnezzar, kings with supreme power. Their people looked upon them as gods. These kings wanted to rule the world. (3) This could refer to both Satan and a great human king, possibly Nebuchadnezzar, because Babylon is pictured as the seat of evil in Revelation 17–18. Pride was Satan's sin as well as Babylon's. Common to all three viewpoints is the truth that pride willfully opposes God and will result in judgment. Israel made the mistake of being too proud to depend on God, and we are vulnerable to that same mistake.

Isa 14:24-27 This prophecy came true as Isaiah predicted (see 2 Kgs 19; Isa 37:21-38).

A Message about Philistia

ISAIAH 14:28-32

This message came to me the year King Ahaz died:*

29 Do not rejoice, you Philistines,
that the rod that struck you is broken—
that the king who attacked you is dead.
For from that snake a more poisonous snake will be born,
a fiery serpent to destroy you!
30 I will feed the poor in my pasture;
the needy will lie down in peace.
But as for you, I will wipe you out with famine
and destroy the few who remain.
31 Wail at the gates! Weep in the cities!
Melt with fear, you Philistines!
A powerful army comes like smoke from the north.
Each soldier rushes forward eager to fight.

32 What should we tell the Philistine messengers?
Tell them,

"The LORD has built Jerusalem*;
its walls will give refuge to his oppressed people."

A Message about Moab

ISAIAH 15:1–16:14

This message came to me concerning Moab:

In one night the town of Ar will be leveled,
and the city of Kir will be destroyed.
2 Your people will go to their temple in Dibon
to mourn.
They will go to their sacred shrines to weep.
They will wail for the fate of Nebo and Medeba,
shaving their heads in sorrow and cutting
off their beards.
3 They will wear burlap as they wander the streets.
From every home and public square will come
the sound of wailing.
4 The people of Heshbon and Elealeh will
cry out;
their voices will be heard as far away
as Jahaz!
The bravest warriors of Moab will cry out
in utter terror.
They will be helpless with fear.
5 My heart weeps for Moab.
Its people flee to Zoar and Eglath-shelishiyah.
Weeping, they climb the road to Luhith.
Their cries of distress can be heard all along
the road to Horonaim.
6 Even the waters of Nimrim are dried up!
The grassy banks are scorched.
The tender plants are gone;
nothing green remains.
7 The people grab their possessions
and carry them across the Ravine of Willows.
8 A cry of distress echoes through the land
of Moab
from one end to the other—
from Eglaim to Beer-elim.
9 The stream near Dibon* runs red with blood,
but I am still not finished with Dibon!
Lions will hunt down the survivors—
both those who try to escape
and those who remain behind.

16:1 Send lambs from Sela as tribute
to the ruler of the land.
Send them through the desert
to the mountain of beautiful Zion.
2 The women of Moab are left like homeless birds
at the shallow crossings of the Arnon River.
3 "Help us," they cry.
"Defend us against our enemies.
Protect us from their relentless attack.
Do not betray us now that we have escaped.
4 Let our refugees stay among you.
Hide them from our enemies until the terror
is past."
When oppression and destruction have ended
and enemy raiders have disappeared,
5 then God will establish one of David's
descendants as king.
He will rule with mercy and truth.
He will always do what is just
and be eager to do what is right.

6 We have heard about proud Moab—
about its pride and arrogance and rage.
But all that boasting has disappeared.
7 The entire land of Moab weeps.
Yes, everyone in Moab mourns

Is 14:28 King Ahaz died in 715 B.C. **Is 14:32** Hebrew *Zion.* **Is 15:9** As in Dead Sea Scrolls, some Greek manuscripts, and Latin Vulgate; Masoretic Text reads *Dimon;* also in 15:9b.

Isa 14:28-31 Isaiah received this message from the Lord in 715 B.C., the year that King Ahaz of Judah died. "The king who attacked you" (Isa 14:29) was not Ahaz but Shalmaneser V or Sargon of Assyria. The "powerful army" from the north (Isa 14:31) refers to the soldiers of Sargon of Assyria.

Isa 15:1 Moab was east of the Dead Sea. The Moabites were descendants of Lot through his incestuous relationship with his older daughter (Gen 19:31-37). Moab had always been Israel's enemy. They oppressed Israel and invaded their land (Judg 3:12-14), fought against Saul (1 Sam 14:47) and against David (2 Sam 8:2, 11-12). Moab would be punished for treating Israel harshly.

Isa 16:1ff Attacked by the Assyrians, Moabite refugees would flee to Sela, which lay in the country of Edom to the south. Desperate Moabites, seeking Judah's protection, would send a tribute of lambs to Jerusalem. Jerusalem would be a safe refuge for a while. Isaiah advised Judah to accept these refugees as a sign of compassion during the enemy's time of devastation.

▸ **ISAIAH 15:1–16:14** ***(cont.)***

for the cakes of raisins from Kir-hareseth.
They are all gone now.
8 The farms of Heshbon are abandoned;
the vineyards at Sibmah are deserted.
The rulers of the nations have broken down Moab—
that beautiful grapevine.
Its tendrils spread north as far as the town of Jazer
and trailed eastward into the wilderness.
Its shoots reached so far west
that they crossed over the Dead Sea.*

9 So now I weep for Jazer and the vineyards of Sibmah;
my tears will flow for Heshbon and Elealeh.
There are no more shouts of joy
over your summer fruits and harvest.
10 Gone now is the gladness,
gone the joy of harvest.
There will be no singing in the vineyards,
no more happy shouts,
no treading of grapes in the winepresses.
I have ended all their harvest joys.
11 My heart's cry for Moab is like a lament on a harp.
I am filled with anguish for Kir-hareseth.*
12 The people of Moab will worship at their pagan shrines,
but it will do them no good.
They will cry to the gods in their temples,
but no one will be able to save them.

13The LORD has already said these things about
Moab in the past. 14But now the LORD says, "Within
three years, counting each day,* the glory of Moab will
be ended. From its great population, only a few of its
people will be left alive."

Is 16:8 Hebrew *the sea.* **Is 16:11** Hebrew *Kir-heres,* a variant spelling of Kir-hareseth. **Is 16:14** Hebrew *Within three years, as a servant bound by contract would count them.*

2. HEZEKIAH'S REFORMS

Hezekiah saw the northern kingdom of Israel destroyed by the Assyrians, but he understood that it was God's judgment that sent his neighbors into exile. He recognized some of the same sins in his own nation, so when he took the throne he immediately began to call the people to repentance. He reopened the Temple, orchestrated a national celebration of Passover, and reformed the nation's religious practices by ordering their idols to be destroyed. This was one of the greatest revivals in history!

Hezekiah Reopens the Temple

2 CHRONICLES 29:3-17

In the very first month of the first year of his reign,
Hezekiah reopened the doors of the Temple of the
LORD and repaired them. 4He summoned the priests
and Levites to meet him at the courtyard east of the
Temple. 5He said to them, "Listen to me, you Levites!
Purify yourselves, and purify the Temple of the LORD,
the God of your ancestors. Remove all the defiled
things from the sanctuary. 6Our ancestors were unfaithful and did what was evil in the sight of the LORD
our God. They abandoned the LORD and his dwelling place; they turned their backs on him. 7They also
shut the doors to the Temple's entry room, and they
snuffed out the lamps. They stopped burning incense
and presenting burnt offerings at the sanctuary of the
God of Israel.

8"That is why the LORD's anger has fallen upon Judah and Jerusalem. He has made them an object of
dread, horror, and ridicule, as you can see with your
own eyes. 9Because of this, our fathers have been
killed in battle, and our sons and daughters and wives
have been captured. 10But now I will make a covenant
with the LORD, the God of Israel, so that his fierce anger will turn away from us. 11My sons, do not neglect
your duties any longer! The LORD has chosen you to
stand in his presence, to minister to him, and to lead
the people in worship and present offerings to him."
12Then these Levites got right to work:

From the clan of Kohath: Mahath son of Amasai and Joel son of Azariah.
From the clan of Merari: Kish son of Abdi and Azariah son of Jehallelel.

Isa 16:10 The treading out of grapes (squeezing the juice from grapes by mashing them with bare feet) was the climax of the harvest season, a time of great joy in the vineyards. But the joy of harvest would soon be ended because the people in their pride ignored God and rebelled against him.

Isa 16:12 When the people of Moab experienced God's wrath, they sought their own idols and gods. Nothing happened because there was no one there to save them. We may seek our own ways of escaping daily troubles—work, friends, pleasure, or even some human-made religious idea. But our only hope lies in God, the only one who can hear and help us.

Isa 16:13-14 Tiglath-pileser III invaded Moab in 732 B.C.; Sennacherib invaded Moab the same year that he invaded Judah, 701 B.C. In these events, the people of Israel saw prophecy fulfilled before their very eyes.

2 Chr 29:11 The Levites, chosen by God to serve in the Temple, had been kept from their duties by Ahaz's wickedness (2 Chr 28:24). But Hezekiah called them back into service, reminding them that the Lord had chosen them to minister.

We may not have to face a wicked king, but pressures or responsibilities can render us inactive and ineffective. When you have been given the responsibility to minister, don't neglect your duty. If you have become inactive in Christian service, either by choice or by circumstance, look for opportunities to minister, and listen to the "Hezekiahs" that God will send your way. Then, like the Levites, be ready for action (2 Chr 29:12-15).

From the clan of Gershon: Joah son of Zimmah
and Eden son of Joah.
13 From the family of Elizaphan: Shimri and Jeiel.
From the family of Asaph: Zechariah and
Mattaniah.
14 From the family of Heman: Jehiel and Shimei.
From the family of Jeduthun: Shemaiah and
Uzziel.

15 These men called together their fellow Levites,
and they all purified themselves. Then they began to
cleanse the Temple of the LORD, just as the king had
commanded. They were careful to follow all the LORD's
instructions in their work. 16 The priests went into the
sanctuary of the Temple of the LORD to cleanse it, and
they took out to the Temple courtyard all the defiled
things they found. From there the Levites carted it all
out to the Kidron Valley.

17 They began the work in early spring, on the
first day of the new year,* and in eight days they had
reached the entry room of the LORD's Temple. Then
they purified the Temple of the LORD itself, which took
another eight days. So the entire task was completed
in sixteen days.

The Temple Rededication

2 CHRONICLES 29:18-36

Then the Levites went to King Hezekiah and gave him
this report: "We have cleansed the entire Temple of the
LORD, the altar of burnt offering with all its utensils,
and the table of the Bread of the Presence with all
its utensils. 19 We have also recovered all the items
discarded by King Ahaz when he was unfaithful and
closed the Temple. They are now in front of the altar
of the LORD, purified and ready for use."

20 Early the next morning King Hezekiah gathered
the city officials and went to the Temple of the LORD.
21 They brought seven bulls, seven rams, and seven
male lambs as a burnt offering, together with seven
male goats as a sin offering for the kingdom, for the
Temple, and for Judah. The king commanded the
priests, who were descendants of Aaron, to sacrifice
the animals on the altar of the LORD.

22 So they killed the bulls, and the priests took the
blood and sprinkled it on the altar. Next they killed
the rams and sprinkled their blood on the altar. And
finally, they did the same with the male lambs. 23 The
male goats for the sin offering were then brought before the king and the assembly of people, who laid
their hands on them. 24 The priests then killed the
goats as a sin offering and sprinkled their blood on
the altar to make atonement for the sins of all Israel.
The king had specifically commanded that this burnt
offering and sin offering should be made for all Israel.

25 King Hezekiah then stationed the Levites at the
Temple of the LORD with cymbals, lyres, and harps.
He obeyed all the commands that the LORD had given
to King David through Gad, the king's seer, and the

2 Chr 29:17 Hebrew *on the first day of the first month.* This day in the ancient Hebrew lunar calendar occurred in March or early April, 715 B.C.

GREAT REVIVALS IN THE BIBLE

The Bible records several great revivals where people in great numbers turned to God and gave up their sinful ways of living. Each revival was characterized by a leader who recognized the nation's spiritual dryness.

Leader	*Reference*	*How the People Responded*
Moses	Exod 34–36	Accepted God's laws and built the Tabernacle
Samuel	1 Sam 7:2-13	Promised to make God first in their lives by destroying their idols
David	2 Sam 6	Brought the Ark of the Covenant to Jerusalem; praised God with singing and musical instruments
Jehoshaphat	2 Chr 20	Decided to trust in God alone to help them, and their discouragement turned to joy
Hezekiah	2 Chr 29–31	Purified the Temple; got rid of idols; brought tithes to God's house
Josiah	2 Chr 34–35	Made a commitment to obey God's commands and remove sinful influences from their lives
Ezra	Ezra 9–10 Hag 1	Stopped associating with those who caused them to compromise their faith; renewed their commitment to God's commands; began rebuilding the Temple
Nehemiah (with Ezra)	Neh 8–10	Fasted, confessed their sins, read God's Word publicly, and promised in writing to again serve God wholeheartedly

2 Chr 29:21 Throughout the Old Testament, the sacrifice was God's appointed way of approaching him and restoring a right relationship with him. Hezekiah's sin offering was a sacrifice given to God for forgiveness of unintentional sins. (For more information on why God required sacrifices and how they were carried out, see the notes on Lev 1, p. 202.)

2 Chr 29:22 The blood sprinkled on the altar represented the innocence of the sacrificed animal taking the place of the person making the offering. The animal died so the sinner could live. This ritual looked forward to the day when Jesus Christ, God's perfect Son, would sacrifice his innocent life on the cross in order that the sinful and guilty human race might be spared the punishment it deserves (Heb 10:1-14).

▸ **2 CHRONICLES 29:18-36** ***(cont.)***

prophet Nathan. 26The Levites then took their positions around the Temple with the instruments of David, and the priests took their positions with the trumpets.

27Then Hezekiah ordered that the burnt offering be placed on the altar. As the burnt offering was presented, songs of praise to the LORD were begun, accompanied by the trumpets and other instruments of David, the former king of Israel. 28The entire assembly worshiped the LORD as the singers sang and the trumpets blew, until all the burnt offerings were finished. 29Then the king and everyone with him bowed down in worship. 30King Hezekiah and the officials ordered the Levites to praise the LORD with the psalms written by David and by Asaph the seer. So they offered joyous praise and bowed down in worship.

31Then Hezekiah declared, "Now that you have consecrated yourselves to the LORD, bring your sacrifices and thanksgiving offerings to the Temple of the LORD." So the people brought their sacrifices and thanksgiving offerings, and all whose hearts were willing brought burnt offerings, too. 32The people brought to the LORD 70 bulls, 100 rams, and 200 male lambs for burnt offerings. 33They also brought 600 cattle and 3,000 sheep and goats as sacred offerings.

34But there were too few priests to prepare all the burnt offerings. So their relatives the Levites helped them until the work was finished and more priests had been purified, for the Levites had been more conscientious about purifying themselves than the priests had been. 35There was an abundance of burnt offerings, along with the usual liquid offerings, and a great deal of fat from the many peace offerings.

So the Temple of the LORD was restored to service. 36And Hezekiah and all the people rejoiced because of what God had done for the people, for everything had been accomplished so quickly.

710 BC

First known lock and key in the palace in Assyria

Preparations for Passover

2 CHRONICLES 30:1-9

King Hezekiah now sent word to all Israel and Judah, and he wrote letters of invitation to the people of Ephraim and Manasseh. He asked everyone to come to the Temple of the LORD at Jerusalem to celebrate the Passover of the LORD, the God of Israel. 2The king, his officials, and all the community of Jerusalem decided to celebrate Passover a month later than usual.* 3They were unable to celebrate it at the prescribed time because not enough priests could be purified by then, and the people had not yet assembled at Jerusalem.

4This plan for keeping the Passover seemed right to the king and all the people. 5So they sent a proclamation throughout all Israel, from Beersheba in the south to Dan in the north, inviting everyone to come to Jerusalem to celebrate the Passover of the LORD, the God of Israel. The people had not been celebrating it in great numbers as required in the Law.

6At the king's command, runners were sent throughout Israel and Judah. They carried letters that said:

> "O people of Israel, return to the LORD, the God of Abraham, Isaac, and Israel,* so that he will return to the few of us who have survived the conquest of the Assyrian kings. 7Do not be like your ancestors and relatives who abandoned the LORD, the God of their ancestors, and became an object of derision, as you yourselves can see. 8Do not be stubborn, as they were, but submit yourselves to the LORD. Come to his Temple, which he has set apart as holy forever. Worship the LORD your God so that his fierce anger will turn away from you.
>
> 9"For if you return to the LORD, your relatives and your children will be treated mercifully by their captors, and they will be able to return to this land. For the LORD your God is gracious and merciful. If you return to him, he will not continue to turn his face from you."

Celebration of Passover

2 CHRONICLES 30:10-27

The runners went from town to town throughout Ephraim and Manasseh and as far as the territory of Zebulun. But most of the people just laughed at the runners and made fun of them. 11However, some

2 Chr 30:2 Hebrew *in the second month.* Passover was normally observed in the first month (of the ancient Hebrew lunar calendar). **2 Chr 30:6** *Israel* is the name that God gave to Jacob.

2 Chr 29:30 A seer was someone who received messages from God for the nation through visions or dreams.

2 Chr 29:31 A thanksgiving offering, one type of peace offering (see Lev 7:12-15), was given as an expression of gratitude to God. As a peace offering, it symbolized restored peace and fellowship with God.

2 Chr 30:1 The Passover celebration commemorated the time when God spared the lives of Israel's firstborn sons in Egypt. God had promised to send a plague to kill all the firstborn sons except in those homes where the blood of a slain lamb had been painted on the doorposts. The Israelites obeyed, and when the destroyer saw the blood, he "passed over" the house and did not harm anyone in it (Exod 12:23). After this plague, Pharaoh freed the Israelites from slavery. This celebration was to be a yearly reminder of how God delivered his people. The careful preparations, both in the Temple and for the festival, show that this was not a temporary or impulsive revival, but a deep-seated change of heart and life.

2 Chr 30:2-3 God's law had a provision that, under certain circumstances, the Passover could be celebrated one month later (Num 9:10-11).

2 Chr 30:6-9 Hezekiah was a king dedicated to God and to the spiritual progress of the nation. He sent letters throughout Judah and Israel urging everyone to return to God. He told them not to be stubborn but to submit to the Lord. To submit means to obey him first, yielding our bodies, minds, wills, and emotions to him. His Holy Spirit must guide and renew every part of us. Only then will we be able to temper our stubborn selfishness.

2 Chr 30:10 Assyria had recently conquered the northern kingdom of Israel, and most of the people had been carried away to foreign lands. Hezekiah sent a proclamation to the few people who remained, inviting them to

people from Asher, Manasseh, and Zebulun humbled themselves and went to Jerusalem.
[12]At the same time, God's hand was on the people in the land of Judah, giving them all one heart to obey the orders of the king and his officials, who were following the word of the LORD. [13]So a huge crowd assembled at Jerusalem in midspring* to celebrate the Festival of Unleavened Bread. [14]They set to work and removed the pagan altars from Jerusalem. They took away all the incense altars and threw them into the Kidron Valley.
[15]On the fourteenth day of the second month, one month later than usual,* the people slaughtered the Passover lamb. This shamed the priests and Levites, so they purified themselves and brought burnt offerings to the Temple of the LORD. [16]Then they took their places at the Temple as prescribed in the Law of Moses, the man of God. The Levites brought the sacrificial blood to the priests, who then sprinkled it on the altar.
[17]Since many of the people had not purified themselves, the Levites had to slaughter their Passover lamb for them, to set them apart for the LORD. [18]Most of those who came from Ephraim, Manasseh, Issachar, and Zebulun had not purified themselves. But King Hezekiah prayed for them, and they were allowed to eat the Passover meal anyway, even though this was contrary to the requirements of the Law. For Hezekiah said, "May the LORD, who is good, pardon those [19]who decide to follow the LORD, the God of their ancestors, even though they are not properly cleansed for the ceremony." [20]And the LORD listened to Hezekiah's prayer and healed the people.
[21]So the people of Israel who were present in Jerusalem joyously celebrated the Festival of Unleavened Bread for seven days. Each day the Levites and priests sang to the LORD, accompanied by loud instruments.* [22]Hezekiah encouraged all the Levites regarding the skill they displayed as they served the LORD. The celebration continued for seven days. Peace offerings were sacrificed, and the people gave thanks to the LORD, the God of their ancestors.
[23]The entire assembly then decided to continue the festival another seven days, so they celebrated joyfully for another week. [24]King Hezekiah gave the people 1,000 bulls and 7,000 sheep and goats for offerings, and the officials donated 1,000 bulls and 10,000 sheep and goats. Meanwhile, many more priests purified themselves.
[25]The entire assembly of Judah rejoiced, including the priests, the Levites, all who came from the land of Israel, the foreigners who came to the festival, and all those who lived in Judah. [26]There was great joy in the city, for Jerusalem had not seen a celebration like this one since the days of Solomon, King David's son. [27]Then the priests and Levites stood and blessed the people, and God heard their prayer from his holy dwelling in heaven.

Hezekiah's Religious Reforms

2 CHRONICLES 31:1-21

When the festival ended, the Israelites who attended went to all the towns of Judah, Benjamin, Ephraim, and Manasseh, and they smashed all the sacred pillars, cut down the Asherah poles, and removed the pagan shrines and altars. After this, the Israelites returned to their own towns and homes.
[2]Hezekiah then organized the priests and Levites into divisions to offer the burnt offerings and peace offerings, and to worship and give thanks and praise to the LORD at the gates of the Temple. [3]The king also

2 Chr 30:13 Hebrew *in the second month.* The second month of the ancient Hebrew lunar calendar usually occurs within the months of April and May. **2 Chr 30:15** Hebrew *On the fourteenth day of the second month.* Passover normally began on the fourteenth day of the first month (see Lev 23:5). **2 Chr 30:21** Or *sang to the LORD with all their strength.*

come to the Passover (2 Chr 30:1), but most responded with scorn and ridicule. People may mock you when you try to promote spiritual renewal and growth. Are you prepared to be ridiculed for your faith? When it comes your way, do not waver. Stand strong in your faith, as Hezekiah did, and God will honor you.

2 Chr 30:11 Most scorned Hezekiah's messengers, but some accepted the invitation. Our efforts to tell others about God often meet with similar reactions. Many people will laugh at an invitation to accept Christ. But this must not stop us from reaching out. If you know and understand that rejecting the gospel is common, you can guard against feelings of personal rejection. Remember that the Holy Spirit convicts and convinces. Our task is to invite others to consider God's actions, his claims, and his promises.

2 Chr 30:14 Just as the priests had purified the Temple (2 Chr 29:4-5), so the people cleared the city of pagan idols and then purified themselves to prepare for worship (2 Chr 30:17-19). Even the good kings of Judah found it difficult to get rid of the idols and altars in the pagan shrines (2 Kgs 14:4; 2 Chr 20:33). Finally, Hezekiah, with the help of his people, completed this task.

2 Chr 30:15 The people were so zealous to celebrate the Passover and bring offerings to the Temple that the priests and Levites were ashamed they did not share the same enthusiasm. The zeal of common people's faith motivated the ministers to take action. Devout laypeople today can motivate professional church staff to rekindle their enthusiasm for God's work. Laypeople should never be shut out of church government or decision making. The church needs their good examples of faith.

2 Chr 30:22 One important purpose of the peace offering was to express gratitude to God for health or for safety in times of crisis.

2 Chr 30:26 It had been more than 200 years since there had been such a celebration in Jerusalem.

2 Chr 31:1ff Why was idol worship so bad? The Israelites had access to the one true God, but they constantly fell into worshiping lifeless idols made of wood or stone. They put aside worshiping the Creator in order to worship the creation. We are just as guilty when God no longer holds first place in our lives. When we think more about wealth, pleasure, prestige, or material possessions than about God, we are actually worshiping them as gods. Because of idol worship, the people of Judah were eventually sent into captivity in foreign lands (2 Chr 36:14-17). We may not be sent into captivity, but discipline awaits all those who continually put earthly desires above spiritual priorities.

2 Chr 31:2-21 The priests had not been supported by the government during the evil kings' reigns. Now that the Temple was repaired, Hezekiah organized the priests and resumed the work of the Temple according to the plan originally set up by David (1 Chr 23:6-24; 24:3-19).

▸ **2 CHRONICLES 31:1-21** ***(cont.)***

made a personal contribution of animals for the daily
morning and evening burnt offerings, the weekly Sabbath festivals, the monthly new moon festivals, and
the annual festivals as prescribed in the Law of the
LORD. 4In addition, he required the people in Jerusalem to bring a portion of their goods to the priests
and Levites, so they could devote themselves fully to
the Law of the LORD.
5When the people of Israel heard these requirements, they responded generously by bringing the
first share of their grain, new wine, olive oil, honey,
and all the produce of their fields. They brought a large
quantity—a tithe of all they produced. 6The people
who had moved to Judah from Israel, and the people of
Judah themselves, brought in the tithes of their cattle,
sheep, and goats and a tithe of the things that had been
dedicated to the LORD their God, and they piled them
up in great heaps. 7They began piling them up in late
spring, and the heaps continued to grow until early
autumn.* 8When Hezekiah and his officials came
and saw these huge piles, they thanked the LORD and
his people Israel!
9"Where did all this come from?" Hezekiah asked
the priests and Levites.
10And Azariah the high priest, from the family of
Zadok, replied, "Since the people began bringing their
gifts to the LORD's Temple, we have had enough to eat
and plenty to spare. The LORD has blessed his people,
and all this is left over."
11Hezekiah ordered that storerooms be prepared
in the Temple of the LORD. When this was done, 12the
people faithfully brought all the tithes and gifts to the
Temple. Conaniah the Levite was put in charge, assisted by his brother Shimei. 13The supervisors under
them were Jehiel, Azaziah, Nahath, Asahel, Jerimoth,
Jozabad, Eliel, Ismakiah, Mahath, and Benaiah. These
appointments were made by King Hezekiah and Azariah, the chief official in the Temple of God.
14Kore son of Imnah the Levite, who was the gatekeeper at the East Gate, was put in charge of distributing the voluntary offerings given to God, the gifts,

2 Chr 31:7 Hebrew *in the third month . . . until the seventh month.* The third month of the ancient Hebrew lunar calendar usually occurs within the months of May and June; the seventh month usually occurs within September and October.

DAVID'S DYNASTY

The Lord promised David that his kingdom would endure and his throne would be established forever (2 Sam 7:16). As a partial fulfillment of this promise, David and his descendants ruled Judah for over 400 years. Jesus Christ was a direct descendant of David and was the ultimate fulfillment of this promise (Acts 2:22-36).

Ruler	*Length of Reign*	*Reference*
David	40 years	1 Chr 10–29
Solomon	40 years	2 Chr 1–9
Rehoboam	17 years	2 Chr 10–12
Abijah	3 years	2 Chr 13
Asa	41 years	2 Chr 14–16
Jehoshaphat	25 years	2 Chr 17–20
Jehoram	8 years	2 Chr 21
Ahaziah	1 year	2 Chr 22:1-9
Athaliah	6 years	2 Chr 22:10–23:21
Joash	40 years	2 Chr 24
Amaziah	29 years	2 Chr 25
Uzziah	52 years	2 Chr 26
Jotham	16 years	2 Chr 27
Ahaz	16 years	2 Chr 28
Hezekiah	29 years	2 Chr 29–32
Manasseh	55 years	2 Chr 33:1-20
Amon	2 years	2 Chr 33:21-25
Josiah	31 years	2 Chr 34–35
Jehoahaz	3 months	2 Chr 36:1-4
Jehoiakim	11 years	2 Chr 36:5-8
Jehoiachin	3 months	2 Chr 36:9-10
Zedekiah	11 years	2 Chr 36:11-16

2 Chr 31:4-8 Hezekiah reinstated the practice of tithing—giving a tenth of one's income to the priests and Levites so they could be free to serve God and minister to the people. The people responded immediately and generously. God's work needs the support of God's people. Does God receive a regular percentage of your income? Generosity makes our giving delightful to us and to God (2 Cor 8–9). How different the church would be today if all believers consistently followed this pattern.

2 Chr 31:20-21 Because Hezekiah did "what was pleasing and good in the sight of the LORD his God," he led the people of Judah in spiritual renewal. His actions serve as a model of renewal for us: (1) He remembered God's compassion (2 Chr 30:9); (2) he kept going despite ridicule (2 Chr 30:10); (3) he aggressively removed evil influences from his life (2 Chr 30:14; 31:1); (4) he interceded for the people, asking for the Lord's pardon (2 Chr 30:15-20); (5) he was open to spontaneity in worship (2 Chr 30:23); (6) he contributed generously to God's work (2 Chr 31:3). If any of these are lacking in your life, consider how they might apply, and renew your commitment to God.

and the things that had been dedicated to the LORD.
15 His faithful assistants were Eden, Miniamin, Jeshua,
Shemaiah, Amariah, and Shecaniah. They distributed
the gifts among the families of priests in their towns
by their divisions, dividing the gifts fairly among
old and young alike. 16 They distributed the gifts to
all males three years old or older, regardless of their
place in the genealogical records. The distribution
went to all who would come to the LORD's Temple to
perform their daily duties according to their divisions.
17 They distributed gifts to the priests who were listed
by their families in the genealogical records, and to
the Levites twenty years old or older who were listed
according to their jobs and their divisions. 18 Food
allotments were also given to the families of all those
listed in the genealogical records, including their little
babies, wives, sons, and daughters. For they had all
been faithful in purifying themselves.
19 As for the priests, the descendants of Aaron, who
were living in the open villages around the towns,
men were appointed by name to distribute portions
to every male among the priests and to all the Levites
listed in the genealogical records.
20 In this way, King Hezekiah handled the distribution throughout all Judah, doing what was pleasing
and good in the sight of the LORD his God. 21 In all
that he did in the service of the Temple of God and in
his efforts to follow God's laws and commands, Hezekiah sought his God wholeheartedly. As a result, he
was very successful.

3. PROVERBS COLLECTED DURING HEZEKIAH'S REIGN

These proverbs were collected by Hezekiah's advisers. The first section was written by Solomon, and the next two sections were written by others. While we all can learn from these proverbs, many were originally directed toward the king or those who dealt with the king. These are particularly helpful for those who are leaders or aspire to become leaders. The book ends with a description of a truly good wife, who is an example of godly wisdom.

More Proverbs of Solomon

PROVERBS 25:1–29:27

These are more proverbs of Solomon, collected by the advisers of King Hezekiah of Judah.

2 It is God's privilege to conceal things
and the king's privilege to discover them.

3 No one can comprehend the height of heaven,
the depth of the earth,
or all that goes on in the king's mind!

4 Remove the impurities from silver,
and the sterling will be ready for the silversmith.
5 Remove the wicked from the king's court,
and his reign will be made secure by justice.

6 Don't demand an audience with the king
or push for a place among the great.
7 It's better to wait for an invitation to the head table
than to be sent away in public disgrace.

Just because you've seen something,
8 don't be in a hurry to go to court.
For what will you do in the end
if your neighbor deals you a shameful defeat?

9 When arguing with your neighbor,
don't betray another person's secret.
10 Others may accuse you of gossip,
and you will never regain your good reputation.

11 Timely advice is lovely,
like golden apples in a silver basket.

12 To one who listens, valid criticism
is like a gold earring or other gold jewelry.

It is God's privilege to conceal things and the king's privilege to discover them.
Proverbs 25:2

Prov 25:1 Hezekiah was one of the few kings of Judah who honored the Lord. By contrast, his father, Ahaz, actually nailed the Temple door shut. Hezekiah restored the Temple, destroyed idol worship centers, and earned the respect of surrounding nations, many of whom brought gifts to God because of him.

Prov 25:2-6 These four proverbs all focus on the king. Proverbs 25:2 indicates the importance of a king's efforts to discover the truth. This is followed by a parable on the value of a king keeping his own counsel and making up his own mind. Then, because a wise king seeks good advisers, he must be aware of the danger posed by wicked people in places of influence. Last, a warning is issued to those within the court that anyone who makes demands on the king's time treads on dangerous ground. Hezekiah began his collection of wisdom with words for himself.

Prov 25:6-7 Jesus made this proverb into a parable (see Luke 14:7-11). We should not seek honors for ourselves. It is better to quietly and faithfully accomplish the work God has given us to do. As others notice the quality of our life, then they will draw attention to us.

▸ **PROVERBS 25:1–29:27** ***(cont.)***

13 Trustworthy messengers refresh like snow in summer.
They revive the spirit of their employer.

14 A person who promises a gift but doesn't give it
is like clouds and wind that bring no rain.

15 Patience can persuade a prince,
and soft speech can break bones.

16 Do you like honey?
Don't eat too much, or it will make you sick!

17 Don't visit your neighbors too often,
or you will wear out your welcome.

18 Telling lies about others
is as harmful as hitting them with an ax,
wounding them with a sword,
or shooting them with a sharp arrow.

19 Putting confidence in an unreliable person in times of trouble
is like chewing with a broken tooth or walking on a lame foot.

20 Singing cheerful songs to a person with a heavy heart
is like taking someone's coat in cold weather
or pouring vinegar in a wound.*

21 If your enemies are hungry, give them food to eat.
If they are thirsty, give them water to drink.

22 You will heap burning coals of shame on their heads,
and the LORD will reward you.

23 As surely as a north wind brings rain,
so a gossiping tongue causes anger!

24 It's better to live alone in the corner of an attic
than with a quarrelsome wife in a lovely home.

25 Good news from far away
is like cold water to the thirsty.

26 If the godly give in to the wicked,
it's like polluting a fountain or muddying a spring.

27 It's not good to eat too much honey,
and it's not good to seek honors for yourself.

28 A person without self-control
is like a city with broken-down walls.

26:1 Honor is no more associated with fools
than snow with summer or rain with harvest.

Prv 25:20 As in Greek version; Hebrew reads *pouring vinegar on soda.*

Prov 25:13 It is often difficult to find people you can really trust. Faithful employees ("trustworthy messengers") are punctual, responsible, honest, and hardworking. Such people are invaluable as they help take some of the pressure off their employer. Find out what your employer needs from you, and do it.

Prov 25:14 Most churches, missions organizations, and Christian groups depend on the gifts of people to keep their ministries going. But many who promise to give fail to follow through. The Bible is very clear about the effect this has on those involved in the ministry. If you make a pledge, keep your promise.

Prov 25:18 Lying about someone is as vicious as an act of physical violence. Its effects can be as permanent as those of a wound. The next time you are tempted to pass on a bit of gossip, imagine yourself wounding the victim of your remarks with a sword. This image may shock you into silence.

Prov 25:21-22 God's form of retaliation is most effective and yet difficult to do. Paul quotes this proverb in Romans 12:19-21. In Matthew 5:44, Jesus encourages us to pray for those who hurt us. By returning good for evil, we are acknowledging God as the balancer of all accounts and trusting him to be the judge.

Prov 25:26 To compromise with the wicked means setting aside your standards of right and wrong. No one is helped by someone who compromises with the wicked.

THE FOUR TONGUES

What we say probably affects people more than any other action we take. It is not surprising, then, to find that Proverbs gives special attention to words and how they are used. Four common speech patterns are described in Proverbs. The first two should be copied; the last two should be avoided. Other verses about our speech include Prov 10:11, 20, 31; 12:6, 17-19; 13:2; 14:3; 19:5, 28; 25:11; 27:2, 5, 14, 17; 29:9.

The Controlled Tongue	Those with this speech pattern think before speaking, know when silence is best, and give wise advice.	Prov 10:19; 11:12-13; 12:16; 13:3; 15:1, 4, 28; 16:23; 17:14, 27-28; 21:23; 24:26
The Caring Tongue	Those with this speech pattern speak truthfully while seeking to encourage.	Prov 10:32; 12:18, 25; 15:23; 16:24; 25:15; 27:9
The Conniving Tongue	Those with this speech pattern are filled with wrong motives, gossip, slander, and a desire to twist truth.	Prov 6:12-14; 8:13; 15:4; 16:28; 18:8; 25:18; 26:20-28
The Careless Tongue	Those with this speech pattern are filled with lies, curses, quick-tempered words—which can lead to rebellion and destruction.	Prov 10:18, 32; 11:9; 12:16, 18; 17:9, 14, 19; 20:19; 25:23

Prov 25:27 Dwelling on the honors you deserve can only be harmful. It can make you bitter, discouraged, or angry, and it will not bring you the rewards that you think should be yours. Pining for what you should have received may make you miss the satisfaction of knowing you did your best.

Prov 25:28 Even though city walls restricted the inhabitants' movements, people were happy to have them. Without walls, they would have been vulnerable to attack by any passing group of marauders. Self-control limits us, to be sure, but it is necessary. An out-of-control life is open to all sorts of attacks by the enemy. Think of self-control as a wall for defense and protection.

2 Like a fluttering sparrow or a darting swallow,
an undeserved curse will not land on its
intended victim.
3 Guide a horse with a whip, a donkey with a bridle,
and a fool with a rod to his back!
4 Don't answer the foolish arguments of fools,
or you will become as foolish as they are.
5 Be sure to answer the foolish arguments of fools,
or they will become wise in their own
estimation.
6 Trusting a fool to convey a message
is like cutting off one's feet or drinking poison!
7 A proverb in the mouth of a fool
is as useless as a paralyzed leg.
8 Honoring a fool
is as foolish as tying a stone to a slingshot.
9 A proverb in the mouth of a fool
is like a thorny branch brandished by a drunk.
10 An employer who hires a fool or a bystander
is like an archer who shoots at random.
11 As a dog returns to its vomit,
so a fool repeats his foolishness.
12 There is more hope for fools
than for people who think they are wise.
13 The lazy person claims, "There's a lion on the
road!
Yes, I'm sure there's a lion out there!"
14 As a door swings back and forth on its hinges,
so the lazy person turns over in bed.
15 Lazy people take food in their hand
but don't even lift it to their mouth.
16 Lazy people consider themselves smarter
than seven wise counselors.
17 Interfering in someone else's argument
is as foolish as yanking a dog's ears.
18 Just as damaging
as a madman shooting a deadly weapon
19 is someone who lies to a friend
and then says, "I was only joking."
20 Fire goes out without wood,
and quarrels disappear when gossip stops.
21 A quarrelsome person starts fights
as easily as hot embers light charcoal or fire
lights wood.
22 Rumors are dainty morsels
that sink deep into one's heart.
23 Smooth* words may hide a wicked heart,
just as a pretty glaze covers a clay pot.
24 People may cover their hatred with pleasant
words,
but they're deceiving you.
25 They pretend to be kind, but don't believe them.
Their hearts are full of many evils.*
26 While their hatred may be concealed by trickery,
their wrongdoing will be exposed in public.
27 If you set a trap for others,
you will get caught in it yourself.
If you roll a boulder down on others,
it will crush you instead.

Prv 26:23 As in Greek version; Hebrew reads *Burning.* **Prv 26:25** Hebrew *seven evils.*

Prov 26:2 "An undeserved curse will not land" means that it has no effect.

Prov 26:4-5 These two verses seem to contradict, but they actually are purposely demonstrating the contradiction between reason and folly. A fool remains a fool whether answered or not. The wise person has a choice to make depending on what the greatest need of the fool may be in that situation. Some fools don't deserve an answer because they are clearly not in a mood to listen, and those who try to answer them will simply stoop to their level. There are other situations where common sense says to answer the fool in order to expose pride and folly.

Prov 26:7 Some people are so dulled that they won't sense the wisdom even if they memorize these proverbs. A mindlessly quoted proverb proves as useless as a paralyzed body part. Only those who want to be wise have the receptive attitude needed to make the most of these wise words. If we want to learn from God, he will respond and pour out his heart to us (Prov 1:23).

Prov 26:8 Sometimes when someone in a group causes discord or dissension, the leader tries to make that person loyal and productive by giving a privilege or responsibility. This usually doesn't work. In fact, it is like tying a stone to the sling of a slingshot—it won't go anywhere and will swing back and hurt you. The dissenter's new power may be just the key to manipulate the group.

Prov 26:9 Normally the first prick of a thorn alerts us, so we remove the thorn before it damages us more. A drunk person may not feel the thorn, and so it will work its way into the flesh. Similarly, fools may not feel the sting of a proverb because they don't see how it applies to their lives. Instead of taking its point to heart, fools will apply it to their church, their employer, their spouse—anyone they're rebelling against. The next time you find yourself saying, "So-and-so should really pay attention to that," stop and ask yourself, "Is there a message in it for me?"

Prov 26:13-16 A person not willing to work has endless excuses to avoid it. But laziness is more dangerous than a prowling lion. The less you do, the less you want to do, and the more useless you become. To overcome laziness, take a few small steps toward change. Set a concrete, realistic goal. Figure out the steps needed to reach it, and follow those steps. Pray for strength and persistence. To keep your excuses from making you useless, stop making useless excuses.

Prov 26:17 Yanking the ears of a dog is a good way to get bitten, and interfering in arguments is a good way to get hurt. Many times both arguers will turn on the person who interferes. It is best simply to keep out of arguments that are none of your business. If you must become involved, try to wait until the arguers have stopped fighting and cooled off a bit. Then maybe you can help them mend their differences and their relationship.

Prov 26:20 Talking about every little irritation and piece of gossip only keeps the fires of anger going. Refusing to discuss them cuts the fuel line and makes the fires die out. Does someone continually irritate you? Decide not to complain about the person, and see if your irritation dies from lack of fuel.

▸ **PROVERBS 25:1–29:27** ***(cont.)***

28 A lying tongue hates its victims,
and flattering words cause ruin.

27:1 Don't brag about tomorrow,
since you don't know what the day will bring.

2 Let someone else praise you, not your own mouth—
a stranger, not your own lips.

3 A stone is heavy and sand is weighty,
but the resentment caused by a fool is even heavier.

4 Anger is cruel, and wrath is like a flood,
but jealousy is even more dangerous.

5 An open rebuke
is better than hidden love!

6 Wounds from a sincere friend
are better than many kisses from an enemy.

7 A person who is full refuses honey,
but even bitter food tastes sweet to the hungry.

8 A person who strays from home
is like a bird that strays from its nest.

9 The heartfelt counsel of a friend
is as sweet as perfume and incense.

10 Never abandon a friend—
either yours or your father's.
When disaster strikes, you won't have to ask your brother for assistance.
It's better to go to a neighbor than to a brother who lives far away.

11 Be wise, my child,* and make my heart glad.
Then I will be able to answer my critics.

12 A prudent person foresees danger and takes precautions.
The simpleton goes blindly on and suffers the consequences.

13 Get security from someone who guarantees a stranger's debt.
Get a deposit if he does it for foreigners.*

14 A loud and cheerful greeting early in the morning
will be taken as a curse!

15 A quarrelsome wife is as annoying
as constant dripping on a rainy day.

16 Stopping her complaints is like trying to stop the wind
or trying to hold something with greased hands.

17 As iron sharpens iron,
so a friend sharpens a friend.

18 As workers who tend a fig tree are allowed to eat the fruit,
so workers who protect their employer's interests will be rewarded.

19 As a face is reflected in water,
so the heart reflects the real person.

20 Just as Death and Destruction* are never satisfied,
so human desire is never satisfied.

21 Fire tests the purity of silver and gold,
but a person is tested by being praised.*

22 You cannot separate fools from their foolishness,
even though you grind them like grain with mortar and pestle.

23 Know the state of your flocks,
and put your heart into caring for your herds,

24 for riches don't last forever,
and the crown might not be passed to the next generation.

Prv 27:11 Hebrew *my son.* **Prv 27:13** As in Greek and Latin versions (see also 20:16); Hebrew reads *for a promiscuous woman.* **Prv 27:20** Hebrew *Sheol and Abaddon.* **Prv 27:21** Or *by flattery.*

Prov 27:6 Who would prefer a friend's wounds to an enemy's kisses? Anyone who considers the source. A friend who has your best interests at heart may have to give you unpleasant advice at times, but you know it is for your own good. An enemy, by contrast, may whisper sweet words and happily send you on your way to ruin. We tend to hear what we want to hear, even if an enemy is the only one who will say it. A friend's advice, no matter how painful, is much more valuable.

Prov 27:15-16 Quarrelsome nagging, a steady stream of unwanted advice, is a form of torture. People nag because they think they're not getting through, but nagging hinders communication more than it helps. When tempted to engage in this destructive habit, stop and examine your motives. Are you more concerned about yourself—getting your way, being right—than about the person you are pretending to help? If you are truly concerned about other people, think of a more effective way to get through to them. Surprise them with words of patience and love, and see what happens.

Prov 27:17 Mental sharpness comes from being around good people. And a meeting of minds can help people see their ideas with new clarity, refine them, and shape them into brilliant insights. This requires partners who can challenge one another and stimulate thought—people who focus on the idea without involving their egos in the discussion; people who know how to attack the thought and not the thinker. Two friends who bring their ideas together can help each other become sharper.

Prov 27:18 With all the problems and concerns a leader has, it can be easy to overlook the very people who most deserve attention—faithful employees or volunteers (those who "tend a fig tree"). The people who stand behind you, who work hard and help you get the job done, deserve to share in your success. Be sure that in all your planning, organizing, and working, you don't forget the people who are helping you the most.

Prov 27:21 Praise tests a person, just as high temperatures test metal. How does praise affect you? Do you work to get it? Do you work harder after you've gotten it? Your attitude toward praise tells a lot about your character. People of high integrity are not swayed by praise. They are attuned to their inner convictions, and they do what they should whether or not they are praised for it.

25 After the hay is harvested and the new crop
appears
and the mountain grasses are gathered in,
26 your sheep will provide wool for clothing,
and your goats will provide the price of a field.
27 And you will have enough goats' milk for yourself,
your family, and your servant girls.

28:1 The wicked run away when no one is chasing
them,
but the godly are as bold as lions.
2 When there is moral rot within a nation, its
government topples easily.
But wise and knowledgeable leaders bring
stability.
3 A poor person who oppresses the poor
is like a pounding rain that destroys the crops.
4 To reject the law is to praise the wicked;
to obey the law is to fight them.
5 Evil people don't understand justice,
but those who follow the LORD understand
completely.
6 Better to be poor and honest
than to be dishonest and rich.
7 Young people who obey the law are wise;
those with wild friends bring shame to their
parents.*
8 Income from charging high interest rates
will end up in the pocket of someone who is
kind to the poor.
9 God detests the prayers
of a person who ignores the law.
10 Those who lead good people along an
evil path
will fall into their own trap,
but the honest will inherit good things.

Prv 28:7 Hebrew *their father.*

DILIGENCE AND LAZINESS

Proverbs makes it clear that diligence—being willing to work hard and do our best at any job given to us—is a vital part of wise living. We work hard, not to become rich, famous, or admired (although those may be by-products), but to serve God with our very best during our lives.

The Diligent	*The Lazy*	*Reference*
Become rich	Are soon poor	**Prov 10:4**
Gather their crops	Sleep during harvest	**Prov 10:5**
	Are an annoyance	**Prov 10:26**
Have plenty of food	Have no sense	**Prov 12:11**
Gain many rewards		**Prov 12:14**
Will become leaders	Will become slaves	**Prov 12:24**
Make good use of resources	Waste good resources	**Prov 12:27**
Will prosper	Want much but get little	**Prov 13:4**
Bring profit	Experience poverty	**Prov 14:23**
Path is open	Path is blocked	**Prov 15:19**
	Are like those who destroy	**Prov 18:9**
	Go hungry	**Prov 19:15**
	Won't feed themselves	**Prov 19:24**
	Won't plow in season	**Prov 20:4**
Stay awake and have food to spare	Love sleep and grow poor	**Prov 20:13**
Make careful plans	Make hasty shortcuts	**Prov 21:5**
Love to give	Desire things but refuse to work for them	**Prov 21:25-26**
	Are full of excuses for not working	**Prov 22:13**
Will serve before kings		**Prov 22:29**
	Sleep too much, which leads to poverty	**Prov 24:30-34**
Reap abundance through hard work	Experience poverty because of laziness	**Prov 28:19**

Prov 27:23-27 Because life is uncertain, we should be all the more diligent in preparing for the future. We should act with foresight, giving responsible attention to our home, our family, and our career. We should be responsible stewards, like a farmer with his lands and herds. Thinking ahead is a duty, not an option, for God's people.

Prov 28:2 For a government or a society to endure, it needs wise, informed leaders—and these are hard to find. Each person's selfishness quickly affects others. A selfish employee who steals from the company ruins its productivity. A selfish driver who drinks before taking the wheel makes the highways unsafe. A selfish spouse who has an adulterous affair often breaks up several families. When people live for themselves with little concern for how their actions affect others, the resulting moral rot contaminates the entire nation. Are you part of the problem or part of the solution?

Prov 28:5 Because justice is part of God's character, a person who follows God treats others justly. Justice begins with concern for what is happening to others. A Christian cannot be indifferent to human suffering because God isn't. And we certainly must not contribute to human suffering through selfish business practices or unfair government policies. Be sure you are more concerned for justice than merely your own interests. You can't claim to follow God and ignore your neighbor.

Prov 28:9 God does not listen to our prayers if we intend to go back to our sin as soon as we get off our knees. When we forsake our sin and follow him, he willingly listens—no matter how bad our sin has been. What closes his ears is not the depth of our sin but our secret intention to do it again. God hears our intentions as clearly as he hears our words.

▸ **PROVERBS 25:1–29:27** ***(cont.)***

11 Rich people may think they are wise,
but a poor person with discernment can see right through them.

12 When the godly succeed, everyone is glad.
When the wicked take charge, people go into hiding.

13 People who conceal their sins will not prosper,
but if they confess and turn from them, they will receive mercy.

14 Blessed are those who fear to do wrong,*
but the stubborn are headed for serious trouble.

15 A wicked ruler is as dangerous to the poor
as a roaring lion or an attacking bear.

16 A ruler with no understanding will oppress his people,
but one who hates corruption will have a long life.

17 A murderer's tormented conscience will drive him into the grave.
Don't protect him!

18 The blameless will be rescued from harm,
but the crooked will be suddenly destroyed.

19 A hard worker has plenty of food,
but a person who chases fantasies ends up in poverty.

20 The trustworthy person will get a rich reward,
but a person who wants quick riches will get into trouble.

21 Showing partiality is never good,
yet some will do wrong for a mere piece of bread.

22 Greedy people try to get rich quick
but don't realize they're headed for poverty.

23 In the end, people appreciate honest criticism
far more than flattery.

24 Anyone who steals from his father and mother
and says, "What's wrong with that?"
is no better than a murderer.

25 Greed causes fighting;
trusting the LORD leads to prosperity.

26 Those who trust their own insight are foolish,
but anyone who walks in wisdom is safe.

27 Whoever gives to the poor will lack nothing,
but those who close their eyes to poverty will be cursed.

28 When the wicked take charge, people go into hiding.
When the wicked meet disaster, the godly flourish.

29:1 Whoever stubbornly refuses to accept criticism
will suddenly be destroyed beyond recovery.

2 When the godly are in authority, the people rejoice.
But when the wicked are in power, they groan.

3 The man who loves wisdom brings joy to his father,
but if he hangs around with prostitutes, his wealth is wasted.

Prv 28:14 Or *those who fear the LORD;* Hebrew reads *those who fear.*

Prov 28:11 Rich people often think they are wonderful; depending on no one, they take credit for all they do. But theirs is a hollow self-esteem. Through dependence on God in their struggles, the poor may develop a richness of spirit that no amount of wealth can provide. The rich person can lose all material wealth, while no one can take away the poor person's character. Don't be jealous of the rich; money may be all they will ever have.

Prov 28:13 It is human nature to hide our sins or overlook our mistakes. But it is hard to learn from a mistake you don't acknowledge making. And what good is a mistake if it doesn't teach you something? To learn from an error you need to admit it, confess it, analyze it, and make adjustments so that it doesn't happen again. Everybody makes mistakes, but only fools repeat them.

Prov 28:13 Something in each of us strongly resists admitting we are wrong. That is why we admire people who openly and graciously admit their mistakes and sins. These people have a strong self-image. They do not always have to be right to feel good about themselves. Be willing to reconsider—to admit you are wrong and to change your plans when necessary. And remember, the first step toward forgiveness is confession.

Prov 28:17-18 The conscience will drive sinners either into guilt, resulting in repentance, or to death itself because of a refusal to repent. It is no act of kindness to try to make sinners feel better; the more guilt they feel, the more likely they are to turn to God and repent. If we interfere with the natural consequences of their actions, we may make it easier for them to continue in sin.

Prov 28:26 For many people, the rugged individualist is a hero. We admire the bold, self-directed men and women who know what they want and fight for it. They are self-reliant, neither giving nor asking advice. What a contrast to God's way. A person can't know the future or predict the consequences of their choices with certainty. And so the totally self-reliant person is doomed to failure. The wise person depends on God.

Prov 28:27 God wants us to identify with the needy, not ignore them. The second part of this proverb could be restated positively: "Those who open their eyes to poor people will be blessed." If we help others when they are in trouble, they will do whatever they can to return the favor (see Prov 11:24-25). Paul promises that God will supply all our needs (Phil 4:19); he usually does this through other people. What can you do today to help God supply someone's need?

Prov 29:1 Warnings rarely come with countdowns. We can't tell when we've had our last chance to change. When we, like the person in this proverb, refuse to consider valid criticism, we leave ourselves open to sudden disaster. The moment we realize that a change is necessary is the best moment to take action. What significant adjustments have been on hold in your life for too long?

4 A just king gives stability to his nation,
but one who demands bribes destroys it.

5 To flatter friends
is to lay a trap for their feet.

6 Evil people are trapped by sin,
but the righteous escape, shouting for joy.

7 The godly care about the rights of the poor;
the wicked don't care at all.

8 Mockers can get a whole town agitated,
but the wise will calm anger.

9 If a wise person takes a fool to court,
there will be ranting and ridicule but no satisfaction.

10 The bloodthirsty hate blameless people,
but the upright seek to help them.*

11 Fools vent their anger,
but the wise quietly hold it back.

12 If a ruler pays attention to liars,
all his advisers will be wicked.

13 The poor and the oppressor have this in common—
the LORD gives sight to the eyes of both.

14 If a king judges the poor fairly,
his throne will last forever.

15 To discipline a child produces wisdom,
but a mother is disgraced by an undisciplined child.

16 When the wicked are in authority, sin flourishes,
but the godly will live to see their downfall.

17 Discipline your children, and they will give you peace of mind
and will make your heart glad.

18 When people do not accept divine guidance,
they run wild.
But whoever obeys the law is joyful.

19 Words alone will not discipline a servant;
the words may be understood, but they are not heeded.

20 There is more hope for a fool
than for someone who speaks without thinking.

21 A servant pampered from childhood
will become a rebel.

22 An angry person starts fights;
a hot-tempered person commits all kinds of sin.

23 Pride ends in humiliation,
while humility brings honor.

24 If you assist a thief, you only hurt yourself.
You are sworn to tell the truth, but you dare not testify.

Prv 29:10 Or *The bloodthirsty hate blameless people, / and they seek to kill the upright;* Hebrew reads *The bloodthirsty hate blameless people; / as for the upright, they seek their life.*

LEADERSHIP

Since many of the proverbs came from King Solomon, it is natural to expect some of his interest to be directed toward leadership. Other verses to study: Prov 24:27; 25:13; 27:18.

Qualities of a Good Leader	*Reference*
Works hard	**Prov 12:24**
Doesn't penalize people for honesty	**Prov 17:26**
Listens before answering	**Prov 18:13**
Open to new ideas	**Prov 18:15**
Listens to both sides of the story	**Prov 18:17**
Stands up under pressure	**Prov 24:10**
Stands up under praise	**Prov 27:21**
What Happens without Good Leadership	
Fools are honored	**Prov 26:8**
A wicked ruler is dangerous	**Prov 28:15**
People groan	**Prov 29:2**
A wicked ruler has wicked advisers	**Prov 29:12**

Prov 29:13 "The LORD gives sight to the eyes of both" means that everyone depends on God for sight. Both the oppressor and the poor have the gift of sight from the same God. God sees and judges both, and his judgment falls on those whose greed or power drives them to oppress the poor.

Prov 29:15 Parents of young children often weary of disciplining them. They feel like all they do is nag, scold, and punish. When you're tempted to give up and let your children do what they want, or when you wonder if you've ruined every chance for a loving relationship with them, remember that kind, firm correction helps them learn, and learning makes them wise. Consistent, loving discipline will ultimately teach them to discipline themselves.

Prov 29:16 When the wicked are in leadership, sin prevails. In any organization—whether a church, a business, a family, or a government—the climate comes from the top. The people become like their leaders. What kind of climate are you setting for the people you lead?

Prov 29:18 "Divine guidance" refers to words from God received by prophets. Where there is ignorance or rejection of God, crime and sin run rampant. Public morality depends on the knowledge of God, but it also depends on keeping God's laws. In order for nations and individuals to function well, people must know God's ways and keep his rules. Having God's Word means little if we are not obeying it.

Prov 29:24 This proverb is saying that a thief's accomplice may not tell the truth when under oath. Thus, by his participation in the crime and his perjury in the courtroom, he will hurt himself. Further, a witness who refuses to report a crime becomes an accomplice.

▸ **PROVERBS 25:1–29:27** ***(cont.)***

25 Fearing people is a dangerous trap,
but trusting the LORD means safety.

26 Many seek the ruler's favor,
but justice comes from the LORD.

27 The righteous despise the unjust;
the wicked despise the godly.

The Sayings of Agur

PROVERBS 30:1-33

The sayings of Agur son of Jakeh contain this message.*

I am weary, O God;
I am weary and worn out, O God.*
2 I am too stupid to be human,
and I lack common sense.
3 I have not mastered human wisdom,
nor do I know the Holy One.
4 Who but God goes up to heaven and comes
back down?
Who holds the wind in his fists?
Who wraps up the oceans in his cloak?
Who has created the whole wide world?
What is his name—and his son's name?
Tell me if you know!
5 Every word of God proves true.
He is a shield to all who come to him for
protection.
6 Do not add to his words,
or he may rebuke you and expose you as a liar.

7 O God, I beg two favors from you;
let me have them before I die.
8 First, help me never to tell a lie.
Second, give me neither poverty nor riches!
Give me just enough to satisfy my needs.
9 For if I grow rich, I may deny you and say, "Who
is the LORD?"
And if I am too poor, I may steal and thus
insult God's holy name.

10 Never slander a worker to the employer,
or the person will curse you, and you will pay
for it.

11 Some people curse their father
and do not thank their mother.
12 They are pure in their own eyes,
but they are filthy and unwashed.
13 They look proudly around,
casting disdainful glances.
14 They have teeth like swords
and fangs like knives.
They devour the poor from the earth
and the needy from among humanity.

15 The leech has two suckers
that cry out, "More, more!"*

There are three things that are never satisfied—
no, four that never say, "Enough!":
16 the grave,*
the barren womb,
the thirsty desert,
the blazing fire.

17 The eye that mocks a father
and despises a mother's instructions
will be plucked out by ravens of the valley
and eaten by vultures.

18 There are three things that amaze me—
no, four things that I don't understand:
19 how an eagle glides through the sky,
how a snake slithers on a rock,
how a ship navigates the ocean,
how a man loves a woman.

20 An adulterous woman consumes a man,
then wipes her mouth and says, "What's wrong
with that?"

Prv 30:1a Or *son of Jakeh from Massa;* or *son of Jakeh, an oracle.* **Prv 30:1b** The Hebrew can also be translated *The man declares this to Ithiel, / to Ithiel and to Ucal.* **Prv 30:15** Hebrew *two daughters who cry out, "Give, give!"* **Prv 30:16** Hebrew *Sheol.*

Prov 29:25 Fear of people can hamper everything you try to do. In extreme forms, it can make you afraid to leave your home. By contrast, fear of God—respect, reverence, and trust—is liberating. Why fear people who can do no eternal harm? Instead, trust God who can turn the harm intended by others into good for those who trust him.

Prov 30:1 The origin of these sayings is not clear. Nothing is known about Agur except that he was a wise teacher who may have come from Lemuel's kingdom (see the note on Prov 31:1, p. 847).

Prov 30:2-4 Because God is infinite, certain aspects of his nature will always remain a mystery. Compare these questions with the questions God asked Job (Job 38–41). Use these questions to probe your own humility and awe before your Creator.

Prov 30:4 Some scholars feel that the son referred to is the Son of God, the pre-incarnate being of the Messiah who, before the foundation of the earth, participated in the Creation. Colossians 1:16-17 teaches that through Christ the world was created.

Prov 30:7-9 Having too much money can be dangerous, but so can having too little. Being poor can, in fact, be hazardous to spiritual as well as physical health. On the other hand, being rich is not the answer. As Jesus pointed out, rich people have trouble getting into God's Kingdom (Matt 19:23-24). Like Paul, we can learn how to live whether we have little or plenty (Phil 4:12), but our lives are more likely to be effective if we have "neither poverty nor riches."

Prov 30:11-14 This sequence of proverbs contains a fourfold description of arrogance. Notice that a life of pride and abuse of others often begins with a lack of appreciation for one's parents. The command to honor one's father and mother does create negative consequences when rejected.

Prov 30:15ff "Three things . . . no, four" is a poetic way of saying the list is not complete. The writer of these proverbs is observing the world with delighted interest. This passage is an invitation to look at nature from the perspective of a keen observer.

21 There are three things that make the earth
tremble—
no, four it cannot endure:
22 a slave who becomes a king,
an overbearing fool who prospers,
23 a bitter woman who finally gets a husband,
a servant girl who supplants her mistress.

24 There are four things on earth that are small
but unusually wise:
25 Ants—they aren't strong,
but they store up food all summer.
26 Hyraxes*—they aren't powerful,
but they make their homes among the rocks.
27 Locusts—they have no king,
but they march in formation.
28 Lizards—they are easy to catch,
but they are found even in kings' palaces.

29 There are three things that walk with stately
stride—
no, four that strut about:
30 the lion, king of animals, who won't turn aside
for anything,
31 the strutting rooster,
the male goat,
a king as he leads his army.

32 If you have been a fool by being proud or
plotting evil,
cover your mouth in shame.

33 As the beating of cream yields butter
and striking the nose causes bleeding,
so stirring up anger causes quarrels.

The Sayings of King Lemuel

PROVERBS 31:1-9

The sayings of King Lemuel contain this message,*
which his mother taught him.

2 O my son, O son of my womb,
O son of my vows,
3 do not waste your strength on women,
on those who ruin kings.

4 It is not for kings, O Lemuel, to guzzle wine.
Rulers should not crave alcohol.
5 For if they drink, they may forget the law
and not give justice to the oppressed.
6 Alcohol is for the dying,
and wine for those in bitter distress.
7 Let them drink to forget their poverty
and remember their troubles no more.

8 Speak up for those who cannot speak for
themselves;
ensure justice for those being crushed.
9 Yes, speak up for the poor and helpless,
and see that they get justice.

A Wife of Noble Character

PROVERBS 31:10-31

10*Who can find a virtuous and capable wife?
She is more precious than rubies.
11 Her husband can trust her,
and she will greatly enrich his life.
12 She brings him good, not harm,
all the days of her life.

13 She finds wool and flax
and busily spins it.
14 She is like a merchant's ship,
bringing her food from afar.
15 She gets up before dawn to prepare breakfast
for her household
and plan the day's work for her servant girls.

16 She goes to inspect a field and buys it;
with her earnings she plants a vineyard.
17 She is energetic and strong,
a hard worker.
18 She makes sure her dealings are profitable;
her lamp burns late into the night.
19 Her hands are busy spinning thread,
her fingers twisting fiber.

Prv 30:26 Or *Coneys*, or *Rock badgers*. **Prv 31:1** Or *of Lemuel, king of Massa;* or *of King Lemuel, an oracle.* **Prv 31:10** Verses 10-31 comprise a Hebrew acrostic poem; each verse begins with a successive letter of the Hebrew alphabet.

Prov 30:24-28 Ants can teach us about preparation; badgers about wise building; locusts about cooperation and order; and lizards about fearlessness. Compare this to Jesus' teaching in Matthew 6:25-34 that an effective way to resist worry involves a careful observation of the birds and the lilies.

Prov 31:1 Little is known about Lemuel except that he was a king who received wise teachings from his mother. His name means "devoted to God." Some believe that Lemuel and Agur were both from the kingdom of Massa in northern Arabia.

Prov 31:4-7 Drunkenness might be understandable among dying people in great pain, but it is inexcusable for national leaders. Alcohol clouds the mind and can lead to injustice and poor decisions. People in leadership who anesthetize themselves with alcohol will eventually compromise their principles.

Prov 31:10-31 Proverbs has a lot to say about women. How fitting that the book ends with a picture of a woman of strong character, great wisdom, many skills, and great compassion.

Some people have the mistaken idea that the ideal woman in the Bible is retiring, servile, and entirely domestic. Not so! This woman is an excellent wife and mother. She is also a manufacturer, importer, manager, realtor, farmer, seamstress, upholsterer, and merchant. Her strength and dignity do not come from her amazing achievements—they are a result of her reverence for God. In our society, where physical appearance counts for so much, it may surprise us to realize that her appearance is never mentioned. Her attractiveness comes entirely from her character.

The woman described in this chapter has outstanding abilities. Her family's social position is high. In fact, she may not be one woman at all—she may be a composite portrait of ideal womanhood. Do not see her as a model to imitate in every detail; your days are not long enough to do everything she does! See her instead as an inspiration to be all you can be. We can't be just like her, but we can learn from her industry, integrity, and resourcefulness.

▸ **PROVERBS 31:10-31** ***(cont.)***

20 She extends a helping hand to the poor
and opens her arms to the needy.
21 She has no fear of winter for her household,
for everyone has warm* clothes.

22 She makes her own bedspreads.
She dresses in fine linen and purple gowns.
23 Her husband is well known at the city gates,
where he sits with the other civic leaders.
24 She makes belted linen garments
and sashes to sell to the merchants.
25 She is clothed with strength and dignity,
and she laughs without fear of the future.
26 When she speaks, her words are wise,
and she gives instructions with kindness.
27 She carefully watches everything in her household
and suffers nothing from laziness.

28 Her children stand and bless her.
Her husband praises her:
29 "There are many virtuous and capable women in the world,
but you surpass them all!"

30 Charm is deceptive, and beauty does not last;
but a woman who fears the LORD will be greatly praised.
31 Reward her for all she has done.
Let her deeds publicly declare her praise.

Prv 31:21 As in Greek and Latin versions; Hebrew reads *scarlet.*

4. PSALMS COLLECTED IN HEZEKIAH'S ERA

This is a loose collection of 57 psalms. Psalms 42–49, along with 84, 85, and 89, are attributed to the descendants of Korah, who served in the Temple. The other psalms in this section are all anonymous, meaning that the Hebrew subtitles don't give any indication of who wrote the psalm. We collected all of them together here because it is as likely a place as any for them to appear. This doesn't mean they are a group that was meant to be read together, or that they were necessarily written at this time. However, it is likely that during Hezekiah's reign many psalms were either composed or rediscovered as part of his revival.

Psalm 42

THEME: A thirst for God. When you feel lonely or depressed, meditate on God's kindness and love.

AUTHOR: The descendants of Korah, who were Temple musicians and assistants

For the choir director: A psalm of the descendants of Korah.*

1 As the deer longs for streams of water,
so I long for you, O God.
2 I thirst for God, the living God.
When can I go and stand before him?
3 Day and night I have only tears for food,
while my enemies continually taunt me, saying,
"Where is this God of yours?"

4 My heart is breaking
as I remember how it used to be:
I walked among the crowds of worshipers,
leading a great procession to the house of God,
singing for joy and giving thanks
amid the sound of a great celebration!
5 Why am I discouraged?
Why is my heart so sad?

Ps 42:TITLE Hebrew *maskil.* This may be a literary or musical term.

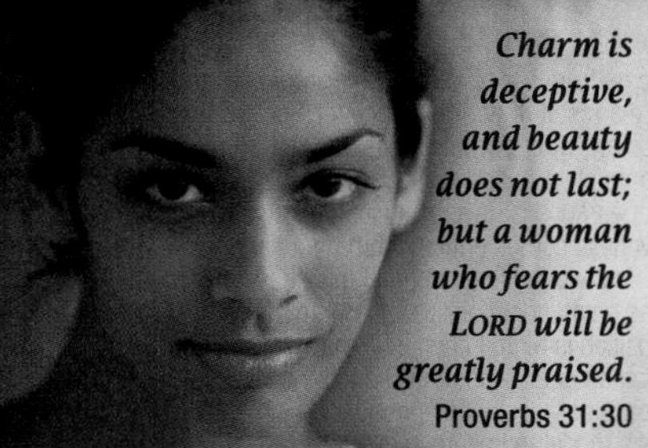

Charm is deceptive, and beauty does not last; but a woman who fears the LORD will be greatly praised.
Proverbs 31:30

Prov 31:31 The book of Proverbs begins with the command to fear the Lord (Prov 1:7) and ends with the picture of a woman who fulfills this command. Her qualities are mentioned throughout the book: hard work, fear of God, respect for spouse, foresight, encouragement, care for others, concern for the poor, wisdom in handling money. These qualities, when coupled with fear of God, lead to enjoyment, success, honor, and worth. Proverbs is practical for us because it shows how to become wise, make good decisions, and live according to God's ideal.

Ps 42:1ff Psalms 42–49 were written by the descendants of Korah. Korah was a Levite who led a rebellion against Moses (Num 16:1-35). He was killed, but his descendants remained faithful to God and continued to serve God in the Temple. David appointed men from the clan of Korah to serve as choir leaders (1 Chr 6:31-38), and they continued to be Temple musicians for hundreds of years (2 Chr 20:18-19).

Ps 42:1-2 As the life of a deer depends upon water, so our lives depend upon God. Those who seek him and long to understand him find eternal life. Feeling separated from God, this psalmist wouldn't rest until he restored his relationship with God because he knew that his very life depended on it. Do you thirst for God?

Ps 42:4-5 The writer of this psalm was discouraged because he was exiled to a place far from Jerusalem and could not worship in the Temple. During these God-given holidays, the nation was to remember all that God had done for them. Many of these festivals are explained in the chart on p. 233.

Ps 42:5-6 Depression is one of the most common emotional ailments. One antidote for depression is to meditate on the record

I will put my hope in God!
I will praise him again—
my Savior and [6]my God!

Now I am deeply discouraged,
but I will remember you—
even from distant Mount Hermon, the source of the Jordan,
from the land of Mount Mizar.
7 I hear the tumult of the raging seas
as your waves and surging tides sweep over me.
8 But each day the LORD pours his unfailing love upon me,
and through each night I sing his songs,
praying to God who gives me life.

9 "O God my rock," I cry,
"Why have you forgotten me?
Why must I wander around in grief,
oppressed by my enemies?"
10 Their taunts break my bones.
They scoff, "Where is this God of yours?"

11 Why am I discouraged?
Why is my heart so sad?
I will put my hope in God!
I will praise him again—
my Savior and my God!

Psalm 43

THEME: Hope in a time of discouragement. In the face of discouragement, our only hope is in God.

AUTHOR: The descendants of Korah (Temple assistants). Psalms 42 and 43 are one psalm in many Hebrew manuscripts.

1 Declare me innocent, O God!
Defend me against these ungodly people.
Rescue me from these unjust liars.
2 For you are God, my only safe haven.
Why have you tossed me aside?
Why must I wander around in grief,
oppressed by my enemies?
3 Send out your light and your truth;
let them guide me.
Let them lead me to your holy mountain,
to the place where you live.
4 There I will go to the altar of God,
to God—the source of all my joy.
I will praise you with my harp,
O God, my God!

5 Why am I discouraged?
Why is my heart so sad?
I will put my hope in God!
I will praise him again—
my Savior and my God!

Psalm 44

THEME: A plea for victory by the battle-weary and defeated. When it seems that God has let you down, don't despair. Instead, remember God's past deliverance and be confident that he will restore you.

AUTHOR: The descendants of Korah (Temple assistants)

For the choir director: A psalm of the descendants of Korah.*

1 O God, we have heard it with our own ears—
our ancestors have told us
of all you did in their day,
in days long ago:
2 You drove out the pagan nations by your power
and gave all the land to our ancestors.
You crushed their enemies
and set our ancestors free.

Ps 44:TITLE Hebrew *maskil.* This may be a literary or musical term.

---

of God's goodness to his people. This will take your mind off the present situation as you focus your thoughts on God's ability to help you rather than on your inability to help yourself. When you feel depressed, take advantage of this psalm's antidepressant: Read the Bible's accounts of God's goodness, and meditate on them.

Ps 43:3 The "holy mountain" is Mount Zion, in Jerusalem, the city that David named as Israel's capital. The Temple was built there as the place for the people to meet God in worship and prayer.

Ps 43:3-4 The psalm writer asked God to send his light and truth to guide him to the holy mountain, the Temple, where he would meet God. God's truth (see 1 Jn 2:27) provides the right path to follow, and God's light (see 1 Jn 1:5) provides the clear vision to follow it. If you feel surrounded by darkness and uncertainty, follow God's light and truth. He will guide you.

Dead Sea Scrolls

The Dead Sea Scrolls are a collection of manuscripts found in a number of regions west of the Dead Sea in 1947 and the years following. The manuscripts are all that remain of the library of a Jewish community known as the Essenes, a group of pious Jews under the leadership of one called "the teacher of righteousness." The community library, of which some 500 documents have been identified, comprise biblical and nonbiblical writings dating from the 1st century B.C. to the 1st century A.D. About 100 scrolls are books of the Old Testament in Hebrew; among these all but the book of Esther are represented. There are several manuscript copies of certain books—notably, Genesis, Deuteronomy, Psalms, and Isaiah. Some of the Dead Sea Scrolls were stored in pottery jars like this one, which helped preserve them for two millennia.

Ps 44:1ff This psalm may have been sung at an occasion like the one in 2 Chronicles 20:18-19, where the faithful Jehoshaphat was surrounded by enemies and the Levites sang to the Lord before the battle.

Ps 44:1-3 "You drove out the pagan nations" refers to the conquest of Canaan (the Promised Land) described in the book of Joshua. God gave the land to the Israelites; they were supposed to enter and drive out anyone who was wicked and opposed to God. Israel was told to settle the land and

▸ **PSALM 44** ***(cont.)***

3 They did not conquer the land with their
swords;
it was not their own strong arm that gave
them victory.
It was your right hand and strong arm
and the blinding light from your face that
helped them,
for you loved them.

4 You are my King and my God.
You command victories for Israel.*
5 Only by your power can we push back our
enemies;
only in your name can we trample our foes.
6 I do not trust in my bow;
I do not count on my sword to save me.
7 You are the one who gives us victory over our
enemies;
you disgrace those who hate us.
8 O God, we give glory to you all day long
and constantly praise your name. *Interlude*

9 But now you have tossed us aside in
dishonor.
You no longer lead our armies to battle.
10 You make us retreat from our enemies
and allow those who hate us to plunder our
land.
11 You have butchered us like sheep
and scattered us among the nations.
12 You sold your precious people for a pittance,
making nothing on the sale.
13 You let our neighbors mock us.
We are an object of scorn and derision
to those around us.
14 You have made us the butt of their jokes;
they shake their heads at us in scorn.
15 We can't escape the constant humiliation;
shame is written across our faces.
16 All we hear are the taunts of our mockers.
All we see are our vengeful enemies.

17 All this has happened though we have not
forgotten you.
We have not violated your covenant.
18 Our hearts have not deserted you.
We have not strayed from your path.
19 Yet you have crushed us in the jackal's desert home.
You have covered us with darkness and death.

20 If we had forgotten the name of our God
or spread our hands in prayer to foreign gods,
21 God would surely have known it,
for he knows the secrets of every heart.
22 But for your sake we are killed every day;
we are being slaughtered like sheep.

23 Wake up, O Lord! Why do you sleep?
Get up! Do not reject us forever.
24 Why do you look the other way?
Why do you ignore our suffering and
oppression?
25 We collapse in the dust,
lying face down in the dirt.
26 Rise up! Help us!
Ransom us because of your unfailing love.

Psalm 45

THEME: A poem to the king (possibly Solomon) on the occasion of his wedding. While this psalm was written for a historic occasion, it is also seen as a prophecy about Christ and his bride, the church, who will praise him throughout all generations.

AUTHOR: The descendants of Korah (Temple assistants)

For the choir director: A love song to be sung to the tune "Lilies." A psalm of the descendants of Korah.*

1 Beautiful words stir my heart.
I will recite a lovely poem about the king,
for my tongue is like the pen of a skillful poet.

2 You are the most handsome of all.
Gracious words stream from your lips.
God himself has blessed you forever.

Ps 44:4 Hebrew *for Jacob.* The names "Jacob" and "Israel" are often interchanged throughout the Old Testament, referring sometimes to the individual patriarch and sometimes to the nation. **Ps 45:TITLE** Hebrew *maskil.* This may be a literary or musical term.

to be a witness to the world of God's power and love. Surrounded by enemies, the psalm writer remembered what God had done for his people and took heart. We can have this same confidence in God when we feel attacked.

Ps 44:6-7 In whom or in what do you trust? Only God is trustworthy. He will never let you down.

Ps 44:9-22 Israel had been defeated despite their faith (Ps 44:17) and obedience (Ps 44:18) to God. The psalm writer could not understand why God allowed this to happen, but he did not give up hope of discovering the answer (Ps 44:17-22). Although he felt his suffering was undeserved, he revealed the real reason for it: He suffered because he was committed to the Lord. Paul quoted the psalm writer's complaint (Rom 8:36) to show that we must always be ready to face death for the cause of Christ. Thus, our suffering may not be a punishment but a battle scar that demonstrates our loyalty.

Ps 44:22-26 The writer cried out to God to save his people because of his unfailing love. Nothing can separate us from God's love, not even death (Rom 8:36-39). When you fear for your life, ask God for deliverance, and remember that even death cannot separate you from him.

Ps 44:23-25 The writer's words suggest that he did not believe God had left him. God was still in control, but he seemed to be asleep, and the writer wondered why. In the New Testament, the disciples wondered why Jesus was asleep when they needed his help during a storm (Mark 4:35-41). In both cases, of course, God was ready to help, but he wanted first to build faith in his followers.

Ps 45:1ff This is called a messianic psalm because it prophetically describes the Messiah's future relationship to the church, his body of believers. Psalm 45:2 expresses God's abundant blessing on his Messiah; Psalm 45:6-8 find their ultimate fulfillment in Christ (Heb 1:8-9). The church is described as the bride of Christ in Revelation 19:7-8; 21:9; 22:17.

3 Put on your sword, O mighty warrior!
You are so glorious, so majestic!
4 In your majesty, ride out to victory,
defending truth, humility, and justice.
Go forth to perform awe-inspiring deeds!
5 Your arrows are sharp, piercing your enemies' hearts.
The nations fall beneath your feet.
6 Your throne, O God,* endures forever and ever.
You rule with a scepter of justice.
7 You love justice and hate evil.
Therefore God, your God, has anointed you,
pouring out the oil of joy on you more than on anyone else.
8 Myrrh, aloes, and cassia perfume your robes.
In ivory palaces the music of strings entertains you.
9 Kings' daughters are among your noble women.
At your right side stands the queen,
wearing jewelry of finest gold from Ophir!
10 Listen to me, O royal daughter; take to heart what I say.
Forget your people and your family far away.
11 For your royal husband delights in your beauty;
honor him, for he is your lord.
12 The princess of Tyre* will shower you with gifts.
The wealthy will beg your favor.
13 The bride, a princess, looks glorious
in her golden gown.
14 In her beautiful robes, she is led to the king,
accompanied by her bridesmaids.
15 What a joyful and enthusiastic procession
as they enter the king's palace!
16 Your sons will become kings like their father.
You will make them rulers over many lands.
17 I will bring honor to your name in every generation.
Therefore, the nations will praise you forever and ever.

Psalm 46

THEME: God is always there to help, providing refuge, security, and peace. God's power is complete and his ultimate victory is certain. He will not fail to rescue those who love him.

AUTHOR: The descendants of Korah (Temple assistants)

*For the choir director: A song of the descendants of Korah, to be sung by soprano voices.**

1 God is our refuge and strength,
always ready to help in times of trouble.
2 So we will not fear when earthquakes come
and the mountains crumble into the sea.
3 Let the oceans roar and foam.
Let the mountains tremble as the waters surge! *Interlude*

4 A river brings joy to the city of our God,
the sacred home of the Most High.

Ps 45:6 Or *Your divine throne.* **Ps 45:12** Hebrew *The daughter of Tyre.* **Ps 46:TITLE** Hebrew *according to alamoth.*

PSALMS THAT HAVE INSPIRED HYMNS

Ps 23	The King of Love My Shepherd Is
	My Shepherd Shall Supply My Need
	The Lord Is My Shepherd
Ps 46	A Mighty Fortress Is Our God
Ps 61	Hiding in Thee (O safe to the Rock that is higher than I . . .)
Ps 87	Glorious Things of Thee Are Spoken
Ps 90	O God, Our Help in Ages Past
Ps 100	All People That on Earth Do Dwell
	Before Jehovah's Awful Throne
Ps 103	Praise to the Lord, the Almighty
Ps 104	O Worship the King, All Glorious Above
Ps 126	Bringing in the Sheaves

Ps 45:8-9 Myrrh is a fragrant gum of an Arabian tree, generally used in perfumes. Aloes, a spice, may have come from sandalwood, a close-grained and fragrant wood often used for storage boxes or chests (see also Prov 7:14-17; Song 4:13-14). Cassia was probably made from flowers of the cinnamon tree. These expensive fragrances were appropriate for a king's wedding. The location of Ophir is unknown but believed to be in either Arabia or Africa. It was famous as a source of gold.

Ps 45:13-17 This beautiful section of poetry pictures Christ's bride, the church, with the richest blessings as she unites forever with him (see Rev 19:6-8; 21:2).

Pss 46–48 Psalms 46–48 are hymns of praise, celebrating deliverance from some great foe. Psalm 46 may have been written when the Assyrian army invaded the land and surrounded Jerusalem (2 Kgs 18:13–19:37).

Ps 46:1-3 The fear of mountains or cities suddenly crumbling into the sea as the result of an earthquake, a nuclear blast, or a terrorist attack haunts many people today. But the psalm writer says that even if the world were to end, we need not fear. In the face of utter destruction, the writer expressed a quiet confidence in God's ability to save him. It seems impossible to consider the end of the world without becoming consumed by fear, but the Bible is clear—God is our refuge even in the midst of total destruction. He is not merely a temporary retreat; he is our eternal refuge and can provide strength in any circumstance.

Ps 46:4-5 Many great cities have rivers flowing through them, sustaining people's lives by making agriculture possible and facilitating trade with other cities. Jerusalem had no river, but it had God, who, like a river, sustained the people's lives. As long as God lived among the people, the city was invincible. But when the people abandoned him, God no longer protected them, and Jerusalem fell to the Babylonian army.

▸ **PSALM 46** ***(cont.)***

5 God dwells in that city; it cannot be destroyed.
From the very break of day, God will protect it.
6 The nations are in chaos,
and their kingdoms crumble!
God's voice thunders,
and the earth melts!
7 The LORD of Heaven's Armies is here among us;
the God of Israel* is our fortress. *Interlude*
8 Come, see the glorious works of the LORD:
See how he brings destruction upon
the world.
9 He causes wars to end throughout the earth.
He breaks the bow and snaps the spear;
he burns the shields with fire.
10 "Be still, and know that I am God!
I will be honored by every nation.
I will be honored throughout the world."
11 The LORD of Heaven's Armies is here
among us;
the God of Israel is our fortress. *Interlude*

Psalm 47

THEME: God is still King of the world. All nations of the earth will eventually recognize his lordship.

AUTHOR: The descendants of Korah (Temple assistants)

For the choir director: A psalm of the descendants of Korah.

1 Come, everyone! Clap your hands!
Shout to God with joyful praise!
2 For the LORD Most High is awesome.
He is the great King of all the earth.
3 He subdues the nations before us,
putting our enemies beneath our feet.
4 He chose the Promised Land as our inheritance,
the proud possession of Jacob's descendants,
whom he loves. *Interlude*
5 God has ascended with a mighty shout.
The LORD has ascended with trumpets blaring.
6 Sing praises to God, sing praises;
sing praises to our King, sing praises!
7 For God is the King over all the earth.
Praise him with a psalm.*
8 God reigns above the nations,
sitting on his holy throne.
9 The rulers of the world have gathered together
with the people of the God of Abraham.
For all the kings of the earth belong to God.
He is highly honored everywhere.

Psalm 48

THEME: God's presence is our joy, security, and salvation. God is praised as the defender of Jerusalem, the holy city of the Jews. He is also our defender and guide forever.

AUTHOR: The descendants of Korah (Temple assistants)

A song. A psalm of the descendants of Korah.

1 How great is the LORD,
how deserving of praise,
in the city of our God,
which sits on his holy mountain!
2 It is high and magnificent;
the whole earth rejoices to see it!
Mount Zion, the holy mountain,*
is the city of the great King!
3 God himself is in Jerusalem's towers,
revealing himself as its defender.
4 The kings of the earth joined forces
and advanced against the city.
5 But when they saw it, they were stunned;
they were terrified and ran away.
6 They were gripped with terror
and writhed in pain like a woman in labor.
7 You destroyed them like the mighty ships of
Tarshish
shattered by a powerful east wind.
8 We had heard of the city's glory,
but now we have seen it ourselves—
the city of the LORD of Heaven's Armies.

Ps 46:7 Hebrew *of Jacob;* also in 46:11. See note on 44:4. **Ps 47:7** Hebrew *maskil.* This may be a literary or musical term. **Ps 48:2** Or *Mount Zion, in the far north;* Hebrew reads *Mount Zion, the heights of Zaphon.*

Ps 46:10 War and destruction are inevitable, but so is God's final victory. At that time, all will stand quietly before the all-powerful Lord. How proper, then, for us to be still now, reverently honoring him and his power and majesty. Take time each day to be still and to honor God.

Ps 47:1ff This psalm may have been written about the same event as Psalm 46—the Assyrian invasion of Judah by Sennacherib (2 Kgs 18:13–19:37).

Ps 47:2 The "LORD Most High" is awesome beyond words, but this didn't keep Bible writers from trying to describe him. And it shouldn't keep us from talking about him either. We can't describe God completely, but we can tell others what he has done for us. Don't let the indescribable aspects of God's greatness prevent you from telling others what you know about him.

Ps 47:9 Abraham was the father of the Israelite nation. The one true God was sometimes called the "God of Abraham" (Exod 3:6; 1 Kgs 18:36). In a spiritual sense, God's promises to Abraham apply to all who believe in God, Jew or Gentile (Rom 4:11-12; Gal 3:7-9). Thus, the God of Abraham is our God too.

Ps 48:2 Why is Mount Zion—Jerusalem—"the city of the great King"? Because the Temple was located in Jerusalem, the city was seen as the center of God's presence in the world. The Bible pictures Jerusalem as the place where believers will gather in the last days (Isa 2:2ff) and as the spiritual home of all believers, where God will live among them (Rev 21:2-3).

Ps 48:8 Because Jerusalem has been destroyed several times since this psalm was written, the phrase God "will make it safe forever" may refer prophetically to the new Jerusalem, where God will judge all nations and live with all believers (Rev 21).

It is the city of our God;
he will make it safe forever. *Interlude*
9 O God, we meditate on your unfailing love
as we worship in your Temple.
10 As your name deserves, O God,
you will be praised to the ends of the earth.
Your strong right hand is filled with victory.
11 Let the people on Mount Zion rejoice.
Let all the towns of Judah be glad
because of your justice.
12 Go, inspect the city of Jerusalem.*
Walk around and count the many towers.
13 Take note of the fortified walls,
and tour all the citadels,
that you may describe them
to future generations.
14 For that is what God is like.
He is our God forever and ever,
and he will guide us until we die.

Psalm 49

THEME: Trusting in worldly possessions is futile. You cannot take possessions with you when you die, and they cannot buy forgiveness from sin.

AUTHOR: The descendants of Korah (Temple assistants)

For the choir director: A psalm of the descendants of Korah.

1 Listen to this, all you people!
Pay attention, everyone in the world!
2 High and low,
rich and poor—listen!
3 For my words are wise,
and my thoughts are filled with insight.
4 I listen carefully to many proverbs
and solve riddles with inspiration from a harp.
5 Why should I fear when trouble comes,
when enemies surround me?
6 They trust in their wealth
and boast of great riches.
7 Yet they cannot redeem themselves
from death*

Ps 48:12 Hebrew *Zion.* **Ps 49:7** Or *no one can redeem the life of another.*

Ps 48:11 The people of Judah were from Israel's largest tribe, which settled in the southern part of Canaan, where Jerusalem was located (Josh 15:1-12). David was from Judah, and he made Jerusalem his capital and the center of the nation's worship. Jesus was also a member of the tribe of Judah. The psalm writer was saying that the day would come when God would bring justice to the land and God's people would get the respect they deserved.

Ps 48:12-13 After an enemy army had unsuccessfully besieged Jerusalem, the people had to make a tour of the city, inspecting its defenses and praising God for the protection he had given. In times of great joy or after God has brought us through some great trial, we ought to inspect our defenses to make sure that the foundations—faith in God, knowledge of his Word, and the fellowship and prayers of the body of believers—remain strong (Eph 2:20-22). Then we should praise God for his protection!

Ps 48:14 We often pray for God's guidance as we struggle with decisions. What we need is both a map that gives us directions and a constant companion who has an intimate knowledge of the way and will make sure we interpret the map correctly. The Bible is such a map, and the Holy Spirit is our constant companion and guide. As you make your way through life, use both the map and your Guide.

Ps 49:1ff The futility of worldliness—riches, pride, fame—resounds from this psalm. Comparable in form to the book of Ecclesiastes, this psalm is one of the few written more to instruct than to praise God.

Ps 49:7-8, 15 In the slave markets of the ancient world, a slave had to be redeemed (someone had to pay the price) in order to go free. Jesus paid such a price so that we could be set free from slavery to sin in order to begin a new life with him (Mark 10:45; Eph 1:7; Heb 9:12).

There is no way for a person to buy eternal life. Only God can redeem a soul. Don't count on wealth and physical comforts to keep you happy because you will never have enough wealth to keep from dying.

"Be still, and know that I am God!"
Psalm 46:10

▶ **PSALM 49** ***(cont.)***

by paying a ransom to God.
8 Redemption does not come so easily,
for no one can ever pay enough
9 to live forever
and never see the grave.

10 Those who are wise must finally die,
just like the foolish and senseless,
leaving all their wealth behind.
11 The grave is their eternal home,
where they will stay forever.
They may name their estates after themselves,
12 but their fame will not last.
They will die, just like animals.
13 This is the fate of fools,
though they are remembered as being wise.*
Interlude

14 Like sheep, they are led to the grave,*
where death will be their shepherd.
In the morning the godly will rule over them.
Their bodies will rot in the grave,
far from their grand estates.
15 But as for me, God will redeem my life.
He will snatch me from the power of the grave.
Interlude

16 So don't be dismayed when the wicked
grow rich
and their homes become ever more
splendid.
17 For when they die, they take nothing
with them.
Their wealth will not follow them into
the grave.
18 In this life they consider themselves fortunate
and are applauded for their success.
19 But they will die like all before them
and never again see the light of day.
20 People who boast of their wealth don't
understand;
they will die, just like animals.

Psalm 84

THEME: God's living presence is our greatest joy. His radiant presence helps us grow in strength, grace, and glory.

AUTHOR: The descendants of Korah (Temple assistants)

*For the choir director: A psalm of the descendants of Korah, to be accompanied by a stringed instrument.**

1 How lovely is your dwelling place,
O LORD of Heaven's Armies.
2 I long, yes, I faint with longing
to enter the courts of the LORD.
With my whole being, body and soul,
I will shout joyfully to the living God.
3 Even the sparrow finds a home,
and the swallow builds her nest and raises
her young
at a place near your altar,
O LORD of Heaven's Armies, my King and
my God!
4 What joy for those who can live in your house,
always singing your praises. *Interlude*
5 What joy for those whose strength comes from
the LORD,
who have set their minds on a pilgrimage
to Jerusalem.
6 When they walk through the Valley of
Weeping,*
it will become a place of refreshing springs.
The autumn rains will clothe it with blessings.
7 They will continue to grow stronger,
and each of them will appear before God
in Jerusalem.*

8 O LORD God of Heaven's Armies, hear my prayer.
Listen, O God of Jacob. *Interlude*
9 O God, look with favor upon the king,
our shield!
Show favor to the one you have anointed.

Ps 49:13 The meaning of the Hebrew is uncertain. **Ps 49:14** Hebrew *Sheol;* also in 49:14b, 15. **Ps 84:TITLE** Hebrew *according to the gittith.* **Ps 84:6** Or *Valley of Poplars;* Hebrew reads *valley of Baca.* **Ps 84:7** Hebrew *Zion.*

Ps 49:10-14 The rich and poor have one similarity: When they die, they leave all they own here on earth. At the moment of death (and all of us will face that moment), both rich and poor are naked and empty-handed before God. The only riches we have at that time are those we have already invested in our eternal heritage. At the time of death, each of us will wish we had invested less on earth, where we must leave it, and more in heaven, where we will retain it forever. To have treasure in heaven, we must place our faith in God, pledge ourselves to obey him, and utilize our resources for the good of his Kingdom. This is a good time to check up on your investments and see where you have invested the most. Then do whatever it takes to place your investments where they really count.

Ps 84:1, 4 The writer longed to get away from the bustling world to meet God inside his dwelling place, his holy Temple. We can meet God anywhere, at any time. But we know that going to a special place designated for worship can help us step aside from the busy mainstream of life so we can quietly meditate and pray. We find joy and strength not only in the prayers, music, lessons, and sermons but also in fellowship with other believers in a special place.

Ps 84:5-7 The pilgrimage to the Temple passed through the barren Valley of Weeping. No specific valley has been identified. The "weeping" may have been a symbolic reference to the times of struggles and tears through which people must pass on their way to meet God. Growing strong in God's presence is often preceded by a journey through barren places in our lives. The person who loves to spend time with God will see adversity as an opportunity to experience God's faithfulness even more deeply. If you are walking through your own Valley of Weeping today, be sure your pilgrimage leads toward God, not away from him.

10 A single day in your courts
is better than a thousand anywhere else!
I would rather be a gatekeeper in the house
of my God
than live the good life in the homes of the
wicked.
11 For the LORD God is our sun and our shield.
He gives us grace and glory.
The LORD will withhold no good thing
from those who do what is right.
12 O LORD of Heaven's Armies,
what joy for those who trust in you.

Psalm 85

THEME: From reverence to restoration. Reverence leads to forgiveness, restoring our love and joy for God.

AUTHOR: The descendants of Korah (Temple assistants)

For the choir director: A psalm of the descendants of Korah.

1 LORD, you poured out blessings on your land!
You restored the fortunes of Israel.*
2 You forgave the guilt of your people—
yes, you covered all their sins. *Interlude*
3 You held back your fury.
You kept back your blazing anger.

4 Now restore us again, O God of our salvation.
Put aside your anger against us once more.
5 Will you be angry with us always?
Will you prolong your wrath to all generations?
6 Won't you revive us again,
so your people can rejoice in you?
7 Show us your unfailing love, O LORD,
and grant us your salvation.

8 I listen carefully to what God the LORD is saying,
for he speaks peace to his faithful people.
But let them not return to their foolish ways.
9 Surely his salvation is near to those who fear him,
so our land will be filled with his glory.
10 Unfailing love and truth have met together.
Righteousness and peace have kissed!
11 Truth springs up from the earth,
and righteousness smiles down from
heaven.
12 Yes, the LORD pours down his blessings.
Our land will yield its bountiful harvest.
13 Righteousness goes as a herald before him,
preparing the way for his steps.

Psalm 87

THEME: The city of God, where all believers will one day gather.

AUTHOR: The descendants of Korah (Temple assistants)

A song. A psalm of the descendants of Korah.

1 On the holy mountain
stands the city founded by the LORD.
2 He loves the city of Jerusalem
more than any other city in Israel.*
3 O city of God,
what glorious things are said of you!
Interlude

4 I will count Egypt* and Babylon among those
who know me—
also Philistia and Tyre, and even distant
Ethiopia.*
They have all become citizens of Jerusalem!
5 Regarding Jerusalem* it will be said,
"Everyone enjoys the rights of citizenship
there."
And the Most High will personally bless
this city.
6 When the LORD registers the nations,
he will say,
"They have all become citizens of Jerusalem."
Interlude

7 The people will play flutes* and sing,
"The source of my life springs from
Jerusalem!"

Ps 85:1 Hebrew *of Jacob.* See note on 44:4. **Ps 87:2** Hebrew *He loves the gates of Zion more than all the dwellings of Jacob.* See note on 44:4. **Ps 87:4a** Hebrew *Rahab,* the name of a mythical sea monster that represents chaos in ancient literature. The name is used here as a poetic name for Egypt. **Ps 87:4b** Hebrew *Cush.* **Ps 87:5** Hebrew *Zion.* **Ps 87:7** Or *will dance.*

Ps 84:11 God does not promise to give us everything we think is good, but he will not withhold what is permanently good. He will give us the means to walk along his paths, but we must do the walking. When we obey him, he will not hold anything back that will help us serve him.

Ps 85:6-7 The writer was asking God to revive his people, bringing them back to spiritual life. God is capable of reviving both churches and individuals. He can pour out his love on us, renewing our love for him. If you need revival in your church, family, or personal spiritual life, ask God to give you a fresh touch of his love.

Ps 85:9-13 As the psalmist cries out for God's intervention, he can almost see, taste, and hear God's response. This describes what God can do for those who welcome his herald—righteousness (Ps 9:13). This psalm illustrates a principle: The greater the presence of righteousness (obedience to God), the clearer the examples of God's blessings. It works equally in the life of a nation or an individual; the more we first seek God's righteousness and his kingdom, as Jesus pointed out, the more we will see everything else taken care of by God (see Matt 6:25-33).

Ps 87:1ff Jerusalem (the holy mountain, Zion) and its Temple here represent the future community of all believers. This psalm looks ahead to the Holy City of God described in Revelation 21:10-27. The honor of living there will be granted to all whose names are recorded in the Lamb's Book of Life (Rev 21:27). It is God's grace that forms and sustains this wonderful community. How could anyone refuse God's offer to be part of this celebration?

Psalm 1

THEME: Life's two roads. The life of the faithful person is contrasted with the life of the faithless person.

AUTHOR: Anonymous

1 Oh, the joys of those who do not
follow the advice of the wicked,
or stand around with sinners,
or join in with mockers.
2 But they delight in the law of the LORD,
meditating on it day and night.
3 They are like trees planted along the riverbank,
bearing fruit each season.
Their leaves never wither,
and they prosper in all they do.
4 But not the wicked!
They are like worthless chaff, scattered
by the wind.
5 They will be condemned at the time of judgment.
Sinners will have no place among the godly.
6 For the LORD watches over the path of the godly,
but the path of the wicked leads to destruction.

Psalm 2

THEME: God's ultimate rule. A psalm written to celebrate the coronation of an Israelite king, but also written for the coronation of Christ, the eternal King.

AUTHOR: Anonymous, possibly David (see Acts 4:25-26)

1 Why are the nations so angry?
Why do they waste their time with futile plans?
2 The kings of the earth prepare for battle;
the rulers plot together
against the LORD
and against his anointed one.
3 "Let us break their chains," they cry,
"and free ourselves from slavery to God."
4 But the one who rules in heaven laughs.
The Lord scoffs at them.

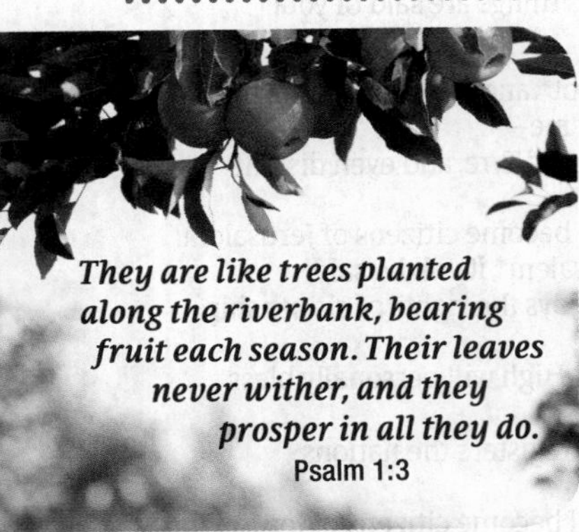

They are like trees planted along the riverbank, bearing fruit each season. Their leaves never wither, and they prosper in all they do.
Psalm 1:3

Ps 1:1 The writer begins this psalm extolling the joys of obeying God and refusing to listen to those who discredit or ridicule him. Our friends and associates can have a profound influence on us, often in very subtle ways. If we insist on friendships with those who mock what God considers important, we might sin by becoming indifferent to God's will. This attitude is the same as mocking. Do your friends build up your faith, or do they tear it down? True friends should help you to draw closer to God, not hinder your relationship with him.

Ps 1:1ff God doesn't judge people on the basis of race, sex, or national origin. He judges them on the basis of their faith in him and their response to his revealed will. Those who diligently try to obey God's will are blessed. They are like healthy, fruit-bearing trees planted along a riverbank with strong roots (Jer 17:7-8), and God promises to watch over them. God's wisdom guides their lives. In contrast, those who don't trust and obey God have meaningless lives that blow away like dust.

Only two paths of life lie before us—God's way of obedience or the way of rebellion and destruction. Be sure to choose God's path, because the path you choose determines how you will spend eternity.

Ps 1:2 You can learn how to follow God by meditating on his Word. This means spending time reading and thinking about what you have read. It means asking yourself how you should change so you will live as God wants. Knowing and thinking about God's Word are the first steps toward applying it to your everyday life. If you want to follow God more closely, you must know what he says.

Ps 1:2 This "law" means all of Scripture: the first five books of Moses, the Prophets, and the other writings. The more we know of the whole scope of God's Word, the more resources we will have to guide us in our daily decisions.

Ps 1:2-3 These two verses hold simple wisdom: The more we delight in obeying God, the more fruitful we are. On the other hand, the more we allow those who ridicule God to affect our thoughts and attitudes, the more we separate ourselves from our source of nourishment. We must have contact with unbelievers if we are to witness to them, but we must not join in or imitate their sinful behavior. If you want despair, spend time with mocking sinners; but if you want God's blessing, make friends with those who love God and his Word.

Ps 1:3 The phrase, "they prosper in all they do," does not mean immunity to failure or difficulties. Nor does it guarantee health, wealth, and happiness. What the Bible means by prosperity is this: When we apply God's wisdom, the fruit (results or by-products) we bear will be good and will receive God's approval. Just as a tree soaks up water and bears luscious fruit, we also are to soak up God's Word, producing actions and attitudes that honor God. To achieve anything worthwhile, we must have God's Word in our hearts.

Ps 1:4 Chaff is the outer shell (or husk) that must be removed to get at the valuable kernels of grain inside. Chaff was removed by a two-part process called threshing and winnowing. After the plants were cut, they were crushed to open up the kernels (threshing), and then the pieces were thrown into the air (winnowing). Chaff is very light and is carried away by even the slightest wind, while the good grain falls back to the earth. Chaff is a symbol of a faithless life that drifts along without direction. Good grain is a symbol of a faithful life that can be used by God. But unlike grain, we can choose the direction we will take.

Ps 2:1ff Several psalms are called "messianic" because of their prophetic descriptions of Jesus the Messiah (Christ)—his life, death, resurrection, and future reign. This psalm is often mentioned in the New Testament (see Acts 4:25-26; 13:33; Heb 1:5-6; 5:5; Rev 2:26-27; 12:5; 19:15).

Ps 2:1ff This psalm might have been written during a conspiracy against Israel by some of the surrounding pagan nations. David had been chosen and anointed by God, and the psalmist knew that God would fulfill his promise to bring the Messiah into the world through David's bloodline (2 Sam 7:16; 1 Chr 17:11-12).

Ps 2:3 People often think they will be free if they can get away from God. Yet, inevitably, everyone serves somebody or something, whether a human king, an organization, or even one's own selfish desires. Just as a fish is not free when it leaves the water and a tree is not free when it leaves the soil, we are not free when we leave the Lord. We can find the one sure route to freedom by wholeheartedly serving God the Creator. God

5 Then in anger he rebukes them,
terrifying them with his fierce fury.
6 For the Lord declares, "I have placed my chosen
king on the throne
in Jerusalem,* on my holy mountain."
7 The king proclaims the LORD's decree:
"The LORD said to me, 'You are my son.*
Today I have become your Father.*
8 Only ask, and I will give you the nations as your
inheritance,
the whole earth as your possession.
9 You will break* them with an iron rod
and smash them like clay pots.'"
10 Now then, you kings, act wisely!
Be warned, you rulers of the earth!
11 Serve the LORD with reverent fear,
and rejoice with trembling.
12 Submit to God's royal son,* or he will become
angry,
and you will be destroyed in the midst
of all your activities—
for his anger flares up in an instant.
But what joy for all who take refuge
in him!

Psalm 10

THEME: Why do the wicked succeed? Although God may seem to be hidden at times, we can be assured that he is aware of every injustice.

AUTHOR: Anonymous, but possibly David. Many ancient manuscripts combine Psalms 9 and 10, and Psalm 9 was written by David.

1 O LORD, why do you stand so far away?
Why do you hide when I am in trouble?
2 The wicked arrogantly hunt down the poor.
Let them be caught in the evil they plan for
others.
3 For they brag about their evil desires;
they praise the greedy and curse the LORD.
4 The wicked are too proud to seek God.
They seem to think that God is dead.
5 Yet they succeed in everything they do.
They do not see your punishment awaiting
them.
They sneer at all their enemies.
6 They think, "Nothing bad will ever happen to us!
We will be free of trouble forever!"
7 Their mouths are full of cursing, lies, and
threats.*
Trouble and evil are on the tips of their
tongues.
8 They lurk in ambush in the villages,
waiting to murder innocent people.
They are always searching for helpless victims.
9 Like lions crouched in hiding,
they wait to pounce on the helpless.
Like hunters they capture the helpless
and drag them away in nets.
10 Their helpless victims are crushed;
they fall beneath the strength of the wicked.
11 The wicked think, "God isn't watching us!
He has closed his eyes and won't even see what
we do!"
12 Arise, O LORD!
Punish the wicked, O God!
Do not ignore the helpless!
13 Why do the wicked get away with despising God?
They think, "God will never call us to account."
14 But you see the trouble and grief they cause.
You take note of it and punish them.

Ps 2:6 Hebrew *on Zion.* **Ps 2:7a** Or *Son;* also in 2:12. **Ps 2:7b** Or *Today I reveal you as my son.* **Ps 2:9** Greek version reads *rule.* Compare Rev 2:27. **Ps 2:12** The meaning of the Hebrew is uncertain. **Ps 10:7** Greek version reads *cursing and bitterness.* Compare Rom 3:14.

can set you free to be the person he created you to be.

Ps 2:4 God laughs, not at the nations, but at their confused thoughts about power. It is the laughter of a father when his three-year-old boasts of outrunning him or beating him in a wrestling match. The father knows the limited strength of his little child, and God knows the boundaries of power of the nations. Every nation is limited, but God is omnipotent. If you have to choose between confidence in God and confidence in any nation, choose God!

Ps 2:4 God is all-powerful. He created the world and knew about the empires of the earth long before they came into being (Dan 2:26-45). But pride and power cause nations and leaders to rebel against God and try to break free of him. Many world leaders boast of their power, rant and rave against God and his people, and promise to take over and form their own empires. But God laughs because any power they have comes from him, and he can also take it from them. We need not fear the boasts of tyrants—they are in God's hands and will be judged by him.

Ps 2:11-12 We must surrender fully and submit to the Son. Christ is not only God's chosen King, but he is also the rightful King of our hearts and lives. To be ready for Christ's return, we must submit to his leadership every day.

Ps 10:1 To the psalm writer, God seemed far away. But even though the writer had honest doubts, he did not stop praying or conclude that God no longer cared. He was not complaining but simply asking God to hurry to his aid. It is during those times when we feel most alone or oppressed that we need to keep praying, telling God about our troubles.

Ps 10:4-6 Some people succeed in everything they do, and they brag that no one, not even God, can keep them down. We may wonder why God allows these people to amass great wealth while they despise him as they do. But why are we upset when the wicked prosper? Are we angry about the damage they are doing or just jealous of their success? To answer these questions, we must gain the right perspective on wickedness and wealth. The wicked will surely be punished because God hates their evil deeds. Wealth is only temporary. It is not necessarily a sign of God's approval on a person's life; nor is lack of it a sign of God's disapproval. Don't let wealth become your obsession. (See Prov 30:7-8 for a prayer you can pray about money.)

Ps 10:11 There is an incompatibility between blind arrogance and the presence of God in our hearts. Proud people depend on themselves rather than on God. This causes God's guiding influences to leave their lives. When God's presence is welcome, there is no room for pride because he makes us aware of our true selves.

▸ **PSALM 10** ***(cont.)***

The helpless put their trust in you.
You defend the orphans.
15 Break the arms of these wicked, evil people!
Go after them until the last one is destroyed.
16 The LORD is king forever and ever!
The godless nations will vanish from the land.
17 LORD, you know the hopes of the helpless.
Surely you will hear their cries and comfort them.
18 You will bring justice to the orphans and the oppressed,
so mere people can no longer terrify them.

Psalm 33

THEME: Because God is Creator, Lord, Savior, and Deliverer, he is worthy of our trust and praise. Because he is faithful and his word is dependable, we can rejoice and sing, giving thanks and praise.

AUTHOR: Anonymous

1 Let the godly sing for joy to the LORD;
it is fitting for the pure to praise him.
2 Praise the LORD with melodies on the lyre;
make music for him on the ten-stringed harp.
3 Sing a new song of praise to him;
play skillfully on the harp, and sing with joy.
4 For the word of the LORD holds true,
and we can trust everything he does.
5 He loves whatever is just and good;
the unfailing love of the LORD fills the earth.
6 The LORD merely spoke,
and the heavens were created.
He breathed the word,
and all the stars were born.
7 He assigned the sea its boundaries
and locked the oceans in vast reservoirs.
8 Let the whole world fear the LORD,
and let everyone stand in awe of him.
9 For when he spoke, the world began!
It appeared at his command.

10 The LORD frustrates the plans of the nations
and thwarts all their schemes.
11 But the LORD's plans stand firm forever;
his intentions can never be shaken.

12 What joy for the nation whose God is the LORD,
whose people he has chosen as his inheritance.

13 The LORD looks down from heaven
and sees the whole human race.
14 From his throne he observes
all who live on the earth.
15 He made their hearts,
so he understands everything they do.
16 The best-equipped army cannot save a king,
nor is great strength enough to save a warrior.
17 Don't count on your warhorse to give you victory—
for all its strength, it cannot save you.

18 But the LORD watches over those who fear him,
those who rely on his unfailing love.
19 He rescues them from death
and keeps them alive in times of famine.

20 We put our hope in the LORD.
He is our help and our shield.
21 In him our hearts rejoice,
for we trust in his holy name.
22 Let your unfailing love surround us, LORD,
for our hope is in you alone.

Ps 10:14 God sees and takes note of each evil deed, encourages us, and listens to our cries (Ps 10:17). He is always with us. We can face the wicked because we do not face them alone. God is by our side.

Ps 33:2-3 David, who some believe wrote this psalm, was an accomplished harpist (1 Sam 16:15-23). His psalms frequently refer to musical instruments. He undoubtedly composed music for many of the psalms, and he commissioned musicians for Temple worship (1 Chr 25).

Ps 33:4 All God's words are true and trustworthy. The Bible is reliable because, unlike people, God does not lie, forget, change his words, or leave his promises unfulfilled. We can trust the Bible because it contains the words of a holy, trustworthy, and unchangeable God.

Ps 33:6-9 This is a poetic summary of the first chapter of Genesis. God is not just the coordinator of natural forces; he is the Lord of creation, the almighty God. Because he is all-powerful, we should revere him in all we do.

Ps 33:11 Are you frustrated by inconsistencies you see in others or even in yourself? God is completely trustworthy—his intentions never change. The Bible promises that whatever is good and perfect comes to us from the Creator, who never changes (Jas 1:17). When you wonder if there is anyone whom you can trust, remember that God is completely consistent. Let him counsel you.

Ps 33:16-17 "Warhorse" refers to military strength. Because God rules and overrules every nation, leaders should never put their trust in their physical power. Military might is not the basis for our hope. Our hope is in God and in his gracious offer to save us if we will trust in him.

Ps 33:18-19 This is not an ironclad guarantee that all believers will be delivered from death and starvation. Thousands of Christian saints have been beaten to death, whipped, fed to lions, or executed (Rom 8:35-36; Heb 11:32-40). God can (and often does) miraculously deliver his followers from pain and death; although sometimes, for purposes known only to him, he chooses not to. When faced with these harsh realities, we must focus on the wise judgments of God. The writer was pleading for God's watchful care and protection. In times of crisis, we can place our hope in God.

Ps 66:5-7 The writer was remembering God's rescue of the Israelites by parting the Red Sea during the Exodus. God saved the Israelites then, and he continues to save his people today.

Psalm 66

THEME: God answers prayer. Individually and as a body of believers, we should praise and worship God.

AUTHOR: Anonymous, written after a great victory in battle

For the choir director: A song. A psalm.

1 Shout joyful praises to God, all the earth!
2 Sing about the glory of his name!
Tell the world how glorious he is.
3 Say to God, "How awesome are your deeds!
Your enemies cringe before your mighty power.
4 Everything on earth will worship you;
they will sing your praises,
shouting your name in glorious songs."
Interlude

5 Come and see what our God has done,
what awesome miracles he performs for people!
6 He made a dry path through the Red Sea,*
and his people went across on foot.
There we rejoiced in him.
7 For by his great power he rules forever.
He watches every movement of the nations;
let no rebel rise in defiance. *Interlude*

8 Let the whole world bless our God
and loudly sing his praises.
9 Our lives are in his hands,
and he keeps our feet from stumbling.
10 You have tested us, O God;
you have purified us like silver.
11 You captured us in your net
and laid the burden of slavery on our backs.
12 Then you put a leader over us.*
We went through fire and flood,
but you brought us to a place of great abundance.

13 Now I come to your Temple with burnt offerings
to fulfill the vows I made to you—
14 yes, the sacred vows that I made
when I was in deep trouble.
15 That is why I am sacrificing burnt offerings to you—
the best of my rams as a pleasing aroma,
and a sacrifice of bulls and male goats.
Interlude

16 Come and listen, all you who fear God,
and I will tell you what he did for me.
17 For I cried out to him for help,
praising him as I spoke.
18 If I had not confessed the sin in my heart,
the Lord would not have listened.
19 But God did listen!
He paid attention to my prayer.
20 Praise God, who did not ignore my prayer
or withdraw his unfailing love from me.

Ps 66:6 Hebrew *the sea.* **Ps 66:12** Or *You made people ride over our heads.*

Psalm 67

THEME: Joy comes from spreading the news about God around the world.

AUTHOR: Anonymous, possibly written for one of the harvest festivals

For the choir director: A song. A psalm, to be accompanied by stringed instruments.

1 May God be merciful and bless us.
May his face smile with favor on us.
Interlude

2 May your ways be known throughout the earth,
your saving power among people everywhere.
3 May the nations praise you, O God.
Yes, may all the nations praise you.
4 Let the whole world sing for joy,
because you govern the nations with justice
and guide the people of the whole world.
Interlude

5 May the nations praise you, O God.
Yes, may all the nations praise you.

Ps 66:10-12 Just as fire purifies silver in the smelting process, trials refine our character. They bring us a new and deeper wisdom, helping us discern truth from falsehood and giving us the discipline to do what we know is right. Above all, these trials help us realize that life is a gift from God to be cherished, not a right to be taken for granted.

Ps 66:13-15 People sometimes make bargains with God, saying, "If you heal me [or get me out of this mess], I'll obey you for the rest of my life." But soon after they recover, the vow is forgotten and the old lifestyle is resumed. This writer made a promise to God, but he remembered the promise and was prepared to carry it out. God always keeps his promises and wants us to follow his example. Be careful to follow through on whatever you promise to do.

Ps 66:18 Our confession of sin must be continual because we continue to do wrong. But true confession requires us to listen to God and to want to stop doing what is wrong. David confessed his sin and prayed, "Cleanse me from these hidden faults. Keep your servant from deliberate sins!" (Ps 19:12-13). When we refuse to repent or when we harbor and cherish certain sins, we place a wall between us and God. We may not be able to remember every sin we have ever committed, but our attitude should be one of confession and obedience.

Ps 67:2 Could the psalm writer have looked across the years and seen the gospel go throughout the earth? This psalm surely speaks of the fulfillment of the great commission (Matt 28:18-20), when Jesus commanded that the gospel be taken to all nations. Count yourself among that great crowd of believers worldwide who know the Savior, praise him for his Good News, and share it so that the harvest will be abundant.

▸ **PSALM 67** ***(cont.)***

6 Then the earth will yield its harvests,
and God, our God, will richly bless us.
7 Yes, God will bless us,
and people all over the world will fear him.

Psalm 71

THEME: God's constant help—from childhood to old age. Our lives are a testimony of what God has done for us.

AUTHOR: Anonymous

1 O LORD, I have come to you for protection;
don't let me be disgraced.
2 Save me and rescue me,
for you do what is right.
Turn your ear to listen to me,
and set me free.
3 Be my rock of safety
where I can always hide.
Give the order to save me,
for you are my rock and my fortress.
4 My God, rescue me from the power of the wicked,
from the clutches of cruel oppressors.
5 O Lord, you alone are my hope.
I've trusted you, O LORD, from childhood.
6 Yes, you have been with me from birth;
from my mother's womb you have cared for me.
No wonder I am always praising you!

7 My life is an example to many,
because you have been my strength and protection.
8 That is why I can never stop praising you;
I declare your glory all day long.
9 And now, in my old age, don't set me aside.
Don't abandon me when my strength is failing.
10 For my enemies are whispering against me.
They are plotting together to kill me.
11 They say, "God has abandoned him.
Let's go and get him,
for no one will help him now."
12 O God, don't stay away.
My God, please hurry to help me.
13 Bring disgrace and destruction on my accusers.
Humiliate and shame those who want to harm me.
14 But I will keep on hoping for your help;
I will praise you more and more.
15 I will tell everyone about your righteousness.
All day long I will proclaim your saving power,
though I am not skilled with words.*
16 I will praise your mighty deeds, O Sovereign LORD.
I will tell everyone that you alone are just.

17 O God, you have taught me from my earliest childhood,
and I constantly tell others about the wonderful things you do.
18 Now that I am old and gray,
do not abandon me, O God.
Let me proclaim your power to this new generation,
your mighty miracles to all who come after me.

19 Your righteousness, O God, reaches to the highest heavens.
You have done such wonderful things.
Who can compare with you, O God?
20 You have allowed me to suffer much hardship,
but you will restore me to life again
and lift me up from the depths of the earth.
21 You will restore me to even greater honor
and comfort me once again.

22 Then I will praise you with music on the harp,
because you are faithful to your promises,
O my God.
I will sing praises to you with a lyre,
O Holy One of Israel.
23 I will shout for joy and sing your praises,
for you have ransomed me.
24 I will tell about your righteous deeds
all day long,
for everyone who tried to hurt me
has been shamed and humiliated.

Ps 71:15 Or *though I cannot count it.*

Ps 67:7 Every verse in this psalm mentions God's relationship with the entire globe. The intended audience of this message spans the world. God repeatedly spoke to and through his people about his love for all nations. Read this psalm with the realization that it was written for and about you and for those around you, whether familiar faces or strangers!

Ps 71:1ff The writer was old and saw his life as an "example," a solemn sign or testimony to others of all God had done for him (Ps 71:7, 18). Remembering our lifetime of blessings will help us to see the consistency of God's grace throughout the years, trust him for the future, and share with others the benefits of following him.

Ps 71:14 As we face the sunset years, we recognize that God has been our constant help in the past. As physical powers wane, we need God even more, and we realize he is still our constant help. We must never despair, but keep on expecting his help no matter how severe our limitations. Hope in him helps us to keep going, to keep serving him.

Ps 71:18 A person is never too old to serve God, never too old to pray. Though age may stop us from certain physical activities, it need not stifle our desire or limit our opportunities to tell others (especially children) about all we have seen God do in our many years of life.

Psalm 91

THEME: God's protection in the midst of danger. God doesn't promise a world free from danger, but he does promise his help whenever we face danger.

AUTHOR: Anonymous

1 Those who live in the shelter of the
Most High
will find rest in the shadow of the Almighty.
2 This I declare about the LORD:
He alone is my refuge, my place of safety;
he is my God, and I trust him.
3 For he will rescue you from every trap
and protect you from deadly disease.
4 He will cover you with his feathers.
He will shelter you with his wings.
His faithful promises are your armor and
protection.
5 Do not be afraid of the terrors of the night,
nor the arrow that flies in the day.
6 Do not dread the disease that stalks in darkness,
nor the disaster that strikes at midday.
7 Though a thousand fall at your side,
though ten thousand are dying around you,
these evils will not touch you.
8 Just open your eyes,
and see how the wicked are punished.
9 If you make the LORD your refuge,
if you make the Most High your shelter,
10 no evil will conquer you;
no plague will come near your home.
11 For he will order his angels
to protect you wherever you go.
12 They will hold you up with their hands
so you won't even hurt your foot on a stone.
13 You will trample upon lions and cobras;
you will crush fierce lions and serpents under
your feet!

14 The LORD says, "I will rescue those who love me.
I will protect those who trust in my name.
15 When they call on me, I will answer;
I will be with them in trouble.
I will rescue and honor them.
16 I will reward them with a long life
and give them my salvation."

Psalm 92

THEME: Be thankful and faithful every day. This psalm was used in Temple services on the Sabbath.

AUTHOR: Anonymous

A psalm. A song to be sung on the Sabbath Day.

1 It is good to give thanks to the LORD,
to sing praises to the Most High.

REASONS TO READ PSALMS

God's Word was written to be studied, understood, and applied, and the book of Psalms lends itself most directly to application. We understand the psalms best when we "stand under" them and allow them to flow over us like a rain shower. We may turn to Psalms looking for something, but sooner or later we will meet Someone. As we read and memorize the psalms, we will gradually discover how much they are already part of us. They put into words our deepest hurts, longings, thoughts, and prayers. They gently push us toward being what God designed us to be—people loving and living for him.

When you want . . .	*Read . . .*
to find comfort	**Ps 23**
to meet God intimately	**Ps 103**
to learn a new prayer	**Ps 136**
to learn a new song	**Ps 92**
to learn more about God	**Ps 24**
to understand yourself more clearly	**Ps 8**
to know how to come to God each day	**Ps 5**
to be forgiven for your sins	**Ps 51**
to feel worthwhile	**Ps 139**
to understand why you should read the Bible	**Ps 119**
to give praise to God	**Ps 145**
to know that God is in control	**Ps 146**
to give thanks to God	**Ps 136**
to please God	**Ps 15**
to know why you should worship God	**Ps 104**

Ps 91:1-6 God is a shelter, a refuge when we are afraid. The writer's faith in God as protector would carry him through all the dangers and fears of life. This should be a picture of our trust—trading all our fears for faith in him, no matter how intense our fears. To do this we must "live" and "rest" with him (Ps 91:1). By entrusting ourselves to his protection and pledging our daily devotion to him, we will be kept safe.

Ps 91:11 One of the functions of angels is to watch over believers (Heb 1:14). There are examples of guardian angels in Scripture (1 Kgs 19:5; Dan 6:22; Matt 18:10; Luke 16:22; Acts 12:7). But there is no indication that one angel is assigned to each believer. Angels can also be God's messengers (Matt 2:13; Acts 27:23-24). Angels are not visible, except on special occasions (Num 22:31; Luke 2:9). Satan quoted Psalm 91:11-12 when he tempted Jesus (Matt 4:6; Luke 4:10-11). It is comforting to know that God watches over us even in times of great stress and fear.

Ps 92:1-2 During the Thanksgiving holiday, we focus on our blessings and express our gratitude to God for them. But thanks should be on our lips every day. We can never say thank you enough to parents, friends, leaders, and especially to God. When thanksgiving becomes an integral part of your life, you will find that your attitude toward life will change. You will become more positive, gracious, loving, and humble.

▸ **PSALM 92** ***(cont.)***

2 It is good to proclaim your unfailing love in the
morning,
your faithfulness in the evening,
3 accompanied by the ten-stringed harp
and the melody of the lyre.
4 You thrill me, LORD, with all you have done for me!
I sing for joy because of what you have done.
5 O LORD, what great works you do!
And how deep are your thoughts.
6 Only a simpleton would not know,
and only a fool would not understand this:
7 Though the wicked sprout like weeds
and evildoers flourish,
they will be destroyed forever.
8 But you, O LORD, will be exalted forever.
9 Your enemies, LORD, will surely perish;
all evildoers will be scattered.
10 But you have made me as strong as a wild ox.
You have anointed me with the finest oil.
11 My eyes have seen the downfall of my enemies;
my ears have heard the defeat of my wicked
opponents.
12 But the godly will flourish like palm trees
and grow strong like the cedars of Lebanon.
13 For they are transplanted to the LORD's own house.
They flourish in the courts of our God.
14 Even in old age they will still produce fruit;
they will remain vital and green.
15 They will declare, "The LORD is just!
He is my rock!
There is no evil in him!"

Psalm 93

THEME: God's unchanging and almighty nature. His creation reminds us of his great power.

AUTHOR: Anonymous

1 The LORD is king! He is robed in majesty.
Indeed, the LORD is robed in majesty and
armed with strength.
The world stands firm
and cannot be shaken.
2 Your throne, O LORD, has stood from time
immemorial.
You yourself are from the everlasting past.
3 The floods have risen up, O LORD.
The floods have roared like thunder;
the floods have lifted their pounding waves.
4 But mightier than the violent raging of the seas,
mightier than the breakers on the shore—
the LORD above is mightier than these!
5 Your royal laws cannot be changed.
Your reign, O LORD, is holy forever and ever.

Psalm 94

THEME: God will keep his people from the severe punishment awaiting the wicked. Since God is holy and just, we can be certain that the wicked will not prevail.

AUTHOR: Anonymous

1 O LORD, the God of vengeance,
O God of vengeance, let your glorious justice
shine forth!
2 Arise, O judge of the earth.
Give the proud what they deserve.
3 How long, O LORD?
How long will the wicked be allowed to gloat?
4 How long will they speak with arrogance?
How long will these evil people boast?
5 They crush your people, LORD,
hurting those you claim as your own.
6 They kill widows and foreigners
and murder orphans.
7 "The LORD isn't looking," they say,
"and besides, the God of Israel* doesn't care."
8 Think again, you fools!
When will you finally catch on?
9 Is he deaf—the one who made your ears?
Is he blind—the one who formed your eyes?
10 He punishes the nations—won't he also
punish you?
He knows everything—doesn't he also know
what you are doing?
11 The LORD knows people's thoughts;
he knows they are worthless!

Ps 94:7 Hebrew *of Jacob.* See note on 44:4.

Ps 92:12-13 Palm trees are known for their long life. To flourish like palm trees means to stand tall and to live long. The cedars of Lebanon grew to 120 feet in height and up to 30 feet in circumference; thus, they were solid, strong, and immovable. The writer saw believers as upright, strong, and unmoved by the winds of circumstance. Those who place their faith firmly in God can have this strength and vitality.

Ps 92:14 Honoring God is not restricted to young people who seem to have unlimited strength and energy. Even in old age, devout believers can produce spiritual fruit. There are many faithful older people who continue to have a fresh outlook and can teach us from a lifetime of experience of serving God. Seek out elderly friends or relatives who can tell you about their experiences with the Lord and challenge you to new heights of spiritual growth.

Ps 93:1ff Jewish tradition claims that the next seven psalms (Pss 93–99) anticipated some of the works of the Messiah. Psalm 93 is said to have been used in post-captivity Temple services and may have been written during Sennacherib's invasion (2 Kgs 18:13–19:37).

Ps 93:5 The atmosphere of God's eternal reign is holiness. Holiness will be the oxygen of heaven. Meanwhile, God's perfect moral character highlights his glory and can be seen everywhere. God will never do anything that is not morally perfect. This reassures us that we can trust him, yet it places a demand on us. Our desire to be holy (dedicated to God and morally clean) is our only suitable response. We must never use unholy means to reach a holy goal because God says, "You must be holy because I, the LORD your God, am holy" (Lev 19:2).

12 Joyful are those you discipline, LORD,
those you teach with your instructions.
13 You give them relief from troubled times
until a pit is dug to capture the wicked.
14 The LORD will not reject his people;
he will not abandon his special possession.
15 Judgment will again be founded on justice,
and those with virtuous hearts will pursue it.

16 Who will protect me from the wicked?
Who will stand up for me against evildoers?
17 Unless the LORD had helped me,
I would soon have settled in the silence
of the grave.
18 I cried out, "I am slipping!"
but your unfailing love, O LORD,
supported me.
19 When doubts filled my mind,
your comfort gave me renewed hope
and cheer.

20 Can unjust leaders claim that God is on their
side—
leaders whose decrees permit injustice?
21 They gang up against the righteous
and condemn the innocent to death.
22 But the LORD is my fortress;
my God is the mighty rock where I hide.
23 God will turn the sins of evil people back
on them.
He will destroy them for their sins.
The LORD our God will destroy them.

Psalm 95

THEME: An invitation to worship God.
AUTHOR: Anonymous

1 Come, let us sing to the LORD!
Let us shout joyfully to the Rock of our salvation.
2 Let us come to him with thanksgiving.
Let us sing psalms of praise to him.
3 For the LORD is a great God,
a great King above all gods.
4 He holds in his hands the depths of the earth
and the mightiest mountains.
5 The sea belongs to him, for he made it.
His hands formed the dry land, too.

6 Come, let us worship and bow down.
Let us kneel before the LORD our maker,
7 for he is our God.
We are the people he watches over,
the flock under his care.

If only you would listen to his voice today!
8 The LORD says, "Don't harden your hearts
as Israel did at Meribah,
as they did at Massah in the wilderness.
9 For there your ancestors tested and tried my
patience,
even though they saw everything I did.
10 For forty years I was angry with them, and I said,
'They are a people whose hearts turn away
from me.
They refuse to do what I tell them.'

JUSTICE IN THE BOOK OF PSALMS

Justice is a major theme in Psalms. The psalmists praise God because he is just; they plead for him to intervene and bring justice where there is oppression and wickedness; they condemn the wicked who trust in their wealth; they extol the righteous who are just toward their neighbors.

Justice in Psalms is more than honesty. It is active intervention on behalf of the helpless, especially the poor. The psalmists do not merely wish the poor could be given what they need, but they plead with God to destroy those nations that are subverting justice and oppressing God's people.

Here are some examples of psalms that speak about justice. As you read them, ask yourself: Who is my neighbor? Does my lifestyle—my work, my play, my buying habits, my giving—help or hurt people who have less than I do? What one thing could I do this week to help a vulnerable person?

Selected psalms that emphasize this theme are Pss 7; 9; 15; 37; 50; 72; 75; 82; 94; 145.

Ps 94:12-13 At times, God must discipline us to help us. This is similar to a loving parent disciplining his children. The discipline is not very enjoyable to the children, but it is essential to teach them right from wrong. The Bible says, "No discipline is enjoyable while it is happening—it's painful! But afterward there will be a peaceful harvest of right living for those who are trained in this way" (Heb 12:11). When you feel God's hand of correction, accept it as proof of his love. Realize that God is urging you to follow his paths instead of stubbornly going your own way.

Ps 95:1-4 Songs, shouts, gratitude, and praise erupted from those gathered to worship the Lord. While Scripture certainly has many examples of stillness and silence in God's presence, there are equally as many examples of exuberant worship. Both peaceful silence and enthusiastic praise are appropriate expressions of worship to our great God.

Ps 95:8 A hardened heart is as useless as a hardened lump of clay or a hardened loaf of bread. Nothing can restore it and make it useful. The writer warns against hardening our hearts as Israel did in the wilderness by continuing to resist God's will (Exod 17:7). The Israelites had been so convinced that God couldn't deliver them that they simply lost their faith in him. When people become so stubbornly set in their ways that their hearts are hardened, they find it impossible to turn to God. This does not happen all at once; it is the result of a series of choices to disregard God's will. If you resist God long enough, God may toss you aside like hardened bread, useless and worthless.

Ps 95:8 The words Meribah ("arguing") and Massah ("testing") refer to the incident at Rephidim (Exod 17:1-7) when the Israelites complained to Moses because they had no water (see also Num 20:1-13).

▸ **PSALM 95** ***(cont.)***

11 So in my anger I took an oath:
'They will never enter my place of rest.'"

Psalm 96

THEME: How to praise God. We can sing about him, tell others about him, worship him, give him glory, bring offerings to him, and live holy lives.

AUTHOR: Anonymous; possibly David because this psalm closely resembles David's hymn of praise in 1 Chronicles 16:23-36

1 Sing a new song to the LORD!
Let the whole earth sing to the LORD!
2 Sing to the LORD; praise his name.
Each day proclaim the good news that he saves.
3 Publish his glorious deeds among the nations.
Tell everyone about the amazing things he does.
4 Great is the LORD! He is most worthy of praise!
He is to be feared above all gods.
5 The gods of other nations are mere idols,
but the LORD made the heavens!
6 Honor and majesty surround him;
strength and beauty fill his sanctuary.

7 O nations of the world, recognize the LORD;
recognize that the LORD is glorious and strong.
8 Give to the LORD the glory he deserves!
Bring your offering and come into his courts.
9 Worship the LORD in all his holy splendor.
Let all the earth tremble before him.
10 Tell all the nations, "The LORD reigns!"
The world stands firm and cannot be shaken.
He will judge all peoples fairly.

11 Let the heavens be glad, and the earth rejoice!
Let the sea and everything in it shout his praise!
12 Let the fields and their crops burst out with joy!
Let the trees of the forest rustle with praise
13 before the LORD, for he is coming!
He is coming to judge the earth.
He will judge the world with justice,
and the nations with his truth.

Psalm 97

THEME: God, our awesome conqueror, is righteous and just.

AUTHOR: Anonymous

1 The LORD is king!
Let the earth rejoice!
Let the farthest coastlands be glad.
2 Dark clouds surround him.
Righteousness and justice are the foundation of his throne.
3 Fire spreads ahead of him
and burns up all his foes.
4 His lightning flashes out across the world.
The earth sees and trembles.
5 The mountains melt like wax before the LORD,
before the Lord of all the earth.
6 The heavens proclaim his righteousness;
every nation sees his glory.
7 Those who worship idols are disgraced—
all who brag about their worthless gods—
for every god must bow to him.
8 Jerusalem* has heard and rejoiced,
and all the towns of Judah are glad
because of your justice, O LORD!
9 For you, O LORD, are supreme over all the earth;
you are exalted far above all gods.

10 You who love the LORD, hate evil!
He protects the lives of his godly people
and rescues them from the power of the wicked.
11 Light shines on the godly,
and joy on those whose hearts are right.
12 May all who are godly rejoice in the LORD
and praise his holy name!

Ps 97:8 Hebrew *Zion.*

Ps 95:11 What keeps us from God's ultimate blessings (entering his "place of rest")? Ungrateful hearts (Ps 95:2), not worshiping or submitting to him (Ps 95:6), hardening our hearts (Ps 95:8), trying God's patience because of stubborn doubts (Ps 95:9). In Hebrews 4:5-11, we are warned not to harden our hearts and to reject the glamour of sin or anything else that would lead us away from God.

Ps 96:1-4 The psalm writer sings out his praises to God, overwhelmed by all that God has done. As we reflect on God's majesty and his goodness to us, we cannot help telling others about him. Witnessing comes naturally when our hearts are full of appreciation for what he has done. God has chosen to use us to "publish his glorious deeds among the nations." Praise for our great God overflows from his creation and should overflow from our lips. How well are you doing at telling others about God's greatness?

Ps 97:2 The dark clouds that surround God symbolize his unapproachable holiness and the inability of people to find him on their own. If he were uncovered, no one could stand before his blazing holiness and glory.

Ps 97:7 People worship all kinds of images and idols. Although God reveals himself and his love through nature and the Bible, there are many who decide to ignore or reject him and pursue goals they believe are more important. The Bible makes it clear that these people are idol worshipers because they give their highest loyalty to something other than God. One day we will stand before God in all his glory and power. Then we will see all our goals and accomplishments for what they really are. How foolish our earthly pursuits will seem then!

Ps 97:10 A sincere purpose to please God will result in an alignment of your desires with God's desires. You will love what God loves and hate what God hates. If you love the Lord, you will hate evil. If you do not despise the actions of people who take advantage of others, if you admire people who only look out for themselves, or if you envy those who get ahead using any means to accomplish their ends, then your primary desire in life is not to please God. Learn to love God's ways and hate evil in every form—not only the obvious sins but also the socially acceptable ones.

Ps 98:1ff This is a psalm of praise anticipating the coming of God to rule his people. Jesus fulfilled this anticipation when he came to save all people from their sins (Ps 98:2-3), and he will come again to judge the world (Ps 98:8-9). God is both perfectly loving and perfectly just. He is merciful when he pun-

Psalm 98

THEME: A song of joy and victory. Because God is victorious over evil, all those who follow him will be victorious with him when he judges the earth.

AUTHOR: Anonymous

A psalm.

1 Sing a new song to the LORD,
for he has done wonderful deeds.
His right hand has won a mighty victory;
his holy arm has shown his saving power!
2 The LORD has announced his victory
and has revealed his righteousness to every nation!
3 He has remembered his promise to love and be faithful to Israel.
The ends of the earth have seen the victory of our God.

4 Shout to the LORD, all the earth;
break out in praise and sing for joy!
5 Sing your praise to the LORD with the harp,
with the harp and melodious song,
6 with trumpets and the sound of the ram's horn.
Make a joyful symphony before the LORD, the King!

7 Let the sea and everything in it shout his praise!
Let the earth and all living things join in.
8 Let the rivers clap their hands in glee!
Let the hills sing out their songs of joy
9 before the LORD.
For the LORD is coming to judge the earth.
He will judge the world with justice,
and the nations with fairness.

Psalm 99

THEME: Praise for God's fairness and holiness. Because God is perfectly just and fair, we can trust him completely.

AUTHOR: Anonymous

1 The LORD is king!
Let the nations tremble!
He sits on his throne between the cherubim.
Let the whole earth quake!
2 The LORD sits in majesty in Jerusalem,*
exalted above all the nations.
3 Let them praise your great and awesome name.
Your name is holy!
4 Mighty King, lover of justice,
you have established fairness.
You have acted with justice
and righteousness throughout Israel.*
5 Exalt the LORD our God!
Bow low before his feet, for he is holy!

6 Moses and Aaron were among his priests;
Samuel also called on his name.
They cried to the LORD for help,
and he answered them.
7 He spoke to Israel from the pillar of cloud,
and they followed the laws and decrees he gave them.
8 O LORD our God, you answered them.
You were a forgiving God to them,
but you punished them when they went wrong.
9 Exalt the LORD our God,
and worship at his holy mountain in Jerusalem,
for the LORD our God is holy!

Psalm 100

THEME: An invitation to enter joyfully into God's presence. His faithfulness extends to our generation and beyond.

AUTHOR: Anonymous

A psalm of thanksgiving.

1 Shout with joy to the LORD, all the earth!
2 Worship the LORD with gladness.
Come before him, singing with joy.
3 Acknowledge that the LORD is God!
He made us, and we are his.*
We are his people, the sheep of his pasture.

Ps 99:2 Hebrew *Zion.* **Ps 99:4** Hebrew *Jacob.* See note on 44:4. **Ps 100:3** As in an alternate reading in the Masoretic Text; the other alternate and some ancient versions read *and not we ourselves.*

ishes, and he overlooks no sin when he loves. Praise him for his promise to save you and to return again.

Ps 99:1 Cherubim are mighty angels that comprise one of several ranks of angels. (For more on angels, see the note on Ps 91:11, p. 861.)

Ps 99:3 Everyone should praise God's great and awesome name because his name points to his divine nature, his personage, and his reputation. But the name of God is often used so carelessly in conversation that we have lost sight of its holiness. How easy it is to treat God lightly in everyday life. If you claim him as your Father, live worthy of the family name. Respect God's name and give him praise by both your words and your life.

Ps 99:5 God's holiness is terribly frightening for sinners, but a wonderful comfort for believers. God is morally perfect and is set apart from people and sin. He has no weaknesses or shortcomings. For sinners, this is frightening because all their inadequacies and evil are exposed by the light of God's holiness. God cannot tolerate, ignore, or excuse sin. For believers, God's holiness gives comfort because, as we worship him, we are lifted from the mire of sin. As we believe in him and humble ourselves before him, we are made holy.

Ps 99:6 The Bible records several instances where Moses, Aaron, and Samuel cried out to God for help (Exod 15:25; 17:4; Num 11:11-15; 12:13; 14:13ff; 16:44-48; 1 Sam 7:5, 9; 15:11).

Ps 100:3 David tells us to acknowledge that the Lord is God! How can we do that? We acknowledge him when we shout out his praises, appreciate his status as our Creator, accept his authority in every detail of life, enthusiastically agree with the guidance he gives us, and express our thanks for his unfailing love.

Ps 100:3 God is our Creator; we did not create ourselves. Many people live as though

▸ **PSALM 100** ***(cont.)***

4 Enter his gates with thanksgiving;
go into his courts with praise.
Give thanks to him and praise his name.
5 For the LORD is good.
His unfailing love continues forever,
and his faithfulness continues to each
generation.

Psalm 102

THEME: The cure for distress. Because God is living, eternal, and unchanging, we can trust him to help his people in this generation just as he helped his people in past generations.

AUTHOR: Anonymous

A prayer of one overwhelmed with trouble, pouring out problems before the LORD.

1 LORD, hear my prayer!
Listen to my plea!
2 Don't turn away from me
in my time of distress.
Bend down to listen,
and answer me quickly when I call to you.
3 For my days disappear like smoke,
and my bones burn like red-hot coals.
4 My heart is sick, withered like grass,
and I have lost my appetite.
5 Because of my groaning,
I am reduced to skin and bones.
6 I am like an owl in the desert,
like a little owl in a far-off wilderness.
7 I lie awake,
lonely as a solitary bird on the roof.
8 My enemies taunt me day after day.
They mock and curse me.
9 I eat ashes for food.
My tears run down into my drink
10 because of your anger and wrath.
For you have picked me up and thrown me out.
11 My life passes as swiftly as the evening shadows.
I am withering away like grass.

12 But you, O LORD, will sit on your throne forever.
Your fame will endure to every generation.
13 You will arise and have mercy on Jerusalem*—
and now is the time to pity her,
now is the time you promised to help.
14 For your people love every stone in her walls
and cherish even the dust in her streets.
15 Then the nations will tremble before the LORD.
The kings of the earth will tremble before
his glory.
16 For the LORD will rebuild Jerusalem.
He will appear in his glory.
17 He will listen to the prayers of the destitute.
He will not reject their pleas.

18 Let this be recorded for future generations,
so that a people not yet born will praise
the LORD.

Ps 102:13 Hebrew *Zion;* also in 102:16.

they are the creator and center of their own little world. This mind-set leads to pride, greed, idolatry, and if everything should be taken away, a loss of hope itself. But when we realize that God created us and gives us all we have, we will want to give to others as God gave to us (2 Cor 9:8). Then, even if all is lost, we still have God and all he gives us.

Ps 100:4 God alone is worthy of being worshiped. What is your attitude toward worship? Do you willingly and joyfully come into God's presence, or are you just going through the motions, reluctantly going to church? This psalm tells us to remember God's goodness and dependability, and then to worship with thanksgiving and praise!

Ps 102:3-4 The writer felt so bad that he lost his appetite. When we face sickness and despair, our days pass blindly, and we don't care about even our basic needs. In these times, God alone is our comfort and strength. Even when we are too weak to fight, we can lean on him. It is often when we recognize our weaknesses that God's greatest strength becomes available.

Ps 102:6-7 These birds are pictures of loneliness and desolation. At times we may need to be alone, and solitude may comfort us. But we must be careful not to spurn those who reach out to us. Don't reject help and conversation. Suffering silently is neither Christian nor particularly healthy. Instead, accept graciously the support and help from family and friends.

HOW GOD IS DESCRIBED IN PSALMS

Most of the psalms speak to God or about God. Because they were composed in a variety of situations, various facets of God's character are mentioned. Here is a sample of God's characteristics as understood and experienced by the psalm writers. As you read these psalms, ask yourself if this is the God you know.

God is . . .	*Reference*
All-knowing and ever-present	**Ps 139**
Beautiful and desirable	**Pss 27; 36; 45**
Creator	**Pss 8; 104; 148**
Good and generous	**Pss 34; 81; 107**
Great and sovereign	**Pss 33; 89; 96**
Holy	**Pss 66; 99; 145**
Loving and faithful	**Pss 23; 42; 51**
Merciful and forgiving	**Pss 32; 111; 130**
Powerful	**Pss 76: 89; 93**
Willing to reveal his will, law, and direction	**Pss 1; 19; 119**
Righteous and just	**Pss 71; 97; 113**
Spirit	**Pss 104; 139; 143**

Ps 102:16-22 Christ's future reign on earth will encompass two events mentioned in these verses. Jerusalem (Zion) will be restored, and the entire world will worship God (Rev 11:15; 21:1-27).

19 Tell them the LORD looked down
from his heavenly sanctuary.
He looked down to earth from heaven
20 to hear the groans of the prisoners,
to release those condemned to die.
21 And so the LORD's fame will be celebrated in Zion,
his praises in Jerusalem,
22 when multitudes gather together
and kingdoms come to worship the LORD.

23 He broke my strength in midlife,
cutting short my days.
24 But I cried to him, "O my God, who lives forever,
don't take my life while I am so young!
25 Long ago you laid the foundation of the earth
and made the heavens with your hands.
26 They will perish, but you remain forever;
they will wear out like old clothing.
You will change them like a garment
and discard them.
27 But you are always the same;
you will live forever.
28 The children of your people
will live in security.
Their children's children
will thrive in your presence."

Psalm 104

THEME: Appreciating God through his creation. He not only creates, but maintains his creation. The Lord's care is the source of our joy.
AUTHOR: Anonymous

1 Let all that I am praise the LORD.

O LORD my God, how great you are!
You are robed with honor and majesty.
2 You are dressed in a robe of light.
You stretch out the starry curtain of the heavens;
3 you lay out the rafters of your home in the rain clouds.
You make the clouds your chariot;
you ride upon the wings of the wind.
4 The winds are your messengers;
flames of fire are your servants.*

5 You placed the world on its foundation
so it would never be moved.
6 You clothed the earth with floods of water,
water that covered even the mountains.
7 At your command, the water fled;
at the sound of your thunder, it hurried away.
8 Mountains rose and valleys sank
to the levels you decreed.
9 Then you set a firm boundary for the seas,
so they would never again cover the earth.

10 You make springs pour water into the ravines,
so streams gush down from the mountains.
11 They provide water for all the animals,
and the wild donkeys quench their thirst.
12 The birds nest beside the streams
and sing among the branches of the trees.
13 You send rain on the mountains from your heavenly home,
and you fill the earth with the fruit of your labor.
14 You cause grass to grow for the livestock
and plants for people to use.
You allow them to produce food from the earth—
15 wine to make them glad,
olive oil to soothe their skin,
and bread to give them strength.

Ps 104:4 Greek version reads *He sends his angels like the winds, / his servants like flames of fire.* Compare Heb 1:7.

Ps 102:25-27 The writer of this psalm felt rejected and tossed aside because of his great troubles (Ps 102:9-10). Problems and heartaches can overwhelm us and cause us to feel that God has rejected us. But God our Creator is eternally with us and will keep all his promises, even though we may feel alone. The world will perish, but God will remain. Hebrews 1:10-12 quotes these verses to show that Jesus Christ, God's Son, was also present and active at the creation of the world.

Ps 104:1ff This psalm is a poetic summary of God's creation of the world as found in the first chapter of Genesis. What God created each day is mentioned as a reason to praise God. On day one, light (Ps 104:1-2; Gen 1:3); day two, the heavens and the waters (Ps 104:2-3; Gen 1:6); day three, land and vegetation (Ps 104:6-18; Gen 1:9-13); day four, the sun, moon, and stars (Ps 104:19-23; Gen 1:14-16); day five, fish and birds (Ps 104:25-26; Gen 1:20-23); and on day six, animals, people, and food to sustain them (Ps 104:21-24, 27-30; Gen 1:24-31). God's act of creation deserves the praise of all people.

Ps 104:5 The earth is built on God's foundations, and he guarantees its permanence. "It would never be moved" by anyone other than God. Even though one day the heavens and the earth will be destroyed (2 Pet 3:10), he will create a new heaven and a new earth that will last forever (Isa 65:17; Rev 21:1). The same power that undergirds the world also provides a firm foundation for believers.

Baking Bread

Carvings (like this one) and reliefs in Egyptian tombs illustrate most of the equipment used in ancient Near Eastern bakeries. Bread-makers used a sieve, which was a wicker strainer that helped separate small impurities from the grain. They also used grindstones, which were a pair of stones shaped so that the top stone turned against the bottom stone, crushing grain into flour. They also used clay jars containing olive oil, water, and liquid leaven to be mixed with the flour to make dough. They used kneading bowls, boards, or tables made of wood to provide space for a thorough mixing of the ingredients. Bread-makers then used pans or ovens to cook the bread.

Bread has always symbolized the basic sustenance of life. That is why Jesus used it to illustrate how we must depend on God to sustain our lives.

▸ **PSALM 104** ***(cont.)***

16 The trees of the LORD are well cared for—
the cedars of Lebanon that he planted.
17 There the birds make their nests,
and the storks make their homes in the cypresses.
18 High in the mountains live the wild goats,
and the rocks form a refuge for the hyraxes.*

19 You made the moon to mark the seasons,
and the sun knows when to set.
20 You send the darkness, and it becomes night,
when all the forest animals prowl about.
21 Then the young lions roar for their prey,
stalking the food provided by God.
22 At dawn they slink back
into their dens to rest.
23 Then people go off to their work,
where they labor until evening.

24 O LORD, what a variety of things you have made!
In wisdom you have made them all.
The earth is full of your creatures.
25 Here is the ocean, vast and wide,
teeming with life of every kind,
both large and small.
26 See the ships sailing along,
and Leviathan,* which you made to play in the sea.

27 They all depend on you
to give them food as they need it.
28 When you supply it, they gather it.
You open your hand to feed them,
and they are richly satisfied.
29 But if you turn away from them, they panic.
When you take away their breath,
they die and turn again to dust.
30 When you give them your breath,* life is created,
and you renew the face of the earth.

31 May the glory of the LORD continue forever!
The LORD takes pleasure in all he has made!
32 The earth trembles at his glance;
the mountains smoke at his touch.

33 I will sing to the LORD as long as I live.
I will praise my God to my last breath!
34 May all my thoughts be pleasing to him,
for I rejoice in the LORD.
35 Let all sinners vanish from the face of the earth;
let the wicked disappear forever.

Let all that I am praise the LORD.

Praise the LORD!

Psalm 105

THEME: God's mighty deeds in bringing Israel to the Promised Land. Remembering his miracles encourages us to keep living close to him.

AUTHOR: Anonymous

1 Give thanks to the LORD and proclaim his greatness.
Let the whole world know what he has done.
2 Sing to him; yes, sing his praises.
Tell everyone about his wonderful deeds.
3 Exult in his holy name;
rejoice, you who worship the LORD.
4 Search for the LORD and for his strength;
continually seek him.
5 Remember the wonders he has performed,
his miracles, and the rulings he has given,
6 you children of his servant Abraham,
you descendants of Jacob, his chosen ones.

7 He is the LORD our God.
His justice is seen throughout the land.
8 He always stands by his covenant—
the commitment he made to a thousand generations.
9 This is the covenant he made with Abraham
and the oath he swore to Isaac.
10 He confirmed it to Jacob as a decree,

Ps 104:18 Or *coneys,* or *rock badgers.* **Ps 104:26** The identification of Leviathan is disputed, ranging from an earthly creature to a mythical sea monster in ancient literature. **Ps 104:30** Or *When you send your Spirit.*

Ps 104:24 Creation is filled with stunning variety, revealing the rich creativity, goodness, and wisdom of our loving God. As you observe your natural surroundings, thank God for his creativity. Take a fresh look at people, seeing God's unique creation with their individual special talents, abilities, and gifts.

Ps 104:26 Here "Leviathan" almost certainly refers to a large and active sea creature.

Ps 104:28-30 Psalm 105 expresses God's sovereignty in history; this psalm tells of his sovereignty over all creation. God has supreme, unlimited power over the entire universe. He creates; he preserves; he governs. As we understand God's power, we realize that he is sufficient to handle our lives.

Ps 104:29 Today many people are arrogant enough to think they don't need God. But our every breath depends on the life he has breathed into us (Gen 2:7; 3:19; Job 33:4; 34:14-15; Dan 5:23). We depend on God for life, and he wants our best. May we desire to learn more of his plans for us each day.

Ps 105:1ff The first 15 verses of this psalm are also found in 1 Chronicles 16:8-22, where it is sung as part of the celebration of David's bringing the Ark of the Covenant to Jerusalem. Three other psalms are also hymns recounting Israel's history: Pss 78; 106; 136.

Ps 105:4-5 If God seems far away, persist in your search for him. God rewards those who sincerely look for him (Heb 11:6). Jesus promised, "Everyone who seeks, finds" (Matt 7:8). The writer suggested a valuable way to find God—become familiar with the way he has helped his people in the past. The Bible records the history of God's people. In searching its pages we will discover a loving God who is waiting for us to find him.

Ps 105:6-11 The nation Israel, the people through whom God revealed his laws to everyone, is descended from Abraham. God chose Abraham and promised that his descendants would live in the land of Canaan (now called Israel) and that they would be too numerous to count (Gen 17:6-8). Abraham's son was Isaac; Isaac's son was Jacob. These three men are considered the patriarchs or

and to the people of Israel as a never-ending
covenant:
11 "I will give you the land of Canaan
as your special possession."

12 He said this when they were few in number,
a tiny group of strangers in Canaan.
13 They wandered from nation to nation,
from one kingdom to another.
14 Yet he did not let anyone oppress them.
He warned kings on their behalf:
15 "Do not touch my chosen people,
and do not hurt my prophets."

16 He called for a famine on the land of Canaan,
cutting off its food supply.
17 Then he sent someone to Egypt ahead of them—
Joseph, who was sold as a slave.
18 They bruised his feet with fetters
and placed his neck in an iron collar.
19 Until the time came to fulfill his dreams,*
the LORD tested Joseph's character.
20 Then Pharaoh sent for him and set him free;
the ruler of the nation opened his prison door.
21 Joseph was put in charge of all the king's
household;
he became ruler over all the king's possessions.
22 He could instruct the king's aides as he pleased
and teach the king's advisers.

23 Then Israel arrived in Egypt;
Jacob lived as a foreigner in the land of Ham.
24 And the LORD multiplied the people of Israel
until they became too mighty for their enemies.
25 Then he turned the Egyptians against the
Israelites,
and they plotted against the LORD's servants.

26 But the LORD sent his servant Moses,
along with Aaron, whom he had chosen.
27 They performed miraculous signs among the
Egyptians,
and wonders in the land of Ham.
28 The LORD blanketed Egypt in darkness,
for they had defied his commands to let his
people go.
29 He turned their water into blood,
poisoning all the fish.
30 Then frogs overran the land
and even invaded the king's bedrooms.
31 When the LORD spoke, flies descended on the
Egyptians,
and gnats swarmed across Egypt.
32 He sent them hail instead of rain,
and lightning flashed over the land.
33 He ruined their grapevines and fig trees
and shattered all the trees.
34 He spoke, and hordes of locusts came—
young locusts beyond number.
35 They ate up everything green in the land,
destroying all the crops in their fields.
36 Then he killed the oldest son in each Egyptian
home,
the pride and joy of each family.

37 The LORD brought his people out of Egypt, loaded
with silver and gold;
and not one among the tribes of Israel even
stumbled.
38 Egypt was glad when they were gone,
for they feared them greatly.
39 The LORD spread a cloud above them as a
covering
and gave them a great fire to light the
darkness.
40 They asked for meat, and he sent them quail;
he satisfied their hunger with manna—bread
from heaven.
41 He split open a rock, and water gushed out
to form a river through the dry wasteland.
42 For he remembered his sacred promise
to his servant Abraham.
43 So he brought his people out of Egypt with joy,
his chosen ones with rejoicing.

Ps 105:19 Hebrew *his word.*

HISTORY IN THE BOOK OF PSALMS

For the original hearers, the historical psalms were vivid reminders of God's past acts on behalf of Israel. These history songs were written for passing on important lessons to succeeding generations. They celebrated the many promises God had made and faithfully kept; they also recounted the faithlessness of the people.

We cannot read this ancient history without reflecting on how consistently God's people failed to learn from the past. They repeatedly turned from fresh examples of God's faithfulness and forgiveness only to plunge back into sin. God can use these psalms to remind us how often we do exactly the same thing: Having every reason to live for God, we choose instead to live for everything but God. If we paid more attention to "his story," we wouldn't make so many mistakes in our own stories.

Selected historical psalms: Pss 68; 78; 95; 105; 106; 111; 114; 135; 136; 149

founders of Israel. God blessed them because of their faith (see Heb 11:8-21).

Ps 105:23-25 Did God cause the Egyptians to hate the Israelites? God is not the author of evil, but the Bible writers don't always distinguish between God's ultimate action and the intermediate steps. Thus, by God blessing the Israelites, the Egyptians came to hate them (Exod 1:8-22). Because God caused the Israelites' blessing, he is also said to have caused the Egyptians' hatred. God used their animosity as a means to lead the Israelites out of Egypt.

▸ **PSALM 105** ***(cont.)***

44 He gave his people the lands of pagan nations,
and they harvested crops that others had planted.
45 All this happened so they would follow his decrees
and obey his instructions.

Praise the LORD!

Psalm 106

THEME: A song of national repentance. God patiently delivers us, in spite of our forgetfulness and self-willed rebellion.

AUTHOR: Anonymous

1 Praise the LORD!

Give thanks to the LORD, for he is good!
His faithful love endures forever.
2 Who can list the glorious miracles of the LORD?
Who can ever praise him enough?
3 There is joy for those who deal justly with others
and always do what is right.

4 Remember me, LORD, when you show favor to your people;
come near and rescue me.
5 Let me share in the prosperity of your chosen ones.
Let me rejoice in the joy of your people;
let me praise you with those who are your heritage.

6 Like our ancestors, we have sinned.
We have done wrong! We have acted wickedly!
7 Our ancestors in Egypt
were not impressed by the LORD's miraculous deeds.
They soon forgot his many acts of kindness to them.
Instead, they rebelled against him at the Red Sea.*
8 Even so, he saved them—
to defend the honor of his name
and to demonstrate his mighty power.
9 He commanded the Red Sea* to dry up.
He led Israel across the sea as if it were a desert.
10 So he rescued them from their enemies
and redeemed them from their foes.
11 Then the water returned and covered their enemies;
not one of them survived.
12 Then his people believed his promises.
Then they sang his praise.

13 Yet how quickly they forgot what he had done!
They wouldn't wait for his counsel!
14 In the wilderness their desires ran wild,
testing God's patience in that dry wasteland.
15 So he gave them what they asked for,
but he sent a plague along with it.
16 The people in the camp were jealous of Moses
and envious of Aaron, the LORD's holy priest.
17 Because of this, the earth opened up;
it swallowed Dathan
and buried Abiram and the other rebels.
18 Fire fell upon their followers;
a flame consumed the wicked.

19 The people made a calf at Mount Sinai*;
they bowed before an image made of gold.
20 They traded their glorious God
for a statue of a grass-eating bull.
21 They forgot God, their savior,
who had done such great things in Egypt—
22 such wonderful things in the land of Ham,
such awesome deeds at the Red Sea.
23 So he declared he would destroy them.
But Moses, his chosen one, stepped between the LORD and the people.
He begged him to turn from his anger and not destroy them.

24 The people refused to enter the pleasant land,
for they wouldn't believe his promise to care for them.
25 Instead, they grumbled in their tents
and refused to obey the LORD.

Ps 106:7 Hebrew *at the sea, the sea of reeds.* **Ps 106:9** Hebrew *sea of reeds;* also in 106:22. **Ps 106:19** Hebrew *at Horeb,* another name for Sinai.

Ps 105:45 God's purpose for saving the Israelites was that they would "follow his decrees and obey his instructions." Too often we use our lives and freedom to please ourselves, but we should honor God. That is God's purpose for our lives and why he gave us his Word.

Ps 106:1ff While Psalm 105 is a summary of God's faithfulness, Psalm 106 is a summary of humanity's sinfulness. Psalm 105 covers events up to the exodus from Egypt (Exod 5–14), and Psalm 106 covers events from the Exodus up to what appears to be the Babylonian captivity (2 Kgs 25).

Ps 106:2 If we ever stopped to list all the mighty acts or miracles in the Bible, we would be astounded. They cover every aspect of life. The more we think about what God has done, the more we can appreciate the miracles he has done for us individually—birth, personal development, salvation, specific guidance, healing, loving friends and family—the list goes on and on. If you think you have never seen a miracle, look closer. You will see God's power and loving intervention on your behalf. God still performs great miracles!

Ps 106:13-15 In the wilderness, the Israelites were so intent on getting the food and water they wanted that they became blind to what God wanted. They were more concerned about immediate physical gratification than lasting spiritual satisfaction. They did not want what was best for them, and they refused to trust in God's care and provision (Num 11:18-33). If you complain enough, God may give you what you ask for, even if it is not the best for you. If you're not getting what you want, perhaps God knows it is not in your best interest. Trust in his care and provision.

Ps 106:23 Moses served as the people's intercessor. This refers to the time when the Lord wanted to destroy the people for worshiping the gold calf (Exod 32:7-14).

26 Therefore, he solemnly swore
that he would kill them in the wilderness,
27 that he would scatter their descendants among
the nations,
exiling them to distant lands.
28 Then our ancestors joined in the worship
of Baal at Peor;
they even ate sacrifices offered to the dead!
29 They angered the LORD with all these things,
so a plague broke out among them.
30 But Phinehas had the courage to intervene,
and the plague was stopped.
31 So he has been regarded as a righteous man
ever since that time.
32 At Meribah, too, they angered the LORD,
causing Moses serious trouble.
33 They made Moses angry,*
and he spoke foolishly.
34 Israel failed to destroy the nations in the land,
as the LORD had commanded them.
35 Instead, they mingled among the pagans
and adopted their evil customs.
36 They worshiped their idols,
which led to their downfall.
37 They even sacrificed their sons
and their daughters to the demons.
38 They shed innocent blood,
the blood of their sons and daughters.
By sacrificing them to the idols of Canaan,
they polluted the land with murder.
39 They defiled themselves by their evil deeds,
and their love of idols was adultery in the
LORD's sight.
40 That is why the LORD's anger burned against
his people,
and he abhorred his own special possession.
41 He handed them over to pagan nations,
and they were ruled by those who hated
them.
42 Their enemies crushed them
and brought them under their cruel power.
43 Again and again he rescued them,
but they chose to rebel against him,
and they were finally destroyed by their sin.
44 Even so, he pitied them in their distress
and listened to their cries.
45 He remembered his covenant with them
and relented because of his unfailing love.
46 He even caused their captors
to treat them with kindness.

47 Save us, O LORD our God!
Gather us back from among the nations,
so we can thank your holy name
and rejoice and praise you.

48 Praise the LORD, the God of Israel,
who lives from everlasting to everlasting!
Let all the people say, "Amen!"

Praise the LORD!

Psalm 107

THEME: Thankfulness to God should constantly be on the lips of those whom he has saved.

AUTHOR: Anonymous

1 Give thanks to the LORD, for he is good!
His faithful love endures forever.
2 Has the LORD redeemed you? Then speak out!
Tell others he has redeemed you from your
enemies.
3 For he has gathered the exiles from many lands,
from east and west,
from north and south.

Ps 106:33 Hebrew *They embittered his spirit.*

Ps 106:34-39 Israel constantly turned away from God. How could they turn from God and worship the idols of the land after the great miracles they had seen? We also have seen God's great miracles but sometimes find ourselves enticed by the world's gods: power, money, convenience, fame, sex, and pleasure. As Israel forgot God, so we are susceptible to forgetting him and giving in to the pressures of an evil world. Remember all that God has done for you so that you won't be drawn away from him by the world's pleasures.

Ps 106:40-42 God allowed trouble to come to the Israelites in order to help them. Our troubles can be helpful because they (1) humble us, (2) wean us from the allurements of the world and drive us back to God, (3) vitalize our prayers, (4) allow us to experience more of God's faithfulness, (5) make us more dependent upon God, (6) encourage us to submit to God's purpose for our lives, and (7) make us more compassionate toward others in trouble.

Ps 106:44-46 This is a beautiful picture of God's great love for his people who deserved only judgment. Fortunately, God's compassion and mercy toward us are not limited by our faithfulness to him. God was merciful to us in sending his Son to die for our sins. If he did this while we were captive to sin, how much more merciful will he be now that we are his children?

Ps 107:1ff This psalm speaks of four different types of people in distress and how God rescues them: wanderers (Ps 107:4-9), prisoners (Ps 107:10-16), the distressed (Ps 107:17-20), and the storm-tossed (Ps 107:23-30). No matter how extreme our calamity, God is able to help us. He is loving and kind to those who are distressed.

Ps 107:1-2 "Has the LORD redeemed you? Then speak out!" God has done so much for us, and we have so much for which to thank him (see Ps 103). He wants us to tell everyone all that he has done. These verses are not so much a mandate to witness as a declaration that when we live in God's presence, we will not be able to keep this glorious experience to ourselves (see also Acts 1:8; 2 Cor 5:18-20). What has God done for you? Is there someone you can tell?

Ps 107:4-9 Lost, hungry, thirsty, and exhausted, these wanderers typify the Israelites in exile. But they also typify anyone who has not found the satisfaction that comes from knowing God. All those who recognize their own lostness can receive the offer of Jesus to satisfy these needs. Jesus is the way (John 14:6), the bread from heaven (John 6:33, 35), the living water (John 4:10-14), and the giver of rest (Matt 11:28-30). Have you received his life-giving offer?

▸ **PSALM 107** ***(cont.)***

4 Some wandered in the wilderness,
lost and homeless.
5 Hungry and thirsty,
they nearly died.
6 "LORD, help!" they cried in their trouble,
and he rescued them from their distress.
7 He led them straight to safety,
to a city where they could live.
8 Let them praise the LORD for his great love
and for the wonderful things he has done
for them.
9 For he satisfies the thirsty
and fills the hungry with good things.

10 Some sat in darkness and deepest gloom,
imprisoned in iron chains of misery.
11 They rebelled against the words of God,
scorning the counsel of the Most High.
12 That is why he broke them with hard labor;
they fell, and no one was there to help them.
13 "LORD, help!" they cried in their trouble,
and he saved them from their distress.
14 He led them from the darkness and deepest
gloom;
he snapped their chains.
15 Let them praise the LORD for his great love
and for the wonderful things he has done
for them.
16 For he broke down their prison gates of bronze;
he cut apart their bars of iron.

17 Some were fools; they rebelled
and suffered for their sins.
18 They couldn't stand the thought of food,
and they were knocking on death's door.
19 "LORD, help!" they cried in their trouble,
and he saved them from their distress.
20 He sent out his word and healed them,
snatching them from the door of death.
21 Let them praise the LORD for his great love
and for the wonderful things he has done
for them.
22 Let them offer sacrifices of thanksgiving
and sing joyfully about his glorious acts.

23 Some went off to sea in ships,
plying the trade routes of the world.
24 They, too, observed the LORD's power in action,
his impressive works on the deepest seas.
25 He spoke, and the winds rose,
stirring up the waves.
26 Their ships were tossed to the heavens
and plunged again to the depths;
the sailors cringed in terror.
27 They reeled and staggered like drunkards
and were at their wits' end.
28 "LORD, help!" they cried in their trouble,
and he saved them from their distress.
29 He calmed the storm to a whisper
and stilled the waves.
30 What a blessing was that stillness
as he brought them safely into harbor!
31 Let them praise the LORD for his great love
and for the wonderful things he has done
for them.
32 Let them exalt him publicly before the
congregation
and before the leaders of the nation.

33 He changes rivers into deserts,
and springs of water into dry, thirsty land.
34 He turns the fruitful land into salty wastelands,
because of the wickedness of those who
live there.
35 But he also turns deserts into pools of water,
the dry land into springs of water.
36 He brings the hungry to settle there
and to build their cities.
37 They sow their fields, plant their vineyards,
and harvest their bumper crops.
38 How he blesses them!
They raise large families there,
and their herds of livestock increase.

39 When they decrease in number and become
impoverished
through oppression, trouble, and sorrow,
40 the LORD pours contempt on their princes,
causing them to wander in trackless
wastelands.
41 But he rescues the poor from trouble
and increases their families like flocks
of sheep.
42 The godly will see these things and be glad,
while the wicked are struck silent.

Ps 107:10-16 Do you know anyone who is in prison? Most people think that those in prison deserve whatever misery they experience as punishment for their crimes. But God loves all men and women no matter how far they have fallen. He wants to reach them with his love and dispel the gloom they face (Matt 25:34-46). Throughout the world, people are imprisoned for their faith; others suffer as victims of injustice. Can you reach out to them? Pray for those in prison. Pray for ministries and Christian chaplains who take God's message of love and forgiveness to prisoners. What can you do to support these efforts?

Ps 107:17-20 Fools and rebels surely bring trouble upon themselves. This psalm offers hope for those who have made a mess of their lives. By receiving God's free gift of forgiveness (Mic 7:18-20; 1 Jn 1:9), anyone can begin a new life and break with the past (see Rom 3:23-26; 2 Cor 5:17). By faith in Christ, we can break addictions, heal memories, and restore broken relationships. If we ask Christ to take control of our lives, he will answer us. His love reaches even those who have rebelled against him.

Ps 107:32 Those who have never truly suffered may not appreciate God as much as those who have matured under hardship. Those who have seen God work in times of distress have a deeper insight into his loving-kindness. If you have experienced great trials, you have the potential for great praise.

43 Those who are wise will take all this to heart;
they will see in our history the faithful love of the LORD.

Psalm 111*

THEME: All that God does is good. Reverence for God is the beginning of wisdom.

AUTHOR: Anonymous

1 Praise the LORD!

I will thank the LORD with all my heart
as I meet with his godly people.
2 How amazing are the deeds of the LORD!
All who delight in him should ponder them.
3 Everything he does reveals his glory and majesty.
His righteousness never fails.
4 He causes us to remember his wonderful works.
How gracious and merciful is our LORD!
5 He gives food to those who fear him;
he always remembers his covenant.
6 He has shown his great power to his people
by giving them the lands of other nations.
7 All he does is just and good,
and all his commandments are trustworthy.
8 They are forever true,
to be obeyed faithfully and with integrity.
9 He has paid a full ransom for his people.
He has guaranteed his covenant with them forever.
What a holy, awe-inspiring name he has!
10 Fear of the LORD is the foundation of true wisdom.
All who obey his commandments will grow in wisdom.

Praise him forever!

Psalm 112*

THEME: The advantages of having faith in God. God guards the minds and actions of those who follow his commands.

AUTHOR: Anonymous

1 Praise the LORD!

How joyful are those who fear the LORD
and delight in obeying his commands.
2 Their children will be successful everywhere;
an entire generation of godly people will be blessed.
3 They themselves will be wealthy,
and their good deeds will last forever.
4 Light shines in the darkness for the godly.
They are generous, compassionate, and righteous.
5 Good comes to those who lend money generously
and conduct their business fairly.
6 Such people will not be overcome by evil.
Those who are righteous will be long remembered.
7 They do not fear bad news;
they confidently trust the LORD to care for them.
8 They are confident and fearless
and can face their foes triumphantly.
9 They share freely and give generously to those in need.
Their good deeds will be remembered forever.
They will have influence and honor.
10 The wicked will see this and be infuriated.
They will grind their teeth in anger;
they will slink away, their hopes thwarted.

Ps 111 This psalm is a Hebrew acrostic poem; after the introductory note of praise, each line begins with a successive letter of the Hebrew alphabet. **Ps 112** This psalm is a Hebrew acrostic poem; after the introductory note of praise, each line begins with a successive letter of the Hebrew alphabet.

Pss 111–118 Psalms 111–118 are called hallelujah psalms. *Hallelujah* means "praise the LORD" and expresses the uplifting and optimistic tone of these songs.

Ps 111:9 The ransom here pictures God's rescue of the Israelites from Egypt and the future return from captivity in Babylon (see Deut 7:8; Jer 31:11). *Ransom* means "to free from captivity by paying a price." All people were being held in slavery by sin until Jesus paid the price to free us—giving his life as a perfect sacrifice. Before Jesus offered himself as a sacrifice for sin, people were not permitted into God's presence (the Most Holy Place); now, all believers can freely approach God's throne through prayer and have God in their lives through the Holy Spirit.

Ps 111:10 The only way to become truly wise is to fear (revere) God. This same thought is expressed in Proverbs 1:7-9. Too often people want to skip this step, thinking they can become wise by life experience and academic knowledge alone. But if we do not acknowledge God as the source of wisdom, then our foundation for making wise decisions is shaky and we are prone to mistakes and foolish choices.

Ps 112:1 Many blessings are available to us—honor, prosperity, security, freedom from fear (Ps 112:2-9)—if we *fear* the Lord and *delight* in obeying his commands. If you expect God's blessings, you must revere him and gladly obey him.

Ps 112:5 Generosity can cure two problems that having money can create. The rich person may abuse others in the desire to accumulate wealth. Generosity will eliminate that abuse. Also, the fear of losing money can be a snare. Generosity shows that we have placed our trust in God, not in our money, for justice and security.

Ps 112:7-8 We all want to live without fear; our heroes are fearless people who take on all dangers and overcome them. The writer teaches us that *fear* of God can lead to a *fearless* life. To fear God means to respect and revere him as the almighty Lord. When we trust God completely to take care of us, we will find that our other fears—even of death itself—will subside.

Psalm 113

THEME: The scope of God's care. God's great mercy is demonstrated by his concern for the poor and the oppressed.

AUTHOR: Anonymous

1 Praise the LORD!

Yes, give praise, O servants of the LORD.
Praise the name of the LORD!
2 Blessed be the name of the LORD
now and forever.
3 Everywhere—from east to west—
praise the name of the LORD.
4 For the LORD is high above the nations;
his glory is higher than the heavens.

5 Who can be compared with the LORD
our God,
who is enthroned on high?
6 He stoops to look down
on heaven and on earth.
7 He lifts the poor from the dust
and the needy from the garbage dump.
8 He sets them among princes,
even the princes of his own people!
9 He gives the childless woman a family,
making her a happy mother.

Praise the LORD!

Psalm 114

THEME: The mighty God who delivered Israel from Egypt. We can celebrate God's great work in our life.

AUTHOR: Anonymous

1 When the Israelites escaped from Egypt—
when the family of Jacob left that foreign
land—
2 the land of Judah became God's sanctuary,
and Israel became his kingdom.
3 The Red Sea* saw them coming and hurried out
of their way!
The water of the Jordan River turned away.
4 The mountains skipped like rams,
the hills like lambs!
5 What's wrong, Red Sea, that made you hurry out
of their way?
What happened, Jordan River, that you turned
away?
6 Why, mountains, did you skip like rams?
Why, hills, like lambs?

7 Tremble, O earth, at the presence of the Lord,
at the presence of the God of Jacob.
8 He turned the rock into a pool of water;
yes, a spring of water flowed from solid rock.

Psalm 115

THEME: God is alive. He is thinking about us and caring for us, and we should put him first in our life.

AUTHOR: Anonymous

1 Not to us, O LORD, not to us,
but to your name goes all the glory
for your unfailing love and faithfulness.
2 Why let the nations say,
"Where is their God?"
3 Our God is in the heavens,
and he does as he wishes.
4 Their idols are merely things of silver and gold,
shaped by human hands.
5 They have mouths but cannot speak,
and eyes but cannot see.
6 They have ears but cannot hear,
and noses but cannot smell.
7 They have hands but cannot feel,
and feet but cannot walk,
and throats but cannot make a sound.
8 And those who make idols are just like them,
as are all who trust in them.

Ps 114:3 Hebrew *the sea;* also in 114:5.

Ps 113:5-9 In God's eyes, a person's value has no relationship to wealth or position on the social ladder. Many people who have excelled in God's work began in poverty or humble beginnings. God supersedes the social orders of this world, often choosing his future leaders and ambassadors from among social outcasts. Do you treat the unwanted in society as though they have value? Demonstrate by your actions that all people are valuable and useful in God's eyes.

Ps 114:7 When God gave the law at Mount Sinai, the mountain trembled in God's presence. Even with our great technology, the seas, rivers, and mountains still present us with formidable challenges. But to God, who controls nature, they are as nothing. When observing the power of an ocean wave or the majesty of a mountain peak, think of God's greatness and glory, which are far more awesome than the natural wonders you can see. To tremble at God's presence means to recognize God's complete power and authority and our frailty by comparison.

Pss 115–118 Psalms 115–118 were traditionally sung at the Passover meal, commemorating Israel's escape from slavery in Egypt (Exod 11–12).

Ps 115:1 The writer asked that God's name, not the nation's, be glorified. Too often we ask God to glorify his name with ours. For example, we may pray for help to do a good job so that our work will be noticed. Or we may ask that a presentation go well so we will get applause. There is nothing wrong with looking good or impressing others; the problem comes when we want to look good no matter what happens to God's reputation in the process. Before you pray, ask yourself, Who will get the credit if God answers my prayer?

Ps 115:4-8 When the psalms were written, many people worshiped idols—statues of wood, stone, or metal. They took pride in what they could see and had contempt for what they couldn't see. Today, we still may value tangible objects (home, clothing, possessions) rather than intangible realities (spiritual growth, salvation, giving to those in need, spending time with loved ones). Those who spend their time obtaining tangible objects are as foolish and empty as the idols themselves. (For more on the foolishness of idols, see Isa 44:9-20.)

9 O Israel, trust the LORD!
He is your helper and your shield.
10 O priests, descendants of Aaron, trust the LORD!
He is your helper and your shield.
11 All you who fear the LORD, trust the LORD!
He is your helper and your shield.

12 The LORD remembers us and will bless us.
He will bless the people of Israel
and bless the priests, the descendants of Aaron.
13 He will bless those who fear the LORD,
both great and lowly.

14 May the LORD richly bless
both you and your children.
15 May you be blessed by the LORD,
who made heaven and earth.
16 The heavens belong to the LORD,
but he has given the earth to all humanity.
17 The dead cannot sing praises to the LORD,
for they have gone into the silence of the grave.
18 But we can praise the LORD
both now and forever!

Praise the LORD!

Psalm 116

THEME: Praise for being saved from certain death. Worship is a thankful response and not a repayment for what God has done.

AUTHOR: Anonymous

1 I love the LORD because he hears my voice
and my prayer for mercy.
2 Because he bends down to listen,
I will pray as long as I have breath!
3 Death wrapped its ropes around me;
the terrors of the grave* overtook me.
I saw only trouble and sorrow.
4 Then I called on the name of the LORD:
"Please, LORD, save me!"
5 How kind the LORD is! How good he is!
So merciful, this God of ours!
6 The LORD protects those of childlike faith;
I was facing death, and he saved me.
7 Let my soul be at rest again,
for the LORD has been good to me.
8 He has saved me from death,
my eyes from tears,
my feet from stumbling.
9 And so I walk in the LORD's presence
as I live here on earth!
10 I believed in you, so I said,
"I am deeply troubled, LORD."
11 In my anxiety I cried out to you,
"These people are all liars!"
12 What can I offer the LORD
for all he has done for me?
13 I will lift up the cup of salvation
and praise the LORD's name for saving me.
14 I will keep my promises to the LORD
in the presence of all his people.

15 The LORD cares deeply
when his loved ones die.
16 O LORD, I am your servant;
yes, I am your servant, born into your
household;
you have freed me from my chains.
17 I will offer you a sacrifice of thanksgiving
and call on the name of the LORD.
18 I will fulfill my vows to the LORD
in the presence of all his people—
19 in the house of the LORD
in the heart of Jerusalem.

Praise the LORD!

Psalm 117

THEME: Another reason for praise—God's love for the whole world. We should praise God for his unlimited love.

AUTHOR: Anonymous

1 Praise the LORD, all you nations.
Praise him, all you people of the earth.
2 For he loves us with unfailing love;
the LORD's faithfulness endures forever.

Praise the LORD!

Ps 116:3 Hebrew *of Sheol.*

Ps 115:12 "The LORD remembers us," says the psalm writer. What a fantastic truth! There are many times when we feel isolated, alone, and abandoned, even by God. In reality, he sees, understands, and thinks about us. When depressed by problems or struggling with self-worth, be encouraged that God keeps you in his thoughts. If he thinks about you, surely his help is near.

Ps 116:1-2 God is so responsive that you can always reach him. He bends down and listens to your voice. This writer's love for the Lord had grown because he had experienced answers to his prayers. If you are discouraged, remember that God is near, listening carefully to every prayer and answering each one in order to give you his best.

Ps 116:15 God stays close to us even in death. When someone we love is nearing death, we may become angry and feel abandoned. But believers (the Lord's loved ones) are precious to God, and he carefully chooses the time when they will be called into his presence. Let this truth provide comfort when you've lost a loved one. God sees, and each life is valuable to him (see Jesus' statement in Matt 10:29).

Ps 117:1-2 Psalm 117 the shortest chapter in the Bible, and it is also the middle chapter. Paul quotes from this psalm in Romans 15:11 to show that God's salvation is for all people, not just the Jews.

Ps 117:1-2 Have you ever said, "I can't think of anything God has done for me. How can I praise him?" This psalm gives two reasons for praising God: his unfailing love toward us and his faithfulness that endures forever. If he did nothing else for us, he would still be worthy of our highest praise.

Psalm 118

THEME: Confidence in God's eternal love. God's love is unchanging in the midst of changing situations. This gives us security.

AUTHOR: Anonymous

1 Give thanks to the LORD, for he is good!
His faithful love endures forever.

2 Let all Israel repeat:
"His faithful love endures forever."
3 Let Aaron's descendants, the priests, repeat:
"His faithful love endures forever."
4 Let all who fear the LORD repeat:
"His faithful love endures forever."

5 In my distress I prayed to the LORD,
and the LORD answered me and set me free.
6 The LORD is for me, so I will have no fear.
What can mere people do to me?
7 Yes, the LORD is for me; he will help me.
I will look in triumph at those who hate me.
8 It is better to take refuge in the LORD
than to trust in people.
9 It is better to take refuge in the LORD
than to trust in princes.

10 Though hostile nations surrounded me,
I destroyed them all with the authority of the LORD.
11 Yes, they surrounded and attacked me,
but I destroyed them all with the authority of the LORD.
12 They swarmed around me like bees;
they blazed against me like a crackling fire.
But I destroyed them all with the authority of the LORD.
13 My enemies did their best to kill me,
but the LORD rescued me.
14 The LORD is my strength and my song;
he has given me victory.

15 Songs of joy and victory are sung in the camp of the godly.
The strong right arm of the LORD has done glorious things!
16 The strong right arm of the LORD is raised in triumph.
The strong right arm of the LORD has done glorious things!
17 I will not die; instead, I will live
to tell what the LORD has done.
18 The LORD has punished me severely,
but he did not let me die.

19 Open for me the gates where the righteous enter,
and I will go in and thank the LORD.
20 These gates lead to the presence of the LORD,
and the godly enter there.
21 I thank you for answering my prayer
and giving me victory!

22 The stone that the builders rejected
has now become the cornerstone.
23 This is the LORD's doing,
and it is wonderful to see.
24 This is the day the LORD has made.
We will rejoice and be glad in it.
25 Please, LORD, please save us.
Please, LORD, please give us success.
26 Bless the one who comes in the name of the LORD.
We bless you from the house of the LORD.
27 The LORD is God, shining upon us.
Take the sacrifice and bind it with cords on the altar.
28 You are my God, and I will praise you!
You are my God, and I will exalt you!

29 Give thanks to the LORD, for he is good!
His faithful love endures forever.

Psalm 119*

THEME: God's word is true and wonderful. Stay true to God and his word no matter how bad the world becomes. Obedience to God's laws is the only way to achieve real happiness.

AUTHOR: Anonymous, some suggest Ezra the priest

Aleph

1 Joyful are people of integrity,
who follow the instructions of the LORD.

Ps 119 This psalm is a Hebrew acrostic poem; there are twenty-two stanzas, one for each successive letter of the Hebrew alphabet. Each of the eight verses within each stanza begins with the Hebrew letter named in its heading.

Ps 118:8 Pilots put confidence in their planes. Commuters place confidence in trains, cars, or buses. Each day we must put our confidence in something or someone. If you are willing to trust a plane or car to get you to your destination, are you willing to trust God to guide you here on earth and to your eternal destination? Do you trust him more than any human being? How futile it is to trust anything or anyone more than God.

Ps 118:22-23 Jesus referred to this verse when he spoke of being rejected by his own people (Matt 21:42; Mark 12:10-11; Luke 20:17). Although he was rejected, Jesus is now the "cornerstone," the most important part of the church (Acts 4:11; Eph 2:20; 1 Pet 2:6-7). The cornerstone is the foundation stone, holding the structure together.

Ps 118:24 There are days when the last thing we want to do is rejoice. Our mood is down, our situation is out of hand, and our sorrow or guilt is overwhelming. We can relate to the writers of the psalms who often felt this way. But no matter how low the writers felt, they were always honest with God. And as they talked to God, their prayers ended in praise. When you don't feel like rejoicing, tell God how you truly feel. You will find that God will give you a reason to rejoice. God has given you this day to live and to serve him—be glad!

Ps 119:1ff This is both the longest psalm and the longest chapter in the Bible. Although it is anonymous, some people think Ezra might have written it after the Temple was

2 Joyful are those who obey his laws
and search for him with all their hearts.
3 They do not compromise with evil,
and they walk only in his paths.
4 You have charged us
to keep your commandments carefully.
5 Oh, that my actions would consistently
reflect your decrees!
6 Then I will not be ashamed
when I compare my life with your commands.
7 As I learn your righteous regulations,
I will thank you by living as I should!
8 I will obey your decrees.
Please don't give up on me!

WHERE TO GET HELP IN THE BOOK OF PSALMS

When you feel . . .	When you're facing . . .	When you want . . .
Afraid: 3; 4; 27; 46; 49; 56; 91; 118	Atheists: 10; 14; 19; 52; 53; 115	Acceptance: 139
Alone: 9; 10; 12; 13; 27; 40; 43	Competition: 133	Answers: 4; 17
"Burned out": 6; 63	Criticism: 35; 56; 120	Confidence: 46; 71
Cheated: 41	Danger: 11	Courage: 11; 42
Confused: 10; 12; 73	Death: 6; 71; 90	Fellowship with God: 5; 16; 25; 27; 37; 133
Depressed: 27; 34; 42; 43; 88; 143	Decisions: 1; 119	Forgiveness: 32; 38; 40; 51; 69; 86; 103; 130
Distressed: 13; 25; 31; 40; 107	Discrimination: 54	Friendship: 16
Elated: 19; 96	Doubts: 34; 37; 94	Godliness: 15; 25
Guilty: 19; 32; 38; 51	Evil people: 10; 35; 36; 49; 52; 109; 140	Guidance: 1; 5; 15; 19; 25; 32; 48
Hateful: 11	Enemies: 3; 25; 35; 41; 56; 59	Healing: 6; 41
Impatient: 13; 27; 37; 40	Heresy: 14	Hope: 16; 17; 18; 23; 27
Insecure: 3; 5; 12; 91	Hypocrisy: 26; 28; 40; 50	Humility: 19; 147
Insulted: 41; 70	Illness: 6; 139	Illumination: 19
Jealous: 37	Lies: 5; 12; 120	Integrity: 24; 25
Like quitting: 29; 43; 145	Old age: 71; 92	Joy: 9; 16; 28; 126
Lost: 23; 139	Persecution: 1; 3; 7; 56	Justice: 2; 7; 14; 26; 37; 49; 58; 82
Overwhelmed: 25; 69; 142	Poverty: 9; 10; 12	Knowledge: 2; 8; 18; 19; 25; 29; 97; 103
Penitent/Sorry: 32; 51; 66	Punishment: 6; 38; 39	Leadership: 72
Proud: 14; 30; 49	Slander/Insults: 7; 15; 35; 43; 120	Miracles: 60; 111
Purposeless: 14; 25; 39; 49; 90	Slaughter: 6; 46; 83	Money: 15; 16; 17; 49
Sad: 13	Sorrow: 23; 34	Peace: 3; 4
Self-confident: 24	Success: 18; 112; 127; 128	Perspective: 2; 11
Tense: 4	Temptation: 38; 141	Prayer: 5; 17; 27; 61
Thankful: 118; 136; 138	Troubles: 34; 55; 86; 102; 142; 145	Protection: 3; 4; 7; 16; 17; 18; 23; 27; 31; 91; 121; 125
Threatened: 3; 11; 17	Verbal cruelty: 35; 120	Provision: 23
Tired/Weak: 6; 13; 18; 28; 40; 49; 86		Rest: 23; 27
Trapped: 7; 17; 42; 88; 142		Salvation: 26; 37; 49; 126
Unimportant: 8; 90; 139		Stability: 11; 33; 46
Vengeful: 3; 7; 109		Vindication: 9; 14; 28; 35; 109
Worried: 37		Wisdom: 1; 16; 19; 64; 111a
Worshipful: 8; 19; 27; 29; 150		

rebuilt (Ezra 6:14-15) as a repetitive meditation on the beauty of God's Word and how it helps us stay pure and grow in faith. Psalm 119 has 22 carefully constructed sections, each corresponding to a different letter in the Hebrew alphabet and each verse beginning with the letter of its section. Almost every verse mentions God's Word. Such repetition was common in the Hebrew culture. People did not have personal copies of the Scriptures to read as we do, so God's people memorized his Word and passed it along orally. The structure of this psalm allowed for easy memorization. Remember, God's Word, the Bible, is the only sure guide for living a pure life.

▶ **PSALM 119** ***(cont.)***

Beth

9 How can a young person stay pure?
By obeying your word.
10 I have tried hard to find you—
don't let me wander from your commands.
11 I have hidden your word in my heart,
that I might not sin against you.
12 I praise you, O LORD;
teach me your decrees.
13 I have recited aloud
all the regulations you have given us.
14 I have rejoiced in your laws
as much as in riches.
15 I will study your commandments
and reflect on your ways.
16 I will delight in your decrees
and not forget your word.

Gimel

17 Be good to your servant,
that I may live and obey your word.
18 Open my eyes to see
the wonderful truths in your instructions.
19 I am only a foreigner in the land.
Don't hide your commands from me!
20 I am always overwhelmed
with a desire for your regulations.
21 You rebuke the arrogant;
those who wander from your commands are cursed.
22 Don't let them scorn and insult me,
for I have obeyed your laws.
23 Even princes sit and speak against me,
but I will meditate on your decrees.
24 Your laws please me;
they give me wise advice.

Daleth

25 I lie in the dust;
revive me by your word.
26 I told you my plans, and you answered.
Now teach me your decrees.
27 Help me understand the meaning of your commandments,
and I will meditate on your wonderful deeds.
28 I weep with sorrow;
encourage me by your word.
29 Keep me from lying to myself;
give me the privilege of knowing your instructions.
30 I have chosen to be faithful;
I have determined to live by your regulations.
31 I cling to your laws.
LORD, don't let me be put to shame!
32 I will pursue your commands,
for you expand my understanding.

He

33 Teach me your decrees, O LORD;
I will keep them to the end.
34 Give me understanding and I will obey your instructions;
I will put them into practice with all my heart.
35 Make me walk along the path of your commands,
for that is where my happiness is found.
36 Give me an eagerness for your laws
rather than a love for money!
37 Turn my eyes from worthless things,
and give me life through your word.*
38 Reassure me of your promise,
made to those who fear you.
39 Help me abandon my shameful ways;
for your regulations are good.
40 I long to obey your commandments!
Renew my life with your goodness.

Ps 119:37 Some manuscripts read *in your ways.*

Ps 119:9 We are drowning in a sea of sexual images and sinful attractions. Everywhere we look we find temptation to fill our minds with thoughts of sexual relationships that God wouldn't approve. The writer asked a question that troubles us all: How do we stay pure in a contaminating environment? We cannot do this on our own but must have counsel and strength more dynamic than the tempting influences around us. Where can we find that strength and wisdom? By reading God's Word and doing what it says.

Ps 119:11 Hiding (keeping) God's Word in our hearts is a deterrent to sin. This alone should inspire us to memorize Scripture. But memorization alone will not keep us from sin; we must also put God's Word to work in our lives, making it a vital guide for everything we do.

Ps 119:12-24 Most of us chafe under rules, for we think they restrict us from doing what we want. At first glance, then, it may seem strange to hear the writer talk of rejoicing in following God's laws as much as in having great riches. But God's laws were given to free us to be all he wants us to be. They restrict us from doing what might cripple us and keep us from being our best. God's guidelines help us follow his path and avoid paths that lead to destruction.

Ps 119:19 The writer said that he is a "foreigner in the land," and so he needed guidance. Almost any long trip requires a map or guide. As we travel through life, the Bible should be our road map, pointing out safe routes, obstacles to avoid, and our final destination. We must recognize ourselves as pilgrims, travelers here on earth who need to study God's map to learn the way. If we ignore the map, we will wander aimlessly through life and risk missing our real destination.

Ps 119:27-28 Our lives are cluttered with rule books, but the authors never come with us to help us follow the rules. But God does. That is the uniqueness of our Bible. God not only provides the guidelines but comes with us personally each day, strengthening us so that we can live according to his will. All we must do is invite him and respond to his direction.

Ps 119:36 In today's world, people most often covet financial gain. Money represents power, influence, and success. For many people, money is a god. They think about little else. True, money can buy certain comforts and offer some security. But far more valuable than wealth is obedience to God, because it is a heavenly treasure rather than an earthly one (Luke 12:33). We should do what God wants, regardless of the financial implications. Make the writer's prayer your own, asking God to turn your heart toward his laws and not toward making money; it's in your own best interest in the long run.

Waw

41 LORD, give me your unfailing love,
the salvation that you promised me.
42 Then I can answer those who taunt me,
for I trust in your word.
43 Do not snatch your word of truth from me,
for your regulations are my only hope.
44 I will keep on obeying your instructions
forever and ever.
45 I will walk in freedom,
for I have devoted myself to your
commandments.
46 I will speak to kings about your laws,
and I will not be ashamed.
47 How I delight in your commands!
How I love them!
48 I honor and love your commands.
I meditate on your decrees.

Zayin

49 Remember your promise to me;
it is my only hope.
50 Your promise revives me;
it comforts me in all my troubles.
51 The proud hold me in utter contempt,
but I do not turn away from your instructions.
52 I meditate on your age-old regulations;
O LORD, they comfort me.
53 I become furious with the wicked,
because they reject your instructions.
54 Your decrees have been the theme of my songs
wherever I have lived.
55 I reflect at night on who you are, O LORD;
therefore, I obey your instructions.
56 This is how I spend my life:
obeying your commandments.

Heth

57 LORD, you are mine!
I promise to obey your words!
58 With all my heart I want your blessings.
Be merciful as you promised.
59 I pondered the direction of my life,
and I turned to follow your laws.
60 I will hurry, without delay,
to obey your commands.
61 Evil people try to drag me into sin,
but I am firmly anchored to your instructions.
62 I rise at midnight to thank you
for your just regulations.
63 I am a friend to anyone who fears you—
anyone who obeys your commandments.
64 O LORD, your unfailing love fills the earth;
teach me your decrees.

Teth

65 You have done many good things for me, LORD,
just as you promised.
66 I believe in your commands;
now teach me good judgment and knowledge.
67 I used to wander off until you disciplined me;
but now I closely follow your word.
68 You are good and do only good;
teach me your decrees.
69 Arrogant people smear me with lies,
but in truth I obey your commandments
with all my heart.
70 Their hearts are dull and stupid,
but I delight in your instructions.
71 My suffering was good for me,
for it taught me to pay attention to your
decrees.
72 Your instructions are more valuable to me
than millions in gold and silver.

Yodh

73 You made me; you created me.
Now give me the sense to follow your
commands.
74 May all who fear you find in me a cause for joy,
for I have put my hope in your word.
75 I know, O LORD, that your regulations are fair;
you disciplined me because I needed it.
76 Now let your unfailing love comfort me,
just as you promised me, your servant.
77 Surround me with your tender mercies so
I may live,
for your instructions are my delight.
78 Bring disgrace upon the arrogant people who
lied about me;
meanwhile, I will concentrate on your
commandments.
79 Let me be united with all who fear you,
with those who know your laws.
80 May I be blameless in keeping your decrees;
then I will never be ashamed.

Kaph

81 I am worn out waiting for your rescue,
but I have put my hope in your word.
82 My eyes are straining to see your promises
come true.
When will you comfort me?
83 I am shriveled like a wineskin in the smoke,
but I have not forgotten to obey your decrees.
84 How long must I wait?
When will you punish those who persecute me?
85 These arrogant people who hate your instructions
have dug deep pits to trap me.

Ps 119:44-46 The writer talks about keeping the laws and yet being free. Contrary to what we often expect, obeying God's laws does not inhibit or restrain us. Instead, it frees us to be what God designed us to be. By seeking God's salvation and forgiveness, we have freedom from sin and the resulting oppressive guilt. By living God's way, we have freedom to fulfill God's plan for our lives.

▸ **PSALM 119** ***(cont.)***

86 All your commands are trustworthy.
Protect me from those who hunt me down
without cause.
87 They almost finished me off,
but I refused to abandon your commandments.
88 In your unfailing love, spare my life;
then I can continue to obey your laws.

Lamedh

89 Your eternal word, O LORD,
stands firm in heaven.
90 Your faithfulness extends to every generation,
as enduring as the earth you created.
91 Your regulations remain true to this day,
for everything serves your plans.
92 If your instructions hadn't sustained me with joy,
I would have died in my misery.
93 I will never forget your commandments,
for by them you give me life.
94 I am yours; rescue me!
For I have worked hard at obeying your
commandments.
95 Though the wicked hide along the way to kill me,
I will quietly keep my mind on your laws.
96 Even perfection has its limits,
but your commands have no limit.

Mem

97 Oh, how I love your instructions!
I think about them all day long.
98 Your commands make me wiser than my
enemies,
for they are my constant guide.
99 Yes, I have more insight than my teachers,
for I am always thinking of your laws.
100 I am even wiser than my elders,
for I have kept your commandments.
101 I have refused to walk on any evil path,
so that I may remain obedient to your word.
102 I haven't turned away from your regulations,
for you have taught me well.
103 How sweet your words taste to me;
they are sweeter than honey.
104 Your commandments give me understanding;
no wonder I hate every false way of life.

Nun

105 Your word is a lamp to guide my feet
and a light for my path.
106 I've promised it once, and I'll promise it again:
I will obey your righteous regulations.
107 I have suffered much, O LORD;
restore my life again as you promised.
108 LORD, accept my offering of praise,
and teach me your regulations.
109 My life constantly hangs in the balance,
but I will not stop obeying your instructions.
110 The wicked have set their traps for me,
but I will not turn from your commandments.
111 Your laws are my treasure;
they are my heart's delight.
112 I am determined to keep your decrees
to the very end.

Samekh

113 I hate those with divided loyalties,
but I love your instructions.
114 You are my refuge and my shield;
your word is my source of hope.
115 Get out of my life, you evil-minded people,
for I intend to obey the commands of my God.
116 LORD, sustain me as you promised, that I may live!
Do not let my hope be crushed.
117 Sustain me, and I will be rescued;
then I will meditate continually on your decrees.
118 But you have rejected all who stray from your
decrees.
They are only fooling themselves.
119 You skim off the wicked of the earth like scum;
no wonder I love to obey your laws!
120 I tremble in fear of you;
I stand in awe of your regulations.

Ayin

121 Don't leave me to the mercy of my enemies,
for I have done what is just and right.
122 Please guarantee a blessing for me.
Don't let the arrogant oppress me!
123 My eyes strain to see your rescue,
to see the truth of your promise fulfilled.
124 I am your servant; deal with me in unfailing love,
and teach me your decrees.

Ps 119:97-104 God's Word makes us wise—wiser than our enemies and wiser than any teachers who ignore it. True wisdom goes beyond amassing knowledge; it is *applying* knowledge in a life-changing way. Intelligent or experienced people are not necessarily wise. Wisdom comes from allowing God's teachings to guide us.

Ps 119:105 To walk safely in the woods at night we need a light so we don't trip over tree roots or fall into holes. In this life, we walk through a dark forest of evil. But the Bible can be our light to show us the way ahead so we won't stumble as we walk. It reveals the entangling roots of false values and philosophies. Study the Bible so you will be able to see your way clear enough to stay on the right path.

Ps 119:113 Undecided people cannot make up their minds between good and evil. But when it comes to obeying God, there is no middle ground; you must take a stand. Either you are obeying him or you are not. Either you are doing what he wants or you are undecided. Choose to obey God, and say with the writer, "I love your instructions."

Ps 119:125 The writer asked God for discernment. Faith comes alive when we apply Scripture to our daily tasks and concerns. We need discernment so we can understand, and we need the desire to apply Scripture where we need help. The Bible is like medicine: It goes to work only when we apply it to the affected areas. As you read the Bible, be alert for lessons, commands, or examples that you can put into practice.

125 Give discernment to me, your servant;
then I will understand your laws.
126 LORD, it is time for you to act,
for these evil people have violated your
instructions.
127 Truly, I love your commands
more than gold, even the finest gold.
128 Each of your commandments is right.
That is why I hate every false way.

Pe

129 Your laws are wonderful.
No wonder I obey them!
130 The teaching of your word gives light,
so even the simple can understand.
131 I pant with expectation,
longing for your commands.
132 Come and show me your mercy,
as you do for all who love your name.
133 Guide my steps by your word,
so I will not be overcome by evil.
134 Ransom me from the oppression of evil
people;
then I can obey your commandments.
135 Look upon me with love;
teach me your decrees.
136 Rivers of tears gush from my eyes
because people disobey your instructions.

Tsadhe

137 O LORD, you are righteous,
and your regulations are fair.
138 Your laws are perfect
and completely trustworthy.
139 I am overwhelmed with indignation,
for my enemies have disregarded
your words.
140 Your promises have been thoroughly tested;
that is why I love them so much.
141 I am insignificant and despised,
but I don't forget your commandments.
142 Your justice is eternal,
and your instructions are perfectly true.
143 As pressure and stress bear down on me,
I find joy in your commands.
144 Your laws are always right;
help me to understand them so I may live.

Qoph

145 I pray with all my heart; answer me, LORD!
I will obey your decrees.
146 I cry out to you; rescue me,
that I may obey your laws.
147 I rise early, before the sun is up;
I cry out for help and put my hope in your
words.
148 I stay awake through the night,
thinking about your promise.
149 In your faithful love, O LORD, hear my cry;
let me be revived by following your
regulations.
150 Lawless people are coming to attack me;
they live far from your instructions.
151 But you are near, O LORD,
and all your commands are true.
152 I have known from my earliest days
that your laws will last forever.

Resh

153 Look upon my suffering and rescue me,
for I have not forgotten your instructions.
154 Argue my case; take my side!
Protect my life as you promised.
155 The wicked are far from rescue,
for they do not bother with your decrees.
156 LORD, how great is your mercy;
let me be revived by following your
regulations.
157 Many persecute and trouble me,
yet I have not swerved from your laws.
158 Seeing these traitors makes me sick at heart,
because they care nothing for your word.
159 See how I love your commandments, LORD.
Give back my life because of your
unfailing love.
160 The very essence of your words is truth;
all your just regulations will stand forever.

Shin

161 Powerful people harass me without cause,
but my heart trembles only at your word.
162 I rejoice in your word
like one who discovers a great treasure.
163 I hate and abhor all falsehood,
but I love your instructions.
164 I will praise you seven times a day
because all your regulations are just.
165 Those who love your instructions have great
peace
and do not stumble.
166 I long for your rescue, LORD,
so I have obeyed your commands.
167 I have obeyed your laws,
for I love them very much.
168 Yes, I obey your commandments and laws
because you know everything I do.

Ps 119:160 One of God's characteristics is truthfulness. He embodies perfect truth; therefore, his Word cannot lie. It is true and dependable for guidance and help (see John 17:14-17). The Bible is completely true and trustworthy.

Ps 119:165 Modern society longs for peace of mind. Here is clear-cut instruction on how to attain this: If we love God and obey his laws, we will have "great peace." Trust in God, who alone stands above the pressures of daily life and gives us full assurance.

▸ **PSALM 119** ***(cont.)***

Taw

169 O LORD, listen to my cry;
give me the discerning mind you promised.
170 Listen to my prayer;
rescue me as you promised.
171 Let praise flow from my lips,
for you have taught me your decrees.
172 Let my tongue sing about your word,
for all your commands are right.
173 Give me a helping hand,
for I have chosen to follow your
commandments.
174 O LORD, I have longed for your rescue,
and your instructions are my delight.
175 Let me live so I can praise you,
and may your regulations help me.
176 I have wandered away like a lost sheep;
come and find me,
for I have not forgotten your commands.

Psalm 120

THEME: A prayer for deliverance from false accusers. All believers must live with the tension of being in the world but not belonging to it.

AUTHOR: Anonymous, some suggest Hezekiah

A song for pilgrims ascending to Jerusalem.

1 I took my troubles to the LORD;
I cried out to him, and he answered my
prayer.
2 Rescue me, O LORD, from liars
and from all deceitful people.
3 O deceptive tongue, what will God do to you?
How will he increase your punishment?
4 You will be pierced with sharp arrows
and burned with glowing coals.

5 How I suffer in far-off Meshech.
It pains me to live in distant Kedar.
6 I am tired of living
among people who hate peace.
7 I search for peace;
but when I speak of peace, they want war!

Psalm 121

THEME: We can depend upon God for help. Pilgrims must travel through lonely country to their destination; they are protected, not by anything created, but by the Creator of everything.

AUTHOR: Anonymous, some suggest Hezekiah

A song for pilgrims ascending to Jerusalem.

1 I look up to the mountains—
does my help come from there?
2 My help comes from the LORD,
who made heaven and earth!

3 He will not let you stumble;
the one who watches over you will not
slumber.
4 Indeed, he who watches over Israel
never slumbers or sleeps.

5 The LORD himself watches over you!
The LORD stands beside you as your
protective shade.
6 The sun will not harm you by day,
nor the moon at night.

7 The LORD keeps you from all harm
and watches over your life.
8 The LORD keeps watch over you as you come
and go,
both now and forever.

Psalm 123

THEME: Look to God for mercy. We are encouraged to be attentive to God's leading.

AUTHOR: Anonymous, some suggest Hezekiah

A song for pilgrims ascending to Jerusalem.

1 I lift my eyes to you,
O God, enthroned in heaven.
2 We keep looking to the LORD our God for his
mercy,
just as servants keep their eyes on their
master,
as a slave girl watches her mistress for the
slightest signal.

Pss 120–134 The next group of psalms (falling within the range of Pss 120–134) are called "pilgrim psalms" or "songs of ascent." They were written at various times, but gathered together in a collection because of common themes. They were sung by those who journeyed ("ascended") to the Temple for the annual festivals. Each psalm is a "step" along the journey. Psalm 120 begins the journey in a distant land in hostile surroundings; Psalm 122 pictures the pilgrims arriving in Jerusalem; and the rest of the psalms move toward the Temple, mentioning various characteristics of God.

Ps 120:5-6 Meshech was a nation far to the north of Israel; Kedar a nation to the southeast. Both were known for being warlike and barbarian. Because the writer couldn't have been in two places at one time, he was lamenting that he felt far from home and surrounded by pagan people.

Ps 120:7 Peacemaking is not always popular. Some people prefer to fight for what they believe in. The glory of battle is in the hope of winning, but someone must be a loser. The glory of peacemaking is that it may actually produce two winners. Peacemaking is God's way, so we should carefully and prayerfully attempt to be peacemakers.

Ps 121:1ff This song expresses assurance and hope in God's protection day and night. He not only made the hills but heaven and earth as well. We should never trust a lesser power than God himself. Not only is he all-powerful, but he also watches over us. Nothing diverts or deters him. We are safe. We never outgrow our need for God's untiring watch over our lives.

Ps 123:1ff The writer lifted his eyes to God, waiting and watching for God to send his mercy. The more he waited, the more he cried out to God because he knew that the evil and proud offered no help—they had only contempt for God.

3 Have mercy on us, LORD, have mercy,
for we have had our fill of contempt.
4 We have had more than our fill of the scoffing of the proud
and the contempt of the arrogant.

Psalm 125

THEME: God is our Protector. The mountains around Jerusalem symbolize God's protection for his people.

AUTHOR: Anonymous, some suggest Hezekiah

A song for pilgrims ascending to Jerusalem.

1 Those who trust in the LORD are as secure as Mount Zion;
they will not be defeated but will endure forever.
2 Just as the mountains surround Jerusalem,
so the LORD surrounds his people, both now and forever.
3 The wicked will not rule the land of the godly,
for then the godly might be tempted to do wrong.
4 O LORD, do good to those who are good,
whose hearts are in tune with you.
5 But banish those who turn to crooked ways, O LORD.
Take them away with those who do evil.

May Israel have peace!

Psalm 128

THEME: God, the true head of the home. (This is called the marriage prayer because it was often sung at Israelite marriages.) God will reward your devotion to him with inner peace.

AUTHOR: Anonymous, some suggest Hezekiah

A song for pilgrims ascending to Jerusalem.

1 How joyful are those who fear the LORD—
all who follow his ways!
2 You will enjoy the fruit of your labor.
How joyful and prosperous you will be!
3 Your wife will be like a fruitful grapevine,
flourishing within your home.
Your children will be like vigorous young olive trees
as they sit around your table.
4 That is the LORD's blessing
for those who fear him.
5 May the LORD continually bless you from Zion.
May you see Jerusalem prosper as long as you live.
6 May you live to enjoy your grandchildren.
May Israel have peace!

Psalm 129

THEME: Confidence in times of persecution. God will bring us through the tough times.

AUTHOR: Anonymous, some suggest Hezekiah

A song for pilgrims ascending to Jerusalem.

1 From my earliest youth my enemies have persecuted me.
Let all Israel repeat this:
2 From my earliest youth my enemies have persecuted me,
but they have never defeated me.
3 My back is covered with cuts,
as if a farmer had plowed long furrows.
4 But the LORD is good;
he has cut me free from the ropes of the ungodly.
5 May all who hate Jerusalem*
be turned back in shameful defeat.
6 May they be as useless as grass on a rooftop,
turning yellow when only half grown,
7 ignored by the harvester,
despised by the binder.
8 And may those who pass by
refuse to give them this blessing:
"The LORD bless you;
we bless you in the LORD's name."

Ps 129:5 Hebrew *Zion.*

Ps 125:1 Have you ever known people who were drawn to every new fad or idea? Such people are unstable and therefore unreliable. The secret to stability is to trust in God, because he never changes. He cannot be shaken by the changes in our world, and he endures forever. The fads and ideas of our world, and our world itself, will not last that long.

Ps 125:3 Although the writer said, "The wicked will not rule the land of the godly," often Israel had to put up with evil rulers. The writer was expressing what will ultimately happen when God executes his final judgment. Human sinfulness often ruins God's ideal on earth, but that doesn't mean God has lost control. Evil prevails only as long as God allows.

Ps 128:1ff A good family life is a reward for following God. The values outlined in God's Word include love, service, honesty, integrity, and prayer. These help all relationships, and they are especially vital to home life. Is your home life heavenly or hectic? Reading and obeying God's Word is a good place to start to make your family all that it should be.

Ps 129:2 The people of Israel were persecuted from their earliest days but never destroyed completely. The same is true of the church. Christians have faced times of severe persecution, but the church has never been destroyed. As Jesus said to Peter, "Now I say to you that you are Peter (which means 'rock'), and upon this rock I will build my church, and all the powers of hell will not conquer it" (Matt 16:18). When you face persecution and discrimination, take courage—the church will never be destroyed.

Ps 129:3 This verse foreshadowed Jesus' unjust punishment before his death. He endured lashes from the whip of his tormentors, which indeed made "furrows" on his back (John 19:1).

Psalm 130

THEME: Assurance of the Lord's forgiveness. God will surely forgive us if we confess our sins to him.

AUTHOR: Anonymous, some suggest Hezekiah

A song for pilgrims ascending to Jerusalem.

1 From the depths of despair, O LORD,
I call for your help.
2 Hear my cry, O Lord.
Pay attention to my prayer.

3 LORD, if you kept a record of our sins,
who, O Lord, could ever survive?
4 But you offer forgiveness,
that we might learn to fear you.

5 I am counting on the LORD;
yes, I am counting on him.
I have put my hope in his word.
6 I long for the Lord
more than sentries long for the dawn,
yes, more than sentries long for the dawn.

7 O Israel, hope in the LORD;
for with the LORD there is unfailing love.
His redemption overflows.
8 He himself will redeem Israel
from every kind of sin.

Psalm 132

THEME: Honor God and he will honor you. The psalmist reflects upon that great day when the Ark of the Covenant was brought to Jerusalem and praises God for his promise to perpetuate David's line.

AUTHOR: Anonymous

A song for pilgrims ascending to Jerusalem.

1 LORD, remember David
and all that he suffered.
2 He made a solemn promise to the LORD.
He vowed to the Mighty One of Israel,*
3 "I will not go home;
I will not let myself rest.
4 I will not let my eyes sleep
nor close my eyelids in slumber
5 until I find a place to build a house for the LORD,
a sanctuary for the Mighty One of Israel."

6 We heard that the Ark was in Ephrathah;
then we found it in the distant countryside
of Jaar.
7 Let us go to the sanctuary of the LORD;
let us worship at the footstool of his throne.
8 Arise, O LORD, and enter your resting place,
along with the Ark, the symbol of your power.
9 May your priests be clothed in godliness;
may your loyal servants sing for joy.
10 For the sake of your servant David,
do not reject the king you have anointed.

11 The LORD swore an oath to David
with a promise he will never take back:
"I will place one of your descendants
on your throne.
12 If your descendants obey the terms of my
covenant
and the laws that I teach them,
then your royal line
will continue forever and ever."

13 For the LORD has chosen Jerusalem*;
he has desired it for his home.
14 "This is my resting place forever," he said.
"I will live here, for this is the home I desired.
15 I will bless this city and make it prosperous;
I will satisfy its poor with food.
16 I will clothe its priests with godliness;
its faithful servants will sing for joy.
17 Here I will increase the power of David;
my anointed one will be a light for
my people.
18 I will clothe his enemies with shame,
but he will be a glorious king."

Ps 132:2 Hebrew *of Jacob;* also in 132:5. See note on 44:4. **Ps 132:13** Hebrew *Zion.*

Ps 130:1-2 In the depths of despair, the writer cried out to God. Despair makes us feel isolated and distant from God, but this is precisely when we need God most. Despair over sin should not lead to self-pity, causing us to think more about ourselves than God. Instead, it should lead to confession and then to God's mercy, forgiveness, and redemption. When we feel overwhelmed by a problem, feeling sorry for ourselves will only increase feelings of hopelessness; but crying out to God will turn our attention to the only one who can really help.

Ps 130:3-4 Keeping a record of sins (or holding a grudge) is like building a wall between you and another person, and it is nearly impossible to talk openly while the wall is there. God doesn't keep a record of our sins; when he forgives, he forgives completely, tearing down any wall between us and him. Therefore, we fear (revere) God, yet we can talk to him about anything. When you pray, realize that God is holding nothing against you. His lines of communication are completely open.

Ps 132:2-5 This refers to David's desire to build the Temple. When David became king, he built a beautiful palace, but he was troubled that the Ark of the Covenant, the symbol of God's presence among his people (Exod 25:10-22), remained in a tent (2 Sam 6:17; 7:1-17). This so bothered David that he couldn't sleep until he corrected the situation. He began to lay the plans for the Temple to house the Ark. (Eventually the Temple was built by his son Solomon.) We must live so close to God that we become restless until God's will is accomplished through us.

Ps 132:11-12 The promise that David's sons would sit on Israel's throne forever (2 Sam 7:8-29) had two parts: (1) David's descendants would perpetually rule over Israel as long as they followed God, and (2) David's royal line would never end. The first part was conditional: As long as the kings obeyed God ("obey the terms of my covenant"), their dynasty continued. The second part of the promise was unconditional: It was fulfilled in Jesus Christ, a descendant of David, who reigns forever.

Ps 132:17-18 The "increase" of David's power refers to one of his mighty descen-

Psalm 134

THEME: Worship God and experience the joy of his blessings.

AUTHOR: Anonymous, some suggest Hezekiah

A song for pilgrims ascending to Jerusalem.

1 Oh, praise the LORD, all you servants of the LORD,
you who serve at night in the house of the LORD.
2 Lift up holy hands in prayer,
and praise the LORD.

3 May the LORD, who made heaven and earth,
bless you from Jerusalem.*

Psalm 135

THEME: A hymn of praise. This psalm contrasts the greatness of God with the powerlessness of idols. Pagans worship idols while God's people worship the living God.

AUTHOR: Anonymous

1 Praise the LORD!

Praise the name of the LORD!
Praise him, you who serve the LORD,
2 you who serve in the house of the LORD,
in the courts of the house of our God.

3 Praise the LORD, for the LORD is good;
celebrate his lovely name with music.
4 For the LORD has chosen Jacob for himself,
Israel for his own special treasure.

5 I know the greatness of the LORD—
that our Lord is greater than any other god.
6 The LORD does whatever pleases him
throughout all heaven and earth,
and on the seas and in their depths.
7 He causes the clouds to rise over the whole earth.
He sends the lightning with the rain
and releases the wind from his storehouses.

8 He destroyed the firstborn in each Egyptian home,
both people and animals.
9 He performed miraculous signs and wonders
in Egypt
against Pharaoh and all his people.
10 He struck down great nations
and slaughtered mighty kings—
11 Sihon king of the Amorites,
Og king of Bashan,
and all the kings of Canaan.
12 He gave their land as an inheritance,
a special possession to his people Israel.

13 Your name, O LORD, endures forever;
your fame, O LORD, is known to every
generation.
14 For the LORD will give justice to his people
and have compassion on his servants.

15 The idols of the nations are merely things
of silver and gold,
shaped by human hands.
16 They have mouths but cannot speak,
and eyes but cannot see.
17 They have ears but cannot hear,
and noses but cannot smell.
18 And those who make idols are just like them,
as are all who trust in them.

19 O Israel, praise the LORD!
O priests—descendants of Aaron—praise
the LORD!
20 O Levites, praise the LORD!
All you who fear the LORD, praise the LORD!

Ps 134:3 Hebrew *Zion.*

PRAISE IN THE BOOK OF PSALMS

Most of the psalms are prayers, and most of the prayers include praise to God. Praise expresses admiration, appreciation, and thanks. Praise in the book of Psalms is often directed to God, and just as often the praise is shared with others. Considering all that God has done, is doing, and will do for us, what could be more natural than outbursts of heartfelt praise?

As you read Psalms, note the praise given to God, not only for what he does—his creation, his blessings, his forgiveness—but also for who he is—loving, just, faithful, forgiving, patient. Note also those times when the praise of God is shared with others and they, too, are encouraged to praise him. In what ways have you recently praised God or told others all that he has done for you?

Selected psalms that emphasize this theme: Pss 8; 19; 30; 65; 84; 96; 100; 136; 145; 150

dants. David's son Solomon was indeed a glorious king (1 Kgs 3:10-14); but these verses look ahead even further to another descendant of David, Jesus the Messiah (Matt 1:17). The power, might, and glory of the Messiah will last forever.

Ps 134:1-3 This psalm is about a very small group—the Levites who served as Temple watchmen. Singing this psalm, the last of the "songs of ascent" (Pss 120–134), the worshipers would ascend the hill where the Temple sat and see the watchmen who protected it day and night. They saw the watchmen's work as an act of praise to God, done reverently and responsibly. Make your job or your responsibility in the church an act of praise by doing it with reverence. Honor God by the quality of your work and the attitude of service you bring to it.

Ps 135:4 That the descendants of Jacob (Israel) were a chosen people reflects God's commission to the nation (Deut 7:6-8) and later to the church (see 1 Pet 2:9). God treasures us. He gives love and mercy to all those who believe in him.

Ps 135:15-18 Those who worshiped idols were as blind and insensitive as the idols themselves. They couldn't see or hear what God had to say. In subtle, imperceptible ways we become like the idols we worship. If the true God is your God, you will become more like him as you worship him. What are your goals? What takes priority in your life? Choose carefully because you will take on the characteristics of whatever you worship.

▸ PSALM 135 *(cont.)*

21 The LORD be praised from Zion,
for he lives here in Jerusalem.

Praise the LORD!

Psalm 136

THEME: The never-ending story of God's love. God deserves our praise because his endless love never fails.

AUTHOR: Anonymous

1 Give thanks to the LORD, for he is good!
His faithful love endures forever.
2 Give thanks to the God of gods.
His faithful love endures forever.
3 Give thanks to the Lord of lords.
His faithful love endures forever.
4 Give thanks to him who alone does mighty
miracles.
His faithful love endures forever.
5 Give thanks to him who made the heavens so
skillfully.
His faithful love endures forever.
6 Give thanks to him who placed the earth among
the waters.
His faithful love endures forever.
7 Give thanks to him who made the heavenly
lights—
His faithful love endures forever.
8 the sun to rule the day,
His faithful love endures forever.
9 and the moon and stars to rule the night.
His faithful love endures forever.
10 Give thanks to him who killed the firstborn
of Egypt.
His faithful love endures forever.
11 He brought Israel out of Egypt.
His faithful love endures forever.
12 He acted with a strong hand and powerful arm.
His faithful love endures forever.
13 Give thanks to him who parted the Red Sea.*
His faithful love endures forever.
14 He led Israel safely through,
His faithful love endures forever.
15 but he hurled Pharaoh and his army into the
Red Sea.
His faithful love endures forever.
16 Give thanks to him who led his people through
the wilderness.
His faithful love endures forever.
17 Give thanks to him who struck down mighty kings.
His faithful love endures forever.
18 He killed powerful kings—
His faithful love endures forever.
19 Sihon king of the Amorites,
His faithful love endures forever.
20 and Og king of Bashan.
His faithful love endures forever.
21 God gave the land of these kings as an
inheritance—
His faithful love endures forever.
22 a special possession to his servant Israel.
His faithful love endures forever.
23 He remembered us in our weakness.
His faithful love endures forever.
24 He saved us from our enemies.
His faithful love endures forever.
25 He gives food to every living thing.
His faithful love endures forever.
26 Give thanks to the God of heaven.
His faithful love endures forever.

Ps 136:13 Hebrew *sea of reeds;* also in 136:15.

Psalm 146

THEME: The help of people versus the help of God. Help from people is temporal and unstable, but help from God is lasting and complete.

AUTHOR: Anonymous

1 Praise the LORD!

Let all that I am praise the LORD.
2 I will praise the LORD as long as I live.
I will sing praises to my God with my dying
breath.
3 Don't put your confidence in powerful people;
there is no help for you there.
4 When they breathe their last, they return to the
earth,
and all their plans die with them.

Ps 136:1ff Repeated throughout this psalm is the phrase "His faithful love endures forever." This psalm may have been a responsive reading, with the congregation saying these words in unison after each sentence. The repetition made this important lesson sink in. God's love includes aspects of love, kindness, mercy, and faithfulness. We never have to worry that God will run out of love because it flows from a well that will never run dry.

Pss 146–150 The last five psalms overflow with praise. Each begins and ends with "Praise the LORD." They show us where, why, and how to praise God. What does praise do? (1) Praise takes our mind off our problems and shortcomings and helps us focus on God. (2) Praise leads us from individual meditation to corporate worship. (3) Praise causes us to consider and appreciate God's character. (4) Praise lifts our perspective from the earthly to the heavenly. (5) Praise prepares our hearts to receive God's love and the power of his Holy Spirit.

Ps 146:3-8 The writer portrays powerful people as inadequate saviors, making false promises they cannot deliver (Ps 146:3). God is the hope and the help of the needy. Jesus affirms his concern for the poor and afflicted in Luke 4:18-21; 7:21-23. He does not separate the physical needs from spiritual needs but attends to both. While God is the hope of the needy, *we* are his instruments to help here on earth.

5 But joyful are those who have the God of Israel*
as their helper,
whose hope is in the LORD their God.
6 He made heaven and earth,
the sea, and everything in them.
He keeps every promise forever.
7 He gives justice to the oppressed
and food to the hungry.
The LORD frees the prisoners.
8 The LORD opens the eyes of the blind.
The LORD lifts up those who are weighed down.
The LORD loves the godly.
9 The LORD protects the foreigners among us.
He cares for the orphans and widows,
but he frustrates the plans of the wicked.
10 The LORD will reign forever.
He will be your God, O Jerusalem,* throughout
the generations.

Praise the LORD!

Psalm 148

THEME: Let all creation praise and worship the Lord.

AUTHOR: Anonymous

1 Praise the LORD!

Praise the LORD from the heavens!
Praise him from the skies!
2 Praise him, all his angels!
Praise him, all the armies of heaven!
3 Praise him, sun and moon!
Praise him, all you twinkling stars!
4 Praise him, skies above!
Praise him, vapors high above the clouds!
5 Let every created thing give praise to the LORD,
for he issued his command, and they came
into being.
6 He set them in place forever and ever.
His decree will never be revoked.
7 Praise the LORD from the earth,
you creatures of the ocean depths,
8 fire and hail, snow and clouds,*
wind and weather that obey him,
9 mountains and all hills,
fruit trees and all cedars,
10 wild animals and all livestock,
small scurrying animals and birds,
11 kings of the earth and all people,
rulers and judges of the earth,
12 young men and young women,
old men and children.

13 Let them all praise the name of the LORD.
For his name is very great;
his glory towers over the earth and heaven!
14 He has made his people strong,
honoring his faithful ones—
the people of Israel who are close to him.

Praise the LORD!

Psalm 149

THEME: A victory celebration. We have the assurance that God truly enjoys his people.

AUTHOR: Anonymous

1 Praise the LORD!

Sing to the LORD a new song.
Sing his praises in the assembly of the faithful.
2 O Israel, rejoice in your Maker.
O people of Jerusalem,* exult in your King.
3 Praise his name with dancing,
accompanied by tambourine and harp.
4 For the LORD delights in his people;
he crowns the humble with victory.
5 Let the faithful rejoice that he honors them.
Let them sing for joy as they lie on their beds.
6 Let the praises of God be in their mouths,
and a sharp sword in their hands—
7 to execute vengeance on the nations
and punishment on the peoples,
8 to bind their kings with shackles
and their leaders with iron chains,
9 to execute the judgment written against them.
This is the glorious privilege of his faithful
ones.

Praise the LORD!

Ps 146:5 Hebrew *of Jacob.* See note on 44:4. **Ps 146:10** Hebrew *Zion.* **Ps 148:8** Or *mist,* or *smoke.* **Ps 149:2** Hebrew *Zion.*

Ps 146:9 God's plans frustrate the "plans of the wicked" because his values are the opposite of society's. Jesus turned society's values upside down when he proclaimed that "many who are the greatest now will be least important then, and those who are seem least important now will be the greatest then" (Matt 19:30). "If you try to hang on to your life, you will lose it. But if you give up your life for my sake, you will save it" (Matt 16:25). Don't be surprised when others don't understand your Christian values; but don't give in to theirs.

Ps 148:5-14 All creation is like a majestic symphony or a great choir composed of many harmonious parts that together offer up songs of praise to the Lord. Each part (independent, yet part of the whole) is caught up and carried along in swelling tides of praise. This is a picture of how we as believers should praise God—individually, yet as part of the great choir of believers worldwide. Are you singing your part well in the worldwide choir of praise?

Ps 149:3-5 Although the Bible invites us to praise God, we often aren't sure how to go about it. Here, several ways are suggested: singing, dancing, and playing musical instruments. God enjoys his people, and we should enjoy praising him.

Ps 149:6-7 The sharp sword symbolizes the completeness of judgment that the Messiah will execute when he returns to punish all evildoers (Rev 1:16).

Psalm 150

THEME: A closing hymn of praise. God's creation praises him everywhere in every way. We should join this rejoicing song of praise.

AUTHOR: Anonymous

1 Praise the LORD!

Praise God in his sanctuary;
praise him in his mighty heaven!
2 Praise him for his mighty works;
praise his unequaled greatness!
3 Praise him with a blast of the ram's horn;
praise him with the lyre and harp!
4 Praise him with the tambourine and dancing;
praise him with strings and flutes!
5 Praise him with a clash of cymbals;
praise him with loud clanging cymbals.
6 Let everything that breathes sing praises to the LORD!

Praise the LORD!

5. MESSAGES FROM ISAIAH FOR MANY NATIONS

Isaiah's prophecies against Ethiopia, Babylon, Jerusalem, and Tyre may have been given between 714 and 701 B.C. During this time Ethiopia allied itself with Assyria in an attempt to gain control of Egypt.

A Message about Ethiopia

ISAIAH 18:1-7

1 Listen, Ethiopia*—land of fluttering sails*
that lies at the headwaters of the Nile,
2 that sends ambassadors
in swift boats down the river.

Go, swift messengers!
Take a message to a tall, smooth-skinned people,
who are feared far and wide
for their conquests and destruction,
and whose land is divided by rivers.
3 All you people of the world,
everyone who lives on the earth—
when I raise my battle flag on the mountain, look!
When I blow the ram's horn, listen!
4 For the LORD has told me this:
"I will watch quietly from my dwelling place—
as quietly as the heat rises on a summer day,
or as the morning dew forms during the harvest."
5 Even before you begin your attack,
while your plans are ripening like grapes,
the LORD will cut off your new growth with pruning shears.
He will snip off and discard your spreading branches.
6 Your mighty army will be left dead in the fields
for the mountain vultures and wild animals.

Is 18:1a Hebrew *Cush.* **Is 18:1b** Or *land of many locusts;* Hebrew reads *land of whirring wings.*

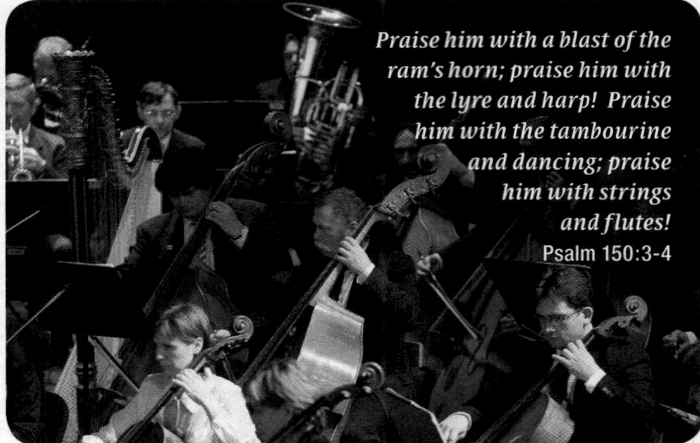
Praise him with a blast of the ram's horn; praise him with the lyre and harp! Praise him with the tambourine and dancing; praise him with strings and flutes!
Psalm 150:3-4

Ps 150:3-5 Music and song were an integral part of Old Testament worship. David introduced music into the Tabernacle and Temple services (1 Chr 16:4-7). The music must have been loud and joyous as evidenced by the list of instruments and the presence of choirs and song leaders. Music was also important in New Testament worship (Eph 5:19; Col 3:16).

Ps 150:6 How could the message be more clear? The writer was telling the individual listeners to praise God. What a fitting way to end this book of praise—with direct encouragement for you to praise God too. Remember to praise him every day!

Ps 150:6 In a way, the book of Psalms parallels our spiritual journey through life. It begins by presenting us with two roads: the way to life and the way to death. If we choose God's way to life, we still face both blessings and troubles, joy and grief, successes and obstacles. Through it all, God is at our side, guiding, encouraging, comforting, and caring. As the wise and faithful person's life draws to an end, it becomes clear that God's road is the right road. Knowing this will cause us to praise God for leading us in the right direction and for assuring us of a place in the perfect world he has in store for those who have faithfully followed him.

Isa 18:1ff This prophecy was probably given in the days of Hezekiah (2 Kgs 19–20). The king of Ethiopia had heard that Assyria's army was marching south toward them. He sent messengers up the Nile asking the surrounding nations to form an alliance. Judah was also asked to join, but Isaiah told the messengers to return home because Judah needed only God's help to repel the Assyrians. Isaiah prophesied that Assyria would be destroyed at the proper time (Isa 37:21-38).

Isa 18:3 This is a signal of Ethiopia's doom and Assyria's victory over Ethiopia (see Isa 20:1-6).

The vultures will tear at the corpses all
summer.
The wild animals will gnaw at the bones
all winter.
7 At that time the LORD of Heaven's Armies
will receive gifts
from this land divided by rivers,
from this tall, smooth-skinned people,
who are feared far and wide for their
conquests and destruction.
They will bring the gifts to Jerusalem,*
where the LORD of Heaven's Armies dwells.

A Message about Egypt

ISAIAH 19:1-25

This message came to me concerning Egypt:

Look! The LORD is advancing against Egypt,
riding on a swift cloud.
The idols of Egypt tremble.
The hearts of the Egyptians melt with fear.

2 "I will make Egyptian fight against Egyptian—
brother against brother,
neighbor against neighbor,
city against city,
province against province.
3 The Egyptians will lose heart,
and I will confuse their plans.
They will plead with their idols for wisdom
and call on spirits, mediums, and those
who consult the spirits of the dead.
4 I will hand Egypt over
to a hard, cruel master.
A fierce king will rule them,"
says the Lord, the LORD of Heaven's Armies.

5 The waters of the Nile will fail to rise and
flood the fields.
The riverbed will be parched and dry.
6 The canals of the Nile will dry up,
and the streams of Egypt will stink
with rotting reeds and rushes.
7 All the greenery along the riverbank
and all the crops along the river
will dry up and blow away.
8 The fishermen will lament for lack of work.
Those who cast hooks into the Nile will groan,
and those who use nets will lose heart.
9 There will be no flax for the harvesters,
no thread for the weavers.
10 They will be in despair,
and all the workers will be sick at heart.

11 What fools are the officials of Zoan!
Their best counsel to the king of Egypt is
stupid and wrong.
Will they still boast to Pharaoh of their wisdom?
Will they dare brag about all their wise
ancestors?
12 Where are your wise counselors, Pharaoh?
Let them tell you what God plans,
what the LORD of Heaven's Armies is going
to do to Egypt.
13 The officials of Zoan are fools,
and the officials of Memphis* are deluded.
The leaders of the people
have led Egypt astray.
14 The LORD has sent a spirit of foolishness on them,
so all their suggestions are wrong.
They cause Egypt to stagger
like a drunk in his vomit.
15 There is nothing Egypt can do.
All are helpless—
the head and the tail,
the noble palm branch and the lowly reed.

16 In that day the Egyptians will be as weak as
women. They will cower in fear beneath the upraised
fist of the LORD of Heaven's Armies. 17 Just to speak

Is 18:7 Hebrew *to Mount Zion.* **Is 19:13** Hebrew *Noph.*

Isa 19:1 Egypt, the nation where God's people were enslaved for 400 years (Exod 1), was hated by the people of Israel. Yet Judah was considering an alliance with Egypt against Assyria (2 Kgs 18:17ff). Isaiah warned against this alliance because God would destroy Assyria in his time.

Isa 19:11-15 Egypt was noted for its wisdom, but here its wise men and counselors were deceived and foolish. True wisdom can come only from God. We must ask him for wisdom to guide our decisions, or we will also be uncertain and misdirected. Are you confused about something in your life now? Ask God for wisdom to deal with it.

Papyrus

The Egyptian bulrush or papyrus has smooth, three-sided stems ordinarily attaining a height of 8 to 10 feet (sometimes even 16 feet), and a thickness of two to three inches at the base with a large tuft of florets at the end. The papyrus formerly grew in great abundance along the banks of the Nile, forming what was almost a dense jungle. The pale, fawn-colored, tassel-like inflorescences at the summit of the stems were used to adorn Egyptian temples and to crown the statues of gods. Papyrus was also used for making small vessels and for making paper.

Significantly, papyrus manuscripts have survived in Egypt for over 2,000 years. Numerous copies of books of the Bible written on papyrus have been recovered. Many of these date to the 1st, 2nd, or 3rd centuries A.D., providing the earliest copies of the New Testament. Scholars use these to make editions of the Greek New Testament, which are then translated. The next time you pick up a modern English Bible, be thankful for all the papyrus manuscripts that have been discovered.

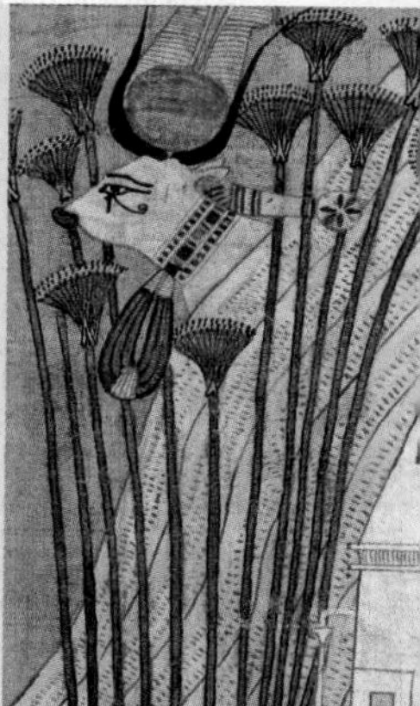

▸ **ISAIAH 19:1-25** ***(cont.)***

the name of Israel will terrorize them, for the LORD of Heaven's Armies has laid out his plans against them.

18In that day five of Egypt's cities will follow the LORD of Heaven's Armies. They will even begin to speak Hebrew, the language of Canaan. One of these cities will be Heliopolis, the City of the Sun.*

19In that day there will be an altar to the LORD in the heart of Egypt, and there will be a monument to the LORD at its border. 20It will be a sign and a witness that the LORD of Heaven's Armies is worshiped in the land of Egypt. When the people cry to the LORD for help against those who oppress them, he will send them a savior who will rescue them. 21The LORD will make himself known to the Egyptians. Yes, they will know the LORD and will give their sacrifices and offerings to him. They will make a vow to the LORD and will keep it. 22The LORD will strike Egypt, and then he will bring healing. For the Egyptians will turn to the LORD, and he will listen to their pleas and heal them.

23In that day Egypt and Assyria will be connected by a highway. The Egyptians and Assyrians will move freely between their lands, and they will both worship God. 24And Israel will be their ally. The three will be together, and Israel will be a blessing to them. 25For the LORD of Heaven's Armies will say, "Blessed be Egypt, my people. Blessed be Assyria, the land I have made. Blessed be Israel, my special possession!"

A Message about Egypt and Ethiopia

ISAIAH 20:1-6

In the year when King Sargon of Assyria sent his commander in chief to capture the Philistine city of Ashdod,* 2the LORD told Isaiah son of Amoz, "Take off the burlap you have been wearing, and remove your sandals." Isaiah did as he was told and walked around naked and barefoot.

3Then the LORD said, "My servant Isaiah has been walking around naked and barefoot for the last three years. This is a sign—a symbol of the terrible troubles I will bring upon Egypt and Ethiopia.* 4For the king of Assyria will take away the Egyptians and Ethiopians* as prisoners. He will make them walk naked and barefoot, both young and old, their buttocks bared, to the shame of Egypt. 5Then the Philistines will be thrown into panic, for they counted on the power of Ethiopia and boasted of their allies in Egypt! 6They will say, 'If this can happen to Egypt, what chance do we have? We were counting on Egypt to protect us from the king of Assyria.'"

A Message about Babylon

ISAIAH 21:1-10

This message came to me concerning Babylon—the desert by the sea*:

Disaster is roaring down on you from the desert,
  like a whirlwind sweeping in from the Negev.

Is 19:18 Or *will be the City of Destruction.* **Is 20:1** Ashdod was captured by Assyria in 711 B.C. **Is 20:3** Hebrew *Cush;* also in 20:5. **Is 20:4** Hebrew *Cushites.* **Is 21:1** Hebrew *concerning the desert by the sea.*

ALLIANCES TODAY

Isaiah warned Judah not to ally with Egypt (Isa 20:5; 30:1-2; 31:1). He knew that trust in any nation or any military might was futile. Judah's only hope was to trust in God. Although we don't consciously put our hope for deliverance in political alliances in quite the same way, we often put our hope in other places.

Government	We rely on government legislation to protect the moral decisions we want made, but legislation cannot change people's hearts.
Science	We enjoy the benefits of science and technology. We look to scientific predictions and analysis before we look to the Bible.
Education	We act as though education and degrees can guarantee our future and success without considering what God plans for our future.
Medical care	We regard medicine as the way to prolong life and preserve its quality—quite apart from faith and moral living.
Financial systems	We place our faith in financial "security"—making as much money as we can for ourselves—forgetting that, while being wise with our money, we must trust God for our needs.

Isa 19:19, 23 After Egypt's chastening, it would turn from idols and worship the one true God. Even more amazing is Isaiah's prophecy that the two chief oppressors of Israel, Egypt and Assyria, would unite in worship. This prophecy will come true "in that day," the future day when Christ comes to reign.

Isa 19:20 When Egypt calls to God for help, he will send a savior to deliver them. Our Savior, Jesus Christ, is available to all who call upon him. We, too, can pray and receive his saving power (John 1:12).

Isa 19:23-25 In Jesus Christ, former enemies may unite in love. In Christ, people and nations that are poles apart politically will bow at his feet as brothers and sisters. Christ breaks down every barrier that threatens relationships (see Eph 2:13-19).

Isa 20:1ff Sargon II was king of Assyria from 722–705 B.C.; this event happened in 711 B.C. Isaiah graphically reminds Judah that they should not count on foreign alliances to protect them.

Isa 20:2 God's command to Isaiah to walk about naked for three years was a humiliating experience. God was using Isaiah to demonstrate the humiliation that Egypt and Ethiopia would experience at the hands of Assyria. But the message was really for Judah: Don't put your trust in foreign governments, or you will experience this kind of shame from your captors. Human governments and institutions can never take God's place.

Isa 20:2 God asked Isaiah to do something that seemed shameful and illogical. At times, God may ask us to take steps we don't understand. We must obey God in complete faith, for he will never ask us to do something wrong.

Isa 21:1ff Some scholars say this prophecy was fulfilled at Babylon's fall in 539 B.C. (see Dan 5). But others say this was a prophecy of Babylon's revolt against Assyria around 700 B.C.

2 I see a terrifying vision:
I see the betrayer betraying,
the destroyer destroying.
Go ahead, you Elamites and Medes,
attack and lay siege.
I will make an end
to all the groaning Babylon caused.
3 My stomach aches and burns with pain.
Sharp pangs of anguish are upon me,
like those of a woman in labor.
I grow faint when I hear what God is planning;
I am too afraid to look.
4 My mind reels and my heart races.
I longed for evening to come,
but now I am terrified of the dark.

5 Look! They are preparing a great feast.
They are spreading rugs for people
to sit on.
Everyone is eating and drinking.
But quick! Grab your shields and prepare
for battle.
You are being attacked!
6 Meanwhile, the Lord said to me,
"Put a watchman on the city wall.
Let him shout out what he sees.
7 He should look for chariots
drawn by pairs of horses,
and for riders on donkeys and camels.
Let the watchman be fully alert."

8 Then the watchman* called out,
"Day after day I have stood on the watchtower,
my lord.
Night after night I have remained
at my post.
9 Now at last—look!
Here comes a man in a chariot
with a pair of horses!"
Then the watchman said,
"Babylon is fallen, fallen!
All the idols of Babylon
lie broken on the ground!"
10 O my people, threshed and winnowed,
I have told you everything the LORD
of Heaven's Armies has said,
everything the God of Israel has told me.

A Message about Edom

ISAIAH 21:11-12

This message came to me concerning Edom*:

Someone from Edom* keeps calling to me,
"Watchman, how much longer until morning?
When will the night be over?"
12 The watchman replies,
"Morning is coming, but night will soon
return.
If you wish to ask again, then come back
and ask."

A Message about Arabia

ISAIAH 21:13-17

This message came to me concerning Arabia:

O caravans from Dedan,
hide in the deserts of Arabia.
14 O people of Tema,
bring water to these thirsty people,
food to these weary refugees.
15 They have fled from the sword,
from the drawn sword,
from the bent bow
and the terrors of battle.

16The Lord said to me, "Within a year, counting each
day,* all the glory of Kedar will come to an end. 17Only
a few of its courageous archers will survive. I, the LORD,
the God of Israel, have spoken!"

Is 21:8 As in Dead Sea Scrolls and Syriac version; Masoretic Text reads *a lion.* **Is 21:11a** Hebrew *Dumah,* which means "silence" or "stillness." It is a wordplay on the word *Edom.* **Is 21:11b** Hebrew *Seir,* another name for Edom. **Is 21:16** Hebrew *Within a year, as a servant bound by contract would count it.* Some ancient manuscripts read *Within three years,* as in 16:14.

Isa 21:5 If the prophecy refers to the fall of Babylon in 539 B.C., this may picture the feast in Daniel 5.

Isa 21:6-7 Watchmen on the city walls often appear in prophetic visions of destruction. They are the first to see trouble coming. The prophet Habakkuk was a watchman (Hab 2:1). The vision of the riders on horses could represent the Medes and Persians attacking Babylon in 539 B.C.

Isa 21:8-9 Babylon was not only a great and powerful city, but it was also filled with horrible sin (idolatry, witchcraft, and temple prostitution). Babylon was, and remains, a symbol of all that stands against God. Despite all its glory and power, Babylon would be destroyed, along with all its idols. They would give no help in time of trouble.

Isa 21:10 Threshing and winnowing were two steps in ancient Israel's farming process. The heads of wheat (often used to symbolize Israel) were first trampled to break open the seeds and expose the valued grain inside (threshing). The seeds were then thrown into the air, and the worthless chaff would blow away while the grain would fall back to the ground (winnowing). Israel would experience this same kind of process: The sinful, rebellious people (worthless chaff) would be taken away, but God would keep the good "grain" to replenish Israel.

Isa 21:11 Edom had been a constant enemy of God's people. It rejoiced when Israel fell to the Assyrians, and this sealed Edom's doom (Isa 34:8ff; 63:4). Seir was another name for Edom because the hill country of Seir was given to Esau and his descendants (see Josh 24:4). Obadiah foretells, in great detail, the destruction of Edom.

Isa 21:13ff The places listed here are all in Arabia. They are border cities that controlled the trade routes throughout the land. This is Isaiah's prediction of disaster.

A Message about Jerusalem

ISAIAH 22:1-14

This message came to me concerning Jerusalem—the Valley of Vision*:

What is happening?
  Why is everyone running to the rooftops?
2 The whole city is in a terrible uproar.
  What do I see in this reveling city?
Bodies are lying everywhere,
  killed not in battle but by famine and disease.
3 All your leaders have fled.
  They surrendered without resistance.
The people tried to slip away,
  but they were captured, too.
4 That's why I said, "Leave me alone to weep;
  do not try to comfort me.
Let me cry for my people
  as I watch them being destroyed."

5 Oh, what a day of crushing defeat!
  What a day of confusion and terror
brought by the Lord, the LORD of Heaven's Armies,
  upon the Valley of Vision!
The walls of Jerusalem have been broken,
  and cries of death echo from the mountainsides.
6 Elamites are the archers,
  with their chariots and charioteers.
  The men of Kir hold up the shields.
7 Chariots fill your beautiful valleys,
  and charioteers storm your gates.
8 Judah's defenses have been stripped away.
  You run to the armory* for your weapons.
9 You inspect the breaks in the walls of Jerusalem.*
  You store up water in the lower pool.
10 You survey the houses and tear some down
  for stone to strengthen the walls.
11 Between the city walls, you build a reservoir
  for water from the old pool.
But you never ask for help from the One who did all this.
  You never considered the One who planned this long ago.

12 At that time the Lord, the LORD of Heaven's Armies,
  called you to weep and mourn.
He told you to shave your heads in sorrow for your sins
  and to wear clothes of burlap to show your remorse.
13 But instead, you dance and play;
  you slaughter cattle and kill sheep.
  You feast on meat and drink wine.
You say, "Let's feast and drink,
  for tomorrow we die!"

14 The LORD of Heaven's Armies has revealed this to me: "Till the day you die, you will never be forgiven for this sin." That is the judgment of the Lord, the LORD of Heaven's Armies.

A Message for Shebna

ISAIAH 22:15-25

This is what the Lord, the LORD of Heaven's Armies, said to me: "Confront Shebna, the palace administrator, and give him this message:

16 "Who do you think you are,
  and what are you doing here,
building a beautiful tomb for yourself—
  a monument high up in the rock?
17 For the LORD is about to hurl you away, mighty man.
  He is going to grab you,

Is 22:1 Hebrew *concerning the Valley of Vision.* **Is 22:8** Hebrew *to the House of the Forest;* see 1 Kgs 7:2-5. **Is 22:9** Hebrew *the city of David.*

Isa 22:1-13 "The Valley of Vision" refers to the city of Jerusalem, where God revealed himself. Jerusalem would be attacked unless God's people returned to him. Instead, they used every means of protection possible except asking God for help. They wanted to trust in their ingenuity, their weapons, and even their pagan neighbors (see 2 Chr 32 for a description of a siege of Jerusalem).

Isa 22:4 Isaiah had warned his people, but they did not repent; thus, they experienced God's judgment. Because he cared about them, Isaiah was hurt by their punishment and mourned for them. Sometimes people we care about ignore our attempts to help, so they suffer the very grief we wanted to spare them. At times like that we grieve because of our concern. God expects us to be involved with others, and this may sometimes require us to suffer with them.

Isa 22:6-7 Elam and Kir were under Assyrian rule. The entire Assyrian army, including its vassals, joined in the attack against Jerusalem.

Isa 22:8-11 The leaders of Judah did what they could to prepare for war: They got weapons, inspected the walls, and stored up water in a reservoir. But all their work was pointless because they never asked God for help. Too often we take steps that, although good in themselves, really won't give us the help we need. We must get the weapons and inspect the walls, but God must guide the work.

Isa 22:13-14 The people said, "Let's feast and drink," because they had given up hope. Attacked on every side (Isa 22:7), they should have repented (Isa 22:12), but they chose to feast instead. The root problem was that Judah did not trust God's power or his promises (see Isa 56:12; 1 Cor 15:32). Today we still see people living without hope. There are two common responses to hopelessness: despair and self-indulgence. But we need not act as if we had no hope. As we face difficulties, our proper response should be to trust God and his promises.

Isa 22:15-25 Shebna, the palace administrator, was just as materialistic as the rest of the people in Jerusalem (Isa 22:13). He may have been in the group favoring an alliance with foreigners, thus ignoring Isaiah's advice. The Lord revealed that Shebna would lose his position and be replaced by Eliakim (Isa 22:20). Eliakim would be the "nail in the wall" driven firmly in place (Isa 22:23). Unfortunately, Eliakim would also fall (Isa 22:25).

[18] crumple you into a ball,
and toss you away into a distant, barren land.
There you will die,
and your glorious chariots will be broken
and useless.
You are a disgrace to your master!

[19]"Yes, I will drive you out of office," says the LORD.
"I will pull you down from your high position. [20]And
then I will call my servant Eliakim son of Hilkiah to
replace you. [21]I will dress him in your royal robes
and will give him your title and your authority. And
he will be a father to the people of Jerusalem and
Judah. [22]I will give him the key to the house of David—the highest position in the royal court. When
he opens doors, no one will be able to close them;
when he closes doors, no one will be able to open
them. [23]He will bring honor to his family name, for
I will drive him firmly in place like a nail in the wall.
[24]They will give him great responsibility, and he will
bring honor to even the lowliest members of his
family.*"

[25]But the LORD of Heaven's Armies also says:
"The time will come when I will pull out the nail
that seemed so firm. It will come out and fall to the
ground. Everything it supports will fall with it. I, the
LORD, have spoken!"

A Message about Tyre

ISAIAH 23:1-18

This message came to me concerning Tyre:

Weep, O ships of Tarshish,
for the harbor and houses of Tyre are gone!
The rumors you heard in Cyprus*
are all true.
[2] Mourn in silence, you people of the coast
and you merchants of Sidon.
Your traders crossed the sea,
[3] sailing over deep waters.
They brought you grain from Egypt*
and harvests from along the Nile.
You were the marketplace of the world.

[4] But now you are put to shame, city of Sidon,
for Tyre, the fortress of the sea, says,
"Now I am childless;
I have no sons or daughters."
[5] When Egypt hears the news about Tyre,
there will be great sorrow.
[6] Send word now to Tarshish!
Wail, you people who live in distant lands!
[7] Is this silent ruin all that is left of your once
joyous city?
What a long history was yours!

Is 22:24 Hebrew *They will hang on him all the glory of his father's house: its offspring and offshoots, all its lesser vessels, from the bowls to all the jars.* **Is 23:1** Hebrew *Kittim;* also in 23:12. **Is 23:3** Hebrew *from Shihor,* a branch of the Nile River.

Isa 23:1ff Isaiah's prophecies against other nations began in the east with Babylon (Isa 13) and ended in the west with Tyre in Phoenicia. Tyre was one of the most famous cities of the ancient world. A major trading center with a large seaport, Tyre was very wealthy and very evil. Tyre was also rebuked by Jeremiah (Jer 25:22, 27; 47:4), Ezekiel (Ezek 26–28), Joel (Joel 3:4-8), Amos (Amos 1:9-10), and Zechariah (Zech 9:3-4). This is another warning against political alliances with unstable neighbors.

Isa 23:5 Why would Egypt experience "great sorrow" when Tyre fell? Egypt depended on Tyre's shipping expertise to promote and carry their products around the world. Egypt would lose an important trading partner with the fall of Tyre.

Chariots

By the second half of the second millennium B.C., the two great powers, the Hittites and the Egyptians, were equipped with horse-drawn chariots, as were many of the small Aramaean and Canaanite city-states of Syro-Palestine. In the first millennium B.C., the Assyrians developed the chariot as one of their principal weapons, and it became an essential element in plains warfare.

In general, the chariot was of very light construction, wood and leather used extensively, and only the necessary fittings being of bronze or iron. The car was usually open at the back, with receptacles for spears. The wheels generally had six spokes. It was drawn typically by two horses. The crew consisted of two to four men. The chariot was obviously of main service in campaigns on flat country but could be a handicap in irregular terrain.

The Israelites usually didn't use chariots in their warfare. And even if they did, they were exhorted to trust in God rather than chariots (Ps 20:7). We need to trust in God for victory in the battles of our lives as well.

▶ **ISAIAH 23:1-18** ***(cont.)***

Think of all the colonists you sent to distant
places.

8 Who has brought this disaster on Tyre,
that great creator of kingdoms?
Her traders were all princes,
her merchants were nobles.
9 The LORD of Heaven's Armies has done it
to destroy your pride
and bring low all earth's nobility.
10 Come, people of Tarshish,
sweep over the land like the flooding Nile,
for Tyre is defenseless.*
11 The LORD held out his hand over the sea
and shook the kingdoms of the earth.
He has spoken out against Phoenicia,*
ordering that her fortresses be destroyed.
12 He says, "Never again will you rejoice,
O daughter of Sidon, for you have been crushed.
Even if you flee to Cyprus,
you will find no rest."

13 Look at the land of Babylonia*—
the people of that land are gone!
The Assyrians have handed Babylon over
to the wild animals of the desert.
They have built siege ramps against its walls,
torn down its palaces,
and turned it to a heap of rubble.

14 Wail, O ships of Tarshish,
for your harbor is destroyed!

15 For seventy years, the length of a king's life, Tyre
will be forgotten. But then the city will come back to
life as in the song about the prostitute:

16 Take a harp and walk the streets,
you forgotten harlot.
Make sweet melody and sing your songs
so you will be remembered again.

17 Yes, after seventy years the LORD will revive Tyre.
But she will be no different than she was before. She
will again be a prostitute to all kingdoms around the
world. 18 But in the end her profits will be given to the
LORD. Her wealth will not be hoarded but will provide
good food and fine clothing for the LORD's priests.

Destruction of the Earth

ISAIAH 24:1-23

1 Look! The LORD is about to destroy the earth
and make it a vast wasteland.
He devastates the surface of the earth
and scatters the people.
2 Priests and laypeople,
servants and masters,
maids and mistresses,
buyers and sellers,
lenders and borrowers,
bankers and debtors—none will be spared.
3 The earth will be completely emptied and looted.
The LORD has spoken!

4 The earth mourns and dries up,
and the crops waste away and wither.
Even the greatest people on earth waste away.
5 The earth suffers for the sins of its people,
for they have twisted God's instructions,
violated his laws,
and broken his everlasting covenant.
6 Therefore, a curse consumes the earth.
Its people must pay the price for their sin.
They are destroyed by fire,
and only a few are left alive.
7 The grapevines waste away,
and there is no new wine.
All the merrymakers sigh and mourn.
8 The cheerful sound of tambourines is stilled;
the happy cries of celebration are heard
no more.
The melodious chords of the harp are silent.
9 Gone are the joys of wine and song;
alcoholic drink turns bitter in the mouth.
10 The city writhes in chaos;
every home is locked to keep out intruders.
11 Mobs gather in the streets, crying out for wine.
Joy has turned to gloom.
Gladness has been banished from the land.

Is 23:10 The meaning of the Hebrew in this verse is uncertain. **Is 23:11** Hebrew *Canaan.* **Is 23:13** Or *Chaldea.*

Isa 23:9 God would destroy Tyre because he hated its people's pride. Pride separates people from God, and he will not tolerate it. As we examine our own lives, we must remember that all true accomplishment comes as a result of our Creator's help. We have no reason to take pride in ourselves.

Isa 23:15-16 Some scholars believe this is a literal 70 years; some say it is symbolic of a long period of time. If it is literal, this may have occurred between 700 and 630 B.C. during the Assyrian captivity of Israel, or it may have been during the 70-year captivity of the Jews in Babylon (605–536 B.C.). During the 70 years, the Jews would forget about Tyre. But when they returned from captivity, they would once again trade with Tyre.

Isa 24–27 These four chapters are often called "Isaiah's Apocalypse." They discuss God's judgment on the entire world for its sin. Isaiah's prophecies were first directed to Judah, then to Israel, then to the surrounding nations, and finally to the whole world. These chapters describe the last days when God will judge the whole world. At that time he will finally and permanently remove evil.

Isa 24:4-5 Not only the people suffered from their sins; even the land suffered the effects of evil and lawbreaking. Today we see the results of sin in our own land: pollution, crime, addiction, poverty. Sin affects every aspect of society so extensively that even those faithful to God suffer. We cannot blame God for these conditions because sin has brought them about. The more we who are believers renounce sin, speak against immoral practices, and share God's Word with others, the more we slow our society's deterioration. We must not give up: Sin is rampant, but we can make a difference.

Isa 24:14-16 The believers who are left behind after God judges Judah will sing

12 The city is left in ruins,
its gates battered down.
13 Throughout the earth the story is the same—
only a remnant is left,
like the stray olives left on the tree
or the few grapes left on the vine after harvest.

14 But all who are left shout and sing for joy.
Those in the west praise the LORD's majesty.
15 In eastern lands, give glory to the LORD.
In the lands beyond the sea, praise the name of the LORD, the God of Israel.
16 We hear songs of praise from the ends of the earth,
songs that give glory to the Righteous One!

But my heart is heavy with grief.
Weep for me, for I wither away.
Deceit still prevails,
and treachery is everywhere.
17 Terror and traps and snares will be your lot,
you people of the earth.
18 Those who flee in terror will fall into a trap,
and those who escape the trap will be caught in a snare.
Destruction falls like rain from the heavens;
the foundations of the earth shake.
19 The earth has broken up.
It has utterly collapsed;
it is violently shaken.
20 The earth staggers like a drunk.
It trembles like a tent in a storm.
It falls and will not rise again,
for the guilt of its rebellion is very heavy.

21 In that day the LORD will punish the gods in the heavens
and the proud rulers of the nations on earth.
22 They will be rounded up and put in prison.
They will be shut up in prison
and will finally be punished.
23 Then the glory of the moon will wane,
and the brightness of the sun will fade,
for the LORD of Heaven's Armies will rule on Mount Zion.
He will rule in great glory in Jerusalem,
in the sight of all the leaders of his people.

Praise for Judgment and Salvation

ISAIAH 25:1-12

1 O LORD, I will honor and praise your name,
for you are my God.
You do such wonderful things!
You planned them long ago,
and now you have accomplished them.
2 You turn mighty cities into heaps of ruins.
Cities with strong walls are turned to rubble.
Beautiful palaces in distant lands disappear
and will never be rebuilt.
3 Therefore, strong nations will declare your glory;
ruthless nations will fear you.
4 But you are a tower of refuge to the poor, O LORD,
a tower of refuge to the needy in distress.
You are a refuge from the storm
and a shelter from the heat.
For the oppressive acts of ruthless people
are like a storm beating against a wall,
5 or like the relentless heat of the desert.
But you silence the roar of foreign nations.
As the shade of a cloud cools relentless heat,
so the boastful songs of ruthless people are stilled.

6 In Jerusalem,* the LORD of Heaven's Armies
will spread a wonderful feast
for all the people of the world.
It will be a delicious banquet
with clear, well-aged wine and choice meat.
7 There he will remove the cloud of gloom,
the shadow of death that hangs over the earth.
8 He will swallow up death forever!*
The Sovereign LORD will wipe away all tears.

Is 25:6 Hebrew *On this mountain;* also in 25:10. **Is 25:8** Greek version reads *Death is swallowed up in victory.* Compare 1 Cor 15:54.

to the glory of God's righteousness. Isaiah grieved because of his world's condition. We, too, can become depressed by the evil all around us. At those times we need to hold on to God's promises for the future and look forward to singing praises to him when he restores heaven and earth.

Isa 24:21 "The gods in the heavens" refer to spiritual forces opposed to God. Nobody, not even the so-called gods, will escape due punishment.

Isa 25:1 Isaiah honored and praised God because he realized that God completes his plans as promised. God also fulfills his promises to you. Think of the prayers he has answered, and praise him for his goodness and faithfulness.

Isa 25:4 The poor suffered because ruthless people oppressed them. But God is concerned for the poor and is a refuge for them. When we are disadvantaged or oppressed, we can turn to God for comfort and help. Jesus states that the Kingdom of God belongs to the poor (Luke 6:20).

Isa 25:6 Here is a marvelous prophecy of "all the people of the world"—Gentiles and Jews together—at God's messianic feast, celebrating the overthrow of evil and the joy of eternity with God. It shows that God intended his saving message to go out to the whole world, not just to the Jews. During the feast, God will end death forever (Isa 25:7-8). The people who participate in this great feast will be those who have been living by faith. That is why they say, "This is our God! We trusted in him, and he saved us!" (Isa 25:9). (See Isa 55 for another presentation of this great feast.)

Isa 25:8 When the Lord speaks, he does what he says. It is comforting to know that God's plans and activities are closely tied to his Word. When we pray according to God's will (as expressed in the Bible), he hears us and answers our requests.

Isa 25:8 Part of this verse (quoted in 1 Cor 15:54) describes Christ's victory over death. God's ultimate victory is when death, our final enemy, is defeated (see also Hos 13:14). Another part of this verse (quoted in Rev 21:4) describes the glorious scene of God's presence with his people.

▸ **ISAIAH 25:1-12** ***(cont.)***

He will remove forever all insults and mockery
against his land and people.
The LORD has spoken!
9 In that day the people will proclaim,
"This is our God!
We trusted in him, and he saved us!
This is the LORD, in whom we trusted.
Let us rejoice in the salvation he brings!"
10 For the LORD's hand of blessing will rest on
Jerusalem.
But Moab will be crushed.
It will be like straw trampled down and left
to rot.
11 God will push down Moab's people
as a swimmer pushes down water with his
hands.
He will end their pride
and all their evil works.
12 The high walls of Moab will be demolished.
They will be brought down to the ground,
down into the dust.

A Song of Praise to the LORD

ISAIAH 26:1-19

In that day, everyone in the land of Judah will sing
this song:

Our city is strong!
We are surrounded by the walls of God's
salvation.
2 Open the gates to all who are righteous;
allow the faithful to enter.
3 You will keep in perfect peace
all who trust in you,
all whose thoughts are fixed on you!
4 Trust in the LORD always,
for the LORD GOD is the eternal Rock.
5 He humbles the proud
and brings down the arrogant city.
He brings it down to the dust.
6 The poor and oppressed trample it underfoot,
and the needy walk all over it.
7 But for those who are righteous,
the way is not steep and rough.
You are a God who does what is right,
and you smooth out the path ahead of them.
8 LORD, we show our trust in you by obeying
your laws;
our heart's desire is to glorify your name.
9 All night long I search for you;
in the morning I earnestly seek for God.
For only when you come to judge the earth
will people learn what is right.
10 Your kindness to the wicked
does not make them do good.
Although others do right, the wicked keep
doing wrong
and take no notice of the LORD's majesty.
11 O LORD, they pay no attention to your
upraised fist.
Show them your eagerness to defend your
people.
Then they will be ashamed.
Let your fire consume your enemies.
12 LORD, you will grant us peace;
all we have accomplished is really from you.
13 O LORD our God, others have ruled us,
but you alone are the one we worship.
14 Those we served before are dead and gone.
Their departed spirits will never return!
You attacked them and destroyed them,
and they are long forgotten.
15 O LORD, you have made our nation great;
yes, you have made us great.
You have extended our borders,
and we give you the glory!
16 LORD, in distress we searched for you.
We prayed beneath the burden of your
discipline.
17 Just as a pregnant woman
writhes and cries out in pain as she gives birth,
so were we in your presence, LORD.
18 We, too, writhe in agony,
but nothing comes of our suffering.

Isa 25:10 Moab was a symbol of all who oppose God and are rebellious to the end. Moab was Israel's enemy for years (see the note on Isa 15:1, p. 833).

Isa 26:1ff People will praise God in the Day of the Lord when Christ establishes his Kingdom (see Isa 12). Isaiah 26 is a psalm of trust, praise, and meditation. Once more, God revealed the future to Isaiah.

Isa 26:3 We can never avoid strife in the world around us, but when we fix our thoughts on God, we can know perfect peace even in turmoil. As we focus our mind on God and his Word, we become steady and stable. Supported by God's unchanging love and mighty power, we are not shaken by the surrounding chaos (see Phil 4:7). Do you want peace? Keep your thoughts on God and your trust in him.

Isa 26:7-8 At times the "path" of the righteous doesn't seem smooth, and it isn't easy to do God's will, but we are never alone when we face tough times. God is there to help us, to comfort us, and to lead us. God does this by giving us a purpose (keeping our mind centered on him, Isa 26:3) and giving us provisions as we travel. God provides us with relationships of family, friends, and mentors. God gives us wisdom to make decisions and faith to trust him. Don't despair; stay on God's path.

Isa 26:10 Even wicked people receive God's benefits, but that doesn't teach them to do what is right. Sometimes God's judgment teaches us more than God's good gifts. If you have been enriched by God's goodness and grace, respond to him with your grateful devotion.

Isa 26:16-19 The people realized the pain of being away from God's presence, and yet they were assured that they would live again. God turned his back on his people when they disobeyed, but a small number never lost hope and continued to seek him. No matter how difficult times may be, we have hope when we keep our trust in him. Can you wait patiently for God to act?

We have not given salvation to the earth,
nor brought life into the world.
19 But those who die in the LORD will live;
their bodies will rise again!
Those who sleep in the earth
will rise up and sing for joy!
For your life-giving light will fall like dew
on your people in the place of the dead!

Restoration for Israel

ISAIAH 26:20–27:13

20 Go home, my people,
and lock your doors!
Hide yourselves for a little while
until the LORD's anger has passed.
21 Look! The LORD is coming from heaven
to punish the people of the earth for their sins.
The earth will no longer hide those who have
been killed.
They will be brought out for all to see.

27:1 In that day the LORD will take his terrible, swift
sword and punish Leviathan,* the swiftly moving
serpent, the coiling, writhing serpent. He will kill the
dragon of the sea.

2 "In that day,
sing about the fruitful vineyard.
3 I, the LORD, will watch over it,
watering it carefully.
Day and night I will watch so no one can
harm it.
4 My anger will be gone.
If I find briers and thorns growing,
I will attack them;
I will burn them up—
5 unless they turn to me for help.
Let them make peace with me;
yes, let them make peace with me."

6 The time is coming when Jacob's descendants
will take root.
Israel will bud and blossom
and fill the whole earth with fruit!

7 Has the LORD struck Israel
as he struck her enemies?
Has he punished her
as he punished them?
8 No, but he exiled Israel to call her to account.
She was exiled from her land
as though blown away in a storm from
the east.
9 The LORD did this to purge Israel's* wickedness,
to take away all her sin.
As a result, all the pagan altars will be crushed
to dust.
No Asherah pole or pagan shrine will be left
standing.
10 The fortified towns will be silent and empty,
the houses abandoned, the streets overgrown
with weeds.
Calves will graze there,
chewing on twigs and branches.
11 The people are like the dead branches of a tree,
broken off and used for kindling beneath the
cooking pots.
Israel is a foolish and stupid nation,
for its people have turned away from God.
Therefore, the one who made them
will show them no pity or mercy.

12 Yet the time will come when the LORD will gather
them together like handpicked grain. One by one he
will gather them—from the Euphrates River* in the
east to the Brook of Egypt in the west. 13 In that day
the great trumpet will sound. Many who were dying
in exile in Assyria and Egypt will return to Jerusalem
to worship the LORD on his holy mountain.

Is 27:1 The identification of Leviathan is disputed, ranging from an earthly creature to a mythical sea monster in ancient literature. **Is 27:9** Hebrew *Jacob's.* See note on 14:1. **Is 27:12** Hebrew *the river.*

Isa 26:19 Some people say there is no life after death. Others believe that there is, but it is not physical life. But Isaiah tells us that our bodies shall rise again. According to 1 Corinthians 15:50-53, all the dead believers will arise with new, imperishable bodies—bodies like the one Jesus had when he was resurrected (see Phil 3:21). Isaiah 26:19 is not the only Old Testament verse to speak about the resurrection of the dead (see also Job 19:26; Ps 16:10; Dan 12:2, 13).

Isa 26:20-21 When God comes to judge the earth, the guilty will find no place to hide. Jesus said that the hidden will be made known because his truth, like a light shining in a dark corner, will reveal it (Matt 10:26). Instead of trying to hide your shameful thoughts and actions from God, confess them to him and receive his forgiveness.

Isa 27:1 "That day" is a reference to the end of the evil world as we know it. In ancient Aramean (Ugaritic) literature, Leviathan was a seven-headed monster, the enemy of God's created order. Thus, Isaiah is comparing God's slaughter of the wicked to the conquering of a great enemy. Although evil is a powerful foe, God will crush it and abolish it from the earth forever.

Isa 27:2-6 The trampled vineyard of Isaiah 5 will be restored in God's new earth. God will protect and care for the vineyard, his people. It will no longer produce worthless fruit but will produce enough good fruit for the whole world. Gentiles will come to know God through Israel.

Isa 27:9 Only God can take away sin, but to be driven out of the land was considered the penalty that would purify God's people. Deuteronomy 28:49-52, 64 explains God's warning about these consequences.

Isa 27:11 Isaiah compares the state of Israel's spiritual life with dead branches of a tree that are broken off and used to make fires. Trees in Scripture often represent spiritual life. The trunk is the channel of strength from God; the branches are the people who serve him. Tree branches sometimes waver and blow in the wind. Like Israel, they may dry up from internal rottenness and become useless for anything except building a fire. What kind of branch are you? If you are withering spiritually, check to see if you are firmly attached to God.

A Message about Jerusalem

ISAIAH 29:1-24

1 "What sorrow awaits Ariel,* the City of David.
Year after year you celebrate your feasts.
2 Yet I will bring disaster upon you,
and there will be much weeping and sorrow.
For Jerusalem will become what her name Ariel means—
an altar covered with blood.
3 I will be your enemy,
surrounding Jerusalem and attacking its walls.
I will build siege towers
and destroy it.
4 Then deep from the earth you will speak;
from low in the dust your words will come.
Your voice will whisper from the ground
like a ghost conjured up from the grave.

5 "But suddenly, your ruthless enemies will be crushed
like the finest of dust.
Your many attackers will be driven away
like chaff before the wind.
Suddenly, in an instant,
6 I, the LORD of Heaven's Armies, will act for you
with thunder and earthquake and great noise,
with whirlwind and storm and consuming fire.
7 All the nations fighting against Jerusalem*
will vanish like a dream!
Those who are attacking her walls
will vanish like a vision in the night.
8 A hungry person dreams of eating
but wakes up still hungry.
A thirsty person dreams of drinking
but is still faint from thirst when morning comes.
So it will be with your enemies,
with those who attack Mount Zion."

9 Are you amazed and incredulous?
Don't you believe it?
Then go ahead and be blind.
You are stupid, but not from wine!
You stagger, but not from liquor!
10 For the LORD has poured out on you a spirit of deep sleep.
He has closed the eyes of your prophets and visionaries.

11 All the future events in this vision are like a sealed
book to them. When you give it to those who can read,
they will say, "We can't read it because it is sealed."
12 When you give it to those who cannot read, they will
say, "We don't know how to read."

13 And so the Lord says,
"These people say they are mine.
They honor me with their lips,
but their hearts are far from me.
And their worship of me
is nothing but man-made rules learned by rote.*
14 Because of this, I will once again astound these hypocrites
with amazing wonders.
The wisdom of the wise will pass away,
and the intelligence of the intelligent will disappear."

15 What sorrow awaits those who try to hide their plans from the LORD,
who do their evil deeds in the dark!
"The LORD can't see us," they say.
"He doesn't know what's going on!"
16 How foolish can you be?
He is the Potter, and he is certainly greater than you, the clay!
Should the created thing say of the one who made it,
"He didn't make me"?
Does a jar ever say,
"The potter who made me is stupid"?

17 Soon—and it will not be very long—
the forests of Lebanon will become a fertile field,
and the fertile field will yield bountiful crops.
18 In that day the deaf will hear words read from a book,
and the blind will see through the gloom and darkness.
19 The humble will be filled with fresh joy from the LORD.
The poor will rejoice in the Holy One of Israel.

Is 29:1 *Ariel* sounds like a Hebrew term that means "hearth" or "altar." **Is 29:7** Hebrew *Ariel.* **Is 29:13** Greek version reads *Their worship is a farce, / for they teach man-made ideas as commands from God.* Compare Mark 7:7.

Isa 29:1 Ariel is a special name for Jerusalem, David's city. It may mean "lion of God" (Jerusalem is strong as a lion) or "altar hearth" (Jerusalem is the place of the altar in the Temple; see Isa 29:2; Ezek 43:15-16).

Isa 29:13-14 The people claimed to be close to God, but they were disobedient and merely went through the motions; therefore, God would bring judgment upon them. Religion had become routine instead of real. Jesus quoted Isaiah's condemnation of Israel's hypocrisy when he spoke to the Pharisees, the religious leaders of his day (Matt 15:7-9; Mark 7:6-7). We are all capable of hypocrisy. Often we slip into routine patterns when we worship, and we neglect to give God our love and devotion. If we want to be called God's people, we must be obedient and worship him honestly and sincerely.

Isa 29:15 Thinking God couldn't see them and didn't know what was happening, the people of Jerusalem tried to hide their plans from him. How strange that so many people think they can hide from God. In Psalm 139 we learn that God has examined us and knows everything about us. Would you be embarrassed if your best friends knew your personal thoughts? Remember that God knows all of them.

Isa 29:17-24 The world described here, under Christ's rule, will be far different from the one we live in today. There will be no more violence or gloom. This new world will be characterized by joy, understanding, justice, and praise to God.

20 The scoffer will be gone,
the arrogant will disappear,
and those who plot evil will be killed.
21 Those who convict the innocent
by their false testimony will disappear.
A similar fate awaits those who use trickery
to pervert justice
and who tell lies to destroy the innocent.

22 That is why the LORD, who redeemed Abraham, says
to the people of Israel,*

"My people will no longer be ashamed
or turn pale with fear.
23 For when they see their many children
and all the blessings I have given them,
they will recognize the holiness of the Holy One
of Israel.
They will stand in awe of the God of Jacob.
24 Then the wayward will gain understanding,
and complainers will accept instruction.

Judah's Worthless Treaty with Egypt

ISAIAH 30:1-7

1 "What sorrow awaits my rebellious children,"
says the LORD.
"You make plans that are contrary to mine.
You make alliances not directed by
my Spirit,
thus piling up your sins.
2 For without consulting me,
you have gone down to Egypt for help.
You have put your trust in Pharaoh's protection.
You have tried to hide in his shade.
3 But by trusting Pharaoh, you will be humiliated,
and by depending on him, you will be
disgraced.
4 For though his power extends to Zoan
and his officials have arrived in Hanes,
5 all who trust in him will be ashamed.
He will not help you.
Instead, he will disgrace you."

6 This message came to me concerning the animals
in the Negev:

The caravan moves slowly
across the terrible desert to Egypt—
donkeys weighed down with riches
and camels loaded with treasure—
all to pay for Egypt's protection.
They travel through the wilderness,
a place of lionesses and lions,
a place where vipers and poisonous
snakes live.
All this, and Egypt will give you nothing
in return.
7 Egypt's promises are worthless!
Therefore, I call her Rahab—
the Harmless Dragon.*

Is 29:22 Hebrew *of Jacob.* See note on 14:1. **Is 30:7** Hebrew *Rahab who sits still.* Rahab is the name of a mythical sea monster that represents chaos in ancient literature. The name is used here as a poetic name for Egypt.

Isa 30:1 The rebellious children are the people of Judah (see Isa 1:2), those who have rebelled against God. The negotiations for an alliance were underway, and Isaiah condemned their twisted plans. The people of Judah sought advice from everyone but God. When we are driven by fear, we tend to search everywhere for comfort, advice, and relief, hoping to find an easy way out of our troubles. Instead, we should consult God. Although he gives emergency help in a crisis, he prefers to be our guide throughout our life. By reading his Word and actively seeking to do his will, we can maintain our bond with him who provides stability no matter what the crisis.

Isa 30:2ff Hezekiah had been seeking a defensive alliance with Egypt against Sennacherib of Assyria (see 2 Kgs 18:21).

Isa 30:6 This message is directed to those who carried bribes to Egypt through the desert in the Negev region.

Isa 30:7 This Harmless Dragon (also called Rahab) was a mythological female sea monster associated with Leviathan (see the note on Isa 27:1, p. 897; see also Job 9:13; 26:12). It was a name associated with Egypt, where hippopotamuses, perhaps a likeness to Rahab, sat on the Nile River and did nothing.

Isaiah Scroll

The Dead Sea Scrolls are one of the most important archaeological discoveries of modern times. In 1947 some Bedouins discovered several scrolls, including a scroll of the book of Isaiah, in jars in a cave overlooking the Dead Sea. The Shrine of the Book in Jerusalem houses this famous Isaiah scroll. It is the best preserved of all the manuscripts discovered at Qumran. It is practically complete and is older by about 1,000 years than any other known Hebrew manuscript of a complete Old Testament book. What a precious discovery!

A Warning for Rebellious Judah

ISAIAH 30:8-17

8 Now go and write down these words.
Write them in a book.
They will stand until the end of time
as a witness
9 that these people are stubborn rebels
who refuse to pay attention to the LORD's
instructions.
10 They tell the seers,
"Stop seeing visions!"
They tell the prophets,
"Don't tell us what is right.
Tell us nice things.
Tell us lies.
11 Forget all this gloom.
Get off your narrow path.
Stop telling us about your
'Holy One of Israel.'"

12 This is the reply of the Holy One of Israel:

"Because you despise what I tell you
and trust instead in oppression
and lies,
13 calamity will come upon you suddenly—
like a bulging wall that bursts and falls.
In an instant it will collapse
and come crashing down.
14 You will be smashed like a piece of pottery—
shattered so completely that
there won't be a piece big enough
to carry coals from a fireplace
or a little water from the well."

15 This is what the Sovereign LORD,
the Holy One of Israel, says:
"Only in returning to me
and resting in me will you be saved.
In quietness and confidence is your strength.
But you would have none of it.
16 You said, 'No, we will get our help from
Egypt.
They will give us swift horses for riding
into battle.'
But the only swiftness you are going to see
is the swiftness of your enemies chasing you!
17 One of them will chase a thousand of you.
Five of them will make all of you flee.
You will be left like a lonely flagpole on a hill
or a tattered banner on a distant
mountaintop."

Blessings for the LORD's People

ISAIAH 30:18-33

18 So the LORD must wait for you to come to him
so he can show you his love and compassion.
For the LORD is a faithful God.
Blessed are those who wait for his help.
19 O people of Zion, who live in Jerusalem,
you will weep no more.
He will be gracious if you ask for help.
He will surely respond to the sound
of your cries.
20 Though the Lord gave you adversity for food
and suffering for drink,
he will still be with you to teach you.
You will see your teacher with your own eyes.
21 Your own ears will hear him.
Right behind you a voice will say,
"This is the way you should go,"
whether to the right or to the left.
22 Then you will destroy all your silver idols
and your precious gold images.
You will throw them out like filthy rags,
saying to them, "Good riddance!"

23 Then the LORD will bless you with rain at planting time. There will be wonderful harvests and
plenty of pastureland for your livestock. 24 The
oxen and donkeys that till the ground will eat good
grain, its chaff blown away by the wind. 25 In that
day, when your enemies are slaughtered and the
towers fall, there will be streams of water flowing
down every mountain and hill. 26 The moon will be
as bright as the sun, and the sun will be seven times
brighter—like the light of seven days in one! So it
will be when the LORD begins to heal his people and
cure the wounds he gave them.

Isa 30:10-11 Some people in Judah may have sought refuge in Egypt. In their desire to find security, they wanted to hear only good news. They did not welcome the truth from God's prophets. Often the truth makes us uncomfortable. We prefer lies and illusions when they make us feel more secure. It is much better to face reality than to live a lie. Don't settle for something that makes you feel comfortable but is not true.

Isa 30:15 God warned Judah that turning to Egypt and other nations for military might could not save them. Only God could do that. They must wait for him "in quietness and confidence." No amount of fast talking or hasty activity could speed up God's grand design. We have nothing to say to God but thank you. Salvation comes from God alone. Because he has saved us, we can trust him and be peacefully confident that he will give us strength to face our difficulties. We should lay aside our well-laid plans and allow him to act.

Isa 30:20 The Lord gave his people adversity for food and suffering for drink, but he promised to be with them, teach them, and guide them during hard times. God expects a lot from us, and many times following him can be painful; but he always acts out of his love for us. Next time you go through a difficult time, try to appreciate the experience and grow from it, learning what God wants to teach you. God may be showing you his love by patiently walking with you through adversity.

Isa 30:21 When the people of Jerusalem left God's path, he would correct them. He will do the same for us. But when we hear his voice of correction, we must be willing to follow it!

27 Look! The LORD is coming from far away,
burning with anger,
surrounded by thick, rising smoke.
His lips are filled with fury;
his words consume like fire.
28 His hot breath pours out like a flood
up to the neck of his enemies.
He will sift out the proud nations for destruction.
He will bridle them and lead them away
to ruin.
29 But the people of God will sing a song of joy,
like the songs at the holy festivals.
You will be filled with joy,
as when a flutist leads a group of pilgrims
to Jerusalem, the mountain of the LORD—
to the Rock of Israel.
30 And the LORD will make his majestic voice heard.
He will display the strength of his
mighty arm.
It will descend with devouring flames,
with cloudbursts, thunderstorms, and huge
hailstones.
31 At the LORD's command, the Assyrians will be
shattered.
He will strike them down with his royal
scepter.
32 And as the LORD strikes them with his rod of
punishment,
his people will celebrate with tambourines
and harps.
Lifting his mighty arm, he will fight the
Assyrians.
33 Topheth—the place of burning—
has long been ready for the Assyrian king;
the pyre is piled high with wood.
The breath of the LORD, like fire from a volcano,
will set it ablaze.

The Futility of Relying on Egypt

ISAIAH 31:1-9

1 What sorrow awaits those who look to Egypt
for help,
trusting their horses, chariots, and
charioteers
and depending on the strength of human
armies
instead of looking to the LORD,
the Holy One of Israel.
2 In his wisdom, the LORD will send great disaster;
he will not change his mind.
He will rise against the wicked
and against their helpers.
3 For these Egyptians are mere humans, not God!
Their horses are puny flesh, not mighty
spirits!
When the LORD raises his fist against them,
those who help will stumble,
and those being helped will fall.
They will all fall down and die together.

4 But this is what the LORD has told me:

"When a strong young lion
stands growling over a sheep it has killed,
it is not frightened by the shouts and noise
of a whole crowd of shepherds.
In the same way, the LORD of Heaven's Armies
will come down and fight on Mount Zion.
5 The LORD of Heaven's Armies will hover over
Jerusalem
and protect it like a bird protecting its nest.
He will defend and save the city;
he will pass over it and rescue it."

6 Though you are such wicked rebels, my people,
come and return to the LORD. 7 I know the glorious day
will come when each of you will throw away the gold
idols and silver images your sinful hands have made.

8 "The Assyrians will be destroyed,
but not by the swords of men.
The sword of God will strike them,
and they will panic and flee.
The strong young Assyrians
will be taken away as captives.
9 Even the strongest will quake with terror,
and princes will flee when they see your
battle flags,"
says the LORD, whose fire burns in Zion,
whose flame blazes from Jerusalem.

Isa 30:27 The judgment of God will be accompanied by thick, rising smoke and words that consume like fire (see Isa 33:14; Luke 12:49; Heb 12:29). Some people who were brought up in a church but dropped out complain about the preaching of the wrath of God. Yet his wrath and anger are very real and are designed for the rebellious and for those who hate God, not for those who are humble and love him. Are you one of God's people? Help others discover God's love so that his wrath will never be an issue for them.

Isa 31:1 It was wrong for Judah to look to other nations for military help. (1) They were trusting in human beings instead of God. Judah sought protection from those who were powerless when compared to God. Both Egypt and Judah would fall as a result of their arrogance. (2) They were serving their own interests instead of God's, and thus they did not even consult him. They violated God's stipulation in Deuteronomy 17:16. (3) They did not want to pay the price of looking to God and repenting of their sinful ways. When we have problems, it is good to seek help, but we must never bypass God or his previous directions to us.

Isa 31:7 Someday these people would throw their idols away, recognizing that they were nothing but human-made objects. Idols such as money, fame, or success are seductive. Instead of contributing to our spiritual development, they rob us of our time, energy, and devotion that ought to be directed toward God. At first our idols seem exciting and promise to take us places, but in the end we will find that we have become their slaves. We need to recognize their worthlessness now, before they rob us of our freedom.

Israel's Ultimate Deliverance

ISAIAH 32:1-20

1 Look, a righteous king is coming!
And honest princes will rule under him.
2 Each one will be like a shelter from the wind
and a refuge from the storm,
like streams of water in the desert
and the shadow of a great rock in a parched land.
3 Then everyone who has eyes will be able to see the truth,
and everyone who has ears will be able to hear it.
4 Even the hotheads will be full of sense and understanding.
Those who stammer will speak out plainly.
5 In that day ungodly fools will not be heroes.
Scoundrels will not be respected.
6 For fools speak foolishness
and make evil plans.
They practice ungodliness
and spread false teachings about the LORD.
They deprive the hungry of food
and give no water to the thirsty.
7 The smooth tricks of scoundrels are evil.
They plot crooked schemes.
They lie to convict the poor,
even when the cause of the poor is just.
8 But generous people plan to do what is generous,
and they stand firm in their generosity.
9 Listen, you women who lie around in ease.
Listen to me, you who are so smug.
10 In a short time—just a little more than a year—
you careless ones will suddenly begin to care.
For your fruit crops will fail,
and the harvest will never take place.
11 Tremble, you women of ease;
throw off your complacency.
Strip off your pretty clothes,
and put on burlap to show your grief.
12 Beat your breasts in sorrow for your bountiful farms
and your fruitful grapevines.
13 For your land will be overgrown with thorns and briers.
Your joyful homes and happy towns will be gone.
14 The palace and the city will be deserted,
and busy towns will be empty.
Wild donkeys will frolic and flocks will graze
in the empty forts* and watchtowers
15 until at last the Spirit is poured out
on us from heaven.
Then the wilderness will become a fertile field,
and the fertile field will yield bountiful crops.
16 Justice will rule in the wilderness
and righteousness in the fertile field.
17 And this righteousness will bring peace.
Yes, it will bring quietness and confidence forever.
18 My people will live in safety, quietly at home.
They will be at rest.
19 Even if the forest should be destroyed
and the city torn down,
20 the LORD will greatly bless his people.
Wherever they plant seed, bountiful crops will spring up.
Their cattle and donkeys will graze freely.

A Message about Assyria

ISAIAH 33:1-24

1 What sorrow awaits you Assyrians, who have destroyed others*
but have never been destroyed yourselves.
You betray others,
but you have never been betrayed.
When you are done destroying,
you will be destroyed.
When you are done betraying,
you will be betrayed.

Is 32:14 Hebrew *the Ophel.* **Is 33:1** Hebrew *What sorrow awaits you, O destroyer.* The Hebrew text does not specifically name Assyria as the object of the prophecy in this chapter.

Isa 32:1 Having suffered much injustice from evil rulers, many in Judah were hungry for a strong king who would rule with justice. This "righteous king" will be Christ. Judah would be destroyed and taken into captivity. But one day, God's Son, a King unlike any other king, will reign in righteousness and rule with justice.

Isa 32:5-6 When the righteous king comes, people's motives will become transparent. Fools will not be regarded as heroes. Those who have opposed God's standards of living will be unable to maintain their deception. In the blazing light of the holy Savior, sin cannot disguise itself and appear good. Christ's revealing light shines into the darkest corners of our hearts, showing sin clearly for what it is. When King Jesus reigns in your heart, there is no place for sin, no matter how well hidden you may think it is.

Isa 32:9-13 The people turned their backs on God and concentrated on their own pleasures. This warning is not just to the women of Jerusalem (see Isa 3:16–4:1) but to all who sit back in their thoughtless complacency, enjoying crops, clothes, land, and cities while an enemy approaches. Wealth and luxury bring false security, lulling us into thinking all is well when disaster is around the corner. By abandoning God's purpose for our life, we also abandon his help.

Isa 32:15-17 God acts from above to change people's conditions here on earth. Only when God's Spirit is among us can we achieve true peace and fruitfulness (Ezek 36:22-38; Gal 5:22-23). The outpouring mentioned here will happen when the worldwide Kingdom of God is established for all eternity (see Joel 2:28-29). But we can also have God's Spirit with us *now*, for he is available to all believers through Christ (John 15:26).

Isa 33:1 Assyria continually broke its promises but demanded that others keep theirs. It is easy to put ourselves in the same selfish position, demanding our rights while ignoring the rights of others. Broken promises shatter trust and destroy relationships. Determine to keep your promises; at the same time, ask forgiveness for past promises you have broken. Treat others with the same fairness that you demand for yourself.

2 But LORD, be merciful to us,
for we have waited for you.
Be our strong arm each day
and our salvation in times of trouble.
3 The enemy runs at the sound of your voice.
When you stand up, the nations flee!
4 Just as caterpillars and locusts strip the fields
and vines,
so the fallen army of Assyria will be stripped!

5 Though the LORD is very great and lives in heaven,
he will make Jerusalem* his home of justice
and righteousness.
6 In that day he will be your sure foundation,
providing a rich store of salvation, wisdom,
and knowledge.
The fear of the LORD will be your treasure.

7 But now your brave warriors weep in public.
Your ambassadors of peace cry in bitter
disappointment.
8 Your roads are deserted;
no one travels them anymore.
The Assyrians have broken their peace treaty
and care nothing for the promises they made
before witnesses.*
They have no respect for anyone.
9 The land of Israel wilts in mourning.
Lebanon withers with shame.
The plain of Sharon is now a wilderness.
Bashan and Carmel have been plundered.

10 But the LORD says: "Now I will stand up.
Now I will show my power and might.
11 You Assyrians produce nothing but dry grass
and stubble.
Your own breath will turn to fire and
consume you.
12 Your people will be burned up completely,
like thornbushes cut down and tossed in a fire.
13 Listen to what I have done, you nations far away!
And you that are near, acknowledge my might!"

14 The sinners in Jerusalem shake with fear.
Terror seizes the godless.
"Who can live with this devouring fire?" they cry.
"Who can survive this all-consuming fire?"
15 Those who are honest and fair,
who refuse to profit by fraud,
who stay far away from bribes,
who refuse to listen to those who plot murder,
who shut their eyes to all enticement to do
wrong—
16 these are the ones who will dwell on high.
The rocks of the mountains will be their
fortress.
Food will be supplied to them,
and they will have water in abundance.

17 Your eyes will see the king in all his splendor,
and you will see a land that stretches into the
distance.
18 You will think back to this time of terror, asking,
"Where are the Assyrian officers
who counted our towers?
Where are the bookkeepers
who recorded the plunder taken from our
fallen city?"
19 You will no longer see these fierce, violent
people
with their strange, unknown language.

20 Instead, you will see Zion as a place of holy
festivals.
You will see Jerusalem, a city quiet and
secure.
It will be like a tent whose ropes are taut
and whose stakes are firmly fixed.
21 The LORD will be our Mighty One.
He will be like a wide river of protection
that no enemy can cross,
that no enemy ship can sail upon.
22 For the LORD is our judge,
our lawgiver, and our king.
He will care for us and save us.
23 The enemies' sails hang loose
on broken masts with useless tackle.
Their treasure will be divided by the people
of God.
Even the lame will take their share!
24 The people of Israel will no longer say,
"We are sick and helpless,"
for the LORD will forgive their sins.

Is 33:5 Hebrew *Zion;* also in 33:14. **Is 33:8** As in Dead Sea Scrolls; Masoretic Text reads *care nothing for the cities.*

Isa 33:2 These are the words of the righteous remnant who were waiting for God to deliver them from their oppression.

Isa 33:4 See 2 Kings 19:20-37; Isaiah 37:21-38 for a description of the victory over Assyria described here.

Isa 33:5 When Christ's Kingdom is established, Jerusalem will be the home of justice and righteousness because the Messiah will reign there. As a light to the world, the new Jerusalem will be the holy city (Rev 21:2).

Isa 33:9 These fruitful, productive areas would become deserts. Lebanon was known for its huge cedars. Sharon was very fertile. Bashan was very productive in grain and cattle. Carmel was thickly forested.

Isa 33:14-16 These sinners realized that they could not live in the presence of the holy God, for he is like a fire that devours evil. Only those who walk uprightly and speak what is right can live with God. Isaiah gives examples of how to demonstrate our righteousness and uprightness: We can reject gain from extortion and bribes, refuse to listen to plots of wrong actions, and shut our eyes to evil. If we are fair and honest in our relationships, we will dwell with God, and he will supply our needs.

A Message for the Nations

ISAIAH 34:1-17

1 Come here and listen, O nations of the earth.
Let the world and everything in it hear
my words.
2 For the LORD is enraged against the nations.
His fury is against all their armies.
He will completely destroy* them,
dooming them to slaughter.
3 Their dead will be left unburied,
and the stench of rotting bodies will fill
the land.
The mountains will flow with their blood.
4 The heavens above will melt away
and disappear like a rolled-up scroll.
The stars will fall from the sky
like withered leaves from a grapevine,
or shriveled figs from a fig tree.

5 And when my sword has finished its work
in the heavens,
it will fall upon Edom,
the nation I have marked for destruction.
6 The sword of the LORD is drenched with blood
and covered with fat—
with the blood of lambs and goats,
with the fat of rams prepared for sacrifice.
Yes, the LORD will offer a sacrifice in the city
of Bozrah.
He will make a mighty slaughter in Edom.
7 Even men as strong as wild oxen will die—
the young men alongside the veterans.
The land will be soaked with blood
and the soil enriched with fat.

8 For it is the day of the LORD's revenge,
the year when Edom will be paid back
for all it did to Israel.*
9 The streams of Edom will be filled with
burning pitch,
and the ground will be covered with fire.
10 This judgment on Edom will never end;
the smoke of its burning will rise forever.
The land will lie deserted from generation to
generation.
No one will live there anymore.
11 It will be haunted by the desert owl and the
screech owl,
the great owl and the raven.*
For God will measure that land carefully;
he will measure it for chaos and destruction.
12 It will be called the Land of Nothing,
and all its nobles will soon be gone.*
13 Thorns will overrun its palaces;
nettles and thistles will grow in its forts.
The ruins will become a haunt for jackals
and a home for owls.
14 Desert animals will mingle there with hyenas,
their howls filling the night.
Wild goats will bleat at one another among
the ruins,
and night creatures* will come there to rest.
15 There the owl will make her nest and lay her eggs.
She will hatch her young and cover them with
her wings.
And the buzzards will come,
each one with its mate.

16 Search the book of the LORD,
and see what he will do.
Not one of these birds and animals will be missing,
and none will lack a mate,
for the LORD has promised this.
His Spirit will make it all come true.
17 He has surveyed and divided the land
and deeded it over to those creatures.
They will possess it forever,
from generation to generation.

Hope for Restoration

ISAIAH 35:1-10

1 Even the wilderness and desert will be glad
in those days.
The wasteland will rejoice and blossom with
spring crocuses.

Is 34:2 The Hebrew term used here refers to the complete consecration of things or people to the LORD, either by destroying them or by giving them as an offering; similarly in 34:5. **Is 34:8** Hebrew *to Zion.* **Is 34:11** The identification of some of these birds is uncertain. **Is 34:12** The meaning of the Hebrew is uncertain. **Is 34:14** Hebrew *Lilith,* possibly a reference to a mythical demon of the night.

Isa 34:5 The Edomites shared a common ancestry with Israel. The Israelites were descended from Jacob; the Edomites from Jacob's twin brother, Esau. Edom was always Israel's bitter enemy. The destruction of Edom mentioned here is a picture of the ultimate end of all who oppose God and his people.

Isa 34:16 Isaiah referred to the prophecies that God commanded him to write down as the "book of the LORD." Whoever lived to see the time of Edom's destruction would have only to look up these prophecies to find agreement between what happened and what was predicted. Prophecy predicts and history reveals what has been in God's mind for all time.

Isa 35:1ff In Isaiah 1–34, Isaiah has delivered a message of judgment on all nations, including Israel and Judah, for rejecting God. Although there have been glimpses of relief and restoration for the remnant of faithful believers, the climate of wrath, fury, judgment, and destruction has prevailed. Now Isaiah breaks through with a vision of beauty and encouragement. God is just as thorough in his mercy as he is severe in his judgment. God's complete moral perfection is revealed by his hatred of all sin, and this leads to judgment. This same moral perfection is revealed in his love for all he has created. This leads to mercy for those who have sinned but who have sincerely loved Jesus and put their trust in him.

Isa 35:1ff This chapter is a beautiful picture of the final Kingdom in which God will establish his justice and destroy all evil. This is the world the redeemed can anticipate after the judgment when creation itself will rejoice in God. Isaiah 34 spoke of great distress when God will judge all people for their actions. Isaiah 35 pictures the days when life will be peaceful at last and everything will be made right. Carmel and Sharon were regions of

2 Yes, there will be an abundance of flowers
and singing and joy!
The deserts will become as green as the mountains of Lebanon,
as lovely as Mount Carmel or the plain of Sharon.
There the LORD will display his glory,
the splendor of our God.
3 With this news, strengthen those who have tired hands,
and encourage those who have weak knees.
4 Say to those with fearful hearts,
"Be strong, and do not fear,
for your God is coming to destroy your enemies.
He is coming to save you."
5 And when he comes, he will open the eyes of the blind
and unplug the ears of the deaf.
6 The lame will leap like a deer,
and those who cannot speak will sing for joy!
Springs will gush forth in the wilderness,
and streams will water the wasteland.
7 The parched ground will become a pool,
and springs of water will satisfy the thirsty land.
Marsh grass and reeds and rushes will flourish
where desert jackals once lived.
8 And a great road will go through that once deserted land.
It will be named the Highway of Holiness.
Evil-minded people will never travel on it.
It will be only for those who walk in God's ways;
fools will never walk there.
9 Lions will not lurk along its course,
nor any other ferocious beasts.
There will be no other dangers.
Only the redeemed will walk on it.
10 Those who have been ransomed by the LORD will return.
They will enter Jerusalem* singing,
crowned with everlasting joy.
Sorrow and mourning will disappear,
and they will be filled with joy and gladness.

Is 35:10 Hebrew *Zion.*

6. MICAH'S PROPHECIES

This section represents the rest of the prophecies of Micah (chapter 1 was given earlier, p. 786). They were probably written shortly before Assyria invaded Judah, around 703 B.C. Micah emphasized the need for justice and peace. Like a lawyer, he set forth God's case against Israel and Judah, their leaders, and their people. He makes several prophecies about Jesus, the Messiah, who will mercifully gather the people again into one nation. Micah makes it clear that God hates unkindness, idolatry, injustice, and empty ritual; he still hates these today. But God is very willing to forgive the sins of any who repent.

Judgment against Wealthy Oppressors

MICAH 2:1-5

1 What sorrow awaits you who lie awake at night,
thinking up evil plans.
You rise at dawn and hurry to carry them out,
simply because you have the power to do so.
2 When you want a piece of land,
you find a way to seize it.
When you want someone's house,
you take it by fraud and violence.
You cheat a man of his property,
stealing his family's inheritance.
3 But this is what the LORD says:
"I will reward your evil with evil;
you won't be able to pull your neck out of the noose.
You will no longer walk around proudly,
for it will be a terrible time."
4 In that day your enemies will make fun of you
by singing this song of despair about you:
"We are finished,
completely ruined!
God has confiscated our land,
taking it from us.
He has given our fields
to those who betrayed us.*"

Mi 2:4 Or *to those who took us captive.*

thick vegetation and fertile soil. They were symbols of productivity and plenty.

Isa 35:8-10 This "Highway of Holiness" is the way that righteous pilgrims will take from the desert of suffering to Zion (Jerusalem). It is found only by following God. Only the redeemed will travel God's highway; they will be protected from wicked travelers and harmful animals. God is preparing a way for his people (those who walk in his ways) to travel to his home, and he will walk with us. God doesn't simply point the way; he is always beside us as we go.

Mic 2:1-2 Micah spoke out against those who planned evil deeds at night and rose at dawn to do them. Thoughts and plans reflect a person's character. What do you think about as you lie down to sleep? Do your desires involve greed or stepping on others to achieve your goals? Evil thoughts lead to evil deeds.

Mic 2:2 Micah warned against those who use their position to take advantage of others. Less than a century earlier, King Ahab of Israel had pouted because he couldn't get Naboth's vineyard. So his wife, Jezebel, had Naboth killed in order to give the garden to Ahab (1 Kgs 21:1-16). This kind of injustice had spread throughout the nation and, like a disease, was destroying the people from the inside out.

▸ **MICAH 2:1-5 *(cont.)***

5 Others will set your boundaries then,
and the LORD's people will have no say
in how the land is divided.

True and False Prophets

MICAH 2:6-11

6 "Don't say such things,"
the people respond.*
"Don't prophesy like that.
Such disasters will never come our way!"

7 Should you talk that way, O family of Israel?*
Will the LORD's Spirit have patience with such behavior?
If you would do what is right,
you would find my words comforting.
8 Yet to this very hour
my people rise against me like an enemy!
You steal the shirts right off the backs
of those who trusted you,
making them as ragged as men
returning from battle.
9 You have evicted women from their pleasant homes
and forever stripped their children of all that
God would give them.
10 Up! Begone!
This is no longer your land and home,
for you have filled it with sin
and ruined it completely.

11 Suppose a prophet full of lies would say to you,
"I'll preach to you the joys of wine and alcohol!"
That's just the kind of prophet you would like!

Hope for Restoration

MICAH 2:12-13

12 "Someday, O Israel, I will gather you;
I will gather the remnant who are left.
I will bring you together again like sheep in a pen,
like a flock in its pasture.
Yes, your land will again
be filled with noisy crowds!
13 Your leader will break out
and lead you out of exile,
out through the gates of the enemy cities,
back to your own land.
Your king will lead you;
the LORD himself will guide you."

Judgment against Israel's Leaders

MICAH 3:1-12

1 I said, "Listen, you leaders of Israel!
You are supposed to know right from wrong,
2 but you are the very ones
who hate good and love evil.

Mi 2:6 Or *the prophets respond;* Hebrew reads *they prophesy.* **Mi 2:7** Hebrew *O house of Jacob?* See note on 1:5a.

Mic 2:5 Those who have been oppressing others will find the tables turned. They will end up not having any share in the decisions to divide the land because they won't have any surviving relatives.

Mic 2:6-7 If these messages seem harsh, remember that God did not want to take revenge on Israel; he wanted to get them back on the right path. The people had rejected what was true and right, and they needed stern discipline. Children may think discipline is harsh, but it helps keep them going in the right direction. If we only want God's comforting messages, we may miss what he has for us. Listen whenever God speaks, even when the message is hard to take.

Mic 2:11 The people liked the false prophets who told them only what they wanted to hear. Micah spoke against prophets who encouraged the people to feel comfortable in their sin. Preachers are popular when they don't ask too much of us and when they tell us our greed or lust might even be good for us. But a true teacher of God speaks the truth, regardless of what the listeners want to hear.

Mic 2:12-13 Micah's prophecy telescopes two great events—Judah's return from captivity in Babylon, and the great gathering of all believers when the Messiah returns. God gave his prophets visions of various future events, but not necessarily the ability to discern when these events would happen. For example, they could not see the long period of time between the Babylonian captivity and the coming of the Messiah, but they could clearly see that the Messiah was coming. The purpose of this prophecy was not to predict exactly *how* and *when* this would occur but *that* it would. This gave the people hope and helped them turn from sin.

Mic 3:1ff Micah denounced the sins of the leaders, including priests and prophets—those responsible for teaching the people right from wrong. The leaders, who should have known the law and taught it to the people, had set the law aside and had become the worst of sinners. They were taking advantage of the very people they were supposed to serve. All sin is bad, but the sin that leads others astray is the worst of all.

Mic 3:1 The dividing line between right and wrong often seems blurred, but spiritual leaders are supposed to help others see it. The Bible is God's guidebook to show us how to distinguish right and wrong. Spiritual leaders must understand the Bible's principles, teach them clearly, and exemplify them in their lives. While leaders cannot force people to do right, they should point them in that direction.

MICAH'S CHARGES OF INJUSTICE

Micah charged the people with injustice of many kinds.

Plotting evil	**Mic 2:1**
Fraud, coveting, violence	**Mic 2:2**
Stealing, dishonesty	**Mic 2:8**
Evicting women from their homes	**Mic 2:9**
Hating good, loving evil	**Mic 3:1-2**
Despising justice, distorting what is right	**Mic 3:9**
Murder and corruption	**Mic 3:10**
Taking bribes	**Mic 3:11**

You skin my people alive
and tear the flesh from their bones.
3 Yes, you eat my people's flesh,
strip off their skin,
and break their bones.
You chop them up
like meat for the cooking pot.
4 Then you beg the LORD for help in times
of trouble!
Do you really expect him to answer?
After all the evil you have done,
he won't even look at you!"

5 This is what the LORD says:
"You false prophets are leading my people
astray!
You promise peace for those who give
you food,
but you declare war on those who refuse
to feed you.
6 Now the night will close around you,
cutting off all your visions.
Darkness will cover you,
putting an end to your predictions.
The sun will set for you prophets,
and your day will come to an end.
7 Then you seers will be put to shame,
and you fortune-tellers will be disgraced.
And you will cover your faces
because there is no answer from God."

8 But as for me, I am filled with power—
with the Spirit of the LORD.
I am filled with justice and strength
to boldly declare Israel's sin and rebellion.
9 Listen to me, you leaders of Israel!
You hate justice and twist all that is right.
10 You are building Jerusalem
on a foundation of murder and corruption.
11 You rulers make decisions based on bribes;
you priests teach God's laws only for a price;
you prophets won't prophesy unless you
are paid.
Yet all of you claim to depend on the LORD.
"No harm can come to us," you say,
"for the LORD is here among us."
12 Because of you, Mount Zion will be plowed like
an open field;
Jerusalem will be reduced to ruins!
A thicket will grow on the heights
where the Temple now stands.

The LORD's Future Reign

MICAH 4:1-5

1 In the last days, the mountain of the LORD's house
will be the highest of all—
the most important place on earth.
It will be raised above the other hills,
and people from all over the world will stream
there to worship.
2 People from many nations will come and say,
"Come, let us go up to the mountain of the LORD,
to the house of Jacob's God.
There he will teach us his ways,
and we will walk in his paths."
For the LORD's teaching will go out from Zion;
his word will go out from Jerusalem.
3 The LORD will mediate between peoples
and will settle disputes between strong nations
far away.
They will hammer their swords into plowshares
and their spears into pruning hooks.
Nation will no longer fight against nation,
nor train for war anymore.
4 Everyone will live in peace and prosperity,
enjoying their own grapevines and fig trees,
for there will be nothing to fear.

Mic 3:2-4 The leaders had no compassion or respect for those they were supposed to serve. They were treating the people miserably in order to satisfy their own desires; then they had the gall to ask for God's help when they found themselves in trouble. We, like the leaders, should not treat God like a light switch to be turned on only as needed. Instead, we should always rely on him.

Mic 3:5-7 Micah remained true to his calling and proclaimed God's words. In contrast, the false prophets' messages were geared to the favors they received. Not all those who claim to have messages from God really do. Micah prophesied that one day the false prophets would be shamed by their actions.

Mic 3:8 Micah attributed the power of his ministry to the Spirit of the Lord. Our power comes from the same source. Jesus told his followers they would receive power to witness about him when the Holy Spirit came on them (Acts 1:8). You can't witness effectively by relying on your own strength because fear will keep you from speaking out for God. Only by relying on the power of the Holy Spirit can you live and witness for him.

Mic 3:11 Micah warned the rulers, priests, and prophets of his day to avoid bribes. Pastors today accept bribes when they allow those who are big contributors to control the church. If fear of losing money or members influences pastors to remain silent when they should speak up for what is right, their churches are in danger. We should remember that Judah was finally destroyed because of the behavior of its religious leaders. A similar warning must be directed at those who have money—never use your resources to influence or manipulate God's ministers because that is bribery.

Mic 3:12 Jerusalem would be destroyed just as Samaria was (Mic 1:6). This happened in 586 B.C. when Nebuchadnezzar and the Babylonian army attacked the city (2 Kgs 25). Although Micah blamed the corrupt leaders, the people were not without fault. They allowed the corruption to continue without turning to God or calling for justice.

Mic 4:1ff The phrase "in the last days" describes the days when God will reign over his perfect Kingdom (see Mic 4:1-8). The "mountain of the LORD's house" is Mount Zion. This will be an era of peace and blessing, a time when nations will not war against each other. We cannot pinpoint its date, but God has promised that it will arrive (see also Isa 2:2; Jer 16:15; Joel 3:1ff; Zech 14:9-11; Mal 3:17-18; Rev 19–22).

Micah 4:9-13 predicted the Babylonian captivity of 586 B.C., even before Babylon became a powerful empire. Just as God promises a time of peace and prosperity, he also promises judgment and punishment for all who refuse to follow him. Both results are certain.

▸ **MICAH 4:1-5** ***(cont.)***
The LORD of Heaven's Armies
has made this promise!
5 Though the nations around us follow their idols,
we will follow the LORD our God forever
and ever.

Israel's Return from Exile

MICAH 4:6-13
6 "In that coming day," says the LORD,
"I will gather together those who are lame,
those who have been exiles,
and those whom I have filled with grief.
7 Those who are weak will survive as a remnant;
those who were exiles will become a strong
nation.
Then I, the LORD, will rule from Jerusalem*
as their king forever."
8 As for you, Jerusalem,
the citadel of God's people,*
your royal might and power
will come back to you again.
The kingship will be restored
to my precious Jerusalem.
9 But why are you now screaming in terror?
Have you no king to lead you?
Have your wise people all died?
Pain has gripped you like a woman in
childbirth.
10 Writhe and groan like a woman in labor,
you people of Jerusalem,*
for now you must leave this city
to live in the open country.
You will soon be sent in exile
to distant Babylon.
But the LORD will rescue you there;
he will redeem you from the grip of your
enemies.
11 Now many nations have gathered against you.
"Let her be desecrated," they say.
"Let us see the destruction of Jerusalem.*"
12 But they do not know the LORD's thoughts
or understand his plan.
These nations don't know
that he is gathering them together
to be beaten and trampled
like sheaves of grain on a threshing floor.
13 "Rise up and crush the nations, O Jerusalem!"*
says the LORD.
"For I will give you iron horns and bronze hooves,
so you can trample many nations to pieces.
You will present their stolen riches to the LORD,
their wealth to the LORD of all the earth."

A Ruler from Bethlehem

MICAH 5:1-6
1*Mobilize! Marshal your troops!
The enemy is laying siege to Jerusalem.
They will strike Israel's leader
in the face with a rod.
2*But you, O Bethlehem Ephrathah,
are only a small village among all the people
of Judah.
Yet a ruler of Israel will come from you,
one whose origins are from the distant past.
3 The people of Israel will be abandoned to their
enemies
until the woman in labor gives birth.
Then at last his fellow countrymen
will return from exile to their own land.
4 And he will stand to lead his flock with the LORD's
strength,
in the majesty of the name of the LORD his God.
Then his people will live there undisturbed,
for he will be highly honored around the world.
5 And he will be the source of peace.

Mi 4:7 Hebrew *Mount Zion.* **Mi 4:8** Hebrew *As for you, Migdal-eder, / the Ophel of the daughter of Zion.* **Mi 4:10** Hebrew *O daughter of Zion.* **Mi 4:11** Hebrew *of Zion.* **Mi 4:13** Hebrew *"Rise up and thresh, O daughter of Zion."* **Mi 5:1** Verse 5:1 is numbered 4:14 in Hebrew text. **Mi 5:2** Verses 5:2-15 are numbered 5:1-14 in Hebrew text.

Mic 4:9-13 Micah predicted the end of the kings. This was a drastic statement to the people of Judah who thought that their kingdom would last forever. Micah also said that Babylon would destroy the land of Judah and carry away its king, but that after a while God would help his people return to their land. This all happened just as Micah prophesied, and these events are recorded in 2 Chronicles 36:9-23; Ezra 1–2.

Mic 4:12 When God reveals the future, his purpose goes beyond satisfying our curiosity. He wants us to change our present behavior because of what we know about the future. Forever begins now; and a glimpse of God's plan for his followers should motivate us to serve him, no matter what the rest of the world may do.

Mic 5:1 This leader was probably King Zedekiah, who was reigning in Jerusalem when Nebuchadnezzar conquered the city (2 Kgs 25:1-2). Zedekiah was the last of the kings in David's line to sit on the throne in Jerusalem. Micah said that the next king in David's line would be the Messiah, who would establish a Kingdom that would never end.

Mic 5:1ff Jerusalem's leaders were obsessed with wealth and position, but Micah prophesied that mighty Jerusalem, with all its wealth and power, would be besieged and destroyed. Its king could not save it. In contrast, Bethlehem, a tiny town, would be the birthplace of the only ruler who could save his people. This deliverer, the Messiah, would be born as a baby in Bethlehem (Luke 2:4-7) and eventually would reign as the eternal King (Rev 19–22).

Mic 5:2 Ephrathah was the district in which Bethlehem was located.

Mic 5:2 This ruler is Jesus, the Messiah. Micah accurately predicted Christ's birthplace hundreds of years before Jesus was born. The promised eternal King in David's line, who would come to live as a man, had been alive forever—"whose origins are from the distant past." Although eternal, the Son entered human history as a human, Jesus of Nazareth.

Mic 5:5 This chapter provides one of the clearest Old Testament prophecies of Christ's coming. The key descriptive phrase is "he will be the source of peace." In one of Christ's final talks he said, "I am leaving you with a gift—peace of mind and heart. And the peace I give is a gift the world cannot give. So don't be troubled or afraid" (John 14:27).

When the Assyrians invade our land
and break through our defenses,
we will appoint seven rulers to watch over us,
eight princes to lead us.
6 They will rule Assyria with drawn swords
and enter the gates of the land of Nimrod.
He will rescue us from the Assyrians
when they pour over the borders to invade
our land.

The Remnant Purified

MICAH 5:7-15

7 Then the remnant left in Israel*
will take their place among the nations.
They will be like dew sent by the LORD
or like rain falling on the grass,
which no one can hold back
and no one can restrain.
8 The remnant left in Israel
will take their place among the nations.
They will be like a lion among the animals of the
forest,
like a strong young lion among flocks of sheep
and goats,
pouncing and tearing as they go
with no rescuer in sight.
9 The people of Israel will stand up to their foes,
and all their enemies will be wiped out.

10 "In that day," says the LORD,
"I will slaughter your horses
and destroy your chariots.
11 I will tear down your walls
and demolish your defenses.
12 I will put an end to all witchcraft,
and there will be no more fortune-tellers.
13 I will destroy all your idols and sacred pillars,
so you will never again worship the work of
your own hands.
14 I will abolish your idol shrines with their
Asherah poles
and destroy your pagan cities.
15 I will pour out my vengeance
on all the nations that refuse to obey me."

Mi 5:7 Hebrew *in Jacob;* also in 5:8. See note on 1:5a.

The LORD's Case against Israel

MICAH 6:1-8

Listen to what the LORD is saying:

"Stand up and state your case against me.
Let the mountains and hills be called to
witness your complaints.
2 And now, O mountains,
listen to the LORD's complaint!
He has a case against his people.
He will bring charges against Israel.

3 "O my people, what have I done to you?
What have I done to make you tired of me?
Answer me!
4 For I brought you out of Egypt
and redeemed you from slavery.
I sent Moses, Aaron, and Miriam to help you.
5 Don't you remember, my people,
how King Balak of Moab tried to have you
cursed
and how Balaam son of Beor blessed you
instead?

Because of Christ's first coming, we have the opportunity to experience peace with God with no more fear of judgment and no more conflict and guilt. Christ's peace gives us assurance even though wars continue. At Christ's second coming, all wars and weapons will be destroyed (Mic 4:3-5).

Mic 5:5 Micah's prophecy of seven rulers and eight princes is a figurative way of saying that the Messiah will raise up many good leaders when he returns to reign. This contrasts with Micah's words about Judah's corrupt leaders (Mic 3). "The Assyrians" symbolically refer to all nations in every age that oppose God's people. These good leaders will help Christ defeat all evil in the world.

Mic 5:6 The land of Nimrod is another name for Assyria, which, in this case, is a symbol of all the evil nations in the world.

Mic 5:10 When God rules in his eternal Kingdom, our strength and deliverance will not be found in military might but in God's almighty power. God will destroy all the weapons that people use for security. Armies will not be needed because God will rule in the heart of every person. Instead of being overwhelmed by fear of invasion or nuclear attack, we should have confidence in God.

Mic 5:12-14 Idols, sacred pillars, and Asherah poles were all part of pagan worship.

Mic 6:1ff Here Micah pictures a courtroom. God, the Judge, tells his people what he requires of them and recites all the ways they have wronged both him and others. Micah 4–5 is full of hope; Micah 6–7 proclaims judgment and appeals to the people to repent.

Mic 6:1-2 God called to the mountains to confirm the people's guilt. The mountains would serve as excellent witnesses, for it was in the high places that the people had built pagan altars and had sacrificed to false gods (1 Kgs 14:23; Jer 17:2-3; Ezek 20:28).

Mic 6:3 The people would never be able to answer this question because God had done nothing wrong. In fact, God had been exceedingly patient with them, had always lovingly guided them, and had given them every opportunity to return to him. If God asked you, "What have I done to you?" how would you reply?

Mic 6:5 The story of Balak and Balaam is found in Numbers 22–24. Acacia Grove was the Israelites' campsite by the Jordan River just before they entered the Promised Land (Josh 2:1). There the people received many of God's instructions about how to live. Gilgal, their first campsite after crossing the Jordan (Josh 4:19), was where the people renewed their covenant with God (Josh 5:3-9). These two places represent God's loving care for his people: his willingness both to protect them and to warn them about potential troubles. In Micah's day, the people had forgotten this covenant and its benefits and had turned away from God.

Mic 6:5 God continued to be kind to his forgetful people, but their short memory and lack of thankfulness condemned them. When people refuse to see how fortunate they are and begin to take God's gifts for granted, they become self-centered. Regularly remember God's goodness and thank him. Remembering God's past protection will help you see his present provision.

▶ **MICAH 6:1-8 *(cont.)***

And remember your journey from Acacia Grove*
to Gilgal,
when I, the LORD, did everything I could
to teach you about my faithfulness."

6 What can we bring to the LORD?
What kind of offerings should we give him?
Should we bow before God
with offerings of yearling calves?
7 Should we offer him thousands of rams
and ten thousand rivers of olive oil?
Should we sacrifice our firstborn children
to pay for our sins?

8 No, O people, the LORD has told you what is good,
and this is what he requires of you:
to do what is right, to love mercy,
and to walk humbly with your God.

Israel's Guilt and Punishment

MICAH 6:9-16

9 Fear the LORD if you are wise!
His voice calls to everyone in Jerusalem:
"The armies of destruction are coming;
the LORD is sending them.*
10 What shall I say about the homes of the wicked
filled with treasures gained by cheating?
What about the disgusting practice
of measuring out grain with dishonest
measures?*
11 How can I tolerate your merchants
who use dishonest scales and weights?
12 The rich among you have become wealthy
through extortion and violence.
Your citizens are so used to lying
that their tongues can no longer tell the truth.

13 "Therefore, I will wound you!
I will bring you to ruin for all your sins.
14 You will eat but never have enough.
Your hunger pangs and emptiness will remain.
And though you try to save your money,
it will come to nothing in the end.
You will save a little,
but I will give it to those who conquer you.
15 You will plant crops
but not harvest them.
You will press your olives
but not get enough oil to anoint yourselves.
You will trample the grapes
but get no juice to make your wine.
16 You keep only the laws of evil King Omri;
you follow only the example of wicked
King Ahab!
Therefore, I will make an example of you,
bringing you to complete ruin.
You will be treated with contempt,
mocked by all who see you."

Misery Turned to Hope

MICAH 7:1-13

1 How miserable I am!
I feel like the fruit picker after the harvest
who can find nothing to eat.
Not a cluster of grapes or a single early fig
can be found to satisfy my hunger.
2 The godly people have all disappeared;
not one honest person is left on the earth.
They are all murderers,
setting traps even for their own brothers.
3 Both their hands are equally skilled at doing evil!
Officials and judges alike demand bribes.
The people with influence get what they want,
and together they scheme to twist justice.
4 Even the best of them is like a brier;
the most honest is as dangerous as a hedge
of thorns.
But your judgment day is coming swiftly now.
Your time of punishment is here, a time of
confusion.
5 Don't trust anyone—
not your best friend or even your wife!

Mi 6:5 Hebrew *Shittim.* **Mi 6:9** Hebrew *"Listen to the rod. / Who appointed it?"* **Mi 6:10** Hebrew *of using the short ephah?* The ephah was a unit for measuring grain.

Mic 6:6-8 Israel responded to God's request by trying to appease him with sacrifices, hoping he would then leave them alone. But sacrifices and other religious rituals aren't enough; God wants changed lives. He wants his people to be fair, just, merciful, and humble. God wants us to be living sacrifices (Rom 12:1-2), not just doing religious deeds, but living rightly (Jer 4:4; Heb 9:14). It is impossible to follow God consistently without his transforming love in our hearts.

Mic 6:8 People have tried all kinds of ways to please God (Mic 6:6-7), but God has made his wishes clear: He wants his people to do what is right, love mercy, and walk humbly with him. In your efforts to please God, examine these areas on a regular basis. Are you fair in your dealings with people? Do you show mercy to those who wrong you? Are you learning humility?

Mic 6:16 Omri reigned over Israel and led the people into idol worship (1 Kgs 16:21-26). Ahab, his son, was Israel's most wicked king (1 Kgs 16:29-33). If the people were following the laws and practices of these kings, they were in bad shape. Such evil was ripe for punishment.

Mic 7:1ff This chapter begins in gloom (Mic 7:1-6) and ends in hope (Mic 7:8-20). Micah watched as society rotted around him. Rulers demanded gifts; judges accepted bribes; corruption was universal. But God promised to lead the people out of the darkness of sin and into his light. Then the people would praise him for his faithfulness. God alone is perfectly faithful.

Mic 7:1-4 Micah could not find an honest person anywhere in the land. Even today, fair-mindedness (uprightness, honesty, integrity) is difficult to find. Society rationalizes sin, and even believers sometimes compromise Christian principles in order to do what they want. It is easy to convince ourselves that we deserve a few breaks, especially when "everyone else" is doing it. But the standards for honesty come from God, not society. We are to be honest because God is truth, and we are to be like him.

Mic 7:5-6 Sin had affected the government leaders and society in general. Deceit and dishonesty had even ruined the family, the

6 For the son despises his father.
The daughter defies her mother.
The daughter-in-law defies her mother-in-law.
Your enemies are right in your own
household!

7 As for me, I look to the LORD for help.
I wait confidently for God to save me,
and my God will certainly hear me.
8 Do not gloat over me, my enemies!
For though I fall, I will rise again.
Though I sit in darkness,
the LORD will be my light.
9 I will be patient as the LORD punishes me,
for I have sinned against him.
But after that, he will take up my case
and give me justice for all I have suffered
from my enemies.
The LORD will bring me into the light,
and I will see his righteousness.
10 Then my enemies will see that the LORD is
on my side.
They will be ashamed that they taunted me,
saying,
"So where is the LORD—
that God of yours?"
With my own eyes I will see their downfall;
they will be trampled like mud in the streets.

11 In that day, Israel, your cities will be rebuilt,
and your borders will be extended.
12 People from many lands will come and
honor you—
from Assyria all the way to the towns
of Egypt,
from Egypt all the way to the Euphrates River,*
and from distant seas and mountains.
13 But the land* will become empty and desolate
because of the wickedness of those who
live there.

The LORD's Compassion on Israel

MICAH 7:14-20

14 O LORD, protect your people with your
shepherd's staff;
lead your flock, your special possession.
Though they live alone in a thicket
on the heights of Mount Carmel,*
let them graze in the fertile pastures of Bashan
and Gilead
as they did long ago.
15 "Yes," says the LORD,
"I will do mighty miracles for you,
like those I did when I rescued you
from slavery in Egypt."
16 All the nations of the world will stand amazed
at what the LORD will do for you.
They will be embarrassed
at their feeble power.
They will cover their mouths in silent awe,
deaf to everything around them.
17 Like snakes crawling from their holes,
they will come out to meet the LORD
our God.
They will fear him greatly,
trembling in terror at his presence.

18 Where is another God like you,
who pardons the guilt of the remnant,
overlooking the sins of his special people?
You will not stay angry with your people forever,
because you delight in showing unfailing love.
19 Once again you will have compassion on us.
You will trample our sins under your feet
and throw them into the depths of the ocean!
20 You will show us your faithfulness and
unfailing love
as you promised to our ancestors Abraham
and Jacob long ago.

Mi 7:12 Hebrew *the river.* **Mi 7:13** Or *earth.* **Mi 7:14** Or *surrounded by a fruitful land.*

core of society. As a result, the only way left to purify the people was God's judgment. This would draw the nation back to God and restore them from the inside out.

Mic 7:7-10 Micah showed great faith in God both personally (Mic 7:7) and on Israel's behalf (Mic 7:8-10) as he proclaimed that (1) he would wait upon God because God hears and saves when help is needed, (2) God would bring his people through when times were tough, (3) Israel must be patient in punishment because God would bring them out of the darkness, and (4) their enemies would be punished. We, too, can have a relationship with God that allows us to have confidence like Micah's. It doesn't take unusual talent; it simply takes faith in God and a willingness to act on that faith.

Mic 7:9 Micah understood that if the people would be patient and obedient while they were being punished, God would forgive them and show his goodness again (Lam 3:39-41). Punishment does not mean rejection. The people were being punished in order to bring them back to God, not to send them away from him. When you face trials because of your sin, do not be angry with God or afraid that he has rejected you. Instead, turn away from your sin, turn to God, and continue to be patient and obedient.

Mic 7:14 Bashan and Gilead were fertile areas east of the Jordan, previously the territory of Reuben, Gad, and the half-tribe of Manasseh.

Mic 7:18 God delights to show his unfailing love! He does not forgive grudgingly but is glad when we repent, and he offers forgiveness to all who come back to him. Today you can confess your sins and receive his loving forgiveness. Don't be too proud to accept God's free offer.

Mic 7:20 In an age when religion was making little difference in people's lives, Micah said that God expected his people to do what is right, love mercy, and walk humbly with him (Mic 6:8). He requires the same of Christians today. In a world that is unjust, we must act justly and do what is right. In a world of tough breaks, we must be merciful. In a world of pride and self-sufficiency, we must walk humbly with God. Only when we live according to God's way will we begin to affect our homes, our society, and our world.

7. THE ASSYRIAN THREAT TO JUDAH

Assyria, the great empire that had destroyed the northern kingdom and scattered their people less than a generation earlier, returned to the region and threatened to do the same to Judah. God used the prophet Isaiah to speak to the nation of Judah, and the people responded with trust in God despite the overwhelming threat of being outmatched on the battlefield. God miraculously delivered the nation of Judah, once again giving testimony to his power over any nation on earth.

Assyria Invades Judah PARALLEL •••

2 KINGS 18:13-18 •••

In the fourteenth year of King Hezekiah's reign,* King
Sennacherib of Assyria came to attack the fortified
towns of Judah and conquered them. 14King Hezekiah
sent this message to the king of Assyria at Lachish: "I
have done wrong. I will pay whatever tribute money
you demand if you will only withdraw." The king of
Assyria then demanded a settlement of more than
eleven tons of silver and one ton of gold.* 15To gather
this amount, King Hezekiah used all the silver stored
in the Temple of the LORD and in the palace treasury.
16Hezekiah even stripped the gold from the doors of
the LORD's Temple and from the doorposts he had overlaid with gold, and he gave it all to the Assyrian king.
17Nevertheless, the king of Assyria sent his commander in chief, his field commander, and his chief
of staff* from Lachish with a huge army to confront
King Hezekiah in Jerusalem. The Assyrians took up a
position beside the aqueduct that feeds water into the
upper pool, near the road leading to the field where
cloth is washed.* 18They summoned King Hezekiah,
but the king sent these officials to meet with them: Eliakim son of Hilkiah, the palace administrator; Shebna
the court secretary; and Joah son of Asaph, the royal
historian.

2 CHRONICLES 32:1-8 •••

After Hezekiah had faithfully carried out this work,
King Sennacherib of Assyria invaded Judah. He laid
siege to the fortified towns, giving orders for his army
to break through their walls. 2When Hezekiah realized
that Sennacherib also intended to attack Jerusalem,
3he consulted with his officials and military advisers, and they decided to stop the flow of the springs
outside the city. 4They organized a huge work crew to

2 Kgs 18:13 The fourteenth year of Hezekiah's reign was 701 B.C. **2 Kgs 18:14** Hebrew *300 talents* [10 metric tons] *of silver and 30 talents* [1 metric ton] *of gold.* **2 Kgs 18:17a** Or *the rabshakeh;* also in 18:19, 26, 27, 28, 37. **2 Kgs 18:17b** Or *bleached.*

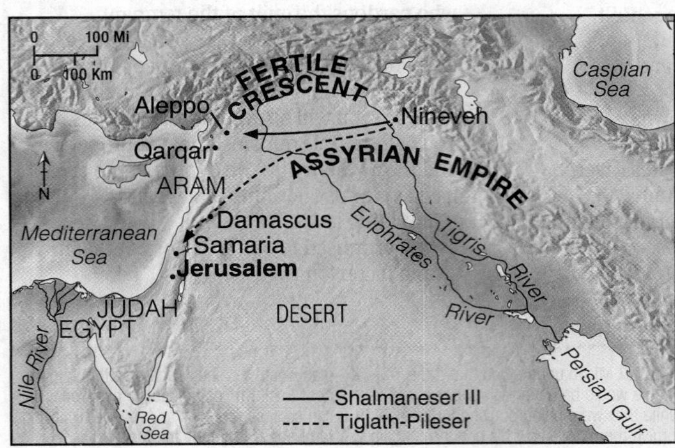

***THE ASSYRIAN EMPIRE** The mighty Assyrian Empire extended from the Persian Gulf, across the Fertile Crescent, and south to Egypt. Shalmaneser III extended the empire toward the Mediterranean Sea by conquering cities as far west as Qarqar. Tiglath-pileser extended the empire south into Aram, Israel, Judah, and Philistia. It was Shalmaneser V who destroyed Samaria, Israel's capital.*

2 Kgs 18:13 This event occurred in 701 B.C., four years after Sennacherib had become Assyria's king. Sennacherib was the son of Sargon II, the king who had deported Israel's people into captivity (see the note on 2 Kgs 17:3, p. 801). To keep Assyria from attacking, the southern kingdom paid tribute annually. But when Sennacherib became king, Hezekiah stopped paying this money, hoping Assyria would ignore him. When Sennacherib and his army retaliated, Hezekiah realized his mistake and paid the tribute money (2 Kgs 18:14), but Sennacherib attacked anyway (2 Kgs 18:19ff). Although Sennacherib attacked Judah, he was not as war-hungry as the previous Assyrian kings, preferring to spend most of his time building and beautifying his capital city, Nineveh. With less frequent invasions, Hezekiah was able to institute many reforms and strengthen the nation.

2 Kgs 18:17 Sending the commander in chief, the field commander, and the chief of staff was like sending the vice president, secretary of state, and the head general of the army to speak to the enemy prior to a battle. All of these men were sent in an effort to impress and discourage the Israelites.

2 Chr 32:1 Assyria was a great empire by Hezekiah's time, controlling most of the Middle East. From a small strip of land located in present-day Iran and Iraq, it began to establish its power under Ashurnasirpal II (883–859 B.C.) and his son Shalmaneser III (859–824 B.C.). Under Tiglath-pileser III (745–727 B.C.), Assyria's boundaries extended to the borders of Israel, making it one of the largest empires in ancient history. Shalmaneser V destroyed the northern kingdom in 722 B.C., and his grandson Sennacherib (705–681 B.C.) tried to bring Judah, the southern kingdom, under his control. Less than a century later, Assyria would lie in ruins (612 B.C.).

2 Chr 32:1 Sennacherib wanted to conquer these cities so he could force them to pay tribute. Forcing captured cities to pay tribute was a way for kings to build their income base. Often Assyria would require an oath of allegiance from a country, including the promise to pay taxes in the form of livestock, wine, battle equipment (horses, chariots, weapons), gold, silver, and anything else that pleased the invading king. Tribute was more important to Assyria than captives because captives cost money. Thus, captives were taken only in cases of extreme rebellion or to repopulate cities that had been destroyed.

stop the flow of the springs, cutting off the brook that ran through the fields. For they said, "Why should the kings of Assyria come here and find plenty of water?"

5Then Hezekiah worked hard at repairing all the broken sections of the wall, erecting towers, and constructing a second wall outside the first. He also reinforced the supporting terraces* in the City of David and manufactured large numbers of weapons and shields. 6He appointed military officers over the people and assembled them before him in the square at the city gate. Then Hezekiah encouraged them by saying: 7"Be strong and courageous! Don't be afraid or discouraged because of the king of Assyria or his mighty army, for there is a power far greater on our side! 8He may have a great army, but they are merely men. We have the LORD our God to help us and to fight our battles for us!" Hezekiah's words greatly encouraged the people.

ISAIAH 36:1-3
In the fourteenth year of King Hezekiah's reign,* King Sennacherib of Assyria came to attack the fortified towns of Judah and conquered them. 2Then the king of Assyria sent his chief of staff* from Lachish with a huge army to confront King Hezekiah in Jerusalem. The Assyrians took up a position beside the aqueduct that feeds water into the upper pool, near the road leading to the field where cloth is washed.*

3These are the officials who went out to meet with them: Eliakim son of Hilkiah, the palace administrator; Shebna the court secretary; and Joah son of Asaph, the royal historian.

Sennacherib Threatens Jerusalem PARALLEL

2 KINGS 18:19-37
Then the Assyrian king's chief of staff told them to give this message to Hezekiah:

"This is what the great king of Assyria says: What are you trusting in that makes you so confident?
20Do you think that mere words can substitute for military skill and strength? Who are you counting on, that you have rebelled against me?
21On Egypt? If you lean on Egypt, it will be like a reed that splinters beneath your weight and pierces your hand. Pharaoh, the king of Egypt, is completely unreliable!

22"But perhaps you will say to me, 'We are trusting in the LORD our God!' But isn't he the one who was insulted by Hezekiah? Didn't Hezekiah tear down his shrines and altars and make everyone in Judah and Jerusalem worship only at the altar here in Jerusalem?

23"I'll tell you what! Strike a bargain with my master, the king of Assyria. I will give you 2,000 horses if you can find that many men to ride on them! 24With your tiny army, how can you think of challenging even the weakest contingent of my master's troops, even with the help of Egypt's chariots and charioteers? 25What's more, do you think we have invaded your land without the LORD's direction? The LORD himself told us, 'Attack this land and destroy it!'"

26Then Eliakim son of Hilkiah, Shebna, and Joah said to the Assyrian chief of staff, "Please speak to us in Aramaic, for we understand it well. Don't speak in Hebrew,* for the people on the wall will hear."

27But Sennacherib's chief of staff replied, "Do you think my master sent this message only to you and your master? He wants all the people to hear it, for when we put this city under siege, they will suffer along with you. They will be so hungry and thirsty that they will eat their own dung and drink their own urine."

28Then the chief of staff stood and shouted in Hebrew to the people on the wall, "Listen to this message from the great king of Assyria! 29This is what the king says: Don't let Hezekiah deceive you. He will never be able to rescue you from my power. 30Don't let him fool you into trusting in the LORD by saying, 'The LORD will surely rescue us. This city will never fall into the hands of the Assyrian king!'

31"Don't listen to Hezekiah! These are the terms the king of Assyria is offering: Make peace with me—open the gates and come out. Then each of you can continue eating from your own grapevine and fig tree and drinking from your own well. 32Then I will arrange to

2 Chr 32:5 Hebrew *the millo.* The meaning of the Hebrew is uncertain. **Is 36:1** The fourteenth year of Hezekiah's reign was 701 B.C. **Is 36:2a** Or *the rabshakeh;* also in 36:4, 11, 12, 22. **Is 36:2b** Or *bleached.* **2 Kgs 18:26** Hebrew *in the dialect of Judah;* also in 18:28.

2 Chr 32:1ff When Hezekiah was confronted with the frightening prospect of an Assyrian invasion, he made two important decisions. He did everything he could to deal with the situation, and he trusted God for the outcome. That is exactly what we must do when faced with difficult or frightening situations. Take all the steps you possibly can to solve the problem or improve the situation. But also commit the situation to God in prayer, trusting him for the solution.

2 Chr 32:3-4 Cities had to be built near reliable water sources. Natural springs were some of Jerusalem's major sources of water. In a brilliant military move, Hezekiah plugged the springs outside the city and channeled the water through an underground tunnel (2 Chr 32:30); therefore, Jerusalem would have water even through a long siege. Hezekiah's tunnel has been discovered along with an inscription describing how it was built: Two groups of workers started digging underground, one in Jerusalem and one at the Gihon Spring, and they met in the middle.

2 Chr 32:7-8 Hezekiah could see with eyes of faith. The number of his opponents meant nothing as long as he was on the Lord's side. Victory is "not by force nor by strength, but by my Spirit, says the LORD of Heaven's Armies" (Zech 4:6). Hezekiah could confidently encourage his men because he had no doubt about where he stood with God. Are you on the Lord's side? You may never face an army, but the battles you face every day can be won with God's strength.

▸ 2 KINGS 18:19-37 *(cont.)*
take you to another land like this one—a land of grain
and new wine, bread and vineyards, olive groves and
honey. Choose life instead of death!
"Don't listen to Hezekiah when he tries to mislead
you by saying, 'The LORD will rescue us!' 33Have the
gods of any other nations ever saved their people
from the king of Assyria? 34What happened to the
gods of Hamath and Arpad? And what about the gods
of Sepharvaim, Hena, and Ivvah? Did any god rescue
Samaria from my power? 35What god of any nation
has ever been able to save its people from my power?
So what makes you think that the LORD can rescue
Jerusalem from me?"
36But the people were silent and did not utter a
word because Hezekiah had commanded them, "Do
not answer him."
37Then Eliakim son of Hilkiah, the palace administrator; Shebna the court secretary; and Joah son of
Asaph, the royal historian, went back to Hezekiah.
They tore their clothes in despair, and they went in
to see the king and told him what the Assyrian chief
of staff had said.

ISAIAH 36:4-22
Then the Assyrian king's chief of staff told them to
give this message to Hezekiah:

701 BC

Sennacherib taunts Hezekiah

"This is what the great king of Assyria says: What
are you trusting in that makes you so confident?
5Do you think that mere words can substitute for
military skill and strength? Who are you counting
on, that you have rebelled against me? 6On Egypt?
If you lean on Egypt, it will be like a reed that
splinters beneath your weight and pierces your
hand. Pharaoh, the king of Egypt, is completely
unreliable!
7"But perhaps you will say to me, 'We are
trusting in the LORD our God!' But isn't he the one
who was insulted by Hezekiah? Didn't Hezekiah
tear down his shrines and altars and make
everyone in Judah and Jerusalem worship only at
the altar here in Jerusalem?
8"I'll tell you what! Strike a bargain with my
master, the king of Assyria. I will give you 2,000
horses if you can find that many men to ride on
them! 9With your tiny army, how can you think
of challenging even the weakest contingent of
my master's troops, even with the help of Egypt's
chariots and charioteers? 10What's more, do
you think we have invaded your land without
the LORD's direction? The LORD himself told us,
'Attack this land and destroy it!'"
11Then Eliakim, Shebna, and Joah said to the Assyrian chief of staff, "Please speak to us in Aramaic, for
we understand it well. Don't speak in Hebrew,* for the
people on the wall will hear."
12But Sennacherib's chief of staff replied, "Do you
think my master sent this message only to you and your
master? He wants all the people to hear it, for when we
put this city under siege, they will suffer along with you.
They will be so hungry and thirsty that they will eat
their own dung and drink their own urine."
13Then the chief of staff stood and shouted in Hebrew to the people on the wall, "Listen to this message
from the great king of Assyria! 14This is what the king
says: Don't let Hezekiah deceive you. He will never
be able to rescue you. 15Don't let him fool you into
trusting in the LORD by saying, 'The LORD will surely
rescue us. This city will never fall into the hands of
the Assyrian king!'
16"Don't listen to Hezekiah! These are the terms the
king of Assyria is offering: Make peace with me—open
the gates and come out. Then each of you can continue eating from your own grapevine and fig tree and
drinking from your own well. 17Then I will arrange to
take you to another land like this one—a land of grain
and new wine, bread and vineyards.
18"Don't let Hezekiah mislead you by saying, 'The
LORD will rescue us!' Have the gods of any other nations

Is 36:11 Hebrew *in the dialect of Judah;* also in 36:13.

Isa 36:4-6 Isaiah 19 describes Isaiah's prophecy of judgment upon Egypt, while Isaiah 30–31 pronounces woe on those from Judah who would ally themselves with Egypt in the face of Assyria's impending attack. Sennacherib of Assyria was taunting Judah for trusting in Egypt. Even the Assyrians knew that Egypt could not help Judah.

Isa 36:5 Hezekiah put great trust in Pharaoh's promise to help Israel against the Assyrians, but promises are only as good as the credibility of the person making them. It was Pharaoh's word against God's. How quickly we seek human advice while we neglect God's eternal promises. When choosing between God's Word and someone else's, whose will you believe?

Isa 36:7 The Assyrian king's chief of staff claimed that Hezekiah had insulted God by tearing down his altars and making the people worship only in Jerusalem. But Hezekiah's reform sought to eliminate idol worship (which occurred mainly on high hills) so that the people worshiped only the true God. Either the Assyrians didn't know about the religion of the true God, or they wanted to deceive the people into thinking they had angered a powerful god.

In the same way, Satan tries to confuse or deceive us. People don't necessarily need to be sinful to be ineffective for God; they need only be confused about what God wants. To avoid Satan's deceit, study God's Word carefully and regularly. When you know what God says, you will not fall for Satan's lies.

Isa 36:10 Sennacherib continued his demoralization campaign by sending his chief of staff to try to convince the people of Judah that God had turned against them and that they should surrender without fighting. But Isaiah had already said that the Assyrians would not destroy Jerusalem, so the people did not need to be afraid of them (Isa 10:24-27; 29:5-8).

Isa 36:11 Aramaic was an international language at this time. See also Isaiah 22:15-25 for Isaiah's prophecies concerning Eliakim and Shebna.

Isa 36:17 Sennacherib's representative tried yet another ploy to demoralize the people. He appealed to the starving city under siege by offering to take them to a land with plenty of food if they surrendered. The Assyrian policy

ever saved their people from the king of Assyria?
19What happened to the gods of Hamath and Arpad?
And what about the gods of Sepharvaim? Did any god
rescue Samaria from my power? 20What god of any
nation has ever been able to save its people from my
power? So what makes you think that the LORD can
rescue Jerusalem from me?"

21But the people were silent and did not utter a
word because Hezekiah had commanded them, "Do
not answer him."

22Then Eliakim son of Hilkiah, the palace administrator; Shebna the court secretary; and Joah son of Asaph, the royal historian, went back to Hezekiah. They tore their clothes in despair, and they went in to see the king and told him what the Assyrian chief of staff had said.

Hezekiah Seeks the LORD's Help PARALLEL •••

2 KINGS 19:1-19 •••

When King Hezekiah heard their report, he tore his
clothes and put on burlap and went into the Temple
of the LORD. 2And he sent Eliakim the palace administrator, Shebna the court secretary, and the leading
priests, all dressed in burlap, to the prophet Isaiah son
of Amoz. 3They told him, "This is what King Hezekiah
says: Today is a day of trouble, insults, and disgrace. It
is like when a child is ready to be born, but the mother
has no strength to deliver the baby. 4But perhaps the
LORD your God has heard the Assyrian chief of staff,*
sent by the king to defy the living God, and will punish him for his words. Oh, pray for those of us who
are left!"

5After King Hezekiah's officials delivered the king's
message to Isaiah, 6the prophet replied, "Say to your
master, 'This is what the LORD says: Do not be disturbed by this blasphemous speech against me from
the Assyrian king's messengers. 7Listen! I myself will
move against him,* and the king will receive a message that he is needed at home. So he will return to
his land, where I will have him killed with a sword.'"

8Meanwhile, the Assyrian chief of staff left Jerusalem and went to consult the king of Assyria, who had left Lachish and was attacking Libnah.

9Soon afterward King Sennacherib received word that King Tirhakah of Ethiopia* was leading an army to fight against him. Before leaving to meet the attack, he sent messengers back to Hezekiah in Jerusalem with this message:

10"This message is for King Hezekiah of Judah.
Don't let your God, in whom you trust, deceive you
with promises that Jerusalem will not be captured
by the king of Assyria. 11You know perfectly well
what the kings of Assyria have done wherever
they have gone. They have completely destroyed
everyone who stood in their way! Why should
you be any different? 12Have the gods of other

2 Kgs 19:4 Or *the rabshakeh;* also in 19:8. **2 Kgs 19:7** Hebrew *I will put a spirit in him.* **2 Kgs 19:9** Hebrew *of Cush.*

for dealing with conquered nations was to resettle the inhabitants and then to move other conquered peoples into the recently conquered area. This provided manpower for their armies and prevented revolts in conquered territories.

Isa 36:19-20 The king's representative said that the gods of the other cities he had conquered had not been able to save their people, so how could the God of Jerusalem save them? The Lord was supposedly the God of Samaria (the northern kingdom), and it fell. But the Lord was the God of Samaria in name only because the people were not worshiping him. That is why prophets foretold the fall of Samaria. But for the Lord's own sake and for the sake of David, the Lord would rescue Jerusalem from the Assyrian army (Isa 37:35).

2 Kgs 19:1-7 Sennacherib, whose armies had captured all the fortified cities of Judah, sent a message to Hezekiah to surrender. Realizing the situation was hopeless, Hezekiah went to the Temple and prayed. God answered Hezekiah's prayer and delivered Judah by sending an army to attack the Assyrian camp, forcing Sennacherib to leave at once. Prayer should be our first response in any crisis. Don't wait until things are hopeless. Pray daily for his guidance. Our problems are God's opportunities.

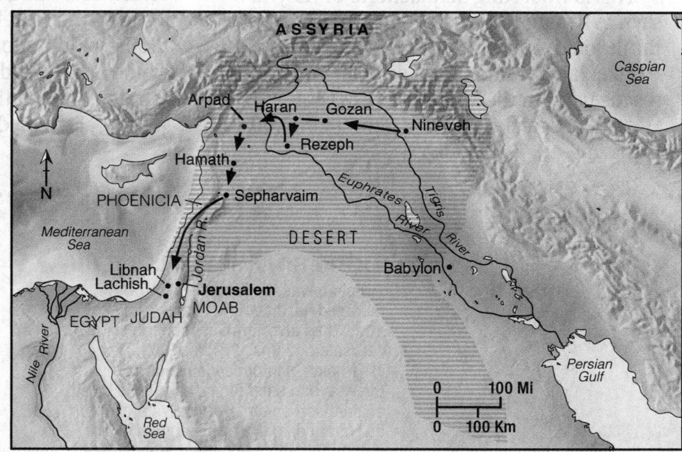

***ASSYRIA ADVANCES** As Sennacherib beautified his capital city, Nineveh, Hezekiah withheld tribute and prepared for battle. The Assyrians advanced toward their rebellious western border, attacking swiftly down the Mediterranean coast. From Lachish, Sennacherib threatened to take Jerusalem, but Isaiah knew his threats would die with him upon his return to Nineveh.*

2 Kgs 19:2 Isaiah the prophet had been working for God since the days of Uzziah—40 years (Isa 6:1). Although Assyria was a world power, it could not conquer Judah as long as Isaiah counseled the kings. Isaiah prophesied during the reigns of Uzziah (Azariah), Jotham, Ahaz, and Hezekiah. Ahaz ignored Isaiah, but Hezekiah listened to his advice.

▸ **2 KINGS 19:1-19** ***(cont.)***

nations rescued them—such nations as Gozan,
Haran, Rezeph, and the people of Eden who were
in Tel-assar? My predecessors destroyed them all!
13 What happened to the king of Hamath and the
king of Arpad? What happened to the kings of
Sepharvaim, Hena, and Ivvah?"

14 After Hezekiah received the letter from the messengers and read it, he went up to the LORD's Temple
and spread it out before the LORD. 15 And Hezekiah
prayed this prayer before the LORD: "O LORD, God of Israel, you are enthroned between the mighty cherubim!
You alone are God of all the kingdoms of the earth.
You alone created the heavens and the earth. 16 Bend
down, O LORD, and listen! Open your eyes, O LORD,
and see! Listen to Sennacherib's words of defiance
against the living God.
17 "It is true, LORD, that the kings of Assyria have
destroyed all these nations. 18 And they have thrown
the gods of these nations into the fire and burned
them. But of course the Assyrians could destroy them!
They were not gods at all—only idols of wood and
stone shaped by human hands. 19 Now, O LORD our
God, rescue us from his power; then all the kingdoms
of the earth will know that you alone, O LORD, are God."

2 CHRONICLES 32:9-19

While King Sennacherib of Assyria was still besieging
the town of Lachish, he sent his officers to Jerusalem
with this message for Hezekiah and all the people
in the city:

10 "This is what King Sennacherib of Assyria
says: What are you trusting in that makes you
think you can survive my siege of Jerusalem?
11 Hezekiah has said, 'The LORD our God will
rescue us from the king of Assyria.' Surely
Hezekiah is misleading you, sentencing you to
death by famine and thirst! 12 Don't you realize
that Hezekiah is the very person who destroyed
all the LORD's shrines and altars? He commanded
Judah and Jerusalem to worship only at the altar
at the Temple and to offer sacrifices on it alone.
13 "Surely you must realize what I and the other
kings of Assyria before me have done to all the
people of the earth! Were any of the gods of those
nations able to rescue their people from my
power? 14 Which of their gods was able to rescue
its people from the destructive power of my
predecessors? What makes you think your God
can rescue you from me? 15 Don't let Hezekiah
deceive you! Don't let him fool you like this! I say
it again—no god of any nation or kingdom has
ever yet been able to rescue his people from me
or my ancestors. How much less will your God
rescue you from my power!"

16 And Sennacherib's officers further mocked the
LORD God and his servant Hezekiah, heaping insult
upon insult. 17 The king also sent letters scorning the
LORD, the God of Israel. He wrote, "Just as the gods of
all the other nations failed to rescue their people from
my power, so the God of Hezekiah will also fail." 18 The
Assyrian officials who brought the letters shouted
this in Hebrew* to the people gathered on the walls
of the city, trying to terrify them so it would be easier
to capture the city. 19 These officers talked about the
God of Jerusalem as though he were one of the pagan
gods, made by human hands.

ISAIAH 37:1-20

When King Hezekiah heard their report, he tore his
clothes and put on burlap and went into the Temple
of the LORD. 2 And he sent Eliakim the palace administrator, Shebna the court secretary, and the leading
priests, all dressed in burlap, to the prophet Isaiah son

2 Chr 32:18 Hebrew *in the dialect of Judah.*

Tirhakah, King of Ethiopia

Tirhakah was the Ethiopian king who marched north to fight against the Assyrian army, thus diverting Sennacherib's siege of Jerusalem (2 Kgs 19:9; Isa 37:9). The report of Tirhakah's intended invasion prompted the Assyrian chief of staff's second threat against Jerusalem, Hezekiah's prayer for deliverance, and the subsequent divine destruction of the Assyrian army (2 Kgs 19:8-37). Tirhakah is almost certainly the Egyptian Taharqa, who ruled from 689–664 B.C. during the 25th (Ethiopian) dynasty. Tirhakah probably served as commander of the army while he was crown prince, so that the reference to him as "king" refers to his then-future position. This image shows Tirhakah sitting under the protection of the Egyptian god Amun.

2 Kgs 19:15-19 Although Hezekiah came boldly to God, he did not take God for granted or approach him flippantly. Instead, Hezekiah acknowledged God's sovereignty and Judah's total dependence on him. Hezekiah's prayer provides a good model for us. We should not be afraid to approach God with our prayers, but we must come to him with respect for who he is and what he can do.

of Amoz. 3They told him, "This is what King Hezekiah
says: Today is a day of trouble, insults, and disgrace. It
is like when a child is ready to be born, but the mother
has no strength to deliver the baby. 4But perhaps the
LORD your God has heard the Assyrian chief of staff,*
sent by the king to defy the living God, and will punish him for his words. Oh, pray for those of us who
are left!"

5After King Hezekiah's officials delivered the king's
message to Isaiah, 6the prophet replied, "Say to your
master, 'This is what the LORD says: Do not be disturbed by this blasphemous speech against me from
the Assyrian king's messengers. 7Listen! I myself will
move against him,* and the king will receive a message that he is needed at home. So he will return to
his land, where I will have him killed with a sword.'"

8Meanwhile, the Assyrian chief of staff left Jerusalem and went to consult the king of Assyria, who had
left Lachish and was attacking Libnah.

9Soon afterward King Sennacherib received word
that King Tirhakah of Ethiopia* was leading an army
to fight against him. Before leaving to meet the attack,
he sent messengers back to Hezekiah in Jerusalem
with this message:

> 10"This message is for King Hezekiah of Judah.
> Don't let your God, in whom you trust, deceive
> you with promises that Jerusalem will not be
> captured by the king of Assyria. 11You know
> perfectly well what the kings of Assyria have done
> wherever they have gone. They have completely
> destroyed everyone who stood in their way! Why
> should you be any different? 12Have the gods
> of other nations rescued them—such nations
> as Gozan, Haran, Rezeph, and the people of
> Eden who were in Tel-assar? My predecessors
> destroyed them all! 13What happened to the
> king of Hamath and the king of Arpad? What
> happened to the kings of Sepharvaim, Hena,
> and Ivvah?"

14After Hezekiah received the letter from the messengers and read it, he went up to the LORD's Temple
and spread it out before the LORD. 15And Hezekiah
prayed this prayer before the LORD: 16"O LORD of Heav-
en's Armies, God of Israel, you are enthroned between
the mighty cherubim! You alone are God of all the
kingdoms of the earth. You alone created the heavens
and the earth. 17Bend down, O LORD, and listen! Open
your eyes, O LORD, and see! Listen to Sennacherib's
words of defiance against the living God.

18"It is true, LORD, that the kings of Assyria have destroyed all these nations. 19And they have thrown the
gods of these nations into the fire and burned them.
But of course the Assyrians could destroy them! They
were not gods at all—only idols of wood and stone
shaped by human hands. 20Now, O LORD our God,
rescue us from his power; then all the kingdoms of
the earth will know that you alone, O LORD, are God.*"

Isaiah Predicts Judah's Deliverance PARALLEL

2 KINGS 19:20-37

Then Isaiah son of Amoz sent this message to Hezekiah: "This is what the LORD, the God of Israel, says:
I have heard your prayer about King Sennacherib of
Assyria. 21And the LORD has spoken this word against
him:

"The virgin daughter of Zion
despises you and laughs at you.
The daughter of Jerusalem
shakes her head in derision as you flee.

22 "Whom have you been defying and ridiculing?
Against whom did you raise your voice?
At whom did you look with such haughty eyes?
It was the Holy One of Israel!
23 By your messengers you have defied the Lord.
You have said, 'With my many chariots
I have conquered the highest mountains—
yes, the remotest peaks of Lebanon.
I have cut down its tallest cedars
and its finest cypress trees.
I have reached its farthest corners
and explored its deepest forests.

Is 37:4 Or *the rabshakeh;* also in 37:8. **Is 37:7** Hebrew *I will put a spirit in him.* **Is 37:9** Hebrew *of Cush.* **Is 37:20** As in Dead Sea Scrolls (see also 2 Kgs 19:19); Masoretic Text reads *you alone are the LORD.*

Isa 37:3 Judah is compared to a woman who is trying to give birth to a child but is too weak to deliver. When the situation seemed hopeless, Hezekiah didn't give up. Instead, he asked the prophet Isaiah to pray that God would help his people. No matter how bad your circumstances seem, don't despair. Turn to God.

Isa 37:4 Hezekiah did exactly what Isaiah had been calling the people to do. He turned to God and watched him come to Judah's aid. Turning to God means believing that God is there and that he is able to help you.

Isa 37:8-10 Although the answer to Hezekiah's prayer was already in motion because Tirhakah was poised to attack, Hezekiah did not know it. He persisted in prayer and faith even though he could not see the answer coming. When we pray, we must have faith that God has already prepared the best answer. Our task is to ask in faith and wait in humility.

Isa 37:16 Cherubim are mighty angels. The phrase "enthroned between the mighty cherubim" refers to the atonement cover on the Ark of the Covenant, which symbolized God's holiness, power, and sovereignty.

2 Kgs 19:21-34 God replied to Sennacherib's taunting words (2 Kgs 18:19-25), indicting him for arrogance. Sennacherib believed his kingdom had grown because of his own efforts and strength. In reality, said God, he succeeded only because of what God had allowed and caused. It is arrogance to think we are solely responsible for our achievements. God, as Creator, rules over nations and people.

▸ **2 KINGS 19:20-37** ***(cont.)***

24 I have dug wells in many foreign lands
and refreshed myself with their water.
With the sole of my foot
I stopped up all the rivers of Egypt!'

25 "But have you not heard?
I decided this long ago.
Long ago I planned it,
and now I am making it happen.
I planned for you to crush fortified cities
into heaps of rubble.
26 That is why their people have so little power
and are so frightened and confused.
They are as weak as grass,
as easily trampled as tender green shoots.
They are like grass sprouting on a housetop,
scorched before it can grow lush and tall.

27 "But I know you well—
where you stay
and when you come and go.
I know the way you have raged against me.
28 And because of your raging against me
and your arrogance, which I have heard
for myself,
I will put my hook in your nose
and my bit in your mouth.
I will make you return
by the same road on which you came."

29Then Isaiah said to Hezekiah, "Here is the proof that
what I say is true:

"This year you will eat only what grows up
by itself,
and next year you will eat what springs up
from that.
But in the third year you will plant crops and
harvest them;
you will tend vineyards and eat their fruit.
30 And you who are left in Judah,
who have escaped the ravages of the siege,
will put roots down in your own soil
and will grow up and flourish.
31 For a remnant of my people will spread out from
Jerusalem,
a group of survivors from Mount Zion.
The passionate commitment of the LORD
of Heaven's Armies*
will make this happen!

32"And this is what the LORD says about the king of
Assyria:

"His armies will not enter Jerusalem.
They will not even shoot an arrow at it.
They will not march outside its gates with their
shields
nor build banks of earth against its walls.
33 The king will return to his own country
by the same road on which he came.
He will not enter this city,
says the LORD.
34 For my own honor and for the sake of my
servant David,
I will defend this city and protect it."

35That night the angel of the LORD went out to the
Assyrian camp and killed 185,000 Assyrian soldiers.
When the surviving Assyrians* woke up the next
morning, they found corpses everywhere. 36Then King
Sennacherib of Assyria broke camp and returned to
his own land. He went home to his capital of Nineveh
and stayed there.
37One day while he was worshiping in the temple of
his god Nisroch, his sons* Adrammelech and Sharezer
killed him with their swords. They then escaped to the
land of Ararat, and another son, Esarhaddon, became
the next king of Assyria.

2 CHRONICLES 32:20-23

Then King Hezekiah and the prophet Isaiah son of
Amoz cried out in prayer to God in heaven. 21And the
LORD sent an angel who destroyed the Assyrian army
with all its commanders and officers. So Sennacherib
was forced to return home in disgrace to his own land.
And when he entered the temple of his god, some of
his own sons killed him there with a sword.
22That is how the LORD rescued Hezekiah and the
people of Jerusalem from King Sennacherib of Assyria and from all the others who threatened them.
So there was peace throughout the land. 23From then
on King Hezekiah became highly respected among all
the surrounding nations, and many gifts for the LORD

2 Kgs 19:31 As in Greek and Syriac versions, Latin Vulgate, and an alternate reading of the Masoretic Text (see also Isa 37:32); the other alternate reads *the LORD.* **2 Kgs 19:35** Hebrew *When they.* **2 Kgs 19:37** As in Greek version and an alternate reading of the Masoretic Text (see also Isa 37:38); the other alternate reading lacks *his sons.*

700 BC

False teeth invented in Italy

2 Kgs 19:28 The Assyrians treated captives with cruelty. They tortured prisoners for entertainment by blinding them, cutting them, or pulling off strips of their skin until they died. If the Assyrians wished to make a captive a slave, they would often put a hook in his nose. God was saying that the Assyrians would be treated the way they had treated others.

2 Kgs 19:31 As long as a tiny spark remains, a fire can be rekindled and fanned into a roaring blaze. Similarly, if just a small remnant of true believers retains the spark of faith, God can rebuild it into a strong nation. And if only a glimmer of faith remains in a heart, God can use it to restore blazing faith in that believer. If you feel that only a spark of faith remains in you, ask God to use it to rekindle a blazing fire of commitment to him.

Isa 37:35 God would defend Jerusalem for the sake of his own honor and for David's sake in remembrance of his promise to David. The Assyrians had insulted God. They would not be his instrument to punish Jerusalem. What Jerusalem could not possibly do, God would do for it. God is prepared to do the impossible if we trust him enough to ask.

Isa 37:38 Isaiah prophesied the death of Sennacherib (Isa 10:12, 33-34; 37:7).

arrived at Jerusalem, with valuable presents for King Hezekiah, too.

ISAIAH 37:21-38

Then Isaiah son of Amoz sent this message to Hezekiah: "This is what the LORD, the God of Israel, says: Because you prayed about King Sennacherib of Assyria, [22]the LORD has spoken this word against him:

"The virgin daughter of Zion
despises you and laughs at you.
The daughter of Jerusalem
shakes her head in derision as you flee.
23 "Whom have you been defying and ridiculing?
Against whom did you raise your voice?
At whom did you look with such haughty eyes?
It was the Holy One of Israel!
24 By your messengers you have defied the Lord.
You have said, 'With my many chariots
I have conquered the highest mountains—
yes, the remotest peaks of Lebanon.
I have cut down its tallest cedars
and its finest cypress trees.
I have reached its farthest heights
and explored its deepest forests.
25 I have dug wells in many foreign lands*
and refreshed myself with their water.
With the sole of my foot,
I stopped up all the rivers of Egypt!'

26 "But have you not heard?
I decided this long ago.
Long ago I planned it,
and now I am making it happen.
I planned for you to crush fortified cities
into heaps of rubble.
27 That is why their people have so little power
and are so frightened and confused.
They are as weak as grass,
as easily trampled as tender green shoots.
They are like grass sprouting on a housetop,
scorched* before it can grow lush and tall.

28 "But I know you well—
where you stay
and when you come and go.
I know the way you have raged against me.
29 And because of your raging against me
and your arrogance, which I have heard for myself,
I will put my hook in your nose
and my bit in your mouth.
I will make you return
by the same road on which you came."

[30]Then Isaiah said to Hezekiah, "Here is the proof that what I say is true:

"This year you will eat only what grows up by itself,
and next year you will eat what springs up from that.
But in the third year you will plant crops and harvest them;
you will tend vineyards and eat their fruit.
31 And you who are left in Judah,
who have escaped the ravages of the siege,
will put roots down in your own soil
and grow up and flourish.
32 For a remnant of my people will spread out from Jerusalem,
a group of survivors from Mount Zion.
The passionate commitment of the LORD of Heaven's Armies
will make this happen!

[33]"And this is what the LORD says about the king of Assyria:

"'His armies will not enter Jerusalem.
They will not even shoot an arrow at it.
They will not march outside its gates with their shields
nor build banks of earth against its walls.
34 The king will return to his own country
by the same road on which he came.
He will not enter this city,'
says the LORD.
35 'For my own honor and for the sake of my servant David,
I will defend this city and protect it.'"

[36]That night the angel of the LORD went out to the
Assyrian camp and killed 185,000 Assyrian soldiers.
When the surviving Assyrians* woke up the next
morning, they found corpses everywhere. [37]Then King
Sennacherib of Assyria broke camp and returned to
his own land. He went home to his capital of Nineveh
and stayed there.

[38]One day while he was worshiping in the temple of
his god Nisroch, his sons Adrammelech and Sharezer
killed him with their swords. They then escaped to the
land of Ararat, and another son, Esarhaddon, became
the next king of Assyria.

Hezekiah's Sickness and Recovery PARALLEL

2 KINGS 20:1-11

About that time Hezekiah became deathly ill, and the
prophet Isaiah son of Amoz went to visit him. He gave
the king this message: "This is what the LORD says: Set
your affairs in order, for you are going to die. You will
not recover from this illness."

[2]When Hezekiah heard this, he turned his face to
the wall and prayed to the LORD, [3]"Remember, O LORD,
how I have always been faithful to you and have served

Is 37:25 As in Dead Sea Scrolls (see also 2 Kgs 19:24); Masoretic Text lacks *in many foreign lands.* **Is 37:27** As in Dead Sea Scrolls and some Greek manuscripts (see also 2 Kgs 19:26); most Hebrew manuscripts read *like a terraced field.* **Is 37:36** Hebrew *When they.*

▸ **2 KINGS 20:1-11** ***(cont.)***

you single-mindedly, always doing what pleases you." Then he broke down and wept bitterly.

4But before Isaiah had left the middle courtyard,* this message came to him from the LORD: 5"Go back to Hezekiah, the leader of my people. Tell him, 'This is what the LORD, the God of your ancestor David, says: I have heard your prayer and seen your tears. I will heal you, and three days from now you will get out of bed and go to the Temple of the LORD. 6I will add fifteen years to your life, and I will rescue you and this city from the king of Assyria. I will defend this city for my own honor and for the sake of my servant David.'"

7Then Isaiah said, "Make an ointment from figs." So Hezekiah's servants spread the ointment over the boil, and Hezekiah recovered!

8Meanwhile, Hezekiah had said to Isaiah, "What sign will the LORD give to prove that he will heal me and that I will go to the Temple of the LORD three days from now?"

9Isaiah replied, "This is the sign from the LORD to prove that he will do as he promised. Would you like the shadow on the sundial to go forward ten steps or backward ten steps?*"

10"The shadow always moves forward," Hezekiah replied, "so that would be easy. Make it go ten steps backward instead." 11So Isaiah the prophet asked the LORD to do this, and he caused the shadow to move ten steps backward on the sundial* of Ahaz!

2 CHRONICLES 32:24-31

About that time Hezekiah became deathly ill. He prayed to the LORD, who healed him and gave him a miraculous sign. 25But Hezekiah did not respond appropriately to the kindness shown him, and he became proud. So the LORD's anger came against him and against Judah and Jerusalem. 26Then Hezekiah humbled himself and repented of his pride, as did the people of Jerusalem. So the LORD's anger did not fall on them during Hezekiah's lifetime.

27Hezekiah was very wealthy and highly honored. He built special treasury buildings for his silver, gold, precious stones, and spices, and for his shields and other valuable items. 28He also constructed many storehouses for his grain, new wine, and olive oil; and he made many stalls for his cattle and pens for his flocks of sheep and goats. 29He built many towns and acquired vast flocks and herds, for God had given him great wealth. 30He blocked up the upper spring of Gihon and brought the water down through a tunnel to the west side of the City of David. And so he succeeded in everything he did.

31However, when ambassadors arrived from Babylon to ask about the remarkable events that had taken place in the land, God withdrew from Hezekiah in order to test him and to see what was really in his heart.

ISAIAH 38:1-8

About that time Hezekiah became deathly ill, and the prophet Isaiah son of Amoz went to visit him. He gave the king this message: "This is what the LORD says: 'Set your affairs in order, for you are going to die. You will not recover from this illness.'"

2When Hezekiah heard this, he turned his face to the wall and prayed to the LORD, 3"Remember, O LORD, how I have always been faithful to you and have served you single-mindedly, always doing what pleases you." Then he broke down and wept bitterly.

4Then this message came to Isaiah from the LORD: 5"Go back to Hezekiah and tell him, 'This is what the LORD, the God of your ancestor David, says: I have heard your prayer and seen your tears. I will add fifteen years to your life, 6and I will rescue you and this city from the king of Assyria. Yes, I will defend this city.

2 Kgs 20:4 As in Greek version and an alternate reading in the Masoretic Text; the other alternate reads *the middle of the city.* **2 Kgs 20:9** Or *The shadow on the sundial has gone forward ten steps; do you want it to go backward ten steps?* **2 Kgs 20:11** Hebrew *the steps.*

2 Kgs 20:5-6 Over a 100-year period of Judah's history (732–640 B.C.), Hezekiah was the only faithful king; but what a difference he made! Because of Hezekiah's faith and prayer, God healed him and saved his city from the Assyrians. You can make a difference, too, even if your faith puts you in the minority. Faith and prayer, if they are sincere and directed toward the one true God, can change any situation.

2 Kgs 20:11 Egyptian sundials in this period were sometimes made in the form of miniature staircases so that the shadows moved up and down the steps.

2 Chr 32:31 A test can bring out a person's true character. God tested Hezekiah to see what he was really like and to show him his own shortcomings and the attitude of his heart. God did not totally abandon Hezekiah, nor did he tempt him to sin or trick him. The test was meant to strengthen Hezekiah, develop his character, and prepare him for the tasks ahead. In times of success, most of us can live good lives. But pressure, trouble, or pain will quickly remove our thin veneer of goodness unless our strength comes from God. What are you like under pressure or when everything is going wrong? Do you give in or turn to God? Those who are consistently in touch with God don't have to worry about what pressure may reveal about them.

2 Chr 32:31 Babylon was slowly and quietly rising to become a world power. At the same time, the Assyrian Empire was slowly declining due to internal strife and a succession of weak kings. When Assyria was finally crushed in 612 B.C., Babylon, under Nebuchadnezzar, moved into its place of prominence. (For more information on Babylon, see the note on 2 Kgs 20:14, p. 922.)

2 Chr 32:31 Why did God withdraw from Hezekiah? After Hezekiah was healed of his sickness, he became proud. When ambassadors came to inquire about his miraculous healing, God stepped back to see how Hezekiah would respond. Unfortunately, Hezekiah's actions revealed his runaway pride. He pointed to his own accomplishments rather than to God (see 2 Kgs 20:12-19). Pride is any attitude that elevates our effort or abilities above God's or treats with disdain his work in us. It causes us to congratulate ourselves for our successes and to look down on other people. God does not object to self-confidence, healthy self-esteem, or good feelings about our accomplishments. He objects to the foolish attitude of taking full credit for what *he* has done or for setting ourselves up as superior to others.

Isa 38:1-5 When Isaiah went to Hezekiah, who was extremely ill, and told him of his impending death, Hezekiah immediately turned to God. God responded to his prayer, allowing Hezekiah to live another 15 years.

7"'And this is the sign from the LORD to prove that
he will do as he promised: 8I will cause the sun's
shadow to move ten steps backward on the sundial*
of Ahaz!'" So the shadow on the sundial moved backward ten steps.

Hezekiah's Poem of Praise

ISAIAH 38:9-22

When King Hezekiah was well again, he wrote this poem:

10 I said, "In the prime of my life,
must I now enter the place of the dead?*
Am I to be robbed of the rest of
my years?"
11 I said, "Never again will I see the LORD GOD
while still in the land of the living.
Never again will I see my friends
or be with those who live in this world.
12 My life has been blown away
like a shepherd's tent in a storm.
It has been cut short,
as when a weaver cuts cloth from a loom.
Suddenly, my life was over.
13 I waited patiently all night,
but I was torn apart as though by lions.
Suddenly, my life was over.
14 Delirious, I chattered like a swallow or
a crane,
and then I moaned like a mourning dove.
My eyes grew tired of looking to heaven for help.
I am in trouble, Lord. Help me!"
15 But what could I say?
For he himself sent this sickness.
Now I will walk humbly throughout my years
because of this anguish I have felt.
16 Lord, your discipline is good,
for it leads to life and health.
You restore my health
and allow me to live!
17 Yes, this anguish was good for me,
for you have rescued me from death
and forgiven all my sins.
18 For the dead* cannot praise you;
they cannot raise their voices in praise.
Those who go down to the grave
can no longer hope in your faithfulness.
19 Only the living can praise you as I do today.
Each generation tells of your faithfulness to
the next.
20 Think of it—the LORD is ready to heal me!
I will sing his praises with instruments
every day of my life
in the Temple of the LORD.

21Isaiah had said to Hezekiah's servants, "Make an
ointment from figs and spread it over the boil, and
Hezekiah will recover."
22And Hezekiah had asked, "What sign will prove
that I will go to the Temple of the LORD?"

Is 38:8 Hebrew *the steps.* **Is 38:10** Hebrew *enter the gates of Sheol?* **Is 38:18** Hebrew *Sheol.*

If you have a desperate need in your life, bring it to the Lord. In response to fervent prayer, God may change the course of your life too.

Isa 38:16-18 Hezekiah realized that his prayer brought deliverance and forgiveness. His words "the dead cannot praise you" may reveal that he was unaware of the blessedness of the future life for those who trust in God (Isa 57:1-2), or he may have meant that dead bodies cannot praise God. In either case, Hezekiah knew that God had spared his life, so in his poem Hezekiah praises God. Hezekiah recognized the good that came from his bitter experience. The next time you have difficult struggles, pray for God's help to gain something beneficial from them.

Isa 38:19 Hezekiah spoke of the significance of passing the joy of the Lord from generation to generation. The heritage of our faith has come to us because of faithful men and women who have carried God's message to us across the centuries. Do you share with your children or other young people the excitement of your relationship with God?

Hezekiah's Tunnel

When Hezekiah was faced with a threat of invasion by the Assyrian army under Sennacherib, he diverted the upper Gihon spring through a conduit or tunnel into an upper cistern or pool. This tunnel can still be seen today. Inside the tunnel there was an inscription which reads, ". . . was being dug out. It was cut in the following manner . . . axes, each man toward his fellow, and while there was three cubits to be cut through, the voice of one man calling to the other was heard, showing that he was deviating to the right. When the tunnel was driven through, the excavators met man to man, axe to axe, and the water flowed for 1,200 cubits from the spring of the reservoir. The height of the rock above the heads of the excavators was 100 cubits." The archaic Hebrew script in the inscription supports a date in Hezekiah's reign (c. 710 B.C.).

Here is a clear case where archaeology confirms the Scripture (2 Chr 32:30). The biblical record can be trusted.

8. THE END OF HEZEKIAH'S REIGN

Hezekiah was a good king who followed God and led the nation of Judah well for most of his reign, but he made a critical error toward the end of his reign, giving envoys from Babylon a guided tour of the riches of the nation. The prophet Isaiah warned Hezekiah that this foolish act would result in his descendants being carried off to Babylon.

Envoys from Babylon PARALLEL

2 KINGS 20:12-19

Soon after this, Merodach-baladan son of Baladan, king
of Babylon, sent Hezekiah his best wishes and a gift,
for he had heard that Hezekiah had been very sick.
13Hezekiah received the Babylonian envoys and showed
them everything in his treasure-houses—the silver, the
gold, the spices, and the aromatic oils. He also took
them to see his armory and showed them everything
in his royal treasuries! There was nothing in his palace
or kingdom that Hezekiah did not show them.
14Then Isaiah the prophet went to King Hezekiah
and asked him, "What did those men want? Where
were they from?"
Hezekiah replied, "They came from the distant land
of Babylon."
15"What did they see in your palace?" Isaiah asked.
"They saw everything," Hezekiah replied. "I showed
them everything I own—all my royal treasuries."
16Then Isaiah said to Hezekiah, "Listen to this
message from the LORD: 17The time is coming when
everything in your palace—all the treasures stored up
by your ancestors until now—will be carried off to
Babylon. Nothing will be left, says the LORD. 18Some
of your very own sons will be taken away into exile.
They will become eunuchs who will serve in the palace
of Babylon's king."
19Then Hezekiah said to Isaiah, "This message you
have given me from the LORD is good." For the king
was thinking, "At least there will be peace and security
during my lifetime."

ISAIAH 39:1-8

Soon after this, Merodach-baladan son of Baladan,
king of Babylon, sent Hezekiah his best wishes and a
gift. He had heard that Hezekiah had been very sick
and that he had recovered. 2Hezekiah was delighted
with the Babylonian envoys and showed them everything in his treasure-houses—the silver, the gold, the
spices, and the aromatic oils. He also took them to see
his armory and showed them everything in his royal
treasuries! There was nothing in his palace or kingdom
that Hezekiah did not show them.
3Then Isaiah the prophet went to King Hezekiah
and asked him, "What did those men want? Where
were they from?"
Hezekiah replied, "They came from the distant land
of Babylon."
4"What did they see in your palace?" asked Isaiah.
"They saw everything," Hezekiah replied. "I showed
them everything I own—all my royal treasuries."
5Then Isaiah said to Hezekiah, "Listen to this message from the LORD of Heaven's Armies: 6'The time
is coming when everything in your palace—all the
treasures stored up by your ancestors until now—will
be carried off to Babylon. Nothing will be left,' says
the LORD. 7'Some of your very own sons will be taken
away into exile. They will become eunuchs who will
serve in the palace of Babylon's king.'"

---

2 Kgs 20:12-19 Hezekiah had been a good and faithful king. But when Isaiah asked him what he had shown the messengers from Babylon, he replied, "I showed them everything I own—all my royal treasuries." Rather than giving credit to God for all his blessings, he tried to impress the foreigners. When God helps us, we must not use his blessings to impress others. A testimony of victory can quickly degenerate into vanity and self-congratulations.

2 Kgs 20:14 Babylon, a city that had rebelled against the Assyrian Empire, was destroyed by Sennacherib in 689 B.C. This event probably occurred shortly before that date. When Sennacherib died in 681 B.C., his son, Esarhaddon, foolishly rebuilt the city of Babylon. Assyria, whose rulers at that time were weak, allowed Babylon plenty of opportunity to become strong. As the Assyrian army marched off to conquer and oppress faraway lands, the city of Babylon grew and expanded into a small nation. After some years, Babylon was strong enough to rebel again. It eventually crushed Assyria (612 B.C.) and became the next world power.

2 Kgs 20:19 Hezekiah was saying that it was good that these terrible events foretold by Isaiah wouldn't happen during his lifetime. Hezekiah's statement seems selfish, shortsighted, and proud. He knew that his nation would be punished for its sins, so he may have been acknowledging and thanking God for choosing not to destroy Judah during his lifetime.

Isa 39:1ff Merodach-baladan, a Babylonian prince, was planning a revolt against Assyria and was forming an alliance. He probably hoped to convince Hezekiah to join this alliance against Assyria. Hezekiah, feeling honored by this attention and perhaps feeling some sympathy for their proposal, showed the Babylonian envoys his treasures. But Isaiah warned the king not to trust Babylon. Someday they would turn on Judah and devour Jerusalem's wealth.

Isa 39:4-7 What was so wrong about showing these Babylonians around? Hezekiah failed to see that the Babylonians would become his next threat and that they, not the Assyrians, would conquer his city. When Isaiah told him that Babylon would someday carry it all away, this was an amazing prophecy because Babylon was struggling for independence under Assyria. Hezekiah's prideful display of his earthly treasures brought its own consequences (2 Kgs 25; Dan 1:1-2).

Isa 39:8 Hezekiah, one of Judah's most faithful kings, worked hard throughout his reign to stamp out idol worship and to purify the worship of the true God at the Jerusalem Temple. Nevertheless he knew his kingdom was not pure. Powerful undercurrents of evil invited destruction, and only God's miraculous interventions preserved Judah from its enemies. Here Hezekiah was grateful that God would preserve peace during his reign. As soon as Hezekiah died, the nation rushed back to its sinful ways under the leadership of Manasseh, Hezekiah's son. He actually rebuilt the centers of idolatry his father had destroyed.

8 Then Hezekiah said to Isaiah, "This message you
have given me from the LORD is good." For the king
was thinking, "At least there will be peace and security
during my lifetime."

Summary of Hezekiah's Reign PARALLEL

2 KINGS 20:20-21

The rest of the events in Hezekiah's reign, including the extent of his power and how he built a pool
and dug a tunnel* to bring water into the city, are
recorded in *The Book of the History of the Kings of*
Judah. 21 Hezekiah died, and his son Manasseh became
the next king.

2 Kgs 20:20 Hebrew *watercourse*.

2 CHRONICLES 32:32-33

The rest of the events in Hezekiah's reign and his acts
of devotion are recorded in *The Vision of the Prophet*
Isaiah Son of Amoz, which is included in *The Book of*
the Kings of Judah and Israel. 33 When Hezekiah died,
he was buried in the upper area of the royal cemetery,
and all Judah and Jerusalem honored him at his death.
And his son Manasseh became the next king.

K. Isaiah's Messages of Hope for God's People

Nearing the end of his ministry, Isaiah now speaks of events that will occur after Judah is carried off into captivity. This includes the decree by Cyrus to release the remnant captives and allow them to return to Jerusalem after he conquered Babylon. But Isaiah also foretells the coming of the suffering Servant, Jesus Christ, and describes his life and death with incredible detail. Isaiah also speaks about the coming of the new heavens and earth, when God's people will be completely restored. Because all believers will participate in this new world to come, we can have confident hope in the future.

1. THE PROMISE OF ISRAEL'S RELEASE FROM CAPTIVITY

In this section, Isaiah announces the good news of God's coming salvation for his people. The Lord is coming to vindicate his own and to judge his enemies. This note of hope would serve to comfort and encourage the people of Judah during difficult times in their history, and would continue to do so during their exile.

Comfort for God's People

ISAIAH 40:1-11

1 "Comfort, comfort my people,"
says your God.
2 "Speak tenderly to Jerusalem.
Tell her that her sad days are gone
and her sins are pardoned.
Yes, the LORD has punished her twice over
for all her sins."

3 Listen! It's the voice of someone
shouting,
"Clear the way through the wilderness
for the LORD!
Make a straight highway through the wasteland
for our God!
4 Fill in the valleys,
and level the mountains and hills.
Straighten the curves,
and smooth out the rough places.
5 Then the glory of the LORD will be revealed,
and all people will see it together.
The LORD has spoken!"*

Is 40:3-5 Greek version reads *He is a voice shouting in the wilderness, / "Prepare the way for the LORD's coming! / Clear a road for our God! / Fill in the valleys, / and level the mountains and hills. / And then the glory of the LORD will be revealed, / and all people will see the salvation sent from God. / The LORD has spoken!"* Compare Matt 3:3; Mark 1:3; Luke 3:4-6.

2 Kgs 20:20 The pool and the tunnel refer to a 1,777-foot tunnel built from the upper spring of Gihon to the pool of Siloam (see 2 Chr 32:30). It was from a water source outside the wall of Jerusalem to a secure reservoir inside the city. This was done so the Assyrian army would not cut off the city's water supply.

Isa 40–66 The book of Isaiah makes a dramatic shift at this point. These chapters discuss the majesty of God, who is coming to rule the earth and judge all people. Instead of warning Israel and Judah of impending judgment, Isaiah here comforts them. Isaiah 40 refers to the restoration after the Exile; Cyrus is the instrument of their deliverance from Babylon (Isa 45). Isaiah also foretells a time when "Babylon"—the future evil world system—will be destroyed and the persecution of God's people will end. God will reunite Israel and Judah and restore them to glory.

Isa 40:1-2 Judah still had 100 years of trouble before Jerusalem would fall, then 70 years of exile. So God tells Isaiah to speak tenderly and comfort Jerusalem.

The seeds of comfort may take root in the soil of adversity. When your life seems to be falling apart, ask God to comfort you. You may not escape adversity, but you may find God's comfort as you face it. Sometimes the only comfort we have is in the knowledge that someday we will be with God. Appreciate the comfort and encouragement found in his Word, his presence, and his people.

Isa 40:3-5 Preparing a straight highway means removing obstacles and rolling out the red carpet for the coming of the Lord. The wasteland is a picture of life's trials and sufferings. We are not immune to these, but our faith need not be hindered by them. Isaiah told the people to prepare to see God work. John the Baptist used these words as he challenged the people to prepare for the coming Messiah (Matt 3:3).

▸ ISAIAH 40:1-11 *(cont.)*

6 A voice said, "Shout!"
I asked, "What should I shout?"

"Shout that people are like the grass.
Their beauty fades as quickly
as the flowers in a field.
7 The grass withers and the flowers fade
beneath the breath of the LORD.
And so it is with people.
8 The grass withers and the flowers fade,
but the word of our God stands forever."

9 O Zion, messenger of good news,
shout from the mountaintops!
Shout it louder, O Jerusalem.*
Shout, and do not be afraid.
Tell the towns of Judah,
"Your God is coming!"
10 Yes, the Sovereign LORD is coming in power.
He will rule with a powerful arm.
See, he brings his reward with him as he
comes.
11 He will feed his flock like a shepherd.
He will carry the lambs in his arms,
holding them close to his heart.
He will gently lead the mother sheep with
their young.

The LORD Has No Equal

ISAIAH 40:12-31

12 Who else has held the oceans in his hand?
Who has measured off the heavens with
his fingers?
Who else knows the weight of the earth
or has weighed the mountains and hills
on a scale?
13 Who is able to advise the Spirit of the LORD?*
Who knows enough to give him advice or
teach him?
14 Has the LORD ever needed anyone's advice?
Does he need instruction about what is good?
Did someone teach him what is right
or show him the path of justice?

15 No, for all the nations of the world
are but a drop in the bucket.
They are nothing more
than dust on the scales.
He picks up the whole earth
as though it were a grain of sand.
16 All the wood in Lebanon's forests
and all Lebanon's animals would not be
enough
to make a burnt offering worthy of our God.
17 The nations of the world are worth nothing
to him.
In his eyes they count for less than nothing—
mere emptiness and froth.

18 To whom can you compare God?
What image can you find to resemble him?
19 Can he be compared to an idol formed in a mold,
overlaid with gold, and decorated with silver
chains?
20 Or if people are too poor for that,
they might at least choose wood that won't
decay
and a skilled craftsman
to carve an image that won't fall down!

21 Haven't you heard? Don't you understand?
Are you deaf to the words of God—
the words he gave before the world began?
Are you so ignorant?
22 God sits above the circle of the earth.
The people below seem like grasshoppers
to him!
He spreads out the heavens like a curtain
and makes his tent from them.
23 He judges the great people of the world
and brings them all to nothing.
24 They hardly get started, barely taking root,
when he blows on them and they wither.
The wind carries them off like chaff.

25 "To whom will you compare me?
Who is my equal?" asks the Holy One.

26 Look up into the heavens.
Who created all the stars?
He brings them out like an army, one after
another,
calling each by its name.

Is 40:9 Or *O messenger of good news, shout to Zion from the mountaintops! Shout it louder to Jerusalem.* **Is 40:13** Greek version reads *Who can know the LORD's thoughts?* Compare Rom 11:34; 1 Cor 2:16.

Isa 40:6-8 People are compared here to grass and flowers that wither away. We are mortal, but God's Word is eternal and unfailing. Public opinion changes and is unreliable, but God's Word is constant. Only in God's eternal Word will we find lasting solutions to our problems and needs.

Isa 40:11 God is often pictured as a shepherd, gently caring for and guiding his flock. He is powerful (Isa 40:10), yet careful and gentle. He is called a shepherd (Ps 23); the good shepherd (John 10:11, 14); the great Shepherd (Heb 13:20); and the Great Shepherd (1 Pet 5:4). Note that the shepherd is caring for the most defenseless members of his society: children and those caring for them. This reinforces the prophetic theme that the truly powerful nation is not the one with a strong military, but rather the one that relies on God's caring strength.

Isa 40:12-31 Isaiah describes God's power to create, his provision to sustain, and his presence to help. God is almighty and all-powerful; but even so, he cares for each of us personally. No person or thing can be compared to God (Isa 40:25). We describe God as best we can with our limited knowledge and language, but we only limit our understanding of him and his power when we compare him to what we experience on earth. What is your concept of God, especially as revealed in his Son, Jesus Christ? Don't limit his work in your life by underestimating him.

Because of his great power and incomparable
strength,
not a single one is missing.
27 O Jacob, how can you say the LORD does not
see your troubles?
O Israel, how can you say God ignores
your rights?
28 Have you never heard?
Have you never understood?
The LORD is the everlasting God,
the Creator of all the earth.
He never grows weak or weary.
No one can measure the depths of his
understanding.
29 He gives power to the weak
and strength to the powerless.
30 Even youths will become weak and tired,
and young men will fall in exhaustion.
31 But those who trust in the LORD will find
new strength.
They will soar high on wings like eagles.
They will run and not grow weary.
They will walk and not faint.

God's Help for Israel

ISAIAH 41:1-29

1 "Listen in silence before me, you lands
beyond the sea.
Bring your strongest arguments.
Come now and speak.
The court is ready for your case.

2 "Who has stirred up this king from the east,
rightly calling him to God's service?
Who gives this man victory over many
nations
and permits him to trample their kings
underfoot?
With his sword, he reduces armies to dust.
With his bow, he scatters them like chaff
before the wind.
3 He chases them away and goes on safely,
though he is walking over unfamiliar ground.
4 Who has done such mighty deeds,
summoning each new generation from the
beginning of time?
It is I, the LORD, the First and the Last.
I alone am he."

5 The lands beyond the sea watch in fear.
Remote lands tremble and mobilize for war.
6 The idol makers encourage one another,
saying to each other, "Be strong!"
7 The carver encourages the goldsmith,
and the molder helps at the anvil.
"Good," they say. "It's coming along fine."
Carefully they join the parts together,
then fasten the thing in place so it won't
fall over.

8 "But as for you, Israel my servant,
Jacob my chosen one,
descended from Abraham my friend,
9 I have called you back from the ends of the earth,
saying, 'You are my servant.'
For I have chosen you
and will not throw you away.
10 Don't be afraid, for I am with you.
Don't be discouraged, for I am your God.
I will strengthen you and help you.
I will hold you up with my victorious
right hand.

11 "See, all your angry enemies lie there,
confused and humiliated.
Anyone who opposes you will die
and come to nothing.
12 You will look in vain
for those who tried to conquer you.
Those who attack you
will come to nothing.
13 For I hold you by your right hand—
I, the LORD your God.

Isa 40:29-31 Even the strongest people get tired at times, but God's power and strength never diminish. He is never too tired or too busy to help and listen. His strength is our source of strength. When you feel all of life crushing you and you cannot go another step, remember that you can call upon God to renew your strength.

Isa 40:31 Trusting in the Lord is the patient expectation that God will fulfill his promises in his Word and strengthen us to rise above life's difficulties. Do you believe God loves you and wants the best for you? Can you relax, confident that his purposes are right? Are you convinced that he has the power to control all of life—and your life as well? Though your faith may be struggling or weak, accept his provisions and care for you.

Isa 41:1ff The "king from the east" is Cyrus II of Persia, who would be king within a century and a half (he is also mentioned by name in Isa 44:28). He conquered Babylon in 539 B.C. and was responsible for the decree releasing the exiled Jews to return to Jerusalem. God could even use a pagan ruler to protect and care for Israel because God is in control of all world politics.

Isa 41:4 Each generation gets caught up in its own problems, but God's plan embraces all generations. When your great-grandparents lived, God worked personally in the lives of his people. When your great-grandchildren live, God will still work personally in the lives of his people. He is the only one who sees 100 years from now as clearly as 100 years ago. When you are concerned about the future, talk with God, who knows the generations of the future as well as he knows the generations of the past.

Isa 41:8-10 God chose Israel through Abraham because he wanted to, not because the people deserved it (Deut 7:6-8; 9:4-6). Although God chose the Israelites to represent him to the world, they failed to do this; so God punished them and sent them into captivity. Now all believers are God's chosen people, and all share the responsibility of representing him to the world. One day God will bring all his faithful people together. We need not fear because: (1) God is with us ("I am with you"); (2) God has established a relationship with us ("I am your God"); and (3) God gives us assurance of his strength, help, and victory over sin and death. Are you aware of all the ways God has helped you?

▶ **ISAIAH 41:1-29** ***(cont.)***

And I say to you,
'Don't be afraid. I am here to help you.
14 Though you are a lowly worm, O Jacob,
don't be afraid, people of Israel, for I will help you.
I am the LORD, your Redeemer.
I am the Holy One of Israel.'
15 You will be a new threshing instrument
with many sharp teeth.
You will tear your enemies apart,
making chaff of mountains.
16 You will toss them into the air,
and the wind will blow them all away;
a whirlwind will scatter them.
Then you will rejoice in the LORD.
You will glory in the Holy One of Israel.

17 "When the poor and needy search for water
and there is none,
and their tongues are parched from thirst,
then I, the LORD, will answer them.
I, the God of Israel, will never abandon them.
18 I will open up rivers for them on the high plateaus.
I will give them fountains of water in the valleys.
I will fill the desert with pools of water.
Rivers fed by springs will flow across the parched ground.
19 I will plant trees in the barren desert—
cedar, acacia, myrtle, olive, cypress, fir, and pine.
20 I am doing this so all who see this miracle
will understand what it means—
that it is the LORD who has done this,
the Holy One of Israel who created it.

21 "Present the case for your idols,"
says the LORD.
"Let them show what they can do,"
says the King of Israel.*
22 "Let them try to tell us what happened long ago
so that we may consider the evidence.
Or let them tell us what the future holds,
so we can know what's going to happen.
23 Yes, tell us what will occur in the days ahead.
Then we will know you are gods.
In fact, do anything—good or bad!
Do something that will amaze and frighten us.
24 But no! You are less than nothing and can do nothing at all.
Those who choose you pollute themselves.

25 "But I have stirred up a leader who will come from the north.
I have called him by name from the east.
I will give him victory over kings and princes.
He will trample them as a potter treads on clay.

26 "Who told you from the beginning
that this would happen?
Who predicted this,
making you admit that he was right?
No one said a word!
27 I was the first to tell Zion,
'Look! Help is on the way!'*
I will send Jerusalem a messenger with good news.
28 Not one of your idols told you this.
Not one gave any answer when I asked.
29 See, they are all foolish, worthless things.
All your idols are as empty as the wind.

The LORD's Chosen Servant

ISAIAH 42:1-9

1 "Look at my servant, whom I strengthen.
He is my chosen one, who pleases me.
I have put my Spirit upon him.
He will bring justice to the nations.
2 He will not shout
or raise his voice in public.
3 He will not crush the weakest reed
or put out a flickering candle.
He will bring justice to all who have been wronged.
4 He will not falter or lose heart
until justice prevails throughout the earth.
Even distant lands beyond the sea will wait for his instruction.*"

Is 41:21 Hebrew *the King of Jacob.* See note on 14:1. **Is 41:27** Or *'Look! They are coming home.'* **Is 42:4** Greek version reads *And his name will be the hope of all the world.* Compare Matt 12:21.

Isa 41:21-24 Israel was surrounded by many nations whose gods supposedly had special powers, such as helping crops grow and providing victory in war. But these gods failed to deliver. A god with limited or no power is not really a god. When we are tempted to put our trust in something other than the living God—money, career, family, or even military power—we should stop and ask some serious questions. Will it come through? Will it unfailingly provide what I am looking for? God delivers. When he makes a promise, he keeps it. He is completely trustworthy.

Isa 42:1-4 These verses are quoted in Matthew 12:18-21 with reference to Christ. The chosen servant reveals a character of gentleness, encouragement, justice, and truth. When you feel broken and bruised or burned out in your spiritual life, God won't step on you or toss you aside as useless but will gently pick you up. God's loving attributes are desperately needed in the world today. Through God's Spirit, we can show sensitivity to people around us, reflecting God's goodness and honesty to them.

Isa 42:1-9 Sometimes called the Servant Song, these verses are about the Servant-Messiah, not the servant Cyrus (described in Isa 41). Both Israel and the Messiah are often called *servant.* Israel, as God's servant, was to help bring the world to a knowledge of God. The Messiah, Jesus, would fulfill this task and show God himself to the world.

5 God, the LORD, created the heavens and stretched
them out.
He created the earth and everything in it.
He gives breath to everyone,
life to everyone who walks the earth.
And it is he who says,
6 "I, the LORD, have called you to demonstrate my
righteousness.
I will take you by the hand and guard you,
and I will give you to my people, Israel,
as a symbol of my covenant with them.
And you will be a light to guide the nations.
7 You will open the eyes of the blind.
You will free the captives from prison,
releasing those who sit in dark dungeons.

8 "I am the LORD; that is my name!
I will not give my glory to anyone else,
nor share my praise with carved idols.
9 Everything I prophesied has come true,
and now I will prophesy again.
I will tell you the future before it happens."

A Song of Praise to the LORD

ISAIAH 42:10-17

10 Sing a new song to the LORD!
Sing his praises from the ends of the earth!
Sing, all you who sail the seas,
all you who live in distant coastlands.
11 Join in the chorus, you desert towns;
let the villages of Kedar rejoice!
Let the people of Sela sing for joy;
shout praises from the mountaintops!
12 Let the whole world glorify the LORD;
let it sing his praise.
13 The LORD will march forth like a mighty hero;
he will come out like a warrior, full of fury.
He will shout his battle cry
and crush all his enemies.

14 He will say, "I have long been silent;
yes, I have restrained myself.
But now, like a woman in labor,
I will cry and groan and pant.
15 I will level the mountains and hills
and blight all their greenery.
I will turn the rivers into dry land
and will dry up all the pools.
16 I will lead blind Israel down a new path,
guiding them along an unfamiliar way.
I will brighten the darkness before them
and smooth out the road ahead of them.
Yes, I will indeed do these things;
I will not forsake them.
17 But those who trust in idols,
who say, 'You are our gods,'
will be turned away in shame.

Israel's Failure to Listen and See

ISAIAH 42:18-25

18 "Listen, you who are deaf!
Look and see, you blind!
19 Who is as blind as my own people, my servant?
Who is as deaf as my messenger?
Who is as blind as my chosen people,
the servant of the LORD?
20 You see and recognize what is right
but refuse to act on it.
You hear with your ears,
but you don't really listen."

21 Because he is righteous,
the LORD has exalted his glorious law.
22 But his own people have been robbed and
plundered,
enslaved, imprisoned, and trapped.
They are fair game for anyone
and have no one to protect them,
no one to take them back home.

THE SERVANT IN ISAIAH

The nation was given a mission to serve God, to be custodian of his Word, and to be a light to the Gentile nations. Because of sin and rebellion, they failed. God sent his Son, Jesus Christ, as Messiah to fulfill that mission on earth.

The nation Israel is called the servant:	Isa 41:8; 42:19; 43:10; 44:1-2, 21; 45:4; 48:20
The Messiah is called the Servant:	Isa 42:1-7; 49:5-7; 50:10; 52:13; 53:11

Isa 42:6-7 Part of Christ's mission on earth was to demonstrate God's righteousness and to be a light for the Gentiles (to all nations). Through Christ, all people have the opportunity to share in his mission. God calls us to be servants of his Son, demonstrating God's righteousness and bringing his light. What a rare privilege it is to help the Messiah fulfill his mission! But we must seek his righteousness (Matt 6:33) before we demonstrate it to others and let his light shine in us before we can be lights ourselves (Matt 5:16; 2 Cor 4:6).

Isa 42:10 Look at all the Lord will do for us and through us (Isa 42:6-9)! Majestic works prompt majestic responses. Do you really appreciate the good things that God does for you and through you? If so, let your praise to him reflect how you really feel.

Isa 42:19-20 How could Israel and Judah be God's servants and yet be so blind? How could they be so close to God and see so little? Jesus condemned the religious leaders of his day for the same disregard of God (John 9:39-41). Yet do we not fail in the same way? Sometimes partial blindness—seeing but not understanding, or knowing what is right but not doing it—can be worse than not seeing at all.

▸ **ISAIAH 42:18-25 *(cont.)***

23 Who will hear these lessons from the past
and see the ruin that awaits you in the future?
24 Who allowed Israel to be robbed and hurt?
It was the LORD, against whom we sinned,
for the people would not walk in his path,
nor would they obey his law.
25 Therefore, he poured out his fury on them
and destroyed them in battle.
They were enveloped in flames,
but they still refused to understand.
They were consumed by fire,
but they did not learn their lesson.

The Savior of Israel

ISAIAH 43:1-13

1 But now, O Jacob, listen to the LORD who created you.
O Israel, the one who formed you says,
"Do not be afraid, for I have ransomed you.
I have called you by name; you are mine.
2 When you go through deep waters,
I will be with you.
When you go through rivers of difficulty,
you will not drown.
When you walk through the fire of oppression,
you will not be burned up;
the flames will not consume you.
3 For I am the LORD, your God,
the Holy One of Israel, your Savior.
I gave Egypt as a ransom for your freedom;
I gave Ethiopia* and Seba in your place.
4 Others were given in exchange for you.
I traded their lives for yours
because you are precious to me.
You are honored, and I love you.

5 "Do not be afraid, for I am with you.
I will gather you and your children from east and west.
6 I will say to the north and south,
'Bring my sons and daughters back to Israel
from the distant corners of the earth.
7 Bring all who claim me as their God,
for I have made them for my glory.
It was I who created them.'"

8 Bring out the people who have eyes but are blind,
who have ears but are deaf.
9 Gather the nations together!
Assemble the peoples of the world!
Which of their idols has ever foretold such things?
Which can predict what will happen tomorrow?
Where are the witnesses of such predictions?
Who can verify that they spoke the truth?

10 "But you are my witnesses, O Israel!" says the LORD.
"You are my servant.
You have been chosen to know me, believe in me,
and understand that I alone am God.
There is no other God—
there never has been, and there never will be.
11 I, yes I, am the LORD,
and there is no other Savior.
12 First I predicted your rescue,
then I saved you and proclaimed it to the world.
No foreign god has ever done this.
You are witnesses that I am the only God,"
says the LORD.
13 "From eternity to eternity I am God.
No one can snatch anyone out of my hand.
No one can undo what I have done."

The LORD's Promise of Victory

ISAIAH 43:14–44:5

This is what the LORD says—your Redeemer, the Holy One of Israel:

"For your sakes I will send an army against Babylon,
forcing the Babylonians* to flee in those ships
they are so proud of.

Is 43:3 Hebrew *Cush.* **Is 43:14** Or *Chaldeans.*

Isa 42:23 We may condemn our predecessors for their failures, but we are twice as guilty if we repeat the same mistakes that we recognize as failures. We may be so ready to direct God's message at others that we can't see how it touches our own lives. Make sure you are willing to take your own advice as you teach or lead.

Isa 43:1ff Isaiah 42 ends with God's sorrow over the spiritual decay of his people. In Isaiah 43, God says that despite the people's spiritual failure, he would show them mercy, bring them back from captivity, and restore them. He would give them an outpouring of love, not wrath. Then the world would know that God alone had done this.

Isa 43:1-4 God created the people of Israel, and they were special to him. God redeemed them and called them by name to be those who belong to him. God protected Israel in times of trouble. We are important to God, too. If we claim to belong to God, we must never do anything that would bring shame to him.

Isa 43:2 Going through rivers of difficulty will either cause you to drown or force you to grow stronger. If you go in your own strength, you are more likely to drown. If you invite the Lord to go with you, he will protect you.

Isa 43:3 God gave other nations to Persia in exchange for returning the Jews to their homeland. Egypt, Ethiopia, and parts of Arabia (Seba) had attacked Persia, and the Persians defeated them.

Isa 43:5-6 Isaiah was speaking primarily of Israel's return from Babylon. But there is a broader meaning: All God's people will be regathered when Christ comes to rule in peace over the earth.

Isa 43:10-11 Israel's task was to be a witness (Isa 44:8), telling the world who God is and what he had done. Believers today share the responsibility of being God's witnesses. Do people know what God is like through your words and example? They cannot see God directly, but they can see him reflected in you.

15 I am the LORD, your Holy One,
Israel's Creator and King.
16 I am the LORD, who opened a way through the waters,
making a dry path through the sea.
17 I called forth the mighty army of Egypt
with all its chariots and horses.
I drew them beneath the waves, and they drowned,
their lives snuffed out like a smoldering candlewick.

18 "But forget all that—
it is nothing compared to what I am going to do.
19 For I am about to do something new.
See, I have already begun! Do you not see it?
I will make a pathway through the wilderness.
I will create rivers in the dry wasteland.
20 The wild animals in the fields will thank me,
the jackals and owls, too,
for giving them water in the desert.
Yes, I will make rivers in the dry wasteland
so my chosen people can be refreshed.
21 I have made Israel for myself,
and they will someday honor me before the whole world.

22 "But, dear family of Jacob, you refuse to ask for my help.
You have grown tired of me, O Israel!
23 You have not brought me sheep or goats for burnt offerings.
You have not honored me with sacrifices,
though I have not burdened and wearied you
with requests for grain offerings and frankincense.
24 You have not brought me fragrant calamus
or pleased me with the fat from sacrifices.
Instead, you have burdened me with your sins
and wearied me with your faults.

25 "I—yes, I alone—will blot out your sins for my own sake
and will never think of them again.
26 Let us review the situation together,
and you can present your case to prove your innocence.
27 From the very beginning, your first ancestor
sinned against me;
all your leaders broke my laws.
28 That is why I have disgraced your priests;
I have decreed complete destruction*
for Jacob
and shame for Israel.

44:1 "But now, listen to me, Jacob my servant,
Israel my chosen one.
2 The LORD who made you and helps you says:
Do not be afraid, O Jacob, my servant,
O dear Israel,* my chosen one.
3 For I will pour out water to quench your thirst
and to irrigate your parched fields.
And I will pour out my Spirit on your descendants,
and my blessing on your children.
4 They will thrive like watered grass,
like willows on a riverbank.
5 Some will proudly claim, 'I belong to the LORD.'
Others will say, 'I am a descendant of Jacob.'
Some will write the LORD's name on their hands
and will take the name of Israel as their own."

Is 43:28 The Hebrew term used here refers to the complete consecration of things or people to the LORD, either by destroying them or by giving them as an offering. **Is 44:2** Hebrew *Jeshurun*, a term of endearment for Israel.

TODAY'S IDOLATRY

Isaiah tells us, "Who but a fool would make his own god—an idol that cannot help him one bit?" (Isa 44:10). We think of idols as statues of wood or stone, but in reality an idol is anything natural that is given sacred value and power. If your answer to any of the following questions is anything or anyone other than God, you may need to check out who or what you are worshiping.

- Who created me?
- Whom do I ultimately trust?
- Whom do I look to for ultimate truth?
- Whom do I look to for security and happiness?
- Who is in charge of my future?

Isa 43:25 How tempting it is to remind someone of a past offense! But when God forgives our sins, he totally forgets them. We never have to fear that he will remind us of them later. Because God forgives our sins, we need to forgive others.

Isa 44:5 The time will come when Israel will be proud of belonging to God. If we are truly God's, we should be unashamed and delighted to let everyone know about our relationship with him (Isa 44:8).

Isa 43:15-21 This section pictures a new exodus for a people once again oppressed, as the Israelites had been as slaves in Egypt before the Exodus. They would cry out to God, and again he would hear and deliver them. A new exodus would take place through a new wilderness. The past miracles were nothing compared to what God would do for his people in the future.

Isa 43:22-24 A sacrifice required both giving up a valuable animal and pleading with God for forgiveness. But the people presented God with sins instead of sacrifices. Can you imagine bringing the best of your sins to God's altar? This ironic picture shows the depths to which Israel had sunk. What do you present to God—your sins or a plea for his forgiveness?

The Foolishness of Idols

ISAIAH 44:6-20

This is what the LORD says—Israel's King and
Redeemer, the LORD of Heaven's Armies:

"I am the First and the Last;
there is no other God.
7 Who is like me?
Let him step forward and prove to you his power.
Let him do as I have done since ancient times
when I established a people and explained its future.
8 Do not tremble; do not be afraid.
Did I not proclaim my purposes for you long ago?
You are my witnesses—is there any other God?
No! There is no other Rock—not one!"

9 How foolish are those who manufacture idols.
These prized objects are really worthless.
The people who worship idols don't know this,
so they are all put to shame.
10 Who but a fool would make his own god—
an idol that cannot help him one bit?
11 All who worship idols will be disgraced
along with all these craftsmen—mere humans—
who claim they can make a god.
They may all stand together,
but they will stand in terror and shame.

12 The blacksmith stands at his forge to make a sharp tool,
pounding and shaping it with all his might.
His work makes him hungry and weak.
It makes him thirsty and faint.
13 Then the wood-carver measures a block of wood
and draws a pattern on it.
He works with chisel and plane
and carves it into a human figure.
He gives it human beauty
and puts it in a little shrine.
14 He cuts down cedars;
he selects the cypress and the oak;
he plants the pine in the forest
to be nourished by the rain.
15 Then he uses part of the wood to make a fire.
With it he warms himself and bakes his bread.
Then—yes, it's true—he takes the rest of it
and makes himself a god to worship!
He makes an idol
and bows down in front of it!
16 He burns part of the tree to roast his meat
and to keep himself warm.
He says, "Ah, that fire feels good."
17 Then he takes what's left
and makes his god: a carved idol!
He falls down in front of it,
worshiping and praying to it.
"Rescue me!" he says.
"You are my god!"

18 Such stupidity and ignorance!
Their eyes are closed, and they cannot see.
Their minds are shut, and they cannot think.
19 The person who made the idol never stops to reflect,
"Why, it's just a block of wood!
I burned half of it for heat
and used it to bake my bread and roast my meat.
How can the rest of it be a god?
Should I bow down to worship a piece of wood?"
20 The poor, deluded fool feeds on ashes.
He trusts something that can't help him at all.
Yet he cannot bring himself to ask,
"Is this idol that I'm holding in my hand a lie?"

Restoration for Jerusalem

ISAIAH 44:21-28

21 "Pay attention, O Jacob,
for you are my servant, O Israel.
I, the LORD, made you,
and I will not forget you.
22 I have swept away your sins like a cloud.
I have scattered your offenses like the morning mist.
Oh, return to me,
for I have paid the price to set you free."
23 Sing, O heavens, for the LORD has done this wondrous thing.
Shout for joy, O depths of the earth!
Break into song,
O mountains and forests and every tree!
For the LORD has redeemed Jacob
and is glorified in Israel.

Isa 44:8-9 The manufactured idols were guilty of false advertising. They made big promises, but they were worthless and helpless. In contrast, God fulfills his claims and delivers on all his promises. God challenges us to be his witnesses. When we share our faith with those who can find no meaning in life or have no hope of eternal life, we are not proclaiming anything shoddy or unreliable. God is real and life with him is best. Pray for boldness in your life to share your faith in Christ with friends, relatives, and neighbors.

Isa 44:9-20 Here Isaiah describes how people make their own gods. How absurd to make a god from the same tree that gives firewood. What are the gods we make—money, fame, power? We deceive ourselves if we expect them to empower our lives.

Isa 44:21 God said that we should serve our Creator (Isa 17:7; 40:28; 43:15; 45:9). Idolaters do the opposite—serving or worshiping what they have made rather than the one who made them. Our Creator paid the price to set us free from our sins against him. By contrast, no idol ever created anybody, and no idol can redeem us from our sins.

24 This is what the LORD says—
your Redeemer and Creator:
"I am the LORD, who made all things.
I alone stretched out the heavens.
Who was with me
when I made the earth?
25 I expose the false prophets as liars
and make fools of fortune-tellers.
I cause the wise to give bad advice,
thus proving them to be fools.
26 But I carry out the predictions of my prophets!
By them I say to Jerusalem, 'People will live here again,'
and to the towns of Judah, 'You will be rebuilt;
I will restore all your ruins!'
27 When I speak to the rivers and say, 'Dry up!'
they will be dry.
28 When I say of Cyrus, 'He is my shepherd,'
he will certainly do as I say.
He will command, 'Rebuild Jerusalem';
he will say, 'Restore the Temple.'"

Cyrus, the LORD's Chosen One

ISAIAH 45:1-13

1 This is what the LORD says to Cyrus, his anointed one,
whose right hand he will empower.
Before him, mighty kings will be paralyzed with fear.
Their fortress gates will be opened,
never to shut again.
2 This is what the LORD says:

"I will go before you, Cyrus,
and level the mountains.*
I will smash down gates of bronze
and cut through bars of iron.
3 And I will give you treasures hidden in the darkness—
secret riches.
I will do this so you may know that I am the LORD,
the God of Israel, the one who calls you by name.
4 "And why have I called you for this work?
Why did I call you by name when you did not know me?
It is for the sake of Jacob my servant,
Israel my chosen one.
5 I am the LORD;
there is no other God.
I have equipped you for battle,
though you don't even know me,
6 so all the world from east to west
will know there is no other God.
I am the LORD, and there is no other.
7 I create the light and make the darkness.
I send good times and bad times.
I, the LORD, am the one who does these things.

8 "Open up, O heavens,
and pour out your righteousness.
Let the earth open wide
so salvation and righteousness can sprout up together.
I, the LORD, created them.

9 "What sorrow awaits those who argue with their Creator.
Does a clay pot argue with its maker?
Does the clay dispute with the one who shapes it, saying,
'Stop, you're doing it wrong!'
Does the pot exclaim,
'How clumsy can you be?'
10 How terrible it would be if a newborn baby said to its father,
'Why was I born?'
or if it said to its mother,
'Why did you make me this way?'"

11 This is what the LORD says—
the Holy One of Israel and your Creator:
"Do you question what I do for my children?
Do you give me orders about the work of my hands?
12 I am the one who made the earth
and created people to live on it.

Is 45:2 As in Dead Sea Scrolls and Greek version; Masoretic Text reads *the swellings.*

Isa 44:25-26 False prophets were people who claimed to bring messages from the gods. Because God is truth, he is the standard for all teachings. We can always trust his Word as absolute truth. His Word is completely accurate, and against it we can measure all other teachings. If you are unsure about a teaching, test it against God's Word. God condemned the false prophets because they gave advice opposite to his.

Isa 44:28 Isaiah, who prophesied from about 740–681 B.C., called Cyrus by name almost 150 years before he ruled (559–530 B.C.)! Later historians said that Cyrus read this prophecy and was so moved that he carried it out. Isaiah also predicted that Jerusalem would fall more than 100 years before it happened (586 B.C.) and that the Temple would be rebuilt about 200 years before it happened. It is clear these prophecies came from God, who knows the future.

Isa 45:1-8 This is the only place in the Bible where a Gentile ruler is said to be "anointed." God is the power over all rulers, and he anoints whom he chooses for his special tasks. Cyrus's kingdom spread across 2,000 miles (the largest of any empire then known), including the territories of both the Assyrian and the Babylonian Empires. Why did God anoint Cyrus? Because God had a special task for him to do for Israel. Cyrus would allow God's city, Jerusalem, to be rebuilt, and he would set the exiles free without expecting anything in return. Few kings of Israel or Judah had done as much for God's people as Cyrus would do.

Isa 45:7 God is ruler over light and darkness, over good times and bad times. Our lives are sprinkled with both types of experiences, and both are needed for us to grow spiritually. When good times come, thank God and use your prosperity for him. When bad times come, don't resent them, but ask what you can learn from this refining experience to make you a better servant of God.

▸ **ISAIAH 45:1-13** ***(cont.)***

With my hands I stretched out the heavens.
All the stars are at my command.
13 I will raise up Cyrus to fulfill my righteous purpose,
and I will guide his actions.
He will restore my city and free my captive
people—
without seeking a reward!
I, the LORD of Heaven's Armies, have spoken!"

Future Conversion of Gentiles

ISAIAH 45:14-25

This is what the LORD says:

"You will rule the Egyptians,
the Ethiopians,* and the Sabeans.
They will come to you with all their merchandise,
and it will all be yours.
They will follow you as prisoners in chains.
They will fall to their knees in front of you
and say,
'God is with you, and he is the only God.
There is no other.'"
15 Truly, O God of Israel, our Savior,
you work in mysterious ways.
16 All craftsmen who make idols will be humiliated.
They will all be disgraced together.
17 But the LORD will save the people of Israel
with eternal salvation.
Throughout everlasting ages,
they will never again be humiliated and
disgraced.
18 For the LORD is God,
and he created the heavens and earth
and put everything in place.
He made the world to be lived in,
not to be a place of empty chaos.
"I am the LORD," he says,
"and there is no other.
19 I publicly proclaim bold promises.
I do not whisper obscurities in some dark
corner.
I would not have told the people of Israel*
to seek me
if I could not be found.
I, the LORD, speak only what is true
and declare only what is right.
20 "Gather together and come,
you fugitives from surrounding nations.
What fools they are who carry around their
wooden idols
and pray to gods that cannot save!
21 Consult together, argue your case.
Get together and decide what to say.
Who made these things known so long ago?
What idol ever told you they would happen?
Was it not I, the LORD?
For there is no other God but me,
a righteous God and Savior.
There is none but me.
22 Let all the world look to me for salvation!
For I am God; there is no other.
23 I have sworn by my own name;
I have spoken the truth,
and I will never go back on my word:
Every knee will bend to me,
and every tongue will confess allegiance
to me.*"
24 The people will declare,
"The LORD is the source of all my righteousness
and strength."
And all who were angry with him
will come to him and be ashamed.

Is 45:14 Hebrew *Cushites.* **Is 45:19** Hebrew *of Jacob.* See note on 14:1. **Is 45:23** Hebrew *will confess;* Greek version reads *will confess and give praise to God.* Compare Rom 14:11.

Isa 45:14 The Sabeans were people from Seba in southern Arabia.

Isa 45:17 Until this time, Israel had anticipated temporal salvation—God would save them from their enemies. Here Isaiah tells of eternal salvation with God.

Isa 45:18-19 God's promises are public, and their fulfillment is sure. So why do we ever doubt him? We never have to be uncertain when we have a God of truth and righteousness.

Isa 45:22 Salvation is for all nations, not just the Israelites. Many times it seems as though Israel had an inside track on salvation. But God makes it clear that his people include all those who follow him. Israel was to be the means through which the whole world would come to know God. Jesus, the Messiah, fulfilled Israel's role and gave all people the opportunity to follow God. (See also Rom 11:11; Gal 3:28; Eph 3:6; Phil 2:10.)

MAJOR IDOLS MENTIONED IN THE BIBLE

Name	*Where They Were Worshiped*	*What They Stood For*	*What the Worship Included*
Bel (Marduk)	Babylon	Weather, war, sun god	Prostitution, child sacrifice
Nebo (son of Marduk)	Babylon	Learning, astronomy, science	Prostitution
Ashtoreth (Asherah)	Canaan	Goddess of love, childbirth, and fertility	Child sacrifice
Chemosh	Moab	National god	Child sacrifice
Molech	Ammon	National god	Child sacrifice
Baal	Canaan	Rain, harvest, symbolized strength and fertility	Prostitution
Dagon	Philistia	Harvest, grain, success in farming	Child sacrifice

25 In the LORD all the generations of Israel will be
justified,
and in him they will boast.

Babylon's False Gods

ISAIAH 46:1-13

1 Bel and Nebo, the gods of Babylon,
bow as they are lowered to the ground.
They are being hauled away on ox carts.
The poor beasts stagger under the weight.
2 Both the idols and their owners are
bowed down.
The gods cannot protect the people,
and the people cannot protect the gods.
They go off into captivity together.
3 "Listen to me, descendants of Jacob,
all you who remain in Israel.
I have cared for you since you were born.
Yes, I carried you before you were born.
4 I will be your God throughout your lifetime—
until your hair is white with age.
I made you, and I will care for you.
I will carry you along and save you.
5 "To whom will you compare me?
Who is my equal?
6 Some people pour out their silver and gold
and hire a craftsman to make a god from it.
Then they bow down and worship it!
7 They carry it around on their shoulders,
and when they set it down, it stays there.
It can't even move!
And when someone prays to it, there is no answer.
It can't rescue anyone from trouble.
8 "Do not forget this! Keep it in mind!
Remember this, you guilty ones.
9 Remember the things I have done in the past.
For I alone am God!
I am God, and there is none like me.
10 Only I can tell you the future
before it even happens.
Everything I plan will come to pass,
for I do whatever I wish.
11 I will call a swift bird of prey from the east—
a leader from a distant land to come and
do my bidding.
I have said what I would do,
and I will do it.
12 "Listen to me, you stubborn people
who are so far from doing right.
13 For I am ready to set things right,
not in the distant future, but right now!
I am ready to save Jerusalem*
and show my glory to Israel.

Prediction of Babylon's Fall

ISAIAH 47:1-15

1 "Come down, virgin daughter of Babylon, and sit
in the dust.
For your days of sitting on a throne have ended.
O daughter of Babylonia,* never again will you be
the lovely princess, tender and delicate.
2 Take heavy millstones and grind flour.

Is 46:13 Hebrew *Zion*. **Is 47:1** Or *Chaldea;* also in 47:5.

Isa 46:1-4 Cyrus would carry out God's judgment against Babylon. Bel was the chief deity of the Babylonians; Nebo was the god of science and learning. These gods, however, needed animals and people to carry them around and could not even save themselves from being taken into captivity. They had no power at all. In contrast, our God created us and cares for us. His love is so enduring that he will care for us throughout our lifetime and even through death.

Isa 46:8-11 Israel was tempted to waver between the Lord God and pagan gods. Isaiah affirms the sole lordship of God. God is unique in his knowledge and in his control of the future. His consistent purpose is to carry out what he has planned. When we are tempted to pursue anything that promises pleasure, comfort, peace, or security apart from God, we must remember our commitment to God.

Isa 46:13 Much of the book of Isaiah speaks of a future deliverance when we all will live with God in perfect peace. God offers not only this future hope but also help for our present needs. His righteousness is near us, and we do not have to wait for his salvation.

Isa 47:1ff Here Isaiah predicted the fall of Babylon more than 150 years before it happened. At this time, Babylon had not yet emerged as the mightiest force on earth, the proud empire that would destroy Judah and Jerusalem. But the Babylonians, Judah's captors, would become captives themselves in 539 B.C. God, not Babylon, has the ultimate power. He used Babylon to punish his sinful people; he would use Medo-Persia to destroy Babylon and free his people.

Millstone

The earliest millstone, the saddle quern, consisted of a rough base stone, slightly concave, and a convex rubbing stone. The base stone varied from 18 to 30 inches across with one end a little thicker than the other. It was known as the underneath portion or "lower millstone." The upper stone, called "the rider portion," varied from 6 to 15 inches long and was flat on one side and convex on the other. It could easily be held in the hand. Grinding was done by pushing the upper stone backward and forward over the grain, which lay on the lower stone. Only a small quantity of grain could be ground at one time using this method.

Jesus used the millstone in a warning he made about people misleading young believers. He said, "If you cause one of these little ones who trusts in me to fall into sin, it would be better for you to have a large millstone tied around your neck and be drowned in the depths of the sea" (Matt 18:6).

▸ **ISAIAH 47:1-15** ***(cont.)***

Remove your veil, and strip off your robe.
Expose yourself to public view.
3 You will be naked and burdened with shame.
I will take vengeance against you without pity."
4 Our Redeemer, whose name is the LORD of Heaven's Armies,
is the Holy One of Israel.
5 "O beautiful Babylon, sit now in darkness and silence.
Never again will you be known as the queen of kingdoms.
6 For I was angry with my chosen people
and punished them by letting them fall into your hands.
But you, Babylon, showed them no mercy.
You oppressed even the elderly.
7 You said, 'I will reign forever as queen of the world!'
You did not reflect on your actions
or think about their consequences.
8 "Listen to this, you pleasure-loving kingdom,
living at ease and feeling secure.
You say, 'I am the only one, and there is no other.
I will never be a widow or lose my children.'
9 Well, both these things will come upon you in a moment:
widowhood and the loss of your children.
Yes, these calamities will come upon you,
despite all your witchcraft and magic.
10 "You felt secure in your wickedness.
'No one sees me,' you said.
But your 'wisdom' and 'knowledge' have led you astray,
and you said, 'I am the only one, and there is no other.'
11 So disaster will overtake you,
and you won't be able to charm it away.
Calamity will fall upon you,
and you won't be able to buy your way out.
A catastrophe will strike you suddenly,
one for which you are not prepared.
12 "Now use your magical charms!
Use the spells you have worked at all these years!
Maybe they will do you some good.
Maybe they can make someone afraid of you.
13 All the advice you receive has made you tired.
Where are all your astrologers,
those stargazers who make predictions each month?
Let them stand up and save you from what the future holds.
14 But they are like straw burning in a fire;
they cannot save themselves from the flame.
You will get no help from them at all;
their hearth is no place to sit for warmth.
15 And all your friends,
those with whom you've done business since childhood,
will go their own ways,
turning a deaf ear to your cries.

God's Stubborn People

ISAIAH 48:1-11

1 "Listen to me, O family of Jacob,
you who are called by the name of Israel
and born into the family of Judah.
Listen, you who take oaths in the name of the LORD
and call on the God of Israel.
You don't keep your promises,
2 even though you call yourself the holy city
and talk about depending on the God of Israel,
whose name is the LORD of Heaven's Armies.
3 Long ago I told you what was going to happen.
Then suddenly I took action,
and all my predictions came true.
4 For I know how stubborn and obstinate you are.
Your necks are as unbending as iron.
Your heads are as hard as bronze.
5 That is why I told you what would happen;
I told you beforehand what I was going to do.
Then you could never say, 'My idols did it.
My wooden image and metal god commanded it to happen!'
6 You have heard my predictions and seen them fulfilled,
but you refuse to admit it.
Now I will tell you new things,
secrets you have not yet heard.

Isa 47:8-9 Caught up in the pursuit of power and pleasure, Babylon believed in its own greatness and claimed to be the only power on earth. Babylon felt completely secure, and Nebuchadnezzar, its king, exalted himself as a "god." But the true God taught Nebuchadnezzar a powerful lesson by taking everything away from him (Dan 4:28-37). Our society is addicted to pleasure and power, but these can quickly vanish. Look at your own life and ask yourself how you can be more responsible with the talents and possessions God has given you. How can you use your life for God's honor rather than your own?

Isa 47:12-15 The people of Babylon sought advice and help from astrologers and stargazers. But like the idols of wood or gold, astrologers could not even deliver themselves from what was to come from the hand of God. Why rely on those who are powerless? The helpless cannot help us. Alternatives to God are destined to fail. If you want help, find it in God, who has proven his power in creation and in history.

Isa 48:1 The people of Judah felt confident because they lived in Jerusalem, the city with God's Temple. They depended on their heritage, their city, and their Temple—but this was false security because they did not depend on God. Do you feel secure because you go to church or live in a Christian country? Heritage, buildings, or nations cannot give us a relationship with God; we must truly depend on him personally, with all our hearts and minds.

7 They are brand new, not things from the past.
So you cannot say, 'We knew that all the time!'
8 "Yes, I will tell you of things that are entirely new,
things you never heard of before.
For I know so well what traitors you are.
You have been rebels from birth.
9 Yet for my own sake and for the honor
of my name,
I will hold back my anger and not wipe
you out.
10 I have refined you, but not as silver is refined.
Rather, I have refined you in the furnace
of suffering.
11 I will rescue you for my sake—
yes, for my own sake!
I will not let my reputation be tarnished,
and I will not share my glory with idols!

Freedom from Babylon

ISAIAH 48:12-22

12 "Listen to me, O family of Jacob,
Israel my chosen one!
I alone am God,
the First and the Last.
13 It was my hand that laid the foundations
of the earth,
my right hand that spread out the heavens
above.
When I call out the stars,
they all appear in order."

14 Have any of your idols ever told you this?
Come, all of you, and listen:
The LORD has chosen Cyrus as his ally.
He will use him to put an end to the empire
of Babylon
and to destroy the Babylonian* armies.
15 "I have said it: I am calling Cyrus!
I will send him on this errand and will help
him succeed.
16 Come closer, and listen to this.
From the beginning I have told you plainly
what would happen."

And now the Sovereign LORD and his Spirit
have sent me with this message.
17 This is what the LORD says—
your Redeemer, the Holy One of Israel:
"I am the LORD your God,
who teaches you what is good for you
and leads you along the paths you should follow.
18 Oh, that you had listened to my commands!
Then you would have had peace flowing like a
gentle river
and righteousness rolling over you like waves
in the sea.
19 Your descendants would have been like the sands
along the seashore—
too many to count!
There would have been no need for your
destruction,
or for cutting off your family name."
20 Yet even now, be free from your captivity!
Leave Babylon and the Babylonians.*
Sing out this message!
Shout it to the ends of the earth!
The LORD has redeemed his servants,
the people of Israel.*
21 They were not thirsty
when he led them through the desert.
He divided the rock,
and water gushed out for them to drink.
22 "But there is no peace for the wicked,"
says the LORD.

Is 48:14 Or *Chaldean.* **Is 48:20a** Or *the Chaldeans.* **Is 48:20b** Hebrew *his servant, Jacob.* See note on 14:1.

Isa 48:9-11 There was nothing in the people's actions, attitudes, or accomplishments to compel God to love and to save them. But for his own sake, to show who he is and what he can do, he saved them. God does not save us because we are good but because he loves us and because of his forgiving nature.

Isa 48:10 Do you find it easy to complain when your life becomes complicated or difficult? Why would a loving God allow all kinds of unpleasant experiences to come to his children? This verse shows us plainly that God tests us in the "furnace of suffering." Rather than complain, our response should be to turn to God in faith for the strength to endure and rejoice in our sufferings (see Rom 5:3; Jas 1:2-4). For without the testing, we will never know what we are capable of doing, nor will we grow. And without the refining, we will not become more pure and more like Christ. If you are facing adversity or suffering, seek God and his refining work in your life.

Isa 48:14-15 That the Lord would choose Cyrus as his "ally" must have shocked his audience. How could the Lord choose a pagan king, an enemy? But it was Cyrus whom God would use to free his people from their captivity in Babylon. Cyrus's mission was to set Israel free by conquering Babylon, then to decree that all Jews could return to their homeland. Who but a prophet of God could predict such an inconceivable but true story almost 200 years before it happened?

Isa 48:17-18 Like a loving parent, God teaches and guides us. We should listen to him because peace and righteousness come to us as we obey his Word. Refusing to pay attention to God's commands invites punishment and threatens that peace and righteousness.

Isa 48:20 Do you see the captives leaving Babylon many years later? No wonder they are shouting with joy, as their ancestors shouted joyfully after they crossed the Red Sea, free from slavery at last! What is holding you captive? Be free! The Lord has redeemed his servants from slavery to sin. When you let him free you from your captivity, you will feel like shouting with joy.

Isa 48:22 Many people cry out for comfort, security, and relief, but they haven't taken the first steps to turn away from sin and open the channels to God. They have not repented and trusted in him. If you want true peace, seek God first. Then he will give you his peace.

2. THE FUTURE REDEEMER

In this section, Isaiah looks forward to the coming of the Redeemer. Salvation would be accomplished through the arrival, suffering, and exaltation of the Lord's Servant—the Messiah, Jesus Christ.

The LORD's Servant Commissioned

ISAIAH 49:1-7

1 Listen to me, all you in distant lands!
Pay attention, you who are far away!
The LORD called me before my birth;
from within the womb he called me by name.
2 He made my words of judgment as sharp
as a sword.
He has hidden me in the shadow of his hand.
I am like a sharp arrow in his quiver.
3 He said to me, "You are my servant, Israel,
and you will bring me glory."
4 I replied, "But my work seems so useless!
I have spent my strength for nothing and
to no purpose.
Yet I leave it all in the LORD's hand;
I will trust God for my reward."
5 And now the LORD speaks—
the one who formed me in my mother's womb
to be his servant,
who commissioned me to bring Israel back
to him.
The LORD has honored me,
and my God has given me strength.
6 He says, "You will do more than restore the
people of Israel to me.
I will make you a light to the Gentiles,
and you will bring my salvation to the ends
of the earth."
7 The LORD, the Redeemer
and Holy One of Israel,
says to the one who is despised and rejected
by the nations,
to the one who is the servant of rulers:
"Kings will stand at attention when you pass by.
Princes will also bow low
because of the LORD, the faithful one,
the Holy One of Israel, who has chosen you."

Promises of Israel's Restoration

ISAIAH 49:8–50:3

This is what the LORD says:
"At just the right time, I will respond to you.*
On the day of salvation I will help you.
I will protect you and give you to the people
as my covenant with them.
Through you I will reestablish the land of Israel
and assign it to its own people again.
9 I will say to the prisoners, 'Come out in freedom,'
and to those in darkness, 'Come into the light.'
They will be my sheep, grazing in green pastures
and on hills that were previously bare.
10 They will neither hunger nor thirst.
The searing sun will not reach them anymore.
For the LORD in his mercy will lead them;
he will lead them beside cool waters.
11 And I will make my mountains into level paths
for them.
The highways will be raised above the valleys.
12 See, my people will return from far away,
from lands to the north and west,
and from as far south as Egypt.*"
13 Sing for joy, O heavens!
Rejoice, O earth!
Burst into song, O mountains!
For the LORD has comforted his people
and will have compassion on them in their
suffering.
14 Yet Jerusalem* says, "The LORD has deserted us;
the Lord has forgotten us."
15 "Never! Can a mother forget her nursing child?
Can she feel no love for the child she has borne?
But even if that were possible,
I would not forget you!
16 See, I have written your name on the palms
of my hands.
Always in my mind is a picture of Jerusalem's
walls in ruins.
17 Soon your descendants will come back,
and all who are trying to destroy you will go away.
18 Look around you and see,
for all your children will come back to you.
As surely as I live," says the LORD,
"they will be like jewels or bridal ornaments
for you to display.
19 "Even the most desolate parts of your
abandoned land
will soon be crowded with your people.

Is 49:8 Greek version reads *I heard you.* Compare 2 Cor 6:2. **Is 49:12** As in Dead Sea Scrolls, which read *from the region of Aswan,* which is in southern Egypt. Masoretic Text reads *from the region of Sinim.* **Is 49:14** Hebrew *Zion.*

Isa 49:1-7 Before the Servant, the Messiah, was born, God had chosen him to bring the light of the gospel (the message of salvation) to the world (see Acts 13:47). Christ offered salvation to all nations, and his apostles began the missionary movement to take this gospel to the ends of the earth. Missionary work today continues Jesus' great commission (Matt 28:18-20), taking the light of the gospel to all nations. Do you support evangelism and missionary efforts with your money? Do you have talent or other resources to help spread the message of Christ? God wants you to be involved. How can you help?

Isa 49:14-15 The people of Israel felt that God had forgotten them in Babylon; but Isaiah pointed out that God would never forget

Your enemies who enslaved you
will be far away.
20 The generations born in exile will return
and say,
'We need more room! It's crowded here!'
21 Then you will think to yourself,
'Who has given me all these descendants?
For most of my children were killed,
and the rest were carried away into exile.
I was left here all alone.
Where did all these people come from?
Who bore these children?
Who raised them for me?'"

22 This is what the Sovereign LORD says:
"See, I will give a signal to the godless nations.
They will carry your little sons back to you in
their arms;
they will bring your daughters on their
shoulders.
23 Kings and queens will serve you
and care for all your needs.
They will bow to the earth before you
and lick the dust from your feet.
Then you will know that I am the LORD.
Those who trust in me will never be put
to shame."

24 Who can snatch the plunder of war from the
hands of a warrior?
Who can demand that a tyrant* let his
captives go?
25 But the LORD says,
"The captives of warriors will be released,
and the plunder of tyrants will be retrieved.
For I will fight those who fight you,
and I will save your children.
26 I will feed your enemies with their own flesh.
They will be drunk with rivers of their own
blood.
All the world will know that I, the LORD,
am your Savior and your Redeemer,
the Mighty One of Israel.*"

50:1 This is what the LORD says:

"Was your mother sent away because
I divorced her?
Did I sell you as slaves to my creditors?
No, you were sold because of your sins.
And your mother, too, was taken because
of your sins.
2 Why was no one there when I came?
Why didn't anyone answer when I called?
Is it because I have no power to rescue?
No, that is not the reason!
For I can speak to the sea and make it dry up!
I can turn rivers into deserts covered with
dying fish.
3 I dress the skies in darkness,
covering them with clothes of mourning."

The LORD's Obedient Servant

ISAIAH 50:4-11

4 The Sovereign LORD has given me his words
of wisdom,
so that I know how to comfort the weary.
Morning by morning he wakens me
and opens my understanding to his will.
5 The Sovereign LORD has spoken to me,
and I have listened.
I have not rebelled or turned away.
6 I offered my back to those who beat me
and my cheeks to those who pulled out
my beard.
I did not hide my face
from mockery and spitting.

7 Because the Sovereign LORD helps me,
I will not be disgraced.
Therefore, I have set my face like a stone,
determined to do his will.
And I know that I will not be put to shame.
8 He who gives me justice is near.
Who will dare to bring charges against
me now?
Where are my accusers?
Let them appear!
9 See, the Sovereign LORD is on my side!
Who will declare me guilty?
All my enemies will be destroyed
like old clothes that have been eaten by moths!

10 Who among you fears the LORD
and obeys his servant?
If you are walking in darkness,
without a ray of light,

Is 49:24 As in Dead Sea Scrolls, Syriac version, and Latin Vulgate (also see 49:25); Masoretic Text reads *a righteous person.* **Is 49:26** Hebrew *of Jacob.* See note on 14:1.

them, as a loving mother would not forget her little child. When we feel that God has forsaken us, we must ask if we have forsaken and forgotten God (see Deut 31:6).

Isa 49:24-25 God would prove to the world that he is God by doing the impossible—causing warriors to set their captives free; and these warriors would even return the plunder they had taken from the captives! God had done this before at the Exodus and would do it again when the exiles returned to Israel. Never should we doubt that God will fulfill his promises. He will even do the impossible to make them come true.

Isa 50:1-2 God promised to fight for Israel, but Israel sold itself into sin. Israel had caused its own problems. The people of Israel forgot God and trusted in other countries to help them. God had not rejected Israel, but Israel had rejected God.

Isa 50:10-11 If we walk by our own light and reject God's, we become self-sufficient, and the result of self-sufficiency is torment. When we place confidence in our own intelligence, appearance, or accomplishments instead of in God, we risk torment later when these strengths fade.

▸ **ISAIAH 50:4-11** ***(cont.)***

trust in the LORD
and rely on your God.
11 But watch out, you who live in your own light
and warm yourselves by your own fires.
This is the reward you will receive from me:
You will soon fall down in great torment.

A Call to Trust the LORD

ISAIAH 51:1-23

1 "Listen to me, all who hope for deliverance—
all who seek the LORD!
Consider the rock from which you were cut,
the quarry from which you were mined.
2 Yes, think about Abraham, your ancestor,
and Sarah, who gave birth to your nation.
Abraham was only one man when I called him.
But when I blessed him, he became a
great nation."

3 The LORD will comfort Israel* again
and have pity on her ruins.
Her desert will blossom like Eden,
her barren wilderness like the garden
of the LORD.
Joy and gladness will be found there.
Songs of thanksgiving will fill the air.

4 "Listen to me, my people.
Hear me, Israel,
for my law will be proclaimed,
and my justice will become a light to the
nations.
5 My mercy and justice are coming soon.
My salvation is on the way.
My strong arm will bring justice to the nations.
All distant lands will look to me
and wait in hope for my powerful arm.
6 Look up to the skies above,
and gaze down on the earth below.
For the skies will disappear like smoke,
and the earth will wear out like a piece
of clothing.
The people of the earth will die like flies,
but my salvation lasts forever.
My righteous rule will never end!
7 "Listen to me, you who know right from wrong,
you who cherish my law in your hearts.
Do not be afraid of people's scorn,
nor fear their insults.
8 For the moth will devour them as it devours
clothing.
The worm will eat at them as it eats wool.
But my righteousness will last forever.
My salvation will continue from generation
to generation."

9 Wake up, wake up, O LORD! Clothe yourself with
strength!
Flex your mighty right arm!
Rouse yourself as in the days of old
when you slew Egypt, the dragon of the Nile.*
10 Are you not the same today,
the one who dried up the sea,
making a path of escape through the depths
so that your people could cross over?
11 Those who have been ransomed by the LORD
will return.
They will enter Jerusalem* singing,
crowned with everlasting joy.
Sorrow and mourning will disappear,
and they will be filled with joy and gladness.

12 "I, yes I, am the one who comforts you.
So why are you afraid of mere humans,
who wither like the grass and disappear?
13 Yet you have forgotten the LORD, your Creator,
the one who stretched out the sky like a canopy
and laid the foundations of the earth.
Will you remain in constant dread of human
oppressors?
Will you continue to fear the anger of your
enemies?
Where is their fury and anger now?
It is gone!
14 Soon all you captives will be released!
Imprisonment, starvation, and death will not
be your fate!

Is 51:3 Hebrew *Zion;* also in 51:16. **Is 51:9** Hebrew *You slew Rahab; you pierced the dragon.* Rahab is the name of a mythical sea monster that represents chaos in ancient literature. The name is used here as a poetic name for Egypt. **Is 51:11** Hebrew *Zion.*

Isa 51:1-2 The faithful remnant may have felt alone because they were few. But God reminded them of their ancestors, the source of their spiritual heritage—Abraham and Sarah. Abraham was only one person, but much came from his faithfulness. If the faithful few would remain faithful, even more could come from them. If we Christians, even a faithful few, remain faithful, think what God can do through us!

Isa 51:7 Isaiah encouraged those who follow God's laws. He gave them hope when they faced people's reproach or insults because of their faith. We need not fear when people insult us for our faith because God is with us and truth will prevail. If people make fun of you or dislike you because you believe in God, remember that they are not against you personally but against God. God will deal with them; you should concentrate on loving and obeying him.

Isa 51:9-10 God had performed many powerful miracles in founding Israel, perhaps none more exciting than making a dry path through the middle of the Red Sea (see Exod 14). Our God is the same God who made that road through the sea. His methods may change, but his love and care do not.

Isa 51:12-16 God's people feared Babylon but not God. They had reason to fear Babylon for the harm it wanted to do, but they should also have realized that God's power is much greater than Babylon's. Babylon was interested in making the people captives; God was interested in setting them free. The people had misplaced their fear and their love. Jerusalem should have feared God's power and loved his mercy.

15 For I am the LORD your God,
who stirs up the sea, causing its waves
to roar.
My name is the LORD of Heaven's Armies.
16 And I have put my words in your mouth
and hidden you safely in my hand.
I stretched out* the sky like a canopy
and laid the foundations of the earth.
I am the one who says to Israel,
'You are my people!'"

17 Wake up, wake up, O Jerusalem!
You have drunk the cup of the LORD's fury.
You have drunk the cup of terror,
tipping out its last drops.
18 Not one of your children is left alive
to take your hand and guide you.
19 These two calamities have fallen on you:
desolation and destruction, famine and war.
And who is left to sympathize with you?
Who is left to comfort you?*
20 For your children have fainted and lie in the
streets,
helpless as antelopes caught in a net.
The LORD has poured out his fury;
God has rebuked them.

21 But now listen to this, you afflicted ones
who sit in a drunken stupor,
though not from drinking wine.
22 This is what the Sovereign LORD,
your God and Defender, says:
"See, I have taken the terrible cup from your
hands.
You will drink no more of my fury.
23 Instead, I will hand that cup to your
tormentors,
those who said, 'We will trample you into
the dust
and walk on your backs.'"

Deliverance for Jerusalem

ISAIAH 52:1-12

1 Wake up, wake up, O Zion!
Clothe yourself with strength.
Put on your beautiful clothes, O holy city
of Jerusalem,
for unclean and godless people will enter your
gates no longer.
2 Rise from the dust, O Jerusalem.
Sit in a place of honor.
Remove the chains of slavery from your neck,
O captive daughter of Zion.
3 For this is what the LORD says:
"When I sold you into exile,
I received no payment.
Now I can redeem you
without having to pay for you."

4This is what the Sovereign LORD says: "Long ago my
people chose to live in Egypt. Now they are oppressed
by Assyria. 5What is this?" asks the LORD. "Why are my
people enslaved again? Those who rule them shout in
exultation. My name is blasphemed all day long.* 6But
I will reveal my name to my people, and they will come
to know its power. Then at last they will recognize that
I am the one who speaks to them."

7 How beautiful on the mountains
are the feet of the messenger who brings
good news,
the good news of peace and salvation,
the news that the God of Israel* reigns!
8 The watchmen shout and sing with joy,
for before their very eyes
they see the LORD returning to Jerusalem.*
9 Let the ruins of Jerusalem break into joyful song,
for the LORD has comforted his people.
He has redeemed Jerusalem.
10 The LORD has demonstrated his holy power
before the eyes of all the nations.
All the ends of the earth will see
the victory of our God.

11 Get out! Get out and leave your captivity,
where everything you touch is unclean.
Get out of there and purify yourselves,
you who carry home the sacred objects
of the LORD.
12 You will not leave in a hurry,
running for your lives.
For the LORD will go ahead of you;
yes, the God of Israel will protect you from
behind.

Is 51:16 As in Syriac version (see also 51:13); Hebrew reads *planted.* **Is 51:19** As in Dead Sea Scrolls and Greek, Latin, and Syriac versions; Masoretic Text reads *How can I comfort you?* **Is 52:5** Greek version reads *The Gentiles continually blaspheme my name because of you.* Compare Rom 2:24. **Is 52:7** Hebrew *of Zion.* **Is 52:8** Hebrew *to Zion.*

Isa 51:17–52:10 Jerusalem was God's holy city, the city with God's Temple. But the people of Judah experienced ruin instead of prosperity, destruction instead of liberty. Because of their sins, the people suffered. But God promised to restore Jerusalem as a holy city where sinners cannot enter. God reigns. Put your entire faith and confidence in his ability to control the course of history—and your life.

Isa 52:7 God says that the feet of those who bring good news are "beautiful." It is a wonderful privilege to be able to share God's Good News with others, his news of redemption, salvation, and peace. To whom do you need to give the Good News?

Isa 52:12 The people would not have to leave in fearful haste because Cyrus, God's anointed (Isa 45:1), would decree that the Jewish exiles could return safely to Jerusalem (Ezra 1:1-4). They had the king's approval, his guaranteed protection. More importantly, the Lord would go ahead to point the way and be behind to protect them.

The LORD's Suffering Servant

ISAIAH 52:13–53:12

13 See, my servant will prosper;
he will be highly exalted.
14 But many were amazed when they saw him.*
His face was so disfigured he seemed hardly human,
and from his appearance, one would scarcely know he was a man.
15 And he will startle* many nations.
Kings will stand speechless in his presence.
For they will see what they had not been told;
they will understand what they had not heard about.*
53:1 Who has believed our message?
To whom has the LORD revealed his powerful arm?
2 My servant grew up in the LORD's presence like a tender green shoot,
like a root in dry ground.
There was nothing beautiful or majestic about his appearance,
nothing to attract us to him.
3 He was despised and rejected—
a man of sorrows, acquainted with deepest grief.
We turned our backs on him and looked the other way.
He was despised, and we did not care.
4 Yet it was our weaknesses he carried;
it was our sorrows* that weighed him down.
And we thought his troubles were a punishment from God,
a punishment for his own sins!
5 But he was pierced for our rebellion,
crushed for our sins.
He was beaten so we could be whole.
He was whipped so we could be healed.
6 All of us, like sheep, have strayed away.
We have left God's paths to follow our own.
Yet the LORD laid on him
the sins of us all.

7 He was oppressed and treated harshly,
yet he never said a word.
He was led like a lamb to the slaughter.
And as a sheep is silent before the shearers,
he did not open his mouth.
8 Unjustly condemned,
he was led away.*
No one cared that he died without descendants,
that his life was cut short in midstream.*
But he was struck down
for the rebellion of my people.
9 He had done no wrong
and had never deceived anyone.
But he was buried like a criminal;
he was put in a rich man's grave.

10 But it was the LORD's good plan to crush him
and cause him grief.
Yet when his life is made an offering for sin,
he will have many descendants.
He will enjoy a long life,
and the LORD's good plan will prosper in his hands.
11 When he sees all that is accomplished by his anguish,
he will be satisfied.

Is 52:14 As in Syriac version; Hebrew reads *you.* **Is 52:15a** Or *cleanse.* **Is 52:15b** Greek version reads *Those who have never been told about him will see, / and those who have never heard of him will understand.* Compare Rom 15:21. **Is 53:4** Or *Yet it was our sicknesses he carried; / it was our diseases.* **Is 53:8a** Greek version reads *He was humiliated and received no justice.* Compare Acts 8:33. **Is 53:8b** Or *As for his contemporaries, / who cared that his life was cut short in midstream?* Greek version reads *Who can speak of his descendants? / For his life was taken from the earth.* Compare Acts 8:33.

Isa 52:13 "My servant," as the term is used here, is the Messiah, our Lord Jesus. He would be highly exalted because of his sacrifice (described in Isa 53).

Isa 52:14-15 This servant, Christ, would be "disfigured"; but through his suffering, he would cleanse the nations (Heb 10:14; 1 Pet 1:2).

Isa 53:1ff This chapter continues to speak of the Messiah, Jesus, who would suffer for the sins of all people. Such a prophecy is astounding! Who would believe that God would choose to save the world through a humble, suffering servant rather than a glorious king? The idea is contrary to human pride and worldly thinking. But God often works in ways we don't expect. The Messiah's strength is shown by humility, suffering, and mercy.

Isa 53:2 There was nothing beautiful or majestic in the physical appearance of this servant. Israel would miscalculate the servant's importance—they would consider him an ordinary man. But even though Jesus would not attract a large following based on his physical appearance, he would bring salvation and healing. Many people miscalculate the importance of Jesus' life and work, and they need faithful Christians to point out his extraordinary nature.

Isa 53:4-5 How could an Old Testament person understand the idea of Christ dying for our sins—actually bearing the punishment that we deserved? The sacrifices suggested this idea, but it is one thing to kill a lamb, and something quite different to think of God's chosen servant as that Lamb. But God was pulling aside the curtain of time to let the people of Isaiah's day look ahead to the suffering of the future Messiah and the resulting forgiveness made available to all people.

Isa 53:6 Isaiah speaks of Israel straying from God and compares them to wandering sheep. Yet God would send the Messiah to bring them back into the fold. We have the hindsight to see and know the identity of the promised Messiah, who has come and died for our sins. But if we know all that Jesus did and still reject him, our sin is much greater than that of the ancient Israelites, who could not see what we have seen. Have you given your life to Jesus Christ, the "good shepherd" (John 10:11-16), or are you still going your own way like a wandering sheep?

Isa 53:7-12 In the Old Testament, people offered animals as sacrifices for their sins. Here, the sinless servant of the Lord offers himself for our sins. He is the Lamb (Isa 53:7) offered for the sins of all people (John 1:29; Rev 5:6-14). The Messiah suffered for our sake, bearing our sins to make us acceptable to God. What can we say to such love? How will we respond to him?

Isa 53:11 This verse tells of the enormous family of believers who will become right with

And because of his experience,
my righteous servant will make it possible
for many to be counted righteous,
for he will bear all their sins.
12 I will give him the honors of a victorious soldier,
because he exposed himself to death.
He was counted among the rebels.
He bore the sins of many and interceded
for rebels.

Future Glory for Jerusalem

ISAIAH 54:1-17

1 "Sing, O childless woman,
you who have never given birth!
Break into loud and joyful song, O Jerusalem,
you who have never been in labor.
For the desolate woman now has more
children
than the woman who lives with her
husband,"
says the LORD.
2 "Enlarge your house; build an addition.
Spread out your home, and spare no expense!
3 For you will soon be bursting at the seams.
Your descendants will occupy other nations
and resettle the ruined cities.

4 "Fear not; you will no longer live in shame.
Don't be afraid; there is no more disgrace
for you.
You will no longer remember the shame
of your youth
and the sorrows of widowhood.
5 For your Creator will be your husband;
the LORD of Heaven's Armies is his name!
He is your Redeemer, the Holy One of Israel,
the God of all the earth.
6 For the LORD has called you back from your
grief—
as though you were a young wife abandoned
by her husband,"
says your God.
7 "For a brief moment I abandoned you,
but with great compassion I will take you back.
8 In a burst of anger I turned my face away for
a little while.
But with everlasting love I will have
compassion on you,"
says the LORD, your Redeemer.

9 "Just as I swore in the time of Noah
that I would never again let a flood cover the
earth,
so now I swear
that I will never again be angry and punish you.
10 For the mountains may move
and the hills disappear,
but even then my faithful love for you will
remain.
My covenant of blessing will never be
broken,"
says the LORD, who has mercy on you.

11 "O storm-battered city,
troubled and desolate!
I will rebuild you with precious jewels
and make your foundations from lapis lazuli.
12 I will make your towers of sparkling rubies,
your gates of shining gems,
and your walls of precious stones.
13 I will teach all your children,
and they will enjoy great peace.
14 You will be secure under a government that
is just and fair.
Your enemies will stay far away.
You will live in peace,
and terror will not come near.
15 If any nation comes to fight you,
it is not because I sent them.
Whoever attacks you will go down in defeat.

16 "I have created the blacksmith
who fans the coals beneath the forge
and makes the weapons of destruction.
And I have created the armies that destroy.
17 But in that coming day
no weapon turned against you will succeed.
You will silence every voice
raised up to accuse you.
These benefits are enjoyed by the servants
of the LORD;
their vindication will come from me.
I, the LORD, have spoken!

God, not by their works, but by the Messiah's great work on the cross. They are justified because they have claimed Christ, the righteous servant, as their Savior and Lord (see Rom 10:9; 2 Cor 5:21). Their life of sin is stripped away, and they are clothed with Christ's goodness (Eph 4:22-24).

Isa 54:1 To be childless at that time was a woman's great shame, a disgrace. Families depended on children for survival, especially when the parents became elderly. Israel (Jerusalem) was unfruitful, like a childless woman, but God would permit her to have many children and change her mourning into singing.

Isa 54:6-8 God said that he had abandoned Israel for a brief moment, so the nation was like a young wife rejected by her husband. But God still called Israel his own. The God we serve is holy, and he cannot tolerate sin. When his people blatantly sinned, God in his righteous anger chose to punish them. Sin separates us from God and brings us pain and suffering. But if we confess our sin and repent, then God will forgive us. Have you ever been separated from a loved one and then experienced joy when that person returned? That is like the joy God experiences when you repent and return to him.

Isa 54:9-13 God made a covenant with Noah that he has never broken (Gen 9:8-17). Likewise, God made a covenant of peace with the people of Israel that the time would come when he would stop pouring out his anger on them; he would teach their citizens and give them prosperity.

Invitation to the LORD's Salvation

ISAIAH 55:1-13

1 "Is anyone thirsty?
Come and drink—
even if you have no money!
Come, take your choice of wine or milk—
it's all free!
2 Why spend your money on food that does not give you strength?
Why pay for food that does you no good?
Listen to me, and you will eat what is good.
You will enjoy the finest food.

3 "Come to me with your ears wide open.
Listen, and you will find life.
I will make an everlasting covenant with you.
I will give you all the unfailing love I promised to David.
4 See how I used him to display my power among the peoples.
I made him a leader among the nations.
5 You also will command nations you do not know,
and peoples unknown to you will come running to obey,
because I, the LORD your God,
the Holy One of Israel, have made you glorious."

6 Seek the LORD while you can find him.
Call on him now while he is near.
7 Let the wicked change their ways
and banish the very thought of doing wrong.
Let them turn to the LORD that he may have mercy on them.
Yes, turn to our God, for he will forgive generously.
8 "My thoughts are nothing like your thoughts,"
says the LORD.
"And my ways are far beyond anything you could imagine.
9 For just as the heavens are higher than the earth,
so my ways are higher than your ways
and my thoughts higher than your thoughts.

10 "The rain and snow come down from the heavens
and stay on the ground to water the earth.
They cause the grain to grow,
producing seed for the farmer
and bread for the hungry.
11 It is the same with my word.
I send it out, and it always produces fruit.
It will accomplish all I want it to,
and it will prosper everywhere I send it.
12 You will live in joy and peace.
The mountains and hills will burst into song,
and the trees of the field will clap their hands!
13 Where once there were thorns, cypress trees will grow.
Where nettles grew, myrtles will sprout up.
These events will bring great honor to the LORD's name;
they will be an everlasting sign of his power and love."

Blessings for All Nations

ISAIAH 56:1-8

This is what the LORD says:

"Be just and fair to all.
Do what is right and good,
for I am coming soon to rescue you
and to display my righteousness among you.
2 Blessed are all those
who are careful to do this.
Blessed are those who honor my Sabbath days of rest
and keep themselves from doing wrong.

3 "Don't let foreigners who commit themselves to the LORD say,
'The LORD will never let me be part of his people.'
And don't let the eunuchs say,
'I'm a dried-up tree with no children and no future.'
4 For this is what the LORD says:
I will bless those eunuchs
who keep my Sabbath days holy
and who choose to do what pleases me
and commit their lives to me.
5 I will give them—within the walls of my house—
a memorial and a name
far greater than sons and daughters could give.

Isa 55:1-6 Food costs money, lasts only a short time, and meets only physical needs. But God offers us free nourishment that feeds our soul. How do we get it? We are to come (Isa 55:1), listen (Isa 55:2), seek, and call on God (Isa 55:6). God's salvation is freely offered, but to nourish our souls we must eagerly receive it. We will starve spiritually without this food as surely as we will starve physically without our daily bread.

Isa 55:3 God's covenant with David promised a permanent homeland for the Israelites, no threat from pagan nations, and no wars (2 Sam 7:10-11). But Israel did not fulfill its part of the covenant to obey God and stay away from idols. Even so, God was ready to renew his covenant again. He is a forgiving God!

Isa 55:6 Isaiah tells us to call on the Lord while he is near. God is not planning to move away from us, but we often move far from him or erect barriers of sin between us. Don't wait until you have drifted far away from God to seek him. Turning to him may be far more difficult later in life. Or God may come to judge the earth before you decide to turn to him. Seek God now, while you can, before it is too late.

Isa 55:8-9 The people of Israel were foolish to act as if they knew what God was thinking and planning. His knowledge and wisdom are far greater than any human's. We are foolish to try to fit God into our mold—to make his plans and purposes conform to ours. Instead, we must strive to fit into *his* plans.

Isa 56:2 God commanded his people to rest and honor him on the Sabbath (Exod 20:8-11). He wants us to serve him every day, but he wants us to make one day special when we rest and focus our thoughts on him. For the Israelites, this special day was the Sabbath (Saturday). Some Christians

For the name I give them is an everlasting one.
It will never disappear!
6 "I will also bless the foreigners who commit
themselves to the LORD,
who serve him and love his name,
who worship him and do not desecrate the
Sabbath day of rest,
and who hold fast to my covenant.
7 I will bring them to my holy mountain
of Jerusalem
and will fill them with joy in my house
of prayer.
I will accept their burnt offerings and sacrifices,
because my Temple will be called a house of
prayer for all nations.
8 For the Sovereign LORD,
who brings back the outcasts of Israel, says:
I will bring others, too,
besides my people Israel."

Sinful Leaders Condemned

ISAIAH 56:9–57:2

9 Come, wild animals of the field!
Come, wild animals of the forest!
Come and devour my people!
10 For the leaders of my people—
the LORD's watchmen, his shepherds—
are blind and ignorant.
They are like silent watchdogs
that give no warning when danger comes.
They love to lie around, sleeping and dreaming.
11 Like greedy dogs, they are never satisfied.
They are ignorant shepherds,
all following their own path
and intent on personal gain.
12 "Come," they say, "let's get some wine and
have a party.
Let's all get drunk.
Then tomorrow we'll do it again
and have an even bigger party!"
57:1 Good people pass away;
the godly often die before their time.
But no one seems to care or wonder why.
No one seems to understand
that God is protecting them from the evil to
come.
2 For those who follow godly paths
will rest in peace when they die.

Idolatrous Worship Condemned

ISAIAH 57:3-13

3 "But you—come here, you witches' children,
you offspring of adulterers and prostitutes!
4 Whom do you mock,
making faces and sticking out your tongues?
You children of sinners and liars!
5 You worship your idols with great passion
beneath the oaks and under every green tree.
You sacrifice your children down in the valleys,
among the jagged rocks in the cliffs.
6 Your gods are the smooth stones in the valleys.
You worship them with liquid offerings and
grain offerings.
They, not I, are your inheritance.
Do you think all this makes me happy?
7 You have committed adultery on every high
mountain.
There you have worshiped idols
and have been unfaithful to me.
8 You have put pagan symbols
on your doorposts and behind your doors.
You have left me
and climbed into bed with these detestable gods.
You have committed yourselves to them.
You love to look at their naked bodies.
9 You have given olive oil to Molech*
with many gifts of perfume.
You have traveled far,
even into the world of the dead,*
to find new gods to love.
10 You grew weary in your search,
but you never gave up.
Desire gave you renewed strength,
and you did not grow weary.
11 "Are you afraid of these idols?
Do they terrify you?

Is 57:9a Or *to the king.* **Is 57:9b** Hebrew *into Sheol.*

set Saturday aside as this special day, but many accept Sunday (the day of the week that Jesus rose from the dead) as the "Lord's Day," a day of rest and honor to God. Do you make Sunday special?

Isa 56:3 Isaiah clearly proclaims the radical message that God's blessings are for all people, even Gentiles and eunuchs, who were often excluded from worship and not even considered citizens in Israel. Whatever your race, social position, work, or financial situation, God's blessings are as much for you as for anyone else. No one must exclude in any way those God chooses to bless.

Isa 56:7 Jesus quoted from this verse when he threw the money changers out of the Temple (Mark 11:17). (See the note on Mark 11:15-17, p. 180.)

Isa 56:9-11 The "watchmen" were the nation's leaders. The leaders of Israel were blind to every danger and thus did not warn when danger was coming. Apathetic about their people's needs, they were more concerned about satisfying their own greed. The privileges of leadership can cause leaders to either sacrifice themselves for the good of their people or to sacrifice their people for their own greed. If you are in a leadership position, use it for the good of your people.

Isa 57:7-8 Marriage is an exclusive relationship in which a man and a woman become one. Adultery breaks this beautiful bond of unity. When the people turned from God and gave their love to idols, God said they were committing spiritual adultery—breaking their exclusive commitment to God. How could people give their love to worthless wood and stone idols instead of to the God who made them and loved them so very much?

Isa 57:9 Molech was an Ammonite god whose worship included child sacrifice.

▸ **ISAIAH 57:3-13** ***(cont.)***

Is that why you have lied to me
and forgotten me and my words?
Is it because of my long silence
that you no longer fear me?
12 Now I will expose your so-called good deeds.
None of them will help you.
13 Let's see if your idols can save you
when you cry to them for help.
Why, a puff of wind can knock them down!
If you just breathe on them, they fall over!
But whoever trusts in me will inherit the land
and possess my holy mountain."

God Forgives the Repentant

ISAIAH 57:14-21

14 God says, "Rebuild the road!
Clear away the rocks and stones
so my people can return from captivity."
15 The high and lofty one who lives in eternity,
the Holy One, says this:
"I live in the high and holy place
with those whose spirits are contrite and humble.
I restore the crushed spirit of the humble
and revive the courage of those with repentant hearts.
16 For I will not fight against you forever;
I will not always be angry.
If I were, all people would pass away—
all the souls I have made.
17 I was angry,
so I punished these greedy people.
I withdrew from them,
but they kept going on their own stubborn way.
18 I have seen what they do,
but I will heal them anyway!
I will lead them.
I will comfort those who mourn,
19 bringing words of praise to their lips.
May they have abundant peace, both near and far,"
says the LORD, who heals them.
20 "But those who still reject me are like the restless sea,
which is never still
but continually churns up mud and dirt.
21 There is no peace for the wicked,"
says my God.

True and False Worship

ISAIAH 58:1-14

1 "Shout with the voice of a trumpet blast.
Shout aloud! Don't be timid.
Tell my people Israel* of their sins!
2 Yet they act so pious!
They come to the Temple every day
and seem delighted to learn all about me.
They act like a righteous nation
that would never abandon the laws of its God.
They ask me to take action on their behalf,
pretending they want to be near me.
3 'We have fasted before you!' they say.
'Why aren't you impressed?
We have been very hard on ourselves,
and you don't even notice it!'

"I will tell you why!" I respond.
"It's because you are fasting to please yourselves.
Even while you fast,
you keep oppressing your workers.
4 What good is fasting
when you keep on fighting and quarreling?
This kind of fasting
will never get you anywhere with me.
5 You humble yourselves
by going through the motions of penance,
bowing your heads
like reeds bending in the wind.
You dress in burlap
and cover yourselves with ashes.
Is this what you call fasting?
Do you really think this will please the LORD?

6 "No, this is the kind of fasting I want:
Free those who are wrongly imprisoned;
lighten the burden of those who work for you.
Let the oppressed go free,
and remove the chains that bind people.
7 Share your food with the hungry,
and give shelter to the homeless.
Give clothes to those who need them,
and do not hide from relatives who need your help.

Is 58:1 Hebrew *Jacob.* See note on 14:1.

Isa 57:12 God says that he will expose their good deeds for what they really were—mere pretensions of doing good. Isaiah warned these people that their good deeds would not save them any more than their weak, worthless idols. We cannot gain our salvation through good works because our sins exclude us from God's presence. Salvation is a gift from God, received only through faith in Christ, not because of good works (Eph 2:8-9).

Isa 57:14-21 Isaiah 57:1-13 speaks of pride and lust; Isaiah 57:14-21 tells how God relates to those who are humble and repentant ("contrite"). The high and holy God came down to our level to save us because it is impossible for us to go up to his level to save ourselves (see 2 Chr 6:18; Ps 51:1-7; Phil 2).

Isa 58:1ff True worship was more than religious ritual, going to the Temple every day, fasting, and listening to Scripture readings. These people missed the point of a living, vital relationship with God. He doesn't want us to act pious when we have unforgiven sin in our hearts and continue our sinful lifestyles. More important even than correct worship and doctrine is genuine compassion for the oppressed, the poor, and the helpless.

Isa 58:6-12 We cannot be saved without faith in Christ, but our faith lacks sincerity if it doesn't reach out to others. Fasting can be beneficial spiritually and physically, but at its best fasting helps only the person doing it.

8 "Then your salvation will come like the dawn,
and your wounds will quickly heal.
Your godliness will lead you forward,
and the glory of the LORD will protect you
from behind.
9 Then when you call, the LORD will answer.
'Yes, I am here,' he will quickly reply.

"Remove the heavy yoke of oppression.
Stop pointing your finger and spreading
vicious rumors!
10 Feed the hungry,
and help those in trouble.
Then your light will shine out from the darkness,
and the darkness around you will be as bright
as noon.
11 The LORD will guide you continually,
giving you water when you are dry
and restoring your strength.
You will be like a well-watered garden,
like an ever-flowing spring.
12 Some of you will rebuild the deserted ruins
of your cities.
Then you will be known as a rebuilder of walls
and a restorer of homes.

13 "Keep the Sabbath day holy.
Don't pursue your own interests on that day,
but enjoy the Sabbath
and speak of it with delight as the LORD's
holy day.
Honor the Sabbath in everything you do on
that day,
and don't follow your own desires or talk idly.
14 Then the LORD will be your delight.
I will give you great honor
and satisfy you with the inheritance I promised
to your ancestor Jacob.
I, the LORD, have spoken!"

Warnings against Sin

ISAIAH 59:1-21

1 Listen! The LORD's arm is not too weak to save you,
nor is his ear too deaf to hear you call.
2 It's your sins that have cut you off from God.
Because of your sins, he has turned away
and will not listen anymore.
3 Your hands are the hands of murderers,
and your fingers are filthy with sin.
Your lips are full of lies,
and your mouth spews corruption.
4 No one cares about being fair and honest.
The people's lawsuits are based on lies.
They conceive evil deeds
and then give birth to sin.
5 They hatch deadly snakes
and weave spiders' webs.
Whoever falls into their webs will die,
and there's danger even in getting near them.
6 Their webs can't be made into clothing,
and nothing they do is productive.
All their activity is filled with sin,
and violence is their trademark.
7 Their feet run to do evil,
and they rush to commit murder.
They think only about sinning.
Misery and destruction always follow them.
8 They don't know where to find peace
or what it means to be just and good.
They have mapped out crooked roads,
and no one who follows them knows a
moment's peace.

9 So there is no justice among us,
and we know nothing about right living.
We look for light but find only darkness.
We look for bright skies but walk in gloom.
10 We grope like the blind along a wall,
feeling our way like people without eyes.
Even at brightest noontime,
we stumble as though it were dark.
Among the living,
we are like the dead.
11 We growl like hungry bears;
we moan like mournful doves.
We look for justice, but it never comes.
We look for rescue, but it is far away from us.
12 For our sins are piled up before God
and testify against us.
Yes, we know what sinners we are.
13 We know we have rebelled and have denied
the LORD.
We have turned our backs on our God.

God says he wants our fasting to go beyond our own personal growth to acts of kindness, charity, justice, and generosity. This truly is pleasing to God.

Isa 58:13-14 The day of rest should be observed and regarded not only because Sabbath-keeping is a commandment but also because it is best for us and it honors God. Keeping the Sabbath shows proper respect to God, our Creator, who also rested on the seventh day (Gen 2:3). It also unifies our family and sets priorities for them. Our day of rest refreshes us spiritually and physically—providing time when we can gather together for worship and reflect on God without the stress of our everyday activities.

Isa 59:1-14 Sin offends our holy God and separates us from him. Because God is holy, he cannot ignore, excuse, or tolerate sin as though it didn't matter. Sin cuts people off from him, forming a wall to isolate God from the people he loves. No wonder this long list of wretched sins makes God angry and forces him to look the other way. People who die with their life of sin unforgiven separate themselves eternally from God. God wants them to live with him forever, but he cannot take them into his holy presence unless their sin is removed. Have you confessed your sin to God, allowing him to remove it? The Lord can save you if you turn to him.

▶ ISAIAH 59:1-21 *(cont.)*

We know how unfair and oppressive
we have been,
carefully planning our deceitful lies.
14 Our courts oppose the righteous,
and justice is nowhere to be found.
Truth stumbles in the streets,
and honesty has been outlawed.
15 Yes, truth is gone,
and anyone who renounces evil is attacked.

The LORD looked and was displeased
to find there was no justice.
16 He was amazed to see that no one intervened
to help the oppressed.
So he himself stepped in to save them with his
strong arm,
and his justice sustained him.
17 He put on righteousness as his body armor
and placed the helmet of salvation on his head.
He clothed himself with a robe of vengeance
and wrapped himself in a cloak of divine
passion.
18 He will repay his enemies for their evil deeds.
His fury will fall on his foes.
He will pay them back even to the ends
of the earth.
19 In the west, people will respect the name
of the LORD;
in the east, they will glorify him.
For he will come like a raging flood tide
driven by the breath of the LORD.*

20 "The Redeemer will come to Jerusalem
to buy back those in Israel
who have turned from their sins,"*
says the LORD.

21 "And this is my covenant with them," says the
LORD. "My Spirit will not leave them, and neither will
these words I have given you. They will be on your lips
and on the lips of your children and your children's
children forever. I, the LORD, have spoken!

Is 59:19 Or *When the enemy comes like a raging flood tide, / the Spirit of the LORD will drive him back.* **Is 59:20** Hebrew *The Redeemer will come to Zion / to buy back those in Jacob / who have turned from their sins.* Greek version reads *The one who rescues will come on behalf of Zion, / and he will turn Jacob away from ungodliness.* Compare Rom 11:26.

3. THE FUTURE KINGDOM

This section deals both with the glory of the Kingdom of God realized through the Messiah and the Good News of his salvation, and with the still-future heavenly Kingdom that all of God's people look forward to in the last days.

Future Glory for Jerusalem

ISAIAH 60:1-22

1 "Arise, Jerusalem! Let your light shine for all
to see.
For the glory of the LORD rises to shine on you.
2 Darkness as black as night covers all the nations
of the earth,
but the glory of the LORD rises and appears
over you.
3 All nations will come to your light;
mighty kings will come to see your radiance.

4 "Look and see, for everyone is coming home!
Your sons are coming from distant lands;
your little daughters will be carried home.
5 Your eyes will shine,
and your heart will thrill with joy,
for merchants from around the world will come
to you.
They will bring you the wealth of many lands.
6 Vast caravans of camels will converge on you,
the camels of Midian and Ephah.
The people of Sheba will bring gold and
frankincense
and will come worshiping the LORD.
7 The flocks of Kedar will be given to you,
and the rams of Nebaioth will be brought for
my altars.
I will accept their offerings,
and I will make my Temple glorious.

Isa 59:15 Because of Israel's willful, persistent rebellion (Isa 56–59), the nation became unable to take action against its sins. Sin fills the vacuum left when God's truth no longer fills our life. Only God can defeat sin.

Isa 59:16-17 God would, in fact, act to rescue the nation from enemy armies (Assyria and Babylon) and to punish wicked Israelites as well. He would also rescue his people from sin. Because redemption is an impossible task for any human, God himself, as the Messiah, would personally step in to help (Rom 11:26-27). Whether we sin once or many times, out of rebellion or out of ignorance, our sin separates us from God and will continue to separate us until we confess and repent of our sin; then God forgives us and removes it.

Isa 59:21 When the Holy Spirit dwells within his people, they change. Their former desires no longer entice them; now their chief aim is to please God. We who are Christians today are the heirs of this prophecy; we are able to respond to God's will and distinguish between good and evil because the Holy Spirit dwells within us (John 14:26; Phil 2:13; Heb 5:14).

Isa 60:1ff As we read these promises, we long for their fulfillment. But we must patiently wait for God's timing. He is in control of history, and he weaves all our lives into his plan.

Isa 60:6-7 The places mentioned belonged to obscure tribes in the Arabian desert hundreds of miles from Israel. All people would come to Jerusalem because God would be living there, and they would be attracted to his light. Don't be discouraged when you look around and see so few people turning to God; one day people throughout the earth will recognize him as the one true God.

8 "And what do I see flying like clouds
to Israel,
like doves to their nests?
9 They are ships from the ends of the earth,
from lands that trust in me,
led by the great ships of Tarshish.
They are bringing the people of Israel home
from far away,
carrying their silver and gold.
They will honor the LORD your God,
the Holy One of Israel,
for he has filled you with splendor.

10 "Foreigners will come to rebuild your towns,
and their kings will serve you.
For though I have destroyed you in my anger,
I will now have mercy on you through
my grace.
11 Your gates will stay open day and night
to receive the wealth of many lands.
The kings of the world will be led as captives
in a victory procession.
12 For the nations that refuse to serve you
will be destroyed.
13 "The glory of Lebanon will be yours—
the forests of cypress, fir, and pine—
to beautify my sanctuary.
My Temple will be glorious!
14 The descendants of your tormentors
will come and bow before you.
Those who despised you
will kiss your feet.
They will call you the City of the LORD,
and Zion of the Holy One of Israel.

15 "Though you were once despised and hated,
with no one traveling through you,
I will make you beautiful forever,
a joy to all generations.
16 Powerful kings and mighty nations
will satisfy your every need,
as though you were a child
nursing at the breast of a queen.
You will know at last that I, the LORD,
am your Savior and your Redeemer,
the Mighty One of Israel.*
17 I will exchange your bronze for gold,
your iron for silver,
your wood for bronze,
and your stones for iron.
I will make peace your leader
and righteousness your ruler.
18 Violence will disappear from your land;
the desolation and destruction of war will end.
Salvation will surround you like city walls,
and praise will be on the lips of all who enter
there.

19 "No longer will you need the sun to shine by day,
nor the moon to give its light by night,
for the LORD your God will be your everlasting
light,
and your God will be your glory.
20 Your sun will never set;
your moon will not go down.
For the LORD will be your everlasting light.
Your days of mourning will come to an end.
21 All your people will be righteous.
They will possess their land forever,
for I will plant them there with my own hands
in order to bring myself glory.
22 The smallest family will become a thousand
people,
and the tiniest group will become a mighty
nation.
At the right time, I, the LORD, will make it
happen."

Is 60:16 Hebrew *of Jacob.* See note on 14:1.

THE SPIRIT IN ISAIAH

Reference	*Main Teaching*
Isa 11:2	The Spirit of the Lord brings wisdom, understanding, counsel, might, knowledge, and the fear of the Lord.
Isa 32:15	The Spirit of the Lord brings abundance.
Isa 34:16	The Spirit of the Lord carries out God's word.
Isa 40:13	The Spirit of the Lord is the Master Counselor.
Isa 42:1	The Messiah, God's Servant, will be given the Spirit.
Isa 44:3-5	Through the Spirit, God's true children will thrive.
Isa 48:16	The Spirit of the Lord sent Isaiah to prophesy.
Isa 61:1	God's servants (Isaiah and then Jesus) were appointed by the Spirit to proclaim the Good News.
Isa 63:10-11	The Spirit of the Lord was grieved because of God's people.
Isa 63:14	The Spirit of the Lord gives rest.

Isa 60:19-20 See Revelation 21:23-24; 22:5, where this beautiful reality is also promised.

Isa 61:1-2 Jesus quoted these words in Luke 4:18-19. As he read to the people in the synagogue, he said, "The Scripture you've just heard has been fulfilled this very day!" (Luke 4:21).

Good News for the Oppressed

ISAIAH 61:1-11

1 The Spirit of the Sovereign LORD is upon me,
for the LORD has anointed me
to bring good news to the poor.
He has sent me to comfort the brokenhearted
and to proclaim that captives will be released
and prisoners will be freed.*
2 He has sent me to tell those who mourn
that the time of the LORD's favor has come,*
and with it, the day of God's anger against
their enemies.
3 To all who mourn in Israel,*
he will give a crown of beauty for ashes,
a joyous blessing instead of mourning,
festive praise instead of despair.
In their righteousness, they will be like great oaks
that the LORD has planted for his own glory.
4 They will rebuild the ancient ruins,
repairing cities destroyed long ago.
They will revive them,
though they have been deserted for many
generations.
5 Foreigners will be your servants.
They will feed your flocks
and plow your fields
and tend your vineyards.
6 You will be called priests of the LORD,
ministers of our God.
You will feed on the treasures of the nations
and boast in their riches.
7 Instead of shame and dishonor,
you will enjoy a double share of honor.
You will possess a double portion of prosperity
in your land,
and everlasting joy will be yours.
8 "For I, the LORD, love justice.
I hate robbery and wrongdoing.
I will faithfully reward my people for their
suffering
and make an everlasting covenant with them.
9 Their descendants will be recognized
and honored among the nations.
Everyone will realize that they are a people
the LORD has blessed."
10 I am overwhelmed with joy in the LORD my God!
For he has dressed me with the clothing of
salvation
and draped me in a robe of righteousness.
I am like a bridegroom in his wedding suit
or a bride with her jewels.
11 The Sovereign LORD will show his justice to the
nations of the world.
Everyone will praise him!
His righteousness will be like a garden in early
spring,
with plants springing up everywhere.

Isaiah's Prayer for Jerusalem

ISAIAH 62:1-12

1 Because I love Zion,
I will not keep still.
Because my heart yearns for Jerusalem,
I cannot remain silent.
I will not stop praying for her
until her righteousness shines like the dawn,
and her salvation blazes like a burning torch.
2 The nations will see your righteousness.
World leaders will be blinded by your glory.
And you will be given a new name
by the LORD's own mouth.
3 The LORD will hold you in his hand for all to see—
a splendid crown in the hand of God.
4 Never again will you be called "The Forsaken City"*
or "The Desolate Land."*
Your new name will be "The City of God's Delight"*
and "The Bride of God,"*
for the LORD delights in you
and will claim you as his bride.
5 Your children will commit themselves to you,
O Jerusalem,
just as a young man commits himself to his bride.
Then God will rejoice over you
as a bridegroom rejoices over his bride.
6 O Jerusalem, I have posted watchmen on your
walls;

Is 61:1 Greek version reads *and the blind will see.* Compare Luke 4:18. **Is 61:2** Or *to proclaim the acceptable year of the LORD.* **Is 61:3** Hebrew *in Zion.* **Is 62:4a** Hebrew *Azubah,* which means "forsaken." **Is 62:4b** Hebrew *Shemamah,* which means "desolate." **Is 62:4c** Hebrew *Hephzibah,* which means "my delight is in her." **Is 62:4d** Hebrew *Beulah,* which means "married."

Isa 61:6 Under the old covenant, God ordained the priests of Israel to stand between him and his people. They brought God's word to the people and the people's needs and sins to God. Under the new covenant, all believers are priests of the Lord (1 Pet 2:5), reading God's Word and seeking to understand it, confessing their sins directly to God, and ministering to others.

Isa 61:8 We suffer for many reasons—our own mistakes, someone else's mistakes, injustice. When we suffer for our own mistakes, we get what we deserve. When we suffer because of others or because of injustice, God is angry. God in his mercy says that his people have suffered enough. God will reward those who suffer because of injustice. He will settle all accounts.

Isa 61:10 "Me" could refer to the Messiah, the person appointed by the Spirit of the Lord (Isa 61:1), or to Zion (Isa 62:1), which symbolizes God's people. The imagery of the bridegroom is often used in Scripture to depict the Messiah (see Matt 9:15), while the imagery of the bride is used to depict God's people (see Rev 19:6-8). We, too, can put on our new clothes—a right relationship with God—by putting our trust in Christ (2 Cor 5:21).

Isa 62:1-7 Many commentators believe Isaiah is speaking here. If so, Isaiah's zeal for his people and his desire to see the work of salvation completed caused him to pray without resting, hoping that Israel would be saved. We should have Isaiah's zeal to see God's will done. This is what we mean when we pray, "May your Kingdom come soon. May your will be done on earth, as it is in heaven" (Matt 6:10). It is good to keep praying persistently for others.

they will pray day and night, continually.
Take no rest, all you who pray to the LORD.
7 Give the LORD no rest until he completes
his work,
until he makes Jerusalem the pride of the
earth.
8 The LORD has sworn to Jerusalem by his own
strength:
"I will never again hand you over to your
enemies.
Never again will foreign warriors come
and take away your grain and new wine.
9 You raised the grain, and you will eat it,
praising the LORD.
Within the courtyards of the Temple,
you yourselves will drink the wine you have
pressed."

10 Go out through the gates!
Prepare the highway for my people to return!
Smooth out the road; pull out the boulders;
raise a flag for all the nations to see.
11 The LORD has sent this message to every land:
"Tell the people of Israel,*
'Look, your Savior is coming.
See, he brings his reward with him as he comes.'"
12 They will be called "The Holy People"
and "The People Redeemed by the LORD."
And Jerusalem will be known as "The
Desirable Place"
and "The City No Longer Forsaken."

Judgment against the LORD's Enemies

ISAIAH 63:1-6

1 Who is this who comes from Edom,
from the city of Bozrah,
with his clothing stained red?
Who is this in royal robes,
marching in his great strength?

"It is I, the LORD, announcing your salvation!
It is I, the LORD, who has the power to save!"

2 Why are your clothes so red,
as if you have been treading out grapes?

3 "I have been treading the winepress alone;
no one was there to help me.
In my anger I have trampled my enemies
as if they were grapes.
In my fury I have trampled my foes.
Their blood has stained my clothes.
4 For the time has come for me to avenge my
people,
to ransom them from their oppressors.
5 I was amazed to see that no one intervened
to help the oppressed.
So I myself stepped in to save them with my
strong arm,
and my wrath sustained me.
6 I crushed the nations in my anger
and made them stagger and fall to the
ground,
spilling their blood upon the earth."

Praise for Deliverance

ISAIAH 63:7-14

7 I will tell of the LORD's unfailing love.
I will praise the LORD for all he has done.
I will rejoice in his great goodness to Israel,
which he has granted according to his mercy
and love.
8 He said, "They are my very own people.
Surely they will not betray me again."
And he became their Savior.

Is 62:11 Hebrew *Tell the daughter of Zion.*

Winepress

The winepress was a sunken area into which the grape harvest was thrown and then trodden with bare feet, amid shouts of joy and traditional vintage work songs (Jer 48:33). The red juice flowed out through spouts into jars. Full winepresses meant prosperity; deserted ones spoke of destitution. The common winepress made a natural landmark (Judg 7:25; Zech 14:10); a privately owned one indicated the special care and efficiency of the vineyard's owner (Isa 5:2; Matt 21:33). Grape treading provided a dramatic metaphor for the ruthless trampling of invading armies (Lam 1:15). This vivid metaphor of battle is mingled with divine judgment (Isa 63:1-6) and anticipates the Lord's final judgment, spoken of as "the great winepress of God's wrath" (Rev 14:18-20). Thankfully, Christians are exempt from this furious judgment. Christ took the judgment on himself: "He was . . . crushed for our sins . . . so we could be whole" (Isa 53:5). This is cause for great thanksgiving.

Isa 62:12 The people of Jerusalem (Zion) will have new names: "The Holy People" and "The People Redeemed by the LORD." Believers today also have new names—Christians. In 1 Peter 2:5, we are called God's "holy priests."

Isa 63:1-4 Edom was a constant enemy of Israel despite its common ancestry in Isaac (Gen 25:23). Edom rejoiced at any trouble Israel faced. The imagery in this passage is of a watchman on the wall of Jerusalem, seeing Edom approaching and fearing that the Edomite king in his red garment is leading an attack. But it turns out to be the Lord, in bloodstained clothes, who has trampled and destroyed Edom. Bozrah is a city in Edom. (For other prophecies against Edom, see Amos 1:11-12; Obad 1:10-11; Mal 1:2-4.)

▸ **ISAIAH 63:7-14** ***(cont.)***

9 In all their suffering he also suffered,
and he personally* rescued them.
In his love and mercy he redeemed them.
He lifted them up and carried them
through all the years.
10 But they rebelled against him
and grieved his Holy Spirit.
So he became their enemy
and fought against them.

11 Then they remembered those days of old
when Moses led his people out of Egypt.
They cried out, "Where is the one who brought
Israel through the sea,
with Moses as their shepherd?
Where is the one who sent his Holy Spirit
to be among his people?
12 Where is the one whose power was displayed
when Moses lifted up his hand—
the one who divided the sea before them,
making himself famous forever?
13 Where is the one who led them through the
bottom of the sea?
They were like fine stallions
racing through the desert, never stumbling.
14 As with cattle going down into a peaceful valley,
the Spirit of the LORD gave them rest.
You led your people, LORD,
and gained a magnificent reputation."

Prayer for Mercy and Pardon

ISAIAH 63:15–64:12

15 LORD, look down from heaven;
look from your holy, glorious home, and see us.
Where is the passion and the might
you used to show on our behalf?
Where are your mercy and compassion now?
16 Surely you are still our Father!
Even if Abraham and Jacob* would disown us,
LORD, you would still be our Father.
You are our Redeemer from ages past.
17 LORD, why have you allowed us to turn from
your path?
Why have you given us stubborn hearts so we
no longer fear you?
Return and help us, for we are your servants,
the tribes that are your special possession.
18 How briefly your holy people possessed your
holy place,
and now our enemies have destroyed it.
19 Sometimes it seems as though we never
belonged to you,
as though we had never been known as your
people.

64:1*Oh, that you would burst from the heavens and
come down!
How the mountains would quake in your
presence!
2*As fire causes wood to burn
and water to boil,
your coming would make the nations tremble.
Then your enemies would learn the reason for
your fame!
3 When you came down long ago,
you did awesome deeds beyond our highest
expectations.
And oh, how the mountains quaked!
4 For since the world began,
no ear has heard
and no eye has seen a God like you,
who works for those who wait for him!
5 You welcome those who gladly do good,
who follow godly ways.
But you have been very angry with us,
for we are not godly.
We are constant sinners;
how can people like us be saved?
6 We are all infected and impure with sin.
When we display our righteous deeds,
they are nothing but filthy rags.
Like autumn leaves, we wither and fall,
and our sins sweep us away like the wind.
7 Yet no one calls on your name
or pleads with you for mercy.
Therefore, you have turned away from us
and turned us over* to our sins.

Is 63:9 Hebrew *and the angel of his presence.* **Is 63:16** Hebrew *Israel.* See note on 14:1. **Is 64:1** In the Hebrew text this verse is included in 63:19. **Is 64:2** Verses 64:2-12 are numbered 64:1-11 in Hebrew text. **Is 64:7** As in Greek, Syriac, and Aramaic versions; Hebrew reads *melted us.*

Isa 63:10 Grieving the Holy Spirit is willfully thwarting his leading by disobedience or rebellion. Isaiah mentions the work of the Holy Spirit more than any other Old Testament writer. (See the note on Eph 4:28-32, p. 1712, for more on grieving the Holy Spirit.)

Isa 63:15–64:7 On behalf of the faithful remnant, Isaiah asks God for two favors: to show mercy and compassion to them and to punish their enemies. Before making these requests, Isaiah recited the Lord's past favors, reminding him of his compassion in former days (Isa 63:7-14).

Isa 64:1-6 God's appearance is so intense that it is like a consuming fire that burns everything in its path. If we are so impure, how can we be saved? Only by God's mercy. The Israelites had experienced God's presence at Mount Sinai (Exod 19:16-19). When God met with Moses, there was a thunderstorm, smoke, and an earthquake. If God were to meet us today, his glory would overwhelm us, especially when we look at our "filthy rags" (Isa 64:6).

Isa 64:6 Sin makes us unclean so that we cannot approach God (Isa 6:5; Rom 3:23) any more than a beggar in filthy rags could dine at a king's table. Our best efforts are still infected with sin. Our only hope, therefore, is faith in Jesus Christ, who can cleanse us and bring us into God's presence (read Rom 3).

This passage can easily be misunderstood. It doesn't mean that God will reject us if we come to him in faith, nor that he despises our efforts to please him. It means that if we come to him demanding acceptance on the basis of our "good" conduct, God will point out that our righteousness is but filthy rags compared to his infinite righteousness. This message is primarily for the unrepentant person, not the true follower of God.

8 And yet, O LORD, you are our Father.
We are the clay, and you are the potter.
We all are formed by your hand.
9 Don't be so angry with us, LORD.
Please don't remember our sins forever.
Look at us, we pray,
and see that we are all your people.
10 Your holy cities are destroyed.
Zion is a wilderness;
yes, Jerusalem is a desolate ruin.
11 The holy and beautiful Temple
where our ancestors praised you
has been burned down,
and all the things of beauty are destroyed.
12 After all this, LORD, must you still refuse to
help us?
Will you continue to be silent and punish us?

Judgment and Final Salvation

ISAIAH 65:1–66:24

The LORD says,

"I was ready to respond, but no one asked for
help.
I was ready to be found, but no one was looking
for me.
I said, 'Here I am, here I am!'
to a nation that did not call on my name.*
2 All day long I opened my arms to a rebellious
people.*
But they follow their own evil paths
and their own crooked schemes.
3 All day long they insult me to my face
by worshiping idols in their sacred gardens.
They burn incense on pagan altars.
4 At night they go out among the graves,
worshiping the dead.
They eat the flesh of pigs
and make stews with other forbidden foods.
5 Yet they say to each other,
'Don't come too close or you will defile me!
I am holier than you!'
These people are a stench in my nostrils,
an acrid smell that never goes away.

6 "Look, my decree is written out* in front of me:
I will not stand silent;
I will repay them in full!
Yes, I will repay them—
7 both for their own sins
and for those of their ancestors,"
says the LORD.
"For they also burned incense on the mountains
and insulted me on the hills.
I will pay them back in full!

8 "But I will not destroy them all,"
says the LORD.
"For just as good grapes are found among a
cluster of bad ones
(and someone will say, 'Don't throw them all
away—
some of those grapes are good!'),
so I will not destroy all Israel.
For I still have true servants there.

Is 65:1 Or *to a nation that did not bear my name.* **Is 65:1-2** Greek version reads *I was found by people who were not looking for me. / I showed myself to those who were not asking for me. / All day long I opened my arms to them, / but they were disobedient and rebellious.* Compare Rom 10:20-21. **Is 65:6** Or *their sins are written out;* Hebrew reads *it stands written.*

Isa 65:1 Israel considered itself to be the only people of God, but the time would come when other nations would seek him. Paul mentions Isaiah's statement in Romans 10:20 and points out that these other nations were the Gentiles. God's people today are those who accept Jesus as Savior and Lord, whether they are Jews or Gentiles. The gospel is for every person. Do not ignore or reject anyone when you share the gospel. You may be surprised at how many are sincerely searching for God.

Isa 65:3-5 God said these people directly disobeyed his laws when they worshiped and sacrificed to idols (Exod 20:1-6), consulted the dead and evil spirits (Lev 19:31), and ate forbidden foods (Lev 11). But they were so perverse that they still thought they were spiritually superior to others. Jesus called such people hypocrites (Matt 23:13-36).

Isa 65:6 God said he would pay back the people for their sins. Judgment is not our job but God's because he alone is just. Who else knows our hearts and minds? Who else knows what is a completely fair reward or punishment? Leave judgment of others up to God. If he gave us what *we* deserve, he might wipe us out. Instead, pray for his mercy.

Isa 65:8-9 God will always preserve a faithful remnant of his people. No matter how bad the world is, there are always a few who remain loyal to him. Jesus made this point in Matthew 13:36-43.

Sharon Plain

Sharon is a section of the plain on the Mediterranean coast of Israel. It extends from Joppa in the south to the Crocodile River, which serves as the northern border and separates it from the plain of Dor. The largest of the coastal plains, it is 50 miles from north to south and 10 miles wide. Its shore is straight and consists of beach and cliffs. There are no natural harbors along its coast, so the plain had no large trading ports. The "spring crocus" (Song 2:1; traditionally the "rose of Sharon") may have been one of several varieties of red flowering plants that grow in the Sharon plain. In the book of Isaiah, along with the regions of Carmel and Lebanon, Sharon is noted for its fertility and luxuriance (Isa 33:9; 35:2). When Isaiah speaks of the final restoration, when the earth will be made new, he refers to the Sharon pastures as the place for flocks (Isa 65:10). How we look forward to the coming of the new heavens and earth (Isa 66:22; Rev 21:1)!

▶ **ISAIAH 65:1–66:24** ***(cont.)***

9 I will preserve a remnant of the people of Israel*
and of Judah to possess my land.
Those I choose will inherit it,
and my servants will live there.
10 The plain of Sharon will again be filled with flocks
for my people who have searched for me,
and the valley of Achor will be a place to pasture herds.
11 "But because the rest of you have forsaken the LORD
and have forgotten his Temple,
and because you have prepared feasts to honor the god of Fate
and have offered mixed wine to the god of Destiny,
12 now I will 'destine' you for the sword.
All of you will bow down before the executioner.
For when I called, you did not answer.
When I spoke, you did not listen.
You deliberately sinned—before my very eyes—
and chose to do what you know I despise."

13 Therefore, this is what the Sovereign LORD says:
"My servants will eat,
but you will starve.
My servants will drink,
but you will be thirsty.
My servants will rejoice,
but you will be sad and ashamed.
14 My servants will sing for joy,
but you will cry in sorrow and despair.
15 Your name will be a curse word among my people,
for the Sovereign LORD will destroy you
and will call his true servants by another name.
16 All who invoke a blessing or take an oath
will do so by the God of truth.
For I will put aside my anger
and forget the evil of earlier days.
17 "Look! I am creating new heavens and a new earth,
and no one will even think about the old ones anymore.
18 Be glad; rejoice forever in my creation!
And look! I will create Jerusalem as a place of happiness.
Her people will be a source of joy.
19 I will rejoice over Jerusalem
and delight in my people.
And the sound of weeping and crying
will be heard in it no more.

20 "No longer will babies die when only a few days old.
No longer will adults die before they have lived a full life.
No longer will people be considered old at one hundred!
Only the cursed will die that young!
21 In those days people will live in the houses they build
and eat the fruit of their own vineyards.
22 Unlike the past, invaders will not take their houses
and confiscate their vineyards.
For my people will live as long as trees,
and my chosen ones will have time to enjoy their hard-won gains.
23 They will not work in vain,
and their children will not be doomed to misfortune.
For they are people blessed by the LORD,
and their children, too, will be blessed.
24 I will answer them before they even call to me.
While they are still talking about their needs,
I will go ahead and answer their prayers!
25 The wolf and the lamb will feed together.
The lion will eat hay like a cow.
But the snakes will eat dust.
In those days no one will be hurt or destroyed
on my holy mountain.
I, the LORD, have spoken!"

66:1 This is what the LORD says:
"Heaven is my throne,
and the earth is my footstool.
Could you build me a temple as good as that?
Could you build me such a resting place?
2 My hands have made both heaven and earth;
they and everything in them are mine.*
I, the LORD, have spoken!

Is 65:9 Hebrew *remnant of Jacob.* See note on 14:1. **Is 66:2** As in Greek, Latin, and Syriac versions; Hebrew reads *these things are.*

Isa 65:10 Sharon is a plain in the western part of Israel. The valley of Achor is in the east, near Jericho. The valley of Achor was also called the Valley of Trouble because Achan was executed there for hiding the devoted goods of battle (Josh 7:10-26). Even in this valley there will be peace: The coming restoration will be complete.

Isa 65:17-25 In Isaiah 65:17-19 we have a pictorial description of the new heavens and the new earth. They are eternal, and in them safety, peace, and plenty will be available to all (see also Isa 66:22-23; 2 Pet 3:13; Rev 21:1). Isaiah 65:20-25 may refer to the reign of Christ on earth because sin and death have not yet been finally destroyed.

Isa 66:1 Even the beautiful Temple in Jerusalem was woefully inadequate for a God who is present everywhere. God cannot be confined to any human structure (see 2 Chr 6:18; Acts 7:49-50). This chapter is a fitting climax to the book. God will lift up the humble, judge all people, destroy the wicked, bring all believers together, and establish the new heavens and the new earth. Let this hope encourage you each day.

Isa 66:2-3 These key verses summarize Isaiah's message. He contrasted humble people, who have a profound reverence for God's messages and their application to life,

"I will bless those who have humble and contrite
hearts,
who tremble at my word.
3 But those who choose their own ways—
delighting in their detestable sins—
will not have their offerings accepted.
When such people sacrifice a bull,
it is no more acceptable than a human
sacrifice.
When they sacrifice a lamb,
it's as though they had sacrificed a dog!
When they bring an offering of grain,
they might as well offer the blood of a pig.
When they burn frankincense,
it's as if they had blessed an idol.
4 I will send them great trouble—
all the things they feared.
For when I called, they did not answer.
When I spoke, they did not listen.
They deliberately sinned before my very eyes
and chose to do what they know I despise."

5 Hear this message from the LORD,
all you who tremble at his words:
"Your own people hate you
and throw you out for being loyal to my name.
'Let the LORD be honored!' they scoff.
'Be joyful in him!'
But they will be put to shame.
6 What is all the commotion in the city?
What is that terrible noise from the Temple?
It is the voice of the LORD
taking vengeance against his enemies.
7 "Before the birth pains even begin,
Jerusalem gives birth to a son.
8 Who has ever seen anything as strange as this?
Who ever heard of such a thing?
Has a nation ever been born in a single day?
Has a country ever come forth in a mere
moment?
But by the time Jerusalem's* birth pains begin,
her children will be born.
9 Would I ever bring this nation to the point of birth
and then not deliver it?" asks the LORD.
"No! I would never keep this nation from being
born,"
says your God.

10 "Rejoice with Jerusalem!
Be glad with her, all you who love her
and all you who mourn for her.
11 Drink deeply of her glory
even as an infant drinks at its mother's
comforting breasts."

12 This is what the LORD says:
"I will give Jerusalem a river of peace and
prosperity.
The wealth of the nations will flow to her.
Her children will be nursed at her breasts,
carried in her arms, and held on her lap.
13 I will comfort you there in Jerusalem
as a mother comforts her child."

14 When you see these things, your heart will rejoice.
You will flourish like the grass!
Everyone will see the LORD's hand of blessing on
his servants—
and his anger against his enemies.
15 See, the LORD is coming with fire,
and his swift chariots roar like a whirlwind.
He will bring punishment with the fury of his
anger
and the flaming fire of his hot rebuke.
16 The LORD will punish the world by fire
and by his sword.
He will judge the earth,
and many will be killed by him.

17 "Those who 'consecrate' and 'purify' themselves in
a sacred garden with its idol in the center—feasting on
pork and rats and other detestable meats—will come
to a terrible end," says the LORD.
18 "I can see what they are doing, and I know what
they are thinking. So I will gather all nations and
peoples together, and they will see my glory. 19 I will
perform a sign among them. And I will send those
who survive to be messengers to the nations—to Tarshish, to the Libyans* and Lydians* (who are famous
as archers), to Tubal and Greece,* and to all the lands
beyond the sea that have not heard of my fame or
seen my glory. There they will declare my glory to the
nations. 20 They will bring the remnant of your people
back from every nation. They will bring them to my
holy mountain in Jerusalem as an offering to the LORD.
They will ride on horses, in chariots and wagons, and

Is 66:8 Hebrew *Zion's*. **Is 66:19a** As in some Greek manuscripts, which read *Put* [that is, *Libya*]; Hebrew reads *Pul*. **Is 66:19b** Hebrew *Lud*. **Is 66:19c** Hebrew *Javan*.

with those who choose their own ways. The sacrifices of the arrogant were only external compliance. In their hearts they were murderers, perverts, and idolaters. God shows mercy to the humble, but he curses the proud and self-sufficient (see Luke 1:51-53). Our society urges us to be assertive and to affirm ourselves. Don't let your freedom and right to choose lead you away from God's pathway to eternal life.

Isa 66:7-9 God will not leave his work of national restoration unfinished. In this image of birth, God shows that he will accomplish what he has promised. It is as unstoppable as the birth of a baby. When all the pain is over, the joy begins.

Isa 66:15-17 This is a vivid picture of the great judgment that will occur at Christ's second coming (2 Thes 1:7-9).

Isa 66:19 God's people will go out as missionaries to all parts of the earth—to Tarshish (Spain), to the Libyans in northern Africa, to the Lydians in western Asia Minor, to northeastern Asia Minor (Tubal), and to Greece.

▸ **ISAIAH 65:1–66:24** ***(cont.)***
on mules and camels," says the LORD. [21]"And I will
appoint some of them to be my priests and Levites. I,
the LORD, have spoken!

22 "As surely as my new heavens and earth will
remain,
so will you always be my people,
with a name that will never disappear,"
says the LORD.
23 "All humanity will come to worship me
from week to week
and from month to month.
24 And as they go out, they will see
the dead bodies of those who have rebelled
against me.
For the worms that devour them will never die,
and the fire that burns them will never go out.
All who pass by
will view them with utter horror."

L. Cycles of Rebellion and Repentance in Judah

After Hezekiah's great reforms, the nation of Judah seemed like it would be set up for a long-term revival. Unfortunately, Hezekiah's son Manasseh was an extremely evil king, taking Judah perhaps farther from God than they had been prior to the reforms of Hezekiah. He even built altars for pagan worship in the Temple! Manasseh had an encounter with God and repented, leading to a restoration of the Temple in his later years, but his son Amon resumed the evil practices that many kings before him had followed. Then Josiah became king and led another great revival, perhaps greater than Hezekiah's. It was a time of great highs and great lows in the spiritual life of God's people.

1. MANASSEH THROUGH JOSIAH

This progression of kings took place over about 85 years, with many spiritual ups and downs. The nation was relatively secure politically, however, with very little opposition and outside threats.

660 BC

Japan founded as a nation

Manasseh Begins His Reign in Judah PARALLEL

2 KINGS 21:1-9
Manasseh was twelve years old when he became
king, and he reigned in Jerusalem fifty-five years. His
mother was Hephzibah. [2]He did what was evil in the
LORD's sight, following the detestable practices of the
pagan nations that the LORD had driven from the land
ahead of the Israelites. [3]He rebuilt the pagan shrines
his father, Hezekiah, had destroyed. He constructed
altars for Baal and set up an Asherah pole, just as King
Ahab of Israel had done. He also bowed before all the
powers of the heavens and worshiped them.
[4]He built pagan altars in the Temple of the LORD,
the place where the LORD had said, "My name will
remain in Jerusalem forever." [5]He built these altars
for all the powers of the heavens in both courtyards of
the LORD's Temple. [6]Manasseh also sacrificed his own
son in the fire.* He practiced sorcery and divination,
and he consulted with mediums and psychics. He
did much that was evil in the LORD's sight, arousing
his anger.
[7]Manasseh even made a carved image of Asherah
and set it up in the Temple, the very place where the
LORD had told David and his son Solomon: "My name
will be honored forever in this Temple and in Jerusalem—the city I have chosen from among all the
tribes of Israel. [8]If the Israelites will be careful to obey
my commands—all the laws my servant Moses gave
them—I will not send them into exile from this land
that I gave their ancestors." [9]But the people refused
to listen, and Manasseh led them to do even more evil
than the pagan nations that the LORD had destroyed
when the people of Israel entered the land.

2 CHRONICLES 33:1-9
Manasseh was twelve years old when he became king,
and he reigned in Jerusalem fifty-five years. [2]He did
what was evil in the LORD's sight, following the detestable practices of the pagan nations that the LORD
had driven from the land ahead of the Israelites. [3]He
rebuilt the pagan shrines his father, Hezekiah, had
broken down. He constructed altars for the images of
Baal and set up Asherah poles. He also bowed before
all the powers of the heavens and worshiped them.
[4]He built pagan altars in the Temple of the LORD,
the place where the LORD had said, "My name will
remain in Jerusalem forever." [5]He built these altars
for all the powers of the heavens in both courtyards
of the LORD's Temple. [6]Manasseh also sacrificed his
own sons in the fire* in the valley of Ben-Hinnom. He

2 Kgs 21:6 *Or also made his son pass through the fire.* **2 Chr 33:6** *Or also made his sons pass through the fire.*

Isa 66:22-24 Isaiah brings his book to a close with great drama. For the faithless there is a sobering portrayal of judgment. For the faithful, there is a glorious picture of rich reward: "So will you always be my people, with a name that will never disappear." The contrast is so striking that it would seem that everyone would want to be God's follower. But we are often just as rebellious, foolish, and reluctant to change as the Israelites. We are just as negligent in feeding the hungry, working for justice, obeying God's Word, and taking up his causes. Make sure you are among those who will be richly blessed.

practiced sorcery, divination, and witchcraft, and he
consulted with mediums and psychics. He did much
that was evil in the LORD's sight, arousing his anger.
7Manasseh even took a carved idol he had made and
set it up in God's Temple, the very place where God had
told David and his son Solomon: "My name will be honored forever in this Temple and in Jerusalem—the city
I have chosen from among all the tribes of Israel. 8If
the Israelites will be careful to obey my commands—
all the laws, decrees, and regulations given through
Moses—I will not send them into exile from this land
that I set aside for your ancestors." 9But Manasseh led
the people of Judah and Jerusalem to do even more evil
than the pagan nations that the LORD had destroyed
when the people of Israel entered the land.

The LORD Speaks to Manasseh PARALLEL

2 KINGS 21:10-16

Then the LORD said through his servants the prophets:
11"King Manasseh of Judah has done many detestable
things. He is even more wicked than the Amorites,
who lived in this land before Israel. He has caused
the people of Judah to sin with his idols.* 12So this
is what the LORD, the God of Israel, says: I will bring
such disaster on Jerusalem and Judah that the ears
of those who hear about it will tingle with horror. 13I
will judge Jerusalem by the same standard I used for
Samaria and the same measure* I used for the family
of Ahab. I will wipe away the people of Jerusalem as
one wipes a dish and turns it upside down. 14Then I
will reject even the remnant of my own people who
are left, and I will hand them over as plunder for their
enemies. 15For they have done great evil in my sight
and have angered me ever since their ancestors came
out of Egypt."
16Manasseh also murdered many innocent people
until Jerusalem was filled from one end to the other
with innocent blood. This was in addition to the sin
that he caused the people of Judah to commit, leading
them to do evil in the LORD's sight.

2 Kgs 21:11 The Hebrew term (literally *round things*) probably alludes to dung; also in 21:21. **2 Kgs 21:13** Hebrew *the same plumb line I used for Samaria and the same plumb bob.*

2 Kgs 21:1ff Manasseh followed the example of his grandfather Ahaz more than that of his father. He adopted the wicked practices of the Babylonians and Canaanites, including sacrificing his own son (2 Kgs 21:6). Manasseh did not listen to the words of God's prophets but willfully led his people into sin.

2 Kgs 21:6 Manasseh was an evil king, and he angered God with his sin. Listed among Manasseh's sins are occult practices—sorcery and divination, and consulting mediums and psychics. These acts are strictly forbidden by God (Lev 19:31; Deut 18:9-13) because they demonstrate a lack of faith in him, involve sinful actions, and open the door to demonic influences. Today, some books, television shows, and games emphasize fortune-telling, séances, and other occult practices. Don't let desire to know the future or the belief that superstition is harmless lead you into condoning occult practices. They are counterfeits of God's power and have as their root a system of beliefs totally opposed to God.

2 Kgs 21:7 Asherah was a Canaanite mother-goddess, a mistress of Baal. Her images were made of wood. The Israelites were expressly forbidden to associate with Asherah practices in any way (Exod 34:13; Deut 12:3).

2 Chr 33:6 Sorcery is using power gained from evil spirits. Divination is predicting the future through omens.

2 Kgs 21:16 Tradition says that during Manasseh's massive slaughter, Isaiah was sawed in two when trying to hide in a hollow log (see Heb 11:37-38). Other prophets may also have been killed at this time.

MANASSEH

Even a brief outline of King Manasseh's evil sickens us, and we wonder how God could ever forgive him. Not only did he intentionally offend God by desecrating Solomon's Temple with idols, but he also worshiped pagan gods and even sacrificed his children to them! Child sacrifice is a vile act of pagan idolatry, an act against both God and people. Such blatant sins require severe correction. • God showed justice to Manasseh in warning and punishing him. He showed mercy in responding to Manasseh's heartfelt repentance by forgiving and restoring him. Given the nature of Manasseh's rebellion, we are not surprised by God's punishment—defeat and exile at the hands of the Assyrians. But Manasseh's repentance and God's forgiveness are unexpected. Manasseh's life was changed. He was given a new start. • How far has God gone to get your attention? Have you ever, like Manasseh, come to your senses and cried out to God for help? Only your repentance and a prayer for a new attitude stand between you and God's complete forgiveness.

Strengths and accomplishments	• Despite the bitter consequences of his sins, he learned from them • Humbly repented of his sins before God
Weaknesses and mistakes	• Challenged God's authority and was defeated • Reversed many of the positive effects of his father Hezekiah's rule • Sacrificed his children to idols
Lessons from his life	• God will go a long way to get someone's attention • Forgiveness is limited, not by the amount of sin, but by our willingness to repent
Vital statistics	• Where: Jerusalem • Occupation: King of Judah • Relatives: Father: Hezekiah. Mother: Hephzibah. Son: Amon.
Key verses	"But while in deep distress, Manasseh sought the LORD his God and sincerely humbled himself before the God of his ancestors. And when he prayed, the LORD listened to him and was moved by his request. So the LORD brought Manasseh back to Jerusalem and to his kingdom. Then Manasseh finally realized that the LORD alone is God!" (2 Chr 33:12-13).

Manasseh's story is told in 2 Kings 21:1-18; 2 Chronicles 32:33–33:20. He is also mentioned in Jeremiah 15:4.

648 BC

Horse racing first held at 33rd Olympics

2 CHRONICLES 33:10-17

The LORD spoke to Manasseh and his people, but they ignored all his warnings. 11 So the LORD sent the commanders of the Assyrian armies, and they took Manasseh prisoner. They put a ring through his nose, bound him in bronze chains, and led him away to Babylon. 12 But while in deep distress, Manasseh sought the LORD his God and sincerely humbled himself before the God of his ancestors. 13 And when he prayed, the LORD listened to him and was moved by his request. So the LORD brought Manasseh back to Jerusalem and to his kingdom. Then Manasseh finally realized that the LORD alone is God!

14 After this Manasseh rebuilt the outer wall of the City of David, from west of the Gihon Spring in the Kidron Valley to the Fish Gate, and continuing around the hill of Ophel. He built the wall very high. And he stationed his military officers in all of the fortified towns of Judah. 15 Manasseh also removed the foreign gods and the idol from the LORD's Temple. He tore down all the altars he had built on the hill where the Temple stood and all the altars that were in Jerusalem, and he dumped them outside the city. 16 Then he restored the altar of the LORD and sacrificed peace offerings and thanksgiving offerings on it. He also encouraged the people of Judah to worship the LORD, the God of Israel. 17 However, the people still sacrificed at the pagan shrines, though only to the LORD their God.

The End of Manasseh's Reign PARALLEL

2 KINGS 21:17-18

The rest of the events in Manasseh's reign and everything he did, including the sins he committed, are recorded in *The Book of the History of the Kings of Judah.* 18 When Manasseh died, he was buried in the palace garden, the garden of Uzza. Then his son Amon became the next king.

2 CHRONICLES 33:18-20

The rest of the events of Manasseh's reign, his prayer to God, and the words the seers spoke to him in the name of the LORD, the God of Israel, are recorded in *The Book of the Kings of Israel.* 19 Manasseh's prayer, the account of the way God answered him, and an account of all his sins and unfaithfulness are recorded in *The Record of the Seers.** It includes a list of the locations where he built pagan shrines and set up Asherah poles and idols before he humbled himself and repented. 20 When Manasseh died, he was buried in his palace. Then his son Amon became the next king.

Amon Rules in Judah PARALLEL

2 KINGS 21:19-26

Amon was twenty-two years old when he became king, and he reigned in Jerusalem two years. His mother was Meshullemeth, the daughter of Haruz from Jotbah. 20 He did what was evil in the LORD's sight, just as his father, Manasseh, had done. 21 He followed the example of his father, worshiping the same idols his father had worshiped. 22 He abandoned the LORD, the God of his ancestors, and he refused to follow the LORD's ways.

23 Then Amon's own officials conspired against him and assassinated him in his palace. 24 But the people of the land killed all those who had conspired against King Amon, and they made his son Josiah the next king.

25 The rest of the events in Amon's reign and what he did are recorded in *The Book of the History of the Kings of Judah.* 26 He was buried in his tomb in the garden of Uzza. Then his son Josiah became the next king.

2 CHRONICLES 33:21-25

Amon was twenty-two years old when he became king, and he reigned in Jerusalem two years. 22 He did what was evil in the LORD's sight, just as his father, Manasseh, had done. He worshiped and sacrificed to all the idols his father had made. 23 But unlike his father, he did not humble himself before the LORD. Instead, Amon sinned even more.

24 Then Amon's own officials conspired against him and assassinated him in his palace. 25 But the people of the land killed all those who had conspired against King Amon, and they made his son Josiah the next king.

2 Chr 33:19 Or *The Record of Hozai.*

---

2 Chr 33:11 Between 652 and 648 B.C., the city of Babylon rebelled against Assyria. The rebellion was crushed, but Assyria may have suspected that Manasseh supported it. That may explain why Manasseh was taken to Babylon for trial rather than to the Assyrian capital of Nineveh.

2 Chr 33:12-13 In a list of corrupt kings, Manasseh would rank near the top. His life was a catalog of evil deeds including idol worship, sacrificing his own children, and Temple desecration. Eventually he realized his sins and cried out to God for forgiveness. And God listened. If God can forgive Manasseh, surely he can forgive anyone. Are you burdened by overpowering guilt? Do you doubt that anyone could forgive what you have done? Take heart—until death, no one is beyond the reach of God's forgiveness.

2 Chr 33:17 Although the people worshiped God alone, they worshiped him in the wrong way. God had told them to make their sacrifices only in certain places (Deut 12:13-14). This kept them from changing their way of worship and protected them against the dangerous influence of pagan religious practices. Unfortunately, the people continued to use these places of worship, not realizing that they were adopting practices God opposed and that these places were against God's law. They were mixing pagan beliefs with worship of God. Blending religious ideas leads to confusion about who God really is. We must take care that subtle secular influences do not distort our worship practices.

Josiah Begins His Reign in Judah PARALLEL

2 KINGS 22:1-2

Josiah was eight years old when he became king, and he reigned in Jerusalem thirty-one years. His mother was Jedidah, the daughter of Adaiah from Bozkath. [2]He did what was pleasing in the LORD's sight and followed the example of his ancestor David. He did not turn away from doing what was right.

2 CHRONICLES 34:1-7

Josiah was eight years old when he became king, and he reigned in Jerusalem thirty-one years. [2]He did what was pleasing in the LORD's sight and followed the example of his ancestor David. He did not turn away from doing what was right.

[3]During the eighth year of his reign, while he was still young, Josiah began to seek the God of his ancestor David. Then in the twelfth year he began to purify Judah and Jerusalem, destroying all the pagan shrines, the Asherah poles, and the carved idols and cast images. [4]He ordered that the altars of Baal be demolished and that the incense altars which stood above them be broken down. He also made sure that the Asherah poles, the carved idols, and the cast images were smashed and scattered over the graves of those who had sacrificed to them. [5]He burned the bones of the pagan priests on their own altars, and so he purified Judah and Jerusalem.

[6]He did the same thing in the towns of Manasseh, Ephraim, and Simeon, even as far as Naphtali, and in the regions* all around them. [7]He destroyed the pagan altars and the Asherah poles, and he crushed the idols into dust. He cut down all the incense altars throughout the land of Israel. Finally, he returned to Jerusalem.

2 Chr 34:6 As in Syriac version. Hebrew reads *in their temples,* or *in their ruins.* The meaning of the Hebrew is uncertain.

2. JEREMIAH BEGINS HIS MINISTRY

Jeremiah was called by God to be a prophet to Judah. He faithfully confronted the leaders and the people with their sin, prophesying both their 70-year captivity in Babylon and their eventual return from exile. After a long prophetic ministry, surviving the fall of Jerusalem, Jeremiah was forcefully taken to Egypt. Yet Jeremiah remained faithful in spite of Jerusalem's destruction. Years of obedience had made him strong and courageous. May we be able to stand through difficult times as did Jeremiah.

627 BC

The Prophecy of Jeremiah

JEREMIAH 1:1-3

These are the words of Jeremiah son of Hilkiah, one of the priests from the town of Anathoth in the land of Benjamin. [2]The LORD first gave messages to Jeremiah during the thirteenth year of the reign of Josiah son of Amon, king of Judah.* [3]The LORD's messages continued throughout the reign of King Jehoiakim, Josiah's son, until the eleventh year of the reign of King Zedekiah, another of Josiah's sons. In August* of that eleventh year the people of Jerusalem were taken away as captives.

Jer 1:2 The thirteenth year of Josiah's reign was 627 B.C. **Jer 1:3** Hebrew *In the fifth month,* of the ancient Hebrew lunar calendar. A number of events in Jeremiah can be cross-checked with dates in surviving Babylonian records and related accurately to our modern calendar. The fifth month in the eleventh year of Zedekiah's reign occurred within the months of August and September 586 B.C. Also see 52:12 and the note there.

Jeremiah begins his ministry

JEREMIAH

Jeremiah served as a prophet to Judah from 627 B.C. until the exile in 586 B.C.

Climate of the times	Society was deteriorating economically, politically, and spiritually. Wars and captivity dominated the world scene. God's word was deemed offensive.
Main message	Repentance from sin would postpone Judah's coming judgment at the hands of Babylon.
Importance of message	Repentance is one of the greatest needs in our immoral world. God's promises to the faithful shine brightly by bringing hope for tomorrow and strength for today.
Contemporary prophets	Habakkuk (612–589 B.C.), Zephaniah (640–621 B.C.)

2 Kgs 22:1-2 In reading the biblical lists of kings, it is rare to find one who obeyed God completely. Josiah was such a person, and he was only eight years old when he began to reign. For 18 years Josiah reigned obediently; then, when he was 26, he began the reforms based on God's laws. Children are the future leaders of our churches and our world. A person's major work for God may have to wait until adulthood, but no one is ever too young to take God seriously and obey him. Josiah's early years laid the base for his later task of reforming Judah. God can use you, regardless of your age.

2 Chr 34:3 In Josiah's day, boys were considered men at age 12. By 16, Josiah understood the responsibility of his office. Even at this young age, he showed greater wisdom than many of the older kings who came before him because he had decided to seek the Lord God and his wisdom. Don't let your age hinder you from serving God.

Jer 1:1-2 After King Solomon's death, the united kingdom of Israel had split into rival northern and southern kingdoms. The northern kingdom was called Israel; the southern, Judah. Jeremiah was from Anathoth, four miles north of Jerusalem in the southern kingdom. He lived and prophesied during the reigns of the last five kings of Judah. This was a chaotic time politically, morally, and spiritually. As Babylon, Egypt, and Assyria battled for world supremacy, Judah found itself caught in the middle. Although Jeremiah prophesied for 40 years, he never saw his people heed his words and turn from their sins.

Jeremiah's Call and First Visions

JEREMIAH 1:4-19

The LORD gave me this message:

5 "I knew you before I formed you in your mother's womb.
Before you were born I set you apart
and appointed you as my prophet to the nations."

6"O Sovereign LORD," I said, "I can't speak for you!
I'm too young!"

7The LORD replied, "Don't say, 'I'm too young,' for you
must go wherever I send you and say whatever I tell you.
8And don't be afraid of the people, for I will be with you
and will protect you. I, the LORD, have spoken!" 9Then
the LORD reached out and touched my mouth and said,

"Look, I have put my words in your mouth!
10 Today I appoint you to stand up
against nations and kingdoms.
Some you must uproot and tear down,
destroy and overthrow.
Others you must build up
and plant."

11Then the LORD said to me, "Look, Jeremiah! What
do you see?"

And I replied, "I see a branch from an almond tree."
12And the LORD said, "That's right, and it means that
I am watching,* and I will certainly carry out all my
plans."

13Then the LORD spoke to me again and asked,
"What do you see now?"

And I replied, "I see a pot of boiling water, spilling
from the north."

14"Yes," the LORD said, "for terror from the north
will boil out on the people of this land. 15Listen! I am
calling the armies of the kingdoms of the north to
come to Jerusalem. I, the LORD, have spoken!

Jer 1:12 The Hebrew word for "watching" *(shoqed)* sounds like the word for "almond tree" *(shaqed).*

Almond Tree

The almond is a peach-like tree with saw-toothed, pointed leaves and gray bark. It grows to a height of 10 to 25 feet. It blooms very early in the year. To the Jews it was a welcome harbinger of spring (Jer 1:11). Depending on where we live, we all look for certain signs of spring. Budding trees and blossoming flowers speak of new life. They are signs of resurrection, which was realized in Christ, who is the resurrection and the life for all who believe (John 11:25).

Jer 1:5 God knew you, as he knew Jeremiah, long before you were born or even conceived. He thought about you and planned for you. When you feel discouraged or inadequate, remember that God has always thought of you as valuable and that he has a purpose in mind for you.

Jer 1:5 Jeremiah was "appointed" by God as his "prophet to the nations." God has a purpose for each Christian, but some people are appointed by God for specific kinds of work. Samson (Judg 13:3-5), David (1 Sam 16:12-13), John the Baptist (Luke 1:13-17), and Paul (Gal 1:15-16) were also called to do particular jobs for God. Whatever work you do should be done for the glory of God (Phil 1:11). If God gives you a specific task, accept it cheerfully and do it with diligence. If God has not given you a specific call or assignment, then seek to fulfill the mission common to all believers—to love, obey, and serve God—until his guidance becomes clear.

Jer 1:6-8 Often people struggle with new challenges because they lack self-confidence, feeling that they have inadequate ability, training, or experience. Jeremiah thought he was "too young" and inexperienced to be God's prophet to the nations. But God promised to be with him. We should not allow feelings of inadequacy to keep us from obeying God. He will always be with us. If God gives you a job to do, he will provide all you need to do it.

Jer 1:8 God promised to be with Jeremiah and take care of him, but not to keep trouble from coming. God did not insulate him from imprisonment, deportation, or insults. God does not keep us from encountering life's storms, but he will see us through them. In fact, God walks through these storms with us and rescues us.

Jer 1:10 God appointed Jeremiah to bring his word to "nations and kingdoms." Jeremiah's work was to warn not only the Jews but all the nations of the world about God's judgment for sin. Don't forget in reading the Old Testament that, while God was consistently working through the people of Judah and Israel, his plan was to communicate to every nation and person. We are included in Jeremiah's message of judgment and hope, and as believers we are to share God's desire to reach the whole world for him.

Jer 1:11-14 The vision of the branch from an almond tree revealed the beginning of God's judgment because the almond tree is among the first to blossom in the spring. God saw the sins of Judah and the nations, and he would carry out swift and certain judgment. The pot of boiling water tipping from the north and spilling over Judah was a picture of Babylon delivering God's scalding judgment against Jeremiah's people.

Jer 1:14-19 The problems we face may not seem as ominous as Jeremiah's, but they are critical to *us* and may overwhelm us. God's promise to Jeremiah and to us is that nothing will defeat us completely; he will help us through the most agonizing problems. Face each day with the assurance that God will be with you and see you through.

Jer 1:16 The people of Judah sinned greatly by continuing to worship other gods. God had commanded them specifically against this

"They will set their thrones
at the gates of the city.
They will attack its walls
and all the other towns of Judah.
16 I will pronounce judgment
on my people for all their evil—
for deserting me and burning incense
to other gods.
Yes, they worship idols made with their
own hands!

17 "Get up and prepare for action.
Go out and tell them everything I tell you to say.
Do not be afraid of them,
or I will make you look foolish in front of them.
18 For see, today I have made you strong
like a fortified city that cannot be captured,
like an iron pillar or a bronze wall.
You will stand against the whole land—
the kings, officials, priests, and people
of Judah.
19 They will fight you, but they will fail.
For I am with you, and I will take care of you.
I, the LORD, have spoken!"

The LORD's Case against His People

JEREMIAH 2:1-13

The LORD gave me another message. He said, 2"Go
and shout this message to Jerusalem. This is what the
LORD says:

JEREMIAH

Endurance is not a common quality. Many people lack the long-term commitment, caring, and willingness that are vital to sticking with a task against all odds. But Jeremiah was a prophet who endured. • Jeremiah's call by God teaches how intimately God knows us. He valued us before anyone else knew we would exist. He cared for us while we were in our mothers' wombs. He planned our lives while our bodies were still being formed. He values us more highly than we value ourselves. • Jeremiah had to depend on God's love as he developed endurance. His audiences were usually antagonistic or apathetic to his messages. He was ignored; his life was often threatened. He saw both the excitement of a spiritual awakening and the sorrow of a national return to idolatry. With the exception of the good king Josiah, Jeremiah watched king after king ignore his warnings and lead the people away from God. He saw fellow prophets murdered. He himself was severely persecuted. Finally, he watched Judah's defeat at the hands of the Babylonians. • Jeremiah responded to all this with God's message and human tears. He felt firsthand God's love for his people and the people's rejection of that love. But even when he was angry with God and tempted to give up, Jeremiah knew he had to keep going. God had called him to endure. He expressed intense feelings but saw beyond the feelings to the God who was soon to execute justice but who afterward would show mercy. • It may be easy for us to identify with Jeremiah's frustrations and discouragement, but we need to realize that this prophet's life is also an encouragement to faithfulness.

Strengths and accomplishments	• Wrote two Old Testament books, Jeremiah and Lamentations • Ministered during the reigns of the last five kings of Judah • Was a catalyst for the great spiritual reformation under King Josiah • Acted as God's faithful messenger in spite of many attempts on his life • Was so deeply sorrowful for the fallen condition of Judah that he earned the title "the weeping prophet"
Lessons from his life	• The majority opinion is not necessarily God's will • Although punishment for sin is severe, there is hope in God's mercy • God will not accept empty or insincere worship • Serving God does not guarantee earthly security
Vital statistics	• Where: Anathoth • Occupation: Prophet • Relative: Father: Hilkiah. • Contemporaries: Josiah, Jehoahaz, Jehoiakim, Jehoiachin, Zedekiah, Baruch
Key verses	"'O Sovereign LORD,' I said, 'I can't speak for you! I'm too young!' The LORD replied, 'Don't say, "I'm too young," for you must go wherever I send you and say whatever I tell you. And don't be afraid of the people, for I will be with you and will protect you. I, the LORD, have spoken!'" (Jer 1:6-8).

Jeremiah's story is told in the book of Jeremiah. He is also mentioned in Ezra 1:1; Daniel 9:2; Matthew 2:17; 16:14; 27:9. See also 2 Chronicles 34–35 for the story of the spiritual revival under Josiah.

(Exod 20:3-6) because idolatry places trust in created things rather than the Creator. Although these people belonged to God, they chose to follow false gods. Many "gods" entice us to turn away from God. Material possessions, dreams for the future, approval of others, and vocational goals compete for our total commitment. Striving after these at the expense of our commitment to God puts our hearts where Judah's was—and God severely punished Judah.

Jer 2:1–3:5 In this section, the marriage analogy sharply contrasts God's love for his people with their love for other gods and reveals Judah's faithlessness. Jeremiah condemned Judah (he sometimes called Judah "Jerusalem," the name of its capital city) for seeking security in worthless, changeable things rather than the unchangeable God. We may be tempted to seek security from possessions, people, or our own abilities, but these will fail us. There is no lasting security apart from the eternal God.

Jer 2:2 We appreciate a friend who remains true to a commitment, and we are disappointed with someone who fails to keep a promise. God was pleased when his people obeyed initially, but he became angry with them when they refused to keep their commitment. Temptations distract us from God. Think about your original commitment to obey God, and ask yourself if you are remaining truly devoted.

▸ **JEREMIAH 2:1-13** ***(cont.)***

"I remember how eager you were to please me
as a young bride long ago,
how you loved me and followed me
even through the barren wilderness.
3 In those days Israel was holy to the LORD,
the first of his children.*
All who harmed his people were declared guilty,
and disaster fell on them.
I, the LORD, have spoken!"

4Listen to the word of the LORD, people of Jacob—all
you families of Israel! 5This is what the LORD says:

"What did your ancestors find wrong with me
that led them to stray so far from me?
They worshiped worthless idols,
only to become worthless themselves.
6 They did not ask, 'Where is the LORD
who brought us safely out of Egypt
and led us through the barren wilderness—
a land of deserts and pits,
a land of drought and death,
where no one lives or even travels?'
7 "And when I brought you into a fruitful land
to enjoy its bounty and goodness,
you defiled my land and
corrupted the possession I had promised you.
8 The priests did not ask,
'Where is the LORD?'
Those who taught my word ignored me,
the rulers turned against me,
and the prophets spoke in the name of Baal,
wasting their time on worthless idols.
9 Therefore, I will bring my case against you,"
says the LORD.
"I will even bring charges against your children's
children
in the years to come.
10 "Go west and look in the land of Cyprus*;
go east and search through the land of Kedar.
Has anyone ever heard of anything
as strange as this?
11 Has any nation ever traded its gods for new ones,
even though they are not gods at all?
Yet my people have exchanged their glorious God*
for worthless idols!
12 The heavens are shocked at such a thing
and shrink back in horror and dismay,"
says the LORD.
13 "For my people have done two evil things:
They have abandoned me—
the fountain of living water.
And they have dug for themselves cracked
cisterns
that can hold no water at all!

The Results of Israel's Sin

JEREMIAH 2:14-22

14 "Why has Israel become a slave?
Why has he been carried away as plunder?
15 Strong lions have roared against him,
and the land has been destroyed.
The towns are now in ruins,
and no one lives in them anymore.
16 Egyptians, marching from their cities of
Memphis* and Tahpanhes,
have destroyed Israel's glory and power.
17 And you have brought this upon yourselves
by rebelling against the LORD your God,
even though he was leading you on the way!

Jer 2:3 Hebrew *the firstfruits of his harvest.* **Jer 2:10** Hebrew *Kittim.* **Jer 2:11** Hebrew *their glory.* **Jer 2:16** Hebrew *Noph.*

Jer 2:3 The phrase, "first of his children," is a comparison with the firstfruits (the first part) of the harvest. Both were to be set apart for God (Deut 26:1-11). That's how God's people declared their allegiance to him. Israel had been a holy, devoted people, as eager to please God as if she were his young bride. This contrasted greatly with the situation in Jeremiah's time.

Jer 2:4-8 The united nation of Israel included both the "families of Israel" and the "people of Jacob" (Judah). Jeremiah knew Israel's history well. The prophets recited history to the people for several reasons: (1) to remind them of God's faithfulness; (2) to make sure the people wouldn't forget (they didn't have Bibles to read); (3) to emphasize God's love for them; (4) to remind the people that there was a time when they had been close to God. We should learn from history so we can build on the successes and avoid repeating the failures of others.

Jer 2:8 Baal was the chief male god of the Canaanite religion. Baal was the god of fertility. Worship of Baal included animal sacrifice and sacred prostitution (male and female) in the high places. Jezebel, the wife of King Ahab, introduced Baal worship into the northern kingdom, and eventually it spread to Judah. The sexual orientation of this worship was a constant temptation to the Israelites, who were called to be holy.

Jer 2:10 God was saying that even pagan nations like Cyprus (in the west) and Kedar (the home of Arab tribes living in the desert east of Palestine) remained loyal to their national gods. But Israel had abandoned the one and only God for a completely worthless object of worship.

Jer 2:13 Who would set aside a fountain of living water for a cracked cistern, a pit that collected rainwater but could not hold it? God told the Israelites they were doing that very thing when they turned from him, the fountain of living water, to the worship of idols. Not only that, but the cisterns they chose were broken and empty. The people had built religious systems in which to store truth, but those systems were worthless. Why should we cling to the broken promises of unstable "cisterns" (money, power, religious systems, or whatever transitory thing we are putting in place of God) when God promises to constantly refresh us with living water (John 4:10)?

Jer 2:16-17 Memphis was near modern Cairo's present location in lower Egypt, and Tahpanhes was in northeastern Egypt. Jeremiah could be speaking of Pharaoh Shishak's previous invasion of Judah in 926 B.C. (1 Kgs 14:25), or he may have been predicting Pharaoh Neco's invasion in 609 B.C. when King Josiah of Judah would be killed (2 Kgs 23:29-30). Jeremiah's point is that the people brought this on themselves by rebelling against God.

Jer 2:22 The stain of sin is more than skin-deep. Israel had stains that could not be washed out, even with the strongest cleansers. Spiritual cleansing must reach deep into the heart—and this is a job that God alone can do. We cannot ignore the effects

18 "What have you gained by your alliances with
Egypt
and your covenants with Assyria?
What good to you are the streams of the Nile*
or the waters of the Euphrates River?*
19 Your wickedness will bring its own punishment.
Your turning from me will shame you.
You will see what an evil, bitter thing it is
to abandon the LORD your God and not
to fear him.
I, the Lord, the LORD of Heaven's Armies,
have spoken!

20 "Long ago I broke the yoke that oppressed you
and tore away the chains of your slavery,
but still you said,
'I will not serve you.'
On every hill and under every green tree,
you have prostituted yourselves by bowing
down to idols.
21 But I was the one who planted you,
choosing a vine of the purest stock—the very
best.
How did you grow into this corrupt wild vine?
22 No amount of soap or lye can make you clean.
I still see the stain of your guilt.
I, the Sovereign LORD, have spoken!

Israel, an Unfaithful Wife

JEREMIAH 2:23–3:5

23 "You say, 'That's not true!
I haven't worshiped the images of Baal!'
But how can you say that?
Go and look in any valley in the land!
Face the awful sins you have done.
You are like a restless female camel
desperately searching for a mate.
24 You are like a wild donkey,
sniffing the wind at mating time.
Who can restrain her lust?
Those who desire her don't need to search,
for she goes running to them!
25 When will you stop running?
When will you stop panting after other gods?
But you say, 'Save your breath.
I'm in love with these foreign gods,
and I can't stop loving them now!'

26 "Israel is like a thief
who feels shame only when he gets caught.
They, their kings, officials, priests, and
prophets—
all are alike in this.
27 To an image carved from a piece of wood they say,
'You are my father.'
To an idol chiseled from a block of stone they say,
'You are my mother.'
They turn their backs on me,
but in times of trouble they cry out to me,
'Come and save us!'
28 But why not call on these gods you have made?
When trouble comes, let them save you
if they can!
For you have as many gods
as there are towns in Judah.
29 Why do you accuse me of doing wrong?
You are the ones who have rebelled,"
says the LORD.
30 "I have punished your children,
but they did not respond to my discipline.

Jer 2:18a Hebrew *of Shihor,* a branch of the Nile River. **Jer 2:18b** Hebrew *the river?*

THE KINGS OF JEREMIAH'S LIFETIME

King	*Story of His Reign*	*Dates of His Reign*	*Character of Reign*	*Jeremiah's Message to the King*
Josiah	2 Kgs 22:1–23:30	640–609 B.C.	Mostly good	Jer 3:6-25
Jehoahaz	2 Kgs 23:31-33	609 B.C.	Evil	Jer 22:11-17
Jehoiakim	2 Kgs 23:34–24:7	609–598 B.C.	Evil	Jer 22:18-23; 25:1-38; 26:1-24; 35:1-19; 36:1-32
Jehoiachin	2 Kgs 24:8-17	598–597 B.C.	Evil	Jer 13:18-27; 22:24-30
Zedekiah	2 Kgs 24:18–25:26	597–586 B.C.	Evil	Jer 21:1-14; 24:8-10; 27:12-22; 32:1-5; 34:1-22; 37:1-21; 38:1-28; 51:59-64

of sin and hope they will go away. Your sin has caused a deep stain that only God can remove if you are willing to let him cleanse you (Isa 1:18; Ezek 36:25).

Jer 2:23-27 The people are compared to animals who search for mates in mating season. Unrestrained, they rush for power, money, alliances with foreign powers, and other gods. The idols did not seek the people; the people sought the idols and ran wildly after them. Then they became so comfortable in their sin that they could not think of giving it up. Their only shame was in getting caught. If we desire something so much that we'll do anything to get it, it is a sign that we are addicted to it and out of tune with God.

Jer 2:30 Being a prophet in Jeremiah's day was risky business. Prophets had to criticize the policies of evil kings, and this made them appear to be traitors. The kings hated the prophets for standing against their policies, and the people often hated the prophets for preaching against their idolatrous lifestyles (see Acts 7:52).

Jer 2:31-32 Forgetting can be dangerous, whether it is intentional or an oversight. Israel deliberately ignored God by focusing its affections on the allurements of the world. The more we focus on the passing pleasures of this life, the easier it becomes to forget God's care, his love, his dependability, his guidance, and most of all, God himself. What pleases you most? Have you been forgetting God lately?

▸ **JEREMIAH 2:23–3:5** ***(cont.)***

You yourselves have killed your prophets
as a lion kills its prey.

31 "O my people, listen to the words of the LORD!
Have I been like a desert to Israel?
Have I been to them a land of darkness?
Why then do my people say, 'At last we are free from God!
We don't need him anymore!'
32 Does a young woman forget her jewelry?
Does a bride hide her wedding dress?
Yet for years on end
my people have forgotten me.
33 "How you plot and scheme to win your lovers.
Even an experienced prostitute could learn from you!
34 Your clothing is stained with the blood of the innocent and the poor,
though you didn't catch them breaking into your houses!
35 And yet you say,
'I have done nothing wrong.
Surely God isn't angry with me!'
But now I will punish you severely
because you claim you have not sinned.
36 First here, then there—
you flit from one ally to another asking for help.
But your new friends in Egypt will let you down,
just as Assyria did before.
37 In despair, you will be led into exile
with your hands on your heads,
for the LORD has rejected the nations you trust.
They will not help you at all.

3:1 "If a man divorces a woman
and she goes and marries someone else,
he will not take her back again,
for that would surely corrupt the land.
But you have prostituted yourself with many lovers,
so why are you trying to come back to me?"
says the LORD.
2 "Look at the shrines on every hilltop.
Is there any place you have not been defiled
by your adultery with other gods?
You sit like a prostitute beside the road waiting for a customer.
You sit alone like a nomad in the desert.
You have polluted the land with your prostitution
and your wickedness.
3 That's why even the spring rains have failed.
For you are a brazen prostitute and completely shameless.
4 Yet you say to me,
'Father, you have been my guide since my youth.
5 Surely you won't be angry forever!
Surely you can forget about it!'
So you talk,
but you keep on doing all the evil you can."

Judah Follows Israel's Example

JEREMIAH 3:6-10

During the reign of King Josiah, the LORD said to me,
"Have you seen what fickle Israel has done? Like a wife
who commits adultery, Israel has worshiped other gods
on every hill and under every green tree. 7I thought,
'After she has done all this, she will return to me.' But
she did not return, and her faithless sister Judah saw
this. 8She saw that I divorced faithless Israel because
of her adultery. But that treacherous sister Judah had
no fear, and now she, too, has left me and given herself to prostitution. 9Israel treated it all so lightly—she
thought nothing of committing adultery by worshiping
idols made of wood and stone. So now the land has
been polluted. 10But despite all this, her faithless sister
Judah has never sincerely returned to me. She has only
pretended to be sorry. I, the LORD, have spoken!"

Jer 2:36 God is not against alliances or working partnerships, but he is against people trusting others for the help that should come from him. This was the problem in Jeremiah's time. After the days of David and Solomon, Israel fell apart because the leaders turned to other nations and gods instead of the true God. They played power politics, thinking that their strong neighbors could protect them. But Judah would soon learn that its alliance with Egypt would be just as disappointing as its former alliance with Assyria (2 Kgs 16:8-9; Isa 7:13-25).

Jer 3:1 This law (see Deut 24:1-4) says that a divorced woman who remarries can never be reunited with her first husband. Judah "divorced" God and "married" other gods. God had every right to permanently disown his wayward people, but in his mercy he was willing to take them back again.

Jer 3:2 "Like a nomad in the desert" means that Judah plotted idolatry as a thief might hide in the wilderness to plunder a passing caravan.

Jer 3:4-5 In spite of their great sin, the people of Israel continued to talk like they were God's children. The only way they could do this was to minimize their sin. When we know we've done something wrong, we want to downplay the error and relieve some of the guilt we feel. As we minimize our sinfulness, we naturally shy away from making changes, and so we keep on sinning. But if we view every wrong attitude and action as a serious offense against God, we will begin to understand what living for God is all about. Is there any sin in your life that you've written off as too small to worry about? God says that we must confess and turn away from every sin.

Jer 3:6–6:30 The northern kingdom, Israel, had fallen to Assyria, and its people had been taken into captivity. The tragic lesson of their fall should have caused the southern kingdom, Judah, to return to God, but Judah paid no attention. Jeremiah urged Judah to return to God to avoid certain disaster. This message came between 627 and 621 B.C., during Josiah's reign. Although Josiah obeyed God's commands, his example apparently did not penetrate the hearts of the people. If the people refused to repent, God said he would destroy the nation because of the evils of Josiah's grandfather, King Manasseh (2 Kgs 23:25-27).

Hope for Wayward Israel

JEREMIAH 3:11–4:2

Then the LORD said to me, "Even faithless Israel is less
guilty than treacherous Judah! 12 Therefore, go and give
this message to Israel.* This is what the LORD says:

"O Israel, my faithless people,
  come home to me again,
for I am merciful.
  I will not be angry with you forever.
13 Only acknowledge your guilt.
  Admit that you rebelled against the LORD
    your God
and committed adultery against him
  by worshiping idols under every green tree.
Confess that you refused to listen to my voice.
  I, the LORD, have spoken!
14 "Return home, you wayward children,"
  says the LORD,
  "for I am your master.
I will bring you back to the land of Israel*—
  one from this town and two from that family—
  from wherever you are scattered.
15 And I will give you shepherds after my own heart,
  who will guide you with knowledge and
    understanding.

16 "And when your land is once more filled with
people," says the LORD, "you will no longer wish for
'the good old days' when you possessed the Ark of the
LORD's Covenant. You will not miss those days or even
remember them, and there will be no need to rebuild
the Ark. 17 In that day Jerusalem will be known as 'The
Throne of the LORD.' All nations will come there to
honor the LORD. They will no longer stubbornly follow their own evil desires. 18 In those days the people
of Judah and Israel will return together from exile
in the north. They will return to the land I gave their
ancestors as an inheritance forever.

19 "I thought to myself,
  'I would love to treat you as my own children!'
I wanted nothing more than to give you this
  beautiful land—
  the finest possession in the world.
I looked forward to your calling me 'Father,'
  and I wanted you never to turn from me.
20 But you have been unfaithful to me, you people
  of Israel!
  You have been like a faithless wife who leaves
    her husband.
  I, the LORD, have spoken."

21 Voices are heard high on the windswept
    mountains,
  the weeping and pleading of Israel's people.
For they have chosen crooked paths
  and have forgotten the LORD their God.

22 "My wayward children," says the LORD,
  "come back to me, and I will heal your
    wayward hearts."

"Yes, we're coming," the people reply,
  "for you are the LORD our God.
23 Our worship of idols on the hills
  and our religious orgies on the mountains
  are a delusion.
Only in the LORD our God
  will Israel ever find salvation.
24 From childhood we have watched
  as everything our ancestors worked for—
their flocks and herds, their sons and daughters—
  was squandered on a delusion.
25 Let us now lie down in shame
  and cover ourselves with dishonor,
for we and our ancestors have sinned
  against the LORD our God.
From our childhood to this day
  we have never obeyed him."

Jer 3:12 Hebrew *toward the north.* **Jer 3:14** Hebrew *to Zion.*

Jer 3:11-13 Israel was not even trying to look as if it were obeying God, but Judah maintained the appearance of faith without a true heart. Believing the right doctrines without heartfelt commitment is like offering sacrifices without true repentance. Judah's false repentance brought Jeremiah's words of condemnation. To live without faith is hopeless; to express sorrow without change is hypocritical. Being sorry for sin is not enough. Repentance demands a change of mind and heart that results in changed behavior.

Jer 3:12-18 The northern kingdom, Israel, was in captivity, being punished for its sins. The people of Judah undoubtedly looked down on these northern neighbors for their blatant heresy and degraded morals. Even so, Jeremiah promised the remnant of Israel God's blessings if they would turn to him. Judah, still secure in its own mind, should have turned to God after seeing the destruction of Israel. But the people of Judah refused, so Jeremiah startled them by reaffirming God's promise to Israel's remnant if they would repent.

Jer 3:15 God promised to give his people leaders (shepherds) who would follow him, filled with knowledge (wisdom) and understanding. God saw Israel's lack of direction, so he promised to provide the right kind of leadership. We look to and trust our leaders for guidance and direction. But if they do not follow God, they will lead us astray. Pray for God-honoring leaders in our nations, communities, and churches—those who will be good examples and bring us God's wisdom.

Jer 3:16-17 In the days of Solomon's reign over a united Israel, the people had a beautiful Temple where they worshiped God. The Temple housed the Ark of the Covenant, the symbol of God's presence with the people. The Ark held the tablets of the Ten Commandments (see Exod 25:10-22). Those days with the Ark wouldn't be missed in the future Kingdom because God's presence by the Holy Spirit would be there personally among his people.

Jer 3:22-25 Jeremiah predicted a day when the nation would be reunited, true worship would be reinstated, and sin would be seen for what it is. Our world glorifies the thrill that comes from wealth, winning, and sexual pleasure, and it ignores the sin that is so often associated with these thrills. It is sad that so few see sin as it really is—a deception. Most people can't see this until they are destroyed by the sin they pursue. The advantage of believing God's Word is that we don't have to learn by hard experience the destructive results of sin.

▸ **JEREMIAH 3:11–4:2** ***(cont.)***

4:1 "O Israel," says the LORD,
"if you wanted to return to me, you could.
You could throw away your detestable idols
and stray away no more.
2 Then when you swear by my name, saying,
'As surely as the LORD lives,'
you could do so
with truth, justice, and righteousness.
Then you would be a blessing to the nations
of the world,
and all people would come and praise my
name."

Coming Judgment against Judah

JEREMIAH 4:3-18

This is what the LORD says to the people of Judah and Jerusalem:

"Plow up the hard ground of your hearts!
Do not waste your good seed among thorns.
4 O people of Judah and Jerusalem,
surrender your pride and power.
Change your hearts before the LORD,*
or my anger will burn like an
unquenchable fire
because of all your sins.
5 "Shout to Judah, and broadcast to Jerusalem!
Tell them to sound the alarm throughout
the land:
'Run for your lives!
Flee to the fortified cities!'
6 Raise a signal flag as a warning for Jerusalem*:
'Flee now! Do not delay!'
For I am bringing terrible destruction upon you
from the north."
7 A lion stalks from its den,
a destroyer of nations.
It has left its lair and is headed your way.
It's going to devastate your land!
Your towns will lie in ruins,
with no one living in them anymore.
8 So put on clothes of mourning
and weep with broken hearts,
for the fierce anger of the LORD
is still upon us.
9 "In that day," says the LORD,
"the king and the officials will tremble in fear.
The priests will be struck with horror,
and the prophets will be appalled."
10 Then I said, "O Sovereign LORD,
the people have been deceived by what
you said,
for you promised peace for Jerusalem.
But the sword is held at their throats!"
11 The time is coming when the LORD will say
to the people of Jerusalem,
"My dear people, a burning wind is blowing in
from the desert,
and it's not a gentle breeze useful for
winnowing grain.
12 It is a roaring blast sent by me!
Now I will pronounce your destruction!"
13 Our enemy rushes down on us like storm clouds!
His chariots are like whirlwinds.
His horses are swifter than eagles.
How terrible it will be, for we are doomed!
14 O Jerusalem, cleanse your heart
that you may be saved.
How long will you harbor
your evil thoughts?
15 Your destruction has been announced
from Dan and the hill country of Ephraim.
16 "Warn the surrounding nations
and announce this to Jerusalem:
The enemy is coming from a distant land,
raising a battle cry against the towns
of Judah.
17 They surround Jerusalem like watchmen around
a field,
for my people have rebelled against me,"
says the LORD.

Jer 4:4 Hebrew *Circumcise yourselves to the LORD, and take away the foreskins of your heart.* **Jer 4:6** Hebrew *Zion.*

Jer 4:1-2 Throughout the Old Testament, God consistently revealed his intentions to bless the nations of the world. His global vision included a central role for the people of Israel as the channel through which God would pour out his blessings on all nations. But their privilege as the chosen people was in jeopardy as long as they insisted on disobedience and idolatry.

Jer 4:3 Jeremiah told the people to plow up the hardness of their hearts as a plow breaks up unplowed ground—soil that has not been tilled for a season. Good kings like Josiah had tried to turn the people back to God, but the people had continued to worship their idols in secret. Their hearts had become hardened to God's will. Unless their hearts were broken and cleaned up, the good seed of God's commands could not take root. Old habits and hidden sins had to be uprooted and rejected. Likewise we must remove our heart-hardening sin if we expect God's Word to take root and grow in our life.

Jer 4:6-7 The destruction from the north came from Babylon when Nabopolassar and his son, Nebuchadnezzar II, attacked (see 2 Chr 36).

Jer 4:10 Jeremiah, deeply moved by God's words, expressed his sorrow and confusion to God. Jeremiah was intercessor for the people. These people had false expectations because of the past promises of blessings, their blindness to their own sin, and the false prophets who kept telling them that all was well.

Jer 4:15 Destruction was announced first from Dan because it was located at the northern border of Israel, then on to the hill country of Ephraim. Thus, the Danites would be the first to see the approaching armies as they invaded from the north. No one would be able to stop the armies because they would be coming as punishment for the people's sin.

18 "Your own actions have brought this upon you.
This punishment is bitter, piercing you to the heart!"

Jeremiah Weeps for His People

JEREMIAH 4:19-22

19 My heart, my heart—I writhe in pain!
My heart pounds within me! I cannot be still.
For I have heard the blast of enemy trumpets
and the roar of their battle cries.
20 Waves of destruction roll over the land,
until it lies in complete desolation.
Suddenly my tents are destroyed;
in a moment my shelters are crushed.
21 How long must I see the battle flags
and hear the trumpets of war?
22 "My people are foolish
and do not know me," says the LORD.
"They are stupid children
who have no understanding.
They are clever enough at doing wrong,
but they have no idea how to do right!"

Jeremiah's Vision of Coming Disaster

JEREMIAH 4:23-31

23 I looked at the earth, and it was empty and formless.
I looked at the heavens, and there was no light.
24 I looked at the mountains and hills,
and they trembled and shook.
25 I looked, and all the people were gone.
All the birds of the sky had flown away.
26 I looked, and the fertile fields had become a wilderness.
The towns lay in ruins,
crushed by the LORD's fierce anger.
27 This is what the LORD says:
"The whole land will be ruined,
but I will not destroy it completely.
28 The earth will mourn
and the heavens will be draped in black
because of my decree against my people.
I have made up my mind and will not change it."
29 At the noise of charioteers and archers,
the people flee in terror.
They hide in the bushes
and run for the mountains.
All the towns have been abandoned—
not a person remains!
30 What are you doing,
you who have been plundered?
Why do you dress up in beautiful clothing
and put on gold jewelry?
Why do you brighten your eyes with mascara?
Your primping will do you no good!
The allies who were your lovers
despise you and seek to kill you.
31 I hear a cry, like that of a woman in labor,
the groans of a woman giving birth to her first child.
It is beautiful Jerusalem*
gasping for breath and crying out,
"Help! I'm being murdered!"

The Sins of Judah

JEREMIAH 5:1-19

1 "Run up and down every street in Jerusalem," says the LORD.
"Look high and low; search throughout the city!
If you can find even one just and honest person,
I will not destroy the city.
2 But even when they are under oath,
saying, 'As surely as the LORD lives,'
they are still telling lies!"
3 LORD, you are searching for honesty.
You struck your people,
but they paid no attention.

Jer 4:31 Hebrew *the daughter of Zion.*

Jer 4:19-31 Jeremiah was anguished by the sure devastation of the coming judgment. This judgment would continue until the people turned from their sin and listened to God. Although this prophecy refers to the future destruction by Babylon, it could also describe the judgment of all sinners at the end of the world. These verses also speak to those in an age of terrorism about overwhelming feelings of dread and the importance of recognizing God's ultimate control over the events of history.

Jer 4:22 Judah was clever at doing wrong but did not know how to do what was right. Right living is more than simply avoiding sin. It requires decision and discipline. We must develop skills in right living because our behavior attracts attention to our God. We should pursue excellence in Christian living with as much effort as we pursue excellence at work.

Jer 4:27 God warned that destruction was certain, but he promised that the faithful remnant would be spared. God is committed to preserving those who are faithful to him.

Jer 5:1 Jerusalem was the capital city and center of worship for Judah. God was willing to spare the city if only one person who was just and honest could be found (he made a similar statement about Sodom; see Gen 18:32). Think how significant your testimony may be in your city or community. You may represent the only witness for God to many people. Are you faithful to that opportunity?

Jer 5:3 Nothing but honesty is acceptable to God. When we pray, sing, speak, or serve, nothing closes the door of God's acceptance more than hypocrisy, lying, or pretense. God sees through us and refuses to listen. To be close to God, be honest with him.

▸ **JEREMIAH 5:1-19** ***(cont.)***

You crushed them,
but they refused to be corrected.
They are determined, with faces set like stone;
they have refused to repent.

4 Then I said, "But what can we expect from
the poor?
They are ignorant.
They don't know the ways of the LORD.
They don't understand God's laws.
5 So I will go and speak to their leaders.
Surely they know the ways of the LORD
and understand God's laws."
But the leaders, too, as one man,
had thrown off God's yoke
and broken his chains.
6 So now a lion from the forest will attack them;
a wolf from the desert will pounce on them.
A leopard will lurk near their towns,
tearing apart any who dare to venture out.
For their rebellion is great,
and their sins are many.

7 "How can I pardon you?
For even your children have turned from me.
They have sworn by gods that are not gods at all!
I fed my people until they were full.
But they thanked me by committing adultery
and lining up at the brothels.
8 They are well-fed, lusty stallions,
each neighing for his neighbor's wife.
9 Should I not punish them for this?" says the LORD.
"Should I not avenge myself against such
a nation?

10 "Go down the rows of the vineyards and destroy
the grapevines,
leaving a scattered few alive.
Strip the branches from the vines,
for these people do not belong to the LORD.
11 The people of Israel and Judah
are full of treachery against me,"
says the LORD.

12 "They have lied about the LORD
and said, 'He won't bother us!
No disasters will come upon us.
There will be no war or famine.
13 God's prophets are all windbags
who don't really speak for him.
Let their predictions of disaster fall on
themselves!'"

14 Therefore, this is what the LORD God of Heaven's
Armies says:

"Because the people are talking like this,
my messages will flame out of your mouth
and burn the people like kindling wood.
15 O Israel, I will bring a distant nation against you,"
says the LORD.
"It is a mighty nation,
an ancient nation,
a people whose language you do not know,
whose speech you cannot understand.
16 Their weapons are deadly;
their warriors are mighty.
17 They will devour the food of your harvest;
they will devour your sons and daughters.
They will devour your flocks and herds;
they will devour your grapes and figs.
And they will destroy your fortified towns,
which you think are so safe.

18 "Yet even in those days I will not blot you out completely," says the LORD. 19 "And when your people ask,
'Why did the LORD our God do all this to us?' you must
reply, 'You rejected him and gave yourselves to foreign
gods in your own land. Now you will serve foreigners
in a land that is not your own.'

A Warning for God's People

JEREMIAH 5:20-31

20 "Make this announcement to Israel,*
and say this to Judah:
21 Listen, you foolish and senseless people,
with eyes that do not see
and ears that do not hear.

Jer 5:20 Hebrew *to the house of Jacob.* The names "Jacob" and "Israel" are often interchanged throughout the Old Testament, referring sometimes to the individual patriarch and sometimes to the nation.

Jer 5:4-5 Even the leaders who knew God's laws and understood his words of judgment had rejected him. They were supposed to teach and guide the people, but instead they led them into sin. Jeremiah observed the poor and ignorant—those who were uninformed of God's ways—and realized they were not learning God's laws from their leaders. Thus, God's search in Jerusalem was complete. There were no true followers in any level of society.

Jer 5:7 God held these people responsible for the sins of their children because the children had followed their parents' example. The sin of leading others, especially our children, astray by our example is one for which God will hold us accountable.

Jer 5:15 Babylon was indeed an ancient nation. The old Babylonian Empire had lasted from about 1900 to 1550 B.C., and earlier kingdoms had been on her soil as early as 3000 B.C. Babylon in Jeremiah's day would shortly rebel against Assyrian domination, form its own army, conquer Assyria, and become the next dominant world power.

Jer 5:21 Have you ever spoken to someone only to realize that the person didn't hear a word you were saying? Jeremiah told the people that their eyes and ears did them no good because they refused to see or hear God's message. The people of Judah and Israel were foolishly deaf when God promised blessings for obedience and destruction for disobedience. When God speaks through his Word or his messengers, we harm ourselves if we fail to listen. God's message will never change us unless we heed it.

22 Have you no respect for me?
Why don't you tremble in my presence?
I, the LORD, define the ocean's sandy shoreline
as an everlasting boundary that the waters
cannot cross.
The waves may toss and roar,
but they can never pass the boundaries I set.
23 But my people have stubborn and rebellious
hearts.
They have turned away and abandoned me.
24 They do not say from the heart,
'Let us live in awe of the LORD our God,
for he gives us rain each spring and fall,
assuring us of a harvest when the time
is right.'
25 Your wickedness has deprived you of these
wonderful blessings.
Your sin has robbed you of all these good
things.

26 "Among my people are wicked men
who lie in wait for victims like a hunter hiding
in a blind.
They continually set traps
to catch people.
27 Like a cage filled with birds,
their homes are filled with evil plots.
And now they are great and rich.
28 They are fat and sleek,
and there is no limit to their wicked deeds.
They refuse to provide justice to orphans
and deny the rights of the poor.
29 Should I not punish them for this?" says the
LORD.
"Should I not avenge myself against such
a nation?
30 A horrible and shocking thing
has happened in this land—
31 the prophets give false prophecies,
and the priests rule with an iron hand.
Worse yet, my people like it that way!
But what will you do when the end comes?

Jerusalem's Last Warning

JEREMIAH 6:1-9

1 "Run for your lives, you people of Benjamin!
Get out of Jerusalem!
Sound the alarm in Tekoa!
Send up a signal at Beth-hakkerem!
A powerful army is coming from the north,
coming with disaster and destruction.
2 O Jerusalem,* you are my beautiful and delicate
daughter—
but I will destroy you!
3 Enemies will surround you, like shepherds
camped around the city.
Each chooses a place for his troops to devour.
4 They shout, 'Prepare for battle!
Attack at noon!'
'No, it's too late; the day is fading,
and the evening shadows are falling.'
5 'Well then, let's attack at night
and destroy her palaces!'"

6 This is what the LORD of Heaven's Armies says:
"Cut down the trees for battering rams.
Build siege ramps against the walls of
Jerusalem.
This is the city to be punished,
for she is wicked through and through.
7 She spouts evil like a fountain.
Her streets echo with the sounds of violence
and destruction.
I always see her sickness and sores.
8 Listen to this warning, Jerusalem,
or I will turn from you in disgust.
Listen, or I will turn you into a heap of ruins,
a land where no one lives."

9 This is what the LORD of Heaven's Armies says:
"Even the few who remain in Israel
will be picked over again,
as when a harvester checks each vine
a second time
to pick the grapes that were missed."

Jer 6:2 Hebrew *Daughter of Zion.*

Jer 5:22-24 What is your attitude when you come into God's presence? We should come with respect and trembling because God sets the boundaries of the roaring ocean and sends the rain, assuring us of plentiful harvests. God had to strip away all the benefits that Judah and Israel had grown to expect from him and give the people another opportunity to turn back to him. God still sometimes uses the same method of blessing or withholding blessing to get our attention. Don't wait until God removes your cherished resources before committing yourself to him as you should.

Jer 5:28-29 People and nations who please God treat the fatherless (orphans) justly and care for the poor. Wicked men in Israel treated the defenseless unjustly, which displeased God greatly. Some defenseless people—orphans, the poor, the homeless, the refugee, and the lonely—are within your reach. What action can you take to help at least one of them?

Jer 6:1 The Lord warned Jeremiah's own tribe of Benjamin to flee—not to the security of the great walled city of Jerusalem because it would be under siege, but toward Tekoa, a town about 12 miles south of Jerusalem. The warning smoke signal was lit at Beth-hakkerem, halfway between Jerusalem and Bethlehem.

Jer 6:3 The shepherds were the leaders of Babylon's armies.

Jer 6:9 The "few who remain in Israel" is not to be confused with the righteous remnant. This remnant refers to those left after the first wave of destruction. Like a grape gatherer, Babylon wouldn't be satisfied until every person was taken. The Babylonians invaded Judah three times until they destroyed the nation and its Temple completely (2 Kgs 24–25).

Judah's Constant Rebellion

JEREMIAH 6:10-15

10 To whom can I give warning?
Who will listen when I speak?
Their ears are closed,
and they cannot hear.
They scorn the word of the LORD.
They don't want to listen at all.
11 So now I am filled with the LORD's fury.
Yes, I am tired of holding it in!

"I will pour out my fury on children playing
in the streets
and on gatherings of young men,
on husbands and wives
and on those who are old and gray.
12 Their homes will be turned over to their
enemies,
as will their fields and their wives.
For I will raise my powerful fist
against the people of this land,"
says the LORD.
13 "From the least to the greatest,
their lives are ruled by greed.
From prophets to priests,
they are all frauds.
14 They offer superficial treatments
for my people's mortal wound.
They give assurances of peace
when there is no peace.
15 Are they ashamed of their disgusting actions?
Not at all—they don't even know how to blush!
Therefore, they will lie among the slaughtered.
They will be brought down when I punish
them,"
says the LORD.

Judah Rejects the LORD's Way

JEREMIAH 6:16-21

16 This is what the LORD says:
"Stop at the crossroads and look around.
Ask for the old, godly way, and walk in it.
Travel its path, and you will find rest for
your souls.
But you reply, 'No, that's not the road we want!'
17 I posted watchmen over you who said,
'Listen for the sound of the alarm.'
But you replied,
'No! We won't pay attention!'
18 "Therefore, listen to this, all you nations.
Take note of my people's situation.
19 Listen, all the earth!
I will bring disaster on my people.
It is the fruit of their own schemes,
because they refuse to listen to me.
They have rejected my word.
20 There's no use offering me sweet frankincense
from Sheba.
Keep your fragrant calamus imported from
distant lands!
I will not accept your burnt offerings.
Your sacrifices have no pleasing aroma
for me."
21 Therefore, this is what the LORD says:
"I will put obstacles in my people's path.
Fathers and sons will both fall over them.
Neighbors and friends will die together."

An Invasion from the North

JEREMIAH 6:22-30

22 This is what the LORD says:
"Look! A great army coming from the north!
A great nation is rising against you from
far-off lands.
23 They are armed with bows and spears.
They are cruel and show no mercy.
They sound like a roaring sea
as they ride forward on horses.
They are coming in battle formation,
planning to destroy you, beautiful Jerusalem.*"
24 We have heard reports about the enemy,
and we wring our hands in fright.
Pangs of anguish have gripped us,
like those of a woman in labor.
25 Don't go out to the fields!
Don't travel on the roads!
The enemy's sword is everywhere
and terrorizes us at every turn!

Jer 6:23 Hebrew *daughter of Zion.*

Jer 6:10 The people became angry and closed their ears. They wanted no part of God's commands because living for God did not appear very exciting. As in Jeremiah's day, people today dislike God's demand for disciplined living. As unsettling as people's responses might be, we must continue to share God's Word. Our responsibility is to present God's Word; their responsibility is to accept it. We must not let what people want to hear determine what we say.

Jer 6:14 "Ignore it and maybe it will go away!" Sound familiar? This was Israel's response to Jeremiah's warnings. They kept listening to predictions of peace because they did not like Jeremiah's condemnation of their sin. But denying the truth never changes it; what God says always happens. Sin is never removed by denying its existence. We must confess to God that we have sinned and ask him to forgive us.

Jer 6:16 The right path for living is "the old, godly way" and has been marked out by God. But the people refused to take God's path, going their own way instead. We face the same decision today—going God's old but true way, or following a new path of our own choosing. Don't be misled. The only way to find peace and "rest for your souls" is to walk on God's path.

Jer 6:20 Sheba, located in southwest Arabia, was a center of trade in incense and spices used in pagan religious rituals.

Jer 6:25 Ominous travel warnings, increased threat levels, and tight security were as much a part of life in ancient Israel as they are in the world today. Terrorism, in one form or another, has been a tactic throughout history. The question raised about

26 Oh, my people, dress yourselves in burlap
and sit among the ashes.
Mourn and weep bitterly, as for the loss
of an only son.
For suddenly the destroying armies will
be upon you!
27 "Jeremiah, I have made you a tester
of metals,*
that you may determine the quality
of my people.
28 They are the worst kind of rebel,
full of slander.
They are as hard as bronze and iron,
and they lead others into corruption.
29 The bellows fiercely fan the flames
to burn out the corruption.
But it does not purify them,
for the wickedness remains.
30 I will label them 'Rejected Silver,'
for I, the LORD, am discarding them."

Jer 6:27 As in Greek version; Hebrew reads *a tester of my people a fortress.*

3. JOSIAH'S SWEEPING REFORMS IN JUDAH

Josiah had already begun instituting changes in Judah—removing pagan idols and shrines, restoring the Temple, worshiping God alone—but while his workers were restoring the Temple, they found a scroll with the Book of the Law (possibly all or part of the book of Deuteronomy). When Josiah read this scroll, he was deeply grieved and called for even more wide-reaching reforms. Before he had read the law, Josiah was doing everything he could think of to bring the people of Judah back to God and restore proper worship, but it wasn't until he found the instructions God had given in Scripture that he realized what God actually wanted from his people. We need to be students of God's Word—the entire Bible—so that we will know how God wants us to live as Christians.

Hilkiah Discovers God's Law PARALLEL

2 KINGS 22:3-20

In the eighteenth year of his reign, King Josiah sent
Shaphan son of Azaliah and grandson of Meshullam, the court secretary, to the Temple of the LORD.
He told him, 4"Go to Hilkiah the high priest and have
him count the money the gatekeepers have collected
from the people at the LORD's Temple. 5Entrust this
money to the men assigned to supervise the Temple's
restoration. Then they can use it to pay workers to
repair the Temple of the LORD. 6They will need to hire
carpenters, builders, and masons. Also have them buy
the timber and the finished stone needed to repair the
Temple. 7But don't require the construction supervisors to keep account of the money they receive, for
they are honest and trustworthy men."
8Hilkiah the high priest said to Shaphan the court
secretary, "I have found the Book of the Law in the
LORD's Temple!" Then Hilkiah gave the scroll to Shaphan, and he read it.
9Shaphan went to the king and reported, "Your officials have turned over the money collected at the
Temple of the LORD to the workers and supervisors
at the Temple." 10Shaphan also told the king, "Hilkiah
the priest has given me a scroll." So Shaphan read it
to the king.

11When the king heard what was written in the
Book of the Law, he tore his clothes in despair. 12Then
he gave these orders to Hilkiah the priest, Ahikam son
of Shaphan, Acbor son of Micaiah, Shaphan the court
secretary, and Asaiah the king's personal adviser: 13"Go
to the Temple and speak to the LORD for me and for
the people and for all Judah. Inquire about the words
written in this scroll that has been found. For the
LORD's great anger is burning against us because our
ancestors have not obeyed the words in this scroll. We
have not been doing everything it says we must do."
14So Hilkiah the priest, Ahikam, Acbor, Shaphan,
and Asaiah went to the New Quarter* of Jerusalem
to consult with the prophet Huldah. She was the wife

Law scroll found in the Temple

2 Kgs 22:14 Or *the Second Quarter,* a newer section of Jerusalem. Hebrew reads *the Mishneh.*

such real or potential dangers forces us to examine our sense of ultimate security. Whether the outlook is bleak or hopeful, do we actually trust in God? Or does our trust last only as long as the threat seems distant?

Jer 6:29-30 Metal is purified by fire. As it is heated, impurities are burned away and only the pure metal remains. As God tested the people of Judah, he could find no purity in their lives. They continued in their sinful ways. Do you see impurities in your life that should be burned away? Confess these to God and allow him to purify you as he sees fit. Take time right now to reflect on the areas of your life that he has already refined; then thank him for what he is doing.

2 Kgs 22:4 The gatekeepers controlled who entered the Temple and supervised the collection of the money.

2 Kgs 22:8 This book may have been the entire Pentateuch (Genesis—Deuteronomy), but it was probably only the book of Deuteronomy. Because of the long line of evil kings, the record of God's laws had been lost. Josiah, who was about 26 years old at this time, wanted religious reform throughout the nation. When God's Word was found, drastic changes had to be made to bring the kingdom in line with God's commands. Today you have God's Word at your fingertips. How much change must you make in order to bring your life into line with it?

2 Kgs 22:11ff When Josiah heard the law, he tore his clothes in despair. He immediately instituted reforms. With just one reading of God's law, he changed the course of the nation. Today many people own Bibles, but few are affected by the truths found in God's Word. The Word of God should cause us, like Josiah, to take action immediately to reform our lives and bring them into harmony with God's will.

2 Kgs 22:14 Huldah was a prophet, as were Miriam (Exod 15:20) and Deborah (Judg 4:4). God freely selects his servants to carry out his will—rich or poor, male or female, king or slave (Joel 2:28-30). Huldah was obviously highly regarded by the people of her time.

▸ 2 KINGS 22:3-20 ***(cont.)***

of Shallum son of Tikvah, son of Harhas, the keeper
of the Temple wardrobe.
15She said to them, "The LORD, the God of Israel, has
spoken! Go back and tell the man who sent you, 16'This
is what the LORD says: I am going to bring disaster on
this city* and its people. All the words written in the
scroll that the king of Judah has read will come true.
17For my people have abandoned me and offered sacrifices to pagan gods, and I am very angry with them
for everything they have done. My anger will burn
against this place, and it will not be quenched.'
18"But go to the king of Judah who sent you to seek
the LORD and tell him: 'This is what the LORD, the God
of Israel, says concerning the message you have just
heard: 19You were sorry and humbled yourself before
the LORD when you heard what I said against this city
and its people—that this land would be cursed and
become desolate. You tore your clothing in despair
and wept before me in repentance. And I have indeed
heard you, says the LORD. 20So I will not send the promised disaster until after you have died and been buried
in peace. You will not see the disaster I am going to
bring on this city.'"

So they took her message back to the king.

2 CHRONICLES 34:8-28

In the eighteenth year of his reign, after he had purified the land and the Temple, Josiah appointed
Shaphan son of Azaliah, Maaseiah the governor of
Jerusalem, and Joah son of Joahaz, the royal historian,
to repair the Temple of the LORD his God. 9They gave
Hilkiah the high priest the money that had been collected by the Levites who served as gatekeepers at
the Temple of God. The gifts were brought by people
from Manasseh, Ephraim, and from all the remnant
of Israel, as well as from all Judah, Benjamin, and the
people of Jerusalem.
10He entrusted the money to the men assigned to
supervise the restoration of the LORD's Temple. Then
they paid the workers who did the repairs and renovation of the Temple. 11They hired carpenters and builders, who purchased finished stone for the walls and
timber for the rafters and beams. They restored what
earlier kings of Judah had allowed to fall into ruin.
12The workers served faithfully under the leadership of Jahath and Obadiah, Levites of the Merarite
clan, and Zechariah and Meshullam, Levites of the
Kohathite clan. Other Levites, all of whom were skilled
musicians, 13were put in charge of the laborers of the
various trades. Still others assisted as secretaries, officials, and gatekeepers.
14While they were bringing out the money collected
at the LORD's Temple, Hilkiah the priest found the
Book of the Law of the LORD that was written by Moses.
15Hilkiah said to Shaphan the court secretary, "I have
found the Book of the Law in the LORD's Temple!" Then
Hilkiah gave the scroll to Shaphan.
16Shaphan took the scroll to the king and reported,
"Your officials are doing everything they were assigned to do. 17The money that was collected at the
Temple of the LORD has been turned over to the supervisors and workmen." 18Shaphan also told the king,
"Hilkiah the priest has given me a scroll." So Shaphan
read it to the king.
19When the king heard what was written in the Law,
he tore his clothes in despair. 20Then he gave these
orders to Hilkiah, Ahikam son of Shaphan, Acbor son
of Micaiah,* Shaphan the court secretary, and Asaiah
the king's personal adviser: 21"Go to the Temple and
speak to the LORD for me and for all the remnant of
Israel and Judah. Inquire about the words written in
the scroll that has been found. For the LORD's great anger has been poured out on us because our ancestors
have not obeyed the word of the LORD. We have not
been doing everything this scroll says we must do."
22So Hilkiah and the other men went to the New
Quarter* of Jerusalem to consult with the prophet
Huldah. She was the wife of Shallum son of Tikvah,
son of Harhas,* the keeper of the Temple wardrobe.
23She said to them, "The LORD, the God of Israel, has
spoken! Go back and tell the man who sent you, 24'This
is what the LORD says: I am going to bring disaster on
this city* and its people. All the curses written in the
scroll that was read to the king of Judah will come
true. 25For my people have abandoned me and offered
sacrifices to pagan gods, and I am very angry with
them for everything they have done. My anger will be
poured out on this place, and it will not be quenched.'
26"But go to the king of Judah who sent you to seek
the LORD and tell him: 'This is what the LORD, the God
of Israel, says concerning the message you have just
heard: 27You were sorry and humbled yourself before
God when you heard his words against this city and its

2 Kgs 22:16 Hebrew *this place;* also in 22:19, 20. **2 Chr 34:20** As in parallel text at 2 Kgs 22:12; Hebrew reads *Abdon son of Micah.* **2 Chr 34:22a** Or *the Second Quarter,* a newer section of Jerusalem. Hebrew reads *the Mishneh.* **2 Chr 34:22b** As in parallel text at 2 Kgs 22:14; Hebrew reads *son of Tokhath, son of Hasrah.* **2 Chr 34:24** Hebrew *this place;* also in 34:27, 28.

---

2 Kgs 22:19 When Josiah realized how corrupt his nation had become, he tore his clothes and wept before God. Then God had mercy on him and the nation. Josiah used the customs of his day to show his repentance. Today, we are unlikely to tear our clothes in sorrow for our sin, but weeping, fasting, and making restitution or apologies (if our sin has involved others) demonstrate our sincerity when we repent. The hardest part of repentance is changing the attitudes that originally produced the sinful behavior.

2 Chr 34:19 It is human nature to treat sin lightly—to make excuses, blame somebody else, or minimize the harm done. Not so with Josiah. He was so appalled at the people's neglect of the law that he tore his clothing to express his grief. True understanding of our sins should lead to "sorrow" that "leads us away from sin" (2 Cor 7:10). Are you always excusing your sin, blaming others, and pretending that it's not so bad? God does not take sin lightly, and he wants us to respond with true remorse as Josiah did.

people. You humbled yourself and tore your clothing
in despair and wept before me in repentance. And I
have indeed heard you, says the LORD. 28So I will not
send the promised disaster until after you have died
and been buried in peace. You yourself will not see
the disaster I am going to bring on this city and its
people.'"
So they took her message back to the king.

Josiah's Religious Reforms PARALLEL

2 KINGS 23:1-20

Then the king summoned all the elders of Judah and
Jerusalem. 2And the king went up to the Temple of
the LORD with all the people of Judah and Jerusalem, along with the priests and the prophets—all the
people from the least to the greatest. There the king
read to them the entire Book of the Covenant that had
been found in the LORD's Temple. 3The king took his
place of authority beside the pillar and renewed the
covenant in the LORD's presence. He pledged to obey
the LORD by keeping all his commands, laws, and decrees with all his heart and soul. In this way, he confirmed all the terms of the covenant that were written
in the scroll, and all the people pledged themselves
to the covenant.
4Then the king instructed Hilkiah the high priest
and the priests of the second rank and the Temple
gatekeepers to remove from the LORD's Temple all the
articles that were used to worship Baal, Asherah, and
all the powers of the heavens. The king had all these
things burned outside Jerusalem on the terraces of the
Kidron Valley, and he carried the ashes away to Bethel.
5He did away with the idolatrous priests, who had been
appointed by the previous kings of Judah, for they had
offered sacrifices at the pagan shrines throughout Judah and even in the vicinity of Jerusalem. They had also
offered sacrifices to Baal, and to the sun, the moon, the
constellations, and to all the powers of the heavens.

JOSIAH

Josiah never knew his great-grandfather Hezekiah, but they were alike in many ways. Both had close, personal relationships with God. Both were passionate reformers, making valiant efforts to lead their people back to God. Both were bright flashes of obedience to God among kings with darkened consciences who seemed bent on outdoing each other in disobedience and evil. • Although Josiah's father and grandfather were exceptionally wicked, his life is an example of God's willingness to provide ongoing guidance to those who set out to be obedient. At a young age, Josiah already understood that there was spiritual sickness in his land. Idols were sprouting in the countryside faster than crops. In a sense, Josiah began his search for God by destroying and cleaning up whatever he recognized as not belonging to the worship of the true God. In the process, God's Word was rediscovered. The king's intentions and the power of God's written revelation were brought together. • As the Book of the Law was read to Josiah, he was shocked, frightened, and humbled. He realized what a great gap existed between his efforts to lead his people to God and God's expectations for his chosen nation. He was overwhelmed by God's holiness and immediately tried to expose his people to that holiness. The people did respond, but the Bible makes it clear that their renewed worship of God was much more out of respect for Josiah than out of personal understanding of their own guilt before God. • How would you describe your relationship with God? Are your feeble efforts at holiness based mostly on a desire to "go along" with a well-liked leader or popular opinion? Or are you, like Josiah, deeply humbled by God's Word, realizing the great gap between your life and the kind of life God expects, and realizing your deep need to be cleansed and renewed by him? Humble obedience pleases God. Good intentions, even reforms, are not enough. You must allow God's Word to truly humble you and change your life.

Strengths and accomplishments	• Was king of Judah • Sought after God and was open to him • Was a reformer like his great-grandfather Hezekiah • Cleaned out the Temple and revived obedience to God's law
Weakness and mistake	• Became involved in a military conflict that he had been warned against
Lessons from his life	• God consistently responds to those with repentant and humble hearts • Even sweeping outward reforms are of little lasting value if there are no changes in people's lives
Vital statistics	• Where: Jerusalem • Occupation: 16th king of Judah, the southern kingdom • Relatives: Father: Amon. Mother: Jedidah. Sons: Jehoahaz, Eliakim. • Contemporaries: Jeremiah, Huldah, Hilkiah, Zephaniah
Key verse	"Never before had there been a king like Josiah, who turned to the LORD with all his heart and soul and strength, obeying all the laws of Moses. And there has never been a king like him since" (2 Kgs 23:25).

Josiah's story is told in 2 Kings 21:24–23:30; 2 Chronicles 33:25–35:27. He is also mentioned in Jeremiah 1:1-3; 22:11, 18.

2 Kgs 23:1-2 For more about the importance and operation of the Temple, see 1 Kings 5–8 and 2 Chronicles 2–7.

2 Kgs 23:4-8 When Josiah realized the terrible state of Judah's religious life, he did something about it. It is not enough to say we believe what is right; we must respond with action, doing what faith requires. This is what James was emphasizing when he wrote, "Can't you see that faith without good deeds is useless?" (Jas 2:20). This means acting differently at home, school, work, and church. Simply talking about obedience is not enough.

▸ 2 KINGS 23:1-20 *(cont.)*

6The king removed the Asherah pole from the LORD's
Temple and took it outside Jerusalem to the Kidron
Valley, where he burned it. Then he ground the
ashes of the pole to dust and threw the dust over the
graves of the people. 7He also tore down the living
quarters of the male and female shrine prostitutes
that were inside the Temple of the LORD, where the
women wove coverings for the Asherah pole.

8Josiah brought to Jerusalem all the priests who
were living in other towns of Judah. He also defiled the
pagan shrines, where they had offered sacrifices—all
the way from Geba to Beersheba. He destroyed the
shrines at the entrance to the gate of Joshua, the governor of Jerusalem. This gate was located to the left of
the city gate as one enters the city. 9The priests who
had served at the pagan shrines were not allowed* to
serve at the LORD's altar in Jerusalem, but they were
allowed to eat unleavened bread with the other priests.

10Then the king defiled the altar of Topheth in the
valley of Ben-Hinnom, so no one could ever again use
it to sacrifice a son or daughter in the fire* as an offering to Molech. 11He removed from the entrance of
the LORD's Temple the horse statues that the former
kings of Judah had dedicated to the sun. They were
near the quarters of Nathan-melech the eunuch, an
officer of the court.*The king also burned the chariots
dedicated to the sun.

12Josiah tore down the altars that the kings of Judah
had built on the palace roof above the upper room of
Ahaz. The king destroyed the altars that Manasseh
had built in the two courtyards of the LORD's Temple.
He smashed them to bits* and scattered the pieces
in the Kidron Valley. 13The king also desecrated the
pagan shrines east of Jerusalem, to the south of the
Mount of Corruption, where King Solomon of Israel
had built shrines for Ashtoreth, the detestable goddess
of the Sidonians; and for Chemosh, the detestable god
of the Moabites; and for Molech,* the vile god of the
Ammonites. 14He smashed the sacred pillars and cut
down the Asherah poles. Then he desecrated these
places by scattering human bones over them.

15The king also tore down the altar at Bethel—the
pagan shrine that Jeroboam son of Nebat had made
when he caused Israel to sin. He burned down the
shrine and ground it to dust, and he burned the Asherah pole. 16Then Josiah turned around and noticed
several tombs in the side of the hill. He ordered that
the bones be brought out, and he burned them on the
altar at Bethel to desecrate it. (This happened just as
the LORD had promised through the man of God when
Jeroboam stood beside the altar at the festival.)

Then Josiah turned and looked up at the tomb of
the man of God* who had predicted these things.
17"What is that monument over there?" Josiah asked.

And the people of the town told him, "It is the tomb
of the man of God who came from Judah and predicted the very things that you have just done to the
altar at Bethel!"

18Josiah replied, "Leave it alone. Don't disturb his
bones." So they did not burn his bones or those of the
old prophet from Samaria.

19Then Josiah demolished all the buildings at the
pagan shrines in the towns of Samaria, just as he had
done at Bethel. They had been built by the various
kings of Israel and had made the LORD* very angry.
20He executed the priests of the pagan shrines on their
own altars, and he burned human bones on the altars
to desecrate them. Finally, he returned to Jerusalem.

2 CHRONICLES 34:29-33

29Then the king summoned all the elders of Judah and
Jerusalem. 30And the king went up to the Temple of
the LORD with all the people of Judah and Jerusalem,
along with the priests and the Levites—all the people
from the greatest to the least. There the king read to
them the entire Book of the Covenant that had been
found in the LORD's Temple. 31The king took his place
of authority beside the pillar and renewed the covenant in the LORD's presence. He pledged to obey the
LORD by keeping all his commands, laws, and decrees
with all his heart and soul. He promised to obey all
the terms of the covenant that were written in the
scroll. 32And he required everyone in Jerusalem and
the people of Benjamin to make a similar pledge. The
people of Jerusalem did so, renewing their covenant
with God, the God of their ancestors.

2 Kgs 23:9 Hebrew *did not come up.* **2 Kgs 23:10** Or *to make a son or daughter pass through the fire.* **2 Kgs 23:11** The meaning of the Hebrew is uncertain. **2 Kgs 23:12** Or *He quickly removed them.* **2 Kgs 23:13** Hebrew *Milcom,* a variant spelling of Molech. **2 Kgs 23:16** As in Greek version; Hebrew lacks *when Jeroboam stood beside the altar at the festival. Then Josiah turned and looked up at the tomb of the man of God.* **2 Kgs 23:19** As in Greek and Syriac versions and Latin Vulgate; Hebrew lacks *the LORD.*

2 Kgs 23:6 This shameful Asherah pole had been set up in God's Temple by the evil King Manasseh (2 Kgs 21:7). Asherah is most often identified as the mistress of Baal. She was a chief goddess of the Canaanites. Her worship glorified sex and war and was accompanied by male prostitution.

2 Kgs 23:13 The Mount of Olives is here called the Mount of Corruption because it had become a favorite spot to build pagan shrines. Solomon built a pagan shrine, and other kings built places of idol worship there too. But God-fearing kings, such as Hezekiah and Josiah, destroyed these pagan worship centers. In New Testament times, Jesus often sat on the Mount of Olives and taught his disciples about serving only God (Matt 24:3ff). (For more background on Ashtoreth, Chemosh, and Molech, see the note on 1 Kgs 11:5-8, p. 671.)

2 Kgs 23:16-18 The prophecies mentioned in this passage appear in 1 Kings 13:21-32.

2 Chr 34:31 When Josiah read the book that Hilkiah discovered (2 Chr 34:14), he responded with repentance and humility and promised to follow God's commands as written in the book. The Bible is God's word to us, "alive and powerful" (Heb 4:12), but we cannot know what God wants us to do if we don't read it. And even reading God's Word is not enough; we must be willing to do what it says. There is not much difference between the book hidden in the Temple and the Bible

[33]So Josiah removed all detestable idols from the entire land of Israel and required everyone to worship the LORD their God. And throughout the rest of his lifetime, they did not turn away from the LORD, the God of their ancestors.

Josiah Celebrates Passover PARALLEL

2 KINGS 23:21-28

King Josiah then issued this order to all the people: "You must celebrate the Passover to the LORD your God, as required in this Book of the Covenant." [22]There had not been a Passover celebration like that since the time when the judges ruled in Israel, nor throughout all the years of the kings of Israel and Judah. [23]This Passover was celebrated to the LORD in Jerusalem in the eighteenth year of King Josiah's reign.

[24]Josiah also got rid of the mediums and psychics, the household gods, the idols,* and every other kind of detestable practice, both in Jerusalem and throughout the land of Judah. He did this in obedience to the laws written in the scroll that Hilkiah the priest had found in the LORD's Temple. [25]Never before had there been a king like Josiah, who turned to the LORD with all his heart and soul and strength, obeying all the laws of Moses. And there has never been a king like him since.

[26]Even so, the LORD was very angry with Judah because of all the wicked things Manasseh had done to provoke him. [27]For the LORD said, "I will also banish Judah from my presence just as I have banished Israel. And I will reject my chosen city of Jerusalem and the Temple where my name was to be honored."

[28]The rest of the events in Josiah's reign and all his deeds are recorded in *The Book of the History of the Kings of Judah.*

2 CHRONICLES 35:1-19

Then Josiah announced that the Passover of the LORD would be celebrated in Jerusalem, and so the Passover lamb was slaughtered on the fourteenth day of the first month.* [2]Josiah also assigned the priests to their duties and encouraged them in their work at the Temple of the LORD. [3]He issued this order to the Levites, who were to teach all Israel and who had been set apart to serve the LORD: "Put the holy Ark in the Temple that was built by Solomon son of David, the king of Israel. You no longer need to carry it back and forth on your shoulders. Now spend your time serving the LORD your God and his people Israel. [4]Report for duty according to the family divisions of your ancestors, following the directions of King David of Israel and the directions of his son Solomon.

[5]"Then stand in the sanctuary at the place appointed for your family division and help the families assigned to you as they bring their offerings to the Temple. [6]Slaughter the Passover lambs, purify yourselves, and prepare to help those who come. Follow all the directions that the LORD gave through Moses."

[7]Then Josiah provided 30,000 lambs and young goats for the people's Passover offerings, along with 3,000 cattle, all from the king's own flocks and herds. [8]The king's officials also made willing contributions to the people, priests, and Levites. Hilkiah, Zechariah, and Jehiel, the administrators of God's Temple, gave the priests 2,600 lambs and young goats and 300 cattle as Passover offerings. [9]The Levite leaders—Conaniah and his brothers Shemaiah and Nethanel, as well as Hashabiah, Jeiel, and Jozabad—gave 5,000 lambs and young goats and 500 cattle to the Levites for their Passover offerings.

[10]When everything was ready for the Passover celebration, the priests and the Levites took their places, organized by their divisions, as the king had commanded. [11]The Levites then slaughtered the Passover lambs and presented the blood to the priests, who sprinkled the blood on the altar while the Levites prepared the animals. [12]They divided the burnt offerings among the people by their family groups, so they could offer them to the LORD as prescribed in the Book of Moses. They did the same with the cattle. [13]Then they roasted the Passover lambs as prescribed; and they boiled the holy offerings in pots, kettles, and pans, and brought them out quickly so the people could eat them.

[14]Afterward the Levites prepared Passover offerings for themselves and for the priests—the descendants

2 Kgs 23:24 The Hebrew term (literally *round things*) probably alludes to dung. **2 Chr 35:1** This day in the ancient Hebrew lunar calendar was April 5, 622 B.C.

hidden on the bookshelf. An unread Bible is as useless as a lost one.

2 Kgs 23:21-23 When Josiah rediscovered the Passover in the Book of the Covenant, he ordered everyone to observe the ceremonies exactly as prescribed. This Passover celebration was to have been a yearly holiday celebrated in remembrance of the entire nation's deliverance from slavery in Egypt (Exod 12), but it had not been kept for many years. As a result, "there had not been a Passover celebration like that since the time when the judges ruled in Israel, nor throughout all the years of the kings of Israel and Judah." A common misconception states that God is against celebration, wanting to take all the fun out of life. In reality, God wants to give us life in its fullness (John 10:10), and those who love him have the most to celebrate.

2 Kgs 23:25 Josiah is remembered as Judah's most obedient king. His obedience followed this pattern: (1) He recognized sin; (2) he eliminated sinful practices; (3) he attacked the causes of sin. This approach for dealing with sin works. Not only must we remove sinful actions, but we must also eliminate causes for sin—those situations, relationships, routines, and patterns of life that lead us to the door of temptation.

2 Kgs 23:25 Both Josiah and Hezekiah (2 Kgs 18:5) are praised for their reverence toward God. Hezekiah was said to be greatest in trusting God (faith), while Josiah is said to be greatest in following the law of God (obedience). May we follow their example through our trust in God and our obedient actions.

2 Chr 35:3 In Moses' day, one of the duties of the Levites was to carry the Ark of the Covenant whenever Israel traveled. The Ark was now permanently housed in the Temple and would no longer be carried about in procession as it had been in the wilderness. Josiah was telling the Levites that they were now free to take on other responsibilities (1 Chr 24).

▸ **2 CHRONICLES 35:1-19** ***(cont.)***

of Aaron—because the priests had been busy from morning till night offering the burnt offerings and the fat portions. The Levites took responsibility for all these preparations.

15 The musicians, descendants of Asaph, were in their assigned places, following the commands that had been given by David, Asaph, Heman, and Jeduthun, the king's seer. The gatekeepers guarded the gates and did not need to leave their posts of duty, for their Passover offerings were prepared for them by their fellow Levites.

16 The entire ceremony for the LORD's Passover was completed that day. All the burnt offerings were sacrificed on the altar of the LORD, as King Josiah had
commanded. 17 All the Israelites present in Jerusalem celebrated Passover and the Festival of Unleavened Bread for seven days. 18 Never since the time of the
prophet Samuel had there been such a Passover. None of the kings of Israel had ever kept a Passover as Josiah did, involving all the priests and Levites, all the people of Jerusalem, and people from all over Judah
and Israel. 19 This Passover celebration took place in
the eighteenth year of Josiah's reign.

M. The Prophecy of Nahum

Nahum's ministry occurred sometime before the fall of Assyria in 612 B.C. He prophesied about the coming destruction of Nineveh, the Assyrian capital. The news of its coming destruction was a relief for Judah, who was subject to Assyrian domination. No longer would Judah be forced to pay tribute as insurance against invasion. Judah was comforted to know that God was still in control. Nineveh is an example that God is sovereign over even those who are seemingly invincible. We can be confident that God's power and justice will one day conquer all evil.

1. NINEVEH'S JUDGE

God is sovereign over the entire world, and he would judge Assyria for their wickedness. No nation is beyond God's reach.

The LORD's Anger against Nineveh

NAHUM 1:1-15

This message concerning Nineveh came as a vision to Nahum, who lived in Elkosh.

2 The LORD is a jealous God,
filled with vengeance and rage.
He takes revenge on all who oppose him
and continues to rage against his enemies!
3 The LORD is slow to get angry, but his power
is great,
and he never lets the guilty go unpunished.
He displays his power in the whirlwind and
the storm.
The billowing clouds are the dust beneath
his feet.
4 At his command the oceans dry up,
and the rivers disappear.
The lush pastures of Bashan and
Carmel fade,
and the green forests of Lebanon wither.
5 In his presence the mountains quake,
and the hills melt away;

2 Chr 35:15 The Temple gatekeepers, who were all Levites, guarded the four main entrances to the Temple and opened the gates each morning. They also did other day-to-day chores, such as cleaning and preparing the offerings for sacrifice and accounting for the gifts given to the Temple. (For more on gatekeepers, see 1 Chr 26:1ff.)

2 Chr 35:17 The Festival of Unleavened Bread was a seven-day celebration beginning the day after Passover. Like Passover, it commemorated the exodus from Egypt. For seven days the people ate bread without yeast, just as their ancestors did while leaving Egypt because it could be made quickly in preparation for their swift departure (Exod 12:14-20). This festival reminded the people that they had left slavery behind and had come to the land God promised them.

Nah 1:1 Nahum, like Jonah, was a prophet to Nineveh, the capital of the Assyrian Empire, and he prophesied between 663 and 612 B.C. Jonah had seen Nineveh repent a century earlier (see the book of Jonah), but the city had fallen back into wickedness. Assyria, the world power controlling the Fertile Crescent, seemed unstoppable. Its ruthless and savage warriors had already conquered Israel, the northern kingdom, and were causing great suffering in Judah. So Nahum proclaimed God's anger against Assyria's evil. Within a few decades, the mighty Assyrian Empire would be toppled by Babylon.

Nah 1:1 Elkosh was a village thought by some to be in southwest Judah.

Nah 1:2 God alone has the right to be jealous and to carry out vengeance. *Jealousy* and *vengeance* may be surprising terms to associate with God. When humans are jealous and take vengeance, they are usually acting in a spirit of selfishness. But it is appropriate for God to insist on our complete allegiance, and it is just for him to punish unrepentant evildoers. His jealousy and vengeance are unmixed with selfishness. Their purpose is to remove sin and restore peace to the world (Deut 4:24; 5:9).

Nah 1:3 God is slow to get angry, but when he is ready to punish, even the earth trembles. Often people avoid God because they see evildoers in the world and hypocrites in the church. They don't realize that because God is slow to anger, he gives his true followers time to share his love and truth with evildoers. But judgment *will* come; God will not allow sin to go unchecked forever. When people wonder why God doesn't punish evil immediately, help them remember that if he did, none of us would be here. We can all be thankful that God gives people time to turn to him.

Nah 1:4 Bashan and Carmel were very fertile areas.

the earth trembles,
and its people are destroyed.
6 Who can stand before his fierce anger?
Who can survive his burning fury?
His rage blazes forth like fire,
and the mountains crumble to dust
in his presence.

7 The LORD is good,
a strong refuge when trouble comes.
He is close to those who trust in him.
8 But he will sweep away his enemies
in an overwhelming flood.
He will pursue his foes
into the darkness of night.
9 Why are you scheming against
the LORD?
He will destroy you with one blow;
he won't need to strike twice!
10 His enemies, tangled like thornbushes
and staggering like drunks,
will be burned up like dry stubble
in a field.
11 Who is this wicked counselor of yours
who plots evil against the LORD?

12 This is what the LORD says:
"Though the Assyrians have many allies,
they will be destroyed and disappear.
O my people, I have punished you before,
but I will not punish you again.
13 Now I will break the yoke of bondage from
your neck
and tear off the chains of Assyrian oppression."

14 And this is what the LORD says concerning the
Assyrians in Nineveh:
"You will have no more children to carry on
your name.
I will destroy all the idols in the temples of
your gods.
I am preparing a grave for you
because you are despicable!"

15* Look! A messenger is coming over the mountains
with good news!
He is bringing a message of peace.
Celebrate your festivals, O people of Judah,
and fulfill all your vows,
for your wicked enemies will never invade your
land again.
They will be completely destroyed!

Na 1:15 Verse 1:15 is numbered 2:1 in Hebrew text.

NAHUM

Nahum served as a prophet to Judah from 663–612 B.C.

Climate of the times	Manasseh, one of Judah's most wicked kings, ruled the land. He openly defied God and persecuted God's people. Assyria, the world power at that time, made Judah one of its vassal states. The people of Judah wanted to be like the Assyrians, who seemed to have all the power and possessions they wanted.
Main message	The mighty empire of Assyria that oppressed God's people would soon tumble.
Importance of message	Those who do evil and oppress others will one day meet a bitter end.
Contemporary prophet	Zephaniah (640–621 B.C.)

Nah 1:6 No person on earth can safely defy God, the Almighty, the Creator of all the universe. God, who controls the sun, the galaxies, and the vast stretches beyond, also controls the rise and fall of nations. How could a small temporal kingdom like Assyria, no matter how powerful, challenge God's awesome power? If only Assyria could have looked ahead to see the desolate mound of rubble that it would become—yet God would still be alive and well! Don't defy God; he will be here forever with greater power than that of all armies and nations combined.

Nah 1:6-8 To people who refuse to believe, God's punishment is like an angry fire. To those who love him, his mercy is a refuge, supplying all their needs without diminishing his supply. But to God's enemies he is an overwhelming flood that will sweep them away. The relationship we have with God is up to us. What kind of relationship will you choose?

Nah 1:11 The one "who plots evil against the LORD" could have been (1) Ashurbanipal (669–627 B.C.), king of Assyria during much of Nahum's life and the one who brought Assyria to the zenith of its power; (2) Sennacherib (705–681 B.C.), who openly defied God (2 Kgs 18:13-35), epitomizing rebellion against God; (3) no one king in particular but the entire evil monarchy. The point is that Nineveh would be destroyed for rebelling against God.

Nah 1:12-15 The good news for Judah, whom Assyria afflicted, was that its conquerors and tormentors would be destroyed and would never rise to torment it again. Nineveh was so completely wiped out that its ruins were not identified until 1845.

2. NINEVEH'S JUDGMENT

The great power that Assyria had over the nations of the world was nothing when faced with the power of God. All of the world's most secure defenses cannot prevent God's judgment on wickedness.

The Fall of Nineveh

NAHUM 2:1-13

1 *Your enemy is coming to crush you, Nineveh.
Man the ramparts! Watch the roads!
Prepare your defenses! Call out your forces!

2 Even though the destroyer has destroyed Judah,
the LORD will restore its honor.
Israel's vine has been stripped of branches,
but he will restore its splendor.

3 Shields flash red in the sunlight!
See the scarlet uniforms of the valiant troops!
Watch as their glittering chariots move into position,
with a forest of spears waving above them.*
4 The chariots race recklessly along the streets
and rush wildly through the squares.
They flash like firelight
and move as swiftly as lightning.
5 The king shouts to his officers;
they stumble in their haste,
rushing to the walls to set up their defenses.
6 The river gates have been torn open!
The palace is about to collapse!
7 Nineveh's exile has been decreed,
and all the servant girls mourn its capture.
They moan like doves
and beat their breasts in sorrow.
8 Nineveh is like a leaking water reservoir!
The people are slipping away.
"Stop, stop!" someone shouts,
but no one even looks back.
9 Loot the silver!
Plunder the gold!
There's no end to Nineveh's treasures—
its vast, uncounted wealth.
10 Soon the city is plundered, empty, and ruined.
Hearts melt and knees shake.
The people stand aghast,
their faces pale and trembling.
11 Where now is that great Nineveh,
that den filled with young lions?
It was a place where people—like lions and their cubs—
walked freely and without fear.
12 The lion tore up meat for his cubs
and strangled prey for his mate.
He filled his den with prey,
his caverns with his plunder.

13 "I am your enemy!"
says the LORD of Heaven's Armies.

Na 2:1 Verses 2:1-13 are numbered 2:2-14 in Hebrew text. **Na 2:3** Greek and Syriac versions read *into position, / the horses whipped into a frenzy.*

The Fall of Nineveh

This inscription has the Babylonian Chronicle for the years 616–609 B.C., including an account of the capture of Assur by the Medes (614 B.C.) and the fall of Nineveh to the Medes, Scythians, and Babylonians. Nahum predicted the fall of Nineveh because it had housed an unalterably proud, selfish, and unholy people. The Assyrians had made Nineveh a splendid and sophisticated metropolis by making merchandise out of other nations and people, either through military might or economic exploitation. Nineveh had played the harlot via such seductions. Accordingly, they who had so maliciously treated others would receive just recompense for their deeds, while the city itself would lie in ruins with none to mourn its demise. Its ruins were not even identified until A.D. 1945. Nahum's prophetic word came true; we can trust God's word.

Nah 2:1ff This chapter predicts the events of 612 B.C., when the combined armies of the Babylonians and the Medes sacked seemingly impregnable Nineveh.

Nah 2:2 Assyria had plundered and crushed the northern kingdom (Israel) and had deported its people in 722 B.C. (2 Kgs 17:3-6; 18:9-11). Assyria had also attacked the southern kingdom (Judah) and had forced it to pay tribute. These two separate kingdoms had been formed after Solomon's reign. A civil dispute with Solomon's son had caused ten of the tribes to set up their own kingdom. They had become the northern kingdom, while the remaining two tribes (Judah and Benjamin) stayed loyal to David's line and became the southern kingdom.

Nah 2:6 This reference to the opening of river gates could refer either to the enemy flowing into Nineveh like a flood (Nah 1:8) or to an actual flood of water. Some scholars suggest that dam gates, which were found in archaeological excavations, were closed to dam up the river. When an enormous amount of water had been accumulated, the gates were opened, allowing the water to flood Nineveh.

Nah 2:12–3:1 The major source of wealth for the Assyrian economy was the plunder taken from other nations. The Assyrians had taken the food of innocent people to maintain their luxurious standard of living, depriving others to supply their excesses. Depriving innocent people to support the luxury of a few is a sin that angers God. As Christians we must stand firm against this common but evil practice.

Nah 2:13 God had given the people of Nineveh a chance to repent, which they did after hearing Jonah (see the book of Jonah). But they had returned to their sin, and its consequences were destroying them. There is a point for people, cities, and nations after which there is no turning back; Assyria had passed that point. We must warn others to repent while there is still time.

Nah 3:4 Nineveh had used its beauty, prestige, and power to seduce other nations. Like a harlot, she had enticed them into false

"Your chariots will soon go up in smoke.
Your young men* will be killed in battle.
Never again will you plunder conquered nations.
The voices of your proud messengers will be heard no more."

The Lord's Judgment against Nineveh

NAHUM 3:1-19

1 What sorrow awaits Nineveh,
the city of murder and lies!
She is crammed with wealth
and is never without victims.
2 Hear the crack of whips,
the rumble of wheels!
Horses' hooves pound,
and chariots clatter wildly.
3 See the flashing swords and glittering spears
as the charioteers charge past!
There are countless casualties,
heaps of bodies—
so many bodies that
people stumble over them.
4 All this because Nineveh,
the beautiful and faithless city,
mistress of deadly charms,
enticed the nations with her beauty.
She taught them all her magic,
enchanting people everywhere.

5 "I am your enemy!"
says the Lord of Heaven's Armies.
"And now I will lift your skirts
and show all the earth your nakedness
and shame.
6 I will cover you with filth
and show the world how vile you really are.
7 All who see you will shrink back and say,
'Nineveh lies in ruins.
Where are the mourners?'
Does anyone regret your destruction?"
8 Are you any better than the city of Thebes,*
situated on the Nile River, surrounded
by water?
She was protected by the river on all sides,
walled in by water.
9 Ethiopia* and the land of Egypt
gave unlimited assistance.
The nations of Put and Libya
were among her allies.
10 Yet Thebes fell,
and her people were led away as captives.
Her babies were dashed to death
against the stones of the streets.
Soldiers threw dice* to get Egyptian officers
as servants.
All their leaders were bound in chains.

11 And you, Nineveh, will also stagger like a
drunkard.
You will hide for fear of the attacking enemy.
12 All your fortresses will fall.
They will be devoured like the ripe figs
that fall into the mouths
of those who shake the trees.
13 Your troops will be as weak
and helpless as women.
The gates of your land will be opened wide
to the enemy
and set on fire and burned.
14 Get ready for the siege!
Store up water!
Strengthen the defenses!
Go into the pits to trample clay,
and pack it into molds,
making bricks to repair the walls.

15 But the fire will devour you;
the sword will cut you down.
The enemy will consume you like locusts,
devouring everything they see.
There will be no escape,
even if you multiply like swarming locusts.
16 Your merchants have multiplied
until they outnumber the stars.
But like a swarm of locusts,
they strip the land and fly away.
17 Your guards* and officials are also like
swarming locusts
that crowd together in the hedges on
a cold day.
But like locusts that fly away when the sun
comes up,
all of them will fly away and disappear.

18 Your shepherds are asleep, O Assyrian king;
your princes lie dead in the dust.

Na 2:13 Hebrew *young lions.* **Na 3:8** Hebrew *No-amon;* also in 3:10. **Na 3:9** Hebrew *Cush.* **Na 3:10** Hebrew *They cast lots.* **Na 3:17** Or *princes.*

friendships. Then when the other nations relaxed, thinking Assyria was a friend, Assyria destroyed and plundered them. Beautiful and impressive on the outside, Nineveh was vicious and deceitful on the inside. Beneath attractive facades sometimes lie seduction and death. Don't let an institution, company, movement, or person seduce you into lowering your standards or compromising your moral principles.

Nah 3:8-10 Thebes was a city in Egypt, the previous world power, that had stood in the path of Assyria's expansion in the south. The Assyrians had conquered Thebes 51 years before this prophecy was given. To Judah, surrounded to the north and south by Assyria, the situation appeared hopeless. But God said that the same atrocities done in Thebes would happen in Nineveh.

Nah 3:8-10 No power on earth can protect us from God's judgment or be a suitable substitute for his power in our lives. Thebes and Assyria put their trust in alliances and military power, but history would show that these were inadequate. Don't insist on learning this through personal experience; instead, learn the lessons history has already taught. Put your trust in God above all else.

▸ **NAHUM 3:1-19** ***(cont.)***

Your people are scattered across the mountains
with no one to gather them together.
19 There is no healing for your wound;
your injury is fatal.
All who hear of your destruction
will clap their hands for joy.
Where can anyone be found
who has not suffered from your continual
cruelty?

N. The Prophecy of Habakkuk

Habakkuk's ministry probably occurred around the time of Assyria's fall in 612 B.C. When Habakkuk was troubled, he brought his concerns directly to God. After receiving God's answers, he responded with a prayer of faith. Habakkuk's example is one that should encourage us as we struggle to move from doubt to faith. We don't have to be afraid to ask questions of God. The problem is not with God and his ways but with our limited understanding of him.

1. HABAKKUK'S COMPLAINTS

Habakkuk looked at the world around him and saw violence and injustice everywhere. He didn't understand why God would allow such things to go on, and so he cried out to God, complaining about the situation and asking God to respond. It might seem presumptuous to ask God to explain himself, but God responded to Habakkuk's honest questions.

Habakkuk's Complaint

HABAKKUK 1:1-4

This is the message that the prophet Habakkuk received in a vision.

2 How long, O LORD, must I call for help?
But you do not listen!
"Violence is everywhere!" I cry,
but you do not come to save.
3 Must I forever see these evil deeds?
Why must I watch all this misery?
Wherever I look,
I see destruction and violence.
I am surrounded by people
who love to argue and fight.
4 The law has become paralyzed,
and there is no justice in the courts.
The wicked far outnumber the righteous,
so that justice has become perverted.

The LORD's Reply

HABAKKUK 1:5-11

The LORD replied,

"Look around at the nations;
look and be amazed!*

Hb 1:5 Greek version reads *Look, you mockers; / look and be amazed and die.* Compare Acts 13:41.

Nah 3:19 All the nations hated to be ruled by the merciless Assyrians, but the nations wanted to be like Assyria—powerful, wealthy, prestigious—and they courted Assyria's friendship. In the same way, we don't like the idea of being ruled harshly, so we do what we can to stay on good terms with a powerful leader. And deep down, we would like to have that power. But power is seductive, so we should not try to get or hold on to it. Those who lust after power will be powerfully destroyed, as was the mighty Assyrian Empire.

Hab 1:1 Habakkuk lived in Judah during the reign of Jehoiakim (2 Kgs 23:36–24:5). He prophesied around the time of the fall of Nineveh (the capital of Assyria) in 612 B.C. but before the Babylonian invasion of Judah in 588 B.C. With Assyria in disarray, Babylon was becoming the dominant world power. This book records the prophet's dialogue with God concerning two questions: Why does God often seem indifferent in the face of evil? and Why do evil people seem to go unpunished? While other prophetic books brought God's word to people, this book brought people's questions to God. A "vision" is a message from God.

HABAKKUK

Habakkuk served as a prophet to Judah from 612–589 B.C.

Climate of the times	Judah's last four kings were wicked men who rejected God and oppressed their own people. Babylon invaded Judah twice before finally destroying it in 586 B.C. It was a time of fear, oppression, persecution, lawlessness, and immorality.
Main message	Habakkuk couldn't understand why God seemed to do nothing about the wickedness in society. Then he realized that faith in God alone would supply the answers to his questions.
Importance of message	Instead of questioning the ways of God, we should realize that he is totally just and we should have faith that he is in control and that one day evil will be utterly destroyed.
Contemporary prophets	Jeremiah (627–586 B.C.), Daniel (605–536 B.C.), Ezekiel (593–571 B.C.)

Hab 1:2-4 Saddened by the violence and corruption he saw around him, Habakkuk poured out his heart to God. Today injustice is still rampant, but don't let your concern cause you to doubt God or rebel against him. Instead, consider the message that God gave Habakkuk and recognize God's long-range plans and purposes. Realize that God is doing right, even when you do not understand why he works as he does.

For I am doing something in your own day,
something you wouldn't believe
even if someone told you about it.
6 I am raising up the Babylonians,*
a cruel and violent people.
They will march across the world
and conquer other lands.
7 They are notorious for their cruelty
and do whatever they like.
8 Their horses are swifter than cheetahs*
and fiercer than wolves at dusk.
Their charioteers charge from far away.
Like eagles, they swoop down to devour
their prey.
9 "On they come, all bent on violence.
Their hordes advance like a desert wind,
sweeping captives ahead of them like sand.
10 They scoff at kings and princes
and scorn all their fortresses.
They simply pile ramps of earth
against their walls and capture them!
11 They sweep past like the wind
and are gone.
But they are deeply guilty,
for their own strength is their god."

Habakkuk's Second Complaint

HABAKKUK 1:12–2:1

12 O LORD my God, my Holy One, you who are
eternal—
surely you do not plan to wipe us out?
O LORD, our Rock, you have sent these
Babylonians to correct us,
to punish us for our many sins.
13 But you are pure and cannot stand the sight of evil.
Will you wink at their treachery?
Should you be silent while the wicked
swallow up people more righteous than they?
14 Are we only fish to be caught and killed?
Are we only sea creatures that have no leader?
15 Must we be strung up on their hooks
and caught in their nets while they rejoice and
celebrate?
16 Then they will worship their nets
and burn incense in front of them.
"These nets are the gods who have made us rich!"
they will claim.
17 Will you let them get away with this forever?
Will they succeed forever in their heartless
conquests?

2:1 I will climb up to my watchtower
and stand at my guardpost.
There I will wait to see what the LORD says
and how he* will answer my complaint.

The LORD's Second Reply

HABAKKUK 2:2-20

Then the LORD said to me,

"Write my answer plainly on tablets,
so that a runner can carry the correct message
to others.

Hb 1:6 Or *Chaldeans.* **Hb 1:8** Or *leopards.* **Hb 2:1** As in Syriac version; Hebrew reads *I.*

Nineveh destroyed

Hab 1:5 God responded to Habakkuk's questions and concerns by stating that he would do amazing acts that would astound Habakkuk. When circumstances around us become almost unbearable, we wonder if God has forgotten us. But remember, he is in control. God has a plan and will judge evildoers in his time. If we are truly humble, we will be willing to accept God's answers and await his timing.

Hab 1:5ff God told the inhabitants of Jerusalem that they would be utterly amazed at what he was about to do. The people would, in fact, see a series of unbelievable events: (1) Their own independent kingdom, Judah, would suddenly become a vassal nation; (2) Egypt, a world power for centuries, would be crushed almost overnight; (3) Nineveh, the capital of the Assyrian Empire, would be so completely ransacked that people would forget where it had been; and (4) the Babylonians would rise to power. Though these words were indeed amazing, the people saw them fulfilled during their lifetime.

Hab 1:6 The Babylonians, who lived northwest of the Persian Gulf, made a rapid rise to power around 630 B.C. They began to assert themselves against the Assyrian Empire and by 605 B.C. had conquered Assyria and Egypt to become the strongest world power. But they were as wicked as the Assyrians, for they loved to collect captives (Hab 1:9), were proud of their warfare tactics (Hab 1:10), and trusted in their military strength (Hab 1:11).

Hab 1:10 Armies were able to take walled cities by building earthen ramps—heaping mounds of earth against the walls.

Hab 1:11 Babylon was proud of its military might, strategies, armies, and weapons. With no regard for humanity, the armies brought home riches, plunder, prisoners, and tribute from the nations they conquered. Such is the essence of idolatry—asking the gods we make to help us get all we want. The essence of Christianity is asking the God who made us to help us give all we can in service to him. The goal of idolatry is self-glory; the aim of Christianity is God's glory.

Hab 1:13 Judah's forthcoming punishment would be at the hands of the Babylonians. Habakkuk was appalled that God would use a nation even more wicked than Judah to punish it. But the Babylonians did not know they were being used by God to help Judah return to him, and Babylon's pride in its victories would be its downfall. Evil is self-destructive, and it is never beyond God's control. God may use whatever unusual instrument he chooses to correct or punish us. When we deserve punishment or correction, how can we complain about the kind of discipline God uses on us?

Hab 2:1 The watchman and watchtower, often used by the prophets to show an attitude of expectation (Isa 21:8, 11; Jer 6:17; Ezek 3:17), are pictures of Habakkuk's attitude of patient waiting and watching for God's response. Stone watchtowers were built on city walls or ramparts so that watchmen could see people (enemies or messengers) approaching their city while still at a distance. Watchtowers were also erected in vineyards to help guard the ripening grapes (Isa 5:2). Habakkuk wanted to be in the best position to receive God's message.

Hab 2:2ff This chapter records God's answers to Habakkuk's questions: (1) How long would evil prevail (Hab 1:2-3)? (2) Why was Babylon chosen to punish Judah (Hab 1:13)? God said that the judgment, though slow to come, was certain. Although God used Babylon against Judah, he knew Babylon's sins and would punish it in due time.

▶ **HABAKKUK 2:2-20** ***(cont.)***

3 This vision is for a future time.
It describes the end, and it will be fulfilled.
If it seems slow in coming, wait patiently,
for it will surely take place.
It will not be delayed.

4 "Look at the proud!
They trust in themselves, and their lives are crooked.
But the righteous will live by their faithfulness to God.*
5 Wealth* is treacherous,
and the arrogant are never at rest.
They open their mouths as wide as the grave,*
and like death, they are never satisfied.
In their greed they have gathered up many nations
and swallowed many peoples.

6 "But soon their captives will taunt them.
They will mock them, saying,
'What sorrow awaits you thieves!
Now you will get what you deserve!
You've become rich by extortion,
but how much longer can this go on?'
7 Suddenly, your debtors will take action.
They will turn on you and take all you have,
while you stand trembling and helpless.
8 Because you have plundered many nations,
now all the survivors will plunder you.
You committed murder throughout the countryside
and filled the towns with violence.

9 "What sorrow awaits you who build big houses
with money gained dishonestly!
You believe your wealth will buy security,
putting your family's nest beyond the reach of danger.
10 But by the murders you committed,
you have shamed your name and forfeited your lives.
11 The very stones in the walls cry out against you,
and the beams in the ceilings echo the complaint.

12 "What sorrow awaits you who build cities
with money gained through murder and corruption!
13 Has not the LORD of Heaven's Armies promised
that the wealth of nations will turn to ashes?
They work so hard,
but all in vain!
14 For as the waters fill the sea,
the earth will be filled with an awareness
of the glory of the LORD.

Hb 2:3b-4 Greek version reads *If the vision is delayed, wait patiently, / for it will surely come and not delay. /* [4] *I will take no pleasure in anyone who turns away. / But the righteous person will live by my faith.* Compare Rom 1:17; Gal 3:11; Heb 10:37-38. **Hb 2:5a** As in Dead Sea Scroll 1QpHab; other Hebrew manuscripts read *Wine.* **Hb 2:5b** Hebrew *as Sheol.*

Hab 2:3 Evil and injustice seem to have the upper hand in the world. Like Habakkuk, Christians often feel angry and discouraged as they see what goes on. Habakkuk complained vigorously to God about the situation. God's answer to Habakkuk is the same answer he would give us, "If it seems slow in coming, wait patiently, for it will surely take place." It isn't easy to be patient, but it helps to remember that God hates sin even more than we do. Punishment of sin will certainly come. As God told Habakkuk, "Wait patiently." We must trust God even when we don't understand why events occur as they do.

Hab 2:4 The wicked Babylonians trusted in themselves and would fall; but the righteous will live by their faithfulness to God. This verse has inspired countless Christians. Paul quotes it in Romans 1:17 and Galatians 3:11. The writer of Hebrews quotes it in 10:38, just before the famous chapter on faith. And it is helpful to all Christians who must live through difficult times without seeing signs of hope. Christians must trust that God is directing all things according to his purposes.

Hab 2:9-13 Babylon's riches had come from the misfortunes of others, but these riches would only be fuel for the fire. The victims and their cities would cry out against Babylon. Money is not evil, but God condemns the love of riches and the evil means of acquiring them (1 Tim 6:10). Be careful not to hunger for wealth so much that you lose your appetite for God. Do not allow money to take the place of family, friends, or God.

Ancient Commentary on Habakkuk

Eleven caves of Qumran have yielded 600 manuscripts, 200 of which are biblical. One of the most interesting finds is this scroll, which preserves the book of Habakkuk with a commentary. In this commentary the enemies of God's people are called the Kittim, who are the Romans. Thus, the Habakkuk commentary was probably written about the time of the Roman capture of Palestine under Pompey in 63 B.C.

Hab 2:18 Idolatry may seem like a sin that modern people do not commit. But idolatry is not just bowing down to idols; it is trusting in what one has made and, therefore, in one's own power as creator and sustainer. If we say we worship God but put our trust in bank accounts, homes, businesses, and organizations, then we are idolaters. Do you trust God more than you trust what your hands have made?

Hab 2:20 Idols have no life, no personhood, no power; they are empty chunks of wood or stone. Temples built to idols are equally empty; no one lives there. But the Lord is in his Temple. He is real, alive, and powerful. He is truly and fully God. Idolaters command their idols to save them, but we who worship the living God come to him in silent awe and reverence. We acknowledge that God is in control and knows what he is doing. Idols remain silent because they cannot answer. The living God, by contrast, speaks through his Word. Approach God reverently and wait silently to hear what he has to say.

15 "What sorrow awaits you who make your
neighbors drunk!
You force your cup on them
so you can gloat over their shameful
nakedness.
16 But soon it will be your turn to be
disgraced.
Come, drink and be exposed!*
Drink from the cup of the LORD's
judgment,
and all your glory will be turned
to shame.
17 You cut down the forests of Lebanon.
Now you will be cut down.
You destroyed the wild animals,
so now their terror will be yours.
You committed murder throughout the
countryside
and filled the towns with violence.
18 "What good is an idol carved by man,
or a cast image that deceives you?
How foolish to trust in your own creation—
a god that can't even talk!
19 What sorrow awaits you who say to wooden idols,
'Wake up and save us!'
To speechless stone images you say,
'Rise up and teach us!'
Can an idol tell you what to do?
They may be overlaid with gold and silver,
but they are lifeless inside.
20 But the LORD is in his holy Temple.
Let all the earth be silent before him."

Hb 2:16 Dead Sea Scrolls and Greek and Syriac versions read *and stagger!*

2. HABAKKUK'S RESPONSE

Upon hearing God's responses to his complaints, Habakkuk responded in precisely the right way: with awe-filled worship and prayer.

Habakkuk's Prayer

HABAKKUK 3:1-19

This prayer was sung by the prophet Habakkuk*:

2 I have heard all about you, LORD.
I am filled with awe by your amazing works.
In this time of our deep need,
help us again as you did in years gone by.
And in your anger,
remember your mercy.

3 I see God moving across the deserts from Edom,*
the Holy One coming from Mount Paran.*
His brilliant splendor fills the heavens,
and the earth is filled with his praise.
4 His coming is as brilliant as the sunrise.
Rays of light flash from his hands,
where his awesome power is hidden.
5 Pestilence marches before him;
plague follows close behind.
6 When he stops, the earth shakes.
When he looks, the nations tremble.
He shatters the everlasting mountains
and levels the eternal hills.
He is the Eternal One!
7 I see the people of Cushan in distress,
and the nation of Midian trembling in terror.
8 Was it in anger, LORD, that you struck the rivers
and parted the sea?
Were you displeased with them?
No, you were sending your chariots of
salvation!
9 You brandished your bow
and your quiver of arrows.
You split open the earth with flowing
rivers.
10 The mountains watched and trembled.
Onward swept the raging waters.
The mighty deep cried out,
lifting its hands to the LORD.
11 The sun and moon stood still in the sky
as your brilliant arrows flew
and your glittering spear flashed.
12 You marched across the land in anger
and trampled the nations in your fury.
13 You went out to rescue your chosen people,
to save your anointed ones.
You crushed the heads of the wicked
and stripped their bones from head to toe.
14 With his own weapons,
you destroyed the chief of those
who rushed out like a whirlwind,
thinking Israel would be easy prey.

Hb 3:1 Hebrew adds *according to shigionoth,* probably indicating the musical setting for the prayer. **Hb 3:3a** Hebrew *Teman.* **Hb 3:3b** Hebrew adds *selah;* also in 3:9, 13. The meaning of this Hebrew term is uncertain; it is probably a musical or literary term.

Hab 3:1ff Habakkuk praised God for answering his questions. Evil will not triumph forever; God is in control, and he can be completely trusted to vindicate those who are faithful to him. We must patiently wait for him to act (Hab 3:16).

Hab 3:2 Habakkuk knew that God was going to discipline the people of Judah and that it wasn't going to be a pleasant experience. But Habakkuk accepted God's will, asking for help and mercy. Habakkuk did not ask to escape the discipline, but he accepted the truth that Judah needed to learn a lesson. God still disciplines in love to bring his children back to him (Heb 12:5-6). Accept God's discipline gladly, and ask him to help you change.

▸ **HABAKKUK 3:1-19** ***(cont.)***

15 You trampled the sea with your horses,
and the mighty waters piled high.

16 I trembled inside when I heard this;
my lips quivered with fear.
My legs gave way beneath me,*
and I shook in terror.
I will wait quietly for the coming day
when disaster will strike the people
who invade us.
17 Even though the fig trees have no blossoms,
and there are no grapes on the vines;
even though the olive crop fails,
and the fields lie empty and barren;
even though the flocks die in the fields,
and the cattle barns are empty,
18 yet I will rejoice in the LORD!
I will be joyful in the God of my
salvation!
19 The Sovereign LORD is my strength!
He makes me as surefooted as a deer,*
able to tread upon the heights.

(For the choir director: This prayer is to be accompanied by stringed instruments.)

Hb 3:16 Hebrew *Decay entered my bones.* **Hb 3:19** Or *He gives me the speed of a deer.*

O. The Prophecy of Zephaniah

Zephaniah's ministry probably took place around the time of Assyria's fall in 612 B.C. Zephaniah warned the people of Judah that if they refused to repent, the entire nation, including the beloved city of Jerusalem, would be lost. The people knew that God would eventually bless them, but Zephaniah made it clear that there would be judgment first, then blessing. This judgment would not be merely punishment for sin, but it would also be a means of purifying the people. Though we live in a fallen world surrounded by evil, we can hope in the perfect Kingdom of God to come, and we can allow any punishment that touches us now to purify us from sin.

Coming Judgment against Judah

ZEPHANIAH 1:1-18

The LORD gave this message to Zephaniah when Josiah son of Amon was king of Judah. Zephaniah was the son of Cushi, son of Gedaliah, son of Amariah, son of Hezekiah.

2 "I will sweep away everything
from the face of the earth," says the LORD.
3 "I will sweep away people and animals alike.
I will sweep away the birds of the sky and the
fish in the sea.
I will reduce the wicked to heaps of rubble,*
and I will wipe humanity from the face of the
earth," says the LORD.
4 "I will crush Judah and Jerusalem with my fist
and destroy every last trace of their Baal
worship.
I will put an end to all the idolatrous priests,
so that even the memory of them will disappear.

Zep 1:3 The meaning of the Hebrew is uncertain.

Hab 3:17-19 Crop failure and the death of animals would devastate Judah. But Habakkuk affirmed that even in the times of starvation and loss, he would still rejoice in the Lord. Habakkuk's feelings were not controlled by the events around him but by faith in God's ability to give him strength. When nothing makes sense, and when troubles seem more than you can bear, remember that God gives strength. Take your eyes off your difficulties and look to God.

Hab 3:19 God will give his followers strength and confidence in difficult times. They will run surefooted as deer across rough and dangerous terrain. At the proper time, God will bring about his justice and completely rid the world of evil. In the meantime, God's people need to live in the strength of his Spirit, confident in his ultimate victory over evil.

Hab 3:19 The note to the choir director was to be used when this passage was sung as a psalm in Temple worship.

Hab 3:19 Habakkuk had asked God why evil people prosper while the righteous suffer. God's answer: They don't, not in the long run. Habakkuk saw his own limitations in contrast to God's unlimited power and control of all the world's events. God is alive and in control of the world and its events. We cannot see all that God is doing, and we cannot see all that God will do. But we can be assured that he is God and will do what is right. Knowing this can give us confidence and hope in a confusing world.

Zeph 1:1 Zephaniah prophesied in the days of Josiah king of Judah (640–609 B.C.). Josiah followed God, and during his reign the Book of the Law was discovered in the Temple. After reading it, Josiah began a great religious revival in Judah (2 Kgs 22:1–23:25). Zephaniah helped fan the revival by warning the people that judgment would come if they did not turn from their sins. Although this great revival turned the nation back to God, it did not fully eliminate idolatry and lasted only a short time. Just four years after Josiah's death, Nebuchadnezzar swept into Palestine and took the first wave of Israelite captives into exile.

Zeph 1:2ff The people of Judah were clearly warned by the highest authority of all—God. They refused to listen, either because they doubted God's prophet and thus did not believe that the message was from God, or because they doubted God himself and thus did not believe that he would do what he said. If we refuse to listen to God's Word, the Bible, we are as shortsighted as the people of Judah, and like them, we will be punished.

Zeph 1:4 When the Israelites arrived in the Promised Land, God had commanded that they completely rid the land of its pagan inhabitants who worshiped idols. But the Israelites failed to do so, and gradually they began to worship the Canaanites' gods. The Canaanites believed in many gods that represented various aspects of life, and the chief god was Baal, symbolizing strength and fertility. God was extremely angry when his people turned from him to Baal.

5 For they go up to their roofs
and bow down to the sun, moon, and stars.
They claim to follow the LORD,
but then they worship Molech,* too.
6 And I will destroy those who used to worship me
but now no longer do.
They no longer ask for the LORD's guidance
or seek my blessings."

7 Stand in silence in the presence of the
Sovereign LORD,
for the awesome day of the LORD's judgment
is near.
The LORD has prepared his people for a great
slaughter
and has chosen their executioners.*
8 "On that day of judgment,"
says the LORD,
"I will punish the leaders and princes of Judah
and all those following pagan customs.
9 Yes, I will punish those who participate in pagan
worship ceremonies,
and those who fill their masters' houses with
violence and deceit.

10 "On that day," says the LORD,
"a cry of alarm will come from the
Fish Gate
and echo throughout the New Quarter
of the city.*
And a great crash will sound from
the hills.
11 Wail in sorrow, all you who live in the
market area,
for all the merchants and traders will be
destroyed.

12 "I will search with lanterns in Jerusalem's
darkest corners
to punish those who sit complacent in
their sins.
They think the LORD will do nothing to them,
either good or bad.
13 So their property will be plundered,
their homes will be ransacked.
They will build new homes
but never live in them.
They will plant vineyards
but never drink wine from them.

Zep 1:5 Hebrew *Malcam,* a variant spelling of Molech; or it could possibly mean *their king.* **Zep 1:7** Hebrew *has prepared a sacrifice and sanctified his guests.* **Zep 1:10** Or *the Second Quarter,* a newer section of Jerusalem. Hebrew reads *the Mishneh.*

ZEPHANIAH

Zephaniah served as a prophet to Judah from 640–621 B.C.

Climate of the times	Josiah was the last good king in Judah. His bold attempts to reform the nation and turn it back to God were probably influenced by Zephaniah.
Main message	A day will come when God, as judge, will severely punish all nations. But after judgment, he will show mercy to all who have been faithful to him.
Importance of message	We will all be judged for our disobedience to God; but if we remain faithful to him, he will show us mercy.
Contemporary prophet	Jeremiah (627–586 B.C.)

Zeph 1:4-6 Idols have been worshiped down through history. More than just a stone statue, an idol can be anything reverenced more than God. Thus, idol worship is prevalent even today: People trust in themselves, money, or power but not in God. Ultimately all idols will prove worthless, and the true God will prevail. Seek God first (Matt 6:33), and have no other gods before him (Exod 20:3).

Zeph 1:5 The people had become polytheistic, worshiping the Lord *and* all the other gods of the land. They added the "best" of pagan worship to the worship of God. But God commands that he alone be worshiped (Exod 20:1-5); thus, the people committed a horrible sin. One of these other gods was Molech, the national god of the Ammonites. The worship of Molech included child sacrifice, an abominable sin. From the time of Moses, the Israelites had been warned about worshiping this false god (Lev 18:21; 20:5), but they refused to take heed. Because of their sins, God would destroy them.

Zeph 1:7 A day of judgment and great slaughter occurred during the lifetime of these people when Babylon invaded the land. The prophet saw these prophecies as future events, but he could not see when or in what order these events would take place. Many think that these prophecies have a double fulfillment—one for the near future (soon after the prophecy was made) and another for the distant future (possibly during the end times). Some scholars believe that these prophecies of judgment refer to events entirely in the future.

Zeph 1:8-9 Following pagan customs involved not only imitating foreign ways but also worshiping foreign gods. Leaders who should have been good examples to the people were adopting foreign practices and thus showing their contempt for the Lord by ignoring his commands against adopting the pagan culture.

Zeph 1:12 God would search the city with lanterns and punish those who deserved punishment. Because they did not search their own hearts and because they were content with the moral chaos around them and indifferent to God, God would use the Babylonians to judge them. Within 20 years, the Babylonians would enter Jerusalem, drag people out of hiding, and take them captive or kill them. No one would escape God's judgment; there would be no place to hide.

Zeph 1:12-14 Some people think of God as an indulgent heavenly grandfather, nice to have around but not a real force in shaping modern life. They don't believe in his power or his coming judgment. But God is holy, and therefore he will actively judge and justly punish everyone who is content to live in sin, indifferent to him, or unconcerned about justice. When people are indifferent to God, they tend to think that he is indifferent to them and their sin. They will be surprised to find that the "terrible day of the LORD is near."

▸ **ZEPHANIAH 1:1-18** ***(cont.)***

14 "That terrible day of the LORD is near.
Swiftly it comes—
a day of bitter tears,
a day when even strong men will cry out.
15 It will be a day when the LORD's anger is poured out—
a day of terrible distress and anguish,
a day of ruin and desolation,
a day of darkness and gloom,
a day of clouds and blackness,
16 a day of trumpet calls and battle cries.
Down go the walled cities
and the strongest battlements!
17 "Because you have sinned against the LORD,
I will make you grope around like the blind.
Your blood will be poured into the dust,
and your bodies will lie rotting on the ground."

18 Your silver and gold will not save you
on that day of the LORD's anger.
For the whole land will be devoured
by the fire of his jealousy.
He will make a terrifying end
of all the people on earth.*

A Call to Repentance

ZEPHANIAH 2:1-3

1 Gather together—yes, gather together,
you shameless nation.
2 Gather before judgment begins,
before your time to repent is blown away like chaff.
Act now, before the fierce fury of the LORD falls
and the terrible day of the LORD's anger begins.
3 Seek the LORD, all who are humble,
and follow his commands.
Seek to do what is right
and to live humbly.
Perhaps even yet the LORD will protect you—
protect you from his anger on that day of destruction.

Judgment against Philistia

ZEPHANIAH 2:4-7

4 Gaza and Ashkelon will be abandoned,
Ashdod and Ekron torn down.
5 And what sorrow awaits you Philistines*
who live along the coast and in the land of Canaan,
for this judgment is against you, too!
The LORD will destroy you
until not one of you is left.
6 The Philistine coast will become a wilderness pasture,
a place of shepherd camps
and enclosures for sheep and goats.
7 The remnant of the tribe of Judah will pasture there.
They will rest at night in the abandoned houses in Ashkelon.
For the LORD their God will visit his people in kindness
and restore their prosperity again.

Judgment against Moab and Ammon

ZEPHANIAH 2:8-11

8 "I have heard the taunts of the Moabites
and the insults of the Ammonites,
mocking my people
and invading their borders.

Zep 1:18 Or *the people living in the land.* **Zep 2:5** Hebrew *Kerethites.*

Zeph 1:14-18 The day of the Lord was near; the Babylonians would soon come and destroy Jerusalem. The day of the Lord is also near for us. God promises a final judgment, a day of worldwide destruction (Rev 20:12-15). The Babylonian conquest occurred just as surely and horribly as Zephaniah had predicted. And God's final day of judgment is also sure—but so is his ability to save. To be spared from judgment, recognize that you have sinned, that your sin will bring judgment, that you cannot save yourself, and that God alone can save you.

Zeph 1:18 Money is not evil in itself, but it is useless to save us. In this life, money can warp our perspective, giving us feelings of security and power. Just as the Israelites' wealth could not save them from the Babylonian invasion, so at the final judgment, our riches will be worthless. Only Christ's redemptive work on our behalf matters for eternity. Christ alone will ransom us if we believe in him. Don't trust money; trust Christ.

Zeph 2:1-3 There was still time for the people to avert God's judgment. They simply had to turn from their sins, humble themselves, and obey God. The Old Testament prophets announced news of destruction, but they also offered the only means of escape and protection—turning from sin and walking with God (see also Mic 6:8).

Zeph 2:4 The four cities mentioned here are in Philistia, the nation southwest of Judah on the coast of the Mediterranean Sea. Age-old enemies of Israel from the days of Joshua, the Philistines were known for their cruelty. God judged these cities for their idolatry and their constant taunting of Israel. These four cities were four of the five capitals. The fifth (Gath) had probably already been destroyed.

Zeph 2:7 All the prophets, even while prophesying doom and destruction, speak of "the remnant"—a small group of God's people who remain faithful to him and whom God will restore to the land. Although God said he would destroy Judah, he also promised to save some, thus keeping his original covenant to preserve Abraham's descendants (Gen 17:4-8). Because God is holy, he cannot allow sin to continue. But God is also faithful to his promises. He cannot stay angry forever with Israel or with you, if you are his child, because he loves his children and always seeks their good.

Zeph 2:8 The Moabites and Ammonites lived to the east of Judah, and they often ridiculed and attacked Judah. These nations worshiped Chemosh and Molech (1 Kgs 11:7). Moab's king once sacrificed his son on the city wall to stop an invasion (2 Kgs 3:26-27). God would judge these nations for their wickedness and for their treatment of his people.

Zeph 2:8-11 Judah had been taunted and mocked by the neighboring nations, Moab and Ammon, but God reminded them that he had "heard the taunts" (Zeph 2:8), and that the taunters would be punished for their pride (Zeph 2:10). At times the whole world

9 Now, as surely as I live,"
says the LORD of Heaven's Armies, the God of Israel,
"Moab and Ammon will be destroyed—
destroyed as completely as Sodom and Gomorrah.
Their land will become a place of stinging nettles,
salt pits, and eternal desolation.
The remnant of my people will plunder them
and take their land."
10 They will receive the wages of their pride,
for they have scoffed at the people of the LORD of Heaven's Armies.
11 The LORD will terrify them
as he destroys all the gods in the land.
Then nations around the world will worship the LORD,
each in their own land.

Judgment against Ethiopia and Assyria

ZEPHANIAH 2:12-15

12 "You Ethiopians* will also be slaughtered
by my sword," says the LORD.

13 And the LORD will strike the lands of the north with his fist,
destroying the land of Assyria.
He will make its great capital, Nineveh, a desolate wasteland,
parched like a desert.
14 The proud city will become a pasture for flocks and herds,
and all sorts of wild animals will settle there.
The desert owl and screech owl will roost on its ruined columns,
their calls echoing through the gaping windows.
Rubble will block all the doorways,
and the cedar paneling will be exposed to the weather.
15 This is the boisterous city,
once so secure.
"I am the greatest!" it boasted.
"No other city can compare with me!"
But now, look how it has become an utter ruin,
a haven for wild animals.
Everyone passing by will laugh in derision
and shake a defiant fist.

Jerusalem's Rebellion and Redemption

ZEPHANIAH 3:1-20

1 What sorrow awaits rebellious, polluted Jerusalem,
the city of violence and crime!
2 No one can tell it anything;
it refuses all correction.
It does not trust in the LORD
or draw near to its God.
3 Its leaders are like roaring lions
hunting for their victims.
Its judges are like ravenous wolves at evening time,
who by dawn have left no trace of their prey.

Zep 2:12 Hebrew *Cushites.*

seems to mock God and those who have faith in him. When you are ridiculed, remember that God hears and will answer. Eventually, in God's timing, justice will be carried out.

Zeph 2:9 The nations of Moab and Ammon trace their roots to Lot's incest with his daughters after escaping the destruction of evil Sodom and Gomorrah (Gen 19). Ironically, Moab and Ammon would be the same kind of perpetual wasteland that God had made those evil cities. Sodom and Gomorrah were so completely destroyed that their exact location is still unknown.

Zeph 2:12 Ethiopia, at the southern end of the Red Sea, controlled Egypt at this time. No one can escape deserved judgment. The Ethiopians were also "slaughtered by my sword" when the Babylonians invaded Egypt in 605 B.C. (See Isa 18; Ezek 30:9 for other prophecies concerning Ethiopia.)

Zeph 2:13 Zephaniah mentioned the large nation to the south and then moved to the nation that invaded from the north, Assyria. Though declining, Assyria was still the strongest military power of the day, dominating the world for three centuries and destroying any nation in its path. Nineveh, the large capital city, was considered impregnable. However, just as Zephaniah predicted, Nineveh was wiped out in 612 B.C. by the Babylonians, who would become the next world power.

Zeph 2:13-15 To predict the destruction of Nineveh before it happened would be equivalent to predicting the destruction of London, Tokyo, Paris, or New York. Nineveh was the ancient Near Eastern center for culture, technology, and beauty. It had great libraries, buildings, and a vast irrigation system that created lush gardens in the city. The city wall was 60 miles long, 100 feet high, and over 30 feet wide and was fortified with 1,500 towers. Yet the entire city was destroyed so completely that its very existence was questioned until it was discovered, with great difficulty, by 19th-century archaeologists. Nineveh had indeed become as desolate and dry as the desert.

Zeph 3:1ff After predicting the destruction of the surrounding nations, Zephaniah returned to the problem at hand—sin in Jerusalem. The city of God, and God's people themselves, had become "polluted"—as sinful as their pagan neighbors. The people pretended to worship and serve God, but in their hearts they had rejected him and continued to be complacent about their sins. They no longer cared about the consequences of turning away from God.

Zeph 3:2 Do you know people who refuse to listen when someone disagrees with their opinions? Their root problem is pride—inflated self-esteem. God's people had become so proud that they would not even listen to God's voice. Do you find it difficult to listen to the spiritual counsel of others or God's words from the Bible? Don't let pride make you unable or unwilling to let God work in your life. You will be more willing to listen when you consider how weak and sinful you really are compared to God.

Zeph 3:3-4 Leading God's people is a privilege and a responsibility. Through Zephaniah, God rebuked many different leaders in Jerusalem—judges, prophets, and priests—because of their callous disobedience, irresponsibility, and sin. If you are a leader in the church, consider yourself in a privileged position, but be careful. God holds you responsible for the purity of your actions, the quality of your example, and the truth of your words.

▸ **ZEPHANIAH 3:1-20** *(cont.)*

4 Its prophets are arrogant liars seeking their
own gain.
Its priests defile the Temple by disobeying
God's instructions.
5 But the LORD is still there in the city,
and he does no wrong.
Day by day he hands down justice,
and he does not fail.
But the wicked know no shame.

6 "I have wiped out many nations,
devastating their fortress walls and
towers.
Their streets are now deserted;
their cities lie in silent ruin.
There are no survivors—
none at all.
7 I thought, 'Surely they will have reverence
for me now!
Surely they will listen to my warnings.
Then I won't need to strike again,
destroying their homes.'
But no, they get up early
to continue their evil deeds.
8 Therefore, be patient," says the LORD.
"Soon I will stand and accuse these evil
nations.
For I have decided to gather the kingdoms
of the earth
and pour out my fiercest anger and fury
on them.
All the earth will be devoured
by the fire of my jealousy.

9 "Then I will purify the speech of all people,
so that everyone can worship the LORD
together.
10 My scattered people who live beyond the rivers
of Ethiopia*
will come to present their offerings.
11 On that day you will no longer need to be
ashamed,
for you will no longer be rebels against me.
I will remove all proud and arrogant people from
among you.
There will be no more haughtiness on my holy
mountain.
12 Those who are left will be the lowly and humble,
for it is they who trust in the name of the LORD.
13 The remnant of Israel will do no wrong;
they will never tell lies or deceive one another.
They will eat and sleep in safety,
and no one will make them afraid."

14 Sing, O daughter of Zion;
shout aloud, O Israel!
Be glad and rejoice with all your heart,
O daughter of Jerusalem!
15 For the LORD will remove his hand of judgment
and will disperse the armies of your enemy.
And the LORD himself, the King of Israel,
will live among you!
At last your troubles will be over,
and you will never again fear disaster.
16 On that day the announcement to Jerusalem will be,
"Cheer up, Zion! Don't be afraid!
17 For the LORD your God is living among you.
He is a mighty savior.
He will take delight in you with gladness.
With his love, he will calm all your fears.*
He will rejoice over you with joyful songs."

18 "I will gather you who mourn for the appointed
festivals;
you will be disgraced no more.*

Zep 3:10 Hebrew *Cush.* **Zep 3:17** Or *He will be silent in his love.* Greek and Syriac versions read *He will renew you with his love.* **Zep 3:18** The meaning of the Hebrew for this verse is uncertain.

Zeph 3:5 Jerusalem's citizens, of all people, had no excuse for their sins. Jerusalem, where the Temple was located, was the religious center of the nation. But even though the people didn't follow God, God was still there in the city, present in the midst of corruption, persecution, and unbelief. No matter how spiritually desolate the world seems, God is here, and he is at work. Ask yourself, What is he doing now, and how can I be part of his work?

Zeph 3:7 We may wonder how the Israelites could have had such clear warnings and still not turn to God. The problem was that they had allowed sin to so harden them that they no longer cared to follow God. They refused to heed God's warnings, and they refused to repent. The more God punished them, the more they sinned. If you are living in disobedience to God now, your heart may grow hard, and you may lose all desire for God.

Zeph 3:8 In the last days, God will judge all people according to what they have done (Rev 20:12). Justice will prevail; evildoers will be punished; and the obedient will be blessed. Don't try to avenge yourself. Be patient, and God's justice will come.

Zeph 3:9 God will purify speech and unify language so that all his people from all nations will be able to worship him together. In the new earth, all believers will be able to understand each other; the confusion of languages at the tower of Babel (Gen 11) will be reversed. God will purify our hearts, so that the words coming from our lips will be pure as well.

Zeph 3:10 The "scattered people" refers to Jews dispersed beyond the rivers of Ethiopia. It symbolizes that all Jews, no matter how far they have been scattered, will return to worship God.

Zeph 3:11-12 God will remove the proud people and leave the lowly and humble. God is opposed to the proud and arrogant of every generation. But those who are lowly and humble, both physically and spiritually, will be rewarded because they trust in God. Self-reliance and arrogance have no place among God's people or in his Kingdom.

Zeph 3:14-18 The Lord himself will remove his hand of judgment, disperse Israel's enemies, and come to live among his people. He will give them gladness. Zephaniah points out that gladness results when we allow God to be with us. We do that by faithfully following him and obeying his commands. Then God rejoices over us with singing. If you want to be happy, draw close to the source of happiness by obeying God.

19 And I will deal severely with all who have
oppressed you.
I will save the weak and helpless ones;
I will bring together
those who were chased away.
I will give glory and fame to my former exiles,
wherever they have been mocked and shamed.
20 On that day I will gather you together
and bring you home again.
I will give you a good name, a name of
distinction,
among all the nations of the earth,
as I restore your fortunes before their very eyes.
I, the LORD, have spoken!"

P. The Era of Judah's Destruction

Judah had rebelled against God for the great majority of their existence as a nation, ignoring his law and worshiping other gods. He loves his people immeasurably, but his love does not preclude judgment. God raised up the Babylonian Empire to be his mighty arm of judgment, and they harrassed Judah for over 20 years before finally destroying Jerusalem and carrying the people off into exile. There were three deportations to Babylon: Daniel was among those taken to Babylon in the first deportation in 605 B.C., Ezekiel was among those taken in the second deportation in 597 B.C., and the nation was finally destroyed in 586 B.C. Jeremiah was active in prophesying to the kings in Judah throughout this time, and he was among the few people of Judah left behind in the wake of Babylon's destruction.

1. EGYPT DOMINATES JUDAH

Pharaoh Neco of Egypt wanted to help the waning Assyrian Empire to hold off Babylonian domination, and so he decided to march north past Judah to assist Assyria in battle. Josiah, however, decided to try to stop Egypt from intervening and was himself killed in battle with Egypt. This led to a four year period when Egypt dominated Judah.

Josiah Dies in Battle PARALLEL

2 KINGS 23:29-30

While Josiah was king, Pharaoh Neco, king of Egypt, went to the Euphrates River to help the king of Assyria. King Josiah and his army marched out to fight him,* but King Neco* killed him when they met at Megiddo. 30Josiah's officers took his body back in a chariot from Megiddo to Jerusalem and buried him in his own tomb. Then the people of the land anointed Josiah's son Jehoahaz and made him the next king.

2 Kgs 23:29a Or *Josiah went out to meet him.* **2 Kgs 23:29b** Hebrew *he.*

2 CHRONICLES 35:20-27

After Josiah had finished restoring the Temple, King Neco of Egypt led his army up from Egypt to do battle

Megiddo

Megiddo is a city in northern Israel right on the main route between Mesopotamia and Egypt. It overlooks the historic route where a pass through Mt. Carmel led from the plain of Sharon into the plain of Jezreel. This strategic position made Megiddo one of the most important commercial and military centers of the world in the second millennium and the early first millennium B.C. From earliest times, the environs have been the scene of major battles. The book of Revelation predicts a great future war that will take place there (Rev 16:16). The world has come to know this as the battle of Armageddon, a future event feared by all. But we can trust that God is in control of the future.

Zeph 3:20 "Before their very eyes" does not necessarily mean that this promise would be fulfilled during Zephaniah's generation. Rather, it means that the restoration will be an obvious work of the Lord.

Zeph 3:20 The message of doom in the beginning of the book becomes a message of hope by the end. There will be a new day when God will bless his people. If the leaders in the church today were to hear a message from a prophet of God, the message would probably resemble the book of Zephaniah. Under Josiah's religious reforms, the people did return to God outwardly, but their hearts were far from him. Zephaniah encouraged the nation to gather together and pray for salvation. We must also ask ourselves: Is our reform merely an outward show, or is it changing our hearts and lives? We need to gather together and pray, to walk humbly with God, to do what is right, and to hear the message of hope regarding the new world to come.

2 Chr 35:20 This event occurred in 609 B.C. Nineveh, the Assyrian capital, had been destroyed three years earlier by the Babylonians. The defeated Assyrians regrouped at Haran and Carchemish, but Babylon sent its army to destroy them once and for all. Pharaoh Neco, who wanted to make Egypt a world power, was worried about Babylon's growing strength, so he marched his army north through Judah to help the Assyrians at Carchemish. But King Josiah of Judah tried to prevent Neco from passing through his land on his way to Carchemish. Josiah may have thought that both nations would turn on him after the battle with Babylon, but instead Josiah was killed, and Judah became a vassal state to Egypt. Neco went on to Carchemish and held off the Babylonians for four years, but in 605 he was soundly defeated, and Babylon moved into the spotlight as the dominant world power.

▶ **2 CHRONICLES 35:20-27** ***(cont.)***
at Carchemish on the Euphrates River, and Josiah and
his army marched out to fight him.* 21But King Neco
sent messengers to Josiah with this message:

"What do you want with me, king of Judah? I
have no quarrel with you today! I am on my way
to fight another nation, and God has told me to
hurry! Do not interfere with God, who is with me,
or he will destroy you."

22But Josiah refused to listen to Neco, to whom
God had indeed spoken, and he would not turn back.
Instead, he disguised himself and led his army into
battle on the plain of Megiddo. 23But the enemy archers hit King Josiah with their arrows and wounded
him. He cried out to his men, "Take me from the battle,
for I am badly wounded!"
24So they lifted Josiah out of his chariot and placed
him in another chariot. Then they brought him back to
Jerusalem, where he died. He was buried there in the
royal cemetery. And all Judah and Jerusalem mourned
for him. 25The prophet Jeremiah composed funeral
songs for Josiah, and to this day choirs still sing these
sad songs about his death. These songs of sorrow have
become a tradition and are recorded in *The Book of
Laments*.
26The rest of the events of Josiah's reign and his
609 BC acts of devotion (carried out according to what was
written in the Law of the LORD), 27from beginning to
end—all are recorded in *The Book of the Kings of Israel
and Judah*.

Neco kills Josiah in battle

2 Chr 35:20 Or *Josiah went out to meet him.* **Jer 47:4** Hebrew *from Caphtor.* **Jer 47:5** Hebrew *the plain.*

Jeremiah's Message about Philistia

JEREMIAH 47:1-7
This is the LORD's message to the prophet Jeremiah
concerning the Philistines of Gaza, before it was captured by the Egyptian army. 2This is what the LORD says:

"A flood is coming from the north
to overflow the land.
It will destroy the land and everything in it—
cities and people alike.
People will scream in terror,
and everyone in the land will wail.
3 Hear the clatter of stallions' hooves
and the rumble of wheels as the chariots
rush by.
Terrified fathers run madly,
without a backward glance at their helpless
children.
4 "The time has come for the Philistines to be
destroyed,
along with their allies from Tyre and Sidon.
Yes, the LORD is destroying the remnant of the
Philistines,
those colonists from the island of Crete.*
5 Gaza will be humiliated, its head shaved bald;
Ashkelon will lie silent.
You remnant from the Mediterranean coast,*
how long will you lament and mourn?
6 "Now, O sword of the LORD,
when will you be at rest again?

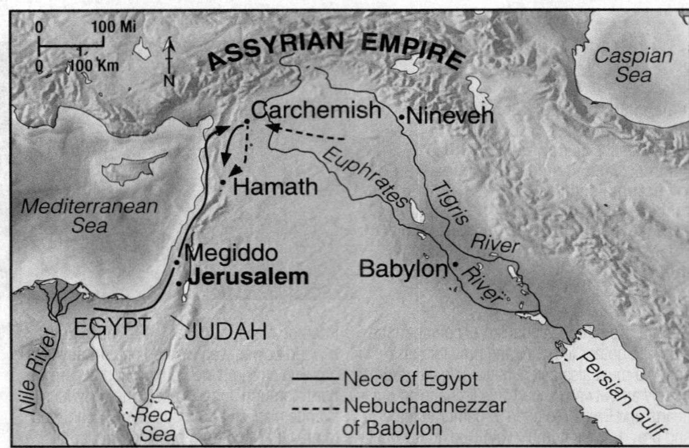

THE BATTLE AT CARCHEMISH *A world war was brewing in 609 B.C. Pharaoh Neco of Egypt set out for the city of Carchemish to join the Assyrians in an attempt to defeat the Babylonians, who were rising to great power. Neco marched his armies through Judah. King Josiah tried to stop Neco at Megiddo, but Josiah was killed. The battle began at Carchemish in 605 B.C., and the Egyptians and Assyrians were soundly defeated, chased to Hamath, and defeated again. Babylon was now the new world power.*

2 Chr 35:21-24 Josiah ignored Neco's message because of who Neco was—king of a pagan nation. The mistaken assumption that Neco could not be part of God's larger plan cost Josiah his life. While not everyone who claims to have a message from God really does, God's messages may come in unexpected ways. God had spoken to pagan kings in the past (Gen 12:17-20; 20:3-7; see also Dan 4:1-3). Don't let prejudice or false assumptions blind you to God's message.

2 Chr 35:25 Though Jeremiah recorded these laments for the death of Josiah, they are not the same as the book of Lamentations.

Jer 47:1 Located on the coastal plain next to Judah, Philistia had always been a thorn in Israel's side. The two nations battled constantly. Other prophets who spoke against Philistia included Isaiah (Isa 14:28-32), Ezekiel (Ezek 25:15-17), Amos (Amos 1:6-8), and Zephaniah (Zeph 2:4-7).

Jer 48:1 The Moabites were descendants of Lot through an incestuous relationship with one of his daughters (Gen 19:30-37). They led the Israelites into idolatry (Num 25:1-3) and joined the bands of raiders Nebuchadnezzar sent into Judah in 602 B.C. Babylon conquered them and they disappeared as a nation.

Go back into your sheath;
rest and be still.
7 "But how can it be still
when the LORD has sent it on a mission?
For the city of Ashkelon
and the people living along the sea
must be destroyed."

Jeremiah's Message about Moab

JEREMIAH 48:1-47

This message was given concerning Moab. This is what the LORD of Heaven's Armies, the God of Israel, says:

"What sorrow awaits the city of Nebo;
it will soon lie in ruins.
The city of Kiriathaim will be humiliated and captured;
the fortress will be humiliated and broken down.
2 No one will ever brag about Moab again,
for in Heshbon there is a plot to destroy her.
'Come,' they say, 'we will cut her off from being a nation.'
The town of Madmen,* too, will be silenced;
the sword will follow you there.
3 Listen to the cries from Horonaim,
cries of devastation and great destruction.
4 All Moab is destroyed.
Her little ones will cry out.*
5 Her refugees weep bitterly,
climbing the slope to Luhith.
They cry out in terror,
descending the slope to Horonaim.
6 Flee for your lives!
Hide* in the wilderness!
7 Because you have trusted in your wealth and skill,
you will be taken captive.
Your god Chemosh, with his priests and officials,
will be hauled off to distant lands!
8 "All the towns will be destroyed,
and no one will escape—
either on the plateaus or in the valleys,
for the LORD has spoken.
9 Oh, that Moab had wings
so she could fly away,*
for her towns will be left empty,
with no one living in them.
10 Cursed are those who refuse to do the LORD's work,
who hold back their swords from shedding blood!

11 "From his earliest history, Moab has lived in peace,
never going into exile.
He is like wine that has been allowed to settle.
He has not been poured from flask to flask,
and he is now fragrant and smooth.
12 But the time is coming soon," says the LORD,
"when I will send men to pour him from his jar.
They will pour him out,
then shatter the jar!
13 At last Moab will be ashamed of his idol Chemosh,
as the people of Israel were ashamed of their gold calf at Bethel.*
14 "You used to boast, 'We are heroes,
mighty men of war.'
15 But now Moab and his towns will be destroyed.
His most promising youth are doomed to slaughter,"
says the King, whose name is the LORD of Heaven's Armies.
16 "Destruction is coming fast for Moab;
calamity threatens ominously.
17 You friends of Moab,
weep for him and cry!
See how the strong scepter is broken,
how the beautiful staff is shattered!
18 "Come down from your glory
and sit in the dust, you people of Dibon,
for those who destroy Moab will shatter Dibon, too.
They will tear down all your towers.
19 You people of Aroer,
stand beside the road and watch.
Shout to those who flee from Moab,
'What has happened there?'
20 "And the reply comes back,
'Moab lies in ruins, disgraced;
weep and wail!
Tell it by the banks of the Arnon River:
Moab has been destroyed!'
21 Judgment has been poured out on the towns of the plateau—
on Holon and Jahaz* and Mephaath,
22 on Dibon and Nebo and Beth-diblathaim,
23 on Kiriathaim and Beth-gamul and Beth-meon,
24 on Kerioth and Bozrah—
all the towns of Moab, far and near.

Jer 48:2 *Madmen* sounds like the Hebrew word for "silence"; it should not be confused with the English word *madmen.* **Jer 48:4** Greek version reads *Her cries are heard as far away as Zoar.* **Jer 48:6** Or *Hide like a wild donkey;* or *Hide like a juniper shrub;* or *Be like* [the town of] *Aroer.* The meaning of the Hebrew is uncertain. **Jer 48:9** Or *Put salt on Moab, / for she will be laid waste.* **Jer 48:13** Hebrew *ashamed when they trusted in Bethel.* **Jer 48:21** Hebrew *Jahzah,* a variant spelling of Jahaz.

Jer 48:7 Chemosh was the main god of the nation of Moab (Num 21:29), and child sacrifice was an important part of his worship (2 Kgs 3:26-27). God's judgment made it clear that human-made resources and gods are no match for the Lord of Heaven's Armies.

Jer 48:13 After Israel divided into northern and southern kingdoms, the northern kingdom set up gold calf idols in Bethel and Dan to keep people from going to worship in Jerusalem, capital of the southern kingdom (1 Kgs 12:25-29).

▸ **JEREMIAH 48:1-47** ***(cont.)***

25 "The strength of Moab has ended.
His arm has been broken," says the LORD.
26 "Let him stagger and fall like a drunkard,
for he has rebelled against the LORD.
Moab will wallow in his own vomit,
ridiculed by all.
27 Did you not ridicule the people of Israel?
Were they caught in the company of thieves
that you should despise them as you do?

28 "You people of Moab,
flee from your towns and live in the caves.
Hide like doves that nest
in the clefts of the rocks.
29 We have all heard of the pride of Moab,
for his pride is very great.
We know of his lofty pride,
his arrogance, and his haughty heart.
30 I know about his insolence,"
says the LORD,
"but his boasts are empty—
as empty as his deeds.
31 So now I wail for Moab;
yes, I will mourn for Moab.
My heart is broken for the men of Kir-hareseth.*

32 "You people of Sibmah, rich in vineyards,
I will weep for you even more than I did
for Jazer.
Your spreading vines once reached as far as the
Dead Sea,*
but the destroyer has stripped you bare!
He has harvested your grapes and summer
fruits.
33 Joy and gladness are gone from fruitful Moab.
The presses yield no wine.
No one treads the grapes with shouts of joy.
There is shouting, yes, but not of joy.

34"Instead, their awful cries of terror can be heard
from Heshbon clear across to Elealeh and Jahaz; from
Zoar all the way to Horonaim and Eglath-shelishiyah.
Even the waters of Nimrim are dried up now.
35"I will put an end to Moab," says the LORD, "for the
people offer sacrifices at the pagan shrines and burn
incense to their false gods. 36My heart moans like a
flute for Moab and Kir-hareseth, for all their wealth
has disappeared. 37The people shave their heads and
beards in mourning. They slash their hands and put on
clothes made of burlap. 38There is crying and sorrow
in every Moabite home and on every street. For I have
smashed Moab like an old, unwanted jar. 39How it is
shattered! Hear the wailing! See the shame of Moab! It
has become an object of ridicule, an example of ruin
to all its neighbors."
40This is what the LORD says:

"Look! The enemy swoops down like an eagle,
spreading his wings over Moab.
41 Its cities will fall,
and its strongholds will be seized.
Even the mightiest warriors will be in anguish
like a woman in labor.
42 Moab will no longer be a nation,
for it has boasted against the LORD.

43 "Terror and traps and snares will be your lot,
O Moab," says the LORD.
44 "Those who flee in terror will fall into a trap,
and those who escape the trap will step
into a snare.
I will see to it that you do not get away,
for the time of your judgment has come,"
says the LORD.
45 "The people flee as far as Heshbon
but are unable to go on.
For a fire comes from Heshbon,
King Sihon's ancient home,
to devour the entire land
with all its rebellious people.

46 "O Moab, they weep for you!
The people of the god Chemosh are destroyed!
Your sons and your daughters
have been taken away as captives.
47 But I will restore the fortunes of Moab
in days to come.
I, the LORD, have spoken!"

This is the end of Jeremiah's prophecy concerning Moab.

Jehoahaz Rules in Judah PARALLEL

2 KINGS 23:31-35

Jehoahaz was twenty-three years old when he became
king, and he reigned in Jerusalem three months. His
mother was Hamutal, the daughter of Jeremiah from
Libnah. 32He did what was evil in the LORD's sight, just
as his ancestors had done.

Jer 48:31 Hebrew *Kir-heres,* a variant spelling of Kir-hareseth; also in 48:36. **Jer 48:32** Hebrew *the sea of Jazer.*

Jer 48:29 Moab was condemned for its pride. God cannot tolerate pride because pride is looking down on others or taking personal credit for what God has done. God does not condemn our taking satisfaction in what we do (Eccl 3:22), but he stands against overestimates of our own importance. Romans 12:3 teaches us to have an honest estimate of ourselves.

Jer 48:31 Kir-hareseth was a stronghold city in Moab. God's compassion reaches to all creation, even to his enemies.

2 Kgs 23:31-34 The people appointed Jehoahaz, one of Josiah's sons, to be Judah's next king. But Neco was not happy with their choice, so he exiled Jehoahaz to Egypt, where he died. Neco then installed Eliakim, another of Josiah's sons, as king of Judah, changing his name to Jehoiakim. Jehoiakim was little more than a puppet ruler. In 605 B.C., Babylon defeated Egypt. Judah then became a vassal state of Babylon (2 Kgs 24:1).

[33]Pharaoh Neco put Jehoahaz in prison at Riblah in the land of Hamath to prevent him from ruling* in Jerusalem. He also demanded that Judah pay 7,500 pounds of silver and 75 pounds of gold* as tribute.
[34]Pharaoh Neco then installed Eliakim, another of Josiah's sons, to reign in place of his father, and he changed Eliakim's name to Jehoiakim. Jehoahaz was taken to Egypt as a prisoner, where he died.
[35]In order to get the silver and gold demanded as tribute by Pharaoh Neco, Jehoiakim collected a tax from the people of Judah, requiring them to pay in proportion to their wealth.

2 CHRONICLES 36:1-4

Then the people of the land took Josiah's son Jehoahaz and made him the next king in Jerusalem.
[2]Jehoahaz* was twenty-three years old when he became king, and he reigned in Jerusalem three months.
[3]Then he was deposed by the king of Egypt, who demanded that Judah pay 7,500 pounds of silver and 75 pounds of gold* as tribute.
[4]The king of Egypt then installed Eliakim, the brother of Jehoahaz, as the next king of Judah and Jerusalem, and he changed Eliakim's name to Jehoiakim. Then Neco took Jehoahaz to Egypt as a prisoner.

Jehoiakim Begins to Rule in Judah PARALLEL

2 KINGS 23:36-37

Jehoiakim was twenty-five years old when he became king, and he reigned in Jerusalem eleven years. His mother was Zebidah, the daughter of Pedaiah from Rumah. [37]He did what was evil in the LORD's sight, just as his ancestors had done.

2 CHRONICLES 36:5

Jehoiakim was twenty-five years old when he became king, and he reigned in Jerusalem eleven years. He did what was evil in the sight of the LORD his God.

Jeremiah's Message for Judah's Kings

JEREMIAH 22:1-5

This is what the LORD said to me: "Go over and speak directly to the king of Judah. Say to him, [2]'Listen to this message from the LORD, you king of Judah, sitting on David's throne. Let your attendants and your people listen, too. [3]This is what the LORD says: Be fair-minded and just. Do what is right! Help those who have been robbed; rescue them from their oppressors. Quit your evil deeds! Do not mistreat foreigners, orphans, and widows. Stop murdering the innocent! [4]If you obey me, there will always be a descendant of David sitting on the throne here in Jerusalem. The king will ride through the palace gates in chariots and on horses, with his parade of attendants and subjects. [5]But if you refuse to pay attention to this warning, I swear by my own name, says the LORD, that this palace will become a pile of rubble.'"

Jeremiah's Message about the Palace

JEREMIAH 22:6-9

Now this is what the LORD says concerning Judah's royal palace:

"I love you as much as fruitful Gilead
and the green forests of Lebanon.
But I will turn you into a desert,
with no one living within your walls.
[7] I will call for wreckers,
who will bring out their tools to
dismantle you.
They will tear out all your fine cedar beams
and throw them on the fire.

[8]"People from many nations will pass by the ruins of this city and say to one another, 'Why did the LORD destroy such a great city?' [9]And the answer will be, 'Because they violated their covenant with the LORD their God by worshiping other gods.'"

Jeremiah's Message about Jehoahaz

JEREMIAH 22:10-12

[10] Do not weep for the dead king or mourn
his loss.
Instead, weep for the captive king being
led away!
For he will never return to see his native land
again.

2 Kgs 23:33a The meaning of the Hebrew is uncertain. **2 Kgs 23:33b** Hebrew *100 talents* [3,400 kilograms] *of silver and 1 talent* [34 kilograms] *of gold.* **2 Chr 36:2** Hebrew *Joahaz,* a variant spelling of Jehoahaz; also in 36:4. **2 Chr 36:3** Hebrew *100 talents* [3,400 kilograms] *of silver and 1 talent* [34 kilograms] *of gold.*

2 Kgs 23:36-37 Josiah followed God, but Jehoiakim, his son, was evil. He killed the prophet Uriah (Jer 26:20-23) and was dishonest, greedy, and unjust with the people (Jer 22:13-19). Jehoiakim also rebelled against Babylon, switching his allegiance to Egypt. This proved to be a crucial mistake. Nebuchadnezzar crushed Jehoiakim's rebellion and took him to Babylon (2 Chr 36:6), but he was eventually allowed to return to Jerusalem, where he died. The Bible does not record the cause of Jehoiakim's death.

2 Kgs 23:37 Many good kings had children who did not follow God. Perhaps it was because of neglect or preoccupation with political and military affairs or because these kings delegated the religious education to others. No doubt many of the children simply rebelled at the way they were raised. Being a strong believer as a parent doesn't guarantee that your children will pick up your beliefs. Children must be taught about faith, and parents dare not leave that task for others to do. Make sure you practice, explain, and teach what you preach.

Jer 22:3 God gave the king the basis for rebuilding the nation—turn from evil and do right. Doing what is right is more than simply believing all the right doctrines about God. It means living in obedience to God. Good deeds do not save us, but they display our faith (Jas 2:17-26).

Jer 22:10-12 Good King Josiah had died at the battle of Megiddo (2 Kgs 23:29); his son Jehoahaz reigned for only three months in 609 B.C. before being taken away to Egypt by Pharaoh Neco. He would be the first ruler to die in exile. The people were told not to waste their tears on the death of Josiah but to cry for the king who was taken into exile and would never return.

▸ JEREMIAH 22:10-12 ***(cont.)***

11For this is what the LORD says about Jehoahaz,* who
succeeded his father, King Josiah, and was taken away
as a captive: "He will never return. 12He will die in a
distant land and will never again see his own country."

A Message about Jehoiakim

JEREMIAH 22:13-23

13 And the LORD says, "What sorrow awaits
Jehoiakim,*
who builds his palace with forced labor.*
He builds injustice into its walls,
for he makes his neighbors work for nothing.
He does not pay them for their labor.
14 He says, 'I will build a magnificent palace
with huge rooms and many windows.
I will panel it throughout with fragrant cedar
and paint it a lovely red.'
15 But a beautiful cedar palace does not make
a great king!
Your father, Josiah, also had plenty to eat
and drink.
But he was just and right in all his dealings.
That is why God blessed him.
16 He gave justice and help to the poor and needy,
and everything went well for him.
Isn't that what it means to know me?"
says the LORD.
17 "But you! You have eyes only for greed and
dishonesty!
You murder the innocent,
oppress the poor, and reign ruthlessly."

18Therefore, this is what the LORD says about Jehoiakim, son of King Josiah:

"The people will not mourn for him, crying to one
another,
'Alas, my brother! Alas, my sister!'
His subjects will not mourn for him, crying,
'Alas, our master is dead! Alas, his splendor
is gone!'
19 He will be buried like a dead donkey—
dragged out of Jerusalem and dumped outside
the gates!
20 Weep for your allies in Lebanon.
Shout for them in Bashan.
Search for them in the regions east of the river.*
See, they are all destroyed.
Not one is left to help you.
21 I warned you when you were prosperous,
but you replied, 'Don't bother me.'
You have been that way since childhood—
you simply will not obey me!
22 And now the wind will blow away your allies.
All your friends will be taken away as captives.
Surely then you will see your wickedness and
be ashamed.
23 It may be nice to live in a beautiful palace
paneled with wood from the cedars of
Lebanon,
but soon you will groan with pangs of anguish—
anguish like that of a woman in labor."

Jeremiah's Escape from Death

JEREMIAH 26:1-24

This message came to Jeremiah from the LORD early
in the reign of Jehoiakim son of Josiah,* king of Judah.
2"This is what the LORD says: Stand in the courtyard
in front of the Temple of the LORD, and make an announcement to the people who have come there to
worship from all over Judah. Give them my entire message; include every word. 3Perhaps they will listen and
turn from their evil ways. Then I will change my mind
about the disaster I am ready to pour out on them
because of their sins.
4"Say to them, 'This is what the LORD says: If you will

Jer 22:11 Hebrew *Shallum*, another name for Jehoahaz. **Jer 22:13a** The brother and successor of the exiled Jehoahaz. See 22:18. **Jer 22:13b** Hebrew *by unrighteousness.* **Jer 22:20** Or *in Abarim.* **Jer 26:1** The first year of Jehoiakim's reign was 608 B.C.

Jer 22:15-16 God passed judgment on King Jehoiakim. His father, Josiah, had been one of Judah's great kings, but Jehoiakim was evil. Josiah had been faithful in his responsibility to be a model of right living, but Jehoiakim had been unfaithful in his responsibility to imitate his father. God's judgment was on unfaithful Jehoiakim. He could not claim his father's blessings when he had not followed his father's God. We may inherit our parents' money, but we cannot inherit their faith. A godly heritage, a good education, or a beautiful home doesn't guarantee moral character. We must have our own relationship with God.

Jer 22:21 Jehoiakim had been hardheaded and hard-hearted since childhood. God warned him, but he refused to listen. His prosperity always took a higher priority than his relationship with God. If you ever find yourself so comfortable that you don't have time for God, stop and ask which is more important—the comforts of this life or a close relationship with God.

Jer 26:1ff Jehoiakim was a materialistic and self-centered king who persecuted and murdered innocent people (Jer 36:22-32; 2 Kgs 23:36–24:6). Jeremiah 26 describes how and why Jeremiah was on trial for his life.

Jer 26:2 God reminded Jeremiah that he wanted his entire message given—"include every word." Jeremiah may have been tempted to leave out the parts that would turn his audience against him, sound too harsh, or make him sound like a traitor. But by God's command, he was not to delete parts of God's message to suit himself, his audience, or the circumstances in which he found himself. Like Jeremiah, we must never ignore or exclude important parts of God's Word to please someone.

Jer 26:2-9 Shiloh was where the Tabernacle had been set up after the conquest of Canaan (Josh 18:1). The Philistines destroyed it in 1050 B.C. God said he would destroy the Temple as Shiloh had been destroyed. When Jeremiah said that Jerusalem, the city of God, would become an object of cursing and the Temple would be destroyed (Jer 26:6), the priests and false prophets were infuriated. The Temple was important to them because the people's reverence for it brought them power. By saying that the Temple would be destroyed, Jeremiah was undermining their authority. Jesus also infuriated the religious leaders of his time by foretelling the destruction of Jerusalem and the Temple (Matt 24:2).

not listen to me and obey my word I have given you,
5and if you will not listen to my servants, the prophets—for I sent them again and again to warn you, but
you would not listen to them—6then I will destroy
this Temple as I destroyed Shiloh, the place where the
Tabernacle was located. And I will make Jerusalem an
object of cursing in every nation on earth.'"

7The priests, the prophets, and all the people listened to Jeremiah as he spoke in front of the LORD's
Temple. 8But when Jeremiah had finished his message, saying everything the LORD had told him to
say, the priests and prophets and all the people at
the Temple mobbed him. "Kill him!" they shouted.
9"What right do you have to prophesy in the LORD's
name that this Temple will be destroyed like Shiloh?
What do you mean, saying that Jerusalem will be destroyed and left with no inhabitants?" And all the
people threatened him as he stood in front of the
Temple.

10When the officials of Judah heard what was happening, they rushed over from the palace and sat
down at the New Gate of the Temple to hold court.
11The priests and prophets presented their accusations to the officials and the people. "This man should
die!" they said. "You have heard with your own ears
what a traitor he is, for he has prophesied against
this city."

12Then Jeremiah spoke to the officials and the
people in his own defense. "The LORD sent me to
prophesy against this Temple and this city," he said.
"The LORD gave me every word that I have spoken.
13But if you stop your sinning and begin to obey the
LORD your God, he will change his mind about this
disaster that he has announced against you. 14As for
me, I am in your hands—do with me as you think best.
15But if you kill me, rest assured that you will be killing
an innocent man! The responsibility for such a deed
will lie on you, on this city, and on every person living
in it. For it is absolutely true that the LORD sent me to
speak every word you have heard."

16Then the officials and the people said to the
priests and prophets, "This man does not deserve the
death sentence, for he has spoken to us in the name
of the LORD our God."

17Then some of the wise old men stood and spoke
to all the people assembled there. 18They said, "Remember when Micah of Moresheth prophesied during the reign of King Hezekiah of Judah. He told the
people of Judah,

'This is what the LORD of Heaven's Armies says:
Mount Zion will be plowed like an open field;
  Jerusalem will be reduced to ruins!
A thicket will grow on the heights
  where the Temple now stands.'*

19But did King Hezekiah and the people kill him for
saying this? No, they turned from their sins and worshiped the LORD. They begged him for mercy. Then the
LORD changed his mind about the terrible disaster he
had pronounced against them. So we are about to do
ourselves great harm."

20At this time Uriah son of Shemaiah from Kiriath-
jearim was also prophesying for the LORD. And he
predicted the same terrible disaster against the city
and nation as Jeremiah did. 21When King Jehoiakim
and the army officers and officials heard what he was
saying, the king sent someone to kill him. But Uriah
heard about the plan and escaped in fear to Egypt.
22Then King Jehoiakim sent Elnathan son of Acbor to
Egypt along with several other men to capture Uriah.
23They took him prisoner and brought him back to
King Jehoiakim. The king then killed Uriah with a
sword and had him buried in an unmarked grave.

24Nevertheless, Ahikam son of Shaphan stood up
for Jeremiah and persuaded the court not to turn him
over to the mob to be killed.

Jer 26:18 Mic 3:12.

Jer 26:11 Jeremiah was branded a traitor because he prophesied the destruction of the city and the Temple. But the "courageous" people advocated a foreign alliance to fight Babylon and retain their independence. The accusations they leveled at Jeremiah were actually true of themselves—they were the traitors because they had turned away from God.

Jer 26:17-19 The wise old men remembered the words of the prophet Micah (Mic 3:12), which were similar to the words Jeremiah spoke. When Micah called the people to repent, they turned from their wickedness. Although these people did not kill Jeremiah, they missed the main point—that the application of the story was for them. They spared Jeremiah, but they did not spare themselves by repenting of their sins. As you recall a great story of the Bible, ask how it can be applied to *your* life.

Jer 26:20-23 Uriah is an otherwise unknown prophet who was executed for faithfully proclaiming God's words. This shows us that God has had other prophets whose words are not included in the Bible.

2. BABYLON'S FIRST INVASION OF JUDAH

In 605 B.C., Babylon defeated Egypt and took control over all of Egypt's vassal states, including Judah. Jehoiakim decided to test the Babylonians, ceasing payment of tribute after the third year, leading to a military response from Babylon. During this time, Jeremiah predicted the 70-year exile for Judah and continued to speak to the kings and the people about God and his coming judgment.

Jehoiakim Rebels against Babylon

2 KINGS 24:1-4

During Jehoiakim's reign, King Nebuchadnezzar of Babylon invaded the land of Judah. Jehoiakim surrendered and paid him tribute for three years but then rebelled. 2Then the LORD sent bands of Babylonian,* Aramean, Moabite, and Ammonite raiders against Judah to destroy it, just as the LORD had promised through his prophets. 3These disasters happened to Judah because of the LORD's command. He had decided to banish Judah from his presence because of the many sins of Manasseh, 4who had filled Jerusalem with innocent blood. The LORD would not forgive this.

Jeremiah Predicts Seventy Years of Captivity

JEREMIAH 25:1-14

This message for all the people of Judah came to Jeremiah from the LORD during the fourth year of Jehoiakim's reign over Judah.* This was the year when King Nebuchadnezzar* of Babylon began his reign.

2Jeremiah the prophet said to all the people in Judah and Jerusalem, 3"For the past twenty-three years—from the thirteenth year of the reign of Josiah son of Amon,* king of Judah, until now—the LORD has been giving me his messages. I have faithfully passed them on to you, but you have not listened.

4"Again and again the LORD has sent you his servants, the prophets, but you have not listened or even paid attention. 5Each time the message was this: 'Turn from the evil road you are traveling and from the evil things you are doing. Only then will I let you live in this land that the LORD gave to you and your ancestors forever. 6Do not provoke my anger by worshiping idols you made with your own hands. Then I will not harm you.'

7"But you would not listen to me," says the LORD. "You made me furious by worshiping idols you made with your own hands, bringing on yourselves all the disasters you now suffer. 8And now the LORD of Heaven's Armies says: Because you have not listened to me, 9I will gather together all the armies of the north under King Nebuchadnezzar of Babylon, whom I have appointed as my deputy. I will bring them all against this land and its people and against the surrounding nations. I will completely destroy* you and make you an object of horror and contempt and a ruin forever. 10I will take away your happy singing and laughter. The joyful voices of bridegrooms and brides will no longer be heard. Your millstones will fall silent, and the lights in your homes will go out. 11This entire land will become a desolate wasteland. Israel and her neighboring lands will serve the king of Babylon for seventy years.

12"Then, after the seventy years of captivity are over, I will punish the king of Babylon and his people for their sins," says the LORD. "I will make the country of the Babylonians* a wasteland forever. 13I will bring upon them all the terrors I have promised in this book—all the penalties announced by Jeremiah against the nations. 14Many nations and great kings will enslave the Babylonians, just as they enslaved my people. I will punish them in proportion to the suffering they cause my people."

The Cup of the LORD's Anger

JEREMIAH 25:15-38

This is what the LORD, the God of Israel, said to me: "Take from my hand this cup filled to the brim with

2 Kgs 24:2 Or *Chaldean.* **Jer 25:1a** The fourth year of Jehoiakim's reign and the accession year of Nebuchadnezzar's reign was 605 B.C. **Jer 25:1b** Hebrew *Nebuchadrezzar,* a variant spelling of Nebuchadnezzar; also in 25:9. **Jer 25:3** The thirteenth year of Josiah's reign was 627 B.C. **Jer 25:9** The Hebrew term used here refers to the complete consecration of things or people to the LORD, either by destroying them or by giving them as an offering. **Jer 25:12** Or *Chaldeans.*

2 Kgs 24:1 Babylon became the new world power after overthrowing Assyria in 612 B.C. and defeating Egypt at the battle of Carchemish in 605 B.C. After defeating Egypt, the Babylonians invaded Judah and brought it under their control. This was the first of three Babylonian invasions of Judah over the next 20 years. The other two invasions occurred in 597 and 586 B.C. With each invasion, captives were taken back to Babylon. Daniel was one of the captives taken during this first invasion (605 B.C.; Dan 1:1-6).

2 Kgs 24:1 For more information on Nebuchadnezzar, see his Profile on p. 1120.

2 Kgs 24:1-4 Nebuchadnezzar took control as king of Babylon in 605 B.C. Earlier that year Nebuchadnezzar had defeated the Egyptians led by Pharaoh Neco at Carchemish. Thus, Babylon had taken control of all Egypt's vassals (including Judah). Later, Nebuchadnezzar invaded the land in order to establish his rule by force.

Jer 25:1ff Jeremiah gave this message in 605 B.C., the year Nebuchadnezzar came to power. From Jeremiah 25:3 we learn that the beginning of Jeremiah's ministry was in 627 B.C. He predicted the 70 years of captivity a full 20 years before they began.

Jer 25:2-6 Imagine preaching the same message for 23 years and continually being rejected! Jeremiah faced this; but because he had committed his life to God, he continued to proclaim the message: "Turn from the evil road you are traveling and from the evil things you are doing." Regardless of the people's response, Jeremiah did not give up. God never stops loving us, even when we reject him. We can thank God that he won't give up on us, and like Jeremiah, we can commit ourselves to never forsaking him. No matter how people respond when you tell them about God, remain faithful to God's high call and continue to witness for him.

Jer 25:12 This event is further described in Daniel 5. The troops of Cyrus the Great entered Babylon in 539 B.C. and killed Belshazzar, the last Babylonian ruler.

Jer 25:15-38 Judah would not be the only nation to drink the cup of God's anger. Here Jeremiah listed other wicked nations that would experience God's wrath at the hands

my anger, and make all the nations to whom I send
you drink from it. 16 When they drink from it, they
will stagger, crazed by the warfare I will send against
them."

17 So I took the cup of anger from the LORD and made
all the nations drink from it—every nation to which the
LORD sent me. 18 I went to Jerusalem and the other towns
of Judah, and their kings and officials drank from the
cup. From that day until this, they have been a desolate
ruin, an object of horror, contempt, and cursing. 19 I gave
the cup to Pharaoh, king of Egypt, his attendants, his
officials, and all his people, 20 along with all the foreigners living in that land. I also gave it to all the kings of
the land of Uz and the kings of the Philistine cities of
Ashkelon, Gaza, Ekron, and what remains of Ashdod.
21 Then I gave the cup to the nations of Edom, Moab,
and Ammon, 22 and the kings of Tyre and Sidon, and
the kings of the regions across the sea. 23 I gave it to
Dedan, Tema, and Buz, and to the people who live in
distant places.* 24 I gave it to the kings of Arabia, the
kings of the nomadic tribes of the desert, 25 and to
the kings of Zimri, Elam, and Media. 26 And I gave it to
the kings of the northern countries, far and near, one
after the other—all the kingdoms of the world. And
finally, the king of Babylon* himself drank from the
cup of the LORD's anger.

27 Then the LORD said to me, "Now tell them, 'This is
what the LORD of Heaven's Armies, the God of Israel,
says: Drink from this cup of my anger. Get drunk and
vomit; fall to rise no more, for I am sending terrible
wars against you.' 28 And if they refuse to accept the
cup, tell them, 'The LORD of Heaven's Armies says: You
have no choice but to drink from it. 29 I have begun
to punish Jerusalem, the city that bears my name.
Now should I let you go unpunished? No, you will
not escape disaster. I will call for war against all the
nations of the earth. I, the LORD of Heaven's Armies,
have spoken!'

30 "Now prophesy all these things, and say to them,

"'The LORD will roar against his own land
  from his holy dwelling in heaven.
He will shout like those who tread grapes;
  he will shout against everyone on earth.
31 His cry of judgment will reach the ends of
    the earth,
  for the LORD will bring his case against all
    the nations.
He will judge all the people of the earth,
  slaughtering the wicked with the sword.
  I, the LORD, have spoken!'"

32 This is what the LORD of Heaven's Armies says:
"Look! Disaster will fall upon nation after
    nation!
A great whirlwind of fury is rising
  from the most distant corners of the earth!"

33 In that day those the LORD has slaughtered will fill
the earth from one end to the other. No one will mourn
for them or gather up their bodies to bury them. They
will be scattered on the ground like manure.

34 Weep and moan, you evil shepherds!
  Roll in the dust, you leaders of the flock!
The time of your slaughter has arrived;
  you will fall and shatter like a fragile vase.
35 You will find no place to hide;
  there will be no way to escape.
36 Listen to the frantic cries of the shepherds.
  The leaders of the flock are wailing in despair,
  for the LORD is ruining their pastures.
37 Peaceful meadows will be turned into a
    wasteland
  by the LORD's fierce anger.
38 He has left his den like a strong lion seeking
    its prey,
  and their land will be made desolate
by the sword of the enemy
  and the LORD's fierce anger.

Baruch Reads the LORD's Messages

JEREMIAH 36:1-20

During the fourth year that Jehoiakim son of Josiah
was king in Judah,* the LORD gave this message to
Jeremiah: 2 "Get a scroll, and write down all my messages against Israel, Judah, and the other nations. Begin with the first message back in the days of Josiah,
and write down every message, right up to the present
time. 3 Perhaps the people of Judah will repent when
they hear again all the terrible things I have planned
for them. Then I will be able to forgive their sins and
wrongdoings."

4 So Jeremiah sent for Baruch son of Neriah, and as
Jeremiah dictated all the prophecies that the LORD
had given him, Baruch wrote them on a scroll. 5 Then
Jeremiah said to Baruch, "I am a prisoner here and
unable to go to the Temple. 6 So you go to the Temple
on the next day of fasting, and read the messages from
the LORD that I have had you write on this scroll. Read
them so the people who are there from all over Judah
will hear them. 7 Perhaps even yet they will turn from
their evil ways and ask the LORD's forgiveness before

Jer 25:23 Or *who clip the corners of their hair.* **Jer 25:26** Hebrew *of Sheshach,* a code name for Babylon. **Jer 36:1** The fourth year of Jehoiakim's reign was 605 B.C.

of Babylon. Finally, Babylon itself would be destroyed because of its sin.

Jer 36:1ff This happened in the summer of 605 B.C., shortly after Nebuchadnezzar's victory over the Egyptian army at Carchemish.

Jer 36:2-4 Most people in ancient times could neither read nor write, so those who could were highly esteemed. These men, called scribes or teachers, held positions of great importance and were very respected for their knowledge. Baruch was Jeremiah's scribe. Writing was often done on vellum or papyrus sheets that were sewn or glued together and stored in long rolls called scrolls. After the Exile, scribes became teachers of the law. In New Testament times, the scribes formed a powerful political party.

▸ **JEREMIAH 36:1-20** *(cont.)*
it is too late. For the LORD has threatened them with
his terrible anger."
8Baruch did as Jeremiah told him and read these
messages from the LORD to the people at the Temple.
9He did this on a day of sacred fasting held in late autumn,* during the fifth year of the reign of Jehoiakim
son of Josiah. People from all over Judah had come to
Jerusalem to attend the services at the Temple on that
day. 10Baruch read Jeremiah's words on the scroll to
all the people. He stood in front of the Temple room
of Gemariah, son of Shaphan the secretary. This room
was just off the upper courtyard of the Temple, near
the New Gate entrance.
11When Micaiah son of Gemariah and grandson
of Shaphan heard the messages from the LORD, 12he
went down to the secretary's room in the palace where
the administrative officials were meeting. Elishama
the secretary was there, along with Delaiah son of
Shemaiah, Elnathan son of Acbor, Gemariah son of
Shaphan, Zedekiah son of Hananiah, and all the other
officials. 13When Micaiah told them about the messages Baruch was reading to the people, 14the officials
sent Jehudi son of Nethaniah, grandson of Shelemiah
and great-grandson of Cushi, to ask Baruch to come
and read the messages to them, too. So Baruch took
the scroll and went to them. 15"Sit down and read the
scroll to us," the officials said, and Baruch did as they
requested.
16When they heard all the messages, they looked
at one another in alarm. "We must tell the king what
we have heard," they said to Baruch. 17"But first, tell us
how you got these messages. Did they come directly
from Jeremiah?"
18So Baruch explained, "Jeremiah dictated them,
and I wrote them down in ink, word for word, on this
scroll."
19"You and Jeremiah should both hide," the officials
told Baruch. "Don't tell anyone where you are!" 20Then
the officials left the scroll for safekeeping in the room
of Elishama the secretary and went to tell the king
what had happened.

King Jehoiakim Burns the Scroll

JEREMIAH 36:21-26
The king sent Jehudi to get the scroll. Jehudi brought it
from Elishama's room and read it to the king as all his
officials stood by. 22It was late autumn, and the king
was in a winterized part of the palace, sitting in front
of a fire to keep warm. 23Each time Jehudi finished
reading three or four columns, the king took a knife
and cut off that section of the scroll. He then threw it
into the fire, section by section, until the whole scroll
was burned up. 24Neither the king nor his attendants
showed any signs of fear or repentance at what they
heard. 25Even when Elnathan, Delaiah, and Gemariah
begged the king not to burn the scroll, he wouldn't
listen.
26Then the king commanded his son Jerahmeel,
Seraiah son of Azriel, and Shelemiah son of Abdeel
to arrest Baruch and Jeremiah. But the LORD had hidden them.

Jeremiah Rewrites the Scroll

JEREMIAH 36:27-32
After the king had burned the scroll on which Baruch
had written Jeremiah's words, the LORD gave Jeremiah
another message. He said, 28"Get another scroll, and
write everything again just as you did on the scroll
King Jehoiakim burned. 29Then say to the king, 'This
is what the LORD says: You burned the scroll because
it said the king of Babylon would destroy this land and
empty it of people and animals. 30Now this is what
the LORD says about King Jehoiakim of Judah: He will
have no heirs to sit on the throne of David. His dead
body will be thrown out to lie unburied—exposed to
the heat of the day and the frost of the night. 31I will
punish him and his family and his attendants for their
sins. I will pour out on them and on all the people of
Jerusalem and Judah all the disasters I promised, for
they would not listen to my warnings.'"
32So Jeremiah took another scroll and dictated again
to his secretary, Baruch. He wrote everything that had
been on the scroll King Jehoiakim had burned in the
fire. Only this time he added much more!

Jer 36:9 Hebrew *in the ninth month,* of the ancient Hebrew lunar calendar (also in 36:22). The ninth month in the fifth year of Jehoiakim's reign occurred within the months of November and December 604 B.C. Also see note on 1:3.

Jer 36:9 A time of fasting (when people abstained from eating food to show their humility and repentance) was often called during times of national emergency. Babylon was destroying city after city and closing in on Jerusalem. As the people came to the Temple, Baruch told them how to avert the coming tragedy, but they refused to listen.

Jer 36:10-32 God told Jeremiah to write his words on a scroll. Because he was not allowed to go to the Temple, Jeremiah asked his scribe, Baruch, to whom he had dictated the scroll to read it to the people gathered there. Baruch then read it to the officials, and finally Jehudi read it to the king himself. Although the king burned the scroll, he could not destroy the word of God. Today many people try to put God's Word aside or say that it contains errors and therefore cannot be trusted. People may reject God's Word, but they cannot destroy it. God's Word will stand forever (Ps 119:89).

Jer 36:25 Only three leaders protested this evil act of burning the scroll containing God's word. This shows how complacent and insensitive to God the people had become. Not only did the king reject God's word, but he tried to destroy it. Speaking out against these actions took courage. Anyone who decides to live for God must be willing to stand for right even if almost everyone else turns away. It is in the climate of darkness and sin that genuine faith shines most brightly.

Jer 36:30 Jehoiakim's son, Jehoiachin, was king for three months before he was taken into captivity, but this did not qualify as sitting "on the throne of David"—an expression that implied permanence. Jehoiakim did not secure a dynasty. Zedekiah, the next ruler, was Jehoiachin's uncle. Thus, the line of mortal human kings descended from David's son Solomon was finished, but in less than 600 years the eternal King would come through the descendants of Solomon's brother Nathan (see also the note on Jer 22:30, p. 1027).

Jeremiah's Message for Baruch

JEREMIAH 45:1-5

The prophet Jeremiah gave a message to Baruch son of Neriah in the fourth year of the reign of Jehoiakim son of Josiah,* after Baruch had written down everything Jeremiah had dictated to him. He said, 2"This is what the LORD, the God of Israel, says to you, Baruch: 3You have said, 'I am overwhelmed with trouble! Haven't I had enough pain already? And now the LORD has added more! I am worn out from sighing and can find no rest.'

4"Baruch, this is what the LORD says: 'I will destroy this nation that I built. I will uproot what I planted. 5Are you seeking great things for yourself? Don't do it! I will bring great disaster upon all these people; but I will give you your life as a reward wherever you go. I, the LORD, have spoken!'"

Jeremiah's Messages about Egypt

JEREMIAH 46:1-28

The following messages were given to Jeremiah the prophet from the LORD concerning foreign nations.

2This message concerning Egypt was given in the fourth year of the reign of Jehoiakim son of Josiah, the king of Judah, on the occasion of the battle of Carchemish* when Pharaoh Neco, king of Egypt, and his army were defeated beside the Euphrates River by King Nebuchadnezzar* of Babylon.

3 "Prepare your shields,
and advance into battle!
4 Harness the horses,
and mount the stallions.
Take your positions.
Put on your helmets.
Sharpen your spears,
and prepare your armor.
5 But what do I see?
The Egyptian army flees in terror.
The bravest of its fighting men run
without a backward glance.
They are terrorized at every turn,"
says the LORD.
6 "The swiftest runners cannot flee;
the mightiest warriors cannot escape.
By the Euphrates River to the north,
they stumble and fall.

7 "Who is this, rising like the Nile at floodtime,
overflowing all the land?
8 It is the Egyptian army,
overflowing all the land,
boasting that it will cover the earth like a flood,
destroying cities and their people.
9 Charge, you horses and chariots;
attack, you mighty warriors of Egypt!
Come, all you allies from Ethiopia, Libya,
and Lydia*
who are skilled with the shield and bow!
10 For this is the day of the Lord, the LORD of
Heaven's Armies,
a day of vengeance on his enemies.
The sword will devour until it is satisfied,
yes, until it is drunk with your blood!
The Lord, the LORD of Heaven's Armies, will
receive a sacrifice today
in the north country beside the Euphrates River.

11 "Go up to Gilead to get medicine,
O virgin daughter of Egypt!
But your many treatments
will bring you no healing.
12 The nations have heard of your shame.
The earth is filled with your cries of despair.
Your mightiest warriors will run into each other
and fall down together."

13Then the LORD gave the prophet Jeremiah this message about King Nebuchadnezzar's plans to attack Egypt.

14 "Shout it out in Egypt!
Publish it in the cities of Migdol, Memphis,*
and Tahpanhes!

Jer 45:1 The fourth year of Jehoiakim's reign was 605 B.C. **Jer 46:2a** This event occurred in 605 B.C., during the fourth year of Jehoiakim's reign (according to the calendar system in which the new year begins in the spring). **Jer 46:2b** Hebrew *Nebuchadrezzar,* a variant spelling of Nebuchadnezzar; also in 46:13, 26. **Jer 46:9** Hebrew *from Cush, Put, and Lud.* **Jer 46:14** Hebrew *Noph;* also in 46:19.

Jer 45:1ff The event relating to this chapter is recorded in Jeremiah 36:1-8. The chapter was written in 605–604 B.C. Baruch was the scribe who recorded Jeremiah's words on a scroll.

Jer 45:5 Baruch had long been serving this unpopular prophet, writing his book of struggles and judgments, and now he was upset. God told Baruch to take his eyes off himself and whatever rewards he thought he deserved. If Baruch did this, God would protect him. It is easy to lose the joy of serving God when we take our eyes off him. The more we look away from God's purposes toward our own sacrifices, the more frustrated we will become. As you serve God, beware of focusing on what you are giving up. When this happens, ask God's forgiveness; then redirect your attention to the incomparable privilege of serving God.

Jer 46:1ff In this chapter, we gain several insights about God and his plan for this world. (1) Although God chose Israel for a special purpose, he loves all people and wants all to come to him. (2) God is holy and will not tolerate sin. (3) God's judgments are not based on prejudice and a desire for revenge but on fairness and justice. (4) God does not delight in judgment but in salvation. (5) God is impartial—he judges everyone by the same standard.

Jer 46:2 At the battle of Carchemish in 605 B.C., Babylon and Egypt, the two major world powers after Assyria's fall, clashed. The Babylonians entered Carchemish by surprise and defeated Egypt. This battle, which passed world leadership to Babylon, was Nebuchadnezzar's first victory, establishing him in his new position as king of the Babylonian Empire. With Egypt's power declining, it was both poor strategy and disobedience to God for Judah to form an alliance with Egypt.

Jer 46:9 The soldiers from Ethiopia and Libya were from eastern and northern Africa. The men of Lydia may have been from Greece.

▸ **JEREMIAH 46:1-28** ***(cont.)***

Mobilize for battle,
for the sword will devour everyone around you.
15 Why have your warriors fallen?
They cannot stand, for the LORD has knocked them down.
16 They stumble and fall over each other
and say among themselves,
'Come, let's go back to our people,
to the land of our birth.
Let's get away from the sword of the enemy!'
17 There they will say,
'Pharaoh, the king of Egypt, is a loudmouth
who missed his opportunity!'
18 "As surely as I live," says the King,
whose name is the LORD of Heaven's Armies,
"one is coming against Egypt
who is as tall as Mount Tabor,
or as Mount Carmel by the sea!
19 Pack up! Get ready to leave for exile,
you citizens of Egypt!
The city of Memphis will be destroyed,
without a single inhabitant.
20 Egypt is as sleek as a beautiful young cow,
but a horsefly from the north is on its way!
21 Egypt's mercenaries have become like
fattened calves.
They, too, will turn and run,
for it is a day of great disaster for Egypt,
a time of great punishment.
22 Egypt flees, silent as a serpent gliding away.
The invading army marches in;
they come against her with axes like woodsmen.
23 They will cut down her people like trees,"
says the LORD,
"for they are more numerous than locusts.
24 Egypt will be humiliated;
she will be handed over to people from
the north."

25The LORD of Heaven's Armies, the God of Israel,
says: "I will punish Amon, the god of Thebes,* and
all the other gods of Egypt. I will punish its rulers
and Pharaoh, too, and all who trust in him. 26I will
hand them over to those who want them killed—to
King Nebuchadnezzar of Babylon and his army. But
afterward the land will recover from the ravages of
war. I, the LORD, have spoken!

27 "But do not be afraid, Jacob, my servant;
do not be dismayed, Israel.
For I will bring you home again from distant lands,
and your children will return from their exile.
Israel* will return to a life of peace and quiet,
and no one will terrorize them.
28 Do not be afraid, Jacob, my servant,
for I am with you," says the LORD.
"I will completely destroy the nations to which
I have exiled you,
but I will not completely destroy you.
I will discipline you, but with justice;
I cannot let you go unpunished."

Jeremiah's Shattered Jar

JEREMIAH 19:1-15

This is what the LORD said to me: "Go and buy a clay
jar. Then ask some of the leaders of the people and of
the priests to follow you. 2Go out through the Gate of
Broken Pots to the garbage dump in the valley of Ben-
Hinnom, and give them this message. 3Say to them,
'Listen to this message from the LORD, you kings of
Judah and citizens of Jerusalem! This is what the LORD
of Heaven's Armies, the God of Israel, says: I will bring
a terrible disaster on this place, and the ears of those
who hear about it will ring!
4"'For Israel has forsaken me and turned this valley
into a place of wickedness. The people burn incense
to foreign gods—idols never before acknowledged by
this generation, by their ancestors, or by the kings of
Judah. And they have filled this place with the blood
of innocent children. 5They have built pagan shrines
to Baal, and there they burn their sons as sacrifices to
Baal. I have never commanded such a horrible deed;
it never even crossed my mind to command such a
thing! 6So beware, for the time is coming, says the
LORD, when this garbage dump will no longer be called
Topheth or the valley of Ben-Hinnom, but the Valley
of Slaughter.
7"'For I will upset the careful plans of Judah and
Jerusalem. I will allow the people to be slaughtered by
invading armies, and I will leave their dead bodies as
food for the vultures and wild animals. 8I will reduce
Jerusalem to ruins, making it a monument to their

Jer 46:25 Hebrew *of No.* **Jer 46:27** Hebrew *Jacob.* See note on 5:20.

Jer 46:17 The Egyptian pharaoh was a "loudmouth" who "missed his opportunity" because, although he had come to help Jerusalem, he beat a hasty retreat when the Babylonians turned on him. Jeremiah had prophesied that Pharaoh Hophra would be killed by his enemies (Jer 44:30). This was fulfilled nearly 20 years later when his co-regent Ahmose led a revolt.

Jer 46:28 God punished his people in order to bring them back to himself, and he punishes us to correct and purify us. No one welcomes punishment, but we should all welcome its results: correction and purity.

Jer 19:6 The valley of Ben-Hinnom was the garbage dump of Jerusalem and the place where children were sacrificed to the god Molech. It is also mentioned in Jeremiah 7:31-32. Topheth was located in the valley and means "fireplace." God declared that the place of sacrifice would become a place of slaughter. The killers of the innocent would be judged by losing their own lives.

Jer 19:7-13 The horrible carnage that Jeremiah predicted happened twice: in 586 B.C. during the Babylonian invasion under Nebuchadnezzar and in A.D. 70 when Titus

stupidity. All who pass by will be astonished and will
gasp at the destruction they see there. 9 I will see to it
that your enemies lay siege to the city until all the food
is gone. Then those trapped inside will eat their own
sons and daughters and friends. They will be driven
to utter despair.'

10 "As these men watch you, Jeremiah, smash the
jar you brought. 11 Then say to them, 'This is what the
LORD of Heaven's Armies says: As this jar lies shattered,
so I will shatter the people of Judah and Jerusalem
beyond all hope of repair. They will bury the bodies
here in Topheth, the garbage dump, until there is no
more room for them. 12 This is what I will do to this
place and its people, says the LORD. I will cause this city
to become defiled like Topheth. 13 Yes, all the houses
in Jerusalem, including the palace of Judah's kings,
will become like Topheth—all the houses where you
burned incense on the rooftops to your star gods, and
where liquid offerings were poured out to your idols.'"

14 Then Jeremiah returned from Topheth, the garbage dump where he had delivered this message, and
he stopped in front of the Temple of the LORD. He
said to the people there, 15 "This is what the LORD of
Heaven's Armies, the God of Israel, says: 'I will bring
disaster upon this city and its surrounding towns as
I promised, because you have stubbornly refused to
listen to me.'"

Jeremiah and Pashhur

JEREMIAH 20:1-6

Now Pashhur son of Immer, the priest in charge of the
Temple of the LORD, heard what Jeremiah was prophesying. 2 So he arrested Jeremiah the prophet and had
him whipped and put in stocks at the Benjamin Gate
of the LORD's Temple.

3 The next day, when Pashhur finally released him,
Jeremiah said, "Pashhur, the LORD has changed your
name. From now on you are to be called 'The Man
Who Lives in Terror.'* 4 For this is what the LORD says:
'I will send terror upon you and all your friends, and
you will watch as they are slaughtered by the swords
of the enemy. I will hand the people of Judah over
to the king of Babylon. He will take them captive to
Babylon or run them through with the sword. 5 And I
will let your enemies plunder Jerusalem. All the famed
treasures of the city—the precious jewels and gold and
silver of your kings—will be carried off to Babylon. 6 As
for you, Pashhur, you and all your household will go as
captives to Babylon. There you will die and be buried,
you and all your friends to whom you prophesied that
everything would be all right.'"

Jeremiah's Complaint

JEREMIAH 20:7-18

7 O LORD, you misled me,
 and I allowed myself to be misled.
You are stronger than I am,
 and you overpowered me.
Now I am mocked every day;
 everyone laughs at me.
8 When I speak, the words burst out.
 "Violence and destruction!" I shout.
So these messages from the LORD
 have made me a household joke.
9 But if I say I'll never mention the LORD
 or speak in his name,
his word burns in my heart like a fire.
 It's like a fire in my bones!
I am worn out trying to hold it in!
 I can't do it!
10 I have heard the many rumors about me.
 They call me "The Man Who Lives in Terror."
They threaten, "If you say anything, we will
 report it."
 Even my old friends are watching me,
 waiting for a fatal slip.
"He will trap himself," they say,
 "and then we will get our revenge on him."
11 But the LORD stands beside me like a great
 warrior.
 Before him my persecutors will stumble.
 They cannot defeat me.

Jer 20:3 Hebrew *Magor-missabib,* which means "surrounded by terror"; also in 20:10.

destroyed Jerusalem. During the Babylonian siege, food became so scarce that people became cannibals, even eating their own children. (See Lev 26:29; Deut 28:53-57 for prophecies concerning this; and see 2 Kgs 6:28-29; Lam 2:20; 4:10 for accounts of actual occurrences.)

Jer 20:1ff This event took place during the reign of Jehoiakim of Judah. Jeremiah preached at the valley of Ben-Hinnom, the center of idolatry in the city. He also preached in the Temple, which should have been the center of true worship. Both places attracted many people; both were places of false worship.

Jer 20:1-3 Pashhur was the official in charge of maintaining order in the Temple (see Jer 29:26 for a description of how leaders in Jeremiah's day understood the responsibility). He was also a priest and had pretended to be a prophet. After hearing Jeremiah's words, Pashhur had him whipped and put in the stocks (locked up) instead of taking his message to heart and acting on it. The truth sometimes stings, but our reaction to the truth shows what we are made of. We can deny the charges and destroy evidence of our misdeeds, or we can take the truth humbly to heart and let it change us. Pashhur may have thought he was a strong leader, but he was really a coward.

Jer 20:4-6 This prophecy of destruction came true in three waves of invasion by Babylon. The first wave had already happened (605 B.C.). Pashhur was probably exiled to Babylon during the second wave in 597 B.C. when Jehoiachin was taken captive. The third invasion occurred in 586 B.C.

Jer 20:7-18 Jeremiah cried out in despair mixed with praise, unburdening his heart to God. He had faithfully proclaimed God's word and had received nothing in return but persecution and sorrow. Yet when he withheld God's word for a while, it became fire in his bones until he could hold it back no longer. When God's living message of forgiveness and love becomes fire in your bones, you also will feel compelled to share it with others, regardless of the results.

▸ **JEREMIAH 20:7-18** ***(cont.)***

They will fail and be thoroughly humiliated.
Their dishonor will never be forgotten.
12 O LORD of Heaven's Armies,
you test those who are righteous,
and you examine the deepest thoughts
and secrets.
Let me see your vengeance against them,
for I have committed my cause to you.
13 Sing to the LORD!
Praise the LORD!
For though I was poor and needy,
he rescued me from my oppressors.
14 Yet I curse the day I was born!
May no one celebrate the day of my birth.
15 I curse the messenger who told my father,
"Good news—you have a son!"
16 Let him be destroyed like the cities of old
that the LORD overthrew without mercy.
Terrify him all day long with battle shouts,
17 because he did not kill me at birth.
Oh, that I had died in my mother's womb,
that her body had been my grave!
18 Why was I ever born?
My entire life has been filled
with trouble, sorrow, and shame.

3. DANIEL IS EXILED TO BABYLON

Babylon asserted their dominance over Judah, conquering them, imprisoning king Jehoiakim, and taking a group of hostages from Jerusalem to Babylon—including Daniel. Daniel was drafted as a counselor to King Nebuchadnezzar. With God's help, Daniel interpreted two of the king's dreams, Daniel's three friends were rescued from certain death in the blazing furnace, and even Nebuchadnezzar acknowledged the power of the God of Judah. Daniel's life is a picture of the triumph of faith. May God grant us this type of faith so that we may also live courageously each day.

Nebuchadnezzar Besie.ges Jerusalem

DANIEL 1:1-2

During the third year of King Jehoiakim's reign in Judah,* King Nebuchadnezzar of Babylon came to Jerusalem and besieged it. 2The Lord gave him victory over King Jehoiakim of Judah and permitted him to take some of the sacred objects from the Temple of God. So Nebuchadnezzar took them back to the land of Babylonia* and placed them in the treasure-house of his god.

Dn 1:1 This event occurred in 605 B.C., during the third year of Jehoiakim's reign (according to the calendar system in which the new year begins in the spring).
Dn 1:2 Hebrew *the land of Shinar.*

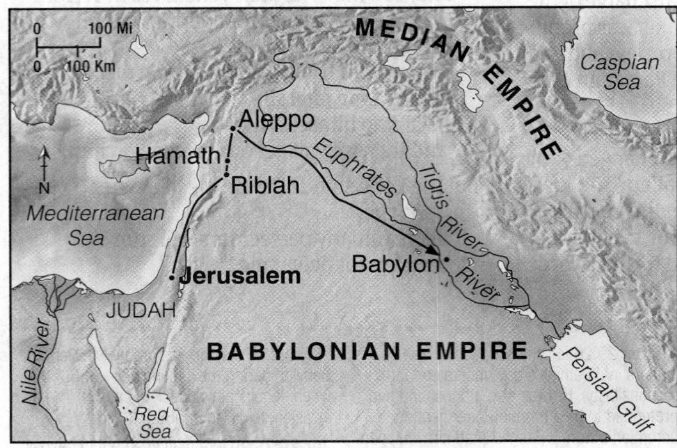

TAKEN TO BABYLON *Daniel, as a captive of Babylonian soldiers, faced a long and difficult march to a new land. The 500-mile trek, under harsh conditions, certainly tested his faith in God.*

Jer 20:14-18 Probably as troubling as the self-loathing that oozes from these verses is the stark contrast between the exuberant confidence of the previous paragraph and the sudden inward turn of revulsion. Yet in Jeremiah's honestly recorded moments of despair we can find hope. If someone with such intimate awareness of God's presence struggled with insecurity, we ought not to be surprised over our own failures and weaknesses. Jeremiah doesn't give us an excuse, but rather an example. No matter how we may feel about ourselves at any moment, God remains unchanged, loving, and present in our lives.

Dan 1:1-2 Born during the middle of Josiah's reign (2 Kgs 22–23), Daniel grew up during the king's reforms. During this time, Daniel probably heard Jeremiah, a prophet he quoted in Daniel 9:2. In 609 B.C. Josiah was killed in a battle against Egypt, and within four years, the southern kingdom of Judah had returned to its evil ways.

In 605 B.C. Nebuchadnezzar became king of Babylon. In September of that year, he swept into Palestine and surrounded Jerusalem, making Judah his vassal state. To demonstrate his dominance, Nebuchadnezzar took many of Jerusalem's wisest men and most beautiful women to Babylon as captives. Daniel was among this group.

Dan 1:1-2 Nebuchadnezzar, the supreme leader of Babylon, was feared throughout the world. When he invaded a country, defeat was certain. After a victory, the Babylonians usually took the most talented and useful people back to Babylon and left only the poor behind to take whatever land they wanted and to live peacefully there (2 Kgs 24:14). This system fostered great loyalty from conquered lands and ensured a steady supply of wise and talented people for civil service.

Dan 1:2 At certain times God allows his work to suffer. In this instance, the Babylonians raided the Temple of God and took the worship articles to the temple of a god in Babylon. This god may have been Bel, also called Marduk, the chief god of the

Daniel in Nebuchadnezzar's Court

DANIEL 1:3-21

Then the king ordered Ashpenaz, his chief of staff, to bring to the palace some of the young men of Judah's royal family and other noble families, who had been brought to Babylon as captives. 4"Select only strong, healthy, and good-looking young men," he said. "Make sure they are well versed in every branch of learning, are gifted with knowledge and good judgment, and are suited to serve in the royal palace. Train these young men in the language and literature of Babylon.*" 5The king assigned them a daily ration of food and wine from his own kitchens. They were to be trained for three years, and then they would enter the royal service.

6Daniel, Hananiah, Mishael, and Azariah were four of the young men chosen, all from the tribe of Judah. 7The chief of staff renamed them with these Babylonian names:

Daniel was called Belteshazzar.
Hananiah was called Shadrach.
Mishael was called Meshach.
Azariah was called Abednego.

8But Daniel was determined not to defile himself by eating the food and wine given to them by the king. He asked the chief of staff for permission not to eat these unacceptable foods. 9Now God had given the chief of staff both respect and affection for Daniel. 10But he responded, "I am afraid of my lord the king, who has ordered that you eat this food and wine. If you become pale and thin compared to the other youths your age, I am afraid the king will have me beheaded."

11Daniel spoke with the attendant who had been appointed by the chief of staff to look after Daniel, Hananiah, Mishael, and Azariah. 12"Please test us for ten days on a diet of vegetables and water," Daniel said. 13"At the end of the ten days, see how we look

Dn 1:4 Or *of the Chaldeans.*

DANIEL

Daniel served as a prophet to the exiles in Babylon from 605–536 B.C.

Climate of the times	The people of Judah were captives in a strange land, feeling hopeless.
Main message	God is sovereign over all human history: past, present, and future.
Importance of message	We should spend less time wondering when future events will happen and more time learning how we should live now.
Contemporary prophets	Jeremiah (627–586 B.C.), Habakkuk (612–589 B.C.), Ezekiel (593–571 B.C.)

Babylonians. Those who loved the Lord must have felt disheartened and discouraged. We feel greatly disappointed when our churches suffer physical damage, split, close down for financial reasons, or are rocked by scandals. We do not know why God allows his church to experience these calamities. But like the people who witnessed the Babylonians' plunder of the Temple, we must trust that God is in control and that he is watching over all who trust in him.

Dan 1:4 The common language of Babylon was Aramaic, while the language of scholarship included the ancient and complicated Babylonian language. The academic program would have included mathematics, astronomy, history, science, and magic. These young men demonstrated not only aptitude but also discipline. This character trait, combined with integrity, served them well in their new culture.

Dan 1:7 Nebuchadnezzar changed the names of Daniel and his friends because he wanted to make them Babylonian—in their own eyes and in the eyes of the Babylonian people. New names would help them to be assimilated into the culture. *Daniel* means "God is my judge" in Hebrew; his new name, *Belteshazzar*, means "Bel, protect his life!" (Bel, also called Marduk, was the chief Babylonian god.) *Hananiah* means "the LORD shows grace"; his new name, *Shadrach*, probably means "under the command of Aku" (the moon god). *Mishael* means "who is like God?"; his new name, *Meshach*, probably means "who is like Aku?" *Azariah* means "the LORD helps"; his new name, *Abednego*, means "servant of Nego/Nebo" (or Nabu, the god of learning and writing). This was how the king attempted to change the religious loyalty of these young men from Judah's God to Babylon's gods.

Dan 1:8 Daniel resolved not to eat this food, either because it was forbidden by Jewish law, such as pork (see Lev 11), or because accepting the king's food and drink was the first step toward depending on his gifts and favors. Although Daniel was in a culture that did not honor God, he still obeyed God's laws.

Dan 1:8 Daniel "was determined" to be devoted to principle and to be committed to a course of action. When Daniel made up his mind not to defile himself, he was being true to a lifelong determination to do what was right and not to give in to the pressures around him. We, too, are often assaulted by pressures to compromise our standards and live more like the world around us. Merely wanting or preferring God's will and way is not enough to stand against the onslaught of temptation. Like Daniel, we must resolve to obey God.

Dan 1:8 It is easier to resist temptation if you have thought through your convictions before the temptation arises. Daniel and his friends made their decision to be faithful to the laws of God *before* they were faced with the king's delicacies, so they did not hesitate to stick with their convictions. We will get into trouble if we have not previously decided where to draw the line. Before such situations arise, decide on your commitments and what you will do. Then when temptation comes, you will be ready to say no.

Dan 1:9 God moved with an unseen hand to change the heart of this Babylonian official. The strong moral conviction of these four young men made an impact. God promises to be with his people in times of trial and temptation (Ps 106:46; Isa 43:2-5; 1 Cor 10:13). His active intervention often comes just when we take a stand for him. Stand for God and trust him to protect you in ways you may not be able to see.

Dan 1:10 Anything short of complete obedience meant execution for the officials who served Nebuchadnezzar. Even in such a small matter as this, the official feared for his life.

Dan 1:12 The Babylonians were trying to change their *thinking* by giving them a Babylonian education, their *loyalty* by changing their names, and their *lifestyle* by changing their diet. Without compromising, Daniel found a way to live by God's standards in a culture that did not honor God. Wisely choosing to negotiate rather than to rebel, Daniel suggested an experimental 10-day diet of vegetables and water instead of the royal foods and wine the king offered. Without compromising, Daniel quickly thought of a practical, creative solution that saved his life and the lives of his companions. As God's people, we may adjust to our culture as long as we do not compromise God's laws.

605 BC
First captivity; Daniel taken to Babylon

▸ **DANIEL 1:3-21** ***(cont.)***
compared to the other young men who are eating the king's food. Then make your decision in light of what you see."
14The attendant agreed to Daniel's suggestion and tested them for ten days.
15At the end of the ten days, Daniel and his three friends looked healthier and better nourished than the young men who had been eating the food assigned by the king.
16So after that, the attendant fed them only vegetables instead of the food and wine provided for the others.
17God gave these four young men an unusual aptitude for understanding every aspect of literature and wisdom. And God gave Daniel the special ability to interpret the meanings of visions and dreams.
18When the training period ordered by the king was completed, the chief of staff brought all the young men to King Nebuchadnezzar.
19The king talked with them, and no one impressed him as much as Daniel, Hananiah, Mishael, and Azariah. So they entered the royal service.
20Whenever the king consulted them in any matter requiring wisdom and balanced judgment, he found them ten times more capable than any of the magicians and enchanters in his entire kingdom.
21Daniel remained in the royal service until the first year of the reign of King Cyrus.*

Nebuchadnezzar's Dream

DANIEL 2:1-23
One night during the second year of his reign,* Nebuchadnezzar had such disturbing dreams that he couldn't sleep.
2He called in his magicians, enchanters, sorcerers, and astrologers,* and he demanded that they tell him what he had dreamed. As they stood before the king,
3he said, "I have had a dream that deeply troubles me, and I must know what it means."
4Then the astrologers answered the king in Aramaic,* "Long live the king! Tell us the dream, and we will tell you what it means."
5But the king said to the astrologers, "I am serious about this. If you don't tell me what my dream was and what it means, you will be torn limb from limb, and your houses will be turned into heaps of rubble!
6But if you tell me what I dreamed and what the dream means, I will give you many wonderful gifts and honors. Just tell me the dream and what it means!"
7They said again, "Please, Your Majesty. Tell us the dream, and we will tell you what it means."
8The king replied, "I know what you are doing! You're stalling for time because you know I am serious when I say,
9'If you don't tell me the dream, you are doomed.' So you have conspired to tell me lies, hoping I will change my mind. But tell me the dream, and then I'll know that you can tell me what it means."
10The astrologers replied to the king, "No one on earth can tell the king his dream! And no king, however great and powerful, has ever asked such a thing of any magician, enchanter, or astrologer!
11The king's demand is impossible. No one except the gods can tell you your dream, and they do not live here among people."
12The king was furious when he heard this, and he

Dn 1:21 Cyrus began his reign (over Babylon) in 539 B.C. **Dn 2:1** The second year of Nebuchadnezzar's reign was 603 B.C. **Dn 2:2** Or *Chaldeans;* also in 2:4, 5, 10. **Dn 2:4** The original text from this point through chapter 7 is in Aramaic.

Dan 1:17 Daniel and his friends learned all they could about their new culture so they could do their work with excellence. But while they learned, they maintained steadfast allegiance to God, and God gave them skill and wisdom. Culture need not be God's enemy. If it does not violate his commands, it can aid in accomplishing his purpose. We who follow God are free to be competent leaders in our culture, but we are required to pledge our allegiance to God first.

Dan 1:20 Nebuchadnezzar put Daniel and his friends on his staff of advisers. This staff included many "magicians and enchanters." These were astrologers who claimed to be able to tell the future through occult practices. They were masters at communicating their message so that it sounded authoritative—as though it came directly from their gods. In addition to knowledge, Daniel and his three friends had wisdom and understanding, given to them by God. Thus, the king was far more pleased with them than with his magicians and enchanters. As we serve others, we must not merely pretend to have God's wisdom. Our wisdom will be genuine when we are rightly related to God.

Dan 1:20 How did the captives survive in a foreign culture? They learned about the culture, achieved excellence in their work, served the people, prayed for God's help, and maintained their integrity. We may feel like foreigners whenever we experience change. Alien cultures come in many forms: a new job, a new school, a new neighborhood. We can use the same principles to help us adapt to our new surroundings without abandoning God.

Dan 1:21 Daniel was one of the first captives taken to Babylon, and he lived to see the first exiles return to Jerusalem in 538 B.C. Throughout this time Daniel honored God, and God honored him. While serving as an adviser to the kings of Babylon, Daniel was God's spokesman to the Babylonian Empire. Babylon was a wicked nation, but it would have been much worse without Daniel's influence.

Dan 2:1-11 Dreams were considered to be messages from the gods, and the astrologers were expected to interpret them. Usually the astrologers could give some sort of interpretation as long as they knew what the dream was about. But this time Nebuchadnezzar demanded to be told the dream also. God sent a series of dreams to Nebuchadnezzar with prophetic messages that could be revealed and understood only by a servant of God. People from other time periods who received dreams from God include Jacob (Gen 28:10-15), Joseph (Gen 37:5-11), Pharaoh's cup-bearer and his baker (Gen 40), Pharaoh (Gen 41), Solomon (1 Kgs 3:5-15), and Joseph (Matt 1:20-24).

Dan 2:10-11 The astrologers told the king that "no one on earth" could know the dreams of another person. What the king asked was humanly impossible. But Daniel could tell what the king had dreamed, and he could also give the interpretation because God was working through him. In daily life, we face many apparently impossible situations that would be hopeless if we had to handle them with our limited strength. But God specializes in working through us to achieve the impossible.

Dan 2:10-11 The astrologers were unable to persuade the king with any amount of logic or rational argument. The king asked for something impossible and didn't want anyone to change his mind. When power goes to a leader's head, whether at work, at home, or in the church, that leader may sometimes demand the impossible from subordinates. At times, he may motivate workers to achieve more than they thought they could. At other times, they may ignore his rantings and rav-

ordered that all the wise men of Babylon be executed.
13And because of the king's decree, men were sent to
find and kill Daniel and his friends.
14When Arioch, the commander of the king's guard,
came to kill them, Daniel handled the situation with
wisdom and discretion. 15He asked Arioch, "Why has
the king issued such a harsh decree?" So Arioch told
him all that had happened. 16Daniel went at once to
see the king and requested more time to tell the king
what the dream meant.
17Then Daniel went home and told his friends
Hananiah, Mishael, and Azariah what had happened.
18He urged them to ask the God of heaven to show
them his mercy by telling them the secret, so they
would not be executed along with the other wise men
of Babylon. 19That night the secret was revealed to
Daniel in a vision. Then Daniel praised the God of
heaven. 20He said,

"Praise the name of God forever and ever,
for he has all wisdom and power.
21 He controls the course of world events;
he removes kings and sets up other kings.
He gives wisdom to the wise
and knowledge to the scholars.
22 He reveals deep and mysterious things
and knows what lies hidden in darkness,
though he is surrounded by light.
23 I thank and praise you, God of my ancestors,
for you have given me wisdom and strength.
You have told me what we asked of you
and revealed to us what the king demanded."

Daniel Interprets the Dream

DANIEL 2:24-45

Then Daniel went in to see Arioch, whom the king had
ordered to execute the wise men of Babylon. Daniel
said to him, "Don't kill the wise men. Take me to the
king, and I will tell him the meaning of his dream."
25Arioch quickly took Daniel to the king and said,
"I have found one of the captives from Judah who will
tell the king the meaning of his dream!"
26The king said to Daniel (also known as Belteshazzar), "Is this true? Can you tell me what my dream
was and what it means?"

NEBUCHADNEZZAR'S DREAM FULFILLED

The large statue in Nebuchadnezzar's dream (Dan 2:24-45) represented the four kingdoms that would dominate as world powers. We recognize these as the Babylonian Empire, the Medo-Persian Empire, the Grecian Empire, and the Roman Empire. All of these will be crushed and brought to an end by the Kingdom of God, which will continue forever.

Part	*Material*	*Empire*	*Period of Domination*
Head	Gold	Babylonian	606–539 B.C.
Chest and Arms	Silver	Medo-Persian	539–331 B.C.
Belly and Thighs	Bronze	Grecian	331–146 B.C.
Legs and Feet	Iron and Clay	Roman	146 B.C.—A.D. 476

ings. Just as Daniel dealt wisely in the situation, we can ask God to give us wisdom to know how to deal with unreasonable bosses.

Dan 2:11 The astrologers admitted that their gods did not "live here among people." Of course their gods didn't—they didn't even exist! This exposed the limitations of the astrologers. They could invent interpretations of dreams but could not tell Nebuchadnezzar *what* he had dreamed. Although his request was unreasonable, Nebuchadnezzar was infuriated by their reply. It was not unusual in these times for astrologers to be in conflict with the king. They sometimes used their craft to gain political power.

Dan 2:11 By answering that the gods "do not live here among people," the astrologers betrayed their concept of the gods. Theirs was a hollow religion, a religion of convenience. They believed in the gods, but that belief made no difference in their conduct. Today, many people profess to believe in God, but it is also a hollow belief. In essence, they are practical atheists because they don't listen to him or do what he says. Do you believe in God? He does live among people, and he wants to change your life.

Dan 2:16-18 Daniel was at a crisis point. Imagine going to see the powerful, temperamental king who had just angrily ordered your death! Daniel did not shrink back in fear but confidently believed God would tell him all the king wanted to know. When the king gave Daniel time to find the answer, Daniel found his three friends and they prayed. When you find yourself in a tight spot, share your needs with trusted friends who also believe in God's power. Prayer is more effective than panic. Panic confirms your hopelessness; prayer confirms your hope in God. Daniel's trust in God saved not only himself but also his three friends and all the other wise men of Babylon.

Dan 2:19-23 After Daniel asked God to reveal Nebuchadnezzar's dream to him, he saw a vision of the dream. Daniel's prayer was answered. Before rushing to Arioch with the news, Daniel took time to give God credit for all wisdom and power, thanking God for answering his request. How do you feel when your prayers are answered? Excited? Surprised? Relieved? There are times when we seek God in prayer and, after having been answered, dash off in our excitement, forgetting to give God credit for the answer. Match your persistence in prayer with gratitude when your requests are answered.

Dan 2:21 If you know that you still have much to learn in life, and if you have ever wished that you knew more about how to deal with people, then look to God for wisdom. While educational institutions provide diplomas at great expense, God gives wisdom freely to all who ask. (See Jas 1:5 for more on asking God for wisdom.)

Dan 2:21 When we see evil leaders who live long and good leaders who die young, we may wonder if God is still in control. Daniel saw evil rulers with almost limitless power, but he knew that God "removes kings and sets up other kings" and that he controls everything that happens. God governs the world according to his purposes. You may be dismayed when you see evil people prosper, but God is in control. Let this knowledge give you confidence and peace no matter what happens.

Dan 2:24 Daniel did not use his success to promote his own self-interest. He thought of others. When striving to succeed or survive, remember the needs of others.

▸ **DANIEL 2:24-45** ***(cont.)***

27Daniel replied, "There are no wise men, enchanters, magicians, or fortune-tellers who can reveal the
king's secret. 28But there is a God in heaven who reveals secrets, and he has shown King Nebuchadnezzar what will happen in the future. Now I will tell
you your dream and the visions you saw as you lay
on your bed.
29"While Your Majesty was sleeping, you dreamed
about coming events. He who reveals secrets has
shown you what is going to happen. 30And it is not
because I am wiser than anyone else that I know the
secret of your dream, but because God wants you to
understand what was in your heart.
31"In your vision, Your Majesty, you saw standing
before you a huge, shining statue of a man. It was a
frightening sight. 32The head of the statue was made
of fine gold. Its chest and arms were silver, its belly
and thighs were bronze, 33its legs were iron, and its
feet were a combination of iron and baked clay. 34As
you watched, a rock was cut from a mountain, but not
by human hands. It struck the feet of iron and clay,
smashing them to bits. 35The whole statue was crushed
into small pieces of iron, clay, bronze, silver, and gold.
Then the wind blew them away without a trace, like
chaff on a threshing floor. But the rock that knocked
the statue down became a great mountain that covered
the whole earth.
36"That was the dream. Now we will tell the king
what it means. 37Your Majesty, you are the greatest of

Dan 2:27-30 Before Daniel told the king anything else, he gave credit to God, explaining that he did not know the dream through his own wisdom but only because God revealed it. How easily we take credit for what God does through us! This robs God of the honor that he alone deserves. Instead, we should be like Daniel and point people to God so that we give him the glory.

Dan 2:31ff The head of gold on the statue in the dream represented Nebuchadnezzar, ruler of the Babylonian Empire. The silver chest and two arms represented the Medo-Persian Empire, which conquered Babylon in 539 B.C. The belly and thighs of bronze were Greece and Macedonia under Alexander the Great, who conquered the Medo-Persian Empire (334–330 B.C.). The legs of iron represented Rome, which conquered the Greeks in 63 B.C. The feet of clay and iron represented the breakup of the Roman Empire, when the territory Rome ruled divided into a mixture of strong and weak nations. The type of metal in each part depicted the strength of the political power it represented. The rock cut out of the mountain depicted God's Kingdom, which would be ruled eternally by the Messiah, the King of kings. The dream revealed Daniel's God as the power behind all earthly kingdoms.

DANIEL

Daniel's early life demonstrates that there is more to being young than making mistakes. No characteristic wins the hearts of adults more quickly than wisdom in the words and actions of a young person. Daniel and his friends had been taken from their homes in Judah and exiled. Their futures were in doubt, but they all had personal traits that qualified them for jobs as servants in the king's palace. They took advantage of the opportunity without letting the opportunity take advantage of them. • Our first hint of Daniel's greatness comes in his quiet refusal to give up his convictions. He had applied God's will to his own life, and he resisted changing the good habits he had formed. Both his physical and spiritual diets were an important part of his relationship with God. He ate carefully and lived prayerfully. One of the benefits of being in training for royal service was eating food from the king's table. Daniel tactfully chose a simpler menu that wouldn't compromise his observance of God's law. • While Daniel carefully limited his food options, he generously indulged in prayer. He was able to communicate with God because he made it a habit. He put into practice his convictions, even when that meant being thrown into a den of hungry lions. His life proved he made the right choice. • Do you hold so strongly to your faith in God that no matter what happens you will do what God says? Such conviction keeps you a step ahead of temptation; such conviction gives you wisdom and stability in changing circumstances. Prayerfully live out your convictions in everyday life and trust God for the results.

Strengths and accomplishments	• Although young when deported, remained true to his faith • Served as an adviser to two Babylonian kings and two Medo-Persian kings • Was a man of prayer and a statesman with the gift of prophecy
Lessons from his life	• Quiet convictions often earn long-term respect • Don't wait until you are in a tough situation to learn about prayer • God can use people wherever they are
Vital statistics	• Where: Judah and the courts of both Babylon and Persia • Occupation: A captive from Israel who became an adviser of kings • Contemporaries: Shadrach, Meshach, Abednego, Nebuchadnezzar, Belshazzar, Darius, Cyrus
Key verse	"This man Daniel, whom the king named Belteshazzar, has exceptional ability and is filled with divine knowledge and understanding. He can interpret dreams, explain riddles, and solve difficult problems. Call for Daniel, and he will tell you what the writing means" (Dan 5:12).

Daniel's story is told in the book of Daniel. He is also mentioned in Ezekiel 14:14, 20; 28:3; Matthew 24:15.

kings. The God of heaven has given you sovereignty, power, strength, and honor. 38He has made you the ruler over all the inhabited world and has put even the wild animals and birds under your control. You are the head of gold.

39"But after your kingdom comes to an end, another kingdom, inferior to yours, will rise to take your place. After that kingdom has fallen, yet a third kingdom, represented by bronze, will rise to rule the world. 40Following that kingdom, there will be a fourth one, as strong as iron. That kingdom will smash and crush all previous empires, just as iron smashes and crushes everything it strikes. 41The feet and toes you saw were a combination of iron and baked clay, showing that this kingdom will be divided. Like iron mixed with clay, it will have some of the strength of iron. 42But while some parts of it will be as strong as iron, other parts will be as weak as clay. 43This mixture of iron and clay also shows that these kingdoms will try to strengthen themselves by forming alliances with each other through intermarriage. But they will not hold together, just as iron and clay do not mix.

44"During the reigns of those kings, the God of heaven will set up a kingdom that will never be destroyed or conquered. It will crush all these kingdoms into nothingness, and it will stand forever. 45That is the meaning of the rock cut from the mountain, though not by human hands, that crushed to pieces the statue of iron, bronze, clay, silver, and gold. The great God was showing the king what will happen in the future. The dream is true, and its meaning is certain."

Nebuchadnezzar Rewards Daniel

DANIEL 2:46-49

Then King Nebuchadnezzar threw himself down before Daniel and worshiped him, and he commanded his people to offer sacrifices and burn sweet incense before him. 47The king said to Daniel, "Truly, your God is the greatest of gods, the Lord over kings, a revealer of mysteries, for you have been able to reveal this secret."

48Then the king appointed Daniel to a high position and gave him many valuable gifts. He made Daniel ruler over the whole province of Babylon, as well as chief over all his wise men. 49At Daniel's request, the king appointed Shadrach, Meshach, and Abednego to be in charge of all the affairs of the province of Babylon, while Daniel remained in the king's court.

Nebuchadnezzar's Gold Statue

DANIEL 3:1-18

King Nebuchadnezzar made a gold statue ninety feet tall and nine feet wide* and set it up on the plain of Dura in the province of Babylon. 2Then he sent messages to the high officers, officials, governors, advisers, treasurers, judges, magistrates, and all the provincial officials to come to the dedication of the statue he had set up. 3So all these officials* came and stood before the statue King Nebuchadnezzar had set up.

4Then a herald shouted out, "People of all races and nations and languages, listen to the king's command! 5When you hear the sound of the horn, flute, zither, lyre, harp, pipes, and other musical instruments,* bow to the ground to worship King Nebuchadnezzar's gold statue. 6Anyone who refuses to obey will immediately be thrown into a blazing furnace."

7So at the sound of the musical instruments,* all the people, whatever their race or nation or language, bowed to the ground and worshiped the gold statue that King Nebuchadnezzar had set up.

8But some of the astrologers* went to the king and informed on the Jews. 9They said to King Nebuchadnezzar, "Long live the king! 10You issued a decree requiring all the people to bow down and worship the gold statue when they hear the sound of the horn, flute,

Dn 3:1 Aramaic *60 cubits* [27 meters] *tall and 6 cubits* [2.7 meters] *wide.* **Dn 3:3** Aramaic *the high officers, officials, governors, advisers, treasurers, judges, magistrates, and all the provincial officials.* **Dn 3:5** The identification of some of these musical instruments is uncertain. **Dn 3:7** Aramaic *the horn, flute, zither, lyre, harp, and other musical instruments.* **Dn 3:8** Aramaic *Chaldeans.*

600 BC

The Temple of Artemis is constructed in Ephesus

Dan 2:44 God's Kingdom will never be destroyed. If you are upset by threats of war and the prosperity of evil leaders, remember that God, not world leaders, decides the outcome of history. Under God's protection, God's Kingdom is indestructible. Those who trust in God are members of his Kingdom and are secure in him.

Dan 2:47 Nebuchadnezzar honored Daniel and Daniel's God. If Daniel had taken the credit himself, the king would have honored only Daniel. Because Daniel gave God the credit, the king honored both of them. Part of our mission in this world is to show unbelievers what God is like. We can do that by acts of love and compassion; and if we give God credit for our actions, they will want to know more about him. Give thanks to God for what he is doing in and through you.

Dan 2:49 After being named ruler over the whole province of Babylon and placed in charge of the wise men, Daniel requested that his companions, Shadrach, Meshach, and Abednego, be appointed as his assistants. Daniel knew that he could not handle such an enormous responsibility without capable assistants, so he chose the best men he knew—his three Hebrew companions. A competent leader never does all the work alone but knows how to delegate and supervise. Moses, Israel's greatest leader, shared the burden of administration with dozens of assistants. (See Exod 18:13-27.)

Dan 3:1 In Babylon's religious culture, statues were frequently worshiped. Nebuchadnezzar hoped to use this huge image (90 feet high by 9 feet wide) as a strategy to unite the nation and solidify his power by centralizing worship. This gold statue may have been inspired by his dream. Instead of having only a head of gold, however, it was gold from head to toe. Nebuchadnezzar wanted his kingdom to last forever. When he made the statue, Nebuchadnezzar showed that his devotion to Daniel's God was short-lived. He neither feared nor obeyed the God who was behind the dream.

Dan 3:6 This blazing furnace was not a small oven for cooking dinner or heating a house; it was a huge industrial furnace that could have been used for baking bricks or smelting metals. The temperatures were hot enough to assure that no one could survive. The roaring flames could be seen leaping from its top opening, and a fiery blast killed the soldiers who went up to the large opening (Dan 3:22).

▶ **DANIEL 3:1-18** ***(cont.)***

zither, lyre, harp, pipes, and other musical instruments.
11That decree also states that those who refuse to obey
must be thrown into a blazing furnace. 12But there
are some Jews—Shadrach, Meshach, and Abednego—
whom you have put in charge of the province of Babylon. They pay no attention to you, Your Majesty. They
refuse to serve your gods and do not worship the gold
statue you have set up."
13Then Nebuchadnezzar flew into a rage and ordered that Shadrach, Meshach, and Abednego be
brought before him. When they were brought in,
14Nebuchadnezzar said to them, "Is it true, Shadrach,
Meshach, and Abednego, that you refuse to serve my
gods or to worship the gold statue I have set up? 15I
will give you one more chance to bow down and worship the statue I have made when you hear the sound
of the musical instruments.* But if you refuse, you
will be thrown immediately into the blazing furnace.
And then what god will be able to rescue you from
my power?"
16Shadrach, Meshach, and Abednego replied,
"O Nebuchadnezzar, we do not need to defend ourselves before you. 17If we are thrown into the blazing
furnace, the God whom we serve is able to save us. He
will rescue us from your power, Your Majesty. 18But

Dn 3:15 Aramaic *the horn, flute, zither, lyre, harp, pipes, and other musical instruments.*

Dan 3:12 We don't know if other Jews refused to fall down and worship the statue, but these three were singled out as public examples. Why didn't the three men just bow to the image and tell God that they didn't mean it? They had determined never to worship another god, and they courageously took their stand. As a result, they were condemned and led away to be executed. The men did not know whether they would be delivered from the fire; all they knew was that they would not fall down and worship an idol. Are you ready to take a stand for God no matter what? When you stand for God, you will stand out. It may be painful, and there may not always be a happy ending. Be prepared to say, "If he rescues me, or if he doesn't, I will serve only God."

Dan 3:13 Nebuchadnezzar flew into a rage when anyone dared to disobey his commands. As the supreme ruler of Babylon, he expected absolute obedience. But his pride had caused him to go beyond his own authority. His demands were unjust and his reactions extreme. If you find yourself angered when people don't follow your directions, ask yourself, Why am I reacting this way? Your ego may be overly involved with your authority.

Dan 3:15 The three men were given one more chance. Here are eight excuses they could have used to bow to the statue and save their lives: (1) We will bow down but not actually worship the idol. (2) We won't become idol worshipers but will worship it this one time, and then ask God for forgiveness. (3) The king has absolute power, and we must obey him. God will understand. (4) The king appointed us—we owe this to him. (5) This is a foreign land, so God will excuse us for following the customs of the land. (6) Our ancestors set up idols in God's Temple! This isn't half as bad! (7) We're not hurting anybody. (8) If we get ourselves killed and some pagans take our high positions, they won't help our people in exile!

Although all these excuses sound sensible at first, they are dangerous rationalizations. To bow down and worship the image would violate God's command in Exodus 20:3: "You must not have any other god but me."

SHADRACH/MESHACH/ABEDNEGO

Friendships make life enjoyable and difficult times bearable. Friendships are tested and strengthened by hardships. Such was the relationship among three young Hebrew men deported to Babylon along with Daniel. Shadrach, Meshach, and Abednego help us think about the real meaning of friendship. As much as these friends meant to each other, they never allowed their friendship to usurp God's place in their lives—not even in the face of death. • Together they silently defied King Nebuchadnezzar's order to fall down and worship his gold statue. They shared a courageous act, while others, eager to get rid of them, told the king that the three Hebrews were being disloyal. While this was not true, Nebuchadnezzar could not spare them without losing face. • This was the moment of truth. Death was about to end their friendship. A small compromise would have allowed them to live and go on enjoying each other, serving God, and serving their people while in this foreign land. But they were wise enough to see that compromise would have poisoned the very conviction that bound them so closely—each had a higher allegiance to God. So they did not hesitate to place their lives in the hands of God. The rest was victory! • When we leave God out of our most important relationships, we tend to expect those relationships to meet needs in us that only God can meet. Friends are helpful, but they cannot meet our deepest spiritual needs. Leaving God out of our relationships indicates how unimportant he really is in our own lives. Our relationship with God should be important enough to touch our other relationships—especially our closest friendships.

Strengths and accomplishments	• Stood with Daniel against eating food from the king's table • Shared a friendship that stood the tests of hardship, success, wealth, and possible death • Unwilling to compromise their convictions even in the face of death
Lessons from their lives	• There is great strength in real friendship • It is important to stand with others with whom we share convictions • God can be trusted even when we can't predict the outcome
Vital statistics	• Where: Babylon • Occupations: King's servants and advisers • Contemporaries: Daniel, Nebuchadnezzar
Key verses	"Shadrach, Meshach, and Abednego replied, 'O Nebuchadnezzar, we do not need to defend ourselves before you. If we are thrown into the blazing furnace, the God whom we serve is able to save us. He will rescue us from your power, Your Majesty. But even if he doesn't, we want to make it clear to you, Your Majesty, that we will never serve your gods or worship the gold statue you have set up'" (Dan 3:16-18).

The story of Shadrach (Hananiah), Meshach (Mishael), and Abednego (Azariah) is told in the book of Daniel.

even if he doesn't, we want to make it clear to you, Your Majesty, that we will never serve your gods or worship the gold statue you have set up."

The Blazing Furnace

DANIEL 3:19-30

Nebuchadnezzar was so furious with Shadrach, Meshach, and Abednego that his face became distorted with rage. He commanded that the furnace be heated seven times hotter than usual. [20]Then he ordered some of the strongest men of his army to bind Shadrach, Meshach, and Abednego and throw them into the blazing furnace. [21]So they tied them up and threw them into the furnace, fully dressed in their pants, turbans, robes, and other garments. [22]And because the king, in his anger, had demanded such a hot fire in the furnace, the flames killed the soldiers as they threw the three men in. [23]So Shadrach, Meshach, and Abednego, securely tied, fell into the roaring flames.

[24]But suddenly, Nebuchadnezzar jumped up in amazement and exclaimed to his advisers, "Didn't we tie up three men and throw them into the furnace?"

"Yes, Your Majesty, we certainly did," they replied.

[25]"Look!" Nebuchadnezzar shouted. "I see four men, unbound, walking around in the fire unharmed! And the fourth looks like a god*!"

[26]Then Nebuchadnezzar came as close as he could to the door of the flaming furnace and shouted: "Shadrach, Meshach, and Abednego, servants of the Most High God, come out! Come here!"

So Shadrach, Meshach, and Abednego stepped out of the fire. [27]Then the high officers, officials, governors, and advisers crowded around them and saw that the fire had not touched them. Not a hair on their heads was singed, and their clothing was not scorched. They didn't even smell of smoke!

[28]Then Nebuchadnezzar said, "Praise to the God of Shadrach, Meshach, and Abednego! He sent his angel to rescue his servants who trusted in him. They defied the king's command and were willing to die rather than serve or worship any god except their own God. [29]Therefore, I make this decree: If any people, whatever their race or nation or language, speak a word against the God of Shadrach, Meshach, and Abednego, they will be torn limb from limb, and their houses will be turned into heaps of rubble. There is no other god who can rescue like this!"

[30]Then the king promoted Shadrach, Meshach, and Abednego to even higher positions in the province of Babylon.

Dn 3:25 Aramaic *like a son of the gods.*

4. JEREMIAH PROPHESIES JUDAH'S DESTRUCTION

The prophecies in this collection were probably given during the time between Babylon's first invasion of Judah in 605 B.C. and their second incursion in 597 B.C. Jeremiah continued to warn the people and leaders of Judah about God's coming judgment on the nation, but they didn't want to hear his message.

Jeremiah Speaks at the Temple

JEREMIAH 7:1-15

The LORD gave another message to Jeremiah. He said, [2]"Go to the entrance of the LORD's Temple, and give this message to the people: 'O Judah, listen to this message from the LORD! Listen to it, all of you who worship here! [3]This is what the LORD of Heaven's Armies, the God of Israel, says:

It would also erase their testimony for God forever. Never again could they talk about the power of their God above all other gods. What excuses do you use for not standing up for him?

Dan 3:16-18 Shadrach, Meshach, and Abednego were pressured to deny God, but they chose to be faithful to him no matter what happened! They trusted God to deliver them, but they were determined to be faithful regardless of the consequences. We should be faithful to serve God whether he intervenes on our behalf or not. Our eternal reward is worth any suffering we may have to endure first.

Dan 3:25 It was obvious to those watching that this fourth person was supernatural. We cannot be certain who the fourth man was. It could have been an angel or a preincarnate appearance of Christ. In either case, God sent a heavenly visitor to accompany these faithful men during their time of great trial.

Dan 3:25-30 God's deliverance of Shadrach, Meshach, and Abednego was a great victory of faith for the Jews in captivity. They were protected from harm, they were comforted in trial, God was glorified, and they were rewarded. Let us determine to be true to God no matter how difficult the pressure or punishment. God's protection transcends anything we could imagine.

Dan 3:27 These young men had been completely untouched by the fire and heat. Only the rope that bound them had been burned. No human can bind us if God wants us to be free. The power available to us is the same that delivered Shadrach, Meshach, and Abednego and raised Christ from the dead (Eph 1:18-20). Trust God in every situation. There are eternal reasons for temporary trials, so be thankful that your destiny is in God's hands, not in human hands.

Dan 3:28-29 Nebuchadnezzar was not making a commitment here to serve the Hebrews' God alone. Instead, he was acknowledging that God is powerful, and he commanded his people not to speak against God. Nebuchadnezzar didn't tell the people to throw away all the other gods but to add this one to the list.

Dan 3:30 Where was Daniel in this story? The Bible doesn't say, but there are several possibilities: (1) He may have been on official business in another part of the kingdom. (2) He may have been present, but because he was a ruler, the officials didn't accuse him of not falling down and worshiping the image. (3) He may have been in the capital city handling the administration while Nebuchadnezzar was away. (4) He may have been considered exempt from bowing down to the image because of his reputation for interpreting dreams through his God. Whether Daniel was there or not, we can be sure that he would not have worshiped the statue.

Jer 7:1–10:25 As this section opens, God sends Jeremiah to the Temple gates to refute the false belief that God would not let harm come to the Temple or to those who

▸ JEREMIAH 7:1-15 *(cont.)*

"'Even now, if you quit your evil ways, I will let you
stay in your own land. 4But don't be fooled by those
who promise you safety simply because the LORD's
Temple is here. They chant, "The LORD's Temple is
here! The LORD's Temple is here!" 5But I will be merciful only if you stop your evil thoughts and deeds and
start treating each other with justice; 6only if you stop
exploiting foreigners, orphans, and widows; only if
you stop your murdering; and only if you stop harming yourselves by worshiping idols. 7Then I will let
you stay in this land that I gave to your ancestors to
keep forever.
8"'Don't be fooled into thinking that you will never
suffer because the Temple is here. It's a lie! 9Do you
really think you can steal, murder, commit adultery,
lie, and burn incense to Baal and all those other new
gods of yours, 10and then come here and stand before
me in my Temple and chant, "We are safe!"—only to go
right back to all those evils again? 11Don't you yourselves admit that this Temple, which bears my name,
has become a den of thieves? Surely I see all the evil
going on there. I, the LORD, have spoken!
12"'Go now to the place at Shiloh where I once put
the Tabernacle that bore my name. See what I did
there because of all the wickedness of my people,
the Israelites. 13While you were doing these wicked
things, says the LORD, I spoke to you about it repeatedly, but you would not listen. I called out to you, but
you refused to answer. 14So just as I destroyed Shiloh,
I will now destroy this Temple that bears my name,
this Temple that you trust in for help, this place that I
gave to you and your ancestors. 15And I will send you
out of my sight into exile, just as I did your relatives,
the people of Israel.*'

Judah's Persistent Idolatry

JEREMIAH 7:16-29

"Pray no more for these people, Jeremiah. Do not weep
or pray for them, and don't beg me to help them, for
I will not listen to you. 17Don't you see what they are
doing throughout the towns of Judah and in the streets

Jer 7:15 Hebrew *of Ephraim*, referring to the northern kingdom of Israel.

Queen of Heaven

The Queen of Heaven is a goddess mentioned by Jeremiah in his denunciations of Judah's idolatry (Jer 7:18; 44:17-19, 25). The goddess is generally identified with Ishtar, a Babylonian deity of war and love (associated with the planet Venus). This illustration pictures an Assyrian cylinder-seal with its impression showing the Queen of Heaven. Probably imported into Judah during Manasseh's reign, this worship was especially attractive to the women of Judah. After the destruction and depopulation of Jerusalem in 586 B.C., a group of exiles fled to Egypt, carrying Jeremiah with them. There he again condemned the idolatry that had brought this disaster. The Old Testament condemns idolatry because it steals peoples' hearts from worshiping the true God. The New Testament condemns idolatry as well (see 1 Jn 5:21). We should heed the Scriptures and worship the true God.

lived near it. Jeremiah rebukes the people for their false and worthless religion, their idolatry, and the shameless behavior of the people and their leaders. Judah, he says, is ripe for judgment and exile. This happened during the reign of Jehoiakim, a puppet of Egypt. The nation, in shock over the death of Josiah, was going through a spiritual reversal that removed much of the good Josiah had done. The themes of this section are false religion, idolatry, and hypocrisy. Jeremiah was almost put to death for this sermon, but he was saved by the officials of Judah (see Jer 26).

Jer 7:2-3 The people followed a worship ritual but maintained a sinful lifestyle. It was religion without personal commitment to God. Attending church, taking communion, teaching church school, singing in the choir—all are empty exercises unless we are truly doing them for God. It is good to do these activities—not because we ought to do them for the church but because we want to do them for God.

Jer 7:9-11 There are several parallels between how the people of Judah viewed their Temple and how many today view their churches. (1) They didn't make the Temple part of their daily living. We may go to beautiful churches well-prepared for worship, but often we don't take the presence of God with us through the week. (2) The image of the Temple became more important than the substance of faith. Going to church and belonging to a group can become more important than a life changed for God. (3) The people used their Temple as a sanctuary. Many use religious affiliation as a hideout, thinking it will protect them from evil and problems.

Jer 7:11-12 Jesus later used these words from Jeremiah 7:11 when he cleared the Temple (Mark 11:17; Luke 19:46). This passage applied to the evil in the Temple in Jesus' day as well as in Jeremiah's. God's Tabernacle had been at Shiloh, but Shiloh had been abandoned (Ps 78:60; Jer 26:6). If God did not preserve Shiloh because the Tabernacle was there, why would he preserve Jerusalem because of the Temple?

Jer 7:15 Israel, the northern kingdom, had been taken into captivity by Assyria in 722 B.C.

Jer 7:18 The "Queen of Heaven" was a name for Ishtar, the Mesopotamian goddess

of Jerusalem? [18]No wonder I am so angry! Watch how the children gather wood and the fathers build sacrificial fires. See how the women knead dough and make cakes to offer to the Queen of Heaven. And they pour out liquid offerings to their other idol gods! [19]Am I the one they are hurting?" asks the LORD. "Most of all, they hurt themselves, to their own shame."

[20]So this is what the Sovereign LORD says: "I will pour out my terrible fury on this place. Its people, animals, trees, and crops will be consumed by the unquenchable fire of my anger."

[21]This is what the LORD of Heaven's Armies, the God of Israel, says: "Take your burnt offerings and your other sacrifices and eat them yourselves! [22]When I led your ancestors out of Egypt, it was not burnt offerings and sacrifices I wanted from them. [23]This is what I told them: 'Obey me, and I will be your God, and you will be my people. Do everything as I say, and all will be well!'

[24]"But my people would not listen to me. They kept doing whatever they wanted, following the stubborn desires of their evil hearts. They went backward instead of forward. [25]From the day your ancestors left Egypt until now, I have continued to send my servants, the prophets—day in and day out. [26]But my people have not listened to me or even tried to hear. They have been stubborn and sinful—even worse than their ancestors.

[27]"Tell them all this, but do not expect them to listen. Shout out your warnings, but do not expect them to respond. [28]Say to them, 'This is the nation whose people will not obey the LORD their God and who refuse to be taught. Truth has vanished from among them; it is no longer heard on their lips. [29]Shave your head in mourning, and weep alone on the mountains. For the LORD has rejected and forsaken this generation that has provoked his fury.'

The Valley of Slaughter

JEREMIAH 7:30–8:3

"The people of Judah have sinned before my very eyes," says the LORD. "They have set up their abominable idols right in the Temple that bears my name, defiling it. [31]They have built pagan shrines at Topheth, the garbage dump in the valley of Ben-Hinnom, and there they burn their sons and daughters in the fire. I have never commanded such a horrible deed; it never even crossed my mind to command such a thing! [32]So beware, for the time is coming," says the LORD, "when that garbage dump will no longer be called Topheth or the valley of Ben-Hinnom, but the Valley of Slaughter. They will bury the bodies in Topheth until there is no more room for them. [33]The bodies of my people will be food for the vultures and wild animals, and no one will be left to scare them away. [34]I will put an end to the happy singing and laughter in the streets of Jerusalem. The joyful voices of bridegrooms and brides will no longer be heard in the towns of Judah. The land will lie in complete desolation.

8:1"In that day," says the LORD, "the enemy will break open the graves of the kings and officials of Judah, and the graves of the priests, prophets, and common people of Jerusalem. [2]They will spread out their bones on the ground before the sun, moon, and stars—the gods my people have loved, served, and worshiped. Their bones will not be gathered up again or buried but will be scattered on the ground like manure. [3]And the people of this evil nation who survive will wish to die rather than live where I will send them. I, the LORD of Heaven's Armies, have spoken!

---

of love and fertility. After the fall of Jerusalem, the refugees from Judah who fled to Egypt continued to worship her (Jer 44:17). A papyrus dating from the 5th century B.C., found at Hermopolis in Egypt, mentions the Queen of Heaven among the gods honored by the Jewish community living there.

Jer 7:19 This verse answers the question, Who gets hurt when we turn away from God? We do! Separating ourselves from God is like keeping a green plant away from sunlight or water. God is our only source of spiritual strength. Cut yourself off from him, and you cut off life itself.

Jer 7:21-23 God had set up a system of sacrifices to encourage the people to joyfully obey him (see the book of Leviticus). He required the people to make these sacrifices, not because the sacrifices themselves pleased him, but because they caused the people to recognize their sin and refocus on living for God. They faithfully made the sacrifices but forgot the reason they were offering them, and thus they disobeyed God. Jeremiah reminded the people that unless they were prepared to obey God in all areas of life, acting out religious rituals was meaningless. (See the chart on p. 809.)

Jer 7:25 From the time of Moses to the end of the Old Testament period, God sent many prophets to Israel and Judah. No matter how bad the circumstances were, God always raised up a prophet to speak against their stubborn spiritual attitudes.

Jer 7:27 Why did God instruct Jeremiah to prophesy and proclaim if the effort would be fruitless? God demonstrates his consistent faithfulness even in the face of human resistance. God was also "going on record" for those beyond Jeremiah's generation. (See 1 Cor 10:1-11 for an explanation of God's detailed recording of the past failures of his people.) The stories are intended to guide us and prevent us from making the same mistakes.

Jer 7:31-32 The shrines of Topheth (meaning "fireplace") were set up in the valley of Ben-Hinnom, where debris and rubbish from the city were thrown away. This altar was used to worship Molech—a god who required child sacrifice (2 Kgs 23:10). Their valley of sacrifice would become their Valley of Slaughter by the Babylonians. At the place where the people had killed their children in sinful idol worship, they themselves would be slaughtered.

Jer 8:1-2 The threat that the graves of Judah's people would be opened was horrible to a people who highly honored the dead and believed that it was the highest desecration to open graves. This would be an ironic punishment for idol worshipers—their bones would be laid out before the sun, moon, and stars—the gods they thought could save them.

Deception by False Prophets

JEREMIAH 8:4-17

"Jeremiah, say to the people, 'This is what the LORD says:

"'When people fall down, don't they get up again?
When they discover they're on the wrong road,
don't they turn back?
5 Then why do these people stay on their self-destructive path?
Why do the people of Jerusalem refuse
to turn back?
They cling tightly to their lies
and will not turn around.
6 I listen to their conversations
and don't hear a word of truth.
Is anyone sorry for doing wrong?
Does anyone say, "What a terrible thing
I have done"?
No! All are running down the path of sin
as swiftly as a horse galloping into battle!
7 Even the stork that flies across the sky
knows the time of her migration,
as do the turtledove, the swallow, and the crane.*
They all return at the proper time each year.
But not my people!
They do not know the LORD's laws.

8 "'How can you say, "We are wise because we have
the word of the LORD,"
when your teachers have twisted it by
writing lies?
9 These wise teachers will fall
into the trap of their own foolishness,
for they have rejected the word of the LORD.
Are they so wise after all?
10 I will give their wives to others
and their farms to strangers.
From the least to the greatest,
their lives are ruled by greed.
Yes, even my prophets and priests are
like that.
They are all frauds.
11 They offer superficial treatments
for my people's mortal wound.
They give assurances of peace
when there is no peace.
12 Are they ashamed of these disgusting actions?
Not at all—they don't even know how
to blush!
Therefore, they will lie among the slaughtered.
They will be brought down when I punish
them,
says the LORD.

Jer 8:7 The identification of some of these birds is uncertain.

OLD TESTAMENT TESTS FOR FALSE PROPHETS

In the Old Testament, various signs or works pointed to a true or false prophet. Many of these can be applied today.

1. **Does the prophet use fortune-telling?**
Divination was expressly forbidden by God (Deut 18:9-14). No true teacher or prophet would use fortune-telling or have any dealings with spirits of the dead (Jer 14:14; Ezek 12:24; Mic 3:7).
2. **Have the prophet's short-term prophecies been fulfilled?**
Deuteronomy 18:22 used this as a test. Do predictions come to pass?
3. **Is the prophet marked by a desire to say only what pleases people?**
Many false prophets told people what they wanted to hear. A true prophet serves God, not people (Jer 8:11; 14:13; 23:17; Ezek 13:10; Mic 3:5).
4. **Does the prophet draw people away from God?**
Many teachers draw people to themselves or to the system or organization they have built (Deut 13:1-3).
5. **Does the prophet's prophecy confirm the Bible's main teaching?**
If a prophecy is inconsistent with or contradictory to Scripture, it is not to be believed.
6. **What is the prophet's moral character?**
False prophets were charged with lying (Jer 8:10; 14:14), drunkenness (Isa 28:7), and immorality (Jer 23:14).
7. **Do other Spirit-led people discern authenticity in this prophet?**
Discernment by others who are led of the Spirit is a key test (1 Kgs 22:7). The New Testament speaks of this a great deal (John 10:4-15; 1 Cor 2:14; 14:29, 32; 1 Jn 4:1-3).

Jer 8:4-6 When people fall down or realize that they are headed in the wrong direction, it only makes sense for them to get up or change directions. But as God watched the nation, he saw people living sinful lives by choice, deceiving themselves that there would be no consequences. They had lost perspective concerning God's will for their lives and were trying to minimize their sin. Are there some indicators that you have fallen down or are heading the wrong way? What are you doing to get back on the right path?

Jer 8:16 Dan was the northernmost tribe in Israel.

Jer 8:18-19 Jeremiah was pleading with God to save his people.

Jer 8:20-22 These words vividly portray Jeremiah's emotion as he watched his people reject God. He responded with anguish to a world dying in sin. We watch that same world still dying in sin, still rejecting God. But how often is our heart broken for our lost friends and neighbors, our lost world? Only when we have Jeremiah's kind of passionate concern will we be moved to help. We must begin by asking God to break our hearts for the world he loves.

Jer 8:22 Gilead was famous for its healing medicine. This is a rhetorical question. The obvious answer is, "Yes—God," but Israel was not applying the "medicine"; they were not obeying the Lord. Although the people's spiritual sickness was very deep, it could be healed. But the people refused the medicine.

13 I will surely consume them.
There will be no more harvests of figs
and grapes.
Their fruit trees will all die.
Whatever I gave them will soon be gone.
I, the LORD, have spoken!'

14 "Then the people will say,
'Why should we wait here to die?
Come, let's go to the fortified towns and die there.
For the LORD our God has decreed our
destruction
and has given us a cup of poison to drink
because we sinned against the LORD.
15 We hoped for peace, but no peace came.
We hoped for a time of healing, but found
only terror.'

16 "The snorting of the enemies' warhorses can
be heard
all the way from the land of Dan in the north!
The neighing of their stallions makes the whole
land tremble.
They are coming to devour the land and
everything in it—
cities and people alike.
17 I will send these enemy troops among you
like poisonous snakes you cannot charm.
They will bite you, and you will die.
I, the LORD, have spoken!"

Jeremiah Weeps for Sinful Judah

JEREMIAH 8:18–9:2

18 My grief is beyond healing;
my heart is broken.
19 Listen to the weeping of my people;
it can be heard all across the land.
"Has the LORD abandoned Jerusalem?*" the
people ask.
"Is her King no longer there?"

"Oh, why have they provoked my anger with their
carved idols
and their worthless foreign gods?" says the
LORD.

20 "The harvest is finished,
and the summer is gone," the people cry,
"yet we are not saved!"

21 I hurt with the hurt of my people.
I mourn and am overcome with grief.
22 Is there no medicine in Gilead?
Is there no physician there?
Why is there no healing
for the wounds of my people?

9:1 *If only my head were a pool of water
and my eyes a fountain of tears,
I would weep day and night
for all my people who have been slaughtered.
2 *Oh, that I could go away and forget my people
and live in a travelers' shack in the desert.
For they are all adulterers—
a pack of treacherous liars.

Judgment for Disobedience

JEREMIAH 9:3-16

3 "My people bend their tongues like bows
to shoot out lies.
They refuse to stand up for the truth.
They only go from bad to worse.
They do not know me,"
says the LORD.

4 "Beware of your neighbor!
Don't even trust your brother!
For brother takes advantage of brother,
and friend slanders friend.
5 They all fool and defraud each other;
no one tells the truth.
With practiced tongues they tell lies;
they wear themselves out with all their
sinning.
6 They pile lie upon lie
and utterly refuse to acknowledge me,"
says the LORD.

7 Therefore, this is what the LORD of Heaven's
Armies says:
"See, I will melt them down in a crucible
and test them like metal.
What else can I do with my people?*
8 For their tongues shoot lies like poisoned
arrows.
They speak friendly words to their neighbors
while scheming in their heart to kill them.
9 Should I not punish them for this?" says the
LORD.
"Should I not avenge myself against such
a nation?"

10 I will weep for the mountains
and wail for the wilderness pastures.
For they are desolate and empty of life;
the lowing of cattle is heard no more;
the birds and wild animals have all fled.

Jer 8:19 Hebrew *Zion?* **Jer 9:1** Verse 9:1 is numbered 8:23 in Hebrew text. **Jer 9:2** Verses 9:2-26 are numbered 9:1-25 in Hebrew text. **Jer 9:7** Hebrew *with the daughter of my people?* Greek version reads *with the evil daughter of my people?*

God could heal their self-inflicted wounds, but he would not force his healing on them.

Jer 9:1-6 Jeremiah felt conflicting emotions concerning his people. Lying, deceit, treachery, adultery, and idolatry had become common sins. He was angered by their sin, but he had compassion, too. He was set apart from them by his mission for God, but he was also one of them. Jesus had similar feelings when he stood before Jerusalem, the city that would reject him (Matt 23:37).

▸ **JEREMIAH 9:3-16** ***(cont.)***

11 "I will make Jerusalem into a heap of ruins,"
says the LORD.
"It will be a place haunted by jackals.
The towns of Judah will be ghost towns,
with no one living in them."

12Who is wise enough to understand all this? Who
has been instructed by the LORD and can explain it to
others? Why has the land been so ruined that no one
dares to travel through it?
13The LORD replies, "This has happened because
my people have abandoned my instructions; they
have refused to obey what I said. 14Instead, they have
stubbornly followed their own desires and worshiped
the images of Baal, as their ancestors taught them.
15So now, this is what the LORD of Heaven's Armies,
the God of Israel, says: Look! I will feed them with
bitterness and give them poison to drink. 16I will
scatter them around the world, in places they and
their ancestors never heard of, and even there I will
chase them with the sword until I have destroyed
them completely."

Weeping in Jerusalem

JEREMIAH 9:17-26

17 This is what the LORD of Heaven's Armies says:
"Consider all this, and call for the mourners.
Send for the women who mourn at funerals.
18 Quick! Begin your weeping!
Let the tears flow from your eyes.
19 Hear the people of Jerusalem* crying in despair,
'We are ruined! We are completely
humiliated!
We must leave our land,
because our homes have been torn down.'"
20 Listen, you women, to the words of the LORD;
open your ears to what he has to say.
Teach your daughters to wail;
teach one another how to lament.
21 For death has crept in through our windows
and has entered our mansions.
It has killed off the flower of our youth:
Children no longer play in the streets,
and young men no longer gather in the
squares.
22 This is what the LORD says:
"Bodies will be scattered across the fields like
clumps of manure,
like bundles of grain after the harvest.
No one will be left to bury them."
23 This is what the LORD says:
"Don't let the wise boast in their wisdom,
or the powerful boast in their power,
or the rich boast in their riches.
24 But those who wish to boast
should boast in this alone:
that they truly know me and understand that
I am the LORD
who demonstrates unfailing love
and who brings justice and righteousness
to the earth,
and that I delight in these things.
I, the LORD, have spoken!

25"A time is coming," says the LORD, "when I will
punish all those who are circumcised in body but
not in spirit—26the Egyptians, Edomites, Ammonites,
Moabites, the people who live in the desert in remote
places,* and yes, even the people of Judah. And like
all these pagan nations, the people of Israel also have
uncircumcised hearts."

Idolatry Brings Destruction

JEREMIAH 10:1-16

Hear the word that the LORD speaks to you, O Israel!
2This is what the LORD says:

"Do not act like the other nations,
who try to read their future in the stars.
Do not be afraid of their predictions,
even though other nations are terrified
by them.
3 Their ways are futile and foolish.
They cut down a tree, and a craftsman carves
an idol.
4 They decorate it with gold and silver
and then fasten it securely with hammer
and nails
so it won't fall over.
5 Their gods are like
helpless scarecrows in a cucumber field!

Jer 9:19 Hebrew *Zion.* **Jer 9:26** Or *in the desert and clip the corners of their hair.*

Jer 9:23-24 People tend to admire three things about others: wisdom, power, and riches. But God puts a higher priority on knowing him personally and living a life that reflects his justice, righteousness, and love. What do you want people to admire most about you?

Jer 9:25-26 Circumcision went back to the time of Abraham. For the people of Israel, it was a symbol of their covenant relationship to God (Gen 17:9-14). Pagan nations also practiced circumcision, but not as the sign of a covenant with God. By Jeremiah's time, the Israelites had forgotten the spiritual significance of circumcision even though they continued to do the physical ritual.

Jer 10:2-3 Most people would like to know the future. Decisions would be easier, failures would be avoided, and successes would be assured. The people of Judah wanted to know the future, too, and they tried to discern it through reading the signs in the sky. God made the earth and the heavens, including stars that people consult and worship (Jer 10:12). No one will discover the future in man-made charts of God's stars. But God, who promises to guide you, knows your future and will be with you all the way. He will not reveal your future to you, but he will walk with you as the future unfolds. Don't trust the stars; trust the one who made the stars.

Jer 10:8 Those who put their trust in a

They cannot speak,
and they need to be carried because they
cannot walk.
Do not be afraid of such gods,
for they can neither harm you nor do you
any good."
6 LORD, there is no one like you!
For you are great, and your name is full
of power.
7 Who would not fear you, O King of nations?
That title belongs to you alone!
Among all the wise people of the earth
and in all the kingdoms of the world,
there is no one like you.
8 People who worship idols are stupid and foolish.
The things they worship are made of wood!
9 They bring beaten sheets of silver from Tarshish
and gold from Uphaz,
and they give these materials to skillful craftsmen
who make their idols.
Then they dress these gods in royal blue and
purple robes
made by expert tailors.
10 But the LORD is the only true God.
He is the living God and the everlasting King!
The whole earth trembles at his anger.
The nations cannot stand up to his wrath.

11Say this to those who worship other gods: "Your
so-called gods, who did not make the heavens and
earth, will vanish from the earth and from under the
heavens."*

12 But God made the earth by his power,
and he preserves it by his wisdom.
With his own understanding
he stretched out the heavens.
13 When he speaks in the thunder,
the heavens roar with rain.
He causes the clouds to rise over the earth.
He sends the lightning with the rain
and releases the wind from his storehouses.
14 The whole human race is foolish and has no
knowledge!
The craftsmen are disgraced by the idols
they make,
for their carefully shaped works are
a fraud.
These idols have no breath or power.
15 Idols are worthless; they are ridiculous lies!
On the day of reckoning they will all be
destroyed.
16 But the God of Israel* is no idol!
He is the Creator of everything that
exists,
including Israel, his own special possession.
The LORD of Heaven's Armies is his name!

The Coming Destruction

JEREMIAH 10:17-22

17 Pack your bags and prepare to leave;
the siege is about to begin.
18 For this is what the LORD says:
"Suddenly, I will fling out
all you who live in this land.
I will pour great troubles upon you,
and at last you will feel my anger."
19 My wound is severe,
and my grief is great.
My sickness is incurable,
but I must bear it.
20 My home is gone,
and no one is left to help me rebuild it.
My children have been taken away,
and I will never see them again.
21 The shepherds of my people have lost their
senses.
They no longer seek wisdom from the LORD.
Therefore, they fail completely,
and their flocks are scattered.
22 Listen! Hear the terrifying roar of great
armies
as they roll down from the north.
The towns of Judah will be destroyed
and become a haunt for jackals.

Jeremiah's Prayer

JEREMIAH 10:23-25

23 I know, LORD, that our lives are not our own.
We are not able to plan our own course.
24 So correct me, LORD, but please be gentle.
Do not correct me in anger, for I would die.

Jer 10:11 The original text of this verse is in Aramaic. **Jer 10:16** Hebrew *the Portion of Jacob.* See note on 5:20.

chunk of wood, even though it is carved well and looks beautiful, are foolish. The simplest person who worships God is wiser than the smartest person who worships a worthless substitute because this person has discerned who God really is. In what or whom do you place your trust?

Jer 10:9 Tarshish was located at the westward limit of the ancient world, perhaps in what is now Spain (see Jon 1:3). It was a source of silver, tin, lead, and iron for Tyre (Ezek 27:12). The location of Uphaz is unknown. Instead, it may be a metallurgical term for "refined gold." No matter how well made or how beautiful idols are, they can never have the power and life of the true and living God.

Jer 10:19-21 In this section, Jeremiah uses the picture of nomads wandering in the wilderness trying to pitch their tents. The "shepherds of my people" are the evil leaders responsible for the distress. "Flocks" are the people of Judah. Instead of guiding the people to God, the leaders were leading them astray.

Jer 10:23-24 God's ability to direct our lives is far superior to our ability. Sometimes we are afraid of God's power and plans because we know his power would easily crush us if he used it against us. Don't be afraid to let God correct your plans. He will give you wisdom if you are willing.

▸ **JEREMIAH 10:23-25** ***(cont.)***

25 Pour out your wrath on the nations that refuse
to acknowledge you—
on the peoples that do not call upon
your name.
For they have devoured your people Israel*;
they have devoured and consumed them,
making the land a desolate wilderness.

Judah's Broken Covenant

JEREMIAH 11:1-17

The LORD gave another message to Jeremiah. He said,
2"Remind the people of Judah and Jerusalem about the
terms of my covenant with them. 3Say to them, 'This is
what the LORD, the God of Israel, says: Cursed is anyone
who does not obey the terms of my covenant! 4For I
said to your ancestors when I brought them out of the
iron-smelting furnace of Egypt, "If you obey me and do
whatever I command you, then you will be my people,
and I will be your God." 5I said this so I could keep my
promise to your ancestors to give you a land flowing
with milk and honey—the land you live in today.'"

Then I replied, "Amen, LORD! May it be so."

6Then the LORD said, "Broadcast this message in the
streets of Jerusalem. Go from town to town throughout
the land and say, 'Remember the ancient covenant, and
do everything it requires. 7For I solemnly warned your
ancestors when I brought them out of Egypt, "Obey
me!" I have repeated this warning over and over to
this day, 8but your ancestors did not listen or even
pay attention. Instead, they stubbornly followed their
own evil desires. And because they refused to obey, I
brought upon them all the curses described in this
covenant.'"

9Again the LORD spoke to me and said, "I have discovered a conspiracy against me among the people
of Judah and Jerusalem. 10They have returned to the
sins of their forefathers. They have refused to listen

Jer 10:25 Hebrew *devoured Jacob.* See note on 5:20.

to me and are worshiping other gods. Israel and Judah have both broken the covenant I made with their
ancestors. 11Therefore, this is what the LORD says: I am
going to bring calamity upon them, and they will not
escape. Though they beg for mercy, I will not listen to
their cries. 12Then the people of Judah and Jerusalem
will pray to their idols and burn incense before them.
But the idols will not save them when disaster strikes!
13Look now, people of Judah; you have as many gods as
you have towns. You have as many altars of shame—
altars for burning incense to your god Baal—as there
are streets in Jerusalem.

14"Pray no more for these people, Jeremiah. Do not
weep or pray for them, for I will not listen to them
when they cry out to me in distress.

15 "What right do my beloved people have
to come to my Temple,
when they have done so many immoral
things?
Can their vows and sacrifices prevent their
destruction?
They actually rejoice in doing evil!
16 I, the LORD, once called them a thriving olive tree,
beautiful to see and full of good fruit.
But now I have sent the fury of their enemies
to burn them with fire,
leaving them charred and broken.

17"I, the LORD of Heaven's Armies, who planted this
olive tree, have ordered it destroyed. For the people of
Israel and Judah have done evil, arousing my anger by
burning incense to Baal."

A Plot against Jeremiah

JEREMIAH 11:18-23

Then the LORD told me about the plots my enemies
were making against me. 19I was like a lamb being led
to the slaughter. I had no idea that they were planning

I know, LORD, that our lives are not our own. We are not able to plan our own course.
Jeremiah 10:23

Jer 11:1–13:27 This section concerns the broken covenant, and a rebuke for those who returned to idols after Josiah's reform. Jeremiah's rebuke prompted a threat against his life by his own countrymen. As Jeremiah suffered, he pondered the prosperity of the wicked. As he brought these words to a close, he used a rotten linen loincloth and filled jars of wine as object lessons of God's coming judgment (see the note on Jer 13:1-11, p. 1016).

Jer 11:14 At first glance this command is shocking: God tells Jeremiah not to pray for the people and says he won't listen to the people if they pray. A time comes when God must dispense justice. Sin brings its own bitter reward. If the people were unrepentant and continued in their sin, neither their prayers nor Jeremiah's would prevent God's judgment. Their only hope was repentance—sorrow for sin, turning from it, and turning to God. How can we keep praying for God's help if we haven't committed our lives to him? God's blessings come when we are committed to him, not when we selfishly hang on to our sinful ways.

Jer 11:18-23 To Jeremiah's surprise, the people of Anathoth, his hometown, were

to kill me! "Let's destroy this man and all his words," they said. "Let's cut him down, so his name will be forgotten forever."

20 O LORD of Heaven's Armies,
you make righteous judgments,
and you examine the deepest thoughts
and secrets.
Let me see your vengeance against them,
for I have committed my cause to you.

21This is what the LORD says about the men of Anathoth who wanted me dead. They had said, "We will
kill you if you do not stop prophesying in the LORD's
name." 22So this is what the LORD of Heaven's Armies
says about them: "I will punish them! Their young men
will die in battle, and their boys and girls will starve
to death. 23Not one of these plotters from Anathoth
will survive, for I will bring disaster upon them when
their time of punishment comes."

Jeremiah Questions the LORD's Justice

JEREMIAH 12:1-4

1 LORD, you always give me justice
when I bring a case before you.
So let me bring you this complaint:
Why are the wicked so prosperous?
Why are evil people so happy?
2 You have planted them,
and they have taken root and prospered.
Your name is on their lips,
but you are far from their hearts.
3 But as for me, LORD, you know my heart.
You see me and test my thoughts.
Drag these people away like sheep to be
butchered!
Set them aside to be slaughtered!
4 How long must this land mourn?
Even the grass in the fields has withered.
The wild animals and birds have disappeared
because of the evil in the land.
For the people have said,
"The LORD doesn't see what's ahead for us!"

The LORD's Reply to Jeremiah

JEREMIAH 12:5-13

5 "If racing against mere men makes you tired,
how will you race against horses?
If you stumble and fall on open ground,
what will you do in the thickets near the Jordan?
6 Even your brothers, members of your own family,
have turned against you.
They plot and raise complaints against you.
Do not trust them,
no matter how pleasantly they speak.
7 "I have abandoned my people, my special
possession.
I have surrendered my dearest ones to their
enemies.
8 My chosen people have roared at me like a lion
of the forest,
so I have treated them with contempt.
9 My chosen people act like speckled vultures,*
but they themselves are surrounded by vultures.
Bring on the wild animals to pick their
corpses clean!
10 "Many rulers have ravaged my vineyard,
trampling down the vines
and turning all its beauty into a barren
wilderness.
11 They have made it an empty wasteland;
I hear its mournful cry.
The whole land is desolate,
and no one even cares.
12 On all the bare hilltops,
destroying armies can be seen.
The sword of the LORD devours people
from one end of the nation to the other.
No one will escape!
13 My people have planted wheat
but are harvesting thorns.
They have worn themselves out,
but it has done them no good.
They will harvest a crop of shame
because of the fierce anger of the LORD."

Jer 12:9 Or *speckled hyenas.*

plotting to kill him. They wanted to silence Jeremiah's message for several reasons: (1) economic—his condemnation of idol worship would hurt the business of the idol makers; (2) religious—the message of doom and gloom made the people feel depressed and guilty; (3) political—he openly rebuked their hypocritical politics; and (4) personal—the people hated him for showing them that they were wrong. Jeremiah had two options: run and hide, or call on God. Jeremiah called, and God answered. Like Jeremiah, we can either run and hide when we face opposition because of our faithfulness to God, or we can call on God for help. Hiding compromises our message; calling on God lets him reinforce it.

Jer 12:1-6 Many people have asked, "Why are the wicked so prosperous?" (See, for example, Job 21:4-21; Hab 1:1-4.) Jeremiah knew that God's justice would ultimately come, but he was impatient because he wanted justice to come quickly. God didn't give a doctrinal answer; instead, he gave a challenge: If Jeremiah couldn't handle this, how would he handle the injustices ahead? It is natural for us to demand fair play and cry for justice against those who take advantage of others. But when we call for justice, we must realize that we ourselves would be in big trouble if God gave each of us what we truly deserve.

Jer 12:5-6 Life was extremely difficult for Jeremiah despite his love for and obedience to God. When he called to God for relief, God's reply in effect was, "If you think this is bad, how are you going to cope when it gets really tough?" God's answers to prayer are not always nice or easy to handle. Any Christian who has experienced war, bereavement, or a serious illness knows this. We are to be committed to God even when the going gets tough and when our prayers for relief are not immediately answered.

A Message for Israel's Neighbors

JEREMIAH 12:14-17

Now this is what the LORD says: "I will uproot from
their land all the evil nations reaching out for the
possession I gave my people Israel. And I will uproot
Judah from among them. 15 But afterward I will return and have compassion on all of them. I will bring
them home to their own lands again, each nation to
its own possession. 16 And if these nations truly learn
the ways of my people, and if they learn to swear by
my name, saying, 'As surely as the LORD lives' (just as
they taught my people to swear by the name of Baal),
then they will be given a place among my people. 17 But
any nation who refuses to obey me will be uprooted
and destroyed. I, the LORD, have spoken!"

Jeremiah's Linen Loincloth

JEREMIAH 13:1-14

This is what the LORD said to me: "Go and buy a linen
loincloth and put it on, but do not wash it." 2 So I
bought the loincloth as the LORD directed me, and
I put it on.

3 Then the LORD gave me another message: 4 "Take
the linen loincloth you are wearing, and go to the Euphrates River.* Hide it there in a hole in the rocks."
5 So I went and hid it by the Euphrates as the LORD
had instructed me.

6 A long time afterward the LORD said to me, "Go
back to the Euphrates and get the loincloth I told you
to hide there." 7 So I went to the Euphrates and dug it
out of the hole where I had hidden it. But now it was
rotting and falling apart. The loincloth was good for
nothing.

8 Then I received this message from the LORD: 9 "This
is what the LORD says: This shows how I will rot away
the pride of Judah and Jerusalem. 10 These wicked
people refuse to listen to me. They stubbornly follow
their own desires and worship other gods. Therefore,
they will become like this loincloth—good for nothing!
11 As a loincloth clings to a man's waist, so I created
Judah and Israel to cling to me, says the LORD. They
were to be my people, my pride, my glory—an honor
to my name. But they would not listen to me.

12 "So tell them, 'This is what the LORD, the God of
Israel, says: May all your jars be filled with wine.' And
they will reply, 'Of course! Jars are made to be filled
with wine!'

13 "Then tell them, 'No, this is what the LORD means:
I will fill everyone in this land with drunkenness—
from the king sitting on David's throne to the priests
and the prophets, right down to the common people
of Jerusalem. 14 I will smash them against each other,
even parents against children, says the LORD. I will
not let my pity or mercy or compassion keep me from
destroying them.'"

A Warning against Pride

JEREMIAH 13:15-27

15 Listen and pay attention!
Do not be arrogant, for the LORD has spoken.
16 Give glory to the LORD your God
before it is too late.
Acknowledge him before he brings darkness
upon you,
causing you to stumble and fall on the
darkening mountains.
For then, when you look for light,
you will find only terrible darkness
and gloom.
17 And if you still refuse to listen,
I will weep alone because of your pride.
My eyes will overflow with tears,
because the LORD's flock will be led away
into exile.

18 Say to the king and his mother,
"Come down from your thrones
and sit in the dust,
for your glorious crowns
will soon be snatched from your heads."
19 The towns of the Negev will close their
gates,
and no one will be able to open them.

Jer 13:4 Hebrew *Perath;* also in 13:5, 6, 7.

Jer 12:14-17 God chose a people through whom to demonstrate his care for the world. The nation of Israel was given much; thus, much was required of her. But she repeatedly failed. The fate of other nations depended on their willingness to demonstrate faith in God whether or not God's chosen people accomplished their task of witness. God's love extends to reach every square inch of the globe.

Jer 13:1 A linen loincloth was one of the more intimate pieces of clothing, clinging close to the body. It was like underwear. Jeremiah's action showed how God would ruin Judah just as Jeremiah had ruined the linen loincloth.

Jer 13:1-11 Actions speak louder than words. Jeremiah often used vivid object lessons to arouse the people's curiosity and get his point across. This lesson of the linen loincloth illustrated Judah's destiny. Although the people had once been close to God, their pride had made them useless. Proud people may look important, but God says their pride makes them good for nothing, completely useless. Pride rots our hearts until we lose our usefulness to God.

Jer 13:15 While it is good to respect our country and our church, our loyalties always carry a hidden danger—arrogance. When is pride harmful? When it causes us to: (1) look down on others; (2) be selfish with our resources; (3) force our solutions on others' problems; (4) think God is blessing us because of our own merits; (5) be content with our plans rather than seeking God's plans.

Jer 13:18 The king was Jehoiachin, and his mother was Nehushta. The king's father, Jehoiakim, had surrendered to Nebuchadnezzar but later rebelled. During Jehoiachin's reign, Nebuchadnezzar's armies besieged Jerusalem, and both Jehoiachin and Nehushta surrendered. Jehoiachin was sent to Babylon and imprisoned (2 Kgs 24:1-15). Jeremiah's prophecy came true.

Jer 13:19 The Negev region is the dry wasteland stretching south from Beersheba. The towns in this area would be closed to any refugees fleeing the invading army.

The people of Judah will be taken away
as captives.
All will be carried into exile.

20 Open up your eyes and see
the armies marching down from the north!
Where is your flock—
your beautiful flock—
that he gave you to care for?
21 What will you say when the LORD takes the
allies you have cultivated
and appoints them as your rulers?
Pangs of anguish will grip you,
like those of a woman in labor!
22 You may ask yourself,
"Why is all this happening to me?"
It is because of your many sins!
That is why you have been stripped
and raped by invading armies.
23 Can an Ethiopian* change the color of his skin?
Can a leopard take away its spots?
Neither can you start doing good,
for you have always done evil.
24 "I will scatter you like chaff
that is blown away by the desert winds.
25 This is your allotment,
the portion I have assigned to you,"
says the LORD,
"for you have forgotten me,
putting your trust in false gods.
26 I myself will strip you
and expose you to shame.
27 I have seen your adultery and lust,
and your disgusting idol worship out in the
fields and on the hills.
What sorrow awaits you, Jerusalem!
How long before you are pure?"

Judah's Terrible Drought

JEREMIAH 14:1-10

This message came to Jeremiah from the LORD, explaining why he was holding back the rain:

2 "Judah wilts;
commerce at the city gates grinds to a halt.
All the people sit on the ground in mourning,
and a great cry rises from Jerusalem.
3 The nobles send servants to get water,
but all the wells are dry.
The servants return with empty pitchers,
confused and desperate,
covering their heads in grief.
4 The ground is parched
and cracked for lack of rain.
The farmers are deeply troubled;
they, too, cover their heads.
5 Even the doe abandons her newborn fawn
because there is no grass in the field.
6 The wild donkeys stand on the bare hills
panting like thirsty jackals.
They strain their eyes looking for grass,
but there is none to be found."

7 The people say, "Our wickedness has caught up
with us, LORD,
but help us for the sake of your own
reputation.
We have turned away from you
and sinned against you again and again.
8 O Hope of Israel, our Savior in times of trouble,
why are you like a stranger to us?
Why are you like a traveler passing through the
land,
stopping only for the night?
9 Are you also confused?
Is our champion helpless to save us?
You are right here among us, LORD.
We are known as your people.
Please don't abandon us now!"

10 So this is what the LORD says to his people:
"You love to wander far from me
and do not restrain yourselves.
Therefore, I will no longer accept you as my
people.
Now I will remember all your wickedness
and will punish you for your sins."

The LORD Forbids Jeremiah to Intercede

JEREMIAH 14:11-18

Then the LORD said to me, "Do not pray for these
people anymore. 12When they fast, I will pay no attention. When they present their burnt offerings and
grain offerings to me, I will not accept them. Instead, I
will devour them with war, famine, and disease."
13Then I said, "O Sovereign LORD, their prophets are
telling them, 'All is well—no war or famine will come.
The LORD will surely send you peace.'"

Jer 13:23 Hebrew *a Cushite.*

Jer 13:23 Not even the threat of captivity could move the people to repent. The people had become so accustomed to doing evil that they had lost their ability to change. God never rejects those who sincerely turn to him. God was warning them to repent before it became impossible to change. We must never put off until tomorrow those changes God wants us to make. Our attitudes and patterns for living can become so set that we will lose all desire to change and will no longer fear the consequences.

Jer 14:1–15:21 This section opens with God sending a drought on Judah and refusing to answer their prayers for rain. It continues with Jeremiah's description of judgment to come.

Jer 14:1ff Drought was a judgment with devastating consequences. As usual, when their backs were to the wall, the people cried out to God. But God rejected their plea because they did not repent; they merely wanted his rescue. Not even Jeremiah's prayers on their behalf would help. Their only hope was to turn to God.

▸ **JEREMIAH 14:11-18** ***(cont.)***

14 Then the LORD said, "These prophets are telling
lies in my name. I did not send them or tell them to
speak. I did not give them any messages. They prophesy of visions and revelations they have never seen
or heard. They speak foolishness made up in their
own lying hearts. 15 Therefore, this is what the LORD
says: I will punish these lying prophets, for they have
spoken in my name even though I never sent them.
They say that no war or famine will come, but they
themselves will die by war and famine! 16 As for the
people to whom they prophesy—their bodies will
be thrown out into the streets of Jerusalem, victims
of famine and war. There will be no one left to bury
them. Husbands, wives, sons, and daughters—all will
be gone. For I will pour out their own wickedness on
them. 17 Now, Jeremiah, say this to them:

"Night and day my eyes overflow with tears.
I cannot stop weeping,
for my virgin daughter—my precious people—
has been struck down
and lies mortally wounded.
18 If I go out into the fields,
I see the bodies of people slaughtered
by the enemy.
If I walk the city streets,
I see people who have died of starvation.
The prophets and priests continue with
their work,
but they don't know what they're doing."

A Prayer for Healing

JEREMIAH 14:19-22

19 LORD, have you completely rejected Judah?
Do you really hate Jerusalem?*
Why have you wounded us past all hope of
healing?
We hoped for peace, but no peace came.
We hoped for a time of healing, but found
only terror.
20 LORD, we confess our wickedness
and that of our ancestors, too.
We all have sinned against you.
21 For the sake of your reputation, LORD, do not
abandon us.
Do not disgrace your own glorious throne.
Please remember us,
and do not break your covenant with us.
22 Can any of the worthless foreign gods send
us rain?
Does it fall from the sky by itself?
No, you are the one, O LORD our God!
Only you can do such things.
So we will wait for you to help us.

Judah's Inevitable Doom

JEREMIAH 15:1-9

Then the LORD said to me, "Even if Moses and Samuel
stood before me pleading for these people, I wouldn't
help them. Away with them! Get them out of my sight!
2 And if they say to you, 'But where can we go?' tell
them, 'This is what the LORD says:

"'Those who are destined for death, to death;
those who are destined for war, to war;
those who are destined for famine, to famine;
those who are destined for captivity,
to captivity.'

3 "I will send four kinds of destroyers against them,"
says the LORD. "I will send the sword to kill, the dogs to
drag away, the vultures to devour, and the wild animals
to finish up what is left. 4 Because of the wicked things
Manasseh son of Hezekiah, king of Judah, did in Jerusalem, I will make my people an object of horror to
all the kingdoms of the earth.

5 "Who will feel sorry for you, Jerusalem?
Who will weep for you?
Who will even bother to ask how you are?
6 You have abandoned me
and turned your back on me,"
says the LORD.
"Therefore, I will raise my fist to destroy you.
I am tired of always giving you another chance.
7 I will winnow you like grain at the gates
of your cities
and take away the children you hold dear.

Jer 14:19 Hebrew *Zion?*

Jer 14:14 What made the people listen to the false prophets? These "prophets" said what the people wanted to hear. False teachers earn fame and money by telling people what they want to hear, but they lead people away from God. If we encourage false teachers, we are as guilty as they are.

Jer 14:19-22 Interceding for the people, Jeremiah asked God if Judah's repentance would bring his help. But God refused to come to their aid (Jer 15:1) because the people were insincere, wicked, and stubborn. They knew he wanted to bless them, and they knew what they needed to do to receive that blessing. They wanted God to do his part, but they did not want to do theirs. It's easy to express sorrow for wrong actions, especially when we want something, but we must be willing to stop doing what is wrong. God will forgive those who are truly repentant, but hypocrites will be severely punished.

Jer 15:1 Moses and Samuel were two of God's greatest prophets. Like Jeremiah, both interceded for the people before God (Exod 32:11; Num 14:11-20; 1 Sam 7:9; 12:17; Ps 99:6). Intercession is often effective. In this case, however, the people were so wicked and stubborn that God knew they would not turn to him.

Jer 15:3-4 The goal of these destroyers would be to destroy the living and devour the dead. Because of Manasseh's evil reign and the people's sin (2 Kgs 21:1-16; 23:26; 24:3), the destruction would be complete. The people may have argued that they should not be held responsible for Manasseh's sins, but they were continuing what Manasseh began. If we follow corrupt leaders knowingly, we can't excuse ourselves by blaming their bad example.

I will destroy my own people,
because they refuse to change their evil ways.
8 There will be more widows
than the grains of sand on the seashore.
At noontime I will bring a destroyer
against the mothers of young men.
I will cause anguish and terror
to come upon them suddenly.
9 The mother of seven grows faint and gasps
for breath;
her sun has gone down while it is still day.
She sits childless now,
disgraced and humiliated.
And I will hand over those who are left
to be killed by the enemy.
I, the LORD, have spoken!"

Jeremiah's Complaint

JEREMIAH 15:10-21

Then I said,

"What sorrow is mine, my mother.
Oh, that I had died at birth!
I am hated everywhere I go.
I am neither a lender who threatens to foreclose
nor a borrower who refuses to pay—
yet they all curse me."

11 The LORD replied,

"I will take care of you, Jeremiah.
Your enemies will ask you to plead on their
behalf
in times of trouble and distress.
12 Can a man break a bar of iron from the north,
or a bar of bronze?
13 At no cost to them,
I will hand over your wealth and treasures
as plunder to your enemies,
for sin runs rampant in your land.
14 I will tell your enemies to take you
as captives to a foreign land.
For my anger blazes like a fire
that will burn forever.*"

15 Then I said,

"LORD, you know what's happening to me.
Please step in and help me. Punish my
persecutors!
Please give me time; don't let me die young.
It's for your sake that I am suffering.
16 When I discovered your words, I devoured
them.
They are my joy and my heart's delight,
for I bear your name,
O LORD God of Heaven's Armies.
17 I never joined the people in their merry
feasts.
I sat alone because your hand was on me.
I was filled with indignation at their sins.
18 Why then does my suffering continue?
Why is my wound so incurable?
Your help seems as uncertain as a seasonal
brook,
like a spring that has gone dry."

19 This is how the LORD responds:

"If you return to me, I will restore you
so you can continue to serve me.
If you speak good words rather than
worthless ones,
you will be my spokesman.
You must influence them;
do not let them influence you!
20 They will fight against you like an attacking
army,
but I will make you as secure as a fortified
wall of bronze.
They will not conquer you,
for I am with you to protect and rescue you.
I, the LORD, have spoken!
21 Yes, I will certainly keep you safe from these
wicked men.
I will rescue you from their cruel hands."

Jeremiah Forbidden to Marry

JEREMIAH 16:1-4

The LORD gave me another message. He said, 2"Do not
get married or have children in this place. 3For this is
what the LORD says about the children born here in
this city and about their mothers and fathers: 4They
will die from terrible diseases. No one will mourn
for them or bury them, and they will lie scattered on
the ground like manure. They will die from war and
famine, and their bodies will be food for the vultures
and wild animals."

Jer 15:14 As in some Hebrew manuscripts (see also 17:4); most Hebrew manuscripts read *will burn against you.*

Jer 15:17-21 Jeremiah accused God of not helping him when he really needed it. Jeremiah had taken his eyes off God's purposes and was feeling sorry for himself. He was angry, hurt, and afraid. In response, God didn't get angry at Jeremiah; he answered by rearranging Jeremiah's priorities. As God's mouthpiece, he was to influence the people, not let them influence him. There are three important lessons in this passage: (1) In prayer we can reveal our deepest thoughts to God; (2) God expects us to trust him, no matter what; (3) we are here to influence others for God.

Jer 16:1–17:18 This section portrays the coming day of disaster. It begins by showing Jeremiah's loneliness. He is a social outcast because of his harsh messages and his celibate lifestyle. He must not marry, have children, or take part in funerals or festivals. The section concludes with another appeal to avoid judgment by turning to God. Babylon had already ransacked the land in 605 B.C., but the people did not heed Jeremiah's words, and the waves of destruction kept coming. The second wave came in 597 B.C., and Judah was completely destroyed in 586 B.C.

Judah's Coming Punishment

JEREMIAH 16:5-13

This is what the LORD says: "Do not go to funerals to
mourn and show sympathy for these people, for I have
removed my protection and peace from them. I have
taken away my unfailing love and my mercy. [6]Both
the great and the lowly will die in this land. No one
will bury them or mourn for them. Their friends will
not cut themselves in sorrow or shave their heads in
sadness. [7]No one will offer a meal to comfort those
who mourn for the dead—not even at the death of a
mother or father. No one will send a cup of wine to
console them.

[8]"And do not go to their feasts and parties. Do not
eat and drink with them at all. [9]For this is what the
LORD of Heaven's Armies, the God of Israel, says: In
your own lifetime, before your very eyes, I will put an
end to the happy singing and laughter in this land.
The joyful voices of bridegrooms and brides will no
longer be heard.

[10]"When you tell the people all these things, they
will ask, 'Why has the LORD decreed such terrible
things against us? What have we done to deserve such
treatment? What is our sin against the LORD our God?'

[11]"Then you will give them the LORD's reply: 'It is
because your ancestors were unfaithful to me. They
worshiped other gods and served them. They abandoned me and did not obey my word. [12]And you are
even worse than your ancestors! You stubbornly follow
your own evil desires and refuse to listen to me. [13]So
I will throw you out of this land and send you into a
foreign land where you and your ancestors have never
been. There you can worship idols day and night—and
I will grant you no favors!'

Hope despite the Disaster

JEREMIAH 16:14-18

"But the time is coming," says the LORD, "when people
who are taking an oath will no longer say, 'As surely as
the LORD lives, who rescued the people of Israel from
the land of Egypt.' [15]Instead, they will say, 'As surely
as the LORD lives, who brought the people of Israel
back to their own land from the land of the north and
from all the countries to which he had exiled them.'
For I will bring them back to this land that I gave their
ancestors.

[16]"But now I am sending for many fishermen who
will catch them," says the LORD. "I am sending for hunters who will hunt them down in the mountains, hills,
and caves. [17]I am watching them closely, and I see every
sin. They cannot hope to hide from me. [18]I will double
their punishment for all their sins, because they have
defiled my land with lifeless images of their detestable
gods and have filled my territory with their evil deeds."

Jeremiah's Prayer of Confidence

JEREMIAH 16:19-21

19 LORD, you are my strength and fortress,
  my refuge in the day of trouble!
Nations from around the world
  will come to you and say,
"Our ancestors left us a foolish heritage,
  for they worshiped worthless idols.
20 Can people make their own gods?
  These are not real gods at all!"

21 The LORD says,
"Now I will show them my power;
  now I will show them my might.
At last they will know and understand
  that I am the LORD.

Judah's Sin and Punishment

JEREMIAH 17:1-4

1 "The sin of Judah
  is inscribed with an iron chisel—
engraved with a diamond point on their stony
    hearts
  and on the corners of their altars.

Jer 16:5-7 In Jeremiah's culture, it was unthinkable not to show grief publicly. The absence of mourning showed the people how complete their devastation would be. So many people would die that it would be impossible to carry out customary mourning rituals for all of them.

Jer 16:8-13 Jeremiah was also told not to participate in parties or other joyful events to show how seriously God took the nation's sins. In both cases (no public grief or joy), Jeremiah's life was to be an attention getter and an illustration of God's truth. Sometimes we think that the only way to communicate is through speaking or teaching, but God can use a wide variety of means to bring his message. Use your creativity.

Jer 16:14-15 The book of Exodus records God's miraculous rescue of his people from Egyptian slavery (Exod 1–15). The people's return from exile would be so momentous that it would overshadow even the exodus from Egypt. Even though his people had been so stubborn, God would once again show his great mercy.

Jer 16:17 Small children think that if they can't see you, then you can't see them. The people of Israel may have wished that hiding from God were as simple as closing their eyes. Although they closed their eyes to their sinful ways, their sins certainly weren't hidden from God. He who sees everything cannot be deceived. Do you have a sinful attitude or activity that you hope God won't notice? He knows about it. The first step of repentance is to acknowledge that God knows about your sins.

Jer 16:19 In this prayer, Jeremiah approached God with three descriptive names: strength, fortress, and refuge. Each name gives a slightly different glimpse of how Jeremiah experienced God's presence, and each is a picture of security and protection. Let God be your strength when you feel weak, your fortress when enemies come against you, and your refuge when you need to retreat from life's pressures.

Jer 17:1 God's people continued to sin even though they had the law, the prophets of God, and history replete with God's miracles. How could they do that? Why do we continue in sin even though we understand the eternal consequences? Jeremiah says the heart is deceitful (Jer 17:9), and their sin is "engraved with a diamond point on their stony hearts." The Hebrews symbolized the various aspects of a person by locating them in certain physical organs. The heart was the organ of reason, intelligence, and will. So deep is our tendency to sin that only God's redemption can deliver us.

2 Even their children go to worship
at their pagan altars and Asherah poles,
beneath every green tree
and on every high hill.
3 So I will hand over my holy mountain—
along with all your wealth and treasures
and your pagan shrines—
as plunder to your enemies,
for sin runs rampant in your land.
4 The wonderful possession I have reserved
for you
will slip from your hands.
I will tell your enemies to take you
as captives to a foreign land.
For my anger blazes like a fire
that will burn forever."

Wisdom from the Lord

JEREMIAH 17:5-10

5 This is what the Lord says:
"Cursed are those who put their trust in mere
humans,
who rely on human strength
and turn their hearts away from the Lord.
6 They are like stunted shrubs in the desert,
with no hope for the future.
They will live in the barren wilderness,
in an uninhabited salty land.

7 "But blessed are those who trust in the Lord
and have made the Lord their hope and
confidence.
8 They are like trees planted along a riverbank,
with roots that reach deep into the water.
Such trees are not bothered by the heat
or worried by long months of drought.
Their leaves stay green,
and they never stop producing fruit.

9 "The human heart is the most deceitful
of all things,
and desperately wicked.
Who really knows how bad it is?
10 But I, the Lord, search all hearts
and examine secret motives.
I give all people their due rewards,
according to what their actions deserve."

Jeremiah's Trust in the Lord

JEREMIAH 17:11-18

11 Like a partridge that hatches eggs she has
not laid,
so are those who get their wealth by unjust
means.
At midlife they will lose their riches;
in the end, they will become poor old fools.
12 But we worship at your throne—
eternal, high, and glorious!
13 O Lord, the hope of Israel,
all who turn away from you will be
disgraced.
They will be buried in the dust of the earth,
for they have abandoned the Lord, the
fountain of living water.

14 O Lord, if you heal me, I will be truly healed;
if you save me, I will be truly saved.
My praises are for you alone!
15 People scoff at me and say,
"What is this 'message from the Lord' you
talk about?
Why don't your predictions come true?"

Jer 17:5-8 Two kinds of people are contrasted here: those who trust in human beings and those who trust in the Lord. The people of Judah were trusting in false gods and military alliances instead of God, and thus they were barren and unfruitful. In contrast, those who trust in the Lord flourish like trees planted along a riverbank (see Ps 1). In times of trouble, those who trust in human beings will be impoverished and spiritually weak, so they will have no strength to draw on. But those who trust in the Lord will have abundant strength, not only for their own needs, but even for the needs of others. Are you satisfied with being unfruitful, or do you, like a well-watered tree, have strength for times of crisis and even some to share as you bear fruit for the Lord?

Jer 17:9-10 God makes it clear why we sin—it's a matter of the heart. Our heart is inclined toward sin from the time we are born. It is easy to fall into the routine of forgetting and forsaking God. But we can still choose whether or not to continue in sin. We can yield to a specific temptation, or we can ask God to help us resist temptation when it comes.

Jer 17:11 There is a right way and a wrong way to do any task. Jeremiah says that the person who becomes rich by unjust means will end up foolish and poor. Whether at work, school, or play, we should strive to be honest in all our dealings. Getting a promotion, passing an exam, or gaining prestige by dishonest means will never bring God's blessing or lasting happiness.

Partridge

The partridge is the most common game bird in the Holy Land. It resembles a chicken in its basic anatomy but has a less chunky body and a longer tail. Two species of partridge inhabit the Holy Land: the sand partridge (found near the Dead Sea, in the Jordan River valley, and in the Sinai desert) and the chukar partridge. The sand partridge is a medium-sized bird with yellow feet. The male has sandy-buff plumage, upper tail feathers penciled and barred with brown, and a chestnut and white undersurface. The female is grayish buff. The chukar partridge resembles the common French partridge of Europe, having a body about 16 inches long. It is covered with beautiful, radiantly colored feathers. The biblical description of the partridge hatching eggs she did not lay (Jer 17:11) seems to be based on the fact that the hen lays at least two clutches of eggs, one for herself and one for the cock to incubate.

▸ **JEREMIAH 17:11-18** ***(cont.)***

16 LORD, I have not abandoned my job
as a shepherd for your people.
I have not urged you to send disaster.
You have heard everything I've said.
17 LORD, don't terrorize me!
You alone are my hope in the day of disaster.
18 Bring shame and dismay on all who persecute me,
but don't let me experience shame and dismay.
Bring a day of terror on them.
Yes, bring double destruction upon them!

Observing the Sabbath

JEREMIAH 17:19-27

This is what the LORD said to me: "Go and stand in the
gates of Jerusalem, first in the gate where the king
goes in and out, and then in each of the other gates.
[20]Say to all the people, 'Listen to this message from the
LORD, you kings of Judah and all you people of Judah
and everyone living in Jerusalem. [21]This is what the
LORD says: Listen to my warning! Stop carrying on
your trade at Jerusalem's gates on the Sabbath day.
[22]Do not do your work on the Sabbath, but make it a
holy day. I gave this command to your ancestors, [23]but
they did not listen or obey. They stubbornly refused
to pay attention or accept my discipline.

[24]"'But if you obey me, says the LORD, and do not
carry on your trade at the gates or work on the Sabbath
day, and if you keep it holy, [25]then kings and their officials will go in and out of these gates forever. There will
always be a descendant of David sitting on the throne
here in Jerusalem. Kings and their officials will always
ride in and out among the people of Judah in chariots
and on horses, and this city will remain forever. [26]And
from all around Jerusalem, from the towns of Judah
and Benjamin, from the western foothills* and the
hill country and the Negev, the people will come with
their burnt offerings and sacrifices. They will bring
their grain offerings, frankincense, and thanksgiving
offerings to the LORD's Temple.

[27]"'But if you do not listen to me and refuse to keep
the Sabbath holy, and if on the Sabbath day you bring
loads of merchandise through the gates of Jerusalem
just as on other days, then I will set fire to these gates.
The fire will spread to the palaces, and no one will be
able to put out the roaring flames.'"

The Potter and the Clay

JEREMIAH 18:1-17

The LORD gave another message to Jeremiah. He said,
[2]"Go down to the potter's shop, and I will speak to you
there." [3]So I did as he told me and found the potter
working at his wheel. [4]But the jar he was making did
not turn out as he had hoped, so he crushed it into a
lump of clay again and started over.

[5]Then the LORD gave me this message: [6]"O Israel,
can I not do to you as this potter has done to his clay?
As the clay is in the potter's hand, so are you in my
hand. [7]If I announce that a certain nation or kingdom
is to be uprooted, torn down, and destroyed, [8]but then
that nation renounces its evil ways, I will not destroy it
as I had planned. [9]And if I announce that I will plant

Jer 17:26 Hebrew *the Shephelah.*

Jer 17:19-27 The people were working on the Sabbath, their day of rest (Exod 20:8-11). Instead of entering the gates of the city on their way to worship, they continued the hustle and bustle of business like any other day. They considered making money more important than keeping God's law. If they would repent and put God first in their lives, God promised them honor among the nations. Over a century later, when Nehemiah led the exiles on their return to Jerusalem, one of his most important reforms was to reinstitute Sabbath observance (Neh 13:15-22).

Jer 18:1-23 The parable in this chapter illustrates God's sovereignty over the nation. God has power over the clay (Judah), and he continues to work with it to make it a useful vessel. But Judah must soon repent, or the clay will harden the wrong way. Then it will be worth nothing and will be broken and destroyed.

Jer 18:6 As the potter molded or shaped a clay pot on the potter's wheel, defects often appeared. The potter had power over the clay—to permit the defects to remain or to reshape the pot. Likewise, God had power to reshape the nation to conform to his purposes. Our strategy should not be to become mindless and passive—one aspect of

GOD'S OBJECT LESSONS IN JEREMIAH

Reference	*Object Lesson*	*Significance*
Jer 1:11-12	Branch from an almond tree	God will carry out his threats of punishment.
Jer 1:13	Pot of boiling water, spilling southward	God will punish Judah.
Jer 13:1-11	A rotten linen loincloth	Because the people refused to listen to God, they had become useless, good for nothing, like a useless linen loincloth.
Jer 18:1-17	Potter's clay	God could destroy his sinful people if he so desired. This is a warning to them to repent before he is forced to bring judgment.
Jer 19:1-12	Shattered clay jars	God would smash Judah just as Jeremiah smashed the clay jars.
Jer 24:1-10	Two baskets of figs	Good figs represent God's remnant. Bad figs are the people left behind.
Jer 27:2-11	Yoke	Any nation who refused to submit to Babylon's yoke of control would be punished.
Jer 43:8-13	Large rocks	The rocks marked the place where Nebuchadnezzar would set his throne when God allowed him to conquer Egypt.
Jer 51:59-64	Scroll sunk in the river	Babylon would sink to rise no more.

and build up a certain nation or kingdom, [10]but then that nation turns to evil and refuses to obey me, I will not bless it as I said I would.

[11]"Therefore, Jeremiah, go and warn all Judah and Jerusalem. Say to them, 'This is what the LORD says: I am planning disaster for you instead of good. So turn from your evil ways, each of you, and do what is right.'"

[12]But the people replied, "Don't waste your breath. We will continue to live as we want to, stubbornly following our own evil desires."

[13]So this is what the LORD says:

"Has anyone ever heard of such a thing,
even among the pagan nations?
My virgin daughter Israel
has done something terrible!
14 Does the snow ever disappear from the
mountaintops of Lebanon?
Do the cold streams flowing from those distant
mountains ever run dry?
15 But my people are not so reliable, for they have
deserted me;
they burn incense to worthless idols.
They have stumbled off the ancient highways
and walk in muddy paths.
16 Therefore, their land will become desolate,
a monument to their stupidity.
All who pass by will be astonished
and will shake their heads in amazement.
17 I will scatter my people before their enemies
as the east wind scatters dust.
And in all their trouble I will turn my back
on them
and refuse to notice their distress."

A Plot against Jeremiah

JEREMIAH 18:18-23

Then the people said, "Come on, let's plot a way to stop Jeremiah. We have plenty of priests and wise men and prophets. We don't need him to teach the word and give us advice and prophecies. Let's spread rumors about him and ignore what he says."

19 LORD, hear me and help me!
Listen to what my enemies are saying.
20 Should they repay evil for good?
They have dug a pit to kill me,
though I pleaded for them
and tried to protect them from your anger.
21 So let their children starve!
Let them die by the sword!
Let their wives become childless widows.
Let their old men die in a plague,
and let their young men be killed in battle!
22 Let screaming be heard from their homes
as warriors come suddenly upon them.
For they have dug a pit for me
and have hidden traps along my path.
23 LORD, you know all about their murderous plots
against me.
Don't forgive their crimes and blot out
their sins.
Let them die before you.
Deal with them in your anger.

The Faithful Recabites

JEREMIAH 35:1-19

This is the message the LORD gave Jeremiah when Jehoiakim son of Josiah was king of Judah: [2]"Go to the
settlement where the families of the Recabites live,
and invite them to the LORD's Temple. Take them into
one of the inner rooms, and offer them some wine."
[3]So I went to see Jaazaniah son of Jeremiah and
grandson of Habazziniah and all his brothers and
sons—representing all the Recabite families. [4]I took
them to the Temple, and we went into the room assigned to the sons of Hanan son of Igdaliah, a man of
God. This room was located next to the one used by the
Temple officials, directly above the room of Maaseiah
son of Shallum, the Temple gatekeeper.
[5]I set cups and jugs of wine before them and invited
them to have a drink, [6]but they refused. "No," they
said, "we don't drink wine, because our ancestor Jehonadab* son of Recab gave us this command: 'You
and your descendants must never drink wine. [7]And
do not build houses or plant crops or vineyards, but
always live in tents. If you follow these commands,
you will live long, good lives in the land.' [8]So we have
obeyed him in all these things. We have never had a

Jer 35:6 Hebrew *Jonadab*, a variant spelling of Jehonadab; also in 35:10, 14, 16, 18, 19. See 2 Kgs 10:15.

clay—but to be willing and receptive to God's impact on us. As we yield to God, he begins reshaping us into valuable vessels.

Jer 18:12 Our society admires assertiveness, independence, and defiance of authority. In a relationship with God these qualities become stubbornness, self-importance, and refusal to listen or change. Left unchecked, stubbornness becomes a way of life hostile to God.

Jer 18:18 Jeremiah's words and actions challenged the people's social and moral behavior. He had openly spoken against the king, the officials, the priests and prophets, the teachers, and the wise (Jer 4:9; 8:8-9). He wasn't afraid to give unpopular criticism. The people could either obey him or silence him. They chose the latter. They did not think they needed Jeremiah; their false prophets told them what they wanted to hear. How do you respond to criticism? Listen carefully—God may be trying to tell you something.

Jer 35:1ff The Recabites' code of conduct resembled that of the Nazirites, who took a special vow of dedication to God (Num 6). For 200 years they had obeyed their ancestor's vow to abstain from wine. While the rest of the nation was breaking its covenant with God, these people were steadfast in their commitment. God wanted the rest of his people to remain as committed to their covenant with him as the Recabites were to their vow. God had Jeremiah tempt the Recabites with wine to demonstrate their commitment and dedication. God knew they wouldn't break their vow.

Jer 35:6 Jehonadab son of Recab had joined Jehu in purging the northern kingdom of Baal worship (2 Kgs 10:15-28).

▸ **JEREMIAH 35:1-19** ***(cont.)***

drink of wine to this day, nor have our wives, our sons,
or our daughters. 9We haven't built houses or owned
vineyards or farms or planted crops. 10We have lived
in tents and have fully obeyed all the commands of
Jehonadab, our ancestor. 11But when King Nebuchadnezzar* of Babylon attacked this country, we were
afraid of the Babylonian and Syrian* armies. So we decided to move to Jerusalem. That is why we are here."
12Then the LORD gave this message to Jeremiah:
13"This is what the LORD of Heaven's Armies, the God
of Israel, says: Go and say to the people in Judah and
Jerusalem, 'Come and learn a lesson about how to obey
me. 14The Recabites do not drink wine to this day because their ancestor Jehonadab told them not to. But
I have spoken to you again and again, and you refuse
to obey me. 15Time after time I sent you prophets,
who told you, "Turn from your wicked ways, and start
doing things right. Stop worshiping other gods so that
you might live in peace here in the land I have given
to you and your ancestors." But you would not listen
to me or obey me. 16The descendants of Jehonadab
son of Recab have obeyed their ancestor completely,
but you have refused to listen to me.'
17"Therefore, this is what the LORD God of Heaven's
Armies, the God of Israel, says: 'Because you refuse to
listen or answer when I call, I will send upon Judah
and Jerusalem all the disasters I have threatened.'"
18Then Jeremiah turned to the Recabites and said,
"This is what the LORD of Heaven's Armies, the God
of Israel, says: 'You have obeyed your ancestor Jehonadab in every respect, following all his instructions.'
19Therefore, this is what the LORD of Heaven's Armies,
the God of Israel, says: 'Jehonadab son of Recab will
always have descendants who serve me.'"

Jeremiah's Message about Ammon

JEREMIAH 49:1-6

This message was given concerning the Ammonites.
This is what the LORD says:

"Are there no descendants of Israel
to inherit the land of Gad?
Why are you, who worship Molech,*
living in its towns?
2 In the days to come," says the LORD,
"I will sound the battle cry against your city
of Rabbah.
It will become a desolate heap of ruins,
and the neighboring towns will be burned.
Then Israel will take back the land
you took from her," says the LORD.

3 "Cry out, O Heshbon,
for the town of Ai is destroyed.
Weep, O people of Rabbah!
Put on your clothes of mourning.
Weep and wail, hiding in the hedges,
for your god Molech, with his priests and
officials,
will be hauled off to distant lands.
4 You are proud of your fertile valleys,
but they will soon be ruined.
You trusted in your wealth,
you rebellious daughter,
and thought no one could ever harm you.
5 But look! I will bring terror upon you,"
says the Lord, the LORD of Heaven's Armies.
"Your neighbors will chase you from your land,
and no one will help your exiles as they flee.
6 But I will restore the fortunes of the Ammonites
in days to come.
I, the LORD, have spoken."

Jeremiah's Messages about Edom

JEREMIAH 49:7-22

This message was given concerning Edom. This is
what the LORD of Heaven's Armies says:

"Is there no wisdom in Teman?
Is no one left to give wise counsel?
8 Turn and flee!
Hide in deep caves, you people of Dedan!
For when I bring disaster on Edom,*
I will punish you, too!
9 Those who harvest grapes
always leave a few for the poor.

Jer 35:11a Hebrew *Nebuchadrezzar,* a variant spelling of Nebuchadnezzar. **Jer 35:11b** Or *Chaldean and Aramean.* **Jer 49:1** Hebrew *Malcam,* a variant spelling of Molech; also in 49:3. **Jer 49:8** Hebrew *Esau;* also in 49:10.

Jer 35:13-17 There is a vivid contrast between the Recabites and the other Israelites. (1) The Recabites kept their vows to a fallible human leader; the people of Israel broke their covenant with their infallible divine Leader. (2) Jehonadab told his family one time not to drink, and they obeyed; God commanded Israel constantly to turn from sin, and they refused. (3) The Recabites obeyed laws that dealt with temporal issues; Israel refused to obey God's laws that dealt with eternal issues. (4) The Recabites had obeyed for hundreds of years; Israel had disobeyed for hundreds of years. (5) The Recabites would be rewarded; Israel would be punished. We often are willing to observe customs merely for the sake of tradition; how much more should we obey God's Word because it is eternal?

Jer 49:1 The Ammonites were descendants of Lot through an incestuous relationship with one of his daughters (as were the Moabites; see Gen 19:30-38). They were condemned for stealing land from God's people and for worshiping the idol Molech, to whom they sacrificed children.

Jer 49:7 The Israelites descended from Jacob, and the Edomites descended from his twin brother, Esau; thus, both nations descended from their father, Isaac. There was constant conflict between these nations, and Edom rejoiced at the fall of Jerusalem (see the book of Obadiah). Teman, a town in the northern part of Edom, was known for its wisdom and was the hometown of Eliphaz, one of Job's friends (Job 2:11). But even the wisdom of Teman could not save Edom from God's wrath.

Jer 49:8 Dedan was a flourishing city that supported caravan travel. God told its inhabitants to flee to the caves or they would also be destroyed. Teman and Dedan were at

If thieves came at night,
they would not take everything.
10 But I will strip bare the land of Edom,
and there will be no place left to hide.
Its children, its brothers, and its neighbors
will all be destroyed,
and Edom itself will be no more.
11 But I will protect the orphans who remain
among you.
Your widows, too, can depend on me for help."

12And this is what the LORD says: "If the innocent
must suffer, how much more must you! You will not
go unpunished! You must drink this cup of judgment!
13For I have sworn by my own name," says the LORD,
"that Bozrah will become an object of horror and a
heap of ruins; it will be mocked and cursed. All its
towns and villages will be desolate forever."

14 I have heard a message from the LORD
that an ambassador was sent to the nations
to say,
"Form a coalition against Edom,
and prepare for battle!"
15 The LORD says to Edom,
"I will cut you down to size among the nations.
You will be despised by all.
16 You have been deceived
by the fear you inspire in others
and by your own pride.
You live in a rock fortress
and control the mountain heights.
But even if you make your nest among the peaks
with the eagles,
I will bring you crashing down,"
says the LORD.
17 "Edom will be an object of horror.
All who pass by will be appalled
and will gasp at the destruction they see there.
18 It will be like the destruction of Sodom and
Gomorrah
and their neighboring towns," says the LORD.
"No one will live there;
no one will inhabit it.
19 I will come like a lion from the thickets of the
Jordan,
leaping on the sheep in the pasture.
I will chase Edom from its land,
and I will appoint the leader of my choice.
For who is like me, and who can challenge me?
What ruler can oppose my will?"
20 Listen to the LORD's plans against Edom
and the people of Teman.
Even the little children will be dragged off like
sheep,
and their homes will be destroyed.
21 The earth will shake with the noise of Edom's fall,
and its cry of despair will be heard all the way
to the Red Sea.*
22 Look! The enemy swoops down like an eagle,
spreading his wings over Bozrah.
Even the mightiest warriors will be in anguish
like a woman in labor.

Jeremiah's Message about Damascus

JEREMIAH 49:23-27

This message was given concerning Damascus. This is what the LORD says:

"The towns of Hamath and Arpad are struck
with fear,
for they have heard the news of their
destruction.
Their hearts are troubled
like a wild sea in a raging storm.
24 Damascus has become feeble,
and all her people turn to flee.
Fear, anguish, and pain have gripped her
as they grip a woman in labor.
25 That famous city, a city of joy,
will be forsaken!
26 Her young men will fall in the streets and die.
Her soldiers will all be killed,"
says the LORD of Heaven's Armies.
27 "And I will set fire to the walls of Damascus
that will burn up the palaces of Ben-hadad."

Jeremiah's Message about Kedar and Hazor

JEREMIAH 49:28-33

This message was given concerning Kedar and the kingdoms of Hazor, which were attacked by King Nebuchadnezzar* of Babylon. This is what the LORD says:

Jer 49:21 Hebrew *sea of reeds.* **Jer 49:28** Hebrew *Nebuchadrezzar,* a variant spelling of Nebuchadnezzar; also in 49:30.

opposite ends of the country, so this shows the completeness of God's destruction of Edom. Bozrah (Jer 49:13) was a town in northern Edom.

Jer 49:16 Edom was located in a rock fortress that today is known as Petra, in southern Jordan. Edom thought it was invincible because of its location. Edom was destroyed because of its pride. Pride destroys nations as well as individuals. It deludes us into thinking that we can take care of ourselves without God's help. Even serving God and others can lead us into pride. Take inventory of your life and service for God; ask God to point out and remove any pride you may be harboring.

Jer 49:23-26 Damascus was the capital of Aram, north of Israel. Assyria defeated this city, then Babylonia attacked and defeated it in 605 B.C. (Amos 1:4-5). It is difficult to attribute the defeat of the army to a particular event, but God utterly destroyed Aram.

Jer 49:28 Kedar and Hazor were nomadic tribes east of Israel and south of Aram, in the desert. In 599 B.C., Nebuchadnezzar destroyed them.

▸ JEREMIAH 49:28-33 *(cont.)*

"Advance against Kedar!
Destroy the warriors from the East!
29 Their flocks and tents will be captured,
and their household goods and camels will be taken away.
Everywhere shouts of panic will be heard:
'We are terrorized at every turn!'
30 Run for your lives," says the LORD.
"Hide yourselves in deep caves, you people of Hazor,
for King Nebuchadnezzar of Babylon has plotted against you
and is preparing to destroy you.
31 "Go up and attack that complacent nation,"
says the LORD.
"Its people live alone in the desert
without walls or gates.
32 Their camels and other livestock will all be yours.
I will scatter to the winds these people
who live in remote places.*
I will bring calamity upon them
from every direction," says the LORD.
33 "Hazor will be inhabited by jackals,
and it will be desolate forever.
No one will live there;
no one will inhabit it."

Jer 49:32 Or *who clip the corners of their hair.*

5. JUDAH CONTINUES TO WEAKEN

Jehoiachin's brief three-month reign in Judah was a time of turmoil, with the Babylonian threat increasing and seemingly no attempt by Judah to return to God in spite of Jeremiah's prophetic work. Jeremiah continued to serve during this time, changing his tone to one of hope for restoration after the Exile and God's sure judgment against Babylon for their own evil deeds.

The End of Jehoiakim's Reign PARALLEL

2 KINGS 24:5-7

The rest of the events in Jehoiakim's reign and all his deeds are recorded in *The Book of the History of the Kings of Judah.* 6When Jehoiakim died, his son Jehoiachin became the next king.

7The king of Egypt did not venture out of his country after that, for the king of Babylon captured the entire area formerly claimed by Egypt—from the Brook of Egypt to the Euphrates River.

2 CHRONICLES 36:6-8

Then King Nebuchadnezzar of Babylon came to Jerusalem and captured it, and he bound Jehoiakim in bronze chains and led him away to Babylon. 7Nebuchadnezzar also took some of the treasures from the Temple of the LORD, and he placed them in his palace* in Babylon.

8The rest of the events in Jehoiakim's reign, including all the evil things he did and everything found against him, are recorded in *The Book of the Kings of Israel and Judah.* Then his son Jehoiachin became the next king.

Jehoiachin Begins to Reign in Judah PARALLEL

2 KINGS 24:8-9

Jehoiachin was eighteen years old when he became king, and he reigned in Jerusalem three months. His mother was Nehushta, the daughter of Elnathan from Jerusalem. 9Jehoiachin did what was evil in the LORD's sight, just as his father had done.

2 CHRONICLES 36:9

Jehoiachin was eighteen* years old when he became king, and he reigned in Jerusalem three months and ten days. Jehoiachin did what was evil in the LORD's sight.

Jeremiah's Message for Jehoiachin

JEREMIAH 22:24-30

"As surely as I live," says the LORD, "I will abandon you, Jehoiachin* son of Jehoiakim, king of Judah. Even if you were the signet ring on my right hand, I would pull you off. 25I will hand you over to those who seek to kill you, those you so desperately fear—to King Nebuchadnezzar* of Babylon and the mighty Babylonian* army. 26I will expel you and your mother from this land, and you will die in a foreign country, not in your native land. 27You will never again return to the land you yearn for.

28 "Why is this man Jehoiachin like a discarded, broken jar?
Why are he and his children to be exiled
to a foreign land?
29 O earth, earth, earth!
Listen to this message from the LORD!

2 Chr 36:7 Or *temple.* **2 Chr 36:9** As in one Hebrew manuscript, some Greek manuscripts, and Syriac version (see also 2 Kgs 24:8); most Hebrew manuscripts read *eight.* **Jer 22:24** Hebrew *Coniah,* a variant spelling of Jehoiachin; also 22:28. **Jer 22:25a** Hebrew *Nebuchadrezzar,* a variant spelling of Nebuchadnezzar. **Jer 22:25b** Or *Chaldean.*

2 Chr 36:6 Nebuchadnezzar was the son of the founder of the new Babylonian Empire. In 605 B.C., the year he became king, Nebuchadnezzar won the battle of Carchemish. That win crushed Assyria (see the note on 2 Chr 35:20, p. 987). (For more information about Nebuchadnezzar, read his Profile on p. 1120.)

2 Chr 36:9 Many Hebrew manuscripts list Jehoiachin as 8 years old here. In 2 Kings 24:8, he is listed as 18 years old, which is most likely accurate because he had wives at that time (see 2 Kgs 24:15).

Jer 22:24-25 A signet ring was extremely valuable because a king used it to authen-

30 This is what the LORD says:
'Let the record show that this man Jehoiachin
was childless.
He is a failure,
for none of his children will succeed him
on the throne of David
to rule over Judah.'

The Righteous Descendant

JEREMIAH 23:1-8

"What sorrow awaits the leaders of my people—the
shepherds of my sheep—for they have destroyed and
scattered the very ones they were expected to care
for," says the LORD.
2Therefore, this is what the LORD, the God of Israel, says to these shepherds: "Instead of caring for
my flock and leading them to safety, you have deserted them and driven them to destruction. Now I
will pour out judgment on you for the evil you have
done to them. 3But I will gather together the remnant of my flock from the countries where I have
driven them. I will bring them back to their own
sheepfold, and they will be fruitful and increase in
number. 4Then I will appoint responsible shepherds
who will care for them, and they will never be afraid
again. Not a single one will be lost or missing. I, the
LORD, have spoken!

5 "For the time is coming,"
says the LORD,
"when I will raise up a righteous descendant*
from King David's line.
He will be a King who rules with wisdom.
He will do what is just and right throughout
the land.
6 And this will be his name:
'The LORD Is Our Righteousness.'*
In that day Judah will be saved,
and Israel will live in safety.

7"In that day," says the LORD, "when people are taking an oath, they will no longer say, 'As surely as the
LORD lives, who rescued the people of Israel from the
land of Egypt.' 8Instead, they will say, 'As surely as the
LORD lives, who brought the people of Israel back to
their own land from the land of the north and from
all the countries to which he had exiled them.' Then
they will live in their own land."

Judgment on False Prophets

JEREMIAH 23:9-32

9 My heart is broken because of the false prophets,
and my bones tremble.
I stagger like a drunkard,
like someone overcome by wine,
because of the holy words
the LORD has spoken against them.
10 For the land is full of adultery,
and it lies under a curse.
The land itself is in mourning—
its wilderness pastures are dried up.
For they all do evil
and abuse what power they have.

11 "Even the priests and prophets
are ungodly, wicked men.
I have seen their despicable acts
right here in my own Temple,"
says the LORD.
12 "Therefore, the paths they take
will become slippery.
They will be chased through the dark,
and there they will fall.
For I will bring disaster upon them
at the time fixed for their punishment.
I, the LORD, have spoken!

13 "I saw that the prophets of Samaria were
terribly evil,
for they prophesied in the name of Baal
and led my people of Israel into sin.
14 But now I see that the prophets of Jerusalem
are even worse!
They commit adultery and love dishonesty.

Jer 23:5 Hebrew *a righteous branch.* **Jer 23:6** Hebrew *Yahweh Tsidqenu.*

ticate important documents. Jehoiachin's sins spoiled his usefulness to God. Even if he were God's own signet ring, God would depose him because of his sins (see Jer 24:1).

Jer 22:30 Zedekiah reigned after Jehoiachin but died before him (Jer 52:10-11). Jehoiachin was the last king of David's line to sit on the throne in Judah (1 Chr 3:15-20). He had seven sons, but not one served as king. Jehoiachin's grandson Zerubbabel ruled after the return from exile (Ezra 2:2), but he was only a governor, not a king.

Jer 23:1-4 Those responsible to lead Israel in God's path were the very ones responsible for Israel's present plight, so God had decreed harsh judgment against them. Leaders are held responsible for those entrusted to their care. Whom has God placed in your care? Remember that you are accountable to God for those you influence and lead.

Jer 23:5-6 Jeremiah contrasted the present corrupt leaders with the coming Messiah, the perfect King, who would come from David's line to reign over Israel.

Jer 23:9-14 How did the nation become so corrupt? A major factor was false prophecy. The false prophets had a large, enthusiastic audience and were very popular because they made the people believe that all was well. By contrast, Jeremiah's message from God was unpopular because it showed the people how bad they were.

There are four warning signs of false prophets—characteristics we need to watch for even today: (1) They may appear to speak God's message, but they do not live according to God's Word. (2) They water down God's message in order to make it more palatable. (3) They encourage their listeners, often subtly, to disobey God. (4) They tend to be arrogant and self-serving, appealing to the desires of their audience instead of being true to God's Word.

Jer 23:14 Sodom and Gomorrah were sinful cities destroyed by God (Gen 19:23-24). In the Bible they typify the ultimate in depraved, sinful behavior and rebellion against God.

▸ **JEREMIAH 23:9-32** ***(cont.)***

They encourage those who are doing evil
so that no one turns away from their sins.
These prophets are as wicked
as the people of Sodom and Gomorrah
once were."

15Therefore, this is what the LORD of Heaven's Armies says concerning the prophets:

"I will feed them with bitterness
and give them poison to drink.
For it is because of Jerusalem's prophets
that wickedness has filled this land."

16This is what the LORD of Heaven's Armies says to his people:

"Do not listen to these prophets when they
prophesy to you,
filling you with futile hopes.
They are making up everything they say.
They do not speak for the LORD!
17 They keep saying to those who despise my word,
'Don't worry! The LORD says you will have
peace!'
And to those who stubbornly follow their own
desires,
they say, 'No harm will come your way!'

18 "Have any of these prophets been in the LORD's
presence
to hear what he is really saying?
Has even one of them cared enough to listen?
19 Look! The LORD's anger bursts out like a storm,
a whirlwind that swirls down on the heads of
the wicked.
20 The anger of the LORD will not diminish
until it has finished all he has planned.
In the days to come
you will understand all this very clearly.

21 "I have not sent these prophets,
yet they run around claiming to speak for me.
I have given them no message,
yet they go on prophesying.
22 If they had stood before me and listened to me,
they would have spoken my words,
and they would have turned my people
from their evil ways and deeds.
23 Am I a God who is only close at hand?" says the
LORD.
"No, I am far away at the same time.
24 Can anyone hide from me in a secret place?
Am I not everywhere in all the heavens and
earth?"
says the LORD.

25"I have heard these prophets say, 'Listen to the
dream I had from God last night.' And then they proceed to tell lies in my name. 26How long will this go
on? If they are prophets, they are prophets of deceit,
inventing everything they say. 27By telling these false
dreams, they are trying to get my people to forget me,
just as their ancestors did by worshiping the idols
of Baal.

28 "Let these false prophets tell their dreams,
but let my true messengers faithfully proclaim
my every word.
There is a difference between straw and grain!
29 Does not my word burn like fire?"
says the LORD.
"Is it not like a mighty hammer
that smashes a rock to pieces?

30"Therefore," says the LORD, "I am against these
prophets who steal messages from each other and
claim they are from me. 31I am against these smooth-
tongued prophets who say, 'This prophecy is from the
LORD!' 32I am against these false prophets. Their imaginary dreams are flagrant lies that lead my people into
sin. I did not send or appoint them, and they have no
message at all for my people. I, the LORD, have spoken!

False Prophecies and False Prophets

JEREMIAH 23:33-40

"Suppose one of the people or one of the prophets or priests asks you, 'What prophecy has the LORD burdened you with now?' You must reply, 'You are the burden!* The LORD says he will abandon you!'

Jer 23:33 As in Greek version and Latin Vulgate; Hebrew reads *What burden?*

Jer 23:20 The people would see the truth of this prophecy when Jerusalem fell.

Jer 23:21-24 In Jeremiah's time, those who claimed to speak for God were often guilty of representing a deity they thought of as limited and localized—a neighborhood god. Their gods frequently had limited interests and shortsighted awareness. God declares his omnipresence with a question: "Am I not everywhere in all the heavens and earth?" We make the same mistake those would-be prophets made when we assume God doesn't know or care about the situations in our lives or when we question his ability to handle things beyond our control. How big is the God you worship?

Jer 23:28 True prophets and false prophets are as different as straw and wheat. Straw is useless for food and cannot compare to nourishing wheat. To share the gospel is a great responsibility because the way we present it and live it will encourage people either to accept it or to reject it. Whether we speak from a pulpit, teach in a class, or share with friends, we must accurately communicate and live out God's Word. As you share God's Word with friends and neighbors, they will look for its effectiveness in your life. Unless it has changed you, why should they let it change them? If you preach it, make sure you live it!

Jer 23:33-40 People mocked Jeremiah by saying sarcastically, "What prophecy has the LORD burdened you with now?" It seemed that Jeremiah brought nothing but God's sad news of condemnation. But this sad news was the truth. If they had accepted it, they would have had to repent and turn to God. Because they did not want to do this, they rejected Jeremiah's message. Have you ever rejected a message or made fun of it because it would require you to change

[34]"If any prophet, priest, or anyone else says, 'I have a prophecy from the LORD,' I will punish that person along with his entire family. [35]You should keep asking each other, 'What is the LORD's answer?' or 'What is the LORD saying?' [36]But stop using this phrase, 'prophecy from the LORD.' For people are using it to give authority to their own ideas, turning upside down the words of our God, the living God, the LORD of Heaven's Armies.

[37]"This is what you should say to the prophets: 'What is the LORD's answer?' or 'What is the LORD saying?' [38]But suppose they respond, 'This is a prophecy from the LORD!' Then you should say, 'This is what the LORD says: Because you have used this phrase, "prophecy from the LORD," even though I warned you not to use it, [39]I will forget you completely.* I will expel you from my presence, along with this city that I gave to you and your ancestors. [40]And I will make you an object of ridicule, and your name will be infamous throughout the ages.'"

Good and Bad Figs

JEREMIAH 24:1-10

After King Nebuchadnezzar* of Babylon exiled Jehoiachin* son of Jehoiakim, king of Judah, to Babylon along with the officials of Judah and all the craftsmen and artisans, the LORD gave me this vision. I saw two baskets of figs placed in front of the LORD's Temple in Jerusalem. [2]One basket was filled with fresh, ripe figs, while the other was filled with bad figs that were too rotten to eat.

[3]Then the LORD said to me, "What do you see, Jeremiah?"

I replied, "Figs, some very good and some very bad, too rotten to eat."

[4]Then the LORD gave me this message: [5]"This is what the LORD, the God of Israel, says: The good figs represent the exiles I sent from Judah to the land of the Babylonians.* [6]I will watch over and care for them, and I will bring them back here again. I will build them up and not tear them down. I will plant them and not uproot them. [7]I will give them hearts that recognize me as the LORD. They will be my people, and I will be their God, for they will return to me wholeheartedly.

[8]"But the bad figs," the LORD said, "represent King Zedekiah of Judah, his officials, all the people left in Jerusalem, and those who live in Egypt. I will treat them like bad figs, too rotten to eat. [9]I will make them an object of horror and a symbol of evil to every nation on earth. They will be disgraced and mocked, taunted and cursed, wherever I scatter them. [10]And I will send war, famine, and disease until they have vanished from the land of Israel, which I gave to them and their ancestors."

A Letter to the Exiles

JEREMIAH 29:1-23

Jeremiah wrote a letter from Jerusalem to the elders, priests, prophets, and all the people who had been exiled to Babylon by King Nebuchadnezzar. [2]This was after King Jehoiachin,* the queen mother, the court officials, the other officials of Judah, and all the craftsmen and artisans had been deported from Jerusalem. [3]He sent the letter with Elasah son of Shaphan and Gemariah son of Hilkiah when they went to Babylon as King Zedekiah's ambassadors to Nebuchadnezzar. This is what Jeremiah's letter said:

> [4]This is what the LORD of Heaven's Armies, the God of Israel, says to all the captives he has exiled to Babylon from Jerusalem: [5]"Build homes, and plan to stay. Plant gardens, and eat the food they produce. [6]Marry and have children. Then find spouses for them so that you may have many grandchildren. Multiply! Do not dwindle away! [7]And work for the peace and prosperity of the city where I sent you into exile. Pray to the LORD for it, for its welfare will determine your welfare."

Jer 23:39 Some Hebrew manuscripts and Greek version read *I will surely lift you up.* **Jer 24:1a** Hebrew *Nebuchadrezzar,* a variant spelling of Nebuchadnezzar. **Jer 24:1b** Hebrew *Jeconiah,* a variant spelling of Jehoiachin. **Jer 24:5** Or *Chaldeans.* **Jer 29:2** Hebrew *Jeconiah,* a variant spelling of Jehoiachin.

your ways? Before dismissing someone who brings sad news, look carefully at your motives.

Jer 24:1 In 597 B.C., Jehoiachin was taken to Babylon, and Zedekiah became king. Often royal officials were exiled to keep them from exerting power and starting a rebellion. Skilled craftsmen and artisans were taken because they were valuable for Babylon's building program. Jeremiah had foretold this event (Jer 22:24-28).

Jer 24:2-10 The fresh, ripe figs represented the exiles to Babylon, not because they themselves were good but because their hearts would respond to God. He would preserve them and bring them back to the land. The bad, rotten figs represented those who remained in Judah or ran away to Egypt. Those people may have arrogantly believed they would be blessed if they remained in the land or escaped to Egypt, but the opposite was true because God would use the captivity to refine the exiles. We may assume we are blessed when life goes well and cursed when it does not. But trouble is a blessing when it makes us stronger, and prosperity is a curse if it entices us away from God. If you are facing trouble, ask God to help you grow stronger for him. If things are going your way, ask God to help you use your prosperity for him.

Jer 24:6 The Lord cared for the exiles in Babylon. Although they were moved to a foreign land, their captivity was not enslavement. The people could function in business and own homes. Some, like Daniel, even held high positions in the government (see Dan 2:48).

Jer 29:4-7 Jeremiah wrote to the captives in Babylon (Jer 29:4-23) instructing them to move ahead with their lives and to pray for the pagan nation that enslaved them. Life cannot grind to a halt during troubled times. In an unpleasant or distressing situation, we must adjust and keep moving. You may find it difficult to pray for those in authority if they are evil, but that is when your prayers are most needed (1 Tim 2:1-2). When you enter times of trouble or sudden change, pray diligently and move ahead, doing whatever you can rather than giving up because of fear and uncertainty.

▸ **JEREMIAH 29:1-23** *(cont.)*

8This is what the LORD of Heaven's Armies, the
God of Israel, says: "Do not let your prophets and
fortune-tellers who are with you in the land of
Babylon trick you. Do not listen to their dreams,
9because they are telling you lies in my name.
I have not sent them," says the LORD.
10This is what the LORD says: "You will be
in Babylon for seventy years. But then I will
come and do for you all the good things I have
promised, and I will bring you home again. 11For
I know the plans I have for you," says the LORD.
"They are plans for good and not for disaster,
to give you a future and a hope. 12In those days
when you pray, I will listen. 13If you look for me
wholeheartedly, you will find me. 14I will be found
by you," says the LORD. "I will end your captivity
and restore your fortunes. I will gather you out of
the nations where I sent you and will bring you
home again to your own land."
15You claim that the LORD has raised up
prophets for you in Babylon. 16But this is what
the LORD says about the king who sits on
David's throne and all those still living here
in Jerusalem—your relatives who were not exiled
to Babylon. 17This is what the LORD of Heaven's
Armies says: "I will send war, famine, and disease
upon them and make them like bad figs, too
rotten to eat. 18Yes, I will pursue them with war,
famine, and disease, and I will scatter them
around the world. In every nation where I send
them, I will make them an object of damnation,
horror, contempt, and mockery. 19For they refuse
to listen to me, though I have spoken to them
repeatedly through the prophets I sent. And you
who are in exile have not listened either," says
the LORD.
20Therefore, listen to this message from the
LORD, all you captives there in Babylon. 21This
is what the LORD of Heaven's Armies, the God
of Israel, says about your prophets—Ahab son
of Kolaiah and Zedekiah son of Maaseiah—who
are telling you lies in my name: "I will turn them
over to Nebuchadnezzar* for execution before
your eyes. 22Their terrible fate will become
proverbial, so that the Judean exiles will curse
someone by saying, 'May the LORD make you like
Zedekiah and Ahab, whom the king of Babylon
burned alive!' 23For these men have done
terrible things among my people. They have
committed adultery with their neighbors' wives
and have lied in my name, saying things I did
not command. I am a witness to this. I, the LORD,
have spoken."

Jer 29:21 Hebrew *Nebuchadrezzar,* a variant spelling of Nebuchadnezzar.

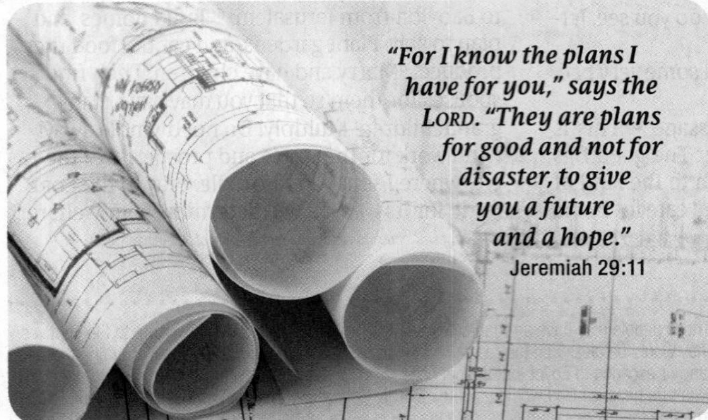

"For I know the plans I have for you," says the LORD. "They are plans for good and not for disaster, to give you a future and a hope."
Jeremiah 29:11

Jer 29:10 Scholars differ on the exact dates of this 70-year period in Babylon. Some say it refers to the years 605–538 B.C., from the first deportation to Babylon to the arrival of the first exiles back in Jerusalem after Cyrus's freedom decree. Others point to the years 586–515 B.C., from the last deportation to Babylon and the destruction of the Temple until its rebuilding. A third possibility is that 70 years is an approximate number meaning a lifetime. All agree that God sent his people to Babylon for a long time, not the short captivity predicted by the false prophets.

Jer 29:11 We're all encouraged by a leader who stirs us to move ahead, someone who believes we can do the task he has given and who will be with us all the way. God is that kind of leader. He knows the future, and his plans for us are good and full of hope. As long as God, who knows the future, provides our agenda and goes with us as we fulfill his mission, we can have boundless hope. This does not mean that we will be spared pain, suffering, or hardship, but that God will see us through to a glorious conclusion.

Jer 29:12-14 God did not forget his people, even though they were captives in Babylon. He planned to give them a new beginning with a new purpose—to turn them into new people. In times of dire circumstances, it may appear as though God has forgotten you. But God may be preparing you, as he did the people of Judah, for a new beginning with him at the center.

Jer 29:13 According to God's wise plan, his people were to have a future and a hope; consequently, they could call upon him in confidence. Although the exiles were in a difficult place and time, they need not despair because they had God's presence, the privilege of prayer, and God's grace. If we seek him wholeheartedly, he will be found. Neither a strange land, sorrow, persecution, nor physical problems can break our fellowship with God.

Jer 29:20-23 Why would Nebuchadnezzar decide to execute these two false prophets? In contrast to Jeremiah's message from God that the people should settle in Babylon and wait faithfully for 70 years to pass, the false prophets were inciting false hopes for a quick return to Jerusalem. This would have sounded like rebellion to the Babylonian king, who would have had little hesitation over killing uncooperative refugees.

Jer 29:21 These false prophets, Ahab and Zedekiah, should not be confused with the kings who had the same names.

Jeremiah's Message for Shemaiah

JEREMIAH 29:24-32

The LORD sent this message to Shemaiah the Nehelamite in Babylon: 25"This is what the LORD of Heaven's
Armies, the God of Israel, says: You wrote a letter on
your own authority to Zephaniah son of Maaseiah, the
priest, and you sent copies to the other priests and
people in Jerusalem. You wrote to Zephaniah,

> 26"The LORD has appointed you to replace
> Jehoiada as the priest in charge of the house of
> the LORD. You are responsible to put into stocks
> and neck irons any crazy man who claims to be
> a prophet. 27So why have you done nothing to
> stop Jeremiah from Anathoth, who pretends to
> be a prophet among you? 28Jeremiah sent a letter
> here to Babylon, predicting that our captivity
> will be a long one. He said, 'Build homes, and
> plan to stay. Plant gardens, and eat the food they
> produce.'"

29But when Zephaniah the priest received Shemaiah's letter, he took it to Jeremiah and read it to
him. 30Then the LORD gave this message to Jeremiah:
31"Send an open letter to all the exiles in Babylon.
Tell them, 'This is what the LORD says concerning
Shemaiah the Nehelamite: Since he has prophesied
to you when I did not send him and has tricked you
into believing his lies, 32I will punish him and his family. None of his descendants will see the good things
I will do for my people, for he has incited you to rebel
against me. I, the LORD, have spoken!'"

Promises of Deliverance

JEREMIAH 30:1-24

The LORD gave another message to Jeremiah. He said,
2"This is what the LORD, the God of Israel, says: Write
down for the record everything I have said to you,
Jeremiah. 3For the time is coming when I will restore
the fortunes of my people of Israel and Judah. I will
bring them home to this land that I gave to their ancestors, and they will possess it again. I, the LORD, have
spoken!"

4This is the message the LORD gave concerning Israel and Judah. 5This is what the LORD says:

"I hear cries of fear;
  there is terror and no peace.
6 Now let me ask you a question:
  Do men give birth to babies?
Then why do they stand there, ashen-faced,
  hands pressed against their sides
  like a woman in labor?
7 In all history there has never been such a time
    of terror.
  It will be a time of trouble for my people
    Israel.*
  Yet in the end they will be saved!
8 For in that day,"
  says the LORD of Heaven's Armies,
"I will break the yoke from their necks
  and snap their chains.
Foreigners will no longer be their masters.
9 For my people will serve the LORD their God
and their king descended from David—
  the king I will raise up for them.

10 "So do not be afraid, Jacob, my servant;
  do not be dismayed, Israel,"
  says the LORD.
"For I will bring you home again from distant
    lands,
  and your children will return from their
    exile.
Israel will return to a life of peace and quiet,
  and no one will terrorize them.
11 For I am with you and will save you,"
  says the LORD.
"I will completely destroy the nations where
    I have scattered you,
  but I will not completely destroy you.
I will discipline you, but with justice;
  I cannot let you go unpunished."

12 This is what the LORD says:
"Your injury is incurable—
  a terrible wound.

Jer 30:7 Hebrew *Jacob;* also in 30:10b, 18. See note on 5:20.

Jer 29:24-28 These verses describe the reaction of Shemaiah, a false prophet exiled in 597 B.C. who had protested about Jeremiah's letter. To discredit Jeremiah, Shemaiah accused him of false prophecy. Although Jeremiah's message was true and his words were from God, the people hated him because he told them to make the most of the exile. Jeremiah's truth from God offered temporary correction and long-range benefit, while the false teachers' lies offered only temporary comfort and long-range punishment.

Jer 30:1ff Jeremiah 30–31 shows that Jeremiah spoke of hope and consolation as well as trouble and gloom. The people would one day be restored to their land, and God would make a new covenant with them to replace the one they had broken. Whereas once they sinned and disobeyed, eventually they would repent and obey.

Jer 30:8-9 Like Isaiah, Jeremiah associated events of the near future and those of the distant future. Reading these prophecies is like looking at several mountain peaks in a range. From a distance they look as though they are next to each other, when actually they are miles apart. Jeremiah presents near and distant events as if they will all happen soon. He sees the exile, but he also sees the future day when Christ will reign forever. The "king descended from David" refers to the Messiah (Luke 1:69).

Jer 30:12-13, 17 The medical language here conveys the idea that sin is terminal. Sinful people cannot be cured by being good or being religious. Beware of putting your confidence in useless cures while your sin spreads and causes you pain. God alone can cure the disease of sin, but you must be willing to let him do it.

▸ **JEREMIAH 30:1-24** ***(cont.)***

13 There is no one to help you
or to bind up your injury.
No medicine can heal you.
14 All your lovers—your allies—have left you
and do not care about you anymore.
I have wounded you cruelly,
as though I were your enemy.
For your sins are many,
and your guilt is great.
15 Why do you protest your punishment—
this wound that has no cure?
I have had to punish you
because your sins are many
and your guilt is great.

16 "But all who devour you will be devoured,
and all your enemies will be sent into exile.
All who plunder you will be plundered,
and all who attack you will be attacked.
17 I will give you back your health
and heal your wounds," says the LORD.
"For you are called an outcast—
'Jerusalem* for whom no one cares.'"

18 This is what the LORD says:
"When I bring Israel home again from captivity
and restore their fortunes,
Jerusalem will be rebuilt on its ruins,
and the palace reconstructed as before.
19 There will be joy and songs of thanksgiving,
and I will multiply my people, not diminish
them;
I will honor them, not despise them.
20 Their children will prosper as they did
long ago.
I will establish them as a nation before me,
and I will punish anyone who hurts them.
21 They will have their own ruler again,
and he will come from their own people.
I will invite him to approach me," says the LORD,
"for who would dare to come unless invited?
22 You will be my people,
and I will be your God."

23 Look! The LORD's anger bursts out like a storm,
a driving wind that swirls down on the heads
of the wicked.
24 The fierce anger of the LORD will not diminish
until it has finished all he has planned.
In the days to come
you will understand all this.

Hope for Restoration

JEREMIAH 31:1-14

"In that day," says the LORD, "I will be the God of all the
families of Israel, and they will be my people. 2This is
what the LORD says:

"Those who survive the coming destruction
will find blessings even in the barren land,
for I will give rest to the people of Israel."

3 Long ago the LORD said to Israel:
"I have loved you, my people, with an everlasting
love.
With unfailing love I have drawn you to myself.
4 I will rebuild you, my virgin Israel.
You will again be happy
and dance merrily with your tambourines.
5 Again you will plant your vineyards on the
mountains of Samaria
and eat from your own gardens there.
6 The day will come when watchmen will shout
from the hill country of Ephraim,
'Come, let us go up to Jerusalem*
to worship the LORD our God.'"

7 Now this is what the LORD says:
"Sing with joy for Israel.*
Shout for the greatest of nations!
Shout out with praise and joy:
'Save your people, O LORD,
the remnant of Israel!'
8 For I will bring them from the north
and from the distant corners of the earth.
I will not forget the blind and lame,
the expectant mothers and women in labor.
A great company will return!
9 Tears of joy will stream down their faces,
and I will lead them home with great care.
They will walk beside quiet streams
and on smooth paths where they will not
stumble.
For I am Israel's father,
and Ephraim is my oldest child.

Jer 30:17 Hebrew *Zion.* **Jer 31:6** Hebrew *Zion;* also in 31:12. **Jer 31:7** Hebrew *Jacob;* also in 31:11. See note on 5:20.

Jer 30:15 Judah protested its punishment, even though the sin that caused the pain was scandalous. But punishment is an opportunity for growth because it makes us aware of sin's consequences. The people should have asked how they could profit from their mistakes. Remember this the next time you are corrected.

Jer 30:18 This prophecy that Jerusalem would be rebuilt was not completely fulfilled by the work of Ezra, Nehemiah, and Zerubbabel. The city was indeed rebuilt after the Captivity, but the final restoration will occur when all believers are gathered in Christ's Kingdom. This restoration will include buildings (Jer 30:18), people (Jer 30:19), and rulers (Jer 30:21).

Jer 30:21 This verse refers to the restoration after the Babylonian captivity as well as to the final restoration under Christ.

Jer 31:1 This promise is to all the families of Israel, not only to the tribe of Judah. The restoration will include all people who trust God.

Jer 31:3 God reaches toward his people with kindness motivated by deep and everlasting love. He is eager to do the best for them if they will only let him. After many words of warning about sin, this reminder of God's magnificent love is a breath of fresh air. Rather than thinking of God with dread,

10 "Listen to this message from the LORD,
you nations of the world;
proclaim it in distant coastlands:
The LORD, who scattered his people,
will gather them and watch over them
as a shepherd does his flock.
11 For the LORD has redeemed Israel
from those too strong for them.
12 They will come home and sing songs of joy
on the heights of Jerusalem.
They will be radiant because of the LORD's
good gifts—
the abundant crops of grain, new wine,
and olive oil,
and the healthy flocks and herds.
Their life will be like a watered garden,
and all their sorrows will be gone.
13 The young women will dance for joy,
and the men—old and young—will join in the
celebration.
I will turn their mourning into joy.
I will comfort them and exchange their sorrow
for rejoicing.
14 The priests will enjoy abundance,
and my people will feast on my good gifts.
I, the LORD, have spoken!"

Rachel's Sadness Turns to Joy

JEREMIAH 31:15-40

This is what the LORD says:

"A cry is heard in Ramah—
deep anguish and bitter weeping.
Rachel weeps for her children,
refusing to be comforted—
for her children are gone."

16 But now this is what the LORD says:
"Do not weep any longer,
for I will reward you," says the LORD.
"Your children will come back to you
from the distant land of the enemy.
17 There is hope for your future," says
the LORD.
"Your children will come again to their
own land.
18 I have heard Israel* saying,
'You disciplined me severely,
like a calf that needs training for the yoke.
Turn me again to you and restore me,
for you alone are the LORD my God.
19 I turned away from God,
but then I was sorry.
I kicked myself for my stupidity!
I was thoroughly ashamed of all I did in my
younger days.'
20 "Is not Israel still my son,
my darling child?" says the LORD.
"I often have to punish him,
but I still love him.
That's why I long for him
and surely will have mercy on him.
21 Set up road signs;
put up guideposts.
Mark well the path
by which you came.
Come back again, my virgin Israel;
return to your towns here.
22 How long will you wander,
my wayward daughter?
For the LORD will cause something new to
happen—
Israel will embrace her God.*"

23 This is what the LORD of Heaven's Armies, the God
of Israel, says: "When I bring them back from captivity,
the people of Judah and its towns will again say, 'The
LORD bless you, O righteous home, O holy mountain!'
24 Townspeople and farmers and shepherds alike will
live together in peace and happiness. 25 For I have
given rest to the weary and joy to the sorrowing."
26 At this, I woke up and looked around. My sleep
had been very sweet.
27 "The day is coming," says the LORD, "when I will
greatly increase the human population and the number of animals here in Israel and Judah. 28 In the past
I deliberately uprooted and tore down this nation. I
overthrew it, destroyed it, and brought disaster upon
it. But in the future I will just as deliberately plant it
and build it up. I, the LORD, have spoken!
29 "The people will no longer quote this proverb:

Jer 31:18 Hebrew *Ephraim,* referring to the northern kingdom of Israel; also in 31:20.

Jer 31:22 Hebrew *a woman will surround a man.*

look carefully and see him lovingly drawing us toward himself.

Jer 31:14 This means that many sacrifices will be made at the Temple so that the priests will have a feast with their portion. It is also a symbol of life and prosperity (Pss 36:8; 63:5; Isa 55:2).

Jer 31:15 Rachel, Jacob's favorite wife, was the symbolic mother of the northern tribes, which were taken into captivity by the Assyrians. Rachel is pictured crying for the exiles at Ramah, a staging point of deportation. This verse is quoted in Matthew 2:18 to describe the grief of the mothers of Bethlehem as the male children were killed. The weeping was great in both cases.

Jer 31:18-20 These words picture grief and mourning. Although Israel, the northern kingdom, had sunk into the most degrading sins, God still loved the people. A remnant would turn to God by repenting of their sins, and God would forgive. God still loves you despite anything you may have done. He will forgive you if you turn back to him.

Jer 31:29-30 The people tried to blame God's judgment on the sins of their parents. One person's sin does indeed affect other people, but all people are still held personally accountable for the sin in their own life (Deut 24:16; Ezek 18:2). What excuses do you use for your sins?

▸ **JEREMIAH 31:15-40** ***(cont.)***

'The parents have eaten sour grapes,
but their children's mouths pucker at the taste.'

30 All people will die for their own sins—those who
eat the sour grapes will be the ones whose mouths
will pucker.
31 "The day is coming," says the LORD, "when I will
make a new covenant with the people of Israel and
Judah. 32 This covenant will not be like the one I made
with their ancestors when I took them by the hand and
brought them out of the land of Egypt. They broke that
covenant, though I loved them as a husband loves his
wife," says the LORD.
33 "But this is the new covenant I will make with the
people of Israel on that day," says the LORD. "I will put
my instructions deep within them, and I will write
them on their hearts. I will be their God, and they will
be my people. 34 And they will not need to teach their
neighbors, nor will they need to teach their relatives,
saying, 'You should know the LORD.' For everyone,
from the least to the greatest, will know me already,"
says the LORD. "And I will forgive their wickedness, and
I will never again remember their sins."

35 It is the LORD who provides the sun to light
the day
and the moon and stars to light the night,
and who stirs the sea into roaring waves.
His name is the LORD of Heaven's Armies,
and this is what he says:
36 "I am as likely to reject my people Israel
as I am to abolish the laws of nature!"
37 This is what the LORD says:
"Just as the heavens cannot be measured
and the foundations of the earth cannot be
explored,
so I will not consider casting them away
for the evil they have done.
I, the LORD, have spoken!

38 "The day is coming," says the LORD, "when all
Jerusalem will be rebuilt for me, from the Tower of
Hananel to the Corner Gate. 39 A measuring line will
be stretched out over the hill of Gareb and across to
Goah. 40 And the entire area—including the graveyard
and ash dump in the valley, and all the fields out to the
Kidron Valley on the east as far as the Horse Gate—
will be holy to the LORD. The city will never again be
captured or destroyed."

Jeremiah's Message about Elam

JEREMIAH 49:34-39

This message concerning Elam came to the prophet
Jeremiah from the LORD at the beginning of the reign
of King Zedekiah of Judah. 35 This is what the LORD of
Heaven's Armies says:

"I will destroy the archers of Elam—
the best of their forces.
36 I will bring enemies from all directions,
and I will scatter the people of Elam to the four
winds.
They will be exiled to countries around the
world.
37 I myself will go with Elam's enemies to shatter it.
In my fierce anger, I will bring great disaster
upon the people of Elam," says the LORD.
"Their enemies will chase them with the sword
until I have destroyed them completely.
38 I will set my throne in Elam," says the LORD,
"and I will destroy its king and officials.
39 But I will restore the fortunes of Elam
in days to come.
I, the LORD, have spoken!"

Jeremiah's Message about Babylon

JEREMIAH 50:1-3

The LORD gave Jeremiah the prophet this message
concerning Babylon and the land of the Babylonians.*
2 This is what the LORD says:

Jer 50:1 Or *Chaldeans;* also in 50:8, 25, 35, 45.

Jer 31:33 God would write his law on their hearts rather than on tablets of stone, as he did the Ten Commandments. In Jeremiah 17:1 their sin was engraved on their hearts so that they wanted above all to disobey. This change seems to describe an experience very much like the new birth, with God taking the initiative. When we turn our life over to God, he, by his Holy Spirit, builds into us the desire to obey him.

Jer 31:33 The old covenant, broken by the people, would be replaced by a new covenant. The foundation of this new covenant is Christ (Heb 8:6). It is revolutionary, involving not only Israel and Judah but even the Gentiles. It offers a unique personal relationship with God himself, with his laws written on individuals' hearts instead of on stone. Jeremiah looked forward to the day when Jesus would come to establish this covenant. But for us today, this covenant is here. We have the wonderful opportunity to make a fresh start and establish a permanent, personal relationship with God (see Jer 29:11; 32:38-40).

Jer 31:35-37 God has the power to do away with the laws of nature or even to do away with his people. But he will do neither. This is not a prediction; it is a promise. This is God's way of saying that he will not reject Israel any more than he will do away with nature's laws.

Jer 31:38-40 These points mark the boundaries of restored Jerusalem in the days of Nehemiah. Gareb and Goah are unknown. The graveyard and ash dump probably refer to the valley of Ben-Hinnom, where children were sacrificed in pagan worship.

Jer 49:34 Nebuchadnezzar attacked Elam, east of Babylon, in 597 B.C. Later, Elam became the nucleus of the Persian Empire (Dan 8:2) and the residence of Darius.

Jer 49:38 The throne represents God's judgment and sovereignty. God would preside over Elam's destruction. He is the King over all kings, including Elam's.

Jer 50:1ff At the height of its power, the Babylonian Empire seemed invincible. But when Babylon had finished serving God's purpose of punishing Judah for her sins, it would be punished and crushed for its own. Babylon was destroyed in 539 B.C. by the Medo-Persians (Dan 5:30-31). Babylon is also used in Scripture as a symbol of all evil. This message can thus apply to the end times when God will wipe out all evil once and for all.

"Tell the whole world,
and keep nothing back.
Raise a signal flag
to tell everyone that Babylon will fall!
Her images and idols* will be shattered.
Her gods Bel and Marduk will be utterly
disgraced.
3 For a nation will attack her from the north
and bring such destruction that no one
will live there again.
Everything will be gone;
both people and animals will flee.

Hope for Israel and Judah

JEREMIAH 50:4-10

4 "In those coming days,"
says the LORD,
"the people of Israel will return home
together with the people of Judah.
They will come weeping
and seeking the LORD their God.
5 They will ask the way to Jerusalem*
and will start back home again.
They will bind themselves to the LORD
with an eternal covenant that will never
be forgotten.

6 "My people have been lost sheep.
Their shepherds have led them astray
and turned them loose in the
mountains.
They have lost their way
and can't remember how to get back
to the sheepfold.
7 All who found them devoured them.
Their enemies said,
'We did nothing wrong in attacking them,
for they sinned against the LORD,
their true place of rest,
and the hope of their ancestors.'

8 "But now, flee from Babylon!
Leave the land of the Babylonians.
Like male goats at the head of the flock,
lead my people home again.
9 For I am raising up an army
of great nations from the north.
They will join forces to attack Babylon,
and she will be captured.
The enemies' arrows will go straight
to the mark;
they will not miss!
10 Babylonia* will be looted
until the attackers are glutted with loot.
I, the LORD, have spoken!

Babylon's Sure Fall

JEREMIAH 50:11-16

11 "You rejoice and are glad,
you who plundered my chosen people.
You frisk about like a calf in a meadow
and neigh like a stallion.
12 But your homeland* will be overwhelmed
with shame and disgrace.
You will become the least of nations—
a wilderness, a dry and desolate land.
13 Because of the LORD's anger,
Babylon will become a deserted wasteland.
All who pass by will be horrified
and will gasp at the destruction they see there.

14 "Yes, prepare to attack Babylon,
all you surrounding nations.
Let your archers shoot at her; spare no arrows.
For she has sinned against the LORD.
15 Shout war cries against her from every side.
Look! She surrenders!
Her walls have fallen.
It is the LORD's vengeance,
so take vengeance on her.
Do to her as she has done to others!

Jer 50:2 The Hebrew term (literally *round things*) probably alludes to dung. **Jer 50:5** Hebrew *Zion;* also in 50:28. **Jer 50:10** Or *Chaldea.* **Jer 50:12** Hebrew *your mother.*

Jer 50:3 The nation from the north was Medo-Persia, an alliance of Media and Persia that would become the next world power. Cyrus took the city of Babylon by surprise and brought the nation to its knees in 539 B.C. (Dan 5:30-31). The complete destruction of the city was accomplished by later Persian kings.

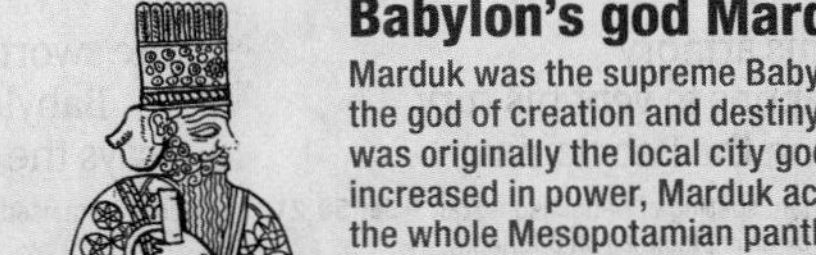

Babylon's god Marduk

Marduk was the supreme Babylonian deity, worshiped as the god of creation and destiny. Marduk (also called Bel) was originally the local city god of Babylon. As Babylon increased in power, Marduk achieved preeminence over the whole Mesopotamian pantheon of deities. The creation epic *Enuma Elish* chronicles his rise to supremacy: Marduk is credited with defeating Tiamat, primeval chaos; he then created the heavens and the earth. Zarpanit was Marduk's consort, and the temple Esagila at Babylon was erected for them. Jeremiah foretold that Marduk would be put to shame for his inability to keep Babylon from destruction (Jer 50:2). Dead idols could never intervene in human affairs, regardless of the creative tales their followers invented about their powers and history. Only the true and living God is worthy of our worship.

▸ **JEREMIAH 50:11-16** ***(cont.)***

16 Take from Babylon all those who plant crops;
send all the harvesters away.
Because of the sword of the enemy,
everyone will run away and rush back to their own lands.

Hope for God's People

JEREMIAH 50:17-20

17 "The Israelites are like sheep
that have been scattered by lions.
First the king of Assyria ate them up.
Then King Nebuchadnezzar* of Babylon cracked their bones."
18 Therefore, this is what the LORD of Heaven's Armies,
the God of Israel, says:
"Now I will punish the king of Babylon and his land,
just as I punished the king of Assyria.
19 And I will bring Israel home again to its own land,
to feed in the fields of Carmel and Bashan,
and to be satisfied once more
in the hill country of Ephraim and Gilead.
20 In those days," says the LORD,
"no sin will be found in Israel or in Judah,
for I will forgive the remnant I preserve.

The LORD's Judgment on Babylon

JEREMIAH 50:21–51:14

21 "Go up, my warriors, against the land of Merathaim
and against the people of Pekod.
Pursue, kill, and completely destroy* them,
as I have commanded you," says the LORD.
22 "Let the battle cry be heard in the land,
a shout of great destruction.
23 Babylon, the mightiest hammer in all the earth,
lies broken and shattered.
Babylon is desolate among the nations!
24 Listen, Babylon, for I have set a trap for you.
You are caught, for you have fought against the LORD.
25 The LORD has opened his armory
and brought out weapons to vent his fury.
The terror that falls upon the Babylonians
will be the work of the Sovereign LORD of Heaven's Armies.
26 Yes, come against her from distant lands.
Break open her granaries.
Crush her walls and houses into heaps of rubble.
Destroy her completely, and leave nothing!
27 Destroy even her young bulls—
it will be terrible for them, too!
Slaughter them all!
For Babylon's day of reckoning has come.
28 Listen to the people who have escaped from Babylon,
as they tell in Jerusalem
how the LORD our God has taken vengeance
against those who destroyed his Temple.
29 "Send out a call for archers to come to Babylon.
Surround the city so none can escape.
Do to her as she has done to others,
for she has defied the LORD, the Holy One of Israel.
30 Her young men will fall in the streets and die.
Her soldiers will all be killed,"
says the LORD.
31 "See, I am your enemy, you arrogant people,"
says the Lord, the LORD of Heaven's Armies.
"Your day of reckoning has arrived—
the day when I will punish you.
32 O land of arrogance, you will stumble and fall,
and no one will raise you up.
For I will light a fire in the cities of Babylon
that will burn up everything around them."
33 This is what the LORD of Heaven's Armies says:
"The people of Israel and Judah have been wronged.
Their captors hold them and refuse to let them go.
34 But the one who redeems them is strong.
His name is the LORD of Heaven's Armies.
He will defend them
and give them rest again in Israel.
But for the people of Babylon
there will be no rest!
35 "The sword of destruction will strike the Babylonians,"
says the LORD.

Jer 50:17 Hebrew *Nebuchadrezzar,* a variant spelling of Nebuchadnezzar. **Jer 50:21** The Hebrew term used here refers to the complete consecration of things or people to the LORD, either by destroying them or by giving them as an offering.

Jer 50:17-20 God would punish wicked Babylon as he punished Assyria for what it had done to Israel. Assyria was crushed by Babylon, which Assyria had once ruled. Babylon in turn would be crushed by Medo-Persia, formerly under its authority. These verses also look to the time when the Messiah will rule and Israel will be fully restored. No sin will then be found in Israel because God's people will seek him and be forgiven.

Jer 50:21 Merathaim was located in southern Babylonia; Pekod was in eastern Babylonia.

Jer 50:32 Pride was Babylon's characteristic sin. Pride comes from feeling self-sufficient or believing that we don't need God. Proud nations or persons will eventually fail because they refuse to recognize God as the ultimate power. Getting rid of pride is not easy, but if we can admit that it often rules us and ask God to forgive us, he will help us overcome it. The best antidote to pride is to focus our attention on the greatness and goodness of God.

"It will strike the people of Babylon—
her officials and wise men, too.
36 The sword will strike her wise counselors,
and they will become fools.
The sword will strike her mightiest warriors,
and panic will seize them.
37 The sword will strike her horses and chariots
and her allies from other lands,
and they will all become like women.
The sword will strike her treasures,
and they all will be plundered.
38 The sword will even strike her water supply,
causing it to dry up.
And why? Because the whole land is filled
with idols,
and the people are madly in love with them.

39 "Soon Babylon will be inhabited by desert
animals and hyenas.
It will be a home for owls.
Never again will people live there;
it will lie desolate forever.
40 I will destroy it as I* destroyed Sodom and
Gomorrah
and their neighboring towns," says
the LORD.
"No one will live there;
no one will inhabit it.

41 "Look! A great army is coming from the north.
A great nation and many kings
are rising against you from far-off lands.
42 They are armed with bows and spears.
They are cruel and show no mercy.
As they ride forward on horses,
they sound like a roaring sea.
They are coming in battle formation,
planning to destroy you, Babylon.
43 The king of Babylon has heard reports about
the enemy,
and he is weak with fright.
Pangs of anguish have gripped him,
like those of a woman in labor.

44 "I will come like a lion from the thickets of the
Jordan,
leaping on the sheep in the pasture.
I will chase Babylon from its land,
and I will appoint the leader of my choice.
For who is like me, and who can challenge me?
What ruler can oppose my will?"
45 Listen to the LORD's plans against Babylon
and the land of the Babylonians.
Even the little children will be dragged off like
sheep,
and their homes will be destroyed.
46 The earth will shake with the shout, "Babylon has
been taken!"
and its cry of despair will be heard around the
world.

51:1 This is what the LORD says:
"I will stir up a destroyer against Babylon
and the people of Babylonia.*
2 Foreigners will come and winnow her,
blowing her away as chaff.
They will come from every side
to rise against her in her day of trouble.
3 Don't let the archers put on their armor
or draw their bows.
Don't spare even her best soldiers!
Let her army be completely destroyed.*
4 They will fall dead in the land of the
Babylonians,*
slashed to death in her streets.
5 For the LORD of Heaven's Armies
has not abandoned Israel and Judah.
He is still their God,
even though their land was filled with sin
against the Holy One of Israel."

6 Flee from Babylon! Save yourselves!
Don't get trapped in her punishment!
It is the LORD's time for vengeance;
he will repay her in full.
7 Babylon has been a gold cup in the LORD's hands,
a cup that made the whole earth drunk.
The nations drank Babylon's wine,
and it drove them all mad.
8 But suddenly Babylon, too, has fallen.
Weep for her.
Give her medicine.
Perhaps she can yet be healed.
9 We would have helped her if we could,
but nothing can save her now.
Let her go; abandon her.
Return now to your own land.
For her punishment reaches to the heavens;
it is so great it cannot be measured.
10 The LORD has vindicated us.
Come, let us announce in Jerusalem*
everything the LORD our God has done.

Jer 50:40 Hebrew *as God.* **Jer 51:1** Hebrew *of Leb-kamai,* a code name for Babylonia. **Jer 51:3** The Hebrew term used here refers to the complete consecration of things or people to the LORD, either by destroying them or by giving them as an offering. **Jer 51:4** Or *Chaldeans;* also in 51:54. **Jer 51:10** Hebrew *Zion;* also in 51:24.

Jer 50:39 Babylon remains a wasteland to this day. (See also Isa 13:19-22.)

Jer 50:44-46 This invader was Cyrus, who attacked Babylon by surprise and overthrew it. The world was shocked that its greatest empire was overthrown so quickly. No earthly power, no matter how great, can last forever.

Jer 51:2 To *winnow* is to separate the wheat from the chaff. When winnowers threw the mixture into the air, the wind blew away the worthless chaff while the wheat settled to the floor. Babylon would be blown away like chaff in the wind. (See also Matt 3:12 where John the Baptist says Jesus will separate the wheat from the chaff.)

▸ **JEREMIAH 50:21–51:14** ***(cont.)***

11 Sharpen the arrows!
Lift up the shields!*
For the LORD has inspired the kings of the Medes
to march against Babylon and destroy her.
This is his vengeance against those who desecrated his Temple.
12 Raise the battle flag against Babylon!
Reinforce the guard and station the watchmen.
Prepare an ambush,
for the LORD will fulfill all his plans against Babylon.
13 You are a city by a great river,
a great center of commerce,
but your end has come.
The thread of your life is cut.
14 The LORD of Heaven's Armies has taken this vow
and has sworn to it by his own name:
"Your cities will be filled with enemies,
like fields swarming with locusts,
and they will shout in triumph over you."

A Hymn of Praise to the LORD

JEREMIAH 51:15-19

15 The LORD made the earth by his power,
and he preserves it by his wisdom.
With his own understanding
he stretched out the heavens.
16 When he speaks in the thunder,
the heavens are filled with water.
He causes the clouds to rise over the earth.
He sends the lightning with the rain
and releases the wind from his storehouses.
17 The whole human race is foolish and has no knowledge!
The craftsmen are disgraced by the idols they make,
for their carefully shaped works are a fraud.
These idols have no breath or power.
18 Idols are worthless; they are ridiculous lies!
On the day of reckoning they will all be destroyed.
19 But the God of Israel* is no idol!
He is the Creator of everything that exists,
including his people, his own special possession.
The LORD of Heaven's Armies is his name!

Babylon's Great Punishment

JEREMIAH 51:20-35

20 "You* are my battle-ax and sword,"
says the LORD.
"With you I will shatter nations
and destroy many kingdoms.
21 With you I will shatter armies—
destroying the horse and rider,
the chariot and charioteer.
22 With you I will shatter men and women,
old people and children,
young men and maidens.
23 With you I will shatter shepherds and flocks,
farmers and oxen,
captains and officers.

24 "I will repay Babylon
and the people of Babylonia*
for all the wrong they have done
to my people in Jerusalem," says the LORD.

25 "Look, O mighty mountain, destroyer of the earth!
I am your enemy," says the LORD.
"I will raise my fist against you,
to knock you down from the heights.
When I am finished,
you will be nothing but a heap of burnt rubble.
26 You will be desolate forever.
Even your stones will never again be used for building.
You will be completely wiped out,"
says the LORD.

27 Raise a signal flag to the nations.
Sound the battle cry!
Mobilize them all against Babylon.
Prepare them to fight against her!
Bring out the armies of Ararat, Minni, and Ashkenaz.
Appoint a commander,
and bring a multitude of horses like swarming locusts!
28 Bring against her the armies of the nations—
led by the kings of the Medes
and all their captains and officers.
29 The earth trembles and writhes in pain,
for everything the LORD has planned against Babylon stands unchanged.
Babylon will be left desolate without a single inhabitant.

Jer 51:11 Greek version reads *Fill up the quivers.* **Jer 51:19** Hebrew *the Portion of Jacob.* See note on 5:20. **Jer 51:20** Possibly Cyrus, whom God used to conquer Babylon. Compare Isa 44:28; 45:1. **Jer 51:24** Or *Chaldea;* also in 51:35.

Jer 51:11 Cyrus, king of Persia, had allied himself with Babylon to defeat Nineveh (capital of the Assyrian Empire) in 612 B.C. Then the Medes joined Persia to defeat Babylon (539 B.C.).

Jer 51:17-19 It is foolish to trust in human-made images rather than in God. It is easy to think that the things we see and touch will bring us more security than God. But things rust, rot, and decay. God is eternal. Why put your trust in something that will disappear within a few years?

30 Her mightiest warriors no longer fight.
They stay in their barracks, their courage gone.
They have become like women.
The invaders have burned the houses
and broken down the city gates.
31 The news is passed from one runner
to the next
as the messengers hurry to tell the king
that his city has been captured.
32 All the escape routes are blocked.
The marshes have been set aflame,
and the army is in a panic.

33 This is what the LORD of Heaven's Armies,
the God of Israel, says:
"Babylon is like wheat on a threshing floor,
about to be trampled.
In just a little while
her harvest will begin."

34 "King Nebuchadnezzar* of Babylon has eaten
and crushed us
and drained us of strength.
He has swallowed us like a great monster
and filled his belly with our riches.
He has thrown us out of our own country.
35 Make Babylon suffer as she made us suffer,"
say the people of Zion.
"Make the people of Babylonia pay for spilling
our blood,"
says Jerusalem.

The LORD's Vengeance on Babylon

JEREMIAH 51:36-44

36 This is what the LORD says to Jerusalem:
"I will be your lawyer to plead your case,
and I will avenge you.
I will dry up her river,
as well as her springs,
37 and Babylon will become a heap of ruins,
haunted by jackals.
She will be an object of horror and contempt,
a place where no one lives.
38 Her people will roar together like strong lions.
They will growl like lion cubs.
39 And while they lie inflamed with all their wine,
I will prepare a different kind of feast
for them.
I will make them drink until they fall asleep,
and they will never wake up again,"
says the LORD.
40 "I will bring them down
like lambs to the slaughter,
like rams and goats to be sacrificed.

41 "How Babylon* is fallen—
great Babylon, praised throughout the earth!
Now she has become an object of horror
among the nations.
42 The sea has risen over Babylon;
she is covered by its crashing waves.
43 Her cities now lie in ruins;
she is a dry wasteland
where no one lives or even passes by.
44 And I will punish Bel, the god of Babylon,
and make him vomit up all he has eaten.
The nations will no longer come and worship him.
The wall of Babylon has fallen!

A Message for the Exiles

JEREMIAH 51:45-53

45 "Come out, my people, flee from Babylon.
Save yourselves! Run from the LORD's fierce
anger.
46 But do not panic; don't be afraid
when you hear the first rumor of approaching
forces.
For rumors will keep coming year by year.
Violence will erupt in the land
as the leaders fight against each other.
47 For the time is surely coming
when I will punish this great city and all
her idols.
Her whole land will be disgraced,
and her dead will lie in the streets.
48 Then the heavens and earth will rejoice,
for out of the north will come destroying armies
against Babylon," says the LORD.

49 "Just as Babylon killed the people of Israel
and others throughout the world,
so must her people be killed.
50 Get out, all you who have escaped the sword!
Do not stand and watch—flee while you can!
Remember the LORD, though you are in a far-off
land,
and think about your home in Jerusalem."

Jer 51:34 Hebrew *Nebuchadrezzar,* a variant spelling of Nebuchadnezzar. **Jer 51:41** Hebrew *Sheshach,* a code name for Babylon.

Jer 51:33 Grain was threshed on a threshing floor, where sheaves were brought from the field. The stalks of grain were distributed on the floor, a large level section of hard ground. There the grain was crushed to separate the kernels from the stalk; then the kernels were beaten with a wooden tool. Sometimes animals pulled a wooden sledge over the grain to break the kernels loose. Babylon would soon be trampled like grain on a threshing floor as God judged it for its sins.

Jer 51:36 This verse may refer to when Cyrus took Babylon by surprise by diverting the river that ran through the city far upstream and walking beneath the city's fortifications on the dry riverbed. More likely it is saying that Babylon will be deprived of life-giving water. Unlike Jerusalem, Babylon will not be restored.

Jer 51:44 Bel is one of the names of Marduk, the chief god of the city of Babylon.

▸ **JEREMIAH 51:45-53** ***(cont.)***

51 "We are ashamed," the people say.
"We are insulted and disgraced
because the LORD's Temple
has been defiled by foreigners."
52 "Yes," says the LORD, "but the time is coming
when I will destroy Babylon's idols.
The groans of her wounded people
will be heard throughout the land.
53 Though Babylon reaches as high as the heavens
and makes her fortifications incredibly strong,
I will still send enemies to plunder her.
I, the LORD, have spoken!

Babylon's Complete Destruction

JEREMIAH 51:54-58

54 "Listen! Hear the cry of Babylon,
the sound of great destruction from the land of
the Babylonians.
55 For the LORD is destroying Babylon.
He will silence her loud voice.
Waves of enemies pound against her;
the noise of battle rings through the city.
56 Destroying armies come against Babylon.
Her mighty men are captured,
and their weapons break in their hands.
For the LORD is a God who gives just punishment;
he always repays in full.
57 I will make her officials and wise men drunk,
along with her captains, officers, and
warriors.
They will fall asleep
and never wake up again!"
says the King, whose name is
the LORD of Heaven's Armies.
58 This is what the LORD of Heaven's Armies says:
"The thick walls of Babylon will be leveled to the
ground,
and her massive gates will be burned.
The builders from many lands have worked
in vain,
for their work will be destroyed by fire!"

6. BABYLON'S SECOND INVASION OF JUDAH

In 597 B.C., Babylon's armies returned to Jerusalem, taking another large group of people from Judah into exile—including King Jehoiachin and the prophet Ezekiel. Babylon set up their own king, Jehoiachin's uncle Mattaniah. They changed his name to Zedekiah, further asserting their dominance over Judah.

Babylon Captures Jerusalem PARALLEL

2 KINGS 24:10-17

During Jehoiachin's reign, the officers of King Nebuchadnezzar of Babylon came up against Jerusalem
and besieged it. 11 Nebuchadnezzar himself arrived
at the city during the siege. 12 Then King Jehoiachin, along with the queen mother, his advisers, his
commanders, and his officials, surrendered to the
Babylonians.
In the eighth year of Nebuchadnezzar's reign, he
took Jehoiachin prisoner. 13 As the LORD had said
beforehand, Nebuchadnezzar carried away all the
treasures from the LORD's Temple and the royal palace. He stripped away* all the gold objects that King

2 Kgs 24:13 Or *He cut apart.*

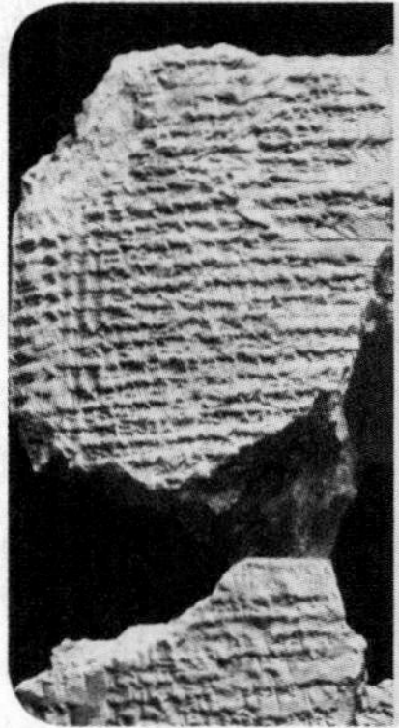

Jehoiachin in Babylon

Jehoiachin was appointed king of Judah by the Babylonians following the revolt and death of his father Jehoiakim. His brief reign of three months and ten days is described in 2 Kings 24. It was marked by evil, and the prophet Jeremiah foretold the end of both his rule and dynasty (Jer 22:24-30). According to Josephus (*Antiquities* 10.99), Nebuchadnezzar changed his mind about the appointment and returned to besiege Jerusalem and carry off the 18-year-old king, with his family and fellow Jews, into exile in Babylon. There Jehoiachin was treated as a royal hostage. On this tablet (dated from 595–570 B.C.) found in Babylon, "Jehoiachin, king of Judah," and his sons are named among the recipients of rations given to prisoners held in Babylon. This tablet affirms the prophetic word of Jeremiah.

Jer 51:51 The people were paralyzed with guilt over their past. The Babylonian armies had desecrated the Temple and the people were ashamed to return to Jerusalem. But God told them to return to the city because he would destroy Babylon for its sins.

2 Kgs 24:10 Babylonian troops were already on the march to crush Jehoiakim's rebellion when he died. After Jehoiakim's death, his son Jehoiachin became king of Judah, only to face the mightiest army on earth just weeks after he was crowned (597 B.C.). During this second of three invasions, the Babylonians looted the Temple and took most of the leaders captive, including the king. Then Nebuchadnezzar placed Zedekiah, another son of Josiah, on the throne. But the Jews didn't recognize him as their true king as long as Jehoiachin was still alive, even though he was a captive in Babylon.

2 Kgs 24:14 The Babylonian policy for taking captives was different from that of the Assyrians, who moved most of the people out and resettled the land with foreigners (see the note on 2 Kgs 17:24, p. 821). The Babylonians took only the strong and skilled, leaving the poor and weak to rule the land, thus elevating them to positions of authority and winning their loyalty. The leaders were taken to Babylonian cities, where they were permitted to live together, find jobs, and become an important part of the society. This policy kept the Jews united and faithful to God throughout the captivity and made it possible for their return in the days of Zerubbabel and Ezra as recorded in the book of Ezra.

Solomon of Israel had placed in the Temple. 14King
Nebuchadnezzar took all of Jerusalem captive, including all the commanders and the best of the soldiers,
craftsmen, and artisans—10,000 in all. Only the poorest people were left in the land.
15Nebuchadnezzar led King Jehoiachin away as a
captive to Babylon, along with the queen mother, his
wives and officials, and all Jerusalem's elite. 16He also
exiled 7,000 of the best troops and 1,000 craftsmen
and artisans, all of whom were strong and fit for war.
17Then the king of Babylon installed Mattaniah, Jehoiachin's* uncle, as the next king, and he changed
Mattaniah's name to Zedekiah.

2 CHRONICLES 36:10

In the spring of the year* King Nebuchadnezzar took Jehoiachin to Babylon. Many treasures from the Temple of the LORD were also taken to Babylon at that time. And Nebuchadnezzar installed Jehoiachin's uncle,* Zedekiah, as the next king in Judah and Jerusalem.

Zedekiah Begins His Reign in Judah PARALLEL

2 KINGS 24:18-20a

Zedekiah was twenty-one years old when he became
king, and he reigned in Jerusalem eleven years. His
mother was Hamutal, the daughter of Jeremiah from
Libnah. 19But Zedekiah did what was evil in the LORD's
sight, just as Jehoiakim had done. 20These things happened because of the LORD's anger against the people
of Jerusalem and Judah, until he finally banished
them from his presence and sent them into exile.

2 CHRONICLES 36:11-14

Zedekiah was twenty-one years old when he became
king, and he reigned in Jerusalem eleven years. 12He
did what was evil in the sight of the LORD his God, and
he refused to humble himself when the prophet Jeremiah spoke to him directly from the LORD. 13He also
rebelled against King Nebuchadnezzar, even though
he had taken an oath of loyalty in God's name. Zedekiah was a hard and stubborn man, refusing to turn
to the LORD, the God of Israel.
14Likewise, all the leaders of the priests and the
people became more and more unfaithful. They followed all the pagan practices of the surrounding
nations, desecrating the Temple of the LORD that had
been consecrated in Jerusalem.

JEREMIAH 52:1-3a

Zedekiah was twenty-one years old when he became king, and he reigned in Jerusalem eleven years. His mother was Hamutal, the daughter of Jeremiah from

2 Kgs 24:17 Hebrew *his.* **2 Chr 36:10a** Hebrew *At the turn of the year.* The first day of this year in the ancient Hebrew lunar calendar was April 13, 597 B.C.
2 Chr 36:10b As in parallel text at 2 Kgs 24:17; Hebrew reads *brother,* or *relative.*

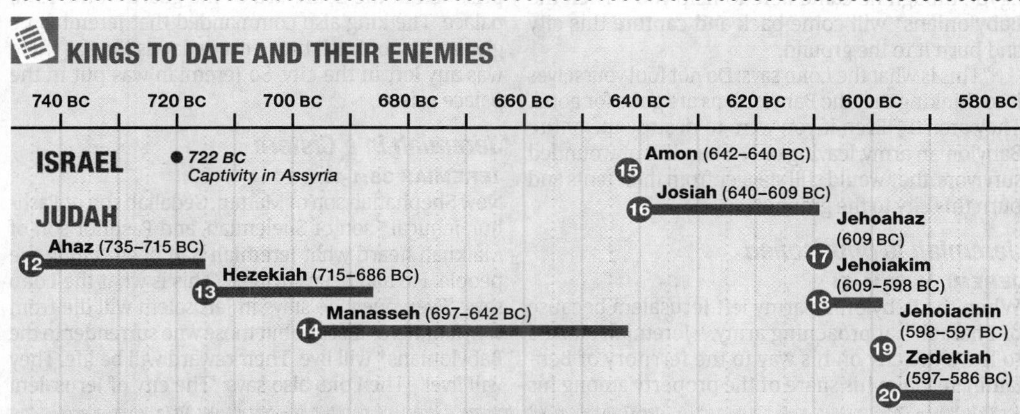

12 Ahaz (16years) Harassed by Pekah (Israel), paid Assyria for protection against Rezin (Aram), also harassed by Edom and Philistia (*2 Kgs 15:38–16:20; 2 Chr 27:9–28:27*).

13 Hezekiah (29 years) Miraculously delivered from Sennacherib's (Assyria) attack, conquered Gaza in Philistia (*2 Kgs 18:1–20:21; 2 Chr 28:27–32:33*).

14 Manasseh (55 years) Taken captive by Assyria, imprisoned in Babylon and later released (*2 Kgs 20:21–21:18; 2 Chr 32:33–33:20*).

15 Amon (2 years) (*2 Kgs 21:18-26; 2 Chr 33:20-24*)

16 Josiah (31 years) Died in battle against Neco (Egypt) (*2 Kgs 22:1–23:30; 2 Chr 33:25–35:27*).

17 Jehoahaz (3 months) Neco (Egypt) (*2 Kgs 23:30-34; 2 Chr 36:1-4*)

18 Jehoiakim (11 years) (*2 Kgs 23:34–24:6; 2 Chr 36:4-8*)

19 Jehoiachin (3 months) Rebelled against Babylon and was taken captive (*2 Kgs 24:6-16; 25:27-30; 2 Chr 36:8-10*).

20 Zedekiah (11 years) Rebelled, completely conquered by Babylon (*2 Kgs 24:17–25:21; 2 Chr 36:10-20*).

▸ **JEREMIAH 52:1-3a** ***(cont.)***
Libnah. [2]But Zedekiah did what was evil in the LORD's sight, just as Jehoiakim had done. [3]These things happened because of the LORD's anger against the people of Jerusalem and Judah, until he finally banished them from his presence and sent them into exile.

Zedekiah Calls for Jeremiah

JEREMIAH 37:1-10
Zedekiah son of Josiah succeeded Jehoiachin* son of Jehoiakim as the king of Judah. He was appointed by King Nebuchadnezzar* of Babylon. [2]But neither King Zedekiah nor his attendants nor the people who were left in the land listened to what the LORD said through Jeremiah.

[3]Nevertheless, King Zedekiah sent Jehucal son of Shelemiah, and Zephaniah the priest, son of Maaseiah, to ask Jeremiah, "Please pray to the LORD our God for us." [4]Jeremiah had not yet been imprisoned, so he could come and go among the people as he pleased.

[5]At this time the army of Pharaoh Hophra* of Egypt appeared at the southern border of Judah. When the Babylonian* army heard about it, they withdrew from their siege of Jerusalem.

[6]Then the LORD gave this message to Jeremiah: [7]"This is what the LORD, the God of Israel, says: The king of Judah sent you to ask me what is going to happen. Tell him, 'Pharaoh's army is about to return to Egypt, though he came here to help you. [8]Then the Babylonians* will come back and capture this city and burn it to the ground.'

[9]"This is what the LORD says: Do not fool yourselves into thinking that the Babylonians are gone for good. They aren't! [10]Even if you were to destroy the entire Babylonian army, leaving only a handful of wounded survivors, they would still stagger from their tents and burn this city to the ground!"

Jeremiah Is Imprisoned

JEREMIAH 37:11-21
When the Babylonian army left Jerusalem because of Pharaoh's approaching army, [12]Jeremiah started to leave the city on his way to the territory of Benjamin, to claim his share of the property among his relatives there.* [13]But as he was walking through the Benjamin Gate, a sentry arrested him and said, "You are defecting to the Babylonians!" The sentry making the arrest was Irijah son of Shelemiah, grandson of Hananiah.

[14]"That's not true!" Jeremiah protested. "I had no intention of doing any such thing." But Irijah wouldn't listen, and he took Jeremiah before the officials. [15]They were furious with Jeremiah and had him flogged and imprisoned in the house of Jonathan the secretary. Jonathan's house had been converted into a prison. [16]Jeremiah was put into a dungeon cell, where he remained for many days.

[17]Later King Zedekiah secretly requested that Jeremiah come to the palace, where the king asked him, "Do you have any messages from the LORD?"

"Yes, I do!" said Jeremiah. "You will be defeated by the king of Babylon."

[18]Then Jeremiah asked the king, "What crime have I committed? What have I done against you, your attendants, or the people that I should be imprisoned like this? [19]Where are your prophets now who told you the king of Babylon would not attack you or this land? [20]Listen, my lord the king, I beg you. Don't send me back to the dungeon in the house of Jonathan the secretary, for I will die there."

[21]So King Zedekiah commanded that Jeremiah not be returned to the dungeon. Instead, he was imprisoned in the courtyard of the guard in the royal palace. The king also commanded that Jeremiah be given a loaf of fresh bread every day as long as there was any left in the city. So Jeremiah was put in the palace prison.

Jeremiah in a Cistern

JEREMIAH 38:1-13
Now Shephatiah son of Mattan, Gedaliah son of Pashhur, Jehucal* son of Shelemiah, and Pashhur son of Malkijah heard what Jeremiah had been telling the people. He had been saying, [2]"This is what the LORD says: 'Everyone who stays in Jerusalem will die from war, famine, or disease, but those who surrender to the Babylonians* will live. Their reward will be life. They will live!' [3]The LORD also says: 'The city of Jerusalem

Jer 37:1a Hebrew *Coniah,* a variant spelling of Jehoiachin. **Jer 37:1b** Hebrew *Nebuchadrezzar,* a variant spelling of Nebuchadnezzar. **Jer 37:5a** Hebrew *army of Pharaoh;* see 44:30. **Jer 37:5b** Or *Chaldean;* also in 37:10, 11. **Jer 37:8** Or *Chaldeans;* also in 37:9, 13. **Jer 37:12** Hebrew *to separate from there in the midst of the people.* **Jer 38:1** Hebrew *Jucal,* a variant spelling of Jehucal; see 37:3. **Jer 38:2** Or *Chaldeans;* also in 38:18, 19, 23.

Jer 37:1ff King Jehoiakim died on the way to Babylon (2 Chr 36:6). His son Jehoiachin was appointed king but was taken captive to Babylon three months later. Nebuchadnezzar then appointed Zedekiah as his vassal in Judah.

Jer 37:2-3 King Zedekiah and his officials did not want to listen to Jeremiah's words, but they wanted the blessings of his prayers. They wanted a superficial religion that wouldn't cost anything. God is not pleased with those who come to him seeking only what they can get rather than seeking to have a relationship with him. We would not accept that kind of relationship with someone else, and we shouldn't expect God to accept it from us.

Jer 37:5 When Nebuchadnezzar besieged Jerusalem in 589 B.C., Pharaoh Hophra marched against him at Zedekiah's invitation. Jerusalem looked to Egypt for help in spite of Jeremiah's warnings. But the Egyptians were no help, for as soon as the Babylonians turned on them, they retreated. Jeremiah's warnings had been correct.

Jer 37:17 Zedekiah teetered between surrender and resistance. Too frightened and weak to exercise authority, he asked Jeremiah to come secretly to the palace, perhaps hoping for some better news from God. Zedekiah was desperate. He wanted to hear a word from the Lord, but he feared the political ramifications of being caught talking to Jeremiah.

will certainly be handed over to the army of the king of Babylon, who will capture it.'"

4So these officials went to the king and said, "Sir, this man must die! That kind of talk will undermine the morale of the few fighting men we have left, as well as that of all the people. This man is a traitor!"

5King Zedekiah agreed. "All right," he said. "Do as you like. I can't stop you."

6So the officials took Jeremiah from his cell and lowered him by ropes into an empty cistern in the prison yard. It belonged to Malkijah, a member of the royal family. There was no water in the cistern, but there was a thick layer of mud at the bottom, and Jeremiah sank down into it.

7But Ebed-melech the Ethiopian,* an important court official, heard that Jeremiah was in the cistern. At that time the king was holding court at the Benjamin Gate, 8so Ebed-melech rushed from the palace to speak with him. 9"My lord the king," he said, "these men have done a very evil thing in putting Jeremiah the prophet into the cistern. He will soon die of hunger, for almost all the bread in the city is gone."

10So the king told Ebed-melech, "Take thirty of my men with you, and pull Jeremiah out of the cistern before he dies."

11So Ebed-melech took the men with him and went to a room in the palace beneath the treasury, where he found some old rags and discarded clothing. He carried these to the cistern and lowered them to Jeremiah on a rope. 12Ebed-melech called down to Jeremiah, "Put these rags under your armpits to protect you from the ropes." Then when Jeremiah was ready, 13they pulled him out. So Jeremiah was returned to the courtyard of the guard—the palace prison—where he remained.

Zedekiah Questions Jeremiah

JEREMIAH 38:14-28

One day King Zedekiah sent for Jeremiah and had him brought to the third entrance of the LORD's Temple. "I want to ask you something," the king said. "And don't try to hide the truth."

15Jeremiah said, "If I tell you the truth, you will kill me. And if I give you advice, you won't listen to me anyway."

16So King Zedekiah secretly promised him, "As surely as the LORD our Creator lives, I will not kill you or hand you over to the men who want you dead."

17Then Jeremiah said to Zedekiah, "This is what the LORD God of Heaven's Armies, the God of Israel, says: 'If you surrender to the Babylonian officers, you and your family will live, and the city will not be burned down. 18But if you refuse to surrender, you will not escape! This city will be handed over to the Babylonians, and they will burn it to the ground.'"

19"But I am afraid to surrender," the king said, "for the Babylonians may hand me over to the Judeans who have defected to them. And who knows what they will do to me!"

20Jeremiah replied, "You won't be handed over to them if you choose to obey the LORD. Your life will be spared, and all will go well for you. 21But if you refuse to surrender, this is what the LORD has revealed to me: 22All the women left in your palace will be brought out and given to the officers of the Babylonian army. Then the women will taunt you, saying,

'What fine friends you have!
  They have betrayed and misled you.
When your feet sank in the mud,
  they left you to your fate!'

23All your wives and children will be led out to the Babylonians, and you will not escape. You will be seized by the king of Babylon, and this city will be burned down."

24Then Zedekiah said to Jeremiah, "Don't tell anyone you told me this, or you will die! 25My officials may hear that I spoke to you, and they may say, 'Tell us what you and the king were talking about. If you don't

Jer 38:7 Hebrew *the Cushite.*

Jer 38:4-5 No wonder Judah was in turmoil: The king agreed with everybody. He listened to Jeremiah (Jer 37:21); then he agreed Jeremiah should be killed (Jer 38:5); and finally he rescued Jeremiah (Jer 38:10). Jeremiah was not popular; his words undermined the morale of the army and the people. Zedekiah couldn't decide between public opinion and God's will. What is most influential in your life—what others say and think or what God wants?

Jer 38:6 Officials put Jeremiah in a cistern to die. A cistern was a large hole in the ground lined with rocks to collect rainwater. The bottom would have been dark, damp, and, in this case, full of mud. Jeremiah could drown, die of exposure, or starve to death in the cistern.

Jer 38:6 Judah's leaders persecuted Jeremiah repeatedly for faithfully proclaiming God's messages. For 40 years of faithful ministry, he received no acclaim, no love, no popular following. He was beaten, jailed, threatened, and even forced to leave his homeland. Only the pagan Babylonians showed him any respect (Jer 39:11-12). God does not guarantee that his servants will escape persecution, even when they are faithful. But God does promise that he will be with them and will give them strength to endure (2 Cor 1:3-7). As you minister to others, recognize that your service is for God and not just for human approval. God rewards our faithfulness, but not always during our lifetime.

Jer 38:7-8 The Benjamin Gate was one of Jerusalem's city gates where legal matters were handled. A palace official, Ebed-melech, had access to the king. When Ebed-melech heard of Jeremiah's plight, he went immediately to deal with the injustice.

Jer 38:9-13 Ebed-melech feared God more than people. He alone among the palace officials stood up against the murder plot. His obedience could have cost him his life. Because he obeyed, he was spared when Jerusalem fell (Jer 39:15-18). You can either go along with the crowd or speak up for God. When someone is treated unkindly or unjustly, for example, reach out to that person with God's love. You may be the only one who does. And, when you are being treated unkindly yourself, be sure to thank God when he sends an "Ebed-melech" your way.

▶ **JEREMIAH 38:14-28 *(cont.)***

tell us, we will kill you.' [26]If this happens, just tell them
you begged me not to send you back to Jonathan's
dungeon, for fear you would die there."
[27]Sure enough, it wasn't long before the king's officials came to Jeremiah and asked him why the king
had called for him. But Jeremiah followed the king's
instructions, and they left without finding out the
truth. No one had overheard the conversation between
Jeremiah and the king. [28]And Jeremiah remained a
prisoner in the courtyard of the guard until the day
Jerusalem was captured.

7. THE BEGINNING OF EZEKIEL'S MINISTRY

Ezekiel prophesied to the exiles in Babylon beginning on July 31, 593 B.C. He had to dispel the false hope that Israel's captivity would be short, explain the reasons for the severe judgments on their nation, and bring a message of future hope. Although the people did not respond positively, they heard the messages and knew the truth. God's people were not left without explanation and direction, and neither are we.

Ezekiel's Vision of Living Beings

EZEKIEL 1:1-28

On July 31* of my thirtieth year,* while I was with the
Judean exiles beside the Kebar River in Babylon, the
heavens were opened and I saw visions of God. [2]This
happened during the fifth year of King Jehoiachin's
captivity. [3](The LORD gave this message to Ezekiel son
of Buzi, a priest, beside the Kebar River in the land of
the Babylonians,* and he felt the hand of the LORD
take hold of him.)
[4]As I looked, I saw a great storm coming from the
north, driving before it a huge cloud that flashed with

Ez 1:1a Hebrew *On the fifth day of the fourth month,* of the ancient Hebrew lunar calendar. A number of dates in Ezekiel can be cross-checked with dates in surviving Babylonian records and related accurately to our modern calendar. This event occurred on July 31, 593 B.C. **Ez 1:1b** Or *in the thirtieth year.* **Ez 1:3** Or *Chaldeans.*

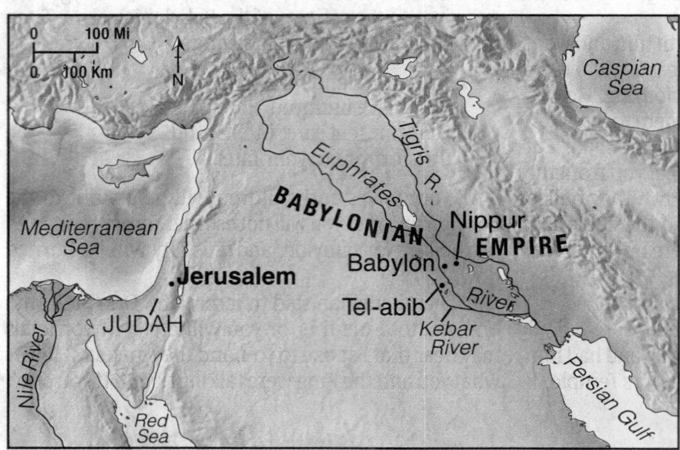

***EXILE IN BABYLON** Ezekiel worked for God right where he was—among the exiles in various colonies near the Kebar River in Babylonia. Jerusalem and its Temple lay over 500 miles away, but Ezekiel helped the people understand that, although they were far from home, they did not need to be far from God.*

Jer 38:27 The officials wanted accurate information, but not God's truth. They wanted to use this information against God, his prophet, and the king. But Jeremiah told the officials only what the king ordered him to say. We must not withhold God's truth from others, but we should withhold information that will be used to bring evil to God's people.

Ezek 1:1 Ezekiel, born and raised in the land of Judah, was preparing to become a priest in God's Temple when the Babylonians attacked in 597 B.C. and carried him away along with 10,000 other captives (2 Kgs 24:10-14). The nation was on the brink of complete destruction. Five years later, when Ezekiel was 30 (the normal age for becoming a priest), God called him to be a prophet. During the first six years when Ezekiel ministered in the land of the Babylonians (Ezek 1:3), Jeremiah was preaching to the Jews still in Judah, and Daniel was serving in Nebuchadnezzar's court. The Kebar River connected to the Euphrates in Babylonia and was the location of a Jewish settlement of exiles.

Ezek 1:1 Why did the Jewish exiles in Babylonia need a prophet? God wanted Ezekiel to (1) help the exiles understand why they had been taken captive, (2) dispel the false hope that the captivity was going to be short, (3) bring a new message of hope, and (4) call the people to a new awareness of their dependence upon God.

Ezek 1:1 God communicated to Ezekiel in visions. A vision is a miraculous revelation of God's truth. These visions seem strange to us because they are apocalyptic. This means that Ezekiel saw symbolic pictures that vividly conveyed an idea. Daniel and John were other Bible writers who used apocalyptic imagery. The people in exile had lost their perspective of God's purpose and presence, and Ezekiel came to them with a vision from God to show God's awesome glory and holiness and to warn the exiles of sin's consequences before it was too late.

Ezek 1:1ff Ezekiel's latest dated message from God (Ezek 29:17) was given in 571 B.C. He was taken captive during the second Babylonian invasion of Judah in 597 B.C. The Babylonians invaded Judah a third and final time in 586 B.C., completely destroying Jerusalem, burning the Temple, and deporting the rest of the people (see 2 Kgs 25). Ezekiel dates all his messages from the year he was taken captive (597). His first prophecy to the exiles occurred four years after he arrived in Babylonia (593 B.C.).

Ezek 1:3 Ezekiel's name means "God is strong" or "God strengthens." In a very real sense, this sums up the basic message of the book: In spite of the captivity, God's sovereign strength prevails, and he will judge his enemies and restore his true people.

Ezek 1:4ff In this first vision, God called Ezekiel to be a prophet (see Ezek 2:5). Nothing in Ezekiel's previous experience had prepared him for such a display of

lightning and shone with brilliant light. There was fire inside the cloud, and in the middle of the fire glowed something like gleaming amber.* 5From the center of the cloud came four living beings that looked human, 6except that each had four faces and four wings. 7Their legs were straight, and their feet had hooves like those of a calf and shone like burnished bronze. 8Under each of their four wings I could see human hands. So each of the four beings had four faces and four wings. 9The wings of each living being touched the wings of the beings beside it. Each one moved straight forward in any direction without turning around.

10Each had a human face in the front, the face of a lion on the right side, the face of an ox on the left side, and the face of an eagle at the back. 11Each had two pairs of outstretched wings—one pair stretched out to touch the wings of the living beings on either side of it, and the other pair covered its body. 12They went in whatever direction the spirit chose, and they moved straight forward in any direction without turning around.

13The living beings looked like bright coals of fire or brilliant torches, and lightning seemed to flash back and forth among them. 14And the living beings darted to and fro like flashes of lightning.

15As I looked at these beings, I saw four wheels touching the ground beside them, one wheel belonging to each. 16The wheels sparkled as if made of beryl. All four wheels looked alike and were made the same; each wheel had a second wheel turning crosswise within it. 17The beings could move in any of the four directions they faced, without turning as they moved. 18The rims of the four wheels were tall and frightening, and they were covered with eyes all around.

19When the living beings moved, the wheels moved with them. When they flew upward, the wheels went up, too. 20The spirit of the living beings was in the wheels. So wherever the spirit went, the wheels and the living beings also went. 21When the beings moved, the wheels moved. When the beings stopped, the wheels stopped. When the beings flew upward, the wheels rose up, for the spirit of the living beings was in the wheels.

22Spread out above them was a surface like the sky, glittering like crystal. 23Beneath this surface the wings of each living being stretched out to touch the others' wings, and each had two wings covering its body. 24As they flew, their wings sounded to me like waves crashing against the shore or like the voice of the Almighty* or like the shouting of a mighty army. When they stopped, they let down their wings. 25As they stood with wings lowered, a voice spoke from beyond the crystal surface above them.

26Above this surface was something that looked like a throne made of blue lapis lazuli. And on this throne high above was a figure whose appearance resembled a man. 27From what appeared to be his waist up, he looked like gleaming amber, flickering like a fire. And from his waist down, he looked like a burning flame, shining with splendor. 28All around him was a glowing halo, like a rainbow shining in the clouds on a rainy day. This is what the glory of the LORD looked like to me. When I saw it, I fell face down on the ground, and I heard someone's voice speaking to me.

Ez 1:4 Or *like burnished metal;* also in 1:27. **Ez 1:24** Hebrew *Shaddai.*

God's glorious presence and power. The huge cloud flashed with lightning and was surrounded by a brilliant light. From the fire in the cloud came four living beings. They showed Ezekiel that Jerusalem's coming destruction was God's punishment of Judah for its sins. (These living beings are also seen in Rev 4:6-7.)

When Ezekiel received this vision, he was far away from the Temple in Jerusalem, the physical symbol of God's presence. Through this vision, he learned that God is present everywhere and that God's activities in heaven are shaping the events on earth.

Ezek 1:5-12 Each of the four living beings had four faces, symbolizing God's perfect nature. Some believe that the lion represented strength; the ox, diligent service; the human, intelligence; and the eagle, divinity. Others see these as the most majestic of God's creatures and say that they therefore represented God's whole creation. The early church fathers saw a connection between these beings and the four Gospels: the lion with Matthew, presenting Christ as the Lion of Judah; the ox with Mark, portraying Christ as the Servant; the human with Luke, portraying Christ as the perfect human; the eagle with John, portraying Christ as the Son of God, exalted and divine. The vision of John in Revelation 4 parallels Ezekiel's vision.

Ezek 1:16-18 Ezekiel described two wheels at right angles to each other, one on a north-south and the other on an east-west axis. Able to move anywhere, these wheels show that God is present everywhere and is able to see all things (Ezek 1:18). God is not restricted to Jerusalem but rules all of life and history. Though the exiles had experienced great change, God was still in control.

Ezek 1:26 This figure "whose appearance resembled a man" revealed God's holiness and prepared Ezekiel for what God was about to tell him. The figure represented God himself on the throne. In a similar way, Christ revealed God in human form and prepared us for his message of salvation. Christ came into history in a real, human body.

Ezek 1:27-28 The glory of the Lord appeared like fire and a glowing halo or rainbow to Ezekiel. Ezekiel fell face down, overwhelmed by the contrast between God's holiness and his own sinfulness and insignificance. Eventually every person will fall before God, either out of reverence and awe for his mercy or out of fear of his judgment. Based on the way you are living today, how will you respond to God's holiness?

Ezek 1:27-28 The four living beings and the four wheels are powerful pictures of judgment, yet the rainbow over the throne symbolizes God's never-ending faithfulness to his people. Just as God sent a rainbow to Noah to symbolize his promise never again to destroy the earth by a flood (Gen 9:8-17), so this rainbow symbolizes God's promise to preserve those who remain faithful to him. The purpose of God's judgment is to correct us and, ultimately, to allow perfect peace and righteousness to reign on the earth forever.

597 BC *Second captivity; Ezekiel taken to Babylon*

Ezekiel's Call and Commission

EZEKIEL 2:1–3:15

"Stand up, son of man," said the voice. "I want to speak with you." 2 The Spirit came into me as he spoke, and he set me on my feet. I listened carefully to his words. 3 "Son of man," he said, "I am sending you to the nation of Israel, a rebellious nation that has rebelled against me. They and their ancestors have been rebelling against me to this very day. 4 They are a stubborn and hard-hearted people. But I am sending you to say to them, 'This is what the Sovereign LORD says!' 5 And whether they listen or refuse to listen—for remember, they are rebels—at least they will know they have had a prophet among them.

6 "Son of man, do not fear them or their words. Don't be afraid even though their threats surround you like nettles and briers and stinging scorpions. Do not be dismayed by their dark scowls, even though they are rebels. 7 You must give them my messages whether they listen or not. But they won't listen, for they are completely rebellious! 8 Son of man, listen to what I say to you. Do not join them in their rebellion. Open your mouth, and eat what I give you."

9 Then I looked and saw a hand reaching out to me. It held a scroll, 10 which he unrolled. And I saw that both sides were covered with funeral songs, words of sorrow, and pronouncements of doom.

3:1 The voice said to me, "Son of man, eat what I am giving you—eat this scroll! Then go and give its message to the people of Israel." 2 So I opened my mouth, and he fed me the scroll. 3 "Fill your stomach with this," he said. And when I ate it, it tasted as sweet as honey in my mouth.

4 Then he said, "Son of man, go to the people of Israel and give them my messages. 5 I am not sending you to a foreign people whose language you cannot understand. 6 No, I am not sending you to people with strange and difficult speech. If I did, they would listen! 7 But the people of Israel won't listen to you any more than they listen to me! For the whole lot of them are hard-hearted and stubborn. 8 But look, I have made you as obstinate and hard-hearted as they are. 9 I have

---

Ezek 2:1 The immortal God addressed Ezekiel by calling him "son of man," emphasizing the distance between them. It is amazing that God chooses to work his divine will on earth through finite, imperfect beings. We are made from the dust of the ground, yet God chooses to place within us his life and breath and to ask us to serve him.

Ezek 2:2 We can only imagine what it was like for Ezekiel to experience this vision. Certainly there was much he did not understand, but Ezekiel knew that each part had significance because it came from God. When God saw Ezekiel's open and obedient attitude, he filled Ezekiel with his Spirit and gave Ezekiel power for the job ahead. God doesn't expect us to understand everything about him. He wants us to be willing and obedient servants, faithful to what we know is true and right.

Ezek 2:3-5 The business world defines success in terms of giving customers what they want. Ezekiel was called to give God's message to the people, whether they would listen or not. The measure of Ezekiel's success would not be how well the people responded, but how well he obeyed God and thus fulfilled God's purpose for him. Isaiah and Jeremiah also prophesied with little positive response (see Isa 6:9-12; Jer 1:17-19). God's truth does not depend on how people respond. God will not judge us for how well others respond to our witness but for how faithful we have been. God always gives us the strength to accomplish what he asks us to do.

Ezek 2:4-5 God called the people "stubborn and hard-hearted" because they refused to admit their sin. Rebelliousness was the nation's primary characteristic at this time. Even when God pointed out their wrongdoing, the people ignored the truth. Is God pointing at some sin in your life? Don't be stubborn—confess your sin and begin to live for God. By obeying him now you will be ready for God's final review of your life (Matt 25:31-46).

EZEKIEL

Ezekiel served as a prophet to the exiles in Babylon from 593–571 B.C.

Climate of the times	Ezekiel and his people are taken to Babylon as captives. The Hebrews become foreigners in a strange land ruled by an authoritarian government.
Main message	Because of the people's sins, God allowed the nation of Judah to be destroyed. But there was still hope—God promised to restore the land to those who remained faithful to him.
Importance of message	God never forgets those who faithfully seek to obey him. They have a glorious future ahead.
Contemporary prophets	Daniel (605–536 B.C.), Habakkuk (612–589 B.C.), Jeremiah (627–586 B.C.)

Ezek 2:6-8 God gave Ezekiel the difficult responsibility of presenting his message to ungrateful and abusive people. Sometimes we must be an example to or share our faith with unkind people. The Lord told Ezekiel not to be afraid, but to speak his words, whether or not the people would listen. He also wants us to tell the Good News, whether it's convenient or not (2 Tim 4:2).

Ezek 2:6-10 Three times God told Ezekiel not to be afraid or dismayed. When God's Spirit is within us, we can lay aside our fears of rejection or ridicule. God's strength is powerful enough to help us live for him even under the heaviest criticism.

Ezek 2:9-10 Ancient books were usually scrolls, one page (up to 30 feet long) rolled up simultaneously from both ends. Normally, scrolls had writing on only one side. But in this case, the warnings overflowed to the scroll's other side, showing the full measure of judgment about to descend on Judah.

Ezek 3:1-3 In his vision, Ezekiel ate God's message and found this spiritual food not only good for him but also sweet as honey (see Rev 10:8-10 for a similar use of this image). If you "digest" God's Word, you will find that not only does it make you stronger in your faith, but its wisdom also sweetens your life. You need to feed yourself spiritually just as you do physically. This means doing more than simply giving God's Word a casual glance. You must make digesting God's Word a regular part of your life.

Ezek 3:8-9 Belief in God is not a crutch for those too weak to stand on their own. God makes his followers strong enough to stand against anything or anyone, including those who hate what is right. Just as God gave Ezekiel tough faith ("as hard as the hardest rock"), he wants to give you the stability, perseverance, and insight you need to live up to the great task he has given you. Give yourself over to God's conditioning and let him get your life in shape.

made your forehead as hard as the hardest rock! So don't be afraid of them or fear their angry looks, even though they are rebels."

10 Then he added, "Son of man, let all my words sink deep into your own heart first. Listen to them carefully for yourself. 11 Then go to your people in exile and say to them, 'This is what the Sovereign LORD says!' Do this whether they listen to you or not."

12 Then the Spirit lifted me up, and I heard a loud rumbling sound behind me. (May the glory of the LORD be praised in his place!)* 13 It was the sound of the wings of the living beings as they brushed against each other and the rumbling of their wheels beneath them.

14 The Spirit lifted me up and took me away. I went in bitterness and turmoil, but the LORD's hold on me was strong. 15 Then I came to the colony of Judean exiles in Tel-abib, beside the Kebar River. I was overwhelmed and sat among them for seven days.

A Watchman for Israel

EZEKIEL 3:16-27

After seven days the LORD gave me a message. He said, 17 "Son of man, I have appointed you as a watchman for Israel. Whenever you receive a message from me, warn people immediately. 18 If I warn the wicked, saying, 'You are under the penalty of death,' but you fail to deliver the warning, they will die in their sins. And I will hold you responsible for their deaths. 19 If you warn them and they refuse to repent and keep on sinning, they will die in their sins. But you will have saved yourself because you obeyed me.

20 "If righteous people turn away from their righteous behavior and ignore the obstacles I put in their way, they will die. And if you do not warn them, they will die in their sins. None of their righteous acts will be remembered, and I will hold you responsible for their deaths. 21 But if you warn righteous people not to sin and they listen to you and do not sin, they will live, and you will have saved yourself, too."

22 Then the LORD took hold of me and said, "Get up and go out into the valley, and I will speak to you there." 23 So I got up and went, and there I saw the glory of the LORD, just as I had seen in my first vision by the Kebar River. And I fell face down on the ground.

24 Then the Spirit came into me and set me on my feet. He spoke to me and said, "Go to your house and shut yourself in. 25 There, son of man, you will be tied with ropes so you cannot go out among the people. 26 And I will make your tongue stick to the roof of your mouth so that you will be speechless and unable to rebuke them, for they are rebels. 27 But when I give you a message, I will loosen your tongue and let you speak. Then you will say to them, 'This is what the Sovereign LORD says!' Those who choose to listen will listen, but those who refuse will refuse, for they are rebels.

Ez 3:12 A possible reading for this verse is *Then the Spirit lifted me up, and as the glory of the LORD rose from its place, I heard a loud rumbling sound behind me.*

Ezek 3:10-11 Ezekiel needed to take God's words to heart before preaching them to others. God's message must sink deep into your heart and show in your actions before you can effectively help others understand and apply the gospel.

Ezek 3:14-15 Ezekiel was bitter and angry—not at God but at the sins and attitudes of the people. Ezekiel's extraordinary vision had ended, and he had to begin the tedious job of prophesying among his people, who cared little about God's messages. Earlier, the people had heard Jeremiah, but they would not listen. Here Ezekiel had to give a similar message, and he expected to be rejected as well. But Ezekiel had the vision of the four living beings and the wheels to back up his message. He had nothing to fear because God was with him. Despite knowing the probable outcome, Ezekiel obeyed God.

As we grow, we will have times of great joy when we feel close to God and times when sins, struggles, or everyday tasks overwhelm us. Like Ezekiel, we should obey God even when we don't feel like it. Don't let feelings hinder your obedience.

Ezek 3:15 Ezekiel sat quietly among the people for seven days. This was the customary period of mourning for the dead (Gen 50:10; 1 Sam 31:13; Job 2:13). Ezekiel was mourning for those who were spiritually dead. Tel-abib was the location of one of the settlements of Jews who were exiled from Jerusalem.

Ezek 3:17-18 A watchman's job was to stand on the city wall and warn the people of approaching danger. Ezekiel's role was to be a spiritual watchman, warning the people of the judgment to come. Some think that the phrase "I will hold you responsible for their deaths" means that just as a watchman on the wall would pay with his life if he failed to warn the city of approaching enemies, Ezekiel would pay with his life if he refused to warn the people of coming judgment. Others believe this phrase simply means that God would hold Ezekiel accountable.

Ezek 3:18-19 God had already told Ezekiel that the people would not listen, so why should he bother to tell them God's message? God wanted the people to know they had been warned. Ezekiel's job was to obey God. We are responsible to tell others about God's judgment and his message of salvation, although we are not held responsible for how they respond. If we refuse to tell others what we know, God will judge us. Remember God's words to Ezekiel when you are tempted to remain silent among those who don't believe.

Ezek 3:18-21 In these verses, God is not talking about loss of salvation but rather about physical death. If the people back in Judah continued in their sins, they and their land and cities would be destroyed by Nebuchadnezzar's armies. If, on the other hand, the people would turn to God, God would spare them. God would hold Ezekiel responsible for his fellow Jews if he failed to warn them of the consequences of their sins. All people are individually responsible to God, but believers have a special responsibility to warn unbelievers of the consequences of rejecting God. If we fail to do this, God will hold us responsible for what happens to them. This should motivate us to begin sharing our faith with others—in word and deed—and to avoid becoming callous or unconcerned in our attitude.

Ezek 3:23 Ezekiel recognized his helplessness before God and fell face down in his presence. Sometimes our prosperity, popularity, or physical strength blinds us to our spiritual helplessness. But nothing we do on our own can accomplish much for God. Only when God is in control of our wills can we accomplish great tasks for him. The first step to being God's person is to admit that you need his help; then you can begin to see what God can really do in your life.

Ezek 3:24-27 Ezekiel was allowed to speak only when God had a message for the people. Thus, the people knew that whatever Ezekiel said was God's message. They did not have to wonder whether Ezekiel was speaking by God's authority or his own.

A Sign of the Coming Siege

EZEKIEL 4:1-17

"And now, son of man, take a large clay brick and set it down in front of you. Then draw a map of the city of Jerusalem on it. 2Show the city under siege. Build a wall around it so no one can escape. Set up the enemy camp, and surround the city with siege ramps and battering rams. 3Then take an iron griddle and place it between you and the city. Turn toward the city and demonstrate how harsh the siege will be against Jerusalem. This will be a warning to the people of Israel.

4"Now lie on your left side and place the sins of Israel on yourself. You are to bear their sins for the number of days you lie there on your side. 5I am requiring you to bear Israel's sins for 390 days—one day for each year of their sin. 6After that, turn over and lie on your right side for 40 days—one day for each year of Judah's sin.

7"Meanwhile, keep staring at the siege of Jerusalem. Lie there with your arm bared and prophesy her destruction. 8I will tie you up with ropes so you won't be able to turn from side to side until the days of your siege have been completed.

9"Now go and get some wheat, barley, beans, lentils, millet, and emmer wheat, and mix them together in a storage jar. Use them to make bread for yourself during the 390 days you will be lying on your side. 10Ration this out to yourself, eight ounces* of food for each day, and eat it at set times. 11Then measure out a jar* of water for each day, and drink it at set times. 12Prepare and eat this food as you would barley cakes. While all the people are watching, bake it over a fire using dried human dung as fuel and then eat the bread." 13Then the LORD said, "This is how Israel will eat defiled bread in the Gentile lands to which I will banish them!"

14Then I said, "O Sovereign LORD, must I be defiled by using human dung? For I have never been defiled before. From the time I was a child until now I have never eaten any animal that died of sickness or was killed by other animals. I have never eaten any meat forbidden by the law."

15"All right," the LORD said. "You may bake your bread with cow dung instead of human dung." 16Then he told me, "Son of man, I will make food very scarce in Jerusalem. It will be weighed out with great care and eaten fearfully. The water will be rationed out drop by drop, and the people will drink it with dismay. 17Lacking food and water, people will look at one another in terror, and they will waste away under their punishment."

Ez 4:10 Hebrew *20 shekels* [228 grams]. **Ez 4:11** Hebrew *1/6 of a hin* [about 1 pint or 0.6 liters].

Ezek 4:1ff Ezekiel acted out the coming siege and fall of Jerusalem before it actually happened. God gave Ezekiel specific instructions about what to do and say and how to do and say it. Each detail had a specific meaning. Often we ignore or disregard the smaller details of God's Word, thinking God probably doesn't care. Like Ezekiel, we should want to obey God completely, even in the details.

Ezek 4:4-17 Ezekiel's unusual actions symbolically portrayed the fate of Jerusalem. He lay on his left side for 390 days to show that Israel would be punished for 390 years; then he lay on his right side for 40 days to show that Judah would be punished for 40 years. Ezekiel was not allowed to move, symbolizing the fact that the people of Jerusalem would be imprisoned within the walls of the city. We know that Ezekiel did not have to lie on his side all day because these verses tell of other tasks God asked him to do during this time. The small amount of food he was allowed to eat represented the normal ration provided to those living in a city under siege by enemy armies. The food that was to be cooked over dried human dung was a symbol of Judah's spiritual uncleanness.

Certainly many people saw these spectacles and, in the process, heard Ezekiel's occasional speeches (Ezek 3:27). How many would be willing to do something so radical? We need to pray for greater boldness in our witness.

Ezek 4:12-14 Ezekiel asked God not to make him use human dung for fuel because it violated the laws for purity (Lev 21–22; Deut 23:12-14). As a priest, Ezekiel would have been careful to keep all these laws. To use human dung for fuel would paint a dramatic picture of ruin. If nothing was left in the city that could be burned, it would be impossible to continue to follow God's laws for sacrifices.

EZEKIEL'S ACTS OF OBEDIENCE

Ezek 2:1	Stood and received God's message
Ezek 3:24-26	Shut himself inside his house
Ezek 3:27	Faithfully proclaimed God's message
Ezek 4:1ff	Drew a map of Jerusalem on a large brick (clay tablet)
Ezek 4:4-5	Lay on his left side for 390 days
Ezek 4:6	Lay on his right side for 40 days
Ezek 4:9-17	Followed specific cooking instructions
Ezek 5:1-4	Shaved his head and beard
Ezek 12:3-7	Left home to demonstrate exile
Ezek 13:1ff	Spoke against false prophets
Ezek 19:1ff	Sang a funeral song concerning the leaders
Ezek 21:2	Prophesied against Israel and the Temple
Ezek 21:19-23	Marked out two routes for Babylon's king
Ezek 24:16-17	Did not mourn his wife's death

8. JEREMIAH'S MESSAGES EARLY IN ZEDEKIAH'S REIGN

Jeremiah gave the following messages in 593 B.C., the fourth year of Zedekiah's reign in Judah.

Jeremiah Wears an Ox Yoke

JEREMIAH 27:1-22

This message came to Jeremiah from the LORD early in the reign of Zedekiah* son of Josiah, king of Judah. 2This is what the LORD said to me: "Make a yoke, and fasten it on your neck with leather straps. 3Then send messages to the kings of Edom, Moab, Ammon, Tyre, and Sidon through their ambassadors who have come to see King Zedekiah in Jerusalem. 4Give them this message for their masters: 'This is what the LORD of Heaven's Armies, the God of Israel, says: 5With my great strength and powerful arm I made the earth and all its people and every animal. I can give these things of mine to anyone I choose. 6Now I will give your countries to King Nebuchadnezzar of Babylon, who is my servant. I have put everything, even the wild animals, under his control. 7All the nations will serve him, his son, and his grandson until his time is up. Then many nations and great kings will conquer and rule over Babylon. 8So you must submit to Babylon's king and serve him; put your neck under Babylon's yoke! I will punish any nation that refuses to be his slave, says the LORD. I will send war, famine, and disease upon that nation until Babylon has conquered it.

9"'Do not listen to your false prophets, fortune-tellers, interpreters of dreams, mediums, and sorcerers who say, "The king of Babylon will not conquer you." 10They are all liars, and their lies will lead to your being driven out of your land. I will drive you out and send you far away to die. 11But the people of any nation that submits to the king of Babylon will be allowed to stay in their own country to farm the land as usual. I, the LORD, have spoken!'"

12Then I repeated this same message to King Zedekiah of Judah. "If you want to live, submit to the yoke of the king of Babylon and his people. 13Why do you insist on dying—you and your people? Why should you choose war, famine, and disease, which the LORD will bring against every nation that refuses to submit to Babylon's king? 14Do not listen to the false prophets who keep telling you, 'The king of Babylon will not conquer you.' They are liars. 15This is what the LORD says: 'I have not sent these prophets! They are telling you lies in my name, so I will drive you from this land. You will all die—you and all these prophets, too.'"

16Then I spoke to the priests and the people and said, "This is what the LORD says: 'Do not listen to your prophets who claim that soon the gold articles taken from my Temple will be returned from Babylon. It is all a lie! 17Do not listen to them. Surrender to the king of Babylon, and you will live. Why should this whole city be destroyed? 18If they really are prophets and speak the LORD's messages, let them pray to the LORD of Heaven's Armies. Let them pray that the articles remaining in the LORD's Temple and in the king's palace and in the palaces of Jerusalem will not be carried away to Babylon!'

19"For the LORD of Heaven's Armies has spoken about the pillars in front of the Temple, the great bronze basin called the Sea, the water carts, and all the other ceremonial articles. 20King Nebuchadnezzar of Babylon left them here when he exiled Jehoiachin* son of Jehoiakim, king of Judah, to Babylon, along with all the other nobles of Judah and Jerusalem. 21Yes, this is what the LORD of Heaven's Armies, the God of Israel, says about the precious things still in the Temple and in the palace of Judah's king: 22'They will all be carried away to Babylon and will stay there until I send for them,' says the LORD. 'Then I will bring them back to Jerusalem again.'"

Jeremiah Condemns Hananiah

JEREMIAH 28:1-17

One day in late summer* of that same year—the fourth year of the reign of Zedekiah, king of Judah—Hananiah son of Azzur, a prophet from Gibeon, addressed me publicly in the Temple while all the priests and people listened. He said, 2"This is what the LORD of Heaven's

Jer 27:1 As in some Hebrew manuscripts and Syriac version (see also 27:3, 12); most Hebrew manuscripts read *Jehoiakim.* **Jer 27:20** Hebrew *Jeconiah,* a variant spelling of Jehoiachin. **Jer 28:1** Hebrew *In the fifth month,* of the ancient Hebrew lunar calendar. The fifth month in the fourth year of Zedekiah's reign occurred within the months of August and September 593 B.C. Also see note on 1:3.

Jer 27:1ff The year was 593 B.C., and Nebuchadnezzar had already invaded Judah once and had taken many captives. Jeremiah wore an ox yoke (a wooden frame used to fasten a team of animals to a plow) as a symbol of bondage. This was an object lesson, telling the people they must put themselves under Babylon's yoke or be destroyed.

Jer 27:5-6 God punished the people of Judah in an unusual way, by appointing a foreign ruler to be his "servant." Nebuchadnezzar was not appointed to proclaim God's message, but to fulfill God's promise of judgment on sin. Because God is in control of all events, he uses whomever he wants. God may use unlikely people or circumstances to correct you. Be ready to accept God's guidance, even if it comes from unexpected sources.

Jer 27:12-18 Zedekiah was in a tough spot. Jeremiah called on him to surrender to Nebuchadnezzar at a time when many of the other leaders wanted him to form an alliance and fight. It would be disgraceful for a king to surrender, and he would look like a coward. This was a great opportunity for the false prophets, who kept saying that the Babylonians would not defeat the great city of Jerusalem and that God would never allow the magnificent, holy Temple to be destroyed.

Jer 27:19-22 When Nebuchadnezzar invaded Judah, first in 605 and then in 597 B.C., he took away many important people living in Jerusalem—including Daniel and Ezekiel. Although these men were captives, they had a profound impact on the exiles and leaders in Babylon. Jeremiah predicted that more people, and even the precious objects in the Temple, would be taken. This happened in 586 B.C. during Babylon's third and last invasion.

▸ **JEREMIAH 28:1-17** ***(cont.)***

Armies, the God of Israel, says: 'I will remove the yoke of the king of Babylon from your necks. [3]Within two years I will bring back all the Temple treasures that King Nebuchadnezzar carried off to Babylon. [4]And I will bring back Jehoiachin* son of Jehoiakim, king of Judah, and all the other captives that were taken to Babylon. I will surely break the yoke that the king of Babylon has put on your necks. I, the LORD, have spoken!'"

[5]Jeremiah responded to Hananiah as they stood in front of all the priests and people at the Temple. [6]He said, "Amen! May your prophecies come true! I hope the LORD does everything you say. I hope he does bring back from Babylon the treasures of this Temple and all the captives. [7]But listen now to the solemn words I speak to you in the presence of all these people. [8]The ancient prophets who preceded you and me spoke against many nations, always warning of war, disaster, and disease. [9]So a prophet who predicts peace must show he is right. Only when his predictions come true can we know that he is really from the LORD."

[10]Then Hananiah the prophet took the yoke off Jeremiah's neck and broke it in pieces. [11]And Hananiah said again to the crowd that had gathered, "This is what the LORD says: 'Just as this yoke has been broken, within two years I will break the yoke of oppression from all the nations now subject to King Nebuchadnezzar of Babylon.'" With that, Jeremiah left the Temple area.

[12]Soon after this confrontation with Hananiah, the LORD gave this message to Jeremiah: [13]"Go and tell Hananiah, 'This is what the LORD says: You have broken a wooden yoke, but you have replaced it with a yoke of iron. [14]The LORD of Heaven's Armies, the God of Israel, says: I have put a yoke of iron on the necks of all these nations, forcing them into slavery under King Nebuchadnezzar of Babylon. I have put everything, even the wild animals, under his control.'"

[15]Then Jeremiah the prophet said to Hananiah, "Listen, Hananiah! The LORD has not sent you, but the people believe your lies. [16]Therefore, this is what the LORD says: 'You must die. Your life will end this very year because you have rebelled against the LORD.'"

[17]Two months later* the prophet Hananiah died.

Jeremiah's Message Sent to Babylon

JEREMIAH 51:59-64

The prophet Jeremiah gave this message to Seraiah son of Neriah and grandson of Mahseiah, a staff officer, when Seraiah went to Babylon with King Zedekiah of Judah. This was during the fourth year of Zedekiah's reign.* [60]Jeremiah had recorded on a scroll all the terrible disasters that would soon come upon Babylon—all the words written here. [61]He said to Seraiah, "When you get to Babylon, read aloud everything on this scroll. [62]Then say, 'LORD, you have said that you will destroy Babylon so that neither people nor animals will remain here. She will lie empty and abandoned forever.' [63]When you have finished reading the scroll, tie it to a stone and throw it into the Euphrates River. [64]Then say, 'In this same way Babylon and her people will sink, never again to rise, because of the disasters I will bring upon her.'"

This is the end of Jeremiah's messages.

Jer 28:4 Hebrew *Jeconiah,* a variant spelling of Jehoiachin. **Jer 28:17** Hebrew *In the seventh month of that same year.* See 28:1 and the note there. **Jer 51:59** The fourth year of Zedekiah's reign was 593 B.C.

9. EZEKIEL PROPHESIES JUDGMENT FOR JUDAH

In words and in mimed actions, the prophet Ezekiel declared the certainty of impending judgment on Jerusalem. God's people, having broken the terms of the Lord's covenant with them at Mount Sinai, now faced the curses of death and destruction that were attached to that covenant. Only after these curses had taken effect could there be any hope for the future.

A Sign of the Coming Judgment

EZEKIEL 5:1-17

"Son of man, take a sharp sword and use it as a razor to shave your head and beard. Use a scale to weigh the hair into three equal parts. [2]Place a third of it at the center of your map of Jerusalem. After acting out the siege, burn it there. Scatter another third across your map and chop it with a sword. Scatter the last third to

Jer 28:6-9 Hananiah had just come up with a prophecy everyone liked. He declared that God would soon bring relief from all their problems and oppressors. Jeremiah had to admit that Hananiah's words echoed his own wishes. He sincerely hoped Hananiah was right. But unfortunately, Hananiah's words were not from God. Positive or negative, God's words are exactly true. We, like Jeremiah, may honestly wish for results or benefits outside God's plans. But if we are going to be faithful to God, there will be times when we must disagree with our own wishes in order to speak the truth and be obedient to God.

Jer 28:8-17 Jeremiah spoke the truth, but it was unpopular; Hananiah spoke lies, but his deceitful words brought false hope and comfort to the people. God had already outlined the marks of a true prophet (Deut 13; 18:20-22): A true prophet's predictions always come true, and his words never contradict previous revelation. Jeremiah's predictions were already coming true, from Hananiah's death to the Babylonian invasions. But the people still preferred to listen to comforting lies rather than painful truth.

Jer 51:59 Jeremiah could not visit Babylon, so he sent the message with Seraiah, the officer who cared for the comforts of the army. Seraiah was probably Baruch's brother (Jer 32:12).

Jer 51:60-64 Here we find again the twin themes of God's sovereignty and his judgment. Babylon had been allowed to oppress the people of Israel, but Babylon itself would be judged. Although God brings good out of evil, he does not allow evil to remain unpunished. The wicked may succeed for a while, but resist the temptation to follow them or you may share in their judgment.

Ezek 5:1-10 Shaving one's head and beard signified mourning, humiliation, and repentance. God told Ezekiel to shave his head and beard and then to divide the hair into

the wind, for I will scatter my people with the sword.
[3]Keep just a bit of the hair and tie it up in your robe.
[4]Then take some of these hairs out and throw them
into the fire, burning them up. A fire will then spread
from this remnant and destroy all of Israel.
[5]"This is what the Sovereign LORD says: This is an
illustration of what will happen to Jerusalem. I placed
her at the center of the nations, [6]but she has rebelled
against my regulations and decrees and has been even
more wicked than the surrounding nations. She has
refused to obey the regulations and decrees I gave
her to follow.

[7]"Therefore, this is what the Sovereign LORD says: You
people have behaved worse than your neighbors and
have refused to obey my decrees and regulations. You
have not even lived up to the standards of the nations
around you. [8]Therefore, I myself, the Sovereign LORD,
am now your enemy. I will punish you publicly while all
the nations watch. [9]Because of your detestable idols,
I will punish you like I have never punished anyone
before or ever will again. [10]Parents will eat their own
children, and children will eat their parents. I will punish you and scatter to the winds the few who survive.
[11]"As surely as I live, says the Sovereign LORD, I

EZEKIEL

Although Ezekiel's visions and prophecies were clear and vivid, very little is known about the prophet's personal life. He was among the thousands of young men deported from Judah to Babylon when King Jehoiachin surrendered. Until those tragic days, Ezekiel was being trained for the priesthood. But during the exile in Babylon, God called Ezekiel to be his prophet during one of Israel's darkest times. • Ezekiel experienced the same kind of shocking encounter with God that Isaiah had reported 150 years earlier. Like Isaiah, Ezekiel was never the same after his personal encounter with God. Although God's messages through both these prophets had many points in common, the conditions under which they lived were very different. Isaiah warned of the coming storm; Ezekiel spoke in the midst of the storm of national defeat that devastated his people. He announced that even Jerusalem would not escape destruction. In addition, during this time Ezekiel had to endure the pain of his wife's death. • God's description of Ezekiel as a watchman on the walls of the city captures the personal nature of his ministry. A watchman's job was dangerous. If he failed at his post, he and the entire city might be destroyed. His own safety depended on the quality of his work. The importance of each person's accountability before God was a central part of Ezekiel's message. He taught the exiles that God expected personal obedience and worship from each of them. • As in Ezekiel's day, it is easy for us today to forget that God has a personal interest in each one of us. We may feel insignificant or out of control when we look at world events. But knowing that God is ultimately in control, that he cares, and that he is willing to be known by us can bring a new sense of purpose to our lives. How do you measure your worth? Are you valuable because of your achievements and potential or because God, your Creator and Designer, declares you valuable?

Strengths and accomplishments	• Was a priest by training, a prophet by God's call • Received vivid visions and delivered powerful messages • Served as God's messenger during Israel's captivity in Babylon • Became a tough and courageous man so he could reach a hard and stubborn people (Ezek 3:8)
Lessons from his life	• Even the repeated failures of his people will not prevent God's plan for the world from being fulfilled • One's response to God determines one's eternal destiny • God has people through whom he can work even in seemingly hopeless situations
Vital statistics	• Where: Babylon • Occupation: Prophet to the captives in Babylon • Relatives: Father: Buzi. Wife: Unknown. • Contemporaries: Daniel, Jehoiachin, Jeremiah, Jehoiakim, Nebuchadnezzar
Key verses	"Then he added, 'Son of man, let all my words sink deep into your own heart first. Listen to them carefully for yourself. Then go to your people in exile and say to them, "This is what the Sovereign LORD says!" Do this whether they listen to you or not'" (Ezek 3:10-11).

Ezekiel's story is told in the book of Ezekiel and 2 Kings 24:10-17.

three parts, symbolizing what was going to happen to the people in Jerusalem (see Ezek 5:12). Along with verbal prophecies, God asked Ezekiel to use dramatic visual images to command the people's attention and to burn an indelible impression on their minds. Just as God gave Ezekiel creative ways to communicate his message to the exiles, we can creatively communicate the Good News about God to a lost generation.

Ezek 5:3-4 The few strands of hair Ezekiel put in his robe symbolized the small remnant of faithful people whom God would preserve. But even some from this remnant would be judged and destroyed because their faith was not genuine. Where will you stand in the coming judgment? Matthew 7:22-23 warns that many who believe they will be saved won't be. Make sure your commitment to the Lord is genuine.

Ezek 5:7 The people's wickedness was so great that they couldn't even be compared favorably with the pagan nations around them, not to mention how they would appear with respect to God's laws.

Ezek 5:11 It was a serious sin to defile the Temple, God's sanctuary, by worshiping idols and practicing evil within its very walls. In the New Testament, we learn that God now makes his home within those who are his. Our bodies are God's temple (see 1 Cor 6:19). We defile God's temple today by allowing gossiping, bitterness, love of money, lying, or any other wrong actions or attitudes to be a part of our lives. By asking the Holy Spirit's help, you can keep from defiling his temple, your body.

▶ **EZEKIEL 5:1-17** ***(cont.)***

will cut you off completely. I will show you no pity at all because you have defiled my Temple with your vile images and detestable sins. 12A third of your people will die in the city from disease and famine. A third of them will be slaughtered by the enemy outside the city walls. And I will scatter a third to the winds, chasing them with my sword. 13Then at last my anger will be spent, and I will be satisfied. And when my fury against them has subsided, all Israel will know that I, the LORD, have spoken to them in my jealous anger.

14"So I will turn you into a ruin, a mockery in the eyes of the surrounding nations and to all who pass by. 15You will become an object of mockery and taunting and horror. You will be a warning to all the nations around you. They will see what happens when the LORD punishes a nation in anger and rebukes it, says the LORD.

16"I will shower you with the deadly arrows of famine to destroy you. The famine will become more and more severe until every crumb of food is gone. 17And along with the famine, wild animals will attack you and rob you of your children. Disease and war will stalk your land, and I will bring the sword of the enemy against you. I, the LORD, have spoken!"

Judgment against Israel's Mountains

EZEKIEL 6:1-14

Again a message came to me from the LORD: 2"Son of man, turn and face the mountains of Israel and prophesy against them. 3Proclaim this message from the Sovereign LORD against the mountains of Israel. This is what the Sovereign LORD says to the mountains and hills and to the ravines and valleys: I am about to bring war upon you, and I will smash your pagan shrines. 4All your altars will be demolished, and your places of worship will be destroyed. I will kill your people in front of your idols.* 5I will lay your corpses in front of your idols and scatter your bones around your altars. 6Wherever you live there will be desolation, and I will destroy your pagan shrines. Your altars will be demolished, your idols will be smashed, your places of worship will be torn down, and all the religious objects you have made will be destroyed. 7The place will be littered with corpses, and you will know that I alone am the LORD.

8"But I will let a few of my people escape destruction, and they will be scattered among the nations of the world. 9Then when they are exiled among the nations, they will remember me. They will recognize how hurt I am by their unfaithful hearts and lustful eyes that long for their idols. Then at last they will hate themselves for all their detestable sins. 10They will know that I alone am the LORD and that I was serious when I said I would bring this calamity on them.

11"This is what the Sovereign LORD says: Clap your hands in horror, and stamp your feet. Cry out because of all the detestable sins the people of Israel have committed. Now they are going to die from war and famine and disease. 12Disease will strike down those who are far away in exile. War will destroy those who are nearby. And anyone who survives will be killed by famine. So at last I will spend my fury on them. 13They will know that I am the LORD when their dead lie scattered among their idols and altars on every hill and mountain and under every green tree and every great shade tree—the places where they offered sacrifices to their idols. 14I will crush them and make their cities desolate from the wilderness in the south to Riblah* in the north. Then they will know that I am the LORD."

Ez 6:4 The Hebrew term (literally *round things*) probably alludes to dung; also in 6:5, 6, 9, 13. **Ez 6:14** As in some Hebrew manuscripts; most Hebrew manuscripts read *Diblah.*

Ezek 5:13 Have you ever seen someone try to discipline a child by saying, "If you do that one more time . . ."? If the parent doesn't follow through, the child learns not to listen. Empty threats backfire. God was going to punish the Israelites for their blatant sins, and he wanted them to know that he would do what he said. The people learned the hard way that God always follows through on his word. Too many people ignore God's warnings, treating them as empty threats. Don't make the mistake of thinking God doesn't really mean what he says.

Ezek 6:1ff This is the beginning of a two-part message. Remember that Ezekiel could speak only when giving messages from God. The message in Ezekiel 6 is that Judah's idolatry will surely call down God's judgment. The message in Ezekiel 7 describes the nature of that judgment—utter destruction of the nation. Nevertheless God in his mercy saved a remnant. Ezekiel prophesies against the mountains of Israel because mountains were sites of the pagan shrines used to worship idols.

Ezek 6:8-10 A ray of light appears in this prophecy of darkness—God would spare a small group, a remnant, of people, but only after they had learned some hard lessons. God sometimes has to break a person in order to bring about true repentance. The people needed to change their attitudes, but they wouldn't until God broke their hearts with humiliation, pain, suffering, and defeat. Does your heart long for God enough to change those areas displeasing him? Or will God have to break your heart?

Ezek 6:11 Prophets often used this threefold description of judgment upon Jerusalem—war, famine, and disease—as a way of saying that the destruction would be complete. War meant death in battle; famine came when enemies besieged a city; disease was always a danger during famine. Don't make the mistake of underestimating the extent of God's judgment. If you ignore the biblical warnings and turn away from God, his punishment awaits you.

Ezek 6:14 The phrase "then they will know that I am the LORD" (or a variation of this phrase) occurs 65 times in the book of Ezekiel. The purpose of God's punishment was not to take revenge but to impress upon the people the truth that the Lord is the only true and living God. People in Ezekiel's day were worshiping human-made idols and calling them gods. Today money, sex, and power have become idols for many. Punishment will come upon all who put other things ahead of God. It is easy to forget that the Lord alone is God, the supreme authority and the only source of eternal love and life. Remember that God may use the difficulties of your life to teach you that he alone is God.

The Coming of the End

EZEKIEL 7:1-13

Then this message came to me from the LORD: [2]"Son of man, this is what the Sovereign LORD says to Israel:

"The end is here!
  Wherever you look—
east, west, north, or south—
  your land is finished.
3 No hope remains,
  for I will unleash my anger against you.
I will call you to account
  for all your detestable sins.
4 I will turn my eyes away and show no pity.
  I will repay you for all your detestable sins.
Then you will know that I am the LORD.

5 "This is what the Sovereign LORD says:
Disaster after disaster
  is coming your way!
6 The end has come.
  It has finally arrived.
  Your final doom is waiting!
7 O people of Israel, the day of your destruction
  is dawning.
  The time has come; the day of trouble
  is near.
Shouts of anguish will be heard on the
  mountains,
  not shouts of joy.
8 Soon I will pour out my fury on you
  and unleash my anger against you.
I will call you to account
  for all your detestable sins.
9 I will turn my eyes away and show no pity.
  I will repay you for all your detestable sins.
Then you will know that it is I, the LORD,
  who is striking the blow.

10 "The day of judgment is here;
  your destruction awaits!
The people's wickedness and pride
  have blossomed to full flower.
11 Their violence has grown into a rod
  that will beat them for their wickedness.
None of these proud and wicked people will
  survive.
  All their wealth and prestige will be
  swept away.
12 Yes, the time has come;
  the day is here!
Buyers should not rejoice over bargains,
  nor sellers grieve over losses,
for all of them will fall
  under my terrible anger.
13 Even if the merchants survive,
  they will never return to their business.
For what God has said applies to everyone—
  it will not be changed!
Not one person whose life is twisted by sin
  will ever recover.

The Desolation of Israel

EZEKIEL 7:14-27

14 "The trumpet calls Israel's army to mobilize,
  but no one listens,
  for my fury is against them all.
15 There is war outside the city
  and disease and famine within.
Those outside the city walls
  will be killed by enemy swords.
Those inside the city
  will die of famine and disease.
16 The survivors who escape to the mountains
  will moan like doves, weeping for
  their sins.
17 Their hands will hang limp,
  their knees will be weak as water.
18 They will dress themselves in burlap;
  horror and shame will cover them.
They will shave their heads
  in sorrow and remorse.

19 "They will throw their money in the streets,
  tossing it out like worthless trash.
Their silver and gold won't save them
  on that day of the LORD's anger.
It will neither satisfy nor feed them,
  for their greed can only trip them up.

Ezek 7:10-11 In chapter 7, Ezekiel predicts the complete destruction of Israel. The wicked and proud will finally get what they deserve. If it seems as though God ignores the evil and proud people of our day, be assured that a day of judgment will come, just as it came for the people of Israel. God is waiting patiently for sinners to repent (see 2 Pet 3:9), but when his judgment comes, "none of these proud and wicked people will survive." What you decide about God now will determine your fate then.

Ezek 7:12-13 The nation of Israel trusted in its prosperity and possessions instead of in God. So God planned to destroy the basis of its prosperity. Whenever we begin to trust in jobs, the economy, a political system, or military might for our security, we put God in the backseat.

Ezek 7:19 God's people had allowed their love of money to lead them into sin. For this, God would destroy them. Money has a strange power; Paul said that "the love of money is the root of all kinds of evil" (1 Tim 6:10). It is ironic that we use a gift of God—money—to buy things that separate us from him. It is tragic that we spend so much money seeking to satisfy ourselves and so little time seeking God, the true source of satisfaction.

Ezek 7:20 God gave the people silver and gold, but they used that silver and gold to make idols. The resources God gives us should be used to do his work and carry out his will, but too often we use them to satisfy our own desires. When we abuse God's gifts or use resources selfishly, we miss the real purpose God had in mind. This is as shortsighted as idolatry.

▸ **EZEKIEL 7:14-27** ***(cont.)***

20 They were proud of their beautiful jewelry
and used it to make detestable idols and vile images.
Therefore, I will make all their wealth
disgusting to them.
21 I will give it as plunder to foreigners,
to the most wicked of nations,
and they will defile it.
22 I will turn my eyes from them
as these robbers invade and defile my treasured land.

23 "Prepare chains for my people,
for the land is bloodied by terrible crimes.
Jerusalem is filled with violence.
24 I will bring the most ruthless of nations
to occupy their homes.
I will break down their proud fortresses
and defile their sanctuaries.
25 Terror and trembling will overcome my people.
They will look for peace but not find it.
26 Calamity will follow calamity;
rumor will follow rumor.
They will look in vain
for a vision from the prophets.
They will receive no teaching from the priests
and no counsel from the leaders.
27 The king and the prince will stand helpless,
weeping in despair,
and the people's hands
will tremble with fear.
I will bring on them
the evil they have done to others,
and they will receive the punishment
they so richly deserve.
Then they will know that I am the LORD."

Idolatry in the Temple

EZEKIEL 8:1-18

Then on September 17,* during the sixth year of King
Jehoiachin's captivity, while the leaders of Judah were
in my home, the Sovereign LORD took hold of me. 2I
saw a figure that appeared to be a man. From what
appeared to be his waist down, he looked like a burning flame. From the waist up he looked like gleaming
amber.* 3He reached out what seemed to be a hand
and took me by the hair. Then the Spirit lifted me
up into the sky and transported me to Jerusalem in a
vision from God. I was taken to the north gate of the
inner courtyard of the Temple, where there is a large
idol that has made the LORD very jealous. 4Suddenly,
the glory of the God of Israel was there, just as I had
seen it before in the valley.

5Then the LORD said to me, "Son of man, look toward the north." So I looked, and there to the north,
beside the entrance to the gate near the altar, stood
the idol that had made the LORD so jealous.

6"Son of man," he said, "do you see what they are
doing? Do you see the detestable sins the people of
Israel are committing to drive me from my Temple?
But come, and you will see even more detestable sins
than these!" 7Then he brought me to the door of the
Temple courtyard, where I could see a hole in the wall.
8He said to me, "Now, son of man, dig into the wall."
So I dug into the wall and found a hidden doorway.

9"Go in," he said, "and see the wicked and detestable sins they are committing in there!" 10So I went in
and saw the walls engraved with all kinds of crawling
animals and detestable creatures. I also saw the various idols* worshiped by the people of Israel. 11Seventy
leaders of Israel were standing there with Jaazaniah
son of Shaphan in the center. Each of them held an
incense burner, from which a cloud of incense rose
above their heads.

12Then the LORD said to me, "Son of man, have
you seen what the leaders of Israel are doing with
their idols in dark rooms? They are saying, 'The LORD
doesn't see us; he has deserted our land!'" 13Then the
LORD added, "Come, and I will show you even more
detestable sins than these!"

14He brought me to the north gate of the LORD's
Temple, and some women were sitting there, weeping

Ez 8:1 Hebrew *on the fifth day of the sixth month,* of the ancient Hebrew lunar calendar. This event occurred on September 17, 592 B.C.; also see note on 1:1. **Ez 8:2** Or *like burnished metal.* **Ez 8:10** The Hebrew term (literally *round things*) probably alludes to dung.

Ezek 7:24 The people of Jerusalem took great pride in their buildings. The Temple itself was a source of pride (see Ezek 24:20-21). This pride would be crushed when the evil and godless Babylonians destroyed Jerusalem's fortresses and sanctuaries. If you are going through a humiliating experience, God may be using that experience to weed out pride in your life.

Ezek 8:1ff This prophecy's date corresponds to 592 B.C. The message of Ezekiel 8–11 is directed specifically toward Jerusalem and its leaders. Chapter 8 records Ezekiel being taken in a vision from Babylon to the Temple in Jerusalem to see the great wickedness being practiced there. The people and their religious leaders were thoroughly corrupt. While Ezekiel's first vision (Ezek 1–3) showed that judgment was from God, this vision showed that their sin was the reason for judgment.

Ezek 8:2 This figure could have been an angel or a manifestation of God himself. In Ezekiel's previous vision, a man with a similar appearance was pictured as God on his throne (Ezek 1:26-28).

Ezek 8:3-5 This "idol that has made the LORD very jealous" could be an image of Asherah, the Canaanite goddess of fertility, whose character encouraged sexual immorality and self-gratification. King Manasseh had placed such an idol in the Temple (2 Kgs 21:7). King Josiah had burned the Asherah pole (2 Kgs 23:6), but there were certainly many other idols around.

Ezek 8:6ff In scene after scene, God revealed to Ezekiel the extent to which the people had embraced idolatry and wickedness. God's Spirit works within us in a similar way, revealing sin that lurks in our lives. How comfortable would you feel if God held an open house in your life today?

Ezek 8:14 Tammuz was the Babylonian god of spring. He was the husband or lover of the goddess Ishtar. The followers of this cult believed that the green vegetation shriveled and died in the hot summer because Tammuz had died and descended into the

for the god Tammuz. 15"Have you seen this?" he asked. "But I will show you even more detestable sins than these!"

16Then he brought me into the inner courtyard of the LORD's Temple. At the entrance to the sanctuary, between the entry room and the bronze altar, there were about twenty-five men with their backs to the sanctuary of the LORD. They were facing east, bowing low to the ground, worshiping the sun!

17"Have you seen this, son of man?" he asked. "Is it nothing to the people of Judah that they commit these detestable sins, leading the whole nation into violence, thumbing their noses at me, and provoking my anger? 18Therefore, I will respond in fury. I will neither pity nor spare them. And though they cry for mercy, I will not listen."

The Slaughter of Idolaters

EZEKIEL 9:1-11

Then the LORD thundered, "Bring on the men appointed to punish the city! Tell them to bring their weapons with them!" 2Six men soon appeared from the upper gate that faces north, each carrying a deadly weapon in his hand. With them was a man dressed in linen, who carried a writer's case at his side. They all went into the Temple courtyard and stood beside the bronze altar.

3Then the glory of the God of Israel rose up from between the cherubim, where it had rested, and moved to the entrance of the Temple. And the LORD called to the man dressed in linen who was carrying the writer's case. 4He said to him, "Walk through the streets of Jerusalem and put a mark on the foreheads of all who weep and sigh because of the detestable sins being committed in their city."

5Then I heard the LORD say to the other men, "Follow him through the city and kill everyone whose forehead is not marked. Show no mercy; have no pity! 6Kill them all—old and young, girls and women and little children. But do not touch anyone with the mark. Begin right here at the Temple." So they began by killing the seventy leaders.

7"Defile the Temple!" the LORD commanded. "Fill its courtyards with corpses. Go!" So they went and began killing throughout the city.

8While they were out killing, I was all alone. I fell face down on the ground and cried out, "O Sovereign LORD! Will your fury against Jerusalem wipe out everyone left in Israel?"

9Then he said to me, "The sins of the people of Israel and Judah are very, very great. The entire land is full of murder; the city is filled with injustice. They are saying, 'The LORD doesn't see it! The LORD has abandoned the land!' 10So I will not spare them or have any pity on them. I will fully repay them for all they have done."

11Then the man in linen clothing, who carried the writer's case, reported back and said, "I have done as you commanded."

---

underworld. Thus, the worshipers wept and mourned his death. In the springtime, when the new vegetation appeared, they rejoiced, believing that Tammuz had come back to life. God was showing Ezekiel that many people were no longer worshiping the true God of life and vegetation. We must also be careful not to spend so much time thinking about the benefits of creation that we lose sight of the Creator.

Ezek 9:1ff This chapter presents a picture of coming judgment. After Ezekiel had seen how corrupt Jerusalem had become, God called one man to spare the small minority that had been faithful. Then he called six men to slaughter the wicked people in the city. God himself ordered this judgment (Ezek 9:5-7).

Ezek 9:2 The writer's case was a common object in Ezekiel's day. It included a long narrow board with a groove to hold the reed brush that was used to write on parchment, papyrus, or dried clay. The board had hollowed out areas for holding cakes of black and red ink that had to be moistened before use.

Ezek 9:3 Cherubim are an order of powerful angelic beings created to glorify God. They are associated with God's absolute holiness and moral perfection. God placed cherubim at the entrance of Eden to keep Adam and Eve out after they sinned (Gen 3:24). Representations of cherubim were used to decorate the Tabernacle and Temple. The lid of the Ark of the Covenant, called the atonement cover, was adorned with two gold cherubim (Exod 37:6-9). It was a symbol of the very presence of God. The cherubim seen by Ezekiel left the Temple along with the glory of God (Ezek 10). Ezekiel then recognized them as the living beings he had seen in his first vision (see Ezek 1).

Ezek 9:4-5 God told the man with the writer's case to put a mark on those who were faithful to God. Their faithfulness was determined by their sorrow over their nation's sin. Those with the mark were spared when the six men began to destroy the wicked people. During the Exodus, the Israelites put a mark of blood on their doorframes to save them from death. In the final days, God will mark the foreheads of those destined for salvation (Rev 7:3), and Satan will mark his followers (Rev 13:16-17), who, like him, are destined for destruction. When God punishes sin, he won't forget his promise to preserve his people.

Ezek 9:6 The spiritual leaders of Israel blatantly promoted their idolatrous beliefs, and the people abandoned God and followed them. Spiritual leaders are especially accountable to God because they are entrusted with the task of teaching the truth (see Jas 3:1). When they pervert the truth, they can lead countless people away from God and even cause a nation to fall. It is not surprising, then, that when God began to judge the nation, he started at the Temple and worked outward (see 1 Pet 4:17). How tragic it is that in the Temple, the one place where they should have been teaching God's truth, these men were teaching lies.

Ezek 9:9-10 The people said that the Lord had abandoned the land and wouldn't see their sin. People have many convenient explanations to make it easier to sin: "It doesn't matter," "Everybody's doing it," or "Nobody will ever know." Do you find yourself making excuses for sin? Rationalizing sin makes it easier to commit, but rationalization does not convince God or cancel the punishment.

The LORD's Glory Leaves the Temple

EZEKIEL 10:1-22

In my vision I saw what appeared to be a throne of blue lapis lazuli above the crystal surface over the heads of the cherubim. 2Then the LORD spoke to the man in linen clothing and said, "Go between the whirling wheels beneath the cherubim, and take a handful of burning coals and scatter them over the city." He did this as I watched.

3The cherubim were standing at the south end of the Temple when the man went in, and the cloud of glory filled the inner courtyard. 4Then the glory of the LORD rose up from above the cherubim and went over to the door of the Temple. The Temple was filled with this cloud of glory, and the courtyard glowed brightly with the glory of the LORD. 5The moving wings of the cherubim sounded like the voice of God Almighty* and could be heard even in the outer courtyard.

6The LORD said to the man in linen clothing, "Go between the cherubim and take some burning coals from between the wheels." So the man went in and stood beside one of the wheels. 7Then one of the cherubim reached out his hand and took some live coals from the fire burning among them. He put the coals into the hands of the man in linen clothing, and the man took them and went out. 8(All the cherubim had what looked like human hands under their wings.)

9I looked, and each of the four cherubim had a wheel beside him, and the wheels sparkled like beryl. 10All four wheels looked alike and were made the same; each wheel had a second wheel turning crosswise within it. 11The cherubim could move in any of the four directions they faced, without turning as they moved. They went straight in the direction they faced, never turning aside. 12Both the cherubim and the wheels were covered with eyes. The cherubim had eyes all over their bodies, including their hands, their backs, and their wings. 13I heard someone refer to the wheels as "the whirling wheels." 14Each of the four cherubim had four faces: the first was the face of an ox,* the second was a human face, the third was the face of a lion, and the fourth was the face of an eagle.

15Then the cherubim rose upward. These were the same living beings I had seen beside the Kebar River. 16When the cherubim moved, the wheels moved with them. When they lifted their wings to fly, the wheels stayed beside them. 17When the cherubim stopped, the wheels stopped. When they flew upward, the wheels rose up, for the spirit of the living beings was in the wheels.

18Then the glory of the LORD moved out from the door of the Temple and hovered above the cherubim. 19And as I watched, the cherubim flew with their wheels to the east gate of the LORD's Temple. And the glory of the God of Israel hovered above them.

20These were the same living beings I had seen beneath the God of Israel when I was by the Kebar River. I knew they were cherubim, 21for each had four faces and four wings and what looked like human hands under their wings. 22And their faces were just like the faces of the beings I had seen at the Kebar, and they traveled straight ahead, just as the others had.

Judgment on Israel's Leaders

EZEKIEL 11:1-13

Then the Spirit lifted me and brought me to the east gateway of the LORD's Temple, where I saw twenty-five prominent men of the city. Among them were Jaazaniah son of Azzur and Pelatiah son of Benaiah, who were leaders among the people.

2The Spirit said to me, "Son of man, these are the men who are planning evil and giving wicked counsel in this city. 3They say to the people, 'Is it not a good time to build houses? This city is like an iron pot. We are safe inside it like meat in a pot.*' 4Therefore, son of man, prophesy against them loudly and clearly."

5Then the Spirit of the LORD came upon me, and he told me to say, "This is what the LORD says to the

Ez 10:5 Hebrew *El-Shaddai.* **Ez 10:14** Hebrew *the face of a cherub;* compare 1:10. **Ez 11:3** Hebrew *This city is the pot, and we are the meat.*

Ezek 10:1ff Ezekiel 8–11 depicts God's glory departing from the Temple. Ezekiel saw the glory of the Lord over the north gate (Ezek 8:3-4). It then moved to the entrance (Ezek 9:3), then the south end of the Temple (Ezek 10:3-4), the east gate (Ezek 10:18-19; 11:1), and finally the mountain east of the Temple (Ezek 11:23), probably the Mount of Olives. Because of the nation's sins, God's glory had departed.

Ezek 10:2 God's perfect holiness demands judgment for sin. The cherubim are mighty angels. The burning coals scattered over the city represent the purging of sin. For Jerusalem, this meant the destruction of all the people who blatantly sinned and refused to repent. Shortly after this prophecy, the Babylonians destroyed Jerusalem by fire (2 Kgs 25:9; 2 Chr 36:19).

Ezek 10:18 God's glory departed from the Temple and was never completely present again until Christ himself visited it in New Testament times. God's holiness required that he leave the Temple because the people had so defiled it. God had to completely destroy what people had perverted in order for true worship to be revived. We must commit ourselves, our families, our churches, and our nation to follow God faithfully so that we never have to experience God's abandoning us.

Ezek 11:1-4 God had abandoned his altar and Temple (Ezek 9–11); here his judgment was complete as his glory stopped above the mountain east of the city (Ezek 11:23). The city gate was where merchants and politicians conducted business, so the 25 men may have represented the nation's rulers. Because of their leadership positions, they were responsible for leading the people astray. They had wrongly said that they were secure from another attack by the Babylonians. "This city is like an iron pot. We are safe inside it like meat in a pot" means they believed that they were the elite, the influential, the ones who would be protected from all harm. Without God, however, our situation is always precarious.

Ezek 11:5 God knew everything about the Israelites, even their thoughts. He also knows everything about us, even the sins we try to hide. Instead of worrying about people noticing how we look or what we do, we should care about what God thinks, for he sees everything. Trying to hide our thoughts and actions from God is futile. "Secret" sins are never secret from God. The only effective way to deal with our sins is to confess them and ask God to help us overcome them.

people of Israel: I know what you are saying, for I know every thought that comes into your minds. 6You have murdered many in this city and filled its streets with the dead.

7"Therefore, this is what the Sovereign LORD says: This city is an iron pot all right, but the pieces of meat are the victims of your injustice. As for you, I will soon drag you from this pot. 8I will bring on you the sword of war you so greatly fear, says the Sovereign LORD. 9I will drive you out of Jerusalem and hand you over to foreigners, who will carry out my judgments against you. 10You will be slaughtered all the way to the borders of Israel. I will execute judgment on you, and you will know that I am the LORD. 11No, this city will not be an iron pot for you, and you will not be like meat safe inside it. I will judge you even to the borders of Israel, 12and you will know that I am the LORD. For you have refused to obey my decrees and regulations; instead, you have copied the standards of the nations around you."

13While I was still prophesying, Pelatiah son of Benaiah suddenly died. Then I fell face down on the ground and cried out, "O Sovereign LORD, are you going to kill everyone in Israel?"

Hope for Exiled Israel

EZEKIEL 11:14-21

Then this message came to me from the LORD: 15"Son of man, the people still left in Jerusalem are talking about you and your relatives and all the people of Israel who are in exile. They are saying, 'Those people are far away from the LORD, so now he has given their land to us!'

16"Therefore, tell the exiles, 'This is what the Sovereign LORD says: Although I have scattered you in the countries of the world, I will be a sanctuary to you during your time in exile. 17I, the Sovereign LORD, will gather you back from the nations where you have been scattered, and I will give you the land of Israel once again.'

18"When the people return to their homeland, they will remove every trace of their vile images and detestable idols. 19And I will give them singleness of heart and put a new spirit within them. I will take away their stony, stubborn heart and give them a tender, responsive heart,* 20so they will obey my decrees and regulations. Then they will truly be my people, and I will be their God. 21But as for those who long for vile images and detestable idols, I will repay them fully for their sins. I, the Sovereign LORD, have spoken!"

The LORD's Glory Leaves Jerusalem

EZEKIEL 11:22-25

Then the cherubim lifted their wings and rose into the air with their wheels beside them, and the glory of the God of Israel hovered above them. 23Then the glory of the LORD went up from the city and stopped above the mountain to the east.

24Afterward the Spirit of God carried me back again to Babylonia,* to the people in exile there. And so ended the vision of my visit to Jerusalem. 25And I told the exiles everything the LORD had shown me.

Ez 11:19 Hebrew *a heart of flesh.* **Ez 11:24** Or *Chaldea.*

Ezek 11:12 From the time they entered the Promised Land, the Israelites were warned not to copy the customs and religious practices of other nations. Disobeying this command and following pagan customs instead of God's laws always got them into trouble. Today, believers are still tempted to conform to the ways of the world. But we must get our standards of right and wrong from God, not from the popular trends of society.

Ezek 11:14ff God promised the exiles in Babylonia that he would continue to be with them even though they were not in Jerusalem. This was a major concern to the Jews because they believed that God was present primarily in the Temple. But God assured them that he would continue to be their God regardless of where they were. In the midst of Ezekiel's burning message of judgment stands a cool oasis—God's promise to restore the faithful few to their homeland. God's arms are now open to receive those who will repent of their sins.

Ezek 11:15-21 God's messages through Ezekiel are full of irony. Here God says that the Jews in captivity are the faithful ones, and those in Jerusalem are the sinful and wicked ones. This was the opposite of the people's perception. Appearances can be deceiving. God will evaluate your life by your faith and obedience, not by your apparent earthly success. Furthermore, we should not judge others by outward appearances.

Ezek 11:16 God was a sanctuary for the righteous remnant. Idolatrous people, even though they worshiped in the Jerusalem Temple (Ezek 11:15), would find no true sanctuary; but the faithful exiles, though they were far from home, would be protected by God. Likewise, our external circumstances do not truly indicate our standing with God. Those who appear safe and secure may be far from him, while those going through difficult times may be safely under God's protection. We can depend on God to keep us safe if we pledge ourselves to his care.

Ezek 11:18-19 "Singleness of heart" indicates a unanimous singleness of purpose. No longer will God's people seek many gods; they will be content with God. Their stubborn hearts of stone will be radically transplanted with tender, responsive hearts (see Jer 32:39; Ezek 18:31; 36:26). This new life can only be the work of the Holy Spirit. It is God's work, but we must recognize and turn from our sin. When we do, God will give us new motives, new guidelines, and new purpose. Have you received your new heart?

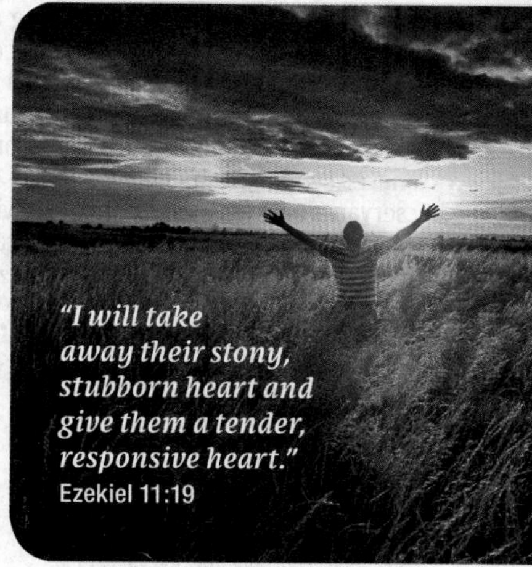
"I will take
away their stony,
stubborn heart and
give them a tender,
responsive heart."
Ezekiel 11:19

Ezek 11:23 God's glory left Jerusalem and stopped above a mountain on the east side of the city—almost certainly the Mount of Olives. Ezekiel 43:1-4 implies that God will return the same way he left, when he comes back to earth to set up his perfect Kingdom.

Signs of the Coming Exile

EZEKIEL 12:1-20

Again a message came to me from the LORD: 2"Son of man, you live among rebels who have eyes but refuse to see. They have ears but refuse to hear. For they are a rebellious people.

3"So now, son of man, pretend you are being sent into exile. Pack the few items an exile could carry, and leave your home to go somewhere else. Do this right in front of the people so they can see you. For perhaps they will pay attention to this, even though they are such rebels. 4Bring your baggage outside during the day so they can watch you. Then in the evening, as they are watching, leave your house as captives do when they begin a long march to distant lands. 5Dig a hole through the wall while they are watching and go out through it. 6As they watch, lift your pack to your shoulders and walk away into the night. Cover your face so you cannot see the land you are leaving. For I have made you a sign for the people of Israel."

7So I did as I was told. In broad daylight I brought my pack outside, filled with the things I might carry into exile. Then in the evening while the people looked on, I dug through the wall with my hands and went out into the night with my pack on my shoulder.

8The next morning this message came to me from the LORD: 9"Son of man, these rebels, the people of Israel, have asked you what all this means. 10Say to them, 'This is what the Sovereign LORD says: These actions contain a message for King Zedekiah in Jerusalem* and for all the people of Israel.' 11Explain that your actions are a sign to show what will soon happen to them, for they will be driven into exile as captives.

12"Even Zedekiah will leave Jerusalem at night through a hole in the wall, taking only what he can carry with him. He will cover his face, and his eyes will not see the land he is leaving. 13Then I will throw my net over him and capture him in my snare. I will bring him to Babylon, the land of the Babylonians,* though he will never see it, and he will die there. 14I will scatter his servants and warriors to the four winds and send the sword after them. 15And when I scatter them among the nations, they will know that I am the LORD. 16But I will spare a few of them from death by war, famine, or disease, so they can confess all their detestable sins to their captors. Then they will know that I am the LORD."

17Then this message came to me from the LORD: 18"Son of man, tremble as you eat your food. Shake with fear as you drink your water. 19Tell the people, 'This is what the Sovereign LORD says concerning those living in Israel and Jerusalem: They will eat their food with trembling and sip their water in despair, for their land will be stripped bare because of their violence. 20The cities will be destroyed and the farmland made desolate. Then you will know that I am the LORD.'"

A New Proverb for Israel

EZEKIEL 12:21-28

Again a message came to me from the LORD: 22"Son of man, you've heard that proverb they quote in Israel: 'Time passes, and prophecies come to nothing.' 23Tell the people, 'This is what the Sovereign LORD says: I will put an end to this proverb, and you will soon stop quoting it.' Now give them this new proverb to replace the old one: 'The time has come for every prophecy to be fulfilled!'

24"There will be no more false visions and flattering predictions in Israel. 25For I am the LORD! If I say it, it will happen. There will be no more delays, you rebels of Israel. I will fulfill my threat of destruction in your own lifetime. I, the Sovereign LORD, have spoken!"

26Then this message came to me from the LORD: 27"Son of man, the people of Israel are saying, 'He's talking about the distant future. His visions won't come true for a long, long time.' 28Therefore, tell them, 'This is what the Sovereign LORD says: No more delay! I will now do everything I have threatened. I, the Sovereign LORD, have spoken!'"

Judgment against False Prophets

EZEKIEL 13:1-16

Then this message came to me from the LORD: 2"Son of man, prophesy against the false prophets of Israel who are inventing their own prophecies. Say to

Ez 12:10 Hebrew *the prince in Jerusalem;* similarly in 12:12. **Ez 12:13** Or *Chaldeans.*

Ezek 12:1ff Ezekiel played the role of a captive being led away to exile, portraying what was about to happen to King Zedekiah and the people remaining in Jerusalem. The exiles knew exactly what Ezekiel was doing because only six years earlier they had made similar preparations as they left Jerusalem for Babylonia. This was to show the people that they should not trust the king or the capital city to save them from the Babylonian army—only God could do that. And the exiles who hoped for an early return from exile would be disappointed. Ezekiel's graphic demonstration was proven correct to the last detail. But when he warned them, many refused to listen.

Ezek 12:10-12 Zedekiah, Judah's last king (597–586 B.C.), was reigning in Jerusalem when Ezekiel gave these messages from God. Ezekiel showed the people what would happen to Zedekiah. Jerusalem would be attacked again, and Zedekiah would join the exiles already in Babylon. Zedekiah would be unable to see because Nebuchadnezzar would have his eyes gouged out (2 Kgs 25:3-7; Jer 52:10-11).

Ezek 12:21-28 These two short messages were warnings that God's words would come true—soon! Less than six years later, Jerusalem would be destroyed. Yet the people were skeptical. Unbelief and false security led them to believe it would never happen. The apostle Peter dealt with this problem in the church (2 Pet 3:9). It is dangerous to say Christ will never return or to regard his coming as so far in the future as to be irrelevant today. All that God says is sure to happen. Don't dare assume that you have plenty of time to get right with God.

Ezek 13:1ff This warning was directed against false prophets, whose messages were not from God but were lies intended to win popularity by saying whatever made the people happy. False prophets did not care about the truth as Ezekiel did. They lulled people into a false sense of security, making Ezekiel's job even more difficult. Beware of

them, 'Listen to the word of the LORD. [3]This is what the Sovereign LORD says: What sorrow awaits the false prophets who are following their own imaginations and have seen nothing at all!'

[4]"O people of Israel, these prophets of yours are like jackals digging in the ruins. [5]They have done nothing to repair the breaks in the walls around the nation. They have not helped it to stand firm in battle on the day of the LORD. [6]Instead, they have told lies and made false predictions. They say, 'This message is from the LORD,' even though the LORD never sent them. And yet they expect him to fulfill their prophecies! [7]Can your visions be anything but false if you claim, 'This message is from the LORD,' when I have not even spoken to you?

[8]"Therefore, this is what the Sovereign LORD says: Because what you say is false and your visions are a lie, I will stand against you, says the Sovereign LORD. [9]I will raise my fist against all the prophets who see false visions and make lying predictions, and they will be banished from the community of Israel. I will blot their names from Israel's record books, and they will never again set foot in their own land. Then you will know that I am the Sovereign LORD.

[10]"This will happen because these evil prophets deceive my people by saying, 'All is peaceful' when there is no peace at all! It's as if the people have built a flimsy wall, and these prophets are trying to reinforce it by covering it with whitewash! [11]Tell these whitewashers that their wall will soon fall down. A heavy rainstorm will undermine it; great hailstones and mighty winds will knock it down. [12]And when the wall falls, the people will cry out, 'What happened to your whitewash?'

[13]"Therefore, this is what the Sovereign LORD says: I will sweep away your whitewashed wall with a storm of indignation, with a great flood of anger, and with hailstones of fury. [14]I will break down your wall right to its foundation, and when it falls, it will crush you. Then you will know that I am the LORD. [15]At last my anger against the wall and those who covered it with whitewash will be satisfied. Then I will say to you: 'The wall and those who whitewashed it are both gone. [16]They were lying prophets who claimed peace would come to Jerusalem when there was no peace. I, the Sovereign LORD, have spoken!'

Judgment against False Women Prophets

EZEKIEL 13:17-23

"Now, son of man, speak out against the women who prophesy from their own imaginations. [18]This is what the Sovereign LORD says: What sorrow awaits you women who are ensnaring the souls of my people, young and old alike. You tie magic charms on their wrists and furnish them with magic veils. Do you think you can trap others without bringing destruction on yourselves? [19]You bring shame on me among my people for a few handfuls of barley or a piece of bread. By lying to my people who love to listen to lies, you kill those who should not die, and you promise life to those who should not live.

[20]"This is what the Sovereign LORD says: I am against all your magic charms, which you use to ensnare my people like birds. I will tear them from your arms, setting my people free like birds set free from a cage. [21]I will tear off the magic veils and save my people from your grasp. They will no longer be your victims. Then you will know that I am the LORD. [22]You have discouraged the righteous with your lies, but I didn't want them to be sad. And you have encouraged the wicked by promising them life, even though they continue in their sins. [23]Because of all this, you will no longer talk of seeing visions that you never saw, nor will you make predictions. For I will rescue my people from your grasp. Then you will know that I am the LORD."

The Idolatry of Israel's Leaders

EZEKIEL 14:1-11

Then some of the leaders of Israel visited me, and while they were sitting with me, [2]this message came to me from the LORD: [3]"Son of man, these leaders have set

---

people who bend the truth in their quest for popularity and power.

Ezek 13:2-3 The false prophets had a large following because they comforted the people and approved of their sinful actions. Lies are often attractive, and liars may have large followings. Today, for example, some spiritual leaders assure us that God promises his followers health and material success. This is comforting, but is it true? God's own Son did not have an easy life on earth. Make sure the messages you believe are consistent with what God teaches in his Word.

Ezek 13:10-12 These false prophets covered their lies (a "flimsy wall") with "whitewash"—a pleasing front. Such superficiality can't hold up under God's scrutiny.

Ezek 13:17 In the Bible, the gift of prophecy was given to women as well as men. Miriam (Exod 15:20), Deborah (Judg 4:4), and Huldah (2 Kgs 22:14) were prophets. But the women mentioned here are more like the medium of 1 Samuel 28:7, and they are condemned for discouraging the righteous (Ezek 13:22).

Ezek 13:18 These magic charms and veils were used in witchcraft practices as good luck charms, but they were used to ensnare the people in idolatry.

Ezek 14:3 God condemned the leaders for setting up idols in their hearts and then daring to come to God's prophet for advice. On the outside, they appeared to worship God, making regular visits to the Temple to offer sacrifices. But they were not sincere. It is easy for us to criticize the Israelites for worshiping idols when they so clearly needed God instead. But we have idols in our hearts when we pursue reputation, acceptance, wealth, or sensual pleasure with the intensity and commitment that should be reserved for serving God.

Ezek 14:3-5 For Hebrew writers, important functions of life were assigned to different physical organs. The heart was considered the core of a person's intellect and spirit. Because all people have someone or something as the object of their heart's devotion, they have the potential for idolatry within them. God wants to recapture the hearts of his people. We must never let anything captivate our allegiance or imagination in such a way that it replaces or weakens our devotion to God.

▶ **EZEKIEL 14:1-11** *(cont.)*

up idols* in their hearts. They have embraced things that will make them fall into sin. Why should I listen to their requests? 4Tell them, 'This is what the Sovereign LORD says: The people of Israel have set up idols in their hearts and fallen into sin, and then they go to a prophet asking for a message. So I, the LORD, will give them the kind of answer their great idolatry deserves. 5I will do this to capture the minds and hearts of all my people who have turned from me to worship their detestable idols.'

6"Therefore, tell the people of Israel, 'This is what the Sovereign LORD says: Repent and turn away from your idols, and stop all your detestable sins. 7I, the LORD, will answer all those, both Israelites and foreigners, who reject me and set up idols in their hearts and so fall into sin, and who then come to a prophet asking for my advice. 8I will turn against such people and make a terrible example of them, eliminating them from among my people. Then you will know that I am the LORD.

9"'And if a prophet is deceived into giving a message, it is because I, the LORD, have deceived that prophet. I will lift my fist against such prophets and cut them off from the community of Israel. 10False prophets and those who seek their guidance will all be punished for their sins. 11In this way, the people of Israel will learn not to stray from me, polluting themselves with sin. They will be my people, and I will be their God. I, the Sovereign LORD, have spoken!'"

The Certainty of the LORD's Judgment

EZEKIEL 14:12-23

Then this message came to me from the LORD: 13"Son of man, suppose the people of a country were to sin against me, and I lifted my fist to crush them, cutting off their food supply and sending a famine to destroy both people and animals. 14Even if Noah, Daniel, and Job were there, their righteousness would save no one but themselves, says the Sovereign LORD.

15"Or suppose I were to send wild animals to invade the country, kill the people, and make the land too desolate and dangerous to pass through. 16As surely as I live, says the Sovereign LORD, even if those three men were there, they wouldn't be able to save their own sons or daughters. They alone would be saved, but the land would be made desolate.

17"Or suppose I were to bring war against the land, and I sent enemy armies to destroy both people and animals. 18As surely as I live, says the Sovereign LORD, even if those three men were there, they wouldn't be able to save their own sons or daughters. They alone would be saved.

19"Or suppose I were to pour out my fury by sending an epidemic into the land, and the disease killed people and animals alike. 20As surely as I live, says the Sovereign LORD, even if Noah, Daniel, and Job were there, they wouldn't be able to save their own sons or daughters. They alone would be saved by their righteousness.

21"Now this is what the Sovereign LORD says: How terrible it will be when all four of these dreadful punishments fall upon Jerusalem—war, famine, wild animals, and disease—destroying all her people and animals. 22Yet there will be survivors, and they will come here to join you as exiles in Babylon. You will see with your own eyes how wicked they are, and then you will feel better about what I have done to Jerusalem. 23When you meet them and see their behavior, you will understand that these things are not being done to Israel without cause. I, the Sovereign LORD, have spoken!"

Jerusalem—a Useless Vine

EZEKIEL 15:1-8

Then this message came to me from the LORD: 2"Son of man, how does a grapevine compare to a tree? Is a vine's wood as useful as the wood of a tree? 3Can its wood be used for making things, like pegs to hang up pots and pans? 4No, it can only be used for fuel, and even as fuel, it burns too quickly. 5Vines are useless both before and after being put into the fire!

6"And this is what the Sovereign LORD says: The people of Jerusalem are like grapevines growing among the trees of the forest. Since they are useless, I have thrown them on the fire to be burned. 7And I will see to it that if they escape from one fire, they will fall into another. When I turn against them, you will know that I am the LORD. 8And I will make the land desolate because my people have been unfaithful to me. I, the Sovereign LORD, have spoken!"

Ez 14:3 The Hebrew term (literally *round things*) probably alludes to dung; also in 14:4, 5, 6, 7.

Ezek 14:6-11 The people of Judah, although eager to accept the messages of false prophets, considered the presence of a few God-fearing men in the nation an insurance policy against disaster. In a pinch, they could always ask God's prophets for advice. We must remember that the relationship our pastors, families, or friends have with God will not protect us from the consequences of our own sins. Establishing a relationship with God is each person's responsibility. Is your faith personal and real, or are you resting in what others have done?

Ezek 14:14-19 Noah, Daniel, and Job were great men in Israel's history, renowned for their relationship with God and for their wisdom (see Gen 6:8-9; Dan 2:47-48; Job 1:1). Daniel had been taken into captivity during Babylon's first invasion of Judah in 605 B.C., eight years before Ezekiel was taken captive. At the time of Ezekiel's message, Daniel occupied a high government position in Babylon. But even these great men of God could not have saved the people of Judah because God had already passed judgment on the nation's pervasive evil.

Ezek 15:1ff The messages given to Ezekiel (Ezek 15–17) provided further evidence that God was going to destroy Jerusalem. The first message was about a vine, useless at first and even more useless after being burned. The people of Jerusalem were useless to God because of their idol worship, and so they would be destroyed and their cities burned. Isaiah also compared the nation of Israel to a vineyard (see Isa 5:1-7). Have you become apathetic and unfruitful to God? How can you begin fulfilling his plan for you?

Jerusalem—an Unfaithful Wife

EZEKIEL 16:1-34

Then another message came to me from the LORD: 2"Son of man, confront Jerusalem with her detestable sins. 3Give her this message from the Sovereign LORD: You are nothing but a Canaanite! Your father was an Amorite and your mother a Hittite. 4On the day you were born, no one cared about you. Your umbilical cord was not cut, and you were never washed, rubbed with salt, and wrapped in cloth. 5No one had the slightest interest in you; no one pitied you or cared for you. On the day you were born, you were unwanted, dumped in a field and left to die.

6"But I came by and saw you there, helplessly kicking about in your own blood. As you lay there, I said, 'Live!' 7And I helped you to thrive like a plant in the field. You grew up and became a beautiful jewel. Your breasts became full, and your body hair grew, but you were still naked. 8And when I passed by again, I saw that you were old enough for love. So I wrapped my cloak around you to cover your nakedness and declared my marriage vows. I made a covenant with you, says the Sovereign LORD, and you became mine.

9"Then I bathed you and washed off your blood, and I rubbed fragrant oils into your skin. 10I gave you expensive clothing of fine linen and silk, beautifully embroidered, and sandals made of fine goatskin leather. 11I gave you lovely jewelry, bracelets, beautiful necklaces, 12a ring for your nose, earrings for your ears, and a lovely crown for your head. 13And so you were adorned with gold and silver. Your clothes were made of fine linen and were beautifully embroidered. You ate the finest foods—choice flour, honey, and olive oil—and became more beautiful than ever. You looked like a queen, and so you were! 14Your fame soon spread throughout the world because of your beauty. I dressed you in my splendor and perfected your beauty, says the Sovereign LORD.

15"But you thought your fame and beauty were your own. So you gave yourself as a prostitute to every man who came along. Your beauty was theirs for the asking. 16You used the lovely things I gave you to make shrines for idols, where you played the prostitute. Unbelievable! How could such a thing ever happen? 17You took the very jewels and gold and silver ornaments I had given you and made statues of men and worshiped them. This is adultery against me! 18You used the beautifully embroidered clothes I gave you to dress your idols. Then you used my special oil and my incense to worship them. 19Imagine it! You set before them as a sacrifice the choice flour, olive oil, and honey I had given you, says the Sovereign LORD.

20"Then you took your sons and daughters—the children you had borne to me—and sacrificed them to your gods. Was your prostitution not enough? 21Must you also slaughter my children by sacrificing them to idols? 22In all your years of adultery and detestable sin, you have not once remembered the days long ago when you lay naked in a field, kicking about in your own blood.

23"What sorrow awaits you, says the Sovereign LORD. In addition to all your other wickedness, 24you built a pagan shrine and put altars to idols in every town square. 25On every street corner you defiled your beauty, offering your body to every passerby in an endless stream of prostitution. 26Then you added lustful Egypt to your lovers, provoking my anger with your increasing promiscuity. 27That is why I struck you with my fist and reduced your boundaries. I handed you over to your enemies, the Philistines, and even they were shocked by your lewd conduct. 28You have prostituted yourself with the Assyrians, too. It seems you can never find enough new lovers! And after your prostitution there, you still were not satisfied. 29You added to your lovers by embracing Babylonia,* the land of merchants, but you still weren't satisfied.

30"What a sick heart you have, says the Sovereign LORD, to do such things as these, acting like a shameless prostitute. 31You build your pagan shrines on every street corner and your altars to idols in every square. In fact, you have been worse than a prostitute, so eager for sin that you have not even demanded

Ez 16:29 Or *Chaldea*.

Ezek 16:1ff This message reminded Jerusalem of its former despised status among the Canaanite nations. Using the imagery of a young baby growing to mature womanhood, God reminded Jerusalem that he raised her from a lowly state to great glory as his bride. Then she betrayed God's trust and prostituted herself by seeking alliances with pagan nations and adopting their customs. If we push God aside for anything, even education, family, career, or pleasure, we are abandoning him in the same way.

Ezek 16:3 Canaan was the name of the territory taken over by the children of Israel and Canaanites were the people who lived there. The Bible often uses this name to refer to all the corrupt pagan nations of the region. The Amorites and Hittites, two Canaanite peoples, were known for their wickedness. But here God implies that his people are no better than the Canaanites.

Ezek 16:15 God cared for and loved Judah, only to have it turn away to other nations and their false gods. The nation had grown to maturity and become famous, but the people forgot who had given them their life (Ezek 16:22). This is a picture of spiritual adultery (called apostasy—turning from the one true God). As you become wise and more mature, don't turn away from the one who truly loves you.

Ezek 16:20-21 The Canaanites practiced child sacrifice long before Israel invaded their land, but God strictly forbid it (Lev 20:1-3). By Ezekiel's time, the people were openly sacrificing their own children (2 Kgs 16:3; 21:6). Jeremiah confirmed that this was a common practice (Jer 7:31; 32:35). Because of such vile acts among the people and priesthood, the Temple became unfit for God to inhabit. When God left the Temple, he was no longer Judah's guide and protector.

Ezek 16:27 The conduct of the Jews was so disgusting that even those who worshiped other gods, including their great enemy the Philistines, would have been ashamed to behave that way. The Jews outdid them in doing evil.

▸ **EZEKIEL 16:1-34** ***(cont.)***

payment. 32Yes, you are an adulterous wife who takes in strangers instead of her own husband. 33Prostitutes charge for their services—but not you! You give gifts to your lovers, bribing them to come and have sex with you. 34So you are the opposite of other prostitutes. You pay your lovers instead of their paying you!

Judgment on Jerusalem's Prostitution

EZEKIEL 16:35-63

"Therefore, you prostitute, listen to this message from the LORD! 36This is what the Sovereign LORD says: Because you have poured out your lust and exposed yourself in prostitution to all your lovers, and because you have worshiped detestable idols,* and because you have slaughtered your children as sacrifices to your gods, 37this is what I am going to do. I will gather together all your allies—the lovers with whom you have sinned, both those you loved and those you hated—and I will strip you naked in front of them so they can stare at you. 38I will punish you for your murder and adultery. I will cover you with blood in my jealous fury. 39Then I will give you to these many nations who are your lovers, and they will destroy you. They will knock down your pagan shrines and the altars to your idols. They will strip you and take your beautiful jewels, leaving you stark naked. 40They will band together in a mob to stone you and cut you up with swords. 41They will burn your homes and punish you in front of many women. I will stop your prostitution and end your payments to your many lovers.

42"Then at last my fury against you will be spent, and my jealous anger will subside. I will be calm and will not be angry with you anymore. 43But first, because you have not remembered your youth but have angered me by doing all these evil things, I will fully repay you for all of your sins, says the Sovereign LORD. For you have added lewd acts to all your detestable sins. 44Everyone who makes up proverbs will say of you, 'Like mother, like daughter.' 45For your mother loathed her husband and her children, and so do you. And you are exactly like your sisters, for they despised their husbands and their children. Truly your mother was a Hittite and your father an Amorite.

46"Your older sister was Samaria, who lived with her daughters in the north. Your younger sister was Sodom, who lived with her daughters in the south. 47But you have not merely sinned as they did. You quickly surpassed them in corruption. 48As surely as I live, says the Sovereign LORD, Sodom and her daughters were never as wicked as you and your daughters. 49Sodom's sins were pride, gluttony, and laziness, while the poor and needy suffered outside her door. 50She was proud and committed detestable sins, so I wiped her out, as you have seen.*

51"Even Samaria did not commit half your sins. You have done far more detestable things than your sisters ever did. They seem righteous compared to you. 52Shame on you! Your sins are so terrible that you make your sisters seem righteous, even virtuous.

53"But someday I will restore the fortunes of Sodom and Samaria, and I will restore you, too. 54Then you will be truly ashamed of everything you have done, for your sins make them feel good in comparison. 55Yes, your sisters, Sodom and Samaria, and all their people will be restored, and at that time you also will be restored. 56In your proud days you held Sodom in contempt. 57But now your greater wickedness has been exposed to all the world, and you are the one who is scorned—by Edom* and all her neighbors and by Philistia. 58This is your punishment for all your lewdness and detestable sins, says the LORD.

59"Now this is what the Sovereign LORD says: I will give you what you deserve, for you have taken your solemn vows lightly by breaking your covenant. 60Yet I will remember the covenant I made with you when you were young, and I will establish an everlasting covenant with you. 61Then you will remember with shame all the evil you have done. I will make your sisters, Samaria and Sodom, to be your daughters, even though they are not part of our covenant. 62And I will reaffirm my covenant with you, and you will know that I am the LORD. 63You will remember your sins and cover your mouth in silent shame when I forgive you of all that you have done. I, the Sovereign LORD, have spoken!"

Ez 16:36 The Hebrew term (literally *round things*) probably alludes to dung. **Ez 16:50** As in a few Hebrew manuscripts and Greek version; Masoretic Text reads *as I have seen.* **Ez 16:57** As in many Hebrew manuscripts and Syriac version; Masoretic Text reads *Aram.*

Ezek 16:44-52 The city of Sodom, a symbol of total corruption, was completely destroyed by God for its wickedness (Gen 19:24-25). Samaria, the capital of what had been the northern kingdom (Israel), was despised and rejected by the Jews in Judah. To be called a sister of Samaria and Sodom was bad enough, but to be called more wicked than they were meant that Judah's sins were an unspeakable abomination and that its doom was inevitable. The reason it was considered worse was not necessarily that Judah's sins were worse but that Judah knew better. In that light, we who live in an age when God's message is made clear to us through the Bible are worse than Judah if we continue in sin (see Matt 11:20-24).

Ezek 16:49 It is easy to judge and condemn Sodom, especially for its terrible sexual sins. Ezekiel reminded Judah that Sodom was destroyed because of its pride, laziness, gluttony, and unconcern for the poor and needy. It is easy to be selective in what we consider gross sin. If we do not commit such horrible sins as adultery, homosexuality, stealing, and murder, we may think we are living good enough lives. But what about sins like pride, laziness, gluttony, and indifference to the needy? These sins may not be as shocking to you as the others, but they are also forbidden by God.

Ezek 16:59-63 Although the people had broken their promises and did not deserve anything but punishment, God would not break his promises. If the people turned back to him, he would again forgive them and renew his covenant. This covenant was put into effect when Jesus paid for everyone's sins by his death on the cross (Heb 10:8-10). No one is beyond the reach of God's forgiveness. Although we don't deserve anything but punishment for our sins, God's arms are still

A Story of Two Eagles

EZEKIEL 17:1-10

Then this message came to me from the LORD: [2]"Son of man, give this riddle, and tell this story to the people of Israel. [3]Give them this message from the Sovereign LORD:

"A great eagle with broad wings and long feathers,
covered with many-colored plumage,
came to Lebanon.
He seized the top of a cedar tree
4 and plucked off its highest branch.
He carried it away to a city filled with merchants.
He planted it in a city of traders.
5 He also took a seedling from the land
and planted it in fertile soil.
He placed it beside a broad river,
where it could grow like a willow tree.
6 It took root there and
grew into a low, spreading vine.
Its branches turned up toward the eagle,
and its roots grew down into the ground.
It produced strong branches
and put out shoots.
7 But then another great eagle came
with broad wings and full plumage.
So the vine now sent its roots and branches
toward him for water,
8 even though it was already planted in good soil
and had plenty of water
so it could grow into a splendid vine
and produce rich leaves and luscious fruit.

9 "So now the Sovereign LORD asks:
Will this vine grow and prosper?
No! I will pull it up, roots and all!
I will cut off its fruit
and let its leaves wither and die.
I will pull it up easily
without a strong arm or a large army.
10 But when the vine is transplanted,
will it thrive?
No, it will wither away
when the east wind blows against it.
It will die in the same good soil
where it had grown so well."

Ez 17:21 Or *his fleeing warriors.* The meaning of the Hebrew is uncertain.

The Riddle Explained

EZEKIEL 17:11-24

Then this message came to me from the LORD: [12]"Say
to these rebels of Israel: Don't you understand the
meaning of this riddle of the eagles? The king of
Babylon came to Jerusalem, took away her king and
princes, and brought them to Babylon. [13]He made a
treaty with a member of the royal family and forced
him to take an oath of loyalty. He also exiled Israel's
most influential leaders, [14]so Israel would not become
strong again and revolt. Only by keeping her treaty
with Babylon could Israel survive.
[15]"Nevertheless, this man of Israel's royal family
rebelled against Babylon, sending ambassadors to
Egypt to request a great army and many horses. Can
Israel break her sworn treaties like that and get away
with it? [16]No! For as surely as I live, says the Sovereign
LORD, the king of Israel will die in Babylon, the land of
the king who put him in power and whose treaty he
disregarded and broke. [17]Pharaoh and all his mighty
army will fail to help Israel when the king of Babylon
lays siege to Jerusalem again and destroys many lives.
[18]For the king of Israel disregarded his treaty and
broke it after swearing to obey; therefore, he will not
escape.
[19]"So this is what the Sovereign LORD says: As surely
as I live, I will punish him for breaking my covenant
and disregarding the solemn oath he made in my
name. [20]I will throw my net over him and capture
him in my snare. I will bring him to Babylon and put
him on trial for this treason against me. [21]And all his
best warriors* will be killed in battle, and those who
survive will be scattered to the four winds. Then you
will know that I, the LORD, have spoken.
[22]"This is what the Sovereign LORD says: I will take
a branch from the top of a tall cedar, and I will plant
it on the top of Israel's highest mountain. [23]It will
become a majestic cedar, sending forth its branches
and producing seed. Birds of every sort will nest in
it, finding shelter in the shade of its branches. [24]And
all the trees will know that it is I, the LORD, who cuts
the tall tree down and makes the short tree grow tall.
It is I who makes the green tree wither and gives the
dead tree new life. I, the LORD, have spoken, and I will
do what I said!"

---

outstretched. He will not break his promise to give us salvation and forgiveness if we repent and turn to him.

Ezek 17:1ff The first eagle in this chapter represents King Nebuchadnezzar of Babylon (see Ezek 17:12), who appointed or "planted" Zedekiah as king in Jerusalem. Zedekiah rebelled against this arrangement and tried to ally with Egypt, the second eagle, to battle against Babylon. This took place while Ezekiel, miles away in Babylon, was describing these events (explained in Ezek 17:10-21). Jeremiah, a prophet in Judah, was also warning Zedekiah not to form this alliance (Jer 2:36-37). Although many miles apart, the prophets had the same message because both spoke for God. God still directs his chosen spokespeople to speak his truth all around the world.

Ezek 17:10 This east wind was the hot, dry wind blowing off the desert, a wind that could wither a flourishing crop. The hot wind of Nebuchadnezzar's armies was about to overcome the nation of Judah.

Ezek 17:22-23 Ezekiel's prophecy of judgment ends in hope. When the people put their hope in foreign alliances, they were disappointed. Only God could give them true hope. God said he would plant a branch, the Messiah, whose Kingdom would grow and become a shelter for all who come to him (see Isa 11:1-5). This prophecy was fulfilled at the coming of Jesus Christ.

The Justice of a Righteous God

EZEKIEL 18:1-32

Then another message came to me from the LORD: 2"Why do you quote this proverb concerning the land of Israel: 'The parents have eaten sour grapes, but their children's mouths pucker at the taste'? 3As surely as I live, says the Sovereign LORD, you will not quote this proverb anymore in Israel. 4For all people are mine to judge—both parents and children alike. And this is my rule: The person who sins is the one who will die.

5"Suppose a certain man is righteous and does what is just and right. 6He does not feast in the mountains before Israel's idols* or worship them. He does not commit adultery or have intercourse with a woman during her menstrual period. 7He is a merciful creditor, not keeping the items given as security by poor debtors. He does not rob the poor but instead gives food to the hungry and provides clothes for the needy. 8He grants loans without interest, stays away from injustice, is honest and fair when judging others, 9and faithfully obeys my decrees and regulations. Anyone who does these things is just and will surely live, says the Sovereign LORD.

10"But suppose that man has a son who grows up to be a robber or murderer and refuses to do what is right. 11And that son does all the evil things his father would never do—he worships idols on the mountains, commits adultery, 12oppresses the poor and helpless, steals from debtors by refusing to let them redeem their security, worships idols, commits detestable sins, 13and lends money at excessive interest. Should such a sinful person live? No! He must die and must take full blame.

14"But suppose that sinful son, in turn, has a son who sees his father's wickedness and decides against that kind of life. 15This son refuses to worship idols on the mountains and does not commit adultery. 16He does not exploit the poor, but instead is fair to debtors and does not rob them. He gives food to the hungry and provides clothes for the needy. 17He helps the poor,* does not lend money at interest, and obeys all my regulations and decrees. Such a person will not die because of his father's sins; he will surely live. 18But the father will die for his many sins—for being cruel, robbing people, and doing what was clearly wrong among his people.

19"'What?' you ask. 'Doesn't the child pay for the parent's sins?' No! For if the child does what is just and right and keeps my decrees, that child will surely live. 20The person who sins is the one who will die. The child will not be punished for the parent's sins, and the parent will not be punished for the child's sins. Righteous people will be rewarded for their own righteous behavior, and wicked people will be punished for their own wickedness. 21But if wicked people turn away from all their sins and begin to obey my decrees and do what is just and right, they will surely live and not die. 22All their past sins will be forgotten, and they will live because of the righteous things they have done.

23"Do you think that I like to see wicked people die? says the Sovereign LORD. Of course not! I want them to turn from their wicked ways and live. 24However, if righteous people turn from their righteous behavior and start doing sinful things and act like other sinners, should they be allowed to live? No, of course not! All their righteous acts will be forgotten, and they will die for their sins.

25"Yet you say, 'The Lord isn't doing what's right!' Listen to me, O people of Israel. Am I the one not doing what's right, or is it you? 26When righteous people turn from their righteous behavior and start doing sinful things, they will die for it. Yes, they will die because of their sinful deeds. 27And if wicked people turn from their wickedness, obey the law, and do what is just and right, they will save their lives. 28They will live because they thought it over and decided to turn from their sins. Such people will not die. 29And yet the people of Israel keep saying, 'The Lord isn't doing what's right!' O people of Israel, it is you who are not doing what's right, not I.

Ez 18:6 The Hebrew term (literally *round things*) probably alludes to dung; also in 18:12, 15. **Ez 18:17** Greek version reads *He refuses to do evil.*

Ezek 18:1ff The people of Judah believed they were being punished for the sins of their ancestors, not their own. They thought this way because this was the teaching of the Ten Commandments (Exod 20:5). But in the corporate life of Israel this belief led to fatalism and irresponsibility. So Ezekiel gave God's new policy because the people had misconstrued the old one. God judges each person individually. Although we often suffer from the effects of sins committed by those who came before us, God does not punish us for someone else's sins, and we can't use their mistakes as an excuse for our sins. Each person is accountable to God.

In addition, some people of Judah used the corporate umbrella of God's blessing as an excuse for disobeying God. They thought that because of their righteous ancestors (Ezek 18:5-9), they would live. God told them that they would not; they were the evil children of righteous parents and, as such, would die (Ezek 18:10-13). But anyone who returned to God would live (Ezek 18:14-18).

Ezek 18:8 The law of Moses had rules about charging interest (Exod 22:25; Lev 25:36; Deut 23:19-20) to prevent God's people from taking advantage of the poor among them.

Ezek 18:12 Allowing people to "redeem their security" refers to lenders letting debtors use at night what they had pledged (often a cloak). Without their cloaks, debtors would be cold at night. (See Exod 22:26; Deut 24:10-13 for the giving of this law.)

Ezek 18:23 God is perfect love, but he also dispenses perfect justice. His perfect love causes him to be merciful to those who recognize their sin and turn back to him, but he cannot overlook those who willfully sin. Wicked people die both physically and spiritually. God takes no joy in their deaths; he would prefer that they turn to him and have eternal life. Likewise, we should not rejoice in the misfortunes of nonbelievers. Instead, we should do all in our power to bring them to faith.

Ezek 18:25 A typical childish response to punishment is to say, "That isn't fair!" In reality, God is fair, but we have broken the rules. It is not God who must live up to our ideas of fairness; instead, we must live up to his. Don't spend your time looking for the loopholes in God's law. Instead, live up to God's standards.

30"Therefore, I will judge each of you, O people of Israel, according to your actions, says the Sovereign LORD. Repent, and turn from your sins. Don't let them destroy you! 31Put all your rebellion behind you, and find yourselves a new heart and a new spirit. For why should you die, O people of Israel? 32I don't want you to die, says the Sovereign LORD. Turn back and live!

A Funeral Song for Israel's Kings

EZEKIEL 19:1-14

"Sing this funeral song for the princes of Israel:

2 "What is your mother?
A lioness among lions!
She lay down among the young lions
and reared her cubs.
3 She raised one of her cubs
to become a strong young lion.
He learned to hunt and devour prey,
and he became a man-eater.
4 Then the nations heard about him,
and he was trapped in their pit.
They led him away with hooks
to the land of Egypt.

5 "When the lioness saw
that her hopes for him were gone,
she took another of her cubs
and taught him to be a strong young lion.
6 He prowled among the other lions
and stood out among them in his strength.
He learned to hunt and devour prey,
and he, too, became a man-eater.
7 He demolished fortresses*
and destroyed their towns and cities.
Their farms were desolated,
and their crops were destroyed.
The land and its people trembled in fear
when they heard him roar.
8 Then the armies of the nations attacked him,
surrounding him from every direction.
They threw a net over him
and captured him in their pit.
9 With hooks, they dragged him into a cage
and brought him before the king of Babylon.
They held him in captivity,
so his voice could never again be heard
on the mountains of Israel.

10 "Your mother was like a vine
planted by the water's edge.
It had lush, green foliage
because of the abundant water.
11 Its branches became strong—
strong enough to be a ruler's scepter.
It grew very tall,
towering above all others.
It stood out because of its height
and its many lush branches.
12 But the vine was uprooted in fury
and thrown down to the ground.
The desert wind dried up its fruit
and tore off its strong branches,
so that it withered
and was destroyed by fire.
13 Now the vine is transplanted to the wilderness,
where the ground is hard and dry.
14 A fire has burst out from its branches
and devoured its fruit.
Its remaining limbs are not
strong enough to be a ruler's scepter.

"This is a funeral song, and it will be used in a funeral."

The Rebellion of Israel

EZEKIEL 20:1-26

On August 14,* during the seventh year of King Jehoiachin's captivity, some of the leaders of Israel came
to request a message from the LORD. They sat down
in front of me to wait for his reply. 2Then this message came to me from the LORD: 3"Son of man, tell
the leaders of Israel, 'This is what the Sovereign LORD
says: How dare you come to ask me for a message?
As surely as I live, says the Sovereign LORD, I will tell
you nothing!'
4"Son of man, bring charges against them and

Ez 19:7 As in Greek version; Hebrew reads *He knew widows.* **Ez 20:1** Hebrew *In the fifth month, on the tenth day,* of the ancient Hebrew lunar calendar. This day was August 14, 591 B.C.; also see note on 1:1.

Ezek 18:30-32 Ezekiel's solution to the problem of inherited guilt is for each person to have a changed life. This is God's work in us and not something we can do for ourselves. The Holy Spirit does it (Ps 51:10-12). If we renounce our lives' direction of sin and rebellion and turn to God, he will give us a new direction, a new love, and a new power to change. You can begin by faith, trusting in God's power to change your heart and mind. Then determine to live each day with him in control (Eph 4:22-24).

Ezek 19:1ff Ezekiel used illustrations to communicate many of his messages. With the picture of the lioness and her cubs, he raised the curiosity of his listeners. The lioness symbolized the nation of Judah, and the two cubs were two of its kings. The first cub was King Jehoahaz, who had been taken captive to Egypt in 609 B.C. by Pharaoh Neco (2 Kgs 23:31-33). The second cub was either King Jehoiachin, who had already been taken into captivity in Babylon (2 Kgs 24:8ff), or King Zedekiah, who soon would be (2 Kgs 25:7). This showed that for Judah, there was no hope for a quick return from exile and no escape from the approaching Babylonian armies.

Ezek 19:11-12 Not even the political and military might of Judah's kings could save the nation. Like branches of a vine, they would be cut off and uprooted by "the desert wind"—the powerful Babylonian army.

Ezek 20:1ff Here Ezekiel gives a panoramic view of Israel's history of rebellion. The emphasis is on God's attempts to bring the nation back to himself and on God's mercy on his constantly rebellious and disobedient people. Ezekiel gives the message that the people alone are responsible for the troubles and judgments they have experienced. God will purge out those who persist in rebellion (Ezek 20:38), while he will bring the faithful into the land of Israel. The reason: that "you will know that I am the LORD" (Ezek 20:42).

▸ **EZEKIEL 20:1-26** ***(cont.)***

condemn them. Make them realize how detestable
the sins of their ancestors really were. [5]Give them
this message from the Sovereign LORD: When I chose
Israel—when I revealed myself to the descendants
of Jacob in Egypt—I took a solemn oath that I, the
LORD, would be their God. [6]I took a solemn oath that
day that I would bring them out of Egypt to a land I
had discovered and explored for them—a good land,
a land flowing with milk and honey, the best of all
lands anywhere. [7]Then I said to them, 'Each of you,
get rid of the vile images you are so obsessed with.
Do not defile yourselves with the idols* of Egypt, for
I am the LORD your God.'

[8]"But they rebelled against me and would not listen. They did not get rid of the vile images they were
obsessed with, or forsake the idols of Egypt. Then I
threatened to pour out my fury on them to satisfy my
anger while they were still in Egypt. [9]But I didn't do it,
for I acted to protect the honor of my name. I would
not allow shame to be brought on my name among
the surrounding nations who saw me reveal myself
by bringing the Israelites out of Egypt. [10]So I brought
them out of Egypt and led them into the wilderness.
[11]There I gave them my decrees and regulations so
they could find life by keeping them. [12]And I gave
them my Sabbath days of rest as a sign between them
and me. It was to remind them that I am the LORD, who
had set them apart to be holy.

[13]"But the people of Israel rebelled against me, and
they refused to obey my decrees there in the wilderness. They wouldn't obey my regulations even though
obedience would have given them life. They also violated my Sabbath days. So I threatened to pour out my
fury on them, and I made plans to utterly consume
them in the wilderness. [14]But again I held back in order
to protect the honor of my name before the nations
who had seen my power in bringing Israel out of Egypt.
[15]But I took a solemn oath against them in the wilderness. I swore I would not bring them into the land I
had given them, a land flowing with milk and honey,
the most beautiful place on earth. [16]For they had rejected my regulations, refused to follow my decrees,
and violated my Sabbath days. Their hearts were given
to their idols. [17]Nevertheless, I took pity on them and
held back from destroying them in the wilderness.

[18]"Then I warned their children not to follow in
their parents' footsteps, defiling themselves with their
idols. [19]'I am the LORD your God,' I told them. 'Follow
my decrees, pay attention to my regulations, [20]and
keep my Sabbath days holy, for they are a sign to remind you that I am the LORD your God.'

[21]"But their children, too, rebelled against me. They
refused to keep my decrees and follow my regulations,
even though obedience would have given them life.
And they also violated my Sabbath days. So again I
threatened to pour out my fury on them in the wilderness. [22]Nevertheless, I withdrew my judgment against
them to protect the honor of my name before the nations that had seen my power in bringing them out
of Egypt. [23]But I took a solemn oath against them in
the wilderness. I swore I would scatter them among
all the nations [24]because they did not obey my regulations. They scorned my decrees by violating my Sabbath days and longing for the idols of their ancestors.
[25]I gave them over to worthless decrees and regulations that would not lead to life. [26]I let them pollute
themselves* with the very gifts I had given them, and
I allowed them to give their firstborn children as offerings to their gods—so I might devastate them and
remind them that I alone am the LORD.

Judgment and Restoration

EZEKIEL 20:27-44

"Therefore, son of man, give the people of Israel this
message from the Sovereign LORD: Your ancestors
continued to blaspheme and betray me, [28]for when
I brought them into the land I had promised them,
they offered sacrifices on every high hill and under
every green tree they saw! They roused my fury as they
offered up sacrifices to their gods. They brought their
perfumes and incense and poured out their liquid
offerings to them. [29]I said to them, 'What is this high
place where you are going?' (This kind of pagan shrine
has been called Bamah—'high place'—ever since.)

[30]"Therefore, give the people of Israel this message

Ez 20:7 The Hebrew term (literally *round things*) probably alludes to dung; also in 20:8, 16, 18, 24, 31, 39. **Ez 20:25-26** Or *I gave them worthless decrees and regulations. . . . I polluted them.*

Ezek 20:12-13 The Sabbath, instituted by God at creation, was entrusted to Israel as a sign that God had created and redeemed them (Exod 20:8-11; Deut 5:12-15). This day of rest was a gift from a loving God, not a difficult obligation. But the people repeatedly violated the Sabbath and ignored God (see also Ezek 20:20-21). It was meant to be a reminder that they were God's special people. Today many Christians celebrate the Lord's Day, Sunday, as their Sabbath. Whatever the day, we must be careful to fulfill God's purpose for the Sabbath. He wants us to rest, to refocus, and to remember him.

Ezek 20:23-24 At the very beginning of Israel's history, God clearly warned the people about the consequences of disobedience (Deut 28:15ff). When the people disobeyed, God let them experience those devastating consequences to remind them of the seriousness of their sins. If you choose to live for yourself, apart from God, you may experience similar destructive consequences. Even through such consequences, God may be drawing you to himself. Let your misfortunes bring you to your senses and to the merciful God before it is too late.

Ezek 20:25 These "worthless" decrees and regulations do not refer to any aspect of the laws of Moses—Ezekiel reinforces that law (Ezek 20:11, 13, 21). Evidently the Jews had taken Exodus 13:12; 22:29, the dedication of firstborn animals and children, as a justification for child sacrifice to the Canaanite god Molech. God gave them over to this delusion to get them to acknowledge him, to jar their consciences, and to revitalize their faith (Ezek 20:26).

from the Sovereign LORD: Do you plan to pollute yourselves just as your ancestors did? Do you intend to keep prostituting yourselves by worshiping vile images? [31]For when you offer gifts to them and give your little children to be burned as sacrifices,* you continue to pollute yourselves with idols to this day. Should I allow you to ask for a message from me, O people of Israel? As surely as I live, says the Sovereign LORD, I will tell you nothing.

[32]"You say, 'We want to be like the nations all around us, who serve idols of wood and stone.' But what you have in mind will never happen. [33]As surely as I live, says the Sovereign LORD, I will rule over you with an iron fist in great anger and with awesome power. [34]And in anger I will reach out with my strong hand and powerful arm, and I will bring you back* from the lands where you are scattered. [35]I will bring you into the wilderness of the nations, and there I will judge you face to face. [36]I will judge you there just as I did your ancestors in the wilderness after bringing them out of Egypt, says the Sovereign LORD. [37]I will examine you carefully and hold you to the terms of the covenant. [38]I will purge you of all those who rebel and revolt against me. I will bring them out of the countries where they are in exile, but they will never enter the land of Israel. Then you will know that I am the LORD.

[39]"As for you, O people of Israel, this is what the Sovereign LORD says: Go right ahead and worship your idols, but sooner or later you will obey me and will stop bringing shame on my holy name by worshiping idols. [40]For on my holy mountain, the great mountain of Israel, says the Sovereign LORD, the people of Israel will someday worship me, and I will accept them. There I will require that you bring me all your offerings and choice gifts and sacrifices. [41]When I bring you home from exile, you will be like a pleasing sacrifice to me. And I will display my holiness through you as all the nations watch. [42]Then when I have brought you home to the land I promised with a solemn oath to give to your ancestors, you will know that I am the LORD. [43]You will look back on all the ways you defiled yourselves and will hate yourselves because of the evil you have done. [44]You will know that I am the LORD, O people of Israel, when I have honored my name by treating you mercifully in spite of your wickedness. I, the Sovereign LORD, have spoken!"

Judgment against the Negev

EZEKIEL 20:45-49

[45]*Then this message came to me from the LORD: [46]"Son of man, turn and face the south* and speak out against it; prophesy against the brushlands of the Negev. [47]Tell the southern wilderness, 'This is what the Sovereign LORD says: Hear the word of the LORD! I will set you on fire, and every tree, both green and dry, will be burned. The terrible flames will not be quenched and will scorch everything from south to north. [48]And everyone in the world will see that I, the LORD, have set this fire. It will not be put out.'"

[49]Then I said, "O Sovereign LORD, they are saying of me, 'He only talks in riddles!'"

The LORD's Sword of Judgment

EZEKIEL 21:1-17

[1]*Then this message came to me from the LORD: [2]"Son of man, turn and face Jerusalem and prophesy against Israel and her sanctuaries. [3]Tell her, 'This is what the LORD says: I am your enemy, O Israel, and I am about to unsheath my sword to destroy your people—the righteous and the wicked alike. [4]Yes, I will cut off both the righteous and the wicked! I will draw my sword against everyone in the land from south to north. [5]Everyone in the world will know that I am the LORD. My sword

Ez 20:31 Or *and make your little children pass through the fire.* **Ez 20:34** Greek version reads *I will welcome you.* Compare 2 Cor 6:17. **Ez 20:45** Verses 20:45-49 are numbered 21:1-5 in Hebrew text. **Ez 20:46** Hebrew *toward Teman.* **Ez 21:1** Verses 21:1-32 are numbered 21:6-37 in Hebrew text.

Ezek 20:35-38 When the Israelites disobeyed God by refusing to enter the Promised Land the first time, God chose to purify his people by forcing them to wander in the wilderness until that entire generation died (Num 14:26-35). Here he promised to purge the nation of its rebellious people again as they crossed the vast wilderness from their captivity in Babylon. Only those who faithfully followed God would be able to return to their land. The purpose of this wilderness judgment would be to purge all those who worshiped idols and to restore those faithful to God.

Ezek 20:39 The Israelites were worshiping idols and giving gifts to God at the same time! They did not believe in their God as the one true God; instead, they worshiped him along with the other gods of the land. Perhaps they enjoyed the immoral pleasures of idol worship; or perhaps they didn't want to miss out on the benefits the idols might give them. Often people believe in God and give him gifts of church attendance or service, while still holding on to their idols of money, power, or pleasure, not wanting to miss out on any possible benefits. But God wants all of our life and all of our devotion; devotion to anything else is idol worship. Beware of trying to please God while also pursuing the pleasures of sin. You must choose one or the other.

Ezek 20:45-47 "The south" refers to Jerusalem and Judah. "The southern wilderness" is the region of the Negev, which is compared to a forest about to be destroyed by fire.

Ezek 20:49 Ezekiel was exasperated and discouraged. Many Israelites were complaining that he spoke only in riddles, so they refused to listen. No matter how important our work or how significant our ministry, we will have moments of discouragement. Apparently God did not answer Ezekiel's plea; instead, he gave Ezekiel another message to proclaim. What has been discouraging you? Have you felt like giving up? Instead, continue doing what God has told you to do. He promises to reward the faithful (Mark 13:13). God's cure for discouragement may be another assignment. In serving others, we may find the renewal we need.

Ezek 21:1ff The short message in Ezekiel 20:45-48 introduces the first of three messages about the judgments that would come upon Jerusalem: (1) the sword of the Lord (Ezek 21:1-7); (2) the sharpened sword (Ezek 21:8-17); (3) the sword of Nebuchadnezzar (Ezek 21:18-22). The city would be destroyed because it was defiled. According to Jewish law, defiled objects were to be passed through fire in order to purify them (see Num 31:22-23; Ps 66:10-12; Prov 17:3). God's judgment is designed to purify; destruction is often a necessary part of that process.

▸ **EZEKIEL 21:1-17** ***(cont.)***
is in my hand, and it will not return to its sheath until
its work is finished.'
6"Son of man, groan before the people! Groan before
them with bitter anguish and a broken heart. 7When
they ask why you are groaning, tell them, 'I groan because of the terrifying news I have heard. When it
comes true, the boldest heart will melt with fear; all
strength will disappear. Every spirit will faint; strong
knees will become as weak as water. And the Sovereign
LORD says: It is coming! It's on its way!'"
8Then the LORD said to me, 9"Son of man, give the
people this message from the Lord:

"A sword, a sword
is being sharpened and polished.
10 It is sharpened for terrible slaughter
and polished to flash like lightning!
Now will you laugh?
Those far stronger than you have fallen
beneath its power!*
11 Yes, the sword is now being sharpened and
polished;
it is being prepared for the executioner.
12 "Son of man, cry out and wail;
pound your thighs in anguish,
for that sword will slaughter my people
and their leaders—
everyone will die!
13 It will put them all to the test.
What chance do they have?*
says the Sovereign LORD.

14 "Son of man, prophesy to them
and clap your hands.
Then take the sword and brandish it twice,
even three times,
to symbolize the great massacre,
the great massacre facing them on every side.
15 Let their hearts melt with terror,
for the sword glitters at every gate.
It flashes like lightning
and is polished for slaughter!
16 O sword, slash to the right,
then slash to the left,
wherever you will,
wherever you want.
17 I, too, will clap my hands,
and I will satisfy my fury.
I, the LORD, have spoken!"

Omens for Babylon's King

EZEKIEL 21:18-27

Then this message came to me from the LORD: 19"Son
of man, make a map and trace two routes on it for the
sword of Babylon's king to follow. Put a signpost on the
road that comes out of Babylon where the road forks
into two—20one road going to Ammon and its capital,
Rabbah, and the other to Judah and fortified Jerusalem. 21The king of Babylon now stands at the fork,
uncertain whether to attack Jerusalem or Rabbah. He
calls his magicians to look for omens. They cast lots by
shaking arrows from the quiver. They inspect the livers
of animal sacrifices. 22The omen in his right hand says,
'Jerusalem!' With battering rams his soldiers will go
against the gates, shouting for the kill. They will put
up siege towers and build ramps against the walls.
23The people of Jerusalem will think it is a false omen,
because of their treaty with the Babylonians. But the
king of Babylon will remind the people of their rebellion. Then he will attack and capture them.
24"Therefore, this is what the Sovereign LORD says:
Again and again you remind me of your sin and your
guilt. You don't even try to hide it! In everything you
do, your sins are obvious for all to see. So now the time
of your punishment has come!
25"O you corrupt and wicked prince of Israel, your
final day of reckoning is here! 26This is what the Sovereign LORD says:

"Take off your jeweled crown,
for the old order changes.
Now the lowly will be exalted,
and the mighty will be brought down.
27 Destruction! Destruction!
I will surely destroy the kingdom.
And it will not be restored until the one
appears
who has the right to judge it.
Then I will hand it over to him.

Ez 21:10 The meaning of the Hebrew is uncertain. **Ez 21:13** The meaning of the Hebrew is uncertain.

Ezek 21:12 Pounding the thighs was a gesture of grief.

Ezek 21:18-23 Ammon evidently rebelled against Babylon about the same time as King Zedekiah of Judah. In 589 B.C. the nations of Judah and Ammon were among those who conspired against Babylon (Jer 27:3). Ezekiel gave this message to the exiles who had heard the news and were again filled with hope of returning to their homeland. Ezekiel said that Babylon's king would march his armies into the region to stop the rebellion. Traveling from the north, he would stop at a fork in the road, one way leading to Rabbah, the capital of Ammon, and the other leading to Jerusalem, the capital of Judah. He had to decide which city to destroy. Just as Ezekiel predicted, King Nebuchadnezzar went to Jerusalem and besieged it.

Ezek 21:21 Nebuchadnezzar had two ways to get advice on the future. One was shaking arrows, much like drawing straws, to see which course of action was right; the second was having priests inspect the liver of a sacrificed animal to see if its shape and size would indicate a decision.

Ezek 21:28 The Ammonites and Israelites were usually fighting each other. God told the Israelites not to ally with foreign nations, but Judah and Ammon united against Babylon in 589 B.C. (Jer 27:3). God first judged Judah when Nebuchadnezzar went to Jerusalem (Ezek 21:22); but Ammon would also be judged, not for allying with Judah, but for watching Jerusalem's destruction with insulting delight.

A Message for the Ammonites

EZEKIEL 21:28-32

"And now, son of man, prophesy concerning the Ammonites and their mockery. Give them this message from the Sovereign LORD:

"A sword, a sword
is drawn for your slaughter.
It is polished to destroy,
flashing like lightning!
29 Your prophets have given false visions,
and your fortune-tellers have told lies.
The sword will fall on the necks of the wicked
for whom the day of final reckoning has come.
30 "Now return the sword to its sheath,
for in your own country,
the land of your birth,
I will pass judgment upon you.
31 I will pour out my fury on you
and blow on you with the fire of my anger.
I will hand you over to cruel men
who are skilled in destruction.
32 You will be fuel for the fire,
and your blood will be spilled in your own land.
You will be utterly wiped out,
your memory lost to history,
for I, the LORD, have spoken!"

The Sins of Jerusalem

EZEKIEL 22:1-16

Now this message came to me from the LORD: 2"Son of
man, are you ready to judge Jerusalem? Are you ready
to judge this city of murderers? Publicly denounce
her detestable sins, 3and give her this message from
the Sovereign LORD: O city of murderers, doomed and
damned—city of idols,* filthy and foul—4you are guilty
because of the blood you have shed. You are defiled
because of the idols you have made. Your day of destruction has come! You have reached the end of your
years. I will make you an object of mockery throughout
the world. 5O infamous city, filled with confusion, you
will be mocked by people far and near.
6"Every leader in Israel who lives within your walls is
bent on murder. 7Fathers and mothers are treated with
contempt. Foreigners are forced to pay for protection.
Orphans and widows are wronged and oppressed
among you. 8You despise my holy things and violate
my Sabbath days of rest. 9People accuse others falsely
and send them to their death. You are filled with idol
worshipers and people who do obscene things. 10Men
sleep with their fathers' wives and have intercourse with
women who are menstruating. 11Within your walls live
men who commit adultery with their neighbors' wives,
who defile their daughters-in-law, or who rape their own
sisters. 12There are hired murderers, loan racketeers, and
extortioners everywhere. They never even think of me
and my commands, says the Sovereign LORD.
13"But now I clap my hands in indignation over your
dishonest gain and bloodshed. 14How strong and courageous will you be in my day of reckoning? I, the LORD,
have spoken, and I will do what I said. 15I will scatter you
among the nations and purge you of your wickedness.
16And when I have been dishonored among the nations
because of you,* you will know that I am the LORD."

The LORD's Refining Furnace

EZEKIEL 22:17-22

Then this message came to me from the LORD: 18"Son
of man, the people of Israel are the worthless slag that
remains after silver is smelted. They are the dross that
is left over—a useless mixture of copper, tin, iron, and
lead. 19So tell them, 'This is what the Sovereign LORD
says: Because you are all worthless slag, I will bring you
to my crucible in Jerusalem. 20Just as copper, iron, lead,
and tin are melted down in a furnace, I will melt you
down in the heat of my fury. 21I will gather you together
and blow the fire of my anger upon you, 22and you will
melt like silver in fierce heat. Then you will know that
I, the LORD, have poured out my fury on you.'"

The Sins of Israel's Leaders

EZEKIEL 22:23-31

Again a message came to me from the LORD: 24"Son
of man, give the people of Israel this message: In the
day of my indignation, you will be like a polluted land,
a land without rain. 25Your princes* plot conspiracies
just as lions stalk their prey. They devour innocent
people, seizing treasures and extorting wealth. They
make many widows in the land. 26Your priests have
violated my instructions and defiled my holy things.

Ez 22:3 The Hebrew term (literally *round things*) probably alludes to dung; also in 22:4. **Ez 22:16** Or *when you have been dishonored among the nations.* **Ez 22:25** As in Greek version; Hebrew reads *prophets.*

Ezek 22:1ff Ezekiel 22 explains why Jerusalem's judgment would come (Ezek 22:2-16), how it would come (Ezek 22:17-22), and who would be affected by it (Ezek 22:23-31).

Ezek 22:6-13 The leaders, whom God chose, were responsible for the moral climate of the nation. The same is true today (see Jas 3:1). Unfortunately, many of the sins mentioned here have been committed in recent years by Christian leaders. We must uphold our leaders in prayer, and leaders must seek accountability to help them maintain their moral and spiritual integrity.

Ezek 22:17-22 Precious metals are refined with intense heat to remove the impurities or slag. When heated, the slag rises to the top of the molten metal and is skimmed off and thrown away. The purpose of the invasion of Jerusalem was to refine the people, but the refining process showed that the people, like worthless slag, had nothing good in them.

Ezek 22:26 The priests were supposed to keep God's worship pure and teach the people right living. But the worship of God had become commonplace to them; they ignored the Sabbath, and they refused to teach the people. They no longer carried out their God-given duties (Lev 10:10-11; Ezek 44:23). When doing God's work becomes no more important than any mundane task, we are no longer giving God the reverence he deserves. Instead of bringing God down to our sinful human level, we should live in ways that reflect his holiness.

▸ **EZEKIEL 22:23-31** ***(cont.)***

They make no distinction between what is holy and what is not. And they do not teach my people the difference between what is ceremonially clean and unclean. They disregard my Sabbath days so that I am dishonored among them. 27Your leaders are like wolves who tear apart their victims. They actually destroy people's lives for money! 28And your prophets cover up for them by announcing false visions and making lying predictions. They say, 'My message is from the Sovereign LORD,' when the LORD hasn't spoken a single word to them. 29Even common people oppress the poor, rob the needy, and deprive foreigners of justice.

30"I looked for someone who might rebuild the wall of righteousness that guards the land. I searched for someone to stand in the gap in the wall so I wouldn't have to destroy the land, but I found no one. 31So now I will pour out my fury on them, consuming them with the fire of my anger. I will heap on their heads the full penalty for all their sins. I, the Sovereign LORD, have spoken!"

The Adultery of Two Sisters

EZEKIEL 23:1-21

This message came to me from the LORD: 2"Son of man, once there were two sisters who were daughters of the same mother. 3They became prostitutes in Egypt. Even as young girls, they allowed men to fondle their breasts. 4The older girl was named Oholah, and her sister was Oholibah. I married them, and they bore me sons and daughters. I am speaking of Samaria and Jerusalem, for Oholah is Samaria and Oholibah is Jerusalem.

5"Then Oholah lusted after other lovers instead of me, and she gave her love to the Assyrian officers. 6They were all attractive young men, captains and commanders dressed in handsome blue, charioteers driving their horses. 7And so she prostituted herself with the most desirable men of Assyria, worshiping their idols* and defiling herself. 8For when she left Egypt, she did not leave her spirit of prostitution behind. She was still as lewd as in her youth, when the Egyptians slept with her, fondled her breasts, and used her as a prostitute.

9"And so I handed her over to her Assyrian lovers,

Ez 23:7 The Hebrew term (literally *round things*) probably alludes to dung; also in 23:30, 37, 39, 49.

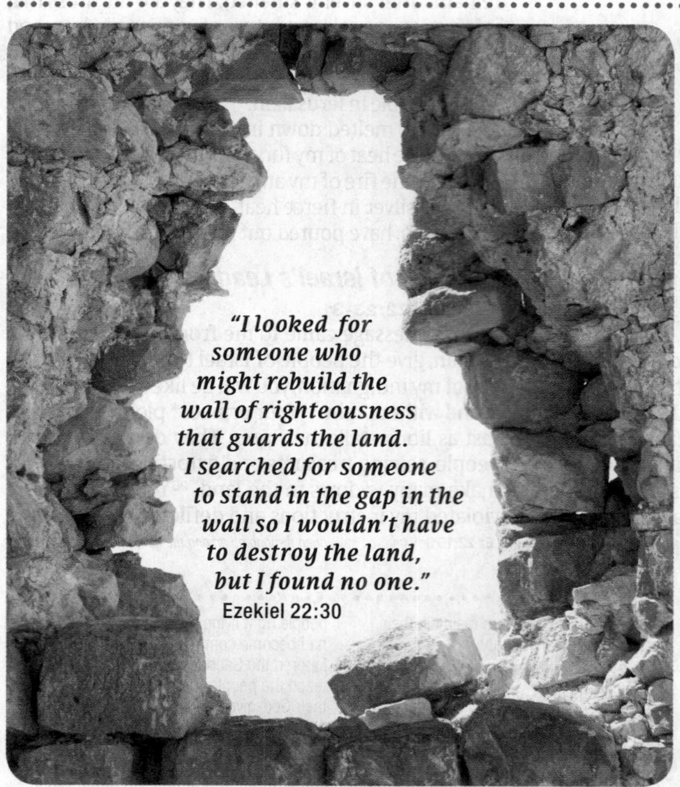
"I looked for someone who might rebuild the wall of righteousness that guards the land. I searched for someone to stand in the gap in the wall so I wouldn't have to destroy the land, but I found no one."
Ezekiel 22:30

Ezek 22:30 The wall spoken of here is not made of stones but of faithful people united in their efforts to resist evil. This wall was in disrepair because there was no one who could lead the people back to God. The feeble attempts to repair the gap—through religious rituals or messages based on opinion rather than God's will—were as worthless as whitewash, only covering the real problems. What the people needed was total spiritual reconstruction! When we give the appearance of loving God without living his way, we are covering up sins that could eventually damage us deeply. Don't use religion as a whitewash; repair your life by applying the principles of God's Word. Then you can join with others to "stand in the gap" and make a difference for God in the world.

Ezek 23:1ff Ezekiel continued his discussion of the reasons for God's judgment by telling a further allegory. He compared the northern and southern kingdoms to two sisters who became prostitutes. The proud citizens of Jerusalem had long scorned their sister city of Samaria, thinking that they were superior. But God called *both* of these cities prostitutes—a shock to the people of Jerusalem, who thought they were righteous. Just as the imagery of this message was shocking and distasteful to the people, so our sins are repugnant to God.

Ezek 23:4-6 Oholah (meaning "her tent"), the northern kingdom of Israel, was lured away from God by the dashing Assyrians. The people of Israel coveted their youth, strength, power, wealth, and pleasure—the same qualities people think will bring happiness today.

whom she desired so much. [10]They stripped her, took away her children as their slaves, and then killed her. After she received her punishment, her reputation was known to every woman in the land.

[11]"Yet even though Oholibah saw what had happened to Oholah, her sister, she followed right in her footsteps. And she was even more depraved, abandoning herself to her lust and prostitution. [12]She fawned over all the Assyrian officers—those captains and commanders in handsome uniforms, those charioteers driving their horses—all of them attractive young men. [13]I saw the way she was going, defiling herself just like her older sister.

[14]"Then she carried her prostitution even further. She fell in love with pictures that were painted on a wall—pictures of Babylonian* military officers, outfitted in striking red uniforms. [15]Handsome belts encircled their waists, and flowing turbans crowned their heads. They were dressed like chariot officers from the land of Babylonia.* [16]When she saw these paintings, she longed to give herself to them, so she sent messengers to Babylonia to invite them to come to her. [17]So they came and committed adultery with her, defiling her in the bed of love. After being defiled, however, she rejected them in disgust.

[18]"In the same way, I became disgusted with Oholibah and rejected her, just as I had rejected her sister, because she flaunted herself before them and gave herself to satisfy their lusts. [19]Yet she turned to even greater prostitution, remembering her youth when she was a prostitute in Egypt. [20]She lusted after lovers with genitals as large as a donkey's and emissions like those of a horse. [21]And so, Oholibah, you relived your former days as a young girl in Egypt, when you first allowed your breasts to be fondled.

The Lord's Judgment of Oholibah

EZEKIEL 23:22-35

"Therefore, Oholibah, this is what the Sovereign Lord says: I will send your lovers against you from every direction—those very nations from which you turned away in disgust. [23]For the Babylonians will come with all the Chaldeans from Pekod and Shoa and Koa. And all the Assyrians will come with them—handsome young captains, commanders, chariot officers, and other high-ranking officers, all riding their horses. [24]They will all come against you from the north* with chariots, wagons, and a great army prepared for attack. They will take up positions on every side, surrounding you with men armed with shields and helmets. And I will hand you over to them for punishment so they can do with you as they please. [25]I will turn my jealous anger against you, and they will deal harshly with you. They will cut off your nose and ears, and any survivors will then be slaughtered by the sword. Your children will be taken away as captives, and everything that is left will be burned. [26]They will strip you of your beautiful clothes and jewels. [27]In this way, I will put a stop to the lewdness and prostitution you brought from Egypt. You will never again cast longing eyes on those things or fondly remember your time in Egypt.

[28]"For this is what the Sovereign Lord says: I will surely hand you over to your enemies, to those you loathe, those you rejected. [29]They will treat you with hatred and rob you of all you own, leaving you stark naked. The shame of your prostitution will be exposed to all the world. [30]You brought all this on yourself by prostituting yourself to other nations, defiling yourself with all their idols. [31]Because you have followed in your sister's footsteps, I will force you to drink the same cup of terror she drank.

[32]"Yes, this is what the Sovereign Lord says:

"You will drink from your sister's cup of terror,
a cup that is large and deep.
It is filled to the brim
with scorn and derision.
[33] Drunkenness and anguish will fill you,
for your cup is filled to the brim with distress and desolation,
the same cup your sister Samaria drank.
[34] You will drain that cup of terror
to the very bottom.
Then you will smash it to pieces
and beat your breast in anguish.
I, the Sovereign Lord, have spoken!

[35]"And because you have forgotten me and turned your back on me, this is what the Sovereign Lord says: You must bear the consequences of all your lewdness and prostitution."

Ez 23:14 Or *Chaldean.* **Ez 23:15** Or *Chaldea;* also in 23:16. **Ez 23:24** As in Greek version; the meaning of the Hebrew is uncertain.

Ezek 23:11ff Oholibah (meaning "my tent is in her") was shown to be worse, because she did not learn from the judgment upon her sister but continued in her lust for the Assyrians and Babylonians. Therefore, her judgment was equally certain. Just as Oholibah was privileged and should have known better, so we are privileged because we know about Christ. We need to be doubly sure that we follow him.

Ezek 23:12 "She fawned over all the Assyrian officers" probably means Judah excessively tried to please Assyria and may refer to Ahaz's paying protection money to Tiglath-pileser III (2 Kgs 16:7-8).

Ezek 23:16 In essence, Hezekiah was giving an invitation to Babylonia when he showed its envoys around (2 Kgs 20:12ff; Isa 39).

Ezek 23:17 At first, Judah made an alliance with Babylonia, but then changed its mind. During the reigns of Jehoiakim and Zedekiah, Judah looked to Egypt for help. Judah's unfaithfulness (its alliances with godless nations) cost it the only real protection it ever had—God.

Ezek 23:22-26 This predicts the last attack on Jerusalem that would destroy the city and bring to Babylonia the third wave of captives in 586 B.C. (2 Kgs 25; Jer 52). The first attack came in 605 B.C., the second in 597 B.C. Pekod, Shoa, and Koa were Babylonian allies.

The LORD's Judgment on Both Sisters

EZEKIEL 23:36-49

The LORD said to me, "Son of man, you must accuse Oholah and Oholibah of all their detestable sins. 37They have committed both adultery and murder—adultery by worshiping idols and murder by burning as sacrifices the children they bore to me. 38Furthermore, they have defiled my Temple and violated my Sabbath day! 39On the very day that they sacrificed their children to their idols, they boldly came into my Temple to worship! They came in and defiled my house.

40"You sisters sent messengers to distant lands to get men. Then when they arrived, you bathed yourselves, painted your eyelids, and put on your finest jewels for them. 41You sat with them on a beautifully embroidered couch and put my incense and my special oil on a table that was spread before you. 42From your room came the sound of many men carousing. They were lustful men and drunkards* from the wilderness, who put bracelets on your wrists and beautiful crowns on your heads. 43Then I said, 'If they really want to have sex with old worn-out prostitutes like these, let them!' 44And that is what they did. They had sex with Oholah and Oholibah, these shameless prostitutes. 45But righteous people will judge these sister cities for what they really are—adulterers and murderers.

46"Now this is what the Sovereign LORD says: Bring an army against them and hand them over to be terrorized and plundered. 47For their enemies will stone them and kill them with swords. They will butcher their sons and daughters and burn their homes. 48In this way, I will put an end to lewdness and idolatry in the land, and my judgment will be a warning to others not to follow their wicked example. 49You will be fully repaid for all your prostitution—your worship of idols. Yes, you will suffer the full penalty. Then you will know that I am the Sovereign LORD."

Ez 23:42 Or *Sabeans.*

10. BABYLON'S FINAL INVASION AND DESTRUCTION OF JERUSALEM

In 586 B.C., Judah's expulsion from the land was completed by Babylon. They sieged Jerusalem, sacked the city, and destroyed the Temple and walls. All but the poorest and weakest people of Judah were either killed or carried off to exile. God's promises of judgment for Judah's sins were fulfilled, but God continued to speak to his people through the prophets and in prayer. Even with his judgment on sin, God is always faithful to his promises.

The Siege of Jerusalem PARALLEL •••

2 KINGS 24:20b–25:2 •••

Zedekiah rebelled against the king of Babylon.

25:1 So on January 15,* during the ninth year of Zedekiah's reign, King Nebuchadnezzar of Babylon led his entire army against Jerusalem. They surrounded the city and built siege ramps against its walls. 2Jerusalem was kept under siege until the eleventh year of King Zedekiah's reign.

JEREMIAH 39:1 •••

In January* of the ninth year of King Zedekiah's reign, King Nebuchadnezzar* came with his army to besiege Jerusalem.

JEREMIAH 52:3b-5 •••

Zedekiah rebelled against the king of Babylon. 4So on January 15,* during the ninth year of Zedekiah's reign, King Nebuchadnezzar* of Babylon led his entire army against Jerusalem. They surrounded the city and built siege ramps against its walls. 5Jerusalem was kept under siege until the eleventh year of King Zedekiah's reign.

The Sign of the Cooking Pot

EZEKIEL 24:1-14

On January 15,* during the ninth year of King Jehoiachin's captivity, this message came to me from the LORD: 2"Son of man, write down today's date, because

2 Kgs 25:1 Hebrew *on the tenth day of the tenth month,* of the ancient Hebrew lunar calendar. A number of events in 2 Kings can be cross-checked with dates in surviving Babylonian records and related accurately to our modern calendar. This day was January 15, 588 B.C. **Jer 39:1a** Hebrew *in the tenth month,* of the ancient Hebrew lunar calendar. A number of events in Jeremiah can be cross-checked with dates in surviving Babylonian records and related accurately to our modern calendar. This event occurred on January 15, 588 B.C.; see 52:4a and the note there. **Jer 39:1b** Hebrew *Nebuchadrezzar,* a variant spelling of Nebuchadnezzar; also in 39:11. **Jer 52:4a** Hebrew *on the tenth day of the tenth month,* of the ancient Hebrew lunar calendar. A number of events in Jeremiah can be cross-checked with dates in surviving Babylonian records and related accurately to our modern calendar. This day was January 15, 588 B.C. **Jer 52:4b** Hebrew *Nebuchadrezzar,* a variant spelling of Nebuchadnezzar; also in 52:12, 28, 29, 30. **Ez 24:1** Hebrew *On the tenth day of the tenth month,* of the ancient Hebrew lunar calendar. This event occurred on January 15, 588 B.C.; also see note on 1:1.

Ezek 23:39 The Israelites went so far as to sacrifice their own children to idols and then to sacrifice to the Lord the same day. This made a mockery of worship. We cannot praise God and willfully sin at the same time. That would be like a person committing adultery and celebrating a wedding anniversary on the same day.

2 Kgs 25:1 Judah was invaded by the Babylonians three times (2 Kgs 24:1, 10; 25:1), just as Israel was invaded by the Assyrians three times. Once again, God demonstrated his mercy in the face of deserved judgment by giving the people repeated opportunities to repent.

Ezek 24:1-14 Ezekiel gave this illustration in 588 B.C., about three years after the first of the previous messages (see Ezek 20:1-2). The people in Judah thought they were the "choice pieces of meat" because they hadn't been taken into captivity in 597 when the Babylonians last invaded the land. Ezekiel used this illustration before (Ezek 11) to show that, although the people thought they were safe and secure inside the cooking pot, this pot would actually be the place of their destruction. He gave this message to the exiles in Babylonia the very day that the Babylonians attacked Jerusalem (Ezek 24:2), beginning a siege that lasted over two years and resulted in the city's destruction. When God's punishment comes, it is relentless.

on this very day the king of Babylon is beginning his
attack against Jerusalem. 3Then give these rebels an
illustration with this message from the Sovereign
LORD:

"Put a pot on the fire,
and pour in some water.
4 Fill it with choice pieces of meat—
the rump and the shoulder
and all the most tender cuts.
5 Use only the best sheep from the flock,
and heap fuel on the fire beneath the pot.
Bring the pot to a boil,
and cook the bones along with the meat.

6 "Now this is what the Sovereign LORD says:
What sorrow awaits Jerusalem,
the city of murderers!
She is a cooking pot
whose corruption can't be cleaned out.
Take the meat out in random order,
for no piece is better than another.
7 For the blood of her murders
is splashed on the rocks.
It isn't even spilled on the ground,
where the dust could cover it!
8 So I will splash her blood on a rock
for all to see,
an expression of my anger
and vengeance against her.

9 "This is what the Sovereign LORD says:
What sorrow awaits Jerusalem,
the city of murderers!
I myself will pile up the fuel beneath her.
10 Yes, heap on the wood!
Let the fire roar to make the pot boil.
Cook the meat with many spices,
and afterward burn the bones.
11 Now set the empty pot on the coals.
Heat it red hot!
Burn away the filth and corruption.
12 But it's hopeless;
the corruption can't be cleaned out.
So throw it into the fire.
13 Your impurity is your lewdness
and the corruption of your idolatry.
I tried to cleanse you,
but you refused.
So now you will remain in your filth
until my fury against you has been satisfied.

14"I, the LORD, have spoken! The time has come, and
I won't hold back. I will not change my mind, and I will
have no pity on you. You will be judged on the basis
of all your wicked actions, says the Sovereign LORD."

The Death of Ezekiel's Wife

EZEKIEL 24:15-27

Then this message came to me from the LORD: 16"Son
of man, with one blow I will take away your dearest
treasure. Yet you must not show any sorrow at her
death. Do not weep; let there be no tears. 17Groan silently, but let there be no wailing at her grave. Do not
uncover your head or take off your sandals. Do not
perform the usual rituals of mourning or accept any
food brought to you by consoling friends."

18So I proclaimed this to the people the next morning, and in the evening my wife died. The next morning I did everything I had been told to do. 19Then the
people asked, "What does all this mean? What are you
trying to tell us?"

20So I said to them, "A message came to me from
the LORD, 21and I was told to give this message to the
people of Israel. This is what the Sovereign LORD says:
I will defile my Temple, the source of your security
and pride, the place your heart delights in. Your sons
and daughters whom you left behind in Judea will
be slaughtered by the sword. 22Then you will do as
Ezekiel has done. You will not mourn in public or
console yourselves by eating the food brought by
friends. 23Your heads will remain covered, and your
sandals will not be taken off. You will not mourn or
weep, but you will waste away because of your sins.
You will mourn privately for all the evil you have done.
24Ezekiel is an example for you; you will do just as he
has done. And when that time comes, you will know
that I am the Sovereign LORD."

25Then the LORD said to me, "Son of man, on the
day I take away their stronghold—their joy and glory,
their heart's desire, their dearest treasure—I will also
take away their sons and daughters. 26And on that day
a survivor from Jerusalem will come to you in Babylon

Ezek 24:6-13 The city of Jerusalem was like a pot so encrusted with sin that it would not come clean. God wanted to cleanse the lives of those who lived in Jerusalem, and he wants to cleanse our lives today. Sometimes he tries to purify us through difficulties and troublesome circumstances. When you face tough times, allow the sin to be burned from your life. Look at your problems as opportunities for your faith to grow. When these times come, unnecessary priorities and diversions are purged away. We can reexamine our lives so that we will do what really counts.

Ezek 24:15-18 God told Ezekiel that his wife would die and that he should not grieve for her. Ezekiel obeyed God fully, even as Hosea did when he was told to marry a prostitute (Hos 1:2-3). In both cases, these unusual events were intended as symbolic acts to illustrate God's relationship with his people. Obeying God can carry a high price, but not obeying God will cost you more—eternal life. We should be wholehearted in our obedience to God as Ezekiel was. We can begin by doing all that God commands us to do, even when we don't feel like it. Are you willing to serve God as completely as Ezekiel did?

Ezek 24:20-24 Ezekiel was not allowed to mourn for his dead wife in order to show his fellow exiles that they were not to mourn publicly over Jerusalem when it was destroyed. Any personal sorrow felt would soon be eclipsed by national sorrow over the horror of the city's total destruction. The individuals would waste away because of their sins, which caused the city's destruction.

▸ **EZEKIEL 24:15-27** ***(cont.)***

and tell you what has happened. 27And when he arrives, your voice will suddenly return so you can talk to
him, and you will be a symbol for these people. Then
they will know that I am the LORD."

Ezekiel's Message for Ammon

EZEKIEL 25:1-7

Then this message came to me from the LORD: 2"Son of
man, turn and face the land of Ammon and prophesy
against its people. 3Give the Ammonites this message
from the Sovereign LORD: Hear the word of the Sovereign LORD! Because you cheered when my Temple
was defiled, mocked Israel in her desolation, and
laughed at Judah as she went away into exile, 4I will
allow nomads from the eastern deserts to overrun
your country. They will set up their camps among you
and pitch their tents on your land. They will harvest
all your fruit and drink the milk from your livestock.
5And I will turn the city of Rabbah into a pasture for
camels, and all the land of the Ammonites into a resting place for sheep and goats. Then you will know that
I am the LORD.

6"This is what the Sovereign LORD says: Because you
clapped and danced and cheered with glee at the destruction of my people, 7I will raise my fist of judgment
against you. I will give you as plunder to many nations.
I will cut you off from being a nation and destroy you
completely. Then you will know that I am the LORD.

Ezekiel's Message for Moab

EZEKIEL 25:8-11

"This is what the Sovereign LORD says: Because the
people of Moab have said that Judah is just like all
the other nations, 9I will open up their eastern flank
and wipe out their glorious frontier towns—Beth-
jeshimoth, Baal-meon, and Kiriathaim. 10And I will
hand Moab over to nomads from the eastern deserts,
just as I handed over Ammon. Yes, the Ammonites
will no longer be counted among the nations. 11In
the same way, I will bring my judgment down on the
Moabites. Then they will know that I am the LORD.

Ezekiel's Message for Edom

EZEKIEL 25:12-14

"This is what the Sovereign LORD says: The people of
Edom have sinned greatly by avenging themselves
against the people of Judah. 13Therefore, says the Sovereign LORD, I will raise my fist of judgment against
Edom. I will wipe out its people and animals with the
sword. I will make a wasteland of everything from Teman to Dedan. 14I will accomplish this by the hand of
my people of Israel. They will carry out my vengeance
with anger, and Edom will know that this vengeance is
from me. I, the Sovereign LORD, have spoken!

Ezekiel's Message for Philistia

EZEKIEL 25:15-17

"This is what the Sovereign LORD says: The people of
Philistia have acted against Judah out of bitter revenge
and long-standing contempt. 16Therefore, this is what
the Sovereign LORD says: I will raise my fist of judgment against the land of the Philistines. I will wipe out
the Kerethites and utterly destroy the people who live
by the sea. 17I will execute terrible vengeance against
them to punish them for what they have done. And
when I have inflicted my revenge, they will know that
I am the LORD."

Jeremiah's Warning for Zedekiah

JEREMIAH 34:1-7

King Nebuchadnezzar of Babylon came with all the
armies from the kingdoms he ruled, and he fought
against Jerusalem and the towns of Judah. At that time
this message came to Jeremiah from the LORD: 2"Go
to King Zedekiah of Judah, and tell him, 'This is what
the LORD, the God of Israel, says: I am about to hand
this city over to the king of Babylon, and he will burn
it down. 3You will not escape his grasp but will be
captured and taken to meet the king of Babylon face
to face. Then you will be exiled to Babylon.

4"'But listen to this promise from the LORD, O Zedekiah, king of Judah. This is what the LORD says: You
will not be killed in war 5but will die peacefully. People
will burn incense in your memory, just as they did for

Ezek 24:27 For some time Ezekiel had not been allowed to speak except when God gave him a message to deliver to the people (Ezek 3:25-27). This restriction would soon end when Jerusalem was destroyed and all Ezekiel's prophecies about Judah and Jerusalem had come true (Ezek 33:21-22).

Ezek 25:1ff The judgments in Ezekiel 25 are not simply vengeful words of Jews against their enemies; they are God's judgments on nations that failed to acknowledge the one true God and fulfill the good purposes God intended for them. The Ammonites were judged because of their joy over the desecration of the Temple (Ezek 25:1-7), the Moabites because they found pleasure in Judah's wickedness (Ezek 25:8-11), the Edomites because of their racial hatred for the Jews (Ezek 25:12-14), and the Philistines because they sought revenge against Judah for defeating them in battle (Ezek 25:15-17).

Ezek 25:5 Rabbah was the capital city of the Ammonites.

Ezek 25:9 These towns were on the northern border of Moab.

Ezek 25:12-14 The Edomites were blood brothers of the Jews, both nations having descended from Isaac (Gen 25:19-26). Edom shared its northern border with Israel, and the two nations were always in conflict. The Edomites hated Israel so much that they rejoiced when Jerusalem, Israel's capital, was destroyed. Teman was in the northern part of Edom; Dedan was in the southern part. Thus, Ezekiel was saying that the entire country would be destroyed.

Ezek 25:16 The Kerethites originated in Crete, from which they take their name. They were either a clan of the Philistines or possibly a separate people who migrated from the Aegean to Palestine about the same time. The Kerethites and Philistines were closely intermixed once they were in Palestine and are often mentioned together.

Jer 34:1ff This chapter describes the fulfillment of many of Jeremiah's predictions. In the book of Jeremiah, many prophecies were both given and quickly fulfilled.

your ancestors, the kings who preceded you. They will mourn for you, crying, "Alas, our master is dead!" This I have decreed, says the LORD.'"

6So Jeremiah the prophet delivered the message to King Zedekiah of Judah. 7At this time the Babylonian army was besieging Jerusalem, Lachish, and Azekah—the only fortified cities of Judah not yet captured.

Freedom for Hebrew Slaves

JEREMIAH 34:8-22

This message came to Jeremiah from the LORD after King Zedekiah made a covenant with the people, proclaiming freedom for the slaves. 9He had ordered all the people to free their Hebrew slaves—both men and women. No one was to keep a fellow Judean in bondage. 10The officials and all the people had obeyed the king's command, 11but later they changed their minds. They took back the men and women they had freed, forcing them to be slaves again.

12So the LORD gave them this message through Jeremiah: 13"This is what the LORD, the God of Israel, says: I made a covenant with your ancestors long ago when I rescued them from their slavery in Egypt. 14I told them that every Hebrew slave must be freed after serving six years. But your ancestors paid no attention to me. 15Recently you repented and did what was right, following my command. You freed your slaves and made a solemn covenant with me in the Temple that bears my name. 16But now you have shrugged off your oath and defiled my name by taking back the men and women you had freed, forcing them to be slaves once again.

17"Therefore, this is what the LORD says: Since you have not obeyed me by setting your countrymen free, I will set you free to be destroyed by war, disease, and famine. You will be an object of horror to all the nations of the earth. 18Because you have broken the terms of our covenant, I will cut you apart just as you cut apart the calf when you walked between its halves to solemnize your vows. 19Yes, I will cut you apart, whether you are officials of Judah or Jerusalem, court officials, priests, or common people—for you have broken your oath. 20I will give you to your enemies, and they will kill you. Your bodies will be food for the vultures and wild animals.

21"I will hand over King Zedekiah of Judah and his officials to the army of the king of Babylon. And although Babylon's king has left Jerusalem for a while, 22I will call the Babylonian armies back again. They will fight against this city and will capture it and burn it down. I will see to it that all the towns of Judah are destroyed, with no one living there."

No Deliverance from Babylon

JEREMIAH 21:1-10

The LORD spoke through Jeremiah when King Zedekiah sent Pashhur son of Malkijah and Zephaniah son of Maaseiah, the priest, to speak with him. They begged Jeremiah, 2"Please speak to the LORD for us and ask him to help us. King Nebuchadnezzar* of

Jer 21:2 Hebrew *Nebuchadrezzar,* a variant spelling of Nebuchadnezzar; also in 21:7.

Jer 34:8-9 Babylon had laid siege to Jerusalem, and the city was about to fall. Zedekiah finally decided to listen to Jeremiah and try to appease God—so he freed the slaves. He thought he could win God's favor with a kind act, but what he needed was a change of heart. The people had been disobeying God's law from the beginning (Exod 21:2-11; Lev 25:39-55; Deut 15:12-18). When the siege was temporarily lifted, the people became bold and returned to their sins (Jer 34:11-17; 37:5, 11).

Jer 34:15-16 The people of Israel had a hard time keeping their promises to God. In the Temple, they would solemnly promise to obey God, but back in their homes and at work they wouldn't do it. God expressed his great displeasure. If you want to please God, make sure you keep your promises. God wants promises kept, not just piously made.

Jer 34:18-20 Cutting a calf in two and walking between the halves was a customary way to ratify a contract (Gen 15:9-10). This action symbolized the judgment on anyone who broke the contract. God was saying, "You have broken the contract you made with me, so you know the judgment awaiting you!"

Jer 21:1-2 King Zedekiah probably was referring to God's deliverance of Jerusalem from Sennacherib, king of Assyria, in the days of Hezekiah (Isa 36–37). But Zedekiah's hopes were dashed. He was Judah's last ruler during the time of the final exile in 586 B.C.

Jer 21:1-2 Pashhur came to the prophet for help. (This is not the same Pashhur as in Jer 20:1.) God still had work for Jeremiah to do. In living out our faith, we may find that rejection, disappointment, or hard work has brought us to the point of despondency. But we are still needed. God has important work for us as well.

Jer 21:1-14 Jeremiah had foretold Jerusalem's destruction. The city's leaders had denied his word and mocked his pronouncements. In desperation, King Zedekiah turned to God for help, but without acknowledging God's warnings or admitting his sin. Too often we expect God to help us in our time of trouble even though we have ignored him in our time of prosperity. But God wants a lasting relationship. Are you trying to build a lasting friendship with God, or are you merely using him occasionally to escape trouble? What would you think of your family or friends if they thought of you only as a temporary resource?

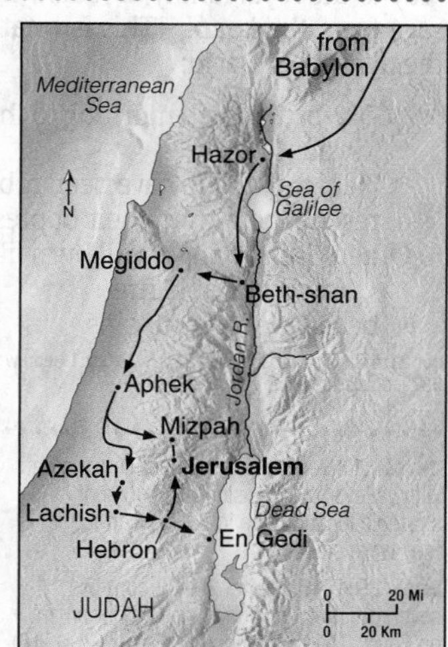

***BABYLON ATTACKS JUDAH** Zedekiah incurred Babylon's wrath by allying with Egypt (Jer 37:5-8) and not surrendering as God told him through Jeremiah (Jer 38:17). Nebuchadnezzar attacked Judah for the third and final time, moving systematically until all its cities fell. Jerusalem withstood siege for several months but was burned (Jer 39), as Jeremiah had predicted.*

▸ **JEREMIAH 21:1-10** ***(cont.)***

Babylon is attacking Judah. Perhaps the LORD will be
gracious and do a mighty miracle as he has done in
the past. Perhaps he will force Nebuchadnezzar to
withdraw his armies."

3Jeremiah replied, "Go back to King Zedekiah and
tell him, 4'This is what the LORD, the God of Israel, says:
I will make your weapons useless against the king of
Babylon and the Babylonians* who are outside your
walls attacking you. In fact, I will bring your enemies
right into the heart of this city. 5I myself will fight
against you with a strong hand and a powerful arm,
for I am very angry. You have made me furious! 6I will
send a terrible plague upon this city, and both people
and animals will die. 7And after all that, says the LORD,
I will hand over King Zedekiah, his staff, and everyone
else in the city who survives the disease, war, and famine. I will hand them over to King Nebuchadnezzar of
Babylon and to their other enemies. He will slaughter
them and show them no mercy, pity, or compassion.'

8"Tell all the people, 'This is what the LORD says:
Take your choice of life or death! 9Everyone who stays
in Jerusalem will die from war, famine, or disease, but
those who go out and surrender to the Babylonians
will live. Their reward will be life! 10For I have decided
to bring disaster and not good upon this city, says the
LORD. It will be handed over to the king of Babylon,
and he will reduce it to ashes.'

Judgment on Judah's Kings

JEREMIAH 21:11-14

"Say to the royal family of Judah, 'Listen to this message from the LORD! 12This is what the LORD says to
the dynasty of David:

"'Give justice each morning to the people
you judge!
Help those who have been robbed;
rescue them from their oppressors.
Otherwise, my anger will burn like an
unquenchable fire
because of all your sins.

13 I will personally fight against the people
in Jerusalem,
that mighty fortress—
the people who boast, "No one can touch us here.
No one can break in here."
14 And I myself will punish you for your sinfulness,
says the LORD.
I will light a fire in your forests
that will burn up everything around you.'"

Ezekiel's Message for Egypt

EZEKIEL 29:1-16

On January 7,* during the tenth year of King Jehoiachin's captivity, this message came to me from the
LORD: 2"Son of man, turn and face Egypt and prophesy
against Pharaoh the king and all the people of Egypt.
3Give them this message from the Sovereign LORD:

"I am your enemy, O Pharaoh, king of Egypt—
you great monster, lurking in the streams of
the Nile.
For you have said, 'The Nile River is mine;
I made it for myself.'
4 I will put hooks in your jaws
and drag you out on the land
with fish sticking to your scales.
5 I will leave you and all your fish
stranded in the wilderness to die.
You will lie unburied on the open ground,
for I have given you as food to the wild animals
and birds.
6 All the people of Egypt will know that I am the
LORD,
for to Israel you were just a staff made of reeds.
7 When Israel leaned on you,
you splintered and broke
and stabbed her in the armpit.
When she put her weight on you, you gave way,
and her back was thrown out of joint.

8"Therefore, this is what the Sovereign LORD says:
I will bring an army against you, O Egypt, and destroy
both people and animals. 9The land of Egypt will

Jer 21:4 Or *Chaldeans;* also in 21:9. **Ez 29:1** Hebrew *On the twelfth day of the tenth month,* of the ancient Hebrew lunar calendar. This event occurred on January 7, 587 B.C.; also see note on 1:1.

Jer 21:13 Jerusalem was built on a plateau with valleys on three sides. Because of its strategic location, the inhabitants thought they were safe.

Ezek 29:1-16 Ezekiel 29–32 contains seven prophecies, all dealing with judgment on Egypt. The first prophecy (Ezekiel 29:1-16) was probably given in 587 B.C. (some prophecies in these chapters occurred much later). Hezekiah, Jehoiakim, and Zedekiah (kings of Judah) had all sought help from Egypt despite God's warnings.

This prophecy was given for three key reasons: (1) Egypt was an ancient enemy of the Jews, having once enslaved them for more than 400 years; (2) Egypt worshiped many gods; (3) Egypt's wealth and power made it seem like a good ally. Egypt offered to help Judah only because of the benefits it hoped to receive from such an alliance. When the Egyptians didn't get what they hoped for, they bailed out of their agreement without regard to any promises they had made.

Ezek 29:2ff Egypt had great artistic treasures, a flourishing civilization, and world-renowned military power. Unfortunately, it was also evil, egotistical, idolatrous, and it treated slaves cruelly. For those sins God condemned Egypt. At the battle of Carchemish in 605 B.C., Babylon crushed Egypt along with Assyria, its rivals for the position of world ruler.

Ezek 29:9-10 The Nile was Egypt's pride and joy, a life-giving river cutting through the middle of the desert. But rather than thanking God, Egypt declared, "The Nile River is mine; I made it." We do the same when we say, "This house is mine; I built it," or "I have brought myself to the place where I am today," or "I have built this church, business, or reputation from the ground up." These statements reveal our pride. Sometimes we take for granted what God has given us, thinking we have made it ourselves. Of course, we have put forth a lot of hard effort, but God supplied the resources, gave us the abilities, and provided us with the opportunities to make it happen. Instead of proclaiming

become a desolate wasteland, and the Egyptians will
know that I am the LORD.

"Because you said, 'The Nile River is mine; I made it,'
10 I am now the enemy of both you and your river. I will
make the land of Egypt a totally desolate wasteland,
from Migdol to Aswan, as far south as the border of
Ethiopia.* 11 For forty years not a soul will pass that
way, neither people nor animals. It will be completely
uninhabited. 12 I will make Egypt desolate, and it will
be surrounded by other desolate nations. Its cities
will be empty and desolate for forty years, surrounded
by other ruined cities. I will scatter the Egyptians to
distant lands.

13 "But this is what the Sovereign LORD also says: At
the end of the forty years I will bring the Egyptians
home again from the nations to which they have been
scattered. 14 I will restore the prosperity of Egypt and
bring its people back to the land of Pathros in southern Egypt from which they came. But Egypt will remain an unimportant, minor kingdom. 15 It will be the
lowliest of all the nations, never again great enough to
rise above its neighbors.

16 "Then Israel will no longer be tempted to trust in
Egypt for help. Egypt's shattered condition will remind
Israel of how sinful she was to trust Egypt in earlier days.
Then Israel will know that I am the Sovereign LORD."

The Broken Arms of Pharaoh

EZEKIEL 30:20-26

On April 29,* during the eleventh year of King Jehoiachin's captivity, this message came to me from the
LORD: 21 "Son of man, I have broken the arm of Pharaoh, the king of Egypt. His arm has not been put in a
cast so that it may heal. Neither has it been bound up

Ez 29:10 Hebrew *from Migdol to Syene as far as the border of Cush.* **Ez 30:20** Hebrew *On the seventh day of the first month,* of the ancient Hebrew lunar calendar. This event occurred on April 29, 587 B.C.; also see note on 1:1.

our own greatness, as the Egyptians did, we should proclaim God's greatness and give him the credit. (Migdol is in the north of Egypt, and Aswan in the south. Thus, this meant all of Egypt.)

Ezek 29:13-16 This 40-year period of desolation in Egypt is hard to pinpoint. Nebuchadnezzar attacked Egypt around 572 B.C. and carried many people off to Babylon, while others fled for safety to surrounding nations. Approximately 33 years later, Cyrus, king of the Persian Empire, conquered Babylon and allowed the nations that Babylon had conquered to return to their homelands. Adding a possible seven-year regrouping and travel period, this could then make up that 40-year time period. Since that time, Egypt has never returned to its previous dominance as a world power.

Ezek 30:20-21 This message came in 587 B.C. while Jerusalem was under attack from Babylon. Judah had rebelled against Babylon and made an alliance with Egypt in spite of God's warnings (Jer 2:36-37). Pharaoh Hophra made a halfhearted attempt to help Jerusalem, but when Nebuchadnezzar's army turned on him, he fled back to Egypt (Jer 37:5-7). This defeat is what Ezekiel meant when he said that God had "broken the arm of Pharaoh."

Ezek 30:21-26 Ezekiel received this prophecy in 587 B.C. God destroyed Egypt's military superiority and gave it to Babylon. God allows nations to rise to power to accomplish a particular purpose, often beyond our immediate understanding. When you read about armies and wars, don't despair. Remember that God is sovereign and in charge of everything, even military might. Besides praying for your military and government leaders, pray that God's greater purposes would be carried out and that his will would be done "on earth, as it is in heaven" (see Matt 6:10).

Elephantine

Elephantine was located on the southern tip of a small island in the Nile River. The Bible is probably referring to the city of Elephantine as Migdol in the phrase "from Migdol to Aswan" (Ezek 29:10; 30:6), that is, from Egypt's northern border to its southern border. The city's name was an Aramaic version of an Egyptian name meaning "city of ivories" and was translated into Greek as Elephantine.

Many Aramaic documents from the 5th century B.C. were discovered at Elephantine. At the time of their writing, Elephantine was a Persian military outpost, manned in part by a group of Jewish mercenaries with their families. The documents, numbering over 100, contained many complete scrolls that were still tied and sealed at the time of their discovery (in the early 1900s), along with numerous broken papyri and fragments. Several centuries older than most of the Dead Sea Scrolls, the documents portray the social, political, and religious life of a Jewish community outside Palestine. Because several points of contact are made with the books of Ezra and Nehemiah, these scroll can help us to understand these books better.

▸ **EZEKIEL 30:20-26** ***(cont.)***

with a splint to make it strong enough to hold a sword.
22 Therefore, this is what the Sovereign LORD says: I am
the enemy of Pharaoh, the king of Egypt! I will break
both of his arms—the good arm along with the broken
one—and I will make his sword clatter to the ground.
23 I will scatter the Egyptians to many lands throughout
the world. 24 I will strengthen the arms of Babylon's king
and put my sword in his hand. But I will break the arms
of Pharaoh, king of Egypt, and he will lie there mortally
wounded, groaning in pain. 25 I will strengthen the arms
of the king of Babylon, while the arms of Pharaoh fall
useless to his sides. And when I put my sword in the
hand of Babylon's king and he brings it against the land
of Egypt, Egypt will know that I am the LORD. 26 I will
scatter the Egyptians among the nations, dispersing
them throughout the earth. Then they will know that
I am the LORD."

Egypt Compared to Fallen Assyria

EZEKIEL 31:1-18

On June 21,* during the eleventh year of King Jehoiachin's captivity, this message came to me from the LORD: 2 "Son of man, give this message to Pharaoh, king of Egypt, and all his hordes:

"To whom would you compare your greatness?
3 You are like mighty Assyria,
which was once like a cedar of Lebanon,
with beautiful branches that cast deep forest shade
and with its top high among the clouds.
4 Deep springs watered it
and helped it to grow tall and luxuriant.
The water flowed around it like a river,
streaming to all the trees nearby.
5 This great tree towered high,
higher than all the other trees around it.
It prospered and grew long thick branches
because of all the water at its roots.
6 The birds nested in its branches,
and in its shade all the wild animals gave birth.
All the great nations of the world
lived in its shadow.
7 It was strong and beautiful,
with wide-spreading branches,
for its roots went deep
into abundant water.
8 No other cedar in the garden of God
could rival it.
No cypress had branches to equal it;
no plane tree had boughs to compare.
No tree in the garden of God
came close to it in beauty.
9 Because I made this tree so beautiful,
and gave it such magnificent foliage,
it was the envy of all the other trees of Eden,
the garden of God.

10 "Therefore, this is what the Sovereign LORD says:
Because Egypt* became proud and arrogant, and because it set itself so high above the others, with its top
reaching to the clouds, 11 I will hand it over to a mighty
nation that will destroy it as its wickedness deserves.
I have already discarded it. 12 A foreign army—the terror of the nations—has cut it down and left it fallen
on the ground. Its branches are scattered across the
mountains and valleys and ravines of the land. All
those who lived in its shadow have gone away and
left it lying there.

13 "The birds roost on its fallen trunk,
and the wild animals lie among its branches.
14 Let the tree of no other nation
proudly exult in its own prosperity,
though it be higher than the clouds
and it be watered from the depths.
For all are doomed to die,
to go down to the depths of the earth.
They will land in the pit
along with everyone else on earth.

15 "This is what the Sovereign LORD says: When Assyria went down to the grave,* I made the deep springs
mourn. I stopped its rivers and dried up its abundant
water. I clothed Lebanon in black and caused the trees
of the field to wilt. 16 I made the nations shake with
fear at the sound of its fall, for I sent it down to the
grave with all the others who descend to the pit. And
all the other proud trees of Eden, the most beautiful
and the best of Lebanon, the ones whose roots went
deep into the water, took comfort to find it there with
them in the depths of the earth. 17 Its allies, too, were all
destroyed and had passed away. They had gone down to
the grave—all those nations that had lived in its shade.
18 "O Egypt, to which of the trees of Eden will you
compare your strength and glory? You, too, will be
brought down to the depths with all these other nations. You will lie there among the outcasts* who have
died by the sword. This will be the fate of Pharaoh and
all his hordes. I, the Sovereign LORD, have spoken!"

Ez 31:1 Hebrew *On the first day of the third month,* of the ancient Hebrew lunar calendar. This event occurred on June 21, 587 B.C.; also see note on 1:1. **Ez 31:10** Hebrew *you.* **Ez 31:15** Hebrew *to Sheol;* also in 31:16, 17. **Ez 31:18** Hebrew *among the uncircumcised.*

Ezek 31:1ff This message was given in 587 B.C. Ezekiel compared Egypt to Assyria, calling Assyria a great cedar tree. The Egyptians were to look at the fall of the mighty nation of Assyria (whose demise they had seen) as an example of what would happen to them. Just like Assyria, Egypt took pride in its strength and beauty; this would be its downfall. She would crash like a mighty tree and be sent to the grave. There is no permanence apart from God, even for a great society with a magnificent culture and military power.

Ezek 31:9 "All the other trees of Eden" may refer to all the other nations of the world, which were jealous of Assyria's power and grandeur.

Ezek 31:11 The "mighty nation" may refer to Babylon (see Dan 2:37-38).

Jeremiah's Land Purchase

JEREMIAH 32:1-15

The following message came to Jeremiah from the LORD in the tenth year of the reign of Zedekiah,* king of Judah. This was also the eighteenth year of the reign of King Nebuchadnezzar.* 2Jerusalem was then under siege from the Babylonian army, and Jeremiah was imprisoned in the courtyard of the guard in the royal palace. 3King Zedekiah had put him there, asking why he kept giving this prophecy: "This is what the LORD says: 'I am about to hand this city over to the king of Babylon, and he will take it. 4King Zedekiah will be captured by the Babylonians* and taken to meet the king of Babylon face to face. 5He will take Zedekiah to Babylon, and I will deal with him there,' says the LORD. 'If you fight against the Babylonians, you will never succeed.'"

6At that time the LORD sent me a message. He said, 7"Your cousin Hanamel son of Shallum will come and say to you, 'Buy my field at Anathoth. By law you have the right to buy it before it is offered to anyone else.'"

8Then, just as the LORD had said he would, my cousin Hanamel came and visited me in the prison. He said, "Please buy my field at Anathoth in the land of Benjamin. By law you have the right to buy it before it is offered to anyone else, so buy it for yourself." Then I knew that the message I had heard was from the LORD.

9So I bought the field at Anathoth, paying Hanamel seventeen pieces* of silver for it. 10I signed and sealed the deed of purchase before witnesses, weighed out the silver, and paid him. 11Then I took the sealed deed and an unsealed copy of the deed, which contained the terms and conditions of the purchase, 12and I handed them to Baruch son of Neriah and grandson of Mahseiah. I did all this in the presence of my cousin Hanamel, the witnesses who had signed the deed, and all the men of Judah who were there in the courtyard of the guardhouse.

13Then I said to Baruch as they all listened, 14"This is what the LORD of Heaven's Armies, the God of Israel, says: 'Take both this sealed deed and the unsealed copy, and put them into a pottery jar to preserve them for a long time.' 15For this is what the LORD of Heaven's Armies, the God of Israel, says: 'Someday people will again own property here in this land and will buy and sell houses and vineyards and fields.'"

Jeremiah's Prayer

JEREMIAH 32:16-25

Then after I had given the papers to Baruch, I prayed to the LORD:

17"O Sovereign LORD! You made the heavens and earth by your strong hand and powerful arm. Nothing is too hard for you! 18You show unfailing love to thousands, but you also bring the consequences of one generation's sin upon the next. You are the great and powerful God, the LORD of Heaven's Armies. 19You have all wisdom and do great and mighty miracles. You see the conduct of all people, and you give them what they deserve. 20You performed miraculous signs and wonders in the land of Egypt—things still remembered to this day! And you have continued to do great miracles in Israel and all around the world. You have made your name famous to this day.

21"You brought Israel out of Egypt with mighty signs and wonders, with a strong hand and powerful arm, and with overwhelming terror. 22You gave the people of Israel this land that you had promised their ancestors long before—a land flowing with milk and honey. 23Our ancestors came and conquered it and lived in it, but they refused to obey you or follow your word. They have not done anything you commanded. That is why you have sent this terrible disaster upon them.

24"See how the siege ramps have been built against the city walls! Through war, famine, and disease, the city will be handed over to the Babylonians, who will conquer it. Everything has happened just as you said. 25And yet, O Sovereign LORD, you have told me to buy the field—paying good money for it before these witnesses—even though the city will soon be handed over to the Babylonians."

Jer 32:1a The tenth year of Zedekiah's reign and the eighteenth year of Nebuchadnezzar's reign was 587 B.C. **Jer 32:1b** Hebrew *Nebuchadrezzar,* a variant spelling of Nebuchadnezzar; also in 32:28. **Jer 32:4** Or *Chaldeans;* also in 32:5, 24, 25, 28, 29, 43. **Jer 32:9** Hebrew *17 shekels,* about 7 ounces or 194 grams in weight.

Jer 32:1-12 God told Jeremiah to buy a field outside Jerusalem. The city had been under siege for a year, and Jeremiah bought land that the soldiers occupied—certainly a poor investment. In addition, Jeremiah was a prisoner in the palace. But Jeremiah was demonstrating his faith in God's promises to bring his people back and to rebuild Jerusalem.

Jer 32:6-17 Trust doesn't come easily. It wasn't easy for Jeremiah to publicly buy land already captured by the enemy. But he trusted God. It wasn't easy for David to believe that he would become king, even after he was anointed. But he trusted God (1 Sam 16–31). It wasn't easy for Moses to believe that he and his people would escape Egypt, even after God spoke to him from a burning bush. But he trusted God (Exod 3:1–4:20). It isn't easy for us to believe that God can fulfill his "impossible" promises either, but we must trust him. God, who worked in the lives of biblical heroes, will work in our lives, too, if we will let him.

Jer 32:17-25 After Jeremiah bought the field, he began to wonder if such a move was wise. He sought relief in prayer from his nagging doubts. In this prayer, Jeremiah affirmed that God is the Creator of heaven and earth (Jer 32:17), the wise Judge, who is aware of our conduct (Jer 32:19), and our Redeemer, who has great power (Jer 32:21). God loves us and sees our situation. Whenever we doubt God's wisdom or wonder if it is practical to obey him, we can review what we already know about him. Such thoughts and prayers will quiet our doubts and calm our fears.

A Prediction of Jerusalem's Fall

JEREMIAH 32:26-35

Then this message came to Jeremiah from the LORD:
27"I am the LORD, the God of all the peoples of the
world. Is anything too hard for me? 28Therefore, this
is what the LORD says: I will hand this city over to the
Babylonians and to Nebuchadnezzar, king of Babylon,
and he will capture it. 29The Babylonians outside the
walls will come in and set fire to the city. They will burn
down all these houses where the people provoked my
anger by burning incense to Baal on the rooftops and
by pouring out liquid offerings to other gods. 30Israel
and Judah have done nothing but wrong since their
earliest days. They have infuriated me with all their
evil deeds," says the LORD. 31"From the time this city
was built until now, it has done nothing but anger me,
so I am determined to get rid of it.

32"The sins of Israel and Judah—the sins of the
people of Jerusalem, the kings, the officials, the priests,
and the prophets—have stirred up my anger. 33My
people have turned their backs on me and have refused to return. Even though I diligently taught them,
they would not receive instruction or obey. 34They
have set up their abominable idols right in my own
Temple, defiling it. 35They have built pagan shrines
to Baal in the valley of Ben-Hinnom, and there they
sacrifice their sons and daughters to Molech. I have
never commanded such a horrible deed; it never even
crossed my mind to command such a thing. What an
incredible evil, causing Judah to sin so greatly!

A Promise of Restoration

JEREMIAH 32:36-44

"Now I want to say something more about this city.
You have been saying, 'It will fall to the king of Babylon
through war, famine, and disease.' But this is what the
LORD, the God of Israel, says: 37I will certainly bring my
people back again from all the countries where I will
scatter them in my fury. I will bring them back to this
very city and let them live in peace and safety. 38They
will be my people, and I will be their God. 39And I will
give them one heart and one purpose: to worship me
forever, for their own good and for the good of all
their descendants. 40And I will make an everlasting
covenant with them: I will never stop doing good for
them. I will put a desire in their hearts to worship me,
and they will never leave me. 41I will find joy doing
good for them and will faithfully and wholeheartedly
replant them in this land.

42"This is what the LORD says: Just as I have brought
all these calamities on them, so I will do all the good I
have promised them. 43Fields will again be bought and
sold in this land about which you now say, 'It has been
ravaged by the Babylonians, a desolate land where
people and animals have all disappeared.' 44Yes, fields
will once again be bought and sold—deeds signed and
sealed and witnessed—in the land of Benjamin and
here in Jerusalem, in the towns of Judah and in the hill
country, in the foothills of Judah* and in the Negev,
too. For someday I will restore prosperity to them. I,
the LORD, have spoken!"

Jer 32:44 Hebrew *the Shephelah.*

Negev

The Negev is the southernmost region of Palestine. The name comes from the root "to be dry, parched," although its basic meaning is "south country" or "south." It is an area with no precise geographical boundaries. From north to south, the Negev covers the area between Beersheba and Kadesh-barnea. From west to east it extends from near the Mediterranean to the Arabah, a distance of 70 miles. This is an arid section of the country, with infrequent and limited rainfall. With limited water resources, there was restricted opportunity for agriculture. A pastoral economy existed based primarily on the raising of sheep, goats, and camels. Jeremiah prophesied that when God would restore his people, even this barren area would be so prosperous that people would buy and sell property there. Even the most barren areas of our lives are not beyond God's healing touch.

Jer 32:35 The most important and grotesque part of Molech worship took place at these pagan shrines, where children were offered in sacrifice to this god.

Jer 32:36-42 God uses his power to accomplish *his* purposes through *his* people. God doesn't give you power to be all *you* want to be, but he gives you power to be all *he* wants you to be. The people of Israel had to learn that trusting God meant radically realigning their purposes and desires with his. God gave them "one heart" toward him (Jer 32:39). We must develop such singleness of heart and action to love God above anything else.

Jer 32:44 The hill country is in western Palestine. The Negev is the southern part of Judah.

Promises of Peace and Prosperity

JEREMIAH 33:1-26

While Jeremiah was still confined in the courtyard of the guard, the LORD gave him this second message: 2"This is what the LORD says—the LORD who made the earth, who formed and established it, whose name is the LORD: 3Ask me and I will tell you remarkable secrets you do not know about things to come. 4For this is what the LORD, the God of Israel, says: You have torn down the houses of this city and even the king's palace to get materials to strengthen the walls against the siege ramps and swords of the enemy. 5You expect to fight the Babylonians,* but the men of this city are already as good as dead, for I have determined to destroy them in my terrible anger. I have abandoned them because of all their wickedness.

6"Nevertheless, the time will come when I will heal Jerusalem's wounds and give it prosperity and true peace. 7I will restore the fortunes of Judah and Israel and rebuild their towns. 8I will cleanse them of their sins against me and forgive all their sins of rebellion. 9Then this city will bring me joy, glory, and honor before all the nations of the earth! The people of the world will see all the good I do for my people, and they will tremble with awe at the peace and prosperity I provide for them.

10"This is what the LORD says: You have said, 'This is a desolate land where people and animals have all disappeared.' Yet in the empty streets of Jerusalem and Judah's other towns, there will be heard once more 11the sounds of joy and laughter. The joyful voices of bridegrooms and brides will be heard again, along with the joyous songs of people bringing thanksgiving offerings to the LORD. They will sing,

'Give thanks to the LORD of Heaven's Armies,
for the LORD is good.
His faithful love endures forever!'

For I will restore the prosperity of this land to what it was in the past, says the LORD.

12"This is what the LORD of Heaven's Armies says: This land—though it is now desolate and has no people and animals—will once more have pastures where shepherds can lead their flocks. 13Once again shepherds will count their flocks in the towns of the hill country, the foothills of Judah,* the Negev, the land of Benjamin, the vicinity of Jerusalem, and all the towns of Judah. I, the LORD, have spoken!

14"The day will come, says the LORD, when I will do for Israel and Judah all the good things I have promised them.

15 "In those days and at that time
I will raise up a righteous descendant* from King David's line.
He will do what is just and right throughout the land.
16 In that day Judah will be saved,
and Jerusalem will live in safety.
And this will be its name:
'The LORD Is Our Righteousness.'*

17For this is what the LORD says: David will have a descendant sitting on the throne of Israel forever. 18And there will always be Levitical priests to offer burnt offerings and grain offerings and sacrifices to me."

19Then this message came to Jeremiah from the LORD: 20"This is what the LORD says: If you can break my covenant with the day and the night so that one does not follow the other, 21only then will my covenant with my servant David be broken. Only then will he no longer have a descendant to reign on his throne. The same is true for my covenant with the Levitical priests who minister before me. 22And as the stars of the sky cannot be counted and the sand on the seashore cannot be measured, so I will multiply the descendants of my servant David and the Levites who minister before me."

23The LORD gave another message to Jeremiah. He said, 24"Have you noticed what people are saying?—'The LORD chose Judah and Israel and then abandoned them!' They are sneering and saying that Israel is not worthy to be counted as a nation. 25But this is what the LORD says: I would no more reject my people than I would change my laws that govern night and day, earth and sky. 26I will never abandon the descendants of Jacob or David, my servant, or change the plan that David's descendants will rule the descendants of Abraham, Isaac, and Jacob. Instead, I will restore them to their land and have mercy on them."

Jer 33:5 Or *Chaldeans.* **Jer 33:13** Hebrew *the Shephelah.* **Jer 33:15** Hebrew *a righteous branch.* **Jer 33:16** Hebrew *Yahweh Tsidqenu.*

Jer 33:1ff God would restore Jerusalem not because the people cried but because it was part of his ultimate plan. The Babylonian disaster did not change God's purposes for his people. Although Jerusalem would be destroyed, it would be restored (after the 70-year captivity and in the end times when the Messiah will rule). God's justice is always tempered by his mercy.

Jer 33:3 God assured Jeremiah that he had only to ask God and God would answer (see also Ps 145:18; Isa 58:9; Matt 7:7). God is ready to answer our prayers, but we must ask for his assistance. Surely God could take care of our needs without our asking. But when we ask, we are acknowledging that he alone is God and that we cannot accomplish in our own strength all that is his domain to do. When we ask, we must humble ourselves, lay aside our willfulness and worry, and determine to obey him.

Jer 33:15-16 These verses refer to both the first and second comings of Christ. At his first coming he would set up his reign in the hearts of believers; at his second coming he will execute justice and righteousness throughout the whole earth. Christ is the "righteous descendant" from King David's line, the man after God's own heart.

Jer 33:18 As Christ fulfills the role of King, he also fulfills the role of Priest, maintaining constant fellowship with God and mediating for the people. This verse does not mean that actual priests will perform sacrifices, for sacrifices will no longer be necessary (Heb 10:4, 11-12). Now that Christ is our High Priest, all believers are priests of God, and we can come before him personally.

Ezekiel's Message for Tyre

EZEKIEL 26:1-14

On February 3, during the twelfth year of King Jehoiachin's captivity,* this message came to me from the LORD: 2"Son of man, Tyre has rejoiced over the fall of Jerusalem, saying, 'Ha! She who was the gateway to the rich trade routes to the east has been broken, and I am the heir! Because she has been made desolate, I will become wealthy!'

3"Therefore, this is what the Sovereign LORD says: I am your enemy, O Tyre, and I will bring many nations against you, like the waves of the sea crashing against your shoreline. 4They will destroy the walls of Tyre and tear down its towers. I will scrape away its soil and make it a bare rock! 5It will be just a rock in the sea, a place for fishermen to spread their nets, for I have spoken, says the Sovereign LORD. Tyre will become the prey of many nations, 6and its mainland villages will be destroyed by the sword. Then they will know that I am the LORD.

7"This is what the Sovereign LORD says: From the north I will bring King Nebuchadnezzar* of Babylon against Tyre. He is king of kings and brings his horses, chariots, charioteers, and great army. 8First he will destroy your mainland villages. Then he will attack you by building a siege wall, constructing a ramp, and raising a roof of shields against you. 9He will pound your walls with battering rams and demolish your towers with sledgehammers. 10The hooves of his horses will choke the city with dust, and the noise of the charioteers and chariot wheels will shake your walls as they storm through your broken gates. 11His horsemen will trample through every street in the city. They will butcher your people, and your strong pillars will topple.

12"They will plunder all your riches and merchandise and break down your walls. They will destroy your lovely homes and dump your stones and timbers and even your dust into the sea. 13I will stop the music of your songs. No more will the sound of harps be heard among your people. 14I will make your island a bare rock, a place for fishermen to spread their nets. You will never be rebuilt, for I, the LORD, have spoken. Yes, the Sovereign LORD has spoken!

The Effect of Tyre's Destruction

EZEKIEL 26:15-21

"This is what the Sovereign LORD says to Tyre: The whole coastline will tremble at the sound of your fall, as the screams of the wounded echo in the continuing slaughter. 16All the seaport rulers will step down from their thrones and take off their royal robes and beautiful clothing. They will sit on the ground trembling with horror at your destruction. 17Then they will wail for you, singing this funeral song:

"O famous island city,
once ruler of the sea,
how you have been destroyed!
Your people, with their naval power,
once spread fear around the world.
18 Now the coastlands tremble at your fall.
The islands are dismayed as you disappear.

19"This is what the Sovereign LORD says: I will make Tyre an uninhabited ruin, like many others. I will bury you beneath the terrible waves of enemy attack. Great seas will swallow you. 20I will send you to the pit to join those who descended there long ago. Your city will lie in ruins, buried beneath the earth, like those in the pit who have entered the world of the dead. You will have no place of respect here in the land of the living. 21I will bring you to a terrible end, and you will exist no more. You will be looked for, but you will never again be found. I, the Sovereign LORD, have spoken!"

The End of Tyre's Glory

EZEKIEL 27:1-25

Then this message came to me from the LORD: 2"Son of man, sing a funeral song for Tyre, 3that mighty gateway to the sea, the trading center of the world. Give Tyre this message from the Sovereign LORD:

Ez 26:1 Hebrew *In the eleventh year, on the first day of the month,* of the ancient Hebrew lunar calendar year. Since an element is missing in the date formula here, scholars have reconstructed this probable reading: *In the eleventh [month of the twelfth] year, on the first day of the month.* This reading would put this message on February 3, 585 B.C.; also see note on 1:1. **Ez 26:7** Hebrew *Nebuchadrezzar,* a variant spelling of Nebuchadnezzar.

Ezek 26:1ff This message came to Ezekiel in 586 B.C. Ezekiel 26–27 is a prophecy against Tyre, the capital of Phoenicia, just north of Israel. Part of the city was on the coastline, and part was on a beautiful island. Tyre rejoiced when Jerusalem fell, because Tyre and Judah always competed for the lucrative trade that came through their lands from Egypt in the south and Mesopotamia to the north. Tyre dominated the sea trading routes, while Judah dominated the land caravan routes. After Judah was defeated, Tyre thought it had all the trade routes to itself. But this gloating didn't last long. In 586 B.C., Nebuchadnezzar attacked the city. It took him 15 years to capture Tyre (586–571) because the city's back side lay on the sea so fresh supplies could be shipped in daily.

Ezek 26:14 After a 15-year siege, Nebuchadnezzar could not conquer the part of Tyre located on the island; thus, certain aspects of the description (Ezek 26:12, 14) exceed the actual damage he inflicted. But the prophecy predicted what would happen to the island settlement later during the conquests of Alexander the Great. Alexander threw the rubble of the mainland city into the sea until it made a bridge to the island. Then he marched across the bridge and destroyed the island (332 B.C.). Today the island city is still a pile of rubble, a testimony to God's judgment.

Ezek 27:1ff Ezekiel 27 is a funeral lament over Tyre's fall. It compares the city to a ship (Ezek 27:1-9), mentions many of its trading partners (Ezek 27:10-25), and then describes how the ship sank (Ezek 27:26-36). Jesus spoke of Tyre in Matthew 11:22 as a city worthy of God's judgment.

Ezek 27:3-4 The beauty of Tyre was the source of its pride, and Tyre's pride guaranteed its judgment. Conceit or pride in our own accomplishments should be a danger signal to us (see Jas 4:13-17). God is not against our taking pleasure or finding satisfaction in what we do; he is against arrogance and inflated self-esteem that looks down on others. We must acknowledge God as the basis and source of our lives.

"You boasted, O Tyre,
'My beauty is perfect!'
4 You extended your boundaries into the sea.
Your builders made your beauty perfect.
5 You were like a great ship
built of the finest cypress from Senir.*
They took a cedar from Lebanon
to make a mast for you.
6 They carved your oars
from the oaks of Bashan.
Your deck of pine from the coasts of
Cyprus*
was inlaid with ivory.
7 Your sails were made of Egypt's finest linen,
and they flew as a banner above you.
You stood beneath blue and purple awnings
made bright with dyes from the coasts
of Elishah.
8 Your oarsmen came from Sidon and Arvad;
your helmsmen were skilled men from
Tyre itself.
9 Wise old craftsmen from Gebal did the
caulking.
Ships from every land came with goods
to barter for your trade.

10"Men from distant Persia, Lydia, and Libya* served
in your great army. They hung their shields and helmets on your walls, giving you great honor. 11Men from
Arvad and Helech stood on your walls. Your towers
were manned by men from Gammad. Their shields
hung on your walls, completing your beauty.

12"Tarshish sent merchants to buy your wares in
exchange for silver, iron, tin, and lead. 13Merchants
from Greece,* Tubal, and Meshech brought slaves and
articles of bronze to trade with you.

14"From Beth-togarmah came riding horses, chariot horses, and mules, all in exchange for your goods.
15Merchants came to you from Dedan.* Numerous
coastlands were your captive markets; they brought
payment in ivory tusks and ebony wood.

16"Syria* sent merchants to buy your rich variety
of goods. They traded turquoise, purple dyes, embroidery, fine linen, and jewelry of coral and rubies.
17Judah and Israel traded for your wares, offering
wheat from Minnith, figs,* honey, olive oil, and balm.

18"Damascus sent merchants to buy your rich variety of goods, bringing wine from Helbon and white
wool from Zahar. 19Greeks from Uzal* came to trade
for your merchandise. Wrought iron, cassia, and fragrant calamus were bartered for your wares.

20"Dedan sent merchants to trade their expensive saddle blankets with you. 21The Arabians and
the princes of Kedar sent merchants to trade lambs
and rams and male goats in exchange for your goods.
22The merchants of Sheba and Raamah came with
all kinds of spices, jewels, and gold in exchange for
your wares.

23"Haran, Canneh, Eden, Sheba, Asshur, and Kilmad
came with their merchandise, too. 24They brought
choice fabrics to trade—blue cloth, embroidery, and
multicolored carpets rolled up and bound with cords.
25The ships of Tarshish were your ocean caravans. Your
island warehouse was filled to the brim!

The Destruction of Tyre

EZEKIEL 27:26-36

26 "But look! Your oarsmen
have taken you into stormy seas!
A mighty eastern gale
has wrecked you in the heart of the sea!
27 Everything is lost—
your riches and wares,
your sailors and pilots,
your ship builders, merchants, and warriors.
On the day of your ruin,
everyone on board sinks into the depths
of the sea.
28 Your cities by the sea tremble
as your pilots cry out in terror.
29 All the oarsmen abandon their ships;
the sailors and pilots on shore come
to stand on the beach.
30 They cry aloud over you
and weep bitterly.
They throw dust on their heads
and roll in ashes.
31 They shave their heads in grief for you
and dress themselves in burlap.
They weep for you with bitter anguish
and deep mourning.
32 As they wail and mourn over you,
they sing this sad funeral song:
'Was there ever such a city as Tyre,
now silent at the bottom of the sea?
33 The merchandise you traded
satisfied the desires of many nations.
Kings at the ends of the earth
were enriched by your trade.
34 Now you are a wrecked ship,
broken at the bottom of the sea.
All your merchandise and crew
have gone down with you.
35 All who live along the coastlands
are appalled at your terrible fate.
Their kings are filled with horror
and look on with twisted faces.
36 The merchants among the nations
shake their heads at the sight of you,*
for you have come to a horrible end
and will exist no more.'"

Ez 27:5 Or *Hermon.* **Ez 27:6** Hebrew *Kittim.* **Ez 27:10** Hebrew *Paras, Lud, and Put.* **Ez 27:13** Hebrew *Javan.* **Ez 27:15** Greek version reads *Rhodes.* **Ez 27:16** Hebrew *Aram;* some manuscripts read *Edom.* **Ez 27:17** The meaning of the Hebrew is uncertain. **Ez 27:19** Hebrew *Vedan and Javan from Uzal.* The meaning of the Hebrew is uncertain. **Ez 27:36** Hebrew *hiss at you.*

Ezekiel's Message for Tyre's King

EZEKIEL 28:1-19

Then this message came to me from the LORD: [2]"Son of man, give the prince of Tyre this message from the Sovereign LORD:

"In your great pride you claim, 'I am a god!
I sit on a divine throne in the heart
of the sea.'
But you are only a man and not a god,
though you boast that you are a god.
3 You regard yourself as wiser than Daniel
and think no secret is hidden from you.
4 With your wisdom and understanding you
have amassed great wealth—
gold and silver for your treasuries.
5 Yes, your wisdom has made you very rich,
and your riches have made you very proud.

6 "Therefore, this is what the Sovereign LORD says:
Because you think you are as wise as a god,
7 I will now bring against you a foreign army,
the terror of the nations.
They will draw their swords against your
marvelous wisdom
and defile your splendor!
8 They will bring you down to the pit,
and you will die in the heart of the sea,
pierced with many wounds.
9 Will you then boast, 'I am a god!'
to those who kill you?
To them you will be no god
but merely a man!
10 You will die like an outcast*
at the hands of foreigners.
I, the Sovereign LORD, have spoken!"

[11]Then this further message came to me from the LORD: [12]"Son of man, sing this funeral song for the king of Tyre. Give him this message from the Sovereign LORD:

"You were the model of perfection,
full of wisdom and exquisite in beauty.
13 You were in Eden,
the garden of God.
Your clothing was adorned with every precious
stone*—
red carnelian, pale-green peridot, white
moonstone,
blue-green beryl, onyx, green jasper,
blue lapis lazuli, turquoise, and emerald—
all beautifully crafted for you
and set in the finest gold.
They were given to you
on the day you were created.
14 I ordained and anointed you
as the mighty angelic guardian.*
You had access to the holy mountain of God
and walked among the stones of fire.

15 "You were blameless in all you did
from the day you were created
until the day evil was found in you.
16 Your rich commerce led you to violence,
and you sinned.
So I banished you in disgrace
from the mountain of God.
I expelled you, O mighty guardian,
from your place among the stones of fire.
17 Your heart was filled with pride
because of all your beauty.
Your wisdom was corrupted
by your love of splendor.
So I threw you to the ground
and exposed you to the curious gaze
of kings.
18 You defiled your sanctuaries
with your many sins and your dishonest
trade.
So I brought fire out from within you,
and it consumed you.
I reduced you to ashes on the ground
in the sight of all who were watching.
19 All who knew you are appalled at your fate.
You have come to a terrible end,
and you will exist no more."

Ez 28:10 Hebrew *will die the death of the uncircumcised.* similarly in 28:16. **Ez 28:13** The identification of some of these gemstones is uncertain. **Ez 28:14** Hebrew *guardian cherub;*

Ezek 28:1ff Previously Ezekiel had prophesied against the city of Tyre (Ezek 26–27). Here he focused his prophecy on Tyre's leader. The chief sin of Tyre's king was pride—believing himself to be a god. But Ezekiel also may have made a broader spiritual application, speaking about the spiritual king of Tyre, Satan, whom the people were really following (see the note on Ezek 28:12-19, below).

Ezek 28:2-3 Daniel, an important official in Nebuchadnezzar's kingdom (Ezek 14:14), was already renowned for his wisdom. Daniel proclaimed that all his wisdom came from God (Dan 2:20-23). By contrast, the king of Tyre thought that he himself was a god. As truly wise people get closer to God, they recognize their need to depend on him for guidance.

Ezek 28:6-10 The enemy army that attacked Tyre was the Babylonian army under Nebuchadnezzar. This attack occurred in 573/572 B.C.

Ezek 28:12-19 Some of the phrases in this passage describing the human king of Tyre may also describe Satan. Great care must be taken to interpret these verses with discernment. It is clear that at times Ezekiel describes this king in terms that could not apply to a mere human. This king had been in the Garden of Eden (Ezek 28:13), had been "ordained and anointed . . . as the mighty angelic guardian" (Ezek 28:14), and had access to the holy mountain of God (Ezek 28:14), but was banished from there (Ezek 28:16-17). Ezekiel, therefore, may have been condemning not only the king of Tyre but Satan as well, who had motivated the king to sin.

Ezekiel's Message for Sidon

EZEKIEL 28:20-24

Then another message came to me from the LORD:
21"Son of man, turn and face the city of Sidon and
prophesy against it. 22Give the people of Sidon this
message from the Sovereign LORD:

"I am your enemy, O Sidon,
and I will reveal my glory by what I do
to you.
When I bring judgment against you
and reveal my holiness among you,
everyone watching will know
that I am the LORD.
23 I will send a plague against you,
and blood will be spilled in your streets.
The attack will come from every direction,
and your people will lie slaughtered within
your walls.
Then everyone will know
that I am the LORD.
24 No longer will Israel's scornful neighbors
prick and tear at her like briers and thorns.
For then they will know
that I am the Sovereign LORD.

Restoration for Israel

EZEKIEL 28:25-26

"This is what the Sovereign LORD says: The people
of Israel will again live in their own land, the land I
gave my servant Jacob. For I will gather them from
the distant lands where I have scattered them. I will
reveal to the nations of the world my holiness among
my people. 26They will live safely in Israel and build
homes and plant vineyards. And when I punish the
neighboring nations that treated them with contempt,
they will know that I am the LORD their God."

The Fall of Jerusalem PARALLEL

2 KINGS 25:3-7

By July 18 in the eleventh year of Zedekiah's reign,* the
famine in the city had become very severe, and the last
of the food was entirely gone. 4Then a section of the
city wall was broken down, and all the soldiers fled.
Since the city was surrounded by the Babylonians,*
they waited for nightfall. Then they slipped through
the gate between the two walls behind the king's garden and headed toward the Jordan Valley.*
5But the Babylonian* troops chased the king and
caught him on the plains of Jericho, for his men had
all deserted him and scattered. 6They took him to the
king of Babylon at Riblah, where they pronounced
judgment upon Zedekiah. 7They made Zedekiah
watch as they slaughtered his sons. Then they gouged
out Zedekiah's eyes, bound him in bronze chains, and
led him away to Babylon.

JEREMIAH 39:2-10

Two and a half years later, on July 18* in the eleventh year of Zedekiah's reign, the Babylonians broke
through the wall, and the city fell. 3All the officers
of the Babylonian army came in and sat in triumph
at the Middle Gate: Nergal-sharezer of Samgar, and
Nebo-sarsekim,* a chief officer, and Nergal-sharezer,
the king's adviser, and all the other officers.
4When King Zedekiah and all the soldiers saw that
the Babylonians had broken into the city, they fled.
They waited for nightfall and then slipped through the
gate between the two walls behind the king's garden
and headed toward the Jordan Valley.*

2 Kgs 25:3 Hebrew *By the ninth day of the [fourth] month* [in the eleventh year of Zedekiah's reign] (compare Jer 52:6 and the note there). This day was July 18, 586 B.C.; also see note on 25:1. **2 Kgs 25:4a** Or *the Chaldeans;* also in 25:13, 25, 26. **2 Kgs 25:4b** Hebrew *the Arabah.* **2 Kgs 25:5** Or *Chaldean;* also in 25:10, 24. **Jer 39:2** Hebrew *On the ninth day of the fourth month.* This day was July 18, 586 B.C.; also see note on 39:1a. **Jer 39:3** Or *Nergal-sharezer, Samgar-nebo, Sarsekim.* **Jer 39:4** Hebrew *the Arabah.*

Ezek 28:20-21 Sidon was another famous seaport, located about 25 miles north of Tyre. God charged this city with contempt for his people. Sidon's economy was bound to Tyre's, so when Tyre fell to Nebuchadnezzar, Sidon was doomed to follow.

Ezek 28:24-26 This promise that God's people will live in complete safety has yet to be fulfilled. While many were allowed to return from exile under Zerubbabel, Ezra, and Nehemiah, and although the political nation is restored today, the inhabitants do not yet live in complete safety (Ezek 28:26). Therefore, this promise will have its ultimate fulfillment when Christ sets up his eternal Kingdom. Then all people who have been faithful to God will dwell together in harmony and complete safety.

The Babylonian Chronicle

This is a Babylonian Chronicle for the years 605–594 B.C. The events recorded include the battle of Carchemish in 605 B.C., the accession of Nebuchadnezzar II as the king of Babylon, the appointment of Zedekiah as king of Judah after the capture of Jerusalem on March 16, 597 B.C., and the removal of the Judeans to exile in Babylon (2 Chr 36:9-21). This is an archaeological find that confirms the reliability of Scripture.

Jer 39:2ff Zedekiah, son of Josiah and last king of Judah, ruled 11 years, from 597 to 586 B.C. Zedekiah's two older brothers, Jehoahaz and Jehoiakim, and his nephew Jehoiachin ruled before him. When Jehoiachin was exiled to Babylon, Nebuchadnezzar made 21-year-old Mattaniah the king, changing his name to Zedekiah. Zedekiah rebelled against Nebuchadnezzar, who captured him, killed his sons in front of him, and then blinded him and took him back to Babylon, where he later died (see 2 Kgs 24–25; 2 Chr 36; and Jer 52).

▶ **JEREMIAH 39:2-10** ***(cont.)***

[5]But the Babylonian* troops chased the king and caught him on the plains of Jericho. They took him to King Nebuchadnezzar of Babylon, who was at Riblah in the land of Hamath. There the king of Babylon pronounced judgment upon Zedekiah. [6]He made Zedekiah watch as they slaughtered his sons and all the nobles of Judah. [7]Then they gouged out Zedekiah's eyes, bound him in bronze chains, and led him away to Babylon.

[8]Meanwhile, the Babylonians burned Jerusalem, including the palace, and tore down the walls of the city. [9]Then Nebuzaradan, the captain of the guard, sent to Babylon the rest of the people who remained in the city as well as those who had defected to him. [10]But Nebuzaradan left a few of the poorest people in Judah, and he assigned them vineyards and fields to care for.

JEREMIAH 52:6-11

By July 18 in the eleventh year of Zedekiah's reign,* the famine in the city had become very severe, and the last of the food was entirely gone. [7]Then a section of the city wall was broken down, and all the soldiers fled. Since the city was surrounded by the Babylonians,* they waited for nightfall. Then they slipped through the gate between the two walls behind the king's garden and headed toward the Jordan Valley.*

[8]But the Babylonian troops chased King Zedekiah and caught him on the plains of Jericho, for his men had all deserted him and scattered. [9]They took him to the king of Babylon at Riblah in the land of Hamath. There the king of Babylon pronounced judgment upon Zedekiah. [10]He made Zedekiah watch as they slaughtered his sons and all the other officials of Judah. [11]Then they gouged out Zedekiah's eyes, bound him in bronze chains, and led him away to Babylon. Zedekiah remained there in prison until the day of his death.

Jeremiah Remains in Judah

JEREMIAH 39:11–40:6

King Nebuchadnezzar had told Nebuzaradan, the captain of the guard, to find Jeremiah. [12]"See that he isn't hurt," he said. "Look after him well, and give him anything he wants." [13]So Nebuzaradan, the captain of the guard; Nebushazban, a chief officer; Nergal-sharezer, the king's adviser; and the other officers of Babylon's king [14]sent messengers to bring Jeremiah out of the prison. They put him under the care of Gedaliah son of Ahikam and grandson of Shaphan, who took him back to his home. So Jeremiah stayed in Judah among his own people.

[15]The LORD had given the following message to Jeremiah while he was still in prison: [16]"Say to Ebed-melech the Ethiopian,* 'This is what the LORD of Heaven's Armies, the God of Israel, says: I will do to this city everything I have threatened. I will send disaster, not prosperity. You will see its destruction, [17]but I will rescue you from those you fear so much. [18]Because you trusted me, I will give you your life as a reward. I will rescue you and keep you safe. I, the LORD, have spoken!' "

40:1 The LORD gave a message to Jeremiah after Nebuzaradan, the captain of the guard, had released him at Ramah. He had found Jeremiah bound in chains among all the other captives of Jerusalem and Judah who were being sent to exile in Babylon.

[2]The captain of the guard called for Jeremiah and said, "The LORD your God has brought this disaster on this land, [3]just as he said he would. For these people have sinned against the LORD and disobeyed him. That is why it happened. [4]But I am going to take off your chains and let you go. If you want to come with me to Babylon, you are welcome. I will see that you are well cared for. But if you don't want to come, you may stay

Jer 39:5 Or *Chaldean;* similarly in 39:8. **Jer 52:6** Hebrew *By the ninth day of the fourth month* [in the eleventh year of Zedekiah's reign]. This day was July 18, 586 B.C.; also see note on 52:4a. **Jer 52:7a** Or *the Chaldeans;* similarly in 52:8, 17. **Jer 52:7b** Hebrew *the Arabah.* **Jer 39:16** Hebrew *the Cushite.*

Jer 39:10 Babylon had a shrewd foreign policy toward conquered lands. They deported the rich and powerful, leaving only the very poor in charge, thus making them grateful to their conquerors. This policy assured that conquered populations would be too loyal and too weak to revolt.

Jer 52:8-9 Riblah was 200 miles north of Jerusalem, located on the Orontes River in the region of Aram (or Syria). This was the Babylonian headquarters for ruling the entire region. Hamath was the district of Aram where the capital, Riblah, was located.

Jer 39:11-12 God had promised to rescue Jeremiah from his trouble (Jer 1:8). The superstitious Babylonians, who highly respected magicians and fortune-tellers, treated Jeremiah as a seer. Because he had been imprisoned by his own people, they assumed he was a traitor and on their side. They undoubtedly knew he had counseled cooperation with Babylon and predicted a Babylonian victory. So the Babylonians freed Jeremiah and protected him.

Jer 39:13-14 What a difference there is between Jeremiah's fate and Zedekiah's! Jeremiah was freed; Zedekiah was imprisoned. Jeremiah was saved because of his faith; Zedekiah was destroyed because of his fear. Jeremiah was treated with respect; Zedekiah was treated with contempt. Jeremiah was concerned for the people; Zedekiah was concerned for himself.

Jer 39:17-18 Ebed-melech had risked his life to save God's prophet Jeremiah (Jer 38:7-13). When Babylon conquered Jerusalem, God protected Ebed-melech from the Babylonians. God has special rewards for his faithful people, but not everyone will receive them in this life (see the note on Jer 38:6, p. 1043).

Jer 40:2-3 The Babylonian captain of the guard, who did not know God, acknowledged that God had given the Babylonians victory. It is strange for people to recognize that God exists and does miracles and yet not personally accept him. Knowing God is more than knowing about him. Be sure you know him personally.

Jer 40:4 Jeremiah was free to go anywhere. In Babylon he would have great comfort and power. In Judah he would continue to face hardship. In Babylon Jeremiah would have been favored by the Babylonians but hated by the Judean exiles. In Judah he would remain poor and unwanted, but the Judean remnant would know he was not a traitor. Jeremiah returned to Judah.

Jer 40:6 Mizpah was a few miles north of Jerusalem. Not thoroughly destroyed by the Babylonians, Mizpah served as a refuge after the destruction of Jerusalem.

2 Kgs 25:13 The bronze basin called the Sea was used to hold the huge reservoir of water for ritual cleansing for the priests. The bronze was so valuable that it was broken up and carried off to Babylon.

here. The whole land is before you—go wherever you like. [5]If you decide to stay, then return to Gedaliah son of Ahikam and grandson of Shaphan. He has been appointed governor of Judah by the king of Babylon. Stay there with the people he rules. But it's up to you; go wherever you like."

Then Nebuzaradan, the captain of the guard, gave Jeremiah some food and money and let him go. [6]So Jeremiah returned to Gedaliah son of Ahikam at Mizpah, and he lived in Judah with the few who were still left in the land.

The Temple Destroyed PARALLEL

2 KINGS 25:8-21

On August 14 of that year,* which was the nineteenth year of King Nebuchadnezzar's reign, Nebuzaradan, the captain of the guard and an official of the Babylonian king, arrived in Jerusalem. [9]He burned down the Temple of the Lord, the royal palace, and all the houses of Jerusalem. He destroyed all the important buildings* in the city. [10]Then he supervised the entire Babylonian army as they tore down the walls of Jerusalem on every side. [11]Nebuzaradan, the captain of the guard, then took as exiles the rest of the people who remained in the city, the defectors who had declared their allegiance to the king of Babylon, and the rest of the population. [12]But the captain of the guard allowed some of the poorest people to stay behind in Judah to care for the vineyards and fields.

[13]The Babylonians broke up the bronze pillars in front of the Lord's Temple, the bronze water carts, and the great bronze basin called the Sea, and they carried all the bronze away to Babylon. [14]They also took all the ash buckets, shovels, lamp snuffers, dishes, and all the other bronze articles used for making sacrifices at the Temple. [15]Nebuzaradan, the captain of the guard, also took the incense burners and basins, and all the other articles made of pure gold or silver.

[16]The weight of the bronze from the two pillars, the Sea, and the water carts was too great to be measured. These things had been made for the Lord's Temple in the days of King Solomon. [17]Each of the pillars was 27 feet* tall. The bronze capital on top of each pillar was 7½ feet* high and was decorated with a network of bronze pomegranates all the way around.

[18]Nebuzaradan, the captain of the guard, took with him as prisoners Seraiah the high priest, Zephaniah the priest of the second rank, and the three chief gatekeepers. [19]And from among the people still hiding in the city, he took an officer who had been in

2 Kgs 25:8 Hebrew *On the seventh day of the fifth month,* of the ancient Hebrew lunar calendar. This day was August 14, 586 B.C.; also see note on 25:1. **2 Kgs 25:9** Or *destroyed the houses of all the important people.* **2 Kgs 25:17a** Hebrew *18 cubits* [8.1 meters]. **2 Kgs 25:17b** As in parallel texts at 1 Kgs 7:16, 2 Chr 3:15, and Jer 52:22, all of which read *5 cubits* [2.3 meters]; Hebrew reads *3 cubits,* which is 4.5 feet or 1.4 meters.

EBED-MELECH

During one of the bleakest moments in Jeremiah's life, God demonstrated his power by providing help from an unexpected source. Ebed-melech, a high-ranking African official in Zedekiah's court, risked his career and perhaps his life to rescue Jeremiah from a muddy cistern. This unsung Ethiopian represents a crowd of quiet heroes throughout Bible history who showed real courage and character. He made the most of his position in life by using it to serve God. • Spineless King Zedekiah had agreed to let Jeremiah's enemies arrange for the prophet's death. Though he had previously consulted with Jeremiah and even arranged for less harsh imprisonment, Zedekiah wavered under pressure. When certain influential voices demanded Jeremiah's life, Zedekiah offered no resistance. The plan involved lowering Jeremiah into an empty cistern and leaving him to die of starvation. • Ebed-melech's response shows us a radical and almost reckless pursuit of justice. He appealed directly to the king who was holding court in a public place. His boldness prodded Zedekiah to reverse his previous decision. Ebed-melech took the king's men, gathered the padding and ropes he would need, and hauled the shivering and slimy prophet out of the pit. The picture wasn't pretty, but the mission succeeded. Jeremiah later had the privilege of informing his Ethiopian rescuer that God would keep him safe during the fall and destruction of Jerusalem. • In whatever place you find yourself in life, continually ask God to help you see and respond to needs that you are uniquely placed to meet. Like Ebed-melech, you may experience fear along the way. But better to fear and act anyway than to live with the disappointment that fear prevented you from serving God and his people.

Strengths and accomplishments	• Took Jeremiah's case before the king and secured his rescue • Organized the extraction of the prophet from the quagmire-filled cistern • Received God's guarantee of safety during the Babylonian destruction of Jerusalem
Lessons from his life	• The places we serve in life can often provide us with unique opportunities to serve God and his people • We can trust God and act in spite of our fear • God does not forget those who take a stand for him • One bold person's actions may stem a tide of evil
Vital statistics	• Where: From Ethiopia, lived in Judah • Occupation: Palace official in Judah • Contemporaries: Jeremiah, Baruch, Zedekiah
Key verse	"Because you trusted me, I will give you your life as a reward. I will rescue you and keep you safe. I, the Lord, have spoken!" (Jer 39:18).

Ebed-melech's story is told in Jeremiah 38–39.

▸ 2 KINGS 25:8-21 ***(cont.)***

charge of the Judean army; five of the king's personal advisers; the army commander's chief secretary, who was in charge of recruitment; and sixty other citizens. [20]Nebuzaradan, the captain of the guard, took them all to the king of Babylon at Riblah. [21]And there at Riblah, in the land of Hamath, the king of Babylon had them all put to death. So the people of Judah were sent into exile from their land.

2 CHRONICLES 36:15-21

The LORD, the God of their ancestors, repeatedly sent his prophets to warn them, for he had compassion on his people and his Temple. [16]But the people mocked these messengers of God and despised their words. They scoffed at the prophets until the LORD's anger could no longer be restrained and nothing could be done.

[17]So the LORD brought the king of Babylon against them. The Babylonians* killed Judah's young men, even chasing after them into the Temple. They had no pity on the people, killing both young men and young women, the old and the infirm. God handed all of them over to Nebuchadnezzar. [18]The king took home to Babylon all the articles, large and small, used in the Temple of God, and the treasures from both the LORD's Temple and from the palace of the king and his officials. [19]Then his army burned the Temple of God, tore down the walls of Jerusalem, burned all the palaces, and completely destroyed everything of value.* [20]The few who survived were taken as exiles to Babylon, and they became servants to the king and his sons until the kingdom of Persia came to power.

[21]So the message of the LORD spoken through Jeremiah was fulfilled. The land finally enjoyed its Sabbath rest, lying desolate until the seventy years were fulfilled, just as the prophet had said.

JEREMIAH 52:12-27

On August 17 of that year,* which was the nineteenth year of King Nebuchadnezzar's reign, Nebuzaradan, the captain of the guard and an official of the Babylonian king, arrived in Jerusalem. [13]He burned down the Temple of the LORD, the royal palace, and all the houses of Jerusalem. He destroyed all the important buildings* in the city. [14]Then he supervised the entire Babylonian* army as they tore down the walls of Jerusalem on every side. [15]Nebuzaradan, the captain of the guard, then took as exiles some of the poorest of the people, the rest of the people who remained in the city, the defectors who had declared their allegiance to the king of Babylon, and the rest of the craftsmen. [16]But Nebuzaradan allowed some of the poorest people to stay behind in Judah to care for the vineyards and fields.

[17]The Babylonians broke up the bronze pillars in front of the LORD's Temple, the bronze water carts, and the great bronze basin called the Sea, and they carried all the bronze away to Babylon. [18]They also took all the ash buckets, shovels, lamp snuffers, basins, dishes, and all the other bronze articles used for making sacrifices at the Temple. [19]Nebuzaradan, the captain of the guard, also took the small bowls, incense burners, basins, pots, lampstands, dishes, bowls used for liquid

2 Chr 36:17 Or *Chaldeans.* **2 Chr 36:19** Or *destroyed all the valuable articles from the Temple.* **Jer 52:12** Hebrew *On the tenth day of the fifth month,* of the ancient Hebrew lunar calendar. This day was August 17, 586 B.C.; also see note on 52:4a. **Jer 52:13** Or *destroyed the houses of all the important people.* **Jer 52:14** Or *Chaldean.*

JUDAH EXILED *Evil permeated Judah, and God's anger flared against his rebellious people. The Babylonian army marched into Jerusalem, burned the Temple, tore down the city's massive walls, and carried off the people into captivity.*

2 Kgs 25:21 Judah, like Israel, was unfaithful to God. So God, as he had warned, allowed Judah to be destroyed and taken away (Deut 28). The book of Lamentations records the prophet Jeremiah's sorrow at seeing Jerusalem destroyed.

2 Chr 36:16 God warned Judah about its sin and continually restored the people to his favor, only to have them turn away. Eventually the situation was beyond remedy. Beware of harboring sin in your heart. The day will come when remedy is no longer possible and God's judgment replaces his mercy. Sin often repeated, but never repented of, invites disaster.

2 Chr 36:21 Leviticus 26:27-45 strikingly predicts captivity and exile, telling how God's people would be torn from their land for disobeying him. One of the laws they had ignored stated that one year in every seven the land should lie fallow, resting from producing crops (Exod 23:10-11). The 70-year captivity allowed the land to rest, making up for all the years the Israelites had not observed this law. We know that God keeps all his promises—not only his promises of blessing, but also his promises of judgment.

offerings, and all the other articles made of pure gold or silver.

20The weight of the bronze from the two pillars, the Sea with the twelve bronze oxen beneath it, and the water carts was too great to be measured. These things had been made for the LORD's Temple in the days of
King Solomon. 21Each of the pillars was 27 feet tall and 18 feet in circumference.* They were hollow, with
walls 3 inches thick.* 22The bronze capital on top of each pillar was 7½ feet* high and was decorated with a network of bronze pomegranates all the way around.
23There were 96 pomegranates on the sides, and a total of 100 on the network around the top.

24Nebuzaradan, the captain of the guard, took with him as prisoners Seraiah the high priest, Zephaniah the priest of the second rank, and the three chief
gatekeepers. 25And from among the people still hiding in the city, he took an officer who had been in charge of the Judean army; seven of the king's personal advisers; the army commander's chief secretary, who was in charge of recruitment; and sixty other citizens.
26Nebuzaradan, the captain of the guard, took them all
to the king of Babylon at Riblah. 27And there at Riblah, in the land of Hamath, the king of Babylon had them all put to death. So the people of Judah were sent into exile from their land.

Jer 52:21a Hebrew *18 cubits* [8.1 meters] *tall and 12 cubits* [5.4 meters] *in circumference.* **Jer 52:21b** Hebrew *4 fingers thick* [8 centimeters]. **Jer 52:22** Hebrew *5 cubits* [2.3 meters].

So the people of Judah were sent into exile from their land.
Jeremiah 52:27

Exile

THE LAND WAS LAID WASTE and it looked like God had abandoned his people. The Temple, designed as the center for proper worship of God and meant to be a light to the nations, had been destroyed by the conquering armies of the Babylonian Empire. Almost all of the people of Judah had been either killed or exiled to Babylon. The northern kingdom of Israel had been wiped out and scattered by Assyria more than a century earlier.

Jeremiah was left behind with the few remaining people from Judah, and he mourned the destruction of the Temple and Jerusalem in poetic form, recorded in the book of Lamentations. When the people asked him what they should do with themselves, he prayed to God and then advised them to remain in the Promised Land and trust God to preserve and protect them. Jeremiah assured the people that God was more powerful than the Babylonian armies and they should rely on him rather than fleeing to Egypt. Unfortunately, like those before them, they chose to ignore the message of the prophet and went to Egypt, where they died.

But all was not lost for God's people. Even in exile, there were

TIMELINE

600 BC | 590 BC | 580 BC | 570 BC | 560 BC

DANIEL (605–535 BC)

EZEKIEL (593–571 BC)

OBADIAH (about 586 BC)

PERSIAN EMPIRE

BABYLONIAN EMPIRE

NEO-BABYLONIAN EMPIRE (626–539 BC)

Nebuchadnezzar II (605–562 BC)

Amel-marduk (561–560 BC)

Nergal-shar-usur (559–556 BC)

***April 2, 561 BC**, Jehoiachin is released from prison*

JUDAH

July–August 586 BC
Jerusalem is destroyed, end of the Kingdom of Judah

***585 BC**, Judeans flee to Egypt*

EGYPT

DYNASTY 26 (664–525 BC)

Apries "Hophra" (589–570 BC)

Amasis II (570–526 BC)

BOOKS

- 2 KINGS
- PSALMS
- JEREMIAH
- LAMENTATIONS
- EZEKIEL
- DANIEL
- OBADIAH

DATES

FROM:
586 BC
TO:
538 BC

THEMES

- Judgment
- Repentance
- Justice
- Promise
- Hope

those who loved God and were loyal to him. The prophets Ezekiel and Daniel are great examples of people who continued to serve God faithfully in Babylon. Ezekiel brought messages of hope and restoration, and Daniel was a bright, shining example of righteousness in the midst of a pagan nation. God protected and preserved the remnant of his people, even when their Babylonian captors were destroyed by the rising Persian Empire.

Daniel was a highly-placed government official in both Babylon and Persia, but his heart was always with his people and his God. One day, he was reading from the prophecies of Jeremiah and realized that the seventy years of exile was coming to an end. His prayer of repentance for the sins of his people and his request for God to restore them to the land is the climax of the Exile. Would God respond and restore his people?

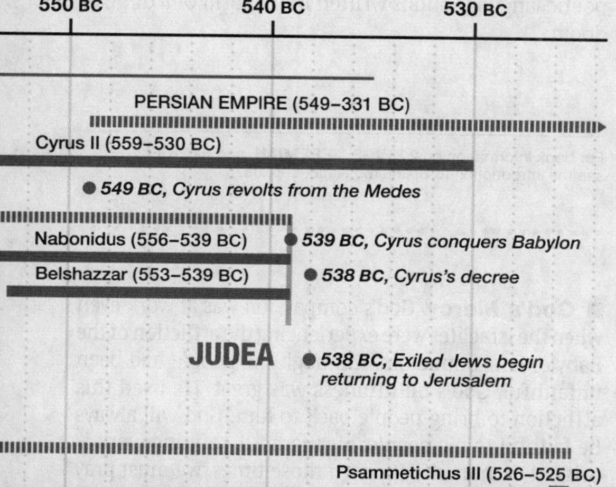

Daniel in the Lions' Den, by Peter Paul Rubens

PEOPLE & CULTURE

- **Destruction of Jerusalem.** The great capital city of the Jews was completely decimated by Babylon. The Temple was destroyed, the king was taken away in chains, and the people were exiled or killed. God had warned his people that he would destroy them if they abandoned him. Now, afterward, the people realized their condition and some confessed their sin. God's warnings to us are justified. He does what he says he will do. His punishment for sin is certain. Only by confessing and renouncing our sin can we turn to him for deliverance.

- **Babylonian Empire.** The instrument of God's judgment was a wicked and violent world power: the Babylonian Empire. Babylon was a vast empire that had wiped out Assyria before them, and had imposed their rule and customs on as much of the world as they could manage. Their conquest of Judah came near the height of their power. While some Israelites were groomed for high-ranking service in the Babylonian Empire, most were simply resettled in cities and towns throughout the empire.

- **Persian Empire.** The Babylonian Empire began to weaken through poor leadership and stretching themselves too thin militarily, and God used the Persian Empire to execute judgment on the Babylonians for their cruelty and for destroying Jerusalem. When Persia conquered Babylon in 539 B.C., they became the dominant world power. One year later, Cyrus (the Persian emperor) initiated his new policy of allowing the people that Babylon had displaced from their land to return home, fulfilling the prophecy of Isaiah decades earlier and setting up the possibility of a return to the Promised Land for God's people.

■ **Prophets.** God continued to speak to Israel and the world through the prophets, even when they were in exile. Jeremiah ministered to the few people who had been left behind in devastated Judah. Ezekiel ministered to the exiles in Babylon through messages of hope for future restoration as well as challenging messages calling for repentance and renewal. And Daniel represented God in the halls of power, first in Babylon and later in the Persian Empire. God continued to speak about his love for his people, his plan for redemption, and his control of world events, and the prophets represented the best of God's people, relying on him in their daily lives and being faithful wherever they found themselves.

BOOKS IN THIS SECTION

LAMENTATIONS

AUTHOR: Jeremiah

AUDIENCE: The exiled people of Judah

PURPOSE: To teach people that to disobey God is to invite disaster, and to show that God suffers when his people suffer

SETTING: Jerusalem had been destroyed by Babylon and her people killed, tortured, or taken captive.

DATE WRITTEN: Soon after the fall of Jerusalem in 586 B.C.

SPECIAL FEATURES: Three strands of Hebrew thought meet in Lamentations—prophecy, ritual, and wisdom. Lamentations is written in the rhythm and style of ancient Jewish funeral songs or chants. It contains five poems corresponding to the five chapters.

DANIEL

AUTHOR: Daniel

AUDIENCE: The other captives in Babylon

PURPOSE: To give a historical account of the faithful Jews who lived in captivity and to show how God is in control of heaven and earth, directing the forces of nature, the destiny of nations, and the care of his people

SETTING: Daniel had been taken captive and deported to Babylon by Nebuchadnezzar in 605 B.C. There he served in the government for about 70 years during the reigns of Nebuchadnezzar, Belshazzar, Darius, and Cyrus.

DATE WRITTEN: Approximately 536 B.C., recording events that occurred from about 605–536 B.C.

SPECIAL FEATURES: Daniel's apocalyptic visions (Dan 7–12) give a glimpse of God's plan for the ages, including a direct prediction of the Messiah.

OBADIAH

AUTHOR: Obadiah. Very little is known about him. His name means "servant of the Lord."

AUDIENCE: The Edomites and the Jews in exile

PURPOSE: To show that God judges those who have harmed his people

SETTING: Historically, Edom had constantly harassed the Jews. Prior to the time this book was written, they had participated in attacks against Judah, and more recently had celebrated Babylon's destruction of Judah.

SPECIAL FEATURES: The book of Obadiah uses vigorous poetic language and is written in the form of a dirge of doom.

For book information on **PSALMS**, see the introduction to United Monarchy, p. 430.

For book information on **2 KINGS**, **JEREMIAH**, and **EZEKIEL** see the introduction to Splintered Nations, p. 687.

MEGATHEMES

■ **Sin's Consequences.** God was angry at the prolonged rebellion by his people. Sin was the cause of their misery, and destruction was the result of their sin. The destruction of the nation shows the vanity of human glory and pride. To continue in rebellion against God is to invite disaster. We must never trust our own leadership, resources, intelligence, or power more than God. If we do, we invite consequences similar to Jerusalem's.

■ **God's Mercy.** God's compassion was at work even when the Israelites were experiencing the affliction of the Babylonian conquerors. Although the people had been unfaithful, God's faithfulness was great. He used this affliction to bring people back to him. God will always be faithful to his people; his merciful, refining work is evident even in affliction. At those times, we must pray for forgiveness and turn to him for deliverance.

■ **Restoration.** The prophets console the people by telling them that the day will come when God will restore those who turn from sin. God will be their King and shepherd. He will give his people a new heart to worship him, and he will reestablish his presence among them through a new Temple. The certainty of future restoration encourages believers in times of trial. But we must be faithful to God because we love him—and not just for what he can do for us. Is your faith in him, or merely in the future benefits?

■ **God Is in Control.** God is all-knowing, and he is in charge of world events. God overrules and removes rebellious leaders who defy him. God will overcome evil; no one is exempt. But he will deliver the faithful who follow him. Although nations vie for world control now, one day Christ's Kingdom will replace and surpass the kingdoms of this world. Our faith is sure because our future is secure in Christ. We must have courage and put our faith in God, who controls everything.

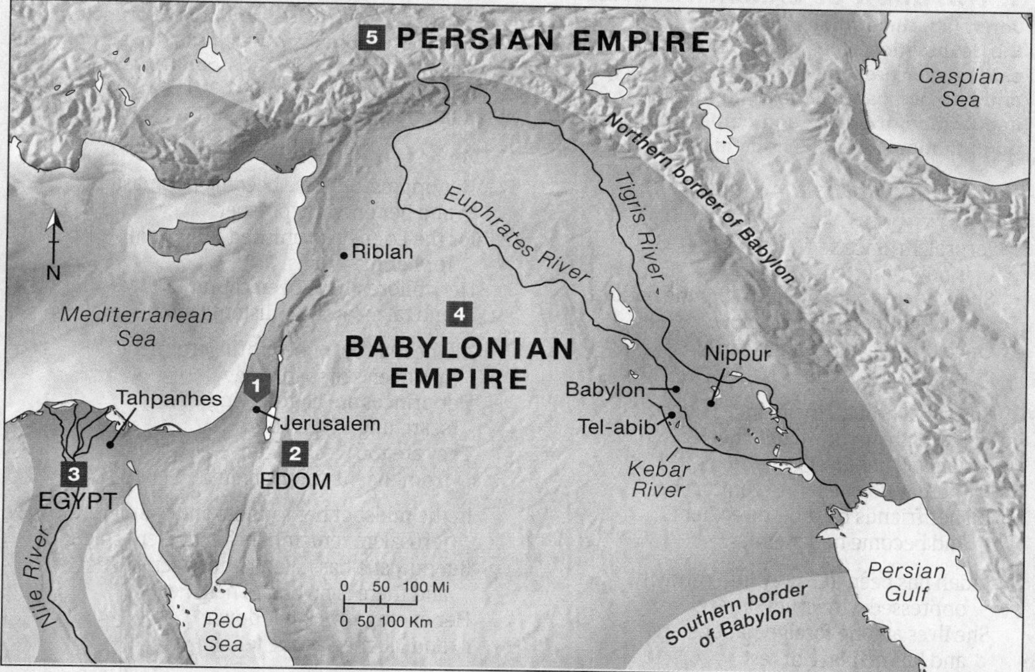

MAP

1 Jerusalem This section begins with Jerusalem lying in ruins, devastated by the total destruction wrought by the armies of Babylon. Jeremiah laments the situation in Jerusalem and the Temple in the book of Lamentations. Babylon appointed a man named Gedaliah to govern the area around Jerusalem, but some of the people of Judah who remained in the land rebelled against him and murdered him (Jer 40:7–41:18).

2 Edom The nation of Edom was a neighbor to Judah, and descended from Jacob's twin brother, Esau. These historic ties, however, did not lead to good relations between the two nations. Edom was a constant enemy to Judah, and they rejoiced in the destruction of Jerusalem. The book of Obadiah records God's judgment against Edom for their opposition to his people.

3 Egypt After murdering Gedaliah, the people were scared of retribution from Babylon. They approached Jeremiah to ask his advice on what to do, and God told Jeremiah to tell the people to stay in Judah because he would protect them and provide for them there. But the people refused to listen and fled to Egypt, getting at least as far as Tahpanhes, and even to southern Egypt (Jer 42–44). There, they again faced God's judgment because they refused to trust in him completely.

4 Babylon Many people from Judah had been carried off to Babylon in three separate deportations over a twenty year period, in 605, 597, and 586 B.C. Daniel and Ezekiel were among these people who were resettled into new lives in the Babylonian Empire. Babylon was the center of world power at the time of the Exile, but in short order they would have a new rival for world domination.

5 Persia In 539 B.C., the Persians swooped down on Babylon and destroyed the capital and seat of power for the Babylonians. The Persian Empire was much larger than Babylon had ever been, extending much farther to the north, east, and west.

A. Jerusalem Destroyed and Sacked

The Babylonians, after years of threats against Jerusalem and multiple deportations, finally decided that they no longer wanted to deal with Judah's rebellion. They brought the full force of their military might against Jerusalem, destroying the city and the Temple and carrying off everything of value as plunder. Only a small, weak group of people were left behind to witness the destruction and desolation of this once-great city. The prophets Jeremiah and Obadiah were among those left behind in Judah.

1. THE BOOK OF LAMENTATIONS

Jeremiah, the author of Lamentations, grieves deeply because of the destruction of Jerusalem and the devastation of his nation. But in the depths of his grief, there shines a ray of hope. God's compassion is ever present. His faithfulness is great. This book shows us the serious consequences of sin and how we can still have hope in the midst of tragedy because God is good. We see the timeless importance of prayer and confession of sin. We will all face tragedy in our lives. But in the midst of our afflictions, there is hope in God.

Jeremiah Mourns for Jerusalem

LAMENTATIONS 1:1-22

1*Jerusalem, once so full of people,
is now deserted.
She who was once great among the nations
now sits alone like a widow.
Once the queen of all the earth,
she is now a slave.

2 She sobs through the night;
tears stream down her cheeks.
Among all her lovers,
there is no one left to comfort her.
All her friends have betrayed her
and become her enemies.

3 Judah has been led away into captivity,
oppressed with cruel slavery.
She lives among foreign nations
and has no place of rest.
Her enemies have chased her down,
and she has nowhere to turn.

4 The roads to Jerusalem* are in mourning,
for crowds no longer come to celebrate
the festivals.
The city gates are silent,
her priests groan,
her young women are crying—
how bitter is her fate!

5 Her oppressors have become her masters,
and her enemies prosper,
for the LORD has punished Jerusalem
for her many sins.
Her children have been captured
and taken away to distant lands.

6 All the majesty of beautiful Jerusalem*
has been stripped away.
Her princes are like starving deer
searching for pasture.
They are too weak to run
from the pursuing enemy.

7 In the midst of her sadness and wandering,
Jerusalem remembers her ancient splendor.
But now she has fallen to her enemy,
and there is no one to help her.
Her enemy struck her down
and laughed as she fell.

8 Jerusalem has sinned greatly,
so she has been tossed away like a filthy rag.
All who once honored her now despise her,
for they have seen her stripped naked and
humiliated.
All she can do is groan
and hide her face.

9 She defiled herself with immorality
and gave no thought to her future.

Lam 1 Each of the first four chapters of this book is an acrostic, laid out in the order of the Hebrew alphabet. The first word of each verse begins with a successive Hebrew letter. Chapters 1, 2, and 4 have one verse for each of the 22 Hebrew letters. Chapter 3 contains 22 stanzas of three verses each. Though chapter 5 has 22 verses, it is not an acrostic. **Lam 1:4** Hebrew *Zion;* also in 1:17. **Lam 1:6** Hebrew *of the daughter of Zion.*

Lam 1:1 This is the prophet Jeremiah's song of sorrow for Jerusalem's destruction. The nation of Judah had been utterly defeated, the Temple destroyed, and captives taken away to Babylon. Jeremiah's tears were for the suffering and humiliation of the people, but he also wept because God had rejected the people for their rebellious ways. Each year this book was read aloud to remind all the Jews that their great city fell because of their stubborn sinfulness.

Lam 1:2 The term *lovers* refers to nations such as Egypt, to whom Judah kept turning for help. As the Babylonians closed in on Jerusalem, the nation of Judah turned away from God and sought help and protection from other nations instead.

Lam 1:9 The warning was loud and clear: If Judah played with fire, its people would get burned. Jerusalem foolishly took a chance and lost, refusing to believe that immoral living brings God's punishment. The ultimate consequence of sin is punishment (Rom 6:23). We can choose to ignore God's warnings, but as surely as judgment came upon Jerusalem, so it will come upon those who defy God. Are you listening to God's Word? Are you obeying it? Obedience is a sure sign of your love for God.

Now she lies in the gutter
with no one to lift her out.
"LORD, see my misery," she cries.
"The enemy has triumphed."
10 The enemy has plundered her completely,
taking every precious thing she owns.
She has seen foreigners violate her sacred Temple,
the place the LORD had forbidden them to enter.
11 Her people groan as they search for bread.
They have sold their treasures for food to stay alive.
"O LORD, look," she mourns,
"and see how I am despised.
12 "Does it mean nothing to you, all you who pass by?
Look around and see if there is any suffering like mine,
which the LORD brought on me
when he erupted in fierce anger.
13 "He has sent fire from heaven that burns in my bones.
He has placed a trap in my path and turned me back.
He has left me devastated,
racked with sickness all day long.
14 "He wove my sins into ropes
to hitch me to a yoke of captivity.
The Lord sapped my strength and turned me over to my enemies;
I am helpless in their hands.
15 "The Lord has treated my mighty men
with contempt.
At his command a great army has come
to crush my young warriors.
The Lord has trampled his beloved city*
like grapes are trampled in a winepress.
16 "For all these things I weep;
tears flow down my cheeks.
No one is here to comfort me;
any who might encourage me are far away.
My children have no future,
for the enemy has conquered us."
17 Jerusalem reaches out for help,
but no one comforts her.
Regarding his people Israel,*
the LORD has said,
"Let their neighbors be their enemies!
Let them be thrown away like a filthy rag!"
18 "The LORD is right," Jerusalem says,
"for I rebelled against him.
Listen, people everywhere;
look upon my anguish and despair,
for my sons and daughters
have been taken captive to distant lands.
19 "I begged my allies for help,
but they betrayed me.
My priests and leaders
starved to death in the city,
even as they searched for food
to save their lives.
20 "LORD, see my anguish!
My heart is broken
and my soul despairs,
for I have rebelled against you.
In the streets the sword kills,
and at home there is only death.
21 "Others heard my groans,
but no one turned to comfort me.
When my enemies heard about my troubles,
they were happy to see what you had done.
Oh, bring the day you promised,
when they will suffer as I have suffered.
22 "Look at all their evil deeds, LORD.
Punish them,
as you have punished me
for all my sins.
My groans are many,
and I am sick at heart."

Lam 1:15 Hebrew *the virgin daughter of Judah.* **Lam 1:17** Hebrew *Jacob.* The names "Jacob" and "Israel" are often interchanged throughout the Old Testament, referring sometimes to the individual patriarch and sometimes to the nation.

Lam 1:14 At first, sin seems to offer freedom. But the liberty to do anything we want gradually becomes a desire to do everything. Then we become captive to sin, bound by its "yoke." Freedom from sin's captivity comes only from God. He gives us freedom—not to do anything we want but to do what he knows is best for us. Strange as it may seem, true freedom comes in obeying God—following his guidance so that we can receive his best.

Lam 1:16 Jeremiah's sorrow expresses the sorrow of the nation. God is the comforter, but because of the people's sins, he had to turn away from them and become their judge. When we suffer the consequences of sin, repentance from the sin that caused the problem is the first and most important way to find relief.

Lam 1:19 Jerusalem's allies could not come to help because, like Jerusalem, they failed to seek God. Though these allies appeared strong, they were actually weak because God was not with them. Dependable assistance can come only from an ally whose power is from God. When you seek wise counsel, go to Christians who get their wisdom from the all-knowing God.

Lam 1:22 Babylon, although sinful, was God's instrument for punishing Judah and its capital, Jerusalem. The people of Jerusalem were pleading for God to punish sinful Babylon as he had punished them ("punish them, as you have punished me"). God would do this, for he had already passed judgment on Babylon (see Jer 50:1-27).

586 BC
Jerusalem destroyed by Babylon

God's Anger at Sin

LAMENTATIONS 2:1-22

1 The Lord in his anger
has cast a dark shadow over beautiful Jerusalem.*
The fairest of Israel's cities lies in the dust,
thrown down from the heights of heaven.
In his day of great anger,
the Lord has shown no mercy even to his Temple.*

2 Without mercy the Lord has destroyed
every home in Israel.*
In his anger he has broken down
the fortress walls of beautiful Jerusalem.*
He has brought them to the ground,
dishonoring the kingdom and its rulers.

3 All the strength of Israel
vanishes beneath his fierce anger.
The Lord has withdrawn his protection
as the enemy attacks.
He consumes the whole land of Israel
like a raging fire.

4 He bends his bow against his people,
as though he were their enemy.
His strength is used against them
to kill their finest youth.
His fury is poured out like fire
on beautiful Jerusalem.*

5 Yes, the Lord has vanquished Israel
like an enemy.
He has destroyed her palaces
and demolished her fortresses.
He has brought unending sorrow and tears
upon beautiful Jerusalem.

6 He has broken down his Temple
as though it were merely a garden shelter.
The LORD has blotted out all memory
of the holy festivals and Sabbath days.
Kings and priests fall together
before his fierce anger.

7 The Lord has rejected his own altar;
he despises his own sanctuary.
He has given Jerusalem's palaces
to her enemies.
They shout in the LORD's Temple
as though it were a day of celebration.

8 The LORD was determined
to destroy the walls of beautiful Jerusalem.
He made careful plans for their destruction,
then did what he had planned.
Therefore, the ramparts and walls
have fallen down before him.

9 Jerusalem's gates have sunk into the ground.
He has smashed their locks and bars.
Her kings and princes have been exiled
to distant lands;
her law has ceased to exist.
Her prophets receive
no more visions from the LORD.

10 The leaders of beautiful Jerusalem
sit on the ground in silence.
They are clothed in burlap
and throw dust on their heads.
The young women of Jerusalem
hang their heads in shame.

11 I have cried until the tears no longer come;
my heart is broken.
My spirit is poured out in agony
as I see the desperate plight of my people.
Little children and tiny babies
are fainting and dying in the streets.

12 They cry out to their mothers,
"We need food and drink!"
Their lives ebb away in the streets
like the life of a warrior wounded in battle.

Lam 2:1a Hebrew *the daughter of Zion;* also in 2:8, 10, 18. **Lam 2:1b** Hebrew *his footstool.* **Lam 2:2a** Hebrew *Jacob;* also in 2:3b. See note on 1:17. **Lam 2:2b** Hebrew *the daughter of Judah;* also in 2:5. **Lam 2:4** Hebrew *on the tent of the daughter of Zion.*

Lam 2:6 King Solomon's Temple in Jerusalem represented God's presence with the people (1 Kgs 8:1-11). The Temple was the central place of worship. Many in Jeremiah's day assumed that God would never allow his Temple to be harmed. Its destruction symbolized God's rejection of his people—that he had withdrawn his presence from them.

Lam 2:7 Our place of worship is not as important to God as our priorities in worship. A church building may be beautiful, but if its people don't sincerely follow God, the church will decay from within. The people of Judah, despite their stunning Temple, had rejected in their daily lives what they proclaimed in their worship rituals. Thus, their worship had turned into a mocking lie. When you worship, are you saying words you don't really mean? Do you pray for help you don't really believe will come? Do you express love for God you don't really have? Earnestly seek God and catch a fresh vision of his love and care. Then worship him wholeheartedly.

Lam 2:9 Four powerful symbols and sources of security were lost: the protection of the gates, the leadership of the kings and princes, the guidance of the law, and the vision of the prophets. With those four factors present, the people were lulled into a false sense of security and felt comfortable with their sins. But after each was removed, the people were confronted with the choice of repenting and returning to God or continuing on this path of suffering. Don't substitute symbols, even good ones, for the reality of a living, personal relationship with God himself.

Lam 2:11 Jeremiah's tears were sincere and full of compassion. Sorrow does not mean that we lack faith or strength. There is nothing wrong with crying—Jesus himself felt sorrow and even wept (John 11:35). How do we react to the tearing down of our society and to moral degradation? This may not be as obvious as an invading enemy army, but the destruction is just as certain. We, too, should be deeply moved when we see the moral decay that surrounds us.

They gasp for life
as they collapse in their mothers' arms.

13 What can I say about you?
Who has ever seen such sorrow?
O daughter of Jerusalem,
to what can I compare your anguish?
O virgin daughter of Zion,
how can I comfort you?
For your wound is as deep as the sea.
Who can heal you?

14 Your prophets have said
so many foolish things, false to the core.
They did not save you from exile
by pointing out your sins.
Instead, they painted false pictures,
filling you with false hope.

15 All who pass by jeer at you.
They scoff and insult beautiful Jerusalem,*
saying,
"Is this the city called 'Most Beautiful
in All the World'
and 'Joy of All the Earth'?"

16 All your enemies mock you.
They scoff and snarl and say,
"We have destroyed her at last!
We have long waited for this day,
and it is finally here!"

17 But it is the LORD who did just as he planned.
He has fulfilled the promises of disaster
he made long ago.
He has destroyed Jerusalem without mercy.
He has caused her enemies to gloat over her
and has given them power over her.

18 Cry aloud* before the Lord,
O walls of beautiful Jerusalem!
Let your tears flow like a river
day and night.
Give yourselves no rest;
give your eyes no relief.

19 Rise during the night and cry out.
Pour out your hearts like water to the Lord.
Lift up your hands to him in prayer,
pleading for your children,
for in every street
they are faint with hunger.

20 "O LORD, think about this!
Should you treat your own people this way?
Should mothers eat their own children,
those they once bounced on their knees?
Should priests and prophets be killed
within the Lord's Temple?

21 "See them lying in the streets—
young and old,
boys and girls,
killed by the swords of the enemy.
You have killed them in your anger,
slaughtering them without mercy.

22 "You have invited terrors from all around,
as though you were calling them to
a day of feasting.
In the day of the LORD's anger,
no one has escaped or survived.
The enemy has killed all the children
whom I carried and raised."

Hope in the Midst of Affliction

LAMENTATIONS 3:1-66

1 I am the one who has seen the afflictions
that come from the rod of the LORD's anger.
2 He has led me into darkness,
shutting out all light.

Lam 2:15 Hebrew *the daughter of Jerusalem.* **Lam 2:18** Hebrew *Their heart cried.*

Lam 2:14 False prophets were everywhere in Jeremiah's day. They gave counterfeit and misleading messages. While Jeremiah warned the people of coming destruction and lengthy captivity, the false prophets said that all was well so the people need not fear. All of Jeremiah's words came true because he was a true prophet of God (Jer 14:14-16).

Lam 2:19 Jeremiah describes Jerusalem's desolation and calls for God's revenge on his enemies (Lam 1). He includes a call for God's people to pour out their hearts in the Lord's presence (Lam 2). The people must turn from their sins; they must sincerely mourn over their wrongs against God (Lam 3:40-42). The people had much to cry about. Because of their stubborn rebellion against God, they had brought great suffering to all, especially to the innocent. Was this suffering God's fault? No, it was the fault of the wayward people. Sinful people brought destruction on themselves, but tragically, sin's consequences affected everyone—good and evil alike.

Lam 2:19 The people's suffering and sin should have brought them to the Lord, weeping for forgiveness. Only when our prideful, independent hearts are broken over sin will God come to our rescue. Just feeling sorry about experiencing sin's consequences does not bring forgiveness. But if we cry out to God in repentance, he will forgive us.

Lam 2:21-22 This horrible scene could have been avoided. Jeremiah had warned the people for years that this day of destruction would come, and it broke his heart to see it fulfilled. We are always shocked when we hear of tragedy striking the innocent. But often innocent bystanders are victims of judgment on a nation. Sin has a way of causing great sorrow and devastation to many.

Lam 3:1ff In Jeremiah's darkest moment, his hope was strengthened with this assurance: God had been faithful and would continue to be faithful. Jeremiah saw both God's judgment and God's steadfast love. In the time of judgment, Jeremiah could still cling to God's love, just as in times of prosperity he had warned of God's judgment.

Lam 3:1ff In the original Hebrew, the first four chapters in Lamentations are acrostic poems. Each verse in each chapter begins with a successive letter of the Hebrew alphabet. Lamentations 3 has 66 verses rather than 22 because it is a triple acrostic: The first three verses begin with the first letter of the Hebrew alphabet, the next three with the second, and so on. This was a typical form of Hebrew poetry. Other examples of acrostics are Psalms 37; 119; 145; Proverbs 31:10-31.

▸ **LAMENTATIONS 3:1-66** ***(cont.)***

3 He has turned his hand against me
again and again, all day long.
4 He has made my skin and flesh grow old.
He has broken my bones.
5 He has besieged and surrounded me
with anguish and distress.
6 He has buried me in a dark place,
like those long dead.

7 He has walled me in, and I cannot escape.
He has bound me in heavy chains.
8 And though I cry and shout,
he has shut out my prayers.
9 He has blocked my way with a high stone wall;
he has made my road crooked.

10 He has hidden like a bear or a lion,
waiting to attack me.
11 He has dragged me off the path and torn me
in pieces,
leaving me helpless and devastated.
12 He has drawn his bow
and made me the target for his arrows.

13 He shot his arrows
deep into my heart.
14 My own people laugh at me.
All day long they sing their mocking songs.
15 He has filled me with bitterness
and given me a bitter cup of sorrow to drink.

16 He has made me chew on gravel.
He has rolled me in the dust.
17 Peace has been stripped away,
and I have forgotten what prosperity is.
18 I cry out, "My splendor is gone!
Everything I had hoped for from the LORD
is lost!"

19 The thought of my suffering and
homelessness
is bitter beyond words.*
20 I will never forget this awful time,
as I grieve over my loss.
21 Yet I still dare to hope
when I remember this:

22 The faithful love of the LORD never ends!*
His mercies never cease.
23 Great is his faithfulness;
his mercies begin afresh each morning.
24 I say to myself, "The LORD is my inheritance;
therefore, I will hope in him!"

25 The LORD is good to those who depend on him,
to those who search for him.
26 So it is good to wait quietly
for salvation from the LORD.
27 And it is good for people to submit at an early age
to the yoke of his discipline:

28 Let them sit alone in silence
beneath the LORD's demands.
29 Let them lie face down in the dust,
for there may be hope at last.
30 Let them turn the other cheek to those who
strike them
and accept the insults of their enemies.

31 For no one is abandoned
by the Lord forever.
32 Though he brings grief, he also shows
compassion
because of the greatness of his unfailing love.
33 For he does not enjoy hurting people
or causing them sorrow.

34 If people crush underfoot
all the prisoners of the land,
35 if they deprive others of their rights
in defiance of the Most High,
36 if they twist justice in the courts—
doesn't the Lord see all these things?

37 Who can command things to happen
without the Lord's permission?

Lam 3:19 Or *is wormwood and gall.* **Lam 3:22** As in Syriac version; Hebrew reads *of the LORD keeps us from destruction.*

Lam 3:21-23 Jeremiah saw one ray of hope in all the sin and sorrow surrounding him: "The faithful love of the LORD never ends. . . . Great is his faithfulness; his mercies begin afresh each morning." God willingly responds with help when we ask. Perhaps there is some sin in your life that you thought God would not forgive. God's steadfast love and mercy are greater than any sin, and he promises forgiveness.

Lam 3:23 Jeremiah knew from personal experience about God's faithfulness. God had promised that punishment would follow disobedience, and it did. But God also had promised future restoration and blessing, and Jeremiah knew that God would keep that promise also. Trusting in God's faithfulness day by day makes us confident in his great promises for the future.

Lam 3:27-33 To submit "to the yoke of his discipline" means to willingly come under God's discipline and learn what he wants to teach. This involves several important factors: (1) silent reflection on what God wants, (2) repentant humility, (3) self-control in the face of adversity, and (4) confident patience, depending on the divine Teacher to bring about loving lessons in our lives. God has several long-term and short-term lessons for you right now. Are you doing your homework?

Lam 3:30 This call to "turn the other cheek" reminds us that sometimes God calls us to suffer criticism and abuse for his purposes. Jesus taught his followers to turn the other cheek (Matt 5:39), and he exemplified this at the highest level just before his crucifixion (Matt 27:27-31; Luke 22:64; John 18:22; 19:3). But this should never be used to justify anyone's continued suffering of spousal or any other kind of abuse. It is a call to absorb violence without striking back in kind, not a command to remain in a violent situation indefinitely.

Lam 3:39-42 Parents discipline children to produce right behavior. God disciplined Judah to produce right living and genuine worship. We must not complain about corrective or instructive discipline in our lives but learn from it, trusting God and being willing to change. We must allow God's correction to bring about the kind of behavior in our life that pleases him.

38 Does not the Most High
send both calamity and good?
39 Then why should we, mere humans, complain
when we are punished for our sins?

40 Instead, let us test and examine our ways.
Let us turn back to the LORD.
41 Let us lift our hearts and hands
to God in heaven and say,
42 "We have sinned and rebelled,
and you have not forgiven us.

43 "You have engulfed us with your anger,
chased us down,
and slaughtered us without mercy.
44 You have hidden yourself in a cloud
so our prayers cannot reach you.
45 You have discarded us as refuse and garbage
among the nations.

46 "All our enemies
have spoken out against us.
47 We are filled with fear,
for we are trapped, devastated, and ruined."
48 Tears stream from my eyes
because of the destruction of my people!

49 My tears flow endlessly;
they will not stop
50 until the LORD looks down
from heaven and sees.
51 My heart is breaking
over the fate of all the women of Jerusalem.

52 My enemies, whom I have never harmed,
hunted me down like a bird.
53 They threw me into a pit
and dropped stones on me.
54 The water rose over my head,
and I cried out, "This is the end!"

55 But I called on your name, LORD,
from deep within the pit.
56 You heard me when I cried, "Listen to my
pleading!
Hear my cry for help!"
57 Yes, you came when I called;
you told me, "Do not fear."

58 Lord, you are my lawyer! Plead my case!
For you have redeemed my life.
59 You have seen the wrong they have done to me,
LORD.
Be my judge, and prove me right.
60 You have seen the vengeful plots
my enemies have laid against me.

61 LORD, you have heard the vile names they call me.
You know all about the plans they have made.
62 My enemies whisper and mutter
as they plot against me all day long.
63 Look at them! Whether they sit or stand,
I am the object of their mocking songs.

64 Pay them back, LORD,
for all the evil they have done.
65 Give them hard and stubborn hearts,
and then let your curse fall on them!
66 Chase them down in your anger,
destroying them beneath the LORD's heavens.

God's Anger Is Satisfied

LAMENTATIONS 4:1-22

1 How the gold has lost its luster!
Even the finest gold has become dull.
The sacred gemstones
lie scattered in the streets!

2 See how the precious children of Jerusalem,*
worth their weight in fine gold,

Lam 4:2 Hebrew *precious sons of Zion.*

Lam 3:52-57 At one point in his ministry, Jeremiah was thrown into an empty cistern, and he was left to die in the mire at the bottom (Jer 38:6-13). But God rescued him. Jeremiah used this experience as a picture of the nation sinking into sin. If they turned to God, he would rescue them.

Lam 4:1ff Lamentations 4 contrasts the situation before the siege of Jerusalem with the situation after the siege. The sights and sounds of prosperity were gone because of the people's sin. This chapter warns us not to assume that when life is going well, it will always stay that way. We must be careful not to glory in our prosperity or we will fall into spiritual poverty.

Lam 4:1-10 When a city was under siege, the city wall—built for protection—sealed the people inside. They could not get out to the fields to get food and water because the enemy was camped around the city. As food in the city ran out, the people watched their enemies harvest and eat the food in the fields. The siege was a test of wills to see which army could outlast the other. Jerusalem was under siege for two years. Life became so harsh that people even ate their own children, and dead bodies were left to rot in the streets. All hope was gone.

Pottery

In the Bible are many references to a potter and his work, usually as a metaphor for the relationship God has with his creation: "O Israel, can I not do to you as this potter has done to his clay? As the clay is in the potter's hand, so are you in my hand" (Jer 18:6). In the Creation story God is portrayed as the potter making man from the ground (Gen 2:7). Jeremiah graphically prophesied the destruction of Jerusalem by breaking a potter's earthen flask into so many pieces that it could not be restored (Jer 19:10-11). Although precious in God's sight, the Jews, at the time of the siege and capture of Jerusalem, were "treated like pots of clay" (Lam 4:2)—an expression of their human frailty. They could be easily broken and destroyed. We should always remember that God, our Father, is the potter, and we are the clay. We are all formed by his hand (Isa 64:8).

▸ **LAMENTATIONS 4:1-22** ***(cont.)***

are now treated like pots of clay
made by a common potter.

3 Even the jackals feed their young,
but not my people Israel.
They ignore their children's cries,
like ostriches in the desert.

4 The parched tongues of their little ones
stick to the roofs of their mouths in thirst.
The children cry for bread,
but no one has any to give them.

5 The people who once ate the richest foods
now beg in the streets for anything they
can get.
Those who once wore the finest clothes
now search the garbage dumps for food.

6 The guilt* of my people
is greater than that of Sodom,
where utter disaster struck in a moment
and no hand offered help.

7 Our princes once glowed with health—
brighter than snow, whiter than milk.
Their faces were as ruddy as rubies,
their appearance like fine jewels.*

8 But now their faces are blacker than soot.
No one recognizes them in the streets.
Their skin sticks to their bones;
it is as dry and hard as wood.

9 Those killed by the sword are better off
than those who die of hunger.
Starving, they waste away
for lack of food from the fields.

10 Tenderhearted women
have cooked their own children.
They have eaten them
to survive the siege.

11 But now the anger of the LORD is satisfied.
His fierce anger has been poured out.
He started a fire in Jerusalem*
that burned the city to its foundations.

12 Not a king in all the earth—
no one in all the world—
would have believed that an enemy
could march through the gates of Jerusalem.

13 Yet it happened because of the sins of her
prophets
and the sins of her priests,
who defiled the city
by shedding innocent blood.

14 They wandered blindly
through the streets,
so defiled by blood
that no one dared touch them.

15 "Get away!" the people shouted at them.
"You're defiled! Don't touch us!"
So they fled to distant lands
and wandered among foreign nations,
but none would let them stay.

16 The LORD himself has scattered them,
and he no longer helps them.
People show no respect for the priests
and no longer honor the leaders.

17 We looked in vain for our allies
to come and save us,
but we were looking to nations
that could not help us.

18 We couldn't go into the streets
without danger to our lives.
Our end was near; our days were numbered.
We were doomed!

19 Our enemies were swifter than eagles in flight.
If we fled to the mountains, they found us.
If we hid in the wilderness,
they were waiting for us there.

20 Our king—the LORD's anointed, the very life
of our nation—
was caught in their snares.

Lam 4:6 Or *punishment.* **Lam 4:7** Hebrew *like lapis lazuli.* **Lam 4:11** Hebrew *in Zion.*

Lam 4:6 The city of Sodom, destroyed by burning sulfur from heaven because of its wickedness (Gen 18:20–19:29), became a symbol of God's ultimate judgment. Yet the guilt of Jerusalem was even greater than that of Sodom! Jeremiah wasn't comparing sins but acknowledging that Sodom had few of the advantages and blessings that the people of Jerusalem had enjoyed from God. Jerusalem's greater guilt was in turning away in spite of the city's countless God-given benefits.

Lam 4:13-15 To be defiled or unclean meant to be unfit to enter the Temple or to worship before God. The priests and prophets should have been the most careful to maintain ceremonial purity so that they could continue to perform their duties before God. But many priests and prophets did evil and were defiled. As the nation's leaders, their example led the people into sin and caused the ultimate downfall of the nation and its capital city, Jerusalem.

Lam 4:17 Judah had asked Egypt to help it fight the Babylonian army. Egypt gave Judah false hope by starting to help, but then it retreated (Jer 37:5-7). Jeremiah warned Judah not to ally itself with Egypt. He told the leaders to rely on God, but they refused to listen.

Lam 4:20 King Zedekiah, although called "the LORD's anointed," had little spiritual depth or leadership power. Instead of putting his faith in God and listening to God's true prophet, Jeremiah, he listened to the false prophets. To make matters worse, the people chose to follow and trust in their king (2 Chr 36:11-16). They chose the path

We had thought that his shadow
would protect us against any nation
on earth!
21 Are you rejoicing in the land of Uz,
O people of Edom?
But you, too, must drink from the cup of the
LORD's anger.
You, too, will be stripped naked in your
drunkenness.
22 O beautiful Jerusalem,* your punishment
will end;
you will soon return from exile.
But Edom, your punishment is just
beginning;
soon your many sins will be exposed.

Jeremiah Pleads for Restoration

LAMENTATIONS 5:1-22

1 LORD, remember what has happened to us.
See how we have been disgraced!
2 Our inheritance has been turned over
to strangers,
our homes to foreigners.
3 We are orphaned and fatherless.
Our mothers are widowed.
4 We have to pay for water to drink,
and even firewood is expensive.
5 Those who pursue us are at our heels;
we are exhausted but are given no rest.
6 We submitted to Egypt and Assyria
to get enough food to survive.
7 Our ancestors sinned, but they have died—
and we are suffering the punishment they
deserved!
8 Slaves have now become our masters;
there is no one left to rescue us.
9 We hunt for food at the risk of our lives,
for violence rules the countryside.
10 The famine has blackened our skin
as though baked in an oven.
11 Our enemies rape the women in Jerusalem*
and the young girls in all the towns
of Judah.
12 Our princes are being hanged by their
thumbs,
and our elders are treated with contempt.
13 Young men are led away to work at millstones,
and boys stagger under heavy loads
of wood.
14 The elders no longer sit in the city gates;
the young men no longer dance and sing.
15 Joy has left our hearts;
our dancing has turned to mourning.
16 The garlands have* fallen from our heads.
Weep for us because we have sinned.
17 Our hearts are sick and weary,
and our eyes grow dim with tears.
18 For Jerusalem* is empty and desolate,
a place haunted by jackals.
19 But LORD, you remain the same forever!
Your throne continues from generation
to generation.
20 Why do you continue to forget us?
Why have you abandoned us for so long?
21 Restore us, O LORD, and bring us back
to you again!
Give us back the joys we once had!
22 Or have you utterly rejected us?
Are you angry with us still?

Lam 4:22 Hebrew *O daughter of Zion.* **Lam 5:11** Hebrew *in Zion.* **Lam 5:16** Or *The crown has.* **Lam 5:18** Hebrew *Mount Zion.*

of complacency, wanting to feel secure rather than following the directives God was giving his people through Jeremiah. But now the source of their confidence—King Zedekiah—was captured.

Lam 4:21-22 Edom was Judah's arch-enemy, even though they had a common ancestor, Isaac (see Gen 25:19-26; 36:1). Edom had actively aided Babylon in the siege of Jerusalem. As a reward, Nebuchadnezzar gave the outlying lands of Judah to Edom. Jeremiah said that the nation of Edom would be judged for treachery against Judah—in essence, against its own relatives. (See also Jer 49:7-22; Ezek 25:12-14; Amos 9:12; Obad 1:1-21.)

Lam 5:1ff At a time of grief, the true believer should turn to God in prayer. Here Jeremiah prayed for mercy for his people. At the end of his prayer, he wondered if God had "utterly rejected" his people because of his great anger toward them. But then he remembered, "You will not stay angry with your people forever, because you delight in showing unfailing love" (Mic 7:18).

Lam 5:14 During peace and prosperity, the leaders and elders of the city would sit at the city gate talking over politics, theology, and philosophy, and conducting business. As Jeremiah prayed, he saw fewer and fewer evidences of either the healthy interaction or the lighthearted dancing of their former lives under God's blessing. They had lost even the everyday events they had assumed would always be there. A lack of continual gratefulness to God often indicates that we are taking the goodness of life for granted.

Lam 5:22 A high calling flouted by low living results in deep suffering. Lamentations gives us a portrait of the bitter suffering the people of Jerusalem experienced when sin caught up with them and God turned his back on them. Every material goal they had lived for collapsed. But although God turned away from them because of their sin, he did not abandon them—that was their great hope. Despite their sinful past, God would restore them if they returned to him. Hope is found only in the Lord. Thus, our grief should turn us toward him, not away from him.

2. THE BOOK OF OBADIAH

When Jerusalem was destroyed by Babylon, the nearby nation of Edom celebrated the demise of Judah. Although these nations had common ancestry (Edom descended from Esau, Israel from his twin brother, Jacob), Edom was a consistent enemy of God's people. Obadiah brings a message of judgment against Edom. God would not ignore the enemies of his people, and justice would be done.

Edom's Judgment Announced

OBADIAH 1:1-9

This is the vision that the Sovereign LORD revealed to Obadiah concerning the land of Edom.

We have heard a message from the LORD
that an ambassador was sent to the nations
to say,
"Get ready, everyone!
Let's assemble our armies and attack Edom!"

2 The LORD says to Edom,
"I will cut you down to size among the nations;
you will be greatly despised.
3 You have been deceived by your own pride
because you live in a rock fortress
and make your home high in the mountains.
'Who can ever reach us way up here?'
you ask boastfully.
4 But even if you soar as high as eagles
and build your nest among the stars,
I will bring you crashing down,"
says the LORD.

5 "If thieves came at night and robbed you
(what a disaster awaits you!),
they would not take everything.
Those who harvest grapes
always leave a few for the poor.
But your enemies will wipe you out
completely!
6 Every nook and cranny of Edom*
will be searched and looted.
Every treasure will be found and taken.

7 "All your allies will turn against you.
They will help to chase you from your land.
They will promise you peace
while plotting to deceive and destroy you.
Your trusted friends will set traps for you,
and you won't even know about it.
8 At that time not a single wise person

Ob 6 Hebrew *Esau;* also in 8b, 9, 18, 19, 21.

Obad 1:1 Obadiah was a prophet from Judah who told of God's judgment against the nation of Edom. There are two commonly accepted dates for this prophecy: (1) between 855 and 840 B.C., when a Philistine/Arab coalition attacked King Jehoram and Jerusalem (2 Chr 21:16ff); (2) 586 B.C., when the Babylonians completely destroyed Jerusalem. Either is possible, but in this Bible we have placed it at the later date. Edom had rejoiced over the misfortunes of both Israel and Judah, although the Edomites and Jews descended from two brothers—Esau and Jacob (Gen 25:19-26). But just as these two brothers were constantly fighting, so were Israel and Edom. God pronounced judgment on Edom for its callous and malicious actions toward his people.

Obad 1:3 Edom was Judah's southern neighbor, sharing a common boundary. But neighbors are not always friends, and Edom liked nothing about Judah. Edom's capital at this time was Sela (perhaps the later city of Petra), a city considered impregnable because it was cut into rock cliffs and set in a canyon that could be entered only through a narrow gap. What Edom perceived as its strengths would be its downfall: (1) safety in their city (Obad 1:3-4)—God would send them plummeting from the heights; (2) pride in their self-sufficiency (Obad 1:4)—God would humble them; (3) wealth (Obad 1:5-6)—thieves would steal all they had; (4) allies (Obad 1:7)—God would cause them to turn against Edom; (5) wisdom (Obad 1:8-9)—the wise would be destroyed.

OBADIAH

Obadiah served as a prophet to Judah possibly around 586 B.C.

Climate of the times	Edom was a constant thorn in Judah's side. The Edomites often participated in attacks initiated by other enemies.
Main message	God will judge Edom for its evil actions toward God's people.
Importance of message	Just as Edom was destroyed and disappeared as a nation, so God will destroy proud and wicked people.
Contemporary prophets	Jeremiah, Ezekiel, Daniel

Obad 1:3 The Edomites felt secure, and they were proud of their self-sufficiency. But they were fooling themselves because there is no lasting security apart from God. Is your security in objects or people? Ask yourself how much lasting security they really offer. Possessions and people can disappear in a moment, but God does not change. Only he can supply true security.

Obad 1:4 The Edomites were proud of their city carved right into the rock. Today Sela, or Petra, is considered one of the marvels of the ancient world, but only as a tourist attraction. The Bible warns that pride is the surest route to self-destruction (Prov 16:18). Just as Petra and Edom fell, so will proud people fall. A humble person is more secure than a proud person because humility gives a more accurate perspective of oneself and the world.

Obad 1:4-9 God did not pronounce these harsh judgments against Edom out of vengeance but in order to bring about justice. God is morally perfect and demands complete justice and fairness. The Edomites were simply getting what they deserved. Because they murdered, they would be murdered. Because they robbed, they would be robbed. Because they took advantage of others, they would be used. Don't talk yourself into sin, thinking that "nobody will know" or "I won't get caught." God knows all our sins, and he will be just.

Obad 1:8 Edom was noted for its wise people. But there is a difference between human wisdom and God's wisdom. The Edomites may have been wise in the ways of the world, but they were foolish because they ignored and even mocked God.

will be left in the whole land of Edom,"
says the LORD.
"For on the mountains of Edom
I will destroy everyone who has understanding.
9 The mightiest warriors of Teman
will be terrified,
and everyone on the mountains of Edom
will be cut down in the slaughter.

Reasons for Edom's Punishment

OBADIAH 1:10-14

10 "Because of the violence you did
to your close relatives in Israel,*
you will be filled with shame
and destroyed forever.
11 When they were invaded,
you stood aloof, refusing to help them.
Foreign invaders carried off their wealth
and cast lots to divide up Jerusalem,
but you acted like one of Israel's enemies.

12 "You should not have gloated
when they exiled your relatives to distant lands.
You should not have rejoiced
when the people of Judah suffered such misfortune.
You should not have spoken arrogantly
in that terrible time of trouble.
13 You should not have plundered the land of Israel
when they were suffering such calamity.
You should not have gloated over their destruction
when they were suffering such calamity.
You should not have seized their wealth
when they were suffering such calamity.
14 You should not have stood at the crossroads,
killing those who tried to escape.
You should not have captured the survivors
and handed them over in their terrible time of trouble.

Edom Destroyed, Israel Restored

OBADIAH 1:15-21

15 "The day is near when I, the LORD,
will judge all godless nations!
As you have done to Israel,
so it will be done to you.
All your evil deeds
will fall back on your own heads.
16 Just as you swallowed up my people
on my holy mountain,
so you and the surrounding nations
will swallow the punishment I pour out on you.
Yes, all you nations will drink and stagger
and disappear from history.

Ob 10 Hebrew *your brother Jacob*. The names "Jacob" and "Israel" are often interchanged throughout the Old Testament, referring sometimes to the individual patriarch and sometimes to the nation.

HISTORY OF THE CONFLICT BETWEEN ISRAEL AND EDOM

The nation of Israel descended from Jacob; the nation of Edom descended from Esau.	Gen 25:23
Jacob and Esau struggled in their mother's womb.	Gen 25:19-26
Esau sold his birthright and blessing to Jacob.	Gen 25:29-34
Edom refused to let the Israelites pass through its land.	Num 20:14-21
Israel's kings had constant conflict with Edom:	
• Saul	1 Sam 14:47
• David	2 Sam 8:13-14
• Solomon	1 Kgs 11:14-22
• Jehoram	2 Kgs 8:20-22; 2 Chr 21:8ff
• Ahaz	2 Chr 28:16
Edom urged Babylon to destroy Jerusalem.	Ps 137:7

Obad 1:9 Eliphaz, one of Job's three friends (Job 2:11), was from Teman, about five miles east of Petra. Teman was named after Esau's grandson (Gen 36:11).

Obad 1:10-11 The Israelites had descended from Jacob, and the Edomites, from his brother, Esau (Gen 25:19-26). Instead of helping Israel and Judah when they were in need, Edom had allowed them to be destroyed and even had plundered what was left behind. Edom, therefore, acted like an enemy and would be punished. Anyone who does not help God's people is God's enemy. If you have withheld your help from someone in a time of need, this is sin (Jas 4:17). Sin includes not only what we do, but also what we refuse to do. Don't ignore or refuse to help those in need.

Obad 1:12 The Edomites were glad to see Judah in trouble. Their hatred made them want the nation destroyed. God wiped out the Edomites for their wrong attitudes and actions. How often do you find yourself rejoicing at the misfortunes of others? Because God alone is the judge, we must never be happy about others' misfortunes, even if we think they deserve them (see Prov 24:17).

Obad 1:12-14 Of all Israel and Judah's neighbors, the Edomites were the only ones not promised any mercy from God. This was because they looted Jerusalem and rejoiced at the misfortunes of Israel and Judah. They betrayed their blood brothers in times of crisis and aided their brothers' enemies. (See also Ps 137:7; Jer 49:7-22; Ezek 25:12-14; Amos 1:11-12.)

Obad 1:15 Why will God's judgment fall on all nations? Edom was not the only nation to rejoice at Judah's fall. All nations and individuals will be judged for the way they have treated God's people. Some nations today treat God's people favorably, while others are hostile toward them. God will judge all people according to the way they treat others, especially believers (Rev 20:12-13). Jesus talked about this in Matthew 25:31-46.

▶ **OBADIAH 1:15-21** ***(cont.)***

17 "But Jerusalem* will become a refuge
for those who escape;
it will be a holy place.
And the people of Israel* will come back
to reclaim their inheritance.
18 The people of Israel will be a raging fire,
and Edom a field of dry stubble.
The descendants of Joseph will be
a flame
roaring across the field, devouring
everything.
There will be no survivors in Edom.
I, the LORD, have spoken!

19 "Then my people living in the Negev
will occupy the mountains of Edom.
Those living in the foothills of Judah*
will possess the Philistine plains
and take over the fields of Ephraim and
Samaria.
And the people of Benjamin
will occupy the land of Gilead.
20 The exiles of Israel will return to their land
and occupy the Phoenician coast as far
north as Zarephath.
The captives from Jerusalem exiled in the north*
will return home and resettle the towns
of the Negev.
21 Those who have been rescued* will go up to*
Mount Zion in Jerusalem
to rule over the mountains of Edom.
And the LORD himself will be king!"

Ob 17a Hebrew *Mount Zion.* **Ob 17b** Hebrew *house of Jacob;* also in 18. See note on 10. **Ob 19** Hebrew *the Shephelah.* **Ob 20** Hebrew *in Sepharad.* **Ob 21a** As in Greek and Syriac versions; Hebrew reads *Rescuers.* **Ob 21b** Or *from.*

B. People Remaining in Judah

Although Babylon completely devastated the city of Jerusalem and destroyed the Temple, they did leave a small group of people behind in the land and appointed Gedaliah to govern them. The prophet Jeremiah was among this group left behind, and he encouraged the people to stay in Judah to enjoy God's protection and blessing. But after murdering Babylon's appointed governor, they ignored Jeremiah's prophecy and fled to Egypt in fear of reprisal from Babylon. God still had not abandoned his people, but they would not trust him and continued to suffer the consequences of their sin.

Gedaliah Governs in Judah PARALLEL

2 KINGS 25:22-26

Then King Nebuchadnezzar appointed Gedaliah son of Ahikam and grandson of Shaphan as governor over the people he had left in Judah. [23]When all the army commanders and their men learned that the king of Babylon had appointed Gedaliah as governor, they went to see him at Mizpah. These included Ishmael son of Nethaniah, Johanan son of Kareah, Seraiah son of Tanhumeth the Netophathite, and Jezaniah* son of the Maacathite, and all their men.

[24]Gedaliah vowed to them that the Babylonian officials meant them no harm. "Don't be afraid of them.

2 Kgs 25:23 As in parallel text at Jer 40:8; Hebrew reads *Jaazaniah,* a variant spelling of Jezaniah. **2 Kgs 25:25** Hebrew *in the seventh month,* of the ancient Hebrew lunar calendar. This month occurred within the months of October and November 586 B.C.; also see note on 25:1.

Obad 1:17-21 The Edomites were routed by Judas Maccabeus in 164 B.C. The nation no longer existed by the first century A.D. At the time of Obadiah's prophecy, Edom may have seemed more likely to survive than Judah. Yet Edom has vanished, and Judah still exists. This demonstrates the absolute certainty of God's word and of the punishment awaiting all who have mistreated God's people.

Obad 1:19 The Negev was the southern part of Judah, a dry, hot region. The foothills were in the western part of Judah.

Obad 1:20 The boundaries of the kingdom would be extended to include Phoenicia as far north as Zarephath, located between Tyre and Sidon on the Mediterranean coast.

Obad 1:21 Obadiah brought God's message of judgment on Edom. God was displeased with both their inward and their outward rebellion. People today are much the same as people in Obadiah's time, filled with arrogance, envy, and dishonesty. We may wonder how much longer evil will continue. Regardless of sin's effects, God is in control. Don't despair or give up hope. Know that when all is said and done, the Lord is still sovereign, and the confidence you place in him will not be in vain.

Obad 1:21 Edom is an example to all the nations that are hostile to God. Nothing can break God's promise to protect his people from complete destruction. In the book of Obadiah we see four aspects of God's message of judgment: (1) Evil will certainly be punished; (2) those faithful to God have hope for a new future; (3) God is sovereign in human history; (4) God's ultimate purpose is to establish his eternal Kingdom. The Edomites had been cruel to God's people. They were arrogant and proud, and they took advantage of others' misfortunes. Any nation that mistreats people who obey God will be punished, regardless of how invincible they appear. Similarly we, as individuals, cannot allow ourselves to feel so comfortable with our wealth or security that we fail to help God's people. This is sin. And because God is just, sin will be punished.

2 Kgs 25:22 In place of the king (Zedekiah) who was deported to Babylon, Nebuchadnezzar appointed a governor (Gedaliah), who would faithfully administer the Babylonian policies.

2 Kgs 25:22-26 This story shows that Israel's last hope of gaining back its land was gone—even the army commanders (now guerrilla rebels) had fled. Judah's earthly kingdom was absolutely demolished. But through prophets like Ezekiel and Daniel, who were also captives, God was able to keep his spiritual Kingdom alive in the hearts of many of the exiles.

Jer 40:13–41:3 Gedaliah, appointed governor of Judah, foolishly ignored the warnings

Live in the land and serve the king of Babylon, and all will go well for you," he promised.

[25]But in midautumn of that year,* Ishmael son of Nethaniah and grandson of Elishama, who was of the royal family, went to Mizpah with ten men and killed Gedaliah. He also killed all the Judeans and Babylonians who were with Gedaliah at Mizpah.

[26]Then all the people of Judah, from the least to the greatest, as well as the army commanders, fled in panic to Egypt, for they were afraid of what the Babylonians would do to them.

JEREMIAH 40:7-12

The leaders of the Judean guerrilla bands in the countryside heard that the king of Babylon had appointed Gedaliah son of Ahikam as governor over the poor people who were left behind in Judah—the men, women, and children who hadn't been exiled to Babylon. [8]So they went to see Gedaliah at Mizpah. These included: Ishmael son of Nethaniah, Johanan and Jonathan sons of Kareah, Seraiah son of Tanhumeth, the sons of Ephai the Netophathite, Jezaniah son of the Maacathite, and all their men.

[9]Gedaliah vowed to them that the Babylonians* meant them no harm. "Don't be afraid to serve them. Live in the land and serve the king of Babylon, and all will go well for you," he promised. [10]"As for me, I will stay at Mizpah to represent you before the Babylonians who come to meet with us. Settle in the towns you have taken, and live off the land. Harvest the grapes and summer fruits and olives, and store them away."

[11]When the Judeans in Moab, Ammon, Edom, and the other nearby countries heard that the king of Babylon had left a few people in Judah and that Gedaliah was the governor, [12]they began to return to Judah from the places to which they had fled. They stopped at Mizpah to meet with Gedaliah and then went into the Judean countryside to gather a great harvest of grapes and other crops.

A Plot against Gedaliah

JEREMIAH 40:13-16

Soon after this, Johanan son of Kareah and the other guerrilla leaders came to Gedaliah at Mizpah. [14]They said to him, "Did you know that Baalis, king of Ammon, has sent Ishmael son of Nethaniah to assassinate you?" But Gedaliah refused to believe them.

[15]Later Johanan had a private conference with Gedaliah and volunteered to kill Ishmael secretly. "Why should we let him come and murder you?" Johanan asked. "What will happen then to the Judeans who have returned? Why should the few of us who are still left be scattered and lost?"

[16]But Gedaliah said to Johanan, "I forbid you to do any such thing, for you are lying about Ishmael."

The Murder of Gedaliah

JEREMIAH 41:1-18

But in midautumn,* Ishmael son of Nethaniah and grandson of Elishama, who was a member of the royal family and had been one of the king's high officials, went to Mizpah with ten men to meet Gedaliah. While they were eating together, [2]Ishmael and his ten men suddenly jumped up, drew their swords, and killed Gedaliah, whom the king of Babylon had appointed governor. [3]Ishmael also killed all the Judeans and the Babylonian* soldiers who were with Gedaliah at Mizpah.

[4]The next day, before anyone had heard about Gedaliah's murder, [5]eighty men arrived from Shechem, Shiloh, and Samaria to worship at the Temple of the LORD. They had shaved off their beards, torn their clothes, and cut themselves, and had brought along grain offerings and frankincense. [6]Ishmael left Mizpah to meet them, weeping as he went. When he reached them, he said, "Oh, come and see what has happened to Gedaliah!"

[7]But as soon as they were all inside the town, Ishmael and his men killed all but ten of them and threw their bodies into a cistern. [8]The other ten had talked Ishmael into letting them go by promising to bring him their stores of wheat, barley, olive oil, and honey that they had hidden away. [9]The cistern where Ishmael dumped the bodies of the men he murdered was the large one dug by King Asa when he fortified Mizpah to protect himself against King Baasha of Israel. Ishmael son of Nethaniah filled it with corpses.

[10]Then Ishmael made captives of the king's daughters and the other people who had been left under Gedaliah's care in Mizpah by Nebuzaradan, the captain of the guard. Taking them with him, he started back toward the land of Ammon.

[11]But when Johanan son of Kareah and the other guerrilla leaders heard about Ishmael's crimes, [12]they took all their men and set out to stop him. They caught up with him at the large pool near Gibeon. [13]The people Ishmael had captured shouted for joy when they saw Johanan and the other guerrilla leaders. [14]And all the captives from Mizpah escaped and began to help Johanan. [15]Meanwhile, Ishmael and eight of his men escaped from Johanan into the land of Ammon.

[16]Then Johanan son of Kareah and the other

Jer 40:9 Or *Chaldeans;* also in 40:10. **Jer 41:1** Hebrew *in the seventh month,* of the ancient Hebrew lunar calendar. This month occurred within the months of October and November 586 B.C.; also see note on 39:1a. **Jer 41:3** Or *Chaldean.*

of assassination. Ishmael, in the line of David, may have been angry that he had been passed over for leadership. This is similar to the chaotic political situation that Ezra and Nehemiah faced when they returned to rebuild the Temple and the city.

Jer 41:4-9 The 80 men came from three cities of the northern kingdom to worship in Jerusalem. Ishmael probably killed them for the money and food they were carrying. Without a king, with no law and no loyalty to God, Judah was subjected to complete anarchy.

Jer 41:16-17 Johanan and his group were already on their way to Egypt, headed south from Gibeon, stopping first at Geruth-kimham, near Bethlehem. Their visit to Jeremiah (Jer 42:1-6) was hypocritical, as he later told them (Jer 42:20).

▸ **JEREMIAH 41:1-18** ***(cont.)***

guerrilla leaders took all the people they had rescued in Gibeon—the soldiers, women, children, and court officials* whom Ishmael had captured after he killed Gedaliah. 17They took them all to the village of Geruth-kimham near Bethlehem, where they prepared to leave for Egypt. 18They were afraid of what the Babylonians* would do when they heard that Ishmael had killed Gedaliah, the governor appointed by the Babylonian king.

Warning to Stay in Judah

JEREMIAH 42:1-22

Then all the guerrilla leaders, including Johanan son of Kareah and Jezaniah* son of Hoshaiah, and all the people, from the least to the greatest, approached 2Jeremiah the prophet. They said, "Please pray to the Lord your God for us. As you can see, we are only a tiny remnant compared to what we were before. 3Pray that the Lord your God will show us what to do and where to go."

4"All right," Jeremiah replied. "I will pray to the Lord your God, as you have asked, and I will tell you everything he says. I will hide nothing from you."

5Then they said to Jeremiah, "May the Lord your God be a faithful witness against us if we refuse to obey whatever he tells us to do! 6Whether we like it or not, we will obey the Lord our God to whom we are sending you with our plea. For if we obey him, everything will turn out well for us."

7Ten days later the Lord gave his reply to Jeremiah. 8So he called for Johanan son of Kareah and the other guerrilla leaders, and for all the people, from the least to the greatest. 9He said to them, "You sent me to the Lord, the God of Israel, with your request, and this is his reply: 10'Stay here in this land. If you do, I will build you up and not tear you down; I will plant you and not uproot you. For I am sorry about all the punishment I have had to bring upon you. 11Do not fear the king of Babylon anymore,' says the Lord. 'For I am with you and will save you and rescue you from his power. 12I will be merciful to you by making him kind, so he will let you stay here in your land.'

13"But if you refuse to obey the Lord your God, and if you say, 'We will not stay here; 14instead, we will go to Egypt where we will be free from war, the call to arms, and hunger,' 15then hear the Lord's message to the remnant of Judah. This is what the Lord of Heaven's Armies, the God of Israel, says: 'If you are determined to go to Egypt and live there, 16the very war and famine you fear will catch up to you, and you will die there. 17That is the fate awaiting every one of you who insists on going to live in Egypt. Yes, you will die from war, famine, and disease. None of you will escape the disaster I will bring upon you there.'

18"This is what the Lord of Heaven's Armies, the God of Israel, says: 'Just as my anger and fury have been poured out on the people of Jerusalem, so they will be poured out on you when you enter Egypt. You will be an object of damnation, horror, cursing, and mockery. And you will never see your homeland again.'

19"Listen, you remnant of Judah. The Lord has told you: 'Do not go to Egypt!' Don't forget this warning I have given you today. 20For you were not being honest when you sent me to pray to the Lord your God for you. You said, 'Just tell us what the Lord our God says, and we will do it!' 21And today I have told you exactly what he said, but you will not obey the Lord your God any better now than you have in the past. 22So you can be sure that you will die from war, famine, and disease in Egypt, where you insist on going."

Jer 41:16 Or *eunuchs.* **Jer 41:18** Or *Chaldeans.* **Jer 42:1** Greek version reads *Azariah;* compare 43:2.

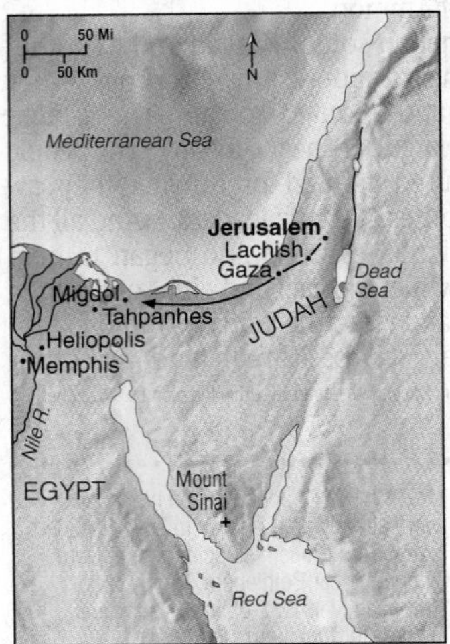

◀ ***ESCAPE TO EGYPT***
With Judah in turmoil after the murder of Gedaliah, the people turned to Jeremiah for guidance. Jeremiah had God's answer, "Stay in this land," but the leaders disobeyed and went to Egypt—taking Jeremiah with them. In Egypt, Jeremiah told them they were in grave danger.

Jer 42:5-6 Johanan and his associates spoke their own curse; Jeremiah merely elaborated on it. It was a tragic mistake to ask for God's guidance with no intention of following it. Be sure never to ask God for something that you know in your heart you really do not want. It is better not to pray than to pray hypocritically. God cannot be deceived.

Jer 43:1-3 Johanan and his tiny band had come to Jeremiah for God's approval of their plan, not for God's direction. This is a recurring problem for some of us—seeking God's approval of our desires rather than asking him for guidance. It is not good to make plans apart from God's guidance, and it is not good to pray unless we are willing to accept God's answer.

Jer 43:4-7 Afraid to obey the Lord, the people headed for Egypt, even forcing Jeremiah to go with them. (They thought that perhaps God would spare them if Jeremiah was with them.) Jeremiah had served as a prophet for 40 years. Many of his words had already come true, and he had turned down an offer to live comfortably in Babylon, returning instead to his beloved people. But the people still rejected Jeremiah's advice. The response of our audience is not necessarily a measure of our success. Jeremiah was doing all God asked, but he had been called to minister to a very stubborn group of people.

Jer 43:10-13 Nebuchadnezzar invaded Egypt in 568–567 B.C. Like Judah, Egypt

Jeremiah Taken to Egypt

JEREMIAH 43:1-13

When Jeremiah had finished giving this message from the LORD their God to all the people, 2Azariah son of Hoshaiah and Johanan son of Kareah and all the other proud men said to Jeremiah, "You lie! The LORD our God hasn't forbidden us to go to Egypt! 3Baruch son of Neriah has convinced you to say this, because he wants us to stay here and be killed by the Babylonians* or be carried off into exile."

4So Johanan and the other guerrilla leaders and all the people refused to obey the LORD's command to stay in Judah. 5Johanan and the other leaders took with them all the people who had returned from the nearby countries to which they had fled. 6In the crowd were men, women, and children, the king's daughters, and all those whom Nebuzaradan, the captain of the guard, had left with Gedaliah. The prophet Jeremiah and Baruch were also included. 7The people refused to obey the voice of the LORD and went to Egypt, going as far as the city of Tahpanhes.

8Then at Tahpanhes, the LORD gave another message to Jeremiah. He said, 9"While the people of Judah are watching, take some large rocks and bury them under the pavement stones at the entrance of Pharaoh's palace here in Tahpanhes. 10Then say to the people of Judah, 'This is what the LORD of Heaven's Armies, the God of Israel, says: I will certainly bring my servant Nebuchadnezzar,* king of Babylon, here to Egypt. I will set his throne over these stones that I have hidden. He will spread his royal canopy over them. 11And when he comes, he will destroy the land of Egypt. He will bring death to those destined for death, captivity to those destined for captivity, and war to those destined for war. 12He will set fire to the temples of Egypt's gods; he will burn the temples and carry the idols away as plunder. He will pick clean the land of Egypt as a shepherd picks fleas from his cloak. And he himself will leave unharmed. 13He will break down the sacred pillars standing in the temple of the sun* in Egypt, and he will burn down the temples of Egypt's gods.'"

Judgment for Idolatry

JEREMIAH 44:1-30

This is the message Jeremiah received concerning the Judeans living in northern Egypt in the cities of Migdol, Tahpanhes, and Memphis,* and in southern Egypt* as well: 2"This is what the LORD of Heaven's Armies, the God of Israel, says: You saw the calamity I brought on Jerusalem and all the towns of Judah. They now lie deserted and in ruins. 3They provoked my anger with all their wickedness. They burned incense and worshiped other gods—gods that neither they nor you nor any of your ancestors had ever even known.

4"Again and again I sent my servants, the prophets, to plead with them, 'Don't do these horrible things that I hate so much.' 5But my people would not listen or turn back from their wicked ways. They kept on burning incense to these gods. 6And so my fury boiled over and fell like fire on the towns of Judah and into the streets of Jerusalem, and they are still a desolate ruin today.

7"And now the LORD God of Heaven's Armies, the God of Israel, asks you: Why are you destroying yourselves? For not one of you will survive—not a man, woman, or child among you who has come here from Judah, not even the babies in your arms. 8Why provoke my anger by burning incense to the idols you have made here in Egypt? You will only destroy yourselves and make yourselves an object of cursing and mockery for all the nations of the earth. 9Have you forgotten the sins of your ancestors, the sins of the kings and queens of Judah, and the sins you and your wives committed in Judah and Jerusalem? 10To this very hour you have

Jer 43:3 Or *Chaldeans.* **Jer 43:10** Hebrew *Nebuchadrezzar,* a variant spelling of Nebuchadnezzar. **Jer 43:13** Or *in Heliopolis.* **Jer 44:1a** Hebrew *Noph.* **Jer 44:1b** Hebrew *in Pathros.*

rebelled against him and was quickly crushed. So much for the great empire on which Judah had constantly placed its hopes!

Jer 44:1ff This message, given while Jeremiah was in Egypt against his will, reminded the people that their idolatry had brought destruction on their land. Jeremiah told them that they would never return to Judah because the escape to Egypt had been against God's advice (Jer 42:9ff). But the people refused to learn any lessons from all the destruction their sins had caused.

Jer 44:9-10 When we forget a lesson or refuse to learn it, we risk repeating our mistakes. The people of Judah struggled with this; to forget their former sins was to repeat them. To fail to learn from failure is to assure future failure. Your past is your school of experience. Let your past mistakes point you to God's way.

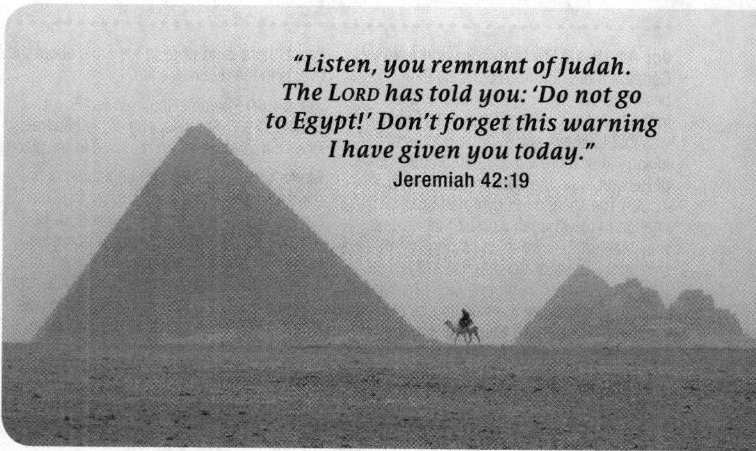
"Listen, you remnant of Judah. The LORD has told you: 'Do not go to Egypt!' Don't forget this warning I have given you today."
Jeremiah 42:19

▸ **JEREMIAH 44:1-30** ***(cont.)***
shown no remorse or reverence. No one has chosen
to follow my word and the decrees I gave to you and
your ancestors before you.
11"Therefore, this is what the LORD of Heaven's
Armies, the God of Israel, says: I am determined to
destroy every one of you! 12I will take this remnant of
Judah—those who were determined to come here and
live in Egypt—and I will consume them. They will fall
here in Egypt, killed by war and famine. All will die,
from the least to the greatest. They will be an object
of damnation, horror, cursing, and mockery. 13I will
punish them in Egypt just as I punished them in Jerusalem, by war, famine, and disease. 14Of that remnant
who fled to Egypt, hoping someday to return to Judah,
there will be no survivors. Even though they long to
return home, only a handful will do so."
15Then all the women present and all the men who
knew that their wives had burned incense to idols—a
great crowd of all the Judeans living in northern Egypt
and southern Egypt*—answered Jeremiah, 16"We will
not listen to your messages from the LORD! 17We will
do whatever we want. We will burn incense and pour
out liquid offerings to the Queen of Heaven just as
much as we like—just as we, and our ancestors, and
our kings and officials have always done in the towns
of Judah and in the streets of Jerusalem. For in those
days we had plenty to eat, and we were well off and
had no troubles! 18But ever since we quit burning incense to the Queen of Heaven and stopped worshiping her with liquid offerings, we have been in great
trouble and have been dying from war and famine."
19"Besides," the women added, "do you suppose
that we were burning incense and pouring out liquid
offerings to the Queen of Heaven, and making cakes
marked with her image, without our husbands knowing it and helping us? Of course not!"
20Then Jeremiah said to all of them, men and
women alike, who had given him that answer, 21"Do
you think the LORD did not know that you and your
ancestors, your kings and officials, and all the people
were burning incense to idols in the towns of Judah
and in the streets of Jerusalem? 22It was because the
LORD could no longer bear all the disgusting things
you were doing that he made your land an object of
cursing—a desolate ruin without inhabitants—as it
is today. 23All these terrible things happened to you
because you have burned incense to idols and sinned
against the LORD. You have refused to obey him and
have not followed his instructions, his decrees, and
his laws."
24Then Jeremiah said to them all, including the
women, "Listen to this message from the LORD, all
you citizens of Judah who live in Egypt. 25This is what
the LORD of Heaven's Armies, the God of Israel, says:
'You and your wives have said, "We will keep our promises to burn incense and pour out liquid offerings to
the Queen of Heaven," and you have proved by your
actions that you meant it. So go ahead and carry out
your promises and vows to her!'
26"But listen to this message from the LORD, all you
Judeans now living in Egypt: 'I have sworn by my great
name,' says the LORD, 'that my name will no longer be
spoken by any of the Judeans in the land of Egypt.
None of you may invoke my name or use this oath: "As
surely as the Sovereign LORD lives." 27For I will watch
over you to bring you disaster and not good. Everyone
from Judah who is now living in Egypt will suffer war
and famine until all of you are dead. 28Only a small
number will escape death and return to Judah from
Egypt. Then all those who came to Egypt will find out
whose words are true—mine or theirs!
29"'And this is the proof I give you,' says the LORD, 'that
all I have threatened will happen to you and that I will
punish you here.' 30This is what the LORD says: 'I will
turn Pharaoh Hophra, king of Egypt, over to his enemies
who want to kill him, just as I turned King Zedekiah
of Judah over to King Nebuchadnezzar* of Babylon.'"

Jer 44:15 Hebrew *in Egypt, in Pathros.* **Jer 44:30** Hebrew *Nebuchadrezzar,* a variant spelling of Nebuchadnezzar.

Jer 44:15-18 The farther we drift from God, the more confused our thinking becomes. Whatever spiritual life was left in the Israelites when they went to Egypt was lost as they sank into the depths of idolatry. (For more information on the "Queen of Heaven," see the note on Jer 7:18, p. 1008.) The escape to Egypt had brought a change in their pagan worship habits, and they blamed their troubles on neglect of their idols. But idol worship had started all their problems in the first place. The people refused to recognize the true source of their problems—departure from God's ways. When calamity forces you to examine your life, take a close look at God's instructions for you and be willing to humbly apply what you find there.

Jer 44:28 After Jeremiah's forced move to Egypt, there is no word in the Bible about the events in the rest of his life.

Jer 44:30 Pharaoh Hophra ruled Egypt 588–569 B.C. Ahmose, one of his generals, killed him and was then crowned in his place.

Ezek 33:21-22 Near the beginning of his ministry, Ezekiel had been unable to speak except to give specific messages from God (Ezek 3:26-27). After Ezekiel's prophecies came true and the false prophets were exposed, Ezekiel was again able to talk freely. No longer needing to prove himself, he was free to offer God's message of restoration and hope.

Ezek 33:30-32 The people refused to act upon Ezekiel's message. When people mock your witness for Christ or ignore your advice, don't give up. You cannot make someone accept the message of salvation. Your part is to be faithful in delivering it.

Ezek 33:31 In your heart, do you really love God? These people gave the appearance of following God, but they loved their money more. Many today also give the outward impression of being religious while remaining inwardly greedy. Jesus warned that we cannot love God and money at the same time (Matt 6:24). It's easy to say, "I surrender all" when we don't have much. It's when we start accumulating wealth that it becomes difficult to avoid loving it.

Ezek 33:32 The people were coming to listen to Ezekiel in order to be entertained. They listened to the message from the Lord but had no intention of putting it into practice. Many people regard church as entertainment. They enjoy the music, the people, and the activities,

C. Exiles in Babylon

Babylon was home for many people from Judah who had been taken there in three separate deportations in 605, 597, and 586 B.C. Among those who had been taken were the prophets Ezekiel and Daniel, who continued to speak for God to his people and to the leaders in Babylon. Even though Judah was suffering exile as judgment for their sins, God had not abandoned them or forgotten his covenant promises to them. Ezekiel and Daniel, along with others like them during this period, are an encouragement to any of God's people today who find themselves in the midst of a culture or nation that is hostile to God.

1. MESSAGES OF HOPE FROM EZEKIEL

After the fall of Jerusalem, Ezekiel delivered messages of future restoration and hope for the people who were captive in Babylon. God is holy, but Jerusalem and the Temple had become defiled. The nation had to be cleansed through 70 years of captivity. But in the midst of the darkness of captivity, Ezekiel tells the people about the future glorious restoration of God's people, who would experience the fullness of God's presence again. We, too, must gain a vision of the glory of God, a fresh sense of his greatness, as we face the struggles of daily life.

Ezekiel's Explanation of Jerusalem's Fall

EZEKIEL 33:21-33

On January 8,* during the twelfth year of our captivity,
a survivor from Jerusalem came to me and said, "The
city has fallen!" 22The previous evening the LORD had
taken hold of me and given me back my voice. So I was
able to speak when this man arrived the next morning.
23Then this message came to me from the LORD:
24"Son of man, the scattered remnants of Judah living
among the ruined cities keep saying, 'Abraham was
only one man, yet he gained possession of the entire
land. We are many; surely the land has been given to us
as a possession.' 25So tell these people, 'This is what the
Sovereign LORD says: You eat meat with blood in it, you
worship idols,* and you murder the innocent. Do you
really think the land should be yours? 26Murderers!
Idolaters! Adulterers! Should the land belong to you?'
27"Say to them, 'This is what the Sovereign LORD says:
As surely as I live, those living in the ruins will die by the
sword. And I will send wild animals to eat those living
in the open fields. Those hiding in the forts and caves
will die of disease. 28I will completely destroy the land
and demolish her pride. Her arrogant power will come
to an end. The mountains of Israel will be so desolate
that no one will even travel through them. 29When I
have completely destroyed the land because of their
detestable sins, then they will know that I am the LORD.'
30"Son of man, your people talk about you in their
houses and whisper about you at the doors. They say
to each other, 'Come on, let's go hear the prophet tell
us what the LORD is saying!' 31So my people come pretending to be sincere and sit before you. They listen
to your words, but they have no intention of doing
what you say. Their mouths are full of lustful words,
and their hearts seek only after money. 32You are very
entertaining to them, like someone who sings love
songs with a beautiful voice or plays fine music on
an instrument. They hear what you say, but they don't
act on it! 33But when all these terrible things happen
to them—as they certainly will—then they will know
a prophet has been among them."

The Shepherds of Israel

EZEKIEL 34:1-10

Then this message came to me from the LORD: 2"Son
of man, prophesy against the shepherds, the leaders
of Israel. Give them this message from the Sovereign
LORD: What sorrow awaits you shepherds who feed
yourselves instead of your flocks. Shouldn't shepherds
feed their sheep? 3You drink the milk, wear the wool,
and butcher the best animals, but you let your flocks
starve. 4You have not taken care of the weak. You have
not tended the sick or bound up the injured. You have
not gone looking for those who have wandered away
and are lost. Instead, you have ruled them with harshness and cruelty. 5So my sheep have been scattered

Ez 33:21 Hebrew *On the fifth day of the tenth month,* of the ancient Hebrew lunar calendar. This event occurred on January 8, 585 B.C.; also see note on 1:1.
Ez 33:25 The Hebrew term (literally *round things*) probably alludes to dung.

but they don't take the messages to heart. They are apathetic toward serving the Lord. Have you reduced church services to the level of entertainment, or does your worship truly have an impact on your life? Listen to God's words and then obey—apply his words and put them into practice in your life.

Ezek 34:1ff Ezekiel called the exiles "Israel," referring to all Jews in captivity from both the northern and southern kingdoms. Ezekiel criticized Israel's leaders for taking care of themselves rather than taking care of their people. He outlined their sins (Ezek 34:1-6) and pronounced judgment upon them (Ezek 34:7-10). Then he promised that a good shepherd (the Messiah) would come who would take care of the people as the other leaders were supposed to have done (Ezek 34:11-31). This beautiful message portrays the fate of the present shepherds, the work of the new shepherd, and the future of the sheep.

Ezek 34:4-6 God would judge the religious leaders because they were selfishly caught up in their own concerns and were neglecting their service to others. Spiritual leaders must be careful not to pursue self-development at the expense of broken, lost people. When we give too much attention to our own needs and ideas, we may push God aside and abandon those who depend on us.

▸ **EZEKIEL 34:1-10** *(cont.)*

without a shepherd, and they are easy prey for any wild animal. [6]They have wandered through all the mountains and all the hills, across the face of the earth, yet no one has gone to search for them.

[7]"Therefore, you shepherds, hear the word of the LORD: [8]As surely as I live, says the Sovereign LORD, you abandoned my flock and left them to be attacked by every wild animal. And though you were my shepherds, you didn't search for my sheep when they were lost. You took care of yourselves and left the sheep to starve. [9]Therefore, you shepherds, hear the word of the LORD. [10]This is what the Sovereign LORD says: I now consider these shepherds my enemies, and I will hold them responsible for what has happened to my flock. I will take away their right to feed the flock, and I will stop them from feeding themselves. I will rescue my flock from their mouths; the sheep will no longer be their prey.

The Good Shepherd

EZEKIEL 34:11-24

"For this is what the Sovereign LORD says: I myself will search and find my sheep. [12]I will be like a shepherd looking for his scattered flock. I will find my sheep and rescue them from all the places where they were scattered on that dark and cloudy day. [13]I will bring them back home to their own land of Israel from among the peoples and nations. I will feed them on the mountains of Israel and by the rivers and in all the places where people live. [14]Yes, I will give them good pastureland on the high hills of Israel. There they will lie down in pleasant places and feed in the lush pastures of the hills. [15]I myself will tend my sheep and give them a place to lie down in peace, says the Sovereign LORD. [16]I will search for my lost ones who strayed away, and I will bring them safely home again. I will bandage the injured and strengthen the weak. But I will destroy those who are fat and powerful. I will feed them, yes—feed them justice!

[17]"And as for you, my flock, this is what the Sovereign LORD says to his people: I will judge between one animal of the flock and another, separating the sheep from the goats. [18]Isn't it enough for you to keep the best of the pastures for yourselves? Must you also trample down the rest? Isn't it enough for you to drink clear water for yourselves? Must you also muddy the rest with your feet? [19]Why must my flock eat what you have trampled down and drink water you have fouled?

[20]"Therefore, this is what the Sovereign LORD says: I will surely judge between the fat sheep and the scrawny sheep. [21]For you fat sheep pushed and butted and crowded my sick and hungry flock until you scattered them to distant lands. [22]So I will rescue my flock, and they will no longer be abused. I will judge between one animal of the flock and another. [23]And I will set over them one shepherd, my servant David. He will feed them and be a shepherd to them. [24]And I, the LORD, will be their God, and my servant David will be a prince among my people. I, the LORD, have spoken!

The LORD's Covenant of Peace

EZEKIEL 34:25-31

"I will make a covenant of peace with my people and drive away the dangerous animals from the land. Then they will be able to camp safely in the wildest places and sleep in the woods without fear. [26]I will bless my people and their homes around my holy hill. And in the proper season I will send the showers they need. There will be showers of blessing. [27]The orchards and fields of my people will yield bumper crops, and everyone will live in safety. When I have broken their chains of slavery and rescued them from those who enslaved them, then they will know that I am the LORD. [28]They will no longer be prey for other nations, and wild animals will no longer devour them. They will live in safety, and no one will frighten them.

[29]"And I will make their land famous for its crops, so my people will never again suffer from famines or the insults of foreign nations. [30]In this way, they will know that I, the LORD their God, am with them. And they will know that they, the people of Israel, are my

Ezek 34:9-10 Those shepherds who failed their flock would be removed from office and held responsible for what happened to the people they were supposed to lead. Christian leaders must heed this warning and care for their flock, or total failure and judgment will be the result (see 1 Cor 9:24-27). True leadership focuses on helping others, not just on getting ahead.

Ezek 34:11-16 God promises to take over as shepherd of his scattered flock. When our leaders fail us, we must not despair but remember that God is in control and that he promises to return and care for his flock. Thus, we know that we can turn to God for help. He is still in control and can transform any tragic situation into good for his Kingdom (see Gen 50:20; Rom 8:28).

BAD SHEPHERDS VERSUS GOOD SHEPHERDS

Bad Shepherds	Good Shepherds
Take care of themselves	Take care of their flock
Worry about their own health	Strengthen the weak and sick, search for the lost
Rule harshly and brutally	Rule lovingly and gently
Abandon and scatter the sheep	Gather and protect the sheep
Keep the best for themselves	Give their best to the sheep

Ezek 34:18-19 A bad shepherd is not only selfish but destructive. A minister who muddies the waters for others by causing unnecessary fears, teaching false ideas, and acting sinfully is a detriment to the flock's spiritual nourishment.

Ezek 34:23-31 In contrast to the present evil shepherds (leaders) of God's people (Ezek 34:1-6), God will send a perfect shepherd, the Messiah ("my servant David"), who will take care of every need his people have and set up a Kingdom of perfect peace and

people, says the Sovereign LORD. [31]You are my flock, the sheep of my pasture. You are my people, and I am your God. I, the Sovereign LORD, have spoken!"

A Message for Edom

EZEKIEL 35:1-15

Again a message came to me from the LORD: [2]"Son of man, turn and face Mount Seir, and prophesy against its people. [3]Give them this message from the Sovereign LORD:

"I am your enemy, O Mount Seir,
  and I will raise my fist against you
  to destroy you completely.
4 I will demolish your cities
  and make you desolate.
Then you will know that I am the LORD.

[5]"Your eternal hatred for the people of Israel led you to butcher them when they were helpless, when I had already punished them for all their sins. [6]As surely as I live, says the Sovereign LORD, since you show no distaste for blood, I will give you a bloodbath of your own. Your turn has come! [7]I will make Mount Seir utterly desolate, killing off all who try to escape and any who return. [8]I will fill your mountains with the dead. Your hills, your valleys, and your ravines will be filled with people slaughtered by the sword. [9]I will make you desolate forever. Your cities will never be rebuilt. Then you will know that I am the LORD.

[10]"For you said, 'The lands of Israel and Judah will be ours. We will take possession of them. What do we care that the LORD is there!' [11]Therefore, as surely as I live, says the Sovereign LORD, I will pay back your angry deeds with my own. I will punish you for all your acts of anger, envy, and hatred. And I will make myself known to Israel* by what I do to you. [12]Then you will know that I, the LORD, have heard every contemptuous word you spoke against the mountains of Israel. For you said, 'They are desolate; they have been given to us as food to eat!' [13]In saying that, you boasted proudly against me, and I have heard it all!

[14]"This is what the Sovereign LORD says: The whole world will rejoice when I make you desolate. [15]You rejoiced at the desolation of Israel's territory. Now I will rejoice at yours! You will be wiped out, you people of Mount Seir and all who live in Edom! Then you will know that I am the LORD.

Restoration for Israel

EZEKIEL 36:1-38

"Son of man, prophesy to Israel's mountains. Give them this message: O mountains of Israel, hear the word of the LORD! [2]This is what the Sovereign LORD says: Your enemies have taunted you, saying, 'Aha! Now the ancient heights belong to us!' [3]Therefore, son of man, give the mountains of Israel this message from the Sovereign LORD: Your enemies have attacked you from all directions, making you the property of many nations and the object of much mocking and slander. [4]Therefore, O mountains of Israel, hear the word of the Sovereign LORD. He speaks to the hills and mountains, ravines and valleys, and to ruined wastes and long-deserted cities that have been destroyed and mocked by the surrounding nations. [5]This is what the Sovereign LORD says: My jealous anger burns against these nations, especially Edom, because they have shown utter contempt for me by gleefully taking my land for themselves as plunder.

[6]"Therefore, prophesy to the hills and mountains, the ravines and valleys of Israel. This is what the Sovereign LORD says: I am furious that you have suffered shame before the surrounding nations. [7]Therefore, this is what the Sovereign LORD says: I have taken a solemn oath that those nations will soon have their own shame to endure.

[8]"But the mountains of Israel will produce heavy crops of fruit for my people—for they will be coming home again soon! [9]See, I care about you, and I will pay attention to you. Your ground will be plowed and your crops planted. [10]I will greatly increase the population of Israel, and the ruined cities will be rebuilt and filled with people. [11]I will increase not only the people, but

585 BC

Greek astronomer Thales predicts an eclipse

Ez 35:11 Hebrew *to them;* Greek version reads *to you.*

justice (see Ps 23; Jer 23:5-6; John 10:11; Heb 13:20-21; Rev 21). *Peace* here means more than the absence of conflict. It is contentment, fulfillment, and security.

Ezek 35:1ff Ezekiel gave another prophecy against Edom (where Mount Seir was located); his first was given earlier (Ezek 25:12-14). In this prophecy, Ezekiel is probably using Edom to represent all the nations opposed to God's people. Ezekiel 36 says that Israel will be restored, while Ezekiel 35 says that Edom (God's enemies) will be made "desolate."

Ezek 35:2 Edom offered to help destroy Jerusalem and rejoiced when the city fell. Edom's long-standing hostility against God's people resulted in God's judgment.

Ezek 35:6-8 Ezekiel prophesied not only against the people of Edom but also against their mountains and land. Their home territory was Mount Seir. Mountains, symbols of strength and power, represented the pride of these people, who thought they could get away with evil. Their desire for revenge turned against them. Edom received the punishment it was so hasty to give out. God has a way of allowing our treatment of others to boomerang on us. So be careful in your judgment of others (Matt 7:1-2).

Ezek 36:1ff In this prophecy, Ezekiel said that Israel would be restored as a nation and would return to its own land. The mountains were symbolic of Israel's strength (see the note on Ezek 35:6-8, above). To the exiles in Babylon, this seemed impossible. This message again emphasized God's sovereignty and trustworthiness. He would first judge the nations used to punish Israel (Ezek 36:1-7) and then restore his people (Ezek 36:8-15).

Ezek 36:2 "The ancient heights" refers to the Promised Land—the land of Israel. Israel's enemies challenged not only their boundaries but also God's promises to Israel.

▸ **EZEKIEL 36:1-38** ***(cont.)***

also your animals. O mountains of Israel, I will bring people to live on you once again. I will make you even more prosperous than you were before. Then you will know that I am the LORD. 12I will cause my people to walk on you once again, and you will be their territory. You will never again rob them of their children.

13"This is what the Sovereign LORD says: The other nations taunt you, saying, 'Israel is a land that devours its own people and robs them of their children!' 14But you will never again devour your people or rob them of their children, says the Sovereign LORD. 15I will not let you hear those other nations insult you, and you will no longer be mocked by them. You will not be a land that causes its nation to fall, says the Sovereign LORD."

16Then this further message came to me from the LORD: 17"Son of man, when the people of Israel were living in their own land, they defiled it by the evil way they lived. To me their conduct was as unclean as a woman's menstrual cloth. 18They polluted the land with murder and the worship of idols,* so I poured out my fury on them. 19I scattered them to many lands to punish them for the evil way they had lived. 20But when they were scattered among the nations, they brought shame on my holy name. For the nations said, 'These are the people of the LORD, but he couldn't keep them safe in his own land!' 21Then I was concerned for my holy name, on which my people brought shame among the nations.

22"Therefore, give the people of Israel this message from the Sovereign LORD: I am bringing you back, but not because you deserve it. I am doing it to protect my holy name, on which you brought shame while you were scattered among the nations. 23I will show how holy my great name is—the name on which you brought shame among the nations. And when I reveal my holiness through you before their very eyes, says the Sovereign LORD, then the nations will know that I am the LORD. 24For I will gather you up from all the nations and bring you home again to your land.

25"Then I will sprinkle clean water on you, and you will be clean. Your filth will be washed away, and you will no longer worship idols. 26And I will give you a new heart, and I will put a new spirit in you. I will take out your stony, stubborn heart and give you a tender, responsive heart.* 27And I will put my Spirit in you so that you will follow my decrees and be careful to obey my regulations.

28"And you will live in Israel, the land I gave your ancestors long ago. You will be my people, and I will be your God. 29I will cleanse you of your filthy behavior. I will give you good crops of grain, and I will send no more famines on the land. 30I will give you great harvests from your fruit trees and fields, and never again will the surrounding nations be able to scoff at your land for its famines. 31Then you will remember your past sins and despise yourselves for all the detestable things you did. 32But remember, says the Sovereign LORD, I am not doing this because you deserve it. O my people of Israel, you should be utterly ashamed of all you have done!

33"This is what the Sovereign LORD says: When I cleanse you from your sins, I will repopulate your cities, and the ruins will be rebuilt. 34The fields that used to lie empty and desolate in plain view of everyone will again be farmed. 35And when I bring you back, people will say, 'This former wasteland is now like the Garden of Eden! The abandoned and ruined cities now have strong walls and are filled with people!' 36Then the surrounding nations that survive will know that

Ez 36:18 The Hebrew term (literally *round things*) probably alludes to dung; also in 36:25. **Ez 36:26** Hebrew *a heart of flesh.*

Ezek 36:21-23 Why did God want to protect his holy name—his reputation—among the nations of the world? God was concerned about the salvation of not only his people but also the whole world. To allow his people to remain in sin and be permanently destroyed by their enemies would lead other nations to conclude that their pagan gods were more powerful than Israel's God (Isa 48:11). Thus, to protect his holy name, God would return a remnant of his people to their land. God will not share his glory with false gods—he alone is the one true God. The people had the responsibility to represent God to the rest of the world. Believers today have that same responsibility. How do you represent God to your world?

Ezek 36:25-27 God promised to restore Israel not only physically but spiritually. To accomplish this, God would give them a new heart for following him and put his Spirit within them (see Ezek 11:19-20; Ps 51:7-11) to transform them and empower them to do his will. Again God promised the new covenant (see Ezek 16:61-63; 34:23-25), ultimately to be fulfilled in Christ. No matter how impure your life is right now, God offers you a fresh start. You can have your sins washed away, receive a new heart for God, and have his Spirit within you—if you accept God's promise. Why try to patch up your old life when you can have a new one?

Ezek 36:31-32 God said his people should be ashamed of their sins. The people had become so callous that they had lost all sensitivity to sin. First they had to "remember" their sins, then be ashamed of them, and finally repent of them (see Jas 4:8-9). As we examine our lives, we may find that we, too, have lost our sensitivity to certain sins. But as we measure ourselves against God's standards of right living, we will be ashamed. To regain sensitivity we must recognize our sin for what it is, be sorry for displeasing God, and ask his forgiveness. The Holy Spirit will guide us, making us responsive and receptive to God's truth (John 14:26; 16:8, 13).

OLD AND NEW COVENANTS

Old covenant	*New covenant*
Placed upon stone	**Placed upon people's hearts**
Based on the law	**Based on a desire to love and serve God**
Must be taught	**Known by all**
Legal relationship with God	**Personal relationship with God**

I, the LORD, have rebuilt the ruins and replanted the wasteland. For I, the LORD, have spoken, and I will do what I say.

37“This is what the Sovereign LORD says: I am ready to hear Israel's prayers and to increase their numbers like a flock. 38They will be as numerous as the sacred flocks that fill Jerusalem's streets at the time of her festivals. The ruined cities will be crowded with people once more, and everyone will know that I am the LORD.”

A Valley of Dry Bones

EZEKIEL 37:1-14

The LORD took hold of me, and I was carried away by the Spirit of the LORD to a valley filled with bones. 2He led me all around among the bones that covered the valley floor. They were scattered everywhere across the ground and were completely dried out. 3Then he asked me, “Son of man, can these bones become living people again?”

“O Sovereign LORD,” I replied, “you alone know the answer to that.”

4Then he said to me, “Speak a prophetic message to these bones and say, ‘Dry bones, listen to the word of the LORD! 5This is what the Sovereign LORD says: Look! I am going to put breath into you and make you live again! 6I will put flesh and muscles on you and cover you with skin. I will put breath into you, and you will come to life. Then you will know that I am the LORD.’”

7So I spoke this message, just as he told me. Suddenly as I spoke, there was a rattling noise all across the valley. The bones of each body came together and attached themselves as complete skeletons. 8Then as I watched, muscles and flesh formed over the bones. Then skin formed to cover their bodies, but they still had no breath in them.

9Then he said to me, “Speak a prophetic message to the winds, son of man. Speak a prophetic message and say, ‘This is what the Sovereign LORD says: Come, O breath, from the four winds! Breathe into these dead bodies so they may live again.’”

10So I spoke the message as he commanded me, and breath came into their bodies. They all came to life and stood up on their feet—a great army.

11Then he said to me, “Son of man, these bones represent the people of Israel. They are saying, ‘We have become old, dry bones—all hope is gone. Our nation is finished.’ 12Therefore, prophesy to them and say, ‘This is what the Sovereign LORD says: O my people, I will open your graves of exile and cause you to rise again. Then I will bring you back to the land of Israel. 13When this happens, O my people, you will know that I am the LORD. 14I will put my Spirit in you, and you will live again and return home to your own land. Then you will know that I, the LORD, have spoken, and I have done what I said. Yes, the LORD has spoken!’”

Reunion of Israel and Judah

EZEKIEL 37:15-28

Again a message came to me from the LORD: 16“Son of man, take a piece of wood and carve on it these words: ‘This represents Judah and its allied tribes.’ Then take another piece and carve these words on it: ‘This represents Ephraim and the northern tribes of Israel.’* 17Now hold them together in your hand as if they were one piece of wood. 18When your people ask you what your actions mean, 19say to them, ‘This is what the Sovereign LORD says: I will take Ephraim and the northern tribes and join them to Judah. I will make them one piece of wood in my hand.’

20“Then hold out the pieces of wood you have inscribed, so the people can see them. 21And give them this message from the Sovereign LORD: I will gather the people of Israel from among the nations. I will bring them home to their own land from the places where they have been scattered. 22I will unify them

Ez 37:16 Hebrew *This is Ephraim's wood, representing Joseph and all the house of Israel.*

Ezek 36:37-38 God said that he was ready to answer Israel's prayers. We cannot expect God to answer our prayers until we have received a new heart from him (Ezek 36:26). Is your heart right with God?

Ezek 37:1ff This vision illustrates the promise of Ezekiel 36—new life and a nation restored, both physically and spiritually. The dry bones are a picture of the Jews in captivity—scattered and dead. The two pieces of wood (Ezek 37:15-17) represent the reunion of the entire nation of Israel that had divided into northern and southern kingdoms after Solomon. The scattered exiles of both Israel and Judah would be released from the “graves” of exile and one day be regathered in their homeland, with the Messiah as their leader. Ezekiel felt he was speaking to the dead as he preached to the exiles because they rarely responded to his message. But these bones responded! And just as God brought life to the dead bones, he would bring life again to his spiritually dead people.

Ezek 37:4-5 The dry bones represented the people's spiritually dead condition. Your church may seem like a heap of dry bones to you, spiritually dead with no hope of vitality. But just as God promised to restore his nation, he can restore any church, no matter how dry or dead it may be. Rather than give up, pray for renewal, for God can restore it to life. The hope and prayer of every church should be that God will put his Spirit into it (Ezek 37:14). In fact, God is at work calling his people back to himself, bringing new life into dead churches.

Ezek 37:16 The first piece of wood was for Judah, being the leading tribe in the southern kingdom. The other was for Ephraim, the leading tribe in the northern kingdom.

Then he asked me, “Son of man, can these bones become living people again?”
Ezekiel 37:3

▶ **EZEKIEL 37:15-28** ***(cont.)***

into one nation on the mountains of Israel. One king will rule them all; no longer will they be divided into two nations or into two kingdoms. 23They will never again pollute themselves with their idols* and vile images and rebellion, for I will save them from their sinful backsliding. I will cleanse them. Then they will truly be my people, and I will be their God.

24"My servant David will be their king, and they will have only one shepherd. They will obey my regulations and be careful to keep my decrees. 25They will live in the land I gave my servant Jacob, the land where their ancestors lived. They and their children and their grandchildren after them will live there forever, generation after generation. And my servant David will be their prince forever. 26And I will make a covenant of peace with them, an everlasting covenant. I will give them their land and increase their numbers,* and I will put my Temple among them forever. 27I will make my home among them. I will be their God, and they will be my people. 28And when my Temple is among them forever, the nations will know that I am the LORD, who makes Israel holy."

A Message for Gog

EZEKIEL 38:1-23

This is another message that came to me from the LORD: 2"Son of man, turn and face Gog of the land of Magog, the prince who rules over the nations of Meshech and Tubal, and prophesy against him. 3Give him this message from the Sovereign LORD: Gog, I am your enemy! 4I will turn you around and put hooks in your jaws to lead you out with your whole army—your horses and charioteers in full armor and a great horde armed with shields and swords. 5Persia, Ethiopia, and Libya* will join you, too, with all their weapons. 6Gomer and all its armies will also join you, along with the armies of Beth-togarmah from the distant north, and many others.

7"Get ready; be prepared! Keep all the armies around you mobilized, and take command of them. 8A long time from now you will be called into action. In the distant future you will swoop down on the land of Israel, which will be enjoying peace after recovering from war and after its people have returned from many lands to the mountains of Israel. 9You and all your allies—a vast and awesome army—will roll down on them like a storm and cover the land like a cloud.

10"This is what the Sovereign LORD says: At that time evil thoughts will come to your mind, and you will devise a wicked scheme. 11You will say, 'Israel is an unprotected land filled with unwalled villages! I will march against her and destroy these people who live in such confidence! 12I will go to those formerly desolate cities that are now filled with people who have returned from exile in many nations. I will capture vast amounts of plunder, for the people are rich with livestock and other possessions now. They think the whole world revolves around them!' 13But Sheba and Dedan and the merchants of Tarshish will ask, 'Do you really think the armies you have gathered can rob them of silver and gold? Do you think you can drive away their livestock and seize their goods and carry off plunder?'

14"Therefore, son of man, prophesy against Gog. Give him this message from the Sovereign LORD: When my people are living in peace in their land, then you will rouse yourself.* 15You will come from your homeland in the distant north with your vast cavalry and your mighty army, 16and you will attack my people Israel, covering their land like a cloud. At that time in the distant future, I will bring you against my land as everyone watches, and my holiness will be displayed by what happens to you, Gog. Then all the nations will know that I am the LORD.

17"This is what the Sovereign LORD asks: Are you the one I was talking about long ago, when I announced through Israel's prophets that in the future I would bring you against my people? 18But this is what the Sovereign LORD says: When Gog invades the land of Israel, my fury will boil over! 19In my jealousy and blazing anger, I promise a mighty shaking in the land of Israel on that day. 20All living things—the fish in the

Ez 37:23 The Hebrew term (literally *round things*) probably alludes to dung. **Ez 37:26** Hebrew reads *I will give them and increase their numbers;* Greek version lacks the entire phrase. **Ez 38:5** Hebrew *Paras, Cush, and Put.* **Ez 38:14** As in Greek version; Hebrew reads *then you will know.*

Ezek 37:24-25 The Messiah was often called David because he is David's descendant. David was a good king, but the Messiah would be the perfect King (Rev 17:14; 19:16).

Ezek 37:26-27 God's promise here goes beyond the physical and geographical restoration of Israel. He promises to breathe new spiritual life into his people so that their hearts and attitudes will be right with him and united with one another. This same process is described throughout God's Word as the cleansing and renewing of our hearts by God's Spirit (Titus 3:4-6).

Ezek 38:1ff Ezekiel 37 reveals how Israel (God's people) would be restored to their land from many parts of the world. Once Israel became strong (Ezek 38), a confederacy of nations from the north would attack, led by Gog (see also Rev 20:8). Their purpose would be to destroy God's people. Gog's allies would come from the mountainous area southeast of the Black Sea and southwest of the Caspian Sea (central Turkey), as well as from the area that is present-day Iran, Ethiopia, Libya, and possibly Russia. Gog could be a person (he sometimes is identified with Gyges, king of Lydia in 660 B.C.), or Gog could also be a symbol of all the evil in the world. Whether symbolic or literal, Gog represents the aggregate military might of all the forces opposed to God.

Many say that the battle Ezekiel described will occur at the end of human history, but there are many differences between the events described here and those in Revelation 20. Regardless of when this battle will occur, the message is clear: God will deliver his people—no enemy can stand before his mighty power.

Ezek 38:13 Sheba and Dedan, great trading centers in Arabia, would in effect say to Gog, "Who are you to usurp our position as the world's trade leaders?" Sheba and Dedan would then join this confederacy. Tarshish was the leading trade center in the west; many believe it was in Spain.

sea, the birds of the sky, the animals of the field, the small animals that scurry along the ground, and all the people on earth—will quake in terror at my presence. Mountains will be thrown down; cliffs will crumble; walls will fall to the earth. 21I will summon the sword against you on all the hills of Israel, says the Sovereign LORD. Your men will turn their swords against each other. 22I will punish you and your armies with disease and bloodshed; I will send torrential rain, hailstones, fire, and burning sulfur! 23In this way, I will show my greatness and holiness, and I will make myself known to all the nations of the world. Then they will know that I am the LORD.

The Slaughter of Gog's Hordes

EZEKIEL 39:1-24

"Son of man, prophesy against Gog. Give him this message from the Sovereign LORD: I am your enemy, O Gog, ruler of the nations of Meshech and Tubal. 2I will turn you around and drive you toward the mountains of Israel, bringing you from the distant north. 3I will knock the bow from your left hand and the arrows from your right hand, and I will leave you helpless. 4You and your army and your allies will all die on the mountains. I will feed you to the vultures and wild animals. 5You will fall in the open fields, for I have spoken, says the Sovereign LORD. 6And I will rain down fire on Magog and on all your allies who live safely on the coasts. Then they will know that I am the LORD.

7"In this way, I will make known my holy name among my people of Israel. I will not let anyone bring shame on it. And the nations, too, will know that I am the LORD, the Holy One of Israel. 8That day of judgment will come, says the Sovereign LORD. Everything will happen just as I have declared it.

9"Then the people in the towns of Israel will go out and pick up your small and large shields, bows and arrows, javelins and spears, and they will use them for fuel. There will be enough to last them seven years! 10They won't need to cut wood from the fields or forests, for these weapons will give them all the fuel they need. They will plunder those who planned to plunder them, and they will rob those who planned to rob them, says the Sovereign LORD.

11"And I will make a vast graveyard for Gog and his hordes in the Valley of the Travelers, east of the Dead Sea.* It will block the way of those who travel there, and they will change the name of the place to the Valley of Gog's Hordes. 12It will take seven months for the people of Israel to bury the bodies and cleanse the land. 13Everyone in Israel will help, for it will be a glorious victory for Israel when I demonstrate my glory on that day, says the Sovereign LORD.

14"After seven months, teams of men will be appointed to search the land for skeletons to bury, so the land will be made clean again. 15Whenever bones are found, a marker will be set up so the burial crews will take them to be buried in the Valley of Gog's Hordes. 16(There will be a town there named Hamonah, which means 'horde.') And so the land will finally be cleansed.

17"And now, son of man, this is what the Sovereign LORD says: Call all the birds and wild animals. Say to them: Gather together for my great sacrificial feast. Come from far and near to the mountains of Israel, and there eat flesh and drink blood! 18Eat the flesh of mighty men and drink the blood of princes as though they were rams, lambs, goats, and bulls—all fattened animals from Bashan! 19Gorge yourselves with flesh until you are glutted; drink blood until you are drunk. This is the sacrificial feast I have prepared for you. 20Feast at my banquet table—feast on horses and charioteers, on mighty men and all kinds of valiant warriors, says the Sovereign LORD.

21"In this way, I will demonstrate my glory to the nations. Everyone will see the punishment I have inflicted on them and the power of my fist when I strike. 22And from that time on the people of Israel will know that I am the LORD their God. 23The nations will then know why Israel was sent away to exile—it was punishment for sin, for they were unfaithful to their God. Therefore, I turned away from them and let their enemies destroy them. 24I turned my face away and punished them because of their defilement and their sins.

Restoration for God's People

EZEKIEL 39:25-29

"So now, this is what the Sovereign LORD says: I will end the captivity of my people*; I will have mercy on all Israel, for I jealously guard my holy reputation! 26They will accept responsibility for* their past shame and

Ez 39:11 Hebrew *the sea.* **Ez 39:25** Hebrew *of Jacob.* **Ez 39:26** A few Hebrew manuscripts read *They will forget.*

Ezek 38:21 God will directly intervene in the defense of Israel, unleashing severe natural disasters on the invaders from the north. In the end, the stricken pagan nations will turn on themselves in confusion and panic. All those who set themselves against God will be destroyed.

Ezek 39:1ff The story of the battle continues. The defeat of the evil forces will be final and complete; they will be destroyed by divine intervention. Because of this victory, God's name will be known throughout the world. His glory will be evident, and the nations will understand that he alone is in charge of human history. God will clearly show his love for his people by restoring them to their homeland.

Ezek 39:12-16 Two themes are intertwined: God's total victory over his enemies, and the need to cleanse the land to make it holy. After the final battle, special crews will be appointed to give proper burial to the bodies of the dead enemies in order for the land to be cleansed. The land would have been defiled by unburied corpses. Those who would come in contact with the corpses out in the open would become ceremonially unclean (according to Num 19:14-16). There will be so many bodies that all kinds of birds will be called in order to help dispose of them (Ezek 39:17-20). This message is exciting for us: With God on our side, we are assured of ultimate victory over his foes because God will fight on our behalf (see also Zeph 3:14-17; Rom 8:38-39).

▸ **EZEKIEL 39:25-29** *(cont.)*
unfaithfulness after they come home to live in peace
in their own land, with no one to bother them. 27When
I bring them home from the lands of their enemies,
I will display my holiness among them for all the nations to see. 28Then my people will know that I am
the LORD their God, because I sent them away to exile
and brought them home again. I will leave none of
my people behind. 29And I will never again turn my
face from them, for I will pour out my Spirit upon the
people of Israel. I, the Sovereign LORD, have spoken!"

A Warning for Pharaoh

EZEKIEL 32:1-16

On March 3,* during the twelfth year of King Jehoiachin's captivity, this message came to me from the
LORD: 2"Son of man, mourn for Pharaoh, king of Egypt,
and give him this message:

"You think of yourself as a strong young lion
among the nations,
but you are really just a sea monster,
heaving around in your own rivers,
stirring up mud with your feet.
3 Therefore, this is what the Sovereign LORD says:
I will send many people
to catch you in my net
and haul you out of the water.
4 I will leave you stranded on the land to die.
All the birds of the heavens will land on you,
and the wild animals of the whole earth
will gorge themselves on you.
5 I will scatter your flesh on the hills
and fill the valleys with your bones.
6 I will drench the earth with your gushing blood
all the way to the mountains,
filling the ravines to the brim.
7 When I blot you out,
I will veil the heavens and darken the stars.
I will cover the sun with a cloud,
and the moon will not give you its light.
8 I will darken the bright stars overhead
and cover your land in darkness.
I, the Sovereign LORD, have spoken!

9"I will disturb many hearts when I bring news of
your downfall to distant nations you have never seen.
10Yes, I will shock many lands, and their kings will be
terrified at your fate. They will shudder in fear for
their lives as I brandish my sword before them on
the day of your fall. 11For this is what the Sovereign
LORD says:

"The sword of the king of Babylon
will come against you.
12 I will destroy your hordes with the swords of
mighty warriors—
the terror of the nations.
They will shatter the pride of Egypt,
and all its hordes will be destroyed.
13 I will destroy all your flocks and herds
that graze beside the streams.
Never again will people or animals
muddy those waters with their feet.
14 Then I will let the waters of Egypt become calm
again,
and they will flow as smoothly as olive oil,
says the Sovereign LORD.
15 And when I destroy Egypt
and strip you of everything you own
and strike down all your people,
then you will know that I am the LORD.
16 Yes, this is the funeral song
they will sing for Egypt.
Let all the nations mourn.
Let them mourn for Egypt and its hordes.
I, the Sovereign LORD, have spoken!"

Egypt Falls into the Pit

EZEKIEL 32:17-32

On March 17,* during the twelfth year, another message came to me from the LORD: 18"Son of man, weep
for the hordes of Egypt and for the other mighty nations.* For I will send them down to the world below
in company with those who descend to the pit. 19Say
to them,

'O Egypt, are you lovelier than the other nations?
No! So go down to the pit and lie there among
the outcasts.*'

Ez 32:1 Hebrew *On the first day of the twelfth month,* of the ancient Hebrew lunar calendar. This event occurred on March 3, 585 B.C.; also see note on 1:1. **Ez 32:17** Hebrew *On the fifteenth day of the month,* presumably in the twelfth month of the ancient Hebrew lunar calendar (see 32:1). This would put this message at the end of King Jehoiachin's twelfth year of captivity, on March 17, 585 B.C.; also see note on 1:1. Greek version reads *On the fifteenth day of the first month,* which would put this message on April 27, 586 B.C., at the beginning of Jehoiachin's twelfth year. **Ez 32:18** The meaning of the Hebrew is uncertain. **Ez 32:19** Hebrew *the uncircumcised;* also in 32:21, 24, 25, 26, 28, 29, 30, 32.

Ezek 39:29 Both in this prophecy and in Joel 2:28-29, God promises to pour out his Spirit on his people. The early church believed this began to be fulfilled at Pentecost, when God's Holy Spirit came to live in all believers (Acts 2:1-18).

Ezek 32:1ff This prophecy was given in 585 B.C., two months after the news of Jerusalem's fall had reached the exiles in Babylon. Ezekiel prophesied numerous judgments upon many wicked nations. These judgments served a positive purpose: They showed that evil forces are continually being overcome and that one day God will overthrow all evil, making the world the perfect place he intended. They also serve as warnings that God alone is sovereign. Even the mightiest rulers, like Pharaoh, will fall before God. All are accountable to him.

Ezek 32:2 Although Pharaoh thought of himself as a strong, young lion, in God's eyes he was nothing but a crocodile ("sea monster") muddying the water. God's judgment would reduce Pharaoh to his true size. Anyone who defies God will face his judgment.

Ezek 32:18 The Hebrews believed in an afterlife for all people, good and bad. Ezekiel predicted that Egypt would share the same fate as that of the evil nations already sent to the "pit." The words here are more poetic than doctrinal (see Job 24:19; Ps 16:10; Isa 38:10, and the note on Matt 25:46, p. 1453). The Egyptians had a preoccupation with the

20The Egyptians will fall with the many who have died
by the sword, for the sword is drawn against them.
Egypt and its hordes will be dragged away to their
judgment. 21Down in the grave* mighty leaders will
mockingly welcome Egypt and its allies, saying, 'They
have come down; they lie among the outcasts, hordes
slaughtered by the sword.'
22"Assyria lies there surrounded by the graves of
its army, those who were slaughtered by the sword.
23Their graves are in the depths of the pit, and they
are surrounded by their allies. They struck terror in
the hearts of people everywhere, but now they have
been slaughtered by the sword.
24"Elam lies there surrounded by the graves of all
its hordes, those who were slaughtered by the sword.
They struck terror in the hearts of people everywhere,
but now they have descended as outcasts to the world
below. Now they lie in the pit and share the shame
of those who have gone before them. 25They have a
resting place among the slaughtered, surrounded by
the graves of all their hordes. Yes, they terrorized the
nations while they lived, but now they lie in shame
with others in the pit, all of them outcasts, slaughtered by the sword.
26"Meshech and Tubal are there, surrounded by the
graves of all their hordes. They once struck terror in the
hearts of people everywhere. But now they are outcasts,
all slaughtered by the sword. 27They are not buried in
honor like their fallen heroes, who went down to the
grave* with their weapons—their shields covering their
bodies* and their swords beneath their heads. Their
guilt rests upon them because they brought terror to
everyone while they were still alive.
28"You too, Egypt, will lie crushed and broken among
the outcasts, all slaughtered by the sword.
29"Edom is there with its kings and princes. Mighty
as they were, they also lie among those slaughtered
by the sword, with the outcasts who have gone down
to the pit.
30"All the princes of the north and the Sidonians are
there with others who have died. Once a terror, they
have been put to shame. They lie there as outcasts
with others who were slaughtered by the sword. They
share the shame of all who have descended to the pit.
31"When Pharaoh and his entire army arrive, he
will take comfort that he is not alone in having his
hordes killed, says the Sovereign LORD. 32Although I
have caused his terror to fall upon all the living, Pharaoh and his hordes will lie there among the outcasts
who were slaughtered by the sword. I, the Sovereign
LORD, have spoken!"

Ezekiel as Israel's Watchman

EZEKIEL 33:1-9

Once again a message came to me from the LORD:
2"Son of man, give your people this message: 'When
I bring an army against a country, the people of that
land choose one of their own to be a watchman.
3When the watchman sees the enemy coming, he
sounds the alarm to warn the people. 4Then if those
who hear the alarm refuse to take action, it is their own
fault if they die. 5They heard the alarm but ignored

Ez 32:21 Hebrew *in Sheol.* **Ez 32:27a** Hebrew *to Sheol.* **Ez 32:27b** The meaning of the Hebrew is uncertain.

"When the watchman sees the enemy coming, he sounds the alarm to warn the people."
Ezekiel 33:3

afterlife and built pyramids to ensure the pharaohs' comfort in the next life. God alone controls our future and life after death.

Ezek 32:21-32 In these verses, Ezekiel conducts a guided tour of the "grave"—the region of the afterlife. In the grave, all of God's enemies are condemned in judgment; many of them experience the fate they so quickly imposed on others. Though Babylon is not mentioned, Ezekiel's readers would have concluded that if all the other nations would be judged for their rebellion against God, Babylon would be judged as well. These words would comfort the captives.

Ezek 32:24-26 Elam was a nation of fierce warriors from the region east of Assyria. Nebuchadnezzar conquered them (Jer 49:34-39), but they eventually rebuilt themselves and became part of Persia. Meshech and Tubal were territories located in the eastern region of Asia Minor, now eastern and central Turkey. In Ezekiel 38–39 they are described as allies of Gog, the chief prince of a confederacy. They are included with the evil nations that will be judged for fighting against God's people.

Ezek 32:30 The princes of the north were probably the princes of the Phoenician city-states.

Ezek 32:32 After reading Ezekiel's prophecies against all these foreign nations, we may wonder if he was blindly loyal to his own nation. But Ezekiel spoke only when God gave him a message (Ezek 3:27). Besides, God's prophets pronounced judgment on God's sinful people just as much as on God's enemies. But if Babylon was God's enemy, why isn't it mentioned in Ezekiel's judgments? Perhaps because (1) God wanted to foster a spirit of cooperation between the exiles and Babylon in order to preserve his people; (2) God was still using Babylon to refine his own people; (3) God wanted to use Daniel, a powerful official in Babylon, to draw the Babylonians to him.

Ezek 33:1ff Ezekiel 33 sets forth a new direction for Ezekiel's prophecies. Up to this point, Ezekiel has pronounced judgment upon Judah (Ezek 1–24) and the surrounding evil nations (Ezek 25–32) for their sins. After Jerusalem fell, he turned from messages of doom and judgment to messages of comfort, hope, and future restoration for God's people (Ezek 33–48). God previously appointed Ezekiel to be a watchman, warning the nation of coming judgment (see Ezek 3:17-21). Here God appointed him to be a watchman again, but this time he was to preach a message of hope. More warnings will come (Ezek 33:23–34:10; 36:1-7), but these are part of the larger picture of hope. God will remember to bless those who are faithful to him. We must pay attention to both aspects of Ezekiel's message: warning and promise. Those who persist in rebelling against God should take warning. Those faithful to God should find encouragement and hope.

▸ **EZEKIEL 33:1-9** ***(cont.)***
it, so the responsibility is theirs. If they had listened
to the warning, they could have saved their lives. [6]But
if the watchman sees the enemy coming and doesn't
sound the alarm to warn the people, he is responsible
for their captivity. They will die in their sins, but I will
hold the watchman responsible for their deaths.'
[7]"Now, son of man, I am making you a watchman
for the people of Israel. Therefore, listen to what I
say and warn them for me. [8]If I announce that some
wicked people are sure to die and you fail to tell them
to change their ways, then they will die in their sins,
and I will hold you responsible for their deaths. [9]But
if you warn them to repent and they don't repent, they
will die in their sins, but you will have saved yourself.

The Watchman's Message

EZEKIEL 33:10-20
"Son of man, give the people of Israel this message: You
are saying, 'Our sins are heavy upon us; we are wasting
away! How can we survive?' [11]As surely as I live, says
the Sovereign LORD, I take no pleasure in the death
of wicked people. I only want them to turn from their
wicked ways so they can live. Turn! Turn from your
wickedness, O people of Israel! Why should you die?
[12]"Son of man, give your people this message: The
righteous behavior of righteous people will not save
them if they turn to sin, nor will the wicked behavior of wicked people destroy them if they repent and
turn from their sins. [13]When I tell righteous people
that they will live, but then they sin, expecting their
past righteousness to save them, then none of their
righteous acts will be remembered. I will destroy
them for their sins. [14]And suppose I tell some wicked
people that they will surely die, but then they turn
from their sins and do what is just and right. [15]For instance, they might give back a debtor's security, return
what they have stolen, and obey my life-giving laws,
no longer doing what is evil. If they do this, then they
will surely live and not die. [16]None of their past sins
will be brought up again, for they have done what is
just and right, and they will surely live.
[17]"Your people are saying, 'The Lord isn't doing
what's right,' but it is they who are not doing what's
right. [18]For again I say, when righteous people turn away
from their righteous behavior and turn to evil, they will
die. [19]But if wicked people turn from their wickedness
and do what is just and right, they will live. [20]O people
of Israel, you are saying, 'The Lord isn't doing what's
right.' But I judge each of you according to your deeds."

582 BC

Pythagoras, Greek philosopher and mathematician, is born

2. EXILES MOURN IN BABYLON

The people who had been taken to Babylon were deeply grieved over the destruction of Jerusalem, and they longed to be restored and to see the Babylonians brought to justice. We, too, can cry out to God in our distress. He is always ready to listen.

Summary of Captives from Jerusalem to Babylon

JEREMIAH 52:28-30
The number of captives taken to Babylon in the seventh year of Nebuchadnezzar's reign* was 3,023.
[29]Then in Nebuchadnezzar's eighteenth year* he
took 832 more. [30]In Nebuchadnezzar's twenty-third
year* he sent Nebuzaradan, the captain of the guard,
who took 745 more—a total of 4,600 captives in all.

Psalm 137

THEME: A person in exile weeps over the bitterness of captivity. Our sorrow can make it difficult to imagine singing joyful songs again.
AUTHOR: Anonymous

[1] Beside the rivers of Babylon, we sat and wept
as we thought of Jerusalem.*
[2] We put away our harps,
hanging them on the branches of poplar
trees.
[3] For our captors demanded a song from us.
Our tormentors insisted on a joyful
hymn:
"Sing us one of those songs of Jerusalem!"
[4] But how can we sing the songs of the LORD
while in a pagan land?

[5] If I forget you, O Jerusalem,
let my right hand forget how to play
the harp.
[6] May my tongue stick to the roof of my
mouth
if I fail to remember you,
if I don't make Jerusalem my greatest joy.

Jer 52:28 This exile in the seventh year of Nebuchadnezzar's reign occurred in 597 B.C. **Jer 52:29** This exile in the eighteenth year of Nebuchadnezzar's reign occurred in 586 B.C. **Jer 52:30** This exile in the twenty-third year of Nebuchadnezzar's reign occurred in 581 B.C. **Psalm 137:1** Hebrew *Zion;* also in 137:3.

Ezek 33:10-12 The exiles were discouraged by their past sins. This is an important turning point in this book—elsewhere in Ezekiel the people had refused to face their sins. Here, they felt heavy guilt for rebelling against God for so many years. Therefore, God assured them of forgiveness if they repented. God wants everyone to turn to him. He looks at what we are and will become, not what we have been. God gives you the opportunity to turn to him if you will. Sincerely follow God, and ask him to forgive you when you fail.

Ezek 33:13 Past good deeds will not save a person who decides to turn to a life of sin. Some people think that if they do enough good deeds, they can hold on to the sins they don't want to give up. But it's useless to try to be good in some areas so you can be deliberately bad in others. God wants wholehearted love and obedience.

Ezek 33:15 While good deeds will not save us, our salvation must lead to righteous actions (see Eph 2:10; Jas 2:14-17).

7 O LORD, remember what the Edomites did
on the day the armies of Babylon captured
Jerusalem.
"Destroy it!" they yelled.
"Level it to the ground!"
8 O Babylon, you will be destroyed.
Happy is the one who pays you back
for what you have done to us.
9 Happy is the one who takes your babies
and smashes them against the rocks!

3. DANIEL AND NEBUCHADNEZZAR

Daniel was a highly-placed advisor in King Nebuchadnezzar's court, and Nebuchadnezzar trusted him to be able to interpret his prophetic dreams. Daniel was able to interpret these dreams because God had given them to Nebuchadnezzar and he told Daniel what they meant. Daniel wasn't a magician or a psychic; he was simply a faithful servant of God who was respected because of his integrity and blessed for his obedience.

Nebuchadnezzar's Dream about a Tree

DANIEL 4:1-18

1*King Nebuchadnezzar sent this message to the people of every race and nation and language throughout the world:

"Peace and prosperity to you!
2"I want you all to know about the miraculous
signs and wonders the Most High God has
performed for me.
3 How great are his signs,
how powerful his wonders!
His kingdom will last forever,
his rule through all generations.
4*"I, Nebuchadnezzar, was living in my
palace in comfort and prosperity. 5But one
night I had a dream that frightened me; I saw
visions that terrified me as I lay in my bed. 6So
I issued an order calling in all the wise men of
Babylon, so they could tell me what my dream
meant. 7When all the magicians, enchanters,
astrologers,* and fortune-tellers came in, I told
them the dream, but they could not tell me
what it meant. 8At last Daniel came in before
me, and I told him the dream. (He was named
Belteshazzar after my god, and the spirit of the
holy gods is in him.)
9"I said to him, 'Belteshazzar, chief of the
magicians, I know that the spirit of the holy gods
is in you and that no mystery is too great for you
to solve. Now tell me what my dream means.
10"'While I was lying in my bed, this is what
I dreamed. I saw a large tree in the middle of
the earth. 11The tree grew very tall and strong,
reaching high into the heavens for all the world to
see. 12It had fresh green leaves, and it was loaded
with fruit for all to eat. Wild animals lived in its
shade, and birds nested in its branches. All the
world was fed from this tree.
13"'Then as I lay there dreaming, I saw a
messenger,* a holy one, coming down from
heaven. 14The messenger shouted,

"Cut down the tree and lop off its branches!
Shake off its leaves and scatter its fruit!
Chase the wild animals from its shade
and the birds from its branches.
15 But leave the stump and the roots in the
ground,
bound with a band of iron and bronze
and surrounded by tender grass.

Dn 4:1 Verses 4:1-3 are numbered 3:31-33 in Aramaic text. **Dn 4:4** Verses 4:4-37 are numbered 4:1-34 in Aramaic text. **Dn 4:7** Or *Chaldeans.* **Dn 4:13** Aramaic *a watcher;* also in 4:23.

This includes restitution for past sins (as exemplified in the story of Zacchaeus, Luke 19:1-10). God expects us to make restitution, whenever necessary, for the wrongs we have committed.

Ps 137:7 The Edomites were related to the Israelites, both nations having descended from Isaac and his father, Abraham. Although Israel shared its southern border with Edom, there was bitter hatred between the two nations. The Edomites did not come to help when the city of Jerusalem was besieged by the Babylonian army. In fact, they rejoiced when the city was destroyed (Jer 49:7-22; Joel 3:19; Obad 1:1-21).

Ps 137:8-9 God destroyed Babylon and its offspring for their proud assault against God and his Kingdom. The Medes and Persians destroyed Babylon in 539 B.C. Many of those who were oppressed lived to see the victory. The phrase about the babies is harsh because the writer is crying out for judgment: "Treat the Babylonians the way they treated us."

Dan 4:2-3 Although Nebuchadnezzar praised Daniel's God, he still did not believe in him completely or submit to him alone (Dan 4:8). Many people attend church and use Christian language, but they really don't honor God with their lives. Profession doesn't always mean possession. Does your life match your profession of faith?

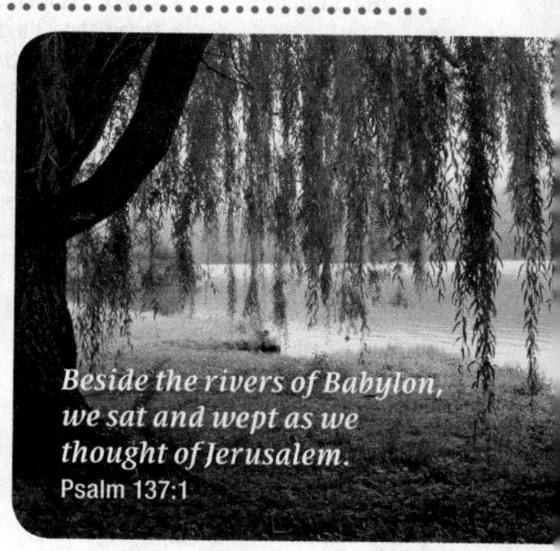
Beside the rivers of Babylon, we sat and wept as we thought of Jerusalem.
Psalm 137:1

▶ **DANIEL 4:1-18** ***(cont.)***

Now let him be drenched with the dew
of heaven,
and let him live with the wild animals
among the plants of the field.
16 For seven periods of time,
let him have the mind of a wild animal
instead of the mind of a human.
17 For this has been decreed by the messengers*;
it is commanded by the holy ones,
so that everyone may know
that the Most High rules over the kingdoms
of the world.
He gives them to anyone he chooses—
even to the lowliest of people."

Dn 4:17 Aramaic *the watchers.*

18"'Belteshazzar, that was the dream that I,
King Nebuchadnezzar, had. Now tell me what it
means, for none of the wise men of my kingdom
can do so. But you can tell me because the spirit
of the holy gods is in you.'

Daniel Explains the Dream

DANIEL 4:19-27

19"Upon hearing this, Daniel (also known
as Belteshazzar) was overcome for a time,
frightened by the meaning of the dream. Then
the king said to him, 'Belteshazzar, don't be
alarmed by the dream and what it means.'
"Belteshazzar replied, 'I wish the events
foreshadowed in this dream would happen

NEBUCHADNEZZAR

Nebuchadnezzar was one world leader who decided he could get more cooperation from the people he conquered by letting them keep their gods. Their lands he took, their riches he robbed, their lives he controlled, but their idols he allowed them to worship—sometimes even worshiping them himself. Nebuchadnezzar's plan worked well, with one glaring exception. When he conquered the little nation of Judah, he met a God who demanded exclusive worship—not just his share among many gods. In a sense, Nebuchadnezzar had always been able to rule the gods. This new God was different; this God dared to claim that he had made Nebuchadnezzar all that he was. One of the great conquerors in history was himself conquered by his Creator. • The Bible allows us to note the ways in which God worked on Nebuchadnezzar. God allowed him victories, but he was accomplishing God's purposes. God allowed him to deport the best young Jewish leaders as his palace servants, while placing close to him a young man named Daniel, who would change the king's life. God allowed Nebuchadnezzar to attempt to kill three of his servants to teach the king that he did not really have power over life and death. God warned him of the dangers in his pride and then allowed Nebuchadnezzar to live through seven years of insanity before restoring him to the throne. God showed the king who was really in control! • These lessons are clear to us today because of our place in history. When our attention shifts to our own lives, we often find ourselves unable to see how God is working. But we do have the advantage of God's Word as our guide for today's challenges. We are commanded to obey God; we are also commanded to trust him. Trusting him covers those times when we are not sure about the outcome. God has entrusted us with this day; have we trusted him with our lives?

Strengths and accomplishments	• Greatest of the Babylonian kings • A foreign ruler God used for his purposes
Weaknesses and mistakes	• Thought of himself as a god • Became extremely proud, which led to a bout of insanity • Tended to forget the demonstrations of God's power he had witnessed
Lessons from his life	• History records the actions of God's willing servants and those who were his unwitting tools • A leader's greatness is affected by the quality of his advisers • Uncontrolled pride is self-destructive
Vital statistics	• Where: Babylon • Occupation: King • Relatives: Father: Nabopolassar. Son: Evil-merodach. Grandson: Belshazzar. • Contemporaries: Jeremiah, Ezekiel, Daniel, Jehoiakim, Jehoiachin
Key verse	"Now I, Nebuchadnezzar, praise and glorify and honor the King of heaven. All his acts are just and true, and he is able to humble the proud" (Dan 4:37).

Nebuchadnezzar's story is told in 2 Kings 24–25; 2 Chronicles 36; Jeremiah 21–52; Daniel 1–4.

Dan 4:17 One of the most difficult lessons to learn is that God is sovereign. He is above all of those who are above us. He limits the power and authority of all the government, business, and religious leaders in the world. Those who live in freedom and with a relatively high degree of autonomy find this difficult to understand. While we may feel as though we are free to do what we please, God is sovereign over all of our plans and desires.

Dan 4:19 When Daniel understood Nebuchadnezzar's dream, he was stunned, and he wondered how to break the news. He told the king he wished what the dream foreshadowed would happen to the king's enemies and not to Nebuchadnezzar. How could Daniel be so deeply grieved at the fate of Nebuchadnezzar—the king who was responsible for the destruction of Daniel's home and nation? Daniel had forgiven Nebuchadnezzar, and so God was able to use Daniel. Very often when we have been wronged by someone, we find it difficult to forget the past. We may even be glad when that person suffers. Forgiveness means putting the past behind us. Can you love someone who has hurt you? Can you serve someone who mistreated you? Ask God to help you forgive, forget, and love. God may use you in an extraordinary way in that person's life!

to your enemies, my lord, and not to you!
[20]The tree you saw was growing very tall and
strong, reaching high into the heavens for all
the world to see. [21]It had fresh green leaves
and was loaded with fruit for all to eat. Wild
animals lived in its shade, and birds nested in its
branches. [22]That tree, Your Majesty, is you. For
you have grown strong and great; your greatness
reaches up to heaven, and your rule to the ends
of the earth.

[23]"'Then you saw a messenger, a holy one,
coming down from heaven and saying, "Cut down
the tree and destroy it. But leave the stump and
the roots in the ground, bound with a band of
iron and bronze and surrounded by tender grass.
Let him be drenched with the dew of heaven. Let
him live with the animals of the field for seven
periods of time."

[24]"'This is what the dream means, Your
Majesty, and what the Most High has declared
will happen to my lord the king. [25]You will be
driven from human society, and you will live
in the fields with the wild animals. You will eat
grass like a cow, and you will be drenched with
the dew of heaven. Seven periods of time will
pass while you live this way, until you learn that
the Most High rules over the kingdoms of the
world and gives them to anyone he chooses.
[26]But the stump and roots of the tree were left in
the ground. This means that you will receive your
kingdom back again when you have learned that
heaven rules.

[27]"'King Nebuchadnezzar, please accept
my advice. Stop sinning and do what is right.
Break from your wicked past and be merciful
to the poor. Perhaps then you will continue
to prosper.'

The Dream's Fulfillment

DANIEL 4:28-33

[28]"But all these things did happen to King
Nebuchadnezzar. [29]Twelve months later he was
taking a walk on the flat roof of the royal palace
in Babylon. [30]As he looked out across the city,
he said, 'Look at this great city of Babylon! By
my own mighty power, I have built this beautiful
city as my royal residence to display my majestic
splendor.'

[31]"While these words were still in his mouth,
a voice called down from heaven, 'O King
Nebuchadnezzar, this message is for you! You
are no longer ruler of this kingdom. [32]You will be
driven from human society. You will live in the
fields with the wild animals, and you will eat grass
like a cow. Seven periods of time will pass while
you live this way, until you learn that the Most
High rules over the kingdoms of the world and
gives them to anyone he chooses.'

[33]"That same hour the judgment was fulfilled,
and Nebuchadnezzar was driven from human
society. He ate grass like a cow, and he was
drenched with the dew of heaven. He lived this
way until his hair was as long as eagles' feathers
and his nails were like birds' claws.

Nebuchadnezzar Praises God

DANIEL 4:34-37

[34]"After this time had passed, I, Nebuchadnezzar,
looked up to heaven. My sanity returned, and
I praised and worshiped the Most High and
honored the one who lives forever.

His rule is everlasting,
  and his kingdom is eternal.
[35] All the people of the earth
  are nothing compared to him.
He does as he pleases
  among the angels of heaven
  and among the people of the earth.
No one can stop him or say to him,
  'What do you mean by doing these things?'

[36]"When my sanity returned to me, so did my
honor and glory and kingdom. My advisers and
nobles sought me out, and I was restored as head
of my kingdom, with even greater honor than
before.

[37]"Now I, Nebuchadnezzar, praise and glorify
and honor the King of heaven. All his acts are
just and true, and he is able to humble the
proud."

Dan 4:23ff Although much of the world thought that Nebuchadnezzar was a mighty (even divine) king, God demonstrated that Nebuchadnezzar was an ordinary man. The king would go insane and become like an animal for a set period of time ("seven periods of time"). God humiliated Nebuchadnezzar to show that almighty God, not Nebuchadnezzar, was Lord of the nations. Whether a person is powerful or weak, self-centered pride will push God from one's life. Pride may be the most dangerous temptation you will face. Don't let anything cause you to forget God.

Dan 4:27-33 Daniel pleaded with Nebuchadnezzar to change his ways, and God gave Nebuchadnezzar 12 months to do it. Unfortunately, there was no repentance in the heart of this proud king, and so the dream was fulfilled.

Dan 4:34 Ancient kings tried to avoid mentioning their weaknesses or defeats in their monuments and official records. From Nebuchadnezzar's records, however, we can infer that for a time during his 43-year reign he did not rule. The Bible explains Nebuchadnezzar's pride and punishment.

Dan 4:36 Nebuchadnezzar's pilgrimage with God is one of the themes of the book of Daniel. He first acknowledged that God revealed mysteries to Daniel (Dan 2:47). Then he praised the God who rescued the three Hebrews (Dan 3:28-29). Although Nebuchadnezzar recognized that God exists and works great miracles, the Scripture text does not say that he acknowledged God as his Lord (Dan 4:30). We may recognize that God exists and does wonderful miracles, but so do many unbelievers! To be a child of God, you must invite him to be Lord of your life.

4. EZEKIEL'S VISION OF RESTORED WORSHIP

Years earlier, Ezekiel had a vision of the Temple in Jerusalem where God's presence departed from the Temple and went into the wilderness (Ezek 10). Since that time, Babylon's armies had returned to Jerusalem and completely destroyed the Temple, which now sat in ruins. But Ezekiel had another vision of a restored Temple, where the glory of the Lord returns and the people of God worship him fully. There is great hope in the midst of judgment.

The New Temple Area

EZEKIEL 40:1-4

On April 28,* during the twenty-fifth year of our captivity—fourteen years after the fall of Jerusalem—the LORD took hold of me. [2]In a vision from God he took me to the land of Israel and set me down on a very high mountain. From there I could see toward the south what appeared to be a city. [3]As he brought me nearer, I saw a man whose face shone like bronze standing beside a gateway entrance. He was holding in his hand a linen measuring cord and a measuring rod.

[4]He said to me, "Son of man, watch and listen. Pay close attention to everything I show you. You have been brought here so I can show you many things. Then you will return to the people of Israel and tell them everything you have seen."

The East Gateway

EZEKIEL 40:5-16

I could see a wall completely surrounding the Temple area. The man took a measuring rod that was 10½ feet* long and measured the wall, and the wall was 10½ feet* thick and 10½ feet high.

[6]Then he went over to the eastern gateway. He climbed the steps and measured the threshold of the gateway; it was 10½ feet front to back.* [7]There were guard alcoves on each side built into the gateway passage. Each of these alcoves was 10½ feet square, with a distance between them of 8¾ feet* along the passage wall. The gateway's inner threshold, which led to the entry room at the inner end of the gateway passage, was 10½ feet front to back. [8]He also measured the entry room of the gateway.* [9]It was 14 feet* across, with supporting columns 3½ feet* thick. This entry room was at the inner end of the gateway structure, facing toward the Temple.

[10]There were three guard alcoves on each side of the gateway passage. Each had the same measurements, and the dividing walls separating them were also identical. [11]The man measured the gateway entrance, which was 17½ feet* wide at the opening and 22¾ feet* wide in the gateway passage. [12]In front of each of the guard alcoves was a 21-inch* curb. The alcoves themselves were 10½ feet* on each side.

[13]Then he measured the entire width of the gateway, measuring the distance between the back walls

Ez 40:1 Hebrew *At the beginning of the year, on the tenth day of the month,* of the ancient Hebrew lunar calendar. This event occurred on April 28, 573 B.C.; also see note on 1:1. **Ez 40:5a** Hebrew *6 long cubits* [3.2 meters], *each being a cubit* [18 inches or 45 centimeters] *and a handbreadth* [3 inches or 8 centimeters] *in length.* **Ez 40:5b** Hebrew *1 rod* [3.2 meters]; also in 40:5c, 7. **Ez 40:6** As in Greek version, which reads *1 rod* [3.2 meters] *deep;* Hebrew reads *1 rod deep, and 1 threshold, 1 rod deep.* **Ez 40:7** Hebrew *5 cubits* [2.7 meters]; also in 40:48. **Ez 40:8** Many Hebrew manuscripts add *which faced inward toward the Temple; it was 1 rod* [10.5 feet or 3.2 meters] *deep. [9]Then he measured the entry room of the gateway.* **Ez 40:9a** Hebrew *8 cubits* [4.2 meters]. **Ez 40:9b** Hebrew *2 cubits* [1.1 meters]. **Ez 40:11a** Hebrew *10 cubits* [5.3 meters]. **Ez 40:11b** Hebrew *13 cubits* [6.9 meters]. **Ez 40:12a** Hebrew *1 cubit* [53 centimeters]. **Ez 40:12b** Hebrew *6 cubits* [3.2 meters].

Ezek 40:1ff To the exiles, the building of the Temple envisioned a time of complete restoration, a time when God would return to his people. The Temple was rebuilt 520–515 B.C. (see Ezra 5–6) but fell short of Ezekiel's plan (Hag 2:3; Zech 4:10). This vision of the Temple has been interpreted in four main ways: (1) This is the Temple Zerubbabel should have built from 520 to 515 B.C. and is the actual blueprint Ezekiel intended. But due to disobedience (Ezek 43:9-10), it was never followed. (2) This is a literal Temple to be rebuilt during the millennial reign of Christ. (3) This Temple is symbolic of the true worship of God by the Christian church right now. (4) This Temple is symbolic of the future and eternal reign of God when his presence and blessing fill the earth.

Whether the Temple is literal or symbolic, it seems clear that this is a vision of God's final perfect Kingdom. This gave hope to the people of Ezekiel's time who had just seen their nation and its Temple destroyed with no hope of rebuilding it in the near future. The details given in this vision gave the people even more hope that what Ezekiel saw had come from God and would surely happen in the future.

Ezek 40:1ff One argument against the view that Ezekiel's Temple is a literal building of the future is the mention of sacrifices (Ezek 40:38-43). If the sacrifices were to be reinstituted in the last days, then Christ's final sacrifice would not have been final. The New Testament makes it clear that Christ died once and for all (Rom 6:10; Heb 9:12; 10:10, 18). Our sins have been removed; no further sacrifice is needed.

In Ezekiel's day, the only kind of worship the people knew was the kind that involved sacrifices and ceremonies as described in Exodus through Deuteronomy. Ezekiel had to explain the new order of worship in terms the people would understand. The next nine chapters tell how the Temple is the focal point of everything, showing that the ideal relationship with God is when all of life centers on him.

Ezek 40:1ff Ezekiel explained God's dwelling place in words and images the people could understand. God wanted them to see the great splendor he had planned for those who lived faithfully. This kind of Temple was never built, but it was a vision intended to typify God's perfect plan for his people—the centrality of worship, the presence of the Lord, the blessings flowing from it, and the orderliness of worship and worship duties. Don't let the details obscure the point of this vision: One day all those who have been faithful to God will enjoy eternal life with him. Let the majesty of this vision lift you and teach you about the God you worship and serve.

Ezek 40:1–43:27 This vision (Ezek 40–43) came to Ezekiel in 573 B.C. It gives the Temple's measurements and then describes how it would be filled with God's glory. Because Ezekiel was a priest, he would have been familiar with the furnishings and ceremonies of Solomon's Temple. As in Revelation 11:1-2, the command to "measure" defines the areas God has marked out for special use. As you read all these details, remember that God is sovereign over all our worship and over the timetable for restoring the faithful to himself.

Ezek 40:3-4 Who was this man? He was obviously not a human being, so he may have been the angel in Ezekiel 9:1-11 or one like him. Some say he may have been Christ himself because he speaks as God had been speaking to Ezekiel, calling him "son of man."

of facing guard alcoves; this distance was 43¾ feet.* 14He measured the dividing walls all along the inside of the gateway up to the entry room of the gateway; this distance was 105 feet.* 15The full length of the gateway passage was 87½ feet* from one end to the other. 16There were recessed windows that narrowed inward through the walls of the guard alcoves and their dividing walls. There were also windows in the entry room. The surfaces of the dividing walls were decorated with carved palm trees.

The Outer Courtyard

EZEKIEL 40:17-19

Then the man brought me through the gateway into the outer courtyard of the Temple. A stone pavement ran along the walls of the courtyard, and thirty rooms were built against the walls, opening onto the pavement. 18This pavement flanked the gates and extended out from the walls into the courtyard the same distance as the gateway entrance. This was the lower pavement. 19Then the man measured across the Temple's outer courtyard between the outer and inner gateways; the distance was 175 feet.*

The North Gateway

EZEKIEL 40:20-23

The man measured the gateway on the north just like the one on the east. 21Here, too, there were three guard alcoves on each side, with dividing walls and an entry room. All the measurements matched those of the east gateway. The gateway passage was 87½ feet long and 43¾ feet wide between the back walls of facing guard alcoves. 22The windows, the entry room, and the palm tree decorations were identical to those in the east gateway. There were seven steps leading up to the gateway entrance, and the entry room was at the inner end of the gateway passage. 23Here on the north side, just as on the east, there was another gateway leading to the Temple's inner courtyard directly opposite this outer gateway. The distance between the two gateways was 175 feet.

The South Gateway

EZEKIEL 40:24-27

Then the man took me around to the south gateway and measured its various parts, and they were exactly the same as in the others. 25It had windows along the walls as the others did, and there was an entry room where the gateway passage opened into the outer courtyard. And like the others, the gateway passage was 87½ feet long and 43¾ feet wide between the back walls of facing guard alcoves. 26This gateway also had a stairway of seven steps leading up to it, and an entry room at the inner end, and palm tree decorations along the dividing walls. 27And here again, directly opposite the outer gateway, was another gateway that led into the inner courtyard. The distance between the two gateways was 175 feet.

Gateways to the Inner Courtyard

EZEKIEL 40:28-37

Then the man took me to the south gateway leading into the inner courtyard. He measured it, and it had the same measurements as the other gateways. 29Its guard alcoves, dividing walls, and entry room were the same size as those in the others. It also had windows along its walls and in the entry room. And like the others, the gateway passage was 87½ feet long and 43¾ feet wide. 30(The entry rooms of the gateways leading into the inner courtyard were 14 feet* across and 43¾ feet wide.) 31The entry room to the south gateway faced into the outer courtyard. It had palm tree decorations on its columns, and there were eight steps leading to its entrance.

32Then he took me to the east gateway leading to the inner courtyard. He measured it, and it had the

Ez 40:13 Hebrew *25 cubits* [13.3 meters]; also in 40:21, 25, 29, 30, 33, 36. **Ez 40:14** Hebrew *60 cubits* [31.8 meters]. Greek version reads *20 cubits* [35 feet or 10.6 meters]. The meaning of the Hebrew in this verse is uncertain. **Ez 40:15** Hebrew *50 cubits* [26.5 meters]; also in 40:21, 25, 29, 33, 36. **Ez 40:19** Hebrew *100 cubits* [53 meters]; also in 40:23, 27, 47. **Ez 40:30** As in 40:9, which reads *8 cubits* [14 feet or 4.2 meters]; here the Hebrew reads *5 cubits* [8¾ feet or 2.7 meters]. Some Hebrew manuscripts and the Greek version lack this entire verse.

Ezekiel's Temple

As a priest, Ezekiel remained keenly interested in the Temple, priesthood, sacrificial regulations, and festivals. A large section at the end of Ezekiel describes the Temple's revived worship (Ezek 40:1–46:24). His vision of the departure of the glory of God, so important in the messages of God's judgment on Jerusalem (Ezek 1; 10–11), now assures the remnant that God did not forsake his people (Ezek 43:2-5). He will return to dwell among them, for the Temple is a symbol of God's presence (Ezek 37:26-28). Some interpreters believe that the Temple, with its ritual as described in Ezekiel 40–46, will be restored in the messianic era before the Last Judgment. Others believe the promises about the Temple are symbolic imagery used to answer Ezekiel's greatest concern: Would God return to be with his people (Ezek 48:35; see John 2:21; Rev 21:22)?

▸ **EZEKIEL 40:28-37** ***(cont.)***

same measurements as the other gateways. [33]Its guard alcoves, dividing walls, and entry room were the same size as those of the others, and there were windows along the walls and in the entry room. The gateway passage measured 87½ feet long and 43¾ feet wide. [34]Its entry room faced into the outer courtyard. It had palm tree decorations on its columns, and there were eight steps leading to its entrance.

[35]Then he took me around to the north gateway leading to the inner courtyard. He measured it, and it had the same measurements as the other gateways. [36]The guard alcoves, dividing walls, and entry room of this gateway had the same measurements as in the others and the same window arrangements. The gateway passage measured 87½ feet long and 43¾ feet wide. [37]Its entry room faced into the outer courtyard, and it had palm tree decorations on the columns. There were eight steps leading to its entrance.

Rooms for Preparing Sacrifices

EZEKIEL 40:38-43

A door led from the entry room of one of the inner gateways into a side room, where the meat for sacrifices was washed. [39]On each side of this entry room were two tables, where the sacrificial animals were slaughtered for the burnt offerings, sin offerings, and guilt offerings. [40]Outside the entry room, on each side of the stairs going up to the north entrance, were two more tables. [41]So there were eight tables in all—four inside and four outside—where the sacrifices were cut up and prepared. [42]There were also four tables of finished stone for preparation of the burnt offerings, each 31½ inches square and 21 inches high.* On these tables were placed the butchering knives and other implements for slaughtering the sacrificial animals. [43]There were hooks, each 3 inches* long, fastened to the foyer walls. The sacrificial meat was laid on the tables.

Rooms for the Priests

EZEKIEL 40:44-46

Inside the inner courtyard were two rooms,* one beside the north gateway, facing south, and the other beside the south* gateway, facing north. [45]And the man said to me, "The room beside the north inner gate is for the priests who supervise the Temple maintenance. [46]The room beside the south inner gate is for the priests in charge of the altar—the descendants of Zadok—for they alone of all the Levites may approach the LORD to minister to him."

The Inner Courtyard and Temple

EZEKIEL 40:47–41:26

Then the man measured the inner courtyard, and it was a square, 175 feet wide and 175 feet across. The altar stood in the courtyard in front of the Temple. [48]Then he brought me to the entry room of the Temple. He measured the walls on either side of the opening to the entry room, and they were 8¾ feet thick. The entrance itself was 24½ feet wide, and the walls on each side of the entrance were an additional 5¼ feet long.* [49]The entry room was 35 feet* wide and 21 feet* deep. There were ten steps leading up to it, with a column on each side.

41:1 After that, the man brought me into the sanctuary of the Temple. He measured the walls on either side of its doorway, and they were 10½ feet* thick. [2]The doorway was 17½ feet* wide, and the walls on each side of it were 8¾ feet* long. The sanctuary itself was 70 feet long and 35 feet wide.*

[3]Then he went beyond the sanctuary into the inner room. He measured the walls on either side of its entrance, and they were 3½ feet* thick. The entrance was 10½ feet wide, and the walls on each side of the entrance were 12¼ feet* long. [4]The inner room of the sanctuary was 35 feet* long and 35 feet wide. "This," he told me, "is the Most Holy Place."

[5]Then he measured the wall of the Temple, and it was 10½ feet thick. There was a row of rooms along the outside wall; each room was 7 feet* wide. [6]These side rooms were built in three levels, one above the other, with thirty rooms on each level. The supports for these side rooms rested on exterior ledges on the Temple wall; they did not extend into the wall. [7]Each level was wider than the one below it, corresponding to the narrowing of the Temple wall as it rose higher. A stairway led up from the bottom level through the middle level to the top level.

[8]I saw that the Temple was built on a terrace, which provided a foundation for the side rooms. This terrace was 10½ feet* high. [9]The outer wall

Ez 40:42 Hebrew *1½ cubits* [80 centimeters] *long and 1½ cubits wide and 1 cubit* [53 centimeters] *high.* **Ez 40:43** Hebrew *a handbreadth* [8 centimeters]. **Ez 40:44a** As in Greek version; Hebrew reads *rooms for singers.* **Ez 40:44b** As in Greek version; Hebrew reads *east.* **Ez 40:48** As in Greek version, which reads *The entrance was 14 cubits* [7.4 meters] *wide, and the walls of the entrance were 3 cubits* [1.6 meters] *on each side;* Hebrew lacks *14 cubits wide, and the walls of the entrance were.* **Ez 40:49a** Hebrew *20 cubits* [10.6 meters]. **Ez 40:49b** As in Greek version, which reads *12 cubits* [21 feet or 6.4 meters]; Hebrew reads *11 cubits* [19¼ feet or 5.8 meters]. **Ez 41:1** Hebrew *6 cubits* [3.2 meters]; also in 41:3, 5. **Ez 41:2a** Hebrew *10 cubits* [5.3 meters]. **Ez 41:2b** Hebrew *5 cubits* [2.7 meters]; also in 41:9, 11. **Ez 41:2c** Hebrew *40 cubits* [21.2 meters] *long and 20 cubits* [10.6 meters] *wide.* **Ez 41:3a** Hebrew *2 cubits* [1.1 meters]. **Ez 41:3b** Hebrew *7 cubits* [3.7 meters]. **Ez 41:4** Hebrew *20 cubits* [10.6 meters]; also in 41:4b, 10. **Ez 41:5** Hebrew *4 cubits* [2.1 meters]. **Ez 41:8** Hebrew *1 rod, 6 cubits* [3.2 meters].

Ezek 40:38-39 The washing of the sacrifices was done according to the standards of preparation established in Leviticus 1:6-9. This washing was part of the process of presenting an acceptable sacrifice to God.

Ezek 41:4 God's holiness is a central theme throughout both the Old and New Testaments. The Most Holy Place was the innermost room in the Temple (Exod 26:33-34). This was where the Ark of the Covenant was kept and where God's glory was said to dwell. This room was entered only once a year by the high priest, who performed a ceremony to atone for the nation's sins.

of the Temple's side rooms was 8¾ feet thick. This left an open area between these side rooms [10]and the row of rooms along the outer wall of the inner courtyard. This open area was 35 feet wide, and it went all the way around the Temple. [11]Two doors opened from the side rooms into the terrace yard, which was 8¾ feet wide. One door faced north and the other south.

[12]A large building stood on the west, facing the Temple courtyard. It was 122½ feet wide and 157½ feet long, and its walls were 8¾ feet* thick. [13]Then the man measured the Temple, and it was 175 feet* long. The courtyard around the building, including its walls, was an additional 175 feet in length. [14]The inner courtyard to the east of the Temple was also 175 feet wide. [15]The building to the west, including its two walls, was also 175 feet wide.

The sanctuary, the inner room, and the entry room of the Temple [16]were all paneled with wood, as were the frames of the recessed windows. The inner walls of the Temple were paneled with wood above and below the windows. [17]The space above the door leading into the inner room, and its walls inside and out, were also paneled. [18]All the walls were decorated with carvings of cherubim, each with two faces, and there was a carving of a palm tree between each of the cherubim. [19]One face—that of a man—looked toward the palm tree on one side. The other face—that of a young lion—looked toward the palm tree on the other side. The figures were carved all along the inside of the Temple, [20]from the floor to the top of the walls, including the outer wall of the sanctuary.

[21]There were square columns at the entrance to the sanctuary, and the ones at the entrance of the Most Holy Place were similar. [22]There was an altar made of wood, 5¼ feet high and 3½ feet across.* Its corners, base, and sides were all made of wood. "This," the man told me, "is the table that stands in the LORD's presence."

[23]Both the sanctuary and the Most Holy Place had double doorways, [24]each with two swinging doors. [25]The doors leading into the sanctuary were decorated with carved cherubim and palm trees, just as on the walls. And there was a wooden roof at the front of the entry room to the Temple. [26]On both sides of the entry room were recessed windows decorated with carved palm trees. The side rooms along the outside wall also had roofs.

Rooms for the Priests

EZEKIEL 42:1-20

Then the man led me out of the Temple courtyard by way of the north gateway. We entered the outer courtyard and came to a group of rooms against the north wall of the inner courtyard. [2]This structure, whose entrance opened toward the north, was 175 feet* long and 87½ feet* wide. [3]One block of rooms overlooked the 35-foot* width of the inner courtyard. Another block of rooms looked out onto the pavement of the outer courtyard. The two blocks were built three levels high and stood across from each other. [4]Between the two blocks of rooms ran a walkway 17½ feet* wide. It extended the entire 175 feet of the complex,* and all the doors faced north. [5]Each of the two upper levels of rooms was narrower than the one beneath it because the upper levels had to allow space for walkways in front of them. [6]Since there were three levels and they did not have supporting columns as in the courtyards, each of the upper levels was set back from the level beneath it. [7]There was an outer wall that separated the rooms from the outer courtyard; it was 87½ feet long. [8]This wall added length to the outer block of rooms, which extended for only 87½ feet, while the inner block—the rooms toward the Temple—extended for 175 feet. [9]There was an eastern entrance from the outer courtyard to these rooms.

[10]On the south* side of the Temple there were two blocks of rooms just south of the inner courtyard between the Temple and the outer courtyard. These rooms were arranged just like the rooms on the north. [11]There was a walkway between the two blocks of rooms just like the complex on the north side of the Temple. This complex of rooms was the same length and width as the other one, and it had the same entrances and doors. The dimensions of each were identical. [12]So there was an entrance in the wall facing the doors of the inner block of rooms, and another on the east at the end of the interior walkway.

[13]Then the man told me, "These rooms that overlook the Temple from the north and south are holy. Here the priests who offer sacrifices to the LORD will eat the most holy offerings. And because these rooms are holy, they will be used to store the sacred offerings—the grain offerings, sin offerings, and guilt offerings. [14]When the priests leave the sanctuary, they must not go directly to the outer courtyard. They must first take off the clothes they wore while ministering,

Ez 41:12 Hebrew *70 cubits* [37.1 meters] *wide and 90 cubits* [47.7 meters] *long, and its walls were 5 cubits* [2.7 meters] *thick.* **Ez 41:13** Hebrew *100 cubits* [53 meters]; also in 41:13b, 14, 15. **Ez 41:22** Hebrew *3 cubits* [1.6 meters] *high and 2 cubits* [1.1 meters] *across.* **Ez 42:2a** Hebrew *100 cubits* [53 meters]; also in 42:8. **Ez 42:2b** Hebrew *50 cubits* [26.5 meters]; also in 42:7, 8. **Ez 42:3** Hebrew *20-cubit* [10.6-meter]. **Ez 42:4a** Hebrew *10 cubits* [5.3 meters]. **Ez 42:4b** As in Greek and Syriac versions, which read *Its length was 100 cubits* [53 meters]; Hebrew reads *and a passage 1 cubit* [18 inches or 53 centimeters] *wide.* **Ez 42:10** As in Greek version; Hebrew reads *east.*

Ezek 41:18 Cherubim are mighty angels.

Ezek 41:22 The dimensions given would fit either the table of the Bread of the Presence (Exod 25:30) or the incense altar (Exod 30:1-3).

Ezek 42:14 Approaching our holy God must not be taken lightly. The holy garments the priests were required to wear may symbolize the importance of having a holy heart when approaching God. The priests had to wear these special clothes in order to minister in the inner rooms of the Temple. Because the garments were holy, the priests had to change their clothes before going back out to the public.

▸ **EZEKIEL 42:1-20** ***(cont.)***

because these clothes are holy. They must put on other
clothes before entering the parts of the building complex open to the public."
15 When the man had finished measuring the inside of the Temple area, he led me out through the
east gateway to measure the entire perimeter. 16 He
measured the east side with his measuring rod, and
it was 875 feet long.* 17 Then he measured the north
side, and it was also 875 feet. 18 The south side was
also 875 feet, 19 and the west side was also 875 feet.
20 So the area was 875 feet on each side with a wall all
around it to separate what was holy from what was
common.

The LORD's Glory Returns

EZEKIEL 43:1-12

After this, the man brought me back around to the
east gateway. 2 Suddenly, the glory of the God of Israel
appeared from the east. The sound of his coming was
like the roar of rushing waters, and the whole landscape shone with his glory. 3 This vision was just like
the others I had seen, first by the Kebar River and then
when he came to destroy Jerusalem. I fell face down
on the ground. 4 And the glory of the LORD came into
the Temple through the east gateway.
5 Then the Spirit took me up and brought me into
the inner courtyard, and the glory of the LORD filled
the Temple. 6 And I heard someone speaking to me
from within the Temple, while the man who had
been measuring stood beside me. 7 The LORD said to
me, "Son of man, this is the place of my throne and
the place where I will rest my feet. I will live here
forever among the people of Israel. They and their
kings will not defile my holy name any longer by
their adulterous worship of other gods or by honoring the relics of their kings who have died. 8 They put
their idol altars right next to mine with only a wall
between them and me. They defiled my holy name
by such detestable sin, so I consumed them in my
anger. 9 Now let them stop worshiping other gods
and honoring the relics of their kings, and I will live
among them forever.
10 "Son of man, describe to the people of Israel the
Temple I have shown you, so they will be ashamed of
all their sins. Let them study its plan, 11 and they will
be ashamed* of what they have done. Describe to
them all the specifications of the Temple—including
its entrances and exits—and everything else about
it. Tell them about its decrees and laws. Write down
all these specifications and decrees as they watch
so they will be sure to remember and follow them.
12 And this is the basic law of the Temple: absolute
holiness! The entire top of the mountain where the
Temple is built is holy. Yes, this is the basic law of
the Temple.

Ez 42:16 As in 45:2 and in Greek version at 42:17, which reads *500 cubits* [265 meters]; Hebrew reads *500 rods* [5,250 feet or 1,590 meters]; similarly in 42:17, 18, 19, 20.
Ez 43:11 As in Greek version; Hebrew reads *if they are ashamed.*

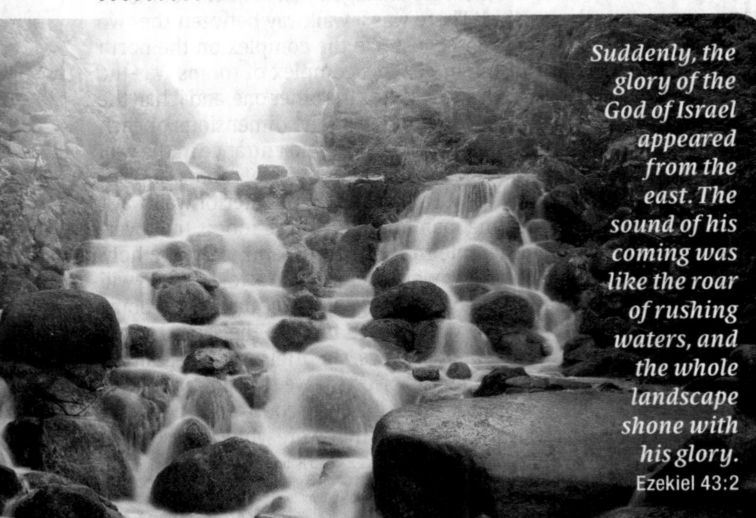

Suddenly, the glory of the God of Israel appeared from the east. The sound of his coming was like the roar of rushing waters, and the whole landscape shone with his glory.
Ezekiel 43:2

Ezek 42:16-20 The perfect symmetry of Ezekiel's Temple may represent the order and harmony in God's future Kingdom.

Ezek 43:1ff This is the culmination of Ezekiel 40–42 because God's glory returns to the Temple. It reverses the negative tone of the book and serves as a fitting end for all the passages dealing with the blessings reserved for the restored remnant. All true believers should long for that moment when God's name will finally be glorified and he will live among his people forever.

Ezek 43:2 In Ezekiel 11:23, God's glory stopped over the Mount of Olives, to the east of Jerusalem, before leaving the city. This prophecy states that his glory would also return from the east.

Ezek 43:2-4 It was completely devastating for Ezekiel when God's glory departed from his Temple (Ezek 11:23), but he was overwhelmed with awe and joy beyond expression when he saw God's glory return.

Ezek 43:3 The Kebar River connected with the Euphrates River and was the location of a Jewish settlement of exiles in Babylonia.

Ezek 43:9-11 God's departure from the city had been a signal for the destruction of the city and the Temple. Now for God to return, his conditions had to be met: Idolatry had to be removed. Some commentators feel these verses indicate that Ezekiel was commanding the people of his day to build this Temple according to the designs and regulations that the angelic architect had given. But the people never repented and the conditions were not met, so the fulfillment was postponed.

Ezek 43:12 The basic law of God's Temple was holiness. In all he does, God is holy, perfect, and blameless. There is no trace of evil or sin in him. Just as God is holy, so we are to be holy (Lev 19:2; 1 Pet 1:15-16). People are holy when they are devoted to God and separated from sin. It is important to understand the concept of holiness in order that we may progress in our Christian growth.

The Altar

EZEKIEL 43:13-27

"These are the measurements of the altar*: There is a gutter all around the altar 21 inches deep and 21 inches wide,* with a curb 9 inches* wide around its edge. And this is the height* of the altar: 14From the gutter the altar rises 3½ feet* to a lower ledge that surrounds the altar and is 21 inches* wide. From the lower ledge the altar rises 7 feet* to the upper ledge that is also 21 inches wide. 15The top of the altar, the hearth, rises another 7 feet higher, with a horn rising up from each of the four corners. 16The top of the altar is square, measuring 21 feet by 21 feet.* 17The upper ledge also forms a square, measuring 24½ feet by 24½ feet,* with a 21-inch gutter and a 10½-inch curb* all around the edge. There are steps going up the east side of the altar."

18Then he said to me, "Son of man, this is what the Sovereign LORD says: These will be the regulations for the burning of offerings and the sprinkling of blood when the altar is built. 19At that time, the Levitical priests of the family of Zadok, who minister before me, are to be given a young bull for a sin offering, says the Sovereign LORD. 20You will take some of its blood and smear it on the four horns of the altar, the four corners of the upper ledge, and the curb that runs around that ledge. This will cleanse and make atonement for the altar. 21Then take the young bull for the sin offering and burn it at the appointed place outside the Temple area.

22"On the second day, sacrifice as a sin offering a young male goat that has no physical defects. Then cleanse and make atonement for the altar again, just as you did with the young bull. 23When you have finished the cleansing ceremony, offer another young bull that has no defects and a perfect ram from the flock. 24You are to present them to the LORD, and the priests are to sprinkle salt on them and offer them as a burnt offering to the LORD.

25"Every day for seven days a male goat, a young bull, and a ram from the flock will be sacrificed as a sin offering. None of these animals may have physical defects of any kind. 26Do this each day for seven days to cleanse and make atonement for the altar, thus setting it apart for holy use. 27On the eighth day, and on each day afterward, the priests will sacrifice on the altar the burnt offerings and peace offerings of the people. Then I will accept you. I, the Sovereign LORD, have spoken!"

The Prince, Levites, and Priests

EZEKIEL 44:1-31

Then the man brought me back to the east gateway in the outer wall of the Temple area, but it was closed. 2And the LORD said to me, "This gate must remain closed; it will never again be opened. No one will ever open it and pass through, for the LORD, the God of Israel, has entered here. Therefore, it must always remain shut. 3Only the prince himself may sit inside this gateway to feast in the LORD's presence. But he may come and go only through the entry room of the gateway."

4Then the man brought me through the north gateway to the front of the Temple. I looked and saw that the glory of the LORD filled the Temple of the LORD, and I fell face down on the ground.

5And the LORD said to me, "Son of man, take careful notice. Use your eyes and ears, and listen to everything I tell you about the regulations concerning the LORD's Temple. Take careful note of the procedures for using the Temple's entrances and exits. 6And give these rebels, the people of Israel, this message from the Sovereign LORD: O people of Israel, enough of your detestable sins! 7You have brought uncircumcised foreigners into my sanctuary—people who have no heart for God. In this way, you defiled my Temple even as you offered me my food, the fat and blood of sacrifices. In addition to all your other detestable sins, you have broken my covenant. 8Instead of safeguarding my sacred rituals, you have hired foreigners to take charge of my sanctuary.

9"So this is what the Sovereign LORD says: No foreigners, including those who live among the people

Ez 43:13a Hebrew *measurements of the altar in long cubits, each being a cubit* [18 inches or 45 centimeters] *and a handbreadth* [3 inches or 8 centimeters] *in length.* **Ez 43:13b** Hebrew *a cubit* [53 centimeters] *deep and a cubit wide.* **Ez 43:13c** Hebrew *1 span* [23 centimeters]. **Ez 43:13d** As in Greek version; Hebrew reads *base.* **Ez 43:14a** Hebrew *2 cubits* [1.1 meters]. **Ez 43:14b** Hebrew *1 cubit* [53 centimeters]; also in 43:14d. **Ez 43:14c** Hebrew *4 cubits* [2.1 meters]; also in 43:15. **Ez 43:16** Hebrew *12 cubits* [6.4 meters] *long and 12 cubits wide.* **Ez 43:17a** Hebrew *14 cubits* [7.4 meters] *long and 14 cubits wide.* **Ez 43:17b** Hebrew *a gutter of 1 cubit* [53 centimeters] *and a curb of ½ a cubit* [27 centimeters].

Ezek 43:18-27 This vision was simultaneously flashing back to Mount Sinai and forward to Mount Calvary. When the people returned from exile, they would seek forgiveness through the sacrificial system instituted in Moses' day. Today, Christ's death has made the forgiveness of our sins possible, making us acceptable to God (Heb 9:9-15). God stands ready to forgive those who come to him in faith.

Ezek 44:2 Why was this east gate to remain closed? Several reasons have been suggested: (1) This was the gate through which God entered the Temple, and no one else could walk where God had (Ezek 43:4); (2) the closed gate indicated that God would never again leave the Temple (Ezek 10:19; 11:23); (3) it would prevent people from worshiping the sun as it rises in the east from within the Temple grounds (Ezek 8:16).

Ezek 44:3 Although Christ is called a prince (Ezek 37:25), this prince is probably not Christ because he offers a sacrifice to God (Ezek 46:4) and he can enter only by the "entry room of the gateway." He is a princely ruler of the city, but he is distinguished from other princes because he will be just and fair (see Ezek 45:9). Some have understood this prince to be a prophetic image that anticipates the coming of Christ, who would offer himself as a sacrifice to God.

Ezek 44:9 Unbelievers would not be allowed to enter the Temple. Ezekiel's vision was for a restored, purified worship in which only those who prepared themselves physically and spiritually could participate. People from other nations are allowed to join in worship by accepting the standards of faith and practice declared in the law (Ezek 47:22-23; see Lev 24:22; Num 15:29).

▸ **EZEKIEL 44:1-31** ***(cont.)***

of Israel, will enter my sanctuary if they have not been circumcised and have not surrendered themselves to the LORD. [10]And the men of the tribe of Levi who abandoned me when Israel strayed away from me to worship idols* must bear the consequences of their unfaithfulness. [11]They may still be Temple guards and gatekeepers, and they may slaughter the animals brought for burnt offerings and be present to help the people. [12]But they encouraged my people to worship idols, causing Israel to fall into deep sin. So I have taken a solemn oath that they must bear the consequences for their sins, says the Sovereign LORD. [13]They may not approach me to minister as priests. They may not touch any of my holy things or the holy offerings, for they must bear the shame of all the detestable sins they have committed. [14]They are to serve as the Temple caretakers, taking charge of the maintenance work and performing general duties.

[15]"However, the Levitical priests of the family of Zadok continued to minister faithfully in the Temple when Israel abandoned me for idols. These men will serve as my ministers. They will stand in my presence and offer the fat and blood of the sacrifices, says the Sovereign LORD. [16]They alone will enter my sanctuary and approach my table to serve me. They will fulfill all my requirements.

[17]"When they enter the gateway to the inner courtyard, they must wear only linen clothing. They must wear no wool while on duty in the inner courtyard or in the Temple itself. [18]They must wear linen turbans and linen undergarments. They must not wear anything that would cause them to perspire. [19]When they return to the outer courtyard where the people are, they must take off the clothes they wear while ministering to me. They must leave them in the sacred rooms and put on other clothes so they do not endanger anyone by transmitting holiness to them through this clothing.

[20]"They must neither shave their heads nor let their hair grow too long. Instead, they must trim it regularly. [21]The priests must not drink wine before entering the inner courtyard. [22]They may choose their wives only from among the virgins of Israel or the widows of the priests. They may not marry other widows or divorced women. [23]They will teach my people the difference between what is holy and what is common, what is ceremonially clean and unclean.

[24]"They will serve as judges to resolve any disagreements among my people. Their decisions must be based on my regulations. And the priests themselves must obey my instructions and decrees at all the sacred festivals, and see to it that the Sabbaths are set apart as holy days.

[25]"A priest must not defile himself by being in the presence of a dead person unless it is his father, mother, child, brother, or unmarried sister. In such cases it is permitted. [26]Even then, he can return to his Temple duties only after being ceremonially cleansed and then waiting for seven days. [27]The first day he returns to work and enters the inner courtyard and the sanctuary, he must offer a sin offering for himself, says the Sovereign LORD.

[28]"The priests will not have any property or possession of land, for I alone am their special possession. [29]Their food will come from the gifts and sacrifices brought to the Temple by the people—the grain offerings, the sin offerings, and the guilt offerings. Whatever anyone sets apart* for the LORD will belong to the priests. [30]The first of the ripe fruits and all the gifts brought to the LORD will go to the priests. The first samples of each grain harvest and the first of your flour must also be given to the priests so the LORD will bless your homes. [31]The priests may not eat meat from any bird or animal that dies a natural death or that dies after being attacked by another animal.

Division of the Land

EZEKIEL 45:1-8

"When you divide the land among the tribes of Israel, you must set aside a section for the LORD as his holy portion. This piece of land will be 8⅓ miles long and 6⅔ miles wide.* The entire area will be holy. [2]A section of this land, measuring 875 feet by 875 feet,* will be set aside for the Temple. An additional strip of land 87½ feet* wide is to be left empty all around it. [3]Within the larger sacred area, measure out a portion of land 8⅓ miles long and 3⅓ miles wide.* Within it the sanctuary of the Most Holy Place will be located. [4]This area will be holy, set aside for the priests who minister to the LORD in the sanctuary. They will use it for their homes, and my Temple will be located within

Ez 44:10 The Hebrew term (literally *round things*) probably alludes to dung; also in 44:12. **Ez 44:29** The Hebrew term used here refers to the complete consecration of things or people to the LORD, either by destroying them or by giving them as an offering. **Ez 45:1** As in Greek version, which reads *25,000 cubits* [13.3 kilometers] *long and 20,000 cubits* [10.6 kilometers] *wide;* Hebrew reads *25,000 cubits long and 10,000 cubits* [3⅓ miles or 5.3 kilometers] *wide.* Compare 45:3, 5; 48:9. **Ez 45:2a** Hebrew *500 cubits* [265 meters] *by 500 cubits, a square.* **Ez 45:2b** Hebrew *50 cubits* [26.5 meters]. **Ez 45:3** Hebrew *25,000 cubits* [13.3 kilometers] *long and 10,000 cubits* [5.3 kilometers] *wide;* also in 45:5.

Ezek 44:15 Zadok's descendants are mentioned because many of the priests in Zadok's line had remained faithful to God, while others had become corrupt. Zadok supported God's choice of Solomon to succeed David and was therefore appointed high priest during his reign (1 Kgs 1:32-35; 2:27, 35). Zadok's descendants were considered the true priestly line throughout the time between the Old and New Testaments.

Ezek 44:20-31 These laws were originally given to God's people in the wilderness. They are recorded in the books of Exodus and Leviticus. They reveal the importance of approaching God respectfully, and they give guidelines for the priests to live above reproach so they could carry out their responsibility to teach the people "the difference between what is holy and what is common, what is ceremonially clean and unclean" (Ezek 44:23).

Ezek 45:1-7 The land allotted to the Temple was in the center of the nation. God is central to life. He must be our first priority.

it. [5]The strip of sacred land next to it, also 8⅓ miles long and 3⅓ miles wide, will be a living area for the Levites who work at the Temple. It will be their possession and a place for their towns.*

[6]"Adjacent to the larger sacred area will be a section of land 8⅓ miles long and 1⅔ miles wide.* This will be set aside for a city where anyone in Israel can live.

[7]"Two special sections of land will be set apart for the prince. One section will share a border with the east side of the sacred lands and city, and the second section will share a border on the west side. Then the far eastern and western borders of the prince's lands will line up with the eastern and western boundaries of the tribal areas. [8]These sections of land will be the prince's allotment. Then my princes will no longer oppress and rob my people; they will assign the rest of the land to the people, giving an allotment to each tribe.

Rules for the Princes

EZEKIEL 45:9-12

"For this is what the Sovereign LORD says: Enough, you princes of Israel! Stop your violence and oppression and do what is just and right. Quit robbing and cheating my people out of their land. Stop expelling them from their homes, says the Sovereign LORD. [10]Use only honest weights and scales and honest measures, both dry and liquid.* [11]The homer* will be your standard unit for measuring volume. The ephah and the bath* will each measure one-tenth of a homer. [12]The standard unit for weight will be the silver shekel.* One shekel will consist of twenty gerahs, and sixty shekels will be equal to one mina.*

Special Offerings and Celebrations

EZEKIEL 45:13–46:18

"You must give this tax to the prince: one bushel of wheat or barley for every 60* you harvest, [14]one percent of your olive oil,* [15]and one sheep or goat for every 200 in your flocks in Israel. These will be the grain offerings, burnt offerings, and peace offerings that will make atonement for the people who bring them, says the Sovereign LORD. [16]All the people of Israel must join in bringing these offerings to the prince. [17]The prince will be required to provide offerings that are given at the religious festivals, the new moon celebrations, the Sabbath days, and all other similar occasions. He will provide the sin offerings, burnt offerings, grain offerings, liquid offerings, and peace offerings to purify the people of Israel, making them right with the LORD.*

[18]"This is what the Sovereign LORD says: In early spring, on the first day of each new year,* sacrifice a young bull with no defects to purify the Temple. [19]The priest will take blood from this sin offering and put it on the doorposts of the Temple, the four corners of the upper ledge of the altar, and the gateposts at the entrance to the inner courtyard. [20]Do this also on the seventh day of the new year for anyone who has sinned through error or ignorance. In this way, you will purify* the Temple.

[21]"On the fourteenth day of the first month,* you must celebrate the Passover. This festival will last for seven days. The bread you eat during that time must be made without yeast. [22]On the day of Passover the prince will provide a young bull as a sin offering for himself and the people of Israel. [23]On each of the seven days of the feast he will prepare a burnt offering to the LORD, consisting of seven young bulls and seven rams without defects. A male goat will also be given each day for a sin offering. [24]The prince will provide a basket of flour as a grain offering and a gallon of olive oil* with each young bull and ram.

[25]"During the seven days of the Festival of Shelters, which occurs every year in early autumn,* the prince will provide these same sacrifices for the sin offering, the burnt offering, and the grain offering, along with the required olive oil.

46:1"This is what the Sovereign LORD says: The east gateway of the inner courtyard will be closed during the six workdays each week, but it will be open on

Ez 45:5 As in Greek version; Hebrew reads *They will have as their possession 20 rooms.* **Ez 45:6** Hebrew *25,000 cubits* [13.3 kilometers] *long and 5,000 cubits* [2.65 kilometers] *wide.* **Ez 45:10** Hebrew *use honest scales, an honest ephah, and an honest bath.* **Ez 45:11a** The *homer* measures about 40 gallons or 182 liters. **Ez 45:11b** The *ephah* is a dry measure; the *bath* is a liquid measure. **Ez 45:12a** The *shekel* weighs about 0.4 ounces or 11 grams. **Ez 45:12b** Elsewhere the *mina* is equated to 50 shekels. **Ez 45:13** Hebrew *1/6 of an ephah from each homer of wheat and 1/6 of an ephah from each homer of barley.* **Ez 45:14** Hebrew *the portion of oil, measured by the bath, is 1/10 of a bath from each cor, which consists of 10 baths or 1 homer, for 10 baths are equivalent to a homer.* **Ez 45:17** Or *to make atonement for the people of Israel.* **Ez 45:18** Hebrew *On the first day of the first month,* of the Hebrew calendar. This day in the ancient Hebrew lunar calendar occurred in March or April. **Ez 45:20** Or *will make atonement for.* **Ez 45:21** This day in the ancient Hebrew lunar calendar occurred in late March, April, or early May. **Ez 45:24** Hebrew *an ephah* [20 quarts or 22 liters] *of flour . . . and a hin* [3.8 liters] *of olive oil.* **Ez 45:25** Hebrew *the festival which begins on the fifteenth day of the seventh month* (see Lev 23:34). This day in the ancient Hebrew lunar calendar occurred in late September, October, or early November.

Ezek 45:9-12 Violence and oppression were two of the major social sins of the nation during this time (see Amos 5:10-13). In the new economy there would be plenty of land for the "prince" (Ezek 45:7-8) and no longer any basis for greed. Therefore, God commanded the princes and the people to do what was just and right, especially in their business dealings. Consider the ways that you measure goods, money, or services. If you are paid for an hour of work, be sure you work for a full hour. If you sell a bushel of apples, make sure it is a full bushel. God is completely trustworthy, and his followers should be too.

Ezek 45:17 The conditions and regulations for these offerings are described in detail in Leviticus 1–7.

Ezek 45:21 The Passover was an annual seven-day festival instituted by God so that his people would remember how he brought them out of slavery in Egypt. On that first Passover night, the Lord passed over the homes marked by lamb's blood; he struck only the unmarked homes (see Exod 11–12).

Ezek 45:25 This annual festival was celebrated in October. It commemorates God's protection of his people as they traveled through the wilderness from Egypt to the Promised Land (see Lev 23:33-43; Deut 16:13-17).

Ezek 46:1-15 Ezekiel continued to describe various aspects of daily worship. While allowing for diversity in worship, God prescribed order and continuity. This continuity gave a healthy rhythm to the spiritual life of his people.

▶ **EZEKIEL 45:13–46:18** ***(cont.)***

Sabbath days and the days of new moon celebrations. 2The prince will enter the entry room of the gateway from the outside. Then he will stand by the gatepost while the priest offers his burnt offering and peace offering. He will bow down in worship inside the gateway passage and then go back out the way he came. The gateway will not be closed until evening. 3The common people will bow down and worship the LORD in front of this gateway on Sabbath days and the days of new moon celebrations.

4"Each Sabbath day the prince will present to the LORD a burnt offering of six lambs and one ram, all with no defects. 5He will present a grain offering of a basket of choice flour to go with the ram and whatever amount of flour he chooses to go with each lamb, and he is to offer one gallon of olive oil* for each basket of flour. 6At the new moon celebrations, he will bring one young bull, six lambs, and one ram, all with no defects. 7With the young bull he must bring a basket of choice flour for a grain offering. With the ram he must bring another basket of flour. And with each lamb he is to bring whatever amount of flour he chooses to give. With each basket of flour he must offer one gallon of olive oil.

8"The prince must enter the gateway through the entry room, and he must leave the same way. 9But when the people come in through the north gateway to worship the LORD during the religious festivals, they must leave by the south gateway. And those who entered through the south gateway must leave by the north gateway. They must never leave by the same gateway they came in, but must always use the opposite gateway. 10The prince will enter and leave with the people on these occasions.

11"So at the special feasts and sacred festivals, the grain offering will be a basket of choice flour with each young bull, another basket of flour with each ram, and as much flour as the prince chooses to give with each lamb. Give one gallon of olive oil with each basket of flour. 12When the prince offers a voluntary burnt offering or peace offering to the LORD, the east gateway to the inner courtyard will be opened for him, and he will offer his sacrifices as he does on Sabbath days. Then he will leave, and the gateway will be shut behind him.

13"Each morning you must sacrifice a one-year-old lamb with no defects as a burnt offering to the LORD. 14With the lamb, a grain offering must also be given to the LORD—about three quarts of flour with a third of a gallon of olive oil* to moisten the choice flour. This will be a permanent law for you. 15The lamb, the grain offering, and the olive oil must be given as a daily sacrifice every morning without fail.

16"This is what the Sovereign LORD says: If the prince gives a gift of land to one of his sons as his inheritance, it will belong to him and his descendants forever. 17But if the prince gives a gift of land from his inheritance to one of his servants, the servant may keep it only until the Year of Jubilee, which comes every fiftieth year.* At that time the land will return to the prince. But when the prince gives gifts to his sons, those gifts will be permanent. 18And the prince may never take anyone's property by force. If he gives property to his sons, it must be from his own land, for I do not want any of my people unjustly evicted from their property."

The Temple Kitchens

EZEKIEL 46:19-24

In my vision, the man brought me through the entrance beside the gateway and led me to the sacred rooms assigned to the priests, which faced toward the north. He showed me a place at the extreme west end of these rooms. 20He explained, "This is where the priests will cook the meat from the guilt offerings and sin offerings and bake the flour from the grain offerings into bread. They will do it here to avoid carrying the sacrifices through the outer courtyard and endangering the people by transmitting holiness to them."

21Then he brought me back to the outer courtyard and led me to each of its four corners. In each corner I saw an enclosure. 22Each of these enclosures was 70 feet long and 52½ feet wide,* surrounded by walls. 23Along the inside of these walls was a ledge of stone with fireplaces under the ledge all the way around. 24The man said to me, "These are the kitchens to be used by the Temple assistants to boil the sacrifices offered by the people."

The River of Healing

EZEKIEL 47:1-12

In my vision, the man brought me back to the entrance of the Temple. There I saw a stream flowing east from beneath the door of the Temple and passing to the right of the altar on its south side. 2The man brought me outside the wall through the north gateway and led me around to the eastern entrance. There I could see the water flowing out through the south side of the east gateway.

3Measuring as he went, he took me along the stream for 1,750 feet* and then led me across. The water was up to my ankles. 4He measured off another 1,750 feet and led me across again. This time the water was up to my knees. After another 1,750 feet, it was up to my waist. 5Then he measured another 1,750 feet, and the river was too deep to walk across. It was deep enough to swim in, but too deep to walk through.

6He asked me, "Have you been watching, son of man?" Then he led me back along the riverbank. 7When I returned, I was surprised by the sight of many trees growing on both sides of the river. 8Then he said to

Ez 46:5 Hebrew *an ephah* [20 quarts or 22 liters] *of choice flour . . . a hin* [3.8 liters] *of olive oil;* similarly in 46:7, 11. **Ez 46:14** Hebrew *1/6 of an ephah* [3.7 liters] *of flour with 1/3 of a hin* [1.3 liters] *of olive oil.* **Ez 46:17** Hebrew *until the Year of Release;* see Lev 25:8-17. **Ez 46:22** Hebrew *40 cubits* [21.2 meters] *long and 30 cubits* [15.9 meters] *wide.* **Ez 47:3** Hebrew *1,000 cubits* [530 meters]; also in 47:4, 5.

me, "This river flows east through the desert into the valley of the Dead Sea.* The waters of this stream will make the salty waters of the Dead Sea fresh and pure.
9There will be swarms of living things wherever the water of this river flows. Fish will abound in the Dead Sea, for its waters will become fresh. Life will flourish wherever this water flows.
10Fishermen will stand along the shores of the Dead Sea. All the way from En-gedi to En-eglaim, the shores will be covered with nets drying in the sun. Fish of every kind will fill the Dead Sea, just as they fill the Mediterranean.*
11But the marshes and swamps will not be purified; they will still be salty.
12Fruit trees of all kinds will grow along both sides of the river. The leaves of these trees will never turn brown and fall, and there will always be fruit on their branches. There will be a new crop every month, for they are watered by the river flowing from the Temple. The fruit will be for food and the leaves for healing."

Boundaries for the Land

EZEKIEL 47:13-23

This is what the Sovereign LORD says: "Divide the land in this way for the twelve tribes of Israel: The descendants of Joseph will be given two shares of land.*
14Otherwise each tribe will receive an equal share. I took a solemn oath and swore that I would give this land to your ancestors, and it will now come to you as your possession.

15"These are the boundaries of the land: The northern border will run from the Mediterranean toward Hethlon, then on through Lebo-hamath to Zedad;
16then it will run to Berothah and Sibraim, which are on the border between Damascus and Hamath, and finally to Hazer-hatticon, on the border of Hauran.
17So the northern border will run from the Mediterranean to Hazar-enan, on the border between Hamath to the north and Damascus to the south.

18"The eastern border starts at a point between Hauran and Damascus and runs south along the Jordan River between Israel and Gilead, past the Dead Sea* and as far south as Tamar.* This will be the eastern border.

19"The southern border will go west from Tamar to the waters of Meribah at Kadesh* and then follow the course of the Brook of Egypt to the Mediterranean. This will be the southern border.

20"On the west side, the Mediterranean itself will be your border from the southern border to the point where the northern border begins, opposite Lebo-hamath.

21"Divide the land within these boundaries among the tribes of Israel.
22Distribute the land as an allotment for yourselves and for the foreigners who have joined you and are raising their families among you. They will be like native-born Israelites to you and will receive an allotment among the tribes.
23These foreigners are to be given land within the territory of the tribe with whom they now live. I, the Sovereign LORD, have spoken!

Ez 47:8 Hebrew *the sea.* **Ez 47:10** Hebrew *the great sea;* also in 47:15, 17, 19, 20. **Ez 47:13** It was important to retain twelve portions of land. Since Levi had no portion, the descendants of Joseph's sons, Ephraim and Manasseh, received land as two tribes. **Ez 47:18a** Hebrew *the eastern sea.* **Ez 47:18b** As in Greek version; Hebrew reads *you will measure.* **Ez 47:19** Hebrew *waters of Meribath-kadesh.*

Ezek 47:1-12 This river is similar to the river mentioned in Revelation 22:1-2. Both are associated with the river in the Garden of Eden (see Gen 2:10). The river symbolizes life from God and the blessings that flow from his throne. It is a gentle, safe, deep river, expanding as it flows.

Ezek 47:8-9 The valley of the Dead Sea is the geological depression in which the Dead Sea lies. The Dead Sea is a body of water so salty that nothing can live in it. The river would freshen the Dead Sea's water so it can support life. This is another picture of the life-giving nature of the water that flows from God's Temple. God's power can transform us no matter how lifeless or corrupt we may be. Even when we feel messed up and beyond hope, his power can heal us.

Ezek 47:10 En-gedi and En-eglaim were on the western shore of the Dead Sea.

Ezek 47:22-23 In the restoration there would be room for foreigners. The regulations of Leviticus 24:22 and Numbers 15:29 provided for this. Isaiah also taught it (Isa 56:3-8). The children of foreigners would even inherit property like Israelites. Anyone accepting the standards and willing to obey would enjoy the blessings of God's rule.

Fishing

Fishing was an active profession in the holy land from early times and is referred to in the Old Testament (Isa 19:8; Jer 16:16; Ezek 47:10). Fishermen formed a distinct class in society. Their work was strenuous and not always rewarding. The Sea of Galilee and the Mediterranean Sea were the two main sites for fishing because fish cannot live in the salty waters of the Dead Sea. Yet Ezekiel 47:10 foresees that this lake would be stocked with fish as one of the blessings of the coming Kingdom.

Several of Jesus' disciples were fishermen. After he called them to follow him, he told them that he would make them fishers of men (Matt 4:18-19; Mark 1:16-17; Luke 5:2-10). All who have been called by Jesus should "catch" others for the Kingdom.

Division of the Land

EZEKIEL 48:1-29

"Here is the list of the tribes of Israel and the territory each is to receive. The territory of Dan is in the extreme north. Its boundary line follows the Hethlon road to Lebo-hamath and then runs on to Hazar-enan on the border of Damascus, with Hamath to the north. Dan's territory extends all the way across the land of Israel from east to west.

2"Asher's territory lies south of Dan's and also extends from east to west. 3Naphtali's land lies south of Asher's, also extending from east to west. 4Then comes Manasseh south of Naphtali, and its territory also extends from east to west. 5South of Manasseh is Ephraim, 6and then Reuben, 7and then Judah, all of whose boundaries extend from east to west.

8"South of Judah is the land set aside for a special purpose. It will be 8⅓ miles* wide and will extend as far east and west as the tribal territories, with the Temple at the center.

9"The area set aside for the LORD's Temple will be 8⅓ miles long and 6⅔ miles wide.* 10For the priests there will be a strip of land measuring 8⅓ miles long by 3⅓ miles wide,* with the LORD's Temple at the center. 11This area is set aside for the ordained priests, the descendants of Zadok who served me faithfully and did not go astray with the people of Israel and the rest of the Levites. 12It will be their special portion when the land is distributed, the most sacred land of all. Next to the priests' territory will lie the land where the other Levites will live.

13"The land allotted to the Levites will be the same size and shape as that belonging to the priests—8⅓ miles long and 3⅓ miles wide. Together these portions of land will measure 8⅓ miles long by 6⅔ miles wide.* 14None of this special land may ever be sold or traded or used by others, for it belongs to the LORD; it is set apart as holy.

15"An additional strip of land 8⅓ miles long by 1⅔ miles wide,* south of the sacred Temple area, will be allotted for public use—homes, pasturelands, and common lands, with a city at the center. 16The city will measure 1½ miles* on each side—north, south, east, and west. 17Open lands will surround the city for 150 yards* in every direction. 18Outside the city there will be a farming area that stretches 3⅓ miles to the east and 3⅓ miles to the west* along the border of the sacred area. This farmland will produce food for the people working in the city. 19Those who come from the various tribes to work in the city may farm it. 20This entire area—including the sacred lands and the city—is a square that measures 8⅓ miles* on each side.

21"The areas that remain, to the east and to the west of the sacred lands and the city, will belong to the prince. Each of these areas will be 8⅓ miles wide, extending in opposite directions to the eastern and western borders of Israel, with the sacred lands and the sanctuary of the Temple in the center. 22So the prince's land will include everything between the territories allotted to Judah and Benjamin, except for the areas set aside for the sacred lands and the city.

23"These are the territories allotted to the rest of the tribes. Benjamin's territory lies just south of the prince's lands, and it extends across the entire land of Israel from east to west. 24South of Benjamin's territory lies that of Simeon, also extending across the land from east to west. 25Next is the territory of Issachar with the same eastern and western boundaries.

26"Then comes the territory of Zebulun, which also extends across the land from east to west. 27The territory of Gad is just south of Zebulun with the same borders to the east and west. 28The southern border of Gad runs from Tamar to the waters of Meribah at Kadesh* and then follows the Brook of Egypt to the Mediterranean.*

29"These are the allotments that will be set aside for each tribe's exclusive possession. I, the Sovereign LORD, have spoken!

The Gates of the City

EZEKIEL 48:30-35

"These will be the exits to the city: On the north wall, which is 1½ miles long, 31there will be three gates, each one named after a tribe of Israel. The first will be named for Reuben, the second for Judah, and the third for Levi. 32On the east wall, also 1½ miles long, the gates will be named for Joseph, Benjamin, and Dan. 33The south wall, also 1½ miles long, will have gates named for Simeon, Issachar, and Zebulun. 34And on the west wall, also 1½ miles long, the gates will be named for Gad, Asher, and Naphtali.

35"The distance around the entire city will be 6 miles.* And from that day the name of the city will be 'The LORD Is There.'*"

Ez 48:8 Hebrew *25,000 cubits* [13.3 kilometers]. **Ez 48:9** As in one Greek manuscript and the Greek reading in 45:1: *25,000 cubits* [13.3 kilometers] *long and 20,000 cubits* [10.6 kilometers] *wide;* Hebrew reads *25,000 cubits long and 10,000 cubits* [3⅓ miles or 5.3 kilometers] *wide.* Similarly in 48:13b. Compare 45:1-5; 48:10-13. **Ez 48:10** Hebrew *25,000 cubits* [13.3 kilometers] *long by 10,000 cubits* [5.3 kilometers] *wide;* also in 48:13a. **Ez 48:13** See note on 48:9. **Ez 48:15** Hebrew *25,000 cubits* [13.3 kilometers] *long by 5,000 cubits* [2.65 kilometers] *wide.* **Ez 48:16** Hebrew *4,500 cubits* [2.4 kilometers]; also in 48:30, 32, 33, 34. **Ez 48:17** Hebrew *250 cubits* [133 meters]. **Ez 48:18** Hebrew *10,000 cubits* [5.3 kilometers] *to the east and 10,000 cubits to the west.* **Ez 48:20** Hebrew *25,000 cubits* [13.3 kilometers]; also in 48:21. **Ez 48:28a** Hebrew *waters of Meribath-kadesh.* **Ez 48:28b** Hebrew *the great sea.* **Ez 48:35a** Hebrew *18,000 cubits* [9.6 kilometers]. **Ez 48:35b** Hebrew *Yahweh Shammah.*

Ezek 48:1ff The land would be divided into 13 parallel portions (one for each tribe plus a sacred district) that would stretch from the Jordan River or Dead Sea to the Mediterranean Sea. The division of the land shows that in God's Kingdom there is a place for all who believe in and obey the one true God (see John 14:1-6).

Ezek 48:35 The book of Ezekiel begins by describing the holiness of God that Israel had despised and ignored. As a result, God's presence departed from the Temple, the city, and the people. The book ends with a detailed vision of the new Temple, the new city, and the new people—all demonstrating God's holiness. The pressures of everyday life may cause us to focus on the here and

5. HOPE FOR EXILED ISRAEL

Here are more signs of hope for Israel during their time in exile. God would use Babylon to judge Egypt for the role they played in the destruction of Judah and for their idolatry. And the exiled king of Israel was released from prison and treated kindly by his captors. While the ultimate restoration of God's people and judgment on their oppressors was still future, God was giving glimpses of hope to his people.

Nebuchadnezzar to Conquer Egypt

EZEKIEL 29:17-21

On April 26, the first day of the new year,* during the
twenty-seventh year of King Jehoiachin's captivity,
this message came to me from the LORD: [18]"Son of
man, the army of King Nebuchadnezzar* of Babylon
fought so hard against Tyre that the warriors' heads
were rubbed bare and their shoulders were raw and
blistered. Yet Nebuchadnezzar and his army won
no plunder to compensate them for all their work.
[19]Therefore, this is what the Sovereign LORD says: I
will give the land of Egypt to Nebuchadnezzar, king
of Babylon. He will carry off its wealth, plundering
everything it has so he can pay his army. [20]Yes, I have
given him the land of Egypt as a reward for his work,
says the Sovereign LORD, because he was working for
me when he destroyed Tyre.

[21]"And the day will come when I will cause the ancient glory of Israel to revive,* and then, Ezekiel, your
words will be respected. Then they will know that I
am the LORD."

A Sad Day for Egypt

EZEKIEL 30:1-19

This is another message that came to me from the
LORD: [2]"Son of man, prophesy and give this message
from the Sovereign LORD:

"Weep and wail
  for that day,
3 for the terrible day is almost here—
  the day of the LORD!
It is a day of clouds and gloom,
  a day of despair for the nations.
4 A sword will come against Egypt,
  and those who are slaughtered will cover
    the ground.
Its wealth will be carried away
  and its foundations destroyed.
The land of Ethiopia* will be ravished.
5 Ethiopia, Libya, Lydia, all Arabia,*
and all their other allies
  will be destroyed in that war.

6 "For this is what the LORD says:
All of Egypt's allies will fall,
  and the pride of her power will end.
From Migdol to Aswan*
  they will be slaughtered by the sword,
  says the Sovereign LORD.
7 Egypt will be desolate,
  surrounded by desolate nations,
and its cities will be in ruins,
  surrounded by other ruined cities.
8 And the people of Egypt will know that
    I am the LORD
  when I have set Egypt on fire
  and destroyed all their allies.
9 At that time I will send swift messengers in ships
  to terrify the complacent Ethiopians.
Great panic will come upon them
  on that day of Egypt's certain destruction.
Watch for it!
  It is sure to come!

10 "For this is what the Sovereign LORD says:
By the power of King Nebuchadnezzar*
    of Babylon,
  I will destroy the hordes of Egypt.
11 He and his armies—the most ruthless of all—
  will be sent to demolish the land.
They will make war against Egypt
  until slaughtered Egyptians cover the ground.
12 I will dry up the Nile River
  and sell the land to wicked men.
I will destroy the land of Egypt and everything
    in it
  by the hands of foreigners.
  I, the LORD, have spoken!

Ez 29:17 Hebrew *On the first day of the first month,* of the ancient Hebrew lunar calendar. This event occurred on April 26, 571 B.C.; also see note on 1:1. **Ez 29:18** Hebrew *Nebuchadrezzar,* a variant spelling of Nebuchadnezzar; also in 29:19. **Ez 29:21** Hebrew *I will cause a horn to sprout for the house of Israel.* **Ez 30:4** Hebrew *Cush;* similarly in 30:9. **Ez 30:5** Hebrew *Cush, Put, Lud, all Arabia, Cub. Cub* is otherwise unknown and may be another spelling for *Lub* (Libya). **Ez 30:6** Hebrew *to Syene.* **Ez 30:10** Hebrew *Nebuchadrezzar,* a variant spelling of Nebuchadnezzar.

571 BC

Ezekiel's prophetic ministry ends

now and thus forget God. That is why worship is so important: It takes our eyes off our current worries, gives us a glimpse of God's holiness, and allows us to look toward his future Kingdom. God's presence makes everything glorious, and worship brings us into his presence.

Ezek 29:17-18 This prophecy was given in 571 B.C. and is actually the latest prophecy in Ezekiel. Nebuchadnezzar had finally conquered Tyre after a long and costly 15-year siege (586–571 B.C.). He had not counted on such an expense, so he went south and conquered Egypt to make up for all he had lost in taking Tyre. Ezekiel placed this prophecy here to describe who would bring this punishment to Egypt. God was using Nebuchadnezzar, an evil man, as an instrument of his judgment on Tyre, Judah, and Egypt—evil nations themselves. When Babylon didn't recognize God's favor, he judged it, too.

Ezek 30:1-19 This is a lament for Egypt and its allies. Because of the Egyptians' pride and idolatry, they would be brought down.

Ezek 30:12 Egypt's pharaohs claimed that they had made the Nile—the river on which the entire nation depended. If God dried up the Nile, the nation would be doomed.

▸ **EZEKIEL 30:1-19** ***(cont.)***

13 "This is what the Sovereign LORD says:
I will smash the idols* of Egypt
and the images at Memphis.*
There will be no rulers left in Egypt;
terror will sweep the land.
14 I will destroy southern Egypt,*
set fire to Zoan,
and bring judgment against Thebes.*
15 I will pour out my fury on Pelusium,*
the strongest fortress of Egypt,
and I will stamp out
the hordes of Thebes.
16 Yes, I will set fire to all Egypt!
Pelusium will be racked with pain;
Thebes will be torn apart;
Memphis will live in constant terror.
17 The young men of Heliopolis and Bubastis*
will die in battle,
and the women* will be taken away as slaves.
18 When I come to break the proud strength of Egypt,
it will be a dark day for Tahpanhes, too.
A dark cloud will cover Tahpanhes,
and its daughters will be led away as captives.
19 And so I will greatly punish Egypt,
and they will know that I am the LORD."

Hope for Israel's Royal Line PARALLEL

2 KINGS 25:27-30

In the thirty-seventh year of the exile of King Jehoiachin of Judah, Evil-merodach ascended to the
Babylonian throne. He was kind to* Jehoiachin and
released him from prison on April 2 of that year.*
28He spoke kindly to Jehoiachin and gave him a
higher place than all the other exiled kings in Babylon. 29He supplied Jehoiachin with new clothes to
replace his prison garb and allowed him to dine in
the king's presence for the rest of his life. 30So the
Babylonian king gave him a regular food allowance
as long as he lived.

JEREMIAH 52:31-34

In the thirty-seventh year of the exile of King Jehoiachin of Judah, Evil-merodach ascended to the
Babylonian throne. He was kind to* Jehoiachin and
released him from prison on March 31 of that year.*
32He spoke kindly to Jehoiachin and gave him a higher
place than all the other exiled kings in Babylon. 33He
supplied Jehoiachin with new clothes to replace his
prison garb and allowed him to dine in the king's
presence for the rest of his life. 34So the Babylonian
king gave him a regular food allowance as long as he
lived. This continued until the day of his death.

Ez 30:13a The Hebrew term (literally *round things*) probably alludes to dung. **Ez 30:13b** Hebrew *Noph;* also in 30:16. **Ez 30:14a** Hebrew *Pathros.* **Ez 30:14b** Hebrew *No;* also in 30:15, 16. **Ez 30:15** Hebrew *Sin;* also in 30:16. **Ez 30:17a** Hebrew *of Awen and Pi-beseth.* **Ez 30:17b** Or *and her cities.* **2 Kgs 25:27a** Hebrew *He raised the head of.* **2 Kgs 25:27b** Hebrew *on the twenty-seventh day of the twelfth month,* of the ancient Hebrew lunar calendar. This day was April 2, 561 B.C.; also see note on 25:1. **Jer 52:31a** Hebrew *He raised the head of.* **Jer 52:31b** Hebrew *on the twenty-fifth day of the twelfth month,* of the ancient Hebrew lunar calendar. This day was March 31, 561 B.C.; also see note on 52:4a.

Belshazzar

Belshazzar was the ruler of Babylon who was killed at the time of its capture in 539 B.C. Belshazzar (whose name means "Bel has protected the king") is named in Babylonian documents alongside his father Nabonidus, who was king of Babylon 556-539 B.C. Other texts give details of Belshazzar's administration and religious interests in Babylon up to the 14th year of his father's reign. He was possibly a grandson of Nebuchadnezzar II and, according to the *Nabonidus Chronicle*, his father entrusted the army and kingship to him around 556 B.C., while Nabonidus campaigned in central Arabia, where he eventually remained for 10 years.

In this illustration Belshazzar is named with his father Nabonidus on a clay barrel cylinder, which records the king's restoration of the temple of the moon-god Sin, at Ur (c. 550 B.C.). This inscription coincides with Daniel's dating of his prophecies (Dan 7:1; 8:1). It helps us date Daniel's writings, which is important for their prophetic messages. We can thus know that Daniel predicted events before they occurred, thereby showing he was a true prophet of God.

Ezek 30:13-19 The list of cities to be destroyed shows the breadth of the destruction; the drying up of the Nile (Ezek 30:12) shows how deep the devastation would reach. Egypt would be completely incapacitated.

2 Kgs 25:27 Evil-merodach, the son of Nebuchadnezzar, became king of the Babylonian Empire in 562 B.C., 24 years after the beginning of the general captivity and 37 years after Jehoiachin was removed from Jerusalem. The new king treated Jehoiachin with kindness, even allowing him to eat at his table (2 Kgs 25:29). Evil-merodach was later killed in a plot by his brother-in-law, Nergal-sharezer, who succeeded him to the throne.

2 Kgs 25:30 The book of 2 Kings opens with Elijah being carried to heaven—the destination awaiting those who follow God. But the book ends with the people of Judah being carried off to foreign lands as humiliated slaves—the result of failing to follow God.

The book of 2 Kings is an illustration of what happens when we make anything more important than God, when we make ruinous alliances, when our consciences become desensitized to right and wrong, and when we are no longer able to discern God's purpose for our lives. We may fail, like the people of Judah and Israel, but God's promises do not. He is always available to help us straighten out our lives and start over. And

6. DANIEL'S FAITHFULNESS TO GOD IN EXILE

Daniel continued to serve God faithfully throughout his life in exile. Even when Babylon was overthrown by Persia, the leaders of the new empire recognized Daniel for his integrity and value as an adviser. He remained faithful to God even when faced with death, and God blessed him for it and rescued him. Daniel recognized that the 70 years of exile God had spoken of through Jeremiah was coming to an end and pleaded with God in prayer for the restoration of his people to Jerusalem. God heard Daniel's prayer. Are you attentive to God's will and fervently praying for it to come true?

Daniel's Vision of Four Beasts

DANIEL 7:1-14

Earlier, during the first year of King Belshazzar's reign
in Babylon,* Daniel had a dream and saw visions as he
lay in his bed. He wrote down the dream, and this is
what he saw.
2In my vision that night, I, Daniel, saw a great storm
churning the surface of a great sea, with strong winds
blowing from every direction. 3Then four huge beasts
came up out of the water, each different from the others.
4The first beast was like a lion with eagles' wings.
As I watched, its wings were pulled off, and it was left
standing with its two hind feet on the ground, like a
human being. And it was given a human mind.
5Then I saw a second beast, and it looked like a bear.
It was rearing up on one side, and it had three ribs in its
mouth between its teeth. And I heard a voice saying to
it, "Get up! Devour the flesh of many people!"
6Then the third of these strange beasts appeared,
and it looked like a leopard. It had four bird's wings
on its back, and it had four heads. Great authority was
given to this beast.
7Then in my vision that night, I saw a fourth beast—
terrifying, dreadful, and very strong. It devoured and
crushed its victims with huge iron teeth and trampled
their remains beneath its feet. It was different from
any of the other beasts, and it had ten horns.
8As I was looking at the horns, suddenly another
small horn appeared among them. Three of the first
horns were torn out by the roots to make room for it.
This little horn had eyes like human eyes and a mouth
that was boasting arrogantly.

9 I watched as thrones were put in place
and the Ancient One* sat down to judge.
His clothing was as white as snow,
his hair like purest wool.
He sat on a fiery throne
with wheels of blazing fire,

Dn 7:1 The first year of Belshazzar's reign (who was co-regent with his father, Nabonidus) was 556 B.C. (or perhaps as late as 553 B.C.). **Dn 7:9** Aramaic *an Ancient of Days;* also in 7:13, 22.

that is just what would happen in the book of Ezra. When the people acknowledged their sins, God was ready and willing to help them return to their land and start again.

Jer 52:31 Babylon's king showed kindness to Jehoiachin. In 561 B.C. Jehoiachin was released from prison and allowed to eat with the king. God continued to show kindness to the descendants of King David, even in exile.

Jer 52:34 In the world's eyes, Jeremiah looked totally unsuccessful. He had no money, family, or friends. He prophesied the destruction of the nation, the capital city, and the Temple, but the political and religious leaders would not accept or follow his advice. No group of people liked him or listened to him. Yet as we look back, we see that he successfully completed the work God gave him to do. Success must never be measured by popularity, fame, or fortune, for these are temporal measures. King Zedekiah, for example, lost everything by pursuing selfish goals. God measures our success with the yardsticks of obedience, faithfulness, and righteousness. If you are faithfully doing the work God has given you, you are successful in his eyes.

Dan 7:1 The book of Daniel is not ordered chronologically; Daniel 7 takes place before Daniel 5. At this time, Belshazzar had just been given a position of authority (553 B.C.), and Daniel was probably in his late sixties. The first six chapters of Daniel present history; the last six chapters are visions relating mainly to the future.

Dan 7:1ff Daniel had a vision of four huge beasts, each representing a world empire. This was similar to Nebuchadnezzar's dream (Dan 2), which covered the political aspects of the empires; Daniel's dream depicted their moral characteristics. These nations, which would reign over Israel, were evil and cruel; but Daniel also saw God's everlasting, indestructible Kingdom arrive and conquer them all.

Dan 7:4-8 The lion with eagles' wings represents Babylon with its swift conquests (statues of winged lions have been recovered from Babylon's ruins). The bear that ravaged the lion is Medo-Persia. The three ribs in its mouth represent the conquests of three major enemies. The leopard is Greece. Its wings show the swiftness of Alexander the Great's campaign as he conquered much of the civilized world in four years (334–330 B.C.). The leopard's four heads are the four divisions of the Greek Empire after Alexander's death.

The fourth beast points to both Rome and the end times. Many Bible scholars believe that the horns correspond to 10 kings who will reign shortly before God sets up his everlasting Kingdom. These 10 kings had still not come to power at the time of John's vision recorded in the book of Revelation (Rev 17:12). The little horn is a future human ruler or the Antichrist (see also 2 Thes 2:3-4). God is illustrating the final end of all worldly kingdoms in contrast to his eternal Kingdom.

Dan 7:7 In the book of Revelation, John also recorded a vision of a scarlet beast that had seven heads and ten horns (Rev 17:3). The angel told John that the ten horns were ten kings (Rev 17:12). Most likely these would be ten rulers who would rule under the Antichrist. The number ten may be literal; or more likely, it symbolizes the totality of the powers on earth that would serve the Antichrist and war against Christ. In John's day, Rome was the world power, but would be followed by other powers. Whatever the identity of the ten kings, they would give their power to the Antichrist and make war against Christ and his followers.

Dan 7:9 Here the prophecy shifts to the end times. This judgment scene is similar to one that the apostle John saw (Rev 1:14-15). The Ancient One is almighty God, who assigns power to kingdoms and who will himself judge those kingdoms in the end.

560 BC *Aesop writes his fables*

▸ **DANIEL 7:1-14** ***(cont.)***

10 and a river of fire was pouring out,
flowing from his presence.
Millions of angels ministered to him;
many millions stood to attend him.
Then the court began its session,
and the books were opened.

11 I continued to watch because I could hear the
little horn's boastful speech. I kept watching until the
fourth beast was killed and its body was destroyed
by fire. 12 The other three beasts had their authority taken from them, but they were allowed to live a
while longer.*
13 As my vision continued that night, I saw someone
like a son of man* coming with the clouds of heaven.
He approached the Ancient One and was led into his
presence. 14 He was given authority, honor, and sovereignty over all the nations of the world, so that people
of every race and nation and language would obey
him. His rule is eternal—it will never end. His kingdom
will never be destroyed.

The Vision Is Explained

DANIEL 7:15-28

I, Daniel, was troubled by all I had seen, and my visions terrified me. 16 So I approached one of those
standing beside the throne and asked him what it all
meant. He explained it to me like this: 17 "These four
huge beasts represent four kingdoms that will arise
from the earth. 18 But in the end, the holy people of
the Most High will be given the kingdom, and they
will rule forever and ever."
19 Then I wanted to know the true meaning of the
fourth beast, the one so different from the others and
so terrifying. It had devoured and crushed its victims
with iron teeth and bronze claws, trampling their remains beneath its feet. 20 I also asked about the ten
horns on the fourth beast's head and the little horn
that came up afterward and destroyed three of the
other horns. This horn had seemed greater than the
others, and it had human eyes and a mouth that was
boasting arrogantly. 21 As I watched, this horn was waging war against God's holy people and was defeating
them, 22 until the Ancient One—the Most High—came
and judged in favor of his holy people. Then the time
arrived for the holy people to take over the kingdom.
23 Then he said to me, "This fourth beast is the
fourth world power that will rule the earth. It will be
different from all the others. It will devour the whole
world, trampling and crushing everything in its path.
24 Its ten horns are ten kings who will rule that empire.
Then another king will arise, different from the other
ten, who will subdue three of them. 25 He will defy the
Most High and oppress the holy people of the Most
High. He will try to change their sacred festivals and
laws, and they will be placed under his control for a
time, times, and half a time.
26 "But then the court will pass judgment, and all his
power will be taken away and completely destroyed.
27 Then the sovereignty, power, and greatness of all

Dn 7:12 Aramaic *for a season and a time.* **Dn 7:13** Or *like a Son of Man.*

Dan 7:10 The book of Revelation records a similar picture of God with angels surrounding his throne. John recorded that there were "thousands and millions" (Rev 5:11-12). In other words, angels too numerous to count surround God's throne and minister to him. Created by God, angels are spiritual beings who help carry out his work on earth.

Dan 7:10 The phrase "the books were opened" refers to judgment. Revelation refers to this final judgment where the "books were opened, including the Book of Life. And the dead were judged according to what they had done, as recorded in the books" (Rev 20:12). The Book of Life is the heavenly registry of those who have accepted Christ's gift of salvation (Rev 3:5). All believers' names are written in the Book of Life and they need not fear judgment. Unbelievers, however, will be judged according to their works, but their works, no matter how good, will not be able to save them.

Dan 7:10 Daniel saw God judging millions of people as they stand before him. We all must stand before almighty God and give an account of our lives. If God judged your life today, what would he say about it? How would he measure it against his will for you? We should live each day with the full awareness that we must appear before God to give account for how we used our life. How will your life measure up?

Dan 7:11-12 The slaying of the beast represents the fall of Rome. While this beast was destroyed, the other beasts were allowed to live for a period of time. The kingdoms (or their cultures) continued to be recognizable in some form; history did not end when God intervened with his judgment.

Dan 7:13-14 This one "like a son of man" is the Messiah. Jesus used this verse to refer to himself (Matt 26:64; Luke 21:27; John 1:51). The clouds of heaven portray the Son of Man as divine; throughout the Bible, clouds represent his majesty and awesome presence. God's glory appeared in a cloud at the giving of the law at Sinai (Exod 16:10; 19:9). The book of Revelation also records Christ coming with the clouds of heaven (Rev 1:7).

Dan 7:18 The "holy people of the Most High" are the true Israel, the people ruled by the Messiah. Jesus Christ gave the Kingdom to the new Israel, his church, made up of all faithful believers. His coming ushered in the Kingdom of God, and all believers are its citizens (see also Dan 7:22, 27). Although God may allow persecution to continue for a while, the destiny of his followers is to possess the Kingdom and be with him forever.

Dan 7:21-22 This "horn" that wages war against God's people is also described in Revelation as the beast who is "allowed to wage war against God's holy people and to conquer them" (Rev 13:7). For a while, the "horn" will defeat God's people. But in reality, those who die for the faith will be the ultimate overcomers, for they will receive great rewards. In the end, the Ancient One himself will defeat the horn.

Dan 7:24 The 10 horns, or 10 kings, are also mentioned in Revelation 17:12. There were also 10 toes in Nebuchadnezzar's vision (Dan 2:41-42). While all do not agree concerning the identity of these 10 kings, they will make war against Christ (Rev 17:12-14), but as the King of kings, he will conquer them. The other king mentioned here is the future man of lawlessness (see 2 Thes 2:3-4).

Dan 7:25 The exact meaning of this "time, times, and half a time" is debated. Many scholars believe that "time" means one year; "times" means two years; and "half a time" means half a year. Thus, this would refer to three and a half years. God's people will be placed under this king's control and the persecution will continue only a relatively short time. God has promised to give his Kingdom to his holy people.

the kingdoms under heaven will be given to the holy people of the Most High. His kingdom will last forever, and all rulers will serve and obey him."

28That was the end of the vision. I, Daniel, was terrified by my thoughts and my face was pale with fear, but I kept these things to myself.

Daniel's Vision of a Ram and Goat

DANIEL 8:1-14

1*During the third year of King Belshazzar's reign, I, Daniel, saw another vision, following the one that had already appeared to me. 2In this vision I was at the fortress of Susa, in the province of Elam, standing beside the Ulai River.*

3As I looked up, I saw a ram with two long horns standing beside the river.* One of the horns was longer than the other, even though it had grown later than the other one. 4The ram butted everything out of his way to the west, to the north, and to the south, and no one could stand against him or help his victims. He did as he pleased and became very great.

5While I was watching, suddenly a male goat appeared from the west, crossing the land so swiftly that he didn't even touch the ground. This goat, which had one very large horn between its eyes, 6headed toward the two-horned ram that I had seen standing beside the river, rushing at him in a rage. 7The goat charged furiously at the ram and struck him, breaking off both his horns. Now the ram was helpless, and the goat knocked him down and trampled him. No one could rescue the ram from the goat's power.

8The goat became very powerful. But at the height of his power, his large horn was broken off. In the large horn's place grew four prominent horns pointing in the four directions of the earth. 9Then from one of the prominent horns came a small horn whose power grew very great. It extended toward the south and the east and toward the glorious land of Israel. 10Its power reached to the heavens, where it attacked the heavenly army, throwing some of the heavenly beings and some of the stars to the ground and trampling them. 11It even challenged the Commander of heaven's army by canceling the daily sacrifices offered to him and by destroying his Temple. 12The army of heaven was restrained from responding to this rebellion. So the daily sacrifice was halted, and truth was overthrown. The horn succeeded in everything it did.*

13Then I heard two holy ones talking to each other. One of them asked, "How long will the events of this vision last? How long will the rebellion that causes desecration stop the daily sacrifices? How long will the Temple and heaven's army be trampled on?"

14The other replied, "It will take 2,300 evenings and mornings; then the Temple will be made right again."

Gabriel Explains the Vision

DANIEL 8:15-27

As I, Daniel, was trying to understand the meaning of this vision, someone who looked like a man stood in front of me. 16And I heard a human voice calling out from the Ulai River, "Gabriel, tell this man the meaning of his vision."

17As Gabriel approached the place where I was standing, I became so terrified that I fell with my

Dn 8:1 The original text from this point through chapter 12 is in Hebrew. See note at 2:4. **Dn 8:2** Or *the Ulai Gate;* also in 8:16. **Dn 8:3** Or *the gate;* also in 8:6. **Dn 8:11-12** The meaning of the Hebrew for these verses is uncertain.

551 BC — *Confucius is born in China*

Dan 8:1 Daniel 7–8 precedes Daniel 5 chronologically; the dream probably occurred in 551 B.C. when Daniel was about 70 years old. Daniel 7–8 corresponds to the first and third years of Belshazzar's reign and belongs chronologically between Daniel 4 and Daniel 5. Daniel 9 took place at approximately the same time as Daniel 6. It gives us more details about the Medo-Persian and Greek Empires, the two world powers that ruled after Babylonia.

Dan 8:2 Susa was one of the capitals of the Babylonian Empire. Located in what is now Iran, Susa was a well-developed city. It was the winter capital of the Persian Empire and a mighty fortress. In his vision, Daniel saw himself in this important location. The earliest known code of law, the Code of Hammurabi, was found there. Susa rivaled Babylon itself in cultural sophistication.

Dan 8:3 The two horns were the kings of Media and Persia (Dan 8:20). The longer horn represented the growing dominance of Persia in the Medo-Persian Empire.

Dan 8:5-7 The goat represented Greece, and its large horn, Alexander the Great (Dan 8:21). This is an amazing prediction because Greece was not yet considered a world power when this prophecy was given. Alexander the Great conquered the world with great speed and military strategy, indicated by the goat's rapid movement. The shattering of both horns symbolized Alexander breaking both parts of the Medo-Persian Empire.

Dan 8:8 Alexander the Great died in his thirties at the height of his power. His kingdom was split into four parts under four generals: Ptolemy I of Egypt and Palestine; Seleucus of Babylonia and Syria; Lysimachus of Asia Minor; and Antipater of Macedonia and Greece.

Dan 8:9 Antiochus IV Epiphanes ("the small horn") attacked Israel ("the glorious land") in the second century B.C. He was the eighth ruler of the Seleucid Empire (Babylonia and Syria). He overthrew Israel's high priest, looted the Temple, and replaced worship of God with a Greek form of worship. A further fulfillment of this prophecy of a powerful horn would occur in the future with the coming of the Antichrist (see Dan 8:17, 19, 23; 11:36; 2 Thes 2:4).

Dan 8:11 The "Commander of heaven's army" here refers to a heavenly authority, perhaps an angel or even God himself (see also Josh 5:13-15).

Dan 8:14 The phrase "evenings and mornings" means evening and morning sacrifices; it refers to the time from the desecration of the altar in the Temple by Antiochus IV Epiphanes to the restoration of Temple worship under Judas Maccabeus in 165 B.C.

Dan 8:16 Gabriel is an angel, the heavenly messenger God used to explain Daniel's visions (Dan 9:21). He also announced the births of John the Baptist (Luke 1:11) and the Messiah (Luke 1:26).

Dan 8:17 The "time of the end," in this case, refers to the whole period from the end of the Exile until the second coming of Christ. Many of the events that would happen under Antiochus IV Epiphanes would be repeated on a broader scale just before Christ's second coming. During these times, God deals with Israel in a radically different way, with divine discipline coming through Gentile nations. This time is sometimes referred to as the "period of the Gentiles" (Luke 21:24).

▸ **DANIEL 8:15-27** ***(cont.)***

face to the ground. "Son of man," he said, "you must understand that the events you have seen in your vision relate to the time of the end."

[18]While he was speaking, I fainted and lay there with my face to the ground. But Gabriel roused me with a touch and helped me to my feet.

[19]Then he said, "I am here to tell you what will happen later in the time of wrath. What you have seen pertains to the very end of time. [20]The two-horned ram represents the kings of Media and Persia. [21]The shaggy male goat represents the king of Greece,* and the large horn between his eyes represents the first king of the Greek Empire. [22]The four prominent horns that replaced the one large horn show that the Greek Empire will break into four kingdoms, but none as great as the first.

[23]"At the end of their rule, when their sin is at its height, a fierce king, a master of intrigue, will rise to power. [24]He will become very strong, but not by his own power. He will cause a shocking amount of destruction and succeed in everything he does. He will destroy powerful leaders and devastate the holy people. [25]He will be a master of deception and will become arrogant; he will destroy many without warning. He will even take on the Prince of princes in battle, but he will be broken, though not by human power.

550 BC

[26]"This vision about the 2,300 evenings and mornings* is true. But none of these things will happen for a long time, so keep this vision a secret."

[27]Then I, Daniel, was overcome and lay sick for several days. Afterward I got up and performed my duties for the king, but I was greatly troubled by the vision and could not understand it.

The Writing on the Wall

DANIEL 5:1-12

Many years later King Belshazzar gave a great feast for 1,000 of his nobles, and he drank wine with them. [2]While Belshazzar was drinking the wine, he gave orders to bring in the gold and silver cups that his predecessor,* Nebuchadnezzar, had taken from the Temple in Jerusalem. He wanted to drink from them with his nobles, his wives, and his concubines. [3]So they brought these gold cups taken from the Temple, the house of God in Jerusalem, and the king and his nobles, his wives, and his concubines drank from them. [4]While they drank from them they praised their idols made of gold, silver, bronze, iron, wood, and stone.

[5]Suddenly, they saw the fingers of a human hand writing on the plaster wall of the king's palace, near the lampstand. The king himself saw the hand as it wrote, [6]and his face turned pale with fright. His knees knocked together in fear and his legs gave way beneath him.

[7]The king shouted for the enchanters, astrologers,* and fortune-tellers to be brought before him. He said to these wise men of Babylon, "Whoever can read this writing and tell me what it means will be dressed in purple robes of royal honor and will have a gold chain placed around his neck. He will become the third highest ruler in the kingdom!"

[8]But when all the king's wise men had come in,

Dn 8:21 Hebrew *of Javan.* **Dn 8:26** Hebrew *about the evenings and mornings;* compare 8:14. **Dn 5:2** Aramaic *father;* also in 5:11, 13, 18. **Dn 5:7** Or *Chaldeans;* also in 5:11.

Cyrus the Great conquers the Medes, founding the Persian Empire

Dan 8:23 This fierce king describes both Antiochus IV Epiphanes and the Antichrist at the end of human history (Rev 13:1-18).

Dan 8:25 This Prince of princes is God himself. No human power could defeat the king whom Daniel saw in his vision, but God would bring him down. Antiochus IV Epiphanes reportedly went insane and died in Persia in 164 B.C. God's power and justice will prevail, so we should never give up our faith or lose hope, no matter how powerful God's enemies may seem.

Dan 5:1 About 66 years have elapsed since Nebuchadnezzar's second strike against Jerusalem in 605 B.C. (Dan 1). He died in 562 B.C. after a reign of 43 years. His son, Evil-merodach, ruled 562–560 B.C. His brother-in-law Neriglissar reigned 560–556 B.C. After a two-month reign by Labashi-marduk in 556 B.C., the Babylonian Empire continued 556–539 B.C. under the command of Nabonidus. Belshazzar was the son of Nabonidus. He coreigned 553–539 B.C. with his father.

Dan 5:1 Archaeologists have recently discovered Belshazzar's name on several documents. He ruled with his father, Nabonidus, staying home to administer the affairs of the kingdom while his father tried to reopen trade routes taken over by Cyrus and the Persians. Belshazzar was in charge of the city of Babylon when it was captured.

Dan 5:7 Belshazzar served as coregent with his father, Nabonidus. Thus, Nabonidus was the first ruler and his son Belshazzar, the second. The person who could read the writing would be given third place, which was the highest position and honor that Belshazzar could offer.

Dan 5:8 Although the writing on the wall contained only three words in Aramaic, a language understood by Babylonians (see Dan 2:4), the people could not determine its prophetic significance. God gave Daniel alone the ability to interpret the message

The Writing on the Wall

Mene, mene, tekel, parsin, **written in Aramaic script, is literally "mina, mina, shekel, half-mina (or half-shekel)." Minas were units of weight measurement for gold and silver. A mina weighed about 50 shekels or 500 grams. Shekels were units of weight, a shekel weighing about 10 grams. There is also a wordplay here: *Mene* can mean "to number," *tekel* means "to weigh," and *parsin* means "to divide." In this context, "to divide" = "halved," thereby indicating that the Babylonian Empire had been evaluated and then given to two peoples, the Medes and Persians.**

This writing on the wall became a prophetic word for the destruction of the Babylonian Empire, which occurred soon thereafter. God's prophetic word is to be believed and heeded.

none of them could read the writing or tell him what it meant. [9]So the king grew even more alarmed, and his face turned pale. His nobles, too, were shaken.

[10]But when the queen mother heard what was happening, she hurried to the banquet hall. She said to Belshazzar, "Long live the king! Don't be so pale and frightened. [11]There is a man in your kingdom who has within him the spirit of the holy gods. During Nebuchadnezzar's reign, this man was found to have insight, understanding, and wisdom like that of the gods. Your predecessor, the king—your predecessor King Nebuchadnezzar—made him chief over all the magicians, enchanters, astrologers, and fortune-tellers of Babylon. [12]This man Daniel, whom the king named Belteshazzar, has exceptional ability and is filled with divine knowledge and understanding. He can interpret dreams, explain riddles, and solve difficult problems. Call for Daniel, and he will tell you what the writing means."

Daniel Explains the Writing

DANIEL 5:13-31

So Daniel was brought in before the king. The king asked him, "Are you Daniel, one of the exiles brought from Judah by my predecessor, King Nebuchadnezzar? [14]I have heard that you have the spirit of the gods within you and that you are filled with insight, understanding, and wisdom. [15]My wise men and enchanters have tried to read the words on the wall and tell me their meaning, but they cannot do it. [16]I am told that you can give interpretations and solve difficult problems. If you can read these words and tell me their meaning, you will be clothed in purple robes of royal honor, and you will have a gold chain placed around your neck. You will become the third highest ruler in the kingdom."

[17]Daniel answered the king, "Keep your gifts or give them to someone else, but I will tell you what the writing means. [18]Your Majesty, the Most High God gave sovereignty, majesty, glory, and honor to your predecessor, Nebuchadnezzar. [19]He made him so great that people of all races and nations and languages trembled before him in fear. He killed those he wanted to kill and spared those he wanted to spare. He honored those he wanted to honor and disgraced those he wanted to disgrace. [20]But when his heart and mind were puffed up with arrogance, he was brought down from his royal throne and stripped of his glory. [21]He was driven from human society. He was given the mind of a wild animal, and he lived among the wild donkeys. He ate grass like a cow, and he was drenched with the dew of heaven, until he learned that the Most High God rules over the kingdoms of the world and appoints anyone he desires to rule over them.

[22]"You are his successor,* O Belshazzar, and you knew all this, yet you have not humbled yourself. [23]For you have proudly defied the Lord of heaven and have had these cups from his Temple brought before you. You and your nobles and your wives and concubines have been drinking wine from them while praising gods of silver, gold, bronze, iron, wood, and stone—gods that neither see nor hear nor know anything at all. But you have not honored the God who gives you the breath of life and controls your destiny! [24]So God has sent this hand to write this message.

[25]"This is the message that was written: MENE, MENE, TEKEL, and PARSIN. [26]This is what these words mean:

Mene means 'numbered'—God has numbered the days of your reign and has brought it to an end.
[27] *Tekel* means 'weighed'—you have been weighed on the balances and have not measured up.
[28] *Parsin** means 'divided'—your kingdom has been divided and given to the Medes and Persians."

Dn 5:22 Aramaic *son.* **Dn 5:28** Aramaic *Peres,* the singular of *Parsin.*

of doom to Babylon. The wise men of the kingdom were ignorant of God's wisdom, no matter how great the reward. Daniel did not rush into the banquet hall with the others. His loyalty was to God, not money.

Dan 5:10 This queen mother was either Nabonidus's wife or the wife of one of his predecessors, possibly even of Nebuchadnezzar. She was not Belshazzar's wife, because his wives were with him in the banquet hall.

Dan 5:17 The king offered Daniel beautiful gifts and great power if he would explain the writing, but Daniel turned him down. Daniel was not motivated by material rewards. His entire life had been characterized by doing right. Daniel was not showing disrespect in refusing the gifts, but he was growing older himself and knew the gifts would do him little good. Besides, being third highest ruler in a kingdom Daniel knew was about to be destroyed was not exactly motivating! Daniel wanted to show that he was giving an unbiased interpretation to the king. Doing right should be our first priority, not gaining power or rewards. Do you love God enough to do what is right, even if it means giving up personal rewards?

Dan 5:21-23 Belshazzar knew Babylonian history, and so he knew how God had humbled Nebuchadnezzar. Nevertheless Belshazzar's feast was open defiance to God's authority as he took the gold cups from God's Temple and drank from them (Dan 5:2-4). No one who understands that God is the Creator of the universe should be foolish enough to challenge him.

Dan 5:22 Often kings would kill the bearer of bad news. But Daniel was not afraid to tell the truth to the king even though it was not what he wanted to hear. We should be just as courageous in telling the truth under pressure.

Dan 5:23-24 Belshazzar used the cups from the Temple for his party, and God condemned him for this act. We must not use for sinful purposes what has been dedicated to God. Today this would include church buildings, financial donations, and anything else that has been set apart for serving God. Be careful how you use what is God's.

Dan 5:27 The writing on the wall was a message for all those who defy God. Although Belshazzar had power and wealth, his kingdom was totally corrupt, and he could not withstand the judgment of God. God's time of judgment comes for all people. If you have forgotten God and slipped into a sinful way of life, turn away from your sin now before he removes any opportunities to repent. Ask God to forgive you, and begin to live by his standards of justice.

Dan 5:28 The Medes and Persians joined forces to overthrow Babylon. This event was predicted in the second phase of Nebuchadnezzar's dream in Daniel 2—the silver chest and arms.

▸ **DANIEL 5:13-31** *(cont.)*
29Then at Belshazzar's command, Daniel was
dressed in purple robes, a gold chain was hung around
his neck, and he was proclaimed the third highest
ruler in the kingdom.
30That very night Belshazzar, the Babylonian* king,
was killed.*
31*And Darius the Mede took over the kingdom at
the age of sixty-two.

Daniel in the Lions' Den

DANIEL 6:1-28
1*Darius the Mede decided to divide the kingdom
into 120 provinces, and he appointed a high officer
to rule over each province. 2The king also chose Daniel and two others as administrators to supervise the
high officers and protect the king's interests. 3Daniel
soon proved himself more capable than all the other
administrators and high officers. Because of Daniel's
great ability, the king made plans to place him over
the entire empire.
4Then the other administrators and high officers
began searching for some fault in the way Daniel was
handling government affairs, but they couldn't find
anything to criticize or condemn. He was faithful,
always responsible, and completely trustworthy. 5So
they concluded, "Our only chance of finding grounds
for accusing Daniel will be in connection with the
rules of his religion."
6So the administrators and high officers went
to the king and said, "Long live King Darius! 7We
are all in agreement—we administrators, officials,
high officers, advisers, and governors—that the king
should make a law that will be strictly enforced. Give
orders that for the next thirty days any person who
prays to anyone, divine or human—except to you,
Your Majesty—will be thrown into the den of lions.
8And now, Your Majesty, issue and sign this law so it
cannot be changed, an official law of the Medes and
Persians that cannot be revoked." 9So King Darius
signed the law.
10But when Daniel learned that the law had been
signed, he went home and knelt down as usual in his
upstairs room, with its windows open toward Jerusalem. He prayed three times a day, just as he had always
done, giving thanks to his God. 11Then the officials
went together to Daniel's house and found him praying and asking for God's help. 12So they went straight
to the king and reminded him about his law. "Did you
not sign a law that for the next thirty days any person
who prays to anyone, divine or human—except to you,
Your Majesty—will be thrown into the den of lions?"
"Yes," the king replied, "that decision stands; it is
an official law of the Medes and Persians that cannot
be revoked."
13Then they told the king, "That man Daniel, one of
the captives from Judah, is ignoring you and your law.
He still prays to his God three times a day."
14Hearing this, the king was deeply troubled, and
he tried to think of a way to save Daniel. He spent the

Dn 5:30a Or *Chaldean.* **Dn 5:30b** The Persians and Medes conquered Babylon in October 539 B.C. **Dn 5:31** Verse 5:31 is numbered 6:1 in Aramaic text. **Dn 6:1** Verses 6:1-28 are numbered 6:2-29 in Aramaic text.

540 BC

Horseback postal service in the Persian Empire

Dan 5:31 Darius and his soldiers entered Babylon by diverting the river that ran through the city, then walking in on the dry riverbed.

Dan 5:31 This Darius is not to be confused with Darius I, mentioned in the books of Ezra, Haggai, and Zechariah; or Darius II (the Persian), mentioned in the book of Nehemiah. Darius the Mede is named only in the book of Daniel. Other records name no king between Belshazzar and Cyrus. Thus, Darius may have been (1) appointed by Cyrus to rule over Babylon as a province of Persia, (2) another name for Cyrus himself or for his son, Cambyses, or (3) a descendant of Xerxes I.

Dan 6:1-3 At this time, Daniel was over 80 years old and one of Darius's top three administrators. Daniel was working with those who did not believe in his God, but he worked more efficiently and capably than all the rest. Thus, he attracted the attention of the pagan king and earned a place of respect. One of the best ways to influence non-Christian employers is to work diligently and responsibly. How well do you represent God to your employer?

Dan 6:3-4 Daniel made enemies at work by doing a good job. Perhaps you have had a similar experience. When you begin to excel, you will find that coworkers may look for ways to hold you back and tear you down. How should you deal with those who would cheer at your downfall and even try to hasten it? Conduct your life above reproach. Then you will have nothing to hide, and your enemies will have a difficult time finding legitimate charges against you. Of course, this will not always save you from attacks, and like Daniel, you will have to rely on God for protection.

Dan 6:4-5 The jealous administrators and officers couldn't find anything about Daniel's life to criticize, so they attacked his religion. If you face jealous critics because of your faith, be glad they're criticizing that part of your life—perhaps they had to focus on your religion as a last resort! Respond by continuing to believe and live as you should. Then remember that God is in control, fighting this battle for you.

Dan 6:8-9 In Babylon, the king's word was the law. In the Medo-Persian Empire, when a law was made, even the king couldn't change it. Darius was an effective government administrator, but he had a fatal flaw—pride. By appealing to his vanity, the men talked Darius into signing a law effectively making himself a god for 30 days. This law could not be broken—not even by an important official like Daniel. Another example of the irrevocable nature of the laws of the Medes and Persians appears in Esther 8:8.

Dan 6:10 Daniel stood alone. Although he knew about the law against praying to anyone except the king, he continued to pray three times a day as he always had. Daniel had a disciplined prayer life. Our prayers are usually interrupted, not by threats, but simply by the pressure of our schedules. Don't let threats or pressures cut into your prayer time. Pray regularly, no matter what, for prayer is your lifeline to God.

Dan 6:10 Daniel made no attempt to hide his daily prayer routine from his enemies in government, even though he knew he would be disobeying the new law. Hiding his daily prayers would have been futile because surely the conspirators would have caught him at something else during the month. Also, hiding would have demonstrated that he was afraid of the other government officials. Daniel continued to pray because he could not look to the king for the guidance and strength that he needed during this difficult time. Only God could provide what he really needed.

rest of the day looking for a way to get Daniel out of
this predicament.
15 In the evening the men went together to the king
and said, "Your Majesty, you know that according to
the law of the Medes and the Persians, no law that the
king signs can be changed."
16 So at last the king gave orders for Daniel to be
arrested and thrown into the den of lions. The king
said to him, "May your God, whom you serve so faithfully, rescue you."
17 A stone was brought and placed over the mouth
of the den. The king sealed the stone with his own
royal seal and the seals of his nobles, so that no one
could rescue Daniel. 18 Then the king returned to his
palace and spent the night fasting. He refused his
usual entertainment and couldn't sleep at all that
night.
19 Very early the next morning, the king got up and
hurried out to the lions' den. 20 When he got there, he
called out in anguish, "Daniel, servant of the living
God! Was your God, whom you serve so faithfully,
able to rescue you from the lions?"
21 Daniel answered, "Long live the king! 22 My God
sent his angel to shut the lions' mouths so that they
would not hurt me, for I have been found innocent in
his sight. And I have not wronged you, Your Majesty."
23 The king was overjoyed and ordered that Daniel
be lifted from the den. Not a scratch was found on
him, for he had trusted in his God.
24 Then the king gave orders to arrest the men who
had maliciously accused Daniel. He had them thrown
into the lions' den, along with their wives and children.
The lions leaped on them and tore them apart before
they even hit the floor of the den.
25 Then King Darius sent this message to the people
of every race and nation and language throughout
the world:

"Peace and prosperity to you!
26 "I decree that everyone throughout my
kingdom should tremble with fear before
the God of Daniel.

For he is the living God,
and he will endure forever.
His kingdom will never be destroyed,
and his rule will never end.
27 He rescues and saves his people;
he performs miraculous signs and
wonders
in the heavens and on earth.
He has rescued Daniel
from the power of the lions."

28 So Daniel prospered during the reign of Darius
and the reign of Cyrus the Persian.*

Dn 6:28 Or *of Darius, that is, the reign of Cyrus the Persian.*

KINGS DANIEL SERVED

Name	*Empire*	*Story told in*	*Memorable events*
Nebuchadnezzar	Babylonia	Dan 1–4	Shadrach, Meshach, and Abednego thrown into blazing furnace; Nebuchadnezzar became insane for 7 years
Belshazzar	Babylonia	Dan 5, 7–8	Daniel read the writing on the wall, which signaled the end of the Babylonian Empire
Darius	Medo-Persia	Dan 6, 9	Daniel thrown into a lions' den
Cyrus	Medo-Persia	Dan 10–12	The exiles return to their homeland in Judah and their capital city, Jerusalem

Dan 6:16 Lions roamed the countryside and forests in Mesopotamia, and the people feared them and greatly respected their power. Some kings hunted lions for sport. The Persians captured lions, keeping them in large parks where they were fed and attended. Lions were also used for executing people. But God has ways of delivering his people (Dan 6:22) that none of us can imagine. It is always premature to give up and give in to the pressure of unbelievers, because God has power they know nothing about. God can even shut the lions' mouths.

Dan 6:16 Even unbelievers witnessed to Daniel's consistency. By his continual service, Daniel had demonstrated his faithful devotion to God. What can unbelievers determine about your life?

Dan 6:21-23 The person who trusts in God and obeys his will is untouchable until God grants permission to take that person. To trust God is to have immeasurable peace. God, who delivered Daniel, will deliver you. Do you trust him with your life?

Dan 6:24 In accordance with Persian custom, this cruel punishment was transferred to those who had conspired against the king by provoking him into an unjust action (see also Esth 7:9-10). The king's great anger resulted in the execution of the evil officials and their families. Evil deeds often backfire on those who plan cruelty.

Dan 6:25-27 Nebuchadnezzar had come to believe that Israel's God was real because of the faithfulness of Daniel and his friends. Here Darius was also convinced of God's power because Daniel was faithful and God rescued him. Although Daniel was captive in a strange land, his devotion to God was a testimony to powerful rulers. If you find yourself in new surroundings, take the opportunity to testify about God's power in your life. Be faithful to God so he can use you to make an impact on others.

Daniel's Prayer for His People

DANIEL 9:1-19

It was the first year of the reign of Darius the Mede,
the son of Ahasuerus, who became king of the
Babylonians.* 2During the first year of his reign, I,
Daniel, learned from reading the word of the LORD, as
revealed to Jeremiah the prophet, that Jerusalem must
lie desolate for seventy years.* 3So I turned to the Lord
God and pleaded with him in prayer and fasting. I also
wore rough burlap and sprinkled myself with ashes.
4I prayed to the LORD my God and confessed:

"O Lord, you are a great and awesome God!
You always fulfill your covenant and keep your
promises of unfailing love to those who love
you and obey your commands. 5But we have
sinned and done wrong. We have rebelled against
you and scorned your commands and regulations.
6We have refused to listen to your servants the
prophets, who spoke on your authority to our
kings and princes and ancestors and to all the
people of the land.

7"Lord, you are in the right; but as you see, our
faces are covered with shame. This is true of all of
us, including the people of Judah and Jerusalem
and all Israel, scattered near and far, wherever you
have driven us because of our disloyalty to you.
8O LORD, we and our kings, princes, and ancestors
are covered with shame because we have sinned
against you. 9But the Lord our God is merciful and
forgiving, even though we have rebelled against
him. 10We have not obeyed the LORD our God,
for we have not followed the instructions he gave
us through his servants the prophets. 11All Israel
has disobeyed your instruction and turned away,
refusing to listen to your voice.

"So now the solemn curses and judgments
written in the Law of Moses, the servant of God,
have been poured down on us because of our sin.
12You have kept your word and done to us and
our rulers exactly as you warned. Never has there
been such a disaster as happened in Jerusalem.
13Every curse written against us in the Law of
Moses has come true. Yet we have refused to seek
mercy from the LORD our God by turning from
our sins and recognizing his truth. 14Therefore,
the LORD has brought upon us the disaster he
prepared. The LORD our God was right to do all
of these things, for we did not obey him.

15"O Lord our God, you brought lasting honor
to your name by rescuing your people from Egypt
in a great display of power. But we have sinned
and are full of wickedness. 16In view of all your
faithful mercies, Lord, please turn your furious
anger away from your city Jerusalem, your holy
mountain. All the neighboring nations mock
Jerusalem and your people because of our sins
and the sins of our ancestors.

17"O our God, hear your servant's prayer! Listen
as I plead. For your own sake, Lord, smile again on
your desolate sanctuary.

18"O my God, lean down and listen to me. Open
your eyes and see our despair. See how your city—
the city that bears your name—lies in ruins. We

Dn 9:1 Or *the Chaldeans.* **Dn 9:2** See Jer 25:11-12; 29:10.

Dan 9:1 The vision in Daniel 9 was given during the same time period as the events of Daniel 6. This Darius is the person mentioned in Daniel 6. The Ahasuerus (or Xerxes) mentioned here is not Esther's husband. The events described in the book of Esther happened about 50 years later.

Dan 9:2-3 Daniel pleaded with God to bring about the promised return of his people to their land. The prophet Jeremiah had written that God would not allow the captives to return to their land for 70 years (Jer 25:11-12; 29:10). Daniel knew of this prophecy and realized that this 70-year period was coming to an end.

Dan 9:3ff In Daniel's prayer for the nation he confessed his own sin, using the pronoun *we* throughout. In times of adversity, it's easy to blame others and excuse our own actions. If any Israelite was righteous, it was Daniel; and yet he confessed his sinfulness and need for God's forgiveness. Instead of looking for others to blame, first examine yourself and confess your own sins to God.

Dan 9:3-19 Daniel knew how to pray. As he prayed, he fasted, confessed his sins, and pleaded that God would reveal his will. He prayed with complete surrender to God and with complete openness to what God was saying to him. When you pray, do you speak openly to God? Examine your attitude. Talk to God with openness, vulnerability, and honesty, and be ready for God's reply.

Dan 9:4-6 The captives from Judah had rebelled against God. Their sins had led to their captivity. But God is merciful even to rebels if they confess their sins and return to him. Don't let your past disobedience keep you from returning to God. He is waiting for you and wants you to return to him.

Dan 9:6 God had sent many prophets to speak to his people through the years, but their messages had been ignored. The truth had been too painful to hear. God still speaks clearly and accurately through the Bible, and he also speaks through preachers, teachers, and concerned friends. Sometimes the truth hurts, and we would rather hear words that soothe, even if they are false. If you are unwilling to accept God's message, maybe you are trying to avoid making a painful change. Don't settle for a soothing lie that will bring harsh judgment. Accepting the truth even if it is painful can only help you.

Dan 9:11-13 Daniel mentioned the curses outlined in Deuteronomy 28. God had given the people of Israel a choice: Obey me and receive blessings, or disobey me and face curses. The affliction was meant to turn the people to God. When we face difficult circumstances, we should ask ourselves if God has reason to send judgment. If we think so, we must seek his forgiveness. Then we can ask him to help us through our troubles.

Dan 9:14 Daniel spoke about how God continually tried to bring Israel back to himself. Yet even after disaster struck them, they refused to obey him. God still uses circumstances, other people, and, most importantly, his Word to bring his people back to him. What would it take for God to get your attention?

Dan 9:17-19 It would be a mistake to read the Bible as dry history and miss the deep personal feelings. In this section, Daniel was crying out to the Lord. He had a deep concern for his nation and his people. So often our prayers are without passion and true compassion for others. Are you willing to pray by pouring out your deep feelings to God?

Dan 9:18 Daniel begged for mercy, not for help, because he knew that his people

make this plea, not because we deserve help, but
because of your mercy.
19“O Lord, hear. O Lord, forgive. O Lord, listen
and act! For your own sake, do not delay, O my God,
for your people and your city bear your name.”

Gabriel's Message about the Anointed One

DANIEL 9:20-27

I went on praying and confessing my sin and the sin
of my people, pleading with the LORD my God for Jerusalem, his holy mountain. 21As I was praying, Gabriel,
whom I had seen in the earlier vision, came swiftly
to me at the time of the evening sacrifice. 22He explained to me, “Daniel, I have come here to give you
insight and understanding. 23The moment you began praying, a command was given. And now I am
here to tell you what it was, for you are very precious
to God. Listen carefully so that you can understand
the meaning of your vision.
24“A period of seventy sets of seven* has been
decreed for your people and your holy city to finish
their rebellion, to put an end to their sin, to atone for
their guilt, to bring in everlasting righteousness, to
confirm the prophetic vision, and to anoint the Most
Holy Place.* 25Now listen and understand! Seven sets
of seven plus sixty-two sets of seven* will pass from the
time the command is given to rebuild Jerusalem until
a ruler—the Anointed One*—comes. Jerusalem will
be rebuilt with streets and strong defenses,* despite
the perilous times.
26“After this period of sixty-two sets of seven,* the
Anointed One will be killed, appearing to have accomplished nothing, and a ruler will arise whose armies
will destroy the city and the Temple. The end will come
with a flood, and war and its miseries are decreed from
that time to the very end. 27The ruler will make a treaty
with the people for a period of one set of seven,* but
after half this time, he will put an end to the sacrifices
and offerings. And as a climax to all his terrible deeds,*
he will set up a sacrilegious object that causes desecration,* until the fate decreed for this defiler is finally
poured out on him.”

Dn 9:24a Hebrew *seventy sevens.* **Dn 9:24b** Or *the Most Holy One.* **Dn 9:25a** Hebrew *Seven sevens plus sixty-two sevens.* **Dn 9:25b** Or *an anointed one;* similarly in 9:26. Hebrew reads *a messiah.* **Dn 9:25c** Or *and a moat,* or *and trenches.* **Dn 9:26** Hebrew *After sixty-two sevens.* **Dn 9:27a** Hebrew *for one seven.* **Dn 9:27b** Hebrew *And on the wing of abominations;* the meaning of the Hebrew is uncertain. **Dn 9:27c** Hebrew *an abomination of desolation.*

deserved God's wrath and punishment. God sends his help, not because we deserve it, but because he wants to show great mercy. If God would refuse to help us because of our sin, how could we complain? But when he sends mercy instead of the punishment we deserve, how can we withhold our praise and thanksgiving?

Dan 9:23 Just as God answered Daniel's prayer, so we can have confidence that God hears and answers our prayers.

Dan 9:24-25 Each day of these 70 weeks (“seventy sets of seven”) may represent one year. The Bible often uses round numbers to make a point, not to give an exact count. For example, Jesus said we are to forgive others “seventy times seven” (Matt 18:22). He did not mean a literal 490 times, but that we should forgive abundantly. Similarly, some scholars see this figure of 70 weeks as a figurative time period. Others interpret this time period as a literal 70 weeks or 490 years, observing that Christ's death came at the end of the 69 weeks (i.e., 483 years later). One interpretation places the 70th week as the seven years of the Great Tribulation, still in the future. Consequently the number would symbolize both the first and second comings of Christ.

Dan 9:25 These “strong defenses” show that Jerusalem will be rebuilt as a complete, fully functioning city.

Dan 9:26 The Messiah, the Anointed One, will be rejected and killed by his own people. His perfect, eternal Kingdom will come later.

Dan 9:26-27 There has been much discussion on the numbers, times, and events in these verses, and there are three basic views: (1) The prophecy was fulfilled in the past at the desecration of the Temple by Antiochus IV Epiphanes in 168–167 B.C. (see Dan 11:31); (2) it was fulfilled in the past at the destruction of the Temple by the Roman general Titus in A.D. 70 when one million Jews were killed; or (3) it is still to be fulfilled in the future under the Antichrist (see Matt 24:15).

Daniel prays for his people

***“O Lord, hear. O Lord, forgive. O Lord, listen and act!
For your own sake, do not delay, O my God,
for your people and your city bear your name.”***
Daniel 9:19

Return & Diaspora

GOD'S PEOPLE HAD LIVED IN EXILE for more than two generations. But then the Persian Empire swept through the entire region and conquered Judah's captors, the Babylonians. Persia's policy on dealing with conquered peoples was different from that of the Babylonians. Babylon removed the people from their lands and tried to get people to assimilate their culture, customs, and religion. Persia, however, had a policy of allowing people to return to their homelands and to resume their own customs and religion. God's people took advantage of this, returning to Jerusalem and beginning to restore their nation.

There were at least three waves of people who returned to Jerusalem from exile. The first and largest group went under the leadership of Zerubbabel immediately after Cyrus issued his decree allowing them to return in 538 B.C. This group resettled in the land around Jerusalem, a region that was now called Judea, and began the work of rebuilding the Temple. They faced opposition from the people who had been living in and around Jerusalem, and that combined with their own complacency meant that it took more than 20 years to finish their

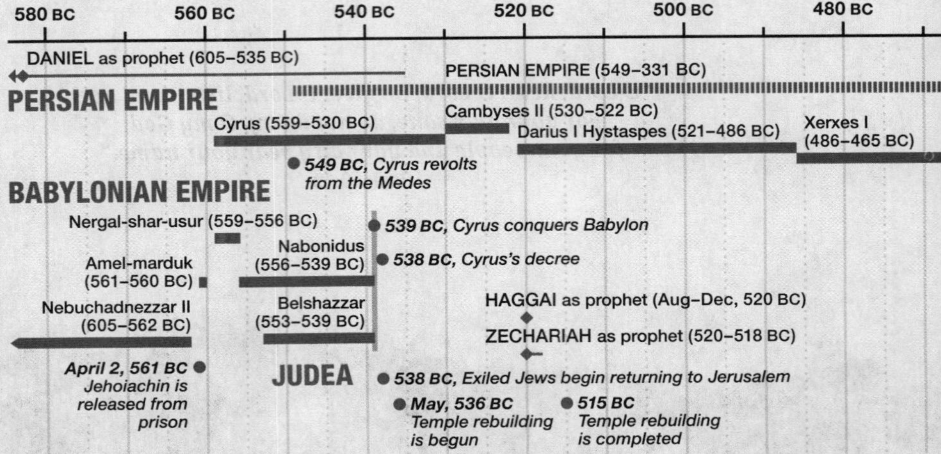

BOOKS

- 1 CHRONICLES
- 2 CHRONICLES
- EZRA
- NEHEMIAH
- ESTHER
- PSALMS
- DANIEL
- JOEL
- HAGGAI
- ZECHARIAH
- MALACHI

DATES

FROM:
538 BC
TO:
6 BC

THEMES

- Restoration
- Leadership
- Priorities
- Prayer
- Repentance
- Hope

work on the Temple. The prophets Haggai and Zechariah were instrumental in getting the people back to that important work.

The second wave of returnees was a smaller group, just about 2,000 families, under the leadership of Ezra in 458 B.C. Ezra was a scribe and a priest, and when he arrived in Judea he found the Temple rebuilt but the people's spiritual lives in ruin. The Israelites had intermarried with the people from surrounding nations and had begun to follow their gods instead of remaining faithful to the Lord. He confronted them with their sin and called them to repentance and renewal.

Nehemiah came with a small group of people in 455 B.C. to encourage the rebuilding of Jerusalem's wall. In spite of strong opposition from the people around Jerusalem, Nehemiah successfully led the Jews in rebuilding the wall around Jerusalem and securing the city for God's people. Nehemiah

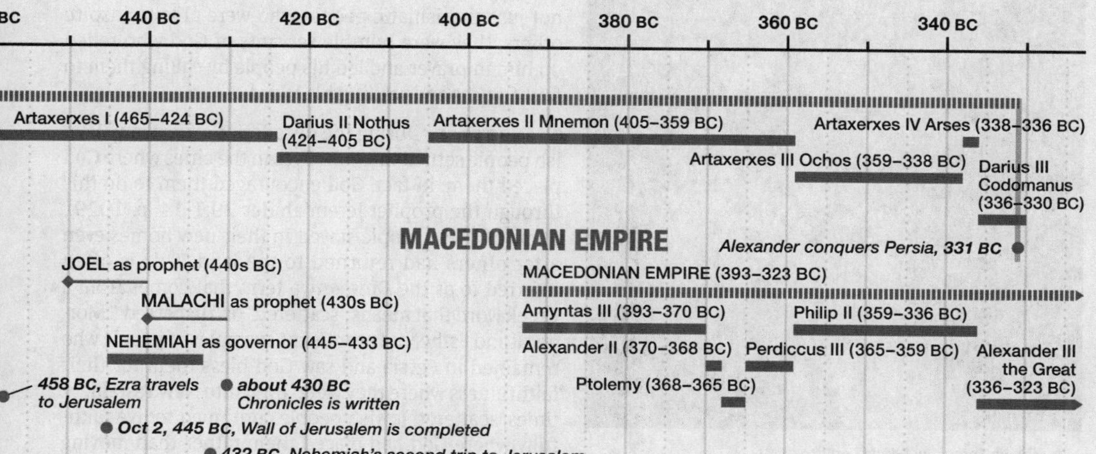

also confronted the people with their sins and called on them to repent and return to the Lord. After him, God also sent the prophets Joel and Malachi to challenge the people on their sinfulness and encourage them to remain faithful to the Lord while they awaited his final salvation.

Not everyone returned to the land from their homes in exile. Daniel served God faithfully throughout the Exile, and as an old man he continued to serve God in the first few years of Persian rule in Babylon. It was at this time that Daniel had some visions about the future of the world and God's people.

Esther became queen of the Persian kingdom in 479 B.C., between the first and second Jewish returns. The story of her life shows God's hand working behind the scenes for his people even when it appears that he is far off. God is sovereign over everything, and he cares for his people wherever they are.

The time of the return and Diaspora shows a consistent picture of a God who shepherds his people and tenderly restores them when they repent. It also provides us with a sense of longing for something more; a sense that God is going to do something huge to finally redeem and restore his people for good.

PEOPLE & CULTURE

■ **Persian Policy.** When Judah was conquered and taken into exile by Babylon, they were removed almost completely from their land and were forced to integrate with Babylonian culture and religion. But the Persian Empire conquered Babylon, and they brought a new policy toward conquered nations. The Persian emperors wanted to ingratiate the people to themselves, and they had a policy of tolerance toward conquered peoples that allowed them to return to their homelands and follow their own religions as part of the Persian Empire. In fact, Persia even funded the rebuilding of the Temple in Jerusalem. This was a significant change for the people of Judah, and they took full advantage of the new Persian policy.

Queen Esther, by Edwin Long

■ **Reconstructing Jerusalem.** Jerusalem had been decimated by the Babylonian conquest. The Temple was destroyed and the walls were in ruins. When the Jewish people returned to the land, one of their first tasks was to rebuild their capital city and the Temple of the Lord. But this was a large and expensive task, and they faced major opposition from the people in the surrounding areas.

■ **Jewish Leaders.** The task of returning to the land of Israel and rebuilding Jerusalem and the Temple was huge, and it required strong leadership. Zerubbabel, Ezra, Nehemiah, Haggai, and Zechariah were a few of the amazing leaders that God used to inspire and challenge his people to accomplish these tasks. These leaders were not just charismatic people who were able to inspire others; they were humble servants of God who relied on him in prayer and led his people by calling them to faithfulness and reading his Word.

■ **Diaspora.** During the decades of exile, many Jewish people settled into new lives in the cities where God placed them; in fact, God encouraged them to do this through the prophet Jeremiah (Jer 29:1-14, p. 1029). Many of these people stayed in their new homes even after others had returned to the land. This is often referred to as the *Diaspora*, a term that comes from a Greek word that means "scattered" or "dispersed." Mordecai and Esther are prominent examples of people who remained in Persia and saw God bless them for their faithfulness where they were. Even into New Testament times, scattered Jewish people continued to live faithfully where God had placed them rather than moving back to Jerusalem and the surrounding areas.

BOOKS IN THIS SECTION

EZRA

AUTHOR: Not stated, but probably Ezra

AUDIENCE: The exiles who returned from captivity

PURPOSE: To show God's faithfulness and the way he kept his promise to restore his people to their land

SETTING: Ezra follows 2 Chronicles as a history of the Jewish people, recording their return to the land after the Captivity.

DATE WRITTEN: Around 450 B.C., recording events from about 538–450 B.C.

NEHEMIAH

AUTHOR: Much of the book is written in the first person, suggesting Nehemiah as the author. Nehemiah probably wrote the book with Ezra serving as editor.

AUDIENCE: The exiles who returned from captivity

PURPOSE: Nehemiah is chronologically the last of the Old Testament historical books. It records the history of the third return to Jerusalem after captivity, telling how the walls were rebuilt and the people were renewed in their faith.

SETTING: Zerubbabel led the first return to Jerusalem in 538 B.C. In 458 B.C., Ezra led the second return. Finally, in 445 B.C., Nehemiah returned with the third group of exiles to rebuild the city walls.

DATE WRITTEN: Approximately 445–432 B.C.

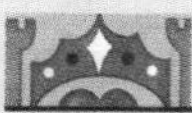

ESTHER

AUTHOR: Unknown

AUDIENCE: The people of Israel

PURPOSE: To demonstrate God's sovereignty and his loving care for his people.

SETTING: Although Esther follows Nehemiah in traditional Bibles, its events happen about 30 years prior to those recorded in Nehemiah. The story is set in the Persian Empire, and most of the action takes place in the king's palace in Susa, the Persian capital.

DATE WRITTEN: Approximately 470 B.C. (Esther became queen in 479 B.C.)

SPECIAL FEATURES: Esther is one of only two books in the Bible named for women.

JOEL

AUTHOR: Joel son of Pethuel

AUDIENCE: The people of Israel

PURPOSE: To warn of God's impending judgment because of sin and to urge the people to turn back to God

SETTING: The people had become prosperous and complacent. Taking God for granted, they had turned to self-centeredness, idolatry, and sin. Joel warned them that this kind of lifestyle would inevitably bring God's judgment.

DATE WRITTEN: Unknown, possibly around 800 B.C. or 430 B.C.

HAGGAI

AUTHOR: Haggai

AUDIENCE: The people living in Jerusalem and those who had returned from exile

PURPOSE: To call the people to complete the rebuilding of the Temple

SETTING: The Temple in Jerusalem had been destroyed in 586 B.C. Cyrus had allowed the Jews to return to their homeland and rebuild their Temple in 538 B.C. They had begun the work but had been unable to complete it. Through the ministry of Haggai and Zechariah, the Temple was completed (520–515 B.C.).

DATE WRITTEN: 520 B.C.

SPECIAL FEATURES: Haggai was the first of the postexilic prophets. The others were Joel, Zechariah, and Malachi. The literary style of this book is simple and direct.

ZECHARIAH

AUTHOR: Zechariah

AUDIENCE: The Jews in Jerusalem who had returned from their captivity in Babylon

PURPOSE: To encourage the rebuilding of the Temple and to give hope to God's people by revealing God's future deliverance through the Messiah

SETTING: The exiles had returned from Babylon to rebuild the Temple, but the work had been thwarted and stalled. Haggai and Zechariah confronted the people with their task and encouraged them to complete it.

DATE WRITTEN: Chapters 1–8 were written approximately 520–518 B.C. Chapters 9–14 were written later.

SPECIAL FEATURES: This book is the most apocalyptic and messianic of all the minor prophets.

The Prophet Malachi, by unknown 18th century artist

MALACHI

AUTHOR: Malachi

AUDIENCE: The people in Jerusalem

PURPOSE: To confront the people with their sins and to restore their relationship with God

SETTING: After Haggai and Zechariah had successfully rebuked the people for their failure to rebuild the Temple, Malachi confronted them with their neglect of the Temple and their false and profane worship.

SPECIAL FEATURES: Malachi's literary style employs a dramatic use of questions asked by God and his people (for example, see Mal 3:7-8).

For book information on **1 CHRONICLES** and **PSALMS**, see the introduction to United Monarchy, p. 430.

For book information on **2 CHRONICLES**, see the introduction to Splintered Nation, p. 687.

For book information on **DANIEL**, see the introduction to Exile, p. 1092.

MEGATHEMES

Rededication. When the people returned to their homeland, they rebuilt the altar and laid a new foundation for the Temple. They reinstated daily sacrifices and annual festivals, and rededicated themselves to a new spiritual worship of God. In rededicating the altar, the people were recommitting themselves to God and his service. To grow spiritually, our commitment must be reviewed and renewed often.

Opposition. Opposition came soon after the people returned to the land and rebuilt the altar. Enemies of the Jews used deceit to hinder the building and eventually forced them to stop. This opposition severely tested their wavering faith. There will always be adversaries who oppose God's work. The life of faith is never easy. But God can overrule all opposition to his service. When we face opposition, we must not falter or withdraw, but keep active and patient.

Prayer. Both Nehemiah and Ezra responded to problems with prayer. When Nehemiah began his work, he recognized the problem, immediately prayed, and then acted on the problem. Prayer is still God's mighty force in solving problems today. Prayer and action go hand in hand. Through prayer, God guides our preparation, teamwork, and diligent efforts to carry out his will.

God's Sovereignty. Several stories from this time period show how circumstances in the lives of the Jewish people came together to allow them to return to Judah and survive in the Diaspora. These "circumstances" were not the result of chance but of God's grand design. God is sovereign over every area of life. With God in charge, we can take courage. He can guide us through the circumstances we face in our lives. As we unite our lives' purposes to God's purpose, we benefit from his sovereign care.

Right Priorities. God had given the Jews the assignment to rebuild the Temple in Jerusalem when they returned from captivity. After 15 years, they still hadn't completed it. They were more concerned about building their own homes than finishing God's work. Haggai and Zechariah told them to get their priorities straight. It is easy to make other priorities more important than doing God's work, but God wants us to follow through and build up his kingdom. Don't stop, and don't make excuses. Set your heart on what is right and do it.

God's Encouragement. The prophets encouraged the people as they worked. They assured them of the divine presence of the Holy Spirit and final victory, and instilled in them the hope that the Messiah was coming and that he would reign. If God gives you a task, don't be afraid to get started. His resources are infinite. God will help you complete it by giving you encouragement from others along the way.

MAP

1 Persian Empire The Persian Empire was massive, stretching farther to the north, east, and west than the Babylonian Empire ever had. After sweeping through the region and taking control of Babylonian territories, the Persian leaders offered conquered peoples the opportunity to return to their homelands to live as semi-independent nations under Persian rule.

2 Babylon Most of the Jewish people had been taken to live in the city of Babylon during the time of their exile, and this is where the largest groups of returnees came from. They gathered in Babylon and traveled along the Euphrates River and then turned south once they reached the inhabited areas closer to the Mediterranean Sea. Zerubbabel led the first group of returnees, followed by Ezra and Nehemiah some years later.

3 Jerusalem When the people arrived back home in the Promised Land, most returnees settled down and built homes in areas around the city of Jerusalem, not in the city itself. There was a lot of rebuilding work to be done in the city, and God used leaders like Ezra, Haggai, Zechariah, and Nehemiah to motivate the people to complete the work of building the Temple and restoring the city walls.

4 Judea The area around Jerusalem came to be called Judea, not to be confused with the name of the nation of Judah that was exiled from the land. There were dozens of towns around the city of Jerusalem that comprised the new region of Judea where the returnees resettled.

5 Samaria While the people of Judah were exiled from the land, many of the people from the northern kingdom of Israel had been left in the land to intermarry with other conquered peoples that the Assyrians brought into the land. These people came to be known as Samaritans, and they lived in the region surrounding the city of Samaria, formerly the capital of the northern kingdom. The Samaritans were established in the land when the Jews came back to resettle Judea.

6 Susa Many Jewish people remained in the cities where God had placed them throughout the Persian Empire. Esther lived in the capital of this vast empire. The story of how God providentially put her in a position to save her people takes place in the palace in Susa.

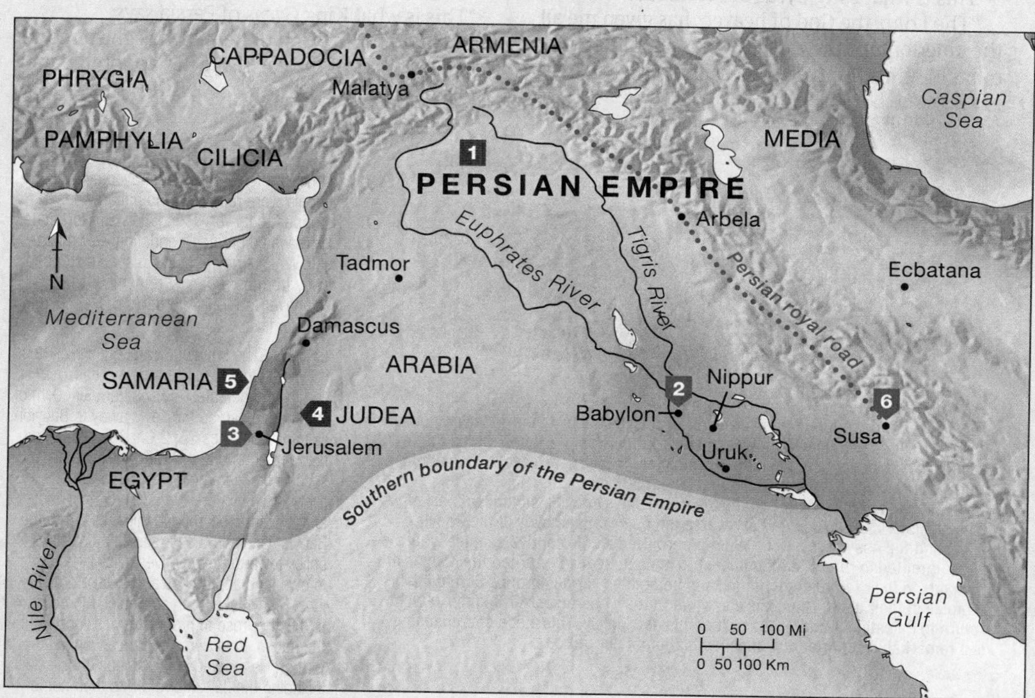

A. God's People Return to Jerusalem

After 70 years in exile, the captives from Judah were allowed to return to their homeland. Babylon, Judah's conqueror, had been themselves conquered by Persia, and King Cyrus of Persia issued an edict allowing the Jews to return to Jerusalem and rebuild their Temple. Isaiah had prophesied about this over 100 years earlier, even calling Cyrus by name. God is not surprised by the events of history! After disciplining his people through the exile in Babylon, God raised up the Persian Empire and Cyrus to free his people from bondage to the Babylonians and to return them to the land he had promised to Abraham, Isaac, and Jacob centuries before. Would the people finally prove faithful to God?

1. THE RETURN LED BY ZERUBBABEL

Nearly 50,000 people made this journey under Zerubbabel's leadership. Upon arrival they began to rebuild the Temple but quickly became discouraged by opposition, and the work stopped well short of completion.

Cyrus Allows the Exiles to Return PARALLEL

2 CHRONICLES 36:22-23

In the first year of King Cyrus of Persia,* the LORD fulfilled the prophecy he had given through Jeremiah.* He stirred the heart of Cyrus to put this proclamation in writing and to send it throughout his kingdom:

23"This is what King Cyrus of Persia says:

"The LORD, the God of heaven, has given me all the kingdoms of the earth. He has appointed me to build him a Temple at Jerusalem, which is in Judah. Any of you who are the LORD's people may go there for this task. And may the LORD your God be with you!"

EZRA 1:1-11

In the first year of King Cyrus of Persia,* the LORD fulfilled the prophecy he had given through Jeremiah.* He stirred the heart of Cyrus to put this proclamation in writing and to send it throughout his kingdom:

2"This is what King Cyrus of Persia says:

"The LORD, the God of heaven, has given me all the kingdoms of the earth. He has appointed me

2 Chr 36:22a The first year of Cyrus's reign over Babylon was 538 B.C. **2 Chr 36:22b** See Jer 25:11-12; 29:10. **Ezr 1:1a** The first year of Cyrus's reign over Babylon was 538 B.C. **Ezr 1:1b** See Jer 25:11-12; 29:10.

Cyrus Cylinder

The Cyrus Cylinder, found in an excavation at Babylon, is a nine-inch-long baked clay barrel inscribed in cuneiform. The inscription was written by Cyrus the Great as an effort to describe and justify his policies. The largely intact text is about 1,000 words in translation and dates to about 536 B.C.

One section of the inscription relates to the Jews and is a significant part of biblical history. Cyrus decided to reverse the deportation policy of the Babylonians and the Assyrians before him. He permitted all the captive peoples who had been uprooted to return to their ancestral homes. He also returned the images of the gods to their former sanctuaries and helped the various groups to rebuild the temples of their gods. Thus, it is clear that Cyrus's decree permitting the Jews to return to Palestine (Ezra 1) was part of this new policy. This piece of archaeology is a remarkable confirmation and illumination of Scripture.

2 Chr 36:22-23 Cyrus made this proclamation 48 years after the Temple was destroyed (2 Chr 36:18-19), in the year after he conquered Babylon. The book of Ezra tells the story of this proclamation and the return of the exiles to Judah.

2 Chr 36:22-23 Second Chronicles focuses on the proper and improper worship of God as symbolized by the Jerusalem Temple. David planned the Temple; Solomon built it and then put on the greatest dedication service the world has ever seen. Worship in the Temple was superbly organized.

But several evil kings defiled the Temple and degraded worship so that the people revered idols more highly than God. Finally, King Nebuchadnezzar of Babylon destroyed the Temple (2 Chr 36:19). The kings were gone, the Temple was destroyed, and the people were removed. The nation was stripped to its very foundation. But fortunately there was a greater foundation—God himself. When everything in life seems stripped away from us, we must remember that we still have God—his Word, his presence, and his promises.

Ezra 1:1 The book of Ezra opens in 538 B.C., 48 years after Nebuchadnezzar destroyed Jerusalem, defeated the southern kingdom of Judah, and carried the Jews away to Babylon as captives (2 Kgs 25; 2 Chr 36). Nebuchadnezzar died in 562 B.C., and because his successors were not strong, Babylon was overthrown by Persia in 539 B.C., just prior to the events recorded in this book. Both the Babylonians and the Persians had a relaxed policy toward their captives, allowing them to own land and homes and to take ordinary jobs. Many Jews such as Daniel, Mordecai, and Esther rose to prominent positions within the nation. King Cyrus of Persia went a step further: He allowed many groups of exiles, including the Jews, to return to their homelands. By doing this, he hoped to win their loyalty and thus provide buffer zones around the borders of his empire. For the Jews this was a day of hope, a new beginning.

Ezra 1:1 Cyrus, king of Persia (539–530 B.C.), had already begun his rise to power in the Near East by unifying the Medes and Persians into a strong empire. As he conquered cities, he treated the inhabitants

to build him a Temple at Jerusalem, which is in Judah. [3]Any of you who are his people may go to Jerusalem in Judah to rebuild this Temple of the LORD, the God of Israel, who lives in Jerusalem. And may your God be with you! [4]Wherever this Jewish remnant is found, let their neighbors contribute toward their expenses by giving them silver and gold, supplies for the journey, and livestock, as well as a voluntary offering for the Temple of God in Jerusalem."

[5]Then God stirred the hearts of the priests and Levites and the leaders of the tribes of Judah and

PROPHECIES FULFILLED BY THE RETURN OF ISRAEL FROM EXILE

God, through his faithful prophets, said that the people of Judah would be taken into captivity because of their sinfulness. But he also promised that they would return to Jerusalem and rebuild the city, the Temple, and the nation.

Reference	*Prophecy*	*Approximate Date*	*Fulfillment Date*	*Significance*
Isa 44:28	Cyrus would be used by God to guarantee the return of a remnant. Jerusalem would be rebuilt and the Temple restored.	688 B.C.	538 B.C.	As God named Cyrus even before he was born, God knows what will happen—he is in control.
Jer 25:12	Babylon would be punished for destroying Jerusalem and exiling God's people.	605 B.C.	539 B.C.	Cyrus the Great conquered Babylon. God may seem to allow evil to go unpunished, but consequences for wrongdoing are inevitable. God will punish evil.
Jer 29:10	The people would spend 70 years in Babylon; then God would bring them back to their homeland.	594 B.C.	538 B.C.	The 70 years of captivity passed (see the third note on Ezra 1:1, below), and God provided the opportunity for Zerubbabel to lead the first group of captives home. God's plans may allow for hardship, but his desire is for our good.
Dan 5:17-31	God had judged the Babylonian Empire. It would be given to the Medes and the Persians, forming a new world power.	539 B.C.	539 B.C.	Belshazzar was killed and Babylon was conquered the same night. God's judgment is accurate and swift. God knows the point of no return in each of our lives. Until then, he allows us the freedom to repent and seek his forgiveness.

with mercy. Although not a servant of Yahweh, God used Cyrus to return the Jews to their homeland. Cyrus may have been shown the prophecy of Isaiah 44:28–45:6, written over a century earlier, which predicted that Cyrus himself would help the Jews return to Jerusalem. Daniel, a prominent government official (Dan 5:29; 6:28), would have been familiar with the prophecy. The book of Daniel has more to say about Cyrus.

Ezra 1:1 Jeremiah prophesied that the Jews would remain in captivity for 70 years (Jer 25:11; 29:10). The 70-year period has been calculated two different ways: (1) from the first captivity in 605 B.C. (2 Kgs 24:1) until the altar was rebuilt by the returned exiles in 537 B.C. (Ezra 3:1-6), or (2) from the destruction of the Temple in 586 B.C. until the exiles finished rebuilding it in 515 B.C. Many scholars prefer the second approach because the Temple was the focus and heartbeat of the nation. Without the Temple, the Jews did not consider themselves reestablished as a nation.

Ezra 1:2 Cyrus was not a Jew, but God worked through him to return the exiled Jews to their homeland. Cyrus gave the proclamation allowing their return, and he gave them protection, money, and the Temple articles taken by Nebuchadnezzar. When you face difficult situations and feel surrounded, outnumbered, overpowered, or outclassed, remember that God's power is not limited to your resources. He is able to use anyone to carry out his plans.

Ezra 1:2-4 This proclamation permitted the Jews to work together to accomplish the huge task of rebuilding the Temple. Some did the actual building, while others operated the supply lines. Significant ventures require teamwork, with certain people serving in the forefront and others providing support. Each function is vital to accomplishing the task. When you're asked to serve, do so faithfully as a team member, no matter who gets the credit.

Ezra 1:5 Cyrus was king over the entire region that had once been Assyria and Babylon. Assyria had deported the Israelites from the northern kingdom (Israel) in 722 B.C. Babylon, the next world power, had taken Israelites captive from the southern kingdom (Judah) in 586 B.C. Therefore, when the Medo-Persian Empire came to power, King Cyrus's proclamation of freedom went to all the original 12 tribes, but only Judah and Benjamin responded and returned to rebuild God's Temple. The 10 tribes of the northern kingdom had been so fractured and dispersed by Assyria, and so much time had elapsed since their captivity, that many may have been unsure of their real heritage. Thus, they were unwilling to share in the vision of rebuilding the Temple.

Ezra 1:5 God moved the hearts of the leaders, family heads, priests, and Levites and gave them a great desire to return to Jerusalem to rebuild the Temple. Major changes begin on the inside as God works on our attitudes, beliefs, and desires. These inner changes lead to faithful actions. After 48 years of captivity, the arrogant Jewish nation had been humbled. When the people's attitudes and desires changed, God ended their punishment and gave them another opportunity to go home and try again. In the New Testament, Paul reminds us that "God is working in you, giving you the desire and the power to do what pleases him" (Phil 2:13). Doing God's will begins with your desires. Are you willing to be humble, to be open to his opportunities, and to move at his direction? Ask God to give you the desire to follow him more closely.

Ezra 1:5-6 Many Jews chose to go to Jerusalem, but many more chose to remain in Babylon rather than return to their homeland. The journey back to Jerusalem was difficult, dangerous, and expensive, lasting over four months. Travel conditions were poor;

▶ EZRA 1:1-11 ***(cont.)***

Benjamin to go to Jerusalem to rebuild the Temple
of the LORD. 6And all their neighbors assisted by giving them articles of silver and gold, supplies for the
journey, and livestock. They gave them many valuable
gifts in addition to all the voluntary offerings.
7King Cyrus himself brought out the articles that
King Nebuchadnezzar had taken from the LORD's
Temple in Jerusalem and had placed in the temple
of his own gods. 8Cyrus directed Mithredath, the
treasurer of Persia, to count these items and present
them to Sheshbazzar, the leader of the exiles returning to Judah.* 9This is a list of the items that were
returned:

gold basins 30
silver basins 1,000
silver incense burners* 29
10 gold bowls 30
silver bowls 410
other items 1,000

11In all, there were 5,400 articles of gold and silver.
Sheshbazzar brought all of these along when the
exiles went from Babylon to Jerusalem.

Ezr 1:8 Hebrew *Sheshbazzar, the prince of Judah.* **Ezr 1:9** The meaning of this Hebrew word is uncertain.

Exiles Who Returned with Zerubbabel

EZRA 2:1-70

Here is the list of the Jewish exiles of the provinces
who returned from their captivity. King Nebuchadnezzar had deported them to Babylon, but now they
returned to Jerusalem and the other towns in Judah
where they originally lived. 2Their leaders were Zerubbabel, Jeshua, Nehemiah, Seraiah, Reelaiah, Mordecai,
Bilshan, Mispar, Bigvai, Rehum, and Baanah.

This is the number of the men of Israel who returned from exile:

3 The family of Parosh 2,172
4 The family of Shephatiah 372
5 The family of Arah 775
6 The family of Pahath-moab (descendants of Jeshua and Joab) 2,812
7 The family of Elam 1,254
8 The family of Zattu 945
9 The family of Zaccai 760
10 The family of Bani 642
11 The family of Bebai 623
12 The family of Azgad 1,222
13 The family of Adonikam 666

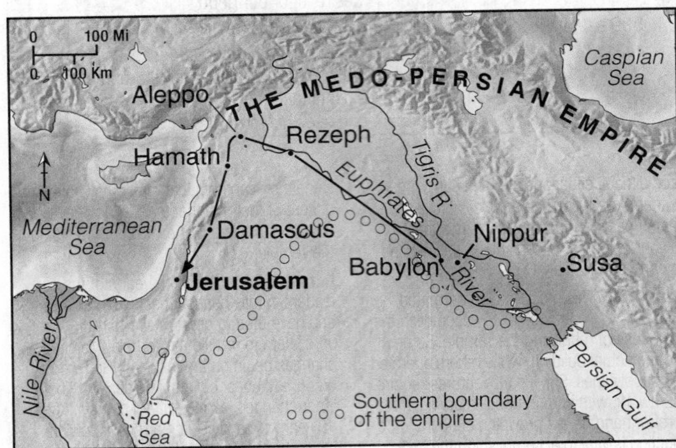

THE JOURNEY HOME *The vast Medo-Persian Empire included all the area on this map and more. A group of exiles began the long trip back to their homeland. Many exiles preferred the comfort and security they had in Babylon to the dangerous trip back to Jerusalem, and so they decided to stay in Babylon.*

Jerusalem and the surrounding countryside were in ruins; and the people living in the area were hostile.

Persian records indicate that many Jews in captivity had accumulated great wealth. Returning to Jerusalem would have meant giving up everything they had and starting over. Many people couldn't bring themselves to do that; they preferred wealth and security to the sacrifice that God's work would require. Their priorities were upside down (Mark 4:18-19). We must not let our comfort, security, or material possessions prevent us from doing what God wants.

Ezra 1:7 When King Nebuchadnezzar ransacked the Temple, he took many of the valuable furnishings with him. What he did not take, he burned (2 Chr 36:18-19). Most of the captured items were made of solid gold (1 Kgs 7:48-50), and Cyrus kindly returned them to the Jews for the Temple they would soon rebuild.

Ezra 1:8 Either Sheshbazzar was the Babylonian name for Zerubbabel, one of the Jewish leaders during the first return (Ezra 2:2; 3:8; 4:3), or he was a government official with responsibility for the returning party. The reasons Sheshbazzar may be identified with Zerubbabel are as follows: (1) Both were called governors (Ezra 5:14; Hag 1:1); (2) both laid the Temple foundation (Ezra 3:8; 5:16); (3) Jews in exile were often given Babylonian names (see Dan 1:7 where Daniel and his companions were given new names).

Ezra 1:9-11 Every article of gold and silver was a witness to God's protection and care. Although many years had passed, God delivered these Temple articles back to his people. We may be discouraged by events in life, but we must never give up our hope in God's promises to us. The turning point may be just ahead.

Ezra 2:2 The Nehemiah listed here is a different person from the one who rebuilt Jerusalem's walls 80 years later, and the Mordecai listed here is not the one who appears in the book of Esther.

Ezra 2:2 This first list is made up of men who were leaders. The same list occurs in Nehemiah 7:7.

Ezra 2:2-35 These people were from the tribes of Judah and Benjamin (Ezra 1:5).

Ezra 2:3-35 This list is the major group of those returning, divided by families (Ezra 2:3-20) or by cities (Ezra 2:21-35). Ezra 2:36 begins listing priests, Levites, and other Temple servants.

14 The family of Bigvai 2,056
15 The family of Adin 454
16 The family of Ater
(descendants of Hezekiah) 98
17 The family of Bezai 323
18 The family of Jorah 112
19 The family of Hashum 223
20 The family of Gibbar 95
21 The people of Bethlehem 123
22 The people of Netophah 56
23 The people of Anathoth 128
24 The people of Beth-azmaveth* 42
25 The people of Kiriath-jearim,* Kephirah,
and Beeroth 743
26 The people of Ramah and Geba 621
27 The people of Micmash 122
28 The people of Bethel and Ai 223
29 The citizens of Nebo 52
30 The citizens of Magbish 156
31 The citizens of West Elam* 1,254
32 The citizens of Harim 320
33 The citizens of Lod, Hadid, and Ono 725
34 The citizens of Jericho 345
35 The citizens of Senaah 3,630

36These are the priests who returned from exile:
The family of Jedaiah
(through the line of Jeshua) 973
37 The family of Immer 1,052
38 The family of Pashhur 1,247
39 The family of Harim 1,017

40These are the Levites who returned from exile:
The families of Jeshua and Kadmiel
(descendants of Hodaviah) 74
41 The singers of the family of Asaph 128
42 The gatekeepers of the families of Shallum,
Ater, Talmon, Akkub, Hatita, and Shobai . . . 139

43The descendants of the following Temple servants returned from exile:
Ziha, Hasupha, Tabbaoth,
44 Keros, Siaha, Padon,
45 Lebanah, Hagabah, Akkub,
46 Hagab, Shalmai,* Hanan,
47 Giddel, Gahar, Reaiah,
48 Rezin, Nekoda, Gazzam,
49 Uzza, Paseah, Besai,
50 Asnah, Meunim, Nephusim,
51 Bakbuk, Hakupha, Harhur,
52 Bazluth, Mehida, Harsha,
53 Barkos, Sisera, Temah,
54 Neziah, and Hatipha.

55The descendants of these servants of King Solomon returned from exile:
Sotai, Hassophereth, Peruda,
56 Jaalah, Darkon, Giddel,
57 Shephatiah, Hattil, Pokereth-hazzebaim, and Ami.

58In all, the Temple servants and the descendants of Solomon's servants numbered 392.

59Another group returned at this time from the
towns of Tel-melah, Tel-harsha, Kerub, Addan, and Immer. However, they could not prove that they or their
families were descendants of Israel. 60This group included the families of Delaiah, Tobiah, and Nekoda—a
total of 652 people.
61Three families of priests—Hobaiah, Hakkoz, and
Barzillai—also returned. (This Barzillai had married a
woman who was a descendant of Barzillai of Gilead,
and he had taken her family name.) 62They searched

Ezr 2:24 As in parallel text at Neh 7:28; Hebrew reads *Azmaveth.* **Ezr 2:25** As in some Hebrew manuscripts and Greek version (see also Neh 7:29); Hebrew reads *Kiriath-arim.* **Ezr 2:31** Or *of the other Elam.* **Ezr 2:46** As in an alternate reading of the Masoretic Text (see also Neh 7:48); the other alternate reads *Shamlai.*

538 BC

Zerubbabel leads 50,000 people back to Jerusalem

THE RETURN FROM EXILE

Babylon, the once-mighty nation that had destroyed Jerusalem and carried the people of Judah into captivity, had itself become a defeated nation. Persia was the new world power, and under its new foreign policy, captured peoples were allowed to return to their homelands. The people of Judah and Israel returned to their land in three successive waves.

Year	*Number of People Returning*	*Persian King*	*Jewish Leader*	*Main Accomplishment*
538 B.C.	50,000	Cyrus	Zerubbabel	They rebuilt the Temple, but only after a 20-year struggle. The work was halted for several years but was finally finished.
458 B.C.	2,000 men and their families	Artaxerxes	Ezra	Ezra confronted the spiritual disobedience of the people, and they repented and established worship at the Temple. But the wall of Jerusalem remained in ruins.
445 B.C.	Small group	Artaxerxes	Nehemiah	The wall was rebuilt, the city was revitalized, and a spiritual awakening followed. But the people still struggled with ongoing disobedience.

Ezra 2:59-63 Genealogies were very important credentials to the Hebrew people. If they could not prove they had descended from Abraham, they were not considered true Jews and were excluded from full participation in Jewish community life. In addition, some privileges were restricted to members of certain tribes. For example, only descendants of Levi (Abraham's great-grandson) could serve in the Temple.

▶ **EZRA 2:1-70** ***(cont.)***

for their names in the genealogical records, but they
were not found, so they were disqualified from serving as priests. 63The governor told them not to eat the
priests' share of food from the sacrifices until a priest
could consult the LORD about the matter by using the
Urim and Thummim—the sacred lots.
64So a total of 42,360 people returned to Judah,
65in addition to 7,337 servants and 200 singers, both
men and women. 66They took with them 736 horses,
245 mules, 67435 camels, and 6,720 donkeys.
68When they arrived at the Temple of the LORD in
Jerusalem, some of the family leaders made voluntary
offerings toward the rebuilding of God's Temple on
its original site, 69and each leader gave as much as
he could. The total of their gifts came to 61,000 gold
coins,* 6,250 pounds* of silver, and 100 robes for
the priests.
70So the priests, the Levites, the singers, the gatekeepers, the Temple servants, and some of the common people settled in villages near Jerusalem. The rest
of the people returned to their own towns throughout
Israel.

Psalm 126

THEME: What does great things. His power not only releases us from sin's captive hold but brings us back to him.

AUTHOR: Anonymous, possibly written to celebrate the exiles' return from captivity (Ezra 1)

A song for pilgrims ascending to Jerusalem.

1 When the LORD brought back his exiles
to Jerusalem,*
it was like a dream!
2 We were filled with laughter,
and we sang for joy.
And the other nations said,
"What amazing things the LORD has done
for them."
3 Yes, the LORD has done amazing things for us!
What joy!
4 Restore our fortunes, LORD,
as streams renew the desert.
5 Those who plant in tears
will harvest with shouts of joy.
6 They weep as they go to plant their seed,
but they sing as they return with the harvest.

Psalm 147

THEME: What gives God joy? Although God created everything, his greatest joy comes from our genuine worship and trust.

AUTHOR: Anonymous, written when the exiles returned to Jerusalem

1 Praise the LORD!

How good to sing praises to our God!
How delightful and how fitting!
2 The LORD is rebuilding Jerusalem
and bringing the exiles back to Israel.
3 He heals the brokenhearted
and bandages their wounds.
4 He counts the stars
and calls them all by name.
5 How great is our Lord! His power is absolute!
His understanding is beyond comprehension!
6 The LORD supports the humble,
but he brings the wicked down into the dust.
7 Sing out your thanks to the LORD;
sing praises to our God with a harp.
8 He covers the heavens with clouds,
provides rain for the earth,

Ezr 2:69a Hebrew *61,000 darics of gold,* about 1,100 pounds or 500 kilograms in weight. **Ezr 2:69b** Hebrew *5,000 minas* [3,000 kilograms]. **Ps 126:1** Hebrew *Zion.*

Ezra 2:63 The governor mentioned here was probably Zerubbabel. The sacred lots were probably the Urim and Thummim, two objects originally carried in the garment worn by the high priest. They were used to determine God's will in important matters. (For more on the Urim and Thummim, see the note on Lev 8:8, p. 210.) The priests' share of food was their allotted portion of meat that was sacrificed on the altar.

Ezra 2:68-69 As the Temple reconstruction progressed, everyone contributed freewill offerings according to their ability. Some were able to give huge gifts and did so generously. Everyone's effort and cooperation were required, and the people gave as much as they could. Often we limit our giving to 10 percent of our income. The Bible emphasizes that we should give from the heart all that we are able (2 Cor 8:12; 9:6). Let your gift be decided by God's call to give generously, not by the amount you have left over.

Ezra 2:69 The money given was enough to start rebuilding the Temple. The people put what resources they had to their best use. They were enthusiastic and sincere, but this Temple would never match the splendor of Solomon's. The amount of money David gathered to start the building of Solomon's Temple was a thousand times more (1 Chr 22:14). Some people wept as they remembered the glorious Temple that had been destroyed (Ezra 3:12).

Ps 126:5-6 God's ability to restore life is beyond our understanding. Forests burn down and are able to grow back. Broken bones heal. Even grief is not a permanent condition. Our tears can be seeds that will grow into a harvest of joy because God is able to bring good out of tragedy. When burdened by sorrow, know that your times of grief will end and that you will again find joy. We must be patient as we wait. God's great harvest of joy is coming!

Ps 147:5 Sometimes we feel as if we don't understand ourselves—what we want, how we feel, what's wrong with us, or what we should do about it. But God's understanding has no limit, and therefore he understands us fully. If you feel troubled and don't understand yourself, remember that God understands you perfectly. Take your mind off yourself and focus on God. Seek to become more and more like him. The more you learn about God and his ways, the better you will understand yourself.

Ps 147:10-11 We may spend a lot of effort trying to sharpen our skills or become physically fit. There is nothing wrong with doing so, and, in fact, our gifts can be used to glorify God. But when we use our gifts with no regard for God, they are indeed worth little. It is our honor and trust that God desires. When he has those, then he will use our gifts and strengths in ways far greater than we can imagine.

and makes the grass grow in mountain
pastures.
9 He gives food to the wild animals
and feeds the young ravens when they cry.
10 He takes no pleasure in the strength of a horse
or in human might.
11 No, the LORD's delight is in those who fear him,
those who put their hope in his
unfailing love.
12 Glorify the LORD, O Jerusalem!
Praise your God, O Zion!
13 For he has strengthened the bars of
your gates
and blessed your children within
your walls.
14 He sends peace across your nation
and satisfies your hunger with the finest
wheat.
15 He sends his orders to the world—
how swiftly his word flies!
16 He sends the snow like white wool;
he scatters frost upon the ground like ashes.
17 He hurls the hail like stones.*
Who can stand against his freezing cold?
18 Then, at his command, it all melts.
He sends his winds, and the ice thaws.
19 He has revealed his words to Jacob,
his decrees and regulations to Israel.
20 He has not done this for any other nation;
they do not know his regulations.

Praise the LORD!

The Altar Is Rebuilt

EZRA 3:1-6

In early autumn,* when the Israelites had settled in
their towns, all the people assembled in Jerusalem
with a unified purpose. 2Then Jeshua son of Jehozadak* joined his fellow priests and Zerubbabel son of
Shealtiel with his family in rebuilding the altar of the
God of Israel. They wanted to sacrifice burnt offerings
on it, as instructed in the Law of Moses, the man of
God. 3Even though the people were afraid of the local
residents, they rebuilt the altar at its old site. Then they
began to sacrifice burnt offerings on the altar to the
LORD each morning and evening.
4They celebrated the Festival of Shelters as prescribed in the Law, sacrificing the number of burnt
offerings specified for each day of the festival.

Ps 147:17 Hebrew *like bread crumbs.* **Ezr 3:1** Hebrew *In the seventh month.* The year is not specified, so it may have been during Cyrus's first year (538 B.C.) or second year (537 B.C.). The seventh month of the ancient Hebrew lunar calendar occurred within the months of September/October 538 B.C. and October/November 537 B.C. **Ezr 3:2** Hebrew *Jozadak*, a variant spelling of Jehozadak; also in 3:8.

Ps 147:19-20 The nation of Israel (the descendants of Jacob) was special to God because God brought his laws to its people, and through its people he sent his Son, Jesus Christ. Now any individual who follows God is just as special to him. In fact, the Bible says that the real nation of Israel is not a specific people or geographic place but the community of all who believe in and obey God (see Gal 3:28-29; 6:15-16).

Ezra 3:2-3 The Jews built the altar as one of their first official acts. It symbolized God's presence and protection. It also demonstrated their purpose as a nation and their commitment to serve God alone. Zerubbabel sacrificed burnt offerings as the law of Moses instructed (Lev 1–7). The sacrifices were essential because they demonstrated that the people were seeking God's guidance, rededicating themselves to living as he commanded, and daily asking him to forgive their sins.

Ezra 3:3 The Jews were afraid they were going to be attacked by the surrounding people—a mixed group whose ancestors had been conquered by the Assyrians. Foreigners had been forced to resettle in the northern kingdom of Israel after Israel was defeated and her people taken captive in 722 B.C. (Ezra 4:1-2). This resettlement procedure was a common tactic of the Assyrians to prevent strong nationalistic uprisings by conquered peoples. Some of the resettled people in Israel had migrated south near Jerusalem, and they may have thought the returning exiles threatened their claim on the land.

Ezra 3:4 The Festival of Shelters lasted seven days (see Lev 23:33-36). During this time the people lived in temporary dwellings (tents, booths, lean-tos) as their ancestors had done years before when they journeyed through the wilderness on their way to the Promised Land. The festival reminded the people of God's past protection and guidance in the wilderness and of his continued love for them.

He sends the snow like white wool; he scatters frost upon the ground like ashes.
Psalm 147:16

▸ **EZRA 3:1-6** ***(cont.)***

5They also offered the regular burnt offerings and the offerings required for the new moon celebrations and the annual festivals as prescribed by the LORD. The people also gave voluntary offerings to the LORD. 6Fifteen days before the Festival of Shelters began,* the priests had begun to sacrifice burnt offerings to the LORD. This was even before they had started to lay the foundation of the LORD's Temple.

The People Begin to Rebuild the Temple

EZRA 3:7-13

Then the people hired masons and carpenters and bought cedar logs from the people of Tyre and Sidon, paying them with food, wine, and olive oil. The logs were brought down from the Lebanon mountains and floated along the coast of the Mediterranean Sea* to Joppa, for King Cyrus had given permission for this.

8The construction of the Temple of God began in midspring,* during the second year after they arrived in Jerusalem. The work force was made up of everyone who had returned from exile, including Zerubbabel son of Shealtiel, Jeshua son of Jehozadak and his fellow priests, and all the Levites. The Levites who were twenty years old or older were put in charge of rebuilding the LORD's Temple. 9The workers at the Temple of God were supervised by Jeshua with his sons and relatives, and Kadmiel and his sons, all descendants of Hodaviah.* They were helped in this task by the Levites of the family of Henadad.

10When the builders completed the foundation of the LORD's Temple, the priests put on their robes and took their places to blow their trumpets. And the Levites, descendants of Asaph, clashed their cymbals to praise the LORD, just as King David had prescribed. 11With praise and thanks, they sang this song to the LORD:

"He is so good!
His faithful love for Israel endures forever!"

Then all the people gave a great shout, praising the LORD because the foundation of the LORD's Temple had been laid.

12But many of the older priests, Levites, and other leaders who had seen the first Temple wept aloud when they saw the new Temple's foundation. The others, however, were shouting for joy. 13The joyful shouting and weeping mingled together in a loud noise that could be heard far in the distance.

Ezr 3:6 Hebrew *On the first day of the seventh month.* This day in the ancient Hebrew lunar calendar occurred in September or October. The Festival of Shelters began on the fifteenth day of the seventh month. **Ezr 3:7** Hebrew *the sea.* **Ezr 3:8** Hebrew *in the second month.* This month in the ancient Hebrew lunar calendar occurred within the months of April and May 536 B.C. **Ezr 3:9** Hebrew *sons of Judah* (i.e., *bene Yehudah*). *Bene* might also be read here as the proper name Binnui; *Yehudah* is probably another name for Hodaviah. Compare 2:40; Neh 7:43; 1 Esdras 5:58.

Ezra 3:5 Almost immediately after arriving in the new land, the returning exiles built an altar. The people began worshiping God through sacrifices even before the Temple foundation was laid. After many years in captivity, they had learned their lesson—they knew that God does not offer special protection to people who ignore him. They had been carried off by the Babylonians when they were relatively strong; here they were few, weak, and surrounded by enemies. If ever they needed to rely on God's power, it was at this time. They realized the importance of obeying God from the heart, and not merely out of habit. If we want God's help when we undertake large tasks, we must make staying close to him our top priority.

Ezra 3:5 These sacrifices were originally set up under the law of Moses (see Lev 1; 6:8-13). The festivals are described in Leviticus 23. At the beginning of every month, they held a special observance (Num 10:10).

Ezra 3:7 When Solomon built the first Temple (2 Chr 2), he also exchanged food and olive oil—plentiful resources in Israel—for wood, a resource Israel lacked. The wood came from Tyre and Sidon that time too.

Ezra 3:8 Why was the Lord's Temple begun first, even before the city wall? The Temple was used for spiritual purposes; the wall, for military and political purposes. God had always been the nation's protector, and the Jews knew that the strongest stone wall would not protect them if God was not with them. They knew that putting their spiritual lives in order was a far higher priority than assuring the national defense.

Ezra 3:8 It took from September (Ezra 3:1; September was the seventh month because the year began in March) to April just to prepare to build the Temple. The exiles took time to make plans because the project was important to them. Preparation may not feel heroic or spiritual, but it is vital to any project meant to be done well.

Ezra 3:10-11 David had given clear instructions concerning the use of music in worship services in the Temple (1 Chr 16; 25).

Ezra 3:10-11 Completing the foundation for the Temple required great effort on the part of all involved. But no one tried to get individual praise for their own hard work. Instead, everyone praised God for what had been done. All good gifts come from God—talents, abilities, strength, and leadership. We should thank God for what has been done in and through us!

Ezra 3:11 The Bible records many songs and musical events. For a list of such events, see the chart on p. 163.

Ezra 3:12 Fifty years after its destruction, the Temple was being rebuilt (536 B.C.). Some of the older people remembered Solomon's Temple, and they wept because the new Temple would not be as glorious as the first one. But the beauty of the building was not nearly as important to God as were the attitudes of the builders and worshipers. God cares more about who we are than what we accomplish. Our world is always changing, and once-magnificent accomplishments decay and disappear. Seek to serve God wholeheartedly. Then you won't need to compare your work with anyone else's.

Ezra 3:12 Because the new Temple was built on the foundation of Solomon's Temple, the two structures were not that different in size. But the old Temple was far more ornate and was surrounded by many buildings and a vast courtyard. Both Temples were constructed of imported cedar wood, but Solomon's was decorated with vast amounts of gold and precious stones. Solomon's Temple took over seven years to build; Zerubbabel's took about four years. Solomon's Temple was at the hub of a thriving city; Zerubbabel's was surrounded by ruins. No wonder the people wept.

Ezra 3:13 The celebration after laying the Temple foundation was marked by contrasts of emotion—shouts of joy and sounds of weeping. Both were appropriate. The Holy Spirit can stimulate us both to rejoice over the goodness of his grace and to grieve over the sins that required him to correct us. When we come into the presence of almighty God, we may feel full of joy and thanksgiving, yet at the same time be sobered by our shortcomings.

Ezra 4:1-3 The enemies of Judah and Benjamin were people who had been relocated in the northern kingdom when Assyria conquered Israel (see 2 Kgs 17 and the note on Ezra 3:3, p. 1155). In an attempt to infiltrate and disrupt the project, these people offered to help in the rebuilding. They wanted to keep a close eye on what the Jews were doing. They

Enemies Oppose the Rebuilding

EZRA 4:1-5
The enemies of Judah and Benjamin heard that the exiles were rebuilding a Temple to the LORD, the God of Israel. [2]So they approached Zerubbabel and the other leaders and said, "Let us build with you, for we worship your God just as you do. We have sacrificed to him ever since King Esarhaddon of Assyria brought us here."

[3]But Zerubbabel, Jeshua, and the other leaders of Israel replied, "You may have no part in this work. We alone will build the Temple for the LORD, the God of Israel, just as King Cyrus of Persia commanded us."

[4]Then the local residents tried to discourage and frighten the people of Judah to keep them from their work. [5]They bribed agents to work against them and to frustrate their plans. This went on during the entire reign of King Cyrus of Persia and lasted until King Darius of Persia took the throne.*

Ezr 4:5 Darius reigned 521–486 B.C.

ZERUBBABEL

God's people had been exiled in Babylon for many years. Many had settled into comfortable lifestyles there and wanted to stay. There were, however, almost 60,000 who had not forgotten Judah. When Babylon was defeated in 539 B.C., the Persian ruler, Cyrus, allowed the Jews to return to Jerusalem and rebuild their Temple. Zerubbabel led the first and largest group back to the Promised Land. • Zerubbabel's leadership was by right and recognition. Not only was he a descendant of David, but he also had personal leadership qualities. When the people arrived in Judah, they were given time to establish living quarters and then were called to begin the work. They began not by laying the city walls or constructing government buildings, but by rebuilding the altar, worshiping God together, and celebrating a feast. Under Zerubbabel's leadership, they established a spiritual foundation for their building efforts. • The Temple foundation was then quickly completed, and another round of celebration followed. But soon two problems arose. A few old men remembered Solomon's glorious Temple and were saddened at how much smaller and less glorious this one was. Also, some enemies of the Jews tried to infiltrate the workforce and stop the building with political pressure. Fear caused the work to grind to a halt. The people went to their homes, and 16 years passed. • We do not know what Zerubbabel did during this time. His discouragement, following those first months of excitement and accomplishment, must have been deep. Those feelings eventually hardened into hopelessness. So God sent the prophets Haggai and Zechariah to be Zerubbabel's encouraging companions. They confronted the people's reluctance and comforted their fears. The work began once again with renewed energy and was completed in four years. • Zerubbabel, like many of us, knew how to start well but found it hard to keep going. His successes depended on the quality of encouragement he received. Zerubbabel let discouragement get the better of him. But when he let God take control, the work was finished. God is always in control. We must not let circumstances or lack of encouragement slow us from doing the tasks God has given us.

Strengths and accomplishments	• Led the first group of Jewish exiles back to Jerusalem from Babylon • Completed the rebuilding of God's Temple • Demonstrated wisdom in the help he accepted and refused
Weaknesses and mistakes	• Needed constant encouragement • Allowed problems and resistance to stop the rebuilding work
Lessons from his life	• Leaders need to provide not only the initial motivation for a project but the continued encouragement necessary to keep the project going • Even leaders must find their own dependable source of encouragement
Vital statistics	• Where: Babylon, Jerusalem • Occupation: Recognized leader of the exiles • Relatives: Father: Shealtiel. Grandfather: Jehoiachin. • Contemporaries: Cyrus, Darius, Zechariah, Haggai
Key verses	"Then he said to me, 'This is what the LORD says to Zerubbabel: It is not by force nor by strength, but by my Spirit, says the LORD of Heaven's Armies. Nothing, not even a mighty mountain, will stand in Zerubbabel's way; it will become a level plain before him! And when Zerubbabel sets the final stone of the Temple in place, the people will shout: "May God bless it! May God bless it!"'" (Zech 4:6-7).

Zerubbabel's story is told in Ezra 2:2–5:2. He is also mentioned in 1 Chronicles 3:19; Nehemiah 7:7; 12:1, 47; Haggai 1:1, 12, 14; 2:4, 21, 23; Zechariah 4:6-10; Matthew 1:12-13; Luke 3:27.

were hoping to keep Jerusalem from becoming strong again. But the Jews saw through their ploy. Such a partnership with unbelievers would have led God's people to compromise their faith.

Ezra 4:1-5 Believers can expect opposition when they do God's work (2 Tim 3:12). Unbelievers and evil spiritual forces are always working against God and his people. The opposition may offer compromising alliances (Ezra 4:2), attempt to discourage and intimidate us (Ezra 4:4-5), or accuse us unjustly (Ezra 4:6). If you expect these tactics, you won't be hindered by them. Move ahead with the work God has planned for you, and trust him to show you how to overcome the obstacles.

Ezra 4:2 These enemies claimed to worship the same God as Zerubbabel and the rest of the Jews. In one sense, this was true; they worshiped God, but they also worshiped many other gods (see 2 Kgs 17:27-29, 32-34, 41). In God's eyes, this was not worship—it was sin and rebellion. True worship involves devotion to God alone (Exod 20:3-5). To these foreigners, God was just another "idol" to be added to their collection. Their real motive was to disrupt the Temple project. Believers today must beware of those who claim to be Christians but whose actions clearly reveal they are using Christianity to serve their own interests.

Ezra 4:4-5 Discouragement and fear are two of the greatest obstacles to completing God's work. Most often they come when you

2. DANIEL'S VISIONS OF THE END

Daniel had many visions of the future, both for the near future of the kingdoms and empires of the world and for the still-future end of all things. His visions are difficult to understand, and even Daniel didn't understand everything he had seen! What is certain is that God knows and is in control of the future, for his people and for the entire world.

Daniel's Vision of a Messenger

DANIEL 10:1–11:1

In the third year of the reign of King Cyrus of Persia,* Daniel (also known as Belteshazzar) had another vision. He understood that the vision concerned events certain to happen in the future—times of war and great hardship.

2When this vision came to me, I, Daniel, had been in mourning for three whole weeks. 3All that time I
had eaten no rich food. No meat or wine crossed my lips, and I used no fragrant lotions until those three weeks had passed.

4On April 23,* as I was standing on the bank of the great Tigris River, 5I looked up and saw a man dressed in linen clothing, with a belt of pure gold around his
waist. 6His body looked like a precious gem. His face flashed like lightning, and his eyes flamed like torches. His arms and feet shone like polished bronze, and his voice roared like a vast multitude of people.

7Only I, Daniel, saw this vision. The men with me saw nothing, but they were suddenly terrified and ran
away to hide. 8So I was left there all alone to see this amazing vision. My strength left me, my face grew
deathly pale, and I felt very weak. 9Then I heard the man speak, and when I heard the sound of his voice, I fainted and lay there with my face to the ground.

10Just then a hand touched me and lifted me, still
trembling, to my hands and knees. 11And the man
said to me, "Daniel, you are very precious to God, so listen carefully to what I have to say to you. Stand up, for I have been sent to you." When he said this to me, I stood up, still trembling.

12Then he said, "Don't be afraid, Daniel. Since the first day you began to pray for understanding and to humble yourself before your God, your request has been heard in heaven. I have come in answer to your
prayer. 13But for twenty-one days the spirit prince* of the kingdom of Persia blocked my way. Then Michael, one of the archangels,* came to help me, and I left him there with the spirit prince of the kingdom of
Persia.* 14Now I am here to explain what will happen to your people in the future, for this vision concerns a time yet to come."

15While he was speaking to me, I looked down at
the ground, unable to say a word. 16Then the one who
looked like a man* touched my lips, and I opened my mouth and began to speak. I said to the one standing in front of me, "I am filled with anguish because of the
vision I have seen, my lord, and I am very weak. 17How
can someone like me, your servant, talk to you, my lord? My strength is gone, and I can hardly breathe."

18Then the one who looked like a man touched
me again, and I felt my strength returning. 19"Don't
be afraid," he said, "for you are very precious to God. Peace! Be encouraged! Be strong!"

As he spoke these words to me, I suddenly felt stronger and said to him, "Please speak to me, my lord, for you have strengthened me."

20He replied, "Do you know why I have come? Soon
I must return to fight against the spirit prince of the

Dn 10:1 The third year of Cyrus's reign was 536 B.C. **Dn 10:4** Hebrew *On the twenty-fourth day of the first month,* of the ancient Hebrew lunar calendar. This date in the book of Daniel can be cross-checked with dates in surviving Persian records and can be related accurately to our modern calendar. This event occurred on April 23, 536 B.C. **Dn 10:13a** Hebrew *the prince;* also in 10:13c, 20. **Dn 10:13b** Hebrew *the chief princes.* **Dn 10:13c** As in one Greek version; Hebrew reads *and I was left there with the kings of Persia.* The meaning of the Hebrew is uncertain. **Dn 10:16** As in most manuscripts of the Masoretic Text; one manuscript of the Masoretic Text and one Greek version read *Then something that looked like a human hand.*

least expect them. Discouragement eats away at our motivation, and fear paralyzes us so we don't act at all. Recognize these common barriers. Remember that God's people in every age have faced these problems and with God's help have overcome them. By standing together with other believers, you can overcome fear and discouragement and fulfill God's purposes for your life.

Dan 10:1ff This is Daniel's final vision (536 B.C.). In it, he was given further insight into the great spiritual battle between God's people and those who want to destroy them. There is also more detailed information on the future, specifically the struggles between the Ptolemies (kings of the south) and the Seleucids (kings of the north).

Dan 10:1ff Prior to this vision, Cyrus allowed the Jews to return to Jerusalem, but Daniel stayed in Babylon. Why didn't Daniel return to Jerusalem? He may have been too old to make the long, hazardous journey (he was over 80); his government duties could have prevented him; or God may have told him to stay behind to complete the work he was called to do.

Dan 10:3 Daniel refrained from eating certain foods and using fragrant lotions because these were signs of feasting and rejoicing.

Dan 10:5-6 The man Daniel saw was a heavenly being. Some commentators believe that this was an appearance of Christ (see Rev 1:13-15), while others think it was an angel (because he required Michael's help; Dan 10:13). In either case, Daniel caught a glimpse of the battle between good and evil supernatural powers.

Dan 10:10-18 Daniel was frightened by this vision, but the messenger reassured him. Daniel lost his speech, but the messenger's touch restored it. Daniel felt weak and helpless, but the messenger's words strengthened him. God can bring us healing when we are hurt, peace when we are troubled, and strength when we are weak. Trust God to minister to you as he did to Daniel.

Dan 10:12-13 Although God sent a messenger to Daniel, a powerful spiritual being ("the spirit prince of the kingdom of Persia") detained the messenger for three weeks. Daniel faithfully continued praying and fasting, and God's messenger eventually arrived, assisted by Michael, the archangel. Answers to our prayers may be hindered by unseen obstacles. Don't expect God's answers to come too easily or too quickly. Prayer may be challenged by evil forces, so pray fervently and pray earnestly. Then expect God to answer at the right time.

kingdom of Persia, and after that the spirit prince of
the kingdom of Greece* will come. 21Meanwhile, I will
tell you what is written in the Book of Truth. (No one
helps me against these spirit princes except Michael,
your spirit prince.* 11:1I have been standing beside
Michael* to support and strengthen him since the
first year of the reign of Darius the Mede.)

Kings of the South and North

DANIEL 11:2-45

"Now then, I will reveal the truth to you. Three more
Persian kings will reign, to be succeeded by a fourth,
far richer than the others. He will use his wealth to stir
up everyone to fight against the kingdom of Greece.*
3"Then a mighty king will rise to power who will
rule with great authority and accomplish everything
he sets out to do. 4But at the height of his power, his
kingdom will be broken apart and divided into four
parts. It will not be ruled by the king's descendants,
nor will the kingdom hold the authority it once had.
For his empire will be uprooted and given to others.
5"The king of the south will increase in power, but
one of his own officials will become more powerful
than he and will rule his kingdom with great strength.
6"Some years later an alliance will be formed between the king of the north and the king of the south.
The daughter of the king of the south will be given
in marriage to the king of the north to secure the alliance, but she will lose her influence over him, and
so will her father. She will be abandoned along with
her supporters. 7But when one of her relatives* becomes king of the south, he will raise an army and
enter the fortress of the king of the north and defeat
him. 8When he returns to Egypt, he will carry back
their idols with him, along with priceless articles of
gold and silver. For some years afterward he will leave
the king of the north alone.
9"Later the king of the north will invade the realm
of the king of the south but will soon return to his own
land. 10However, the sons of the king of the north will
assemble a mighty army that will advance like a flood
and carry the battle as far as the enemy's fortress.
11"Then, in a rage, the king of the south will rally
against the vast forces assembled by the king of the
north and will defeat them. 12After the enemy army
is swept away, the king of the south will be filled with
pride and will execute many thousands of his enemies.
But his success will be short lived.
13"A few years later the king of the north will return
with a fully equipped army far greater than before.
14At that time there will be a general uprising against
the king of the south. Violent men among your own
people will join them in fulfillment of this vision, but
they will not succeed. 15Then the king of the north will
come and lay siege to a fortified city and capture it.
The best troops of the south will not be able to stand
in the face of the onslaught.
16"The king of the north will march onward un-
opposed; none will be able to stop him. He will pause
in the glorious land of Israel,* intent on destroying
it. 17He will make plans to come with the might of his
entire kingdom and will form an alliance with the king
of the south. He will give him a daughter in marriage
in order to overthrow the kingdom from within, but
his plan will fail.
18"After this, he will turn his attention to the coast-
land and conquer many cities. But a commander from
another land will put an end to his insolence and cause

Dn 10:20 Hebrew *of Javan.* **Dn 10:21** Hebrew *against these except Michael, your prince.* **Dn 11:1** Hebrew *him.* **Dn 11:2** Hebrew *of Javan.* **Dn 11:7** Hebrew *a branch from her roots.* **Dn 11:16** Hebrew *the glorious land.*

Dan 10:20-21 The heavenly warfare was to be directed against Persia and then Greece. Each of these nations was to have power over God's people. Both Persia and Greece were represented by evil "spirit princes," or demons. But God is in control of the past, present, and future, and he has all events recorded in his "Book of Truth."

Dan 11:2 The angelic messenger was revealing Israel's future (see Dan 10:20-21). Only God can reveal future events so clearly. God's work not only deals with the sweeping panorama of history but also focuses on the intricate details of people's lives. And his plans—whether for nations or individuals—are unshakable.

Dan 11:2 The fourth Persian king may have been Xerxes I (also called Ahasuerus, 486–465 B.C.), who launched an all-out effort against Greece in 480 (Esth 1:1).

Dan 11:2ff Babylon was defeated by Medo-Persia. Medo-Persia was defeated by Greece under Alexander the Great, who conquered most of the Mediterranean and Middle Eastern lands. After Alexander's death, the empire was divided into four parts. The Ptolemies gained control of the southern section of Palestine, and the Seleucids took the northern part. Daniel 11:2-20 shows the conflict between the Ptolemies and the Seleucids over control of Palestine in 300–200 B.C. Daniel 11:21-35 describes the persecution of Israel under Antiochus IV Epiphanes. The prophecy then shifts to the end times (Dan 11:36-45). Antiochus IV fades from view, and the Antichrist of the last days becomes the center of attention.

Dan 11:3 This mighty king of Greece was Alexander the Great, who conquered Medo-Persia and built a huge empire in only four years.

Dan 11:4-5 Eventually Alexander the Great's empire was divided into four nations. These four weaker nations were comprised of the following regions: (1) Egypt, (2) Babylonia and Syria, (3) Asia Minor, and (4) Macedonia and Greece. The king of Egypt ("the king of the south") was Ptolemy I or perhaps a reference to the Ptolemaic dynasty in general.

Dan 11:6-7 These prophecies seem to have been fulfilled many years later in the Seleucid wars between Egypt and Syria. In 252 B.C., Ptolemy II of Egypt ("the south") gave his daughter Berenice in marriage to Antiochus II of Syria ("the north") to finalize a peace treaty between their two lands. But Berenice was murdered in Antioch by Antiochus II's former wife, Laodice. Berenice's brother, Ptolemy III, ascended the Egyptian throne and declared war against the Seleucids to avenge his sister's murder.

Dan 11:9-11 The king of Syria ("the north") was Seleucus II, and the king of Egypt ("the south") was Ptolemy IV.

Dan 11:13-16 This king of the north may have been Antiochus III (the Great). He defeated many Egyptian cities and established himself in Israel ("the glorious land"). He was later defeated by the Romans at Magnesia (Dan 11:18).

Dan 11:17 The invader, Antiochus III, tried to bring peace between Egypt and Syria by having his daughter marry Ptolemy V Epiphanes of Egypt, but the plan failed.

▸ DANIEL 11:2-45 ***(cont.)***

him to retreat in shame. 19He will take refuge in his own fortresses but will stumble and fall and be seen no more.

20"His successor will send out a tax collector to maintain the royal splendor. But after a very brief reign, he will die, though not from anger or in battle.

21"The next to come to power will be a despicable man who is not in line for royal succession. He will slip in when least expected and take over the kingdom by flattery and intrigue. 22Before him great armies will be swept away, including a covenant prince. 23With deceitful promises, he will make various alliances. He will become strong despite having only a handful of followers. 24Without warning he will enter the richest areas of the land. Then he will distribute among his followers the plunder and wealth of the rich—something his predecessors had never done. He will plot the overthrow of strongholds, but this will last for only a short while.

25"Then he will stir up his courage and raise a great army against the king of the south. The king of the south will go to battle with a mighty army, but to no avail, for there will be plots against him. 26His own household will cause his downfall. His army will be swept away, and many will be killed. 27Seeking nothing but each other's harm, these kings will plot against each other at the conference table, attempting to deceive each other. But it will make no difference, for the end will come at the appointed time.

28"The king of the north will then return home with great riches. On the way he will set himself against the people of the holy covenant, doing much damage before continuing his journey.

29"Then at the appointed time he will once again invade the south, but this time the result will be different. 30For warships from western coastlands* will scare him off, and he will withdraw and return home. But he will vent his anger against the people of the holy covenant and reward those who forsake the covenant.

31"His army will take over the Temple fortress, pollute the sanctuary, put a stop to the daily sacrifices, and set up the sacrilegious object that causes desecration.* 32He will flatter and win over those who have violated the covenant. But the people who know their God will be strong and will resist him.

33"Wise leaders will give instruction to many, but these teachers will die by fire and sword, or they will be jailed and robbed. 34During these persecutions, little help will arrive, and many who join them will not be sincere. 35And some of the wise will fall victim to persecution. In this way, they will be refined and cleansed and made pure until the time of the end, for the appointed time is still to come.

36"The king will do as he pleases, exalting himself and claiming to be greater than every god, even blaspheming the God of gods. He will succeed, but only until the time of wrath is completed. For what has been determined will surely take place. 37He will have no respect for the gods of his ancestors, or for the god loved by women, or for any other god, for he will boast that he is greater than them all. 38Instead of these, he will worship the god of fortresses—a god his ancestors never knew—and lavish on him gold, silver, precious stones, and expensive gifts. 39Claiming this foreign god's help, he will attack the strongest fortresses. He will honor those who submit to him, appointing them

Dn 11:30 Hebrew *from Kittim.* **Dn 11:31** Hebrew *the abomination of desolation.*

534 BC *Tragedy emerges as a form of Greek drama*

Dan 11:20 The successor to Antiochus III was Seleucus IV. He sent Heliodorus to collect money from the Temple treasury in Jerusalem.

Dan 11:21 Seleucus IV was succeeded by his brother, Antiochus IV Epiphanes, who found favor with the Romans.

Dan 11:22 The "great armies" refer to the way all opposition against Antiochus IV will be broken. The covenant prince may be the high priest Onias III, who was assassinated by Menelaus in 170 B.C.

Dan 11:27 These two treacherous kings were probably Antiochus IV of Syria and Ptolemy VI of Egypt. Treachery and deceit are a power broker's way to position oneself over someone else. When two power brokers try to gain the upper hand, it is a mutually weakening and self-destructive process. It is also futile because God ultimately holds all power in *his* hands.

Dan 11:29-31 Antiochus IV again invaded "the south," but enemy ships caused him to retreat. On his way back, he plundered Jerusalem, desecrated the Temple, and stopped the Jews' daily sacrifices. The Temple was desecrated when he sacrificed pigs on an altar erected in honor of Zeus. According to Jewish law, pigs were unclean and were not to be touched or eaten. To sacrifice a pig to a false god in the Temple was the worst kind of insult an enemy could level against the Jews. This happened in 168–167 B.C.

Dan 11:32 This reference to those who have violated the covenant may include Menelaus, the high priest, who was won over by Antiochus and who conspired with him against the Jews who were loyal to God. The "people who know their God" may refer to the Maccabees and their sympathizers, but a further fulfillment may lie in the future.

Dan 11:33-34 Those who are wise will teach many, but they will also face great persecution. Difficult times show up our weaknesses and our inability to cope. We want answers, leadership, and clear direction. During these times, God's Word begins to interest even those who would never look at it otherwise. We should look for opportunities to share God's Word in hard times. We must also be prepared to face persecution and rejection as we teach and preach.

Dan 11:35 God's messenger described a time of trial when even wise believers would fall victim to persecution. If we persevere in our faith, any such experience will only refine us and make us stronger. Are you facing trials? Recognize them as opportunities to strengthen your faith. If you remain steadfast in these experiences, you will be stronger in your faith and closer to God.

Dan 11:36-39 These verses could refer to Antiochus IV Epiphanes, Titus (the Roman general), or the Antichrist. Some of these events may have been fulfilled in the past, and some have yet to be fulfilled.

Dan 11:37 The "god loved by women" may refer to Tammuz, a Babylonian fertility god. Tammuz is also mentioned in Ezekiel 8:14. In other words, this person won't recognize any deity or religions at all, not even pagan ones. Instead, he will proclaim himself to be divine and the ultimate power.

Dan 11:38 The "god of fortresses" is believed by some to be Jupiter or Zeus. The implication is that this king will make war his god. More than all his predecessors, he will wage war and glorify its horrors.

to positions of authority and dividing the land among
them as their reward.*
40“Then at the time of the end, the king of the south
will attack the king of the north. The king of the north
will storm out with chariots, charioteers, and a vast
navy. He will invade various lands and sweep through
them like a flood. 41He will enter the glorious land of
Israel,* and many nations will fall, but Moab, Edom,
and the best part of Ammon will escape. 42He will
conquer many countries, and even Egypt will not escape. 43He will gain control over the gold, silver, and
treasures of Egypt, and the Libyans and Ethiopians*
will be his servants.
44“But then news from the east and the north will
alarm him, and he will set out in great anger to destroy
and obliterate many. 45He will stop between the glorious holy mountain and the sea and will pitch his royal
tents. But while he is there, his time will suddenly run
out, and no one will help him.

The Time of the End

DANIEL 12:1-13

“At that time Michael, the archangel* who stands
guard over your nation, will arise. Then there will be
a time of anguish greater than any since nations first
came into existence. But at that time every one of
your people whose name is written in the book will
be rescued. 2Many of those whose bodies lie dead
and buried will rise up, some to everlasting life and
some to shame and everlasting disgrace. 3Those who
are wise will shine as bright as the sky, and those who
lead many to righteousness will shine like the stars
forever. 4But you, Daniel, keep this prophecy a secret;
seal up the book until the time of the end, when many
will rush here and there, and knowledge will increase.”
5Then I, Daniel, looked and saw two others standing
on opposite banks of the river. 6One of them asked the
man dressed in linen, who was now standing above
the river, “How long will it be until these shocking
events are over?”
7The man dressed in linen, who was standing above
the river, raised both his hands toward heaven and
took a solemn oath by the One who lives forever, saying, “It will go on for a time, times, and half a time.
When the shattering of the holy people has finally
come to an end, all these things will have happened.”
8I heard what he said, but I did not understand what
he meant. So I asked, “How will all this finally end,
my lord?”
9But he said, “Go now, Daniel, for what I have said
is kept secret and sealed until the time of the end.
10Many will be purified, cleansed, and refined by these

Dn 11:39 Or *at a price.* **Dn 11:41** Hebrew *the glorious land.* **Dn 11:43** Hebrew *Cushites.* **Dn 12:1** Hebrew *the great prince.*

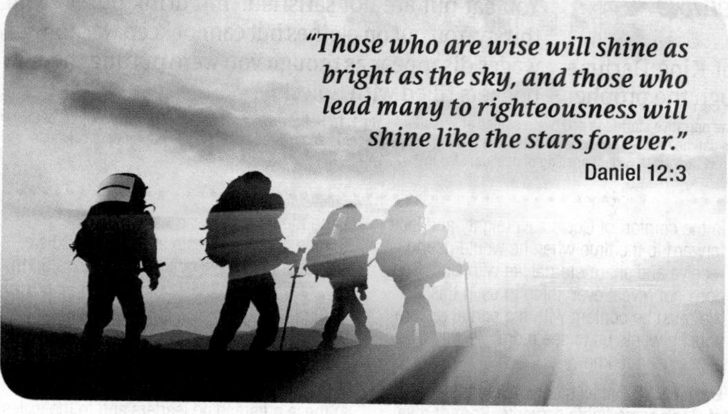
“Those who are wise will shine as bright as the sky, and those who lead many to righteousness will shine like the stars forever.”
Daniel 12:3

Dan 11:40 The Antichrist of the last days becomes the center of attention from this point through the rest of the book of Daniel.

Dan 11:45 “The glorious holy mountain” is Mount Zion or the city of Jerusalem.

Dan 12:1 Great suffering is in store for God’s people throughout the years ahead. Jeremiah (Jer 30:7) and Jesus (Matt 24:21ff) also use this way of describing the future. Yet the great suffering is tempered by a great promise of hope for true believers.

Dan 12:2 This is a clear reference to the resurrection of both the righteous and the wicked, although the eternal destiny of each will be quite different. Up to this point in time, teaching about the resurrection of the dead was not common, although every Israelite had the belief of being included in the restoration of the new Kingdom one day. This reference to a bodily resurrection of both the saved and the lost was a sharp departure from common belief. (See also Job 19:25-26; Ps 16:10; Isa 26:19 for other Old Testament references to the resurrection of the dead.)

Dan 12:3 Many people try to be stars in the world of entertainment, only to find their stardom temporary. God tells us how we can be eternal “stars”—by being wise and leading many to God’s righteousness. If we share our Lord with others, we can be true stars—radiantly beautiful in God’s sight!

Dan 12:4 Closing and sealing up the book meant that it was to be kept safe and preserved. This was to be done so that believers of all times could look back on God’s work in history and find hope. Daniel did not understand the exact meaning of the times and events in his vision. The whole book will not be understood until the climax of earth’s history.

Dan 12:7 “Time, times, and half a time” may add up to three-and-a-half years and may be taken as either literal or figurative.

Dan 12:7 “The holy people” seem to be shattered again and again throughout history. God’s recurring purpose in this is to break the pride and self-sufficiency of his rebellious people and to bring them to accept him as their Lord.

Dan 12:10 Trials and persecutions make very little sense to us when we experience them, but they can purify us if we are willing to learn from them. After you come through a difficult time, seek to learn from it so that it can help you in the future. See Romans 5:3-5 for more on God’s purpose in our sufferings.

525 BC

Polo played as a sport in Persia

▸ **DANIEL 12:1-13** ***(cont.)***

trials. But the wicked will continue in their wickedness, and none of them will understand. Only those who are wise will know what it means.

11“From the time the daily sacrifice is stopped and the sacrilegious object that causes desecration* is set up to be worshiped, there will be 1,290 days. 12And blessed are those who wait and remain until the end of the 1,335 days!

13“As for you, go your way until the end. You will rest, and then at the end of the days, you will rise again to receive the inheritance set aside for you.”

Dn 12:11 Hebrew *the abomination of desolation.*

B. Haggai, Zechariah, and the Rebuilding of the Temple

When the exiles first returned from Babylon, they set about rebuilding the Temple right away, but because of opposition from the people around them the work came to a standstill. The people went about their daily lives, forgetting about the Temple. God sent the prophets Haggai and Zechariah to the people. Through the ministry of these prophets, the people changed their actions and attitudes, got back to their work on the Temple, and completed the task. We need to be on guard to keep our priorities straight and pay attention to the people God puts in our lives to remind us of the need to put God first.

Haggai and Zechariah Prophesy

EZRA 4:24–5:1

So the work on the Temple of God in Jerusalem had stopped, and it remained at a standstill until the second year of the reign of King Darius of Persia.*

5:1At that time the prophets Haggai and Zechariah son of Iddo prophesied to the Jews in Judah and Jerusalem. They prophesied in the name of the God of Israel who was over them.

520 BC

Haggai and Zechariah serve as prophets

Haggai's Call to Rebuild the Temple

HAGGAI 1:1-11

On August 29* of the second year of King Darius's reign, the LORD gave a message through the prophet Haggai to Zerubbabel son of Shealtiel, governor of Judah, and to Jeshua* son of Jehozadak, the high priest.

2“This is what the LORD of Heaven's Armies says: The people are saying, ‘The time has not yet come to rebuild the house of the LORD.’”

3Then the LORD sent this message through the prophet Haggai: 4“Why are you living in luxurious houses while my house lies in ruins? 5This is what the LORD of Heaven's Armies says: Look at what's happening to you! 6You have planted much but harvest little. You eat but are not satisfied. You drink but are still thirsty. You put on clothes but cannot keep warm. Your wages disappear as though you were putting them in pockets filled with holes!

Ezr 4:24 The second year of Darius's reign was 520 B.C. The narrative started in 4:1-5 is resumed at verse 24. **Hg 1:1a** Hebrew *On the first day of the sixth month,* of the ancient Hebrew lunar calendar. A number of dates in Haggai can be cross-checked with dates in surviving Persian records and related accurately to our modern calendar. This event occurred on August 29, 520 B.C. **Hg 1:1b** Hebrew *Joshua,* a variant spelling of Jeshua; also in 1:12, 14.

Dan 12:11 “The sacrilegious object that causes desecration” set up in the Temple refers to the altar of Zeus, where Antiochus IV Epiphanes sacrificed a pig. Some think it will have another fulfillment in the Antichrist and one of his horrible acts of evil (Matt 24:15). However, this and the predictions at the early part of the chapter may refer specifically to Antiochus IV Epiphanes, and the rest of the prophecy may refer to the end times.

Dan 12:11-12 Either these are further calculations relating to the persecution of the Jews under Antiochus IV Epiphanes, or they refer to the end times. The abolishing of the daily sacrifices means the removal of worship of the true God, as well as oppression of believers. There is much speculation about these numbers. The point is that this time of persecution has an end; God is in control of it, and he will be victorious over evil.

Dan 12:13 The promise of resurrection was reaffirmed to Daniel. He would one day see the fulfillment of his words, but he was not to spend the rest of his life wondering what his visions might mean. Instead, he was to rest in the comfort of God's sovereignty and look forward to the time when he would rise to receive and share eternal life with God. God does not reveal everything to us in this life. We must be content with the partial picture until he wants us to see more. He will tell us all we need to know.

Dan 12:13 Daniel stands tall in the gallery of God's remarkable servants. Born of royal heritage, yet taken into captivity when only a teenager, Daniel determined to remain faithful to God in the land of his captivity. Even at great personal cost, Daniel spent his entire lifetime advising his captors with unusual wisdom. God chose him as his servant to record some of the events of the captivity and some significant events concerning the future. As an old man, having been faithful to God throughout his years, Daniel was assured by God that he would rise from the dead and receive his portion in God's eternal Kingdom. Faithfulness to God has a rich reward, not necessarily in this life, but most certainly in the life to come.

Ezra 4:24 Ezra resumes his chronological account here. It may have been 10 years since the Israelites had worked on the Temple. It did not begin again until 520 B.C., the second year of Darius's reign (Ezra 5:1ff).

Hag 1:1 Zerubbabel, governor of Judah, and Jeshua, the high priest, were key leaders in rebuilding the Temple. They had already reestablished the altar, but work on the Temple had slowed. Haggai gave a message to these outstanding leaders and to the exiles who had returned from Babylon, encouraging them to complete the rebuilding of the Temple in Jerusalem.

Hag 1:1ff The Jews who had returned from Babylon in 538 B.C. to rebuild the Temple in Jerusalem were not able to finish their work because they were hindered by their enemies. After opposition put a halt to progress, no further work had been done on the Temple for over 10 years. In August 520 B.C., Haggai delivered a message to encourage the people to rebuild the Temple. Haggai was probably born in captivity in Babylon and returned to Jerusalem with Zerubbabel in 538 B.C. (Ezra 1–2). Haggai and Zechariah, two prophets who encouraged the Temple rebuilding, are mentioned in Ezra 5:1.

7"This is what the LORD of Heaven's Armies says:
Look at what's happening to you! 8Now go up into the
hills, bring down timber, and rebuild my house. Then I
will take pleasure in it and be honored, says the LORD.
9You hoped for rich harvests, but they were poor. And
when you brought your harvest home, I blew it away.
Why? Because my house lies in ruins, says the LORD
of Heaven's Armies, while all of you are busy building
your own fine houses. 10It's because of you that the
heavens withhold the dew and the earth produces
no crops. 11I have called for a drought on your fields
and hills—a drought to wither the grain and grapes
and olive trees and all your other crops, a drought to
starve you and your livestock and to ruin everything
you have worked so hard to get."

Obedience to God's Call

HAGGAI 1:12-15

Then Zerubbabel son of Shealtiel, and Jeshua son of
Jehozadak, the high priest, and the whole remnant
of God's people began to obey the message from the
LORD their God. When they heard the words of the
prophet Haggai, whom the LORD their God had sent,
the people feared the LORD. 13Then Haggai, the LORD's
messenger, gave the people this message from the
LORD: "I am with you, says the LORD!"
14So the LORD sparked the enthusiasm of Zerubbabel son of Shealtiel, governor of Judah, and the enthusiasm of Jeshua son of Jehozadak, the high priest,
and the enthusiasm of the whole remnant of God's
people. They began to work on the house of their God,
the LORD of Heaven's Armies, 15on September 21* of
the second year of King Darius's reign.

The New Temple's Diminished Splendor

HAGGAI 2:1-9

Then on October 17 of that same year,* the LORD
sent another message through the prophet Haggai.
2"Say this to Zerubbabel son of Shealtiel, governor
of Judah, and to Jeshua* son of Jehozadak, the high
priest, and to the remnant of God's people there in
the land: 3'Does anyone remember this house—this
Temple—in its former splendor? How, in comparison,
does it look to you now? It must seem like nothing at

Hg 1:15 Hebrew *on the twenty-fourth day of the sixth month,* of the ancient Hebrew lunar calendar. This event occurred on September 21, 520 B.C.; also see note on 1:1a. **Hg 2:1** Hebrew *on the twenty-first day of the seventh month,* of the ancient Hebrew lunar calendar. This event (in the second year of Darius's reign) occurred on October 17, 520 B.C.; also see note on 1:1a. **Hg 2:2** Hebrew *Joshua,* a variant spelling of Jeshua; also in 2:4.

HAGGAI

Haggai served as a prophet to Judah about 520 B.C., after the return from exile.

Climate of the times	The people of Judah had been exiled to Babylon in 586 B.C., and Jerusalem and the Temple had been destroyed. Under Cyrus, king of Persia, the Jews were allowed to return to Judah and rebuild their Temple.
Main message	The people returned to Jerusalem to begin rebuilding the Temple, but they hadn't finished. Haggai's message encouraged the people to finish rebuilding God's Temple.
Importance of message	The Temple lay half-finished while the people lived in beautiful homes. Haggai warned them against putting their possessions and jobs ahead of God. We must put God first in our lives.
Contemporary prophet	Zechariah (520–480 B.C.)

Hag 1:2-15 Haggai encouraged the people to finish rebuilding the Temple. Opposition from hostile neighbors had caused them to feel discouraged and to neglect the Temple and thus neglect God. But Haggai's message turned them around and motivated them to pick up their tools and continue the work they had begun.

Hag 1:3-6 God asked his people how they could live in luxury when his house was lying in ruins. The Temple was the focal point of Judah's relationship with God, but it was still demolished. Instead of rebuilding the Temple, the people put their energies into beautifying their own homes. But the harder the people worked for themselves, the less they had, because they ignored their spiritual lives. The same happens to us. If we put God first, he will provide for our deepest needs. If we put him in any other place, all our efforts will be futile. Caring only for your physical needs while ignoring your relationship with God will lead to ruin.

Hag 1:6 Because the people had not given God first place in their lives, their work was not fruitful or productive, and their material possessions did not satisfy. While they concentrated on building and beautifying their own homes, God's blessing was withheld because they no longer put him first. Moses had predicted that this would be the result if the people neglected God (Deut 28:38-45).

Hag 1:9 Judah's problem was confused priorities. Like Judah, our priorities involving occupation, family, and God's work are often confused. Jobs, homes, vacations, and leisure activities may rank higher on our list of importance than God. What is most important to you? Where is God on your list of priorities?

Hag 1:11 Grain, grapes for wine, and olives for oil were Israel's major crops. The people depended on these for security while neglecting the worship of God. As a result, God would send a drought to destroy their livelihood and call them back to himself.

Hag 1:14-15 The people began rebuilding the Temple just 23 days after Haggai's first message. Rarely did a prophet's message produce such a quick response. How often we hear a sermon and respond, "That was an excellent point—I ought to do that," only to leave church and forget to act. These people put their words into action. When you hear a sermon or lesson from God's Word, ask what you should do about it, and then make plans to put it into practice.

Hag 2:1-9 This is Haggai's second message. It was given during the Festival of Shelters in October 520 B.C. The older people could remember the incredible beauty of Solomon's Temple, destroyed 66 years earlier. Many were discouraged because the rebuilt Temple was inferior to Solomon's. But Haggai encouraged them with God's message that the glory of this Temple would surpass that of its predecessor. The most important part of the Temple is God's presence. Some 500 years later, Jesus Christ would walk in the Temple courts.

▸ **HAGGAI 2:1-9** ***(cont.)***

all! 4But now the LORD says: Be strong, Zerubbabel. Be
strong, Jeshua son of Jehozadak, the high priest. Be
strong, all you people still left in the land. And now get
to work, for I am with you, says the LORD of Heaven's
Armies. 5My Spirit remains among you, just as I promised when you came out of Egypt. So do not be afraid.'
6"For this is what the LORD of Heaven's Armies says:
In just a little while I will again shake the heavens and
the earth, the oceans and the dry land. 7I will shake all
the nations, and the treasures of all the nations will be
brought to this Temple. I will fill this place with glory,
says the LORD of Heaven's Armies. 8The silver is mine,
and the gold is mine, says the LORD of Heaven's Armies.
9The future glory of this Temple will be greater than
its past glory, says the LORD of Heaven's Armies. And
in this place I will bring peace. I, the LORD of Heaven's
Armies, have spoken!"

Zechariah's Call to Return to the LORD

ZECHARIAH 1:1-6

In November* of the second year of King Darius's
reign, the LORD gave this message to the prophet Zechariah son of Berekiah and grandson of Iddo:
2"I, the LORD, was very angry with your ancestors.
3Therefore, say to the people, 'This is what the LORD
of Heaven's Armies says: Return to me, and I will
return to you, says the LORD of Heaven's Armies.'
4Don't be like your ancestors who would not listen
or pay attention when the earlier prophets said to
them, 'This is what the LORD of Heaven's Armies
says: Turn from your evil ways, and stop all your
evil practices.'
5"Where are your ancestors now? They and the
prophets are long dead. 6But everything I said
through my servants the prophets happened to your
ancestors, just as I said. As a result, they repented
and said, 'We have received what we deserved from
the LORD of Heaven's Armies. He has done what he
said he would do.'"

Blessings Promised for Obedience

HAGGAI 2:10-19

On December 18* of the second year of King Darius's
reign, the LORD sent this message to the prophet Haggai: 11"This is what the LORD of Heaven's Armies says.
Ask the priests this question about the law: 12'If one
of you is carrying some meat from a holy sacrifice in

Zec 1:1 Hebrew *In the eighth month.* A number of dates in Zechariah can be cross-checked with dates in surviving Persian records and related accurately to our modern calendar. This month of the ancient Hebrew lunar calendar occurred within the months of October and November 520 B.C. **Hg 2:10** Hebrew *On the twenty-fourth day of the ninth month,* of the ancient Hebrew lunar calendar (similarly in 2:18). This event occurred on December 18, 520 B.C.; also see note on 1:1a.

Hag 2:4 "Be strong . . . and now get to work, for I am with you." Judah's people had returned to worshiping God, and God had promised to bless their efforts. But now it was time for them to work. We must be people of prayer, Bible study, and worship, but eventually we must get out and *do* the work God has prepared for us. He wants to change the world through us, his ambassadors. God has given you a job to do in the church, at your place of employment, and at home. The time has come to take courage and get going because God is with you!

Hag 2:5 The Israelites had been led from captivity in Egypt to their Promised Land. They were God's chosen people, guided and cared for by his Holy Spirit. Although God had punished them for their sins, he kept his promise and never left them (Exod 29:45-46). No matter what difficulties we face or how frustrating our work may be, God's Spirit is with us.

Hag 2:6-9 The focus shifts from the local Temple being rebuilt in Jerusalem to the worldwide reign of the Messiah on earth. The words "in just a little while" are not limited to the immediate historical context; they refer to God's control of history—he can act anytime he chooses. God will act in his time (see also Heb 12:26-27).

Hag 2:7 When God promised to shake all the nations with his judgment, he was speaking of both his present judgment on evil nations and future judgment during the last days.

Hag 2:8-9 God wanted the Temple to be rebuilt, and he had the gold and silver to do it, but he needed willing hands. God has chosen to do his work through people. He provides the resources, but willing hands must do the work. Are your hands available for God's work in the world?

Zech 1:1 Born in Babylon during the Exile, Zechariah was a fairly young man when he returned to Jerusalem in 538 B.C. King Cyrus of Persia had defeated Babylon in 539 B.C. and had decreed that captives in exile could return to their homelands. Zechariah and Haggai were among the first to leave. Zechariah, a prophet and a priest, began ministering at the same time as the prophet Haggai (520–518 B.C.). His first prophecy was delivered two months after Haggai's first prophecy.

Like Haggai, Zechariah encouraged the people to continue rebuilding the Temple, whose reconstruction had been halted for nearly 10 years. Zechariah combated the people's spiritual apathy, despair over pressures from their enemies, and discouragement about the smaller scale of the new Temple foundation. Neglect of our spiritual priorities can be just as devastating today to fulfilling God's purpose.

Zech 1:2-6 The familiar phrase "Like father, like son" implies that children turn out like their parents. But here, God warned Israel not

ZECHARIAH

Zechariah served as a prophet to Judah about 520 B.C., after the return from exile.

Climate of the times	The exiles had returned from captivity to rebuild their Temple. But work on the Temple had stalled, and the people were ignoring their service to God.
Main message	Zechariah, like Haggai, encouraged the people to finish rebuilding the Temple. His visions gave the people hope. He told the people of a future king who would one day establish an eternal Kingdom.
Importance of message	Even in times of discouragement and despair, God is working out his plan. God protects and guides us; we must trust and follow him.
Contemporary prophet	Haggai (approximately 520 B.C.)

his robes and his robe happens to brush against some bread or stew, wine or olive oil, or any other kind of food, will it also become holy?'"

The priests replied, "No."

[13]Then Haggai asked, "If someone becomes ceremonially unclean by touching a dead person and then touches any of these foods, will the food be defiled?"

And the priests answered, "Yes."

[14]Then Haggai responded, "That is how it is with this people and this nation, says the LORD. Everything they do and everything they offer is defiled by their sin. [15]Look at what was happening to you before you began to lay the foundation of the LORD's Temple. [16]When you hoped for a twenty-bushel crop, you harvested only ten. When you expected to draw fifty gallons from the winepress, you found only twenty. [17]I sent blight and mildew and hail to destroy everything you worked so hard to produce. Even so, you refused to return to me, says the LORD.

[18]"Think about this eighteenth day of December, the day* when the foundation of the LORD's Temple was laid. Think carefully. [19]I am giving you a promise now while the seed is still in the barn.* You have not yet harvested your grain, and your grapevines, fig trees, pomegranates, and olive trees have not yet produced their crops. But from this day onward I will bless you."

The Temple Building Resumes

EZRA 5:2

Zerubbabel son of Shealtiel and Jeshua son of Jehozadak* responded by starting again to rebuild the Temple of God in Jerusalem. And the prophets of God were with them and helped them.

Promises for Zerubbabel

HAGGAI 2:20-23

On that same day, December 18,* the LORD sent this second message to Haggai: [21]"Tell Zerubbabel, the governor of Judah, that I am about to shake the heavens and the earth. [22]I will overthrow royal thrones and destroy the power of foreign kingdoms. I will overturn their chariots and riders. The horses will fall, and their riders will kill each other.

[23]"But when this happens, says the LORD of Heaven's Armies, I will honor you, Zerubbabel son of Shealtiel, my servant. I will make you like a signet ring on my finger, says the LORD, for I have chosen you. I, the LORD of Heaven's Armies, have spoken!"

A Man among the Myrtle Trees

ZECHARIAH 1:7-17

Three months later, on February 15,* the LORD sent another message to the prophet Zechariah son of Berekiah and grandson of Iddo.

520 BC

Public libraries open in Athens, Greece

Hg 2:18 Or *On this eighteenth day of December, think about the day.* **Hg 2:19** Hebrew *Is the seed yet in the barn?* **Ezr 5:2** Aramaic *Jozadak,* a variant spelling of Jehozadak. **Hg 2:20** Hebrew *On the twenty-fourth day of the [ninth] month;* see note on 2:10. **Zec 1:7** Hebrew *On the twenty-fourth day of the eleventh month, the month of Shebat, in the second year of Darius.* This event occurred on February 15, 519 B.C.; also see note on 1:1.

to be like their forefathers, who disobeyed him and reaped the consequences—his punishment. We are responsible before God for our actions. We can't use our heredity or environment as excuses for our sins. We are free to choose, and individually we must return to God and follow him.

Zech 1:5-6 The words God had spoken through his prophets a century earlier, before the Captivity, also applied to Zechariah's generation, and they are still relevant for us. Because God's Word endures, we must read, study, and apply what is preserved for us in Scripture. Learn the lessons of God's Word so you will not repeat the mistakes of others.

Hag 2:10-19 The point of this message (delivered in December 520 B.C.) is that holiness will not rub off on others, but contamination will. As the people began to obey, God promised to encourage and prosper them. But they needed to understand that activities in the Temple would not clean up their sin; only repentance and obedience could do that. If we insist on harboring wrong attitudes and sins or on maintaining close relationships with sinful people, we will be defiled. Holy living will come only when we are empowered by God's Holy Spirit.

Hag 2:14 A young child eating spaghetti sauce very soon gets a red face, hands, and clothes. Sin and selfish attitudes produce the same result—they stain everything they touch. Even good deeds done for God can be tainted by sinful attitudes. The only remedy is God's cleansing.

Hag 2:16 For many years, the grain had only given 50 percent of the expected yield, and wine had done even worse.

Hag 2:18-19 The people re-laid the Temple foundation, and immediately God blessed them. He did not wait for the project to be completed. God often sends his encouragement and approval with our first few obedient steps. He is eager to bless us!

Ezra 5:2 "The prophets of God were with them and helped them." God sometimes sends prophets to encourage and strengthen his people. To accomplish this, Haggai and Zechariah not only preached but also got involved in the labor. In the church today God appoints prophetic voices to help us with our work (Eph 4:11-13). Their ministry should have the same effect upon us as Haggai's and Zechariah's had on Israel. "One who prophesies strengthens others, encourages them, and comforts them" (1 Cor 14:3). In turn, we should encourage those who bring God's words to us.

Hag 2:20-23 Haggai's final message acknowledged that he was merely the messenger who brings the word of the Lord. It is addressed to Zerubbabel, the governor of Judah.

Hag 2:23 A signet ring was used to guarantee the authority and authenticity of a letter. It served as a signature when pressed in soft wax on a written document. God was reaffirming and guaranteeing his promise of a Messiah through David's line (Matt 1:12).

Hag 2:23 God closed his message to Zerubbabel with this tremendous affirmation: "I have chosen you." Such a proclamation applies to us as well: Each of us has been chosen by God (Eph 1:4). This truth should make us see how much God loves us; in turn it should motivate us to work for him. When you feel down, remind yourself: God has chosen me!

Hag 2:23 Haggai's message to the people sought to get their priorities straight, help them quit worrying, and motivate them to rebuild the Temple. Like them, we often place a higher priority on our personal comfort than on God's work and true worship. But God is pleased and promises strength and guidance when we give him first place in our life.

Zech 1:7-17 The man among the myrtle trees was the angel of the Lord (Zech 1:11). The horses and their colors were symbols of God's involvement in world governments. The full meaning of the colors is unknown, although the red horse is often associated with war and the white horse with final victory.

▸ **ZECHARIAH 1:7-17** ***(cont.)***

8In a vision during the night, I saw a man sitting on a
red horse that was standing among some myrtle trees
in a small valley. Behind him were riders on red, brown,
and white horses. 9I asked the angel who was talking
with me, "My lord, what do these horses mean?"
"I will show you," the angel replied.
10The rider standing among the myrtle trees then
explained, "They are the ones the LORD has sent out
to patrol the earth."
11Then the other riders reported to the angel of
the LORD, who was standing among the myrtle trees,
"We have been patrolling the earth, and the whole
earth is at peace."
12Upon hearing this, the angel of the LORD prayed
this prayer: "O LORD of Heaven's Armies, for seventy
years now you have been angry with Jerusalem and the
towns of Judah. How long until you again show mercy
to them?" 13And the LORD spoke kind and comforting
words to the angel who talked with me.
14Then the angel said to me, "Shout this message for
all to hear: 'This is what the LORD of Heaven's Armies
says: My love for Jerusalem and Mount Zion is passionate and strong. 15But I am very angry with the other
nations that are now enjoying peace and security. I
was only a little angry with my people, but the nations
inflicted harm on them far beyond my intentions.
16"'Therefore, this is what the LORD says: I have
returned to show mercy to Jerusalem. My Temple
will be rebuilt, says the LORD of Heaven's Armies, and
measurements will be taken for the reconstruction of
Jerusalem.*'
17"Say this also: 'This is what the LORD of Heaven's
Armies says: The towns of Israel will again overflow
with prosperity, and the LORD will again comfort Zion
and choose Jerusalem as his own.'"

Four Horns and Four Blacksmiths

ZECHARIAH 1:18-21

18*Then I looked up and saw four animal horns.
19"What are these?" I asked the angel who was talking with me.
He replied, "These horns represent the nations that
scattered Judah, Israel, and Jerusalem."
20Then the LORD showed me four blacksmiths.
21"What are these men coming to do?" I asked.
The angel replied, "These four horns—these nations—
scattered and humbled Judah. Now these blacksmiths
have come to terrify those nations and throw them down
and destroy them."

Future Prosperity of Jerusalem

ZECHARIAH 2:1-5

*When I looked again, I saw a man with a measuring
line in his hand. 2"Where are you going?" I asked.
He replied, "I am going to measure Jerusalem, to
see how wide and how long it is."

Zec 1:16 Hebrew *and the measuring line will be stretched out over Jerusalem.* **Zec 1:18** Verses 1:18-21 are numbered 2:1-4 in Hebrew text. **Zec 2:1** Verses 2:1-13 are numbered 2:5-17 in Hebrew text.

Zech 1:11 The angel of the Lord saw that all the nations were secure and at peace, while Israel was still oppressed and despised. But God was planning a change. He had released his people, and he would allow them to return and rebuild his Temple.

Zech 1:12 Seventy years was the time that God had decreed for Israel to remain in captivity (Jer 25:11; 29:10). This time was over, and the angel asked God to act swiftly to complete the promised return of his people to Jerusalem.

Zech 1:13 God's people had lived under his judgment for 70 years during their captivity in Babylon. But here God spoke words of comfort and assurance. God promises that when we return to him, he will heal us (Hos 6:1). If you feel wounded and crushed by the events of your life, turn to God so he can heal and comfort you.

Zech 1:15 Although the pagan nations afflicted God's people beyond his intentions, God was not powerless to stop them. God used these nations to punish his sinful people. When the nations went beyond his plans by trying to destroy Israel as a nation, he intervened.

Zech 1:18-21 The horns were the four world powers that oppressed Israel—Egypt, Assyria, Babylon, and Medo-Persia. The four blacksmiths (Zech 1:20) were the nations used to overthrow Israel's enemies. God raised them up to judge the oppressors of his people.

Zech 2:1 The man with the measuring line symbolizes the hope of a rebuilt Jerusalem and a restored people. The man would be measuring to mark out the boundaries for a foundation (see Zech 1:16; Jer 31:38-40).

Zech 2:6-7 Many of the captive Israelites did not return to Jerusalem because they had become accustomed to the security and wealth they had in Babylon. But Zechariah instructed them to leave Babylon quickly. This was an urgent request because Babylon would be destroyed and its decadent culture would cause God's people to forget their spiritual priorities. A vast majority of the Israelites rejected these warnings and remained in Babylon.

Zech 2:8 Believers are precious to God (Ps 116:15); they are his very own children (Ps 103:13). Treating any believer unkindly is the same as treating God that way. As Jesus told his disciples, when we help others we are helping him; when we neglect or abuse them, we are neglecting or abusing him (Matt 25:34-46). Be careful, therefore, how you treat fellow believers—that is the way you are treating God.

Zech 2:9-12 *Me* (Zech 2:9) may refer to the Messiah, who, in the end, will judge all who have oppressed God's people. God promises to live among his people, and he says that many nations will come to know him (John 1:14; Rev 21:3).

Zech 2:11-12 God did not forget his words to Abraham, "All the families on earth will be blessed through you" (Gen 12:3). Abraham, the father of the nation of Israel, was promised that his descendants would bless the whole world. Since the coming of Jesus, the Messiah, this promise is being fulfilled—people from all nations are coming to God through him.

Zech 3:1 Jeshua was Israel's high priest when the remnant returned to Jerusalem and began rebuilding the walls (Hag 1:1, 12; 2:4).

Zech 3:1-3 Satan accused Jeshua, who here represents the nation of Israel. The accusations were accurate—Jeshua stood in "filthy" clothes (sins). Yet God revealed his mercy, stating that he chose to save his people in spite of their sin. Satan is always accusing people of their sins before God (Job 1:6). But he greatly misunderstands the breadth of God's mercy and forgiveness toward those who believe in him. Satan the Accuser will ultimately be destroyed (Rev 12:10), while everyone who is a believer will be saved (John 3:16). To be prepared, we can ask God to remove our clothing of sin and dress us with his goodness.

3Then the angel who was with me went to meet a second angel who was coming toward him. 4The other angel said, "Hurry, and say to that young man, 'Jerusalem will someday be so full of people and livestock that there won't be room enough for everyone! Many will live outside the city walls. 5Then I, myself, will be a protective wall of fire around Jerusalem, says the LORD. And I will be the glory inside the city!'"

The Exiles Are Called Home

ZECHARIAH 2:6-13

The LORD says, "Come away! Flee from Babylon in the land of the north, for I have scattered you to the four winds. 7Come away, people of Zion, you who are exiled in Babylon!"

8After a period of glory, the LORD of Heaven's Armies sent me* against the nations who plundered you. For he said, "Anyone who harms you harms my most precious possession.* 9I will raise my fist to crush them, and their own slaves will plunder them." Then you will know that the LORD of Heaven's Armies has sent me.

10The LORD says, "Shout and rejoice, O beautiful Jerusalem,* for I am coming to live among you. 11Many nations will join themselves to the LORD on that day, and they, too, will be my people. I will live among you, and you will know that the LORD of Heaven's Armies sent me to you. 12The land of Judah will be the LORD's special possession in the holy land, and he will once again choose Jerusalem to be his own city. 13Be silent before the LORD, all humanity, for he is springing into action from his holy dwelling."

Cleansing for the High Priest

ZECHARIAH 3:1-10

Then the angel showed me Jeshua* the high priest standing before the angel of the LORD. The Accuser,

Zec 2:8a The meaning of the Hebrew is uncertain. **Zec 2:8b** Hebrew *Anyone who touches you touches the pupil of his eye.* **Zec 2:10** Hebrew *O daughter of Zion.*
Zec 3:1a Hebrew *Joshua,* a variant spelling of Jeshua; also in 3:3, 4, 6, 8, 9.

ZECHARIAH'S VISIONS

Vision	*Reference*	*Significance*
Zechariah sees messengers reporting to God that the surrounding nations that have oppressed Judah are living in careless and sinful ease.	**Zech 1:7-17**	Israel was asking, "Why isn't God punishing the wicked?" Wicked nations may prosper, but not forever. God will bring upon them the judgment they deserve.
Zechariah sees four horns, representing the four world powers that oppressed and scattered the people of Judah and Israel. Then he sees four blacksmiths who will throw down the horns.	**Zech 1:18-21**	God will do what he promised. After the evil nations have carried out his will in punishing his people, God will destroy these nations for their sin.
Zechariah sees a man measuring the city of Jerusalem. The city will one day be full of people, and God himself will be a wall around the city.	**Zech 2:1-13**	The city will be restored in God's future Kingdom. God will keep his promise to protect his people.
Zechariah sees Jeshua the high priest standing before God. Jeshua's filthy clothes are exchanged for fine new clothes; God rejects Satan's accusations against Jeshua.	**Zech 3:1-10**	The story of Jeshua the high priest pictures how the filthy clothes of sin are replaced with the pure linen of God's righteousness. Christ has taken our clothes of sin and replaced them with God's righteousness. (See Eph 4:24; 1 Jn 1:9.)
Zechariah sees a lampstand that is continually kept burning by an unlimited reservoir of oil. This picture reminds the people that it is only through God's Spirit that they will succeed, not by their own might and resources.	**Zech 4:1-14**	The Spirit of God is given without measure. The work of God is not accomplished in human strength.
Zechariah sees a flying scroll, which represents God's curse.	**Zech 5:1-4**	By God's word and Spirit, every person will be judged. The individual's sin is the focus here, not the sins of the nation. God's curse is a symbol of destruction; all sin will be judged and removed.
Zechariah sees a vision of a woman in a basket. She represents the wickedness of the nations. The angel packed the woman back into the basket and sent her to Babylon.	**Zech 5:5-11**	Sins of the individual were judged in the last vision (Zech 5:1-4); now sin is being removed from society. Sin has to be eradicated in order to clean up the nation and the individual.
Zechariah sees a vision of four chariots. Their horses represent God's judgment on the world—one is sent north, the direction from which most of Judah's enemies came. The other horses are patrolling the world, ready to execute judgment at God's command.	**Zech 6:1-8**	Judgment will come upon those who oppress God's people—it will come in God's time and at his command.

▸ ZECHARIAH 3:1-10 *(cont.)*

Satan,* was there at the angel's right hand, making accusations against Jeshua. 2And the LORD said to Satan, "I, the LORD, reject your accusations, Satan. Yes, the LORD, who has chosen Jerusalem, rebukes you. This man is like a burning stick that has been snatched from the fire."

3Jeshua's clothing was filthy as he stood there before the angel. 4So the angel said to the others standing there, "Take off his filthy clothes." And turning to Jeshua he said, "See, I have taken away your sins, and now I am giving you these fine new clothes."

5Then I said, "They should also place a clean turban on his head." So they put a clean priestly turban on his head and dressed him in new clothes while the angel of the LORD stood by.

6Then the angel of the LORD spoke very solemnly to Jeshua and said, 7"This is what the LORD of Heaven's Armies says: If you follow my ways and carefully serve me, then you will be given authority over my Temple and its courtyards. I will let you walk among these others standing here.

8"Listen to me, O Jeshua the high priest, and all you other priests. You are symbols of things to come. Soon I am going to bring my servant, the Branch. 9Now look at the jewel I have set before Jeshua, a single stone with seven facets.* I will engrave an inscription on it, says the LORD of Heaven's Armies, and I will remove the sins of this land in a single day.

10"And on that day, says the LORD of Heaven's Armies, each of you will invite your neighbor to sit with you peacefully under your own grapevine and fig tree."

A Lampstand and Two Olive Trees

ZECHARIAH 4:1-14

Then the angel who had been talking with me returned and woke me, as though I had been asleep. 2"What do you see now?" he asked.

I answered, "I see a solid gold lampstand with a bowl of oil on top of it. Around the bowl are seven

Zec 3:1b Hebrew *The satan;* similarly in 3:2. **Zec 3:9** Hebrew *seven eyes.*

Olive Press

Oil was extracted from olives by a simple process. For the finest-quality oil, olives were picked before fully ripe and then crushed by hand with a stone mortar and pestle and the oil was manually collected. For the majority of uses, this fine oil wasn't necessary, and pickers would beat the olive trees with long poles to collect the fallen, ripe olives in baskets. Next, the olives were trodden out, probably in the same vat used for grapes (which were harvested approximately four weeks later). An oil mill or oil press (pictured) was then used to get the most oil from the olives as possible. As the oil dripped through the press, it was collected in a stone vat and allowed to settle and purify. When refined, the oil was stored in skins or jars. Oil was used in keeping lamps lit. In Zechariah's vision, the angel showed him a lampstand full of oil in the restored Temple. Whatever the oil represents—it could be the Spirit (see Zech 4:2-6)—we need a sufficient amount to keep our spiritual lamps lit.

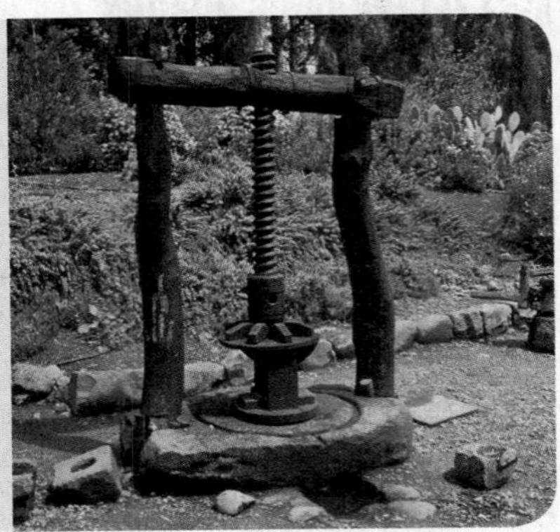

Zech 3:2 God punished Judah through the fire of great trials, but he rescued the nation before it was completely destroyed, like "a burning stick that has been snatched from the fire."

Zech 3:2-4 Zechariah's vision graphically portrays how we receive God's mercy. We do nothing ourselves. God removes our filthy clothes (sins), then provides us with fine, new clothes (the righteousness and holiness of God; 2 Cor 5:21; Eph 4:24; Rev 19:8). All we need to do is repent and ask God to forgive us. When Satan tries to make you feel dirty and unworthy, remember that the clean clothes of Christ's righteousness make you worthy to draw near to God.

Zech 3:5-7 The Greek name for Jeshua is Jesus, meaning "the LORD saves." He is seen here as a symbol of Jesus, the Messiah.

Zech 3:7-10 There was no priesthood during the Exile, so it had to be reinstated upon the return to the land. In this vision, Jeshua is installed as high priest. One of the high priest's duties was to offer a sacrifice on the Day of Atonement to make amends for all the sins of the people. The priest was the mediator between God and the nation. Thus, he represented the coming Messiah (Isa 11:1), who would change the entire order of God's dealing with people's sin (Heb 10:8-14 explains this in detail). Jesus, the Messiah, was the High Priest who offered, once for all, the sacrifice of himself to take away our sins. In the new order, every Christian is a priest, offering a holy, cleansed life to God (1 Pet 2:9; Rev 5:10).

Zech 3:8-9 The "Branch" refers to the Messiah. The meaning of the stone with seven facets is unclear. It could mean (1) the Branch himself as the foundation stone of the Temple, (2) the rock struck by Moses that produced water for the Israelites (Num 20:7-11), or (3) the renewed spiritual priesthood of the church (1 Pet 2:5). These verses were fulfilled hundreds of years later by Jesus Christ. God said, "I will remove the sins of this land in a single day," and this was fulfilled in Christ who "suffered for our sins once for all time . . . to bring you safely home to God" (1 Pet 3:18). You cannot remove your sins by your own effort. You must allow God to remove them through Christ.

Zech 3:10 God promises that each person will have their own place of security during Christ's reign (see also Mic 4:4).

Zech 4:1-3 The gold lampstand with a bowl and seven lamps on it represents a steady supply of oil, signifying that God's power would be reflected in the light. Oil was obtained from crushed olives and used in bowls with wicks to produce light. The two

lamps, each having seven spouts with wicks. [3]And
I see two olive trees, one on each side of the bowl."
[4]Then I asked the angel, "What are these, my lord?
What do they mean?"
[5]"Don't you know?" the angel asked.
"No, my lord," I replied.
[6]Then he said to me, "This is what the LORD says to
Zerubbabel: It is not by force nor by strength, but by
my Spirit, says the LORD of Heaven's Armies. [7]Nothing,
not even a mighty mountain, will stand in Zerubbabel's way; it will become a level plain before him! And
when Zerubbabel sets the final stone of the Temple
in place, the people will shout: 'May God bless it! May
God bless it!'*"
[8]Then another message came to me from the LORD:
[9]"Zerubbabel is the one who laid the foundation of
this Temple, and he will complete it. Then you will
know that the LORD of Heaven's Armies has sent me.
[10]Do not despise these small beginnings, for the LORD
rejoices to see the work begin, to see the plumb line
in Zerubbabel's hand."
(The seven lamps* represent the eyes of the LORD
that search all around the world.)
[11]Then I asked the angel, "What are these two olive
trees on each side of the lampstand, [12]and what are the
two olive branches that pour out golden oil through
two gold tubes?"
[13]"Don't you know?" he asked.
"No, my lord," I replied.
[14]Then he said to me, "They represent the two heavenly beings who stand in the court of the Lord of all
the earth."

A Flying Scroll

ZECHARIAH 5:1-4

I looked up again and saw a scroll flying through the
air.
[2]"What do you see?" the angel asked.
"I see a flying scroll," I replied. "It appears to be
about 30 feet long and 15 feet wide.*"
[3]Then he said to me, "This scroll contains the curse
that is going out over the entire land. One side of the
scroll says that those who steal will be banished from
the land; the other side says that those who swear
falsely will be banished from the land. [4]And this is
what the LORD of Heaven's Armies says: I am sending this curse into the house of every thief and into
the house of everyone who swears falsely using my
name. And my curse will remain in that house and
completely destroy it—even its timbers and stones."

A Woman in a Basket

ZECHARIAH 5:5-11

Then the angel who was talking with me came forward
and said, "Look up and see what's coming."
[6]"What is it?" I asked.
He replied, "It is a basket for measuring grain,* and it's
filled with the sins* of everyone throughout the land."
[7]Then the heavy lead cover was lifted off the basket,
and there was a woman sitting inside it. [8]The angel
said, "The woman's name is Wickedness," and he
pushed her back into the basket and closed the heavy
lid again.
[9]Then I looked up and saw two women flying toward us, gliding on the wind. They had wings like a

Zec 4:7 Hebrew *'Grace, grace to it.'* **Zec 4:10** Or *The seven facets* (see 3:9); Hebrew reads *These seven.* **Zec 5:2** Hebrew *20 cubits* [9 meters] *long and 10 cubits* [4.5 meters] *wide.* **Zec 5:6a** Hebrew *an ephah* [20 quarts or 22 liters]; also in 5:7, 8, 9, 10, 11. **Zec 5:6b** As in Greek version; Hebrew reads *the appearance.*

olive trees stood for the priestly and royal offices.

Zech 4:6 Zerubbabel was given the responsibility of rebuilding the Temple in Jerusalem (Ezra 3:2, 8; Hag 1:1; 2:23). While the prophets Haggai and Zechariah gave the moral and spiritual encouragement to resume work on the Temple, Zerubbabel saw that the task was carried out. As the work was being completed, the prophets encouraged Zerubbabel and told him of a time when spiritual apathy and foreign oppression would forever be abolished.

Zech 4:6 Many people believe that to survive in this world a person must be tough, strong, unbending, and harsh. But God says, "Not by force nor by strength, but by my Spirit." The key words are "by my Spirit." It is only through God's Spirit that anything of lasting value is accomplished. The returned exiles were indeed weak—harassed by their enemies, tired, discouraged, and poor. But actually they had God on their side! As you live for God, determine not to trust in your own strength or abilities. Instead, depend on God and work in the power of his Spirit! (See also Hos 1:7.)

Zech 4:9 The Temple was completed in 516 B.C. (Ezra 6:14-15).

Zech 4:10 Many of the older Jews were disheartened when they realized this new Temple would not match the size and splendor of the previous Temple built during King Solomon's reign. But bigger and more beautiful is not always better. What you do for God may seem small and insignificant at the time, but God rejoices in what is right, not necessarily in what is big. Be faithful in the small opportunities. Begin where you are and do what you can, and leave the results to God.

Zech 4:14 The two heavenly beings may be Jeshua and Zerubbabel, dedicated for this special task. Also note that in Revelation 11:3, two witnesses arise to prophesy to the nations during the time of tribulation. These witnesses will be killed but will rise again.

Zech 5:1-9 The judgment of the flying scroll was leveled against those who violated God's law, specifically by stealing and lying (Zech 5:1-4). The woman in a basket personified wickedness; this vision showed that wickedness would be not only severely punished (the vision of the flying scroll) but also banished (the vision of the woman in a basket; Zech 5:6-9).

Zech 5:9-11 The woman in a basket was carried away "to the land of Babylonia," which had become a symbol for the center of world idolatry and wickedness. This woman was a picture to Zechariah that wickedness and sin would be taken away from Israel and one day sin would be removed from the entire earth. When Christ died, he removed sin's power and penalty. When we trust Christ to forgive us, he removes the penalty of sin and gives us the power to overcome sin in our lives. When Christ returns, he will remove all sin from the earth, allowing people to live in eternal safety and security.

▸ **ZECHARIAH 5:5-11** ***(cont.)***

stork, and they picked up the basket and flew into the sky.
10"Where are they taking the basket?" I asked the angel.
11He replied, "To the land of Babylonia,* where they will build a temple for the basket. And when the temple is ready, they will set the basket there on its pedestal."

Four Chariots

ZECHARIAH 6:1-8

Then I looked up again and saw four chariots coming from between two bronze mountains. 2The first
chariot was pulled by red horses, the second by black
horses, 3the third by white horses, and the fourth by
powerful dappled-gray horses. 4"And what are these,
my lord?" I asked the angel who was talking with me.
5The angel replied, "These are the four spirits* of
heaven who stand before the Lord of all the earth. They
are going out to do his work. 6The chariot with black
horses is going north, the chariot with white horses is
going west,* and the chariot with dappled-gray horses
is going south."
7The powerful horses were eager to set out to patrol
the earth. And the LORD said, "Go and patrol the earth!"
So they left at once on their patrol.
8Then the LORD summoned me and said, "Look,
those who went north have vented the anger of my
Spirit* there in the land of the north."

The Crowning of Jeshua

ZECHARIAH 6:9-15

Then I received another message from the LORD:
10"Heldai, Tobijah, and Jedaiah will bring gifts of
silver and gold from the Jews exiled in Babylon. As
soon as they arrive, meet them at the home of Josiah
son of Zephaniah. 11Accept their gifts, and make a
crown* from the silver and gold. Then put the crown
on the head of Jeshua* son of Jehozadak, the high
priest. 12Tell him, 'This is what the LORD of Heaven's
Armies says: Here is the man called the Branch. He will
branch out from where he is and build the Temple of
the LORD. 13Yes, he will build the Temple of the LORD.
Then he will receive royal honor and will rule as king
from his throne. He will also serve as priest from his
throne,* and there will be perfect harmony between
his two roles.'
14"The crown will be a memorial in the Temple of
the LORD to honor those who gave it—Heldai,* Tobijah,
Jedaiah, and Josiah* son of Zephaniah."
15People will come from distant lands to rebuild the
Temple of the LORD. And when this happens, you will
know that my messages have been from the LORD of
Heaven's Armies. All this will happen if you carefully
obey what the LORD your God says.

Tattenai's Letter to King Darius

EZRA 5:3-17

But Tattenai, governor of the province west of the
Euphrates River,* and Shethar-bozenai and their
colleagues soon arrived in Jerusalem and asked,
"Who gave you permission to rebuild this Temple
and restore this structure?" 4They also asked for
the names of all the men working on the Temple.
5But because their God was watching over them,
the leaders of the Jews were not prevented from
building until a report was sent to Darius and he
returned his decision.
6This is a copy of the letter that Tattenai the

Zec 5:11 Hebrew *the land of Shinar.* **Zec 6:5** Or *the four winds.* **Zec 6:6** Hebrew *is going after them.* **Zec 6:8** Hebrew *have given my Spirit rest.* **Zec 6:11a** As in Greek and Syriac versions; Hebrew reads *crowns.* **Zec 6:11b** Hebrew *Joshua,* a variant spelling of Jeshua. **Zec 6:13** Or *There will be a priest by his throne.* **Zec 6:14a** As in Syriac version (compare 6:10); Hebrew reads *Helem.* **Zec 6:14b** As in Syriac version (compare 6:10); Hebrew reads *Hen.* **Ezr 5:3** Aramaic *the province beyond the river;* also in 5:6.

Zech 6:1-8 The four chariots were similar to the four horsemen in the first vision. These chariots represent the four angels of God's judgment on the earth.

Zech 6:6, 8 The black horses that went north executed God's judgment in the north country. God is angry with sin and with the wicked (Ps 7:11), and his anger is expressed in judgment. As much as we like to concentrate on God's love and mercy, anger and judgment are also part of his righteous character. If you have unconfessed or habitual sin in your life, confess it and turn away from it. Confession brings God's mercy, but refusing to repent invites his judgment.

Zech 6:9-15 This vision is about the Messiah, the King-Priest. In the days of the kings and after the Exile, Judah's government was to be ruled by two distinct persons—the king, ruling the nation's political life, and the high priest, ruling its religious life. Kings and priests had often been corrupt. God was telling Zechariah that someone worthy of the crown would come to rule as both king ("rule as king from his throne") and priest ("serve as priest from his throne"). This was an unlikely combination for that day.

Zech 6:15 Some of God's promises are conditional—we must obey him to receive them. The rebuilding of the Temple required careful obedience. God would protect the people as long as they obeyed. Casual or occasional obedience, the result of a halfhearted or divided commitment, would not lead to blessing. Many of God's blessings come to us as a result of diligent obedience. Inconsistent obedience can't produce consistent blessing.

Ezra 5:3-5 The non-Jews who lived nearby attempted to hinder the construction of the Temple. But while the legal debate went on and the decision was under appeal, the Jews continued to rebuild. When we are doing God's work, others may try to delay, confuse, or frustrate us, but we can proceed confidently. God will accomplish his purposes in our world, no matter who attempts to block them. Just as he watched over the Jewish elders, he watches over you. Concentrate on God's purpose, and don't be sidetracked by intrigues or slander.

Ezra 5:6-17 This letter, in comparison with the previous one (Ezra 4:11-16), at least stated the facts correctly and asked a fair question. The earlier letter accused the Jews of preparing the foundation for the entire city, rather than reporting that they were doing only what they had been permitted by Cyrus to do. Perhaps the opposition simply thought that sending this letter to Babylon would create enough concern to stop the Jews from rebuilding the Temple. But God had other plans. We can't predict how God will get his purposes accomplished, but we can certainly trust he will succeed!

governor, Shethar-bozenai, and the other officials
of the province west of the Euphrates River sent to
King Darius:

7"To King Darius. Greetings.
8"The king should know that we went to the
construction site of the Temple of the great God
in the province of Judah. It is being rebuilt with
specially prepared stones, and timber is being
laid in its walls. The work is going forward with
great energy and success.
9"We asked the leaders, 'Who gave you
permission to rebuild this Temple and restore
this structure?' 10And we demanded their names
so that we could tell you who the leaders were.
11"This was their answer: 'We are the servants
of the God of heaven and earth, and we are
rebuilding the Temple that was built here many
years ago by a great king of Israel. 12But because
our ancestors angered the God of heaven, he
abandoned them to King Nebuchadnezzar of
Babylon,* who destroyed this Temple and exiled
the people to Babylonia. 13However, King Cyrus
of Babylon,* during the first year of his reign,
issued a decree that the Temple of God should
be rebuilt. 14King Cyrus returned the gold and
silver cups that Nebuchadnezzar had taken
from the Temple of God in Jerusalem and had
placed in the temple of Babylon. These cups
were taken from that temple and presented to
a man named Sheshbazzar, whom King Cyrus
appointed as governor of Judah. 15The king
instructed him to return the cups to their place
in Jerusalem and to rebuild the Temple of God
there on its original site. 16So this Sheshbazzar
came and laid the foundations of the Temple
of God in Jerusalem. The people have been
working on it ever since, though it is not yet
completed.'
17"Therefore, if it pleases the king, we request
that a search be made in the royal archives of
Babylon to discover whether King Cyrus ever
issued a decree to rebuild God's Temple in
Jerusalem. And then let the king send us his
decision in this matter."

Ezr 5:12 Aramaic *Nebuchadnezzar the Chaldean.* **Ezr 5:13** King Cyrus of Persia is here identified as the king of Babylon because Persia had conquered the Babylonian Empire.

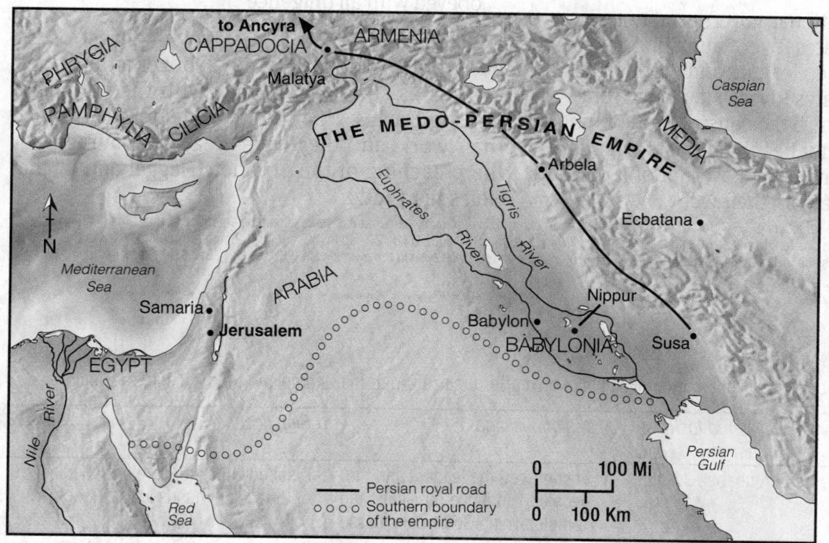

◀ ***THE MEDO-PERSIAN EMPIRE*** *The Medo-Persian Empire included the lands of Media and Persia, much of the area shown on this map and more. The Jewish exiles were concentrated in the area around Nippur in the Babylonian province. The decree by King Cyrus that allowed the Israelites to return to their homeland and rebuild the Temple was discovered in the palace at Ecbatana.*

Ezra 5:11 While rebuilding the Temple, the workers were confronted by the Persia-appointed governor, demanding to know who gave permission for their construction project (Ezra 5:3). This could have been intimidating, but, as we learn from the letter, they boldly replied, "We are the servants of the God of heaven and earth."

It is not always easy to speak up for our faith in an unbelieving world, but we must. The way to deal with pressure and intimidation is to recognize that we are workers for God. Our allegiance is to him first, people second. When we contemplate the reactions and criticisms of hostile people, we can become paralyzed with fear. If we try to offend no one or to please everyone, we won't be effective. God is our leader, and his rewards are most important. So don't be intimidated. Let others know by your words and actions whom you really serve.

Ezra 5:13-17 Cyrus is called king of Persia in Ezra 1:1 and king of Babylon in Ezra 5:13. Because Persia had just conquered Babylon, Cyrus was king of both nations. Babylon is more important to this story because it was the location of the Hebrews' 70-year captivity. The Babylon in Ezra 5:17 may refer to the city of Babylon, which was the capital of the nation of Babylon.

Darius Approves the Rebuilding

EZRA 6:1-14a

So King Darius issued orders that a search be made in the Babylonian archives, which were stored in the treasury. 2But it was at the fortress at Ecbatana in the province of Media that a scroll was found. This is what it said:

"Memorandum:

3"In the first year of King Cyrus's reign, a decree was sent out concerning the Temple of God at Jerusalem.

"Let the Temple be rebuilt on the site where Jews used to offer their sacrifices, using the original foundations. Its height will be ninety feet, and its width will be ninety feet.* 4Every three layers of specially prepared stones will be topped by a layer of timber. All expenses will be paid by the royal treasury. 5Furthermore, the gold and silver cups, which were taken to Babylon by Nebuchadnezzar from the Temple of God in Jerusalem, must be returned to Jerusalem and put back where they belong. Let them be taken back to the Temple of God."

6So King Darius sent this message:

"Now therefore, Tattenai, governor of the province west of the Euphrates River,* and Shethar-bozenai, and your colleagues and other officials west of the Euphrates River—stay away from there! 7Do not disturb the construction of the Temple of God. Let it be rebuilt on its original site, and do not hinder the governor of Judah and the elders of the Jews in their work.

8"Moreover, I hereby decree that you are to help these elders of the Jews as they rebuild this Temple of God. You must pay the full construction costs, without delay, from my taxes collected in the province west of the Euphrates River so that the work will not be interrupted.

9"Give the priests in Jerusalem whatever is needed in the way of young bulls, rams, and male lambs for the burnt offerings presented to the God of heaven. And without fail, provide them with as much wheat, salt, wine, and olive oil as they need each day. 10Then they will be able to offer acceptable sacrifices to the God of heaven and pray for the welfare of the king and his sons.

11"Those who violate this decree in any way will have a beam pulled from their house. Then they will be tied to it and flogged, and their house will be reduced to a pile of rubble.* 12May the God who has chosen the city of Jerusalem as the place to honor his name destroy any king or nation that violates this command and destroys this Temple.

"I, Darius, have issued this decree. Let it be obeyed with all diligence."

13Tattenai, governor of the province west of the Euphrates River, and Shethar-bozenai and their colleagues complied at once with the command of King Darius. 14So the Jewish elders continued their work, and they were greatly encouraged by the preaching of the prophets Haggai and Zechariah son of Iddo.

Ezr 6:3 Aramaic *Its height will be 60 cubits* [27.6 meters], *and its width will be 60 cubits.* It is commonly held that this verse should be emended to read: "Its height will be 30 cubits [45 feet, or 13.8 meters], its length will be 60 cubits [90 feet, or 27.6 meters], and its width will be 20 cubits [30 feet, or 9.2 meters]"; compare 1 Kgs 6:2. The emendation regarding the width is supported by the Syriac version. **Ezr 6:6** Aramaic *the province beyond the river;* also in 6:6b, 8, 13. **Ezr 6:11** Aramaic *a dunghill.*

THE POSTEXILIC PROPHETS

God used these men both to confront and comfort his people after their return to their homeland from exile in Babylon.

Who?	*When?*	*Ministered to These Contemporary Leaders*	*Main Message*	*Significance*
Haggai	520 B.C.	Zerubbabel, Joshua	Encouraged the leaders and the people to continue rebuilding the Temple, which God would bless	Disobedience and careless obedience of God's commands lead to judgment.
Zechariah	520 B.C.	Zerubbabel, Joshua	Challenged the people's careless worship, which God would not bless	Encouragement for today's effort sometimes requires that we remember God has a plan and purpose for tomorrow. Meanwhile the challenge is to live for him today.
Joel	440 B.C. (?)	Specific leaders aren't mentioned	Encouraged faithfulness to God in light of his coming day of judgment and salvation	God is in control of everything that happens. We need to trust him and look forward to his ultimate justice.
Malachi	430 B.C.	The priests are the only leaders mentioned	Emphasized God's command to rebuild his Temple	God expects our obedience to him to affect our attitude toward him and our treatment of one another.

A Call to Justice and Mercy

ZECHARIAH 7:1-14

On December 7* of the fourth year of King Darius's
reign, another message came to Zechariah from the
LORD. 2The people of Bethel had sent Sharezer and
Regemmelech,* along with their attendants, to seek
the LORD's favor. 3They were to ask this question of the
prophets and the priests at the Temple of the LORD of
Heaven's Armies: "Should we continue to mourn and
fast each summer on the anniversary of the Temple's
destruction,* as we have done for so many years?"
4The LORD of Heaven's Armies sent me this message
in reply: 5"Say to all your people and your priests, 'During these seventy years of exile, when you fasted and
mourned in the summer and in early autumn,* was it
really for me that you were fasting? 6And even now in
your holy festivals, aren't you eating and drinking just
to please yourselves? 7Isn't this the same message the
LORD proclaimed through the prophets in years past
when Jerusalem and the towns of Judah were bustling
with people, and the Negev and the foothills of Judah*
were well populated?'"
8Then this message came to Zechariah from the
LORD: 9"This is what the LORD of Heaven's Armies says:
Judge fairly, and show mercy and kindness to one another. 10Do not oppress widows, orphans, foreigners,
and the poor. And do not scheme against each other.
11"Your ancestors refused to listen to this message.
They stubbornly turned away and put their fingers in
their ears to keep from hearing. 12They made their
hearts as hard as stone, so they could not hear the
instructions or the messages that the LORD of Heaven's
Armies had sent them by his Spirit through the earlier
prophets. That is why the LORD of Heaven's Armies was
so angry with them.
13"Since they refused to listen when I called to
them, I would not listen when they called to me, says
the LORD of Heaven's Armies. 14As with a whirlwind, I
scattered them among the distant nations, where they
lived as strangers. Their land became so desolate that
no one even traveled through it. They turned their
pleasant land into a desert."

Promised Blessings for Jerusalem

ZECHARIAH 8:1-23

Then another message came to me from the LORD of
Heaven's Armies: 2"This is what the LORD of Heaven's
Armies says: My love for Mount Zion is passionate and
strong; I am consumed with passion for Jerusalem!
3"And now the LORD says: I am returning to Mount
Zion, and I will live in Jerusalem. Then Jerusalem will
be called the Faithful City; the mountain of the LORD
of Heaven's Armies will be called the Holy Mountain.
4"This is what the LORD of Heaven's Armies says:
Once again old men and women will walk Jerusalem's
streets with their canes and will sit together in the city
squares. 5And the streets of the city will be filled with
boys and girls at play.
6"This is what the LORD of Heaven's Armies says: All
this may seem impossible to you now, a small remnant
of God's people. But is it impossible for me? says the
LORD of Heaven's Armies.
7"This is what the LORD of Heaven's Armies says: You
can be sure that I will rescue my people from the east

Zec 7:1 Hebrew *On the fourth day of the ninth month, the month of Kislev,* of the ancient Hebrew lunar calendar. This event occurred on December 7, 518 B.C.; also see note on 1:1. **Zec 7:2** Or *Bethel-sharezer had sent Regemmelech.* **Zec 7:3** Hebrew *mourn and fast in the fifth month.* The Temple had been destroyed in the fifth month of the ancient Hebrew lunar calendar (August 586 B.C.); see 2 Kgs 25:8. **Zec 7:5** Hebrew *fasted and mourned in the fifth and seventh months.* The fifth month of the ancient Hebrew lunar calendar usually occurs within the months of July and August. The seventh month usually occurs within the months of September and October; both the Day of Atonement and the Festival of Shelters were celebrated in the seventh month. **Zec 7:7** Hebrew *the Shephelah.*

Ezra 6:1-2 Many clay and papyrus documents recording business transactions and historical data have been discovered in this area (near present-day Syria). A great library and archives with thousands of such records was also discovered at Ebla in Syria.

Zech 7:1ff The fourth year of King Darius's reign was 518 B.C. For the previous 70 years, the people had been holding a fast in August to remember the destruction of Jerusalem. Because Jerusalem was being rebuilt, they came to the Temple to ask if they had to continue this annual fast. God did not answer their question directly. Instead, he told them that their acts of justice and mercy were more important than their fasting. What he wanted from his people was true justice in their dealings and mercy and compassion for the weak.

Zech 7:5-7 The Israelites had lost their sincere desire for a loving relationship with God. Zechariah told them that they had been fasting without a proper attitude of repentance or worship. They fasted and mourned during their exile with no thought of God or their sins that had caused it in the first place. When you go to church, pray, or have fellowship with other believers, are you doing these things from habit or for what you can get out of them? God says that an attitude of worship without a sincere desire to know and love him will lead to ruin.

Zech 7:7 The Negev was the southern part of Judah.

Zech 7:11-12 Zechariah explained to the people that their ancestors brought God's great wrath on themselves by hardening their hearts. Any sin seems more natural the second time—as we become hardened, each repetition is easier. Ignoring or refusing God's warning hardens you each time you do wrong. Read God's Word and apply it to your life. Sensitivity and submission to God's Word can soften your heart and allow you to live as you should.

Zech 8:3 One day Christ will reign in his Kingdom on earth. There all his people will live with him. This truth should encourage us to look forward to the Messiah's reign.

Zech 8:4-5 In troubled times, the very old and very young are the first to suffer and die. But both groups are plentiful in this vision, filling the streets with their normal everyday activities. This is a sign of the complete peace and prosperity of God's new earth.

Zech 8:6 The remnant was the small group of exiles who had returned from Babylon to rebuild Jerusalem and the Temple. Struggling to survive in the land, they became discouraged over the opposition they often faced from hostile neighbors. It was hard to believe that one day God himself would reign from this city and that their land would enjoy great peace and prosperity. Our God is all-powerful; he can do anything! When confronting seemingly impossible tasks or situations, remember that "with God everything is possible" (Matt 19:26).

▸ **ZECHARIAH 8:1-23** ***(cont.)***

and from the west. 8I will bring them home again to live safely in Jerusalem. They will be my people, and I will be faithful and just toward them as their God.

9"This is what the LORD of Heaven's Armies says: Be strong and finish the task! Ever since the laying of the foundation of the Temple of the LORD of Heaven's Armies, you have heard what the prophets have been saying about completing the building. 10Before the work on the Temple began, there were no jobs and no money to hire people or animals. No traveler was safe from the enemy, for there were enemies on all sides. I had turned everyone against each other.

11"But now I will not treat the remnant of my people as I treated them before, says the LORD of Heaven's Armies. 12For I am planting seeds of peace and prosperity among you. The grapevines will be heavy with fruit. The earth will produce its crops, and the heavens will release the dew. Once more I will cause the remnant in Judah and Israel to inherit these blessings. 13Among the other nations, Judah and Israel became symbols of a cursed nation. But no longer! Now I will rescue you and make you both a symbol and a source of blessing. So don't be afraid. Be strong, and get on with rebuilding the Temple!

14"For this is what the LORD of Heaven's Armies says: I was determined to punish you when your ancestors angered me, and I did not change my mind, says the LORD of Heaven's Armies. 15But now I am determined to bless Jerusalem and the people of Judah. So don't be afraid. 16But this is what you must do: Tell the truth to each other. Render verdicts in your courts that are just and that lead to peace. 17Don't scheme against each other. Stop your love of telling lies that you swear are the truth. I hate all these things, says the LORD."

18Here is another message that came to me from the LORD of Heaven's Armies. 19"This is what the LORD of Heaven's Armies says: The traditional fasts and times of mourning you have kept in early summer, midsummer, autumn, and winter* are now ended. They will become festivals of joy and celebration for the people of Judah. So love truth and peace.

20"This is what the LORD of Heaven's Armies says: People from nations and cities around the world will travel to Jerusalem. 21The people of one city will say to the people of another, 'Come with us to Jerusalem to ask the LORD to bless us. Let's worship the LORD of Heaven's Armies. I'm determined to go.' 22Many peoples and powerful nations will come to Jerusalem to seek the LORD of Heaven's Armies and to ask for his blessing.

23"This is what the LORD of Heaven's Armies says: In those days ten men from different nations and languages of the world will clutch at the sleeve of one Jew. And they will say, 'Please let us walk with you, for we have heard that God is with you.'"

Judgment against Israel's Enemies

ZECHARIAH 9:1-8

This is the message* from the LORD against the land of Aram* and the city of Damascus, for the eyes of humanity, including all the tribes of Israel, are on the LORD.

2 Doom is certain for Hamath,
  near Damascus,
and for the cities of Tyre and Sidon,
  though they are so clever.
3 Tyre has built a strong fortress
  and has made silver and gold
  as plentiful as dust in the streets!

Zec 8:19 Hebrew *in the fourth, fifth, seventh, and tenth months.* The fourth month of the ancient Hebrew lunar calendar usually occurs within the months of June and July. The fifth month usually occurs within the months of July and August. The seventh month usually occurs within the months of September and October. The tenth month usually occurs within the months of December and January. **Zec 9:1a** Hebrew *An Oracle: The message.* **Zec 9:1b** Hebrew *land of Hadrach.*

Zech 8:8 The covenant relationship will be renewed, and the whole community will be filled with the presence of God. This promise of forgiveness and restoration extends to all God's people wherever they may be found. (For other references to this promise, see Exod 6:6-7; 19:5-6; 29:45; Lev 26:12; Deut 7:6; Jer 31:1, 33.)

Zech 8:9 God had to give the Temple workers a little push to get them moving. They had heard the prophets' words of encouragement; at this time they needed to stop listening only and get to work. We need to listen to what God says, but after he has made our course of action plain, we need to "be strong" and do what he wants.

Zech 8:13-15 For more than 15 years, God and his prophets had been urging the people to finish building the Temple. Here again, God encouraged them with visions of the future. We may be tempted to slow down for many reasons: People aren't responding; we feel physically or emotionally drained; the workers are uncooperative; the work is distasteful, too difficult, or not worth the effort. God's promises about the future should encourage us now. He knows what the results of our labors will be, and thus he can give us a perspective that will help us continue in our work for him.

Zech 8:14-17 God promised to give his people rich rewards, reassuring them that despite the punishments they had endured, he would not change his mind to bless them. But he also said they had a job to do: "This is what you must do." God will be faithful, but we also have responsibilities: to tell the truth, exercise justice, and live peacefully. If you expect God to do his part, be sure to do yours.

Zech 8:19-22 There will come a time when fasting for sins will be replaced by feasting and joy. People from all nations will "seek the LORD of Heaven's Armies." Zechariah 2:11 also promises this.

Zech 8:23 In the past, Jerusalem had often borne the brunt of cruel jokes from other nations (Zech 8:13). The city was not respected; its citizens had sinned so much that God let them be kicked around by their enemies. But eventually, says Zechariah, Jerusalem will be a holy place—highly respected throughout the world because its people will have a change of heart toward God. People from other nations will see how God has rewarded his people for their faithfulness and want to be included in their great blessings.

Zech 9:1-17 Zechariah 9–14 contains two messages delivered late in Zechariah's life. They point to the Messiah and his second coming. Some of these prophecies were fulfilled before the Messiah came, perhaps by Alexander the Great; others were fulfilled during the Messiah's time on earth; and others will be fulfilled when he returns. Those who oppressed Jerusalem—Aram, Philistia, Phoenicia—would be crushed. Zion's promised King would come—first as a servant on a donkey's colt, later as a powerful ruler and judge.

4 But now the Lord will strip away Tyre's
possessions
and hurl its fortifications into the sea,
and it will be burned to the ground.
5 The city of Ashkelon will see Tyre fall
and will be filled with fear.
Gaza will shake with terror,
as will Ekron, for their hopes will be dashed.
Gaza's king will be killed,
and Ashkelon will be deserted.
6 Foreigners will occupy the city of Ashdod.
I will destroy the pride of the Philistines.
7 I will grab the bloody meat from their mouths
and snatch the detestable sacrifices from their
teeth.
Then the surviving Philistines will worship
our God
and become like a clan in Judah.*
The Philistines of Ekron will join my people,
as the ancient Jebusites once did.
8 I will guard my Temple
and protect it from invading armies.
I am watching closely to ensure
that no more foreign oppressors overrun my
people's land.

Zion's Coming King

ZECHARIAH 9:9-17

9 Rejoice, O people of Zion!*
Shout in triumph, O people of Jerusalem!
Look, your king is coming to you.
He is righteous and victorious,*
yet he is humble, riding on a donkey—
riding on a donkey's colt.
10 I will remove the battle chariots from Israel*
and the warhorses from Jerusalem.
I will destroy all the weapons used in battle,
and your king will bring peace to the
nations.
His realm will stretch from sea to sea
and from the Euphrates River* to the ends
of the earth.*
11 Because of the covenant I made with you,
sealed with blood,
I will free your prisoners
from death in a waterless dungeon.
12 Come back to the place of safety,
all you prisoners who still have hope!
I promise this very day
that I will repay two blessings for each of your
troubles.

Zec 9:7 Hebrew *and will become a leader in Judah.* **Zec 9:9a** Hebrew *O daughter of Zion!* **Zec 9:9b** Hebrew *and is being vindicated.* **Zec 9:10a** Hebrew *Ephraim,* referring to the northern kingdom of Israel; also in 9:13. **Zec 9:10b** Hebrew *the river.* **Zec 9:10c** Or *the end of the land.*

Zech 9:5-7 Zechariah mentions four key cities in Philistia: Ashkelon, Gaza, and Ekron would be destroyed, and Ashdod would be overtaken by foreigners. This would happen because of their great evil and idolatry. But those left in the land would be adopted into Israel as a new clan, as the Jebusites had been. (When David conquered Jerusalem, he did not wipe out the Jebusites, but absorbed them into Judah.)

Zech 9:8 Several centuries after Zechariah's day, Antiochus IV Epiphanes would invade Israel; and in A.D. 70, Titus, a Roman general, would completely destroy the Temple. This promise, therefore, may have been conditional upon the people's obedience. The day will come, however, when God's people will never again have to worry about invading enemies (Joel 3:17).

Zech 9:9 The triumphal entry of Jesus riding into Jerusalem (Matt 21:1-11) was predicted here more than 500 years before it happened. Just as this prophecy was fulfilled when Jesus came to earth, so the prophecies of his second coming are just as certain to come true. We are to be ready for his return, for he is coming!

Zech 9:10 When we view two distant mountains, they appear to be close together, perhaps even to touch each other. But as we approach them, we can see that they are, in fact, far apart, even separated by a huge valley. This is the situation with many Old Testament prophecies. Zechariah 9:9 was clearly fulfilled in Christ's first coming, but Zechariah 9:10 can now be seen to refer to his second coming. At that time all nations will be subject to Christ, and his rule will extend over the whole earth. In Philippians 2:9-11, we are told that at that time every knee will bow to Christ and every tongue will confess him as Lord.

Zech 9:11 Covenants in Old Testament times were sealed or confirmed with blood, much as we would sign our name to a contract. The old covenant was sealed by the blood of sacrifices, pointing ahead to the blood Christ would shed at Calvary, his "signature" that confirmed God's new covenant with his people. Because God had made a covenant with these people, he delivered them from the "waterless dungeon," the cistern-like prison of exile.

Gaza

Gaza is a city near the Palestinian coast, about 50 miles west-southwest of Jerusalem. It has been occupied almost continuously since ancient times. Modern Gaza continues to play an important part in the conflict between Arabs and Israelis. Gaza was named the southern boundary of Israel during the time of Solomon, whose dominion extended over all the kingdoms west of the Euphrates River, from Tiphsah to Gaza (1 Kgs 4:24). Hezekiah defeated the Philistines as far as Gaza (2 Kgs 18:8). Jeremiah 47 records a prophecy against the Philistines, which the Lord gave him before Pharaoh attacked Gaza. Amos gives specific prophecies of judgment against Gaza (Amos 1:6-7). Zechariah 9:5 gives an oracle of judgment in which it is said that Gaza will "shake with terror" and that its king will perish.

▸ **ZECHARIAH 9:9-17** ***(cont.)***

13 Judah is my bow,
and Israel is my arrow.
Jerusalem* is my sword,
and like a warrior, I will brandish it against the Greeks.*
14 The LORD will appear above his people;
his arrows will fly like lightning!
The Sovereign LORD will sound the ram's horn
and attack like a whirlwind from the southern desert.
15 The LORD of Heaven's Armies will protect his people,
and they will defeat their enemies by hurling great stones.
They will shout in battle as though drunk with wine.
They will be filled with blood like a bowl,
drenched with blood like the corners of the altar.
16 On that day the LORD their God will rescue his people,
just as a shepherd rescues his sheep.
They will sparkle in his land
like jewels in a crown.
17 How wonderful and beautiful they will be!
The young men will thrive on abundant grain,
and the young women will flourish on new wine.

The LORD Will Restore His People

ZECHARIAH 10:1–11:3

1 Ask the LORD for rain in the spring,
for he makes the storm clouds.
And he will send showers of rain
so every field becomes a lush pasture.
2 Household gods give worthless advice,
fortune-tellers predict only lies,
and interpreters of dreams pronounce
falsehoods that give no comfort.
So my people are wandering like lost sheep;
they are attacked because they have no shepherd.
3 "My anger burns against your shepherds,
and I will punish these leaders.*
For the LORD of Heaven's Armies has arrived
to look after Judah, his flock.
He will make them strong and glorious,
like a proud warhorse in battle.
4 From Judah will come the cornerstone,
the tent peg,
the bow for battle,
and all the rulers.
5 They will be like mighty warriors in battle,
trampling their enemies in the mud under their feet.
Since the LORD is with them as they fight,
they will overthrow even the enemy's horsemen.
6 "I will strengthen Judah and save Israel*;
I will restore them because of my compassion.
It will be as though I had never rejected them,
for I am the LORD their God, who will hear their cries.
7 The people of Israel* will become like mighty warriors,
and their hearts will be made happy as if by wine.
Their children, too, will see it and be glad;
their hearts will rejoice in the LORD.
8 When I whistle to them, they will come running,
for I have redeemed them.
From the few who are left,
they will grow as numerous as they were before.
9 Though I have scattered them like seeds among the nations,
they will still remember me in distant lands.

Zec 9:13a Hebrew *Zion.* **Zec 9:13b** Hebrew *the sons of Javan.* **Zec 10:3** Or *these male goats.* **Zec 10:6** Hebrew *save the house of Joseph.* **Zec 10:7** Hebrew *of Ephraim.*

Zech 9:14-17 After Solomon's reign, the kingdom was divided into the northern kingdom (called Israel or Ephraim) and the southern kingdom (called Judah, with Jerusalem as the capital). This prophecy says that all Israel, north and south, will someday be reunited. Zechariah 9:1-8 tells how God will help his people avoid war; here (Zech 9:14-17) God explains that he will come to help his people when war is inevitable. The Jews will triumph over the Greeks (Zech 9:14-16); it is also a figurative picture of the ultimate future victory over evil by God's people.

Zech 10:2 We often create idols of money, power, fame, or success, and then we expect them to give us happiness and security. But these idols can't supply what we need any more than a stone image can make it rain. How foolish it is to trust in idols. Instead, trust God's promises for your future.

Zech 10:4 Zechariah's prophecy, more than 500 years before Christ's first coming, called Christ the "cornerstone" (see also Isa 28:16), the "nail in the wall" (Isa 22:23), the "bow for battle," and a ruler who was a man of action (see also Gen 49:10; Mic 5:2). This Messiah would be strong, stable, victorious, and trustworthy—in all ways, the answer to Israel's problems. Only in the Messiah will all the promises to God's people be fulfilled.

Zech 10:6 Judah refers to the southern kingdom, and Israel refers to the northern kingdom. One day God will unite all his people. This verse tells about God's reuniting of the Jews (see also Jer 31:10). This was a startling idea. The people of the northern kingdom of Israel were so completely absorbed into other cultures after their captivity in 722 B.C. that a regathering could only be accomplished by God.

Zech 10:6, 12 God promises to strengthen his people. When we stay closely connected to God, his Spirit will enable us to do his will, despite the obstacles. When we stray from God, we will be cut off from our power source.

They and their children will survive
and return again to Israel.
10 I will bring them back from Egypt
and gather them from Assyria.
I will resettle them in Gilead and Lebanon
until there is no more room for them all.
11 They will pass safely through the sea
of distress,*
for the waves of the sea will be held back,
and the waters of the Nile will dry up.
The pride of Assyria will be crushed,
and the rule of Egypt will end.
12 By my power* I will make my people strong,
and by my authority they will go wherever
they wish.
I, the LORD, have spoken!"

11:1 Open your doors, Lebanon,
so that fire may devour your cedar forests.
2 Weep, you cypress trees, for all the ruined
cedars;
the most majestic ones have fallen.
Weep, you oaks of Bashan,
for the thick forests have been cut down.
3 Listen to the wailing of the shepherds,
for their rich pastures are destroyed.
Hear the young lions roaring,
for their thickets in the Jordan Valley are
ruined.

The Good and Evil Shepherds

ZECHARIAH 11:4-17

This is what the LORD my God says: "Go and care for
the flock that is intended for slaughter. 5The buyers
slaughter their sheep without remorse. The sellers say,
'Praise the LORD! Now I'm rich!' Even the shepherds
have no compassion for them. 6Likewise, I will no longer have pity on the people of the land," says the LORD.
"I will let them fall into each other's hands and into
the hands of their king. They will turn the land into a
wilderness, and I will not rescue them."

7So I cared for the flock intended for slaughter—the flock that was oppressed. Then I took two
shepherd's staffs and named one Favor and the other
Union. 8I got rid of their three evil shepherds in a
single month.

But I became impatient with these sheep, and they
hated me, too. 9So I told them, "I won't be your shepherd any longer. If you die, you die. If you are killed,
you are killed. And let those who remain devour each
other!"

10Then I took my staff called Favor and cut it in
two, showing that I had revoked the covenant I had
made with all the nations. 11That was the end of my
covenant with them. The suffering flock was watching me, and they knew that the LORD was speaking
through my actions.

12And I said to them, "If you like, give me my wages,
whatever I am worth; but only if you want to." So they
counted out for my wages thirty pieces of silver.

13And the LORD said to me, "Throw it to the
potter*"—this magnificent sum at which they valued
me! So I took the thirty coins and threw them to the
potter in the Temple of the LORD.

14Then I took my other staff, Union, and cut it in
two, showing that the bond of unity between Judah
and Israel was broken.

Zec 10:11 Or *the sea of Egypt,* referring to the Red Sea. **Zec 10:12** Hebrew *In the LORD.* **Zec 11:13** Syriac version reads *into the treasury;* also in 11:13b. Compare Matt 27:6-10.

Zech 10:10 This pictured return from Egypt and Assyria was a symbolic way of saying that the people would be returned from all the countries where they had been dispersed. Egypt and Assyria evoked memories of slavery and separation.

Zech 10:11 The "sea of distress" refers to the Red Sea, through which the Israelites were miraculously delivered from Egypt. As the Israelites returned once again from Egypt and other lands, they would be protected by God's miraculous power.

Zech 11:4-17 In this message, God told Zechariah to act out the roles of two different kinds of shepherds. The first type of shepherd demonstrated how God would reject his people (the sheep) because they rejected him (Zech 11:4-14). The second type of shepherd demonstrated how God would let his people fall into the clutches of evil shepherds (Zech 11:15-17). (See Ezek 34 for a detailed portrayal of the evil shepherds of Israel.)

Zech 11:4 God told Zechariah to take a job as shepherd of a flock of sheep being fattened for slaughter. The Messiah would shepherd God's people during a time of spiritual and political confusion. The flock represented the people feeding on their own greed and evil desires until they were ripe for God's judgment.

Zech 11:7 Zechariah took two shepherd's staffs and named them "Favor" and "Union." He broke the first one ("Favor") to show that God's gracious covenant with his people was broken. He broke the second one ("Union") to show that "the bond of unity between Judah and Israel was broken" (Zech 11:14).

Zech 11:8 The identity of the three evil shepherds is not known. But God knew they were unfit to shepherd his people, and so he removed them.

Zech 11:12 To pay this shepherd 30 pieces of silver was an insult—this was the price paid to an owner for a slave gored by an ox (Exod 21:32). This is also the amount Judas received for betraying Jesus (Matt 27:3-10). The priceless Messiah was sold for the price of a slave.

Zech 11:13 Potters were in the lowest social class. "This magnificent sum" (a sarcastic comment) was so little that it could be thrown to the potters. It is significant that the 30 pieces of silver paid to Judas for betraying Jesus were returned to the Temple and used to buy a potter's field (Matt 27:3-10).

Zech 11:14 Because the people had rejected the Messiah, God would reject them—symbolized by Zechariah breaking the staff called "Union." Not long after Zechariah's time, the Jews began to divide into numerous factions: Pharisees, Sadducees, Essenes, Herodians, and Zealots. The discord among these groups was a key factor leading to the destruction of Jerusalem in A.D. 70.

▸ **ZECHARIAH 11:4-17** ***(cont.)***

15Then the LORD said to me, "Go again and play the part of a worthless shepherd. 16This illustrates how I will give this nation a shepherd who will not care for those who are dying, nor look after the young,* nor heal the injured, nor feed the healthy. Instead, this shepherd will eat the meat of the fattest sheep and tear off their hooves.

17 "What sorrow awaits this worthless shepherd
who abandons the flock!
The sword will cut his arm
and pierce his right eye.
His arm will become useless,
and his right eye completely blind."

Future Deliverance for Jerusalem

ZECHARIAH 12:1-14

This* message concerning the fate of Israel came from the LORD: "This message is from the LORD, who stretched out the heavens, laid the foundations of the earth, and formed the human spirit. 2I will make Jerusalem like an intoxicating drink that makes the nearby nations stagger when they send their armies to besiege Jerusalem and Judah. 3On that day I will make Jerusalem an immovable rock. All the nations will gather against it to try to move it, but they will only hurt themselves.

4"On that day," says the LORD, "I will cause every horse to panic and every rider to lose his nerve. I will watch over the people of Judah, but I will blind all the horses of their enemies. 5And the clans of Judah will say to themselves, 'The people of Jerusalem have found strength in the LORD of Heaven's Armies, their God.'

6"On that day I will make the clans of Judah like a flame that sets a woodpile ablaze or like a burning torch among sheaves of grain. They will burn up all the neighboring nations right and left, while the people living in Jerusalem remain secure.

7"The LORD will give victory to the rest of Judah first, before Jerusalem, so that the people of Jerusalem and the royal line of David will not have greater honor than the rest of Judah. 8On that day the LORD will defend the people of Jerusalem; the weakest among them will be as mighty as King David! And the royal descendants will be like God, like the angel of the LORD who goes before them! 9For on that day I will begin to destroy all the nations that come against Jerusalem.

10"Then I will pour out a spirit* of grace and prayer on the family of David and on the people of Jerusalem. They will look on me whom they have pierced and mourn for him as for an only son. They will grieve bitterly for him as for a firstborn son who has died. 11The sorrow and mourning in Jerusalem on that day will be like the great mourning for Hadad-rimmon in the valley of Megiddo.

Zec 11:16 Or *the scattered.* **Zec 12:1** Hebrew *An Oracle: This.* **Zec 12:10** Or *the Spirit.*

Zech 11:15-17 Israel would not only reject the true shepherd, it would accept instead a worthless shepherd. This shepherd would serve his own concerns rather than the concerns of his flock and would destroy rather than defend them. Condemnation is his rightful fate because he trusted his arm (military might) and his right eye (intellect). God would destroy both areas.

Zech 11:17 It is a great tragedy for God's people when their leaders fail to care for them adequately. God holds leaders particularly accountable for the condition of his people. The New Testament tells church leaders, "Not many of you should become teachers in the church, for we who teach will be judged more strictly" (Jas 3:1). If God puts you in a position of leadership, remember that it is also a place of great responsibility.

Zech 12:1-14 This chapter pictures the final siege against the people of Jerusalem.

Zech 12:3-4 This speaks of a great future battle against Jerusalem. Some say it is Armageddon, the last great battle on earth. Those who oppose God's people will not prevail forever. Eventually, evil, pain, and oppression will be abolished once and for all.

Zech 12:7 As water flows downhill, so a city's influence usually flows to its surrounding countryside. But this time, the countryside of Judah would have priority over Jerusalem so that the people of Jerusalem would not become proud. Don't think that you must witness to only "important" people—professional athletes, movie stars, and prominent businesspeople. Christ came to seek and save the lost (Luke 19:10), even the "down-and-out" lost. We must be careful to avoid spiritual pride, or we, like Jerusalem, may be the last to know what God is doing.

Zech 12:10 The Holy Spirit was poured out at Pentecost, 50 days after Christ's resurrection (see Acts 2). Zechariah calls the Spirit "a spirit of grace and prayer." It is this Spirit who convicts us of sin, reveals to us God's righteousness and judgment, and helps us as we pray. "And the Holy Spirit helps us in our weakness. For example, we don't know what God wants us to pray for. But the Holy Spirit prays for us with groanings that cannot be expressed in words" (Rom 8:26). Ask God to fill you with his Spirit.

Zech 12:10-14 Eventually *all* people will realize that Jesus, the man who was pierced and killed, is indeed the Messiah. There will be an awakening, with sorrow for sin and genuine revival. The crucified Messiah will be clearly revealed (Phil 2:10; Rev 5:13).

Zech 12:11 Hadad-rimmon could refer to the place near the plain of Megiddo,

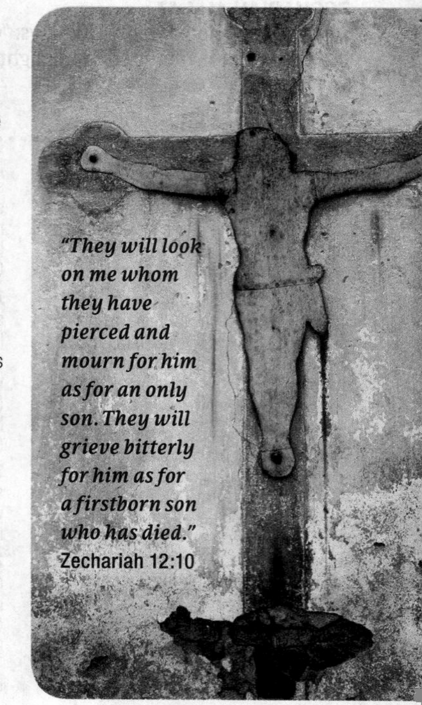
"They will look on me whom they have pierced and mourn for him as for an only son. They will grieve bitterly for him as for a firstborn son who has died."
Zechariah 12:10

12"All Israel will mourn, each clan by itself, and
with the husbands separate from their wives. The
clan of David will mourn alone, as will the clan of
Nathan, 13the clan of Levi, and the clan of Shimei.
14Each of the surviving clans from Judah will mourn
separately, and with the husbands separate from
their wives.

A Fountain of Cleansing

ZECHARIAH 13:1-6

"On that day a fountain will be opened for the dynasty of David and for the people of Jerusalem, a fountain to cleanse them from all their sins and impurity.

2"And on that day," says the LORD of Heaven's Armies, "I will erase idol worship throughout the land,
so that even the names of the idols will be forgotten. I
will remove from the land both the false prophets and
the spirit of impurity that came with them. 3If anyone
continues to prophesy, his own father and mother will
tell him, 'You must die, for you have prophesied lies in
the name of the LORD.' And as he prophesies, his own
father and mother will stab him.
4"On that day people will be ashamed to claim the
prophetic gift. No one will pretend to be a prophet
by wearing prophet's clothes. 5He will say, 'I'm no
prophet; I'm a farmer. I began working for a farmer as
a boy.' 6And if someone asks, 'Then what about those
wounds on your chest?*' he will say, 'I was wounded
at my friends' house!'

Zec 13:6 Hebrew *wounds between your hands?*

The Scattering of the Sheep

ZECHARIAH 13:7-9

7 "Awake, O sword, against my shepherd,
the man who is my partner,"
says the LORD of Heaven's Armies.
"Strike down the shepherd,
and the sheep will be scattered,
and I will turn against the lambs.
8 Two-thirds of the people in the land
will be cut off and die," says the LORD.
"But one-third will be left in the land.
9 I will bring that group through the fire
and make them pure.
I will refine them like silver
and purify them like gold.
They will call on my name,
and I will answer them.
I will say, 'These are my people,'
and they will say, 'The LORD is our God.'"

The LORD Will Rule the Earth

ZECHARIAH 14:1-21

Watch, for the day of the LORD is coming when your
possessions will be plundered right in front of you!
2I will gather all the nations to fight against Jerusalem. The city will be taken, the houses looted, and
the women raped. Half the population will be taken
into captivity, and the rest will be left among the ruins
of the city.

where King Josiah was killed. The people greatly mourned Josiah's death (see 2 Chr 35:22-25).

Zech 12:12-14 These verses are saying that all Israel will mourn—king, prophet, priest, and people. Each family will go into private mourning, husbands and wives by themselves, to face their sorrow.

Zech 13:1ff There will be a never-ending supply of God's mercy, forgiveness, and cleansing power. This picture of a fountain is similar to the never-ending stream flowing out from the Temple (Ezek 47:1). The fountain is used in Scripture to symbolize God's forgiveness. In John 4, Jesus tells of his "living water" that satisfies completely. Are you spiritually thirsty? Do you need to experience God's forgiveness? Drink from the fountain—ask Jesus to forgive you and give you his salvation.

Zech 13:2-6 This chapter pictures the final days of the earth as we know it. For God's new era to begin, there must be a cleansing—all evil must be abolished. Therefore, idols will be banished, and false prophets will be ashamed of themselves and no longer try to deceive God's people.

Zech 13:7 Just before his arrest, Jesus quoted from this verse, referring to himself and his disciples (Matt 26:31-32). He knew beforehand that his disciples would scatter when he was arrested. The Roman "sword" was the military power that put Christ to death.

Zech 13:8-9 This "third" was a remnant, a small part of the whole. Throughout the history of Israel, whenever the whole nation seemed to turn against God, God said that a righteous remnant still trusted and followed him. These believers were refined like silver and gold through the fire of their difficult circumstances. Determine to be part of God's remnant, that small part of the whole that is obedient to him. Obey God no matter what the rest of the world does. This may mean trials and troubles at times; but as fire purifies gold and silver, you will be purified and made more like Christ.

Zech 14:1 Many times in the Bible we are encouraged to watch for the day of the Lord. What if you knew exactly when this would happen? Would you live differently? Christ could return at any moment. Be ready for him by studying the Scriptures carefully and by making sure that you live as he intends—in obedience and spiritual readiness.

Zech 14:1-21 This chapter portrays the eventual triumph of the Messiah over all the earth and his reign over God's people. But the chronological order of these future events is not clear. They show that God has various ways of dealing with his people. Now we are to watch as the events unfold and God provides an escape for his people.

▸ **ZECHARIAH 14:1-21** ***(cont.)***

3Then the LORD will go out to fight against those
nations, as he has fought in times past. 4On that day
his feet will stand on the Mount of Olives, east of
Jerusalem. And the Mount of Olives will split apart,
making a wide valley running from east to west. Half
the mountain will move toward the north and half
toward the south. 5You will flee through this valley,
for it will reach across to Azal.* Yes, you will flee
as you did from the earthquake in the days of King
Uzziah of Judah. Then the LORD my God will come,
and all his holy ones with him.*

6On that day the sources of light will no longer
shine,* 7yet there will be continuous day! Only the
LORD knows how this could happen. There will be
no normal day and night, for at evening time it will
still be light.

8On that day life-giving waters will flow out from
Jerusalem, half toward the Dead Sea and half toward
the Mediterranean,* flowing continuously in both
summer and winter.

9And the LORD will be king over all the earth. On
that day there will be one LORD—his name alone
will be worshiped.

10All the land from Geba, north of Judah, to Rimmon, south of Jerusalem, will become one vast plain.
But Jerusalem will be raised up in its original place
and will be inhabited all the way from the Benjamin Gate over to the site of the old gate, then to the
Corner Gate, and from the Tower of Hananel to the
king's winepresses. 11And Jerusalem will be filled,
safe at last, never again to be cursed and destroyed.

12And the LORD will send a plague on all the nations that fought against Jerusalem. Their people
will become like walking corpses, their flesh rotting
away. Their eyes will rot in their sockets, and their
tongues will rot in their mouths. 13On that day they
will be terrified, stricken by the LORD with great
panic. They will fight their neighbors hand to hand.
14Judah, too, will be fighting at Jerusalem. The wealth
of all the neighboring nations will be captured—
great quantities of gold and silver and fine clothing.
15This same plague will strike the horses, mules,
camels, donkeys, and all the other animals in the
enemy camps.

16In the end, the enemies of Jerusalem who survive the plague will go up to Jerusalem each year
to worship the King, the LORD of Heaven's Armies,
and to celebrate the Festival of Shelters. 17Any nation in the world that refuses to come to Jerusalem
to worship the King, the LORD of Heaven's Armies,
will have no rain. 18If the people of Egypt refuse to
attend the festival, the LORD will punish them with
the same plague that he sends on the other nations

Zec 14:5a The meaning of the Hebrew is uncertain. **Zec 14:5b** As in Greek version; Hebrew reads *with you.* **Zec 14:6** Hebrew *there will be no light, no cold or frost.* The meaning of the Hebrew is uncertain. **Zec 14:8** Hebrew *half toward the eastern sea and half toward the western sea.*

Mount of Olives

The Mount of Olives (Zech 14:4; Mark 11:1) gained its name from its extensive olive groves, which were renowned in antiquity. The Mount of Olives is a prominent ridge running north–south in the Judean mountains, lying due east of Jerusalem and the Kidron Valley. Three summits with two intervening valleys distinguish the mountain. The northern summit is Mount Scopus. To its south is a small saddle through which the ancient Roman road to Jericho passed. The central hill is the traditional Mount of Olives. Another saddle to the south contains the modern road to Bethany. The southern hill, overlooking Jebusite Jerusalem and the City of David, is called the Mount of Offense since here Solomon built pagan temples for his foreign wives. Jesus gave his famous prophetic discourse from the Mount of Olives (Matt 24; Mark 13; Luke 21). We should heed Jesus' warnings and be prepared for his second coming.

Zech 14:4 On the Mount of Olives, Jesus spoke with his disciples about the end times (Matt 24). Near this mountain, an angel promised that Jesus would return in the same manner as he had left (Acts 1:11; see also Ezek 11:23).

Zech 14:5 Only God's people will escape God's punishment (Matt 24:16-20). In this time of confusion, God will clearly know who his people are. (See the note on Amos 1:1, p. 770, concerning the earthquake in King Uzziah's day.)

Zech 14:10 Jerusalem is honored as the city of God and the focal point of all the world's worship. Jerusalem's elevation is a dramatic way of showing God's supremacy.

Zech 14:16 This Festival of Shelters is the only festival still appropriate during the Messiah's reign. The Passover was fulfilled in Christ's death; the Day of Atonement, in acceptance of Christ's salvation; the Festival of First Harvest, in his resurrection; and Pentecost, with the arrival of the Holy Spirit. But the Festival of Shelters, a festival of thanksgiving, celebrates the harvest of

who refuse to go. [19]Egypt and the other nations will all be punished if they don't go to celebrate the Festival of Shelters.

[20]On that day even the harness bells of the horses will be inscribed with these words: HOLY TO THE LORD. And the cooking pots in the Temple of the LORD will be as sacred as the basins used beside the altar. [21]In fact, every cooking pot in Jerusalem and Judah will be holy to the LORD of Heaven's Armies. All who come to worship will be free to use any of these pots to boil their sacrifices. And on that day there will no longer be traders* in the Temple of the LORD of Heaven's Armies.

The Temple's Dedication

EZRA 6:14b-18

The Temple was finally finished, as had been commanded by the God of Israel and decreed by Cyrus, Darius, and Artaxerxes, the kings of Persia. [15]The Temple was completed on March 12,* during the sixth year of King Darius's reign.

[16]The Temple of God was then dedicated with great joy by the people of Israel, the priests, the Levites, and the rest of the people who had returned from exile. [17]During the dedication ceremony for the Temple of God, 100 young bulls, 200 rams, and 400 male lambs were sacrificed. And 12 male goats were presented as a sin offering for the twelve tribes of Israel. [18]Then the priests and Levites were divided into their various divisions to serve at the Temple of God in Jerusalem, as prescribed in the Book of Moses.

Celebration of Passover

EZRA 6:19-22

On April 21* the returned exiles celebrated Passover. [20]The priests and Levites had purified themselves and were ceremonially clean. So they slaughtered the Passover lamb for all the returned exiles, for their fellow priests, and for themselves. [21]The Passover meal was eaten by the people of Israel who had returned from exile and by the others in the land who had turned from their immoral customs to worship the LORD, the God of Israel. [22]Then they celebrated the Festival of Unleavened Bread for seven days. There was great joy throughout the land because the LORD had caused the king of Assyria* to be favorable to them, so that he helped them to rebuild the Temple of God, the God of Israel.

Opposition under King Xerxes

EZRA 4:6

Years later when Xerxes* began his reign, the enemies of Judah wrote a letter of accusation against the people of Judah and Jerusalem.

515 BC

Zec 14:21 Hebrew *Canaanites.* **Ezr 6:15** Aramaic *on the third day of the month Adar,* of the ancient Hebrew lunar calendar. A number of events in Ezra can be cross-checked with dates in surviving Persian records and related accurately to our modern calendar. This day was March 12, 515 B.C. **Ezr 6:19** Hebrew *On the fourteenth day of the first month,* of the ancient Hebrew lunar calendar. This day was April 21, 515 B.C.; also see note on 6:15. **Ezr 6:22** King Darius of Persia is here identified as the king of Assyria because Persia had conquered the Babylonian Empire, which included the earlier Assyrian Empire. **Ezr 4:6** Hebrew *Ahasuerus,* another name for Xerxes. He reigned 486–465 B.C.

Second Temple completed in Jerusalem

human souls for the Lord. Jesus may have alluded to it in John 4:35.

Zech 14:20-21 In the future, even such common objects as horses' bells and cooking pots will be holy. This vision of a restored, holy Jerusalem stands in contrast to its broken walls and unpleasant living conditions. One day God would fulfill the people's dreams for Jerusalem beyond what they could imagine. God wants to do much more for us than we can imagine (Eph 3:20). As we walk with him, we will discover this day by day.

Zech 14:21 Zechariah was speaking to a people who were enduring hardships: They were being harassed by neighbors; they were discouraged over their small numbers and seemingly inadequate Temple; and their worship was apathetic. But God said, "My love for Jerusalem and Mount Zion is passionate and strong" (Zech 1:14). He promised to restore their land, their city, and their Temple. Like other prophets, Zechariah blended prophecies of the present, near future, and final days into one sweeping panorama. Through his message we learn that our hope is found in God and his Messiah, who are in complete control of the world.

Ezra 6:14 Ezra carefully pointed out that rebuilding the Temple was commanded first by God and then by the kings, who were his instruments. How ironic and wonderful that God's work was carried on by the discovery of a lost paragraph in a pagan library. All the opposition of powerful forces was stopped by a clause in a legal document. God's will is supreme over all rulers, all historical events, and all hostile forces. He can deliver us in ways we can't imagine. If we trust in his power and love, no opposition can stop us.

Ezra 6:15 The Temple was completed in 515 B.C.

Ezra 6:16-22 Feasting and celebration were in order at the great Temple dedication. This celebration was similar to the one that Solomon had when he dedicated the Temple (1 Kgs 8:63), although Solomon offered more than 200 times as many cattle and sheep. This "Book of Moses" was probably Leviticus. The priests and Levites were organized into groups in order to "serve at the Temple of God . . . as prescribed in the Book of Moses." There is a time to celebrate, but there is also a time to work. Both are proper and necessary when worshiping God, and both are pleasing to him.

Ezra 6:19 The Passover was an annual celebration commemorating Israel's deliverance from Egypt. After a series of plagues failed to convince Pharaoh to free the Israelites, God said that he would send the death angel to kill the firstborn in every household. But the angel would pass over every home that had the blood of a specified type of lamb on the sides and top of the doorframe. (See Exod 12:1-30 for the story of this event and the establishment of the Passover celebration.)

Ezra 6:22 There are many ways to pray for God's help. Have you ever considered that God would change the attitude of a person or group of people? God is infinitely powerful; his insight and wisdom transcend the laws of human nature. While you must always change your attitude as a first step, remember that he can change the attitude of others.

Ezra 4:6 This verse fits chronologically between Ezra 6 and Ezra 7. It is part of a collection of verses summarizing the opposition the Jews faced as they were rebuilding Jerusalem and the Temple; Ezra 4:7-23 refers to the events between Ezra 7 and Nehemiah 1. Ezra grouped them together to highlight the persistent opposition to God's people over the years and God's ability to overcome it.

C. The Book of Esther

Not all of the Jews returned to Jerusalem when Cyrus issued his decree allowing them to do so. Many Jews stayed in Persia and throughout the world where they had settled during the Exile. Esther is one such woman. The book of Esther is an example of God's divine guidance and care over our lives. God's sovereignty and power are seen throughout this book. Although we may question certain circumstances in our lives, we must have faith that God is in control, working through both the pleasant and difficult times so that we can serve him effectively.

1. ESTHER BECOMES QUEEN

King Xerxes gave a lavish banquet for key leaders in Persia, but Queen Vashti refused to show off her beauty for the guests, so Xerxes deposed her and searched for a new queen. Esther, a young Jewish woman, was chosen to be queen.

The King's Banquet

ESTHER 1:1-9

These events happened in the days of King Xerxes,*
who reigned over 127 provinces stretching from
India to Ethiopia.* 2At that time Xerxes ruled his
empire from his royal throne at the fortress of Susa.
3In the third year of his reign, he gave a banquet for
all his nobles and officials. He invited all the military
officers of Persia and Media as well as the princes
and nobles of the provinces. 4The celebration lasted
180 days—a tremendous display of the opulent
wealth of his empire and the pomp and splendor
of his majesty.

5When it was all over, the king gave a banquet for
all the people, from the greatest to the least, who were
in the fortress of Susa. It lasted for seven days and
was held in the courtyard of the palace garden. 6The
courtyard was beautifully decorated with white cotton
curtains and blue hangings, which were fastened with
white linen cords and purple ribbons to silver rings
embedded in marble pillars. Gold and silver couches
stood on a mosaic pavement of porphyry, marble,
mother-of-pearl, and other costly stones.

7Drinks were served in gold goblets of many designs, and there was an abundance of royal wine, reflecting the king's generosity. 8By edict of the king, no
limits were placed on the drinking, for the king had
instructed all his palace officials to serve each man
as much as he wanted.

9At the same time, Queen Vashti gave a banquet for
the women in the royal palace of King Xerxes.

Queen Vashti Deposed

ESTHER 1:10-22

On the seventh day of the feast, when King Xerxes was
in high spirits because of the wine, he told the seven
eunuchs who attended him—Mehuman, Biztha, Harbona, Bigtha, Abagtha, Zethar, and Carcas—11to bring
Queen Vashti to him with the royal crown on her head.
He wanted the nobles and all the other men to gaze on

Est 1:1a Hebrew *Ahasuerus,* another name for Xerxes; also throughout the book of Esther. Xerxes reigned 486–465 B.C. **Est 1:1b** Hebrew *to Cush.*

500 BC *Earliest copies of Sun Tzu's The Art of War*

Esth 1:1 Esther's story begins in 483 B.C., 103 years after Nebuchadnezzar had taken the Jews into captivity (2 Kgs 25), 54 years after Zerubbabel led the first group of exiles back to Jerusalem (Ezra 1–2), and 25 years before Ezra led the second group to Jerusalem (Ezra 7). Esther lived in the kingdom of Persia, the dominant kingdom in the Middle East after Babylon's fall in 539 B.C. Esther's parents must have been among those exiles who chose not to return to Jerusalem, even though Cyrus, the Persian king, had issued a decree allowing them to do so. The Jewish exiles had great freedom in Persia, and many remained because they had established themselves there or were fearful of the dangerous journey back to their homeland.

Esth 1:1 Xerxes the Great was Persia's fifth king (486–465 B.C.). He was proud and impulsive, as we see from the events in Esther 1. His winter palace was in Susa, where he held the banquet (Esth 1:3-7). Persian kings often held great banquets before going to war. In 481 B.C., Xerxes launched an attack against Greece. After his fleet won a great victory at Thermopylae, he was defeated at Salamis in 480 B.C. and had to return to Persia. Esther became queen in 479 B.C.

Esth 1:2 In this context, *fortress* means "palace."

Esth 1:4 The celebration lasted 180 days (about six months) because its real purpose was to plan the battle strategy for invading Greece and to demonstrate that the king had sufficient wealth to carry it out. Waging war was not only for survival; it was a means of acquiring more wealth, territory, and power.

Esth 1:5-7 Persia was a world power, and the king, as the center of that power, was one of the wealthiest people in the world. Persian kings loved to flaunt their wealth, even wearing precious gemstones in their beards. Jewelry was a sign of rank for Persian men. Even soldiers wore great amounts of gold jewelry into battle.

Esth 1:9 Ancient Greek documents call Xerxes's wife Amestris, probably a Greek form of Vashti. Vashti was deposed in 483/482 B.C., but she is mentioned again in ancient records as the queen mother during the reign of her son, Artaxerxes, who succeeded Xerxes. Toward the end of Xerxes's reign, either Esther died or Vashti was able through her son to regain the influence she had lost.

Esth 1:10 Some advisers and government officials were castrated in order to prevent them from having children and then rebelling and trying to establish a dynasty of their own. A castrated official was called a *eunuch.*

Esth 1:10-11 Xerxes made a rash, half-drunk decision, based purely on feelings. His self-restraint and practical wisdom were weakened by too much wine. Poor decisions are made when people don't think clearly. Base your decisions on careful thinking, not on the emotions of the moment. Impulsive decision-making leads to severe complications.

Esth 1:12 Queen Vashti refused to parade before the king's all-male party, possibly because it was against Persian custom for a woman to appear before a public gathering of men. This conflict between Persian custom and the king's command put her in a difficult situation, and she chose to refuse her half-drunk husband, hoping he would come to his senses later. Some have suggested that

her beauty, for she was a very beautiful woman. 12But
when they conveyed the king's order to Queen Vashti,
she refused to come. This made the king furious, and
he burned with anger.
13He immediately consulted with his wise advisers,
who knew all the Persian laws and customs, for he
always asked their advice. 14The names of these men
were Carshena, Shethar, Admatha, Tarshish, Meres,
Marsena, and Memucan—seven nobles of Persia and
Media. They met with the king regularly and held the
highest positions in the empire.
15"What must be done to Queen Vashti?" the king
demanded. "What penalty does the law provide for a
queen who refuses to obey the king's orders, properly
sent through his eunuchs?"
16Memucan answered the king and his nobles,
"Queen Vashti has wronged not only the king but
also every noble and citizen throughout your empire. 17Women everywhere will begin to despise
their husbands when they learn that Queen Vashti
has refused to appear before the king. 18Before this
day is out, the wives of all the king's nobles throughout Persia and Media will hear what the queen did
and will start treating their husbands the same way.
There will be no end to their contempt and anger.
19"So if it please the king, we suggest that you issue
a written decree, a law of the Persians and Medes that
cannot be revoked. It should order that Queen Vashti
be forever banished from the presence of King Xerxes,
and that the king should choose another queen more
worthy than she. 20When this decree is published
throughout the king's vast empire, husbands everywhere, whatever their rank, will receive proper respect
from their wives!"
21The king and his nobles thought this made good
sense, so he followed Memucan's counsel. 22He sent
letters to all parts of the empire, to each province in
its own script and language, proclaiming that every
man should be the ruler of his own home and should
say whatever he pleases.*

Est 1:22 *Or and should speak in the language of his own people.*

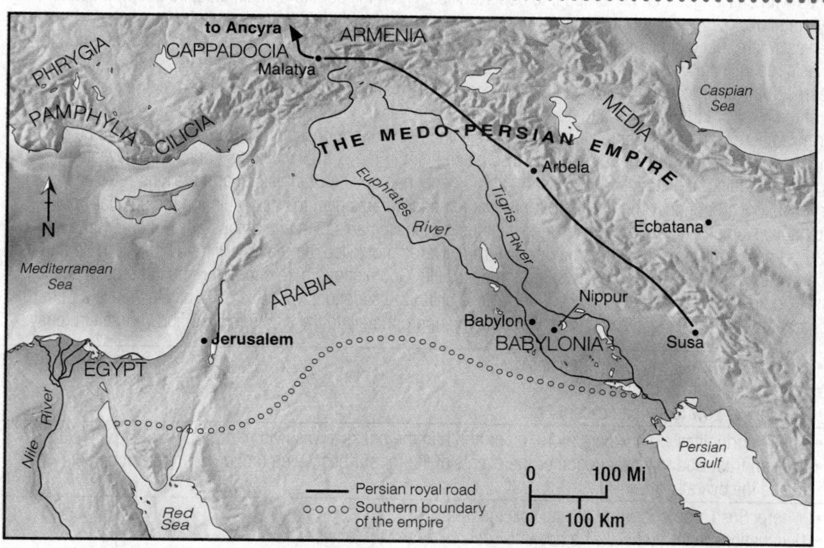

THE WORLD OF ESTHER'S DAY *Esther lived in the capital of the vast Medo-Persian Empire, which incorporated the provinces of Media and Persia, as well as the previous empires of Assyria and Babylon. Esther, a Jew, was chosen by King Xerxes to be his queen. The story of how she saved her people takes place at the palace in Susa.*

490 BC ***Greeks repel Persia in the Battle of Marathon***

Vashti was pregnant with Artaxerxes, who was born in 483 B.C., and that she did not want to be seen in public in that state.

Whatever the reason, her action was a breach of protocol that also placed Xerxes in a difficult situation. Once he made the command, as a Persian king he could not reverse it (see the note on Esth 1:19, below). While preparing to invade Greece, Xerxes had invited important officials from all over his land to see his power, wealth, and authority. If it was perceived that he had no authority over his own wife, his military credibility would be damaged—the greatest criterion of success for an ancient king. In addition, King Xerxes was accustomed to getting what he wanted.

Esth 1:13-15 Xerxes, like most leaders past and present, kept a handful of advisers whom he consulted on almost all matters. Often a king's success rose or fell on the wisdom of these men. Daniel was such an adviser under Darius and Cyrus (Dan 6:28).

Esth 1:15 Middle Eastern kings often did not have close personal relationships with their wives. Xerxes demonstrates this because (1) he had a harem (Esth 2:3); (2) he showed no respect for Vashti's personhood (Esth 1:10-12); (3) Esther, when she became queen, did not see him for long periods of time (Esth 4:11).

Esth 1:16-21 Perhaps the men's thinking had been clouded by drinking. Obviously this law would not cause the women of the country to respect their husbands. Respect between men and women comes from mutual regard and appreciation for each other as those created in God's image, not from legal pronouncements and orders. Forced obedience is a poor substitute for the love and respect wives and husbands should have for each other.

Esth 1:19 A Persian king was thought to be a god by many of his people; therefore, when he issued a law or command, it stood forever (see the notes on Esth 8:8, p. 1192, and Dan 6:8-9, p. 1140). The law could never be canceled, even if it was ill-advised; but if necessary, a new law could be issued to neutralize the effects of the old law.

Esther Becomes Queen

ESTHER 2:1-20

But after Xerxes' anger had subsided, he began
thinking about Vashti and what she had done and
the decree he had made. 2So his personal attendants
suggested, "Let us search the empire to find beautiful young virgins for the king. 3Let the king appoint
agents in each province to bring these beautiful young
women into the royal harem at the fortress of Susa.
Hegai, the king's eunuch in charge of the harem, will
see that they are all given beauty treatments. 4After
that, the young woman who most pleases the king will
be made queen instead of Vashti." This advice was very
appealing to the king, so he put the plan into effect.

5At that time there was a Jewish man in the fortress
of Susa whose name was Mordecai son of Jair. He was
from the tribe of Benjamin and was a descendant of
Kish and Shimei. 6His family* had been among those
who, with King Jehoiachin* of Judah, had been exiled
from Jerusalem to Babylon by King Nebuchadnezzar. 7This man had a very beautiful and lovely young
cousin, Hadassah, who was also called Esther. When
her father and mother died, Mordecai adopted her
into his family and raised her as his own daughter.

8As a result of the king's decree, Esther, along with
many other young women, was brought to the king's
harem at the fortress of Susa and placed in Hegai's care.
9Hegai was very impressed with Esther and treated her

Est 2:6a Hebrew *He.* **Est 2:6b** Hebrew *Jeconiah*, a variant spelling of Jehoiachin.

MORDECAI

Following Jerusalem's last stand against Nebuchadnezzar, Mordecai's family was deported to Babylonia. He was probably born in Susa, a city that became one of Persia's capitals after Cyrus conquered Babylon. Mordecai then inherited an official position among the Jewish captives that kept him around the palace even after the Babylonians were driven out. At one time, when Mordecai overheard plans to assassinate King Xerxes, he reported the plot and saved the king's life. • Mordecai's life was filled with challenges that he turned into opportunities. When his aunt and uncle died, he adopted Esther, their daughter and his young cousin, probably because his own parents were dead and he felt responsible for her. Later, when she was drafted into Xerxes's harem and chosen to be queen, Mordecai continued to advise her. Shortly after this, he found himself in conflict with Xerxes's recently appointed second-in-command, Haman. Although willing to serve the king, Mordecai refused to worship the king's representative. Haman was furious with Mordecai. So he planned to have Mordecai and all the Jews killed. His plan became a law of the Medes and Persians, and it looked as though the Jews were doomed. • Mordecai, willing to be God's servant wherever he was, responded by contacting Esther and telling her that one reason God had allowed her to be queen might well be to save her people from this threat. But God had also placed him in the right place years earlier. God revealed to the king through his nighttime reading of historical documents that Mordecai had once saved his life, and the king realized he had never thanked Mordecai. The great honor then given to Mordecai ruined Haman's plan to impale him on the specially built pole he had set up. God had woven an effective counterstrategy against which Haman's plan could not stand. • Later, Mordecai instituted the Festival of Purim, commemorating when the Jews were delivered, not killed, on the day Haman had fixed. He had a lengthy career of service to the king on behalf of the Jews. In Mordecai's life, God blended both character and circumstances to accomplish great things. God has not changed the way he works. He is using the situations you face each day to weave a pattern of godliness into your character. Pause and ask God to help you respond appropriately to the situations you find yourself in today.

Strengths and accomplishments	• Exposed an assassination plot against the king • Cared enough to adopt his cousin • Refused to bow to anyone except God
Lessons from his life	• The opportunities we have are more important than the ones we wish we had • We can trust God to weave together the events of life for our best, even though we may not be able to see the overall pattern
Vital statistics	• Where: Susa, one of several capital cities in Persia • Occupation: Jewish official who became second in rank to Xerxes • Relatives: Adopted daughter: Esther. Father: Jair. • Contemporaries: Xerxes, Haman
Key verse	"Mordecai the Jew became the prime minister, with authority next to that of King Xerxes himself. He was very great among the Jews, who held him in high esteem, because he continued to work for the good of his people and to speak up for the welfare of all their descendants" (Esth 10:3).

Mordecai's story is told in the book of Esther.

Esth 2:1 The phrase "he began thinking about Vashti" may mean that the king began to miss his queen and what she had done for him. But he also remembered that in his anger he had banished her from his presence with a decree that couldn't be rescinded.

Esth 2:3, 14-17 Persian kings collected not only vast amounts of jewelry but also great numbers of women. These young virgins were taken from their homes and were required to live in a separate building near the palace called a *harem.* Their sole purpose was to serve the king and to await his call for sexual pleasure. They rarely saw the king, and their lives were restricted and boring. If rejected, Esther would be one of many girls the king had seen once and forgotten. But Esther's presence and beauty pleased the king enough that he crowned her queen in place of Vashti. The queen held a more influential position than a concubine, and she was given more freedom and authority than others in the harem. But even as queen, Esther had few rights—especially because

kindly. He quickly ordered a special menu for her and
provided her with beauty treatments. He also assigned
her seven maids specially chosen from the king's palace, and he moved her and her maids into the best
place in the harem.
10Esther had not told anyone of her nationality and
family background, because Mordecai had directed
her not to do so. 11Every day Mordecai would take a
walk near the courtyard of the harem to find out about
Esther and what was happening to her.
12Before each young woman was taken to the king's
bed, she was given the prescribed twelve months of
beauty treatments—six months with oil of myrrh, followed by six months with special perfumes and ointments. 13When it was time for her to go to the king's
palace, she was given her choice of whatever clothing
or jewelry she wanted to take from the harem. 14That
evening she was taken to the king's private rooms,
and the next morning she was brought to the second
harem,* where the king's wives lived. There she would
be under the care of Shaashgaz, the king's eunuch in
charge of the concubines. She would never go to the
king again unless he had especially enjoyed her and
requested her by name.
15Esther was the daughter of Abihail, who was Mordecai's uncle. (Mordecai had adopted his younger
cousin Esther.) When it was Esther's turn to go to the
king, she accepted the advice of Hegai, the eunuch
in charge of the harem. She asked for nothing except
what he suggested, and she was admired by everyone
who saw her.
16Esther was taken to King Xerxes at the royal palace in early winter* of the seventh year of his reign.
17And the king loved Esther more than any of the other
young women. He was so delighted with her that he set
the royal crown on her head and declared her queen
instead of Vashti. 18To celebrate the occasion, he gave
a great banquet in Esther's honor for all his nobles and
officials, declaring a public holiday for the provinces
and giving generous gifts to everyone.
19Even after all the young women had been transferred to the second harem* and Mordecai had become a palace official,* 20Esther continued to keep
her family background and nationality a secret. She
was still following Mordecai's directions, just as she
did when she lived in his home.

Mordecai's Loyalty to the King

ESTHER 2:21-23

21One day as Mordecai was on duty at the king's gate,
two of the king's eunuchs, Bigthana* and Teresh—
who were guards at the door of the king's private
quarters—became angry at King Xerxes and plotted to assassinate him. 22But Mordecai heard about
the plot and gave the information to Queen Esther.
She then told the king about it and gave Mordecai

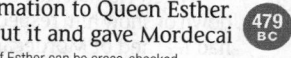

Est 2:14 Or *to another part of the harem.* **Est 2:16** Hebrew *in the tenth month, the month of Tebeth.* A number of dates in the book of Esther can be cross-checked with dates in surviving Persian records and related accurately to our modern calendar. This month of the ancient Hebrew lunar calendar occurred within the months of December 479 B.C. and January 478 B.C. **Est 2:19a** The meaning of the Hebrew is uncertain. **Est 2:19b** Hebrew *and Mordecai was sitting in the gate of the king.* **Est 2:21** Hebrew *Bigthan;* compare 6:2.

479 BC

Esther becomes queen of Persia

she had been chosen to replace a woman who had become too assertive.

Esth 2:5-6 Mordecai was a Jew. The Jewish population had increased since their exile over 100 years earlier. They had been given great freedom and were allowed to run their own businesses and hold positions in government (Esth 2:19; Dan 6:3).

Esth 2:6 The Bible says that Mordecai's family had been carried into exile from Jerusalem by Nebuchadnezzar. If this referred to Mordecai himself, he would have been over 100 years old at the time of this story. Most likely this means that Mordecai's great-grandparents had been carried into captivity, rather than Mordecai himself.

Esth 2:10 With virtually no rights and little access to the king, it was better for Esther not to reveal her identity. While boldness in stating our identity as God's people is our responsibility, at times a good strategy is to keep quiet until we have won the right to be heard. This is especially true when dealing with those in authority over us. But we can always let them see the difference God makes in our lives.

Esth 2:17 God placed Esther on the throne even before the Jews faced the possibility of complete destruction (Esth 3:5ff), so that when trouble came, a person would already be in the position to help. No human effort could thwart God's plan to send the Messiah to earth as a Jew. If you are changing jobs, position, or location and can't see God's purpose in your situation, understand that God is in control. He may be placing you in a position so you can help when the need arises.

GOD BEHIND THE SCENES IN THE BOOK OF ESTHER

Why was God's name hidden in the book of Esther? There were many gods in the Middle East and Persian Empire. Usually, their names were mentioned in official documents in order to control the peoples who worshiped those particular gods. The Jews were unique in being the people of one God. A story about them was naturally a story about God, for even the name "Jew" carried with it the connotation of one who worshiped Yahweh. Although God's name is not mentioned in the Hebrew text of Esther, he makes himself known in these ways:

Indirect References	**Esth 2:17**	Esther, who worshiped God, became queen.
	Esth 4:14	God's existence and his power over the affairs of people are assumed.
	Esth 4:16	Fasting was a distinct spiritual activity usually connected with prayer.
Divine Incidents	**Esth 2:21-23**	Mordecai overhears a death plot and saves the king's life.
The book of Esther is filled with divine interventions	**Esth 6:1**	Xerxes can't sleep and decides to read a history book.
	Esth 6:2	Xerxes reads the exact page needed for the moment, reminding him of an unpaid reward to Mordecai.
	Esth 7:9-10	Haman's plan is exactly reversed—the intended victims are the victors.

▸ **ESTHER 2:21-23 *(cont.)***
credit for the report. 23When an investigation was
made and Mordecai's story was found to be true, the
two men were impaled on a sharpened pole. This
was all recorded in *The Book of the History of King
Xerxes' Reign*.

2. THE JEWS ARE THREATENED

Mordecai, Esther's uncle, refused to bow down to Haman with everyone else; Mordecai would only bow to God. Haman was infuriated by this affront, and he blamed not only Mordecai but all Jews. He created a plot to destroy the Jews and received the king's approval. Neither of them were aware that Queen Esther was also a Jew.

Haman's Plot against the Jews

ESTHER 3:1-15
Some time later King Xerxes promoted Haman son
of Hammedatha the Agagite over all the other nobles,
making him the most powerful official in the empire.
2All the king's officials would bow down before Haman to show him respect whenever he passed by, for
so the king had commanded. But Mordecai refused
to bow down or show him respect.
3Then the palace officials at the king's gate asked
Mordecai, "Why are you disobeying the king's command?" 4They spoke to him day after day, but still he
refused to comply with the order. So they spoke to Haman about this to see if he would tolerate Mordecai's
conduct, since Mordecai had told them he was a Jew.
5When Haman saw that Mordecai would not bow
down or show him respect, he was filled with rage. 6He
had learned of Mordecai's nationality, so he decided
it was not enough to lay hands on Mordecai alone.
Instead, he looked for a way to destroy all the Jews
throughout the entire empire of Xerxes.
7So in the month of April,* during the twelfth year
of King Xerxes' reign, lots were cast in Haman's presence (the lots were called *purim*) to determine the best
day and month to take action. And the day selected
was March 7, nearly a year later.*
8Then Haman approached King Xerxes and said,
"There is a certain race of people scattered through
all the provinces of your empire who keep themselves
separate from everyone else. Their laws are different
from those of any other people, and they refuse to
obey the laws of the king. So it is not in the king's
interest to let them live. 9If it please the king, issue a
decree that they be destroyed, and I will give 10,000
large sacks* of silver to the government administrators to be deposited in the royal treasury."
10The king agreed, confirming his decision by
removing his signet ring from his finger and giving

Est 3:7a Hebrew *in the first month, the month of Nisan.* This month of the ancient Hebrew lunar calendar occurred within the months of April and May 474 B.C.; also see note on 2:16. **Est 3:7b** As in 3:13, which reads *the thirteenth day of the twelfth month, the month of Adar;* Hebrew reads *in the twelfth month,* of the ancient Hebrew lunar calendar. The date selected was March 7, 473 B.C.; also see note on 2:16. **Est 3:9** Hebrew *10,000 talents,* about 375 tons or 340 metric tons in weight.

Esth 3:2 Mordecai's determination came from his faith in God. He did not take a poll first to determine the safest or most popular course of action; he had the courage to stand alone. Doing what is right will not always make you popular. Those who do right will be in the minority, but to obey God is more important than to obey people (Acts 5:29).

Esth 3:2-4 Mordecai refused to kneel down before Haman. Jews did bow down to government authorities, at times, as a sign of respect (Gen 23:7; 1 Sam 24:8), but Haman's ancestors were ancient enemies of the Jews. Israel had been commanded by God to "destroy the Amalekites and erase their memory from under heaven" (Deut 25:17-19; see also Exod 17:16). Mordecai was not about to kneel before wicked Haman and, by his act, acknowledge Haman as a god. Daniel's three friends had the same convictions (Dan 3). We must worship God alone. We should never let any person, institution, or government take God's place. When people demand loyalties or duties from you that do not honor God, don't give in. It may be time to take a stand.

Esth 3:5-6 Why did Haman want to destroy all Jews just because of one man's action? (1) Haman was an Agagite (Esth 3:1), a descendant of Agag, king of the Amalekites (1 Sam 15:20). The Amalekites were ancient enemies of the Israelites (see Exod 17:16; Deut 25:17-19). Haman's hatred was directed not just at Mordecai but at all the Jews. (2) As second-in-command in the Persian Empire (Esth 3:1), Haman loved his power and authority and the reverence shown him. The Jews looked to God as their final authority, not to any man. Haman realized that the only way to fulfill his self-centered desires was to kill all those who disregarded his authority. His quest for personal power and his hatred of the Jewish race consumed him.

Esth 3:5-6 Haman enjoyed the power and prestige of his position, and he was enraged when Mordecai did not respond with the expected reverential bow. Haman's anger was not directed just toward Mordecai, but toward what Mordecai stood for—the Jews' dedication to God as the only authority worthy of reverence. Haman's attitude was prejudiced: He hated a group of people because of a difference in belief or culture. Prejudice grows out of personal pride—considering oneself better than others. In the end, Haman was punished for his arrogant attitude (Esth 7:9-10). God will harshly judge those who are prejudiced or whose pride causes them to look down on others.

Esth 3:7 Haman cast lots to determine the best day to carry out his decree. Little did he know that he was playing into the hands of God, for the day of death was set for almost a year away, giving Esther time to make her plea to the king. The Persian word for "lots" was *purim*, which became the name for the holiday celebrated by the Jews when they were delivered, not killed, on the day appointed by Haman.

Esth 3:9 Haman must have hoped to acquire this tremendous sum of money by plundering the homes and businesses of the Jews who would be killed through his decree.

Esth 3:10-12 Officials in the ancient world used signet rings as personal signatures. The ring's surface had a raised imprint made of metal, wood, or bone; Xerxes's was probably made of silver or gold. Each individual had his own imprint. Letters were sealed by pressing the ring into soft wax, and official documents were certified by using the royal signet. By giving Haman his signet ring, Xerxes gave him his personal signature and with it the authority to do whatever he wished. Little did the king realize that his own ring would sign the death warrant for his queen, Esther.

it to Haman son of Hammedatha the Agagite, the enemy of the Jews. [11]The king said, "The money and the people are both yours to do with as you see fit."

[12]So on April 17* the king's secretaries were summoned, and a decree was written exactly as Haman dictated. It was sent to the king's highest officers, the governors of the respective provinces, and the nobles of each province in their own scripts and languages. The decree was written in the name of King Xerxes and sealed with the king's signet ring. [13]Dispatches were sent by swift messengers into all the provinces of the empire, giving the order that all Jews—young and old, including women and children—must be killed, slaughtered, and annihilated on a single day. This was scheduled to happen on March 7 of the next year.* The property of the Jews would be given to those who killed them.

[14]A copy of this decree was to be issued as law in every province and proclaimed to all peoples, so that they would be ready to do their duty on the appointed day. [15]At the king's command, the decree went out by swift messengers, and it was also proclaimed in the fortress of Susa. Then the king and Haman sat down to drink, but the city of Susa fell into confusion.

Mordecai Requests Esther's Help

ESTHER 4:1-17

When Mordecai learned about all that had been done, he tore his clothes, put on burlap and ashes, and went out into the city, crying with a loud and bitter wail. [2]He went as far as the gate of the palace, for no one was allowed to enter the palace gate while wearing clothes of mourning. [3]And as news of the king's decree reached all the provinces, there was great mourning among the Jews. They fasted, wept, and wailed, and many people lay in burlap and ashes.

[4]When Queen Esther's maids and eunuchs came and told her about Mordecai, she was deeply distressed. She sent clothing to him to replace the burlap, but he refused it. [5]Then Esther sent for Hathach, one of the king's eunuchs who had been appointed as her attendant. She ordered him to go to Mordecai and

Est 3:12 Hebrew *On the thirteenth day of the first month,* of the ancient Hebrew lunar calendar. This day was April 17, 474 B.C.; also see note on 2:16. **Est 3:13** Hebrew *on the thirteenth day of the twelfth month, the month of Adar,* of the ancient Hebrew lunar calendar. The date selected was March 7, 473 B.C.; also see note on 2:16.

ESTHER

We treasure security, even though we know that security in this life carries no guarantees—possessions can be destroyed, beauty fades, relationships can be broken, death is inevitable. Real security, then, must be found beyond this life. Only when our security rests on God and his unchanging nature can we face the challenges that life is sure to bring our way.

Esther's beauty and character won Xerxes's heart, and he made her his queen. But even in her favored position she was risking her life by attempting to see the king when he had not requested her presence. There was no guarantee that the king would even see her. Although she was queen, she was still not secure. But, cautiously and courageously, Esther decided to risk her life by approaching the king on behalf of her people. • She made her plans carefully. The Jews were asked to fast and pray with her before she went to the king. Then on the chosen day she went before him, and he *did* ask her to come forward and speak. But instead of issuing her request directly, she invited him and Haman to a banquet. Xerxes was astute enough to realize she had something on her mind. Esther then conveyed the importance of the matter by insisting on a second banquet. • In the meantime, God was working behind the scenes. He caused Xerxes to read the historical records of the kingdom late one night, and the king discovered that Mordecai had once saved his life. Xerxes lost no time in honoring Mordecai for that act. During the second banquet, Esther told the king of Haman's plot against the Jews, and Haman was doomed. There is grim justice in Haman's death on the impaling pole he had set up for Mordecai, and it seems fitting that the day on which the Jews were to be slaughtered became the day their enemies died. Esther's risk confirmed that God was the source of her security. • How much of your security lies in your possessions, position, or reputation? God has not placed you in your present position for your own benefit. He put you there to serve him. As in Esther's case, this may involve risking your security. Are you willing to let God be your ultimate security?

Strengths and accomplishments	• She combined courage with careful planning • She was open to advice and willing to act • She was more concerned for others than for her own security
Lessons from her life	• Serving God often demands that we risk our own security • God has a purpose for the situations in which he places us • Courage, while often vital, does not replace careful planning
Vital statistics	• Where: Persian Empire • Occupation: Xerxes's wife, queen of Persia • Relatives: Cousin: Mordecai. Husband: Xerxes. Father: Abihail.
Key verse	"Go and gather together all the Jews of Susa and fast for me. Do not eat or drink for three days, night or day. My maids and I will do the same. And then, though it is against the law, I will go in to see the king. If I must die, I must die" (Esth 4:16).

Esther's story is told in the book of Esther.

Esth 3:13 Haman's death decree was against all Jews in the Persian Empire; thus, it would have included the land of Israel. If his decree had been carried out, all of God's chosen people could have been exterminated, and God's plan to send his Son to earth as a Jew could have been ruined. But God's plans cannot be stopped. Haman was doomed to fail.

▶ **ESTHER 4:1-17** ***(cont.)***
find out what was troubling him and why he was in
mourning. [6]So Hathach went out to Mordecai in the
square in front of the palace gate.
[7]Mordecai told him the whole story, including the
exact amount of money Haman had promised to
pay into the royal treasury for the destruction of the
Jews. [8]Mordecai gave Hathach a copy of the decree
issued in Susa that called for the death of all Jews. He
asked Hathach to show it to Esther and explain the
situation to her. He also asked Hathach to direct her
to go to the king to beg for mercy and plead for her
people. [9]So Hathach returned to Esther with Mordecai's message.
[10]Then Esther told Hathach to go back and relay this
message to Mordecai: [11]"All the king's officials and
even the people in the provinces know that anyone
who appears before the king in his inner court without
being invited is doomed to die unless the king holds
out his gold scepter. And the king has not called for
me to come to him for thirty days." [12]So Hathach* gave
Esther's message to Mordecai.
[13]Mordecai sent this reply to Esther: "Don't think for
a moment that because you're in the palace you will
escape when all other Jews are killed. [14]If you keep
quiet at a time like this, deliverance and relief for the
Jews will arise from some other place, but you and
your relatives will die. Who knows if perhaps you were
made queen for just such a time as this?"
[15]Then Esther sent this reply to Mordecai: [16]"Go and
gather together all the Jews of Susa and fast for me. Do
not eat or drink for three days, night or day. My maids
and I will do the same. And then, though it is against
the law, I will go in to see the king. If I must die, I must
die." [17]So Mordecai went away and did everything as
Esther had ordered him.

Est 4:12 As in Greek version; Hebrew reads *they.*

3. ESTHER INTERCEDES FOR THE JEWS

Haman continued to burn with hate for Mordecai and the Jews, and even had a pole built to have Mordecai publicly impaled. In a stunning reversal, Haman was forced to publicly honor Mordecai, and then Esther revealed to King Xerxes that Haman's plot against her people would endanger her as well. Xerxes had Haman impaled on the very pole he had set up for Mordecai!

Esther's Request to the King

ESTHER 5:1-8
On the third day of the fast, Esther put on her royal
robes and entered the inner court of the palace, just
across from the king's hall. The king was sitting on
his royal throne, facing the entrance. [2]When he saw
Queen Esther standing there in the inner court, he
welcomed her and held out the gold scepter to her.
So Esther approached and touched the end of the
scepter.

Esth 4:11–5:2 Esther risked her life by coming before the king. Her courageous act gives us a model to follow in approaching a difficult or dangerous task. Like Esther, we can: (1) Calculate the cost. Esther realized her life was at stake. (2) Set priorities. She believed that the safety of the Jewish race was more important than her life. (3) Prepare. She gathered support and fasted. (4) Determine a course of action and move ahead boldly. She didn't think too long about it, not allowing the interlude to lessen her commitment to what she had to do.

Do you have to face a hostile audience, confront a friend on a delicate subject, or talk to your family about changes to be made? Rather than dreading difficult situations or putting them off, take action with confidence by following Esther's inspiring example.

Esth 4:13 Although Esther was the queen and shared some of the king's power and wealth, she still needed God's protection and wisdom. No one is secure in one's own strength in any political system. It is foolish to believe that wealth or position can make us impervious to danger. Deliverance and safety come only from God.

Esth 4:13-14 After the decree to kill the Jews was given, Mordecai and Esther could have despaired, decided to save only themselves, or just waited for God's intervention. Instead, they saw that God had placed them in their positions for a purpose, so they seized the moment and acted. When it is within our reach to save others, we must do so. In a life-threatening situation, don't withdraw, behave selfishly, wallow in despair, or wait for God to fix everything. Instead, ask God for his direction, and *act!* God may have placed you where you are "for just such a time as this."

Esth 4:14 God is not specifically mentioned in the book of Esther, but it is obvious that Mordecai expected a divine deliverance. While the book of Esther does not mention God by name or title, his presence fills the pages. Esther and Mordecai believed in God's care, and because they acted at the right time, God used them to save his people.

When you face challenges in life, seek to know what God wants you to do, and then do it, confident that he will do his part. You don't know ahead of time how he will accomplish his will. Trust God and prepare to be surprised by the ways he demonstrates his trustworthiness.

Esth 4:16 By calling for a fast, Esther was asking the Jews to pray for God's help on her dangerous mission. In the Old Testament, prayer always accompanied fasting (see Exod 34:28; Deut 9:9; Ezra 8:21-23). An important

"Who knows if perhaps you were made queen for just such a time as this?"
Esther 4:14

3Then the king asked her, "What do you want, Queen Esther? What is your request? I will give it to you, even if it is half the kingdom!"
4And Esther replied, "If it please the king, let the king and Haman come today to a banquet I have prepared for the king."
5The king turned to his attendants and said, "Tell Haman to come quickly to a banquet, as Esther has requested." So the king and Haman went to Esther's banquet.
6And while they were drinking wine, the king said to Esther, "Now tell me what you really want. What is your request? I will give it to you, even if it is half the kingdom!"
7Esther replied, "This is my request and deepest wish.
8If I have found favor with the king, and if it pleases the king to grant my request and do what I ask, please come with Haman tomorrow to the banquet I will prepare for you. Then I will explain what this is all about."

Haman's Plan to Kill Mordecai

ESTHER 5:9-14

Haman was a happy man as he left the banquet! But when he saw Mordecai sitting at the palace gate, not

HAMAN

The most arrogant people are often those who must measure their self-worth by the power or influence they think they have over others. Haman was an extremely arrogant leader. He recognized the king as his superior but could not accept anyone as an equal. When one man, Mordecai, refused to bow in submission to him, Haman wanted to destroy him. He became consumed with hatred for Mordecai. He was already filled with racial hatred for all the Jewish people because of the long-standing hatred between the Jews and Haman's ancestors, the Amalekites. Mordecai's dedication to God and his refusal to give homage to any human person challenged Haman's self-centered religion. Haman saw the Jews as a threat to his power, and he decided to kill them all. • God was preparing Haman's downfall and the protection of his people long before Haman came to power under Xerxes. Esther, a Jew, became queen, and Mordecai's role in exposing an assassination plot indebted the king to him. Not only was Haman prevented from killing Mordecai; he also had to suffer the humiliation of publicly honoring him. Within hours, Haman died on the pole he had built to impale Mordecai, and his plan to wipe out the Jews was thwarted. In contrast to Esther, who risked everything for God and won, Haman risked everything for an evil purpose and lost. • Our initial response to the story about Haman is to say that he got what he deserved. But the Bible leads us to ask deeper questions: How much of Haman is in me? Do I desire to control others? Am I threatened when others don't appreciate me as I think they should? Do I want revenge when my pride is attacked? Confess these attitudes to God, and ask him to replace them with an attitude of forgiveness. Otherwise, God's justice will settle the matter.

Strength and accomplishment	• Achieved great power, second in rank to Persia's king Xerxes
Weaknesses and mistakes	• The desire to control others and receive honor was his highest goal • Was blinded by arrogance and self-importance • Orchestrated the plan to slaughter God's people throughout the empire
Lessons from his life	• Hatred will be punished • Pride and self-importance will be punished • An insatiable thirst for power and prestige is self-destructive
Vital statistics	• Where: Susa, the capital of Persia • Occupation: Second in rank in the empire • Relative: Wife: Zeresh. • Contemporaries: Xerxes, Mordecai, Esther
Key verses	"When Haman saw that Mordecai would not bow down or show him respect, he was filled with rage. He had learned of Mordecai's nationality, so he decided it was not enough to lay hands on Mordecai alone. Instead, he looked for a way to destroy all the Jews throughout the entire empire of Xerxes" (Esth 3:5-6).

Haman's story is told in the book of Esther.

function of a community of believers is mutual support in difficult times. When you are experiencing struggles, turn to fellow believers for support by sharing your trials with them and gaining strength from the bond that unites you. Ask them to pray for you. And when others need your support, give it willingly.

Esth 4:16 "Save your own skin" and "Watch out for number one" are mottos that reflect our world's selfish outlook on life. Esther's attitude stands in bold contrast to this. She knew what she had to do, and she knew it could cost her life. And yet she responded, "If I must die, I must die." We should have the same commitment to do what is right despite the possible consequences. Do you try to save yourself by remaining silent rather than standing up for what is right? Decide to do what God wants, and trust him for the outcome.

Esth 4:17–5:1 God was in control, yet Mordecai and Esther had to act. We cannot understand how both can be true at the same time, and yet they are. God chooses to work through those willing to act for him. We should pray as if it all depended on God and act as if it all depended on us. We should avoid two extremes: doing nothing, and feeling that we must do everything.

Esth 5:9 Hatred and bitterness are like weeds with long roots that grow in the heart and corrupt all of life. Haman was so consumed with hatred toward Mordecai that he could not even enjoy the honor of being invited to Esther's party. Hebrews 12:15 warns us to "watch out that no poisonous root of bitterness grows up to trouble you, corrupting many." Don't let hatred and its resulting bitterness build up in your heart. Like Haman, you will find it backfiring against you (see Esth 6:13; 7:9-10). If the mere mention of someone's name provokes you to anger, confess your bitterness as sin.

▸ **ESTHER 5:9-14** ***(cont.)***

standing up or trembling nervously before him, Haman became furious. 10However, he restrained himself
and went on home.

Then Haman gathered together his friends and Zeresh, his wife, 11and boasted to them about his great
wealth and his many children. He bragged about the
honors the king had given him and how he had been
promoted over all the other nobles and officials.

12Then Haman added, "And that's not all! Queen
Esther invited only me and the king himself to the
banquet she prepared for us. And she has invited me
to dine with her and the king again tomorrow!" 13Then
he added, "But this is all worth nothing as long as I see
Mordecai the Jew just sitting there at the palace gate."

14So Haman's wife, Zeresh, and all his friends suggested, "Set up a sharpened pole that stands seventy-
five feet* tall, and in the morning ask the king to
impale Mordecai on it. When this is done, you can
go on your merry way to the banquet with the king."
This pleased Haman, and he ordered the pole set up.

The King Honors Mordecai

ESTHER 6:1-14

That night the king had trouble sleeping, so he ordered an attendant to bring the book of the history
of his reign so it could be read to him. 2In those records he discovered an account of how Mordecai had
exposed the plot of Bigthana and Teresh, two of the
eunuchs who guarded the door to the king's private
quarters. They had plotted to assassinate King Xerxes.

3"What reward or recognition did we ever give Mordecai for this?" the king asked.

His attendants replied, "Nothing has been done
for him."

4"Who is that in the outer court?" the king inquired.
As it happened, Haman had just arrived in the outer
court of the palace to ask the king to impale Mordecai
on the pole he had prepared.

5So the attendants replied to the king, "Haman is
out in the court."

"Bring him in," the king ordered. 6So Haman came
in, and the king said, "What should I do to honor a
man who truly pleases me?"

Haman thought to himself, "Whom would the king
wish to honor more than me?" 7So he replied, "If the
king wishes to honor someone, 8he should bring out
one of the king's own royal robes, as well as a horse
that the king himself has ridden—one with a royal
emblem on its head. 9Let the robes and the horse be
handed over to one of the king's most noble officials.
And let him see that the man whom the king wishes to
honor is dressed in the king's robes and led through
the city square on the king's horse. Have the official
shout as they go, 'This is what the king does for someone he wishes to honor!' "

10"Excellent!" the king said to Haman. "Quick! Take
the robes and my horse, and do just as you have said
for Mordecai the Jew, who sits at the gate of the palace.
Leave out nothing you have suggested!"

11So Haman took the robes and put them on Mordecai, placed him on the king's own horse, and led him
through the city square, shouting, "This is what the
king does for someone he wishes to honor!" 12After-
ward Mordecai returned to the palace gate, but Haman
hurried home dejected and completely humiliated.

13When Haman told his wife, Zeresh, and all his
friends what had happened, his wise advisers and his
wife said, "Since Mordecai—this man who has humiliated you—is of Jewish birth, you will never succeed
in your plans against him. It will be fatal to continue
opposing him."

14While they were still talking, the king's eunuchs
arrived and quickly took Haman to the banquet Esther
had prepared.

The King Executes Haman

ESTHER 7:1-10

So the king and Haman went to Queen Esther's banquet. 2On this second occasion, while they were drinking wine, the king again said to Esther, "Tell me what
you want, Queen Esther. What is your request? I will
give it to you, even if it is half the kingdom!"

3Queen Esther replied, "If I have found favor with the
king, and if it pleases the king to grant my request, I ask
that my life and the lives of my people will be spared.
4For my people and I have been sold to those who would
kill, slaughter, and annihilate us. If we had merely been

Est 5:14 Hebrew *50 cubits* [22.5 meters].

Ignoring bitterness, hiding it from others, or making superficial changes in behavior is not enough. If bitterness isn't completely removed, it will grow back, making matters worse.

Esth 5:14 Haman's family and friends, who were as arrogant as he, suggested that the sharpened pole be 75 feet high, probably built on the city wall or some prominent building. They wanted to make sure that all the people of the city saw Mordecai's death and would be reminded of the consequences of disobeying Haman. Ironically, this impaling pole later allowed everyone to see Haman's death.

Esth 6:1-2 Unable to sleep, the king decided to review the history of his reign, and his servants read to him about Mordecai's good deed. This might seem coincidental, but God is always at work. God has been working quietly and patiently throughout your life as well. The events that have come together for good are not mere coincidence; they are the result of God's sovereign control over the course of people's lives (Rom 8:28).

Esth 6:7-9 Haman had wealth, but he craved something even his money couldn't buy—respect. He could buy the trappings of success and power, but his lust for popularity had become an obsession. Don't let your desire for approval, applause, and popularity drive you to immoral actions.

Esth 6:10-13 Mordecai had exposed a plot to assassinate Xerxes—thus, he had saved the king's life (Esth 2:21-23). Although his good deed was recorded in the history books, Mordecai had gone unrewarded. But God was saving Mordecai's reward for the right time. Just as Haman was about to impale Mordecai unjustly, the king was ready to give the reward. Although God promises to reward our good deeds, we sometimes feel our "pay-

sold as slaves, I could remain quiet, for that would be too trivial a matter to warrant disturbing the king."
5"Who would do such a thing?" King Xerxes demanded. "Who would be so presumptuous as to touch you?"
6Esther replied, "This wicked Haman is our adversary and our enemy." Haman grew pale with fright before the king and queen. 7Then the king jumped to his feet in a rage and went out into the palace garden.

Haman, however, stayed behind to plead for his life with Queen Esther, for he knew that the king intended to kill him. 8In despair he fell on the couch where Queen Esther was reclining, just as the king was returning from the palace garden.

The king exclaimed, "Will he even assault the queen right here in the palace, before my very eyes?" And as soon as the king spoke, his attendants covered Haman's face, signaling his doom.
9Then Harbona, one of the king's eunuchs, said, "Haman has set up a sharpened pole that stands seventy-five feet* tall in his own courtyard. He intended to use it to impale Mordecai, the man who saved the king from assassination."

"Then impale Haman on it!" the king ordered. 10So they impaled Haman on the pole he had set up for Mordecai, and the king's anger subsided.

Est 7:9 Hebrew *50 cubits* [22.5 meters].

A Decree to Help the Jews

ESTHER 8:1-17

On that same day King Xerxes gave the property of Haman, the enemy of the Jews, to Queen Esther. Then Mordecai was brought before the king, for Esther had told the king how they were related. 2The king took

HOW GOD WORKS IN THE WORLD

	What God wants done—he works through . . .			
	Natural Order	**Miracles**	**Providence**	
God's Action	God set into action through Creation a normal working of his universe. He also revealed his expectations of people through his Word and people's consciences.	God breaks into the natural order to respond to the expressed needs of people.	God overrules the natural order to accomplish an act that people may or may not have requested.	**GOD'S WILL** ↓
Examples from Esther	God gave Esther natural beauty.	God allowed Esther to speak to the king.	God allowed Mordecai to overhear a plot.	
	Esther planned a way to save her people.	The people prayed and fasted.	Mordecai trusted God to accomplish what was impossible in human terms.	↑
	What people want done—we either . . .			
	Plan	**Pray**	**Trust and Obey**	
Action We Can Take	Can make plans based on the order and dependability of God's creation. Know and obey his words.	Can ask God to intervene in certain affairs while realizing that our knowledge and perspective are limited.	Can trust that God is in control even when circumstances seem to indicate that he is not.	**PEOPLE'S WILL**
	or . . .			
	Disobey	**Demand**	**Despair**	
Mistakes We Can Make	Can violate the natural order, disobey God's commands.	Can assume that we understand what is needed and expect God to agree and answer our prayers that way.	Can assume God doesn't answer prayer or respond to our needs and live as though there is nothing but the natural order.	

off" is too far away. Be patient. God steps in when it will do the most good.

Esth 7:6-10 Haman's hatred and evil plotting turned against him when the king discovered his true intentions. He was impaled on the pole he had set up for someone else. Proverbs 26:27 teaches that if you set a trap for others, you will get caught in it yourself. What happened to Haman shows the often violent results of setting any kind of trap for others.

Esth 7:8 A veil was placed over the face of someone condemned to death because Persian kings refused to look upon the face of a condemned person.

Esth 8:1-7 While we should not expect earthly rewards for being faithful to God, they often come—and in unexpected ways. Esther and Mordecai were faithful, even to the point of risking their lives to save others. They were willing to give up everything, and God rewarded in proportion to their all-out commitment and in ways they could not have foreseen.

▸ **ESTHER 8:1-17** ***(cont.)***

off his signet ring—which he had taken back from Haman—and gave it to Mordecai. And Esther appointed Mordecai to be in charge of Haman's property.

3Then Esther went again before the king, falling down at his feet and begging him with tears to stop the evil plot devised by Haman the Agagite against the Jews. 4Again the king held out the gold scepter to Esther. So she rose and stood before him.

5Esther said, "If it please the king, and if I have found favor with him, and if he thinks it is right, and if I am pleasing to him, let there be a decree that reverses the orders of Haman son of Hammedatha the Agagite, who ordered that Jews throughout all the king's provinces should be destroyed. 6For how can I endure to see my people and my family slaughtered and destroyed?"

7Then King Xerxes said to Queen Esther and Mordecai the Jew, "I have given Esther the property of Haman, and he has been impaled on a pole because he tried to destroy the Jews. 8Now go ahead and send a message to the Jews in the king's name, telling them whatever you want, and seal it with the king's signet ring. But remember that whatever has already been written in the king's name and sealed with his signet ring can never be revoked."

473 BC

9So on June 25* the king's secretaries were summoned, and a decree was written exactly as Mordecai dictated. It was sent to the Jews and to the highest officers, the governors, and the nobles of all the 127 provinces stretching from India to Ethiopia.* The decree was written in the scripts and languages of all the peoples of the empire, including that of the Jews. 10The decree was written in the name of King Xerxes and sealed with the king's signet ring. Mordecai sent the dispatches by swift messengers, who rode fast horses especially bred for the king's service.

11The king's decree gave the Jews in every city authority to unite to defend their lives. They were allowed to kill, slaughter, and annihilate anyone of any nationality or province who might attack them or their children and wives, and to take the property of their enemies. 12The day chosen for this event throughout all the provinces of King Xerxes was March 7 of the next year.*

13A copy of this decree was to be issued as law in every province and proclaimed to all peoples, so that the Jews would be ready to take revenge on their enemies on the appointed day. 14So urged on by the king's command, the messengers rode out swiftly on fast horses bred for the king's service. The same decree was also proclaimed in the fortress of Susa.

15Then Mordecai left the king's presence, wearing the royal robe of blue and white, the great crown of gold, and an outer cloak of fine linen and purple. And the people of Susa celebrated the new decree. 16The Jews were filled with joy and gladness and were honored everywhere. 17In every province and city, wherever the king's decree arrived, the Jews rejoiced and had a great celebration and declared a public festival and holiday. And many of the people of the land became Jews themselves, for they feared what the Jews might do to them.

Est 8:9a Hebrew *on the twenty-third day of the third month, the month of Sivan,* of the ancient Hebrew lunar calendar. This day was June 25, 474 B.C.; also see note on 2:16. **Est 8:9b** Hebrew *to Cush.* **Est 8:12** Hebrew *the thirteenth day of the twelfth month, the month of Adar,* of the ancient Hebrew lunar calendar. The date selected was March 7, 473 B.C.; also see note on 2:16.

Festival of Purim originates

4. THE JEWS ARE DELIVERED

Although God is not mentioned, it is clear that he was active throughout the story of Esther, orchestrating events to protect his people from their enemies even in the land of Persia. Because they depended on him and prayed for deliverance, he saved them when they were being attacked, and Mordecai was promoted to a position of great power in the empire. This great deliverance became memorialized in the annual Jewish festival of Purim.

The Victory of the Jews

ESTHER 9:1-19

So on March 7* the two decrees of the king were put into effect. On that day, the enemies of the Jews had hoped to overpower them, but quite the opposite happened. It was the Jews who overpowered their enemies. 2The Jews gathered in their cities throughout all the king's provinces to attack anyone who tried to harm them. But no one could make a stand against them, for everyone was afraid of them. 3And all the nobles of the provinces, the highest officers, the governors, and the royal officials helped the Jews for fear of Mordecai. 4For Mordecai had been promoted in the king's palace, and his fame

Est 9:1 Hebrew *on the thirteenth day of the twelfth month, the month of Adar,* of the ancient Hebrew lunar calendar. This day was March 7, 473 B.C.; also see note on 2:16.

Esth 8:8 Haman's message had been sealed with the king's signet ring and could not be reversed, even by the king. It was part of the famed "law of the Medes and Persians." Now the king gave permission for whatever other decree Mordecai could devise that would offset the first, without actually canceling it.

Esth 8:12 This was the day set by Haman for the extermination of the Jews (Esth 3:13).

Esth 8:15-17 Everyone wants to be a hero and receive praise, honor, and wealth. But few are willing to pay the price. Mordecai served the government faithfully for years, bore Haman's hatred and oppression, and risked his life for his people. He was faithful in obscurity. The price to be paid by God's heroes is long-term commitment, whether or not they receive recognition. Are you ready and willing to pay the price?

spread throughout all the provinces as he became more and more powerful.

5So the Jews went ahead on the appointed day and struck down their enemies with the sword. They killed and annihilated their enemies and did as they pleased with those who hated them. 6In the fortress of Susa itself, the Jews killed 500 men. 7They also killed Parshandatha, Dalphon, Aspatha, 8Poratha, Adalia, Aridatha, 9Parmashta, Arisai, Aridai, and Vaizatha—10the ten sons of Haman son of Hammedatha, the enemy of the Jews. But they did not take any plunder.

11That very day, when the king was informed of the number of people killed in the fortress of Susa, 12he called for Queen Esther. He said, "The Jews have killed 500 men in the fortress of Susa alone, as well as Haman's ten sons. If they have done that here, what has happened in the rest of the provinces? But now, what more do you want? It will be granted to you; tell me and I will do it."

13Esther responded, "If it please the king, give the Jews in Susa permission to do again tomorrow as they have done today, and let the bodies of Haman's ten sons be impaled on a pole."

14So the king agreed, and the decree was announced in Susa. And they impaled the bodies of Haman's ten sons. 15Then the Jews at Susa gathered together on March 8* and killed 300 more men, and again they took no plunder.

16Meanwhile, the other Jews throughout the king's provinces had gathered together to defend their lives. They gained relief from all their enemies, killing 75,000 of those who hated them. But they did not take any plunder. 17This was done throughout the provinces on March 7, and on March 8 they rested,* celebrating their victory with a day of feasting and gladness. 18(The Jews at Susa killed their enemies on March 7 and again on March 8, then rested on March 9,* making that their day of feasting and gladness.) 19So to this day, rural Jews living in remote villages celebrate an annual festival and holiday on the appointed day in late winter,* when they rejoice and send gifts of food to each other.

The Festival of Purim

ESTHER 9:20-32

Mordecai recorded these events and sent letters to the Jews near and far, throughout all the provinces of King Xerxes, 21calling on them to celebrate an annual festival on these two days.* 22He told them to celebrate these days with feasting and gladness and by giving gifts of food to each other and presents to the poor. This would commemorate a time when the Jews gained relief from their enemies, when their sorrow was turned into gladness and their mourning into joy.

23So the Jews accepted Mordecai's proposal and adopted this annual custom. 24Haman son of Hammedatha the Agagite, the enemy of the Jews, had plotted to crush and destroy them on the date determined by casting lots (the lots were called *purim*). 25But when Esther came before the king, he issued a decree causing Haman's evil plot to backfire, and Haman and his sons were impaled on a sharpened pole. 26That is why this celebration is called Purim, because it is the ancient word for casting lots.

So because of Mordecai's letter and because of what they had experienced, 27the Jews throughout the realm agreed to inaugurate this tradition and to pass it on to their descendants and to all who became Jews. They declared they would never fail to celebrate these two prescribed days at the appointed time each year. 28These days would be remembered and kept from generation to generation and celebrated by every family throughout the provinces and cities of the empire. This Festival of Purim would never cease to be celebrated among the Jews, nor would the memory of what happened ever die out among their descendants.

29Then Queen Esther, the daughter of Abihail, along with Mordecai the Jew, wrote another letter putting

Est 9:15 Hebrew *the fourteenth day of the month of Adar,* of the Hebrew lunar calendar. This day was March 8, 473 B.C.; also see note on 2:16. **Est 9:17** Hebrew *on the thirteenth day of the month of Adar, and on the fourteenth day they rested.* These days were March 7 and 8, 473 B.C.; also see note on 2:16. **Est 9:18** Hebrew *killed their enemies on the thirteenth day and the fourteenth day, and then rested on the fifteenth day,* of the Hebrew month of Adar. **Est 9:19** Hebrew *on the fourteenth day of the month of Adar.* This day of the Hebrew lunar calendar occurs in February or March. **Est 9:21** Hebrew *on the fourteenth and fifteenth days of Adar,* of the Hebrew lunar calendar.

Esth 9:5-16 Haman had decreed that on March 7 anyone could kill the Jews and take their property. Mordecai's decree could not reverse Haman's because no law signed by the king could be repealed. Instead, Mordecai had the king sign a new law giving Jews the right to fight back. When the dreaded day arrived, there was much fighting, but the Jews killed only those who wanted to kill them, and they did not take their enemies' possessions, even though they could have (Esth 8:11; 9:10, 16). There were no additional riots after the two-day slaughter, so obviously selfish gain or revenge was not a primary motive of the Jews. They simply wanted to defend themselves and their families from those who hated them.

Esth 9:11 Here the word *fortress* seems to refer to the fortified city of Susa. The king appears to be more concerned about Esther's wishes than the slaughter of his subjects.

Esth 9:19-22 People tend to have short memories when it comes to God's faithfulness. To help counter this, Mordecai wrote down these events and encouraged an annual holiday to commemorate the historic days of Purim. Jews still celebrate Purim today. Celebrations of feasting, gladness, and gift-giving are important ways to remember God's specific acts. Today the festivities of Christmas and Easter help us remember the birth and resurrection of Jesus Christ. Don't let the celebration or the exchanging of gifts hide the meaning of these great events.

Esth 9:29-31 Among Jews, women were expected to be quiet, to serve in the home, and to stay on the fringe of religious and political life. But Esther was a Jewish woman who broke through the cultural norms, stepping outside her expected role to risk her life to help God's people. Whatever your place in life, God can use you. Be open, available, and ready because God may use you to do what others are afraid to even consider.

▸ **ESTHER 9:20-32** ***(cont.)***

the queen's full authority behind Mordecai's letter
to establish the Festival of Purim. 30Letters wishing
peace and security were sent to the Jews throughout
the 127 provinces of the empire of Xerxes. 31These
letters established the Festival of Purim—an annual
celebration of these days at the appointed time, decreed by both Mordecai the Jew and Queen Esther.
(The people decided to observe this festival, just as
they had decided for themselves and their descendants to establish the times of fasting and mourning.)
32So the command of Esther confirmed the practices
of Purim, and it was all written down in the records.

The Greatness of Xerxes and Mordecai

ESTHER 10:1-3

King Xerxes imposed a tribute throughout his
empire, even to the distant coastlands. 2His great
achievements and the full account of the greatness
of Mordecai, whom the king had promoted, are recorded in *The Book of the History of the Kings of
Media and Persia.* 3Mordecai the Jew became the
prime minister, with authority next to that of King
Xerxes himself. He was very great among the Jews,
who held him in high esteem, because he continued
to work for the good of his people and to speak up
for the welfare of all their descendants.

D. The Return Led by Ezra

Ezra returned to the land with a second group of exiles, 80 years after Zerubbabel. Ezra found the Temple rebuilt but the lives of the people in shambles. Intermarriage with foreigners opposed to God threatened the spiritual future of the nation. So Ezra prayed for guidance and then followed through with action. Christians today must also strive to keep their lives pure, refusing to let the sinful allurements of the world around them compromise their lifestyle.

Opposition to the Returned Jews under Artaxerxes

EZRA 4:7-23

460 BC *Hippocrates, the father of modern medicine, is born*

Even later, during the reign of King Artaxerxes of
Persia,* the enemies of Judah, led by Bishlam, Mithredath, and Tabeel, sent a letter to Artaxerxes in the
Aramaic language, and it was translated for the king.
8*Rehum the governor and Shimshai the court secretary wrote the letter, telling King Artaxerxes about
the situation in Jerusalem. 9They greeted the king for
all their colleagues—the judges and local leaders, the
people of Tarpel, the Persians, the Babylonians, and
the people of Erech and Susa (that is, Elam). 10They
also sent greetings from the rest of the people whom
the great and noble Ashurbanipal* had deported and
relocated in Samaria and throughout the neighboring
lands of the province west of the Euphrates River.*
11This is a copy of their letter:

Ezr 4:7 Artaxerxes reigned 465–424 B.C. **Ezr 4:8** The original text of 4:8–6:18 is in Aramaic. **Ezr 4:10a** Aramaic *Osnappar,* another name for Ashurbanipal. **Ezr 4:10b** Aramaic *the province beyond the river;* also in 4:11, 16, 17, 20.

Esth 10:3 Mordecai enjoyed a good reputation among the Jews because he was still their friend when he rose to a place of power. Corruption and abuse of authority often characterize those in power. But power used to lift the fallen and ease the burden of the oppressed is power used well. People placed by God in positions of power or political influence must not turn their backs on those in need.

Esth 10:3 No archaeological records of Mordecai's being prime minister and second-in-command have been discovered, but during this time there is a strange gap in ancient Persian records. The records indicate that another man held that position in 465 B.C., about seven years after Mordecai was first appointed. One tablet has been discovered naming Mardukaya as an official in the early years of Xerxes's reign; some believe this was Mordecai.

Esth 10:3 In the book of Esther, we clearly see God at work in the lives of individuals and in the affairs of a nation. Even when it looks as if the world is in the hands of evil people, God is still in control, protecting those who are his. Although we may not understand everything happening around us, we must trust in God's protection and retain our integrity by doing what we know is right. Esther, who risked her life by appearing before the king, became a heroine. Mordecai, who was effectively condemned to death, rose to become the second highest ranking official in the nation. No matter how hopeless our condition, or how much we would like to give up, we need not despair. God is in control of our world.

Ezra 4:7 This letter sent to King Artaxerxes may have been inscribed on a clay tablet, a fragment of pottery, or sheets of parchment.

THE PERSIAN KINGS OF EZRA'S DAY

Name	*Date of Reign*	*Relationship to Israel*
Cyrus	559–530 B.C.	Conquered Babylon. Established a policy of returning exiles to their homelands. Sent Zerubbabel to Jerusalem, financed his project, and returned the gold and silver articles that Nebuchadnezzar had taken from the Temple. He probably knew Daniel.
Darius	522–486 B.C.	Supported construction of the Temple in Jerusalem.
Xerxes (Ahasuerus)	486–465 B.C.	Was Esther's husband. Allowed the Jews to protect themselves against Haman's attempt to eliminate their people.
Artaxerxes I	465–424 B.C.	Had Nehemiah as his cup-bearer. Allowed both Ezra and Nehemiah to return to Jerusalem.

"To King Artaxerxes, from your loyal subjects in the province west of the Euphrates River.

[12]"The king should know that the Jews who came here to Jerusalem from Babylon are rebuilding this rebellious and evil city. They have already laid the foundation and will soon finish its walls. [13]And the king should know that if this city is rebuilt and its walls are completed, it will be much to your disadvantage, for the Jews will then refuse to pay their tribute, customs, and tolls to you.

[14]"Since we are your loyal subjects* and do not want to see the king dishonored in this way, we have sent the king this information. [15]We suggest that a search be made in your ancestors' records, where you will discover what a rebellious city this has been in the past. In fact, it was destroyed because of its long and troublesome history of revolt against the kings and countries who controlled it. [16]We declare to the king that if this city is rebuilt and its walls are completed, the province west of the Euphrates River will be lost to you."

[17]Then King Artaxerxes sent this reply:

"To Rehum the governor, Shimshai the court secretary, and their colleagues living in Samaria and throughout the province west of the Euphrates River. Greetings.

[18]"The letter you sent has been translated and read to me. [19]I ordered a search of the records and have found that Jerusalem has indeed been a hotbed of insurrection against many kings. In fact, rebellion and revolt are normal there! [20]Powerful kings have ruled over Jerusalem and the entire province west of the Euphrates River, receiving tribute, customs, and tolls. [21]Therefore, issue orders to have these men stop their work. That city must not be rebuilt except at my express command. [22]Be diligent, and don't neglect this matter, for we must not permit the situation to harm the king's interests."

[23]When this letter from King Artaxerxes was read to Rehum, Shimshai, and their colleagues, they hurried to Jerusalem. Then, with a show of strength, they forced the Jews to stop building.

Ezra Arrives in Jerusalem

EZRA 7:1-10

Many years later, during the reign of King Artaxerxes of Persia,* there was a man named Ezra. He was the son* of Seraiah, son of Azariah, son of Hilkiah, [2]son of Shallum, son of Zadok, son of Ahitub, [3]son of Amariah, son of Azariah, son* of Meraioth, [4]son of Zerahiah, son of Uzzi, son of Bukki, [5]son of Abishua, son of Phinehas, son of Eleazar, son of Aaron the high priest.* **458 BC**

Ezr 4:14 Aramaic *Since we eat the salt of the palace.* **Ezr 7:1a** Artaxerxes reigned 465–424 B.C. **Ezr 7:1b** Or *descendant;* see 1 Chr 6:14. **Ezr 7:3** Or *descendant;* see 1 Chr 6:6-10. **Ezr 7:5** Or *the first priest.*

Ezra 4:10 Ashurbanipal (669–627 B.C.) was the Assyrian king who completed the relocation of Israelite captives. He was the last of the strong Assyrian kings. After his death the nation quickly declined. Babylon conquered Assyria in 612 B.C.

Ezra 4:19-20 Artaxerxes said that Jerusalem had been "a hotbed of insurrection against many kings." By reading the historical records, he learned that mighty kings had come from Jerusalem, and he may have feared that another would arise if the city were rebuilt. Solomon had ruled a huge empire (1 Kgs 4:21), and Jerusalem's kings had rebelled against mighty powers. For example, Zedekiah rebelled against Nebuchadnezzar despite his oath of loyalty (2 Chr 36:13). Artaxerxes did not want to aid the rebuilding of a rebellious city and nation.

Ezra 4:23 Setbacks and standstills are painful and discouraging to God's workers. These exiles had received a double dose (see Ezra 4:1-5, 6-22). Leaders should do everything to keep work from grinding to a halt; yet circumstances sometimes really are beyond our control. When you have been brought to a standstill, remember to still stand strong in the Lord.

Ezra 7:1 Ezra traveled to Jerusalem in 458 B.C.

The Court of Ashurbanipal

Much of what we know about the culture of ancient Mesopotamia—historical facts, religion, legends, and lore—comes from the cuneiform literature collected by Ashurbanipal and deposited in a large library he built in Nineveh, his capital. The remains of this library, discovered over a century ago, continue to have an impact on biblical knowledge. Without doubt, this library has been his most significant memorial. This relief from Nineveh shows two ambassadors from Susa at the court of Ashurbanipal.

Ashurbanipal was evidently the Assyrian monarch who sent alien people into Samaria (Ezra 4:10). Deportation of conquered peoples was standard Assyrian policy, which accounts for the assimilation and disappearance of the ten tribes of the northern kingdom of Israel after its fall to Sargon II. The Assyrian king is called Osnappar, a transliteration of the Hebrew spelling (see the textual note at Ezra 4:10). The consonantal similarity of the Hebrew word to Ashurbanipal's Assyrian name, plus the list of conquered peoples mentioned in the text, points to Ashurbanipal as the most likely identification.

Ezra leads another group of returning exiles to Jerusalem

▸ **EZRA 7:1-10** ***(cont.)***
6This Ezra was a scribe who was well versed in the Law
of Moses, which the LORD, the God of Israel, had given
to the people of Israel. He came up to Jerusalem from
Babylon, and the king gave him everything he asked
for, because the gracious hand of the LORD his God
was on him. 7Some of the people of Israel, as well as
some of the priests, Levites, singers, gatekeepers, and
Temple servants, traveled up to Jerusalem with him in
the seventh year of King Artaxerxes' reign.
8Ezra arrived in Jerusalem in August* of that year.
9He had arranged to leave Babylon on April 8, the first
day of the new year,* and he arrived at Jerusalem on
August 4,* for the gracious hand of his God was on
him. 10This was because Ezra had determined to study
and obey the Law of the LORD and to teach those decrees and regulations to the people of Israel.

Artaxerxes' Letter to Ezra

EZRA 7:11-26
King Artaxerxes had given a copy of the following letter to Ezra, the priest and scribe who studied and taught the commands and decrees of the LORD to Israel:

12*"From Artaxerxes, the king of kings, to Ezra
the priest, the teacher of the law of the God of
heaven. Greetings.
13"I decree that any of the people of Israel in
my kingdom, including the priests and Levites,

Ezr 7:8 Hebrew *in the fifth month.* This month in the ancient Hebrew lunar calendar occurred within the months of August and September 458 B.C. **Ezr 7:9a** Hebrew *on the first day of the first month,* of the ancient Hebrew lunar calendar. This day was April 8, 458 B.C.; also see note on 6:15. **Ezr 7:9b** Hebrew *on the first day of the fifth month,* of the ancient Hebrew lunar calendar. This day was August 4, 458 B.C.; also see note on 6:15. **Ezr 7:12** The original text of 7:12-26 is in Aramaic.

EZRA

It is not personal achievement but personal commitment to live for God that is important. Achievements are simply examples of what God can do through someone's life. The most effective leaders spoken of in the Bible had little awareness of the impact their lives had on others. They were too busy obeying God to keep track of their successes. Ezra fits that description. • About 80 years after the rebuilding of the Temple under Zerubbabel, Ezra led a second group of exiles to Judah, about 2,000 men and their families. King Artaxerxes gave Ezra a letter instructing him to carry out a program of religious education. Along with the letter came significant power. But long before Ezra's mission began, God had shaped him in three important ways so that he would use the power well. First, as a scribe, Ezra dedicated himself to carefully studying God's Word. Second, he intended to apply and obey personally the commands he discovered in God's Word. Third, he was committed to teaching others God's Word and its application to life. • Knowing Ezra's priorities, it is not surprising to note his actions when he arrived in Jerusalem. The people had disobeyed God's command not to marry women of foreign nations. On a cold and rainy day, Ezra addressed the people and made it clear that they had sinned. Because of the sins of many, all were under God's condemnation. Confession, repentance, and action were needed. The people admitted their sin and devised a plan to deal with the problem. • This initial effort on Ezra's part set the stage for what Nehemiah would later accomplish. Ezra continued his ministry under Nehemiah, and God used the two of them to start a spiritual movement that swept the nation following the rebuilding of Jerusalem. • Ezra achieved great things and made a significant impact because he had the right starting place for his actions and his life: God's Word. He studied it seriously and applied it faithfully. He taught others what he learned. He is, therefore, a great model for anyone who wants to live for God.

Strengths and accomplishments	• Committed to study, follow, and teach God's Word • Led the second group of exiles from Babylon to Jerusalem • Concerned about keeping the details of God's commands • Worked alongside Nehemiah during the last spiritual awakening recorded in the Old Testament
Lessons from his life	• A willingness to know and practice God's Word will have a direct effect on how God uses a person's life • The starting place for serving God is a personal commitment to serve him today, even before knowing what that service will be
Vital statistics	• Where: Babylon, Jerusalem • Occupations: Scribe among the exiles in Babylon, king's envoy, teacher • Relative: Father: Seraiah. • Contemporaries: Nehemiah, Artaxerxes
Key verse	"Ezra had determined to study and obey the Law of the LORD and to teach those decrees and regulations to the people of Israel" (Ezra 7:10).

Ezra's story is told in Ezra 7:1–10:16; Nehemiah 8:1–12:36.

Ezra 7:6 Eighty years after the first exiles returned to Jerusalem (Ezra 2:1), Ezra himself returned to his homeland. This was his first trip, and it took four months. The Temple had been standing for about 58 years. Up to this point in the narrative, Ezra had remained in Babylon, probably compiling a record of the events that had taken place.

Why did he have to ask the king if he could return? Ezra wanted to lead many Jews back to Jerusalem, and he needed a decree from the king stating that any Jew who wanted to return could do so. This decree would be like a passport in case they ran into opposition along the way. The king's generous decree showed that God was blessing Ezra (Ezra 7:6, 28). It also indicated that Ezra was probably a prominent man in Artaxerxes's kingdom. He was willing to give up this position in order to return to his homeland and teach the Israelites God's laws.

Ezra 7:6-10 Ezra demonstrates how a gifted Bible teacher can move God's people forward. He was effective because he was a well-versed student of the law of the Lord and because he was determined to obey those laws. He taught through both his speaking

may volunteer to return to Jerusalem with you.
14I and my council of seven hereby instruct you
to conduct an inquiry into the situation in Judah
and Jerusalem, based on your God's law, which is in
your hand. 15We also commission you to take with
you silver and gold, which we are freely presenting
as an offering to the God of Israel who lives in
Jerusalem.
16"Furthermore, you are to take any silver and
gold that you may obtain from the province of
Babylon, as well as the voluntary offerings of
the people and the priests that are presented
for the Temple of their God in Jerusalem.
17These donations are to be used specifically
for the purchase of bulls, rams, male lambs,
and the appropriate grain offerings and liquid
offerings, all of which will be offered on the altar
of the Temple of your God in Jerusalem. 18Any
silver and gold that is left over may be used in
whatever way you and your colleagues feel is the
will of your God.
19"But as for the cups we are entrusting to you
for the service of the Temple of your God, deliver
them all to the God of Jerusalem. 20If you need
anything else for your God's Temple or for any
similar needs, you may take it from the royal
treasury.
21"I, Artaxerxes the king, hereby send this
decree to all the treasurers in the province west
of the Euphrates River*: 'You are to give Ezra, the
priest and teacher of the law of the God of heaven,
whatever he requests of you. 22You are to give him
up to 7,500 pounds* of silver, 500 bushels* of
wheat, 550 gallons of wine, 550 gallons of olive
oil,* and an unlimited supply of salt. 23Be careful
to provide whatever the God of heaven demands
for his Temple, for why should we risk bringing
God's anger against the realm of the king and his
sons? 24I also decree that no priest, Levite, singer,
gatekeeper, Temple servant, or other worker in
this Temple of God will be required to pay tribute,
customs, or tolls of any kind.'
25"And you, Ezra, are to use the wisdom your
God has given you to appoint magistrates and
judges who know your God's laws to govern all
the people in the province west of the Euphrates
River. Teach the law to anyone who does not know
it. 26Anyone who refuses to obey the law of your
God and the law of the king will be punished
immediately, either by death, banishment,
confiscation of goods, or imprisonment."

Ezra Praises the Lord

EZRA 7:27-28

Praise the LORD, the God of our ancestors, who made
the king want to beautify the Temple of the LORD in

Ezr 7:21 Aramaic *the province beyond the river;* also in 7:25. **Ezr 7:22a** Aramaic *100 talents* [3,400 kilograms]. **Ezr 7:22b** Aramaic *100 cors* [18.2 kiloliters]. **Ezr 7:22c** Aramaic *100 baths* [2.1 kiloliters] *of wine, 100 baths of olive oil.*

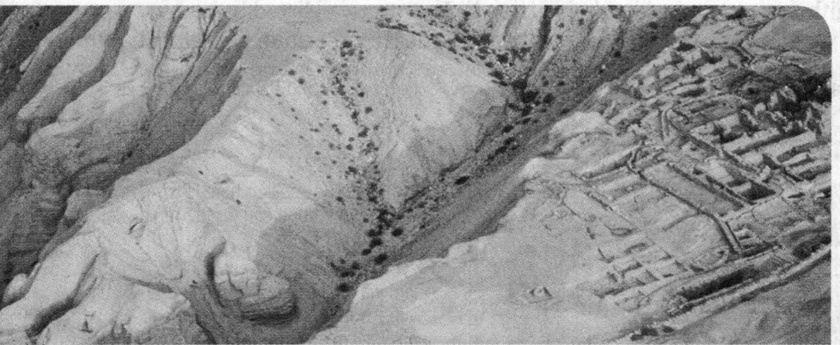

Scribes at Qumran

With the restoration of Judaism under Ezra and Nehemiah, the term *scribe* described those who gathered together, made copies, studied, and interpreted the Torah (Jewish law). They became, in essence, a separate profession of teachers (although unpaid), able to preserve accurately the law of Moses and interpret it to meet conditions in postexilic times. In the initial period, Ezra himself appears as the ideal "scribe who studied and taught the commands and decrees of the LORD to Israel" (Ezra 7:11). At Qumran there were scribes who made copies of Old Testament texts, interpreted them, and applied them to their communal life. We can be thankful that scribes throughout history have made copies of Scripture for future generations to read and trust.

and his example. Like Ezra, we should determine both to study and to obey God's Word.

Ezra 7:14 The council of seven was Artaxerxes's supreme court (see Esth 1:14).

Ezra 7:14 When Nebuchadnezzar destroyed the Temple, he took a vast amount of plunder that may have included a copy of the Book of the Law (2 Chr 36:18). It is also possible that the Jews brought this book into exile and their conquerors confiscated and read it. Foreign leaders who worshiped many gods liked to have records of the gods of other nations for military and political reasons.

Ezra 7:24 Why did Artaxerxes exempt Temple workers from paying taxes? He recognized that the priests and Levites filled an important role in society as spiritual leaders, so he freed them of tax burdens. While the Bible does not teach tax exemption for religious employees, Artaxerxes, a pagan king, recognized and supported the principle. Today, churches have the responsibility to keep such burdens off the shoulders of spiritual workers.

Ezra 7:27 In Ezra's doxology, he acknowledges that God "made the king want to beautify the Temple." God can change a king's heart (see Prov 21:1). When we face life's challenges, we often must work diligently and with extraordinary effort, realizing that God oversees all our work. Recognize his hand in your success, and remember to praise him for his help and protection.

Ezra 7:27-28 Ezra praised God for all that God had done for him and through him. Ezra had honored God throughout his life, and God chose to honor him. Ezra could have assumed that his own greatness and charisma had won over the king and his princes, but he gave the credit to God. We, too, should be grateful to God for our success and not think that we did it in our own power.

▸ **EZRA 7:27-28** ***(cont.)***

Jerusalem! 28 And praise him for demonstrating such unfailing love to me by honoring me before the king, his council, and all his mighty nobles! I felt encouraged because the gracious hand of the LORD my God was on me. And I gathered some of the leaders of Israel to return with me to Jerusalem.

Exiles Who Returned with Ezra

EZRA 8:1-14

Here is a list of the family leaders and the genealogies of those who came with me from Babylon during the reign of King Artaxerxes:

2 From the family of Phinehas: Gershom.
From the family of Ithamar: Daniel.
From the family of David: Hattush, 3 a descendant of Shecaniah.
From the family of Parosh: Zechariah and 150 other men were registered.
4 From the family of Pahath-moab: Eliehoenai son of Zerahiah and 200 other men.
5 From the family of Zattu*: Shecaniah son of Jahaziel and 300 other men.
6 From the family of Adin: Ebed son of Jonathan and 50 other men.
7 From the family of Elam: Jeshaiah son of Athaliah and 70 other men.
8 From the family of Shephatiah: Zebadiah son of Michael and 80 other men.
9 From the family of Joab: Obadiah son of Jehiel and 218 other men.
10 From the family of Bani*: Shelomith son of Josiphiah and 160 other men.
11 From the family of Bebai: Zechariah son of Bebai and 28 other men.
12 From the family of Azgad: Johanan son of Hakkatan and 110 other men.
13 From the family of Adonikam, who came later*: Eliphelet, Jeuel, Shemaiah, and 60 other men.
14 From the family of Bigvai: Uthai, Zaccur,* and 70 other men.

Ezra's Journey to Jerusalem

EZRA 8:15-36

I assembled the exiles at the Ahava Canal, and we
camped there for three days while I went over the
lists of the people and the priests who had arrived.
I found that not one Levite had volunteered to come
along. 16 So I sent for Eliezer, Ariel, Shemaiah, Elnathan,
Jarib, Elnathan, Nathan, Zechariah, and Meshullam,
who were leaders of the people. I also sent for Joiarib
and Elnathan, who were men of discernment. 17 I sent
them to Iddo, the leader of the Levites at Casiphia, to
ask him and his relatives and the Temple servants to
send us ministers for the Temple of God at Jerusalem.
18 Since the gracious hand of our God was on us, they
sent us a man named Sherebiah, along with eighteen of
his sons and brothers. He was a very astute man and a
descendant of Mahli, who was a descendant of Levi son
of Israel.* 19 They also sent Hashabiah, together with
Jeshaiah from the descendants of Merari, and twenty
of his sons and brothers, 20 and 220 Temple servants.
The Temple servants were assistants to the Levites—a
group of Temple workers first instituted by King David
and his officials. They were all listed by name.
21 And there by the Ahava Canal, I gave orders for

Ezr 8:5 As in some Greek manuscripts (see also 1 Esdras 8:32); Hebrew lacks *Zattu.* **Ezr 8:10** As in some Greek manuscripts (see also 1 Esdras 8:36); Hebrew lacks *Bani.* **Ezr 8:13** Or *who were the last of his family.* **Ezr 8:14** As in Greek and Syriac versions and an alternate reading of the Masoretic Text; the other alternate reads *Zabbud.* **Ezr 8:18** *Israel* is the name that God gave to Jacob.

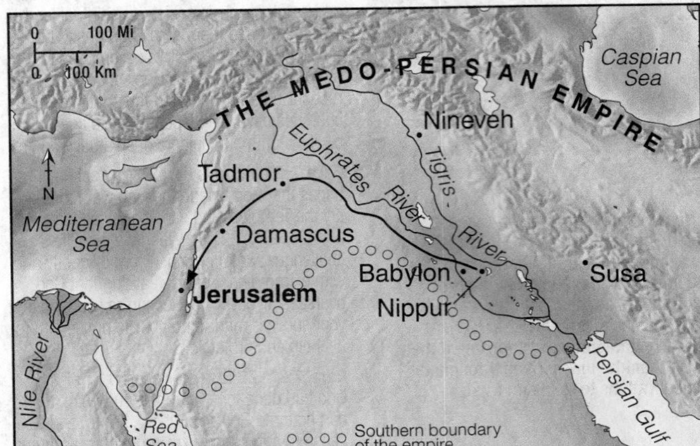

EZRA'S JOURNEY ***Ezra led a second group of exiles back to Judah and Jerusalem about 80 years after the first group. He traveled the dangerous route without military escort (Ezra 8:22), but the people prayed and, under Ezra's godly leadership, arrived safely in Jerusalem after several months.***

Ezra 7:28 The speaker here is Ezra. He writes in the first person for the remainder of the book (Ezra 8–10).

Ezra 8:15 Ezra's progress back to Jerusalem was halted while he waited to recruit Levites. God had called these men to a special service, and yet few were willing to volunteer when their services were needed. God has gifted each of us with abilities so we can make a contribution to his Kingdom work (Rom 12:4-8). Don't wait to be recruited, but look for opportunities to volunteer. Don't hinder God's work by holding back. "God has given each of you a gift from his great variety of spiritual gifts. Use them well to serve one another" (1 Pet 4:10).

Ezra 8:21 Ezra and the people traveled approximately 900 miles on foot. The trip took them through dangerous and difficult territory and lasted about four months. They prayed that God would give them a safe journey. Our journeys today may not be as difficult and dangerous as Ezra's, but we should recognize our need to ask God for guidance and protection.

all of us to fast and humble ourselves before our God.
We prayed that he would give us a safe journey and
protect us, our children, and our goods as we traveled.
22 For I was ashamed to ask the king for soldiers and
horsemen* to accompany us and protect us from
enemies along the way. After all, we had told the king,
"Our God's hand of protection is on all who worship
him, but his fierce anger rages against those who
abandon him." 23 So we fasted and earnestly prayed
that our God would take care of us, and he heard our
prayer.

24 I appointed twelve leaders of the priests—Sherebiah, Hashabiah, and ten other priests—25 to be in
charge of transporting the silver, the gold, the gold
bowls, and the other items that the king, his council,
his officials, and all the people of Israel had presented
for the Temple of God. 26 I weighed the treasure as I
gave it to them and found the totals to be as follows:

24 tons* of silver,
7,500 pounds* of silver articles,
7,500 pounds of gold,
27 20 gold bowls, equal in value to 1,000 gold coins,*
2 fine articles of polished bronze, as precious as gold.

28 And I said to these priests, "You and these treasures have been set apart as holy to the LORD. This
silver and gold is a voluntary offering to the LORD, the
God of our ancestors. 29 Guard these treasures well
until you present them to the leading priests, the Levites, and the leaders of Israel, who will weigh them
at the storerooms of the LORD's Temple in Jerusalem."
30 So the priests and the Levites accepted the task of
transporting these treasures of silver and gold to the
Temple of our God in Jerusalem.

31 We broke camp at the Ahava Canal on April 19*
and started off to Jerusalem. And the gracious hand
of our God protected us and saved us from enemies
and bandits along the way. 32 So we arrived safely in
Jerusalem, where we rested for three days.

33 On the fourth day after our arrival, the silver, gold,
and other valuables were weighed at the Temple of
our God and entrusted to Meremoth son of Uriah the
priest and to Eleazar son of Phinehas, along with Jozabad son of Jeshua and Noadiah son of Binnui—both
of whom were Levites. 34 Everything was accounted
for by number and weight, and the total weight was
officially recorded.

35 Then the exiles who had come out of captivity
sacrificed burnt offerings to the God of Israel. They
presented twelve bulls for all the people of Israel, as
well as ninety-six rams and seventy-seven male lambs.
They also offered twelve male goats as a sin offering.
All this was given as a burnt offering to the LORD. 36 The
king's decrees were delivered to his highest officers
and the governors of the province west of the Euphrates River,* who then cooperated by supporting the
people and the Temple of God.

Ezra's Prayer concerning Intermarriage

EZRA 9:1-15

When these things had been done, the Jewish leaders came to me and said, "Many of the people of Israel, and even some of the priests and Levites, have not kept themselves separate from the other peoples living in the land. They have taken up the detestable practices of the Canaanites, Hittites, Perizzites, Jebusites,

Ezr 8:22 Or *charioteers.* **Ezr 8:26a** Hebrew *650 talents* [22 metric tons]. **Ezr 8:26b** Hebrew *100 talents* [3,400 kilograms]; also in 8:26c. **Ezr 8:27** Hebrew *1,000 darics,* about 19 pounds or 8.6 kilograms in weight. **Ezr 8:31** Hebrew *on the twelfth day of the first month,* of the ancient Hebrew lunar calendar. This day was April 19, 458 B.C.; also see note on 6:15. **Ezr 8:36** Hebrew *the province beyond the river.*

Ezra 8:21-23 Before making all the physical preparations for the journey, Ezra made spiritual preparations. Their prayers and fasting prepared them spiritually and showed their dependence on God for protection, their faith that God was in control, and their affirmation that they were not strong enough to make the trip without him. When we take time to put God first in any endeavor, we are preparing well for whatever lies ahead.

Ezra 8:23 Ezra knew God's promises to protect his people, but he didn't take them for granted. He also knew that God's blessings are appropriated through prayer, so Ezra and the people humbled themselves by fasting and praying. And their prayers were answered. Fasting humbled them because going without food was a reminder of their complete dependence on God. Fasting also gave them more time to pray and meditate on God.

Too often we pray glibly and superficially. Serious prayer, by contrast, requires concentration. It puts us in touch with God's will and can really change us. Without serious prayer, we reduce God to a quick-service pharmacist with painkillers for our every ailment.

Ezra 8:26 This was a large amount of treasure to transport, with or without a detachment of soldiers for protection.

Ezra 8:28-29 Every object used in Temple service was dedicated to God; each was considered a holy treasure to be guarded carefully and set apart for his special use. *Stewardship* means taking special care of whatever God has entrusted to you. This means considering what God has given to you as being from him and for *his* use. What has God entrusted to your care?

Ezra 9:1-2 Since the time of the judges, Israelite men had married pagan women and then adopted their religious practices (Judg 3:5-7). Even Israel's great king Solomon was guilty of this sin (1 Kgs 11:1-8). Although this practice was forbidden in God's law (Exod 34:11-16; Deut 7:1-4), it happened in Ezra's day and again only a generation after him (Neh 13:23-27). Opposition to mixed marriage was not racial prejudice because Jews and non-Jews of this area were of the same Semitic background. The reasons were strictly spiritual. A person who married a pagan was inclined to adopt that person's pagan beliefs and practices. If the Israelites were insensitive enough to disobey God in something as important as marriage, they wouldn't be strong enough to stand firm against their spouses' idolatry. Until the Israelites finally stopped this practice, idolatry remained a constant problem.

▸ **EZRA 9:1-15** ***(cont.)***

Ammonites, Moabites, Egyptians, and Amorites. 2For the men of Israel have married women from these people and have taken them as wives for their sons. So the holy race has become polluted by these mixed marriages. Worse yet, the leaders and officials have led the way in this outrage."

3When I heard this, I tore my cloak and my shirt, pulled hair from my head and beard, and sat down utterly shocked. 4Then all who trembled at the words of the God of Israel came and sat with me because of this outrage committed by the returned exiles. And I sat there utterly appalled until the time of the evening sacrifice.

5At the time of the sacrifice, I stood up from where I had sat in mourning with my clothes torn. I fell to my knees and lifted my hands to the LORD my God. 6I prayed,

"O my God, I am utterly ashamed; I blush to lift up my face to you. For our sins are piled higher than our heads, and our guilt has reached to the heavens. 7From the days of our ancestors until now, we have been steeped in sin. That is why we and our kings and our priests have been at the mercy of the pagan kings of the land. We have been killed, captured, robbed, and disgraced, just as we are today.

8"But now we have been given a brief moment of grace, for the LORD our God has allowed a few of us to survive as a remnant. He has given us security in this holy place. Our God has brightened our eyes and granted us some relief from our slavery. 9For we were slaves, but in his unfailing love our God did not abandon us in our slavery. Instead, he caused the kings of Persia to treat us favorably. He revived us so we could rebuild the Temple of our God and repair its ruins. He has given us a protective wall in Judah and Jerusalem.

10"And now, O our God, what can we say after all of this? For once again we have abandoned your commands! 11Your servants the prophets warned us when they said, 'The land you are entering to possess is totally defiled by the detestable practices of the people living there. From one end to the other, the land is filled with corruption. 12Don't let your daughters marry their sons! Don't take their daughters as wives for your sons. Don't ever promote the peace and prosperity of those nations. If you follow these instructions, you will be strong and will enjoy the good things the land produces, and you will leave this prosperity to your children forever.'

13"Now we are being punished because of our wickedness and our great guilt. But we have actually been punished far less than we deserve, for you, our God, have allowed some of us to survive as a remnant. 14But even so, we are again breaking your commands and intermarrying with people who do these detestable things. Won't your anger be enough to destroy us, so that even this little remnant no longer survives? 15O LORD, God of Israel, you are just. We come before you in our guilt as nothing but an escaped remnant, though in such a condition none of us can stand in your presence."

The People Confess Their Sin

EZRA 10:1-17

While Ezra prayed and made this confession, weeping and lying face down on the ground in front of the Temple

457 BC *The Golden Age begins in Athens, Greece*

Ezra 9:2 Some Israelites had married pagan spouses and lost track of God's purpose for them. The New Testament says that believers should not "team up with those who are unbelievers" (2 Cor 6:14). Such marriages cannot have unity in the most important issue in life—commitment and obedience to God. Because marriage involves two people becoming one, faith may become an issue, and one spouse may have to compromise beliefs for the sake of unity. Many people discount this problem only to regret it later. Don't allow emotion or passion to blind you to the importance of marrying someone with whom you can be united spiritually.

Ezra 9:3-5 Tearing one's clothes and pulling hair from one's head or beard were signs of self-abasement or humility. They expressed sorrow for sin.

Ezra 9:5-15 After learning about the sins of the people, Ezra fell to his knees in prayer. His heartfelt prayer provides a good perspective on sin. He recognized (1) that sin is serious (Ezra 9:6); (2) that no one sins without affecting others (Ezra 9:7); (3) that he was not sinless, although he didn't have a pagan wife (Ezra 9:10ff); and (4) that God's love and mercy had spared the nation when they had done nothing to deserve it (Ezra 9:8-9, 15). It is easy to view sin lightly in a world that sees sin as inconsequential, but we should view sin as seriously as Ezra did.

Ezra 9:5-15 Ezra confessed the sins of his people. Although he had not sinned in the way his people had, he identified with their sins. With weeping, he expressed shame for sin, fear of the consequences, and desire that the people would come to their senses and repent. His prayer moved the people to tears (Ezra 10:1). Ezra demonstrated the need for a holy community around the rebuilt Temple. We need a holy community in our local churches, too. Even when we sin in the worst imaginable way, we can turn to God with prayers of repentance.

Ezra 9:9 Building a wall was not only a matter of civic pride or architectural beauty, it was essential for security and defense against robbers and marauders (see Ezra 9:7). God in his kindness had given them new life and protection.

Ezra 9:15 Ezra recognized that if God gave the people the justice they deserved, they would not be able to stand before him. Often we cry out for justice when we feel abused and unfairly treated. In those moments, we forget the reality of our own sin and the righteous judgment we deserve. How fortunate we are that God gives us mercy and grace rather than only justice. The next time you ask God for fair treatment, pause to think what would happen if God gave you what you really deserve. Plead instead for his mercy.

Ezra 10:1 Ezra set the standard of repentance by his own behavior. His weeping brought others to the point of sorrow. Some may respond when we *tell* them what to do, but more will follow if we *show* them what to do and participate ourselves. In this case, Ezra's actions actually motivated a leader to make a significant stand. We can never predict who will follow or benefit from our example.

of God, a very large crowd of people from Israel—men, women, and children—gathered and wept bitterly with him. 2Then Shecaniah son of Jehiel, a descendant of Elam, said to Ezra, "We have been unfaithful to our God, for we have married these pagan women of the land. But in spite of this there is hope for Israel. 3Let us now make a covenant with our God to divorce our pagan wives and to send them away with their children. We will follow the advice given by you and by the others who respect the commands of our God. Let it be done according to the Law of God. 4Get up, for it is your duty to tell us how to proceed in setting things straight. We are behind you, so be strong and take action."

5So Ezra stood up and demanded that the leaders of the priests and the Levites and all the people of Israel swear that they would do as Shecaniah had said. And they all swore a solemn oath. 6Then Ezra left the front of the Temple of God and went to the room of Jehohanan son of Eliashib. He spent the night* there without eating or drinking anything. He was still in mourning because of the unfaithfulness of the returned exiles.

7Then a proclamation was made throughout Judah and Jerusalem that all the exiles should come to Jerusalem. 8Those who failed to come within three days would, if the leaders and elders so decided, forfeit all their property and be expelled from the assembly of the exiles.

9Within three days, all the people of Judah and Benjamin had gathered in Jerusalem. This took place on December 19,* and all the people were sitting in the square before the Temple of God. They were trembling both because of the seriousness of the matter and because it was raining. 10Then Ezra the priest stood and said to them: "You have committed a terrible sin. By marrying pagan women, you have increased Israel's guilt. 11So now confess your sin to the LORD, the God of your ancestors, and do what he demands. Separate yourselves from the people of the land and from these pagan women."

12Then the whole assembly raised their voices and answered, "Yes, you are right; we must do as you say!" 13Then they added, "This isn't something that can be done in a day or two, for many of us are involved in this extremely sinful affair. And this is the rainy season, so we cannot stay out here much longer. 14Let our leaders act on behalf of us all. Let everyone who has a pagan wife come at a scheduled time, accompanied by the leaders and judges of his city, so that the fierce anger of our God concerning this affair may be turned away from us."

15Only Jonathan son of Asahel and Jahzeiah son of Tikvah opposed this course of action, and they were supported by Meshullam and Shabbethai the Levite.

16So this was the plan they followed. Ezra selected leaders to represent their families, designating each of the representatives by name. On December 29,* the leaders sat down to investigate the matter. 17By March 27, the first day of the new year,* they had finished dealing with all the men who had married pagan wives.

Those Guilty of Intermarriage

EZRA 10:18-44

These are the priests who had married pagan wives:
From the family of Jeshua son of Jehozadak* and his brothers: Maaseiah, Eliezer, Jarib, and Gedaliah.
19They vowed to divorce their wives, and they each acknowledged their guilt by offering a ram as a guilt offering.
20From the family of Immer: Hanani and Zebadiah.
21From the family of Harim: Maaseiah, Elijah, Shemaiah, Jehiel, and Uzziah.
22From the family of Pashhur: Elioenai, Maaseiah, Ishmael, Nethanel, Jozabad, and Elasah.

23These are the Levites who were guilty: Jozabad, Shimei, Kelaiah (also called Kelita), Pethahiah, Judah, and Eliezer.

24This is the singer who was guilty: Eliashib.

Ezr 10:6 As in parallel text at 1 Esdras 9:2; Hebrew reads *He went.* **Ezr 10:9** Hebrew *on the twentieth day of the ninth month,* of the ancient Hebrew lunar calendar. This day was December 19, 458 B.C.; also see note on 6:15. **Ezr 10:16** Hebrew *On the first day of the tenth month,* of the ancient Hebrew lunar calendar. This day was December 29, 458 B.C.; also see note on 6:15. **Ezr 10:17** Hebrew *By the first day of the first month,* of the ancient Hebrew lunar calendar. This day was March 27, 457 B.C.; also see note on 6:15. **Ezr 10:18** Hebrew *Jozadak,* a variant spelling of Jehozadak.

Ezra 10:3 Why were the men commanded to send away their wives and children? Although the measure was extreme, intermarriage to pagans was strictly forbidden (Deut 7:3-4). Even the priests and Levites had intermarried, which could be compared today to a Christian marrying a devil worshiper. Although a severe solution, it only involved 113 of the approximately 29,000 families.

Ezra's strong act, though very difficult for some, was necessary to preserve Israel as a nation committed to God. Some of the exiles of the northern kingdom of Israel had lost both their spiritual and physical identity through intermarriage. Their pagan spouses had caused the people to worship idols. Ezra did not want this to happen to the exiles of the southern kingdom of Judah.

Ezra 10:3-4, 11 Following Ezra's earnest prayer, the people confessed their sin to God. Then they asked for direction in restoring their relationship with God. True repentance does not end with words of confession—that would be mere lip service. It must lead to changed attitudes and behavior. When you sin and are truly sorry, confess this to God, ask his forgiveness, and accept his grace and mercy. Then, as an act of thankfulness for your forgiveness, make the needed corrections.

Ezra 10:8 To forfeit one's property meant to be disinherited, to lose one's legal right to own land. This was to ensure that no pagan children would inherit Israel's land. In addition, the person who refused to come to Jerusalem would be expelled from the assembly of the exiles and not be allowed to worship in the Temple. The Jews considered this a horrible punishment.

Ezra 10:11 As believers in Christ, all our sins are forgiven. His death cleansed us from all sin. Why do we then still confess our sins? Confession is more than appropriating Christ's forgiveness for what we have done wrong. Confession is agreeing with God that our thoughts, words, and actions are wrong and contrary to his will. It is recommitting ourselves to do his will and renouncing any acts of disobedience. We do not have to confess sins that were previously confessed. Confession involves turning away from all known sin and asking God for fresh power to live for him.

▸ **EZRA 10:18-44** ***(cont.)***

These are the gatekeepers who were guilty: Shallum, Telem, and Uri.

25 These are the other people of Israel who were guilty:
From the family of Parosh: Ramiah, Izziah, Malkijah, Mijamin, Eleazar, Hashabiah,* and Benaiah.
26 From the family of Elam: Mattaniah, Zechariah, Jehiel, Abdi, Jeremoth, and Elijah.
27 From the family of Zattu: Elioenai, Eliashib, Mattaniah, Jeremoth, Zabad, and Aziza.
28 From the family of Bebai: Jehohanan, Hananiah, Zabbai, and Athlai.
29 From the family of Bani: Meshullam, Malluch, Adaiah, Jashub, Sheal, and Jeremoth.
30 From the family of Pahath-moab: Adna, Kelal, Benaiah, Maaseiah, Mattaniah, Bezalel, Binnui, and Manasseh.
31 From the family of Harim: Eliezer, Ishijah, Malkijah, Shemaiah, Shimeon, 32 Benjamin, Malluch, and Shemariah.
33 From the family of Hashum: Mattenai, Mattattah, Zabad, Eliphelet, Jeremai, Manasseh, and Shimei.
34 From the family of Bani: Maadai, Amram, Uel,
35 Benaiah, Bedeiah, Keluhi, 36 Vaniah, Meremoth, Eliashib, 37 Mattaniah, Mattenai, and Jaasu.
38 From the family of Binnui*: Shimei, 39 Shelemiah, Nathan, Adaiah, 40 Macnadebai, Shashai, Sharai,
41 Azarel, Shelemiah, Shemariah, 42 Shallum, Amariah, and Joseph.
43 From the family of Nebo: Jeiel, Mattithiah, Zabad, Zebina, Jaddai, Joel, and Benaiah.

44 Each of these men had a pagan wife, and some even had children by these wives.*

Ezr 10:25 As in parallel text at 1 Esdras 9:26; Hebrew reads *Malkijah.* **Ezr 10:37-38** As in Greek version; Hebrew reads *Jaasu,* [38]*Bani, Binnui.* **Ezr 10:44** Or *and they sent them away with their children.* The meaning of the Hebrew is uncertain.

E. Nehemiah's Return and Reforms

Nehemiah left a comfortable job as an assistant to the king of Persia in order to help the demoralized people of Jerusalem. His new work involved motivating the people to rebuild the city's walls in spite of their neighbors' opposition. But Nehemiah's work was not just with bricks and mortar; he also mediated a financial crisis, initiated religious reforms, and reorganized civic responsibilities in Jerusalem. Nehemiah demonstrates that with faith, prayer, integrity, and God's help, God's servants can succeed.

448 BC

The Parthenon is built in Athens, Greece

1. REBUILDING THE WALL

Despite the fact that the returned exiles had been in Jerusalem for many years, the walls of the city remained unrepaired, leaving its people defenseless and vulnerable. Upon hearing this news, Nehemiah seeks permission from the Persian king to go to Jerusalem. Arriving in Jerusalem, he mobilizes the people to begin rebuilding the wall. Faced with opposition, both from without and from within, Nehemiah perseveres until the project is completed and the city resettled. Seemingly impossible tasks can be accomplished when God is helping those who honor him and when their efforts are united.

Nehemiah's Concern for Jerusalem

NEHEMIAH 1:1-11

These are the memoirs of Nehemiah son of Hacaliah.

In late autumn, in the month of Kislev, in the twentieth year of King Artaxerxes' reign,* I was at the fortress of Susa.
2 Hanani, one of my brothers, came to visit me with some other men who had just arrived from Judah. I asked them about the Jews who had returned there from captivity and about how things were going in Jerusalem.

Neh 1:1 Hebrew *In the month of Kislev of the twentieth year.* A number of dates in the book of Nehemiah can be cross-checked with dates in surviving Persian records and related accurately to our modern calendar. This month of the ancient Hebrew lunar calendar occurred within the months of November and December 446 B.C. The *twentieth year* probably refers to the reign of King Artaxerxes I; compare 2:1; 5:14.

Ezra 10:44 The book of Ezra opens with God's Temple in ruins and the people of Judah captive in Babylon. Ezra tells of the return of God's people, the rebuilding of the Temple, and the restoration of the sacrificial worship system. Similarly, God is able to restore and rebuild the lives of people today. No one is so far away from God that restoration is not possible. Repentance is all that is required. No matter how far we have strayed or how long it has been since we have worshiped God, he is able to restore our relationship to him and rebuild our lives.

Neh 1:1 Nehemiah wasn't the first of the exiles to return to Jerusalem. Zerubbabel had led the first group back in 538 B.C., more than 90 years earlier (Ezra 1–2). Ezra followed with a second group in 458 B.C. (Ezra 7), and here Nehemiah was ready to lead the third major return to Jerusalem (445 B.C.). When he arrived after a three-month journey, he saw the completed Temple and became acquainted with others who had returned to their homeland.

But Nehemiah also found a disorganized group of people and a defenseless city with no walls to protect it. Before the Exile, Israel had its own language, king, army, and identity. At this time it had none of these. What the Jews lacked most was leadership; there was no one to show them where to start and what direction to take as they tried to rebuild their city. As soon as Nehemiah arrived, he began a back-to-the-basics program. He helped care for the people's physical needs by setting up a fair system of government and rebuilding Jerusalem's walls. He also cared for their spiritual needs by rebuilding broken lives. Nehemiah is a model of com-

3They said to me, "Things are not going well for
those who returned to the province of Judah. They
are in great trouble and disgrace. The wall of Jerusalem has been torn down, and the gates have been
destroyed by fire."
4When I heard this, I sat down and wept. In fact,
for days I mourned, fasted, and prayed to the God of
heaven. 5Then I said,

"O LORD, God of heaven, the great and awesome
God who keeps his covenant of unfailing love
with those who love him and obey his commands,
6listen to my prayer! Look down and see me
praying night and day for your people Israel.
I confess that we have sinned against you. Yes,
even my own family and I have sinned! 7We have
sinned terribly by not obeying the commands,

HOW NEHEMIAH USED PRAYER

Reference	*Occasion*	*Summary of His Prayer*	*What Prayer Accomplished*	*Our Prayers*
Neh 1:4-11	After receiving the bad news about the state of Jerusalem's walls	Recognized God's holiness. Asked for a hearing. Confessed sin. Asked for specific help in approaching the king.	Included God in his plans and concerns. Prepared his heart and gave God room to work.	How often do you pour out your heart to God? How often do you give him a specific request to answer?
Neh 2:4	During his conversation with the king	"Here's where you can help, God!"	Put the expected results in God's hands	Giving God credit for what happens before it happens keeps us from taking more credit than we should.
Neh 4:4-5	After being taunted and ridiculed by Tobiah and Sanballat	"They're mocking you, God. You decide what to do with them!"	Expressed anger to God but did not take matters into his own hands	We are prone to do exactly the opposite—take matters into our own hands and not tell God how we feel.
Neh 4:9	After threats of attack by enemies	"We are in your hands, God. We'll keep our weapons handy in case you want us to use them."	Showed trust in God even while taking necessary precautions	Trusting God does not mean we do nothing. Action does not mean we do not trust.
Neh 6:9, 14	Responding to threats	"O Lord God, please strengthen me!"	Showed his reliance on God for emotional and mental stability	How often do you ask God for help when under pressure?
Neh 13:29	Reflecting on the actions of his enemies	Asked God to deal with the enemies and their evil plans	Took away the compulsion to get revenge, and entrusted justice to God	When did you last settle a desire for revenge by turning the matter over to God?
Neh 5:19; 13:14, 22, 31	Reflecting on his own efforts to serve God	"Remember me, God."	Kept clear in mind his own motives for action	How many of your actions today will be done with the purpose of pleasing God?

mitted, God-honoring leadership, and his book contains many useful lessons for today.

Neh 1:2-4 Nehemiah was concerned about Jerusalem because it was the Jews' holy city. As Judah's capital city, it represented Jewish national identity, and it was blessed with God's special presence in the Temple. Jewish history centered around the city from the time of Abraham's gifts to Melchizedek, king of Salem (Gen 14:17-20), to the days when Solomon built the glorious Temple (1 Kgs 7:51), and throughout the history of the kings. Nehemiah loved his homeland even though he had lived his whole life in Babylon. He wanted to return to Jerusalem to reunite the Jews and to remove the shame of Jerusalem's broken-down walls. This would bring glory to God and restore the reality and power of God's presence among his people.

Neh 1:4 Nehemiah broke down and wept when he heard that Jerusalem's walls still had not been rebuilt. Why did this upset him? Walls mean little in most present-day cities, but in Nehemiah's day they were as essential as we would consider electrical power or a police force. They offered safety from raids and symbolized strength and peace. Nehemiah also mourned for his people, the Jews, who had been stifled by a previous edict that had kept them from rebuilding their walls (Ezra 4:6-23).

Neh 1:4 Nehemiah was deeply grieved about the condition of Jerusalem, but he didn't just brood about it. After his initial grief, he prayed, pouring his heart out to God (Neh 1:5-11), and he looked for ways to improve the situation. Nehemiah put all his resources of knowledge, experience, and organization into determining what should be done. When tragic news comes to you, first pray. Then seek ways to move beyond grief to specific action that helps those who need it.

Neh 1:5 God's "covenant of unfailing love" refers to God's promise to love the descendants of Abraham. (See also Deut 7:7-9.)

Neh 1:5ff Nehemiah fasted and prayed for several days, expressing his sorrow for Israel's sin and his desire that Jerusalem would again come alive with the worship of the one true God. Nehemiah demonstrated the elements of effective prayer: (1) praise, (2) thanksgiving, (3) repentance, (4) specific requests, and (5) commitment.

Heartfelt prayers like Nehemiah's can help clarify (1) any problem you may be facing, (2) God's great power to help you, and (3) the job you have to do. By the end of his prayer time, Nehemiah knew what action he had to take (Neh 1:11). When God's people pray, difficult decisions fall into proper perspective, and appropriate actions follow.

▶ **NEHEMIAH 1:1-11** ***(cont.)***

decrees, and regulations that you gave us through
your servant Moses.
8"Please remember what you told your servant
Moses: 'If you are unfaithful to me, I will scatter
you among the nations. 9But if you return to me
and obey my commands and live by them, then
even if you are exiled to the ends of the earth, I
will bring you back to the place I have chosen for
my name to be honored.'
10"The people you rescued by your great power
and strong hand are your servants. 11O Lord,
please hear my prayer! Listen to the prayers of
those of us who delight in honoring you. Please
grant me success today by making the king
favorable to me.* Put it into his heart to be kind
to me."

In those days I was the king's cup-bearer.

Nehemiah Goes to Jerusalem

NEHEMIAH 2:1-10

Early the following spring, in the month of Nisan,*
during the twentieth year of King Artaxerxes' reign,
I was serving the king his wine. I had never before
appeared sad in his presence. 2So the king asked me,
"Why are you looking so sad? You don't look sick to
me. You must be deeply troubled."
Then I was terrified, 3but I replied, "Long live the
king! How can I not be sad? For the city where my
ancestors are buried is in ruins, and the gates have
been destroyed by fire."
4The king asked, "Well, how can I help you?"
With a prayer to the God of heaven, 5I replied, "If it
please the king, and if you are pleased with me, your
servant, send me to Judah to rebuild the city where
my ancestors are buried."
6The king, with the queen sitting beside him, asked,
"How long will you be gone? When will you return?"

Neh 1:11 Hebrew *today in the sight of this man.* **Neh 2:1** Hebrew *In the month of Nisan.* This month of the ancient Hebrew lunar calendar occurred within the months of April and May 445 B.C.

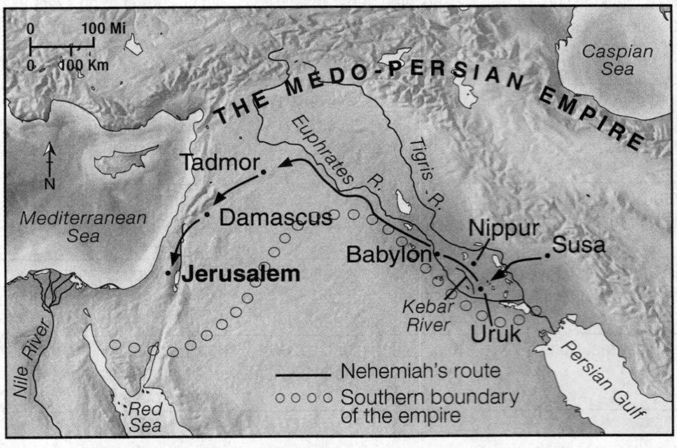

NEHEMIAH GOES TO JERUSALEM ***Nehemiah worked in Susa as a cup-bearer for the king of the vast Medo-Persian Empire. When he heard that the rebuilding projects in Jerusalem were progressing slowly, he asked the king if he could go there to help his people complete the task of rebuilding their city's walls. The king agreed to let him go; so he left as soon as possible, traveling along much the same route Ezra had taken.***

Neh 1:11 Nehemiah was in a unique position to speak to the king. He was the trusted cup-bearer, who ensured the safety and quality of the king's food and drink. Nehemiah was concerned, prayerful, and prepared as he looked for the right opportunity to tell the king about God's people. Each of us is unique and capable of serving no matter what our position. Just as Nehemiah used his place as the king's trusted servant to intercede for his people, we can use our present positions to serve God.

Neh 1:11 Nehemiah prayed for success in this venture, not just for the strength to cope with his problems (see also Neh 2:20). Yet the success he prayed for was not for personal advantage, position, or acclaim. He requested success for God's work. When God's purposes are at work, don't hesitate to ask for success.

Neh 2:2 The king noticed Nehemiah's sad appearance. It surprised Nehemiah to be singled out for attention and it frightened him because it was dangerous to show sorrow before the king, who could execute anyone who displeased him. In fact, anyone wearing mourning clothes was barred from the palace (Esth 4:2).

Neh 2:2-3 Nehemiah wasn't ashamed to admit his fear, but he refused to allow fear to stop him from doing what God had called him to do. He acknowledged the king's position and clearly stated the reasons for his own sorrow. When we allow fear to rule us, we make fear more powerful than God. Is there a task God wants you to do, but fear is holding you back? God is greater than all your fears. Recognizing why you are afraid is the first step in committing your fear to God. Realize that if God has called you to a task, he will help you accomplish it.

Neh 2:4 With little time to think, Nehemiah immediately prayed. Eight times in this book we read that he prayed spontaneously (Neh 2:4; 4:4-5, 9; 5:19; 6:14; 13:14, 22, 29). Nehemiah prayed at any time, even while talking with others. He knew that God is always in charge, is always present, and hears and answers every prayer. Nehemiah could confidently pray throughout the day because he had established an intimate relationship with God during times of extended prayer (Neh 1:4-7). If we want to reach God with our emergency prayers, we need to take time to cultivate a strong relationship with God through times of in-depth prayer.

Neh 2:6 The king asked Nehemiah how long he would be gone. The Bible does not record Nehemiah's immediate answer, but he ended up staying in Jerusalem for 12 years (Neh 5:14; 13:6).

Neh 2:7-8 After his prayer, Nehemiah asked the king for permission to go to Judah. As soon as he got a positive answer, he began asking for additional help. Sometimes when we have needs, we hesitate to ask the right people for help because we are afraid to approach them. Not Nehemiah! He went directly to the person who could help him the most. Don't be reluctant to ask those who are most able to help. They may be more interested and approachable than you think. God's answers to prayer may come as a result of our asking others.

Neh 2:8 Nehemiah had position, power, and many good organizational skills, but

After I told him how long I would be gone, the king
agreed to my request.
7 I also said to the king, "If it please the king, let
me have letters addressed to the governors of the
province west of the Euphrates River,* instructing
them to let me travel safely through their territories
on my way to Judah. 8 And please give me a letter addressed to Asaph, the manager of the king's forest,
instructing him to give me timber. I will need it to
make beams for the gates of the Temple fortress, for
the city walls, and for a house for myself." And the
king granted these requests, because the gracious
hand of God was on me.
9 When I came to the governors of the province
west of the Euphrates River, I delivered the king's
letters to them. The king, I should add, had sent
along army officers and horsemen* to protect me.
10 But when Sanballat the Horonite and Tobiah the
Ammonite official heard of my arrival, they were
very displeased that someone had come to help the
people of Israel.

Nehemiah Inspects Jerusalem's Wall

NEHEMIAH 2:11-20

So I arrived in Jerusalem. Three days later, 12 I slipped
out during the night, taking only a few others with me.
I had not told anyone about the plans God had put
in my heart for Jerusalem. We took no pack animals
with us except the donkey I was riding. 13 After dark
I went out through the Valley Gate, past the Jackal's
Well,* and over to the Dung Gate to inspect the broken
walls and burned gates. 14 Then I went to the Fountain
Gate and to the King's Pool, but my donkey couldn't
get through the rubble. 15 So, though it was still dark,
I went up the Kidron Valley* instead, inspecting the
wall before I turned back and entered again at the
Valley Gate.
16 The city officials did not know I had been out
there or what I was doing, for I had not yet said anything to anyone about my plans. I had not yet spoken
to the Jewish leaders—the priests, the nobles, the officials, or anyone else in the administration. 17 But now
I said to them, "You know very well what trouble we
are in. Jerusalem lies in ruins, and its gates have been
destroyed by fire. Let us rebuild the wall of Jerusalem
and end this disgrace!" 18 Then I told them about how
the gracious hand of God had been on me, and about
my conversation with the king.
They replied at once, "Yes, let's rebuild the wall!" So
they began the good work.
19 But when Sanballat, Tobiah, and Geshem the
Arab heard of our plan, they scoffed contemptuously.
"What are you doing? Are you rebelling against the
king?" they asked.
20 I replied, "The God of heaven will help us succeed. We, his servants, will start rebuilding this wall.
But you have no share, legal right, or historic claim in
Jerusalem."

Neh 2:7 Hebrew *the province beyond the river;* also in 2:9. **Neh 2:9** Or *charioteers.* **Neh 2:13** Or *Serpent's Well.* **Neh 2:15** Hebrew *the valley.*

he acknowledged that God's gracious hand was upon him. He knew that without God's strength, his efforts would be in vain. Do you acknowledge God as your power source and the giver of your gifts?

Neh 2:9-10, 19 When Nehemiah arrived in Judah, opposition greeted him. Opposition to the rebuilding of Jerusalem had been going on for 90 years by those who settled in the area when the Jews were taken captive. In every generation there are those who hate God's people and try to block God's purpose. When you attempt to do God's work, some will oppose you; some will even hope you fail. If you expect opposition, you will be prepared rather than surprised (1 Jn 3:13). Knowing that God is behind your task is the best incentive to move ahead in the face of opposition.

Neh 2:10 Sanballat was governor of Samaria, and Tobiah was probably governor of Transjordan under the Persians. Why were these government officials so concerned about the arrival of Nehemiah and his small band of exiles? There are several possible reasons. (1) When Zerubbabel first returned with his group (Ezra 1–2), his refusal to accept help from the Samaritans had caused bad relations. (2) Nehemiah was no ordinary exile; he was the king's personal adviser and cup-bearer, arriving in Jerusalem with the king's approval to build and fortify the city. If anyone could rebuild Jerusalem, he could. A rebuilt Jerusalem was a threat to the authority of the Samaritan officials who had been in charge of the land since Judah's exile. (3) This was the third group to return from exile. The increasing number of people in Jerusalem made Sanballat and Tobiah angry. They did not want returning exiles taking control of the land and threatening their secure position.

Neh 2:11-17 Nehemiah arrived quietly in Jerusalem and spent several days carefully observing and assessing the damage to the walls. Following this time of thoughtful consideration, he confidently presented his plan. Nehemiah demonstrated an excellent approach to problem solving. He got first-hand information and carefully considered the situation. Then he presented a realistic strategy. Before jumping into a project, follow Nehemiah's example and plan ahead. Check your information to make sure your ideas will work—be realistic. Then you will be able to present your plan with confidence.

Neh 2:11-17 Nehemiah kept his mission a secret and surveyed the walls by moonlight to avoid unhealthy gossip about his arrival and to prevent enemies from being alerted to his plans. Only after planning carefully would he be ready to go public with his mission from God. A premature announcement could have caused rivalry among the Jews as to the best way to begin. In this case, Nehemiah didn't need tedious planning sessions; he needed one plan that would bring quick action.

Neh 2:17-18 Spiritual renewal often begins with one person's vision. Nehemiah had a vision, and he shared it with enthusiasm, inspiring Jerusalem's leaders to rebuild the walls.

We frequently underestimate people and don't challenge them with our dreams for God's work in the world. When God plants an idea in your mind to accomplish something for him, share it with others and trust the Holy Spirit to impress them with similar thoughts. Don't regard yourself as the only one through whom God is working. Often God uses one person to express the vision and others to turn it into reality. When you encourage and inspire others, you put teamwork into action to accomplish God's goals.

Neh 2:19 Sanballat and Tobiah labeled the rebuilding of Jerusalem's walls as rebellion against the king, probably threatening to report the builders as traitors. These enemies also ridiculed Nehemiah, saying that the walls could never be rebuilt because the damage was too extensive. Nehemiah did not tell them he already had permission from the king to rebuild. Instead, he simply said he had God's approval—that was enough.

Rebuilding the Wall of Jerusalem

NEHEMIAH 3:1-32

Then Eliashib the high priest and the other priests
started to rebuild at the Sheep Gate. They dedicated
it and set up its doors, building the wall as far as the
Tower of the Hundred, which they dedicated, and
the Tower of Hananel. 2People from the town of Jericho worked next to them, and beyond them was Zaccur son of Imri.
3The Fish Gate was built by the sons of Hassenaah.
They laid the beams, set up its doors, and installed its
bolts and bars. 4Meremoth son of Uriah and grandson
of Hakkoz repaired the next section of wall. Beside
him were Meshullam son of Berekiah and grandson of
Meshezabel, and then Zadok son of Baana. 5Next were
the people from Tekoa, though their leaders refused
to work with the construction supervisors.
6The Old City Gate* was repaired by Joiada son of
Paseah and Meshullam son of Besodeiah. They laid the
beams, set up its doors, and installed its bolts and bars.
7Next to them were Melatiah from Gibeon, Jadon from
Meronoth, people from Gibeon, and people from Mizpah, the headquarters of the governor of the province
west of the Euphrates River.* 8Next was Uzziel son of
Harhaiah, a goldsmith by trade, who also worked on
the wall. Beyond him was Hananiah, a manufacturer
of perfumes. They left out a section of Jerusalem as
they built the Broad Wall.*
9Rephaiah son of Hur, the leader of half the district
of Jerusalem, was next to them on the wall. 10Next
Jedaiah son of Harumaph repaired the wall across
from his own house, and next to him was Hattush
son of Hashabneiah. 11Then came Malkijah son of Harim and Hasshub son of Pahath-moab, who repaired
another section of the wall and the Tower of the Ovens. 12Shallum son of Hallohesh and his daughters
repaired the next section. He was the leader of the
other half of the district of Jerusalem.
13The Valley Gate was repaired by the people from
Zanoah, led by Hanun. They set up its doors and installed its bolts and bars. They also repaired the 1,500
feet* of wall to the Dung Gate.
14The Dung Gate was repaired by Malkijah son of
Recab, the leader of the Beth-hakkerem district. He
rebuilt it, set up its doors, and installed its bolts and
bars.
15The Fountain Gate was repaired by Shallum* son
of Col-hozeh, the leader of the Mizpah district. He
rebuilt it, roofed it, set up its doors, and installed its
bolts and bars. Then he repaired the wall of the pool
of Siloam* near the king's garden, and he rebuilt the
wall as far as the stairs that descend from the City of

Neh 3:6 Or *The Mishneh Gate,* or *The Jeshanah Gate.* **Neh 3:7** Hebrew *the province beyond the river.* **Neh 3:8** Or *They fortified Jerusalem up to the Broad Wall.* **Neh 3:13** Hebrew *1,000 cubits* [450 meters]. **Neh 3:15a** As in Syriac version; Hebrew reads *Shallun.* **Neh 3:15b** Hebrew *pool of Shelah,* another name for the pool of Siloam.

Neh 3:1 The high priest is the first person mentioned who pitched in and helped with the work. Spiritual leaders must lead not only by word but also by action. The Sheep Gate was the gate used to bring sheep into the city to the Temple for sacrifices. Nehemiah had the priests repair this gate and section of the wall, respecting the priests' area of interest and at the same time emphasizing the priority of worship.

Neh 3:1ff All the citizens of Jerusalem did their part on the huge job of rebuilding the city wall. Similarly, the work of the church requires every member's effort in order for the body of Christ to function effectively (1 Cor 12:12-27). The body needs you! Are you doing your part? Find a place to serve God, and start contributing whatever time, talent, and money are needed.

Neh 3:1ff Jerusalem was a large city, and because many roads converged there, it required many gates. The wall on each side of these heavy wooden gates was taller and thicker so soldiers could stand guard to defend the gates against attack. Sometimes two stone towers guarded the gate. In times of peace, the city gates were hubs of activity—city council was held there, and shopkeepers set up their wares at the entrance. Building the city walls and gates was not only a military priority but also a boost for trade and commerce.

Neh 3:3 One of the main roads through Jerusalem entered the city through the Fish Gate (2 Chr 33:14). The fish market was near the gate, and merchants from Tyre, the Sea of Galilee, and other fishing areas entered this gate to sell their goods.

Neh 3:5 The leaders from Tekoa were lazy and wouldn't help. These men were the only ones who did not support the building project in Jerusalem. Every group, even churches, will have those who think they are too wise or important to work hard. Gentle encouragement doesn't seem to help. Sometimes the best policy is to ignore them. They may think they are getting away with something, but their inactivity will be remembered by all who worked hard.

Neh 3:12 Shallum's daughters helped with the difficult work of repairing the city walls. Rebuilding Jerusalem's walls was a matter of national emergency for the Jews, not just a civic beautification project. Nearly everyone was dedicated to the task and willing to work at it.

Neh 3:14 The Dung Gate was the gate through which the people carried their garbage to be burned in the Valley of Hinnom.

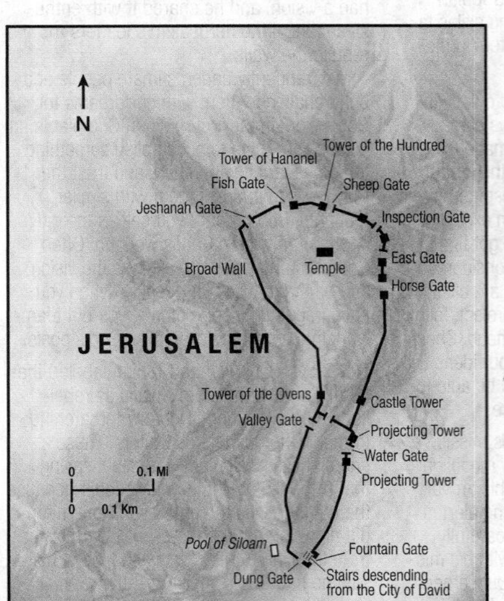

◀ THE RESTORATION OF THE CITY WALLS
Nehemiah takes us on a counterclockwise tour around Jerusalem (beginning with the Sheep Gate). He describes for us each section, gate, and tower on the wall and who worked to rebuild it.

David. [16]Next to him was Nehemiah son of Azbuk, the leader of half the district of Beth-zur. He rebuilt the wall from a place across from the tombs of David's family as far as the water reservoir and the House of the Warriors.

[17]Next to him, repairs were made by a group of Levites working under the supervision of Rehum son of Bani. Then came Hashabiah, the leader of half the district of Keilah, who supervised the building of the wall on behalf of his own district. [18]Next down the line were his countrymen led by Binnui* son of Henadad, the leader of the other half of the district of Keilah.

[19]Next to them, Ezer son of Jeshua, the leader of Mizpah, repaired another section of wall across from the ascent to the armory near the angle in the wall. [20]Next to him was Baruch son of Zabbai, who zealously repaired an additional section from the angle to the door of the house of Eliashib the high priest. [21]Meremoth son of Uriah and grandson of Hakkoz rebuilt another section of the wall extending from the door of Eliashib's house to the end of the house.

[22]The next repairs were made by the priests from the surrounding region. [23]After them, Benjamin and Hasshub repaired the section across from their house, and Azariah son of Maaseiah and grandson of Ananiah repaired the section across from his house. [24]Next was Binnui son of Henadad, who rebuilt another section of the wall from Azariah's house to the angle and the corner. [25]Palal son of Uzai carried on the work from a point opposite the angle and the tower that projects up from the king's upper house beside the court of the guard. Next to him were Pedaiah son of Parosh, [26]with the Temple servants living on the hill of Ophel, who repaired the wall as far as a point across from the Water Gate to the east and the projecting tower. [27]Then came the people of Tekoa, who repaired another section across from the great projecting tower and over to the wall of Ophel.

Neh 3:18 As in a few Hebrew manuscripts, some Greek manuscripts, and Syriac version (see also 3:24; 10:9); most Hebrew manuscripts read *Bavvai.*

NEHEMIAH

God is in the business of working through his people to accomplish seemingly impossible tasks. God often shapes people to prepare them for his purposes by using their personality characteristics, experiences, and training. Usually the people have no idea what God has in store for them. God prepared and positioned Nehemiah to accomplish one of the Bible's "impossible" tasks. • Nehemiah was a common man in a unique position. He was secure and successful as cup-bearer to the Persian king, Artaxerxes. Nehemiah had little power, but he had great influence. The king trusted him. He was also a man of God, concerned about the fate of Jerusalem. • Seventy years earlier, Zerubbabel had managed to rebuild God's Temple. Thirteen years had passed since Ezra had returned to Jerusalem and helped the people with their spiritual needs. Now Nehemiah was needed. Jerusalem's wall was still in ruins, and the news broke his heart. As he talked to God, a plan began to take form in Nehemiah's mind about his own role in the rebuilding of the city walls. He willingly left the security of his home and job in Persia to follow God on an "impossible" mission. And the rest is history. • From beginning to end, Nehemiah prayed for God's help. He never hesitated to ask God to remember him, closing his autobiography with these words: "Remember this in my favor, O my God" (Neh 13:31). Throughout the "impossible" task, Nehemiah displayed unusual leadership. The wall around Jerusalem was rebuilt in record time, despite resistance. Even Israel's enemies grudgingly and fearfully admitted that God was with these builders. Not only that, but God worked through Nehemiah to bring about a spiritual awakening among the people of Judah. • You may not have Nehemiah's unique abilities or feel that you are in a position where you can do anything great for God, but there are two ways you can become useful to God. First, be a person who talks to God. Welcome him into your thoughts and share yourself with him—your concerns, feelings, and dreams. Second, be a person who walks with God. Put what you learn from his Word into action. God may have an "impossible" mission that he wants to do through you.

Strengths and accomplishments	• A man of character, persistence, and prayer • Brilliant planner, organizer, and motivator • Under his leadership, the wall around Jerusalem was rebuilt in 52 days • As political leader, led the nation to religious reform and spiritual awakening
Lessons from his life	• The first step in any venture is to pray • People under God's direction can accomplish "impossible" tasks • There are two parts to real service for God: talking with him and walking with him
Vital statistics	• Where: Persia, Jerusalem • Occupations: King's cup-bearer, city builder, governor of Judah • Relative: Father: Hacaliah. Brother: Hanani. • Contemporaries: Ezra, Artaxerxes, Tobiah, Sanballat
Key verse	"Then I told them about how the gracious hand of God had been on me, and about my conversation with the king. They replied at once, 'Yes, let's rebuild the wall!' So they began the good work" (Neh 2:18).

Nehemiah's story is told in the book of Nehemiah.

▸ **NEHEMIAH 3:1-32** ***(cont.)***

28Above the Horse Gate, the priests repaired the wall. Each one repaired the section immediately across from his own house. 29Next Zadok son of Immer also rebuilt the wall across from his own house, and beyond him was Shemaiah son of Shecaniah, the gatekeeper of the East Gate. 30Next Hananiah son of Shelemiah and Hanun, the sixth son of Zalaph, repaired another section, while Meshullam son of Berekiah rebuilt the wall across from where he lived. 31Malkijah, one of the goldsmiths, repaired the wall as far as the housing for the Temple servants and merchants, across from the Inspection Gate. Then he continued as far as the upper room at the corner. 32The other goldsmiths and merchants repaired the wall from that corner to the Sheep Gate.

Enemies Oppose the Rebuilding

NEHEMIAH 4:1-23

1*Sanballat was very angry when he learned that we were rebuilding the wall. He flew into a rage and mocked the Jews, 2saying in front of his friends and the Samarian army officers, "What does this bunch of poor, feeble Jews think they're doing? Do they think they can build the wall in a single day by just offering a few sacrifices?* Do they actually think they can make something of stones from a rubbish heap—and charred ones at that?"

3Tobiah the Ammonite, who was standing beside him, remarked, "That stone wall would collapse if even a fox walked along the top of it!"

4Then I prayed, "Hear us, our God, for we are being mocked. May their scoffing fall back on their own heads, and may they themselves become captives in a foreign land! 5Do not ignore their guilt. Do not blot out their sins, for they have provoked you to anger here in front of* the builders."

6At last the wall was completed to half its height around the entire city, for the people had worked with enthusiasm.

7*But when Sanballat and Tobiah and the Arabs, Ammonites, and Ashdodites heard that the work was going ahead and that the gaps in the wall of Jerusalem were being repaired, they were furious. 8They all made plans to come and fight against Jerusalem and throw us into confusion. 9But we prayed to our God and guarded the city day and night to protect ourselves.

Neh 4:1 Verses 4:1-6 are numbered 3:33-38 in Hebrew text. **Neh 4:2** The meaning of the Hebrew is uncertain. **Neh 4:5** Or *for they have thrown insults in the face of.* **Neh 4:7** Verses 4:7-23 are numbered 4:1-17 in Hebrew text.

Neh 3:28 The Horse Gate was at the far eastern point of the wall, facing the Kidron Valley.

Neh 3:28 Each priest also repaired the wall in front of his own house, in addition to other sections. If each person was responsible for the part of the wall closest to his own house, (1) he would be more motivated to build it quickly and properly, (2) he wouldn't waste time traveling to more distant parts of the wall, (3) he could defend his own home if the wall were attacked, and (4) he would be able to make the building a family effort. Nehemiah blended self-interest with the group's objectives, helping everyone to feel that the wall project was their own. If you are part of a group working on a large project, make sure everyone sees the importance and meaning of their own jobs. This will ensure high-quality work and personal satisfaction.

Neh 3:31 The Inspection Gate was in the northern part of the eastern wall.

Neh 4:1 Sanballat was governor of Samaria, the region just north of Judea, where Jerusalem was located. Sanballat may have hoped to become governor of Judea as well, but Nehemiah's arrival spoiled his plans. (For his other reasons for opposing Nehemiah, see the note on Neh 2:10, p. 1205.) Sanballat tried to scare Nehemiah away or at least discourage him by scorn (Neh 4:2; 6:6), threats (Neh 4:8), and bluffs (Neh 6:7).

Neh 4:1-2 Almost 300 years before Nehemiah's time, the northern kingdom of Israel was conquered, and most of the people were carried away captive (722 B.C.). Sargon of Assyria repopulated Israel with captives from other lands. These captives eventually intermarried with the few Israelites who remained in the land to form a mixed race of people who became known as Samaritans. The Jews who returned to Jerusalem and the southern region of Judea during the days of Ezra and Nehemiah would have nothing to do with Samaritans, whom they considered to be racially impure. Relations between both groups grew progressively worse—400 years later, the Jews and Samaritans hated each other (John 4:9).

Neh 4:1-5 Ridicule can cut deeply, causing discouragement and despair. Sanballat and Tobiah used ridicule to try to dissuade the Jews from building the wall. Instead of trading insults, Nehemiah prayed, and the work continued. When you are mocked for your faith or criticized for doing what you know is right, refuse to respond in the same way or to become discouraged. Tell God how you feel and remember his promise to be with you. This will give you encouragement and strength to carry on.

Neh 4:4-5 Nehemiah is not praying for revenge but for God's justice to be carried out. His prayer is similar to many of David's (see the note on Ps 7:1-6, p. 523 and the chart on p. 1203).

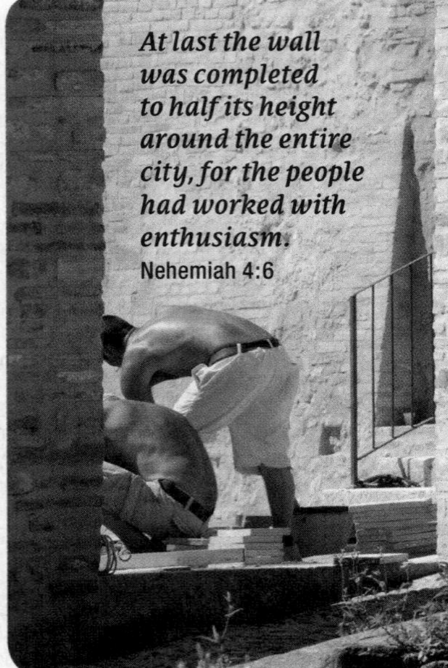
At last the wall was completed to half its height around the entire city, for the people had worked with enthusiasm.
Nehemiah 4:6

Neh 4:6 The work of rebuilding the wall progressed well because the people had set their hearts and minds on accomplishing the task. They did not lose faith or give up, but they persevered in the work. If God has called you to a task, determine to complete it, even if you face opposition or discouragement. The rewards of work well done will be worth the effort.

Neh 4:9 Nehemiah constantly combined prayer with preparation and planning. His people trusted God and at the same time kept vigilant watch over what had been

[10]Then the people of Judah began to complain, "The
workers are getting tired, and there is so much rubble
to be moved. We will never be able to build the wall
by ourselves."
[11]Meanwhile, our enemies were saying, "Before they
know what's happening, we will swoop down on them
and kill them and end their work."
[12]The Jews who lived near the enemy came and told
us again and again, "They will come from all directions
and attack us!"* [13]So I placed armed guards behind
the lowest parts of the wall in the exposed areas. I stationed the people to stand guard by families, armed
with swords, spears, and bows.
[14]Then as I looked over the situation, I called together the nobles and the rest of the people and said
to them, "Don't be afraid of the enemy! Remember
the Lord, who is great and glorious, and fight for your
brothers, your sons, your daughters, your wives, and
your homes!"
[15]When our enemies heard that we knew of their
plans and that God had frustrated them, we all returned to our work on the wall. [16]But from then on,
only half my men worked while the other half stood
guard with spears, shields, bows, and coats of mail. The
leaders stationed themselves behind the people of Judah [17]who were building the wall. The laborers carried
on their work with one hand supporting their load and
one hand holding a weapon. [18]All the builders had a
sword belted to their side. The trumpeter stayed with
me to sound the alarm.
[19]Then I explained to the nobles and officials and
all the people, "The work is very spread out, and we
are widely separated from each other along the wall.
[20]When you hear the blast of the trumpet, rush to
wherever it is sounding. Then our God will fight for us!"
[21]We worked early and late, from sunrise to sunset.
And half the men were always on guard. [22]I also told
everyone living outside the walls to stay in Jerusalem. That way they and their servants could help with
guard duty at night and work during the day. [23]During
this time, none of us—not I, nor my relatives, nor my
servants, nor the guards who were with me—ever took
off our clothes. We carried our weapons with us at all
times, even when we went for water.*

Nehemiah Defends the Oppressed

NEHEMIAH 5:1-19

About this time some of the men and their wives
raised a cry of protest against their fellow Jews. [2]They
were saying, "We have such large families. We need
more food to survive."
[3]Others said, "We have mortgaged our fields, vineyards, and homes to get food during the famine."
[4]And others said, "We have had to borrow money
on our fields and vineyards to pay our taxes. [5]We belong to the same family as those who are wealthy, and

Neh 4:12 The meaning of the Hebrew is uncertain. **Neh 4:23** Or *Each carried his weapon in his right hand.* Hebrew reads *Each his weapon the water.* The meaning of the Hebrew is uncertain.

entrusted to them. Too often we pray without looking for what God wants us to do. We show God we are serious when we combine prayer with thought, preparation, and effort.

Neh 4:10-14 Accomplishing any large task is tiring. There are always pressures that foster discouragement—the task seems impossible, it can never be finished, or too many factors are working against us. The only cure for fatigue and discouragement is focusing on God's purposes. Nehemiah reminded the workers of their calling, their goal, and God's protection. If you are overwhelmed by an assignment, tired and discouraged, remember God's purpose for your life and his special purpose for the project.

Neh 4:10-15 The people working on the walls faced the continual threat of terrorist attacks from those who didn't want to see Jerusalem rebuilt. Threats demoralize. The tension created by the possibility of sudden assaults adds to fatigue. Nehemiah took wise, practical steps to counter the threats: (1) He stationed guards at obvious weak points. (2) He reminded the workers to keep weapons close at hand and to fight for God, their families, and the nation if an attack came. (3) He established duty rotations so that some stood guard while others worked. The preparations for defense and the continuation of the work reversed the effects of terrorism and demoralized the enemies. Obstacles and foes can make us work smarter and live wiser or make us give up our purpose and our way of living. If they accomplish the latter, they have won even if they haven't actually attacked us. But if we adjust our way of living wisely while continuing resolutely to live under God's instructions, the opposition will fail.

Neh 4:16 The workers were spread out along the wall, so Nehemiah devised a plan of defense that would unite and protect his people—half the men worked while the other half stood guard. Christians need to help one another in the same way because we can become so afraid of possible dangers that we can't get anything done. By looking out for each other, we will be free to put forth our best efforts, confident that others are ready to offer help when needed. Don't cut yourself off from others; instead, join together for mutual benefit. You need them as much as they need you.

Neh 4:18-20 To further relieve the anxieties of the people, Nehemiah set up a communication system. The man who sounded the trumpet stayed with Nehemiah, and the people knew what to do if they heard it. We have no record that the trumpet was ever used, but simply knowing it would issue a warning when needed was reassuring. The system also put doubt into the minds of those trying to terrorize the workforce since the people on the wall were no longer passive targets. The promise of open, immediate communication helped the group counter the enemy threats and accomplish the reconstruction of the wall in record time.

Neh 4:23 Although the exact meaning of the Hebrew phrase "even when we went for water" is unclear (it has also been translated, "in his right hand" or "at his right hand at night"), the point is that each man always had his weapon close at hand. The guards were prepared and took their responsibilities seriously.

Neh 5:1-5 Who were these bitterly resented Jews? They were either (1) Jews who had become wealthy in exile and brought this wealth with them to Jerusalem, or (2) descendants of Jews who had arrived almost a century earlier during the first return under Zerubbabel (Ezra 1–2) and had established lucrative businesses.

Neh 5:7-9 Many of the returned exiles were suffering at the hands of some of their rich countrymen. These people would lend large sums of money; then, when the debtors missed a payment, they would take over their fields. Left with no means of income, the debtors were forced to sell their children into slavery, a common practice of this time. Nehemiah was angry with these Jews, who were taking advantage of their own people in order to enrich themselves. These practices violated the law set forth in Exodus 22:25.

▸ **NEHEMIAH 5:1-19** ***(cont.)***
our children are just like theirs. Yet we must sell our
children into slavery just to get enough money to live.
We have already sold some of our daughters, and we
are helpless to do anything about it, for our fields and
vineyards are already mortgaged to others."
[6]When I heard their complaints, I was very angry.
[7]After thinking it over, I spoke out against these nobles and officials. I told them, "You are hurting your
own relatives by charging interest when they borrow
money!" Then I called a public meeting to deal with
the problem.
[8]At the meeting I said to them, "We are doing all
we can to redeem our Jewish relatives who have had
to sell themselves to pagan foreigners, but you are
selling them back into slavery again. How often must
we redeem them?" And they had nothing to say in
their defense.
[9]Then I pressed further, "What you are doing is not
right! Should you not walk in the fear of our God in
order to avoid being mocked by enemy nations? [10]I
myself, as well as my brothers and my workers, have
been lending the people money and grain, but now
let us stop this business of charging interest. [11]You
must restore their fields, vineyards, olive groves, and
homes to them this very day. And repay the interest
you charged when you lent them money, grain, new
wine, and olive oil."
[12]They replied, "We will give back everything and
demand nothing more from the people. We will do as
you say." Then I called the priests and made the nobles
and officials swear to do what they had promised.
[13]I shook out the folds of my robe and said, "If you
fail to keep your promise, may God shake you like this
from your homes and from your property!"
The whole assembly responded, "Amen," and they
praised the LORD. And the people did as they had
promised.
[14]For the entire twelve years that I was governor of
Judah—from the twentieth year to the thirty-second
year of the reign of King Artaxerxes*—neither I nor
my officials drew on our official food allowance. [15]The
former governors, in contrast, had laid heavy burdens
on the people, demanding a daily ration of food and
wine, besides forty pieces* of silver. Even their assistants took advantage of the people. But because I
feared God, I did not act that way.
[16]I also devoted myself to working on the wall and
refused to acquire any land. And I required all my
servants to spend time working on the wall. [17]I asked
for nothing, even though I regularly fed 150 Jewish
officials at my table, besides all the visitors from other
lands! [18]The provisions I paid for each day included
one ox, six choice sheep or goats, and a large number of poultry. And every ten days we needed a large
supply of all kinds of wine. Yet I refused to claim the
governor's food allowance because the people already
carried a heavy burden.
[19]Remember, O my God, all that I have done for
these people, and bless me for it.

Continued Opposition to Rebuilding

NEHEMIAH 6:1-14
Sanballat, Tobiah, Geshem the Arab, and the rest of
our enemies found out that I had finished rebuilding
the wall and that no gaps remained—though we had
not yet set up the doors in the gates. [2]So Sanballat
and Geshem sent a message asking me to meet them
at one of the villages* in the plain of Ono.
But I realized they were plotting to harm me, [3]so
I replied by sending this message to them: "I am

Neh 5:14 That is, 445–433 B.C. **Neh 5:15** Hebrew *40 shekels* [1 pound, or 456 grams]. **Neh 6:2** As in Greek version; Hebrew reads *at Kephirim.*

Neh 5:9-11 God's concern for the poor is revealed in almost every book of the Bible. Here, Nehemiah insisted that fairness to the poor and oppressed was central to following God. The books of Moses clearly spelled out the Israelites' responsibility to care for the poor (Exod 22:22-27; Lev 25:35-37; Deut 14:28-29; 15:7-11). The way we help those in need ought to mirror God's love and concern.

Neh 5:10 Nehemiah told the rich Jews to stop charging interest on their loans to their needy brothers. God never intended people to profit from others' misfortune. In contrast to the values of this world, God says that caring for one another is more important than personal gain. When a Christian brother or sister suffers, we all suffer (1 Cor 12:26). We should help needy believers, not exploit them. The Jerusalem church was praised for working together to eliminate poverty (Acts 4:34-35). Remember, "Whoever gives to the poor will lack nothing" (Prov 28:27). Make it a practice to help those in need around you.

Neh 5:13 This symbolic act was a curse. Nehemiah shook out the folds of his robe and pronounced that anyone who did not keep his promise would likewise be shaken out and emptied, losing all he had.

Neh 5:14-15 This comment by Nehemiah is a parenthetical statement, comparing his 12 years as governor with the unjust proceedings in the land before he arrived. The governor was appointed by the Persian king, not elected by the people.

Neh 5:16 Nehemiah led the entire construction project, but he also worked on the wall alongside the others. He was not a bureaucrat in a well-guarded office but a leader who got involved in the day-to-day work. He did not use his position to lord it over his people. A good leader keeps in touch with the work to be done. Those who lead best lead by what they *do* as well as by what they say.

Neh 6:1ff Sanballat and Tobiah were desperate. The wall was almost complete, and their efforts to stop its construction were failing. So they tried a new approach, centering their attacks on Nehemiah's character. They attacked him personally with rumors (Neh 6:6), deceit (Neh 6:10-13), and false reports (Neh 6:17). Personal attacks hurt, and when the criticism is unjustified, it is easy to despair. When you are doing God's work, you may receive attacks on your character. Follow Nehemiah's example by trusting God to accomplish the task and by overlooking unjustified insults.

Neh 6:2 The plain of Ono was about 20 miles northwest of Jerusalem. If Sanballat and Geshem could get Nehemiah to agree to meet them there, they could ambush him on the way.

engaged in a great work, so I can't come. Why should
I stop working to come and meet with you?"
[4]Four times they sent the same message, and each
time I gave the same reply. [5]The fifth time, Sanballat's
servant came with an open letter in his hand, [6]and
this is what it said:

"There is a rumor among the surrounding nations, and Geshem* tells me it is true, that you and the Jews are planning to rebel and that is why you are building the wall. According to his reports, you plan to be their king.
[7]He also reports that you have appointed prophets in Jerusalem to proclaim about you, 'Look! There is a king in Judah!'

"You can be very sure that this report will get back to the king, so I suggest that you come and talk it over with me."

[8]I replied, "There is no truth in any part of your
story. You are making up the whole thing."
[9]They were just trying to intimidate us, imagining
that they could discourage us and stop the work. So I
continued the work with even greater determination.*
[10]Later I went to visit Shemaiah son of Delaiah
and grandson of Mehetabel, who was confined to
his home. He said, "Let us meet together inside the
Temple of God and bolt the doors shut. Your enemies
are coming to kill you tonight."
[11]But I replied, "Should someone in my position
run from danger? Should someone in my position
enter the Temple to save his life? No, I won't do it!"
[12]I
realized that God had not spoken to him, but that he
had uttered this prophecy against me because Tobiah
and Sanballat had hired him.
[13]They were hoping to
intimidate me and make me sin. Then they would be
able to accuse and discredit me.

[14]Remember, O my God, all the evil things that Tobiah and Sanballat have done. And remember Noadiah the prophet and all the prophets like her who have tried to intimidate me.

The Builders Complete the Wall

NEHEMIAH 6:15–7:3

So on October 2* the wall was finished—just fifty-
two days after we had begun.
[16]When our enemies
and the surrounding nations heard about it, they were
frightened and humiliated. They realized this work
had been done with the help of our God.
[17]During those fifty-two days, many letters went
back and forth between Tobiah and the nobles of Judah.
[18]For many in Judah had sworn allegiance to him
because his father-in-law was Shecaniah son of Arah,
and his son Jehohanan was married to the daughter
of Meshullam son of Berekiah.
[19]They kept telling me
about Tobiah's good deeds, and then they told him
everything I said. And Tobiah kept sending threatening letters to intimidate me.

7:1 After the wall was finished and I had set up the
doors in the gates, the gatekeepers, singers, and
Levites were appointed.
[2]I gave the responsibility of
governing Jerusalem to my brother Hanani, along
with Hananiah, the commander of the fortress, for he
was a faithful man who feared God more than most.

Neh 6:6 Hebrew *Gashmu,* a variant spelling of Geshem. **Neh 6:9** As in Greek version; Hebrew reads *But now to strengthen my hands.* **Neh 6:15** Hebrew *on the twenty-fifth day of the month Elul,* of the ancient Hebrew lunar calendar. This day was October 2, 445 B.C.; also see note on 1:1.

Neh 6:7 During these days, prophets such as Malachi proclaimed the coming of the Messiah (Mal 3:1-3). Sanballat, with his usual flair for stirring up trouble, tried to turn Nehemiah's people against him by saying that Nehemiah was trying to set himself up as the king. Sanballat also tried to turn the local officials against Nehemiah by threatening to report to the king of Persia that Nehemiah was starting a revolt. The fact that Sanballat had an open, or unsealed, letter delivered to Nehemiah shows that he wanted to make sure the letter's contents were made public. But Sanballat's accusations were untrue and did not divert Nehemiah from his task.

Neh 6:9 When opposition builds up against you or God's work, it is tempting to pray, "God, get me out of this situation." But Nehemiah prayed for strength. He showed tremendous determination and character to remain steadfast in his responsibility. When we pray for strength, God always answers.

Neh 6:10 Shemaiah warned Nehemiah of danger and told him to hide in the Temple. Nehemiah wisely tested the message, exposing it as another trick of the enemy. People may misuse God's name by saying they know God's will when they have other motives. Examine self-proclaimed messengers from God to see if they stand up to the test of being consistent with what is revealed in God's Word.

Neh 6:10-13 Nehemiah did not have the full support of the people. Shemaiah (Neh 6:10), Noadiah (Neh 6:14), and many of the officials (Neh 6:17) were working against him. When Nehemiah was attacked personally, he refused to give in to fear and flee to the Temple. According to God's law, it would have been wrong for Nehemiah to go into the Temple to hide because he wasn't a priest (Num 18:22). If he had run for his life, he would have undermined the courage he was trying to instill in the people. Leaders are targets for attacks. Make it a practice to pray for those in authority (1 Tim 2:1-2). Ask God to give them strength to stand against personal attacks and temptation. They need God-given courage to overcome fear.

Neh 6:15 Daniel, who was among the first group of captives taken from Jerusalem to Babylon (605 B.C.), predicted the rebuilding of the city (Dan 9:25). Here his prophecy comes true. He, like Nehemiah, was a Jew who held a prominent position in the kingdom where he had been exiled (Dan 5:29–6:3).

Neh 6:15 They said it couldn't be done. The job was too big and the problems were too great. But God's men and women, joined together for special tasks, can solve huge problems and accomplish great goals. The vision that Nehemiah saw through humble tears in Persia became a reality with God's help every step of the way. Don't let the size of a task or the length of time needed to accomplish it keep you from doing it. With God's help, it can be done.

Neh 7:2 Faithfulness and fear of God were the key character traits that qualified these men to govern Jerusalem. Faithful people can be trusted to carry out their work; God-fearing people can be expected to do so in line with God's priorities. These men had both qualities. If you are in a position of selecting leaders, look for faithfulness and reverence as two of the most important qualifications. Although other qualities may seem more impressive, faithfulness and reverence pass the test of time.

▸ **NEHEMIAH 6:15–7:3** ***(cont.)***

3I said to them, "Do not leave the gates open during the hottest part of the day.* And even while the gatekeepers are on duty, have them shut and bar the doors. Appoint the residents of Jerusalem to act as guards, everyone on a regular watch. Some will serve at sentry posts and some in front of their own homes."

Nehemiah Registers the People

NEHEMIAH 7:4-73a

At that time the city was large and spacious, but the population was small, and none of the houses had been rebuilt. 5So my God gave me the idea to call together all the nobles and leaders of the city, along with the ordinary citizens, for registration. I had found the genealogical record of those who had first returned to Judah. This is what was written there:

6Here is the list of the Jewish exiles of the provinces who returned from their captivity. King Nebuchadnezzar had deported them to Babylon, but now they returned to Jerusalem and the other towns in Judah where they originally lived. 7Their leaders were Zerubbabel, Jeshua, Nehemiah, Seraiah,* Reelaiah,* Nahamani, Mordecai, Bilshan, Mispar,* Bigvai, Rehum,* and Baanah.

This is the number of the men of Israel who returned from exile:

8 The family of Parosh 2,172
9 The family of Shephatiah 372
10 The family of Arah 652
11 The family of Pahath-moab
(descendants of Jeshua and Joab) 2,818
12 The family of Elam 1,254
13 The family of Zattu 845
14 The family of Zaccai 760
15 The family of Bani* 648
16 The family of Bebai 628
17 The family of Azgad 2,322
18 The family of Adonikam 667
19 The family of Bigvai 2,067
20 The family of Adin 655
21 The family of Ater
(descendants of Hezekiah) 98
22 The family of Hashum 328
23 The family of Bezai 324
24 The family of Jorah* 112
25 The family of Gibbar* 95
26 The people of Bethlehem and Netophah . . . 188
27 The people of Anathoth 128
28 The people of Beth-azmaveth 42
29 The people of Kiriath-jearim, Kephirah,
and Beeroth 743
30 The people of Ramah and Geba 621
31 The people of Micmash 122
32 The people of Bethel and Ai 123

Neh 7:3 Or *Keep the gates of Jerusalem closed until the sun is hot.* **Neh 7:7a** As in parallel text at Ezra 2:2; Hebrew reads *Azariah.* **Neh 7:7b** As in parallel text at Ezra 2:2; Hebrew reads *Raamiah.* **Neh 7:7c** As in parallel text at Ezra 2:2; Hebrew reads *Mispereth.* **Neh 7:7d** As in parallel text at Ezra 2:2; Hebrew reads *Nehum.* **Neh 7:15** As in parallel text at Ezra 2:10; Hebrew reads *Binnui.* **Neh 7:24** As in parallel text at Ezra 2:18; Hebrew reads *Hariph.* **Neh 7:25** As in parallel text at Ezra 2:20; Hebrew reads *Gibeon.*

Neh 7:3 City gates were usually opened at sunrise, enabling merchants to enter and set up their tent-stores. Nehemiah didn't want Jerusalem to be caught unprepared by an enemy attack, so he ordered the gates closed until well after sunrise when the people were sure to be awake and alert.

Neh 7:3 The wall was complete, but the work was not finished. Nehemiah assigned each family the task of protecting the section of wall next to their home. It is tempting to relax our guard and rest on past accomplishments after we have completed a large task. But we must continue to serve and to take care of all that God has entrusted to us. Following through after a project is completed is as vital as doing the project itself.

Neh 7:5ff Nehemiah found the genealogical record. Because this genealogy is almost identical to Ezra's (Ezra 2), most likely Ezra's list was stored in the Temple archives and was the one Nehemiah found.

GOING HOME: TWO GREAT JOURNEYS OF ISRAEL

What about the Journeys?	The Exodus	The Return from Exile
Where were they?	Egypt (430 years)	Babylon (70 years)
How many people?	About 1 million	60,000
How long did the journey take them?	40 years and 2 attempts	100 years and 3 journeys
Who led them?	Moses/Aaron/Joshua	Zerubbabel/Ezra/Nehemiah
What was their purpose?	To reclaim the Promised Land	To rebuild the Temple and city of Jerusalem
What obstacles did they face?	Red Sea/wilderness/enemies	Ruins/limited resources/enemies
What failures did they experience?	Complaining/disobedience/retreat—all of which turned a journey of a few weeks into a 40-year ordeal	Fear/discouragement/apathy—all of which turned a project of a few years into one that required a century to complete
What successes did they have?	Eventually entered the Promised Land	Eventually rebuilt Jerusalem's Temple and wall
What lessons did they learn?	God will build his nation. God is both faithful and just. God will accomplish great acts to make his promises come true.	God will preserve his nation. God will continue to have a chosen people, a home for them, and a plan to offer himself to them.

33 The people of West Nebo* 52
34 The citizens of West Elam* 1,254
35 The citizens of Harim 320
36 The citizens of Jericho....................345
37 The citizens of Lod, Hadid, and Ono..........721
38 The citizens of Senaah 3,930

39These are the priests who returned from exile:
The family of Jedaiah
(through the line of Jeshua) 973
40 The family of Immer 1,052
41 The family of Pashhur 1,247
42 The family of Harim.................. 1,017

43These are the Levites who returned from exile:
The families of Jeshua and Kadmiel
(descendants of Hodaviah*)............. 74
44 The singers of the family of Asaph 148
45 The gatekeepers of the families
of Shallum, Ater, Talmon, Akkub,
Hatita, and Shobai 138

46The descendants of the following Temple
servants returned from exile:
Ziha, Hasupha, Tabbaoth,
47 Keros, Siaha,* Padon,
48 Lebanah, Hagabah, Shalmai,
49 Hanan, Giddel, Gahar,
50 Reaiah, Rezin, Nekoda,
51 Gazzam, Uzza, Paseah,
52 Besai, Meunim, Nephusim,*
53 Bakbuk, Hakupha, Harhur,
54 Bazluth,* Mehida, Harsha,
55 Barkos, Sisera, Temah,
56 Neziah, and Hatipha.

57The descendants of these servants of King
Solomon returned from exile:
Sotai, Hassophereth, Peruda,*
58 Jaalah,* Darkon, Giddel,
59 Shephatiah, Hattil, Pokereth-hazzebaim,
and Ami.*

60In all, the Temple servants and the descendants
of Solomon's servants numbered 392.

61Another group returned at this time
from the towns of Tel-melah, Tel-harsha,
Kerub, Addan,* and Immer. However, they
could not prove that they or their families
were descendants of Israel. 62This group
included the families of Delaiah, Tobiah, and
Nekoda—a total of 642 people.
63Three families of priests—Hobaiah, Hakkoz,
and Barzillai—also returned. (This Barzillai
had married a woman who was a descendant
of Barzillai of Gilead, and he had taken her
family name.) 64They searched for their names
in the genealogical records, but they were not
found, so they were disqualified from serving
as priests. 65The governor told them not to eat
the priests' share of food from the sacrifices
until a priest could consult the LORD about the
matter by using the Urim and Thummim—the
sacred lots.
66So a total of 42,360 people returned to
Judah, 67in addition to 7,337 servants and
245 singers, both men and women. 68They took
with them 736 horses, 245 mules,* 69435 camels,
and 6,720 donkeys.
70Some of the family leaders gave gifts for the
work. The governor gave to the treasury 1,000
gold coins,* 50 gold basins, and 530 robes for the
priests. 71The other leaders gave to the treasury
a total of 20,000 gold coins* and some 2,750
pounds* of silver for the work. 72The rest of the
people gave 20,000 gold coins, about 2,500
pounds* of silver, and 67 robes for the priests.
73So the priests, the Levites, the gatekeepers,
the singers, the Temple servants, and some of
the common people settled near Jerusalem. The
rest of the people returned to their own towns
throughout Israel.

Neh 7:33 Or *of the other Nebo.* **Neh 7:34** Or *of the other Elam.* **Neh 7:43** As in parallel text at Ezra 2:40; Hebrew reads *Hodevah.* **Neh 7:47** As in parallel text at Ezra 2:44; Hebrew reads *Sia.* **Neh 7:52** As in parallel text at Ezra 2:50; Hebrew reads *Nephushesim.* **Neh 7:54** As in parallel text at Ezra 2:52; Hebrew reads *Bazlith.* **Neh 7:57** As in parallel text at Ezra 2:55; Hebrew reads *Sotai, Sophereth, Perida.* **Neh 7:58** As in parallel text at Ezra 2:56; Hebrew reads *Jaala.* **Neh 7:59** As in parallel text at Ezra 2:57; Hebrew reads *Amon.* **Neh 7:61** As in parallel text at Ezra 2:59; Hebrew reads *Addon.* **Neh 7:68** As in some Hebrew manuscripts (see also Ezra 2:66); most Hebrew manuscripts lack this verse. Verses 7:69-73 are numbered 7:68-72 in Hebrew text. **Neh 7:70** Hebrew *1,000 darics of gold,* about 19 pounds or 8.6 kilograms in weight. **Neh 7:71a** Hebrew *20,000 darics of gold,* about 375 pounds or 170 kilograms in weight; also in 7:72. **Neh 7:71b** Hebrew *2,200 minas* [1,300 kilograms]. **Neh 7:72** Hebrew *2,000 minas* [1,200 kilograms].

Neh 7:61 Genealogies were greatly valued because it was vitally important to prove oneself a descendant of Abraham and, therefore, part of God's chosen people (Gen 12:1-3; 15; Exod 19:5-6; Deut 11:22-28). A lost genealogy put one's status as a Jew at risk.

Neh 7:64-65 "Sacred lots" referred to the Urim and Thummim, a means of learning God's will (Exod 28:30). If someone's name wasn't in the genealogies, he could still be admitted as a priest if the Urim and Thummim proved him to be a Jew and a Levite. It is not clear whether the Urim and Thummim were the originals that had survived the destruction of Jerusalem or if they were new. The "priests' share of food" was meat dedicated to God as part of the sacrifice. Only true priests could eat it.

2. REFORMING THE PEOPLE

When Nehemiah arrived in Jerusalem he found more than just broken walls; he found broken lives. In response, Nehemiah gathers the people together to hear Ezra read God's law. The people repent and promise to change their lives by obeying God's words. No matter where we live, backsliding is an ever-present danger. We must constantly check our behavior against God's standards in the Bible so that we do not slide back into sinful ways of living.

Ezra Reads the Law

NEHEMIAH 7:73b–8:12

In October,* when the Israelites had settled in their
towns, 8:1all the people assembled with a unified purpose at the square just inside the Water Gate. They
asked Ezra the scribe to bring out the Book of the Law
of Moses, which the LORD had given for Israel to obey.
2So on October 8* Ezra the priest brought the Book
of the Law before the assembly, which included the
men and women and all the children old enough to
understand. 3He faced the square just inside the Water
Gate from early morning until noon and read aloud
to everyone who could understand. All the people
listened closely to the Book of the Law.
4Ezra the scribe stood on a high wooden platform
that had been made for the occasion. To his right stood
Mattithiah, Shema, Anaiah, Uriah, Hilkiah, and Maaseiah. To his left stood Pedaiah, Mishael, Malkijah,
Hashum, Hashbaddanah, Zechariah, and Meshullam. 5Ezra stood on the platform in full view of all
the people. When they saw him open the book, they
all rose to their feet.
6Then Ezra praised the LORD, the great God, and
all the people chanted, "Amen! Amen!" as they lifted
their hands. Then they bowed down and worshiped
the LORD with their faces to the ground.
7The Levites—Jeshua, Bani, Sherebiah, Jamin, Akkub, Shabbethai, Hodiah, Maaseiah, Kelita, Azariah,
Jozabad, Hanan, and Pelaiah—then instructed the
people in the Law while everyone remained in their
places. 8They read from the Book of the Law of God
and clearly explained the meaning of what was being
read, helping the people understand each passage.
9Then Nehemiah the governor, Ezra the priest and
scribe, and the Levites who were interpreting for the
people said to them, "Don't mourn or weep on such a

Neh 7:73 Hebrew *in the seventh month.* This month of the ancient Hebrew lunar calendar occurred within the months of October and November 445 B.C. **Neh 8:2** Hebrew *on the first day of the seventh month,* of the ancient Hebrew lunar calendar. This day was October 8, 445 B.C.; also see note on 1:1.

Law Scroll

Nehemiah read from the Law, which is known as the Pentateuch, a word formed by two Greek words, *pente* (five) and *teuchos* (case)—five scrolls in a case—the first five books of the Old Testament: Genesis, Exodus, Leviticus, Numbers, and Deuteronomy. Moses wrote this portion of God's Word (Exod 17:14; 24:4; 34:27; Num 33:1-2; Deut 31:9, 22). The Pentateuch begins with the creation of the universe and records God's dealings with mankind in the Garden of Eden, his preparation of a seed-bearing line (the patriarchal stories), and the formation of the nation of Israel. A substantial portion of the Pentateuch consists of laws governing the religious and civil life of Israel. We should read this section of Scripture and treasure it as much as the Jews have throughout the centuries, for it constitutes the foundation upon which all other Scripture rests.

Neh 8:1 This is the first mention of Ezra in this book. He had arrived in Jerusalem from Babylon 13 years before Nehemiah (458 B.C.; see Ezra 7:6-9). Given the fact that the first seven chapters are taken with the account of Nehemiah's trip to Jerusalem and the three-month monumental construction task, Ezra's appearance at this point in the book emphasizes that the special role he had all along now came to the forefront. Nehemiah led the rebuilding of the wall; Ezra led the spiritual revival of the nation.

Neh 8:1 Ezra and Nehemiah were contemporaries (Neh 8:9), although Ezra was probably much older. Nehemiah, as governor, was the political leader; and Ezra, as priest and scribe, was the religious leader. A scribe in these days was a combination lawyer, notary public, scholar, and consultant. Scribes were among the most educated people, so they were teachers. No doubt the Jews would have liked to set up the kingdom again as in the days of David, but this would have signaled rebellion against the king of Persia to whom they were subject. The best alternative was to divide the leadership between Nehemiah and Ezra.

Neh 8:1-5 The Book of the Law of Moses was probably the Pentateuch, the first five books of the Bible. The people rose to their feet in respect and anticipation. They listened attentively to Ezra as he read God's Word, and their lives were changed. Because we hear the Bible so often, we can become dulled to its words and immune to its teachings. Instead, we should listen carefully to every verse and ask the Holy Spirit to help us answer the question, How does this apply to my life?

Neh 8:9 Ezra, not Nehemiah, was the official religious leader. It is significant that Nehemiah was a layman, not a member of the religious establishment or a prophet. He was motivated by his relationship with God, and he devoted his life to doing God's will in a secular world. Such people are crucial to God's work in all aspects of life. No matter what your work or role in life, view it as God's

day as this! For today is a sacred day before the LORD
your God." For the people had all been weeping as they
listened to the words of the Law.
10 And Nehemiah* continued, "Go and celebrate
with a feast of rich foods and sweet drinks, and share
gifts of food with people who have nothing prepared.
This is a sacred day before our Lord. Don't be dejected
and sad, for the joy of the LORD is your strength!"
11 And the Levites, too, quieted the people, telling
them, "Hush! Don't weep! For this is a sacred day."
12 So the people went away to eat and drink at a festive meal, to share gifts of food, and to celebrate with
great joy because they had heard God's words and
understood them.

The Festival of Shelters

NEHEMIAH 8:13-18

On October 9* the family leaders of all the people,
together with the priests and Levites, met with Ezra
the scribe to go over the Law in greater detail. 14 As
they studied the Law, they discovered that the LORD
had commanded through Moses that the Israelites
should live in shelters during the festival to be held
that month.* 15 He had said that a proclamation should
be made throughout their towns and in Jerusalem,
telling the people to go to the hills to get branches
from olive, wild olive,* myrtle, palm, and other leafy
trees. They were to use these branches to make shelters in which they would live during the festival, as
prescribed in the Law.
16 So the people went out and cut branches and used
them to build shelters on the roofs of their houses, in
their courtyards, in the courtyards of God's Temple,
or in the squares just inside the Water Gate and the
Ephraim Gate. 17 So everyone who had returned from
captivity lived in these shelters during the festival,
and they were all filled with great joy! The Israelites
had not celebrated like this since the days of Joshua*
son of Nun.
18 Ezra read from the Book of the Law of God on
each of the seven days of the festival. Then on the
eighth day they held a solemn assembly, as was required by law.

The People Confess Their Sins

NEHEMIAH 9:1-37

On October 31* the people assembled again, and this
time they fasted and dressed in burlap and sprinkled
dust on their heads. 2 Those of Israelite descent separated themselves from all foreigners as they confessed
their own sins and the sins of their ancestors. 3 They
remained standing in place for three hours* while the
Book of the Law of the LORD their God was read aloud
to them. Then for three more hours they confessed
their sins and worshiped the LORD their God. 4 The
Levites—Jeshua, Bani, Kadmiel, Shebaniah, Bunni,
Sherebiah, Bani, and Kenani—stood on the stairway
of the Levites and cried out to the LORD their God
with loud voices.
5 Then the leaders of the Levites—Jeshua, Kadmiel,
Bani, Hashabneiah, Sherebiah, Hodiah, Shebaniah,
and Pethahiah—called out to the people: "Stand up
and praise the LORD your God, for he lives from everlasting to everlasting!" Then they prayed:

"May your glorious name be praised! May it be
exalted above all blessing and praise!
6 "You alone are the LORD. You made the skies
and the heavens and all the stars. You made
the earth and the seas and everything in them.
You preserve them all, and the angels of heaven
worship you.

Neh 8:10 Hebrew *he.* **Neh 8:13** Hebrew *On the second day,* of the seventh month of the ancient Hebrew lunar calendar. This day was October 9, 445 B.C.; also see notes on 1:1 and 8:2. **Neh 8:14** Hebrew *in the seventh month.* This month of the ancient Hebrew lunar calendar usually occurs within the months of September and October. See Lev 23:39-43. **Neh 8:15** Or *pine;* Hebrew reads *oil tree.* **Neh 8:17** Hebrew *Jeshua,* a variant spelling of Joshua. **Neh 9:1** Hebrew *On the twenty-fourth day of that same month,* the seventh month of the ancient Hebrew lunar calendar. This day was October 31, 445 B.C.; also see notes on 1:1 and 8:2. **Neh 9:3** Hebrew *for a quarter of a day.*

special calling to serve him. God can accomplish his purposes through you, beginning right where you are.

Neh 8:9-10 The people wept openly when they heard God's laws and realized how far they were from obeying them. But Ezra told them they should be filled with joy because the day was sacred. It was time to celebrate and to give gifts to those in need.

Celebration is not to be self-centered. Ezra connected celebration with giving. This gave those in need an opportunity to celebrate as well. Often when we celebrate and give to others (even when we don't feel like it), we are strengthened spiritually and filled with joy. Enter into celebrations that honor God, and allow him to fill you with his joy.

Neh 8:13ff After Ezra read God's laws to the people, they studied them further and then acted upon them. A careful reading of Scripture always calls for a response to these questions: What should we do with this knowledge? How should our lives change? We must do something about what we have learned if it is to have real significance for our lives.

Neh 8:14-17 During the seven-day Festival of Shelters, the people lived in shelters made of branches. This practice was instituted as a reminder of their rescue from Egypt and the time spent in shelters in the wilderness (Lev 23:43). They were to think about God's protection and guidance during their years of wandering and the fact that God would still protect and guide them if they obeyed him. This was a time to remember their origins. It is helpful to remember our beginnings in order to appreciate where we are today. Think back on your life to see where God has led you. Then thank God for his continuing work to protect you and provide for your needs.

Neh 9:1 Fasting, wearing burlap, and sprinkling dust on the head were public signs of sorrow and repentance.

Neh 9:2-3 The Hebrews practiced open confession, admitting their sins to one another. Reading and studying God's Word should precede confession (see Neh 8:18) because God can show us where we are sinning. Honest confession should precede worship, because we cannot have a right relationship with God if we hold on to certain sins.

▸ **NEHEMIAH 9:1-37** ***(cont.)***

7"You are the LORD God, who chose Abram and brought him from Ur of the Chaldeans and renamed him Abraham. 8When he had proved himself faithful, you made a covenant with him to give him and his descendants the land of the Canaanites, Hittites, Amorites, Perizzites, Jebusites, and Girgashites. And you have done what you promised, for you are always true to your word.

9"You saw the misery of our ancestors in Egypt, and you heard their cries from beside the Red Sea.* 10You displayed miraculous signs and wonders against Pharaoh, his officials, and all his people, for you knew how arrogantly they were treating our ancestors. You have a glorious reputation that has never been forgotten. 11You divided the sea for your people so they could walk through on dry land! And then you hurled their enemies into the depths of the sea. They sank like stones beneath the mighty waters. 12You led our ancestors by a pillar of cloud during the day and a pillar of fire at night so that they could find their way.

13"You came down at Mount Sinai and spoke to them from heaven. You gave them regulations and instructions that were just, and decrees and commands that were good. 14You instructed them concerning your holy Sabbath. And you commanded them, through Moses your servant, to obey all your commands, decrees, and instructions.

15"You gave them bread from heaven when they were hungry and water from the rock when they were thirsty. You commanded them to go and take possession of the land you had sworn to give them.

16"But our ancestors were proud and stubborn, and they paid no attention to your commands. 17They refused to obey and did not remember the miracles you had done for them. Instead, they became stubborn and appointed a leader to take them back to their slavery in Egypt! But you are a God of forgiveness, gracious and merciful, slow to become angry, and rich in unfailing love. You did not abandon them, 18even when they made an idol shaped like a calf and said, 'This is your god who brought you out of Egypt!' They committed terrible blasphemies.

19"But in your great mercy you did not abandon them to die in the wilderness. The pillar of cloud still led them forward by day, and the pillar of fire showed them the way through the night. 20You sent your good Spirit to instruct them, and you did not stop giving them manna from heaven or water for their thirst. 21For forty years you sustained them in the wilderness, and they lacked nothing. Their clothes did not wear out, and their feet did not swell!

22"Then you helped our ancestors conquer kingdoms and nations, and you placed your people in every corner of the land.* They took over the land of King Sihon of Heshbon and the land of King Og of Bashan. 23You made their descendants as numerous as the stars in the sky and brought them into the land you had promised to their ancestors.

24"They went in and took possession of the land. You subdued whole nations before them. Even the Canaanites, who inhabited the land, were powerless! Your people could deal with these nations and their kings as they pleased. 25Our ancestors captured fortified cities and fertile land. They took over houses full of good things, with cisterns already dug and vineyards and olive groves and fruit trees in abundance. So they ate until they were full and grew fat and enjoyed themselves in all your blessings.

26"But despite all this, they were disobedient and rebelled against you. They turned their backs on your Law, they killed your prophets who warned them to return to you, and they committed terrible blasphemies. 27So you handed them over to their enemies, who made them suffer. But in their time of trouble they cried to you, and you heard them from heaven. In your great mercy, you sent them liberators who rescued them from their enemies.

28"But as soon as they were at peace, your people again committed evil in your sight, and once more you let their enemies conquer them. Yet whenever your people turned and cried to you again for help, you listened once more from heaven. In your wonderful mercy, you rescued them many times!

29"You warned them to return to your Law, but they became proud and obstinate and

Neh 9:9 Hebrew *sea of reeds.* **Neh 9:22** The meaning of the Hebrew is uncertain.

Neh 9:7-38 Many prayers and speeches in the Bible include a long summary of Israel's history because individuals did not have their own copies of the Bible as we do today. This summary of God's past works reminded the people of their great heritage and God's promises.

Remembering our personal history can certainly help us to avoid repeating our mistakes so that we can serve God better. Reviewing our past helps us understand how to improve our behavior. It shows us the pattern to our spiritual growth. Learn from your past so that you will become the kind of person God wants you to be.

Neh 9:16-21 Seeing how God continued to be with his people shows that his patience is amazing! In spite of our repeated failings, pride, and stubbornness, he is always ready to forgive (Neh 9:17), and his Spirit is always ready to instruct (Neh 9:20). Realizing the extent of God's forgiveness helps us forgive those who fail us, even "seventy times seven" if necessary (Matt 18:21-22).

disobeyed your commands. They did not follow
your regulations, by which people will find life
if only they obey. They stubbornly turned their
backs on you and refused to listen. [30]In your
love, you were patient with them for many years.
You sent your Spirit, who warned them through
the prophets. But still they wouldn't listen! So
once again you allowed the peoples of the land
to conquer them. [31]But in your great mercy, you
did not destroy them completely or abandon
them forever. What a gracious and merciful
God you are!

[32]"And now, our God, the great and mighty
and awesome God, who keeps his covenant
of unfailing love, do not let all the hardships
we have suffered seem insignificant to you.
Great trouble has come upon us and upon our
kings and leaders and priests and prophets
and ancestors—all of your people—from the
days when the kings of Assyria first triumphed
over us until now. [33]Every time you punished
us you were being just. We have sinned greatly,
and you gave us only what we deserved. [34]Our
kings, leaders, priests, and ancestors did not
obey your Law or listen to the warnings in your
commands and laws. [35]Even while they had their
own kingdom, they did not serve you, though
you showered your goodness on them. You gave
them a large, fertile land, but they refused to turn
from their wickedness.

[36]"So now today we are slaves in the land
of plenty that you gave our ancestors for their
enjoyment! We are slaves here in this good land.
[37]The lush produce of this land piles up in the
hands of the kings whom you have set over us
because of our sins. They have power over us and
our livestock. We serve them at their pleasure,
and we are in great misery."

The People Agree to Obey

NEHEMIAH 9:38–10:27

[38]*The people responded, "In view of all this,* we are
making a solemn promise and putting it in writing.
On this sealed document are the names of our leaders
and Levites and priests."

10:1*The document was ratified and sealed with the
following names:

The governor:
Nehemiah son of Hacaliah, and also Zedekiah.

[2]The following priests:
Seraiah, Azariah, Jeremiah, [3]Pashhur, Amariah,
Malkijah, [4]Hattush, Shebaniah, Malluch, [5]Harim,
Meremoth, Obadiah, [6]Daniel, Ginnethon, Baruch,
[7]Meshullam, Abijah, Mijamin, [8]Maaziah, Bilgai,
and Shemaiah. These were the priests.

[9]The following Levites:
Jeshua son of Azaniah, Binnui from the family
of Henadad, Kadmiel, [10]and their fellow Levites:
Shebaniah, Hodiah, Kelita, Pelaiah, Hanan,
[11]Mica, Rehob, Hashabiah, [12]Zaccur, Sherebiah,
Shebaniah, [13]Hodiah, Bani, and Beninu.

[14]The following leaders:
Parosh, Pahath-moab, Elam, Zattu, Bani,
[15]Bunni, Azgad, Bebai, [16]Adonijah, Bigvai, Adin,
[17]Ater, Hezekiah, Azzur, [18]Hodiah, Hashum,
Bezai, [19]Hariph, Anathoth, Nebai, [20]Magpiash,
Meshullam, Hezir, [21]Meshezabel, Zadok, Jaddua,
[22]Pelatiah, Hanan, Anaiah, [23]Hoshea, Hananiah,
Hasshub, [24]Hallohesh, Pilha, Shobek, [25]Rehum,
Hashabnah, Maaseiah, [26]Ahiah, Hanan, Anan,
[27]Malluch, Harim, and Baanah.

The Vow of the People

NEHEMIAH 10:28-39

Then the rest of the people—the priests, Levites,
gatekeepers, singers, Temple servants, and all who

Neh 9:38a Verse 9:38 is numbered 10:1 in Hebrew text. **Neh 9:38b** Or *In spite of all this.* **Neh 10:1** Verses 10:1-39 are numbered 10:2-40 in Hebrew text.

Neh 9:28-31 Israel was devastated by times of intense rebellion and sin. Yet when the people repented and returned to God, he delivered them. God puts no limit on the number of times we can come to him to obtain mercy, but we must come in order to obtain it, recognizing our need and asking him for help. This miracle of grace should inspire us to say, "What a gracious and merciful God you are!" If there is a recurring problem or difficulty in your life, continue to ask God for help, and be willing and ready to make changes in your attitude and behavior that will correct that situation.

Neh 9:35 Sometimes the way we take for granted the very blessings God has showered on us leads us to forget him (Neh 9:28). We are often tempted to rely on wealth for security rather than on God who makes it possible. As you see what happened to the Israelites, look at your own life. Do your blessings make you thankful to God and draw you closer to him, or do they make you feel self-sufficient and forgetful of God?

Neh 9:36 The Israelites were in the strange position of being slaves in their own land, having to turn over a part of their resources each year to a foreign king. How ironic, since God had given the land to them. This was certainly a bitter reminder of the lasting consequences of sin.

Neh 9:38 This "solemn promise" between the people and God had six provisions. They agreed to (1) not marry non-Jewish neighbors (Neh 10:30), (2) observe the Sabbath (Neh 10:31), (3) observe every seventh year as a Sabbath year (Neh 10:31), (4) pay a Temple tax (Neh 10:32-33), (5) supply wood for the burnt offerings in the Temple (Neh 10:34), and (6) give dues to the Temple (Neh 10:35-38). After years of decadence and exile, the people once again took seriously their responsibility to follow God and keep his laws wholeheartedly.

Neh 10:28ff The wall was completed, and the covenant God had made with his people in the days of Moses was restored (Deut 8). This promise has principles that are important for us today. Our relationship with God must go far beyond church attendance and regular devotions. It should affect our relationships (Neh 10:30), our time (Neh 10:31), and our material resources (Neh 10:32-39). When you choose to follow God, you promise to serve him in this way. The Israelites had fallen away from their original commitment. We must keep our promise to God in times of adversity or prosperity.

▸ **NEHEMIAH 10:28-39** ***(cont.)***

had separated themselves from the pagan people of the land in order to obey the Law of God, together with their wives, sons, daughters, and all who were old enough to understand—[29]joined their leaders and bound themselves with an oath. They swore a curse on themselves if they failed to obey the Law of God as issued by his servant Moses. They solemnly promised to carefully follow all the commands, regulations, and decrees of the LORD our Lord:

[30]"We promise not to let our daughters marry the pagan people of the land, and not to let our sons marry their daughters.

[31]"We also promise that if the people of the land should bring any merchandise or grain to be sold on the Sabbath or on any other holy day, we will refuse to buy it. Every seventh year we will let our land rest, and we will cancel all debts owed to us.

[32]"In addition, we promise to obey the command to pay the annual Temple tax of one-eighth of an ounce of silver* for the care of the Temple of our God. [33]This will provide for the Bread of the Presence; for the regular grain offerings and burnt offerings; for the offerings on the Sabbaths, the new moon celebrations, and the annual festivals; for the holy offerings; and for the sin offerings to make atonement for Israel. It will provide for everything necessary for the work of the Temple of our God.

[34]"We have cast sacred lots to determine when—at regular times each year—the families of the priests, Levites, and the common people should bring wood to God's Temple to be burned on the altar of the LORD our God, as is written in the Law.

[35]"We promise to bring the first part of every harvest to the LORD's Temple year after year—whether it be a crop from the soil or from our fruit trees. [36]We agree to give God our oldest sons and the firstborn of all our herds and flocks, as prescribed in the Law. We will present them to the priests who minister in the Temple of our God. [37]We will store the produce in the storerooms of the Temple of our God. We will bring the best of our flour and other grain offerings, the best of our fruit, and the best of our new wine and olive oil. And we promise to bring to the Levites a tenth of everything our land produces, for it is the Levites who collect the tithes in all our rural towns.

[38]"A priest—a descendant of Aaron—will be with the Levites as they receive these tithes. And a tenth of all that is collected as tithes will be delivered by the Levites to the Temple of our God and placed in the storerooms. [39]The people and the Levites must bring these offerings of grain, new wine, and olive oil to the storerooms and place them in the sacred containers near the ministering priests, the gatekeepers, and the singers.

"We promise together not to neglect the Temple of our God."

Neh 10:32 Hebrew *tax of 1/3 of a shekel* [4 grams].

Neh 10:30 If God's chosen people were going to witness for him in a pagan world, they needed united, God-fearing families. They also needed to avoid any enticements to worship the idols of the people who lived around them. This was why God prohibited marriage between Israelites and the pagan inhabitants of the land (Deut 7:3-4). But Israelites and pagans often intermarried anyway, and the results were disastrous for the families and for the nation. Time after time, marrying foreigners led God's people into idolatry (1 Kgs 11:1-11). Whenever the nation turned its back on God, it also lost its prosperity and influence for good.

Neh 10:31 The promise to forgive the sin of trading inside the city on the Sabbath was an application of the fourth commandment. The people recognized that the lure of money would conflict with the need for a day of rest, keeping the Sabbath holy. By deciding to honor God first, the Israelites would be refusing to make money their god. Our culture often makes us choose between convenience and profit on the one hand, and putting God first on the other. Look at your work and worship habits: Is God really first?

Neh 10:31 Canceling all debts every seventh year was a part of the law (see Exod 23:10-11 and Deut 15:1-2). The people were reciting and promising to obey God's law and keep the covenant.

Neh 10:32 The Temple had been rebuilt under Ezra's leadership many years earlier (Ezra 6:14-15). So the Temple tax, offerings, and festivals had been restored.

Neh 10:35-36 These practices were instituted at the time of the Exodus from Egypt (see the note on Exod 13:12-14, p. 158). The people needed to relearn the importance of dedicating the first part of their yield and their firstborn sons and animals to God. Nehemiah was simply reinstating these practices from the early days of the nation (Exod 13:1-2; Num 3:40-51). Although this principle was not carried over to New Testament times, the concept of giving God the first portion of our time, treasure, and talent still remains. Do you give God your first and best or merely what is left over?

Neh 10:37-39 According to God's law, the people were to give a tenth of their produce to the Temple for the support of the Levites (those who cared for the Temple and the religious observances). A tenth of what the Levites received or produced went to the priests for their support. The principle at work was to ensure the support of the house of God and his workers. We must not overlook our responsibility to God's workers today.

Jerusalem in the Time of Nehemiah ▶

When Nehemiah came to Jerusalem to rebuild the walls in 445 B.C., the Jewish people had been back in the city for nearly 100 years. This picture gives a good idea of what the city probably looked like after Nehemiah's work of rebuilding the city walls was complete.

Jerusalem in the Time of Nehemiah

See also Jerusalem from Solomon to Hezekiah, p. 707

Nehemiah's restoration project included only the wall around the City of David, and not the larger wall that had existed around Hezekiah's time. Many of the landmarks Nehemiah mentions were destroyed during Herod the Great's renovations (37–4 B.C.), but Nehemiah appears to describe features of the wall in counterclockwise order, beginning and ending with the Sheep Gate (*Neh 3:1, 32*).

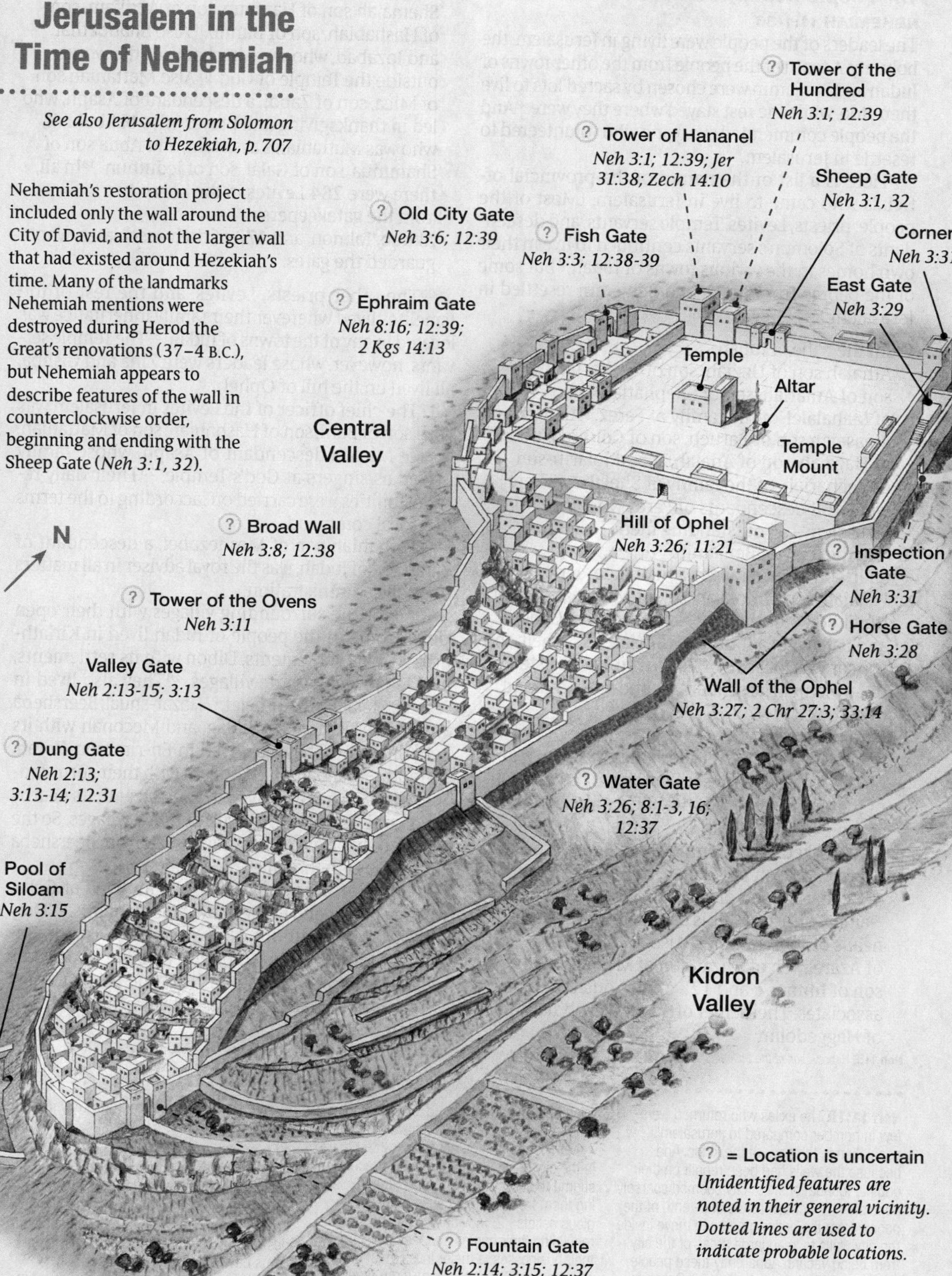

? = Location is uncertain

Unidentified features are noted in their general vicinity. Dotted lines are used to indicate probable locations.

The People Occupy Jerusalem

NEHEMIAH 11:1-36

The leaders of the people were living in Jerusalem, the
holy city. A tenth of the people from the other towns of
Judah and Benjamin were chosen by sacred lots to live
there, too, while the rest stayed where they were. 2And
the people commended everyone who volunteered to
resettle in Jerusalem.

3Here is a list of the names of the provincial officials who came to live in Jerusalem. (Most of the
people, priests, Levites, Temple servants, and descendants of Solomon's servants continued to live in their
own homes in the various towns of Judah, 4but some
of the people from Judah and Benjamin resettled in
Jerusalem.)

From the tribe of Judah:
Athaiah son of Uzziah, son of Zechariah,
son of Amariah, son of Shephatiah, son
of Mahalalel, of the family of Perez. 5Also
Maaseiah son of Baruch, son of Col-hozeh, son
of Hazaiah, son of Adaiah, son of Joiarib, son
of Zechariah, of the family of Shelah.* 6There
were 468 descendants of Perez who lived in
Jerusalem—all outstanding men.
7From the tribe of Benjamin:
Sallu son of Meshullam, son of Joed, son of
Pedaiah, son of Kolaiah, son of Maaseiah, son of
Ithiel, son of Jeshaiah. 8After him were Gabbai
and Sallai and a total of 928 relatives. 9Their chief
officer was Joel son of Zicri, who was assisted by
Judah son of Hassenuah, second-in-command
over the city.
10From the priests:
Jedaiah son of Joiarib; Jakin; 11and Seraiah son
of Hilkiah, son of Meshullam, son of Zadok, son
of Meraioth, son of Ahitub, the supervisor of the
Temple of God. 12Also 822 of their associates,
who worked at the Temple. Also Adaiah son
of Jeroham, son of Pelaliah, son of Amzi, son
of Zechariah, son of Pashhur, son of Malkijah,
13along with 242 of his associates, who were
heads of their families. Also Amashsai son
of Azarel, son of Ahzai, son of Meshillemoth,
son of Immer, 14and 128 of his* outstanding
associates. Their chief officer was Zabdiel son
of Haggedolim.
15From the Levites:
Shemaiah son of Hasshub, son of Azrikam, son
of Hashabiah, son of Bunni. 16Also Shabbethai
and Jozabad, who were in charge of the work
outside the Temple of God. 17Also Mattaniah son
of Mica, son of Zabdi, a descendant of Asaph, who
led in thanksgiving and prayer. Also Bakbukiah,
who was Mattaniah's assistant, and Abda son of
Shammua, son of Galal, son of Jeduthun. 18In all,
there were 284 Levites in the holy city.
19From the gatekeepers:
Akkub, Talmon, and 172 of their associates, who
guarded the gates.

20The other priests, Levites, and the rest of the
Israelites lived wherever their family inheritance was
located in any of the towns of Judah. 21The Temple servants, however, whose leaders were Ziha and Gishpa,
all lived on the hill of Ophel.

22The chief officer of the Levites in Jerusalem was
Uzzi son of Bani, son of Hashabiah, son of Mattaniah,
son of Mica, a descendant of Asaph, whose family
served as singers at God's Temple. 23Their daily responsibilities were carried out according to the terms
of a royal command.

24Pethahiah son of Meshezabel, a descendant of
Zerah son of Judah, was the royal adviser in all matters
of public administration.

25As for the surrounding villages with their open
fields, some of the people of Judah lived in Kiriath-
arba with its settlements, Dibon with its settlements,
and Jekabzeel with its villages. 26They also lived in
Jeshua, Moladah, Beth-pelet, 27Hazar-shual, Beersheba
with its settlements, 28Ziklag, and Meconah with its
settlements. 29They also lived in En-rimmon, Zorah,
Jarmuth, 30Zanoah, and Adullam with their surrounding villages. They also lived in Lachish with its nearby
fields and Azekah with its surrounding villages. So the
people of Judah were living all the way from Beersheba
in the south to the valley of Hinnom.

31Some of the people of Benjamin lived at Geba,
Micmash, Aija, and Bethel with its settlements. 32They
also lived in Anathoth, Nob, Ananiah, 33Hazor, Ramah, Gittaim, 34Hadid, Zeboim, Neballat, 35Lod, Ono,
and the Valley of Craftsmen.* 36Some of the Levites
who lived in Judah were sent to live with the tribe of
Benjamin.

Neh 11:5 Hebrew *son of the Shilonite.* **Neh 11:14** As in Greek version; Hebrew reads *their.* **Neh 11:35** Or *and Ge-harashim.*

Neh 11:1ff The exiles who returned were few in number compared to Jerusalem's population in the days of the kings. And because the walls had been rebuilt on their original foundations, the city seemed sparsely populated. Nehemiah asked one-tenth of the people from the outlying areas to move inside the city walls to keep large areas of the city from being vacant. Apparently these people did not want to move into the city. Only a few people volunteered (Neh 11:1-2), and Nehemiah determined by sacred lot who among the remaining people would have to move.

Many of them may not have wanted to live in the city because (1) non-Jews attached a stigma to Jerusalem residents, often excluding them from trade because of their religious beliefs; (2) moving into the city meant rebuilding their homes and reestablishing their businesses, a major investment of time and money; (3) living in Jerusalem required stricter obedience to God's Word because of greater social pressure and proximity to the Temple.

Neh 12:35-36 How could the priests have used musical instruments? David had instituted music as a part of worship in the Temple, and so his instruments had probably been stored there. Although Nebuchadnezzar destroyed the Temple, he took many Temple items back to Babylon with him (2 Chr 36:18). These were most likely preserved in

A History of the Priests and Levites

NEHEMIAH 12:1-26

Here is the list of the priests and Levites who returned
with Zerubbabel son of Shealtiel and Jeshua the high
priest:

Seraiah, Jeremiah, Ezra,
2 Amariah, Malluch, Hattush,
3 Shecaniah, Harim,* Meremoth,
4 Iddo, Ginnethon,* Abijah,
5 Miniamin, Moadiah,* Bilgah,
6 Shemaiah, Joiarib, Jedaiah,
7 Sallu, Amok, Hilkiah, and Jedaiah.

These were the leaders of the priests and their associates in the days of Jeshua.

8 The Levites who returned with them were Jeshua,
Binnui, Kadmiel, Sherebiah, Judah, and Mattaniah,
who with his associates was in charge of the songs of
thanksgiving. 9 Their associates, Bakbukiah and Unni,
stood opposite them during the service.

10 Jeshua the high priest was the father of Joiakim.
Joiakim was the father of Eliashib.
Eliashib was the father of Joiada.
11 Joiada was the father of Johanan.*
Johanan was the father of Jaddua.

12 Now when Joiakim was high priest, the family leaders of the priests were as follows:

Meraiah was leader of the family of Seraiah.
Hananiah was leader of the family of Jeremiah.
13 Meshullam was leader of the family of Ezra.
Jehohanan was leader of the family of Amariah.
14 Jonathan was leader of the family of Malluch.*
Joseph was leader of the family of Shecaniah.*
15 Adna was leader of the family of Harim.
Helkai was leader of the family of Meremoth.*
16 Zechariah was leader of the family of Iddo.
Meshullam was leader of the family of Ginnethon.
17 Zicri was leader of the family of Abijah.
There was also a* leader of the family of Miniamin.
Piltai was leader of the family of Moadiah.
18 Shammua was leader of the family of Bilgah.
Jehonathan was leader of the family of Shemaiah.
19 Mattenai was leader of the family of Joiarib.
Uzzi was leader of the family of Jedaiah.
20 Kallai was leader of the family of Sallu.*
Eber was leader of the family of Amok.
21 Hashabiah was leader of the family of Hilkiah.
Nethanel was leader of the family of Jedaiah.

22 A record of the Levite families was kept during
the years when Eliashib, Joiada, Johanan, and Jaddua
served as high priest. Another record of the priests
was kept during the reign of Darius the Persian.* 23 A
record of the heads of the Levite families was kept in
The Book of History down to the days of Johanan, the
grandson* of Eliashib.

24 These were the family leaders of the Levites: Hashabiah, Sherebiah, Jeshua, Binnui,* Kadmiel, and other
associates, who stood opposite them during the ceremonies of praise and thanksgiving, one section responding
to the other, as commanded by David, the man of God.
25 This included Mattaniah, Bakbukiah, and Obadiah.

Meshullam, Talmon, and Akkub were the gatekeepers in charge of the storerooms at the gates.
26 These all served in the days of Joiakim son of Jeshua,
son of Jehozadak,* and in the days of Nehemiah the
governor and of Ezra the priest and scribe.

Dedication of Jerusalem's Wall

NEHEMIAH 12:27-43

For the dedication of the new wall of Jerusalem, the
Levites throughout the land were asked to come to
Jerusalem to assist in the ceremonies. They were to
take part in the joyous occasion with their songs of
thanksgiving and with the music of cymbals, harps,
and lyres. 28 The singers were brought together from
the region around Jerusalem and from the villages of
the Netophathites. 29 They also came from Beth-gilgal
and the rural areas near Geba and Azmaveth, for the
singers had built their own settlements around Jerusalem. 30 The priests and Levites first purified themselves;
then they purified the people, the gates, and the wall.

31 I led the leaders of Judah to the top of the wall
and organized two large choirs to give thanks. One of
the choirs proceeded southward* along the top of the
wall to the Dung Gate. 32 Hoshaiah and half the leaders
of Judah followed them, 33 along with Azariah, Ezra,
Meshullam, 34 Judah, Benjamin, Shemaiah, and Jeremiah. 35 Then came some priests who played trumpets,
including Zechariah son of Jonathan, son of Shemaiah,

Neh 12:3 Hebrew *Rehum;* compare 7:42; 12:15; Ezra 2:39. **Neh 12:4** As in some Hebrew manuscripts and Latin Vulgate (see also 12:16); most Hebrew manuscripts read *Ginnethoi.* **Neh 12:5** Hebrew *Mijamin, Maadiah;* compare 12:17. **Neh 12:11** Hebrew *Jonathan;* compare 12:22. **Neh 12:14a** As in Greek version (see also 10:4; 12:2); Hebrew reads *Malluchi.* **Neh 12:14b** As in many Hebrew manuscripts, some Greek manuscripts, and Syriac version (see also 12:3); most Hebrew manuscripts read *Shebaniah.* **Neh 12:15** As in some Greek manuscripts (see also 12:3); Hebrew reads *Meraioth.* **Neh 12:17** Hebrew lacks the name of this family leader. **Neh 12:20** Hebrew *Sallai;* compare 12:7. **Neh 12:22** *Darius the Persian* is probably Darius II, who reigned 423–404 B.C., or possibly Darius III, who reigned 336–331 B.C. **Neh 12:23** Hebrew *descendant;* compare 12:10-11. **Neh 12:24** Hebrew *son of* (i.e., *ben*), which should probably be read here as the proper name Binnui; compare Ezra 3:9 and the note there. **Neh 12:26** Hebrew *Jozadak*, a variant spelling of Jehozadak. **Neh 12:31** Hebrew *to the right.*

Babylon and given back to the Israelites by Cyrus when they returned to their land (Ezra 1:7-11).

Neh 12:35-36 The trumpet that earlier was a tool to rally the workers against a potential threat (Neh 4:18) now became one of the instruments used to celebrate the completion of a task, the rededication of the people, and praise to God. Not only had he written powerful psalms, King David also had instituted music as part of worship in the Temple. Although Nebuchadnezzar had destroyed the Temple, he couldn't destroy worship or the music that served that purpose so well. The reconstruction of the Temple and the walls signaled the worship band to start playing again with gusto!

▸ **NEHEMIAH 12:27-43** ***(cont.)***

son of Mattaniah, son of Micaiah, son of Zaccur, a descendant of Asaph. 36 And Zechariah's colleagues were Shemaiah, Azarel, Milalai, Gilalai, Maai, Nethanel, Judah, and Hanani. They used the musical instruments prescribed by David, the man of God. Ezra the scribe led this procession. 37 At the Fountain Gate they went straight up the steps on the ascent of the city wall toward the City of David. They passed the house of David and then proceeded to the Water Gate on the east.

38 The second choir giving thanks went northward* around the other way to meet them. I followed them, together with the other half of the people, along the top of the wall past the Tower of the Ovens to the Broad Wall, 39 then past the Ephraim Gate to the Old City Gate,* past the Fish Gate and the Tower of Hananel, and on to the Tower of the Hundred. Then we continued on to the Sheep Gate and stopped at the Guard Gate.

40 The two choirs that were giving thanks then proceeded to the Temple of God, where they took their places. So did I, together with the group of leaders who were with me. 41 We went together with the trumpet-playing priests—Eliakim, Maaseiah, Miniamin, Micaiah, Elioenai, Zechariah, and Hananiah—42 and the singers—Maaseiah, Shemaiah, Eleazar, Uzzi, Jehohanan, Malkijah, Elam, and Ezer. They played and sang loudly under the direction of Jezrahiah the choir director.

43 Many sacrifices were offered on that joyous day, for God had given the people cause for great joy. The women and children also participated in the celebration, and the joy of the people of Jerusalem could be heard far away.

Provisions for Temple Worship

NEHEMIAH 12:44-47

On that day men were appointed to be in charge of the storerooms for the offerings, the first part of the harvest, and the tithes. They were responsible to collect from the fields outside the towns the portions required by the Law for the priests and Levites. For all the people of Judah took joy in the priests and Levites and their work. 45 They performed the service of their God and the service of purification, as commanded by David and his son Solomon, and so did the singers and the gatekeepers. 46 The custom of having choir directors to lead the choirs in hymns of praise and thanksgiving to God began long ago in the days of David and Asaph. 47 So now, in the days of Zerubbabel and of Nehemiah, all Israel brought a daily supply of food for the singers, the gatekeepers, and the Levites. The Levites, in turn, gave a portion of what they received to the priests, the descendants of Aaron.

Nehemiah's Various Reforms

NEHEMIAH 13:1-31

On that same day, as the Book of Moses was being read to the people, the passage was found that said no Ammonite or Moabite should ever be permitted to enter the assembly of God.* 2 For they had not provided the Israelites with food and water in the wilderness. Instead, they hired Balaam to curse them, though our God turned the curse into a blessing. 3 When this passage of the Law was read, all those of foreign descent were immediately excluded from the assembly.

4 Before this had happened, Eliashib the priest, who had been appointed as supervisor of the storerooms of the Temple of our God and who was also a relative of Tobiah, 5 had converted a large storage room and placed it at Tobiah's disposal. The room had previously been used for storing the grain offerings, the frankincense, various articles for the Temple, and the tithes of grain, new wine, and olive oil (which were prescribed for the Levites, the singers, and the gatekeepers), as well as the offerings for the priests.

6 I was not in Jerusalem at that time, for I had returned to King Artaxerxes of Babylon in the thirty-second year of his reign,* though I later asked his permission to return. 7 When I arrived back in Jerusalem, I learned about Eliashib's evil deed in providing

Neh 12:38 Hebrew *to the left.* **Neh 12:39** Or *the Mishneh Gate,* or *the Jeshanah Gate.* **Neh 13:1** See Deut 23:3-6. **Neh 13:6** King Artaxerxes of Persia is here identified as the king of Babylon because Persia had conquered the Babylonian Empire. The thirty-second year of Artaxerxes was 433 B.C.

Neh 12:44 Further arrangements were made for supporting those who served at the Temple. The storerooms were administered by men who made sure the tithes and contributions were collected and distributed appropriately. These storerooms had to be large to hold all the grain presented by the people. This storeroom administration was an important responsibility.

Neh 12:44-47 The dedication of the city wall was characterized by joy, praise, and singing (Neh 12:24, 27-29, 35-36, 40-43). Nehemiah repeatedly mentioned David, who began the custom of using choirs in worship. In David's day, Israel was a vigorous, God-fearing nation. These exiles who had returned wanted their rebuilt Jerusalem to be the hub of a renewed nation, strengthened by God; therefore, they dedicated themselves and their city to God.

Neh 13:3 "Those of foreign descent" refers to the Ammonites and Moabites, two nations who were bitter enemies of Israel (Neh 13:1). God's law clearly stated that these two peoples should never be allowed in the Temple (Deut 23:3-5). This had nothing to do with racial prejudice because God clearly loved all people, including foreigners (Deut 10:18). He allowed foreigners to make sacrifices (Num 15:15-16), and he desires all nations to know and love him (Isa 42:6). But while God wants all to come to him, he warns believers to stay away from those bent on evil (Prov 24:1). In their celebration and rededication, they had to show they were serious about following God's law.

Neh 13:6-7 Nehemiah had to return to Babylon in 433 B.C., 12 years after he had arrived in Jerusalem. Either he was recalled by Artaxerxes, or he was fulfilling an agreement to return. It is not known exactly how long he remained in Babylon, but when he returned to Jerusalem (Neh 13:7), he found that one of his major opponents in rebuilding the wall, Tobiah, had been given his own room at the Temple. He was an Ammonite (Neh 4:3) and thus forbidden to enter the Temple. Eliashib the priest had married Tobiah's daughter, so Tobiah used his influence with his son-in-law to get this special room. Nehemiah 2, 4, and 6 tell about Tobiah's opposition to Nehemiah and Nehemiah's appropriate action.

Tobiah with a room in the courtyards of the Temple of God. [8]I became very upset and threw all of Tobiah's belongings out of the room. [9]Then I demanded that the rooms be purified, and I brought back the articles for God's Temple, the grain offerings, and the frankincense.

[10]I also discovered that the Levites had not been given their prescribed portions of food, so they and the singers who were to conduct the worship services had all returned to work their fields. [11]I immediately confronted the leaders and demanded, "Why has the Temple of God been neglected?" Then I called all the Levites back again and restored them to their proper duties. [12]And once more all the people of Judah began bringing their tithes of grain, new wine, and olive oil to the Temple storerooms.

[13]I assigned supervisors for the storerooms: Shelemiah the priest, Zadok the scribe, and Pedaiah, one of the Levites. And I appointed Hanan son of Zaccur and grandson of Mattaniah as their assistant. These men had an excellent reputation, and it was their job to make honest distributions to their fellow Levites.

[14]Remember this good deed, O my God, and do
not forget all that I have faithfully done for the
Temple of my God and its services.

[15]In those days I saw men of Judah treading out their winepresses on the Sabbath. They were also bringing in grain, loading it on donkeys, and bringing their wine, grapes, figs, and all sorts of produce to Jerusalem to sell on the Sabbath. So I rebuked them for selling their produce on that day. [16]Some men from Tyre, who lived in Jerusalem, were bringing in fish and all kinds of merchandise. They were selling it on the Sabbath to the people of Judah—and in Jerusalem at that!

[17]So I confronted the nobles of Judah. "Why are you profaning the Sabbath in this evil way?" I asked. [18]"Wasn't it just this sort of thing that your ancestors did that caused our God to bring all this trouble upon us and our city? Now you are bringing even more wrath upon Israel by permitting the Sabbath to be desecrated in this way!"

[19]Then I commanded that the gates of Jerusalem should be shut as darkness fell every Friday evening,* not to be opened until the Sabbath ended. I sent some of my own servants to guard the gates so that no merchandise could be brought in on the Sabbath day. [20]The merchants and tradesmen with a variety of wares camped outside Jerusalem once or twice. [21]But I spoke sharply to them and said, "What are you doing out here, camping around the wall? If you do this again, I will arrest you!" And that was the last time they came on the Sabbath. [22]Then I commanded the Levites to purify themselves and to guard the gates in order to preserve the holiness of the Sabbath.

Remember this good deed also, O my God! Have
compassion on me according to your great and
unfailing love.

[23]About the same time I realized that some of the men of Judah had married women from Ashdod, Ammon, and Moab. [24]Furthermore, half their children spoke the language of Ashdod or of some other people and could not speak the language of Judah at all. [25]So I confronted them and called down curses on them. I beat some of them and pulled out their hair. I made them swear in the name of God that they would not let their children intermarry with the pagan people of the land.

[26]"Wasn't this exactly what led King Solomon of Israel into sin?" I demanded. "There was no king from any nation who could compare to him, and God loved him and made him king over all Israel. But even he was led into sin by his foreign wives. [27]How could you even think of committing this sinful deed and acting unfaithfully toward God by marrying foreign women?"

[28]One of the sons of Joiada son of Eliashib the high

Neh 13:19 Hebrew *on the day before the Sabbath.*

Neh 13:10 Because the Levites were no longer supported, they had returned to their farms to support themselves, neglecting their Temple duties and the spiritual welfare of the people. Spiritual workers deserve their pay, and their support ought to be enough to care for their needs. They shouldn't have to suffer (or leave) because believers don't adequately assess and meet their needs.

Neh 13:16 Tyre was a large Phoenician city and port on the Mediterranean Sea.

Neh 13:17 God had commanded Israel not to work on the Sabbath, but to rest in remembrance of Creation and the Exodus (Exod 20:8-11; Deut 5:12-15). The Sabbath rest, lasting from sunset Friday to sunset Saturday, was to be honored and observed by all Jews, servants, visiting foreigners, and even farm animals. Jerusalem's busy Sabbath trade directly violated God's law, so Nehemiah commanded that the city gates be shut and traders be sent home every Friday afternoon as the Sabbath hours approached.

Neh 13:24 Ashdod was on the Mediterranean coast, in the region controlled by the Philistines. Ammon and Moab were across the Jordan to the east. These nations were abhorrent to those who knew Israel's history.

Neh 13:25 Nehemiah was filled with righteous indignation at the blatant way the Jews were breaking God's laws and disregarding the covenant they had previously reaffirmed (Neh 10:30). The people had promised not to allow their children to marry pagans. But during Nehemiah's absence, the people had been intermarrying, breaking their solemn promise with God. Nehemiah's severe treatment of these people shows the contrast between his great faithfulness to God and the people's neglect, disobedience, and disloyalty (see also Ezra 10:3).

Neh 13:26 Nehemiah used the example of Solomon's mistakes to teach his people. If one of the greatest kings of Israel fell because of the influence of unbelievers, others could too. Nehemiah saw this principle in Solomon's example: Your gifts and strengths won't be of much benefit if you fail to deal with your weaknesses. A tendency to sin must be recognized and dealt with swiftly; otherwise, it may overpower you and bring you down. One excellent reason for reading the Bible is to learn from the mistakes of God's people.

▸ **NEHEMIAH 13:1-31** ***(cont.)***

priest had married a daughter of Sanballat the Horonite, so I banished him from my presence.

29Remember them, O my God, for they have
defiled the priesthood and the solemn vows of
the priests and Levites.

30So I purged out everything foreign and assigned
tasks to the priests and Levites, making certain that
each knew his work. 31I also made sure that the supply of wood for the altar and the first portions of the
harvest were brought at the proper times.

Remember this in my favor, O my God.

F. The Genealogies of Israel

These genealogies are the official family records of the nation of Israel. They give us an overview of the history of God's work from Creation through the captivity of his people. These records served to teach the exiles returning from Babylon about their spiritual heritage as a nation and to inspire them to renew their faithfulness to God. Although these lists show the racial heritage of the Jews, they contain the spiritual heritage for every believer. We are a part of the community of faith that has existed from generation to generation since the dawn of man.

1. ANCESTRY OF THE NATION

The first section of this genealogy traces the origin of Israel all the way from Adam through Abraham. It then traces the royal lines of two nations: Edom, descended from Isaac's son Esau, and Israel, descended from Isaac's son Jacob. Israel had a great heritage to be celebrated and remembered as they returned from exile. Perhaps a reminder of their past would also help the returning Jews from repeating the mistakes of their ancestors.

From Adam to Noah's Sons

1 CHRONICLES 1:1-4

The descendants of Adam were Seth, Enosh, 2Kenan,
Mahalalel, Jared, 3Enoch, Methuselah, Lamech,
4and Noah.
The sons of Noah were* Shem, Ham, and Japheth.

1 Chr 1:4 As in Greek version (see also Gen 5:3-32); Hebrew lacks *The sons of Noah were.*

Descendants of Japheth

1 CHRONICLES 1:5-7

5The descendants of Japheth were Gomer, Magog,
Madai, Javan, Tubal, Meshech, and Tiras.
6The descendants of Gomer were Ashkenaz,
Riphath,* and Togarmah.

1 Chr 1:6 As in some Hebrew manuscripts and Greek version (see also Gen 10:3); most Hebrew manuscripts read *Diphath.*

Neh 13:31 "Remember this in my favor" means "look favorably upon me for all that I have done."

Neh 13:31 Nehemiah's life story provides many principles of effective leadership that are still valid today: (1) Have a clear purpose and keep evaluating it in light of God's will. Nothing prevented Nehemiah from staying on track. (2) Be straightforward and honest. Everyone knew exactly what Nehemiah needed, and he spoke the truth even when it made his goal harder to achieve. (3) Live above reproach. The accusations against Nehemiah were empty and false. (4) Be a person of constant prayer, deriving power and wisdom from your contact with God. Everything Nehemiah did glorified God.

Leadership appears glamorous at times, but it is often lonely, thankless, and filled with pressures to compromise values and standards. Nehemiah was able to accomplish a huge task against incredible odds because he learned that there is no success without risk of failure, no reward without hard work, no opportunity without criticism, and no true leadership without trust in God. This book is about rebuilding the wall of a great city, but it is also about spiritual renewal, rebuilding a people's dependence on God. When we take our eyes off God, our lives begin to crumble.

1 Chr 1:1 This record of names demonstrates that God is interested not only in nations but also in individuals. Although billions of people have lived since Adam, God knows and remembers the face and name of each person. Each of us is more than a name on a list; we are special persons whom God knows and loves. As we recognize and accept his love, we discover both our uniqueness as individuals and our solidarity with the rest of his family.

1 Chr 1:1ff This long list of names was compiled after the people of Judah, the southern kingdom, were taken captive to Babylon. As the exiles looked forward to the day when they would return to their homeland, one of their biggest fears was that the records of their heritage would be lost. The Jews placed great importance upon their heritage because they wanted to be able to prove that they were descendants of Abraham, the father of the Jewish people. Only then could a person enjoy the benefits of the special blessings God promised to Abraham and his descendants (see the notes on Gen 12:1-3, p. 30, and Gen 17:2-8, p. 37, about these special blessings).

This list reconstructed the family tree for both Judah, the southern kingdom, and Israel, the northern kingdom, before their captivities and served as proof for those who claimed to be Abraham's descendants. (For more information about why the Bible includes genealogies, read the notes on Gen 5:1ff, p. 16; Matt 1:1, p. 1278; Luke 3:23-38, p. 1279.)

1 Chr 1:1ff There is more to this long genealogy than meets the eye. It holds importance for us today because it supports the Old Testament promise that Jesus the Messiah would be a descendant of Abraham and David. This promise is recorded in Genesis 12:1-3; 2 Samuel 7:12-13.

1 Chr 1:1, 4 Adam's story is found in Genesis 1–5. See his Profile on p. 8. Noah's story is found in Genesis 6–9. See his Profile on p. 19.

1 Chr 1:5-9 A biblical genealogy may skip several generations. These lists were not meant to be exhaustive but rather to give adequate information about the various family lines.

1 Chr 1:10 Nimrod is also mentioned in Genesis 10:8-9.

[7]The descendants of Javan were Elishah, Tarshish, Kittim, and Rodanim.

Descendants of Ham

1 CHRONICLES 1:8-16

[8]The descendants of Ham were Cush, Mizraim,* Put, and Canaan.
[9]The descendants of Cush were Seba, Havilah,
Sabtah, Raamah, and Sabteca. The descendants of
Raamah were Sheba and Dedan. [10]Cush was also
the ancestor of Nimrod, who was the first heroic
warrior on earth.
[11]Mizraim was the ancestor of the Ludites,
Anamites, Lehabites, Naphtuhites, [12]Pathrusites,
Casluhites, and the Caphtorites, from whom the
Philistines came.*

1 Chr 1:8 Or *Egypt;* also in 1:11. **1 Chr 1:12** Hebrew *Casluhites, from whom the Philistines came, Caphtorites.* See Jer 47:4; Amos 9:7.

1 Chr 1:11-12 The Philistines had been Israel's constant enemy from the days of the judges. King David finally weakened them, and by this time they were no longer a threat. (For more information on the Philistines, see the notes on Judg 13:1, p. 396; 1 Sam 4:1, p. 423.)

WHO'S WHO IN THE BIBLE

The writer of Chronicles reproduced a thorough history of Israel in one list of people (1 Chr 1–8). Some listed in this genealogy are also mentioned elsewhere. Many have exciting stories that can be traced through the Bible. Look up some of the names here that intrigue you. You may be surprised at what you discover!

Name	*Key Life Lesson*	*Other References*
Adam (1 Chr 1:1)	Our sins have far greater implications than we realize.	Gen 1:26–3:24
Noah (1 Chr 1:4)	Great rewards come from obeying God.	Gen 6–9
Abraham (1 Chr 1:27)	Faith alone makes one right in God's eyes.	Gen 11:26–25:10
Isaac (1 Chr 1:28)	Seeking peace brings true respect.	Gen 21–35
Esau (1 Chr 1:35)	It is never too late to put away bitterness and forgive.	Gen 25:20–36:43
Amalek (1 Chr 1:36)	There are evil men and nations who seek to harm God's people.	Exod 17:8-16
Israel (Jacob) (1 Chr 2:1)	While our sins may haunt us, God will honor our faith.	Gen 25:20–50:13
Judah (1 Chr 2:3)	God can change the hearts of even the most wicked people.	Gen 37–50
Tamar (1 Chr 2:4)	God works his purposes even through sinful events.	Gen 38
Perez (1 Chr 2:5)	Your background does not matter to God.	Gen 38:27-30
Boaz (1 Chr 2:12)	Those who are kind to others will receive kindness themselves.	The book of Ruth
Jesse (1 Chr 2:13)	Never take lightly the impact you may have on your children.	1 Sam 16
David (1 Chr 2:15)	True greatness is having a heart for God.	1–2 Sam; 1 Kgs 1–2
Joab (1 Chr 2:16)	Those who seek power die with nothing.	2 Sam 2:13—1 Kgs 2:34
Amnon (1 Chr 3:1)	Giving in to lust leads only to tragedy.	2 Sam 13
Absalom (1 Chr 3:2)	Those seeking to oust a God-appointed leader will have a difficult battle.	2 Sam 13–18
Adonijah (1 Chr 3:2)	God must determine what is rightfully ours.	1 Kgs 1–2
Bathsheba (1 Chr 3:5)	One wrong act does not disqualify us from accomplishing things for God.	2 Sam 11–12; 1 Kgs 1–2
Solomon (1 Chr 3:5)	Human wisdom is foolishness without God.	1 Kgs 1–11
Reuben (1 Chr 5:1)	What is gained from a moment of passion is only perceived; what is lost is real and permanent.	Gen 35:22; 37; 49:3-4
Aaron (1 Chr 6:3)	Don't expect God's leaders to be perfect, but don't let them get away with sin either.	Exod 4—Num 20
Nadab (1 Chr 6:3)	Pretending to be God's representative is dangerous business.	Lev 10
Eleazar (1 Chr 6:3)	Those who are consistent in their faith are the best models to follow.	Num 20:25-29; 26–34; Josh 24:33
Korah (1 Chr 6:22)	Rebelling against God's leaders is rebelling against God and will always be unsuccessful.	Num 16
Joshua (1 Chr 7:27)	Real courage comes from God.	The book of Joshua
Saul (1 Chr 8:33)	Those who say they follow God but don't live like it waste their God-given potential.	1 Sam 8–31
Jonathan (1 Chr 8:33)	True friends always think of the other person, not just themselves.	1 Sam 14–31

▸ 1 CHRONICLES 1:8-16 *(cont.)*

13 Canaan's oldest son was Sidon, the ancestor of
the Sidonians. Canaan was also the ancestor of
the Hittites,* 14 Jebusites, Amorites, Girgashites,
15 Hivites, Arkites, Sinites, 16 Arvadites, Zemarites,
and Hamathites.

Descendants of Shem

1 CHRONICLES 1:17-27

17 The descendants of Shem were Elam, Asshur,
Arphaxad, Lud, and Aram.
The descendants of Aram were* Uz, Hul, Gether,
and Mash.*
18 Arphaxad was the father of Shelah.
Shelah was the father of Eber.
19 Eber had two sons. The first was named Peleg
(which means "division"), for during his lifetime
the people of the world were divided into different
language groups. His brother's name was Joktan.
20 Joktan was the ancestor of Almodad, Sheleph,
Hazarmaveth, Jerah, 21 Hadoram, Uzal, Diklah,
22 Obal,* Abimael, Sheba, 23 Ophir, Havilah, and
Jobab. All these were descendants of Joktan.
24 So this is the family line descended from Shem:
Arphaxad, Shelah,* 25 Eber, Peleg, Reu, 26 Serug,
Nahor, Terah, 27 and Abram, later known as
Abraham.

Descendants of Abraham

1 CHRONICLES 1:28-33

28 The sons of Abraham were Isaac and Ishmael.
29 These are their genealogical records:
The sons of Ishmael were Nebaioth (the oldest),
Kedar, Adbeel, Mibsam, 30 Mishma, Dumah,
Massa, Hadad, Tema, 31 Jetur, Naphish, and
Kedemah. These were the sons of Ishmael.

32 The sons of Keturah, Abraham's concubine, were
Zimran, Jokshan, Medan, Midian, Ishbak, and
Shuah.
The sons of Jokshan were Sheba and Dedan.
33 The sons of Midian were Ephah, Epher, Hanoch,
Abida, and Eldaah.
All these were descendants of Abraham through his
concubine Keturah.

Descendants of Isaac

1 CHRONICLES 1:34

34 Abraham was the father of Isaac. The sons
of Isaac were Esau and Israel.*

Descendants of Esau

1 CHRONICLES 1:35-37

35 The sons of Esau were Eliphaz, Reuel, Jeush,
Jalam, and Korah.
36 The descendants of Eliphaz were Teman, Omar,
Zepho,* Gatam, Kenaz, and Amalek, who was
born to Timna.*
37 The descendants of Reuel were Nahath, Zerah,
Shammah, and Mizzah.

Original Peoples of Edom

1 CHRONICLES 1:38-42

38 The descendants of Seir were Lotan,
Shobal, Zibeon, Anah, Dishon, Ezer, and
Dishan.
39 The descendants of Lotan were Hori and
Hemam.* Lotan's sister was named Timna.
40 The descendants of Shobal were Alvan,*
Manahath, Ebal, Shepho,* and Onam.
The descendants of Zibeon were Aiah and
Anah.
41 The son of Anah was Dishon.
The descendants of Dishon were Hemdan,*
Eshban, Ithran, and Keran.
42 The descendants of Ezer were Bilhan, Zaavan,
and Akan.*
The descendants of Dishan* were Uz and Aran.

1 Chr 1:13 Hebrew *ancestor of Heth.* **1 Chr 1:17a** As in one Hebrew manuscript and some Greek manuscripts (see also Gen 10:23); most Hebrew manuscripts lack *The descendants of Aram were.* **1 Chr 1:17b** As in parallel text at Gen 10:23; Hebrew reads *and Meshech.* **1 Chr 1:22** As in some Hebrew manuscripts and Syriac version (see also Gen 10:28); most Hebrew manuscripts read *Ebal.* **1 Chr 1:24** Some Greek manuscripts read *Arphaxad, Cainan, Shelah.* See notes on Gen 10:24; 11:12-13. **1 Chr 1:34** *Israel* is the name that God gave to Jacob. **1 Chr 1:36a** As in many Hebrew manuscripts and a few Greek manuscripts (see also Gen 36:11); most Hebrew manuscripts read *Zephi.* **1 Chr 1:36b** As in some Greek manuscripts (see also Gen 36:12); Hebrew reads *Kenaz, Timna, and Amalek.* **1 Chr 1:39** As in parallel text at Gen 36:22; Hebrew reads *and Homam.* **1 Chr 1:40a** As in many Hebrew manuscripts and a few Greek manuscripts (see also Gen 36:23); most Hebrew manuscripts read *Alian.* **1 Chr 1:40b** As in some Hebrew manuscripts (see also Gen 36:23); most Hebrew manuscripts read *Shephi.* **1 Chr 1:41** As in many Hebrew manuscripts and some Greek manuscripts (see also Gen 36:26); most Hebrew manuscripts read *Hamran.* **1 Chr 1:42a** As in many Hebrew and Greek manuscripts (see also Gen 36:27); most Hebrew manuscripts read *Jaakan.* **1 Chr 1:42b** Hebrew *Dishon;* compare 1:38 and parallel text at Gen 36:28.

---

1 Chr 1:13-16 Canaan was the ancestor of the Canaanites, who inhabited the Promised Land (also called Canaan) before the Israelites entered under Joshua's leadership. God helped the Israelites drive out the Canaanites, a wicked and idolatrous people. The land's name was then changed to Israel. The book of Joshua tells that story.

1 Chr 1:19 At one time, everyone spoke a single language. But some people became proud of their accomplishments and gathered to build a monument to themselves—the tower of Babel. The building project was brought to an abrupt conclusion when God caused the people to speak different languages. Without the ability to communicate with one another, the people could not be unified. God showed them that their great efforts were useless without him. Pride in our achievements must not lead us to conclude that we no longer need God. Genesis 11:1-9 tells this story.

1 Chr 1:24-27 Abraham's story is found in Genesis 11:26–25:10. See his Profile on p. 31.

1 Chr 1:28-31 Ishmael's story is found in Genesis 16; 21. See his Profile on p. 37.

1 Chr 1:34 Israel is another name for Jacob, which God gave to him (Gen 32:28). It means "someone who struggles with God." Israel's (Jacob's) 12 sons became the nation of Israel. Esau's descendants became the nation of Edom, a constant enemy of Israel. To learn more about the lives of Isaac and his two sons, Jacob and Esau, read their stories in Genesis 21–36, 46–49. See also their Profiles: Isaac, p. 44, Esau, p. 52, Jacob, p. 55.

Rulers of Edom

1 CHRONICLES 1:43-54

These are the kings who ruled in the land of Edom before any king ruled over the Israelites*:

Bela son of Beor, who ruled from his city of
Dinhabah.
44 When Bela died, Jobab son of Zerah from Bozrah
became king in his place.
45 When Jobab died, Husham from the land of the
Temanites became king in his place.
46 When Husham died, Hadad son of Bedad became
king in his place and ruled from the city of Avith.
He was the one who destroyed the Midianite
army in the land of Moab.
47 When Hadad died, Samlah from the city of
Masrekah became king in his place.
48 When Samlah died, Shaul from the city of
Rehoboth-on-the-River became king in his place.
49 When Shaul died, Baal-hanan son of Acbor
became king in his place.
50 When Baal-hanan died, Hadad became king in
his place and ruled from the city of Pau.* His
wife was Mehetabel, the daughter of Matred and
granddaughter of Me-zahab. 51 Then Hadad died.

The clan leaders of Edom were Timna, Alvah,*
Jetheth, 52 Oholibamah, Elah, Pinon, 53 Kenaz,
Teman, Mibzar, 54 Magdiel, and Iram. These are
the clan leaders of Edom.

Descendants of Israel

1 CHRONICLES 2:1-2

1 The sons of Israel* were Reuben, Simeon, Levi,
Judah, Issachar, Zebulun, 2 Dan, Joseph, Benjamin,
Naphtali, Gad, and Asher.

Descendants of Judah

1 CHRONICLES 2:3-8

3 Judah had three sons from Bathshua, a Canaanite
woman. Their names were Er, Onan, and Shelah.
But the LORD saw that the oldest son, Er, was
a wicked man, so he killed him. 4 Later Judah
had twin sons from Tamar, his widowed daughter-
in-law. Their names were Perez and Zerah. So
Judah had five sons in all.
5 The sons of Perez were Hezron and Hamul.
6 The sons of Zerah were Zimri, Ethan, Heman,
Calcol, and Darda*—five in all.
7 The son of Carmi (a descendant of Zimri) was
Achan,* who brought disaster on Israel by
taking plunder that had been set apart for
the LORD.*
8 The son of Ethan was Azariah.

From Judah's Grandson Hezron to David

1 CHRONICLES 2:9-17

9 The sons of Hezron were Jerahmeel, Ram, and
Caleb.*
10 Ram was the father of Amminadab.
Amminadab was the father of Nahshon, a leader
of Judah.
11 Nahshon was the father of Salmon.*
Salmon was the father of Boaz.
12 Boaz was the father of Obed.
Obed was the father of Jesse.
13 Jesse's first son was Eliab, his second was
Abinadab, his third was Shimea, 14 his fourth
was Nethanel, his fifth was Raddai, 15 his
sixth was Ozem, and his seventh was
David.

1 Chr 1:43 Or *before an Israelite king ruled over them.* **1 Chr 1:50** As in many Hebrew manuscripts, some Greek manuscripts, Syriac version, and Latin Vulgate (see also Gen 36:39); most Hebrew manuscripts read *Pai.* **1 Chr 1:51** As in parallel text at Gen 36:40; Hebrew reads *Aliah.* **1 Chr 2:1** *Israel* is the name that God gave to Jacob. **1 Chr 2:6** As in many Hebrew manuscripts, some Greek manuscripts, and Syriac version (see also 1 Kgs 4:31); Hebrew reads *Dara.* **1 Chr 2:7a** Hebrew *Achar;* compare Josh 7:1. *Achar* means "disaster." **1 Chr 2:7b** The Hebrew term used here refers to the complete consecration of things or people to the LORD, either by destroying them or by giving them as an offering. **1 Chr 2:9** Hebrew *Kelubai,* a variant spelling of Caleb; compare 2:18. **1 Chr 2:11** As in Greek version (see also Ruth 4:20); Hebrew reads *Salma.*

---

1 Chr 1:36 Amalek, Esau's grandson, was the son of his father's concubine (Gen 36:12). He was the ancestor of the wicked tribe known as the Amalekites, the first people to attack the Israelites on their way to the Promised Land. (For more about the Amalekites, read the note on Exod 17:8, p. 165.)

1 Chr 1:43-54 Why are we given information in this genealogy about the descendants of Edom, who were Israel's enemies? Esau, ancestor of the Edomites, was Isaac's oldest son and thus a direct descendant of Abraham. As Abraham's first grandson, he deserved a place in the Jewish records. It was through Esau's marriages to pagan women that the nation of Edom began. This genealogy shows the ancestry of enemy nations; they were not a part of the direct lineage of King David, and thus of the Messiah. This listing further identified Israel's special identity and role.

1 Chr 2:1-2 The story of Israel's (Jacob's) sons is found in Genesis 29:32–50:26. See also the Profiles of Joseph, p. 71, Reuben, p. 73, and Judah, p. 85.

1 Chr 2:3 This long genealogy not only lists names but gives us insights into some of the people. Here, almost as an epitaph, the genealogy states that Er "was a wicked man," so the Lord killed him. Now, thousands of years later, this is all we know of the man. Each of us is forging a reputation, developing personal qualities by which we will be remembered. How would God summarize your life up to now? Some defiantly claim that how they live is their own business. But Scripture teaches that the way you live today will determine how you will be remembered by others and how you will be judged by God. What you do now *does* matter.

1 Chr 2:7 Achan took plunder in direct disobedience to God's instructions following the destruction of Jericho. His greed led to the defeat of Israel at Ai and the death of Achan and his entire family (see Josh 7).

1 Chr 2:12 Boaz was Ruth's husband and an ancestor of both David and Jesus. Boaz's story is found in the book of Ruth. See his Profile on p. 42.

1 Chr 2:15 David is one of the best-known people of the Bible. He was certainly not perfect, but he exemplified what it means to seek God first in all areas of life. God called David "a man after my own heart" (Acts 13:22) because David's greatest desire was to serve and worship God. We can please God in the same way by making God our first consideration in all our desires and plans. David's story is found in 1 Samuel 16:1—1 Kings 2:10; 1 Chronicles 10:14–29:30. David's Profile is on p. 485.

▶ **1 CHRONICLES 2:9-17** ***(cont.)***

16Their sisters were named Zeruiah and
Abigail. Zeruiah had three sons named Abishai,
Joab, and Asahel. 17Abigail married a man named
Jether, an Ishmaelite, and they had a son named
Amasa.

Other Descendants of Hezron

1 CHRONICLES 2:18-24

18Hezron's son Caleb had sons from his wife Azubah
and from Jerioth.* Her sons were named Jesher,
Shobab, and Ardon. 19After Azubah died, Caleb
married Ephrathah,* and they had a son named
Hur. 20Hur was the father of Uri. Uri was the father
of Bezalel.
21When Hezron was sixty years old, he married
Gilead's sister, the daughter of Makir. They had
a son named Segub. 22Segub was the father of
Jair, who ruled twenty-three towns in the land
of Gilead. 23(But Geshur and Aram captured the
Towns of Jair* and also took Kenath and its sixty
surrounding villages.) All these were descendants
of Makir, the father of Gilead.
24Soon after Hezron died in the town of Caleb-
ephrathah, his wife Abijah gave birth to a son
named Ashhur (the father of* Tekoa).

Descendants of Hezron's Son Jerahmeel

1 CHRONICLES 2:25-41

25The sons of Jerahmeel, the oldest son of Hezron,
were Ram (the firstborn), Bunah, Oren, Ozem, and
Ahijah. 26Jerahmeel had a second wife named
Atarah. She was the mother of Onam.
27The sons of Ram, the oldest son of Jerahmeel, were
Maaz, Jamin, and Eker.
28The sons of Onam were Shammai and Jada.
The sons of Shammai were Nadab and Abishur.
29The sons of Abishur and his wife Abihail were
Ahban and Molid.
30The sons of Nadab were Seled and Appaim. Seled
died without children, 31but Appaim had a son
named Ishi. The son of Ishi was Sheshan. Sheshan
had a descendant named Ahlai.
32The sons of Jada, Shammai's brother, were Jether
and Jonathan. Jether died without children, 33but
Jonathan had two sons named Peleth and Zaza.
These were all descendants of Jerahmeel.
34Sheshan had no sons, though he did have
daughters. He also had an Egyptian servant named
Jarha. 35Sheshan gave one of his daughters to be
the wife of Jarha, and they had a son named Attai.
36 Attai was the father of Nathan.
Nathan was the father of Zabad.
37 Zabad was the father of Ephlal.
Ephlal was the father of Obed.
38 Obed was the father of Jehu.
Jehu was the father of Azariah.
39 Azariah was the father of Helez.
Helez was the father of Eleasah.
40 Eleasah was the father of Sismai.
Sismai was the father of Shallum.
41 Shallum was the father of Jekamiah.
Jekamiah was the father of Elishama.

Descendants of Hezron's Son Caleb

1 CHRONICLES 2:42-50a

42The descendants of Caleb, the brother of
Jerahmeel, included Mesha (the firstborn), who
became the father of Ziph. Caleb's descendants
also included the sons of Mareshah, the father of
Hebron.*
43The sons of Hebron were Korah, Tappuah,
Rekem, and Shema. 44Shema was the father
of Raham. Raham was the father of Jorkeam.
Rekem was the father of Shammai. 45The son
of Shammai was Maon. Maon was the father
of Beth-zur.
46Caleb's concubine Ephah gave birth to Haran,
Moza, and Gazez. Haran was the father of Gazez.
47The sons of Jahdai were Regem, Jotham, Geshan,
Pelet, Ephah, and Shaaph.
48Another of Caleb's concubines, Maacah, gave birth
to Sheber and Tirhanah. 49She also gave birth to
Shaaph (the father of Madmannah) and Sheva
(the father of Macbenah and Gibea). Caleb also
had a daughter named Acsah.
50These were all descendants of Caleb.

Descendants of Caleb's Son Hur

1 CHRONICLES 2:50b-55

The sons of Hur, the oldest son of Caleb's wife
Ephrathah, were Shobal (the founder of Kiriath-
jearim), 51Salma (the founder of Bethlehem),
and Hareph (the founder of Beth-gader).
52The descendants of Shobal (the founder
of Kiriath-jearim) were Haroeh, half the
Manahathites, 53and the families of Kiriath-
jearim—the Ithrites, Puthites, Shumathites,
and Mishraites, from whom came the people
of Zorah and Eshtaol.
54The descendants of Salma were the people of
Bethlehem, the Netophathites, Atroth-beth-joab,

1 Chr 2:18 Or *Caleb had a daughter named Jerioth from his wife, Azubah.* The meaning of the Hebrew is uncertain. **1 Chr 2:19** Hebrew *Ephrath,* a variant spelling of Ephrathah; compare 2:50 and 4:4. **1 Chr 2:23** Or *captured Havvoth-jair.* **1 Chr 2:24** Or *the founder of;* also in 2:42, 45, 49. **1 Chr 2:42** Or *who founded Hebron.* The meaning of the Hebrew is uncertain.

---

1 Chr 2:16 Joab's story is found in 2 Samuel 2–3; 10–20; 24; 1 Kings 1–2; 1 Chronicles 11:4-9; 19–21. His Profile is on p. 520. Abishai's story is found in 1 Samuel 26; 2 Samuel 2–3; 10; 15–21; 23; 1 Chronicles 18:12; 19. Abishai's Profile is on p. 525.

1 Chr 2:18 This is not the Caleb who spied out the Promised Land with Joshua. (Caleb the spy is listed in 1 Chr 4:15.)

the other half of the Manahathites, the Zorites,
55and the families of scribes living at Jabez—the
Tirathites, Shimeathites, and Sucathites. All these
were Kenites who descended from Hammath,
the father of the family of Recab.*

Descendants of David

1 CHRONICLES 3:1-9

These are the sons of David who were born in Hebron:

The oldest was Amnon, whose mother was
Ahinoam from Jezreel.
The second was Daniel, whose mother was
Abigail from Carmel.
2 The third was Absalom, whose mother was
Maacah, the daughter of Talmai, king of
Geshur.
The fourth was Adonijah, whose mother was
Haggith.
3 The fifth was Shephatiah, whose mother was
Abital.
The sixth was Ithream, whose mother was Eglah,
David's wife.
4These six sons were born to David in Hebron, where
he reigned seven and a half years.

Then David reigned another thirty-three years in
Jerusalem. 5The sons born to David in Jerusalem included Shammua,* Shobab, Nathan, and Solomon.
Their mother was Bathsheba,* the daughter of Ammiel. 6David also had nine other sons: Ibhar, Elishua,*
Elpelet,* 7Nogah, Nepheg, Japhia, 8Elishama, Eliada,
and Eliphelet.
9These were the sons of David, not including his
sons born to his concubines. Their sister was named
Tamar.

Descendants of Solomon

1 CHRONICLES 3:10-16

10The descendants of Solomon were Rehoboam,
Abijah, Asa, Jehoshaphat, 11Jehoram,* Ahaziah,
Joash, 12Amaziah, Uzziah,* Jotham, 13Ahaz,
Hezekiah, Manasseh, 14Amon, and Josiah.
15The sons of Josiah were Johanan (the oldest),
Jehoiakim (the second), Zedekiah (the third),
and Jehoahaz* (the fourth).
16The successors of Jehoiakim were his son
Jehoiachin and his brother Zedekiah.*

Descendants of Jehoiachin

1 CHRONICLES 3:17-24

17The sons of Jehoiachin,* who was taken prisoner
by the Babylonians, were Shealtiel, 18Malkiram,
Pedaiah, Shenazzar, Jekamiah, Hoshama, and
Nedabiah.
19The sons of Pedaiah were Zerubbabel and Shimei.
The sons of Zerubbabel were Meshullam and
Hananiah. (Their sister was Shelomith.) 20His
five other sons were Hashubah, Ohel, Berekiah,
Hasadiah, and Jushab-hesed.
21The sons of Hananiah were Pelatiah and Jeshaiah.
Jeshaiah's son was Rephaiah. Rephaiah's son was
Arnan. Arnan's son was Obadiah. Obadiah's son
was Shecaniah.
22The descendants of Shecaniah were Shemaiah
and his sons, Hattush, Igal, Bariah, Neariah, and
Shaphat—six in all.
23The sons of Neariah were Elioenai, Hizkiah, and
Azrikam—three in all.
24The sons of Elioenai were Hodaviah, Eliashib,
Pelaiah, Akkub, Johanan, Delaiah, and Anani—
seven in all.

1 Chr 2:55 Or *the founder of Beth-recab.* **1 Chr 3:5a** As in Syriac version (see also 14:4; 2 Sam 5:14); Hebrew reads *Shimea.* **1 Chr 3:5b** Hebrew *Bathshua,* a variant spelling of Bathsheba. **1 Chr 3:6a** As in some Hebrew and Greek manuscripts (see also 14:5-7 and 2 Sam 5:15); most Hebrew manuscripts read *Elishama.* **1 Chr 3:6b** Hebrew *Eliphelet;* compare parallel text at 14:5-7. **1 Chr 3:11** Hebrew *Joram,* a variant spelling of Jehoram. **1 Chr 3:12** Hebrew *Azariah,* a variant spelling of Uzziah. **1 Chr 3:15** Hebrew *Shallum,* another name for Jehoahaz. **1 Chr 3:16** Hebrew *The sons of Jehoiakim were his son Jeconiah* [a variant spelling of Jehoiachin] *and his son Zedekiah.* **1 Chr 3:17** Hebrew *Jeconiah,* a variant spelling of Jehoiachin.

---

1 Chr 3:1 Abigail's story is found in 1 Samuel 25. Her Profile is on p. 466.

1 Chr 3:2 Absalom's story is found in 2 Samuel 13–18. His Profile is on p. 511.

1 Chr 3:5 Bathsheba's story is found in 2 Samuel 11–12; 1 Kings 1, and her Profile is on p. 544. The story of her son, Solomon, who became Israel's third king, is found in 1 Kings 1–11; 2 Chronicles 1–9. Solomon's Profile is on p. 607.

1 Chr 3:9 The tragic story of Tamar, David's daughter, is found in 2 Samuel 13–14.

1 Chr 3:10-14 Many of Solomon's descendants ruled the nation of Judah. Rehoboam's story is found in 2 Chronicles 10–12, and his Profile is on p. 697. Jehoshaphat's story is found in 2 Chronicles 17–20, and his Profile is on p. 714. Uzziah's story is found in 2 Chronicles 26, and his Profile is on p. 763. Hezekiah's story is found in 2 Kings 18–20, and his Profile is on p. 799. Josiah's story is found in 2 Kings 22–23, and his Profile is on p. 971.

1 Chr 3:15 Jehoiakim's story is found in Jeremiah 22–28; 35; 36. Zedekiah's story is found in Jeremiah 21–39.

1 Chr 3:19-20 Zerubbabel was the leader of the first exiles to return from Babylon. His story is found in the book of Ezra. His Profile is on p. 1157.

2. THE TRIBES OF ISRAEL

After tracing Israel's royal line from Judah, the genealogy goes back in time to trace the lineage of all 12 tribes of Israel, including the descendants of the tribe of Judah who were not in the royal line. Every Israelite is important in God's story, just as every member of Christ's body is important today.

Other Descendants of Judah

1 CHRONICLES 4:1-20

1 The descendants of Judah were Perez, Hezron,
Carmi, Hur, and Shobal.
2 Shobal's son Reaiah was the father of Jahath. Jahath
was the father of Ahumai and Lahad. These were
the families of the Zorathites.
3 The descendants of* Etam were Jezreel, Ishma,
Idbash, their sister Hazzelelponi, 4 Penuel
(the father of* Gedor), and Ezer (the father of
Hushah). These were the descendants of Hur
(the firstborn of Ephrathah), the ancestor of
Bethlehem.
5 Ashhur (the father of Tekoa) had two wives,
named Helah and Naarah. 6 Naarah gave birth
to Ahuzzam, Hepher, Temeni, and Haahashtari.
7 Helah gave birth to Zereth, Izhar,* Ethnan, 8 and
Koz, who became the ancestor of Anub, Zobebah,
and all the families of Aharhel son of Harum.
9 There was a man named Jabez who was more
honorable than any of his brothers. His mother
named him Jabez* because his birth had been
so painful. 10 He was the one who prayed to the
God of Israel, "Oh, that you would bless me and
expand my territory! Please be with me in all that
I do, and keep me from all trouble and pain!"
And God granted him his request.
11 Kelub (the brother of Shuhah) was the father of
Mehir. Mehir was the father of Eshton. 12 Eshton
was the father of Beth-rapha, Paseah, and
Tehinnah. Tehinnah was the father of Ir-nahash.
These were the descendants of Recah.
13 The sons of Kenaz were Othniel and Seraiah.
Othniel's sons were Hathath and Meonothai.*
14 Meonothai was the father of Ophrah. Seraiah
was the father of Joab, the founder of the Valley
of Craftsmen,* so called because they were
craftsmen.
15 The sons of Caleb son of Jephunneh were Iru,
Elah, and Naam. The son of Elah was Kenaz.
16 The sons of Jehallelel were Ziph, Ziphah, Tiria,
and Asarel.
17 The sons of Ezrah were Jether, Mered, Epher, and
Jalon. One of Mered's wives became* the mother
of Miriam, Shammai, and Ishbah (the father of
Eshtemoa). 18 He married a woman from Judah,
who became the mother of Jered (the father of
Gedor), Heber (the father of Soco), and Jekuthiel
(the father of Zanoah). Mered also married Bithia,
a daughter of Pharaoh, and she bore him children.

1 Chr 4:3 As in Greek version; Hebrew reads *father of.* The meaning of the Hebrew is uncertain. **1 Chr 4:4** Or *the founder of;* also in 4:5, 12, 14, 17, 18, and perhaps other instances where the text reads *the father of.* **1 Chr 4:7** As in an alternate reading in the Masoretic Text (see also Latin Vulgate); the other alternate and the Greek version read *Zohar.* **1 Chr 4:9** *Jabez* sounds like a Hebrew word meaning "distress" or "pain." **1 Chr 4:13** As in some Greek manuscripts and Latin Vulgate; Hebrew lacks *and Meonothai.* **1 Chr 4:14** Or *Joab, the father of Ge-harashim.* **1 Chr 4:17** Or *Jether's wife became;* Hebrew reads *She became.*

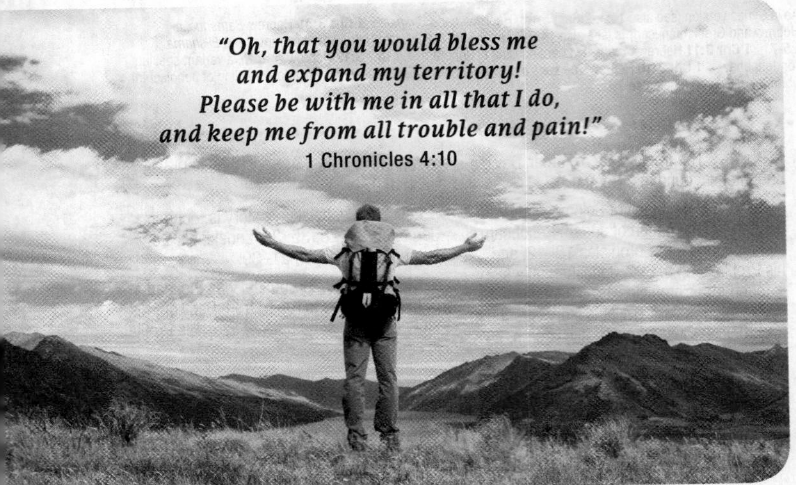
"Oh, that you would bless me
and expand my territory!
Please be with me in all that I do,
and keep me from all trouble and pain!"
1 Chronicles 4:10

1 Chr 4:9-10 Jabez is remembered for a prayer request rather than a heroic act. In his prayer, he asked God to (1) bless him, (2) help him in his work ("expand my territory"), (3) be with him in all he did, and (4) keep him from trouble and pain. Jabez acknowledged God as the true center of his life. When we pray for God's blessing, we should also ask him to take his rightful position as Lord over our work, our family time, and our recreation. Obeying him in daily responsibilities *is* heroic living.

1 Chr 4:10 Jabez prayed specifically to be protected from trouble and pain. We live in a fallen world filled with sin, and it is important to ask God to keep us safe from the unavoidable evil that comes our way. But we must also avoid evil motives, desires, and actions that begin within us. Therefore, not only must we seek God's protection from evil, but we must also ask God to guard our thoughts and actions. We can begin to utilize his protection by filling our mind with positive thoughts and attitudes.

1 Chr 4:13 Othniel was Israel's first judge. He reformed the nation and brought peace to the land. His story is found in Judges 1:9-15; 3:5-11.

1 Chr 4:15 Caleb was one of the 12 scouts that Moses sent into the Promised Land. He and Joshua were the only two scouts to return with a positive report, believing in God's promise to help the Israelites conquer the land. Caleb's story is told in Numbers 13–14; Joshua 14–15. His Profile is on p. 252.

19 Hodiah's wife was the sister of Naham. One of
her sons was the father of Keilah the Garmite,
and another was the father of Eshtemoa the
Maacathite.
20 The sons of Shimon were Amnon, Rinnah,
Ben-hanan, and Tilon.
The descendants of Ishi were Zoheth and Ben-zoheth.

Descendants of Judah's Son Shelah

1 CHRONICLES 4:21-23

21 Shelah was one of Judah's sons. The descendants
of Shelah were Er (the father of Lecah); Laadah
(the father of Mareshah); the families of linen
workers at Beth-ashbea; 22 Jokim; the men of
Cozeba; and Joash and Saraph, who ruled over
Moab and Jashubi-lehem. These names all come
from ancient records. 23 They were the pottery
makers who lived in Netaim and Gederah. They
lived there and worked for the king.

Descendants of Simeon

1 CHRONICLES 4:24-43

24 The sons of Simeon were Jemuel,* Jamin, Jarib,
Zohar,* and Shaul.
25 The descendants of Shaul were Shallum, Mibsam,
and Mishma.
26 The descendants of Mishma were Hammuel,
Zaccur, and Shimei.
27 Shimei had sixteen sons and six daughters,
but none of his brothers had large families. So
Simeon's tribe never grew as large as the tribe
of Judah.
28 They lived in Beersheba, Moladah, Hazar-shual,
29 Bilhah, Ezem, Tolad, 30 Bethuel, Hormah, Ziklag,
31 Beth-marcaboth, Hazar-susim, Beth-biri, and
Shaaraim. These towns were under their control
until the time of King David. 32 Their descendants
also lived in Etam, Ain, Rimmon, Token, and
Ashan—five towns 33 and their surrounding
villages as far away as Baalath.* This was their
territory, and these names are listed in their
genealogical records.
34 Other descendants of Simeon included Meshobab,
Jamlech, Joshah son of Amaziah, 35 Joel, Jehu
son of Joshibiah, son of Seraiah, son of Asiel,
36 Elioenai, Jaakobah, Jeshohaiah, Asaiah, Adiel,
Jesimiel, Benaiah, 37 and Ziza son of Shiphi, son
of Allon, son of Jedaiah, son of Shimri, son of
Shemaiah.

38 These were the names of some of the leaders of
Simeon's wealthy clans. Their families grew, 39 and they
traveled to the region of Gerar,* in the east part of the
valley, seeking pastureland for their flocks. 40 They
found lush pastures there, and the land was quiet and
peaceful.

Some of Ham's descendants had been living in that
region. 41 But during the reign of King Hezekiah of Judah, these leaders of Simeon invaded the region and
completely destroyed* the homes of the descendants
of Ham and of the Meunites. No trace of them remains
today. They killed everyone who lived there and took
the land for themselves, because they wanted its good
pastureland for their flocks. 42 Five hundred of these
invaders from the tribe of Simeon went to Mount Seir,
led by Pelatiah, Neariah, Rephaiah, and Uzziel—all
sons of Ishi. 43 They destroyed the few Amalekites who
had survived, and they have lived there ever since.

Descendants of Reuben

1 CHRONICLES 5:1-10

The oldest son of Israel* was Reuben. But since he dishonored his father by sleeping with one of his father's
concubines, his birthright was given to the sons of his
brother Joseph. For this reason, Reuben is not listed
in the genealogical records as the firstborn son. 2 The
descendants of Judah became the most powerful tribe
and provided a ruler for the nation,* but the birthright
belonged to Joseph.

3 The sons of Reuben, the oldest son of Israel, were
Hanoch, Pallu, Hezron, and Carmi.
4 The descendants of Joel were Shemaiah, Gog,
Shimei, 5 Micah, Reaiah, Baal, 6 and Beerah. Beerah
was the leader of the Reubenites when they were
taken into captivity by King Tiglath-pileser* of
Assyria.
7 Beerah's* relatives are listed in their genealogical
records by their clans: Jeiel (the leader),
Zechariah, 8 and Bela son of Azaz, son of Shema,
son of Joel.
The Reubenites lived in the area that stretches from
Aroer to Nebo and Baal-meon. 9 And since they
had so many livestock in the land of Gilead, they

1 Chr 4:24a As in Syriac version (see also Gen 46:10; Exod 6:15); Hebrew reads *Nemuel.* **1 Chr 4:24b** As in parallel texts at Gen 46:10 and Exod 6:15; Hebrew reads *Zerah.* **1 Chr 4:33** As in some Greek manuscripts (see also Josh 19:8); Hebrew reads *Baal.* **1 Chr 4:39** As in Greek version; Hebrew reads *Gedor.* **1 Chr 4:41** The Hebrew term used here refers to the complete consecration of things or people to the LORD, either by destroying them or by giving them as an offering. **1 Chr 5:1** *Israel* is the name that God gave to Jacob. **1 Chr 5:2** Or *and from Judah came a prince.* **1 Chr 5:6** Hebrew *Tilgath-pilneser,* a variant spelling of Tiglath-pileser; also in 5:26. **1 Chr 5:7** Hebrew *His.*

1 Chr 5:1 Reuben's sin of incest was recorded for all future generations to read. The purpose of this epitaph was not to smear Reuben's name but to show that painful memories aren't the only results of sin. The real consequences of sin are ruined lives. As the oldest son, Reuben was the rightful heir to both a double portion of his father's estate and the leadership of Abraham's descendants, who had grown into a large tribe. But his sin stripped away his rights and privileges and destroyed his family. Before you give in to temptation, consider the disastrous consequences sin may produce in your life and the lives of others.

1 Chr 5:2 This ruler from the tribe of Judah refers to David and his royal line and to Jesus the Messiah, David's greatest descendant.

▶ **1 CHRONICLES 5:1-10** ***(cont.)***
spread east toward the edge of the desert that
stretches to the Euphrates River.
10 During the reign of Saul, the Reubenites defeated
the Hagrites in battle. Then they moved into the
Hagrite settlements all along the eastern edge
of Gilead.

Descendants of Gad

1 CHRONICLES 5:11-17
11 Next to the Reubenites, the descendants of Gad
lived in the land of Bashan as far east as Salecah.
12 Joel was the leader in the land of Bashan, and
Shapham was second-in-command, followed by
Janai and Shaphat.
13 Their relatives, the leaders of seven other clans,
were Michael, Meshullam, Sheba, Jorai, Jacan,
Zia, and Eber. 14 These were all descendants of
Abihail son of Huri, son of Jaroah, son of Gilead,
son of Michael, son of Jeshishai, son of Jahdo, son
of Buz. 15 Ahi son of Abdiel, son of Guni, was the
leader of their clans.

16 The Gadites lived in the land of Gilead, in Bashan
and its villages, and throughout all the pasturelands of
Sharon. 17 All of these were listed in the genealogical
records during the days of King Jotham of Judah and
King Jeroboam of Israel.

The Tribes East of the Jordan

1 CHRONICLES 5:18-26
There were 44,760 capable warriors in the armies of
Reuben, Gad, and the half-tribe of Manasseh. They
were all skilled in combat and armed with shields,
swords, and bows. 19 They waged war against the Hagrites, the Jeturites, the Naphishites, and the Nodabites.
20 They cried out to God during the battle, and he answered their prayer because they trusted in him. So
the Hagrites and all their allies were defeated. 21 The
plunder taken from the Hagrites included 50,000
camels, 250,000 sheep and goats, 2,000 donkeys, and
100,000 captives. 22 Many of the Hagrites were killed
in the battle because God was fighting against them.
The people of Reuben, Gad, and Manasseh lived in
their land until they were taken into exile.

23 The half-tribe of Manasseh was very large and
spread through the land from Bashan to Baal-hermon,
Senir, and Mount Hermon. 24 These were the leaders of
their clans: Epher,* Ishi, Eliel, Azriel, Jeremiah, Hodaviah, and Jahdiel. These men had a great reputation as
mighty warriors and leaders of their clans.

25 But these tribes were unfaithful to the God of their
ancestors. They worshiped the gods of the nations
that God had destroyed. 26 So the God of Israel caused
King Pul of Assyria (also known as Tiglath-pileser) to
invade the land and take away the people of Reuben,
Gad, and the half-tribe of Manasseh as captives. The
Assyrians exiled them to Halah, Habor, Hara, and the
Gozan River, where they remain to this day.

The Priestly Line

1 CHRONICLES 6:1-15
1 *The sons of Levi were Gershon, Kohath, and Merari.
2 The descendants of Kohath included Amram, Izhar,
Hebron, and Uzziel.
3 The children of Amram were Aaron, Moses, and
Miriam.
The sons of Aaron were Nadab, Abihu, Eleazar, and
Ithamar.
4 Eleazar was the father of Phinehas.
Phinehas was the father of Abishua.
5 Abishua was the father of Bukki.
Bukki was the father of Uzzi.
6 Uzzi was the father of Zerahiah.
Zerahiah was the father of Meraioth.
7 Meraioth was the father of Amariah.
Amariah was the father of Ahitub.

1 Chr 5:24 As in Greek version and Latin Vulgate; Hebrew reads *and Epher.* **1 Chr 6:1** Verses 6:1-15 are numbered 5:27-41 in Hebrew text.

1 Chr 5:18-22 The armies of Reuben, Gad, and Manasseh succeeded in battle because they trusted God. Although they had instinct and skill as soldiers, they prayed and sought God's direction. The natural and developed abilities God gives us are meant to be used for him, but they should never replace our dependence on him. When we trust in our own cleverness, skill, and strength rather than in God, we open the door for pride. When facing difficult situations, seek God's purpose and ask for his guidance and strength. Psalm 20:7 says, "Some nations boast of their chariots and horses, but we boast in the name of the LORD our God."

1 Chr 5:22 The exile mentioned here refers to the exile of the 10 northern tribes (the northern kingdom of Israel) to Assyria in 722 B.C. These tribes never returned to their homeland. This story is found in 2 Kings 15:29–17:41.

1 Chr 5:24-25 As warriors and leaders, these men had established excellent reputations for their great skill and leadership qualities. But in God's eyes they failed in the most important quality—being faithful to God. If you try to measure up to society's standards for fame and success, you may neglect your true purpose—to please and obey God. In the end, God alone examines our hearts and determines our final standing. How is your present reputation with God?

1 Chr 6:1ff The tribe of Levi was set apart to serve God in the Tabernacle (Num 3–4), and later in the Temple (1 Chr 23–26). Aaron, Levi's descendant (1 Chr 6:3), became Israel's first high priest. God required all future priests to be descendants of Aaron. The rest of the Levites assisted the priests in various Tabernacle or Temple duties; they taught the people God's Word and encouraged them to obey it.

1 Chr 6:3 The people listed here played major roles in the drama of the Exodus. Aaron's story is found in the books of Exodus, Leviticus, and Numbers. His Profile is on p. 184. Moses was one of the greatest prophets and leaders in Israel's history. His story is found in the books of Exodus, Leviticus, Numbers, and Deuteronomy. His Profile is on p.148. The story of Miriam, Moses and Aaron's sister, is found in Exodus 2; 15:20-21; Numbers 12; 20:1. Her Profile is on p. 249. Nadab and Abihu were killed for disobeying God (Lev 10). Eleazar became Israel's high priest after Aaron (Num 20:24-28), and Ithamar played an important role in organizing the worship services of the Tabernacle (Num 4:28, 33; 7:8).

8 Ahitub was the father of Zadok.
Zadok was the father of Ahimaaz.
9 Ahimaaz was the father of Azariah.
Azariah was the father of Johanan.
10 Johanan was the father of Azariah, the high priest
at the Temple* built by Solomon in Jerusalem.
11 Azariah was the father of Amariah.
Amariah was the father of Ahitub.
12 Ahitub was the father of Zadok.
Zadok was the father of Shallum.
13 Shallum was the father of Hilkiah.
Hilkiah was the father of Azariah.
14 Azariah was the father of Seraiah.
Seraiah was the father of Jehozadak, 15 who went
into exile when the LORD sent the people of
Judah and Jerusalem into captivity under
Nebuchadnezzar.

The Levite Clans

1 CHRONICLES 6:16-30

16 *The sons of Levi were Gershon,* Kohath, and
Merari.
17 The descendants of Gershon included Libni and
Shimei.
18 The descendants of Kohath included Amram,
Izhar, Hebron, and Uzziel.
19 The descendants of Merari included Mahli and
Mushi.

The following were the Levite clans, listed according to their ancestral descent:

20 The descendants of Gershon included Libni, Jahath,
Zimmah, 21 Joah, Iddo, Zerah, and Jeatherai.
22 The descendants of Kohath included Amminadab,
Korah, Assir, 23 Elkanah, Abiasaph,* Assir,
24 Tahath, Uriel, Uzziah, and Shaul.
25 The descendants of Elkanah included Amasai,
Ahimoth, 26 Elkanah, Zophai, Nahath, 27 Eliab,
Jeroham, Elkanah, and Samuel.*
28 The sons of Samuel were Joel* (the older) and
Abijah (the second).
29 The descendants of Merari included Mahli, Libni,
Shimei, Uzzah, 30 Shimea, Haggiah, and Asaiah.

The Temple Musicians

1 CHRONICLES 6:31-48

David assigned the following men to lead the music at
the house of the LORD after the Ark was placed there.
32 They ministered with music at the Tabernacle* until
Solomon built the Temple of the LORD in Jerusalem.
They carried out their work, following all the regulations handed down to them. 33 These are the men who
served, along with their sons:

Heman the musician was from the clan of Kohath.
His genealogy was traced back through Joel,
Samuel, 34 Elkanah, Jeroham, Eliel, Toah, 35 Zuph,
Elkanah, Mahath, Amasai, 36 Elkanah, Joel,
Azariah, Zephaniah, 37 Tahath, Assir, Abiasaph,
Korah, 38 Izhar, Kohath, Levi, and Israel.*
39 Heman's first assistant was Asaph from the clan
of Gershon.* Asaph's genealogy was traced back
through Berekiah, Shimea, 40 Michael, Baaseiah,
Malkijah, 41 Ethni, Zerah, Adaiah, 42 Ethan,
Zimmah, Shimei, 43 Jahath, Gershon, and Levi.
44 Heman's second assistant was Ethan from the
clan of Merari. Ethan's genealogy was traced
back through Kishi, Abdi, Malluch, 45 Hashabiah,
Amaziah, Hilkiah, 46 Amzi, Bani, Shemer, 47 Mahli,
Mushi, Merari, and Levi.

48 Their fellow Levites were appointed to various other
tasks in the Tabernacle, the house of God.

Aaron's Descendants

1 CHRONICLES 6:49-53

Only Aaron and his descendants served as priests.
They presented the offerings on the altar of burnt offering and the altar of incense, and they performed all

1 Chr 6:10 Hebrew *the house.* **1 Chr 6:16a** Verses 6:16-81 are numbered 6:1-66 in Hebrew text. **1 Chr 6:16b** Hebrew *Gershom,* a variant spelling of Gershon (see 6:1); also in 6:17, 20, 43, 62, 71. **1 Chr 6:23** Hebrew *Ebiasaph,* a variant spelling of Abiasaph (also in 6:37); compare parallel text at Exod 6:24. **1 Chr 6:27** As in some Greek manuscripts (see also 6:33-34); Hebrew lacks *and Samuel.* **1 Chr 6:28** As in some Greek manuscripts and the Syriac version (see also 6:33 and 1 Sam 8:2); Hebrew lacks *Joel.* **1 Chr 6:32** Hebrew *the Tabernacle, the Tent of Meeting.* **1 Chr 6:38** *Israel* is the name that God gave to Jacob. **1 Chr 6:39** Hebrew lacks *from the clan of Gershon;* see 6:43.

---

1 Chr 6:28 When Samuel became God's leader and spokesman, Israel was on the brink of collapse. The last few chapters of the book of Judges give a vivid picture of the moral decay and the resulting decline of the nation. But with God's help, Samuel almost single-handedly brought the nation from ruin to revival. He unified the people by showing them that God was their common Leader and that any nation that focused on him would find and fulfill its true purpose. For the rest of Samuel's story, and to see how he set up rules for governing a nation based on spiritual principles, read the book of 1 Samuel. His Profile is on p. 426.

1 Chr 6:31 David did much to bring music into worship. He established song leaders and choirs to perform regularly at the Temple (1 Chr 25). As a young man, David was hired to play the harp for King Saul (1 Sam 16:15-23). He also wrote many of the songs found in the book of Psalms.

1 Chr 6:31ff The builders and craftsmen had completed the Temple, and the priests and Levites had been given their responsibilities for taking care of it. Then it was time for another group of people—the musicians—to exercise their talents for God. Some of those who served with music are recorded here. You don't have to be an ordained minister to have an important place in the body of believers. Builders, craftsmen, worship assistants, choir members, and song leaders all have significant contributions to make. God has given you a unique combination of talents. Use them to serve and honor him.

1 Chr 6:49 Aaron and his descendants strictly followed the details of worship commanded by God through Moses. They did not choose only those commands they wanted to obey. Note what happened to Uzzah when important details in handling the Ark of the Covenant were neglected (1 Chr 13:6-10). We should not try to obey God selectively, choosing those commands we will obey and those we will ignore. God's Word has authority over every aspect of our lives, not just selected areas.

1 Chr 6:49 For more information on priests, see the note on Leviticus 8:1ff, p. 210.

▶ **1 CHRONICLES 6:49-53** ***(cont.)***

the other duties related to the Most Holy Place. They made atonement for Israel by doing everything that Moses, the servant of God, had commanded them.

50 The descendants of Aaron were Eleazar, Phinehas, Abishua, 51 Bukki, Uzzi, Zerahiah, 52 Meraioth, Amariah, Ahitub, 53 Zadok, and Ahimaaz.

Territory for the Levites

1 CHRONICLES 6:54-81

This is a record of the towns and territory assigned by means of sacred lots to the descendants of Aaron, who were from the clan of Kohath. 55 This territory included Hebron and its surrounding pasturelands in Judah, 56 but the fields and outlying areas belonging to the city were given to Caleb son of Jephunneh. 57 So the descendants of Aaron were given the following towns, each with its pasturelands: Hebron (a city of refuge),* Libnah, Jattir, Eshtemoa, 58 Holon,* Debir, 59 Ain,* Juttah,* and Beth-shemesh. 60 And from the territory of Benjamin they were given Gibeon,* Geba, Alemeth, and Anathoth, each with its pasturelands. So thirteen towns were given to the descendants of Aaron. 61 The remaining descendants of Kohath received ten towns from the territory of the half-tribe of Manasseh by means of sacred lots.

62 The descendants of Gershon received by sacred lots thirteen towns from the territories of Issachar, Asher, Naphtali, and from the Bashan area of Manasseh, east of the Jordan.

63 The descendants of Merari received by sacred lots twelve towns from the territories of Reuben, Gad, and Zebulun.

64 So the people of Israel assigned all these towns and pasturelands to the Levites. 65 The towns in the territories of Judah, Simeon, and Benjamin, mentioned above, were assigned to them by means of sacred lots.

66 The descendants of Kohath were given the following towns from the territory of Ephraim, each with its pasturelands: 67 Shechem (a city of refuge in the hill country of Ephraim),* Gezer, 68 Jokmeam, Beth-horon, 69 Aijalon, and Gath-rimmon. 70 The remaining descendants of Kohath were assigned the towns of Aner and Bileam from the territory of the half-tribe of Manasseh, each with its pasturelands.

71 The descendants of Gershon received the towns of Golan (in Bashan) and Ashtaroth from the territory of the half-tribe of Manasseh, each with its pasturelands. 72 From the territory of Issachar, they were given Kedesh, Daberath, 73 Ramoth, and Anem, each with its pasturelands. 74 From the territory of Asher, they received Mashal, Abdon, 75 Hukok, and Rehob, each with its pasturelands. 76 From the territory of Naphtali, they were given Kedesh in Galilee, Hammon, and Kiriathaim, each with its pasturelands.

77 The remaining descendants of Merari received the towns of Jokneam, Kartah,* Rimmon,* and Tabor from the territory of Zebulun, each with its pasturelands. 78 From the territory of Reuben, east of the Jordan River opposite Jericho, they received Bezer (a desert town), Jahaz,* 79 Kedemoth, and Mephaath, each with its pasturelands. 80 And from the territory of Gad, they received Ramoth in Gilead, Mahanaim, 81 Heshbon, and Jazer, each with its pasturelands.

Descendants of Issachar

1 CHRONICLES 7:1-5

1 The four sons of Issachar were Tola, Puah, Jashub, and Shimron.

2 The sons of Tola were Uzzi, Rephaiah, Jeriel, Jahmai, Ibsam, and Shemuel. Each of them was the leader of an ancestral clan. At the time of King David, the total number of mighty warriors listed in the records of these clans was 22,600.

3 The son of Uzzi was Izrahiah. The sons of Izrahiah were Michael, Obadiah, Joel, and Isshiah. These five became the leaders of clans. 4 All of them had many wives and many sons, so the total number of men available for military service among their descendants was 36,000.

5 The total number of mighty warriors from all the clans of the tribe of Issachar was 87,000. All of them were listed in their genealogical records.

1 Chr 6:57 As in parallel text at Josh 21:13; Hebrew reads *were given the cities of refuge: Hebron, and the following towns, each with its pasturelands.* **1 Chr 6:58** As in parallel text at Josh 21:15; Masoretic Text reads *Hilez;* other manuscripts read *Hilen.* **1 Chr 6:59a** As in parallel text at Josh 21:16; Hebrew reads *Ashan.* **1 Chr 6:59b** As in Syriac version (see also Josh 21:16); Hebrew lacks *Juttah.* **1 Chr 6:60** As in parallel text at Josh 21:17; Hebrew lacks *Gibeon.* **1 Chr 6:66-67** As in parallel text at Josh 21:21. Hebrew text reads *were given the cities of refuge: Shechem in the hill country of Ephraim, and the following towns, each with its pasturelands.* **1 Chr 6:77a** As in Greek version (see also Josh 21:34); Hebrew lacks *Jokneam, Kartah.* **1 Chr 6:77b** As in Greek version (see also Josh 19:13); Hebrew reads *Rimmono.* **1 Chr 6:78** Hebrew *Jahzah,* a variant spelling of Jahaz.

1 Chr 6:54 The tribe of Levi was not given a specific area of land as were the other tribes. Instead, the Levites were to live throughout the land in order to aid the people of every tribe in their worship of God. Thus, the Levites were given towns or pasturelands within the allotted areas of the other tribes (Josh 13:14, 33).

1 Chr 6:57ff God had told the tribes to designate specific cities to be cities of refuge (Num 35). These cities were to provide refuge for a person who accidentally killed someone. This instruction may have seemed unimportant when it was given—the Israelites hadn't even entered the Promised Land. Sometimes God gives us instructions that do not seem relevant to us at the moment. But later we can see the importance of those instructions. Don't discard the lessons of the Bible because certain details seem irrelevant. Obey God now—in the future you will have a clearer understanding of the reasons for his instructions.

1 Chr 6:61 The Israelites cast lots in order to take the decision-making process out of human hands and put it into God's hands. Casting lots was like drawing straws or throwing dice. Lots were cast only after seeking God's guidance in prayer. (For more information on casting lots, see the note on Josh 18:8, p. 362.)

1 Chr 7:27 Joshua was one of Israel's great leaders, leading the people into the Promised Land. His story is told in the book of Joshua. His Profile is on p. 339.

Descendants of Benjamin

1 CHRONICLES 7:6-12

6 Three of Benjamin's sons were Bela, Beker, and
Jediael.
7 The five sons of Bela were Ezbon, Uzzi, Uzziel,
Jerimoth, and Iri. Each of them was the leader
of an ancestral clan. The total number of mighty
warriors from these clans was 22,034, as listed
in their genealogical records.
8 The sons of Beker were Zemirah, Joash, Eliezer,
Elioenai, Omri, Jeremoth, Abijah, Anathoth,
and Alemeth. 9 Each of them was the leader
of an ancestral clan. The total number of
mighty warriors and leaders from these clans
was 20,200, as listed in their genealogical
records.
10 The son of Jediael was Bilhan. The sons of Bilhan
were Jeush, Benjamin, Ehud, Kenaanah, Zethan,
Tarshish, and Ahishahar. 11 Each of them was the
leader of an ancestral clan. From these clans the
total number of mighty warriors ready for war
was 17,200.
12 The sons of Ir were Shuppim and Huppim.
Hushim was the son of Aher.

Descendants of Naphtali

1 CHRONICLES 7:13

13 The sons of Naphtali were Jahzeel,* Guni, Jezer,
and Shillem.* They were all descendants of
Jacob's concubine Bilhah.

Descendants of Manasseh

1 CHRONICLES 7:14-19

14 The descendants of Manasseh through his
Aramean concubine included Asriel. She also
bore Makir, the father of Gilead. 15 Makir found
wives for* Huppim and Shuppim. Makir had a
sister named Maacah. One of his descendants
was Zelophehad, who had only daughters.
16 Makir's wife, Maacah, gave birth to a son whom
she named Peresh. His brother's name was
Sheresh. The sons of Peresh were Ulam and
Rakem. 17 The son of Ulam was Bedan. All these
were considered Gileadites, descendants of
Makir son of Manasseh.
18 Makir's sister Hammoleketh gave birth to Ishhod,
Abiezer, and Mahlah.
19 The sons of Shemida were Ahian, Shechem, Likhi,
and Aniam.

Descendants of Ephraim

1 CHRONICLES 7:20-29

20 The descendants of Ephraim were Shuthelah,
Bered, Tahath, Eleadah, Tahath, 21 Zabad,
Shuthelah, Ezer, and Elead. These two were killed
trying to steal livestock from the local farmers
near Gath. 22 Their father, Ephraim, mourned
for them a long time, and his relatives came to
comfort him. 23 Afterward Ephraim slept with his
wife, and she became pregnant and gave birth
to a son. Ephraim named him Beriah* because
of the tragedy his family had suffered. 24 He had
a daughter named Sheerah. She built the towns
of Lower and Upper Beth-horon and Uzzen-
sheerah.
25 The descendants of Ephraim included Rephah,
Resheph, Telah, Tahan, 26 Ladan, Ammihud,
Elishama, 27 Nun, and Joshua.

28 The descendants of Ephraim lived in the territory
that included Bethel and its surrounding towns to the
south, Naaran to the east, Gezer and its villages to
the west, and Shechem and its surrounding villages
to the north as far as Ayyah and its towns. 29 Along the
border of Manasseh were the towns of Beth-shan,*
Taanach, Megiddo, Dor, and their surrounding villages. The descendants of Joseph son of Israel* lived
in these towns.

1 Chr 7:13a As in parallel text at Gen 46:24; Hebrew reads *Jahziel,* a variant spelling of Jahzeel. **1 Chr 7:13b** As in some Hebrew and Greek manuscripts (see also Gen 46:24; Num 26:49); most Hebrew manuscripts read *Shallum.* **1 Chr 7:15** Or *Makir took a wife from.* The meaning of the Hebrew is uncertain. **1 Chr 7:23** *Beriah* sounds like a Hebrew term meaning "tragedy" or "misfortune." **1 Chr 7:29a** Hebrew *Beth-shean,* a variant spelling of Beth-shan. **1 Chr 7:29b** *Israel* is the name that God gave to Jacob.

Dor

Dor was a fortified Palestinian city situated along the Mediterranean coast, south of Mount Carmel and eight miles north of Caesarea. It is mentioned occasionally in connection with events in the period of the judges and the united monarchy (Josh 17:11; Judg 1:27; 1 Chr 7:29). Dor is probably the same city as Naphoth-dor (Josh 11:2; 12:23; 17:11; 1 Kgs 4:11). During the Israelites' conquest of Canaan, the king of Dor joined Jabin's confederacy against Joshua (Josh 11:2), but was defeated (Josh 12:23). The city was assigned to Manasseh's tribe, but the tribe failed to dispossess its inhabitants (Judg 1:27).

Descendants of Asher

1 CHRONICLES 7:30-40

30 The sons of Asher were Imnah, Ishvah, Ishvi, and
Beriah. They had a sister named Serah.
31 The sons of Beriah were Heber and Malkiel (the
father of Birzaith).
32 The sons of Heber were Japhlet, Shomer, and
Hotham. They had a sister named Shua.
33 The sons of Japhlet were Pasach, Bimhal, and
Ashvath.
34 The sons of Shomer were Ahi,* Rohgah, Hubbah,
and Aram.
35 The sons of his brother Helem* were Zophah,
Imna, Shelesh, and Amal.
36 The sons of Zophah were Suah, Harnepher, Shual,
Beri, Imrah, 37 Bezer, Hod, Shamma, Shilshah,
Ithran,* and Beera.
38 The sons of Jether were Jephunneh, Pispah,
and Ara.
39 The sons of Ulla were Arah, Hanniel, and Rizia.
40 Each of these descendants of Asher was the head of
an ancestral clan. They were all select men—mighty
warriors and outstanding leaders. The total number
of men available for military service was 26,000, as
listed in their genealogical records.

Descendants of Benjamin

1 CHRONICLES 8:1-28

1 Benjamin's first son was Bela, the second was
Ashbel, the third was Aharah, 2 the fourth was
Nohah, and the fifth was Rapha.
3 The sons of Bela were Addar, Gera, Abihud,*
4 Abishua, Naaman, Ahoah, 5 Gera, Shephuphan,
and Huram.
6 The sons of Ehud, leaders of the clans living at
Geba, were exiled to Manahath. 7 Ehud's sons were
Naaman, Ahijah, and Gera. Gera, who led them
into exile, was the father of Uzza and Ahihud.*
8 After Shaharaim divorced his wives Hushim and
Baara, he had children in the land of Moab. 9 His
wife Hodesh gave birth to Jobab, Zibia, Mesha,
Malcam, 10 Jeuz, Sakia, and Mirmah. These sons
all became the leaders of clans.
11 Shaharaim's wife Hushim had already given
birth to Abitub and Elpaal. 12 The sons of Elpaal
were Eber, Misham, Shemed (who built the
towns of Ono and Lod and their nearby villages),
13 Beriah, and Shema. They were the leaders of
the clans living in Aijalon, and they drove out the
inhabitants of Gath.
14 Ahio, Shashak, Jeremoth, 15 Zebadiah, Arad, Eder,
16 Michael, Ishpah, and Joha were the sons of
Beriah.
17 Zebadiah, Meshullam, Hizki, Heber, 18 Ishmerai,
Izliah, and Jobab were the sons of Elpaal.
19 Jakim, Zicri, Zabdi, 20 Elienai, Zillethai, Eliel,
21 Adaiah, Beraiah, and Shimrath were the sons
of Shimei.
22 Ishpan, Eber, Eliel, 23 Abdon, Zicri, Hanan,
24 Hananiah, Elam, Anthothijah, 25 Iphdeiah, and
Penuel were the sons of Shashak.
26 Shamsherai, Shehariah, Athaliah, 27 Jaareshiah,
Elijah, and Zicri were the sons of Jeroham.
28 These were the leaders of the ancestral clans; they
were listed in their genealogical records, and they all
lived in Jerusalem.

The Family of Saul

1 CHRONICLES 8:29–9:1a

29 Jeiel* (the father of* Gibeon) lived in the town of
Gibeon. His wife's name was Maacah, 30 and his
oldest son was named Abdon. Jeiel's other sons
were Zur, Kish, Baal, Ner,* Nadab, 31 Gedor, Ahio,
Zechariah,* 32 and Mikloth, who was the father
of Shimeam.* All these families lived near each
other in Jerusalem.
33 Ner was the father of Kish.
Kish was the father of Saul.
Saul was the father of Jonathan, Malkishua,
Abinadab, and Esh-baal.
34 Jonathan was the father of Merib-baal.
Merib-baal was the father of Micah.
35 Micah was the father of Pithon, Melech, Tahrea,*
and Ahaz.
36 Ahaz was the father of Jadah.*
Jadah was the father of Alemeth, Azmaveth,
and Zimri.
Zimri was the father of Moza.

1 Chr 7:34 Or *The sons of Shomer, his brother, were.* **1 Chr 7:35** Possibly another name for *Hotham;* compare 7:32. **1 Chr 7:37** Possibly another name for *Jether;* compare 7:38. **1 Chr 8:3** Possibly *Gera the father of Ehud;* compare 8:6. **1 Chr 8:7** Or *Gera, that is Heglam, was the father of Uzza and Ahihud.* **1 Chr 8:29a** As in some Greek manuscripts (see also 9:35); Hebrew lacks *Jeiel.* **1 Chr 8:29b** Or *the founder of.* **1 Chr 8:30** As in some Greek manuscripts (see also 9:36); Hebrew lacks *Ner.* **1 Chr 8:31** As in parallel text at 9:37; Hebrew reads *Zeker,* a variant spelling of Zechariah. **1 Chr 8:32** As in parallel text at 9:38; Hebrew reads *Shimeah,* a variant spelling of Shimeam. **1 Chr 8:35** As in parallel text at 9:41; Hebrew reads *Tarea,* a variant spelling of Tahrea. **1 Chr 8:36** As in parallel text at 9:42; Hebrew reads *Jehoaddah,* a variant spelling of Jadah.

1 Chr 8:8-10 These verses list Shaharaim's children by Hodesh after he had divorced his first two wives, Hushim and Baara. Divorce and polygamy are sometimes recorded in the Old Testament without critical comments. This does not mean that God takes divorce lightly. Malachi 2:15-16 says to "remain loyal to the wife of your youth. 'For I hate divorce!' says the LORD, the God of Israel." Jesus explained that although divorce was allowed, it was not God's will: "Moses permitted divorce only as a concession to your hard hearts, but it was not what God had originally intended" (Matt 19:8). Don't assume that God approves of an act because it isn't vigorously condemned in every related Bible reference.

1 Chr 8:33 Saul, Israel's first king, was very inconsistent. His story is found in 1 Samuel 9–31, and his Profile is on p. 438. Saul's son Jonathan was the opposite. Although Jonathan was the rightful heir to the throne, he realized that David was God's choice to be Israel's next king. Instead of being jealous, Jonathan was David's friend and even helped him escape from Saul's attempts at murder. Jonathan's story is told in 1 Samuel 14–31. His Profile is on p. 455.

[37] Moza was the father of Binea.
Binea was the father of Rephaiah.*
Rephaiah was the father of Eleasah.
Eleasah was the father of Azel.
[38] Azel had six sons: Azrikam, Bokeru, Ishmael,
Sheariah, Obadiah, and Hanan. These were the
sons of Azel.
[39] Azel's brother Eshek had three sons: the first was
Ulam, the second was Jeush, and the third was
Eliphelet. [40] Ulam's sons were all mighty warriors
and expert archers. They had many sons and
grandsons—150 in all.

All these were descendants of Benjamin.

9:1 So all Israel was listed in the genealogical records
in *The Book of the Kings of Israel.*

1 Chr 8:37 As in parallel text at 9:43; Hebrew reads *Raphah,* a variant spelling of Rephaiah.

3. RETURNEES FROM EXILE IN BABYLON

This genealogy was compiled for the sake of these people returning to the Promised Land from their exile. It was important to these families that they were able to trace their lineage back to the original nation of Israel, to remind them of their spiritual heritage and the promises that God had made to their ancestors.

The Returning Exiles

1 CHRONICLES 9:1b-9

The people of Judah were exiled to Babylon because
they were unfaithful to the LORD. [2] The first of the
exiles to return to their property in their former
towns were priests, Levites, Temple servants, and
other Israelites. [3] Some of the people from the tribes
of Judah, Benjamin, Ephraim, and Manasseh came and
settled in Jerusalem.

[4] One family that returned was that of Uthai son of
Ammihud, son of Omri, son of Imri, son of Bani,
a descendant of Perez son of Judah.
[5] Others returned from the Shilonite clan, including
Asaiah (the oldest) and his sons.
[6] From the Zerahite clan, Jeuel returned with his
relatives.

In all, 690 families from the tribe of Judah returned.

[7] From the tribe of Benjamin came Sallu son of
Meshullam, son of Hodaviah, son of Hassenuah;
[8] Ibneiah son of Jeroham; Elah son of Uzzi, son
of Micri; and Meshullam son of Shephatiah, son
of Reuel, son of Ibnijah.
[9] These men were all leaders of clans, and they were
listed in their genealogical records. In all, 956 families
from the tribe of Benjamin returned.

The Returning Priests

1 CHRONICLES 9:10-13

[10] Among the priests who returned were Jedaiah,
Jehoiarib, Jakin, [11] Azariah son of Hilkiah, son of
Meshullam, son of Zadok, son of Meraioth, son
of Ahitub. Azariah was the chief officer of the
house of God.
[12] Other returning priests were Adaiah son of
Jeroham, son of Pashhur, son of Malkijah, and
Maasai son of Adiel, son of Jahzerah, son of
Meshullam, son of Meshillemith, son of Immer.
[13] In all, 1,760 priests returned. They were heads of
clans and very able men. They were responsible for
ministering at the house of God.

The Returning Levites

1 CHRONICLES 9:14-34

[14] The Levites who returned were Shemaiah son
of Hasshub, son of Azrikam, son of Hashabiah,
a descendant of Merari; [15] Bakbakkar; Heresh;
Galal; Mattaniah son of Mica, son of Zicri, son of
Asaph; [16] Obadiah son of Shemaiah, son of Galal,
son of Jeduthun; and Berekiah son of Asa, son of
Elkanah, who lived in the area of Netophah.
[17] The gatekeepers who returned were Shallum,
Akkub, Talmon, Ahiman, and their relatives.

---

1 Chr 9:1 Although not every person in Judah was unfaithful, the entire nation was carried away into captivity. Everyone was affected by the sin of a few. Even if we don't participate in a certain widespread wrongdoing, we still will be affected by those who do. It is not enough to say, "I didn't do it." We must speak out against the sins of our society.

1 Chr 9:1ff Chronologically, this chapter could be placed after the end of 2 Chronicles because it records the names of the exiles who returned from the Babylonian captivity. But the writer placed it at the very beginning of 1 Chronicles to show his concern for their need, as a nation, to return to what made them great in the first place—obedience to God.

1 Chr 9:10-11 When we think of doing God's work, usually preaching, teaching, singing, and other kinds of up-front leadership come to mind. But Azariah was chief officer in charge of the house of God, and he was singled out for special mention. Whatever role you have in church, it is important to God. He appreciates your service and the attitude you have as you do it.

1 Chr 9:17-18 Gatekeepers guarded the four main entrances to the Temple and opened the gates each morning for those who wanted to worship. In addition, they did other day-to-day chores to keep the Temple running smoothly—cleaning, preparing the offerings for sacrifice, and accounting for the gifts designated to the Temple (1 Chr 9:22-32).

Gatekeepers had to be reliable, honest, and trustworthy. The people in our churches who handle the offerings and care for the materials and functions of the building follow in a great tradition, and we should honor them for their reliability and service.

▸ 1 CHRONICLES 9:14-34 ***(cont.)***
Shallum was the chief gatekeeper. 18Prior to
this time, they were responsible for the King's
Gate on the east side. These men served as
gatekeepers for the camps of the Levites.
19Shallum was the son of Kore, a descendant of
Abiasaph,* from the clan of Korah. He and his
relatives, the Korahites, were responsible for
guarding the entrance to the sanctuary, just as
their ancestors had guarded the Tabernacle in
the camp of the LORD.

20Phinehas son of Eleazar had been in charge
of the gatekeepers in earlier times, and the LORD
had been with him. 21And later Zechariah son of
Meshelemiah was responsible for guarding the
entrance to the Tabernacle.*

22In all, there were 212 gatekeepers in those days,
and they were listed according to the genealogies
in their villages. David and Samuel the seer had appointed their ancestors because they were reliable
men. 23These gatekeepers and their descendants, by
their divisions, were responsible for guarding the entrance to the house of the LORD when that house was
a tent. 24The gatekeepers were stationed on all four
sides—east, west, north, and south. 25Their relatives
in the villages came regularly to share their duties for
seven-day periods.

26The four chief gatekeepers, all Levites, were
trusted officials, for they were responsible for the
rooms and treasuries at the house of God. 27They
would spend the night around the house of God, since
it was their duty to guard it and to open the gates every
morning.

28Some of the gatekeepers were assigned to care
for the various articles used in worship. They checked
them in and out to avoid any loss. 29Others were responsible for the furnishings, the items in the sanctuary, and the supplies, such as choice flour, wine,
olive oil, frankincense, and spices. 30But it was the
priests who blended the spices. 31Mattithiah, a Levite
and the oldest son of Shallum the Korahite, was entrusted with baking the bread used in the offerings.
32And some members of the clan of Kohath were in
charge of preparing the bread to be set on the table
each Sabbath day.

33The musicians, all prominent Levites, lived at the
Temple. They were exempt from other responsibilities since they were on duty at all hours. 34All these
men lived in Jerusalem. They were the heads of Levite
families and were listed as prominent leaders in their
genealogical records.

King Saul's Family Tree

1 CHRONICLES 9:35-44
35Jeiel (the father of* Gibeon) lived in the town of
Gibeon. His wife's name was Maacah, 36and his
oldest son was named Abdon. Jeiel's other sons
were Zur, Kish, Baal, Ner, Nadab, 37Gedor, Ahio,
Zechariah, and Mikloth. 38Mikloth was the father
of Shimeam. All these families lived near each
other in Jerusalem.
39 Ner was the father of Kish.
Kish was the father of Saul.
Saul was the father of Jonathan, Malkishua,
Abinadab, and Esh-baal.
40 Jonathan was the father of Merib-baal.
Merib-baal was the father of Micah.
41 The sons of Micah were Pithon, Melech, Tahrea,
and Ahaz.*
42 Ahaz was the father of Jadah.*
Jadah was the father of Alemeth, Azmaveth, and
Zimri.
Zimri was the father of Moza.
43 Moza was the father of Binea.
Binea's son was Rephaiah.
Rephaiah's son was Eleasah.
Eleasah's son was Azel.
44Azel had six sons, whose names were Azrikam,
Bokeru, Ishmael, Sheariah, Obadiah, and Hanan.
These were the sons of Azel.

1 Chr 9:19 Hebrew *Ebiasaph*, a variant spelling of Abiasaph; compare Exod 6:24. **1 Chr 9:21** Hebrew *Tent of Meeting.* **1 Chr 9:35** Or *the founder of.* **1 Chr 9:41** As in Syriac version and Latin Vulgate (see also 8:35); Hebrew lacks *and Ahaz.* **1 Chr 9:42** As in some Hebrew manuscripts and Greek version (see also 8:36); Hebrew reads *Jarah.*

1 Chr 9:22-32 The priests put a great deal of time and care into worship. Not only did they perform rather complicated tasks (described in Lev 1–9), but they also took care of many pieces of equipment. Everything relating to worship was carefully prepared and maintained so they and all the people could enter worship with their minds and hearts focused on God. In our busy world, it is easy to rush into our one-hour-a-week worship services without preparing ourselves for worship beforehand. We reflect and worry about the week's problems, we pray about whatever comes into our minds, and we do not meditate on the words we are singing. But God wants our worship to be conducted "properly and in order" (1 Cor 14:40). Just as we prepare to meet a business associate or invited guests, we should carefully prepare to meet our King in worship.

1 Chr 9:33-34 Worship was the primary focus of many Israelites, whose vocation centered on the house of the Lord. Worship (appreciating God for his nature and worth) should occupy the core of our lives and not just a few minutes once a week. We, too, can worship at any time if we stay aware of God's presence and guidance in all situations and if we maintain an attitude of serving him. Build your life around the worship of God rather than making worship just another activity in a busy schedule.

G. The Book of Joel

Joel is very difficult to place chronologically because he doesn't mention any kings or other clear historical information. The two most likely time periods for Joel's ministry are either during the time that Joash was king in Judah (around 835 B.C.) or during the time of the return from exile. In this Bible, we have placed Joel in the later chronology, but the message for us today is the same no matter when Joel prophesied: God's judgment on sin is sure, but his mercy and redemption are just as certain for those who love and serve him.

1. THE DAY OF THE LOCUSTS

Joel describes a devastating locust plague that afflicted Judah and Jerusalem. This plague represents God's judgment against sin, and the prophet calls on the people to repent and turn to God for mercy.

Mourning over the Locust Plague

JOEL 1:1-20

The LORD gave this message to Joel son of Pethuel.
2 Hear this, you leaders of the people.
Listen, all who live in the land.
In all your history,
has anything like this happened before?
3 Tell your children about it in the years to come,
and let your children tell their children.
Pass the story down from generation to generation.
4 After the cutting locusts finished eating the crops,
the swarming locusts took what was left!
After them came the hopping locusts,
and then the stripping locusts,* too!
5 Wake up, you drunkards, and weep!
Wail, all you wine-drinkers!
All the grapes are ruined,
and all your sweet wine is gone.
6 A vast army of locusts* has invaded my land,
a terrible army too numerous to count.
Its teeth are like lions' teeth,
its fangs like those of a lioness.
7 It has destroyed my grapevines
and ruined my fig trees,
stripping their bark and destroying it,
leaving the branches white and bare.
8 Weep like a bride dressed in black,
mourning the death of her husband.
9 For there is no grain or wine
to offer at the Temple of the LORD.
So the priests are in mourning.
The ministers of the LORD are weeping.
10 The fields are ruined,
the land is stripped bare.

Jl 1:4 The precise identification of the four kinds of locusts mentioned here is uncertain. **Jl 1:6** Hebrew *A nation.*

JOEL

Joel served as a prophet to Israel after the return from exile, around 440 B.C.

Climate of the times	The people had returned from a 70-year exile from the land, but they continued to struggle with being faithful to God.
Main message	A plague of locusts had come to discipline the nation. Joel called the people to turn back to God before an even greater judgment occurred.
Importance of message	God judges all people for their sins, but he is merciful to those who turn to him and offers them eternal salvation.
Contemporary prophet	Malachi (about 430 B.C.)

Joel 1:1 The book of Joel does not mention when Joel lived, but many believe that he prophesied to the nation of Judah during the reign of King Joash (835–796 B.C.). In this Bible, we have placed Joel at a later date, after God's people had returned from exile and were reestablishing themselves in the land he had promised them. The date of Joel's book is not nearly so important as its timeless message: Sin brings God's judgment; yet with God's justice there is also great mercy.

Joel 1:3 God urged parents to pass their history down to their children, telling over and over the important lessons they learned. One of the greatest gifts you can give young people is your life's story to help them repeat your successes and avoid your mistakes.

Joel 1:4 A locust plague can be as devastating as an invading army. Locusts gather in swarms too numerous to count (Joel 1:6) and fly several feet above the ground, seeming to darken the sun as they pass by (Joel 2:2). When they land, they devour almost every piece of vegetation (Joel 1:7-12), covering and entering everything in their path (Joel 2:9).

Joel 1:4 Joel's detailed description has caused many to believe that he was referring to an actual locust plague that had come or was about to come upon the land. Another view is that the locusts symbolize an invading enemy army. In either case, the locusts represent devastation, and Joel's point was that God would punish the people because of their sin. Joel calls this judgment the "day of the LORD" (see the note on Joel 1:15, p. 1240).

Joel 1:5 The people's physical and moral senses were dulled, making them oblivious to sin. Joel called them to awaken from their complacency and admit their sins before it was too late. Otherwise everything would be destroyed, even the grapes that caused their drunkenness. Our times of peace and prosperity can lull us to sleep. We must never let material abundance hinder our spiritual readiness.

Joel 1:9 Because of the devastation, there was no grain to make fine flour for the grain offerings and no wine for the drink offerings (see Lev 1–2 for a detailed explanation of these offerings).

▸ **JOEL 1:1-20 *(cont.)***

The grain is destroyed,
the grapes have shriveled,
and the olive oil is gone.
11 Despair, all you farmers!
Wail, all you vine growers!
Weep, because the wheat and barley—
all the crops of the field—are ruined.
12 The grapevines have dried up,
and the fig trees have withered.
The pomegranate trees, palm trees, and apple trees—
all the fruit trees—have dried up.
And the people's joy has dried up with them.

13 Dress yourselves in burlap and weep, you priests!
Wail, you who serve before the altar!
Come, spend the night in burlap,
you ministers of my God.
For there is no grain or wine
to offer at the Temple of your God.
14 Announce a time of fasting;
call the people together for a solemn meeting.
Bring the leaders
and all the people of the land
into the Temple of the LORD your God,
and cry out to him there.
15 The day of the LORD is near,
the day when destruction comes from the Almighty.
How terrible that day will be!
16 Our food disappears before our very eyes.
No joyful celebrations are held in the house of our God.
17 The seeds die in the parched ground,
and the grain crops fail.
The barns stand empty,
and granaries are abandoned.
18 How the animals moan with hunger!
The herds of cattle wander about confused,
because they have no pasture.
The flocks of sheep and goats bleat in misery.

19 LORD, help us!
The fire has consumed the wilderness pastures,
and flames have burned up all the trees.
20 Even the wild animals cry out to you
because the streams have dried up,
and fire has consumed the wilderness pastures.

Locusts Invade like an Army

JOEL 2:1-11

1 Sound the alarm in Jerusalem*!
Raise the battle cry on my holy mountain!
Let everyone tremble in fear
because the day of the LORD is upon us.
2 It is a day of darkness and gloom,
a day of thick clouds and deep blackness.
Suddenly, like dawn spreading across the mountains,
a great and mighty army appears.
Nothing like it has been seen before
or will ever be seen again.

3 Fire burns in front of them,
and flames follow after them.
Ahead of them the land lies
as beautiful as the Garden of Eden.
Behind them is nothing but desolation;
not one thing escapes.
4 They look like horses;
they charge forward like warhorses.*
5 Look at them as they leap along the mountaintops.
Listen to the noise they make—like the rumbling of chariots,
like the roar of fire sweeping across a field of stubble,
or like a mighty army moving into battle.
6 Fear grips all the people;
every face grows pale with terror.

Jl 2:1 Hebrew *Zion;* also in 2:15, 23. **Jl 2:4** Or *like charioteers.*

Joel 1:13 Mourners at a funeral would wear burlap clothing. Used here, it would be a sign of repentance.

Joel 1:14 A fast was a period of time when no food was eaten and people approached God with humility, sorrow for sin, and urgent prayer. In the Old Testament, people often would fast during times of calamity in order to focus their attention on God and to demonstrate their change of heart and their true devotion (see, for example, Judg 20:26; 1 Kgs 21:27; Ezra 8:21; Jon 3:5). This solemn meeting was a public religious gathering, called so that everyone could repent and pray to God for mercy.

Joel 1:15 The "day of the LORD" is a common phrase in the Old Testament and in the book of Joel (see Joel 2:1, 11, 31; 3:14). It always refers to some extraordinary happening, whether a present event (like a locust plague), an event in the near future (like a military threat against Jerusalem or the defeat of enemy nations), or the final period of history when God will defeat all the forces of evil.

Even when the day of the Lord refers to a present event, it also foreshadows the final day of the Lord. This final event of history has two aspects to it: (1) the last judgment on all evil and sin and (2) the final reward for faithful believers. Righteousness and truth will prevail, but not before much suffering (Zech 14:1-3). If you trust the Lord, looking toward this final day should give you hope, because then all who are faithful will be united forever with God.

Joel 1:15-19 Without God, destruction is sure. Those who have not personally accepted God's love and forgiveness will stand before him with no appeal. Be sure to avail yourself of God's love and mercy while you have the opportunity (Joel 2:32).

Joel 2:1ff Joel was still describing the devastating effects of the locust plague (see Joel 2:25). The alarm showed that the crisis was at hand. However, Joel implied that the locust plague would be only the forerunner of an even greater crisis if the people didn't turn from their sins.

Joel 2:3 The Garden of Eden was Adam and Eve's first home (Gen 2:8). Known for its beauty, it is used here to describe the beauty of the land prior to the devastation.

7 The attackers march like warriors
and scale city walls like soldiers.
Straight forward they march,
never breaking rank.
8 They never jostle each other;
each moves in exactly the right position.
They break through defenses
without missing a step.
9 They swarm over the city
and run along its walls.
They enter all the houses,
climbing like thieves through the windows.
10 The earth quakes as they advance,
and the heavens tremble.
The sun and moon grow dark,
and the stars no longer shine.

11 The LORD is at the head of the column.
He leads them with a shout.
This is his mighty army,
and they follow his orders.
The day of the LORD is an awesome, terrible
thing.
Who can possibly survive?

A Call to Repentance

JOEL 2:12-17

12 That is why the LORD says,
"Turn to me now, while there is time.
Give me your hearts.
Come with fasting, weeping, and mourning.
13 Don't tear your clothing in your grief,
but tear your hearts instead."
Return to the LORD your God,
for he is merciful and compassionate,
slow to get angry and filled with unfailing love.
He is eager to relent and not punish.
14 Who knows? Perhaps he will give you a reprieve,
sending you a blessing instead of this curse.
Perhaps you will be able to offer grain and wine
to the LORD your God as before.

15 Blow the ram's horn in Jerusalem!
Announce a time of fasting;
call the people together
for a solemn meeting.
16 Gather all the people—
the elders, the children, and even the babies.
Call the bridegroom from his quarters
and the bride from her private room.
17 Let the priests, who minister in the LORD's
presence,
stand and weep between the entry room to the
Temple and the altar.
Let them pray, "Spare your people, LORD!
Don't let your special possession become an
object of mockery.
Don't let them become a joke for unbelieving
foreigners who say,
'Has the God of Israel left them?'"

The LORD's Promise of Restoration

JOEL 2:18-27

18 Then the LORD will pity his people
and jealously guard the honor of his land.
19 The LORD will reply,
"Look! I am sending you grain and new wine and
olive oil,
enough to satisfy your needs.
You will no longer be an object of mockery
among the surrounding nations.
20 I will drive away these armies from the north.
I will send them into the parched wastelands.
Those in the front will be driven into the
Dead Sea,
and those at the rear into the Mediterranean.*
The stench of their rotting bodies will rise over
the land."

Surely the LORD has done great things!
21 Don't be afraid, my people.
Be glad now and rejoice,
for the LORD has done great things.

Jl 2:20 Hebrew *into the eastern sea, . . . into the western sea.*

Joel 2:12-13 God told the people to turn to him while there was still time. Destruction would soon be upon them. Time is also running out for us. Because we don't know when our life will end, we should trust and obey God now while we can. Don't let anything hinder you from turning to him.

Joel 2:13 Deep remorse was often shown by tearing one's clothes. But God didn't want an outward display of penitence without true inward repentance (1 Sam 16:7; Matt 23:1-36). Be sure your attitude toward God is correct, not just your outward actions.

Joel 2:18 Joel reached a turning point in his message, moving from prophesying about an outpouring of God's judgment to prophesying about an outpouring of God's forgiveness and blessing. But this would come only if the people began to live as God wanted them to, giving up their sins. Where there is repentance, there is hope. This section of the book inspires that hope. Without it, Joel's prophecy could bring only despair. This promise of forgiveness should have encouraged the people to repent.

Joel 2:20 Some scholars think Joel prophesied earlier in Judah's history and was prophesying about the invasion from the north by the armies of Assyria and Babylon, typified by the locusts.

Joel 2:21 Joel contrasts the fear of God's judgment (Joel 2:1) with the joy of God's intervention (Joel 2:21). On the day of the Lord, sin will bring judgment, and only God's forgiveness will bring rejoicing. Unless you repent, your sin will result in punishment. Let God intervene in your life. Then you will be able to rejoice in that day because you will have nothing to fear. Before, there were fasting, plagues, and funeral dirges; then, there will be feasting, harvesting, and songs of praise. When God rules, his restoration will be complete. In the meantime, we must remember that God does not promise that all his followers will be prosperous now. When God pardons, he restores our relationship with him, but this does not guarantee individual wealth. Instead, God promises to meet the deepest needs of those who love him by loving us, forgiving us, giving us purpose in life, and giving us a caring Christian community.

▸ **JOEL 2:18-27** ***(cont.)***

22 Don't be afraid, you animals of the field,
for the wilderness pastures will soon be green.
The trees will again be filled with fruit;
fig trees and grapevines will be loaded down
once more.
23 Rejoice, you people of Jerusalem!
Rejoice in the LORD your God!
For the rain he sends demonstrates his
faithfulness.
Once more the autumn rains will come,
as well as the rains of spring.
24 The threshing floors will again be piled high with
grain,
and the presses will overflow with new wine
and olive oil.
25 The LORD says, "I will give you back what
you lost
to the swarming locusts, the hopping
locusts,
the stripping locusts, and the cutting locusts.*
It was I who sent this great destroying army
against you.
26 Once again you will have all the food you want,
and you will praise the LORD your God,
who does these miracles for you.
Never again will my people be disgraced.
27 Then you will know that I am among my people
Israel,
that I am the LORD your God, and there is no
other.
Never again will my people be disgraced.

Jl 2:25 The precise identification of the four kinds of locusts mentioned here is uncertain.

2. THE DAY OF THE LORD

The locust plague was only a foretaste of the judgment to come in the day of the Lord. This is a timeless call to repentance with the promise of blessing. Just as the people faced the tragedy of their crops being destroyed, we, too, will face tragic judgment if we live in sin. But God's grace is available to us both now and in that coming day.

The LORD's Promise of His Spirit

JOEL 2:28-32

28* "Then, after doing all those things,
I will pour out my Spirit upon all people.
Your sons and daughters will prophesy.
Your old men will dream dreams,
and your young men will see visions.
29 In those days I will pour out my Spirit
even on servants—men and women alike.
30 And I will cause wonders in the heavens and
on the earth—
blood and fire and columns of smoke.
31 The sun will become dark,
and the moon will turn blood red
before that great and terrible* day of the
LORD arrives.
32 But everyone who calls on the name of the LORD
will be saved,

Jl 2:28 Verses 2:28-32 are numbered 3:1-5 in Hebrew text. **Jl 2:31** Greek version reads *glorious.*

"I will pour out my Spirit upon all people. Your sons and daughters will prophesy. Your old men will dream dreams, and your young men will see visions."
Joel 2:28

Joel 2:26-27 If the Jews would never again experience a disaster like this locust plague ("never again will my people be disgraced"), how do we explain the Jews' slavery under the Greeks and Romans and their persecution under Hitler? It is important not to take these verses out of context. This is still part of the "blessings" section of Joel's prophecy. Only if the people truly repented would they avoid a disaster like the one Joel had described. God's blessings are promised only to those who sincerely and consistently follow him. God does promise that after the final day of judgment, his people will never again experience this kind of disaster (Zech 14:9-11; Rev 21).

Joel 2:28-32 Peter quoted this passage (see Acts 2:16-21); the outpouring of the Spirit predicted by Joel occurred on Pentecost. While in the past God's Spirit seemed available to kings, prophets, and judges, Joel envisioned a time when the Spirit would be available to every believer. Ezekiel also spoke of an outpouring of the Spirit (Ezek 39:28-29). God's Spirit is available today to anyone who calls on the Lord for salvation (Joel 2:32).

Joel 2:30 These "wonders" would give a hint or a picture of a coming event.

Joel 2:31-32 The "day of the LORD" is used here as God's appointed time to judge the nations (see the note on Joel 1:15, p. 1240). Judgment and mercy go hand in hand.

for some on Mount Zion in Jerusalem will escape,
just as the LORD has said.
These will be among the survivors
whom the LORD has called.

Judgment against Enemy Nations

JOEL 3:1-16

1*"At the time of those events," says the LORD,
"when I restore the prosperity of Judah
and Jerusalem,
2 I will gather the armies of the world
into the valley of Jehoshaphat.*
There I will judge them
for harming my people, my special
possession,
for scattering my people among the nations,
and for dividing up my land.
3 They threw dice* to decide which of my people
would be their slaves.
They traded boys to obtain prostitutes
and sold girls for enough wine to get drunk.

4"What do you have against me, Tyre and Sidon and
you cities of Philistia? Are you trying to take revenge
on me? If you are, then watch out! I will strike swiftly
and pay you back for everything you have done. 5You
have taken my silver and gold and all my precious
treasures, and have carried them off to your pagan
temples. 6You have sold the people of Judah and Jerusalem to the Greeks,* so they could take them far
from their homeland.
7"But I will bring them back from all the places
to which you sold them, and I will pay you back for
everything you have done. 8I will sell your sons and
daughters to the people of Judah, and they will sell
them to the people of Arabia,* a nation far away. I, the
LORD, have spoken!"

9 Say to the nations far and wide:
"Get ready for war!
Call out your best warriors.
Let all your fighting men advance for the
attack.
10 Hammer your plowshares into swords
and your pruning hooks into spears.
Train even your weaklings to be warriors.
11 Come quickly, all you nations everywhere.
Gather together in the valley."

And now, O LORD, call out your warriors!

12 "Let the nations be called to arms.
Let them march to the valley of Jehoshaphat.
There I, the LORD, will sit
to pronounce judgment on them all.
13 Swing the sickle,
for the harvest is ripe.*
Come, tread the grapes,
for the winepress is full.
The storage vats are overflowing
with the wickedness of these people."

14 Thousands upon thousands are waiting in the
valley of decision.
There the day of the LORD will soon arrive.
15 The sun and moon will grow dark,
and the stars will no longer shine.
16 The LORD's voice will roar from Zion
and thunder from Jerusalem,
and the heavens and the earth will shake.
But the LORD will be a refuge for his people,
a strong fortress for the people of Israel.

Jl 3:1 Verses 3:1-21 are numbered 4:1-21 in Hebrew text. **Jl 3:2** *Jehoshaphat* means "the LORD judges." **Jl 3:3** Hebrew *They cast lots.* **Jl 3:6** Hebrew *to the peoples of Javan.* **Jl 3:8** Hebrew *to the Sabeans.* **Jl 3:13** Greek version reads *for the harvest time has come.* Compare Mark 4:29.

Joel had said that if the people repented, the Lord would save them from judgment (Joel 2:12-14). In this day of judgment and catastrophe, therefore, some will be saved. God's intention is not to destroy but to heal and to save. However, we must accept his salvation or we will certainly perish with the unrepentant.

Joel 3:1-2 The phrase "at the time of those events" refers to the time when those who call on the Lord will be saved (Joel 2:32). God will not only bless believers with everything they need, but he will also bless them by destroying all evil and ending the pain and suffering on earth. This prophecy has three fulfillments: immediate, ongoing, and final. Its immediate and ongoing interpretation could apply to the partial restoration of the people to their land after the exile to Babylon. The final fulfillment would come in the great battle that precedes the Messiah's reign over the earth (Rev 20:7-9).

Joel 3:2 The geographic location of the valley of Jehoshaphat is not known, and some suggest it is being used as a symbol for the place where the Lord is to judge. Some think it may be a future valley created by the splitting of the Mount of Olives when the Messiah returns (Zech 14:4). The most important fact for us is that the name means "the LORD judges."

Joel 3:4 Tyre and Sidon were major cities in Phoenicia to the northwest of Israel; Philistia was the nation southwest of Judah. Phoenicia and Philistia were small countries that rejoiced at the fall of Judah and Israel because they would benefit from the increased trade. God would judge them for their wrong attitude.

Joel 3:6 Jews were sold to Greeks, a pagan and unclean people.

Joel 3:8 The "people of Arabia" are also referred to as Sabeans, who came from Sheba, a nation in southwestern Arabia. One of Sheba's queens had visited Solomon centuries earlier (1 Kgs 10:1-13). The Sabeans controlled the eastern trade routes.

Joel 3:14 Joel described multitudes waiting in the "valley of decision" (the valley of judgment of Joel 3:2, 12). Billions of people have lived on earth, and every one of them—dead, living, and yet to be born—will face judgment. Look around you. See your friends—those with whom you work and live. Have they received God's forgiveness? Have they been warned about sin's consequences? If we understand the severity of God's final judgment, we will want to take God's offer of hope to those we know.

Blessings for God's People

JOEL 3:17-21

17 "Then you will know that I, the LORD your God,
live in Zion, my holy mountain.
Jerusalem will be holy forever,
and foreign armies will never conquer her again.
18 In that day the mountains will drip with sweet wine,
and the hills will flow with milk.
Water will fill the streambeds of Judah,
and a fountain will burst forth from the LORD's Temple,
watering the arid valley of acacias.*
19 But Egypt will become a wasteland
and Edom will become a wilderness,
because they attacked the people of Judah
and killed innocent people in their land.
20 "But Judah will be filled with people forever,
and Jerusalem will endure through all generations.
21 I will pardon my people's crimes,
which I have not yet pardoned;
and I, the LORD, will make my home
in Jerusalem* with my people."

Jl 3:18 Hebrew *valley of Shittim.* **Jl 3:21** Hebrew *Zion.*

H. The Book of Malachi

Malachi rebuked the people and the priests for neglecting the worship of God and failing to live according to his will. The priests were corrupt; how could they lead the people? They had become stumbling blocks instead of spiritual leaders. The men were divorcing their wives and marrying pagan women; how could they have godly children? Their relationship to God had become inconsequential. If our relationship with God is unimportant, we need to take stock of ourselves by setting aside our sinful habits, putting the Lord first, and giving God our best each day.

The LORD's Love for Israel

MALACHI 1:1-5

This is the message* that the LORD gave to Israel through the prophet Malachi.*

2"I have always loved you," says the LORD.
But you retort, "Really? How have you loved us?"
And the LORD replies, "This is how I showed my
love for you: I loved your ancestor Jacob, 3but I rejected
his brother, Esau, and devastated his hill country. I
turned Esau's inheritance into a desert for jackals."
4Esau's descendants in Edom may say, "We have
been shattered, but we will rebuild the ruins."
But the LORD of Heaven's Armies replies, "They may
try to rebuild, but I will demolish them again. Their
country will be known as 'The Land of Wickedness,'
and their people will be called 'The People with Whom
the LORD Is Forever Angry.' 5When you see the destruction
for yourselves, you will say, 'Truly, the LORD's greatness
reaches far beyond Israel's borders!'"

Mal 1:1a Hebrew *An Oracle: The message.* **Mal 1:1b** *Malachi* means "my messenger."

Joel 3:17 The last word will be God's; his ultimate sovereignty will be revealed in the end. We cannot predict when that end will come, but we can have confidence in his control over the world's events. The world's history, as well as our own pilgrimage, is in God's hands. We can be secure in his love and trust him to guide our decisions.

Joel 3:18 The picture of this restored land is one of perfect beauty, similar to the Garden of Eden. The life-giving fountain flowing from the Lord's Temple illustrates the blessings that come from God. Those who trust in him will be forever fruitful. (See also Ezek 47:1-12; Rev 22:1-2.)

Joel 3:19 Egypt and Edom were two of Israel's most persistent enemies. They represent all the nations hostile to God's people. God's promise that they would be destroyed is also a promise that all evil in the world will one day be destroyed.

Joel 3:20-21 The word *Judah* is used here to refer to all God's people—anyone who has called on the name of the Lord. There is full assurance of victory and peace for those who trust in God (Joel 2:32).

Joel 3:21 Joel began with a prophecy about the destruction of the land and ended with a prophecy about its restoration. He began by stressing the need for repentance and ended with the promise of forgiveness that repentance brings. Joel was trying to convince the people to wake up (Joel 1:5), get rid of their complacency, and realize the danger of living apart from God. His message to us is that there is still time; anyone who calls on God's name can be saved (Joel 2:12-14, 32). Those who turn to God will enjoy the blessings mentioned in Joel's prophecy; those who refuse will face destruction.

Mal 1:1 Malachi, the last Old Testament prophet, preached after Haggai, Zechariah, and Nehemiah—about 430 B.C. The Temple had been rebuilt for almost a century, and the people were losing their enthusiasm for worship. Apathy and disillusionment had set in because the exciting messianic prophecies of Isaiah, Jeremiah, and Micah had not been fulfilled. Many of the sins that had brought the downfall of Jerusalem in 586 B.C. were still being practiced in Judah. Malachi confronted the hypocrites with their sins by portraying a graphic dialogue between a righteous God and his hardened people.

Mal 1:2 God's first message through Malachi was "I have always loved you." Although this message applied specifically to Israel, it is a message of hope for all people in all times. Unfortunately, many people are cynical about God's love, using political and economic progress as a measure of success. Because the government was corrupt and the economy poor, the Israelites assumed that God didn't love them. They were wrong. God loves all people because he made them; however, his eternal rewards go only to those who are faithful to him.

Mal 1:2-5 The phrase "I rejected . . . Esau" does not refer to Esau's eternal destiny. It simply means that God chose Jacob, not his brother Esau, to be the one through whom the nation of Israel and the Messiah would come (see Rom 9:10-13). God allowed Esau to father a nation, but this nation, Edom, later

Unworthy Sacrifices

MALACHI 1:6-14

The LORD of Heaven's Armies says to the priests: "A son honors his father, and a servant respects his master. If I am your father and master, where are the honor and respect I deserve? You have shown contempt for my name!

"But you ask, 'How have we ever shown contempt for your name?'

[7]"You have shown contempt by offering defiled sacrifices on my altar.

"Then you ask, 'How have we defiled the sacrifices?*'

"You defile them by saying the altar of the LORD deserves no respect. [8]When you give blind animals as sacrifices, isn't that wrong? And isn't it wrong to offer animals that are crippled and diseased? Try giving gifts like that to your governor, and see how pleased he is!" says the LORD of Heaven's Armies.

[9]"Go ahead, beg God to be merciful to you! But when you bring that kind of offering, why should he show you any favor at all?" asks the LORD of Heaven's Armies.

[10]"How I wish one of you would shut the Temple doors so that these worthless sacrifices could not be offered! I am not pleased with you," says the LORD of Heaven's Armies, "and I will not accept your offerings. [11]But my name is honored* by people of other nations from morning till night. All around the world they offer* sweet incense and pure offerings in honor of my name. For my name is great among the nations," says the LORD of Heaven's Armies.

[12]"But you dishonor my name with your actions. By bringing contemptible food, you are saying it's all right to defile the Lord's table. [13]You say, 'It's too hard to serve the LORD,' and you turn up your noses at my commands," says the LORD of Heaven's Armies. "Think of it! Animals that are stolen and crippled and sick are being presented as offerings! Should I accept from you such offerings as these?" asks the LORD.

Mal 1:7 As in Greek version; Hebrew reads *defiled you?* **Mal 1:11a** Or *will be honored.* **Mal 1:11b** Or *will offer.*

MALACHI

Malachi served as a prophet to Judah about 430 B.C. He was the last of the Old Testament prophets.

Climate of the times	The city of Jerusalem and the Temple had been rebuilt for almost a century, but the people had become complacent in their worship of God.
Main message	The people's relationship with God was broken because of their sin, and they would soon be punished. But the few who repented would receive God's blessing, highlighted in his promise to send a Messiah.
Importance of message	Hypocrisy, neglecting God, and careless living have devastating consequences. Serving and worshiping God must be the primary focus of our life, both now and in eternity.
Contemporary prophet	Joel (about 440 B.C.)

became one of Israel's chief enemies. (See Gen 25:19-26 for the story of Jacob and Esau.) Because God chose Jacob and his descendants as the nation through whom the world would be blessed, God cared for them in a special way. Ironically, they rejected God after he chose them.

Mal 1:6ff God charged the priests with failing to honor him (to the point of despising his name) and failing to be good spiritual examples to the people. The Temple had been rebuilt in 516 B.C., and worship was being conducted there, but the priests did not worship God properly. They were not following his laws for the sacrifices. Ezra the priest had sparked a great revival around 458 B.C. But by Malachi's time, the nation's leaders had once again fallen away from God, and the people right along with them. The worship of God was no longer from heartfelt adoration; instead, it was simply a burdensome job for the priests.

Mal 1:6-8 God's law required that only perfect animals be offered to God (see, for example, Lev 1:3). But these priests were allowing the people to offer blind, crippled, and diseased animals. God accused them of dishonoring him by offering imperfect sacrifices, and he was greatly displeased. The New Testament says that our lives should be living sacrifices to God (Rom 12:1). If we give God only our leftover time, money, and energy, we repeat the same sin as these worshipers, who didn't want to bring anything valuable to God. What we give God reflects our true attitude toward him.

Mal 1:7-8 The people sacrificed to God wrongly through (1) expedience—being as cheap as possible, (2) neglect—not caring how they offered the sacrifice, and (3) outright disobedience—sacrificing their own way and not as God had commanded. Their methods of giving showed their real attitudes toward God. How about your attitude? Do expedience, neglect, or disobedience characterize your giving?

Mal 1:10 As intermediaries between God and the people, priests were responsible for reflecting God's attitudes and character. By accepting imperfect sacrifices, they were leading the people to believe that God accepted those sacrifices as well. But God says, "I am not pleased with you." As Christians, we are often in the same position as these priests because we reflect God to our friends and family. What image of God's character and attitudes do they see in you? If you casually accept sin, you are like these priests in Malachi's day, and God is not pleased with you.

Mal 1:11 A theme that can be heard throughout the Old Testament is affirmed in this book: "My name is honored by people of other nations." God had a chosen people, the Jews, through whom he planned to save and bless the entire world. Today God still wants to save and bless the world through all who believe in him—Jews and Gentiles. Christians are now his chosen people, and our offering to the Lord is our life. Are you available to God to be used in making his name honored by the nations? This mission begins in our home and in our neighborhood, but it doesn't stop there. We must work and pray so that God's name will be honored everywhere.

Mal 1:13 Worship was "too hard" according to these priests. Some people think that following God is supposed to make life more comfortable. They are looking for a God of convenience. The truth is that it takes commitment and hard work to live by God's high standards. We may have to face poverty or suffering. But if serving God is more important to us than anything else, what we give up is nothing compared to what we gain—eternal life with God.

430 BC

Malachi serves as a prophet

▶ **MALACHI 1:6-14** ***(cont.)***

14"Cursed is the cheat who promises to give a fine ram from his flock but then sacrifices a defective one to the Lord. For I am a great king," says the LORD of Heaven's Armies, "and my name is feared among the nations!

A Warning to the Priests

MALACHI 2:1-9

"Listen, you priests—this command is for you! 2Listen
to me and make up your minds to honor my name,"
says the LORD of Heaven's Armies, "or I will bring a terrible curse against you. I will curse even the blessings
you receive. Indeed, I have already cursed them, because you have not taken my warning to heart. 3I will
punish your descendants and splatter your faces with
the manure from your festival sacrifices, and I will
throw you on the manure pile. 4Then at last you will
know it was I who sent you this warning so that my
covenant with the Levites can continue," says the LORD
of Heaven's Armies.
5"The purpose of my covenant with the Levites was
to bring life and peace, and that is what I gave them.
This required reverence from them, and they greatly
revered me and stood in awe of my name. 6They
passed on to the people the truth of the instructions
they received from me. They did not lie or cheat; they
walked with me, living good and righteous lives, and
they turned many from lives of sin.
7"The words of a priest's lips should preserve
knowledge of God, and people should go to him for
instruction, for the priest is the messenger of the
LORD of Heaven's Armies. 8But you priests have left
God's paths. Your instructions have caused many to
stumble into sin. You have corrupted the covenant I
made with the Levites," says the LORD of Heaven's Armies. 9"So I have made you despised and humiliated
in the eyes of all the people. For you have not obeyed
me but have shown favoritism in the way you carry
out my instructions."

A Call to Faithfulness

MALACHI 2:10-17

Are we not all children of the same Father? Are we not all created by the same God? Then why do we betray each other, violating the covenant of our ancestors?

Petra

Malachi's first prophecy pertained to the Lord's judgment of Edom, where Petra is located. Petra was the capital of the Nabateans, who first appeared in history in 312 B.C. The Nabateans were of Arabic origin; they occupied the old land of Edom and made Petra their capital. Petra lay in an impressive valley about 1,000 yards wide among the mountains of western Edom, some 60 miles north of the Gulf of Aqaba. The only access to the valley is through a narrow gorge called the Siq. On all sides, massive cliffs of reddish sandstone arise. Today, ruins of many temples, houses, tombs, and other structures hewn out of reddish sandstone remain. A Roman basilica and theater are still to be seen. The place continued through Roman times and later had a Christian church and a bishop. It fell into ruins during the days of the Muslim conquest in the 7th century A.D.

Mal 2:1-2 God warned the priests that if they did not honor his name, he would punish them. Like these priests, we, too, are called to honor God's name—to worship him. This means acknowledging God for who he is—the almighty Creator of the universe, who alone is perfect and who reaches down to sinful people with perfect love. According to this definition, are you honoring God's name?

Mal 2:1-2 The priests didn't take seriously God's priority, even though he had reminded them through his word many times. How do you find out what is most important to God? Begin by loving him with all your heart, soul, and strength (Deut 6:5). This means listening to what God says in his Word and then setting your heart, mind, and will on doing what he says. When we love God, his Word becomes a shining light that guides our daily activities. The priests in Malachi's day had stopped loving God, and thus they did not know nor care what he wanted.

Mal 2:4-6 The Levites "walked with [God]," and "turned many from lives of sin" (Mal 2:6). Levi was the ancestor of the tribe of Levites, the tribe set apart for service to God (Num 1:47-54). The Levites became God's ministers, first in the Tabernacle, then in the Temple. In these verses, God was addressing the priests who were from this tribe, admonishing them for corrupting the laws he gave their ancestor Levi and not following his example.

Mal 2:7-8 Malachi was angry at the priests because, although they were to be God's messengers, they did not know God's will. And this lack of knowledge caused them to lead God's people astray. Their ignorance was willful and inexcusable. Pastors and leaders of God's people *must* know God's Word—what it says, what it means, and how it applies to daily life. How much time do you spend in God's Word?

Mal 2:9 The priests had allowed influential and favored people to break the law. The priests were so dependent on these people for support that they could not afford to confront them when they did wrong. In your church, are certain people allowed to do wrong without criticism? There should be no double standard based on wealth or position. Let your standards be those presented in God's Word. Playing favorites is contemptible in God's sight (see Jas 2:1-9).

11Judah has been unfaithful, and a detestable thing
has been done in Israel and in Jerusalem. The men of
Judah have defiled the LORD's beloved sanctuary by
marrying women who worship idols. 12May the LORD
cut off from the nation of Israel* every last man who
has done this and yet brings an offering to the LORD
of Heaven's Armies.
13Here is another thing you do. You cover the LORD's
altar with tears, weeping and groaning because he
pays no attention to your offerings and doesn't accept
them with pleasure. 14You cry out, "Why doesn't the
LORD accept my worship?" I'll tell you why! Because
the LORD witnessed the vows you and your wife made
when you were young. But you have been unfaithful
to her, though she remained your faithful partner, the
wife of your marriage vows.
15Didn't the LORD make you one with your wife? In
body and spirit you are his.* And what does he want?
Godly children from your union. So guard your heart;
remain loyal to the wife of your youth. 16"For I hate
divorce!" says the LORD, the God of Israel. "To divorce
your wife is to overwhelm her with cruelty,*" says the
LORD of Heaven's Armies. "So guard your heart; do not
be unfaithful to your wife."
17You have wearied the LORD with your words.
"How have we wearied him?" you ask.
You have wearied him by saying that all who do
evil are good in the LORD's sight, and he is pleased
with them. You have wearied him by asking, "Where
is the God of justice?"

The Coming Day of Judgment

MALACHI 3:1-5

"Look! I am sending my messenger, and he will
prepare the way before me. Then the Lord you are
seeking will suddenly come to his Temple. The messenger of the covenant, whom you look for so eagerly, is surely coming," says the LORD of Heaven's
Armies.
2"But who will be able to endure it when he comes?
Who will be able to stand and face him when he appears? For he will be like a blazing fire that refines
metal, or like a strong soap that bleaches clothes.
3He will sit like a refiner of silver, burning away the
dross. He will purify the Levites, refining them like
gold and silver, so that they may once again offer acceptable sacrifices to the LORD. 4Then once more the
LORD will accept the offerings brought to him by the
people of Judah and Jerusalem, as he did in the past.
5"At that time I will put you on trial. I am eager to
witness against all sorcerers and adulterers and liars.
I will speak against those who cheat employees of
their wages, who oppress widows and orphans, or who
deprive the foreigners living among you of justice,
for these people do not fear me," says the LORD of
Heaven's Armies.

Mal 2:12 Hebrew *from the tents of Jacob.* The names "Jacob" and "Israel" are often interchanged throughout the Old Testament, referring sometimes to the individual patriarch and sometimes to the nation. **Mal 2:15** Or *Didn't the one LORD make us and preserve our life and breath?* or *Didn't the one LORD make her, both flesh and spirit?* The meaning of the Hebrew is uncertain. **Mal 2:16** Hebrew *to cover one's garment with violence.*

Mal 2:10-16 The people were being unfaithful. Though not openly saying they rejected God, they were living as if he did not exist. Men were marrying pagan women who worshiped idols. Divorce was common, occurring for no reason other than a desire for change. People acted as if they could do anything without being punished. And they wondered why God refused to accept their offerings and bless them (Mal 2:13)! We cannot successfully separate our dealings with God from the rest of our life. He must be Lord of all.

Mal 2:11-12 After the Temple had been rebuilt and the walls completed, the people were excited to see past prophecies coming true. But as time passed, the prophecies about the destruction of God's enemies and a coming Messiah were not immediately fulfilled. The people became discouraged, and they grew complacent about obeying all of God's laws. This complacency gradually led to blatant sin, such as marriage to those who worshiped idols. Ezra and Nehemiah also had confronted this problem years earlier (Ezra 9–10; Neh 13:23-31).

Mal 2:14 The people were complaining about their adverse circumstances when they had only themselves to blame. People often try to avoid guilt feelings by shifting the blame. But this doesn't solve the problem. When you face problems, look first at yourself. If you changed your attitude or behavior, would the problem be solved?

Mal 2:14-15 Divorce in these times was practiced exclusively by men. They were disloyal to their wives and ignored the wedding vows they had made before God, thus corrupting his purpose for them to rear godly children who love the Lord. Not only were men unfaithful to their wives, but they also were ignoring the fact that this bonding relationship was an illustration of their union with God.

Mal 2:15-16 "Guard your heart; remain loyal to the wife of your youth" means to have the same commitment to marriage that God has to his promises for his people. Our passion should be reserved exclusively for our spouse.

Mal 2:17–3:6 God was tired of the way the people had cynically twisted his truths. He would punish those who insisted that because God was silent, he approved of their actions or at least would never punish them. God would also punish those who professed a counterfeit faith while acting sinfully (see Mal 3:5).

Mal 3:1 There are two messengers in this verse. The first is usually understood to be John the Baptist (Matt 11:10; Luke 7:27). The second messenger is Jesus, the Messiah, for whom both Malachi and John the Baptist prepared the way.

Mal 3:2-3 In the process of refining metals, the raw metal is heated with fire until it melts. The impurities separate from it and rise to the surface. They are skimmed off, leaving the pure metal. Without this heating and melting, there could be no purifying. As the impurities are skimmed off the top, the reflection of the worker appears in the clear, pure surface. As God purifies us, his reflection in our life will become more and more clear to those around us. God says that the Levites (Israel's leaders) should be especially open to his purification process in their lives.

The strong soap was alkali used to whiten cloth, also used here as a symbol of the purifying process.

A Call to Repentance

MALACHI 3:6-15

"I am the LORD, and I do not change. That is why you descendants of Jacob are not already destroyed. 7Ever since the days of your ancestors, you have scorned my decrees and failed to obey them. Now return to me, and I will return to you," says the LORD of Heaven's Armies.

"But you ask, 'How can we return when we have never gone away?'

8"Should people cheat God? Yet you have cheated me!

"But you ask, 'What do you mean? When did we ever cheat you?'

"You have cheated me of the tithes and offerings due to me. 9You are under a curse, for your whole nation has been cheating me. 10Bring all the tithes into the storehouse so there will be enough food in my Temple. If you do," says the LORD of Heaven's Armies, "I will open the windows of heaven for you. I will pour out a blessing so great you won't have enough room to take it in! Try it! Put me to the test! 11Your crops will be abundant, for I will guard them from insects and disease.* Your grapes will not fall from the vine before they are ripe," says the LORD of Heaven's Armies. 12"Then all nations will call you blessed, for your land will be such a delight," says the LORD of Heaven's Armies.

13"You have said terrible things about me," says the LORD.

"But you say, 'What do you mean? What have we said against you?'

14"You have said, 'What's the use of serving God? What have we gained by obeying his commands or by trying to show the LORD of Heaven's Armies that we are sorry for our sins? 15From now on we will call the arrogant blessed. For those who do evil get rich, and those who dare God to punish them suffer no harm.'"

Mal 3:11 Hebrew *from the devourer.*

The LORD's Promise of Mercy

MALACHI 3:16-18

Then those who feared the LORD spoke with each other, and the LORD listened to what they said. In his presence, a scroll of remembrance was written to record the names of those who feared him and always thought about the honor of his name.

Plato, famous philosopher, is born

Mal 3:7 God's patience seems endless! Throughout history, his people have disobeyed, even scorned, his laws, but he has always been willing to accept them back. Here the people have the nerve to imply that they never disobeyed ("How can we return when we have never gone away?")! Many people have turned their backs on forgiveness and restoration because they have refused to admit their sin. Don't follow their example. God is ready to return to us if we are willing to return to him.

Mal 3:8-12 Malachi urged the people to stop holding back their tithes, to stop cheating God. The tithing system began during the time of Moses (Lev 27:30-34; Deut 14:22). The Levites received some of the tithe because they could not possess land of their own (Num 18:20-21). During Malachi's day, the people were not giving tithes, so the Levites went to work to earn a living, thereby neglecting their God-given responsibilities to care for the Temple and for the service of worship. Everything we have is from God; so when we refuse to return to him a part of what he has given, we rob him. Do you selfishly want to keep 100 percent of what God gives, or are you willing to return at least 10 percent to help advance God's Kingdom?

Mal 3:8-12 The people of Malachi's day ignored God's command to give a tithe of their income to his Temple. They may have feared losing what they had worked so hard to get, but in this they misjudged God. "Give, and you will receive," he says (Luke 6:38). When we give, we must remember that the blessings God promises are not always material and may not be experienced completely here on earth, but we will certainly receive them in our future life with him.

GIVING A TENTH

Many ancient peoples observed the practice of tithing—that is, giving a tenth of their earnings (or produce, harvest, etc.) back to a leader or a god. Malachi reminded the people of God's command to tithe. The first instance is Abraham's tithe to Melchizedek.

The Israelites were required to tithe of their crops, fruit, and herds.	**Lev 27:30-33**
The Levites were given the tithe as their support.	**Num 18:21, 24**
The Levites, in turn, gave "a tithe of the tithe" to support the priests.	**Num 18:26-29; Neh 10:38-39**
The Israelites were to bring their tithes to Jerusalem, and offering them came in the form of a ritual meal in which Levites were invited to share. If Jerusalem was too far for a person to transport the tithe, he could take the tithe there in the form of money. Every third year the tithe could be offered in one's local area, but the person was still to go to Jerusalem to worship.	**Deut 12:5-7, 11-19; 14:22-29; 26:12-15**
God promises blessings for those who faithfully tithe, and he says that refusing to tithe is like robbing him.	**Mal 3:8-12**
Tithing, without love for or obedience to God, amounts to nothing more than a meaningless ritual.	**Matt 23:23; Luke 11:42**

Mal 3:10 The "storehouse" was a place in the Temple for storing grain and other food given as tithes. The priests lived off these gifts. We also need to give from the plenty that God has given us in order to support those who serve God by ministering to the spiritual needs of others.

Mal 3:13-15 These verses describe the people's arrogant attitude toward God. When we ask, "What's the use of serving God?" we are really asking, "What good does it do for *me*?" Our focus is selfish. Our real question should be, "What good does it do for God?" We must serve God just because he is God and deserves to be served.

Mal 3:16 God will remember those who remain faithful to him, and who love, fear, honor, and respect him.

Mal 3:17 God's special treasure are those faithful to him. This fulfills the promise he

17“They will be my people,” says the LORD of Heav-
en’s Armies. “On the day when I act in judgment, they
will be my own special treasure. I will spare them as
a father spares an obedient child. 18Then you will
again see the difference between the righteous and
the wicked, between those who serve God and those
who do not.”

The Coming Day of Judgment

MALACHI 4:1-6

1*The LORD of Heaven’s Armies says, “The day of judgment is coming, burning like a furnace. On that day
the arrogant and the wicked will be burned up like
straw. They will be consumed—roots, branches, and all.
2“But for you who fear my name, the Sun of Righteousness will rise with healing in his wings.* And
you will go free, leaping with joy like calves let out to
pasture. 3On the day when I act, you will tread upon
the wicked as if they were dust under your feet,” says
the LORD of Heaven’s Armies.
4“Remember to obey the Law of Moses, my servant—all the decrees and regulations that I gave him
on Mount Sinai* for all Israel.
5“Look, I am sending you the prophet Elijah before the great and dreadful day of the LORD arrives.
6His preaching will turn the hearts of fathers to their
children, and the hearts of children to their fathers.
Otherwise I will come and strike the land with a curse.”

Mal 4:1 Verses 4:1-6 are numbered 3:19-24 in Hebrew text. **Mal 4:2** Or *the sun of righteousness will rise with healing in its wings.* **Mal 4:4** Hebrew *Horeb*, another name for Sinai.

made in the covenant to his people (Exod 19:5). According to 1 Peter 2:9, believers are God’s very own possession. Have you committed your life to God for safekeeping?

Mal 4:2 In the day of the Lord, God’s wrath toward the wicked will burn like a furnace (Mal 4:1). But he will be like the healing warmth of the sun to those who love and obey him. John the Baptist prophesied that with the coming of Jesus, the dawn was about to break with light for those in sin’s darkness (Luke 1:76-79). In Isaiah 60:20; Revelation 21:23-24, we learn that no light will be needed in God’s holy city because God himself will be the light.

Mal 4:2ff These last verses of the Old Testament are filled with hope. Regardless of how life looks now, God controls the future, and everything will be made right. We who have loved and served God look forward to a joyful celebration. This hope for the future becomes ours when we trust God with our lives.

Mal 4:4 These decrees and regulations, given to Moses at Mount Sinai, were the foundation of the nation’s civil, moral, and ceremonial life (Exod 20; Deut 4:5-6). We still must obey the moral laws because they apply to all generations.

Mal 4:5-6 Elijah was one of the greatest prophets who ever lived (his story is recorded in 1 Kgs 17—2 Kgs 2). With Malachi’s death, the voice of God’s prophets would be silent for 400 years. Then a prophet would come, like Elijah, to herald the Messiah’s coming (Matt 17:10-13; Luke 1:17). This prophet was John the Baptist. John prepared people’s hearts for Jesus by urging people to repent of their sins. Christ’s coming would bring not only unity and peace but also judgment on those who refused to turn from their sins.

“I will open the windows of heaven for you. I will pour out a blessing so great you won’t have enough room to take it in! Try it! Put me to the test!”
Malachi 3:10

Mal 4:6 Malachi gives us practical guidelines about commitment to God: God deserves the best we have to offer (Mal 1:7-10). We must be willing to change our wrong ways of living (Mal 2:1-2). We should make our family a lifelong priority (Mal 2:13-16). We should be sensitive to God’s refining process in our life (Mal 3:3). We should tithe our income (Mal 3:8-12). There is no room for pride (Mal 3:13-15).

Malachi closes his messages by pointing to that great final day of judgment. For those who are committed to God, judgment day will be a day of joy because it will usher in eternity in God’s presence. Those who have ignored God will be “straw,” to be burned up (Mal 4:1). To help the people prepare for that day of judgment, God would send a prophet like Elijah (John the Baptist), who would prepare the way for Jesus, the Messiah. The New Testament begins with this prophet calling the people to turn from their sins to God. Such a commitment to God demands great sacrifice on our part, but we can be sure it will be worth it all in the end.

The Time Between the Old & New Testaments

THE ERA OF THE RETURN & DIASPORA doesn't end with the book of Malachi. It actually continues through the 400 years that are sometimes referred to as the intertestamental period. Many people mistakenly assume that because there was no Scripture written during this time, that nothing significant was going on with God's people. In fact, there was a great deal going on in Judea and throughout the world. Jewish communities in Judea grew and spread throughout the region,

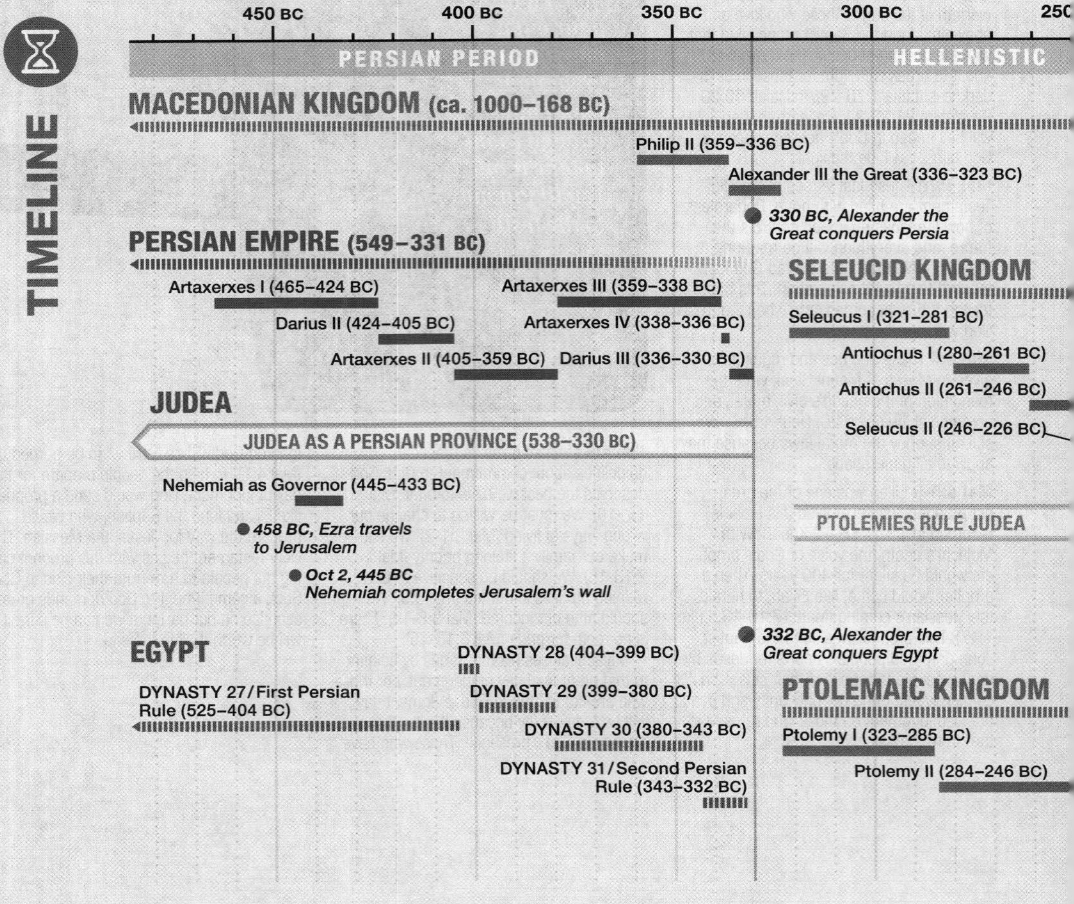

TIMELINE

450 BC | 400 BC | 350 BC | 300 BC | 250 BC

PERSIAN PERIOD | HELLENISTIC

MACEDONIAN KINGDOM (ca. 1000–168 BC)

Philip II (359–336 BC)

Alexander III the Great (336–323 BC)

330 BC, Alexander the Great conquers Persia

PERSIAN EMPIRE (549–331 BC)

Artaxerxes I (465–424 BC)

Darius II (424–405 BC)

Artaxerxes II (405–359 BC)

Artaxerxes III (359–338 BC)

Artaxerxes IV (338–336 BC)

Darius III (336–330 BC)

SELEUCID KINGDOM

Seleucus I (321–281 BC)

Antiochus I (280–261 BC)

Antiochus II (261–246 BC)

Seleucus II (246–226 BC)

JUDEA

JUDEA AS A PERSIAN PROVINCE (538–330 BC)

Nehemiah as Governor (445–433 BC)

458 BC, Ezra travels to Jerusalem

Oct 2, 445 BC Nehemiah completes Jerusalem's wall

PTOLEMIES RULE JUDEA

EGYPT

DYNASTY 27/First Persian Rule (525–404 BC)

DYNASTY 28 (404–399 BC)

DYNASTY 29 (399–380 BC)

DYNASTY 30 (380–343 BC)

DYNASTY 31/Second Persian Rule (343–332 BC)

332 BC, Alexander the Great conquers Egypt

PTOLEMAIC KINGDOM

Ptolemy I (323–285 BC)

Ptolemy II (284–246 BC)

extending north to Galilee and beyond. Meanwhile, Jewish communities were also thriving throughout the known world—Rome, Egypt, Greece, Turkey, Arabia, Libya, and beyond. The Jews who returned to Judea and those in the Diaspora experienced both prosperity and suffering during this turbulent time when world power shifted drastically several times.

Alexander the Great in the Temple of Jerusalem, by Sebastiano Conca

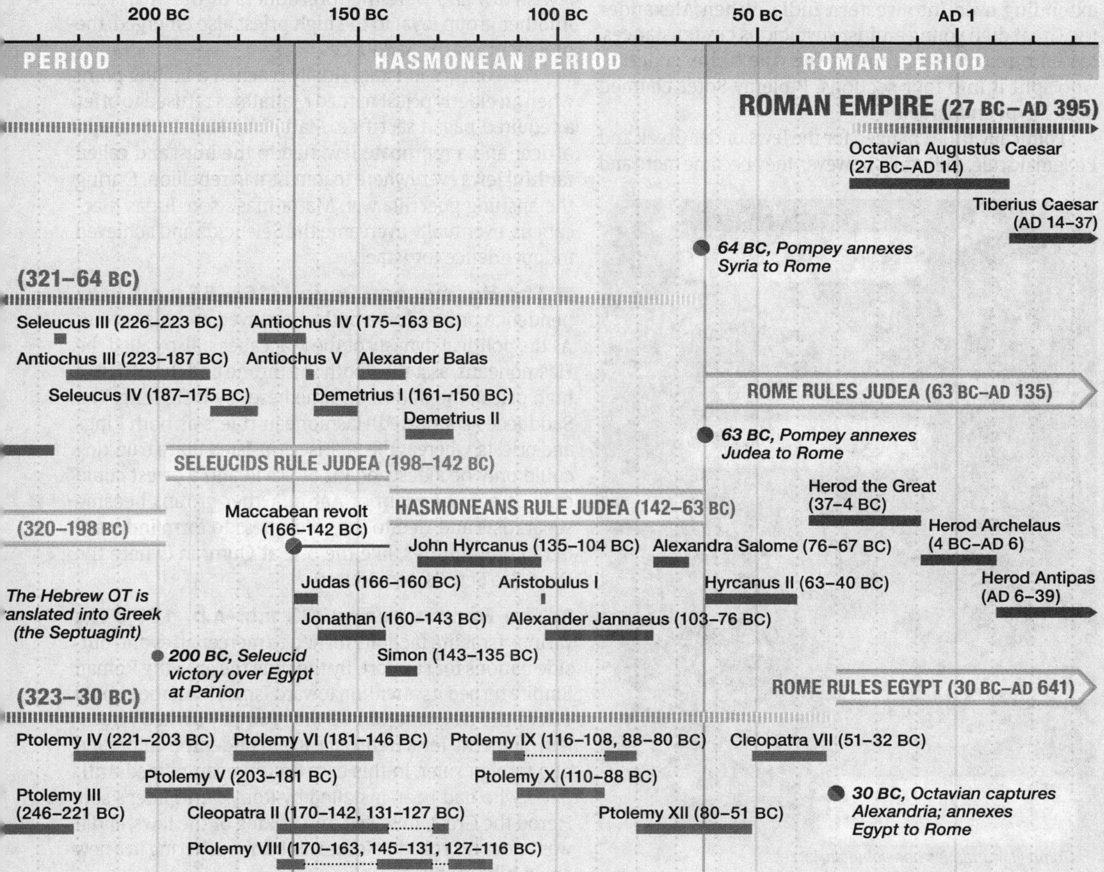

200 BC | 150 BC | 100 BC | 50 BC | AD 1

PERIOD | HASMONEAN PERIOD | ROMAN PERIOD

ROMAN EMPIRE (27 BC–AD 395)

Octavian Augustus Caesar (27 BC–AD 14)

Tiberius Caesar (AD 14–37)

64 BC, Pompey annexes Syria to Rome

(321–64 BC)

Seleucus III (226–223 BC)

Antiochus IV (175–163 BC)

Antiochus III (223–187 BC)

Antiochus V

Alexander Balas

Seleucus IV (187–175 BC)

Demetrius I (161–150 BC)

Demetrius II

ROME RULES JUDEA (63 BC–AD 135)

63 BC, Pompey annexes Judea to Rome

SELEUCIDS RULE JUDEA (198–142 BC)

Herod the Great (37–4 BC)

Maccabean revolt (166–142 BC)

HASMONEANS RULE JUDEA (142–63 BC)

Herod Archelaus (4 BC–AD 6)

(320–198 BC)

John Hyrcanus (135–104 BC)

Alexandra Salome (76–67 BC)

The Hebrew OT is ranslated into Greek (the Septuagint)

Judas (166–160 BC)

Aristobulus I

Hyrcanus II (63–40 BC)

Herod Antipas (AD 6–39)

Jonathan (160–143 BC)

Alexander Jannaeus (103–76 BC)

200 BC, Seleucid victory over Egypt at Panion

Simon (143–135 BC)

(323–30 BC)

ROME RULES EGYPT (30 BC–AD 641)

Ptolemy IV (221–203 BC)

Ptolemy VI (181–146 BC)

Ptolemy IX (116–108, 88–80 BC)

Cleopatra VII (51–32 BC)

Ptolemy V (203–181 BC)

Ptolemy X (110–88 BC)

Ptolemy III (246–221 BC)

30 BC, Octavian captures Alexandria; annexes Egypt to Rome

Cleopatra II (170–142, 131–127 BC)

Ptolemy XII (80–51 BC)

Ptolemy VIII (170–163, 145–131, 127–116 BC)

■ **The Persian Period (539–330 B.C.).** When the Persians wrested the position of world dominance from the Babylonians, they encouraged the Jews to return home to Judea and rebuild their Temple. The Jews dwelt in relative peace. However, several key developments began to reshape their practice of religion. Likely as a result of their many years in exile, the Jews had begun to worship in local synagogues spread throughout the Persian Empire. They continued this new practice in their own land, even after the Temple was rebuilt. Worship in the synagogues centered on the study of the Law, and teachers of religious law became the influential preservers and interpreters of the law.

During this time, the Israelites also came into contact with the Samaritans. Descendants of Israelites who had been left behind during the Babylonian exile, the Samaritans had intermarried with Babylonians, Syrians, and others. Their worship was syncretistic, incorporating elements of pagan religions with worship of Yahweh, the God of Israel. While the Jews rebuilt the Temple in Jerusalem, the Samaritans built a rival temple in the north.

■ **The Hellenistic Period (330–165 B.C.).** With the fall of Persia to Alexander the Great, the Greek Empire became the largest the world had ever seen, extending even into western India. When Alexander the Great died young amidst suspicious circumstances, his empire continued under the rule of his generals, who split it into four sections. Ptolemy Soter claimed both Egypt and Israel.

Politically, little changed for the Jews under Greek and Ptolemaic rule. Culturally, however, they became more and more influenced by Greek (Hellenistic) civilization. The Ptolemaic dynasty promoted Greek thought and language by all possible means in order to preserve and strengthen their empire culturally. Thousands of Jews were forcibly resettled in Alexandria, Egypt. Although Jews both at home and abroad resisted adapting to Greek religion, they couldn't escape all aspects of Hellenistic influence. They soon began to speak Greek, the trade language of the empire. More significantly, a group of Jewish scholars during this time began to translate the Old Testament from its original Hebrew into Greek. Called the Septuagint, this Greek translation came to be widely used by Jews everywhere.

Tomb of Mattathias ben Johanan, Israel

In 198 B.C., the Seleucid section of the empire overthrew the Ptolemies in Judea. For the first time, Israel came under the rule of a leader who tried to stamp out Judaism completely. Antiochus Epiphanes desecrated the Temple, forbade sacrifices to Yahweh, outlawed circumcision, forced Jews to eat pork, and canceled Sabbaths and feast days. Some Jews attempted to conciliate Antiochus and cooperate with his demands; others resisted. These two groups were known as the Hellenists and the Hasidim. The Hellenists embraced and promoted Greek culture. The Hasidim (meaning, "pious ones") closely practiced Jewish law and were the forerunners of the Pharisees. Another group loyal to the high priest also emerged, the precursors of the Sadducees.

The conflict in Israel finally reached a boiling point when an elderly priest named Mattathias refused to offer a required pagan sacrifice. Mattathias killed a Seleucid officer and a reprobate Jew, fled to the hills, and called faithful Jews everywhere to join him in rebellion. During the ensuing guerrilla war, Mattathias's son, Judas Maccabeus, eventually overcame the Seleucids and achieved independence for Israel.

■ **The Hasmonean Period (165–63 B.C.).** Independence proved to be both short-lived and disastrous. As the political dynasty of the Maccabees, also called the Hasmoneans, assumed both the throne and the office of high priest, the nation became beset by infighting. The Sadducees supported Hasmonean rulers as both kings and priests, whereas the Pharisees insisted that a true king could only be a descendant of David and a priest could only be a descendant of Aaron. Other groups became separatists and fled to the wilderness to form independent communities, like the one at Qumran (where the Dead Sea Scrolls were found).

■ **The Roman Period (63 B.C.–A.D. 135).** The various Israelite factions turned to mercenaries and outside nations for support. By the time the growing Roman Empire turned its attention toward Israel, the nation could offer little resistance. In 63 B.C., Pompey sacked Jerusalem. Soon the Jews were once again under the command of a foreign ruler, in this case an Idumean named Antipater who had been installed by Rome. Antipater's son, Herod the Great, followed him as king of the Jews, and it was under his rule that Jesus was born—ushering in a new era in biblical history.

New Testament

Jesus Christ

JESUS WAS BORN into a world that had changed drastically from the time his people, the people of Israel, had returned from exile some five hundred years earlier. Politics, culture, language, and the religious practices in Israel had all undergone great shifts. The time was ripe for God to send his Son into the world to be the Messiah, Savior, and King. But he wouldn't come in the way that everyone expected.

Israel had been waiting for their Messiah, and there were many expectations about what he would do for them and how it would look. He was supposed to be a mighty leader who would reestablish Israel's hold on the land God had given to their ancestor Abraham, expelling the Romans and recalling the glory of the age of David and Solomon. The Messiah was expected to be the climax of Israel's story, the ultimate fulfillment of all God's promises to his people. Nobody expected the Messiah to come as the baby of a humble peasant girl from a small, unimportant town in Galilee. Nobody expected him to gather a small group of disciples and walk around the country telling stories and challenging the religious authorities.

But Jesus is the climax of God's story! He is the ultimate fulfillment of all God's promises to his people! The four Gospels tell the story of how

TIMELINE

15 BC | 10 BC | 5 BC | AD 1 | AD 5 | AD 10

ROME

Octavian Augustus Caesar (27 BC–AD 14)

JEWISH TERRITORIES

Herod Antipas rules as tetrarch of Galilee and Perea (4 BC–AD 39)

Herod the Great as king of the Jews (37–4 BC)

Annas as high priest (AD 6–15)

Herod Archelaus rules Judea and Samaria (4 BC–AD 6)

LIFE OF JESUS

6 BC *Birth of Jesus in Bethlehem*

AD 6 *Jesus in the Temple at age 12*

BOOKS	DATES	THEMES
■ MATTHEW ■ MARK ■ LUKE ■ JOHN ■ ACTS	FROM: **6 BC** TO: **AD 30**	■ Incarnation ■ Jesus' Teaching ■ Jesus' Miracles ■ Resurrection

this man from the margins of Israel's society displayed God's power through mighty miracles and through teaching with authority. They tell the story of how this unlikely Messiah gave the world far more than any military or political or religious leader ever could have. They tell the story of God with us, the eternal Son of God made flesh to live among his people and offer them salvation and eternal life—far more than the meager earthly kingdom they were hoping for.

In order to understand the story of Jesus the Messiah, we need to get the lay of the land. Who were the key people and social structures in Israel at this time? Where and with whom did Jesus spend his time? Who were the people who flocked to see him? Who were the ones threatened by his popularity?

PEOPLE & CULTURE

■ **Greek Influence.** A few centuries earlier, the Greek Empire had conquered most of the known world, and along with their rule they brought their culture and language to the Jewish people. Jesus was born into a world that was still heavily influenced by Greek thought, and virtually everyone would have known the Greek language in addition to their local language (in Jesus' case, likely Aramaic).

■ **Roman Rule.** The Roman Empire was in control of the entire world of the Gospels, and had been for nearly a century. There were several levels of Roman government, as can be seen in the Herod family, Pontius

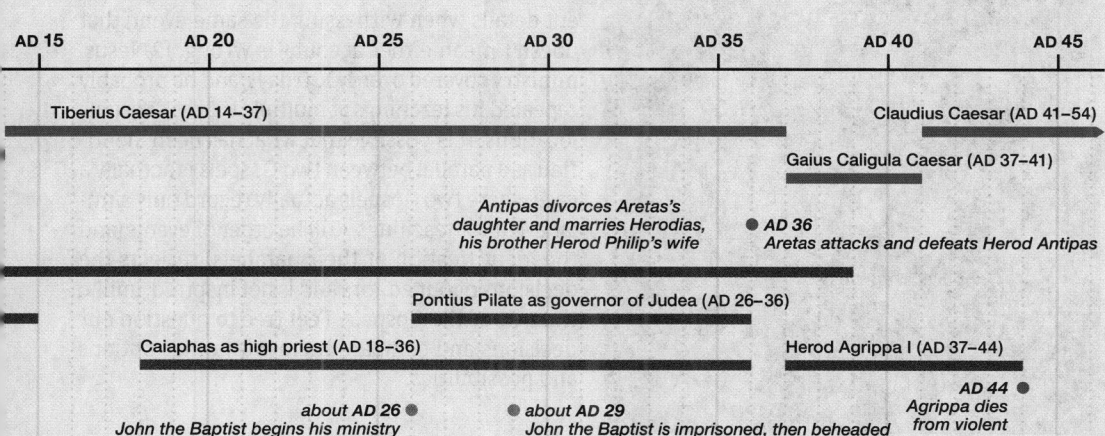

AD 15 | AD 20 | AD 25 | AD 30 | AD 35 | AD 40 | AD 45

Tiberius Caesar (AD 14–37)

Claudius Caesar (AD 41–54)

Gaius Caligula Caesar (AD 37–41)

Antipas divorces Aretas's daughter and marries Herodias, his brother Herod Philip's wife

AD 36 Aretas attacks and defeats Herod Antipas

Pontius Pilate as governor of Judea (AD 26–36)

Caiaphas as high priest (AD 18–36)

Herod Agrippa I (AD 37–44)

AD 44 Agrippa dies from violent illness

about AD 26 John the Baptist begins his ministry

about AD 29 John the Baptist is imprisoned, then beheaded

about AD 27 Jesus begins his ministry

Passover, about AD 30 Jesus' death and resurrection

Pilate, and the Roman soldiers who make appearances throughout the Gospels. Rome collected taxes, enforced peace (sometimes with brutal violence), and allowed many religious freedoms that were not always permitted under Greek rule.

■ **Jewish Groups.** There were several prominent Jewish groups during this period in history. The Pharisees and Sadducees bridged political and religious leadership, the teachers of religious law and priests were primarily responsible for the religious life of the people, and other groups such as the Zealots and the Essenes were radicals—though in very different ways. Zealots wanted to take political power by force, while Essenes separated themselves from the world in an effort to live pure lives marked by ritual holiness. Ordinary Jewish people were able to worship regularly in local synagogues, led by the mainstream religious leaders in their community. They would journey to Jerusalem only to worship in the Temple for special life events and religious festivals.

■ **John the Baptist.** John didn't really fit into any of the major Jewish groups of his day. He was a herald of the coming Kingdom of God, calling everyone to repentance and preparing the way for Jesus and his ministry. Many people traveled into the wilderness to hear his message and be baptized, including a number of people who would eventually follow Jesus.

■ **Jesus and the Disciples.** Jesus was born into an ordinary family and grew up in an ordinary town, but his life was far from ordinary. He chose a very diverse group of disciples—some followers of John the Baptist, at least one Zealot, a man who collected taxes for Rome, and a handful of uneducated fishermen. Jesus taught these disciples what it meant to follow him and prepared them to be his ambassadors on earth after his resurrection and ascension.

"Life of Jesus" versus "Gospels"

We need to remember that the story of Jesus' life is given to us in four canonical Gospels—literally accounts of the "Good News." As important as it is to understand the events of Jesus' life and see them in chronological order, ultimately God gave us the Gospels so that we would be able to hear his Good News with clarity. Rearranging the Gospels into chronological order can sometimes highlight places where individual Gospel writers have placed a particular story out of chronological order to highlight a theological truth about Jesus and his purposes. So pay attention to parts that seem to be located differently in one Gospel compared to another. It may indicate something about the different Gospel writers' goals.

You also might notice some differences in the way a particular story from Jesus' life is told, especially when the accounts from different Gospels are placed together as they are in the *Chronological Life Application Study Bible*. Several things should be kept in mind as you notice the differences: (1) Different people often notice different details when witnessing the same event; that doesn't mean either account is wrong. (2) Jesus' ministry covered over 1,000 days, and he probably repeated his teachings at multiple times in various locations. It is possible that what has been identified as a parallel between two Gospels is actually a case where two Gospels actually record only similar events or teachings. (3) The order of events (and the identification of their parallels) reflects the decisions of our editors and is not inspired, unlike the text of the Gospels. Feel free to question our decisions and compare them with other options and possibilities.

BOOKS IN THIS SECTION

MATTHEW

AUTHOR: Matthew (Levi), a former tax collector who became one of Jesus' 12 disciples

AUDIENCE: Jews

PURPOSE: To prove that Jesus is the Messiah, the eternal King

DATE WRITTEN: Approximately A.D. 60–65

SPECIAL FEATURES: Matthew is filled with messianic language ("Son of David" is used throughout) and Old Testament references (53 quotes and 76 other references). This Gospel's purpose was to present the clear evidence that Jesus is the predicted Messiah, the Savior.

LUKE

AUTHOR: Luke, a doctor (Col 4:14), a Greek (Gentile) Christian. He is the only known Gentile (non-Jewish) author in the New Testament. Luke was a close friend and companion of Paul. He also wrote Acts, and the two books go together.

AUDIENCE: Theophilus and other Gentiles

PURPOSE: To present an accurate account of the life of Christ, and to present Christ as the perfect human and Savior

DATE WRITTEN: About A.D. 60

SPECIAL FEATURES: This is the most comprehensive of the Gospels. The general vocabulary and writing style show that the author was educated. He makes frequent references to illnesses and diagnoses. Luke stresses Jesus' relationship with people; emphasizes prayer, miracles, and angels; records inspired hymns of praise; gives a prominent place to women.

MARK

AUTHOR: John Mark. He was not one of the 12 disciples, but he accompanied Paul on his first missionary journey (Acts 13:13) and is traditionally associated with Peter.

AUDIENCE: Christians in Rome, where the Gospel was written

PURPOSE: To present the person, work, and teachings of Jesus

DATE WRITTEN: Approximately A.D. 55–60

SPECIAL FEATURES: Mark was probably the first Gospel written. The other Gospels quote all but 31 verses of Mark. Mark records more miracles than any other Gospel.

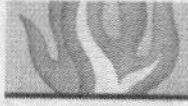

JOHN

AUTHOR: John the apostle, son of Zebedee, brother of James, called a "Son of Thunder"

AUDIENCE: New Christians and searching non-Christians

PURPOSE: To prove conclusively that Jesus is the Son of God and that all who believe in him will have eternal life

DATE WRITTEN: Probably A.D. 85–90

SPECIAL FEATURES: Of the eight miracles recorded, six are unique (among the Gospels) to John, as is the "Upper Room Discourse" (John 14–17). Over 90 percent of John is unique to his Gospel—John does not contain a genealogy or any record of Jesus' birth, childhood, temptation, transfiguration, appointment of the disciples, nor any account of Jesus' parables, ascension, or great commission.

For book information on **ACTS**, see the introduction to The Church, p. 1505.

MEGATHEMES

■ **Jesus Christ: King, Messiah, Servant, Savior, Son of God.** In each of the four Gospels, Jesus Christ is the central focus, but each Gospel highlights a slightly different aspect of his significance. Matthew presents Jesus as the King of kings and the long-awaited Jewish Messiah. Mark presents Jesus as the Servant of God. Luke presents Jesus as the Savior of the entire world, and John presents Jesus as the unique Son of God who reveals the Father to us. All of these portraits of Jesus are important (and true), and the differences between the Gospel accounts can be attributed to the different elements of Jesus' character and ministry that they are highlighting.

■ **Jesus' Teachings.** In addition to learning about who Jesus is, the four Gospels give us direct access to what Jesus taught throughout his ministry. Jesus spoke often about the Kingdom of God (or Kingdom of Heaven), and how it differs from the kingdom of this world. He often taught using parables, giving profound truths through ordinary stories. He taught his disciples about the Holy Spirit, who would come to indwell and empower them after his death and resurrection. His teachings form an important foundation for the things his followers would write in the rest of the New Testament. The teachings of Jesus are alternatively challenging and comforting; make sure that you allow all of what he taught to penetrate your heart and life.

■ **Jesus' Miracles.** Jesus demonstrated power over sickness, nature, demons, and even death many times in his ministry. But this wasn't just a way to show everyone how powerful he was, or a flashy way to gain more followers—Jesus' miracles show his profound love and compassion for people. Certainly his miracles are proof that he is the Son of God, but they also prove that he sees the needs of his people and has both the power and the will to help them. This is no less true today—become a person of prayer and watch God transform you and the world around you through his power.

■ **Spreading the Gospel.** Jesus went all over the land of Israel spreading the message of the Kingdom of God, but even that wasn't enough. Several times, Jesus went beyond the borders of his nation to share the Good News with Gentiles and even the hated Samaritans. And his message was given to all sorts of people—blind beggars, wealthy merchants, social outcasts, powerful religious leaders, fishermen, Roman soldiers, widows, children, immoral people, and scrupulous Pharisees. The Good News is for all people, and eternal life is offered to all who will believe in the Son and the Father who sent him. What part can you play in spreading this Good News to all people?

■ **Resurrection.** The story of Jesus' life doesn't end with his death—in many ways it only begins there. His resurrection shouts loudly about the power of God and the Good News that our sins have been forgiven, and death has been defeated. Allow the truth of the Resurrection to penetrate your life, and see what God will do in and through you as you follow Jesus.

MAP ▶

1 Bethlehem Jesus was born in Bethlehem, a village just a few miles south of Jerusalem in Judea (Luke 2:1-38; Matt 2:1-22).

2 Nazareth Jesus grew up in Nazareth (Matt 2:23; Luke 2:39-40), a small village in the southern part of Galilee, 65 miles north of Jerusalem. When he began his ministry, he preached here but was rejected in his hometown (Matt 13:53-58; Mark 6:1-6; Luke 4:16-30).

3 Jordan River Jesus was baptized by John the Baptist in the Jordan River (Matt 3:13-17; Mark 1:9-11; Luke 4:1-13).

4 Cana Jesus' first recorded miracle was at a wedding in this Galilean village (John 2:1-12).

5 Jerusalem Jesus traveled to Jerusalem right at the beginning of his ministry (John 2:13–4:3), and he concluded his ministry here as well. Jerusalem was the center of religious and political power in the region, as it was home to the Jewish Temple and the Roman governor. Many of the most important events in Jesus' life happened in and around Jerusalem, including his crucifixion and resurrection. His last week was all spent in this area, with some time spent in Bethany, Bethphage, and the Garden of Gethsemane on the Mount of Olives.

6 Samaria Instead of shunning this region, as most Jews at this time did, Jesus chose to travel through Samaria and minister to the people he met there (John 4:4-42). Many people in Sychar believed in him as a result of his ministry. The people of Samaria were half Jewish, the result of intentional mixing of peoples when they were exiled centuries earlier, and their worship practices were different from the Jews even though they were also based on the Pentateuch (Genesis—Deuteronomy).

7 Galilee Jesus spent most of his time during his ministry traveling throughout the region of Galilee. He spent a lot of time preaching in towns around the Sea of Galilee, including Capernaum, Bethsaida, and Korazin. He performed many miracles in Galilee, including the calming of the storm (Matt 8:23-27; Mark 1:40-45; Luke 5:12-16) and raising a widow's son from the dead (Luke 7:11-17). He also delivered the Sermon on the Mount in Galilee (Matt 5:1–7:29). While there were synagogues in every town and a large Jewish population, there were also many Gentiles and Roman military personnel in this region, which was at Israel's northern border.

8 Beyond Israel Jesus didn't limit his ministry to the borders of Israel. He ventured out into Phoenicia, visiting Tyre (Matt 15:21-28; Mark 7:24-30) and Sidon (Matt 15:29-31; Mark 8:1-10). He also went to the Decapolis region west of Galilee, where he fed 4,000 people (Matt 15:32-39; Mark 8:1-10).

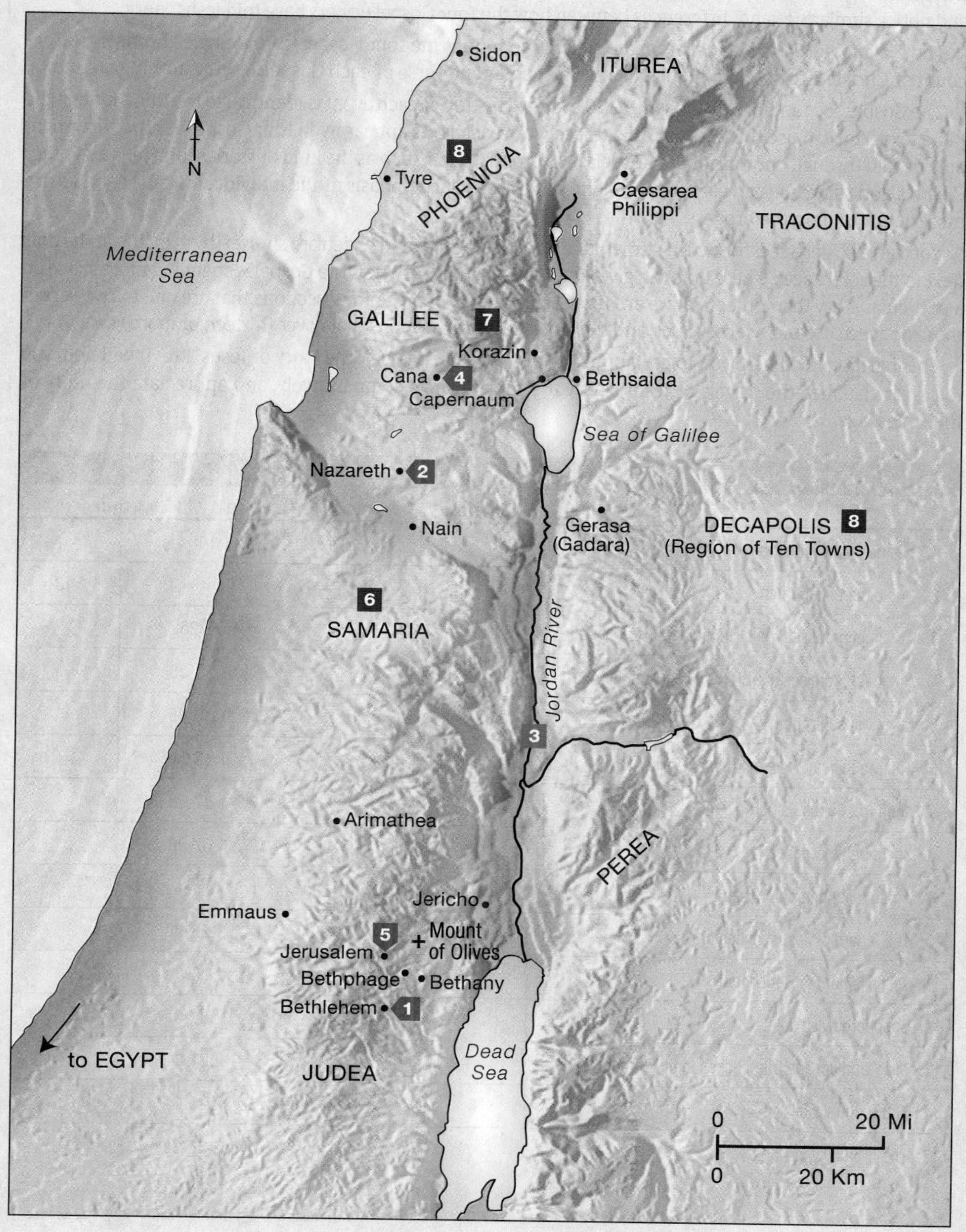

250 EVENTS IN THE LIFE OF CHRIST

A Harmony of the Gospels

All four books in the Bible that tell the story of Jesus Christ—Matthew, Mark, Luke, and John—stand alone, emphasizing a unique aspect of Jesus' life. When these are blended into one complete account, as we have done in the *Chronological Life Application Study Bible*, we can see how these different accounts relate to one another and notice similarities and differences between how the four Gospel writers have told Jesus' story.

The *Chronological Life Application Study Bible* combines the four Gospels into a single chronological account of Christ's life on earth. It includes every chapter and verse of each Gospel, leaving nothing out.

The Gospel accounts are divided into 250 events. The title of each event is identical to the title found in the Bible text. You can use this chart to quickly see which accounts appear in all four Gospels, and which might only be told through only one of the Gospels. Look for patterns, such as the kind of stories John tells that other Gospels don't, and you can gain fresh insight into the special emphasis of the individual Gospels—and learn more about Jesus in the process.

You can also get a feel for which stories take up a lot of space, and which are shorter, by glancing at the dots next to the references. These dots can give you a quick handle on when one Gospel is spending more space on a particular story than others. There are three sizes of dots, representing sections that are one to five verses, those between six and twelve verses, and the largest dots for sections that cover thirteen or more verses.

This harmony will help you to get a quick, at-a-glance overview of the story of Jesus' life. It will help you to better visualize the travels of Jesus, study the four Gospels comparatively, and appreciate the unity of their message.

A. THE BIRTH AND PREPARATION OF JESUS CHRIST

	MATTHEW	MARK	LUKE	JOHN
1. The nature of a Gospel		• 1:1a	• 1:1-4	
2. God became a human				⬤ 1:1-18
3. An angel promises the birth of John to Zechariah			⬤ 1:5-25	
4. An angel promises the Birth of Jesus to Mary			⬤ 1:26-38	
5. Mary visits Elizabeth			● 1:39-45	
6. The Magnificat: Mary's Song of Praise			● 1:46-56	
7. John the Baptist is born			● 1:57-66	
8. Zechariah's prophecy			⬤ 1:67-80	
9. An angel appears to Joseph	● 1:18-25			
10. The record of Jesus' ancestors	⬤ 1:1-17		⬤ 3:23-38	
11. Jesus is born in Bethlehem			● 2:1-7	
12. Shepherds visit Jesus			⬤ 2:8-20	
13. Mary and Joseph bring Jesus to the Temple			• 2:21-24	
14. The prophecy of Simeon			● 2:25-35	
15. The prophecy of Anna			• 2:36-38	

• 1-5 verses | ● 6-12 verses | ⬤ 13+ verses

	MATTHEW	MARK	LUKE	JOHN
16. Visitors arrive from Eastern lands	2:1-12			
17. The escape to Egypt	2:13-18			
18. The Return from Egypt	2:19-22			
19. Jesus' Childhood in Nazareth	2:23		2:39-40	
20. Jesus speaks with the religious teachers			2:41-52	
21. John the Baptist prepares the way for Jesus	3:1-12	1:1b-8	3:1-18	1:19-28
22. The baptism of Jesus	3:13-17	1:9-11	3:21-22	
23. Satan tempts Jesus in the wilderness	4:1-11	1:12-13	4:1-13	
24. John the Baptist proclaims Jesus as the Messiah				1:29-34
25. The first disciples follow Jesus				1:35-51
26. Jesus turns water into wine				2:1-12

B. MESSAGE AND MINISTRY OF JESUS CHRIST

	MATTHEW	MARK	LUKE	JOHN
Jesus Begins His Ministry in Jerusalem				
27. Jesus clears the Temple				2:13-22
28. Nicodemus visits Jesus at night				2:23–3:21
29. John the Baptist tells more about Jesus				3:22-36
30. Herod puts John in prison			3:19-20	
31. Jesus leaves Judea	4:12	1:14		4:1-3
Jesus Ministers in Samaria				
32. Jesus talks to a woman at the well				4:4-26
33. Jesus tells about the spiritual harvest				4:27-38
34. Many Samaritans believe in Jesus				4:39-42
Jesus Ministers in Galilee				
35. Jesus preaches in Galilee	4:13-17	1:15	4:14-15	4:43-45
36. Jesus heals a government official's son				4:46-54
37. Four fishermen follow Jesus	4:18-22	1:16-20	5:1-11	
38. Jesus teaches with authority		1:21-28	4:31-37	
39. Jesus heals Peter's mother-in-law and many others	8:14-17	1:29-34	4:38-41	
40. Jesus preaches throughout Galilee	4:23-25	1:35-39	4:42-44	
41. Jesus heals a man with leprosy	8:1-4	1:40-45	5:12-16	
42. Jesus heals a paralyzed man	9:1-8	2:1-12	5:17-26	

	MATTHEW	MARK	LUKE	JOHN
43. Jesus eats with sinners at Matthew's house	9:9-13	2:13-17	5:27-32	
44. Religious leaders ask Jesus about fasting	9:14-17	2:18-22	5:33-39	
45. Jesus heals a lame man by a pool				5:1-15
46. Jesus claims to be the Son of God				5:16-30
47. Jesus supports his claim				5:31-47
48. The disciples pick wheat on the Sabbath	12:1-8	2:23-28	6:1-5	
49. Jesus heals a man's hand on the Sabbath	12:9-14	3:1-6	6:6-11	
50. Large crowds follow Jesus	12:15-21	3:7-12	6:17-19	
51. Jesus chooses the twelve disciples		3:13-19	6:12-16	
52. Jesus gives the Beatitudes	5:1-12		6:20-26	
53. Jesus teaches about salt and light	5:13-16			
54. Jesus teaches about the law	5:17-20			
55. Jesus teaches about anger	5:21-26			
56. Jesus teaches about lust	5:27-30			
57. Jesus teaches about divorce	5:31-32			
58. Jesus teaches about vows	5:33-37			
59. Jesus teaches about revenge	5:38-42			
60. Jesus teaches about loving enemies	5:43-48		6:27-36	
61. Jesus teaches about giving to the needy	6:1-4			
62. Jesus teaches about prayer	6:5-15			
63. Jesus teaches about fasting	6:16-18			
64. Jesus teaches about money	6:19-24			
65. Jesus teaches about worry	6:25-34			
66. Jesus teaches about judging others	7:1-6		6:37-42	
67. Jesus teaches about asking, seeking, knocking	7:7-11			
68. The golden rule	7:12			
69. Jesus teaches about the way to heaven	7:13-14			
70. Jesus teaches about fruit of people's lives	7:15-29		6:43-49	
71. A Roman officer demonstrates faith	8:5-13		7:1-10	
72. Jesus raises a widow's son from the dead			7:11-17	
73. Jesus eases John's doubt	11:1-19		7:18-35	

1-5 verses | 6-12 verses | 13+ verses

	MATTHEW	MARK	LUKE	JOHN
74. Jesus promises rest for the soul	11:20-30			
75. A sinful woman anoints Jesus			7:36-50	
76. Women accompany Jesus and the disciples			8:1-3	
77. Religious leaders accuse Jesus of getting his power from Satan	12:22-37	3:20-30	11:14-23	
78. Religious leaders ask Jesus for a miraculous sign	12:38-45		11:24-32	
79. Jesus describes his true family	12:46-50	3:31-35	8:19-21	
80. The parable of the four soils	13:1-23	4:1-20	8:4-15	
81. Parable of the lamp		4:21-25	8:16-18	
82. Jesus tells the parable of the growing seed		4:26-29		
83. Jesus tells the parable of the weeds	13:24-30			
84. Jesus tells the parables of the mustard seed and the yeast	13:31-33	4:30-32	13:18-21	
85. Why Jesus taught using parables	13:34-35	4:33-34		
86. Jesus explains the parable of the weeds	13:36-43			
87. Jesus tells the parable of hidden treasure	13:44			
88. Jesus tells the parable of the pearl merchant	13:45-46			
89. Jesus tells the parable of the fishing net	13:47-52			
90. Jesus calms a storm	8:23-27	4:35-41	8:22-25	
91. Jesus sends demons into a herd of pigs	8:28-34	5:1-20	8:26-39	
92. Jesus heals a bleeding woman and restores a girl to life	9:18-26	5:21-43	8:40-56	
93. Jesus heals the blind and mute	9:27-34			
94. Jesus is rejected in Nazareth	13:53-58	6:1-6a	4:16-30	
95. Jesus urges the disciples to pray for workers	9:35-38			
96. Jesus sends out the twelve disciples	10:1-15	6:6b-13	9:1-6	
97. Jesus prepares the disciples for persecution	10:16-42			
98. Herod kills John the Baptist	14:3-12	6:17-29		
99. Herod mistakes Jesus for John the Baptist back from the dead	14:1-2	6:14-16	9:7-9	
100. Jesus feeds five thousand	14:13-21	6:30-44	9:10-17	6:1-15
101. Jesus walks on water	14:22-33	6:45-52		6:16-21
102. Jesus heals all who touch him	14:34-36	6:53-56		
103. Jesus is the true bread from heaven				6:22-40
104. The people disagree that Jesus is from heaven				6:41-59

	MATTHEW	MARK	LUKE	JOHN
105. Many disciples desert Jesus				6:60-71
106. Jesus teaches about inner purity	15:1-20	7:1-23		
Jesus' Ministry Beyond Galilee				
107. Jesus sends a demon out of a girl	15:21-28	7:24-30		
108. Jesus heals many people	15:29-31	7:31-37		
109. Jesus feeds four thousand	15:32-39	8:1-10		
Jesus Resumes His Ministry in Galilee				
110. Leaders demand a miraculous sign	16:1-4	8:11-13		
111. Jesus warns against wrong teaching	16:5-12	8:14-21		
112. Jesus restores sight to a blind man		8:22-26		
113. Peter says Jesus is the Messiah	16:13-20	8:27-30	9:18-21	
114. Jesus predicts his death for the first time	16:21-28	8:31–9:1	9:22-27	
115. Jesus is transfigured on the mountain	17:1-13	9:2-13	9:28-36	
116. Jesus heals a demon-possessed boy	17:14-20	9:14-29	9:37-43a	
117. Jesus predicts his death the second time	17:22-23	9:30-32	9:43b-45	
118. Peter finds the coin in the fish's mouth	17:24-27			
119. The disciples argue about who would be the greatest	18:1-5	9:33-37	9:46-48	
120. The disciples forbid another to use Jesus' name		9:38-41	9:49-50	
121. Warning against causing sin	18:6-10	9:42-50		
122. Jesus tells the parable of the lost sheep	18:12-14			
123. Jesus teaches how to treat a believer who sins	18:15-20			
124. Jesus tells the parable of the unforgiving debtor	18:21-35			
125. Jesus' brothers ridicule him				7:1-9
Jesus Turns Toward Jerusalem				
126. Jesus travels to Judea	19:1-2	10:1	9:51	
127. Jesus passes through Samaria			9:52-56	
128. Jesus teaches about the cost of following him	8:18-22		9:57-62	
129. Jesus teaches openly at the Temple				7:10-31
130. Religious leaders attempt to arrest Jesus				7:32-53
131. Jesus forgives an adulterous woman				8:1-11
132. Jesus is the light of the world				8:12-20

1-5 verses | 6-12 verses | 13+ verses

	MATTHEW	MARK	LUKE	JOHN
133. Jesus warns of coming judgment				8:21-30
134. Jesus speaks about God's true children				8:31-47
135. Jesus states he is eternal				8:48-59
136. Jesus sends out seventy-two messengers			10:1-16	
137. The seventy-two messengers return			10:17-24	
138. Jesus tells the parable of the Good Samaritan			10:25-37	
139. Jesus visits Martha and Mary			10:38-42	
140. Jesus teaches his disciples about prayer			11:1-13	
141. Jesus teaches about the light within			11:33-36	
142. Jesus criticizes the religious leaders			11:37-54	
143. Jesus speaks against hypocrisy			12:1-12	
144. Jesus tells the parable of the rich fool			12:13-21	
145. Jesus warns about worry			12:22-34	
146. Jesus warns about preparing for his coming			12:35-48	
147. Jesus warns about coming division			12:49-53	
148. Jesus warns about the future crisis			12:54-59	
149. Jesus calls the people to repent			13:1-9	
150. Jesus heals the crippled woman			13:10-17	
151. Jesus heals the man who was born blind				9:1-12
152. Religious leaders question the blind man				9:13-34
153. Jesus teaches about spiritual blindness				9:35-41
154. Jesus is the good shepherd				10:1-21
155. Religious leaders surround Jesus at the Temple				10:22-42
156. Jesus teaches about entering the Kingdom			13:22-30	
157. Jesus grieves over Jerusalem	23:37-39		13:31-35	
158. Jesus heals a man with swollen limbs			14:1-6	
159. Jesus teaches about humility			14:7-14	
160. Jesus tells the parable of the great feast			14:15-24	
161. Jesus teaches about the cost of being a disciple			14:25-35	
162. Jesus tells the parable of the lost sheep			15:1-7	
163. Jesus tells the parable of the lost coin			15:8-10	

	MATTHEW	MARK	LUKE	JOHN
164. Jesus tells the parable of the lost son			15:11-32	
165. Jesus tells the parable of the shrewd manager			16:1-18	
166. Jesus tells about the rich man and the beggar			16:19-31	
167. Jesus tells about forgiveness and faith			17:1-10	
168. Lazarus becomes sick and dies				11:1-16
169. Jesus comforts Mary and Martha				11:17-37
170. Jesus raises Lazarus from the dead				11:38-44
171. Religious leaders plot to kill Jesus				11:45-57
172. Jesus heals ten men with leprosy			17:11-19	
173. Jesus teaches about the coming of the Kingdom of God			17:20-37	
174. Jesus tells the parable of the persistent widow			18:1-8	
175. Jesus tells the parable of two men who prayed			18:9-14	
176. Jesus teaches about marriage and divorce	19:3-12	10:2-12		
177. Jesus blesses the children	19:13-15	10:13-16	18:15-17	
178. Jesus speaks to the rich young man	19:16-30	10:17-31	18:18-30	
179. Jesus tells the parable of the vineyard workers	20:1-16			
180. Jesus predicts his death the third time	20:17-19	10:32-34	18:31-34	
181. Jesus teaches about serving others	20:20-28	10:35-45		
182. Jesus heals two blind beggars	20:29-34	10:46-52	18:35-43	
183. Jesus brings salvation to Zacchaeus's home			19:1-10	
184. Jesus tells the parable of the king's ten servants			19:11-27	
185. A woman anoints Jesus with perfume	26:6-13	14:3-9		12:1-11
Jesus' Ministry in Jerusalem				
186. Jesus rides into Jerusalem on a donkey	21:1-11	11:1-11	19:28-40	12:12-19
187. Jesus grieves over Jerusalem again			19:41-44	
188. Jesus clears the Temple again	21:12-17	11:15-19	19:45-48	
189. Jesus explains why he must die				12:20-36
190. Most of the people do not believe in Jesus				12:37-43
191. Jesus summarizes his message				12:44-50
192. Jesus curses a fig tree	21:18-22	11:12-14, 20-25		
193. Religious leaders challenge Jesus' authority	21:23-27	11:27-33	20:1-8	

● 1-5 verses ● 6-12 verses ● 13+ verses

	MATTHEW	MARK	LUKE	JOHN
194. Jesus tells the parable of the two sons	21:28-32			
195. Jesus tells the parable of the evil farmers	21:33-46	12:1-12	20:9-19	
196. Jesus tells the parable of the wedding dinner	22:1-14			
197. Religious leaders question Jesus about paying taxes	22:15-22	12:13-17	20:20-26	
198. Religious leaders question Jesus about the Resurrection	22:23-33	12:18-27	20:27-40	
199. Religious leaders question Jesus about the greatest commandment	22:34-40	12:28-34		
200. Religious leaders cannot answer Jesus' question	22:41-46	12:35-37	20:41-44	
201. Jesus warns against the religious leaders	23:1-12	12:38-40	20:45-47	
202. Jesus condemns the religious leaders	23:13-36			
203. A poor widow gives all she has		12:41-44	21:1-4	
204. Jesus teaches about being watchful for his return	24:1-51	13:1-37	21:5-38	
205. Jesus tells the parable of the ten bridesmaids	25:1-13			
206. Jesus tells the parable of the loaned money	25:14-30			
207. Jesus tells about the final judgment	25:31-46			

III. THE DEATH AND RESURRECTION OF JESUS

	MATTHEW	MARK	LUKE	JOHN
208. Religious leaders plot to kill Jesus	26:1-5	14:1-2	22:1-2	
209. Judas agrees to betray Jesus	26:14-16	14:10-11	22:3-6	
210. The disciples prepare for the Passover	26:17-19	14:12-16	22:7-13	
211. Jesus washes the disciples' feet				13:1-20
212. Jesus and the disciples share the Last Supper	26:20-30	14:17-26	22:14-30	13:21-30
213. Jesus predicts Peter's denial	26:31-35	14:27-31	22:31-38	13:31-38
214. Jesus is the way to the Father				14:1-14
215. Jesus promises the Holy Spirit				14:15-31
216. Jesus teaches about the vine and the branches				15:1-17
217. Jesus warns about the world's hatred				15:18–16:4
218. Jesus teaches about the Holy Spirit				16:5-15
219. Jesus teaches about using his name in prayer				16:16-33
220. Jesus prays for himself				17:1-5
221. Jesus prays for his disciples				17:6-19
222. Jesus prays for future believers				17:20-26
223. Jesus agonizes in the garden	26:36-46	14:32-42	22:39-46	

	MATTHEW	MARK	LUKE	JOHN
224. Jesus is betrayed and arrested	26:47-56	14:43-52	22:47-53	18:1-11
225. Annas questions Jesus				18:12-24
226. Caiaphas questions Jesus	26:57-68	14:53-65	22:54a, 63-65	
227. Peter denies knowing Jesus	26:69-75	14:66-72	22:54b-62	18:25-27
228. The council of religious leaders condemns Jesus	27:1-2	15:1	22:66-71	
229. Judas hangs himself	27:3-10			
230. Jesus stands trial before Pilate	27:11-14	15:2-5	23:1-7	18:28-37
231. Jesus stands trial before Herod			23:8-12	
232. Pilate hands Jesus over to be crucified	27:15-26	15:6-15	23:13-25	18:38–19:16
233. Roman soldiers mock Jesus	27:27-31	15:16-20		
234. Jesus is led away to be crucified	27:32	15:21	23:26-31	
235. Jesus is placed on the cross	27:33-44	15:22-32	23:32-43	19:17-27
236. Jesus dies on the cross	27:45-56	15:33-41	23:44-49	19:28-37
237. Jesus is laid in the tomb	27:57-61	15:42-47	23:50-56	19:38-42
238. Guards are posted at the tomb	27:62-66			
239. Jesus rises from the dead	28:1-8	16:1-8	24:1-11	20:1-2
240. Peter and John run to the tomb			24:12	20:3-10
241. Jesus appears to the women	28:9-10	16:9-11		20:11-18
242. Religious leaders bribe the guards	28:11-15			
243. Jesus appears to two believers traveling on the road		16:12-13	24:13-35	
244. Jesus appears to his disciples		16:14	24:36-43	20:19-23
245. Jesus appears to Thomas				20:24-31
246. Jesus appears to seven disciples				21:1-14
247. Jesus challenges Peter				21:15-25
248. Jesus gives the great commission	28:16-20	16:15-18		
249. Jesus appears to the disciples in Jerusalem			24:44-49	
250. Jesus ascends into heaven		16:19-20	24:50-53	

● 1-5 verses ● 6-12 verses ● 13+ verses

THE PARABLES OF JESUS

I. Teaching Parables

A. About the Kingdom of God

1. The Four Soils (Matt 13:1-23; Mark 4:1-20; Luke 8:4-15)
2. The Lamp (Mark 4:21-25; Luke 8:16-18)
3. The Growing Seed (Mark 4:26-29)
4. The Weeds (Matt 13:24-30)
5. The Mustard Seed and the Yeast (Matt 13:31-33; Mark 4:30-32; Luke 13:18-21)
6. The Hidden Treasure (Matt 13:44)
7. The Pearl Merchant (Matt 13:45-46)
8. The Fishing Net (Matt 13:47-52)

B. About Service and Obedience

1. The Servant's Role (Luke 17:7-10)
2. The Vineyard Workers (Matt 20:1-16)
3. The King's Ten Servants (Luke 19:11-27)
4. The Loaned Money (Matt 25:14-30)

C. About Prayer

1. The Friend at Midnight (Luke 11:5-8)
2. The Persistent Widow (Luke 18:1-8)

D. About Neighbors

1. The Good Samaritan (Luke 10:25-37)

E. About Humility

1. The Wedding Feast (Luke 14:7-11)
2. Two Men Who Prayed (Luke 18:9-14)

F. About Wealth

1. The Rich Fool (Luke 12:13-21)
2. The Great Feast (Luke 14:15-24)
3. The Shrewd Manager (Luke 16:1-18)

II. Gospel Parables

A. About God's Love

1. The Lost Sheep (Matt 18:12-14; Luke 15:1-7)
2. The Lost Coin (Luke 15:8-10)
3. The Lost Son (Luke 15:11-32)

B. About Thankfulness

1. The Forgiven Debts (Luke 7:41-43)

III. Parables of Judgment and the Future

A. About Christ's Return

1. The Wise and Faithful Servants (Matt 24:45-51; Luke 12:42-48)
2. The Traveling Owner of the House (Mark 13:34-37)
3. The Ten Bridesmaids (Matt 25:1-13)

B. About God's Values

1. The Unforgiving Debtor (Matt 18:21-35)
2. The Unproductive Fig Tree (Luke 13:6-9)
3. The Two Sons (Matt 21:28-32)
4. The Evil Farmers (Matt 21:33-46; Mark 12:1-12; Luke 20:9-19)
5. The Wedding Dinner (Matt 22:1-14)

COMPARISON OF THE FOUR GOSPELS

All four Gospels present the life and teachings of Jesus. Each book, however, focuses on a unique facet of Jesus and his character. To understand more about the specific characteristics of Jesus, read any one of the four Gospels.

	MATTHEW	MARK	LUKE	JOHN
Jesus is . . .	The promised King	The Servant of God	The Son of Man	The Son of God
The original readers were . . .	Jews	Gentiles, Romans	Greeks	Christians throughout the world
Significant themes . . .	Jesus is the Messiah because he fulfilled Old Testament prophecy	Jesus backed up his words with action	Jesus was fully God but also fully human	Belief in Jesus is required for salvation
Character of the writer . . .	Teacher	Storyteller	Historian	Theologian
Greatest emphasis is on . . .	Jesus' sermons and words	Jesus' miracles and actions	Jesus' humanity	The principles of Jesus' teaching

A. The Birth and Preparation of Jesus Christ

Jesus is the eternal Son of God, and yet he chose to be born as a human. The nation of Israel had been waiting for centuries for their Messiah, but when he arrived as an infant, very few recognized him. The King of Israel, the Servant Savior, the God of the universe was born as a humble infant, grew up in the small village of Nazareth, and began his ministry by submitting to the baptism of John.

The Nature of a Gospel PARALLEL

MARK 1:1a

This is the Good News about Jesus the Messiah, the Son of God.*

LUKE 1:1-4

Many people have set out to write accounts about the
events that have been fulfilled among us. [2]They used
the eyewitness reports circulating among us from the
early disciples.* [3]Having carefully investigated everything from the beginning, I also have decided to write
a careful account for you, most honorable Theophilus,
[4]so you can be certain of the truth of everything you
were taught.

God Became a Human

JOHN 1:1-18

1 In the beginning the Word already existed.
The Word was with God,
and the Word was God.
2 He existed in the beginning with God.
3 God created everything through him,
and nothing was created except
through him.

Mk 1:1 Some manuscripts do not include *the Son of God.* **Lk 1:2** Greek *from those who from the beginning were servants of the word.*

Mark 1:1 When you experience the excitement of a big event, you naturally want to tell someone. Telling the story can bring back that original thrill as you relive the experience. Reading Mark's first words, you can sense his excitement. Picture yourself in the crowd as Jesus heals and teaches. Imagine yourself as one of the disciples. Respond to his words of love and encouragement. And remember that Jesus came for us who live today as well as for those who lived 2,000 years ago.

Mark 1:1 Mark was not one of the 12 disciples of Jesus, but he probably knew Jesus personally. Mark wrote his Gospel in the form of a fast-paced story, like a popular novel. The book portrays Jesus as a man who backed up his words with action that constantly proved who he is—the Son of God. Because Mark wrote his Gospel for Christians in Rome, where many gods were worshiped, he wanted his readers to know that Jesus is the one true Son of God.

Mark gave the "punch line" of his Gospel in the very first verse, but both Jesus' enemies and his disciples would not get it until Jesus' resurrection. For us who read Mark today, the message is clear that we must not ignore or reject Jesus Christ.

Luke 1:1-2 Luke tells Jesus' story from the unique perspective of a Gentile, a physician, and the first historian of the early church. Though not an eyewitness of Jesus' ministry, Luke nevertheless was concerned that eyewitness accounts be preserved accurately and that the foundations of Christian belief be transmitted intact to the next generation. Many of Jesus' parables are found in Luke. In addition, more than any other Gospel, it gives specific instances of Jesus' concern for women.

Luke 1:1-4 There was a lot of interest in Jesus, and many people had written firsthand accounts about him. Luke used these accounts and all other available resources as material for an accurate and complete account of Jesus' life, teachings, and ministry. Because truth was important to Luke, he relied heavily on eyewitness accounts. Christianity doesn't say, "Close your eyes and believe," but rather, "Check it out for yourself." The Bible encourages you to investigate its claims thoroughly (John 1:46; 21:24; Acts 17:11) because your conclusion about Jesus is a life-and-death matter.

Luke 1:1-4 The book of Acts, also written by Luke, is likewise addressed to Theophilus. Theophilus means "one who loves God," so this preface may be a general dedication to all Christian readers. Or, Theophilus may have been Luke's patron, who helped to finance the book's writing. More likely, Theophilus was a Roman acquaintance of Luke's with a strong interest in the new Christian religion.

Luke 1:3-4 As a medical doctor, Luke knew the importance of being thorough. He used his skills in observation and analysis to thoroughly investigate the stories about Jesus. You can read Luke's account of Jesus' life with confidence that it was written by a clear thinker and a thoughtful researcher. Because the Good News is founded on historical truth, our spiritual growth must involve careful, disciplined, and thorough investigation of God's Word so that we can understand how God has acted in history. If this kind of study is not part of your life, find a pastor, teacher, or even a book to help you get started and to guide you in this important part of Christian growth.

John 1:1 What Jesus taught and what he did are tied inseparably to who he is. John shows Jesus as fully human and fully God. Although Jesus took upon himself full humanity and lived as a man, he never ceased to be the eternal God who has always existed, the Creator and Sustainer of all things, and the source of eternal life. This is the truth about Jesus, and the foundation of all truth. If we cannot or do not believe this basic truth, we will not have enough faith to trust our eternal destiny to him. That is why John wrote this Gospel—to build faith and confidence in Jesus Christ so that we may bleieve that he truly was and is the Son of God (John 20:30-31).

John 1:1 John wrote to believers everywhere, both Jews and non-Jews (Gentiles). As one of Jesus' 12 disciples, John writes with credibility and the details of an eyewitness. His book is not a biography (like the book of Luke); it is a thematic presentation of Jesus' life. Many in John's original audience had a Greek background. Greek culture encouraged worship of many mythological gods, whose supernatural characteristics were as important to Greeks as genealogies were to Jews. John shows that Jesus is not only different from but superior to these gods of mythology.

John 1:1ff What does John mean by "the Word"? The Word was a term used by theologians and philosophers, both Jews and Greeks, in many different ways. In Hebrew Scripture, the Word was an agent of creation (Ps 33:6), the source of God's message to his people through the prophets (Hos 4:1), and God's law, his standard of holiness (Ps 119:11). In Greek philosophy, the Word was the principle of reason that governed the world, or the thought still in the mind, while in Hebrew thought, the Word was another expression for God. John's description shows clearly that he is speaking of Jesus (see especially John 1:14)—a human being he knew and loved, but at the same time the Creator of the universe, the ultimate revelation of God, the living picture of God's holiness, the one who "holds all creation together" (Col 1:17). To Jewish readers, to say this man Jesus "was God" was blasphemous. To Greek readers, "the Word became human" (John 1:14) was unthinkable. To John, this new understanding of the Word was the Good News of Jesus Christ.

[4] The Word gave life to everything that was
created,*
and his life brought light to everyone.
[5] The light shines in the darkness,
and the darkness can never extinguish it.*

[6]God sent a man, John the Baptist,* [7]to tell about
the light so that everyone might believe because of
his testimony. [8]John himself was not the light; he was
simply a witness to tell about the light. [9]The one who
is the true light, who gives light to everyone, was coming into the world.
[10]He came into the very world he created, but the
world didn't recognize him. [11]He came to his own
people, and even they rejected him. [12]But to all who
believed him and accepted him, he gave the right to
become children of God. [13]They are reborn—not with
a physical birth resulting from human passion or plan,
but a birth that comes from God.
[14]So the Word became human* and made his home
among us. He was full of unfailing love and faithfulness.* And we have seen his glory, the glory of the
Father's one and only Son.
[15]John testified about him when he shouted to the
crowds, "This is the one I was talking about when I
said, 'Someone is coming after me who is far greater
than I am, for he existed long before me.' "

Jn 1:3-4 Or *and nothing that was created was created except through him. The Word gave life to everything.* **Jn 1:5** Or *and the darkness has not understood it.* **Jn 1:6** Greek *a man named John.* **Jn 1:14a** Greek *became flesh.* **Jn 1:14b** Or *grace and truth;* also in 1:17.

John 1:3 When God created, he made something from nothing. Because we are created beings, we have no basis for pride. Remember that you exist only because God made you, and you have special gifts only because God gave them to you. With God you are something valuable and unique; apart from God you are nothing, and if you try to live without him, you will be abandoning the purpose for which you were made.

John 1:3-5 Do you ever feel that your life is too complex for God to understand? Remember, God created the entire universe, and nothing is too difficult for him. God created you; he is alive today, and his love is bigger than any problem you may face.

John 1:4-5 "The darkness can never extinguish it" means the darkness of evil never has and never will overcome God's light. Jesus Christ is the Creator of life, and his life brings light to humankind. In his light, we see ourselves as we really are (sinners in need of a Savior). When we follow Jesus, the true Light, we can avoid walking blindly and falling into sin. He lights the path ahead of us so we can see how to live. He removes the darkness of sin from our lives. In what ways have you allowed the light of Christ to shine into your life? Let Christ guide your life, and you'll never need to stumble in darkness.

John 1:6-8 For more information on John the Baptist, see his Profile on p. 1292.

John 1:8 We, like John the Baptist, are not the source of God's light; we merely reflect that light. Jesus Christ is the true Light; he helps us see our way to God and shows us how to walk along that way. We are never to present ourselves as the light to others, but are always to point them to Jesus, the Light.

John 1:10-11 Although Jesus created the world, the people he created didn't recognize him. Even the people chosen by God to prepare the rest of the world for the Messiah rejected him, although the entire Old Testament pointed to his coming.

John 1:12-13 All who welcome Jesus Christ as Lord of their lives are reborn spiritually, receiving new life from God. Through faith in Jesus, this new birth changes us from the inside out—rearranging our attitudes, desires, and motives. Being born makes you physically alive and places you in your parents' family. Being born of God makes you spiritually alive and puts you in God's family. Have you asked Jesus to make you a new person? This fresh start in life is available to all who believe in him.

John 1:14 "The Word became human." By doing so, Jesus became (1) the perfect teacher—in Jesus' life we see how God thinks and therefore how we should think (Phil 2:5-11); (2) the perfect example—as a model of what we are to become, he shows us how to live and gives us the power to live that way (1 Pet 2:21); (3) the perfect sacrifice—Jesus came as a sacrifice for all sins, and his death satisfied God's requirements for the removal of sin (Col 1:15-22).

John 1:14 "The Father's one and only Son" emphasizes Jesus' uniqueness. He is unlike believers, who are all called "children of God." Jesus is one of a kind and enjoys a unique relationship with God.

John 1:14 When Jesus was conceived, God became a man. He was not part man and part God; he was completely human and completely divine (Col 2:9). Jesus is the perfect expression of God in human form. The two most common errors people make about Jesus are to minimize his humanity or to minimize his divinity. Jesus is both God and man.

One and Only God

The most exciting and significant discovery of biblical manuscripts since the Dead Sea Scrolls was discovered in the Dishna Plain, east of the Nile River in Egypt. Several of these manuscripts are known as the Bodmer biblical papyri, which include two *early manuscripts of John's Gospel (P66 and P75)*.

John 1:18 is an important verse in showing that Jesus was called "God" in Scripture, but there is a difference in the Greek manuscripts of this verse. The Greek *monogenes theos* (one and only God) was attested in some early manuscripts, but many later manuscripts read *monogenes huios* (one and only Son) instead. However, the discovery of two second-century papyri, P66 and P75, both of which read *theos,* tipped the balance. It is now clear that *monogenes theos* is the earlier reading and most likely to be original. This is translated as "the unique One, who is himself God" in the NLT.

▶ **JOHN 1:1-18** ***(cont.)***

16From his abundance we have all received one
gracious blessing after another.* 17For the law was
given through Moses, but God's unfailing love and
faithfulness came through Jesus Christ. 18No one has
ever seen God. But the unique One, who is himself
God,* is near to the Father's heart. He has revealed
God to us.

An Angel Promises the Birth of John to Zechariah

LUKE 1:5-25

When Herod was king of Judea, there was a Jewish
priest named Zechariah. He was a member of the
priestly order of Abijah, and his wife, Elizabeth, was
also from the priestly line of Aaron. 6Zechariah and
Elizabeth were righteous in God's eyes, careful to obey
all of the Lord's commandments and regulations.
7They had no children because Elizabeth was unable
to conceive, and they were both very old.

8One day Zechariah was serving God in the Temple,
for his order was on duty that week. 9As was the custom of the priests, he was chosen by lot to enter the
sanctuary of the Lord and burn incense. 10While the
incense was being burned, a great crowd stood outside, praying.

11While Zechariah was in the sanctuary, an angel
of the Lord appeared to him, standing to the right

Jn 1:16 Or *received the grace of Christ rather than the grace of the law;* Greek reads *received grace upon grace.* **Jn 1:18** Some manuscripts read *But the one and only Son.*

John 1:17 Law and grace (the combination of "God's unfailing love and faithfulness") are both aspects of God's nature that he uses in dealing with us. Moses emphasized God's law and justice, while Jesus Christ came to highlight God's mercy, love, faithfulness, and forgiveness. Moses could only be the giver of the law, while Jesus came to fulfill the law (Matt 5:17). The nature and will of God were revealed in the law; now the nature and will of God are revealed in Jesus Christ. Rather than coming through cold stone tablets, God's revelation now comes through a person. As we get to know Jesus better, our understanding of God will increase.

John 1:18 God communicated through various people in the Old Testament, usually prophets who were told to give specific messages. But no one ever saw God. Jesus is both God and the Father's unique Son. In Jesus, God revealed his nature and essence in a way that could be seen and touched. In Jesus, God became a man who lived on earth.

Luke 1:5 This was Herod the Great, confirmed by the Roman Senate as king of the Jews. Only half-Jewish himself and eager to please his Roman superiors, Herod expanded and beautified the Jerusalem Temple—but he placed a Roman eagle over the entrance. When he helped the Jews, it was for political purposes and not because he cared about their God. Later, Herod the Great would order a massacre of infants in a futile attempt to kill the infant Jesus, whom some were calling the new "king of the Jews" (Matt 2:2).

Luke 1:5 A Jewish priest was a minister of God who worked at the Temple managing its upkeep, teaching the people the Scriptures, and directing the worship services. At this time there were about 20,000 priests throughout the country—far too many to minister in the Temple at one time. Therefore the priests were divided into 24 separate groups of about 1,000 each, according to David's instructions (1 Chr 24:3-19).

Zechariah was a member of the order of Abijah, on duty this particular week. Each morning a priest was to enter the Holy Place in the Temple and burn incense. The priests would cast lots to decide who would enter the inner sanctuary, and one day the lot fell to Zechariah. But it was not by chance that Zechariah was on duty and that he was chosen that day to enter the Holy Place—perhaps a once-in-a-lifetime opportunity. God was guiding the events of history to prepare the way for Jesus to come to earth.

Luke 1:6 Zechariah and Elizabeth didn't merely go through the motions in following God's laws; they backed up their outward compliance with inward obedience. Unlike the religious leaders whom Jesus called hypocrites, Zechariah and Elizabeth did not stop with the letter of the law. Their obedience was from the heart, and that is why they are called "righteous in God's eyes."

Luke 1:7 God answers prayer in his own way and in his own time. He worked in an "impossible" situation—Elizabeth's age and barrenness—to bring about the fulfillment of all the prophecies concerning the Messiah. When you pray, be open to what God can do in impossible situations. And you must wait for God to work in his way and in his time.

ZECHARIAH

Zechariah, a Jewish priest, was told before anyone else that God was setting in motion his own visit to earth. Zechariah and his wife, Elizabeth, shared the pain of not having children, and in Jewish culture this was considered not having God's blessing. Zechariah and Elizabeth were old, and they had stopped even asking for children. • One day while on duty at the Temple in Jerusalem, Zechariah was chosen to enter the Holy Place to offer incense to God for the people. Suddenly, much to his surprise and terror, an angel appeared and promised him a son. But this good news was eclipsed by his doubts. He feared he was too old to father the child the angel had promised. As a result, God prevented Zechariah from speaking until his son, John, was born. • Like so many of God's most faithful servants, he passed quietly from the scene once his part was done. He becomes our hero for those times when we doubt God and yet are willing to obey. We gain hope from Zechariah's story that God can do great things through anyone who is available to him.

Strengths and accomplishments	• Known as a righteous man • Was a priest of God • One of the few people directly addressed by an angel • Fathered John the Baptist
Weakness and mistake	• Momentarily doubted the angel's promise of a son because of his own old age
Lessons from his life	• Physical limitations do not limit God • God accomplishes his will, often in unexpected ways
Vital statistics	• Occupation: Priest • Relatives: Wife: Elizabeth. Son: John the Baptist.
Key verses	"Zechariah and Elizabeth were righteous in God's eyes, careful to obey all of the Lord's commandments and regulations. They had no children because Elizabeth was unable to conceive, and they were both very old" (Luke 1:6-7).

Zechariah's story is told in Luke 1.

of the incense altar. 12Zechariah was shaken and
overwhelmed with fear when he saw him. 13But the
angel said, "Don't be afraid, Zechariah! God has heard
your prayer. Your wife, Elizabeth, will give you a son,
and you are to name him John. 14You will have great
joy and gladness, and many will rejoice at his birth,
15for he will be great in the eyes of the Lord. He must
never touch wine or other alcoholic drinks. He will
be filled with the Holy Spirit, even before his birth.*
16And he will turn many Israelites to the Lord their
God. 17He will be a man with the spirit and power of
Elijah. He will prepare the people for the coming of
the Lord. He will turn the hearts of the fathers to their
children,* and he will cause those who are rebellious
to accept the wisdom of the godly."
18Zechariah said to the angel, "How can I be sure
this will happen? I'm an old man now, and my wife is
also well along in years."
19Then the angel said, "I am Gabriel! I stand in the
very presence of God. It was he who sent me to bring
you this good news! 20But now, since you didn't believe
what I said, you will be silent and unable to speak until
the child is born. For my words will certainly be fulfilled at the proper time."
21Meanwhile, the people were waiting for Zechariah to come out of the sanctuary, wondering why he
was taking so long. 22When he finally did come out,
he couldn't speak to them. Then they realized from
his gestures and his silence that he must have seen a
vision in the sanctuary.
23When Zechariah's week of service in the Temple
was over, he returned home. 24Soon afterward his
wife, Elizabeth, became pregnant and went into seclusion for five months. 25"How kind the Lord is!" she
exclaimed. "He has taken away my disgrace of having
no children."

Lk 1:15 Or *even from birth.* **Lk 1:17** See Mal 4:5-6.

Luke 1:9 Incense was burned in the Temple twice daily (Exod 30:7-8). When the people saw the smoke from the burning incense, they prayed. The smoke drifting heavenward symbolized their prayers ascending to God's throne.

Luke 1:11-12 Angels are spirit beings who live in God's presence and do his will. Only two angels are mentioned by name in Scripture—Michael and Gabriel—but there are many who act as God's messengers. Here, Gabriel (Luke 1:19) delivered a special message to Zechariah. This was not a dream or a vision. The angel appeared in visible form and spoke audible words to the priest.

Luke 1:13 While burning incense on the altar, Zechariah was also praying, most likely for the coming of the Messiah to his people. How odd it must have seemed that the angel would say that his prayer was answered and Zechariah would soon have a son. Yet the greatest desire of Zechariah's heart—to have a son—would come true. At the same time, the answer to the nation's prayer for the Messiah would also come true. Zechariah's son would grow up to prepare the way for the Messiah.

Luke 1:13 John means "the LORD is gracious," and Jesus means "the LORD saves." Both names were prescribed by God, not chosen by human parents. Throughout the Gospels, God acts graciously and saves his people. He will not withhold salvation from anyone who sincerely comes to him.

Luke 1:15 John was set apart for special service to God. He may have been forbidden to drink wine as part of the Nazirite vow, an ancient vow of consecration to God (see Num 6:1-8). Samson (Judg 13) was under the Nazirite vow, and Samuel may have been also (1 Sam 1:11).

Luke 1:15 This is Luke's first mention of the Holy Spirit, the third Person of the Trinity; Luke refers to the Holy Spirit more than any other Gospel writer. Because Luke also wrote the book of Acts, we know he was thoroughly informed about the work of the Holy Spirit. Luke recognized and emphasized the Holy Spirit's work in directing the beginnings of Christianity and in guiding the early church. The presence of the Spirit was God's gift to the entire church at Pentecost. Prior to that, God's Spirit was given to the faithful for special tasks. We need the Holy Spirit's help to do God's work effectively.

Luke 1:17 John's role was to be almost identical to that of an Old Testament prophet: to encourage people to turn away from sin and back to God. John is often compared to the great prophet Elijah, who was known for standing up to evil rulers (Mal 4:5; Matt 11:14; 17:10-13). See Elijah's Profile on p. 719.

Luke 1:18-20 When told he would have a son, Zechariah doubted the angel's word. From Zechariah's human perspective, his doubts were understandable—but with God, anything is possible. What God promises, he delivers. And God delivers on time! You can have complete confidence that God will keep his promises. Their fulfillment may not be the next day, but they will be "at the proper time." If you are waiting for God to answer some request or to fill some need, remain patient.

Luke 1:21 The people were waiting outside for Zechariah to come out and pronounce the customary blessing upon them as found in Numbers 6:24-26.

Luke 1:25 Zechariah and Elizabeth were both godly people, yet they were suffering. Children were considered a blessing, and childlessness was seen as a curse. Zechariah and Elizabeth had been childless for many years, and at this time they were too old to expect any change in their situation. They felt humiliated and hopeless. But God was waiting for the right time to encourage them and take away their disgrace.

DOUBTERS IN THE BIBLE

Many of the people God used to accomplish great things started out as real doubters. With all of them, God showed great patience. Honest doubt was not a bad starting point as long as they didn't stay there. How great a part does doubt have in your willingness to trust God?

Doubter	*Doubtful Moment*	*Reference*
Abraham	When told he would be a father in old age	Gen 17:17
Sarah	When she heard she would be a mother in old age	Gen 18:12
Moses	When told to return to Egypt to lead the people	Exod 3:10-15
Israelites	Whenever they faced difficulties in the wilderness	Exod 16:1-3
Gideon	When told he would be a judge and leader	Judg 6:14-23
Zechariah	When told he would be a father in old age	Luke 1:18
Thomas	When told Jesus had risen from the dead	John 20:24-25

An Angel Promises the Birth of Jesus to Mary

LUKE 1:26-38

In the sixth month of Elizabeth's pregnancy, God sent
the angel Gabriel to Nazareth, a village in Galilee, 27to
a virgin named Mary. She was engaged to be married
to a man named Joseph, a descendant of King David.
28Gabriel appeared to her and said, "Greetings, favored
woman! The Lord is with you!*"
29Confused and disturbed, Mary tried to think what
the angel could mean. 30"Don't be afraid, Mary," the
angel told her, "for you have found favor with God!
31You will conceive and give birth to a son, and you
will name him Jesus. 32He will be very great and will
be called the Son of the Most High. The Lord God
will give him the throne of his ancestor David. 33And
he will reign over Israel* forever; his Kingdom will
never end!"
34Mary asked the angel, "But how can this happen?
I am a virgin."
35The angel replied, "The Holy Spirit will come upon
you, and the power of the Most High will overshadow
you. So the baby to be born will be holy, and he will
be called the Son of God. 36What's more, your relative
Elizabeth has become pregnant in her old age! People
used to say she was barren, but she has conceived a
son and is now in her sixth month. 37For nothing is
impossible with God.*"

Lk 1:28 Some manuscripts add *Blessed are you among women.* **Lk 1:33** Greek *over the house of Jacob.* **Lk 1:37** Some manuscripts read *For the word of God will never fail.*

Luke 1:26 Gabriel appeared not only to Zechariah and to Mary but also to the prophet Daniel more than 500 years earlier (Dan 8:15-17; 9:21). Each time Gabriel appeared, he brought important messages from God.

Luke 1:26 Nazareth, Joseph and Mary's hometown, was a long way from Jerusalem, the center of Jewish life and worship. Located on a major trade route, Nazareth was frequently visited by Gentile merchants and Roman soldiers. It was known for its independent and aloof attitude. Jesus was born in Bethlehem but grew up in Nazareth. Nevertheless, the people of Nazareth would reject him as the Messiah (Luke 4:22-30).

Luke 1:27-28 Mary was young, poor, and female—all characteristics that, to the people of her day, would make her seem unusable by God for any major task. But God chose Mary for one of the most important acts of obedience he has ever demanded of anyone. You may feel that your ability, experience, or education makes you an unlikely candidate for God's service. Don't limit God's choices. He can use you if you trust him.

Luke 1:30-31 God's favor does not automatically bring instant success or fame. His blessing on Mary, the honor of being the mother of the Messiah, would lead to much pain: her peers would ridicule her; her fiancé would come close to leaving her; her son would be rejected and murdered. But through her son would come the world's only hope, and this is why Mary has been praised by countless generations. Her submission was part of God's plan to bring about our salvation. If sorrow weighs you down and dims your hope, think of Mary and wait patiently for God to finish working out his plan.

Luke 1:31 Jesus, a Greek form of the Hebrew name Joshua, was a common name meaning "the LORD saves." Just as Joshua had led Israel into the Promised Land (see Josh 1:1-2), so Jesus would lead his people into eternal life. The symbolism of his name was not lost on the people of his day, who took names seriously and saw them as a source of power. In Jesus' name, people were healed, demons were banished, and sins were forgiven.

Luke 1:32-33 Centuries earlier, God had promised David that David's kingdom would last forever (2 Sam 7:16). This promise was fulfilled in the coming of Jesus, a direct descendant of David, whose Kingdom will never end.

Luke 1:34 The birth of Jesus to a virgin is a miracle that many people find hard to believe. These three facts can aid our faith: (1) Luke was a medical doctor, and he knew perfectly well how babies are made. It would have been just as hard for him to believe in a virgin birth as it is for us, yet he reports it as fact. (2) Luke was a painstaking researcher who based his Gospel on eyewitness accounts. Tradition holds that he talked with Mary about the events he recorded in the first two chapters. This is Mary's story, not a fictional invention. (3) Christians and Jews, who worship God as the Creator of the universe, should have no doubts that God has the power to create a child in a virgin's womb.

Luke 1:35 Why is the Virgin Birth important to the Christian faith? Jesus was born without the sin that entered the world through Adam. He was born holy, just as Adam was created sinless. In contrast to Adam, who disobeyed God, Jesus obeyed God and was thus able to face sin's consequences in our place and make us acceptable to God (Rom 5:14-19). Jesus Christ, God's Son, had to be free from the sinful nature passed on to all other human beings by Adam. Because Jesus was born of a woman, he was a human being; but as the Son of God, Jesus was born without any trace of human sin. Jesus is both fully human and fully divine. Because Jesus lived as a man, human beings know that he fully understands their experiences and struggles (Heb 4:15-16). Because he is God, he has

GOD'S UNUSUAL METHODS OF COMMUNICATING

One of the best ways to understand God's willingness to communicate to people is to note the various methods, some of them quite unexpected, that he has used to give his message.

Person/Group	*Method*	*Reference*
Jacob, Zechariah, Mary, shepherds	Angels	Gen 32:22-32; Luke 1:13, 30; 2:10
Jacob, Joseph, a baker, a cup-bearer, Pharaoh, Isaiah, Joseph, the wise men	Dreams	Gen 28:10-22; 37:5-10; 40:5; 41:7-8; Isa 1:1; Matt 1:20; 2:12-13
Belshazzar	Writing on the wall	Dan 5:5-9
Balaam	Talking donkey	Num 22:21-35
People of Israel	Pillars of cloud and fire	Exod 13:21-22
Jonah	Being swallowed by a fish	Jon 2
Abraham, Moses, those present at Jesus' baptism, Paul	Verbally	Gen 12:1-4; Exod 7:8; Matt 3:13-17; Acts 18:9
Moses	Fire	Exod 3:2
Us	God's Son	Heb 1:1-2

38 Mary responded, "I am the Lord's servant. May everything you have said about me come true." And then the angel left her.

Mary Visits Elizabeth

LUKE 1:39-45

A few days later Mary hurried to the hill country of Judea, to the town
40 where Zechariah lived. She entered the house and greeted Elizabeth.
41 At the sound of Mary's greeting, Elizabeth's child leaped within her, and Elizabeth was filled with the Holy Spirit.
42 Elizabeth gave a glad cry and exclaimed to Mary, "God has blessed you above all women, and your child is blessed.
43 Why am I so honored, that the mother of my Lord should visit me?
44 When I heard your greeting, the baby in my womb jumped for joy.
45 You are blessed because you believed that the Lord would do what he said."

The Magnificat: Mary's Song of Praise

LUKE 1:46-56

Mary responded,

"Oh, how my soul praises the Lord.
47 How my spirit rejoices in God my Savior!
48 For he took notice of his lowly servant girl,

ELIZABETH

In societies like Israel, in which a woman's value was largely measured by the children she bore, barrenness often led to personal hardship and public shame. For Elizabeth, a childless old age was a painful and lonely time but still she remained faithful to God. • Both Elizabeth and Zechariah came from priestly families. For two weeks each year, Zechariah went to the Temple in Jerusalem for his priestly duties. After one of those trips, Zechariah returned home excited but speechless. He had to write down his good news: Their faded dream would become an exciting reality! Soon Elizabeth became pregnant, and she knew her child was a long-hoped-for gift from God. • Seventy miles to the north, in Nazareth, Elizabeth's relative Mary also unexpectedly became pregnant. Within days after hearing that she would bear the Messiah, Mary went to visit Elizabeth. They were instantly bound together by the unique gifts God had given them. • When her baby was born, Elizabeth insisted on his God-given name: John. Things had worked out even better than she could have planned. We, too, need to remember that God is in control of every situation. When did you last pause to recognize God's timing in the events of your life?

Strengths and accomplishments	• Known as a deeply spiritual woman • Never doubted God's ability to fulfill his promise • The first woman besides Mary to hear of the coming Savior
Lessons from her life	• God does not forget those who are faithful to him • God's timetable and methods do not have to conform to what we expect
Vital statistics	• Occupation: Homemaker • Relatives: Husband: Zechariah. Son: John the Baptist. Relative: Mary.
Key verses	"Why am I so honored, that the mother of my Lord should visit me? When I heard your greeting, the baby in my womb jumped for joy" (Luke 1:43-44).

Elizabeth's story is told in Luke 1:5-80.

the power and authority to deliver people from sin (Col 2:13-15). People can tell Jesus all their thoughts, feelings, and needs. He has been where they are, and he has the ability to help.

Luke 1:38 A young unmarried girl who became pregnant risked disaster. Unless the father of the child agreed to marry her, she would probably remain unmarried for life. If her own father rejected her, she could be forced into begging or prostitution in order to earn her living. And Mary, with her story about becoming pregnant by the Holy Spirit, risked being considered crazy as well. Still Mary said, despite the possible risks, "May everything you have said about me come true." When Mary said that, she didn't know about the tremendous opportunity she would have. She only knew that God was asking her to serve him, and she willingly obeyed. Don't wait to see the bottom line before offering your life to God. Offer yourself willingly, even when the outcome seems disastrous.

Luke 1:38 God's announcement of the birth of a special child was met with various responses throughout Scripture. Sarah, Abraham's wife, laughed (Gen 18:9-15). Zechariah doubted (Luke 1:18). By contrast, Mary graciously submitted. She believed the angel's words and agreed to bear the child, even under humanly impossible circumstances. God is able to do the impossible. Our response to his demands should not be laughter or doubt but willing acceptance.

Luke 1:41-43 Apparently the Holy Spirit told Elizabeth that Mary's child was the Messiah, because Elizabeth called her young relative "the mother of my Lord" as she greeted her. As Mary rushed off to visit her relative, she must have been wondering if the events of the last few days had been real. Elizabeth's greeting must have strengthened her faith. Mary's pregnancy may have seemed impossible, but her wise relative believed in the Lord's faithfulness and rejoiced in Mary's blessed condition.

Luke 1:42-43 Even though she herself was pregnant with a long-awaited son, Elizabeth could have envied Mary, whose son would be even greater than her own. Instead, she was filled with joy that the mother of her Lord would visit her. Have you ever envied people whom God has apparently singled out for special blessing? A cure for jealousy is to rejoice with those individuals, realizing that God uses his people in ways best suited to his purpose.

Luke 1:46-55 This song is often called the Magnificat, the first word in the Latin translation of this passage. Mary's song has often been used as the basis for choral music and hymns. Like Hannah, the mother of Samuel (1 Sam 2:1-10), Mary glorified God in song for what he was going to do for the world through her. Notice that in both songs, God is pictured as a champion of the poor, the oppressed, and the despised.

Luke 1:48 When Mary said, "From now on all generations will call me blessed," was she being proud? No, she was recognizing and accepting the gift God had given her. Pride is refusing to accept God's gifts or taking credit for what God has done; humility is accepting the gifts and using them to praise and serve God. Don't deny, belittle, or ignore your gifts. Thank God for them and use them to his glory.

▸ **LUKE 1:46-56 *(cont.)***

and from now on all generations will call me
blessed.
49 For the Mighty One is holy,
and he has done great things for me.
50 He shows mercy from generation to generation
to all who fear him.
51 His mighty arm has done tremendous things!
He has scattered the proud and haughty ones.
52 He has brought down princes from their thrones
and exalted the humble.
53 He has filled the hungry with good things
and sent the rich away with empty hands.
54 He has helped his servant Israel
and remembered to be merciful.
55 For he made this promise to our ancestors,
to Abraham and his children forever."

56Mary stayed with Elizabeth about three months
and then went back to her own home.

John the Baptist Is Born

LUKE 1:57-66

When it was time for Elizabeth's baby to be born, she
gave birth to a son. 58And when her neighbors and
relatives heard that the Lord had been very merciful
to her, everyone rejoiced with her.

59When the baby was eight days old, they all came
for the circumcision ceremony. They wanted to name
him Zechariah, after his father. 60But Elizabeth said,
"No! His name is John!"

61"What?" they exclaimed. "There is no one in all your
family by that name." 62So they used gestures to ask
the baby's father what he wanted to name him. 63He
motioned for a writing tablet, and to everyone's surprise
he wrote, "His name is John." 64Instantly Zechariah could
speak again, and he began praising God.

65Awe fell upon the whole neighborhood, and the
news of what had happened spread throughout the
Judean hills. 66Everyone who heard about it reflected
on these events and asked, "What will this child turn
out to be?" For the hand of the Lord was surely upon
him in a special way.

Zechariah's Prophecy

LUKE 1:67-80

Then his father, Zechariah, was filled with the Holy
Spirit and gave this prophecy:

68 "Praise the Lord, the God of Israel,
because he has visited and redeemed his people.
69 He has sent us a mighty Savior*
from the royal line of his servant David,
70 just as he promised
through his holy prophets long ago.
71 Now we will be saved from our enemies
and from all who hate us.
72 He has been merciful to our ancestors
by remembering his sacred covenant—
73 the covenant he swore with an oath
to our ancestor Abraham.
74 We have been rescued from our enemies
so we can serve God without fear,
75 in holiness and righteousness
for as long as we live.

76 "And you, my little son,
will be called the prophet of the Most High,
because you will prepare the way for the Lord.
77 You will tell his people how to find salvation
through forgiveness of their sins.
78 Because of God's tender mercy,
the morning light from heaven is about
to break upon us,*

Lk 1:69 Greek *has raised up a horn of salvation for us.* **Lk 1:78** Or *the Morning Light from Heaven is about to visit us.*

Luke 1:54-55 God kept his promise to Abraham to be merciful to God's people forever (Gen 22:16-18). Christ's birth fulfilled the promise, and Mary understood this. She was not surprised when her special son eventually announced that he was the Messiah. She had known Jesus' mission from before his birth.

Luke 1:56 Because travel was difficult, long visits were customary. Mary must have been a great help to Elizabeth, who was experiencing the discomforts of a first pregnancy in old age.

Luke 1:59 The circumcision ceremony was an important event to the family of a Jewish baby boy. God commanded circumcision when he was beginning to form his holy nation (Gen 17:4-14), and he had reaffirmed it through Moses (Lev 12:1-3). This ceremony was a time of joy when friends and family members would celebrate the baby's becoming part of God's covenant nation.

Luke 1:59 Family lines and family names were important to the Jews. The people naturally assumed the child would receive Zechariah's name or at least a family name. They were surprised, therefore, that both Elizabeth and Zechariah wanted to name the boy John. This was the name the angel had given them (see Luke 1:13).

Luke 1:62 Zechariah's relatives talked to him by gestures because he was apparently deaf as well as speechless and had not heard what his wife had said.

Luke 1:67-79 Zechariah praised God with his first words after months of silence. In a song that is often called the Benedictus after the first words in the Latin translation of this passage, Zechariah prophesied the coming of a Savior who would redeem his people and predicted that his son, John, would prepare the Messiah's way. All the Old Testament prophecies were coming true—no wonder Zechariah praised God!

Luke 1:72-73 This was God's promise to Abraham to bless all peoples through him (see Gen 12:3). It would be fulfilled through the Messiah, Abraham's descendant.

Luke 1:76 Zechariah had just recalled hundreds of years of God's sovereign work in history, beginning with Abraham and going on into eternity. Then, in tender contrast, he personalized the story. His son had been chosen for a key role in the drama of the ages. Although God has unlimited power, he chooses to work through frail humans who begin as helpless babies. Don't minimize what God can do through those who are faithful to him.

Luke 1:80 Why did John live out in the wilderness? Prophets used the isolation of the uninhabited wilderness to enhance their spiritual growth and to focus their message on God. By being in the wilderness, John remained separate from the economic and political powers so that he

79 to give light to those who sit in darkness and
in the shadow of death,
and to guide us to the path of peace."

80John grew up and became strong in spirit. And he lived in the wilderness until he began his public ministry to Israel.

An Angel Appears to Joseph

MATTHEW 1:18-25

This is how Jesus the Messiah was born. His mother, Mary, was engaged to be married to Joseph. But before the marriage took place, while she was still a virgin, she became pregnant through the power of the Holy Spirit.
19Joseph, her fiancé, was a good man and did not want to disgrace her publicly, so he decided to break the engagement* quietly.
20As he considered this, an angel of the Lord appeared to him in a dream. "Joseph, son of David," the angel said, "do not be afraid to take Mary as your wife. For the child within her was conceived by the Holy Spirit. 21And she will have a son, and you are to name him Jesus,* for he will save his people from their sins."

Mt 1:19 Greek *to divorce her.* **Mt 1:21** *Jesus* means "The LORD saves."

JOSEPH

The strength of what we believe is measured by how much we are willing to suffer for those beliefs. Joseph was a man with strong beliefs. He was prepared to do what was right, despite the pain he knew it would cause. But Joseph not only tried to do what was right, he also tried to do it in the right way. • When Mary told Joseph about her pregnancy, Joseph knew the child was not his. Joseph decided he had to break the engagement, but he was determined to do it in a way that would not cause public shame to Mary. He intended to act with justice and love. • At this point, God sent a messenger to Joseph to confirm Mary's story and open another way of obedience for Joseph—to take Mary as his wife. Joseph obeyed God, married Mary, and honored her virginity until the baby was born. • We do not know how long Joseph lived his role as Jesus' earthly father—he is last mentioned when Jesus was 12 years old. But Joseph trained his son in the trade of carpentry and took the whole family on the yearly trip to Jerusalem for the Passover, providing good spiritual leadership for his family. • Joseph knew Jesus was someone special from the moment he heard the angel's words. His strong belief in that fact and his willingness to follow God's leading empowered him to be Jesus' chosen earthly father.

Strengths and accomplishments	• A man of integrity • Jesus' legal and earthly father • Sensitive to God's guidance and ready to do God's will
Lessons from his life	• God honors integrity • Being obedient to God leads to more guidance from him • Feelings are not accurate measures of the rightness or wrongness of an action
Vital statistics	• Where: Nazareth, Bethlehem • Occupation: Carpenter • Relatives: Wife: Mary. Children: Jesus, James, Joses, Judas, Simon, and daughters.
Key verse	"Joseph, her fiancé, was a good man and did not want to disgrace her publicly, so he decided to break the engagement quietly" (Matt 1:19).

Joseph's story is told in Matthew 1:16–2:23; Luke 1:26–2:52.

could aim his message against them. He also remained separate from the hypocritical religious leaders of his day. His message was different from theirs, and his life proved it.

Matt 1:18 Jewish marriage involved three basic steps. First, the two families agreed to the union. Second, a public announcement was made. At this point, the couple was "engaged." This was similar to engagement today except that their relationship could be broken only through death or divorce (even though sexual relations were not yet permitted). Third, the couple was married and began living together. Because Mary and Joseph were engaged, Mary's apparent unfaithfulness carried a severe social stigma. According to Jewish civil law, Joseph had a right to divorce her, and the Jewish authorities could have had her stoned to death (Deut 22:23-24). On the importance of the Virgin Birth, see note on Luke 1:35, p. 1274.

Matt 1:19 Joseph was faced with a difficult choice after discovering that Mary was pregnant. Perhaps Joseph thought he had only two options: divorce Mary quietly or have her stoned. But God gave a third option—marry her (Matt 1:20-23). In view of the circumstances, this had not occurred to Joseph. But God often shows us that there are more options available than we think. Although Joseph seemed to be doing the right thing by breaking the engagement, only God's guidance helped him make the best decision. But that did not make it an easy decision. Consenting to marry Mary surely cast doubt on his own innocence regarding the pregnancy, as well as leaving them both with a social stigma they would carry for the rest of their lives. Yet Joseph chose to obey the angel's command (Matt 1:24). When our decisions affect the lives of others, we must always seek God's wisdom and then be willing to follow through no matter how difficult it may be.

Matt 1:20 The conception and birth of Jesus Christ are supernatural events beyond human logic or reasoning. Because of this, God sent angels to help certain people understand the significance of what was happening (see Matt 2:13, 19; Luke 1:11, 26; 2:9).

Angels are spiritual beings created by God who help carry out his work on earth. They bring God's messages to people (Luke 1:26), protect God's people (Dan 6:22), offer encouragement (Gen 16:7ff), give guidance (Exod 14:19), carry out punishment (2 Sam 24:16), patrol the earth (Zech 1:9-14), and fight the forces of evil (2 Kgs 6:16-18; Rev 20:1-2). There are both good and bad angels (Rev 12:7), but because bad angels are allied with the devil, or Satan, they have considerably less power and authority than good angels. Eventually the main role of angels will be to offer continuous praise to God (Rev 7:11-12).

Matt 1:20-23 The angel declared to Joseph that Mary's child was conceived by the Holy Spirit and would be a son. This reveals an important truth about Jesus—he is both God and human. The infinite, unlimited God took on the limitations of humanity so he could live and die for the salvation of all who would believe in him.

Jesus means "the LORD saves." Jesus came to earth to save us because we can't save ourselves from sin and its consequences. No matter how good we are, we can't eliminate the sinful nature present in all of us. Only Jesus can do that. Jesus

▶ **MATTHEW 1:18-25 *(cont.)***

22 All of this occurred to fulfill the Lord's message through his prophet:

23 "Look! The virgin will conceive a child!
She will give birth to a son,
and they will call him Immanuel,*
which means 'God is with us.'"

24 When Joseph woke up, he did as the angel of the
Lord commanded and took Mary as his wife. 25 But he
did not have sexual relations with her until her son
was born. And Joseph named him Jesus.

The Record of Jesus' Ancestors PARALLEL

MATTHEW 1:1-17

This is a record of the ancestors of Jesus the Messiah, a descendant of David* and of Abraham:

2 Abraham was the father of Isaac.
Isaac was the father of Jacob.
Jacob was the father of Judah and his brothers.
3 Judah was the father of Perez and Zerah (whose mother was Tamar).
Perez was the father of Hezron.
Hezron was the father of Ram.*
4 Ram was the father of Amminadab.
Amminadab was the father of Nahshon.
Nahshon was the father of Salmon.
5 Salmon was the father of Boaz (whose mother was Rahab).
Boaz was the father of Obed (whose mother was Ruth).
Obed was the father of Jesse.
6 Jesse was the father of King David.
David was the father of Solomon (whose mother was Bathsheba, the widow of Uriah).
7 Solomon was the father of Rehoboam.
Rehoboam was the father of Abijah.
Abijah was the father of Asa.*
8 Asa was the father of Jehoshaphat.
Jehoshaphat was the father of Jehoram.*
Jehoram was the father* of Uzziah.
9 Uzziah was the father of Jotham.
Jotham was the father of Ahaz.
Ahaz was the father of Hezekiah.
10 Hezekiah was the father of Manasseh.
Manasseh was the father of Amon.*
Amon was the father of Josiah.
11 Josiah was the father of Jehoiachin* and his brothers (born at the time of the exile to Babylon).
12 After the Babylonian exile:
Jehoiachin was the father of Shealtiel.
Shealtiel was the father of Zerubbabel.

Mt 1:23 Isa 7:14; 8:8, 10 (Greek version). **Mt 1:1** Greek *Jesus the Messiah, son of David.* **Mt 1:3** Greek *Aram,* a variant spelling of Ram; also in 1:4. See 1 Chr 2:9-10. **Mt 1:7** Greek *Asaph,* a variant spelling of Asa; also in 1:8. See 1 Chr 3:10. **Mt 1:8a** Greek *Joram,* a variant spelling of Jehoram; also in 1:8b. See 1 Kgs 22:50 and note at 1 Chr 3:11. **Mt 1:8b** Or *ancestor;* also in 1:11. **Mt 1:10** Greek *Amos,* a variant spelling of Amon; also in 1:10b. See 1 Chr 3:14. **Mt 1:11** Greek *Jeconiah,* a variant spelling of Jehoiachin; also in 1:12. See 2 Kgs 24:6 and note at 1 Chr 3:16.

didn't come to help people save themselves; he came to be their Savior from the power and penalty of sin. Thank Jesus for his death on the cross for your sin, and then ask him to take control of your life. Your new life begins at that moment.

Jesus would fulfill the prophecy of Isaiah, for he would be Immanuel ("God is with us," see Isa 7:14). Jesus was God in the flesh; thus, God was literally among us, "with us." Through the Holy Spirit, Christ is present today in the life of every believer. Perhaps not even Isaiah understood how far-reaching the meaning of Immanuel would be.

Matt 1:24 Joseph changed his plans quickly after learning that Mary had not been unfaithful to him (Matt 1:19). He obeyed God and proceeded with the marriage plans. Although others may have disapproved of his decision, Joseph went ahead with what he knew was right. Sometimes we avoid doing what is right because of what others might think. Like Joseph, we must choose to obey God rather than seek the approval of others.

Matt 1:1 Presenting this record of ancestors (called a genealogy) was one of the most interesting ways that Matthew could begin a book for a Jewish audience. Because a person's family line proved his or her standing as one of God's chosen people, Matthew began by showing that Jesus was a descendant of Abraham, the father of all Jews, and a direct descendant of David, fulfilling Old Testament prophecies about the Messiah's line. The facts of this ancestry were carefully preserved. This is the first of many proofs recorded by Matthew to show that Jesus is the true Messiah.

Matt 1:1ff More than 400 years had passed since the last Old Testament prophecies, and faithful Jews all over the world were still waiting for the Messiah (Luke 3:15). Matthew wrote this book to Jews to present Jesus as King and Messiah, the promised descendant of David who would reign forever (Isa 11:1-5). The Gospel of Matthew links the Old and New Testaments and contains many references that show how Jesus fulfilled Old Testament prophecy.

Matt 1:1ff Jesus entered human history when the land of Palestine was controlled by Rome and considered an insignificant outpost of the vast and mighty Roman Empire. The presence of Roman soldiers in Israel gave the Jews military peace, but at the price of oppression, slavery, injustice, and immorality. Into this kind of world came the promised Messiah.

Matt 1:1-17 In the first 17 verses we meet 46 people whose lifetimes span 2,000 years. All were ancestors of Jesus, but they varied considerably in personality, spirituality, and experience. Some were heroes of faith—like Abraham, Isaac, Ruth, and David. Some had shady reputations—like Rahab and Tamar. Many were very ordinary—like Hezron, Ram, Nahshon, and Akim. And others were evil—like Manasseh and Abijah. God's work in history is not limited by human failures or sins, and he works through ordinary people. Just as God used all kinds of people to bring his Son into the world, he uses all kinds today to accomplish his will. And God wants to use you.

Matt 1:3-6 Matthew's inclusion of four particular women (Tamar, Rahab, Ruth, and Bathsheba) reveals his concern to do more than relay historical data. These women raise both ethnic and ethical questions. At least two of them were not Israelites by birth and all four of them had reputations that could have made them unmentionable in an ancestral tree. Yet this was the line into which God's Son was born. Jesus' genealogy makes it clear, not that there were a few disreputable people in his family, but that all of them were sinners. God sent his Son as Savior of all people—Jews, Gentiles, men, and women. No matter what the sins of the people, God's plan was never thwarted. It continues to unfold. That plan includes you.

Matt 1:11 The exile to Babylon occurred in 586 B.C. when Nebuchadnezzar, king of Babylon, conquered Judah, destroyed Jerusalem, and took thousands of people captive.

13 Zerubbabel was the father of Abiud.
Abiud was the father of Eliakim.
Eliakim was the father of Azor.
14 Azor was the father of Zadok.
Zadok was the father of Akim.
Akim was the father of Eliud.
15 Eliud was the father of Eleazar.
Eleazar was the father of Matthan.
Matthan was the father of Jacob.
16 Jacob was the father of Joseph, the husband of Mary.
Mary gave birth to Jesus, who is called the Messiah.

17 All those listed above include fourteen generations from Abraham to David, fourteen from David to the Babylonian exile, and fourteen from the Babylonian exile to the Messiah.

LUKE 3:23-38

Jesus was about thirty years old when he began his public ministry.

Jesus was known as the son of Joseph.
Joseph was the son of Heli.
24 Heli was the son of Matthat.
Matthat was the son of Levi.
Levi was the son of Melki.
Melki was the son of Jannai.
Jannai was the son of Joseph.
25 Joseph was the son of Mattathias.
Mattathias was the son of Amos.
Amos was the son of Nahum.
Nahum was the son of Esli.
Esli was the son of Naggai.
26 Naggai was the son of Maath.
Maath was the son of Mattathias.
Mattathias was the son of Semein.
Semein was the son of Josech.
Josech was the son of Joda.
27 Joda was the son of Joanan.
Joanan was the son of Rhesa.
Rhesa was the son of Zerubbabel.
Zerubbabel was the son of Shealtiel.
Shealtiel was the son of Neri.
28 Neri was the son of Melki.
Melki was the son of Addi.
Addi was the son of Cosam.
Cosam was the son of Elmadam.
Elmadam was the son of Er.
29 Er was the son of Joshua.
Joshua was the son of Eliezer.
Eliezer was the son of Jorim.
Jorim was the son of Matthat.
Matthat was the son of Levi.
30 Levi was the son of Simeon.
Simeon was the son of Judah.

Matt 1:16 Because Mary was a virgin when she became pregnant, Matthew lists Joseph only as the husband of Mary, not the father of Jesus. Matthew's genealogy gives Jesus' legal (or royal) lineage through Joseph. Mary's ancestral line is recorded in Luke 3:23-38. Both Mary and Joseph were direct descendants of David.

Matthew traced the genealogy back to Abraham, while Luke traced it back to Adam. Matthew wrote to the Jews, so Jesus was shown as a descendant of their father, Abraham. Luke wrote to the Gentiles, so he emphasized Jesus as the Savior of all people.

Matt 1:17 Matthew breaks Israel's history into three sets of 14 generations, but there were probably more generations than those listed here. Genealogies often compressed history, meaning that not every generation of ancestors was specifically listed. Thus, the phrase "the father of" can also be translated "the ancestor of."

Luke 3:23 Imagine the Savior of the world working in a small-town carpenter's shop until he was 30 years old! It seems incredible that Jesus would have been content to remain in Nazareth all that time, but he patiently trusted his Father's timing for his life and ministry. Thirty was the prescribed age for priests to begin their ministry (Num 4:3). Joseph was 30 years old when he began serving the king of Egypt (Gen 41:46), and David was 30 years old when he began to reign over Judah (2 Sam 5:4). Age 30, then, was a good time to begin an important task in the Jewish culture. Like Jesus, we need to resist the temptation to jump ahead before receiving the Spirit's direction. Are you waiting and wondering what your next step should be? Don't jump ahead—trust God's timing.

The Adoration of the Shepherds, by Bartolomé Murillo.

Luke 3:23-38 Matthew's genealogy goes back to Abraham and shows that Jesus was related to all Jews (Matt 1). Luke's genealogy goes back to Adam, showing that Jesus is related to all human beings. This is consistent with Luke's picture of Jesus as the Savior of the whole world.

▸ LUKE 3:23-38 *(cont.)*

Judah was the son of Joseph.
Joseph was the son of Jonam.
Jonam was the son of Eliakim.
31 Eliakim was the son of Melea.
Melea was the son of Menna.
Menna was the son of Mattatha.
Mattatha was the son of Nathan.
Nathan was the son of David.
32 David was the son of Jesse.
Jesse was the son of Obed.
Obed was the son of Boaz.
Boaz was the son of Salmon.*
Salmon was the son of Nahshon.
33 Nahshon was the son of Amminadab.
Amminadab was the son of Admin.
Admin was the son of Arni.*
Arni was the son of Hezron.
Hezron was the son of Perez.
Perez was the son of Judah.
34 Judah was the son of Jacob.
Jacob was the son of Isaac.
Isaac was the son of Abraham.
Abraham was the son of Terah.
Terah was the son of Nahor.
35 Nahor was the son of Serug.
Serug was the son of Reu.
Reu was the son of Peleg.
Peleg was the son of Eber.
Eber was the son of Shelah.
36 Shelah was the son of Cainan.
Cainan was the son of Arphaxad.
Arphaxad was the son of Shem.
Shem was the son of Noah.
Noah was the son of Lamech.
37 Lamech was the son of Methuselah.
Methuselah was the son of Enoch.
Enoch was the son of Jared.
Jared was the son of Mahalalel.
Mahalalel was the son of Kenan.
38 Kenan was the son of Enosh.*
Enosh was the son of Seth.
Seth was the son of Adam.
Adam was the son of God.

Jesus Is Born in Bethlehem

LUKE 2:1-7

At that time the Roman emperor, Augustus, decreed
that a census should be taken throughout the Roman
Empire. [2](This was the first census taken when Quirinius was governor of Syria.) [3]All returned to their
own ancestral towns to register for this census. [4]And
because Joseph was a descendant of King David, he
had to go to Bethlehem in Judea, David's ancient home.
He traveled there from the village of Nazareth in Galilee. [5]He took with him Mary, his fiancée, who was now
obviously pregnant.

[6]And while they were there, the time came for her
baby to be born. [7]She gave birth to her first child, a
son. She wrapped him snugly in strips of cloth and
laid him in a manger, because there was no lodging
available for them.

Lk 3:32 Greek *Sala,* a variant spelling of Salmon; also in 3:32b. See Ruth 4:20. **Lk 3:33** Some manuscripts read *Amminadab was the son of Aram. Arni* and *Aram* are alternate spellings of Ram. See 1 Chr 2:9-10. **Lk 3:38** Greek *Enos,* a variant spelling of Enosh; also in 3:38b. See Gen 5:6.

6 BC

Jesus is born

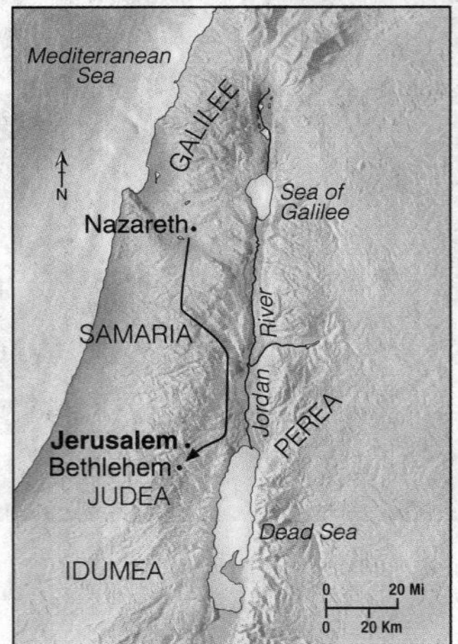

***THE JOURNEY TO BETHLEHEM** Caesar's decree for a census of the entire Roman Empire made it necessary for Joseph and Mary to leave their hometown, Nazareth, and journey the 70 miles to the Judean village of Bethlehem.*

Luke 2:1 Luke is the only Gospel writer who related the events he recorded to world history. His account was addressed to a predominantly Greek audience that would have been interested in and familiar with the political situation. Palestine was under the rule of the Roman Empire with Emperor Caesar Augustus, the first Roman emperor, in charge. The Roman rulers, considered to be like gods, stood in contrast to the tiny baby in a manger who was truly God in the flesh.

Luke 2:1 A Roman census (registration) was taken to aid military conscription or tax collection. The Jews weren't required to serve in the Roman army, but they could not avoid paying taxes. Augustus's decree went out in God's perfect timing and according to God's perfect plan to bring his Son into the world.

Luke 2:1-6 The Romans ruled the civilized world at this time. By contrast, Joseph controlled very little. Against his better judgment and political convictions, he complied with the Roman order to make a long trip just to pay his taxes. His fiancée, who had to go with him, was about to give birth.

The Romans were in control insofar as human authority can get its way by exerting human power. But the Romans did not recognize their limitations. In reality, God controls the world. In all times and places, he works his will. By the decree of Emperor Augustus, Jesus was born in the very town prophesied for his birth (Mic 5:2), even though his parents did not live there. Joseph and Mary were both descendants of David. The Old Testament is filled with prophecies that the Messiah would be born in David's royal line (see, for example, Isa 11:1; Jer 33:15; Ezek 37:24; Hos 3:5). Rome made the decree, just as God intended.

Luke 2:4-5 Sometimes we think to ourselves, "I'm being obedient, so why aren't things going better?" We face discomfort or inconvenience and immediately think either that we have misread God's will or that God has made a mistake. But watch this quiet couple as they head toward Bethlehem. God did not soften Joseph's bumpy road, but strengthened him. God did not provide a luxurious inn for Joseph and Mary, but brought his Son into the world in humble surroundings. When we do God's will, we are not guaranteed comfort and convenience. But we are promised that everything, even discomfort and inconvenience, has meaning in God's plan. He will guide you and provide all you need. Like Joseph, live each day by faith, trusting that God is in charge.

Shepherds Visit Jesus

LUKE 2:8-20

That night there were shepherds staying in the
fields nearby, guarding their flocks of sheep.
9Suddenly, an angel of the Lord appeared among
them, and the radiance of the Lord's glory surrounded them. They were terrified, 10but the angel
reassured them. "Don't be afraid!" he said. "I bring
you good news that will bring great joy to all people.
11The Savior—yes, the Messiah, the Lord—has been
born today in Bethlehem, the city of David! 12And
you will recognize him by this sign: You will find
a baby wrapped snugly in strips of cloth, lying in
a manger."
13Suddenly, the angel was joined by a vast host
of others—the armies of heaven—praising God and
saying,

14 "Glory to God in highest heaven,
and peace on earth to those with whom God
is pleased."

15When the angels had returned to heaven, the
shepherds said to each other, "Let's go to Bethlehem!
Let's see this thing that has happened, which the Lord
has told us about."
16They hurried to the village and found Mary and
Joseph. And there was the baby, lying in the manger.
17After seeing him, the shepherds told everyone what
had happened and what the angel had said to them
about this child. 18All who heard the shepherds' story
were astonished, 19but Mary kept all these things in
her heart and thought about them often. 20The shepherds went back to their flocks, glorifying and praising God for all they had heard and seen. It was just as
the angel had told them.

Luke 2:7 Strips of cloth were used to keep a baby warm and give him a sense of security. These cloths were believed to protect his internal organs. The custom of wrapping infants this way is still practiced in many Middle Eastern countries.

Luke 2:7 This mention of the manger is the basis for the traditional belief that Jesus was born in a stable. Stables were often caves with feeding troughs (mangers) carved into the rock walls. Despite popular Christmas card pictures, the surroundings were dark and dirty. This was not the atmosphere the Jews expected as the birthplace of the Messiah-King. They thought their promised Messiah would be born in royal surroundings. We should not limit God by our expectations. He is at work wherever he is needed in our sin-darkened and dirty world.

Luke 2:7 Although our first picture of Jesus is as a baby in a manger, it must not be our last. The Christ child in the manger is the subject of a beautiful Christmas scene, but we must not leave him there. This tiny, helpless baby lived an amazing life, died for us, rose from the dead, ascended to heaven, and will return to earth as King of kings. Christ will rule the world and judge all people according to their decisions about him. Do you still picture Jesus as a baby in a manger—or is he your Lord? Make sure you don't underestimate Jesus. Let him grow up in your life.

Luke 2:8 God continued to reveal the news about his Son, but not to those we might expect. Luke records that Jesus' birth was announced to shepherds in the fields. These may have been the shepherds who supplied the lambs for the Temple sacrifices that were performed for the forgiveness of sin. Here the angels invited these shepherds to greet the Lamb of God (John 1:36), who would take away the sins of the world forever.

Luke 2:8-15 What a birth announcement! The shepherds were terrified, but their fear turned to joy as the angels announced the Messiah's birth. First the shepherds ran to see the baby; then they spread the word. Jesus is your Messiah, your Savior. Do you look forward to meeting him in prayer and in his Word each day? Have you discovered a Lord so wonderful that you can't help sharing your joy with your friends?

Luke 2:9-10 The greatest event in history had just happened! The Messiah had been born! For ages the Jews had waited for this, and when it finally occurred, the announcement came to humble shepherds. The Good News about Jesus is that he comes to all, including the plain and the ordinary. He comes to anyone with a heart humble enough to accept him. Whoever you are, whatever you do, you can have Jesus in your life. Don't think you need extraordinary qualifications—he accepts you as you are.

Luke 2:11-14 Some of the Jews were waiting for a savior to deliver them from Roman rule; others hoped the Christ (Messiah) would deliver them from physical ailments. But Jesus, while healing their illnesses and establishing a spiritual Kingdom, delivered them from sin. His work is more far-reaching than anyone could imagine. Christ paid the price for sin and opened the way to peace with God. He offers us more than temporary political or physical changes—he offers us new hearts that will last for eternity.

Luke 2:14 The story of Jesus' birth resounds with music that has inspired composers for 2,000 years. The angels' song, often called the Gloria after its first word in the Latin translation, is the basis for many modern choral works, traditional Christmas carols, and ancient liturgical chants.

Shepherds and Sheep

Shepherds played an important role in the world of Israel. Their work was to find grass and water for the sheep and to protect them from wild animals and tend to their sicknesses and wounds. It required them to spend long hours exposed to the natural elements. It was not an easy life. It was to the shepherds that the angels first announced the birth of Jesus. This was especially appropriate since Jesus' famous ancestor, David, had centuries earlier watched his family's sheep in those same fields near Bethlehem. It also reminds us that the coming of Jesus was good news for all people, not just for those already privileged by wealth and power. The important role of the shepherd is used often in the New Testament to teach us about Jesus. He is the Good Shepherd who gives his life for the sheep (John 10:1-18).

Mary and Joseph Bring Jesus to the Temple

LUKE 2:21-24

Eight days later, when the baby was circumcised, he was named Jesus, the name given him by the angel even before he was conceived.

[22]Then it was time for their purification offering, as required by the law of Moses after the birth of a child; so his parents took him to Jerusalem to present him to the Lord. [23]The law of the Lord says, "If a woman's first child is a boy, he must be dedicated to the LORD."* [24]So they offered the sacrifice required in the law of the Lord—"either a pair of turtledoves or two young pigeons."*

The Prophecy of Simeon

LUKE 2:25-35

At that time there was a man in Jerusalem named Simeon. He was righteous and devout and was eagerly waiting for the Messiah to come and rescue Israel. The Holy Spirit was upon him [26]and had revealed to him that he would not die until he had seen the Lord's Messiah. [27]That day the Spirit led him to the Temple. So when Mary and Joseph came to present the baby Jesus to the Lord as the law required, [28]Simeon was there. He took the child in his arms and praised God, saying,

29 "Sovereign Lord, now let your servant die in peace,
as you have promised.
30 I have seen your salvation,
31 which you have prepared for all people.
32 He is a light to reveal God to the nations,
and he is the glory of your people Israel!"

[33]Jesus' parents were amazed at what was being said about him. [34]Then Simeon blessed them, and he said to Mary, the baby's mother, "This child is destined to cause many in Israel to fall, but he will be a joy to many others. He has been sent as a sign from God, but many will oppose him. [35]As a result, the deepest thoughts of many hearts will be revealed. And a sword will pierce your very soul."

The Prophecy of Anna

LUKE 2:36-38

Anna, a prophet, was also there in the Temple. She was the daughter of Phanuel from the tribe of Asher, and she was very old. Her husband died when they had been married only seven years. [37]Then she lived

Lk 2:23 Exod 13:2. **Lk 2:24** Lev 12:8.

Luke 2:21-24 Jewish families went through several ceremonies soon after a baby's birth: (1) Circumcision. Every boy was circumcised and named on the eighth day after birth (Lev 12:3; Luke 1:59-60). Circumcision symbolized the Jews' separation from Gentiles and their unique relationship with God (see the note on Luke 1:59). (2) Redemption of the firstborn. A firstborn son was presented to God one month after birth (Exod 13:2, 11-16; Num 18:15-16). The ceremony included buying back—"redeeming"—the child from God through an offering. This way, the parents acknowledged that the child belonged to God, who alone has the power to give life. (3) Purification of the mother. For 40 days after the birth of a son and 80 days after the birth of a daughter, the mother was ceremonially unclean and could not enter the Temple. At the end of her time of separation, the parents were to bring a lamb for a burnt offering and a dove or pigeon for a sin offering. The priest would sacrifice these animals and declare her to be clean. If a lamb was too expensive, the parents could bring a second dove or pigeon instead. This is what Mary and Joseph did.

Jesus was God's Son, but his family carried out these ceremonies according to God's law. Jesus was not born above the law; instead, he fulfilled it perfectly.

Luke 2:28-32 When Mary and Joseph brought Jesus to the Temple to be dedicated to God, they met an old man who told them what their child would become. Simeon's song is often called the Nunc Dimittis, from the first words of its Latin translation. Simeon could die in peace because he had seen the Messiah.

TO FEAR OR NOT TO FEAR

People in the Bible who were confronted by God or his angels all had one consistent response—fear. To each of them, God's response was always the same—don't be afraid. As soon as they sensed that God accepted them and wanted to communicate with them, their fear subsided.

Person	*Reference*	*Person*	*Reference*
Abraham	Gen 15:1	**Zechariah**	Luke 1:13
Moses	Num 21:34 Deut 3:2	**Mary**	Luke 1:30
		Shepherds	Luke 2:10
Joshua	Josh 8:1	**Peter**	Luke 5:10
Jeremiah	Lam 3:57	**Paul**	Acts 27:23-24
Daniel	Dan 10:12, 19	**John**	Rev 1:17-18

Luke 2:32 The Jews were well acquainted with the Old Testament prophecies that spoke of the Messiah's blessings to their nation. They did not always give equal attention to the prophecies stating that he would bring salvation to the entire world, not just the Jews (see, for example, Isa 49:6). Many thought that Christ had come to save only his own people. Luke made sure his Greek audience understood that Christ had come to save all who believe, Gentiles as well as Jews.

Luke 2:33 Joseph and Mary were amazed when this old man took their son into his arms and spoke such stunning words. Simeon said that Jesus was a gift from God, and he recognized Jesus as the Messiah who would be a light to the entire world. This was at least the second time that Mary had been greeted with a prophecy about her son; the first time was when Elizabeth had welcomed her as the mother of her Lord (Luke 1:42-45).

Luke 2:34-35 Simeon prophesied that Jesus would have a paradoxical effect on Israel. Some would fall because of him (see Isa 8:14-15), while others would rise (see Mal 4:2). With Jesus, there would be no neutral ground: People would either joyfully accept him or totally reject him. As Jesus' mother, Mary would be grieved by the widespread rejection he would face. This is the first note of sorrow in Luke's Gospel.

Luke 2:36 Although Simeon and Anna were very old, they had never lost their hope that they would see the Messiah. Led by the Holy Spirit, they were among the first to bear witness to Jesus. In the Jewish culture, elders

as a widow to the age of eighty-four.* She never left the Temple but stayed there day and night, worshiping God with fasting and prayer. 38She came along just as Simeon was talking with Mary and Joseph, and she began praising God. She talked about the child to everyone who had been waiting expectantly for God to rescue Jerusalem.

Visitors Arrive from Eastern Lands

MATTHEW 2:1-12

Jesus was born in Bethlehem in Judea, during the reign of King Herod. About that time some wise men* from eastern lands arrived in Jerusalem, asking, 2"Where is the newborn king of the Jews? We saw his star as it rose,* and we have come to worship him."

Lk 2:37 Or *She had been a widow for eighty-four years.* **Mt 2:1** Or *royal astrologers;* Greek reads *magi;* also in 2:7, 16. **Mt 2:2** Or *star in the east.*

MARY

Motherhood is a painful privilege. Young Mary of Nazareth had the unique privilege of being mother to the very Son of God. Mary was the only human present at Jesus' birth who also witnessed his death. She saw him arrive as her baby son, and she watched him die as her Savior. • Mary found Gabriel's unexpected visit to be both puzzling and frightening at first, but what she heard next was the most amazing news: Her child would be the Messiah, God's promised Savior. Mary did not doubt the message but rather asked how pregnancy would be possible. Gabriel told her the baby would be God's Son. Her answer was perfect: "I am the Lord's servant. May everything you have said about me come true" (Luke 1:38). Later her song of joy shows us how well she knew God, for her thoughts were filled with his words from the Old Testament. • When Mary took the eight-day-old Jesus to the Temple to be dedicated to God, she was met by two devout people, Simeon and Anna, who recognized the child as the Messiah and praised God. Simeon directed some words to Mary that must have come to her mind many times in the years that followed: "A sword will pierce your very soul" (Luke 2:35). A big part of her painful privilege of motherhood would be to see her son rejected and crucified by the people he came to save. • We can imagine that even if she had known all she would suffer as Jesus' mother, Mary would still have given the same response. Are you, like Mary, available to be used by God?

Strengths and accomplishments	• The mother of Jesus, the Messiah • Willing to be available to God • Knew and applied Old Testament Scriptures
Lessons from her life	• God's best servants are often ordinary people who make themselves available to him • A person's character is revealed by his or her response to the unexpected
Vital statistics	• Where: Nazareth, Bethlehem • Occupation: Homemaker • Relatives: Husband: Joseph. Relatives: Zechariah and Elizabeth. Children: Jesus, James, Joseph, Judas, Simon, and daughters.
Key verse	"Mary responded, 'I am the Lord's servant. May everything you have said about me come true.'" (Luke 1:38).

Mary's story is told throughout the Gospels. She is also mentioned in Acts 1:14.

were respected; thus, because of Simeon's and Anna's ages, their prophecies carried extra weight. In contrast, our society values youthfulness over wisdom, and contributions by the elderly are often ignored. As Christians, we should reverse those values wherever we can. Encourage older people to share their wisdom and experience. Listen carefully when they speak. Offer them your friendship, and help them find ways to continue to serve God.

Luke 2:36-37 Anna was called a prophet, indicating that she was unusually close to God. Prophets did not necessarily predict the future. Their main role was to speak for God, proclaiming his truth.

Matt 2:1 Bethlehem is a small town five miles south of Jerusalem. It sits on a high ridge more than 2,000 feet above sea level. It is mentioned in more detail in the Gospel of Luke. Luke also explains why Joseph and Mary were in Bethlehem when Jesus was born, rather than in Nazareth, their hometown.

Matt 2:1 The land of Israel was divided into four political districts and several lesser territories. Judea was to the south, Samaria in the middle, Galilee to the north, and Idumea to the southwest. Bethlehem of Judea (also called Judah, Matt 2:6) had been prophesied as the Messiah's birthplace (Mic 5:2). Jerusalem was also in Judea and was the seat of government for Herod the Great, king over all four political districts. After Herod's death, the districts were divided among three separate rulers (see the note on Matt 2:19-22). Although he was a ruthless, evil man who murdered many in his own family, Herod the Great supervised the renovation of the Temple, making it much larger and more beautiful. This made him popular with many Jews. Jesus would visit Jerusalem many times because the great Jewish festivals were held there.

Matt 2:1-2 Not much is known about these "wise men." We don't know where they came from or how many there were. Tradition says they were men of high position from Parthia, near the site of ancient Babylon. How did they know that the star represented the Messiah? (1) They could have been Jews who remained in Babylon after the Exile and knew the Old Testament predictions of the Messiah's coming. (2) They may have been eastern astrologers who studied ancient manuscripts from around the world. Because of the Jewish exile centuries earlier, they would have had copies of the Old Testament in their land. (3) They may have had a special message from God directing them to the Messiah. Some scholars say these wise men were each from a different land, representing the entire world bowing before Jesus. These men from faraway lands recognized Jesus as the Messiah when most of God's chosen people in Israel did not. Matthew pictures Jesus as the King over the whole world, not just Judea.

Matt 2:1-2 The wise men traveled thousands of miles to see the king of the Jews. When they finally found him, they responded with joy, worship, and gifts. This is so different from the approach people often take today. We expect God to come looking for us, to explain himself, prove who he is, and give us gifts. But those who are wise still seek and worship Jesus today, not for what they can get, but for who he is.

Matt 2:2 The wise men said they saw Jesus' star. Balaam referred to a coming "star . . . from Jacob" (Num 24:17). Some say this star may have been a conjunction of Jupiter, Saturn, and Mars in 6 B.C., and others offer other explanations. But couldn't God, who created the heavens, have created a special star to signal the arrival of his Son? Whatever the nature of the star, these wise men traveled thousands of miles searching for a king, and they found him.

▸ **MATTHEW 2:1-12 *(cont.)***

[3]King Herod was deeply disturbed when he heard
this, as was everyone in Jerusalem. [4]He called a meeting of the leading priests and teachers of religious
law and asked, "Where is the Messiah supposed to
be born?"
[5]"In Bethlehem in Judea," they said, "for this is what
the prophet wrote:

[6] 'And you, O Bethlehem in the land of Judah,
are not least among the ruling cities*
of Judah,
for a ruler will come from you
who will be the shepherd for my people
Israel.'*"

[7]Then Herod called for a private meeting with the
wise men, and he learned from them the time when
the star first appeared. [8]Then he told them, "Go to
Bethlehem and search carefully for the child. And
when you find him, come back and tell me so that I
can go and worship him, too!"
[9]After this interview the wise men went their way.
And the star they had seen in the east guided them to
Bethlehem. It went ahead of them and stopped over
the place where the child was. [10]When they saw the

Mt 2:6a Greek *the rulers.* **Mt 2:6b** Mic 5:2; 2 Sam 5:2.

Matt 2:3 Herod the Great was quite disturbed when the wise men asked about a newborn king of the Jews because (1) Herod was not the rightful heir to the throne of David; therefore, many Jews hated him as a usurper. If Jesus really was an heir, trouble would arise. (2) Herod was ruthless, and because of his many enemies, he was suspicious that someone would try to overthrow him. (3) Herod didn't want the Jews, a religious people, to unite around a religious figure. (4) If these wise men were of Jewish descent and from Parthia (the most powerful region next to Rome), they would have welcomed a Jewish king who could swing the balance of power away from Rome. The land of Israel, far from Rome, would have been easy prey for a nation trying to gain more control.

The text tells us that not only was Herod disturbed, but so was everyone in Jerusalem. When Jesus was born into the world, people immediately began to react. His presence did not soothe and comfort most people; instead, it startled and disturbed them. In some he awakened spiritual longings; in others, fear and insecurity. Things have not changed that much. Jesus still disturbs people. If it is true that God entered our world when Jesus was born, we dare not sit idly by ignoring and rationalizing our inaction. We must acknowledge Jesus as the rightful King of our lives.

Matt 2:4-6 The leading priests and teachers of religious law were aware of Micah 5:2 and other prophecies about the Messiah. Matthew repeatedly highlighted their knowledge and unbelief. The wise men's news troubled Herod because he knew that the Jewish people expected the Messiah to come soon (Luke 3:15). Most Jews expected the Messiah to be a great military and political deliverer, like Alexander the Great. Herod's counselors would have told Herod this. No wonder this ruthless man took no chances and ordered all the baby boys in Bethlehem killed (Matt 2:16)!

Matt 2:6 Most religious leaders believed in a literal fulfillment of all Old Testament prophecy; therefore, they believed the Messiah would be born in Bethlehem as foreseen by the prophet Micah seven centuries earlier (Mic 5:2). Ironically, when Jesus was born, these same religious leaders became his greatest enemies. When the Messiah for whom they had been waiting finally came, they didn't recognize him.

Matt 2:8 Herod did not want to worship Christ—he was lying. This was a trick to get the wise men to return to him and reveal the whereabouts of the newborn king. Herod's plan was to kill Jesus.

Matt 2:11 Jesus was probably one or two years old when the wise men found him. By this time, Mary and Joseph were married, living in a house, and intending to stay in Bethlehem for a while. For more on Joseph and Mary's stay there, see the note on Luke 2:39, p. 1286.

HEROD

Herod the Great was the father of the Herodian family and is remembered as a builder of cities and the lavish rebuilder of the Temple in Jerusalem. But he also destroyed people. He showed little greatness in either his personal actions or his character. He was ruthless in ruling his territory. His suspicions and jealousy led to the murder of several of his children and the death of his wife Mariamne. • Herod's title, king of the Jews, was granted by Rome but never accepted by the Jewish people. He was only partly Jewish, and although Israel benefited from Herod's lavish efforts to repair the Temple in Jerusalem, he also rebuilt various pagan temples. Herod's costly attempt to gain the loyalty of the people failed because it was superficial. His only loyalty was to himself. • Herod was constantly worried about losing his position. His actions when hearing from the wise men about their search for the new king are consistent with his character. He planned to locate and kill the child before he could become a threat. The murder of innocent children that followed is a tragic lesson in what can happen when actions are motivated by selfishness.

Strengths and accomplishments	• Rome appointed him king of the Jews • Was an effective, though ruthless, ruler for 30 years • Sponsored a great variety of large building projects
Weaknesses and mistakes	• Treated those around him with fear, suspicion, and jealousy • Had several of his children and at least one wife killed • Ordered the killing of the baby boys in Bethlehem
Lessons from his life	• Great power brings neither peace nor security • No one can prevent God's plans from being carried out • Superficial loyalty does not impress people or God
Vital statistics	• Occupation: King of Judea from 37 to 4 B.C. • Relatives: Father: Antipater. Sons: Archelaus, Antipater, Antipas, Philip, and others. Wives: Doris, Mariamne, and others. • Contemporaries: Zechariah, Elizabeth, Mary, Joseph, Mark Antony, Augustus
Key verse	"Herod was furious when he realized that the wise men had outwitted him. He sent soldiers to kill all the boys in and around Bethlehem who were two years old and under" (Matt 2:16).

Herod the Great is mentioned in Matthew 2:1-22 and Luke 1:5.

star, they were filled with joy! [11]They entered the house and saw the child with his mother, Mary, and they bowed down and worshiped him. Then they opened their treasure chests and gave him gifts of gold, frankincense, and myrrh.

[12]When it was time to leave, they returned to their own country by another route, for God had warned them in a dream not to return to Herod.

The Escape to Egypt

MATTHEW 2:13-18

After the wise men were gone, an angel of the Lord appeared to Joseph in a dream. "Get up! Flee to Egypt with the child and his mother," the angel said. "Stay there until I tell you to return, because Herod is going to search for the child to kill him."

[14]That night Joseph left for Egypt with the child and Mary, his mother, [15]and they stayed there until Herod's death. This fulfilled what the Lord had spoken through the prophet: "I called my Son out of Egypt."*

[16]Herod was furious when he realized that the wise men had outwitted him. He sent soldiers to kill all the boys in and around Bethlehem who were two years old and under, based on the wise men's report of the star's first appearance. [17]Herod's brutal action fulfilled what God had spoken through the prophet Jeremiah:

[18] "A cry was heard in Ramah—
weeping and great mourning.
Rachel weeps for her children,
refusing to be comforted,
for they are dead."*

The Return from Egypt

MATTHEW 2:19-22

When Herod died, an angel of the Lord appeared in a dream to Joseph in Egypt. [20]"Get up!" the angel said. "Take the child and his mother back to the land of Israel, because those who were trying to kill the child are dead."

[21]So Joseph got up and returned to the land of

Mt 2:15 Hos 11:1. **Mt 2:18** Jer 31:15.

Matt 2:11 The wise men gave these expensive gifts as worthy acknowledgement for a future king. Bible students have seen in the gifts symbols of Christ's identity and what he would accomplish. Gold was a gift for royalty; frankincense was a gift for deity; and myrrh was a spice used to anoint a body for burial. These gifts may have provided the financial resources for the trip to Egypt and back.

Matt 2:11 The wise men brought gifts and worshiped Jesus for who he was. This is the essence of true worship—honoring Christ for who he is and being willing to give him what is valuable to you. Worship God because he is the perfect, just, and almighty Creator of the universe, worthy of the best you have to give.

Matt 2:12 After finding Jesus and worshiping him, the wise men were warned by God not to return through Jerusalem as they had intended. Finding Jesus may mean that your life must take a different direction, one that is responsive and obedient to God's Word. In what ways has Jesus affected the direction of your life?

Matt 2:13 This was the second dream or vision that Joseph received from God. Joseph's first dream revealed that Mary's child would be the Messiah (Matt 1:20-21). His second dream told him how to protect the child's life. Although Joseph was not Jesus' natural father, he was Jesus' legal father and was responsible for his safety and well-being. Divine guidance comes only to prepared hearts. Joseph remained receptive to God's guidance.

Matt 2:14-15 Going to Egypt was not unusual because there were colonies of Jews in several major Egyptian cities. These colonies had developed during the time of the great captivity (see Jer 43–44). There is an interesting parallel between this flight to Egypt and Israel's history. As an infant nation, Israel went to Egypt, just as Jesus did as a child. God led Israel out (Hos 11:1); God brought Jesus back. Both events show God working to save his people.

Matt 2:16 Herod, the king of the Jews, killed all the boys under two years of age in an obsessive attempt to kill Jesus, the newborn king. He stained his hands with blood, but he did not harm Jesus. Herod was king by a human appointment; Jesus was King by a divine appointment. No one can thwart God's plans.

Matt 2:16 Herod was afraid that this newborn king would one day take his throne. He completely misunderstood the reason for Christ's coming. Jesus didn't want Herod's throne; he wanted to be king of Herod's life. Jesus wanted to give Herod eternal life, not take away his present life. Today people are often afraid that Christ wants to take things away when, in reality, he wants to give them real freedom, peace, and joy. Don't fear Christ—give him the throne of your life.

Matt 2:17-18 Rachel had been the favored wife of Jacob, one of the great men of God in the Old Testament. As such, she was considered the mother of a nation. From Jacob's 12 sons had come the 12 tribes of Israel. Rachel was buried near Bethlehem (Gen 35:19). For more about the significance of this verse, see the note on Jeremiah 31:15, p. 1033, from which this verse was quoted.

Matt 2:19-22 Herod the Great died in 4 B.C. of an incurable disease. Rome trusted him but didn't trust his sons. Herod knew that Rome wouldn't give his successor as much power, so he divided his kingdom into three parts, one for each son. Archelaus received Judea, Samaria, and Idumea; Herod Antipas received Galilee and Perea; Herod Philip II received Traconitis. Archelaus, a violent man, began his reign by slaughtering 3,000 influential people. Nine years later, he was banished. God didn't want Joseph's family to go into the region of this evil ruler.

4 BC **Herod the Great dies**

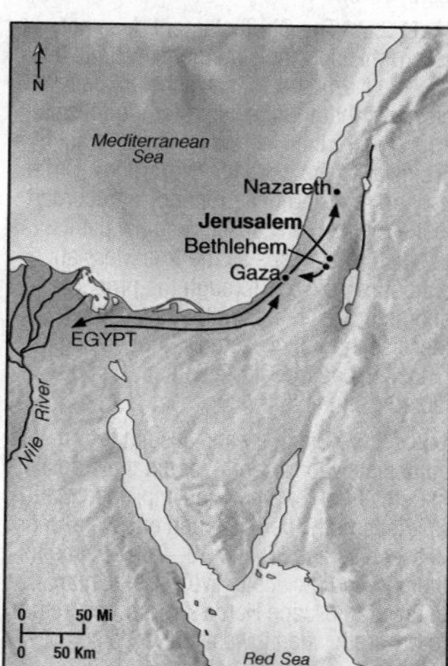

***THE FLIGHT TO EGYPT** Herod planned to kill the baby Jesus, whom he perceived to be a threat to his position. Warned in a dream, Joseph took his family to Egypt until Herod's death, which occurred a year or two later. Then God led them to return to Nazareth in Galilee.*

▸ **MATTHEW 2:19-22 *(cont.)***

Israel with Jesus and his mother. 22But when he learned that the new ruler of Judea was Herod's son Archelaus, he was afraid to go there. Then, after being warned in a dream, he left for the region of Galilee.

Jesus' Childhood in Nazareth PARALLEL

MATTHEW 2:23

So the family went and lived in a town called Nazareth. This fulfilled what the prophets had said: "He will be called a Nazarene."

LUKE 2:39-40

When Jesus' parents had fulfilled all the requirements of the law of the Lord, they returned home to Nazareth in Galilee. 40There the child grew up healthy and strong. He was filled with wisdom, and God's favor was on him.

Jesus Speaks with the Religious Teachers

LUKE 2:41-52

Every year Jesus' parents went to Jerusalem for the Passover festival. 42When Jesus was twelve years old, they attended the festival as usual. 43After the celebration was over, they started home to Nazareth, but Jesus stayed behind in Jerusalem. His parents didn't miss him at first, 44because they assumed he was among the other travelers. But when he didn't show up that evening, they started looking for him among their relatives and friends.

45When they couldn't find him, they went back to Jerusalem to search for him there. 46Three days later they finally discovered him in the Temple, sitting among the religious teachers, listening to them and asking questions. 47All who heard him were amazed at his understanding and his answers.

48His parents didn't know what to think. "Son," his

Matt 2:23 Nazareth sat in the hilly area of southern Galilee near the crossroads of great caravan trade routes. The town itself was rather small. The Roman garrison in charge of Galilee was housed there. The people of Nazareth had constant contact with people from all over the world, so world news reached them quickly. The people of Nazareth had an attitude of independence that many of the Jews despised. This may have been why Nathanael commented "Nazareth! . . . Can anything good come from Nazareth?" (John 1:46).

Matt 2:23 The Old Testament does not record this specific statement, "He will be called a Nazarene." Many scholars believe, however, that Matthew is referring to Isaiah 11:1, where the Hebrew word for "branch" is similar to the word for "Nazarene." Or he may be referring to a prophecy unrecorded in the Bible. In any case, Matthew paints the picture of Jesus as the true Messiah announced by God through the prophets; and he makes the point that Jesus, the Messiah, had unexpectedly humble beginnings, just as the Old Testament had predicted (see Mic 5:2).

Luke 2:39 Did Mary and Joseph return immediately to Nazareth, or did they remain in Bethlehem for a time (as implied in Matt 2)? Apparently there is a gap of several years between verses 38 and 39—ample time for them to find a place to live in Bethlehem, flee to Egypt to escape Herod's wrath, and return to Nazareth when it was safe to do so.

Luke 2:41-42 According to God's law, every male was required to go to Jerusalem three times a year for the great festivals (Deut 16:16). In the spring, the Passover was celebrated, followed immediately by the weeklong Festival of Unleavened Bread. Passover commemorated the night of the Jews' escape from Egypt when God had killed the Egyptian firstborn but had passed over Israelite homes (see Exod 12:21-36). Passover was the most important of the three annual festivals.

AD 1 **Saddles first used in Europe**

GOSPEL ACCOUNTS FOUND ONLY IN MATTHEW

Matthew records nine events that are not mentioned in any of the other Gospels. In each case, Matthew's choice seems to relate to his purpose in communicating the gospel to Jewish people. Five cases are fulfillments of prophecies (marked with asterisks). The other four would have been of particular interest to the Jews of Matthew's day.

Passage	*Subject*
1:20-24	Joseph's dream*
2:1-12	The visit of the wise men
2:13-15	Escape to Egypt*
2:16-18	Slaughter of the male children*
27:3-10	The death of Judas*
27:19	The dream of Pilate's wife
27:52	The other resurrections
28:11-15	The bribery of the guards
28:19-20	The baptism emphasis in the great commission*

Luke 2:43-45 At age 12, Jesus was considered almost an adult, so he probably didn't spend a lot of time with his parents during the festival. Those who attended these festivals often traveled in caravans for protection from robbers along the Palestine roads. The women and children usually would travel at the front of the caravan, with the men bringing up the rear. A 12-year-old boy conceivably could have been in either group, so both Mary and Joseph probably assumed that Jesus was with the other one. But when the caravan left Jerusalem, Jesus stayed behind, absorbed in his discussion with the religious leaders.

Luke 2:46-47 The Temple courts were famous throughout Judea as a place of learning. At the time of the Passover, the greatest rabbis of the land would assemble to teach and to discuss great truths among themselves. The coming Messiah might have been a popular discussion topic, for many people were expecting him soon. Jesus would have been eager to listen and to ask probing questions. It was not his youth but the depth of his wisdom that astounded these teachers.

Luke 2:48 Mary had to let go of her child and let him become a man, God's Son, the Messiah. Fearful that she hadn't been careful enough with this God-given child, she searched frantically for him. But she was looking for a boy, not the young man who was in the Temple astounding the religious leaders with his questions. Letting go of people or projects we have nurtured can be very difficult. It is both sweet and painful to see our children growing into adults, our students into teachers, our subordinates into managers, our inspirations into institutions. But when the time comes we must step back and let go—in spite of the hurt. Then our protégés can exercise their wings, take flight, and soar to the heights God intended for them.

mother said to him, "why have you done this to us? Your father and I have been frantic, searching for you everywhere."

49"But why did you need to search?" he asked. "Didn't you know that I must be in my Father's house?"* 50But they didn't understand what he meant.

51Then he returned to Nazareth with them and was obedient to them. And his mother stored all these things in her heart.

52Jesus grew in wisdom and in stature and in favor with God and all the people.

John the Baptist Prepares the Way for Jesus PARALLEL ••••

MATTHEW 3:1-12 ••••

In those days John the Baptist came to the Judean wilderness and began preaching. His message was,
2"Repent of your sins and turn to God, for the King-
dom of Heaven is near.*" 3The prophet Isaiah was
speaking about John when he said,

"He is a voice shouting in the wilderness,
'Prepare the way for the LORD's coming!
Clear the road for him!'"*

Lk 2:49 Or *"Didn't you realize that I should be involved with my Father's affairs?"* **Mt 3:2** Or *has come,* or *is coming soon.* **Mt 3:3** Isa 40:3 (Greek version).

Luke 2:49-50 This is the first mention of Jesus' awareness that he was God's Son. But even though he knew his real Father, Jesus did not reject his earthly parents. He went back to Nazareth with them and lived under their authority for another 18 years. God's people do not despise human relationships or family responsibilities. If the Son of God obeyed his human parents, how much more should we honor our family members! Don't use commitment to God's work to justify neglecting your family.

Luke 2:50 Jesus' parents didn't understand what he meant about his Father's house. They didn't realize he was making a distinction between his earthly father and his heavenly Father. Jesus knew that he had a unique relationship with God. Although Mary and Joseph knew he was God's Son, they didn't understand what his mission would involve. Besides, they had to raise him, along with his brothers and sisters (Matt 13:55-56), as a normal child. They knew he was unique, but they did not know what was going on in his mind.

Luke 2:52 The Bible does not record any events of the next 18 years of Jesus' life, but Jesus undoubtedly was learning and maturing. As the oldest in a large family, he would have assisted Joseph in his carpentry work. Since there is no mention of Joseph after this time, he may have died, leaving Jesus to provide for the family. The normal routines of daily life gave Jesus a solid understanding of the Judean people.

Luke 2:52 The second chapter of Luke shows us that although Jesus was unique, he had a normal childhood and adolescence. In terms of development, he went through the same progression we do. He grew physically and mentally, he related to other people, and he was loved by God. A full human life is balanced. Thus it was important to Jesus—and it should be important to all believers—to develop fully and harmoniously in each of these key areas: physical, mental, social, and spiritual.

Matt 3:1-2 John the Baptist bursts onto the scene thirty years after the birth of Jesus. His theme was "Repent of your sins." The people needed to repent—make a 180-degree turn—from the kind of self-centeredness that leads to wrong actions, such as lying, cheating, stealing, gossiping, taking revenge, abusing, and indulging in sexual immorality. A person who turns from sin stops rebelling and begins following God's way of living prescribed in his Word. The first step in turning to God is to admit your sin, as John urged. Then God will receive you and help you live the way he wants. Remember that only God can get rid of sin. He doesn't expect us to clean up our life before we come to him.

Matt 3:2 The Kingdom of Heaven began when God himself entered human history as a man. Today Jesus Christ reigns in the hearts of believers, but the Kingdom of Heaven will not be fully realized until all evil in the world is judged and removed. Christ came to earth first as a suffering servant; he will come again as king and judge to rule victoriously over all the earth.

Matt 3:3 The prophecy quoted is Isaiah 40:3. Isaiah was one of the greatest prophets of the Old Testament and one of the most quoted in the New. Like Isaiah, John was a prophet who urged the people to confess their sins and live for God. Both prophets taught that the message of repentance is good news to those who listen and seek the healing forgiveness of God's love, but terrible news to those who refuse to listen and thus cut off their only hope.

Matt 3:3 John the Baptist prepared the way for Jesus by preparing others to welcome him. People who do not know Jesus need to get ready to meet him. We can prepare them by explaining their need for forgiveness, demonstrating Christ's teachings by our conduct, and telling them how Christ can give their lives meaning. We can "clear the road for him" by correcting misconceptions that might be hindering people from coming to Christ. Someone you know may be open to a relationship with Christ. How are you helping those around you to welcome Jesus?

AD 6 *Jesus visits Temple as a boy*

Egypt in Jesus' Day The Sphinx and the great pyramids dominated the landscape when Jesus was there as an infant, but they were just as much cultural artifacts then as they are today. It had been centuries since the classical Egyptian culture had been conquered, and Greco-Roman customs and culture dominated the area at this time. The people there spoke Greek and were under Roman rule, just like Judea and Galilee.

▶ **MATTHEW 3:1-12 *(cont.)***

4John's clothes were woven from coarse camel hair,
and he wore a leather belt around his waist. For food
he ate locusts and wild honey. 5People from Jerusalem
and from all of Judea and all over the Jordan Valley
went out to see and hear John. 6And when they confessed their sins, he baptized them in the Jordan River.
7But when he saw many Pharisees and Sadducees
coming to watch him baptize,* he denounced them.
"You brood of snakes!" he exclaimed. "Who warned
you to flee God's coming wrath? 8Prove by the way you
live that you have repented of your sins and turned to
God. 9Don't just say to each other, 'We're safe, for we
are descendants of Abraham.' That means nothing, for
I tell you, God can create children of Abraham from
these very stones. 10Even now the ax of God's judgment

Mt 3:7 Or *coming to be baptized.*

John the Baptist begins his ministry

Matt 3:4 John was markedly different from other religious leaders of his day. While many were greedy, selfish, and preoccupied with winning the praise of the people, John was concerned only with the praise of God. Having separated himself from the evil and hypocrisy of his day, John lived differently from other people to show that his message was new. John not only preached God's law, he lived it. Do you practice what you preach? Could people discover what you believe by observing the way you live?

Matt 3:4-6 John must have presented a strange image! Many people came to hear this preacher, who wore odd clothes and ate unusual food. Some probably came simply out of curiosity and ended up turning from their sins as they listened to his powerful message. People may be curious about your Christian lifestyle and values. You can use their simple curiosity as an opener to share how Christ makes a difference in you.

Matt 3:5 Why did John attract so many people? He was a true prophet from God, and he publicly blasted both Herod and the religious leaders, daring words that fascinated the common people. But John also had a strong message for his audience: They, too, were sinners and needed to turn from their sins. His words were powerful and true. The people were expecting a prophet like Elijah (Mal 4:5; Luke 1:17), and John seemed to be the one!

Matt 3:6 When you wash dirty hands, the results are immediately visible. But turning from sins (repentance) happens inside with a cleansing that isn't seen right away. So John used a symbolic action that people could see: baptism. The Jews used baptism to initiate converts, so John's audience was familiar with the rite. Here, baptism was used as a sign of repentance and forgiveness. Turning from sins implies a change in behavior, turning from sin toward God. Have you turned from sin in your life? Can others see the difference it makes in you? A changed life with new and different behavior makes your repentance real and visible.

Matt 3:6 The Jordan River is about 70 miles long, its main section stretching between the Sea of Galilee and the Dead Sea. Jerusalem lies about 20 miles west of the Jordan. This river was Israel's eastern border, and many significant events in the nation's history took place there. It was by the Jordan River that the Israelites renewed their covenant with God before entering the Promised Land (Josh 1–2). Here John the Baptist calls them to renew their covenant with God again, this time through baptism.

THE PHARISEES AND SADDUCEES

The Pharisees and Sadducees were the two major religious leadership groups in Israel at the time of Jesus. The Pharisees were more religiously minded, while the Sadducees were more politically minded. Although the groups disliked and distrusted each other, they became allies in their common hatred for Jesus.

Name	*Positive Characteristics*	*Negative Characteristics*
PHARISEES	• Were committed to obeying God's law • Were admired by the people for their piety • Believed in a bodily resurrection and eternal life • Believed in angels and demons	• Behaved as though their own religious rules were just as important as God's law • Their piety was often hypocritical, and they admonished others to live up to standards they themselves could not live up to • Were more concerned with appearing to be good than obeying God
SADDUCEES	• Believed strongly in the Law of Moses and in Levitical purity • Were more practically minded than the Pharisees	• Relied on logic while placing little importance on faith • Did not believe all the Old Testament was God's Word • Did not believe in a bodily resurrection or eternal life • Did not believe in angels or demons • Were willing to compromise their values in order to maintain their status and power

Matt 3:7 The Jewish religious leaders were divided into several groups. Two of the most prominent groups were the Pharisees and the Sadducees. The Pharisees separated themselves from anything non-Jewish and carefully followed both the Old Testament laws and the oral traditions handed down through the centuries. The Sadducees believed the Pentateuch alone (Genesis—Deuteronomy) to be God's Word. They were descended mainly from priestly nobility, while the Pharisees came from all classes of people. The two groups disliked each other greatly, and both opposed Jesus. John the Baptist criticized the Pharisees for being legalistic and hypocritical, following the letter of the law while ignoring its true intent. He criticized the Sadducees for using religion to advance their political position. For more information on these two groups, see the chart on p. 1313.

Matt 3:8 John the Baptist called people to more than words or ritual; he told them to change their behavior. "Prove by the way you live that you have repented of your sins" means that God looks beyond our words and religious activities to see if our conduct backs up what we say, and he judges our words by the actions that accompany them. Do your actions match your words?

Matt 3:9-10 Just as a fruit tree is expected to bear fruit, God's people should produce a crop of good deeds. God has no use for people who call themselves Christians but who live otherwise. Like many people in John's day who were God's people in name only, we are of no value if we are Christians in name only. If others can't see our faith in the way we treat them, we may not be God's people at all.

is poised, ready to sever the roots of the trees. Yes, every tree that does not produce good fruit will be chopped down and thrown into the fire.

[11]"I baptize with* water those who repent of their sins and turn to God. But someone is coming soon who is greater than I am—so much greater that I'm not worthy even to be his slave and carry his sandals. He will baptize you with the Holy Spirit and with fire.* [12]He is ready to separate the chaff from the wheat with his winnowing fork. Then he will clean up the threshing area, gathering the wheat into his barn but burning the chaff with never-ending fire."

MARK 1:1b-8

It began [2]just as the prophet Isaiah had written:

"Look, I am sending my messenger ahead
of you,
and he will prepare your way.*
[3] He is a voice shouting in the wilderness,
'Prepare the way for the LORD's coming!
Clear the road for him!'*"

[4]This messenger was John the Baptist. He was in the wilderness and preached that people should be baptized to show that they had repented of their sins and

Mt 3:11a Or *in.* **Mt 3:11b** Or *in the Holy Spirit and in fire.* **Mk 1:2** Mal 3:1. **Mk 1:3** Isa 40:3 (Greek version).

Matt 3:10 God's message hasn't changed since the Old Testament: People will be judged for their unproductive lives. God calls us to be active in our obedience. John compared people who claim they believe God but don't live for God to unproductive trees that will be cut down. To be productive for God, we must obey his teachings, resist temptation, actively serve and help others, and share our faith. How productive are you for God?

Matt 3:11 John baptized people as a sign that they had asked God to forgive their sins and had decided to live as he wanted them to live. Baptism was an outward sign of commitment. To be effective, it had to be accompanied by an inward change of attitude leading to a changed life.

Matt 3:12 A winnowing fork is a pitchfork used to toss wheat in the air to separate grain from chaff. The grain is the part of the plant that is useful; chaff is the worthless outer shell. Because it is useless, chaff is burned; grain, however, is gathered. "Winnowing" is often used as a picture of God's judgment.

Mark 1:2-3 Isaiah was one of the greatest prophets of the Old Testament. The second half of the book of Isaiah is devoted to the promise of salvation. Isaiah wrote about the coming of the Messiah, Jesus Christ, and the man who would announce his coming, John the Baptist. John's call to "clear the road for him" meant that people should give up their selfish way of living, renounce their sins, seek God's forgiveness, and establish a relationship with God by believing and obeying his words as found in Scripture (Isa 1:18-20; 57:15).

Mark 1:2-3 Mark 1:2-3 is a composite quotation, taken first from Malachi 3:1 and then from Isaiah 40:3.

Mark 1:2-4 Hundreds of years earlier, the prophet Isaiah had predicted that John the Baptist and Jesus would come. Isaiah's words comforted many people as they looked forward to the Messiah, and knowing that God keeps his promises can comfort you, too. As you read the book of Mark, realize that it is more than just a story; it is part of God's Word. In it God is revealing to you his plans for human history—and offering the Good News of his salvation to you.

Nazareth Jesus spent his childhood in Nazareth, a village in the southern hills of Galilee about seventy miles from Jerusalem. Though it was close to some roads and major trade routes, the village itself was not on the main road. Nazareth was somewhat outside of the mainstream of Jewish life in that time, providing the background for Nathanael's remark to Philip, "Can anything good come from Nazareth?" (John 1:46).

Mark 1:3 John the Baptist prepared the way for Jesus. People who do not know Jesus need to be prepared to meet him. We can "prepare the way" by explaining their need for forgiveness, demonstrating Christ's teaching by our conduct, and telling them how Christ can give their lives meaning. We can "clear the road for him" by correcting misconceptions that might be hindering people from approaching Christ. Someone you know may be open to a relationship with Christ. What can you do to prepare the way for this person?

Mark 1:4 Why does the Gospel of Mark begin with the story of John the Baptist and not mention the story of Jesus' birth? Important Roman officials of this day were always preceded by an announcer or herald. When the herald arrived in town, the people knew that someone of prominence would soon arrive. Because Mark's audience was primarily Roman Christians, he began his book with John the Baptist, whose mission it was to announce the coming of Jesus, the most important man who ever lived. Roman Christians would have been less interested in Jesus' birth than in this messenger who prepared the way.

Mark 1:4 In John's ministry, baptism was a visible sign that a person had decided to change his or her life, giving up a sinful and selfish way of living and turning to God. John took a known custom and gave it new meaning. The Jews often baptized non-Jews who had converted to Judaism. But to baptize a Jew as a sign of repentance was a radical departure from Jewish custom. The early church took baptism a step further, associating it with Jesus' death and resurrection (see, for example, Rom 6:3-4; 1 Pet 3:21).

▶ **MARK 1:1b-8** ***(cont.)***

turned to God to be forgiven. 5All of Judea, including all the people of Jerusalem, went out to see and hear John. And when they confessed their sins, he baptized them in the Jordan River. 6His clothes were woven from coarse camel hair, and he wore a leather belt around his waist. For food he ate locusts and wild honey.

7John announced: "Someone is coming soon who is greater than I am—so much greater that I'm not even worthy to stoop down like a slave and untie the straps of his sandals. 8I baptize you with* water, but he will baptize you with the Holy Spirit!"

LUKE 3:1-18

It was now the fifteenth year of the reign of Tiberius, the Roman emperor. Pontius Pilate was governor over Judea; Herod Antipas was ruler* over Galilee; his brother Philip was ruler* over Iturea and Traconitis; Lysanias was ruler over Abilene. 2Annas and Caiaphas were the high priests. At this time a message from God came to John son of Zechariah, who was living in the wilderness. 3Then John went from place to place on both sides of the Jordan River, preaching that people should be baptized to show that they had repented of their sins and turned to God to be forgiven. 4Isaiah had spoken of John when he said,

"He is a voice shouting in the wilderness,
'Prepare the way for the LORD's coming!
Clear the road for him!
5 The valleys will be filled,
and the mountains and hills made level.
The curves will be straightened,
and the rough places made smooth.
6 And then all people will see
the salvation sent from God.'"*

7When the crowds came to John for baptism, he said, "You brood of snakes! Who warned you to flee

Mk 1:8 Or *in;* also in 1:8b. **Lk 3:1a** Greek *Herod was tetrarch.* Herod Antipas was a son of King Herod. **Lk 3:1b** Greek *tetrarch;* also in 3:1c. **Lk 3:4-6** Isa 40:3-5 (Greek version).

Mark 1:5 Jesus came at a time in history when the entire civilized world was relatively peaceful under Roman rule, travel was easy, and there was a common language. The news about Jesus' life, death, and resurrection could spread quickly throughout the vast Roman Empire.

In Israel, people were ready for Jesus, too, and they flocked to hear John, the wilderness preacher. There had been no God-sent prophets for 400 years, since the days of Malachi (who wrote the last book of the Old Testament). Anticipation was growing that a great prophet, or the Messiah prophesied in the Old Testament, would soon come (see Luke 3:15).

Mark 1:5 The purpose of John's preaching was to prepare people to accept Jesus as God's Son. When John challenged the people to confess sin individually, he signaled the start of a new way to relate to God.

Is change needed in your life before you can hear and understand Jesus' message? You have to admit that you need forgiveness before you can accept it. To prepare to receive Christ, repent. Turn away from the world's dead-end attractions, sinful temptations, and harmful attitudes, and turn to God. He can give you a new start.

Mark 1:6 John dressed much like the prophet Elijah (2 Kgs 1:8) in order to distinguish himself from the religious leaders, whose flowing robes reflected their great pride in their position (Mark 12:38). John's striking appearance reinforced his striking message.

Mark 1:7-8 Although John was the first genuine prophet in 400 years, Jesus the Messiah would be infinitely greater than he. John was pointing out how insignificant he was compared to the one who was coming. John was not even worthy of being his slave. What John began, Jesus finished. What John prepared, Jesus fulfilled.

Mark 1:8 John said Jesus would baptize them with the Holy Spirit, sending the Holy Spirit to live within each believer. John's baptism with water prepared a person to receive Christ's message. This baptism demonstrated repentance, humility, and willingness to turn from sin. This was the beginning of the spiritual process. When Jesus baptizes with the Holy Spirit, the entire person is transformed by the Spirit's power. Jesus offers to us both forgiveness of sin and the power to live for him.

Luke 3:1 Tiberius, the Roman emperor, ruled from A.D. 14 to 37. Pilate was the Roman governor responsible for the province of Judea; Herod Antipas and Philip were half brothers and sons of the cruel Herod the Great, who had been dead more than 20 years. Antipas, Philip, Pilate, and Lysanias apparently had equal powers in governing their separate territories. All were subject to Rome and responsible for keeping peace in their respective lands.

Luke 3:2 Jewish law provided for only one high priest. He was appointed from Aaron's line and held his position for life. By this time, however, the religious system had been corrupted, and the Roman government was appointing its own religious leaders to maintain greater control over the Jews. Apparently the Roman authorities had deposed the Jewish-appointed Annas and had replaced him with Annas's son-in-law, Caiaphas. Nevertheless Annas retained his title (see Acts 4:6) and probably also much of the power it carried. Because the Jews believed the high priest's position to be for life, they would have continued to call Annas their high priest.

Luke 3:2 Pilate, Herod, and Caiaphas were the most powerful leaders in Palestine, but they were upstaged by a wilderness prophet from rural Judea. God chose to speak through the loner, John the Baptist, who has gone down in history as greater than any of the rulers of his day. How often people judge others by the superficial standards of power, wealth, and beauty, and miss the truly great people through whom God works! Greatness is measured not by what you have but by your faith in God. Like John, give yourself entirely to God so God's power can work through you.

Luke 3:3 To turn to God to receive forgiveness from sins implies turning away from sins. We can't just say we believe and then live any way we choose (see Luke 3:7-8); neither can we simply live a morally correct life without a personal relationship with God because that cannot bring forgiveness from sin. Determine to rid your life of any sins God points out, and then determine to live in a way that pleases him.

Luke 3:4-5 In John's day, before a king would take a trip, messengers would tell those he was planning to visit to prepare the roads for him. Similarly John told his listeners to make their lives ready so the Lord could come to them. This does not mean that you must get rid of all your sin or wrongdoing before you can accept Christ; rather, when you accept him, he takes care of all your sinfulness. To "prepare the way" means clearing aside the baggage of the past and the doubts of the present in order to let the King come into your life. He'll take it from there.

Luke 3:6 Luke was written to a non-Jewish audience. The quote from Isaiah shows that salvation is for "all people," not just the Jews (Isa 40:3-5; 52:10). John the Baptist called everyone to prepare to meet Jesus. That includes you, no matter what your nationality, social standing, religious affiliation, or political position. God is calling to all people. Don't let feelings of being an outsider cause you to hold back. No one who wants to follow Jesus is an outsider in God's Kingdom.

God's coming wrath? [8]Prove by the way you live that you have repented of your sins and turned to God. Don't just say to each other, 'We're safe, for we are descendants of Abraham.' That means nothing, for I tell you, God can create children of Abraham from these very stones. [9]Even now the ax of God's judgment is poised, ready to sever the roots of the trees. Yes, every tree that does not produce good fruit will be chopped down and thrown into the fire."

[10]The crowds asked, "What should we do?"

[11]John replied, "If you have two shirts, give one to the poor. If you have food, share it with those who are hungry."

[12]Even corrupt tax collectors came to be baptized and asked, "Teacher, what should we do?"

[13]He replied, "Collect no more taxes than the government requires."

[14]"What should we do?" asked some soldiers.

John replied, "Don't extort money or make false accusations. And be content with your pay."

[15]Everyone was expecting the Messiah to come soon, and they were eager to know whether John

Luke 3:7-9 Some people wanted to be baptized by John so they could escape eternal punishment, but they were not really repenting from sin nor were they willing to change the way they lived. John had harsh words for such people. He knew that God values reformation above ritual. Confession of sins and a changed life are inseparable. Faith without deeds is dead (Jas 2:14-26). Jesus also spoke harsh words to the respectable religious leaders who lacked the willingness to repent. They wanted to be known as religious authorities and they wanted eternal life, but they didn't want to repent of their sins. Thus, their lives were unproductive. Turning from sin must be tied to action. Following Jesus means more than saying the right words; it means acting on what he says.

Luke 3:8 Many of John's hearers were shocked when he said that being Abraham's descendants was not enough to ensure salvation. The religious leaders relied more on family lines than on faith for their standing with God. For them, religion was inherited. But a personal relationship with God cannot be handed down from parents to children. Everyone has to make a personal decision of whether or not to trust Christ. Don't rely on someone else's faith for your salvation. Have you made that personal decision to trust Christ?

Luke 3:11-14 John's message demanded at least three specific responses: (1) Share what you have with those who need it, (2) whatever your job is, do it well and with fairness, and (3) be content with your earnings. John had not been commissioned to bring comforting messages to those who lived sinful lives; he was calling the people to right living as he prepared the way for their Messiah. What changes can you make in sharing what you have, doing your work honestly and well, and being content?

Luke 3:12 Tax collectors were notorious for their dishonesty. Romans gathered funds for their government by farming out the collection privilege. Tax collectors earned their own living by adding a sizable sum—whatever they could get away with—to the total and keeping this money for themselves. Unless the people revolted and risked Roman retaliation, they had to pay whatever was demanded. Obviously the people hated the tax collectors, who were generally corrupt and greedy. Yet, said John, God would accept even these men; God desires to pour out mercy on those who confess their sins and then to give them strength to live changed lives.

Luke 3:12-14 John's message took root in unexpected places—among the poor, the dishonest, and even the hated occupation army. These people were painfully aware of their needs and they were honestly seeking to know what to do to change their lives. Did anyone follow John's advice? Surely some did, and their softened hearts became ready to receive the message of the One who was to come.

Luke 3:14 These soldiers were the Roman troops sent to keep peace in this distant province. Many of them oppressed the poor and used their power to take advantage of all the people. John called them to turn from their sins and change their ways.

Luke 3:15 Israel had not seen a prophet for more than 400 years. It was widely believed that when the Messiah would come, prophecy would reappear (Joel 2:28-29; Mal 3:1; 4:5). When John burst onto the scene, the people were excited. He was obviously a great prophet, and they were sure that the eagerly awaited age of the Messiah had come. Some, in fact, thought John himself was the Messiah. John spoke like the prophets of old, saying that the people must turn from their sin to God to avoid punishment and to experience his mercy and approval. This is a message for all times and places, but John spoke it with particular urgency; he was preparing the people for the coming Messiah.

The Jordan River

The Jordan River follows a north–south route, descending gradually from the Huleh Lake to the Dead Sea. Prior to Jesus' baptism in the Jordan River, it was already quite important in Israel's history. The Israelites passed across the Jordan upon entry into the Promised Land (Josh 3:14-17). The prophet Elijah sought refuge from Ahab king of Israel by the brook of Kerith east of the Jordan (1 Kgs 17:1-5). Elijah was translated up to heaven in a whirlwind after crossing the Jordan on dry ground with Elisha (2 Kgs 2:6-12). Naaman, the Syrian general, bathed in the Jordan at the command of Elisha and his leprosy was healed (2 Kgs 5:8-14). Elisha made the ax head float here (2 Kgs 6:1-7).

▸ **LUKE 3:1-18** ***(cont.)***

might be the Messiah. [16]John answered their questions by saying, "I baptize you with* water; but someone is coming soon who is greater than I am—so much greater that I'm not even worthy to be his slave and untie the straps of his sandals. He will baptize you with the Holy Spirit and with fire.* [17]He is ready to separate the chaff from the wheat with his winnowing fork. Then he will clean up the threshing area, gathering the wheat into his barn but burning the chaff with never-ending fire." [18]John used many such warnings as he announced the Good News to the people.

JOHN 1:19-28

This was John's testimony when the Jewish leaders sent priests and Temple assistants* from Jerusalem to ask John, "Who are you?" [20]He came right out and said, "I am not the Messiah."

[21]"Well then, who are you?" they asked. "Are you Elijah?"

"No," he replied.

"Are you the Prophet we are expecting?"*

"No."

[22]"Then who are you? We need an answer for those who sent us. What do you have to say about yourself?"

Lk 3:16a Or *in.* **Lk 3:16b** Or *in the Holy Spirit and in fire.* **Jn 1:19** Greek *and Levites.* **Jn 1:21** Greek *Are you the Prophet?* See Deut 18:15, 18; Mal 4:5-6.

Luke 3:16 John's baptism with water symbolized the washing away of sins. His baptism followed his message of repentance and reformation. Jesus' baptism with fire equips one with power to do God's will. The baptism with the Holy Spirit was first given at Pentecost (Acts 2) when the Holy Spirit came upon believers in the form of tongues of fire, empowering them to proclaim Jesus' resurrection in many languages. The baptism with fire also symbolizes the work of the Holy Spirit in bringing God's judgment on those who refuse to repent.

Luke 3:17 John warned of impending judgment by comparing those who refuse to live for God to chaff, the useless outer husk of the grain. By contrast, John compared those who repent and reform their lives to the nourishing wheat itself. Those who refuse to be used by God will be discarded because they have no value in furthering God's work. Those who repent and believe, however, hold great value in God's eyes because they are beginning a new life of productive service for him.

John 1:19 The priests and Temple assistants (also called Levites) were respected religious leaders in Jerusalem. Priests served in the Temple, and Temple assistants helped them. The Pharisees (John 1:24) were a group that both John the Baptist and Jesus often denounced. Many of them outwardly obeyed God's laws to look pious, while inwardly their hearts were filled with pride and greed. The Pharisees believed that their own oral traditions were just as important as God's inspired Word.

These leaders came to see John the Baptist for several reasons: (1) Their duty as guardians of the faith included investigating any new teaching or movement (Deut 13:1-5; 18:20-22). (2) They wanted to find out if John had the credentials of a prophet. (3) John had quite a following, and it was growing. They were probably jealous and wanted to see why this man was so popular.

John 1:21-23 In the religious leaders' minds, there were four options regarding John the Baptist's identity: He was (1) the Prophet foretold by Moses (Deut 18:15), (2) Elijah (Mal 4:5), (3) the Messiah, or (4) a false prophet. John denied being the first three personages. Instead, he called himself, in the words of the Old Testament prophet Isaiah, "The voice of someone shouting, 'Clear the way through the wilderness for the LORD!'" (Isa 40:3). The leaders kept pressing John to say who he was because people were expecting the Messiah to come (Luke 3:15). But John emphasized only why he had come—to prepare the way for the Messiah. The Pharisees missed the

JOHN THE BAPTIST

John the Baptist was unique. He wore odd clothes and ate strange food and preached an unusual message to the Judeans who went out to the wastelands to see him. But John did not aim at uniqueness for its own sake. Instead, he aimed at obedience. The angel who had announced John's birth to Zechariah had made it clear that this child was to be a Nazirite—one set apart for God's service. He knew he had a specific role to play in the world—announcing the coming of the Savior—and he put all his energies into this task. • This wild-looking man spoke with almost irresistible authority. People were moved by his words because he spoke the truth, challenging them to turn from their sins and baptizing them as a symbol of their repentance. They responded by the hundreds. But even as people crowded to him, he pointed beyond himself, never forgetting that his main role was to announce the coming of the Savior. • God has given each of us a purpose for living, and we can trust him to guide us. John focused his life on the truth he knew from the Scriptures. Likewise, we can discover in God's Word the truths he wants us to know. And as these truths work in us, others will be drawn to him. God can use you in a way he can use no one else. Let him know your willingness to follow him today.

Strengths and accomplishments	• The God-appointed messenger to announce the arrival of Jesus • A preacher whose theme was repentance • Known for his remarkable lifestyle • Uncompromising
Lessons from his life	• God does not guarantee an easy or safe life to those who serve him • Standing for the truth is more important than life itself
Vital statistics	• Where: Judea • Occupation: Prophet • Relatives: Father: Zechariah. Mother: Elizabeth. Relative: Jesus. • Contemporaries: Herod, Herodias
Key verse	"I tell you the truth, of all who have ever lived, none is greater than John the Baptist. Yet even the least person in the Kingdom of Heaven is greater than he is!" (Matt 11:11).

John's story is told in all four Gospels. His coming was predicted in Isaiah 40:3 and Malachi 4:5; and he is mentioned in Acts 1:5, 22; 10:37; 11:16; 13:24, 25; 18:25; 19:3-4.

23John replied in the words of the prophet Isaiah:

"I am a voice shouting in the wilderness,
'Clear the way for the LORD's coming!'"*

24Then the Pharisees who had been sent 25asked
him, "If you aren't the Messiah or Elijah or the Prophet,
what right do you have to baptize?"
26John told them, "I baptize with* water, but right
here in the crowd is someone you do not recognize.
27Though his ministry follows mine, I'm not even
worthy to be his slave and untie the straps of his
sandal."
28This encounter took place in Bethany, an area east
of the Jordan River, where John was baptizing.

The Baptism of Jesus PARALLEL

MATTHEW 3:13-17

Then Jesus went from Galilee to the Jordan River to
be baptized by John. 14But John tried to talk him out
of it. "I am the one who needs to be baptized by you,"
he said, "so why are you coming to me?"
15But Jesus said, "It should be done, for we must
carry out all that God requires.*" So John agreed to
baptize him.
16After his baptism, as Jesus came up out of the
water, the heavens were opened* and he saw the Spirit
of God descending like a dove and settling on him.
17And a voice from heaven said, "This is my dearly
loved Son, who brings me great joy."

Jn 1:23 Isa 40:3. **Jn 1:26** Or *in;* also in 1:31, 33. **Mt 3:15** Or *for we must fulfill all righteousness.* **Mt 3:16** Some manuscripts read *opened to him.*

point. They wanted to know who John was, but John wanted to prepare them to recognize who Jesus was.

John 1:25-26 John was baptizing Jews. The Essenes (a strict, monastic sect of Judaism) practiced baptism for purification, but normally only non-Jews (Gentiles) were baptized when they converted to Judaism. When the Pharisees questioned John's authority to baptize, they were asking who gave John the right to treat God's chosen people like Gentiles. John said, "I baptize with water"—he was merely helping the people perform a symbolic act of repentance. But soon one would come who would truly forgive sins, something only the Son of God—the Messiah—could do.

John 1:27 John the Baptist said he was not even worthy to be Christ's slave. But according to Luke 7:28, Jesus said that John was the greatest of all prophets. If such a great person felt inadequate even to be Christ's slave, how much more should we lay aside our pride to serve him! When we truly understand who Jesus is, our pride and self-importance melt away.

Matt 3:13-15 John had been explaining that Jesus' baptism would be much greater than his, when suddenly Jesus came to him and asked to be baptized! John felt unqualified. He wanted Jesus to baptize him. Why did Jesus ask to be baptized? It was not for repentance of sin, because Jesus never sinned. "We must carry out all that God requires" refers to accomplishing God's mission. Jesus saw his baptism as advancing God's work. Jesus was baptized because (1) he was confessing sin on behalf of the nation, as Nehemiah, Ezra, Moses, and Daniel had done; (2) he was showing support for what John was doing; (3) he was inaugurating his public ministry; (4) he was identifying with the penitent people of God, not with the critical Pharisees who were only watching. Jesus, the perfect man, didn't need baptism for sin, but he accepted baptism in obedient service to the Father, and God showed his approval.

Matt 3:15 Put yourself in John's shoes. Your work is going well, people are taking notice, everything is growing. But you know that the purpose of your work is to prepare the people for Jesus (John 1:35-37). Then Jesus arrives, and his coming tests your integrity. Will you be able to turn your followers over to him? John passed the test by publicly baptizing Jesus. Soon he would say, "He must become greater and greater, and I must become less and less" (John 3:30). Can we, like John, put our egos and profitable work aside in order to point others to Jesus? Are we willing to lose some of our status so that everyone will benefit?

Matt 3:16-17 The doctrine of the Trinity, which appeared later in church history, teaches that God is three persons and yet one in essence. In this passage, all three persons of the Trinity are present and active. God the Father speaks; God the Son is baptized; God the Holy Spirit descends on Jesus. God is one, yet in three persons at the same time. This is one of God's incomprehensible mysteries.

The Heavens Were Opened

Two British archaeologists went to Oxyrhynchus, Egypt, from 1898 to 1913 in search of ancient manuscripts. Among the thousands of manuscripts they unearthed was a manuscript known as P. Oxyrhynchus 405, which became *the earliest available manuscript of Matthew's record of Jesus' baptism.*

There is a one-word difference in Matthew 3:16 among the available manuscripts, with some expanding the reading to "were opened to him" in an attempt to harmonize the beginning of the verse to the end, which states that Jesus (not the crowd gathered there) saw God's Spirit descending upon him. The early manuscript found in Oxyrhynchus confirms the NLT reading in Matthew 3:16, omitting the Greek word for "to him," and reading simply "the heavens were opened."

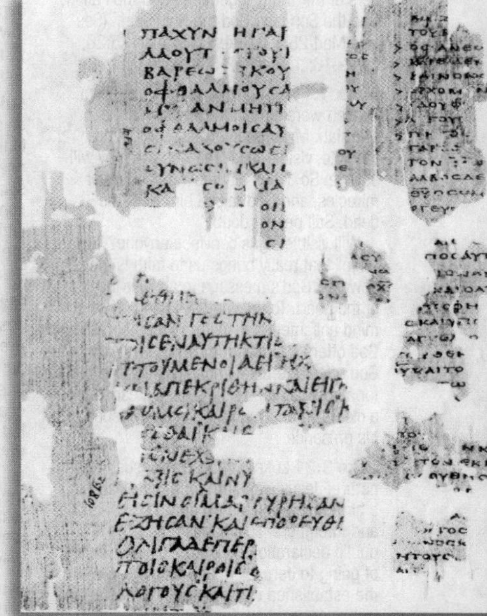

MARK 1:9-11
One day Jesus came from Nazareth in Galilee, and John
baptized him in the Jordan River. [10]As Jesus came up
out of the water, he saw the heavens splitting apart and
the Holy Spirit descending on him* like a dove. [11]And a
voice from heaven said, "You are my dearly loved Son,
and you bring me great joy."

LUKE 3:21-22
One day when the crowds were being baptized, Jesus
himself was baptized. As he was praying, the heavens opened, [22]and the Holy Spirit, in bodily form, descended on him like a dove. And a voice from heaven
said, "You are my dearly loved Son, and you bring me
great joy.*"

Satan Tempts Jesus in the Wilderness PARALLEL

MATTHEW 4:1-11
Then Jesus was led by the Spirit into the wilderness to be tempted there by the devil. [2]For forty
days and forty nights he fasted and became very
hungry.
[3]During that time the devil* came and said to him,
"If you are the Son of God, tell these stones to become
loaves of bread."
[4]But Jesus told him, "No! The Scriptures say,

'People do not live by bread alone,
but by every word that comes from the mouth
of God.'*"

Mk 1:10 Or *toward him,* or *into him.* **Lk 3:22** Some manuscripts read *my Son, and today I have become your Father.* **Mt 4:3** Greek *the tempter.* **Mt 4:4** Deut 8:3.

Mark 1:9 Jesus grew up in Nazareth, where he had lived since he was a young boy (Matt 2:22-23). Nazareth was a small town in Galilee, located about halfway between the Sea of Galilee and the Mediterranean Sea. The city was despised and avoided by many Jews (John 1:46). Nazareth was a crossroads for trade routes and had contact with many cultures.

Mark 1:10-11 The Spirit descended like a dove on Jesus, and the voice from heaven proclaimed the Father's approval of Jesus as his divine Son. Here we see all three members of the Trinity together—God the Father, God the Son, and God the Holy Spirit. (See also Matt 28:19; Luke 1:35; John 15:26; Eph 2:18; 1 Thes 1:2-5; 1 Pet 1:2.)

Mark 1:11 The dove and the voice from heaven were signs that Jesus was the Messiah. Many people want something tangible, visible, and "real" before they will believe. So Jesus did healings and other miracles, and God raised him from the dead. Still people doubt.

Will visible signs convince anyone? The "sign" that really brings us to faith is the power of God's message to answer the cry of the heart. To the confused, God offers a mind enlightened by faith. To the depressed, God offers a reason for joy. To the lonely, God offers eternal companionship. Don't look for a spectacular visible sign; instead, seek a cleansed and renewed life as evidence of his presence.

Luke 3:21 Luke emphasizes Jesus' human nature. Jesus was born to humble parents, a birth unannounced except to shepherds and foreigners. This baptism was the first public declaration of Jesus' ministry. Instead of going to Jerusalem and identifying with the established religious leaders, Jesus went to a river and identified with those who were repenting of sin. When Jesus, at age 12, had visited the Temple, he had understood his mission (Luke 2:49). Eighteen years later, at his baptism, he began carrying it out. And as Jesus prayed, God spoke and confirmed his decision to act. God was breaking into human history through Jesus.

Luke 3:21-22 Theologians have long been troubled by Jesus' allowing himself to be baptized by John. After all, this baptism was for sinners. Why, then, did Jesus do it? He did it because he is both God and human—he underwent baptism and even death as only a human could; he lived a sinless life and rose from the dead as only God could. This baptism by John in the Jordan River was another step in his identification with us sinful people; and the arrival of the dove signifies God's approval. Now Jesus would officially begin his ministry as God's beloved Son walking the dusty roads of Israel. When you are hurting, depressed, broken, remember: You have a Savior who understands your humanity. When you sin, remember: He has paid the price for your disobedience.

Luke 3:21-22 The mystery of the Trinity is on display here—Father, Son, and Holy Spirit. In the traditional words of the church, the one God exists in three persons but one substance, coeternal and coequal. No explanation can adequately portray the power and intricacy of this unique relationship. There are no perfect analogies in nature because there is no other relationship like the Trinity.

Matt 4:1 This time of testing showed that Jesus really was the Son of God, able to overcome the devil and his temptations. A person has not shown true obedience if he or she has never had an opportunity to disobey. We read in Deuteronomy 8:2 that God led Israel into the wilderness to humble and to test them. God wanted to see whether or not his people would really obey him. We, too, will be tested. Because we know that testing will come, we should be alert and ready for it. Remember, your convictions are only strong if they hold up under pressure!

Matt 4:1ff This temptation by the devil shows us that Jesus was human, and it gave Jesus the opportunity to reaffirm God's plan for his ministry. Jesus' temptation was an important demonstration of his sinlessness. He could face temptation and not give in.

Matt 4:1ff Jesus wasn't tempted inside the Temple or at his baptism but in the wilderness, where he was tired, alone, and hungry, and thus most vulnerable. The devil often tempts us when we are under physical or emotional stress (for example, lonely, tired, weighing big decisions, or faced with uncertainty). But he also likes to tempt us through our strengths, where we are most susceptible to pride (see the note on Luke 4:3ff, p. 1296). We must guard at all times against his attacks.

Matt 4:1-10 The devil's temptations focused on three crucial areas: (1) physical needs and desires, (2) possessions and power, and (3) pride (see 1 Jn 2:15-16 for a similar list). But Jesus did not give in. Hebrews 4:15 says that Jesus "faced all of the same testings we do, yet he did not sin." He knows firsthand what we are experiencing, and he is willing and able to help us in our struggles. When you are tempted, turn to him for strength.

Matt 4:3-4 Jesus was hungry and weak after fasting for 40 days, but he chose not to use his divine power to satisfy his natural desire for food. Food, hunger, and eating are good, but the timing was wrong. Jesus was in the wilderness to fast, not to eat. We also may be tempted to satisfy a perfectly normal desire in a wrong way or at the wrong time. If we indulge in sex before marriage or if we steal to get food, we are trying to satisfy God-given desires in wrong ways. Remember, many of your desires are normal and good, but God wants you to satisfy them in the right way and at the right time.

Matt 4:3-4 Jesus was able to resist all of the devil's temptations because he not only knew Scripture, but he also obeyed it. Knowing Bible verses is an important step in helping us resist the devil's attacks, but we must also obey the Bible. Note that Satan had memorized Scripture, but he failed to obey it. Knowing and obeying the Bible helps us follow God's desires rather than the devil's.

Matt 4:5 The Temple was the religious center of the Jewish nation and the place where the people expected the Messiah to arrive (Mal 3:1). Herod the Great had renovated the Temple in the hope of gaining the Jews'

5Then the devil took him to the holy city, Jerusalem, to the highest point of the Temple, 6and said,
"If you are the Son of God, jump off! For the Scriptures say,

'He will order his angels to protect you.
And they will hold you up with their hands
so you won't even hurt your foot
on a stone.'*"

7Jesus responded, "The Scriptures also say, 'You
must not test the LORD your God.'*"
8Next the devil took him to the peak of a very high
mountain and showed him all the kingdoms of the
world and their glory. 9"I will give it all to you," he said,
"if you will kneel down and worship me."

10"Get out of here, Satan," Jesus told him. "For the
Scriptures say,

'You must worship the LORD your God
and serve only him.'*"

11Then the devil went away, and angels came and
took care of Jesus.

MARK 1:12-13
The Spirit then compelled Jesus to go into the wilderness, 13where he was tempted by Satan for forty days.
He was out among the wild animals, and angels took
care of him.

LUKE 4:1-13
Then Jesus, full of the Holy Spirit, returned from
the Jordan River. He was led by the Spirit in the

Mt 4:6 Ps 91:11-12. **Mt 4:7** Deut 6:16. **Mt 4:10** Deut 6:13.

confidence. The Temple was the tallest building in the area, and this "highest point" was probably the corner wall that jutted out of the hillside, overlooking the valley below. From this spot, Jesus could see all of Jerusalem behind him and the country for miles in front of him.

Matt 4:5-7 God is not our magician in the sky ready to perform on request. In response to Satan's temptations, Jesus said not to test God (Deut 6:16). Maybe you want to ask God to do something to prove his existence or his love for you. Jesus once taught through a parable that people who don't believe what is written in the Bible won't believe even if someone were to come back from the dead to warn them (Luke 16:31)! God wants us to live by faith, not by magic. Don't try to manipulate God by asking for signs.

Matt 4:6 The devil used Scripture to try to convince Jesus to sin! Sometimes friends or associates will present attractive and convincing reasons why you should try something you know is wrong. They may even find Bible verses that seem to support their viewpoint. Study the Bible carefully, especially the broader contexts of specific verses, so that you understand God's principles for living and what he wants for your life. Only if you really understand what the whole Bible says will you be able to recognize errors of interpretation when people take verses out of context and twist them to say what they want them to say.

Matt 4:8-9 Did the devil have the power to give Jesus the nations of the world? Doesn't God, the creator of the world, have control over these nations? Yes, but for now, Satan does have a measure of power over the world and he based his offer on this temporary control and free rein over the earth because of humanity's sinfulness. The temptation before Jesus was to take the world as a political ruler right then, without carrying out his plan to save the world from sin. Satan was trying to distort Jesus' perspective by making him focus on worldly power and not on God's plans.

Matt 4:8-10 The devil offered the whole world to Jesus if Jesus would only kneel down and worship him. Today the devil offers us the world by trying to entice us with materialism and power. We can resist temptations the same way Jesus did. If you find yourself craving something that the world offers, quote Jesus' words to the devil: "You must worship the LORD your God and serve only him."

Matt 4:11 Angels, like these who waited on Jesus, have a significant role as God's messengers. These spiritual beings were involved in Jesus' life on earth by (1) announcing Jesus' birth to Mary, (2) reassuring Joseph, (3) naming Jesus, (4) announcing Jesus' birth to the shepherds, (5) protecting Jesus by sending his family to Egypt, and (6) ministering to Jesus in Gethsemane. For more on angels, see the note on Matthew 1:20, p. 1277.

Mark 1:12-13 Satan is an angel who rebelled against God. He is real, not symbolic, and is constantly working against God and those who obey him. Satan tempted Eve in the garden and persuaded her to sin; he tempted Jesus in the wilderness and did not persuade him to fall. To be tempted is not a sin. Tempting others or giving in to temptation is sin. Satan's temptations are real, and he is always trying to get us to live his way or our way rather than God's way. When temptations seem especially strong, or when you think you can rationalize giving in, consider whether Satan may be trying to block God's purposes for your life or for someone else's life.

Mark 1:12-13 To identify fully with human beings, Jesus had to endure Satan's temptations. Although Jesus is God, he is also man. And as fully human, he was not exempt from Satan's attacks. Because Jesus faced temptations and overcame them, he can assist us in two important ways: (1) as an example of how to face temptation without sinning, and (2) as a helper who knows just what we need because he went through the same experience (Heb 4:15).

Luke 4:1 Sometimes we feel that if the Holy Spirit leads us, it will always be "beside peaceful streams" (Ps 23:2). But that is not necessarily true. He led Jesus into the wilderness for a long and difficult time of testing, and he may also lead us into difficult situations. When facing trials, first make sure you haven't brought them on yourself through sin or unwise choices. If you find no sin to confess or unwise behavior to change, then ask God to strengthen you for your test. Finally, be careful to follow faithfully wherever the Holy Spirit leads.

Luke 4:1-2 The devil, who tempted Adam and Eve in the garden, also tempted Jesus in the wilderness. Jesus was a prime target for the devil's temptations. Satan had succeeded with Adam and Eve, and he hoped to succeed with Jesus as well.

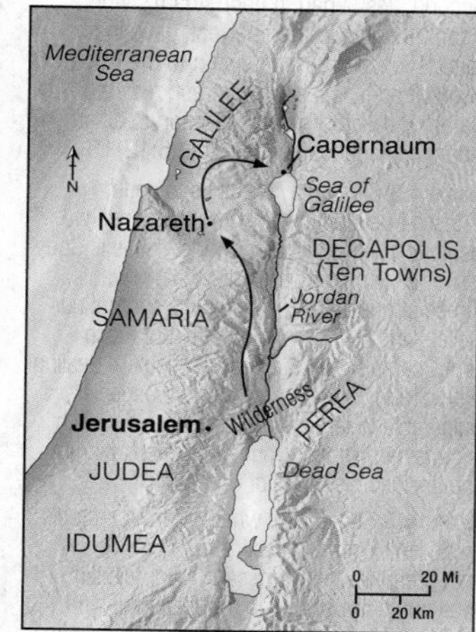

JESUS' TEMPTATION AND RETURN TO GALILEE *Satan tempted Jesus in the rough Judean wilderness before returning to his boyhood home, Nazareth. John's Gospel tells of Jesus' journeys in Galilee, Samaria, and Judea (see John 1–4) before he moved to Capernaum to set up his base of operations (see Matt 4:12-13).*

▸ LUKE 4:1-13 *(cont.)*
wilderness,* 2where he was tempted by the devil for
forty days. Jesus ate nothing all that time and became
very hungry.
3Then the devil said to him, "If you are the Son of
God, tell this stone to become a loaf of bread."
4But Jesus told him, "No! The Scriptures say, 'People
do not live by bread alone.'*"
5Then the devil took him up and revealed to him all
the kingdoms of the world in a moment of time. 6"I
will give you the glory of these kingdoms and authority
over them," the devil said, "because they are mine to
give to anyone I please. 7I will give it all to you if you
will worship me."
8Jesus replied, "The Scriptures say,
'You must worship the LORD your God
and serve only him.'*"
9Then the devil took him to Jerusalem, to the highest point of the Temple, and said, "If you are the Son
of God, jump off! 10For the Scriptures say,

'He will order his angels to protect and
guard you.
11 And they will hold you up with their hands
so you won't even hurt your foot on a stone.'*"

12Jesus responded, "The Scriptures also say, 'You
must not test the LORD your God.'*"
13When the devil had finished tempting Jesus, he
left him until the next opportunity came.

Lk 4:1 Some manuscripts read *into the wilderness.* **Lk 4:4** Deut 8:3. **Lk 4:8** Deut 6:13. **Lk 4:10-11** Ps 91:11-12. **Lk 4:12** Deut 6:16.

Luke 4:1-13 Knowing and obeying God's Word is an effective weapon against temptation, the only offensive weapon provided in the Christian's "armor" (Eph 6:17). Jesus used Scripture to counter Satan's attacks, and so should we. But to use it effectively, we must have faith in God's promises because Satan also knows Scripture and is adept at twisting it to suit his purposes. Obeying the Scriptures is more important than simply having a verse to quote, so read them daily and apply them to your life. Then your "sword" will always be sharp.

Luke 4:2 Why was it necessary for Jesus to be tempted? First, temptation is part of the human experience. For Jesus to be fully human, for him to understand us completely, he had to face temptation (see Heb 4:15). Second, Jesus had to undo Adam's work. Adam, though created perfect, gave in to temptation and passed sin on to the whole human race. Jesus, by contrast, resisted Satan. His victory offers salvation to all of Adam's descendants (see Rom 5:12-19).

Luke 4:3 Satan may tempt us to doubt Christ's true identity. He knows that once we begin to question whether or not Jesus is God, it's far easier to get us to do what he wants. Times of questioning can help us sort out our beliefs and strengthen our faith, but those times can also be dangerous. If you are dealing with doubt, be aware that you are especially vulnerable to temptation. Even as you search for answers, protect yourself by meditating on the unshakable truths of God's Word.

Luke 4:3 Sometimes what we are tempted to do isn't wrong in itself. Turning a stone into bread wasn't necessarily bad. The sin was not in the act but in the reason behind it. The devil was trying to get Jesus to take a shortcut, to solve Jesus' immediate problem at the expense of his long-range goals, to seek comfort at the sacrifice of his discipline. Satan often works that way—persuading us to take action, even right action, for the wrong reason or at the wrong time. The fact that something is not wrong in itself does not mean that it is good for you at a given time. Many people sin by attempting to fulfill legitimate desires outside of God's will or ahead of his timetable. First ask: Is the Holy Spirit leading me to do this, or is Satan trying to get me off the track?

THE TEMPTATIONS

As if going through a final test of preparation, Jesus was tempted by Satan in the wilderness. Matthew lists three specific parts of the Temptation. They are familiar because we face the same kinds of temptations. Temptation is often the combination of a real need and a possible doubt that creates an inappropriate desire. Jesus demonstrates both the importance and the effectiveness of knowing and applying Scripture to combat temptation.

Temptation	Make bread	Dare God to rescue you (based on misapplied Scripture, Ps 91:11-12)	Worship me! (Satan)
Real needs used as basis for temptation	Physical need: hunger	Emotional need: security	Psychological need: significance, power, achievement
Possible doubts that made the temptations real	Would God provide food?	Would God protect?	Would God rule?
Potential weaknesses Satan sought to exploit	Hunger, impatience, need to "prove his sonship"	Pride, insecurity, need to test God	Desire for quick power, easy solutions, need to prove equality with God
Jesus' answer	Deut 8:3 "Depend on God" Focus: God's purpose	Deut 6:16 "Don't test God" Focus: God's plan	Deut 6:13 "No compromise with evil" Focus: God's person

Luke 4:3ff Often we are tempted not through our weaknesses but through our strengths. The devil tempted Jesus where he was strong. Jesus had power over stones, the kingdoms of the world, and even angels, and Satan wanted him to use that power without regard for his mission. When we give in to the devil and wrongly use our strengths, we become proud and self-reliant. Trusting in our own powers, we feel little need of God. To avoid this trap, we must realize that all our strengths are God's gifts to us, and we must dedicate those strengths to his service.

Luke 4:6-7 The devil arrogantly hoped to succeed in his rebellion against God by diverting Jesus from his mission and winning his worship. "This world is mine, not God's," he was saying, "and if you hope to do anything worthwhile here, you'll need to follow my instructions." Jesus didn't argue with Satan about who owns the world, but he refused to validate Satan's claim by worshiping him. Jesus knew that he would redeem the world through giving

John the Baptist Proclaims Jesus as the Messiah

JOHN 1:29-34

The next day John saw Jesus coming toward him and
said, "Look! The Lamb of God who takes away the sin
of the world! 30He is the one I was talking about when
I said, 'A man is coming after me who is far greater
than I am, for he existed long before me.' 31I did not
recognize him as the Messiah, but I have been baptizing with water so that he might be revealed to Israel."
32Then John testified, "I saw the Holy Spirit descending like a dove from heaven and resting upon him. 33I
didn't know he was the one, but when God sent me
to baptize with water, he told me, 'The one on whom
you see the Spirit descend and rest is the one who will
baptize with the Holy Spirit.' 34I saw this happen to
Jesus, so I testify that he is the Chosen One of God.*"

The First Disciples Follow Jesus

JOHN 1:35-51

The following day John was again standing with two
of his disciples. 36As Jesus walked by, John looked at

Jn 1:34 Some manuscripts read *the Son of God.*

up his life on the cross, not through making an alliance with a corrupt angel.

Luke 4:9-11 Here the devil misinterpreted Scripture. The intention of Psalm 91 is to show God's protection of his people, not to incite them to use God's power for sensational or foolish displays.

Luke 4:13 Christ's defeat of the devil in the wilderness was decisive but not final. Throughout his ministry, Jesus would confront Satan in many forms. Too often we see temptation as once and for all. In reality, we need to be constantly on guard against the devil's ongoing attacks. Where are you most susceptible to temptation right now? How are you preparing to withstand it?

Luke 4:13 What would it take for you to "sell out"? What is there in life that would cause you to compromise your faith? Whatever it is—sexual temptation, financial inducement, fear of alienating or offending someone—it will be placed in your path at some point. The enemy wants to destroy believers or at least neutralize them through sin, shame, and guilt. When that temptation rears its seductive head, do what Jesus did: rely on the Word of God and stand fast in your commitment to worship God alone, above all else. No matter the cost or the sacrifice, no matter how appealing the come-on, believers must follow Jesus' example and stand strong.

John 1:29 Every morning and evening, a lamb was sacrificed in the Temple for the sins of the people (Exod 29:38-42). Isaiah 53:7 prophesied that the Messiah, God's servant, would be led to the slaughter like a lamb. To pay the penalty for sin, a life had to be given—and God chose to provide the sacrifice himself. The sins of the world were removed when Jesus died as the perfect sacrifice. This is the way our sins are forgiven (1 Cor 5:7). The "sin of the world" means everyone's sin, the sin of each individual. Jesus paid the price of your sin by his death. You can receive forgiveness by confessing your sin to him and asking for his forgiveness.

John 1:30 Although John the Baptist was a well-known preacher who attracted large crowds, he was content for Jesus to take the higher place. This is true humility, the basis for greatness in preaching, teaching, or any other work we do for Christ. When you are content to do what God wants you to do and let Jesus Christ be honored for it, God will do great things through you.

John 1:31-34 At Jesus' baptism, John the Baptist declared Jesus to be the Messiah. At that time God had given John a sign to show him that Jesus truly had been sent from God (John 1:33). John and Jesus were related (see Luke 1:36), so John probably knew who he was. But it wasn't until Jesus' baptism that John understood that Jesus was the Messiah. Jesus' baptism is described in Matthew 3:13-17; Mark 1:9-11; and Luke 3:21-22.

John 1:33 John the Baptist's baptism with water was preparatory because it was for repentance and symbolized the washing away of sins. Jesus, by contrast, would baptize with the Holy Spirit. He would send the Holy Spirit upon all believers, empowering them to live and to teach the message of salvation. This outpouring of the Spirit came after Jesus had risen from the dead and ascended into heaven (see John 20:22; Acts 2).

John 1:34 John the Baptist's job was to point people to Jesus, their long-awaited Messiah. Today people are looking for someone to give them security in an insecure world. Our job is to point them to Christ and to show that he is the one whom they seek.

John 1:35ff These new disciples used several names for Jesus: Lamb of God (John 1:36), Rabbi (John 1:38), Messiah (John 1:41), Son of God (John 1:49), and King of Israel (John 1:49). As they got to know Jesus, their appreciation for him grew. The more time we spend getting to know Christ, the more we will understand and appreciate who he is. We may be drawn to him for his teaching, but we will come to know him as the Son of God. Although these disciples made this verbal shift in a few days, they would not fully understand Jesus until three years later (Acts 2). What they so easily professed had to be worked out in experience. We may find that words of faith come easily, but deep appreciation for Christ comes with living by faith.

Ancient Manuscripts of John

Manuscript discoveries in the past 100 years have shed new light on some verses in the Bible, including John 1:34. Did John the Baptist say about Jesus, "I testify that he is the Son of God" or "I testify that he is the Chosen One of God"? Some manuscripts say one thing, and some say the other. Since not all of the manuscripts agree, translators have to weigh the evidence to consider which reading is likely to be original. The title "Chosen One of God" is more unusual, so perhaps it could be what John originally wrote, which a scribe then accidentally changed to the more usual title "Son of God" when copying the manuscript; but we cannot be certain. Therefore, this is a case where either reading could be original. Two early papyrus manuscripts found in Egypt support "Chosen One of God." The NLT has "Chosen One of God" in the text, and "the Son of God" in the textual note. Although the manuscripts available to us are often small and fragmentary, God has provided hundreds and hundreds of manuscripts to compare and study, so we can ultimately be certain that the Bible we have today is complete and accurate.

▶ **JOHN 1:35-51 *(cont.)***
him and declared, "Look! There is the Lamb of God!"
37When John's two disciples heard this, they followed
Jesus.
38Jesus looked around and saw them following.
"What do you want?" he asked them.
They replied, "Rabbi" (which means "Teacher"),
"where are you staying?"
39"Come and see," he said. It was about four o'clock
in the afternoon when they went with him to the place
where he was staying, and they remained with him
the rest of the day.
40Andrew, Simon Peter's brother, was one of these
men who heard what John said and then followed
Jesus. 41Andrew went to find his brother, Simon, and
told him, "We have found the Messiah" (which means
"Christ"*).
42Then Andrew brought Simon to meet Jesus. Looking intently at Simon, Jesus said, "Your name is Simon,
son of John—but you will be called Cephas" (which
means "Peter"*).
43The next day Jesus decided to go to Galilee. He
found Philip and said to him, "Come, follow me."
44Philip was from Bethsaida, Andrew and Peter's
hometown.
45Philip went to look for Nathanael and told him,
"We have found the very person Moses* and the
prophets wrote about! His name is Jesus, the son of
Joseph from Nazareth."
46"Nazareth!" exclaimed Nathanael. "Can anything
good come from Nazareth?"
"Come and see for yourself," Philip replied.
47As they approached, Jesus said, "Now here is a
genuine son of Israel—a man of complete integrity."
48"How do you know about me?" Nathanael asked.
Jesus replied, "I could see you under the fig tree
before Philip found you."
49Then Nathanael exclaimed, "Rabbi, you are the
Son of God—the King of Israel!"
50Jesus asked him, "Do you believe this just because I told you I had seen you under the fig tree?
You will see greater things than this." 51Then he said,
"I tell you the truth, you will all see heaven open and
the angels of God going up and down on the Son of
Man, the one who is the stairway between heaven
and earth.*"

Jn 1:41 *Messiah* (a Hebrew term) and *Christ* (a Greek term) both mean "the anointed one." **Jn 1:42** The names *Cephas* (from Aramaic) and *Peter* (from Greek) both mean "rock." **Jn 1:45** Greek *Moses in the law.* **Jn 1:51** Greek *going up and down on the Son of Man;* see Gen 28:10-17. "Son of Man" is a title Jesus used for himself.

John 1:37 One of the two disciples was Andrew (John 1:40). The other probably was John, the writer of this book. Why did these disciples leave John the Baptist? Because that's what John wanted them to do—he was pointing the way to Jesus, the one John had prepared them to follow.

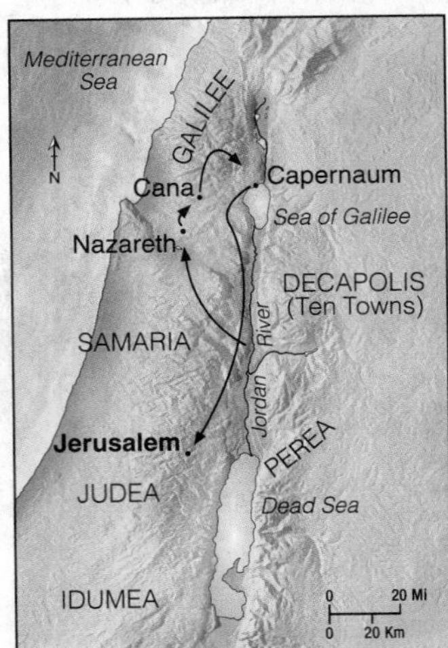

***JESUS' FIRST TRAVELS** After John baptized him in the Jordan River and Satan tempted him in the wilderness, Jesus returned to Galilee (see "Jesus' Temptation and Return to Galilee," p. 1295). He visited Nazareth, Cana, and Capernaum, and then returned to Jerusalem for the Passover.*

These were Jesus' first disciples, along with Simon Peter (John 1:42) and Nathanael (John 1:45).

John 1:38 When the two disciples began to follow Jesus, he asked them, "What do you want?" Following Christ is not enough; we must follow him for the right reasons. To follow Christ for our own purposes would be asking Christ to follow us—to align with us to support and advance our cause, not his. We must examine our motives for following him. Are we seeking his glory or ours?

John 1:40-42 Andrew accepted John the Baptist's testimony about Jesus and immediately went to tell his brother, Simon, about him. There was no question in Andrew's mind that Jesus was the Messiah. Not only did he tell his brother, but he was also eager to introduce others to Jesus (see John 12:20-22). How many people in your life have heard you talk about your relationship with Jesus?

John 1:42 Jesus saw not only who Simon was, but who he would become. That is why he gave him a new name—Cephas in Aramaic, Peter in Greek (the name means "a rock"). Peter is not presented as rock-solid throughout the Gospels, but he became a solid rock in the days of the early church, as we learn in the book of Acts. By giving Simon a new name, Jesus introduced a change in character. For more on Simon Peter, see his Profile on p. 1473.

John 1:46 The Jews despised Nazareth because a Roman army garrison was located there. Some have speculated that an aloof attitude or a poor reputation in morals and religion on the part of the people of Nazareth led to Nathanael's harsh comment. Nathanael's hometown was Cana, about four miles from Nazareth.

John 1:46 When Nathanael heard that the Messiah was from Nazareth, he was surprised. Philip responded, "Come and see for yourself." Fortunately for Nathanael, he went to meet Jesus and became a disciple. If he had stuck to his prejudice without investigating further, he would have missed the Messiah! Don't let people's stereotypes about Christ cause them to miss his power and love. Invite them to come and see who Jesus really is.

John 1:47-49 Jesus knew about Nathanael before the two ever met. Jesus also knows what we are really like. An honest person will feel comfortable with the thought that Jesus knows him or her through and through. A dishonest person will feel uncomfortable. You can't pretend to be something you're not. God knows the real you and wants you to follow him.

John 1:51 This is a reference to Jacob's dream recorded in Genesis 28:12. As the unique God-man, Jesus would be the ladder between heaven and earth. Jesus is not saying that this would be a physical experience (seeing the ladder with their eyes) like the Transfiguration, but that they would have spiritual insight into Jesus' true nature and purpose for coming.

John 2:1-2 Jesus was on a mission to save the world, the greatest mission in the history of humankind. Yet he took time to attend a wedding and take part in its festivities. We may be tempted to think we should not take time out from our "important" work for social

Jesus Turns Water into Wine

JOHN 2:1-12

The next day* there was a wedding celebration in the
village of Cana in Galilee. Jesus' mother was there,
2and Jesus and his disciples were also invited to the
celebration. 3The wine supply ran out during the festivities, so Jesus' mother told him, "They have no more
wine."
4"Dear woman, that's not our problem," Jesus replied. "My time has not yet come."
5But his mother told the servants, "Do whatever
he tells you."
6Standing nearby were six stone water jars, used
for Jewish ceremonial washing. Each could hold
twenty to thirty gallons.* 7Jesus told the servants,
"Fill the jars with water." When the jars had been
filled, 8he said, "Now dip some out, and take it to
the master of ceremonies." So the servants followed
his instructions.
9When the master of ceremonies tasted the water
that was now wine, not knowing where it had come
from (though, of course, the servants knew), he called
the bridegroom over. 10"A host always serves the best
wine first," he said. "Then, when everyone has had a
lot to drink, he brings out the less expensive wine.
But you have kept the best until now!"
11This miraculous sign at Cana in Galilee was the
first time Jesus revealed his glory. And his disciples
believed in him.
12After the wedding he went to Capernaum for
a few days with his mother, his brothers, and his
disciples.

Jn 2:1 Greek *On the third day;* see 1:35, 43. **Jn 2:6** Greek *2 or 3 measures* [75 to 113 liters].

B. Message and Ministry of Jesus

For about three years Jesus traveled and ministered to people throughout Israel and the neighboring areas. Jesus spent much of his time teaching, confronting the religious leaders who had distorted God's laws, and providing new teaching through parables and about himself. He demonstrated his identity as the Son of God and his power over everything through many miracles, healing the sick and casting out demons. Jesus gave people a view of God that they had never seen before—God incarnate, walking and talking among them.

1. JESUS BEGINS HIS MINISTRY IN JERUSALEM

Jesus launched his public ministry by attending the annual Passover celebration in Jerusalem. While there, he immediately came into conflict with the religious leaders of the day, clearing the Temple because of corruption in his Father's house. But he wasn't rejected by all the religious leaders—one of them came to visit him at night to learn more about this new teacher.

occasions. But maybe these social occasions are part of our mission. Jesus valued these wedding festivities because they involved people, and he came to be with people. Our mission can often be accomplished in joyous times of celebration with others. Bring balance to your life by inviting Jesus into times of pleasure as well as times of work.

John 2:1-3 Weddings in Jesus' day were week-long festivals. Banquets would be prepared for many guests, and the week would be spent celebrating the new life of the married couple. Often the whole town was invited, and everybody would come—it was considered an insult to refuse an invitation to a wedding. To accommodate many people, careful planning was needed. To run out of wine was more than embarrassing; it broke the strong, unwritten laws of hospitality. Jesus was about to respond to a heartfelt need.

John 2:4 Mary was probably not asking Jesus to do a miracle; she was simply hoping that her son would help solve this major problem and find some wine. Tradition says that Joseph, Mary's husband, was dead, so she probably was used to asking for her son's help in certain situations. Jesus' answer to Mary is difficult to understand, but maybe that is the point. Although Mary did not understand what Jesus was going to do, she trusted him to do what was right. Those who believe in Jesus but run into situations they cannot understand must continue to trust that he will work in the best way.

John 2:5 Mary submitted to Jesus' way of doing things. She recognized that Jesus was more than her human son—he was the Son of God. When we bring our problems to Christ, we may think we know how he should take care of them. But he may have a completely different plan. Like Mary, we should submit and allow him to deal with the problem as he sees best.

John 2:6 The six stone water jars were normally used for ceremonial washing. When full, the pots would hold 20 to 30 gallons. According to the Jews' ceremonial laws, people became symbolically unclean by touching objects of everyday life. Before eating, the Jews would pour water over their hands to cleanse themselves of any bad influences associated with what they had touched.

John 2:10 People look everywhere but to God for excitement and meaning. For some reason, they expect God to be dull and lifeless. Just as the wine Jesus made was the best, so life in him is better than life on our own. Why wait until everything else runs out before trying God? Why save the best until last?

John 2:11 When the disciples saw Jesus' miracle, they believed. The miracle showed his power over nature and revealed the way he would go about his ministry—helping others, speaking with authority, and being in personal touch with people.

Miracles are not merely superhuman events, but events that demonstrate God's power. Almost every miracle Jesus did was a renewal of fallen Creation—restoring sight, making the lame walk, even restoring life to the dead. Believe in Christ not because he is a superman but because he is the God who continues his creation, even in those of us who are poor, weak, crippled, orphaned, blind, deaf, or have some other desperate need.

John 2:12 Capernaum became Jesus' home base during his ministry in Galilee. Located on a major trade route, it was an important city in the region, with a Roman garrison and a customs station. At Capernaum, Matthew was called to be a disciple (Matt 9:9). The city was also the home of several other disciples (Matt 4:13-19) and a high-ranking government official (John 4:46). It had at least one major synagogue. Although Jesus made this city his base of operations in Galilee, he condemned it for the people's unbelief (Matt 11:23; Luke 10:15).

Jesus Clears the Temple

JOHN 2:13-22

It was nearly time for the Jewish Passover celebration, so Jesus went to Jerusalem. 14In the Temple area
he saw merchants selling cattle, sheep, and doves for
sacrifices; he also saw dealers at tables exchanging
foreign money. 15Jesus made a whip from some ropes
and chased them all out of the Temple. He drove out
the sheep and cattle, scattered the money changers'
coins over the floor, and turned over their tables.
16Then, going over to the people who sold doves, he
told them, "Get these things out of here. Stop turning
my Father's house into a marketplace!"

17Then his disciples remembered this prophecy
from the Scriptures: "Passion for God's house will
consume me."*

18But the Jewish leaders demanded, "What are you
doing? If God gave you authority to do this, show us a
miraculous sign to prove it."

19"All right," Jesus replied. "Destroy this temple, and
in three days I will raise it up."

20"What!" they exclaimed. "It has taken forty-six
years to build this Temple, and you can rebuild it in
three days?" 21But when Jesus said "this temple," he
meant his own body. 22After he was raised from the
dead, his disciples remembered he had said this, and
they believed both the Scriptures and what Jesus
had said.

Nicodemus Visits Jesus at Night

JOHN 2:23–3:21

Because of the miraculous signs Jesus did in Jerusalem at the Passover celebration, many began to trust
in him. 24But Jesus didn't trust them, because he knew
human nature. 25No one needed to tell him what mankind is really like.

3:1 There was a man named Nicodemus, a Jewish religious leader who was a Pharisee. 2After dark one

Jn 2:17 Or *"Concern for God's house will be my undoing."* Ps 69:9.

John 2:13 The Passover celebration took place yearly at the Temple in Jerusalem. Every Jewish male was expected to make a pilgrimage to Jerusalem during this time (Deut 16:16). This was a week-long festival—the Passover was one day, and the Festival of Unleavened Bread lasted the rest of the week. The entire week commemorated the freeing of the Jews from slavery in Egypt (Exod 12:1-13).

John 2:13 Jerusalem was both the religious and the political seat of Palestine, and the place where the Messiah was expected to arrive. The Temple was located there, and many Jewish families from all over the world would travel to Jerusalem during the key festivals. The Temple was on an imposing site, a hill overlooking the city. Solomon had built the first Temple on this same site almost 1,000 years earlier (959 B.C.), but his Temple had been destroyed by the Babylonians (2 Kgs 25). The Temple had been rebuilt in 515 B.C., and Herod the Great had enlarged and remodeled it.

John 2:14 The Temple area was always crowded during Passover with thousands of out-of-town visitors. The religious leaders crowded it even further by allowing money changers and merchants to set up booths in the Court of the Gentiles. They rationalized this practice as a convenience for the worshipers and as a way to make money for Temple upkeep. But the religious leaders did not seem to care that the Court of the Gentiles was so full of merchants that foreigners found it difficult to worship. And worship was the main purpose for visiting the Temple. No wonder Jesus was angry!

John 2:14 The Temple tax had to be paid in local currency, so foreigners had to have their money changed. But the money changers often charged exorbitant exchange rates. The people were also required to make sacrifices for sins. Because of the long journey, many could not bring their own animals. Some who brought animals had them rejected for imperfections. So animal merchants conducted a flourishing business in the Temple courtyard. The price of sacrificial animals was much higher in the Temple area than elsewhere. Jesus was angry at the dishonest, greedy practices of the money changers and merchants, and he particularly disliked their presence on the Temple grounds. They were making a mockery of God's house of worship.

John 2:14ff John records this first clearing, or cleansing, of the Temple. A second clearing occurred at the end of Jesus' ministry, about three years later (see Matt 21:12-17; Mark 11:15-19; Luke 19:45-48).

John 2:14-16 God's Temple was being misused by people who had turned it into a marketplace. They had forgotten, or didn't care, that God's house is a place of worship, not a place for making a profit. Our attitude toward the church is wrong if we see it as a place for personal contacts or business advantage. Make sure you attend church to worship God.

John 2:15-16 Jesus was obviously angry at the merchants who exploited those who had come to God's house to worship. There is a difference between uncontrolled rage and righteous indignation—yet both are called anger. We must be very careful how we use the powerful emotion of anger. It is right to be angry about injustice and sin; it is wrong to be angry over trivial personal offenses.

John 2:15-16 Jesus made a whip and chased out the money changers. Does his example permit us to use violence against wrongdoers? Certain authority is granted to some, but not to all. For example, the authority to use weapons and restrain people is granted to police officers, but not to the general public. The authority to imprison people is granted to judges, but not to individual citizens. Jesus had God's authority, something we cannot have. While we want to live like Christ, we should never try to claim his authority where it has not been given to us.

John 2:17 Jesus took the evil acts in the Temple as an insult against God, and thus, he did not deal with them halfheartedly. He was consumed with righteous anger against such flagrant disrespect for God.

John 2:19-20 The Jews understood Jesus to mean the Temple out of which he had just driven the merchants and money changers. This was the Temple Zerubbabel had built over 500 years earlier, but Herod the Great had begun remodeling it, making it much larger and far more beautiful. It had been 46 years since this remodeling had started (20 B.C.), and it still wasn't completely finished. They understood Jesus' words to mean that this imposing building could be torn down and rebuilt in three days, and they were startled.

John 2:21-22 Jesus was not talking about the Temple made of stones, but about his body. His listeners didn't realize it, but Jesus was greater than the Temple (Matt 12:6). His words would take on meaning for his disciples after his resurrection. That Christ so perfectly fulfilled this prediction became the strongest proof for his claims to be God.

John 2:23-25 The Son of God knows all about human nature. Jesus was well aware of the truth of Jeremiah 17:9: "The human heart is the most deceitful of all things, and desperately wicked. Who really knows how bad it is?" Jesus was discerning, and he knew that the faith of some followers was superficial. Some of the same people claiming to believe in Jesus at this time would later yell, "Crucify him!" It's easy to believe when it's exciting and everyone else believes the same way. But keep your faith firm even when it isn't popular to follow Christ.

evening, he came to speak with Jesus. "Rabbi," he said, "we all know that God has sent you to teach us. Your miraculous signs are evidence that God is with you."
[3]Jesus replied, "I tell you the truth, unless you are born again,* you cannot see the Kingdom of God."
[4]"What do you mean?" exclaimed Nicodemus. "How can an old man go back into his mother's womb and be born again?"
[5]Jesus replied, "I assure you, no one can enter the Kingdom of God without being born of water and the Spirit.* [6]Humans can reproduce only human life, but the Holy Spirit gives birth to spiritual life.* [7]So don't be surprised when I say, 'You* must be born again.'

Jn 3:3 Or *born from above;* also in 3:7. **Jn 3:5** Or *and spirit.* The Greek word for *Spirit* can also be translated *wind;* see 3:8. **Jn 3:6** Greek *what is born of the Spirit is spirit.* **Jn 3:7** The Greek word for *you* is plural; also in 3:12.

NICODEMUS

God specializes in finding and changing people we consider out of reach. It took a while for Nicodemus to come out of the dark, but God was patient with this "undercover" believer. • Afraid of being discovered, Nicodemus made an appointment to see Jesus at night. Daylight conversations between Pharisees and Jesus tended to be antagonistic, but Nicodemus really wanted to learn. He got a lot more than he probably expected—a challenge to a new life! We know very little about Nicodemus, but we know that he left that evening's encounter a changed man. He came away with a whole new understanding of both God and himself. • Nicodemus next appears as part of the Jewish high council (John 7:50). As the group discussed ways to eliminate Jesus, Nicodemus raised the question of justice. Although his objection was overruled, he had spoken up. He had begun to change. • Our last picture of Nicodemus shows him joining Joseph of Arimathea in asking for Jesus' body in order to provide for its burial (John 19:39). Nicodemus was making a bold move, risking everything. He was continuing to grow. • God looks for steady growth, not instant perfection. How well does your present level of spiritual growth match up with how long you have known Jesus?

Strengths and accomplishments	• One of the few religious leaders who believed in Jesus • A member of the powerful Jewish high council • A Pharisee who was attracted by Jesus' character and miracles • Joined with Joseph of Arimathea in burying Jesus
Weakness and mistake	• Limited by his fear of being publicly exposed as Jesus' follower
Lessons from his life	• Unless we are born again, we can never be part of the Kingdom of God • God is able to change those we might consider unreachable • God is patient, but persistent • If we are available, God can use us
Vital statistics	• Where: Jerusalem • Occupation: Religious leader • Contemporaries: Jesus, Annas, Caiaphas, Pilate, Joseph of Arimathea
Key verse	"'What do you mean?' exclaimed Nicodemus. 'How can an old man go back into his mother's womb and be born again?'" (John 3:4).

Nicodemus's story is told in John 3:1-21; 7:50-52; 19:39-40.

John 3:1ff Nicodemus came to Jesus personally, although he could have sent one of his assistants. He wanted to examine Jesus for himself to separate fact from rumor. Perhaps Nicodemus was afraid of what his peers, the Pharisees, would say about his visit, so he came after dark. Later, when he understood that Jesus was truly the Messiah, he spoke up boldly in his defense (John 7:50-51). Like Nicodemus, we must examine Jesus for ourselves—others cannot do it for us. Then, if we believe he is who he says, we will want to speak up for him.

John 3:1 Nicodemus was a Pharisee and a member of the ruling council (called the high council, or the Sanhedrin). The Pharisees were a group of religious leaders whom Jesus and John the Baptist often criticized for being hypocrites (see note on Matt 3:7, p. 1288, for more on the Pharisees). Most Pharisees were intensely jealous of Jesus because he undermined their authority and challenged their views. But Nicodemus was searching, and he believed that Jesus had some answers. A learned teacher himself, he came to Jesus to be taught. No matter how intelligent and well educated you are, you must come to Jesus with an open mind and heart so he can teach you the truth about God.

John 3:3 What did Nicodemus know about the Kingdom? From the Bible he knew it would be ruled by God, it would be restored on earth, and it would incorporate God's people. Jesus revealed to this devout Pharisee that the Kingdom would come to the whole world (John 3:16), not just the Jews, and that Nicodemus wouldn't be a part of it unless he was personally born again (John 3:5). This was a revolutionary concept: The Kingdom is personal, not national or ethnic, and its entrance requirements are repentance and spiritual rebirth. Jesus later taught that God's Kingdom has already begun in the hearts of believers (Luke 17:21). It will be fully realized when Jesus returns again to judge the world and abolish evil forever (Rev 21–22).

John 3:5-6 "Being born of water and the Spirit" could refer to (1) the contrast between physical birth (water) and spiritual birth (Spirit), or (2) being regenerated by the Spirit and signifying that rebirth by Christian baptism. The water may also represent the cleansing action of God's Holy Spirit (Titus 3:5). Nicodemus undoubtedly would have been familiar with God's promise in Ezekiel 36:25-26. Jesus was explaining the importance of a spiritual rebirth, saying that people don't enter the Kingdom by living a better life, but by being spiritually reborn.

John 3:6 Who is the Holy Spirit? God is three persons in one—the Father, the Son, and the Holy Spirit. God became a man in Jesus so that Jesus could die for our sins. Jesus rose from the dead to offer salvation to all people through spiritual renewal and rebirth. When Jesus ascended into heaven, his physical presence left the earth, but he promised to send the Holy Spirit so that his spiritual presence would still be among humankind (see Luke 24:49). The Holy Spirit first became available to all believers at Pentecost (Acts 2). Whereas in Old Testament days the Holy Spirit empowered specific individuals for specific purposes, now all believers have the power of the Holy Spirit available to them. For more on the Holy Spirit, read John 14:16-28; Romans 8:9; 1 Corinthians 12:13; and 2 Corinthians 1:22.

▸ JOHN 2:23–3:21 *(cont.)*

8The wind blows wherever it wants. Just as you can hear the wind but can't tell where it comes from or where it is going, so you can't explain how people are born of the Spirit."

9"How are these things possible?" Nicodemus asked.

10Jesus replied, "You are a respected Jewish teacher, and yet you don't understand these things? 11I assure you, we tell you what we know and have seen, and yet you won't believe our testimony. 12But if you don't believe me when I tell you about earthly things, how can you possibly believe if I tell you about heavenly things? 13No one has ever gone to heaven and returned. But the Son of Man* has come down from heaven. 14And as Moses lifted up the bronze snake on a pole in the wilderness, so the Son of Man must be lifted up, 15so that everyone who believes in him will have eternal life.*

16"For God loved the world so much that he gave his one and only Son, so that everyone who believes in him will not perish but have eternal life. 17God sent his Son into the world not to judge the world, but to save the world through him.

18"There is no judgment against anyone who believes in him. But anyone who does not believe in him has already been judged for not believing in God's one and only Son. 19And the judgment is based on this fact: God's light came into the world, but people loved the darkness more than the light, for their actions were evil. 20All who do evil hate the light and refuse to go near it for fear their sins will be exposed. 21But those who do what is right come to the light so others can see that they are doing what God wants.*"

John the Baptist Tells More about Jesus

JOHN 3:22-36

Then Jesus and his disciples left Jerusalem and went into the Judean countryside. Jesus spent some time with them there, baptizing people.

23At this time John the Baptist was baptizing at Aenon, near Salim, because there was plenty of water there; and people kept coming to him for baptism. 24(This was before John was thrown into prison.) 25A debate broke out between John's disciples and a certain Jew* over ceremonial cleansing. 26So John's disciples came to him and said, "Rabbi, the man you met on the other side of the Jordan River, the one you identified as the Messiah, is also baptizing people. And everybody is going to him instead of coming to us."

27John replied, "No one can receive anything unless God gives it from heaven. 28You yourselves know how

Jn 3:13 Some manuscripts add *who lives in heaven.* "Son of Man" is a title Jesus used for himself. **Jn 3:15** Or *everyone who believes will have eternal life in him.* **Jn 3:21** Or *can see God at work in what he is doing.* **Jn 3:25** Some manuscripts read *some Jews.*

John 3:8 Jesus explained that we cannot control the work of the Holy Spirit. He works in ways we cannot predict or understand. Just as you did not control your physical birth, so you cannot control your spiritual birth. It is a gift from God through the Holy Spirit (Rom 8:16; 1 Cor 2:10-12; 1 Thes 1:5-6).

John 3:10-11 This Jewish teacher of the Bible knew the Old Testament thoroughly, but he didn't understand what it said about the Messiah. Knowledge is not salvation. You should know the Bible, but even more important, you should understand the God whom the Bible reveals and the salvation that God offers.

John 3:14-15 When the Israelites were wandering in the wilderness, God sent a plague of snakes to punish the people for their rebellious attitudes. Those doomed to die from snakebite could be healed by obeying God's command to look up at the elevated bronze snake and by believing that God would heal them if they did (see Num 21:8-9). Similarly, our salvation happens when we look up to Jesus, believing he will save us. God has provided this way for us to be healed of sin's deadly bite.

John 3:16 The message of the Good News comes to a focus in this verse. God's love is not static or self-centered; it reaches out and draws others in. Here God sets the pattern of true love, the basis for all love relationships: When you love someone dearly, you are willing to give freely to the point of self-sacrifice. God paid dearly with the life of his Son, the highest price he could pay. Jesus accepted our punishment, paid the price for our sins, and then offered us the new life that he had bought for us. When we share the Good News with others, our love must be like Jesus'—willingly giving up our own comfort and security so that others might join us in receiving God's love.

John 3:16 Some people are repulsed by the idea of eternal life because their lives are miserable. But eternal life is not an extension of a person's miserable, mortal life. It is God's life embodied in Christ, given to all believers now as a guarantee that they will live forever. In eternal life there is no death, sickness, enemy, evil, or sin. When we don't know Christ, we make choices as though this life is all we have. In reality, this life is just the introduction to eternity. Receive this new life by faith and begin to evaluate all that happens from an eternal perspective.

John 3:16 To "believe" is more than intellectual agreement that Jesus is God. It means putting our trust and confidence in him that he alone can save us. It is to put Christ in charge of our present plans and eternal destiny. Believing is both trusting his words as reliable, and relying on him for the power to change. If you have never trusted Christ, let this promise of everlasting life be yours—and believe.

John 3:18 People often try to protect themselves from their fears by putting their faith in something they do or have: good deeds, skill or intelligence, money or possessions. But only God can save us from the one thing that we really need to fear—eternal condemnation. We believe in God by recognizing the insufficiency of our own efforts to find salvation and by asking him to do his work in us. When Jesus talks about unbelievers, he means those who reject or ignore him completely, not those who have momentary doubts.

John 3:19-21 Many people don't want their lives exposed to God's light because they are afraid of what will be revealed. They don't want to be changed. Don't be surprised when these same people are threatened by your desire to obey God and do what is right, because they are afraid that the light in you may expose some of the darkness in their lives. Rather than giving in to discouragement, keep praying that they will come to see how much better it is to live in light than in darkness.

John 3:25ff Some people look for points of disagreement so they can sow seeds of discord, discontent, and doubt. John the Baptist ended this theological argument by focusing on his devotion to Christ. It is divisive to try to force others to believe our way. Instead, let's witness about what Christ has done for us. How can anyone argue with us about that?

plainly I told you, 'I am not the Messiah. I am only
here to prepare the way for him.' 29It is the bridegroom who marries the bride, and the best man is
simply glad to stand with him and hear his vows.
Therefore, I am filled with joy at his success. 30He
must become greater and greater, and I must become
less and less.

31"He has come from above and is greater than
anyone else. We are of the earth, and we speak of
earthly things, but he has come from heaven and
is greater than anyone else.* 32He testifies about
what he has seen and heard, but how few believe
what he tells them! 33Anyone who accepts his testimony can affirm that God is true. 34For he is sent
by God. He speaks God's words, for God gives him
the Spirit without limit. 35The Father loves his
Son and has put everything into his hands. 36And
anyone who believes in God's Son has eternal life.
Anyone who doesn't obey the Son will never experience eternal life but remains under God's angry
judgment."

Herod Puts John in Prison

LUKE 3:19-20

John also publicly criticized Herod Antipas, the
ruler of Galilee,* for marrying Herodias, his brother's wife, and for many other wrongs he had done.
20So Herod put John in prison, adding this sin to his
many others.

Jesus Leaves Judea PARALLEL

MATTHEW 4:12

When Jesus heard that John had been arrested,
he left Judea and returned to Galilee.

MARK 1:14

Later on, after John was arrested, Jesus went into
Galilee, where he preached God's Good News.*

JOHN 4:1-3

Jesus* knew the Pharisees had heard that he was baptizing and making more disciples than John 2(though
Jesus himself didn't baptize them—his disciples did).
3So he left Judea and returned to Galilee.

Jn 3:31 Some manuscripts do not include *and is greater than anyone else.* **Lk 3:19** Greek *Herod the tetrarch.* **Mk 1:14** Some manuscripts read *the Good News of the Kingdom of God.* **Jn 4:1** Some manuscripts read *The Lord.*

John 3:26 John the Baptist's disciples were disturbed because people were following Jesus instead of John. It is easy to grow jealous of the popularity of another person's ministry. But we must remember that our true mission is to influence people to follow Christ, not us.

John 3:27 Why did John the Baptist continue to baptize after Jesus came onto the scene? Why didn't he become a disciple too? John explained that because God had given him his work, he had to continue it until God called him to do something else. John's main purpose was to point people to Christ. Even with Jesus beginning his own ministry, John could still turn people to Jesus.

John 3:30 John's willingness to decrease in importance shows unusual humility. Pastors and other Christian leaders can be tempted to focus more on the success of their ministries than on Christ. Beware of those who put more emphasis on their own achievements than on God's Kingdom.

John 3:31-35 Jesus' testimony was trustworthy because he had come from heaven and was speaking of what he had seen there. His words were the very words of God. Your whole spiritual life depends on your answer to one question: Who is Jesus Christ? If you accept Jesus as only a prophet or teacher, you have to reject his teaching, for he claimed to be God's Son, even God himself. The heartbeat of John's Gospel is the dynamic truth that Jesus Christ is God's Son, the Messiah, the Savior, who existed from the beginning and will continue to live forever. This same Jesus has invited us to accept him and live with him eternally. When we understand who Jesus is, we are compelled to believe what he said.

John 3:34 God's Spirit was upon Jesus without measure or limit. Thus, Jesus was the highest revelation of God to humanity (Heb 1:2).

John 3:36 Jesus says that those who believe in him have (not *will have*) eternal life. To receive eternal life is to join in God's life, which by nature is eternal. Thus, eternal life begins at the moment of spiritual rebirth.

John 3:36 John, the author of this Gospel, has been demonstrating that Jesus is the true Son of God. Jesus sets before us the greatest choice in life. We are responsible to decide today whom we will obey (Josh 24:15), and God wants us to choose him and life (Deut 30:15-20). God's angry judgment refers to his final rejection of those who reject him. To put off the choice is to choose not to follow Christ. Indecision is a fatal decision.

Luke 3:19-20 This is Herod Antipas (see p. 1362 for his Profile). Herodias was Herod's niece and also his brother's wife. She would later treacherously plot John the Baptist's death (Matt 14:1-12). The Herods were a murderous and deceitful family. Rebuking a tyrannical official who could imprison and execute him was extremely dangerous, yet that is what John did. He was focused on eternal matters, not safety and comfort for today.

John 4:1-3 Already opposition was rising against Jesus, especially from the Pharisees. They resented Jesus' popularity as well as his message, which challenged much of their teachings. Because Jesus was just beginning his ministry, it wasn't yet time to confront these leaders openly; so he left Jerusalem and traveled north toward Galilee.

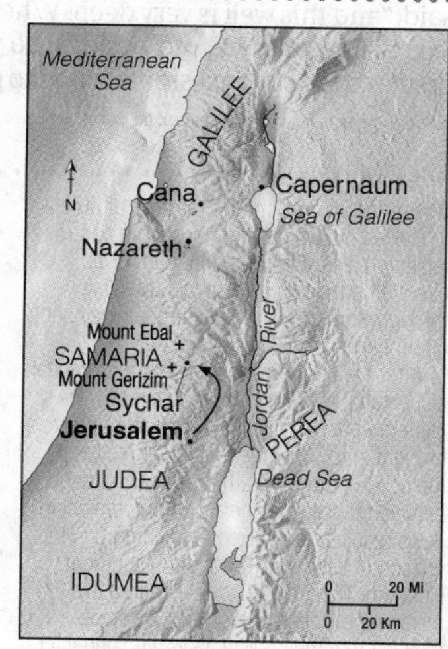

***THE VISIT IN SAMARIA** Jesus went to Jerusalem for the Passover, cleared the Temple, and talked with Nicodemus, a religious leader, about eternal life. He then left Jerusalem and traveled in Judea. On his way to Galilee, he visited Sychar and other villages in Samaria. Unlike most Jews of the day, he did not try to avoid the region of Samaria.*

2. JESUS MINISTERS IN SAMARIA

On his way home from Jerusalem, Jesus stopped in Samaria—an area most Jewish people avoided. Jesus didn't have any concern for the prejudices of people around him. Instead, he chose to minister to everyone who was willing to recognize him for who he really was.

Jesus Talks to a Woman at the Well

JOHN 4:4-26

He had to go through Samaria on the way. [5]Eventu-
ally he came to the Samaritan village of Sychar, near
the field that Jacob gave to his son Joseph. [6]Jacob's
well was there; and Jesus, tired from the long walk,
sat wearily beside the well about noontime. [7]Soon a
Samaritan woman came to draw water, and Jesus said
to her, "Please give me a drink." [8]He was alone at the
time because his disciples had gone into the village
to buy some food.
[9]The woman was surprised, for Jews refuse to have
anything to do with Samaritans.* She said to Jesus,
"You are a Jew, and I am a Samaritan woman. Why are
you asking me for a drink?"
[10]Jesus replied, "If you only knew the gift God has
for you and who you are speaking to, you would ask
me, and I would give you living water."
[11]"But sir, you don't have a rope or a bucket," she
said, "and this well is very deep. Where would you get
this living water? [12]And besides, do you think you're
greater than our ancestor Jacob, who gave us this well?
How can you offer better water than he and his sons
and his animals enjoyed?"
[13]Jesus replied, "Anyone who drinks this water will
soon become thirsty again. [14]But those who drink the
water I give will never be thirsty again. It becomes
a fresh, bubbling spring within them, giving them
eternal life."
[15]"Please, sir," the woman said, "give me this water!
Then I'll never be thirsty again, and I won't have to
come here to get water."
[16]"Go and get your husband," Jesus told her.
[17]"I don't have a husband," the woman replied.
Jesus said, "You're right! You don't have a husband—
[18]for you have had five husbands, and you aren't even
married to the man you're living with now. You certainly spoke the truth!"
[19]"Sir," the woman said, "you must be a prophet.
[20]So tell me, why is it that you Jews insist that Jerusalem is the only place of worship, while we Samaritans
claim it is here at Mount Gerizim,* where our ancestors worshiped?"
[21]Jesus replied, "Believe me, dear woman, the time

Jn 4:9 Some manuscripts do not include this sentence. **Jn 4:20** Greek *on this mountain.*

John 4:4 To go from the territory of Judea to Galilee meant passing through a central territory called Samaria. Most Jews did everything they could to avoid traveling through Samaria. The reason goes way back into their history.

After the northern kingdom, with its capital at Samaria, fell to the Assyrians, many Jews were deported to Assyria, and foreigners were brought in to settle the land and help keep the peace (2 Kgs 17:24). The intermarriage between those foreigners and the remaining Jews resulted in a mixed race, impure in the opinion of Jews who lived in the southern kingdom. Thus, the pure Jews hated this mixed race, called Samaritans, because they felt that their fellow Jews who had intermarried had betrayed their people and nation. The Samaritans had set up an alternate center for worship on Mount Gerizim (John 4:20) to parallel the Temple at Jerusalem, but it had been destroyed 150 years earlier. While there was long-standing prejudice between Jews and Samaritans, Jesus did not live by such restrictions. The route through Samaria was shorter, and that was the route he took.

John 4:5-7 Jacob's well was on the property originally owned by Jacob (Gen 33:18-19). It was not a spring-fed well but one into which water seeped from rain and dew, collecting at the bottom. Wells were almost always located outside the city along the main road. Twice each day, morning and evening, women came to draw water. This woman came at noon, however, probably to avoid meeting people who knew her reputation. Jesus gave this woman an extraordinary message about fresh and pure water that would quench her spiritual thirst forever.

John 4:7-9 This woman (1) was a Samaritan, a member of the hated mixed race, (2) was known to be living in sin, and (3) was in a public place. No respectable Jewish man would talk to a woman under such circumstances. But Jesus did. The Good News is for every person, no matter what his or her race, social position, or past sins. We must be prepared to share it at any time, in any place. Jesus crossed all barriers to share the Good News, and we who follow him must do no less.

John 4:10 What did Jesus mean by "living water"? In the Old Testament, many verses speak of thirsting after God as one thirsts for water (Ps 42:1; Isa 55:1; Jer 2:13; Zech 13:1). God is called the fountain of life (Ps 36:9) and the fountain of living water (Jer 17:13). In saying he would bring living water that could forever quench a person's thirst for God, Jesus was claiming to be the Messiah. Only the Messiah could give this gift that satisfies the soul's desire.

John 4:13-15 Many spiritual functions parallel physical functions. As our bodies hunger and thirst, so do our souls. But our souls need spiritual food and water. The woman confused the two kinds of water, perhaps because no one had ever before talked with her about her spiritual hunger and thirst. We would not think of depriving our bodies of food and water when they hunger or thirst. Why then should we deprive our souls? The living Word, Jesus Christ, and the written Word, the Bible, can satisfy our hungry and thirsty souls.

John 4:15 The woman mistakenly believed that if she received the water Jesus offered, she would not have to return to the well each day. She was interested in Jesus' message because she thought it could make her life easier. But if that were always the case, people would accept Christ's message for the wrong reasons. Christ did not come to take away challenges, but to change us on the inside and to empower us to deal with problems from God's perspective.

John 4:16-20 When this woman discovered that Jesus knew all about her private life, she quickly changed the subject. Often people become uncomfortable when the conversation hits too close to home, and they try to talk about something else. As we witness, we should gently guide the conversation back to Christ. His presence exposes sin and makes people squirm, but only Christ can forgive sins and give new life.

John 4:20-24 The woman brought up a popular theological issue—the correct place to worship. But her question was a smoke screen to keep Jesus away from her deepest need. Jesus directed the conversation to a much more important point: The location of worship is not nearly as important as the attitude of the worshipers.

is coming when it will no longer matter whether you worship the Father on this mountain or in Jerusalem.
22You Samaritans know very little about the one you worship, while we Jews know all about him, for salvation comes through the Jews.
23But the time is coming—indeed it's here now—when true worshipers will worship the Father in spirit and in truth. The Father is looking for those who will worship him that way.
24For God is Spirit, so those who worship him must worship in spirit and in truth."

25The woman said, "I know the Messiah is coming—the one who is called Christ. When he comes, he will explain everything to us."

26Then Jesus told her, "I AM the Messiah!"*

Jesus Tells about the Spiritual Harvest

JOHN 4:27-38

Just then his disciples came back. They were shocked to find him talking to a woman, but none of them had the nerve to ask, "What do you want with her?" or "Why are you talking to her?"
28The woman left her water jar beside the well and ran back to the village, telling everyone,
29"Come and see a man who told me everything I ever did! Could he possibly be the Messiah?"
30So the people came streaming from the village to see him.

31Meanwhile, the disciples were urging Jesus, "Rabbi, eat something."

32But Jesus replied, "I have a kind of food you know nothing about."

33"Did someone bring him food while we were gone?" the disciples asked each other.

34Then Jesus explained: "My nourishment comes from doing the will of God, who sent me, and from finishing his work.
35You know the saying, 'Four months between planting and harvest.' But I say, wake up and look around. The fields are already ripe* for harvest.
36The harvesters are paid good wages, and the fruit they harvest is people brought to eternal life. What joy awaits both the planter and the harvester alike!
37You know the saying, 'One plants and another harvests.' And it's true.
38I sent you to harvest where you didn't plant; others had already done the work, and now you will get to gather the harvest."

Jn 4:26 Or *"The 'I AM' is here"*; or *"I am the LORD"*; Greek reads *"I am, the one speaking to you."* See Exod 3:14. **Jn 4:35** Greek *white.*

John 4:22 When Jesus said, "Salvation comes through the Jews," he meant that only through the Jewish Messiah would the whole world find salvation. God had promised that through the Jewish race the whole earth would be blessed (Gen 12:3). The Old Testament prophets had called the Jews to be a light to the other nations of the world, bringing them to a knowledge of God; and they had predicted the Messiah's coming. The woman at the well may have known of these passages and was expecting the Messiah, but she didn't realize that she was talking to him!

John 4:24 "God is Spirit" means he is not a physical being limited to one place. He is present everywhere, and he can be worshiped anywhere, at any time. It is not where we worship that counts, but how we worship. Is your worship genuine and true? Do you have the Holy Spirit's help? How does the Holy Spirit help us worship? The Holy Spirit prays for us (Rom 8:26), teaches us the words of Christ (John 14:26), and tells us we are loved (Rom 5:5).

John 4:34 Jesus was speaking about his spiritual nourishment. It includes more than Bible study, prayer, and attending church. Spiritual nourishment also comes from doing God's will and helping to bring his work of salvation to completion. We are nourished not only by what we take in, but also by what we give out for God. In John 17:4, Jesus refers to completing God's work on earth.

John 4:35 Sometimes Christians excuse themselves from witnessing by saying that their family or friends aren't ready to believe. Jesus, however, makes it clear that around us a continual harvest waits to be reaped. Don't let Jesus find you making excuses. Look around. You will find people ready to hear God's Word.

John 4:36-38 The wages Jesus offers are the joy of working for him and seeing the harvest of believers. These wages come to planter and harvester alike because both find joy in seeing new believers come into Christ's Kingdom. The phrase "others had already done the work" (John 4:38) may refer to the Old Testament prophets and to John the Baptist, who paved the way for the Good News.

Samaria

Samaria was an area of land that was allotted to Ephraim and half the tribe of Manasseh in the days of Joshua (Josh 16:1–17:18). After the death of Solomon and the revolt of the 10 northern tribes, the inhabitants of Samaria followed the idolatry introduced by Jeroboam, refusing to go to Jerusalem to worship at the Temple. Years later, after the 10 tribes had been carried away into captivity, the king of Assyria put into this province a colony of various nations that soon intermingled and intermarried with the original people, causing a strange medley of religions. Second Kings 17:33 says, "Though they worshiped the LORD, they continued to follow their own gods." This conglomerate of people became known as Samaritans. They adopted the Pentateuch (Genesis—Deuteronomy) as their Scriptures and set up a place of worship on Mount Gerizim (Deut 11:26-29). But they were far from having accurate knowledge about the truth, even though they knew about a coming Messiah.

When a remnant of Jews returned from Babylonian captivity, they refused to allow the Samaritans any part in rebuilding the Temple or the city of Jerusalem, even though the Samaritans claimed to have the same God as the Jews. This refusal led to a bitter animosity between the two groups, which was succinctly summed up by John: "Jews refuse to have anything to do with Samaritans" (John 4:9). Jews wouldn't talk to them and generally avoided going through their neighborhoods. But Jesus wasn't bound by these prejudices.

Many Samaritans Believe in Jesus

JOHN 4:39-42

Many Samaritans from the village believed in Jesus because the woman had said, "He told me everything I ever did!" [40]When they came out to see him, they begged him to stay in their village. So he stayed for two days, [41]long enough for many more to hear his message and believe. [42]Then they said to the woman, "Now we believe, not just because of what you told us, but because we have heard him ourselves. Now we know that he is indeed the Savior of the world."

3. JESUS MINISTERS IN GALILEE

The majority of Jesus' ministry took place in Galilee, the northern region of Israel around the Sea of Galilee. Here Jesus performed many miracles, taught extensively (including the Sermon on the Mount), and spent a lot of time investing in the lives of his twelve chosen disciples. He traveled regularly throughout this region, going from town to town sharing his message with all who would listen.

Jesus Preaches in Galilee PARALLEL ●●●●

MATTHEW 4:13-17 ●○○○

He went first to Nazareth, then left there and moved to Capernaum, beside the Sea of Galilee, in the region of Zebulun and Naphtali. [14]This fulfilled what God said through the prophet Isaiah:

15 "In the land of Zebulun and of Naphtali,
beside the sea, beyond the Jordan River,
in Galilee where so many Gentiles live,
16 the people who sat in darkness
have seen a great light.
And for those who lived in the land where death
casts its shadow,
a light has shined."*

[17]From then on Jesus began to preach, "Repent of your sins and turn to God, for the Kingdom of Heaven is near.*"

MARK 1:15 ○●○○

"The time promised by God has come at last!" he announced. "The Kingdom of God is near! Repent of your sins and believe the Good News!"

LUKE 4:14-15 ○○●○

Then Jesus returned to Galilee, filled with the Holy Spirit's power. Reports about him spread quickly through the whole region. [15]He taught regularly in their synagogues and was praised by everyone.

Mt 4:15-16 Isa 9:1-2 (Greek version). **Mt 4:17** Or *has come,* or *is coming soon.*

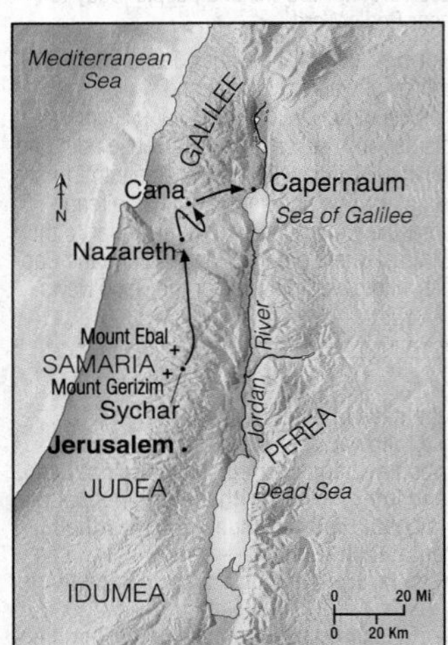

***JESUS RETURNS TO GALILEE** Jesus stayed in Sychar for two days, then went on to Galilee. He visited Nazareth and various towns in Galilee before arriving in Cana. From there he spoke the word of healing, and a government official's son in Capernaum was healed. The Gospel of Matthew tells us Jesus then settled in Capernaum (Matt 4:12-13).*

John 4:39 The Samaritan woman immediately shared her experience with others. Despite her reputation, many took her invitation and came out to meet Jesus. Perhaps we're ashamed of sins in our past. But Christ changes us. As people see these changes, they become curious. Use these opportunities to introduce them to Christ.

Matt 4:13 Jesus moved from Nazareth, his hometown, to Capernaum, about 20 miles farther north. Capernaum became Jesus' home base during his ministry in Galilee. Jesus probably moved (1) to get away from intense opposition in Nazareth, (2) to have an impact on the greatest number of people (Capernaum was a busy city, and Jesus' message could reach more people and spread more quickly), and (3) to utilize extra resources and support for his ministry.

Jesus' move fulfilled the prophecy of Isaiah 9:1-2, which states that the Messiah would be a light to the land of Zebulun and Naphtali, the region of Galilee where Capernaum was located. Zebulun and Naphtali were two of the original 12 tribes of Israel.

Matt 4:14-16 By quoting from the book of Isaiah, Matthew continues to tie Jesus' ministry to the Old Testament. This was helpful for his Jewish readers, who were familiar with these Scriptures. In addition, it shows the unity of God's purposes as he works with his people throughout all the ages.

Matt 4:17 The "Kingdom of Heaven" has the same meaning as the "Kingdom of God" in Mark and Luke. Matthew uses this phrase because the Jews, out of their intense reverence and respect, did not pronounce God's name. The Kingdom of Heaven is still near because it has arrived in our hearts. See the note on Matthew 3:2, p. 1287, for more on the Kingdom of Heaven.

Matt 4:17 Jesus started his ministry with the same message people had heard John the Baptist say: "Repent of your sins." The message is the same today as when Jesus and John gave it. Becoming a follower of Christ means turning away from our self-centeredness and "self" control and turning our lives over to Christ's direction and control.

Luke 4:15 Synagogues were very important in Jewish religious life. During the Exile when the Jews no longer had their Temple, synagogues were established as places of worship on the Sabbath and as schools for young boys during the week. Synagogues continued to exist even after the Temple was rebuilt. A synagogue could be set up in any town with at least 10 Jewish families. It was administered by one leader and an assistant. At the synagogue, the leader often would invite a visiting rabbi to read from the Scriptures and to teach. Itinerant rabbis, like Jesus, were always welcome to speak to those gathered each Sabbath in the synagogues. The apostle Paul also took advantage of this practice (see Acts 13:5; 14:1).

JOHN 4:43-45

At the end of the two days, Jesus went on to Galilee. 44He himself had said that a prophet is not honored in his own hometown. 45Yet the Galileans welcomed him, for they had been in Jerusalem at the Passover celebration and had seen everything he did there.

Jesus Heals a Government Official's Son

JOHN 4:46-54

As he traveled through Galilee, he came to Cana, where he had turned the water into wine. There was a government official in nearby Capernaum whose son was very sick. 47When he heard that Jesus had come from Judea to Galilee, he went and begged Jesus to come to Capernaum to heal his son, who was about to die.

48Jesus asked, "Will you never believe in me unless you see miraculous signs and wonders?"

49The official pleaded, "Lord, please come now before my little boy dies."

50Then Jesus told him, "Go back home. Your son will live!" And the man believed what Jesus said and started home.

51While the man was on his way, some of his servants met him with the news that his son was alive and well. 52He asked them when the boy had begun to get better, and they replied, "Yesterday afternoon at one o'clock his fever suddenly disappeared!" 53Then the father realized that that was the very time Jesus had told him, "Your son will live." And he and his entire household believed in Jesus. 54This was the second miraculous sign Jesus did in Galilee after coming from Judea.

Some Fishermen Follow Jesus PARALLEL

MATTHEW 4:18-22

One day as Jesus was walking along the shore of the Sea of Galilee, he saw two brothers—Simon, also called Peter, and Andrew—throwing a net into the water, for they fished for a living. 19Jesus called out to them, "Come, follow me, and I will show you how to fish for people!" 20And they left their nets at once and followed him.

John 4:46-49 This government official was probably an officer in Herod's service. He had walked 20 miles to see Jesus and addressed him as "Lord," putting himself under Jesus even though he had legal authority over Jesus.

John 4:48 This miracle was more than a favor to one official; it was a sign to all the people. John's Gospel was written to all humankind to urge faith in Christ. Here a government official had faith that Jesus could do what he claimed. The official believed; then he saw a miraculous sign.

John 4:50 This government official not only believed Jesus could heal, he also obeyed by returning home, thus demonstrating his faith. It isn't enough for us to say we believe that Jesus can take care of our problems. We need to act as if he can. When you pray about a need or problem, live as though you believe Jesus can do what he says.

John 4:51 Jesus' miracles were not mere illusions. Although the official's son was 20 miles away, he was healed when Jesus spoke the word. Distance was no problem because Christ has mastery over space. We can never put so much space between ourselves and Christ that he can no longer help us.

John 4:53 Notice how the official's faith grew. First, he believed enough to ask Jesus to help his son. Second, he believed Jesus' assurance that his son would live, and he acted on it. Third, he and his whole house believed in Jesus. Faith is a gift that grows as we use it.

Matt 4:18-20 These men already knew Jesus. He had talked to Peter and Andrew previously (John 1:35-42) and had been preaching in the area. When Jesus called them, they knew what kind of man he was and were willing to follow him. Jesus told Peter and Andrew to leave their fishing business and begin fishing "for people," helping others find God. Jesus was calling them away from their productive trade to be productive spiritually. We all need to fish for souls. If we practice Christ's teachings and share the Good News with others, we will be able to draw those around us to Christ like a fisherman who pulls fish into his boat with nets.

Matt 4:18 The Sea of Galilee is really a large lake. About 30 fishing towns surrounded it during Jesus' day, and Capernaum was the largest.

Fishing Boats

Fishermen have been working in Palestine from early times, and the profession of fishing is referred to in both the Old and New Testaments (Isa 19:8; Jer 16:16; Ezek 47:10; John 21:3-10). Fishermen formed a distinct class in society. Several fishermen were among Jesus' disciples, including two pairs of brothers: Peter and Andrew, and John and James (see Matt 4:18-22; Mark 1:16-20; Luke 5:2-11). Their work was strenuous and not always rewarding (Luke 5:5; John 21:3). Pictured are some modern fishing boats on the Sea of Galilee, where Jesus' disciples fished. Jesus used the metaphor "fishers of men" for his disciples to indicate that they would "catch" people for the Kingdom (Matt 4:19; Mark 1:17; Luke 5:10).

▸ **MATTHEW 4:18-22 *(cont.)***

21A little farther up the shore he saw two other brothers, James and John, sitting in a boat with their father, Zebedee, repairing their nets. And he called them to come, too. 22They immediately followed him, leaving the boat and their father behind.

MARK 1:16-20

One day as Jesus was walking along the shore of the Sea of Galilee, he saw Simon* and his brother Andrew throwing a net into the water, for they fished for a living. 17Jesus called out to them, "Come, follow me, and I will show you how to fish for people!" 18And they left their nets at once and followed him.

19A little farther up the shore Jesus saw Zebedee's sons, James and John, in a boat repairing their nets. 20He called them at once, and they also followed him, leaving their father, Zebedee, in the boat with the hired men.

LUKE 5:1-11

One day as Jesus was preaching on the shore of the Sea of Galilee,* great crowds pressed in on him to listen to the word of God. 2He noticed two empty boats at the water's edge, for the fishermen had left them and were washing their nets. 3Stepping into one of the boats, Jesus asked Simon,* its owner, to push it out into the water. So he sat in the boat and taught the crowds from there.

4When he had finished speaking, he said to Simon, "Now go out where it is deeper, and let down your nets to catch some fish."

5"Master," Simon replied, "we worked hard all last night and didn't catch a thing. But if you say so, I'll let the nets down again." 6And this time their nets were so full of fish they began to tear! 7A shout for help brought their partners in the other boat, and soon both boats were filled with fish and on the verge of sinking.

8When Simon Peter realized what had happened, he fell to his knees before Jesus and said, "Oh, Lord, please leave me—I'm too much of a sinner to be around you." 9For he was awestruck by the number of fish they had caught, as were the others with him. 10His partners, James and John, the sons of Zebedee, were also amazed.

Jesus replied to Simon, "Don't be afraid! From now on you'll be fishing for people!" 11And as soon as they landed, they left everything and followed Jesus.

Jesus Teaches with Authority PARALLEL

MARK 1:21-28

Jesus and his companions went to the town of Capernaum. When the Sabbath day came, he went into the synagogue and began to teach. 22The people were amazed at his teaching, for he taught with real authority—quite unlike the teachers of religious law.

Mk 1:16 *Simon* is called "Peter" in 3:16 and thereafter. **Lk 5:1** Greek *Lake Gennesaret,* another name for the Sea of Galilee. **Lk 5:3** *Simon* is called "Peter" in 6:14 and thereafter.

Matt 4:21-22 James and his brother, John, along with Peter and Andrew, were the first disciples that Jesus called to work with him. Jesus' call motivated these men to get up and leave their jobs—immediately. They didn't make excuses about why it wasn't a good time. They left at once and followed. Jesus calls each of us to follow him. When Jesus asks us to serve him, we must be like the disciples and do it at once.

Mark 1:16-20 We often assume that Jesus' disciples were great men of faith from the first time they met Jesus. But they had to grow in their faith just as all believers do (Mark 14:48-50, 66-72; John 14:1-9; 20:26-29). This is apparently not the only time Jesus called Peter (Simon), James, and John to follow him (see John 1:35-42 for another time). Although it took time for Jesus' call and his message to get through, the disciples followed. In the same way, we may question and falter, but we must never stop following Jesus.

Mark 1:17 Fishing was a major industry around the Sea of Galilee. Fishing with nets was the most common method. Jesus called the disciples to fish for people with the same energy they had used to fish for food. The gospel would be like a net, lifting people from dark waters into the light of day and transforming their lives. How can God use you to fish for people's souls? How can you train new converts to find new seas and cast new nets where waters have never been fished before? The gospel makes missionaries of all God's people. Where are you casting your net?

Luke 5:2 Fishermen on the Sea of Galilee used nets, often bell-shaped ones with lead weights around the edges. A net would be thrown flat onto the water, and the lead weights would cause it to sink around the fish. Then the fishermen would pull on a cord, drawing the net around the fish. Nets had to be kept in good condition, so they would be washed to remove weeds and then mended.

Luke 5:8 Simon Peter was awestruck at this miracle, and his first response was to realize his own insignificance in comparison to this man's greatness. Peter knew that Jesus had healed the sick and driven out demons, but he was amazed that Jesus cared about his day-to-day routine and understood his needs. God is interested not only in saving us but also in helping us in our daily activities.

Luke 5:11 God has two requirements for coming to him. Like Peter, we must recognize our own sinfulness. Then, like these fishermen, we must realize that we can't save ourselves and that we need help. If we know that Jesus is the only one who can help us, we will be ready to leave everything and follow him.

Luke 5:11 This was the disciples' second call. After the first call (John 1:35-51), Peter and Andrew had gone back to fishing. They continued to watch Jesus, however, as he established his authority in the synagogue, healed the sick, and drove out demons. Here he also established his authority in their lives—he met them on their level and helped them in their work. From this point on, they left their nets and remained with Jesus. For us, following Jesus means more than just acknowledging him as Savior. We must leave our past behind and commit our future to him.

Mark 1:21 Jesus had recently moved to Capernaum from Nazareth (Matt 4:12-13). Capernaum was a thriving town with great wealth as well as great sin and decadence. Because it was the headquarters for many Roman troops, pagan influences from all over the Roman Empire were pervasive. This was an ideal place for Jesus to challenge both Jews and non-Jews with the Good News of God's Kingdom.

Mark 1:21-22 Because the Temple in Jerusalem was too far away for many Jews to attend regularly for worship, many towns had synagogues serving both as places of worship and as schools. Beginning in the days of Ezra, about 450 B.C., a group of 10 Jewish families could start a synagogue. There, during the week, Jewish boys were taught the

[23]Suddenly, a man in the synagogue who was possessed by an evil* spirit began shouting, [24]"Why are you interfering with us, Jesus of Nazareth? Have you come to destroy us? I know who you are—the Holy One of God!"

[25]Jesus cut him short. "Be quiet! Come out of the man," he ordered. [26]At that, the evil spirit screamed, threw the man into a convulsion, and then came out of him.

[27]Amazement gripped the audience, and they began to discuss what had happened. "What sort of new teaching is this?" they asked excitedly. "It has such authority! Even evil spirits obey his orders!" [28]The news about Jesus spread quickly throughout the entire region of Galilee.

LUKE 4:31-37

Then Jesus went to Capernaum, a town in Galilee, and taught there in the synagogue every Sabbath day. [32]There, too, the people were amazed at his teaching, for he spoke with authority.

[33]Once when he was in the synagogue, a man possessed by a demon—an evil* spirit—began shouting at Jesus, [34]"Go away! Why are you interfering with us, Jesus of Nazareth? Have you come to destroy us? I know who you are—the Holy One of God!"

[35]Jesus cut him short. "Be quiet! Come out of the man," he ordered. At that, the demon threw the man to the floor as the crowd watched; then it came out of him without hurting him further.

[36]Amazed, the people exclaimed, "What authority and power this man's words possess! Even evil spirits obey him, and they flee at his command!" [37]The news about Jesus spread through every village in the entire region.

Jesus Heals Peter's Mother-in-Law and Many Others PARALLEL

MATTHEW 8:14-17

When Jesus arrived at Peter's house, Peter's mother-in-law was sick in bed with a high fever. [15]But when Jesus touched her hand, the fever left her. Then she got up and prepared a meal for him.

[16]That evening many demon-possessed people were brought to Jesus. He cast out the evil spirits with a simple command, and he healed all the sick. [17]This fulfilled the word of the Lord through the prophet Isaiah, who said,

"He took our sicknesses
and removed our diseases."*

Mk 1:23 Greek *unclean;* also in 1:26, 27. **Lk 4:33** Greek *unclean;* also in 4:36. **Mt 8:17** Isa 53:4.

Old Testament law and Jewish religion. Girls could not attend. Each Saturday, the Sabbath, the Jewish men would gather to listen to a rabbi teach from the Scriptures. Because there was no permanent rabbi or teacher, it was customary for the synagogue leader to ask visiting teachers to speak. This is why Jesus often taught in the synagogues in the towns he visited. While the Jewish teachers often quoted from well-known rabbis to give their words more authority, Jesus didn't need to. Because Jesus is God, he knew exactly what the Scriptures said and meant. He was the ultimate authority.

Mark 1:23ff Some people dismiss all accounts of demon possession as a primitive way to describe mental illness. Throughout history mental illness has often been wrongly diagnosed as demon possession, but clearly a hostile outside force controlled this man. Mark emphasized Jesus' conflict with evil powers to show his superiority over them, so he recorded many stories about Jesus driving out evil spirits. Jesus didn't have to conduct an elaborate exorcism ritual. His word was enough to send out the evil spirit.

Mark 1:23-24 The evil spirit knew at once that Jesus was the Holy One sent from God. By including this event in his Gospel, Mark was establishing Jesus' credentials, showing that even the spiritual underworld recognized Jesus as the Messiah.

Mark 1:23 Evil spirits, or demons, are ruled by Satan. They work to tempt people to sin. They were not created by Satan because God is the creator of all. Rather, they are fallen angels who joined Satan in his rebellion. Though not all disease comes from Satan, demons can cause a person to become mute, deaf, blind, or insane. But in every case where demons confronted Jesus, they lost their power. Thus, God limits what evil spirits can do; they can do nothing without his permission. During Jesus' life on earth, demons were allowed to be very active to demonstrate once and for all Christ's power and authority over them.

Luke 4:33 A man possessed by a demon was in the synagogue where Jesus was teaching. This man made his way into the place of worship and verbally abused Jesus. It is naive to think that we will be sheltered from evil in the church. Satan is happy to invade our presence wherever and whenever he can. But Jesus' authority is much greater than Satan's, and where Jesus is present, demons cannot stay for long.

Luke 4:34-36 The people were amazed at Jesus' authority to drive out demons—evil spirits ruled by Satan and sent to harass people, tempt them to sin, and ultimately destroy them. Demons are fallen angels who have joined Satan in rebellion against God. Jesus faced many demons during his time on earth, and he always exerted authority over them. Not only did the evil spirit leave this man; Luke records that the man was not even injured.

While we may not often see cases of demon possession today, it does still exist. There is no doubt that evil permeates our world. We need not be fearful, however. Jesus' power is far greater than Satan's. The first step toward conquering fear of evil is to recognize Jesus' authority and power. He has overcome all evil, including Satan himself.

Matt 8:14-15 Peter's mother-in-law gives us a beautiful example to follow. Her response to Jesus' touch was to wait on Jesus and his disciples—immediately. Has God ever helped you through a dangerous or difficult situation? If so, ask him how you can express your gratitude. Because God has promised us all the rewards of his Kingdom, we should look for ways to serve him and his followers now.

Matt 8:16-17 Matthew continues to show Jesus' kingly nature. Through a single touch, Jesus healed (Matt 8:3, 15); when he spoke a single word, evil spirits fled his presence (Matt 8:16). Jesus has authority over all evil powers and all earthly disease. He also has power and authority to conquer sin. Sickness and evil are consequences of living in a fallen world. But in the future, when God removes all sin, there will be no more sickness and death. Jesus' healing miracles were a taste of what the whole world will one day experience in God's Kingdom.

MARK 1:29-34
After Jesus left the synagogue with James and John,
they went to Simon and Andrew's home. 30Now Simon's mother-in-law was sick in bed with a high fever.
They told Jesus about her right away. 31So he went to
her bedside, took her by the hand, and helped her sit
up. Then the fever left her, and she prepared a meal
for them.
32That evening after sunset, many sick and
demon-possessed people were brought to Jesus.
33The whole town gathered at the door to watch. 34So
Jesus healed many people who were sick with various
diseases, and he cast out many demons. But because
the demons knew who he was, he did not allow them
to speak.

LUKE 4:38-41
After leaving the synagogue that day, Jesus went to
Simon's home, where he found Simon's mother-in-law
very sick with a high fever. "Please heal her," everyone begged. 39Standing at her bedside, he rebuked
the fever, and it left her. And she got up at once and
prepared a meal for them.
40As the sun went down that evening, people
throughout the village brought sick family members
to Jesus. No matter what their diseases were, the touch
of his hand healed every one. 41Many were possessed
by demons; and the demons came out at his command, shouting, "You are the Son of God!" But because
they knew he was the Messiah, he rebuked them and
refused to let them speak.

Mark 1:29-31 Each Gospel writer had a slightly different perspective as he wrote; thus, the comparable stories in the Gospels often highlight different details. In Matthew, Jesus touched the woman's hand. In Mark, he helped her up. In Luke, he spoke to the fever and it left her. The accounts do not conflict. Just as four people might witness the same event and all recount different details, so each Gospel writer simply emphasized different details of this story.

Mark 1:34 Why didn't Jesus want the demons to reveal who he was? (1) By commanding the demons to remain silent, Jesus proved his authority and power over them. (2) Jesus wanted the people to believe he was the Messiah because of what he said and did, not because of the demons' words. (3) Jesus wanted to reveal his identity as the Messiah according to his timetable, not Satan's. The demons called Jesus "Son of God" or "the Holy One sent from God" (Luke 4:34) because they knew he was the Christ. But Jesus was going to show himself to be the suffering servant before he became the great King. To reveal his identity as King too soon would stir up the crowds with the wrong expectations of what he had come to do.

Luke 4:40 The people came to Jesus when the sun was setting because this was the Sabbath (Luke 4:31), their day of rest. Sabbath lasted from sunset on Friday to sunset on Saturday. The people didn't want to break the law that prohibited travel on the Sabbath, so they waited until the sun set before coming to Jesus. Then, as Luke the physician notes, they came with all kinds of diseases, and Jesus healed each one.

Luke 4:40 When you've faced a particularly difficult time, what helped you most? While some may have said kind words, most likely it was the presence and touch of a friend. A hug, an arm around your shoulder, or even just a hand laid gently on top of yours—these simple, wordless gestures mean so much to those in pain. In healing the sick and the demon possessed, Jesus had already demonstrated that he could heal with just a word (Luke 4:39). Yet here in Capernaum, Luke records that the touch of Jesus' hand healed the sick. Why not just speak a word and heal the whole crowd at once? Why go to all the trouble of treating each person individually, face-to-face? Perhaps because human touch is so very important. Does someone need a touch from you today?

Matt 4:23-24 Jesus preached the gospel—the Good News—to everyone who wanted to hear it. The Good News is that the Kingdom of Heaven has come, that God is with us, and that he cares for us. Christ can heal us, not just of physical sickness, but of spiritual sickness as well. There's

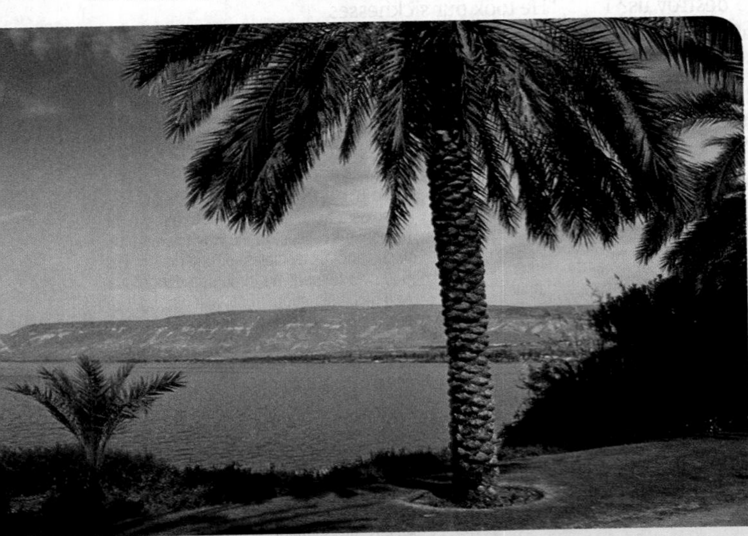

Sea of Galilee

The Sea of Galilee is a large body of water in Palestine. It has had many names in its history. In the Old Testament the Sea of Galilee was known as the Sea of Kinnereth (Num 34:11), named for the town on its border (Josh 19:35). Later, the name was changed to Lake of Gennesaret (Luke 5:1). It derived the name Sea of Tiberias (John 6:1; 21:1) from the town of Tiberias on its southwestern shore. The most familiar name, the Sea of Galilee, was due to its connection with the province of Galilee to its west (Matt 4:18). The Sea of Galilee, which is fed by the Jordan River, lies in the lower section of the Jordan Valley about 60 miles north of Jerusalem. The climate of the Sea of Galilee is semitropical. The lake is 13 miles long and 6 miles wide; its greatest depth is 200 feet. Its shape resembles a harp, and some scholars think the name Kinnereth comes from the Hebrew word meaning "harp." The lake has an abundant supply of fish.

Most of the events in Jesus' ministry took place around the Sea of Galilee, especially around Gennesaret, the most densely populated area of Palestine. Jesus is said to have lived in Capernaum (Matt 4:13), and he did many miracles there. Because the area west of the lake was a health resort, Jesus found many sick people there and healed them.

Jesus Preaches throughout Galilee PARALLEL

MATTHEW 4:23-25

Jesus traveled throughout the region of Galilee, teaching in the synagogues and announcing the Good News about the Kingdom. And he healed every kind of disease and illness. [24]News about him spread as far as Syria, and people soon began bringing to him all who were sick. And whatever their sickness or disease, or if they were demon possessed or epileptic or paralyzed—he healed them all. [25]Large crowds followed him wherever he went—people from Galilee, the Ten Towns,* Jerusalem, from all over Judea, and from east of the Jordan River.

MARK 1:35-39

Before daybreak the next morning, Jesus got up and went out to an isolated place to pray. [36]Later Simon and the others went out to find him. [37]When they found him, they said, "Everyone is looking for you."

[38]But Jesus replied, "We must go on to other towns as well, and I will preach to them, too. That is why I came." [39]So he traveled throughout the region of Galilee, preaching in the synagogues and casting out demons.

LUKE 4:42-44

Early the next morning Jesus went out to an isolated place. The crowds searched everywhere for him, and when they finally found him, they begged him not to leave them. [43]But he replied, "I must preach the Good News of the Kingdom of God in other towns, too, because that is why I was sent." [44]So he continued to travel around, preaching in synagogues throughout Judea.*

Jesus Heals a Man with Leprosy PARALLEL

MATTHEW 8:1-4

Large crowds followed Jesus as he came down the mountainside. [2]Suddenly, a man with leprosy approached him and knelt before him. "Lord," the man said, "if you are willing, you can heal me and make me clean."

[3]Jesus reached out and touched him. "I am willing," he said. "Be healed!" And instantly the leprosy disappeared. [4]Then Jesus said to him, "Don't tell anyone about this. Instead, go to the priest and let him examine you. Take along the offering required in the law of Moses for those who have been healed of leprosy.* This will be a public testimony that you have been cleansed."

Mt 4:25 Greek *Decapolis.* **Lk 4:44** Some manuscripts read *Galilee.* **Mt 8:4** See Lev 14:2-32.

no sin or problem too great or too small for him to handle. Jesus' words were good news because they offered freedom, hope, peace of heart, and eternal life with God.

Matt 4:23 Jesus was teaching, preaching, and healing. These were the three main aspects of his ministry. Teaching shows Jesus' concern for understanding; preaching shows his concern for commitment; and healing shows his concern for wholeness. His miracles of healing authenticated his teaching and preaching, proving that he truly was from God.

Matt 4:23 Jesus soon developed a powerful preaching ministry and often spoke in the synagogues. Most towns that had 10 or more Jewish families had a synagogue. The building served as a religious gathering place on the Sabbath and as a school during the week. The leader of the synagogue was not a preacher as much as an administrator. His job was to find and invite rabbis to teach and preach. It was customary to invite visiting rabbis like Jesus to speak.

Matt 4:25 The "Ten Towns" (Greek *Decapolis*) was a league of 10 Gentile cities east of the Sea of Galilee, joined together for better trade and mutual defense. The word about Jesus was out, and Jews and Gentiles were coming long distances to hear him.

Mark 1:35-37 Were the disciples impatient that Jesus prayed in solitude while so much ministry waited to be done? How would you have responded if you had been the one to find Jesus in prayer? It's easy to be so caught up with ministry that you neglect times of solitude, individual worship, and prayer. Perhaps you need to redesign your schedule. It is vitally important to (1) seek the Lord before your busy schedule takes over your thoughts; (2) withdraw from noise and demands so you can focus on God; (3) take Jesus' attitude of regular communion with the Father; (4) reflect on the priorities Jesus had for his life; (5) determine to pray on a more regular basis, not just in times of crisis. If prayer was important for Jesus, then it must be important for his followers. Pray—even if you have to get up very early in the morning to do it!

Mark 1:39 The Romans divided the land of Israel into three separate regions: Galilee, Samaria, and Judea. Galilee was the northernmost region, an area about 60 miles long and 30 miles wide. Jesus did much of his ministry in this area, an ideal place for him to teach because there were over 250 towns concentrated there, with many synagogues.

Luke 4:42 Jesus had to get up very early just to get some time alone. If Jesus needed solitude for prayer and refreshment, how much more is this true for us? Don't become so busy that life turns into a flurry of activity, leaving no room for quiet fellowship alone with God. No matter how much you have to do, you should always have time for prayer.

Luke 4:43 The Kingdom of God is Good News! It was Good News to the Jews because they had been awaiting the coming of the promised Messiah ever since the Babylonian captivity. It is Good News for us also because it means freedom from the slavery of sin and selfishness. The Kingdom of God is here and now because the Holy Spirit lives in the hearts of believers. Yet it is also in the future because Jesus will return to reign over a perfect Kingdom, where sin and evil will no longer exist.

Matt 8:2-3 Leprosy was a terrifying disease because there was no known cure. In Jesus' day, the Greek word for "leprosy" was used for a variety of similar diseases, and some forms were contagious. If a person contracted the contagious type, a priest declared him a leper and banished him from his home and city. The leper was sent to live in a community with other lepers until he either got better or died. Yet when the leper begged Jesus to heal him, Jesus reached out and touched him, even though his skin was covered with the dread disease.

Sin is also an incurable disease—and we all have it. Only Christ's healing touch can miraculously take away our sins and restore us to real living. But first, just like the leper, we must realize our inability to cure ourselves and ask for Christ's saving help.

Matt 8:4 The law required a healed leper to be examined by the priest (Lev 14). Jesus wanted this man to give his story firsthand to the priest to prove that his leprosy was completely gone so that he could be restored to his community.

MARK 1:40-45

A man with leprosy came and knelt in front of Jesus, begging to be healed. "If you are willing, you can heal me and make me clean," he said.

[41]Moved with compassion,* Jesus reached out and touched him. "I am willing," he said. "Be healed!" [42]Instantly the leprosy disappeared, and the man was healed. [43]Then Jesus sent him on his way with a stern warning: [44]"Don't tell anyone about this. Instead, go to the priest and let him examine you. Take along the offering required in the law of Moses for those who have been healed of leprosy.* This will be a public testimony that you have been cleansed."

[45]But the man went and spread the word, proclaiming to everyone what had happened. As a result, large crowds soon surrounded Jesus, and he couldn't publicly enter a town anywhere. He had to stay out in the secluded places, but people from everywhere kept coming to him.

LUKE 5:12-16

In one of the villages, Jesus met a man with an advanced case of leprosy. When the man saw Jesus, he bowed with his face to the ground, begging to be healed. "Lord," he said, "if you are willing, you can heal me and make me clean."

[13]Jesus reached out and touched him. "I am willing," he said. "Be healed!" And instantly the leprosy disappeared. [14]Then Jesus instructed him not to tell anyone what had happened. He said, "Go to the priest and let him examine you. Take along the offering required in the law of Moses for those who have been healed of leprosy.* This will be a public testimony that you have been cleansed."

[15]But despite Jesus' instructions, the report of his power spread even faster, and vast crowds came to hear him preach and to be healed of their diseases. [16]But Jesus often withdrew to the wilderness for prayer.

Jesus Heals a Paralyzed Man PARALLEL

MATTHEW 9:1-8

Jesus climbed into a boat and went back across the lake to his own town. [2]Some people brought to him a paralyzed man on a mat. Seeing their faith, Jesus said to the paralyzed man, "Be encouraged, my child! Your sins are forgiven."

[3]But some of the teachers of religious law said to themselves, "That's blasphemy! Does he think he's God?"

[4]Jesus knew* what they were thinking, so he asked them, "Why do you have such evil thoughts in your hearts? [5]Is it easier to say 'Your sins are forgiven,' or 'Stand up and walk'? [6]So I will prove to you that the Son of Man* has the authority on earth to

Mk 1:41 Some manuscripts read *Moved with anger.* **Mk 1:44** See Lev 14:2-32. **Lk 5:14** See Lev 14:2-32. **Mt 9:4** Some manuscripts read *saw.* **Mt 9:6** "Son of Man" is a title Jesus used for himself.

Mark 1:40-41 In keeping with the law in Leviticus 13 and 14, Jewish leaders declared people with leprosy unclean. This meant that lepers were unfit to participate in any religious or social activity. Because the law said that contact with any unclean person made that person unclean, too, some people even threw rocks at lepers to keep them at a safe distance. Even the mention of this disabling disease terrified people. How astounding it was, then, when Jesus reached out and touched this man who had leprosy.

The real value of a person is inside, not outside. Although a person's body may be diseased or deformed, the person inside is no less valuable to God. In a sense, we are all people with leprosy because we have all been deformed by the ugliness of sin. By sending his Son, Jesus, God has touched us, giving us the opportunity to be healed.

Luke 5:12 Leprosy had a similar emotional impact and terror associated with it as AIDS does today. (Sometimes called Hansen's disease, leprosy still exists in a less contagious form that can be treated.) The priests monitored the disease, banishing lepers who were in a contagious stage to prevent the spread of infection and readmitting lepers whose disease was in remission. Because leprosy destroys the nerve endings, lepers often would unknowingly damage their fingers, toes, and noses. This man had an advanced case, so he undoubtedly had lost much bodily tissue. Still, he believed that Jesus could heal him of every trace of the disease. And Jesus did just that, reaching out to touch this untouchable, contagious man in order to restore him. For more on the power of touch, see the second note on Luke 4:40, p. 1310.

Luke 5:16 People were flocking to hear Jesus preach and to have their diseases healed, but Jesus made sure he often withdrew to quiet, solitary places to pray. Many things clamor for our attention, and we often run ourselves ragged attending to them. Like Jesus, however, we should take time to withdraw to a quiet and deserted place to pray. Strength comes from God, and we can only be strengthened by spending time with him.

Matt 9:1 "His own town" was Capernaum, a good choice for Jesus' base of operations. It was a wealthy city due to fishing and trade. Situated on the Sea of Galilee in a densely populated area, Capernaum housed the Roman garrison that kept peace in the region. The city was a cultural melting pot, greatly influenced by Greek and Roman manners, dress, architecture, and politics.

Matt 9:2 Among the first words Jesus said to the paralyzed man were "Your sins are forgiven." Then he healed the man. We must be careful not to concentrate more on God's power to heal physical sickness than on his power to forgive spiritual sickness in the form of sin. Jesus saw that in addition to physical health, this man needed spiritual health. Spiritual health comes only from Jesus' healing touch.

Matt 9:2 Both the man's body and his spirit were paralyzed—he could not walk, and he did not know Jesus. But the man's spiritual state was what Jesus addressed first. If God does not heal us or someone we love, we need to remember that physical healing is not Christ's only concern. We will all be completely healed in Christ's coming Kingdom; but first we have to come to know Jesus.

Matt 9:3 Blaspheming is claiming to be God and applying his characteristics to yourself. The religious leaders rightly saw that Jesus was claiming to be God. What they did not understand was that he is God and thus has the authority to heal and to forgive sins.

Matt 9:5-6 It's easy to tell someone his sins are forgiven; it's a lot more difficult to reverse a case of paralysis! Jesus backed up his words by healing the man's legs. Jesus' action showed that his words were true; he had the power to forgive as well as to heal. Talk is cheap, and our words lack meaning if our actions do not back them up. We can say we love God or others, but if we are not taking practical steps to demonstrate that love, our words are empty and meaningless. How well do your actions back up what you say?

forgive sins." Then Jesus turned to the paralyzed
man and said, "Stand up, pick up your mat, and go
home!"
[7]And the man jumped up and went home! [8]Fear
swept through the crowd as they saw this happen.
And they praised God for sending a man with such
great authority.*

MARK 2:1-12

When Jesus returned to Capernaum several days
later, the news spread quickly that he was back home.
[2]Soon the house where he was staying was so packed
with visitors that there was no more room, even outside the door. While he was preaching God's word
to them, [3]four men arrived carrying a paralyzed man
on a mat. [4]They couldn't bring him to Jesus because
of the crowd, so they dug a hole through the roof
above his head. Then they lowered the man on his
mat, right down in front of Jesus. [5]Seeing their faith,
Jesus said to the paralyzed man, "My child, your sins
are forgiven."

Mt 9:8 Greek *for giving such authority to human beings.*

Mark 2:3 The paralyzed man's need moved his friends to action, and they brought him to Jesus. When you recognize someone's need, do you act? Many people have physical and spiritual needs you can meet, either by yourself or with others who are also concerned. Human need moved these four men; let it also move you to compassionate action.

Mark 2:4 The crowd that had gathered made it impossible to bring the paralyzed man close to Jesus. Successful churches or busy Christians can be oblivious to needy people who want to see Jesus. In some churches, if the crowd is too thick or too disinterested, a needy person will simply wander away. How sad when the people in a church are so preoccupied with their own relationships and agendas that they don't even see those who are trying to get in. That should never happen. Where Jesus is present, may the faces of the faithful reflect his love, may their hands extend to greet all newcomers and seekers as friends, and may they open a way for others to come in.

Mark 2:4 Houses in Bible times were built of stone. They had flat roofs made of mud mixed with straw. Outside stairways led to the roofs. These friends may have carried the paralyzed man up the outside stairs to the roof. They then could easily have taken apart the mud and straw mixture to make a hole through which to lower their friend to Jesus.

PROMINENT JEWISH RELIGIOUS AND POLITICAL GROUPS

Name and selected references	*Description*	*Agreement with Jesus*	*Disagreement with Jesus*
PHARISEES Matt 5:20 Matt 23:1-36 Luke 6:2 Luke 7:36-47	Strict group of religious Jews who advocated obedience to the most minute portions of the Jewish law and traditions. Very influential in the synagogues.	Respect for the law, belief in the resurrection of the dead, committed to obeying God's will.	Rejected Jesus' claim to be the Messiah. Despised Jesus because he did not follow all their traditions and associated with notoriously wicked people.
SADDUCEES Matt 3:7 Matt 16:11-12 Mark 12:18	Wealthy, upper class, Jewish priestly party. Rejected the authority of the Scriptures beyond the five books of Moses. Profited from business in the Temple. They, along with the Pharisees, were one of the two major parties of the Jewish high council.	Showed great respect for the five books of Moses, as well as the sanctity of the Temple.	Denied the resurrection of the dead. Thought the Temple could also be used as a place to transact business.
TEACHERS OF RELIGIOUS LAW Matt 7:29 Mark 2:6 Mark 2:16	Professional interpreters of the law—who especially emphasized the traditions. Many teachers of religious law were Pharisees.	Respect for the law. Committed to obeying God.	Denied Jesus' authority to interpret the law. Rejected Jesus as the Messiah because he did not obey all of their traditions.
SUPPORTERS OF HEROD Matt 22:16 Mark 3:6 Mark 12:13	A Jewish political party of King Herod's supporters.	Unknown. In the Gospels they tried to trap Jesus with questions and plotted to kill him.	Afraid of Jesus causing political instability. Saw Jesus as a threat to their political future at a time when they were trying to regain from Rome some of their lost political power.
ZEALOTS Luke 6:15 Acts 1:13	A fiercely dedicated group of Jewish patriots determined to end Roman rule in Israel.	Concerned about the future of Israel. Believed in the Messiah but did not recognize Jesus as the one sent by God.	Believed that the Messiah must be a political leader who would deliver Israel from Roman occupation.
ESSENES none	Jewish monastic group practicing ritual purity and personal holiness.	Emphasized justice, honesty, commitment.	Believed ceremonial rituals made them righteous.

▶ **MARK 2:1-12 (cont.)**

6But some of the teachers of religious law who were
sitting there thought to themselves, 7"What is he saying? This is blasphemy! Only God can forgive sins!"
8Jesus knew immediately what they were thinking,
so he asked them, "Why do you question this in your
hearts? 9Is it easier to say to the paralyzed man 'Your
sins are forgiven,' or 'Stand up, pick up your mat, and
walk'? 10So I will prove to you that the Son of Man*
has the authority on earth to forgive sins." Then Jesus
turned to the paralyzed man and said, 11"Stand up,
pick up your mat, and go home!"
12And the man jumped up, grabbed his mat, and
walked out through the stunned onlookers. They were
all amazed and praised God, exclaiming, "We've never
seen anything like this before!"

LUKE 5:17-26

One day while Jesus was teaching, some Pharisees and teachers of religious law were sitting nearby. (It seemed that these men showed up from every village in all Galilee and Judea, as well as from Jerusalem.) And the Lord's healing power was strongly with Jesus.

18Some men came carrying a paralyzed man on a
sleeping mat. They tried to take him inside to Jesus,
19but they couldn't reach him because of the crowd.
So they went up to the roof and took off some tiles.
Then they lowered the sick man on his mat down
into the crowd, right in front of Jesus. 20Seeing their
faith, Jesus said to the man, "Young man, your sins
are forgiven."
21But the Pharisees and teachers of religious law
said to themselves, "Who does he think he is? That's
blasphemy! Only God can forgive sins!"
22Jesus knew what they were thinking, so he asked
them, "Why do you question this in your hearts? 23Is it
easier to say 'Your sins are forgiven,' or 'Stand up and
walk'? 24So I will prove to you that the Son of Man*
has the authority on earth to forgive sins." Then Jesus
turned to the paralyzed man and said, "Stand up, pick
up your mat, and go home!"
25And immediately, as everyone watched, the man
jumped up, picked up his mat, and went home praising
God. 26Everyone was gripped with great wonder and
awe, and they praised God, exclaiming, "We have seen
amazing things today!"

Jesus Eats with Sinners at Matthew's House PARALLEL

MATTHEW 9:9-13

As Jesus was walking along, he saw a man named Matthew sitting at his tax collector's booth. "Follow me and be my disciple," Jesus said to him. So Matthew got up and followed him.

10Later, Matthew invited Jesus and his disciples to
his home as dinner guests, along with many tax collectors and other disreputable sinners. 11But when the

Mk 2:10 "Son of Man" is a title Jesus used for himself. Lk 5:24 "Son of Man" is a title Jesus used for himself.

Mark 2:6-7 The teachers of religious law were in a perfect position, sitting where they could observe and criticize. Some Christians follow their example. Is the music at church too fast or too loud? Is the sermon too long or too short? Do people aggravate you by sitting in your pew or dressing too casually? How much time do you spend worshiping in church and how much time do you spend complaining and criticizing? How about trying a little healthy activism—the kind that gets involved to work with fellow believers toward real progress on common goals, such as sharing the Good News, helping the needy, and building strong and caring disciples of Christ. Are you criticizing the church or changing the world?

Mark 2:8-11 Before saying, "Stand up" to the paralyzed man, Jesus said, "Your sins are forgiven." To the Jewish leaders this statement was blasphemous—claiming to do something only God can do. According to the law, the punishment for this sin was death (Lev 24:15-16). In labeling Jesus' claim to forgive sins as blasphemous, the religious leaders showed they did not understand that Jesus is God, and that he has God's power to heal both the body and the soul. Forgiveness of sins was a sign that the messianic age had come (Isa 40:2; Joel 2:32; Mic 7:18-19; Zech 13:1).

Mark 2:10 This is the first time Mark refers to Jesus as the "Son of Man," a title emphasizing that Jesus is fully human. The title "Son of God" (see, for example, John 20:31) emphasizes that he is fully God. As God's Son, Jesus has the authority to forgive sin and help us overcome it. As a man, he can identify with our deepest needs and sufferings (see also the note on Mark 8:31, p. 1377).

Luke 5:17 The religious leaders spent much time defining and discussing the huge body of religious tradition that had been accumulating for more than 400 years since the Jews' return from exile. They were so concerned with these man-made traditions, in fact, that they often lost sight of Scripture. Here these leaders felt threatened because Jesus challenged their sincerity and the people were flocking to him.

Luke 5:18-20 It wasn't the paralyzed man's faith that impressed Jesus but the faith of his friends. Jesus responded to their faith and healed the man. For better or worse, our faith affects others. We cannot make another person a Christian, but we can do much through our words, actions, and love to give him or her a chance to respond. Look for opportunities to bring your friends to the living Christ.

Luke 5:24 God offers the same forgiveness given to the paralytic to all who believe. Forgiveness means that a relationship has been renewed despite a wrong that has been done. But the act cannot be erased or changed. God's forgiveness, however, goes far beyond human forgiveness, for it includes the "putting away" of sin in two ways: (1) Both the law and justice are satisfied because Jesus paid the penalty that sin deserved; thus, sins can no longer be held against a believer. (2) The guilt caused by sin is removed and replaced with Christ's righteousness. Believers are so forgiven that, in God's eyes, it is as if they had never sinned. Do you carry a heavy burden for sins you have committed? Confess all to Christ and receive ultimate forgiveness.

Matt 9:9 Matthew was a Jew who was appointed by the Romans to be the area's tax collector. He collected taxes from the citizens as well as from merchants passing through town. Tax collectors were expected to take a commission on the taxes they collected, but most of them overcharged and kept the profits. Thus, tax collectors were hated by the Jews because of their reputation for cheating and because of their support of Rome.

Matt 9:9 When Jesus called Matthew to be one of his disciples, Matthew got up and followed, leaving a lucrative career. When God calls you to follow or obey him, do you do it with as much abandon as Matthew? Sometimes the decision to follow Christ requires difficult or painful choices. Like Matthew, we must decide to leave behind those things that would keep us from following Christ.

Pharisees saw this, they asked his disciples, "Why does
your teacher eat with such scum?*"
12 When Jesus heard this, he said, "Healthy people
don't need a doctor—sick people do." 13 Then he
added, "Now go and learn the meaning of this Scripture: 'I want you to show mercy, not offer sacrifices.'*
For I have come to call not those who think they are
righteous, but those who know they are sinners."

MARK 2:13-17

Then Jesus went out to the lakeshore again and
taught the crowds that were coming to him. 14 As
he walked along, he saw Levi son of Alphaeus sitting at his tax collector's booth. "Follow me and be
my disciple," Jesus said to him. So Levi got up and
followed him.
15 Later, Levi invited Jesus and his disciples to his
home as dinner guests, along with many tax collectors
and other disreputable sinners. (There were many
people of this kind among Jesus' followers.) 16 But
when the teachers of religious law who were Pharisees* saw him eating with tax collectors and other
sinners, they asked his disciples, "Why does he eat
with such scum?*"
17 When Jesus heard this, he told them, "Healthy
people don't need a doctor—sick people do. I have
come to call not those who think they are righteous,
but those who know they are sinners."

Mt 9:11 Greek *with tax collectors and sinners?* **Mt 9:13** Hos 6:6 (Greek version). **Mk 2:16a** Greek *the scribes of the Pharisees.* **Mk 2:16b** Greek *with tax collectors and sinners?*

MATTHEW

Matthew had a clear idea of how much it would cost to follow Jesus, yet he did not hesitate a moment. When he left his tax-collecting booth, he guaranteed himself unemployment. For several of the other disciples, there was always fishing to return to; but for Matthew, there was no turning back. • Two changes happened to Matthew when he decided to follow Jesus. First, Jesus gave him a new life. He not only belonged to a new group, but he also belonged to the Son of God. He was not just accepting a different way of life; he was now an accepted person. For a despised tax collector, that change must have been wonderful! Second, Jesus gave Matthew a new purpose for his skills. When he followed Jesus, the only tool he took from his past job was his pen. Jesus' call eventually allowed him to put his skills to their finest work. The Gospel that bears his name came as a result. • Each of us, from the beginning, is one of God's works in progress. Much of what God has for us he gives long before we are able to consciously respond to him. He trusts us with skills and abilities ahead of schedule. He has made each of us capable of being his servant. When we trust him with what he has given us, we begin a life of real adventure. Matthew couldn't have known that God would use the very skills he had sharpened as a tax collector to record the greatest story ever lived. And God has no less meaningful a purpose for each one of us. Have you recognized Jesus saying to you, "Follow me"? What has been your response?

Strengths and accomplishments	• Was one of Jesus' 12 disciples • Responded immediately to Jesus' call • Invited many friends to his home to meet Jesus • Authored the Gospel of Matthew • Clarified for his Jewish audience Jesus' fulfillment of Old Testament prophecies
Lessons from his life	• Jesus accepts people from every level of society • With new life, our God-given skills can be put to a greater purpose
Vital statistics	• Where: Capernaum • Occupations: Tax collector, disciple of Jesus • Relative: Father: Alphaeus • Contemporaries: Jesus, Pilate, Herod, other disciples
Key verse	"As Jesus was walking along, he saw a man named Matthew sitting at his tax collector's booth. 'Follow me and be my disciple,' Jesus said to him. So Matthew got up and followed him" (Matt 9:9).

Matthew's story is told in the Gospels. He is also mentioned in Acts 1:13.

Matt 9:10-13 When he visited Matthew, Jesus hurt his own reputation among the religious elites in order to reach out to those who were lost. Matthew's reputation hadn't yet caught up with his new life as a disciple, but he became a bridge for Jesus' message to Matthew's past associates. We should not be afraid to reach out to people who are living in sin. God's message changes people—and their friends, too!

Matt 9:11-12 The Pharisees constantly tried to trap Jesus, and they thought his association with these "lowlifes" was the perfect opportunity. They were more concerned with their own appearance of holiness than with helping people, with criticism than encouragement, with outward respectability than practical help. But God is concerned for all people, including the sinful and hurting ones. The Christian life is not a popularity contest! Following Jesus' example, we should share the Good News with the poor, immoral, lonely, and outcast, not just the rich, moral, popular, and powerful.

Matt 9:13 Those who are sure that they are good enough can't be saved because the first step in following Jesus is acknowledging our need and admitting that we don't have all the answers. For more on "I want you to show mercy, not offer sacrifices," see the chart on p. 809.

Mark 2:14 Levi is another name for Matthew, the disciple who wrote the Gospel of Matthew. See Matthew's Profile above for more information.

Mark 2:14 Capernaum (Mark 2:1) was a key military center for Roman troops as well as a thriving business community. Several major highways intersected in Capernaum, with merchants passing through from as far away as Egypt to the south and Mesopotamia to the north.

Mark 2:16-17 The self-righteous Pharisees were indignant that Jesus would eat a meal with such sinners. But Jesus gladly associated with sinners because he loved them and knew that they needed to hear what he had to say. Jesus spent time with whoever needed or wanted to hear his message—poor, rich, bad, good. We, too, must befriend those who need Christ, even if they do not seem to be ideal companions. Are there people you have been neglecting because of their reputation? They may be the ones who most need to see and hear the message of Christ's love in and from you.

LUKE 5:27-32
Later, as Jesus left the town, he saw a tax collector
named Levi sitting at his tax collector's booth. "Follow
me and be my disciple," Jesus said to him. 28So Levi
got up, left everything, and followed him.
29Later, Levi held a banquet in his home with Jesus
as the guest of honor. Many of Levi's fellow tax collectors and other guests also ate with them. 30But the
Pharisees and their teachers of religious law complained bitterly to Jesus' disciples, "Why do you eat
and drink with such scum?*"
31Jesus answered them, "Healthy people don't need
a doctor—sick people do. 32I have come to call not
those who think they are righteous, but those who
know they are sinners and need to repent."

Religious Leaders Ask Jesus about Fasting PARALLEL

MATTHEW 9:14-17
One day the disciples of John the Baptist came to Jesus
and asked him, "Why don't your disciples fast* like we
do and the Pharisees do?"
15Jesus replied, "Do wedding guests mourn while
celebrating with the groom? Of course not. But someday the groom will be taken away from them, and
then they will fast.
16"Besides, who would patch old clothing with new
cloth? For the new patch would shrink and rip away
from the old cloth, leaving an even bigger tear than
before.
17"And no one puts new wine into old wineskins.
For the old skins would burst from the pressure,
spilling the wine and ruining the skins. New wine
is stored in new wineskins so that both are preserved."

MARK 2:18-22
Once when John's disciples and the Pharisees were
fasting, some people came to Jesus and asked, "Why
don't your disciples fast like John's disciples and the
Pharisees do?"
19Jesus replied, "Do wedding guests fast while celebrating with the groom? Of course not. They can't
fast while the groom is with them. 20But someday the
groom will be taken away from them, and then they
will fast.
21"Besides, who would patch old clothing with new
cloth? For the new patch would shrink and rip away
from the old cloth, leaving an even bigger tear than
before.
22"And no one puts new wine into old wineskins.
For the wine would burst the wineskins, and the wine
and the skins would both be lost. New wine calls for
new wineskins."

Lk 5:30 Greek *with tax collectors and sinners?* **Mt 9:14** Some manuscripts read *fast often.*

Luke 5:28-29 Levi left a lucrative, though probably dishonest, tax-collecting business to follow Jesus. Then he responded as Jesus would want all his followers to do. He held a banquet for his fellow tax collectors and other notorious "sinners" so they could meet Jesus too. Levi, who left behind a material fortune in order to gain a spiritual fortune, was proud to be associated with Jesus.

Luke 5:30-32 The Pharisees wrapped their sin in respectability. They made themselves appear good by publicly doing good deeds and pointing at the sins of others. Jesus chose to spend time not with these proud, self-righteous religious leaders, but with people who sensed their own sin and knew that they were not good enough for God. In order to come to God, we must repent; in order to renounce our sin, we must first acknowledge it.

Matt 9:14 John's disciples fasted (went without food) as a sign of mourning for sin and preparation for the Messiah's coming. Jesus' disciples did not need to fast because he is the Messiah and was with them! Jesus did not condemn fasting—he himself fasted (Matt 4:2). He emphasized that fasting must be done for the right reasons.

Matt 9:14 John the Baptist's message was harsh, and it focused on the law. When people look at God's law and compare themselves to it, they realize how far they fall short and how badly they need to repent. Jesus' message focused on life, the result of turning from sin and turning to him. John's disciples had the right start, but they needed to take the next step and trust in Jesus. Where is your focus—on the law or on Christ?

Matt 9:15 The arrival of the Kingdom of Heaven was like a wedding feast with Jesus as the groom. His disciples, therefore, were filled with joy. It would not be right to mourn or fast when the groom was present.

Matt 9:17 In Bible times wine was not kept in glass bottles but in goatskins sewn around the edges to form watertight bags. New wine expanded as it fermented, stretching its wineskin. After the wine had aged, the stretched skin would burst if more new wine was poured into it. New wine, therefore, was always put into new wineskins.

Jesus used this description to explain that he had not come to patch up the old religious system of Judaism with its rules and traditions. His purpose was to bring in something new, though it had been prophesied for centuries. This new message, the Good News, said that Jesus Christ, God's Son, came to earth to offer all people forgiveness of sins and reconciliation with God. The Good News did not fit into the old rigid legalistic system of religion. It needed a fresh start. The message will always remain "new" because it must be accepted and applied in every generation. When we follow Christ, we must be prepared for new ways to live, new ways to look at people, and new ways to serve.

Mark 2:18ff John the Baptist had two goals: to lead people to repent of their sin, and to prepare them for Christ's coming. John's message was sobering, so he and his followers fasted. Fasting is both an outward sign of humility and regret for sin, and an inner discipline that clears the mind and keeps the spirit alert. Fasting empties the body of food; repentance empties the life of sin. Jesus' disciples did not need to fast to prepare for his coming because he was already with them. But he did not condemn fasting. He himself fasted for 40 days (Matt 4:2). Nevertheless, Jesus emphasized fasting with the right motives. The Pharisees fasted twice a week to show others how holy they were. Jesus explained that if people fast only to impress others, they will be twisting the purpose of fasting (Matt 5:16-18).

Mark 2:19 Jesus compared himself to a groom. In the Bible, the image of a bride is often used for God's people and the image of a groom for the God who loves them (Isa 62:5; Matt 25:1-13; Rev 21:2).

Mark 2:22 The Pharisees had become rigid, like old wineskins. They could not accept faith in Jesus that would not be contained by man-made ideas or rules. Our hearts, like a wineskin, can become rigid and prevent us from accepting the new life that Christ offers. Keep your heart pliable and open to accepting the life-changing truths of Christ.

LUKE 5:33-39
One day some people said to Jesus, "John the Baptist's
disciples fast and pray regularly, and so do the disciples of the Pharisees. Why are your disciples always
eating and drinking?"
34Jesus responded, "Do wedding guests fast while
celebrating with the groom? Of course not. 35But
someday the groom will be taken away from them,
and then they will fast."
36Then Jesus gave them this illustration: "No one
tears a piece of cloth from a new garment and uses it
to patch an old garment. For then the new garment
would be ruined, and the new patch wouldn't even
match the old garment.
37"And no one puts new wine into old wineskins.
For the new wine would burst the wineskins, spilling
the wine and ruining the skins. 38New wine must be
stored in new wineskins. 39But no one who drinks the
old wine seems to want the new wine. 'The old is just
fine,' they say."

Jesus Heals a Lame Man by a Pool

JOHN 5:1-15
Afterward Jesus returned to Jerusalem for one
of the Jewish holy days. 2Inside the city, near the
Sheep Gate, was the pool of Bethesda,* with five
covered porches. 3Crowds of sick people—blind,
lame, or paralyzed—lay on the porches.* 5One of
the men lying there had been sick for thirty-eight
years. 6When Jesus saw him and knew he had been
ill for a long time, he asked him, "Would you like
to get well?"
7"I can't, sir," the sick man said, "for I have no one
to put me into the pool when the water bubbles up.
Someone else always gets there ahead of me."
8Jesus told him, "Stand up, pick up your mat, and
walk!"
9Instantly, the man was healed! He rolled up his
sleeping mat and began walking! But this miracle
happened on the Sabbath, 10so the Jewish leaders
objected. They said to the man who was cured, "You
can't work on the Sabbath! The law doesn't allow you
to carry that sleeping mat!"
11But he replied, "The man who healed me told me,
'Pick up your mat and walk.'"
12"Who said such a thing as that?" they demanded.
13The man didn't know, for Jesus had disappeared
into the crowd. 14But afterward Jesus found him in
the Temple and told him, "Now you are well; so stop
sinning, or something even worse may happen to you."

Jn 5:2 Other manuscripts read *Beth-zatha;* still others read *Bethsaida.* **Jn 5:3** Some manuscripts add an expanded conclusion to verse 3 and all of verse 4: *waiting for a certain movement of the water, 4for an angel of the Lord came from time to time and stirred up the water. And the first person to step in after the water was stirred was healed of whatever disease he had.*

Luke 5:35 Jesus knew his death was coming. After that time, fasting would be in order. Although he was fully human, Jesus knew he was God and why he had come—to die for the sins of the world.

Luke 5:36-39 Like old wineskins, the Pharisees were too rigid to accept Jesus, who could not be contained in their traditions or rules. Christianity required new approaches, new traditions, new structures. Our church programs and ministries should not be so structured that they have no room for a fresh touch of the Spirit, a new method, or a new idea. We, too, must be careful that our hearts do not become rigid, hindering us from accepting new ways of thinking that Christ brings. We need to keep our hearts pliable so we can accept Jesus' life-changing message.

John 5:1 Three festivals (or "holy days") required all Jewish males to come to Jerusalem: (1) the Festivals of Passover and Unleavened Bread, (2) the Festival of Pentecost (also called the Festival of Harvest or the Festival of Weeks), and (3) the Festival of Shelters.

John 5:6 After 38 years, this man's problem had become a way of life. No one had ever helped him. He had no hope of ever being healed. The man's situation looked hopeless. But no matter how trapped you feel in your infirmities, God can minister to your deepest needs. Don't let a problem or hardship cause you to lose hope. God may have special work for you to do in spite of your condition, or even because of it. Many have ministered effectively to hurting people because they have triumphed over their own hurts.

John 5:10 According to the Pharisees, carrying a mat on the Sabbath was work and was therefore unlawful. It did not break an Old Testament law, but it broke the Pharisees' interpretation of God's command to "remember to observe the Sabbath day by keeping it holy" (Exod 20:8). This was just one of hundreds of rules they had added to the Old Testament law.

John 5:10 A man who hadn't walked for 38 years had been healed, but the Pharisees were more concerned about their petty rules than the life and health of a human being. The Jewish leaders saw both a mighty miracle of healing and a broken rule. They threw the miracle aside and focused on the broken rule, which was more important to them than the miracle. It is easy to get so caught up in our man-made structures and rules that we forget the people involved. Are your guidelines for living God-made or man-made? Are they helping people, or have they become needless stumbling blocks?

John 5:14 This man had been lame or paralyzed, and suddenly he could walk. This was a great miracle. But he needed an even greater miracle—to have his sins forgiven. The man was delighted to be physically healed, but he had to turn from his sins and seek God's forgiveness to be spiritually healed. God's forgiveness is the greatest gift you will ever receive. Don't neglect his gracious offer.

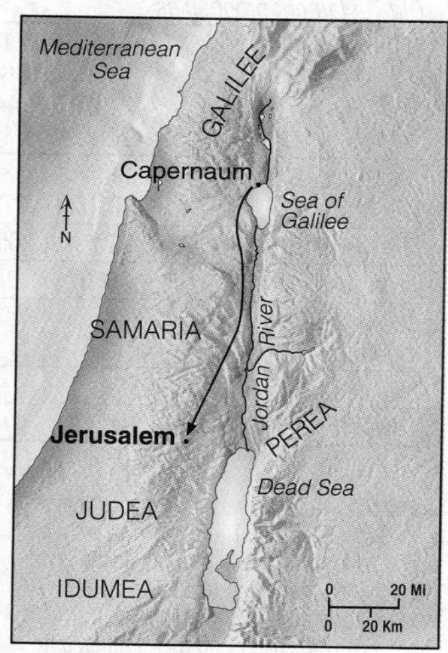

JESUS TEACHES IN JERUSALEM
After Jesus ministered throughout Galilee, especially in Capernaum, he headed down to Jerusalem for an annual festival (John 5:1). Early in his ministry, he had called certain men to follow him, but it wasn't until after this trip to Jerusalem that he chose his 12 disciples from among them.

▶ **JOHN 5:1-15** ***(cont.)***
15Then the man went and told the Jewish leaders that it was Jesus who had healed him.

Jesus Claims to Be the Son of God

JOHN 5:16-30
So the Jewish leaders began harassing* Jesus for breaking the Sabbath rules. 17But Jesus replied, "My Father is
always working, and so am I." 18So the Jewish leaders
tried all the harder to find a way to kill him. For he
not only broke the Sabbath, he called God his Father,
thereby making himself equal with God.
19So Jesus explained, "I tell you the truth, the Son
can do nothing by himself. He does only what he sees
the Father doing. Whatever the Father does, the Son
also does. 20For the Father loves the Son and shows
him everything he is doing. In fact, the Father will
show him how to do even greater works than healing
this man. Then you will truly be astonished. 21For just
as the Father gives life to those he raises from the dead,
so the Son gives life to anyone he wants. 22In addition,
the Father judges no one. Instead, he has given the Son
absolute authority to judge, 23so that everyone will
honor the Son, just as they honor the Father. Anyone
who does not honor the Son is certainly not honoring
the Father who sent him.
24"I tell you the truth, those who listen to my message and believe in God who sent me have eternal life.
They will never be condemned for their sins, but they
have already passed from death into life.
25"And I assure you that the time is coming, indeed
it's here now, when the dead will hear my voice—the
voice of the Son of God. And those who listen will live.
26The Father has life in himself, and he has granted
that same life-giving power to his Son. 27And he has
given him authority to judge everyone because he is

Jn 5:16 Or *persecuting.*

THE CLAIMS OF CHRIST

Those who read the life of Christ are faced with one unavoidable question: Was Jesus God? Part of any reasonable conclusion has to include the fact that he did claim to be God. We have no other choice but to agree or disagree with his claim. Eternal life is at stake in the choice.

Jesus claimed to be:	**Matthew**	**Mark**	**Luke**	**John**
The fulfillment of Old Testament prophecies	5:17; 26:31, 53-56	14:21	4:16-21; 7:18-23; 18:31; 22:37; 24:44	2:22; 5:45-47; 6:45; 7:40; 10:34-36; 13:18; 15:25; 20:9
The Son of Man	8:20; 12:8; 16:27; 19:28; 20:18-19; 24:27, 30, 44; 25:31; 26:2, 45, 64	2:10; 8:31, 38; 9:9; 10:45; 14:41, 62	6:22; 7:33-34; 12:8-10; 17:22-26, 30; 18:8, 31; 19:10; 21:36	1:51; 3:13-14; 6:27, 53, 62; 12:23-34
The Son of God	11:27; 14:33; 16:16-17; 27:43	3:11-12; 14:61-62	8:28; 10:22	1:18; 3:35-36; 5:18-28; 6:40; 10:36; 11:4; 17:1; 19:7
The Messiah/the Christ	23:8-10; 26:63-64	8:29-30	4:41; 23:1-2; 24:25-27	4:25-26; 10:24-25; 11:27
Teacher/Master	26:18			13:13-14
One with authority to forgive		2:5-12	7:48-49	
Lord		5:19		13:13-14; 20:28-29
Savior			19:10	3:17; 10:9

John 5:17ff Jesus was identifying himself with God, his Father. There could be no doubt as to his claim to be God. Jesus does not leave us the option to believe in God while ignoring God's Son (John 5:23). The Pharisees also called God their Father, but they realized Jesus was claiming a unique relationship with him. In response to Jesus' claim, the Pharisees had two choices: to believe him, or to accuse him of blasphemy. They chose the second.

John 5:17 If God stopped every kind of work on the Sabbath, nature would fall into chaos, and sin would overrun the world. Genesis 2:2 says that God rested on the seventh day, but this can't mean that he stopped doing good. Jesus wanted to teach that when the opportunity to do good presents itself, it should not be ignored, even on the Sabbath.

John 5:19-23 Because of his unity with God, Jesus lived as God wanted him to live. Because of our identification with Jesus, we must honor him and live as he wants us to live. The question "What would Jesus do?" may help us make the right choices.

John 5:24 Eternal life—living forever with God—begins when you accept Jesus Christ as Savior. At that moment, new life begins in you (2 Cor 5:17). It is a completed transaction. You still will face physical death, but when Christ returns again, your body will be resurrected to live forever (1 Cor 15).

John 5:25 In saying that the dead will hear his voice, Jesus was talking about the spiritually dead who hear, understand, and accept him. Those who accept Jesus, the Word, will have eternal life. Jesus was also talking about the physically dead. He raised several dead people while he was on earth, and at his second coming, "the Christians who have died" will rise to meet him (1 Thes 4:16).

John 5:26 God is the source and creator of life, for there is no life apart from God, here or hereafter. The life in us is a gift from him (see Deut 30:20; Ps 36:9). Because Jesus has eternally existed with God, he, too, is "the life" (John 14:6) through whom we may live eternally (see 1 Jn 5:11).

John 5:27 The Old Testament mentioned three signs of the coming Messiah. In this chapter, John shows that Jesus has fulfilled all three signs. Authority to judge is given to the Son of Man.* [28]Don't be so surprised! Indeed, the time is coming when all the dead in their graves will hear the voice of God's Son, [29]and they will rise again. Those who have done good will rise to experience eternal life, and those who have continued in evil will rise to experience judgment. [30]I can do nothing on my own. I judge as God tells me. Therefore, my judgment is just, because I carry out the will of the one who sent me, not my own will.

Jesus Supports His Claim

JOHN 5:31-47

"If I were to testify on my own behalf, my testimony would not be valid. [32]But someone else is also testifying about me, and I assure you that everything he says about me is true. [33]In fact, you sent investigators to listen to John the Baptist, and his testimony about me was true. [34]Of course, I have no need of human witnesses, but I say these things so you might be saved. [35]John was like a burning and shining lamp, and you were excited for a while about his message. [36]But I have a greater witness than John—my teachings and my miracles. The Father gave me these works to accomplish, and they prove that he sent me. [37]And the Father who sent me has testified about me himself. You have never heard his voice or seen him face to face, [38]and you do not have his message in your hearts, because you do not believe me—the one he sent to you.

[39]"You search the Scriptures because you think they give you eternal life. But the Scriptures point to me! [40]Yet you refuse to come to me to receive this life.

[41]"Your approval means nothing to me, [42]because I know you don't have God's love within you. [43]For I have come to you in my Father's name, and you have rejected me. Yet if others come in their own name, you gladly welcome them. [44]No wonder you can't believe! For you gladly honor each other, but you don't care about the honor that comes from the one who alone is God.*

[45]"Yet it isn't I who will accuse you before the Father. Moses will accuse you! Yes, Moses, in whom you put your hopes. [46]If you really believed Moses, you would believe me, because he wrote about me. [47]But since you don't believe what he wrote, how will you believe what I say?"

The Disciples Pick Wheat on the Sabbath PARALLEL •••

MATTHEW 12:1-8 •••

At about that time Jesus was walking through some grainfields on the Sabbath. His disciples were hungry, so they began breaking off some heads of grain and eating them. [2]But some Pharisees saw them do it and protested, "Look, your disciples are breaking the law by harvesting grain on the Sabbath."

[3]Jesus said to them, "Haven't you read in the Scriptures what David did when he and his companions were hungry? [4]He went into the house of God, and he and his companions broke the law by eating the sacred loaves of bread that only the priests are allowed to eat. [5]And haven't you read in the law of Moses that the priests on duty in the Temple may work on the Sabbath? [6]I tell you, there is one here who is even greater

Jn 5:27 "Son of Man" is a title Jesus used for himself. **Jn 5:44** Some manuscripts read *from the only One.*

---

him as the Son of Man (cf. John 5:27 with Dan 7:13-14). The lame and sick are healed (cf. John 5:20-21 with Isa 35:6; Jer 31:8-9). The dead are raised to life (cf. John 5:21, 28 with Deut 32:39; 1 Sam 2:6; 2 Kgs 5:7).

John 5:29 Those who have rebelled against Christ will be resurrected too, but they will hear God's judgment against them and will be sentenced to eternity apart from him. There are those who wish to live well on earth, ignore God, and then see death as final rest. Jesus does not allow unbelieving people to see death as the end of it all. There is a judgment to face.

John 5:31ff Jesus claimed to be equal with God (John 5:18), to give eternal life (John 5:24), to be the source of life (John 5:26), and to judge sin (John 5:27). These statements make it clear that Jesus was claiming to be divine—an almost unbelievable claim, but one that was supported by another witness, John the Baptist.

John 5:39-40 The religious leaders knew what the Bible said but failed to apply its words to their lives. They knew the teachings of the Scriptures but failed to see the Messiah to whom the Scriptures pointed. They knew the rules but missed the Savior. Entrenched in their own religious system, they refused to let the Son of God change their lives. Don't become so involved in "religion" that you miss Christ.

John 5:41 Whose praise do you seek? The religious leaders enjoyed great prestige in Israel, but their stamp of approval meant nothing to Jesus. He was concerned about God's approval. This is a good principle for us. If even the highest officials in the world approve of our actions and God does not, we should be concerned. But if God approves, even though others don't, we should be content.

John 5:45 The Pharisees prided themselves on being the true followers of their ancestor Moses. They were trying to follow every one of his laws to the letter, and they even added some of their own. Jesus' warning that Moses would accuse them stung them to fury. Moses wrote about Jesus (Gen 3:15; Num 21:9; 24:17; Deut 18:15), yet the religious leaders refused to believe Jesus when he came.

Matt 12:4 This story is recorded in 1 Samuel 21:1-6. The Bread of the Presence was replaced every week, and the old loaves were eaten by the priests. The loaves given to David were the old loaves that had just been replaced with fresh ones. Although the priests were the only ones allowed to eat this bread, God did not punish David because his need for food was more important than the priestly regulations. Jesus was saying, "If you condemn me, you must also condemn David," something the religious leaders could never do without causing a great uproar among the people. Jesus was not condoning disobedience to God's laws. Instead, he was emphasizing discernment and compassion in enforcing the laws.

Matt 12:5 The Ten Commandments require that the Sabbath be kept holy (Exod 20:8-11). The Pharisees had interpreted that as a long list of actions that could not be done on the Sabbath, forcing the people to "rest." That was the letter of the law. But because the purpose of the Sabbath is to rest and to worship God, the priests were allowed to work by performing sacrifices and conducting worship services. This "Sabbath work" was serving and worshiping God. Jesus always emphasized the intent of the law, the meaning behind the letter. The Pharisees had lost the spirit of the law and were rigidly demanding that the letter (and their interpretation of it) be obeyed.

MATTHEW 12:1-8 *(cont.)*
than the Temple! 7But you would not have condemned
my innocent disciples if you knew the meaning of
this Scripture: 'I want you to show mercy, not offer
sacrifices.'* 8For the Son of Man* is Lord, even over
the Sabbath!"

MARK 2:23-28
One Sabbath day as Jesus was walking through some
grainfields, his disciples began breaking off heads of
grain to eat. 24But the Pharisees said to Jesus, "Look,
why are they breaking the law by harvesting grain on
the Sabbath?"
25Jesus said to them, "Haven't you ever read in the
Scriptures what David did when he and his companions were hungry? 26He went into the house of God
(during the days when Abiathar was high priest) and
broke the law by eating the sacred loaves of bread that
only the priests are allowed to eat. He also gave some
to his companions."
27Then Jesus said to them, "The Sabbath was made
to meet the needs of people, and not people to meet
the requirements of the Sabbath. 28So the Son of Man
is Lord, even over the Sabbath!"

LUKE 6:1-5
One Sabbath day as Jesus was walking through some
grainfields, his disciples broke off heads of grain,
rubbed off the husks in their hands, and ate the grain.
2But some Pharisees said, "Why are you breaking the
law by harvesting grain on the Sabbath?"
3Jesus replied, "Haven't you read in the Scriptures
what David did when he and his companions were
hungry? 4He went into the house of God and broke the
law by eating the sacred loaves of bread that only the
priests can eat. He also gave some to his companions."
5And Jesus added, "The Son of Man* is Lord, even over
the Sabbath."

Jesus Heals a Man's Hand on the Sabbath PARALLEL

MATTHEW 12:9-14
Then Jesus went over to their synagogue, 10where he
noticed a man with a deformed hand. The Pharisees
asked Jesus, "Does the law permit a person to work by
healing on the Sabbath?" (They were hoping he would
say yes, so they could bring charges against him.)
11And he answered, "If you had a sheep that fell

Mt 12:7 Hos 6:6 (Greek version). **Mt 12:8** "Son of Man" is a title Jesus used for himself. **Lk 6:5** "Son of Man" is a title Jesus used for himself.

Matt 12:6 The Pharisees were so concerned about religious rituals that they missed the whole purpose of the Temple—to bring people to God. And because Jesus Christ is even greater than the Temple, he is that much greater at bringing people to God! God is far more important than the created instruments of worship. If we become more concerned with the means of worship than the one we worship, we will miss God even as we think we are worshiping him.

Matt 12:7 Jesus repeated to the Pharisees words the Jewish people had heard time and again throughout their history (1 Sam 15:22-23; Ps 40:6-8; Isa 1:11-17; Jer 7:21-23; Hos 6:6). Our heart attitude toward God comes first. Only then can we properly obey and observe religious regulations and rituals.

Matt 12:8 When Jesus said he was master of the Sabbath, he claimed to be greater than the law and above the law. To the Pharisees, this was heresy. They did not realize that Jesus, the divine Son of God, had created the Sabbath. The Creator is always greater than his creation; thus, Jesus had the authority to overrule their traditions and regulations.

Mark 2:23 Jesus and his disciples were not stealing when they picked the grain. Leviticus 19:9-10 and Deuteronomy 23:25 say that farmers were to leave the edges of their fields unharvested so that some of their crops could be picked by travelers and by the poor. Just as walking on a sidewalk is not trespassing on private property, so picking heads of grain at the edge of a field was not stealing.

Mark 2:24 God's law said that crops should not be harvested on the Sabbath (Exod 34:21). This law prevented farmers from becoming greedy and ignoring God on the Sabbath. It also protected laborers from being overworked.

The Pharisees interpreted the action of Jesus and his disciples—picking the grain and eating it as they walked through the fields—as harvesting; and so they judged Jesus a lawbreaker. But Jesus and the disciples clearly were not harvesting the grain for personal gain; they were simply looking for something to eat. The Pharisees were so focused on the words of the rule that they missed its intent.

Mark 2:25-28 Jesus used the example of David to point out how ridiculous the Pharisees' accusations were. God created the Sabbath for our benefit; we are restored both physically and spiritually when we take time to rest and to focus on God. For the Pharisees, Sabbath rules had become more important than Sabbath rest. Both David and Jesus understood that the intent of God's law is to promote love for God and others.

The Christian faith involves many rules that are meant to be governed by love. That makes love the highest rule, but it also moves Christians toward personal sacrifice, discipline, and responsibility—scarce resources in today's world. When confronted with rules of your own or others' making, ask: (1) Does the rule serve God's purposes? (2) Does the rule reveal God's character? (3) Does the rule help people get into God's family or keep them out? (4) Does the rule have biblical roots that can be supported in the context of all of Scripture? Good rules pass all four tests.

Mark 2:26 The "sacred loaves of bread" (called the Bread of the Presence) were set before God on a table in the Holy Place in the Tabernacle (and later in the Temple). Every Sabbath, 12 freshly baked loaves of bread were set out, and the priests ate the old loaves. See Exodus 25:30 and Leviticus 24:5-9 for more about the Bread of the Presence.

Luke 6:1-2 The Pharisees had established 39 categories of actions forbidden on the Sabbath, based on interpretations of God's law and on Jewish custom. Harvesting was one of those forbidden actions. By picking wheat and rubbing it in their hands, the disciples were technically harvesting, according to the Pharisees. Jesus and the disciples were picking grain because they were hungry, not because they wanted to harvest the grain for a profit. They were not working on the Sabbath. The Pharisees, however, could not (and did not want to) see beyond their law's technicalities. They had no room for compassion, and they were determined to accuse Jesus of wrongdoing.

Matt 12:10-12 The Pharisees placed their laws above human need. They were so concerned about Jesus breaking one of their rules that they did not care about the man's deformed hand. What is your attitude toward others? If your convictions don't allow you to help certain people, your convictions may not be in tune with God's Word. Don't allow rule keeping to blind you to human need.

Matt 12:10 As they pointed to the man with the deformed hand, the Pharisees tried to trick Jesus by asking him if it was legal to heal on the Sabbath. Their Sabbath rules

into a well on the Sabbath, wouldn't you work to pull
it out? Of course you would. 12And how much more
valuable is a person than a sheep! Yes, the law permits
a person to do good on the Sabbath."
13Then he said to the man, "Hold out your hand." So
the man held out his hand, and it was restored, just like
the other one! 14Then the Pharisees called a meeting
to plot how to kill Jesus.

MARK 3:1-6

Jesus went into the synagogue again and noticed a man
with a deformed hand. 2Since it was the Sabbath, Jesus'
enemies watched him closely. If he healed the man's
hand, they planned to accuse him of working on the
Sabbath.
3Jesus said to the man with the deformed hand,
"Come and stand in front of everyone." 4Then he
turned to his critics and asked, "Does the law permit
good deeds on the Sabbath, or is it a day for doing
evil? Is this a day to save life or to destroy it?" But they
wouldn't answer him.
5He looked around at them angrily and was deeply
saddened by their hard hearts. Then he said to the
man, "Hold out your hand." So the man held out his
hand, and it was restored! 6At once the Pharisees went
away and met with the supporters of Herod to plot
how to kill Jesus.

LUKE 6:6-11

On another Sabbath day, a man with a deformed right
hand was in the synagogue while Jesus was teaching. 7The teachers of religious law and the Pharisees
watched Jesus closely. If he healed the man's hand, they
planned to accuse him of working on the Sabbath.
8But Jesus knew their thoughts. He said to the man
with the deformed hand, "Come and stand in front
of everyone." So the man came forward. 9Then Jesus
said to his critics, "I have a question for you. Does the
law permit good deeds on the Sabbath, or is it a day
for doing evil? Is this a day to save life or to destroy it?"
10He looked around at them one by one and then
said to the man, "Hold out your hand." So the man
held out his hand, and it was restored! 11At this, the
enemies of Jesus were wild with rage and began to
discuss what to do with him.

Large Crowds Follow Jesus PARALLEL

MATTHEW 12:15-21

But Jesus knew what they were planning. So he left
that area, and many people followed him. He healed

---

said that people could be helped on the Sabbath only if their lives were in danger. Jesus healed on the Sabbath several times, and none of those healings were in response to emergencies. If Jesus had waited until another day, he would have been submitting to the Pharisees' authority, showing that their petty rules were equal to God's law. If he healed the man on the Sabbath, the Pharisees could claim that because Jesus broke their rules, his power was not from God. But Jesus made it clear how ridiculous and petty their rules were. God is a God of people, not rules. The best time to reach out is when someone needs help.

Matt 12:14 The Pharisees plotted Jesus' death because they were proud, fearful, and outraged. Jesus had overruled their authority (Luke 6:11) and had exposed their evil attitudes in front of the entire crowd in the synagogue. Jesus had shown that the Pharisees were more loyal to their religious system than to God.

Mark 3:2 Already many of the religious leaders had turned against Jesus and become his "enemies." They were jealous of his popularity, his miracles, and the authority in his teaching and actions. They valued their status in the community and their opportunity for personal gain so much that they lost sight of their goal as religious leaders—to point people toward God. Of all people, the Pharisees should have recognized the Messiah, but they refused to acknowledge him because they were not willing to give up their treasured position and power. When Jesus exposed their attitudes, he became their enemy instead of their Messiah, and they began looking for ways to turn the people against him.

Mark 3:5 Jesus was angry about the Pharisees' uncaring attitudes. Anger itself is not wrong. It depends on what makes us angry and what we do with our anger. Too often we express our anger in selfish and harmful ways. By contrast, Jesus expressed his anger by correcting a problem—healing the man's hand. Use your anger to find constructive solutions rather than to tear people down.

Mark 3:6 The Pharisees were a Jewish religious group that zealously followed the Old Testament laws as well as their own religious traditions. They were highly respected in the community, but they hated Jesus because he challenged their proud attitudes and dishonorable motives. The supporters of Herod were a Jewish political party that hoped to restore Herod the Great's line to the throne. Jesus was a threat to them as well because he challenged their political ambitions. These two groups were normally at odds, but they joined forces against Jesus.

Mark 3:6 The Pharisees had accused Jesus of breaking their law that said medical attention could be given to no one on the Sabbath except in matters of life and death. Ironically, the Pharisees themselves were breaking God's law by plotting murder.

Luke 6:6-7 According to the tradition of the religious leaders, no healing could be done on the Sabbath. Healing, they said, was practicing medicine, and people could not practice their professions on the Sabbath. The religious leaders were more concerned about protecting their traditions than freeing a person from painful suffering. They were more concerned with negatives: what rules should not be broken and what activities should not be done. Jesus was positive: doing good and helping those in need.

Which would an objective observer say is more characteristic of your Christianity—the positives or the negatives? Are you more concerned about what people shouldn't be doing than you are about advancing God's Kingdom? Is your way of being a Christian the only way? And what about your church? The Pharisees thought their religious system had all the answers. They could not accept Jesus because he did not fit into their system. Beware of thinking that you or your church has all the answers. No religious system is big enough to contain Christ completely or to fulfill perfectly all his desires for the world. Christianity is the most positive force to ever hit this planet. Make sure you don't let it degenerate into a bunch of negatives.

Luke 6:11 Jesus' enemies were furious. Not only had he read their minds; he also had flouted their traditions and exposed the hatred in their hearts. Ironically, their hatred, combined with their zeal for the law, drove them to plot murder—an act that was clearly against their law.

Matt 12:15 Up to this point, Jesus had been aggressively confronting the Pharisees' hypocrisy. Here he decided to withdraw from the synagogue before a major confrontation developed because it was not yet time for him to die. Jesus had many lessons still to teach his disciples and the people.

▸ MATTHEW 12:15-21 *(cont.)*

all the sick among them, [16]but he warned them not to reveal who he was. [17]This fulfilled the prophecy of Isaiah concerning him:

18 "Look at my Servant, whom I have chosen.
He is my Beloved, who pleases me.
I will put my Spirit upon him,
and he will proclaim justice to the nations.
19 He will not fight or shout
or raise his voice in public.
20 He will not crush the weakest reed
or put out a flickering candle.
Finally he will cause justice to be victorious.
21 And his name will be the hope
of all the world."*

MARK 3:7-12

Jesus went out to the lake with his disciples, and a large crowd followed him. They came from all over Galilee, Judea, [8]Jerusalem, Idumea, from east of the Jordan River, and even from as far north as Tyre and Sidon. The news about his miracles had spread far and wide, and vast numbers of people came to see him.

[9]Jesus instructed his disciples to have a boat ready so the crowd would not crush him. [10]He had healed many people that day, so all the sick people eagerly pushed forward to touch him. [11]And whenever those possessed by evil* spirits caught sight of him, the spirits would throw them to the ground in front of him shrieking, "You are the Son of God!" [12]But Jesus sternly commanded the spirits not to reveal who he was.

LUKE 6:17-19

When they came down from the mountain, the disciples stood with Jesus on a large, level area, surrounded by many of his followers and by the crowds. There were people from all over Judea and from Jerusalem and from as far north as the seacoasts of Tyre and Sidon. [18]They had come to hear him and to be healed of their diseases; and those troubled by evil* spirits were healed. [19]Everyone tried to touch him, because healing power went out from him, and he healed everyone.

Jesus Chooses the Twelve Disciples PARALLEL

MARK 3:13-19

Afterward Jesus went up on a mountain and called out the ones he wanted to go with him. And they came to him. [14]Then he appointed twelve of them and called them his apostles.* They were to accompany him, and he would send them out to preach, [15]giving them authority to cast out demons. [16]These are the twelve he chose:

Mt 12:18-21 Isa 42:1-4 (Greek version for 42:4). **Mk 3:11** Greek *unclean;* also in 3:30. **Lk 6:18** Greek *unclean.* **Mk 3:14** Some manuscripts do not include *and called them his apostles.*

Matt 12:16 Jesus did not want those he healed to tell others about his miracles because he didn't want people coming to him for the wrong reasons. That would hinder his teaching ministry and arouse false hopes about an earthly kingdom. But the news of Jesus' miracles spread anyway, and many came to see for themselves (see Mark 3:7-8).

Matt 12:17-21 The people expected the Messiah to be a king. This quotation from Isaiah's prophecy (Isa 42:1-4) showed that the Messiah was indeed a king, but it illustrated what kind of king—a gentle ruler who brings justice to the nations. Like the crowd in Jesus' day, we may want Christ to rule as a king and bring great and visible victories in our life. But often Christ's work is quiet, and it happens according to his perfect timing, not ours.

Mark 3:7-11 Many people followed Jesus but didn't understand his true purpose for coming. Some people came for miracles, some came to hear his teaching, but they didn't understand the way of the cross. Knowing about Jesus, or even believing that he is God's Son, does not guarantee salvation. The evil spirits knew that Jesus was the Son of God, but they had no intention of following him. We must also follow and obey him (see Jas 2:17).

Mark 3:12 Jesus warned the evil spirits not to reveal his identity because he did not want them to reinforce a popular misconception. The huge crowds were looking for a political and military leader who would free them from Rome's control, and they thought that the Messiah predicted by the Old Testament prophets would be this kind of man. Jesus wanted to teach the people about the kind of Messiah he really was—one who was far different from their expectations. Christ's Kingdom is spiritual. It begins with the overthrow of sin in people's hearts, not with the overthrow of governments.

Luke 6:19 Once word of Jesus' healing power spread, crowds gathered just to touch him. For many, he had become a magician or a symbol of good fortune. Instead of desiring God's pardon and love, they only wanted physical healing or a chance to see spectacular events. Some people still see God as a cosmic magician and consider prayer as a way to get God to do his tricks. But God is not a magician—he is the Master. Prayer is not a way for us to control God; it is a way for us to put ourselves under his control.

Mark 3:13 What does it mean to hear the "call" of God? First, God calls you to faith in Jesus. You will know this call by the growing desire in your heart to find peace with God speedily. Respond to him—answer with a grateful, "Yes, Lord, I need you!"

Second, God calls you to service in Jesus' name. Wherever you are (and sometimes you need to move), whatever you're doing (and sometimes you need to upgrade your skills), God has a place of service for you. Jesus calls you and he wants you. Answer this call thoughtfully, seriously, in consultation with other Christians, saying, "Yes, Lord, I love you and will follow you!"

Mark 3:14 From the hundreds of people who followed him from place to place, Jesus chose 12 to be his apostles. Apostle means "messenger" or "authorized representative." Why did Jesus choose 12 apostles? The number 12 corresponds to the 12 tribes of Israel (Matt 19:28), showing the continuity between the old religious system and the new one based on Jesus' message. Many people followed Jesus, but these 12 received the most intense training.

Jesus did not choose these 12 to be his close companions because of their faith; their faith often faltered. He didn't choose them because of their talent and ability; no one stood out with unusual ability. The disciples represented a wide range of backgrounds and life experiences, but apparently they had no more leadership potential than those who were not chosen. The one characteristic they all shared was their willingness to obey Jesus. After Jesus' ascension, they were filled with the Holy Spirit and empowered to carry out special roles in the growth of the early church. We should not disqualify ourselves from service to Christ because we

Simon (whom he named Peter),
[17] James and John (the sons of Zebedee, but Jesus nicknamed them "Sons of Thunder"*),
[18] Andrew,
Philip,
Bartholomew,
Matthew,
Thomas,
James (son of Alphaeus),
Thaddaeus,
Simon (the zealot*),
[19] Judas Iscariot (who later betrayed him).

LUKE 6:12-16

One day soon afterward Jesus went up on a mountain
to pray, and he prayed to God all night. [13]At daybreak
he called together all of his disciples and chose twelve
of them to be apostles. Here are their names:

[14] Simon (whom he named Peter),
Andrew (Peter's brother),
James,
John,
Philip,
Bartholomew,
[15] Matthew,
Thomas,
James (son of Alphaeus),
Simon (who was called the zealot),
[16] Judas (son of James),
Judas Iscariot (who later betrayed him).

Jesus Gives the Beatitudes PARALLEL

MATTHEW 5:1-12

One day as he saw the crowds gathering, Jesus went
up on the mountainside and sat down. His disciples
gathered around him, [2]and he began to teach them.

[3] "God blesses those who are poor and realize their need for him,*
for the Kingdom of Heaven is theirs.
[4] God blesses those who mourn,
for they will be comforted.

Mk 3:17 Greek *whom he named Boanerges, which means Sons of Thunder.* **Mk 3:18** Greek *the Cananean,* an Aramaic term for Jewish nationalists. **Mt 5:3** Greek *poor in spirit.*

do not have the expected credentials. Being a good disciple is simply a matter of following Jesus with a willing heart.

Luke 6:12 The Gospel writers note that before every important event in Jesus' life, he would take time to go off by himself and pray. This time Jesus was preparing to choose his inner circle, the 12 apostles. Make sure that all your important decisions are grounded in prayer.

Luke 6:13-16 Jesus selected "ordinary" men with a mixture of backgrounds and personalities to be his disciples. Today, God calls "ordinary" people together to build his church, teach salvation's message, and serve others out of love. Alone we may feel unqualified to serve Christ effectively, but together we make up a group strong enough to serve God in any way. Ask for patience to accept the diversity of people in your church, and build on the variety of strengths represented in your group.

Luke 6:13 Jesus had many disciples (learners), but he chose only 12 apostles (messengers). The apostles were his inner circle; he gave them special training and sent them out with his own authority. These were the ones who started the Christian church. In the Gospels these 12 are usually called the disciples, but in the book of Acts they are called apostles.

Luke 6:14-16 The disciples are not always listed by the same names. For example, Simon is sometimes called Peter or Cephas. Matthew is also known as Levi. Bartholomew is thought to be the same person as Nathanael (John 1:45). Judas the son of James is also called Thaddaeus.

Matt 5:1ff Matthew 5–7 is called the Sermon on the Mount because Jesus gave it on a hillside near Capernaum. This "sermon" probably covered several days of preaching. In it, Jesus proclaimed his attitude toward the law. Position, authority, and money are not important in his Kingdom—what matters is faithful obedience from the heart. The Sermon on the Mount challenged the proud and legalistic religious leaders of the day. It called them back to the messages of the Old Testament prophets, who, like Jesus, taught that heartfelt obedience is more important than legalistic observance.

Matt 5:1-2 Enormous crowds were following Jesus—he was the talk of the town, and everyone wanted to see him. The disciples, who were the closest associates of this popular man, were certainly tempted to feel important, proud, and possessive. Being with Jesus gave them not only prestige but also opportunity for receiving money and power.

The crowds were gathering once again. But before speaking to them, Jesus pulled his disciples aside and warned them about the temptations they would face as his associates. Don't expect fame and fortune, Jesus was saying, but mourning, hunger, and persecution. Nevertheless, Jesus assured his disciples that they would be rewarded—but perhaps not in this life. There may be times when following Jesus will bring us great popularity. If we don't live by Jesus' words in this sermon, we will find ourselves using God's message only to promote our personal interests.

Matt 5:3-12 The Beatitudes can be understood in at least four ways: (1) They are a code of ethics for the disciples and a standard of conduct for all believers. (2) They contrast Kingdom values (what is eternal) with worldly values (what is temporary). (3) They contrast the superficial "faith" of the Pharisees with the real faith that Christ demands. (4) They show how the Old Testament expectations will be fulfilled in the new Kingdom. These Beatitudes are not multiple choice—pick what you like and leave the rest. They must be taken as a whole. They describe what we should be like as Christ's followers.

Matt 5:3-12 Each beatitude tells how to be blessed by God. Being blessed means more than happiness. It implies the fortunate or enviable state of those who are in God's Kingdom. The Beatitudes don't promise laughter, pleasure, or earthly prosperity. Being "blessed" by God means the experience of hope and joy, independent of outward circumstances. To find hope and joy, the deepest form of happiness, follow Jesus no matter what the cost.

Matt 5:3-12 With Jesus' announcement that the Kingdom was near (Matt 4:17), people were naturally asking, "How do I qualify to be in God's Kingdom?" Jesus said that God's Kingdom is organized differently from worldly kingdoms. In the Kingdom of Heaven, wealth and power and authority are unimportant. Kingdom people seek different blessings and benefits, and they have different attitudes. Are your attitudes a carbon copy of the world's selfishness, pride, and lust for power, or do they reflect the humility and self-sacrifice of Jesus, your king?

Matt 5:3-5 Jesus began his sermon with words that seem to contradict each other. But God's way of living usually contradicts the world's. If you want to live for God, you must be ready to say and do what seems strange to the world. You must be willing to give when others take, to love when others hate, to help when others abuse. By giving up your own rights in order to serve others, you will one day receive everything God has in store for you.

THE TWELVE DISCIPLES

Jesus' faithful disciples were ordinary men who became extraordinary because of Jesus Christ. Despite their confusion and lack of understanding during his lifetime, they became powerful witnesses to his resurrection. Their lives were transformed by God's power. The story of Jesus' disciples does not end with the Gospels. It continues in the book of Acts and many of the letters.

Name	*Occupation*	*Outstanding characteristics*	*Major events in his life*
SIMON PETER (son of John)	Fisherman	Impulsive; later—bold in preaching about Jesus	One of three in core group of disciples; recognized Jesus as the Messiah; denied Christ and repented; preached Pentecost sermon; a leader of the Jerusalem church; baptized Gentiles; wrote 1 and 2 Peter.
JAMES (son of Zebedee), he and his brother, John, were called the "Sons of Thunder"	Fisherman	Ambitious, short-tempered, judgmental, deeply committed to Jesus	Also in core group; he and his brother, John, asked Jesus for places of honor in his Kingdom; wanted to call fire down to destroy a Samaritan village; first disciple to be martyred.
JOHN (son of Zebedee), James's brother, and "the disciple Jesus loved"	Fisherman	Ambitious, judgmental; later—very loving	Third disciple in core group; asked Jesus for a place of honor in his Kingdom; wanted to call down fire on a Samaritan village; a leader of the Jerusalem church; wrote the Gospel of John, 1, 2, 3 John, and Revelation.
ANDREW (Peter's brother)	Fisherman	Eager to bring others to Jesus	Accepted John the Baptist's testimony about Jesus; told Peter about Jesus; he and Philip told Jesus that Greeks wanted to see him.
PHILIP	Fisherman	Questioning attitude	Told Nathanael about Jesus; wondered how Jesus could feed the 5,000; asked Jesus to show his followers God the Father; he and Andrew told Jesus that Greeks wanted to see him.
NATHANAEL (perhaps known also as Bartholomew)	Unknown	Honest and straightforward	Initially rejected Jesus because Jesus was from Nazareth but acknowledged him as the "Son of God" and "King of Israel" when they met.
MATTHEW (Levi)	Tax collector	Despised outcast because of his dishonest career	Abandoned his corrupt (and financially profitable) way of life to follow Jesus; invited Jesus to a party with his notorious friends; wrote the Gospel of Matthew.
THOMAS (the Twin)	Unknown	Courage and doubt	Suggested the disciples go with Jesus to Bethany—even if it meant death; asked Jesus about where he was going; refused to believe Jesus was risen until he could see Jesus alive and touch his wounds.
JAMES (son of Alphaeus)	Unknown	Unknown	Became one of Jesus' disciples.
THADDAEUS (Judas son of James)	Unknown	Unknown	Asked Jesus why he would reveal himself to his followers and not to the world.
SIMON THE ZEALOT	Unknown	Fierce patriotism	Became a disciple of Jesus.
JUDAS ISCARIOT	Unknown	Treacherous and greedy	Became one of Jesus' disciples; betrayed Jesus; committed suicide.

What Jesus said about him	*A key lesson from his life*	*Selected references*
Named him Peter, "rock"; called him "Satan" when he urged Jesus to reject the cross; said he would fish for people; he received revelation from God; said he would deny Jesus; said he would later be crucified for his faith.	Christians falter at times, but when they return to Jesus, he forgives them and strengthens their faith	Matt 4:18-20 Mark 8:29-33 Luke 22:31-34 John 21:15-19 Acts 2:14-41 Acts 10:1–11:18
Called James and John "Sons of Thunder"; said he would fish for people; said he would drink the cup Jesus drank.	Christians must be willing to die for Jesus.	Mark 3:17 Mark 10:35-40 Luke 9:52-56 Acts 12:1-2
Called John and James "Sons of Thunder"; said he would fish for people; said he would drink the cup Jesus drank; told to take care of Jesus' mother after Jesus' death.	The transforming power of the love of Christ is available to all.	Mark 1:19-20 Mark 10:35-40 Luke 9:52-56 John 19:26-27 John 21:20-24
Said he would fish for people.	Christians are to tell other people about Jesus.	Matt 4:18-20 John 1:35-42 John 6:8-9 John 12:20-22
Asked if Philip realized that to know and see him was to know and see the Father.	God uses our questions to teach us.	Matt 10:3 John 1:43-46 John 6:2-7 John 12:20-22 John 14:8-11
Called him "a true son of Israel" and "an honest man."	Jesus respects honesty in people—even if they challenge him because of it.	Mark 3:18 John 1:45-51 John 21:1-13
Called him to be a disciple.	Christianity is not for people who think they're already good; it is for people who know they've failed and want help.	Matt 9:9-13 Mark 2:15-17 Luke 5:27-32
Said Thomas believed because he actually saw Jesus after the Resurrection.	Even when Christians experience serious doubts, Jesus reaches out to them to restore their faith.	Matt 10:3 John 14:5 John 20:24-29 John 21:1-13
Unknown	Unknown	Matt 10:3 Mark 3:18 Luke 6:15
Unknown	Christians follow Jesus because they believe in him; they do not always understand the details of God's plan.	Matt 10:3 Mark 3:18 Luke 6:16 John 14:22
Unknown	If we are willing to give up our plans for the future, we can participate in Jesus' plans.	Matt 10:4 Mark 3:18 Luke 6:15
Called him "a devil"; said Judas would betray Jesus.	It is not enough to be familiar with Jesus' teachings. Jesus' true followers love and obey him.	Matt 10:4; 26:20-25 Luke 6:16; 22:47-48 John 12:4-8

▶ MATTHEW 5:1-12 *(cont.)*

5 God blesses those who are humble,
for they will inherit the whole earth.
6 God blesses those who hunger and thirst
for justice,*
for they will be satisfied.
7 God blesses those who are merciful,
for they will be shown mercy.
8 God blesses those whose hearts are pure,
for they will see God.
9 God blesses those who work for peace,
for they will be called the children of God.
10 God blesses those who are persecuted
for doing right,
for the Kingdom of Heaven is theirs.

11"God blesses you when people mock you and persecute you and lie about you* and say all sorts of evil
things against you because you are my followers. 12Be
happy about it! Be very glad! For a great reward awaits
you in heaven. And remember, the ancient prophets
were persecuted in the same way."

LUKE 6:20-26

Then Jesus turned to his disciples and said,

"God blesses you who are poor,
for the Kingdom of God is yours.
21 God blesses you who are hungry now,
for you will be satisfied.
God blesses you who weep now,
for in due time you will laugh.

Mt 5:6 Or *for righteousness.* **Mt 5:11** Some manuscripts do not include *and lie about you.*

KEY LESSONS FROM THE SERMON ON THE MOUNT

In his longest recorded sermon, Jesus began by describing the traits he was looking for in his followers. He said that God blesses those who live out these traits. Each beatitude is almost a direct contradiction of society's typical way of life. In the last beatitude, Jesus even points out that a serious effort to develop these traits is bound to create opposition. The best example of each trait is found in Jesus himself. If our goal is to become like him, applying the Beatitudes will challenge the way we live each day.

Beatitudes—the traits	Old Testament anticipation	Clashing worldly values	God's reward	How to develop this attitude
Realizing need for God (Matt 5:3)	Isa 57:15	Pride and personal independence	Kingdom of Heaven	Jas 4:7-10
Mourning (Matt 5:4)	Isa 61:1-2	Happiness at any cost	Will be comforted	Ps 51; Jas 4:7-10
Humility (Matt 5:5)	Ps 37:5-11; Isa 57:15	Power	Will inherit the earth	Matt 11:28-30; Jas 4:7-10
A hunger and thirst for justice (Matt 5:6)	Isa 11:4-5; 42:1-4	Pursuing personal needs	Will be satisfied	John 16:8-11; Phil 3:7-11
Mercy (Matt 5:7)	Ps 41:1	Strength without feeling	Will be shown mercy	Eph 4:32
Pure in heart (Matt 5:8)	Pss 24:3-4; 51:10	Deception is acceptable	Will see God	1 Jn 3:1-3
Working for peace (Matt 5:9)	Isa 57:18-19; 60:17	Personal peace is pursued without concern for the world's chaos	Will be called children of God	Rom 12:9-21; Heb 12:10-11
Experience persecution (Matt 5:10)	Isa 52:13; 53:12	Weak commitments	Kingdom of Heaven	2 Tim 3:12

Matt 5:11-12 Jesus said to be happy when we're persecuted for our faith. Persecution can be good because (1) it takes our eyes off earthly rewards, (2) it strips away superficial belief, (3) it strengthens the faith of those who endure, and (4) our attitude through it serves as an example to others who follow. We can be comforted knowing that God's greatest prophets were persecuted (Elijah, Jeremiah, Daniel). The fact that we are being persecuted proves that we have been faithful; faithless people would be unnoticed. In the future God will reward the faithful by receiving them into his eternal Kingdom, where there is no more persecution.

Luke 6:20ff This may be Luke's account of the sermon that Matthew records in Matthew 5–7, or it may be that Jesus gave similar sermons on several different occasions. Some believe that this was not one sermon, but a composite based on Jesus' customary teachings.

Luke 6:20-23 These verses are called the *Beatitudes,* from the Latin word meaning "blessing." They describe what it means to be Christ's follower, give standards of conduct, and contrast Kingdom values with worldly values, showing what Christ's followers can expect from the world and what God will give them. In addition, they contrast fake piety with true humility. They also show how Old Testament expectations are fulfilled in God's Kingdom.

Luke 6:21 Some believe that the hunger about which Jesus spoke is a hunger for righteousness (Matt 5:6). Others say this is physical hunger. In any case, in a nation where riches were seen as a sign of God's favor, Jesus startled his hearers by pronouncing blessings on the hungry. In doing so, however, he was in line with an ancient tradition. The Old Testament is filled with texts proclaiming God's concern for the poor and needy. (See, for example, 1 Sam 2:5; Ps 146:7; Isa 58:6-7; Luke 1:53, Jesus' own mother's prayer.)

22What blessings await you when people hate you and
exclude you and mock you and curse you as evil because you follow the Son of Man. 23When that happens,
be happy! Yes, leap for joy! For a great reward awaits
you in heaven. And remember, their ancestors treated
the ancient prophets that same way.

24 "What sorrow awaits you who are rich,
for you have your only happiness now.
25 What sorrow awaits you who are fat and
prosperous now,
for a time of awful hunger awaits you.
What sorrow awaits you who laugh now,
for your laughing will turn to mourning
and sorrow.
26 What sorrow awaits you who are praised
by the crowds,
for their ancestors also praised false prophets."

Jesus Teaches about Salt and Light

MATTHEW 5:13-16

"You are the salt of the earth. But what good is salt
if it has lost its flavor? Can you make it salty again?
It will be thrown out and trampled underfoot as
worthless.
14"You are the light of the world—like a city on a
hilltop that cannot be hidden. 15No one lights a lamp
and then puts it under a basket. Instead, a lamp is
placed on a stand, where it gives light to everyone
in the house. 16In the same way, let your good deeds
shine out for all to see, so that everyone will praise
your heavenly Father.

Jesus Teaches about the Law

MATTHEW 5:17-20

"Don't misunderstand why I have come. I did not
come to abolish the law of Moses or the writings of
the prophets. No, I came to accomplish their purpose. 18I tell you the truth, until heaven and earth disappear, not even the smallest detail of God's law will
disappear until its purpose is achieved. 19So if you
ignore the least commandment and teach others to
do the same, you will be called the least in the Kingdom of Heaven. But anyone who obeys God's laws
and teaches them will be called great in the Kingdom of Heaven.

Luke 6:24 If you are trying to find fulfillment only through riches, wealth may be the only reward you will ever get—and it does not last. We should not seek comfort now at the expense of eternal life.

Luke 6:26 Many false prophets lived during Old Testament times. They were praised by kings and crowds because their predictions—prosperity and victory in war—were exactly what the people wanted to hear. But popularity is no guarantee of truth, and human flattery does not bring God's approval. Sadness lies ahead for those who chase after the crowd's praise rather than God's truth.

Matt 5:13 If a seasoning has no flavor, it has no value. If Christians make no effort to affect the world around them, they are of little value to God. If we are too much like the world, we are worthless. Christians should not blend in with everyone else. Instead, we should affect others positively, just as seasoning brings out the best flavor in food.

Matt 5:14-16 Can you hide a city that is sitting on top of a mountain? Its light at night can be seen for miles. If we live for Christ, we will glow like lights, showing others what Christ is like. We hide our light by (1) being quiet when we should speak, (2) going along with the crowd, (3) denying the light, (4) letting sin dim our light, (5) not explaining our light to others, or (6) ignoring the needs of others. Be a beacon of truth—don't shut your light off from the rest of the world.

Matt 5:17-20 If Jesus did not come to abolish the law, does that mean all the Old Testament laws still apply to us today? In the Old Testament, the law can be understood to have three dimensions: ceremonial, civil, and moral.

(1) The ceremonial law related specifically to Israel's worship (see Lev 1:2-3, for example). Its primary purpose was to point forward to Jesus Christ; these laws, therefore, were no longer necessary after Jesus' death and resurrection. While we are no longer bound by ceremonial law, the principles behind them—to worship and love a holy God—still apply. Jesus was often accused by the Pharisees of violating ceremonial law.

(2) The civil law applied to daily living in Israel (see Deut 24:10-11, for example). Because modern society and culture are so radically different from that time and setting, all of these guidelines cannot be followed specifically. But the principles behind the commands are timeless and should guide our conduct. Jesus demonstrated these principles by example.

(3) The moral law (such as the Ten Commandments) is the direct command of God, and it requires strict obedience (see Exod 20:13, for example). The moral law reveals the nature and will of God, and it still applies today. Jesus obeyed the moral law completely.

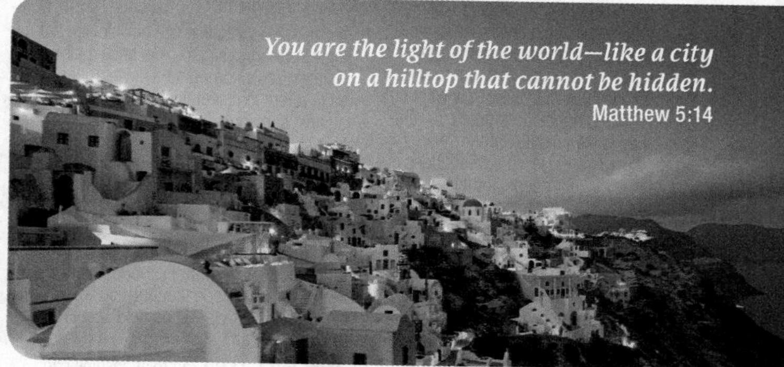

You are the light of the world—like a city on a hilltop that cannot be hidden.
Matthew 5:14

Matt 5:17 God's laws were given to help people love God with all their hearts and minds. Throughout Israel's history, however, these laws had often been misquoted and misapplied. By Jesus' time, religious leaders had turned the laws into a confusing mass of rules. When Jesus talked about a new way to understand God's law, he was actually trying to bring people back to its original purpose. Jesus did not speak against the law itself but against the abuses and excesses to which it had been subjected (see John 1:17).

Matt 5:19 Some of those in the crowd were experts at telling others what to do, but they themselves missed the central point of God's laws. Jesus made it clear that obeying God's laws is more important than explaining them. It's much easier to study God's laws and tell others to obey them than to put them into practice. How are you doing at obeying God yourself?

▸ **MATTHEW 5:17-20 *(cont.)***

20“But I warn you—unless your righteousness is better than the righteousness of the teachers of religious law and the Pharisees, you will never enter the Kingdom of Heaven!

Jesus Teaches about Anger

MATTHEW 5:21-26

“You have heard that our ancestors were told, ‘You must not murder. If you commit murder, you are subject to judgment.’* 22But I say, if you are even angry with someone,* you are subject to judgment! If you call someone an idiot,* you are in danger of being brought before the court. And if you curse someone,* you are in danger of the fires of hell.*

23“So if you are presenting a sacrifice* at the altar in the Temple and you suddenly remember that someone has something against you, 24leave your sacrifice there at the altar. Go and be reconciled to that person. Then come and offer your sacrifice to God.

25“When you are on the way to court with your adversary, settle your differences quickly. Otherwise, your accuser may hand you over to the judge, who will hand you over to an officer, and you will be thrown into prison. 26And if that happens, you surely won't be free again until you have paid the last penny.*

Jesus Teaches about Lust

MATTHEW 5:27-30

“You have heard the commandment that says, ‘You must not commit adultery.’* 28But I say, anyone who even looks at a woman with lust has already committed adultery with her in his heart. 29So if your eye—even your good eye*—causes you to lust, gouge it out and throw it away. It is better for you to lose one part of your body than for your whole body to be thrown into hell. 30And if your hand—even your stronger hand*—causes you to sin, cut it off and throw it away. It is better for you to lose one part of your body than for your whole body to be thrown into hell.

Mt 5:21 Exod 20:13; Deut 5:17. **Mt 5:22a** Some manuscripts add *without cause.* **Mt 5:22b** Greek uses an Aramaic term of contempt: *If you say to your brother, ‘Raca.’* **Mt 5:22c** Greek *if you say, ‘You fool.’* **Mt 5:22d** Greek *Gehenna;* also in 5:29, 30. **Mt 5:23** Greek *gift;* also in 5:24. **Mt 5:26** Greek *the last kodrantes* [i.e., quadrans]. **Mt 5:27** Exod 20:14; Deut 5:18. **Mt 5:29** Greek *your right eye.* **Mt 5:30** Greek *your right hand.*

Matt 5:20 The Pharisees were exacting and scrupulous in their attempts to follow their laws. So how could Jesus reasonably call us to greater righteousness than theirs? The Pharisees' weakness was that they were content to obey the laws outwardly without allowing God to change their hearts (or attitudes). They looked pious, but they were far from the Kingdom of Heaven. God judges our hearts as well as our deeds, for it is in the heart that our real allegiance lies.

Jesus was saying that his listeners needed a different kind of righteousness altogether (out of love for God), not just a more intense version of the Pharisees' obedience (which was mere legal compliance). Our righteousness must (1) come from what God does in us, not what we can do by ourselves, (2) be God-centered, not self-centered, (3) be based on reverence for God, not approval from people, and (4) go beyond keeping the law to living by the principles behind the law. We should be just as concerned about our attitudes that people don't see as about our actions that they do see.

Matt 5:21-22 When Jesus said, “But I say,” he was not doing away with the law or adding his own beliefs. Rather, he was giving a fuller understanding of why God made that law in the first place. For example, Moses said, “You must not murder” (Exod 20:13); Jesus taught that we should not even become angry enough to murder, for then we have already committed murder in our hearts. The Pharisees read this law and, not having literally murdered anyone, felt that they had obeyed it. Yet they were angry enough with Jesus that they would soon plot his death, though they would not do the dirty work themselves. We miss the intent of God's Word when we read his rules for living without trying to understand why he made them. When do you keep God's rules but close your eyes to his intent?

Matt 5:21-22 Killing is a terrible sin, but anger is a great sin, too, because it also violates God's command to love. Anger in this case refers to a seething, brooding bitterness against someone. It is a dangerous emotion that always threatens to leap out of control, leading to violence, emotional hurt, increased mental stress, and spiritual damage. Anger keeps us from developing a spirit pleasing to God. Have you ever been proud that you didn't strike out and say what was really on your mind? Self-control is good, but Christ wants us to practice thought-control as well. Jesus said that we will be held accountable even for our attitudes.

Matt 5:23-24 Broken relationships can hinder our relationship with God. If we have a problem or grievance with a friend, we should resolve the problem as soon as possible. We are hypocrites if we claim to love God while we hate others. Our attitudes toward others reflect our relationship with God (1 Jn 4:20).

Matt 5:25-26 In Jesus' day, someone who couldn't pay a debt was thrown into prison until the debt was paid. Unless someone came to pay the debt, the prisoner would probably die there. It is practical advice to resolve our differences with our enemies before their anger causes more trouble (Prov 25:8-10). You may not get into a disagreement that takes you to court, but even small conflicts mend more easily if you try to make peace right away. In a broader sense, these verses advise us to get things right with our brothers and sisters before we have to stand before God.

Matt 5:27-28 The Old Testament law said that it is wrong for a person to have sex with someone other than his or her spouse (Exod 20:14). But Jesus said that the desire to have sex with someone other than your spouse is mental adultery and thus sin. Jesus emphasized that if the act is wrong, then so is the intention. To be faithful to your spouse with your body but not your mind is to break the trust so vital to a strong marriage. Jesus is condemning not natural interest in the opposite sex or even healthy sexual desire but the deliberate and repeated filling of one's mind with fantasies that would be evil if acted out.

Matt 5:27-28 Some think that if lustful thoughts are sin, why shouldn't a person go ahead and do the lustful actions, too? Acting out sinful desires is harmful in several ways: (1) It causes people to excuse sin rather than to stop sinning; (2) it destroys marriages; (3) it is deliberate rebellion against God's Word; (4) it always hurts someone else in addition to the sinner. Sinful actions are more dangerous than sinful desires, and that is why desires should not be acted out. Nevertheless, sinful desires are just as damaging to obedience. Left unchecked, wrong desires will result in wrong actions and turn people away from God.

Matt 5:29-30 When Jesus said to get rid of your hand or your eye, he was speaking figuratively. He didn't mean literally to gouge out your eye because even a blind person can lust. But if that were the only choice, it would be better to go into heaven with one eye or hand than to go to hell with two. We sometimes tolerate sins in our life that, left unchecked, could eventually destroy us. It is better to experience the pain of removal (getting rid of a bad habit or something we treasure, for instance) than to allow the sin to bring judgment and condemnation. Examine your life for anything that causes you to sin, and take every necessary action to remove it.

Jesus Teaches about Divorce

MATTHEW 5:31-32

"You have heard the law that says, 'A man can divorce his wife by merely giving her a written notice of divorce.'* [32]But I say that a man who divorces his wife, unless she has been unfaithful, causes her to commit adultery. And anyone who marries a divorced woman also commits adultery.

Jesus Teaches about Vows

MATTHEW 5:33-37

"You have also heard that our ancestors were told, 'You must not break your vows; you must carry out the vows you make to the LORD.'* [34]But I say, do not make any vows! Do not say, 'By heaven!' because heaven is God's throne. [35]And do not say, 'By the earth!' because the earth is his footstool. And do not say, 'By Jerusalem!' for Jerusalem is the city of the great King. [36]Do not even say, 'By my head!' for you can't turn one hair white or black. [37]Just say a simple, 'Yes, I will,' or 'No, I won't.' Anything beyond this is from the evil one.

Jesus Teaches about Revenge

MATTHEW 5:38-42

"You have heard the law that says the punishment must match the injury: 'An eye for an eye, and a tooth for a tooth.'* [39]But I say, do not resist an evil person! If someone slaps you on the right cheek, offer the other cheek also. [40]If you are sued in court and your shirt is taken from you, give your coat, too. [41]If a soldier demands that you carry his gear for a mile,* carry it two miles. [42]Give to those who ask, and don't turn away from those who want to borrow.

Mt 5:31 Deut 24:1. **Mt 5:33** Num 30:2. **Mt 5:38** Greek *the law that says: 'An eye for an eye and a tooth for a tooth.'* Exod 21:24; Lev 24:20; Deut 19:21. **Mt 5:41** Greek *milion* [4,854 feet or 1,478 meters].

SIX WAYS TO THINK LIKE CHRIST

More often than not, we avoid the extreme sins but regularly commit the types of sins with which Jesus was most concerned. In these six examples, our real struggle with sin is exposed. Jesus pointed out what kind of lives would be required of his followers. Are you living as Jesus taught?

Reference	Example	It's not enough to . . .	We must also . . .
Matt 5:21-22	Murder	Avoid killing	Avoid anger and hatred
Matt 5:23-26	Sacrifices	Offer regular gifts	Have right relationships with God and others
Matt 5:27-30	Adultery	Avoid adultery	Keep our hearts from lusting and be faithful
Matt 5:31-32	Divorce	Be legally married	Live out marriage commitments
Matt 5:33-37	Vows	Keep a vow	Avoid casual and irresponsible commitments to God
Matt 5:38-47	Revenge	Seek justice for ourselves	Show mercy and love to others

Matt 5:31-32 Divorce is as hurtful and destructive today as in Jesus' day. God intends marriage to be a lifetime commitment (Gen 2:24). When entering into marriage, people should never consider divorce an option for solving problems or as a way out of a relationship that seems dead. In these verses, Jesus is also attacking those who purposefully abuse the marriage contract, using divorce to satisfy their lustful desire to marry someone else. Are your actions today helping your marriage grow stronger, or are you tearing it apart?

Matt 5:32 Jesus said that divorce is not permissible except for unfaithfulness. This does not mean that divorce should automatically occur when a spouse commits adultery. The word translated "unfaithful" implies a sexually immoral lifestyle, not a confessed and repented act of adultery. Those who discover that their partner has been unfaithful should first make every effort to forgive, reconcile, and restore their relationship. We are always to look for reasons to restore the marriage relationship rather than for excuses to leave it.

Matt 5:33ff Here, Jesus was emphasizing the importance of telling the truth. People were breaking vows and using sacred language casually and carelessly. Keeping vows and promises is important; it builds trust and makes committed human relationships possible. The Bible condemns making vows or taking oaths casually, giving your word while knowing that you won't keep it, or swearing falsely in God's name (Exod 20:7; Lev 19:12; Num 30:1-2; Deut 19:16-20). Vows are needed in certain situations only because we live in a sinful society that breeds distrust.

Matt 5:33-37 Vows were common, but Jesus told his followers not to use them—their word alone should be enough (see Jas 5:12). Are you known as a person of your word? Truthfulness seems so rare that we feel we must end our statements with "I promise." If we tell the truth all the time, we will have less pressure to back up our words with an oath or promise.

Matt 5:38 God's purpose behind this law was an expression of mercy. The law was given to judges and said, in effect, "Make the punishment fit the crime." It was not a guide for personal revenge (Exod 21:23-25; Lev 24:19-20; Deut 19:21). These laws were given to limit vengeance and help the court administer punishment that was neither too strict nor too lenient. Some people, however, were using this phrase to justify their vendettas against others. People still try to excuse their acts of revenge by saying, "I was just doing to him what he did to me."

Matt 5:38-42 When we are wronged, often our first reaction is to get even. Instead, Jesus said we should do good to those who wrong us! Our desire should not be to keep score but to love and forgive. This is not natural—it is supernatural. Only God can give us the strength to love as he does. Instead of planning vengeance, pray for those who hurt you.

Matt 5:39-42 To many Jews of Jesus' day, these statements were offensive. Any Messiah who would turn the other cheek was not the military leader they wanted to lead a revolt against Rome. Since they were under Roman oppression, they wanted retaliation against their enemies, whom they hated. But Jesus suggested a new, radical response to injustice: Instead of demanding rights, give them up freely! According to Jesus, it is more important to give justice and mercy than to receive it.

Jesus Teaches about Loving Enemies PARALLEL

MATTHEW 5:43-48

"You have heard the law that says, 'Love your neighbor'* and hate your enemy. [44]But I say, love your enemies!* Pray for those who persecute you! [45]In that way, you will be acting as true children of your Father in heaven. For he gives his sunlight to both the evil and the good, and he sends rain on the just and the unjust alike. [46]If you love only those who love you, what reward is there for that? Even corrupt tax collectors do that much. [47]If you are kind only to your friends,* how are you different from anyone else? Even pagans do that. [48]But you are to be perfect, even as your Father in heaven is perfect."

LUKE 6:27-36

"But to you who are willing to listen, I say, love your enemies! Do good to those who hate you. [28]Bless those who curse you. Pray for those who hurt you. [29]If someone slaps you on one cheek, offer the other cheek also. If someone demands your coat, offer your shirt also. [30]Give to anyone who asks; and when things are taken away from you, don't try to get them back. [31]Do to others as you would like them to do to you.

[32]"If you love only those who love you, why should you get credit for that? Even sinners love those who love them! [33]And if you do good only to those who do good to you, why should you get credit? Even sinners do that much! [34]And if you lend money only to those who can repay you, why should you get credit? Even sinners will lend to other sinners for a full return.

[35]"Love your enemies! Do good to them. Lend to them without expecting to be repaid. Then your reward from heaven will be very great, and you will truly be acting as children of the Most High, for he is kind to those who are unthankful and wicked. [36]You must be compassionate, just as your Father is compassionate."

Jesus Teaches about Giving to the Needy

MATTHEW 6:1-4

"Watch out! Don't do your good deeds publicly, to be admired by others, for you will lose the reward from your Father in heaven. [2]When you give to someone in need, don't do as the hypocrites do—blowing trumpets in the synagogues and streets to call attention to their acts of charity! I tell you the truth, they have received all the reward they will ever get. [3]But when you give to

Mt 5:43 Lev 19:18. **Mt 5:44** Some manuscripts add *Bless those who curse you. Do good to those who hate you.* Compare Luke 6:27-28. **Mt 5:47** Greek *your brothers.*

Matt 5:43-44 By telling us not to retaliate, Jesus keeps us from taking the law into our own hands. By loving and praying for our enemies, we can overcome evil with good.

The Pharisees interpreted Leviticus 19:18 as teaching that they should love only those who love in return, and Psalms 139:19-22 and 140:9-11 as meaning that they should hate their enemies. But Jesus says we are to love our enemies. If you love your enemies and treat them well, you will truly show that Jesus is Lord of your life. This is possible only for those who give themselves fully to God, because only he can deliver people from natural hatred and selfishness. We must trust the Holy Spirit to help us show love to those for whom we may not feel love.

Matt 5:48 How can we be perfect? (1) In character: In this life we cannot be flawless, but we can aspire to be as much like Christ as possible. (2) In holiness: Like the Pharisees, we are to separate ourselves from the world's sinful values. But unlike the Pharisees, we are to be devoted to God's desires rather than our own and carry his love and mercy into the world. (3) In maturity: We can't achieve Christlike character and holy living all at once, but we must grow toward maturity and wholeness. Just as we expect different behavior from a baby, a child, a teenager, and an adult, so God expects different behavior from us, depending on our stage of spiritual development. (4) In love: We can seek to love others as completely as God loves us.

We can be perfect if our behavior is appropriate for our maturity level—perfect, yet with much room to grow. Our tendency to sin must never deter us from striving to be more like Christ. Christ calls all of his disciples to excel, to rise above mediocrity, and to mature in every area, becoming like him.

Luke 6:27 The Jews despised the Romans because they oppressed God's people, but Jesus told them to love these enemies. Such words turned many away from Christ. Jesus wasn't talking about having affection for enemies; he was talking about an act of the will. You can't "fall into" this kind of love—it takes conscious effort. Loving our enemies means acting in their best interests. We can pray for them, and we can think of ways to help them. Jesus loves the whole world, even though the world is in rebellion against God. Jesus asks us to follow his example by loving our enemies. Grant your enemies the same respect and rights as you desire for yourself.

Matt 6:2 The term hypocrites, as used here, describes people who do good acts for appearances only—not out of compassion or other good motives. Their actions may be good, but their motives are hollow. These

JESUS AND THE OLD TESTAMENT LAW

What seems to be a case of Jesus contradicting the laws of the Old Testament deserves a careful look. It is too easy to overlook how much mercy was written into the Old Testament laws. The chart shows several examples. What God designed as a system of justice with mercy had been distorted over the years into a license for revenge. It was this misapplication of the law that Jesus attacked.

Reference	Examples of Old Testament mercy in justice:
Lev 19:18	"Do not seek revenge or bear a grudge against a fellow Israelite, but love your neighbor as yourself. I am the LORD."
Prov 24:28-29	"Don't testify against your neighbors without cause; don't lie about them. And don't say, 'Now I can pay them back for what they've done to me! I'll get even with them!'"
Prov 25:21-22	"If your enemies are hungry, give them food to eat. If they are thirsty, give them water to drink. You will heap burning coals of shame on their heads, and the LORD will reward you."
Lam 3:30-31	"Let them turn the other cheek to those who strike them and accept the insults of their enemies. For no one is abandoned by the Lord forever."

someone in need, don't let your left hand know what
your right hand is doing. 4 Give your gifts in private,
and your Father, who sees everything, will reward you.

Jesus Teaches about Prayer

MATTHEW 6:5-15

"When you pray, don't be like the hypocrites who love
to pray publicly on street corners and in the synagogues where everyone can see them. I tell you the
truth, that is all the reward they will ever get. 6 But
when you pray, go away by yourself, shut the door behind you, and pray to your Father in private. Then your
Father, who sees everything, will reward you.

7 "When you pray, don't babble on and on as people
of other religions do. They think their prayers are answered merely by repeating their words again and
again. 8 Don't be like them, for your Father knows
exactly what you need even before you ask him! 9 Pray
like this:

Our Father in heaven,
may your name be kept holy.
10 May your Kingdom come soon.
May your will be done on earth,
as it is in heaven.
11 Give us today the food we need,*
12 and forgive us our sins,
as we have forgiven those who sin against us.
13 And don't let us yield to temptation,*
but rescue us from the evil one.*

14 "If you forgive those who sin against you, your
heavenly Father will forgive you. 15 But if you refuse to forgive others, your Father will not forgive
your sins.

Mt 6:11 Or *Give us today our food for the day;* or *Give us today our food for tomorrow.* **Mt 6:13a** Or *And keep us from being tested.* **Mt 6:13b** Or *from evil.* Some manuscripts add *For yours is the kingdom and the power and the glory forever. Amen.*

empty acts are their only reward, but God will reward those who are sincere in their faith.

Matt 6:3 When Jesus says not to let your left hand know what your right hand is doing, he is teaching that our motives for giving to God and to others must be pure. It is easy to give with mixed motives, to do something for someone if it will benefit us in return. But believers should avoid all scheming and give for the pleasure of giving and as a response to God's love. Why do you give?

Matt 6:3-4 It's easier to do what's right when we gain recognition and praise. But we should do our good deeds quietly or in secret, with no thought of reward. Jesus says to check our motives in three areas: generosity (Matt 6:4), prayer (Matt 6:6), and fasting (Matt 6:18). Those acts should not be self-centered but God-centered, done not to make us look good but to make God look good. The reward God promises is not material, and it is never given to those who seek it. Doing something only for ourselves is not a loving sacrifice. With your next good deed, ask, would I still do this if no one would ever know I did it?

Matt 6:5-6 Some people, especially the religious leaders, wanted to be seen as "holy," and public prayer was one way to get attention. Jesus saw through their self-righteous acts, however, and taught that the essence of prayer is not public style but private communication with God. There is a place for public prayer, but to pray only where others will notice you indicates that your real audience is not God.

Matt 6:6 Some have concluded that Jesus' directions about private prayer call into question all public prayer. Jesus' own practice indicates this wasn't his intention. The Gospels record Jesus at prayer both privately (Matt 14:23) and publicly (Matt 14:18-19). Again, Jesus was drawing attention to the motives behind actions. The point really wasn't a choice between public and private prayer but between heartfelt and hypocritical prayer. When asked to pray in public, focus on addressing God, not on how you're coming across to others.

Matt 6:7-8 Repeating the same words over and over like a magic incantation is no way to ensure that God will hear your prayer. It's not wrong to come to God many times with the same requests—Jesus encourages persistent prayer. But he condemns the shallow repetition of words that are not offered with a sincere heart. We can never pray too much if our prayers are honest and sincere. Before you start to pray, make sure you mean what you say.

Matt 6:9 This is often called the Lord's Prayer because Jesus gave it to the disciples as a model for them (and us) to keep in mind as we pray. Jesus provided a pattern to be imitated as well as duplicated. We should praise God, pray for his work in the world, pray for our daily needs, and pray for help in our daily struggles. To what extent do you use the items in the Lord's Prayer to guide your own prayer times?

Matt 6:9 The phrase "Our Father in heaven" indicates that God is not only majestic and holy but also personal and loving. The first line of this model prayer is a statement of praise and a commitment to hallow, or honor, God's holy name. We can honor God's name by being careful to use it respectfully. If we use God's name lightly, we aren't remembering God's holiness.

Matt 6:10 The phrase "May your Kingdom come soon" is a reference to God's spiritual reign, not Israel's freedom from Rome. God's Kingdom was announced in the covenant with Abraham (Matt 8:11; Luke 13:28), is present in Christ's reign in believers' hearts (Luke 17:21), and will be complete when all evil is destroyed and God establishes the new heaven and earth (Rev 21:1).

Matt 6:10 When we pray "May your will be done," we are not resigning ourselves to fate but praying that God's perfect purpose will be accomplished in this world as well as in the next. And how does God accomplish his will on earth? He does it largely through people willing to obey him. This part of the prayer allows us to offer ourselves as doers of God's will, asking him to guide, lead, and give us the means to accomplish his purposes.

Matt 6:11 When we pray "Give us today the food we need," we are acknowledging that God is our sustainer and provider. It is a misconception to think that we provide for our needs ourselves. We must trust God daily to provide what he knows we need.

Matt 6:13 God sometimes allows us to be tested by temptation. As disciples, we should pray for God's help during these trying times and for deliverance from Satan ("the evil one") and his deceit. All Christians struggle with temptation. Sometimes it is so subtle that we don't even realize what is happening to us. God has promised that he won't allow us to be tempted beyond what we can bear (1 Cor 10:13). Ask God to help you recognize temptation, and to strengthen you to overcome it and choose God's way instead. For more on temptation, see the notes on Matthew 4:1, p. 1294.

Matt 6:14-15 Jesus gives a startling warning about forgiveness: If we refuse to forgive others, God will also refuse to forgive us. Why? Because when we don't forgive others, we are denying our common ground as sinners in need of God's forgiveness. God's forgiveness of sin is not the direct result of our forgiving others, but it is based on our realizing what forgiveness means (see Eph 4:32). It is easy to ask God for forgiveness but difficult to grant it to others. Whenever we ask God to forgive us for sin, we should ask, have I forgiven the people who have wronged me?

Jesus Teaches about Fasting

MATTHEW 6:16-18

"And when you fast, don't make it obvious, as the hypocrites do, for they try to look miserable and disheveled so people will admire them for their fasting. I tell you the truth, that is the only reward they will ever get. 17But when you fast, comb your hair and wash your face. 18Then no one will notice that you are fasting, except your Father, who knows what you do in private. And your Father, who sees everything, will reward you.

Jesus Teaches about Money

MATTHEW 6:19-24

"Don't store up treasures here on earth, where moths eat them and rust destroys them, and where thieves break in and steal. 20Store your treasures in heaven, where moths and rust cannot destroy, and thieves do not break in and steal. 21Wherever your treasure is, there the desires of your heart will also be.

22"Your eye is a lamp that provides light for your body. When your eye is good, your whole body is filled with light. 23But when your eye is bad, your whole body is filled with darkness. And if the light you think you have is actually darkness, how deep that darkness is!

24"No one can serve two masters. For you will hate one and love the other; you will be devoted to one and despise the other. You cannot serve both God and money.

Jesus Teaches about Worry

MATTHEW 6:25-34

"That is why I tell you not to worry about everyday life—whether you have enough food and drink, or enough clothes to wear. Isn't life more than food, and your body more than clothing? 26Look at the birds. They don't plant or harvest or store food in barns, for your heavenly Father feeds them. And aren't you far more valuable to him than they are? 27Can all your worries add a single moment to your life?

28"And why worry about your clothing? Look at the lilies of the field and how they grow. They don't work or make their clothing, 29yet Solomon in all his glory was not dressed as beautifully as they are. 30And if God cares so wonderfully for wildflowers that are here today and thrown into the fire tomorrow, he will certainly care for you. Why do you have so little faith?

31"So don't worry about these things, saying, 'What will we eat? What will we drink? What will we wear?' 32These things dominate the thoughts of unbelievers, but your heavenly Father already knows all your needs. 33Seek the Kingdom of God* above all else, and live righteously, and he will give you everything you need.

Mt 6:33 Some manuscripts do not include *of God.*

Matt 6:16 Fasting—going without food in order to spend time in prayer—is noble and difficult. It gives us time to pray, teaches self-discipline, reminds us that we can live with a lot less, and helps us appreciate God's gifts. Jesus was not condemning fasting but rather hypocrisy—fasting in order to gain public approval. Fasting was mandatory for the Jewish people once a year on the Day of Atonement (Lev 23:32). The Pharisees voluntarily fasted twice a week to impress the people with their "holiness." Jesus commended acts of self-sacrifice done quietly and sincerely. He wanted people to adopt spiritual disciplines for the right reasons, not from a selfish desire for praise.

Matt 6:20 Storing treasures in heaven is not limited to tithing but is accomplished by all acts of obedience to God. There is a sense in which giving our money to God's work is like investing in heaven. But we should seek to please God not only in our giving but also in fulfilling God's purposes in all we do.

Matt 6:21 Jesus made it clear that having the wrong treasures results in a heart that is in the wrong place. What we treasure the most controls us, whether we admit it or not. If possessions or money become too important to us, we must re-establish control or get rid of something. Jesus calls for a decision that allows us to live contentedly with whatever we have because we have chosen eternal values over temporary, earthly treasures.

Matt 6:22-23 Spiritual vision is our capacity to see clearly what God wants us to do and to see the world from his point of view. But this spiritual insight can easily be clouded. Self-serving desires, interests, and goals block that vision. Serving God is the best way to restore it. A "good" eye is one that is fixed on God.

Matt 6:24 Jesus says we can have only one master. We live in a materialistic society where many people serve money. They spend all their lives collecting and storing it, only to die and leave it behind. Their desire for money and what it can buy far outweighs their commitment to God and spiritual matters. You will spend much of your time and energy thinking about whatever you store up. Don't fall into the materialistic trap, because "the love of money is the root of all kinds of evil" (1 Tim 6:10). Can you honestly say that God, and not money, is your master? One test is to ask yourself which one occupies more of your thoughts, time, and efforts.

Matt 6:24 Jesus contrasted heavenly values with earthly values when he explained that our first loyalty should be to those things that do not fade, cannot be stolen or used up, and never wear out. We should not be fascinated with our possessions, lest they possess us. God alone deserves to be our master. Either we store our treasures with God (Matt 6:20-21), focus our "eyes" on him (Matt 6:22-23), and serve him alone—or else we do not serve him at all. Where does your ultimate allegiance lie?

Matt 6:25 Because of the ill effects of worry, Jesus tells us not to worry about those needs that God promises to supply. Worry may (1) damage your health, (2) disrupt your productivity, (3) negatively affect the way you treat others, and (4) reduce your ability to trust in God. How many ill effects of worry are you experiencing? Here is the difference between worry and genuine concern—worry immobilizes, but concern moves you to action.

Matt 6:33 To "seek the Kingdom of God above all else" means to put God first in your life, to fill your thoughts with his desires, to take his character for your pattern, and to serve and obey him in everything. What is really important to you? People, objects, goals, and other desires all compete for priority. Any of these can quickly become most important to you if you don't actively choose to give God first place in every area of your life.

Matt 6:34 Planning for tomorrow is time well spent; worrying about tomorrow is time wasted. Sometimes it's difficult to tell the difference. Careful planning is thinking ahead about goals, steps, and schedules, and trusting in God's guidance. When done well, planning can help alleviate worry.

34"So don't worry about tomorrow, for tomorrow will bring its own worries. Today's trouble is enough for today.

Jesus Teaches about Judging Others PARALLEL

MATTHEW 7:1-6

"Do not judge others, and you will not be judged. 2For you will be treated as you treat others.* The standard you use in judging is the standard by which you will be judged.*

3"And why worry about a speck in your friend's eye* when you have a log in your own? 4How can you think of saying to your friend,* 'Let me help you get rid of that speck in your eye,' when you can't see past the log in your own eye? 5Hypocrite! First get rid of the log in your own eye; then you will see well enough to deal with the speck in your friend's eye.

6"Don't waste what is holy on people who are unholy.* Don't throw your pearls to pigs! They will trample the pearls, then turn and attack you."

LUKE 6:37-42

"Do not judge others, and you will not be judged. Do not condemn others, or it will all come back against you. Forgive others, and you will be forgiven. 38Give, and you will receive. Your gift will return to you in full—pressed down, shaken together to make room for more, running over, and poured into your lap. The amount you give will determine the amount you get back.*"

39Then Jesus gave the following illustration: "Can one blind person lead another? Won't they both fall into a ditch? 40Students* are not greater than their teacher. But the student who is fully trained will become like the teacher.

41"And why worry about a speck in your friend's eye* when you have a log in your own? 42How can you think of saying, 'Friend,* let me help you get rid of that speck in your eye,' when you can't see past the log in your own eye? Hypocrite! First get rid of the log in your own eye; then you will see well enough to deal with the speck in your friend's eye."

Mt 7:2a Or *For God will judge you as you judge others.* **Mt 7:2b** Or *The measure you give will be the measure you get back.* **Mt 7:3** Greek *your brother's eye;* also in 7:5. **Mt 7:4** Greek *your brother.* **Mt 7:6** Greek *Don't give the sacred to dogs.* **Lk 6:38** Or *The measure you give will be the measure you get back.* **Lk 6:40** Or *Disciples.* **Lk 6:41** Greek *your brother's eye;* also in 6:42. **Lk 6:42** Greek *Brother.*

SEVEN REASONS NOT TO WORRY

Matt 6:25	The same God who created life in you can be trusted with the details of your life.
Matt 6:26	Worrying about the future hampers your efforts for today.
Matt 6:27	Worrying is more harmful than helpful.
Matt 6:28-30	God does not ignore those who depend on him.
Matt 6:31-32	Worrying shows a lack of faith in and understanding of God.
Matt 6:33	Worrying keeps us from the real challenges that God wants us to pursue.
Matt 6:34	Living one day at a time keeps us from being consumed with worry.

Worriers, by contrast, are consumed by fear and find it difficult to trust God. They let their plans interfere with their relationship with God. Don't let worries about tomorrow affect your relationship with God today.

Matt 7:1-2 Jesus tells us to examine our own motives and conduct instead of judging others. The traits that bother us in others are often the habits we have ourselves. Our bad habits and behavior patterns are the very ones that we most want to change in others. Do you find it easy to magnify others' faults while excusing your own? If you are ready to criticize someone, check to see if you deserve the same criticism. Judge yourself first, and then lovingly forgive and help your neighbor.

Matt 7:1-5 Jesus' statement, "Do not judge others," is against the kind of hypocritical, judgmental attitude that tears others down in order to build oneself up. It is not a blanket statement to overlook wrong behavior but a call to be discerning rather than negative. Jesus said to expose false prophets (Matt 7:15-23), and Paul taught that we should exercise church discipline (1 Cor 5:1-2) and trust God to be the final judge (1 Cor 4:3-5).

Matt 7:6 Pigs were unclean animals according to God's law (Deut 14:8). Anyone who touched an unclean animal became "ceremonially unclean" and could not go to the Temple to worship until the uncleanness was removed. Jesus says that we should not entrust holy teachings to unholy or unclean people. It is futile to try to teach holy concepts to people who don't want to listen and will only tear apart what we say. We should not stop giving God's Word to unbelievers, but we should be wise and discerning in our witnessing, so that we will not be wasting our time.

Luke 6:37-38 A forgiving spirit demonstrates that a person has received God's forgiveness. Jesus used the picture of measuring grain in a basket to ensure a full amount. If we are critical rather than compassionate, we will also receive criticism. But if we treat others generously, graciously, and compassionately, these qualities will come back to us in full measure. We are to love others, not judge them.

Luke 6:39-40 Make sure you're following the right teachers and leaders, because you will go no farther than they do. Look for leaders who will show you more about faith and whose guidance you can trust.

Luke 6:41 Jesus doesn't mean we should ignore wrongdoing, but we should not be so worried about others' sins that we overlook our own. We often rationalize our sins by pointing out the same mistakes in others. What kinds of "specks" in others' eyes are the easiest for you to criticize? Remember your own "logs" when you feel like criticizing, and you may find that you have less to say.

Luke 6:42 We should not be so afraid of the label *hypocrite* that we stand still in our Christian life, hiding our faith and making no attempts to grow. A person who tries to do right but often fails is not a hypocrite. Neither are those who fulfill their duty even when they don't feel like doing it. Often it is necessary and good to set aside our desires in order to do what needs to be done. It is not hypocrisy to be weak in faith. A hypocrite is a person who only puts on religious behavior in order to gain attention, approval, or admiration from others.

Jesus Teaches about Asking, Seeking, Knocking

MATTHEW 7:7-11

"Keep on asking, and you will receive what you ask for. Keep on seeking, and you will find. Keep on knocking, and the door will be opened to you. [8]For everyone who asks, receives. Everyone who seeks, finds. And to everyone who knocks, the door will be opened.

[9]"You parents—if your children ask for a loaf of bread, do you give them a stone instead? [10]Or if they ask for a fish, do you give them a snake? Of course not! [11]So if you sinful people know how to give good gifts to your children, how much more will your heavenly Father give good gifts to those who ask him.

The Golden Rule

MATTHEW 7:12

"Do to others whatever you would like them to do to you. This is the essence of all that is taught in the law and the prophets.

Jesus Teaches about the Way to Heaven

MATTHEW 7:13-14

"You can enter God's Kingdom only through the narrow gate. The highway to hell* is broad, and its gate is wide for the many who choose that way. [14]But the gateway to life is very narrow and the road is difficult, and only a few ever find it.

Jesus Teaches about Fruit in People's Lives PARALLEL

MATTHEW 7:15-29

"Beware of false prophets who come disguised as harmless sheep but are really vicious wolves. [16]You can identify them by their fruit, that is, by the way they act. Can you pick grapes from thornbushes, or figs from thistles? [17]A good tree produces good fruit, and a bad tree produces bad fruit. [18]A good tree can't produce bad fruit, and a bad tree can't produce good fruit. [19]So every tree that does not produce good fruit is chopped down and thrown into the fire. [20]Yes, just as you can identify a tree by its fruit, so you can identify people by their actions.

[21]"Not everyone who calls out to me, 'Lord! Lord!' will enter the Kingdom of Heaven. Only those who actually do the will of my Father in heaven will enter. [22]On judgment day many will say to me, 'Lord! Lord! We prophesied in your name and cast out demons in your name and performed many miracles in your name.' [23]But I will reply, 'I never knew you. Get away from me, you who break God's laws.'

Mt 7:13 Greek *The road that leads to destruction.*

Matt 7:7-8 Jesus tells us to persist in pursuing God. People often give up after a few halfhearted efforts and conclude that God cannot be found. But knowing God takes faith, focus, and follow-through, and Jesus assures us that we will be rewarded. Don't give up in your efforts to seek God. Continue to ask him for more knowledge, patience, wisdom, love, and understanding. He will give them to you.

Matt 7:9-10 The children in Jesus' example asked their father for bread and fish—good and necessary items. If the children had asked for a poisonous snake, would the wise father have granted the request? God knows that sometimes we are praying for "snakes," and he does not give us what we ask for, even though we persist in our prayers. Nor will God give us "stones" or "snakes" instead of what we need. As we learn to know God better as a loving Father, we learn to ask for what is good for us.

Matt 7:11 Christ is showing us the heart of God the Father. God is not selfish, begrudging, or stingy, and we don't have to beg or grovel as we come with our requests. He is a loving Father, who understands, cares, and comforts. If humans can be kind, imagine how kind God, the creator of kindness, can be.

Matt 7:11 Jesus used the expression "you sinful people" to contrast sinful and fallible human beings with the holy and perfect God.

Matt 7:12 This is commonly known as the Golden Rule. In many religions it is stated negatively: "Don't do to others what you don't want done to you." By stating it positively, Jesus made it more significant. It is not very hard to refrain from harming others; it is much more difficult to take the initiative in doing something good for them. The Golden Rule, as Jesus formulated it, is the foundation of active goodness and mercy—the kind of love God shows to us every day. Think of a good and merciful action you can do today.

Matt 7:13-14 The gate that leads to eternal life (John 10:7-9) is called "narrow." This does not mean that it is difficult to become a Christian but that there is only one way to eternal life with God and that only a few decide to walk that road. Believing in Jesus is the only way to heaven because he alone died for our sins and made us right before God. Living his way may not be popular, but it is true and right.

Matt 7:15 False prophets were common in Old Testament times. They prophesied only what the king and the people wanted to hear, claiming it was God's message. Jesus indicates that false prophets were just as prevalent in his time. False teachers are also common today. Jesus says to beware of those whose words sound religious but who are motivated by money, fame, or power. You can tell who they are because in their teaching they minimize Christ and glorify themselves.

Matt 7:20 We should evaluate teachers' words by examining their lives. Just as trees are consistent in the kind of fruit they produce, good teachers consistently exhibit good behavior and high moral character as they seek to live out the truths of Scripture. This does not mean we should have witch-hunts, throwing out Sunday school teachers, pastors, and others who are less than perfect. Every one of us is subject to sin, and we must show the same mercy to others that we expect for ourselves. When Jesus talks about worthless trees, he means teachers who deliberately teach false doctrine. We must examine the teachers' motives, the direction they are taking, and the results they are seeking.

Matt 7:21 Some self-professed athletes can "talk" a great game, but that tells you nothing about their athletic skills. And not everyone who talks about heaven belongs to God's Kingdom. Jesus is more concerned about our walk than our talk. He wants us to do right, not just say the right words. What you do cannot be separated from what you believe.

Matt 7:21-23 Jesus exposed those people who sounded religious but had no personal relationship with him. On "judgment day" only our relationship with Christ—our acceptance of him as Savior and our obedience to him—will matter. Many people think that if they are "good" people and say religious things, they will be rewarded with eternal life. In reality, faith in Christ is what will count at the judgment.

Matt 7:22 "Judgment day" is the final day of reckoning when God will settle all accounts, judging sin and rewarding faith.

24"Anyone who listens to my teaching and follows it
is wise, like a person who builds a house on solid rock.
25Though the rain comes in torrents and the floodwaters rise and the winds beat against that house, it
won't collapse because it is built on bedrock. 26But
anyone who hears my teaching and doesn't obey it
is foolish, like a person who builds a house on sand.
27When the rains and floods come and the winds
beat against that house, it will collapse with a mighty
crash."
28When Jesus had finished saying these things, the
crowds were amazed at his teaching, 29for he taught
with real authority—quite unlike their teachers of
religious law.

LUKE 6:43-49

"A good tree can't produce bad fruit, and a bad tree
can't produce good fruit. 44A tree is identified by its
fruit. Figs are never gathered from thornbushes, and
grapes are not picked from bramble bushes. 45A good
person produces good things from the treasury of a
good heart, and an evil person produces evil things
from the treasury of an evil heart. What you say flows
from what is in your heart.
46"So why do you keep calling me 'Lord, Lord!' when
you don't do what I say? 47I will show you what it's like
when someone comes to me, listens to my teaching,
and then follows it. 48It is like a person building a
house who digs deep and lays the foundation on solid
rock. When the floodwaters rise and break against
that house, it stands firm because it is well built. 49But
anyone who hears and doesn't obey is like a person
who builds a house without a foundation. When the
floods sweep down against that house, it will collapse
into a heap of ruins."

A Roman Officer Demonstrates Faith PARALLEL

MATTHEW 8:5-13

When Jesus returned to Capernaum, a Roman officer* came and pleaded with him, 6"Lord, my young
servant* lies in bed, paralyzed and in terrible pain."
7Jesus said, "I will come and heal him."
8But the officer said, "Lord, I am not worthy to have
you come into my home. Just say the word from where
you are, and my servant will be healed. 9I know this
because I am under the authority of my superior officers, and I have authority over my soldiers. I only need
to say, 'Go,' and they go, or 'Come,' and they come. And
if I say to my slaves, 'Do this,' they do it."
10When Jesus heard this, he was amazed. Turning
to those who were following him, he said, "I tell you
the truth, I haven't seen faith like this in all Israel!

Mt 8:5 Greek *a centurion;* similarly in 8:8, 13. **Mt 8:6** Or *child;* also in 8:13.

Matt 7:24 To build "on solid rock" means to be a hearing, responding disciple, not a phony, superficial one. Practicing obedience becomes the solid foundation to weather the storms of life. See James 1:22-27 for more on putting into practice what we hear.

Matt 7:24-27 The two lives Jesus compares at the end of the Sermon on the Mount have several points in common: They both build, they both hear Jesus' teaching, and they both experience the same set of circumstances in life. The difference between them isn't caused by ignorance but by one ignoring what Jesus said. Externally, their lives may look similar; but the lasting, structural differences will be revealed by the storms of life. The immediate differences in your life when you follow Jesus may not be obvious, but eventually they will turn out to affect even your eternal destiny. To what degree does your life reflect the directions Jesus gave in this sermon?

Matt 7:26-27 Like a house of cards, the fool's life crumbles. Most people do not deliberately seek to build on a false or inferior foundation; instead, they just don't think about life's purpose. Many people are headed for destruction, not out of stubbornness but out of thoughtlessness. Part of our responsibility as believers is to help others stop and think about where their lives are headed and to point out the consequences of ignoring Christ's message.

Matt 7:29 The teachers of religious law (religious scholars) often cited traditions and quoted authorities to support their arguments and interpretations. But Jesus spoke with a new authority—his own. He didn't need to quote anyone because he was the original Word (John 1:1).

Luke 6:45 Jesus reminds us that our speech and actions reveal our true underlying beliefs, attitudes, and motivations. The good impressions we try to make cannot last if we are being deceptive. What is in your heart will come out in your speech and behavior.

Luke 6:46-49 Why would people build a house without a foundation? Perhaps to save time and avoid the hard work of preparing the stone. Possibly because the waterfront scenery is more attractive or because beach houses have higher social status than cliff houses. Perhaps because they want to join their friends who have already settled in sandy areas. Maybe because they haven't heard about the violent storms coming, or they have discounted the reports because they think disaster can't happen to them. Whatever their reason, those with no foundation are shortsighted, and they will be sorry. Obeying God is like building a house on a strong, solid foundation that stands firm when storms come. When life is calm, our foundations don't seem to matter. But when crises come, our foundations are tested. Be sure your life is built on the solid foundation of knowing and trusting Jesus Christ.

Matt 8:5-6 The Roman officer could have let many obstacles stand between him and Jesus—pride, doubt, money, language, distance, time, self-sufficiency, power, race. But he didn't. If he did not let these barriers block his approach to Jesus, we don't need to either. What keeps you from Christ?

Matt 8:8-12 This Roman officer (also called a centurion) was a career military officer in the Roman army with control over 100 soldiers. Roman soldiers, of all people, were hated by the Jews for their oppression, control, and ridicule. Yet this man's genuine faith amazed Jesus! This hated Gentile's faith put to shame the pompous piety of many of the Jewish religious leaders.

Matt 8:10-12 Jesus told the crowd that many religious Jews who should be in the Kingdom would be excluded because of their lack of faith. Entrenched in their religious traditions, they could not accept Christ and his new message. We must be careful not to become so set in our religious habits that we expect God to work only in specified ways. Don't limit God by your mind-set and lack of faith.

▸ **MATTHEW 8:5-13 *(cont.)***
11And I tell you this, that many Gentiles will come
from all over the world—from east and west—and sit
down with Abraham, Isaac, and Jacob at the feast in
the Kingdom of Heaven. 12But many Israelites—those
for whom the Kingdom was prepared—will be thrown
into outer darkness, where there will be weeping and
gnashing of teeth."
13Then Jesus said to the Roman officer, "Go back
home. Because you believed, it has happened." And
the young servant was healed that same hour.

LUKE 7:1-10
When Jesus had finished saying all this to the people,
he returned to Capernaum. 2At that time the highly
valued slave of a Roman officer* was sick and near
death. 3When the officer heard about Jesus, he sent
some respected Jewish elders to ask him to come and
heal his slave. 4So they earnestly begged Jesus to help
the man. "If anyone deserves your help, he does," they
said, 5"for he loves the Jewish people and even built
a synagogue for us."
6So Jesus went with them. But just before they
arrived at the house, the officer sent some friends
to say, "Lord, don't trouble yourself by coming to my
home, for I am not worthy of such an honor. 7I am
not even worthy to come and meet you. Just say the
word from where you are, and my servant will be
healed. 8I know this because I am under the authority of my superior officers, and I have authority over
my soldiers. I only need to say, 'Go,' and they go, or
'Come,' and they come. And if I say to my slaves, 'Do
this,' they do it."
9When Jesus heard this, he was amazed. Turning to
the crowd that was following him, he said, "I tell you,
I haven't seen faith like this in all Israel!" 10And when
the officer's friends returned to his house, they found
the slave completely healed.

Jesus Raises a Widow's Son from the Dead

LUKE 7:11-17
Soon afterward Jesus went with his disciples to the
village of Nain, and a large crowd followed him. 12A
funeral procession was coming out as he approached
the village gate. The young man who had died was a

Lk 7:2 Greek *a centurion;* similarly in 7:6.

Matt 8:11-12 Faithful people of God from "all over the world" will be gathered to feast with the Messiah (Isa 25:6-8). The Jews should have known that when the Messiah came, his blessings would be for Gentiles, too (see Isa 66:12, 19). But this message came as a shock because they were too wrapped up in their own affairs and destiny. In claiming God's promises, we must not apply them so personally or culturally that we forget to see what God wants to do to reach all the people he loves.

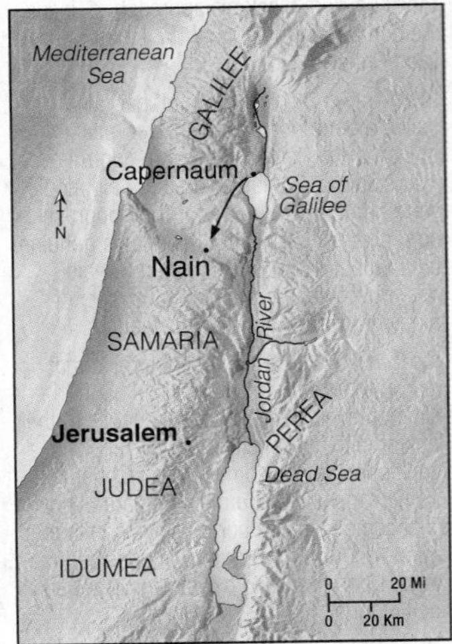

***JESUS RAISES A WIDOW'S SON FROM THE DEAD** Jesus traveled to Nain and met a funeral procession leaving the village. A widow's only son had died, but Jesus brought the young man back to life. This miracle, recorded only in Luke, reveals Jesus' compassion for people's needs.*

Matt 8:11-12 Matthew emphasizes this universal theme—Jesus' message is for everyone. The Old Testament prophets knew this (see Isa 56:3, 6-8; 66:12, 19; Mal 1:11), but many New Testament Jewish leaders chose to ignore it. Further, no one can become part of God's Kingdom on the basis of heritage or connections Each individual must choose to accept or reject the Good News. Having Christian parents is a wonderful blessing, but it won't guarantee you eternal life. You must believe in and follow Christ.

Luke 7:1ff This passage marks a turning point in Luke's account of Jesus' ministry. Up to this point, Jesus had dealt exclusively with the Jews; here he begins to include the Gentiles. Notice the main characters in this short drama: the Jewish elders, a Roman officer, and the officer's slave—very different racial and religious backgrounds, and vastly different standings on the social ladder. Jesus broke through all those barriers, all the way to the sick man's need. The gospel travels well across ethnic, racial, national, and religious barriers. Are you willing to work through them as well? Jesus was no respecter of artificial divisions, and we should follow his example. Reach out to those whom Jesus came to save.

Luke 7:2 This Roman officer was a centurion, meaning he was a captain in charge of 100 men. The officer heard about Jesus and obviously also heard about Jesus' healing power. He sent a request through some of the Jewish elders on behalf of his slave. He may have heard about the healing of the Roman official's son (which probably occurred earlier, see John 4:46-54). He knew Jesus had the power to heal his slave.

Luke 7:3 Matthew 8:5 says the Roman officer visited Jesus himself, while Luke 7:3 says he sent Jewish elders to present his request to Jesus. In those days, dealing with a person's messengers was considered the same as dealing with the one who had sent them. Thus, in dealing with the messengers, Jesus was dealing with the officer. For his Jewish audience, Matthew emphasized the Roman soldier's faith. For his Gentile audience, Luke highlighted the good relationship between the Jewish elders and the Roman officer. This army captain daily delegated work and sent groups on missions, so this was how he chose to get his message to Jesus.

Luke 7:9 The Roman officer didn't come to Jesus, and he didn't expect Jesus to come to him. Just as this officer did not need to be present to have his orders carried out, so Jesus didn't need to be present to heal. The officer's faith was especially amazing because he was a Gentile who had not been brought up to know a loving God.

Luke 7:11-17 This story illustrates salvation. The whole world was dead in sin (Eph 2:1), just as the widow's son was dead. Being dead, we could do nothing to help ourselves—we couldn't even ask for help. But God had compassion on us, and he sent Jesus to raise us to life with him (Eph 2:4-7). The dead man did not earn his second chance at life, and we cannot earn our new life in Christ. But we can accept God's gift of life, praise God for it, and use our lives to do his will.

widow's only son, and a large crowd from the village
was with her. 13When the Lord saw her, his heart overflowed with compassion. "Don't cry!" he said. 14Then
he walked over to the coffin and touched it, and the
bearers stopped. "Young man," he said, "I tell you, get
up." 15Then the dead boy sat up and began to talk! And
Jesus gave him back to his mother.
16Great fear swept the crowd, and they praised
God, saying, "A mighty prophet has risen among us,"
and "God has visited his people today." 17And the news
about Jesus spread throughout Judea and the surrounding countryside.

Jesus Eases John's Doubt PARALLEL

MATTHEW 11:1-19

When Jesus had finished giving these instructions to
his twelve disciples, he went out to teach and preach
in towns throughout the region.
2John the Baptist, who was in prison, heard about
all the things the Messiah was doing. So he sent his
disciples to ask Jesus, 3"Are you the Messiah we've
been expecting,* or should we keep looking for someone else?"
4Jesus told them, "Go back to John and tell him what
you have heard and seen—5the blind see, the lame walk,
the lepers are cured, the deaf hear, the dead are raised to
life, and the Good News is being preached to the poor.
6And tell him, 'God blesses those who do not turn away
because of me.*'"
7As John's disciples were leaving, Jesus began talking about him to the crowds. "What kind of man did
you go into the wilderness to see? Was he a weak reed,
swayed by every breath of wind? 8Or were you expecting to see a man dressed in expensive clothes? No,
people with expensive clothes live in palaces. 9Were
you looking for a prophet? Yes, and he is more than
a prophet. 10John is the man to whom the Scriptures
refer when they say,

Mt 11:3 Greek *Are you the one who is coming?* **Mt 11:6** Or *who are not offended by me.*

Luke 7:11-15 The widow's situation was serious. She had lost her husband, and now her only son had died—her last means of support. The crowd of mourners would go home, and she would be left penniless and alone. The widow was probably past the age of childbearing and would not marry again. Unless a relative came to her aid, her future was bleak. She would be an easy prey for swindlers, and she would likely be reduced to begging for food. In fact, as Luke repeatedly emphasizes, this woman was just the kind of person Jesus had come to help—and help her he did. Jesus has great compassion on your pain, and he has the power to bring hope out of any tragedy.

Luke 7:12 Honoring the dead was important in Jewish tradition. A funeral procession, with relatives of the dead person following the body that was wrapped and carried on a kind of stretcher, would make its way through town, and bystanders would be expected to join the procession. In addition, hired mourners would cry aloud and draw attention to the procession. The family's mourning would continue for 30 days.

Luke 7:16 The people thought of Jesus as a prophet because, like the Old Testament prophets, he boldly proclaimed God's message and sometimes raised the dead. Both Elijah and Elisha raised children from the dead (1 Kgs 17:17-24; 2 Kgs 4:18-37). The people were correct in thinking that Jesus was a prophet, but he is much more—he is God himself.

Matt 11:2-3 John had been put in prison by Herod. Herod had married his own sister-in-law, and John publicly rebuked Herod's flagrant sin (Matt 14:3-5). See John's Profile on p. 1292 and Herod's Profile on p. 1362.

Matt 11:4-6 As John sat in prison, he began to have some doubts about whether Jesus really was the Messiah. If John's purpose was to prepare people for the coming Messiah (Matt 3:3), and if Jesus really was that Messiah, then why was John in prison when he could have been preaching to the crowds, preparing their hearts?

Jesus answered John's doubts by pointing to the acts of healing the blind, lame, and deaf, curing lepers, raising the dead, and preaching the Good News to the poor. With so much evidence, Jesus' identity was obvious. If you sometimes doubt your salvation, the forgiveness of your sins, or God's work in your life, look at the evidence in Scripture and the changes in your life. When you doubt, don't turn away from Christ; turn to him.

Funeral Procession

The Bible tells us several things about the common burial practices of the Jews. Placing the body in the ground or in a cave was the preferred method for burial. One of the worst indignities was to be left unburied or become food for predators (Deut 28:26; 1 Kgs 11:15). If possible, the deceased were to be buried on the day of death (Deut 21:23). While embalming was not practiced, the body was dressed in special burial clothes and sprinkled with various perfumes (Mark 15:46; Luke 23:56–24:1).

Intense weeping surrounded funerals during biblical times. This wasn't simply spontaneous grief but was part of the funeral ritual (Matt 11:17). In ancient Israel, groups of paid mourners emerged who could wail on ritual cue. Much of the funeral service centered on these professional mourners who sang psalms and delivered elaborate eulogies for the dead (2 Chr 35:25; Jer 9:17-22). The Hebrews had a deep appreciation of human life and health, which were considered God's greatest gifts (Ps 91:16), which led to a particular emphasis on mourning death. In Luke 7, a young man's life had been cut short. His mother was mourning, as were those in the funeral procession. But they were met by Jesus, who raised the boy back to life and gave him to a thankful mother.

▶ **MATTHEW 11:1-19 *(cont.)***

'Look, I am sending my messenger ahead of you,
and he will prepare your way before you.'*

[11]"I tell you the truth, of all who have ever lived, none is greater than John the Baptist. Yet even the least person in the Kingdom of Heaven is greater than he is!
[12]And from the time John the Baptist began preaching until now, the Kingdom of Heaven has been forcefully advancing,* and violent people are attacking it. [13]For before John came, all the prophets and the law of Moses looked forward to this present time. [14]And if you are willing to accept what I say, he is Elijah, the one the prophets said would come.* [15]Anyone with ears to hear should listen and understand!

[16]"To what can I compare this generation? It is like children playing a game in the public square. They complain to their friends,

[17] 'We played wedding songs,
and you didn't dance,
so we played funeral songs,
and you didn't mourn.'

[18]For John didn't spend his time eating and drinking, and you say, 'He's possessed by a demon.' [19]The Son of Man,* on the other hand, feasts and drinks, and you say, 'He's a glutton and a drunkard, and a friend of tax collectors and other sinners!' But wisdom is shown to be right by its results."

LUKE 7:18-35

The disciples of John the Baptist told John about everything Jesus was doing. So John called for two of his disciples, [19]and he sent them to the Lord to ask him, "Are you the Messiah we've been expecting,* or should we keep looking for someone else?"

[20]John's two disciples found Jesus and said to him, "John the Baptist sent us to ask, 'Are you the Messiah we've been expecting, or should we keep looking for someone else?'"

[21]At that very time, Jesus cured many people of their diseases, illnesses, and evil spirits, and he restored sight to many who were blind. [22]Then he told John's disciples, "Go back to John and tell him what you have seen and heard—the blind see, the lame walk, the lepers are cured, the deaf hear, the dead are raised to life, and the Good News is being preached to the poor.
[23]And tell him, 'God blesses those who do not turn away because of me.*'"

[24]After John's disciples left, Jesus began talking about him to the crowds. "What kind of man did you go into the wilderness to see? Was he a weak reed, swayed by every breath of wind? [25]Or were you expecting to see a man dressed in expensive clothes? No, people who wear beautiful clothes and live in luxury are found in palaces. [26]Were you looking for a prophet? Yes, and he is more than a prophet. [27]John is the man to whom the Scriptures refer when they say,

'Look, I am sending my messenger ahead of you,
and he will prepare your way before you.'*

[28]I tell you, of all who have ever lived, none is greater than John. Yet even the least person in the Kingdom of God is greater than he is!"

[29]When they heard this, all the people—even the tax

Mt 11:10 Mal 3:1. **Mt 11:12** Or *the Kingdom of Heaven has suffered from violence.* **Mt 11:14** See Mal 4:5. **Mt 11:19** "Son of Man" is a title Jesus used for himself. **Lk 7:19** Greek *Are you the one who is coming?* Also in 7:20. **Lk 7:23** Or *who are not offended by me.* **Lk 7:27** Mal 3:1.

Matt 11:11 No person ever fulfilled his God-given purpose better than John. Yet in God's coming Kingdom all members will have a greater spiritual heritage than John because they will have seen and known Christ and his finished work on the cross.

Matt 11:12 There are three common views about the meaning of this verse: (1) Jesus may have been referring to a vast movement toward God, the momentum that began with John's preaching. (2) He may have been reflecting the Jewish activists' expectation that God's Kingdom would come through a violent overthrow of Rome. (3) Or he may have meant that entering God's Kingdom takes courage, unwavering faith, determination, and endurance because of the growing opposition leveled at Jesus' followers. In any case, Jesus was pointing out that John's ministry had ushered in the Kingdom of Heaven.

Matt 11:14 John was not a resurrected Elijah, but he took on Elijah's prophetic role—boldly confronting sin and pointing people to God (Mal 3:1). See Elijah's Profile on p. 719.

Matt 11:16-19 Jesus condemned the attitude of his generation. No matter what he said or did, they took the opposite view. They were cynical and skeptical because he challenged their comfortable, secure, and self-centered lives. Too often we justify our inconsistencies because listening to God may require us to change the way we live.

Luke 7:18-23 John was confused because the reports he received about Jesus were unexpected and incomplete. John's doubts were natural, and Jesus didn't rebuke him for them. Instead, he responded in a way that John would understand: Jesus explained that he had accomplished what the Messiah was supposed to accomplish. God can handle our doubts, and he welcomes our questions. Do you have questions about Jesus—about who he is or what he expects of you? Admit them to yourself and to God, and begin looking for answers. Only as you face your doubts honestly can you begin to resolve them.

Luke 7:20-22 The proofs listed here for Jesus being the Messiah are significant. They consist of observable deeds, not theories—actions that Jesus' contemporaries saw and reported for us to read today. The prophets had said that the Messiah would do these very acts (see Isa 35:5-6; 61:1). These physical proofs helped John—and will help all of us—to recognize who Jesus is.

Luke 7:28 Of all people, no one fulfilled his God-given purpose better than John. Yet in God's Kingdom, all who come after John have a greater spiritual heritage because they have clearer knowledge of the purpose of Jesus' death and resurrection. John was the last to function like the Old Testament prophets, the last to prepare the people for the coming messianic age. Jesus was not contrasting John with other Christians; he was contrasting life before Christ with life in the fullness of Christ's Kingdom.

Luke 7:29-30 The common people, including the tax collectors (who embodied evil in most people's minds) heard John's message and repented. In contrast, the Pharisees and experts in the law—religious leaders—rejected his words. Wanting to live their own way, they justified their own point of view and refused to listen to other ideas. They "rejected God's plan for them." They were so close to Jesus, and yet so far away. The truth stood before them, and they rejected it. What have you done with the truth you read in God's Word?

collectors—agreed that God's way was right,* for they
had been baptized by John. 30 But the Pharisees and
experts in religious law rejected God's plan for them,
for they had refused John's baptism.

31 "To what can I compare the people of this generation?" Jesus asked. "How can I describe them? 32 They
are like children playing a game in the public square.
They complain to their friends,

'We played wedding songs,
and you didn't dance,
so we played funeral songs,
and you didn't weep.'

33 For John the Baptist didn't spend his time eating
bread or drinking wine, and you say, 'He's possessed
by a demon.' 34 The Son of Man,* on the other hand,
feasts and drinks, and you say, 'He's a glutton and a
drunkard, and a friend of tax collectors and other
sinners!' 35 But wisdom is shown to be right by the lives
of those who follow it.*"

Jesus Promises Rest for the Soul

MATTHEW 11:20-30

Then Jesus began to denounce the towns where he
had done so many of his miracles, because they hadn't
repented of their sins and turned to God. 21 "What
sorrow awaits you, Korazin and Bethsaida! For if the
miracles I did in you had been done in wicked Tyre and
Sidon, their people would have repented of their sins
long ago, clothing themselves in burlap and throwing
ashes on their heads to show their remorse. 22 I tell
you, Tyre and Sidon will be better off on judgment
day than you.

23 "And you people of Capernaum, will you be honored in heaven? No, you will go down to the place of
the dead.* For if the miracles I did for you had been
done in wicked Sodom, it would still be here today. 24 I
tell you, even Sodom will be better off on judgment
day than you."

25 At that time Jesus prayed this prayer: "O Father,
Lord of heaven and earth, thank you for hiding these
things from those who think themselves wise and
clever, and for revealing them to the childlike. 26 Yes,
Father, it pleased you to do it this way!

27 "My Father has entrusted everything to me. No
one truly knows the Son except the Father, and no
one truly knows the Father except the Son and those
to whom the Son chooses to reveal him."

28 Then Jesus said, "Come to me, all of you who are
weary and carry heavy burdens, and I will give you rest.
29 Take my yoke upon you. Let me teach you, because I
am humble and gentle at heart, and you will find rest

Lk 7:29 Or *praised God for his justice.* **Lk 7:34** "Son of Man" is a title Jesus used for himself. **Lk 7:35** Or *But wisdom is justified by all her children.* **Mt 11:23** Greek *to Hades.*

Luke 7:31-35 The religious leaders hated both John and Jesus, but they did not bother to be consistent in their faultfinding. They criticized John the Baptist because he fasted and drank no wine; they criticized Jesus because he ate heartily and drank wine with tax collectors and sinners. Their real objection to both men, of course, had nothing to do with dietary habits. What the Pharisees and experts in the law couldn't stand was being exposed for their hypocrisy.

Luke 7:33-35 The Pharisees weren't troubled by their inconsistency toward John the Baptist and Jesus. They were good at justifying their "wisdom." Most of us can find compelling reasons to do or believe whatever suits our purposes. If we do not examine our ideas in the light of God's truth, however, we may be just as obviously self-serving as the Pharisees.

Matt 11:21-24 Tyre, Sidon, and Sodom were ancient cities with a long-standing reputation for wickedness (Gen 18–19; Ezek 27–28). Each was destroyed by God for its evil. The people of Bethsaida, Korazin, and Capernaum saw Jesus firsthand, and yet they stubbornly refused to repent of their sins and believe in him. Jesus said that if those wicked cities had seen him, they would have repented. Because Bethsaida, Korazin, and Capernaum saw Jesus and didn't believe, they would suffer even greater punishment than would those who hadn't seen him. Similarly, nations and cities with churches on every corner and Bibles in every home will have no excuse on judgment day if they do not repent and believe.

Matt 11:25 Jesus mentioned two kinds of people in his prayer: the "wise and clever"—arrogant in their own knowledge—and the "childlike"—humbly open to receive the truth of God's Word. Are you wise in your own eyes, or do you seek the truth with childlike faith, realizing that only God holds all the answers?

Matt 11:27 In the Old Testament, "to know" someone meant more than head knowledge; it implied an intimate relationship. The communion between God the Father and God the Son is the core of their relationship. For anyone else to know God, God must reveal himself to that person, by the Son's choice. How fortunate we are that Jesus has clearly revealed God to us, as well as his truth and how we can know him.

Matt 11:28-30 A yoke is a heavy wooden harness that fits over the shoulders of an ox or oxen. It is attached to a piece of equipment the oxen are to pull. A person may be carrying heavy burdens of sin, excessive demands of religious leaders (Matt 23:4; Acts 15:10), oppression and persecution, or weariness in the search for God. Jesus frees people from all these burdens. The rest that Jesus promises is love, healing, and peace with God, not the end of all labor. A relationship with God changes meaningless, wearisome toil into spiritual productivity and purpose.

Yoke

A yoke was a wooden bar that allowed two (or more) animals to be teamed up (yoked) so that they might effectively work together (Num 19:2; 1 Kgs 19:19; Job 1:3). The Bible frequently uses yoke language metaphorically to refer to work or slavery (Lev 26:13). The yoke of slavery was applied not only by foreign oppressors but often by Israel's own kings (1 Kgs 12:4-14; 2 Chr 10:4-14). In prophetic writings, the yoke of slavery was generally associated with divine judgment (Lam 1:14), so that deliverance was represented as God breaking the yoke ("chains," "heavy loads") that had enslaved Israel (Isa 9:4; 10:27; 14:25; 58:6; Jer 2:20; 5:5). In the New Testament Jesus transforms "yoke" into a positive term by calling on us to take up his yoke, which is not burdensome, and he will give us rest for our souls (Matt 11:29-30). Have you tied yourself to Jesus?

▸ **MATTHEW 11:20-30 *(cont.)***

for your souls. 30For my yoke is easy to bear, and the
burden I give you is light."

A Sinful Woman Anoints Jesus' Feet

LUKE 7:36-50

One of the Pharisees asked Jesus to have dinner with
him, so Jesus went to his home and sat down to eat.*
37When a certain immoral woman from that city
heard he was eating there, she brought a beautiful
alabaster jar filled with expensive perfume. 38Then
she knelt behind him at his feet, weeping. Her tears
fell on his feet, and she wiped them off with her hair.
Then she kept kissing his feet and putting perfume
on them.
39When the Pharisee who had invited him saw this,
he said to himself, "If this man were a prophet, he
would know what kind of woman is touching him.
She's a sinner!"
40Then Jesus answered his thoughts. "Simon," he
said to the Pharisee, "I have something to say to you."
"Go ahead, Teacher," Simon replied.
41Then Jesus told him this story: "A man loaned
money to two people—500 pieces of silver* to one
and 50 pieces to the other. 42But neither of them could
repay him, so he kindly forgave them both, canceling their debts. Who do you suppose loved him more
after that?"
43Simon answered, "I suppose the one for whom he
canceled the larger debt."
"That's right," Jesus said. 44Then he turned to the
woman and said to Simon, "Look at this woman kneeling here. When I entered your home, you didn't offer
me water to wash the dust from my feet, but she has
washed them with her tears and wiped them with
her hair. 45You didn't greet me with a kiss, but from
the time I first came in, she has not stopped kissing
my feet. 46You neglected the courtesy of olive oil to
anoint my head, but she has anointed my feet with
rare perfume.
47"I tell you, her sins—and they are many—have been
forgiven, so she has shown me much love. But a person
who is forgiven little shows only little love." 48Then Jesus
said to the woman, "Your sins are forgiven."
49The men at the table said among themselves,
"Who is this man, that he goes around forgiving sins?"

Lk 7:36 Or *and reclined.* **Lk 7:41** Greek *500 denarii.* A denarius was equivalent to a laborer's full day's wage.

Matt 11:30 In what sense is Jesus' yoke easy? The yoke emphasizes the challenges, work, and difficulties of partnering with Christ in life. Responsibilities, even the effort of staying true to God, weigh us down. But Jesus' yoke remains easy compared to the crushing alternative.

Jesus doesn't offer a life of luxurious ease—the yoke is still an oxen's tool for working hard. But it's a shared yoke, with weight falling on bigger shoulders than yours. Someone with more pulling power is alongside helping. Suddenly you are participating in life's responsibilities with a great partner—and now that frown can turn into a smile, and that gripe into a song.

Luke 7:36ff A similar incident occurred later in Jesus' ministry (see Matt 26:6-13; Mark 14:3-9; John 12:1-11).

Luke 7:38 Although the woman was not an invited guest, she entered the house anyway and knelt behind Jesus at his feet. In Jesus' day, it was customary to recline while eating. Dinner guests would lie on couches with their heads near the table, propping themselves up on one elbow and stretching their feet out behind them. The woman could easily anoint Jesus' feet without approaching the table.

JESUS AND WOMEN

As a non-Jew recording the words and works of Jesus' life, Luke demonstrates a special sensitivity to other "outsiders" with whom Jesus came into contact. For instance, Luke records five events involving women that are not mentioned in the other Gospels. In first-century Jewish culture, women were usually treated as second-class citizens with few of the rights men had. But Jesus crossed those barriers, and Luke showed the special care Jesus had for women. Jesus treated all people with equal respect. These passages below tell of his encounters with women.

Jesus talks to a Samaritan woman at the well.	John 4:1-26
Jesus raises a widow's son from the dead.	Luke 7:11-17
A sinful woman anoints Jesus' feet.	Luke 7:36-50
Jesus forgives an adulterous woman.	John 8:1-11
A group of women travels with Jesus.	Luke 8:1-3
Jesus visits Mary and Martha.	Luke 10:38-42
Jesus heals a crippled woman.	Luke 13:10-17
Jesus heals the daughter of a Gentile woman.	Mark 7:24-30
Weeping women follow Jesus on his way to the cross.	Luke 23:27-31
Jesus' mother and other women gather at the cross.	John 19:25-27
Jesus appears to Mary Magdalene.	Mark 16:9-11
Jesus appears to other women after his resurrection.	Matt 28:8-10

Luke 7:44ff Again Luke contrasts the Pharisees with sinners—and again the sinners come out ahead. Simon had committed several social errors by neglecting to wash Jesus' feet (a courtesy extended to guests because sandaled feet got very dirty), anoint his head with oil, and offer him the kiss of greeting. Did Simon perhaps feel that he was too good for Jesus? Was he trying to give Jesus a subtle put-down? Whatever the case, the contrast is vivid. The sinful woman lavished tears, expensive perfume, and kisses on her Savior. In this story it is the grateful immoral woman, not the religious leader, whose sins were forgiven. Although God's grace through faith is what saves us, not acts of love or generosity, this woman's act demonstrated her true faith, and Jesus honored her.

Luke 7:47 Overflowing love is the natural response to forgiveness and the appropriate consequence of faith. But only those who realize the depth of their sin can appreciate the complete forgiveness that God offers them. Jesus has rescued all of his followers from eternal death, whether they were once extremely wicked or conventionally good. Do you appreciate the wideness

[50]And Jesus said to the woman, "Your faith has saved you; go in peace."

Women Accompany Jesus and the Disciples

LUKE 8:1-3

Soon afterward Jesus began a tour of the nearby towns and villages, preaching and announcing the Good News about the Kingdom of God. He took his twelve disciples with him, [2]along with some women who had been cured of evil spirits and diseases. Among them were Mary Magdalene, from whom he had cast out seven demons; [3]Joanna, the wife of Chuza, Herod's business manager; Susanna; and many others who were contributing from their own resources to support Jesus and his disciples.

Religious Leaders Accuse Jesus of Getting His Power from Satan PARALLEL •••

MATTHEW 12:22-37 •○○

Then a demon-possessed man, who was blind and couldn't speak, was brought to Jesus. He healed the man so that he could both speak and see. [23]The crowd was amazed and asked, "Could it be that Jesus is the Son of David, the Messiah?"

[24]But when the Pharisees heard about the miracle, they said, "No wonder he can cast out demons. He gets his power from Satan,* the prince of demons."

[25]Jesus knew their thoughts and replied, "Any kingdom divided by civil war is doomed. A town or family splintered by feuding will fall apart. [26]And if Satan is casting out Satan, he is divided and fighting against himself. His own kingdom will not survive. [27]And if I am empowered by Satan, what about your own exorcists? They cast out demons, too, so they will condemn you for what you have said. [28]But if I am casting out demons by the Spirit of God, then the Kingdom of God has arrived among you. [29]For who is powerful enough to enter the house of a strong man like Satan and plunder his goods? Only someone even stronger—someone who could tie him up and then plunder his house.

[30]"Anyone who isn't with me opposes me, and anyone who isn't working with me is actually working against me.

[31]"So I tell you, every sin and blasphemy can be forgiven—except blasphemy against the Holy Spirit, which will never be forgiven. [32]Anyone who speaks against the Son of Man can be forgiven, but anyone who speaks against the Holy Spirit will never be forgiven, either in this world or in the world to come.

[33]"A tree is identified by its fruit. If a tree is good, its fruit will be good. If a tree is bad, its fruit will be bad. [34]You brood of snakes! How could evil men like you speak what is good and right? For whatever is in your heart determines what you say. [35]A good person produces good things from the treasury of a good heart, and an evil person produces evil things from the treasury of an evil heart. [36]And I tell you this, you

Mt 12:24 Greek *Beelzeboul;* also in 12:27. Other manuscripts read *Beezeboul;* Latin version reads *Beelzebub.*

of God's mercy? Are you grateful for his forgiveness?

Luke 7:49-50 The Pharisees believed that only God could forgive sins, so they wondered why this man, Jesus, was saying that the woman's sins were forgiven. They did not grasp the fact that Jesus was indeed God. (See also Luke 5:17-26.)

Luke 8:2-3 Jesus lifted women up from degradation and servitude to the joy of fellowship and service. In Jewish culture, women were not supposed to learn from rabbis. By allowing these women to travel with him, Jesus was showing that all people are equal under God. These women supported Jesus' ministry with their own money. They owed a great debt to him because he had driven demons out of some and had healed others.

Luke 8:2-3 Here we catch a glimpse of a few of the people behind the scenes in Jesus' ministry. The ministry of those in the foreground is supported by those whose work is less visible but essential. Offer your resources to God, whether or not you will be on center stage.

Matt 12:24 The Pharisees were trying to discredit him by using an emotional argument. Refusing to believe that Jesus came from God, they said he was in league with Satan. Jesus easily exposed the foolishness of their argument.

Matt 12:25 In the Incarnation, Jesus gave up the complete and unlimited use of his supernatural abilities. But he still had profound insight into human nature. His discernment stopped the religious leaders' attempts to trick him. The resurrected Christ knows all our thoughts. This can be both comforting and threatening: He knows what we really mean when we speak to him, and he knows any selfish motives because we cannot hide from him.

Matt 12:29 At Jesus' birth, Satan's power and control were disrupted. In the wilderness Jesus overcame Satan's temptations, and at the Resurrection he defeated Satan's ultimate weapon—death. Eventually Satan will be constrained forever (Rev 20:10), and evil will no longer pervade the earth. Jesus has complete power and authority over Satan and all his forces.

Matt 12:30 It is impossible to be neutral about Christ. Anyone who is not actively following him has chosen to reject him. Any person who tries to remain neutral in the struggle of good against evil is choosing to be separated from God, who alone is good. To refuse to follow Christ is to choose to be on Satan's team.

Matt 12:31-32 The Pharisees had blasphemed against the Spirit by attributing the power by which Christ did miracles to Satan (Matt 12:24) instead of the Holy Spirit. The unpardonable sin is the deliberate refusal to acknowledge God's power in Christ. It indicates an intentional and irreversible hardness of heart. Sometimes believers worry that they have accidentally committed this unforgivable sin. But only those who have turned their backs on God and rejected all faith have any need to worry. Jesus said they can't be forgiven—not because their sin is worse than any other but because they will never ask for forgiveness. Those who reject the prompting of the Holy Spirit remove themselves from the only force that can lead them to repentance and restoration to God.

Matt 12:34-36 Jesus reminds us that what we say reveals what is in our hearts. What kinds of words come from your mouth? That is an indication of what is in your heart. But you can't solve your heart problem just by cleaning up your speech. You must allow the Holy Spirit to fill you with new attitudes and motives; then your speech will be cleansed at its source.

▸ MATTHEW 12:22-37 *(cont.)*

must give an account on judgment day for every idle word you speak. 37The words you say will either acquit you or condemn you."

MARK 3:20-30

One time Jesus entered a house, and the crowds began to gather again. Soon he and his disciples couldn't even find time to eat. 21When his family heard what was happening, they tried to take him away. "He's out of his mind," they said.

22But the teachers of religious law who had arrived from Jerusalem said, "He's possessed by Satan,* the prince of demons. That's where he gets the power to cast out demons."

23Jesus called them over and responded with an illustration. "How can Satan cast out Satan?" he asked. 24"A kingdom divided by civil war will collapse. 25Similarly, a family splintered by feuding will fall apart. 26And if Satan is divided and fights against himself, how can he stand? He would never survive. 27Let me illustrate this further. Who is powerful enough to enter the house of a strong man like Satan and plunder his goods? Only someone even stronger—someone who could tie him up and then plunder his house.

28"I tell you the truth, all sin and blasphemy can be forgiven, 29but anyone who blasphemes the Holy Spirit will never be forgiven. This is a sin with eternal consequences." 30He told them this because they were saying, "He's possessed by an evil spirit."

LUKE 11:14-23

One day Jesus cast out a demon from a man who couldn't speak, and when the demon was gone, the man began to speak. The crowds were amazed, 15but some of them said, "No wonder he can cast out demons. He gets his power from Satan,* the prince of demons." 16Others, trying to test Jesus, demanded that he show them a miraculous sign from heaven to prove his authority.

17He knew their thoughts, so he said, "Any kingdom divided by civil war is doomed. A family splintered by feuding will fall apart. 18You say I am empowered by Satan. But if Satan is divided and fighting against himself, how can his kingdom survive? 19And if I am empowered by Satan, what about your own exorcists? They cast out demons, too, so they will condemn you for what you have said. 20But if I am casting out demons by the power of God,* then the Kingdom of God has arrived among you. 21For when a strong man like Satan is fully armed and guards his palace, his possessions are safe—22until someone even stronger attacks and overpowers him, strips him of his weapons, and carries off his belongings.

23"Anyone who isn't with me opposes me, and anyone who isn't working with me is actually working against me."

Mk 3:22 Greek *Beelzeboul;* other manuscripts read *Beezeboul;* Latin version reads *Beelzebub.* **Lk 11:15** Greek *Beelzeboul;* also in 11:18, 19. Other manuscripts read *Beezeboul;* Latin version reads *Beelzebub.* **Lk 11:20** Greek *by the finger of God.*

Mark 3:21 With the crowds pressing in on him, Jesus didn't even take time to eat. Because of this, his friends and family came to take charge of him, thinking he had gone "over the edge" as a religious fanatic (see also Mark 3:31-32). They were concerned for him, but they missed the point of his ministry. Even those who were closest to Jesus were slow to understand who he was and what he had come to do.

Mark 3:21 The family may be the most difficult place to be a witness for Jesus. To be the first or only Christian may go against the grain. Your faith may be misinterpreted as criticism. Your zeal may be misunderstood. You may be accused of being a hypocrite because other areas of your life still fall short of Christ's ideals. Uncommitted people may view your new commitment to the Bible as unreasonable bigotry.

Family members require the most patience. They see you at your worst when your guard is down. Remember that Christ's family rejected and ridiculed him. Jesus knows what you face by trying to be a witness for him in your own family. Stay true to your faith. Don't respond negatively to the attacks that may come. Over time, your love for your family will have a positive effect.

Mark 3:22-27 These teachers of the law brought a nonsensical accusation against Jesus. They tried to say that Jesus was driving out demons by the power of the prince of demons—in other words, that Jesus' power came from Satan, not God. They wanted the people to believe that Jesus himself was possessed (Mark 3:30). This would disprove his claim to be the Messiah and place him instead in league with the devil.

The more effective you are in your Christian life, the more extreme will be the attacks of the enemy. Even the most ridiculous accusation will convince some when it's cleverly packaged to sound sincere and concerned. Stand firm for the truth, even when clever attacks come.

Mark 3:27 Although God permits Satan to work in our world, God is still in control. Because he is God, Jesus has power over Satan and is able to drive out demons, thus ending their terrible work in people's lives. One day Satan will be bound forever (Rev 20:10).

Mark 3:28-29 Christians sometimes wonder if they have committed this sin of blaspheming the Holy Spirit. Christians need not worry because this sin is defined as attributing to the devil the work of the Holy Spirit. It reveals a heart attitude of unbelief and unrepentance. Deliberate, ongoing rejection of the work of the Holy Spirit is blasphemy because it is rejecting God himself. The religious leaders accused Jesus of blasphemy, but ironically they were the guilty ones when they looked Jesus in the face and accused him of being possessed by Satan.

Luke 11:15-20 Some of the Pharisees' followers were exorcists too—that is, they drove out demons. The Pharisees' accusations were becoming more desperate. To accuse Jesus of being empowered by Satan, the prince of demons, because Jesus was driving out demons was also to say that the Pharisees' own exorcists were doing Satan's work. Jesus turned the religious leaders' accusation against them. He first dismissed their claim as absurd (Why would the devil drive out his own demons?). Then he engaged in a little irony ("What about your own exorcists?"). Finally, he concluded that his work of driving out demons proved that the Kingdom of God had arrived.

Satan, who had controlled the kingdom of this world for thousands of years (see note on Matt 4:8-9, p. 1295), was now being overpowered by Jesus and the Kingdom of Heaven. Jesus' Kingdom began to come into power at Jesus' birth and grew as he resisted the wilderness temptations. It established itself through his teachings and healings, blossomed in victory at his resurrection and at Pentecost, and will become permanent and universal at his second coming.

Luke 11:21-22 Jesus may have been referring to Isaiah 49:24-26. Regardless of how great Satan's power is, Jesus is stronger still.

Religious Leaders Ask Jesus for a Miraculous Sign PARALLEL

MATTHEW 12:38-45

One day some teachers of religious law and Pharisees
came to Jesus and said, "Teacher, we want you to show
us a miraculous sign to prove your authority."
39But Jesus replied, "Only an evil, adulterous generation would demand a miraculous sign; but the only
sign I will give them is the sign of the prophet Jonah.
40For as Jonah was in the belly of the great fish for
three days and three nights, so will the Son of Man
be in the heart of the earth for three days and three
nights.
41"The people of Nineveh will stand up against
this generation on judgment day and condemn it,
for they repented of their sins at the preaching of
Jonah. Now someone greater than Jonah is here—
but you refuse to repent. 42The queen of Sheba* will
also stand up against this generation on judgment
day and condemn it, for she came from a distant
land to hear the wisdom of Solomon. Now someone greater than Solomon is here—but you refuse
to listen.
43"When an evil* spirit leaves a person, it goes into
the desert, seeking rest but finding none. 44Then it
says, 'I will return to the person I came from.' So it
returns and finds its former home empty, swept,
and in order. 45Then the spirit finds seven other
spirits more evil than itself, and they all enter the
person and live there. And so that person is worse
off than before. That will be the experience of this
evil generation."

LUKE 11:24-32

"When an evil* spirit leaves a person, it goes into the
desert, searching for rest. But when it finds none, it
says, 'I will return to the person I came from.' 25So it
returns and finds that its former home is all swept
and in order. 26Then the spirit finds seven other spirits more evil than itself, and they all enter the person and live there. And so that person is worse off
than before."
27As he was speaking, a woman in the crowd called
out, "God bless your mother—the womb from which
you came, and the breasts that nursed you!"
28Jesus replied, "But even more blessed are all who
hear the word of God and put it into practice."

Mt 12:42 Greek *The queen of the south.* **Mt 12:43** Greek *unclean.* **Lk 11:24** Greek *unclean.*

He will overpower Satan and dispose of him for eternity (see Rev 20:2, 10).

Luke 11:23 How does this verse relate to Luke 9:50: "Anyone who is not against you is for you"? In chapter 9, Jesus was talking about a person who was driving out demons in Jesus' name. Those who fight evil, he was saying, are on the same side as the one driving out demons in Jesus' name. Here, by contrast, he was talking about the conflict between God and the devil. In this battle, a person who is not on God's side is on Satan's. There is no neutral ground. Since God has already won the battle, why be on the losing side? If you aren't actively for Christ, you are against him.

Matt 12:38-40 The Pharisees were asking for another miraculous sign, but they were not sincerely seeking to know Jesus. Jesus knew they had already seen enough miraculous proof to convince them that he was the Messiah if they would just open their hearts. But they had already decided not to believe in him, and more miracles would not change that.

Many people have said, "If I could just see a real miracle, then I could really believe in God." But Jesus' response to the Pharisees applies to us. We have plenty of evidence—Jesus' birth, death, resurrection, and ascension, and centuries of his work in believers around the world. Instead of looking for additional evidence or miracles, accept what God has already given and move forward. He may use your life as evidence to reach another person.

Matt 12:39-41 Jonah was a prophet sent to the Assyrian city of Nineveh (see the book of Jonah). Because Assyria was such a cruel and warlike nation, Jonah tried to run from his assignment and ended up spending three days in the belly of a huge fish. When Jonah got out, he grudgingly went to Nineveh, preached God's message, and saw the city repent. By contrast, when Jesus came to his people, they refused to repent. Here Jesus is clearly saying that his resurrection will prove he is the Messiah. Three days after his death, Jesus will come back to life, just as Jonah was given a new chance at life after three days in the fish.

Matt 12:41-42 In Jonah's day, Nineveh was the capital of the Assyrian Empire, and it was as evil as it was powerful (Jon 1:2). But the entire city repented at Jonah's preaching. The queen of Sheba traveled far to see Solomon, king of Israel, and learn about his great wisdom (1 Kgs 10:1-10; also see the note on Luke 11:31-32, p. 1344, for more on the queen of Sheba). These Gentiles recognized the truth about God when it was presented to them, unlike the religious leaders, who ignored the truth even though it stared them in the face. How have you responded to the evidence and truth that you have?

Matt 12:43-45 Jesus was describing the attitude of the nation of Israel and the religious leaders in particular. Just cleaning up one's life without filling it with God leaves plenty of room for Satan to enter. The book of Ezra records how the people rid themselves of idolatry but failed to replace it with love for God and obedience to him. Ridding our life of sin is the first step. We must also take the second step: filling our life with God's Word and the Holy Spirit. Unfilled and complacent people are easy targets for Satan.

Luke 11:24-26 Jesus was illustrating an unfortunate human tendency: Our desire to reform often does not last long. In Israel's history, almost as soon as a good king would pull down idols, a bad king would set them up again. It is not enough to be emptied of evil; we must then be filled with the power of the Holy Spirit to accomplish God's new purpose in our life (see also Matt 12:43-45; Gal 5:22).

Luke 11:27-28 Jesus was speaking to people who put an extremely high value on family ties. Their genealogies were important guarantees that they were part of God's chosen people. A man's value came from his ancestors, and a woman's value came from the sons she bore. Jesus' response to the woman meant that a person's obedience to God is more important than the place on the family tree. Consistent obedience is more important than the honor of bearing a respected son.

▸ **LUKE 11:24-32 *(cont.)***
29As the crowd pressed in on Jesus, he said, "This
evil generation keeps asking me to show them a miraculous sign. But the only sign I will give them is the
sign of Jonah. 30What happened to him was a sign to
the people of Nineveh that God had sent him. What
happens to the Son of Man* will be a sign to these
people that he was sent by God.
31"The queen of Sheba* will stand up against this
generation on judgment day and condemn it, for she
came from a distant land to hear the wisdom of Solomon. Now someone greater than Solomon is here—
but you refuse to listen. 32The people of Nineveh will
also stand up against this generation on judgment day
and condemn it, for they repented of their sins at the
preaching of Jonah. Now someone greater than Jonah
is here—but you refuse to repent."

Jesus Describes His True Family PARALLEL

MATTHEW 12:46-50
As Jesus was speaking to the crowd, his mother
and brothers stood outside, asking to speak to him.
47Someone told Jesus, "Your mother and your brothers
are outside, and they want to speak to you."*
48Jesus asked, "Who is my mother? Who are my
brothers?" 49Then he pointed to his disciples and said,
"Look, these are my mother and brothers. 50Anyone
who does the will of my Father in heaven is my brother
and sister and mother!"

MARK 3:31-35
Then Jesus' mother and brothers came to see him.
They stood outside and sent word for him to come
out and talk with them. 32There was a crowd sitting
around Jesus, and someone said, "Your mother and
your brothers* are outside asking for you."
33Jesus replied, "Who is my mother? Who are my
brothers?" 34Then he looked at those around him
and said, "Look, these are my mother and brothers.
35Anyone who does God's will is my brother and sister
and mother."

LUKE 8:19-21
Then Jesus' mother and brothers came to see him,
but they couldn't get to him because of the crowd.
20Someone told Jesus, "Your mother and your brothers
are outside, and they want to see you."
21Jesus replied, "My mother and my brothers are all
those who hear God's word and obey it."

The Parable of the Four Soils PARALLEL

MATTHEW 13:1-23
Later that same day Jesus left the house and sat beside
the lake. 2A large crowd soon gathered around him, so

Lk 11:30 "Son of Man" is a title Jesus used for himself. **Lk 11:31** Greek *The queen of the south.* **Mt 12:47** Some manuscripts do not include verse 47. Compare Mark 3:32 and Luke 8:20. **Mk 3:32** Some manuscripts add *and sisters.*

Luke 11:29-32 The cruel, warlike men of Nineveh, capital of Assyria, repented when Jonah preached to them—and Jonah did not even care about them. The pagan queen of Sheba praised the God of Israel when she heard Solomon's wisdom, and Solomon was full of faults. By contrast, Jesus, the perfect Son of God, came to people whom he loved dearly—but they rejected him. Thus, God's chosen people made themselves more liable to judgment than either a notoriously wicked nation or a powerful pagan queen. Compare Luke 10:12-15, where Jesus says the evil cities of Sodom, Tyre, and Sidon will be judged less harshly than the cities in Judea and Galilee that rejected Jesus' message.

Luke 11:29-30 What was the sign of Jonah? God had asked Jonah to preach repentance to the Gentiles (non-Jews). Jesus was affirming Jonah's message. Salvation is not only for Jews but for all people. Matthew 12:40 adds another explanation: Jesus would die and rise after three days, just as the prophet Jonah was rescued after three days in the belly of the great fish.

Luke 11:31-32 The people of Nineveh and the queen of Sheba had turned to God with far less evidence than Jesus was giving his listeners—and far less than we have today. We have eyewitness reports of the risen Jesus, the continuing power of the Holy Spirit unleashed at Pentecost, easy access to the Bible, and knowledge of 2,000 years of Christ's acts through his church. With the knowledge and insight available to us, our response to Christ ought to be even more complete and wholehearted.

Matt 12:46-50 Jesus was not denying his responsibility to his earthly family. On the contrary, he criticized the religious leaders for not following the Old Testament command to honor their parents (Matt 15:1-9). He provided for his mother's security as he hung on the cross (John 19:25-27). His mother and brothers were present in the upper room at Pentecost (Acts 1:14). Instead, Jesus was pointing out that spiritual relationships are as binding as physical ones, and he was paving the way for a new community of believers (the universal church), our spiritual family.

Mark 3:31-35 Jesus' mother was Mary (Luke 1:30-31), and his brothers were probably the other children Mary and Joseph had after Jesus (see also Mark 6:3). Some Christians believe the ancient tradition that Jesus was Mary's only child. If this is true, the "brothers" were possibly cousins (cousins were often called brothers in those days). Some have offered yet another suggestion: When Joseph married Mary, he was a widower, and these were his children by his first marriage. Most likely, however, these were Jesus' half brothers (see Mark 6:3-4).

Jesus' family did not yet fully understand his ministry, as can be seen in Mark 3:21. Jesus explained that in our spiritual family, the relationships are ultimately more important and longer lasting than those formed by our physical families.

Mark 3:33-35 God's family is accepting and doesn't exclude anyone. Although Jesus cared for his mother and brothers, he also cared for all those who loved him. Jesus did not show partiality; he allowed everyone the privilege of obeying God and becoming part of his family. In our increasingly computerized, impersonal world, warm relationships among members of God's family take on major importance. The church should give the loving, personalized care that many people find nowhere else.

Luke 8:21 Jesus' true family is comprised of those who hear and obey his words. Hearing without obeying is not enough. As Jesus loved his mother (see John 19:25-27), so he loves us. Christ offers us an intimate family relationship with him (Rom 8:14-16).

Matt 13:2-3 Jesus used many stories, or parables (Matt 13:34), when speaking to the crowds. These stories compare something familiar to something unfamiliar, helping us understand spiritual truth by using everyday objects and relationships. Jesus' parables compel listeners to discover truth, while at the same time concealing the truth from those too lazy or too stubborn to see it. To those who are honestly searching, the truth becomes clear.

he got into a boat. Then he sat there and taught as the
people stood on the shore. 3He told many stories in
the form of parables, such as this one:

"Listen! A farmer went out to plant some seeds.
4As he scattered them across his field, some seeds
fell on a footpath, and the birds came and ate them.
5Other seeds fell on shallow soil with underlying
rock. The seeds sprouted quickly because the soil
was shallow. 6But the plants soon wilted under the
hot sun, and since they didn't have deep roots, they
died. 7Other seeds fell among thorns that grew up
and choked out the tender plants. 8Still other seeds
fell on fertile soil, and they produced a crop that was
thirty, sixty, and even a hundred times as much as
had been planted! 9Anyone with ears to hear should
listen and understand."

10His disciples came and asked him, "Why do you
use parables when you talk to the people?"

11He replied, "You are permitted to understand
the secrets* of the Kingdom of Heaven, but others
are not. 12To those who listen to my teaching, more
understanding will be given, and they will have an
abundance of knowledge. But for those who are not
listening, even what little understanding they have
will be taken away from them. 13That is why I use
these parables,

For they look, but they don't really see.
They hear, but they don't really listen or
understand.

14This fulfills the prophecy of Isaiah that says,

'When you hear what I say,
you will not understand.
When you see what I do,
you will not comprehend.
15 For the hearts of these people are hardened,
and their ears cannot hear,
and they have closed their eyes—
so their eyes cannot see,
and their ears cannot hear,
and their hearts cannot understand,
and they cannot turn to me
and let me heal them.'*

16"But blessed are your eyes, because they see; and
your ears, because they hear. 17I tell you the truth,
many prophets and righteous people longed to see
what you see, but they didn't see it. And they longed
to hear what you hear, but they didn't hear it.

18"Now listen to the explanation of the parable
about the farmer planting seeds: 19The seed that fell
on the footpath represents those who hear the message about the Kingdom and don't understand it. Then
the evil one comes and snatches away the seed that
was planted in their hearts. 20The seed on the rocky
soil represents those who hear the message and immediately receive it with joy. 21But since they don't
have deep roots, they don't last long. They fall away
as soon as they have problems or are persecuted for
believing God's word. 22The seed that fell among the
thorns represents those who hear God's word, but all
too quickly the message is crowded out by the worries of this life and the lure of wealth, so no fruit is
produced. 23The seed that fell on good soil represents
those who truly hear and understand God's word and
produce a harvest of thirty, sixty, or even a hundred
times as much as had been planted!"

Mt 13:11 Greek *the mysteries.* **Mt 13:14-15** Isa 6:9-10 (Greek version).

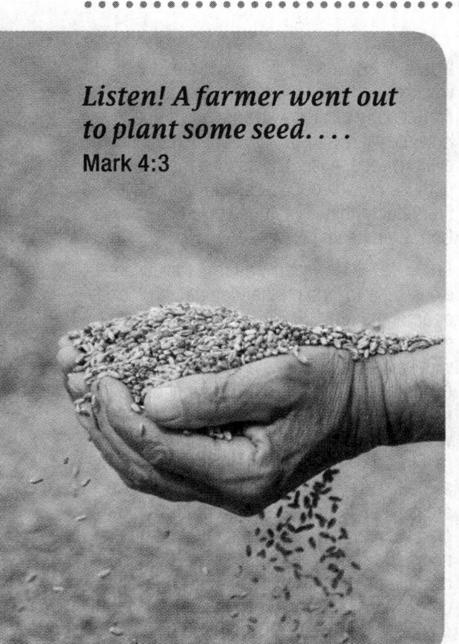

Listen! A farmer went out to plant some seed. . . .
Mark 4:3

Matt 13:8 This parable should encourage spiritual "farmers"—those who teach, preach, and seek to lead others to the Lord. The farmer sowed good seed, but not all the seed sprouted; even the plants that grew had varying yields. Don't be discouraged if you do not always see results as you faithfully teach the Word. Belief cannot be forced to follow a mathematical formula (i.e., a 4:1 ratio of seeds planted to seeds sprouted). Rather, it is a miracle of God's Holy Spirit using your words to produce faith in Christ.

Matt 13:9-10 Human ears hear many sounds, but there is a deeper kind of listening that results in spiritual understanding. When speaking in parables, Jesus was not hiding truth from sincere seekers, because those who were receptive to spiritual truth understood the illustrations. To others they were only stories without meaning.

Matt 13:12 This phrase means that we are responsible to use well what we have. When people reject Jesus, their hardness of heart drives away or renders useless even the little understanding they had.

Matt 13:22 How easy it is to agree with Christ but with no intention of obeying. It is easy to denounce the worries of this life and the deceitfulness of wealth and still do nothing to change our ways. In light of eternal life with God, are your present worries justified? If you had everything you could want but forfeited eternal life with God, would those things be so desirable?

Matt 13:23 The four types of soil represent different responses to God's message. People respond differently because they are in different states of readiness. Some are hardened, others are shallow, others are contaminated by distracting worries, and some are receptive. How has God's Word taken root in your life?

MARK 4:1-20

Once again Jesus began teaching by the lakeshore. A very large crowd soon gathered around him, so he got into a boat. Then he sat in the boat while all the people remained on the shore. 2He taught them by telling many stories in the form of parables, such as this one:

3"Listen! A farmer went out to plant some seed. 4As he scattered it across his field, some of the seed fell on a footpath, and the birds came and ate it. 5Other seed fell on shallow soil with underlying rock. The seed sprouted quickly because the soil was shallow. 6But the plant soon wilted under the hot sun, and since it didn't have deep roots, it died. 7Other seed fell among thorns that grew up and choked out the tender plants so they produced no grain. 8Still other seeds fell on fertile soil, and they sprouted, grew, and produced a crop that was thirty, sixty, and even a hundred times as much as had been planted!" 9Then he said, "Anyone with ears to hear should listen and understand."

10Later, when Jesus was alone with the twelve disciples and with the others who were gathered around, they asked him what the parables meant.

11He replied, "You are permitted to understand the secret* of the Kingdom of God. But I use parables for everything I say to outsiders, 12so that the Scriptures might be fulfilled:

'When they see what I do,
they will learn nothing.
When they hear what I say,
they will not understand.
Otherwise, they will turn to me
and be forgiven.'*"

13Then Jesus said to them, "If you can't understand the meaning of this parable, how will you understand all the other parables? 14The farmer plants seed by taking God's word to others. 15The seed that fell on the footpath represents those who hear the message, only to have Satan come at once and take it away. 16The seed on the rocky soil represents those who hear the message and immediately receive it with joy. 17But since they don't have deep roots, they don't last long. They fall away as soon as they have problems or are persecuted for believing God's word. 18The seed that fell among the thorns represents others who hear God's word, 19but all too quickly the message is crowded out by the worries of this life, the lure of wealth, and the desire for other things, so no fruit is produced. 20And the seed that fell on good soil represents those who hear and accept God's word and produce a harvest of thirty, sixty, or even a hundred times as much as had been planted!"

LUKE 8:4-15

One day Jesus told a story in the form of a parable to a large crowd that had gathered from many towns to hear him: 5"A farmer went out to plant his seed. As he scattered it across his field, some seed fell on a footpath, where it was stepped on, and the birds ate it. 6Other seed fell among rocks. It began to grow, but the plant soon wilted and died for lack of moisture. 7Other seed fell among thorns that grew up with it and choked out the tender plants. 8Still other seed fell on fertile soil. This seed grew and produced a crop that was a hundred times as much as had been planted!" When he had said this, he called out, "Anyone with ears to hear should listen and understand."

9His disciples asked him what this parable meant.

Mk 4:11 Greek *mystery.* **Mk 4:12** Isa 6:9-10 (Greek version).

Mark 4:2 Jesus taught the people by telling stories called parables, using familiar scenes to explain spiritual truths. This method of teaching compels the listener to think. It conceals the truth from those who are too stubborn or prejudiced to hear what is being taught. Most parables have one main point, so we must be careful not to go beyond what Jesus intended to teach.

Mark 4:3 Seed was planted by hand. As the farmer walked across the field, he threw handfuls of seed onto the ground from a large bag slung across his shoulders. The plants did not grow in neat rows as they do with today's machine planting. No matter how skillful, no farmer could keep some of his seed from falling on the footpath, from being scattered among rocks and thorns, or from being carried off by the wind. So the farmer would throw the seed liberally, and enough would fall on good ground to ensure the harvest.

Mark 4:9 The hearing Jesus wants from us is not the kind we use when we listen to background music or when someone starts to recount a long story we've already heard. To truly "hear" Jesus' words is to believe them, to use them immediately in decisions and attitudes, and to base life on them—your recreation and work, family plans and money matters, praying and singing. To hear Jesus' words is to make Jesus your true Lord. What is Jesus saying to you?

Mark 4:14-20 This parable should encourage spiritual "sowers"—those who teach, preach, and lead others. The farmer sowed good seed, but not all the seed sprouted, and even the plants that grew had varying yields. Don't be discouraged if you do not always see results as you faithfully teach the Word. Some people do not understand God's truth because they are not ready for it. God reveals truth to people who will act on it and make it visible in their lives. When you talk with people about God, be aware that they will not understand if they are not yet ready. Be patient, taking every chance to tell them more about God and praying that the Holy Spirit will open their minds and hearts to receive the truth and act on it. Productivity is in God's hands.

Mark 4:19 Worries of this life, the lure of wealth, and the desire for things plagued first-century disciples just as they do us today. How easy it is for our daily routines to become overcrowded. A life packed with materialistic pursuits crowds out God's Word and leaves us unfruitful for him. Stay free so you can hear God when he speaks.

Luke 8:5-8 Why would a farmer allow precious seed to land on the footpath, on rocks, or among thorns? This was not an irresponsible farmer scattering seeds at random. He was using the acceptable method of the day for seeding a large field—tossing it by handfuls as he walked through the field. His goal was to get as much seed as possible to take root in good soil, but waste was inevitable as some fell or was blown into less productive areas. That some of the seed produced no crop was not the fault of the faithful farmer nor of the seed. The yield depended on the condition of the soil where the seed fell. It is our responsibility to spread the seed (God's message), but we should not give up when some of our efforts fail.

10He replied, "You are permitted to understand the
secrets* of the Kingdom of God. But I use parables
to teach the others so that the Scriptures might be
fulfilled:

'When they look, they won't really see.
When they hear, they won't understand.'*

11"This is the meaning of the parable: The seed is
God's word. 12The seeds that fell on the footpath represent those who hear the message, only to have the
devil come and take it away from their hearts and
prevent them from believing and being saved. 13The
seeds on the rocky soil represent those who hear the
message and receive it with joy. But since they don't
have deep roots, they believe for a while, then they fall
away when they face temptation. 14The seeds that fell
among the thorns represent those who hear the message, but all too quickly the message is crowded out
by the cares and riches and pleasures of this life. And
so they never grow into maturity. 15And the seeds that
fell on the good soil represent honest, good-hearted
people who hear God's word, cling to it, and patiently
produce a huge harvest."

Jesus Tells the Parable of the Lamp PARALLEL

MARK 4:21-25

Then Jesus asked them, "Would anyone light a lamp
and then put it under a basket or under a bed? Of
course not! A lamp is placed on a stand, where its
light will shine. 22For everything that is hidden will
eventually be brought into the open, and every secret
will be brought to light. 23Anyone with ears to hear
should listen and understand."

24Then he added, "Pay close attention to what you
hear. The closer you listen, the more understanding
you will be given*—and you will receive even more.
25To those who listen to my teaching, more understanding will be given. But for those who are not listening, even what little understanding they have will
be taken away from them."

LUKE 8:16-18

"No one lights a lamp and then covers it with a bowl
or hides it under a bed. A lamp is placed on a stand,
where its light can be seen by all who enter the house.
17For all that is secret will eventually be brought into
the open, and everything that is concealed will be
brought to light and made known to all.
18"So pay attention to how you hear. To those who
listen to my teaching, more understanding will be
given. But for those who are not listening, even what
they think they understand will be taken away from
them."

Jesus Tells the Parable of the Growing Seed

MARK 4:26-29

Jesus also said, "The Kingdom of God is like a farmer
who scatters seed on the ground. 27Night and day,
while he's asleep or awake, the seed sprouts and
grows, but he does not understand how it happens.

Lk 8:10a Greek *mysteries.* **Lk 8:10b** Isa 6:9 (Greek version). **Mk 4:24** Or *The measure you give will be the measure you get back.*

Luke 8:10 Why didn't the crowds understand Jesus' words? Perhaps they were looking for a military leader or a political Messiah and could not fit his gentle teaching style into their preconceived ideas. Perhaps they were afraid of pressure from religious leaders and did not want to look too deeply into Jesus' words. God told Isaiah that people would listen without understanding and watch without learning anything (Isa 6:9), and that kind of reaction confronted Jesus. The story of the farmer was an accurate picture of the people's reaction to the rest of his stories.

Luke 8:11-15 "Footpath" people, like many of the religious leaders, refuse to believe God's message. "Rocky soil" people, like many in the crowds who followed Jesus, believe his message but never get around to doing anything about it. "Thorn patch" people, overcome by worries and the lure of materialism, leave no room in their lives for God. "Good soil" people, in contrast to all the other groups, follow Jesus no matter what the cost. Which type of soil are you?

Mark 4:21 Many Christians today are hidden from sight, reluctant to be identified as Christians. Such a Christian is like a brand-new light that never leaves the carton it came in. If a lamp doesn't help people see, it isn't worth much. Does your life show other people how to find God and how to live for him? If not, ask what "baskets" have hidden your light. Complacency, resentment, embarrassment, stubbornness of heart, or disobedience could keep you from shining. What do you need to do to let your light shine?

Mark 4:24-25 The light of Jesus' truth is revealed to us, not hidden. But we may not be able to see or to use all of that truth right now. Only as we put God's teachings into practice will we understand and see more of the truth. The truth is clear, but our ability to understand is imperfect. As we obey, we will sharpen our vision and increase our understanding (see Jas 1:22-25).

Mark 4:25 Jesus' words may have been directed to the Jews who had no understanding of Jesus and would lose even what they had—their privileged status as God's people. Or Jesus might have meant that when people reject him, their hardness of heart drives away or renders useless even the little understanding they had; thus, any opportunity to share in God's Kingdom will eventually be taken away completely. To understand Jesus' message, people must listen and respond. Those who listen casually, for whatever reason, will miss the point.

Luke 8:16-17 When the light of the truth about Jesus illuminates us, we have the duty to shine that light to help others. Our witness for Christ should be public, not hidden. We should not keep the benefits for ourselves alone but pass them on to others. In order to be helpful, we need to be well placed. Seek opportunities to shine your light when unbelievers need help to see.

Luke 8:18 Applying God's Word helps us grow. This is a principle of growth in physical, mental, and spiritual life. For example, a muscle, when exercised, will grow stronger, but an unused muscle will grow weak and flabby. If you are not growing stronger, you are growing weaker; it is impossible for you to stand still. How are you using what God has taught you?

Mark 4:26-29 God promises that his harvest will be magnificent and prolific—the best fruit ever grown. Your witness may be weak and your efforts may seem to influence so few, but the Word of God is a powerful growth agent. Keep your eyes on the great harvest to come and don't let bad soil or weeds discourage you from faithful service and witness.

▸ **MARK 4:26-29 *(cont.)***

28The earth produces the crops on its own. First a leaf
blade pushes through, then the heads of wheat are
formed, and finally the grain ripens. 29And as soon
as the grain is ready, the farmer comes and harvests
it with a sickle, for the harvest time has come."

Jesus Tells the Parable of the Weeds

MATTHEW 13:24-30

Here is another story Jesus told: "The Kingdom of
Heaven is like a farmer who planted good seed in his
field. 25But that night as the workers slept, his enemy
came and planted weeds among the wheat, then
slipped away. 26When the crop began to grow and
produce grain, the weeds also grew.
27"The farmer's workers went to him and said, 'Sir,
the field where you planted that good seed is full of
weeds! Where did they come from?'
28"'An enemy has done this!' the farmer exclaimed.
"'Should we pull out the weeds?' they asked.
29"'No,' he replied, 'you'll uproot the wheat if you
do. 30Let both grow together until the harvest. Then I
will tell the harvesters to sort out the weeds, tie them
into bundles, and burn them, and to put the wheat
in the barn.'"

Jesus Tells the Parables of the Mustard Seed and the Yeast PARALLEL •••

MATTHEW 13:31-33 •••

Here is another illustration Jesus used: "The Kingdom
of Heaven is like a mustard seed planted in a field. 32It
is the smallest of all seeds, but it becomes the largest
of garden plants; it grows into a tree, and birds come
and make nests in its branches."
33Jesus also used this illustration: "The Kingdom
of Heaven is like the yeast a woman used in making bread. Even though she put only a little yeast in
three measures of flour, it permeated every part of
the dough."

MARK 4:30-32 •••

Jesus said, "How can I describe the Kingdom of God?
What story should I use to illustrate it? 31It is like a
mustard seed planted in the ground. It is the smallest
of all seeds, 32but it becomes the largest of all garden
plants; it grows long branches, and birds can make
nests in its shade."

LUKE 13:18-21 •••

Then Jesus said, "What is the Kingdom of God like?
How can I illustrate it? 19It is like a tiny mustard seed
that a man planted in a garden; it grows and becomes
a tree, and the birds make nests in its branches."
20He also asked, "What else is the Kingdom of
God like? 21It is like the yeast a woman used in making bread. Even though she put only a little yeast in
three measures of flour, it permeated every part of
the dough."

Why Jesus Taught in Parables PARALLEL ••

MATTHEW 13:34-35 ••

Jesus always used stories and illustrations like these
when speaking to the crowds. In fact, he never spoke
to them without using such parables. 35This fulfilled
what God had spoken through the prophet:

"I will speak to you in parables.
I will explain things hidden since the creation
of the world.*"

MARK 4:33-34 ••

Jesus used many similar stories and illustrations to
teach the people as much as they could understand.
34In fact, in his public ministry he never taught without using parables; but afterward, when he was alone
with his disciples, he explained everything to them.

Mt 13:35 Some manuscripts do not include *of the world.* Ps 78:2.

Matt 13:24ff Jesus gives the meaning of this parable in Matthew 13:36-43. All the parables in this chapter teach us about God and his Kingdom. They explain what the Kingdom is really like as opposed to our expectations of it. The Kingdom of Heaven is not a geographic location but a spiritual realm where God rules and where we share in his eternal life. We join that Kingdom when we trust in Christ as Savior.

Matt 13:30 The young weeds and the young blades of wheat look the same and can't be distinguished until they are grown and ready for harvest. Weeds (unbelievers) and wheat (believers) must live side by side in this world. God allows unbelievers to remain for a while, just as a farmer allows weeds to remain in his field so the surrounding wheat isn't uprooted with them. At the harvest, however, the weeds will be uprooted and thrown away. God's harvest (judgment) of all people is coming. We are to make ourselves ready by making sure that our faith is sincere.

Matt 13:31-32 The mustard seed was the smallest seed a farmer used. Jesus used this parable to show that the Kingdom has small beginnings but will grow and produce great results.

Matt 13:33 In other Bible passages, yeast is used as a symbol of evil or uncleanness. Here it is a positive symbol of growth. Although yeast looks like a minor ingredient, it permeates the whole loaf. Although the Kingdom began small and was nearly invisible, it would soon grow and have a great impact on the world.

Mark 4:30-32 Jesus used this parable to explain that although Christianity had very small beginnings, it would grow into a worldwide community of believers. When you feel alone in your stand for Christ, realize that God has faithful followers in every part of the world. Your faith, no matter how small, can join with that of others to accomplish great things.

Luke 13:18-21 The general expectation among Jesus' hearers was that the Messiah would come as a great king and leader, freeing the nation from Rome and restoring Israel's former glory. But Jesus said his Kingdom was beginning quietly. Like the tiny mustard seed that grows into an enormous tree, or the spoonful of yeast that makes the bread dough double in size, the Kingdom of God would eventually push outward until the whole world was changed.

Matt 13:40-43 At the end of the world, angels will separate the evil from the good. There are true and false believers in churches today, but we should be cautious in our judgments because only Christ is qualified to make the final separation. If you start judging, you may damage some of the good "plants." It's more important to judge our own response to God than to analyze others' responses.

Jesus Explains the Parable of the Weeds

MATTHEW 13:36-43

Then, leaving the crowds outside, Jesus went into the house. His disciples said, "Please explain to us the story of the weeds in the field."

37 Jesus replied, "The Son of Man* is the farmer who plants the good seed. 38 The field is the world, and the good seed represents the people of the Kingdom. The weeds are the people who belong to the evil one. 39 The enemy who planted the weeds among the wheat is the devil. The harvest is the end of the world,* and the harvesters are the angels.

40 "Just as the weeds are sorted out and burned in the fire, so it will be at the end of the world. 41 The Son of Man will send his angels, and they will remove from his Kingdom everything that causes sin and all who do evil. 42 And the angels will throw them into the fiery furnace, where there will be weeping and gnashing of teeth. 43 Then the righteous will shine like the sun in their Father's Kingdom. Anyone with ears to hear should listen and understand!

Jesus Tells the Parable of the Hidden Treasure

MATTHEW 13:44

"The Kingdom of Heaven is like a treasure that a man discovered hidden in a field. In his excitement, he hid it again and sold everything he owned to get enough money to buy the field.

Jesus Tells the Parable of the Pearl Merchant

MATTHEW 13:45-46

"Again, the Kingdom of Heaven is like a merchant on the lookout for choice pearls. 46 When he discovered a pearl of great value, he sold everything he owned and bought it!

Jesus Tells the Parable of the Fishing Net

MATTHEW 13:47-52

"Again, the Kingdom of Heaven is like a fishing net that was thrown into the water and caught fish of every kind. 48 When the net was full, they dragged it up onto the shore, sat down, and sorted the good fish into crates, but threw the bad ones away. 49 That is the way it will be at the end of the world. The angels will come and separate the wicked people from the righteous, 50 throwing the wicked into the fiery furnace, where there will be weeping and gnashing of teeth. 51 Do you understand all these things?"

"Yes," they said, "we do."

52 Then he added, "Every teacher of religious law who becomes a disciple in the Kingdom of Heaven is like a homeowner who brings from his storeroom new gems of truth as well as old."

Jesus Calms the Storm PARALLEL •••

MATTHEW 8:23-27 •○○

Then Jesus got into the boat and started across the lake with his disciples. 24 Suddenly, a fierce storm struck the

Mt 13:37 "Son of Man" is a title Jesus used for himself. **Mt 13:39** Or *the age;* also in 13:40, 49.

Matt 13:42 Jesus often uses these terms to refer to the coming judgment. The weeping indicates sorrow or remorse, and gnashing of teeth shows extreme anxiety or pain. Those who say they don't care what happens to them after they die don't realize what they are saying. They will be punished for living in selfishness and indifference to God.

Matt 13:43 Those who will shine like the sun in God's Kingdom stand in contrast to those who receive his judgment. A similar illustration is used in Daniel 12:3.

Matt 13:44-46 The Kingdom of Heaven is more valuable than anything else we can have, and a person must be willing to give up everything to obtain it. The man who discovered the treasure hidden in the field stumbled upon it by accident but knew its value when he found it. Although the transaction cost the man everything, he paid nothing for the priceless treasure itself. It came free, with the field. Nothing is more precious than the Kingdom of Heaven; yet God gives it to us as a gift. The parable of the pearl of great value reinforces the same point.

Matt 13:47-49 The parable of the fishing net has the same meaning as the parable of the wheat and weeds. We are to obey God and tell others about his grace and goodness, but we cannot dictate who is part of the Kingdom of Heaven and who is not. This sorting will be done at the last judgment by those infinitely more qualified than we.

Matt 13:52 Anyone who understands God's real purpose in the law as revealed in the Old Testament has a real treasure. The Old Testament points the way to Jesus, the Messiah. Jesus always upheld its authority and relevance. But there is a double benefit for those who understand Jesus' teaching about the Kingdom of Heaven. This was a new treasure that Jesus was revealing. Both the old and new teaching give practical guidelines for faith and for living in the world. The teachers of religious law, however, were trapped in the old and blind to the new.

Matt 8:23 The boat used here was probably the kind familiar to many of Jesus' disciples who were fishermen. Josephus, an ancient historian, wrote that there were usually more than 300 fishing boats on the Sea of Galilee at one time. This boat was large enough to hold Jesus and his 12 disciples and was powered by both oars and sails. During a storm, however, the sails were taken down to keep them from ripping and to make the boat easier to control.

Matt 8:24 The Sea of Galilee is an unusual body of water. It is relatively small (13 miles long, 7 miles wide), but it is 150-200 feet deep, and the shoreline is 680 feet below sea level. Sudden storms can appear over the surrounding mountains with little warning, stirring the water into violent 20-foot waves. The disciples had not foolishly set out in a storm. They had been caught without warning, and their danger was great.

Suddenly, a fierce storm struck the lake, with waves breaking into the boat. But Jesus was sleeping.

Matthew 8:24

▸ **MATTHEW 8:23-27** ***(cont.)***

lake, with waves breaking into the boat. But Jesus was sleeping. 25The disciples went and woke him up, shouting, "Lord, save us! We're going to drown!"

26Jesus responded, "Why are you afraid? You have so little faith!" Then he got up and rebuked the wind and waves, and suddenly there was a great calm.

27The disciples were amazed. "Who is this man?" they asked. "Even the winds and waves obey him!"

MARK 4:35-41

As evening came, Jesus said to his disciples, "Let's cross to the other side of the lake." 36So they took Jesus in the boat and started out, leaving the crowds behind (although other boats followed). 37But soon a fierce storm came up. High waves were breaking into the boat, and it began to fill with water.

38Jesus was sleeping at the back of the boat with his head on a cushion. The disciples woke him up, shouting, "Teacher, don't you care that we're going to drown?"

39When Jesus woke up, he rebuked the wind and said to the waves, "Silence! Be still!" Suddenly the wind stopped, and there was a great calm. 40Then he asked them, "Why are you afraid? Do you still have no faith?"

41The disciples were absolutely terrified. "Who is this man?" they asked each other. "Even the wind and waves obey him!"

LUKE 8:22-25

One day Jesus said to his disciples, "Let's cross to the other side of the lake." So they got into a boat and started out. 23As they sailed across, Jesus settled down for a nap. But soon a fierce storm came down on the lake. The boat was filling with water, and they were in real danger.

24The disciples went and woke him up, shouting, "Master, Master, we're going to drown!"

When Jesus woke up, he rebuked the wind and the raging waves. Suddenly the storm stopped and all was calm. 25Then he asked them, "Where is your faith?"

The disciples were terrified and amazed. "Who is this man?" they asked each other. "When he gives a command, even the wind and waves obey him!"

Jesus Sends Demons into a Herd of Pigs PARALLEL

MATTHEW 8:28-34

When Jesus arrived on the other side of the lake, in the region of the Gadarenes,* two men who were possessed by demons met him. They lived in a cemetery

Mt 8:28 Other manuscripts read *Gerasenes;* still others read *Gergesenes.* Compare Mark 5:1; Luke 8:26.

Matt 8:25 Although the disciples had witnessed many miracles, they panicked in this storm. As experienced sailors, they knew its danger; what they did not know was that Christ could control the forces of nature. We often encounter storms in our life where we feel God can't or won't work. When we truly understand who God is, however, we will realize that he controls both the storms of nature and the storms of the troubled heart. Jesus' power that calmed this storm can also help us deal with the problems we face. Jesus is willing to help if we only ask him. We should never discount his power even in terrible trials.

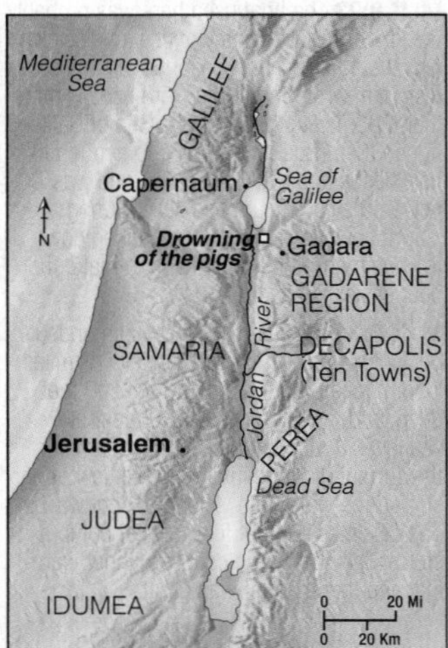

JESUS' MIRACULOUS POWER DISPLAYED *Jesus finished the sermon he had given on a hillside near Galilee and returned to Capernaum. As he and his disciples crossed the Sea of Galilee, Jesus calmed a fierce storm. Then, in the Gentile Gadarene region, Jesus commanded demons to come out of two men.*

Mark 4:35-38 The "lake" is the Sea of Galilee, a body of water 680 feet below sea level and surrounded by hills. Winds blowing across the land intensify close to the sea, often causing violent and unexpected storms. The disciples were seasoned fishermen who had spent their lives fishing on this huge lake, but during this squall they panicked.

Mark 4:37 The Christian life may have more stormy weather than calm seas. The disciples needed rest, but they encountered a terrible storm. As Christ's follower, be prepared for the storms that will surely come. Do not surrender to the stress, but remain resilient and recover from setbacks. With faith in Christ, you can pray, trust, and move ahead. When a squall approaches, lean into the wind and trust God.

Mark 4:41 The disciples lived with Jesus, but they underestimated him. They did not see that his power applied to their very own situation. Jesus has been with his people for 2,000 years, and yet we, like the disciples, underestimate his power to handle crises in our lives. The disciples did not yet know enough about Jesus. We cannot make the same excuse.

Luke 8:23-25 When caught in the storms of life, it is easy to think that God has lost control and that we're at the mercy of the winds of fate. In reality, God is sovereign. He controls the history of the world as well as our personal destinies. Just as Jesus calmed the waves, he can calm whatever storms you may face.

Matt 8:28 The region of the Gadarenes is located southeast of the Sea of Galilee, near the town of Gadara, one of the most important cities of the region. Gadara was a member of the Ten Towns (see the note on Mark 5:20, p. 1352), towns with independent governments that were largely inhabited by Gentiles.

Matt 8:28 Demon-possessed people are under the control of one or more demons. Demons are fallen angels who joined Satan in his rebellion against God and are now evil spirits under Satan's control. They help Satan tempt people to sin and have great destructive powers. But whenever they are confronted by Jesus, they lose their power. These demons recognized Jesus as God's Son (Mark 8:29), but they didn't think they had to obey him. Just believing is not enough (see Jas 2:19 for a discussion of belief and demons). Faith is more than belief. By faith, you accept what Jesus has done for you, receive him as the only one who can save you from sin, and live out your faith by obeying his commands.

Matt 8:28 Matthew says there were two demon-possessed men, while Mark and Luke refer only to one. Apparently Mark and Luke mention only the man who did the talking.

and were so violent that no one could go through
that area.
[29]They began screaming at him, "Why are you interfering with us, Son of God? Have you come here to
torture us before God's appointed time?"
[30]There happened to be a large herd of pigs feeding
in the distance. [31]So the demons begged, "If you cast
us out, send us into that herd of pigs."
[32]"All right, go!" Jesus commanded them. So the
demons came out of the men and entered the pigs,
and the whole herd plunged down the steep hillside
into the lake and drowned in the water.
[33]The herdsmen fled to the nearby town, telling
everyone what happened to the demon-possessed
men. [34]Then the entire town came out to meet Jesus,
but they begged him to go away and leave them alone.

MARK 5:1-20

So they arrived at the other side of the lake, in the
region of the Gerasenes.* [2]When Jesus climbed out of
the boat, a man possessed by an evil* spirit came out
from a cemetery to meet him. [3]This man lived among
the burial caves and could no longer be restrained,
even with a chain. [4]Whenever he was put into chains
and shackles—as he often was—he snapped the chains
from his wrists and smashed the shackles. No one
was strong enough to subdue him. [5]Day and night
he wandered among the burial caves and in the hills,
howling and cutting himself with sharp stones.
[6]When Jesus was still some distance away, the man
saw him, ran to meet him, and bowed low before him.
[7]With a shriek, he screamed, "Why are you interfering with me, Jesus, Son of the Most High God? In the
name of God, I beg you, don't torture me!" [8]For Jesus
had already said to the spirit, "Come out of the man,
you evil spirit."
[9]Then Jesus demanded, "What is your name?"
And he replied, "My name is Legion, because there
are many of us inside this man." [10]Then the evil spirits
begged him again and again not to send them to some
distant place.
[11]There happened to be a large herd of pigs feeding
on the hillside nearby. [12]"Send us into those pigs," the
spirits begged. "Let us enter them."
[13]So Jesus gave them permission. The evil spirits
came out of the man and entered the pigs, and the
entire herd of about 2,000 pigs plunged down the
steep hillside into the lake and drowned in the water.
[14]The herdsmen fled to the nearby town and the
surrounding countryside, spreading the news as they
ran. People rushed out to see what had happened.
[15]A crowd soon gathered around Jesus, and they saw
the man who had been possessed by the legion of

Mk 5:1 Other manuscripts read *Gadarenes;* still others read *Gergesenes.* See Matt 8:28; Luke 8:26. **Mk 5:2** Greek *unclean;* also in 5:8, 13.

Matt 8:28 According to Jewish ceremonial laws, the men Jesus encountered were unclean in three ways: They were Gentiles (non-Jews), they were demon possessed, and they lived in a cemetery. Jesus helped them anyway. We should not turn our backs on people who are "unclean" or repulsive to us or who violate our moral standards and religious beliefs. Instead, we must realize that every human individual is a unique creation of God, needing to be touched by his love.

Matt 8:29 The Bible tells us that at the end of the world the devil and his angels will be thrown into the lake of fire that burns with sulfur (Rev 20:10). When the demons asked if Jesus had come to torture them "before God's appointed time," they showed they knew their ultimate fate.

Matt 8:32 When the demons entered the pigs, they drove the animals into the sea. The demons' action proved their destructive intent—if they could not destroy the men, they would destroy the pigs. Jesus' action, by contrast, shows the value he places on each human life.

Matt 8:34 Why did the people ask Jesus to leave? Unlike their own pagan gods, Jesus could not be contained, controlled, or appeased. They feared Jesus' supernatural power, a power that they had never before witnessed. And they were upset about losing a herd of pigs more than they were glad about the deliverance of the demon-possessed men. Are you more concerned about property and programs than people? Human beings are created in God's image and have eternal value. How foolish and yet how easy it is to value possessions, investments, and even animals above human life. Would you rather have Jesus leave you than finish his work in you?

Mark 5:1-2 Although we cannot be sure why demon possession occurs, we know that evil spirits can use the human body to distort and destroy a person's relationship with God and likeness to him. Even today, demons are dangerous, powerful, and destructive. While it is important to recognize their evil activity, we should avoid any curiosity about or involvement with demonic forces or the occult (Deut 18:10-12). If we resist the devil and his influences, he will flee from us (Jas 4:7).

Mark 5:7 The demon screamed at Jesus, "Why are you interfering with me?" It was a shriek of fear, defense, and rebellion against God. No one today would like to admit to being demon possessed, but most of our society, like the demon, is screaming at God, the church, and Christian values: "Why are you interfering with me? Get out of my life!" When people reject Jesus Christ and his authority, they put themselves on the side of the demons and are heading in the same direction. Every person must ask: Will I choose autonomy and self-will, leading to destruction; or will I choose Christ's loving leadership over my life, giving me forgiveness, healing from sin, cleansing, and true freedom? The answer has eternal implications.

Mark 5:9 The evil spirit said its name was Legion. A legion was the largest unit of the Roman army, consisting of 3,000 to 6,000 soldiers. This man was possessed by many demons.

Mark 5:10 Mark often highlights the supernatural struggle between Jesus and Satan. The demons' goal was to control the humans they inhabited; Jesus' goal was to give people freedom from sin and Satan's control. The demons knew they had no power over Jesus, so they simply begged not to be sent to some distant place ("the bottomless pit" in Luke 8:31). Jesus granted their request to enter into the herd of pigs (Mark 5:13), but ended their destructive work in people. Perhaps Jesus let the demons destroy the pigs to demonstrate his own superiority over a very powerful yet destructive force. He could have sent them to hell, but he did not because the time for judgment had not yet come. In the end, the devil and all his demons will be sent into eternal fire (Matt 25:41).

Mark 5:11 According to Old Testament law (Lev 11:7), pigs were unclean animals. This meant that they could not be eaten or even touched by a Jew. This incident took place southeast of the Sea of Galilee in the region of the Gerasenes, a Gentile region, which explains how a herd of pigs could be involved.

▶ **MARK 5:1-20 *(cont.)***
demons. He was sitting there fully clothed and perfectly sane, and they were all afraid. 16Then those who
had seen what happened told the others about the
demon-possessed man and the pigs. 17And the crowd
began pleading with Jesus to go away and leave them
alone.
18As Jesus was getting into the boat, the man who
had been demon possessed begged to go with him.
19But Jesus said, "No, go home to your family, and tell
them everything the Lord has done for you and how
merciful he has been." 20So the man started off to visit
the Ten Towns* of that region and began to proclaim
the great things Jesus had done for him; and everyone
was amazed at what he told them.

LUKE 8:26-39
So they arrived in the region of the Gerasenes,* across
the lake from Galilee. 27As Jesus was climbing out
of the boat, a man who was possessed by demons
came out to meet him. For a long time he had been

Mk 5:20 Greek *Decapolis.* **Lk 8:26** Other manuscripts read *Gadarenes;* still others read *Gergesenes;* also in 8:37. See Matt 8:28; Mark 5:1.

Mark 5:17 After such a wonderful miracle of saving a man's life, the people still wanted Jesus to leave because they were undoubtedly afraid of his supernatural power. They may have also feared that Jesus would continue destroying their pigs—their livelihood. They would rather give up Jesus than lose their source of income and security.

Mark 5:19 Jesus told this man to tell his friends about the miraculous healing. Most of the time, Jesus urged those he healed to keep quiet. Why the difference? (1) Jesus knew the man would be an effective witness to those who knew his previous condition and could attest to the miraculous healing. (2) Jesus wanted to expand his ministry by introducing his message into this Gentile area. (3) Jesus knew that the Gentiles, since they were not expecting a Messiah, would not divert his ministry by trying to crown him king. (In fact, the people in this region had asked him to go away.)

Mark 5:19-20 This man had been demon possessed but became a living example of Jesus' power. He wanted to go with Jesus, but Jesus told him to go home and share his story with his friends. If you have experienced Jesus' power in your life, are you, like this man, enthusiastically sharing the good news with those around you? Just as we would tell others about a doctor who cured a physical disease, we should tell about Christ who cures our sin.

Mark 5:20 These Ten Towns were located southeast of the Sea of Galilee. Ten cities, each with its own independent government, formed an alliance for protection and for increased trade opportunities. These cities had been settled several centuries earlier by Greek traders and immigrants. Although Jews also lived in the area, they were not in the majority. Many people from the Ten Towns followed Jesus (Matt 4:25).

Luke 8:27-28 These demons recognized Jesus and his authority immediately. They knew who Jesus was and what his great power could do to them. Demons, Satan's messengers, are powerful and destructive. Still active today, they attempt to distort and destroy people's relationship with God. Demons and demon possession are real. It is vital that believers recognize the power of Satan and his demons, but we shouldn't let curiosity lead us to get involved with

THE TOUCH OF JESUS

What kind of people did Jesus associate with? Whom did he consider important enough to touch? Here we see many of the people Jesus came to know. Some reached out to him; he reached out to them all. Regardless of how great or unknown, rich or poor, young or old, sinner or saint—Jesus cares equally for all. No person is beyond the loving touch of Jesus.

Jesus talked with . . .	Reference
A despised tax collector	Matthew 9:9
An insane hermit	Mark 5:1-20
The Roman governor	John 18:28-39
A father and his young son	Mark 9:17-27
A prominent religious leader	John 3:1-21
A homemaker	Luke 10:38-42
An expert in religious law	Matthew 22:35-40
A criminal	Luke 23:40-43
A synagogue leader	Mark 5:22-23, 35-43
Fishermen	Matthew 4:18-22
A king	Luke 23:7-11
Two poor widows	Luke 7:11-17; 21:1-4
A Roman captain	Luke 7:1-10
A group of children	Mark 10:13-16
A prophet	Matthew 3:13-15
An adulterous woman	John 8:1-11
The Jewish high council	Luke 22:66-71
A sick woman	Mark 5:25-34
A rich man	Mark 10:17-23
A blind beggar	Mark 10:46-52
Jewish political leaders	Mark 12:13-17
A group of women	Luke 8:2-3
The high priest	Matthew 26:62-68
An outcast with leprosy	Luke 17:11-19
A government official	John 4:46-53
A young girl	Mark 5:41-42
A traitor	John 13:1-2, 21-27
A helpless and paralyzed man	Mark 2:1-12
An angry mob of soldiers and guards	John 18:3-12
A woman from a foreign land	Mark 7:25-30
A doubting follower	John 20:24-29
An enemy who hated him	Acts 9:1-9
A Samaritan woman	John 4:1-30

homeless and naked, living in a cemetery outside the town.

28As soon as he saw Jesus, he shrieked and fell down in front of him. Then he screamed, "Why are you interfering with me, Jesus, Son of the Most High God? Please, I beg you, don't torture me!" 29For Jesus had already commanded the evil* spirit to come out of him. This spirit had often taken control of the man. Even when he was placed under guard and put in chains and shackles, he simply broke them and rushed out into the wilderness, completely under the demon's power.

30Jesus demanded, "What is your name?"

"Legion," he replied, for he was filled with many demons. 31The demons kept begging Jesus not to send them into the bottomless pit.*

32There happened to be a large herd of pigs feeding on the hillside nearby, and the demons begged him to let them enter into the pigs.

So Jesus gave them permission. 33Then the demons came out of the man and entered the pigs, and the entire herd plunged down the steep hillside into the lake and drowned.

34When the herdsmen saw it, they fled to the nearby town and the surrounding countryside, spreading the news as they ran. 35People rushed out to see what had happened. A crowd soon gathered around Jesus, and they saw the man who had been freed from the demons. He was sitting at Jesus' feet, fully clothed and perfectly sane, and they were all afraid. 36Then those who had seen what happened told the others how the demon-possessed man had been healed. 37And all the people in the region of the Gerasenes begged Jesus to go away and leave them alone, for a great wave of fear swept over them.

So Jesus returned to the boat and left, crossing back to the other side of the lake. 38The man who had been freed from the demons begged to go with him. But Jesus sent him home, saying, 39"No, go back to your family, and tell them everything God has done for you." So he went all through the town proclaiming the great things Jesus had done for him.

Jesus Heals a Bleeding Woman and Restores a Girl to Life PARALLEL •••

MATTHEW 9:18-26 •○○

As Jesus was saying this, the leader of a synagogue came and knelt before him. "My daughter has just died," he said, "but you can bring her back to life again if you just come and lay your hand on her."

19So Jesus and his disciples got up and went with him. 20Just then a woman who had suffered for twelve years with constant bleeding came up behind him. She touched the fringe of his robe, 21for she thought, "If I can just touch his robe, I will be healed."

22Jesus turned around, and when he saw her he said, "Daughter, be encouraged! Your faith has made you well." And the woman was healed at that moment.

23When Jesus arrived at the official's home, he saw the noisy crowd and heard the funeral music. 24"Get out!" he told them. "The girl isn't dead; she's only asleep." But the crowd laughed at him. 25After the crowd was put outside, however, Jesus went in and took the girl by the hand, and she stood up!

Lk 8:29 Greek *unclean.* **Lk 8:31** Or *the abyss,* or *the underworld.*

---

demonic forces (Deut 18:10-12). Demons are powerless against those who trust in Jesus. If we resist the devil, he will leave us alone (Jas 4:7).

Luke 8:29-31 The demons begged Jesus to spare them from the bottomless pit, which is also mentioned in Revelation 9:1 and 20:1-3 as the place of confinement for Satan and his messengers. The demons, of course, knew all about this place of confinement, and they didn't want to go there.

Luke 8:33 Why didn't Jesus just destroy these demons—or send them to the bottomless pit? Because the time for such work had not yet come. He healed many people of the destructive effects of demon possession, but he did not yet destroy demons. The same question could be asked today—why doesn't Jesus stop all the evil in the world? His time for that has not yet come. But it will come. The book of Revelation portrays the future victory of Jesus over Satan, his demons, and all evil.

Luke 8:33-37 A man had been freed from the devil's power, but the people in the town thought only about their livestock. People have always tended to value financial gain above needy people. Much injustice and oppression, both at home and abroad, is the direct result of some individual's or company's urge to get rich. People are continually being sacrificed to the god of money. Don't think more highly of "pigs" than of people.

Matt 9:18 Mark and Luke say this man's name was Jairus (Mark 5:22; Luke 8:41). As leader of the synagogue, Jairus was responsible for administration—looking after the building, supervising worship, running the school on weekdays, and finding rabbis to teach on the Sabbath. For more information on synagogues, read the note on Mark 1:21-22, p. 1308.

Matt 9:20-22 This woman had suffered for 12 years with a hemorrhage (perhaps a menstrual disorder). In our times of desperation, we don't have to worry about the correct way to reach out to God. Like this woman, we can simply reach out in faith. He will respond.

Matt 9:22 God changed a situation that had been a problem for years. Like the leper and the demon-possessed men (see note on Matt 8:2-3, p. 1311, and the second note on Matt 8:28, p. 1350), this woman was considered unclean. For 12 years, she, too, had been one of the "untouchables" and had not been able to lead a normal life. But Jesus changed that and restored her. Sometimes we are tempted to give up on people or situations that have not changed for many years. God can change what seems unchangeable, giving new purpose and hope.

Matt 9:23-26 The synagogue leader didn't come to Jesus until his daughter was dead—it was too late for anyone else to help. But Jesus simply went to the girl and raised her! In our lives, Christ can make a difference when it seems too late for anyone else to help. He can bring healing to broken relationships, release from addicting habits, and forgiveness and healing to emotional scars. If your situation looks hopeless, remember that Christ can do the impossible.

▸ **MATTHEW 9:18-26** ***(cont.)***

26The report of this miracle swept through the entire
countryside.

MARK 5:21-43

Jesus got into the boat again and went back to the
other side of the lake, where a large crowd gathered
around him on the shore. 22Then a leader of the local
synagogue, whose name was Jairus, arrived. When he
saw Jesus, he fell at his feet, 23pleading fervently with
him. "My little daughter is dying," he said. "Please
come and lay your hands on her; heal her so she can
live."

24Jesus went with him, and all the people followed,
crowding around him. 25A woman in the crowd had
suffered for twelve years with constant bleeding.
26She had suffered a great deal from many doctors,
and over the years she had spent everything she had
to pay them, but she had gotten no better. In fact,
she had gotten worse. 27She had heard about Jesus,
so she came up behind him through the crowd and
touched his robe. 28For she thought to herself, "If I
can just touch his robe, I will be healed." 29Imme-
diately the bleeding stopped, and she could feel in
her body that she had been healed of her terrible
condition.

30Jesus realized at once that healing power had gone
out from him, so he turned around in the crowd and
asked, "Who touched my robe?"

31His disciples said to him, "Look at this crowd
pressing around you. How can you ask, 'Who touched
me?'"

32But he kept on looking around to see who had
done it. 33Then the frightened woman, trembling at
the realization of what had happened to her, came
and fell to her knees in front of him and told him
what she had done. 34And he said to her, "Daughter,
your faith has made you well. Go in peace. Your suffering is over."

35While he was still speaking to her, messengers
arrived from the home of Jairus, the leader of the synagogue. They told him, "Your daughter is dead. There's
no use troubling the Teacher now."

36But Jesus overheard* them and said to Jairus,
"Don't be afraid. Just have faith."

37Then Jesus stopped the crowd and wouldn't let
anyone go with him except Peter, James, and John (the
brother of James). 38When they came to the home of
the synagogue leader, Jesus saw much commotion
and weeping and wailing. 39He went inside and asked,
"Why all this commotion and weeping? The child isn't
dead; she's only asleep."

40The crowd laughed at him. But he made them all
leave, and he took the girl's father and mother and his
three disciples into the room where the girl was lying.
41Holding her hand, he said to her, *"Talitha koum,"*
which means "Little girl, get up!" 42And the girl, who
was twelve years old, immediately stood up and walked
around! They were overwhelmed and totally amazed.
43Jesus gave them strict orders not to tell anyone what
had happened, and then he told them to give her something to eat.

LUKE 8:40-56

On the other side of the lake the crowds welcomed
Jesus, because they had been waiting for him. 41Then

Mk 5:36 Or *ignored.*

Mark 5:22 Jesus went back across the Sea of Galilee, probably landing at Capernaum. Jairus was the elected leader of the local synagogue, responsible for supervising worship, running the weekly school, and caring for the building. Many synagogue leaders had close ties to the Pharisees. It is likely, therefore, that some synagogue rulers had been pressured not to support Jesus. For Jairus to bow before Jesus was a significant and perhaps daring act of respect and worship.

Mark 5:25-34 This woman had a seemingly incurable condition causing her to bleed constantly. This may have been a menstrual or uterine disorder that would have made her ritually unclean (Lev 15:25-27) and excluded her from most social contact. She desperately wanted Jesus to heal her, but she knew that her bleeding would cause Jesus to become unclean under Jewish law if she touched him. Sometimes we feel that our problems will keep us from God. But he is always ready to help, no matter how impossible the problem seems to us. We should never allow our fear to keep us from approaching him.

Mark 5:31 It was virtually impossible to get close to Jesus, but one woman fought her way desperately through the crowd in order to touch him. As soon as she did, she was healed. What a difference between the crowds who are curious about Jesus and the few who reach out and touch him! Today, many people are vaguely familiar with Jesus, but nothing in their lives is changed or bettered by this passing acquaintance. It is only faith that releases God's healing power. Move beyond curiosity. Reach out to Christ in faith. That touch will change your life forever.

Mark 5:35-36 Jairus's crisis made him feel confused, afraid, and without hope. Jesus' words to Jairus in the midst of crisis speak to us as well: "Don't be afraid. Just have faith." In Jesus, there is both hope and promise. The next time you feel hopeless and afraid, look at your problem from Jesus' point of view. Then don't be afraid; just have faith.

Mark 5:38 Loud weeping and wailing were customary at a person's death. Lack of them was the ultimate disgrace and disrespect. Some people, usually women, made mourning a profession and were paid by the dead person's family to weep over the body. On the day of death, the body was carried through the streets, followed by mourners, family members, and friends.

Mark 5:39-40 The mourners laughed at Jesus when he said, "The child isn't dead; she's only asleep." The girl was dead, but Jesus used the image of sleep to indicate that her condition was temporary and that she would be restored.

Jesus tolerated the crowd's abuse in order to teach an important lesson about maintaining hope and trust in him. Today, most of the world laughs at Christ's claims. When you are belittled for expressing faith in Jesus and hope for eternal life, remember that unbelievers don't see from God's perspective. For a clear statement about life after death, see 1 Thessalonians 4:13-14.

Mark 5:41-42 Jesus not only demonstrated great power, but he also showed tremendous compassion. Jesus' power over nature, evil spirits, and death was motivated by compassion—for a demon-possessed man who lived among tombs, a diseased woman, and the family of a dead girl. The rabbis of the day considered such people unclean. Polite society avoided them. But Jesus reached out and helped.

Luke 8:41 It would have been quite unusual for a respected synagogue leader to fall at the feet of an itinerant preacher and beg

a man named Jairus, a leader of the local synagogue, came and fell at Jesus' feet, pleading with him to come home with him. 42His only daughter,* who was about twelve years old, was dying.

As Jesus went with him, he was surrounded by the crowds. 43A woman in the crowd had suffered for twelve years with constant bleeding,* and she could find no cure. 44Coming up behind Jesus, she touched the fringe of his robe. Immediately, the bleeding stopped.

45"Who touched me?" Jesus asked.

Everyone denied it, and Peter said, "Master, this whole crowd is pressing up against you."

46But Jesus said, "Someone deliberately touched me, for I felt healing power go out from me." 47When the woman realized that she could not stay hidden, she began to tremble and fell to her knees in front of him. The whole crowd heard her explain why she had touched him and that she had been immediately healed. 48"Daughter," he said to her, "your faith has made you well. Go in peace."

49While he was still speaking to her, a messenger arrived from the home of Jairus, the leader of the synagogue. He told him, "Your daughter is dead. There's no use troubling the Teacher now."

50But when Jesus heard what had happened, he said to Jairus, "Don't be afraid. Just have faith, and she will be healed."

51When they arrived at the house, Jesus wouldn't let anyone go in with him except Peter, John, James, and the little girl's father and mother. 52The house was filled with people weeping and wailing, but he said, "Stop the weeping! She isn't dead; she's only asleep."

53But the crowd laughed at him because they all knew she had died. 54Then Jesus took her by the hand and said in a loud voice, "My child, get up!" 55And at that moment her life* returned, and she immediately stood up! Then Jesus told them to give her something to eat. 56Her parents were overwhelmed, but Jesus insisted that they not tell anyone what had happened.

Lk 8:42 Or *His only child, a daughter.* **Lk 8:43** Some manuscripts add *having spent everything she had on doctors.* **Lk 8:55** Or *her spirit.*

him to heal his daughter. Jesus honored this man's humble faith (Luke 8:50, 54-56).

Luke 8:45-46 Certainly Jesus knew who had touched him—he knew that someone had intentionally touched him in order to receive some sort of healing. Jesus wanted the woman to step forward and identify herself. To let her slip away would have meant a lost opportunity for Jesus to teach her that his cloak did not have magical properties. Rather, her faith in him had healed her. He may also have wanted to teach the crowds a lesson. According to Jewish law, a man who touched a menstruating woman became ceremonially unclean (Lev 15:19-28). This was true whether her bleeding was normal or, as in this woman's case, the result of an abnormal condition. To protect themselves from such defilement, Jewish men carefully avoided touching, speaking to, or even looking at women. By contrast, Jesus proclaimed to hundreds of people that this "unclean" woman had touched him—and then he healed her. In Jesus' mind, this suffering woman was not to be overlooked. As God's creation, she deserved attention and respect.

Luke 8:50 People with children can readily put themselves emotionally in Jairus's place. His daughter had died while they were on the way home. Luke did not record it, but the poor man probably cried out in anguish. Jesus surely felt the father's very human grief. Jesus said, "Don't be afraid. Just have faith." Again, Luke didn't record Jairus's reaction to these words, but he must have had at least some flicker of hope because he did complete his mission in bringing Jesus to his house. When you experience intense grief over the loss of a loved one, breakup of a marriage, loss of a job, or rejection of a close friend, don't abandon hope. Don't turn away from the one Person who can help you. Do what Jairus did: Don't be afraid; just have faith. Your hope is found in the resurrected Lord, the one with power over life and death.

Luke 8:56 Jesus told the parents not to talk about their daughter's healing because he knew the facts would speak for themselves. Jesus was concerned for his ministry. He did not want to be known as just a miracle worker; he wanted people to listen to his words that could heal their broken spiritual lives.

Early Manuscripts of the Gospels

There are literally thousands of manuscripts of the Bible available to scholars today. These are all handwritten copies of parts of the Bible, some containing almost all of the New Testament, and others representing just a verse or two. Some of them were created by careful, professional scribes (like P75, a late second-century manuscript containing Luke and John, pictured at right), and some are small fragments (like P103, a second-century manuscript with a few verses from Matthew, pictured at left). There are many differences between these handwritten copies, but the vast majority of them are insignificant details like the spelling of the names of Jesus' half-brothers in Matt 13:55 (see NLT textual note on Matt 13:55). We can have great confidence that God has preserved the Bible for us in spite of these differences in manuscripts.

Jesus Heals the Blind and Mute

MATTHEW 9:27-34

After Jesus left the girl's home, two blind men followed along behind him, shouting, "Son of David, have mercy on us!"

28They went right into the house where he was staying, and Jesus asked them, "Do you believe I can make you see?"

"Yes, Lord," they told him, "we do."

29Then he touched their eyes and said, "Because
of your faith, it will happen." 30Then their eyes were
opened, and they could see! Jesus sternly warned
them, "Don't tell anyone about this." 31But instead,
they went out and spread his fame all over the region.

32When they left, a demon-possessed man who
couldn't speak was brought to Jesus. 33So Jesus cast
out the demon, and then the man began to speak. The crowds were amazed. "Nothing like this has ever happened in Israel!" they exclaimed.

34But the Pharisees said, "He can cast out demons because he is empowered by the prince of demons."

Jesus Is Rejected in Nazareth PARALLEL

MATTHEW 13:53-58

When Jesus had finished telling these stories and
illustrations, he left that part of the country. 54He re-
turned to Nazareth, his hometown. When he taught there in the synagogue, everyone was amazed and said, "Where does he get this wisdom and the power
to do miracles?" 55Then they scoffed, "He's just the
carpenter's son, and we know Mary, his mother, and
his brothers—James, Joseph,* Simon, and Judas. 56All
his sisters live right here among us. Where did he
learn all these things?" 57And they were deeply offended and refused to believe in him.

Then Jesus told them, "A prophet is honored everywhere except in his own hometown and among his
own family." 58And so he did only a few miracles there because of their unbelief.

MARK 6:1-6a

Jesus left that part of the country and returned with
his disciples to Nazareth, his hometown. 2The next
Sabbath he began teaching in the synagogue, and

Mt 13:55 Other manuscripts read *Joses;* still others read *John.*

Matt 9:27 "Son of David" was a popular way of addressing Jesus as the Messiah because it was known that the Messiah would be a descendant of David (Isa 9:7). This is the first time the title is used in Matthew. Jesus' ability to give sight to the blind was prophesied in Isaiah 29:18; 35:5; 42:7.

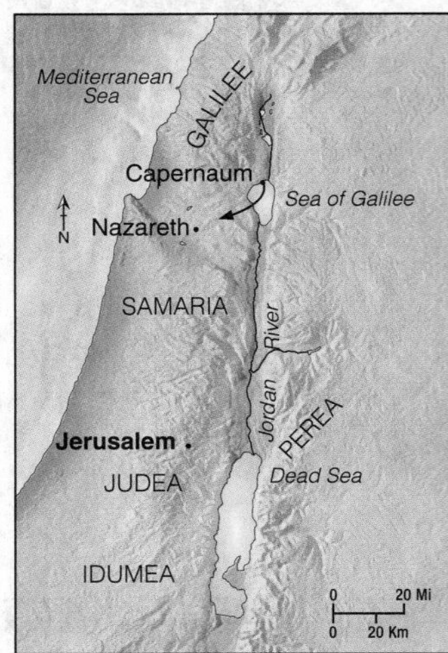

***NAZARETH REJECTS JESUS** After Jesus healed the demon-possessed men in the Gadarene region (Matt 8:28-34), he crossed the Sea of Galilee to Capernaum. From there he traveled to Nazareth, where he had grown up, but the people refused to believe he was the Christ.*

Matt 9:27-30 Jesus didn't respond immediately to the blind men's pleas. He waited to see if they had faith. Not all who say they want help really believe God can help them. Jesus may have waited and questioned these men to emphasize and increase their faith. When you think that God is too slow in answering your prayers, consider that he might be testing you as he did the blind men. Do you believe that God can help you? Do you really want his help?

Matt 9:28 These blind men were persistent. They went right into the house where Jesus was staying. They knew Jesus could heal them, and they would let nothing stop them from finding him. That's real faith in action. If you believe Jesus is the answer to your every need, don't let anything or anyone stop you from reaching out to him.

Matt 9:30 Jesus told them to keep quiet about his healings because he did not want to be known only as a miracle worker. He healed because he had compassion on people, but he also wanted to bring spiritual healing to a sin-sick world.

Matt 9:32 While Jesus was on earth, demonic forces were especially active. Although we cannot always be sure why or how demon possession occurs, it causes both physical and mental problems. In this case, the demon made the man unable to talk. For more on demons and demon possession, read the second note on Matthew 8:28, p. 1350 and the notes on Mark 1:23, p. 1309.

Matt 9:34 In Matthew 9, the Pharisees accuse Jesus of four different sins: blasphemy, befriending outcasts, impiety, and serving Satan. Matthew shows how Jesus was maligned by those who should have received him most gladly. Why did the Pharisees do this? (1) Jesus bypassed their religious authority. (2) He weakened their control over the people. (3) He challenged their cherished beliefs. (4) He exposed their insincere motives.

While the Pharisees questioned, debated, and dissected Jesus, people were being healed and lives changed right in front of them. Their skepticism was based not on insufficient evidence but on jealousy of Jesus' popularity.

Matt 13:55 The residents of Jesus' hometown had known him since he was a young child and were acquainted with his family; they could not bring themselves to believe in his message. They were too close to the situation. Jesus had come to them as a prophet, one who challenged them to respond to unpopular spiritual truth. They did not listen to the timeless message because they could not see beyond the man.

Matt 13:57 Jesus was not the first prophet to be rejected in his own country. Jeremiah experienced rejection in his hometown, even by members of his own family (Jer 12:5-6).

Matt 13:58 Jesus did few miracles in his hometown "because of their unbelief." Unbelief blinds people to the truth and robs them of hope. These people missed the Messiah.

Mark 6:4 Jesus said that a prophet (in other words, a worker for God) is never honored in his hometown. But that doesn't make his work any less important. A person doesn't need to be respected or honored to be useful to God. If friends, neighbors, or family don't respect your Christian work, don't let their rejection keep you from serving God.

many who heard him were amazed. They asked, "Where did he get all this wisdom and the power to perform such miracles?" [3]Then they scoffed, "He's just a carpenter, the son of Mary* and the brother of James, Joseph,* Judas, and Simon. And his sisters live right here among us." They were deeply offended and refused to believe in him.

[4]Then Jesus told them, "A prophet is honored everywhere except in his own hometown and among his relatives and his own family." [5]And because of their unbelief, he couldn't do any miracles among them except to place his hands on a few sick people and heal them. [6]And he was amazed at their unbelief.

LUKE 4:16-30

When he came to the village of Nazareth, his boyhood home, he went as usual to the synagogue on the Sabbath and stood up to read the Scriptures. [17]The scroll of Isaiah the prophet was handed to him. He unrolled the scroll and found the place where this was written:

18 "The Spirit of the LORD is upon me,
for he has anointed me to bring Good News
to the poor.
He has sent me to proclaim that captives will
be released,
that the blind will see,
that the oppressed will be set free,
19 and that the time of the LORD's favor has
come.*"

[20]He rolled up the scroll, handed it back to the attendant, and sat down. All eyes in the synagogue looked at him intently. [21]Then he began to speak to them. "The Scripture you've just heard has been fulfilled this very day!"

[22]Everyone spoke well of him and was amazed by the gracious words that came from his lips. "How can this be?" they asked. "Isn't this Joseph's son?"

[23]Then he said, "You will undoubtedly quote me this proverb: 'Physician, heal yourself'—meaning, 'Do miracles here in your hometown like those you did in Capernaum.' [24]But I tell you the truth, no prophet is accepted in his own hometown.

[25]"Certainly there were many needy widows in Israel in Elijah's time, when the heavens were closed for three and a half years, and a severe famine devastated the land. [26]Yet Elijah was not sent to any of them. He was sent instead to a foreigner—a widow of Zarephath in the land of Sidon. [27]And there were many lepers in Israel in the time of the prophet Elisha, but the only one healed was Naaman, a Syrian."

[28]When they heard this, the people in the synagogue were furious. [29]Jumping up, they mobbed him and forced him to the edge of the hill on which the town was built. They intended to push him over the cliff, [30]but he passed right through the crowd and went on his way.

Jesus Urges the Disciples to Pray for Workers

MATTHEW 9:35-38

Jesus traveled through all the towns and villages of that area, teaching in the synagogues and announcing the Good News about the Kingdom. And he healed every kind of disease and illness. [36]When he saw the crowds, he had compassion on them because they were confused and helpless, like sheep without a shepherd. [37]He said to his disciples, "The harvest is great, but the workers are few. [38]So pray to the Lord who is in charge of the harvest; ask him to send more workers into his fields."

Mk 6:3a Some manuscripts read *He's just the son of the carpenter and of Mary.* **Mk 6:3b** Most manuscripts read *Joses;* see Matt 13:55. **Lk 4:18-19** Or *and to proclaim the acceptable year of the LORD.* Isa 61:1-2 (Greek version); 58:6.

Mark 6:5 Jesus could have done greater miracles in Nazareth, but he chose not to because of the people's pride and unbelief. The miracles he did had little effect on the people because they did not accept his message nor believe that he was from God. Therefore, Jesus looked elsewhere, seeking those who would respond to his miracles and message.

Luke 4:17-21 Jesus was quoting from Isaiah 61:1-2. Isaiah pictures the deliverance of Israel from exile in Babylon as a Year of Jubilee when all debts are cancelled, all slaves are freed, and all property is returned to original owners (Lev 25). But the release from Babylonian exile had not brought the expected fulfillment; they were still a conquered and oppressed people. So Isaiah must have been referring to a future messianic age. Jesus boldly announced, "The Scripture you've just heard has been fulfilled this very day!" Jesus was proclaiming himself as the one who would bring this Good News to pass, but he would do so in a way that the people were not yet able to grasp.

Luke 4:24 Even Jesus himself was not accepted as a prophet in his hometown. Many people have a similar attitude. Don't be surprised if your Christian life and faith are not easily understood or accepted by those who know you well. Because they know your background, your failures, and your foibles, they may not see past those to the new person you have become. Let God work in your life, pray to be a positive witness for him, and be patient.

Luke 4:25-28 Jesus' remarks angered the people of Nazareth because he was saying that God sometimes chose to reach Gentiles rather than Jews. Jesus implied that his hearers were as unbelieving as the citizens of the northern kingdom of Israel in the days of Elijah and Elisha, a time notorious for its great wickedness.

Matt 9:36 Jesus was overwhelmed with compassionate pity for the people. His response echoes the deep inner mercy of God, often described in the Old Testament. Ezekiel also compared Israel to sheep without a shepherd (Ezek 34:5-6). Jesus came to be the "good shepherd," the one who could show people how to avoid life's pitfalls (see John 10:14).

Matt 9:37-38 Jesus looked at the crowds following him and referred to them as a field ripe for harvest. Many people are ready to give their lives to Christ if someone will show them how. Jesus commands us to pray that people will respond to this need for workers. Often, when we pray for something, God answers our prayers by using us. Be prepared for God to use you to show another person the way to him.

Jesus Sends Out the Twelve Disciples PARALLEL

MATTHEW 10:1-15

Jesus called his twelve disciples together and gave
them authority to cast out evil* spirits and to heal
every kind of disease and illness. 2Here are the names
of the twelve apostles:

first, Simon (also called Peter),
then Andrew (Peter's brother),
James (son of Zebedee),
John (James's brother),
3 Philip,
Bartholomew,
Thomas,
Matthew (the tax collector),
James (son of Alphaeus),
Thaddaeus,*
4 Simon (the zealot*),
Judas Iscariot (who later betrayed him).

5Jesus sent out the twelve apostles with these instructions: "Don't go to the Gentiles or the Samaritans,
6but only to the people of Israel—God's lost sheep. 7Go
and announce to them that the Kingdom of Heaven is
near.* 8Heal the sick, raise the dead, cure those with
leprosy, and cast out demons. Give as freely as you
have received!

9"Don't take any money in your money belts—no
gold, silver, or even copper coins. 10Don't carry a traveler's bag with a change of clothes and sandals or even
a walking stick. Don't hesitate to accept hospitality,
because those who work deserve to be fed.

11"Whenever you enter a city or village, search for
a worthy person and stay in his home until you leave
town. 12When you enter the home, give it your blessing. 13If it turns out to be a worthy home, let your blessing stand; if it is not, take back the blessing. 14If any
household or town refuses to welcome you or listen
to your message, shake its dust from your feet as you
leave. 15I tell you the truth, the wicked cities of Sodom
and Gomorrah will be better off than such a town on
the judgment day."

MARK 6:6b-13

Then Jesus went from village to village, teaching
the people. 7And he called his twelve disciples together and began sending them out two by two, giving them authority to cast out evil* spirits. 8He told

Mt 10:1 Greek *unclean.* **Mt 10:3** Other manuscripts read *Lebbaeus;* still others read *Lebbaeus who is called Thaddaeus.* **Mt 10:4** Greek *the Cananean,* an Aramaic term for Jewish nationalists. **Mt 10:7** Or *has come,* or *is coming soon.* **Mk 6:7** Greek *unclean.*

Matt 10:1 Jesus called his 12 disciples. He didn't draft them, force them, or ask them to volunteer; he chose them to serve him in a special way. Christ calls us today. He doesn't twist our arms and make us do something we don't want to do. We can choose to join him or remain behind. When Christ calls you to follow him, how do you respond?

Matt 10:2-4 The list of Jesus' 12 disciples doesn't give us many details—probably because there weren't many impressive details to tell. Jesus called people from all walks of life—fishermen, political activists, tax collectors. He called common people and uncommon leaders, rich and poor, educated and uneducated. Today, many people think only certain kinds of people are fit to follow Christ, but this was not the attitude of the Master himself. God can use anyone, no matter how insignificant at first appearance. When you feel small and useless, remember that God uses ordinary people to do his extraordinary work.

Matt 10:3 Bartholomew is probably another name for Nathanael, whom we meet in John 1:45-51. Thaddaeus is also known as Judas son of James. The disciples are also listed in Mark 3:16-19; Luke 6:14-16; and Acts 1:13.

Matt 10:4 Simon the zealot may have been a member of the Zealots, a radical political party working for the violent overthrow of Roman rule in Israel.

Matt 10:5-6 Why didn't Jesus send the disciples to the Gentiles or the Samaritans? A Gentile is anyone who is not a Jew. The Samaritans were a race that resulted from intermarriage between Jews and Gentiles after the Old Testament captivities (see 2 Kgs 17:24). Jesus asked his disciples to go only to the Jews because he came first to the Jews (Rom 1:16). God had chosen them to tell the rest of the world about him. Jewish disciples and apostles preached the Good News of the risen Christ all around the Roman Empire, and soon Gentiles were pouring into the church. The Bible clearly teaches that God's message of salvation is for all people, regardless of race, gender, or national origin (Gen 12:3; Isa 25:6; 56:3-7; Mal 1:11; Acts 10:34-35; Rom 3:29-30; Gal 3:28).

Matt 10:7 The Jews were waiting for the Messiah to usher in his Kingdom. They hoped for a political and military kingdom that would free them from Roman rule and bring back the days of glory under David and Solomon. But Jesus was talking about a spiritual Kingdom. The Good News today is that the Kingdom is still near. Jesus, the Messiah, has already begun his Kingdom on earth in the hearts of his followers. One day the Kingdom will be fully realized. Then evil will be destroyed and all people will live in peace with one another.

Matt 10:8 Jesus gave the disciples a principle to guide their actions as they ministered to others: "Give as freely as you have received!" Because God has showered us with his blessings, we should give generously to others of our time, love, and possessions.

Matt 10:10 Jesus said that those who minister are to be cared for. The disciples could expect food and shelter in return for the spiritual service they provided. Who ministers to you? Make sure you take care of the pastors, missionaries, and teachers who serve God by serving you (see 1 Cor 9:9-10; 1 Tim 5:17).

Matt 10:14 Why did Jesus tell his disciples to shake the dust off their feet if a city or home didn't welcome them? When leaving Gentile cities, pious Jews often shook the dust from their feet to show their separation from Gentile practices. If the disciples shook the dust of a Jewish town from their feet, it would show their separation from Jews who rejected their Messiah. This gesture was to show the people that they were making a wrong choice—that the opportunity to choose Christ might not present itself again. Are you receptive to teaching from God? If you ignore the Spirit's prompting, you may not get another chance.

Matt 10:15 The cities of Sodom and Gomorrah were destroyed by fire from heaven because of their wickedness (Gen 19:24-25). Those who reject the Good News when they hear it will be worse off than the wicked people of these destroyed cities, who never heard the Good News at all.

Mark 6:7 The disciples were sent out in pairs. Individually they could have reached more areas of the country, but this was not Christ's plan. The advantages in going out by twos: (1) They could strengthen and encourage each other. (2) They could provide comfort in rejection. (3) They could give each other counsel, and make fewer mistakes. (4) They could stir each other to action as a counter to idleness or indifference. Our strength comes from God, but he meets many of our needs through our teamwork with others. As you serve Christ, don't try to go it alone.

them to take nothing for their journey except a walking stick—no food, no traveler's bag, no money.* 9He
allowed them to wear sandals but not to take a change
of clothes.
10"Wherever you go," he said, "stay in the same house
until you leave town. 11But if any place refuses to welcome you or listen to you, shake its dust from your feet
as you leave to show that you have abandoned those
people to their fate."
12So the disciples went out, telling everyone they
met to repent of their sins and turn to God. 13And they
cast out many demons and healed many sick people,
anointing them with olive oil.

LUKE 9:1-6
One day Jesus called together his twelve disciples* and
gave them power and authority to cast out all demons
and to heal all diseases. 2Then he sent them out to tell
everyone about the Kingdom of God and to heal the
sick. 3"Take nothing for your journey," he instructed
them. "Don't take a walking stick, a traveler's bag, food,
money,* or even a change of clothes. 4Wherever you
go, stay in the same house until you leave town. 5And
if a town refuses to welcome you, shake its dust from
your feet as you leave to show that you have abandoned those people to their fate."
6So they began their circuit of the villages, preaching the Good News and healing the sick.

Jesus Prepares the Disciples for Persecution

MATTHEW 10:16-42
"Look, I am sending you out as sheep among wolves.
So be as shrewd as snakes and harmless as doves. 17But
beware! For you will be handed over to the courts and
will be flogged with whips in the synagogues. 18You

Mk 6:8 Greek *no copper coins in their money belts.* **Lk 9:1** Greek *the Twelve;* other manuscripts read *the twelve apostles.* **Lk 9:3** Or *silver coins.*

Mark 6:8-9 Mark records that the disciples were instructed to take nothing with them except walking sticks, while Matthew and Luke record that Jesus told them not to take walking sticks. One explanation is that Matthew and Luke were referring to a club used for protection, whereas Mark was talking about a shepherd's crook. Or, Jesus may have meant that they were not to take an extra pair of sandals, walking stick, or bag. In any case, the point in all three accounts is the same—the disciples were to leave at once, without extensive preparation, trusting in God's care rather than in their own resources.

Mark 6:11 When the disciples shook the dust from their feet after leaving a Jewish town, it was a vivid sign that they wished to remain separate from people who had rejected Jesus and his message. Jesus made it clear that all who heard the gospel were responsible for what they did with it. The disciples were not to blame if the message was rejected, as long as they had faithfully and carefully presented it. We are not responsible when others reject Christ's message of salvation, but we do have the responsibility to share the Good News clearly and faithfully.

Luke 9:1-6 Note Jesus' methods of leadership. He empowered his disciples (Luke 9:1), gave them specific instructions so they knew what to do (Luke 9:3-4), told them how to deal with tough times (Luke 9:5), and held them accountable (Luke 9:10). As you lead others, study the Master Leader's pattern. Which of these elements do you need to incorporate into your leadership?

Luke 9:2 Jesus announced his Kingdom by both preaching and healing, and he sent his disciples out to do the same. If he had limited himself to preaching, people might have seen his Kingdom as spiritual only. If he had healed without preaching, people might not have realized the spiritual importance of his mission. Most of his listeners expected a Messiah who would bring wealth and power to their nation; they preferred material benefits to spiritual discernment. The truth about Jesus is that he is both God and man, both spiritual and physical; and the salvation that he offers is both for the soul and the body. Any group or teaching that emphasizes soul at the expense of body, or body at the expense of soul, is in danger of distorting Jesus' Good News.

Luke 9:3-4 Why were the disciples instructed to depend on others while they went from town to town preaching the Good News? Their purpose was to blanket Judea with Jesus' message, and by traveling light they could move quickly. Their dependence on others had other good effects as well: (1) It clearly showed that the Messiah had not come to offer wealth to his followers. (2) It forced the disciples to rely on God's power and not on their own provision. (3) It involved the villagers and made them more eager to hear the message. This was an excellent approach for the disciples' short-term mission; it was not intended, however, to be a permanent way of life for them (see Luke 22:35-36).

Luke 9:4 The disciples were told to stay in only one home in each town because they were not to offend their hosts by moving to a home that was more comfortable or socially prominent. To remain in one home was not a burden for the homeowner, because the disciples' stay in each community was short. (See also Luke 10:7.)

Matt 10:16 The opposition of the Pharisees would be like ravaging wolves. The disciples' only hope would be to look to their Shepherd for protection. We may face similar hostility. Like the disciples, we are not to be sheep-like in our attitude but sensible and prudent. We are not to be gullible pawns, but neither are we to be deceitful connivers. We must find a balance between wisdom and vulnerability to accomplish God's work.

Matt 10:17-18 Later the disciples experienced these hardships (Acts 5:40; 12:1-3), not only from without (governments, courts), but also from within (friends, family; Matt 10:21). Living for God often brings on persecution, but with it comes the opportunity to tell the Good News of salvation. In times of persecution, we can be confident because Jesus has "overcome the world" (John 16:33). And those who endure to the end will be saved (Matt 10:22).

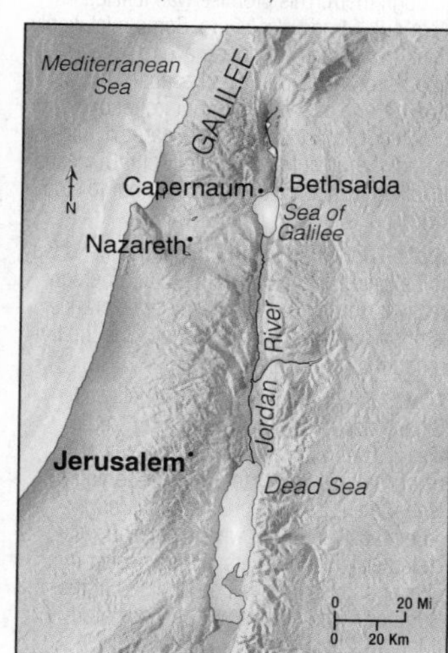

***PREACHING IN GALILEE** After returning to his hometown, Nazareth, from Capernaum, Jesus preached in the villages of Galilee and sent his disciples out to preach as well. After meeting back in Capernaum, they left by boat to rest, only to be met by the crowds who followed the boat along the shore.*

▶ **MATTHEW 10:16-42** ***(cont.)***
will stand trial before governors and kings because
you are my followers. But this will be your opportunity
to tell the rulers and other unbelievers about me.*
19When you are arrested, don't worry about how to
respond or what to say. God will give you the right
words at the right time. 20For it is not you who will be
speaking—it will be the Spirit of your Father speaking
through you.
21"A brother will betray his brother to death, a
father will betray his own child, and children will
rebel against their parents and cause them to be
killed. 22And all nations will hate you because you
are my followers.* But everyone who endures to the
end will be saved. 23When you are persecuted in one
town, flee to the next. I tell you the truth, the Son
of Man* will return before you have reached all the
towns of Israel.
24"Students* are not greater than their teacher,
and slaves are not greater than their master. 25Students are to be like their teacher, and slaves are to
be like their master. And since I, the master of the
household, have been called the prince of demons,*
the members of my household will be called by even
worse names!
26"But don't be afraid of those who threaten you.
For the time is coming when everything that is covered will be revealed, and all that is secret will be
made known to all. 27What I tell you now in the darkness, shout abroad when daybreak comes. What I
whisper in your ear, shout from the housetops for
all to hear!
28"Don't be afraid of those who want to kill your
body; they cannot touch your soul. Fear only God, who
can destroy both soul and body in hell.* 29What is the
price of two sparrows—one copper coin*? But not a
single sparrow can fall to the ground without your
Father knowing it. 30And the very hairs on your head
are all numbered. 31So don't be afraid; you are more
valuable to God than a whole flock of sparrows.
32"Everyone who acknowledges me publicly here
on earth, I will also acknowledge before my Father in
heaven. 33But everyone who denies me here on earth,
I will also deny before my Father in heaven.

Mt 10:18 Or *But this will be your testimony against the rulers and other unbelievers.* **Mt 10:22** Greek *on account of my name.* **Mt 10:23** "Son of Man" is a title Jesus used for himself. **Mt 10:24** Or *Disciples.* **Mt 10:25** Greek *Beelzeboul;* other manuscripts read *Beezeboul;* Latin version reads *Beelzebub.* **Mt 10:28** Greek *Gehenna.* **Mt 10:29** Greek *one assarion* [i.e., one "as," a Roman coin equal to 1/16 of a denarius].

Matt 10:19-20 Jesus told the disciples that when arrested for preaching the Good News, they should not worry about what to say in their defense—God's Spirit would speak through them. This promise was fulfilled in Acts 4:8-14 and elsewhere. Some mistakenly think this means we don't have to prepare to present the Good News because God will take care of everything. Scripture teaches, however, that we are to make carefully prepared, thoughtful statements (Col 4:6). Jesus is telling us not to stop preparing but to stop worrying.

Matt 10:22 Enduring to the end is not a way to be saved but the evidence that a person really is committed to Jesus. Perseverance is not a means to earn salvation; it is the by-product of a truly devoted life.

Matt 10:25 The prince of demons was Satan, also known as Beelzebub ("lord of flies"). The Pharisees accused Jesus of using Satan's power to drive out demons (see Matt 12:24). Good is sometimes labeled evil. If Jesus, who is perfect, was called evil, his followers should expect that similar accusations will be directed at them. But those who endure will be vindicated (Matt 10:22).

Matt 10:29-31 Jesus said that God is aware of everything that happens even to sparrows, and you are far more valuable to him than they are. You are so valuable that God sent his only Son to die for you (John 3:16). Because God places such value on you, you need never fear personal threats or difficult trials. These can't shake God's love or dislodge his Spirit from within you.

This doesn't mean, however, that God will take away all your troubles (see Matt 10:16).

COUNTING THE COST OF FOLLOWING CHRIST

Who may oppose us?	Natural response	Possible pressures	Needed truth
GOVERNMENT Matt 10:18-19		Threats (Matt 10:26)	→ The truth will be revealed (Matt 10:26)
		Physical harm (Matt 10:28)	→ Our soul cannot be harmed (Matt 10:28)
RELIGIOUS PEOPLE Matt 10:17	Fear and worry	Public ridicule (Matt 10:22)	→ God himself will acknowledge us if we acknowledge him (Matt 10:32)
FAMILY Matt 10:21		Rejection by loved ones (Matt 10:34-37)	→ God's love can sustain us (Matt 10:31)

The real test of value is how well something holds up under the wear, tear, and stress of everyday life. Those who stand up for Christ in spite of their troubles truly have lasting value and will receive great rewards (see Matt 5:11-12).

Matt 10:32 Anyone who acknowledges Jesus Christ (that is, publicly confesses faith in or declares allegiance to him) will be acknowledged by Christ before his Father in heaven. Jesus' followers would face earthly courts of law where they would have to publicly claim allegiance to Jesus Christ, usually at their peril (Matt 10:17-25). Genuine discipleship always involves acknowledging Jesus Christ, whether or not we face pressure and persecution.

Matt 10:34 Jesus did not come to bring the kind of peace that glosses over deep differences just for the sake of superficial harmony. Conflict and disagreement will arise between those who choose to follow Christ and those who don't. Yet we can look forward to the day when all conflict will be resolved. For other verses on Jesus as peacemaker, see Isaiah 9:6; Matthew 5:9; John 14:27.

Matt 10:34-39 Christian commitment may separate friends and loved ones. In saying this, Jesus was not encouraging disobedience to parents or conflict at home. Rather, he was showing that his presence demands a decision. Because some will follow Christ and some won't, conflict will inevitably arise. As we take up our cross and follow him, our

[34]"Don't imagine that I came to bring peace to the earth! I came not to bring peace, but a sword.

35 'I have come to set a man against his father,
a daughter against her mother,
and a daughter-in-law against her mother-in-law.
36 Your enemies will be right in your own
household!'*

[37]"If you love your father or mother more than you love me, you are not worthy of being mine; or if you love your son or daughter more than me, you are not worthy of being mine. [38]If you refuse to take up your cross and follow me, you are not worthy of being mine. [39]If you cling to your life, you will lose it; but if you give up your life for me, you will find it.

[40]"Anyone who receives you receives me, and anyone who receives me receives the Father who sent me. [41]If you receive a prophet as one who speaks for God,* you will be given the same reward as a prophet. And if you receive righteous people because of their righteousness, you will be given a reward like theirs. [42]And if you give even a cup of cold water to one of the least of my followers, you will surely be rewarded."

Herod Kills John the Baptist PARALLEL

MATTHEW 14:3-12

For Herod had arrested and imprisoned John as a favor to his wife Herodias (the former wife of Herod's brother Philip). [4]John had been telling Herod, "It is against God's law for you to marry her." [5]Herod wanted to kill John, but he was afraid of a riot, because all the people believed John was a prophet.

[6]But at a birthday party for Herod, Herodias's daughter performed a dance that greatly pleased him, [7]so he promised with a vow to give her anything she wanted. [8]At her mother's urging, the girl said, "I want the head of John the Baptist on a tray!" [9]Then the king regretted what he had said; but because of the vow he had made in front of his guests, he issued the necessary orders. [10]So John was beheaded in the prison, [11]and his head was brought on a tray and given to the girl, who took it to her mother. [12]Later, John's disciples came for his body and buried it. Then they went and told Jesus what had happened.

MARK 6:17-29

For Herod had sent soldiers to arrest and imprison John as a favor to Herodias. She had been his brother Philip's wife, but Herod had married her. [18]John had been telling Herod, "It is against God's law for you to marry your brother's wife." [19]So Herodias bore a grudge against John and wanted to kill him. But without Herod's approval she was powerless, [20]for Herod respected John; and knowing that he was a good and holy man, he protected him. Herod was greatly disturbed whenever he talked with John, but even so, he liked to listen to him.

[21]Herodias's chance finally came on Herod's birthday. He gave a party for his high government officials, army officers, and the leading citizens of Galilee.

Mt 10:35-36 Mic 7:6. **Mt 10:41** Greek *receive a prophet in the name of a prophet.*

different values, morals, and goals will set us apart from others. Christ calls us to a higher mission than to find comfort and tranquility in this life. Love of family is a law of God, but even this love can be self-serving and used as an excuse not to serve God or do his work. Don't neglect your family, but remember that your commitment to God is even more important. God should be your first priority.

Matt 10:38 To take up our cross and follow Jesus means to be willing to publicly identify with him, to experience certain opposition, and to be willing to face even suffering and death for his sake.

Matt 10:39 This verse is a positive and negative statement of the same truth: Clinging to this life may cause us to forfeit the best from Christ in this world and in the next. The more we love this life's rewards (leisure, power, popularity, financial security), the more we will discover how empty they really are. The best way to enjoy life, therefore, is to loosen our greedy grasp on earthly rewards so that we can be free to follow Christ. In doing so, we will inherit eternal life and begin at once to experience the benefits of following Christ.

Matt 10:42 How much we love God can be measured by how well we treat others. Jesus' example of giving a cup of cold water to a thirsty child is a good model of unselfish service. A child usually can't or won't return a favor. God notices every good deed we do or don't do as if he were the one receiving it. Is there something unselfish you can do for someone else today? Although no one else may see you, God will notice.

Matt 14:3-12 Herod Antipas was one of three rulers over the four districts of Palestine. His territory included the regions of Galilee and Perea. He was the son of Herod the Great, who ordered the killing of the babies in Bethlehem (Matt 2:16). He heard Jesus' case before Jesus' crucifixion (Luke 23:6-12).

Matt 14:3-12 For more information on John the Baptist, see his Profile on p. 1292.

Mark 6:17-19 Palestine was divided into four territories, each with a different ruler. Herod Antipas, called Herod in the Gospels, was ruler over Galilee; his brother Philip ruled over Trachonitis and Iturea. Philip's wife was Herodias, but she had left him to marry Herod Antipas. When John confronted the two for committing adultery, Herodias formulated a plot to kill him. Instead of trying to get rid of her sin, Herodias tried to get rid of the one who brought it to public attention. This is also exactly what the religious leaders were trying to do to Jesus.

Mark 6:18 Christians today face a world of moral compromise. Secular power sets standards that correspond to majority vote; Christian standards, however, begin and end with God's Word. To be faithful to God's Word, we must stand up against what is morally wrong. Responsible Christians must choose their battles. Start with prayer for wisdom, then prayer for courage. Once your battle is chosen, speak and act as a faithful follower of the living God. Witness with strength; move mountains by faith; overcome in love. Show the compromised world a little of John's stubbornness, fortitude, and faith.

Mark 6:20 Herod arrested John the Baptist under pressure from his wife and advisers. Though Herod respected John's integrity, in the end Herod had John killed because of pressure from his peers and family. What you do under pressure often shows what you are really like.

▶ **MARK 6:17-29** ***(cont.)***

22Then his daughter, also named Herodias,* came in
and performed a dance that greatly pleased Herod and
his guests. "Ask me for anything you like," the king said
to the girl, "and I will give it to you." 23He even vowed, "I
will give you whatever you ask, up to half my kingdom!"
24She went out and asked her mother, "What should
I ask for?"
Her mother told her, "Ask for the head of John the
Baptist!"
25So the girl hurried back to the king and told him,
"I want the head of John the Baptist, right now, on a
tray!"
26Then the king deeply regretted what he had said;
but because of the vows he had made in front of his
guests, he couldn't refuse her. 27So he immediately
sent an executioner to the prison to cut off John's
head and bring it to him. The soldier beheaded John
in the prison, 28brought his head on a tray, and gave it
to the girl, who took it to her mother. 29When John's
disciples heard what had happened, they came to
get his body and buried it in a tomb.

Herod Mistakes Jesus for John the Baptist Back from the Dead PARALLEL •••

MATTHEW 14:1-2 •••

When Herod Antipas, the ruler of Galilee,* heard
about Jesus, 2he said to his advisers, "This must be
John the Baptist raised from the dead! That is why he
can do such miracles."

Mk 6:22 Some manuscripts read *the daughter of Herodias herself.* **Mt 14:1** Greek *Herod the tetrarch.* Herod Antipas was a son of King Herod and was ruler over Galilee.

HERod ANTIPAS

Most people dislike having their sins pointed out, especially in public. The shame of being exposed is often stronger than the guilt from the sin. • Herod's ruthless ambition was public knowledge, as was his illegal marriage to his brother's wife, Herodias. John the Baptist made Herod's sin a public issue. John had been preaching in the wilderness, and thousands flocked to hear him. Herodias wanted John silenced, so Herod imprisoned John. • Herod liked John. John was probably one of the few people he met who spoke only the truth to him. But the truth about his sin was a bitter pill to swallow, and he didn't want John constantly reminding the people of their leader's sinfulness. Eventually Herodias forced his hand, and John was executed. • Upon hearing about Jesus, Herod was immediately reminded of John. He didn't want to repeat the mistake he had made with John, so he tried (unsuccessfully) to threaten Jesus just before Jesus' final journey to Jerusalem. When the two met briefly during Jesus' trial, Jesus would not speak to Herod. Herod responded with spite and mocking. Having rejected the messenger, it was easy to reject the Messiah. • For each person, God reveals himself in unique ways. He uses his Word, various circumstances, our minds, or other people to get our attention. He is persuasive and persistent but never forces himself on us. To miss or resist God's message is a tragedy. How aware are you of God's attempts to enter your life? Have you welcomed him?

Strengths and accomplishments	• Built the city of Tiberias and oversaw other architectural projects • Ruled the region of Galilee for the Romans
Weaknesses and mistakes	• Consumed with his quest for power • Put off decisions or made wrong ones under pressure • Divorced his wife to marry the wife of his half brother, Philip • Imprisoned John the Baptist and later ordered his execution • Had a minor part in the execution of Jesus
Lessons from his life	• A life motivated by ambition is usually characterized by self-destruction • Opportunities to do good usually come to us in the form of choices to be made
Vital statistics	• Where: Jerusalem • Occupation: Roman ruler of the regions of Galilee and Perea • Relatives: Father: Herod the Great. Mother: Malthace. First wife: daughter of Aretas IV. Second wife: Herodias. • Contemporaries: John the Baptist, Jesus, Pilate
Key verse	"Herod was greatly disturbed whenever he talked with John, but even so, he liked to listen to him" (Mark 6:20).

Herod Antipas's story is told in the Gospels. He is also mentioned in Acts 4:27; 13:1.

Mark 6:22-23 As a ruler under Roman authority, Herod had no kingdom to give. The offer of half his kingdom was Herod's way of saying that he would give Herodias's daughter almost anything she wanted. When Herodias asked for John's head, Herod would have been greatly embarrassed in front of his guests if he had denied her request. Words are powerful. Because they can lead to great sin, we should use them with great care.

Mark 6:14-15 Herod, along with many others, wondered who Jesus really was. Unable to accept Jesus' claim to be God's Son, many people made up their own explanations for his power and authority. Herod thought that Jesus was John the Baptist come back to life, while those who were familiar with the Old Testament thought he was Elijah (Mal 4:5). Still others believed that Jesus was a teaching prophet in the tradition of Moses, Isaiah, or Jeremiah. Today people still have to make up their minds about Jesus. Some think that if they can name what he is—prophet, teacher, good man—they can weaken the power of his claim on their lives. But what they think does not change who Jesus is.

Luke 9:7-8 People found accepting Jesus as the Son of God so difficult that they tried to come up with other solutions—most of which sound quite unbelievable to us. Many thought that Jesus must be someone who had come back to life, perhaps John the Baptist or another prophet. Some suggested that he was Elijah, the great prophet who had not died but had been taken to heaven in a chariot of fire (2 Kgs 2:1-11). Very few found the correct answer, as Peter did (Luke 9:20). Many people today still have difficulty accepting Jesus as the fully human yet fully divine Son of God. People are still trying to find alternate explanations—a great prophet, a radical political leader, a self-deceived rabble-rouser. None of these explanations can account for Jesus' miracles or especially his resurrection. In the end, the attempts to explain away Jesus are far more difficult to believe than the truth.

MARK 6:14-16
Herod Antipas, the king, soon heard about Jesus, because everyone was talking about him. Some were saying,* "This must be John the Baptist raised from the dead. That is why he can do such miracles."
15Others said, "He's the prophet Elijah." Still others said, "He's a prophet like the other great prophets of the past."
16When Herod heard about Jesus, he said, "John, the man I beheaded, has come back from the dead."

LUKE 9:7-9
When Herod Antipas, the ruler of Galilee,* heard about everything Jesus was doing, he was puzzled. Some were saying that John the Baptist had been raised from the dead. 8Others thought Jesus was Elijah or one of the other prophets risen from the dead.
9"I beheaded John," Herod said, "so who is this man about whom I hear such stories?" And he kept trying to see him.

Jesus Feeds Five Thousand PARALLEL

MATTHEW 14:13-21
As soon as Jesus heard the news, he left in a boat to a remote area to be alone. But the crowds heard where he was headed and followed on foot from many towns.
14Jesus saw the huge crowd as he stepped from the boat, and he had compassion on them and healed their sick.
15That evening the disciples came to him and said, "This is a remote place, and it's already getting late. Send the crowds away so they can go to the villages and buy food for themselves."
16But Jesus said, "That isn't necessary—you feed them."
17"But we have only five loaves of bread and two fish!" they answered.
18"Bring them here," he said. 19Then he told the people to sit down on the grass. Jesus took the five loaves and two fish, looked up toward heaven, and blessed them. Then, breaking the loaves into pieces, he gave the bread to the disciples, who distributed it to the people. 20They all ate as much as they wanted, and afterward, the disciples picked up twelve baskets of leftovers. 21About 5,000 men were fed that day, in addition to all the women and children!

MARK 6:30-44
The apostles returned to Jesus from their ministry tour and told him all they had done and taught. 31Then Jesus said, "Let's go off by ourselves to a quiet place and rest awhile." He said this because there were so many people coming and going that Jesus and his apostles didn't even have time to eat.
32So they left by boat for a quiet place, where they could be alone. 33But many people recognized them and saw them leaving, and people from many towns ran ahead along the shore and got there ahead of them. 34Jesus saw the huge crowd as he stepped from the boat, and he had compassion on them because they were like sheep without a shepherd. So he began teaching them many things.
35Late in the afternoon his disciples came to him

Mk 6:14 Some manuscripts read *He was saying.* **Lk 9:7** Greek *Herod the tetrarch.* Herod Antipas was a son of King Herod and was ruler over Galilee.

REAL LEADERSHIP

Mark gives us some of the best insights into Jesus' character.

Herod as a leader	Jesus as a leader
Selfish	Compassionate
Murderer	Healer
Immoral	Just and good
Political opportunist	Servant
King over small territory	King over all creation

Matt 14:13-14 Jesus sought solitude after the news of John's death. Sometimes we may need to deal with our grief alone. Jesus did not dwell on his grief but returned to the ministry he came to do.

Matt 14:14 Jesus performed some miracles as signs of his identity. He used other miracles to teach important truths. But here we read that he healed people because he "had compassion on them." Jesus was—and is—a loving, caring, and feeling person. When you are suffering, remember that Jesus hurts with you. He has compassion on you.

Matt 14:19-21 Jesus multiplied five loaves and two fish to feed over 5,000 people. What he was originally given seemed insufficient, but in his hands it became more than enough. We often feel that our contribution to Jesus is meager, but he can use and multiply whatever we give him, whether it is talent, time, or treasure. It is when we give them to Jesus that our resources are multiplied.

Matt 14:21 The text states that there were 5,000 men present, besides women and children. Therefore, the total number of people Jesus fed could have been 10,000 to 15,000. The number of men is listed separately because in the Jewish culture of the day, men and women usually ate separately when in public. The children ate with the women.

Mark 6:30 Mark uses the word apostles here and in Mark 3:14. Apostle means "one sent" as messenger, authorized agent, or missionary. The word became an official title for Jesus' 12 disciples after his death and resurrection (Acts 1:25-26; Eph 2:20).

Mark 6:31 After the disciples had returned from their mission, Jesus took them away to rest. Doing God's work is very important, but Jesus recognized that to do it effectively they needed periodic rest and renewal. Jesus and his disciples, however, did not always find it easy to get the rest they needed!

Mark 6:34 This crowd was as pitiful as a flock of sheep without a shepherd. Sheep are easily scattered; without a shepherd they are in grave danger. Jesus was the Shepherd who could teach them what they needed to know and keep them from straying from God. See Psalm 23; Isaiah 40:11; Ezekiel 34:5-24; and John 10:11-16 for descriptions of the Good Shepherd.

▸ **MARK 6:30-44 *(cont.)***

and said, "This is a remote place, and it's already getting late. 36Send the crowds away so they can go to the nearby farms and villages and buy something to eat."

37But Jesus said, "You feed them."

"With what?" they asked. "We'd have to work for months to earn enough money* to buy food for all these people!"

38"How much bread do you have?" he asked. "Go and find out."

They came back and reported, "We have five loaves of bread and two fish."

39Then Jesus told the disciples to have the people sit down in groups on the green grass. 40So they sat down in groups of fifty or a hundred.

41Jesus took the five loaves and two fish, looked up toward heaven, and blessed them. Then, breaking the loaves into pieces, he kept giving the bread to the disciples so they could distribute it to the people. He also divided the fish for everyone to share. 42They all ate as much as they wanted, 43and afterward, the disciples picked up twelve baskets of leftover bread and fish. 44A total of 5,000 men and their families were fed from those loaves!

LUKE 9:10-17

When the apostles returned, they told Jesus everything they had done. Then he slipped quietly away with them toward the town of Bethsaida. 11But the crowds found out where he was going, and they followed him. He welcomed them and taught them about the Kingdom of God, and he healed those who were sick.

12Late in the afternoon the twelve disciples came to him and said, "Send the crowds away to the nearby villages and farms, so they can find food and lodging for the night. There is nothing to eat here in this remote place."

13But Jesus said, "You feed them."

"But we have only five loaves of bread and two fish," they answered. "Or are you expecting us to go and buy enough food for this whole crowd?" 14For there were about 5,000 men there.

Jesus replied, "Tell them to sit down in groups of about fifty each." 15So the people all sat down. 16Jesus took the five loaves and two fish, looked up toward heaven, and blessed them. Then, breaking the loaves into pieces, he kept giving the bread and fish to the disciples so they could distribute it to the people. 17They all ate as much as they wanted, and afterward, the disciples picked up twelve baskets of leftovers!

JOHN 6:1-15

After this, Jesus crossed over to the far side of the Sea of Galilee, also known as the Sea of Tiberias. 2A huge crowd kept following him wherever he went, because they saw his miraculous signs as he healed the sick. 3Then Jesus climbed a hill and sat down with his disciples around him. 4(It was nearly time for the Jewish Passover celebration.) 5Jesus soon saw a huge crowd

Mk 6:37 Greek *It would take 200 denarii.* A denarius was equivalent to a laborer's full day's wage.

Mark 6:37-42 When Jesus asked the disciples to provide food for over 5,000 people, they were amazed and said it would take a small fortune to feed such a crowd. How do you react when you are given an impossible task? A situation that seems impossible with human resources is simply an opportunity for God. The disciples did everything they could by gathering the available food and organizing the people into groups. Then, in answer to prayer, God did the impossible. When facing a seemingly impossible task, do what you can and ask God to do the rest. He may see fit to make the impossible happen.

Mark 6:37-42 Why did Jesus bother to feed these people? He could just as easily have sent them on their way. But Jesus does not ignore needs. He is concerned with every aspect of our lives—the physical as well as the spiritual.

We might well ask why the church has taken so lightly the command, "You feed them." Jesus' compassion for these hungry people is recorded in all four Gospels. For people who are desperately hungry, there is no better way for us to show God's love than to help to provide for their physical needs. As we work to bring wholeness to people's lives, we must never ignore the fact that all of us have both physical and spiritual needs. It is impossible to minister effectively to the spiritual need without considering the physical need. (See also Jas 2:14-17.)

Luke 9:10-11 Jesus had tried to slip quietly away from the crowds, but they found out where he was going and followed him. Instead of showing impatience at this interruption, Jesus welcomed the people and ministered to their needs. How do you see people who interrupt your schedule—as nuisances or as the reason for your life and ministry?

Luke 9:11 The Kingdom of God was a focal point of Jesus' teaching. He explained that it was not just a future Kingdom; it was among them, embodied in him, the Messiah. Even though the Kingdom will not be complete until Jesus comes again in glory, we do not have to wait to experience it. The Kingdom of God begins in the hearts of those who believe in Jesus (Luke 17:21). It is as present with us today as it was with the Judeans over 2,000 years ago.

Luke 9:13-14 When the disciples expressed concern about where the crowd of thousands would eat, Jesus offered a surprising solution: "You feed them." The disciples protested, focusing their attention on what they didn't have (food and money). Do you think God would ask you to do something that you and he together couldn't handle? Don't let your lack of resources blind you to God's power.

Luke 9:16-17 Don't miss the fact that Jesus fed the hungry crowd as well as taught them about the Kingdom of God (Luke 9:11). As we work to bring wholeness to people's lives, we must never ignore the fact that all of us have both physical and spiritual needs. It is impossible to minister effectively to one type of need without considering the other.

John 6:5 If anyone knew where to get food, it would have been Philip because he was from Bethsaida, a town about nine miles away (John 1:44). Jesus was testing Philip to strengthen his faith. By asking for a human solution (knowing that there was none), Jesus highlighted the powerful and miraculous act that he was about to perform.

John 6:5-7 When Jesus asked Philip where they could buy a great amount of bread, Philip started assessing the probable cost. Jesus wanted to teach him that financial resources are not the most important ones. We can limit what God does in us by assuming what is and what is not possible. Is there some impossible task that you believe God wants you to do? Don't let your estimate of

of people coming to look for him. Turning to Philip,
he asked, "Where can we buy bread to feed all these
people?" 6He was testing Philip, for he already knew
what he was going to do.
7Philip replied, "Even if we worked for months, we
wouldn't have enough money* to feed them!"
8Then Andrew, Simon Peter's brother, spoke up.
9"There's a young boy here with five barley loaves
and two fish. But what good is that with this huge
crowd?"
10"Tell everyone to sit down," Jesus said. So they
all sat down on the grassy slopes. (The men alone
numbered about 5,000.) 11Then Jesus took the
loaves, gave thanks to God, and distributed them
to the people. Afterward he did the same with the
fish. And they all ate as much as they wanted. 12Af-
ter everyone was full, Jesus told his disciples, "Now
gather the leftovers, so that nothing is wasted." 13So
they picked up the pieces and filled twelve baskets
with scraps left by the people who had eaten from
the five barley loaves.
14When the people saw him* do this miraculous
sign, they exclaimed, "Surely, he is the Prophet we have
been expecting!"* 15When Jesus saw that they were
ready to force him to be their king, he slipped away
into the hills by himself.

Jesus Walks on Water PARALLEL ●●●

MATTHEW 14:22-33 ●○○
Immediately after this, Jesus insisted that his disciples
get back into the boat and cross to the other side of the
lake, while he sent the people home. 23After sending
them home, he went up into the hills by himself to
pray. Night fell while he was there alone.
24Meanwhile, the disciples were in trouble far
away from land, for a strong wind had risen, and they
were fighting heavy waves. 25About three o'clock in
the morning* Jesus came toward them, walking on the
water. 26When the disciples saw him walking on the
water, they were terrified. In their fear, they cried out,
"It's a ghost!"
27But Jesus spoke to them at once. "Don't be afraid,"
he said. "Take courage. I am here!*"
28Then Peter called to him, "Lord, if it's really you,
tell me to come to you, walking on the water."
29"Yes, come," Jesus said.
So Peter went over the side of the boat and walked
on the water toward Jesus. 30But when he saw the
strong* wind and the waves, he was terrified and began to sink. "Save me, Lord!" he shouted.
31Jesus immediately reached out and grabbed him.
"You have so little faith," Jesus said. "Why did you
doubt me?"

Jn 6:7 Greek *Two hundred denarii would not be enough.* A denarius was equivalent to a laborer's full day's wage. **Jn 6:14a** Some manuscripts read *Jesus.* **Jn 6:14b** See Deut 18:15, 18; Mal 4:5-6. **Mt 14:25** Greek *In the fourth watch of the night.* **Mt 14:27** Or *The 'I AM' is here;* Greek reads *I am.* See Exod 3:14. **Mt 14:30** Some manuscripts do not include *strong.*

what can't be done keep you from taking on the task. God can do the miraculous; trust him to provide the resources.

John 6:7-9 The disciples are contrasted with the youngster who brought what he had. They certainly had more resources than the boy, but they knew they didn't have enough, so they didn't give anything at all. The boy gave what little he had, and it made all the difference. If we offer nothing to God, he will have nothing to use. But he can take what little we have and turn it into something great.

John 6:8-9 In performing his miracles, Jesus sometimes decided to work through people. Here he took what a young child offered and used it to accomplish one of the most spectacular miracles recorded in the Gospels. Age is no barrier to Christ. Never think you are too young or old to be of service to him.

John 6:13 There is a lesson in the leftovers. God gives in abundance. He takes whatever we can offer him in time, ability, or resources and multiplies its effectiveness beyond our wildest expectations. If you take the first step in making yourself available to God, he will show you how greatly you can be used to advance the work of his Kingdom.

John 6:14 "The Prophet" is the one prophesied by Moses (Deut 18:15).

Matt 14:23 Seeking solitude was an important priority for Jesus (see also Matt 14:13). He made room in his busy schedule to be alone with the Father. Spending time with God in prayer nurtures a vital relationship with him and equips us to meet life's challenges and struggles. Develop the discipline of spending time alone with God. It will help you grow spiritually and become more and more like Christ.

Matt 14:28 Peter was not putting Jesus to the test, something we are told not to do (Matt 4:7). Instead, he was the only one in the boat to react in faith. His impulsive request led him to experience a rather unusual demonstration of God's power. Peter started to sink because he took his eyes off Jesus and focused on the high waves around him. His faith wavered when he realized what he was doing. We probably will not walk on water, but we may walk through tough situations. If we focus on the waves of difficult circumstances around us without faith in Jesus to help, we, too, may despair and sink. To maintain your faith when situations are difficult, focus on Jesus' power rather than on your inadequacies.

Matt 14:30-31 Although we start out with good intentions, sometimes our faith falters. This doesn't necessarily mean we have failed. When Peter's faith faltered, he reached out to Christ, the only one who could help. He was afraid, but he still looked to Christ. When you are apprehensive about the troubles around you and doubt Christ's presence or ability to help, remember that he is always with you and is the only one who can really help.

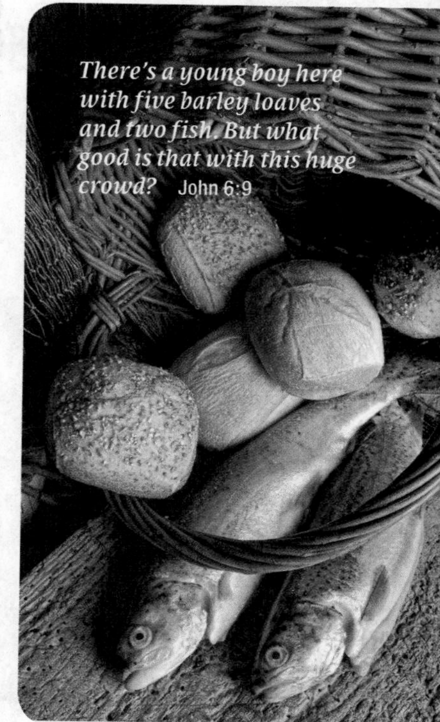
There's a young boy here with five barley loaves and two fish. But what good is that with this huge crowd? John 6:9

▸ **MATTHEW 14:22-33 *(cont.)***

32When they climbed back into the boat, the wind stopped. 33Then the disciples worshiped him. "You really are the Son of God!" they exclaimed.

MARK 6:45-52
Immediately after this, Jesus insisted that his disciples get back into the boat and head across the lake to Bethsaida, while he sent the people home. 46After telling everyone good-bye, he went up into the hills by himself to pray.

47Late that night, the disciples were in their boat in the middle of the lake, and Jesus was alone on land. 48He saw that they were in serious trouble, rowing hard and struggling against the wind and waves. About three o'clock in the morning* Jesus came toward them, walking on the water. He intended to go past them, 49but when they saw him walking on the water, they cried out in terror, thinking he was a ghost. 50They were all terrified when they saw him.

But Jesus spoke to them at once. "Don't be afraid," he said. "Take courage! I am here!*" 51Then he climbed into the boat, and the wind stopped. They were totally amazed, 52for they still didn't understand the significance of the miracle of the loaves. Their hearts were too hard to take it in.

JOHN 6:16-21
That evening Jesus' disciples went down to the shore to wait for him. 17But as darkness fell and Jesus still hadn't come back, they got into the boat and headed across the lake toward Capernaum. 18Soon a gale swept down upon them, and the sea grew very rough. 19They had rowed three or four miles* when suddenly they saw Jesus walking on the water toward the boat. They were terrified, 20but he called out to them, "Don't be afraid. I am here!*" 21Then they were eager to let him in the boat, and immediately they arrived at their destination!

Jesus Heals All Who Touch Him PARALLEL

MATTHEW 14:34-36
After they had crossed the lake, they landed at Gennesaret. 35When the people recognized Jesus, the news of his arrival spread quickly throughout the whole area, and soon people were bringing all their sick to be healed. 36They begged him to let the sick touch at least the fringe of his robe, and all who touched him were healed.

MARK 6:53-56
After they had crossed the lake, they landed at Gennesaret. They brought the boat to shore 54and climbed out. The people recognized Jesus at once, 55and they

Mk 6:48 Greek *About the fourth watch of the night.* **Mk 6:50** Or *The 'I AM' is here;* Greek reads *I am.* See Exod 3:14. **Jn 6:19** Greek *25 or 30 stadia* [4.6 or 5.5 kilometers]. **Jn 6:20** Or *The 'I AM' is here;* Greek reads *I am.* See Exod 3:14.

Mark 6:49-50 The disciples were afraid, but Jesus' presence calmed their fears. When you experience fear, do you try to deal with it yourself, or do you let Jesus deal with it? In times of fear and uncertainty, it is calming to know that Christ is always with you (Matt 28:20). To recognize Christ's presence is the antidote for fear.

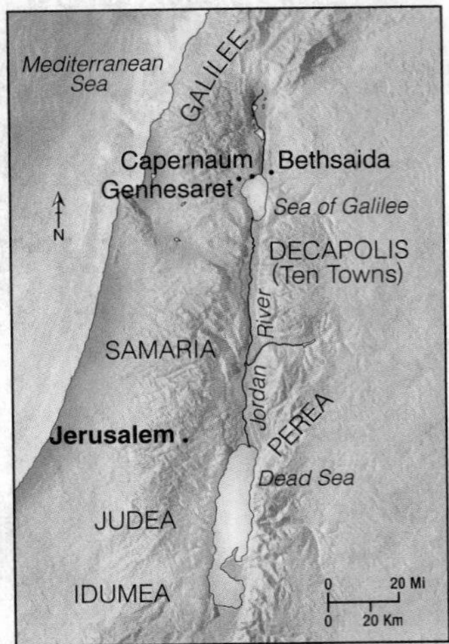

***JESUS WALKS ON THE SEA** The miraculous feeding of the 5,000 occurred on the shores of the Sea of Galilee near Bethsaida. Jesus then sent his disciples across the lake. Several hours later they encountered a storm, and Jesus came to them—walking on the water. The boat then landed at Gennesaret.*

Mark 6:52 The disciples still did not understand the real purpose for Jesus' coming to earth. Their disbelief took the form of misunderstanding. Even after watching Jesus miraculously feed 5,000 people, they still could not take the final step of faith and believe that he was God's Son. If they had, they would not have been amazed that Jesus could walk on water.

Is your heart hardened against Jesus? Even Christians can be hard-hearted to Jesus' words. We can be informed about what his Word says, and we can be amazed at how he has worked in other people's lives, but we can refuse to believe he will come to our aid in our time of trouble. Such a reaction is not unbelief, but willful, hard-hearted rejection of Christ's ability to help. Instead, "take courage," and trust that he is there for you.

John 6:18 The Sea of Galilee is 680 feet below sea level, 150-200 feet deep, and surrounded by hills. These physical features make it subject to sudden windstorms that would cause extremely high waves. Such storms were expected on this lake, but they were nevertheless frightening. When Jesus came to the disciples during a storm, walking on the water (three-and-a-half miles from shore), he told them not to be afraid. We often face spiritual and emotional storms and feel tossed about like a small boat on a big lake. In spite of terrifying circumstances, if we trust our lives to Christ for his safekeeping, he will give us peace in any storm.

John 6:18-19 The disciples, terrified, probably thought they were seeing a ghost (Mark 6:49). But if they had thought about all they had already seen Jesus do, they could have accepted this miracle. They were frightened—they didn't expect Jesus to come, and they weren't prepared for his help.

Matt 14:35-36 The people recognized Jesus as a great healer, but how many understood who he truly was? They came to Jesus for physical healing, but did they come for spiritual healing? They came to prolong their lives on earth, not to seek eternal life. People may follow Jesus to learn valuable lessons from his life or in the hope of finding relief from pain. But we miss Jesus' whole message if we seek him only to heal our bodies but not our souls, if we look to him for help only in this life rather than for his eternal plan for us. Only when we understand the real Jesus Christ can we appreciate how he can truly change our lives.

Matt 14:36 Jewish men wore fringe on the lower edges of their robes according to God's command (Deut 22:12). By Jesus' day, elaborate versions of this fringe were seen as a sign of holiness (Matt 23:5). There is no indication that the fringe on Jesus' robe was anything more than typical. It was natural that

ran throughout the whole area, carrying sick people
on mats to wherever they heard he was. 56Wherever
he went—in villages, cities, or the countryside—they
brought the sick out to the marketplaces. They begged
him to let the sick touch at least the fringe of his robe,
and all who touched him were healed.

Jesus Is the True Bread from Heaven

JOHN 6:22-40

The next day the crowd that had stayed on the far
shore saw that the disciples had taken the only boat,
and they realized Jesus had not gone with them. 23Sev-
eral boats from Tiberias landed near the place where
the Lord had blessed the bread and the people had
eaten. 24So when the crowd saw that neither Jesus nor
his disciples were there, they got into the boats and
went across to Capernaum to look for him. 25They
found him on the other side of the lake and asked,
"Rabbi, when did you get here?"

26Jesus replied, "I tell you the truth, you want to be
with me because I fed you, not because you understood
the miraculous signs. 27But don't be so concerned
about perishable things like food. Spend your energy
seeking the eternal life that the Son of Man* can give
you. For God the Father has given me the seal of his
approval."

28They replied, "We want to perform God's works,
too. What should we do?"

29Jesus told them, "This is the only work God wants
from you: Believe in the one he has sent."

30They answered, "Show us a miraculous sign if you
want us to believe in you. What can you do? 31After
all, our ancestors ate manna while they journeyed
through the wilderness! The Scriptures say, 'Moses
gave them bread from heaven to eat.'*"

32Jesus said, "I tell you the truth, Moses didn't give
you bread from heaven. My Father did. And now he offers you the true bread from heaven. 33The true bread
of God is the one who comes down from heaven and
gives life to the world."

34"Sir," they said, "give us that bread every day."

35Jesus replied, "I am the bread of life. Whoever comes
to me will never be hungry again. Whoever believes in
me will never be thirsty. 36But you haven't believed in
me even though you have seen me. 37However, those
the Father has given me will come to me, and I will never
reject them. 38For I have come down from heaven to do
the will of God who sent me, not to do my own will. 39And
this is the will of God, that I should not lose even one of
all those he has given me, but that I should raise them
up at the last day. 40For it is my Father's will that all who
see his Son and believe in him should have eternal life.
I will raise them up at the last day."

The People Disagree That Jesus Is from Heaven

JOHN 6:41-59

Then the people* began to murmur in disagreement
because he had said, "I am the bread that came down
from heaven." 42They said, "Isn't this Jesus, the son of
Joseph? We know his father and mother. How can he
say, 'I came down from heaven'?"

43But Jesus replied, "Stop complaining about what
I said. 44For no one can come to me unless the Father

Jn 6:27 "Son of Man" is a title Jesus used for himself. **Jn 6:31** Exod 16:4; Ps 78:24. **Jn 6:41** Greek *Jewish people;* also in 6:52.

people seeking healing should reach out and touch the fringe of his robe. But as one sick woman learned, healing came from faith and not from Jesus' robe (Matt 9:19-22).

Mark 6:53 Gennesaret was a small, fertile plain located on the west side of the Sea of Galilee. Capernaum, Jesus' home, sat at the northern edge of this plain.

John 6:26 Jesus criticized the people who followed him only for the physical and temporal benefits and not for the satisfying of their spiritual hunger. Many people use religion to gain prestige, comfort, or even political votes. But those are self-centered motives. True believers follow Jesus simply because they know he has the truth and his way leads to life.

John 6:28-29 Many sincere seekers of God are puzzled about what he wants them to do. The religions of the world are people's attempts to answer this question. But Jesus' reply is brief and simple: We must believe on him whom God has sent. Satisfying God does not come from the work we do, but from whom we believe. The first step involves accepting that Jesus is who he claims to be. All spiritual development is built on this affirmation. Declare to Jesus, "You are the Messiah, the Son of the living God" (Matt 16:16), and embark on a life of belief that satisfies your Creator.

John 6:35 People eat bread to satisfy physical hunger and to sustain physical life. We can satisfy spiritual hunger and sustain spiritual life only by a right relationship with Jesus Christ. No wonder he called himself the Bread of Life. But bread must be eaten to sustain life, and Christ must be invited into our daily walk to sustain spiritual life.

John 6:37-38 Jesus did not work independently of God the Father, but in union with him. This should give us even more assurance of being welcomed into God's presence and being protected by him. Jesus' purpose was to do the will of God, not to satisfy his human desires. When we follow Jesus, we should have the same purpose.

John 6:39 Jesus said he would not lose even one person whom the Father had given him. Thus, anyone who makes a sincere commitment to believe in Jesus Christ as Savior is secure in God's promise of eternal life. Christ will not let his people be overcome by Satan and lose their salvation (see also John 17:12; Phil 1:6).

John 6:40 Those who put their faith in Christ will be resurrected from physical death to eternal life with God when Christ comes again (see 1 Cor 15:52; 1 Thes 4:16).

John 6:41 Some of the people grumbled in disagreement because they could not accept Jesus' claim of divinity. They saw him only as a carpenter from Nazareth. They refused to believe that Jesus was God's divine Son, and they could not tolerate his message. Many people reject Christ because they say they cannot believe he is the Son of God. In reality, the demands that Christ makes for their loyalty and obedience are what they can't accept. So to protect themselves from the message, they reject the messenger.

John 6:44 God, not people, plays the most active role in salvation. When someone chooses to believe in Jesus Christ as Savior, he or she does so only in response to the urging of God's Holy Spirit. God does the urging; then we decide whether or not to believe. Thus, no one can believe in Jesus without God's help.

▸ **JOHN 6:41-59** ***(cont.)***

who sent me draws them to me, and at the last day I will raise them up. 45As it is written in the Scriptures,* 'They will all be taught by God.' Everyone who listens to the Father and learns from him comes to me. 46(Not that anyone has ever seen the Father; only I, who was sent from God, have seen him.)

47"I tell you the truth, anyone who believes has eternal life. 48Yes, I am the bread of life! 49Your ancestors ate manna in the wilderness, but they all died. 50Anyone who eats the bread from heaven, however, will never die. 51I am the living bread that came down from heaven. Anyone who eats this bread will live forever; and this bread, which I will offer so the world may live, is my flesh."

52Then the people began arguing with each other about what he meant. "How can this man give us his flesh to eat?" they asked.

53So Jesus said again, "I tell you the truth, unless you eat the flesh of the Son of Man and drink his blood, you cannot have eternal life within you. 54But anyone who eats my flesh and drinks my blood has eternal life, and I will raise that person at the last day. 55For my flesh is true food, and my blood is true drink. 56Anyone who eats my flesh and drinks my blood remains in me, and I in him. 57I live because of the living Father who sent me; in the same way, anyone who feeds on me will live because of me. 58I am the true bread that came down from heaven. Anyone who eats this bread will not die as your ancestors did (even though they ate the manna) but will live forever."

59He said these things while he was teaching in the synagogue in Capernaum.

Many Disciples Desert Jesus

JOHN 6:60-71

Many of his disciples said, "This is very hard to understand. How can anyone accept it?"

61Jesus was aware that his disciples were complaining, so he said to them, "Does this offend you? 62Then what will you think if you see the Son of Man ascend to heaven again? 63The Spirit alone gives eternal life. Human effort accomplishes nothing. And the very words I have spoken to you are spirit and life. 64But some of you do not believe me." (For Jesus knew from

Jn 6:45 Greek *in the prophets.* Isa 54:13.

John 6:45 Jesus was alluding to an Old Testament view of the messianic Kingdom in which all people are taught directly by God (Isa 54:13; Jer 31:31-34). He was stressing the importance of not merely hearing, but learning. We are taught by God through the Bible, our experiences, the thoughts the Holy Spirit brings, and relationships with other Christians. Are you open to God's teaching?

John 6:47ff The religious leaders frequently asked Jesus to prove to them why he was better than the prophets they already had. Jesus here referred to the manna that Moses had given their ancestors in the wilderness (see Exod 16). This bread was physical and temporal. The people ate it, and it sustained them for a day. But they had to get more bread every day, and this bread could not keep them from dying. Jesus, who is much greater than Moses, offers himself as the spiritual bread from heaven that satisfies completely and leads to eternal life.

John 6:51 How can Jesus give us his flesh as bread to eat? To eat living bread means to accept Christ into our lives and become united with him. We are united with Christ in two ways: (1) by believing in his death (the sacrifice of his flesh) and resurrection and (2) by devoting ourselves to living as he requires, depending on his teaching for guidance, and trusting in the Holy Spirit for power.

John 6:56 This was a shocking message—to eat flesh and drink blood sounded cannibalistic. The idea of drinking any blood, let alone human blood, was repugnant to the religious leaders because the law forbade it (Lev 17:10-11). Jesus was not talking about literal blood, of course. He was saying that his life had to become their own, but they could not accept this concept. The Gospel writers as well as the apostle Paul used the body and blood imagery in talking about Communion (see 1 Cor 11:23-26).

John 6:63, 65 The Holy Spirit gives spiritual life; without the work of the Holy Spirit, we cannot even see our need for new life (John 14:17). All spiritual renewal begins and ends with God. He reveals truth to us, lives within us, and then enables us to respond to that truth.

Synagogue in Capernaum

Capernaum was a city in Galilee that served as the headquarters of Jesus' early ministry. Matthew tells us that Capernaum was located near the Sea of Galilee, in the territory of Zebulun and Naphtali (Matt 4:13). Two stories found in the Gospels help to identify its specific location along the Sea. The story of Jesus' call to Matthew to leave the customs post controlling the taxation of the area gives an idea that it might be a border town (Matt 9:9). The story of the centurion (Matt 8:5ff) points to a small garrison of about 100 men usually stationed at such a frontier town. Jesus performed many miracles at Capernaum (Mark 1:34): the healing of the centurion's servant (Matt 8:5-13), the healing of Peter's mother-in-law (Mark 1:30-31), and the exorcism of an evil spirit (Mark 1:23-26). But in spite of these miracles, many people in Capernaum rejected Jesus (Matt 11:23). The story in John 6 is another example of how the people at the synagogue in Capernaum did not accept Jesus' teaching.

the beginning which ones didn't believe, and he knew
who would betray him.) 65Then he said, "That is why
I said that people can't come to me unless the Father
gives them to me."
66At this point many of his disciples turned away
and deserted him. 67Then Jesus turned to the Twelve
and asked, "Are you also going to leave?"
68Simon Peter replied, "Lord, to whom would we
go? You have the words that give eternal life. 69We
believe, and we know you are the Holy One of God.*"
70Then Jesus said, "I chose the twelve of you, but
one is a devil." 71He was speaking of Judas, son of
Simon Iscariot, one of the Twelve, who would later
betray him.

Jesus Teaches about Inner Purity PARALLEL

MATTHEW 15:1-20

Some Pharisees and teachers of religious law now
arrived from Jerusalem to see Jesus. They asked him,
2"Why do your disciples disobey our age-old tradition? For they ignore our tradition of ceremonial hand
washing before they eat."
3Jesus replied, "And why do you, by your traditions,
violate the direct commandments of God? 4For instance, God says, 'Honor your father and mother,'*
and 'Anyone who speaks disrespectfully of father
or mother must be put to death.'* 5But you say it is
all right for people to say to their parents, 'Sorry, I
can't help you. For I have vowed to give to God what
I would have given to you.' 6In this way, you say they
don't need to honor their parents.* And so you cancel
the word of God for the sake of your own tradition.
7You hypocrites! Isaiah was right when he prophesied
about you, for he wrote,

8 'These people honor me with their lips,
but their hearts are far from me.
9 Their worship is a farce,
for they teach man-made ideas as commands
from God.'*"

10Then Jesus called to the crowd to come and hear.
"Listen," he said, "and try to understand. 11It's not
what goes into your mouth that defiles you; you are
defiled by the words that come out of your mouth."
12Then the disciples came to him and asked, "Do
you realize you offended the Pharisees by what you
just said?"

Jn 6:69 Other manuscripts read *you are the Christ, the Holy One of God;* still others read *you are the Christ, the Son of God;* and still others read *you are the Christ, the Son of the living God.* **Mt 15:4a** Exod 20:12; Deut 5:16. **Mt 15:4b** Exod 21:17 (Greek version); Lev 20:9 (Greek version). **Mt 15:6** Greek *their father;* other manuscripts read *their father or their mother.* **Mt 15:8-9** Isa 29:13 (Greek version).

John 6:66 Why did Jesus' words cause many of his followers to desert him? (1) They may have realized that he wasn't going to be the conquering Messiah-King they expected. (2) He refused to give in to their self-centered requests. (3) He emphasized faith, not deeds. (4) His teachings were difficult to understand, and some of his words were offensive. As we grow in our faith, we may be tempted to turn away because Jesus' lessons are difficult. Will your response be to give up, ignore certain teachings, or reject Christ? Instead, ask God to show you what the teachings mean and how they apply to your life. Then have the courage to act on God's truth.

John 6:67 There is no middle ground with Jesus. When he asked the disciples if they would also leave, he was showing that they could either accept or reject him. Jesus was not trying to repel people with his teachings. He was simply telling the truth. The more the people heard Jesus' real message, the more they divided into two camps—the honest seekers who wanted to understand more, and those who rejected Jesus because they didn't like what they had heard.

John 6:67-68 After many of Jesus' followers had deserted him, he asked the 12 disciples if they were also going to leave. Peter replied, "To whom would we go?" In his straightforward way, Peter answered for all of us—there is no other way. Though there are many philosophies and self-styled authorities, Jesus alone has the words of eternal life. People look everywhere for eternal life and miss Christ, the only source. Stay with him, especially when you are confused or feel alone.

John 6:70 In response to Jesus' message, some people left; others stayed and truly believed; and some, like Judas, stayed but tried to use Jesus for personal gain. Many people today turn away from Christ. Others pretend to follow, going to church for status, approval of family and friends, or business contacts. But there are only two real responses to Jesus—you either accept him or reject him. How have you responded to Christ?

John 6:71 For more information on Judas, see his Profile on p. 1454.

Matt 15:1-2 The Pharisees and teachers of religious law came from Jerusalem, the center of Jewish authority, to scrutinize Jesus' activities. Over the centuries since the Jews' return from Babylonian captivity, hundreds of religious traditions had been added to God's laws. The Pharisees and teachers of religious law considered them all equally important. Many traditions are not bad in themselves. Certain religious traditions can add richness and meaning to life. But we must not assume that because our traditions have been practiced for years, they should be elevated to a sacred standing. God's principles never change, and his law doesn't need additions. Traditions should help us understand God's laws better, not become laws themselves.

Matt 15:5-6 This was the practice of *Corban* (literally, "offering"; see Mark 7:11). Anyone who made a Corban vow was required to dedicate money to God's Temple that otherwise would have gone to support his parents. Corban had become a religiously acceptable way to neglect parents, circumventing the child's responsibility to them. Although the action—giving money to God—seemed worthy and no doubt conferred prestige on the giver, many people who took the Corban vow were disregarding God's command to care for needy parents. These religious leaders were ignoring God's clear command to honor their parents.

Matt 15:8-9 The prophet Isaiah also criticized hypocrites (Isa 29:13), and Jesus applied Isaiah's words to these religious leaders. The Pharisees knew a lot about God, but they didn't know God. When we claim to honor God while our heart is far from him, our worship means nothing. It is not enough to study about religion or even to study the Bible; it is not enough to act religious. Our actions and our attitudes must be sincere. If they are not, Isaiah's words also describe us.

Matt 15:11 Jesus was referring to the Jewish regulations concerning food and drink. This verse could be paraphrased as follows: "You aren't made unclean by eating non-kosher food! It is what you say and think that makes you unclean!" This statement offended the Pharisees, who were very concerned about what people ate and drank.

▶ **MATTHEW 15:1-20 *(cont.)***

13Jesus replied, "Every plant not planted by my heavenly Father will be uprooted, 14so ignore them. They are
blind guides leading the blind, and if one blind person
guides another, they will both fall into a ditch."
15Then Peter said to Jesus, "Explain to us the parable that says people aren't defiled by what they eat."
16"Don't you understand yet?" Jesus asked. 17"Anything you eat passes through the stomach and then
goes into the sewer. 18But the words you speak come
from the heart—that's what defiles you. 19For from the
heart come evil thoughts, murder, adultery, all sexual
immorality, theft, lying, and slander. 20These are what
defile you. Eating with unwashed hands will never
defile you."

MARK 7:1-23

One day some Pharisees and teachers of religious law
arrived from Jerusalem to see Jesus. 2They noticed
that some of his disciples failed to follow the Jewish
ritual of hand washing before eating. 3(The Jews, especially the Pharisees, do not eat until they have poured
water over their cupped hands,* as required by their
ancient traditions. 4Similarly, they don't eat anything
from the market until they immerse their hands* in
water. This is but one of many traditions they have
clung to—such as their ceremonial washing of cups,
pitchers, and kettles.*)
5So the Pharisees and teachers of religious law
asked him, "Why don't your disciples follow our age-
old tradition? They eat without first performing the
hand-washing ceremony."
6Jesus replied, "You hypocrites! Isaiah was right
when he prophesied about you, for he wrote,

'These people honor me with their lips,
but their hearts are far from me.
7 Their worship is a farce,
for they teach man-made ideas as commands
from God.'*

8For you ignore God's law and substitute your own
tradition."
9Then he said, "You skillfully sidestep God's law in
order to hold on to your own tradition. 10For instance,
Moses gave you this law from God: 'Honor your father
and mother,'* and 'Anyone who speaks disrespectfully
of father or mother must be put to death.'* 11But you
say it is all right for people to say to their parents, 'Sorry,
I can't help you. For I have vowed to give to God what

Mk 7:3 Greek *have washed with the fist.* **Mk 7:4a** Some manuscripts read *sprinkle themselves.* **Mk 7:4b** Some manuscripts add *and dining couches.* **Mk 7:7** Isa 29:13 (Greek version). **Mk 7:10a** Exod 20:12; Deut 5:16. **Mk 7:10b** Exod 21:17 (Greek version); Lev 20:9 (Greek version).

Matt 15:13-14 Jesus told his disciples to leave the Pharisees alone because the Pharisees were blind to God's truth. Anyone who listened to their teaching would risk spiritual blindness as well. Not all religious leaders clearly see God's truth. Make sure that those you listen to and learn from are those with good spiritual eyesight—they teach and follow the principles of Scripture.

Matt 15:15 Later Peter would be faced with the issue of clean and unclean food (see the notes on Matt 15:11, p. 1369, and Acts 10:12, p. 1533). Then he would learn that nothing should be a barrier to proclaiming the Good News to the Gentiles (non-Jews).

Matt 15:16-20 We work hard to keep our outward appearance attractive, but what is deep down in our hearts (where others can't see) is more important to God. What are you like inside? When people become Christians, God makes them different on the inside. He will continue the process of change inside them if they only ask. God wants us to have healthy thoughts and motives, not just healthy bodies.

Mark 7:1ff The religious leaders sent some investigators from their headquarters in Jerusalem to check up on Jesus. The delegation didn't like what they found, however, because Jesus scolded them for keeping the law and the traditions in order to look holy instead of to honor God. The prophet Isaiah accused the religious leaders of his day of doing the same thing (Isa 29:13). Jesus used Isaiah's words to accuse these men.

Mark 7:3-4 Mark explained these Jewish rituals because he was writing to a non-Jewish audience. Before each meal, devout Jews performed a short ceremony, washing their hands and arms in a specific way. The disciples did not have dirty hands, but they were simply not carrying out this traditional cleansing. The Pharisees thought this ceremony cleansed them from any contact they might have had with anything considered unclean. Jesus said they were wrong in thinking they were acceptable to God just because they were clean on the outside.

Mark 7:4 Christians become like Pharisees when they worry that contact with unbelievers may leave them tainted—avoiding "worldly" places where sinners hang out or rejecting books or speakers whose ideas do not conform to theirs. Some Christians and some Pharisees have a lot in common: Both would try to stop Jesus from working certain places or talking to certain people. Jesus wants us to go out into the world and make contact. Jesus didn't intend for us to withdraw, purify ourselves, and never reach out.

Mark 7:6-7 Hypocrisy is pretending to be something you are not and have no intention of being. Jesus called the Pharisees hypocrites because they worshiped God for the wrong reasons. Their worship was not motivated by love but by a desire to attain profit, to appear holy, and to increase their status. We become hypocrites when we (1) pay more attention to reputation than to character, (2) carefully follow certain religious practices while allowing our hearts to remain distant from God, and (3) emphasize our virtues but others' sins.

Mark 7:8-9 The Pharisees had added hundreds of their own rules and regulations to God's holy laws, and then they tried to force people to follow these rules. These men claimed to know God's will in every detail of life. There are still religious leaders today who add rules and regulations to God's Word, causing much confusion among believers. It is idolatry to claim that your interpretation of God's Word is as important as God's Word itself. It is especially dangerous to set up unbiblical standards for others to follow. Instead, look to Christ for guidance about your own behavior, and let him lead others in the details of their lives.

Mark 7:8-9 Jesus wasn't against all tradition, but he was against those who made their traditions as important—if not more important—than God's Word. Good traditions shine a spotlight on God's Word, move us to obedient service, and help our hearts sing. They explain and reinforce the teachings of God. God's Word should always be the focus, and tradition a means of bringing that Word to life. Celebrate your traditions with the prayer that Christ would be exalted. Change your traditions if they become more important than God's Word.

Mark 7:10-11 The Pharisees used God as an excuse to avoid helping their families. They thought it was more important to put money in the Temple treasury than to help their needy parents, although God's law specifically says to honor fathers and mothers (Exod 20:12) and to care for those in need (Lev 25:35-43). We should give money and

I would have given to you.'* [12]In this way, you let them disregard their needy parents. [13]And so you cancel the word of God in order to hand down your own tradition. And this is only one example among many others."

[14]Then Jesus called to the crowd to come and hear. "All of you listen," he said, "and try to understand. [15]It's not what goes into your body that defiles you; you are defiled by what comes from your heart.*"

[17]Then Jesus went into a house to get away from the crowd, and his disciples asked him what he meant by the parable he had just used. [18]"Don't you understand either?" he asked. "Can't you see that the food you put into your body cannot defile you? [19]Food doesn't go into your heart, but only passes through the stomach and then goes into the sewer." (By saying this, he declared that every kind of food is acceptable in God's eyes.)

[20]And then he added, "It is what comes from inside that defiles you. [21]For from within, out of a person's heart, come evil thoughts, sexual immorality, theft, murder, [22]adultery, greed, wickedness, deceit, lustful desires, envy, slander, pride, and foolishness. [23]All these vile things come from within; they are what defile you."

Mk 7:11 Greek *'What I would have given to you is Corban' (that is, a gift).* Compare 4:9, 23. **Mk 7:15** Some manuscripts add verse 16, *Anyone with ears to hear should listen and understand.*

4. JESUS' MINISTRY BEYOND GALILEE

Jesus didn't limit his ministry to the people of Israel. He went beyond the borders of his nation, ministering to Gentiles in cities to the north and east of Galilee. His message was not only for one group of people, but for the entire world.

Jesus Sends a Demon Out of a Girl PARALLEL

MATTHEW 15:21-28

Then Jesus left Galilee and went north to the region of Tyre and Sidon. [22]A Gentile* woman who lived there came to him, pleading, "Have mercy on me, O Lord, Son of David! For my daughter is possessed by a demon that torments her severely."

[23]But Jesus gave her no reply, not even a word. Then his disciples urged him to send her away. "Tell her to go away," they said. "She is bothering us with all her begging."

[24]Then Jesus said to the woman, "I was sent only to help God's lost sheep—the people of Israel."

[25]But she came and worshiped him, pleading again, "Lord, help me!"

[26]Jesus responded, "It isn't right to take food from the children and throw it to the dogs."

[27]She replied, "That's true, Lord, but even dogs are allowed to eat the scraps that fall beneath their masters' table."

[28]"Dear woman," Jesus said to her, "your faith is great. Your request is granted." And her daughter was instantly healed.

Mt 15:22 Greek *Canaanite.*

---

time to God, but we must never use God as an excuse to neglect our responsibilities. Helping those in need is one of the most important ways to honor God.

Mark 7:18-19 As they interpreted the dietary laws (Lev 11), the Jews believed they could be clean before God because of what they refused to eat. Jesus pointed out that sin begins in the attitudes and intentions of the inner person. Jesus did not degrade the law, but he paved the way for the change (made clear in Acts 10:9-29) when God removed the cultural restrictions regarding food. While being concerned about what we put into our bodies is a good, healthy practice, very few people are as stringent about what they put into their minds through reading or watching television. Jesus was more concerned about mind-set and thought processes than about food laws. Do you worry about what foods you eat, but put "junk food" into your mind?

Mark 7:20-23 An evil action begins with a single thought. Allowing our mind to dwell on lust, envy, hatred, or revenge will lead to sin. Don't defile yourself by focusing on evil. Instead, follow Paul's advice in Philippians 4:8 and think about what is true, honorable, right, pure, lovely, and admirable.

Matt 15:23 Puzzled by Jesus' silence, the disciples asked him to get rid of the woman because she was bothering them with her persistent begging. They showed no compassion for her or sensitivity to her needs. It is possible to become so occupied with spiritual matters that we become oblivious to the needs around us. This may be true especially if we are prejudiced against needy people or if they cause us inconvenience. Instead of being annoyed, be aware of the opportunities that surround you, and make an effort to look for ways to minister to others.

Matt 15:24 Jesus' words do not contradict the truth that God's message is for all people (Ps 22:27; Isa 56:7; Matt 28:19; Rom 15:9-12). After all, when Jesus said these words, he was in Gentile territory on a mission to Gentile people. He ministered to Gentiles on many other occasions also. Jesus was simply telling the woman that Jews were to have the first opportunity to accept him as the Messiah because God wanted them to present the message of salvation to the rest of the world (see Gen 12:3). Jesus was not rejecting the Gentile woman. He may have wanted to test her faith, or he may have wanted to use the situation as another opportunity to teach that faith is available to all people.

Matt 15:26-28 "Dogs" was a term the Jews commonly applied to Gentiles because the Jews considered these pagan people no more likely than dogs to receive God's blessing. Jesus was not degrading the woman by using this term; he was reflecting the Jews' attitude so as to contrast it with his own. The woman did not argue. Instead, using Jesus' choice of words, she agreed to be considered a dog as long as she could receive God's blessing for her daughter. Ironically, many Jews would lose God's blessing and salvation because they rejected Jesus, and many Gentiles would find salvation because they recognized and accepted him.

MARK 7:24-30
Then Jesus left Galilee and went north to the region of
Tyre.* He didn't want anyone to know which house he
was staying in, but he couldn't keep it a secret. [25]Right
away a woman who had heard about him came and
fell at his feet. Her little girl was possessed by an evil*
spirit, [26]and she begged him to cast out the demon
from her daughter.
Since she was a Gentile, born in Syrian Phoenicia,
[27]Jesus told her, "First I should feed the children—my
own family, the Jews.* It isn't right to take food from
the children and throw it to the dogs."
[28]She replied, "That's true, Lord, but even the dogs
under the table are allowed to eat the scraps from the
children's plates."
[29]"Good answer!" he said. "Now go home, for the
demon has left your daughter." [30]And when she arrived home, she found her little girl lying quietly in
bed, and the demon was gone.

Jesus Heals Many People PARALLEL

MATTHEW 15:29-31
Jesus returned to the Sea of Galilee and climbed a hill
and sat down. [30]A vast crowd brought to him people
who were lame, blind, crippled, those who couldn't
speak, and many others. They laid them before Jesus,
and he healed them all. [31]The crowd was amazed!
Those who hadn't been able to speak were talking,
the crippled were made well, the lame were walking,
and the blind could see again! And they praised the
God of Israel.

MARK 7:31-37
Jesus left Tyre and went up to Sidon before going back
to the Sea of Galilee and the region of the Ten Towns.*
[32]A deaf man with a speech impediment was brought
to him, and the people begged Jesus to lay his hands
on the man to heal him.
[33]Jesus led him away from the crowd so they could
be alone. He put his fingers into the man's ears. Then,
spitting on his own fingers, he touched the man's
tongue. [34]Looking up to heaven, he sighed and said,
"Ephphatha," which means, "Be opened!" [35]Instantly
the man could hear perfectly, and his tongue was freed
so he could speak plainly!
[36]Jesus told the crowd not to tell anyone, but the
more he told them not to, the more they spread the
news. [37]They were completely amazed and said again
and again, "Everything he does is wonderful. He even
makes the deaf to hear and gives speech to those who
cannot speak."

Jesus Feeds Four Thousand PARALLEL

MATTHEW 15:32-39
Then Jesus called his disciples and told them, "I feel
sorry for these people. They have been here with me

Mk 7:24 Some manuscripts add *and Sidon.* **Mk 7:25** Greek *unclean.* **Mk 7:27** Greek *Let the children eat first.* **Mk 7:31** Greek *Decapolis.*

Mark 7:24 Jesus traveled about 30 miles to Tyre. The cities of Tyre and Sidon were port cities on the Mediterranean Sea north of Israel. Both had flourishing trade and were very wealthy. They were proud, historic Canaanite cities.

In David's day, Tyre was on friendly terms with Israel (2 Sam 5:11), but soon afterward the city became known for its wickedness. Its king even claimed to be God (Ezek 28:1-19). Tyre rejoiced when Jerusalem was destroyed in 586 B.C., because without Israel's competition, Tyre's trade and profits would increase. It was into this evil and materialistic culture that Jesus brought his message.

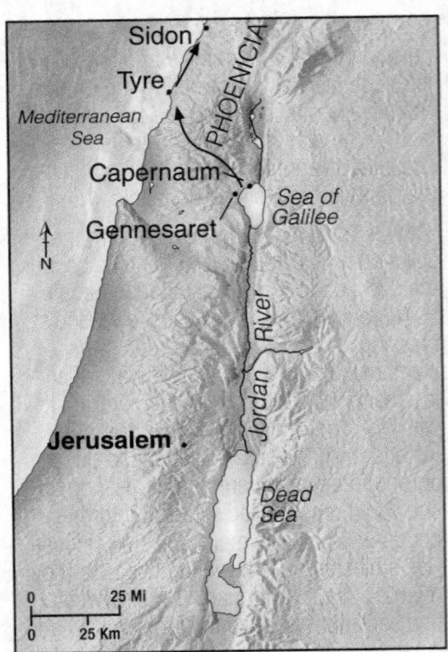

***MINISTRY IN PHOENICIA** Jesus' ministry was to all people—first to Jews but also to Gentiles. Jesus took his disciples from Galilee to Tyre and Sidon, large cities in Phoenicia, where he healed a Gentile woman's daughter.*

Mark 7:26 This woman is called a Gentile, born in Syrian Phoenicia. Mark's designation refers to her political background. His Roman audience would have easily identified her by the part of the empire that was her home.

Mark 7:27-28 On the surface, Jesus' words may seem harsh and unsympathetic, but the woman recognized them as a wide-open door to God's throne. The woman took the title that was created by Jews as a derogatory name for Gentiles and turned it into an analogy for her status as an expectant beggar at Jesus' feet. Her attitude was hopeful, not prickly or hypersensitive. She knew what she wanted and she believed Jesus could provide. We could learn from this woman's singular purpose and optimistic resilience. Jesus really does want to meet our needs. When we pray, we're talking to a friend.

Mark 7:29 This miracle shows that Jesus' power over demons is so great that he doesn't need to be present physically in order to free someone. His power transcends any distance.

Matt 15:29-31 Jesus healed all who were brought to him. Jesus is still able to heal people who are suffering physically, emotionally, and spiritually, and we can be the ones who bring suffering people to him. Whom do you know that needs Christ's healing touch? You can bring them to Jesus through prayer or through explaining to them the reason for the hope that you have (1 Pet 3:15). Then let Christ do the healing.

Mark 7:34 When Jesus said, "Be opened!" he used language that this deaf man would understand. The healing message was personal and unique. Whoever thought spittle might be the conduit of a miracle? If there is only one means of witness in your church (sermons, for instance), many people likely will not hear. Churches need lots of different methods to meet diverse needs. Let musicians play, singers sing, actors act, and writers write. Let each creative Christian tell the story. Jesus used spit and mud; surely we can find windows to the minds and hearts of people as well.

Matt 15:32ff This feeding of 4,000 is a separate event from the feeding of the 5,000 (Matt 14:13-21), confirmed by Mark 8:19-20. This was the beginning of Jesus' expanded ministry to the Gentiles.

Matt 15:33 Jesus had already fed more than 5,000 people with five loaves and two fish. Here, in a similar situation, the disciples

for three days, and they have nothing left to eat. I don't want to send them away hungry, or they will faint along the way."
33The disciples replied, "Where would we get enough food here in the wilderness for such a huge crowd?"
34Jesus asked, "How much bread do you have?"
They replied, "Seven loaves, and a few small fish."
35So Jesus told all the people to sit down on the
ground. 36Then he took the seven loaves and the fish, thanked God for them, and broke them into pieces. He gave them to the disciples, who distributed the food to the crowd.
37They all ate as much as they wanted. Afterward, the disciples picked up seven large baskets of
leftover food. 38There were 4,000 men who were fed that day, in addition to all the women and children.
39Then Jesus sent the people home, and he got into a boat and crossed over to the region of Magadan.

MARK 8:1-10

About this time another large crowd had gathered, and the people ran out of food again. Jesus called his disciples and told them, 2"I feel sorry for these people. They have been here with me for three days, and they have nothing left to eat. 3If I send them home hungry, they will faint along the way. For some of them have come a long distance."
4His disciples replied, "How are we supposed to find enough food to feed them out here in the wilderness?"
5Jesus asked, "How much bread do you have?"
"Seven loaves," they replied.
6So Jesus told all the people to sit down on the ground. Then he took the seven loaves, thanked God for them, and broke them into pieces. He gave them to his disciples, who distributed the bread to the crowd.
7A few small fish were found, too, so Jesus also blessed these and told the disciples to distribute them.
8They ate as much as they wanted. Afterward, the disciples picked up seven large baskets of leftover
food. 9There were about 4,000 people in the crowd that day, and Jesus sent them home after they had
eaten. 10Immediately after this, he got into a boat with his disciples and crossed over to the region of Dalmanutha.

5. JESUS RESUMES HIS MINISTRY IN GALILEE

After a brief time outside of Israel, Jesus returned to his home region of Galilee. During this period of his ministry, he began to prepare his disciples for his death, revealing to them for the first time that he was going to be killed, but that he would also be resurrected. It was at this time that he was transfigured on a mountaintop, revealing his glory to three of his closest disciples. Jesus was revealing more and more of himself to his followers.

Leaders Demand a Miraculous Sign PARALLEL

MATTHEW 16:1-4

One day the Pharisees and Sadducees came to test Jesus, demanding that he show them a miraculous sign from heaven to prove his authority.
2He replied, "You know the saying, 'Red sky at night means fair weather tomorrow; 3red sky in the morning means foul weather all day.' You know how to interpret the weather signs in the sky, but you don't know how to interpret the signs of the times!* 4Only an evil, adulterous generation would demand a miraculous

Mt 16:2-3 Several manuscripts do not include any of the words in 16:2-3 after *He replied.*

were again perplexed. How easily we throw up our hands in despair when faced with difficult situations. Like the disciples, we often forget that if God has cared for us in the past, he will do the same now. When facing a difficult situation, remember that God cares for you and trust him to work faithfully again.

Mark 8:1ff This is a different miracle from the feeding of the 5,000 described in Mark 6. At that time, those fed were mostly Jews. This time Jesus was ministering to a non-Jewish crowd in the Gentile region of the Ten Towns. Jesus' actions and message were beginning to have an impact on large numbers of Gentiles. That Jesus would compassionately minister to non-Jews was very reassuring to Mark's primarily Roman audience.

Mark 8:1-3 Do you ever feel that God is so busy with important concerns that he can't possibly be aware of your needs? Just as Jesus was concerned about these people's need for food, he is concerned about our daily needs. At another time Jesus said, "Your heavenly Father already knows all your needs" (Matt 6:32). Do you have concerns that you think would not interest God? Nothing is too large for him to handle and no need too small to escape his interest.

Mark 8:4 How could the disciples experience so many of Jesus' miracles and yet be so slow to comprehend who he was? They had already seen Jesus feed over 5,000 people with five loaves and two fish (Mark 6:35-44), yet here they doubted whether he could feed another large group.

Mark 8:6 Jesus gave thanks for the food, and he serves as a model for us. Life is a gift, and the nourishment life requires, while it comes from the work of many hands, conveys God's material blessing. Mealtime provides an opportunity to thank God for daily needs met, for taste and beauty, and for human company and divine companionship. Giving thanks keeps us from regarding a plate of food as a trough, our stomachs as bottomless pits, and our gathering to eat as a bothersome interruption. Keep up the good tradition of praying and thanking God before your meals. Let your gratefulness to God be genuine.

Matt 16:1 The Pharisees and Sadducees were Jewish religious leaders of two different parties, and their views were diametrically opposed on many issues. The Pharisees carefully followed their religious rules and traditions, believing that this was the way to God. They also believed in the authority of all Scripture and in the resurrection of the dead. The Sadducees accepted only the books of Moses as Scripture and did not believe in life after death. In Jesus, however, these two groups had a common enemy, and they joined forces to try to kill him. For more information on the Pharisees and Sadducees, see the charts on p. 1288 and p. 1313.

Matt 16:1 The Pharisees and Sadducees demanded a sign from heaven. Although

▸ **MATTHEW 16:1-4** ***(cont.)***

sign, but the only sign I will give them is the sign of
the prophet Jonah.*" Then Jesus left them and went
away.

MARK 8:11-13

When the Pharisees heard that Jesus had arrived, they
came and started to argue with him. Testing him, they
demanded that he show them a miraculous sign from
heaven to prove his authority.
[12]When he heard this, he sighed deeply in his spirit
and said, "Why do these people keep demanding a
miraculous sign? I tell you the truth, I will not give
this generation any such sign." [13]So he got back into
the boat and left them, and he crossed to the other
side of the lake.

Jesus Warns against Wrong Teaching PARALLEL

MATTHEW 16:5-12

Later, after they crossed to the other side of the lake,
the disciples discovered they had forgotten to bring
any bread. [6]"Watch out!" Jesus warned them. "Beware
of the yeast of the Pharisees and Sadducees."
[7]At this they began to argue with each other because they hadn't brought any bread. [8]Jesus knew
what they were saying, so he said, "You have so little
faith! Why are you arguing with each other about
having no bread? [9]Don't you understand even yet?
Don't you remember the 5,000 I fed with five loaves,
and the baskets of leftovers you picked up? [10]Or the
4,000 I fed with seven loaves, and the large baskets
of leftovers you picked up? [11]Why can't you understand that I'm not talking about bread? So again I
say, 'Beware of the yeast of the Pharisees and Sadducees.'"
[12]Then at last they understood that he wasn't speaking about the yeast in bread, but about the deceptive
teaching of the Pharisees and Sadducees.

MARK 8:14-21

But the disciples had forgotten to bring any food.
They had only one loaf of bread with them in the boat.
[15]As they were crossing the lake, Jesus warned them,
"Watch out! Beware of the yeast of the Pharisees and
of Herod."
[16]At this they began to argue with each other because they hadn't brought any bread. [17]Jesus knew
what they were saying, so he said, "Why are you arguing about having no bread? Don't you know or
understand even yet? Are your hearts too hard to
take it in? [18]'You have eyes—can't you see? You have
ears—can't you hear?'* Don't you remember anything
at all? [19]When I fed the 5,000 with five loaves of
bread, how many baskets of leftovers did you pick
up afterward?"

Mt 16:4 Greek *the sign of Jonah.* **Mk 8:18** Jer 5:21.

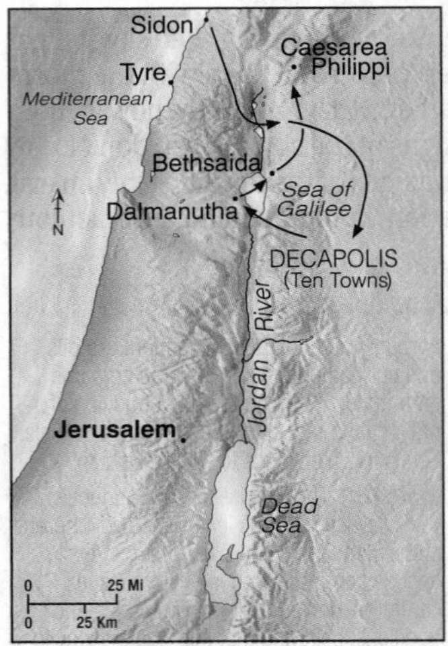

***CONTINUED MINISTRY** After taking a roundabout way back to Galilee through Decapolis (the Ten Towns), Jesus returned to Dalmanutha where Jewish leaders questioned his authority. From there he went to Bethsaida and then on to Caesarea Philippi. Here he talked with his disciples about his authority and coming events.*

Matt 16:1-4... Jesus could have easily impressed them, he refused. He knew that even a miracle on demand would not convince them he was the Messiah because they had already decided not to believe in him.

Matt 16:4 By using the sign of Jonah, who was inside a great fish for three days, Jesus was predicting his death and resurrection (see also Matt 12:38-42).

Matt 16:4 Many people, like these Jewish leaders, say they want to see a miracle so that they can believe. But Jesus knew that miracles never convince the skeptical. Jesus had been healing, raising people from the dead, and feeding thousands, and still people wanted him to prove himself. Do you doubt Christ because you haven't seen a miracle? Do you expect God to prove himself to you personally before you believe? Jesus says, "Blessed are those who believe without seeing me" (John 20:29). We have miracles recorded in the Old and New Testaments, 2,000 years of church history, and the witness of thousands. With all this evidence, those who won't believe are either too proud or too stubborn. If you simply step forward in faith and believe, then you will begin to see the miracles that God can do in your life!

Mark 8:11 The Pharisees had tried to explain away Jesus' previous miracles by claiming they were done by luck, coincidence, or evil power. Here they demanded a sign from heaven—something only God could do. Jesus refused their demand because he knew that even this kind of miracle would not convince them. They had already decided not to believe. Hearts can become so hard that even the most convincing facts and demonstrations will not change them.

Matt 16:12 Yeast is put into bread to make it rise, and it takes only a little to affect a whole batch of dough. Jesus used yeast as an example of how a small amount of evil can affect a large group of people. The wrong teachings of the Pharisees and Sadducees were leading many people astray. Beware of the tendency to say, "How can this little wrong possibly affect anyone?"

Mark 8:15 Mark mentions the yeast of the Pharisees and of Herod, while Matthew talks about the yeast of the Pharisees and Sadducees. Mark's audience, mostly non-Jews, would have known about Herod but not necessarily about the Jewish religious sect of the Sadducees. Thus, Mark quoted the part of Jesus' statement that his readers would understand. This reference to Herod may mean the supporters of Herod, a group of Jews who supported the king. Many supporters of Herod were also Sadducees. Yeast in this passage symbolizes evil. Just as only a small amount of yeast is needed to make a batch of bread rise, so the hard-heartedness of the religious and political leaders could permeate and contaminate the entire society and make it rise up against Jesus.

"Twelve," they said.
[20]"And when I fed the 4,000 with seven loaves, how
many large baskets of leftovers did you pick up?"
"Seven," they said.
[21]"Don't you understand yet?" he asked them.

Jesus Restores Sight to a Blind Man

MARK 8:22-26

When they arrived at Bethsaida, some people brought
a blind man to Jesus, and they begged him to touch
the man and heal him. [23]Jesus took the blind man by
the hand and led him out of the village. Then, spitting
on the man's eyes, he laid his hands on him and asked,
"Can you see anything now?"
[24]The man looked around. "Yes," he said, "I see
people, but I can't see them very clearly. They look like
trees walking around."
[25]Then Jesus placed his hands on the man's eyes
again, and his eyes were opened. His sight was completely restored, and he could see everything clearly.
[26]Jesus sent him away, saying, "Don't go back into the
village on your way home."

Peter Says Jesus Is the Messiah PARALLEL

MATTHEW 16:13-20

When Jesus came to the region of Caesarea Philippi,
he asked his disciples, "Who do people say that the
Son of Man is?"*
[14]"Well," they replied, "some say John the Baptist,
some say Elijah, and others say Jeremiah or one of the
other prophets."
[15]Then he asked them, "But who do you say I am?"
[16]Simon Peter answered, "You are the Messiah,* the
Son of the living God."
[17]Jesus replied, "You are blessed, Simon son of
John,* because my Father in heaven has revealed this
to you. You did not learn this from any human being.
[18]Now I say to you that you are Peter (which means
'rock'),* and upon this rock I will build my church,
and all the powers of hell* will not conquer it. [19]And
I will give you the keys of the Kingdom of Heaven.
Whatever you forbid* on earth will be forbidden in
heaven, and whatever you permit* on earth will be
permitted in heaven."

Mt 16:13 "Son of Man" is a title Jesus used for himself. **Mt 16:16** Or *the Christ. Messiah* (a Hebrew term) and *Christ* (a Greek term) both mean "the anointed one." **Mt 16:17** Greek *Simon bar-Jonah;* see John 1:42; 21:15-17. **Mt 16:18a** Greek *that you are Peter.* **Mt 16:18b** Greek *and the gates of Hades.* **Mt 16:19a** Or *bind,* or *lock.* **Mt 16:19b** Or *loose,* or *open.*

GOSPEL ACCOUNTS FOUND ONLY IN MARK

Section	Topic	Significance
Mark 4:26-29	Story of the growing seed	We must share the Good News of Jesus with other people, but only God makes it grow in their lives.
Mark 7:31-37	Jesus healed a deaf man who could hardly talk	Jesus cares about our physical as well as spiritual needs.
Mark 8:22-26	Jesus healed the blind man at Bethsaida	Jesus is considerate because he made sure this man's sight was fully restored.

Mark 8:17-18 Jesus rebuked the disciples for their hard hearts. Today the Hardhearts believe: (1) that poverty is always caused by laziness; helping the poor only enables them; (2) that worship is best conducted in one way—our way—which has worked very well for forty years, thank you, and need not be changed; (3) that evangelism doesn't apply; people will never change anyway, so we don't need to do it. Joining the Hardhearts requires only one pledge: You must refuse to listen to Jesus' questions. Don't be a Hardheart. Be open to Christ's truth. Let him soften your heart.

Mark 8:25 Why did Jesus touch the man a second time before he could see? This miracle was not too difficult for Jesus, but he chose to do it in stages, possibly to show the disciples that some healing would be gradual rather than instantaneous or to demonstrate that spiritual truth is not always perceived clearly at first. Before Jesus left, however, the man was healed completely.

Matt 16:13 Caesarea Philippi was located several miles north of the Sea of Galilee, in the territory ruled by Philip. The influence of Greek and Roman culture was everywhere, and pagan temples and idols abounded. When Philip became ruler, he rebuilt and renamed the city after the emperor (Caesar) and himself. The city was originally called Caesarea, the same name as the capital city of Philip's brother Herod's territory.

Matt 16:13-17 The disciples answered Jesus' question with the common view—that Jesus was one of the great prophets come back to life. This belief may have stemmed from Deuteronomy 18:18, where God said he would raise up a prophet from among the people. (John the Baptist's Profile is on p. 1292; Elijah's Profile is on p. 719; and Jeremiah's Profile is on p. 959.) Peter, however, confessed Jesus as divine and as the promised and long-awaited Messiah. If Jesus were to ask you this question, how would you answer? Is he your Lord and Messiah?

Matt 16:18 The rock on which Jesus would build his church has been identified as (1) Jesus himself (his work of salvation by dying for us on the cross); (2) Peter (the first great leader in the church at Jerusalem); (3) the confession of faith that Peter gave and that all subsequent true believers would give. It seems most likely that the rock refers to Peter as the leader of the church. Just as Peter had revealed the true identity of Christ, so Jesus revealed Peter's identity and role.

Later, Peter reminds Christians that they are the church built on the foundation of the apostles and prophets, with Jesus Christ as the cornerstone (1 Pet 2:4-6). All believers are joined into this church by faith in Jesus Christ as Savior, the same faith that Peter expressed here (see also Eph 2:20-21). Jesus praised Peter for his confession of faith. It is faith like Peter's that is the foundation of Christ's Kingdom.

Matt 16:19 The meaning of this verse has been a subject of debate for centuries. Some say the "keys" represent the authority to carry out church discipline, legislation, and administration (Matt 18:15-18), while others say the keys give the authority to announce the forgiveness of sins (John 20:23). Still others say the keys may be the opportunity to bring people to the Kingdom of Heaven by presenting them with the message of salvation found in God's Word (Acts 15:7-9). The religious leaders thought they held the keys of the Kingdom, and they tried to shut some people out. We cannot decide to open or close the Kingdom of Heaven for others, but God uses us to help others find the way inside. To all who believe in Christ and obey his words, the Kingdom doors are swung wide open.

▸ **MATTHEW 16:13-20 *(cont.)***

20Then he sternly warned the disciples not to tell anyone that he was the Messiah.

MARK 8:27-30

Jesus and his disciples left Galilee and went up to the villages near Caesarea Philippi. As they were walking along, he asked them, "Who do people say I am?"

28"Well," they replied, "some say John the Baptist, some say Elijah, and others say you are one of the other prophets."

29Then he asked them, "But who do you say I am?"

Peter replied, "You are the Messiah.*"

30But Jesus warned them not to tell anyone about him.

LUKE 9:18-21

One day Jesus left the crowds to pray alone. Only his disciples were with him, and he asked them, "Who do people say I am?"

19"Well," they replied, "some say John the Baptist, some say Elijah, and others say you are one of the other ancient prophets risen from the dead."

20Then he asked them, "But who do you say I am?"

Peter replied, "You are the Messiah* sent from God!"

21Jesus warned his disciples not to tell anyone who he was.

Jesus Predicts His Death the First Time PARALLEL

MATTHEW 16:21-28

From then on Jesus* began to tell his disciples plainly that it was necessary for him to go to Jerusalem, and that he would suffer many terrible things at the hands of the elders, the leading priests, and the teachers of religious law. He would be killed, but on the third day he would be raised from the dead.

22But Peter took him aside and began to reprimand

Mk 8:29 Or *the Christ. Messiah* (a Hebrew term) and *Christ* (a Greek term) both mean "the anointed one." **Lk 9:20** Or *the Christ. Messiah* (a Hebrew term) and *Christ* (a Greek term) both mean "the anointed one." **Mt 16:21** Some manuscripts read *Jesus the Messiah.*

Mark 8:27 Caesarea Philippi was an especially pagan city known for its worship of Greek gods and its temples devoted to the ancient god Pan. The ruler, Philip, referred to in Mark 6:17, changed the city's name from Caesarea to Caesarea Philippi so that it would not be confused with the coastal city of Caesarea (Acts 8:40), the capital of the territory ruled by his brother Herod Antipas. This pagan city where many gods were recognized was a fitting place for Jesus to ask the disciples to recognize him as the Son of God.

Mark 8:28 For the story of John the Baptist, see Mark 1:1-11 and 6:14-29. For the story of Elijah, see 1 Kings 17–20 and 2 Kings 1–2.

Mark 8:29 Jesus asked the disciples who other people thought he was; then he asked them the same question. It is not enough to know what others say about Jesus: You must know, understand, and accept for yourself that he is the Messiah. You must move from curiosity to commitment, from admiration to adoration.

Mark 8:30 Why did Jesus warn his own disciples not to tell anyone the truth about him? Jesus knew they needed more instruction about the work he would accomplish through his death and resurrection. Without more teaching, the disciples would have only half the picture. When they confessed Jesus as the Christ, they still didn't know all that it meant.

Luke 9:18-20 The Christian faith goes beyond knowing what others believe. It requires us to hold beliefs for ourselves. When Jesus asks, "Who do you say I am?" he wants us to take a stand. Who do you say Jesus is?

Luke 9:21 Jesus told his disciples not to tell anyone that he was the Christ because at this point they didn't fully understand the significance of that confession—nor would anyone else. Everyone still expected the Messiah to come as a conquering king. But even though Jesus was the Messiah, he still had to suffer, be rejected by the leaders, be killed, and rise from the dead. When the disciples saw all this happen to Jesus, they would understand what the Messiah had come to do. Only then would they be equipped to share the Good News that the Messiah had come and brought his Kingdom to people's hearts.

Matt 16:21 The phrase "From then on" marks a turning point. In Matthew 4:17 it signaled Jesus' announcement of the Kingdom of Heaven. Here it points to his new emphasis on his death and resurrection. The disciples still didn't grasp Jesus' true purpose because of their preconceived notions about what the Messiah should be. This is the first of three times that Jesus predicted his death (see Matt 17:22-23; 20:18 for others).

Matt 16:21-28 This passage corresponds to Daniel's prophecies: The Messiah would be cut off (Dan 9:26); there would be a period of trouble (Dan 9:27); and the king would come in glory (Dan 7:13-14). The disciples would endure the same suffering as their King and, like him, would be rewarded in the end.

Matt 16:22 Peter, Jesus' friend and devoted follower who had just eloquently proclaimed Jesus' true identity, sought to protect him from the suffering he prophesied. But if Jesus hadn't suffered and died, Peter would have died in his sins. Great temptations can come from those who love us and seek to protect us. Be cautious of advice from a friend who says, "Surely God doesn't want you to face this." Often our most difficult temptations come from those who are only trying to protect us from discomfort.

Ancient Roman Key

The "keys of the Kingdom of Heaven" are a symbolic description of the authority given by Jesus to Peter: "And I will give you the keys of the Kingdom of Heaven. Whatever you forbid on earth will be forbidden in heaven, and whatever you permit on earth will be permitted in heaven" (Matt 16:19). Many ancient peoples believed that heaven and hell were closed by gates to which certain deities and angelic beings had keys. In Roman mythology, for example, Pluto kept the key to Hades. Jewish writings near the time of Jesus give God the key to the abode of the dead. In the book of Revelation, John sees Christ holding the keys of death and the grave (Greek *Hades*) (Rev 1:18). In Matthew's Gospel, the keys symbolize the authority to open and shut the Kingdom of Heaven.

him* for saying such things. "Heaven forbid, Lord," he
said. "This will never happen to you!"
23 Jesus turned to Peter and said, "Get away from
me, Satan! You are a dangerous trap to me. You are
seeing things merely from a human point of view, not
from God's."
24 Then Jesus said to his disciples, "If any of you
wants to be my follower, you must turn from your
selfish ways, take up your cross, and follow me. 25 If
you try to hang on to your life, you will lose it. But
if you give up your life for my sake, you will save
it. 26 And what do you benefit if you gain the whole
world but lose your own soul?* Is anything worth
more than your soul? 27 For the Son of Man will come
with his angels in the glory of his Father and will
judge all people according to their deeds. 28 And I
tell you the truth, some standing here right now will
not die before they see the Son of Man coming in
his Kingdom."

MARK 8:31–9:1

Then Jesus began to tell them that the Son of Man*
must suffer many terrible things and be rejected by
the elders, the leading priests, and the teachers of
religious law. He would be killed, but three days later
he would rise from the dead. 32 As he talked about
this openly with his disciples, Peter took him aside
and began to reprimand him for saying such things.*
33 Jesus turned around and looked at his disciples,
then reprimanded Peter. "Get away from me, Satan!"
he said. "You are seeing things merely from a human
point of view, not from God's."
34 Then, calling the crowd to join his disciples, he
said, "If any of you wants to be my follower, you must
turn from your selfish ways, take up your cross, and

Mt 16:22 Or *began to correct him.* **Mt 16:26** Or *your self?* also in 16:26b. **Mk 8:31** "Son of Man" is a title Jesus used for himself. **Mk 8:32** Or *began to correct him.*

Matt 16:23 In his wilderness temptations, Jesus heard the message that he could achieve greatness without dying (Matt 4:9). Here he heard the same message from Peter. Peter had just recognized Jesus as Messiah; here, however, he forsook God's perspective and evaluated the situation from a human one. Satan is always trying to get us to leave God out of the picture. Jesus rebuked Peter for this attitude.

Matt 16:24 When Jesus used this picture of his followers taking up their crosses to follow him, the disciples knew what he meant. Crucifixion was a common Roman method of execution, and condemned criminals had to carry their cross through the streets to the execution site. Following Jesus, therefore, meant a true commitment, the risk of death, and no turning back (see Matt 10:39).

Matt 16:25 The possibility of losing their lives was very real for the disciples as well as for Jesus. Real discipleship implies real commitment—pledging our whole existence to his service. If we try to save our physical life from death, pain, or discomfort, we may risk losing eternal life. If we protect ourselves from the pain God calls us to suffer, we begin to die spiritually and emotionally. Our lives turn inward, and we lose our intended purpose. When we give our life in service to Christ, however, we discover the real purpose of living.

Matt 16:26 When we don't know Christ, we make choices as though there were no afterlife. In reality, this life is just the introduction to eternity. How we live this brief span determines our eternal state. What we accumulate on earth has no value in gaining eternal life. Even the highest social or civic honors cannot earn us entrance into heaven. Evaluate your lifestyle from an eternal perspective, and you will find your values and decisions changing.

Matt 16:27 Jesus Christ has been given the authority to judge all the earth (Rom 14:9-11; Phil 2:9-11). Although his judgment is already working in our lives, there is a future, final judgment when Christ returns (Matt 25:31-46) and everyone's life will be reviewed and evaluated. This will not be confined to unbelievers; Christians, too, will face a judgment. Their eternal destiny is secure, but Jesus will look at how they handled gifts, opportunities, and responsibilities in order to determine their heavenly rewards. At the time of judgment, God will deliver the righteous and condemn the wicked. We should not judge others' salvation; that is God's work.

Matt 16:28 Because all the disciples died before Christ's return, many believe that Jesus' words were fulfilled at the Transfiguration when Peter, James, and John saw his glory (Matt 17:1-3). Others say this statement refers to the Resurrection (Matt 28; Mark 16; Luke 24; John 20) and the Ascension of Jesus (Acts 1). Still others believe that Pentecost (Acts 2) and the beginning of Christ's church fulfilled Jesus' words. In any case, certain disciples were eyewitnesses to the power and glory of Christ's Kingdom.

Mark 8:31 The name for Jesus, Son of Man, is Jesus' most common title for himself. It comes from Daniel 7:13, where the Son of Man is a heavenly figure who, in the end times, has authority and power. The name refers to Jesus as the Messiah, the representative man, the human agent of God who is vindicated by God. In this passage, Son of Man is linked closely with Peter's confession of Jesus as the Christ and confirms its messianic significance.

From this point on, Jesus spoke plainly and directly to his disciples about his death and resurrection. He began to prepare them for what was going to happen to him by telling them three times that he would soon die (Mark 8:31; 9:31; 10:33-34).

Mark 8:32-33 In this moment, Peter was not considering God's purposes but only his own natural human desires and feelings. Peter wanted Christ to be king, but not the suffering servant prophesied in Isaiah 53. He was ready to receive the glory of following the Messiah but not the persecution.

The Christian life is not a paved road to wealth and ease. It often involves hard work, persecution, deprivation, and deep suffering. Peter saw only part of the picture. Don't repeat his mistake. Instead, focus on the good that God can bring out of apparent evil and the Resurrection that follows the Crucifixion.

Mark 8:33 Peter was often the spokesman for all the disciples. In singling him out, Jesus may have been addressing all of them indirectly. Unknowingly, the disciples were trying to prevent Jesus from going to the cross and thus fulfilling his mission on earth. Satan also tempted Jesus to avoid the way of the cross (Matt 4). Whereas Satan's motives were evil, the disciples were motivated by love and admiration for Jesus. Nevertheless, the disciples' job was not to guide and protect Jesus but to follow him. Only after Jesus' death and resurrection would they fully understand why he had to die.

Mark 8:34 The Gentiles, Mark's original audience, knew what taking up the cross meant. Death on a cross was a form of execution used by Rome for dangerous criminals. A prisoner carried his own cross to the place of execution, signifying submission to Rome's power.

Jesus used the image of carrying a cross to illustrate the ultimate submission required of his followers. He is not against pleasure, nor was he saying that we should seek pain needlessly. Jesus was talking about the heroic effort needed to follow him moment by moment, to do his will even when the work is difficult and the future looks bleak.

▸ **MARK 8:31–9:1 *(cont.)***
follow me. [35]If you try to hang on to your life, you will
lose it. But if you give up your life for my sake and for
the sake of the Good News, you will save it. [36]And what
do you benefit if you gain the whole world but lose
your own soul?* [37]Is anything worth more than your
soul? [38]If anyone is ashamed of me and my message
in these adulterous and sinful days, the Son of Man
will be ashamed of that person when he returns in the
glory of his Father with the holy angels."

[9:1]Jesus went on to say, "I tell you the truth, some
standing here right now will not die before they see
the Kingdom of God arrive in great power!"

LUKE 9:22-27
"The Son of Man* must suffer many terrible things,"
he said. "He will be rejected by the elders, the leading priests, and the teachers of religious law. He will be killed, but on the third day he will be raised from the dead."

[23]Then he said to the crowd, "If any of you wants to
be my follower, you must turn from your selfish ways,
take up your cross daily, and follow me. [24]If you try to
hang on to your life, you will lose it. But if you give up
your life for my sake, you will save it. [25]And what do
you benefit if you gain the whole world but are yourself
lost or destroyed? [26]If anyone is ashamed of me and
my message, the Son of Man will be ashamed of that
person when he returns in his glory and in the glory
of the Father and the holy angels. [27]I tell you the truth,
some standing here right now will not die before they
see the Kingdom of God."

Jesus Is Transfigured on the Mountain PARALLEL

MATTHEW 17:1-13
Six days later Jesus took Peter and the two brothers,
James and John, and led them up a high mountain to
be alone. [2]As the men watched, Jesus' appearance was
transformed so that his face shone like the sun, and his

Mk 8:36 Or *your self?* also in 8:37. **Lk 9:22** "Son of Man" is a title Jesus used for himself.

Mark 8:35 We should be willing to lose our life for the sake of the Good News, not because our life is useless but because nothing—not even life itself—can compare to what we gain with Christ. Jesus wants us to choose to follow him rather than lead a life of sin and self-satisfaction. He wants us to stop trying to control our own destiny and let him direct us. This makes good sense because, as the Creator, Christ knows better than we do what real life is about. He asks for submission, not self-hatred; he asks us only to lose our self-centered determination to be in charge.

Mark 8:36-37 Many people spend all their energy seeking pleasure. But Jesus said that worldliness—which is centered on possessions, position, or power—is ultimately worthless. Whatever you have on earth is only temporary; it cannot be exchanged for your soul. If you work hard at getting what you want, you might eventually have a "pleasurable" life, but in the end you will find it hollow and empty. Are you willing to make the pursuit of God more important than the selfish pursuits? Follow Jesus, and you will know what it means to live abundantly now and to have eternal life as well.

Mark 8:38 Jesus constantly turns the world's perspective upside down with talk of first and last, saving and losing. Here he gives us a choice. We can reject Jesus now and be rejected by him at his second coming, or we can accept him now and be accepted by him then. Rejecting Christ may help us escape shame for the time being, but it will guarantee an eternity of shame later.

Mark 9:1 What did Jesus mean when he said that some of the disciples would see the Kingdom of God arrive in power? There are several possibilities. He could have been foretelling his transfiguration, his resurrection and ascension, the coming of the Holy Spirit at Pentecost, or his second coming. The Transfiguration is a strong possibility because Mark immediately tells that story. In the Transfiguration (Mark 9:2-8), Peter, James, and John saw Jesus glorified as the Son of God (2 Pet 1:16).

Luke 9:22 This was the turning point in Jesus' instruction to his disciples. From this point on he began teaching clearly and specifically what they could expect, so that they would not be surprised when it happened. He explained that he would not now be the conquering Messiah because he first had to suffer, die, and rise again. But one day he would return in great glory to set up his eternal Kingdom.

Luke 9:23 To "take up your cross" meant to carry one's own cross to the place of crucifixion. Many Galileans had been killed that way by the Romans—and Jesus would face it as well. With this word picture, Christ presented a clear and challenging description of the Christian life. Being his disciple means putting aside selfish desires, shouldering one's "cross" every day, and following him. It is simple and yet so demanding. For the original Twelve, this meant literal suffering and death. For believers today, it means understanding that we belong to him and that we live to serve his purposes. Consider this: Do you think of your relationship with God primarily in terms of what's in it for you (which is considerable) or in terms of what you can do for him? Are you willing to deny yourself, take up your cross daily, and follow him? Anything less is not discipleship; it is merely superficial lip service. (See also note on Luke 14:27, p. 1409.)

Luke 9:24-25 If this present life is most important to you, you will do everything you can to protect it. You will not want to do anything that might endanger your safety, health, or comfort. By contrast, if following Jesus is most important, you may find yourself in unsafe, unhealthy, and uncomfortable places. You may risk death, but you will not fear it because you know that Jesus will raise you to eternal life. Nothing material can compensate for the loss of eternal life. Jesus' disciples are not to use their lives on earth merely to please themselves; they should spend their lives serving God and others.

Luke 9:26 Luke's Greek audience would have had difficulty understanding a God who could die, just as Jesus' Jewish audience would have been perplexed by a Messiah who would let himself be captured and killed. Both would be ashamed of Jesus if they did not look past his death to his glorious resurrection and second coming. Then they would see Jesus not as a loser but as the Lord of the universe, who through his death had brought salvation to those who believe.

Luke 9:27 When Jesus said some would not die without seeing the Kingdom, he may have been referring to: (1) Peter, James, and John, who would witness the Transfiguration eight days later; (2) all who would witness the Resurrection and Ascension; (3) all who would take part in the spread of the church after Pentecost. Jesus' listeners would not have to wait for another, future Messiah. The Kingdom was among them, and would soon come in power.

Matt 17:1ff The Transfiguration was a vision, a brief glimpse of the true glory of the King (Matt 16:27-28). This was a special revelation of Jesus' divinity to three of the disciples, and it was God's divine affirmation of everything Jesus had done and was about to do.

Matt 17:3 The Transfiguration was a foretaste of heaven; the participants were doing something worth noting—talking together. In God's world, interactions count highly. People are individuals, with minds, hearts, and opinions. People are also part of a wider whole, connected by relationships built on sharing

clothes became as white as light. 3Suddenly, Moses and
Elijah appeared and began talking with Jesus.
4Peter exclaimed, "Lord, it's wonderful for us
to be here! If you want, I'll make three shelters as
memorials*—one for you, one for Moses, and one
for Elijah."
5But even as he spoke, a bright cloud overshadowed
them, and a voice from the cloud said, "This is my
dearly loved Son, who brings me great joy. Listen to
him." 6The disciples were terrified and fell face down
on the ground.
7Then Jesus came over and touched them. "Get up,"
he said. "Don't be afraid." 8And when they looked up,
Moses and Elijah were gone, and they saw only Jesus.
9As they went back down the mountain, Jesus
commanded them, "Don't tell anyone what you have
seen until the Son of Man* has been raised from
the dead."
10Then his disciples asked him, "Why do the teachers of religious law insist that Elijah must return before
the Messiah comes?*"
11Jesus replied, "Elijah is indeed coming first to get
everything ready. 12But I tell you, Elijah has already
come, but he wasn't recognized, and they chose to
abuse him. And in the same way they will also make
the Son of Man suffer." 13Then the disciples realized
he was talking about John the Baptist.

MARK 9:2-13

Six days later Jesus took Peter, James, and John, and
led them up a high mountain to be alone. As the
men watched, Jesus' appearance was transformed,
3and his clothes became dazzling white, far whiter than
any earthly bleach could ever make them. 4Then Elijah and Moses appeared and began talking with Jesus.
5Peter exclaimed, "Rabbi, it's wonderful for us to be
here! Let's make three shelters as memorials*—one
for you, one for Moses, and one for Elijah." 6He said
this because he didn't really know what else to say,
for they were all terrified.
7Then a cloud overshadowed them, and a voice
from the cloud said, "This is my dearly loved Son.
Listen to him." 8Suddenly, when they looked around,
Moses and Elijah were gone, and they saw only Jesus
with them.
9As they went back down the mountain, he told
them not to tell anyone what they had seen until the
Son of Man* had risen from the dead. 10So they kept
it to themselves, but they often asked each other what
he meant by "rising from the dead."
11Then they asked him, "Why do the teachers of

Mt 17:4 Greek *three tabernacles.* **Mt 17:9** "Son of Man" is a title Jesus used for himself. **Mt 17:10** Greek *that Elijah must come first?* **Mk 9:5** Greek *three tabernacles.* **Mk 9:9** "Son of Man" is a title Jesus used for himself.

between whole persons. Friendship is the key. Make time and opportunities to talk with others. Good conversations act as training for eternity.

Matt 17:3-5 Moses and Elijah were the two greatest prophets in the Old Testament. Moses represents the law, or the old covenant. He wrote the Pentateuch, and he predicted the coming of a great prophet (Deut 18:15-19). Elijah represents the prophets who foretold the coming of the Messiah (Mal 4:5-6). Moses' and Elijah's presence with Jesus confirmed Jesus' messianic mission: to fulfill God's law and the words of God's prophets. Just as God's voice in the cloud over Mount Sinai gave authority to his law (Exod 19:9), God's voice at the Transfiguration gave authority to Jesus' words.

Matt 17:4 Peter wanted to build three memorials for these three great men. Peter had the right idea about Christ, but his timing was wrong. Peter wanted to act, but this was a time for worship and adoration. He wanted to memorialize the moment, but he was supposed to learn and move on.

Matt 17:5 Jesus is more than just a great leader, a good example, a good influence, or a great prophet. He is the Son of God. When you understand this profound truth, the only adequate response is worship. When you have a correct understanding of Christ, you will obey him.

Matt 17:9 Jesus told Peter, James, and John not to tell anyone what they had seen until after his resurrection because Jesus knew that they didn't fully understand it and could not explain what they didn't understand. Their question (Matt 17:10ff) revealed their misunderstandings. They knew that Jesus was the Messiah, but they had much more to learn about the significance of his death and resurrection.

Matt 17:10-12 Based on Malachi 4:5-6, the teachers of the Old Testament law believed that Elijah must appear before the Messiah would appear. Jesus referred to John the Baptist as fulfilling this role, rather than a reappearance of the Old Testament prophet Elijah. John the Baptist took on Elijah's prophetic role, boldly confronting sin and pointing people to God. Malachi had prophesied that a prophet like Elijah would come (Mal 4:5).

Mark 9:2 We don't know why Jesus singled out Peter, James, and John for this special revelation of his glory and purity. Perhaps they were the ones most ready to understand and accept this great truth. These three disciples were the inner circle of the group of 12. They were among the first to hear Jesus' call (Mark 1:16-19). They headed the Gospel lists of disciples (Mark 3:16). And they were present at certain healings where others were excluded (Luke 8:51).

Mark 9:2 Jesus took the disciples to either Mount Hermon or Mount Tabor. A mountain was often associated with closeness to God and readiness to receive his words. God had appeared to both Moses (Exod 24:12-18) and Elijah (1 Kgs 19:8-18) on mountains.

Mark 9:3ff The Transfiguration revealed Christ's divine nature. God's voice exalted Jesus above Moses and Elijah as the long-awaited Messiah with full divine authority. Moses represented the law, and Elijah, the prophets. Their appearance showed Jesus as the fulfillment of both the Old Testament law and the prophetic promises.

Jesus was neither a reincarnation of Elijah or Moses nor merely one of the prophets. As God's only Son, he far surpasses them in authority and power. Many voices try to tell us how to live and how to know God personally. Some of these are helpful, but many are not. We must first listen to the Bible and then evaluate all other authorities in light of God's revelation.

Mark 9:9-10 Jesus told Peter, James, and John not to speak about what they had seen because they would not fully understand it until Jesus had risen from the dead. Then they would realize that only through dying could Jesus show his power over death and his authority to be King of all. The disciples would not be powerful witnesses for God until they had grasped this truth.

It was natural for the disciples to be confused about Jesus' death and resurrection because they could not see into the future. We, on the other hand, have God's revealed Word, the Bible, to give us the full meaning of Jesus' death and resurrection. We have no excuse for our unbelief.

Mark 9:11-13 When Jesus said that Elijah had already come, he was speaking of John the Baptist (Matt 17:11-13), who had fulfilled the role prophesied for Elijah.

▶ **MARK 9:2-13** ***(cont.)***
religious law insist that Elijah must return before the
Messiah comes?*"
[12]Jesus responded, "Elijah is indeed coming first
to get everything ready. Yet why do the Scriptures say
that the Son of Man must suffer greatly and be treated
with utter contempt? [13]But I tell you, Elijah has already
come, and they chose to abuse him, just as the Scriptures predicted."

LUKE 9:28-36
About eight days later Jesus took Peter, John, and
James up on a mountain to pray. [29]And as he was praying, the appearance of his face was transformed, and
his clothes became dazzling white. [30]Suddenly, two
men, Moses and Elijah, appeared and began talking
with Jesus. [31]They were glorious to see. And they were
speaking about his exodus from this world, which was
about to be fulfilled in Jerusalem.
[32]Peter and the others had fallen asleep. When they
woke up, they saw Jesus' glory and the two men standing with him. [33]As Moses and Elijah were starting to
leave, Peter, not even knowing what he was saying,
blurted out, "Master, it's wonderful for us to be here!
Let's make three shelters as memorials*—one for you,
one for Moses, and one for Elijah." [34]But even as he was
saying this, a cloud overshadowed them, and terror
gripped them as the cloud covered them.
[35]Then a voice from the cloud said, "This is my Son,
my Chosen One.* Listen to him." [36]When the voice
finished, Jesus was there alone. They didn't tell anyone
at that time what they had seen.

Mk 9:11 Greek *that Elijah must come first?* **Lk 9:33** Greek *three tabernacles.* **Lk 9:35** Some manuscripts read *This is my dearly loved Son.*

Mark 9:12-13 It was difficult for the disciples to grasp the idea that their Messiah would have to suffer. The Jews who studied the Old Testament prophecies expected the Messiah to be a great king like David, who would overthrow the enemy, Rome. Their vision was limited to their own time and experience. They did not understand that the values of God's eternal Kingdom were different from the values of the world. They wanted relief from their present problems, but deliverance from sin is far more important than deliverance from physical suffering or political oppression. Our understanding and appreciation of Jesus must go beyond what he can do for us here and now.

Luke 9:29-30 Jesus took Peter, James, and John to the top of a mountain to show them who he really was—not merely a great prophet, but God's own Son. Moses, representing the law, and Elijah, representing the prophets, appeared with Jesus. Then God's voice singled out Jesus as the long-awaited Messiah, who possessed divine authority. Jesus would fulfill both the law and the prophets (Matt 5:17).

Luke 9:33 When Peter suggested making three shelters, he may have been thinking of the Festival of Shelters, where shelters were set up to commemorate the Exodus, God's deliverance of the Israelites from slavery in Egypt. Peter wanted to keep Moses and Elijah with them, but this was not what God wanted. Peter's desire to build memorials for Jesus, Moses, and Elijah may also show his understanding that real faith is built on three cornerstones: the law, the prophets, and Jesus. But Peter grew in his understanding, and eventually he would write of Jesus as the "cornerstone" of the church (1 Pet 2:6).

Luke 9:35 As God's Son, Jesus has God's power and authority; thus, his words should be our final authority. If a person's teaching is true, it will agree with Jesus' teachings. Don't be hasty to seek advice and guidance merely from human sources and thereby neglect Christ's message. Test everything you hear

JAMES

Jesus singled out three of his disciples for special training. James, his brother John, and Peter made up this inner circle. Each eventually played a key role in the early church. Peter became a great speaker, John became a major writer, and James was the first of the 12 disciples to die for his faith. • The fact that his name is always mentioned before John's indicates that James was the older brother. Zebedee, their father, owned a fishing business in which they worked alongside Peter and Andrew. When Andrew and John left Galilee to see John the Baptist, James stayed back with the boats and fishing nets. Later, when Jesus called them, James was as eager as his partners to follow. • James enjoyed being in the inner circle of Jesus' disciples, but he misunderstood Jesus' purpose. He and his brother even tried to secure their role in his Kingdom by asking Jesus to promise them each a special position. Like the other disciples, James had a limited view of what Jesus was doing on earth, picturing only an earthly kingdom that would overthrow Rome and restore Israel's former glory. But above all, James wanted to be with Jesus. He had found the right leader, even though he was still on the wrong timetable. Jesus' death and resurrection swiftly corrected his view. • James was the first of the 12 disciples to die for the gospel. He was willing to die because he knew Jesus had conquered death, the doorway to eternal life. Our expectations about life will be limited if this life is all we can see. Jesus promised eternal life to those willing to trust him. If we believe this promise, he will give us the courage to stand for him even during dangerous times.

Strengths and accomplishments	• One of the 12 disciples • One of a special inner circle of three with Peter and John • Witness to the Transfiguration • First of the 12 disciples to be killed for his faith
Weaknesses and mistakes	• Two outbursts from James indicate struggles with temper (Luke 9:54) and selfishness (Mark 10:37); both times, he and his brother, John, spoke as one
Lesson from his life	• Loss of life is not too heavy a price to pay for following Jesus
Vital statistics	• Where: Galilee • Occupations: Fisherman, disciple • Relatives: Father: Zebedee. Mother: Salome. Brother: John. • Contemporaries: Jesus, Pilate, Herod Agrippa
Key verses	"Then James and John, the sons of Zebedee, came over and spoke to him. 'Teacher,' they said, 'we want you to do us a favor. . . . When you sit on your glorious throne, we want to sit in places of honor next to you, one on your right and the other on your left'" (Mark 10:35, 37).

James's story is told in the Gospels. He is also mentioned in Acts 1:13; 12:2.

Jesus Heals a Demon-Possessed Boy PARALLEL

MATTHEW 17:14-20

At the foot of the mountain, a large crowd was waiting
for them. A man came and knelt before Jesus and said,
15"Lord, have mercy on my son. He has seizures and
suffers terribly. He often falls into the fire or into the
water. 16So I brought him to your disciples, but they
couldn't heal him."

17Jesus said, "You faithless and corrupt people! How
long must I be with you? How long must I put up with
you? Bring the boy here to me." 18Then Jesus rebuked
the demon in the boy, and it left him. From that moment the boy was well.

19Afterward the disciples asked Jesus privately,
"Why couldn't we cast out that demon?"

20"You don't have enough faith," Jesus told them.
"I tell you the truth, if you had faith even as small as a
mustard seed, you could say to this mountain, 'Move
from here to there,' and it would move. Nothing would
be impossible.*"

MARK 9:14-29

When they returned to the other disciples, they saw
a large crowd surrounding them, and some teachers
of religious law were arguing with them. 15When the
crowd saw Jesus, they were overwhelmed with awe,
and they ran to greet him.

16"What is all this arguing about?" Jesus asked.

17One of the men in the crowd spoke up and said,
"Teacher, I brought my son so you could heal him.
He is possessed by an evil spirit that won't let him
talk. 18And whenever this spirit seizes him, it throws
him violently to the ground. Then he foams at the
mouth and grinds his teeth and becomes rigid.* So
I asked your disciples to cast out the evil spirit, but
they couldn't do it."

19Jesus said to them,* "You faithless people! How
long must I be with you? How long must I put up with
you? Bring the boy to me."

20So they brought the boy. But when the evil spirit
saw Jesus, it threw the child into a violent convulsion,
and he fell to the ground, writhing and foaming at
the mouth.

21"How long has this been happening?" Jesus asked
the boy's father.

He replied, "Since he was a little boy. 22The spirit
often throws him into the fire or into water, trying to
kill him. Have mercy on us and help us, if you can."

23"What do you mean, 'If I can'?" Jesus asked. "Anything is possible if a person believes."

24The father instantly cried out, "I do believe, but
help me overcome my unbelief!"

25When Jesus saw that the crowd of onlookers was
growing, he rebuked the evil* spirit. "Listen, you spirit
that makes this boy unable to hear and speak," he said.
"I command you to come out of this child and never
enter him again!"

26Then the spirit screamed and threw the boy into
another violent convulsion and left him. The boy appeared to be dead. A murmur ran through the crowd
as people said, "He's dead." 27But Jesus took him by
the hand and helped him to his feet, and he stood up.

28Afterward, when Jesus was alone in the house with
his disciples, they asked him, "Why couldn't we cast
out that evil spirit?"

Mt 17:20 Some manuscripts add verse 21, *But this kind of demon won't leave except by prayer and fasting.* Compare Mark 9:29. **Mk 9:18** Or *becomes weak.* **Mk 9:19** Or *said to his disciples.* **Mk 9:25** Greek *unclean.*

---

against Jesus' words and you will not be led astray. If we believe he is God's Son, then we surely will want to do what he says.

Matt 17:17 The disciples had been given the authority to do the healing, but they had not yet learned how to appropriate the power of God. Jesus' frustration is with the unbelieving and unresponsive generation. His disciples were merely a reflection of that attitude in this instance. Jesus' purpose was not to criticize the disciples but to encourage them to greater faith.

Matt 17:17-20 The disciples had been unable to cast out this demon, and they asked Jesus why. He said their faith was too small. It is the power of God, plus our faith, that moves mountains. The mustard seed was the smallest particle imaginable. Jesus said that even faith as small or undeveloped as a mustard seed would have been sufficient. Perhaps the disciples had tried to cast out the demon with their own ability rather than God's. There is great potential in even a little faith when we trust in God's power to act. If we feel weak or powerless as Christians, we should examine our faith, making sure we are trusting God's power, not our own ability to produce results.

Matt 17:20 Jesus wasn't condemning the disciples for substandard faith; he was trying to show how important faith would be in their future ministry. If you are facing a problem that seems as big and immovable as a mountain, turn your eyes from the mountain and look to Christ for more faith. Only then will you be able to overcome the obstacles that may stand in your way.

Mark 9:18 As the three disciples came down from the mountain with Jesus, they passed from a reassuring experience of God's presence to a frightening experience of evil. The beauty they had just seen must have made the ugliness seem even uglier. As our spiritual vision improves and allows us to see and understand God better, we will also be able to see and understand evil better. We would be overcome by its horror if we did not have Jesus to take us through it safely. Don't be afraid to confront evil and suffering, no matter how ugly or horrible. Jesus goes with you.

Mark 9:18 Why couldn't the disciples cast out the evil spirit? In Mark 6:13 we read that they cast out demons while on their mission to the villages. Perhaps they had special authority only for that trip, or perhaps their faith was faltering. Mark tells this story to show that the battle with Satan is a difficult, ongoing struggle. Victory over sin and temptation comes through faith in Jesus Christ, not through our own efforts.

Mark 9:23 Jesus' words do not mean that we can automatically obtain anything we want if we just think positively. Jesus meant that anything is possible if we believe, because nothing is too difficult for God. We cannot have everything we pray for as if by magic; but with faith, we can have everything we need to serve him.

Mark 9:24 The attitude of trust and confidence that the Bible calls belief or faith (Heb 11:1-6) is not something we can obtain without help. Faith is a gift from God (Eph 2:8-9). No matter how much faith we have, we never reach the point of being self-sufficient. Faith is not stored away like money in the bank. Growing in faith is a constant process of daily renewing our trust in Jesus.

▸ **MARK 9:14-29 *(cont.)***

29Jesus replied, "This kind can be cast out only by prayer.*"

LUKE 9:37-43a

The next day, after they had come down the mountain, a large crowd met Jesus. 38A man in the crowd called out to him, "Teacher, I beg you to look at my son, my only child. 39An evil spirit keeps seizing him, making him scream. It throws him into convulsions so that he foams at the mouth. It batters him and hardly ever leaves him alone. 40I begged your disciples to cast out the spirit, but they couldn't do it."

41Jesus said, "You faithless and corrupt people! How long must I be with you and put up with you?" Then he said to the man, "Bring your son here."

42As the boy came forward, the demon knocked him to the ground and threw him into a violent convulsion. But Jesus rebuked the evil* spirit and healed the boy. Then he gave him back to his father. 43Awe gripped the people as they saw this majestic display of God's power.

Jesus Predicts His Death the Second Time

PARALLEL

MATTHEW 17:22-23

After they gathered again in Galilee, Jesus told them, "The Son of Man is going to be betrayed into the hands of his enemies. 23He will be killed, but on the third day he will be raised from the dead." And the disciples were filled with grief.

MARK 9:30-32

Leaving that region, they traveled through Galilee. Jesus didn't want anyone to know he was there, 31for he wanted to spend more time with his disciples and teach them. He said to them, "The Son of Man is going to be betrayed into the hands of his enemies. He will be killed, but three days later he will rise from the dead." 32They didn't understand what he was saying, however, and they were afraid to ask him what he meant.

LUKE 9:43b-45

While everyone was marveling at everything he was doing, Jesus said to his disciples, 44"Listen to me and remember what I say. The Son of Man is going to be betrayed into the hands of his enemies." 45But they didn't know what he meant. Its significance was hidden from them, so they couldn't understand it, and they were afraid to ask him about it.

Peter Finds the Coin in the Fish's Mouth

MATTHEW 17:24-27

On their arrival in Capernaum, the collectors of the Temple tax* came to Peter and asked him, "Doesn't your teacher pay the Temple tax?"

25"Yes, he does," Peter replied. Then he went into the house.

But before he had a chance to speak, Jesus asked him, "What do you think, Peter?* Do kings tax their own people or the people they have conquered?*"

26"They tax the people they have conquered," Peter replied.

"Well, then," Jesus said, "the citizens are free! 27However, we don't want to offend them, so go down to the lake and throw in a line. Open the mouth of the first fish you catch, and you will find a large silver coin.* Take it and pay the tax for both of us."

Mk 9:29 Some manuscripts read *by prayer and fasting.* **Lk 9:42** Greek *unclean.* **Mt 17:24** Greek *the two-drachma [tax];* also in 17:24b. See Exod 30:13-16; Neh 10:32-33. **Mt 17:25a** Greek *Simon?* **Mt 17:25b** Greek *their sons or others?* **Mt 17:27** Greek *a stater* [a Greek coin equivalent to four drachmas].

Mark 9:29 The disciples would often face difficult situations that could be resolved only through prayer. Prayer is the key that unlocks faith in our life. Effective prayer needs both the attitude of complete dependence and the action of asking. Prayer demonstrates our reliance on God as we humbly invite him to fill us with faith and power. There is no substitute for prayer, especially in circumstances that seem impossible.

Luke 9:37-39 Peter, James, and John experienced a wonderful moment on the mountain, and they probably didn't want to leave. Sometimes we, too, have such an inspiring experience that we want to stay where we are—away from the reality and problems of our daily lives. Knowing that struggles await us in the valley encourages us to linger on the mountaintop. Yet staying on top of a mountain prohibits our ministering to others. Instead of becoming spiritual giants, we would soon become dwarfed by our self-centeredness. We need times of retreat and renewal but only so we can return to minister to the world. Our faith must make sense off the mountain as well as on it.

Matt 17:22-23 Once again Jesus predicted his death (see also Matt 16:21); but more importantly, he told of his resurrection. Unfortunately, the disciples heard only the first part of Jesus' words and became discouraged. They couldn't understand why Jesus wanted to go back to Jerusalem, where he would walk right into trouble.

The disciples didn't fully comprehend the purpose of Jesus' death and resurrection until Pentecost (Acts 2). They didn't know that Jesus' death and resurrection would make his Kingdom possible. We shouldn't get upset at ourselves for being unable to understand everything about Jesus. After all, the disciples spent three years with him, saw his miracles, heard his words, and still had difficulty understanding. Despite their questions and doubts, however, they believed. We should do no less.

Mark 9:30-31 Leaving Caesarea Philippi, Jesus began his last tour through the region of Galilee.

Luke 9:45 The disciples didn't understand Jesus' words about his death. They still thought of Jesus as only an earthly king, and they were concerned about their places in the Kingdom he would set up. So they ignored Jesus' words about his death and began arguing about who would be the greatest (Luke 9:46ff).

Matt 17:24 All Jewish males had to pay a Temple tax to support Temple upkeep (Exod 30:11-16). Tax collectors set up booths to collect these taxes. Only Matthew records this incident—perhaps because he had been a tax collector himself.

Matt 17:24-27 Peter answered a question without really knowing the answer, putting Jesus and the disciples in an awkward position. Jesus used this situation, however, to emphasize his kingly role. Just as kings pay no taxes and collect none from their family, Jesus, the King, owed no taxes. But Jesus supplied the tax payment for both himself and Peter rather than offend those who didn't understand his kingship. Although Jesus supplied the tax money, Peter had to go and

The Disciples Argue about Who Would Be the Greatest PARALLEL •••

MATTHEW 18:1-5 •••
About that time the disciples came to Jesus and asked,
"Who is greatest in the Kingdom of Heaven?"
2Jesus called a little child to him and put the child
among them. 3Then he said, "I tell you the truth, unless
you turn from your sins and become like little children, you will never get into the Kingdom of Heaven.
4So anyone who becomes as humble as this little child
is the greatest in the Kingdom of Heaven.
5"And anyone who welcomes a little child like this
on my behalf* is welcoming me."

MARK 9:33-37 •••
After they arrived at Capernaum and settled in a house,
Jesus asked his disciples, "What were you discussing
out on the road?" 34But they didn't answer, because they
had been arguing about which of them was the greatest.
35He sat down, called the twelve disciples over to him,
and said, "Whoever wants to be first must take last
place and be the servant of everyone else."
36Then he put a little child among them. Taking the
child in his arms, he said to them, 37"Anyone who welcomes a little child like this on my behalf* welcomes
me, and anyone who welcomes me welcomes not only
me but also my Father who sent me."

LUKE 9:46-48 •••
Then his disciples began arguing about which of them
was the greatest. 47But Jesus knew their thoughts, so
he brought a little child to his side. 48Then he said to
them, "Anyone who welcomes a little child like this on
my behalf* welcomes me, and anyone who welcomes
me also welcomes my Father who sent me. Whoever
is the least among you is the greatest."

The Disciples Forbid Another to Use Jesus' Name PARALLEL ••

MARK 9:38-41 ••
John said to Jesus, "Teacher, we saw someone using
your name to cast out demons, but we told him to stop
because he wasn't in our group."
39"Don't stop him!" Jesus said. "No one who performs

Mt 18:5 Greek *in my name.* **Mk 9:37** Greek *in my name.* **Lk 9:48** Greek *in my name.*

get it. Ultimately all that we have comes to us from God's supply, but he may want us to be active in the process.

Matt 17:24-27 As God's people, we are foreigners on earth because our loyalty is always to our real King—Jesus. Still we have to cooperate with the authorities and be responsible citizens. An ambassador to another country keeps the local laws in order to represent well the one who sent him. We are Christ's ambassadors (2 Cor 5:20). Are you being a good foreign ambassador for him to this world?

Matt 18:1-4 Jesus used a child to help his self-centered disciples get the point. We are not to be childish (like the disciples, arguing over petty issues) but childlike, with humble and sincere hearts. In what areas of your life do you tend to struggle with childishness? In what ways are you making progress with childlikeness?

Matt 18:3-4 The disciples had become so preoccupied with the organization of Jesus' earthly kingdom that they had lost sight of its divine purpose. Instead of seeking a place of service, they sought positions of advantage. It is easy to lose our eternal perspective and compete for promotions or status in the church. It is difficult, but healthy, to identify with "children"—weak and dependent people with no status or influence.

Mark 9:34 The disciples, caught up in their constant struggle for personal success, were embarrassed to answer Jesus' question. It is always painful to compare our motives with Christ's. It is not wrong for believers to be industrious or ambitious, but when ambition pushes aside obedience and service, it becomes sin. We are all like the disciples and even like the Pharisees in this regard. Pride or insecurity can cause us to overvalue position and prestige. In God's Kingdom, such motives are destructive. The only safe ambition is directed toward Christ's Kingdom, not our own advancement. We must renounce pride and status seeking. They are Satan's tools, not Christ's.

Mark 9:35 Serving others is real leadership. Jesus described leadership from a new perspective. Instead of using people, we are to serve them. Jesus' mission was to serve others and to give his life away. A real leader has a servant's heart. Servant leaders appreciate others' worth and realize that they're not above any job. If you see something that needs to be done, don't wait to be asked; take the initiative and do it like a faithful servant. Don't approach life expecting high positions, honors, and special privileges. Look instead for ways to help others.

Mark 9:36-37 Jesus taught the disciples to welcome children. This was a new approach in a society where children were usually treated as second-class citizens. It is important not only to treat children well but also to teach them about Jesus. Children's ministries should never be regarded as less important than those for adults.

Luke 9:48 Our care for others is a measure of our greatness. How much concern do you show for others? This is a vital question that can accurately measure your greatness in God's eyes. How have you expressed your care for others lately, especially the helpless, the needy, the poor—those who can't return your love and concern? Your honest answer to that question will give you a good idea of your real greatness.

Mark 9:38-40 Jesus was not saying that being indifferent or neutral toward him is as good as being committed. As he explained in Matthew 12:30, "Anyone who isn't with me opposes me, and anyone who isn't

Then he said to them, "Anyone who welcomes a little child like this on my behalf welcomes me, and anyone who welcomes me also welcomes my Father who sent me. Whoever is the least among you is the greatest."
Luke 9:48

working with me is actually working against me." In both cases, Jesus was pointing out that neutrality toward him is not possible. Nevertheless, his followers will not all resemble each other or belong to the same groups. People who are on Jesus' side have the same goal of building up the Kingdom of God, and they should not let their differences interfere with this goal. Those who share a common faith in Christ should cooperate. People don't have to be just like us to be following Jesus with us.

▸ **MARK 9:38-41 *(cont.)***

a miracle in my name will soon be able to speak evil of
me. 40Anyone who is not against us is for us. 41If anyone
gives you even a cup of water because you belong to
the Messiah, I tell you the truth, that person will surely
be rewarded."

LUKE 9:49-50

John said to Jesus, "Master, we saw someone using
your name to cast out demons, but we told him to stop
because he isn't in our group."
50But Jesus said, "Don't stop him! Anyone who is not
against you is for you."

Jesus Warns against Temptation PARALLEL

MATTHEW 18:6-10

"But if you cause one of these little ones who trusts in
me to fall into sin, it would be better for you to have a
large millstone tied around your neck and be drowned
in the depths of the sea.
7"What sorrow awaits the world, because it tempts
people to sin. Temptations are inevitable, but what
sorrow awaits the person who does the tempting.
8So if your hand or foot causes you to sin, cut it off
and throw it away. It's better to enter eternal life
with only one hand or one foot than to be thrown
into eternal fire with both of your hands and feet.
9And if your eye causes you to sin, gouge it out and
throw it away. It's better to enter eternal life with
only one eye than to have two eyes and be thrown
into the fire of hell.*
10"Beware that you don't look down on any of
these little ones. For I tell you that in heaven their
angels are always in the presence of my heavenly
Father.*"

MARK 9:42-50

"But if you cause one of these little ones who trusts
in me to fall into sin, it would be better for you to be
thrown into the sea with a large millstone hung around
your neck. 43If your hand causes you to sin, cut it off.
It's better to enter eternal life with only one hand than
to go into the unquenchable fires of hell* with two
hands.* 45If your foot causes you to sin, cut it off. It's
better to enter eternal life with only one foot than to
be thrown into hell with two feet.* 47And if your eye
causes you to sin, gouge it out. It's better to enter the
Kingdom of God with only one eye than to have two
eyes and be thrown into hell, 48'where the maggots
never die and the fire never goes out.'*
49"For everyone will be tested with fire.* 50Salt is
good for seasoning. But if it loses its flavor, how do
you make it salty again? You must have the qualities
of salt among yourselves and live in peace with each
other."

Mt 18:9 Greek *the Gehenna of fire.* **Mt 18:10** Some manuscripts add verse 11, *And the Son of Man came to save those who are lost.* Compare Luke 19:10. **Mk 9:43a** Greek *Gehenna;* also in 9:45, 47. **Mk 9:43b** Some manuscripts add verse 44, *'where the maggots never die and the fire never goes out.'* See 9:48. **Mk 9:45** Some manuscripts add verse 46, *'where the maggots never die and the fire never goes out.'* See 9:48. **Mk 9:48** Isa 66:24. **Mk 9:49** Greek *salted with fire;* other manuscripts add *and every sacrifice will be salted with salt.*

Luke 9:49-50 The disciples were jealous. Nine of them together had been unable to cast out a single evil spirit (Luke 9:40), but when they saw a man who was not one of their group casting out demons, they told him to stop. Our pride is hurt when someone else succeeds where we have failed, but Jesus says there is no room for such jealousy in the spiritual warfare of his Kingdom. Share Jesus' open-arms attitude toward Christian workers outside your group. Rejoice when they are able to bring people to Christ.

Matt 18:6 Children are trusting by nature. Because they trust adults, they are easily led to faith in Christ. God holds parents and other adults accountable for how they influence these little ones. Jesus warned that anyone who turns little children away from faith in him will receive severe punishment.

Matt 18:7ff Jesus warned the disciples about two ways to cause others to sin: tempting them (Matt 18:7-9) and neglecting or demeaning them (Matt 18:10). As leaders, we are to help young people or new believers avoid anything or anyone that could cause them to stumble in their faith and lead them to sin. We must never take lightly the spiritual education and protection of those young in age or young in the faith.

Matt 18:8-9 We must remove stumbling blocks that cause us to sin. This does not mean to cut off a part of the body. For the church it means that any person, program, or teaching that threatens the spiritual growth of the body must be removed. For the individual, any relationship, practice, or activity that leads to sin should be stopped. Jesus says it would be better to go to heaven with one hand than to hell with both. Sin, of course, affects more than our hands; it affects our minds and hearts.

Mark 9:42 Luke 9:48 states, "Whoever is the least among you is the greatest." In Jesus' eyes, whoever welcomes a child welcomes Jesus. By contrast, harming others or failing to care for them is a sin, even if they are unimportant people in the world's eyes. It is possible for thoughtless, selfish people to gain a measure of worldly greatness, but lasting greatness is measured by God's standards. What do you use as your measure—personal achievement or unselfish service?

Mark 9:42 This caution against harming little ones in the faith applies both to what we do individually as teachers and examples and to what we allow to fester in our Christian fellowship. Our thoughts and actions must be motivated by love (1 Cor 13), and we must be careful about judging others (Matt 7:1-5; Rom 14:1–15:4). However, we also have a responsibility to confront flagrant sin within the church (1 Cor 5:12-13).

Mark 9:43ff This startling language is not meant to promote self-mutilation but instead stresses the importance of cutting sin out of your life. Painful self-discipline is required of Jesus' true followers. Giving up a relationship, job, or habit that is against God's will may seem just as painful as cutting off a hand, but Christ is worth any possible loss or discomfort. Nothing should stand in the way of faith. We must be ruthless in removing sin from our lives now in order to avoid suffering for eternity. Make your choices from an eternal perspective.

Mark 9:50 Jesus used salt to illustrate three qualities that should be found in his people: (1) We should remember God's faithfulness, just as salt, when used with a sacrifice, recalled God's covenant with his people (Lev 2:13). (2) We should make a difference in the "flavor" of the world we live in, just as salt changes meat's flavor (see Matt 5:13). (3) We should counteract the moral decay in society, just as salt preserves food from decay. When we lose this desire to "salt" the earth with the love and message of God, we become useless to him.

Jesus Tells the Parable of the Lost Sheep

MATTHEW 18:12-14

"If a man has a hundred sheep and one of them wanders away, what will he do? Won't he leave the ninety-nine others on the hills and go out to search for the one that is lost? [13]And if he finds it, I tell you the truth, he will rejoice over it more than over the ninety-nine that didn't wander away! [14]In the same way, it is not my heavenly Father's will that even one of these little ones should perish.

Jesus Teaches How to Treat a Believer Who Sins

MATTHEW 18:15-20

"If another believer* sins against you,* go privately and point out the offense. If the other person listens and confesses it, you have won that person back. [16]But if you are unsuccessful, take one or two others with you and go back again, so that everything you say may be confirmed by two or three witnesses. [17]If the person still refuses to listen, take your case to the church. Then if he or she won't accept the church's decision, treat that person as a pagan or a corrupt tax collector.

[18]"I tell you the truth, whatever you forbid* on earth will be forbidden in heaven, and whatever you permit* on earth will be permitted in heaven.

[19]"I also tell you this: If two of you agree here on earth concerning anything you ask, my Father in heaven will do it for you. [20]For where two or three gather together as my followers,* I am there among them."

Jesus Tells the Parable of the Unforgiving Debtor

MATTHEW 18:21-35

Then Peter came to him and asked, "Lord, how often should I forgive someone* who sins against me? Seven times?"

[22]"No, not seven times," Jesus replied, "but seventy times seven!*

Mt 18:15a Greek *If your brother.* **Mt 18:15b** Some manuscripts do not include *against you.* **Mt 18:18a** Or *bind,* or *lock.* **Mt 18:18b** Or *loose,* or *open.* **Mt 18:20** Greek *gather together in my name.* **Mt 18:21** Greek *my brother.* **Mt 18:22** Or *seventy-seven times.*

Matt 18:12-14 Just as a shepherd is concerned enough about one lost sheep to go search the hills for it, so God is concerned about every human being he has created (he "does not want anyone to be destroyed," 2 Pet 3:9). If you come in contact with children in your neighborhood who need Christ, steer them toward him by your example, your words, and your acts of kindness.

Matt 18:15-17 These are Jesus' guidelines for dealing with those who sin against us. They were meant for (1) Christians, not unbelievers, (2) sins committed against you and not others, and (3) conflict resolution in the context of the church, not the community at large. Jesus' words are not a license for a frontal attack on every person who hurts or slights us. They are not a license to start a destructive gossip campaign or to call for a church trial. They are designed to reconcile those who disagree so that all Christians can live in harmony.

When someone wrongs us, we often do the opposite of what Jesus recommends. We turn away in hatred or resentment, seek revenge, or engage in gossip. By contrast, we should go to that person first, as difficult as that may be. Then we should forgive that person as often as is needed (Matt 18:21-22). This will create a much better chance of restoring the relationship.

Matt 18:17 These guidelines are only for people who are believers, and so they are to be dealt with in the confines of the church, a local Christian community. If the person is unrepentant, they are to be considered an outsider, just like a pagan or a corrupt tax collector—wicked transgressors of the law. This kind of church discipline was essentially exclusion from the community (see Acts 5:1-6; Rom 16:17; 1 Cor 5:1-13; 2 Cor 6:14-18; Gal 5:7-12; 2 Thes 3:14-15), and it is rooted in the conviction that God's people are to be holy and that sin corrupts fellowship, both between people and between the people and God. The goal is not vindictive retribution or a public display or power, but the restoration of the wayward to holiness and fellowship (Matt 18:10-15; Gal 6:1; Jas 5:19-20).

When you are confronted with the difficult task of confronting a brother or sister in Christ with their sin, make sure that you are focused on restoring godliness and fellowship rather than simply trying to make someone pay for the wrong they have done.

Matt 18:18 This forbidding and permitting refers to the decisions of the church in conflicts. Among believers, there should not be any need for a court of appeals beyond the church. Ideally, the church's decisions should be God-guided and based on discernment of his Word. Believers have the responsibility, therefore, to bring their problems to the church, and the church has the responsibility to use God's guidance in seeking to resolve conflicts. Handling problems God's way will have an impact now and for eternity.

Matt 18:19-20 Jesus looked ahead to a new day when he would be present with his followers not in body, but through his Holy Spirit. In the body of believers (the church), the sincere agreement of two people in prayer is more powerful than the superficial agreement of thousands because Christ's Holy Spirit is with them. Two or more believers, filled with the Holy Spirit, will pray according to God's will, not their own.

Matt 18:22 The rabbis taught that people should forgive those who offend them—but only three times. Peter, trying to be especially generous, asked Jesus if seven (the "perfect" number) was enough times to forgive someone. But Jesus answered, "Seventy times seven," meaning that we shouldn't even keep track of how many times we forgive someone. We should always forgive those who are truly repentant, no matter how many times they ask.

If a man has a hundred sheep and one of them wanders away, what will he do? Won't he leave the ninety-nine others on the hills and go out to search for the one that is lost?
Matthew 18:12

▸ **MATTHEW 18:21-35 *(cont.)***

23“Therefore, the Kingdom of Heaven can be compared to a king who decided to bring his accounts up
to date with servants who had borrowed money from
him. 24In the process, one of his debtors was brought
in who owed him millions of dollars.* 25He couldn't
pay, so his master ordered that he be sold—along with
his wife, his children, and everything he owned—to
pay the debt.

26“But the man fell down before his master and
begged him, ‘Please, be patient with me, and I will
pay it all.’ 27Then his master was filled with pity for
him, and he released him and forgave his debt.

28“But when the man left the king, he went to a fellow servant who owed him a few thousand dollars.*
He grabbed him by the throat and demanded instant
payment.

29“His fellow servant fell down before him and
begged for a little more time. ‘Be patient with me, and
I will pay it,’ he pleaded. 30But his creditor wouldn't
wait. He had the man arrested and put in prison until
the debt could be paid in full.

31“When some of the other servants saw this,
they were very upset. They went to the king and told
him everything that had happened. 32Then the king
called in the man he had forgiven and said, ‘You evil
servant! I forgave you that tremendous debt because
you pleaded with me. 33Shouldn't you have mercy
on your fellow servant, just as I had mercy on you?’
34Then the angry king sent the man to prison to be
tortured until he had paid his entire debt.

35“That's what my heavenly Father will do to you if
you refuse to forgive your brothers and sisters* from
your heart.”

Jesus' Brothers Ridicule Him

JOHN 7:1-9

After this, Jesus traveled around Galilee. He wanted
to stay out of Judea, where the Jewish leaders were
plotting his death. 2But soon it was time for the Jewish
Festival of Shelters, 3and Jesus' brothers said to him,
“Leave here and go to Judea, where your followers can
see your miracles! 4You can't become famous if you
hide like this! If you can do such wonderful things,
show yourself to the world!” 5For even his brothers
didn't believe in him.

6Jesus replied, “Now is not the right time for me to
go, but you can go anytime. 7The world can't hate you,
but it does hate me because I accuse it of doing evil.
8You go on. I'm not going* to this festival, because my
time has not yet come.” 9After saying these things,
Jesus remained in Galilee.

Mt 18:24 Greek *10,000 talents* [375 tons or 340 metric tons of silver]. **Mt 18:28** Greek *100 denarii.* A denarius was equivalent to a laborer's full day's wage. **Mt 18:35** Greek *your brother.* **Jn 7:8** Some manuscripts read *not yet going.*

Matt 18:30 In Bible times, serious consequences awaited those who could not pay their debts. A person lending money could seize the borrower who couldn't pay and force him or his family to work until the debt was paid. The debtor could also be thrown into prison, or his family could be sold into slavery to help pay off the debt. It was hoped that the debtor, while in prison, would sell off his landholdings or that relatives would pay the debt. If not, the debtor could remain in prison for life.

Matt 18:35 Because God has forgiven all our sins, we should not withhold forgiveness from others. As we realize how completely Christ has forgiven us, it should produce an attitude of forgiveness toward others. When we don't forgive others, we are setting ourselves above Christ's law of love.

John 7:2 The Festival of Shelters is described in Leviticus 23:33ff. This event occurred in October, about six months after the Passover celebration mentioned in John 6:2-5. The festival commemorated the days when the Israelites wandered in the wilderness and lived in shelters (Lev 23:43).

John 7:3-5 Jesus' brothers had a difficult time believing in him. Some of these brothers would eventually become leaders in the church (James, for example), but for several years they were embarrassed by Jesus. After Jesus died and rose again, they finally believed. We today have every reason to believe because we have the full record of Jesus' miracles, death, and resurrection. We also have the evidence of what the Good News has done in people's lives through the centuries. Don't miss this opportunity to believe in God's Son.

JESUS AND FORGIVENESS

Jesus not only taught frequently about forgiveness, he also demonstrated his own willingness to forgive. Here are several examples that should be an encouragement to recognize his willingness to forgive us also.

Jesus forgave . . .	Reference
The paralyzed man lowered on a mat through the roof	Matt 9:2-8
The woman caught in adultery	John 8:3-11
The woman who anointed his feet with perfume	Luke 7:44-50
Peter, for denying he knew Jesus	John 18:15-18, 25-27; 21:15-19
The criminal on the cross	Luke 23:39-43
The people who crucified him	Luke 23:34

John 7:7 Because the world hated Jesus, we who follow him can expect that many people will hate us as well. If circumstances are going too well, ask if you are following Christ as you should. We can be grateful when life goes well, but we must make sure it is not at the cost of following Jesus halfheartedly or not at all.

Luke 9:51 Although Jesus knew he would face persecution and death in Jerusalem, he was determined to go there. That kind of resolve should characterize our lives as well. When God gives us a course of action, we must move steadily toward our destination, regardless of the potential hazards that await us there.

Luke 9:53 After Assyria invaded Israel, the northern kingdom, and resettled it with its own people (2 Kgs 17:24-41), the mixed race that developed became known as Samaritans. “Purebred” Jews hated these “half-breeds,” and the Samaritans in turn hated the Jews. So many tensions arose

6. JESUS TURNS TOWARD JERUSALEM

Jesus had a very specific mission during his time on earth, and he knew that it would culminate in Jerusalem. When the time was finally right, he made his way toward Jerusalem, but he continued to teach and minister along the way, healing people and delivering some of his most treasured parables.

Jesus Travels to Judea PARALLEL ●●●

MATTHEW 19:1-2
When Jesus had finished saying these things, he left Galilee and went down to the region of Judea east of the Jordan River. [2]Large crowds followed him there, and he healed their sick.

MARK 10:1
Then Jesus left Capernaum and went down to the region of Judea and into the area east of the Jordan River. Once again crowds gathered around him, and as usual he was teaching them.

LUKE 9:51
As the time drew near for him to ascend to heaven, Jesus resolutely set out for Jerusalem.

Jesus Passes Through Samaria

LUKE 9:52-56
He sent messengers ahead to a Samaritan village to prepare for his arrival. [53]But the people of the village did not welcome Jesus because he was on his way to Jerusalem. [54]When James and John saw this, they said to Jesus, "Lord, should we call down fire from heaven to burn them up*?" [55]But Jesus turned and rebuked them.* [56]So they went on to another village.

Jesus Teaches about the Cost of Following Him PARALLEL ●●

MATTHEW 8:18-22
When Jesus saw the crowd around him, he instructed his disciples to cross to the other side of the lake.
[19]Then one of the teachers of religious law said to him, "Teacher, I will follow you wherever you go."
[20]But Jesus replied, "Foxes have dens to live in, and birds have nests, but the Son of Man* has no place even to lay his head."
[21]Another of his disciples said, "Lord, first let me return home and bury my father."
[22]But Jesus told him, "Follow me now. Let the spiritually dead bury their own dead.*"

LUKE 9:57-62
As they were walking along, someone said to Jesus, "I will follow you wherever you go."
[58]But Jesus replied, "Foxes have dens to live in, and birds have nests, but the Son of Man has no place even to lay his head."

Lk 9:54 Some manuscripts add *as Elijah did.* **Lk 9:55** Some manuscripts add an expanded conclusion to verse 55 and an additional sentence in verse 56: *And he said, "You don't realize what your hearts are like. [56]For the Son of Man has not come to destroy people's lives, but to save them."* **Mt 8:20** "Son of Man" is a title Jesus used for himself. **Mt 8:22** Greek *Let the dead bury their own dead.*

between the two peoples that Jewish travelers between Galilee and southern Judea often would walk around rather than through Samaritan territory, even though this would lengthen their trip considerably. Jesus held no such prejudices, and he sent messengers ahead to get things ready in a Samaritan village. But the village refused to welcome these Jewish travelers who were headed for Jerusalem.

Luke 9:54 When the Samaritan village did not welcome Jesus and his disciples, James and John didn't want to stop at shaking the dust from their feet (Luke 9:5). They wanted to retaliate by calling down fire from heaven on the people as Elijah had done on the servants of a wicked king of Israel (2 Kgs 1). When others reject or scorn us, we may feel like retaliating. But we must remember that judgment belongs to God, and we must not expect him to use his power to carry out personal vendettas.

Matt 8:19-20 Following Jesus is not always easy or comfortable. Often it means great cost and sacrifice, with no earthly rewards or security. You may find that following Christ costs you popularity, friendships, leisure time, or treasured habits. But while the cost of following Christ is high, the value of being Christ's disciple is even higher. Discipleship is an investment that lasts for eternity and yields incredible rewards.

Matt 8:21-22 It is possible that this disciple was not asking permission to go to his father's funeral but rather to put off following Jesus until his elderly father died. Perhaps he was the firstborn son and wanted to be sure to claim his inheritance. Perhaps he didn't want to face his father's wrath if he left the family business to follow an itinerant preacher. Whether his concern was financial security, family approval, or something else, he did not want to commit himself to Jesus just yet. Jesus, however, would not accept his excuse.

Jesus was always direct with those who wanted to follow him. He made sure they counted the cost and set aside any conditions they might have for following him. As God's Son, Jesus did not hesitate to demand complete loyalty. Even family loyalty was not to take priority over the demands of obedience. His direct challenge forces us to ask ourselves about our own priorities in following him. The decision to follow Jesus should not be put off, even though other loyalties compete for our attention. Nothing should be placed above a total commitment to living for him.

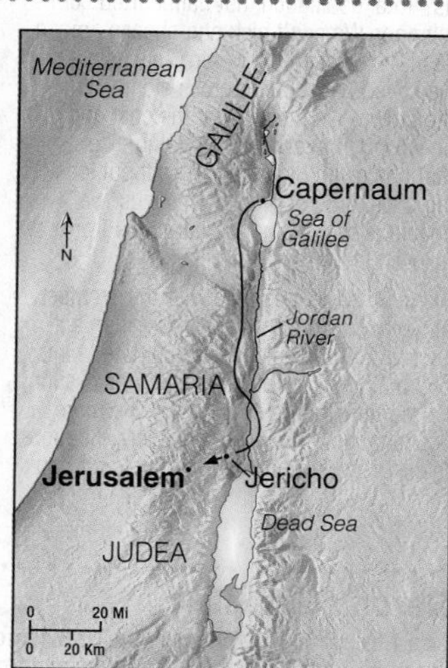

***JESUS TRAVELS TO JUDEA** Jesus quietly left Capernaum, heading toward the borders of Judea before crossing the Jordan River. He preached there before going to Jericho.*

▸ **LUKE 9:57-62 *(cont.)***

59He said to another person, "Come, follow me."
The man agreed, but he said, "Lord, first let me return home and bury my father."
60But Jesus told him, "Let the spiritually dead bury
their own dead!* Your duty is to go and preach about
the Kingdom of God."
61Another said, "Yes, Lord, I will follow you, but first
let me say good-bye to my family."
62But Jesus told him, "Anyone who puts a hand to
the plow and then looks back is not fit for the Kingdom of God."

Jesus Teaches Openly at the Temple

JOHN 7:10-31

But after his brothers left for the festival, Jesus also
went, though secretly, staying out of public view. 11The
Jewish leaders tried to find him at the festival and
kept asking if anyone had seen him. 12There was a lot
of grumbling about him among the crowds. Some
argued, "He's a good man," but others said, "He's nothing but a fraud who deceives the people." 13But no
one had the courage to speak favorably about him in
public, for they were afraid of getting in trouble with
the Jewish leaders.
14Then, midway through the festival, Jesus went
up to the Temple and began to teach. 15The people*
were surprised when they heard him. "How does
he know so much when he hasn't been trained?"
they asked.
16So Jesus told them, "My message is not my own;
it comes from God who sent me. 17Anyone who wants
to do the will of God will know whether my teaching
is from God or is merely my own. 18Those who speak
for themselves want glory only for themselves, but
a person who seeks to honor the one who sent him
speaks truth, not lies. 19Moses gave you the law, but
none of you obeys it! In fact, you are trying to kill me."
20The crowd replied, "You're demon possessed!
Who's trying to kill you?"

Lk 9:60 Greek *Let the dead bury their own dead.* **Jn 7:15** Greek *Jewish people.*

Luke 9:59 Luke does not say whether the father was already dead or just terminally ill. Jesus was saying that true discipleship requires instant action. Jesus did not teach people to forsake responsibilities to family, but he often gave commands to people in light of their real motives. Following Jesus has a cost, and each of us must be ready to serve, even when it requires sacrifice.

Luke 9:62 What does Jesus want from us? Total dedication, not halfhearted commitment. We can't pick and choose among Jesus' ideas and follow him selectively; we have to accept the cross along with the crown. We must count the cost and be willing to abandon everything else that has given us security—without looking back. With our focus on Jesus, we should allow nothing to distract us from following him.

John 7:10 Jesus came with the greatest gift ever offered, so why did he often act secretly? The religious leaders hated him, and many would refuse his gift of salvation, no matter what he said or did. The more Jesus taught and worked publicly, the more these leaders would cause trouble for him and his followers. So it was necessary for Jesus to teach and work as quietly as possible. Many people today have the privilege of teaching, preaching, and worshiping publicly with little persecution. These believers should be grateful and make the most of their opportunities to proclaim the Good News.

John 7:13 The Jewish religious leaders had a great deal of power over the common people. Apparently these leaders couldn't do much to Jesus at this time, but they threatened anyone who might publicly support him. One of the reprisals for believing in Jesus was excommunication from the synagogue (John 9:22). To a Jew, this was a severe punishment.

John 7:13 Everyone was talking about Jesus! But when it came time to speak up for him in public, no one said a word. All were afraid. Fear can stifle our witness. Although many people talk about Christ in church, when it comes to making a public statement about their faith, they are often embarrassed. Jesus says that he will acknowledge us before God if we acknowledge him before others (Matt 10:32). Be courageous! Speak up for Christ!

John 7:16-18 Those who attempt to know God's will and do it will know intuitively that Jesus was telling the truth about himself. Have you ever listened to religious speakers and wondered if they were telling the truth? Test them: Their words should agree with, not contradict, the Bible; and their words should point to God and his will, not to themselves.

John 7:19 The Pharisees spent their days trying to achieve holiness by keeping the meticulous rules that they had added to God's laws. Jesus' accusation that they didn't keep Moses' laws stung them deeply. In spite of their pompous pride in themselves and their rules, they did not even fulfill a legalistic religion, for they were living far below what the law of Moses required. Murder was certainly against the law. Jesus' followers should do more than the moral law requires, not by adding to its requirements, but by going beyond the mere dos and don'ts of the law to the spirit of the law.

John 7:20 Most of the people were probably not aware of the plot to kill Jesus (John 5:18). There was a small group looking for the right opportunity to kill him, but most were still trying to decide what they believed about him.

Herod's Temple ▸

Apart from 100 references in the New Testament, our main sources about Herod's reconstruction of the Temple in Jerusalem come from the Jewish historian Josephus and from the Middoth (a section of the Jewish rabbinic writings). There are considerable differences in detail between the two, which rules out certainty in attempted reconstructions. Since Josephus was alive while the Temple was still standing (he was born about A.D. 37 and died in the early second century), he is probably more reliable than the Middoth (around A.D. 150), which appears to exaggerate occasionally. Archaeological research has been helpful in determining the positions of the outer walls and gates.

Herod's Temple followed the basic plan of its predecessors, although its porch was much larger. It was built in the contemporary Greco-Roman architectural style and must therefore be very different from Zerubbabel's reconstruction of the Temple. Work began in 20 B.C.; and while the main sanctuary was quickly erected (it was in full operation in 10 years), the total project was not completed until A.D. 64, only six years before it was destroyed by the Romans.

Herod's Temple

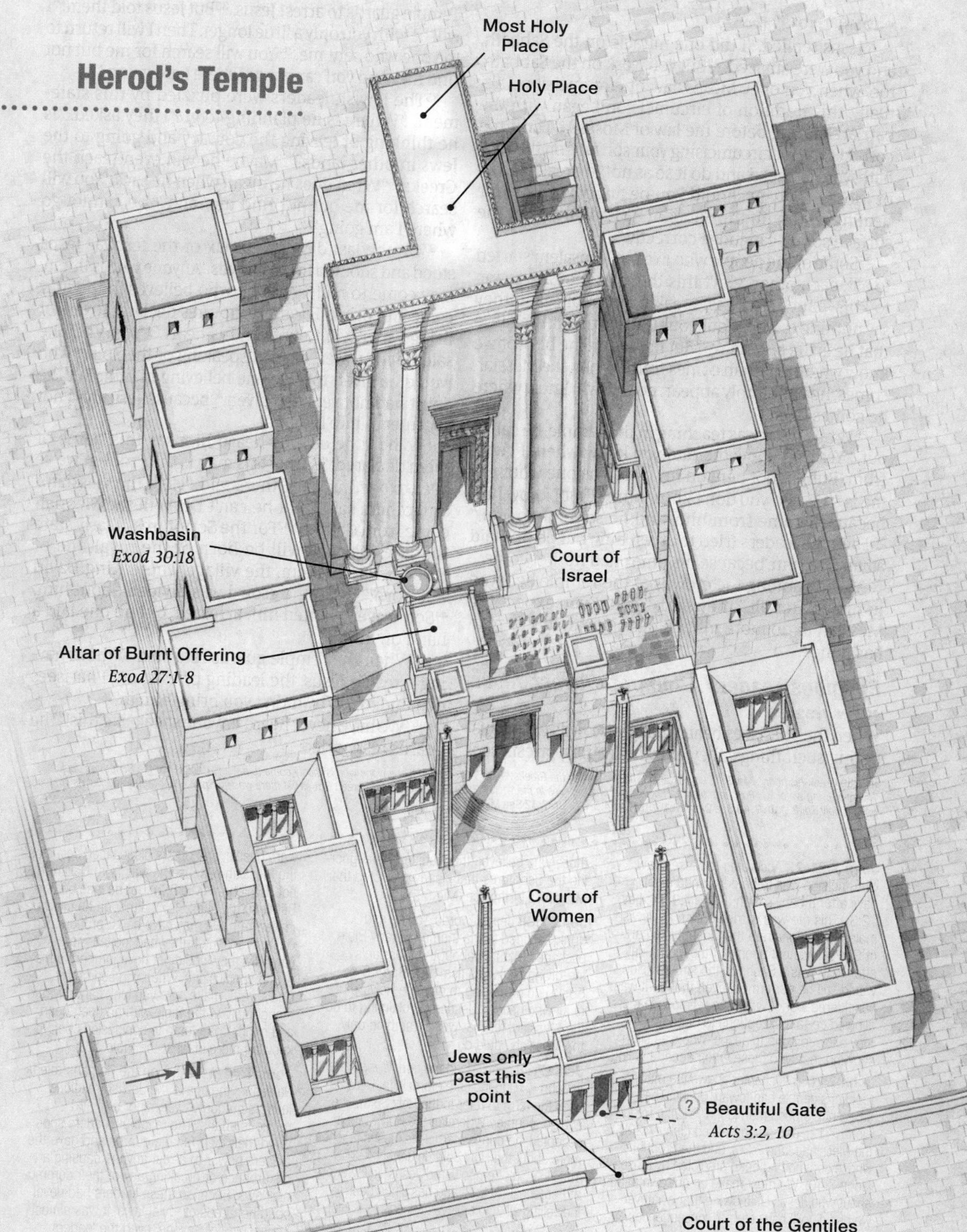
Most Holy Place
Holy Place
Washbasin
Exod 30:18
Court of Israel
Altar of Burnt Offering
Exod 27:1-8
Court of Women
N
Jews only past this point
? Beautiful Gate
Acts 3:2, 10
Court of the Gentiles
Acts 21:28-29; Eph 2:14

▸ **JOHN 7:10-31** ***(cont.)***

21Jesus replied, "I did one miracle on the Sabbath, and you were amazed. 22But you work on the Sabbath, too, when you obey Moses' law of circumcision. (Actually, this tradition of circumcision began with the patriarchs, long before the law of Moses.) 23For if the correct time for circumcising your son falls on the Sabbath, you go ahead and do it so as not to break the law of Moses. So why should you be angry with me for healing a man on the Sabbath? 24Look beneath the surface so you can judge correctly."

25Some of the people who lived in Jerusalem started to ask each other, "Isn't this the man they are trying to kill? 26But here he is, speaking in public, and they say nothing to him. Could our leaders possibly believe that he is the Messiah? 27But how could he be? For we know where this man comes from. When the Messiah comes, he will simply appear; no one will know where he comes from."

28While Jesus was teaching in the Temple, he called out, "Yes, you know me, and you know where I come from. But I'm not here on my own. The one who sent me is true, and you don't know him. 29But I know him because I come from him, and he sent me to you." 30Then the leaders tried to arrest him; but no one laid a hand on him, because his time* had not yet come.

31Many among the crowds at the Temple believed in him. "After all," they said, "would you expect the Messiah to do more miraculous signs than this man has done?"

Religious Leaders Attempt to Arrest Jesus

JOHN 7:32-53

When the Pharisees heard that the crowds were whispering such things, they and the leading priests sent Temple guards to arrest Jesus. 33But Jesus told them, "I will be with you only a little longer. Then I will return to the one who sent me. 34You will search for me but not find me. And you cannot go where I am going."

35The Jewish leaders were puzzled by this statement. "Where is he planning to go?" they asked. "Is he thinking of leaving the country and going to the Jews in other lands?* Maybe he will even teach the Greeks! 36What does he mean when he says, 'You will search for me but not find me,' and 'You cannot go where I am going'?"

37On the last day, the climax of the festival, Jesus stood and shouted to the crowds, "Anyone who is thirsty may come to me! 38Anyone who believes in me may come and drink! For the Scriptures declare, 'Rivers of living water will flow from his heart.'"* 39(When he said "living water," he was speaking of the Spirit, who would be given to everyone believing in him. But the Spirit had not yet been given,* because Jesus had not yet entered into his glory.)

40When the crowds heard him say this, some of them declared, "Surely this man is the Prophet we've been expecting."* 41Others said, "He is the Messiah." Still others said, "But he can't be! Will the Messiah come from Galilee? 42For the Scriptures clearly state that the Messiah will be born of the royal line of David, in Bethlehem, the village where King David was born."* 43So the crowd was divided about him. 44Some even wanted him arrested, but no one laid a hand on him.

45When the Temple guards returned without having arrested Jesus, the leading priests and Pharisees demanded, "Why didn't you bring him in?"

46"We have never heard anyone speak like this!" the guards responded.

Jn 7:30 Greek *his hour.* **Jn 7:35** Or *the Jews who live among the Greeks?* **Jn 7:37-38** Or *"Let anyone who is thirsty come to me and drink. 38For the Scriptures declare, 'Rivers of living water will flow from the heart of anyone who believes in me.'"* **Jn 7:39** Some manuscripts read *But as yet there was no Spirit.* Still others read *But as yet there was no Holy Spirit.* **Jn 7:40** See Deut 18:15, 18; Mal 4:5-6. **Jn 7:42** See Mic 5:2.

John 7:21-23 According to Moses' law, circumcision was to be performed eight days after a baby's birth (Gen 17:9-14; Lev 12:3). This rite was carried out on all Jewish males to demonstrate their identity as part of God's covenant people. If the eighth day after birth was a Sabbath, the circumcision would still be performed (even though it was considered work). While the religious leaders allowed certain exceptions to Sabbath laws, they allowed none to Jesus, who was simply showing mercy to those who needed healing.

John 7:26 This chapter shows the many reactions people had toward Jesus. They called him a good man (John 7:12), a fraud (John 7:12), demon possessed (John 7:20), the Messiah (John 7:26), and the Prophet whose coming had been predicted by Moses (John 7:40). We must make up our own minds about who Jesus is, knowing that whatever we decide will have eternal consequences.

John 7:27 There was a popular tradition that the Messiah would simply appear. But those who believed this tradition were ignoring the Scriptures that clearly predicted the Messiah's birthplace (Mic 5:2).

John 7:38 Jesus' words, "come and drink," alluded to the theme of many Bible passages that talk about the Messiah's life-giving blessings (Isa 12:2-3; 44:3-4; 58:11). In promising to give the Holy Spirit to all who believe, Jesus was claiming to be the Messiah, for that was something only the Messiah could do.

John 7:38 Jesus used the term *living water* in John 4:10 to indicate eternal life. Here he uses the term to refer to the Holy Spirit. The two go together: Wherever the Holy Spirit is accepted, he brings eternal life. Jesus teaches more about the Holy Spirit in John 14–16. The Holy Spirit empowered Jesus' followers at Pentecost (Acts 2) and has since been indwelling all who believe in Jesus as Savior.

John 7:40-44 The crowd was asking questions about Jesus. Some believed, others were hostile, and others disqualified Jesus as the Messiah because he was from Nazareth, not Bethlehem (Mic 5:2). But he was born in Bethlehem (Luke 2:1-7), although he grew up in Nazareth. He may have had a pronounced Galilean accent. If they had looked more carefully, they would not have jumped to the wrong conclusions. When you search for God's truth, make sure you look carefully and thoughtfully at the Bible with an open heart and mind. Don't jump to conclusions before knowing more of what the Bible says.

John 7:44-46 Although the Romans ruled Palestine, they gave the Jewish religious leaders authority over minor civil and religious affairs. The religious leaders supervised their own Temple guards and gave the officers power to arrest anyone causing a disturbance or breaking any of their ceremonial laws. Because these leaders had developed hundreds of trivial laws, it was almost impossible for anyone, even the leaders themselves, not to break, neglect, or ignore

47"Have you been led astray, too?" the Pharisees
mocked. 48"Is there a single one of us rulers or Pharisees who believes in him? 49This foolish crowd follows
him, but they are ignorant of the law. God's curse is
on them!"
50Then Nicodemus, the leader who had met with
Jesus earlier, spoke up. 51"Is it legal to convict a man
before he is given a hearing?" he asked.
52They replied, "Are you from Galilee, too? Search
the Scriptures and see for yourself—no prophet ever
comes* from Galilee!"

[The most ancient Greek manuscripts do not include John 7:53–8:11.]

53Then the meeting broke up, and everybody went
home.

Jn 7:52 Some manuscripts read *the prophet does not come.*

Jesus Forgives an Adulterous Woman

JOHN 8:1-11

Jesus returned to the Mount of Olives, 2but early the
next morning he was back again at the Temple. A
crowd soon gathered, and he sat down and taught
them. 3As he was speaking, the teachers of religious
law and the Pharisees brought a woman who had been
caught in the act of adultery. They put her in front of
the crowd.
4"Teacher," they said to Jesus, "this woman was
caught in the act of adultery. 5The law of Moses says
to stone her. What do you say?"
6They were trying to trap him into saying something
they could use against him, but Jesus stooped down
and wrote in the dust with his finger. 7They kept demanding an answer, so he stood up again and said,
"All right, but let the one who has never sinned throw

at least a few of them some of the time. But these Temple guards couldn't find one reason to arrest Jesus. And as they listened to Jesus to try to find evidence, they couldn't help hearing the wonderful words he said.

John 7:46-49 The Jewish leaders saw themselves as an elite group who alone had the truth. They resisted the truth about Christ because it wasn't theirs to begin with. It is easy to think that we have the truth and that those who disagree with us do not have any truth at all. But God's truth is available to everyone. Don't copy the Pharisees' self-centered and narrow attitude.

John 7:50-52 This passage offers additional insight into Nicodemus, the Pharisee who visited Jesus at night (John 3). Apparently Nicodemus had become a secret believer. Since most of the Pharisees hated Jesus and wanted to kill him, Nicodemus risked his reputation and high position even though he only spoke up indirectly for Jesus. His statement was bold, and the Pharisees immediately became suspicious. After Jesus' death, Nicodemus brought spices for his body (John 19:39). That is the last time he is mentioned in Scripture.

John 7:51 Nicodemus confronted the Pharisees with their failure to keep their own laws. The Pharisees were losing ground—the Temple guards came back impressed by Jesus (John 7:46), and one of the Pharisees' own, Nicodemus, was defending him. With their hypocritical motives being exposed and their prestige slowly eroding, they began to move to protect themselves. Pride would interfere with their ability to reason, and soon they would become obsessed with getting rid of Jesus just to save face. What was good and right no longer mattered.

John 8:3-6 The Jewish leaders had already disregarded the law by arresting the woman without the man. The law required that both parties to adultery be stoned (Lev 20:10; Deut 22:22). The leaders were using the woman as a trap so they could trick Jesus. If Jesus said the woman should not be stoned, they would accuse him of violating Moses' law. If he urged them to execute her, they would report him to the Romans, who did not permit the Jews to carry out their own executions (John 18:31).

John 8:7 This is a significant statement about judging others. Because Jesus upheld the legal penalty for adultery, stoning, he could not be accused of being against the law. But by saying that only a sinless person could throw the first stone, he highlighted the importance of compassion and forgiveness. When others are caught in sin, are you quick to pass judgment? To do so is to act as though you have never sinned. It is God's role to judge, not ours. Our role is to show forgiveness and compassion to a repentant sinner.

Early Manuscripts on the Woman Caught in Adultery

An early papyrus manuscript of the Gospel of John called P66 was found in Egypt in the 1950s. It was created in the middle of the second century by a careful, professional scribe. This early manuscript and a host of others do not include John 7:53–8:11, the story of the woman caught in adultery. The passage is found in later manuscripts (with some variations) and in different positions in the Gospels: here as John 7:53–8:11, though sometimes with asterisks; after John 21:25; after Luke 21:38; after Luke 24:53; and after John 7:36. If the passage wasn't in the original, that doesn't mean it didn't really happen. Jesus did many things that aren't recorded in the Gospels (John 21:25); it might have come from oral tradition.

Try reading John 7:52 and 8:12 (skipping 7:53–8:11) as a continuous narrative. John 8:12ff contains Jesus' rebuttal to the Pharisees, who had boldly told Nicodemus that the Scriptures make no mention of any prophet, much less the Christ, being raised in Galilee (John 7:52). Jesus made a declaration in which he implied that the Scriptures did speak of the Christ coming from Galilee. In John 8:12 he said, "I am the light of the world. If you follow me, you won't have to walk in darkness, because you will have the light that leads to life." This statement was drawn from Isaiah 9:1-2, which speaks about the Messiah coming to the Galilean Gentiles as a light to those who walk in darkness and live in a land of deep darkness; he came to give them the light that leads to life.

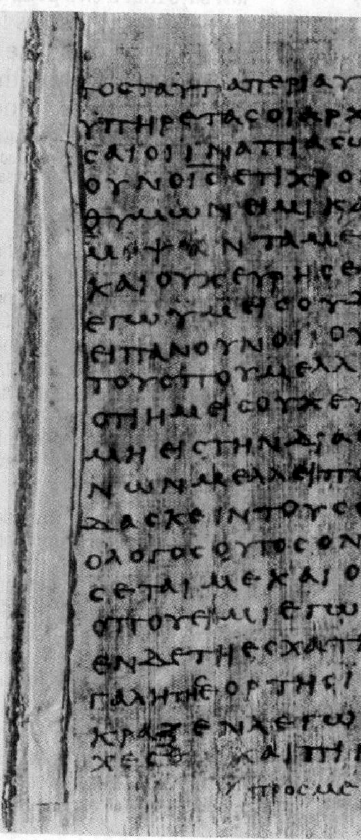

▶ **JOHN 8:1-11** ***(cont.)***

the first stone!" 8Then he stooped down again and
wrote in the dust.
9When the accusers heard this, they slipped away
one by one, beginning with the oldest, until only Jesus
was left in the middle of the crowd with the woman.
10Then Jesus stood up again and said to the woman,
"Where are your accusers? Didn't even one of them
condemn you?"
11"No, Lord," she said.
And Jesus said, "Neither do I. Go and sin no more."

Jesus Is the Light of the World

JOHN 8:12-20

Jesus spoke to the people once more and said, "I am
the light of the world. If you follow me, you won't have
to walk in darkness, because you will have the light
that leads to life."
13The Pharisees replied, "You are making those
claims about yourself! Such testimony is not valid."
14Jesus told them, "These claims are valid even
though I make them about myself. For I know where I
came from and where I am going, but you don't know
this about me. 15You judge me by human standards,
but I do not judge anyone. 16And if I did, my judgment
would be correct in every respect because I am not
alone. The Father* who sent me is with me. 17Your own
law says that if two people agree about something, their
witness is accepted as fact.* 18I am one witness, and
my Father who sent me is the other."
19"Where is your father?" they asked.
Jesus answered, "Since you don't know who I am,
you don't know who my Father is. If you knew me,
you would also know my Father." 20Jesus made these
statements while he was teaching in the section of
the Temple known as the Treasury. But he was not arrested, because his time* had not yet come.

Jesus Warns of Coming Judgment

JOHN 8:21-30

Later Jesus said to them again, "I am going away. You
will search for me but will die in your sin. You cannot
come where I am going."
22The people* asked, "Is he planning to commit suicide? What does he mean, 'You cannot come where I
am going'?"
23Jesus continued, "You are from below; I am from
above. You belong to this world; I do not. 24That is
why I said that you will die in your sins; for unless
you believe that I AM who I claim to be,* you will die
in your sins."
25"Who are you?" they demanded.
Jesus replied, "The one I have always claimed to be.*
26I have much to say about you and much to condemn,
but I won't. For I say only what I have heard from the
one who sent me, and he is completely truthful." 27But
they still didn't understand that he was talking about
his Father.
28So Jesus said, "When you have lifted up the Son
of Man on the cross, then you will understand that I
AM he.* I do nothing on my own but say only what the
Father taught me. 29And the one who sent me is with
me—he has not deserted me. For I always do what
pleases him." 30Then many who heard him say these
things believed in him.

Jn 8:16 Some manuscripts read *The One.* **Jn 8:17** See Deut 19:15. **Jn 8:20** Greek *his hour.* **Jn 8:22** Greek *Jewish people;* also in 8:31, 48, 52, 57. **Jn 8:24** Greek *unless you believe that I am.* See Exod 3:14. **Jn 8:25** Or *Why do I speak to you at all?* **Jn 8:28** Greek *When you have lifted up the Son of Man, then you will know that I am.* "Son of Man" is a title Jesus used for himself.

John 8:9 When Jesus said that only someone who had not sinned should throw the first stone, the leaders slipped quietly away, from oldest to youngest. Evidently the older men were more aware of their sins than the younger. Age and experience often temper youthful self-righteousness. But whatever your age, take an honest look at your life. Recognize your sinful nature, and look for ways to help others rather than hurt them.

John 8:11 Jesus didn't condemn the woman accused of adultery, but neither did he ignore or condone her sin. He told her to leave her life of sin. Jesus stands ready to forgive any sin in your life, but confession and repentance mean a change of heart. With God's help we can accept Christ's forgiveness and stop our wrongdoing.

John 8:12 Jesus was speaking in the Treasury—the part of the Temple where the offerings were put (John 8:20) and where candles burned to symbolize the pillar of fire that led the people of Israel through the wilderness (Exod 13:21-22). The pillar of fire represented God's presence, protection, and guidance. In this context, Jesus called himself "the light of the world" because he is God's presence, protection, and guidance. See also the note on John 1:4-5, p. 1271. Is Jesus the light of your world?

John 8:12 What does it mean to follow Christ? As a soldier follows his captain, so we should follow Christ, our commander. As a slave follows his master, so we should follow Christ, our Lord. As we follow the advice of a trusted counselor, so we should follow Jesus' commands to us in Scripture. As we follow the laws of our nation, so we should follow the laws of the Kingdom of Heaven.

John 8:13-14 The Pharisees thought Jesus was either a lunatic or a liar. Jesus provided them with a third alternative: He was telling the truth. Because most of the Pharisees refused to consider the third alternative, they never recognized him as Messiah and Lord. If you are seeking to know who Jesus is, do not close any door before looking through it honestly. Only with an open mind will you know the truth that he is Messiah and Lord.

John 8:13-18 The Pharisees argued that Jesus' claim was legally invalid because he had no other witnesses. Jesus responded that his confirming witness was God himself. Jesus and the Father made two witnesses, the number required by the law (Deut 19:15).

John 8:20 The Temple treasury was located in the Court of the Women. Thirteen collection boxes were set up in this area to receive money offerings. Seven of the boxes were for the Temple tax; the other six were for freewill offerings. On another occasion, a widow placed her money in one of these boxes, and Jesus taught a profound lesson from her action (Luke 21:1-4).

John 8:24 People will die in their sins if they reject Christ because they are rejecting the only way to be rescued from sin. Sadly, many are so taken up with the values of this world that they are blind to the priceless gift Christ offers. Where are you looking? Don't focus on this world's values and miss what is most valuable—eternal life with God.

John 8:32 Jesus himself is the truth that sets us free (John 8:36). He is the source of

Jesus Speaks about God's True Children

JOHN 8:31-47

Jesus said to the people who believed in him, "You are truly my disciples if you remain faithful to my teachings. 32And you will know the truth, and the truth will set you free."

33"But we are descendants of Abraham," they said. "We have never been slaves to anyone. What do you mean, 'You will be set free'?"

34Jesus replied, "I tell you the truth, everyone who sins is a slave of sin. 35A slave is not a permanent member of the family, but a son is part of the family forever. 36So if the Son sets you free, you are truly free. 37Yes, I realize that you are descendants of Abraham. And yet some of you are trying to kill me because there's no room in your hearts for my message. 38I am telling you what I saw when I was with my Father. But you are following the advice of your father."

39"Our father is Abraham!" they declared.

"No," Jesus replied, "for if you were really the children of Abraham, you would follow his example.* 40Instead, you are trying to kill me because I told you the truth, which I heard from God. Abraham never did such a thing. 41No, you are imitating your real father."

They replied, "We aren't illegitimate children! God himself is our true Father."

42Jesus told them, "If God were your Father, you would love me, because I have come to you from God. I am not here on my own, but he sent me. 43Why can't you understand what I am saying? It's because you can't even hear me! 44For you are the children of your father the devil, and you love to do the evil things he does. He was a murderer from the beginning. He has always hated the truth, because there is no truth in him. When he lies, it is consistent with his character; for he is a liar and the father of lies. 45So when I tell the truth, you just naturally don't believe me! 46Which of you can truthfully accuse me of sin? And since I am telling you the truth, why don't you believe me? 47Anyone who belongs to God listens gladly to the words of God. But you don't listen because you don't belong to God."

Jesus States He Is Eternal

JOHN 8:48-59

The people retorted, "You Samaritan devil! Didn't we say all along that you were possessed by a demon?"

49"No," Jesus said, "I have no demon in me. For I honor my Father—and you dishonor me. 50And though I have no wish to glorify myself, God is going to glorify me. He is the true judge. 51I tell you the truth, anyone who obeys my teaching will never die!"

52The people said, "Now we know you are possessed by a demon. Even Abraham and the prophets died, but you say, 'Anyone who obeys my teaching will never die!' 53Are you greater than our father Abraham? He died, and so did the prophets. Who do you think you are?"

54Jesus answered, "If I want glory for myself, it doesn't count. But it is my Father who will glorify me. You say, 'He is our God,*' 55but you don't even know him. I know him. If I said otherwise, I would be as great a liar as you! But I do know him and obey him. 56Your father Abraham rejoiced as he looked forward to my coming. He saw it and was glad."

57The people said, "You aren't even fifty years old. How can you say you have seen Abraham?*"

Jn 8:39 Some manuscripts read *if you are really the children of Abraham, follow his example.* **Jn 8:54** Some manuscripts read *your God.* **Jn 8:57** Some manuscripts read *How can you say Abraham has seen you?*

---

truth, the perfect standard of what is right. He frees us from continued slavery to sin, from self-deception, and from deception by Satan. He shows us clearly the way to eternal life with God. Thus, Jesus does not give us freedom to do what we want, but freedom to follow God. As we seek to serve God, Jesus' perfect truth frees us to be all that God meant us to be.

John 8:34-35 Sin has a way of enslaving us, controlling us, dominating us, and dictating our actions. Jesus can free you from this slavery that keeps you from becoming the person God created you to be. If sin is restraining, mastering, or enslaving you, Jesus can break its power over your life.

John 8:41 Jesus made a distinction between illegitimate children and true children. The religious leaders were descendants of Abraham (founder of the Jewish nation) and therefore claimed to be children of God. But their actions showed them to be true children of Satan, for they lived under Satan's guidance. True children of Abraham (faithful followers of God) would not act as they did. Your church membership and family connections will not make you a true child of God. Your true father is the one you imitate and obey.

John 8:43 The religious leaders were unable to understand because they refused to listen. Satan used their stubbornness, pride, and prejudices to keep them from believing in Jesus.

John 8:44-45 The attitudes and actions of these leaders clearly identified them as followers of Satan. They may not have been conscious of this, but their hatred of truth, their lies, and their murderous intentions indicated how much control the devil had over them. They were his tools in carrying out his plans; they spoke the very same language of lies. Satan still uses people in his attempt to obstruct God's work (Gen 4:8; Rom 5:12; 1 Jn 3:12).

John 8:46-47 In a number of places Jesus intentionally challenged his listeners to test him. He welcomed those who wanted to question his claims and character as long as they were willing to follow through on what they discovered. Jesus' challenge exposes the two most frequent reasons why people won't believe him: They never accept his challenge to test him, or they test him but are not willing to believe what they discover. Have you made either of those mistakes?

John 8:51 When Jesus said those who obey won't die, he was talking about spiritual death, not physical death. But even physical death will eventually be overcome. Those who follow Christ will be raised to live eternally with him.

John 8:56 God told Abraham, the father of the Jewish nation, that through him all nations would be blessed (Gen 12:1-7; 15:1-21). Abraham had been able to see this through the eyes of faith. Jesus, a descendant of Abraham, blessed all people through his death, resurrection, and offer of salvation.

▸ **JOHN 8:48-59 *(cont.)***

58Jesus answered, "I tell you the truth, before Abraham was even born, I AM!*" 59At that point they picked up stones to throw at him. But Jesus was hidden from them and left the Temple.

Jesus Sends Out Seventy-Two Messengers

LUKE 10:1-16

The Lord now chose seventy-two* other disciples and sent them ahead in pairs to all the towns and places he planned to visit. 2These were his instructions to them: "The harvest is great, but the workers are few. So pray to the Lord who is in charge of the harvest; ask him to send more workers into his fields. 3Now go, and remember that I am sending you out as lambs among wolves. 4Don't take any money with you, nor a traveler's bag, nor an extra pair of sandals. And don't stop to greet anyone on the road.

5"Whenever you enter someone's home, first say, 'May God's peace be on this house.' 6If those who live there are peaceful, the blessing will stand; if they are not, the blessing will return to you. 7Don't move around from home to home. Stay in one place, eating and drinking what they provide. Don't hesitate to accept hospitality, because those who work deserve their pay.

8"If you enter a town and it welcomes you, eat whatever is set before you. 9Heal the sick, and tell them, 'The Kingdom of God is near you now.' 10But if a town refuses to welcome you, go out into its streets and say, 11'We wipe even the dust of your town from our feet to show that we have abandoned you to your fate. And know this—the Kingdom of God is near!' 12I assure you, even wicked Sodom will be better off than such a town on judgment day.

13"What sorrow awaits you, Korazin and Bethsaida! For if the miracles I did in you had been done in wicked Tyre and Sidon, their people would have repented of their sins long ago, clothing themselves in burlap and throwing ashes on their heads to show their remorse. 14Yes, Tyre and Sidon will be better off on judgment day than you. 15And you people of Capernaum, will you be honored in heaven? No, you will go down to the place of the dead.*"

16Then he said to the disciples, "Anyone who accepts your message is also accepting me. And anyone who rejects you is rejecting me. And anyone who rejects me is rejecting God, who sent me."

The Seventy-Two Messengers Return

LUKE 10:17-24

When the seventy-two disciples returned, they joyfully reported to him, "Lord, even the demons obey us when we use your name!"

Jn 8:58 Or *before Abraham was even born, I have always been alive;* Greek reads *before Abraham was, I am.* See Exod 3:14. **Lk 10:1** Some manuscripts read *seventy;* also in 10:17. **Lk 10:15** Greek *to Hades.*

John 8:58 This is one of the most powerful statements uttered by Jesus. Not only did Jesus say that he existed before Abraham, undeniably proclaiming his divinity, but he also applied God's holy name (I AM—Exod 3:14) to himself. This claim demands a response. It cannot be ignored. The Jewish leaders tried to stone Jesus for blasphemy because he claimed equality with God. But Jesus is God. How have you responded to Jesus, the Son of God?

John 8:59 In accordance with the law given in Leviticus 24:16, the religious leaders were ready to stone Jesus for claiming to be God. They well understood what Jesus was claiming, and because they didn't believe he was God, they charged him with blasphemy. It is ironic that they were really the blasphemers, cursing and attacking the very God they claimed to serve!

Luke 10:1-2 Far more than 12 people had been following Jesus. Here Jesus designated a group of 72 to prepare a number of towns for his later visit. These disciples were not unique in their qualifications. They were not better educated, more capable, or of higher status than Jesus' other followers. What prepared them for this mission was that they had been equipped with Jesus' power and a vision to reach all the people. It is important to dedicate our skills to God's Kingdom, but we must also be equipped with his power and have a clear vision of what he wants us to do.

Luke 10:2 Christian service has no unemployment. God has work enough for everyone. Jesus encouraged the disciples not just to do the work but also to pray for workers. Part of every Christian's job is to pray for new workers and to help newcomers learn the ropes. Whatever your role in God's work, pray today for more helpers. Some people, as soon as they understand the gospel, want to go convert others immediately. Jesus gave a different approach: Begin by mobilizing people to pray. And before praying for unsaved people, pray that other concerned disciples will join you in reaching out to them. God will lead you to an important responsibility, but prayer comes first.

Luke 10:3 Jesus said he was sending his disciples out "as lambs among wolves." They would have to be careful because they would surely meet with opposition. We, too, are sent into the world like lambs among wolves. Be alert, and remember to face your enemies not with aggression but with love and gentleness.

Luke 10:7 Jesus' direction to stay in one house avoided certain problems. Shifting from house to house could offend the families who first took them in. Some families might begin to compete for the disciples' presence, and some might think they weren't good enough to hear their message. If the disciples appeared not to appreciate the hospitality offered them, the town might not accept Jesus when he followed them there. In addition, by staying in one place, the disciples would not have to worry continually about getting good accommodations. They could settle down and focus on their appointed task. (See also Luke 9:4.)

Luke 10:7 Jesus told his disciples to accept hospitality graciously because their work entitled them to it. Ministers of the Good News deserve to be supported, and our responsibility is to make sure they have what they need. There are several ways to encourage those who serve God in his church: See that they have an adequate salary; see that they are supported emotionally—plan special times to express appreciation for something they have done; lift their spirits with special surprises from time to time. Our ministers deserve to know we are giving to them cheerfully and generously.

Luke 10:8-9 Jesus gave two rules for the disciples to follow as they traveled. They were to eat what was set before them—that is, they were to accept hospitality without being picky—and they were to heal the sick. Because of the healings, people would be willing to listen to the Good News.

Luke 10:12 Sodom was an evil city that God had destroyed because of its great sinfulness (Gen 19). The city's name is often used to symbolize wickedness and immorality. Sodom will suffer on judgment day, but cities who saw the Messiah and rejected him will suffer even more.

Luke 10:13 Korazin was a city near the Sea of Galilee, probably about two miles north

18"Yes," he told them, "I saw Satan fall from heaven
like lightning! 19Look, I have given you authority over
all the power of the enemy, and you can walk among
snakes and scorpions and crush them. Nothing will
injure you. 20But don't rejoice because evil spirits
obey you; rejoice because your names are registered
in heaven."
21At that same time Jesus was filled with the joy of
the Holy Spirit, and he said, "O Father, Lord of heaven
and earth, thank you for hiding these things from
those who think themselves wise and clever, and for
revealing them to the childlike. Yes, Father, it pleased
you to do it this way.
22"My Father has entrusted everything to me. No
one truly knows the Son except the Father, and no
one truly knows the Father except the Son and those
to whom the Son chooses to reveal him."
23Then when they were alone, he turned to the disciples and said, "Blessed are the eyes that see what
you have seen. 24I tell you, many prophets and kings
longed to see what you see, but they didn't see it. And
they longed to hear what you hear, but they didn't
hear it."

Jesus Tells the Parable of the Good Samaritan

LUKE 10:25-37

One day an expert in religious law stood up to test Jesus by asking him this question: "Teacher, what should I do to inherit eternal life?"

of Capernaum. Tyre and Sidon were cities destroyed by God as punishment for their wickedness (see Ezek 26–28).

Luke 10:15 Capernaum was Jesus' base for his Galilean ministry. The city was located at an important crossroads used by traders and the Roman army, so a message proclaimed in Capernaum was likely to go far. Many people of Capernaum did not understand Jesus' miracles or believe his teaching, however, and the city was included among those who would be judged for rejecting him.

Luke 10:17-20 The disciples had seen tremendous results as they ministered in Jesus' name and with his authority. They were elated by the victories they had witnessed, and Jesus shared their enthusiasm. He helped them get their priorities right, however, by reminding them of their most important victory—that their names were registered in heaven. This honor was more important than any of their accomplishments. As we see God's wonders at work in and through us, we should not lose sight of the greatest wonder of all—our heavenly citizenship.

Luke 10:18-19 Jesus may have been looking ahead to his victory over Satan at the cross. John 12:31-32 indicates that Satan would be judged and driven out at the time of Jesus' death. On the other hand, Jesus may have been warning his disciples against pride. Perhaps he was referring to Isaiah 14:12-17, which begins, "How you are fallen from heaven, O shining star, son of the morning!" Some interpreters identify this verse with Satan and explain that Satan's pride led to all the evil we see on earth today. To Jesus' disciples, who were thrilled with their power over evil spirits ("snakes and scorpions"), he may have been giving this stern warning: "Yours is the kind of pride that led to Satan's downfall. Be careful!"

Luke 10:21 Jesus thanked God that spiritual truth was for everyone and not just for the elite. Many of life's rewards seem to go to the intelligent, the rich, the good looking, or the powerful, but the Kingdom of God is equally available to all, regardless of position or abilities. We come to Jesus not through strength

The Good Samaritan, by Vincent Van Gogh.

or brains but through childlike trust. Jesus is not opposed to engaging in scholarly pursuits; he is opposed to spiritual pride (being wise in one's own eyes). Join Jesus in thanking God that we all have equal access to him. Trust in God's grace, not in your personal qualifications, for your citizenship in the Kingdom.

Luke 10:22 Christ's mission was to reveal God the Father to people. His words brought difficult ideas down to earth. He explained God's love through stories, teachings, and most of all, his life. By examining Jesus' actions, principles, and attitudes, we can understand God more clearly.

Luke 10:23-24 Old Testament men of God, such as David and Isaiah, made many God-inspired predictions that Jesus fulfilled. As Peter later wrote, these prophets wondered what their words meant and when they would be fulfilled (1 Pet 1:10-13). The disciples had the fantastic opportunity of being eyewitnesses to the fulfillment of those prophecies. For many months, however, they took Jesus for granted, not really listening to him or obeying him. We also have a privileged position: the legacy of 2,000 years of church history, the availability of the Bible in hundreds of languages and translations, and access to many excellent pastors and speakers. Yet often we take these for granted. Remember, with privilege comes responsibility. Because we are privileged to know so much about Christ, we must be careful to follow him.

▶ **LUKE 10:25-37 *(cont.)***
26Jesus replied, "What does the law of Moses say?
How do you read it?"
27The man answered, "'You must love the LORD your God with all your heart, all your soul, all your strength, and all your mind.' And, 'Love your neighbor as yourself.'"*
28"Right!" Jesus told him. "Do this and you will live!"
29The man wanted to justify his actions, so he asked Jesus, "And who is my neighbor?"
30Jesus replied with a story: "A Jewish man was traveling from Jerusalem down to Jericho, and he was attacked by bandits. They stripped him of his clothes, beat him up, and left him half dead beside the road.
31"By chance a priest came along. But when he saw the man lying there, he crossed to the other side of the
road and passed him by. 32A Temple assistant* walked over and looked at him lying there, but he also passed by on the other side.
33"Then a despised Samaritan came along, and when he saw the man, he felt compassion for him.
34Going over to him, the Samaritan soothed his wounds with olive oil and wine and bandaged them. Then he put the man on his own donkey and took him to an inn, where he took care of him. 35The next
day he handed the innkeeper two silver coins,* telling him, 'Take care of this man. If his bill runs higher than this, I'll pay you the next time I'm here.'
36"Now which of these three would you say was a neighbor to the man who was attacked by bandits?" Jesus asked.
37The man replied, "The one who showed him mercy."

Then Jesus said, "Yes, now go and do the same."

Lk 10:27 Deut 6:5; Lev 19:18. **Lk 10:32** Greek *A Levite.* **Lk 10:35** Greek *two denarii.* A denarius was equivalent to a laborer's full day's wage.

A COLLECTION OF ATTITUDES ABOUT OTHERS' NEEDS

Confronting the needs of others brings out various attitudes in us. Jesus used the story of the good but despised Samaritan to make clear what attitude was acceptable to him. If we are honest, we often will find ourselves in the place of the expert in religious law, needing to learn again who our neighbor is. Note these different attitudes toward the wounded man.

To the expert in religious law	the wounded man was a subject to discuss.
To the bandits	the wounded man was someone to use and exploit.
To the religious men	the wounded man was a problem to be avoided.
To the innkeeper	the wounded man was a customer to serve for a fee.
To the Samaritan	the wounded man was a human being worth being cared for and loved.
To Jesus	all of them and all of us were worth dying for.

Luke 10:27 This expert in religious law was quoting Deuteronomy 6:5 and Leviticus 19:18. He correctly understood that the law demanded total devotion to God and love for one's neighbor. Jesus talked more about these laws elsewhere (see Matt 19:16-22 and Mark 10:17-22).

Luke 10:27-37 The legal expert viewed the wounded man as a topic for discussion. To the bandits, he was an object to exploit; to the priest, a problem to avoid; and to the Temple assistant, an object of curiosity. Only the Samaritan treated him as a person to love. From the illustration we learn three principles about loving our neighbor: (1) Lack of love is often easy to justify, even though it is never right; (2) our neighbor is anyone of any race, creed, or social background who is in need; (3) love means acting to meet the person's need. Wherever you live, needy people are close by. There is no good reason for refusing to help.

Luke 10:29 We all have neighbors, but we live in a time when we can go weeks or months without ever crossing paths with them. At the same time, we communicate almost every day with people who live miles away, sometimes hundreds or even thousands of miles. We can begin to wonder the same thing—"who's my neighbor?" Is it everyone? Is it no one?

The story of the Good Samaritan happens on a road between two cities. People are coming and going. The beaten man isn't close to anyone's home; he's nobody's neighbor. Everyone has somewhere else to be. Yet, it's out there in the middle of nowhere that the man finds his neighbor. Jesus' story shows us that being neighbors is not a matter of proximity or familiarity. The neighborhood is anywhere mercy is shown. Neighbors don't have to live nearby or be people we know. Strangers can be our neighbors.

Luke 10:33 A deep hatred existed between Jews and Samaritans. The Jews saw themselves as pure descendants of Abraham, while the Samaritans were a mixed race produced when Jews from the northern kingdom intermarried with other peoples after Israel's exile (see also the note on Luke 9:53, p. 1386). To this legal expert, the person least likely to act correctly would be the Samaritan. In fact, he did not even say the word *Samaritan* in answer to Jesus' question. This expert's attitude betrayed his lack of the very thing that he had earlier said the law commanded—love.

Luke 10:37 For the people listening to Jesus, a neighbor would have been identified as a fellow Israelite. But for Jesus, the neighbor in this story was a Samaritan, a hated enemy of the Israelites.

It's easy to put up fences around our neighborhoods. This can make for a lot of outsiders. People who don't go to our church.

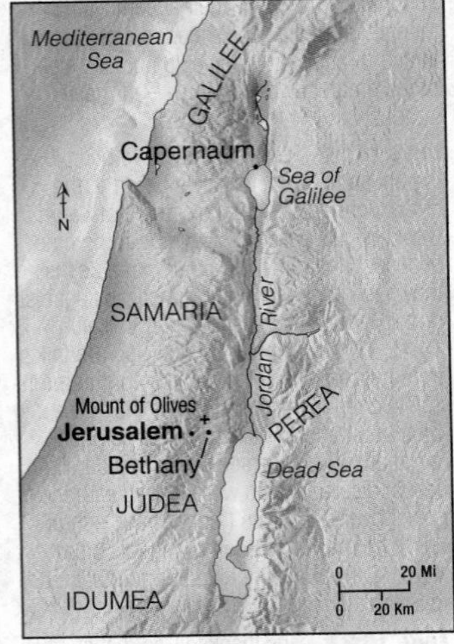

JESUS VISITS MARY AND MARTHA
Jesus had been in Jerusalem for the Festival of Shelters (John 7:2ff). He then visited his friends Mary and Martha in Bethany, a tiny village on the eastern slope of the Mount of Olives.

Jesus Visits Martha and Mary

LUKE 10:38-42

As Jesus and the disciples continued on their way to Jerusalem, they came to a certain village where a woman named Martha welcomed him into her home.
39Her sister, Mary, sat at the Lord's feet, listening to what he taught. 40But Martha was distracted by the big dinner she was preparing. She came to Jesus and said, "Lord, doesn't it seem unfair to you that my sister just sits here while I do all the work? Tell her to come and help me."

41But the Lord said to her, "My dear Martha, you are worried and upset over all these details! 42There is only one thing worth being concerned about. Mary has discovered it, and it will not be taken away from her."

Jesus Teaches His Disciples about Prayer

LUKE 11:1-13

Once Jesus was in a certain place praying. As he finished, one of his disciples came to him and said, "Lord, teach us to pray, just as John taught his disciples."
2Jesus said, "This is how you should pray:*

"Father, may your name be kept holy.
May your Kingdom come soon.
3 Give us each day the food we need,*
4 and forgive us our sins,
as we forgive those who sin against us.
And don't let us yield to temptation.*"

5Then, teaching them more about prayer, he used this story: "Suppose you went to a friend's house at

Lk 11:2 Some manuscripts add additional phrases from the Lord's Prayer as it reads in Matt 6:9-13. **Lk 11:3** Or *Give us each day our food for the day;* or *Give us each day our food for tomorrow.* **Lk 11:4** Or *And keep us from being tested.*

People who make choices we disagree with. People who don't look or act like we do. But Jesus tears down those fences and points to an "outsider" who shows mercy. Jesus says mercy driven by love is the centerpiece of the neighborhood. Sometimes the edges get blurry, but Jesus gave us a clear focal point to center our lives on.

Luke 10:38-42 Mary and Martha both loved Jesus. On this occasion they were both serving him. But Martha thought Mary's style of serving was inferior to hers. She didn't realize that in her desire to serve, she was actually neglecting her guest. Are you so busy doing things for Jesus that you're not spending any time with him? Don't let your service become self-serving. Jesus did not blame Martha for being concerned about household chores. He was only asking her to set priorities. Service to Christ can degenerate into mere busywork that is totally devoid of devotion to God.

Luke 11:2-13 Notice the order in this prayer. First, Jesus praised God; then he made his requests. Praising God first puts us in the right frame of mind to tell him about our needs. Too often our prayers are more like shopping lists than conversations. These verses focus on three aspects of prayer: its content (Luke 11:2-4), our persistence (Luke 11:5-10), and God's faithfulness (Luke 11:11-13).

Luke 11:3 God's provision is daily, not all at once. We cannot store it up and then cut off communication with God. And we dare not be self-satisfied. If you are running low on strength, ask yourself, How long have I been away from the Source?

Luke 11:4 When Jesus taught his disciples to pray, he made forgiveness the cornerstone of their relationship with God. God has forgiven our sins; we must now forgive those who have wronged us. To remain unforgiving shows we have not understood that we ourselves deeply need to be forgiven. Think of some people who have wronged you. Have you forgiven them? How will God deal with you if he treats you as you treat others?

MARTHA

Many older brothers and sisters have an irritating tendency to take charge, a habit developed while growing up. We can easily see this pattern in Martha, the older sister of Mary and Lazarus. She was used to being in control. • The fact that Martha, Mary, and Lazarus are remembered for their hospitality takes on added significance when we note that hospitality was a social requirement in their culture. It was considered shameful to turn anyone away from your door. Apparently Martha's family met this requirement very well. • Martha worried about details. She wished to please, to serve, to do the right thing. Perhaps as the oldest she feared shame if her home did not measure up to expectations. She tried to do everything she could to make sure that wouldn't happen. As a result, she found it hard to relax and enjoy her guests and even harder to accept Mary's lack of cooperation in all the preparations. But Jesus provided a gentle corrective to Martha's priorities as a hostess. The personal attention she gave her guests should be more important than the comforts she tried to provide for them. • Later, following her brother Lazarus's death, Martha rushed out to meet Jesus and expressed her inner conflict of disappointment and hope at his late arrival. Jesus pointed out that her hope was too limited. He was not only Lord over death; he was the resurrection and the life! Moments later, Martha again spoke without thinking, pointing out that four-day-old corpses are well on their way to decomposition. Her awareness of details sometimes kept her from seeing the whole picture, but Jesus was consistently patient with her. • In our last picture of Martha, she is once again serving a meal to Jesus and his disciples. She has not stopped serving. But the Bible records her silence this time. She has begun to learn what her younger sister already knew—that worship begins with silence and listening.

Strengths and accomplishments	• Known as a hospitable homemaker • Believed in Jesus with growing faith • Had a strong desire to do everything exactly right
Weaknesses and mistakes	• Expected others to agree with her priorities • Was overly concerned with details • Limited Jesus' power to this life
Lessons from her life	• Getting caught up in details can make us forget the main reasons for our actions • There is a proper time to listen to Jesus and a proper time to work for him
Vital statistics	• Where: Bethany • Relatives: Sister: Mary. Brother: Lazarus.
Key verse	"But Martha was distracted by the big dinner she was preparing. She came to Jesus and said, 'Lord, doesn't it seem unfair to you that my sister just sits here while I do all the work? Tell her to come and help me'" (Luke 10:40).

Martha's story is told in Luke 10:38-42 and John 11:17-45.

▸ **LUKE 11:1-13 *(cont.)***

midnight, wanting to borrow three loaves of bread. You say to him, [6]'A friend of mine has just arrived for a visit, and I have nothing for him to eat.' [7]And suppose he calls out from his bedroom, 'Don't bother me. The door is locked for the night, and my family and I are all in bed. I can't help you.' [8]But I tell you this—though he won't do it for friendship's sake, if you keep knocking long enough, he will get up and give you whatever you need because of your shameless persistence.*

[9]"And so I tell you, keep on asking, and you will receive what you ask for. Keep on seeking, and you will find. Keep on knocking, and the door will be opened to you. [10]For everyone who asks, receives. Everyone who seeks, finds. And to everyone who knocks, the door will be opened.

[11]"You fathers—if your children ask* for a fish, do you give them a snake instead? [12]Or if they ask for an egg, do you give them a scorpion? Of course not! [13]So if you sinful people know how to give good gifts to your children, how much more will your heavenly Father give the Holy Spirit to those who ask him."

Jesus Teaches about the Light Within

LUKE 11:33-36

"No one lights a lamp and then hides it or puts it under a basket.* Instead, a lamp is placed on a stand, where its light can be seen by all who enter the house.

[34]"Your eye is a lamp that provides light for your body. When your eye is good, your whole body is filled with light. But when it is bad, your body is filled with darkness. [35]Make sure that the light you think you have is not actually darkness. [36]If you are filled with light, with no dark corners, then your whole life will be radiant, as though a floodlight were filling you with light."

Jesus Criticizes the Religious Leaders

LUKE 11:37-54

As Jesus was speaking, one of the Pharisees invited him home for a meal. So he went in and took his place at the table.* [38]His host was amazed to see that he sat down to eat without first performing the hand-washing ceremony required by Jewish custom. [39]Then the Lord said to him, "You Pharisees are so careful to clean the outside of the cup and the dish, but inside you are filthy—full of greed and wickedness! [40]Fools! Didn't God make the inside as well as the outside? [41]So clean the inside by giving gifts to the poor, and you will be clean all over.

[42]"What sorrow awaits you Pharisees! For you are careful to tithe even the tiniest income from your herb gardens,* but you ignore justice and the love of God. You should tithe, yes, but do not neglect the more important things.

[43]"What sorrow awaits you Pharisees! For you love to sit in the seats of honor in the synagogues and receive respectful greetings as you walk in the marketplaces. [44]Yes, what sorrow awaits you! For you are like hidden graves in a field. People walk over them without knowing the corruption they are stepping on."

[45]"Teacher," said an expert in religious law, "you have insulted us, too, in what you just said."

[46]"Yes," said Jesus, "what sorrow also awaits you experts in religious law! For you crush people with

Lk 11:8 Or *in order to avoid shame,* or *so his reputation won't be damaged.* **Lk 11:11** Some manuscripts add *for bread, do you give them a stone? Or [if they ask].* **Lk 11:33** Some manuscripts do not include *or puts it under a basket.* **Lk 11:37** Or *and reclined.* **Lk 11:42** Greek *tithe the mint, the rue, and every herb.*

Luke 11:8 Persistence, or boldness, in prayer overcomes our insensitivity, not God's. To practice persistence does more to change our heart and mind than his, and it helps us understand and express the intensity of our need. Persistence in prayer helps us recognize God's work.

Luke 11:13 Even though good fathers make mistakes, they treat their children well. How much better our perfect heavenly Father treats his children! The most important gift he could ever give us is the Holy Spirit (Acts 2:1-4), whom he promised to give all believers after his death, resurrection, and return to heaven (John 15:26).

Luke 11:33-36 The lamp is Christ; the eye represents spiritual understanding and insight. Evil desires make the eye less sensitive and blot out the light of Christ's presence. If you have a hard time seeing God at work in the world and in your life, check your vision. Are any sinful desires blinding you to Christ?

Luke 11:37-39 The hand-washing ceremony was done not for health reasons but as a symbol of washing away any contamination from touching anything unclean. Not only did the Pharisees make a public show of their washing, but they also commanded everyone else to follow a practice originally intended only for the priests.

Luke 11:41 The Pharisees loved to think of themselves as "clean," but their stinginess toward God and the poor proved that they were not as clean as they thought. How do you use the resources God has entrusted to you? Are you generous in meeting the needs around you? Your generosity reveals much about the purity of your heart.

Luke 11:42 It is easy to rationalize not helping others because we have already given to the church, but a person who follows Jesus should share with needy neighbors as well. While tithing is important to the life of the church, our compassion must not stop there. Where we can help, we should help.

Luke 11:42-52 Jesus criticized the Pharisees and the experts in religious law harshly: they washed their outsides but not their insides; they remembered to give a tenth of even their garden herbs but neglected justice; they loved praise and attention; they loaded people down with burdensome religious demands; they would not accept the truth about Jesus; and they prevented others from believing the truth. They went wrong by focusing on outward appearances and ignoring the inner condition of their hearts. People do the same when their service comes from a desire to be seen rather than from a pure heart that is full of love for others. People may sometimes be fooled, but God isn't. Don't be a Christian on the outside only. Bring your inner life under God's control and your outer life will naturally reflect him.

Luke 11:44 The Old Testament laws said a person who touched a grave was unclean (Num 19:16). Jesus accused the Pharisees of making others unclean by their spiritual rottenness. Like unmarked graves hidden in a field, the Pharisees corrupted everyone who came in contact with them.

Luke 11:46 These "religious demands" were the details the Pharisees had added to God's law. To the commandment "Remember to observe the Sabbath day by keeping it holy" (Exod 20:8), for example, they had added instructions regarding how far a person could walk on the Sabbath, which

unbearable religious demands, and you never lift a finger to ease the burden. 47What sorrow awaits you! For you build monuments for the prophets your own ancestors killed long ago. 48But in fact, you stand as witnesses who agree with what your ancestors did. They killed the prophets, and you join in their crime by building the monuments! 49This is what God in his wisdom said about you:* 'I will send prophets and apostles to them, but they will kill some and persecute the others.'

50"As a result, this generation will be held responsible for the murder of all God's prophets from the creation of the world—51from the murder of Abel to the murder of Zechariah, who was killed between the altar and the sanctuary. Yes, it will certainly be charged against this generation.

52"What sorrow awaits you experts in religious law! For you remove the key to knowledge from the people. You don't enter the Kingdom yourselves, and you prevent others from entering."

53As Jesus was leaving, the teachers of religious law and the Pharisees became hostile and tried to provoke him with many questions. 54They wanted to trap him into saying something they could use against him.

Jesus Speaks against Hypocrisy

LUKE 12:1-12

Meanwhile, the crowds grew until thousands were milling about and stepping on each other. Jesus turned first to his disciples and warned them, "Beware of the yeast of the Pharisees—their hypocrisy. 2The time is coming when everything that is covered up will be revealed, and all that is secret will be made known to all. 3Whatever you have said in the dark will be heard in the light, and what you have whispered behind closed doors will be shouted from the housetops for all to hear!

4"Dear friends, don't be afraid of those who want to kill your body; they cannot do any more to you after that. 5But I'll tell you whom to fear. Fear God, who has the power to kill you and then throw you into hell.* Yes, he's the one to fear.

6"What is the price of five sparrows—two copper coins*? Yet God does not forget a single one of them. 7And the very hairs on your head are all numbered. So don't be afraid; you are more valuable to God than a whole flock of sparrows.

8"I tell you the truth, everyone who acknowledges me publicly here on earth, the Son of Man* will also

Lk 11:49 Greek *Therefore, the wisdom of God said.* **Lk 12:5** Greek *Gehenna.* **Lk 12:6** Greek *two assaria* [Roman coins equal to 1/16 of a denarius]. **Lk 12:8** "Son of Man" is a title Jesus used for himself.

kinds of knots could be tied, and how much weight could be carried. Healing a person was considered unlawful work on the Sabbath although rescuing a trapped animal was permitted (Luke 14:5). No wonder Jesus condemned their additions to the law.

Luke 11:49 God's prophets have been persecuted and murdered throughout history. But this generation was rejecting more than a human prophet—they were rejecting God himself. This quotation is not from the Old Testament. Jesus, the greatest prophet of all, was directly giving them God's message.

Luke 11:51 Abel's death is recorded in Genesis 4:8. For more about him, see his Profile on p. 14. Zechariah's death is recorded in 2 Chronicles 24:20-22 (the Hebrew canon is arranged differently from our English Bibles, and 2 Chronicles is the last book in the Hebrew arrangement). Why would all these sins come upon this particular generation? Because they were rejecting the Messiah himself, the one to whom all their history and prophecy were pointing.

Luke 11:52 How did the legal experts remove the "key to knowledge"? Through their erroneous interpretations of Scripture and their added man-made rules, they made God's truth hard to understand and practice. On top of that, these men were bad examples, arguing their way out of the demanding rules they placed on others. Caught up in a religion of their own making, they could no longer lead the people to God. They had closed the door of God's love to the people and had thrown away the key.

Luke 11:53-54 The teachers of religious law and the Pharisees hoped to arrest Jesus for blasphemy, heresy, and lawbreaking. They were enraged by Jesus' words about them, but they couldn't arrest him for merely speaking words. They had to find a legal way to get rid of Jesus.

Luke 12:1-2 As Jesus watched the huge crowds waiting to hear him, he warned his disciples against hypocrisy—trying to appear holy when one's heart is far from God. The Pharisees could not keep their attitudes hidden forever. Their selfishness would act like yeast, and soon they would expose themselves for what they really were—power-hungry impostors, not devoted religious leaders. It is easy to be angry at the blatant hypocrisy of the Pharisees, but each of us must resist the temptation to settle for the appearance of respectability when our hearts are far from God.

Luke 12:1-2 What are the signs of hypocrisy? (1) Hypocrisy is knowing the truth but not obeying it. People can say they follow Jesus but not be obedient to his Word. (2) Hypocrisy is living a self-serving life. People may desire leadership only because they love position and control, not because they want to serve others. (3) Hypocrisy reduces faith to rigid rules. People can end up worshiping their own rules and regulations about what they think God wants instead of worshiping God himself. (4) Hypocrisy is outward conformity without inner reality. People can obey the details but still be disobedient in general behavior. For example, a person may carefully tithe his income, but be rude and obnoxious to his coworkers.

Many non-Christians use the supposed (or real) hypocrisy of Christians as an excuse to stay away from God and the church. Look carefully at your life. You are not perfect; therefore, at times an action or behavior might provide the ammunition for someone to label you a hypocrite. However, you must discern your own heart. Consider the signs of hypocrisy noted above. Then ask God to help you live rightly.

Luke 12:4-5 Fear of opposition or ridicule can weaken our witness for Christ. Often we cling to peace and comfort, even at the cost of our walk with God. Jesus reminds us here that we should fear God who controls eternal, not merely temporal, consequences. Don't allow fear of a person or group to keep you from standing up for Christ.

Luke 12:7 Our true value is God's estimate of our worth, not our peers' estimate. Other people evaluate and categorize us according to how we perform, what we achieve, and how we look. But God cares for us, as he does for all of his creatures, because we belong to him. Thus, we can face life without fear; we are very valuable to God.

Luke 12:8-9 We deny Jesus when we hope no one will find out we are Christians, decide not to speak up for what is right, are silent about our relationship with God, blend into society, and accept our culture's non-Christian values. By contrast, we acknowledge him when we live moral, upright, Christ-honoring lives, look for opportunities to share our faith with others, help others in need, take a stand for justice, love others, acknowledge our loyalty to Christ, and use our lives and resources to carry out his desires rather than our own.

▶ **LUKE 12:1-12 *(cont.)***

acknowledge in the presence of God's angels. [9]But
anyone who denies me here on earth will be denied
before God's angels. [10]Anyone who speaks against the
Son of Man can be forgiven, but anyone who blasphemes the Holy Spirit will not be forgiven.
[11]"And when you are brought to trial in the synagogues and before rulers and authorities, don't
worry about how to defend yourself or what to say,
[12]for the Holy Spirit will teach you at that time what
needs to be said."

Jesus Tells the Parable of the Rich Fool

LUKE 12:13-21

Then someone called from the crowd, "Teacher,
please tell my brother to divide our father's estate
with me."
[14]Jesus replied, "Friend, who made me a judge over
you to decide such things as that?" [15]Then he said,
"Beware! Guard against every kind of greed. Life is
not measured by how much you own."
[16]Then he told them a story: "A rich man had a fertile
farm that produced fine crops. [17]He said to himself,
'What should I do? I don't have room for all my crops.'
[18]Then he said, 'I know! I'll tear down my barns and
build bigger ones. Then I'll have room enough to store
all my wheat and other goods. [19]And I'll sit back and
say to myself, "My friend, you have enough stored away
for years to come. Now take it easy! Eat, drink, and
be merry!"'
[20]"But God said to him, 'You fool! You will die
this very night. Then who will get everything you
worked for?'
[21]"Yes, a person is a fool to store up earthly wealth
but not have a rich relationship with God."

Jesus Warns about Worry

LUKE 12:22-34

Then, turning to his disciples, Jesus said, "That is why I
tell you not to worry about everyday life—whether you
have enough food to eat or enough clothes to wear. [23]For
life is more than food, and your body more than clothing. [24]Look at the ravens. They don't plant or harvest
or store food in barns, for God feeds them. And you
are far more valuable to him than any birds! [25]Can all
your worries add a single moment to your life? [26]And
if worry can't accomplish a little thing like that, what's
the use of worrying over bigger things?

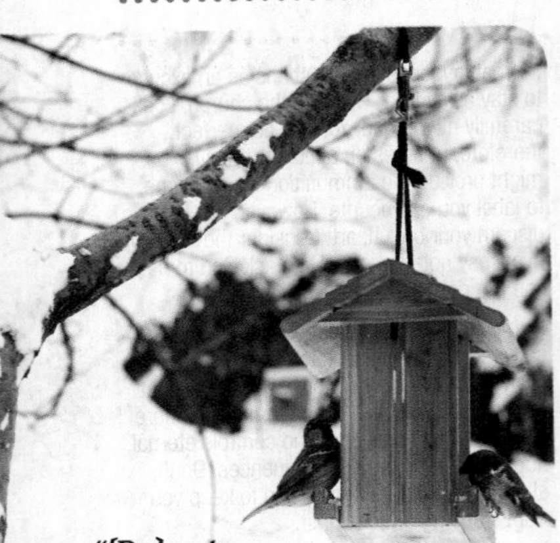

"[Do] not . . . worry about everyday life—whether you have enough food to eat or enough clothes to wear." Luke 12:22

Luke 12:10 Jesus said that blasphemy against the Holy Spirit is unforgivable. This has worried many sincere Christians, but it does not need to. The unforgivable sin is attributing to Satan the work that the Holy Spirit accomplishes (see notes on Matt 12:31-32, p. 1341; Mark 3:28-29, p. 1342). Thus, it is the deliberate and ongoing rejection of the Holy Spirit's work and even of God himself. A person who has committed this sin is far from God and totally unaware of any sin at all. If you fear you have committed this sin, be assured that your very concern shows that you have not sinned in this way.

Luke 12:11-12 The disciples knew they could never get the upper hand in a religious dispute with the well-educated Jewish leaders. Nevertheless, they would not be left unprepared. Jesus promised that the Holy Spirit would give them the appropriate words in their time of need. The disciples' testimony might not make them look impressive, but it would still point out God's work in the world through Jesus' life. We need to pray for opportunities to witness for Christ, and then trust him to help us with our words. This promise of the Spirit's help, however, does not compensate for lack of preparation. Remember that these disciples had three years of personal instruction and practical application. We need to study God's Word. Then God will bring his truths to mind when we most need them, helping us present them in the most effective way.

Luke 12:13ff Problems like this were often brought to rabbis for them to settle. Jesus' response, though not directed to the topic, is not a change of subject. Rather, Jesus is pointing to a broader issue—a correct attitude toward the accumulation of wealth. Life is more than material goods; far more important is our relationship with God. Jesus put his finger on this questioner's heart. When we bring problems to God in prayer, he often responds in the same way, showing us how we need to change and grow in our attitude toward the problem. His answer is often not the one we were looking for, but it is more effective in helping us trace God's hand in our lives.

Luke 12:15 Jesus says that the good life has nothing to do with being wealthy, so be on guard against greed (desire for what we don't have). This is the exact opposite of what society usually says. Advertisers spend millions of dollars to entice us to think that if we buy more and more of their products, we will be happier, more fulfilled, more comfortable. How do you respond to the constant pressure to buy? Learn to tune out expensive enticements and concentrate instead on the truly fulfilled life—living in a relationship with God and doing his work.

Luke 12:16-21 The rich man in Jesus' story died before he could begin to use what was stored in his big barns. Planning for retirement—preparing for life before death—is wise, but neglecting life after death is disastrous. If you accumulate wealth only to enrich yourself, with no concern for helping others, you will enter eternity empty-handed.

Luke 12:18-20 Why do you save money? Are you saving for retirement? to buy more expensive cars or "toys"? to be secure? Jesus challenges us to think beyond earthbound goals and to use what we have been given for God's Kingdom. Faith, service, and obedience are the way to become rich toward God.

Luke 12:22-34 Jesus commands us not to worry. But how can we avoid it? Only faith can free us from the anxiety caused by greed and covetousness. Working and planning responsibly is good; dwelling on all the ways our planning could go wrong is bad. Worry is pointless because it can't fill any of our needs; worry is foolish because the Creator of the universe loves us and knows what we need. He promises to meet all our real needs but not necessarily all our desires.

27"Look at the lilies and how they grow. They don't work or make their clothing, yet Solomon in all his glory was not dressed as beautifully as they are. 28And if God cares so wonderfully for flowers that are here today and thrown into the fire tomorrow, he will certainly care for you. Why do you have so little faith?

29"And don't be concerned about what to eat and what to drink. Don't worry about such things. 30These things dominate the thoughts of unbelievers all over the world, but your Father already knows your needs. 31Seek the Kingdom of God above all else, and he will give you everything you need.

32"So don't be afraid, little flock. For it gives your Father great happiness to give you the Kingdom.

33"Sell your possessions and give to those in need. This will store up treasure for you in heaven! And the purses of heaven never get old or develop holes. Your treasure will be safe; no thief can steal it and no moth can destroy it. 34Wherever your treasure is, there the desires of your heart will also be.

Jesus Warns about Preparing for His Coming

LUKE 12:35-48

"Be dressed for service and keep your lamps burning, 36as though you were waiting for your master to return from the wedding feast. Then you will be ready to open the door and let him in the moment he arrives and knocks. 37The servants who are ready and waiting for his return will be rewarded. I tell you the truth, he himself will seat them, put on an apron, and serve them as they sit and eat! 38He may come in the middle of the night or just before dawn.* But whenever he comes, he will reward the servants who are ready.

39"Understand this: If a homeowner knew exactly when a burglar was coming, he would not permit his house to be broken into. 40You also must be ready all the time, for the Son of Man will come when least expected."

41Peter asked, "Lord, is that illustration just for us or for everyone?"

42And the Lord replied, "A faithful, sensible servant is one to whom the master can give the responsibility of managing his other household servants and feeding them. 43If the master returns and finds that the servant has done a good job, there will be a reward. 44I tell you the truth, the master will put that servant in charge of all he owns. 45But what if the servant thinks, 'My master won't be back for a while,' and he begins beating the other servants, partying, and getting drunk? 46The master will return unannounced and unexpected, and he will cut the servant in pieces and banish him with the unfaithful.

47"And a servant who knows what the master wants, but isn't prepared and doesn't carry out those instructions, will be severely punished. 48But someone who does not know, and then does something wrong, will be punished only lightly. When someone has been

Lk 12:38 Greek *in the second or third watch.*

Overcoming worry requires: (1) Simple trust in God, your heavenly Father. This trust is expressed by praying to him rather than worrying. (2) Perspective on your problems. This can be gained by developing a strategy for addressing and correcting your problems. (3) A support team to help. Find some believers who will pray for you to find wisdom and strength to deal with your worries.

Luke 12:31 Seeking the Kingdom of God above all else means making Jesus the Lord and King of your life. He must control every area—your work, play, plans, relationships. Is the Kingdom only one of your many concerns or is it central to all you do? Are you holding back any areas of your life from God's control? As Lord and Creator, he wants to help provide what you need as well as guide how you use what he provides.

Luke 12:33 Money seen as an end in itself quickly traps us and cuts us off from both God and the needy. The key to using money wisely is to see how much we can use for God's purposes, not how much we can accumulate for ourselves. Does God's love touch your wallet? Does your money free you to help others? If so, you are storing up lasting treasures in heaven. If your financial goals and possessions hinder you from giving generously, loving others, or serving God, sell what you must to bring your life into line with his purposes.

Luke 12:34 If you concentrate your money in your business, your thoughts will center on making the business profitable. If you direct it toward other people, you will become concerned with their welfare. Where do you put your time, money, and energy? What do you think about most? How should you change the way you use your resources in order to reflect Kingdom values more accurately?

Luke 12:35-40 Jesus repeatedly said that he would leave this world but would return at some future time (see Matt 24–25; John 14:1-3). He also said that a Kingdom was being prepared for his followers. Many Greeks envisioned this as a heavenly, idealized, spiritual Kingdom. Jews—like Isaiah and John, the writer of Revelation—saw it as a restored earthly Kingdom.

Luke 12:40 Christ's return at an unexpected time is not a trap, a trick by which God hopes to catch us off guard. In fact, God is delaying his return so more people will have the opportunity to follow him (see 2 Pet 3:9). Before Christ's return, we have time to live out our beliefs and to reflect Jesus' love as we relate to others.

People who are ready for their Lord's return are not hypocritical but sincere (Luke 12:1), not fearful but ready to witness (Luke 12:4-9), not worried but trusting (Luke 12:25-26), not greedy but generous (Luke 12:34), not lazy but diligent (Luke 12:37). May your life be more like Christ's so that when he comes, you will be ready to greet him joyfully.

Luke 12:42-44 Jesus promises a reward for those who have been faithful to the Master. While we sometimes experience immediate and material rewards for our obedience to God, this is not always the case. If so, we would be tempted to boast about our achievements and only do good for what we get. Jesus said that if we look for rewards now, we will lose them later (see Mark 8:36). Our heavenly rewards will be the most accurate reflection of what we have done on earth, and they will be far greater than we can imagine.

Luke 12:48 Jesus has told us how to live until he comes: We must watch for him, work diligently, and obey his commands. Such attitudes are especially necessary for leaders. Watchful and faithful leaders will be given increased opportunities and responsibilities. The more resources, talents, and understanding we have, the more we are required to use them effectively. God will not hold us responsible for gifts he has not given us, but all of us have been given enough gifts and duties to keep us busy until Jesus returns.

▶ **LUKE 12:35-48 *(cont.)***
given much, much will be required in return; and when
someone has been entrusted with much, even more
will be required.

Jesus Warns about Coming Division

LUKE 12:49-53
"I have come to set the world on fire, and I wish it
were already burning! 50I have a terrible baptism of
suffering ahead of me, and I am under a heavy burden
until it is accomplished. 51Do you think I have come
to bring peace to the earth? No, I have come to divide
people against each other! 52From now on families will
be split apart, three in favor of me, and two against—or
two in favor and three against.

53 'Father will be divided against son
and son against father;
mother against daughter
and daughter against mother;
and mother-in-law against daughter-in-law
and daughter-in-law against mother-in-law.'*"

Jesus Warns about the Future Crisis

LUKE 12:54-59
Then Jesus turned to the crowd and said, "When you
see clouds beginning to form in the west, you say, 'Here
comes a shower.' And you are right. 55When the south
wind blows, you say, 'Today will be a scorcher.' And it
is. 56You fools! You know how to interpret the weather
signs of the earth and sky, but you don't know how to
interpret the present times.

57"Why can't you decide for yourselves what
is right? 58When you are on the way to court with
your accuser, try to settle the matter before you get
there. Otherwise, your accuser may drag you before
the judge, who will hand you over to an officer, who
will throw you into prison. 59And if that happens, you
won't be free again until you have paid the very last
penny.*"

Jesus Calls the People to Repent

LUKE 13:1-9
About this time Jesus was informed that Pilate had
murdered some people from Galilee as they were offering sacrifices at the Temple. 2"Do you think those
Galileans were worse sinners than all the other people
from Galilee?" Jesus asked. "Is that why they suffered?
3Not at all! And you will perish, too, unless you repent
of your sins and turn to God. 4And what about the
eighteen people who died when the tower in Siloam
fell on them? Were they the worst sinners in Jerusalem? 5No, and I tell you again that unless you repent,
you will perish, too."

6Then Jesus told this story: "A man planted a fig tree
in his garden and came again and again to see if there
was any fruit on it, but he was always disappointed.
7Finally, he said to his gardener, 'I've waited three years,
and there hasn't been a single fig! Cut it down. It's just
taking up space in the garden.'

8"The gardener answered, 'Sir, give it one more
chance. Leave it another year, and I'll give it special
attention and plenty of fertilizer. 9If we get figs next
year, fine. If not, then you can cut it down.'"

Jesus Heals the Crippled Woman

LUKE 13:10-17
One Sabbath day as Jesus was teaching in a synagogue,
11he saw a woman who had been crippled by an evil

Lk 12:53 Mic 7:6. **Lk 12:59** Greek *last lepton* [the smallest Jewish coin].

Luke 12:50 The "baptism of suffering" to which Jesus referred was his coming crucifixion. Jesus was dreading the physical pain, of course, but even worse would be the spiritual pain of complete separation from God that would accompany his death for the sins of the world.

Luke 12:51-53 In these strange and unsettling words, Jesus revealed that his coming often results in conflict. Because he demands a response, families may be split apart when some choose to follow him and others refuse to do so. Jesus allows no middle ground. He demands loyalty and commitment, sometimes to the point of severing other relationships. Are you willing to risk your family's disapproval in order to follow the Lord?

Luke 12:54-57 For most of recorded history, the world's principal occupation was farming. The farmer depended directly on the weather for his livelihood. He needed just the right amounts of sun and rain—not too much, not too little—to make his living, and he grew skilled at interpreting natural signs. Jesus was announcing an earthshaking event that would be much more important than the year's crops—the coming of God's Kingdom. Just as dark clouds forewarn of a rainstorm, there were signs that the Kingdom would soon arrive. But Jesus' hearers, though skilled at interpreting weather signs, were intentionally ignoring the signs of the times.

Luke 13:1-5 Pilate may have killed the Galileans because he thought they were rebelling against Rome; those killed by the tower in Siloam may have been working for the Romans on an aqueduct there. The Pharisees, who were opposed to using force to deal with Rome, would have said that the Galileans killed by Pilate deserved to die for rebelling. The Zealots, a group of anti-Roman terrorists, would have said the aqueduct workers deserved to die for cooperating. Jesus dismissed the idea that accidents or human cruelties were God's judgment on especially bad sinners. Neither the Galileans nor the workers should be blamed for their calamities. Whether a person is killed in a tragic accident or miraculously survives is not a measure of righteousness. Everyone has to die. Jesus did not explain why some live while others die tragically; instead he pointed to everyone's need for repentance. No matter how or when it occurs, death is not the end. Jesus promises that those who believe in him will not perish but have eternal life (John 3:16).

Luke 13:6-9 In the Old Testament, a fruitful tree was often used as a symbol of godly living (see, e.g., Ps 1:3 and Jer 17:7-8). Jesus pointed out what would happen to the other kind of tree—the kind that took valuable time and space and still produced nothing for the patient gardener. By this illustration Jesus warned his listeners that God would not tolerate forever their lack of productivity. (Luke 3:9 records John the Baptist's version of the same message.) Have you been enjoying God's special treatment without giving anything in return? If so, respond to the Gardener's patient care and begin to bear the fruit God has created you to produce.

Luke 13:10-17 Why was healing considered work? The religious leaders saw healing as part of a doctor's profession, and practicing

spirit. She had been bent double for eighteen years and was unable to stand up straight. [12]When Jesus saw her, he called her over and said, "Dear woman, you are healed of your sickness!" [13]Then he touched her, and instantly she could stand straight. How she praised God!

[14]But the leader in charge of the synagogue was indignant that Jesus had healed her on the Sabbath day. "There are six days of the week for working," he said to the crowd. "Come on those days to be healed, not on the Sabbath."

[15]But the Lord replied, "You hypocrites! Each of you works on the Sabbath day! Don't you untie your ox or your donkey from its stall on the Sabbath and lead it out for water? [16]This dear woman, a daughter of Abraham, has been held in bondage by Satan for eighteen years. Isn't it right that she be released, even on the Sabbath?"

[17]This shamed his enemies, but all the people rejoiced at the wonderful things he did.

Jesus Heals the Man Who Was Born Blind

JOHN 9:1-12

As Jesus was walking along, he saw a man who had been blind from birth. [2]"Rabbi," his disciples asked him, "why was this man born blind? Was it because of his own sins or his parents' sins?"

[3]"It was not because of his sins or his parents' sins," Jesus answered. "This happened so the power of God could be seen in him. [4]We must quickly carry out the tasks assigned us by the one who sent us.* The night is coming, and then no one can work. [5]But while I am here in the world, I am the light of the world."

[6]Then he spit on the ground, made mud with the saliva, and spread the mud over the blind man's eyes. [7]He told him, "Go wash yourself in the pool of Siloam" (Siloam means "sent"). So the man went and washed and came back seeing!

[8]His neighbors and others who knew him as a blind beggar asked each other, "Isn't this the man who used to sit and beg?" [9]Some said he was, and others said, "No, he just looks like him!"

But the beggar kept saying, "Yes, I am the same one!"

[10]They asked, "Who healed you? What happened?"

[11]He told them, "The man they call Jesus made mud and spread it over my eyes and told me, 'Go to the pool of Siloam and wash yourself.' So I went and washed, and now I can see!"

[12]"Where is he now?" they asked.

"I don't know," he replied.

Jn 9:4 Other manuscripts read *I must quickly carry out the tasks assigned me by the one who sent me*; still others read *We must quickly carry out the tasks assigned us by the one who sent me.*

SEVEN SABBATH MIRACLES

Over the centuries, the Jewish religious leaders had added rule after rule to God's law. For example, God's law said the Sabbath is a day of rest (Exod 20:10-11). But the religious leaders added to that law, creating one that said they must not heal on the Sabbath because that would be considered "work." Seven times Jesus healed people on the Sabbath. In doing this, he was challenging these religious leaders to look beyond their rules to their true purpose—to honor God by helping those in need. Would God have been pleased if Jesus had ignored these people?

Jesus sends a demon out of a man	Mark 1:21-28
Jesus heals Peter's mother-in-law	Mark 1:29-31
Jesus heals a lame man by the pool of Bethesda	John 5:1-18
Jesus heals a man with a deformed hand	Mark 3:1-6
Jesus restores a crippled woman	Luke 13:10-17
Jesus heals a man with swollen arms and legs	Luke 14:1-6
Jesus heals a man born blind	John 9:1-16

one's profession on the Sabbath was prohibited. The synagogue leader could not see beyond the law to Jesus' compassion in healing this crippled woman. Jesus shamed him and the other leaders by pointing out their hypocrisy. They would untie their animals and care for them on the Sabbath, but they refused to rejoice when a human being was freed from Satan's bondage.

Luke 13:16 In our fallen world, disease and disability are common. Their causes are many and often multiple—inadequate nutrition, contact with a source of infection, lowered defenses, and even direct attack by Satan. Whatever the immediate cause of our illness, we can trace its original source to Satan, the author of all the evil in our world. The Good News is that Jesus is more powerful than the devil or any disease. He often brings physical healing in this life; and when he returns, he will put an end to all disease and disability.

John 9:1ff In chapter 9, we see four different reactions to Jesus. The neighbors revealed surprise and skepticism; the Pharisees showed disbelief and prejudice; the parents believed but kept quiet for fear of excommunication; and the healed man showed consistent, growing faith. Each reaction to Jesus allowed the man to reach a clearer understanding of the one who had healed him.

John 9:2-3 A common belief in Jewish culture was that calamity or suffering was the result of some great sin. But Christ used this man's suffering to teach about faith and to glorify God. We live in a fallen world where good behavior is not always rewarded and bad behavior not always punished. Therefore, innocent people sometimes suffer. Regardless of the reasons for our suffering, Jesus has the power to help us deal with it. When you suffer from a disease, tragedy, or disability, try not to ask "Why did this happen to me?" or "What did I do wrong?" Instead, ask God to give you strength for the trial and a clearer perspective on what is happening.

John 9:6 When Jesus spit on the ground and made mud in order to repair the man's eyes, he was working with original materials. Genesis 2:7 states that God formed Adam's body from the dust of the ground. Jesus was demonstrating a creator's awareness of the materials he first used to shape the human body.

John 9:7 The pool of Siloam was built by Hezekiah. His workers constructed an underground tunnel from a spring outside the city walls to carry water into the city. Thus, the people could always get water without fear of being attacked. This was especially important during times of siege (see 2 Kgs 20:20; 2 Chr 32:30).

Religious Leaders Question the Blind Man

JOHN 9:13-34

Then they took the man who had been blind to the Pharisees, 14because it was on the Sabbath that Jesus had made the mud and healed him. 15The Pharisees asked the man all about it. So he told them, "He put the mud over my eyes, and when I washed it away, I could see!"

16Some of the Pharisees said, "This man Jesus is not from God, for he is working on the Sabbath." Others said, "But how could an ordinary sinner do such miraculous signs?" So there was a deep division of opinion among them.

17Then the Pharisees again questioned the man who had been blind and demanded, "What's your opinion about this man who healed you?"

The man replied, "I think he must be a prophet."

18The Jewish leaders still refused to believe the man had been blind and could now see, so they called in his parents. 19They asked them, "Is this your son? Was he born blind? If so, how can he now see?"

20His parents replied, "We know this is our son and that he was born blind, 21but we don't know how he can see or who healed him. Ask him. He is old enough to speak for himself." 22His parents said this because they were afraid of the Jewish leaders, who had announced that anyone saying Jesus was the Messiah would be expelled from the synagogue. 23That's why they said, "He is old enough. Ask him."

24So for the second time they called in the man who had been blind and told him, "God should get the glory for this,* because we know this man Jesus is a sinner."

25"I don't know whether he is a sinner," the man replied. "But I know this: I was blind, and now I can see!"

26"But what did he do?" they asked. "How did he heal you?"

27"Look!" the man exclaimed. "I told you once. Didn't you listen? Why do you want to hear it again? Do you want to become his disciples, too?"

28Then they cursed him and said, "You are his disciple, but we are disciples of Moses! 29We know God spoke to Moses, but we don't even know where this man comes from."

30"Why, that's very strange!" the man replied. "He healed my eyes, and yet you don't know where he comes from? 31We know that God doesn't listen to sinners, but he is ready to hear those who worship him and do his will. 32Ever since the world began, no one has been able to open the eyes of someone born blind. 33If this man were not from God, he couldn't have done it."

34"You were born a total sinner!" they answered. "Are you trying to teach us?" And they threw him out of the synagogue.

Jesus Teaches about Spiritual Blindness

JOHN 9:35-41

When Jesus heard what had happened, he found the man and asked, "Do you believe in the Son of Man?*"

36The man answered, "Who is he, sir? I want to believe in him."

37"You have seen him," Jesus said, "and he is speaking to you!"

38"Yes, Lord, I believe!" the man said. And he worshiped Jesus.

39Then Jesus told him,* "I entered this world to render judgment—to give sight to the blind and to show those who think they see* that they are blind."

40Some Pharisees who were standing nearby heard him and asked, "Are you saying we're blind?"

41"If you were blind, you wouldn't be guilty," Jesus replied. "But you remain guilty because you claim you can see.

Jn 9:24 Or *Give glory to God, not to Jesus;* Greek reads *Give glory to God.* **Jn 9:35** Some manuscripts read *the Son of God?* "Son of Man" is a title Jesus used for himself. **Jn 9:38-39a** Some manuscripts do not include *"Yes, Lord, I believe!" the man said. And he worshiped Jesus. Then Jesus told him.* **Jn 9:39b** Greek *those who see.*

John 9:13-17 While the Pharisees conducted investigations and debated about Jesus, people were being healed and lives were being changed. The Pharisees' skepticism was based not on insufficient evidence but on jealousy of Jesus' popularity and his influence on the people.

John 9:14-16 The Jewish Sabbath, Saturday, was the weekly holy day of rest. The Pharisees had made a long list of specific dos and don'ts regarding the Sabbath. Kneading the mud and healing the man were considered work and therefore were forbidden. Jesus may have purposely made the clay in order to emphasize his teaching about the Sabbath—that it is right to care for others' needs even if it involves working on a day of rest.

John 9:25 By now the man who had been blind had heard the same questions over and over. He did not know how or why he was healed, but he knew that his life had been miraculously changed and he was not afraid to tell the truth. You don't need to know all the answers in order to share Christ with others. It is important to tell them how he has changed your life. Then trust that God will use your words to help others believe in him too.

John 9:28, 34 The man's new faith was severely tested by some of the authorities. He was cursed and evicted from the synagogue. Persecution may come when you follow Jesus. You may lose friends; you may even lose your life. But no one can ever take away the eternal life that Jesus gives you.

John 9:38 This man gained not only physical sight but also spiritual sight as he recognized Jesus first as a prophet (John 9:17), then as his Lord. When you turn to Christ, you begin to see him differently. The longer you walk with him, the better you will understand who he is. Peter tells us to "grow in the grace and knowledge of our Lord and Savior Jesus Christ" (2 Pet 3:18). If you want to know more about Jesus, keep trusting him in every area of life.

John 9:40-41 The Pharisees were shocked that Jesus thought they were spiritually blind. Jesus countered by saying that it was only blindness (stubbornness and stupidity) that could excuse their behavior. To those who remained open and recognized how sin had truly blinded them from knowing the truth, he gave spiritual understanding and insight. But he rejected those who had become complacent, self-satisfied, and blind.

John 10:1 At night, sheep were often gathered into a sheepfold to protect them from thieves, weather, or wild animals. Sheepfolds were caves, sheds, or open areas surrounded by walls made of stones or branches. The shepherd often slept across the doorway of the fold to protect the sheep. Just as a shepherd cares for his sheep, Jesus, the

Jesus Is the Good Shepherd

JOHN 10:1-21

"I tell you the truth, anyone who sneaks over the wall
of a sheepfold, rather than going through the gate,
must surely be a thief and a robber! [2]But the one who
enters through the gate is the shepherd of the sheep.
[3]The gatekeeper opens the gate for him, and the sheep
recognize his voice and come to him. He calls his own
sheep by name and leads them out. [4]After he has gathered his own flock, he walks ahead of them, and they
follow him because they know his voice. [5]They won't
follow a stranger; they will run from him because they
don't know his voice."

[6]Those who heard Jesus use this illustration didn't
understand what he meant, [7]so he explained it to
them: "I tell you the truth, I am the gate for the sheep.
[8]All who came before me* were thieves and robbers.
But the true sheep did not listen to them. [9]Yes, I am
the gate. Those who come in through me will be
saved.* They will come and go freely and will find
good pastures. [10]The thief's purpose is to steal and
kill and destroy. My purpose is to give them a rich
and satisfying life.

[11]"I am the good shepherd. The good shepherd
sacrifices his life for the sheep. [12]A hired hand will
run when he sees a wolf coming. He will abandon
the sheep because they don't belong to him and he
isn't their shepherd. And so the wolf attacks them
and scatters the flock. [13]The hired hand runs away
because he's working only for the money and doesn't
really care about the sheep.

[14]"I am the good shepherd; I know my own sheep,
and they know me, [15]just as my Father knows me
and I know the Father. So I sacrifice my life for the
sheep. [16]I have other sheep, too, that are not in this
sheepfold. I must bring them also. They will listen
to my voice, and there will be one flock with one
shepherd.

[17]"The Father loves me because I sacrifice my life
so I may take it back again. [18]No one can take my
life from me. I sacrifice it voluntarily. For I have the
authority to lay it down when I want to and also to

Jn 10:8 Some manuscripts do not include *before me.* **Jn 10:9** Or *will find safety.*

Good Shepherd, cares for his flock (those who follow him). The prophet Ezekiel, in predicting the coming of the Messiah, called him a shepherd (Ezek 34:23).

John 10:7 In the sheepfold, the shepherd functioned as a gate, letting the sheep in and protecting them. Jesus is the gate to God's salvation for us. He offers access to safety and security. Christ is our protector. Some people resent that Jesus is the gate, the only way of access to God. But Jesus is God's Son—why should we seek any other way or want to customize a different approach to God? (See also notes on John 14:6, p. 1461.)

John 10:10 In contrast to the thief who takes life, Jesus gives life. The life he gives right now is abundantly rich and full. It is eternal, yet it begins immediately. Life in Christ is lived on a higher plane because of his overflowing forgiveness, love, and guidance. Have you taken Christ's offer of life?

John 10:11-12 A hired hand tends the sheep for money, while the shepherd does it out of love. The shepherd owns the sheep and is committed to them. Jesus is not merely doing a job; he is committed to love us and even lay down his life for us. False teachers and false prophets do not have this commitment.

John 10:16 The "other sheep" were non-Jews. Jesus came to save Gentiles as well as Jews. This is an insight into his worldwide mission—to die for the sins of the world. People tend to want to restrict God's blessings to their own group, but Jesus refuses to be limited by the fences we build.

John 10:17-18 Jesus' death and resurrection, as part of God's plan for the salvation of the world, were under God's full control. No one could kill Jesus without his consent.

THE NAMES OF JESUS

In different settings, Jesus gave himself names that pointed to special roles he was ready to fulfill for people. Some of these refer back to the Old Testament promises of the Messiah. Others were ways to help people understand him.

Reference	*Name*	*Significance*
John 6:27	**Son of Man**	Jesus' favorite reference for himself. It emphasized his humanity; but the way he used it was a claim of divinity.
John 6:35	**Bread of Life**	Refers to his life-giving role—that he is the only source of eternal life.
John 8:12	**Light of the World**	Light is a symbol of spiritual truth. Jesus is the universal answer for people's need for spiritual truth.
John 10:7	**Gate for the sheep**	Jesus is the only way into God's Kingdom.
John 10:11	**Good Shepherd**	Jesus appropriated the prophetic images of the Messiah pictured in the Old Testament. This is a claim of divinity, focusing on Jesus' love and guidance.
John 11:25	**The resurrection and the life**	Not only is Jesus the source of life, he is the power over death.
John 14:6	**The Way, the Truth, and the Life**	Jesus is the method, the message, and the meaning for all people. With this title, he summarized his purpose in coming to earth.
John 15:1, 5	**The true grapevine**	This title has an important second part, "you are the branches." As in so many of his other names, Jesus reminds us that just as branches gain life from the vine and cannot live apart from it, so we are completely dependent on Christ for spiritual life.

▸ **JOHN 10:1-21 *(cont.)***
take it up again. For this is what my Father has commanded."
[19]When he said these things, the people* were again
divided in their opinions about him. [20]Some said, "He's
demon possessed and out of his mind. Why listen to
a man like that?" [21]Others said, "This doesn't sound
like a man possessed by a demon! Can a demon open
the eyes of the blind?"

Religious Leaders Surround Jesus at the Temple

JOHN 10:22-42
It was now winter, and Jesus was in Jerusalem at
the time of Hanukkah, the Festival of Dedication.
[23]He was in the Temple, walking through the section
known as Solomon's Colonnade. [24]The people surrounded him and asked, "How long are you going
to keep us in suspense? If you are the Messiah, tell
us plainly."
[25]Jesus replied, "I have already told you, and you
don't believe me. The proof is the work I do in my
Father's name. [26]But you don't believe me because you
are not my sheep. [27]My sheep listen to my voice; I know
them, and they follow me. [28]I give them eternal life,
and they will never perish. No one can snatch them
away from me, [29]for my Father has given them to me,
and he is more powerful than anyone else.* No one
can snatch them from the Father's hand. [30]The Father
and I are one."
[31]Once again the people picked up stones to kill
him. [32]Jesus said, "At my Father's direction I have done
many good works. For which one are you going to
stone me?"
[33]They replied, "We're stoning you not for any good
work, but for blasphemy! You, a mere man, claim to
be God."
[34]Jesus replied, "It is written in your own Scriptures* that God said to certain leaders of the people, 'I say, you are gods!'* [35]And you know that the
Scriptures cannot be altered. So if those people who
received God's message were called 'gods,' [36]why do
you call it blasphemy when I say, 'I am the Son of
God'? After all, the Father set me apart and sent me
into the world. [37]Don't believe me unless I carry out
my Father's work. [38]But if I do his work, believe in
the evidence of the miraculous works I have done,
even if you don't believe me. Then you will know
and understand that the Father is in me, and I am
in the Father."

Jn 10:19 Greek *Jewish people;* also in 10:24, 31. **Jn 10:29** Other manuscripts read *for what my Father has given me is more powerful than anything;* still others read *for regarding that which my Father has given me, he is greater than all.* **Jn 10:34a** Greek *your own law.* **Jn 10:34b** Ps 82:6.

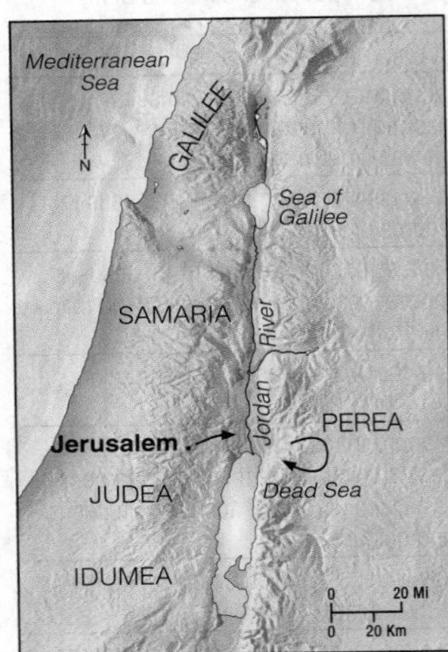

***MINISTRY EAST OF THE JORDAN** Jesus had been in Jerusalem for the Festival of Shelters (John 7:2). He then preached in various towns, probably in Judea, before returning to Jerusalem for Hanukkah. He again angered the religious leaders, who tried to arrest him, but he left the city and went to the region east of the Jordan to preach.*

John 10:19-20 If Jesus had been merely a man, his claims to be God would have proven him insane. If he had been demon possessed, he couldn't have healed the blind man. But his miracles proved his words true—he really was God. The Jewish leaders were in a quandary. But they could not see beyond their own prejudices, so they looked at Jesus only from their limited, human perspective.

John 10:22-23 Hanukkah commemorated the cleansing of the Temple under Judas Maccabeus in 164 B.C. after Antiochus Epiphanes had defiled it by sacrificing a pig on the altar of burnt offering. The festival was celebrated toward the end of December.

John 10:23 Solomon's Colonnade was a roofed walkway supported by large stone columns, just inside the walls of the Temple courtyard.

John 10:24 Many people asking for proof do so for the wrong reasons. Most of these questioners didn't want to follow Jesus in the way that required them to submit to his leadership. They hoped that Jesus would declare himself Messiah for their own distorted reasons. They, along with the disciples and everyone else in the Jewish nation, would have been delighted to have him drive out the Romans. Many of them didn't think he was going to do that, however. These doubters hoped he would identify himself so they could accuse him of telling lies (as the Pharisees did in John 8:13).

John 10:28-29 Just as a shepherd protects his sheep, Jesus protects his people from eternal harm. While believers can expect to suffer on earth, Satan cannot harm their souls or take away their eternal life with God. There are many reasons to be afraid here on earth because this is the devil's domain (1 Pet 5:8). But if you choose to follow Jesus, he will give you everlasting safety.

John 10:30 This is the clearest statement of Jesus' divinity he ever made. Jesus and his Father are not the same person, but they are one in essence and nature. Thus, Jesus is not merely a good teacher—he is God. His claim to be God was unmistakable. The religious leaders wanted to kill him because their laws said that anyone claiming to be God should die. Nothing could persuade them that Jesus' claim was true.

John 10:31 The Jewish leaders attempted to carry out the directive found in Leviticus 24:16 regarding those who blaspheme (claim to be God). They intended to stone Jesus.

John 10:34-36 Jesus referred to Psalm 82:6, where the Israelite rulers and judges are called "gods" (see also Exod 4:16; 7:1). If God called the Israelite leaders gods because they were agents of God's revelation and will, how could it be blasphemy for Jesus to call himself the Son of God? Jesus was rebuking the religious leaders because he is the Son of God in a unique, unparalleled relationship of oneness with the Father.

John 10:35 "The Scriptures cannot be altered" is a clear statement of the truth of the Bible. If we accept Christ as Lord, we also must accept his testimony to the Bible as God's Word.

39Once again they tried to arrest him, but he got away and left them. 40He went beyond the Jordan River near the place where John was first baptizing and stayed there awhile. 41And many followed him. "John didn't perform miraculous signs," they remarked to one another, "but everything he said about this man has come true." 42And many who were there believed in Jesus.

Jesus Teaches about Entering the Kingdom

LUKE 13:22-30

Jesus went through the towns and villages, teaching as he went, always pressing on toward Jerusalem. 23Someone asked him, "Lord, will only a few be saved?"

He replied, 24"Work hard to enter the narrow door to God's Kingdom, for many will try to enter but will fail. 25When the master of the house has locked the door, it will be too late. You will stand outside knocking and pleading, 'Lord, open the door for us!' But he will reply, 'I don't know you or where you come from.' 26Then you will say, 'But we ate and drank with you, and you taught in our streets.' 27And he will reply, 'I tell you, I don't know you or where you come from. Get away from me, all you who do evil.'

28"There will be weeping and gnashing of teeth, for you will see Abraham, Isaac, Jacob, and all the prophets in the Kingdom of God, but you will be thrown out. 29And people will come from all over the world—from east and west, north and south—to take their places in the Kingdom of God. 30And note this: Some who seem least important now will be the greatest then, and some who are the greatest now will be least important then.*"

Jesus Grieves over Jerusalem PARALLEL

MATTHEW 23:37-39

"O Jerusalem, Jerusalem, the city that kills the prophets and stones God's messengers! How often I have wanted to gather your children together as a hen protects her chicks beneath her wings, but you wouldn't let me. 38And now, look, your house is abandoned and desolate.* 39For I tell you this, you will never see me again until you say, 'Blessings on the one who comes in the name of the LORD!'*"

LUKE 13:31-35

At that time some Pharisees said to him, "Get away from here if you want to live! Herod Antipas wants to kill you!"

32Jesus replied, "Go tell that fox that I will keep on casting out demons and healing people today and tomorrow; and the third day I will accomplish my purpose. 33Yes, today, tomorrow, and the next day I must proceed on my way. For it wouldn't do for a prophet of God to be killed except in Jerusalem!

34"O Jerusalem, Jerusalem, the city that kills the prophets and stones God's messengers! How often

Lk 13:30 Greek *Some are last who will be first, and some are first who will be last.* **Mt 23:38** Some manuscripts do not include *and desolate.* **Mt 23:39** Ps 118:26.

Luke 13:22 This is the second time Luke reminds us that Jesus was intentionally going to Jerusalem (see also Luke 9:51). Jesus knew he was on his way to die, but he continued preaching to large crowds. The prospect of death did not deter Jesus from his mission.

Luke 13:24-25 Finding salvation requires more concentrated effort than most people are willing to put forth. Obviously we cannot save ourselves—there is no way we can work ourselves into God's favor. We "work hard to enter" through the narrow door by earnestly desiring to know Jesus and diligently striving to follow him whatever the cost. We dare not put off making this decision because the door will not stay open forever.

Luke 13:26-27 The people were eager to know who would be in God's Kingdom. Jesus explained that, although many people know something about God, only a few have acknowledged their sins and accepted his forgiveness. We may not necessarily see the people we expect to find in the Kingdom of God. Some perfectly respectable religious leaders claiming allegiance to Jesus will not be there because they were not true followers and secretly were morally corrupt. Just listening to Jesus' words or admiring his miracles is not enough. We must turn from sin and trust in God to save us.

Luke 13:29 God's Kingdom will include people from every part of the world. Israel's rejection of Jesus as Messiah would not stop God's plan. True Israel includes all people who believe in Christ. This was an important fact for Luke to stress as he was directing his Good News to a Gentile audience (see also Rom 4:16-25; Gal 3:6-9).

Luke 13:30 God's Kingdom will have many surprises. Some who are despised now will be greatly honored then; some influential people here will be left outside the gates. Many truly great people in God's eyes are virtually ignored by the rest of the world. What matters to God is not a person's earthly popularity, status, wealth, heritage, or power but rather commitment to Christ. How do your values match those of the Bible? Put God in first place, and you will join people from all over the world who will take their places at the feast in the Kingdom of Heaven.

Matt 23:37 Jesus wanted to gather his people together as a hen protects her chicks under her wings, but they wouldn't let him. Jesus also wants to protect us if we will just come to him. Many times we hurt and don't know where to turn. We reject Christ's help because we don't think he can give us what we need. But who knows our needs better than our Creator? Those who turn to Jesus will find that he helps and comforts as no one else can.

Matt 23:37 Jerusalem was the capital city of God's chosen people; the ancestral home of David, Israel's greatest king; and the location of the Temple, the earthly dwelling place of God. It was intended to be the center of worship of the true God and a symbol of justice to all people. But Jerusalem had become blind to God and insensitive to human need. Here we see the depth of Jesus' feelings for lost people and for his beloved city, which would soon be destroyed.

Luke 13:31-33 The Pharisees weren't interested in protecting Jesus from danger; they were trying to trap him themselves. The Pharisees urged Jesus to leave because they wanted to stop him from going to Jerusalem, not because they feared Herod. But Jesus' life, work, and death would not be determined by Herod or the Pharisees. His life was planned and directed by God himself, and his mission would unfold in God's time and according to God's plan.

Luke 13:33 Why was Jesus focusing on Jerusalem? Jerusalem, the city of God, symbolized the entire nation. It was Israel's largest city, the nation's spiritual and political capital, and Jews from around the world frequently visited it. But Jerusalem had a history of rejecting God's prophets (1 Kgs 19:10; 2 Chr 24:19; Jer 2:30; 26:20-23). It would reject the Messiah, just as it had rejected his forerunners.

▸ **LUKE 13:31-35** ***(cont.)***
I have wanted to gather your children together as a hen protects her chicks beneath her wings, but you wouldn't let me. 35And now, look, your house is abandoned. And you will never see me again until you say, 'Blessings on the one who comes in the name of the LORD!'*"

Jesus Heals a Man with Swollen Limbs

LUKE 14:1-6
One Sabbath day Jesus went to eat dinner in the home of a leader of the Pharisees, and the people were watching him closely. 2There was a man there whose arms and legs were swollen.* 3Jesus asked the Pharisees and experts in religious law, "Is it permitted in the law to heal people on the Sabbath day, or not?" 4When they refused to answer, Jesus touched the sick man and healed him and sent him away. 5Then he turned to them and said, "Which of you doesn't work on the Sabbath? If your son* or your cow falls into a pit, don't you rush to get him out?" 6Again they could not answer.

Jesus Teaches about Humility

LUKE 14:7-14
When Jesus noticed that all who had come to the dinner were trying to sit in the seats of honor near the head of the table, he gave them this advice: 8"When you are invited to a wedding feast, don't sit in the seat of honor. What if someone who is more distinguished than you has also been invited? 9The host will come and say, 'Give this person your seat.' Then you will be embarrassed, and you will have to take whatever seat is left at the foot of the table!

10"Instead, take the lowest place at the foot of the table. Then when your host sees you, he will come and say, 'Friend, we have a better place for you!' Then you will be honored in front of all the other guests. 11For those who exalt themselves will be humbled, and those who humble themselves will be exalted."

12Then he turned to his host. "When you put on a luncheon or a banquet," he said, "don't invite your friends, brothers, relatives, and rich neighbors. For they will invite you back, and that will be your only reward. 13Instead, invite the poor, the crippled, the lame, and the blind. 14Then at the resurrection of the righteous, God will reward you for inviting those who could not repay you."

Jesus Tells the Parable of the Great Feast

LUKE 14:15-24
Hearing this, a man sitting at the table with Jesus exclaimed, "What a blessing it will be to attend a banquet* in the Kingdom of God!"

16Jesus replied with this story: "A man prepared a great feast and sent out many invitations. 17When the banquet was ready, he sent his servant to tell the guests, 'Come, the banquet is ready.' 18But they all began making excuses. One said, 'I have just bought a field and must inspect it. Please excuse me.' 19Another said, 'I have just bought five pairs of oxen, and I want to try them out. Please excuse me.' 20Another said, 'I now have a wife, so I can't come.'

Lk 13:35 Ps 118:26. **Lk 14:2** Or *who had dropsy.* **Lk 14:5** Some manuscripts read *donkey.* **Lk 14:15** Greek *to eat bread.*

Luke 14:1-6 Earlier Jesus had been invited to a Pharisee's home for discussion (Luke 7:36). This time a prominent Pharisee invited Jesus to his home specifically to trap him into saying or doing something for which he could be arrested. It may be surprising to see Jesus on the Pharisees' turf after he had denounced them so many times. But he was not afraid to face them, even though he knew that their purpose was to trick him into breaking their laws.

Luke 14:7-11 Jesus advised people not to rush for the best places at a feast. People today are just as eager to raise their social status, whether by being with the right people, dressing for success, or driving the right car. Whom do you try to impress? Rather than aiming for prestige, look for a place where you can serve. If God wants you to serve on a wider scale, he will invite you to take a higher place.

Luke 14:7-14 Jesus taught two lessons here. First, he spoke to the guests, telling them not to seek places of honor. Service is more important in God's Kingdom than status. Second, he told the host not to be exclusive about whom he invited. God opens his Kingdom to everyone.

Luke 14:11 How can we humble ourselves? Some people try to give the appearance of humility in order to manipulate others. Others think that humility means putting themselves down. Truly humble people compare themselves only with Christ, realize their sinfulness, and understand their limitations. On the other hand, they also recognize their gifts and strengths and are willing to use them as Christ directs. Humility is not self-degradation; it is realistic self-assessment and commitment to serve.

Luke 14:15-24 The man sitting at the table with Jesus envisioned the glory of God's Kingdom, but he did not yet understand how to have a share in it. In Jesus' story, many people turned down the invitation to the banquet because the timing was inconvenient. We, too, may resist or delay responding to God's invitation, and our excuses may sound reasonable—work duties, family responsibilities, financial needs, or other reasons. Nevertheless, God's invitation is the most important event in your life, no matter how inconveniently it may be timed. Are you making excuses to avoid responding to God's call?

Luke 14:16ff The custom was to issue two invitations to a party: the first to announce the event and the second to tell the guests that everything was ready. The guests in Jesus' story insulted the host by making excuses when he issued the second invitation. In Israel's history, God's first invitation came from Moses and the prophets; the second came from his Son. The religious leaders accepted the first invitation. They believed that God had called them to be his people, but they insulted God by refusing to accept his Son. Thus, as the master in the story sent his servant into the streets to invite the needy to his banquet, so God sent his Son to a whole world of needy people to tell them that God's Kingdom had arrived and was ready for them.

Luke 14:16ff In this chapter we read Jesus' words against seeking status and in favor of hard work and even suffering. Let us not lose sight of the end result of all our humility and self-sacrifice—a joyous banquet with our Lord! God never asks us to suffer for the sake of suffering. He never asks us to give up something good unless he plans to replace it with something even better. Jesus is not calling us to join him in a labor camp but at a feast—the wedding feast of the Lamb (Rev 19:6-9), when God and his beloved church will be joined forever.

[21]"The servant returned and told his master what they had said. His master was furious and said, 'Go quickly into the streets and alleys of the town and invite the poor, the crippled, the blind, and the lame.' [22]After the servant had done this, he reported, 'There is still room for more.' [23]So his master said, 'Go out into the country lanes and behind the hedges and urge anyone you find to come, so that the house will be full. [24]For none of those I first invited will get even the smallest taste of my banquet.'"

Jesus Teaches about the Cost of Being a Disciple

LUKE 14:25-35

A large crowd was following Jesus. He turned around and said to them, [26]"If you want to be my disciple, you must hate everyone else by comparison—your father and mother, wife and children, brothers and sisters—yes, even your own life. Otherwise, you cannot be my disciple. [27]And if you do not carry your own cross and follow me, you cannot be my disciple.

[28]"But don't begin until you count the cost. For who would begin construction of a building without first calculating the cost to see if there is enough money to finish it? [29]Otherwise, you might complete only the foundation before running out of money, and then everyone would laugh at you. [30]They would say, 'There's the person who started that building and couldn't afford to finish it!'

[31]"Or what king would go to war against another king without first sitting down with his counselors to discuss whether his army of 10,000 could defeat the 20,000 soldiers marching against him? [32]And if he can't, he will send a delegation to discuss terms of peace while the enemy is still far away. [33]So you cannot become my disciple without giving up everything you own.

[34]"Salt is good for seasoning. But if it loses its flavor, how do you make it salty again? [35]Flavorless salt is good neither for the soil nor for the manure pile. It is thrown away. Anyone with ears to hear should listen and understand!"

Jesus Tells the Parable of the Lost Sheep

LUKE 15:1-7

Tax collectors and other notorious sinners often came to listen to Jesus teach. [2]This made the Pharisees and teachers of religious law complain that he

KEY CHARACTERISTICS OF CHRIST IN THE GOSPELS

Characteristic	Reference
Jesus is the Son of God	Matt 16:15-16; Mark 1:1; Luke 22:70-71; John 8:24-30
Jesus is God who became human	John 1:1-2, 14; 20:28
Jesus is the Christ, the Messiah	Matt 26:63-64; Mark 14:61-62; Luke 9:20; John 4:25-26
Jesus came to help sinners	Matt 9:13; Luke 5:32
Jesus has power to forgive sins	Mark 2:9-12; Luke 24:47
Jesus has authority over death	Matt 28:5-6; Mark 5:22-24, 35-42; Luke 24:5-6; John 11:1-44
Jesus has power to give eternal life	John 10:28; 17:2
Jesus healed the sick	Matt 8:5-13; Mark 1:32-34; Luke 5:12-15; John 9:1-7
Jesus taught with authority	Matt 7:29; Mark 1:21-22
Jesus was compassionate	Matt 9:36; Mark 1:41; 8:2
Jesus experienced sorrow	Matt 26:38; John 11:35
Jesus never disobeyed God	Matt 3:15; John 8:46

Luke 14:27 Jesus' audience was well aware of what it meant to carry one's own cross. When the Romans led a criminal to his execution site, he was forced to carry the cross on which he would die. This showed his submission to Rome and warned observers that they had better submit too. Jesus made this statement to get the crowds to think through their enthusiasm for him. He encouraged those who were superficial either to go deeper or to turn back. Following Christ means total submission to him—perhaps even to the point of death. (See also note on Luke 9:23, p. 1378.)

Luke 14:28-30 When a builder doesn't count the cost or estimates it inaccurately, the building may be left uncompleted. Will you abandon the Christian life after a little while because you did not count the cost of commitment to Jesus? What are those costs? Christians may face loss of social status or wealth. They may have to give up control of their money, their time, or their career. They may be hated, separated from their family, and even put to death. Following Christ does not mean a trouble-free life. We must carefully count the cost of becoming Christ's disciples so that we will firmly hold to our faith and won't be tempted later to turn back.

Luke 14:34 Salt can lose its flavor. When it gets wet and then dries, nothing is left but a tasteless residue. Many Christians blend into the world and avoid the cost of standing up for Christ. But Jesus says if Christians lose their distinctive saltiness, they become worthless. Just as salt flavors and preserves food, we are to preserve the good in the world and bring new flavor to life. This requires careful planning, willing sacrifice, and unswerving commitment to Christ's Kingdom. But if we fail to be "salty," we fail to represent Christ in the world. How salty are you?

Luke 15:2 Why were the Pharisees and teachers of religious law bothered that Jesus associated with these people? The religious leaders were always careful to stay "clean" according to Old Testament law. In fact, they went well beyond the law in their avoidance of certain people and situations and in their ritual washings. By contrast, Jesus took their concept of "cleanness" lightly. He risked defilement by touching those who had leprosy and by neglecting to wash in the Pharisees' prescribed manner, and he showed complete disregard for their sanctions against associating with certain classes of people. He came to offer salvation to sinners and to show that God loves them. Jesus didn't worry about the accusations. Instead, he continued going to those who needed him, regardless of the effect these rejected people might have on his reputation. How are you following Jesus' example?

▸ **LUKE 15:1-7 *(cont.)***

was associating with such sinful people—even eating
with them!
3So Jesus told them this story: 4"If a man has a
hundred sheep and one of them gets lost, what will
he do? Won't he leave the ninety-nine others in the
wilderness and go to search for the one that is lost
until he finds it? 5And when he has found it, he will
joyfully carry it home on his shoulders. 6When he arrives, he will call together his friends and neighbors,
saying, 'Rejoice with me because I have found my lost
sheep.' 7In the same way, there is more joy in heaven
over one lost sinner who repents and returns to God
than over ninety-nine others who are righteous and
haven't strayed away!

Jesus Tells the Parable of the Lost Coin

LUKE 15:8-10

"Or suppose a woman has ten silver coins* and loses
one. Won't she light a lamp and sweep the entire house
and search carefully until she finds it? 9And when she
finds it, she will call in her friends and neighbors and
say, 'Rejoice with me because I have found my lost coin.'
10In the same way, there is joy in the presence of God's
angels when even one sinner repents."

Jesus Tells the Parable of the Lost Son

LUKE 15:11-32

To illustrate the point further, Jesus told them this
story: "A man had two sons. 12The younger son told
his father, 'I want my share of your estate now before
you die.' So his father agreed to divide his wealth between his sons.
13"A few days later this younger son packed all his
belongings and moved to a distant land, and there he
wasted all his money in wild living. 14About the time
his money ran out, a great famine swept over the land,
and he began to starve. 15He persuaded a local farmer
to hire him, and the man sent him into his fields to
feed the pigs. 16The young man became so hungry that
even the pods he was feeding the pigs looked good to
him. But no one gave him anything.
17"When he finally came to his senses, he said to
himself, 'At home even the hired servants have food
enough to spare, and here I am dying of hunger! 18I will
go home to my father and say, "Father, I have sinned
against both heaven and you, 19and I am no longer
worthy of being called your son. Please take me on as
a hired servant."'
20"So he returned home to his father. And while he
was still a long way off, his father saw him coming.

Lk 15:8 Greek *ten drachmas*. A drachma was the equivalent of a full day's wage.

Oil Lamp

Israelite lamps developed from those in general use among the Canaanites in the second millennium B.C. Their shape was similar to a shell or saucer with a lip. Lamps of stone, metal, and shells were used, although the majority were made of pottery. A multitude of clay lamps, fashioned in a variety of designs, have been excavated in Palestine. Most lamps were fueled by olive oil, and the average lamp could hold enough oil to burn through the night. Small, round, wheel-made lamps of simple design were prevalent in the time of Christ. This would have been the type of lamp used by the woman searching the house for her gold coin (Luke 15:8). With wicks trimmed, the lamps of the foolish bridesmaids (Matt 25:1-13) would probably have lasted approximately five hours, from dark until about midnight.

Luke 15:3-6 It may seem foolish for the shepherd to leave 99 sheep to go search for just one. But the shepherd knew that the 99 would be safe in the sheepfold, whereas the lost sheep was in danger. Because each sheep was of high value, the shepherd knew that it was worthwhile to search diligently for the lost one. God's love for the individual is so great that he seeks out each one and rejoices when one is found. Jesus associated with sinners because he wanted to bring the lost sheep—considered by others to be beyond hope—the Good News of God's Kingdom. Before you were a believer, God sought you; and he is still seeking those who are yet lost.

Luke 15:4-5 We may be able to understand a God who would forgive sinners who come to him for mercy. But a God who tenderly searches for sinners and then joyfully forgives them must possess an extraordinary love! This is the kind of love that prompted Jesus to come to earth to search for lost people and save them. This is the kind of extraordinary love that God has for you.

Luke 15:8-10 In that culture, women received 10 silver coins as a wedding gift. Besides their monetary value, these coins held sentimental value like that of a wedding ring, and to lose one would be extremely distressing. Just as a woman would rejoice at finding her lost coin, so the angels rejoice over a repentant sinner. Each individual is precious to God. He grieves over every loss and rejoices whenever one of his children is found and brought into the Kingdom. Perhaps we would have more joy in our churches if we shared Jesus' love and concern for the lost, diligently seeking them and rejoicing when they come to the Savior.

Luke 15:12 The younger son's share of the estate would have been one-third, with the older son receiving two-thirds (Deut 21:17). In most cases they would have received this at their father's death, although fathers sometimes chose to divide up their inheritance early and retire from managing their estates. What is unusual here is that the younger one initiated the division of the estate. This showed arrogant disregard for his father's authority as head of the family.

Luke 15:15-16 According to Moses' law, pigs were unclean animals (Lev 11:2-8; Deut 14:8). This meant that pigs could not be eaten or used for sacrifices. To protect themselves from defilement, Jews would not even touch pigs. For a Jew to stoop to feeding pigs was a great humiliation, and for this young man to eat food that the pigs had touched was to be degraded beyond belief. The younger son had truly sunk to the depths.

Luke 15:17 The younger son, like many who are rebellious and immature, wanted to be free to live as he pleased, and he had to hit bottom before he came to his senses. It often takes great sorrow and tragedy to cause people to look to the only One who can help them—Jesus. Are you trying to live life your own way, selfishly pushing aside any responsibility or commit-

Filled with love and compassion, he ran to his son,
embraced him, and kissed him. 21His son said to
him, 'Father, I have sinned against both heaven and
you, and I am no longer worthy of being called your
son.*'

22"But his father said to the servants, 'Quick! Bring
the finest robe in the house and put it on him. Get
a ring for his finger and sandals for his feet. 23And
kill the calf we have been fattening. We must celebrate with a feast, 24for this son of mine was dead
and has now returned to life. He was lost, but now
he is found.' So the party began.

25"Meanwhile, the older son was in the fields working. When he returned home, he heard music and
dancing in the house, 26and he asked one of the servants what was going on. 27'Your brother is back,' he
was told, 'and your father has killed the fattened calf.
We are celebrating because of his safe return.'

28"The older brother was angry and wouldn't go in.
His father came out and begged him, 29but he replied,
'All these years I've slaved for you and never once refused to do a single thing you told me to. And in all that
time you never gave me even one young goat for a feast
with my friends. 30Yet when this son of yours comes
back after squandering your money on prostitutes,
you celebrate by killing the fattened calf!'

31"His father said to him, 'Look, dear son, you have
always stayed by me, and everything I have is yours.
32We had to celebrate this happy day. For your brother
was dead and has come back to life! He was lost, but
now he is found!'"

Jesus Tells the Parable of the Shrewd Manager

LUKE 16:1-18

Jesus told this story to his disciples: "There was a certain
rich man who had a manager handling his affairs. One
day a report came that the manager was wasting his
employer's money. 2So the employer called him in and
said, 'What's this I hear about you? Get your report in
order, because you are going to be fired.'

3"The manager thought to himself, 'Now what? My
boss has fired me. I don't have the strength to dig
ditches, and I'm too proud to beg. 4Ah, I know how
to ensure that I'll have plenty of friends who will give
me a home when I am fired.'

5"So he invited each person who owed money to his
employer to come and discuss the situation. He asked
the first one, 'How much do you owe him?' 6The man
replied, 'I owe him 800 gallons of olive oil.' So the
manager told him, 'Take the bill and quickly change
it to 400 gallons.*'

7"'And how much do you owe my employer?' he
asked the next man. 'I owe him 1,000 bushels of
wheat,' was the reply. 'Here,' the manager said, 'take
the bill and change it to 800 bushels.*'

8"The rich man had to admire the dishonest rascal
for being so shrewd. And it is true that the children of
this world are more shrewd in dealing with the world
around them than are the children of the light. 9Here's
the lesson: Use your worldly resources to benefit others
and make friends. Then, when your earthly possessions
are gone, they will welcome you to an eternal home.*

Lk 15:21 Some manuscripts add *Please take me on as a hired servant.* **Lk 16:6** Greek *100 baths . . . 50 [baths].* **Lk 16:7** Greek *100 korous . . . 80 [korous].* **Lk 16:9** Or *you will be welcomed into eternal homes.*

ment that gets in your way? Stop and look before you hit bottom. You will save yourself and your family much grief.

Luke 15:20 In the two preceding stories, the seeker actively looked for the coin and the sheep, which could not return by themselves. In this story, the father watched and waited. He was dealing with a human being with a will of his own, but he was ready to greet his son if he returned. In the same way, God's love is constant, patient, and welcoming. He will search for us and give us opportunities to respond, but he will not force us to come to him. Like the father in this story, God waits patiently for us to come to our senses.

Luke 15:24 The sheep was lost because it foolishly wandered away (Luke 15:4); the coin was lost through no fault of its own (Luke 15:8); and the son left out of selfishness (Luke 15:12). God's great love reaches out and finds sinners no matter why or how they got lost.

Luke 15:25-31 The older brother found great difficulty in accepting his younger brother when he returned, and it is just as difficult to accept "younger brothers and sisters" today. People who repent after leading notoriously sinful lives are often held in suspicion; churches are sometimes unwilling to admit them to membership. Instead, we should rejoice like the angels in heaven when an unbeliever repents and turns to God. Like the father, accept repentant sinners wholeheartedly and give them the support and encouragement that they need to grow in Christ.

Luke 15:30 In the story of the lost son, the father's response is contrasted with the older brother's. The father forgave because he was filled with love. The son refused to forgive because he was bitter. His resentment rendered him just as lost to the father's love as his younger brother had been. Don't let anything keep you from forgiving others. If you are refusing to forgive people, you are missing a wonderful opportunity to experience joy and share it with others. Make your joy grow: Forgive somebody who has hurt you.

Luke 15:32 In Jesus' story, the older brother represents the Pharisees, who were angry and resentful that sinners were being welcomed into God's Kingdom. "After all," the Pharisees must have thought, "we have sacrificed and done so much for God." How easy it is to resent God's gracious forgiveness of others whom we consider to be far worse sinners than ourselves. But if our self-righteousness gets in the way of rejoicing when others come to Jesus, we are no better than the Pharisees.

Luke 16:1-8 Our use of money is a good test of the lordship of Christ. Money belongs to God, not us; let us use our resources wisely. Money can be used for good or evil; let us use ours for good. Money has a lot of power; let us use it carefully and thoughtfully. We must use our material goods in a way that will foster faith and obedience (see Luke 12:33-34).

Luke 16:9 We are to make wise use of the financial opportunities we have, not to earn heaven but to help people find Christ. If we use our money to help those in need or to help others find Christ, our earthly investment will bring eternal benefit. When we obey God's will, the unselfish use of possessions will follow.

▸ **LUKE 16:1-18** ***(cont.)***

[10]"If you are faithful in little things, you will be faithful in large ones. But if you are dishonest in little things, you won't be honest with greater responsibilities. [11]And if you are untrustworthy about worldly wealth, who will trust you with the true riches of heaven? [12]And if you are not faithful with other people's things, why should you be trusted with things of your own?

[13]"No one can serve two masters. For you will hate one and love the other; you will be devoted to one and despise the other. You cannot serve both God and money."

[14]The Pharisees, who dearly loved their money, heard all this and scoffed at him. [15]Then he said to them, "You like to appear righteous in public, but God knows your hearts. What this world honors is detestable in the sight of God.

[16]"Until John the Baptist, the law of Moses and the messages of the prophets were your guides. But now the Good News of the Kingdom of God is preached, and everyone is eager to get in.* [17]But that doesn't mean that the law has lost its force. It is easier for heaven and earth to disappear than for the smallest point of God's law to be overturned.

[18]"For example, a man who divorces his wife and marries someone else commits adultery. And anyone who marries a woman divorced from her husband commits adultery."

Jesus Tells about the Rich Man and the Beggar

LUKE 16:19-31

Jesus said, "There was a certain rich man who was splendidly clothed in purple and fine linen and who lived each day in luxury. [20]At his gate lay a poor man named Lazarus who was covered with sores. [21]As Lazarus lay there longing for scraps from the rich man's table, the dogs would come and lick his open sores.

[22]"Finally, the poor man died and was carried by the angels to be with Abraham.* The rich man also died and was buried, [23]and his soul went to the place of the dead.* There, in torment, he saw Abraham in the far distance with Lazarus at his side.

[24]"The rich man shouted, 'Father Abraham, have some pity! Send Lazarus over here to dip the tip of his finger in water and cool my tongue. I am in anguish in these flames.'

[25]"But Abraham said to him, 'Son, remember that during your lifetime you had everything you wanted, and Lazarus had nothing. So now he is here being comforted, and you are in anguish. [26]And besides, there is a great chasm separating us. No one can cross over to you from here, and no one can cross over to us from there.'

[27]"Then the rich man said, 'Please, Father Abraham, at least send him to my father's home. [28]For I have five brothers, and I want him to warn them so they don't end up in this place of torment.'

Lk 16:16 Or *everyone is urged to enter in.* **Lk 16:22** Greek *into Abraham's bosom.* **Lk 16:23** Greek *to Hades.*

Luke 16:10-11 Our integrity is often put on the line in money matters. God calls us to be honest even in small details we could easily ignore. Heaven's riches are far more valuable than earthly wealth. But if we are not trustworthy with our money here (no matter how much or little we have), we will be unfit to handle the vast riches of God's Kingdom. See that you maintain your integrity in all matters, whether big or small.

Luke 16:13 Money can easily take God's place in your life. It can become your master. How can you tell if you are a slave to money? Ask yourself: Do I think and worry about it frequently? Do I give up doing what I should do or would like to do in order to make more money? Do I spend a great deal of my time caring for my possessions? Is it hard for me to give money away? Am I in debt?

Money is a hard and deceptive master. Wealth promises power and control, but often it cannot deliver. Great fortunes can be made—and lost—overnight, and no amount of money can provide health, happiness, or eternal life. How much better it is to let God be your master. His servants have peace of mind and security, both now and forever.

Luke 16:14 Because the Pharisees loved money, they took exception to Jesus' teaching. We live in an age that measures people's worth by how much money they make. Do you scoff at Jesus' warnings against serving money? Do you try to explain them away? Do you apply them to someone else? Unless we take Jesus' statements seriously, we may be acting like Pharisees ourselves.

Luke 16:15 The Pharisees acted piously to get praise from others, but God knew what was in their hearts. They considered their wealth to be a sign of God's approval. God detested their wealth because it caused them to abandon true spirituality. Though prosperity may earn people's praise, it must never substitute for devotion and service to God.

Luke 16:16-17 John the Baptist's ministry was the dividing line between the Old and New Testaments (John 1:15-18). With the arrival of Jesus came the realization of all the prophets' hopes. Jesus emphasized that his Kingdom fulfilled the law (the Old Testament); it did not cancel it (Matt 5:17). His was not a new system but the culmination of the old. The same God who worked through Moses was working through Jesus.

Luke 16:18 Most religious leaders of Jesus' day permitted a man to divorce his wife for nearly any reason. Jesus' teaching about divorce went beyond Moses' (Deut 24:1-4). Stricter than any of the then-current schools of thought, Jesus' teachings shocked his hearers (see Matt 19:10) just as they shake today's readers. Jesus says in no uncertain terms that marriage is a lifetime commitment. To leave your spouse for another person may be legal, but it is adultery in God's eyes. Remember that God intends marriage to be a permanent commitment.

Luke 16:19-31 The Pharisees considered wealth to be a proof of a person's righteousness. Jesus startled them with this story in which a diseased beggar is rewarded and a rich man is punished. The rich man did not go to hell because of his wealth but because he was selfish, refusing to feed Lazarus, take him in, or care for him. The rich man was hard-hearted in spite of his great blessings. The amount of money we have is not as important as the way we use it. What is your attitude toward your money and possessions? Do you hoard them selfishly, or do you use them to help others?

Luke 16:20 This Lazarus is merely a character in a story and should not be confused with the Lazarus whom Jesus raised from the dead (see John 11).

Luke 16:29-31 The rich man thought that his five brothers would surely believe a messenger who had been raised from the dead. But Jesus said that if they did not believe Moses and the prophets, who spoke constantly of caring for the poor, not even a resurrection would convince them. Notice the irony in Jesus' statement; on his way to Jerusalem to die, he was fully aware that even when he

29"But Abraham said, 'Moses and the prophets have
warned them. Your brothers can read what they wrote.'
30"The rich man replied, 'No, Father Abraham! But if
someone is sent to them from the dead, then they will
repent of their sins and turn to God.'
31"But Abraham said, 'If they won't listen to Moses
and the prophets, they won't listen even if someone
rises from the dead.'"

Jesus Tells about Forgiveness and Faith

LUKE 17:1-10

One day Jesus said to his disciples, "There will always
be temptations to sin, but what sorrow awaits the person who does the tempting!
2It would be better to be
thrown into the sea with a millstone hung around your
neck than to cause one of these little ones to fall into
sin. 3So watch yourselves!

"If another believer* sins, rebuke that person; then
if there is repentance, forgive. 4Even if that person
wrongs you seven times a day and each time turns
again and asks forgiveness, you must forgive."
5The apostles said to the Lord, "Show us how to
increase our faith."
6The Lord answered, "If you had faith even as small
as a mustard seed, you could say to this mulberry tree,
'May you be uprooted and thrown into the sea,' and
it would obey you!
7"When a servant comes in from plowing or taking care of sheep, does his master say, 'Come in and
eat with me'? 8No, he says, 'Prepare my meal, put on
your apron, and serve me while I eat. Then you can
eat later.' 9And does the master thank the servant
for doing what he was told to do? Of course not.
10In the same way, when you obey me you should
say, 'We are unworthy servants who have simply
done our duty.'"

Lazarus Becomes Sick and Dies

JOHN 11:1-16

A man named Lazarus was sick. He lived in Bethany with his sisters, Mary and Martha.
2This is the
Mary who later poured the expensive perfume on
the Lord's feet and wiped them with her hair.* Her
brother, Lazarus, was sick. 3So the two sisters sent a
message to Jesus telling him, "Lord, your dear friend
is very sick."

Lk 17:3 Greek *If your brother.* **Jn 11:2** This incident is recorded in chapter 12.

had risen from the dead, most of the religious leaders would not accept him. They were set in their ways, and neither Scripture nor God's Son himself would shake them loose.

Luke 17:1-3 Jesus warned about God's wrath for those who offend, abuse, or lead astray the little ones. How appropriate such a warning is when corruption enters our homes every day in many television programs or on the Internet. While Christians must guard against physical abuse, they also must be aware of and work against the mental and spiritual corruption that unfiltered television and unsupervised Internet surfing can bring.

Jesus' warning envisions an additional group, however. The "little ones" can be new disciples. Indifference to the training and treatment of new Christians can leave them theologically vulnerable. Make the follow-through care of recent converts and new members a high priority in your church.

Luke 17:3-4 To rebuke does not mean to point out every sin we see; it means to bring sin to a person's attention with the purpose of restoring that person's relationship with God and with fellow humans. When you feel you must rebuke another Christian for a sin, check your attitudes before you speak. Do you love that person? Are you willing to forgive? Unless rebuke is tied to forgiveness, it will not help the sinning person.

Luke 17:5-6 The disciples' request was genuine; they wanted the faith necessary for such radical forgiveness. But the amount of faith is not as important as its genuineness. What is faith? It is complete trust in and loyalty to God that results in a willingness to do his will. Faith is not something we use to put on a show for others. It is complete and humble obedience to God's will, a readiness to do whatever he calls us to do. The amount of faith isn't as important as the right kind of faith—faith in our all-powerful God.

Luke 17:6 A mustard seed is small, but it is alive and growing. Almost invisible at first, the seed will begin to spread, first under the ground and then above ground. Like a tiny seed, a small amount of genuine faith in God will take root and grow. Although each change will be gradual and imperceptible, soon this faith will have produced major results that will uproot and destroy competing loyalties. We don't need more faith; a tiny seed of faith is enough if it is alive and growing.

Luke 17:7-10 If we have obeyed God, we have only done our duty, and we should regard it as a privilege. Do you sometimes feel that you deserve extra credit for serving God? Remember, obedience is not something extra we do; it is our duty. Jesus is not suggesting that our service is meaningless or useless, nor is he advocating doing away with rewards. He is attacking unwarranted self-esteem and spiritual pride.

John 11:1 The village of Bethany was about two miles east of Jerusalem on the road to Jericho. It was near enough to Jerusalem for Jesus to be in danger, but far enough away so as not to attract attention prematurely.

John 11:3 As their brother grew very sick, Mary and Martha turned to Jesus for help. They believed in his ability to help because they had seen his miracles. We, too, know of Jesus' miracles. When we need extraordinary help, Jesus offers extraordinary resources. We should not hesitate to ask him for assistance.

Millstone

A hand mill is made of two circular stones used for grinding grain. The grinding of grain using concave stones with flat grinding pieces is depicted in ancient art dating from at least the Neolithic period (8300–4500 B.C.). The stone commonly used was black basalt because its rough and porous surface provided good cutting edges. The normal type of hand mill could be operated by one person, but sometimes two people were required (Matt 24:41). The hand mill was so important in the life of the people that it was illegal to take someone's millstone as a pledge against the payment of a debt, for this would deprive the family of the means of making flour for bread (Deut 24:6). These stones were heavy enough to kill a man when thrown on his head, as in the case of Abimelech (Judg 9:53). If tied to the neck, they were also heavy enough to drown a person in the sea (Luke 17:2).

▸ **JOHN 11:1-16 *(cont.)***

[4]But when Jesus heard about it he said, "Lazarus's sickness will not end in death. No, it happened for the glory of God so that the Son of God will receive glory from this." [5]So although Jesus loved Martha, Mary, and Lazarus, [6]he stayed where he was for the next two days. [7]Finally, he said to his disciples, "Let's go back to Judea."

[8]But his disciples objected. "Rabbi," they said, "only a few days ago the people* in Judea were trying to stone you. Are you going there again?"

[9]Jesus replied, "There are twelve hours of daylight every day. During the day people can walk safely. They can see because they have the light of this world. [10]But at night there is danger of stumbling because they have no light." [11]Then he said, "Our friend Lazarus has fallen asleep, but now I will go and wake him up."

[12]The disciples said, "Lord, if he is sleeping, he will soon get better!" [13]They thought Jesus meant Lazarus was simply sleeping, but Jesus meant Lazarus had died.

[14]So he told them plainly, "Lazarus is dead. [15]And for your sakes, I'm glad I wasn't there, for now you will really believe. Come, let's go see him."

[16]Thomas, nicknamed the Twin,* said to his fellow disciples, "Let's go, too—and die with Jesus."

Jesus Comforts Mary and Martha

JOHN 11:17-37

When Jesus arrived at Bethany, he was told that Lazarus had already been in his grave for four days. [18]Bethany was only a few miles* down the road from Jerusalem, [19]and many of the people had come to console Martha and Mary in their loss. [20]When Martha got word that Jesus was coming, she went to meet him. But Mary stayed in the house. [21]Martha said to Jesus, "Lord, if only you had been here, my brother would not have died. [22]But even now I know that God will give you whatever you ask."

[23]Jesus told her, "Your brother will rise again."

[24]"Yes," Martha said, "he will rise when everyone else rises, at the last day."

[25]Jesus told her, "I am the resurrection and the life.* Anyone who believes in me will live, even after dying. [26]Everyone who lives in me and believes in me will never ever die. Do you believe this, Martha?"

[27]"Yes, Lord," she told him. "I have always believed you are the Messiah, the Son of God, the one who has come into the world from God." [28]Then she returned to Mary. She called Mary aside from the mourners and told her, "The Teacher is here and wants to see you." [29]So Mary immediately went to him.

[30]Jesus had stayed outside the village, at the place where Martha met him. [31]When the people who were at the house consoling Mary saw her leave so hastily, they assumed she was going to Lazarus's grave to weep. So they followed her there. [32]When Mary arrived and saw Jesus, she fell at his feet and said, "Lord, if only you had been here, my brother would not have died."

[33]When Jesus saw her weeping and saw the other people wailing with her, a deep anger welled up within him,* and he was deeply troubled. [34]"Where have you put him?" he asked them.

Jn 11:8 Greek *Jewish people;* also in 11:19, 31, 33, 36, 45, 54. **Jn 11:16** Greek *Thomas, who was called Didymus.* **Jn 11:18** Greek *was about 15 stadia* [about 2.8 kilometers]. **Jn 11:25** Some manuscripts do not include *and the life.* **Jn 11:33** Or *he was angry in his spirit.*

John 11:4 Any trial a believer faces can ultimately bring glory to God because God can bring good out of any bad situation (Gen 50:20; Rom 8:28). When trouble comes, do you grumble, complain, and blame God, or do you see your problems as opportunities to honor him?

John 11:5-7 Jesus loved this family and often stayed with them. He knew their pain but did not respond immediately. His delay had a specific purpose. God's timing, especially his delays, may make us think he is not answering or is not answering the way we want. But he will meet all our needs according to his perfect schedule and purpose (Phil 4:19). Patiently await his timing.

John 11:9-10 "Daylight" symbolizes the knowledge of God's will and reliance on his guidance, and "night," the absence of this knowledge combined with self-reliance. When we move ahead in darkness, we will be likely to stumble.

John 11:14-15 If Jesus had been with Lazarus during the final moments of Lazarus's sickness, he might have healed him rather than let him die. But Lazarus died so that Jesus' power over death could be shown to his disciples and others. The raising of Lazarus was an essential display of his power, and the resurrection from the dead is a crucial belief of the Christian faith. Jesus not only raised himself from the dead (John 10:18), but he also has the power to raise others.

John 11:16 We often remember Thomas as "the doubter" because he doubted Jesus' resurrection (John 20:25). But here he demonstrated love and courage. The disciples knew the dangers of going with Jesus to Jerusalem, and they tried to talk him out of it. Thomas merely expressed what all of them felt. When their objections failed, they were willing to go, even though it appeared they might have to die with Jesus. They may not have understood why Jesus would be killed, but they were loyal. There are unknown dangers in doing God's work. It is wise to consider the high cost of being Jesus' disciple.

John 11:25-26 Jesus has power over life and death as well as power to forgive sins. This is because he is the creator of life (see John 14:6). He who is life can surely restore life. Whoever believes in Christ has a spiritual life that death cannot conquer or diminish in any way. When we realize his power and how wonderful his offer to us really is, how can we not commit our lives to him? To those of us who believe, what wonderful assurance and certainty we have: "Since I live, you also will live" (John 14:19).

John 11:27 Martha is best known for being too busy to sit down and talk with Jesus (Luke 10:38-42). But here we see her as a woman of deep faith. Her statement of faith is exactly the response that Jesus wants from us.

John 11:33-37 John stresses that we have a God who cares. When Jesus saw the weeping and wailing, he too wept openly. Perhaps he empathized with their grief, or perhaps he was troubled at their unbelief. In either case, Jesus showed that he cares enough for us to weep with us in our sorrow. This portrait contrasts with the Greek concept of God that was popular in that day—a God with no emotions and no messy involvement with humans. Here we see many of Jesus' emotions—compassion, indignation, sorrow, even frustration. He often expressed deep emotion, and we must never be afraid to reveal our true feelings to him. He understands them, for he experienced them. Be honest, and don't try to hide anything from your Savior. He cares.

They told him, "Lord, come and see." 35Then Jesus wept. 36The people who were standing nearby said, "See how much he loved him!" 37But some said, "This man healed a blind man. Couldn't he have kept Lazarus from dying?"

Jesus Raises Lazarus from the Dead

JOHN 11:38-44

Jesus was still angry as he arrived at the tomb, a cave with a stone rolled across its entrance. 39"Roll the stone aside," Jesus told them.

But Martha, the dead man's sister, protested, "Lord, he has been dead for four days. The smell will be terrible."

40Jesus responded, "Didn't I tell you that you would see God's glory if you believe?" 41So they rolled the stone aside. Then Jesus looked up to heaven and said, "Father, thank you for hearing me. 42You always hear me, but I said it out loud for the sake of all these people standing here, so that they will believe you sent me." 43Then Jesus shouted, "Lazarus, come out!" 44And the dead man came out, his hands and feet bound in graveclothes, his face wrapped in a headcloth. Jesus told them, "Unwrap him and let him go!"

Religious Leaders Plot to Kill Jesus

JOHN 11:45-57

Many of the people who were with Mary believed in Jesus when they saw this happen. 46But some went to the Pharisees and told them what Jesus had done. 47Then the leading priests and Pharisees called the high council* together. "What are we going to do?" they asked each other. "This man certainly performs many miraculous signs. 48If we allow him to go on like this, soon everyone will believe in him. Then the Roman army will come and destroy both our Temple* and our nation."

49Caiaphas, who was high priest at that time,* said, "You don't know what you're talking about! 50You don't realize that it's better for you that one man should die for the people than for the whole nation to be destroyed."

51He did not say this on his own; as high priest at that time he was led to prophesy that Jesus would die for the entire nation. 52And not only for that nation, but to bring together and unite all the children of God scattered around the world.

53So from that time on, the Jewish leaders began to plot Jesus' death. 54As a result, Jesus stopped his public ministry among the people and left Jerusalem. He went to a place near the wilderness, to the village of Ephraim, and stayed there with his disciples.

55It was now almost time for the Jewish Passover celebration, and many people from all over the country arrived in Jerusalem several days early so they could go through the purification ceremony before Passover began. 56They kept looking for Jesus, but as they stood around in the Temple, they said to each other, "What

Jn 11:47 Greek *the Sanhedrin.* **Jn 11:48** Or *our position;* Greek reads *our place.* **Jn 11:49** Greek *that year;* also in 11:51.

John 11:38 Tombs at this time were usually caves carved in the limestone rock of a hillside. A tomb was often large enough for people to walk inside. Several bodies would be placed in one tomb. After burial, a large stone was rolled across the entrance to the tomb.

John 11:38 Jesus was angry when he approached the tomb of Lazarus. Why was Jesus angry (see also John 11:33)? There are two main possibilities: (1) Jesus was angry that Mary and the others at the tomb were weeping and wailing excessively, like those who have no hope of a future resurrection (1 Thes 4:13), in contrast to Martha's response of faith (John 11:20-27); (2) Jesus was angry about the power of sin and death in the world. The fact that Jesus wept himself (John 11:35) and was still angry when he arrived at the tomb is a good indication that the second explanation is correct. Jesus was angry about the devastating effects of sin and death in the world, and he felt the loss keenly at the tomb of his friend, Lazarus. This wasn't the way God designed life to be! But we can find hope in the fact that Christ has overcome death (John 11:25-26), and live in light of that.

John 11:43-33 Jesus spoke to a dead man, and not only did that dead man hear his voice—he responded! This reminds us that Jesus is the Word (John 1:1-18), who was present and active in creation when everything was called forth by the simple words of God (Gen 1:3-31; John 1:3-4).

John 11:44 Jesus raised others from the dead, including Jairus's daughter (Matt 9:18-26; Mark 5:42-43; Luke 8:40-56) and a widow's son (Luke 7:11-15).

John 11:45-53 Even when confronted point-blank with the power of Jesus' deity, some refused to believe. These eyewitnesses not only rejected Jesus; they plotted his murder. They were so hardened that they preferred to reject God's Son rather than admit that they were wrong. They preferred closure instead of being open to God's marvelous power. Beware of pride.

John 11:48 The Jewish leaders knew that if they didn't stop Jesus, the Romans would lash out against all of them. Rome gave partial freedom to the Jews as long as they were quiet and obedient. Jesus' miracles often caused a disturbance. The leaders feared that Rome's displeasure would bring additional hardship to their nation.

John 11:51 John regarded Caiaphas's statement as a prophecy. As high priest, Caiaphas was used by God to explain Jesus' death even though Caiaphas didn't realize what he was doing.

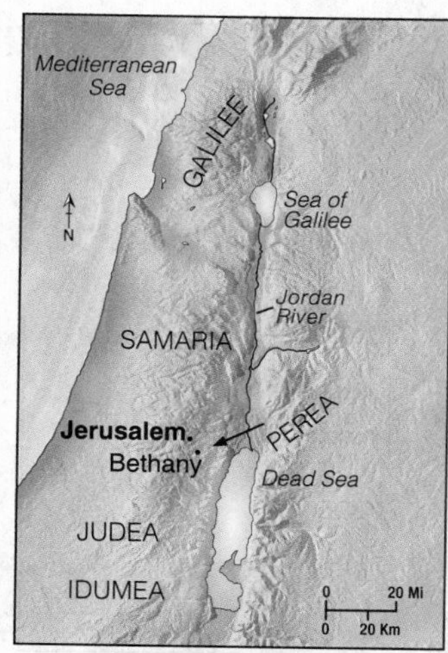

***JESUS RAISES LAZARUS** Jesus had been preaching in the villages beyond the Jordan, probably in Perea, when he received the news of Lazarus's sickness. Jesus did not leave immediately, but waited two days before returning to Judea. He knew Lazarus would be dead when he arrived in Bethany, but he was going to do a great miracle.*

▶ **JOHN 11:45-57 *(cont.)***
do you think? He won't come for Passover, will he?"
57Meanwhile, the leading priests and Pharisees had
publicly ordered that anyone seeing Jesus must report
it immediately so they could arrest him.

Jesus Heals Ten Men with Leprosy

LUKE 17:11-19

As Jesus continued on toward Jerusalem, he reached
the border between Galilee and Samaria. 12As he entered a village there, ten lepers stood at a distance,
13crying out, "Jesus, Master, have mercy on us!"
14He looked at them and said, "Go show yourselves
to the priests."* And as they went, they were cleansed
of their leprosy.
15One of them, when he saw that he was healed,
came back to Jesus, shouting, "Praise God!" 16He fell
to the ground at Jesus' feet, thanking him for what he
had done. This man was a Samaritan.
17Jesus asked, "Didn't I heal ten men? Where are
the other nine? 18Has no one returned to give glory
to God except this foreigner?" 19And Jesus said to the
man, "Stand up and go. Your faith has healed you.*"

Jesus Teaches about the Coming of the Kingdom of God

LUKE 17:20-37

One day the Pharisees asked Jesus, "When will the
Kingdom of God come?"
Jesus replied, "The Kingdom of God can't be detected by visible signs.* 21You won't be able to say,
'Here it is!' or 'It's over there!' For the Kingdom of God
is already among you.*"
22Then he said to his disciples, "The time is coming
when you will long to see the day when the Son of
Man returns,* but you won't see it. 23People will tell
you, 'Look, there is the Son of Man,' or 'Here he is,' but
don't go out and follow them. 24For as the lightning
flashes and lights up the sky from one end to the
other, so it will be on the day when the Son of Man
comes. 25But first the Son of Man must suffer terribly* and be rejected by this generation.
26"When the Son of Man returns, it will be like it
was in Noah's day. 27In those days, the people enjoyed
banquets and parties and weddings right up to the
time Noah entered his boat and the flood came and
destroyed them all.
28"And the world will be as it was in the days of
Lot. People went about their daily business—eating and drinking, buying and selling, farming and
building—29until the morning Lot left Sodom. Then
fire and burning sulfur rained down from heaven and
destroyed them all. 30Yes, it will be 'business as usual'
right up to the day when the Son of Man is revealed.
31On that day a person out on the deck of a roof must
not go down into the house to pack. A person out in
the field must not return home. 32Remember what
happened to Lot's wife! 33If you cling to your life, you

Lk 17:14 See Lev 14:2-32. **Lk 17:19** Or *Your faith has saved you.* **Lk 17:20** Or *by your speculations.* **Lk 17:21** Or *is within you,* or *is in your grasp.* **Lk 17:22** Or *long for even one day with the Son of Man.* "Son of Man" is a title Jesus used for himself. **Lk 17:25** Or *suffer many things.*

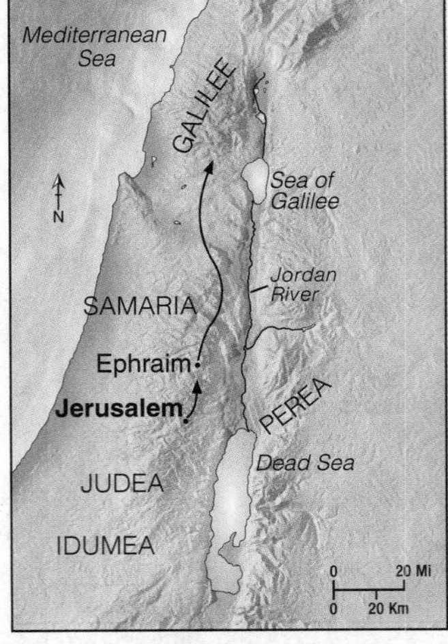

***TIME WITH THE DISCIPLES** Lazarus's return to life became the last straw for the religious leaders, who were bent on killing Jesus. So Jesus stopped his public ministry and took his disciples away from Jerusalem to Ephraim. From there they returned to Galilee for a while.*

Luke 17:11-14 Because leprosy was contagious, people who had leprosy were required to stay away from other people and to announce their presence if they had to come near. Sometimes leprosy would go into remission. If a leper thought his leprosy had gone away, he was supposed to present himself to a priest, who could declare him clean (Lev 14). Jesus sent the 10 lepers to the priest before they were healed—and they went! They responded in faith, and Jesus healed them on the way. Is your trust in God so strong that you act on what he says even before you see evidence that it will work?

Luke 17:16 Jesus healed all 10 lepers, but only one returned to thank him. It is possible to receive God's great gifts with an ungrateful spirit—9 of the 10 men did so. Only the thankful man, however, learned that his faith had played a role in his healing; and only grateful Christians grow in understanding God's grace. God does not demand that we thank him, but he is pleased when we do so. And he uses our responsiveness to teach us more about himself.

Luke 17:16 Not only was this man a leper, but he was also a Samaritan—a race despised by the Jews as idolatrous half-breeds (see note on Luke 10:33, p. 1396). Once again Luke is pointing out that God's grace is for everybody.

Luke 17:20-21 The Pharisees asked when God's Kingdom would come, not knowing that it had already arrived. The Kingdom of God is not like an earthly kingdom with geographical boundaries. Instead, it begins with the work of God's Spirit in people's lives and in relationships. We must resist looking to institutions or programs for evidence of the progress of God's Kingdom. Instead, we should look for what God is doing in people's hearts.

Luke 17:23-24 Many will claim to be the Messiah, and many will claim that the Son of Man has returned—and people will believe them. Jesus warns us never to take such reports seriously, no matter how convincing they may sound. When Jesus returns, his power and presence will be evident to everyone. No one will need to spread the message because all will see for themselves.

Luke 17:23-36 Life will be going on as usual on the day Christ returns. No warning will sound. Most people will be going about their everyday tasks, indifferent to the demands of God. They will be as surprised by Christ's return as the people in Noah's day were by the Flood (Gen 6–8) or the people in Lot's day by the destruction of Sodom (Gen 19). We don't know the time of Christ's return, but we do know that he is coming.

will lose it, and if you let your life go, you will save it.
[34]That night two people will be asleep in one bed;
one will be taken, the other left. [35]Two women will be
grinding flour together at the mill; one will be taken,
the other left.*"

[37]"Where will this happen, Lord?"* the disciples
asked.

Jesus replied, "Just as the gathering of vultures shows there is a carcass nearby, so these signs indicate that the end is near."*

Jesus Tells the Parable of the Persistent Widow

LUKE 18:1-8

One day Jesus told his disciples a story to show that
they should always pray and never give up. [2]"There
was a judge in a certain city," he said, "who neither
feared God nor cared about people. [3]A widow of that
city came to him repeatedly, saying, 'Give me justice in
this dispute with my enemy.' [4]The judge ignored her
for a while, but finally he said to himself, 'I don't fear
God or care about people, [5]but this woman is driving
me crazy. I'm going to see that she gets justice, because
she is wearing me out with her constant requests!'"

[6]Then the Lord said, "Learn a lesson from this unjust judge. [7]Even he rendered a just decision in the
end. So don't you think God will surely give justice
to his chosen people who cry out to him day and
night? Will he keep putting them off? [8]I tell you, he
will grant justice to them quickly! But when the Son
of Man* returns, how many will he find on the earth
who have faith?"

Lk 17:35 Some manuscripts add verse 36, *Two men will be working in the field; one will be taken, the other left.* Compare Matt 24:40. **Lk 17:37a** Greek *"Where, Lord?"* **Lk 17:37b** Greek *"Wherever the carcass is, the vultures gather."* **Lk 18:8** "Son of Man" is a title Jesus used for himself.

He may come today, tomorrow, or centuries in the future. Whenever Christ comes, we must be morally and spiritually ready. Live as if Jesus were returning today.

Luke 17:26-35 Jesus warned against false security. We are to abandon the values and attachments of this world in order to be ready for Christ's return. His return will happen suddenly, and when he comes, there will be no second chances. Some will be taken to be with him; the rest will be left behind.

Luke 17:33 Those clinging to this life are those seeking to escape physical persecution. Those who live for themselves display these common attitudes: (1) Materialism—I want it and work hard to get it. All that I see is real. Unseen things are merely ideas and dreams. (2) Individualism—I work hard for me, and you work hard for you. I may make it; you may not. That's your problem, not mine. (3) Skepticism—anything I'm not convinced about can't be important. Everything important to know I can figure out. Those who have these attitudes may protect themselves, but they will lose the spiritual dimension to their lives. Keep your commitment to Christ at full strength. Then you'll be ready when he returns.

Luke 17:37 To answer the disciples' question, Jesus quoted a familiar proverb. One vulture circling overhead does not mean much, but a gathering of vultures means that a carcass is nearby. Likewise, one sign of the end may not be significant, but when many signs occur, the Second Coming is near.

Luke 18:1 To persist in prayer and not give up does not mean endless repetition or painfully long prayer sessions. Constant prayer means keeping our requests continually before God as we live for him day by day, believing he will answer. When we live by faith, we are not to give up. God may delay answering, but his delays always have good reasons. As we persist in prayer, we grow in character, faith, and hope.

Luke 18:3 Widows and orphans were among the most vulnerable of all God's people, and both Old Testament prophets and New Testament apostles insisted that these needy people be properly cared for (e.g., Exod 22:22-24; Isa 1:17; 1 Tim 5:3; Jas 1:27).

Luke 18:6-7 If godless judges respond to constant pressure, how much more will a great and loving God respond to us? If we know he loves us, we can believe he will hear our cries for help.

CAIAPHAS

Caiaphas was the leader of the Sadducees. Educated and wealthy, they were politically influential in the nation. As the elite group, they were on fairly good terms with Rome. They hated Jesus because he endangered their secure lifestyles and taught a message they could not accept. A kingdom in which leaders served had no appeal to them. • For Caiaphas, whether Jesus should die was not in question; the only point to be settled was when his death should take place. Jesus had to be captured and tried, they needed Roman approval before they could carry out the death sentence. Caiaphas's plans were unexpectedly helped by Judas's offer to betray Christ. • Caiaphas did not realize that his schemes were actually part of a wonderful plan God was carrying out. Caiaphas thought he had won the battle as Jesus hung on the cross, but he did not count on the Resurrection! • Caiaphas represents those people who will not believe because they think it will cost them too much to accept Jesus as Lord. They choose the fleeting power, prestige, and pleasures of this life instead of the eternal life God offers those who receive his Son. What is your choice?

Strength and accomplishment	• High priest for 18 years
Weaknesses and mistakes	• One of those most directly responsible for Jesus' death • Planned Jesus' capture, carried out his illegal trial, and pressured Pilate to approve the Crucifixion • Kept up religious appearances while compromising with Rome • Involved in the later persecution of Christians
Lessons from his life	• When we cover selfish motives with spiritual objectives and words, God still sees our intentions
Vital statistics	• Where: Jerusalem • Occupation: High priest • Relative: Father-in-law: Annas • Contemporaries: Jesus, Pilate, Herod Antipas
Key verses	"Caiaphas, who was high priest at that time, said, 'You don't know what you're talking about! You don't realize that it's better for you that one man should die for the people than for the whole nation to be destroyed'" (John 11:49-50).

Caiaphas is mentioned in Matthew 26:57; Luke 3:2; John 11:49; 18:13-14, 24; and Acts 4:6.

Jesus Tells the Parable of Two Men Who Prayed

LUKE 18:9-14

Then Jesus told this story to some who had great
confidence in their own righteousness and scorned
everyone else: [10]"Two men went to the Temple to pray.
One was a Pharisee, and the other was a despised tax
collector. [11]The Pharisee stood by himself and prayed
this prayer*: 'I thank you, God, that I am not a sinner
like everyone else. For I don't cheat, I don't sin, and I
don't commit adultery. I'm certainly not like that tax
collector! [12]I fast twice a week, and I give you a tenth
of my income.'

[13]"But the tax collector stood at a distance and
dared not even lift his eyes to heaven as he prayed.
Instead, he beat his chest in sorrow, saying, 'O God,
be merciful to me, for I am a sinner.' [14]I tell you, this
sinner, not the Pharisee, returned home justified
before God. For those who exalt themselves will
be humbled, and those who humble themselves
will be exalted."

Jesus Teaches about Marriage and Divorce PARALLEL

MATTHEW 19:3-12

Some Pharisees came and tried to trap him with this
question: "Should a man be allowed to divorce his wife
for just any reason?"

[4]"Haven't you read the Scriptures?" Jesus replied.
"They record that from the beginning 'God made them
male and female.'*" [5]And he said, "'This explains why
a man leaves his father and mother and is joined to
his wife, and the two are united into one.'* [6]Since they
are no longer two but one, let no one split apart what
God has joined together."

[7]"Then why did Moses say in the law that a man
could give his wife a written notice of divorce and
send her away?"* they asked.

[8]Jesus replied, "Moses permitted divorce only as a
concession to your hard hearts, but it was not what God
had originally intended. [9]And I tell you this, whoever
divorces his wife and marries someone else commits
adultery—unless his wife has been unfaithful.*"

Lk 18:11 Some manuscripts read *stood and prayed this prayer to himself.* **Mt 19:4** Gen 1:27; 5:2. **Mt 19:5** Gen 2:24. **Mt 19:7** See Deut 24:1. **Mt 19:9** Some manuscripts add *And anyone who marries a divorced woman commits adultery.* Compare Matt 5:32.

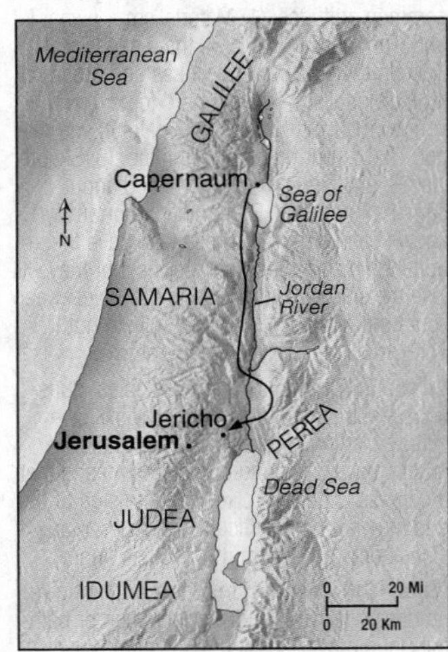

***LAST TRIP FROM GALILEE** Jesus left Galilee for the last time—he would not return before his death. He passed through Samaria, met and healed 10 lepers, and continued to Jerusalem. He spent some time east of the Jordan before going to Jericho (Luke 19:1).*

Luke 18:10 The people who lived near Jerusalem often would go to the Temple to pray. The Temple was the center of their worship.

Luke 18:11-14 The Pharisee did not go to the Temple to pray but to announce to all within earshot how good he was. The tax collector went recognizing his sin and begging for mercy. Self-righteousness is dangerous. It leads to pride, causes us to despise others, and prevents us from learning anything from God. The tax collector's prayer should be our prayer because we all need God's mercy every day. Don't let pride in your achievements cut you off from God.

Matt 19:3-12 The Pharisees were trying to trick Jesus by having him choose sides in a theological controversy. Two schools of thought represented two opposing views of divorce. One group supported divorce for almost any reason. The other believed that divorce could be allowed only for marital unfaithfulness. This conflict hinged on how each group interpreted Deuteronomy 24:1-4. In his answer, however, Jesus focused on marriage rather than divorce. He pointed out that God intended marriage to be permanent and gave four reasons for the importance of marriage (Matt 19:4-6).

Matt 19:4-6 Today, many homosexuals want to "marry" with the blessing of the church. Reasons for homosexual feelings and desires are complex and serious. Christians should not trivialize the situation or flippantly condemn the homosexual person. But Jesus made God's ideal very plain: At creation he approved one kind of marriage bond, man to woman. These become one flesh—one before God. See Romans 1:24-27 and accompanying notes, p. 1647.

Where does that leave homosexual marriage? At best, it is a human invention without any biblical precedent. God created man and woman. Heterosexual monogamy is God's plan for marriage—the best plan, the only one.

Matt 19:7-8 This law is found in Deuteronomy 24:1-4. In Moses' day as well as in Jesus' day, the practice of marriage fell far short of God's intention. The same is true today. Jesus said that Moses gave this law only because of the people's hard hearts—permanent marriage was God's intention. But because sinful human nature made divorce inevitable, Moses instituted some laws to help its victims. These were civil laws designed especially to protect the women who, in that culture, were quite vulnerable when living alone. Because of Moses' law, a man could no longer just throw his wife out—he had to write a formal letter of dismissal. This was a radical step toward civil rights, for it made men think twice about divorce. God designed marriage to be indissoluble. Instead of looking for reasons to leave each other, husbands and wives should concentrate on how to stay together (Matt 19:3-9).

Matt 19:10-12 Although divorce was relatively easy in Old Testament times (Matt 19:7), it is not what God originally intended. Couples should decide against divorce from the start and build their marriage on mutual commitment. There are also many good reasons for not marrying, one being to have more time to work for God's Kingdom. Don't assume that God wants everyone to marry. For many it may be better if they don't. Be sure that you prayerfully seek God's will before you make the lifelong commitment of marriage.

Matt 19:12 A "eunuch" is an emasculated male—a man with no testicles. Jesus' point here is that some people have physical limitations that prevent their marrying, while others choose not to marry because, in their particular situation, they can serve God better as single people. Jesus was not teaching us to avoid marriage because it is inconvenient or takes away our freedom; that would be selfishness. A good reason to remain single is to use the time and freedom to serve God. Paul elaborates on this in 1 Corinthians 7.

10Jesus' disciples then said to him, "If this is the case, it is better not to marry!"

11"Not everyone can accept this statement," Jesus said. "Only those whom God helps. 12Some are born as eunuchs, some have been made eunuchs by others, and some choose not to marry* for the sake of the Kingdom of Heaven. Let anyone accept this who can."

MARK 10:2-12

Some Pharisees came and tried to trap him with this question: "Should a man be allowed to divorce his wife?"

3Jesus answered them with a question: "What did Moses say in the law about divorce?"

4"Well, he permitted it," they replied. "He said a man can give his wife a written notice of divorce and send her away."*

5But Jesus responded, "He wrote this commandment only as a concession to your hard hearts. 6But 'God made them male and female'* from the beginning of creation. 7'This explains why a man leaves his father and mother and is joined to his wife,* 8and the two are united into one.'* Since they are no longer two but one, 9let no one split apart what God has joined together."

10Later, when he was alone with his disciples in the house, they brought up the subject again. 11He told them, "Whoever divorces his wife and marries someone else commits adultery against her. 12And if a woman divorces her husband and marries someone else, she commits adultery."

Jesus Blesses the Children PARALLEL

MATTHEW 19:13-15

One day some parents brought their children to Jesus so he could lay his hands on them and pray for them. But the disciples scolded the parents for bothering him.

14But Jesus said, "Let the children come to me. Don't stop them! For the Kingdom of Heaven belongs to those who are like these children." 15And he placed his hands on their heads and blessed them before he left.

MARK 10:13-16

One day some parents brought their children to Jesus so he could touch and bless them. But the disciples scolded the parents for bothering him.

14When Jesus saw what was happening, he was angry with his disciples. He said to them, "Let the children come to me. Don't stop them! For the Kingdom

Mt 19:12 Greek *and some make themselves eunuchs.* **Mk 10:4** See Deut 24:1. **Mk 10:6** Gen 1:27; 5:2. **Mk 10:7** Some manuscripts do not include *and is joined to his wife.* **Mk 10:7-8** Gen 2:24.

Mark 10:2 The Pharisees were trying to trap Jesus with their question. If he supported divorce, he would be upholding the Pharisees' procedures, and they doubted that he would do that. If Jesus spoke against divorce, however, some members of the crowd would dislike his position; some may have even used the law to their advantage to divorce their wives. More importantly, he might incur the wrath of Herod, who had already killed John the Baptist for speaking out against divorce and adultery (Mark 6:17-28). This is what the Pharisees wanted.

The Pharisees saw divorce as a legal issue rather than a spiritual one. Jesus used this test as an opportunity to review God's intended purpose for marriage and to expose the Pharisees' selfish motives. They were not thinking about what God intended for marriage and were quoting Moses unfairly and out of context. Jesus showed these legal experts how superficial their knowledge really was.

Mark 10:5-9 God allowed divorce as a concession to people's sinfulness. Unfortunately, the Pharisees used Deuteronomy 24:1 as a proof text for the sanctioning of divorce. Jesus explained that divorce is not God's ideal; instead, God wants married people to consider their marriage permanent. Don't enter marriage with the option of getting out. Your marriage is more likely to be happy if from the outset you are committed to permanence. Don't be hardhearted like these Pharisees; but be determined, with God's help, to stay together.

That said, we know that in our world divorce is sometimes necessary (for physical survival, for well-being of children, etc.). Jesus clearly gave God's ideal for marriage in Genesis priority over Moses' permission for divorce. Jesus did not cancel Moses' teaching, however. See Matthew 5:32 and 19:9, where Jesus permitted divorce when the spouse had been unfaithful; and 1 Corinthians 7:15, where Paul recognized divorce when the unbelieving partner leaves the marriage. Divorce is wrong; it severs a holy union. But divorce is permitted. Jesus did not elaborate on the permissible reasons, but his high view of marriage surely requires that divorce be a last resort to avoid greater disaster.

Mark 10:6-9 Women were often treated as property. Marriage and divorce were regarded as transactions similar to buying and selling land. But Jesus condemned this attitude, clarifying God's original intention—that marriage bring oneness (Gen 2:24). Jesus held up God's ideal for marriage and told his followers to live by that ideal.

Matt 19:13-15 The disciples must have forgotten what Jesus had said about children (Matt 18:4-6). Jesus wanted little children to come to him because he loved them and because of their guileless trust in God. All people need childlike faith in God. The receptiveness of little children was a great contrast to the stubbornness of the religious leaders, who let their education and sophistication stand in the way of the simple faith needed to believe in Jesus.

Mark 10:13-16 Jesus was often criticized for spending too much time with the wrong people—children, tax collectors, and sinners (Matt 9:11; Luke 15:1-2; 19:7). Some, including the disciples, thought Jesus should be spending more time with important leaders and the devout because this was the way to improve his position and avoid criticism. But Jesus didn't need to improve his position. He was God, and he wanted to speak to those who needed him most.

Mark 10:14 To feel secure, all children need is a loving look and gentle touch from someone who cares. They believe us because they trust us. Jesus said that people should trust in him with this kind of childlike faith. We do not have to understand all the mysteries of the universe; it should be enough to know that God loves us and provides forgiveness for our sin.

▸ **MARK 10:13-16** ***(cont.)***

of God belongs to those who are like these children.
15I tell you the truth, anyone who doesn't receive the
Kingdom of God like a child will never enter it." 16Then
he took the children in his arms and placed his hands
on their heads and blessed them.

LUKE 18:15-17

One day some parents brought their little children to Jesus so he could touch and bless them. But when the disciples saw this, they scolded the parents for bothering him.

16Then Jesus called for the children and said to the
disciples, "Let the children come to me. Don't stop
them! For the Kingdom of God belongs to those who
are like these children. 17I tell you the truth, anyone
who doesn't receive the Kingdom of God like a child
will never enter it."

Jesus Speaks to the Rich Young Man PARALLEL

MATTHEW 19:16-30

Someone came to Jesus with this question: "Teacher,* what good deed must I do to have eternal life?"

17"Why ask me about what is good?" Jesus replied.
"There is only One who is good. But to answer your question—if you want to receive eternal life, keep* the commandments."

18"Which ones?" the man asked.

And Jesus replied: "'You must not murder. You must not commit adultery. You must not steal. You must not
testify falsely. 19Honor your father and mother. Love
your neighbor as yourself.'*"

20"I've obeyed all these commandments," the young
man replied. "What else must I do?"

21Jesus told him, "If you want to be perfect, go and sell all your possessions and give the money to the poor, and you will have treasure in heaven. Then come, follow me."

22But when the young man heard this, he went away
sad, for he had many possessions.

23Then Jesus said to his disciples, "I tell you the
truth, it is very hard for a rich person to enter the
Kingdom of Heaven. 24I'll say it again—it is easier for
a camel to go through the eye of a needle than for a rich person to enter the Kingdom of God!"

25The disciples were astounded. "Then who in the
world can be saved?" they asked.

26Jesus looked at them intently and said, "Humanly
speaking, it is impossible. But with God everything is possible."

27Then Peter said to him, "We've given up everything to follow you. What will we get?"

28Jesus replied, "I assure you that when the world
is made new* and the Son of Man* sits upon his

Mt 19:16 Some manuscripts read *Good Teacher.* **Mt 19:17** Some manuscripts read *continue to keep.* **Mt 19:18-19** Exod 20:12-16; Deut 5:16-20; Lev 19:18. **Mt 19:28a** Or *in the regeneration.* **Mt 19:28b** "Son of Man" is a title Jesus used for himself.

Mark 10:15 How can you "receive the Kingdom of God like a child"? Adults considering the Christian faith for the first time will have life experiences that take them way past the ability to be as innocent as children. Jesus does not ask us to put aside our experiences, but he does require a change of attitude: adult self-sufficiency must recognize its need for the sovereign God; adult moral defensiveness must humble itself before the holy God; and adult skeptical toughness must soften before the loving God. Children do not feel supremely powerful, perfectly righteous, or totally autonomous. These are adult fantasies. Coming to Jesus means to accept his goodness on your behalf, confess your need, and commit your life to his tender guidance.

Luke 18:15-16 It was customary for a mother to bring her children to a rabbi for a blessing, and that is why these mothers gathered around Jesus. The disciples, however, thought the children were unworthy of the Master's time—less important than whatever else he was doing. But Jesus welcomed them because little children have the kind of faith and trust needed to enter God's Kingdom. It is important that we introduce our children to Jesus.

Luke 18:17 How does someone "receive the Kingdom of God like a child"? It means having the simple, trusting attitude that children show to adults on whom they depend. Jesus wants his people to enjoy prayer by delighting in his company. Find ways in a busy day to read the Bible enthusiastically, seek God's help in any problem, rely on him for guidance, and trust him explicitly. Children do all that with adults who love them. How much more should believers have that attitude toward Jesus, who loves them.

Matt 19:16 To this man seeking assurance of eternal life, Jesus pointed out that salvation does not come from good deeds unaccompanied by love for God. The man needed a whole new starting point. Instead of adding another commandment to keep or good deed to perform, the young man needed to submit humbly to the lordship of Christ.

Matt 19:17ff In response to the young man's question about what good deed he needed to do in order to be assured of eternal life, Jesus told him to keep God's Ten Commandments. Jesus then listed six of them, all referring to relationships with others. When the young man replied that he had kept the commandments, Jesus told him that he must do something more—sell everything he owned and give the money to the poor. Jesus' statement exposed the man's weakness. In reality, his wealth was his god, his idol, and he would not give it up. Thus, he violated the first and greatest commandment (Exod 20:3; Matt 22:36-40).

Matt 19:21 When Jesus told this young man that he would "be perfect" if he gave everything he had to the poor, Jesus wasn't speaking in the temporal, human sense. He was explaining how to be justified and made whole or complete in God's sight.

Matt 19:22 We cannot love God with all our heart and yet keep our money to ourselves. Loving him totally means using our money in ways that please him.

Matt 19:24-26 Because it is impossible for a camel to go through the eye of a needle, it appears impossible for a rich person to get into the Kingdom of Heaven. The disciples were astounded. They thought that if anyone could be saved, it would be the rich, whom their culture considered especially blessed by God. Jesus explained, however, that "with God everything is possible." Even rich people can enter the Kingdom if God brings them in. Faith in Christ, not in self or riches, is what counts. On what are you counting for salvation?

Matt 19:27 In the Bible, God gives rewards to his people according to his justice. In the Old Testament, obedience often brought reward in this life (Deut 28), but obedience and immediate reward are not always linked. If they were, good people would always be rich, and suffering would always be a sign of sin. As believers, our reward is God's presence and power through his indwelling Holy Spirit. Later, in eternity, we will be rewarded for our faith and service. If material rewards in this life came to us for every faithful deed, we would be tempted to boast about our achievements and act out of wrong motivations.

glorious throne, you who have been my followers will also sit on twelve thrones, judging the twelve tribes of Israel. 29And everyone who has given up houses or brothers or sisters or father or mother or children or property, for my sake, will receive a hundred times as much in return and will inherit eternal life. 30But many who are the greatest now will be least important then, and those who seem least important now will be the greatest then.*"

MARK 10:17-31

As Jesus was starting out on his way to Jerusalem, a man came running up to him, knelt down, and asked, "Good Teacher, what must I do to inherit eternal life?"

18"Why do you call me good?" Jesus asked. "Only God is truly good. 19But to answer your question, you know the commandments: 'You must not murder. You must not commit adultery. You must not steal. You must not testify falsely. You must not cheat anyone. Honor your father and mother.'*"

20"Teacher," the man replied, "I've obeyed all these commandments since I was young."

21Looking at the man, Jesus felt genuine love for him. "There is still one thing you haven't done," he told him. "Go and sell all your possessions and give the money to the poor, and you will have treasure in heaven. Then come, follow me."

22At this the man's face fell, and he went away sad, for he had many possessions.

23Jesus looked around and said to his disciples, "How hard it is for the rich to enter the Kingdom of God!" 24This amazed them. But Jesus said again, "Dear children, it is very hard* to enter the Kingdom of God. 25In fact, it is easier for a camel to go through the eye of a needle than for a rich person to enter the Kingdom of God!"

26The disciples were astounded. "Then who in the world can be saved?" they asked.

27Jesus looked at them intently and said, "Humanly speaking, it is impossible. But not with God. Everything is possible with God."

28Then Peter began to speak up. "We've given up everything to follow you," he said.

29"Yes," Jesus replied, "and I assure you that everyone who has given up house or brothers or sisters or mother or father or children or property, for my sake and for the Good News, 30will receive now in return a hundred times as many houses, brothers, sisters, mothers, children, and property—along with persecution. And in the world to come that person will have eternal life. 31But many who are the greatest now will be least important then, and those who seem least important now will be the greatest then.*"

Mt 19:30 Greek *But many who are first will be last; and the last, first.* **Mk 10:19** Exod 20:12-16; Deut 5:16-20. **Mk 10:24** Some manuscripts read *very hard for those who trust in riches.* **Mk 10:31** Greek *But many who are first will be last; and the last, first.*

Matt 19:29 Jesus assured the disciples that anyone who gives up something valuable for his sake will be repaid many times over in this life, although not necessarily in the same form. For example, a person may be rejected by his or her family for accepting Christ, but he or she will gain the larger family of believers.

Matt 19:30 Jesus turned the world's values upside down. Consider the most powerful or well-known people in our world—how many got where they are by being humble, self-effacing, and gentle? Not many! But in the life to come, the last will be first. Don't forfeit eternal rewards for temporary benefits. Be willing to make sacrifices now for greater rewards later. Be willing to accept human disapproval, knowing that you have God's approval.

Mark 10:17-23 This man wanted to be sure he would get eternal life, so he asked what he could do. He said he'd never once broken any of the laws Jesus mentioned (Mark 10:19), and perhaps he had even kept the Pharisees' additional regulations as well. But Jesus lovingly broke through the man's pride with a challenge that brought out his true motives: "Go and sell all your possessions and give the money to the poor." This challenge exposed the barrier that could keep this man out of the Kingdom: his love of money. Money represented his pride of accomplishment and self-effort. Ironically, his attitude made him unable to keep the first commandment: to let nothing be more important than God (Exod 20:3). He could not meet the one requirement Jesus gave—to turn his whole heart and life over to God. The man came to Jesus wondering what he could do; he left seeing what he was unable to do. What barriers are keeping you from turning your life over to Christ?

Mark 10:18 When Jesus asked this question, he was saying, "Do you really know the one to whom you are talking?" Because only God is truly good, the man was calling Jesus "God," whether or not he realized it.

Mark 10:21 What does your money mean to you? Although Jesus wanted this man to sell everything and give his money to the poor, this does not mean that all believers should sell all their possessions. Most of his followers did not sell everything, although they used their possessions to serve others. Instead, this incident shows us that we must not let our possessions or money keep us from following Jesus. We must remove all barriers to serving him fully. If Jesus asked, could you give up your house? your car? your level of income? your position on the ladder of promotion? Your reaction may show your attitude toward money—whether it is your servant or your master.

Mark 10:21 Jesus showed genuine love for this man, even though he knew that the man might not follow him. Love is able to give tough advice; it doesn't hedge on the truth. Christ loved us enough to die for us, and he also loves us enough to talk straight to us. If his love were superficial, he would give us only his approval; but because his love is complete, he gives us life-changing challenges.

Mark 10:23 Jesus said it was very difficult for the rich to enter the Kingdom of God because the rich, having their basic physical needs met, often become self-reliant. When they feel empty, they buy something new to try to fill the void that only God can fill. Their abundance and self-sufficiency become their deficiency. The person who has everything on earth can still lack what is most important—eternal life.

Mark 10:26 The disciples were amazed. Was not wealth a blessing from God, a reward for being good? This misconception is still common today. Although many believers enjoy material prosperity, many others live in poverty. Wealth is not a sign of faith or of partiality on God's part.

Mark 10:31 Jesus explained that in the world to come, the values of this world will be reversed. Those who seek status and importance here will have none in heaven. Those who are humble here will be great in heaven. The corrupt condition of our society encourages confusion in values. We are bombarded by messages that tell us how to be important and how to feel good, and Jesus' teaching about service to others seems alien. But those who have humbly served others are most qualified to be great in heaven.

LUKE 18:18-30
Once a religious leader asked Jesus this question:
"Good Teacher, what should I do to inherit eternal
life?"
19"Why do you call me good?" Jesus asked him.
"Only God is truly good. 20But to answer your question, you know the commandments: 'You must not
commit adultery. You must not murder. You must not
steal. You must not testify falsely. Honor your father
and mother.'*"
21The man replied, "I've obeyed all these commandments since I was young."
22When Jesus heard his answer, he said, "There is
still one thing you haven't done. Sell all your possessions and give the money to the poor, and you will have
treasure in heaven. Then come, follow me."
23But when the man heard this he became very sad,
for he was very rich.
24When Jesus saw this,* he said, "How hard it is for
the rich to enter the Kingdom of God! 25In fact, it is
easier for a camel to go through the eye of a needle
than for a rich person to enter the Kingdom of God!"
26Those who heard this said, "Then who in the
world can be saved?"
27He replied, "What is impossible for people is possible with God."
28Peter said, "We've left our homes to follow you."
29"Yes," Jesus replied, "and I assure you that everyone who has given up house or wife or brothers or
parents or children, for the sake of the Kingdom of
God, 30will be repaid many times over in this life, and
will have eternal life in the world to come."

Jesus Tells the Parable of the Vineyard Workers

MATTHEW 20:1-16
"For the Kingdom of Heaven is like the landowner
who went out early one morning to hire workers for
his vineyard. 2He agreed to pay the normal daily wage*
and sent them out to work.
3"At nine o'clock in the morning he was passing
through the marketplace and saw some people standing around doing nothing. 4So he hired them, telling
them he would pay them whatever was right at the end
of the day. 5So they went to work in the vineyard. At
noon and again at three o'clock he did the same thing.
6"At five o'clock that afternoon he was in town
again and saw some more people standing around.
He asked them, 'Why haven't you been working
today?'
7"They replied, 'Because no one hired us.'
"The landowner told them, 'Then go out and join
the others in my vineyard.'
8"That evening he told the foreman to call the workers in and pay them, beginning with the last workers
first. 9When those hired at five o'clock were paid, each
received a full day's wage. 10When those hired first
came to get their pay, they assumed they would receive
more. But they, too, were paid a day's wage. 11When
they received their pay, they protested to the owner,
12'Those people worked only one hour, and yet you've
paid them just as much as you paid us who worked all
day in the scorching heat.'
13"He answered one of them, 'Friend, I haven't been
unfair! Didn't you agree to work all day for the usual

Lk 18:20 Exod 20:12-16; Deut 5:16-20. **Lk 18:24** Some manuscripts read *When Jesus saw how sad the man was.* **Mt 20:2** Greek *a denarius,* the payment for a full day's labor; similarly in 20:9, 10, 13.

For the Kingdom of Heaven is like the landowner who went out early one morning to hire workers for his vineyard.
Matthew 20:1

Luke 18:18ff This leader sought reassurance, some way of knowing for sure that he had eternal life. He wanted Jesus to measure and grade his qualifications or to give him some task he could do to assure his own immortality. So Jesus gave him a task—the one thing the rich man knew he could not do. "Then who in the world can be saved?" the bystanders asked. None can by their own achievements, Jesus' answer implied: "What is impossible for people is possible with God." Salvation cannot be earned—it is God's gift (see Eph 2:8-10).

Luke 18:22-23 This man's wealth made his life comfortable and gave him power and prestige. By telling him to sell everything he owned, Jesus was touching the very basis of his security and identity. The man did not understand that he would be even more secure if he followed Jesus than he was with all his wealth. Jesus does not ask believers to sell everything they have, although this may be his will for some. He does ask us all, however, to get rid of anything that has become more important in life than God. If your possessions take first place in your life, it would be better for you to get rid of them.

Luke 18:26-30 Peter and the other disciples had paid a high price—leaving their homes and jobs—to follow Jesus. But Jesus reminded Peter that following him has its benefits as well as its sacrifices. Any believer who has had to give up something to follow Christ will be repaid in this life as well as in the next. For example, if you must give up a secure job, you will find that God offers a secure relationship with himself now and forever. If you must give up your family's approval, you will gain the love of the family of God. The disciples had begun to pay the price of following Jesus, and he said they would be rewarded. Don't dwell on what you have given up; think about what you have gained and give thanks for it.

wage? [14]Take your money and go. I wanted to pay this last worker the same as you. [15]Is it against the law for me to do what I want with my money? Should you be jealous because I am kind to others?'

[16]"So those who are last now will be first then, and those who are first will be last."

Jesus Predicts His Death the Third Time PARALLEL

MATTHEW 20:17-19

As Jesus was going up to Jerusalem, he took the twelve disciples aside privately and told them what was going to happen to him. [18]"Listen," he said, "we're going up to Jerusalem, where the Son of Man* will be betrayed to the leading priests and the teachers of religious law. They will sentence him to die. [19]Then they will hand him over to the Romans* to be mocked, flogged with a whip, and crucified. But on the third day he will be raised from the dead."

MARK 10:32-34

They were now on the way up to Jerusalem, and Jesus was walking ahead of them. The disciples were filled with awe, and the people following behind were overwhelmed with fear. Taking the twelve disciples aside, Jesus once more began to describe everything that was about to happen to him. [33]"Listen," he said, "we're going up to Jerusalem, where the Son of Man* will be betrayed to the leading priests and the teachers of religious law. They will sentence him to die and hand him over to the Romans.* [34]They will mock him, spit on him, flog him with a whip, and kill him, but after three days he will rise again."

LUKE 18:31-34

Taking the twelve disciples aside, Jesus said, "Listen, we're going up to Jerusalem, where all the predictions of the prophets concerning the Son of Man will come true. [32]He will be handed over to the Romans,* and he will be mocked, treated shamefully, and spit upon. [33]They will flog him with a whip and kill him, but on the third day he will rise again."

[34]But they didn't understand any of this. The significance of his words was hidden from them, and they failed to grasp what he was talking about.

Mt 20:18 "Son of Man" is a title Jesus used for himself. **Mt 20:19** Greek *the Gentiles.* **Mk 10:33a** "Son of Man" is a title Jesus used for himself. **Mk 10:33b** Greek *the Gentiles.* **Lk 18:32** Greek *the Gentiles.*

Matt 20:1ff Jesus further clarified the membership rules of the Kingdom of Heaven: Entrance is by God's grace alone. In this parable, God is the landowner and believers are the workers. This parable speaks especially to those who feel superior because of heritage, position, or having spent so much time with Christ; and to new believers, it is a reassurance of God's grace.

Matt 20:15 This parable is not about rewards but about salvation. It is a strong teaching about grace, God's generosity. We shouldn't begrudge those who turn to God in the last moments of life because in reality, no one deserves eternal life.

Many people we don't expect to see in the Kingdom will be there. The criminal who repented as he was dying (Luke 23:40-43) will be there along with people who have believed and served God for many years. Do you resent God's gracious acceptance of the despised, the outcast, and the sinners who have turned to him for forgiveness? Have you ever been jealous of what God has given to another person? Instead, focus on God's gracious benefits to you, and be thankful for what you have.

Matt 20:17-19 Jesus predicted his death and resurrection for the third time (see Matt 16:21; 17:22-23). But the disciples still didn't accept and believe what he meant. They continued to argue over their positions in Christ's Kingdom (Matt 20:20-28).

Mark 10:33-34 Jesus' death and resurrection should have come as no surprise to the disciples. Here he clearly explained what would happen to him. Unfortunately, they didn't really hear what he was saying. Jesus said he was the Messiah, but they thought the Messiah would be a conquering king. He spoke to them of resurrection, but they heard only his words about death. Because Jesus often spoke in parables, the disciples may have thought that his words on death and resurrection were another parable that they weren't astute enough to understand. But Jesus' predictions of his death and resurrection show that these events were God's plan from the beginning, not accidents.

Luke 18:31-34 Some predictions about what would happen to Jesus are found in Psalm 41:9 (betrayal); Psalm 22:16-18 and Isaiah 53:4-7 (crucifixion); Psalm 16:10 (resurrection). The disciples didn't understand Jesus, apparently because they were focusing on what he had said about his death and were ignoring what he had said about his resurrection. Even though Jesus had spoken plainly, they would not grasp the significance of his words until they saw the risen Christ face to face.

Roman Whips and Scourges

Jesus predicted that he would be scourged and crucified (Luke 18:32-33). Scourging was a particularly brutal punishment, and the Romans usually reserved it for slaves or foreigners as well as for those condemned to death. Normally, criminals were scourged after they had been condemned to death; it is therefore unusual to find the scourging of Jesus taking place before his condemnation. Pilate may have hoped to soften the people's hearts by Jesus' suffering so that they would not demand the death penalty (Luke 23:16, 22; John 19:1). But Jesus' scourging just added to his suffering. After being beaten by whips with metal barbs (to tear open the flesh), he suffered crucifixion.

Jesus Teaches about Serving Others PARALLEL ••

MATTHEW 20:20-28 ••

Then the mother of James and John, the sons of Zebedee, came to Jesus with her sons. She knelt respectfully to ask a favor. [21]"What is your request?" he asked.

She replied, "In your Kingdom, please let my two sons sit in places of honor next to you, one on your right and the other on your left."

[22]But Jesus answered by saying to them, "You don't know what you are asking! Are you able to drink from the bitter cup of suffering I am about to drink?"

"Oh yes," they replied, "we are able!"

[23]Jesus told them, "You will indeed drink from my bitter cup. But I have no right to say who will sit on my right or my left. My Father has prepared those places for the ones he has chosen."

[24]When the ten other disciples heard what James and John had asked, they were indignant. [25]But Jesus called them together and said, "You know that the rulers in this world lord it over their people, and officials flaunt their authority over those under them. [26]But among you it will be different. Whoever wants to be a leader among you must be your servant, [27]and whoever wants to be first among you must become your slave. [28]For even the Son of Man came not to be served but to serve others and to give his life as a ransom for many."

MARK 10:35-45 ••

Then James and John, the sons of Zebedee, came over and spoke to him. "Teacher," they said, "we want you to do us a favor."

[36]"What is your request?" he asked.

[37]They replied, "When you sit on your glorious throne, we want to sit in places of honor next to you, one on your right and the other on your left."

[38]But Jesus said to them, "You don't know what you are asking! Are you able to drink from the bitter cup of suffering I am about to drink? Are you able to be baptized with the baptism of suffering I must be baptized with?"

[39]"Oh yes," they replied, "we are able!"

Then Jesus told them, "You will indeed drink from my bitter cup and be baptized with my baptism of suffering. [40]But I have no right to say who will sit on my right or my left. God has prepared those places for the ones he has chosen."

[41]When the ten other disciples heard what James and John had asked, they were indignant. [42]So Jesus called them together and said, "You know that the rulers in this world lord it over their people, and officials flaunt their authority over those under them. [43]But among you it will be different. Whoever wants to be a leader among you must be your servant, [44]and whoever wants to be first among you must be the slave

---

Matt 20:20 The mother of James and John came to Jesus and "knelt respectfully to ask a favor." She gave Jesus worship, but her real motive was to get something from him. Too often this happens in our churches and in our lives. We play religious games, expecting God to give us something in return. True worship, however, adores and praises Christ for who he is and for what he has done.

Matt 20:20 The mother of James and John asked Jesus to give her sons special positions in his Kingdom. Parents naturally want to see their children promoted and honored, but this desire is dangerous if it causes them to stand in the way of God's specific will for their children. God may have different work in mind for them—perhaps not as glamorous but just as important. Thus, parents' desires for their children's advancement must be held in check as they pray that God's will be done in their children's lives.

Matt 20:20 According to Matthew 27:56, the mother of James and John was at the cross when Jesus was crucified. Some have suggested that she was the sister of Mary, the mother of Jesus. A close family relationship may have prompted her to make this request for her sons.

Matt 20:22 James, John, and their mother failed to grasp Jesus' previous teachings on rewards (Matt 19:16-30) and eternal life (Matt 20:1-16). They failed to understand the suffering they must face before living in the glory of God's Kingdom. The "cup" was the suffering and crucifixion that Christ faced. Both James and John would also face great suffering. James would be put to death for his faith, and John would be exiled.

Matt 20:23 Jesus was showing that he was under the authority of the Father, who alone makes the decisions about leadership in heaven. Such rewards are not granted as favors. They are for those who have maintained their commitment to Jesus in spite of severe trials.

Matt 20:24 The other disciples were upset with James and John for trying to grab the top positions. All the disciples wanted to be the greatest (Matt 18:1), but Jesus taught them that the greatest person in God's Kingdom is the servant of all. Authority is given, not for self-importance, ambition, or respect, but for useful service to God and his creation.

Matt 20:27 Jesus described leadership from a new perspective. Instead of using people, we are to serve them. Jesus' mission was to serve others and to give his life away. A real leader has a servant's heart. Servant leaders appreciate others' worth and realize that they're not above any job. If you see something that needs to be done, don't wait to be asked. Take the initiative and do it like a faithful servant.

Matt 20:28 A "ransom" was the price paid to release a slave from bondage. Jesus often told his disciples that he must die, but here he told them why—to redeem all people from the bondage of sin and death. The disciples thought that as long as Jesus was alive, he could save them. But Jesus revealed that only his death would save them and the world.

Mark 10:35 Mark records that John and James went to Jesus with their request; in Matthew, their mother also made the request. Apparently mother and sons were in agreement in requesting honored places in Christ's Kingdom.

Mark 10:37 The disciples, like most Jews of that day, had the wrong idea of the Messiah's Kingdom as predicted by the Old Testament prophets. They thought Jesus would establish an earthly kingdom that would free Israel from Rome's oppression. James and John wanted honored places in it. But Jesus' Kingdom is not of this world; it is not centered in palaces and on thrones but rather in the hearts and lives of his followers. The disciples did not understand this until after Jesus' resurrection.

Mark 10:38-39 James and John said they were willing to face any trial for Christ. Both did suffer: James died as a martyr (Acts 12:2), and John was forced to live in exile (Rev 1:9). It is easy to say we will endure anything for Christ, and yet most of us complain about the most minor problems. We may say that we are willing to suffer for Christ, but are we willing to suffer the minor irritations that sometimes come with serving others?

Mark 10:42-45 James and John wanted the highest positions in Jesus' Kingdom. But Jesus told them that true greatness comes in serving others. Peter, one of the disciples who had heard this message, expands the thought in 1 Peter 5:1-4.

of everyone else. 45For even the Son of Man came not
to be served but to serve others and to give his life as
a ransom for many."

Jesus Heals Two Blind Beggars PARALLEL ●●●

MATTHEW 20:29-34 ●○○
As Jesus and the disciples left the town of Jericho, a
large crowd followed behind. 30Two blind men were
sitting beside the road. When they heard that Jesus
was coming that way, they began shouting, "Lord, Son
of David, have mercy on us!"
31"Be quiet!" the crowd yelled at them.
But they only shouted louder, "Lord, Son of David,
have mercy on us!"
32When Jesus heard them, he stopped and called,
"What do you want me to do for you?"
33"Lord," they said, "we want to see!" 34Jesus felt
sorry for them and touched their eyes. Instantly they
could see! Then they followed him.

MARK 10:46-52 ○●○
Then they reached Jericho, and as Jesus and his disciples left town, a large crowd followed him. A blind
beggar named Bartimaeus (son of Timaeus) was sitting beside the road. 47When Bartimaeus heard that
Jesus of Nazareth was nearby, he began to shout,
"Jesus, Son of David, have mercy on me!"
48"Be quiet!" many of the people yelled at him.
But he only shouted louder, "Son of David, have
mercy on me!"
49When Jesus heard him, he stopped and said, "Tell
him to come here."
So they called the blind man. "Cheer up," they said.
"Come on, he's calling you!" 50Bartimaeus threw aside
his coat, jumped up, and came to Jesus.
51"What do you want me to do for you?" Jesus
asked.
"My rabbi,*" the blind man said, "I want to see!"
52And Jesus said to him, "Go, for your faith has
healed you." Instantly the man could see, and he followed Jesus down the road.*

LUKE 18:35-43 ○○●
As Jesus approached Jericho, a blind beggar was sitting beside the road. 36When he heard the noise of
a crowd going past, he asked what was happening.
37They told him that Jesus the Nazarene* was going

Mk 10:51 Greek uses the Hebrew term *Rabboni.* **Mk 10:52** Or *on the way.* **Lk 18:37** Or *Jesus of Nazareth.*

Businesses, organizations, and institutions measure greatness by personal achievement. In Christ's Kingdom, however, service is the way to get ahead. The desire to be on top will hinder, not help. Rather than seeking to have your needs met, look for ways that you can minister to the needs of others.

Mark 10:45 This verse reveals not only the motive for Jesus' ministry but also the basis for our salvation. A ransom was the price paid to release a slave. Jesus paid a ransom for us because we could not pay it ourselves. His death released all of us from our slavery to sin. The disciples thought Jesus' life and power would save them from Rome; Jesus said his death would save them from sin, an even greater slavery than Rome's. See 1 Peter 1:18-19 for more about the ransom Jesus paid for us.

Matt 20:29-34 Matthew records that there were two blind men, while Mark and Luke mention only one. This is probably the same event, but Mark and Luke singled out the more vocal of the two men.

Matt 20:32-33 Although Jesus was concerned about the coming events in Jerusalem, he demonstrated what he had just told the disciples about service (Matt 20:28) by stopping to care for the blind men.

Mark 10:46 Jericho was a popular resort city rebuilt by Herod the Great in the Judean desert, not far from the Jordan River crossing. Jesus was on his way to Jerusalem (Mark 10:32), and after crossing over from Perea, he would naturally enter Jericho.

Mark 10:46 Beggars were a common sight in most towns. Because most occupations of that day required physical labor, anyone with a crippling disease or disability was at a severe disadvantage and was usually forced to beg, even though God's laws commanded care for such needy people (Lev 25:35-38). Blindness was considered a curse from God for sin (John 9:2), but Jesus refuted this idea when he reached out to heal the blind.

Mark 10:47 We do not know how long Bartimaeus had been blind, but it only took a moment for him to decide to call on Jesus for help. Jesus met many spiritually blind people—religious leaders, family members, people in the crowd. Though their eyes were fine, they could not see the truth about Jesus. But blind Bartimaeus heard the report that Jesus was coming and boldly cried out.

In coming to Jesus, we need Bartimaeus's boldness. We must overcome our reticence and doubts and take the step to call on him. Bartimaeus had not seen Jesus' miracles, but he responded in faith to what he had heard. We have heard Jesus described in the Gospels. May we be like those Peter wrote about: "You love him even though you have never seen him. Though you do not see him now, you trust him; and you rejoice with a glorious, inexpressible joy" (1 Pet 1:8).

Luke 18:35 Beggars often would wait along the roads near cities because that was where they could contact the most people. Usually disabled in some way, beggars were unable to earn a living. Medical help was not available for their problems, and people tended to ignore their obligation to care for the needy (Lev 25:35-38). Thus, beggars had little hope of escaping their degrading way of life. But this blind beggar took hope in the Messiah. He shamelessly cried out for Jesus' attention, and Jesus said that his faith allowed him to see. No matter how desperate your situation may seem, if you call out to Jesus in faith, he will help you.

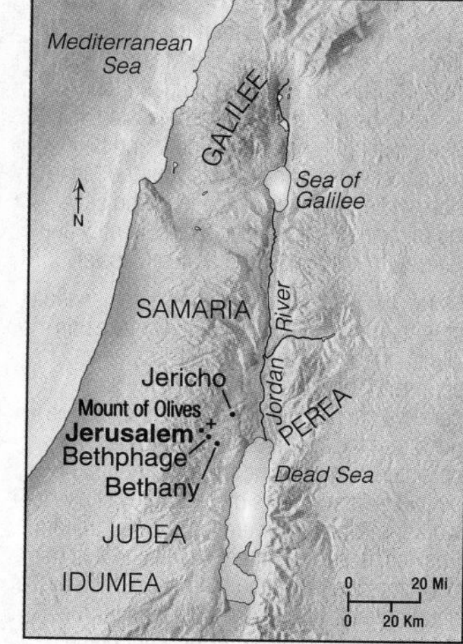

***JESUS NEARS JERUSALEM** From Jericho, Jesus headed toward acclaim, then crucifixion, in Jerusalem. During his last week, he stayed outside the city in Bethany, a village on the eastern slope of the Mount of Olives, entering Jerusalem each day to teach, eat the Passover meal, and finally be crucified.*

▸ LUKE 18:35-43 *(cont.)*

by. 38So he began shouting, "Jesus, Son of David, have
mercy on me!"
39"Be quiet!" the people in front yelled at him.
But he only shouted louder, "Son of David, have
mercy on me!"
40When Jesus heard him, he stopped and ordered
that the man be brought to him. As the man came
near, Jesus asked him, 41"What do you want me to
do for you?"
"Lord," he said, "I want to see!"
42And Jesus said, "All right, receive your sight! Your
faith has healed you." 43Instantly the man could see,
and he followed Jesus, praising God. And all who saw
it praised God, too.

Jesus Brings Salvation to Zacchaeus's Home

LUKE 19:1-10

Jesus entered Jericho and made his way through the
town. 2There was a man there named Zacchaeus. He
was the chief tax collector in the region, and he had
become very rich. 3He tried to get a look at Jesus, but
he was too short to see over the crowd. 4So he ran
ahead and climbed a sycamore-fig tree beside the
road, for Jesus was going to pass that way.
5When Jesus came by, he looked up at Zacchaeus and
called him by name. "Zacchaeus!" he said. "Quick, come
down! I must be a guest in your home today."
6Zacchaeus quickly climbed down and took Jesus to
his house in great excitement and joy. 7But the people
were displeased. "He has gone to be the guest of a
notorious sinner," they grumbled.
8Meanwhile, Zacchaeus stood before the Lord and
said, "I will give half my wealth to the poor, Lord, and
if I have cheated people on their taxes, I will give them
back four times as much!"
9Jesus responded, "Salvation has come to this home
today, for this man has shown himself to be a true son
of Abraham. 10For the Son of Man* came to seek and
save those who are lost."

Jesus Tells the Parable of the King's Ten Servants

LUKE 19:11-27

The crowd was listening to everything Jesus said. And
because he was nearing Jerusalem, he told them a
story to correct the impression that the Kingdom of

Lk 19:10 "Son of Man" is a title Jesus used for himself.

Luke 18:38 The blind man called Jesus "Son of David," a title for the Messiah (Isa 11:1-3). This means that he understood Jesus to be the long-awaited Messiah. It is interesting to note that a poor and blind beggar could see that Jesus was the Messiah, while the religious leaders who saw his miracles were blinded to his identity and refused to recognize him as the Messiah.

Luke 19:1-10 To finance their great world empire, the Romans levied heavy taxes on all nations under their control. The Jews opposed these taxes because they supported a secular government and its pagan gods, but they were still forced to pay. Tax collectors were among the most unpopular people in Israel. Jews by birth, they chose to work for Rome and were considered traitors. Besides, it was common knowledge that tax collectors were making themselves rich by gouging their fellow Jews. No wonder the people muttered when Jesus went home with the tax collector Zacchaeus. But despite the fact that Zacchaeus was both a cheater and a turncoat, Jesus loved him; and in response, this tax collector was converted. In every society, certain groups of people are considered "untouchable" because of their political views, their immoral behavior, or their lifestyle. We should not give in to social pressure to avoid these people. Jesus loves them, and they need to hear his Good News.

Luke 19:8 Judging from the crowd's reaction to him, Zacchaeus must have been a very crooked tax collector. After he met Jesus, however, he realized that his life needed straightening out. By giving to the poor and making restitution—with generous interest—to those he had cheated, Zacchaeus demonstrated inner change by outward action. Following Jesus in your head or heart alone is not enough. You must show your faith by changed behavior. Has your faith resulted in action? What changes do you need to make?

GOSPEL ACCOUNTS FOUND ONLY IN LUKE

Luke 1:5-80	Special events leading up to the births of John the Baptist and Jesus
Luke 2:1-52	Events from Jesus' childhood
Luke 3:19-20	Herod puts John in prison
Luke 4:16-30	Jesus is rejected at Nazareth
Luke 5:1-11	Jesus provides a miraculous catch of fish
Luke 7:11-17	Jesus raises a widow's son from the dead
Luke 7:36-50	A sinful woman anoints Jesus' feet
Luke 8:1-3	Women travel with Jesus
Luke 10:1–18:14	Events, miracles, and teachings during the months prior to Christ's death
Luke 19:1-27	Jesus meets Zacchaeus and later tells the parable of the king's 10 servants
Luke 23:6-12	Jesus' trial before Herod
Luke 24:44-49	Some of Jesus' last words before his ascension

Luke 19:9-10 When Jesus said Zacchaeus was a son of Abraham and yet was lost, he must have shocked his hearers in at least two ways: They would not have liked to acknowledge that this unpopular tax collector was a fellow son of Abraham, and they would not have wished to admit that sons of Abraham could be lost. But a person is not saved because of a good heritage or condemned by a bad one; faith is more important than genealogy. Jesus came to save all the lost, regardless of their background or previous way of life. Through faith, the lost can be forgiven and made new.

Luke 19:11ff The people still hoped for a political leader who would set up an earthly kingdom and get rid of Roman domination. Jesus' story showed that his Kingdom would not take this form right away. First, he would

God would begin right away. 12He said, "A nobleman
was called away to a distant empire to be crowned
king and then return. 13Before he left, he called together ten of his servants and divided among them
ten pounds of silver,* saying, 'Invest this for me while
I am gone.' 14But his people hated him and sent a delegation after him to say, 'We do not want him to be
our king.'
15"After he was crowned king, he returned and called
in the servants to whom he had given the money. He
wanted to find out what their profits were. 16The first
servant reported, 'Master, I invested your money and
made ten times the original amount!'
17" 'Well done!' the king exclaimed. 'You are a good
servant. You have been faithful with the little I entrusted to you, so you will be governor of ten cities
as your reward.'
18"The next servant reported, 'Master, I invested your
money and made five times the original amount.'
19" 'Well done!' the king said. 'You will be governor
over five cities.'
20"But the third servant brought back only the original amount of money and said, 'Master, I hid your
money and kept it safe. 21I was afraid because you are
a hard man to deal with, taking what isn't yours and
harvesting crops you didn't plant.'
22" 'You wicked servant!' the king roared. 'Your own
words condemn you. If you knew that I'm a hard
man who takes what isn't mine and harvests crops I
didn't plant, 23why didn't you deposit my money in
the bank? At least I could have gotten some interest
on it.'
24"Then, turning to the others standing nearby,
the king ordered, 'Take the money from this servant,
and give it to the one who has ten pounds.'
25" 'But, master,' they said, 'he already has ten
pounds!'
26" 'Yes,' the king replied, 'and to those who use well
what they are given, even more will be given. But from
those who do nothing, even what little they have will
be taken away. 27And as for these enemies of mine who
didn't want me to be their king—bring them in and
execute them right here in front of me.' "

A Woman Anoints Jesus with Perfume PARALLEL •••

MATTHEW 26:6-13 •••

Meanwhile, Jesus was in Bethany at the home of
Simon, a man who had previously had leprosy. 7While
he was eating,* a woman came in with a beautiful alabaster jar of expensive perfume and poured it over
his head.

Lk 19:13 Greek *ten minas;* one mina was worth about three months' wages. **Mt 26:7** Or *reclining.*

go away for a while, and his followers would need to be faithful and productive during his absence. Upon his return, Jesus would inaugurate a Kingdom more powerful and just than anything they could expect or imagine.

Luke 19:11ff This story showed Jesus' followers what they were to do during the time between Jesus' departure and his second coming. Because we live in that time period, it applies directly to us. We have been given excellent resources to build and expand God's Kingdom. Jesus expects us to use these talents so that they multiply and the Kingdom grows. He asks each of us to account for what we do with his gifts. While awaiting the coming of the Kingdom of God in glory, we must do Christ's work.

Luke 19:20-27 Why was the king so hard on this man who had not increased the money? He punished the man because (1) he didn't share his master's interest in the Kingdom, (2) he didn't trust his master's intentions, (3) his only concern was for himself, and (4) he did nothing productive with the money. Like the king in this story, God has given you gifts to use for the benefit of his Kingdom. Do you want the Kingdom to grow? Do you trust God to govern it fairly? Are you as concerned for others' welfare as you are for your own? Are you willing to use faithfully what he has entrusted to you?

Matt 26:6-13 Matthew and Mark put this event just before the Last Supper, while John has it just before the Triumphal Entry. Of the three, John places this event in the most likely chronological order. We must remember that the main purpose of the Gospel writers was to give an accurate record of Jesus' message, not to present an exact chronological account of his life. Matthew and Mark may have wanted to contrast the complete devotion of Mary with the betrayal of Judas, the next event they record in their Gospels.

Alabaster Vase

Alabaster vases were used in ancient Egypt and Palestine to store perfumes, oils, and other cosmetic materials. Perfumes were put on clothes (Ps 45:8; Song 4:11) and sprinkled on couches or beds (Prov 7:17). Perfumes and spices also played an important role in the burial of the dead. They were used in embalming (Gen 50:2-3) and were sprinkled on the bier or burned in the fire at some funerals (2 Chr 16:14). Mary took a 12-ounce alabaster jar of expensive perfume and anointed Jesus with it. Jesus understood this as a symbolic act foreshadowing the anointing of his body when it was buried (John 12:1-8). Indeed, Nicodemus brought a mixture of myrrh and aloes to be used in wrapping the body of Jesus when he was buried (John 19:39-40). These were precious gifts, given to the Lord Jesus out of heartfelt love.

Matt 26:7 This woman was Mary, the sister of Martha and Lazarus, who lived in Bethany (John 12:1-3). Alabaster jars were carved from a translucent gypsum. These jars were used to hold perfumed oil.

▸ **MATTHEW 26:6-13** ***(cont.)***

8The disciples were indignant when they saw this.
"What a waste!" they said. 9"It could have been sold
for a high price and the money given to the poor."
10But Jesus, aware of this, replied, "Why criticize
this woman for doing such a good thing to me? 11You
will always have the poor among you, but you will not
always have me. 12She has poured this perfume on me
to prepare my body for burial. 13I tell you the truth,
wherever the Good News is preached throughout the
world, this woman's deed will be remembered and
discussed."

MARK 14:3-9

Meanwhile, Jesus was in Bethany at the home of
Simon, a man who had previously had leprosy. While
he was eating,* a woman came in with a beautiful
alabaster jar of expensive perfume made from essence of nard. She broke open the jar and poured the
perfume over his head.
4Some of those at the table were indignant. "Why
waste such expensive perfume?" they asked. 5"It could
have been sold for a year's wages* and the money
given to the poor!" So they scolded her harshly.
6But Jesus replied, "Leave her alone. Why criticize
her for doing such a good thing to me? 7You will always have the poor among you, and you can help them
whenever you want to. But you will not always have
me. 8She has done what she could and has anointed
my body for burial ahead of time. 9I tell you the truth,
wherever the Good News is preached throughout the
world, this woman's deed will be remembered and
discussed."

JOHN 12:1-11

Six days before the Passover celebration began, Jesus
arrived in Bethany, the home of Lazarus—the man he
had raised from the dead. 2A dinner was prepared in
Jesus' honor. Martha served, and Lazarus was among
those who ate* with him. 3Then Mary took a twelve-
ounce jar* of expensive perfume made from essence
of nard, and she anointed Jesus' feet with it, wiping
his feet with her hair. The house was filled with the
fragrance.

Mk 14:3 Or *reclining.* **Mk 14:5** Greek *for 300 denarii.* A denarius was equivalent to a laborer's full day's wage. **Jn 12:2** Or *who reclined.* **Jn 12:3** Greek *took 1 litra* [327 grams].

MARY

Hospitality is an art. Making sure a guest is welcomed, warmed, and well fed requires creativity, organization, and teamwork. Their ability to accomplish these goals makes Mary and her sister, Martha, one of the best hospitality teams in the Bible. Their frequent guest was Jesus Christ. • For Mary, hospitality meant giving more attention to the guest himself than to the needs he might have. She let her older sister, Martha, take care of those details. Mary's approach to events shows her to be mainly a "responder." She did little preparation—her role was participation. Unlike her sister, who had to learn to stop and listen, Mary needed to learn that action is often appropriate and necessary. • We first meet Mary during a visit Jesus paid to her home. She simply sat at his feet and listened. When Martha became irritated at her sister's lack of help, Jesus stated that Mary's choice to enjoy his company was the most appropriate response at the time. Our last glimpse of Mary shows her to have become a woman of thoughtful and worshipful action. Again she was at Jesus' feet, washing them with perfume and wiping them with her hair. Jesus said her act of worship would be told everywhere as an example of costly service. • Are you so busy planning and running your life that you neglect precious time with Jesus? Or do you respond to him by listening to his Word and then finding ways to worship him with your life?

Strengths and accomplishments	• Perhaps the only person who understood and accepted Jesus' coming death, taking time to anoint his body while he was still living • Learned when to listen and when to act
Lessons from her life	• The busyness of serving God can become a barrier to knowing him personally • Small acts of obedience and service have widespread effects
Vital statistics	• Where: Bethany • Relatives: Sister: Martha. Brother: Lazarus.
Key verses	"'She has poured this perfume on me to prepare my body for burial. I tell you the truth, wherever the Good News is preached throughout the world, this woman's deed will be remembered and discussed'" (Matt 26:12-13).

Mary's story is told in Matthew 26:6-13; Mark 14:3-9; Luke 10:38-42; John 11:17-45; 12:1-11.

Matt 26:8 All the disciples were indignant, but John's Gospel singles out Judas Iscariot as especially so (John 12:4-6).

Matt 26:11 Here Jesus brought back to mind Deuteronomy 15:11: "There will always be some in the land who are poor." This statement does not justify ignoring the needs of the poor. Scripture continually exhorts us to care for the needy. The passage in Deuteronomy continues: "That is why I am commanding you to share freely with the poor and with other Israelites in need." Rather, by saying this, Jesus highlighted the special sacrifice Mary made for him.

Mark 14:3 Bethany is located on the eastern slope of the Mount of Olives (Jerusalem is on the western side). This town was the home of Jesus' friends Lazarus, Mary, and Martha, who were also present at this dinner (John 11:2). The woman who anointed Jesus' feet was Mary, Lazarus and Martha's sister (John 12:1-3).

Mark 14:4-5 Whereas Mark says "some of those at the table," John specifically mentions Judas (John 12:4-5). Judas's indignation over Mary's act of worship was based not on concern for the poor but on greed. Because Judas was the treasurer of Jesus' ministry and had embezzled funds (John 12:6), he no doubt wanted the perfume sold so that he could benefit from the proceeds.

Mark 14:6-7 Jesus was not saying that we should neglect the poor, nor was he justifying indifference to them. (For Jesus' teaching about the poor, see Matt 6:2-4; Luke 6:20-21; 14:13, 21; 18:22.) Jesus was praising Mary for her unselfish act of worship. The essence of worshiping Christ is to regard him with utmost love, respect,

[4]But Judas Iscariot, the disciple who would soon betray him, said, [5]"That perfume was worth a year's wages.* It should have been sold and the money given to the poor." [6]Not that he cared for the poor—he was a thief, and since he was in charge of the disciples' money, he often stole some for himself.

[7]Jesus replied, "Leave her alone. She did this in preparation for my burial. [8]You will always have the poor among you, but you will not always have me."

[9]When all the people* heard of Jesus' arrival, they flocked to see him and also to see Lazarus, the man Jesus had raised from the dead. [10]Then the leading priests decided to kill Lazarus, too, [11]for it was because of him that many of the people had deserted them* and believed in Jesus.

Jn 12:5 Greek *worth 300 denarii.* A denarius was equivalent to a laborer's full day's wage. **Jn 12:9** Greek *Jewish people;* also in 12:11. **Jn 12:11** Or *had deserted their traditions;* Greek reads *had deserted.*

7. JESUS' MINISTRY IN JERUSALEM

Jesus' final week before he was crucified was spent in and around Jerusalem. Beginning with the Triumphal Entry, Jesus continued to teach his followers and challenge the corrupt religious authorities who had rejected his message.

Jesus Rides into Jerusalem on a Donkey PARALLEL ●●●●

MATTHEW 21:1-11 ●○○○

As Jesus and the disciples approached Jerusalem, they came to the town of Bethphage on the Mount of Olives. Jesus sent two of them on ahead. [2]"Go into the village over there," he said. "As soon as you enter it, you will see a donkey tied there, with its colt beside it. Untie them and bring them to me. [3]If anyone asks what you are doing, just say, 'The Lord needs them,' and he will immediately let you take them."

[4]This took place to fulfill the prophecy that said,

[5] "Tell the people of Jerusalem,*
'Look, your King is coming to you.
He is humble, riding on a donkey—
riding on a donkey's colt.'"*

[6]The two disciples did as Jesus commanded. [7]They brought the donkey and the colt to him and threw their garments over the colt, and he sat on it.*

[8]Most of the crowd spread their garments on the road ahead of him, and others cut branches from the trees and spread them on the road. [9]Jesus was in the center of the procession, and the people all around him were shouting,

"Praise God* for the Son of David!
Blessings on the one who comes in the name of the LORD!
Praise God in highest heaven!"*

[10]The entire city of Jerusalem was in an uproar as he entered. "Who is this?" they asked.

[11]And the crowds replied, "It's Jesus, the prophet from Nazareth in Galilee."

Mt 21:5a Greek *Tell the daughter of Zion.* Isa 62:11. **Mt 21:5b** Zech 9:9. **Mt 21:7** Greek *over them, and he sat on them.* **Mt 21:9a** Greek *Hosanna,* an exclamation of praise that literally means "save now"; also in 21:9b, 15. **Mt 21:9b** Pss 118:25-26; 148:1.

and devotion and to be willing to sacrifice to him what is most precious.

John 12:3 Essence of nard was a fragrant ointment imported from the mountains of India. Thus, it was very expensive. The amount Mary used was worth a year's wages.

John 12:4-6 Judas often dipped into the disciples' money bag for his own use. Quite likely, Jesus knew what Judas was doing (John 2:24-25; 6:64), but he never did or said anything about it. Similarly, when we choose the way of sin, God may not immediately do anything to stop us, but this does not mean he approves of our actions. What we deserve will come.

John 12:5-6 Judas used a pious phrase to hide his true motives. But Jesus knew what was in his heart. Judas's life had become a lie, and the devil was gaining more and more control over him (John 13:27). Satan is the father of lies, and a lying character opens the door to his influence. Jesus' knowledge of us should make us want to keep our actions consistent with our words. Because we have nothing to fear with him, we should have nothing to hide.

John 12:7-8 This act and Jesus' response do not teach us to ignore the poor so we can spend money extravagantly for Christ. This was a unique act for a specific occasion—an anointing that anticipated Jesus' burial and a public declaration of faith in him as Messiah. Jesus' words should have taught Judas a valuable lesson about the worth of money. Unfortunately, Judas did not take heed; soon he would sell his Master's life for 30 pieces of silver.

John 12:10-11 The leading priests' blindness and hardness of heart caused them to sink ever deeper into sin. They rejected the Messiah and planned to kill him, and then they plotted to murder Lazarus as well. One sin leads to another. From the Jewish leaders' point of view, they could accuse Jesus of blasphemy because he claimed equality with God. But Lazarus had done nothing of the kind. They wanted Lazarus dead simply because he was a living witness to Jesus' power. This is a warning to us to avoid sin. Sin leads to more sin, a downward spiral that can be stopped only by repentance and the power of the Holy Spirit to change our behavior.

Matt 21:2-5 Matthew mentions a donkey and a colt, while the other Gospels mention only the colt. This was the same event, but Matthew focuses on the prophecy in Zechariah 9:9, where a donkey and a colt are mentioned. He shows how Jesus' actions fulfilled the prophet's words, thus giving another indication that Jesus was indeed the Messiah. When Jesus entered Jerusalem on a donkey's colt, he affirmed his messianic royalty as well as his humility. On the practical side, what better way to lead an unbroken colt for its first ride down a crowded road than to have its mother with it?

Matt 21:8 This verse is one of the few places where the Gospels record that Jesus' glory is recognized on earth. Jesus boldly rode as the King of peace, and the crowd gladly joined him. But these same people would bow to political pressure and desert him in just a few days. Today we celebrate this event on Palm Sunday. That day should remind us to guard against superficial acclaim for Christ.

MARK 11:1-11
As Jesus and his disciples approached Jerusalem, they
came to the towns of Bethphage and Bethany on the
Mount of Olives. Jesus sent two of them on ahead. 2"Go
into that village over there," he told them. "As soon as
you enter it, you will see a young donkey tied there that
no one has ever ridden. Untie it and bring it here. 3If
anyone asks, 'What are you doing?' just say, 'The Lord
needs it and will return it soon.'"
4The two disciples left and found the colt standing
in the street, tied outside the front door. 5As they were
untying it, some bystanders demanded, "What are you
doing, untying that colt?" 6They said what Jesus had
told them to say, and they were permitted to take it.
7Then they brought the colt to Jesus and threw their
garments over it, and he sat on it.
8Many in the crowd spread their garments on the
road ahead of him, and others spread leafy branches
they had cut in the fields. 9Jesus was in the center of
the procession, and the people all around him were
shouting,

"Praise God!*
Blessings on the one who comes in the name
of the LORD!
10 Blessings on the coming Kingdom of our
ancestor David!
Praise God in highest heaven!"*

11So Jesus came to Jerusalem and went into the
Temple. After looking around carefully at everything,
he left because it was late in the afternoon. Then he
returned to Bethany with the twelve disciples.

LUKE 19:28-40
After telling this story, Jesus went on toward Jerusalem, walking ahead of his disciples. 29As he came to
the towns of Bethphage and Bethany on the Mount
of Olives, he sent two disciples ahead. 30"Go into that
village over there," he told them. "As you enter it, you
will see a young donkey tied there that no one has
ever ridden. Untie it and bring it here. 31If anyone
asks, 'Why are you untying that colt?' just say, 'The
Lord needs it.'"
32So they went and found the colt, just as Jesus
had said. 33And sure enough, as they were untying
it, the owners asked them, "Why are you untying
that colt?"
34And the disciples simply replied, "The Lord needs
it." 35So they brought the colt to Jesus and threw their
garments over it for him to ride on.
36As he rode along, the crowds spread out their garments on the road ahead of him. 37When he reached
the place where the road started down the Mount of
Olives, all of his followers began to shout and sing as
they walked along, praising God for all the wonderful
miracles they had seen.

Mk 11:9 Greek *Hosanna,* an exclamation of praise that literally means "save now"; also in 11:10. **Mk 11:9-10** Pss 118:25-26; 148:1.

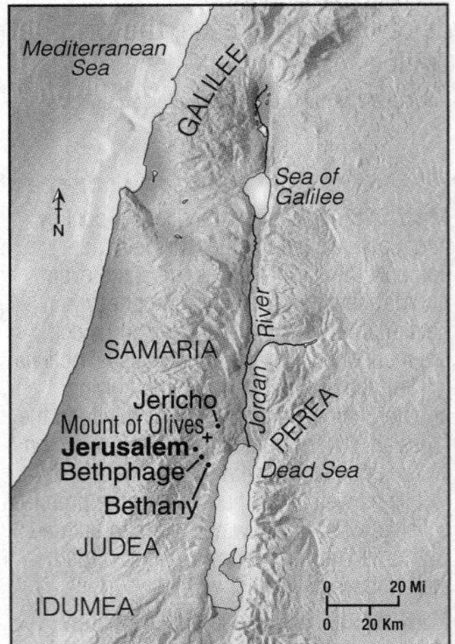

***PREPARATION FOR THE TRIUMPHAL ENTRY** On their way from Jericho, Jesus and the disciples neared Bethphage, on the slope of the Mount of Olives, just outside Jerusalem. Following Jesus' instructions, two disciples went into the village to bring back a donkey and its colt. Jesus rode into Jerusalem on the colt, an unmistakable sign of his kingship.*

Mark 11:1-2 This was Sunday of the week that Jesus would be crucified, and the great Passover festival was about to begin. Jews came to Jerusalem from all over the Roman world during this week-long celebration to remember the great exodus from Egypt (see Exod 12:37-51). Many in the crowds had heard of or seen Jesus and were hoping he would come to the Temple (John 11:55-57).

Jesus did come, not as a warring king on a horse or in a chariot, but as a gentle and peaceable King on a donkey's colt, just as Zechariah 9:9 had predicted. Jesus knew that those who would hear him teach at the Temple would return to their homes throughout the world and announce the coming of the Messiah.

Mark 11:9-10 The people exclaimed "Praise God!" because they recognized that Jesus was fulfilling the prophecy in Zechariah 9:9 (see also Ps 24:7-10; 118:26). They spoke of David's kingdom because of God's words to David in 2 Samuel 7:12-14. The crowd correctly saw Jesus as the fulfillment of these prophecies, but they did not understand where Jesus' kingship would lead him. This same crowd cried out "Crucify him!" when Jesus stood on trial only a few days later.

Mark 11:10 Like those who witnessed Jesus' victory parade into Jerusalem, we have expectations for what we think God should do to make life better, safer, and more enjoyable. Like excited spectators, we can't wait to see suffering stopped, injustice corrected, and prosperity begun. Like the people on the road to Jerusalem that day, we have much to learn about Jesus' death and resurrection. We must not let our personal desires catch us up in the celebration and shouting lest we miss the meaning of true discipleship. In our excitement and celebration, we must remember that following Christ involves hardships. It may include suffering, even death.

Luke 19:30-35 By this time Jesus was extremely well known. Everyone coming to Jerusalem for the Passover festival had heard of him, and for a time, the popular mood was favorable toward him. "The Lord needs it" was all the disciples had to say, and the colt's owners gladly turned their animal over to them.

Luke 19:35-38 Christians celebrate this event on Palm Sunday. The people lined the road praising God, waving palm branches, and throwing their cloaks in front of the colt as it passed before them. "Long live the King" was the meaning behind their joyful shouts because they knew that Jesus was intentionally fulfilling the prophecy in Zechariah 9:9: "Look, your king is coming to you. He is righteous and victorious, yet he is humble, riding on a donkey—riding on a donkey's colt." To announce that he was indeed the Messiah, Jesus chose a time when all Israel would be gathered at Jerusalem, a place where huge

[38] "Blessings on the King who comes in the name
of the LORD!
Peace in heaven, and glory in highest heaven!"*

[39]But some of the Pharisees among the crowd said, "Teacher, rebuke your followers for saying things like that!"

[40]He replied, "If they kept quiet, the stones along the road would burst into cheers!"

JOHN 12:12-19

The next day, the news that Jesus was on the way to Jerusalem swept through the city. A large crowd of Passover visitors [13]took palm branches and went down the road to meet him. They shouted,

"Praise God!*
Blessings on the one who comes in the name
of the LORD!
Hail to the King of Israel!"*

[14]Jesus found a young donkey and rode on it, fulfilling the prophecy that said:

[15] "Don't be afraid, people of Jerusalem.*
Look, your King is coming,
riding on a donkey's colt."*

[16]His disciples didn't understand at the time that this was a fulfillment of prophecy. But after Jesus entered into his glory, they remembered what had happened and realized that these things had been written about him.

[17]Many in the crowd had seen Jesus call Lazarus from the tomb, raising him from the dead, and they were telling others* about it. [18]That was the reason so many went out to meet him—because they had heard about this miraculous sign. [19]Then the Pharisees said to each other, "There's nothing we can do. Look, everyone* has gone after him!"

Jesus Grieves over Jerusalem Again

LUKE 19:41-44

But as he came closer to Jerusalem and saw the city ahead, he began to weep. [42]"How I wish today that you of all people would understand the way to peace. But now it is too late, and peace is hidden from your eyes. [43]Before long your enemies will build ramparts against your walls and encircle you and close in on you from every side. [44]They will crush you into the ground, and your children with you. Your enemies will not leave a single stone in place, because you did not accept your opportunity for salvation."

Jesus Clears the Temple Again

PARALLEL

MATTHEW 21:12-17

Jesus entered the Temple and began to drive out all the people buying and selling animals for sacrifice. He

Lk 19:38 Pss 118:26; 148:1. **Jn 12:13a** Greek *Hosanna,* an exclamation of praise adapted from a Hebrew expression that means "save now." **Jn 12:13b** Ps 118:25-26; Zeph 3:15. **Jn 12:15a** Greek *daughter of Zion.* **Jn 12:15b** Zech 9:9. **Jn 12:17** Greek *were testifying.* **Jn 12:19** Greek *the world.*

crowds could see him, and a way of proclaiming his mission that was unmistakable. The people went wild. They were sure their liberation was at hand.

Luke 19:38 The people who were praising God for giving them a king had the wrong idea about Jesus. They expected him to be a national leader who would restore their nation to its former glory; thus, they were deaf to the words of their prophets and blind to Jesus' real mission. When it became apparent that Jesus was not going to fulfill their hopes, many people turned against him.

Luke 19:39-40 The Pharisees thought the crowd's words were sacrilegious and blasphemous. They didn't want someone challenging their power and authority, and they didn't want a revolt that would bring the Roman army down on them. So they asked Jesus to keep his people quiet. But Jesus said that if the people were quiet, the stones would burst into cheers. Why? Not because Jesus was setting up a powerful political kingdom but because he was establishing God's eternal Kingdom, a reason for the greatest celebration of all.

John 12:13 Jesus began his last week on earth by riding into Jerusalem on a donkey under a canopy of palm branches with crowds hailing him as their king. To announce that he was indeed the Messiah, Jesus chose a time when all Israel would be gathered at Jerusalem, a place where huge crowds could see him, and a way of proclaiming his mission that was unmistakable.

John 12:16 After Jesus' resurrection, the disciples understood for the first time many of the prophecies that they had missed along the way. Jesus' words and actions took on new meaning and made more sense. In retrospect, the disciples saw how Jesus had led them into a deeper and better understanding of his truth. Stop now and think about the events in your life leading up to where you are now. How has God led you to this point? As you grow older, you will look back and see God's involvement more clearly than you do now.

John 12:18 The people flocked to Jesus because they had heard about his great miracle in raising Lazarus from the dead. Their adoration was short-lived and their commitment shallow, for in a few days they would do nothing to stop his crucifixion. Devotion based only on curiosity or popularity fades quickly.

Luke 19:41-44 The Jewish leaders had rejected their King (Luke 19:47). They had gone too far. They had refused God's offer of salvation in Jesus Christ when they were visited by God himself, and soon their nation would suffer. God did not turn away from the Jewish people who obeyed him, however, and he continues to offer salvation to the people he loves, both Jews and Gentiles. Eternal life is within your reach; accept it while the opportunity is still offered.

Luke 19:43-44 About 40 years after Jesus said these words, they came true. In A.D. 66, the Jews revolted against Roman control. Three years later Titus, son of the emperor Vespasian, was sent to crush the rebellion. Roman soldiers attacked Jerusalem and broke through the northern wall but still couldn't take the city. Finally, they laid siege to it, and in A.D. 70 they were able to enter the severely weakened city and burn it. About 600,000 Jews were killed during Titus's onslaught.

Matt 21:12 This is the second time Jesus cleared the Temple (see John 2:13-17). Merchants and money changers set up their booths in the Court of the Gentiles in the Temple, crowding out the Gentiles who had come from all over the civilized world to worship God. The merchants sold sacrificial animals at high prices, taking advantage of those who had come long distances. The money changers exchanged all international currency for the special Temple coins—the only money the merchants would accept. They often deceived foreigners who didn't know the exchange rates. Their commercialism in God's house frustrated people's attempts at worship. This, of course, greatly angered Jesus. Any practice that interferes with worshiping God should be stopped.

▶ **MATTHEW 21:12-17** ***(cont.)***

knocked over the tables of the money changers and the chairs of those selling doves. 13He said to them, "The Scriptures declare, 'My Temple will be called a house of prayer,' but you have turned it into a den of thieves!"*

14The blind and the lame came to him in the Temple, and he healed them. 15The leading priests and the teachers of religious law saw these wonderful miracles and heard even the children in the Temple shouting, "Praise God for the Son of David."

But the leaders were indignant. 16They asked Jesus, "Do you hear what these children are saying?"

"Yes," Jesus replied. "Haven't you ever read the Scriptures? For they say, 'You have taught children and infants to give you praise.'*" 17Then he returned to Bethany, where he stayed overnight.

MARK 11:15-19

When they arrived back in Jerusalem, Jesus entered the Temple and began to drive out the people buying and selling animals for sacrifices. He knocked over the tables of the money changers and the chairs of those selling doves, 16and he stopped everyone from using the Temple as a marketplace.* 17He said to them, "The Scriptures declare, 'My Temple will be called a house of prayer for all nations,' but you have turned it into a den of thieves."*

18When the leading priests and teachers of religious law heard what Jesus had done, they began planning how to kill him. But they were afraid of him because the people were so amazed at his teaching.

19That evening Jesus and the disciples left* the city.

LUKE 19:45-48

Then Jesus entered the Temple and began to drive out the people selling animals for sacrifices. 46He said to them, "The Scriptures declare, 'My Temple will be a house of prayer,' but you have turned it into a den of thieves."*

47After that, he taught daily in the Temple, but the leading priests, the teachers of religious law, and the other leaders of the people began planning how to kill him. 48But they could think of nothing, because all the people hung on every word he said.

Jesus Explains Why He Must Die

JOHN 12:20-36

Some Greeks who had come to Jerusalem for the Passover celebration 21paid a visit to Philip, who was from Bethsaida in Galilee. They said, "Sir, we want to meet Jesus." 22Philip told Andrew about it, and they went together to ask Jesus.

23Jesus replied, "Now the time has come for the Son of Man* to enter into his glory. 24I tell you the truth, unless a kernel of wheat is planted in the soil and dies, it remains alone. But its death will produce many new kernels—a plentiful harvest of new lives. 25Those

Mt 21:13 Isa 56:7; Jer 7:11. **Mt 21:16** Ps 8:2. **Mk 11:16** Or *from carrying merchandise through the Temple.* **Mk 11:17** Isa 56:7; Jer 7:11. **Mk 11:19** Greek *they left;* other manuscripts read *he left.* **Lk 19:46** Isa 56:7; Jer 7:11. **Jn 12:23** "Son of Man" is a title Jesus used for himself.

Mark 11:15-17 Jesus became angry, but he did not sin. There is a place for righteous indignation. Christians are right to be upset about sin and injustice and should take a stand against them. Unfortunately, believers are often passive about these important issues and instead get angry over personal insults and petty irritations. Make sure your anger is directed toward the right issues.

Mark 11:15-17 Money changers and merchants did big business during Passover. Their stalls were set up in the Temple's Court of the Gentiles, making it all but impossible for non-Jews to spend any time in worship (Isa 56:6-7). Jesus became angry because God's house had become a place of extortion and a barrier to Gentiles who wanted to worship.

Luke 19:47 Who were the "other leaders of the people"? This group probably included wealthy leaders in politics, commerce, and law. They had several reasons for wanting to get rid of Jesus. He had damaged business in the Temple by driving the merchants out. In addition, he was preaching against injustice, and his teachings often favored the poor over the rich. Furthermore, his great popularity was in danger of attracting Rome's attention, and the leaders of Israel wanted as little as possible to do with Rome.

John 12:20-21 These Greeks probably were converts to the Jewish faith. They may have gone to Philip because, though he was a Jew, he had a Greek name.

John 12:23-25 This is a beautiful picture of the necessary sacrifice of Jesus. Unless a kernel of wheat is planted in the soil, it will not become a blade of wheat producing many more seeds. Jesus had to die to pay the penalty for our sin, but also to show his power over death. His resurrection proves he has eternal life. Because Jesus is God, Jesus can give this same eternal life to all who believe in him.

John 12:25 We must be so committed to living for Christ that we should "care nothing" for our lives by comparison. This does not mean that we long to die or that we are careless or destructive with the life God has given, but that we are willing to die if doing so will glorify Christ. We must disown the tyrannical rule of our own self-centeredness. By laying aside our striving for advantage, security, and pleasure, we can serve God lovingly and freely. Releasing control of our lives and transferring control to Christ bring eternal life and genuine joy.

History of the Temple in Jerusalem ▶

The Temple in Jerusalem has a significant history. The first Temple was erected in the time of Solomon (959 B.C.). The Babylonian army laid final siege to Jerusalem in 588 B.C., completely decimating the city. The Temple and Solomon's palace were burnt down, the Temple treasures were completely plundered, the city walls were demolished, and the citizens were deported in large numbers. Jeremiah had predicted Jerusalem's doom and 70-year captivity (Jer 25:11; 29:10). The second Temple in Jerusalem was built in the time of Zerubbabel (515 B.C.). In 40 B.C., with the aid of the Parthians, Antigonus attacked and seized Jerusalem, forcing Herod to escape. He journeyed to Rome, where the Senate appointed him "king of the Jews." Armed with this new authority and two Roman legions, Herod recaptured Jerusalem in 37 B.C. and reigned there for 33 years (until 4 B.C.). During this time he beautified the city and enlarged the Temple. Herod's reconstruction of the Temple began in 20 B.C., and it was not completed until around A.D. 64. Six years later, the Roman general Titus laid siege to Jerusalem and destroyed the Temple. Jesus had predicted this 40 years earlier (in A.D. 30).

Jerusalem in the First Century A.D.

See Jerusalem in the Time of Nehemiah, p. 1219

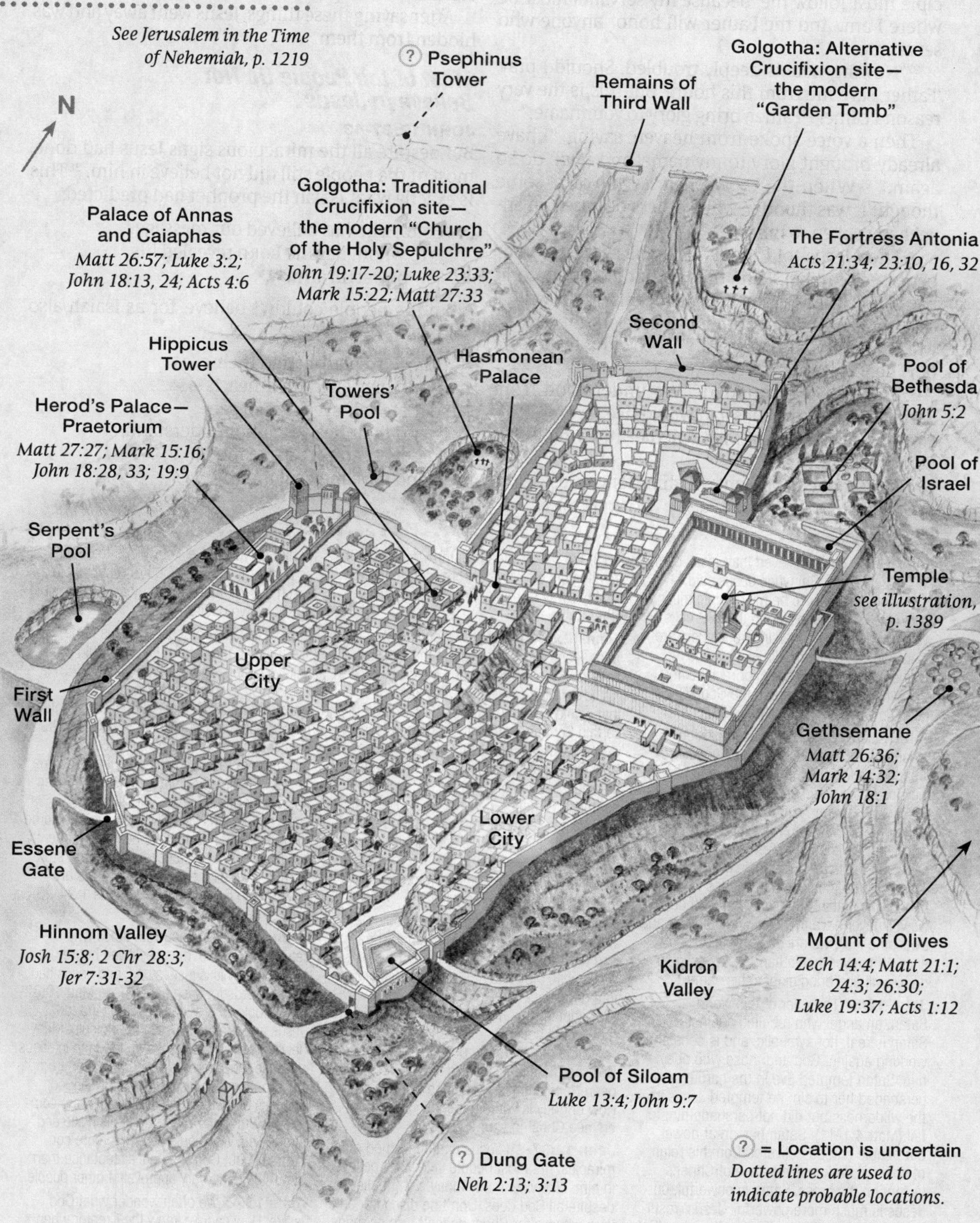

N
? Psephinus Tower
Remains of Third Wall
Golgotha: Alternative Crucifixion site—the modern "Garden Tomb"
Golgotha: Traditional Crucifixion site—the modern "Church of the Holy Sepulchre"
John 19:17-20; Luke 23:33; Mark 15:22; Matt 27:33
Palace of Annas and Caiaphas
Matt 26:57; Luke 3:2; John 18:13, 24; Acts 4:6
The Fortress Antonia
Acts 21:34; 23:10, 16, 32
Second Wall
Hippicus Tower
Hasmonean Palace
Towers' Pool
Herod's Palace—Praetorium
Matt 27:27; Mark 15:16; John 18:28, 33; 19:9
Pool of Bethesda
John 5:2
Pool of Israel
Serpent's Pool
Temple
see illustration, p. 1389
Upper City
First Wall
Gethsemane
Matt 26:36; Mark 14:32; John 18:1
Lower City
Essene Gate
Hinnom Valley
Josh 15:8; 2 Chr 28:3; Jer 7:31-32
Kidron Valley
Mount of Olives
Zech 14:4; Matt 21:1; 24:3; 26:30; Luke 19:37; Acts 1:12
Pool of Siloam
Luke 13:4; John 9:7
? Dung Gate
Neh 2:13; 3:13
? = Location is uncertain
Dotted lines are used to indicate probable locations.

▸ **JOHN 12:20-36** ***(cont.)***
who love their life in this world will lose it. Those
who care nothing for their life in this world will keep
it for eternity. 26Anyone who wants to be my disciple must follow me, because my servants must be
where I am. And the Father will honor anyone who
serves me.
27"Now my soul is deeply troubled. Should I pray,
'Father, save me from this hour'? But this is the very
reason I came! 28Father, bring glory to your name."
Then a voice spoke from heaven, saying, "I have
already brought glory to my name, and I will do so
again." 29When the crowd heard the voice, some
thought it was thunder, while others declared an angel had spoken to him.
30Then Jesus told them, "The voice was for your
benefit, not mine. 31The time for judging this world
has come, when Satan, the ruler of this world, will be
cast out. 32And when I am lifted up from the earth, I
will draw everyone to myself." 33He said this to indicate
how he was going to die.
34The crowd responded, "We understood from
Scripture* that the Messiah would live forever. How
can you say the Son of Man will die? Just who is this
Son of Man, anyway?"
35Jesus replied, "My light will shine for you just a little
longer. Walk in the light while you can, so the darkness
will not overtake you. Those who walk in the darkness
cannot see where they are going. 36Put your trust in
the light while there is still time; then you will become
children of the light."
After saying these things, Jesus went away and was
hidden from them.

Most of the People Do Not Believe in Jesus

JOHN 12:37-43
But despite all the miraculous signs Jesus had done,
most of the people still did not believe in him. 38This
is exactly what Isaiah the prophet had predicted:

"LORD, who has believed our message?
To whom has the LORD revealed his
powerful arm?"*

39But the people couldn't believe, for as Isaiah also
said,

40 "The Lord has blinded their eyes
and hardened their hearts—
so that their eyes cannot see,
and their hearts cannot understand,
and they cannot turn to me
and have me heal them."*

Jn 12:34 Greek *from the law.* **Jn 12:38** Isa 53:1. **Jn 12:40** Isa 6:10.

John 12:26 Many believed that Jesus came for the Jews only. But when Jesus said, "Anyone who wants to be my disciple must follow me," he was talking to these Greeks as well. No matter who the sincere seekers are, Jesus welcomes them. His message is for everyone. Don't allow social or racial differences to become barriers to the Good News. Take the Good News to all people.

John 12:27 Jesus knew his crucifixion lay ahead, and because he was human, he dreaded it. He knew he would have to take the sins of the world on himself, and he knew this would separate him from his Father. He wanted to be delivered from this horrible death, but he knew that God sent him into the world to die for our sins, in our place. Jesus said no to his human desires in order to obey his Father and glorify him. Although we will never have to face such a difficult and awesome task, we are still called to obedience. Whatever the Father asks, we should do his will and bring glory to his name.

John 12:31 The ruler of this world is Satan, an angel who rebelled against God. Satan is real, not symbolic, and is constantly working against God and those who obey him. Satan tempted Eve in the garden and persuaded her to sin; he tempted Jesus in the wilderness but did not persuade him to fall (Matt 4:1-11). Satan has great power, but people can be delivered from his reign of spiritual darkness because of Christ's victory on the cross. Satan is powerful, but Jesus is much more powerful. Jesus' resurrection shattered Satan's deathly power (Col 1:13-14). To overcome Satan we need faithful allegiance to God's Word, determination to stay away from sin, and the support of other believers.

John 12:32-34 The crowd could not believe what Jesus was saying about the Messiah. They envisioned a victorious Messiah who would set up a political, earthly kingdom that would never end. From their reading of certain Scriptures, they thought the Messiah would never die (Ps 89:35-36; 110:4; Isa 9:7). Other passages, however, showed that he would die (Isa 53:5-9). Jesus' words did not mesh with their concept of the Messiah. First he had to suffer and die—then he would one day set up his eternal Kingdom. What kind of Messiah, or Savior, are you seeking? Beware of trying to force Jesus into your own mold—he won't fit.

John 12:35-36 Jesus said he would be with them in person for only a short time, and they should take advantage of his presence while they had it. Like a light shining in a dark place, he would point out the way they should walk. If they walked in his light, they would become "children of the light," revealing the truth and pointing people to God. As Christians, we are to be Christ's light bearers, letting his light shine through us. How brightly is your light shining? Can others see Christ in your actions?

John 12:37-38 Jesus had performed many miracles, but most people still didn't believe in him. Likewise, many today won't believe despite all God does. Don't be discouraged if your witness for Christ doesn't turn as many to him as you'd like. Your job is to continue as a faithful witness. You are responsible to reach out to others, but they are responsible for their own decisions.

John 12:39-41 People in Jesus' time, like those in the time of Isaiah, would not believe despite the evidence (John 12:37). As a result, God hardened their hearts. Does that mean God intentionally prevented these people from believing in him? No, he simply confirmed their own choices. After a lifetime of resisting God, they had become so set in their ways that they wouldn't even try to understand Jesus' message. For such people, it is virtually impossible to come to God—their hearts have been permanently hardened. Other instances of constant stubbornness leading to hardened hearts are recorded in Exodus 9:12; Romans 1:24-28; and 2 Thessalonians 2:8-12.

John 12:42-43 Along with those who refused to believe, many believed but refused to admit it. This is just as bad, and Jesus had strong words for such people (see Matt 10:32-33). People who will not take a stand for Jesus are afraid of rejection or ridicule. Many Jewish leaders wouldn't admit to faith in Jesus because they feared excommunication from the synagogue (which was their livelihood) and loss of their prestigious place in the community. But the praise of others is fickle and short-lived. We should be much more concerned about God's eternal acceptance than about the temporary approval of other people.

John 12:45 We often wonder what God is like. How can we know the Creator when

[41]Isaiah was referring to Jesus when he said this, because he saw the future and spoke of the Messiah's
glory. [42]Many people did believe in him, however, including some of the Jewish leaders. But they wouldn't
admit it for fear that the Pharisees would expel them
from the synagogue. [43]For they loved human praise
more than the praise of God.

Jesus Summarizes His Message

JOHN 12:44-50

Jesus shouted to the crowds, "If you trust me, you are
trusting not only me, but also God who sent me. [45]For
when you see me, you are seeing the one who sent me.
[46]I have come as a light to shine in this dark world, so
that all who put their trust in me will no longer remain
in the dark. [47]I will not judge those who hear me but
don't obey me, for I have come to save the world and
not to judge it. [48]But all who reject me and my message
will be judged on the day of judgment by the truth I
have spoken. [49]I don't speak on my own authority. The
Father who sent me has commanded me what to say
and how to say it. [50]And I know his commands lead to
eternal life; so I say whatever the Father tells me to say."

Jesus Curses a Fig Tree PARALLEL

MATTHEW 21:18-22

In the morning, as Jesus was returning to Jerusalem,
he was hungry, [19]and he noticed a fig tree beside the
road. He went over to see if there were any figs, but
there were only leaves. Then he said to it, "May you
never bear fruit again!" And immediately the fig tree
withered up.
[20]The disciples were amazed when they saw this
and asked, "How did the fig tree wither so quickly?"
[21]Then Jesus told them, "I tell you the truth, if you
have faith and don't doubt, you can do things like this
and much more. You can even say to this mountain,
'May you be lifted up and thrown into the sea,' and it
will happen. [22]You can pray for anything, and if you
have faith, you will receive it."

MARK 11:12-14, 20-25

The next morning as they were leaving Bethany,
Jesus was hungry. [13]He noticed a fig tree in full leaf
a little way off, so he went over to see if he could find
any figs. But there were only leaves because it was
too early in the season for fruit. [14]Then Jesus said to
the tree, "May no one ever eat your fruit again!" And
the disciples heard him say it. . . .

[20]The next morning as they passed by the fig tree he
had cursed, the disciples noticed it had withered from
the roots up. [21]Peter remembered what Jesus had said
to the tree on the previous day and exclaimed, "Look,
Rabbi! The fig tree you cursed has withered and died!"
[22]Then Jesus said to the disciples, "Have faith
in God. [23]I tell you the truth, you can say to this

---

he doesn't make himself visible? Jesus said plainly that those who see him see God because he is God. If you want to know what God is like, study the person and words of Jesus Christ.

John 12:48 The purpose of Jesus' first mission on earth was not to judge people, but to show them the way to find salvation and eternal life. But when he comes again, one of his main purposes will be to judge people for how they lived on earth. Not accepting and obeying Christ is what will condemn them. On the day of judgment, those who accepted Jesus and lived his way will be raised to eternal life (1 Cor 15:51-57; 1 Thes 4:15-18; Rev 21:1-7), but those who rejected Jesus and lived any way they pleased will face eternal punishment (Rev 20:11-15). Decide now which side you'll be on, for the consequences of your decision last forever.

Matt 21:21 Many have wondered about Jesus' statement that if we have faith and don't doubt, we can move mountains. Jesus, of course, was not suggesting that his followers use prayer as "magic" and perform capricious "mountain moving" acts. Instead, he was making a strong point about the disciples' (and our) lack of faith. What kinds of mountains do you face? Have you talked to God about them? How strong is your faith?

Matt 21:22 This verse is not a guarantee that we can get anything we want simply by asking Jesus and believing. God does not grant requests that would hurt us or others or that would violate his own nature or will. Jesus' statement is not a blank check. To be fulfilled, our requests must be in harmony with the principles of God's Kingdom. The stronger our belief, the more likely our prayers will be in line with God's will, and then God will be happy to grant them.

Mark 11:12-14, 20-25 In the Gospel of Mark, two independent incidents are related: the cursing of the fig tree and the clearing of the Temple. The cursing of the fig tree was an acted-out parable tied to the clearing of the Temple. Just as the fig tree looked good from a distance but was fruitless on close examination, so the Temple looked impressive at first glance, but its sacrifices and other activities were hollow because they were not done to worship God sincerely (see Matt 21:43). The fig tree showed promise of fruit, but it produced none. Jesus was showing his anger at religious life without substance. If you claim to have faith without putting it to work in your life, you are like the barren fig tree. Genuine faith has great potential; ask God to help you bear fruit for his Kingdom.

Mark 11:13-14 Fig trees, a popular source of inexpensive food in Israel, require three years from the time they are planted until they can bear fruit. Each tree yields a great amount of fruit twice a year, in late spring and in early autumn. The figs normally grow as the leaves fill out, but this tree, though full of leaves, had no figs. The tree looked promising but offered no fruit. Jesus' harsh words to the fig tree could be applied to the nation of Israel. Fruitful in appearance only, Israel was spiritually barren.

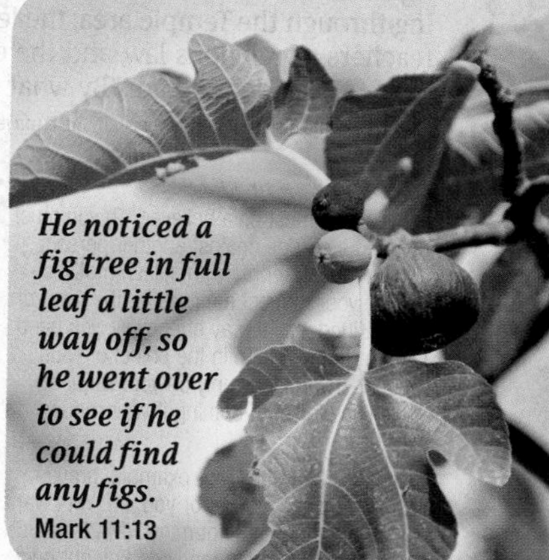
He noticed a fig tree in full leaf a little way off, so he went over to see if he could find any figs.
Mark 11:13

Mark 11:22-23 The kind of prayer that moves mountains is prayer for the fruitfulness of God's Kingdom. It would seem impossible to move a mountain into the sea, so Jesus used that illustration to show that God can do the impossible. God will answer your prayers but not as a result of your positive mental attitude. Other conditions must be

▸ **MARK 11:12-14, 20-25** ***(cont.)***

mountain, 'May you be lifted up and thrown into the sea,' and it will happen. But you must really believe it will happen and have no doubt in your heart. [24]I tell you, you can pray for anything, and if you believe that you've received it, it will be yours. [25]But when you are praying, first forgive anyone you are holding a grudge against, so that your Father in heaven will forgive your sins, too.*"

Religious Leaders Challenge Jesus' Authority PARALLEL

MATTHEW 21:23-27

When Jesus returned to the Temple and began teaching, the leading priests and elders came up to him. They demanded, "By what authority are you doing all these things? Who gave you the right?"

[24]"I'll tell you by what authority I do these things if you answer one question," Jesus replied. [25]"Did John's authority to baptize come from heaven, or was it merely human?"

They talked it over among themselves. "If we say it was from heaven, he will ask us why we didn't believe John. [26]But if we say it was merely human, we'll be mobbed because the people believe John was a prophet." [27]So they finally replied, "We don't know."

And Jesus responded, "Then I won't tell you by what authority I do these things."

MARK 11:27-33

Again they entered Jerusalem. As Jesus was walking through the Temple area, the leading priests, the teachers of religious law, and the elders came up to him. [28]They demanded, "By what authority are you doing all these things? Who gave you the right to do them?"

[29]"I'll tell you by what authority I do these things if you answer one question," Jesus replied. [30]"Did John's authority to baptize come from heaven, or was it merely human? Answer me!"

[31]They talked it over among themselves. "If we say it was from heaven, he will ask why we didn't believe John. [32]But do we dare say it was merely human?" For they were afraid of what the people would do, because everyone believed that John was a prophet. [33]So they finally replied, "We don't know."

And Jesus responded, "Then I won't tell you by what authority I do these things."

LUKE 20:1-8

One day as Jesus was teaching the people and preaching the Good News in the Temple, the leading priests, the teachers of religious law, and the elders came up to him. [2]They demanded, "By what authority are you doing all these things? Who gave you the right?"

[3]"Let me ask you a question first," he replied. [4]"Did John's authority to baptize come from heaven, or was it merely human?"

[5]They talked it over among themselves. "If we say it was from heaven, he will ask why we didn't believe John. [6]But if we say it was merely human, the people will stone us because they are convinced John was a prophet." [7]So they finally replied that they didn't know.

[8]And Jesus responded, "Then I won't tell you by what authority I do these things."

Mk 11:25 Some manuscripts add verse 26, *But if you refuse to forgive, your Father in heaven will not forgive your sins.* Compare Matt 6:15.

met: (1) You must be a believer; (2) you must not hold a grudge against another person; (3) you must not pray with selfish motives; and (4) your request must be for the good of God's Kingdom. To pray effectively, you need faith in God, not faith in the object of your request. If you focus only on your request, you will be left with nothing if your request is refused.

Mark 11:24 Jesus, our example, prayed, "Everything is possible for you. . . . Yet I want your will to be done, not mine" (Mark 14:36). Our prayers are often motivated by our own interests and desires. We like to hear that we can have anything. But Jesus prayed with God's interests in mind. When we pray, we can express our desires, but we should want his will above ours. Check yourself to see if your prayers focus on your interests or God's.

Mark 11:25 Forgiving others is tough work—so much so that many people would rather do something totally distasteful than offer forgiveness to someone who has wronged them. For a person to pray while bearing a grudge, however, is like a tree sprouting leaves and bearing no fruit (Mark 11:13). True faith changes the heart. Real prayer dismantles pride and vengeance, filling the holes with love. Real faith seeks peace. For our churches to have prayer power, there must be harmony and forgiveness evident in the body of believers. Let go of hurts, abandon grudges, and forgive others.

Matt 21:25 For more information on John the Baptist, see Matthew 3 and his Profile on p. 1292.

Mark 11:27-33 The religious leaders were in a quandary. They had wanted to trap Jesus with a question that would show him to be either a blasphemer or a weird fanatic. Instead, Jesus had countered their question with a question about John the Baptist. Now they would have to try to save face. They had not stood up for John or tried to get him released—John had irritated them just as Jesus was doing (see Matt 3:7-10). Always cloaked in self-interest, these religious leaders were only concerned about position and reputation; they weren't looking for the truth. In John 3:19, Jesus summed up this attitude: "People loved the darkness more than the light, for their actions were evil." People who reject Jesus' claims have a greater problem than intellectual doubt; they are rebelling against Christ's control of their lives. They try to ask tricky questions, but don't really want an answer. Sincere seekers, however, will find the truth (Matt 7:7-8).

Luke 20:1-8 This group of leaders wanted to get rid of Jesus, so they tried to trap him with their question. If Jesus would answer that his authority came from God—if he stated openly that he was the Messiah and the Son of God—they would accuse him of blasphemy and bring him to trial. Jesus did not let himself be caught. Instead, he turned the question on them. Thus, he exposed their motives and avoided their trap.

Matt 21:30 The son who said he would obey and then didn't represented many of the people of Israel in Jesus' day, particularly the religious leaders. They said they wanted to do God's will, but they constantly disobeyed. They were phony, just going through the motions. It is dangerous to pretend to obey God when our heart is far from him because

Jesus Tells the Parable of the Two Sons

MATTHEW 21:28-32

"But what do you think about this? A man with two
sons told the older boy, 'Son, go out and work in the
vineyard today.' 29The son answered, 'No, I won't go,'
but later he changed his mind and went anyway.
30Then the father told the other son, 'You go,' and he
said, 'Yes, sir, I will.' But he didn't go.
31"Which of the two obeyed his father?"
They replied, "The first."*
Then Jesus explained his meaning: "I tell you the
truth, corrupt tax collectors and prostitutes will get
into the Kingdom of God before you do. 32For John the
Baptist came and showed you the right way to live, but
you didn't believe him, while tax collectors and prostitutes did. And even when you saw this happening, you
refused to believe him and repent of your sins.

Jesus Tells the Parable of the Evil Farmers PARALLEL

MATTHEW 21:33-46

"Now listen to another story. A certain landowner
planted a vineyard, built a wall around it, dug a pit for
pressing out the grape juice, and built a lookout tower.
Then he leased the vineyard to tenant farmers and
moved to another country. 34At the time of the grape
harvest, he sent his servants to collect his share of the
crop. 35But the farmers grabbed his servants, beat one,
killed one, and stoned another. 36So the landowner
sent a larger group of his servants to collect for him,
but the results were the same.
37"Finally, the owner sent his son, thinking, 'Surely
they will respect my son.'
38"But when the tenant farmers saw his son coming,
they said to one another, 'Here comes the heir to this
estate. Come on, let's kill him and get the estate for
ourselves!' 39So they grabbed him, dragged him out of
the vineyard, and murdered him.
40"When the owner of the vineyard returns,"
Jesus asked, "what do you think he will do to those
farmers?"
41The religious leaders replied, "He will put the
wicked men to a horrible death and lease the vineyard to others who will give him his share of the crop
after each harvest."
42Then Jesus asked them, "Didn't you ever read this
in the Scriptures?

'The stone that the builders rejected
has now become the cornerstone.
This is the LORD's doing,
and it is wonderful to see.'*

43I tell you, the Kingdom of God will be taken away
from you and given to a nation that will produce the
proper fruit. 44Anyone who stumbles over that stone
will be broken to pieces, and it will crush anyone it
falls on.*"
45When the leading priests and Pharisees heard this
parable, they realized he was telling the story against
them—they were the wicked farmers. 46They wanted
to arrest him, but they were afraid of the crowds, who
considered Jesus to be a prophet.

MARK 12:1-12

Then Jesus began teaching them with stories: "A man
planted a vineyard. He built a wall around it, dug
a pit for pressing out the grape juice, and built a
lookout tower. Then he leased the vineyard to tenant farmers and moved to another country. 2At the
time of the grape harvest, he sent one of his servants
to collect his share of the crop. 3But the farmers
grabbed the servant, beat him up, and sent him back
empty-handed. 4The owner then sent another servant, but they insulted him and beat him over the
head. 5The next servant he sent was killed. Others
he sent were either beaten or killed, 6until there
was only one left—his son whom he loved dearly.
The owner finally sent him, thinking, 'Surely they
will respect my son.'
7"But the tenant farmers said to one another,
'Here comes the heir to this estate. Let's kill him
and get the estate for ourselves!' 8So they grabbed
him and murdered him and threw his body out of
the vineyard.
9"What do you suppose the owner of the vineyard
will do?" Jesus asked. "I'll tell you—he will come and

Mt 21:29-31 Other manuscripts read *"The second."* In still other manuscripts the first son says "Yes" but does nothing, the second son says "No" but then repents and goes, and the answer to Jesus' question is that the second son obeyed his father. **Mt 21:42** Ps 118:22-23. **Mt 21:44** This verse is not included in some early manuscripts. Compare Luke 20:18.

God knows our true intentions. Our actions must match our words.

Matt 21:37 In trying to reach us with his love, God finally sent his own Son. Jesus' perfect life, his words of truth, and his sacrifice of love are meant to cause us to listen to him and to follow him as Lord. If we ignore God's gracious gift of his Son, we reject God himself.

Matt 21:44 Jesus used this metaphor to show that one truth can affect people in different ways, depending on how they relate to it (see Isa 8:14-15; 28:16; Dan 2:34, 44-45). Ideally they will build on it, but many will trip over it. And at the Last Judgment, God's enemies will be crushed by it. In the end, Christ offers mercy and forgiveness now and promises judgment later. We should choose him now!

Mark 12:1ff In this parable, the man who planted the vineyard is God; the vineyard is the nation Israel; the tenant farmers are Israel's religious leaders; the servants are the prophets and priests who remained faithful to God; the son is Jesus; and the others are the Gentiles. The religious leaders not only frustrated their nation's purpose but also killed those who were trying to fulfill it. They were so jealous and possessive that they ignored the welfare of the very people they were supposed to be bringing to God. By telling this story, Jesus exposed the religious leaders' plot to kill him and warned that their sins would be punished.

▶ **MARK 12:1-12 *(cont.)***

kill those farmers and lease the vineyard to others.
10Didn't you ever read this in the Scriptures?

'The stone that the builders rejected
has now become the cornerstone.
11 This is the LORD's doing,
and it is wonderful to see.'*"

12The religious leaders* wanted to arrest Jesus because they realized he was telling the story against
them—they were the wicked farmers. But they were
afraid of the crowd, so they left him and went away.

LUKE 20:9-19

Now Jesus turned to the people again and told them
this story: "A man planted a vineyard, leased it to tenant farmers, and moved to another country to live for
several years. 10At the time of the grape harvest, he sent
one of his servants to collect his share of the crop. But
the farmers attacked the servant, beat him up, and sent
him back empty-handed. 11So the owner sent another
servant, but they also insulted him, beat him up, and
sent him away empty-handed. 12A third man was sent,
and they wounded him and chased him away.

13"'What will I do?' the owner asked himself. 'I
know! I'll send my cherished son. Surely they will
respect him.'

14"But when the tenant farmers saw his son, they
said to each other, 'Here comes the heir to this estate. Let's kill him and get the estate for ourselves!'
15So they dragged him out of the vineyard and murdered him.

"What do you suppose the owner of the vineyard
will do to them?" Jesus asked. 16"I'll tell you—he will
come and kill those farmers and lease the vineyard
to others."

"How terrible that such a thing should ever happen," his listeners protested.

17Jesus looked at them and said, "Then what does
this Scripture mean?

'The stone that the builders rejected
has now become the cornerstone.'*

18Everyone who stumbles over that stone will be broken to pieces, and it will crush anyone it falls on."

19The teachers of religious law and the leading
priests wanted to arrest Jesus immediately because
they realized he was telling the story against them—
they were the wicked farmers. But they were afraid of
the people's reaction.

Jesus Tells the Parable of the Wedding Dinner

MATTHEW 22:1-14

Jesus also told them other parables. He said, 2"The
Kingdom of Heaven can be illustrated by the story of
a king who prepared a great wedding feast for his son.
3When the banquet was ready, he sent his servants to
notify those who were invited. But they all refused
to come!

4"So he sent other servants to tell them, 'The feast
has been prepared. The bulls and fattened cattle have
been killed, and everything is ready. Come to the banquet!' 5But the guests he had invited ignored them and
went their own way, one to his farm, another to his
business. 6Others seized his messengers and insulted
them and killed them.

7"The king was furious, and he sent out his army to
destroy the murderers and burn their town. 8And he
said to his servants, 'The wedding feast is ready, and
the guests I invited aren't worthy of the honor. 9Now
go out to the street corners and invite everyone you
see.' 10So the servants brought in everyone they could
find, good and bad alike, and the banquet hall was
filled with guests.

11"But when the king came in to meet the guests, he
noticed a man who wasn't wearing the proper clothes
for a wedding. 12'Friend,' he asked, 'how is it that you
are here without wedding clothes?' But the man had
no reply. 13Then the king said to his aides, 'Bind his
hands and feet and throw him into the outer darkness, where there will be weeping and gnashing of
teeth.'

14"For many are called, but few are chosen."

Mk 12:10-11 Ps 118:22-23. **Mk 12:12** Greek *They.* **Lk 20:17** Ps 118:22.

Mark 12:10-11 Jesus referred to himself as the stone rejected by the builders. Although he would be rejected by most of the Jewish leaders, he would become the cornerstone of a new "building," the church (Acts 4:11-12). The cornerstone was used as a base to make sure the other stones of the building were straight and level. Likewise, Jesus' life and teaching would be the church's foundation.

Luke 20:9-16 The characters in this story are easily identified. Even the religious leaders understood it. Jesus' parable indirectly answered the religious leaders' question about his authority; it also showed them that he knew about their plan to kill him.

Luke 20:17-19 Quoting Psalm 118:22, Jesus showed the unbelieving leaders that even their rejection of the Messiah had been prophesied in Scripture. Ignoring the cornerstone was dangerous. A person could trip or be crushed (punished and judged). Jesus' comments were veiled, but the religious leaders had no trouble interpreting them. They immediately wanted to arrest him.

Matt 22:1-14 In that culture, two invitations were expected when banquets were given. The first asked the guests to attend; the second announced that all was ready. In this story the king invited his guests three times, and each time they rejected his invitation. God wants us to join him at his banquet, which will last for eternity. That's why he sends us invitations again and again. Have you accepted his invitation?

Matt 22:11-12 It was customary for wedding guests to be given wedding clothes to wear to the banquet. It was unthinkable to refuse to wear these clothes. That would insult the host, who could only assume that the guest was arrogant and thought he didn't need these clothes, or that he didn't want to take part in the wedding celebration. The wedding clothes picture the righteousness needed to enter God's Kingdom—the total acceptance in God's eyes that Christ gives every believer. Christ has provided these clothes of righteousness for everyone, but each person must choose to put them on

Religious Leaders Question Jesus about Paying Taxes PARALLEL

MATTHEW 22:15-22

Then the Pharisees met together to plot how to trap Jesus into saying something for which he could be arrested. 16They sent some of their disciples, along with the supporters of Herod, to meet with him. "Teacher," they said, "we know how honest you are. You teach the way of God truthfully. You are impartial and don't play favorites. 17Now tell us what you think about this: Is it right to pay taxes to Caesar or not?"

18But Jesus knew their evil motives. "You hypocrites!" he said. "Why are you trying to trap me? 19Here, show me the coin used for the tax." When they handed him a Roman coin,* 20he asked, "Whose picture and title are stamped on it?"

21"Caesar's," they replied.

"Well, then," he said, "give to Caesar what belongs to Caesar, and give to God what belongs to God."

22His reply amazed them, and they went away.

MARK 12:13-17

Later the leaders sent some Pharisees and supporters of Herod to trap Jesus into saying something for which he could be arrested. 14"Teacher," they said, "we know how honest you are. You are impartial and don't play favorites. You teach the way of God truthfully. Now tell us—is it right to pay taxes to Caesar or not? 15Should we pay them, or shouldn't we?"

Jesus saw through their hypocrisy and said, "Why are you trying to trap me? Show me a Roman coin,* and I'll tell you." 16When they handed it to him, he asked, "Whose picture and title are stamped on it?"

"Caesar's," they replied.

17"Well, then," Jesus said, "give to Caesar what belongs to Caesar, and give to God what belongs to God."

His reply completely amazed them.

LUKE 20:20-26

Watching for their opportunity, the leaders sent spies pretending to be honest men. They tried to get Jesus to say something that could be reported to the Roman governor so he would arrest Jesus. 21"Teacher," they said, "we know that you speak and teach what is right and are not influenced by what others think. You teach the way of God truthfully. 22Now tell us—is it right for us to pay taxes to Caesar or not?"

23He saw through their trickery and said, 24"Show me a Roman coin.* Whose picture and title are stamped on it?"

"Caesar's," they replied.

25"Well then," he said, "give to Caesar what belongs to Caesar, and give to God what belongs to God."

26So they failed to trap him by what he said in front of the people. Instead, they were amazed by his answer, and they became silent.

Mt 22:19 Greek *a denarius.* **Mk 12:15** Greek *a denarius.* **Lk 20:24** Greek *a denarius.*

in order to enter the King's banquet (eternal life). There is an open invitation, but we must be ready. For more on the imagery of clothes of righteousness and salvation, see Psalm 132:16; Isaiah 61:10; Zechariah 3:3-5; Revelation 3:4-5; 19:7-8.

Matt 22:17 Anyone who avoided paying taxes faced harsh penalties. The Jews hated to pay taxes to Rome because the money supported their oppressors and symbolized their subjection. Much of the tax money also went to maintain the pagan temples and luxurious lifestyles of Rome's upper class. The Pharisees and supporters of Herod hoped to trap Jesus with this tax question. A "yes" would mean he supported Rome, which would turn the people against him. A "no" would bring accusations of treason and rebellion against Rome and could lead to civil penalties.

Matt 22:21 Jesus avoided this trap by showing that we have dual citizenship (1 Pet 2:17). Our citizenship in the nation requires that we pay money for the services and benefits we receive. Our citizenship in the Kingdom of Heaven requires that we pledge to God our ultimate obedience and commitment.

Mark 12:13 The Pharisees were primarily a religious group concerned with ritual purity; the supporters of Herod were a Jewish political group that approved of Herod's compromises with Rome. The Pharisees did not like Jesus because he exposed their hypocrisy. The supporters of Herod also saw Jesus as a threat. They had lost political control when, as a result of reported unrest, Rome deposed Archelaus (Herod's son with authority over Judea) and replaced him with a Roman governor. The supporters of Herod feared that Jesus would cause still more instability in Judea and that Rome might react by never allowing the Roman leaders to step down and be replaced by a descendant of Herod.

Luke 20:20-26 Jesus turned his enemies' attempt to trap him into a powerful lesson: As God's followers, we have legitimate obligations to both God and the government. But it is important to keep our priorities straight. When the two authorities conflict, our duty to God always must come before our duty to the government.

Luke 20:22 This was a loaded question. The Jews were enraged at having to pay taxes to Rome, thus supporting the pagan government and its gods. They hated the system that allowed tax collectors to charge exorbitant rates and keep the extra for themselves. If Jesus said they should pay taxes, they would call him a traitor to their nation and their religion. But if he said they should not, they could report him to Rome as a rebel. Jesus' questioners thought they had him this time, but he outwitted them again.

Luke 20:24 This Roman coin was a denarius, the usual pay for one day's work.

Coin of Tiberius Caesar

The image on the coin shown to Jesus by the religious leaders was that of Tiberius Caesar. He was reigning during the days of Jesus' ministry. Tiberius was made Augustus's co-regent in A.D. 13 and succeeded him the following year. When he became emperor, he changed his name to Tiberius Caesar Augustus. He reigned from A.D. 14–37. Tiberius's administration was characterized by wisdom, intelligence, prudence, and duty. He continued his predecessor's policy of striving for peace and security.

Religious Leaders Question Jesus about the Resurrection PARALLEL

MATTHEW 22:23-33

That same day Jesus was approached by some
Sadducees—religious leaders who say there is no
resurrection from the dead. They posed this question: [24]"Teacher, Moses said, 'If a man dies without
children, his brother should marry the widow and
have a child who will carry on the brother's name.'*
[25]Well, suppose there were seven brothers. The oldest
one married and then died without children, so his
brother married the widow. [26]But the second brother
also died, and the third brother married her. This
continued with all seven of them. [27]Last of all, the
woman also died. [28]So tell us, whose wife will she
be in the resurrection? For all seven were married
to her."

[29]Jesus replied, "Your mistake is that you don't know
the Scriptures, and you don't know the power of God.
[30]For when the dead rise, they will neither marry nor
be given in marriage. In this respect they will be like
the angels in heaven.

[31]"But now, as to whether there will be a resurrection of the dead—haven't you ever read about this in
the Scriptures? Long after Abraham, Isaac, and Jacob
had died, God said,* [32]'I am the God of Abraham, the
God of Isaac, and the God of Jacob.'* So he is the God
of the living, not the dead."

[33]When the crowds heard him, they were astounded
at his teaching.

MARK 12:18-27

Then Jesus was approached by some Sadducees—
religious leaders who say there is no resurrection
from the dead. They posed this question: [19]"Teacher,
Moses gave us a law that if a man dies, leaving a wife
without children, his brother should marry the widow
and have a child who will carry on the brother's name.*
[20]Well, suppose there were seven brothers. The oldest
one married and then died without children. [21]So the
second brother married the widow, but he also died
without children. Then the third brother married her.
[22]This continued with all seven of them, and still there
were no children. Last of all, the woman also died. [23]So
tell us, whose wife will she be in the resurrection? For
all seven were married to her."

[24]Jesus replied, "Your mistake is that you don't
know the Scriptures, and you don't know the power
of God. [25]For when the dead rise, they will neither
marry nor be given in marriage. In this respect they
will be like the angels in heaven.

[26]"But now, as to whether the dead will be raised—
haven't you ever read about this in the writings of
Moses, in the story of the burning bush? Long after Abraham, Isaac, and Jacob had died, God said to
Moses,* 'I am the God of Abraham, the God of Isaac,
and the God of Jacob.'* [27]So he is the God of the living,
not the dead. You have made a serious error."

LUKE 20:27-40

Then Jesus was approached by some Sadducees—religious leaders who say there is no resurrection from

Mt 22:24 Deut 25:5-6. **Mt 22:31** Greek *read about this? God said.* **Mt 22:32** Exod 3:6. **Mk 12:19** See Deut 25:5-6. **Mk 12:26a** Greek *in the story of the bush? God said to him.* **Mk 12:26b** Exod 3:6.

Matt 22:23ff After the Pharisees and supporters of Herod had failed to trap Jesus, the Sadducees smugly stepped in to try. They did not believe in the resurrection because the Pentateuch (Genesis—Deuteronomy) has no direct teaching on it. The Pharisees had never been able to come up with a convincing argument from the Pentateuch for the resurrection, and the Sadducees thought they had trapped Jesus for sure. But Jesus was about to show them otherwise (see Matt 22:31-32 for Jesus' answer).

Matt 22:24 The law said that when a woman's husband died without having a son, the man's brother had a responsibility to marry and care for the widow (Deut 25:5-6). This law protected women who were left alone, because in that culture they usually had no other means to support themselves.

Matt 22:29-30 The Sadducees asked Jesus what marriage would be like in heaven. Jesus said it was more important to understand God's power than know what heaven will be like. In every generation and culture, ideas of eternal life tend to be based on images and experiences of present life. Jesus answered that these faulty ideas are caused by ignorance of God's Word. We must not make up our own ideas about eternity and heaven by thinking of it and God in human terms. We should concentrate more on our relationship with God than about what heaven will look like. Eventually we will find out, and it will be far beyond our greatest expectations.

Matt 22:31-32 Because the Sadducees accepted only the Pentateuch as God's divine Word, Jesus answered them from the book of Exodus (Exod 3:6). God would not have said, "I am . . . the God of Abraham, the God of Isaac, and the God of Jacob" if he thought of Abraham, Isaac, and Jacob as dead. From God's perspective, they are alive. Jesus' use of the present tense pointed to the resurrection and the eternal life that all believers enjoy in him.

Mark 12:19 According to Old Testament law, when a man died without a son, his brother had to marry the widow and produce children to care for her and allow the family line to continue. The first son of this marriage was considered the heir of the dead man (Deut 25:5-6).

Mark 12:24 What life will be like after the resurrection is far beyond our ability to understand or imagine (Isa 64:4; 1 Cor 2:9). We need not be afraid of eternal life because of the unknowns, however. Instead of wondering what God's coming Kingdom will be like, we should concentrate on our relationship with Christ right now because in the new Kingdom, we will be with him. If we learn to love and trust Christ now, we will not be afraid of what he has in store for us then.

Mark 12:25-27 Jesus' statement does not mean that people will not recognize their spouses in heaven. It simply means that we must not think of heaven as an extension of life as we now know it. Our relationships in this life are limited by time, death, and sin. We don't know everything about our resurrection life, but Jesus affirms that relationships will be different from what we are used to here and now.

Luke 20:27-38 The Sadducees, a group of conservative religious leaders, honored only the Pentateuch—Genesis through Deuteronomy—as Scripture. They also did not believe in a resurrection of the dead because they could find no mention of it in those books. The Sadducees decided to try their hand at tricking Jesus, so they brought him a question that they probably had used

the dead. 28They posed this question: "Teacher, Moses
gave us a law that if a man dies, leaving a wife but no
children, his brother should marry the widow and
have a child who will carry on the brother's name.*
29Well, suppose there were seven brothers. The oldest
one married and then died without children. 30So the
second brother married the widow, but he also died.
31Then the third brother married her. This continued
with all seven of them, who died without children.
32Finally, the woman also died. 33So tell us, whose wife
will she be in the resurrection? For all seven were married to her!"

34Jesus replied, "Marriage is for people here on
earth. 35But in the age to come, those worthy of being
raised from the dead will neither marry nor be given
in marriage. 36And they will never die again. In this
respect they will be like angels. They are children of
God and children of the resurrection.

37"But now, as to whether the dead will be raised—
even Moses proved this when he wrote about the
burning bush. Long after Abraham, Isaac, and Jacob
had died, he referred to the Lord* as 'the God of Abraham, the God of Isaac, and the God of Jacob.'* 38So
he is the God of the living, not the dead, for they are
all alive to him."

39"Well said, Teacher!" remarked some of the
teachers of religious law who were standing there.
40And then no one dared to ask him any more
questions.

Religious Leaders Question Jesus about the Greatest Commandment PARALLEL

MATTHEW 22:34-40

But when the Pharisees heard that he had silenced the
Sadducees with his reply, they met together to question him again. 35One of them, an expert in religious
law, tried to trap him with this question: 36"Teacher,
which is the most important commandment in the law
of Moses?"

37Jesus replied, "'You must love the LORD your God
with all your heart, all your soul, and all your mind.'*
38This is the first and greatest commandment. 39A
second is equally important: 'Love your neighbor as
yourself.'* 40The entire law and all the demands of the
prophets are based on these two commandments."

MARK 12:28-34

One of the teachers of religious law was standing there
listening to the debate. He realized that Jesus had answered well, so he asked, "Of all the commandments,
which is the most important?"

29Jesus replied, "The most important commandment is this: 'Listen, O Israel! The LORD our God is
the one and only LORD. 30And you must love the LORD
your God with all your heart, all your soul, all your
mind, and all your strength.'* 31The second is equally
important: 'Love your neighbor as yourself.'* No other
commandment is greater than these."

32The teacher of religious law replied, "Well said,

Lk 20:28 See Deut 25:5-6. **Lk 20:37a** Greek *when he wrote about the bush. He referred to the Lord.* **Lk 20:37b** Exod 3:6. **Mt 22:37** Deut 6:5. **Mt 22:39** Lev 19:18. **Mk 12:29-30** Deut 6:4-5. **Mk 12:31** Lev 19:18.

successfully to stump the Pharisees. After addressing their question about marriage, Jesus answered their real question about the resurrection. Basing his answer on the writings of Moses—an authority they respected—he upheld belief in the resurrection.

Luke 20:37-38 Jesus answered the Sadducees' question, then he went beyond it to the real issue. People may ask you tough religious questions, such as "How can a loving God allow people to starve?" "If God knows what I'm going to do, do I have any free choice?" If they do, follow Jesus' example. First, answer them to the best of your ability; then look for the real issue: hurt over a personal tragedy, for example, or difficulty in making a decision. Often the spoken question is only a test, not of your ability to answer hard questions, but of your willingness to listen and care.

Matt 22:34 We might think the Pharisees would have been glad to see the Sadducees silenced. The question that the Sadducees had always used to trap them was finally answered by Jesus. But the Pharisees were too proud to be impressed. Jesus' answer gave them a theological victory over the Sadducees, but they were more interested in defeating Jesus than in learning the truth.

Matt 22:35-40 The Pharisees, who had classified over 600 laws, often tried to distinguish the more important from the less important. So one of them, an "expert in religious law," asked Jesus to identify the most important law. Jesus quoted from Deuteronomy 6:5 and Leviticus 19:18. By fulfilling these two commands, a person keeps all the others. They summarize the Ten Commandments and the other Old Testament moral laws.

Matt 22:37-40 Jesus said that if we truly love God and our neighbor, we will naturally keep the commandments. This is looking at God's law positively. Rather than worrying about all we should not do, we should concentrate on all we can do to show our love for God and others.

Mark 12:28 By Jesus' time, the Jews had accumulated hundreds of laws—613 of them. Some religious leaders tried to distinguish between major and minor laws, and some taught that all laws were equally binding and that it was dangerous to make any distinctions. This teacher's question could have provoked controversy among these groups, but Jesus' answer summarized all of God's laws.

Mark 12:29-31 God's laws are not burdensome. They can be reduced to two simple principles: Love God and love others. According to Jesus, these two commandments summarize all God's laws. Let them rule your thoughts, decisions, and actions. When you are uncertain about what to do, ask yourself which course of action best demonstrates love for God and love for others.

Mark 12:32-34 This Pharisee had grasped the intent of God's law—that true obedience comes from the heart. Because all the Old Testament commands lead to Christ, his next step was faith in Jesus himself. This, however, was the most difficult step to take. We do not know if this Pharisee ever became a true believer, but we must remember that being "close" to being a Christian is infinitely far away if a person never commits to Christ. Salvation cannot rest on intellectual knowledge alone. You must repent, follow Christ, and be made a new person by his Holy Spirit. Don't be content with being close; take the step and make the commitment.

▸ **MARK 12:28-34 *(cont.)***

Teacher. You have spoken the truth by saying that
there is only one God and no other. 33And I know it
is important to love him with all my heart and all my
understanding and all my strength, and to love my
neighbor as myself. This is more important than to
offer all of the burnt offerings and sacrifices required
in the law."

34Realizing how much the man understood, Jesus
said to him, "You are not far from the Kingdom of
God." And after that, no one dared to ask him any
more questions.

Religious Leaders Cannot Answer Jesus' Question PARALLEL

MATTHEW 22:41-46

Then, surrounded by the Pharisees, Jesus asked them
a question: 42"What do you think about the Messiah?
Whose son is he?"

They replied, "He is the son of David."

43Jesus responded, "Then why does David, speaking
under the inspiration of the Spirit, call the Messiah
'my Lord'? For David said,

44 'The LORD said to my Lord,
Sit in the place of honor at my right hand
until I humble your enemies beneath
your feet.'*

45Since David called the Messiah 'my Lord,' how can
the Messiah be his son?"

46No one could answer him. And after that, no one
dared to ask him any more questions.

MARK 12:35-37

Later, as Jesus was teaching the people in the Temple,
he asked, "Why do the teachers of religious law claim
that the Messiah is the son of David? 36For David
himself, speaking under the inspiration of the Holy
Spirit, said,

Mt 22:44 Ps 110:1.

Matt 22:41-45 The Pharisees, Sadducees, and supporters of Herod had asked their questions. Then Jesus turned the tables and asked them a penetrating question—who they thought the Messiah was. The Pharisees knew that the Messiah would be a descendant of David, but they did not understand that he would be God himself. Jesus quoted from Psalm 110:1 to show that the Messiah would be greater than David. (Heb 1:13 uses the same text as proof of Christ's deity.) The most important question we will ever answer is what we believe about Christ. Other theological questions are irrelevant until we believe that Jesus is who he said he is.

Luke 20:41-44 The central issue of life is what we believe about Jesus. Other spiritual questions are irrelevant unless we first decide to believe that Jesus is who he said

WHAT JESUS SAID ABOUT LOVE

In Mark 12:28 a teacher of religious law asked Jesus which of all the commandments was the most important to follow. Jesus mentioned two commandments—one from Deuteronomy 6:5 and the other from Leviticus 19:18. Both had to do with love. Why is love so important? Jesus said that all of the commandments were given for two simple reasons: to help us love God and love others as we should.

What else did Jesus say about love?	Reference
God loves us	John 3:16
We are to love God	Matt 22:37
Because God loves us, he cares for us	Matt 6:25-34
God wants everyone to know how much he loves them	John 17:23
God loves even those who hate him; we are to do the same	Matt 5:43-47; Luke 6:35
God seeks out even those most alienated from him	Luke 15
God must be our first love	Matt 6:24; 10:37
We love God when we obey him	John 14:21; 15:10
God loves Jesus, his Son	John 5:20; 10:17
Jesus loves God	John 14:31
Those who refuse Jesus don't have God's love	John 5:41-44
Jesus loves us just as God loves Jesus	John 15:9
Jesus proved his love for us by dying on the cross so that we could live eternally with him	John 3:14-15; 15:13-14
The love between God and Jesus is the perfect example of how we are to love others	John 17:21-26
We are to love one another (John 13:34-35) and demonstrate that love	Matt 5:40-42; 10:42
We are not to love the praise of people (John 12:43), selfish recognition (Matt 23:6-7), earthly belongings (Luke 6:20-31), or anything more than God	Luke 16:13
Jesus' love extends to each individual	Mark 10:21; John 10:11-15
Jesus wants us to love him through both good and difficult times	Matt 26:31-35
Jesus wants our love to be genuine	John 21:15-17

'The LORD said to my Lord,
Sit in the place of honor at my right hand
until I humble your enemies beneath
your feet.'*

37 Since David himself called the Messiah 'my Lord,'
how can the Messiah be his son?" The large crowd
listened to him with great delight.

LUKE 20:41-44

Then Jesus presented them with a question. "Why is
it," he asked, "that the Messiah is said to be the son
of David? 42 For David himself wrote in the book of
Psalms:

'The LORD said to my Lord,
Sit in the place of honor at my right hand
43 until I humble your enemies,
making them a footstool under your feet.'*

44 Since David called the Messiah 'Lord,' how can the
Messiah be his son?"

Jesus Warns against the Religious Leaders PARALLEL

MATTHEW 23:1-12

Then Jesus said to the crowds and to his disciples,
2 "The teachers of religious law and the Pharisees
are the official interpreters of the law of Moses.*
3 So practice and obey whatever they tell you, but
don't follow their example. For they don't practice
what they teach. 4 They crush people with unbearable
religious demands and never lift a finger to ease the
burden.

5 "Everything they do is for show. On their arms they
wear extra wide prayer boxes with Scripture verses inside, and they wear robes with extra long tassels.* 6 And
they love to sit at the head table at banquets and in the
seats of honor in the synagogues. 7 They love to receive
respectful greetings as they walk in the marketplaces,
and to be called 'Rabbi.'*

8 "Don't let anyone call you 'Rabbi,' for you have only
one teacher, and all of you are equal as brothers and
sisters.* 9 And don't address anyone here on earth as
'Father,' for only God in heaven is your spiritual Father. 10 And don't let anyone call you 'Teacher,' for you
have only one teacher, the Messiah. 11 The greatest
among you must be a servant. 12 But those who exalt
themselves will be humbled, and those who humble
themselves will be exalted."

MARK 12:38-40

Jesus also taught: "Beware of these teachers of religious law! For they like to parade around in flowing
robes and receive respectful greetings as they walk
in the marketplaces. 39 And how they love the seats of
honor in the synagogues and the head table at banquets. 40 Yet they shamelessly cheat widows out of
their property and then pretend to be pious by making long prayers in public. Because of this, they will
be more severely punished."

LUKE 20:45-47

Then, with the crowds listening, he turned to his disciples and said, 46 "Beware of these teachers of religious law! For they like to parade around in flowing
robes and love to receive respectful greetings as
they walk in the marketplaces. And how they love
the seats of honor in the synagogues and the head

Mk 12:36 Ps 110:1. **Lk 20:42-43** Ps 110:1. **Mt 23:2** Greek *and the Pharisees sit in the seat of Moses.* **Mt 23:5** Greek *They enlarge their phylacteries and lengthen their tassels.* **Mt 23:7** *Rabbi,* from Aramaic, means "master" or "teacher." **Mt 23:8** Greek *brothers.*

he is. The Pharisees and Sadducees could not do this. They remained confused over Jesus' identity.

Matt 23:2-3 The Pharisees' traditions and their interpretations and applications of the laws had become as important to them as God's law itself. Their laws were not all bad—some were beneficial. Problems arose when the religious leaders held that man-made rules were equal to God's laws; told the people to obey these rules but did not do so themselves; or obeyed the rules, not to honor God, but to make themselves look good. Usually Jesus did not condemn what the Pharisees taught but what they were—hypocrites.

Matt 23:5 These "prayer boxes" were leather boxes containing Scripture verses. Very religious people wore these boxes on their foreheads and arms in order to obey Deuteronomy 6:8 and Exodus 13:9, 16. But the prayer boxes had been made extra wide and had become more important for the status they gave than for the truth they contained.

Matt 23:5-7 Jesus again exposed the hypocritical attitudes of the religious leaders. They knew the Scriptures but did not live by them. They didn't care about being holy—just looking holy in order to receive people's admiration and praise. Today, like the Pharisees, many people say they know the Bible but do not let it change their lives. They say they follow Jesus, but they don't live by his standards of love. We must make sure that our actions match our beliefs.

Matt 23:5-7 People desire positions of leadership not only in business but also in the church. It is dangerous when love for position grows stronger than loyalty to God. This is what happened to the Pharisees and teachers of religious law. Jesus condemned leaders who serve themselves rather than others.

Matt 23:11-12 Jesus challenged society's norms. To him, greatness comes from serving—giving of yourself to honor God and help others. Service keeps us aware of others' needs, and it stops us from focusing only on ourselves. Jesus came as a servant. What kind of greatness do you seek?

Mark 12:38-40 Jesus again exposed the religious leaders' impure motives. The teachers received no pay, so they depended on the hospitality extended by devout Jews. Some of them used this custom to exploit people, cheating the poor out of everything they had and taking advantage of the rich. Through their pious actions they hoped to gain status, recognition, and respect.

Mark 12:38-40 Jesus warned against trying to make a good impression. These teachers of religious law were religious hypocrites who had no love for God. True followers of Christ are not distinguished by showy spirituality. Reading the Bible, praying in public, or following church rituals can be phony if the motive for doing them is to be noticed or honored. Let your actions be consistent with your beliefs. Live for Christ, even when no one is looking.

Luke 20:45-47 The teachers of religious law loved the benefits associated with their position, and they sometimes cheated the poor in order to get even more benefits. Every job has its rewards, but gaining rewards should never become more important than doing the job faithfully. God will punish people who use their position of responsibility to cheat others. Use whatever resources you have been given to help others and not just yourself.

▸ **LUKE 20:45-47 *(cont.)***
table at banquets. 47Yet they shamelessly cheat widows out of their property and then pretend to be pious by making long prayers in public. Because of this, they will be severely punished."

Jesus Condemns the Religious Leaders

MATTHEW 23:13-36
"What sorrow awaits you teachers of religious law and you Pharisees. Hypocrites! For you shut the door of the Kingdom of Heaven in people's faces. You won't go in yourselves, and you don't let others enter either.*
15"What sorrow awaits you teachers of religious law and you Pharisees. Hypocrites! For you cross land and sea to make one convert, and then you turn that person into twice the child of hell* you yourselves are!
16"Blind guides! What sorrow awaits you! For you say that it means nothing to swear 'by God's Temple,' but that it is binding to swear 'by the gold in the Temple.'
17Blind fools! Which is more important—the gold or the Temple that makes the gold sacred?
18And you say that to swear 'by the altar' is not binding, but to swear 'by the gifts on the altar' is binding.
19How blind! For which is more important—the gift on the altar or the altar that makes the gift sacred?
20When you swear 'by the altar,' you are swearing by it and by everything on it.
21And when you swear 'by the Temple,' you are swearing by it and by God, who lives in it.
22And when you swear 'by heaven,' you are swearing by the throne of God and by God, who sits on the throne.
23"What sorrow awaits you teachers of religious law and you Pharisees. Hypocrites! For you are careful to tithe even the tiniest income from your herb gardens,* but you ignore the more important aspects of the law—justice, mercy, and faith. You should tithe, yes, but do not neglect the more important things.
24Blind guides! You strain your water so you won't accidentally swallow a gnat, but you swallow a camel!*
25"What sorrow awaits you teachers of religious law and you Pharisees. Hypocrites! For you are so careful to clean the outside of the cup and the dish, but inside you are filthy—full of greed and self-indulgence!
26You blind Pharisee! First wash the inside of the cup and the dish,* and then the outside will become clean, too.
27"What sorrow awaits you teachers of religious law and you Pharisees. Hypocrites! For you are like

Mt 23:13 Some manuscripts add verse 14, *What sorrow awaits you teachers of religious law and you Pharisees. Hypocrites! You shamelessly cheat widows out of their property and then pretend to be pious by making long prayers in public. Because of this, you will be severely punished.* Compare Mark 12:40 and Luke 20:47. **Mt 23:15** Greek *of Gehenna;* also in 23:33. **Mt 23:23** Greek *tithe the mint, the dill, and the cumin.* **Mt 23:24** See Lev 11:4, 23, where gnats and camels are both forbidden as food. **Mt 23:26** Some manuscripts do not include *and the dish.*

Luke 20:47 How strange to think that the teachers of religious law would receive the worst punishment. But behind their appearance of holiness and respectability, they were arrogant, crafty, selfish, and uncaring. Jesus exposed their evil hearts. He showed that despite their pious words, they were neglecting God's laws and doing as they pleased. Religious deeds do not cancel sin. Jesus said that God's most severe judgment awaited these teachers because they should have been living examples of mercy and justice.

Matt 23:13-14 Being a religious leader in Jerusalem was very different from being a pastor in secular society today. Israel's history, culture, and daily life centered around its relationship with God. The religious leaders were the best known, most powerful, and most respected of all leaders. Jesus made these stinging accusations because the leaders' hunger for more power, money, and status had made them lose sight of God, and their blindness was spreading to the whole nation.

Matt 23:15 The Pharisees' converts were attracted to religion, not to God. By getting caught up in the details of their additional laws and regulations, they completely missed God, to whom the laws pointed. A religion of works puts pressure on people to surpass others in what they know and do. Thus, a hypocritical teacher was likely to have students who were even more hypocritical. We must make sure we are not creating Pharisees by emphasizing outward obedience at the expense of inner renewal.

THE SEVEN SORROWS

Jesus mentioned seven ways to guarantee God's anger when he told the religious leaders, "What sorrow awaits you." These seven statements were strong and unforgettable. They are still applicable anytime we become so involved in perfecting the practice of religion that we forget that God is also concerned with mercy, real love, and forgiveness.

Matt 23:13	Not letting others enter the Kingdom of Heaven and not entering yourselves
Matt 23:15	Converting people away from God to be like yourselves
Matt 23:16-22	Blindly leading God's people to follow man-made traditions instead of God's Word
Matt 23:23-24	Involving yourself in every last detail and ignoring what is really important: justice, mercy, and faith
Matt 23:25-26	Keeping up appearances while your private world is corrupt
Matt 23:27-28	Acting spiritual to cover up sin
Matt 23:29-36	Pretending to have learned from past history, but your present behavior shows you have learned nothing

Matt 23:23-24 It's possible to obey the details of the laws but still be disobedient in our general behavior. For example, we could be very precise and faithful about giving 10 percent of our money to God but refuse to give one minute of our time in helping others. Tithing is important, but giving a tithe does not exempt us from fulfilling God's other directives.

Matt 23:24 The Pharisees strained their water so they wouldn't accidentally swallow a gnat—an unclean insect according to the law. Meticulous about the details of ceremonial cleanliness, they nevertheless had lost their perspective on inner purity—in essence, they would then swallow a camel and not even notice. They were ceremonially clean on the outside but had corrupt hearts.

Matt 23:25-28 Jesus condemned the

whitewashed tombs—beautiful on the outside but
filled on the inside with dead people's bones and all
sorts of impurity. 28Outwardly you look like righteous
people, but inwardly your hearts are filled with hypocrisy and lawlessness.
29"What sorrow awaits you teachers of religious law
and you Pharisees. Hypocrites! For you build tombs for
the prophets your ancestors killed, and you decorate
the monuments of the godly people your ancestors
destroyed. 30Then you say, 'If we had lived in the days
of our ancestors, we would never have joined them in
killing the prophets.'
31"But in saying that, you testify against yourselves
that you are indeed the descendants of those who
murdered the prophets. 32Go ahead and finish what
your ancestors started. 33Snakes! Sons of vipers! How
will you escape the judgment of hell?
34"Therefore, I am sending you prophets and wise
men and teachers of religious law. But you will kill
some by crucifixion, and you will flog others with
whips in your synagogues, chasing them from city
to city. 35As a result, you will be held responsible for
the murder of all godly people of all time—from the
murder of righteous Abel to the murder of Zechariah son of Berekiah, whom you killed in the Temple
between the sanctuary and the altar. 36I tell you the
truth, this judgment will fall on this very generation."

A Poor Widow Gives All She Has PARALLEL ••

MARK 12:41-44 ••
Jesus sat down near the collection box in the Temple
and watched as the crowds dropped in their money.
Many rich people put in large amounts. 42Then a poor
widow came and dropped in two small coins.*
43Jesus called his disciples to him and said, "I tell
you the truth, this poor widow has given more than
all the others who are making contributions. 44For
they gave a tiny part of their surplus, but she, poor
as she is, has given everything she had to live on."

LUKE 21:1-4 ••
While Jesus was in the Temple, he watched the rich
people dropping their gifts in the collection box. 2Then
a poor widow came by and dropped in two small coins.*
3"I tell you the truth," Jesus said, "this poor widow
has given more than all the rest of them. 4For they have
given a tiny part of their surplus, but she, poor as she
is, has given everything she has."

Jesus Teaches about Being Watchful for His Return PARALLEL •••

MATTHEW 24:1-51 •••
As Jesus was leaving the Temple grounds, his disciples
pointed out to him the various Temple buildings. 2But
he responded, "Do you see all these buildings? I tell

Mk 12:42 Greek *two lepta, which is a kodrantes* [i.e., a quadrans]. **Lk 21:2** Greek *two lepta* [the smallest of Jewish coins].

Pharisees and religious leaders for outwardly appearing upright and holy but inwardly remaining full of corruption and greed. Living our Christianity merely as a show for others is like washing only the outside of a cup. When we are clean on the inside, our cleanliness on the outside won't be a sham.

Matt 23:34-36 These prophets, wise men, and teachers were probably leaders in the early church who would be persecuted, scourged, and killed, as Jesus predicted. The people of Jesus' generation said they would not act as their fathers did in killing the prophets whom God had sent to them (Matt 23:30), but they were about to kill the Messiah himself and his faithful followers. Thus, they would become guilty of all the righteous blood shed through the centuries.

Matt 23:35 Jesus summarized the history of Old Testament martyrdom. Abel was the first martyr (Gen 4); Zechariah was the last martyr mentioned in the Hebrew Bible, which is arranged differently from our English Bibles and ends with 2 Chronicles. Zechariah is a classic example of a man of God who was killed by those who claimed to be God's people (see 2 Chr 24:20-21).

Mark 12:41-44 This widow gave all she had to live on, in contrast to the way most people handle their money. When we consider giving a certain percentage of our income a great accomplishment, we resemble those who gave "a tiny part of their surplus." Here, Jesus was admiring generous and sacrificial giving. As believers, we should consider increasing our giving—whether of money, time, or talents—to a point beyond convenience or calculation.

Luke 21:1-2 Jesus was in the area of the Temple called the Court of the Women. In this area were seven boxes in which worshipers could deposit their Temple tax and six boxes for freewill offerings, like the one this woman gave. This widow was not only poor but had few resources for making money. Her small gift was a sacrifice, but she gave it willingly.

Matt 24:1-2 Although no one knows exactly what this Temple looked like, it must have been beautiful. Herod had helped the Jews remodel and beautify it, no doubt to stay on friendly terms with his subjects. Next to the inner Temple, where the sacred objects were kept and the sacrifices offered, there was a large area called the Court of the Gentiles (where the money changers and merchants had their booths). Outside these courts were long porches. Solomon's Colonnade was 1,562 feet long, decorated with 160 columns stretching along its 921-foot length. Gazing at this glorious and massive structure, the disciples found Jesus' words about its destruction difficult to believe. But the Temple was indeed destroyed only 40 years later when the Romans sacked Jerusalem in A.D. 70.

Wailing Wall

Jesus predicted that the Temple would be completely destroyed (Matt 24:2), which occured 40 years later when the Roman general Titus sacked Jerusalem and razed the Temple. Josephus described it like this: "As soon as the army had no more people to slay or to plunder, . . . Caesar gave orders that they should now demolish the entire city and temple" (*War* 7.1.1). Only one outer wall of the Temple remained, now known as the Wailing Wall. Located in the Old City of Jerusalem at the western side of the Temple Mount, it is one of the most sacred places in Judaism. It has been a site for Jewish prayer and pilgrimages for centuries.

▸ **MATTHEW 24:1-51** ***(cont.)***

you the truth, they will be completely demolished. Not one stone will be left on top of another!"

3Later, Jesus sat on the Mount of Olives. His disciples came to him privately and said, "Tell us, when will all this happen? What sign will signal your return and the end of the world?*"

4Jesus told them, "Don't let anyone mislead you, 5for many will come in my name, claiming, 'I am the Messiah.' They will deceive many. 6And you will hear of wars and threats of wars, but don't panic. Yes, these things must take place, but the end won't follow immediately. 7Nation will go to war against nation, and kingdom against kingdom. There will be famines and earthquakes in many parts of the world. 8But all this is only the first of the birth pains, with more to come.

9"Then you will be arrested, persecuted, and killed. You will be hated all over the world because you are my followers.* 10And many will turn away from me and betray and hate each other. 11And many false prophets will appear and will deceive many people. 12Sin will be rampant everywhere, and the love of many will grow cold. 13But the one who endures to the end will be saved. 14And the Good News about the Kingdom will be preached throughout the whole world, so that all nations* will hear it; and then the end will come.

15"The day is coming when you will see what Daniel the prophet spoke about—the sacrilegious object that causes desecration* standing in the Holy Place." (Reader, pay attention!) 16"Then those in Judea must flee to the hills. 17A person out on the deck of a roof must not go down into the house to pack. 18A person out in the field must not return even to get a coat. 19How terrible it will be for pregnant women and for nursing mothers in those days. 20And pray that your flight will not be in winter or on the Sabbath. 21For there will be greater anguish than at any time since the world began. And it will never be so great again. 22In fact, unless that time of calamity is shortened, not a single person will survive. But it will be shortened for the sake of God's chosen ones.

23"Then if anyone tells you, 'Look, here is the Messiah,' or 'There he is,' don't believe it. 24For false messiahs and false prophets will rise up and perform great signs and wonders so as to deceive, if possible, even God's chosen ones. 25See, I have warned you about this ahead of time.

26"So if someone tells you, 'Look, the Messiah is out in the desert,' don't bother to go and look. Or, 'Look, he is hiding here,' don't believe it! 27For as the lightning flashes in the east and shines to the west, so it will be when the Son of Man* comes. 28Just as the gathering of vultures shows there is a carcass nearby, so these signs indicate that the end is near.*

29"Immediately after the anguish of those days,

Mt 24:3 Or *the age?* **Mt 24:9** Greek *on account of my name.* **Mt 24:14** Or *all peoples.* **Mt 24:15** Greek *the abomination of desolation.* See Dan 9:27; 11:31; 12:11. **Mt 24:27** "Son of Man" is a title Jesus used for himself. **Mt 24:28** Greek *Wherever the carcass is, the vultures gather.*

Matt 24:3ff Jesus was sitting on the Mount of Olives, the very place where the prophet Zechariah had predicted that the Messiah would stand when he came to establish his Kingdom (Zech 14:4). It was a fitting place for the disciples to ask Jesus when he would come in power and what they could expect then. Jesus' reply emphasized the events that would take place before the end of the age. He pointed out that his disciples should be less concerned with knowing the exact date and more concerned with being prepared—living God's way consistently so that no matter when Jesus came, they would be ready.

Matt 24:4 The disciples asked Jesus for the sign of his coming and of the end of the age. Jesus' first response was "Don't let anyone mislead you." The fact is that whenever we look for signs, we become very susceptible to being deceived. There are many "false prophets" (Matt 24:11, 24) around with counterfeit signs of spiritual power and authority. The only sure way to keep from being deceived is to focus on Christ and his words. Don't look for special signs, and don't look at other people. Look at Christ.

Matt 24:9-13 You may not be facing intense persecution now, but Christians in other parts of the world are. As you hear about Christians suffering for their faith, remember that they are your brothers and sisters in Christ. Pray for them. Ask God what you can do to help them in their troubles. When one part of the body suffers, the whole body suffers. But when all the parts join together to ease the suffering, the whole body benefits (1 Cor 12:26).

Matt 24:11 The Old Testament frequently mentions false prophets (see 2 Kgs 3:13; Isa 44:25; Jer 23:16; Ezek 13:2-3; Mic 3:5; Zech 13:2). False prophets claimed to receive messages from God, but they preached a "health and wealth" message. They said what the people wanted to hear, even when the nation was not following God as it should. There were false prophets in Jesus' day, and we have them today. They are the popular leaders who tell people what they want to hear, such as "God wants you to be rich," "Do whatever your desires tell you," or "There is no such thing as sin or hell." Jesus said false teachers would come, and he warned his disciples, as he warns us, not to listen to their dangerous words.

Matt 24:12 With false teaching and loose morals comes a particularly destructive disease—the loss of true love for God and others. Sin cools your love for God and others by turning your focus on yourself. You cannot truly love if you think only of yourself.

Matt 24:14 Jesus said that before he returns, the Good News about the Kingdom (the message of salvation) would be preached throughout the world. This was the disciples' mission—and it is ours today. Jesus talked about the end times and final judgment to show his followers the urgency of spreading the Good News of salvation to everyone.

Matt 24:21-22 Jesus, talking about the end times, telescoped near future and far future events, as did the Old Testament prophets. Many of these persecutions have already occurred; more are yet to come. But God is in control of even the length of persecutions. He will not forget his people. This is all we need to know about the future to motivate us to live rightly now.

Matt 24:23-24 Jesus' warnings about false teachers still hold true. Upon close examination it becomes clear that many nice-sounding messages don't agree with God's message in the Bible. Only a solid foundation in God's Word can equip us to perceive the errors and distortions in false teaching.

Matt 24:24-28 In times of persecution even strong believers will find it difficult to be loyal. To keep from being deceived by false messiahs, we must understand that Jesus' return will be unmistakable (Mark 13:26); no one will doubt that it is he. If you have to be told that the Messiah has come, then he hasn't (Matt 24:27). Christ's coming will be obvious to everyone.

the sun will be darkened,
the moon will give no light,
the stars will fall from the sky,
and the powers in the heavens will be shaken.*
30And then at last, the sign that the Son of Man is coming will appear in the heavens, and there will be deep
mourning among all the peoples of the earth. And
they will see the Son of Man coming on the clouds
of heaven with power and great glory.* 31And he will
send out his angels with the mighty blast of a trumpet,
and they will gather his chosen ones from all over
the world*—from the farthest ends of the earth and
heaven.
32"Now learn a lesson from the fig tree. When its
branches bud and its leaves begin to sprout, you know
that summer is near. 33In the same way, when you see
all these things, you can know his return is very near,
right at the door. 34I tell you the truth, this generation*
will not pass from the scene until all these things take
place. 35Heaven and earth will disappear, but my words
will never disappear.
36"However, no one knows the day or hour when
these things will happen, not even the angels in heaven
or the Son himself.* Only the Father knows.
37"When the Son of Man returns, it will be like it
was in Noah's day. 38In those days before the flood,
the people were enjoying banquets and parties and
weddings right up to the time Noah entered his boat.
39People didn't realize what was going to happen until
the flood came and swept them all away. That is the
way it will be when the Son of Man comes.
40"Two men will be working together in the field;
one will be taken, the other left. 41Two women will
be grinding flour at the mill; one will be taken, the
other left.
42"So you, too, must keep watch! For you don't know
what day your Lord is coming. 43Understand this: If a
homeowner knew exactly when a burglar was coming,
he would keep watch and not permit his house to be
broken into. 44You also must be ready all the time, for
the Son of Man will come when least expected.
45"A faithful, sensible servant is one to whom the
master can give the responsibility of managing his
other household servants and feeding them. 46If the
master returns and finds that the servant has done a
good job, there will be a reward. 47I tell you the truth,
the master will put that servant in charge of all he
owns. 48But what if the servant is evil and thinks, 'My
master won't be back for a while,' 49and he begins
beating the other servants, partying, and getting
drunk? 50The master will return unannounced and
unexpected, 51and he will cut the servant to pieces
and assign him a place with the hypocrites. In that
place there will be weeping and gnashing of teeth."

MARK 13:1-37

As Jesus was leaving the Temple that day, one of his
disciples said, "Teacher, look at these magnificent
buildings! Look at the impressive stones in the walls."
2Jesus replied, "Yes, look at these great buildings.
But they will be completely demolished. Not one stone
will be left on top of another!"
3Later, Jesus sat on the Mount of Olives across the
valley from the Temple. Peter, James, John, and Andrew
came to him privately and asked him, 4"Tell us, when
will all this happen? What sign will show us that these
things are about to be fulfilled?"

Mt 24:29 See Isa 13:10; 34:4; Joel 2:10. **Mt 24:30** See Dan 7:13. **Mt 24:31** Greek *from the four winds.* **Mt 24:34** Or *this age,* or *this nation.* **Mt 24:36** Some manuscripts do not include *or the Son himself.*

Matt 24:30 The nations of the earth will mourn because unbelievers will suddenly realize they have chosen the wrong side. Everything they have scoffed about will be happening, and it will be too late for them.

Matt 24:36 It is good that we don't know exactly when Christ will return. If we knew the precise date, we might be tempted to be lazy in our work for Christ. Worse yet, we might plan to keep sinning and then turn to God right at the end. Heaven is not our only goal; we have work to do here. And we must keep on doing it until death or until we see the unmistakable return of our Savior.

Matt 24:40-42 Christ's second coming will be swift and sudden. There will be no opportunity for last-minute repentance or bargaining. The choice we have already made will determine our eternal destiny.

Matt 24:44 Jesus' purpose in telling about his return is not to stimulate predictions and calculations about the date but to warn us to be prepared. Will you be ready? The only safe choice is to obey him today (Matt 24:46).

Matt 24:45-47 Jesus asks us to spend the time of waiting taking care of his people and doing his work here on earth, both within the church and outside it. This is the best way to prepare for Christ's return.

Matt 24:51 "Weeping and gnashing of teeth" is a phrase used to describe despair. God's coming judgment is as certain as Jesus' return to earth.

Mark 13:1-2 About 15 years before Jesus was born (20 B.C.), Herod the Great began to remodel and rebuild the Temple, which had stood for nearly 500 years since the days of Ezra (Ezra 6:14-15). Herod made the Temple one of the most beautiful buildings in Jerusalem—not to honor God, but to appease the Jews whom he ruled. The magnificent building project was not completely finished until A.D. 64. Jesus' prophecy that not one stone would be left on another was fulfilled in A.D. 70, when the Romans completely destroyed the Temple and the entire city of Jerusalem.

Mark 13:3ff The disciples wanted to know when the Temple would be destroyed. Jesus gave them a prophetic picture of that time, including events leading up to it. He also talked about future events connected with his return to earth to judge all people. Jesus predicted both near and distant events without putting them in chronological order. Some of the disciples lived to see the destruction of Jerusalem in A.D. 70. This event would assure them that everything else Jesus predicted would also happen.

Jesus warned his followers about the future so that they could learn how to live in the present. Many predictions Jesus made in this passage have not yet been fulfilled. He did not make them so that we would guess when they might be fulfilled but to help us to be spiritually alert and prepared at all times as we wait for his return.

Mark 13:3-4 The Mount of Olives rises above Jerusalem to the east. From its slopes a person can look down into the city and see the Temple. Zechariah 14:1-4 predicts that the Messiah will stand on this very mountain when he returns to set up his eternal Kingdom.

▸ **MARK 13:1-37 *(cont.)***

5Jesus replied, "Don't let anyone mislead you, 6for many will come in my name, claiming, 'I am the Messiah.'* They will deceive many. 7And you will hear of wars and threats of wars, but don't panic. Yes, these things must take place, but the end won't follow immediately. 8Nation will go to war against nation, and kingdom against kingdom. There will be earthquakes in many parts of the world, as well as famines. But this is only the first of the birth pains, with more to come.

9"When these things begin to happen, watch out! You will be handed over to the local councils and beaten in the synagogues. You will stand trial before governors and kings because you are my followers. But this will be your opportunity to tell them about me.* 10For the Good News must first be preached to all nations.* 11But when you are arrested and stand trial, don't worry in advance about what to say. Just say what God tells you at that time, for it is not you who will be speaking, but the Holy Spirit.

12"A brother will betray his brother to death, a father will betray his own child, and children will rebel against their parents and cause them to be killed. 13And everyone will hate you because you are my followers.* But the one who endures to the end will be saved.

14"The day is coming when you will see the sacrilegious object that causes desecration* standing where he* should not be." (Reader, pay attention!) "Then those in Judea must flee to the hills. 15A person out on the deck of a roof must not go down into the house to pack. 16A person out in the field must not return even to get a coat. 17How terrible it will be for pregnant women and for nursing mothers in those days. 18And pray that your flight will not be in winter. 19For there will be greater anguish in those days than at any time since God created the world. And it

Mk 13:6 Greek *claiming, 'I am.'* **Mk 13:9** Or *But this will be your testimony against them.* **Mk 13:10** Or *all peoples.* **Mk 13:13** Greek *on account of my name.* **Mk 13:14a** Greek *the abomination of desolation.* See Dan 9:27; 11:31; 12:11. **Mk 13:14b** Or *it.*

Mark 13:5-7 What are the signs of the end times? There have been people in every generation since Christ's resurrection claiming to know exactly when Jesus would return. No one has been right yet, however, because Christ will return on God's timetable, not ours. Jesus predicted that before his return many believers would be misled by false teachers claiming to have revelations from God.

According to Scripture, one clear sign of Christ's return will be his unmistakable appearance in the clouds, which will be seen by all people (Mark 13:26; Rev 1:7). In other words, you do not have to wonder whether a certain person is the Messiah or whether these are the "end times." When Jesus returns, you will know beyond a doubt because it will be evident to all. Beware of groups who claim special knowledge of Christ's return because no one knows when that time will be (Mark 13:32). Be cautious about saying, "This is it!" Rather, be bold in your total commitment; have your heart and life ready for Christ's return.

Mark 13:9-11 As the early church began to grow, most of the disciples experienced the kind of persecution Jesus was talking about. Since the time of Christ, Christians have been persecuted in their own lands and on foreign mission fields. Though you may be safe from persecution now, your vision of God's Kingdom must not be limited by what happens only to you. A glance at a newspaper will reveal that many Christians in other parts of the world daily face hardships and persecution. Persecutions are an opportunity for Christians to witness for Christ to those opposed to him. God's desire is that the Good News be proclaimed to everyone in spite of persecution.

Mark 13:11 Jesus was teaching the kind of attitude we should have when we must take a stand for the Good News. We don't have to be fearful or defensive about our faith because the Holy Spirit will be present to give us the right words to say.

Mark 13:13 To believe in Jesus and endure to the end will take perseverance because our faith will be challenged and opposed. Severe trials will sift true Christians from fair-weather believers. Enduring to the end does not earn salvation for us but marks us as already saved. The assurance of our salvation will keep us strong in times of persecution.

Mark 13:14 The "sacrilegious object that causes desecration" refers to the desecration of the Temple by God's enemies. This happened repeatedly in Israel's history: in 597 B.C. when Nebuchadnezzar looted the Temple and took Judean captives to Babylon (2 Chr 36); in 168 B.C. when Antiochus Epiphanes sacrificed a pig to Zeus on the sacred Temple altar (Dan 9:27; 11:30-31); in A.D. 70 when the Roman general Titus placed an idol on the site of the burned-out Temple after the destruction of Jerusalem. Just a few years after Jesus gave this warning, in A.D. 38, the emperor Caligula made plans to put his own statue in the Temple, but he died before this could be carried out.

Mark 13:17 Some Christian couples who are contemplating pregnancy have been discouraged by this verse. They wonder if kids should be brought into a world filled with sin, evil, and terror. Jesus was not making a general warning against pregnancy, however. Many times in history have had risks and drawbacks; no place or time is perfect. We must remember that God will look out for the welfare of our children as he has looked out for us.

JESUS' PROPHECIES IN THE OLIVET DISCOURSE

In Mark 13, often called the Olivet discourse, Jesus talked a lot about two things: the end times and his second coming. In sharing these prophecies with them, Jesus was not trying to encourage his disciples to speculate about exactly when he would return. Instead, he is urging all his followers to be watchful and prepared for his coming. If we serve Jesus faithfully now, we will be ready when he returns.

Type of Prophecy	*Old Testament References*	*Other New Testament References*
The Last Days		
Mark 13:1-23	Dan 9:26-27	John 15:18-21
Luke 21:5-24	Joel 2:2	1 Tim 4:1-2
Matt 24:1-28	Dan 11:31	Rev 11:2
The Second Coming of Christ		
Mark 13:24-27	Isa 13:6-10	Rev 6:12
Luke 21:25-28	Ezek 32:7-8	Mark 14:62
Matt 24:29-31	Dan 7:13-14	1 Thes 4:16

will never be so great again. 20In fact, unless the Lord
shortens that time of calamity, not a single person
will survive. But for the sake of his chosen ones he
has shortened those days.
21"Then if anyone tells you, 'Look, here is the Messiah,' or 'There he is,' don't believe it. 22For false messiahs and false prophets will rise up and perform signs
and wonders so as to deceive, if possible, even God's
chosen ones. 23Watch out! I have warned you about
this ahead of time!
24"At that time, after the anguish of those days,

the sun will be darkened,
  the moon will give no light,
25 the stars will fall from the sky,
  and the powers in the heavens will be shaken.*

26Then everyone will see the Son of Man* coming on
the clouds with great power and glory.* 27And he will
send out his angels to gather his chosen ones from all
over the world*—from the farthest ends of the earth
and heaven.
28"Now learn a lesson from the fig tree. When
its branches bud and its leaves begin to sprout, you
know that summer is near. 29In the same way, when
you see all these things taking place, you can know
that his return is very near, right at the door. 30I tell
you the truth, this generation* will not pass from the
scene before all these things take place. 31Heaven
and earth will disappear, but my words will never
disappear.
32"However, no one knows the day or hour when
these things will happen, not even the angels in heaven
or the Son himself. Only the Father knows. 33And since
you don't know when that time will come, be on guard!
Stay alert*!
34"The coming of the Son of Man can be illustrated
by the story of a man going on a long trip. When he
left home, he gave each of his slaves instructions about
the work they were to do, and he told the gatekeeper
to watch for his return. 35You, too, must keep watch!
For you don't know when the master of the household
will return—in the evening, at midnight, before dawn,
or at daybreak. 36Don't let him find you sleeping when
he arrives without warning. 37I say to you what I say
to everyone: Watch for him!"

LUKE 21:5-38
Some of his disciples began talking about the majestic stonework of the Temple and the memorial decorations on the walls. But Jesus said, 6"The time is
coming when all these things will be completely demolished. Not one stone will be left on top of another!"
7"Teacher," they asked, "when will all this happen?
What sign will show us that these things are about to
take place?"

Mk 13:24-25 See Isa 13:10; 34:4; Joel 2:10. **Mk 13:26a** "Son of Man" is a title Jesus used for himself. **Mk 13:26b** See Dan 7:13. **Mk 13:27** Greek *from the four winds.* **Mk 13:30** Or *this age,* or *this nation.* **Mk 13:33** Some manuscripts add *and pray.*

Mark 13:20 The "chosen ones" are God's chosen people, those who are saved. See Romans 8:29-30 and Ephesians 1:4-5 for more on God's choice.

Mark 13:22-23 Is it possible for Christians to be deceived? Yes. So convincing will be the arguments and proofs from deceivers in the end times that it will be difficult not to fall away from Christ. If we are prepared, Jesus says, we can remain faithful. But if we are not prepared, we will turn away. To penetrate the disguises of false teachers we can ask: (1) Have their predictions come true, or do they have to revise them to fit what's already happened? (2) Does any teaching utilize a small section of the Bible to the neglect of the whole? (3) Does the teaching contradict what the Bible says about God? (4) Are the practices meant to glorify the teacher or Christ? (5) Do the teachings promote hostility toward other Christians?

Mark 13:31 Jesus tells us that even though the earth will pass away, the truth of his words will never be changed or abolished. God and his Word provide the only stability in our unstable world. How shortsighted people are who spend all their time and energy learning about this temporary world and accumulating its possessions, while neglecting the Bible and its eternal truths!

Mark 13:32 When Jesus said that even he did not know the time of the end, he was affirming his humanity. Of course God the Father knows the time, and Jesus and the Father are one. But when Jesus became a man, he voluntarily gave up the unlimited use of his divine attributes.

The emphasis of this verse is not on Jesus' lack of knowledge, but rather on the fact that no one knows. It is God the Father's secret to be revealed when he wills. No one can predict by Scripture or science the exact day of Jesus' return. Jesus is teaching that preparation, not calculation, is needed.

Mark 13:33-34 Months of planning go into a wedding, the birth of a baby, a career change, a speaking engagement, the purchase of a home. Do you place the same importance on preparing for Christ's return, the most important event in your life? Its results will last for eternity. You dare not postpone your preparations because you do not know when his return will occur. The way to prepare is to study God's Word and live by its instructions each day. Only then will you be ready.

Mark 13:35-37 Mark 13 tells us how to live while we wait for Christ's return: (1) We are not to be misled by confusing claims or speculative interpretations of what will happen (Mark 13:5-6). (2) We should not be afraid to tell people about Christ, despite what they might say or do to us (Mark 13:9-11). (3) We must stand firm by faith and not be surprised by persecution (Mark 13:13). (4) We must be morally alert, obedient to the commands for living found in God's Word. This chapter was not given to promote discussions on prophetic timetables but to stimulate right living for God in a world where he is largely ignored.

Luke 21:5-6 The Temple the disciples were admiring was not Solomon's Temple—that had been destroyed by the Babylonians early in the sixth century B.C. This Temple had been built by Ezra after the return from exile later in the sixth century B.C., desecrated by the Seleucids in the second century B.C., reconsecrated by the Maccabees soon afterward, and enormously expanded by Herod the Great over a 46-year period. It was a beautiful, imposing structure with a significant history, but Jesus said that it would be completely destroyed. This happened in A.D. 70 when the Roman army burned Jerusalem.

Luke 21:7ff Jesus did not leave his disciples unprepared for the difficult years ahead. He warned them about false messiahs, natural disasters, and persecutions; however, he assured the disciples that he would be with them to protect them and make his Kingdom known through them. In the end, Jesus promised that he would return in power and glory to save them. Jesus' warnings and promises to his disciples also apply to us as we look forward to his return.

▸ **LUKE 21:5-38** ***(cont.)***

[8]He replied, "Don't let anyone mislead you, for many will come in my name, claiming, 'I am the Messiah,'* and saying, 'The time has come!' But don't believe them. [9]And when you hear of wars and insurrections, don't panic. Yes, these things must take place first, but the end won't follow immediately." [10]Then he added, "Nation will go to war against nation, and kingdom against kingdom. [11]There will be great earthquakes, and there will be famines and plagues in many lands, and there will be terrifying things and great miraculous signs from heaven.

[12]"But before all this occurs, there will be a time of great persecution. You will be dragged into synagogues and prisons, and you will stand trial before kings and governors because you are my followers. [13]But this will be your opportunity to tell them about me.* [14]So don't worry in advance about how to answer the charges against you, [15]for I will give you the right words and such wisdom that none of your opponents will be able to reply or refute you! [16]Even those closest to you—your parents, brothers, relatives, and friends—will betray you. They will even kill some of you. [17]And everyone will hate you because you are my followers.* [18]But not a hair of your head will perish! [19]By standing firm, you will win your souls.

[20]"And when you see Jerusalem surrounded by armies, then you will know that the time of its destruction has arrived. [21]Then those in Judea must flee to the hills. Those in Jerusalem must get out, and those out in the country should not return to the city. [22]For those will be days of God's vengeance, and the prophetic words of the Scriptures will be fulfilled. [23]How terrible it will be for pregnant women and for nursing mothers in those days. For there will be disaster in the land and great anger against this people. [24]They will be killed by the sword or sent away as captives to all the nations of the world. And Jerusalem will be trampled down by the Gentiles until the period of the Gentiles comes to an end.

[25]"And there will be strange signs in the sun, moon, and stars. And here on earth the nations will be in turmoil, perplexed by the roaring seas and strange tides. [26]People will be terrified at what they see coming upon the earth, for the powers in the heavens will be shaken. [27]Then everyone will see the Son of Man*

Lk 21:8 Greek *claiming, 'I am.'* **Lk 21:13** Or *This will be your testimony against them.* **Lk 21:17** Greek *on account of my name.* **Lk 21:27a** "Son of Man" is a title Jesus used for himself.

Masada

Jesus warned that the destruction of Jerusalem would lead to a mass migration out of Jerusalem (Luke 21:20-21). Some of those who left Jerusalem went to Masada, a towering rock fortress (1,400 feet high) on the western shore of the Dead Sea. When the first Jewish revolt began in A.D. 66, a number of Zealots took over Masada, which had been occupied by a small Roman garrison. After the destruction of Jerusalem (A.D. 70), the Romans removed all pockets of Jewish resistance until only the fortress of Masada remained. When Flavius Silva became the Roman procurator, he determined to bring to an end the last of the revolt. The Zealots at Masada, 960 of them according to Jewish historian Josephus, were led by Eleazar. Silva's troops surrounded the stronghold to prevent even a single Zealot from escaping to stir up a new revolt. Rather than be taken by the Romans, the Jews planned and carried out a mass suicide. In tears, the men killed their wives and children, then killed themselves. Only two women survived to tell the Romans (who entered Masada the next day) the story of the suicide.

Luke 21:12-13 These persecutions soon began. Luke recorded many of them in the book of Acts. Paul wrote from prison that he suffered gladly because it helped him know Christ better and do Christ's work for the church (Phil 3:10; Col 1:24). The early church thrived despite intense persecution. In fact, late in the second century the church father Tertullian wrote, "The blood of Christians is seed," because opposition helped spread Christianity.

Luke 21:14-19 Jesus warned that in the coming persecutions his followers would be betrayed by their family members and friends. Christians of every age have had to face this possibility. It is reassuring to know that even when we feel completely abandoned, the Holy Spirit will stay with us. He will comfort us, protect us, and give us the words we need. This assurance can give us the courage and hope to stand firm for Christ no matter how difficult the situation.

Luke 21:18 Jesus was not saying that believers would be exempt from physical harm or death during the persecutions. Remember that many of the disciples were eventually martyred. Rather he was saying that none of his followers would suffer spiritual or eternal loss. On earth, everyone will die, but believers in Jesus will be saved for eternal life.

Luke 21:24 The "period of the Gentiles" began with Babylon's destruction of Jerusalem in 586 B.C. and the exile of the Jewish people. Israel was no longer an independent nation but was under the control of Gentile rulers. In Jesus' day, Israel was governed by the Roman Empire, and a Roman general

coming on a cloud with power and great glory.* 28So
when all these things begin to happen, stand and look
up, for your salvation is near!"
29Then he gave them this illustration: "Notice the
fig tree, or any other tree. 30When the leaves come
out, you know without being told that summer is near.
31In the same way, when you see all these things taking place, you can know that the Kingdom of God is
near. 32I tell you the truth, this generation will not pass
from the scene until all these things have taken place.
33Heaven and earth will disappear, but my words will
never disappear.
34"Watch out! Don't let your hearts be dulled by
carousing and drunkenness, and by the worries of
this life. Don't let that day catch you unaware, 35like a
trap. For that day will come upon everyone living on
the earth. 36Keep alert at all times. And pray that you
might be strong enough to escape these coming horrors and stand before the Son of Man."
37Every day Jesus went to the Temple to teach, and
each evening he returned to spend the night on the
Mount of Olives. 38The crowds gathered at the Temple
early each morning to hear him.

Jesus Tells the Parable of the Ten Bridesmaids

MATTHEW 25:1-13

"Then the Kingdom of Heaven will be like ten bridesmaids* who took their lamps and went to meet the
bridegroom. 2Five of them were foolish, and five were
wise. 3The five who were foolish didn't take enough
olive oil for their lamps, 4but the other five were wise
enough to take along extra oil. 5When the bridegroom
was delayed, they all became drowsy and fell asleep.
6"At midnight they were roused by the shout, 'Look,
the bridegroom is coming! Come out and meet him!'
7"All the bridesmaids got up and prepared their
lamps. 8Then the five foolish ones asked the others,
'Please give us some of your oil because our lamps
are going out.'
9"But the others replied, 'We don't have enough for
all of us. Go to a shop and buy some for yourselves.'
10"But while they were gone to buy oil, the bridegroom came. Then those who were ready went in with
him to the marriage feast, and the door was locked.
11Later, when the other five bridesmaids returned,
they stood outside, calling, 'Lord! Lord! Open the door
for us!'
12"But he called back, 'Believe me, I don't know you!'
13"So you, too, must keep watch! For you do not
know the day or hour of my return.

Jesus Tells the Parable of the Loaned Money

MATTHEW 25:14-30

"Again, the Kingdom of Heaven can be illustrated by the
story of a man going on a long trip. He called together
his servants and entrusted his money to them while
he was gone. 15He gave five bags of silver* to one, two
bags of silver to another, and one bag of silver to the
last—dividing it in proportion to their abilities. He then
left on his trip.

Lk 21:27b See Dan 7:13. **Mt 25:1** Or *virgins;* also in 25:7, 11. **Mt 25:15** Greek *talents;* also throughout the story. A talent is equal to 75 pounds or 34 kilograms.

would destroy the city in A.D. 70. Jesus was saying that the domination of God's people by his enemies would continue until God decided to end it. The "period of the Gentiles" refers not just to the repeated destructions of Jerusalem but also to the continuing and mounting persecution of God's people until the end.

Luke 21:28 The picture of the coming persecutions and natural disasters is gloomy, but ultimately it is a cause not for worry but for great joy. As believers see these events happening, they will know that the return of their Messiah is near, and they can look forward to his reign of justice and peace. Rather than being terrified by what is happening in our world, we should confidently await Christ's return to bring justice and restoration to his people.

Luke 21:34-36 Jesus told the disciples to keep a constant watch for his return. Although nearly 2,000 years have passed since he spoke these words, their truth remains: Christ is coming again, and we need to watch and be spiritually fit. This means working faithfully at the tasks God has given us. Don't let your mind and spirit be dulled by careless living, drinking, or foolishly pursuing pleasure. Don't let the cares of this life weigh you down. Be ready to move at God's command.

Luke 21:36 Only days after telling the disciples to pray that they might escape persecution, Jesus himself asked God to spare him the agonies of the cross, if that was God's will (Luke 22:41-42). It is abnormal to want to suffer, but as Jesus' followers, we must be willing to suffer if by doing so we can help build God's Kingdom. We have two wonderful promises to help us as we suffer: God will always be with us (Matt 28:20), and he will one day rescue us and give us eternal life (Rev 21:1-4).

Matt 25:1ff Jesus told the following parables to clarify further what it means to be ready for his return and how to live until he comes. The story of the 10 bridesmaids (Matt 25:1-13) teaches that we are responsible for our own individual spiritual condition. The story of the three servants (Matt 25:14-30) shows the necessity of using well what God has entrusted to us. The parable of the sheep and goats (Matt 25:31-46) stresses the importance of serving others in need. No parable by itself completely describes our preparation. Instead, each paints one part of the whole picture.

Matt 25:1ff This parable is about a wedding. On the wedding day the bridegroom went to the bride's house for the ceremony; then the bride and groom, along with a great procession, returned to the groom's house, where a feast took place, often lasting a full week.

These 10 bridesmaids were waiting to join the procession, and they hoped to take part in the marriage feast. But when the groom didn't come at the expected time, five of them were out of lamp oil. By the time they had purchased extra oil, it was too late to join the feast.

When Jesus returns to take his people to heaven, we must be ready. Spiritual preparation cannot be bought or borrowed at the last minute. Our relationship with God must be our own.

Matt 25:15 The master divided the money among his servants according to their abilities. None received more or less than they could handle. If they failed in their assignments, their excuse could not be that they were overwhelmed. Failure would indicate only laziness or hatred toward the master. The bags of silver represent any kind of resource we are given. God gives us time, gifts, and other resources according to our abilities, and he expects us to invest them wisely until he returns. The issue is not how much we have but how well we use what we have.

▸ **MATTHEW 25:14-30** ***(cont.)***

16"The servant who received the five bags of silver began to invest the money and earned five more. 17The servant with two bags of silver also went to work and earned two more. 18But the servant who received the one bag of silver dug a hole in the ground and hid the master's money.

19"After a long time their master returned from his trip and called them to give an account of how they had used his money. 20The servant to whom he had entrusted the five bags of silver came forward with five more and said, 'Master, you gave me five bags of silver to invest, and I have earned five more.'

21"The master was full of praise. 'Well done, my good and faithful servant. You have been faithful in handling this small amount, so now I will give you many more responsibilities. Let's celebrate together!*'

22"The servant who had received the two bags of silver came forward and said, 'Master, you gave me two bags of silver to invest, and I have earned two more.'

23"The master said, 'Well done, my good and faithful servant. You have been faithful in handling this small amount, so now I will give you many more responsibilities. Let's celebrate together!'

24"Then the servant with the one bag of silver came and said, 'Master, I knew you were a harsh man, harvesting crops you didn't plant and gathering crops you didn't cultivate. 25I was afraid I would lose your money, so I hid it in the earth. Look, here is your money back.'

26"But the master replied, 'You wicked and lazy servant! If you knew I harvested crops I didn't plant and gathered crops I didn't cultivate, 27why didn't you deposit my money in the bank? At least I could have gotten some interest on it.'

28"Then he ordered, 'Take the money from this servant, and give it to the one with the ten bags of silver. 29To those who use well what they are given, even more will be given, and they will have an abundance. But from those who do nothing, even what little they have will be taken away. 30Now throw this useless servant into outer darkness, where there will be weeping and gnashing of teeth.'

Jesus Tells about the Final Judgment

MATTHEW 25:31-46

"But when the Son of Man* comes in his glory, and all the angels with him, then he will sit upon his glorious throne. 32All the nations* will be gathered in his presence, and he will separate the people as a

Mt 25:21 Greek *Enter into the joy of your master* [or *your Lord*]; also in 25:23. **Mt 25:31** "Son of Man" is a title Jesus used for himself. **Mt 25:32** Or *peoples.*

Sheep and Goats

Sheep represented the livelihood of pastoral peoples, providing food to eat, milk to drink, wool for clothing, and hides and bones for other uses. Additionally, sheep could be bartered for goods, and they were used as sacrificial animals. The sheep common to Israel is usually white and has a broad tail.

The Palestinian goat is a cud-chewing animal of lighter build than the sheep. It has cloven hoofs, large eyes, floppy ears, and backward-arching horns on both males and females. Almost every part of the goat was used by the Israelites. Goats were sheared in the late spring, and their hair was used for weaving tent cloth. The Tabernacle at Mt. Sinai was made of goat hair cloth. The whole goat was used as a sacrifice.

Matt 25:21 Jesus is coming back—we know this is true. Does this mean we must quit our jobs in order to serve God? No, it means we are to use our time, talents, and treasures diligently in order to serve God completely in whatever we do. For a few people, this may mean changing professions. For most of us, it means doing our daily work out of love for God.

Matt 25:24-30 This last man was thinking only of himself. He hoped to play it safe and protect himself from his hard master, but he was judged for his self-centeredness. We must not make excuses to avoid doing what God calls us to do. If God truly is our Master, we must obey willingly. Our time, abilities, and money aren't ours in the first place—we are caretakers, not owners. When we ignore, squander, or abuse what we are given, we are rebellious and deserve to be punished.

Matt 25:29-30 This parable describes the consequences of two attitudes toward Christ's return. The person who diligently prepares for it by investing time and talents to serve God will be rewarded. The person who has no heart for the work of the Kingdom will be punished. God rewards faithfulness. Those who bear no fruit for God's Kingdom cannot expect to be treated the same as those who are faithful.

Matt 25:31-46 God will separate his obedient followers from pretenders and unbelievers. The real evidence of our belief is the way we act. To treat all people we encounter as if they were Jesus is no easy task. What we do for others demonstrates what we really think about Jesus' words to us: Feed the hungry, give the homeless a place to stay, look after the sick. How well do your actions separate you from pretenders and unbelievers?

Matt 25:32 Jesus used sheep and goats to picture the division between believers and unbelievers. Sheep and goats often grazed together but were separated when it came time to shear the sheep. Ezekiel 34:17-24 also refers to the separation of sheep and goats.

Matt 25:34-40 This parable describes acts of mercy we all can do every day. These acts do not depend on wealth, ability, or intelligence; they are simple acts freely given and freely received. We have no excuse to neglect those who have deep needs, and we cannot hand over this responsibility to the church or government. Jesus demands our personal involvement in caring for others' needs (Isa 58:7).

Matt 25:40 There has been much discussion about the identity of the "brothers and sisters." Some have said they are the Jews; others say they are all Christians; still others say they are suffering people everywhere. Such a debate is much like the lawyer's earlier question to Jesus, "Who is my neighbor?" (Luke 10:29). The point of this parable is not the who, but the what—the importance of serving where service is needed. The focus of this parable is that we should love every person and serve anyone we can. Such love for others glorifies God by reflecting our love for him.

shepherd separates the sheep from the goats. [33]He
will place the sheep at his right hand and the goats
at his left.
[34]"Then the King will say to those on his right,
'Come, you who are blessed by my Father, inherit the
Kingdom prepared for you from the creation of the
world. [35]For I was hungry, and you fed me. I was thirsty,
and you gave me a drink. I was a stranger, and you
invited me into your home. [36]I was naked, and you
gave me clothing. I was sick, and you cared for me. I
was in prison, and you visited me.'
[37]"Then these righteous ones will reply, 'Lord, when
did we ever see you hungry and feed you? Or thirsty
and give you something to drink? [38]Or a stranger and
show you hospitality? Or naked and give you clothing? [39]When did we ever see you sick or in prison
and visit you?'
[40]"And the King will say, 'I tell you the truth, when
you did it to one of the least of these my brothers and
sisters,* you were doing it to me!'
[41]"Then the King will turn to those on the left and
say, 'Away with you, you cursed ones, into the eternal
fire prepared for the devil and his demons.* [42]For I
was hungry, and you didn't feed me. I was thirsty, and
you didn't give me a drink. [43]I was a stranger, and you
didn't invite me into your home. I was naked, and you
didn't give me clothing. I was sick and in prison, and
you didn't visit me.'
[44]"Then they will reply, 'Lord, when did we ever see
you hungry or thirsty or a stranger or naked or sick or
in prison, and not help you?'
[45]"And he will answer, 'I tell you the truth, when you
refused to help the least of these my brothers and
sisters, you were refusing to help me.'
[46]"And they will go away into eternal punishment,
but the righteous will go into eternal life."

Mt 25:40 Greek *my brothers.* **Mt 25:41** Greek *his angels.*

C. Death and Resurrection of Jesus

Jesus was betrayed by a disciple, arrested by the religious leaders, and killed by the Romans. But first, he washed his disciples' feet, shared his last meal with them, and promised that he would always be with them through the Spirit. His suffering and cruel death was not the end of the story, though. He rose from the dead! Jesus is alive; he defeated sin and death!

Religious Leaders Plot to Kill Jesus PARALLEL

MATTHEW 26:1-5

When Jesus had finished saying all these things, he
said to his disciples, [2]"As you know, Passover begins
in two days, and the Son of Man* will be handed over
to be crucified."
[3]At that same time the leading priests and elders
were meeting at the residence of Caiaphas, the high
priest, [4]plotting how to capture Jesus secretly and kill
him. [5]"But not during the Passover celebration," they
agreed, "or the people may riot."

Mt 26:2 "Son of Man" is a title Jesus used for himself.

MARK 14:1-2

It was now two days before Passover and the Festival of Unleavened Bread. The leading priests and
the teachers of religious law were still looking for an

Matt 25:46 Eternal punishment takes place in hell (the lake of fire, or *Gehenna*), the place of punishment after death for all those who refuse to repent. In the Hebrew, three words were used in connection with eternal punishment: (1) *Sheol*, or "the grave," was used in the Hebrew Old Testament to mean the place of the dead, generally thought to be under the earth. (In the Hebrew, this word occurs in Job 24:19; Ps 16:10; Isa 38:10.) (2) *Hades* is the Greek word for the underworld, the realm of the dead. It is the word used in the New Testament for *Sheol.* (In the Greek, this word occurs in Matt 16:18; Rev 1:18; 20:13-14.) (3) *Gehenna*, or "hell," was named after the valley of Ben-Hinnom near Jerusalem, where children were sacrificed by fire to the pagan gods (see 2 Kgs 23:10; 2 Chr 28:3). This is the place of eternal fire (Matt 5:22; 10:28; Mark 9:43; Luke 12:5; Jas 3:6; Rev 19:20) prepared for the devil, his angels, and all those who do not believe in God (Matt 25:46; Rev 20:9-10). This is the final and eternal state of the wicked after the resurrection and the Last Judgment.

When Jesus warns against unbelief, he is trying to save us from agonizing, eternal punishment.

Matt 26:3 Caiaphas was the ruling high priest during Jesus' ministry. He was the son-in-law of Annas, the previous high priest. The Roman government had taken over the process of appointing all political and religious leaders. Caiaphas served for 18 years, longer than most high priests, suggesting that he was gifted at cooperating with the Romans. He was the first to recommend Jesus' death in order to "save" the nation (John 11:49-50).

Matt 26:3-5 This was a deliberate plot to kill Jesus. Without this plot, there would have been no groundswell of popular opinion against him. In fact, because of Jesus' popularity, the religious leaders were afraid to arrest him during the Passover. They did not want their actions to incite a riot.

Mark 14:1 The Passover commemorated the night the Israelites were freed from Egypt (Exod 12), when God "passed over" homes marked by the blood of a lamb while killing firstborn sons in unmarked homes. The day of Passover was followed by a seven-day festival called the Festival of Unleavened Bread. This, too, recalled the Israelites' quick escape from Egypt when they didn't have time to let their bread rise, so they baked it without yeast (leaven). On this holiday, Jewish families still gather for a special meal that includes lamb, wine, bitter herbs, and unleavened bread.

Mark 14:2 The Jews were preparing to observe Passover, a time of remembrance for families to celebrate when the blood of lambs had saved their ancestors. But some of the religious leaders had another agenda. Jesus had disrupted their security, revealed their sham, and opposed their authority. Now they would put him away. But the world is controlled by our all-wise God, not puny politicians. God would turn the religious leaders' murder plot into the greatest blessing that mankind would ever know. Another Lamb would be slain, and his blood would save all people. When grief or disaster seem to be dominating, remember that your life is in God's hands and remember what Jesus did for you.

▸ **MARK 14:1-2** *(cont.)*
opportunity to capture Jesus secretly and kill him.
2"But not during the Passover celebration," they
agreed, "or the people may riot."

LUKE 22:1-2
The Festival of Unleavened Bread, which is also called
Passover, was approaching. 2The leading priests and
teachers of religious law were plotting how to kill
Jesus, but they were afraid of the people's reaction.

Judas Agrees to Betray Jesus PARALLEL

MATTHEW 26:14-16
Then Judas Iscariot, one of the twelve disciples, went
to the leading priests 15and asked, "How much will
you pay me to betray Jesus to you?" And they gave
him thirty pieces of silver. 16From that time on,
Judas began looking for an opportunity to betray
Jesus.

MARK 14:10-11
Then Judas Iscariot, one of the twelve disciples, went to
the leading priests to arrange to betray Jesus to them.
11They were delighted when they heard why he had
come, and they promised to give him money. So he
began looking for an opportunity to betray Jesus.

LUKE 22:3-6
Then Satan entered into Judas Iscariot, who was one
of the twelve disciples, 4and he went to the leading
priests and captains of the Temple guard to discuss
the best way to betray Jesus to them. 5They were delighted, and they promised to give him money. 6So
he agreed and began looking for an opportunity to
betray Jesus so they could arrest him when the crowds
weren't around.

JUDAS ISCARIOT

It is easy to overlook the fact that Jesus chose Judas to be his disciple. With the other disciples, Judas shared a persistent misunderstanding of Jesus' mission. They all expected Jesus to make the right political moves. When he kept talking about dying, they all felt varying degrees of anger, fear, and disappointment. • The exact motivation behind Judas's betrayal is unknown. Judas accepted payment to set Jesus up for the religious leaders. He identified Jesus for the guards in the dimly lit garden of Gethsemane. It is possible that he was trying to force Jesus' hand: Would Jesus now rebel against Rome? • Judas tried to undo the evil he had done by returning the money to the priests, but it was too late. How sad that Judas ended his life in despair without ever experiencing the gift of reconciliation God could give even to him through Jesus Christ. • In betraying Jesus, Judas made the greatest mistake in history. But Judas didn't lose his relationship with Jesus; rather, he never found Jesus in the first place. He is called "the one headed for destruction" (John 17:12) because he was never saved. • Judas does us a favor if he makes us think a second time about our commitment to God and the presence of God's Spirit within us. Are we true disciples and followers, or uncommitted pretenders? We can choose despair and death, or we can choose repentance, forgiveness, hope, and eternal life. Will we accept Jesus' free gift?

Strengths and accomplishments	• He was chosen as one of the 12 disciples • He was in charge of the disciples' funds
Weaknesses and mistakes	• He was greedy (John 12:6) • He betrayed Jesus • He committed suicide instead of seeking forgiveness
Lessons from his life	• Evil plans and motives leave us open to being used by Satan for even greater evil • God's plan and his purposes are worked out even in the worst possible events
Vital statistics	• Where: Possibly from the town of Kerioth • Occupation: Disciple of Jesus • Relative: Father: Simon • Contemporaries: Jesus, Pilate, Herod, the other 11 disciples
Key verses	"Then Satan entered into Judas Iscariot, who was one of the twelve disciples, and he went to the leading priests and captains of the Temple guard to discuss the best way to betray Jesus to them" (Luke 22:3-4).

Judas's story is told in the Gospels. He is also mentioned in Acts 1:18-19.

Luke 22:1 All Jewish males over the age of 12 were required to go to Jerusalem for the Passover festival, which was followed by a seven-day celebration called the Festival of Unleavened Bread. For these festivals, Jews from all over the Roman Empire would converge on Jerusalem to celebrate one of the most important events in their history. To learn more about the Passover and the Festival of Unleavened Bread, see the note on Mark 14:1, p. 1453.

Matt 26:14-15 Why would Judas want to betray Jesus? Judas, like the other disciples, expected Jesus to start a political rebellion and overthrow Rome. As treasurer, Judas certainly assumed (as did the other disciples—see Mark 10:35-37) that he would be given an important position in Jesus' new government. But when Jesus praised Mary for pouring out perfume worth a year's salary, Judas may have realized that Jesus' Kingdom was not physical or political but spiritual. Judas's greedy desire for money and status could not be realized if he followed Jesus, so he betrayed Jesus in exchange for money and favor from the religious leaders.

Matt 26:15 Matthew alone records the exact amount of money Judas accepted to betray Jesus—30 silver coins, the price of a slave (Exod 21:32). The religious leaders had planned to wait until after the Passover to take Jesus, but with Judas's unexpected offer, they accelerated their plans.

Luke 22:3 Satan's part in the betrayal of Jesus does not remove any of the responsibility from Judas. Disillusioned because Jesus was talking about dying rather than about setting up his Kingdom, Judas may have been trying to force Jesus' hand and make him use his power to prove he was the Messiah. Or perhaps Judas, not understanding Jesus' mission, no longer believed that Jesus was God's chosen one. Whatever Judas thought, Satan assumed that Jesus' death would end his mission and thwart

Disciples Prepare for the Passover PARALLEL

MATTHEW 26:17-19

On the first day of the Festival of Unleavened Bread,
the disciples came to Jesus and asked, "Where do you
want us to prepare the Passover meal for you?"
18"As you go into the city," he told them, "you will see
a certain man. Tell him, 'The Teacher says: My time has
come, and I will eat the Passover meal with my disciples
at your house.'" 19So the disciples did as Jesus told them
and prepared the Passover meal there.

MARK 14:12-16

On the first day of the Festival of Unleavened Bread,
when the Passover lamb is sacrificed, Jesus' disciples
asked him, "Where do you want us to go to prepare
the Passover meal for you?"
13So Jesus sent two of them into Jerusalem with these
instructions: "As you go into the city, a man carrying
a pitcher of water will meet you. Follow him. 14At the
house he enters, say to the owner, 'The Teacher asks:
Where is the guest room where I can eat the Passover
meal with my disciples?' 15He will take you upstairs to
a large room that is already set up. That is where you
should prepare our meal." 16So the two disciples went
into the city and found everything just as Jesus had said,
and they prepared the Passover meal there.

LUKE 22:7-13

Now the Festival of Unleavened Bread arrived, when
the Passover lamb is sacrificed. 8Jesus sent Peter and
John ahead and said, "Go and prepare the Passover
meal, so we can eat it together."
9"Where do you want us to prepare it?" they asked
him.
10He replied, "As soon as you enter Jerusalem, a
man carrying a pitcher of water will meet you. Follow him. At the house he enters, 11say to the owner,
'The Teacher asks: Where is the guest room where I
can eat the Passover meal with my disciples?' 12He
will take you upstairs to a large room that is already
set up. That is where you should prepare our meal."
13They went off to the city and found everything just
as Jesus had said, and they prepared the Passover
meal there.

Jesus Washes the Disciples' Feet

JOHN 13:1-20

Before the Passover celebration, Jesus knew that his
hour had come to leave this world and return to his

God's plan. Like Judas, he did not know that Jesus' death and resurrection were the most important parts of God's plan all along.

Matt 26:17 The Passover took place on one night and at one meal, but the Festival of Unleavened Bread, which was celebrated with it, continued for a week. The people removed all yeast from their homes in commemoration of their ancestors' exodus from Egypt, when they did not have time to let the bread dough rise. Thousands of people poured into Jerusalem from all over the Roman Empire for this festival. For more information on how the Passover was celebrated, see the notes on Mark 14:1, p. 1453, and in Exodus 12, p. 155.

Mark 14:13 The two men Jesus sent were Peter and John (Luke 22:8).

Mark 14:14-15 Many homes had large upstairs rooms, sometimes with stairways both inside and outside the house. The preparations for the Passover would have included setting the table and buying and preparing the Passover lamb, unleavened bread, sauces, and other ceremonial food and drink.

Luke 22:7-8 The Passover meal included the sacrifice of a lamb because of the association with the Jews' exodus from Egypt. When the Jews were getting ready to leave, God told them to kill a lamb and paint its blood on the doorframes of their houses. They then were to prepare the meat for food. Peter and John had to buy and prepare the lamb as well as the unleavened bread, herbs, wine, and other ceremonial food.

Luke 22:10 Ordinarily women, not men, would go to the well and bring home the water. So this man with the water pitcher would have stood out in the crowd.

John 13:1 Jesus knew he would be betrayed by one of his disciples, denied by another, and deserted by all of them for a time. Still "he loved them to the very end." God knows us completely, as Jesus knew his disciples (John 2:24-25; 6:64). He knows the sins we have committed and the ones we will yet commit. Still, he loves us. How do you respond to that kind of love?

John 13:1ff John 13–17 tells us what Jesus said to his disciples on the night before his death. These words were all spoken in one evening when, with only the disciples as his audience, he gave final instructions to prepare them for his death and resurrection, events that would change their lives forever.

John 13:1-17 Jesus was the model servant, and he showed his servant attitude to his disciples. Washing guests' feet was a job for a household servant to carry out when guests arrived. But Jesus wrapped a towel around his waist, as the lowliest slave would do, and washed and dried his disciples' feet. If even he, God in the flesh, is willing to serve, we his followers must also be servants, willing to serve in any way that glorifies God. Are you willing to follow Christ's example of serving? Whom can you serve today? There is a special blessing for those who not only agree that humble service is Christ's way, but who also follow through and do it (John 13:17).

UPPER ROOM AND GETHSEMANE ▶
Jesus and the disciples ate the traditional Passover meal in an upper room in the city and then went to the Mount of Olives into a garden called Gethsemane. In the cool of the evening, Jesus prayed for strength to face the trial and suffering ahead.

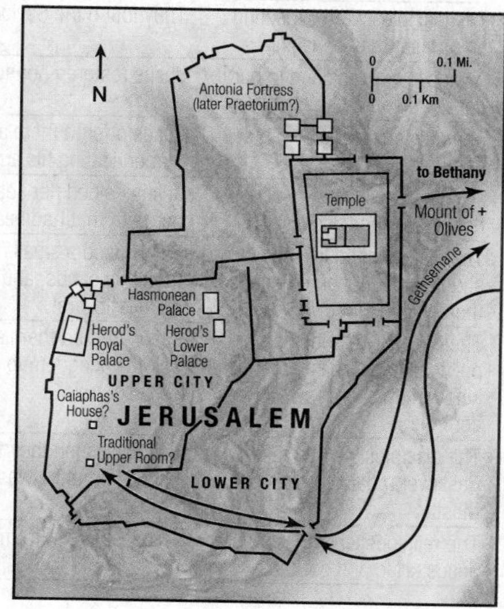

▸ **JOHN 13:1-20 *(cont.)***
Father. He had loved his disciples during his ministry
on earth, and now he loved them to the very end.*
2It was time for supper, and the devil had already
prompted Judas,* son of Simon Iscariot, to betray
Jesus. 3Jesus knew that the Father had given him authority over everything and that he had come from
God and would return to God. 4So he got up from the
table, took off his robe, wrapped a towel around his
waist, 5and poured water into a basin. Then he began
to wash the disciples' feet, drying them with the towel
he had around him.
6When Jesus came to Simon Peter, Peter said to him,
"Lord, are you going to wash my feet?"
7Jesus replied, "You don't understand now what I
am doing, but someday you will."
8"No," Peter protested, "you will never ever wash
my feet!"
Jesus replied, "Unless I wash you, you won't belong
to me."
9Simon Peter exclaimed, "Then wash my hands and
head as well, Lord, not just my feet!"
10Jesus replied, "A person who has bathed all over
does not need to wash, except for the feet,* to be entirely clean. And you disciples are clean, but not all of
you." 11For Jesus knew who would betray him. That is
what he meant when he said, "Not all of you are clean."
12After washing their feet, he put on his robe again
and sat down and asked, "Do you understand what
I was doing? 13You call me 'Teacher' and 'Lord,' and
you are right, because that's what I am. 14And since
I, your Lord and Teacher, have washed your feet, you
ought to wash each other's feet. 15I have given you an
example to follow. Do as I have done to you. 16I tell you
the truth, slaves are not greater than their master. Nor
is the messenger more important than the one who
sends the message. 17Now that you know these things,
God will bless you for doing them.
18"I am not saying these things to all of you; I know
the ones I have chosen. But this fulfills the Scripture that says, 'The one who eats my food has turned
against me.'* 19I tell you this beforehand, so that when
it happens you will believe that I AM the Messiah.*
20I tell you the truth, anyone who welcomes my messenger is welcoming me, and anyone who welcomes
me is welcoming the Father who sent me."

Jesus and the Disciples Share the Last Supper PARALLEL ●●●●

MATTHEW 26:20-30 ●○○○
When it was evening, Jesus sat down at the table*
with the twelve disciples.* 21While they were eating, he said, "I tell you the truth, one of you will
betray me."

Jn 13:1 Or *he showed them the full extent of his love.* **Jn 13:2** Or *the devil had already intended for Judas.* **Jn 13:10** Some manuscripts do not include *except for the feet.* **Jn 13:18** Ps 41:9. **Jn 13:19** Or *that the 'I AM' has come;* or *that I am the LORD;* Greek reads *that I am.* See Exod 3:14. **Mt 26:20a** Or *Jesus reclined.* **Mt 26:20b** Some manuscripts read *the Twelve.*

GREAT EXPECTATIONS

Wherever he went, Jesus did the unexpected as well as exceeded people's expectations.

What was expected	What Jesus did	Reference
A man looked for healing.	Jesus also forgave his sins.	Mark 2:1-12
The disciples were expecting an ordinary day of fishing.	They found the Savior.	Luke 5:1-11
A widow was resigned to bury her dead son.	Jesus restored her son to life.	Luke 7:11-17
The religious leaders wanted a miracle.	Jesus offered them a sign authenticating his authority.	Matt 12:38-45
A woman who wanted to be healed touched Jesus.	Jesus helped her see it was her faith that had healed her.	Mark 5:25-34
The disciples thought the crowd should be sent home because there was no food.	Jesus used a small meal to feed thousands, and there were leftovers!	John 6:1-15
The crowds were looking for a political leader to set up a new kingdom to overthrow Rome's control.	Jesus offered them an eternal, spiritual kingdom to overthrow sin's control.	A theme throughout the Gospels
The disciples wanted to eat the Passover meal with Jesus, their Master.	Jesus washed their feet, showing that he was also their servant.	John 13:1-17
The religious leaders wanted Jesus killed and got their wish.	But Jesus rose from the dead!	John 11:53; 19:30; 20:1-29

John 13:6-7 Imagine being Peter and watching Jesus wash the others' feet, all the while moving closer to you. Seeing his Master behave like a slave must have confused Peter. He still did not understand Jesus' teaching that to be a leader, a person must be a servant. This is not a comfortable passage for leaders who find it hard to serve those beneath them. How do you treat those who work under you (whether children, employees, or volunteers)?

John 13:8-9 When Jesus responded, "Unless I wash you, you won't belong to me," he may have meant (1) that unless he washed away Peter's sins by his death on the cross, then Peter could have no relationship with him, or (2) that unless Peter submitted to him and allowed Jesus to minister in this way, Peter would never learn the lesson of humility. Either way, Peter seemed to grasp the significance of Jesus' words, for he then wanted to be bathed completely: "Then wash my hands and head as well, Lord, not just my feet!"

John 13:12ff Jesus did not wash his disciples' feet just to get them to be nice to each other. His far greater goal was to extend his mission on earth after he was gone. These men were to move into the world serving God, serving each other, and serving all people to whom they took the message of salvation.

22Greatly distressed, each one asked in turn, "Am I
the one, Lord?"
23He replied, "One of you who has just eaten from
this bowl with me will betray me. 24For the Son of
Man must die, as the Scriptures declared long ago.
But how terrible it will be for the one who betrays
him. It would be far better for that man if he had
never been born!"
25Judas, the one who would betray him, also asked,
"Rabbi, am I the one?"
And Jesus told him, "You have said it."
26As they were eating, Jesus took some bread and
blessed it. Then he broke it in pieces and gave it to
the disciples, saying, "Take this and eat it, for this is
my body."
27And he took a cup of wine and gave thanks to
God for it. He gave it to them and said, "Each of you
drink from it, 28for this is my blood, which confirms the covenant* between God and his people.
It is poured out as a sacrifice to forgive the sins of
many. 29Mark my words—I will not drink wine again
until the day I drink it new with you in my Father's
Kingdom."
30Then they sang a hymn and went out to the Mount
of Olives.

MARK 14:17-26

In the evening Jesus arrived with the twelve disciples.*
18As they were at the table* eating, Jesus said, "I tell
you the truth, one of you eating with me here will betray me."
19Greatly distressed, each one asked in turn, "Am
I the one?"
20He replied, "It is one of you twelve who is eating from this bowl with me. 21For the Son of Man*
must die, as the Scriptures declared long ago. But
how terrible it will be for the one who betrays him.
It would be far better for that man if he had never
been born!"
22As they were eating, Jesus took some bread and
blessed it. Then he broke it in pieces and gave it to the
disciples, saying, "Take it, for this is my body."

Mt 26:28 Some manuscripts read *the new covenant.* **Mk 14:17** Greek *the Twelve.* **Mk 14:18** Or *As they reclined.* **Mk 14:21** "Son of Man" is a title Jesus used for himself.

Matt 26:26 Each name we use for this sacrament brings out a different dimension to it. It is the Lord's Supper because it commemorates the Passover meal Jesus ate with his disciples; it is the Eucharist (thanksgiving) because in it we thank God for Christ's work for us; it is Communion because through it we commune with God and with other believers. As we eat the bread and drink the cup, we should be quietly reflective—recalling Jesus' death and his promise to come again, grateful for God's wonderful gift to us, and joyful as we meet with Christ and the body of believers.

Matt 26:28 How does Jesus' blood relate to the new covenant? People under the old covenant (those who lived before Jesus) could approach God only through a priest and an animal sacrifice. Now all people can come directly to God through faith because Jesus' death has made us acceptable in God's eyes (Rom 3:21-24).

The old covenant was a shadow of the new (Jer 31:31; Heb 8:1ff), pointing forward to the day when Jesus himself would be the final and ultimate sacrifice for sin. Rather than an unblemished lamb slain on the altar, the perfect Lamb of God was slain on the cross, a sinless sacrifice, so that our sins could be forgiven once and for all. All those who believe in Christ receive that forgiveness.

Matt 26:29 Again Jesus assured his disciples of victory over death and of their future with him. The next few hours would bring apparent defeat, but soon they would experience the power of the Holy Spirit and witness the great spread of the Good News. And one day they would all be together again in God's new Kingdom.

Matt 26:30 It is possible that the hymn the disciples sang was from Psalms 115–118, the traditional psalms sung as part of the Passover meal.

A Very Early Manuscript of Matthew

P64 is a codex from the late second century A.D. containing Matthew and Luke. In Matthew 26:20, the four earliest manuscripts (P64 and three others) read "the Twelve" instead of "the twelve disciples," which is found in most other manuscripts (see the NLT textual note). The early evidence shows that the word "disciples" could have been a later addition. This is typical of the kind of variant often seen in the manuscripts of the Bible: although there is a difference of one word, the meaning is completely unchanged.

Mark 14:19 Judas, the very man who would betray Jesus, was at the table with the others. Judas had already determined to betray Jesus, but in cold-blooded hypocrisy he shared the fellowship of this meal. It is easy to become enraged or shocked by what Judas did; yet professing commitment to Christ and then denying him with one's life is also betraying him. Denying Christ's love is to disobey him; denying his truth is to distrust him; denying his deity is to reject his authority. Do your words and actions match?

Mark 14:20 It was often the practice to eat from a common bowl. Meat or bread was dipped into a bowl filled with sauce often made from fruit.

Mark 14:22-25 Mark records the origin of the Last Supper, which is still celebrated in worship services today. Jesus and his disciples ate a meal, sang psalms, read Scripture, and prayed. Then Jesus took two traditional parts of the Passover meal, the passing of bread and the drinking of wine, and gave them new meaning as representations of his body and blood. He used the bread and wine to explain the significance of what he was about to do on the cross. For more on the significance of the Last Supper, see 1 Corinthians 11:23-29.

▶ **MARK 14:17-26 *(cont.)***

23And he took a cup of wine and gave thanks to God for it. He gave it to them, and they all drank from it. 24And he said to them, "This is my blood, which confirms the covenant* between God and his people. It is poured out as a sacrifice for many. 25I tell you the truth, I will not drink wine again until the day I drink it new in the Kingdom of God."

26Then they sang a hymn and went out to the Mount of Olives.

LUKE 22:14-30

When the time came, Jesus and the apostles sat down together at the table.* 15Jesus said, "I have been very eager to eat this Passover meal with you before my suffering begins. 16For I tell you now that I won't eat this meal again until its meaning is fulfilled in the Kingdom of God."

17Then he took a cup of wine and gave thanks to God for it. Then he said, "Take this and share it among yourselves. 18For I will not drink wine again until the Kingdom of God has come."

19He took some bread and gave thanks to God for it. Then he broke it in pieces and gave it to the disciples, saying, "This is my body, which is given for you. Do this to remember me."

20After supper he took another cup of wine and said, "This cup is the new covenant between God and his people—an agreement confirmed with my blood, which is poured out as a sacrifice for you.*

21"But here at this table, sitting among us as a friend, is the man who will betray me. 22For it has been determined that the Son of Man* must die. But what sorrow awaits the one who betrays him." 23The disciples began to ask each other which of them would ever do such a thing.

24Then they began to argue among themselves about who would be the greatest among them. 25Jesus told them, "In this world the kings and great men lord it over their people, yet they are called 'friends of the people.' 26But among you it will be different. Those who are the greatest among you should take the lowest rank, and the leader should be like a servant.

Mk 14:24 Some manuscripts read *the new covenant.* **Lk 22:14** Or *reclined together.* **Lk 22:19-20** Some manuscripts do not include 22:19b-20, *which is given for you . . . which is poured out as a sacrifice for you.* **Lk 22:22** "Son of Man" is a title Jesus used for himself.

Mark 14:23 Whatever name your church uses for this event (Communion, Lord's Supper, or Eucharist) and on whatever schedule you celebrate it, the importance is that through celebrating Communion together believers experience the presence of Christ. The celebration of Communion: (1) Humbles us before God—we confess our sin and restate our need for Christ to guide us; (2) reminds us that we are forgiven—we remember that his shed blood paid the price; (3) expresses our oneness in Christ—we are unified in our faith; (4) encourages us to recommit—we are reminded to pledge ourselves to serve him who died for us.

Mark 14:24 Jesus' death for us on the cross seals a new covenant between God and us. The old covenant involved forgiveness of sins through the blood of an animal sacrifice (Exod 24:6-8). But instead of a spotless lamb on the altar, Jesus offered himself, the spotless Lamb of God, as a sacrifice that would forgive sin once and for all. Jesus was the final sacrifice for sins, and his blood sealed the new covenant between God and us. Now all of us can come to God through Jesus, in full confidence that God will hear us and save us from our sins.

Luke 22:14-18 The Passover commemorated Israel's escape from Egypt when the blood of a lamb painted on their doorframes had saved their firstborn sons from death. This event foreshadowed Jesus' work on the cross. As the spotless Lamb of God, his blood would be spilled in order to save his people from the penalty of death brought by sin.

Luke 22:17, 20 Luke mentions two cups of wine, while Matthew and Mark mention only one. In the traditional Passover meal, wine is served four times. Christ spoke the words about his body and his blood when he offered the fourth and last cup.

Luke 22:17-20 Christians differ in their interpretation of the meaning of the commemoration of the Lord's Supper. There are three main views: (1) The bread and wine actually become Christ's body and blood. (2) The bread and wine remain unchanged, yet Christ is spiritually present by faith in and through them. (3) The bread and wine, which remain unchanged, are lasting memorials of Christ's sacrifice. No matter which view they favor, all Christians agree that the Lord's Supper commemorates Christ's death on the cross for our sins and points to the coming of his Kingdom in glory. When we partake of it, we show our deep gratitude for Christ's work on our behalf, and our faith is strengthened.

Luke 22:19 Jesus asked the disciples to eat the broken bread to remember him. He wanted them to remember his sacrifice, the basis for forgiveness of sins, and also his friendship, which they could continue to enjoy through the work of the Holy Spirit. Although the exact meaning of Communion has been strongly debated throughout church history, Christians still take bread and wine in order to remember their Lord and Savior, Jesus Christ. Do not neglect participating in the Lord's Supper. Let it remind you of what Christ did for you.

Luke 22:20 In Old Testament times, God agreed to forgive people's sins if they would bring animals for the priests to sacrifice. When this sacrificial system was inaugurated, the covenant between God and his people was sealed with the blood of animals (Exod 24:8). But animal blood did not in itself remove sin (only God can forgive sin), and animal sacrifices had to be repeated day after day and year after year. Jesus instituted a "new covenant" (agreement) between God and his people. Under this new covenant, Jesus would die in the place of sinners. Unlike the blood of animals, his blood (because he is God) would remove the sins of all who put their faith in him. Jesus' sacrifice would never have to be repeated; it would be good for all eternity (Heb 9:23-28). The prophets looked forward to this new covenant that would fulfill the old sacrificial agreement (Jer 31:31-34), and John the Baptist called Jesus "the Lamb of God who takes away the sin of the world" (John 1:29).

Luke 22:21 From the accounts of Mark and John, we know that the betrayer was Judas Iscariot. Although the other disciples were confused by Jesus' words, Judas knew what Jesus meant.

Luke 22:24 The most important event in human history was about to take place, and the disciples were still arguing about their prestige in the Kingdom! Looking back, we see that this was no time to worry about status. But the disciples, wrapped up in their own concerns, did not perceive what Jesus had been trying to tell them about his approaching death and resurrection. What are your major concerns today? As you look back 20 years from now, will these worries look petty and inappropriate? Get your eyes off yourself and get ready for Christ's coming into human history for the second time.

Luke 22:24-27 The world's system of leadership is very different from leadership in God's Kingdom. Worldly leaders

27Who is more important, the one who sits at the
table or the one who serves? The one who sits at the
table, of course. But not here! For I am among you as
one who serves.
28"You have stayed with me in my time of trial.
29And just as my Father has granted me a Kingdom, I
now grant you the right 30to eat and drink at my table
in my Kingdom. And you will sit on thrones, judging
the twelve tribes of Israel."

JOHN 13:21-30

Now Jesus was deeply troubled,* and he exclaimed, "I
tell you the truth, one of you will betray me!"
22The disciples looked at each other, wondering
whom he could mean. 23The disciple Jesus loved was
sitting next to Jesus at the table.* 24Simon Peter motioned to him to ask, "Who's he talking about?" 25So
that disciple leaned over to Jesus and asked, "Lord,
who is it?"
26Jesus responded, "It is the one to whom I give the
bread I dip in the bowl." And when he had dipped it,
he gave it to Judas, son of Simon Iscariot. 27When Judas had eaten the bread, Satan entered into him. Then
Jesus told him, "Hurry and do what you're going to
do." 28None of the others at the table knew what Jesus
meant. 29Since Judas was their treasurer, some thought
Jesus was telling him to go and pay for the food or to

Jn 13:21 Greek *was troubled in his spirit.* **Jn 13:23** Greek *was reclining on Jesus' bosom.* The "disciple Jesus loved" was probably John.

JOHN

Being loved is the most powerful motivation in the world! Our ability to love is often shaped by our experience of love. We usually love others as we have been loved. John, Jesus' disciple, expressed his relationship to the Son of God by calling himself "the disciple Jesus loved" (John 21:20). Because his own experience of Jesus' love was so strong and personal, John was sensitive to those words and actions of Jesus that illustrated how the one who is love loved others. • Jesus knew John fully and loved him fully. He gave John and his brother James the nickname "Sons of Thunder" (Mark 3:17), perhaps from an occasion when the brothers asked Jesus for permission to "call down fire from heaven" on a village that had refused to welcome Jesus and the disciples (Luke 9:54). In John's Gospel and letters, we see the great God of love, while the thunder of God's justice bursts from the pages of Revelation. • Jesus confronts each of us as he confronted John. We cannot know the depth of Jesus' love unless we are willing to face the fact that he knows us completely. Otherwise we are fooled into believing he must love the people we pretend to be, not the sinners we actually are. John and all the disciples convince us that God is able and willing to accept us as we are. Being aware of God's love is a great motivator for change. His love is not given in exchange for our efforts; his love frees us to really live. Have you accepted that love?

Strengths and accomplishments	• One of John the Baptist's disciples before following Jesus • One of the 12 disciples and, with Peter and James, one of the inner three that were closest to Jesus • Wrote five New Testament books: the Gospel of John; 1, 2, and 3 John; Revelation
Weaknesses and mistakes	• Along with James, shared a tendency for outbursts of selfishness and anger • Asked for a special position in Jesus' Kingdom
Lessons from his life	• Those who realize how much they are loved are able to love much • When God changes a life, he does not take away personality characteristics, but puts them to effective use in his service
Vital statistics	• Occupations: Fisherman, disciple • Relatives: Father: Zebedee. Mother: Salome. Brother: James. • Contemporaries: Jesus, Pilate, Herod
Key verses	"Dear friends, I am not writing a new commandment for you; rather it is an old one you have had from the very beginning. This old commandment—to love one another—is the same message you heard before. Yet it is also new. Jesus lived the truth of this commandment, and you also are living it. For the darkness is disappearing, and the true light is already shining" (1 Jn 2:7-8).

John's story is told throughout the Gospels, Acts, and Revelation.

are often selfish and arrogant as they claw their way to the top. But among Christians, the leader is to be the one who serves best. There are different styles of leadership—some lead through public speaking, some through administering, some through relationships—but every Christian leader needs a servant's heart. Ask the people you lead how you can serve them better.

Luke 22:28-30 Jesus gave the disciples great honors and great responsibilities in this passage. The disciples sit with Christ at his table in his Kingdom, and they would sit on thrones as judges over Israel. Why did Jesus give them such honorable positions? The only qualification that Luke suggests are in Jesus' words, "You have stayed with me in my time of trial." The disciples had simply stuck it out. Jesus did not recognize their service or their humility or their leadership or their wisdom. They simply stuck with Jesus and persevered.

We believe that we are saved by grace through faith, but it's easy to think that God's honor roll will list those who accomplished the most for God's Kingdom. But the disciples were promised great places in God's Kingdom for simply having stayed with Jesus. If you're losing hope in producing something worthwhile for God, or if you're hanging on to God by threads, be encouraged and hold on. Being faithful sometimes simply means staying with Jesus, persevering and sticking it out.

John 13:22 Judas was not the obvious betrayer. After all, he was the one the disciples trusted to keep the money (John 12:6; 13:29).

John 13:26 The honored guest at a meal was often singled out like this.

▸ JOHN 13:21-30 *(cont.)*
give some money to the poor. 30So Judas left at once,
going out into the night.

Jesus Predicts Peter's Denial PARALLEL ●●●●

MATTHEW 26:31-35 ●○○○
On the way, Jesus told them, "Tonight all of you will
desert me. For the Scriptures say,

'God will strike* the Shepherd,
and the sheep of the flock will be
scattered.'

32But after I have been raised from the dead, I will go
ahead of you to Galilee and meet you there."
33Peter declared, "Even if everyone else deserts you,
I will never desert you."
34Jesus replied, "I tell you the truth, Peter—this very
night, before the rooster crows, you will deny three
times that you even know me."
35"No!" Peter insisted. "Even if I have to die with
you, I will never deny you!" And all the other disciples
vowed the same.

MARK 14:27-31 ○●○○
On the way, Jesus told them, "All of you will desert me.
For the Scriptures say,

'God will strike* the Shepherd,
and the sheep will be scattered.'

28But after I am raised from the dead, I will go ahead
of you to Galilee and meet you there."
29Peter said to him, "Even if everyone else deserts
you, I never will."
30Jesus replied, "I tell you the truth, Peter—this very
night, before the rooster crows twice, you will deny
three times that you even know me."
31"No!" Peter declared emphatically. "Even if I have
to die with you, I will never deny you!" And all the
others vowed the same.

LUKE 22:31-38 ○○●○
"Simon, Simon, Satan has asked to sift each of you
like wheat. 32But I have pleaded in prayer for you, Simon, that your faith should not fail. So when you have
repented and turned to me again, strengthen your
brothers."
33Peter said, "Lord, I am ready to go to prison with
you, and even to die with you."
34But Jesus said, "Peter, let me tell you something.
Before the rooster crows tomorrow morning, you will
deny three times that you even know me."
35Then Jesus asked them, "When I sent you out to
preach the Good News and you did not have money,
a traveler's bag, or an extra pair of sandals, did you
need anything?"
"No," they replied.
36"But now," he said, "take your money and a traveler's bag. And if you don't have a sword, sell your cloak
and buy one! 37For the time has come for this prophecy about me to be fulfilled: 'He was counted among
the rebels.'* Yes, everything written about me by the
prophets will come true."
38"Look, Lord," they replied, "we have two swords
among us."
"That's enough," he said.

JOHN 13:31-38 ○○○●
As soon as Judas left the room, Jesus said, "The time
has come for the Son of Man* to enter into his glory,
and God will be glorified because of him. 32And since
God receives glory because of the Son,* he will soon
give glory to the Son. 33Dear children, I will be with
you only a little longer. And as I told the Jewish leaders,
you will search for me, but you can't come where I am

Mt 26:31 Greek *I will strike.* Zech 13:7. **Mk 14:27** Greek *I will strike.* Zech 13:7. **Lk 22:37** Isa 53:12. **Jn 13:31** "Son of Man" is a title Jesus used for himself. **Jn 13:32** Some manuscripts do not include *And since God receives glory because of the Son.*

Matt 26:35 All the disciples declared that they would die before denying Jesus. A few hours later, however, they all scattered. Talk is cheap. It is easy to say we are devoted to Christ, but our claims are meaningful only when they are tested in the crucible of persecution. How strong is your faith? Is it strong enough to stand up under intense trial?

Mark 14:31 Peter was so emphatic. It is easy to say we are devoted to Christ, but our claims are meaningful only when they are tested in the crucible of persecution. We need the Holy Spirit, not boastfulness and human resolve. We must never discount our vulnerability to pride, greed, or even indifference.

Luke 22:31-32 Satan wanted to crush Simon Peter and the other disciples like grains of wheat. He hoped to find only chaff and blow it away. But Jesus assured Peter that his faith, although it would falter, would not be destroyed. It would be renewed, and Peter would become a powerful leader.

Luke 22:33-34 Jesus told the disciples that one of them would betray him and that sorrow awaited the traitor (Luke 22:21-22). Jesus then told Peter that he would deny that he knew Jesus. Later, however, Peter would repent and receive a commission to feed Jesus' lambs (John 21:15). Betraying and denying—one is just about as bad as the other. But Judas and Peter had entirely different fates because one repented.

Luke 22:35-38 Here Jesus reversed his earlier advice regarding how to travel (Luke 9:3). The disciples were to bring bags, money, and swords. They would be facing hatred and persecution and would need to be prepared. When Jesus said, "That's enough," he may have meant it was not time to think of using swords. In either case, mention of a sword vividly communicated the trials they would soon face.

John 13:31-38 John describes these few moments in clear detail. We can see that Jesus knew exactly what was going to happen. He knew about Judas and about Peter, but he did not change the situation, nor did he stop loving them. In the same way, Jesus knows exactly what you will do to hurt him. Yet he still loves you unconditionally and will forgive you whenever you ask him. Judas couldn't understand this, and his life ended tragically. Peter understood, and despite his shortcomings, his life ended triumphantly because he never let go of his faith in the one who loved him.

John 13:34 To love others was not a new commandment (see Lev 19:18), but to love others as much as Christ loved others was revolutionary. Now we are to love others based on Jesus' sacrificial love for us. Such love will not only bring unbelievers to Christ, it will also keep believers strong and united in a world hostile to God. Jesus was a living example of God's love, as we are to be living examples of Jesus' love.

going. 34So now I am giving you a new commandment:
Love each other. Just as I have loved you, you should
love each other. 35Your love for one another will prove
to the world that you are my disciples."
36Simon Peter asked, "Lord, where are you going?"
And Jesus replied, "You can't go with me now, but
you will follow me later."
37"But why can't I come now, Lord?" he asked. "I'm
ready to die for you."
38Jesus answered, "Die for me? I tell you the truth,
Peter—before the rooster crows tomorrow morning,
you will deny three times that you even know me.

Jesus Is the Way to the Father

JOHN 14:1-14

"Don't let your hearts be troubled. Trust in God, and
trust also in me. 2There is more than enough room in
my Father's home.* If this were not so, would I have
told you that I am going to prepare a place for you?*
3When everything is ready, I will come and get you, so
that you will always be with me where I am. 4And you
know the way to where I am going."
5"No, we don't know, Lord," Thomas said. "We have
no idea where you are going, so how can we know
the way?"
6Jesus told him, "I am the way, the truth, and the
life. No one can come to the Father except through
me. 7If you had really known me, you would know
who my Father is.* From now on, you do know him
and have seen him!"
8Philip said, "Lord, show us the Father, and we will
be satisfied."
9Jesus replied, "Have I been with you all this time,
Philip, and yet you still don't know who I am? Anyone
who has seen me has seen the Father! So why are you
asking me to show him to you? 10Don't you believe
that I am in the Father and the Father is in me? The
words I speak are not my own, but my Father who lives

Jn 14:2a Or *There are many rooms in my Father's house.* **Jn 14:2b** Or *If this were not so, I would have told you that I am going to prepare a place for you.* Some manuscripts read *If this were not so, I would have told you. I am going to prepare a place for you.* **Jn 14:7** Some manuscripts read *If you have really known me, you would know who my Father is.*

John 13:34-35 Jesus says that our Christ-like love will show we are his disciples. Do people see petty bickering, jealousy, and division in your church? Or do they know you are Jesus' followers by your love for one another?

Love is more than simply warm feelings; it is an attitude that reveals itself in action. How can we love others as Jesus loves us? By helping when it's not convenient, by giving when it hurts, by devoting energy to others' welfare rather than our own, by absorbing hurts from others without complaining or fighting back. This kind of loving is hard to do. That is why people notice when you do it and know you are empowered by a supernatural source. The Bible has another beautiful description of love in 1 Corinthians 13.

John 13:37-38 Peter proudly told Jesus that he was ready to die for him. But Jesus corrected him. He knew Peter would deny that he knew Jesus that very night to protect himself (John 18:15-18, 25-27). In our enthusiasm, it is easy to make promises, but God knows the extent of our commitment. Paul tells us not to think of ourselves more highly than we ought (Rom 12:3). Instead of bragging, demonstrate your commitment step by step as you grow in your knowledge of God's Word and in your faith.

John 14:1-3 Jesus' words show that the way to eternal life, though unseen, is secure—as secure as your trust in Jesus. He has already prepared the way to eternal life. The only issue that may still be unsettled is your willingness to believe.

John 14:2-3 There are few verses in Scripture that describe eternal life, but these few verses are rich with promises. Here Jesus says, "I am going to prepare a place for you," and "I will come and get you." We can look forward to eternal life because Jesus has promised it to all who believe in him. Although the details of eternity are unknown, we need not fear because Jesus is preparing for us and will spend eternity with us.

John 14:5-6 This is one of the most basic and important passages in Scripture. How can we know the way to God? Only through Jesus. Jesus is the way because he is both God and man. By uniting our lives with his, we are united with God. Trust Jesus to take you to the Father, and all the benefits of being God's child will be yours.

John 14:6 Jesus says he is the only way to God the Father. Some people may argue that this way is too narrow. In reality, it is wide enough for the whole world, if the world chooses to accept it. Instead of worrying about how limited it sounds to have only one way, we should be saying, "Thank you, God, for providing a sure way to get to you!"

John 14:6 As the way, Jesus is our path to the Father. As the truth, he is the reality of all God's promises. As the life, he joins his divine life to ours, both now and eternally. Jesus is, in truth, the only living way to the Father.

John 14:9 Jesus is the visible, tangible image of the invisible God. He is the complete revelation of what God is like. Jesus explained to Philip, who wanted to see the Father, that to know Jesus is to know God. The search for God, for truth and reality, ends in Christ. (See also Col 1:15; Heb 1:1-4.)

Jesus told him, "I am the way, the truth, and the life. No one can come to the Father except through me."
John 14:6

▸ **JOHN 14:1-14** ***(cont.)***
in me does his work through me. 11 Just believe that I
am in the Father and the Father is in me. Or at least
believe because of the work you have seen me do.
12 "I tell you the truth, anyone who believes in me
will do the same works I have done, and even greater
works, because I am going to be with the Father.
13 You can ask for anything in my name, and I will do
it, so that the Son can bring glory to the Father. 14 Yes,
ask me for anything in my name, and I will do it!

Jesus Promises the Holy Spirit

JOHN 14:15-31
"If you love me, obey* my commandments. 16 And I will
ask the Father, and he will give you another Advocate,*
who will never leave you. 17 He is the Holy Spirit, who
leads into all truth. The world cannot receive him,
because it isn't looking for him and doesn't recognize
him. But you know him, because he lives with you now
and later will be in you.* 18 No, I will not abandon you
as orphans—I will come to you. 19 Soon the world will
no longer see me, but you will see me. Since I live, you
also will live. 20 When I am raised to life again, you will
know that I am in my Father, and you are in me, and
I am in you. 21 Those who accept my commandments
and obey them are the ones who love me. And because
they love me, my Father will love them. And I will love
them and reveal myself to each of them."
22 Judas (not Judas Iscariot, but the other disciple
with that name) said to him, "Lord, why are you going to reveal yourself only to us and not to the world
at large?"
23 Jesus replied, "All who love me will do what I say.
My Father will love them, and we will come and make
our home with each of them. 24 Anyone who doesn't
love me will not obey me. And remember, my words
are not my own. What I am telling you is from the
Father who sent me. 25 I am telling you these things
now while I am still with you. 26 But when the Father
sends the Advocate as my representative—that is, the
Holy Spirit—he will teach you everything and will
remind you of everything I have told you.

Jn 14:15 Other manuscripts read *you will obey;* still others read *you should obey.* **Jn 14:16** Or *Comforter,* or *Encourager,* or *Counselor.* Greek reads *Paraclete;* also in 14:26. **Jn 14:17** Some manuscripts read *and is in you.*

John 14:12-13 Raising the dead is about as amazing as you can get; how could the disciples do greater things than that? The "even greater works" would come because the disciples, working in the power of the Holy Spirit, would carry the Good News of God's Kingdom out of Palestine and into the whole world.

John 14:14 When Jesus says we can ask for anything, we must remember that our asking must be in his name—that is, according to God's character and will. God will not grant requests contrary to his nature or his will, and we cannot use his name as a magic formula to fulfill our selfish desires. If we are sincerely following God and seeking to do his will, then our requests will be in line with what he wants. (See also John 15:16; 16:23.)

John 14:15-16 Jesus was soon going to leave the disciples, but he would remain with them. How could this be? The Advocate—the Spirit of God himself—would come after Jesus was gone to care for and guide the disciples. The regenerating power of the Spirit came on the disciples just before Jesus' ascension (John 20:22), and the Spirit was poured out on all the believers at Pentecost (Acts 2), shortly after Jesus had ascended to heaven. The Holy Spirit is the very presence of God within us and all believers, helping us live as God wants and building Christ's church on earth. By faith we can appropriate the Spirit's power each day.

John 14:16 The word translated "Advocate" combines the ideas of comfort and counsel. The word could also be translated "Comforter," "Encourager," or "Counselor." The Holy Spirit is a powerful person on our side, working for and with us.

John 14:17ff The following verses teach these truths about the Holy Spirit: He will never leave us (John 14:16); the world at large cannot receive him (John 14:17); he lives with us and in us (John 14:17); he teaches us (John 14:26); he reminds us of Jesus' words (John 14:26; 15:26); he convicts us of sin, shows us God's righteousness, and announces God's judgment on evil (John 16:8); he guides us into truth and gives insight into future events (John 16:13); he brings glory to Christ (John 16:14). The Holy Spirit has been active among people from the beginning of time, but after Pentecost (Acts 2) he came to live in all believers. Many people are unaware of the Holy Spirit's activities, but to those who hear Christ's words and understand the Spirit's power, the Spirit gives a whole new way to look at life.

John 14:18 When Jesus said, "I will come to you," he meant it. Although Jesus ascended to heaven, he sent the Holy Spirit to live in believers, and to have the Holy Spirit is to have Jesus himself.

John 14:19-21 Sometimes people wish they knew the future so they could prepare for it. God has chosen not to give us this knowledge. He alone knows what will happen, but he tells us all we need to know to prepare for the future. When we live by his standards, he will not leave us; he will come to us, he will be in us, and he will show himself to us. God knows what will happen, and because he will be with us through it all, we need not fear. We don't have to know the future to have faith in God; we have to have faith in God to be secure about the future.

John 14:21 Jesus said that his followers show their love for him by obeying him. Love is more than lovely words; it is commitment and conduct. If you love Christ, then prove it by obeying what he says in his Word.

John 14:22-23 Because the disciples were still expecting Jesus to establish an earthly kingdom and overthrow Rome, they found it hard to understand why he did not tell the world at large that he was the Messiah. Not everyone, however, could understand Jesus' message. Ever since Pentecost, the Good News of the Kingdom has been proclaimed in the whole world, and yet not everyone is receptive to it. Jesus saves the deepest revelations of himself for those who love and obey him.

John 14:26 Jesus promised the disciples that the Holy Spirit would help them remember what he had been teaching them. This promise ensures the validity of the New Testament. The disciples were eyewitnesses of Jesus' life and teachings, and the Holy Spirit helped them remember without taking away their individual perspectives. We can be confident that the Gospels are accurate records of what Jesus taught and did (see 1 Cor 2:10-14). The Holy Spirit can help us in the same way. As we study the Bible, we can trust him to plant truth in our minds, convince us of God's will, and remind us when we stray from it.

John 14:27 The end result of the Holy Spirit's work in our lives is deep and lasting peace. Unlike worldly peace, which is usually defined as the absence of conflict, this peace is confident assurance in any circumstance. With Christ's peace, we have no need to fear the present or the future. Sin, fear, uncertainty, doubt, and numerous other forces are at war within us. The peace of God moves into our hearts and lives to restrain these hostile forces and offer comfort in place of conflict. Jesus says he will

27"I am leaving you with a gift—peace of mind
and heart. And the peace I give is a gift the world
cannot give. So don't be troubled or afraid. 28Re-
member what I told you: I am going away, but I will
come back to you again. If you really loved me, you
would be happy that I am going to the Father, who
is greater than I am. 29I have told you these things
before they happen so that when they do happen,
you will believe.
30"I don't have much more time to talk to you, because the ruler of this world approaches. He has no
power over me, 31but I will do what the Father requires
of me, so that the world will know that I love the Father.
Come, let's be going.

Jesus Teaches about the Vine and the Branches

JOHN 15:1-17

"I am the true grapevine, and my Father is the gardener.
2He cuts off every branch of mine that doesn't produce
fruit, and he prunes the branches that do bear fruit so
they will produce even more. 3You have already been
pruned and purified by the message I have given you.
4Remain in me, and I will remain in you. For a branch
cannot produce fruit if it is severed from the vine, and
you cannot be fruitful unless you remain in me.
5"Yes, I am the vine; you are the branches. Those
who remain in me, and I in them, will produce much
fruit. For apart from me you can do nothing. 6Anyone

give us that peace if we are willing to accept it from him. If your life is full of stress, allow the Holy Spirit to fill you with Christ's peace (see Phil 4:6-7 for more on experiencing God's peace).

John 14:28 As God the Son, Jesus willingly submits to God the Father. On earth, Jesus also submitted to many of the physical limitations of his humanity (Phil 2:6).

John 14:30-31 Although Satan, the ruler of this world, was unable to overpower Jesus (Matt 4), he still had the arrogance to try. Satan's power exists only because God allows him to act. But because Jesus is sinless, Satan has no power over him. If we obey Jesus and align ourselves closely with God's purposes, Satan has no power over us.

John 14:31 "Come, let's be going" suggests that John 15–17 may have been spoken en route to the Garden of Gethsemane. Another view is that Jesus was asking the disciples to get ready to leave the upper room, but they did not actually do so until 18:1.

John 15:1 The grapevine is a prolific plant; a single vine supports numerous branches and bears many grapes. In the Old Testament, grapes symbolized Israel's fruitfulness in doing God's work on the earth (Ps 80:8; Isa 5:1-7; Ezek 19:10-14). In the Passover meal, the fruit of the vine symbolized God's goodness to his people.

John 15:1ff Christ is the vine, and God is the gardener who cares for the branches to make them fruitful. The branches are all those who claim to be followers of Christ. The fruitful branches are true believers who by their living union with Christ produce much fruit. But those who become unproductive—those who turn back from following Christ after making a superficial commitment—will be separated from the vine. Unproductive followers are as good as dead and will be cut off and tossed aside.

John 15:2-3 Jesus makes a distinction between two kinds of pruning: cutting off and cutting back branches. Fruitful branches are cut back to promote growth. In other words, God must sometimes discipline us to strengthen our character and faith. But branches that don't bear fruit are cut off at the trunk not only because they are worthless but also because they often infect the rest of the tree. People who don't bear fruit for God or who try to block the efforts of God's followers will be cut off from his life-giving power.

John 15:5 "Fruit" refers to a number of different things that will be evident in a believer's life. In this chapter, answered prayer, joy, and love are mentioned as fruit (John 15:7, 11-12). Galatians 5:22-24 and 2 Peter 1:5-8 describe additional fruit: qualities of Christian character.

John 15:5-6 Remaining in Christ means believing that he is God's Son (1 Jn 4:15), receiving him as Savior and Lord (John 1:12), doing what God says (1 Jn 3:24), continuing to believe the Good News (1 Jn 2:24), and relating in love to the community of believers, Christ's body (John 15:12).

John 15:5-8 Many people try to be good, honest people who do what is right. But Jesus says that the only way to live a truly good life is to stay close to him, like a branch attached to the vine. Apart from Christ our efforts are unfruitful. Are you receiving the nourishment and life offered by Christ, the vine? If not, you are missing a special gift he has for you.

Grapevine

The grapevine is mentioned frequently in Scripture both in a literal and a figurative sense. Probably originating in the Ararat region (Gen 9:20), the vine was also cultivated in ancient Egypt, where tomb murals depict the wine-making process. Moses described the vineyards in the Promised Land (Deut 6:11). Excellent grapes from the valleys and plains (Num 13:20-24; Judg 14:5; 15:5) provided fruit and wine to enhance the diet of the Hebrews.

Jesus frequently used the vineyard as a background for his parables (Matt 20:1-16; 21:28-43; Mark 12:1-11; Luke 13:6-9; 20:9-18). Wine-making methods were commonly known and understood, so using an illustration of placing new wine in old wineskins was immediately familiar and significant. Jesus described himself as the true grapevine and his followers as branches united to the vine (John 15:1-11). Just as branches are dependent on the vine for their life supply, so Christians need Christ's life-giving flow to enable them to bear spiritual fruit in their lives.

▸ **JOHN 15:1-17** ***(cont.)***

who does not remain in me is thrown away like a useless branch and withers. Such branches are gathered into a pile to be burned. [7]But if you remain in me and my words remain in you, you may ask for anything you want, and it will be granted! [8]When you produce much fruit, you are my true disciples. This brings great glory to my Father.

[9]"I have loved you even as the Father has loved me. Remain in my love. [10]When you obey my commandments, you remain in my love, just as I obey my Father's commandments and remain in his love. [11]I have told you these things so that you will be filled with my joy. Yes, your joy will overflow! [12]This is my commandment: Love each other in the same way I have loved you. [13]There is no greater love than to lay down one's life for one's friends. [14]You are my friends if you do what I command. [15]I no longer call you slaves, because a master doesn't confide in his slaves. Now you are my friends, since I have told you everything the Father told me. [16]You didn't choose me. I chose you. I appointed you to go and produce lasting fruit, so that the Father will give you whatever you ask for, using my name. [17]This is my command: Love each other.

Jesus Warns about the World's Hatred

JOHN 15:18–16:4

"If the world hates you, remember that it hated me first. [19]The world would love you as one of its own if you belonged to it, but you are no longer part of the world. I chose you to come out of the world, so it hates you. [20]Do you remember what I told you? 'A slave is not greater than the master.' Since they persecuted me, naturally they will persecute you. And if they had listened to me, they would listen to you. [21]They will do all this to you because of me, for they have rejected the one who sent me. [22]They would not be guilty if I had not come and spoken to them. But now they have no excuse for their sin. [23]Anyone who hates me also hates my Father. [24]If I hadn't done such miraculous signs among them that no one else could do, they would not be guilty. But as it is, they have seen everything I did, yet they still hate me and my Father. [25]This fulfills what is written in their Scriptures*: 'They hated me without cause.'

[26]"But I will send you the Advocate*—the Spirit of truth. He will come to you from the Father and will testify all about me. [27]And you must also testify about me because you have been with me from the beginning of my ministry.

16:1"I have told you these things so that you won't abandon your faith. [2]For you will be expelled from the synagogues, and the time is coming when those who kill you will think they are doing a holy service for God. [3]This is because they have never known the Father or me. [4]Yes, I'm telling you these things now, so that when they happen, you will remember my warning. I didn't tell you earlier because I was going to be with you for a while longer.

Jn 15:25 Greek *in their law.* Pss 35:19; 69:4. **Jn 15:26** Or *Comforter,* or *Encourager,* or *Counselor.* Greek reads *Paraclete.*

John 15:8 When a vine produces "much fruit," God is glorified, for daily he sent the sunshine and rain to make the crops grow, and constantly he nurtured each tiny plant and prepared it to blossom. What a moment of glory for the Lord of the harvest when the harvest is brought into the barns, mature and ready for use! He made it all happen! This farming analogy shows how God is glorified when people come into a right relationship with him and begin to "produce much fruit" in their lives.

John 15:11 When things are going well, we feel elated. When hardships come, we might sink into depression. But true joy transcends the rolling waves of circumstance. Joy comes from a consistent relationship with Jesus Christ. When our lives are intertwined with his, he will help us walk through adversity without sinking into debilitating lows and manage prosperity without moving into deceptive highs. The joy of living with Jesus Christ daily will keep us levelheaded, no matter how high or low our circumstances.

John 15:12-13 We are to love each other as Jesus loved us, and he loved us enough to give his life for us. We may not have to die for someone, but there are other ways to practice sacrificial love: listening, helping, encouraging, giving. Think of someone in particular who needs this kind of love today. Give all the love you can, and then try to give a little more.

John 15:15 Because Jesus Christ is Lord and Master, he should call us servants; instead, he calls us friends. How comforting and reassuring to be chosen as Christ's friends! We owe him our unqualified obedience, but Jesus asks us to obey him because we love him.

John 15:16 Jesus made the first choice—to love us and to die for us, to invite us to live with him forever. We make the next choice—to accept or reject his offer. Without his choice, we would have no choice to make.

John 15:17 Christians will get plenty of hatred from the world; from each other we need love and support. Do you allow small problems to get in the way of loving other believers? Jesus commands that you love them, and he will give you the strength to do it.

John 15:26 Once again Jesus offers hope. The Holy Spirit gives strength to endure the unreasonable hatred and evil in our world and the hostility many have toward Christ. This is especially comforting for those facing persecution.

John 15:26 Jesus uses two names for the Holy Spirit. "Advocate" conveys the helping, encouraging, and strengthening work of the Spirit. "Spirit of truth" points to the teaching, illuminating, and reminding work of the Spirit. The Holy Spirit ministers to both the head and the heart, and both dimensions are important.

John 16:1-16 In his last moments with his disciples, Jesus warned them about further persecution; told them where, when, and why he was going; and assured them that they would not be left alone, but that the Spirit would come. Jesus knew what lay ahead, and he did not want the disciples' faith shaken or destroyed. God wants you to know you are not alone. You have the Holy Spirit to comfort you, teach you truth, and help you.

John 16:2 Saul (who later became Paul), under the authority of the high priest, went through the land hunting down and persecuting Christians, convinced that he was doing the right thing (Acts 9:1-2; 26:9-11).

John 16:5 Although the disciples had asked Jesus about his death (John 13:36; 14:5), they had never wondered about its meaning. They were mostly concerned about themselves. If Jesus went away, what would become of them?

Jesus Teaches about the Holy Spirit

JOHN 16:5-15

"But now I am going away to the one who sent me, and not one of you is asking where I am going. 6Instead, you grieve because of what I've told you. 7But in fact, it is best for you that I go away, because if I don't, the Advocate* won't come. If I do go away, then I will send him to you. 8And when he comes, he will convict the world of its sin, and of God's righteousness, and of the coming judgment. 9The world's sin is that it refuses to believe in me. 10Righteousness is available because I go to the Father, and you will see me no more. 11Judgment will come because the ruler of this world has already been judged.

12"There is so much more I want to tell you, but you can't bear it now. 13When the Spirit of truth comes, he will guide you into all truth. He will not speak on his own but will tell you what he has heard. He will tell you about the future. 14He will bring me glory by telling you whatever he receives from me. 15All that belongs to the Father is mine; this is why I said, 'The Spirit will tell you whatever he receives from me.'

Jesus Teaches about Using His Name in Prayer

JOHN 16:16-33

"In a little while you won't see me anymore. But a little while after that, you will see me again."

17Some of the disciples asked each other, "What does he mean when he says, 'In a little while you won't see me, but then you will see me,' and 'I am going to the Father'? 18And what does he mean by 'a little while'? We don't understand."

19Jesus realized they wanted to ask him about it, so he said, "Are you asking yourselves what I meant? I said in a little while you won't see me, but a little while after that you will see me again. 20I tell you the truth, you will weep and mourn over what is going to happen to me, but the world will rejoice. You will grieve, but your grief will suddenly turn to wonderful joy. 21It will be like a woman suffering the pains of labor. When her child is born, her anguish gives way to joy because she has brought a new baby into the world. 22So you have sorrow now, but I will see you again; then you will rejoice, and no one can rob you of that joy. 23At that time you won't need to ask me for anything. I tell you the truth, you will ask the Father directly, and he will grant your request because you use my name. 24You haven't done this before. Ask, using my name, and you will receive, and you will have abundant joy.

25"I have spoken of these matters in figures of speech, but soon I will stop speaking figuratively and will tell you plainly all about the Father. 26Then you will ask in my name. I'm not saying I will ask the Father on your behalf, 27for the Father himself loves you dearly because you love me and believe that I came from God.* 28Yes, I came from the Father into the world, and now I will leave the world and return to the Father."

29Then his disciples said, "At last you are speaking plainly and not figuratively. 30Now we understand that you know everything, and there's no need to question you. From this we believe that you came from God."

Jn 16:7 Or *Comforter,* or *Encourager,* or *Counselor.* Greek reads *Paraclete.* **Jn 16:27** Some manuscripts read *from the Father.*

John 16:7 Unless Jesus did what he came to do, there would be no Good News. If he did not die, he could not remove our sins; he could not rise again and defeat death. If he did not go back to the Father, the Holy Spirit would not come. Christ's presence on earth was limited to one place at a time. His leaving meant he could be present to the whole world through the Holy Spirit.

John 16:8-11 Three important tasks of the Holy Spirit are (1) convicting the world of its sin and calling it to repentance, (2) revealing the standard of God's righteousness to anyone who believes because Christ would no longer be physically present on earth, and (3) demonstrating Christ's judgment over Satan.

John 16:9 According to Jesus, not believing in him is sin.

John 16:10-11 Christ's death on the cross made a personal relationship with God available to us. When we confess our sin, God declares us righteous and delivers us from judgment for our sins.

John 16:13 The truth into which the Holy Spirit guides us is the truth about Christ. The Spirit also helps us through patient practice to discern right from wrong.

John 16:13 Jesus said the Holy Spirit would tell them "about the future"—the nature of their mission, the opposition they would face, and the final outcome of their efforts. They didn't fully understand these promises until the Holy Spirit came after Jesus' death and resurrection. Then the Holy Spirit revealed truths to the disciples that they wrote down in the books that now form the New Testament.

John 16:16 Jesus was referring to his death, now only a few hours away, and his resurrection three days later.

John 16:20 What a contrast between the disciples and the world! The world rejoiced as the disciples wept, but the disciples would see Jesus again (in three days) and rejoice. The world's values are often the opposite of God's values. This can cause Christians to feel like misfits. But even if life is difficult now, one day we will rejoice. Keep your eye on the future and on God's promises!

John 16:23-27 Jesus is talking about a new relationship between the believer and God. Previously, people approached God through priests. After Jesus' resurrection, any believer could approach God directly. A new day has dawned and now all believers are priests, talking with God personally and directly (see Heb 10:19-23). We can approach God not because of our own merit but because Jesus, our great High Priest, has made us acceptable to God.

John 16:30 The disciples believed Jesus' words because they were convinced that he knew everything. But their belief was only a first step toward the great faith they would receive when the Holy Spirit came to live in them.

▸ **JOHN 16:16-33 *(cont.)***

[31]Jesus asked, "Do you finally believe? [32]But the time
is coming—indeed it's here now—when you will be
scattered, each one going his own way, leaving me
alone. Yet I am not alone because the Father is with
me. [33]I have told you all this so that you may have peace
in me. Here on earth you will have many trials and
sorrows. But take heart, because I have overcome the
world."

Jesus Prays for Himself

JOHN 17:1-5

After saying all these things, Jesus looked up to heaven
and said, "Father, the hour has come. Glorify your Son
so he can give glory back to you. [2]For you have given
him authority over everyone. He gives eternal life to
each one you have given him. [3]And this is the way to
have eternal life—to know you, the only true God, and
Jesus Christ, the one you sent to earth. [4]I brought glory
to you here on earth by completing the work you gave
me to do. [5]Now, Father, bring me into the glory we
shared before the world began.

Jesus Prays for His Disciples

JOHN 17:6-19

"I have revealed you* to the ones you gave me from
this world. They were always yours. You gave them to
me, and they have kept your word. [7]Now they know

Jn 17:6 Greek *have revealed your name;* also in 17:26.

MAJOR EVENTS OF PASSION WEEK

Sunday through Wednesday Jesus spent each night in Bethany, just two miles east of Jerusalem on the opposite slope of the Mount of Olives. He probably stayed at the home of Mary, Martha, and Lazarus. Jesus spent Thursday night praying in the Garden of Gethsemane. Friday and Saturday nights Jesus' body lay in the garden tomb.

Day	*Event*	*References*
Sunday	Triumphal Entry into Jerusalem	Matt 21:1-11; Mark 11:1-10; Luke 19:29-40; John 12:12-19
Monday	Jesus clears the Temple	Matt 21:12-13; Mark 11:15-17; Luke 19:45-46
Tuesday	Jesus' authority challenged in the Temple	Matt 21:23-27; Mark 11:27-33; Luke 20:1-8
	Jesus teaches in stories and confronts the Jewish leaders	Matt 21:28–23:36; Mark 12:1-40; Luke 20:9-47
	Greeks ask to see Jesus	John 12:20-26
	The Olivet discourse	Matt 24; Mark 13; Luke 21:5-38
	Judas agrees to betray Jesus	Matt 26:14-16; Mark 14:10-11; Luke 22:3-6
Wednesday	The Bible does not say what Jesus did on this day; he probably remained in Bethany with his disciples	
Thursday	The Last Supper	Matt 26:26-29; Mark 14:22-25; Luke 22:14-20
	Jesus speaks to the disciples in the upper room	John 13–17
	Jesus struggles in Gethsemane	Matt 26:36-46; Mark 14:32-42; Luke 22:39-46; John 18:1
	Jesus is betrayed and arrested	Matt 26:47-56; Mark 14:43-52; Luke 22:47-53; John 18:2-12
Friday	Jesus is tried by Jewish and Roman authorities and is denied by Peter	Matt 26:57–27:2, 11-31; Mark 14:53–15:20; Luke 22:54–23:25; John 18:13–19:16
	Jesus is crucified	Matt 27:31-56; Mark 15:20-41; Luke 23:26-49; John 19:17-30
Sunday	The Resurrection	Matt 28:1-10; Mark 16:1-11; Luke 24:1-12; John 20:1-18

John 16:31-33 As Christians, we should expect continuing tension with an unbelieving world that is "out of sync" with Christ, his Good News, and his people. At the same time, we can expect our relationship with Christ to produce peace and comfort because we are "in sync" with him.

John 16:32 The disciples scattered after Jesus was arrested (see Mark 14:50). Jesus accepted their statement of faith even though he knew their weakness. He knew they would have to grow into people whose words and lives matched even to the point of death. He takes us through the same process. How well are you living out what you say you believe about Jesus?

John 16:33 Jesus summed up all he had told them this night, tying together themes from John 14:27-29; 16:1-4; and 16:9-11. With these words he told his disciples to take courage. In spite of the inevitable struggles they would face, they would not be alone. Jesus does not abandon us to our struggles either. If we remember that the ultimate victory has already been won, we can claim the peace of Christ in the most troublesome times.

John 17:1ff This entire chapter is Jesus' prayer. From it we learn that the world is a tremendous battleground where the forces under Satan's power and those under God's authority are at war. Satan and his forces are motivated by bitter hatred for Christ and his forces. Jesus prayed for his disciples, including those of us who follow him today. He prayed that God would keep his chosen

that everything I have is a gift from you, 8for I have
passed on to them the message you gave me. They
accepted it and know that I came from you, and they
believe you sent me.
9"My prayer is not for the world, but for those you
have given me, because they belong to you. 10All who
are mine belong to you, and you have given them to
me, so they bring me glory. 11Now I am departing
from the world; they are staying in this world, but I
am coming to you. Holy Father, you have given me
your name;* now protect them by the power of your
name so that they will be united just as we are. 12Dur-
ing my time here, I protected them by the power of
the name you gave me.* I guarded them so that not
one was lost, except the one headed for destruction,
as the Scriptures foretold.
13"Now I am coming to you. I told them many
things while I was with them in this world so they
would be filled with my joy. 14I have given them your
word. And the world hates them because they do
not belong to the world, just as I do not belong to
the world. 15I'm not asking you to take them out of
the world, but to keep them safe from the evil one.
16They do not belong to this world any more than I
do. 17Make them holy by your truth; teach them your
word, which is truth. 18Just as you sent me into the
world, I am sending them into the world. 19And I give
myself as a holy sacrifice for them so they can be
made holy by your truth.

Jesus Prays for Future Believers

JOHN 17:20-26

"I am praying not only for these disciples but also for
all who will ever believe in me through their message. 21I pray that they will all be one, just as you and
I are one—as you are in me, Father, and I am in you.
And may they be in us so that the world will believe
you sent me.
22"I have given them the glory you gave me, so
they may be one as we are one. 23I am in them and
you are in me. May they experience such perfect
unity that the world will know that you sent me and
that you love them as much as you love me. 24Father,
I want these whom you have given me to be with me
where I am. Then they can see all the glory you gave
me because you loved me even before the world
began!
25"O righteous Father, the world doesn't know you,
but I do; and these disciples know you sent me. 26I
have revealed you to them, and I will continue to do
so. Then your love for me will be in them, and I will
be in them."

Jn 17:11 Some manuscripts read *you have given me these [disciples].* **Jn 17:12** Some manuscripts read *I protected those you gave me, by the power of your name.*

believers safe from Satan's power, setting them apart and making them pure and holy, uniting them through his truth.

John 17:3 How do we get eternal life? Jesus tells us clearly here—by knowing God the Father through his Son, Jesus Christ. Eternal life requires entering into a personal relationship with God in Jesus Christ. When we admit our sin and turn away from it, Christ's love lives in us by the Holy Spirit.

John 17:5 Jesus was asking his Father to restore him to his original place of honor and authority, where he was since before creation. Jesus' resurrection and ascension—and Stephen's dying exclamation (Acts 7:56)—attest that Jesus did return to his exalted position at the right hand of God.

John 17:10 What did Jesus mean when he said "they bring me glory"? God's glory is the revelation of his character and presence. The lives of Jesus' disciples reveal his character, and he is present to the world through them. Does your life reveal Jesus' character and presence?

John 17:11 Jesus was asking that the disciples be united in harmony and love as the Father, Son, and Holy Spirit are united—the strongest of all unions. (See notes on John 17:21-23, below.)

John 17:12 Judas was "the one headed for destruction," who was lost because he betrayed Jesus and never sought forgiveness (see Ps 41:9).

John 17:13 Joy is a common theme in Christ's teachings—he wants us to be joyful (see John 15:11; 16:24). The key to immeasurable joy is living in intimate contact with Christ, the source of all joy. When we do, we will experience God's special care and protection and see the victory God brings even when defeat seems certain.

John 17:14 The world hates Christians because their values differ from the world's. Because Christ's followers don't cooperate with the world by joining in their sin, they are living accusations against the world's immorality. The world follows Satan's agenda, and Satan is the avowed enemy of Jesus and his people.

John 17:17 A follower of Christ becomes pure and holy through believing and obeying the Word of God (Heb 4:12). Although we have already accepted forgiveness through Christ's sacrificial death (Heb 7:26-27), applying God's Word every day will have a purifying effect on our minds and hearts. Scripture points out sin, motivates us to confess, renews our relationship with Christ, and guides us back to the right path.

John 17:18 Jesus didn't ask God to take believers out of the world but instead to use them in the world. Because Jesus sends us into the world, we should not try to escape from it, nor should we avoid all relationships with non-Christians. We are called to be salt and light (Matt 5:13-16), and we are to do the work that God sent us to do.

John 17:20 Jesus prayed for all who would follow him, including you and others you know. He prayed for unity (John 17:11), protection from the evil one (John 17:15), and holiness (John 17:17). Knowing that Jesus prayed for us should give us confidence as we work for his Kingdom.

John 17:21-23 Jesus' great desire for his disciples was that they would become one. He wanted them unified as a powerful witness to the reality of God's love. Are you helping to unify the body of Christ, the church? You can pray for other Christians, avoid gossip, build others up, work together in humility, give your time and money, exalt Christ, and refuse to get sidetracked arguing over divisive matters.

John 17:21-23 Jesus prayed for unity among believers based on the believers' unity with him and the Father. Christians can know unity among themselves if they are living in union with God; each branch living in union with the vine is united with all other branches doing the same.

Jesus Agonizes in the Garden PARALLEL

MATTHEW 26:36-46

Then Jesus went with them to the olive grove called
Gethsemane, and he said, "Sit here while I go over there
to pray." 37 He took Peter and Zebedee's two sons, James
and John, and he became anguished and distressed. 38 He
told them, "My soul is crushed with grief to the point of
death. Stay here and keep watch with me."
39 He went on a little farther and bowed with his face
to the ground, praying, "My Father! If it is possible, let
this cup of suffering be taken away from me. Yet I want
your will to be done, not mine."
40 Then he returned to the disciples and found them
asleep. He said to Peter, "Couldn't you watch with me
even one hour? 41 Keep watch and pray, so that you will
not give in to temptation. For the spirit is willing, but
the body is weak!"
42 Then Jesus left them a second time and prayed,
"My Father! If this cup cannot be taken away* unless
I drink it, your will be done." 43 When he returned to
them again, he found them sleeping, for they couldn't
keep their eyes open.
44 So he went to pray a third time, saying the same
things again. 45 Then he came to the disciples and said,
"Go ahead and sleep. Have your rest. But look—the time
has come. The Son of Man is betrayed into the hands of
sinners. 46 Up, let's be going. Look, my betrayer is here!"

MARK 14:32-42

They went to the olive grove called Gethsemane, and
Jesus said, "Sit here while I go and pray." 33 He took Peter, James, and John with him, and he became deeply
troubled and distressed. 34 He told them, "My soul is
crushed with grief to the point of death. Stay here and
keep watch with me."
35 He went on a little farther and fell to the ground.
He prayed that, if it were possible, the awful hour
awaiting him might pass him by. 36 "Abba, Father,"*
he cried out, "everything is possible for you. Please
take this cup of suffering away from me. Yet I want
your will to be done, not mine."
37 Then he returned and found the disciples asleep.
He said to Peter, "Simon, are you asleep? Couldn't you
watch with me even one hour? 38 Keep watch and pray,
so that you will not give in to temptation. For the spirit
is willing, but the body is weak."
39 Then Jesus left them again and prayed the same
prayer as before. 40 When he returned to them again,
he found them sleeping, for they couldn't keep their
eyes open. And they didn't know what to say.
41 When he returned to them the third time, he
said, "Go ahead and sleep. Have your rest. But no—
the time has come. The Son of Man is betrayed into
the hands of sinners. 42 Up, let's be going. Look, my
betrayer is here!"

Mt 26:42 Greek *If this cannot pass.* **Mk 14:36** *Abba* is an Aramaic term for "father."

Matt 26:37-38 Jesus was in great anguish over his approaching physical pain, separation from the Father, and death for the sins of the world. The divine course was set, but he, in his human nature, still struggled (Heb 5:7-9). Because of the anguish Jesus experienced, he can relate to our suffering. Jesus' strength to obey came from his relationship with God the Father, who is also the source of our strength (John 17:11, 15-16, 21, 26).

Matt 26:39 Jesus was not rebelling against his Father's will when he asked that the cup of suffering and separation be taken away. In fact, he reaffirmed his desire to do God's will by saying, "Yet I want your will to be done, not mine." His prayer reveals to us his terrible suffering. His agony was worse than death because he paid for all sin by being separated from God. The sinless Son of God took our sins upon himself to save us from suffering and separation.

Matt 26:39 In times of suffering people sometimes wish they knew the future, or they wish they could understand the reason for their anguish. Jesus knew what lay ahead of him, and he knew the reason. Even so, his struggle was intense—more wrenching than any struggle we will ever have to face. What does it take to be able to say, "I want your will to be done"? It takes firm trust in God's plans; it takes prayer and obedience each step of the way.

Matt 26:40-41 Jesus used Peter's drowsiness to warn him about the kinds of temptation he would soon face. The way to overcome temptation is to keep alert and pray. Keeping alert means being aware of the possibilities of temptation, sensitive to the subtleties, and spiritually equipped to fight it. Because temptation strikes where we are most vulnerable, we can't resist it alone. Prayer is essential because God's strength can shore up our defenses and defeat Satan's power.

Mark 14:35-36 Jesus expressed his true feelings, but he did not deny or rebel against God's will. He reaffirmed his desire to do what God wanted. Jesus' prayer highlights the terrible suffering he had to endure—an agony so much more magnified because he had to take on the sins of the whole world. This "cup" was the agony of alienation from God, his Father, at the cross (Heb 5:7-9). The sinless Son of God took on our sins and was separated for a while from God so that we could be eternally saved.

Mark 14:36 While praying, Jesus was aware of what doing the Father's will would cost him. He understood the suffering he was about to encounter, and he did not want to endure the horrible experience. But Jesus prayed, "Yet I want your will to be done, not

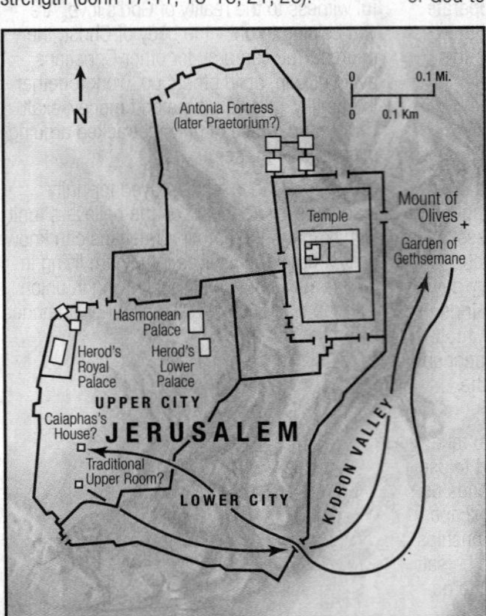

◀ ***FROM THE LAST SUPPER TO GETHSEMANE***
Jesus, who would soon be the final Passover Lamb, ate the traditional Passover meal with his disciples in the upper room of a house in Jerusalem. During the meal they partook of bread and wine, which would be the elements of future Communion celebrations, and then went out to the Garden of Gethsemane on the Mount of Olives.

LUKE 22:39-46

Then, accompanied by the disciples, Jesus left the upstairs room and went as usual to the Mount of Olives. 40There he told them, "Pray that you will not give in to temptation."

41He walked away, about a stone's throw, and knelt down and prayed, 42"Father, if you are willing, please take this cup of suffering away from me. Yet I want your will to be done, not mine." 43Then an angel from heaven appeared and strengthened him. 44He prayed more fervently, and he was in such agony of spirit that his sweat fell to the ground like great drops of blood.*

45At last he stood up again and returned to the disciples, only to find them asleep, exhausted from grief. 46"Why are you sleeping?" he asked them. "Get up and pray, so that you will not give in to temptation."

Jesus Is Betrayed and Arrested PARALLEL

MATTHEW 26:47-56

And even as Jesus said this, Judas, one of the twelve disciples, arrived with a crowd of men armed with swords and clubs. They had been sent by the leading priests and elders of the people. 48The traitor, Judas, had given them a prearranged signal: "You will know which one to arrest when I greet him with a kiss." 49So Judas came straight to Jesus. "Greetings, Rabbi!" he exclaimed and gave him the kiss.

50Jesus said, "My friend, go ahead and do what you have come for."

Then the others grabbed Jesus and arrested him. 51But one of the men with Jesus pulled out his sword and struck the high priest's slave, slashing off his ear.

52"Put away your sword," Jesus told him. "Those who use the sword will die by the sword. 53Don't you realize that I could ask my Father for thousands* of angels to protect us, and he would send them instantly? 54But if I did, how would the Scriptures be fulfilled that describe what must happen now?"

55Then Jesus said to the crowd, "Am I some dangerous revolutionary, that you come with swords and clubs to arrest me? Why didn't you arrest me in the Temple? I was there teaching every day. 56But this is all happening to fulfill the words of the prophets as recorded in the Scriptures." At that point, all the disciples deserted him and fled.

MARK 14:43-52

And immediately, even as Jesus said this, Judas, one of the twelve disciples, arrived with a crowd of men

Lk 22:43-44 Verses 43 and 44 are not included in many ancient manuscripts. **Mt 26:53** Greek *twelve legions.*

mine." Anything worth having costs something. What does your commitment to God cost you?

Mark 14:38 You may not face execution for your faith, but you probably face many problems that wear you down. You deal with irritating people whom you must love and serve; you face the burden of unfinished tasks or lack of obvious results; you cope with helpers who let you down or fail to comprehend. Remember that in times of great stress, you are vulnerable to temptation, even if you have a willing spirit. Jesus explained how to resist: (1) Keep watch (Mark 14:34)—stay awake and be morally vigilant. (2) Pray to God (Mark 14:35)—this is how you maintain your vigilance. (3) Seek support of friends and loved ones (Mark 14:33, 37, 40-41)—this is how you build up your resistance and help others; when one is weak, others are strong. (4) Focus on the purpose God has given you (Mark 14:36)—this is how you do God's will and not your own.

Luke 22:39 The Mount of Olives was located just to the east of Jerusalem. Jesus went up the southwestern slope to an olive grove called Gethsemane, which means "oil press."

Luke 22:40 Jesus asked the disciples to pray that they would not fall into temptation because he knew that he would soon be leaving them. Jesus also knew that they would need extra strength to face the temptations ahead—temptations to run away or to deny their relationship with him. They were about to see Jesus die. Would they still think

BETRAYED!

Scripture records a number of occasions on which a person or group was betrayed. The tragedies caused by these violations of trust are a strong lesson about the importance of keeping our commitments.

Delilah betrayed Samson to the Philistines	Judg 16:16-21
Absalom betrayed David, his father	2 Sam 15:10-16
Jehu betrayed Joram and killed him	2 Kgs 9:14-24
Officials betrayed Joash and killed him	2 Kgs 12:20-21
Judas betrayed Jesus	Matt 26:45-56

he was the Messiah? The disciples' strongest temptation would undoubtedly be to think they had been deceived.

Luke 22:44 Only Luke tells us that Jesus' sweat resembled drops of blood. Jesus was in extreme agony, but he did not give up or give in. He went ahead with the mission for which he had come.

Luke 22:46 These disciples were asleep. How tragic it is that many Christians act as though they are sound asleep when it comes to devotion to Christ and service for him. Don't be found insensitive to or unprepared for Christ's work.

Matt 26:51-53 The man who cut off the servant's ear was Peter (John 18:10). Peter was trying to prevent what he saw as defeat. He didn't realize that Jesus had to die in order to gain victory. But Jesus demonstrated perfect commitment to his Father's will. His Kingdom would not be advanced with swords but with faith and obedience.

Matt 26:55 Although the religious leaders could have arrested Jesus at any time, they came at night because they were afraid of the crowds that followed him each day (see Matt 26:5).

Matt 26:56 A few hours earlier, this band of men had said they would rather die than desert their Lord (see note on Matt 26:35, p. 1460).

Mark 14:43-45 Judas was given a contingent of police and soldiers (John 18:3) in order to seize Jesus and bring him before the religious court for trial. The religious leaders had issued a warrant for Jesus' arrest, and Judas was acting as Jesus' official accuser.

▸ MARK 14:43-52 *(cont.)*
armed with swords and clubs. They had been sent
by the leading priests, the teachers of religious law,
and the elders. 44The traitor, Judas, had given them a
prearranged signal: "You will know which one to arrest
when I greet him with a kiss. Then you can take him
away under guard." 45As soon as they arrived, Judas
walked up to Jesus. "Rabbi!" he exclaimed, and gave
him the kiss.
46Then the others grabbed Jesus and arrested him.
47But one of the men with Jesus pulled out his sword
and struck the high priest's slave, slashing off his ear.
48Jesus asked them, "Am I some dangerous revolutionary, that you come with swords and clubs to arrest me? 49Why didn't you arrest me in the Temple?
I was there among you teaching every day. But these
things are happening to fulfill what the Scriptures
say about me."
50Then all his disciples deserted him and ran away.
51One young man following behind was clothed only
in a long linen shirt. When the mob tried to grab him,
52he slipped out of his shirt and ran away naked.

LUKE 22:47-53
But even as Jesus said this, a crowd approached, led
by Judas, one of the twelve disciples. Judas walked
over to Jesus to greet him with a kiss. 48But Jesus
said, "Judas, would you betray the Son of Man with
a kiss?"
49When the other disciples saw what was about to
happen, they exclaimed, "Lord, should we fight? We
brought the swords!" 50And one of them struck at the
high priest's slave, slashing off his right ear.
51But Jesus said, "No more of this." And he touched
the man's ear and healed him.
52Then Jesus spoke to the leading priests, the captains of the Temple guard, and the elders who had
come for him. "Am I some dangerous revolutionary,"
he asked, "that you come with swords and clubs to
arrest me? 53Why didn't you arrest me in the Temple?
I was there every day. But this is your moment, the
time when the power of darkness reigns."

JOHN 18:1-11
After saying these things, Jesus crossed the Kidron Valley with his disciples and entered a grove of olive trees.
2Judas, the betrayer, knew this place, because Jesus
had often gone there with his disciples. 3The leading
priests and Pharisees had given Judas a contingent
of Roman soldiers and Temple guards to accompany
him. Now with blazing torches, lanterns, and weapons,
they arrived at the olive grove.
4Jesus fully realized all that was going to happen to
him, so he stepped forward to meet them. "Who are
you looking for?" he asked.
5"Jesus the Nazarene,"* they replied.
"I AM he,"* Jesus said. (Judas, who betrayed him,
was standing with them.) 6As Jesus said "I AM he," they
all drew back and fell to the ground! 7Once more he
asked them, "Who are you looking for?"
And again they replied, "Jesus the Nazarene."
8"I told you that I AM he," Jesus said. "And since I am
the one you want, let these others go." 9He did this to
fulfill his own statement: "I did not lose a single one
of those you have given me."*
10Then Simon Peter drew a sword and slashed
off the right ear of Malchus, the high priest's slave.
11But Jesus said to Peter, "Put your sword back into
its sheath. Shall I not drink from the cup of suffering
the Father has given me?"

Jn 18:5a Or *Jesus of Nazareth;* also in 18:7. **Jn 18:5b** Or *"The 'I AM' is here"*; or *"I am the LORD"*; Greek reads *I am;* also in 18:6, 8. See Exod 3:14. **Jn 18:9** See John 6:39 and 17:12.

Mark 14:50 Just hours earlier, these disciples had vowed never to desert Jesus (Mark 14:31).

Mark 14:51-52 Tradition says that this young man may have been John Mark, the writer of this Gospel. The incident is not mentioned in any of the other accounts.

Luke 22:47 A kiss was and still is the traditional greeting among men in certain parts of the world. In this case, it was also the agreed-upon signal to point out Jesus (Matt 26:48). It is ironic that a gesture of greeting would be the means of betrayal. It was a hollow gesture because of Judas's treachery. Have any of your religious practices become empty gestures? We still betray Christ when our acts of service or giving are insincere or carried out merely for show.

Luke 22:53 The religious leaders had not arrested Jesus in the Temple for fear of a riot. Instead, they came secretly at night, under the influence of the power of darkness, Satan himself. Although it looked as if Satan was getting the upper hand, everything was proceeding according to God's plan. It was time for Jesus to die.

John 18:3 The Jewish religious leaders were given authority by the Romans to make arrests for minor infractions. The Roman soldiers may not have participated in the arrest but accompanied the Temple guards to make sure matters didn't get out of control.

John 18:4-5 John does not record Judas's kiss of greeting (Matt 26:49; Mark 14:45; Luke 22:47-48), but Judas's kiss marked a turning point for the disciples. With Jesus' arrest, each one's life would be radically different. For the first time, Judas openly betrayed Jesus before the other disciples. For the first time, Jesus' loyal disciples ran away from him (Matt 26:56). The band of disciples would undergo severe testing before they were transformed from hesitant followers to dynamic leaders.

John 18:5-6 The men may have been startled by the boldness of Jesus' question or by the words "I AM he," a declaration of his divinity (Exod 3:14). Or perhaps they were overcome by his obvious power and authority.

John 18:10-11 Trying to protect Jesus, Peter pulled a sword and wounded the high priest's slave. But Jesus told Peter to put away his sword and allow God's plan to unfold. At times it is tempting to take matters into our own hands, to force the issue. Most often such moves lead to sin. Instead, we must trust God to work out his plan. Think of it—if Peter had had his way, Jesus would not have gone to the cross, and God's plan of redemption would have been thwarted.

John 18:11 "The cup" refers to the suffering, isolation, and death that Jesus would have to endure in order to atone for the sins of the world.

John 18:12-13 Jesus was immediately taken to the high priest's residence, even though this was the middle of the night. The religious leaders were in a hurry—

Annas Questions Jesus

JOHN 18:12-24

So the soldiers, their commanding officer, and the
Temple guards arrested Jesus and tied him up. 13First
they took him to Annas, the father-in-law of Caiaphas,
the high priest at that time.* 14Caiaphas was the one
who had told the other Jewish leaders, "It's better that
one man should die for the people."

15Simon Peter followed Jesus, as did another of the
disciples. That other disciple was acquainted with the
high priest, so he was allowed to enter the high priest's
courtyard with Jesus. 16Peter had to stay outside the
gate. Then the disciple who knew the high priest spoke
to the woman watching at the gate, and she let Peter
in. 17The woman asked Peter, "You're not one of that
man's disciples, are you?"

"No," he said, "I am not."

18Because it was cold, the household servants and
the guards had made a charcoal fire. They stood
around it, warming themselves, and Peter stood with
them, warming himself.

19Inside, the high priest began asking Jesus about
his followers and what he had been teaching them.
20Jesus replied, "Everyone knows what I teach. I have
preached regularly in the synagogues and the Temple,
where the people* gather. I have not spoken in secret.
21Why are you asking me this question? Ask those
who heard me. They know what I said."

22Then one of the Temple guards standing nearby
slapped Jesus across the face. "Is that the way to answer the high priest?" he demanded.

23Jesus replied, "If I said anything wrong, you must
prove it. But if I'm speaking the truth, why are you
beating me?"

24Then Annas bound Jesus and sent him to Caiaphas, the high priest.

Jn 18:13 Greek *that year.* **Jn 18:20** Greek *Jewish people;* also in 18:38.

they wanted to complete the execution before the Sabbath and get on with the Passover celebration. This residence was a palace whose outer walls enclosed a courtyard where servants and soldiers could warm themselves around a fire.

John 18:13 Both Annas and Caiaphas had been high priests. Annas was Israel's high priest from A.D. 6–15, when he was deposed by Roman rulers. Caiaphas, Annas's son-in-law, was appointed high priest from A.D. 18–36/37. According to Jewish law, the office of high priest was held for life. Many Jews, therefore, still considered Annas the high priest and still called him by that title. But although Annas retained much authority among the Jews, Caiaphas made the final decisions.

Both Caiaphas and Annas cared more about their political ambitions than about their responsibility to lead the people to God. Though religious leaders, they had become evil. As the nation's spiritual leaders, they should have been sensitive to God's revelation. They should have known that Jesus was the Messiah about whom the Scriptures spoke, and they should have pointed the people to him. But when deceitful men and women pursue evil, they want to eliminate all opposition. Instead of honestly evaluating Jesus' claims based on their knowledge of Scripture, these religious leaders sought to further their own selfish ambitions and were even willing to kill God's Son, if that's what it took.

John 18:15-16 The other disciple probably is John, the author of this Gospel. He knew the high priest and identified himself to the woman at the door. Because of his connections, John got himself and Peter into the courtyard. But Peter refused to identify himself as Jesus' follower. Peter's experiences in the next few hours would change his life. For more information about Peter, see his Profile on p. 1473.

JESUS' TRIAL

Jesus' trial was actually a series of hearings, carefully controlled to accomplish the death of Jesus. The verdict was predetermined, but certain "legal" procedures were necessary. A lot of effort went into condemning and crucifying an innocent man. Jesus went through an unfair trial in our place so that we would not have to face a fair trial and receive the well-deserved punishment for our sins.

Event	Probable Reasons	References
Trial before Annas (powerful ex-high priest)	Although no longer the high priest, he may have still wielded much power	John 18:13-23
Trial before Caiaphas (the ruling high priest)	To gather evidence for the full high council hearing to follow	Matt 26:57-68 Mark 14:53-65 Luke 22:54, 63-65 John 18:24
Trial before the high council (Sanhedrin)	Formal religious trial and condemnation to death	Matt 27:1 Mark 15:1 Luke 22:66-71
Trial before Pilate (highest Roman authority)	All death sentences needed Roman approval	Matt 27:2, 11-14 Mark 15:1-5 Luke 23:1-6 John 18:28-38
Trial before Herod (ruler of Galilee)	A courteous and guilt-sharing act by Pilate because Jesus was from Galilee, Herod's district	Luke 23:7-12
Trial before Pilate	Pilate's last effort to avoid condemning an obviously innocent man	Matt 27:15-26 Mark 15:6-15 Luke 23:13-25 John 18:39–19:16

John 18:19ff During the night, Jesus had a pretrial hearing before Annas before being taken to Caiaphas and the entire high council (Mark 14:53-65). The religious leaders knew they had no grounds for charging Jesus, so they tried to build evidence against him by using false witnesses (Mark 14:55-59).

Caiaphas Questions Jesus PARALLEL

MATTHEW 26:57-68

Then the people who had arrested Jesus led him to the home of Caiaphas, the high priest, where the teachers of religious law and the elders had gathered. 58 Meanwhile, Peter followed him at a distance and came to the high priest's courtyard. He went in and sat with the guards and waited to see how it would all end.

59 Inside, the leading priests and the entire high council* were trying to find witnesses who would lie about Jesus, so they could put him to death. 60 But even though they found many who agreed to give false witness, they could not use anyone's testimony. Finally, two men came forward 61 who declared, "This man said, 'I am able to destroy the Temple of God and rebuild it in three days.'"

62 Then the high priest stood up and said to Jesus, "Well, aren't you going to answer these charges? What do you have to say for yourself?" 63 But Jesus remained silent. Then the high priest said to him, "I demand in the name of the living God—tell us if you are the Messiah, the Son of God."

64 Jesus replied, "You have said it. And in the future you will see the Son of Man seated in the place of power at God's right hand* and coming on the clouds of heaven."*

65 Then the high priest tore his clothing to show his horror and said, "Blasphemy! Why do we need other witnesses? You have all heard his blasphemy. 66 What is your verdict?"

"Guilty!" they shouted. "He deserves to die!"

67 Then they began to spit in Jesus' face and beat him with their fists. And some slapped him, 68 jeering, "Prophesy to us, you Messiah! Who hit you that time?"

MARK 14:53-65

They took Jesus to the high priest's home where the leading priests, the elders, and the teachers of religious law had gathered. 54 Meanwhile, Peter followed him at a distance and went right into the high priest's courtyard. There he sat with the guards, warming himself by the fire.

55 Inside, the leading priests and the entire high council* were trying to find evidence against Jesus, so they could put him to death. But they couldn't find any. 56 Many false witnesses spoke against him, but they contradicted each other. 57 Finally, some men stood up and gave this false testimony: 58 "We heard him say, 'I will destroy this Temple made with human hands, and in three days I will build another, made without human hands.'" 59 But even then they didn't get their stories straight!

Mt 26:59 Greek *the Sanhedrin.* **Mt 26:64a** Greek *seated at the right hand of the power.* See Ps 110:1. **Mt 26:64b** See Dan 7:13. **Mk 14:55** Greek *the Sanhedrin.*

Matt 26:57 Because of their haste to complete the trial and see Jesus die before the Sabbath, less than 24 hours away, the religious leaders met in Caiaphas's home at night instead of waiting for daylight and meeting in the Temple.

Matt 26:59 The high council was the most powerful religious and political body of the Jewish people. Although the Romans controlled Israel's government, they gave the people power to handle religious disputes and some civil disputes, so the high council made many of the local decisions affecting daily life. But a death sentence had to be approved by the Romans (John 18:31).

Matt 26:60-61 The high council tried to find witnesses who would distort some of Jesus' teachings. Finally, they found two witnesses who distorted Jesus' words about the Temple (see John 2:19). They claimed that Jesus had said he could destroy the Temple—a blasphemous boast. Actually Jesus had said, "Destroy this temple, and in three days I will raise it up" (John 2:19). Jesus, of course, had been talking about his body, not the building. Ironically, the religious leaders were about to destroy Jesus' body just as he had said, and three days later he would rise from the dead.

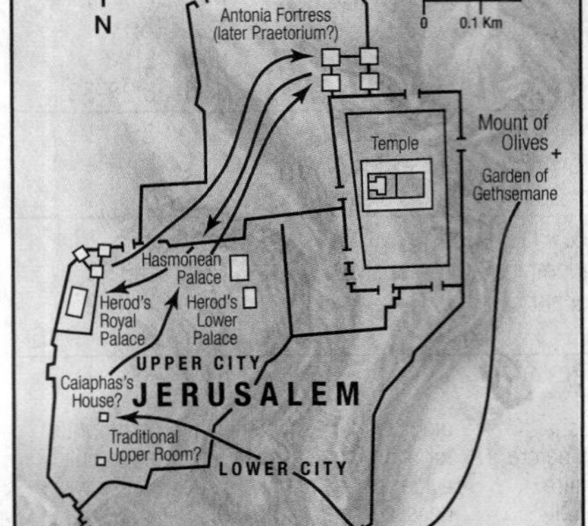

◀ ***JESUS' TRIAL***
After Judas singled Jesus out for arrest, the mob took Jesus first to Caiaphas, the high priest. This trial, a mockery of justice, ended at daybreak with their decision to kill him; but the Jews needed Rome's permission for the death sentence. Jesus was taken to Pilate (who was probably in the Praetorium), then to Herod (Luke 23:5-12), and back to Pilate, who sentenced him to die.

Matt 26:64 Jesus declared his royalty in no uncertain terms. In calling himself the Son of Man, Jesus was claiming to be the Messiah, as his listeners well knew. He knew this declaration would be his undoing, but he did not panic. He was calm, courageous, and determined.

Matt 26:65-66 The high priest accused Jesus of blasphemy—calling himself God. To the Jews, this was a great crime, punishable by death (Lev 24:16). The religious leaders refused even to consider that Jesus' words might be true. They had decided to kill Jesus, and in so doing, they sealed their own fate as well as his. Like the members of the high council, you must decide whether Jesus' words are blasphemy or truth. Your decision has eternal implications.

Mark 14:53ff This trial by the high council had two phases. A small group met at night (John 18:12-24), and then the full high council met at daybreak (Luke 22:66-71). They tried Jesus for religious offenses, such as calling himself the Son of God, which, according to law, was blasphemy. The trial was fixed: These religious leaders had already decided to kill Jesus (Luke 22:2).

Mark 14:55 The Romans controlled Israel, but the Jews were given some authority over religious and minor civil disputes. The Jewish ruling body, the high council, was

60Then the high priest stood up before the others
and asked Jesus, "Well, aren't you going to answer
these charges? What do you have to say for yourself?"
61But Jesus was silent and made no reply. Then the
high priest asked him, "Are you the Messiah, the Son
of the Blessed One?"
62Jesus said, "I AM.* And you will see the Son of Man
seated in the place of power at God's right hand* and
coming on the clouds of heaven.*"
63Then the high priest tore his clothing to show his
horror and said, "Why do we need other witnesses?
64You have all heard his blasphemy. What is your
verdict?"
"Guilty!" they all cried. "He deserves to die!"
65Then some of them began to spit at him, and
they blindfolded him and beat him with their fists.
"Prophesy to us," they jeered. And the guards slapped
him as they took him away.

LUKE 22:54a, 63-65
So they arrested him and led him to the high priest's
home. . . .
63The guards in charge of Jesus began mocking
and beating him. 64They blindfolded him and said,
"Prophesy to us! Who hit you that time?" 65And they
hurled all sorts of terrible insults at him.

Peter Denies Knowing Jesus

PARALLEL

MATTHEW 26:69-75
Meanwhile, Peter was sitting outside in the courtyard.
A servant girl came over and said to him, "You were
one of those with Jesus the Galilean."

Mk 14:62a Or *The 'I AM' is here;* or *I am the LORD.* See Exod 3:14. **Mk 14:62b** Greek *at the right hand of the power.* See Ps 110:1. **Mk 14:62c** See Dan 7:13.

PETER

Jesus' first words to Simon Peter were "Come, follow me" (Mark 1:17). His last words to him were "Follow me" (John 21:22). Every step of the way between those two challenges, Peter never failed to follow—even though he often stumbled. • When Jesus entered Peter's life, this plain fisherman became a new person with new goals and new priorities. He did not become a perfect person, however, and he never stopped being Simon Peter. We may wonder what Jesus saw in Simon that made him greet this potential disciple with a new name: Peter—the "rock." Impulsive Peter certainly didn't act like a rock much of the time. But when Jesus chose his followers, he wasn't looking for models; he was looking for real people. He chose people who could be changed by his love, and then he sent them out to communicate that his acceptance was available to anyone—even to those who often fail. • We may wonder what Jesus sees in us when he calls us to follow him. But we know Jesus accepted Peter, and in spite of his failures, Peter went on to do great things for God. Are you willing to keep following Jesus even when you fail?

Strengths and accomplishments	• Became the recognized leader among Jesus' disciples—one of the inner group of three • Was the first great voice of the gospel during and after Pentecost • Probably knew Mark and gave him information for the Gospel of Mark • Wrote 1 and 2 Peter
Weaknesses and mistakes	• Often spoke without thinking; was brash and impulsive • During Jesus' trial, denied three times that he even knew Jesus • Later found it hard to treat Gentile Christians as equals
Lessons from his life	• Enthusiasm has to be backed up by faith and understanding, or it fails • God's faithfulness can compensate for our greatest unfaithfulness • It is better to be a follower who sometimes fails than one who fails to follow
Vital statistics	• Occupations: Fisherman, disciple • Relatives: Father: John. Brother: Andrew. • Contemporaries: Jesus, Pilate, Herod
Key verse	"Now I say to you that you are Peter (which means 'rock'), and upon this rock I will build my church, and all the powers of hell will not conquer it" (Matt 16:18).

Peter's story is told in the Gospels and the book of Acts. He is mentioned in Galatians 1:18 and 2:7-14; and he wrote the books of 1 and 2 Peter.

made up of 71 of Israel's religious leaders. It was assumed that these men would be just. Instead, they showed great injustice in the trial of Jesus, even to the point of making up lies to use against him (Mark 14:57).

Mark 14:60-64 To the first question, Jesus made no reply because it was based on confusing and erroneous evidence. Not answering was wiser than trying to clarify the fabricated accusations. But if Jesus had refused to answer the second question, it could have been taken as a denial of his mission. Instead, his answer predicted a powerful role reversal. Sitting at God's right hand in the place of power, he would come to judge his accusers, and they would have to answer his questions (Ps 110:1; Rev 20:11-13).

Matt 26:69ff There were three stages to Peter's denial. First, he acted confused and tried to divert attention from himself by changing the subject. Second, using an oath he denied that he knew Jesus. Third, he swore that he did not know Jesus. Believers who deny Christ often begin doing so subtly by pretending not to know him. When opportunities to discuss religious issues come up, they walk away or pretend they don't know the answers. With only a little more pressure, they can be induced to flatly deny their relationship with Christ. If you find yourself subtly diverting conversation so you don't have to talk about Christ, watch out. You may be on the road to denying him.

▸ **MATTHEW 26:69-75 *(cont.)***

70But Peter denied it in front of everyone. "I don't know what you're talking about," he said.

71Later, out by the gate, another servant girl noticed him and said to those standing around, "This man was with Jesus of Nazareth.*"

72Again Peter denied it, this time with an oath. "I don't even know the man," he said.

73A little later some of the other bystanders came over to Peter and said, "You must be one of them; we can tell by your Galilean accent."

74Peter swore, "A curse on me if I'm lying—I don't know the man!" And immediately the rooster crowed.

75Suddenly, Jesus' words flashed through Peter's mind: "Before the rooster crows, you will deny three times that you even know me." And he went away, weeping bitterly.

MARK 14:66-72

Meanwhile, Peter was in the courtyard below. One of the servant girls who worked for the high priest came
by 67and noticed Peter warming himself at the fire. She looked at him closely and said, "You were one of those with Jesus of Nazareth.*"

68But Peter denied it. "I don't know what you're talking about," he said, and he went out into the entryway. Just then, a rooster crowed.*

69When the servant girl saw him standing there, she began telling the others, "This man is definitely one
of them!" 70But Peter denied it again.

A little later some of the other bystanders confronted Peter and said, "You must be one of them, because you are a Galilean."

71Peter swore, "A curse on me if I'm lying—I don't know this man you're talking about!" 72And immediately the rooster crowed the second time.

Suddenly, Jesus' words flashed through Peter's mind: "Before the rooster crows twice, you will deny three times that you even know me." And he broke down and wept.

LUKE 22:54b-62

And Peter followed at a distance. 55The guards lit a fire in the middle of the courtyard and sat around it, and Peter joined them there. 56A servant girl noticed him in the firelight and began staring at him. Finally she said, "This man was one of Jesus' followers!"

57But Peter denied it. "Woman," he said, "I don't even know him!"

58After a while someone else looked at him and said, "You must be one of them!"

"No, man, I'm not!" Peter retorted.

59About an hour later someone else insisted, "This must be one of them, because he is a Galilean, too."

60But Peter said, "Man, I don't know what you are talking about." And immediately, while he was still speaking, the rooster crowed.

61At that moment the Lord turned and looked at Peter. Suddenly, the Lord's words flashed through Peter's mind: "Before the rooster crows tomorrow morning, you will deny three times that you even know me."
62And Peter left the courtyard, weeping bitterly.

JOHN 18:25-27

Meanwhile, as Simon Peter was standing by the fire warming himself, they asked him again, "You're not one of his disciples, are you?"

He denied it, saying, "No, I am not."

26But one of the household slaves of the high priest,

Mt 26:71 Or *Jesus the Nazarene.* **Mk 14:67** Or *Jesus the Nazarene.* **Mk 14:68** Some manuscripts do not include *Just then, a rooster crowed.*

Matt 26:72-74 That Peter denied that he knew Jesus, using an oath and swearing, does not mean he used foul language. This was the kind of swearing that a person does in a court of law. Peter was swearing that he did not know Jesus and was invoking a curse on himself if his words were untrue. In effect he was saying, "May God strike me dead if I am lying."

Mark 14:66-67 Caiaphas's home, where Jesus was tried (Mark 14:53), was part of a huge palace with several courtyards. John was apparently acquainted with the high priest, and he was let into the courtyard along with Peter (John 18:15-16).

Mark 14:71 It is easy to get angry at the high council and the Roman governor for their injustice in condemning Jesus, but Peter and the rest of the disciples also contributed to Jesus' pain by deserting him (Mark 14:50). While most of us may not be like the Jewish and Roman leaders, we are like the disciples because all of us have been guilty of denying Christ as Lord in vital areas of our lives. We may pride ourselves that we have not committed certain sins, but we are all guilty of sin. Don't try to excuse yourself by pointing at others whose sins seem worse than yours.

Luke 22:55 Peter's experiences in the next few hours would change his life. He would change from a halfhearted follower to a repentant disciple, and finally to the kind of person Christ could use to build his church. For more information on Peter, see his Profile on p. 1473.

Luke 22:62 Peter wept bitterly, not only because he realized that he had denied his Lord, the Messiah, but also because he had turned away from a very dear friend, a person who had loved and taught him for three years. Peter had said that he would never deny Christ, despite Jesus' prediction (Mark 14:29-31; Luke 22:33-34). But when frightened, he went against all he had boldly promised. Unable to stand up for his Lord for even 12 hours, he had failed as a disciple and as a friend. We need to be aware of our own breaking points and not become overconfident or self-sufficient. If we fail him, we must remember that Christ can use those who recognize their failure. From this humiliating experience Peter learned much that would help him later when he assumed leadership of the young church.

John 18:25 The other three Gospels say that Peter's three denials happened near a fire in the courtyard outside Caiaphas's palace. John places the first denial outside Annas's home and the other two denials outside Caiaphas's home. This was very likely the same courtyard. The high priest's compound was large, and Annas and Caiaphas undoubtedly lived near each other.

John 18:25-27 Imagine standing outside while Jesus, your Lord and Master, is questioned. Imagine watching this man, whom you have come to believe is the long-awaited Messiah, being abused and beaten. Naturally Peter was confused and afraid. It is a serious sin to deny Christ, but Jesus forgave Peter (John 21:15-17). No sin is too great for Jesus to forgive if you are truly repentant. He will forgive even your worst sin if you turn from it and ask his pardon.

John 18:27 This fulfilled Jesus' words to Peter after Peter promised he would never deny him (Mark 14:31; John 13:38).

a relative of the man whose ear Peter had cut off, asked, "Didn't I see you out there in the olive grove with Jesus?" [27]Again Peter denied it. And immediately a rooster crowed.

The Council of Religious Leaders Condemns Jesus PARALLEL

MATTHEW 27:1-2

Very early in the morning the leading priests and the elders of the people met again to lay plans for putting Jesus to death. [2]Then they bound him, led him away, and took him to Pilate, the Roman governor.

MARK 15:1

Very early in the morning the leading priests, the elders, and the teachers of religious law—the entire high council*—met to discuss their next step. They bound Jesus, led him away, and took him to Pilate, the Roman governor.

LUKE 22:66-71

At daybreak all the elders of the people assembled, including the leading priests and the teachers of religious law. Jesus was led before this high council,* [67]and they said, "Tell us, are you the Messiah?"

But he replied, "If I tell you, you won't believe me. [68]And if I ask you a question, you won't answer. [69]But from now on the Son of Man will be seated in the place of power at God's right hand.*"

[70]They all shouted, "So, are you claiming to be the Son of God?"

And he replied, "You say that I am."

[71]"Why do we need other witnesses?" they said. "We ourselves heard him say it."

Judas Hangs Himself

MATTHEW 27:3-10

When Judas, who had betrayed him, realized that Jesus had been condemned to die, he was filled with remorse. So he took the thirty pieces of silver back to the leading priests and the elders. [4]"I have sinned," he declared, "for I have betrayed an innocent man."

"What do we care?" they retorted. "That's your problem."

Mk 15:1 Greek *the Sanhedrin;* also in 15:43. **Lk 22:66** Greek *before their Sanhedrin.* **Lk 22:69** See Ps 110:1.

HOW JESUS' TRIAL WAS ILLEGAL

The religious leaders were not interested in giving Jesus a fair trial. In their minds, Jesus had to die. This blind obsession led them to pervert the justice they were appointed to protect. These are some examples of the actions taken by the religious leaders that were illegal according to their own laws.

1. Even before the trial began, it had been determined that Jesus must die (Mark 14:1; John 11:50). There was no "innocent until proven guilty" approach.
2. False witnesses were sought to testify against Jesus (Matt 26:59). Usually the religious leaders went through an elaborate system of screening witnesses to ensure justice.
3. No defense for Jesus was sought or allowed (Luke 22:67-71).
4. The trial was conducted at night (Mark 14:53-65; 15:1), which was illegal according to the religious leaders' own laws.
5. The high priest put Jesus under oath, but then incriminated him for what he said (Matt 26:63-66).
6. Cases involving such serious charges were to be tried only in the high council's regular meeting place, not in the high priest's home (Mark 14:53-65).

Matt 27:1-2 The Jewish leaders had arrested Jesus on theological grounds—blasphemy. Because this charge would be thrown out of a Roman court, however, they had to come up with a political reason for Jesus' death. Their strategy was to show Jesus as a rebel who claimed to be a king and thus a threat to Caesar.

Matt 27:2 Pilate was the Roman governor for the regions of Samaria and Judea from A.D. 26 to 36. Jerusalem was located in Judea. Pilate took special pleasure in demonstrating his authority over the Jews; for example, he impounded money from the Temple treasuries to build an aqueduct. Pilate was not popular, but the religious leaders had no other way to get rid of Jesus than to go to him. Ironically, when Jesus, a Jew, came before him for trial, Pilate found him innocent. He could not find a single fault in Jesus, nor could he contrive one.

Mark 15:1 Why did the Jewish leaders send Jesus to Pilate, the Roman governor? The Romans had taken away the Jews' right to inflict capital punishment; so in order for Jesus to be condemned to death, he had to be sentenced by a Roman leader. The Jewish leaders wanted Jesus executed on a cross, a method of death that they believed brought a curse from God (see Deut 21:23). They hoped to persuade the people that Jesus was cursed, not blessed, by God.

Luke 22:70 Jesus in effect agreed that he was the Son of God when he simply turned the high priest's question around by saying, "You say that I am." And Jesus identified himself with God by using a familiar title for God found in the Old Testament: "I AM" (Exod 3:14). The high priest recognized Jesus' claim and could now accuse him of blasphemy. For any other human this claim would have been blasphemy, but in this case, Jesus spoke the truth. Blasphemy, the sin of claiming to be God or of attacking God's authority and majesty in any way, was punishable by death. The Jewish leaders had the evidence they wanted.

Matt 27:3-4 Jesus' formal accuser wanted to drop his charges, but the religious leaders refused to halt the trial. When he betrayed Jesus, perhaps Judas was trying to force Jesus' hand to get him to lead a revolt against Rome. This did not work, of course. Whatever his reason, Judas changed his mind, but it was too late. Many of the plans we set into motion cannot be reversed. It is best to think of the potential consequences before we launch into an action we may later regret.

Matt 27:4 The priests' job was to teach people about God and act as intercessors for them, helping administer the sacrifices to cover their sins. Judas returned to the priests, exclaiming that he had sinned. Rather than helping him find forgiveness, however, the priests said, "That's your problem." Not only had they rejected the Messiah, they had rejected their role as priests.

▸ **MATTHEW 27:3-10 *(cont.)***
5Then Judas threw the silver coins down in the
Temple and went out and hanged himself.
6The leading priests picked up the coins. "It wouldn't
be right to put this money in the Temple treasury," they
said, "since it was payment for murder."* 7After some
discussion they finally decided to buy the potter's field,
and they made it into a cemetery for foreigners. 8That
is why the field is still called the Field of Blood. 9This
fulfilled the prophecy of Jeremiah that says,

"They took* the thirty pieces of silver—
the price at which he was valued by the people
of Israel,
10 and purchased the potter's field,
as the LORD directed.*"

Jesus Stands Trial before Pilate PARALLEL ●●●●

MATTHEW 27:11-14 ○●○○
Now Jesus was standing before Pilate, the Roman governor. "Are you the king of the Jews?" the governor
asked him.
Jesus replied, "You have said it."
12But when the leading priests and the elders made
their accusations against him, Jesus remained silent.
13"Don't you hear all these charges they are bringing
against you?" Pilate demanded. 14But Jesus made no
response to any of the charges, much to the governor's
surprise.

MARK 15:2-5 ○●●○
Pilate asked Jesus, "Are you the king of the Jews?"
Jesus replied, "You have said it."
3Then the leading priests kept accusing him of
many crimes, 4and Pilate asked him, "Aren't you going
to answer them? What about all these charges they
are bringing against you?" 5But Jesus said nothing,
much to Pilate's surprise.

LUKE 23:1-7 ○●●○
Then the entire council took Jesus to Pilate, the
Roman governor. 2They began to state their case:
"This man has been leading our people astray by
telling them not to pay their taxes to the Roman
government and by claiming he is the Messiah,
a king."
3So Pilate asked him, "Are you the king of the
Jews?"
Jesus replied, "You have said it."
4Pilate turned to the leading priests and to the
crowd and said, "I find nothing wrong with this
man!"
5Then they became insistent. "But he is causing
riots by his teaching wherever he goes—all over Judea, from Galilee to Jerusalem!"
6"Oh, is he a Galilean?" Pilate asked. 7When they
said that he was, Pilate sent him to Herod Antipas,
because Galilee was under Herod's jurisdiction,
and Herod happened to be in Jerusalem at the time.

Mt 27:6 Greek *since it is the price for blood.* **Mt 27:9** Or *I took.* **Mt 27:9-10** Greek *as the LORD directed me.* Zech 11:12-13; Jer 32:6-9.

Matt 27:5 According to Matthew, Judas hanged himself. Acts 1:18, however, says that he fell and burst open. The best explanation is that the limb from which he was hanging broke, and the resulting fall split open his body.

Matt 27:6 These leading priests felt no guilt in giving Judas money to betray an innocent man, but when Judas returned the money, the priests couldn't accept it because it was wrong to accept payment for murder! Their hatred for Jesus had caused them to lose all sense of right and wrong.

Matt 27:9-10 This prophecy is found specifically in Zechariah 11:12-13 but may also have been taken from Jeremiah 18:1-4; 19:1-11; or 32:6-15. In ancient times, Jeremiah was considered the collector of some of the prophets' writings, so perhaps his name is cited rather than Zechariah.

Matt 27:12 Standing before Pilate, the religious leaders accused Jesus of a different crime than the ones for which they had arrested him. They arrested him for blasphemy (claiming to be God), but that charge would mean nothing to the Romans. So the religious leaders had to accuse Jesus of crimes that would have concerned the Roman government, such as encouraging the people not to pay taxes, claiming to be a king, and causing riots.

Matt 27:14 Jesus' silence fulfilled the words of the prophet (Isa 53:7). Pilate was amazed that Jesus didn't try to defend himself. He recognized the obvious plot against Jesus and wanted to let him go, but Pilate was already under pressure from Rome to keep peace in his territory. The last thing he needed was a rebellion over this quiet and seemingly insignificant man.

Mark 15:3-4 The Jewish leaders had to fabricate new accusations against Jesus when they brought him before Pilate. The charge of blasphemy would mean nothing to the Roman governor, so they accused Jesus of three other crimes: encouraging the people to not pay their taxes to Rome, claiming he was a king—"the King of the Jews," and causing riots all over the countryside. Tax evasion, treason, and terrorism—all these would be cause for Pilate's concern (see also Luke 23:2). These accusations were not true, but the religious leaders were so determined to kill Jesus that they were willing to lie in order to do so.

Mark 15:5 Why didn't Jesus answer Pilate's questions? It would have been futile to answer, and the time had come to give his life to save the world. Jesus had no reason to try to prolong the trial or save himself. His was the ultimate example of self-assurance and peace, which no ordinary criminal could imitate. Nothing would stop him from completing the work he had come to earth to do (Isa 53:7).

Luke 23:1 Pilate was the Roman governor of Judea (the region where Jerusalem was located) from A.D. 26–36. He had a reputation for seeming to take special pleasure in harassing the Jews. For example, Pilate had taken money from the Temple treasury and had used it to build an aqueduct. And he had insulted the Jewish religion by bringing imperial images into the city. As Pilate well knew, such acts could backfire. If the people were to lodge a formal complaint against his administration, Rome might remove him from his post. Pilate was already beginning to feel insecure in his position when the Jewish leaders brought Jesus to trial. Would he continue to badger the Jews and risk his political future, or would he give in to their demands and condemn a man who, he was quite sure, was innocent? This was the question facing Pilate that springtime Friday morning nearly 2,000 years ago. For more about Pilate, see his Profile on p. 1479.

Luke 23:7 Herod Antipas was in Jerusalem that weekend for the Passover celebration. (This was the Herod who had killed John the Baptist.) Pilate hoped to pass Jesus off on Herod because he knew that Jesus had lived and worked in Galilee. Herod was curious about Jesus and enjoyed making fun of him, but he was not much help. Herod sent Jesus back to Pilate with the same verdict: "not

JOHN 18:28-37

Jesus' trial before Caiaphas ended in the early hours of the morning. Then he was taken to the headquarters of the Roman governor.* His accusers didn't go inside because it would defile them, and they wouldn't be allowed to celebrate the Passover. [29]So Pilate, the governor, went out to them and asked, "What is your charge against this man?"

[30]"We wouldn't have handed him over to you if he weren't a criminal!" they retorted.

[31]"Then take him away and judge him by your own law," Pilate told them.

"Only the Romans are permitted to execute someone," the Jewish leaders replied. [32](This fulfilled Jesus' prediction about the way he would die.*)

[33]Then Pilate went back into his headquarters and called for Jesus to be brought to him. "Are you the king of the Jews?" he asked him.

[34]Jesus replied, "Is this your own question, or did others tell you about me?"

[35]"Am I a Jew?" Pilate retorted. "Your own people and their leading priests brought you to me for trial. Why? What have you done?"

Jn 18:28 Greek *to the Praetorium;* also in 18:33. **Jn 18:32** See John 12:32-33.

THE SIX STAGES OF JESUS' TRIAL

Although Jesus' trial lasted less than 18 hours, he was taken to six different hearings.

Before Jewish Authorities	Preliminary hearing before Annas (John 18:12-24)	Because the office of high priest was for life, Annas was still the "official" high priest in the eyes of the Jews, even though the Romans had appointed another. Thus, Annas still carried much weight in the high council.
	Hearing before Caiaphas (Matt 26:57-68)	Like the hearing before Annas, this hearing was conducted at night in secrecy. It was full of illegalities that made a mockery of justice (see chart on p. 1475).
	Trial before the high council (Matt 27:1-2)	Just after daybreak, 70 members of the high council met to rubber-stamp their approval of the previous hearings to make them appear legal. The purpose of this trial was not to determine justice, but to justify their own preconceptions of Jesus' guilt.
Before Roman Authorities	First hearing before Pilate (Luke 23:1-5)	The religious leaders had condemned Jesus to death on religious grounds, but only the Roman government could grant the death penalty. Thus, they took Jesus to Pilate, the Roman governor, and accused him of treason and rebellion, crimes for which the Roman government gave the death penalty. Pilate saw at once that Jesus was innocent, but he was afraid about the uproar being caused by the religious leaders.
	Hearing before Herod (Luke 23:6-12)	Because Jesus' home was in the region of Galilee, Pilate sent Jesus to Herod Antipas, the ruler of Galilee, who was in Jerusalem for the Passover celebration. Herod was eager to see Jesus do a miracle, but when Jesus remained silent, Herod wanted nothing to do with him and sent him back to Pilate.
	Last hearing before Pilate (Luke 23:13-25)	Pilate didn't like the religious leaders. He wasn't interested in condemning Jesus because he knew Jesus was innocent. However, he knew that another uprising in his district might cost him his job. First he tried to compromise with the religious leaders by having Jesus beaten, an illegal action in itself. But finally he gave in and handed Jesus over to be executed. Pilate's self-interest was stronger than his sense of justice.

guilty." For more about Herod Antipas, see his Profile on p. 1362.

John 18:28 By Jewish law, entering the house of a Gentile would cause a Jewish person to be ceremonially defiled. As a result, he could not take part in worship at the Temple or celebrate the festivals until he was restored to a state of "cleanness." Afraid of being defiled, these men stayed outside the house where they had taken Jesus for trial. They kept the ceremonial requirements of their religion while harboring murder and treachery in their hearts.

John 18:30 Pilate knew what was going on; he knew that the religious leaders hated Jesus, and he did not want to act as their executioner. They could not sentence him to death themselves—permission had to come from a Roman leader. But Pilate initially refused to sentence Jesus without sufficient evidence. Jesus' life became a pawn in a political power struggle.

John 18:31ff Pilate made four attempts to deal with Jesus: (1) He tried to put the responsibility on someone else (John 18:31); (2) he tried to find a way of escape so he could release Jesus (John 18:39); (3) he tried to compromise by having Jesus flogged rather than handing him over to die (John 19:1-3); and (4) he tried a direct appeal to the sympathy of the accusers (John 19:15). Everyone has to decide what to do with Jesus. Pilate tried to let everyone else decide for him—and in the end, he lost.

John 18:32 This prediction is recorded in Matthew 20:19 and John 12:32, 35. Crucifixion was a common method of execution for criminals who were not Roman citizens.

John 18:34 If Pilate was asking this question in his role as the Roman governor, he would have been inquiring whether Jesus was setting up a rebel government. But the Jews were using the word *king* to mean their religious ruler, the Messiah. Israel was a captive nation, under the authority of the Roman Empire. A rival king might have threatened Rome; a Messiah could have been simply a religious leader.

▸ **JOHN 18:28-37 *(cont.)***
36Jesus answered, "My Kingdom is not an earthly
kingdom. If it were, my followers would fight to keep
me from being handed over to the Jewish leaders. But
my Kingdom is not of this world."
37Pilate said, "So you are a king?"
Jesus responded, "You say I am a king. Actually, I was
born and came into the world to testify to the truth. All
who love the truth recognize that what I say is true."

Jesus Stands Trial Before Herod

LUKE 23:8-12
Herod was delighted at the opportunity to see Jesus,
because he had heard about him and had been hoping
for a long time to see him perform a miracle. 9He asked
Jesus question after question, but Jesus refused to answer. 10Meanwhile, the leading priests and the teachers
of religious law stood there shouting their accusations.
11Then Herod and his soldiers began mocking and
ridiculing Jesus. Finally, they put a royal robe on him
and sent him back to Pilate. 12(Herod and Pilate, who
had been enemies before, became friends that day.)

Pilate Hands Jesus Over to Be Crucified PARALLEL ●●●●

MATTHEW 27:15-26 ●○○○
Now it was the governor's custom each year during
the Passover celebration to release one prisoner to the
crowd—anyone they wanted. 16This year there was a
notorious prisoner, a man named Barabbas.* 17As the
crowds gathered before Pilate's house that morning,
he asked them, "Which one do you want me to release
to you—Barabbas, or Jesus who is called the Messiah?"
18(He knew very well that the religious leaders had
arrested Jesus out of envy.)
19Just then, as Pilate was sitting on the judgment
seat, his wife sent him this message: "Leave that innocent man alone. I suffered through a terrible nightmare about him last night."
20Meanwhile, the leading priests and the elders persuaded the crowd to ask for Barabbas to be released
and for Jesus to be put to death. 21So the governor
asked again, "Which of these two do you want me to
release to you?"
The crowd shouted back, "Barabbas!"
22Pilate responded, "Then what should I do with
Jesus who is called the Messiah?"
They shouted back, "Crucify him!"
23"Why?" Pilate demanded. "What crime has he
committed?"
But the mob roared even louder, "Crucify him!"
24Pilate saw that he wasn't getting anywhere and
that a riot was developing. So he sent for a bowl of
water and washed his hands before the crowd, saying,
"I am innocent of this man's blood. The responsibility
is yours!"

Mt 27:16 Some manuscripts read *Jesus Barabbas;* also in 27:17.

The Earliest Manuscript of John

P52 is a small fragment containing John 18:31-34, 37-38. It is noteworthy because of its early date: ca. A.D. 100–125. It is the earliest manuscript of John's Gospel, only about 20 to 30 years removed from the original writing.

John 18:36-37 Pilate asked Jesus a straightforward question, and Jesus answered clearly. Jesus is a King, but one whose Kingdom is not of this world. There seems to have been no question in Pilate's mind that Jesus spoke the truth and was innocent of any crime. It also seems apparent that while recognizing the truth, Pilate chose to reject it. It is a tragedy when we fail to recognize the truth. It is a greater tragedy when we recognize the truth but fail to heed it.

Luke 23:12 Herod was the part-Jewish ruler of Galilee and Perea. Pilate was the Roman governor of Judea and Samaria. Those four provinces, together with several others, had been united under Herod the Great. But when Herod died in 4 B.C., the kingdom was divided among his sons. Archelaus, the son who had received Judea and Samaria, was removed from office within 10 years, and his provinces were then ruled by a succession of Roman governors, of whom Pilate was the fifth.

Herod Antipas had two advantages over Pilate: He came from a hereditary part-Jewish monarchy, and he had held his position much longer. But Pilate had two advantages over Herod: He was a Roman citizen and an envoy of the emperor, and his position was created to replace that of Herod's ineffective half brother. It is not surprising that the two men were uneasy around each other. Jesus' trial, however, brought them together. Because Pilate recognized Herod's authority over Galilee, he stopped feeling threatened by the Roman politician. And because neither man knew what to do in this predicament, their common problem united them.

Matt 27:19 For a leader who was supposed to administer justice, Pilate proved to be more concerned about political expediency than about doing what was right. He had several opportunities to make the right decision. His conscience told him Jesus was innocent; Roman law said an innocent man should not be put to death; and his wife had a nightmare that caused her to encourage her husband to let Jesus go. Pilate had no good excuse to condemn Jesus, but he was afraid of the crowd.

Matt 27:21 Crowds are fickle. They loved Jesus on Sunday because they thought he was going to inaugurate his Kingdom. Then they hated him on Friday when his power appeared broken. In the face of the mass uprising against Jesus, his friends were afraid to speak up.

Matt 27:24 At first Pilate hesitated to give the religious leaders permission to crucify Jesus. He perceived that they were simply jealous of a teacher who was more popular with the people than they were. But when the Jews threatened to report Pilate to Caesar (John 19:12), Pilate became afraid. Historical records indicate that the Jews had already threatened to lodge a formal complaint against Pilate for his stubborn flouting of their traditions—and such a complaint would most likely have led to his recall by Rome. His job was in jeopardy. The Roman government could not afford to put large numbers of

25And all the people yelled back, "We will take responsibility for his death—we and our children!"*
26So Pilate released Barabbas to them. He ordered
Jesus flogged with a lead-tipped whip, then turned
him over to the Roman soldiers to be crucified.

MARK 15:6-15

Now it was the governor's custom each year during the Passover celebration to release one prisoner—anyone the people requested.
7One of the prisoners
at that time was Barabbas, a revolutionary who had committed murder in an uprising.
8The crowd went
to Pilate and asked him to release a prisoner as usual.
9"Would you like me to release to you this 'King of the Jews'?" Pilate asked.
10(For he realized by now
that the leading priests had arrested Jesus out of envy.)
11But at this point the leading priests stirred up
the crowd to demand the release of Barabbas instead of Jesus.
12Pilate asked them, "Then what should I do
with this man you call the king of the Jews?"
13They shouted back, "Crucify him!"
14"Why?" Pilate demanded. "What crime has he
committed?"

But the mob roared even louder, "Crucify him!"
15So to pacify the crowd, Pilate released Barabbas
to them. He ordered Jesus flogged with a lead-tipped whip, then turned him over to the Roman soldiers to be crucified.

Mt 27:25 Greek *"His blood be on us and on our children."*

PILATE

In Jesus' day, any death sentence had to be approved by the Roman official in charge of the administrative district. Pontius Pilate was governor of the province of Judea, where Jerusalem was located. When the Jewish leaders had Jesus in their power and wanted to kill him, they had to obtain Pilate's permission. So it happened that early one morning Pilate found a crowd at his door demanding a man's death. • Pilate's relationship with the Jews had always been stormy. His Roman toughness and fairness had been weakened by cynicism, compromises, and mistakes. On several occasions his actions had deeply offended the religious leaders. The resulting riots and chaos must have made Pilate wonder what he had gotten himself into. He was trying to control people who treated their Roman conquerors without respect. Jesus' trial was another episode in Pilate's ongoing problems. • For Pilate, there was never a doubt about Jesus' innocence. Three separate times he declared Jesus not guilty. He couldn't understand why these people wanted to kill Jesus, but his fear of the Jews' political pressure made him decide to allow Jesus' crucifixion. Because of the people's threat to inform the emperor that Pilate hadn't eliminated a rebel against Rome, Pilate went against what he knew was right. In desperation, he chose to do wrong. • We share a common humanity with Pilate. At times we know what is right but choose what is wrong. He had his moment in history, and now we have ours. What have we done with our opportunities and responsibilities? What judgment have we passed on Jesus?

Strength and accomplishment	• Roman governor of Judea
Weaknesses and mistakes	• His constant political struggles made him a cynical and uncaring compromiser, susceptible to pressure • Although he realized Jesus was innocent, he bowed to the public demand for his execution
Lessons from his life	• Great evil can happen when truth is at the mercy of political pressures • Resisting the truth leaves a person without purpose or direction
Vital statistics	• Where: Judea • Occupation: Roman governor of Judea • Contemporaries: Jesus, Caiaphas, Herod
Key verses	"'What is truth?' Pilate asked. Then he went out again to the people and told them, 'He is not guilty of any crime. But you have a custom of asking me to release one prisoner each year at Passover. Would you like me to release this "King of the Jews"?'" (John 18:38-39).

Pilate's story is told in the Gospels. He is also mentioned in Acts 3:13; 4:27; 13:28; 1 Timothy 6:13.

troops in all the regions under their control, so one of Pilate's main duties was to do whatever was necessary to maintain peace.

Matt 27:24 In making no decision, Pilate made the decision to let the crowds crucify Jesus. Although he washed his hands, the guilt remained. Washing your hands of a tough situation doesn't cancel your guilt. It merely gives you a false sense of peace. Don't make excuses—take responsibility for the decisions you make.

Mark 15:7 Barabbas was arrested for his part in a rebellion against the Roman government, and although he had committed a murder, he may have been a hero among the Jews. The fiercely independent Jews hated to be ruled by pagan Romans. They hated paying taxes to support the despised government and its gods. Most of the Roman authorities who had to settle Jewish disputes hated the Jews in return. The time was ripe for rebellion.

Mark 15:10 The Jewish leaders hated Pilate, but they went to him for the favor of condemning Jesus to crucifixion. Pilate could see that this was a frame-up. Why else would these people, who hated him and the Roman Empire he represented, ask him to convict one of their fellow Jews of treason and give him the death penalty?

Mark 15:13 Crucifixion was the Roman penalty for rebellion. Only slaves or those who were not Roman citizens could be crucified. If Jesus died by crucifixion, he would die the death of a rebel and slave, not of the king he claimed to be. This is just what the Jewish religious leaders wanted and the reason they whipped the mob into a frenzy. In addition, crucifixion would put the responsibility for killing Jesus on the Romans.

Luke 23:13-25 Pilate wanted to release Jesus, but the crowd loudly demanded his death; so Pilate sentenced Jesus to die. No doubt Pilate did not want to risk losing his position, which may already have been shaky, by allowing a riot to occur in his province. As a career politician, he knew the importance of compromise, and he saw Jesus more as a political threat than as a human being with rights and dignity.

When the stakes are high, it is difficult to

LUKE 23:13-25
Then Pilate called together the leading priests and
other religious leaders, along with the people, 14and he
announced his verdict. "You brought this man to me,
accusing him of leading a revolt. I have examined him
thoroughly on this point in your presence and find
him innocent. 15Herod came to the same conclusion
and sent him back to us. Nothing this man has done
calls for the death penalty. 16So I will have him flogged,
and then I will release him."*

18Then a mighty roar rose from the crowd, and with
one voice they shouted, "Kill him, and release Barabbas to us!" 19(Barabbas was in prison for taking part in
an insurrection in Jerusalem against the government,
and for murder.) 20Pilate argued with them, because
he wanted to release Jesus. 21But they kept shouting,
"Crucify him! Crucify him!"

22For the third time he demanded, "Why? What
crime has he committed? I have found no reason to
sentence him to death. So I will have him flogged, and
then I will release him."

23But the mob shouted louder and louder, demanding that Jesus be crucified, and their voices prevailed.
24So Pilate sentenced Jesus to die as they demanded.
25As they had requested, he released Barabbas, the man
in prison for insurrection and murder. But he turned
Jesus over to them to do as they wished.

JOHN 18:38–19:16
"What is truth?" Pilate asked. Then he went out again
to the people and told them, "He is not guilty of any
crime. 39But you have a custom of asking me to release
one prisoner each year at Passover. Would you like me
to release this 'King of the Jews'?"

40But they shouted back, "No! Not this man. We
want Barabbas!" (Barabbas was a revolutionary.)

19:1 Then Pilate had Jesus flogged with a lead-tipped
whip. 2The soldiers wove a crown of thorns and put it
on his head, and they put a purple robe on him. 3"Hail!
King of the Jews!" they mocked, as they slapped him
across the face.

4Pilate went outside again and said to the people, "I
am going to bring him out to you now, but understand
clearly that I find him not guilty." 5Then Jesus came
out wearing the crown of thorns and the purple robe.
And Pilate said, "Look, here is the man!"

Lk 23:16 Some manuscripts add verse 17, *Now it was necessary for him to release one prisoner to them during the Passover celebration.* Compare Matt 27:15; Mark 15:6; John 18:39.

---

stand up for what is right, and it is easy to see our opponents as problems to be solved rather than as people to be respected. Had Pilate been a man of real courage, he would have released Jesus no matter what the consequences. But the crowd roared, and Pilate buckled. We are like Pilate when we know what is right but decide not to do it. When you have a difficult decision to make, don't discount the effects of peer pressure. Realize beforehand that the right decision could have unpleasant consequences: social rejection, career derailment, public ridicule. Then think of Pilate and resolve to stand up for what is right no matter what other people pressure you to do.

Luke 23:15 Jesus was tried six times by both Jewish and Roman authorities, but he was never convicted of a crime deserving death. Today, no one can find fault in Jesus. But just like Pilate, Herod, and the religious leaders, many still refuse to acknowledge him as Lord.

Luke 23:18-19 Barabbas had been part of a rebellion against the Roman government (Mark 15:7). As a political insurgent, he was no doubt a hero among some of the Jews. How ironic it is that Barabbas, who was released, was guilty of the very crime Jesus was accused of (Luke 23:14).

Luke 23:18-19 Who was Barabbas? Jewish men had names that identified them with their fathers. Simon Peter, for example, is called Simon son of John (Matt 16:17). Barabbas is never identified by his given name, and this name is not much help either—*bar-abbas* means "son of Abba" (or "son of daddy"). He could have been anybody's son—and that's just the point. Barabbas, son of an unnamed father, committed a crime. Because Jesus died in his place, this man was set free. We, too, are sinners and criminals who have broken God's holy law. Like Barabbas, we deserve to die. But Jesus has died in our place, for our sins, and we have been set free. We don't have to be very important people to accept our freedom in Christ. In fact, thanks to Jesus, God adopts us all as his own sons and daughters and gives us the right to call him our dear Father (see Gal 4:4-6).

Luke 23:22 When Pilate said he would have Jesus flogged, he was referring to a punishment that could have killed Jesus. The usual procedure was to bare the upper half of the victim's body and tie his hands to a pillar before whipping him with a three-pronged whip. The number of lashes was determined by the severity of the crime; up to 40 were permitted under Jewish law. After being flogged, Jesus also endured other agonies as recorded in Matthew and Mark. He was slapped, struck with fists, and mocked. A crown of thorns was placed on his head, and he was beaten with a stick and stripped before being hung on the cross.

Luke 23:23-24 Pilate did not want to give Jesus the death sentence. He thought the Jewish leaders were simply jealous men who wanted to get rid of a rival. But the last thing he needed was a riot in Jerusalem at Passover time, when the city was crowded with Jews from all over the empire. So Pilate turned Jesus over to the mob to do with as they pleased.

John 18:38 Pilate was cynical; he thought that all truth was relative. To many government officials, truth was whatever the majority of people agreed with or whatever helped advance their own personal power and political goals. When there is no standard or acknowledgement of truth, there is no basis for moral right and wrong. Justice becomes whatever works or whatever helps those in power. In Jesus and his Word, we have a standard for truth and for our moral behavior.

John 18:40 Barabbas was a rebel against Rome, and although he had committed murder, he was probably a hero among the Jews. The Jews hated being governed by Rome and paying taxes to the despised government. Barabbas, who had led a rebellion and failed, was released instead of Jesus, the only one who could truly help Israel.

John 19:1ff To grasp the full picture of Jesus' crucifixion, read the accounts from all four Gospel writers together. Each writer adds meaningful details, but each has the same message—Jesus died on the cross, in fulfillment of Old Testament prophecy, so that we could be saved from our sins and be given eternal life.

John 19:2-5 The soldiers went beyond their orders to whip Jesus—they also mocked his claim to royalty by placing a crown on his head and a royal robe on his shoulders.

John 19:7 The truth finally came out—the religious leaders had not brought Jesus to Pilate because he was causing rebellion against Rome, but because they thought he had broken their religious laws. Blasphemy, one of the most serious crimes in Jewish law, deserved the death penalty. Accusing Jesus of blasphemy would give credibility to their case in the eyes of Jews; accusing Jesus of

6When they saw him, the leading priests and
Temple guards began shouting, "Crucify him! Crucify him!"
"Take him yourselves and crucify him," Pilate said.
"I find him not guilty."
7The Jewish leaders replied, "By our law he ought
to die because he called himself the Son of God."
8When Pilate heard this, he was more frightened
than ever. 9He took Jesus back into the headquarters*
again and asked him, "Where are you from?" But
Jesus gave no answer. 10"Why don't you talk to me?"
Pilate demanded. "Don't you realize that I have the
power to release you or crucify you?"
11Then Jesus said, "You would have no power over
me at all unless it were given to you from above.
So the one who handed me over to you has the
greater sin."
12Then Pilate tried to release him, but the Jewish
leaders shouted, "If you release this man, you are no
'friend of Caesar.'* Anyone who declares himself a
king is a rebel against Caesar."
13When they said this, Pilate brought Jesus out to
them again. Then Pilate sat down on the judgment seat
on the platform that is called the Stone Pavement (in
Hebrew, *Gabbatha*). 14It was now about noon on the
day of preparation for the Passover. And Pilate said to
the people,* "Look, here is your king!"
15"Away with him," they yelled. "Away with him!
Crucify him!"
"What? Crucify your king?" Pilate asked.
"We have no king but Caesar," the leading priests
shouted back.
16Then Pilate turned Jesus over to them to be crucified.
So they took Jesus away.

Roman Soldiers Mock Jesus PARALLEL

MATTHEW 27:27-31

Some of the governor's soldiers took Jesus into their
headquarters* and called out the entire regiment.
28They stripped him and put a scarlet robe on him.
29They wove thorn branches into a crown and put
it on his head, and they placed a reed stick in his
right hand as a scepter. Then they knelt before him in
mockery and taunted, "Hail! King of the Jews!" 30And
they spit on him and grabbed the stick and struck him
on the head with it. 31When they were finally tired
of mocking him, they took off the robe and put his
own clothes on him again. Then they led him away
to be crucified.

Jn 19:9 Greek *the Praetorium.* **Jn 19:12** "Friend of Caesar" is a technical term that refers to an ally of the emperor. **Jn 19:14** Greek *Jewish people;* also in 19:20.
Mt 27:27 Or *into the Praetorium.*

treason would give credibility to their case in the eyes of the Romans. They didn't care which accusation Pilate listened to as long as he would cooperate with them in killing Jesus.

John 19:10 Throughout the trial we see that Jesus was in control, not Pilate or the religious leaders. Pilate vacillated, the Jewish leaders reacted out of hatred and anger, but Jesus remained composed. He knew the truth, he knew God's plan, and he knew the reason for his trial. Despite the pressure and persecution, Jesus remained unmoved. It was really Pilate and the religious leaders who were on trial, not Jesus. When you are questioned or ridiculed because of your faith, remember that while you may be on trial before your accusers, they are on trial before God.

John 19:11 When Jesus said the man who delivered him to Pilate was guiltier than Pilate, he was not excusing Pilate for reacting to the political pressure placed on him. Pilate was responsible for his decision about Jesus. Caiaphas and the other religious leaders were guilty of a greater sin because they premeditated Jesus' murder.

John 19:13 The Stone Pavement was part of the Tower of Antonia bordering the northwest corner of the Temple complex.

John 19:15 The Jewish leaders were so desperate to get rid of Jesus that, despite their intense hatred for Rome, they shouted, "We have no king but Caesar." How ironic that they feigned allegiance to Rome while rejecting their own Messiah! Their own words condemned them; God was to be their only true King, and they had abandoned every trace of loyalty to him. The priests had truly lost their reason for existence—instead of turning people to God, they claimed allegiance to Rome in order to kill their Messiah.

Matt 27:27 A regiment was a division of the Roman legion, containing about 200 men.

Roman Soldiers

With the military intervention of Pompey in the internal affairs of Judea in 63 B.C., Rome established its presence in Palestine. Roman military presence is visible throughout the Gospels (Mark 15:16; Luke 3:14; 7:1-8). During the New Testament period, service in the Roman legions was open to all Roman citizens; a professional volunteer army had replaced a conscripted militia. The permanent standing army was made up of legions recruited from the ranks of citizens. Experienced officers of the rank of consul commanded the legions. On special occasions, particularly at the great Jewish festivals, when riots and disorders could be anticipated, the provincial governor would take up residence in Jerusalem, accompanied by a substantial contingent of troops.

MARK 15:16-20 ••

The soldiers took Jesus into the courtyard of the governor's headquarters (called the Praetorium) and called out the entire regiment. [17]They dressed him in a purple robe, and they wove thorn branches into a crown and put it on his head. [18]Then they saluted him and taunted, "Hail! King of the Jews!" [19]And they struck him on the head with a reed stick, spit on him, and dropped to their knees in mock worship. [20]When they were finally tired of mocking him, they took off the purple robe and put his own clothes on him again. Then they led him away to be crucified.

Jesus Is Led Away to Be Crucified PARALLEL •••

MATTHEW 27:32 •••

Along the way, they came across a man named Simon, who was from Cyrene,* and the soldiers forced him to carry Jesus' cross.

MARK 15:21 •••

A passerby named Simon, who was from Cyrene,* was coming in from the countryside just then, and the soldiers forced him to carry Jesus' cross. (Simon was the father of Alexander and Rufus.)

LUKE 23:26-31 •••

As they led Jesus away, a man named Simon, who was from Cyrene,* happened to be coming in from the countryside. The soldiers seized him and put the cross on him and made him carry it behind Jesus. [27]A large crowd trailed behind, including many grief-stricken women. [28]But Jesus turned and said to them, "Daughters of Jerusalem, don't weep for me, but weep for yourselves and for your children. [29]For the days are coming when they will say, 'Fortunate indeed are the women who are childless, the wombs that have not borne a child and the breasts that have never nursed.' [30]People will beg the mountains, 'Fall on us,' and plead with the hills, 'Bury us.'* [31]For if these things are done when the tree is green, what will happen when it is dry?*"

Jesus Is Placed on the Cross PARALLEL ••••

MATTHEW 27:33-44 ••••

And they went out to a place called Golgotha (which means "Place of the Skull"). [34]The soldiers gave him wine mixed with bitter gall, but when he had tasted it, he refused to drink it.

[35]After they had nailed him to the cross, the soldiers gambled for his clothes by throwing dice.* [36]Then they sat around and kept guard as he hung there. [37]A sign was fastened above Jesus' head, announcing the charge against him. It read: "This is Jesus, the King of the Jews." [38]Two revolutionaries* were crucified with him, one on his right and one on his left.

[39]The people passing by shouted abuse, shaking their heads in mockery. [40]"Look at you now!" they yelled at him. "You said you were going to destroy

Mt 27:32 *Cyrene* was a city in northern Africa. **Mk 15:21** *Cyrene* was a city in northern Africa. **Lk 23:26** *Cyrene* was a city in northern Africa. **Lk 23:30** Hos 10:8. **Lk 23:31** Or *If these things are done to me, the living tree, what will happen to you, the dry tree?* **Mt 27:35** Greek *by casting lots.* A few late manuscripts add *This fulfilled the word of the prophet: "They divided my garments among themselves and cast lots for my robe."* See Ps 22:18. **Mt 27:38** Or *criminals;* also in 27:44.

Mark 15:19 The brutal guards, the power-hungry governor, and the conniving religious leaders had the upper hand. But they did not know the true power and authority of the man they were torturing and had condemned to death. Worldly powers and philosophies that mock Jesus' lordship will not be so arrogant when Jesus returns in judgment (see Phil 2:10-11). When you feel that unjust people with control and viewpoints hostile to Christianity are carrying the day, rest assured that Jesus holds the highest place and will return in glory.

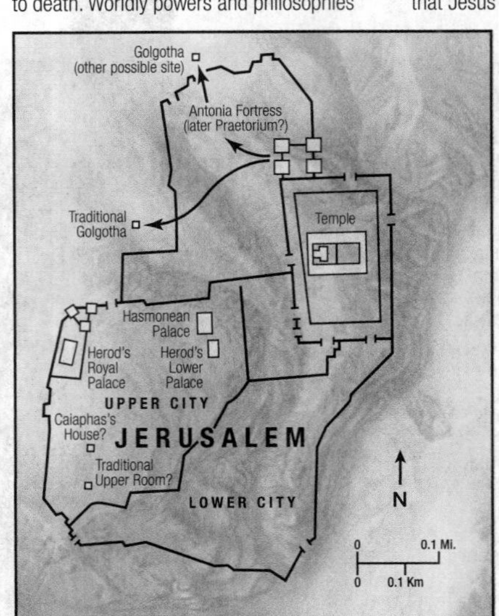

Matt 27:32 Condemned prisoners had to carry their own crosses to the execution site. Jesus, weakened from the beatings he had received, was physically unable to carry his cross any farther. Thus, a bystander, Simon, was forced to do so. Simon was from Cyrene, in northern Africa, and was probably one of the thousands of Jews visiting Jerusalem for the Passover.

◀ ***JESUS LED AWAY TO DIE*** *As Jesus was led away through the streets of Jerusalem, he could no longer carry his cross, and Simon of Cyrene was given the burden. Jesus was crucified, along with common criminals, on a hill outside Jerusalem.*

Mark 15:21 Colonies of Jews existed outside Judea. Simon had made a Passover pilgrimage to Jerusalem all the way from Cyrene in North Africa. His sons, Alexander and Rufus, are mentioned here probably because they became well known in the early church (Rom 16:13).

Luke 23:27-29 Luke alone mentions the tears of the Jewish women while Jesus was being led through the streets to his execution. Jesus told them not to weep for him but for themselves. He knew that in only about 40 years, Jerusalem and the Temple would be destroyed by the Romans.

Luke 23:31 This proverb is difficult to interpret. Some feel it means that if the innocent Jesus (green tree) suffered at the hands of the Romans, what would happen to the guilty Jews (dry tree)?

Matt 27:33 Some scholars say Golgotha ("Place of the Skull") derives its name from its appearance. Golgotha may have been a regular place of execution in a prominent public place outside the city. Executions held there would serve as a deterrent to criminals.

Matt 27:34 Jesus was offered wine mixed with gall to help reduce his pain, but he refused to drink it. Gall is generally under-the Temple and rebuild it in three days. Well then, if you are the Son of God, save yourself and come down from the cross!"

[41]The leading priests, the teachers of religious law, and the elders also mocked Jesus. [42]"He saved others," they scoffed, "but he can't save himself! So he is the King of Israel, is he? Let him come down from the cross right now, and we will believe in him! [43]He trusted God, so let God rescue him now if he wants him! For he said, 'I am the Son of God.'" [44]Even the revolutionaries who were crucified with him ridiculed him in the same way.

MARK 15:22-32

And they brought Jesus to a place called Golgotha (which means "Place of the Skull"). [23]They offered him wine drugged with myrrh, but he refused it.

[24]Then the soldiers nailed him to the cross. They divided his clothes and threw dice* to decide who would get each piece. [25]It was nine o'clock in the morning when they crucified him. [26]A sign announced the charge against him. It read, "The King of the Jews." [27]Two revolutionaries* were crucified with him, one on his right and one on his left.*

[29]The people passing by shouted abuse, shaking their heads in mockery. "Ha! Look at you now!" they yelled at him. "You said you were going to destroy the Temple and rebuild it in three days. [30]Well then, save yourself and come down from the cross!"

[31]The leading priests and teachers of religious law also mocked Jesus. "He saved others," they scoffed, "but he can't save himself! [32]Let this Messiah, this King of Israel, come down from the cross so we can see it and believe him!" Even the men who were crucified with Jesus ridiculed him.

LUKE 23:32-43

Two others, both criminals, were led out to be executed with him. [33]When they came to a place called The Skull,* they nailed him to the cross. And the criminals were also crucified—one on his right and one on his left.

Mk 15:24 Greek *cast lots.* See Ps 22:18. **Mk 15:27a** Or *Two criminals.* **Mk 15:27b** Some manuscripts add verse 28, *And the Scripture was fulfilled that said, "He was counted among those who were rebels."* See Isa 53:12; also compare Luke 22:37. **Lk 23:33** Sometimes rendered *Calvary,* which comes from the Latin word for "skull."

THE SEVEN LAST WORDS OF JESUS ON THE CROSS

The statements that Jesus made from the cross have been treasured by all who have followed him as Lord. They demonstrate both his humanity and his divinity. They also capture the last moments of all that Jesus went through to gain our forgiveness.

"Father, forgive them, for they don't know what they are doing."	Luke 23:34
"I assure you, today you will be with me in paradise."	Luke 23:43
Speaking to Mary and John: "Dear woman, here is your son. . . . Here is your mother."	John 19:26-27
"My God, my God, why have you abandoned me?"	Matt 27:46; Mark 15:34
"I am thirsty."	John 19:28
"It is finished!"	John 19:30
"Father, I entrust my spirit into your hands!"	Luke 23:46

stood to be a narcotic that was used to deaden pain. Jesus would suffer fully conscious and with a clear mind.

Matt 27:40 This accusation was used against Jesus in his trial by the high council (Matt 26:61). It is ironic that Jesus was in the very process of fulfilling his own prophecy. Because Jesus is the Son of God, who always obeys the will of the Father, he did not come down from the cross.

Matt 27:44 Later one of these criminals repented. Jesus promised that the repentant criminal would join him in paradise (Luke 23:39-43).

Mark 15:24 Throwing dice was a way of making a decision by chance. The soldiers gambled to decide who would receive Jesus' clothing. Roman soldiers had the right to take for themselves the clothing of those crucified. This act fulfilled the prophecy of Psalm 22:18.

Mark 15:25 Crucifixion was a feared and shameful form of execution. The victim was forced to carry his cross along the longest possible route to the crucifixion site as a warning to bystanders. There were several shapes for crosses and several different methods of crucifixion. Jesus was nailed to the cross; condemned men were sometimes tied to their crosses with ropes. In either case, death came by suffocation as the person lost strength and the weight of the body made breathing more and more difficult.

Mark 15:26 A sign stating the condemned man's crime was often placed on a cross as a warning. Because Jesus was never found guilty, the only accusation placed on his sign was the "crime" of being King of the Jews.

Mark 15:31 Jesus could have saved himself, but he endured this suffering because of his love for us. He could have chosen not to take the pain and humiliation; he could have killed those who mocked him. But he suffered through it all because he loved even his enemies. We had a significant part in the drama that dark afternoon because our sins were on the cross too. Jesus died on that cross for us, and the penalty for our sins was paid by his death. The only adequate response we can make is to confess our sins and gratefully accept the fact that Jesus paid for them so we wouldn't have to. Don't insult God with indifference toward the greatest act of genuine love in history.

Mark 15:32 When James and John had asked Jesus for the places of honor next to him in his Kingdom, Jesus had told them that they didn't know what they were asking (Mark 10:35-39). Here, as Jesus was preparing to inaugurate his Kingdom through his death, the places on his right and on his left were taken by dying men—criminals. As Jesus explained to his two power-hungry disciples, a person who wants to be close to Jesus must be prepared to suffer and die as he himself was doing. The way to the Kingdom is the way of the cross. If we want the glory of the Kingdom, we must be willing to be united with the crucified Christ.

Luke 23:32-33 This place was probably a hill outside Jerusalem along a main road. The Romans executed criminals publicly as examples to the people.

▸ **LUKE 23:32-43** ***(cont.)***

34 Jesus said, "Father, forgive them, for they don't
know what they are doing."* And the soldiers gambled
for his clothes by throwing dice.*
35 The crowd watched and the leaders scoffed. "He
saved others," they said, "let him save himself if he is
really God's Messiah, the Chosen One." 36 The soldiers
mocked him, too, by offering him a drink of sour wine.
37 They called out to him, "If you are the King of the Jews,
save yourself!" 38 A sign was fastened above him with
these words: "This is the King of the Jews."
39 One of the criminals hanging beside him scoffed,
"So you're the Messiah, are you? Prove it by saving yourself—and us, too, while you're at it!"
40 But the other criminal protested, "Don't you fear
God even when you have been sentenced to die? 41 We
deserve to die for our crimes, but this man hasn't done
anything wrong." 42 Then he said, "Jesus, remember me
when you come into your Kingdom."
43 And Jesus replied, "I assure you, today you will be
with me in paradise."

JOHN 19:17-27

Carrying the cross by himself, he went to the place
called Place of the Skull (in Hebrew, *Golgotha*). 18 There
they nailed him to the cross. Two others were crucified with him, one on either side, with Jesus between
them. 19 And Pilate posted a sign on the cross that read,
"Jesus of Nazareth,* the King of the Jews." 20 The place
where Jesus was crucified was near the city, and the
sign was written in Hebrew, Latin, and Greek, so that
many people could read it.
21 Then the leading priests objected and said to Pilate, "Change it from 'The King of the Jews' to 'He said,
I am King of the Jews.'"
22 Pilate replied, "No, what I have written, I have
written."
23 When the soldiers had crucified Jesus, they divided his clothes among the four of them. They also
took his robe, but it was seamless, woven in one piece
from top to bottom. 24 So they said, "Rather than tearing it apart, let's throw dice* for it." This fulfilled the
Scripture that says, "They divided my garments among

Lk 23:34a This sentence is not included in many ancient manuscripts. **Lk 23:34b** Greek *by casting lots.* See Ps 22:18. **Jn 19:19** Or *Jesus the Nazarene.* **Jn 19:24a** Greek *cast lots.*

מלך היהודים

REX IVDAEORVM

ΟΒΑϹΙΛΕΥϹΤΩΝΙΟΥΔΑΙΩΝ

The Inscription on the Cross

The inscription was written on a placard, which usually consisted of a board smeared with white gypsum and bearing in black letters the name of the condemned criminal and the offense for which he was being executed. This was usually hung about the criminal's neck on the way to the execution and subsequently affixed to the cross over his head. The inscription written for Jesus in Hebrew, Latin, and Greek was "Jesus of Nazareth, the King of the Jews." It is here reproduced in styles current in the first century A.D. The inscription, written in three languages, could be read by all who passed by: Jews (who could read Hebrew), Romans (who could read Latin), and Hellenists (anyone who could read Greek).

Luke 23:34 Jesus asked God to forgive the people who were putting him to death—Jewish leaders, Roman politicians and soldiers, bystanders—and God answered that prayer by opening up the way of salvation even to Jesus' murderers. Jesus was suffering the most horrible, painful death ever devised by sinful man, and he looked at the people responsible for his suffering and prayed for their forgiveness. The Roman officer and soldiers who witnessed the Crucifixion said, "This man truly was the Son of God!" (Matt 27:54). Soon many priests were converted to the Christian faith (Acts 6:7). Because we are all sinners, we all played a part in putting Jesus to death. The Good News is that God is gracious. He will forgive us and give us new life through his Son.

Luke 23:38 This sign was meant to be ironic. A king, stripped and executed in public view, had obviously lost his kingdom forever. But Jesus, who turns the world's wisdom upside down, was just coming into his Kingdom. His death and resurrection would strike the deathblow to Satan's rule and establish Christ's eternal authority over the earth. Few people reading the sign that bleak afternoon understood its real meaning, but the sign was absolutely true. All was not lost. Jesus is King of the Jews—and of the Gentiles and the whole universe.

Luke 23:39-43 As this man was about to die, he turned to Christ for forgiveness, and Christ accepted him. This shows that our deeds don't save us—our faith in Christ does. It is never too late to turn to God. Even in his misery, Jesus had mercy on this criminal who decided to believe in him. Our lives will be much more useful and fulfilling if we turn to God early, but even those who repent at the very last moment will be with God in paradise.

Luke 23:42-43 The dying criminal is an interesting contrast to Jesus' followers during his ministry. Although the disciples continued to love Jesus, their hopes for the Kingdom were shattered. Most of them had gone into hiding. As one of his followers sadly said two days later, "We had hoped he was the Messiah who had come to rescue Israel" (Luke 24:21). By contrast, the criminal looked at the man who was dying next to him and said, "Jesus, remember me when you come into your Kingdom." By all appearances, the Kingdom was finished. How awe-inspiring is the faith of this man who alone saw beyond the present shame to the coming glory!

John 19:19 Few people reading the sign that bleak afternoon understood its real meaning, but the sign was absolutely true. All was not lost. Jesus was King of the Jews—as well as the Gentiles and the whole universe. It might not have looked that way to those standing there that day, but Jesus, who turns the world's wisdom upside down, was just coming into his Kingdom. His death and resurrection would strike the deathblow to Satan's rule and would establish Jesus' eternal authority over the earth.

themselves and threw dice for my clothing."* So that
is what they did.
25Standing near the cross were Jesus' mother, and
his mother's sister, Mary (the wife of Clopas), and Mary
Magdalene. 26When Jesus saw his mother standing
there beside the disciple he loved, he said to her, "Dear
woman, here is your son." 27And he said to this disciple, "Here is your mother." And from then on this
disciple took her into his home.

Jesus Dies on the Cross PARALLEL ••••

MATTHEW 27:45-56

At noon, darkness fell across the whole land until
three o'clock. 46At about three o'clock, Jesus called
out with a loud voice, *"Eli, Eli,* lema sabachthani?"*
which means "My God, my God, why have you abandoned me?"*
47Some of the bystanders misunderstood and
thought he was calling for the prophet Elijah. 48One
of them ran and filled a sponge with sour wine, holding it up to him on a reed stick so he could drink. 49But
the rest said, "Wait! Let's see whether Elijah comes to
save him."*
50Then Jesus shouted out again, and he released
his spirit. 51At that moment the curtain in the sanctuary of the Temple was torn in two, from top to
bottom. The earth shook, rocks split apart, 52and
tombs opened. The bodies of many godly men and
women who had died were raised from the dead.
53They left the cemetery after Jesus' resurrection,
went into the holy city of Jerusalem, and appeared
to many people.
54The Roman officer* and the other soldiers at the
crucifixion were terrified by the earthquake and all

Jn 19:24b Ps 22:18. **Mt 27:46a** Some manuscripts read *Eloi, Eloi.* **Mt 27:46b** Ps 22:1. **Mt 27:49** Some manuscripts add *And another took a spear and pierced his side, and out flowed water and blood.* Compare John 19:34. **Mt 27:54** Greek *The centurion.*

John 19:20 The sign was written in three languages: Hebrew for the native Jews, Latin for the Roman occupation forces, and Greek for foreigners and Jews visiting from other lands. In a double irony, the multilingual sign declared that Jesus was Lord of all.

John 19:25-27 Even while dying on the cross, Jesus was concerned about his family. He instructed John to care for Mary, Jesus' mother. Our families are precious gifts from God, and we should value and care for them under all circumstances. Neither Christian work nor key responsibilities in any job or position excuse us from caring for our families. What can you do today to show your love to your family?

John 19:27 Jesus asked his close friend John to care for his mother, Mary, whose husband, Joseph, must have been dead by this time. Why didn't Jesus assign this task to his brothers? As the oldest son, Jesus entrusted his mother to a person who stayed with him at the cross—and that was John.

Matt 27:45 We do not know how this darkness occurred, but it is clear that God caused it. Nature testified to the gravity of Jesus' death, while Jesus' friends and enemies alike fell silent in the encircling gloom. The darkness on that Friday afternoon was both physical and spiritual.

Matt 27:47 The bystanders misinterpreted Jesus' words and thought he was calling for Elijah. Because Elijah had ascended into heaven without dying (2 Kgs 2:11), they thought he would return again to rescue them from great trouble (Mal 4:5). At their annual Passover meal, each family set an extra place for Elijah in expectation of his return.

Matt 27:52-53 Christ's death was accompanied by at least four miraculous events: darkness, the tearing in two of the curtain in the Temple, an earthquake, and dead people rising from their tombs. Jesus' death, therefore, could not have gone unnoticed. Everyone knew something significant had happened.

Crucifixion

Crucifixion was universally recognized as the most horrible type of execution. The condemned criminal was scourged and forced to carry the crossbeam to the spot where a stake had already been erected. A tablet stating the crime was often placed around the offender's neck and was fastened to the cross after the execution. The victim was commonly tied or sometimes nailed to the crossbeam (with the nails in the wrist, since the bones in the hand could not take the weight). The beam was then raised and fixed to the upright pole. For a particularly slow, agonizing death, they might drive blocks or pins into the stake for a seat or a step to support the feet. Death came about either through loss of blood circulation followed by coronary failure or through the collapse of the lungs, causing suffocation. That could take days, so often the victim's legs would be broken below the knees with a club, causing massive shock and eliminating any further possibility of easing pressure on the wrists.

▸ **MATTHEW 27:45-56 *(cont.)***
that had happened. They said, "This man truly was
the Son of God!"
55And many women who had come from Galilee
with Jesus to care for him were watching from a distance. 56Among them were Mary Magdalene, Mary
(the mother of James and Joseph), and the mother of
James and John, the sons of Zebedee.

MARK 15:33-41
At noon, darkness fell across the whole land until
three o'clock. 34Then at three o'clock Jesus called
out with a loud voice, *"Eloi, Eloi, lema sabachthani?"*
which means "My God, my God, why have you abandoned me?"*
35Some of the bystanders misunderstood and
thought he was calling for the prophet Elijah. 36One
of them ran and filled a sponge with sour wine, holding it up to him on a reed stick so he could drink.
"Wait!" he said. "Let's see whether Elijah comes to
take him down!"
37Then Jesus uttered another loud cry and breathed
his last. 38And the curtain in the sanctuary of the Temple
was torn in two, from top to bottom.
39When the Roman officer* who stood facing him*
saw how he had died, he exclaimed, "This man truly
was the Son of God!"
40Some women were there, watching from a
distance, including Mary Magdalene, Mary (the
mother of James the younger and of Joseph*), and
Salome. 41They had been followers of Jesus and had
cared for him while he was in Galilee. Many other
women who had come with him to Jerusalem were
also there.

LUKE 23:44-49
By this time it was about noon, and darkness fell
across the whole land until three o'clock. 45The light
from the sun was gone. And suddenly, the curtain
in the sanctuary of the Temple was torn down the
middle. 46Then Jesus shouted, "Father, I entrust my
spirit into your hands!"* And with those words he
breathed his last.
47When the Roman officer* overseeing the execution saw what had happened, he worshiped God and
said, "Surely this man was innocent.*" 48And when
all the crowd that came to see the crucifixion saw
what had happened, they went home in deep sorrow.* 49But Jesus' friends, including the women who
had followed him from Galilee, stood at a distance
watching.

JOHN 19:28-37
Jesus knew that his mission was now finished, and to
fulfill Scripture he said, "I am thirsty."* 29A jar of sour

Mk 15:34 Ps 22:1. **Mk 15:39a** Greek *the centurion;* similarly in 15:44, 45. **Mk 15:39b** Some manuscripts add *heard his cry and.* **Mk 15:40** Greek *Joses;* also in 15:47. See Matt 27:56. **Lk 23:46** Ps 31:5. **Lk 23:47a** Greek *the centurion.* **Lk 23:47b** Or *righteous.* **Lk 23:48** Greek *went home beating their breasts.* **Jn 19:28** See Pss 22:15; 69:21.

Mark 15:34 Jesus did not ask this question in surprise or despair. He was quoting the first line of Psalm 22. The whole psalm is a prophecy expressing the deep agony of the Messiah's death for the world's sin. Jesus knew that he would be temporarily separated from God the moment he took upon himself the sins of the world. This separation was what he had dreaded as he prayed in Gethsemane. The physical agony was horrible, but the spiritual alienation from God was the ultimate torture.

Mark 15:37 Jesus' loud cry may have been his last words, "It is finished!" (John 19:30).

Luke 23:44 Darkness covered the entire land for about three hours in the middle of the day. All nature seemed to mourn over the stark tragedy of the death of God's Son.

Luke 23:45 This significant event symbolized Christ's work on the cross. The Temple had three parts: the courts for all the people; the Holy Place, where only priests could enter; and the Most Holy Place, where the high priest alone could enter once a year to atone for the sins of the people. It was in the Most Holy Place that the Ark of the Covenant, and God's presence with it, rested. The curtain that was torn was the one that closed off the Most Holy Place from view. At Christ's death, the barrier between God and humanity was split in two. Now all people can approach God directly through Christ (Heb 9:1-14; 10:19-22).

WHY DID JESUS HAVE TO DIE?

The Problem	We have all done things that are wrong, and we have failed to obey God's laws. Because of this, we have been separated from God our creator. Separation from God is death; but, by ourselves, we can do nothing to become united with God.
Why Jesus Could Help	Jesus was not only a man; he was God's unique Son. Because Jesus never disobeyed God and never sinned, only he can bridge the gap between a sinless God and sinful people.
The Solution	Jesus freely offered his life for us, dying on the cross in our place, taking all our wrongdoing upon himself, and saving us from the consequences of sin—including God's judgment and death.
The Results	Jesus took our past, present, and future sins upon himself so that we could have new life. Because all our wrongdoing is forgiven, we are reconciled to God. Furthermore, Jesus' resurrection from the dead is the proof that his substitutionary sacrifice on the cross was acceptable to God, and his resurrection has become the source of new life for those who believe that Jesus is the Son of God. All who believe in him may have this new life and live it in union with him.

John 19:29 This sour wine was a cheap wine that the Roman soldiers drank while waiting for those crucified to die.

John 19:30 Until this time, a complicated system of sacrifices had atoned for sins. Sin separates people from God, and only through the sacrifice of an animal, a substitute, could people be forgiven and become clean before God. But people sin continually, so frequent sacrifices were required. Jesus, however, became the final and ultimate sacrifice for sin. The word *finished* is the same as "paid in full." Jesus came to finish God's work of salvation (John 4:34;

wine was sitting there, so they soaked a sponge in it,
put it on a hyssop branch, and held it up to his lips.
30When Jesus had tasted it, he said, "It is finished!"
Then he bowed his head and released his spirit.
31It was the day of preparation, and the Jewish leaders didn't want the bodies hanging there the next day,
which was the Sabbath (and a very special Sabbath,
because it was the Passover). So they asked Pilate to
hasten their deaths by ordering that their legs be
broken. Then their bodies could be taken down. 32So
the soldiers came and broke the legs of the two men
crucified with Jesus. 33But when they came to Jesus,
they saw that he was already dead, so they didn't break
his legs. 34One of the soldiers, however, pierced his
side with a spear, and immediately blood and water
flowed out. 35(This report is from an eyewitness giving an accurate account. He speaks the truth so that
you also can believe.*) 36These things happened in
fulfillment of the Scriptures that say, "Not one of his
bones will be broken,"* 37and "They will look on the
one they pierced."*

Jesus Is Laid in the Tomb PARALLEL ●●●●

MATTHEW 27:57-61 ●○○○

As evening approached, Joseph, a rich man from Arimathea who had become a follower of Jesus, 58went
to Pilate and asked for Jesus' body. And Pilate issued
an order to release it to him. 59Joseph took the body
and wrapped it in a long sheet of clean linen cloth.
60He placed it in his own new tomb, which had been
carved out of the rock. Then he rolled a great stone
across the entrance and left. 61Both Mary Magdalene
and the other Mary were sitting across from the tomb
and watching.

MARK 15:42-47 ○●○○

This all happened on Friday, the day of preparation,*
the day before the Sabbath. As evening approached,
43Joseph of Arimathea took a risk and went to Pilate
and asked for Jesus' body. (Joseph was an honored
member of the high council, and he was waiting for
the Kingdom of God to come.) 44Pilate couldn't believe that Jesus was already dead, so he called for the
Roman officer and asked if he had died yet. 45The officer confirmed that Jesus was dead, so Pilate told Joseph he could have the body. 46Joseph bought a long
sheet of linen cloth. Then he took Jesus' body down
from the cross, wrapped it in the cloth, and laid it in
a tomb that had been carved out of the rock. Then
he rolled a stone in front of the entrance. 47Mary
Magdalene and Mary the mother of Joseph saw where
Jesus' body was laid.

Jn 19:35 Some manuscripts read *can continue to believe.* **Jn 19:36** Exod 12:46; Num 9:12; Ps 34:20. **Jn 19:37** Zech 12:10. **Mk 15:42** Greek *It was the day of preparation.*

17:4), to pay the full penalty for our sins. With his death, the complex sacrificial system ended because Jesus took all sin upon himself. Now we can freely approach God because of what Jesus did for us. Those who believe in Jesus' death and resurrection can live eternally with God and escape the penalty that comes from sin.

John 19:31 It was against God's law to leave the body of a dead person exposed overnight (Deut 21:23), and it was also against the law to work after sundown on Friday, when the Sabbath began. This is why the religious leaders urgently wanted to get Jesus' body off the cross and buried by sundown.

John 19:31-35 These Romans were experienced soldiers. They knew from many previous crucifixions whether a man was dead or alive. There was no question that Jesus was dead when they checked him, so they decided not to break his legs as they had done to the other victims. Piercing his side and seeing the sudden flow of blood and water (indicating that the sac surrounding the heart and the heart itself had been pierced) was further proof of his death. Some people say Jesus didn't really die, that he only passed out—and that's how he came back to life. But we have the witness of an impartial party, the Roman soldiers, that Jesus died on the cross (see Mark 15:44-45).

John 19:32 The Roman soldiers would break victims' legs to hasten the death process. When a person hung on a cross, death came by suffocation, but the victim could push against the cross with his legs to hold up his body and keep breathing. With broken legs, he would suffocate almost immediately.

John 19:34-35 The graphic details of Jesus' death are especially important in John's record because he was an eyewitness.

John 19:36-37 Jesus died as the lambs for the Passover meal were being slain. Not a bone was to be broken in these sacrificial lambs (Exod 12:46; Num 9:12). Jesus, the Lamb of God, was the perfect sacrifice for the sins of the world (1 Cor 5:7).

Matt 27:57-58 Joseph of Arimathea was a secret disciple of Jesus. He was a religious leader, an honored member of the high council (Mark 15:43). Joseph courageously asked to take Jesus' body from the cross and to bury it. The disciples who publicly followed Jesus had fled, but this Jewish leader, who followed Jesus in secret, came forward and did what was right.

Matt 27:60 The tomb where Jesus was laid was probably a man-made cave cut out of one of the many limestone hills in the area. These caves were often large enough to walk into.

Mark 15:42ff The Sabbath began at sundown on Friday and ended at sundown on Saturday. Jesus died just a few hours before sundown on Friday. It was against Jewish law to do physical work or to travel on the Sabbath. It was also against Jewish law to let a dead body remain exposed overnight (Deut 21:23). Joseph came to bury Jesus' body before the Sabbath began. If Jesus had died on the Sabbath when Joseph was unavailable, his body would have been taken down by the Romans. Had the Romans taken Jesus' body, no Jews could have confirmed his death, and opponents could have disputed his resurrection.

Mark 15:44 Pilate was surprised that Jesus had died so quickly, so he asked an officer to verify the report. Today, in an effort to deny the Resurrection, there are those who say that Jesus didn't really die. His death, however, was confirmed by the officer, Pilate, Joseph of Arimathea, the religious leaders, and the women who witnessed his burial. Jesus experienced actual physical death on the cross.

Mark 15:46 Joseph wrapped Jesus' body, placed it in the tomb, and rolled a heavy stone across the entrance. The religious leaders also watched where Jesus was buried. They stationed guards by the tomb and sealed the stone to make sure that no one would steal Jesus' body and claim he had risen from the dead (Matt 27:62-66).

LUKE 23:50-56
Now there was a good and righteous man named Joseph. He was a member of the Jewish high council,
51but he had not agreed with the decision and actions of the other religious leaders. He was from the
town of Arimathea in Judea, and he was waiting for
the Kingdom of God to come. 52He went to Pilate
and asked for Jesus' body. 53Then he took the body
down from the cross and wrapped it in a long sheet
of linen cloth and laid it in a new tomb that had been
carved out of rock. 54This was done late on Friday
afternoon, the day of preparation,* as the Sabbath
was about to begin.
55As his body was taken away, the women from Galilee followed and saw the tomb where his body was
placed. 56Then they went home and prepared spices
and ointments to anoint his body. But by the time they
were finished the Sabbath had begun, so they rested
as required by the law.

JOHN 19:38-42
Afterward Joseph of Arimathea, who had been a secret
disciple of Jesus (because he feared the Jewish leaders),
asked Pilate for permission to take down Jesus' body.
When Pilate gave permission, Joseph came and took
the body away. 39With him came Nicodemus, the man
who had come to Jesus at night. He brought about
seventy-five pounds* of perfumed ointment made
from myrrh and aloes. 40Following Jewish burial custom, they wrapped Jesus' body with the spices in long

Lk 23:54 Greek *It was the day of preparation.* **Jn 19:39** Greek *100 litras* [32.7 kilograms].

Luke 23:55 The Galilean women followed Joseph to the tomb, so they knew exactly where to find Jesus' body when they returned after the Sabbath with their spices and perfumes. These women could not do "great" things for Jesus—they were not permitted to stand up before the Jewish high council or the Roman governor and testify on his behalf—but they did what they could. They stayed at the cross when most of the disciples had fled, and they got ready to anoint their Lord's body. Because of their devotion, they were the first to know about the Resurrection. As believers, we may feel we can't do much for Jesus. But we are called to take advantage of the opportunities given us, doing what we can do and not worrying about what we cannot do.

John 19:38-39 Four people were changed in the process of Jesus' death. The criminal dying on the cross beside Jesus asked to be included in his Kingdom (Luke 23:39-43). The Roman officer proclaimed that Jesus was surely the Son of God (Mark 15:39). Joseph and Nicodemus, members of the Jewish high council and secret followers of Jesus (John 7:50-52), came out of hiding. These men were changed more by Jesus' death than by his life. They realized who Jesus was, and that realization brought out their belief, proclamation, and action. When confronted with Jesus and his death, we also should be changed—to believe, proclaim, and act.

John 19:38-42 Joseph of Arimathea and Nicodemus were secret followers of Jesus. They were afraid to make this allegiance known because of their positions in the Jewish community. Joseph was a leader and honored member of the Jewish high council. Nicodemus, also a member of the high council, had come to Jesus by night (John 3:1) and later tried to defend him before the other religious leaders (John 7:50-52). Yet they risked their reputations to provide for Jesus' burial. Are you a secret believer? Do you hide your faith from your friends and fellow workers? This is an appropriate time to step out of hiding and let others know whom you follow.

MARY MAGDALENE

The absence of women among the 12 disciples has bothered a few people. But it is clear that there were many women among Jesus' followers. It is also clear that Jesus did not treat women as others in his culture did; he treated them with dignity, as people with worth. • Mary of Magdala was an early follower of Jesus who certainly deserves to be called a disciple. An energetic, impulsive, caring woman, she not only traveled with Jesus, but also contributed to the needs of the group. She was present at the Crucifixion and was on her way to anoint Jesus' body on Sunday morning when she discovered the empty tomb. Mary was the first to see Jesus after his resurrection. • Mary Magdalene is a heartwarming example of thankful living. Her life was miraculously freed by Jesus when he drove seven demons out of her. In every glimpse we have of her, she was acting out her appreciation for the freedom Christ had given her. That freedom allowed her to stand under Christ's cross when all the disciples except John were hiding in fear. After Jesus' death, she intended to give his body every respect. Like the rest of Jesus' followers, she never expected his bodily resurrection—but she was overjoyed to discover it. • Mary's faith was not complicated, but it was direct and genuine. She was more eager to believe and obey than to understand everything. Jesus honored her childlike faith by appearing to her first and by entrusting her with the first message of his resurrection.

Strengths and accomplishments	• Contributed to the needs of Jesus and his disciples • One of the few faithful followers present at Jesus' death on the cross • First to see the risen Christ
Weakness and mistake	• Jesus had to drive seven demons out of her
Lessons from her life	• Those who are obedient grow in understanding • Women are vital to Jesus' ministry • Jesus relates to women as he created them—as equal reflectors of God's image
Vital statistics	• Where: Magdala, Jerusalem • Occupation: We are not told, but she seems to have been wealthy • Contemporaries: Jesus, the 12 disciples, Mary, Martha, Lazarus, Jesus' mother Mary
Key verse	"After Jesus rose from the dead early on Sunday morning, the first person who saw him was Mary Magdalene, the woman from whom he had cast out seven demons" (Mark 16:9).

Mary Magdalene's story is told in Matthew 27–28; Mark 15–16; Luke 23–24; and John 19–20. She is also mentioned in Luke 8:2.

sheets of linen cloth. [41]The place of crucifixion was near a garden, where there was a new tomb, never used before. [42]And so, because it was the day of preparation for the Jewish Passover* and since the tomb was close at hand, they laid Jesus there.

Guards Are Posted at the Tomb

MATTHEW 27:62-66

The next day, on the Sabbath,* the leading priests and Pharisees went to see Pilate. [63]They told him, "Sir, we remember what that deceiver once said while he was still alive: 'After three days I will rise from the dead.' [64]So we request that you seal the tomb until the third day. This will prevent his disciples from coming and stealing his body and then telling everyone he was raised from the dead! If that happens, we'll be worse off than we were at first."

[65]Pilate replied, "Take guards and secure it the best you can." [66]So they sealed the tomb and posted guards to protect it.

Jesus Rises from the Dead PARALLEL

MATTHEW 28:1-8

Early on Sunday morning,* as the new day was dawning, Mary Magdalene and the other Mary went out to visit the tomb.

[2]Suddenly there was a great earthquake! For an angel of the Lord came down from heaven, rolled aside the stone, and sat on it. [3]His face shone like lightning, and his clothing was as white as snow. [4]The guards shook with fear when they saw him, and they fell into a dead faint.

[5]Then the angel spoke to the women. "Don't be afraid!" he said. "I know you are looking for Jesus, who

Jn 19:42 Greek *because of the Jewish day of preparation.* **Mt 27:62** Or *On the next day, which is after the Preparation.* **Mt 28:1** Greek *After the Sabbath, on the first day of the week.*

John 19:42 As they buried Jesus, Nicodemus and Joseph had to hurry to avoid working on the Sabbath, which began Friday evening at sundown.

Matt 27:64-66 The religious leaders took Jesus' resurrection claims more seriously than the disciples did. The disciples didn't remember Jesus' teaching about his resurrection (Matt 20:17-19); but the religious leaders remembered and took steps they thought would prevent it (or at least a fabrication of it). Because of his claims, they were almost as afraid of Jesus after his death as when he was alive. They tried to take every precaution that his body would remain in the tomb. Because the tomb was hewn out of rock in the side of a hill, there was only one entrance. The tomb was sealed by stringing a cord across the stone that was rolled over the entrance. The cord was sealed at each end with clay. But the religious leaders took a further precaution, asking that guards be placed at the tomb's entrance. The Pharisees failed to understand that no rock, seal, guard, or army could prevent the Son of God from rising again.

Matt 28:1 The other Mary was not Jesus' mother. She could have been the wife of Clopas (John 19:25). Or, she may have been Jesus' aunt, the mother of James and John (Matt 27:56).

Matt 28:2 The stone was not rolled aside so Jesus could get out, but so others could get in and see that Jesus had indeed risen from the dead, just as he had promised.

Matt 28:5-7 The angel who announced the good news of the Resurrection to the women gave them four messages: (1) "Don't be afraid." The reality of the Resurrection brings joy, not fear. When you are afraid, remember the empty tomb. (2) "He isn't here." Jesus is not dead and is not to be looked for among the dead. He is alive, with his people. (3) "Come, see." The women could check the evidence themselves. The tomb was empty then, and it is empty today. The Resurrection is a historical fact. (4) "Go quickly and tell." They were to spread the joy of the Resurrection. We, too, are to spread the great news about Jesus' resurrection.

The Tomb of Christ

The same kind of rock-hewn tomb in which Jesus was buried has been excavated in Palestine. One type was a burial tunnel cut vertically into the wall of the chamber, which left an oblong pit at the center to give a standing man headroom. Projecting rock ledges around the chamber walls would hold the wrapped bodies. Smaller versions of this have also been found consisting of one or more chambers with a low, square entry to crawl through. The closing stone was either like an enormous cork, slotting into the small entry as into the neck of a bottle, or it was a rough boulder. It is clear that such a tomb would match the Gospel descriptions of the place where Joseph put the body of Jesus (see Matt 27:57-61; Mark 15:42-47; Luke 23:50-56; John 19:38-42; 20:1-10).

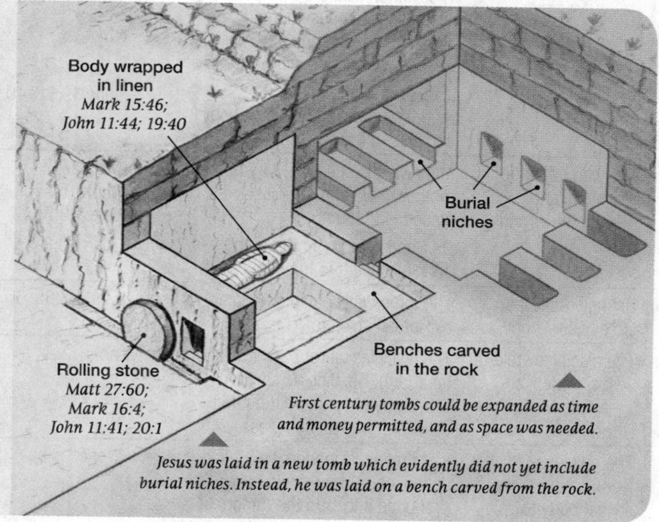
Body wrapped in linen
Mark 15:46; John 11:44; 19:40
Burial niches
Benches carved in the rock
Rolling stone
Matt 27:60; Mark 16:4; John 11:41; 20:1
First century tombs could be expanded as time and money permitted, and as space was needed.
Jesus was laid in a new tomb which evidently did not yet include burial niches. Instead, he was laid on a bench carved from the rock.

▸ **MATTHEW 28:1-8** ***(cont.)***
was crucified. 6He isn't here! He is risen from the dead,
just as he said would happen. Come, see where his body
was lying. 7And now, go quickly and tell his disciples
that he has risen from the dead, and he is going ahead
of you to Galilee. You will see him there. Remember
what I have told you."
8The women ran quickly from the tomb. They were
very frightened but also filled with great joy, and they
rushed to give the disciples the angel's message.

MARK 16:1-8
Saturday evening, when the Sabbath ended, Mary
Magdalene, Mary the mother of James, and Salome
went out and purchased burial spices so they could
anoint Jesus' body. 2Very early on Sunday morning,*
just at sunrise, they went to the tomb. 3On the way
they were asking each other, "Who will roll away the
stone for us from the entrance to the tomb?" 4But as
they arrived, they looked up and saw that the stone,
which was very large, had already been rolled aside.
5When they entered the tomb, they saw a young
man clothed in a white robe sitting on the right side.
The women were shocked, 6but the angel said, "Don't
be alarmed. You are looking for Jesus of Nazareth,*
who was crucified. He isn't here! He is risen from
the dead! Look, this is where they laid his body. 7Now
go and tell his disciples, including Peter, that Jesus
is going ahead of you to Galilee. You will see him
there, just as he told you before he died."

Mk 16:2 Greek *on the first day of the week;* also in 16:9. **Mk 16:6** Or *Jesus the Nazarene.*

Matt 28:6 Jesus' resurrection is the key to the Christian faith. Why? (1) Just as he promised, Jesus rose from the dead. We can be confident, therefore, that he will accomplish all he has promised. (2) Jesus' bodily resurrection shows us that the living Christ is ruler of God's eternal Kingdom, not a false prophet or impostor. (3) We can be certain of our resurrection because he was resurrected. Death is not the end—there is future life. (4) The power that brought Jesus back to life is available to us to bring our spiritually dead selves back to life. (5) The Resurrection is the basis for the church's witness to the world. Jesus is more than just a human leader; he is the Son of God.

Mark 16:1-2 The women purchased the spices on Saturday evening after the Sabbath had ended so they could go to the tomb early the next morning and anoint Jesus' body as a sign of love, devotion, and respect. Bringing spices to the tomb was like bringing flowers to a grave today. These women faced two overwhelming problems as they set out to honor Jesus' body, however: the Roman guards and the huge rock in the tomb's doorway. Impossible obstacles. So what did these women expect to accomplish that early Sunday morning? Yet urged on by love and gratitude, they walked on—even as they wondered the same questions aloud.

The church's mission—to send the gospel to all the world—is fraught with overwhelming obstacles. Any one of them appears devastating. Against human stubbornness, disease, danger, terrorism, loneliness, sin, greed, and even church strife and corruption, what can a few missionaries hope to accomplish? Yet like these solitary women, we go out with love and gratitude for Jesus and leave the big obstacles to God.

Mark 16:5 Mark says that one angel met the women at the tomb, while Luke mentions two angels. Each Gospel writer chose to highlight different details as he explained the same story, just as eyewitnesses to a news story each may highlight a different aspect of that event. Mark probably emphasized only the angel who spoke. The unique emphasis of each Gospel shows that the four accounts were written independently. This should give us confidence that all four are true and reliable.

Mark 16:7 The angel made special mention of Peter to show that, in spite of Peter's denials, Jesus had not disowned or deserted him. Jesus had great responsibilities for Peter to fulfill in the church that was not yet in existence.

Mark 16:7 The angel told the disciples to meet Jesus in Galilee "as he told you"

EVIDENCE THAT JESUS ACTUALLY DIED AND AROSE

This evidence demonstrates Jesus' uniqueness in history and proves that he is God's Son. No one else was able to predict his own resurrection and then accomplish it.

Proposed Explanations for Empty Tomb	Evidence against These Explanations	References
Jesus was only unconscious and later revived.	A Roman soldier told Pilate that Jesus was dead.	Mark 15:44-45
	The Roman soldiers did not break Jesus' legs because he had already died, and one of them pierced Jesus' side with a spear.	John 19:32-34
	Joseph of Arimathea and Nicodemus wrapped Jesus' body and placed it in the tomb.	John 19:38-40
The women made a mistake and went to the wrong tomb.	Mary Magdalene and Mary the mother of Joseph saw Jesus placed in the tomb.	Matt 27:59-61 Mark 15:47 Luke 23:55
	On Sunday morning Peter and John also went to the same tomb.	John 20:3-9
Unknown thieves stole Jesus' body.	The tomb was sealed and guarded by Roman soldiers	Matt 27:65-66
The disciples stole Jesus' body.	The disciples were ready to die for their faith. Stealing Jesus' body would have been admitting that their faith was meaningless.	Acts 12:2
The religious leaders stole Jesus' body to produce it later.	If the religious leaders had taken Jesus' body, they would have produced it to stop the rumors of his resurrection.	None

[8]The women fled from the tomb, trembling and bewildered, and they said nothing to anyone because they were too frightened.*

[*Shorter Ending of Mark*]

Then they briefly reported all this to Peter and his companions. Afterward Jesus himself sent them out from east to west with the sacred and unfailing message of salvation that gives eternal life. Amen.

LUKE 24:1-11

But very early on Sunday morning* the women went to the tomb, taking the spices they had prepared. [2]They found that the stone had been rolled away from the entrance. [3]So they went in, but they didn't find the body of the Lord Jesus. [4]As they stood there puzzled, two men suddenly appeared to them, clothed in dazzling robes.

[5]The women were terrified and bowed with their faces to the ground. Then the men asked, "Why are you looking among the dead for someone who is alive? [6]He isn't here! He is risen from the dead! Remember what he told you back in Galilee, [7]that the Son of Man* must be betrayed into the hands of sinful men and be crucified, and that he would rise again on the third day."

[8]Then they remembered that he had said this. [9]So they rushed back from the tomb to tell his eleven disciples—and everyone else—what had happened. [10]It was Mary Magdalene, Joanna, Mary the mother of James, and several other women who told the apostles

Mk 16:8 The most reliable early manuscripts of the Gospel of Mark end at verse 8. Other manuscripts include various endings to the Gospel. A few include both the "shorter ending" and the "longer ending." The majority of manuscripts include the "longer ending" immediately after verse 8. **Lk 24:1** Greek *But on the first day of the week, very early in the morning.* **Lk 24:7** "Son of Man" is a title Jesus used for himself.

(see Mark 14:28). This is where Jesus had called most of them and had said they would "fish for people" (Matt 4:19), and it would be where this mission would be restated (John 21).

Luke 24:1-9 The two angels (appearing as "two men . . . clothed in dazzling robes") asked the women why they were looking in a tomb for someone who was alive. Often we run into people who are looking for God among the dead. They study the Bible as a mere historical document and go to church as if going to a memorial service. But Jesus is not among the dead—he lives! He reigns in the hearts of Christians, and he is the head of his church. Do you look for Jesus among the living? Do you expect him to be active in the world and in the church? Look for signs of his power—they are all around you.

Luke 24:6-7 The angels reminded the women that Jesus had accurately predicted all that had happened to him (Luke 9:22, 44; 18:31-33).

Luke 24:6-7 The resurrection of Jesus from the dead is the central fact of Christian history. On it, the church is built; without it, there would be no Christian church today. Jesus' resurrection is unique. Other religions have strong ethical systems, concepts about paradise and the afterlife, and various holy scriptures. Only Christianity has a God who became human, literally died for his people, and was raised again in power and glory to rule his people forever.

Why is the Resurrection so important? (1) Because Christ was raised from the dead, we know that the Kingdom of Heaven has broken into earth's history. Our world is now headed for redemption, not disaster. God's mighty power is at work destroying sin, creating new lives, and preparing us for Jesus' second coming. (2) Because of the Resurrection, we know that death has been conquered and we, too, will be raised from the dead to live forever with Christ. (3) The Resurrection gives authority to the church's witness in the world. Look at the early evangelistic sermons in the book of Acts: The apostles' most important message was the proclamation that Jesus Christ had been raised from the dead! (4) The Resurrection gives meaning to the church's sacrament of the Lord's Supper. Like Jesus' followers on the Emmaus road, we break bread with our risen Lord, who comes in power to save us. (5) The Resurrection helps us find meaning even in great tragedy. No matter what happens to us as we walk with the Lord, the Resurrection gives us hope for the future. (6) The Resurrection assures us that Christ is alive and ruling his Kingdom. He is not a legend; he is alive and real. (7) God's power that brought Jesus back from the dead is available to us so that we can live for him in an evil world.

Christians can look very different from one another, and they can hold widely varying beliefs about politics, lifestyle, and even theology. But one central belief unites and inspires all true Christians: Jesus Christ rose from the dead! (For more on the importance of the Resurrection, see 1 Cor 15:3-7, 12-58.)

He isn't here! He is risen from the dead!

Luke 24:6

▸ **LUKE 24:1-11** *(cont.)*
what had happened. 11But the story sounded like nonsense to the men, so they didn't believe it.

JOHN 20:1-2
Early on Sunday morning,* while it was still dark, Mary Magdalene came to the tomb and found that the stone had been rolled away from the entrance.
2She ran and found Simon Peter and the other disciple, the one whom Jesus loved. She said, "They have taken the Lord's body out of the tomb, and we don't know where they have put him!"

Peter and John Run to the Tomb PARALLEL

LUKE 24:12
However, Peter jumped up and ran to the tomb to look. Stooping, he peered in and saw the empty linen wrappings; then he went home again, wondering what had happened.

JOHN 20:3-10
Peter and the other disciple started out for the tomb.
4They were both running, but the other disciple outran
Peter and reached the tomb first. 5He stooped and
looked in and saw the linen wrappings lying there,
but he didn't go in. 6Then Simon Peter arrived and
went inside. He also noticed the linen wrappings
lying there, 7while the cloth that had covered Jesus'
head was folded up and lying apart from the other
wrappings. 8Then the disciple who had reached the
tomb first also went in, and he saw and believed—9for
until then they still hadn't understood the Scriptures
that said Jesus must rise from the dead. 10Then they
went home.

Jn 20:1 Greek *On the first day of the week.*

Jesus Appears to the Women PARALLEL

MATTHEW 28:9-10
And as they went, Jesus met them and greeted them. And they ran to him, grasped his feet, and worshiped him.
10Then Jesus said to them, "Don't be afraid! Go tell my brothers to leave for Galilee, and they will see me there."

MARK 16:9-11 [*Longer Ending of Mark*]
After Jesus rose from the dead early on Sunday morning, the first person who saw him was Mary Magdalene, the woman from whom he had cast out seven demons. 10She went to the disciples, who were grieving and weeping, and told them what had happened. 11But when she told them that Jesus was alive and she had seen him, they didn't believe her.

JOHN 20:11-18
Mary was standing outside the tomb crying, and as
she wept, she stooped and looked in. 12She saw two
white-robed angels, one sitting at the head and the other at the foot of the place where the body of Jesus
had been lying. 13"Dear woman, why are you crying?" the angels asked her.

"Because they have taken away my Lord," she replied, "and I don't know where they have put him."

14She turned to leave and saw someone standing there. It was Jesus, but she didn't recognize him.
15"Dear woman, why are you crying?" Jesus asked her. "Who are you looking for?"

She thought he was the gardener. "Sir," she said, "if you have taken him away, tell me where you have put him, and I will go and get him."

16"Mary!" Jesus said.

She turned to him and cried out, "Rabboni!" (which is Hebrew for "Teacher").

Luke 24:11 People who hear about the Resurrection for the first time may need time before they can comprehend this amazing story. Like the disciples, they may pass through four stages of belief: At first, they may think it is a fairy tale, impossible to believe. Then, like Peter (see Luke 24:12), they may check out the facts but still be puzzled about what happened. (3) Only when they encounter Jesus personally will they be able to accept the fact of the Resurrection. Finally, as they commit themselves to Jesus and devote their lives to serving him, they will begin fully to understand the reality of his presence with them.

John 20:1 Other women came to the tomb along with Mary Magdalene. The other Gospel accounts give their names. For more information on Mary Magdalene, see her Profile on p. 1488.

Luke 24:12 From John 20:3-4, we learn that another disciple ran to the tomb with Peter. That other disciple was almost certainly John, the author of the fourth Gospel.

John 20:6-7 The linen wrappings were left as if Jesus' body had simply vacated them. The cloth that covered Jesus' head was still rolled up in the shape of a head, and it was at about the right distance from the wrappings that had enveloped Jesus' body. A grave robber couldn't possibly have made off with Jesus' body and left the linens as if they were still shaped around it.

John 20:9 As further proof that the disciples did not fabricate this story, we find that Peter and John were surprised that Jesus was not in the tomb. When John saw the linen wrappings looking like an empty cocoon from which Jesus had emerged, he believed that Jesus had risen. It wasn't until after they had seen the empty tomb that they remembered what the Scriptures and Jesus had said—he would die, but he would also rise again!

Matt 28:10 By "brothers," Jesus probably meant his disciples. This showed that he had forgiven them, even after they had denied and deserted him. Jesus told the women to pass a message on to the disciples—that he would meet them in Galilee, as he had previously told them (Mark 14:28). But the disciples, afraid of the religious leaders, stayed hidden behind locked doors in Jerusalem (John 20:19). So Jesus met them first there (Luke 24:36) and then later in Galilee (John 21).

John 20:14-16 Mary didn't recognize Jesus at first. Her grief had blinded her; she couldn't see him because she didn't expect to see him. Then he spoke her name, and immediately she recognized him. Imagine the love that flooded her heart when she heard her Savior saying her name. Jesus is near you, and he is calling your name. Can you, like Mary, regard him as your Lord?

John 20:17 Mary did not want to lose Jesus again. She had not yet understood the Resurrection. Perhaps she thought this was his promised second coming (John 14:3). But Jesus did not want to be detained at the tomb. If he did not ascend to heaven, the Holy Spirit could not come. Both he and Mary had important work to do.

John 20:18 Mary did not meet the risen Christ until she had discovered the empty

17 “Don't cling to me,” Jesus said, “for I haven't yet ascended to the Father. But go find my brothers and tell them, ‘I am ascending to my Father and your Father, to my God and your God.’”

18 Mary Magdalene found the disciples and told them, “I have seen the Lord!” Then she gave them his message.

Religious Leaders Bribe the Guards

MATTHEW 28:11-15

As the women were on their way, some of the guards went into the city and told the leading priests what had happened. 12 A meeting with the elders was called, and they decided to give the soldiers a large bribe. 13 They told the soldiers, “You must say, ‘Jesus' disciples came during the night while we were sleeping, and they stole his body.’ 14 If the governor hears about it, we'll stand up for you so you won't get in trouble.” 15 So the guards accepted the bribe and said what they were told to say. Their story spread widely among the Jews, and they still tell it today.

Jesus Appears to Two Believers Traveling on the Road PARALLEL

MARK 16:12-13 *[Longer Ending of Mark]*

Afterward he appeared in a different form to two of his followers who were walking from Jerusalem into the country. 13 They rushed back to tell the others, but no one believed them.

LUKE 24:13-35

That same day two of Jesus' followers were walking to the village of Emmaus, seven miles* from Jerusalem. 14 As they walked along they were talking about everything that had happened. 15 As they talked and discussed these things, Jesus himself suddenly came and began walking with them. 16 But God kept them from recognizing him.

17 He asked them, “What are you discussing so intently as you walk along?”

They stopped short, sadness written across their faces. 18 Then one of them, Cleopas, replied, “You must be the only person in Jerusalem who hasn't heard about all the things that have happened there the last few days.”

19 “What things?” Jesus asked.

“The things that happened to Jesus, the man from Nazareth,” they said. “He was a prophet who did powerful miracles, and he was a mighty teacher in the eyes of God and all the people. 20 But our leading priests and other religious leaders handed him over to be condemned to death, and they crucified him. 21 We had hoped he was the Messiah who had come to rescue Israel. This all happened three days ago.

Lk 24:13 Greek *60 stadia* [11.1 kilometers].

---

tomb. She responded with joy and obedience by going to tell the disciples. We cannot meet Christ until we discover that he is indeed alive, that his tomb is empty. Are you filled with joy by this Good News, and do you share it with others?

Matt 28:11-15 Jesus' resurrection was already causing a great stir in Jerusalem. A group of women was moving quickly through the streets, looking for the disciples to tell them the amazing news that Jesus was alive. At the same time, a group of religious leaders was plotting how to cover up the Resurrection.

Today there is still a great stir over the Resurrection, and there are still only two choices: to believe that Jesus rose from the dead, or to be closed to the truth—denying it, ignoring it, or trying to explain it away.

Luke 24:13ff The two followers returning to Emmaus at first missed the significance of history's greatest event because they were too focused on their disappointments and problems. In fact, they didn't recognize Jesus when he was walking beside them. To compound the problem, they were walking in the wrong direction—away from the fellowship of believers in Jerusalem. We are likely to miss Jesus and withdraw from the strength found in other believers when we become preoccupied with our dashed hopes and frustrated plans. Only when we are looking for Jesus in our midst will we experience the power and help he can bring.

The Nazareth Decree

A document comprising 20 lines of Greek inscribed on a slab of white marble was discovered in Nazareth in the latter part of the nineteenth century. The statement was a decree of Caesar assigning the death penalty to anyone breaking the seal of a tomb and stealing the body. The decree was issued by Claudius in about A.D. 50. Because Claudius had issued some other decrees against those who followed Christ, it is believed that the “Nazareth Decree” was aimed at early Christians who were proclaiming that Jesus Christ had risen from the dead. The rabbis of the time claimed that “Jesus' disciples came . . . and they stole his body” (Matt 28:13). Whatever his viewpoint on the matter, Claudius did not wish to encourage theories about the disappearance of bodies from tombs. The Nazareth Decree thus becomes a pointer to the resurrection of Christ, which was at that time upsetting the Roman world. Claudius apparently took steps to curb the spread of these disturbing ideas.

Luke 24:18 The news about Jesus' crucifixion had spread throughout Jerusalem. Because this was Passover week, Jews visiting the city from all over the Roman Empire now knew about his death. This was not a small, insignificant event, affecting only the disciples—the whole nation was interested.

Luke 24:21 These followers from Emmaus had been counting on Jesus to redeem Israel, that is, to rescue the nation from its enemies. Most Jews believed that the Old Testament prophecies pointed to a military and political Messiah; they didn't realize that the Messiah had come to redeem people from slavery to sin. When Jesus died, therefore, they lost all hope. They didn't understand that Jesus' death offered the greatest hope possible.

▸ **LUKE 24:13-35** ***(cont.)***

22“Then some women from our group of his followers were at his tomb early this morning, and they
came back with an amazing report. 23They said his
body was missing, and they had seen angels who told
them Jesus is alive! 24Some of our men ran out to see,
and sure enough, his body was gone, just as the women
had said.”

25Then Jesus said to them, “You foolish people!
You find it so hard to believe all that the prophets
wrote in the Scriptures. 26Wasn't it clearly predicted
that the Messiah would have to suffer all these things
before entering his glory?” 27Then Jesus took them
through the writings of Moses and all the prophets,
explaining from all the Scriptures the things concerning himself.

28By this time they were nearing Emmaus and the
end of their journey. Jesus acted as if he were going on,
29but they begged him, “Stay the night with us, since
it is getting late.” So he went home with them. 30As
they sat down to eat,* he took the bread and blessed
it. Then he broke it and gave it to them. 31Suddenly,
their eyes were opened, and they recognized him. And
at that moment he disappeared!

32They said to each other, “Didn't our hearts burn
within us as he talked with us on the road and explained the Scriptures to us?” 33And within the hour
they were on their way back to Jerusalem. There they
found the eleven disciples and the others who had
gathered with them, 34who said, “The Lord has really
risen! He appeared to Peter.*”

35Then the two from Emmaus told their story of
how Jesus had appeared to them as they were walking
along the road, and how they had recognized him as
he was breaking the bread.

Jesus Appears to His Disciples PARALLEL •••

MARK 16:14 ••• [*Longer Ending of Mark*]

Still later he appeared to the eleven disciples as they were eating together. He rebuked them for their stubborn unbelief because they refused to believe those who had seen him after he had been raised from the dead.*

LUKE 24:36-43 •••

And just as they were telling about it, Jesus himself
was suddenly standing there among them. “Peace be
with you,” he said. 37But the whole group was startled
and frightened, thinking they were seeing a ghost!

Lk 24:30 Or *As they reclined.* **Lk 24:34** Greek *Simon.* **Mk 16:14** Some early manuscripts add: *And they excused themselves, saying, “This age of lawlessness and unbelief is under Satan, who does not permit God's truth and power to conquer the evil [unclean] spirits. Therefore, reveal your justice now.” This is what they said to Christ. And Christ replied to them, “The period of years of Satan's power has been fulfilled, but other dreadful things will happen soon. And I was handed over to death for those who have sinned, so that they may return to the truth and sin no more, and so they may inherit the spiritual, incorruptible, and righteous glory in heaven.”*

Luke 24:24 These followers knew that the tomb was empty but didn't understand that Jesus had risen, and they were filled with sadness. Despite the women's witness, which was verified by some of the disciples, and despite the biblical prophecies of this very event, they still didn't believe. Today the Resurrection still catches people by surprise. In spite of 2,000 years of evidence and witness, many people refuse to believe. What more will it take? For these disciples it took the living Jesus in their midst. For many people today, it takes meeting Christians who display the transforming love of the resurrected Christ in their midst.

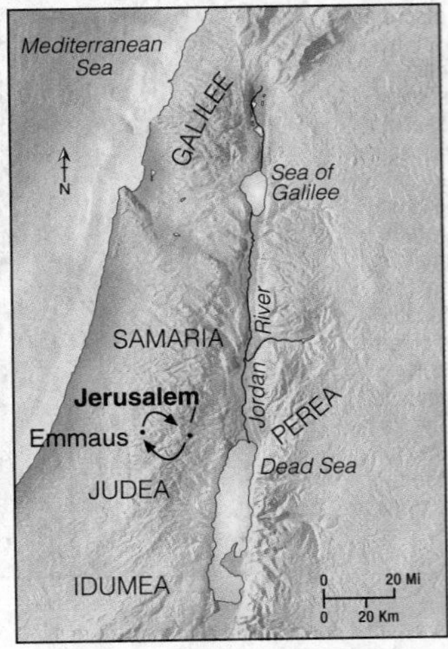

***ON THE ROAD TO EMMAUS** After Jesus' death, two of his followers were walking from Jerusalem back toward Emmaus when a stranger joined them. During dinner in Emmaus, Jesus revealed himself to them and then disappeared. They immediately returned to Jerusalem to tell the disciples the good news that Jesus was alive!*

Luke 24:25 Even though these Jewish men knew the biblical prophecies well, they failed to understand that Christ's suffering was his path to glory. They could not understand why God had not intervened to save Jesus from the cross. They were so caught up in the world's admiration of political power and military might that they were blind to God's Kingdom values—that the last will be first, and that life grows out of death. The world has not changed its values. The suffering servant is no more popular today than he was 2,000 years ago. But we have not only the witness of the Old Testament prophets; we also have the witness of the New Testament apostles and the history of the Christian church testifying to Jesus' victory over death. Will we confront the values of our culture and put our faith in Jesus? Or will we foolishly continue to ignore this Good News?

Luke 24:25-27 After the two followers had explained their sadness and confusion, Jesus responded by going to Scripture and applying it to his ministry. When we are puzzled by questions or problems, we, too, can go to Scripture and find authoritative help. If we, like these two, do not understand what the Bible means, we can turn to other believers who know the Bible and have the wisdom to apply it to our situations.

Luke 24:27 Beginning with the promised offspring in Genesis (Gen 3:15) and going through the suffering servant in Isaiah (Isa 53), the pierced one in Zechariah (Zech 12:10), and the messenger of the covenant in Malachi (Mal 3:1), Jesus reintroduced these disciples to the Old Testament. Christ is the thread woven throughout all the Scriptures, the central theme that binds them together. Following are several key passages Jesus may have mentioned on this walk to Emmaus: Genesis 3; 12; Psalms 22; 69; 110; Isaiah 53; Jeremiah 31; Zechariah 9; 13; Malachi 3.

Luke 24:33-34 Paul also mentions that Jesus appeared to Peter alone (1 Cor 15:5). This appearance is not further described in the Gospels. Jesus showed individual concern for Peter because Peter felt completely unworthy after denying his Lord. But Peter repented, and Jesus approached him and forgave him. Soon God would use Peter in building Christ's church (see the first half of the book of Acts).

Luke 24:36-43 Jesus' body wasn't a figment of the imagination or the appearance of a ghost—the disciples touched him, and he ate food. Jesus' resurrection was literal and

38“Why are you frightened?” he asked. “Why are
your hearts filled with doubt? 39Look at my hands.
Look at my feet. You can see that it’s really me. Touch
me and make sure that I am not a ghost, because
ghosts don’t have bodies, as you see that I do.” 40As
he spoke, he showed them his hands and his feet.
41Still they stood there in disbelief, filled with joy
and wonder. Then he asked them, “Do you have anything here to eat?” 42They gave him a piece of broiled
fish, 43and he ate it as they watched.

JOHN 20:19-23

That Sunday evening* the disciples were meeting
behind locked doors because they were afraid of the
Jewish leaders. Suddenly, Jesus was standing there
among them! “Peace be with you,” he said. 20As he
spoke, he showed them the wounds in his hands and
his side. They were filled with joy when they saw the
Lord! 21Again he said, “Peace be with you. As the Father
has sent me, so I am sending you.” 22Then he breathed
on them and said, “Receive the Holy Spirit. 23If you
forgive anyone’s sins, they are forgiven. If you do not
forgive them, they are not forgiven.”

Jesus Appears to Thomas

JOHN 20:24-31

One of the twelve disciples, Thomas (nicknamed the
Twin),* was not with the others when Jesus came.
25They told him, “We have seen the Lord!”
But he replied, “I won’t believe it unless I see the nail
wounds in his hands, put my fingers into them, and
place my hand into the wound in his side.”
26Eight days later the disciples were together again,
and this time Thomas was with them. The doors were
locked; but suddenly, as before, Jesus was standing
among them. “Peace be with you,” he said. 27Then he
said to Thomas, “Put your finger here, and look at my
hands. Put your hand into the wound in my side. Don’t
be faithless any longer. Believe!”
28“My Lord and my God!” Thomas exclaimed.

Jn 20:19 Greek *In the evening of that day, the first day of the week.* **Jn 20:24** Greek *Thomas, who was called Didymus.*

JESUS’ APPEARANCES AFTER HIS RESURRECTION

The truth of Christianity rests heavily on the Resurrection. If Jesus rose from the grave, who saw him? How trustworthy were the witnesses? Those who claimed to have seen the risen Jesus went on to turn the world upside down. Most of them also died for being followers of Christ. People rarely die for a halfhearted belief. These are the people who saw the risen Jesus.

Mary Magdalene	Mark 16:9-11; John 20:11-18
The other women at the tomb	Matt 28:8-10
Peter in Jerusalem	Luke 24:34; 1 Cor 15:5
The 2 travelers on the road	Mark 16:12-13; Luke 24:13-35
10 disciples behind closed doors	Mark 16:14; Luke 24:36-43; John 20:19-25
All the disciples, with Thomas (excluding Judas Iscariot)	John 20:26-29; 1 Cor 15:5
7 disciples while fishing	John 21:1-14
11 disciples on the mountain	Matt 28:16-20
A crowd of 500	1 Cor 15:6
Jesus’ brother James	1 Cor 15:7
Those who watched Jesus ascend into heaven	Luke 24:50-51; Acts 1:6-12

physical—he was not a disembodied spirit. On the other hand, his body wasn’t a restored human body like Lazarus’s (John 11)—he was able to appear and disappear. Jesus’ resurrected body was immortal. This is the kind of body we will be given at the resurrection of the dead (see 1 Cor 15:42-50).

John 20:21 Jesus again identified himself with his Father. He told the disciples by whose authority he did his work. Then he passed on to his disciples the job of spreading the Good News of salvation around the world. Whatever God has asked you to do, remember that your authority comes from God, and Jesus has demonstrated by words and actions how to accomplish the job he has given you. As the Father sent Jesus, Jesus sends his followers . . . and that includes you.

John 20:22 This may have been a special filling of the Holy Spirit for the disciples, a foretaste of what all believers would experience from the time of Pentecost (Acts 2) and forever after. To do God’s work, we need the guidance and power of the Holy Spirit. We must avoid trying to do his work in our own strength.

John 20:22 There is life in the breath of God. Man was created but did not come alive until God breathed into him the breath of life (Gen 2:7). God’s first breath made man different from all other forms of creation. Now, through the breath of Jesus, God imparted eternal, spiritual life. With this inbreathing came the power to do God’s will on earth.

John 20:23 Jesus was giving the disciples their Spirit-powered and Spirit-guided mission—to preach the Good News about Jesus so people’s sins might be forgiven. The disciples did not have the power to forgive sins (only God can forgive sins), but Jesus gave them the privilege of telling new believers that their sins have been forgiven because they have accepted Jesus’ message (see note on Matt 16:19, p. 1375). All believers have this same privilege. We can announce forgiveness of sins with certainty when we ourselves have found repentance and faith.

John 20:24-29 Have you ever wished you could actually see Jesus, touch him, and hear his words? Are there times you want to sit down with him and get his advice? Thomas wanted Jesus’ physical presence. But God’s plan is wiser. He has not limited himself to one physical body; he wants to be present with you at all times. Even now he is with you in the form of the Holy Spirit. You can talk to him, and you can find his words to you in the pages of the Bible. He can be as real to you as he was to Thomas.

John 20:25-28 Jesus wasn’t hard on Thomas for his doubts. Despite his skepticism, Thomas was still loyal to the believers and to Jesus himself. Some people need to doubt before they believe. If doubt leads to questions, and questions lead to answers, and if the answers are accepted, then doubt has done good work. It is when doubt becomes stubbornness and stubbornness becomes a prideful lifestyle that doubt harms faith. When you doubt, don’t stop there. Let your doubt deepen your faith as you continue to search for the answers.

▸ **JOHN 20:24-31** ***(cont.)***

29 Then Jesus told him, "You believe because you
have seen me. Blessed are those who believe without
seeing me."
30 The disciples saw Jesus do many other miraculous
signs in addition to the ones recorded in this book.
31 But these are written so that you may continue to
believe* that Jesus is the Messiah, the Son of God,
and that by believing in him you will have life by the
power of his name.

Jesus Appears to Seven Disciples

JOHN 21:1-14

Later, Jesus appeared again to the disciples beside the
Sea of Galilee.* This is how it happened. 2 Several of
the disciples were there—Simon Peter, Thomas (nicknamed the Twin),* Nathanael from Cana in Galilee, the
sons of Zebedee, and two other disciples.
3 Simon Peter said, "I'm going fishing."
"We'll come, too," they all said. So they went out in
the boat, but they caught nothing all night.
4 At dawn Jesus was standing on the beach, but the
disciples couldn't see who he was. 5 He called out, "Fel-
lows,* have you caught any fish?"
"No," they replied.
6 Then he said, "Throw out your net on the right-
hand side of the boat, and you'll get some!" So they
did, and they couldn't haul in the net because there
were so many fish in it.
7 Then the disciple Jesus loved said to Peter, "It's the

Jn 20:31 Some manuscripts read *that you may believe.* **Jn 21:1** Greek *Sea of Tiberias,* another name for the Sea of Galilee. **Jn 21:2** Greek *Thomas, who was called Didymus.* **Jn 21:5** Greek *Children.*

THOMAS

Thomas, so often remembered as "Doubting Thomas," deserves to be respected for his faith. He was a doubter, but his doubts had a purpose—he wanted to know the truth. Thomas did not idolize his doubts; he gladly believed when given reasons to do so. He expressed his doubts fully and had them answered completely. Doubting was only his way of responding, not his way of life. • Although our glimpses of Thomas are brief, his character comes through with consistency. He struggled to be faithful to what he knew, despite what he felt. At one point, when it was plain to everyone that Jesus' life was in danger, only Thomas put into words what most were feeling: "Let's go, too—and die with Jesus" (John 11:16). He didn't hesitate to follow Jesus. • We don't know why Thomas was absent the first time Jesus appeared to the disciples after the Resurrection, but he was reluctant to believe their witness to Christ's resurrection. Not even 10 friends could change his mind! • Doubt isn't necessarily a bad thing. Doubt encourages rethinking. Its purpose is more to sharpen the mind than to change it. Doubt can be used to pose the question, get an answer, and push for a decision. But doubt was never meant to be a permanent condition. Doubt is one foot lifted, poised to step forward or backward. There is no motion until the foot comes down. • When you experience doubt, take encouragement from Thomas. He didn't stay in his doubt but allowed Jesus to bring him to belief. Take encouragement also from the fact that countless other followers of Christ have struggled with doubts. The answers God gave them may help you, too. Don't settle into doubts, but move on from them to decision and belief. Find another believer with whom you can share your doubts. Silent doubts rarely find answers.

Strengths and accomplishments	• One of Jesus' 12 disciples • Intense both in doubt and belief • A loyal and honest man
Weaknesses and mistakes	• Along with the others, abandoned Jesus at his arrest • Refused to believe the others' claims to have seen Christ and demanded proof • Struggled with a pessimistic outlook
Lessons from his life	• Jesus does not reject doubts that are honest and directed toward belief • Better to doubt out loud than to disbelieve in silence
Vital statistics	• Where: Galilee, Judea, Samaria • Occupation: Disciple of Jesus • Contemporaries: Jesus, other disciples, Herod, Pilate
Key verses	"Then he said to Thomas, 'Put your finger here, and look at my hands. Put your hand into the wound in my side. Don't be faithless any longer. Believe!' 'My Lord and my God!' Thomas exclaimed" (John 20:27-28).

Thomas's story is told in the Gospels. He is also mentioned in Acts 1:13.

John 20:29 Some people think they would believe in Jesus if they could see a definite sign or miracle. But Jesus says we are blessed if we can believe without seeing. We have all the proof we need in the words of the Bible and the testimony of believers. A physical appearance would not make Jesus any more real to us than he is now.

John 20:30-31 To understand the life and mission of Jesus more fully, all we need to do is study the Gospels. John tells us that his Gospel records only a few of the many events in Jesus' life on earth. But the Good News includes everything we need to know to believe that Jesus is the Messiah, the Son of God, through whom we receive eternal life.

John 21:1ff This chapter tells how Jesus commissioned Peter. Perhaps Peter needed special encouragement after his denial—he may have felt completely worthless. Verses 1-14 set the scene for Jesus' conversation with Peter.

John 21:7 Only John ("the disciple Jesus loved") recognized Jesus in the dim morning light, undoubtedly because Jesus had performed a similar miracle earlier (Luke 5:1-11).

John 21:15-17 In this beach scene, Jesus led Peter through an experience that would remove the cloud of his denial. Peter had denied Jesus three times. Three times Jesus asked Peter if he loved him. When Peter answered yes, Jesus told him to feed his sheep. It is one thing to say you love Jesus, but the real test is willingness to serve him. Peter had repented, and here Jesus was asking him to commit his life. Peter's life changed when he finally realized who Jesus was. His occupation changed from fisherman to evangelist; his identity changed from impetuous to "rock"; and his relationship to Jesus changed—he was forgiven, and he finally understood the significance of Jesus' words about his death and resurrection.

John 21:15-17 Jesus asked Peter three times if he loved him. The first time Jesus said, "Do you love (Greek *agape*: "volitional, self-sacrificial love") me more than these?"

Lord!" When Simon Peter heard that it was the Lord,
he put on his tunic (for he had stripped for work),
jumped into the water, and headed to shore. 8The others stayed with the boat and pulled the loaded net to
the shore, for they were only about a hundred yards*
from shore. 9When they got there, they found breakfast waiting for them—fish cooking over a charcoal
fire, and some bread.
10"Bring some of the fish you've just caught," Jesus
said. 11So Simon Peter went aboard and dragged the
net to the shore. There were 153 large fish, and yet
the net hadn't torn.
12"Now come and have some breakfast!" Jesus said.
None of the disciples dared to ask him, "Who are you?"
They knew it was the Lord. 13Then Jesus served them
the bread and the fish. 14This was the third time Jesus
had appeared to his disciples since he had been raised
from the dead.

Jesus Challenges Peter

JOHN 21:15-25

After breakfast Jesus asked Simon Peter, "Simon son
of John, do you love me more than these?*"
"Yes, Lord," Peter replied, "you know I love you."
"Then feed my lambs," Jesus told him.
16Jesus repeated the question: "Simon son of John,
do you love me?"
"Yes, Lord," Peter said, "you know I love you."
"Then take care of my sheep," Jesus said.
17A third time he asked him, "Simon son of John,
do you love me?"
Peter was hurt that Jesus asked the question a third
time. He said, "Lord, you know everything. You know
that I love you."
Jesus said, "Then feed my sheep.
18"I tell you the truth, when you were young, you
were able to do as you liked; you dressed yourself
and went wherever you wanted to go. But when you
are old, you will stretch out your hands, and others*
will dress you and take you where you don't want to
go." 19Jesus said this to let him know by what kind
of death he would glorify God. Then Jesus told him,
"Follow me."
20Peter turned around and saw behind them the
disciple Jesus loved—the one who had leaned over to
Jesus during supper and asked, "Lord, who will betray
you?" 21Peter asked Jesus, "What about him, Lord?"
22Jesus replied, "If I want him to remain alive until I
return, what is that to you? As for you, follow me." 23So
the rumor spread among the community of believers*
that this disciple wouldn't die. But that isn't what Jesus
said at all. He only said, "If I want him to remain alive
until I return, what is that to you?"
24This disciple is the one who testifies to these
events and has recorded them here. And we know
that his account of these things is accurate.
25Jesus also did many other things. If they were all
written down, I suppose the whole world could not
contain the books that would be written.

Jesus Gives the Great Commission PARALLEL

MATTHEW 28:16-20

Then the eleven disciples left for Galilee, going to the
mountain where Jesus had told them to go. 17When
they saw him, they worshiped him—but some of them
doubted!
18Jesus came and told his disciples, "I have been

Jn 21:8 Greek *200 cubits* [90 meters]. **Jn 21:15** Or *more than these others do?* **Jn 21:18** Some manuscripts read *and another one.* **Jn 21:23** Greek *the brothers.*

The second time, Jesus focused on Peter alone and used the same Greek word. The third time, Jesus used the Greek word *phileo* (signifying "affection, affinity, or brotherly love") and asked, in effect, "Are you even my friend?" Peter responded each time with the Greek word *phileo.* Jesus doesn't settle for quick, superficial answers. He has a way of getting to the heart of the matter. Peter had to face his true feelings and motives when Jesus confronted him. How would you respond if Jesus asked you, "Do you love me? Do you really love me? Are you even my friend?"

John 21:18-19 This was a prediction of Peter's death by crucifixion. Tradition indicates that Peter was crucified for his faith—upside down because he did not feel worthy of dying in the same way his Lord had. Despite what Peter's future held, Jesus told him to follow him. We may be uncertain and fearful about our future, but if we know God is in control, we can confidently follow Christ.

John 21:21-22 Peter asked Jesus how John would die. Jesus replied that Peter should not concern himself with that. We tend to compare our lives to others, whether to rationalize our own level of devotion to Christ or to question God's justice. Jesus responds to us as he did to Peter: "What is that to you? As for you, follow me."

John 21:23 Early church history reports that after John spent several years as an exile on the island of Patmos, he returned to Ephesus where he died as an old man, near the end of the first century.

John 21:25 John's stated purpose for writing his Gospel was to show that Jesus was the Son of God (John 20:31). He clearly and systematically presented the evidence for Jesus' claims. When evidence is presented in the courtroom, those who hear it must make a choice. Those who read the Gospel of John must also make a choice—is Jesus the Son of God, or isn't he? You are the jury. The evidence has been clearly presented. You must decide. Read John's Gospel and believe!

Matt 28:18 God gave Jesus authority over heaven and earth. On the basis of that authority, Jesus told his disciples to make more disciples as they preached, baptized, and taught. With this same authority, Jesus still commands us to tell others the Good News and make them disciples for the Kingdom.

Matt 28:18-20 When someone is dying or leaving us, last words are very important. Jesus left the disciples with these last words of instruction: They were under his authority; they were to make more disciples; they were to baptize and teach these new disciples to obey Christ; Christ would be with them always. In previous missions Jesus had sent his disciples only to the Jews (Matt 10:5-6), but their mission from now on would be worldwide. Jesus is Lord of the earth, and he died for the sins of people from all nations.

We are to go—whether it is next door or to another country—and make disciples. It is not an option but a command to all who call Jesus "Lord." We are not all evangelists in the formal sense, but we have all received gifts that we can use to help fulfill the great commission. As we obey, we have comfort in the knowledge that Jesus is always with us.

▸ **MATTHEW 28:16-20 *(cont.)***
given all authority in heaven and on earth. [19]Therefore, go and make disciples of all the nations,* baptizing them in the name of the Father and the Son and the Holy Spirit. [20]Teach these new disciples to obey all the commands I have given you. And be sure of this: I am with you always, even to the end of the age."

MARK 16:15-18 [*Longer Ending of Mark*]
And then he told them, "Go into all the world and preach the Good News to everyone. [16]Anyone who believes and is baptized will be saved. But anyone who refuses to believe will be condemned. [17]These miraculous signs will accompany those who believe: They will cast out demons in my name, and they will speak in new languages.* [18]They will be able to handle snakes with safety, and if they drink anything poisonous, it won't hurt them. They will be able to place their hands on the sick, and they will be healed."

Jesus Appears to the Disciples in Jerusalem PARALLEL

LUKE 24:44-49
Then he said, "When I was with you before, I told you that everything written about me in the law of Moses and the prophets and in the Psalms must be fulfilled." [45]Then he opened their minds to understand the Scriptures. [46]And he said, "Yes, it was written long ago that the Messiah would suffer and die and rise from the dead on the third day. [47]It was also written that this message would be proclaimed in the authority of his name to all the nations,* beginning in Jerusalem: 'There is forgiveness of sins for all who repent.' [48]You are witnesses of all these things.

[49]"And now I will send the Holy Spirit, just as my Father promised. But stay here in the city until the Holy Spirit comes and fills you with power from heaven."

Mt 28:19 Or *all peoples.* **Mk 16:17** Or *new tongues;* some manuscripts do not include *new.* **Lk 24:47** Or *all peoples.*

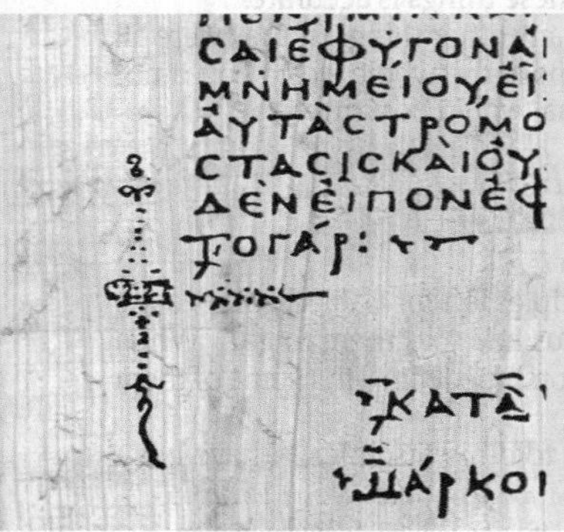

The Ending of the Gospel of Mark

Codex Vaticanus, a fourth-century manuscript of the entire Bible, was in the Vatican Library for many centuries until it was rediscovered in the mid-1800s. Codex Vaticanus provides one of the earliest and best witnesses to the text of the New Testament.

Both Codex Vaticanus and Codex Sinaiticus (another fourth-century manuscript) conclude Mark's Gospel at 16:8, and Codex Vaticanus even has a flourish that clearly marks the ending there (pictured). This is a surprising ending because it does not include an actual resurrection appearance of Jesus, only the angel's report that he had risen. It is also unusual in that the women who heard this report are said to have told no one about it. An ending to Mark may have gotten lost—the last page of the original manuscript being torn away. Various other endings to Mark were added later, three of which are noted in the NLT: (1) Mark 16:9-20, the traditional, longer ending; (2) the longer ending with an expansion at 16:14; (3) a short addition after Mark 16:8.

Matt 28:19 Jesus' words affirm the reality of the Trinity. Some people accuse theologians of making up the concept of the Trinity and reading it into Scripture. As we see here, the concept comes directly from Jesus himself. He did not say baptize them in the names, but in the name of the Father, Son, and Holy Spirit. The word *Trinity* does not occur in Scripture, but it well describes the three-in-one nature of the Father, Son, and Holy Spirit.

Matt 28:19 The disciples were to baptize people because baptism unites believers with Jesus Christ in their death to sin and their resurrection to new life. Baptism symbolizes submission to Christ, a willingness to live God's way, and identification with God's covenant people.

Matt 28:20 How is Jesus "with" us? Jesus was with the disciples physically until he ascended into heaven and then spiritually through the Holy Spirit (Acts 1:4). The Holy Spirit would be Jesus' presence that would never leave them (John 14:26). Jesus continues to be with us today through his Spirit.

Matt 28:20 The Old Testament prophecies and genealogies in the book of Matthew present Jesus' credentials for being King of the world—not a military or political leader, as the disciples had originally hoped, but a spiritual King who can overcome all evil and rule in the heart of every person. If we refuse to serve the King faithfully, we are disloyal subjects, fit only to be banished from the Kingdom. We must make Jesus King of our life and worship him as our Savior, King, and Lord.

Mark 16:15 Jesus told his disciples to go into all the world, telling everyone that he had paid the penalty for sin and that those who believe in him can be forgiven and live eternally with God. Christians today in all parts of the world are telling this Good News to people who haven't heard about Christ. The driving power that carries missionaries around the world and sets Christ's church in motion is the faith that comes from the Resurrection. Do you ever feel as though you don't have the skill or determination to be a witness for Christ? You must personally realize that Jesus rose from the dead and lives for you today. As you grow in your relationship with Christ, he will give you both the opportunities and the inner strength to tell his message.

Mark 16:16 It is not the water of baptism that saves but God's grace accepted through faith in Christ. Because of Jesus' response to the criminal on the cross who died with him, we know it is possible to be saved without being baptized (Luke 23:43). Baptism alone, without faith, does not guarantee that a person will go to heaven. Those who refuse to accept Jesus as their Savior will be condemned, regardless of whether or not they have been baptized.

Mark 16:18 There are times when God intervenes miraculously to protect his followers. Occasionally he gives them special powers. Paul handled a snake safely (Acts 28:5), and the disciples healed the sick (Matt 10:1; Acts 3:7-8). This does not mean, however, that we should test God by putting ourselves in dangerous situations or tempting the laws of nature. No one should build a religion on a portion of Scripture. God calls us to live as new citizens in the eternal Kingdom and to witness by word and service to God's love and power. Our witness should center on Jesus, not on superhero-type stunts.

ACTS 1:4-5
Once when he was eating with them, he commanded them, "Do not leave Jerusalem until the Father sends you the gift he promised, as I told you before. [5]John baptized with* water, but in just a few days you will be baptized with the Holy Spirit."

Acts 1:5 Or *in;* also in 1:5b.

Jesus Ascends into Heaven PARALLEL

MARK 16:19-20 [*Longer Ending of Mark*]
When the Lord Jesus had finished talking with them, he was taken up into heaven and sat down in the place of honor at God's right hand. [20]And the disciples went everywhere and preached, and the Lord worked

Luke 24:44 Many days may have elapsed between verses 43 and 44 because Jesus and his followers traveled to Galilee and back before he returned to heaven (Matt 28:16; John 21). In his second book, Acts, Luke makes it clear that Jesus spent 40 days with his disciples between his resurrection and ascension.

Luke 24:44-46 "Everything written about me in the law of Moses and the prophets and in the Psalms" refers to the entire Old Testament. In other words, the entire Old Testament points to the Messiah. For example, his role as prophet was foretold in Deuteronomy 18:15-20; his sufferings were prophesied in Psalm 22 and Isaiah 53; his resurrection was predicted in Psalm 16:9-11 and Isaiah 53:10-11.

Luke 24:45 Jesus opened these people's minds to understand the Scriptures. The Holy Spirit still does this in our life today when we study the Bible. Have you ever wondered how to understand a difficult Bible passage? Besides reading surrounding passages, asking other people, and consulting reference works, pray that the Holy Spirit will open your mind to understand, giving you the needed insight to put God's Word into action in your life.

Luke 24:47 Luke wrote to the Greek-speaking world. He wanted them to know that Christ's message of God's love and forgiveness should go to all the world. We must never ignore the worldwide scope of Christ's Good News. God wants all the world to hear the Good News of salvation.

Acts 1:4-5 The Trinity is a description of the unique relationship of God the Father, the Son, and the Holy Spirit. If Jesus had stayed on earth, his physical presence would have limited the spread of the Good News because physically he could be in only one place at a time. After Christ was taken up int85 heaven, he would be spiritually present everywhere through the Holy Spirit. The Holy Spirit was sent so that God would be with and within his followers after Christ had returned to heaven. The Spirit would comfort them, guide them to know his truth, remind them of Jesus' words, give them the right words to say, and fill them with power (see John 14–16).

Acts 1:5 At Pentecost (Acts 2:1-4) the Holy Spirit was given to all who believed in Jesus. We receive the Holy Spirit (are baptized with him) when we receive Jesus Christ as our Savior. The baptism of the Holy Spirit must be understood in light of his total work in Christians.

(1) The Spirit marks the beginning of the Christian experience. We cannot be Christians without his Spirit (Rom 8:9); we cannot be joined to Christ without his Spirit (1 Cor 6:17); we cannot be adopted as his children without his Spirit (Rom 8:14-17; Gal 4:6-7); we cannot be in the body of Christ except by baptism in the Spirit (1 Cor 12:13).

(2) The Spirit is the power of our new lives. He begins a lifelong process of change making us more like Christ (Gal 3:3; Phil 1:6). When we receive Christ by faith, we begin an immediate personal relationship with God. The Holy Spirit works in us to help us become like Christ.

(3) The Spirit unites the Christian community in Christ (Eph 2:19-22). The Holy Spirit can be experienced by all, and he works through all (1 Cor 12:11; Eph 4:4).

Mark 16:19 When Jesus ascended into heaven, his physical presence left the disciples (Acts 1:9). Jesus' sitting at God's right hand signifies the completion of his work, his authority as God, and his coronation as King.

Mark 16:20 Mark's Gospel emphasizes Christ's power as well as his servanthood. Jesus' life and teaching turned the world upside down and continue to do so. The world sees power as a way to gain control over others. But Jesus, with all authority and power in heaven and earth, chose to serve others. He held children in his arms, healed the sick, washed the disciples' feet, and died for the sins of the world. Jesus' followers today receive this same power to serve. As believers, we are called to be servants of Christ. As Christ served, so we are to serve.

Therefore, go and make disciples of all the nations, baptizing them in the name of the Father and the Son and the Holy Spirit.
Matthew 28:19

▸ **MARK 16:19-20** ***(cont.)***
through them, confirming what they said by many
miraculous signs.

LUKE 24:50-53
Then Jesus led them to Bethany, and lifting his hands
to heaven, he blessed them. 51While he was blessing
them, he left them and was taken up to heaven. 52So
they worshiped him and then returned to Jerusalem
filled with great joy. 53And they spent all of their time
in the Temple, praising God.

ACTS 1:6-11
So when the apostles were with Jesus, they kept asking
him, "Lord, has the time come for you to free Israel and
restore our kingdom?"

7He replied, "The Father alone has the authority
to set those dates and times, and they are not for you
to know. 8But you will receive power when the Holy
Spirit comes upon you. And you will be my witnesses,
telling people about me everywhere—in Jerusalem,
throughout Judea, in Samaria, and to the ends of
the earth."

9After saying this, he was taken up into a cloud while
they were watching, and they could no longer see him.
10As they strained to see him rising into heaven, two
white-robed men suddenly stood among them. 11"Men
of Galilee," they said, "why are you standing here staring into heaven? Jesus has been taken from you into
heaven, but someday he will return from heaven in
the same way you saw him go!"

Luke 24:50-53 As the disciples stood and watched, Jesus began rising into the air, and soon he disappeared into heaven. Seeing Jesus leave must have been frightening, but the disciples knew that Jesus would keep his promise to send the Holy Spirit to be with them. This same Jesus, who lived with the disciples, who died and was buried, and who rose from the dead, loves us and promises to be with us always. We can get to know him better by studying the Scriptures, praying, and allowing the Holy Spirit to make us more like Jesus.

Luke 24:51 Jesus' physical presence left the disciples when he returned to heaven (Acts 1:9), but the Holy Spirit soon came to comfort them and empower them to spread the Good News of salvation (Acts 2:1-4). Today Jesus' work of salvation is complete, and he is sitting at God's right hand, where he has authority over heaven and earth.

Luke 24:53 Luke's Gospel portrays Jesus as a perfect life lived according to God's plan. As a child, he was obedient to his parents and amazed the religious leaders in the Temple with his knowledge of the Scriptures. As an adult, he served God and others through preaching and healing. Finally, as a condemned man, he suffered without complaint. This portrayal of Jesus was well suited to Luke's Greek audience, who often discussed the meaning of perfection. They placed a high value on the individual being an example, and ever striving to attain even greater excellence. The Greeks, however, had a difficult time understanding the spiritual importance of the physical world. To them, the spiritual was always more important than the physical. To help them understand the God-man who united the spiritual and the physical, Luke emphasized that Jesus was not a phantom but a real human being who healed people and fed them because he was concerned with their physical health as well as the state of their souls.

As believers living according to God's plan, we, too, should obey our Lord in every detail as we seek to bring wholeness to people's bodies and souls. If others want to know how to live a perfect life, we can point them to Jesus.

Acts 1:6 During the years of Jesus' ministry on earth, the disciples continually wondered about his Kingdom. When would it come? What would be their role? In the traditional view, the Messiah would be an earthly conqueror who would free Israel from Rome. But the Kingdom Jesus spoke about was, first of all, a spiritual Kingdom established in the hearts and lives of believers (Luke 17:21). God's presence and power dwell in believers in the person of the Holy Spirit.

Acts 1:6-7 Like other Jews, the disciples chafed under their Roman rulers. They wanted Jesus to free Israel from Roman power and then become their king. Jesus replied that God the Father sets the timetable for all events—worldwide, national, and personal. If you want changes in your life that God hasn't yet made, don't become impatient. Instead, trust God's timetable.

Acts 1:8 The "power" believers receive from the Holy Spirit includes courage, boldness, confidence, insight, ability, and authority. The disciples would need all these gifts to fulfill their mission. If you believe in Jesus Christ as your Savior, you can experience the power of the Holy Spirit in your life.

Acts 1:8 Jesus had instructed his disciples to witness to people of all nations about him (Matt 28:19-20). But they were told to wait first for the Holy Spirit (Luke 24:49). God has important work for us to do as well, but we must do it by the power of the Holy Spirit. We often like to get on with the job, even if it means running ahead of God. But waiting is sometimes part of God's plan. Are you waiting and listening for God's complete instructions, or are you running ahead of his plans? We need God's timing and power to be truly effective.

Acts 1:8 This verse describes a series of ever-widening circles. The Good News was to spread, geographically, from Jerusalem, into Judea and Samaria, and finally to the ends of the earth. It would begin with the devout Jews in Jerusalem and Judea, spread to the mixed race in Samaria, and finally, be offered to Gentiles all over the world. God's Good News has not reached its final destination if someone in your family, your workplace, your school, or your community hasn't heard the Good News about Jesus Christ. Make sure that you are contributing in some way to the ever-widening circle of God's loving message.

Acts 1:9-11 After 40 days with his disciples (Acts 1:3), Jesus returned to heaven. It was important for the disciples to see Jesus taken up into heaven; they knew without a doubt that he was God and that his home was in heaven. The two white-robed men were angels who proclaimed to the disciples that one day Jesus would return in the same way he had gone—bodily and visibly. History is not haphazard or cyclical; it is moving toward a specific point—the return of Jesus Christ to judge and rule over the earth. We should be ready for his sudden return (1 Thes 5:2), not by standing around "staring into heaven," but by working hard to share the Good News so that others will be able to share in God's great blessings.

MESSIANIC PROPHECIES AND FULFILLMENTS

For the Gospel writers, one of the main reasons for believing in Jesus was the way his life fulfilled the Old Testament prophecies about the Messiah. Following is a list of some of the main prophecies.

	Old Testament Prophecies	*New Testament Fulfillment*
1. Messiah was to be born in Bethlehem	Mic 5:2	Matt 2:1-6 Luke 2:1-20
2. Messiah was to be born of a virgin	Isa 7:14	Matt 1:18-25 Luke 1:26-38
3. Messiah was to be a prophet like Moses	Deut 18:15, 18-19	John 7:40
4. Messiah was to enter Jerusalem in triumph	Zech 9:9	Matt 21:1-9 John 12:12-16
5. Messiah was to be rejected by his own people	Isa 53:1, 3	Matt 26:3-4 John 12:37-43 Acts 4:1-12
6. Messiah was to be betrayed by one of his followers	Ps 118:22 Ps 41:9	Matt 26:14-16, 47-50 Luke 22:19-23
7. Messiah was to be tried and condemned	Isa 53:8	Matt 27:1-2 Luke 23:1-25
8. Messiah was to be silent before his accusers	Isa 53:7	Matt 27:12-14 Mark 15:3-4 Luke 23:8-10
9. Messiah was to be struck and spat on by his enemies	Isa 50:6	Matt 26:67; 27:30 Mark 14:65
10. Messiah was to be mocked and insulted	Ps 22:7-8	Matt 27:39-44 Luke 23:11, 35
11. Messiah was to die by crucifixion	Ps 22:14, 16-17	Matt 27:31 Mark 15:20, 25
12. Messiah was to suffer with criminals and pray for his enemies	Isa 53:12	Matt 27:38 Mark 15:27-28 Luke 23:32-34
13. Messiah was to be given sour wine	Ps 69:21	Matt 27:34 John 19:28-30
14. Others were to throw dice for Messiah's garments	Ps 22:18	Matt 27:35 John 19:23-24
15. Messiah's bones were not to be broken	Exod 12:46	John 19:31-36
16. Messiah was to die as a sacrifice for sin	Isa 53:5-6, 8, 10-12	John 1:29; 11:49-52 Acts 10:43; 13:38-39
17. Messiah was to be raised from the dead	Ps 16:10	Matt 28:1-10 Acts 2:22-32
18. Messiah is now at God's right hand	Ps 110:1	Mark 16:19 Luke 24:50-51

The Church

JESUS ASCENDED TO HEAVEN, but he didn't leave his followers alone. Just a few days later, on the day of Pentecost, God sent the Holy Spirit to empower them to be witnesses for Jesus. They were never the same: from that day forward, the Spirit drove them to preach the Good News, demonstrate the power of God, and push the message of salvation through Jesus to the very ends of the earth.

The church began in Jerusalem, but it quickly spread throughout the Roman world when new believers traveled home to all corners of the empire after being converted by Peter's sermon during Pentecost. Then the Jerusalem church grew daily through the bold witness of Peter and John and the love of the believers. The infant church was not without problems, however, with external opposition (resulting in imprisonment, beatings, and death) and internal deceit and complaining.

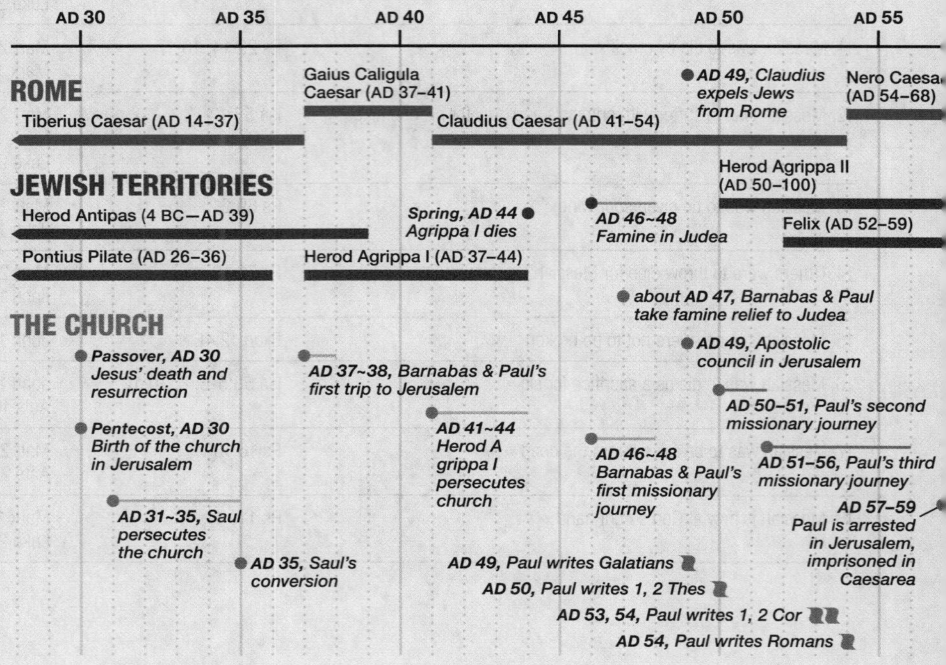

BOOKS

- ACTS
- ROM
- 1 COR
- 2 COR
- GAL
- EPH
- PHIL
- COL
- 1 THESS
- 2 THESS
- 1 TIM
- 2 TIM
- TITUS
- PHLM
- HEB
- JAS
- 1 PET
- 2 PET
- 1 JN
- 2 JN
- 3 JN
- JUDE
- REV

DATES

FROM:
AD 30
TO:
Present

THEMES

- Holy Spirit
- Good News
- Opposition
- Mission
- Hope

Instead of stopping Christianity, opposition and persecution served as catalysts for its spread because the believers took the message with them wherever they fled. Soon there were converts throughout Samaria and even in Ethiopia.

Then we meet a bright young Jew, zealous for the law and intent on ridding Judaism of the Jesus heresy. But on the way to Damascus to arrest believers, Saul was converted when he was confronted in person by the risen Christ.

Meanwhile, the church continued to thrive throughout Judea, Galilee, and Samaria. God sent Peter a vision insisting that he take the gospel to the "unclean" Gentiles. Peter understood, and he faithfully

Pentecost, by Titian

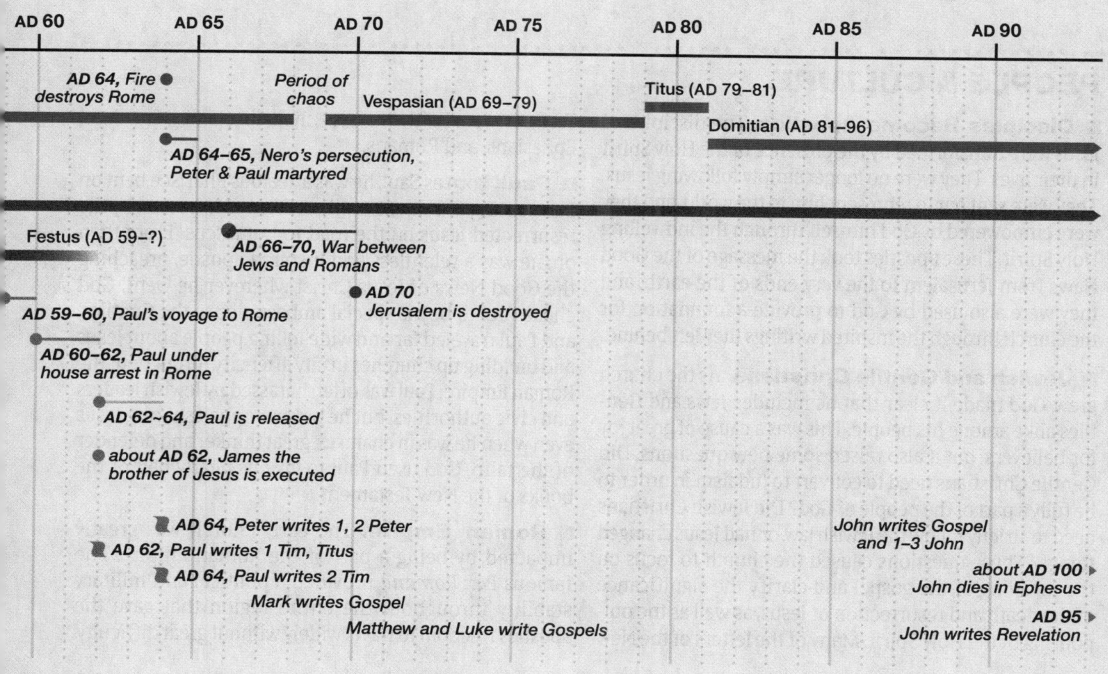

AD 60 | AD 65 | AD 70 | AD 75 | AD 80 | AD 85 | AD 90

AD 64, Fire destroys Rome

Period of chaos

Vespasian (AD 69–79)

Titus (AD 79–81)

Domitian (AD 81–96)

AD 64–65, Nero's persecution, Peter & Paul martyred

Festus (AD 59–?)

AD 66–70, War between Jews and Romans

AD 70 Jerusalem is destroyed

AD 59–60, Paul's voyage to Rome

AD 60–62, Paul under house arrest in Rome

AD 62–64, Paul is released

about AD 62, James the brother of Jesus is executed

AD 64, Peter writes 1, 2 Peter

AD 62, Paul writes 1 Tim, Titus

AD 64, Paul writes 2 Tim

Mark writes Gospel

Matthew and Luke write Gospels

John writes Gospel and 1–3 John

about AD 100 John dies in Ephesus

AD 95 John writes Revelation

shared the truth with Cornelius, whose entire household became believers. This was startling news to the Jerusalem church; but when Peter told his story, they praised God for his plan for all people to hear the Good News. This pushed the church into even wider circles as the message was preached to Greeks in Antioch, where Barnabas brought Paul to encourage the believers.

Soon, the Antioch church commissioned Paul and Barnabas for a missionary tour, sending the gospel to Cyprus and south Galatia with great success. But the Jewish-Gentile controversy still smoldered, and with so many Gentiles responding to Christ, the controversy threatened to divide the church. So a council met in Jerusalem to rule on the relationship of Gentile Christians to the Old Testament laws. After hearing both sides, James (Jesus' half brother and the leader of the Jerusalem church) resolved the issue and sent messengers to the churches with the decision.

After the council, Paul continued his missionary work, pushing the gospel to new cities and regions of the Roman Empire and strengthening the churches he had already visited. Paul continually faced opposition, and ultimately he was arrested in Jerusalem and transferred to Rome to await a hearing before Caesar. According to tradition, he was released and returned to his missionary work, continuing to invest in the next generation of church leaders, but was arrested again and ultimately martyred for his faith during the persecution of Christians under Emperor Nero.

God was at work preparing his church to continue to thrive even after the apostles passed from the scene. Paul, Peter, James, and John wrote letters to churches and individuals under the inspiration of the Holy Spirit. Matthew, John, Mark (influenced by Peter), and Luke (influenced by Paul) wrote down the stories and teachings of Jesus and the early church. These writings (along with Jude and Hebrews) became the New Testament and have guided the church in being faithful to Jesus ever since.

The story of God's church and her mission to take the Good News of Jesus to the ends of the earth continues today. Has Jesus captured your heart? What is your part in the story?

PEOPLE & CULTURE

■ **Disciples Become Apostles.** The disciples of Jesus were transformed by the presence of the Holy Spirit in their lives. They were no longer simply following Jesus. They were sent out to represent him to the world, and they were empowered by God himself through the indwelling Holy Spirit. These apostles took the message of the Good News from Jerusalem to the very ends of the earth, and they were also used by God to provide a foundation for the church through the inspired writings they left behind.

■ **Jewish and Gentile Christians.** As the church grew, God made it clear that he includes Jews and Gentiles alike among his people. This was a cause of great joy for believers, but it also raised some new questions. Did Gentile Christians need to convert to Judaism in order to be fully a part of the people of God? Did Jewish Christians need to strictly follow the Jewish law, or had Jesus changed things? These questions caused the church to focus on the meaning of the gospel and clarify the significance of the death and resurrection of Jesus, as well as the outpouring of the Holy Spirit. Many of the letters of the New Testament deal with this issue, including James, Galatians, Ephesians, and Romans.

■ **Paul.** Born as Saul, he was a zealous Pharisee bent on persecuting Christians until confronted in person by the resurrected Jesus on the road to Damascus. From then on, he was a relentless and inspired apostle, preaching the Good News of Jesus Christ wherever he went. God chose Paul to be his special ambassador to the Gentiles, and Paul traveled far and wide telling people about Jesus and building up churches in city after city throughout the Roman Empire. Paul was often harassed by Jewish leaders and civic authorities, but he never stopped sharing Jesus even when he was in chains. A great thinker and defender of the faith, God used Paul to give us nearly half of the books of the New Testament.

■ **Roman Empire.** The early church was greatly impacted by being a part of the Roman Empire. The famous *Pax Romana* provided a political and military stability throughout the entire region that gave the apostles freedom to travel widely without great difficulty.

Additionally, the Roman investments in infrastructure like roads and consistent shipping lanes sped missionaries on their way. The universal language of Greek gave them the ability to communicate clearly wherever they found themselves, and the security of Roman citizenship protected Paul and other early believers from unfair treatment by authorities. Even the association early Christians had with Judaism was a benefit, since Judaism was an officially recognized religion by the Roman government. God used all of these political factors to help his church spread rapidly in the first century.

BOOKS IN THIS SECTION

ACTS

AUTHOR: Luke (a Gentile physician)

AUDIENCE: Theophilus

PURPOSE: To give an accurate account of the birth and growth of the Christian church

SETTING: Acts is the connecting link between Christ's life and the life of the church, between the Gospels and the Letters.

SPECIAL FEATURE: Acts is a sequel to the Gospel of Luke. Because Acts ends so abruptly, Luke may have planned to write a third book, continuing the story.

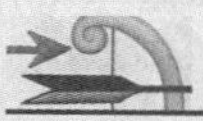

ROMANS

AUTHOR: Paul

AUDIENCE: The Christians in Rome

PURPOSE: To introduce Paul to the Romans and to give a sample of his message before he arrives in Rome

DATE WRITTEN: About A.D. 54, from Corinth

SPECIAL FEATURE: Paul wrote Romans as an organized and carefully presented statement of his faith—it does not have the form of a typical letter.

1 CORINTHIANS

AUTHOR: Paul

AUDIENCE: The church in Corinth

PURPOSE: To identify problems in the Corinthian church, to offer solutions, and to teach the believers how to live for Christ in a corrupt society

DATE WRITTEN: Approximately A.D. 53, during Paul's three-year ministry in Ephesus, during his third missionary journey

SPECIAL FEATURE: This is a strong, straight-forward letter.

2 CORINTHIANS

AUTHOR: Paul

AUDIENCE: The church in Corinth

PURPOSE: To affirm Paul's ministry, defend his authority as an apostle, and refute the false teachers in Corinth

DATE WRITTEN: Approximately A.D. 54, from Macedonia

SPECIAL FEATURES: This is an intensely personal and autobiographical letter. In 1 Corinthians, Paul used strong words to correct and teach. Most of the church had responded in the right spirit; there were, however, those who were denying Paul's authority and questioning his motives.

GALATIANS

AUTHOR: Paul

AUDIENCE: The churches in southern Galatia, founded on Paul's first missionary journey (including Iconium, Lystra, Derbe)

PURPOSE: To refute the Judaizers (who taught that Gentile believers must obey the Jewish law in order to be saved), and to call Christians to faith and freedom in Christ

DATE WRITTEN: Approximately A.D. 49, from Antioch, prior to the Jerusalem council

SETTING: Paul writes an impassioned letter responding to the most pressing controversy in the early church: the relationship of new believers, particularly Gentiles, to the Jewish laws.

EPHESIANS

AUTHOR: Paul

AUDIENCE: The church at Ephesus, then circulated to neighboring local churches

PURPOSE: To strengthen the believers in Ephesus in their Christian faith by explaining the nature and purpose of the church, the body of Christ

DATE WRITTEN: Approximately A.D. 60, from Rome, during Paul's imprisonment there

SPECIAL FEATURE: The letter was not written to confront any heresy or problem in the churches. It was sent with Tychicus to strengthen and encourage the churches in the area.

PHILIPPIANS

AUTHOR: Paul

AUDIENCE: The church at Philippi

PURPOSE: To thank the Philippians for the gift they had sent Paul and to strengthen these believers by showing them that true joy comes from Jesus Christ alone

DATE WRITTEN: Approximately A.D. 60, from Rome, during Paul's imprisonment there

SETTING: The Philippian church had sent a gift to Paul in prison. He wrote this letter to thank them for their gift and to encourage them in their faith.

COLOSSIANS

AUTHOR: Paul

AUDIENCE: The church at Colosse, a city in Asia Minor

PURPOSE: To combat errors in the church and to show that believers have everything they need in Christ

DATE WRITTEN: Approximately A.D. 60, during Paul's imprisonment in Rome

SETTING: Paul had never visited Colosse. Evidently the church had been founded by other converts from Paul's missionary travels. The church had been infiltrated by people attempting to combine elements of paganism and secular philosophy with Christian doctrine. Paul confronts these false teachings and affirms the sufficiency of Christ.

1 THESSALONIANS

AUTHOR: Paul

AUDIENCE: The church at Thessalonica

PURPOSE: To strengthen the Thessalonian Christians in their faith and give them the assurance of Christ's return

DATE WRITTEN: Approximately A.D. 50 from Corinth

SETTING: The church at Thessalonica was very young, having been established only two or three years before this letter was written. The Thessalonian Christians needed to mature in their faith.

2 THESSALONIANS

AUTHOR: Paul

AUDIENCE: The church at Thessalonica

PURPOSE: To clear up the confusion about the second coming of Christ

DATE WRITTEN: Approximately A.D. 50, a few months after 1 Thessalonians, from Corinth

SETTING: This follow-up to 1 Thessalonians clears up some misunderstandings. In this letter, Paul indicates various events that must precede the second coming of Christ.

1 TIMOTHY

AUTHOR: Paul

AUDIENCE: Timothy, Paul's son in the faith

PURPOSE: To give encouragement and instruction to Timothy, a young leader

DATE WRITTEN: Approximately A.D. 62, probably just prior to Paul's final imprisonment in Rome

SPECIAL FEATURES: This is a personal letter and a handbook of church administration and discipline. Timothy led the church in Ephesus.

2 TIMOTHY

AUTHOR: Paul

AUDIENCE: Timothy, Paul's son in the faith

PURPOSE: To give final instructions and encouragement to Timothy, pastor of the church at Ephesus

DATE WRITTEN: Approximately A.D. 64, from prison in Rome, where Paul awaited imminent execution

SPECIAL FEATURES: Because this is Paul's last letter, it reveals his heart and his priorities—sound doctrine, steadfast faith, confident endurance, and lasting love.

TITUS

AUTHOR: Paul

AUDIENCE: Titus, a Greek

PURPOSE: To advise Titus in his responsibility of supervising the churches on the island of Crete

DATE WRITTEN: Approximately A.D. 62, around the same time 1 Timothy was written when Paul traveled between his Roman imprisonments

SETTING: Paul sent Titus to organize and oversee the churches on Crete. This letter tells Titus how to do this job.

PHILEMON

AUTHOR: Paul

AUDIENCE: Philemon, a wealthy member of the Colossian church

PURPOSE: To convince Philemon to forgive his runaway slave, Onesimus, and to accept him as a brother in the faith

DATE WRITTEN: Approximately A.D. 60, during Paul's first imprisonment in Rome

SPECIAL FEATURE: This is a personal letter to a friend.

HEBREWS

AUTHOR: Unknown. Paul, Luke, Barnabas, Apollos, Silas, Philip, Priscilla, and others have been suggested. Whoever it was speaks of Timothy as "brother" (Heb 13:23).

AUDIENCE: Hebrew Christians who may have been considering a return to Judaism

PURPOSE: To present the sufficiency and superiority of Christ

DATE WRITTEN: Probably before A.D. 70, because Jewish sacrifices and ceremonies are discussed, but no mention is made of the Temple's destruction

SETTING: These Jewish Christians were probably undergoing fierce persecution, socially and physically, both from Jews and from Romans. They needed to be reassured that Christianity was true and that Jesus was indeed the Messiah.

Apostle Paul Preaching on the Ruins, by Giovanni Paolo Pannini

JAMES

AUTHOR: James, Jesus' half brother, a leader in the Jerusalem church

AUDIENCE: First-century Jewish Christians residing in Gentile communities

PURPOSE: To expose hypocritical practices and to teach right Christian behavior

DATE WRITTEN: Probably A.D. 48, prior to the Jerusalem council held in A.D. 49

SETTING: James expresses concern for persecuted Christians who were once part of the Jerusalem church.

1 PETER

AUTHOR: Peter

AUDIENCE: Jewish Christians driven out of Jerusalem and scattered throughout Asia Minor

PURPOSE: To offer encouragement to suffering Christians

DATE WRITTEN: Approximately A.D. 62–64, possibly from Rome

SETTING: Throughout the Roman Empire, Christians were being tortured and killed for their faith, and the church in Jerusalem was being scattered.

2 PETER

AUTHOR: Peter

AUDIENCE: The church at large

PURPOSE: To warn Christians about false teachers and to exhort them to grow in their faith and knowledge of Christ

DATE WRITTEN: Approximately A.D. 64, likely from Rome

SETTING: Peter knew that his time on earth was limited, so he wrote about what was on his heart, warning believers about the presence of false teachers and reminding them of the unchanging truth of the gospel.

1 JOHN

AUTHOR: The apostle John

AUDIENCE: This pastoral letter was likely sent to several Gentile congregations.

PURPOSE: To reassure Christians in their faith and to counter false teachings

DATE WRITTEN: Probably between A.D. 85 and 90, from Ephesus

SETTING: John was an older man and perhaps the only surviving apostle at this time. As an eyewitness of Christ, he wrote to give a new generation confidence in God and in their faith.

2 JOHN

AUTHOR: The apostle John

AUDIENCE: To "the chosen lady" and her children—probably a local church

PURPOSE: To emphasize the basics of following Christ—truth and love—and to warn against false teachers

DATE WRITTEN: Approximately A.D. 90 from Ephesus

SETTING: This church had developed a strong relationship with John. John was warning them of the false teachers who were becoming prevalent in the area.

3 JOHN

AUTHOR: The apostle John

AUDIENCE: Gaius, a prominent Christian in one of the churches known to John

PURPOSE: To commend Gaius for his hospitality and to encourage him in his Christian life

DATE WRITTEN: Approximately A.D. 90 from Ephesus

SETTING: Church leaders traveled from town to town helping to establish new congregations. They depended on the hospitality of fellow believers like Gaius.

JUDE

AUTHOR: Jude, half brother of Jesus and brother of James

AUDIENCE: Jewish Christians

PURPOSE: To remind the church of the need for constant vigilance—to keep strong in the faith and to oppose heresy

DATE WRITTEN: Difficult to determine; as early as A.D. 65, but likely around A.D. 90

SETTING: From the beginning, the church has been threatened by false teaching; we must always be on our guard.

REVELATION

AUTHOR: The apostle John

AUDIENCE: The seven churches in Asia and all believers everywhere

PURPOSE: To reveal the full identity of Christ and to give warning and hope to believers

DATE WRITTEN: Approximately A.D. 95 from Patmos

SETTING: The persecution of Christians under Emperor Domitian (A.D. 90–95) was underway, and John had been exiled to the island of Patmos. John had a vision of the glorified Christ and what would take place in the future—judgment and the ultimate triumph of God over evil.

Twin Beaches of Patmos, the island where John was exiled

MEGATHEMES

■ **Holy Spirit.** When Jesus ascended to heaven, he did not leave his church alone. The disciples were empowered by God's Holy Spirit. Nothing that the church has ever accomplished has been because of human effort; the indwelling Spirit is the driving force behind everything we do. He is the promised Advocate and Guide sent by Jesus and the Father. The Holy Spirit's work demonstrated that Christianity was supernatural. Thus, the church became more Holy Spirit conscious than problem conscious. By faith, every believer has the Holy Spirit's power to do Christ's work.

■ **Church Growth.** Here we see the history of a dynamic, growing community of believers from Jerusalem to Syria, Africa, Asia, and Europe. In the first century, Christianity spread from believing Jews to non-Jews in no less than 39 cities and 30 countries or regions. When the Holy Spirit works, there is movement, excitement, and growth. He gives us the motivation, energy, and ability to get the gospel to the whole world. How do you fit into God's plan for spreading Christianity? What is your place in this movement?

■ **Witnessing.** Peter, John, Philip, Paul, Barnabas, and thousands more witnessed to their new faith in Christ. By personal testimony, preaching, or defense before authorities, they told the story with boldness and courage to groups of all sizes. We are God's people, chosen to be part of his plan to reach the world. In love and by faith, we can have the Holy Spirit's help as we witness or preach. Witnessing is also beneficial to us because it strengthens our faith as we confront those who challenge it.

■ **Opposition.** Through imprisonment, beatings, plots, and riots, Christians were persecuted by both Jews and Gentiles. But the opposition became a catalyst for the spread of Christianity. Growth during times of oppression showed that Christianity was not the work of humans, but of God. God can work through any opposition. When persecution from hostile unbelievers comes, realize that it has come because you have been a faithful witness and you have looked for the opportunity to present the Good News about Christ. Seize the opportunities that opposition brings.

■ **Church Controversy.** There wasn't always universal agreement among Christians about the implications of faith in Christ for practical living or theology. The famous Jerusalem Council decided the controversial question of the place of the Jewish law in the lives of Gentile Christians, and we get glimpses of some other debates that arose through the letters of Paul, James, Peter, and John. The way the apostles handled these controversies is a model for us today. They were careful to ensure that the truth about Christ was clear, relying on the Holy Spirit to keep their focus on the gospel and not to allow cultural or personal ideas to distort the simple message.

■ **Theological Development.** As the church grew and spread throughout the world, the Holy Spirit inspired the apostles in their teaching ministries, particularly in the writings that eventually became our New Testament. In these documents, God has revealed more about himself, his work in the world, and the life he calls his followers to live. We need to be constantly immersed in the Word of God to have a firm grasp of who God is and who he calls us to be as his children.

■ **Hope.** The earliest Christians often faced difficulties. Oppression, poverty, persecution, famine, and imprisonment were more common than material peace, security, and prosperity. But even under such difficult earthly circumstances, the presence of the Holy Spirit and the hope of final restoration gave them great joy and strength. No matter what difficulties we might face in this life, the hope of eternal life with God helps us to respond with love, joy, and peace. Come, Lord Jesus!

MAP

1 Judea Jesus ascended to heaven from the Mount of Olives, outside Jerusalem, and he told his followers to stay in the area to await the indwelling of the Holy Spirit, which occurred at Pentecost. Peter gave a powerful sermon that was heard by Jews from across the empire. The Jerusalem church grew, but Stephen was martyred for his faith by Jewish leaders who did not believe in Jesus (Acts 1:1–7:60).

2 Samaria After Stephen's death, the persecution of Christians intensified, but it caused the believers to leave Jerusalem and spread the gospel to other cities in the empire. Philip took the gospel into Samaria, and even to a man from Ethiopia, who he met by a divine appointment on the road to Gaza (Acts 8:1-40).

3 Damascus Paul (Saul) began his story as a persecutor of Christians, only to be confronted by Jesus himself on the road to Damascus. He became a believer and continued to Damascus, where he preached the Good News rather than persecuting people for it. But his new faith created some new enemies who threatened his life, so he returned to his hometown of Tarsus for safety (Acts 9:1-30).

4 Antioch Barnabas sought out Paul in Tarsus and brought him to the church in Antioch of Syria, a thriving church where they worked together (Acts 11:19–12:25). Around the same time, Peter had received a vision that led him to Caesarea, where he presented the gospel to a Gentile family, who became believers (Acts 10:1–11:18).

5 Cyprus The church in Antioch became the home base for the earliest missionary activity. Paul and Barnabas were dedicated for God's work of spreading the gospel to other cities. They set off on their first missionary journey, heading first to Cyprus, where Barnabas was from (Acts 13:1-12).

6 Galatia After sharing the Good News all over the island of Cyprus, Paul and Barnabas headed to the region of Galatia and ministered in several cities there as well. They saw many people come to believe in the Lord Jesus, and established churches in Antioch of Pisidia, Lystra, Derbe, and Iconium (Acts 13:13–14:28).

7 Jerusalem Controversy erupted between Jewish Christians and Gentile Christians over the relationship of Gentile Christians to the Jewish law. This led to a special council, with delegates from the churches in Antioch and Jerusalem meeting in Jerusalem. Together, they resolved the conflict and the news was taken back to Antioch (Acts 15:1-35).

8 Macedonia Paul embarked on a second missionary journey, this time with Silas. He revisited the churches in Galatia and planned to head toward Ephesus, but the Holy Spirit had other plans. So he turned north toward Bithynia and Pontus but again was told not to go. He then received the "Macedonian call," and followed the Spirit's direction into the cities of Macedonia (Acts 15:36–17:14).

9 Achaia Paul traveled from Macedonia to Athens and Corinth in Achaia, then traveled by ship to Ephesus before returning to Caesarea, Jerusalem, and finally back to Antioch (Acts 17:15–18:22). During his stay in Corinth, he wrote two letters to the Christians in Thessalonica.

10 Ephesus Paul's third missionary journey took him back through Cilicia and Galatia, this time straight to Ephesus in Asia, where he stayed for over two years. He visited other cities in Asia before going back to Macedonia and Achaia. During this time he wrote his letters to the church in Corinth and Rome. He then returned to Jerusalem by ship, despite knowing that he would be arrested there (Acts 18:23–23:30).

11 Caesarea Paul was arrested in Jerusalem and taken to Caesarea under Roman guard. Paul always took advantage of any opportunity to share the gospel, and he did so before many Gentile leaders during his more than two-year stay in prison there. But Paul appealed his case to Caesar, so he would be sent to Rome (Acts 23:31–26:32).

12 Rome After storms, layovers in Crete, and shipwreck on the island of Malta, Paul arrived in Sicily and finally in Italy, where he traveled by land, under guard, to his long-awaited destination: Rome, the capital of the empire (Acts 27:1–28:31). While he was in prison waiting for this trial, he wrote many letters to churches and co-workers in the ministry of the Good News. Paul was released from prison in Rome, but after about two more years of ministry he was arrested again and martyred for his faith.

13 Patmos Many other apostles were working for the Good News throughout the world during Paul's journeys. Peter served Jewish Christians throughout the Roman Empire, and he was martyred in Rome around the same time as Paul. John traveled some as well, and settled in Ephesus where he taught and mentored many Christians and churches in the area. Eventually, he was arrested and exiled to the island of Patmos, where he received a vision recorded in the book of Revelation.

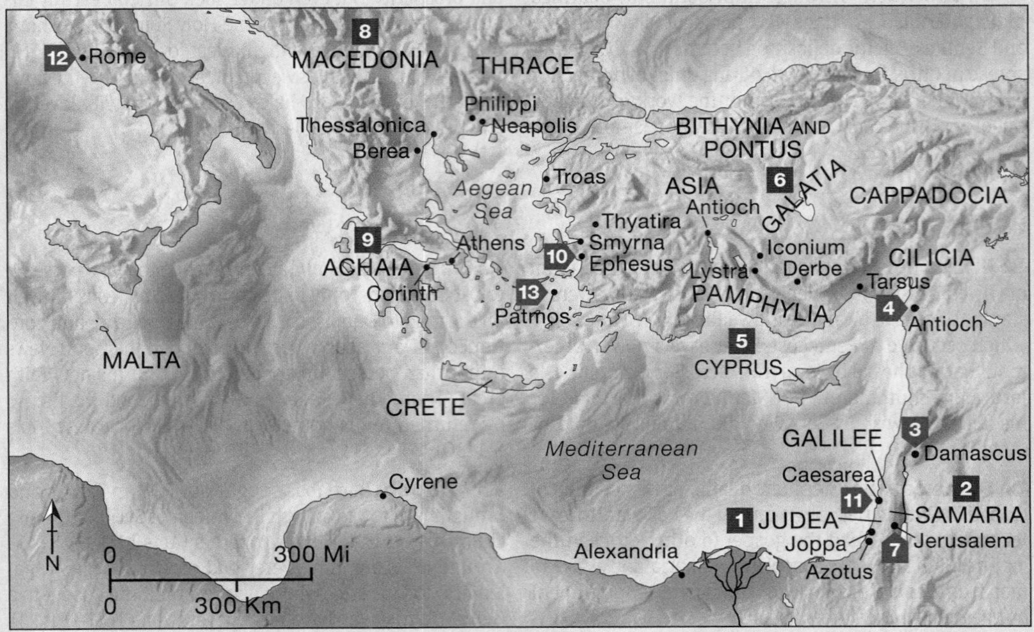

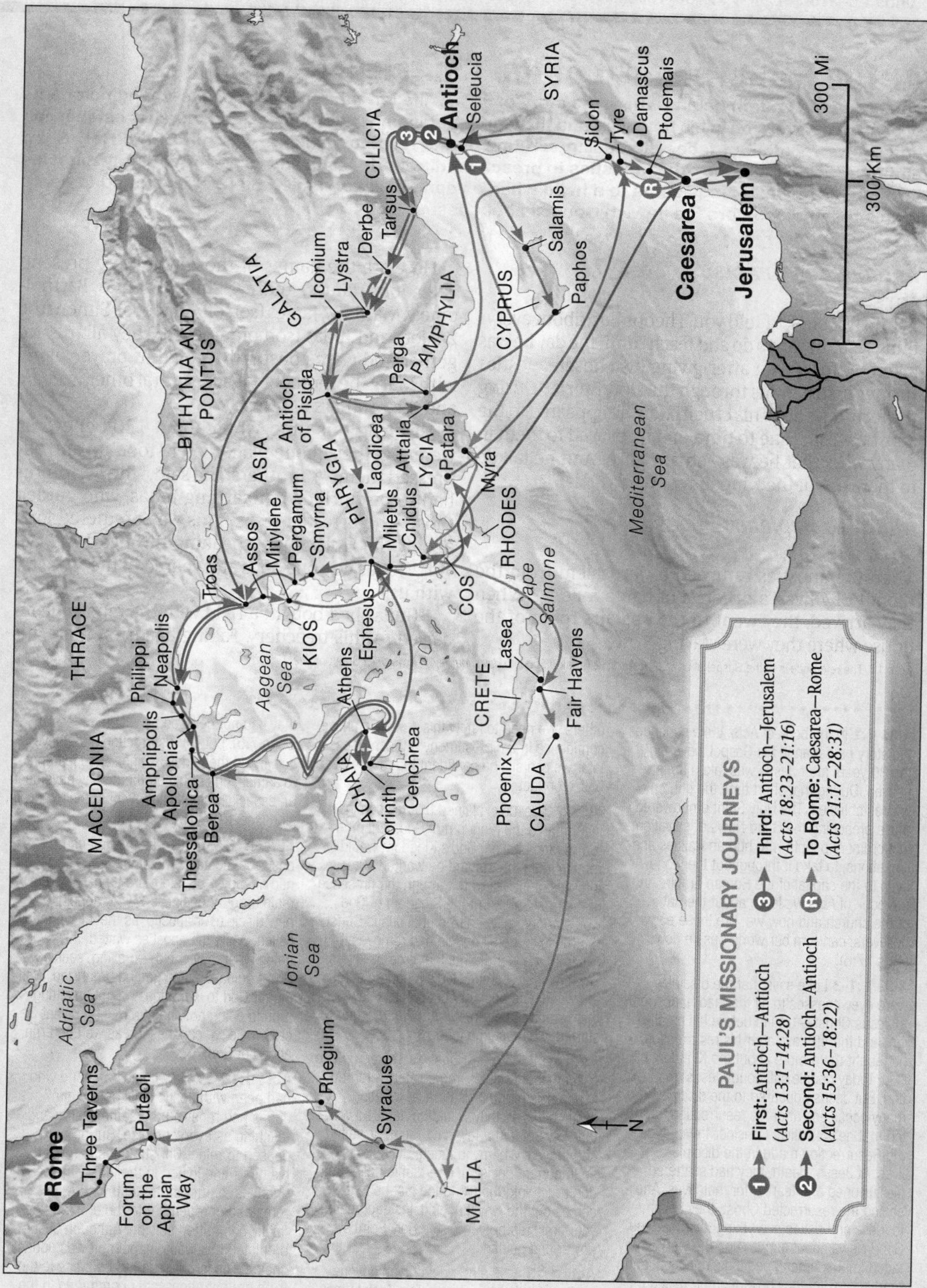

Paul's missionary journeys covered tremendous distances as he tirelessly spread the gospel across much of the Roman Empire. His combined trips, by land and sea, equal more than 13,000 air miles.

A. The Establishment of the Church

The era of the church begins where the story of Jesus' life left off, reporting the life-changing effects of Jesus' resurrection in his followers and the world. Beginning in Jerusalem, the church is established and grows rapidly but faces increasing scrutiny by the religious leaders. The gift of the Holy Spirit empowers Peter and the other apostles to preach boldly about Jesus and to perform mighty miracles through his power. Things come to a head when a young believer named Stephen is stoned to death for his testimony before the Jewish Council about Jesus.

Introduction to Acts

ACTS 1:1-3

In my first book* I told you, Theophilus, about everything Jesus began to do and teach [2]until the day he was
taken up to heaven after giving his chosen apostles
further instructions through the Holy Spirit. [3]During
the forty days after his crucifixion, he appeared to the
apostles from time to time, and he proved to them in
many ways that he was actually alive. And he talked
to them about the Kingdom of God.

Matthias Replaces Judas

ACTS 1:12-26

Then the apostles returned to Jerusalem from the
Mount of Olives, a distance of half a mile.* [13]When
they arrived, they went to the upstairs room of the
house where they were staying.

Here are the names of those who were present:
Peter, John, James, Andrew, Philip, Thomas, Bartholomew, Matthew, James (son of Alphaeus), Simon (the
Zealot), and Judas (son of James). [14]They all met together and were constantly united in prayer, along
with Mary the mother of Jesus, several other women,
and the brothers of Jesus.

[15]During this time, when about 120 believers*
were together in one place, Peter stood up and addressed them. [16]"Brothers," he said, "the Scriptures
had to be fulfilled concerning Judas, who guided
those who arrested Jesus. This was predicted long
ago by the Holy Spirit, speaking through King David. [17]Judas was one of us and shared in the ministry
with us."

[18](Judas had bought a field with the money he received for his treachery. Falling headfirst there, his

Acts 1:1 The reference is to the Gospel of Luke. **Acts 1:12** Greek *a Sabbath day's journey.* **Acts 1:15** Greek *brothers.*

Acts 1:1 In the book of Acts, Luke continues the story he began in his Gospel, covering the 30 years after Jesus was taken up into heaven. During that short time the church was established. The Holy Spirit empowered those preaching the Good News of salvation, just ordinary people with human frailties and limitations, to take it throughout the world, even to the capital of the Roman Empire. In the book of Acts we learn about the nature of the church and how we, like these early believers, can turn our world upside down (Acts 17:6).

Acts 1:1-3 Luke says that the disciples were eyewitnesses to all that had happened to Jesus Christ—his life before his crucifixion, and the 40 days after his resurrection as he taught them more about the Kingdom of God. Today people still doubt Jesus' resurrection. But Jesus appeared to the disciples on many occasions after his resurrection, proving that he was alive. Consider the change the Resurrection made in the disciples' lives. At Jesus' death, they had scattered, disillusioned and fearing for their lives. After seeing the resurrected Christ, they became fearless and risked everything to spread the Good News about him around the world. They faced imprisonment, beatings, rejection, and martyrdom, yet they never compromised their mission. These men would not have risked—and in some cases, given—their lives for something they knew was a fraud. They knew Jesus was alive, and the early church was fired up with their enthusiasm to tell others. We need to know this so we can have confidence in their testimony; 20 centuries later we can still be confident that our faith is based on fact.

Acts 1:3 Jesus explained that his coming inaugurated the Kingdom of God. When he returned to heaven, God's Kingdom would remain in the hearts and be worked out in the lives of all believers through the presence of the Holy Spirit. But the Kingdom of God would not be fully realized until Jesus Christ returns to judge all people and remove all evil from the world. Until that time believers are to work to spread God's Kingdom across the world. The book of Acts records how this work was begun. What the early church started, we must continue.

Acts 1:12-13 After Christ was taken up into heaven, the disciples immediately returned to Jerusalem and had a prayer meeting. Jesus had said they would be baptized with the Holy Spirit in a few days, so they waited and prayed. When you face a difficult task, an important decision, or a baffling dilemma, don't rush into the work and just hope it comes out the way it should. Instead, make your first step prayer for the Holy Spirit's power and guidance.

Acts 1:13 A "Zealot" could mean anyone zealous for the Jewish law. The Zealots may have been a radical political party working for the violent overthrow of Roman rule in Israel.

Acts 1:14 At this time, Jesus' brothers were with the disciples. During Jesus' lifetime, they had not believed he was the Messiah (John 7:5), but his resurrection must have convinced them. Jesus' special appearance to James, one of his brothers, may have been an especially significant event in their conversion (see 1 Cor 15:7).

Acts 1:15-26 This was the first church business meeting. The small group of 11 had already grown to more than 120. The main order of business was to appoint a new disciple, or apostle, as the 11 were now called. While the apostles waited, they were doing what they could—praying, seeking God's guidance, and getting organized. Waiting for God to work does not mean sitting around doing nothing. We must do what we can, while we can, as long as we don't run ahead of God.

Acts 1:16-17 How could someone who had been with Jesus daily betray him? Judas had received the same calling and teaching as everyone else. But he had chosen to reject Christ. Judas hardened his heart and joined in the plot with Jesus' enemies to put him to death. Judas remained unrepentant to the end, and he finally committed suicide. Although Jesus predicted this would happen, it was Judas's choice. Those privileged to be *close* to the truth are not necessarily *committed* to the truth. See Judas's Profile on p. 1454 for more information on his life.

Acts 1:18 Matthew says that Judas hanged himself (Matt 27:5); Acts says that he fell.

body split open, spilling out all his intestines. 19The
news of his death spread to all the people of Jerusalem,
and they gave the place the Aramaic name *Akeldama,*
which means "Field of Blood.")
20Peter continued, "This was written in the book of
Psalms, where it says, 'Let his home become desolate,
with no one living in it.' It also says, 'Let someone else
take his position.'*
21"So now we must choose a replacement for Judas
from among the men who were with us the entire time
we were traveling with the Lord Jesus—22from the time
he was baptized by John until the day he was taken
from us. Whoever is chosen will join us as a witness
of Jesus' resurrection."
23So they nominated two men: Joseph called Barsabbas (also known as Justus) and Matthias. 24Then
they all prayed, "O Lord, you know every heart. Show
us which of these men you have chosen 25as an apostle
to replace Judas in this ministry, for he has deserted
us and gone where he belongs." 26Then they cast lots,
and Matthias was selected to become an apostle with
the other eleven.

The Holy Spirit Comes

ACTS 2:1-13

On the day of Pentecost* all the believers were meeting
together in one place. 2Suddenly, there was a sound
from heaven like the roaring of a mighty windstorm,

Acts 1:20 Pss 69:25; 109:8. **Acts 2:1** The Festival of Pentecost came 50 days after Passover (when Jesus was crucified).

LUKE

Although we know few facts about his life, Luke has left us a strong impression of himself by what he wrote. In his Gospel, he emphasizes Jesus Christ's compassion. He vividly recorded both the power demonstrated by Christ's life and the care with which Christ treated people. Luke highlighted the relationships Jesus had with women. His writing in Acts is full of sharp verbal pictures of real people caught up in the greatest events of history. • Luke was also a doctor. He had a traveling medical practice as Paul's companion. Since the gospel was often welcomed with whips and stones, the doctor was undoubtedly seldom without patients. It is even possible that Paul's "thorn in the flesh" was some kind of physical ailment that needed Luke's regular attention (see 2 Cor 12:7). • God also made special use of Luke as the historian of the early church. Repeatedly, the details of Luke's descriptions have been proven accurate. The first words in his Gospel indicate his interest in the truth. • Luke's compassion reflected his Lord's. Luke's skill as a doctor helped Paul. His passion for the facts as he recorded the life of Christ, the spread of the early church, and the lives of Christianity's first missionaries gives us dependable sources for the basis of our faith. He accomplished all this while staying out of the spotlight. Perhaps his greatest example is the challenge to greatness even when we are not the center of attention.

Strengths and accomplishments	• A humble, faithful, and useful companion of Paul • A well-educated and trained physician • A careful and exact historian • Writer of the Gospel of Luke and the book of Acts
Lessons from his life	• The words we leave behind will be a lasting picture of who we are • Excellence is shown by how we work when no one is noticing
Vital statistics	• Where: Probably met Paul in Troas • Occupations: Doctor, historian, traveling companion • Contemporaries: Paul, Timothy, Silas, Peter
Key verses	"Many people have set out to write accounts about the events that have been fulfilled among us. They used the eyewitness reports circulating among us from the early disciples. Having carefully investigated everything from the beginning, I also have decided to write a careful account for you, most honorable Theophilus, so you can be certain of the truth of everything you were taught" (Luke 1:1-4).

Luke includes himself in the "we" sections of Acts 16–28. He is also mentioned in Luke 1:3; Acts 1:1; Colossians 4:14; 2 Timothy 4:11; Philemon 1:24.

The traditional explanation is that when Judas hanged himself, the rope or branch broke, Judas fell, and his body burst open.

Acts 1:21-22 Many consistently followed Jesus throughout his ministry on earth. The 12 disciples were his inner circle, but others shared the disciples' deep love for and commitment to Jesus.

Acts 1:21-25 The apostles had to choose a replacement for Judas Iscariot. They outlined specific criteria for making the choice. After finalists were chosen, the apostles prayed, asking God to guide the selection process. This gives us a good example of how to proceed when we are making important decisions. Set up criteria consistent with the Bible, examine the alternatives, and pray for wisdom and guidance to reach a good decision.

Acts 1:26 The disciples became apostles. The word *disciple* means "follower or learner," and *apostle* means "messenger or missionary." These men now had the special assignment of spreading the Good News of Jesus' death and resurrection.

Acts 2:1 Held 50 days after Passover, Pentecost was also called the Festival of First Harvest. It was one of three major annual festivals (Deut 16:16), a festival of thanksgiving for the harvested crops. Jesus was crucified at Passover time, and he ascended 40 days after his resurrection. The Holy Spirit came 50 days after the Resurrection, 10 days after the Ascension. Jews of many nations had gathered in Jerusalem for this festival. Thus, Peter's speech (Acts 2:14ff) was given to an international audience, and it resulted in a worldwide harvest of new believers—the first converts to Christianity.

▸ **ACTS 2:1-13** ***(cont.)***

and it filled the house where they were sitting. [3]Then, what looked like flames or tongues of fire appeared and settled on each of them. [4]And everyone present was filled with the Holy Spirit and began speaking in other languages,* as the Holy Spirit gave them this ability.

[5]At that time there were devout Jews from every nation living in Jerusalem. [6]When they heard the loud noise, everyone came running, and they were bewildered to hear their own languages being spoken by the believers.

[7]They were completely amazed. "How can this be?" they exclaimed. "These people are all from Galilee, [8]and yet we hear them speaking in our own native languages! [9]Here we are—Parthians, Medes, Elamites, people from Mesopotamia, Judea, Cappadocia, Pontus, the province of Asia, [10]Phrygia, Pamphylia, Egypt, and the areas of Libya around Cyrene, visitors from Rome [11](both Jews and converts to Judaism), Cretans, and Arabs. And we all hear these people speaking in our own languages about the wonderful things God has done!" [12]They stood there amazed and perplexed. "What can this mean?" they asked each other.

[13]But others in the crowd ridiculed them, saying, "They're just drunk, that's all!"

Peter Preaches to the Crowd

ACTS 2:14-41

Then Peter stepped forward with the eleven other apostles and shouted to the crowd, "Listen carefully, all of you, fellow Jews and residents of Jerusalem! Make no mistake about this. [15]These people are not drunk, as some of you are assuming. Nine o'clock in the morning is much too early for that. [16]No, what you see was predicted long ago by the prophet Joel:

[17] 'In the last days,' God says,
  'I will pour out my Spirit upon all people.
Your sons and daughters will prophesy.
  Your young men will see visions,
  and your old men will dream dreams.

Acts 2:4 Or *in other tongues.*

Acts 2:3-4 This was a fulfillment of John the Baptist's words about the Holy Spirit's baptizing with fire (Luke 3:16) and of the prophet Joel's words about the outpouring of the Holy Spirit (Joel 2:28-29).

Why tongues of fire? Tongues symbolize speech and the communication of the Good News. Fire symbolizes God's purifying presence, which burns away the undesirable elements of our lives and sets our hearts aflame to ignite the lives of others. On Mount Sinai, God confirmed the validity of the Old Testament law with fire from heaven (Exod 19:16-18). At Pentecost, God confirmed the validity of the Holy Spirit's ministry by sending fire. At Mount Sinai, fire came down on one place; at Pentecost, fire came down on many believers, symbolizing that God's presence is available to all who believe in him.

Acts 2:3-4 God made his presence known to this group of believers in a spectacular way—roaring wind (Acts 2:2), fire, and his Holy Spirit. Would you like God to reveal himself to you in such recognizable ways? He may do so, but be wary of forcing your expectations on God. In 1 Kings 19:10-13, Elijah also needed a message from God. First came a great wind, then an earthquake, and finally a fire. But God's message came in a "gentle whisper." God may use dramatic methods to work in your life—or he may speak in gentle whispers. Wait patiently and always listen.

Acts 2:4-11 These people literally spoke in other languages as the Spirit gave them ability—a miraculous attention-getter for the international crowd gathered in town for the festival. All the nationalities represented recognized their own languages being spoken. More than miraculous speaking drew people's attention, however; they saw the presence and power of the Holy Spirit. The apostles continued to minister in the Holy Spirit's power wherever they went.

Acts 2:7-8 Christianity is not limited to any race or group of people. Christ offers salvation to all people without regard to nationality. Visitors in Jerusalem were surprised to hear the apostles and other believers speaking in languages other than their own, but they need not have been. God works all kinds of miracles to spread the Good News, using many languages as he calls all kinds of people to become his followers. No matter what your race, color, nationality, or language, God speaks to you. Are you listening?

Acts 2:9-11 Why are all these places mentioned? This is a list of many lands from which Jews had come to the festivals in Jerusalem. These Jews were not originally from Palestine because their ancestors had been dispersed to other parts of the world through captivities and persecutions. Very likely, some of the Jews who responded to Peter's message returned to their homelands with God's Good News of salvation. Thus, God prepared the way for the spread of the Good News. As you read Acts, you will see how the way was often prepared for Paul and other messengers by people who had become believers at Pentecost. The church at Rome, for example, was probably begun by such Jewish believers.

Acts 2:12 When the gathered crowd recognized that something supernatural was taking place, they naturally wanted an explanation. At this point, Peter stepped forward and explained the truth about God. This should be the pattern in our lives as well. Hopefully we are living in such a way that people will see Christ in us. If we do shine and sparkle (Matt 5:14; Phil 2:15) and if we are "salty" (Matt 5:13), we will get the attention of others. They will surely want to know what is so attractive and different about us. Then we can explain our "Christian hope" (1 Pet 3:15). What is different about your life? What supernatural evidence would cause someone to stop you and say, "What can this mean?"

Acts 2:14 Peter had been an unstable leader during Jesus' ministry, letting his bravado be his downfall, even denying that he knew Jesus (John 18:15-18, 25-27). But Christ had forgiven and restored him (John 21). This was a new Peter, humble but bold. His confidence came from the Holy Spirit, who made him a powerful and dynamic speaker. Have you ever felt as if you've made such bad mistakes that God could never forgive and use you? No matter what sins you have committed, God promises to forgive you and make you useful for his Kingdom. Allow him to forgive you and use you effectively to serve him.

Acts 2:14ff Peter tells the people that they should listen to the testimony of the believers because Old Testament prophecies had been fulfilled: that very morning with the pouring out of the Spirit (Acts 2:16-21) and because Jesus has shown himself to be both Lord and Messiah (Acts 2:25-36). Further, the risen Christ could change their lives (Acts 2:37-40).

Acts 2:16-21 Not everything mentioned in Joel 2:28-29 was happening that particular morning. The "last days" include all the days between Christ's first and second comings and is another way of saying "from now on." "That great and glorious day of the LORD" (Acts 2:20) denotes the whole Christian age. Even Moses yearned for the Lord to put his Spirit upon everyone (Num 11:29). At Pentecost the Holy Spirit was released throughout the entire world—to men, women, slaves, Jews, Gentiles. Now everyone can receive the Spirit. This was a revolutionary thought for first-century Jews.

18 In those days I will pour out my Spirit
even on my servants—men and women
alike—
and they will prophesy.
19 And I will cause wonders in the heavens above
and signs on the earth below—
blood and fire and clouds of smoke.
20 The sun will become dark,
and the moon will turn blood red
before that great and glorious day of the
LORD arrives.
21 But everyone who calls on the name of the LORD
will be saved.'*

22"People of Israel, listen! God publicly endorsed
Jesus the Nazarene* by doing powerful miracles, wonders, and signs through him, as you well know. 23But
God knew what would happen, and his prearranged
plan was carried out when Jesus was betrayed. With
the help of lawless Gentiles, you nailed him to a cross
and killed him. 24But God released him from the horrors of death and raised him back to life, for death
could not keep him in its grip. 25King David said this
about him:

'I see that the LORD is always with me.
I will not be shaken, for he is right beside me.
26 No wonder my heart is glad,
and my tongue shouts his praises!
My body rests in hope.
27 For you will not leave my soul among the dead*
or allow your Holy One to rot in the grave.

Acts 2:17-21 Joel 2:28-32. **Acts 2:22** Or *Jesus of Nazareth.* **Acts 2:27** Greek *in Hades;* also in 2:31.

Acts 2:23 Everything that happened to Jesus was under God's control. His plans were never disrupted by the Roman government or the Jewish officials. This was especially comforting to those facing oppression during the time of the early Christian church.

Acts 2:24 Peter spoke forthrightly about the Resurrection. As Peter preached, the events of Christ's death and resurrection were still hot news, less than two months old. Christ's execution had been carried out in public before many witnesses. His empty tomb was available for inspection just a short distance away. If Christ had not truly died, Peter's message would have been laughed at or ignored. If Christ had not been resurrected, authorities could have produced his body and put an end to this new faith. But Peter and the apostles had witnessed the risen Christ. Changed men, they announced the news with great passion and conviction.

Our faith and our credibility also rest on the truth of the empty tomb. Why? For a number of important reasons. According to the apostle Paul (see 1 Cor 15), the resurrection of Christ means that he is the Son of God and that his word can be trusted. It means that his sacrifice for sin was acceptable to God, so we can be completely forgiven. It means that our Savior is alive and active, able to help us in times of need. It also means that one day we, too, will conquer death. The Christian faith rests on the basic fact of the empty tomb. Don't neglect this essential part of the gospel when you share your faith with others.

Acts 2:25-32 Peter quoted from Psalm 16:8-11—a psalm written by David. He explained that David was not writing about himself because David died and was buried (Acts 2:29). Instead, he was writing as a prophet (Acts 2:30) who spoke of the Messiah who would be resurrected. The emphasis here is that Jesus' body was not left to rot in the grave but was, in fact, resurrected and glorified.

Then, what looked like flames or tongues of fire appeared and settled on each of them.
Acts 2:3

▸ **ACTS 2:14-41 *(cont.)***

28 You have shown me the way of life,
and you will fill me with the joy of your
presence.'*

29"Dear brothers, think about this! You can be sure
that the patriarch David wasn't referring to himself,
for he died and was buried, and his tomb is still here
among us. 30But he was a prophet, and he knew God
had promised with an oath that one of David's own descendants would sit on his throne. 31David was looking
into the future and speaking of the Messiah's resurrection. He was saying that God would not leave him
among the dead or allow his body to rot in the grave.

32"God raised Jesus from the dead, and we are all
witnesses of this. 33Now he is exalted to the place of
highest honor in heaven, at God's right hand. And the
Father, as he had promised, gave him the Holy Spirit to
pour out upon us, just as you see and hear today. 34For
David himself never ascended into heaven, yet he said,

'The LORD said to my Lord,
"Sit in the place of honor at my right hand
35 until I humble your enemies,
making them a footstool under your feet."'*

36"So let everyone in Israel know for certain that
God has made this Jesus, whom you crucified, to be
both Lord and Messiah!"

37Peter's words pierced their hearts, and they said to
him and to the other apostles, "Brothers, what should
we do?"

38Peter replied, "Each of you must repent of your
sins and turn to God, and be baptized in the name of
Jesus Christ for the forgiveness of your sins. Then you
will receive the gift of the Holy Spirit. 39This promise
is to you, and to your children, and even to the Gentiles*—all who have been called by the Lord our God."
40Then Peter continued preaching for a long time,
strongly urging all his listeners, "Save yourselves from
this crooked generation!"

41Those who believed what Peter said were baptized
and added to the church that day—about 3,000 in all.

The Believers Form a Community

ACTS 2:42-47

All the believers devoted themselves to the apostles'
teaching, and to fellowship, and to sharing in meals
(including the Lord's Supper*), and to prayer.

43A deep sense of awe came over them all, and
the apostles performed many miraculous signs and
wonders. 44And all the believers met together in one
place and shared everything they had. 45They sold
their property and possessions and shared the money
with those in need. 46They worshiped together at the
Temple each day, met in homes for the Lord's Supper, and shared their meals with great joy and generosity*—47all the while praising God and enjoying
the goodwill of all the people. And each day the Lord
added to their fellowship those who were being saved.

Peter Heals a Crippled Beggar

ACTS 3:1-11

Peter and John went to the Temple one afternoon
to take part in the three o'clock prayer service. 2As
they approached the Temple, a man lame from birth

Acts 2:25-28 Ps 16:8-11 (Greek version). **Acts 2:34-35** Ps 110:1. **Acts 2:39** Or *and to people far in the future;* Greek reads *and to those far away.* **Acts 2:42** Greek *the breaking of bread;* also in 2:46. **Acts 2:46** Or *and sincere hearts.*

Acts 2:37 After Peter's powerful, Spirit-filled message, the people were deeply moved and asked, "What should we do?" This is the basic question we must ask. It is not enough to be sorry for our sins. We must repent, ask God to forgive us, and then live like forgiven people. Has God spoken to you through his Word or through the words of another believer? Like Peter's audience, ask God what you should do, and then obey.

Acts 2:38-39 If you want to follow Christ, you must "repent of your sins and turn to God, and be baptized in the name of Jesus Christ." To repent means to turn from sin, to change the direction of your life from selfishness and rebellion against God's laws. At the same time, you must turn to Christ, depending on him for forgiveness, mercy, guidance, and purpose. We cannot save ourselves—only God can save us. Baptism identifies us with Christ and with the community of believers. It is a condition of discipleship and a sign of faith.

Acts 2:40-43 About 3,000 people became new believers when Peter preached the Good News about Christ. These new Christians were united with the other believers, taught by the apostles, and included in the prayer meetings and fellowship. New believers in Christ need to be in groups where they can learn God's Word, pray, and mature in the faith. If you have just begun a relationship with Christ, seek out other believers for fellowship, prayer, and teaching. This is the way to grow.

Acts 2:44 Recognizing the other believers as brothers and sisters in the family of God, the Christians in Jerusalem shared all they had so that all could benefit from God's gifts. It is tempting—especially if we have material wealth—to cut ourselves off from one another, concerning ourselves with only our interests and enjoying only our own little piece of the world. But as part of God's spiritual family, it is our responsibility to help one another in every way possible. God's family works best when its members work together.

Acts 2:46 A common misconception about the first Christians (who were Jews) was that they rejected the Jewish religion. But these believers saw Jesus' message and resurrection as the fulfillment of everything they knew and believed from the Old Testament. The Jewish believers at first did not separate themselves from the rest of the Jewish community. They still went to the Temple and synagogues for worship and instruction in the Scriptures. But their belief in Jesus created great friction with Jews who didn't believe that Jesus was the Messiah. Thus, believing Jews were forced to meet in private homes for Communion, prayer, and teaching about Christ. By the end of the first century, many of these Jewish believers were excommunicated from their synagogues.

Acts 2:47 A healthy Christian community attracts people to Christ. The Jerusalem church's zeal for worship and brotherly love was contagious. A healthy, loving church will grow in numbers. What are you doing to make your church the kind of place that will attract others to Christ?

Acts 3:1 The Jews observed three times of prayer—morning (9:00 a.m.), afternoon (3:00 p.m.), and evening (sunset). At these times devout Jews and Gentiles who believed in God often would go to the Temple to pray. Peter and John were going to the Temple for the afternoon prayer service.

Acts 3:2 The Beautiful Gate was an entrance to the Temple, not to the city. It was one of the favored entrances, and many people passed

was being carried in. Each day he was put beside the
Temple gate, the one called the Beautiful Gate, so he
could beg from the people going into the Temple.
3When he saw Peter and John about to enter, he asked
them for some money.
4Peter and John looked at him intently, and Peter
said, "Look at us!" 5The lame man looked at them eagerly, expecting some money. 6But Peter said, "I don't
have any silver or gold for you. But I'll give you what I
have. In the name of Jesus Christ the Nazarene,* get
up and* walk!"
7Then Peter took the lame man by the right hand
and helped him up. And as he did, the man's feet and
ankles were instantly healed and strengthened. 8He
jumped up, stood on his feet, and began to walk! Then,
walking, leaping, and praising God, he went into the
Temple with them.
9All the people saw him walking and heard him
praising God. 10When they realized he was the lame
beggar they had seen so often at the Beautiful Gate,
they were absolutely astounded! 11They all rushed out
in amazement to Solomon's Colonnade, where the
man was holding tightly to Peter and John.

Peter Preaches in the Temple

ACTS 3:12-26

Peter saw his opportunity and addressed the crowd.
"People of Israel," he said, "what is so surprising about
this? And why stare at us as though we had made this
man walk by our own power or godliness? 13For it is the
God of Abraham, Isaac, and Jacob—the God of all our
ancestors—who has brought glory to his servant Jesus
by doing this. This is the same Jesus whom you handed
over and rejected before Pilate, despite Pilate's decision
to release him. 14You rejected this holy, righteous one
and instead demanded the release of a murderer. 15You
killed the author of life, but God raised him from the
dead. And we are witnesses of this fact!
16"Through faith in the name of Jesus, this man was
healed—and you know how crippled he was before.
Faith in Jesus' name has healed him before your very
eyes.
17"Friends,* I realize that what you and your leaders
did to Jesus was done in ignorance. 18But God was
fulfilling what all the prophets had foretold about
the Messiah—that he must suffer these things. 19Now
repent of your sins and turn to God, so that your sins

Acts 3:6a Or *Jesus Christ of Nazareth.* **Acts 3:6b** Some manuscripts do not include *get up and.* **Acts 3:17** Greek *Brothers.*

---

through it on their way to worship. Giving money to beggars was considered praiseworthy in the Jewish religion. So the beggar wisely placed himself where he would be seen by the most people who were on their way to worship at the Temple.

Acts 3:5-6 The lame man asked for money, but Peter gave him something much better—the use of his legs. We often ask God to solve a small problem, but he wants to give us a whole new life and help for *all* our problems. He may say, "I've got something even better for you." You may ask God for what you want, but don't be surprised when he gives you what you really *need.*

Acts 3:6 "In the name of Jesus Christ" means "by the authority of Jesus Christ." The apostles were doing this healing through the Holy Spirit's power, not their own.

Acts 3:7-10 In his excitement, the formerly lame man began to jump and walk around. He also praised God! Then others were awed by God's power. Don't forget to thank people who help you, but also remember to praise God for his care and protection.

Acts 3:11 Solomon's Colonnade was part of the Temple complex built by King Herod the Great in an attempt to strengthen his relationship with the Jews. A colonnade is an entrance or porch supported by columns. Jesus taught and performed miracles in the Temple many times. When the apostles went to the Temple, they were undoubtedly in close proximity to the same religious leaders who had conspired to put Jesus to death.

Acts 3:11ff Peter had an audience, and he capitalized on the opportunity to share Jesus Christ. He clearly presented his message by telling (1) who Jesus was, (2) how the Jews had rejected him, (3) why their rejection was fatal, and (4) what they needed to do to change the situation. Peter told the crowd that they still had a choice; God still offered them the opportunity to believe and receive Jesus as their Messiah and as their Lord. Displays of God's mercy and grace, such as the healing of this lame man, often create teachable moments. Pray to have courage like Peter to see these opportunities and to use them to speak up for Christ.

Acts 3:13-15 Pilate had decided to release Jesus, but the people had clamored to have Barabbas, a murderer, released instead (see Luke 23:13-25). When Peter said, "You killed," he meant it literally. Jesus' trial and death had occurred right there in Jerusalem only weeks earlier. It wasn't an event of the distant past—most of these people had heard about it, and some may very well have taken part in condemning Jesus.

Acts 3:15 The religious leaders thought they had put an end to Jesus when they crucified him. But their confidence was shaken when Peter told them that Jesus was alive again and that this time they could not harm him. Peter's message emphasized that (1) the people and their religious leaders had killed Jesus (Acts 3:17), (2) God had brought him back to life, and (3) the apostles had been witnesses of this fact. After pointing out the sin and injustice of these leaders, Peter showed the significance of the Resurrection: God's triumph and power over death.

Acts 3:16 Jesus, not the apostles, received the glory for the healing of the lame man. In those days a man's name represented his character; it stood for his authority and power. By using Jesus' name, Peter showed who gave him the authority and power to heal. The apostles did not emphasize what *they* could do but what God could do through them. Jesus' name is not to be used as magic—it must be used in faith. When we pray in Jesus' name, we must remember that it is Christ himself, not merely the sound of his name, who gives our prayers their power.

Acts 3:18 Some of these prophecies are in Psalm 22; Isaiah 50:6; Isaiah 53. Peter was explaining the kind of Messiah God had sent to earth. The Jews had expected a great ruler, not a suffering servant.

Acts 3:19 John the Baptist had prepared the way for Jesus by preaching that people should turn from their sins. The apostles' message of salvation also included the call to repent—acknowledging personal sin and turning from it. Many people want the benefits of being identified with Christ without admitting their own disobedience and repenting. The key to forgiveness is confessing your sin and turning from it (see Acts 2:38).

Acts 3:19-20 When we repent, God promises not only to cleanse us of our sins but to bring spiritual refreshment. Turning away from sin may at first seem painful because it is hard to break old habits and give up certain sins. But God will give you a better way. As Hosea promised, "Oh, that we might know the LORD! Let us press on to know him. He will respond to us as surely as the arrival of dawn or the coming of rains in early spring" (Hos 6:3). Do you feel a need to be refreshed?

▸ **ACTS 3:12-26** ***(cont.)***

may be wiped away. [20]Then times of refreshment
will come from the presence of the Lord, and he will
again send you Jesus, your appointed Messiah. [21]For
he must remain in heaven until the time for the final
restoration of all things, as God promised long ago
through his holy prophets. [22]Moses said, 'The LORD
your God will raise up for you a Prophet like me from
among your own people. Listen carefully to everything he tells you.'* [23]Then Moses said, 'Anyone who
will not listen to that Prophet will be completely cut
off from God's people.'*
[24]"Starting with Samuel, every prophet spoke about
what is happening today. [25]You are the children of
those prophets, and you are included in the covenant
God promised to your ancestors. For God said to Abraham, 'Through your descendants* all the families on
earth will be blessed.' [26]When God raised up his servant, Jesus, he sent him first to you people of Israel,
to bless you by turning each of you back from your
sinful ways."

Peter and John before the Council

ACTS 4:1-22

While Peter and John were speaking to the people,
they were confronted by the priests, the captain of
the Temple guard, and some of the Sadducees. [2]These
leaders were very disturbed that Peter and John were
teaching the people that through Jesus there is a resurrection of the dead. [3]They arrested them and, since it
was already evening, put them in jail until morning.
[4]But many of the people who heard their message
believed it, so the number of believers now totaled
about 5,000 men, not counting women and children.*
[5]The next day the council of all the rulers and elders
and teachers of religious law met in Jerusalem. [6]Annas
the high priest was there, along with Caiaphas, John,
Alexander, and other relatives of the high priest. [7]They
brought in the two disciples and demanded, "By what
power, or in whose name, have you done this?"
[8]Then Peter, filled with the Holy Spirit, said to
them, "Rulers and elders of our people, [9]are we being
questioned today because we've done a good deed

Acts 3:22 Deut 18:15. **Acts 3:23** Deut 18:19; Lev 23:29. **Acts 3:25** Greek *your seed;* see Gen 12:3; 22:18. **Acts 4:4** Greek *5,000 adult males.*

Acts 3:21 The time when God will bring the "final restoration of all things" refers to the Second Coming, the Last Judgment, and the removal of sin and its effects from the world.

Acts 3:21-22 Most Jews thought that Joshua was this Prophet predicted by Moses (Deut 18:15). Peter was saying that the Prophet was Jesus Christ. Peter wanted to show that their long-awaited Messiah had come! He and all the apostles were calling the Jewish nation to realize what they had done to their Messiah, to repent, and to believe. From this point on in Acts, we see many Jews rejecting the Good News. So the message went also to the Gentiles, many of whom were open to receive Jesus.

Acts 3:24 The prophet Samuel had lived during the transition between the judges and the kings of Israel, and he had been seen as the first in a succession of prophets. Samuel anointed David king, founding David's royal line, from which the Messiah eventually came. All the prophets pointed to a future Messiah. For more on Samuel, see his Profile on p. 426.

Acts 3:25 God had promised Abraham that he would bless the world through Abraham's descendants, the Jewish race (Gen 12:3), from which the Messiah would come. God intended the Jewish nation to be a separate and holy nation that would teach the world about God, introduce the Messiah, and then carry on his work in the world. But the nation failed to pursue its mission to tell the world about God. Here, too, in apostolic times as well as in the time Jesus spent on earth, the Jews rejected their Messiah.

Acts 4:1 These priests had special influence and were often close relatives of the high priest. The captain of the Temple guard was the leader of the guards who were stationed around the Temple to ensure order. The Sadducees were members of a small but powerful Jewish religious sect that did not believe in the resurrection of the dead. They were the religious leaders who stood to gain financially by cooperating with the Romans. Most of those who planned and carried out Jesus' arrest and crucifixion were from these three groups.

Acts 4:2-3 Peter and John spoke to the people during the afternoon prayer time. The Sadducees moved in quickly to investigate. Because they did not believe in the Resurrection, they were understandably disturbed with what the apostles were saying. Peter and John were refuting one of their fundamental beliefs and thus threatening their authority as religious teachers. Even though the nation was under Roman rule, the Sadducees had almost unlimited power over the Temple grounds. Thus, they were able to arrest Peter and John for no other reason than teaching something that contradicted their beliefs.

Acts 4:3 Depending on where we live, seldom will sharing the Good News send us to jail as it did Peter and John. Still, we run risks in trying to win others to Christ. We might be willing to face a night in jail if it would bring 5,000 people to Christ, but shouldn't we also be willing to suffer for the sake of even one? What do you risk in witnessing—rejection, persecution? Whatever the risks, realize that nothing done for God is ever wasted.

Acts 4:5-6 The rulers, elders, and teachers of religious law made up the Jewish high council—the same council that had condemned Jesus to death (Luke 22:66). It had 70 members plus the current high priest, who presided over the group. The Sadducees held a majority in this ruling group. These were the wealthy, intellectual, and powerful men of Jerusalem. Jesus' followers stood before the same high council that Jesus had.

Acts 4:6 Annas had been deposed as high priest by the Romans, who then had appointed Caiaphas, Annas's son-in-law, in his place. Because the Jews considered the office of high priest a lifetime position, they still called Annas by that title and gave him respect and authority within the high council. Annas and Caiaphas had played significant roles in Jesus' trial (John 18:24, 28). They were not pleased that the man they thought they had sacrificed for the good of the nation (John 11:49-51) had followers who were just as persistent and promised to be just as troublesome as he had been.

Acts 4:7 The high council asked Peter and John by what power they had healed the man (Acts 3:6-7) and by what authority they preached (Acts 3:12-26). The actions and words of Peter and John threatened these religious leaders, who, for the most part, were more interested in their reputations and positions than in God. Through the help of the Holy Spirit (Mark 13:11), Peter spoke boldly before the council, actually putting the council on trial by showing them that the one they had crucified had risen again. Instead of being defensive, the apostles went on the offensive, boldly speaking out for God and presenting the Good News to these leaders.

Acts 4:11 The cornerstone unites two walls at the corner of a building and holds the building together. Peter said that the Jews rejected Christ, but now Christ had become the cornerstone of the church (Ps 118:22; Mark 12:10; 1 Pet 2:7). Without him there would be no church because it wouldn't be able to stand.

for a crippled man? Do you want to know how he was
healed? 10Let me clearly state to all of you and to all
the people of Israel that he was healed by the powerful
name of Jesus Christ the Nazarene,* the man you crucified but whom God raised from the dead. 11For Jesus
is the one referred to in the Scriptures, where it says,

'The stone that you builders rejected
has now become the cornerstone.'*

12There is salvation in no one else! God has given no
other name under heaven by which we must be saved."
13The members of the council were amazed when
they saw the boldness of Peter and John, for they could
see that they were ordinary men with no special training in the Scriptures. They also recognized them as
men who had been with Jesus. 14But since they could
see the man who had been healed standing right there
among them, there was nothing the council could say.
15So they ordered Peter and John out of the council
chamber* and conferred among themselves.
16"What should we do with these men?" they asked
each other. "We can't deny that they have performed
a miraculous sign, and everybody in Jerusalem knows
about it. 17But to keep them from spreading their propaganda any further, we must warn them not to speak
to anyone in Jesus' name again." 18So they called the
apostles back in and commanded them never again
to speak or teach in the name of Jesus.
19But Peter and John replied, "Do you think God
wants us to obey you rather than him? 20We cannot
stop telling about everything we have seen and heard."
21The council then threatened them further, but
they finally let them go because they didn't know how
to punish them without starting a riot. For everyone
was praising God 22for this miraculous sign—the healing of a man who had been lame for more than forty
years.

The Believers Pray for Courage

ACTS 4:23-31

As soon as they were freed, Peter and John returned
to the other believers and told them what the leading
priests and elders had said. 24When they heard the
report, all the believers lifted their voices together in
prayer to God: "O Sovereign Lord, Creator of heaven
and earth, the sea, and everything in them—25you
spoke long ago by the Holy Spirit through our ancestor David, your servant, saying,

'Why were the nations so angry?
Why did they waste their time with futile plans?
26 The kings of the earth prepared for battle;
the rulers gathered together
against the LORD
and against his Messiah.'*

27"In fact, this has happened here in this very city!
For Herod Antipas, Pontius Pilate the governor, the
Gentiles, and the people of Israel were all united
against Jesus, your holy servant, whom you anointed.
28But everything they did was determined beforehand
according to your will. 29And now, O Lord, hear their
threats, and give us, your servants, great boldness in
preaching your word. 30Stretch out your hand with

Acts 4:10 Or *Jesus Christ of Nazareth.* **Acts 4:11** Ps 118:22. **Acts 4:15** Greek *the Sanhedrin.* **Acts 4:25-26** Or *his anointed one;* or *his Christ.* Ps 2:1-2.

Acts 4:12 Many people react negatively to the fact that there is no other name than that of Jesus to call on for salvation. Yet this is not something the church decided; it is the specific teaching of Jesus himself (John 14:6). If God designated Jesus to be the Savior of the world, no one else can be his equal. Christians are to be open-minded on many issues but not on how we are saved from sin. No other religious teacher could die for our sins; no other religious teacher came to earth as God's only Son; no other religious teacher rose from the dead. Our focus should be on Jesus, whom God provided as the way to have an eternal relationship with himself. There is no other name or way!

Acts 4:13 Knowing that Peter and John were untrained, the council was amazed at what being with Jesus had done for them. A changed life convinces people of Christ's power. One of your greatest testimonies is the difference others see in your life and attitudes since you have believed in Christ.

Acts 4:13-18 Although the evidence was overwhelming and irrefutable (changed lives and a healed man), the religious leaders refused to believe in Christ and continued trying to suppress the truth. Don't be surprised if some people reject you and your positive witness for Christ. When minds are closed, even the clearest presentation of the facts can't open them. But don't give up, either. Pray for those people and continue to spread the Good News.

Acts 4:20 We may sometimes be afraid to share our faith in Christ because people may feel uncomfortable or reject us. But Peter and John's zeal for the Lord was so strong that they could not keep quiet, even when threatened. If your courage to witness for God has weakened, pray that your boldness may increase. Remember Jesus' promise: "Everyone who acknowledges me publicly here on earth, I will also acknowledge before my Father in heaven" (Matt 10:32).

Acts 4:24-30 Notice how the believers prayed. First, they praised God; then they told God their specific problem and asked for his help. They did not ask God to remove the problem but to help them deal with it. We can follow this model when we pray. We may ask God to remove our problems, and he may choose to do so. But we must recognize that often he will leave a problem but give us the strength and courage to deal with it.

Acts 4:27 Herod Antipas had been appointed by the Romans to rule over the territory of Galilee. Pontius Pilate was the Roman governor over Judea; he bowed to pressure from the crowd and sentenced Jesus to death. See Herod's Profile on p. 1362 and Pilate's Profile on p. 1479.

Acts 4:28 God is the sovereign Lord of all events who rules history to fulfill his purposes. What his will determines, his power carries out. No leader, army, government, or council can stand in God's way.

Acts 4:29-31 Boldness is not reckless impulsiveness. Boldness requires courage to press on through our fears and do what we know is right. How can we be more bold? Like the disciples, we need to pray with others. To gain boldness, you can (1) pray for the power of the Holy Spirit to give you courage, (2) look for opportunities in your family and neighborhood to talk about Christ, (3) realize that rejection, social discomfort, and embarrassment are not necessarily persecution, and (4) start where you are by being bolder in small ways.

▸ **ACTS 4:23-31** ***(cont.)***

healing power; may miraculous signs and wonders be done through the name of your holy servant Jesus."

31 After this prayer, the meeting place shook, and they were all filled with the Holy Spirit. Then they preached the word of God with boldness.

The Believers Share Their Possessions

ACTS 4:32-37

All the believers were united in heart and mind. And they felt that what they owned was not their own, so they shared everything they had. 33 The apostles testified powerfully to the resurrection of the Lord Jesus, and God's great blessing was upon them all. 34 There were no needy people among them, because those who owned land or houses would sell them 35 and bring the money to the apostles to give to those in need.

36 For instance, there was Joseph, the one the apostles nicknamed Barnabas (which means "Son of Encouragement"). He was from the tribe of Levi and came from the island of Cyprus. 37 He sold a field he owned and brought the money to the apostles.

Ananias and Sapphira

ACTS 5:1-11

But there was a certain man named Ananias who, with his wife, Sapphira, sold some property. 2 He brought part of the money to the apostles, claiming it was the full amount. With his wife's consent, he kept the rest.

3 Then Peter said, "Ananias, why have you let Satan fill your heart? You lied to the Holy Spirit, and you kept some of the money for yourself. 4 The property was yours to sell or not sell, as you wished. And after selling it, the money was also yours to give away. How could you do a thing like this? You weren't lying to us but to God!"

5 As soon as Ananias heard these words, he fell to the floor and died. Everyone who heard about it was terrified. 6 Then some young men got up, wrapped him in a sheet, and took him out and buried him.

7 About three hours later his wife came in, not knowing what had happened. 8 Peter asked her, "Was this the price you and your husband received for your land?"

"Yes," she replied, "that was the price."

9 And Peter said, "How could the two of you even think of conspiring to test the Spirit of the Lord like this? The young men who buried your husband are just outside the door, and they will carry you out, too."

10 Instantly, she fell to the floor and died. When the young men came in and saw that she was dead, they carried her out and buried her beside her husband. 11 Great fear gripped the entire church and everyone else who heard what had happened.

The Apostles Heal Many

ACTS 5:12-16

The apostles were performing many miraculous signs and wonders among the people. And all the believers were meeting regularly at the Temple in the area known

---

Acts 4:32 Differences of opinion are inevitable among human personalities and can actually be helpful if handled well. But spiritual unity is essential—loyalty, commitment, and love for God and his Word. Without spiritual unity, the church could not survive. Paul wrote the letter of 1 Corinthians to urge the church in Corinth toward greater unity.

Acts 4:32 These Christians didn't feel that what they had was their own, so they were able to give and share, eliminating poverty among them. They would not let a brother or sister suffer when others had plenty. How do you feel about your possessions? We should adopt the attitude that everything we have comes from God, and we are only sharing what is already his.

Acts 4:32-35 The early church was able to share possessions and property as a result of the unity brought by the Holy Spirit working in and through the believers' lives. This way of living is different from communism because (1) the sharing was voluntary; (2) it didn't involve all private property but only as much as was needed; (3) it was not a membership requirement in order to be a part of the church. The spiritual unity and generosity of these early believers attracted others to them. This organizational structure is not a biblical command, but it offers vital principles for us to follow.

Acts 4:36 Barnabas (Joseph) was a respected leader of the church. He was a Levite by birth, a member of the Jewish tribe that carried out Temple duties. But his family had moved to Cyprus, so Barnabas didn't serve in the Temple. He traveled with Paul on Paul's first missionary journey (Acts 13:1ff). For more information on Barnabas, see his Profile on p. 1543.

Acts 5:1ff In Acts 5:1–8:3 we see both internal and external problems facing the early church. Inside, the church had dishonesty (Acts 5:1-11), greed (Acts 5:3), and administrative headaches (Acts 6:1-7). Outside, the church was being pressured by persecution. While church leaders were careful and sensitive in dealing with the internal problems, they could not do much to prevent the external pressures. Through it all, the leaders kept their focus on what was most important—spreading the Good News of Jesus Christ.

Acts 5:3 Even after the Holy Spirit had come, the believers were not immune to Satan's temptations. Although Christ had defeated Satan at the cross, Satan was still actively trying to make the believers stumble—as he does today (Eph 6:12; 1 Pet 5:8). Satan's overthrow is inevitable, but it will not occur until the last days, when Christ returns to judge the world (Rev 20:10).

Acts 5:3ff The sin Ananias and Sapphira committed was not stinginess or holding back part of the money—it was their choice whether or not to sell the land and how much to give. Their sin was lying to God and God's people, saying they gave the whole amount but holding back some for themselves and trying to make themselves appear more generous than they really were. This act was judged harshly because dishonesty, greed, and covetousness are destructive in a church, preventing the Holy Spirit from working effectively. All lying is bad, but when we lie to try to deceive God and his people about our relationship with him, we destroy our testimony for Christ.

Acts 5:11 Some read the account of Ananias and Sapphira being struck down and accuse God of being harsh. "I thought God was supposed to be loving and forgiving. I thought all that wrath stuff was for Old Testament times." With an emphasis on grace and mercy, it's easy to overlook the equally important truth of God's holiness. We must remember that God has not changed (Mal 3:6). He still hates sin as much as he ever did. God's judgment of Ananias and Sapphira produced shock and fear among the believers, making them realize how seriously God regards sin in the church.

as Solomon's Colonnade. [13]But no one else dared to join them, even though all the people had high regard for them. [14]Yet more and more people believed and were brought to the Lord—crowds of both men and women. [15]As a result of the apostles' work, sick people were brought out into the streets on beds and mats so that Peter's shadow might fall across some of them as he went by. [16]Crowds came from the villages around Jerusalem, bringing their sick and those possessed by evil* spirits, and they were all healed.

The Apostles Meet Opposition

ACTS 5:17-42

The high priest and his officials, who were Sadducees, were filled with jealousy. [18]They arrested the apostles and put them in the public jail. [19]But an angel of the Lord came at night, opened the gates of the jail, and brought them out. Then he told them, [20]"Go to the Temple and give the people this message of life!"

[21]So at daybreak the apostles entered the Temple, as they were told, and immediately began teaching.

When the high priest and his officials arrived, they convened the high council*—the full assembly of the elders of Israel. Then they sent for the apostles to be brought from the jail for trial. [22]But when the Temple guards went to the jail, the men were gone. So they returned to the council and reported, [23]"The jail was securely locked, with the guards standing outside, but when we opened the gates, no one was there!"

[24]When the captain of the Temple guard and the leading priests heard this, they were perplexed, wondering where it would all end. [25]Then someone arrived with startling news: "The men you put in jail are standing in the Temple, teaching the people!"

[26]The captain went with his Temple guards and arrested the apostles, but without violence, for they were afraid the people would stone them. [27]Then they brought the apostles before the high council, where the high priest confronted them. [28]"Didn't we tell you never again to teach in this man's name?" he demanded. "Instead, you have filled all Jerusalem with your teaching about him, and you want to make us responsible for his death!"

[29]But Peter and the apostles replied, "We must obey God rather than any human authority. [30]The God of our ancestors raised Jesus from the dead after you killed him by hanging him on a cross.* [31]Then God put him in the place of honor at his right hand as Prince and Savior. He did this so the people of Israel would repent of their sins and be forgiven. [32]We are witnesses of these things and so is the Holy Spirit, who is given by God to those who obey him."

[33]When they heard this, the high council was furious and decided to kill them. [34]But one member, a Pharisee

Acts 5:16 Greek *unclean.* **Acts 5:21** Greek *Sanhedrin;* also in 5:27, 41. **Acts 5:30** Greek *on a tree.*

Acts 5:14 What makes Christianity attractive? It is easy to be drawn to churches because of programs, good speakers, size, beautiful facilities, or fellowship. People were attracted to the early church, however, by expressions of God's power at work; the generosity, sincerity, honesty, and unity of the members; and the character of the leaders. Have our standards slipped? God wants to add believers to his church, not just newer and better programs or larger and fancier facilities.

Acts 5:15-16 People who passed within Peter's shadow were healed, not by Peter's shadow, but by God's power working through Peter. What did these miraculous healings do for the early church? (1) They attracted new believers; (2) they confirmed the truth of the apostles' teaching; and (3) they demonstrated that the power of the Messiah, who had been crucified and risen, was now with his followers.

Acts 5:17-18 The apostles experienced power to do miracles, great boldness in preaching, and God's presence in their lives; yet they were not free from hatred and persecution. They were arrested, put in jail, beaten, and slandered by community leaders. Faith in God does not make troubles disappear; it makes troubles appear less frightening because it puts them in the right perspective. Don't expect everyone to react favorably when you share something as dynamic as your faith in Christ. Some will be jealous, afraid, or threatened. Expect some negative reactions, and remember that you must be more concerned about serving God than about the reactions of people (see Acts 5:29).

Acts 5:19 The angel of the Lord gave the apostles a command that, when followed, would lead to a brutal flogging (Acts 5:40). If that strikes you as odd, it is probably because of the prevailing idea among many believers that obedience inevitably leads to blessing (defined as "a problem-free, blissful existence"). Serious students of the Bible know that obeying God often results in pain and suffering. They also recognize that being persecuted for Christ is a deeper kind of blessing. What biblical commands, if obeyed, might result in discomfort for you today? Will you commit to live them out anyway?

Acts 5:21 Suppose someone threatened to kill you if you didn't stop talking about God. You might be tempted to keep quiet. But after being threatened by powerful leaders, arrested, jailed, and miraculously released, the apostles went back to preaching. This was nothing less than God's power working through them (Acts 4:13)! When we are convinced of the truth of Christ's resurrection and have experienced the presence and power of his Holy Spirit, we will also have the confidence to speak out for Christ.

Acts 5:21 The Temple at daybreak was a busy place. Many people stopped at the Temple to pray and worship at sunrise. The apostles were already there, ready to tell them the Good News of new life in Jesus Christ. Also at daybreak, the 70 men of the high council (also called the Sanhedrin) were gathering, preparing to question the apostles. This was going to be no small trial. The religious leaders would do anything to stop these apostles from challenging their authority, threatening their secure position, and exposing their hypocritical motives to the people.

Acts 5:29 The apostles knew their priorities. While we should try to live at peace with everyone (Rom 12:18), conflict with the world and its authorities is sometimes inevitable for a Christian (John 15:18). There will be situations where you cannot obey both God and people. Then you must obey God and trust his Word. Let Jesus' words in Luke 6:22 encourage you: "What blessings await you when people hate you and exclude you and mock you and curse you as evil because you follow the Son of Man."

Acts 5:34 In the Jewish high council, the Pharisees were the other major party with the Sadducees (Acts 5:17). The Pharisees were the strict keepers of the law—not only God's law but hundreds of other rules they had added to God's law. They were careful about outward purity, but many had hearts full of impure motives. Jesus confronted the Pharisees often during his ministry on earth. Oddly enough, a Pharisee named Gamaliel became an unexpected ally for the apostles, although he probably did not support their teachings. He was a distinguished member of the high council and a teacher. While Gamaliel may

ACTS 5:17-42 *(cont.)*
named Gamaliel, who was an expert in religious law
and respected by all the people, stood up and ordered
that the men be sent outside the council chamber for
a while. 35Then he said to his colleagues, "Men of Israel,
take care what you are planning to do to these men!
36Some time ago there was that fellow Theudas, who
pretended to be someone great. About 400 others
joined him, but he was killed, and all his followers
went their various ways. The whole movement came
to nothing. 37After him, at the time of the census, there
was Judas of Galilee. He got people to follow him, but
he was killed, too, and all his followers were scattered.
38"So my advice is, leave these men alone. Let them
go. If they are planning and doing these things merely
on their own, it will soon be overthrown. 39But if it is
from God, you will not be able to overthrow them.
You may even find yourselves fighting against God!"
40The others accepted his advice. They called in the
apostles and had them flogged. Then they ordered
them never again to speak in the name of Jesus, and
they let them go.
41The apostles left the high council rejoicing that
God had counted them worthy to suffer disgrace for
the name of Jesus.* 42And every day, in the Temple
and from house to house, they continued to teach and
preach this message: "Jesus is the Messiah."

Seven Men Chosen to Serve

ACTS 6:1-7
But as the believers* rapidly multiplied, there were
rumblings of discontent. The Greek-speaking believers complained about the Hebrew-speaking believers,
saying that their widows were being discriminated
against in the daily distribution of food.
2So the Twelve called a meeting of all the believers.
They said, "We apostles should spend our time teaching the word of God, not running a food program. 3And
so, brothers, select seven men who are well respected
and are full of the Spirit and wisdom. We will give
them this responsibility. 4Then we apostles can spend
our time in prayer and teaching the word."
5Everyone liked this idea, and they chose the following: Stephen (a man full of faith and the Holy Spirit),

Acts 5:41 Greek *for the name.* **Acts 6:1** Greek *disciples;* also in 6:2, 7.

have saved the apostles' lives, his real intentions probably were to prevent a division in the council and to avoid arousing the Romans. The apostles were popular among the people, and killing them might start a riot. Gamaliel's advice to the council gave the apostles some breathing room to continue their work. The council decided to wait, hoping that this would all fade away harmlessly. They couldn't have been more wrong. Ironically, Paul, who became one of the greatest apostles, had been one of Gamaliel's students (Acts 22:3).

Acts 5:39 Gamaliel presented some sound advice about reacting to religious movements. Unless adherents in these groups endorse obviously dangerous doctrines or practices, it is often wiser to be tolerant rather than repressive. Sometimes only time will tell if they are presenting merely human ideas or if God is trying to say something through them. The next time a group promotes differing religious ideas, consider Gamaliel's advice, just in case you "find yourselves fighting against God."

Acts 5:40-42 Peter and John had been warned repeatedly not to preach, but they continued in spite of the threats. We, too, should live as Christ has asked us to, sharing our faith no matter what the cost. We may not be beaten or thrown in jail, but we may be ridiculed, ostracized, or slandered. To what extent are you willing to suffer for the sake of sharing the Good News with others?

Acts 5:41 Have you ever thought of persecution as a blessing, as something worth rejoicing about? This beating suffered by Peter and John was the first time any of the apostles had been physically abused for their faith. These men knew how Jesus had suffered, and they praised God that he had allowed them to be persecuted like their Lord. If you are mocked or persecuted for your faith, it isn't because you're doing something wrong but because God has counted you "worthy to suffer disgrace for the name of Jesus."

Acts 5:42 Home Bible studies are not new. As the believers needed to grow in their new faith, home Bible studies met their needs, as well as serving as a means to introduce new people to the Christian faith. During later times of persecution, meeting in homes became the primary method of passing on Bible knowledge. Christians throughout the world still use this approach when under persecution and as a way to build up believers.

Acts 6:1 When we read the descriptions of the early church—the miracles, the sharing and generosity, the fellowship—we may wish we could have been a part of this "perfect" church. In reality, the early church had problems just as we do today. No church has ever been or will ever be perfect until Christ and his followers are united at his second coming. All churches have problems. If your church's shortcomings distress you, ask yourself: Would a perfect church allow me to be a member? Then do what you can to make your church better. A church does not have to be perfect to advance the cause of Christ.

Acts 6:1ff Another internal problem developed in the early church between the Hebrew-speaking Christians (probably local Jews who had been converted) and the Greek-speaking Christians (probably Jews from other lands who had been converted at Pentecost). The Greek-speaking Christians complained that their widows were being unfairly treated. To correct the situation, the apostles put seven respected Greek-speaking men in charge of the food distribution program. This solved the problem and allowed the apostles to keep their focus on teaching and preaching the Good News about Jesus.

Acts 6:2 "The Twelve" are the 11 original disciples plus Matthias, who had been chosen to replace Judas Iscariot (Acts 1:26).

Acts 6:2-4 As the early church increased in size, so did its needs. One great need was to organize the distribution of food to the poor. The apostles needed to focus on preaching, so they chose others to administer the food program. Each person has a vital part to play in the life of the church (see 1 Cor 12). If you are in a position of leadership and find yourself overwhelmed by responsibilities, determine *your* God-given abilities and priorities and then find others to help. If you are not in leadership, you have gifts that God can use in various areas of the church's ministry. Offer these gifts in service to him.

Acts 6:3 This administrative task was not taken lightly. Notice the requirements for the men who were to handle the food program: They were to be well respected and full of the Holy Spirit and wisdom. People who carry heavy responsibilities and work closely with others should have these qualities. We must look for spiritually mature and wise men and women to lead our churches.

Acts 6:4 The apostles' priorities were correct. The ministry of the Word should never be neglected because of administrative burdens. Pastors should not try, or be expected to try, to do everything. Instead, the work of the church should be spread out among its members.

Philip, Procorus, Nicanor, Timon, Parmenas, and Nicolas of Antioch (an earlier convert to the Jewish faith). [6]These seven were presented to the apostles, who prayed for them as they laid their hands on them.

[7]So God's message continued to spread. The number of believers greatly increased in Jerusalem, and many of the Jewish priests were converted, too.

Stephen Is Arrested

ACTS 6:8-15

Stephen, a man full of God's grace and power, performed amazing miracles and signs among the people. [9]But one day some men from the Synagogue of Freed Slaves, as it was called, started to debate with him. They were Jews from Cyrene, Alexandria, Cilicia, and the province of Asia. [10]None of them could stand against the wisdom and the Spirit with which Stephen spoke.

[11]So they persuaded some men to lie about Stephen, saying, "We heard him blaspheme Moses, and even God." [12]This roused the people, the elders, and the teachers of religious law. So they arrested Stephen and brought him before the high council.*

[13]The lying witnesses said, "This man is always speaking against the holy Temple and against the law of Moses. [14]We have heard him say that this Jesus of Nazareth* will destroy the Temple and change the customs Moses handed down to us."

Acts 6:12 Greek *Sanhedrin;* also in 6:15. **Acts 6:14** Or *Jesus the Nazarene.*

STEPHEN

Around the world, the gospel has often taken root in places prepared by the blood of martyrs. But before people can *give* their lives for the gospel, they must first *live* their lives for the gospel. One way God trains his servants is to present them with opportunities for service. Their desire to serve Christ is translated into the reality of serving others. • Long before violent persecution broke out against Christians, there was already social ostracism. The believers depended on each other for support. The sharing of homes, food, and resources was both a practical and necessary mark of the early church, but this didn't proceed perfectly at first. People were being overlooked. There were complaints. Those selected to help manage were chosen for their integrity, wisdom, and sensitivity to God. • Stephen was named one of the managers of food distribution in the early church. And besides being a good administrator, Stephen was also a powerful speaker. This is clear from the defense he made before the Jewish high council. He presented a summary of the Jews' own history and made powerful applications that stung his listeners. During his defense Stephen must have known he was speaking his own death sentence. Members of the council could not stand to have their evil motives exposed. They stoned him to death while he prayed for their forgiveness. His final words show how much like Jesus he had become in just a short time. His death had a lasting impact on young Saul (Paul) of Tarsus, who would move from being a violent persecutor of Christians to being one of the greatest champions of the gospel the church has known. • Stephen's life is a continual challenge to all Christians. Because he was the first to die for the faith, his sacrifice raises questions: How many risks do we take in being Jesus' followers? Would we be willing to die for him? Are we really willing to live for him?

Strengths and accomplishments	• One of seven leaders chosen to supervise food distribution to the needy in the early church • Known for his spiritual qualities of faith, wisdom, grace, and power; also known for the Spirit's presence in his life • Outstanding leader, teacher, and debater • First to give his life for the gospel
Lessons from his life	• Real understanding of God always leads to practical and compassionate actions toward people
Vital statistics	• Occupation: Organizer of food distribution • Contemporaries: Paul, Caiaphas, Gamaliel, the apostles
Key verses	"As they stoned him, Stephen prayed, 'Lord Jesus, receive my spirit.' He fell to his knees, shouting, 'Lord, don't charge them with this sin!' And with that, he died" (Acts 7:59-60).

Stephen's story is told in Acts 6:3–8:2. He is also mentioned in Acts 11:19; 22:20.

Acts 6:7 Jesus had told the apostles that they were to witness first in Jerusalem (Acts 1:8). In a short time, their message had infiltrated the entire city and all levels of society. Even some Jewish priests were being converted, an obvious violation of the wishes of the high council that would endanger their position.

Acts 6:7 The word of God spread like ripples on a pond where, from a single center, each wave touches the next, spreading wider and farther. The Good News still spreads this way today. You don't have to change the world single-handedly; it is enough just to be part of the wave, touching those around you, who in turn will touch others until all have felt the movement. Don't ever feel that your part is insignificant or unimportant.

Acts 6:9 This was a group of Jewish slaves who had been freed by Rome and had formed their own synagogue in Jerusalem.

Acts 6:11 These men lied about Stephen, causing him to be arrested and brought before the Jewish high council. The Sadducees, the dominant party in the council, accepted and studied only the writings of Moses (Genesis—Deuteronomy). In their view, to speak blasphemy against Moses was a crime. But from Stephen's speech (Acts 7), we learn that this accusation was false. Stephen based his review of Israel's history on Moses' writings.

Acts 6:14 When Stephen was brought before the council of religious leaders, the accusation against him was the same that the religious leaders had used against Jesus (Matt 26:59-61). The group falsely accused Stephen of wanting to change Moses' customs, because they knew that the Sadducees, who controlled the council, believed only in Moses' laws.

Acts 6:6 Spiritual leadership is serious business and must not be taken lightly by the church or its leaders. In the early church, the chosen men were commissioned (by prayer and laying on of hands) by the apostles. Laying hands on someone, an ancient Jewish practice, was a way to set a person apart for special service (see Num 27:23; Deut 34:9).

▸ **ACTS 6:8-15** ***(cont.)***

15 At this point everyone in the high council stared at Stephen, because his face became as bright as an angel's.

Stephen Addresses the Council

ACTS 7:1–8:1a

Then the high priest asked Stephen, "Are these accusations true?"

2 This was Stephen's reply: "Brothers and fathers, listen to me. Our glorious God appeared to our ancestor Abraham in Mesopotamia before he settled in
Haran.* 3 God told him, 'Leave your native land and your relatives, and come into the land that I will show
you.'* 4 So Abraham left the land of the Chaldeans and lived in Haran until his father died. Then God brought him here to the land where you now live.

5 "But God gave him no inheritance here, not even one square foot of land. God did promise, however, that eventually the whole land would belong to Abraham and his descendants—even though he had no
children yet. 6 God also told him that his descendants would live in a foreign land, where they would be
oppressed as slaves for 400 years. 7 'But I will punish the nation that enslaves them,' God said, 'and in the end they will come out and worship me here in this place.'*

8 "God also gave Abraham the covenant of circumcision at that time. So when Abraham became the father of Isaac, he circumcised him on the eighth day. And the practice was continued when Isaac became the father of Jacob, and when Jacob became the father of the twelve patriarchs of the Israelite nation.

9 "These patriarchs were jealous of their brother Joseph, and they sold him to be a slave in Egypt. But God
was with him 10 and rescued him from all his troubles. And God gave him favor before Pharaoh, king of Egypt. God also gave Joseph unusual wisdom, so that Pharaoh appointed him governor over all of Egypt and put him in charge of the palace.

11 "But a famine came upon Egypt and Canaan. There was great misery, and our ancestors ran out of food.
12 Jacob heard that there was still grain in Egypt, so
he sent his sons—our ancestors—to buy some. 13 The second time they went, Joseph revealed his identity to his brothers,* and they were introduced to Pharaoh.

Acts 7:2 *Mesopotamia* was the region now called Iraq. *Haran* was a city in what is now called Syria. **Acts 7:3** Gen 12:1. **Acts 7:5-7** Gen 12:7; 15:13-14; Exod 3:12.
Acts 7:13 Other manuscripts read *Joseph was recognized by his brothers.*

The Rosetta Stone

Since Moses received a quality Egyptian education, he would have been able to read hieroglyphs. But over time, the ability to read hieroglyphs was lost. No one could read them until the Rosetta Stone was discovered in 1799 by Napoleon's army near Rosetta on the Nile River. The stone records a decree of King Ptolemy V in three languages. At the top of the stone are 14 lines of hieroglyphs, then 32 lines of an Egyptian script called Demotic, and then 54 lines of Greek. The Greek was easy to read, but not the hieroglyphs. Eventually, it was recognized that the signs were used for sounds as well as for words, unearthing the key to deciphering hieroglyphs. This discovery gave birth to modern knowledge of ancient Egyptian language.

The education Moses received in Egypt, including his knowledge of hieroglyphics, was great preparation for the tasks God had in mind for him. God used him—not only to lead the Israelites out of Egypt—but to write the first five books of the Bible, the Pentateuch (Genesis, Exodus, Leviticus, Numbers, Deuteronomy).

Acts 7:1 This high priest was probably Caiaphas, the same man who had earlier questioned and condemned Jesus (John 18:24).

Acts 7:2ff Stephen launched into a long speech about Israel's relationship with God. From Old Testament history he showed that the Jews had constantly rejected God's message and his prophets and that this council had rejected the Messiah, God's Son. He made three main points: (1) Israel's history is the history of God's acts in the world; (2) people worshiped God long before there was a Temple, because God does not live in a Temple; and (3) Jesus' death was just one more example of Israel's rebellion against and rejection of God.

Acts 7:2ff Stephen didn't really defend himself. Instead, he took the offensive, seizing the opportunity to summarize his teaching about Jesus. Stephen was accusing these religious leaders of failing to obey God's laws—the laws they prided themselves in following so meticulously. This was the same accusation that Jesus had leveled against them. When we witness for Christ, we don't need to be on the defensive. Instead, we can simply share our faith.

Acts 7:8 Circumcision was a sign of the promise or covenant God made with Abraham and the entire nation of Israel (Gen 17:9-13). Because Stephen summarized Israel's history, he told how this covenant fared during that time. Stephen pointed out that God always had kept his side of the promise, but Israel had failed again and again to uphold its end. Although the Jews in Stephen's day still circumcised their baby boys, they failed to obey God. The people's hearts were far from God. Their lack of faith and lack of obedience showed that they had failed to keep their part of the covenant.

Acts 7:8 The Jewish rite of circumcision, like Israel's regular sacrifices and annual feasts, was intended to be a very meaningful event. Those who participated thoughtfully would be reminded of profound spiritual truths. But we know that it is difficult to avoid merely going through the motions of our central religious rites, like the Lord's Supper. We are often guilty of participating passively and mindlessly. Make it your goal to give God your full attention (body, soul, and spirit) the next time you pray, take Communion, or take part in a church ceremony.

[14]Then Joseph sent for his father, Jacob, and all his
relatives to come to Egypt, seventy-five persons in all.
[15]So Jacob went to Egypt. He died there, as did our
ancestors. [16]Their bodies were taken to Shechem and
buried in the tomb Abraham had bought for a certain
price from Hamor's sons in Shechem.

[17]"As the time drew near when God would fulfill
his promise to Abraham, the number of our people in
Egypt greatly increased. [18]But then a new king came to
the throne of Egypt who knew nothing about Joseph.
[19]This king exploited our people and oppressed them,
forcing parents to abandon their newborn babies so
they would die.

[20]"At that time Moses was born—a beautiful child in
God's eyes. His parents cared for him at home for three
months. [21]When they had to abandon him, Pharaoh's
daughter adopted him and raised him as her own son.
[22]Moses was taught all the wisdom of the Egyptians,
and he was powerful in both speech and action.

[23]"One day when Moses was forty years old, he decided to visit his relatives, the people of Israel. [24]He
saw an Egyptian mistreating an Israelite. So Moses
came to the man's defense and avenged him, killing
the Egyptian. [25]Moses assumed his fellow Israelites
would realize that God had sent him to rescue them,
but they didn't.

[26]"The next day he visited them again and saw two
men of Israel fighting. He tried to be a peacemaker.
'Men,' he said, 'you are brothers. Why are you fighting
each other?'

[27]"But the man in the wrong pushed Moses aside.
'Who made you a ruler and judge over us?' he asked.
[28]'Are you going to kill me as you killed that Egyptian
yesterday?' [29]When Moses heard that, he fled the
country and lived as a foreigner in the land of Midian. There his two sons were born.

[30]"Forty years later, in the desert near Mount Sinai,
an angel appeared to Moses in the flame of a burning
bush. [31]When Moses saw it, he was amazed at the
sight. As he went to take a closer look, the voice of
the LORD called out to him, [32]'I am the God of your
ancestors—the God of Abraham, Isaac, and Jacob.'
Moses shook with terror and did not dare to look.

[33]"Then the LORD said to him, 'Take off your sandals, for you are standing on holy ground. [34]I have
certainly seen the oppression of my people in Egypt. I
have heard their groans and have come down to rescue
them. Now go, for I am sending you back to Egypt.'*

[35]"So God sent back the same man his people had
previously rejected when they demanded, 'Who made
you a ruler and judge over us?' Through the angel who
appeared to him in the burning bush, God sent Moses
to be their ruler and savior. [36]And by means of many
wonders and miraculous signs, he led them out of
Egypt, through the Red Sea, and through the wilderness for forty years.

[37]"Moses himself told the people of Israel, 'God will
raise up for you a Prophet like me from among your
own people.'* [38]Moses was with our ancestors, the
assembly of God's people in the wilderness, when the
angel spoke to him at Mount Sinai. And there Moses
received life-giving words to pass on to us.*

[39]"But our ancestors refused to listen to Moses.
They rejected him and wanted to return to Egypt.
[40]They told Aaron, 'Make us some gods who can lead
us, for we don't know what has become of this Moses,
who brought us out of Egypt.' [41]So they made an idol
shaped like a calf, and they sacrificed to it and celebrated over this thing they had made. [42]Then God
turned away from them and abandoned them to serve
the stars of heaven as their gods! In the book of the
prophets it is written,

'Was it to me you were bringing sacrifices and
offerings
during those forty years in the wilderness,
Israel?
[43] No, you carried your pagan gods—
the shrine of Molech,
the star of your god Rephan,
and the images you made to worship them.
So I will send you into exile
as far away as Babylon.'*

Acts 7:31-34 Exod 3:5-10. **Acts 7:37** Deut 18:15. **Acts 7:38** Some manuscripts read *to you.* **Acts 7:42-43** Amos 5:25-27 (Greek version).

Acts 7:17 Stephen's review of Jewish history gives a clear testimony of God's faithfulness and sovereignty. Despite the continued failures of his chosen people and the swirling world events, God was working out his plan. When faced by a confusing array of circumstances, remember that (1) God is in control—nothing surprises him; (2) this world is not all there is—it will pass away, but God is eternal; (3) God is just, and he will make things right—punishing the wicked and rewarding the faithful; (4) God wants to use you (like Joseph, Moses, and Stephen) to make a difference in the world.

Acts 7:37 The Jews originally thought this "Prophet" was Joshua. But Moses was prophesying about the coming Messiah (Deut 18:15). Peter also quoted this verse in referring to the Messiah (Acts 3:22).

Acts 7:38 Stephen used the word *ekklesia* (translated "assembly") to describe the congregation or people of God in the wilderness. This word was later used by the first-century Christians to describe their own community or "assembly," and is often translated as "church." Stephen's point was that the giving of the law through Moses to the Jews was the sign of the covenant. By obedience, then, they would continue to be God's covenant people. But because they disobeyed (Acts 7:39), they broke the covenant and forfeited their right to be the chosen people.

Acts 7:38 From Galatians 3:19 and Hebrews 2:2, it appears that God had given the law to Moses through angels. Exodus 31:18 says God wrote the Ten Commandments himself ("written by the finger of God"). Apparently God used angelic messengers as mediators to deliver his law to Moses.

Acts 7:43 Here Stephen gave more details of the idolatry referred to in Acts 7:40. These were idols worshiped by Israel during their wilderness wanderings (Exod 32:4). Molech was the god associated with child sacrifice, and Rephan was an Egyptian god. Amos also named Assyrian deities worshiped by Israel (Amos 5:25-27).

▶ ACTS 7:1–8:1a *(cont.)*

44 “Our ancestors carried the Tabernacle* with them
through the wilderness. It was constructed according
to the plan God had shown to Moses. 45 Years later,
when Joshua led our ancestors in battle against the
nations that God drove out of this land, the Tabernacle
was taken with them into their new territory. And it
stayed there until the time of King David.

46 “David found favor with God and asked for the
privilege of building a permanent Temple for the God
of Jacob.* 47 But it was Solomon who actually built it.
48 However, the Most High doesn't live in temples made
by human hands. As the prophet says,

49 ‘Heaven is my throne,
    and the earth is my footstool.
Could you build me a temple as good as that?’
    asks the LORD.
‘Could you build me such a resting place?
50 Didn't my hands make both heaven and
        earth?’*

51 “You stubborn people! You are heathen* at heart
and deaf to the truth. Must you forever resist the Holy
Spirit? That's what your ancestors did, and so do you!
52 Name one prophet your ancestors didn't persecute!
They even killed the ones who predicted the coming of
the Righteous One—the Messiah whom you betrayed
and murdered. 53 You deliberately disobeyed God's law,
even though you received it from the hands of angels.”

54 The Jewish leaders were infuriated by Stephen's
accusation, and they shook their fists at him in rage.*
55 But Stephen, full of the Holy Spirit, gazed steadily
into heaven and saw the glory of God, and he saw Jesus
standing in the place of honor at God's right hand.
56 And he told them, “Look, I see the heavens opened
and the Son of Man standing in the place of honor at
God's right hand!”

57 Then they put their hands over their ears and
began shouting. They rushed at him 58 and dragged
him out of the city and began to stone him. His accusers took off their coats and laid them at the feet of a
young man named Saul.*

59 As they stoned him, Stephen prayed, “Lord Jesus,
receive my spirit.” 60 He fell to his knees, shouting,
“Lord, don't charge them with this sin!” And with that,
he died.

8:1 Saul was one of the witnesses, and he agreed completely with the killing of Stephen.

Acts 7:44 Greek *the tent of witness.* **Acts 7:46** Some manuscripts read *the house of Jacob.* **Acts 7:49-50** Isa 66:1-2. **Acts 7:51** Greek *uncircumcised.* **Acts 7:54** Greek *they were grinding their teeth against him.* **Acts 7:58** *Saul* is later called Paul; see 13:9.

Acts 7:44-50 Stephen had been accused of speaking against the Temple (Acts 6:13). Although he recognized the importance of the Temple, he knew that it was not more important than God. God is not limited; he lives not only in a house of worship but also in those who are open to receive him (Isa 66:1-2). Solomon knew this when he prayed at the dedication of the Temple (2 Chr 6:18). God wants to live in us. Is he living in you?

Acts 7:52 Indeed, many prophets were persecuted and killed: Uriah (Jer 26:20-23); Jeremiah (Jer 38:1-6); Isaiah (tradition says he was killed by King Manasseh; see 2 Kgs 21:16); Amos (Amos 7:10-13); Zechariah (not the author of the Bible book but the son of Jehoiada the priest; see 2 Chr 24:20-22); Elijah (1 Kgs 19:1-2). Jesus also told a parable about how the Jews had constantly rejected God's messages and persecuted his messengers (Luke 20:9-19).

Acts 7:55-58 Stephen saw the glory of God and Jesus, the Messiah, standing at God's right hand. Stephen's words are similar to Jesus' words spoken before the high council (Matt 26:64; Mark 14:62; Luke 22:69). Stephen's vision supported Jesus' claim and angered the Jewish leaders who had condemned Jesus to death for blasphemy. They would not tolerate Stephen's words, so they dragged him out and killed him. People may not kill us for witnessing about Christ, but they may let us know they don't want to hear the truth and try to silence us. Keep honoring God in your conduct and words; though many may turn against you and your message, some will follow Christ. Remember, Stephen's death had a profound impact on Paul, who later became the world's greatest missionary. Even those who oppose you now may later turn to Christ.

Acts 7:58 Saul is also called Paul (see Acts 13:9), the great missionary who wrote many of the letters in the New Testament. Saul was his Hebrew name; Paul, his Greek name, was used as he began his ministry to the Gentiles. When Luke introduces him, Paul was going everywhere persecuting Jesus' followers. This is in great contrast to the Paul about whom Luke wrote for most of the book of Acts, describing him as a devoted follower of Christ and a gifted preacher. Paul was uniquely qualified to talk to the Jews about Jesus because he had once persecuted those who believed in him and understood how the opposition felt. Paul is a powerful example of a person who was thought to be impossible for God to reach and change.

Acts 7:59 The penalty for blasphemy—speaking irreverently about God—was death by stoning (Lev 24:14). The religious leaders, who were furious, had Stephen stoned without a trial. They did not understand that Stephen's words were true because they were not seeking the truth. They only wanted support for their own views.

Acts 7:60 As Stephen died, he spoke words very similar to Jesus' words on the cross (Luke 23:34). The members of the early church were persecuted for telling the good news of Jesus' death, burial, and resurrection. Sometimes, as in the case of Stephen, they were even put to death. Christ had promised his followers that living for him would lead to trouble (see Luke 21:12-19). This is still true. If we boldly live out our faith, the light of our lives will expose the sinfulness of others. Our words of truth will pierce their souls. Some will be convicted and yield to the leading of the Spirit. Others will become angry and hardened in their hatred of the truth. As Jesus said, “They will do all this to you because of me, for they have rejected the one who sent me” (John 15:21).

THE EFFECTS OF STEPHEN'S DEATH

Stephen's death was not in vain. Below are some of the events that were by-products (either directly or indirectly) of the persecution that began with Stephen's martyrdom.

1. Philip's evangelistic tour (Acts 8:4-40)
2. Paul's (Saul's) conversion (Acts 9:1-30)
3. Peter's missionary tour (Acts 9:32–11:18)
4. The church in Antioch of Syria founded (Acts 11:19ff)

B. Expansion of the Church

After Stephen's martyrdom, intense persecution against those who believed in Jesus caused them to flee the city and go all over the regions of Judah and Samaria. But the Holy Spirit was still active among these faithful people, and they continued to spread the Good News about Jesus wherever they went. And so this persecution in Jerusalem caused the church to grow even more, with new people learning about and following Jesus every day. The Gospel spread to the half-Jewish population of Samaria, and God sent Peter to preach even to the Gentiles. This Good News was for everyone, Jew and Gentile alike. Even the former persecutor of the church, Saul, had a life-changing experience with Jesus Christ.

Persecution Scatters the Believers

ACTS 8:1b-3

A great wave of persecution began that day, sweeping
over the church in Jerusalem; and all the believers
except the apostles were scattered through the regions
of Judea and Samaria. 2(Some devout men came and
buried Stephen with great mourning.) 3But Saul was
going everywhere to destroy the church. He went from
house to house, dragging out both men and women to
throw them into prison.

Philip Preaches in Samaria

ACTS 8:4-25

But the believers who were scattered preached the
Good News about Jesus wherever they went. 5Philip,
for example, went to the city of Samaria and told the
people there about the Messiah. 6Crowds listened intently to Philip because they were eager to hear his
message and see the miraculous signs he did. 7Many
evil* spirits were cast out, screaming as they left their
victims. And many who had been paralyzed or lame
were healed. 8So there was great joy in that city.
9A man named Simon had been a sorcerer there
for many years, amazing the people of Samaria and
claiming to be someone great. 10Everyone, from the
least to the greatest, often spoke of him as "the Great
One—the Power of God." 11They listened closely to
him because for a long time he had astounded them
with his magic.
12But now the people believed Philip's message

Acts 8:7 Greek *unclean.*

We shouldn't be surprised or abandon our faith when we are persecuted.

Acts 8:1-4 Persecution pushed the Christians beyond Jerusalem and into Judea and Samaria, thus fulfilling the second part of Jesus' command (see Acts 1:8). The persecution helped spread the Good News. God would bring great results from the believers' suffering.

Acts 8:4 Persecution forced the believers out of their homes in Jerusalem, and along with them went the Good News. Sometimes we have to become uncomfortable before we'll move. We may not want to experience it, but discomfort may be best for us because God may be working through our hurts. When you are tempted to complain about uncomfortable or painful circumstances, stop and ask if God might be preparing you for a special task.

Acts 8:5 This is not the apostle Philip (see John 1:43-44) but a Greek-speaking Jew, "full of the Spirit and wisdom" (Acts 6:3), who was one of the seven men chosen to help with the food distribution program in the church (Acts 6:5).

Acts 8:5 Israel had been divided into three main regions: Galilee in the north, Samaria in the middle, and Judea in the south. The city of Samaria (in the region of Samaria) had been the capital of the northern kingdom of Israel in the days of the divided kingdom before it was conquered by Assyria in 722 B.C. During that war, the Assyrian king had taken many captives, leaving only the poorest people in the land and resettling it with foreigners. These foreigners had intermarried with the Jews who were left, and the mixed race became known as Samaritans. The Samaritans were considered half-breeds by the "pure" Jews in the southern kingdom of Judah, and the two groups hated each other intensely. But Jesus himself went into Samaria (John 4), and he commanded his followers to spread the Good News there (Acts 1:8).

Acts 8:7 Jesus encountered and drove out many evil spirits during his ministry on earth. Evil spirits, or demons, are ruled by Satan. Most scholars believe that demons are fallen angels who joined Satan in his rebellion against God. They can cause a person to be mute, deaf, blind, or insane and also tempt people to sin. Although they can be powerful, they are not able to read our minds and cannot be everywhere at once. Demons are real and active, but Jesus has given his followers authority over them. Although Satan is allowed to work in our world, God is in complete control. He can drive demons out and end their destructive work in people's lives. Eventually Satan and his demons will be thrown into the lake of fire, forever ending their evil work in the world (Rev 20:10).

Acts 8:9-11 In the days of the early church, sorcerers and magicians were numerous and influential. They worked wonders, performed healings and exorcisms, and practiced astrology. Their wonders may simply have been magic tricks, or the sorcerers may have been empowered by Satan (Matt 24:24; 2 Thes 2:9). Simon had done so many wonders that some even thought that he was the Messiah; but his powers did not come from God (see Acts 8:18-24).

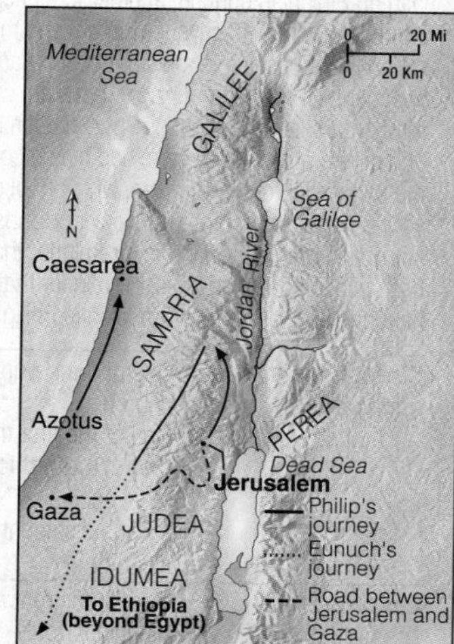

***PHILIP'S MINISTRY** To escape persecution in Jerusalem, Philip fled to Samaria, where he continued preaching the gospel. While he was there, an angel commanded him to meet an Ethiopian official on the road between Jerusalem and Gaza. The man became a believer before continuing on to Ethiopia. Philip then went from Azotus to Caesarea.*

▶ **ACTS 8:4-25** ***(cont.)***

of Good News concerning the Kingdom of God and the name of Jesus Christ. As a result, many men and women were baptized. [13]Then Simon himself believed and was baptized. He began following Philip wherever he went, and he was amazed by the signs and great miracles Philip performed.

[14]When the apostles in Jerusalem heard that the people of Samaria had accepted God's message, they sent Peter and John there. [15]As soon as they arrived, they prayed for these new believers to receive the Holy Spirit. [16]The Holy Spirit had not yet come upon any of them, for they had only been baptized in the name of the Lord Jesus. [17]Then Peter and John laid their hands upon these believers, and they received the Holy Spirit.

[18]When Simon saw that the Spirit was given when the apostles laid their hands on people, he offered them money to buy this power. [19]"Let me have this power, too," he exclaimed, "so that when I lay my hands on people, they will receive the Holy Spirit!"

[20]But Peter replied, "May your money be destroyed with you for thinking God's gift can be bought! [21]You can have no part in this, for your heart is not right with God. [22]Repent of your wickedness and pray to the Lord. Perhaps he will forgive your evil thoughts, [23]for I can see that you are full of bitter jealousy and are held captive by sin."

PHILIP

Jesus' last words to his followers were a command to take the gospel everywhere, but it took intense persecution to scatter the believers from Jerusalem and into Judea and Samaria, where Jesus had instructed them to go. Philip, one of the men in charge of food distribution, left Jerusalem and, like most Jewish Christians, spread the gospel wherever he went; but unlike most of them, he did not limit his audience to other Jews. He went directly to Samaria—the last place many Jews would go due to age-old prejudice. • The Samaritans responded in large numbers. When word got back to Jerusalem, Peter and John were sent to evaluate Philip's ministry. They quickly became involved themselves, seeing firsthand God's acceptance of those who previously were considered unacceptable. • In the middle of all this success and excitement, God directed Philip out to the desert for an unlikely appointment with an Ethiopian eunuch, another foreigner, who had been in Jerusalem. Philip went immediately. His effectiveness in sharing the gospel with this man placed a Christian in a significant position in a distant country and may well have had an effect on an entire continent. • Philip ended up in Caesarea, where events allowed him to be Paul's host many years later. Paul, whose persecution had been instrumental in pushing Philip and others out of Jerusalem, had himself become an effective believer. Philip began the conversion of the Gentiles, which Paul continued across the entire Roman Empire. • Whether or not you are a follower of Christ, Philip's life presents a challenge. To those still outside the gospel, he is a reminder that the gospel is for you also. To those who have accepted Christ, he is a reminder that we are not free to disqualify anyone from hearing about Jesus. How much like Philip would your neighbors say you are?

Strengths and accomplishments	• One of the seven organizers of food distribution in the early church • One of the first traveling missionaries • One of the first to obey Jesus' command to take the gospel to all people • A careful student of the Bible who could explain its meaning clearly
Lessons from his life	• God finds great and various uses for those willing to obey wholeheartedly • The gospel is universal Good News • The whole Bible, not just the New Testament, helps us understand more about Jesus • Both mass response (the Samaritans) and individual response (the man from Ethiopia) to the gospel are valuable
Vital statistics	• Occupations: Organizer of food distribution, evangelist • Relatives: Four daughters. • Contemporaries: Paul, Stephen, the apostles
Key verse	"So beginning with this same Scripture, Philip told him the Good News about Jesus" (Acts 8:35).

Philip's story is told in Acts 6:1-7; 8:5-40; 21:8-10.

Acts 8:14 Peter and John were sent to Samaria to find out whether or not the Samaritans were truly becoming believers. The Jewish Christians, even the apostles, were still unsure whether Gentiles (non-Jews) and half-Jews could receive the Holy Spirit. John once asked Jesus if they should call fire down from heaven to burn up a Samaritan village that refused to welcome them; Jesus rebuked him (Luke 9:51-55). It wasn't until Peter's experience with Cornelius (Acts 10) that the apostles became fully convinced that the Holy Spirit was for all people. Here John and Peter went to the Samaritans to pray with them.

Acts 8:15-17 This was a crucial moment for the spread of the Good News and for the growth of the church. Peter and John had to go to Samaria to help keep this new group of believers from becoming separated from other believers. When Peter and John saw the Lord working in these people, they were assured that the Holy Spirit worked through *all* believers—Gentiles and mixed races as well as "pure" Jews.

Acts 8:15-17 Many scholars believe that God chose to give this dramatic filling of his Spirit as a sign at this special moment in history—the spread of the Good News into Samaria through the powerful, effective preaching of believers. Normally, the Holy Spirit enters a person's life at conversion. But this was a special event. The pouring out of the Spirit would happen again with Cornelius and his family (Acts 10:44-47), a sign that the uncircumcised Gentiles could receive the Good News.

Acts 8:18-23 "Everything has a price" seems to be true in our world of bribes, wealth, and materialism. Simon thought he could buy the Holy Spirit's power, but Peter harshly rebuked him. Why? The only way to receive God's power is to do what Peter told Simon to do—repent, ask God for forgiveness, and be filled with his Spirit. No amount of money can buy salvation, forgiveness of sin, or God's power. These are only gained by repentance and belief in Christ as Savior. In addition, Simon apparently wanted that ability for selfish reasons: to have power, to make money, or to gain prestige. God doesn't give us abilities to enhance our own lives. He

24"Pray to the Lord for me," Simon exclaimed, "that
these terrible things you've said won't happen to me!"
25After testifying and preaching the word of the
Lord in Samaria, Peter and John returned to Jerusalem.
And they stopped in many Samaritan villages along
the way to preach the Good News.

Philip and the Ethiopian Eunuch

ACTS 8:26-40

As for Philip, an angel of the Lord said to him, "Go
south* down the desert road that runs from Jerusalem
to Gaza." 27So he started out, and he met the treasurer
of Ethiopia, a eunuch of great authority under the
Kandake, the queen of Ethiopia. The eunuch had gone
to Jerusalem to worship, 28and he was now returning.
Seated in his carriage, he was reading aloud from the
book of the prophet Isaiah.
29The Holy Spirit said to Philip, "Go over and walk
along beside the carriage."
30Philip ran over and heard the man reading from
the prophet Isaiah. Philip asked, "Do you understand
what you are reading?"
31The man replied, "How can I, unless someone
instructs me?" And he urged Philip to come up into
the carriage and sit with him.
32The passage of Scripture he had been reading
was this:

"He was led like a sheep to the slaughter.
And as a lamb is silent before the shearers,
he did not open his mouth.
33 He was humiliated and received no justice.
Who can speak of his descendants?
For his life was taken from the earth."*

34The eunuch asked Philip, "Tell me, was the
prophet talking about himself or someone else?" 35So
beginning with this same Scripture, Philip told him
the Good News about Jesus.
36As they rode along, they came to some water, and
the eunuch said, "Look! There's some water! Why can't
I be baptized?"* 38He ordered the carriage to stop,
and they went down into the water, and Philip baptized him.
39When they came up out of the water, the Spirit of
the Lord snatched Philip away. The eunuch never saw
him again but went on his way rejoicing. 40Meanwhile,
Philip found himself farther north at the town of Azotus. He preached the Good News there and in every
town along the way until he came to Caesarea.

Saul's Conversion

ACTS 9:1-19a

Meanwhile, Saul was uttering threats with every breath
and was eager to kill the Lord's followers.* So he went
to the high priest. 2He requested letters addressed to

Acts 8:26 Or *Go at noon.* **Acts 8:32-33** Isa 53:7-8 (Greek version). **Acts 8:36** Some manuscripts add verse 37, *"You can," Philip answered, "if you believe with all your heart." And the eunuch replied, "I believe that Jesus Christ is the Son of God."* **Acts 9:1** Greek *disciples.*

AD 35

Saul's conversion on the Damascus road

grants us gifts so that we may bring him glory by building up others. When you find yourself wishing for an ability that would put you into the limelight or somehow enrich you personally, check your motives. Instead of sitting around wishing for talents you don't have, spend your time serving God and others with the gifts you *do* possess.

Acts 8:24 The last time a parent or friend rebuked you, were you hurt, angry, or defensive? Learn a lesson from Simon and his reaction to what Peter told him. He exclaimed, "Pray to the Lord for me." If you are rebuked for a serious mistake, it is for your good. Admit your error, repent quickly, and ask for prayer.

Acts 8:26 Philip was having a successful preaching ministry to great crowds in Samaria (Acts 8:5-8), but he obediently left that ministry to travel on a desert road. Because Philip went where God sent him, Ethiopia was opened up to the Good News. Follow God's leading, even if it seems like a demotion. At first you may not understand his plans, but the results will prove that God's way is right.

Acts 8:27 Ethiopia is located in Africa south of Egypt. The eunuch was obviously very dedicated to God because he had traveled such a long distance to worship in Jerusalem. The Jews had contact with Ethiopia in ancient days (Ps 68:31; Jer 38:7), so this man may have been a Gentile convert to Judaism. Because he was in charge of the treasury of Ethiopia, this man's conversion brought Christianity into the power structures of another government. This is the beginning of the witness "to the ends of the earth" (Acts 1:8). See the prophecy in Isaiah 56:3-8 for words about foreigners and eunuchs.

Acts 8:29-35 Philip found the Ethiopian man reading Scripture. Taking advantage of this opportunity to explain the Good News, Philip asked the man if he understood what he was reading. Philip (1) followed the Spirit's leading, (2) began the discussion from where the man was (immersed in the prophecies of Isaiah), and (3) explained how Jesus Christ fulfilled Isaiah's prophecies. When we share the Good News, we should start where the other person's concerns are focused. Then we can show how God's Word applies to those concerns.

Acts 8:35 Some think that the Old Testament is not relevant today, but Philip led this man to faith in Jesus Christ by using the Old Testament. Jesus Christ is found in the pages of both the Old and New Testaments. God's entire Word is applicable to all people in all ages. Don't avoid or neglect to use the Old Testament. It, too, is God's Word.

Acts 8:38 Baptism was a sign of identification with Christ and with the Christian community. Although Philip was the only witness, it was still important for the eunuch to take this step.

Acts 8:39-40 Why was Philip suddenly transported to a different city? This miraculous sign showed the urgency of bringing the Gentiles to belief in Christ. Azotus is Ashdod, one of the ancient Philistine capitals. Philip probably lived in Caesarea for the next 20 years (Acts 21:8).

Acts 9:2 Saul (later called Paul) was so zealous for his Jewish beliefs that he began a persecution campaign against anyone who believed in Christ ("followers of the Way"). Why would the Jews in Jerusalem want to persecute Christians as far away as Damascus? There are several possibilities: (1) to seize the Christians who had fled, (2) to prevent the spread of Christianity to other major cities, (3) to keep the Christians from causing any trouble with Rome, (4) to advance Saul's career and build his reputation as a true Pharisee, zealous for the law, (5) to unify the factions of Judaism by giving them a common enemy.

Acts 9:2-5 As Saul traveled to Damascus, pursuing Christians, he was confronted by the risen Christ and brought face to face with the truth of the Good News. Sometimes God breaks into a life in a spectacular manner, and sometimes conversion is a quiet experience. Beware of people who insist that you must have a particular type of conversion experience. The right way to come to faith in Jesus is whatever way God brings you.

▶ **ACTS 9:1-19a** ***(cont.)***

the synagogues in Damascus, asking for their cooperation in the arrest of any followers of the Way he found there. He wanted to bring them—both men and women—back to Jerusalem in chains.

[3]As he was approaching Damascus on this mission, a light from heaven suddenly shone down around him. [4]He fell to the ground and heard a voice saying to him, "Saul! Saul! Why are you persecuting me?"

[5]"Who are you, lord?" Saul asked.

And the voice replied, "I am Jesus, the one you are persecuting! [6]Now get up and go into the city, and you will be told what you must do."

[7]The men with Saul stood speechless, for they heard the sound of someone's voice but saw no one! [8]Saul picked himself up off the ground, but when he opened his eyes he was blind. So his companions led him by the hand to Damascus. [9]He remained there blind for three days and did not eat or drink.

[10]Now there was a believer* in Damascus named Ananias. The Lord spoke to him in a vision, calling, "Ananias!"

"Yes, Lord!" he replied.

[11]The Lord said, "Go over to Straight Street, to the house of Judas. When you get there, ask for a man from Tarsus named Saul. He is praying to me right now. [12]I have shown him a vision of a man named Ananias coming in and laying hands on him so he can see again."

[13]"But Lord," exclaimed Ananias, "I've heard many people talk about the terrible things this man has done to the believers* in Jerusalem! [14]And he is authorized by the leading priests to arrest everyone who calls upon your name."

[15]But the Lord said, "Go, for Saul is my chosen instrument to take my message to the Gentiles and to kings, as well as to the people of Israel. [16]And I will show him how much he must suffer for my name's sake."

[17]So Ananias went and found Saul. He laid his hands on him and said, "Brother Saul, the Lord Jesus, who appeared to you on the road, has sent me so that you might regain your sight and be filled with the Holy Spirit." [18]Instantly something like scales fell from Saul's eyes, and he regained his sight. Then he got up and was baptized. [19]Afterward he ate some food and regained his strength.

Saul in Damascus and Jerusalem

ACTS 9:19b-31

Saul stayed with the believers* in Damascus for a few days. [20]And immediately he began preaching about Jesus in the synagogues, saying, "He is indeed the Son of God!"

Acts 9:10 Greek *disciple;* also in 9:26, 36. **Acts 9:13** Greek *God's holy people;* also in 9:32, 41. **Acts 9:19** Greek *disciples;* also in 9:26, 38.

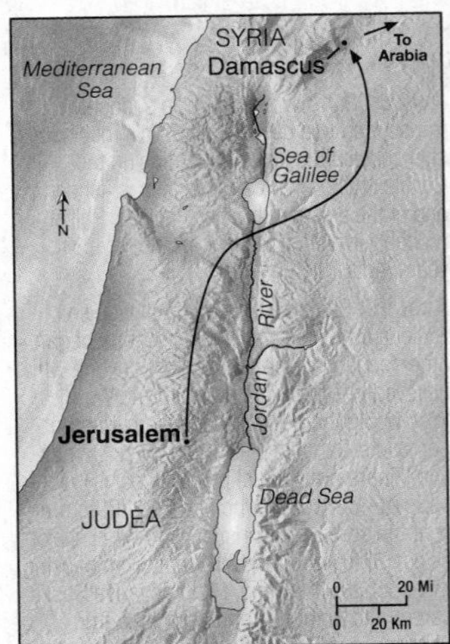

SAUL TRAVELS TO DAMASCUS *Many Christians fled Jerusalem when persecution began after Stephen's death, seeking refuge in other cities and countries. Saul tracked them down, even traveling 150 miles to Damascus in Syria to bring Christians back in chains to Jerusalem. But as he neared the ancient city, he discovered that God had other plans for him (Acts 9:15).*

Acts 9:3 Damascus, a key commercial city, was located about 150 miles northeast of Jerusalem in the Roman province of Syria. Several trade routes linked Damascus to other cities throughout the Roman world. Saul may have thought that by stamping out Christianity in Damascus, he could prevent its spread to other areas.

Acts 9:3-5 Paul refers to this experience as the start of his new life in Christ (1 Cor 9:1; 15:8; Gal 1:15-16). At the center of this wonderful experience was Jesus Christ. Paul did not see a vision; he saw the risen Christ himself (Acts 9:17). Paul acknowledged Jesus as Lord, confessed his own sin, surrendered his life to Christ, and resolved to obey him. True conversion comes from a personal encounter with Jesus Christ and leads to a new life in relationship with him.

Acts 9:5 Saul thought he was pursuing heretics, but he was persecuting Jesus himself. Anyone who persecutes believers today is also guilty of persecuting Jesus (see Matt 25:40, 45) because believers are the body of Christ on earth.

Acts 9:13-14 "Not him, Lord; that's impossible. He could never become a Christian!" In essence, that's what Ananias said when God told him of Saul's conversion. After all, Saul had pursued believers to their death. Despite these understandable feelings, Ananias obeyed God and ministered to Saul. We must not limit God—he can do anything. We must obey and follow God's leading, even when he leads us to difficult people and places.

Acts 9:15-16 Faith in Christ brings great blessings but often great suffering, too. Paul would suffer for his faith (see 2 Cor 11:23-27). God calls us to commitment, not to comfort. He promises to be with us through suffering and hardship, not to spare us from them.

Acts 9:17 Ananias found Saul, as he had been instructed, and greeted him as "Brother Saul." Ananias feared this meeting because Saul had come to Damascus to capture the believers and take them as prisoners to Jerusalem (Acts 9:2). In obedience to the Holy Spirit, Ananias greeted Saul lovingly. It is not always easy to love others, especially when we are afraid of them or doubt their motives. Nevertheless we must follow Jesus' command (John 13:34) and Ananias's example, showing loving acceptance to other believers.

Acts 9:17-18 Although Acts makes no mention of a special filling of the Holy Spirit for Saul, his changed life and subsequent accomplishments bear strong witness to the Holy Spirit's presence and power in him. Evidently, the Holy Spirit had filled Saul when he received his sight and was baptized. (See the second note on Acts 8:15-17, p. 1528, for more on the filling of the Holy Spirit.)

Acts 9:20 Immediately after receiving his sight and spending some time with the believers in Damascus, Saul went to the synagogue to tell the Jews about Jesus Christ. Some Christians counsel new believers to wait until they are thoroughly grounded in their faith before attempting to share the Good News.

21All who heard him were amazed. "Isn't this the same man who caused such devastation among Jesus' followers in Jerusalem?" they asked. "And didn't he come here to arrest them and take them in chains to the leading priests?"

22Saul's preaching became more and more powerful, and the Jews in Damascus couldn't refute his proofs that Jesus was indeed the Messiah.
23After a while some of the Jews plotted together to kill him.
24They were watching for him day and night at the city gate so they could murder him, but Saul was told about their plot.
25So during the night, some of the other believers* lowered him in a large basket through an opening in the city wall.

26When Saul arrived in Jerusalem, he tried to meet with the believers, but they were all afraid of him. They did not believe he had truly become a believer!
27Then Barnabas brought him to the apostles and told them how Saul had seen the Lord on the way to Damascus and how the Lord had spoken to Saul. He also told them that Saul had preached boldly in the name of Jesus in Damascus.

28So Saul stayed with the apostles and went all around Jerusalem with them, preaching boldly in the name of the Lord.
29He debated with some Greek-speaking Jews, but they tried to murder him.
30When the believers* heard about this, they took him down to Caesarea and sent him away to Tarsus, his hometown.

31The church then had peace throughout Judea, Galilee, and Samaria, and it became stronger as the believers lived in the fear of the Lord. And with the encouragement of the Holy Spirit, it also grew in numbers.

Peter Heals Aeneas and Raises Dorcas

ACTS 9:32-43

Meanwhile, Peter traveled from place to place, and he came down to visit the believers in the town of Lydda.
33There he met a man named Aeneas, who had been

Acts 9:25 Greek *his disciples.* **Acts 9:30** Greek *brothers.*

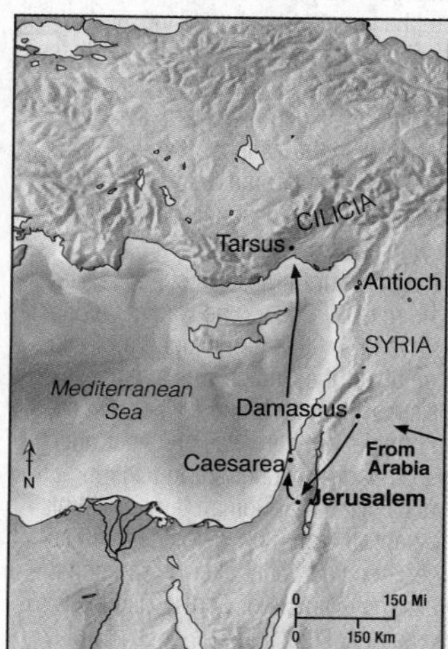

***SAUL'S RETURN TO TARSUS** At least three years elapsed between Acts 9:22 and 9:26. After time alone in Arabia (see Gal 1:16-18), Saul (Paul) returned to Damascus and then to Jerusalem. The apostles were reluctant to believe that this former persecutor could have become one of them. Saul escaped to Caesarea, where he caught a ship and returned to Tarsus.*

Saul spent time with other believers to learn about Jesus before beginning his worldwide ministry, but he did not wait to witness. Although we should not rush into a ministry unprepared, we do not need to wait before telling others what has happened to us.

Acts 9:21-22 Saul's arguments were powerful because he was a brilliant scholar. Even more convincing, however, was his changed life. People knew that what Saul taught was real because they could see the evidence in the way he lived. It is important to know what the Bible teaches and how to defend the faith, but your life should back up your words.

Acts 9:23 According to Galatians 1:17-18, Paul left Damascus and traveled to Arabia, the desert region just southeast of Damascus, where he lived for three years. It is unclear whether his three-year stay occurred between Acts 9:22 and Acts 9:23 or between Acts 9:25 and Acts 9:26. Some commentators say that "after a while" could mean a long period of time. They suggest that when Paul returned to Damascus, the governor under Aretas ordered his arrest (2 Cor 11:32) in an effort to keep peace with influential Jews.

The other possibility is that Paul's night escape occurred during his first stay in Damascus, just after his conversion, when the Pharisees were especially upset over his defection from their ranks. He would have fled to Arabia to spend time alone with God and to let the Jewish religious leaders cool down. Regardless of which theory is correct, there was a period of at least three years between Paul's conversion (Acts 9:3-6) and his trip to Jerusalem (Acts 9:26).

Acts 9:26-27 It is difficult to change your reputation, and Saul had a terrible reputation with the Christians. But Barnabas, a Jewish convert (mentioned in Acts 4:36), became the bridge between Saul and the apostles. New Christians (especially those with tarnished reputations) need sponsors, people who will come alongside, encourage, teach, and introduce them to other believers. In what ways can you become a Barnabas to new believers?

Acts 9:27 Galatians 1:18-19 explains that Saul was in Jerusalem only 15 days and that he met only with Peter and James.

Acts 9:29-30 In these short sentences we can see two characteristics of Saul (Paul), even as a new believer in Christ: He was bold, and he stirred up controversy. These would characterize Saul's ministry for the rest of his life.

Acts 9:30 Saul's visit to Tarsus helped quiet conflicts with the Jews and allowed him time to prove his commitment. After Saul, the most zealous persecutor, was converted, the church enjoyed a brief time of peace.

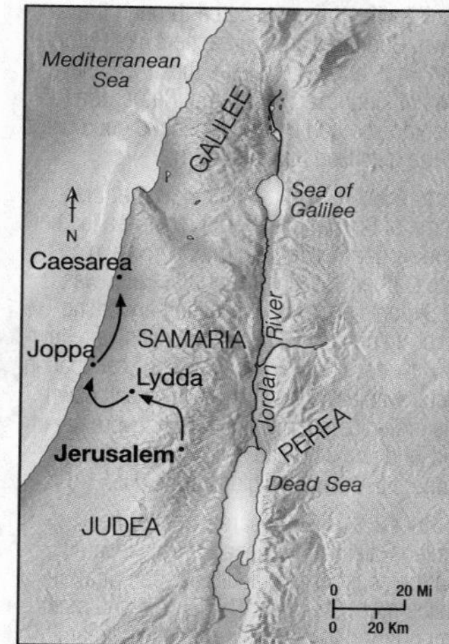

***PETER'S MINISTRY** Peter traveled to the ancient crossroads town of Lydda, where he healed crippled Aeneas. The believers in Joppa, an old port city, sent for him after a wonderful woman died. Peter went and brought her back to life. While in Joppa, Peter had a vision that led him to take the gospel to Cornelius, a Gentile, in Caesarea.*

▸ **ACTS 9:32-43** ***(cont.)***
paralyzed and bedridden for eight years. 34Peter said
to him, "Aeneas, Jesus Christ heals you! Get up, and roll
up your sleeping mat!" And he was healed instantly.
35Then the whole population of Lydda and Sharon saw
Aeneas walking around, and they turned to the Lord.
36There was a believer in Joppa named Tabitha
(which in Greek is Dorcas*). She was always doing kind
things for others and helping the poor. 37About this
time she became ill and died. Her body was washed for
burial and laid in an upstairs room. 38But the believers
had heard that Peter was nearby at Lydda, so they sent
two men to beg him, "Please come as soon as possible!"
39So Peter returned with them; and as soon as he
arrived, they took him to the upstairs room. The room
was filled with widows who were weeping and showing him the coats and other clothes Dorcas had made
for them. 40But Peter asked them all to leave the room;
then he knelt and prayed. Turning to the body he said,
"Get up, Tabitha." And she opened her eyes! When
she saw Peter, she sat up! 41He gave her his hand and
helped her up. Then he called in the widows and all the
believers, and he presented her to them alive.
42The news spread through the whole town, and
many believed in the Lord. 43And Peter stayed a long
time in Joppa, living with Simon, a tanner of hides.

Cornelius Calls for Peter

ACTS 10:1-8
In Caesarea there lived a Roman army officer* named
Cornelius, who was a captain of the Italian Regiment.
2He was a devout, God-fearing man, as was everyone
in his household. He gave generously to the poor and
prayed regularly to God. 3One afternoon about three

Acts 9:36 The names *Tabitha* in Aramaic and *Dorcas* in Greek both mean "gazelle." **Acts 10:1** Greek *a centurion;* similarly in 10:22.

Acts 9:36 The important harbor city of Joppa sits 125 feet above sea level overlooking the Mediterranean Sea. Joppa was the town into which the cedars of Lebanon had been floated to be shipped to Jerusalem for use in the Temple construction (2 Chr 2:16; Ezra 3:7). The prophet Jonah had left the port of Joppa on his ill-fated trip (Jon 1:3).

AD 37 *Caligula becomes the Roman emperor*

Acts 9:36-42 Tabitha made an enormous impact on her community, "always doing kind things for others and helping the poor," by making coats and other garments (Acts 9:39). When she died, the room was filled with mourners, very likely many of the people she had helped. And when she was brought back to life, the news raced through the town. God uses great preachers like Peter and Paul, but he also uses those who have gifts of kindness like Tabitha. Rather than wishing you had other gifts, make good use of the gifts God has given you.

Acts 9:43 In Joppa, Peter stayed at the home of Simon, a tanner of hides—a leather-worker. Leatherworkers made animal hides into leather. It is significant that Peter was at Simon's house because leatherworking involved contact with dead animals, and Jewish law considered it an "unclean" occupation. Peter was already beginning to break down his prejudice against people who were not of his kind and who had customs that did not adhere to Jewish religious traditions.

Acts 10:1 This Caesarea, sometimes called Palestinian Caesarea, was located on the coast of the Mediterranean Sea, 32 miles north of Joppa. The largest and most important port city on the Mediterranean in Palestine, Caesarea served as the capital of the Roman province of Judea. This was the first city to have Gentile Christians and a non-Jewish church.

Acts 10:1 This Roman officer was a centurion—a commander of 100 soldiers. Although stationed in Caesarea, Cornelius would probably return soon to Rome. Thus, his conversion was a major stepping-stone

CORNELIUS

The early days of Christianity were exciting as God's Spirit moved and people's lives were changed. Converts were pouring in from surprising backgrounds. Even the dreaded Saul became a Christian (Paul), and non-Jews were responding to the Good News about Jesus. Among the first of these was the Roman captain Cornelius. • Because of frequent outbreaks of violence, Roman soldiers had to be stationed throughout Israel to keep the peace. But most Romans, hated as conquerors, did not get along well in the nation. As an army officer, Cornelius was in a difficult position. He represented Rome, but his home was in Caesarea. During his years in Israel, he himself had been conquered by the God of Israel. He had a reputation as a godly man who put his faith into action, and he was respected by the Jews. • Four significant aspects of Cornelius's character are noted in Acts: (1) He actively sought God, (2) he revered God, (3) he was generous in meeting other people's needs, and (4) he prayed. God told him to send for Peter, because Peter would give him more knowledge about the God he was already seeking to please. • When Peter entered Cornelius's home, Peter broke a whole list of Jewish rules. Peter confessed he wasn't comfortable, but here was an eager audience, and he couldn't hold back his message. He had no sooner started sharing the gospel when God gave overwhelming approval by filling that Roman family with his Holy Spirit. Peter saw he had no choice but to baptize them and welcome them as equals in the growing Christian church. Another step had been taken in carrying the gospel to the whole world. • Cornelius is a welcome example of God's willingness to use extraordinary means to reach those who desire to know him. He does not play favorites, and he does not hide from those who want to find him. God sent his Son because he loves the whole world—and that includes Peter, Cornelius, and you.

Strengths and accomplishments	• Well-respected by the Jews even though he was an officer in the occupying army • He responded to God and encouraged his family to do the same
Lessons from his life	• God reaches those who want to know him • The gospel is for all people • There are people everywhere eager to believe
Vital statistics	• Where: Caesarea • Occupation: Roman army officer • Contemporaries: Peter, Philip, the apostles
Key verse	"He was a devout, God-fearing man, as was everyone in his household. He gave generously to the poor and prayed regularly to God" (Acts 10:2).

Cornelius's story is told in Acts 10:1–11:18.

o'clock, he had a vision in which he saw an angel of
God coming toward him. "Cornelius!" the angel said.
[4]Cornelius stared at him in terror. "What is it, sir?"
he asked the angel.
And the angel replied, "Your prayers and gifts to the
poor have been received by God as an offering! [5]Now
send some men to Joppa, and summon a man named
Simon Peter. [6]He is staying with Simon, a tanner who
lives near the seashore."
[7]As soon as the angel was gone, Cornelius called
two of his household servants and a devout soldier,
one of his personal attendants. [8]He told them what
had happened and sent them off to Joppa.

Peter Visits Cornelius

ACTS 10:9-33

The next day as Cornelius's messengers were nearing
the town, Peter went up on the flat roof to pray. It was
about noon, [10]and he was hungry. But while a meal
was being prepared, he fell into a trance. [11]He saw
the sky open, and something like a large sheet was let
down by its four corners. [12]In the sheet were all sorts
of animals, reptiles, and birds. [13]Then a voice said to
him, "Get up, Peter; kill and eat them."
[14]"No, Lord," Peter declared. "I have never eaten anything that our Jewish laws have declared impure and
unclean.*"
[15]But the voice spoke again: "Do not call something
unclean if God has made it clean." [16]The same vision
was repeated three times. Then the sheet was suddenly
pulled up to heaven.
[17]Peter was very perplexed. What could the vision
mean? Just then the men sent by Cornelius found Simon's house. Standing outside the gate, [18]they asked
if a man named Simon Peter was staying there.
[19]Meanwhile, as Peter was puzzling over the vision,
the Holy Spirit said to him, "Three men have come
looking for you. [20]Get up, go downstairs, and go with
them without hesitation. Don't worry, for I have sent
them."
[21]So Peter went down and said, "I'm the man you
are looking for. Why have you come?"
[22]They said, "We were sent by Cornelius, a Roman
officer. He is a devout and God-fearing man, well respected by all the Jews. A holy angel instructed him
to summon you to his house so that he can hear your
message." [23]So Peter invited the men to stay for the
night. The next day he went with them, accompanied
by some of the brothers from Joppa.
[24]They arrived in Caesarea the following day. Cornelius was waiting for them and had called together
his relatives and close friends. [25]As Peter entered his
home, Cornelius fell at his feet and worshiped him.
[26]But Peter pulled him up and said, "Stand up! I'm a
human being just like you!" [27]So they talked together
and went inside, where many others were assembled.
[28]Peter told them, "You know it is against our laws
for a Jewish man to enter a Gentile home like this or
to associate with you. But God has shown me that I
should no longer think of anyone as impure or unclean. [29]So I came without objection as soon as I was
sent for. Now tell me why you sent for me."
[30]Cornelius replied, "Four days ago I was praying
in my house about this same time, three o'clock in

Acts 10:14 Greek *anything common and unclean.*

for spreading the Good News to the empire's capital city.

Acts 10:2 What will happen to the heathen who have never heard about Christ? This question about God's justice is often asked. Cornelius wasn't a believer in Christ, but he was seeking God and was reverent and generous. Therefore, God sent Peter to tell Cornelius about Christ. This shows that God "rewards those who sincerely seek him" (Heb 11:6). Cornelius's story demonstrates God's willingness to use extraordinary means to reach those who desire to know him. Those who sincerely seek God will find him! God made Cornelius's knowledge complete.

Acts 10:3 Cornelius had a vision featuring a heavenly messenger. God spoke to other Bible characters through a variety of means—the burning bush of Moses (Exod 3:1-4); the talking donkey of Balaam (Num 22:21-30); the gentle whisper heard by Elijah (1 Kgs 19:11-14); the strange object lessons of Jeremiah (Jer 13:1-11). Simply put, God speaks to his people in remarkably different ways—through the written Scriptures, through the words of others, through circumstances and events. It is up to us to listen, to be perceptive, to be alert. What is God trying to say to you today?

Acts 10:12 According to Jewish law, certain foods were forbidden to be eaten (see Lev 11). The food laws made it difficult for Jews to eat with Gentiles without risking defilement. In fact, the Gentiles themselves were often seen as "unclean." Peter's vision meant that he should not look upon the Gentiles as inferior people whom God would not redeem. Before having the vision, Peter would have thought that a Gentile Roman officer could not become a follower of Christ. Afterward he understood that it was his responsibility to go with the messengers into a Gentile home and tell Cornelius the Good News of salvation in Jesus Christ.

Acts 10:15-16 Steeped in Jewish tradition and filled with certain biases, Peter was convinced his views on the Gentiles were correct. It took a three-part heavenly vision from God to change Peter's mind. One of the most basic and practical lessons from this encounter is that when God speaks, we must not challenge what he says. Doubting God is the rebellion of Eden. When God says something is so, we must not debate with him. The right response is humble submission to his revealed truth. Are you trying to argue with God over some point that he has already made clear?

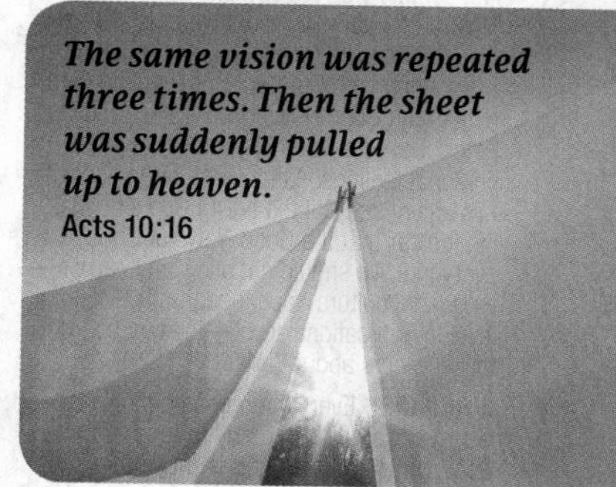
The same vision was repeated three times. Then the sheet was suddenly pulled up to heaven.
Acts 10:16

Acts 10:21-22 Cornelius was religious, devoted, generous, respected, and sincere (Acts 10:1-2). However, he was still spiritually separated from God. Because he needed to understand the gospel, God sent Peter to present to him the truth about salvation. Be careful not to equate earnestness with righteousness before God. We are brought into right standing with God by faith in Christ alone. Have you trusted in Jesus? Are you sharing with others—even those who seem religious—the truth that Christ is the only way to God?

▸ **ACTS 10:9-33** ***(cont.)***

the afternoon. Suddenly, a man in dazzling clothes was standing in front of me. 31He told me, 'Cornelius, your prayer has been heard, and your gifts to the poor have been noticed by God! 32Now send messengers to Joppa, and summon a man named Simon Peter. He is staying in the home of Simon, a tanner who lives near the seashore.' 33So I sent for you at once, and it was good of you to come. Now we are all here, waiting before God to hear the message the Lord has given you."

The Gentiles Hear the Good News

ACTS 10:34-43

Then Peter replied, "I see very clearly that God shows no favoritism. 35In every nation he accepts those who fear him and do what is right. 36This is the message of Good News for the people of Israel—that there is peace with God through Jesus Christ, who is Lord of all. 37You know what happened throughout Judea, beginning in Galilee, after John began preaching his message of baptism. 38And you know that God anointed Jesus of Nazareth with the Holy Spirit and with power. Then Jesus went around doing good and healing all who were oppressed by the devil, for God was with him.

39"And we apostles are witnesses of all he did throughout Judea and in Jerusalem. They put him to death by hanging him on a cross,* 40but God raised him to life on the third day. Then God allowed him to appear, 41not to the general public,* but to us whom God had chosen in advance to be his witnesses. We were those who ate and drank with him after he rose from the dead. 42And he ordered us to preach everywhere and to testify that Jesus is the one appointed by God to be the judge of all—the living and the dead. 43He is the one all the prophets testified about, saying that everyone who believes in him will have their sins forgiven through his name."

The Gentiles Receive the Holy Spirit

ACTS 10:44-48

Even as Peter was saying these things, the Holy Spirit fell upon all who were listening to the message. 45The Jewish believers* who came with Peter were amazed that the gift of the Holy Spirit had been poured out on the Gentiles, too. 46For they heard them speaking in other tongues* and praising God.

Then Peter asked, 47"Can anyone object to their being baptized, now that they have received the Holy Spirit just as we did?" 48So he gave orders for them to be baptized in the name of Jesus Christ. Afterward Cornelius asked him to stay with them for several days.

Peter Explains His Actions

ACTS 11:1-18

Soon the news reached the apostles and other believers* in Judea that the Gentiles had received the

Acts 10:39 Greek *on a tree.* **Acts 10:41** Greek *the people.* **Acts 10:45** Greek *The faithful ones of the circumcision.* **Acts 10:46** Or *in other languages.* **Acts 11:1** Greek *brothers.*

Acts 10:34-35 Perhaps the greatest barrier to the spread of the Good News in the first century was the Jewish–Gentile conflict. Most of the early believers were Jewish, and they thought it scandalous even to think of associating with Gentiles. But God told Peter to take the Good News to a Roman, and Peter obeyed despite his background and personal feelings. (Later Peter struggled with this again; see Gal 2:11-14.) God was making it clear that the Good News of Christ is for everyone! We should not allow any barrier—language, culture, race, geography, economic level, or educational level—to keep us from telling others about Christ.

Acts 10:35 Every nation has people who are restless for God, ready to receive the Good News—but someone must take it to them. Seeking God is not enough—people must find him. How then shall seekers find God without someone to point the way? Is God asking you to show someone the way to him? (See Rom 10:14-15.)

Acts 10:37-43 Peter's brief and powerful sermon contains a concise statement of the Good News: Jesus' perfect life of servanthood; his death on the cross; his resurrection, personally witnessed and experienced by Peter; Jesus' fulfillment of the Scriptures; the necessity of personal faith in him. A sermon or witness for Christ does not need to be long to be effective. It should be Spirit-led and should center on Christ, the way and the truth and the life.

Acts 10:43 Two examples of prophets testifying about Jesus and his forgiveness of sins are Isaiah 52:13–53:12; Ezekiel 36:25-26.

Acts 10:45 Cornelius and Peter were very different people. Cornelius was wealthy, a Gentile, and a military man. Peter was a Jewish fisherman turned preacher. But God's plan included both of them. In Cornelius's house that day, a new chapter in Christian history was written as a Jewish Christian leader and a Gentile Christian convert each discovered something significant about the other. Cornelius needed Peter in order to hear the Good News and know the way of salvation. Peter needed Cornelius in order to know that Gentiles were included in God's plan. You and another believer may also need each other to understand how God works!

Acts 10:47-48 In this case, the people were baptized after they received the Holy Spirit, publicly declaring their allegiance to Christ and identification with the Christian community.

Acts 10:48 Cornelius wanted Peter to stay with him for several days. He was a new believer and realized his need for teaching and fellowship. Are you as eager to learn more about Christ? Recognize your need to be with mature Christians, and strive to learn from them.

Acts 11:1-3 A Gentile was anyone who was not a Jew. Most Jewish believers thought that God offered salvation only to the Jews because God had given his law to them (Exod 19–20). A group in Jerusalem believed that Gentiles could be saved, but only if they followed all the Jewish laws and traditions—in essence, if they first became Jews before becoming Christians. Both groups were mistaken. God chose the Jews and taught them his laws so they could bring the message of salvation to all people (see Gen 12:3; Ps 22:27; Isa 42:4; 49:6; 56:3-7; 60:1-3; Jer 16:19-21; Zech 2:11; Mal 1:11; Rom 15:9-12).

Acts 11:2-18 When Peter brought the news of Cornelius's conversion back to Jerusalem, the believers were shocked that Peter had eaten with Gentiles. After they heard the whole story, they praised God (Acts 11:18). Their reactions teach us how to handle disagreements with other Christians. Before judging the behavior of fellow believers, it is important to hear them out. The Holy Spirit may have something important to teach us through them.

word of God. 2But when Peter arrived back in Jerusalem, the Jewish believers* criticized him. 3"You
entered the home of Gentiles* and even ate with
them!" they said.
4Then Peter told them exactly what had happened.
5"I was in the town of Joppa," he said, "and while I
was praying, I went into a trance and saw a vision.
Something like a large sheet was let down by its four
corners from the sky. And it came right down to me.
6When I looked inside the sheet, I saw all sorts of tame
and wild animals, reptiles, and birds. 7And I heard a
voice say, 'Get up, Peter; kill and eat them.'
8"'No, Lord,' I replied. 'I have never eaten anything
that our Jewish laws have declared impure or unclean.*'
9"But the voice from heaven spoke again: 'Do not
call something unclean if God has made it clean.'
10This happened three times before the sheet and all
it contained was pulled back up to heaven.
11"Just then three men who had been sent from
Caesarea arrived at the house where we were staying.
12The Holy Spirit told me to go with them and not
to worry that they were Gentiles. These six brothers
here accompanied me, and we soon entered the
home of the man who had sent for us. 13He told
us how an angel had appeared to him in his home
and had told him, 'Send messengers to Joppa, and
summon a man named Simon Peter. 14He will tell
you how you and everyone in your household can
be saved!'
15"As I began to speak," Peter continued, "the Holy
Spirit fell on them, just as he fell on us at the beginning. 16Then I thought of the Lord's words when
he said, 'John baptized with* water, but you will be
baptized with the Holy Spirit.' 17And since God gave
these Gentiles the same gift he gave us when we believed in the Lord Jesus Christ, who was I to stand
in God's way?"
18When the others heard this, they stopped ob-
jecting and began praising God. They said, "We can
see that God has also given the Gentiles the privilege
of repenting of their sins and receiving eternal life."

The Church in Antioch of Syria

ACTS 11:19-30

Meanwhile, the believers who had been scattered during the persecution after Stephen's death traveled as
far as Phoenicia, Cyprus, and Antioch of Syria. They
preached the word of God, but only to Jews. 20How-
ever, some of the believers who went to Antioch from
Cyprus and Cyrene began preaching to the Gentiles*
about the Lord Jesus. 21The power of the Lord was with

Acts 11:2 Greek *those of the circumcision.* **Acts 11:3** Greek *of uncircumcised men.* **Acts 11:8** Greek *anything common or unclean.* **Acts 11:16** Or *in;* also in 11:16b.
Acts 11:20 Greek *the Hellenists* (i.e., those who speak Greek); other manuscripts read *the Greeks.*

AD 41 **Herod Agrippa appointed king of Judea**

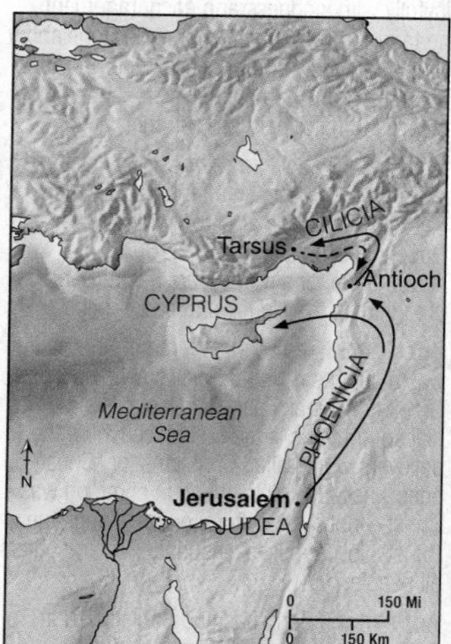

BARNABAS AND SAUL IN ANTIOCH
Persecution scattered the believers into Phoenicia, Cyprus, and Antioch, and the gospel went with them. Most spoke only to Jews, but in Antioch, some Gentiles were converted. The church sent Barnabas to investigate, and he was pleased with what he found. Barnabas went to Tarsus to bring Saul (Paul) back to Antioch.

Acts 11:8 God had promised throughout Scripture that he would reach the nations. This began with his general promise to Abraham (Gen 12:3; 18:18) and became very specific in Malachi's statement: "But my name is honored by people of other nations from morning till night" (Mal 1:11). But this was an extremely difficult truth for Jews, even Jewish believers, to accept. The Jewish believers understood how certain prophecies were fulfilled in Christ, but they overlooked other Old Testament teachings. Too often we are inclined to accept only the parts of God's Word that appeal to us and support our own agendas, ignoring the teachings we don't like. We must accept all of God's Word as absolute truth.

Acts 11:12ff Peter's defense for eating with Gentiles was a simple restatement of what had happened. He brought six witnesses with him to back him up, and then he quoted Jesus' promise about the coming of the Holy Spirit (Acts 11:16). These Gentiles' lives had been changed, and that was all the evidence Peter and the other believers needed. Changed lives are an equally powerful evidence today.

Acts 11:16 Jesus had also demonstrated clearly that he and his message were for all people. He had preached in Samaria (John 4:1-42); in the region of the Gerasenes, populated by Greeks (Mark 5:1-20); and he even had reached out to Romans (Luke 7:1-10). The apostles shouldn't have been surprised that they were called to do the same.

Acts 11:18 The intellectual questions ended, and the theological discussion stopped with the report that God had given the Holy Spirit to the Gentiles. This was a turning point for the early church. They had to accept those whom God had chosen, even if they were Gentiles. But joy over the conversion of Gentiles was not unanimous. This continued to be a struggle for some Jewish Christians throughout the first century.

Acts 11:20-21 In Antioch, Christianity was launched on its worldwide mission and there the believers aggressively preached to the Gentiles (non-Jews who did not worship God). Philip had preached in Samaria, but the Samaritans were part Jewish (Acts 8:5); Peter had preached to Cornelius, but he already worshiped God (Acts 10:2). Believers who were scattered after the outbreak of persecution in Jerusalem spread the Good News to other Jews in the lands they fled to (Acts 11:19). The seeds of this missionary work had been sown after Stephen's death. At this time, the believers began actively sharing the Good News with Gentiles.

▶ **ACTS 11:19-30** ***(cont.)***
them, and a large number of these Gentiles believed
and turned to the Lord.
22When the church at Jerusalem heard what had
happened, they sent Barnabas to Antioch. 23When
he arrived and saw this evidence of God's blessing, he
was filled with joy, and he encouraged the believers
to stay true to the Lord. 24Barnabas was a good man,
full of the Holy Spirit and strong in faith. And many
people were brought to the Lord.
25Then Barnabas went on to Tarsus to look for Saul.
26When he found him, he brought him back to Antioch. Both of them stayed there with the church for a
full year, teaching large crowds of people. (It was at Antioch that the believers* were first called Christians.)
27During this time some prophets traveled from
Jerusalem to Antioch. 28One of them named Agabus
stood up in one of the meetings and predicted by the
Spirit that a great famine was coming upon the entire Roman world. (This was fulfilled during the reign
of Claudius.) 29So the believers in Antioch decided
to send relief to the brothers and sisters* in Judea,

Acts 11:26 Greek *disciples;* also in 11:29. **Acts 11:29** Greek *the brothers.*

HEROD AGRIPPA I

For good or evil, families have a lasting and powerful influence on their children. Traits and qualities are passed on to the next generation, often with the mistakes and sins of the parents being repeated by the children. Four generations of the Herod family are mentioned in the Bible. Each leader left his evil mark: Herod the Great murdered Bethlehem's baby boys; Herod Antipas was involved in Jesus' trial and John the Baptist's execution; Herod Agrippa I murdered the apostle James; and Herod Agrippa II was one of Paul's judges. • Herod Agrippa I related fairly well to his Jewish subjects. He had a Jewish grandmother of royal blood (Mariamne), which allowed the people to accept him—though grudgingly. As a youth, Agrippa I had been temporarily imprisoned by the emperor Tiberias; but Rome now trusted him, and he got along well with the emperors Caligula and Claudius. • The Christian movement created an unexpected opportunity for Herod to gain new favor with the Jews. Gentiles began to be accepted into the church in large numbers. Many Jews had been tolerating this new movement as a sect within Judaism, but its rapid growth alarmed them. Persecution of Christians was revived, and even the apostles were not spared. James was killed, and Peter was thrown into prison. • But soon Herod made a fatal error. During a visit to Caesarea, the people called him a god, and he accepted their praise. Herod was immediately struck with a painful disease, and he died within a week. • Like his grandfather and uncle before him, and his son after him, Herod Agrippa I came close to the truth but missed it. Because religion was important to him only as an aspect of politics, he had no reverence and no qualms about taking praise that only God should receive. His mistake is a common one. Whenever we become proud of our own abilities and accomplishments, not recognizing them as gifts from God, we repeat Herod's sin.

Claudius becomes the Roman emperor

Strength and accomplishment	• Capable administrator and negotiator
Weaknesses and mistakes	• Arranged the murder of the apostle James • Imprisoned Peter with plans to execute him • Allowed the people to praise him as a god
Lessons from his life	• Those who set themselves against God are doomed to ultimate failure • Family traits can influence children toward great good or great evil
Vital statistics	• Where: Jerusalem • Occupation: Roman-appointed king of the Jews • Relatives: Grandfather: Herod the Great. Father: Aristobulus. Uncle: Herod Antipas. Sister: Herodias. Wife: Cypros. Son: Herod Agrippa II. Daughters: Bernice, Mariamne, Drusilla. • Contemporaries: Emperors Tiberias, Caligula, and Claudius; James, Peter, the apostles
Key verse	"Instantly, an angel of the Lord struck Herod with a sickness, because he accepted the people's worship instead of giving the glory to God. So he was consumed with worms and died" (Acts 12:23).

Herod Agrippa I's story is told in Acts 12:1-23.

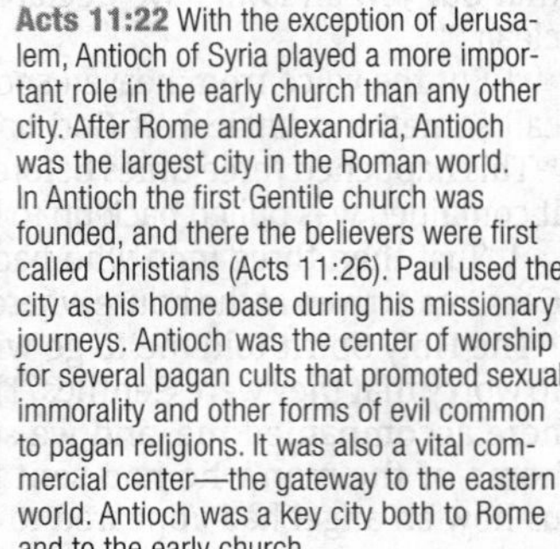

Acts 11:22 With the exception of Jerusalem, Antioch of Syria played a more important role in the early church than any other city. After Rome and Alexandria, Antioch was the largest city in the Roman world. In Antioch the first Gentile church was founded, and there the believers were first called Christians (Acts 11:26). Paul used the city as his home base during his missionary journeys. Antioch was the center of worship for several pagan cults that promoted sexual immorality and other forms of evil common to pagan religions. It was also a vital commercial center—the gateway to the eastern world. Antioch was a key city both to Rome and to the early church.

Acts 11:22-26 Barnabas presents a wonderful example of how to help new Christians. He demonstrated strong faith; he ministered joyfully with kindness and encouragement; he taught new believers further lessons about God (see Acts 9:26-30). Remember Barnabas when you see new believers, and think of ways to help them grow in their faith.

Acts 11:25 Saul had been sent to his home in Tarsus for protection after his conversion had caused an uproar among the Jewish leaders in Jerusalem (Acts 9:26-30). He stayed there for several years before Barnabas brought him to help the church at Antioch.

Acts 11:26 The young church at Antioch was a curious mixture of Jews (who spoke Greek or Aramaic) and Gentiles. It is significant that this is the first place where the believers were called Christians (or "Christ-ones") because all they had in common was Christ—not race, culture, or even language. Christ's love crosses all boundaries and unites all people.

Acts 11:26 Barnabas and Saul stayed at Antioch for a full year teaching the new believers. They could have left for other cities, but they saw the importance of follow-up and training. Have you helped someone believe in Christ? Spend time teaching and encouraging that person. Are you a new believer? Remember, you are just beginning your Christian life. Your faith needs to grow and mature through consistent Bible study and teaching.

Acts 11:27-28 Prophets were found not only in the Old Testament but also in the early church. Their role was to present God's will to the people and to instruct them in God's

everyone giving as much as they could. 30This they did, entrusting their gifts to Barnabas and Saul to take to the elders of the church in Jerusalem.

James Is Killed and Peter Is Imprisoned

ACTS 12:1-5

About that time King Herod Agrippa* began to persecute some believers in the church. 2He had the apostle James (John's brother) killed with a sword. 3When Herod saw how much this pleased the Jewish people, he also arrested Peter. (This took place during the Passover celebration.*) 4Then he imprisoned him, placing him under the guard of four squads of four soldiers each. Herod intended to bring Peter out for public trial after the Passover. 5But while Peter was in prison, the church prayed very earnestly for him.

Peter's Miraculous Escape from Prison

ACTS 12:6-19

The night before Peter was to be placed on trial, he was asleep, fastened with two chains between two soldiers. Others stood guard at the prison gate. 7Suddenly, there was a bright light in the cell, and an angel of the Lord stood before Peter. The angel struck him on the side to awaken him and said, "Quick! Get up!" And the chains fell off his wrists. 8Then the angel told him, "Get dressed and put on your sandals." And he did. "Now put on your coat and follow me," the angel ordered.

9So Peter left the cell, following the angel. But all the time he thought it was a vision. He didn't realize it was actually happening. 10They passed the first and second guard posts and came to the iron gate leading to the city, and this opened for them all by itself. So they passed through and started walking down the street, and then the angel suddenly left him.

11Peter finally came to his senses. "It's really true!" he said. "The Lord has sent his angel and saved me from Herod and from what the Jewish leaders* had planned to do to me!"

12When he realized this, he went to the home of

Acts 12:1 Greek *Herod the king.* He was the nephew of Herod Antipas and a grandson of Herod the Great. **Acts 12:3** Greek *the days of unleavened bread.* **Acts 12:11** Or *the Jewish people.*

Word. Sometimes, like Agabus, they also had the gift of predicting the future.

Acts 11:28-29 Serious food shortages occurred during the reign of the Roman emperor Claudius (A.D. 41–54) because of a drought that had extended across much of the Roman Empire for many years. It is significant that the church in Antioch assisted the church in Jerusalem. The daughter church had grown enough to be able to help the established church.

Acts 11:29 The people of Antioch were motivated to give generously because they cared about the needs of others. This is the cheerful giving that the Bible commends (2 Cor 9:7). Reluctant giving reflects a lack of concern for people. Focus your concern on the needy, and you will be motivated to give.

Acts 12:1 King Herod Agrippa I was the son of Aristobulus and grandson of Herod the Great. His sister was Herodias, who had been responsible for the death of John the Baptist (see Mark 6:17-28). Herod Agrippa I was part Jewish. The Romans had appointed him to rule over most of Palestine, including the territories of Galilee, Perea, Judea, and Samaria. He persecuted the Christians in order to please the Jewish leaders who opposed them, hoping that would solidify his position. Agrippa I died suddenly in A.D. 44 (see Acts 12:20-23). His death was also recorded by the historian Josephus.

Acts 12:2 James and John were two of Jesus' original 12 disciples. They had asked Jesus for special recognition in his Kingdom (Mark 10:35-40). Jesus had said that to be a part of his Kingdom would mean suffering with him (drink from the same cup; Mark 10:38-39). James and John did indeed suffer—Herod executed James, and later John was exiled (see Rev 1:9).

Herod Agrippa I

Granted the title "king" by Caligula, Herod Agrippa I ruled over Palestine (Judea and Samaria) from A.D. 41–44. Pictured is a Roman coin with his image on it. Agrippa I is mentioned in the New Testament for his persecution of the early church in order to gain favor with the Jews (Acts 12:1-19). He killed the apostle James, the son of Zebedee, and imprisoned Peter. When Peter was released by an angel, Agrippa put the guards to death. But cruelty came back upon him soon thereafter; he died a miserable death in A.D. 44. Accounts of this incident are recorded both by Josephus (*Antiquities* 19.9.1.274–275; *War* 2.11.5.214–215) and by the Scriptures (Acts 12:20-23). The incident occurred at Caesarea. He was wearing a sparkling silver robe, and the people flattered him by calling him a god. He accepted their praise, was suddenly struck with a mortal illness, and died a horrible death. A dreadful end awaits those who blaspheme God.

Acts 12:2-11 Why did God allow James to die and yet miraculously save Peter? Life is full of difficult questions like this. Why is one child physically disabled and another child athletically gifted? Why do people die before realizing their potential? Questions like these we cannot possibly answer in this life because we do not see all that God sees. He has chosen to allow evil in this world for a time. But we can trust God's leading because he has promised to destroy all evil eventually. In the meantime, we know that God will help us use our suffering to strengthen us and glorify him. For more on this question, see the notes on Job 1:1ff, p. 94; Job 2:10, p. 96; Job 3:23-26, p. 98.

Acts 12:3-5 Herod had Peter arrested during the Passover celebration. This was a strategic move, since more Jews were in the city than usual, and Herod could impress the most people. Herod's plan undoubtedly was to execute Peter, but the believers were praying for Peter's safety. The earnest prayer of the church significantly affected the outcome of these events. Prayer changes things, so pray often and with confidence.

Acts 12:7 God sent an angel to rescue Peter. Angels are God's messengers. They are divinely created beings with supernatural power, and they sometimes take on human appearance in order to talk to people. Angels should not be worshiped, because they are not divine. They are God's servants, just as we are.

Acts 12:12 John Mark wrote the Gospel of Mark. His mother's house was large enough to accommodate a meeting of many believers. An upstairs room in this house may have been the location of Jesus' Last Supper with his disciples (Luke 22:8ff).

AD 43 *London is founded*

▸ ACTS 12:6-19 ***(cont.)***

Mary, the mother of John Mark, where many were
gathered for prayer. 13He knocked at the door in the
gate, and a servant girl named Rhoda came to open it.
14When she recognized Peter's voice, she was so overjoyed that, instead of opening the door, she ran back
inside and told everyone, "Peter is standing at the door!"
15"You're out of your mind!" they said. When she
insisted, they decided, "It must be his angel."
16Meanwhile, Peter continued knocking. When
they finally opened the door and saw him, they were
amazed. 17He motioned for them to quiet down and
told them how the Lord had led him out of prison.
"Tell James and the other brothers what happened,"
he said. And then he went to another place.
18At dawn there was a great commotion among the
soldiers about what had happened to Peter. 19Herod
Agrippa ordered a thorough search for him. When he
couldn't be found, Herod interrogated the guards and
sentenced them to death. Afterward Herod left Judea
to stay in Caesarea for a while.

The Death of Herod Agrippa

ACTS 12:20-25

Now Herod was very angry with the people of Tyre and
Sidon. So they sent a delegation to make peace with
him because their cities were dependent upon Herod's
country for food. The delegates won the support of
Blastus, Herod's personal assistant, 21and an appointment with Herod was granted. When the day arrived,
Herod put on his royal robes, sat on his throne, and
made a speech to them. 22The people gave him a great

GREAT ESCAPES IN THE BIBLE

Who Escaped	*Reference*	*What Happened*	*What the Escape Accomplished*	*Application*
Jacob	Gen 31:1-55	Fled from his father-in-law, Laban, after almost 20 years of service	Allowed Jacob to return home for Isaac's death and for reconciliation with Esau, his brother	A time away from home often puts the really important things into perspective.
Moses	Exod 2:11-15	Fled Egypt after killing an Egyptian in defense of a fellow Israelite	Saved his own life and began another part of God's training	God fits even our mistakes into his plan.
Israelites	Exod 12:28-42	Escaped Egypt after 430 years, most of that time in slavery	God confirmed his choice of Abraham's descendants.	God will not forget his promises.
Spies	Josh 2:1-24	Escaped searchers in Jericho by hiding in Rahab's house	Prepared the destruction of Jericho and preserved Rahab, who would become one of David's ancestors—as well as an ancestor of Jesus	God's plan weaves lives together in a pattern beyond our understanding.
Ehud	Judg 3:15-30	Escaped undetected after assassinating the Moabite king Eglon	Broke the control of Moab over Israel and began 80 years of peace	Punishments by God are often swift and deadly.
Samson	Judg 16:1-3	Escaped a locked city by ripping the gates from their hinges	Merely postponed Samson's self-destruction because of his lack of self-control	Without dependence on God and his guidance, even great ability is wasted.
Elijah	1 Kgs 19:1-18	Fled into the wilderness out of fear of Queen Jezebel	Preserved Elijah's life but also displayed his human weakness	Even at moments of real success, our personal weaknesses are our greatest challenges.
Saul (Paul)	Acts 9:23-25	Lowered over the wall in a basket to get out of Damascus	Saved this new Christian for great service to God	God has a purpose for every life, which leads to a real adventure for those willing to cooperate.
Peter	Acts 12:1-11	Freed from prison by an angel	Saved Peter for God's further plans for his life	God can use extraordinary means to carry out his plan—often when we least expect it.
Paul and Silas	Acts 16:22-40	Chains loosened and doors opened by an earthquake, but they chose not to leave the prison	Pointed out the powerlessness of humans before God	When our dependence and attention are focused on God rather than our problems, he is able to offer help in unexpected ways.

ovation, shouting, "It's the voice of a god, not of a man!"
[23]Instantly, an angel of the Lord struck Herod with a sickness, because he accepted the people's worship instead of giving the glory to God. So he was consumed with worms and died.
[24]Meanwhile, the word of God continued to spread, and there were many new believers.
[25]When Barnabas and Saul had finished their mission to Jerusalem, they returned,* taking John Mark with them.

Acts 12:25 Or *mission, they returned to Jerusalem.* Other manuscripts read *mission, they returned from Jerusalem;* still others read *mission, they returned from Jerusalem to Antioch.*

C. Paul's First Missionary Journey

Paul begins his great missionary work to the Gentiles, and we begin to see the spread of the church around the world. The first missionary-sending church, the church in Antioch of Syria, commissioned Paul and Barnabas to travel with the Good News of Jesus. On this first missionary journey, Paul and Barnabas go to Cyprus and through many cities in Galatia and surrounding areas. The gospel is spreading farther and farther.

Barnabas and Saul Are Commissioned

ACTS 13:1-3

Among the prophets and teachers of the church at Antioch of Syria were Barnabas, Simeon (called "the black man"*), Lucius (from Cyrene), Manaen (the childhood companion of King Herod Antipas*), and Saul. [2]One day as these men were worshiping the Lord and fasting, the Holy Spirit said, "Dedicate Barnabas and Saul

Acts 13:1a Greek *who was called Niger.* **Acts 13:1b** Greek *Herod the tetrarch.*

Acts 12:13-15 The prayers of the group of believers were answered, even as they prayed. But when the answer arrived at the door, they didn't believe it. We should be people of faith who believe that God answers the prayers of those who seek his will. When you pray, believe you'll get an answer. And when the answer comes, don't be surprised; be thankful!

Acts 12:17 This James was Jesus' brother, who became a leader in the Jerusalem church (Acts 15:13; Gal 1:19). The James who was killed (Acts 12:2) was John's brother and one of the original 12 disciples.

Acts 12:19 Under Roman law, guards who allowed a prisoner to escape were subject to the same punishment the prisoner was to receive. Thus, these 16 guards were sentenced to death.

Acts 12:19 The Jews considered Jerusalem their capital, but the Romans made Caesarea their headquarters in Palestine. That is where Herod Agrippa I lived.

Acts 12:20 These coastal cities, Tyre and Sidon, were free and self-governing but economically dependent on Judea. We don't know why Herod had quarreled with them, but now representatives from those cities were trying to appease him through his personal assistant.

Acts 12:23 Herod died a horrible death accompanied by intense pain; he was literally eaten alive, from the inside out, by worms. Pride is a serious sin, and in this case, God chose to punish it immediately. God does not immediately punish all sin, but he will judge everyone (Heb 9:27). Accept Christ's offer of forgiveness today. No one can afford to wait.

Acts 12:25 John Mark was Barnabas's cousin (Col 4:10). His mother, Mary, often would open her home to the apostles (Acts 12:12), so John Mark would have been exposed to most of the great men and teachings of the early church. Later, John Mark joined Paul and Barnabas on their first missionary journey, but for unknown reasons, he left them in the middle of the trip. Paul criticized John Mark for abandoning the mission (Acts 15:37-39). But Mark wrote the Gospel that bears his name, and he was later acclaimed by Paul as a vital help in the growth of the early church (2 Tim 4:11).

Acts 13:1 What variety there is in the church! The common thread among these five men was their deep faith in Christ. We must never exclude anyone whom Christ has called to follow him. Like the early church, if believers today do their part to reach out to all who are lost, church congregations will eventually be comprised of people from different racial and cultural backgrounds. When this happens, we most often see our propensity to label and categorize. We are most comfortable with those who are just like us. Clearly, at the root of these tendencies is the ugly sin of prejudice. The more we understand the gospel and embrace God's version of the body of Christ, the more we will begin to transcend these differences. More than merely getting along, we will be able to honestly and authentically say from our hearts that we love each other.

Acts 13:2-3 The church dedicated Barnabas and Saul to the work God had for them. To *dedicate* means "to set apart" for a special purpose. We, too, should dedicate our pastors, missionaries, and Christian workers for their tasks. We can also dedicate ourselves to use our time, money, and talents for God's work. Ask God what he wants you to set apart for him.

Acts 13:2-3 This was the beginning of Saul's (Paul; see Acts 13:9) first missionary journey. The church was involved in sending Paul and Barnabas, but it was God's plan. Why did Paul and Barnabas go where they did? (1) The Holy Spirit led them. (2) They followed the communication routes of the Roman Empire, making travel easier. (3) They visited key population and cultural centers to reach as many people as possible. (4) They went to cities with synagogues, speaking first to the Jews in hopes that they would see Jesus as the Messiah and help spread the Good News to everyone.

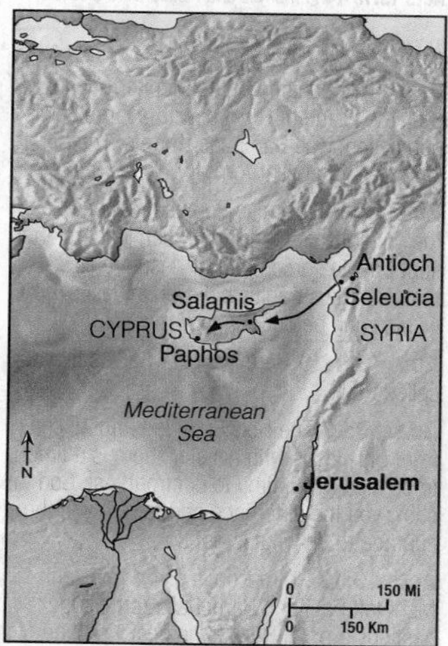

***MINISTRY IN CYPRUS** The leaders of the church in Antioch chose Paul and Barnabas to take the gospel westward. Along with John Mark, they boarded ship at Seleucia and set out across the Mediterranean for Cyprus. They preached in Salamis, the largest city, and went across the island to Paphos.*

▸ **ACTS 13:1-3** ***(cont.)***

for the special work to which I have called them." [3]So after more fasting and prayer, the men laid their hands on them and sent them on their way.

Paul's First Missionary Journey

ACTS 13:4-12

So Barnabas and Saul were sent out by the Holy Spirit. They went down to the seaport of Seleucia and then sailed for the island of Cyprus. [5]There, in the town of Salamis, they went to the Jewish synagogues and preached the word of God. John Mark went with them as their assistant.

[6]Afterward they traveled from town to town across the entire island until finally they reached Paphos, where they met a Jewish sorcerer, a false prophet named Bar-Jesus. [7]He had attached himself to the governor, Sergius Paulus, who was an intelligent man. The governor invited Barnabas and Saul to visit him, for he wanted to hear the word of God. [8]But Elymas, the sorcerer (as his name means in Greek), interfered and urged the governor to pay no attention to what Barnabas and Saul said. He was trying to keep the governor from believing.

[9]Saul, also known as Paul, was filled with the Holy Spirit, and he looked the sorcerer in the eye. [10]Then he said, "You son of the devil, full of every sort of deceit and fraud, and enemy of all that is good! Will you never stop perverting the true ways of the Lord? [11]Watch now, for the Lord has laid his hand of punishment upon you, and you will be struck blind. You will not see the sunlight for some time." Instantly mist and darkness came over the man's eyes, and he began groping around begging for someone to take his hand and lead him.

[12]When the governor saw what had happened, he became a believer, for he was astonished at the teaching about the Lord.

Paul Preaches in Antioch of Pisidia

ACTS 13:13-43

Paul and his companions then left Paphos by ship for Pamphylia, landing at the port town of Perga. There John Mark left them and returned to Jerusalem. [14]But Paul and Barnabas traveled inland to Antioch of Pisidia.*

Acts 13:13-14 *Pamphylia* and *Pisidia* were districts in what is now Turkey.

Paul begins his first missionary journey

Acts 13:4 Located in the Mediterranean Sea, the island of Cyprus, with a large Jewish population, was Barnabas's home. Their first stop was in familiar territory.

Acts 13:6-7 Sergius Paulus functioned as the governor of the island. Such leaders often kept private sorcerers. Bar-Jesus realized that if Sergius Paulus believed in Jesus, he would soon be out of a job.

Acts 13:9-10 Here is where Saul is first called Paul.

Acts 13:10 The Holy Spirit led Paul to confront Bar-Jesus with his sin. There is a time to be nice and a time to confront. Ask God to show you the difference and to give you the courage to do what is right.

Acts 13:13 No reason is given why John Mark left Paul and Barnabas. Some suggestions are: (1) He was homesick; (2) he resented the change in leadership from Barnabas (his cousin) to Paul; (3) he became ill (an illness that may have affected all of them; see Gal 4:13); (4) he was unable to withstand the rigors and dangers of the missionary journey; (5) he may have planned to go only that far but had not communicated this to Paul and Barnabas. Paul implicitly accused John Mark of lacking courage and commitment, refusing to take him along on another journey (see Acts 15:37-38). It is clear from Paul's later letters, however, that he grew to respect Mark (Col 4:10) and that he needed Mark in his work (2 Tim 4:11).

Acts 13:14 Antioch of Pisidia was a different city from Antioch of Syria, where there was already a flourishing church (Acts 11:26). This Antioch, in the region of Pisidia, was a hub of good roads and trade, with a large Jewish population.

MISSIONARIES OF THE NEW TESTAMENT AND THEIR JOURNEYS

Name	*Journey's Purpose*	*Scripture Reference*
Philip	One of the first to preach the gospel outside Jerusalem	Acts 8:4-40
Peter and John	Visited new Samaritan believers to encourage them	Acts 8:14-25
Paul (journey to Damascus)	Set out to capture Christians but was captured by Christ	Acts 9:1-25
Peter	Led by God to one of the first Gentile families to become Christians—Cornelius's family	Acts 9:32–10:48
Barnabas	Went to Antioch as an encourager; traveled on to Tarsus to bring Paul back to Antioch; took famine relief to Jerusalem	Acts 11:25-30
Barnabas, Paul, John Mark	Left Antioch for Cyprus, Pamphylia, and Galatia on the first missionary journey	Acts 13:1–14:28
Barnabas and John Mark	Left Antioch for Cyprus after a disagreement with Paul	Acts 15:36-41
Paul, Silas, Timothy, Luke	Left Antioch to revisit churches in Galatia; then traveled on to Asia, Macedonia, and Achaia on the second missionary journey	Acts 15:36–18:22
Apollos	Left Alexandria for Ephesus; learned the complete gospel story from Priscilla and Aquila; preached in Athens and Corinth	Acts 18:24-28
Paul, Timothy, Erastus	Revisited churches in Galatia, Asia, Macedonia, and Achaia on the third major missionary journey	Acts 18:23; 19:1–21:14

Acts 13:14 When they went to a new city to witness for Christ, Paul and Barnabas would go first to the synagogue. The Jews who were there believed in God and diligently studied the Scriptures. Tragically, many could not accept Jesus as the promised Messiah

On the Sabbath they went to the synagogue for the
services. 15 After the usual readings from the books of
Moses* and the prophets, those in charge of the service
sent them this message: "Brothers, if you have any word
of encouragement for the people, come and give it."
16 So Paul stood, lifted his hand to quiet them, and
started speaking. "Men of Israel," he said, "and you
God-fearing Gentiles, listen to me.
17 "The God of this nation of Israel chose our ancestors and made them multiply and grow strong during their stay in Egypt. Then with a powerful arm he
led them out of their slavery. 18 He put up with them*
through forty years of wandering in the wilderness.
19 Then he destroyed seven nations in Canaan and gave
their land to Israel as an inheritance. 20 All this took
about 450 years.
"After that, God gave them judges to rule until the
time of Samuel the prophet. 21 Then the people begged
for a king, and God gave them Saul son of Kish, a man
of the tribe of Benjamin, who reigned for forty years.
22 But God removed Saul and replaced him with David,
a man about whom God said, 'I have found David son
of Jesse, a man after my own heart. He will do everything I want him to do.'*
23 "And it is one of King David's descendants, Jesus,
who is God's promised Savior of Israel! 24 Before he

Acts 13:15 Greek *from the law.* **Acts 13:18** Some manuscripts read *He cared for them;* compare Deut 1:31. **Acts 13:22** 1 Sam 13:14.

JOHN MARK

Mistakes are effective teachers. Their consequences have a way of making lessons painfully clear. But those who learn from their mistakes are wise. John Mark was a good learner who just needed some time and encouragement. • Mark was eager to do the right thing, but he had trouble staying with a task. In his Gospel, Mark mentions a young man (probably referring to himself) who fled in such fear during Jesus' arrest that he left his clothes behind. This tendency to run showed up later when Paul and Barnabas took him as their assistant on their first missionary journey. At their second stop, Mark left them and returned to Jerusalem. It was a decision Paul did not easily accept. In preparing for their second journey two years later, Barnabas again suggested Mark as a traveling companion, but Paul flatly refused. As a result, the team was divided. Barnabas took Mark with him, and Paul chose Silas. Barnabas was patient with Mark, and the young man repaid his investment. Paul and Mark were later reunited, and the older apostle became a close friend of the young disciple. • Mark was a valuable companion to three early Christian leaders: Barnabas, Paul, and Peter. The material in Mark's Gospel seems to have come mostly from Peter. Mark's role as an assistant allowed him to be an observer. He heard Peter's accounts of the years with Jesus over and over, and he was likely the first to put Jesus' life in writing. • Barnabas played a key role in Mark's life. He stood beside the young man despite his failure, giving him patient encouragement. Mark challenges us to learn from our mistakes and appreciate the patience of others. Is there a "Barnabas" in your life you need to thank for encouraging you?

Strengths and accomplishments	• Wrote the Gospel of Mark • Persisted beyond his youthful mistakes • Was an assistant and traveling companion to three of the greatest early missionaries
Weaknesses and mistakes	• Probably fled in panic when Jesus was arrested • Left Paul and Barnabas for unknown reasons during the first missionary journey
Lessons from his life	• Personal maturity usually comes from a combination of time and mistakes • Mistakes are not usually as important as what can be learned from them • Encouragement can change a person's life
Vital statistics	• Where: Jerusalem • Occupations: Missionary-in-training, Gospel writer, traveling companion • Relatives: Mother: Mary. Cousin: Barnabas. • Contemporaries: Paul, Peter, Timothy, Luke, Silas
Key verse	"Only Luke is with me. Bring Mark with you when you come, for he will be helpful to me in my ministry" (Paul writing in 2 Tim 4:11).

John Mark's story is told in Acts 12:25–13:13; 15:36-39. He is also mentioned in Colossians 4:10; 2 Timothy 4:11; Philemon 1:24; 1 Peter 5:13.

because they had the wrong idea of what the Messiah should be. He was not, as they desired, a military king who would overthrow Rome's control but a servant-king who would defeat sin in people's hearts. (Only later, when Christ returns, will he judge the nations of the world.) Paul and Barnabas did not separate themselves from the synagogues but tried to show clearly that the very Scriptures the Jews studied pointed to Jesus.

Acts 13:14-15 What happened in a synagogue service? First, the Shema was recited (this is Deut 6:4, which Jews repeated several times daily). Certain prayers were spoken; then there was a reading from the Law (Genesis—Deuteronomy), a reading from the Prophets intending to illustrate the Law, and a sermon. Those in charge of the service decided who would lead the service and give the sermon. A different person was chosen to lead each week. Since it was customary for the synagogue leader to invite visiting rabbis to speak, Paul and Barnabas usually had an open door when they first went to a synagogue. But as soon as they spoke about Jesus as Messiah, the door would often slam shut. They were usually not invited back by the religious leaders, and sometimes they would be thrown out of town!

Acts 13:16ff Paul's message to the Jews in the synagogue in Antioch began with an emphasis on God's covenant with Israel. This was a point of agreement because all Jews were proud to be God's chosen people. Then Paul explained how the Good News fulfilled the covenant. Some Jews found this message hard to swallow.

Acts 13:23-31 Because Paul was speaking to devout Jews, he began by reminding them about the covenant, Abraham, David, and other familiar themes. Later, when speaking to the Greek philosophers in Athens (Acts 17:22-32), he would begin by talking about what he had observed in their city. In both cases, he centered the sermon around Christ and emphasized the Resurrection. When you share the Good News, begin where your audience is—then tell them about Christ.

▸ **ACTS 13:13-43 *(cont.)***

came, John the Baptist preached that all the people of
Israel needed to repent of their sins and turn to God
and be baptized. 25As John was finishing his ministry
he asked, 'Do you think I am the Messiah? No, I am not!
But he is coming soon—and I'm not even worthy to be
his slave and untie the sandals on his feet.'
26"Brothers—you sons of Abraham, and also you God-
fearing Gentiles—this message of salvation has been
sent to us! 27The people in Jerusalem and their leaders
did not recognize Jesus as the one the prophets had
spoken about. Instead, they condemned him, and in doing this they fulfilled the prophets' words that are read
every Sabbath. 28They found no legal reason to execute
him, but they asked Pilate to have him killed anyway.
29"When they had done all that the prophecies said
about him, they took him down from the cross* and
placed him in a tomb. 30But God raised him from the
dead! 31And over a period of many days he appeared to
those who had gone with him from Galilee to Jerusalem. They are now his witnesses to the people of Israel.
32"And now we are here to bring you this Good News.
The promise was made to our ancestors, 33and God has
now fulfilled it for us, their descendants, by raising
Jesus. This is what the second psalm says about Jesus:

'You are my Son.
Today I have become your Father.*'

34For God had promised to raise him from the dead,
not leaving him to rot in the grave. He said, 'I will give
you the sacred blessings I promised to David.'* 35An-
other psalm explains it more fully: 'You will not allow
your Holy One to rot in the grave.'* 36This is not a
reference to David, for after David had done the will
of God in his own generation, he died and was buried
with his ancestors, and his body decayed. 37No, it was
a reference to someone else—someone whom God
raised and whose body did not decay.
38*"Brothers, listen! We are here to proclaim that
through this man Jesus there is forgiveness for your
sins. 39Everyone who believes in him is declared right
with God—something the law of Moses could never
do. 40Be careful! Don't let the prophets' words apply
to you. For they said,

41 'Look, you mockers,
be amazed and die!
For I am doing something in your own day,
something you wouldn't believe
even if someone told you about it.'*"

42As Paul and Barnabas left the synagogue that day,
the people begged them to speak about these things
again the next week. 43Many Jews and devout converts
to Judaism followed Paul and Barnabas, and the two
men urged them to continue to rely on the grace of God.

Paul Turns to the Gentiles

ACTS 13:44-52

The following week almost the entire city turned out
to hear them preach the word of the Lord. 45But when
some of the Jews saw the crowds, they were jealous; so
they slandered Paul and argued against whatever he said.
46Then Paul and Barnabas spoke out boldly and
declared, "It was necessary that we first preach the

Acts 13:29 Greek *from the tree.* **Acts 13:33** Or *Today I reveal you as my Son.* Ps 2:7. **Acts 13:34** Isa 55:3. **Acts 13:35** Ps 16:10. **Acts 13:38** English translations divide verses 38 and 39 in various ways. **Acts 13:41** Hab 1:5 (Greek version).

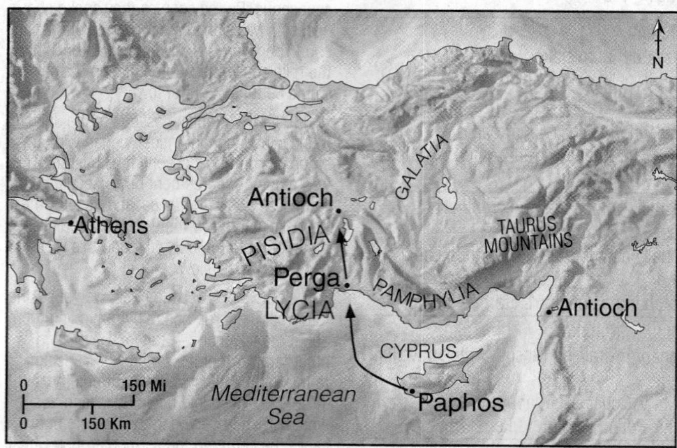

***MINISTRY IN PAMPHYLIA AND GALATIA** Paul, Barnabas, and John Mark left Paphos and landed at Perga in the humid region of Pamphylia, a narrow strip of land between the sea and the Taurus Mountains. John Mark left them in Perga, but Paul and Barnabas traveled up the steep road into the higher elevation of Pisidia in Galatia. When the Jews rejected his message, Paul preached to Gentiles, and the Jews drove Paul and Barnabas out of the Pisidian city of Antioch.*

Acts 13:38-39 This is the focus of the Good News: Forgiveness of sins and freedom from guilt are available through faith in Christ to all people—including you. Have you received this forgiveness? Are you refreshed each day by the thought that you are right with God?

Acts 13:42-45 The Jewish leaders undoubtedly brought theological arguments against Paul and Barnabas, but Luke tells us that the real reason for their hostility was that "they were jealous." When we see others succeeding where we haven't or receiving the affirmation we crave, it is hard to rejoice with them. Jealousy is a natural reaction. But how tragic it is when our jealous feelings make us try to stop God's work. If a work is God's work, rejoice in it—no matter who is doing it.

Acts 13:46 Why was it necessary for the Good News to go first to the Jews? God planned that through the Jewish nation all the world would know of God (Gen 12:3). Paul, a Jew himself, loved his people (Rom 9:1-5) and wanted to give them every opportunity to join him in proclaiming God's salvation. Unfortunately, many Jews did not recognize Jesus as Messiah, and they did not understand that God was offering salvation

word of God to you Jews. But since you have rejected
it and judged yourselves unworthy of eternal life, we
will offer it to the Gentiles. 47For the Lord gave us this
command when he said,

'I have made you a light to the Gentiles,
to bring salvation to the farthest corners
of the earth.'*"

48When the Gentiles heard this, they were very
glad and thanked the Lord for his message; and all
who were chosen for eternal life became believers. 49So the Lord's message spread throughout that
region.

50Then the Jews stirred up the influential religious
women and the leaders of the city, and they incited
a mob against Paul and Barnabas and ran them out
of town. 51So they shook the dust from their feet as
a sign of rejection and went to the town of Iconium.
52And the believers* were filled with joy and with the
Holy Spirit.

Acts 13:47 Isa 49:6. **Acts 13:52** Greek *the disciples.*

BARNABAS

Every group needs an "encourager" because everyone needs encouragement at one time or another. However, the value of encouragement is often missed because it tends to be private rather than public. In fact, people most need encouragement when they feel most alone. A man named Joseph was such an encourager that he earned the nickname "Son of Encouragement," or Barnabas, from the Jerusalem Christians. • Barnabas was drawn to people he could encourage, and he was a great help to those around him. It is delightful that wherever Barnabas encouraged Christians, non-Christians flocked to become believers! • Barnabas's actions were crucial to the early church. In a way, we can thank him for most of the New Testament. God used his relationship with Paul at one point and with Mark at another to keep these two men going when either might have failed. Barnabas did wonders with encouragement! • When Paul arrived in Jerusalem for the first time following his conversion, the local Christians were understandably reluctant to welcome him. They thought his story was a trick to capture more Christians. But Barnabas proved willing to risk his life to meet with Paul and then convince the others that their former enemy was now a vibrant believer in Jesus. We can only wonder what might have happened to Paul without Barnabas. • It was Barnabas who encouraged Mark to go with him and Paul to Antioch. Mark joined them on their first missionary journey but decided during the trip to return home. Later, Barnabas wanted to invite Mark to join them for another journey, but Paul would not agree. As a result, the partners went separate ways, Barnabas with Mark and Paul with Silas. This actually doubled the missionary effort. Barnabas's patient encouragement was a huge boost for the effectiveness of Mark's eventual ministry. Paul and Mark were later reunited in missionary efforts. • As Barnabas's life shows, we are often presented with situations where there is someone who needs encouragement. But our tendency is to criticize instead. It may be important at times to point out someone's shortcomings, but before we have the right to do this, we must build that person's trust through encouragement. Will you take the opportunity to encourage those with whom you come in contact today?

Strengths and accomplishments	• One of the first to sell possessions to help the Christians in Jerusalem • First to travel with Paul as a missionary team • As an encourager, he was one of the most influential people in the early days of Christianity • Called an apostle
Weakness and mistake	• Like Peter, temporarily stayed aloof from Gentile believers until Paul corrected him
Lessons from his life	• Encouragement is one of the most effective ways to help • Sooner or later, true obedience to God will involve risk • There is always someone who needs encouragement
Vital statistics	• Where: Cyprus, Jerusalem, Antioch • Occupations: Missionary, teacher • Relatives: Aunt: Mary. Cousin: John Mark. • Contemporaries: Peter, Silas, Paul, Herod Agrippa I
Key verses	"When he arrived and saw this evidence of God's blessing, he was filled with joy, and he encouraged the believers to stay true to the Lord. Barnabas was a good man, full of the Holy Spirit and strong in faith. And many people were brought to the Lord" (Acts 11:23-24).

Barnabas's story is told in Acts 4:36-37; 9:27–15:39. He is also mentioned in 1 Corinthians 9:6; Galatians 2:1, 9, 13; Colossians 4:10.

to anyone, Jew or Gentile, who comes to him through faith in Christ.

Acts 13:47 God had planned for Israel to be this light (Isa 49:6). Through Israel came Jesus, the light of the nations (Luke 2:32). This light would spread out and enlighten the Gentiles.

Acts 13:50 Instead of accepting the truth, the Jewish leaders stirred up opposition and ran Paul and Barnabas out of town. When confronted by a disturbing truth, people often turn away and refuse to listen. When God's Spirit points out needed changes in our lives, we must listen to him. Otherwise we may be pushing the truth so far away that it no longer affects us.

Acts 13:51 Often Jews would shake the dust off their feet when leaving a Gentile town on the way back to their own land. This symbolized cleansing themselves from the contamination of those who did not worship God. For Paul and Barnabas to do this to Jews demonstrated that Jews who rejected the Good News were not truly part of Israel and were no better than pagans. Jesus had told his disciples to shake from their feet the dust of any town that would not accept or listen to them (Mark 6:11). The disciples were not to blame if the message was rejected, as long as they had faithfully presented it. When we

Paul and Barnabas in Iconium

ACTS 14:1-7

The same thing happened in Iconium.* Paul and Barnabas went to the Jewish synagogue and preached
with such power that a great number of both Jews and
Greeks became believers. 2Some of the Jews, however,
spurned God's message and poisoned the minds of the
Gentiles against Paul and Barnabas. 3But the apostles
stayed there a long time, preaching boldly about the
grace of the Lord. And the Lord proved their message
was true by giving them power to do miraculous signs
and wonders. 4But the people of the town were divided
in their opinion about them. Some sided with the Jews,
and some with the apostles.
5Then a mob of Gentiles and Jews, along with their
leaders, decided to attack and stone them. 6When
the apostles learned of it, they fled to the region of
Lycaonia—to the towns of Lystra and Derbe and the
surrounding area. 7And there they preached the Good
News.

Paul and Barnabas in Lystra and Derbe

ACTS 14:8-20

While they were at Lystra, Paul and Barnabas came
upon a man with crippled feet. He had been that way
from birth, so he had never walked. He was sitting
9and listening as Paul preached. Looking straight at
him, Paul realized he had faith to be healed. 10So Paul
called to him in a loud voice, "Stand up!" And the man
jumped to his feet and started walking.
11When the crowd saw what Paul had done, they
shouted in their local dialect, "These men are gods
in human form!" 12They decided that Barnabas was
the Greek god Zeus and that Paul was Hermes, since
he was the chief speaker. 13Now the temple of Zeus
was located just outside the town. So the priest of the
temple and the crowd brought bulls and wreaths of
flowers to the town gates, and they prepared to offer
sacrifices to the apostles.
14But when the apostles Barnabas and Paul heard
what was happening, they tore their clothing in
dismay and ran out among the people, shouting,
15"Friends,* why are you doing this? We are merely
human beings—just like you! We have come to bring
you the Good News that you should turn from these
worthless things and turn to the living God, who made
heaven and earth, the sea, and everything in them.
16In the past he permitted all the nations to go their
own ways, 17but he never left them without evidence
of himself and his goodness. For instance, he sends

Acts 14:1 *Iconium,* as well as *Lystra* and *Derbe* (14:6), were towns in what is now Turkey. **Acts 14:15** Greek *Men.*

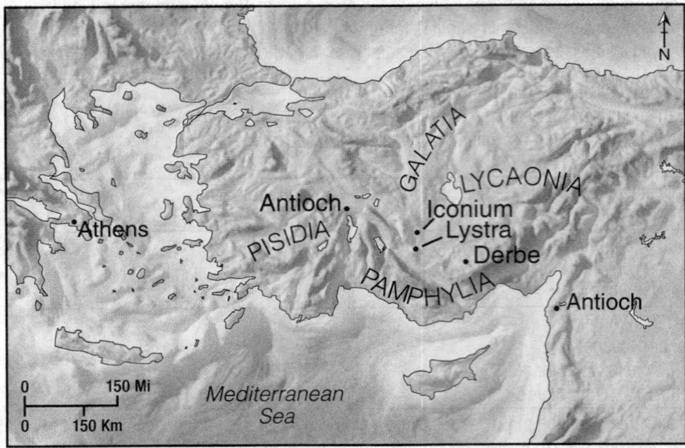

CONTINUED MINISTRY IN GALATIA *Paul and Barnabas, thrown out of Antioch in Pisidia, descended the mountains, going east into Lycaonia. They went first to Iconium, a commercial center on the road between Asia and Syria. After preaching there, they had to flee to Lystra, 25 miles south. Paul was stoned in Lystra, but he and Barnabas traveled the 50 miles to Derbe, a border town. The pair then boldly retraced their steps.*

share Christ carefully and sensitively, God does not hold us responsible for the other person's decision.

Acts 14:3-4 We may wish we could perform a miraculous act that would convince everyone once and for all that Jesus is the Lord. But we see here that even if we could perform a miracle, it wouldn't convince everyone. God gave these men power to do great wonders as confirmation of the message of grace, but people were still divided. Don't spend your time and energy wishing for miracles. Sow the seeds of the Good News on the best ground you can find in the best way you can, and leave the convincing to the Holy Spirit.

Acts 14:6 Iconium (Acts 14:1), Lystra, and Derbe were three cities Paul visited in the southern part of the region of Galatia. Paul probably wrote a letter to these churches—the letter to the Galatians—because many Jewish Christians were claiming that non-Jewish Christians couldn't be saved unless they followed Jewish laws and customs. Paul's letter refuted this and brought the believers back to a right understanding of faith in Jesus (see Gal 3:3, 5). Paul may have written his letter soon after leaving the region (see the note on Acts 14:28, p. 1546).

Acts 14:11-12 Zeus and Hermes (to the Greeks, known as Jupiter and Mercury to the Romans) were two popular gods in the Roman world. People from Lystra claimed that these gods had once visited their city. According to legend, no one had offered them hospitality except an old couple, so Zeus and Hermes had killed the rest of the people and rewarded the old couple. When the citizens of Lystra saw the miracles of Paul and Barnabas, they assumed that the gods were revisiting them. Remembering the story of what had happened to the previous citizens, they immediately honored Paul and Barnabas and showered them with gifts.

Acts 14:15-18 Responding to the people of Lystra, Paul and Barnabas reminded them that God never leaves himself "without evidence of himself and his goodness." Rain and good crops, for example, are evidence of his goodness. Later Paul wrote that this evidence in nature leaves people without an excuse for unbelief (Rom 1:20). When in doubt about God, look around and you will see abundant evidence that he is at work in the world.

you rain and good crops and gives you food and joyful hearts." [18]But even with these words, Paul and Barnabas could scarcely restrain the people from sacrificing to them.

[19]Then some Jews arrived from Antioch and Iconium and won the crowds to their side. They stoned Paul and dragged him out of town, thinking he was dead. [20]But as the believers* gathered around him, he got up and went back into the town. The next day he left with Barnabas for Derbe.

Acts 14:20 Greek *disciples;* also in 14:22, 28.

Paul and Barnabas Return to Antioch of Syria

ACTS 14:21-28

After preaching the Good News in Derbe and making many disciples, Paul and Barnabas returned to Lystra, Iconium, and Antioch of Pisidia, [22]where they strengthened the believers. They encouraged them to continue in the faith, reminding them that we must suffer many hardships to enter the Kingdom of God. [23]Paul and Barnabas also appointed elders in every

Hermes

Hermes was a Greek god, the son of Zeus by Maia. He was called Mercury in the Roman pantheon of deities. In Greek mythology, Hermes was the messenger of the gods and the escort of the dead to Hades. He was the god of fertility, the patron of music, the guardian of travelers, and the god of eloquent speech. The people in Lystra acclaimed Paul as Hermes because of his miraculous work and role as chief speaker. The Lystrians thought Paul was a god visiting them in bodily form (Acts 14:11-12). We know that the only time God appeared in human form is when God became incarnate in Jesus Christ (John 1:1, 14; Col 2:19). He alone is worthy of our worship.

Acts 14:21-22 Paul and Barnabas returned to visit the believers in all the cities where they had recently been threatened and physically attacked. These men knew the dangers they faced, yet they believed that they had a responsibility to encourage the new believers. No matter how inconvenient or uncomfortable the task may seem, we must always support new believers who need our help and encouragement. It was not convenient or comfortable for Jesus to go to the cross for us!

Acts 14:23 Part of the reason that Paul and Barnabas risked their lives to return to these cities was to organize the churches' leadership. They were not just following up on a loosely knit group; they were helping the believers get organized with spiritual leaders who could help them grow. Churches grow under Spirit-led leaders, both laypersons and pastors. Pray for your church leaders and support them; and if God puts his finger on you, humbly accept the responsibility of a leadership role in your church.

Acts 14:18-19 Only days after the people in Lystra had thought that Paul and Barnabas were gods and wanted to offer sacrifices to them, they stoned Paul and left him for dead. That's human nature. Jesus understood how fickle crowds can be (John 2:24-25). When many people approve of us, we feel good, but that should never cloud our thinking or affect our decisions. We should not live to please the crowd—especially in our spiritual lives. Be like Jesus. Know the nature of the crowd and don't put your trust in it. Put your trust in God alone.

Acts 14:18-20 Paul and Barnabas were persistent in their preaching of the Good News, considering the cost to themselves to be nothing in comparison with obedience to Christ. They had just narrowly escaped being stoned in Iconium (Acts 14:1-7), but Jews from Antioch and Iconium tracked Paul down, stoned him, and left him for dead. But Paul got up and went back into the city to preach the Good News. That's commitment! Being a disciple of Christ calls for total commitment. As Christians, we no longer belong to ourselves but to our Lord, for whom we are called to suffer.

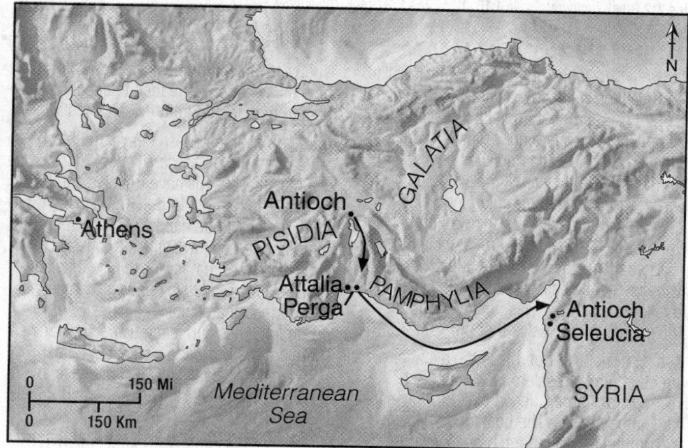

***THE END OF THE FIRST JOURNEY** From Antioch in Pisidia, Paul and Barnabas went down the mountains back to Pamphylia on the coast. Stopping first in Perga, where they had landed, they went west to Attalia, the main port that sent goods from Asia to Syria and Egypt. There they found a ship bound for Seleucia, the port of Antioch in Syria. This ended their first missionary journey.*

▸ **ACTS 14:21-28** ***(cont.)***

church. With prayer and fasting, they turned the elders over to the care of the Lord, in whom they had put their trust. 24Then they traveled back through Pisidia to Pamphylia. 25They preached the word in Perga, then went down to Attalia.

26Finally, they returned by ship to Antioch of Syria, where their journey had begun. The believers there had entrusted them to the grace of God to do the work they had now completed. 27Upon arriving in Antioch, they called the church together and reported everything God had done through them and how he had opened the door of faith to the Gentiles, too. 28And they stayed there with the believers for a long time.

D. The Epistle of James

This epistle was written by James, the half brother of Jesus who had become a believer after Jesus' resurrection and developed into the central leader in the church of Jerusalem. James had a strong ministry among Jewish believers, and his leadership in the early church was vital to maintaining doctrinal purity and unity among the growing and diverse church. This letter addresses many issues about how faith in Jesus needs to affect our behavior, and it addresses some misunderstandings about the relationship between salvation by faith in Jesus and the need for believers to live godly lives. James was probably written around the time of Paul's first missionary journey, before the Jerusalem Council. This letter could be considered a how-to book on Christian living. Confrontation, challenges, and a call to commitment await you. Read James and become a doer of the Word, not just a hearer.

AD 48

James writes a letter to Christians

Greetings from James

JAMES 1:1

This letter is from James, a slave of God and of the Lord Jesus Christ.

I am writing to the "twelve tribes"—Jewish believers scattered abroad.

Greetings!

Faith and Endurance

JAMES 1:2-18

Dear brothers and sisters,* when troubles come your way, consider it an opportunity for great joy. 3For you know that when your faith is tested, your endurance has a chance to grow. 4So let it grow, for when your endurance is fully developed, you will be perfect and complete, needing nothing.

5If you need wisdom, ask our generous God, and he will give it to you. He will not rebuke you for asking. 6But when you ask him, be sure that your faith is in God alone. Do not waver, for a person with divided loyalty is as unsettled as a wave of the sea that is blown and tossed by the wind. 7Such people should not expect to receive anything from the Lord. 8Their loyalty is divided between God and the world, and they are unstable in everything they do.

9Believers who are* poor have something to boast

Jas 1:2 Greek *brothers;* also in 1:16, 19. **Jas 1:9** Greek *The brother who is.*

Acts 14:28 Paul probably wrote his letter to the Galatians while he was staying in Antioch (A.D. 48 or 49) after completing his first missionary journey. There are several theories as to what part of Galatia Paul was addressing, but most agree that Iconium, Lystra, and Derbe were part of that region for which the letter was intended. Galatians was probably written before the Jerusalem council (Acts 15), because in the letter the question of whether Gentile believers should be required to follow Jewish law was not yet resolved. The council met to solve that problem.

Jas 1:1 The writer of this letter, a leader of the church in Jerusalem (see Acts 12:17; 15:13), was James, Jesus' half brother, not James the apostle. The book of James was one of the earliest letters, probably written before A.D. 50. After Stephen was martyred (Acts 7:55–8:3), persecution increased, and Christians in Jerusalem were scattered throughout the Roman world. There were thriving Jewish-Christian communities in Rome, Alexandria, Cyprus, and cities in Greece and Asia Minor. Because these early believers did not have the support of established Christian churches, James wrote to them as a concerned leader, to encourage them in their faith during those difficult times.

Jas 1:2-3 James doesn't say *if* trouble comes your way but *when* it does. He assumes that we will have troubles and that it is possible to profit from them. The point is not to pretend to be happy when we face pain but to have a positive outlook ("consider it an opportunity for great joy") because of what troubles can produce in our lives. James tells us to turn our hardships into times of learning. Tough times can teach us perseverance. There are many other passages that deal with perseverance (also called patience and steadfastness) (see Rom 2:7; 5:3-5; 8:24-25; 2 Cor 6:3-7; 2 Pet 1:2-9).

Jas 1:2-4 We can't really know the depth of our character until we see how we react under pressure. It is easy to be kind to others when everything is going well, but can we still be kind when others are treating us unfairly? God wants to make us mature and complete, not to keep us from all pain. Instead of complaining about our struggles, we should see them as opportunities for growth. Thank God for promising to be with you in rough times. Ask him to help you solve your problems or to give you the strength to endure them. Then be patient. God will not leave you alone with your problems; he will stay close and help you grow.

Jas 1:5 By "wisdom," James is talking not only about knowledge but about the ability to make wise decisions in difficult circumstances. Whenever we need wisdom, we can pray to God, and he will generously supply what we need. Christians don't have to grope around in the dark, hoping to stumble upon answers. We can ask for God's wisdom to guide our choices.

Jas 1:5 The wisdom that we need has three distinct characteristics:

(1) *It is practical.* The wisdom from God relates to life even during the most trying times. It is not a wisdom isolated from suffering and trials. This wisdom is the tool by which trials are overcome. An intelligent person may have profound ideas, but a wise person puts profound ideas into action. Intelligence will allow someone to describe several reasons why the car broke down. The

about, for God has honored them. [10]And those who are rich should boast that God has humbled them. They will fade away like a little flower in the field. [11]The hot sun rises and the grass withers; the little flower droops and falls, and its beauty fades away. In the same way, the rich will fade away with all of their achievements.

[12]God blesses those who patiently endure testing and temptation. Afterward they will receive the crown of life that God has promised to those who love him. [13]And remember, when you are being tempted, do not say, "God is tempting me." God is never tempted to do wrong,* and he never tempts anyone else. [14]Temptation comes from our own desires, which entice us and drag us away. [15]These desires give birth to sinful actions. And when sin is allowed to grow, it gives birth to death.

[16]So don't be misled, my dear brothers and sisters. [17]Whatever is good and perfect comes down to us from God our Father, who created all the lights in the heavens.* He never changes or casts a shifting shadow.* [18]He chose to give birth to us by giving us his true word. And we, out of all creation, became his prized possession.*

Listening and Doing

JAMES 1:19-27

Understand this, my dear brothers and sisters: You must all be quick to listen, slow to speak, and slow

Jas 1:13 Or *God should not be put to a test by evil people.* **Jas 1:17a** Greek *from above, from the Father of lights.* **Jas 1:17b** Some manuscripts read *He never changes, as a shifting shadow does.* **Jas 1:18** Greek *we became a kind of firstfruit of his creatures.*

wise person chooses the most likely reason and proceeds to take action.

(2) *It is divine.* God's wisdom goes beyond common sense. Common sense does not lead us to choose joy in the middle of trials. This wisdom begins with respect for God, leads to living by God's direction, and results in the ability to tell right from wrong. James 3 describes that wisdom at length.

(3) *It is Christlike.* Asking for wisdom is ultimately asking to be like Christ. The Bible identifies Christ as the "wisdom of God" (1 Cor 1:24; 2:1-7).

Jas 1:6 We must believe not only in the existence of God but also in his loving care. This includes relying on God and expecting that he will hear and answer when we pray. We must put away our critical attitude when we come to him. God does not grant every thoughtless or selfish request. We must have confidence that God will align our desires with his purposes. (For more on this concept, read the note on Matt 21:22, p. 1435.)

Jas 1:6 A person with divided loyalty is not completely convinced that God's way is best. He treats God's Word like any human advice and retains the option to disobey. He vacillates between allegiance to subjective feelings, the world's ideas, and God's commands. If your faith is new, weak, or struggling, remember that you can trust God. Then be loyal by committing yourself wholeheartedly to God.

Jas 1:6-8 If you have ever seen the constant rolling of huge waves at sea, you know how restless they are—subject to the forces of wind, gravity, and tide. Divided loyalty leaves a person as unsettled as the restless waves. If you want to stop being tossed about, rely on God to show you what is best for you. Ask him for wisdom, and trust that he will give it to you. Then your decisions will be sure and solid.

Jas 1:9 Christianity brings a new dignity to the poor and not-so-influential people of this world. That dignity is most apparent in the church, where there are not (or should not be) any class distinctions. All believers share the distinction and dignity of being changed by the gospel and being charged with the mission of taking that same Good News to the rest of the world. Believers know they have dignity before God because Christ died for them. Mary, the mother of Jesus, is a great example of this truth. The dignity that she displayed when she realized what God had done for her is seen in her prayer of praise, called the *Magnificat* (Luke 1:46-55). Whatever our social or economic situation, James challenges us to see beyond it to our eternal advantages. What we can have in Jesus Christ outweighs anything in this life. Knowing him gives us our high position, where we find our true dignity.

Jas 1:9-11 The poor should be glad that riches mean nothing to God; otherwise these people would be considered unworthy. The rich should be glad that money means nothing to God because money is easily lost. We find true wealth by developing our spiritual lives, not by developing our financial assets. God is interested in what is lasting (our souls), not in what is temporary (our money and possessions). See Mark 4:18-19 for Jesus' words on this subject. Strive to treat each person as Christ would.

Jas 1:10-11 If wealth, power, and status mean nothing to God, why do we attribute so much importance to them and so much honor to those who possess them? Do your material possessions give you goals and your only reason for living? If they were gone, what would be left? What you have in your heart matters to God and endures for eternity.

Jas 1:12 The crown of life is like the victory wreath given to winning athletes (see 1 Cor 9:25). God's crown of life is not glory and honor here on earth but the reward of eternal life—living with God forever. The way to be in God's winners' circle is by loving him and staying faithful even under pressure.

Jas 1:12-15 Temptation comes from evil desires inside us, not from God. It begins with an evil thought and becomes sin when we dwell on the thought and allow it to become an action. Like a snowball rolling downhill, sin grows more destructive the more we let it have its way. The best time to stop a temptation is before it is too strong or moving too fast to control. (See Matt 4:1-11; 1 Cor 10:13; 2 Tim 2:22 for more about escaping temptation.)

Jas 1:13-14 People who live for God often wonder why they still have temptations. Does God tempt them? God *tests* people, but he does not *tempt* them by trying to seduce them to sin. God allows Satan to tempt people in order to refine their faith and to help them grow in their dependence on Christ. We can resist the temptation to sin by turning to God for strength and choosing to obey his Word.

Jas 1:13-15 It is easy to blame others and make excuses for evil thoughts and wrong actions. We use excuses such as: (1) It's the other person's fault; (2) I couldn't help it; (3) everybody's doing it; (4) it was just a mistake; (5) nobody's perfect; (6) the devil made me do it; (7) I was pressured into it; (8) I didn't know it was wrong; or (9) God is tempting me. A person who makes excuses is trying to shift the blame to something or someone else. As a Christian, accept responsibility for your wrongs, confess them, and ask God for forgiveness.

Jas 1:17 The Bible often compares goodness with light and evil with shadow and darkness. (For other passages where God is pictured as light, see Ps 27:1; Isa 60:19-22; John 1:1-14.)

Jas 1:19 When we talk too much and listen too little, we communicate to others that we think our ideas are much more important than theirs. James wisely advises us to reverse this process. Put a mental stopwatch on your conversations, and keep track of how much you talk and how much you listen. When people talk with you, do they feel that their viewpoints and ideas have value?

Jas 1:19-20 These verses speak of anger that erupts when our ego is bruised: "*I* am hurt"; "*My* opinions are not being heard." When injustice and sin occur, we *should* become angry because others are being hurt. But we should not become angry when we fail to win an argument or when we feel offended or neglected. Selfish anger never helps anybody.

▸ **JAMES 1:19-27** ***(cont.)***

to get angry. [20]Human anger* does not produce the righteousness* God desires. [21]So get rid of all the filth and evil in your lives, and humbly accept the word God has planted in your hearts, for it has the power to save your souls.

[22]But don't just listen to God's word. You must do what it says. Otherwise, you are only fooling yourselves. [23]For if you listen to the word and don't obey, it is like glancing at your face in a mirror. [24]You see yourself, walk away, and forget what you look like. [25]But if you look carefully into the perfect law that sets you free, and if you do what it says and don't forget what you heard, then God will bless you for doing it.

[26]If you claim to be religious but don't control your tongue, you are fooling yourself, and your religion is worthless. [27]Pure and genuine religion in the sight of God the Father means caring for orphans and widows in their distress and refusing to let the world corrupt you.

A Warning against Prejudice

JAMES 2:1-13

My dear brothers and sisters,* how can you claim to have faith in our glorious Lord Jesus Christ if you favor some people over others?

[2]For example, suppose someone comes into your meeting* dressed in fancy clothes and expensive jewelry, and another comes in who is poor and dressed in dirty clothes. [3]If you give special attention and a good seat to the rich person, but you say to the poor one, "You can stand over there, or else sit on the floor"—well, [4]doesn't this discrimination show that your judgments are guided by evil motives?

[5]Listen to me, dear brothers and sisters. Hasn't God chosen the poor in this world to be rich in faith? Aren't they the ones who will inherit the Kingdom he promised to those who love him? [6]But you dishonor the poor! Isn't it the rich who oppress you and drag you into court? [7]Aren't they the ones who slander Jesus Christ, whose noble name* you bear?

Jas 1:20a Greek *A man's anger.* **Jas 1:20b** Or *the justice.* **Jas 2:1** Greek *brothers;* also in 2:5, 14. **Jas 2:2** Greek *your synagogue.* **Jas 2:7** Greek *slander the noble name.*

Jas 1:21 James advises us to get rid of all that is wrong in our lives and "humbly accept" the salvation message we have received, because it alone can save us.

Jas 1:22-25 It is important to *listen* to what God's Word says, but it is much more important to obey it and to *do* what it says. We can measure the effectiveness of our Bible study time by the effect it has on our behavior and attitudes. Do you put into action what you have studied?

Jas 1:25 It seems paradoxical that a law could give us freedom, but God's law offers us a true reflection of our sinful condition and gives us the opportunity to ask for God's forgiveness (see Rom 7:7-8). As Christians, we are saved by God's grace, and salvation frees us from sin's control. As believers, we are free to live as God created us to live. Of course, this does not mean that we are free to do as we please (see 1 Pet 2:16); rather, we are now free to obey God.

Jas 1:26 See the notes in James 3, pp. 1550-1551, for more on controlling the tongue. No matter how spiritual we may think we are, we all could control our speech more effectively.

Jas 1:27 In the first century, orphans and widows had very little means of economic support. Unless a family member was willing to care for them, they were reduced to begging, selling themselves as slaves, or starving. By caring for these people, the church put God's Word into practice. When we give with no thought of receiving, we show what it means to truly serve others.

Jas 1:27 To keep ourselves from letting the world corrupt us, we need to commit ourselves to Christ's ethical and moral system, not the world's. We are not to adapt to the world's value system, which is based on money, power, and pleasure. True faith means nothing if we are contaminated with such values.

SHOWING FAVORITISM

Why it is wrong to show favoritism to the wealthy:

1. It is inconsistent with Christ's teachings.
2. It results from evil thoughts.
3. It insults people made in God's image.
4. It is a by-product of selfish motives.
5. It goes against the biblical definition of love.
6. It shows a lack of mercy to those less fortunate.
7. It is hypocritical.
8. It is a sin.

Jas 2:1ff In this chapter James argues against favoritism and for the necessity of good deeds. He presents three principles of faith: (1) Commitment is an essential part of faith. You cannot be a Christian simply by affirming the right doctrines or agreeing with biblical facts (Jas 2:19). You must commit your mind and heart to Christ. (2) Right actions are the natural by-products of true faith. A genuine Christian will have a changed life (Jas 2:18). (3) Faith without good deeds doesn't do anybody any good—it is useless (Jas 2:14-17). James's teachings are consistent with Paul's teaching that we receive salvation by faith alone. Paul emphasizes the *purpose* of faith: to bring salvation. James emphasizes the *results* of faith: a changed life.

Jas 2:1-7 James condemns acts of favoritism. Often we treat a well-dressed, impressive-looking person better than someone who looks shabby. We do this because we would rather identify with successful people than with apparent failures. The irony, as James reminds us, is that the supposed winners may have gained their impressive lifestyle at our expense. In addition, the rich find it difficult to identify with the Lord Jesus, who came as a humble servant. Are you easily impressed by status, wealth, or fame? Are you partial to the "haves" while ignoring the "have nots"? This attitude is sinful. God views all people as equals, and if he favors anyone, it is the poor and the powerless. We should follow his example.

Jas 2:2-4 Why is it wrong to judge a person based on economic status? Wealth may indicate intelligence, wise decisions, and hard work. On the other hand, it may only mean that a person had the good fortune of being born into a wealthy family. Or it may be the sign of greed, dishonesty, or selfishness. By honoring someone who dresses well, we are making appearance

8Yes indeed, it is good when you obey the royal law as found in the Scriptures: "Love your neighbor as yourself."* 9But if you favor some people over others, you are committing a sin. You are guilty of breaking the law.

10For the person who keeps all of the laws except one is as guilty as a person who has broken all of God's laws. 11For the same God who said, "You must not commit adultery," also said, "You must not murder."* So if you murder someone but do not commit adultery, you have still broken the law.

12So whatever you say or whatever you do, remember that you will be judged by the law that sets you free. 13There will be no mercy for those who have not shown mercy to others. But if you have been merciful, God will be merciful when he judges you.

Faith without Good Deeds Is Dead

JAMES 2:14-26

What good is it, dear brothers and sisters, if you say you have faith but don't show it by your actions? Can that kind of faith save anyone? 15Suppose you see a brother or sister who has no food or clothing, 16and you say, "Good-bye and have a good day; stay warm and eat well"—but then you don't give that person any food or clothing. What good does that do?

17So you see, faith by itself isn't enough. Unless it produces good deeds, it is dead and useless.

18Now someone may argue, "Some people have faith; others have good deeds." But I say, "How can you show me your faith if you don't have good deeds? I will show you my faith by my good deeds."

19You say you have faith, for you believe that there is one God.* Good for you! Even the demons believe

Jas 2:8 Lev 19:18. **Jas 2:11** Exod 20:13-14; Deut 5:17-18. **Jas 2:19** Some manuscripts read *that God is one;* see Deut 6:4.

more important than character. Sometimes we do this because: (1) poverty makes us uncomfortable; we don't want to face our responsibilities to those who have less than we do; (2) we want to be wealthy and hope to use the rich person as a means to that end; (3) we want the rich person to join our church and help support it financially. All these motives are selfish, stemming from the view that we are superior to the poor person but feel inferior to the rich person. If we say that Christ is our Lord, then we must live as he requires, showing no favoritism and loving all people regardless of whether they are rich or poor.

Jas 2:2-4 We are often partial to the rich because we mistakenly assume that riches are a sign of God's blessing and approval. But God does not promise us earthly rewards or riches; in fact, Christ calls us to be ready to suffer for him and give up everything in order to hold on to eternal life (Matt 6:19-21; 19:28-30; Luke 12:14-34; Rom 8:15-21; 1 Tim 6:17-19). We will have untold riches in eternity if we are faithful in our present life (Luke 6:35; John 12:23-25; Gal 6:7-10; Titus 3:4-8).

Jas 2:5 When James speaks about the poor, he is talking about those who have no money and also about those whose simple values are despised by much of our affluent society. Perhaps the "poor" people prefer serving to managing, human relationships to financial security, peace to power. This does not mean that the poor will automatically go to heaven and the rich to hell. Poor people are usually more aware of their powerlessness. Thus, it is often easier for them to acknowledge their need for salvation. For the rich, one of the greatest barriers to salvation is pride. For the poor, bitterness can often bar the way to acceptance of salvation.

Jas 2:8 The "royal law" was given by our great King, Jesus Christ, who said, "Love each other in the same way I have loved you" (John 15:12). This law, originally summarized in Leviticus 19:18, is the basis of all the laws for how people should relate to one another. Christ reinforced this truth in Matthew 22:37-40, and Paul taught it in Romans 13:8; Galatians 5:14.

Jas 2:8-9 We must treat all people as we would want to be treated. We should not ignore the rich, because then we would be withholding our love. But we must not favor them for what they can do for us while ignoring the poor who can offer us seemingly so little in return.

Jas 2:10 Christians must not use this verse to justify sinning. We dare not say, "Because I can't keep every demand of God, why even try?" James reminds us that if we've broken just one law, we are sinners. We can't decide to keep part of God's law and ignore the rest. You can't break the law a little bit; if you have broken it at all, you need Christ to pay for your sin. Measure yourself, not someone else, against God's standards. Ask for forgiveness where you need it, and then renew your effort to put your faith into practice.

Jas 2:12 As Christians, we are saved by God's free gift (grace) through faith, not by keeping the law. But as Christians, we are also required to obey Christ. The apostle Paul taught that "we must all stand before Christ to be judged" (2 Cor 5:10) for our conduct. God's grace does not cancel our duty to obey him; it gives our obedience a new basis. The law is no longer an external set of rules, but it is a "law that sets you free"—one we joyfully and willingly carry out, because we love God and have the power of his Holy Spirit (see Jas 1:25).

Jas 2:13 Only God in his mercy can forgive our sins. We can't earn forgiveness by forgiving others. But when we withhold forgiveness from others after having received it ourselves, we show that we don't understand or appreciate God's mercy toward us (see Matt 6:14-15; 18:21ff; Eph 4:31-32).

Jas 2:14 When someone claims to have faith, what that person may have is intellectual assent—agreement with a set of Christian teachings—and as such it would be incomplete faith. True faith transforms our conduct as well as our thoughts. If our life remains unchanged, we don't truly believe the truths we claim to believe.

Jas 2:17 We cannot earn our salvation by serving and obeying God. But such actions show that our commitment to God is real. Deeds of loving service are not a substitute for, but rather a verification of, our faith in Christ.

Jas 2:18 At first glance, this verse seems to contradict Romans 3:28, "We are made right with God through faith and not by obeying the law." But deeper investigation shows that the teachings of James and Paul are not at odds. While it is true that our good deeds can never earn salvation, true faith always results in a changed life and good deeds. Paul speaks against those who try to be saved by deeds instead of true faith; James speaks against those who confuse mere intellectual assent with true faith. After all, even demons know who Jesus is, but they don't obey him (Jas 2:19). True faith involves a commitment of your whole self to God.

▸ **JAMES 2:14-26** ***(cont.)***

this, and they tremble in terror. 20 How foolish! Can't you see that faith without good deeds is useless?

21 Don't you remember that our ancestor Abraham was shown to be right with God by his actions when he offered his son Isaac on the altar? 22 You see, his faith and his actions worked together. His actions made his faith complete. 23 And so it happened just as the Scriptures say: "Abraham believed God, and God counted him as righteous because of his faith."* He was even called the friend of God.* 24 So you see, we are shown to be right with God by what we do, not by faith alone.

25 Rahab the prostitute is another example. She was shown to be right with God by her actions when she hid those messengers and sent them safely away by a different road. 26 Just as the body is dead without breath,* so also faith is dead without good works.

Controlling the Tongue

JAMES 3:1-12

Dear brothers and sisters,* not many of you should become teachers in the church, for we who teach will be judged more strictly. 2 Indeed, we all make many mistakes. For if we could control our tongues, we would be perfect and could also control ourselves in every other way.

3 We can make a large horse go wherever we want by means of a small bit in its mouth. 4 And a small rudder makes a huge ship turn wherever the pilot chooses to go, even though the winds are strong. 5 In the same way, the tongue is a small thing that makes grand speeches.

But a tiny spark can set a great forest on fire. 6 And the tongue is a flame of fire. It is a whole world of wickedness, corrupting your entire body. It can set your whole life on fire, for it is set on fire by hell itself.*

7 People can tame all kinds of animals, birds, reptiles, and fish, 8 but no one can tame the tongue. It is restless and evil, full of deadly poison. 9 Sometimes it praises our Lord and Father, and sometimes it curses those who have been made in the image of God. 10 And so blessing and cursing come pouring out of the same mouth. Surely, my brothers and sisters, this is not right! 11 Does a spring of water bubble out with both fresh water and bitter water? 12 Does a fig tree produce olives, or a grapevine produce figs? No, and you can't draw fresh water from a salty spring.*

True Wisdom Comes from God

JAMES 3:13-18

If you are wise and understand God's ways, prove it by living an honorable life, doing good works with the humility that comes from wisdom. 14 But if you are bitterly jealous and there is selfish ambition in your heart, don't cover up the truth with boasting and lying. 15 For

Jas 2:23a Gen 15:6. **Jas 2:23b** See Isa 41:8. **Jas 2:26** Or *without spirit.* **Jas 3:1** Greek *brothers;* also in 3:10. **Jas 3:6** Or *for it will burn in hell* (Greek *Gehenna*). **Jas 3:12** Greek *from salt.*

Jas 2:21-24 James says that Abraham was "shown to be right with God" for what he did because he believed God (Rom 4:1-5). James's and Paul's messages are not contradicting but complementing each other. Let's not conclude that the truth is a blending of these two statements. We are not justified by what we do in any way. True faith always results in good deeds, but the deeds do not justify us. Faith brings us salvation; active obedience demonstrates that our faith is genuine.

Jas 2:25 Rahab lived in Jericho, a city the Israelites conquered as they entered the Promised Land (Josh 2). When Israel's spies came to the city, she hid them and helped them escape. In this way she demonstrated faith in God's purpose for Israel. As a result, she and her family were saved when the city was destroyed. Hebrews 11:31 lists Rahab among the heroes of faith.

Jas 3:1 Teaching was a highly valued and respected profession in Jewish culture, and many Jews who embraced Christianity wanted to become teachers. James warned that although it is good to aspire to teach, the responsibility is great because a teacher's words and example affect others' spiritual lives. If you are in a teaching or leadership role, how are you affecting those you lead?

Jas 3:2-3 What you say and what you don't say are both important. To use proper speech you must not only say the right words at the right time but also not say what you shouldn't. Examples of an untamed tongue include gossiping, putting others down, bragging, manipulating, false teaching, exaggerating, complaining, flattering, and lying. Before you speak, ask: "Is what I want to say true? Is it necessary? Is it kind?"

Jas 3:6 James compares the damage the tongue can do to a raging fire—the tongue's wickedness has its source in hell itself. The uncontrolled tongue can do terrible damage. Satan uses the tongue to divide people and pit them against one another. Idle and hateful words are damaging because they spread destruction quickly, and no one can stop the results once they are spoken. We dare not be careless with what we say, thinking we can apologize later, because even if we do, the scars remain. A few words spoken in anger can destroy a relationship that took years to build. Before you speak, remember that words are like fire—you can neither control nor reverse the damage they can do.

Jas 3:8 If no human being can tame the tongue, why bother trying? Even though we may not achieve perfect control of our tongues, the Holy Spirit will help us learn self-control. Remember that we are not fighting the tongue's fire in our own strength. The Holy Spirit will give us increasing power to monitor and control what we say, so that when we are offended, the Spirit will remind us of God's love, and we won't react in a hateful manner. When we are criticized, the Spirit will heal the hurt and help us to not lash out.

Jas 3:9-12 Our contradictory speech often puzzles us. At times our words are right and pleasing to God, but at other times they are violent and destructive. Which of these speech patterns reflects our true identity? We were made in God's image, but the tongue gives us a picture of our basic sinful nature. God works to change us from the inside out. When the Holy Spirit purifies a heart, he gives self-control so that the person will speak words that please God.

Jas 3:13-18 Have you ever known anyone who claimed to be wise but who acted foolishly? True wisdom can be measured by a person's character. Just as you can identify a tree by the type of fruit it produces, you can evaluate your wisdom by the way you act. Foolishness leads to disorder, but wisdom leads to peace and goodness. Are you tempted to escalate the conflict, pass on the gossip, or fan the fire of discord? Careful, winsome speech and wise, loving words are the seeds of peace. God loves peacemakers (Matt 5:9).

Jas 3:14-15 Bitter jealousy and selfish ambition are inspired by the devil. It is easy for us to be drawn into wrong desires by the

jealousy and selfishness are not God's kind of wisdom. Such things are earthly, unspiritual, and demonic. [16]For wherever there is jealousy and selfish ambition, there you will find disorder and evil of every kind.

[17]But the wisdom from above is first of all pure. It is also peace loving, gentle at all times, and willing to yield to others. It is full of mercy and good deeds. It shows no favoritism and is always sincere. [18]And those who are peacemakers will plant seeds of peace and reap a harvest of righteousness.*

Drawing Close to God

JAMES 4:1-10

What is causing the quarrels and fights among you? Don't they come from the evil desires at war within you? [2]You want what you don't have, so you scheme and kill to get it. You are jealous of what others have, but you can't get it, so you fight and wage war to take it away from them. Yet you don't have what you want because you don't ask God for it. [3]And even when you ask, you don't get it because your motives are all wrong—you want only what will give you pleasure.

[4]You adulterers!* Don't you realize that friendship with the world makes you an enemy of God? I say it again: If you want to be a friend of the world, you make yourself an enemy of God. [5]What do you think the Scriptures mean when they say that the spirit God has placed within us is filled with envy?* [6]But he gives us even more grace to stand against such evil desires. As the Scriptures say,

"God opposes the proud
but favors the humble."*

[7]So humble yourselves before God. Resist the devil, and he will flee from you. [8]Come close to God, and God will come close to you. Wash your hands, you

Jas 3:18 Or *of good things,* or *of justice.* **Jas 4:4** Greek *You adulteresses!* **Jas 4:5** Or *that God longs jealously for the human spirit he has placed within us?* or *that the Holy Spirit, whom God has placed within us, opposes our envy?* **Jas 4:6** Prov 3:34 (Greek version).

SPEECH

When our speech is motivated by	*It is full of*
Satan	Bitter jealousy
	Selfish ambition
	Earthly concerns and desires
	Unspiritual thoughts and ideas
	Disorder
	Evil
God and his wisdom	Purity
	Peace
	Consideration for others
	Submission
	Mercy
	Sincerity, impartiality
	Goodness

pressures of society and sometimes even by well-meaning Christians. By listening to the advice to "Assert yourself," "Go for it," "Set high goals," we can be drawn into greed and destructive competitiveness. Seeking God's wisdom delivers us from the need to compare ourselves to others and to want what they have.

Jas 4:1-3 Quarrels and fights among believers are always harmful. James explains that these conflicts result from evil desires battling within us: We want more possessions, more money, higher status, more recognition. When we don't get what we want, we fight in order to have it. Instead of aggressively grabbing what we want, we should submit ourselves to God, ask God to help us get rid of our selfish desires, and trust him to give us what we really need.

Jas 4:2-3 James mentions the most common problems in prayer: not asking, asking for the wrong things, or asking for the wrong reasons. Do you talk to God at all? When you do, what do you talk about? Do you ask only to satisfy your desires? Do you seek God's approval for what you already plan to do? Your prayers will become powerful when you allow God to change your desires so that they perfectly correspond to his will for you (1 Jn 3:21-22).

Jas 4:3-4 There is nothing wrong with wanting a pleasurable life. God gives us good gifts that he wants us to enjoy (Jas 1:17; Eph 4:7; 1 Tim 4:4-5). But having friendship with the world involves seeking pleasure at others' expense or at the expense of obeying God. Pleasure that keeps us from pleasing God is sinful; pleasure from God's rich bounty is good.

Jas 4:4-6 The cure for evil desires is humility (see Prov 16:18-19; 1 Pet 5:5-6). Pride makes us self-centered and leads us to conclude that we deserve all we can see, touch, or imagine. It creates greedy appetites for far more than we need. We can be released from our self-centered desires by humbling ourselves before God, realizing that all we really need is his approval. When the Holy Spirit fills us, we see that this world's seductive attractions are only cheap substitutes for what God has to offer.

Jas 4:5 This verse may mean that because of our fallen nature, we have a tendency toward envy. James is not quoting a specific verse or passage—he is summing up a teaching of Scripture. (See Rom 6:6-8; Gal 5:17-21 for more on the human tendency toward envy and discontent.)

Jas 4:7 Although God and the devil are at war, we don't have to wait until the end to see who will win. God has already defeated Satan (Rev 12:10-12), and when Christ returns, the devil and all he stands for will be eliminated forever (Rev 20:10-15). Satan is here now, and he is trying to win us over to his evil cause. With the Holy Spirit's power, we can resist the devil, and he will flee from us.

Jas 4:7-10 How can you come close to God? James gives five ways: (1) Humble yourselves before God (Jas 4:7). Yield to his authority and will, commit your life to him and his control, and be willing to follow him. (2) Resist the devil (Jas 4:7). Don't allow Satan to entice and tempt you. (3) Lead a pure life (Jas 4:8). Be cleansed from sin, replacing your desire to sin with your desire to experience God's purity. (4) Let there be sorrow and deep grief for your sins (Jas 4:9). Don't be afraid to express deep heartfelt sorrow for what you have done. (5) Humble yourselves before the Lord, and he will lift you up in honor (Jas 4:10; 1 Pet 5:6).

▸ **JAMES 4:1-10** ***(cont.)***

sinners; purify your hearts, for your loyalty is divided
between God and the world. [9]Let there be tears for
what you have done. Let there be sorrow and deep
grief. Let there be sadness instead of laughter, and
gloom instead of joy. [10]Humble yourselves before the
Lord, and he will lift you up in honor.

Warning against Judging Others

JAMES 4:11-12

Don't speak evil against each other, dear brothers and
sisters.* If you criticize and judge each other, then you
are criticizing and judging God's law. But your job is
to obey the law, not to judge whether it applies to you.
[12]God alone, who gave the law, is the Judge. He alone
has the power to save or to destroy. So what right do
you have to judge your neighbor?

Warning about Self-Confidence

JAMES 4:13-17

Look here, you who say, "Today or tomorrow we are going
to a certain town and will stay there a year. We will do
business there and make a profit." [14]How do you know
what your life will be like tomorrow? Your life is like
the morning fog—it's here a little while, then it's gone.
[15]What you ought to say is, "If the Lord wants us to, we
will live and do this or that." [16]Otherwise you are boasting about your own plans, and all such boasting is evil.
[17]Remember, it is sin to know what you ought to do
and then not do it.

Jas 4:11 Greek *brothers.*

Jas 4:10 Bowing in humility before the Lord means recognizing that our worth comes from God alone. To be humble involves leaning on his power and his guidance, and not going our own independent way. Although we do not deserve God's favor, he wants to lift us up and give us worth and dignity, despite our human shortcomings.

Jas 4:11-12 Jesus summarized the law as love for God and neighbor (Matt 22:37-40), and Paul said that love demonstrated toward a neighbor would fully satisfy the law (Rom 13:6-10). When we fail to love, we are actually breaking God's law. Examine your attitude and actions toward others. Do you build people up or tear them down? When you're ready to criticize someone, remember God's law of love and say something good instead. Saying something beneficial to others will cure you of finding fault and increase your ability to obey God's law of love.

Jas 4:13-16 It is good to have goals, but goals can disappoint us if we leave God out of them. There is no point in making plans as though God does not exist because the future is in his hands. The beginning of good planning is to ask: "What would I like to be doing 10 years from now? One year from now? Tomorrow? How will I react if God steps in and rearranges my plans?" We can plan ahead, but we must hold on to our plans loosely. If we put God's desires at the center of our planning, he will never disappoint us.

Jas 4:14 Life is short no matter how many years we live. Don't be deceived into thinking that you have lots of remaining time to live for Christ, to enjoy your loved ones, or to do what you know you should. Live for God today! Then, no matter when your life ends, you will have fulfilled God's plan for you.

Jas 4:17 We tend to think that *doing* wrong is sin. But James tells us that sin is also *not doing* right. (These two kinds of sin are sometimes called sins of commission and sins of omission.) It is a sin to lie; it can also be a sin to know the truth and not tell it. It is a sin to speak evil of someone; it is also a sin to avoid that person when you know your friendship is needed. You should be willing to help as the Holy Spirit guides you. If God has directed you to do a kind act, to render a service, or to restore a relationship, do it. You will experience a renewed and refreshed vitality to your Christian faith.

FAITH THAT WORKS

The book of James offers a larger number of similarities to the Sermon on the Mount than any other book in the New Testament. James relied heavily on Jesus' teachings.

Lesson	*Reference*
When troubles come your way, consider it an opportunity for great joy.	**Jas 1:2** Matt 5:10-12
When your endurance is fully developed, you will be perfect and complete, needing nothing.	**Jas 1:4** Matt 5:48
Ask God, and he will answer.	**Jas 1:5; 5:15** Matt 7:7-11
Believers who are poor (who don't amount to much by the world's standards) should be glad, for God has honored them.	**Jas 1:9** Matt 5:3
Watch out for your anger; it can be dangerous.	**Jas 1:19-20** Matt 5:22
Be merciful to others, as God is merciful to you.	**Jas 2:13** Matt 5:7; 6:14
Your faith must express itself in your actions.	**Jas 2:14-17** Matt 7:21-23
Blessed are the peacemakers; they plant seeds of peace and reap a harvest of righteousness.	**Jas 3:17-18** Matt 5:9
Friendship with the world makes you an enemy of God.	**Jas 4:4** Matt 6:24
When you humble yourself and realize your dependence on God, he will lift you up.	**Jas 4:10** Matt 5:3-5
Don't speak evil against each other. If you do, you are criticizing and judging God's law.	**Jas 4:11** Matt 7:1-2
Treasures on earth will only rot away and be eaten by moths. Store up eternal treasures in heaven.	**Jas 5:2-3** Matt 6:19
Be patient in suffering, as God's prophets were patient.	**Jas 5:10** Matt 5:12
Be honest in your speech; just say a simple yes or no so that you will not sin.	**Jas 5:12** Matt 5:33-37

Jas 5:1-6 James proclaims the worthlessness of riches, not the worthlessness of the rich. Today's money will be worthless when Christ returns, so we should spend our time accumulating the kind of treasures that will be worthwhile in God's eternal Kingdom.

Warning to the Rich

JAMES 5:1-6

Look here, you rich people: Weep and groan with anguish because of all the terrible troubles ahead of you.
2Your wealth is rotting away, and your fine clothes are
moth-eaten rags. 3Your gold and silver have become
worthless. The very wealth you were counting on will eat away your flesh like fire. This treasure you have accumulated will stand as evidence against you on
the day of judgment. 4For listen! Hear the cries of the
field workers whom you have cheated of their pay. The wages you held back cry out against you. The cries of those who harvest your fields have reached the ears of the LORD of Heaven's Armies.
5You have spent your years on earth in luxury,
satisfying your every desire. You have fattened
yourselves for the day of slaughter. 6You have condemned and killed innocent people,* who do not resist you.*

Patience and Endurance

JAMES 5:7-12

Dear brothers and sisters,* be patient as you wait for the Lord's return. Consider the farmers who patiently wait for the rains in the fall and in the spring. They
eagerly look for the valuable harvest to ripen. 8You,
too, must be patient. Take courage, for the coming of the Lord is near.
9Don't grumble about each other, brothers and sisters, or you will be judged. For look—the Judge is standing at the door!
10For examples of patience in suffering, dear brothers and sisters, look at the prophets who spoke
in the name of the Lord. 11We give great honor to those who endure under suffering. For instance, you know about Job, a man of great endurance. You can see how the Lord was kind to him at the end, for the Lord is full of tenderness and mercy.
12But most of all, my brothers and sisters, never take an oath, by heaven or earth or anything else. Just say a simple yes or no, so that you will not sin and be condemned.

The Power of Prayer

JAMES 5:13-18

Are any of you suffering hardships? You should pray. Are
any of you happy? You should sing praises. 14Are any of
you sick? You should call for the elders of the church to come and pray over you, anointing you with oil in
the name of the Lord. 15Such a prayer offered in faith
will heal the sick, and the Lord will make you well. And if you have committed any sins, you will be forgiven.

Jas 5:6a Or *killed the Righteous One.* **Jas 5:6b** Or *Don't they resist you?* or *Doesn't God oppose you?* or *Aren't they now accusing you before God?* **Jas 5:7** Greek *brothers;* also in 5:9, 10, 12, 19.

Money is not the problem; Christian leaders need money to live and to support their families; missionaries need money to help them spread the Good News; churches need money to do their work effectively. It is the *love* of money that leads to evil (1 Tim 6:10) and causes some people to oppress others in order to get more. This is a warning to all Christians who are tempted to adopt worldly standards rather than God's standards (Rom 12:1-2) as well as an encouragement to all those who are oppressed by the rich. (See Matt 6:19-21 to see what Jesus says about riches.)

Jas 5:6 "Innocent people" refers to defenseless persons, probably poor laborers. Poor people who could not pay their debts were thrown in prison or forced to sell all their possessions. At times, they were even forced to sell their family members into slavery. With no opportunity to work off their debts, poor people often died of starvation. God called this murder. Hoarding money, exploiting employees, and living self-indulgently will not escape God's notice.

Jas 5:7-8 The farmer must wait patiently for his crops to grow; he cannot hurry the process. But he does not take the summer off and hope that all goes well in the fields. There is much work to do to ensure a good harvest. In the same way, we must wait patiently for Christ's return. We cannot make him come back any sooner. But while we wait, there is much work that we can do to advance God's Kingdom. Both the farmer and the Christian must live by faith, looking toward the future reward for their labors. Don't live as if Christ will never come. Work faithfully to build his Kingdom. The King will come when the time is right.

Jas 5:9 When things go wrong, we tend to grumble against and blame others for our miseries (see the second note on Gen 3:11-13, p. 12). Blaming others is easier than owning our share of the responsibility, but it can be both destructive and sinful. Before you judge others for their shortcomings, remember that Christ the Judge will come to evaluate each of us (Matt 7:1-5; 25:31-46). He will not let us get away with shifting the blame to others.

Jas 5:10-11 Many prophets suffered and were persecuted, such as Moses, Elijah, and Jeremiah. For a complete list of those persecuted, see the chart on pp. 730-731. For more on the topic of suffering, see the notes on Job 1:1ff, p. 94; Job 2:10, p. 96; Job 3:23-26, p. 98; Job 4:7-8, p. 98; Job 42:17, p. 133 and Job's Profile on p. 97.

Jas 5:12 People with a reputation for exaggeration or lying often can't get anyone to believe them on their word alone. Christians should never become like that. Always be honest so that others will believe your simple yes or no. By avoiding lies, half-truths, and omissions of the truth, you will become known as a trustworthy person.

Jas 5:14-15 James is referring to someone who is physically ill. In Scripture, oil was both a medicine (see the parable of the Good Samaritan in Luke 10:30-37) and a symbol of the Spirit of God (as used in anointing kings, see 1 Sam 16:1-13). Thus, oil can represent both the physical and the spiritual spheres of life. Christians should not separate the physical and the spiritual. Jesus Christ is Lord over both the body and the spirit.

Jas 5:14-15 People in the church are not alone. Members of Christ's body should be able to count on others for support and prayer, especially when they are sick or suffering. The elders should be on call to respond to the illness of any member, and the church should be sensitive to the needs of all its members.

Jas 5:15 The "prayer offered in faith" does not refer to the faith of the sick person but to the faith of the people praying. God heals, faith doesn't, and all prayers are subject to God's will. But prayer is part of God's healing process.

▸ **JAMES 5:13-18** ***(cont.)***

16Confess your sins to each other and pray for each
other so that you may be healed. The earnest prayer
of a righteous person has great power and produces
wonderful results. 17Elijah was as human as we are,
and yet when he prayed earnestly that no rain would
fall, none fell for three and a half years! 18Then, when
he prayed again, the sky sent down rain and the earth
began to yield its crops.

Restore Wandering Believers

JAMES 5:19-20

My dear brothers and sisters, if someone among you
wanders away from the truth and is brought back,
20you can be sure that whoever brings the sinner back
will save that person from death and bring about the
forgiveness of many sins.

E. Controversy over Circumcision: Galatians and the Jerusalem Council

Paul's mission among the Gentiles began to raise some serious questions about the relationship between faith in Jesus and the religious practices of Judaism. Jesus was Jewish, and the early church sprang out of Judaism and was centered in Jerusalem. For some early Christians, this seemed to indicate that Gentiles should become Jewish in order to be fully part of the Christian faith. Some went so far as to send out missionaries to speak against Paul and to claim that the Good News he was sharing was incomplete; people needed to become circumcised and follow aspects of the Jewish law in order to truly follow Christ. Paul reacted strongly against this idea, and the book of Galatians is one such response. This was such an important issue that many key leaders of the church, including Paul, James, John, and Peter, gathered in Jerusalem to discuss and decide on what God wanted his church to look like.

1. AUTHENTICITY OF THE GOSPEL

In response to attacks from false teachers, Paul wrote to defend his apostleship and the authority of the gospel that he preached among the Gentiles. Some people from Jerusalem were claiming to have a more complete version of the gospel, and that Paul was not really a reliable apostle. Paul gives an impassioned account of his call from God and evidence that he is just as much an apostle as Peter or anyone else. God had given Paul his stamp of approval, and anyone who preached a different gospel was teaching a false gospel.

Greetings from Paul

GALATIANS 1:1-5

This letter is from Paul, an apostle. I was not appointed
by any group of people or any human authority, but by
Jesus Christ himself and by God the Father, who raised
Jesus from the dead.
2All the brothers and sisters* here join me in sending this letter to the churches of Galatia.

Gal 1:2 Greek *brothers;* also in 1:11.

The earnest prayer of a righteous person has great power and produces wonderful results.
James 5:16

Jas 5:16 Christ has made it possible for us to go directly to God for forgiveness. But confessing our sins to each other still has an important place in the life of the church. (1) If we have sinned against an individual, we must ask that person to forgive us. (2) If our sin has affected the church, we must confess it publicly. (3) If we need loving support as we struggle with a sin, we should confess that sin to those who are able to provide that support. (4) If we doubt God's forgiveness, after confessing a sin to him, we may wish to confess that sin to a fellow believer for assurance of God's pardon. In Christ's Kingdom, every believer is a priest to other believers (1 Pet 2:9).

Jas 5:16-18 The Christian's most powerful resource is communion with God through prayer. The results are often greater than we thought were possible. Some people see prayer as a last resort to be tried when all else fails. This approach is backward. Prayer should come first. Because God's power is

[3]May God our Father and the Lord Jesus Christ* give
you grace and peace. [4]Jesus gave his life for our sins,
just as God our Father planned, in order to rescue us
from this evil world in which we live. [5]All glory to God
forever and ever! Amen.

There Is Only One Good News

GALATIANS 1:6-10

I am shocked that you are turning away so soon from God, who called you to himself through the loving mercy of Christ.* You are following a different way

Gal 1:3 Some manuscripts read *God the Father and our Lord Jesus Christ.* **Gal 1:6** Some manuscripts read *through loving mercy.*

infinitely greater than ours, it only makes sense to rely on it—especially because God encourages us to do so.

Jas 5:17 For more about the great prophet Elijah, read his Profile on p. 719.

Jas 5:19-20 Clearly this person who has wandered from the truth is a believer who has fallen into sin—one who is no longer living a life consistent with Christian beliefs. Christians disagree over whether or not it is possible for people to lose their salvation, but all agree that those who fall away from their faith are in serious trouble and need to repent. James urges Christians to help backsliders return to God. By taking the initiative, praying for them, and acting in love, we can meet such individuals where they are and bring them back to God and his forgiveness.

Jas 5:20 The book of James emphasizes faith in action. Right living is the evidence and result of faith. The church must serve with compassion, speak lovingly and truthfully, live in obedience to God's commands, and love one another. The body of believers ought to be an example of heaven on earth, drawing people to Christ through love for God and each other. If we truly believe God's Word, we will live it day by day. God's Word is not merely something we read or think about, but something we do. Belief, faith, and trust must have hands and feet—ours!

Gal 1:1 Paul and Barnabas had just completed their first missionary journey (Acts 13:2–14:28). They had visited Iconium, Lystra, and Derbe, cities in the Roman province of Galatia (present-day Turkey). Upon returning to Antioch of Syria, Paul was accused by some Jewish Christians of diluting Christianity to make it more appealing to Gentiles. These Jewish Christians disagreed with Paul's statements that Gentiles did not have to follow many of the religious laws that the Jews had obeyed for centuries. Some of Paul's accusers had even followed him to those Galatian cities and had told the Gentile converts they had to be circumcised and follow all the Jewish laws and customs in order to be saved. According to these people, Gentiles had to first become Jews in order to become Christians.

In response to this threat, Paul wrote this letter to the Galatian churches. In it, he explains that following the Old Testament laws, or the Jewish laws, will not bring salvation. A person is saved by grace through faith. Paul wrote this letter about A.D. 49, shortly before the meeting of the Jerusalem council, which settled the law-versus-grace controversy (Acts 15).

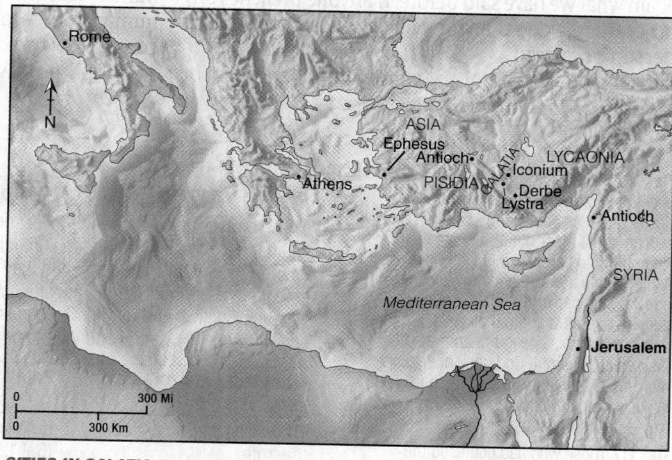

***CITIES IN GALATIA** Paul visited several cities in Galatia on each of his three missionary journeys. On his first journey he went through Antioch in Pisidia, Iconium, Lystra, and Derbe, and then retraced his steps; on his second journey he went by land from Antioch of Syria through the four cities in Galatia; on his third journey he also went through those cities on the main route to Ephesus.*

Gal 1:1 Paul explained his apostleship in these words, not to separate himself from the original Twelve, but to show that his apostleship rested on the same basis as theirs. If the believers in Galatia questioned Paul's apostleship, then they also should question the apostleship of Peter, John, James, and all the others—and such questioning would be absurd. All the apostles were called by Jesus Christ and God the Father, and they answered to God as their final authority.

Gal 1:1 For more information about Paul's life, see his Profile on p. 1571. Paul had been a Christian for about 15 years at this time.

Gal 1:2 In Paul's time, Galatia was the Roman province located in the center section of present-day Turkey. Much of the region rests on a large and fertile plateau, and large numbers of people had moved to the region because of its favorable agriculture. One of Paul's goals during his missionary journeys was to visit regions with large population centers in order to reach as many people as possible.

Gal 1:3-5 God's plan all along was to save us by Jesus' death and resurrection. We have been rescued from the power of this present evil world—a world ruled by Satan and full of cruelty, tragedy, temptation, and deception. Being rescued from this evil world doesn't mean that we are taken out of it but that we are no longer enslaved to it. You were saved to live for God. Does your life reflect your gratitude for being rescued? Have you transferred your loyalty from this world to Christ?

Gal 1:6 Some people were preaching "a different way." They were teaching that to be saved, Gentile believers had to follow Jewish laws and customs, especially the rite of circumcision. Faith in Christ was not enough. This message undermined the truth that salvation is a gift, not a reward for certain deeds. Jesus Christ has made this gift available to all people, not just to Jews. Beware of people who say that we need more than simple faith in Christ to be saved. When people set up additional requirements for salvation, they deny the power of Christ's death on the cross (see Gal 3:1-5).

▸ **GALATIANS 1:6-10** ***(cont.)***

that pretends to be the Good News [7]but is not the Good News at all. You are being fooled by those who deliberately twist the truth concerning Christ.

[8]Let God's curse fall on anyone, including us or even an angel from heaven, who preaches a different kind of Good News than the one we preached to you. [9]I say again what we have said before: If anyone preaches any other Good News than the one you welcomed, let that person be cursed.

[10]Obviously, I'm not trying to win the approval of people, but of God. If pleasing people were my goal, I would not be Christ's servant.

Paul's Message Comes from Christ

GALATIANS 1:11-24

Dear brothers and sisters, I want you to understand that the gospel message I preach is not based on mere human reasoning. [12]I received my message from no human source, and no one taught me. Instead, I received it by direct revelation from Jesus Christ.*

[13]You know what I was like when I followed the

Gal 1:12 Or *by the revelation of Jesus Christ.*

Gal 1:7 The Bible says there is only one way to be forgiven of sin: by believing in Jesus Christ as Savior and Lord. No other person, method, or ritual can give eternal life. Attempting to be open-minded and tolerant, some people assert that all religions are equally valid paths to God. In a free society, people have the right to their religious opinions, but this doesn't guarantee that their ideas are right. God does not accept man-made religion as a substitute for faith in Jesus Christ. He has provided just one way—Jesus Christ (John 14:6).

Gal 1:7 Those who had confused the Galatian believers and perverted the Good News were zealous Jewish Christians who believed that the Old Testament practices, such as circumcision and dietary restrictions, were required of all believers. Because these teachers wanted to turn the Gentile Christians into Jews, they were called "Judaizers."

Most of the Galatian Christians were Greeks who were unfamiliar with Jewish laws and customs. The Judaizers were an extreme faction of Jewish Christians. Both groups believed in Christ, but their lifestyles differed considerably. We do not know why the Judaizers may have traveled no small distance to teach their mistaken notions to the new Gentile converts. They may have been motivated by (1) a sincere wish to integrate Judaism with the new Christian faith, (2) a sincere love for their Jewish heritage, or (3) a jealous desire to destroy Paul's authority. Whether or not these Judaizers were sincere, their teaching threatened these new churches and had to be countered. When Paul said that their teaching twisted and changed the Good News, he was not rejecting everything Jewish. He himself was a Jew who worshiped in the Temple and attended the religious festivals. But he was concerned that *nothing* get in the way of the simple truth of his message—that salvation, for Jews and Gentiles alike, is through faith in Jesus Christ alone. Sometime after the letter to the Galatians was sent, Paul met with the apostles in Jerusalem to discuss this matter further (see Acts 15).

Gal 1:7 A twisting of the truth is more difficult to spot than an outright lie. The Judaizers were twisting the truth about Christ. They claimed to follow him, but they denied that Jesus' work on the cross was sufficient for salvation. There will always be people who twist the Good News. Either they do not understand what the Bible teaches, or they are uncomfortable with the truth as it stands. How can we tell when people are twisting the truth? Before accepting the teachings of any group, find out what the group teaches about Jesus Christ. If their teaching does not match the truth in God's Word, then it is not true.

Gal 1:8-9 Paul strongly denounced the Judaizers' twisting of the Good News of Christ. He said that God's curse should fall on anyone, even an angel from heaven, who came preaching a different kind of Good News. If an angel came preaching another message, he would not be from heaven, no matter how he looked. In 2 Corinthians 11:14-15, Paul warned that Satan disguises himself as an angel of light. Here he invoked a curse on any angel who spreads a false teaching—a fitting response to an emissary of hell. Paul extended that curse to include himself if he should twist the Good News. His message must never change, for the truth of the Good News never changes. Paul used strong language because he was dealing with a life-and-death issue.

Gal 1:10 Do you spend your life trying to please everybody? Paul had to speak harshly to the Christians in Galatia because they were in serious danger. He did not apologize for his straightforward words, knowing that he could not serve Christ faithfully if he allowed the Galatian Christians to remain on the wrong track. Whose approval are you seeking—others' or God's? Pray for the courage to seek God's approval above anyone else's.

Gal 1:11ff Why should the Galatians have listened to Paul instead of the Judaizers? Paul answered this implicit question by furnishing his credentials: His message was received directly from Christ (Gal 1:12); he had been an exemplary Jew (Gal 1:13-14); he had had a special conversion experience (Gal 1:15-16; see also Acts 9:1-9); he had

JUDAIZERS VERSUS PAUL

As the debate raged between the Gentile Christians and the Judaizers, Paul found it necessary to write to the churches in Galatia. The Judaizers were trying to undermine Paul's authority, and they taught a false gospel. In reply, Paul defended his authority as an apostle and the truth of his message. The debate over Jewish laws and Gentile Christians was officially resolved at the Jerusalem council (Acts 15), yet it continued to be a point of contention after that time.

What the Judaizers said about Paul	Paul's defense
They said he was perverting the truth.	He received his message from Christ himself (Gal 1:11-12).
They said he was a traitor to the Jewish faith.	Paul had been one of the most dedicated Jews of his time. Yet, in the midst of one of his most zealous acts, God transformed him through a revelation of the Good News about Jesus (Gal 1:13-16; Acts 9:1-30).
They said he compromised and watered down his message for the Gentiles.	The other apostles declared that the message Paul preached was the true gospel (Gal 2:1-10).
They said he was disregarding the law of Moses.	Far from degrading the law, Paul puts the law in its proper place. He says it shows people where they have sinned, and it points them to Christ (Gal 3:19-29).

Jewish religion—how I violently persecuted God's
church. I did my best to destroy it. [14]I was far ahead
of my fellow Jews in my zeal for the traditions of my
ancestors.
[15]But even before I was born, God chose me and
called me by his marvelous grace. Then it pleased him
[16]to reveal his Son to me* so that I would proclaim the
Good News about Jesus to the Gentiles.
When this happened, I did not rush out to consult
with any human being.* [17]Nor did I go up to Jerusalem
to consult with those who were apostles before I was.
Instead, I went away into Arabia, and later I returned
to the city of Damascus.
[18]Then three years later I went to Jerusalem to get
to know Peter,* and I stayed with him for fifteen days.
[19]The only other apostle I met at that time was James,
the Lord's brother. [20]I declare before God that what I
am writing to you is not a lie.
[21]After that visit I went north into the provinces
of Syria and Cilicia. [22]And still the Christians in the
churches in Judea didn't know me personally. [23]All
they knew was that people were saying, "The one who

Gal 1:16a Or *in me.* **Gal 1:16b** Greek *with flesh and blood.* **Gal 1:18** Greek *Cephas.*

been confirmed and accepted in his ministry by the other apostles (Gal 1:18-19; 2:1-9). Paul also presented his credentials to the Corinthian and Philippian churches (2 Cor 11–12; Phil 3:4-9).

Gal 1:12 There are two possible meanings consistent with the grammar of the phrase, "direct revelation from Jesus Christ." (1) This was a revelation by Christ to Paul that spelled out the gospel message, or (2) it was a personal revelation by Christ of his true identity that suddenly confirmed the gospel message against which Paul had been in bitter conflict. Within each meaning the fact remains that God provided the revelation and its content was the gospel.

Gal 1:13-14 Paul had been one of the most religious Jews of his day, scrupulously keeping the law and relentlessly persecuting Christians (see Acts 9:1-2). Before his conversion Paul had been even more zealous for the law than the Judaizers. He had surpassed his contemporaries in religious knowledge and practice. Paul had been sincere in his zeal—but wrong. When he met Jesus Christ, his life changed. He then directed all his energies toward building up the Christian church.

Gal 1:14 To be fully Jewish, a person must have descended from Abraham. In addition, a faithful Jew adhered to the Jewish laws and traditions. Gentiles (Gal 1:16) are non-Jews, whether in nationality or religion. In Paul's day, Jews thought of all Gentiles as pagans. Jews avoided Gentiles, believing that contact with Gentiles brought spiritual corruption. Although Gentiles could become Jews in religion by undergoing circumcision and by following Jewish laws and customs, they were never fully accepted.

Many Jews had difficulty understanding that God's message is for Jews and Gentiles alike. Some Jews thought that Gentiles had to become Jews before they could become Christians. But God planned to save both Jews and Gentiles. He had revealed this plan through Old Testament prophets (see, for example, Gen 12:3; Isa 42:6; 66:19), and he had fulfilled it through Jesus Christ; he was proclaiming it to the Gentiles through Paul.

Gal 1:15-16 Because God was guiding his ministry, Paul wasn't doing anything that God hadn't already planned and given him power to do. Similarly, God appointed Jeremiah to be his spokesman even before Jeremiah was born (Jer 1:5). God knows you intimately as well, and he chose you to be his even before you were born (see Ps 139). He wants you to draw close to him and to fulfill the purpose he has for your life.

Gal 1:15-24 Paul tells of his conversion to show that his message came directly from God. God commissioned him to preach the Good News to the Gentiles. After his call, Paul did not consult with anyone; instead, he spent three years in Arabia. Then he spoke with Peter and James, but he had no other contact with Jewish Christians for several more years. During those years, Paul preached to the Gentiles the message God had given him. His message did not come from human insight; it came from God.

Gal 1:18 This was Paul's first visit to Jerusalem as a Christian, as recorded in Acts 9:26-30.

Gal 1:21 Because of opposition in Jerusalem (see Acts 9:29-30), Paul had gone to Syria and Cilicia. In those remote areas, he had no opportunity to receive instruction from the apostles.

Gal 1:23 Paul was making the point that his authority and ministry were recognized by people who had never even seen him; yet the Galatians had met him, listened to him, and believed his message, only to turn around and doubt him! The Judean Christians only knew what people were saying: that the one who had persecuted believers was now preaching the faith he had tried to destroy. Instead of doubting Paul's credibility, the churches in Judea had believed and glorified God.

Syria and Cilicia

The photo shows the ancient site of Dura-Europos in Syria. The Roman province of Syria included Cilicia, a strip of territory in the southeastern corner of Asia Minor. The northern boundary reached to the Euphrates River. The province of Syria and Cilicia (Acts 15:23, 41; Gal 1:21) was governed by an imperial legate who commanded a strong force of legionary troops. One such governor, Quirinius, governed Syria at the time of the census of Caesar Augustus; this census brought Joseph and Mary to Bethlehem for the birth of Jesus (Luke 2:2). Paul ministered in Syria and Cilicia early in his missionary career, and over the following centuries the population of Damascus was Christianized. Christianity spread throughout the Roman province of Syria, giving rise to the Old Syrian Church, which remains to this day. We should be thankful that Christianity has been established for nearly 2,000 years in important places in the world, and we should do our best to spread the faith to other parts yet unreached.

▶ **GALATIANS 1:11-24** ***(cont.)***
used to persecute us is now preaching the very faith
he tried to destroy!" 24 And they praised God because
of me.

The Apostles Accept Paul

GALATIANS 2:1-10
Then fourteen years later I went back to Jerusalem
again, this time with Barnabas; and Titus came along,
too. 2 I went there because God revealed to me that I
should go. While I was there I met privately with those
considered to be leaders of the church and shared
with them the message I had been preaching to the
Gentiles. I wanted to make sure that we were in agreement, for fear that all my efforts had been wasted and I
was running the race for nothing. 3 And they supported
me and did not even demand that my companion Titus
be circumcised, though he was a Gentile.*
4 Even that question came up only because of some
so-called Christians there—false ones, really*—who
were secretly brought in. They sneaked in to spy on
us and take away the freedom we have in Christ Jesus.
They wanted to enslave us and force us to follow their
Jewish regulations. 5 But we refused to give in to them
for a single moment. We wanted to preserve the truth
of the gospel message for you.
6 And the leaders of the church had nothing to add
to what I was preaching. (By the way, their reputation
as great leaders made no difference to me, for God has
no favorites.) 7 Instead, they saw that God had given
me the responsibility of preaching the gospel to the
Gentiles, just as he had given Peter the responsibility of
preaching to the Jews. 8 For the same God who worked
through Peter as the apostle to the Jews also worked
through me as the apostle to the Gentiles.
9 In fact, James, Peter,* and John, who were known
as pillars of the church, recognized the gift God had
given me, and they accepted Barnabas and me as their
co-workers. They encouraged us to keep preaching
to the Gentiles, while they continued their work with
the Jews. 10 Their only suggestion was that we keep on
helping the poor, which I have always been eager to do.

Gal 2:3 Greek *a Greek.* **Gal 2:4** Greek *some false brothers.* **Gal 2:9** Greek *Cephas;* also in 2:11, 14.

Gal 1:24 Paul's changed life had brought praise from those who saw him or heard about him. His new life had astonished them. They had praised God because only God could have turned this zealous persecutor of Christians into a Christian himself. You may not have had as dramatic a change as Paul, but still your new life should honor God in every way. When people look at you, do they recognize that God has made changes in you? If not, perhaps you are not living as you should.

Gal 2:1 Paul was converted around A.D. 35. The 14 years he mentions are probably calculated from the time of his conversion. Therefore, this trip to Jerusalem was not his first. Most likely, he made his first trip to Jerusalem around A.D. 38 (see Acts 9:26-30) and other trips to Jerusalem in approximately A.D. 44 (Acts 11:29-30; Gal 2:1-10), A.D. 49/50 (Acts 15), A.D. 52 (Acts 18:22), and A.D. 57 (Acts 21:15ff). Paul probably visited Jerusalem on several other occasions as well.

Gal 2:1 Barnabas and Titus were two of Paul's close friends. Barnabas and Paul visited Galatia together on their first missionary journey. Paul wrote a personal letter to Titus, a faithful believer and church leader serving on the island of Crete. For more information on Barnabas, see his Profile on p. 1543. For more information on Titus, see the letter Paul wrote to him (the book of Titus).

Gal 2:1 After his conversion, Paul spent many years preparing for the ministry to which God had called him. This preparation period included time alone with God (Gal 1:16-17), as well as time conferring with other Christians. Often new Christians, in their zeal, want to begin a full-time ministry without investing the necessary time studying the Bible and learning from qualified teachers. We need not wait to share Christ with our friends, but we may need more preparation before embarking on a special ministry, whether volunteer or paid. While we wait for God's timing, we should continue to study, learn, and grow.

Gal 2:2 God told Paul, through a revelation, to confer with the church leaders in Jerusalem about the message he was preaching to the Gentiles so they would understand and approve of what he was doing. The essence of Paul's message to both Jews and Gentiles was that God's salvation is offered to all people regardless of race, sex, nationality, wealth, social standing, educational level, or anything else. Anyone can be forgiven by trusting in Christ (see Rom 10:8-13).

Gal 2:2-3 Even though God had specifically sent him to the Gentiles (Acts 9:15-16), Paul needed to discuss his message with the leaders of the Jerusalem church (Acts 15). This meeting prevented a major split in the church, and it formally acknowledged the apostles' approval of Paul's preaching. Sometimes we avoid conferring with others because we fear that problems or arguments may develop. Instead, we should openly discuss our plans and actions with friends, counselors, and advisers. Good communication helps everyone understand the situation better, it reduces gossip, and it builds unity in the church.

Gal 2:3-5 When Paul took Titus, a Greek Christian, to Jerusalem, the Judaizers ("false" Christians) said that Titus should be circumcised. Paul adamantly refused to give in to their demands. The apostles agreed that circumcision was an unnecessary rite for Gentile converts. Several years later, Paul circumcised Timothy, another Greek Christian (Acts 16:3). But Timothy was half Jewish. Paul did not deny Jews the right to be circumcised; he was simply saying that Gentiles should not be asked to become Jews before becoming Christians.

Gal 2:4 These false Christians were most likely from the party of the Pharisees (Acts 15:5). These were the strictest religious leaders of Judaism, some of whom had been converted. We don't know if these were representatives of well-meaning converts or of those trying to pervert Christianity. Most commentators agree that neither Peter nor James had any part in this conspiracy.

Gal 2:5 We normally think of taking a stand against those who might lead us into immoral behavior, but Paul had to take a hard line against the most moral of people. We must not give in to those who make the keeping of man-made standards a condition for salvation, even when such people are morally upright or in respected positions.

Gal 2:6 It's easy to rate people on the basis of their official status and to be intimidated by powerful individuals. But Paul was not intimidated by these "great leaders" because all believers are equal in Christ. We should show respect for our spiritual leaders, but our ultimate allegiance must be to Christ. We are to serve him with our whole being. God doesn't rate us according to our status; he looks at the attitude of our hearts (1 Sam 16:7). We should encourage leaders who show humility and a heartfelt desire to please God.

Gal 2:7-9 The church leaders ("pillars")—James (the half brother of Jesus, not the apostle John's brother), Peter, and John—realized that God was using Paul to reach the Gentiles, just as Peter was being used so greatly to reach the Jews. After hearing Paul's message, they gave Paul and

Paul Confronts Peter

GALATIANS 2:11-21

But when Peter came to Antioch, I had to oppose him to
his face, for what he did was very wrong. 12When he first
arrived, he ate with the Gentile Christians, who were
not circumcised. But afterward, when some friends of
James came, Peter wouldn't eat with the Gentiles anymore. He was afraid of criticism from these people who
insisted on the necessity of circumcision. 13As a result,
other Jewish Christians followed Peter's hypocrisy, and
even Barnabas was led astray by their hypocrisy.
14When I saw that they were not following the truth
of the gospel message, I said to Peter in front of all the
others, "Since you, a Jew by birth, have discarded the
Jewish laws and are living like a Gentile, why are you
now trying to make these Gentiles follow the Jewish
traditions?
15"You and I are Jews by birth, not 'sinners' like the
Gentiles. 16Yet we know that a person is made right
with God by faith in Jesus Christ, not by obeying the
law. And we have believed in Christ Jesus, so that we
might be made right with God because of our faith in
Christ, not because we have obeyed the law. For no one
will ever be made right with God by obeying the law."*

Gal 2:16 Some translators hold that the quotation extends through verse 14; others through verse 16; and still others through verse 21.

THE MARKS OF THE TRUE GOSPEL AND OF FALSE GOSPELS

Marks of a false gospel	
Gal 2:21	Treats Christ's death as meaningless
Gal 3:12	Says people must obey the law in order to be saved
Gal 4:10	Tries to find favor with God by observing certain rituals
Gal 5:4	Counts on keeping laws to be right with God
Marks of the true gospel	
Gal 1:11-12	Teaches that the source of the gospel is God
Gal 2:20	Knows that life is obtained through death; we trust in the Son of God who loved us and died for us so that we might die to sin and live for him
Gal 3:14	Explains that all believers have the Holy Spirit through faith
Gal 3:21-22	Declares that we cannot be saved by keeping laws; the only way of salvation is through faith in Christ, which is available to all
Gal 3:26-28	Says that all believers are one in Christ, so there is no basis for discrimination of any kind
Gal 5:24-25	Proclaims that we are free from the grip of sin and that the Holy Spirit's power fills and guides us

Barnabas their approval to continue working among the Gentiles.

Gal 2:10 The apostles were referring to the poor of Jerusalem. While many Gentile converts were financially comfortable, the Jerusalem church had suffered from the effects of a severe famine in Palestine (see Acts 11:28-30) and was struggling. So on his journeys, Paul had gathered funds for the Jewish Christians (Acts 24:17; Rom 15:25-29; 1 Cor 16:1-4; 2 Cor 8). The need for believers to care for the poor is a constant theme in Scripture. But often we do nothing, caught up in meeting our own needs and desires. Perhaps we don't see enough poverty to remember the needs of the poor. The world is filled with poor people, here and in other countries. What can you do to help?

Gal 2:11 This was Antioch of Syria (distinguished from Antioch in Pisidia), a major trade center in the ancient world. Heavily populated by Greeks, it eventually became a strong Christian center. In Antioch the believers were first called Christians (Acts 11:26). Antioch of Syria became the headquarters for the Gentile church and was Paul's base of operations.

Gal 2:11ff The Judaizers accused Paul of watering down the Good News to make it easier for Gentiles to accept, while Paul accused the Judaizers of nullifying the truth of the Good News by adding conditions to it. The basis of salvation was the issue: Is salvation through Christ alone, or does it come through Christ and adherence to the law? The argument came to a climax when Peter, Paul, the Judaizers, and some Gentile Christians all gathered together in Antioch to share a meal. Peter probably thought that by staying away from the Gentiles, he was promoting harmony—he did not want to offend James and the Jewish Christians. James had a very prominent position and would later preside over the Jerusalem council (Acts 15). But Paul charged that Peter's action violated the Good News. By joining the Judaizers, Peter was supporting their claim that Christ was not sufficient for salvation. Compromise is an important element in getting along with others, but we should never compromise the truth of God's Word. If we feel we have to change our Christian beliefs to match those of our companions, we are on dangerous ground.

Gal 2:11-12 Although Peter was a leader of the church, he was acting like a hypocrite. He knew better, yet he was driven by fear of what James and the others would think. Proverbs 29:25 says, "Fearing people is a dangerous trap." Paul knew that he had to confront Peter before his actions damaged the church. So, Paul publicly opposed Peter. Note that Paul did not go to the other leaders, nor did he write letters to the churches telling them not to follow Peter's example. Instead, he opposed Peter face to face. Sometimes sincere Christians, even Christian leaders, make mistakes. And it may take other sincere Christians to get them back on track. If you are convinced that someone is doing harm to himself/herself or the church, try the direct approach. There is no place for backstabbing in the body of Christ.

Gal 2:15-16 If the Jewish laws cannot justify us, why should we still obey the Ten Commandments and other Old Testament laws? We know that Paul was not saying the law is bad, because in another letter he wrote, "The law itself is holy, and its commands are holy and right and good" (Rom 7:12). Instead, he is saying that the law can never make us acceptable to God. The law still has an important role to play in the life of a Christian. The law (1) guards us from sin by showing us God's values in the world; (2) convicts us of sin, leaving us the opportunity to ask for God's forgiveness; and (3) drives us to trust in the sufficiency of Christ, because we can never keep the Ten Commandments perfectly. The law cannot possibly save us. But after we become Christians, it can be an aid in guiding us to live as God desires.

▸ **GALATIANS 2:11-21** *(cont.)*

[17]But suppose we seek to be made right with God through faith in Christ and then we are found guilty because we have abandoned the law. Would that mean Christ has led us into sin? Absolutely not! [18]Rather, I am a sinner if I rebuild the old system of law I already tore down. [19]For when I tried to keep the law, it condemned me. So I died to the law—I stopped trying to meet all its requirements—so that I might live for God. [20]My old self has been crucified with Christ.* It is no longer I who live, but Christ lives in me. So I live in this earthly body by trusting in the Son of God, who loved me and gave himself for me. [21]I do not treat the grace of God as meaningless. For if keeping the law could make us right with God, then there was no need for Christ to die.

Gal 2:20 Some English translations put this sentence in verse 19.

2. SUPERIORITY OF THE GOSPEL

The Galatians were beginning to believe the claims of the false teachers and turning from the gospel Paul had preached to a form of legalism. Paul reminds them that they began their life in Christ and received the Holy Spirit by faith, not by keeping the Law. He then argues strongly, appealing to the Old Testament and the life of Abraham, that the Good News revealed in Christ is far superior to the set of rules and regulations that the false teachers wanted people to submit to. The Law served a purpose in God's plan, but in light of the Good News of Jesus Christ, it was no longer the way to be a part of God's family. All people—Jew, Gentile, slave, free, male, and female—are children of God in Christ.

The Law and Faith in Christ

GALATIANS 3:1-14

Oh, foolish Galatians! Who has cast an evil spell on you? For the meaning of Jesus Christ's death was made as clear to you as if you had seen a picture of his death on the cross. [2]Let me ask you this one question: Did you receive the Holy Spirit by obeying the law of Moses? Of course not! You received the Spirit because you believed the message you heard about Christ. [3]How foolish can you be? After starting your Christian lives in the Spirit, why are you now trying to become perfect by your own human effort? [4]Have you experienced* so much for nothing? Surely it was not in vain, was it?

[5]I ask you again, does God give you the Holy Spirit and work miracles among you because you obey the law? Of course not! It is because you believe the message you heard about Christ.

Gal 3:4 Or *Have you suffered.*

Gal 2:17-19 Through studying the Old Testament Scriptures, Paul realized that he could not be saved by obeying God's laws. The prophets knew that God's plan of salvation did not rest on keeping the law (see the chart on p. 1561 for references). Because we have all been infected by sin, we cannot keep God's laws perfectly. Fortunately, God has provided a way of salvation that depends on Jesus Christ, not on our own efforts. Even though we know this truth, we must guard against the temptation of using service, good deeds, charitable giving, or any other effort as a substitute for faith.

Gal 2:19-20 How have our old selves been crucified with Christ? *Legally,* God looks at us as if we had died with Christ. Because our sins died with him, we are no longer condemned (Col 2:13-15). *Relationally,* we have become one with Christ, and his experiences are ours. The Christian life began when, in unity with him, we each died to our old life (see Rom 6:5-11). In our daily lives, we must regularly crucify sinful desires that keep us from following Christ. This, too, is a kind of dying with him (Luke 9:23-25).

And yet the focus of Christianity is not on dying but on living. Because we have been crucified with Christ, we have also been raised with him (Rom 6:5). *Legally,* we have been reconciled with God (2 Cor 5:19) and are free to grow into Christ's likeness (Rom 8:29). And *in our daily lives,* we have Christ's resurrection power as we continue to fight sin (Eph 1:19-20). We are no longer alone, for Christ lives in us—he is our power for living and our hope for the future (Col 1:27).

Gal 2:21 Believers today may still be in danger of acting as if there was no need for Christ to die. How? By replacing Jewish legalism with their own brand of Christian legalism—they are giving people extra laws to obey. By believing they can earn God's favor by what they do, they are not trusting completely in Christ's work on the cross. By struggling to appropriate God's power to change them (sanctification), they are not resting in God's power to save them (justification). If we could be saved by being good, then Christ would not have had to die. But the cross is the only way to salvation.

Gal 3:1 The Galatian believers had become fascinated by the false teachers' arguments, almost as though an evil spell had been cast on them. Magic was common in Paul's day (Acts 8:9-11; 13:6-7). Magicians used both optical illusions and Satan's power to perform miracles, and people were drawn into the magicians' mysterious rites without recognizing their dangerous source.

Gal 3:2-3 Some of the believers in Galatia may have been in Jerusalem at Pentecost and received the Holy Spirit there. They knew that they hadn't received God's Spirit by obeying the Jewish laws. Paul stressed that just as they began their Christian lives in the power of the Spirit, so they should grow by the Spirit's power. The Galatians had taken a step backward when they had decided to insist on keeping the Jewish laws. We must realize that we grow spiritually because of God's work in us by his Spirit, not by following special rules.

Gal 3:5 The Galatians knew that they had received the Holy Spirit when they believed, not when they obeyed the law. People still feel insecure in their faith because faith alone seems too easy. People still try to get closer to God by following rules. While certain disciplines (Bible study, prayer) and service may help us grow, they must not take the place of the Holy Spirit in us or become ends in themselves. By asking these questions, Paul hoped to get the Galatians to focus again on Christ as the foundation of their faith.

Gal 3:5 The Holy Spirit gives Christians great power to live for God. Some Christians want more than this. They want to live in a state of perpetual excitement. The tedium of everyday living leads them to conclude that something is wrong spiritually. Often the Holy Spirit's greatest work is teaching us to persist, to keep on doing what is right even when it no longer seems interesting or exciting. The Galatians quickly turned from Paul's Good News to the teachings of the newest teach-

6 In the same way, "Abraham believed God, and God counted him as righteous because of his faith."* 7 The real children of Abraham, then, are those who put their faith in God.

8 What's more, the Scriptures looked forward to this time when God would declare the Gentiles to be righteous because of their faith. God proclaimed this good news to Abraham long ago when he said, "All nations will be blessed through you."* 9 So all who put their faith in Christ share the same blessing Abraham received because of his faith.

10 But those who depend on the law to make them right with God are under his curse, for the Scriptures say, "Cursed is everyone who does not observe and obey all the commands that are written in God's Book of the Law."* 11 So it is clear that no one can be made right with God by trying to keep the law. For the Scriptures say, "It is through faith that a righteous person has life."* 12 This way of faith is very different from the way of law, which says, "It is through obeying the law that a person has life."*

13 But Christ has rescued us from the curse pronounced by the law. When he was hung on the cross, he took upon himself the curse for our wrongdoing. For it is written in the Scriptures, "Cursed is everyone who is hung on a tree."* 14 Through Christ Jesus, God has blessed the Gentiles with the same blessing he promised to Abraham, so that we who are believers might receive the promised* Holy Spirit through faith.

The Law and God's Promise

GALATIANS 3:15-22

Dear brothers and sisters,* here's an example from everyday life. Just as no one can set aside or amend an irrevocable agreement, so it is in this case. 16 God gave the promises to Abraham and his child.* And notice that the Scripture doesn't say "to his children,*" as if it meant many descendants. Rather, it says "to his child"—and that, of course, means Christ. 17 This is what I am trying to say: The agreement God made with Abraham could not be canceled 430 years later when God gave the law to Moses. God would be breaking his

Gal 3:6 Gen 15:6. **Gal 3:8** Gen 12:3; 18:18; 22:18. **Gal 3:10** Deut 27:26. **Gal 3:11** Hab 2:4. **Gal 3:12** Lev 18:5. **Gal 3:13** Deut 21:23 (Greek version). **Gal 3:14** Some manuscripts read *the blessing of the.* **Gal 3:15** Greek *Brothers.* **Gal 3:16a** Greek *seed;* also in 3:16c, 19. See notes on Gen 12:7 and 13:15. **Gal 3:16b** Greek *seeds.*

DO WE STILL HAVE TO OBEY THE OLD TESTAMENT LAWS?

When Paul says that non-Jews (Gentiles) are no longer bound by these laws, he is not saying that the Old Testament laws are of no value to us today. One way to think about Old Testament laws is to think about three categories:

Ceremonial law	This kind of law relates specifically to Israel's worship (see, for example, Lev 1:1-13). Its primary purpose was to point forward to Jesus Christ. Therefore, these laws were no longer necessary after Jesus' death and resurrection. While we are no longer bound by ceremonial laws, the principles behind them—to worship and love a holy God—still apply. The Jewish Christians often accused the Gentile Christians of violating the ceremonial law.
Civil law	This type of law dictated Israel's daily living (see Deut 24:10-11, for example). Because modern society and culture are so radically different, some of these guidelines cannot be followed specifically. But the principles behind the commands should guide our conduct. At times, Paul asked Gentile Christians to follow some of these laws, not because they had to, but in order to promote unity.
Moral law	This sort of law is the direct command of God—for example, the Ten Commandments (Exod 20:1-17). It requires strict obedience. It reveals the nature and will of God, and it still applies to us today. We are to obey this moral law, not to obtain salvation, but to live in ways pleasing to God.

ers in town; what they needed was the Holy Spirit's gift of persistence. If the Christian life seems ordinary, you may need the Spirit to stir you up. Every day offers a challenge to live for Christ.

Gal 3:6-9 The main argument of the Judaizers was that Gentiles had to become Jews in order to become Christians. Paul exposed the flaw in this argument by showing that real children of Abraham are those who have faith, not those who keep the law. Abraham himself was saved by his faith (Gen 15:6). All believers in every age and from every nation share Abraham's blessing. This is a comforting promise, a great heritage for us, and a solid foundation for living.

Gal 3:10 Paul quoted Deuteronomy 27:26 to prove that, contrary to what the Judaizers claimed, the law cannot justify and save—it can only condemn. Breaking even one commandment brings a person under condemnation. And because everyone has broken commandments, everyone stands condemned. The law can do nothing to reverse the condemnation (Rom 3:20-24). But Christ took the curse of the law upon himself when he hung on the cross. He did this so we wouldn't have to bear our own punishment. The only condition is that we accept Christ's death on our behalf as the means to be saved (Col 1:20-23).

Gal 3:11 Trying to be right with God by our own effort doesn't work. Good intentions such as "I'll do better next time" or "I'll never do that again" usually end in failure. Paul points to Habakkuk's declaration (Hab 2:4) that by trusting God—believing in his provision for our sins and living each day in his power—we can break this cycle of failure.

Gal 3:17 In the same way that we claim Jesus' death as God's provision for our salvation, Abraham believed in God and his promises, although they would not be made fully evident until centuries later on the cross. God promised, and Abraham answered in faith, even during the trial of God asking him to sacrifice his son. This is the heart of Christian faith. God promises to save us when we trust in Christ and take him at his word, just as Abraham did. We know in greater detail how God worked out his plan of grace in Christ. We have much less excuse for our unbelief!

▶ **GALATIANS 3:15-22 *(cont.)***

promise. 18For if the inheritance could be received
by keeping the law, then it would not be the result of
accepting God's promise. But God graciously gave it
to Abraham as a promise.
19Why, then, was the law given? It was given alongside the promise to show people their sins. But the
law was designed to last only until the coming of the
child who was promised. God gave his law through
angels to Moses, who was the mediator between God
and the people. 20Now a mediator is helpful if more
than one party must reach an agreement. But God,
who is one, did not use a mediator when he gave his
promise to Abraham.
21Is there a conflict, then, between God's law and
God's promises?* Absolutely not! If the law could
give us new life, we could be made right with God by
obeying it. 22But the Scriptures declare that we are
all prisoners of sin, so we receive God's promise of
freedom only by believing in Jesus Christ.

God's Children through Faith

GALATIANS 3:23–4:7

Before the way of faith in Christ was available to us, we
were placed under guard by the law. We were kept in
protective custody, so to speak, until the way of faith
was revealed.
24Let me put it another way. The law was our guardian until Christ came; it protected us until we could
be made right with God through faith. 25And now that
the way of faith has come, we no longer need the law
as our guardian.
26For you are all children* of God through faith
in Christ Jesus. 27And all who have been united with
Christ in baptism have put on Christ, like putting on
new clothes.* 28There is no longer Jew or Gentile,* slave
or free, male and female. For you are all one in Christ
Jesus. 29And now that you belong to Christ, you are the
true children* of Abraham. You are his heirs, and God's
promise to Abraham belongs to you.

4:1 Think of it this way. If a father dies and leaves an
inheritance for his young children, those children are
not much better off than slaves until they grow up,
even though they actually own everything their father
had. 2They have to obey their guardians until they
reach whatever age their father set. 3And that's the
way it was with us before Christ came. We were like
children; we were slaves to the basic spiritual principles* of this world.
4But when the right time came, God sent his Son,

Gal 3:21 Some manuscripts read *and the promises?* **Gal 3:26** Greek *sons.* **Gal 3:27** Greek *have put on Christ.* **Gal 3:28** Greek *Jew or Greek.* **Gal 3:29** Greek *seed.* **Gal 4:3** Or *powers;* also in 4:9.

Gal 3:18-19 The law has two functions. On the positive side, it reveals the nature and will of God and shows people how to live. On the negative side, it points out people's sins and shows them that it is impossible to please God by trying to obey all his laws completely. God's promise to Abraham dealt with Abraham's faith; the law focuses on actions. The covenant with Abraham shows that faith is the only way to be saved; the law shows how to obey God in grateful response. Faith does not annul the law; but the more we know God, the more we see how sinful we are. Then we are driven to depend on our faith in Christ alone for our salvation.

Gal 3:19-20 When God gave his promise to Abraham, he did it by himself alone, without angels or Moses as mediators. Although it is not mentioned in Exodus, Jews believed that the Ten Commandments had been given to Moses by angels (Stephen referred to this in his speech; see Acts 7:38, 53). Paul was showing the superiority of salvation and growth by faith over trying to be saved by keeping the Jewish laws. Christ is the best and only way given by God for us to come to him (1 Tim 2:5).

Gal 3:21-22 Before faith in Christ delivered us, we were imprisoned by sin, beaten down by past mistakes, and choked by desires that we knew were wrong. God knew we were sin's prisoners, but he provided a way of escape—faith in Jesus Christ. Without Christ, everyone is held in sin's grasp, and only those who place their faith in Christ ever get out of it. Look to Christ—he is reaching out to set you free.

Gal 3:24-25 The picture of the law as a guardian is similar to a tutor giving a young child supervision and guidance. We no longer need that kind of supervision. The law teaches us the *need* for salvation; God's grace *gives* us that salvation. The Old Testament still applies today. In it, God reveals his nature, his will for humanity, his moral laws, and his guidelines for living. But we cannot be saved by keeping that law; we must trust in Christ.

Gal 3:28 Some Jewish males greeted each new day by praying, "Lord, I thank you that I am not a Gentile, a slave, or a woman." The role of women was enhanced by Christianity. Faith in Christ transcends these differences and makes all believers one in Christ. Make sure you do not impose distinctions that Christ has removed. Because all believers are his heirs, no one is more privileged than or superior to anyone else.

Gal 3:28 It's our natural inclination to feel uncomfortable around people who are different from us and to gravitate toward those who are similar to us. But when we allow our differences to separate us from our fellow believers, we are disregarding clear biblical teaching. Make a point to seek out and appreciate people who are not just like you and your friends. You may find that you have a lot in common with them.

Gal 3:29 The original promise to Abraham was intended for the whole world, not just for Abraham's physical descendants (see Gen 12:3). All believers participate in this promise and are blessed as children of Abraham.

Gal 4:3-7 Paul uses the illustration of slavery to show that before Christ came and died for sins, people were in bondage to the law. Thinking they could be saved by it, they became enslaved to trying—and failing—to keep it. But we who were once slaves are now God's very own children who have an intimate relationship with him. Because of Christ, there is no reason to be afraid of God. We can come boldly into his presence, knowing that he will welcome us as his family members.

Gal 4:4 "When the right time came," God sent Jesus to earth to die for our sins. For centuries the Jews had been wondering when their Messiah would come—but God's timing was perfect. We may sometimes wonder if God will ever respond to our prayers. But we must never doubt him or give up hope. At the right time he will respond. Are you waiting for God's timing? Trust his judgment and trust that he has your best interests in mind.

Gal 4:4-5 Jesus was born of a woman—he was human. He was born as a Jew—he was subject to God's law and fulfilled it perfectly. Thus, Jesus was the perfect sacrifice because, although he was fully human, he never sinned. His death bought freedom for us who were enslaved to sin so that we could be adopted into God's family.

born of a woman, subject to the law. 5God sent him
to buy freedom for us who were slaves to the law, so
that he could adopt us as his very own children.* 6And
because we* are his children, God has sent the Spirit
of his Son into our hearts, prompting us to call out,
"Abba, Father."* 7Now you are no longer a slave but
God's own child.* And since you are his child, God
has made you his heir.

Paul's Concern for the Galatians

GALATIANS 4:8-20

Before you Gentiles knew God, you were slaves to so-
called gods that do not even exist. 9So now that you
know God (or should I say, now that God knows you),
why do you want to go back again and become slaves
once more to the weak and useless spiritual principles
of this world? 10You are trying to earn favor with God
by observing certain days or months or seasons or
years. 11I fear for you. Perhaps all my hard work with
you was for nothing. 12Dear brothers and sisters,* I
plead with you to live as I do in freedom from these
things, for I have become like you Gentiles—free from
those laws.

You did not mistreat me when I first preached to
you. 13Surely you remember that I was sick when I
first brought you the Good News. 14But even though
my condition tempted you to reject me, you did not
despise me or turn me away. No, you took me in and
cared for me as though I were an angel from God or
even Christ Jesus himself. 15Where is that joyful and
grateful spirit you felt then? I am sure you would have
taken out your own eyes and given them to me if it
had been possible. 16Have I now become your enemy
because I am telling you the truth?

17Those false teachers are so eager to win your favor,
but their intentions are not good. They are trying to
shut you off from me so that you will pay attention
only to them. 18If someone is eager to do good things
for you, that's all right; but let them do it all the time,
not just when I'm with you.

19Oh, my dear children! I feel as if I'm going
through labor pains for you again, and they will continue until Christ is fully developed in your lives. 20I
wish I were with you right now so I could change
my tone. But at this distance I don't know how else
to help you.

Gal 4:5 Greek *sons;* also in 4:6. **Gal 4:6a** Greek *you.* **Gal 4:6b** *Abba* is an Aramaic term for "father." **Gal 4:7** Greek *son;* also in 4:7b. **Gal 4:12** Greek *brothers;* also in 4:28, 31.

Gal 4:5-7 Under Roman law, an adopted child was guaranteed all legal rights to his father's property, even if he was formerly a slave. He was not a second-class son; he was equal to all other sons, biological or adopted, in his father's family. As adopted children of God, we share with Jesus all rights to God's resources. As God's heirs, we can claim what he has provided for us—our full identity as his children (see Rom 8:15-17).

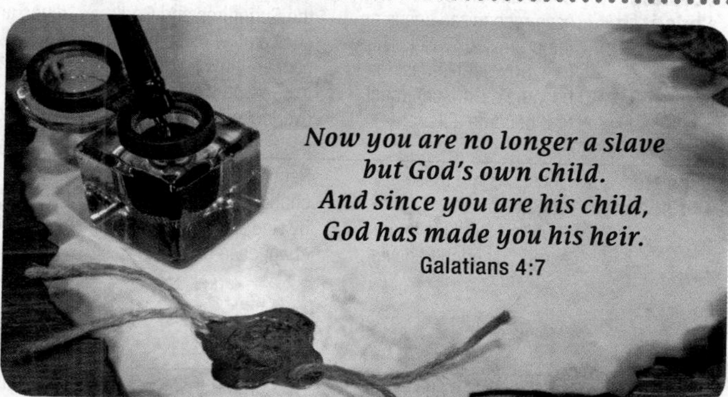
Now you are no longer a slave
but God's own child.
And since you are his child,
God has made you his heir.
Galatians 4:7

Gal 4:13-14 Paul's illness was a sickness that he was enduring while he visited the Galatian churches. The world is often callous to people's pain and misery. Paul commended the Galatians for not scorning him, even though his condition was a trial to them (he didn't explain what was wrong with him). Such caring was what Jesus meant when he called us to serve the homeless, hungry, sick, and imprisoned as if they were Jesus himself (Matt 25:34-40). Do you avoid those in pain or those facing difficulty—or are you willing to care for them as if they were Jesus Christ himself?

Gal 4:15 Have you lost your joy? Paul sensed that the Galatians had lost the joy of their salvation because of legalism. Legalism can take away joy because (1) it makes people feel guilty rather than loved; (2) it produces self-hatred rather than humility; (3) it stresses performance over relationship; (4) it points out how far short we fall rather than how far we've come because of what Christ did for us. If you feel guilty and inadequate, check your focus. Are you living by faith in Christ or by trying to live up to the demands and expectations of others?

Gal 4:16 Paul did not gain great popularity when he rebuked the Galatians for turning away from their first faith in Christ. Human nature hasn't changed much—we still get angry when we're scolded. But don't write off someone who challenges you. There may be truth in what is said. Receive the reproof with humility, and carefully think it over. If you discover that you need to change an attitude or action, take steps to do it.

Gal 4:17 The false teachers claimed to be religious authorities and experts in Judaism and Christianity. Appealing to the believers' desire to do what was right, they drew quite a following. Paul said that they were wrong and that their motives were selfish. False teachers are often respectable and persuasive. That is why all teachings should be checked against the Bible.

Gal 4:19 Paul led many people to Christ and helped them mature spiritually. Perhaps one reason for his success as a spiritual father was the deep concern he felt for his spiritual children; he compared his pain over their faithlessness to the pain of childbirth. We should have the same intense care for those to whom we are spiritual parents. When you lead people to Christ, remember to stand by them to help them grow.

Abraham's Two Children

GALATIANS 4:21-31

Tell me, you who want to live under the law, do you
know what the law actually says? 22The Scriptures
say that Abraham had two sons, one from his slave
wife and one from his freeborn wife.* 23The son of
the slave wife was born in a human attempt to bring
about the fulfillment of God's promise. But the son of
the freeborn wife was born as God's own fulfillment
of his promise.

24These two women serve as an illustration of God's
two covenants. The first woman, Hagar, represents
Mount Sinai where people received the law that enslaved them. 25And now Jerusalem is just like Mount
Sinai in Arabia,* because she and her children live in
slavery to the law. 26But the other woman, Sarah, represents the heavenly Jerusalem. She is the free woman,
and she is our mother. 27As Isaiah said,

"Rejoice, O childless woman,
  you who have never given birth!
Break into a joyful shout,
  you who have never been in labor!
For the desolate woman now has more children
  than the woman who lives with her husband!"*

28And you, dear brothers and sisters, are children
of the promise, just like Isaac. 29But you are now being
persecuted by those who want you to keep the law, just

Gal 4:22 See Gen 16:15; 21:2-3. **Gal 4:25** Greek *And Hagar, which is Mount Sinai in Arabia, is now like Jerusalem;* other manuscripts read *And Mount Sinai in Arabia is now like Jerusalem.* **Gal 4:27** Isa 54:1.

THREE DISTORTIONS OF CHRISTIANITY

Almost from the beginning there were forces at work within Christianity that would have destroyed or sidetracked the movement. Of these, three created many problems then and have continued to reappear in other forms even today. The three aberrations are contrasted to true Christianity.

Group	*Their Definition of a Christian*	*Their Genuine Concern*	*The Danger*	*Application Question*
Judaized Christianity	Christians are Jews who have recognized Jesus as the promised Savior. Therefore, any Gentile desiring to become a Christian must first become a Jew.	Having a high regard for the Scriptures and God's choice of Jews as his people, they did not want to see God's commands overlooked or broken.	Adds human traditions and standards to God's law. Also subtracts from the Scriptures God's clear concern for all nations.	Do you appreciate God's choice of a unique people through whom he offered forgiveness and eternal life to all peoples?
Legalized Christianity	Christians are those who live by a long list of "don'ts." God's favor is earned by good behavior.	Recognized that real change brought about by God should lead to changes in behavior.	Makes God's love something to earn rather than to accept freely. Reduces Christianity to a set of impossible rules and transforms the Good News into bad news.	As important as change in action is, can you see that God may be desiring different changes in you than in others?
Lawless Christianity	Christians live above the law. They need no guidelines. God's Word is not as important as our personal sense of God's guidance.	Recognized that forgiveness from God cannot be based on our ability to live up to his perfect standards. It must be received by faith as a gift made possible by Christ's death on the cross.	Forgets that Christians are still human and fail consistently when trying to live only by what they "feel" God wants.	Do you recognize the ongoing need for God's expressed commands as you live out your gratitude for his great salvation?
True Christianity	Christians are those who believe inwardly and outwardly that Jesus' death has allowed God to offer them forgiveness and eternal life as a gift. They have accepted that gift through faith and are seeking to live a life of obedient gratitude for what God has done for them.	Christianity is both private and public, with heart-belief and mouth-confession. Our relationship to God and the power he provides result in obedience. Having received forgiveness and eternal life, we are now daily challenged to live that life with his help.	Avoids the above dangers.	How would those closest to you describe your Christianity? Do they think you live so that God will accept you, or do they know that you live because God has accepted you in Christ?

as Ishmael, the child born by human effort, persecuted Isaac, the child born by the power of the Spirit.
[30]But what do the Scriptures say about that? "Get rid of the slave and her son, for the son of the slave woman will not share the inheritance with the free woman's son."*
[31]So, dear brothers and sisters, we are not children of the slave woman; we are children of the free woman.

Gal 4:30 Gen 21:10.

3. FREEDOM OF THE GOSPEL

Paul continues his reminder to the Galatians that their faith in Christ is superior to the legalism of the false teachers by reminding them that belonging to Christ means that we are free to obey him joyfully. Why would anyone want to return to the slavery of bondage to a set of rules and regulations? As Christians, we are not boxed in but set free by the power of the Holy Spirit. To preserve our freedom, we must stay close to Christ and resist any who promote subtle ways for us to think we are earning our salvation.

Freedom in Christ

GALATIANS 5:1-15

So Christ has truly set us free. Now make sure that you stay free, and don't get tied up again in slavery to the law.
[2]Listen! I, Paul, tell you this: If you are counting on circumcision to make you right with God, then Christ will be of no benefit to you.
[3]I'll say it again. If you are trying to find favor with God by being circumcised, you must obey every regulation in the whole law of Moses.
[4]For if you are trying to make yourselves right with God by keeping the law, you have been cut off from Christ! You have fallen away from God's grace.
[5]But we who live by the Spirit eagerly wait to receive by faith the righteousness God has promised to us.
[6]For when we place our faith in Christ Jesus, there is no benefit in being circumcised or being uncircumcised. What is important is faith expressing itself in love.
[7]You were running the race so well. Who has held you back from following the truth?
[8]It certainly isn't God, for he is the one who called you to freedom.
[9]This false teaching is like a little yeast that spreads through the whole batch of dough!
[10]I am trusting the Lord to keep you from believing false teachings. God will judge that person, whoever he is, who has been confusing you.
[11]Dear brothers and sisters,* if I were still preaching that you must be circumcised—as some say I do—why am I still being persecuted? If I were no longer preaching salvation through the cross of Christ, no one would be offended.
[12]I just wish that those troublemakers who want to mutilate you by circumcision would mutilate themselves.*
[13]For you have been called to live in freedom, my brothers and sisters. But don't use your freedom to satisfy your sinful nature. Instead, use your freedom

Gal 5:11 Greek *Brothers;* similarly in 5:13. **Gal 5:12** Or *castrate themselves,* or *cut themselves off from you;* Greek reads *cut themselves off.*

Gal 4:21ff People are saved because of their faith in Christ, not because of what they do. Paul contrasted those who are enslaved to the law (represented by Hagar, the slave wife) with those who are freed from the law (represented by Sarah, the freeborn wife). Hagar's abuse of Sarah (Gen 16:4) was like the persecution that the Gentile Christians were getting from the Judaizers, who insisted on keeping the law in order to be saved. Eventually Sarah triumphed because God kept his promise to give her a son, just as those who worship Christ in faith will also triumph.

Gal 4:24 Paul explained that what happened to Sarah and Hagar is an allegory or picture of the relationship between God and people. Paul was using a type of argument that was common in his day and that was probably being used against him by his opponents.

Gal 5:1 Christ died to set us free from sin and from a long list of laws and regulations. Christ came to set us free—not free to do whatever we want because that would lead us back into slavery to our selfish desires. Rather, thanks to Christ, we are now free and able to do what was impossible before—to live unselfishly. Those who appeal to their freedom so that they can have their own way or indulge their own desires are falling back into sin. But it is also wrong to put a burden of law-keeping on Christians. We must stand against those who would enslave us with rules, methods, or special conditions for being saved or growing in Christ.

Gal 5:2-4 Trying to be saved by keeping the law and being saved by grace are two entirely different approaches. "Christ will be of no benefit to you" means that Christ's provision for our salvation will not help us if we are trying to save ourselves. Obeying the law does not make it any easier for God to save us. All we can do is accept his gracious gift through faith. Our deeds of service must never be used to try to earn God's love or favor.

Gal 5:3-4 Circumcision was a symbol of having the right background and doing everything required by religion. No amount of work, discipline, or moral behavior can save us. If a person were counting on finding favor with God by being circumcised, he would also have to obey the rest of God's law completely. Trying to save ourselves by keeping all God's laws only separates us from God.

Gal 5:6 We are saved by faith, not by deeds. But love for others and for God is the response of those whom God has forgiven. God's forgiveness is complete, and Jesus said that those who are forgiven much love much (Luke 7:47). Because faith expresses itself through love, you can check your love for others as a way to monitor your faith.

Gal 5:9 A little yeast causes a whole lump of dough to rise. It only takes one wrong person to infect all the others.

Gal 5:11 Persecution proved that Paul was preaching the true Good News. If he had taught what the false teachers were teaching, no one would be offended. But because he was teaching the truth, he was persecuted by both Jews and Judaizers. Have friends or loved ones rejected you because you have taken a stand for Christ? Jesus said not to be surprised if the world hates you, because it hated him (John 15:18-19). Just as Paul continued to faithfully proclaim the message about Christ, you should continue doing the ministry God has given you—in spite of the obstacles others may put in your way.

Gal 5:13 Paul distinguishes between freedom to sin and freedom to serve. Freedom or license to sin is no freedom at all, because it enslaves you to Satan, others, or your own sinful nature. Christians, by contrast, should not be slaves to sin, because they are free to do right and to glorify God through loving service to others.

▸ **GALATIANS 5:1-15** ***(cont.)***

to serve one another in love. 14 For the whole law can be summed up in this one command: "Love your neighbor as yourself."* 15 But if you are always biting and devouring one another, watch out! Beware of destroying one another.

Living by the Spirit's Power

GALATIANS 5:16-26

So I say, let the Holy Spirit guide your lives. Then you won't be doing what your sinful nature craves. 17 The sinful nature wants to do evil, which is just the opposite of what the Spirit wants. And the Spirit gives us desires that are the opposite of what the sinful nature desires. These two forces are constantly fighting each other, so you are not free to carry out your good intentions. 18 But when you are directed by the Spirit, you are not under obligation to the law of Moses.

19 When you follow the desires of your sinful nature, the results are very clear: sexual immorality, impurity, lustful pleasures, 20 idolatry, sorcery, hostility, quarreling, jealousy, outbursts of anger, selfish ambition, dissension, division, 21 envy, drunkenness, wild parties, and other sins like these. Let me tell you again, as I have before, that anyone living that sort of life will not inherit the Kingdom of God.

22 But the Holy Spirit produces this kind of fruit in our lives: love, joy, peace, patience, kindness, goodness, faithfulness, 23 gentleness, and self-control. There is no law against these things!

Gal 5:14 Lev 19:18.

Gal 5:14-15 When we believers lose the motivation of love, we become critical of others. We stop looking for good in them and see only their faults. Soon we lose our unity. Have you talked behind someone's back? Have you focused on others' shortcomings instead of their strengths? Remind yourself of Jesus' command to love others as you love yourself (Matt 22:39). When you begin to feel critical of someone, make a list of that person's positive qualities. When problems need to be addressed, confront in love rather than gossip.

Gal 5:16-18 If your desire is to have the qualities listed in Galatians 5:22-23, then you know that the Holy Spirit is leading you. At the same time, be careful not to confuse your subjective feelings with the Spirit's leading. Being led by the Holy Spirit involves the desire to hear, the readiness to obey God's Word, and the sensitivity to discern between your feelings and his promptings. Live each day controlled and guided by the Holy Spirit. Then the words of Christ will be in your mind, the love of Christ will be behind your actions, and the power of Christ will help you control your selfish desires.

Gal 5:17 Paul describes the two forces fighting within us—the Holy Spirit and the sinful nature (our evil desires or inclinations that stem from our body; see also Gal 5:16, 19, 24). Paul is not saying that these forces are equal—the Holy Spirit is infinitely stronger. But if we rely on our own wisdom, we will make wrong choices. If we try to follow the Spirit by our own human effort, we will fail. Our only way to freedom from our evil desires is through the empowering of the Holy Spirit (see Rom 8:9; Eph 4:23-24; Col 3:3-8).

Gal 5:19-21 We all have evil desires, and we can't ignore them. In order for us to follow the Holy Spirit's guidance, we must deal with them decisively (crucify them; Gal 5:24). These desires include obvious sins, such as sexual immorality and demonic activities. They also include less obvious sins, such as hostility, jealousy, and selfish ambition. Those who ignore such sins or refuse to deal with them reveal that they have not received the gift of the Spirit that leads to a transformed life.

Gal 5:22-23 The fruit of the Spirit is the spontaneous work of the Holy Spirit in us. The Spirit produces these character traits that are found in the nature of Christ. They are the by-products of Christ's control—we can't obtain them by trying to get them without his help. If we want the fruit of the Spirit to grow in us, we must join our life to his (see John 15:4-5). We must know him, love him, remember him, and imitate him. As a result, we will fulfill the intended purpose of the law—to love God and our neighbors. Which of these qualities do you want the Spirit to produce in you?

VICES AND VIRTUES

The Bible mentions many specific actions and attitudes that are either right or wrong. Look at the list included here. Are there a number of characteristics from the wrong column that are influencing you?

VICES *(Neglecting God and others)*	**VIRTUES** *(The by-products of living for God)*
Sexual immorality (Gal 5:19)	Love (Gal 5:22)
Impurity (Gal 5:19)	Joy (Gal 5:22)
Lust (Col 3:5)	Peace (Gal 5:22)
Hostility (Gal 5:20)	Patience (Gal 5:22)
Quarreling (Gal 5:20)	Kindness (Gal 5:22)
Anger (Gal 5:20)	Goodness (Gal 5:22)
Selfish ambition (Gal 5:20)	Faithfulness (Gal 5:22)
Dissension (Gal 5:20)	Gentleness (Gal 5:23)
Arrogance (2 Cor 12:20)	Self-control (Gal 5:23)
Envy (Gal 5:21)	
Murder (Rev 22:12-15)	
Idolatry (Gal 5:20; Eph 5:5)	
Sorcery (Gal 5:20)	
Drunkenness (Gal 5:21)	
Wild parties (Luke 15:13; Gal 5:21)	
Cheating (1 Cor 6:8)	
Adultery (1 Cor 6:9-10)	
Homosexuality (1 Cor 6:9-10)	
Greed (1 Cor 6:9-10; Eph 5:5)	
Stealing (1 Cor 6:9-10)	
Lying (Rev 22:12-16)	

24Those who belong to Christ Jesus have nailed the
passions and desires of their sinful nature to his cross
and crucified them there. 25Since we are living by the
Spirit, let us follow the Spirit's leading in every part of
our lives. 26Let us not become conceited, or provoke
one another, or be jealous of one another.

We Harvest What We Plant

GALATIANS 6:1-10

Dear brothers and sisters, if another believer* is overcome by some sin, you who are godly* should gently
and humbly help that person back onto the right path.
And be careful not to fall into the same temptation
yourself. 2Share each other's burdens, and in this way
obey the law of Christ. 3If you think you are too important to help someone, you are only fooling yourself.
You are not that important.
4Pay careful attention to your own work, for then
you will get the satisfaction of a job well done, and you
won't need to compare yourself to anyone else. 5For we
are each responsible for our own conduct.
6Those who are taught the word of God should
provide for their teachers, sharing all good things
with them.
7Don't be misled—you cannot mock the justice of
God. You will always harvest what you plant. 8Those
who live only to satisfy their own sinful nature will
harvest decay and death from that sinful nature. But
those who live to please the Spirit will harvest everlasting life from the Spirit. 9So let's not get tired of
doing what is good. At just the right time we will reap
a harvest of blessing if we don't give up. 10Therefore,
whenever we have the opportunity, we should do good
to everyone—especially to those in the family of faith.

Gal 6:1a Greek *Brothers, if a man.* **Gal 6:1b** Greek *spiritual.*

Gal 5:23 Because the God who sent the law also sent the Spirit, the by-products of the Spirit-filled life are in perfect harmony with the intent of God's law. A person who exhibits the fruit of the Spirit fulfills the law far better than a person who observes the rituals but exhibits little love from the heart.

Gal 5:24 In order to accept Christ as Savior, we need to turn from our sins and willingly nail our sinful nature to the cross. This doesn't mean that we will never see traces of its evil desires again. As Christians we still have the capacity to sin, but we have been set free from sin's power over us and no longer have to give in to it. We must daily commit our sinful tendencies to God's control, daily crucify them, and moment by moment draw on the Spirit's power to overcome them (see Gal 2:20; 6:14).

Gal 5:25 God is interested in every part of our life, not just the spiritual part. As we live by the Holy Spirit's power, we need to submit every aspect of our life to God: emotional, physical, social, intellectual, vocational. Paul says that because we're saved, we should live like it! The Holy Spirit is the source of your new life, so keep in step with his leading. Don't let anything or anyone else determine your values and standards in any area of your life.

Gal 5:26 Everyone needs a certain amount of approval from others. But those who go out of their way to secure honors or to win popularity become conceited and show they are not following the Holy Spirit's leading. Those who look to God for approval won't need to envy others. Because we are God's sons and daughters, we have his Holy Spirit as the loving guarantee of his approval. Seek to please God, and the approval of others won't seem so important.

Gal 6:1-3 Christians should never think that they are totally independent and don't need help from others, and no one should feel excused from the task of helping others. The body of Christ—the church—functions only when the members work together for the common good. Do you know someone who needs help? Is there a Christian brother or sister who needs correction or encouragement? Humbly and gently reach out to that person, offering to lift the load (John 13:34-35).

Gal 6:4 When you do your very best, you feel good about the results. There is no need to compare yourself with others. People make comparisons for many reasons. Some point out others' flaws in order to feel better about themselves. Others simply want reassurance that they are doing well. When you are tempted to compare, look at Jesus Christ. His example will inspire you to do your very best, and his loving acceptance will comfort you when you fall short of your expectations.

Gal 6:6 Paul says that students should take care of the material needs of their teachers (1 Cor 9:7-12). It is easy to receive the benefit of good Bible teaching and then to take our spiritual leaders for granted, ignoring their financial and physical needs. We should care for our teachers, not grudgingly or reluctantly, but with a generous spirit, showing honor and appreciation for all they have done (1 Tim 5:17-18).

Gal 6:7-8 It would certainly be a surprise if you planted corn and pumpkins came up. It's a natural law to harvest what we plant. It's true in other areas too. If you gossip about your friends, you will lose their friendship. Every action has results. If you plant to please your own desires, you'll harvest a crop of sorrow and evil. If you plant to please God, you'll harvest joy and everlasting life. What kind of seeds are you planting?

Gal 6:9-10 It is discouraging to continue to do right and receive no word of thanks or see no tangible results. But Paul challenged the Galatians—and he challenges us—to keep on doing good and to trust God for the results. In due time, we will reap a harvest of blessing.

OUR WRONG DESIRES VERSUS THE FRUIT OF THE SPIRIT

The will of the Holy Spirit is in constant opposition to our sinful desires. The two are on opposite sides of the spiritual battle.

Our wrong desires are	The fruit of the Spirit is
Evil	Good
Destructive	Productive
Easy to ignite	Difficult to ignite
Difficult to stifle	Easy to stifle
Self-centered	Self-giving
Oppressive and possessive	Liberating and nurturing
Decadent	Uplifting
Sinful	Holy
Deadly	Abundant life

Paul's Final Advice

GALATIANS 6:11-18

NOTICE WHAT LARGE LETTERS I USE AS I WRITE THESE
CLOSING WORDS IN MY OWN HANDWRITING.
12 Those who are trying to force you to be circumcised want to look good to others. They don't want to
be persecuted for teaching that the cross of Christ
alone can save. 13 And even those who advocate circumcision don't keep the whole law themselves. They
only want you to be circumcised so they can boast
about it and claim you as their disciples.
14 As for me, may I never boast about anything except
the cross of our Lord Jesus Christ. Because of that
cross,* my interest in this world has been crucified,
and the world's interest in me has also died. 15 It doesn't
matter whether we have been circumcised or not. What
counts is whether we have been transformed into a new
creation. 16 May God's peace and mercy be upon all who
live by this principle; they are the new people of God.*
17 From now on, don't let anyone trouble me with
these things. For I bear on my body the scars that show
I belong to Jesus.
18 Dear brothers and sisters,* may the grace of our
Lord Jesus Christ be with your spirit. Amen.

Gal 6:14 Or *Because of him.* **Gal 6:16** Greek *this principle, and upon the Israel of God.* **Gal 6:18** Greek *Brothers.*

4. RESOLUTION AT THE JERUSALEM COUNCIL

The issue of requiring believers to be circumcised and follow the food laws and other Jewish regulations became a major controversy in the early church. The apostles didn't want to create disunity among the body of Christ, and so they came together to discuss why it was causing arguments and to clarify for everyone that they were unified in spreading the Good News of Jesus all over the world. Peter, Paul, and James all spoke about the fact that God had clearly accepted Gentiles as his own children through faith in Christ and had given the Holy Spirit to them as a clear sign. They all agreed that Gentiles were not required to become Jewish in order to be a part of God's people and sent a letter to encourage the Gentile believers and confirm that they were fully accepted by all of the apostles.

The Council at Jerusalem

ACTS 15:1-21

While Paul and Barnabas were at Antioch of Syria,
some men from Judea arrived and began to teach
the believers*: "Unless you are circumcised as required by the law of Moses, you cannot be saved."
2 Paul and Barnabas disagreed with them, arguing vehemently. Finally, the church decided to send Paul

Acts 15:1 Greek *brothers;* also in 15:3, 23, 32, 33, 36, 40.

Paul's Handwriting

Paul's comment about "what large letters I use" is interesting to note. The point is that they indicate an extraordinary difference between Paul's handwriting and that of the amanuensis (the secretary). As was typical in ancient times, the author of a document usually dictated the body of the epistle to an amanuensis and then took stylus in hand to personally write out the concluding remarks. We know that Paul used an amanuensis for the epistle to the Romans, namely Tertius (see Rom 16:22), and we can assume that he did so for at least four other epistles because he specifically mentions that he provided the concluding salutation in his own handwriting (1 Cor 16:21; here in Gal 6:11; Col 4:18; 2 Thes 3:17). If we had the autographs of these epistles, we would see Paul's actual handwriting! Instead, we have very early copies, so we have to imagine what that handwriting looked like.

Gal 6:11 Up to this point, Paul had probably dictated the letter to a secretary. Here he takes the pen into his own hand to write his final, personal greetings. Paul did this in other letters as well, to add emphasis to his words and to validate that the letter was genuine.

Gal 6:13 Some of the Judaizers were emphasizing circumcision as proof of holiness, but were ignoring the other Jewish laws. People often choose a certain principle or prohibition and make it the measure of faith. Some may condemn drunkenness but ignore gluttony. Others may despise promiscuity but tolerate prejudice. The Bible in its entirety is our rule of faith and practice. We cannot pick and choose the mandates we will follow.

Gal 6:14 The world is full of enticements. Daily we are confronted with subtle cultural pressures and overt propaganda. The only way to escape these destructive influences is to ask God to help crucify our interest in them, just as Paul did. How much do the interests of this world matter to you? (See Gal 2:20; 5:24 for more on this concept.)

Gal 6:15 It is easy to get caught up with the externals. Beware of those who emphasize actions that we should or shouldn't do, with no concern for the inward condition of the heart. Living a good life without an inward change leads to a shallow or empty spiritual walk. What matters to God is that we be completely changed from the inside out (2 Cor 5:17).

Gal 6:18 Paul's letter to the Galatians boldly declares the freedom of the Christian. Doubtless these early Christians in Galatia wanted to grow in the Christian life, but they were being misled by those who said this could be done only by keeping certain Jewish laws.

How strange it would be for a prisoner who had been set free to walk back into the cell and refuse to leave! How strange for an animal, released from a trap, to go back inside it! How sad for a believer to be freed

and Barnabas to Jerusalem, accompanied by some local believers, to talk to the apostles and elders about
this question. 3The church sent the delegates to Jerusalem, and they stopped along the way in Phoenicia
and Samaria to visit the believers. They told them—
much to everyone's joy—that the Gentiles, too, were
being converted.
4When they arrived in Jerusalem, Barnabas and
Paul were welcomed by the whole church, including
the apostles and elders. They reported everything
God had done through them. 5But then some of the
believers who belonged to the sect of the Pharisees
stood up and insisted, "The Gentile converts must
be circumcised and required to follow the law of
Moses."
6So the apostles and elders met together to resolve
this issue. 7At the meeting, after a long discussion,
Peter stood and addressed them as follows: "Brothers,
you all know that God chose me from among you some
time ago to preach to the Gentiles so that they could
hear the Good News and believe. 8God knows people's
hearts, and he confirmed that he accepts Gentiles
by giving them the Holy Spirit, just as he did to us.
9He made no distinction between us and them, for
he cleansed their hearts through faith. 10So why are
you now challenging God by burdening the Gentile
believers* with a yoke that neither we nor our ancestors were able to bear? 11We believe that we are all
saved the same way, by the undeserved grace of the
Lord Jesus."
12Everyone listened quietly as Barnabas and Paul
told about the miraculous signs and wonders God had
done through them among the Gentiles.
13When they had finished, James stood and said,
"Brothers, listen to me. 14Peter* has told you about the
time God first visited the Gentiles to take from them a

Acts 15:10 Greek *disciples.* **Acts 15:14** Greek *Symeon.*

from the bondage of sin, only to return to rigid conformity and to a set of rules and regulations!

If you believe in Jesus Christ, you have been set free. Instead of going back into some form of slavery, whether to legalism or to sin, use your freedom to live for Christ and serve him as he desires.

Acts 15:1 The question of whether Gentile believers should obey the law of Moses in order to be saved was extremely critical at this point in Christianity's history and could have potentially split the early church if not handled carefully. The controversy had intensified with the success of the new Gentile churches. The Judaizers in the Jerusalem church were led by converted Pharisees (Acts 15:5) who preferred a legalistic religion to one based on faith alone. If the Judaizers had won, the Gentiles would have been required to be circumcised and, in effect, converted to Judaism. This would have confined Christianity to simply being another sect within Judaism.

There is something of a "Pharisee" in each one of us. We may unwittingly mistake upholding tradition, structure, and legal requirements for obeying God. Make sure the gospel brings freedom and life, not rules and ceremonies, to those you are trying to reach.

Acts 15:2ff The delegates to the council at Jerusalem came from the churches in Jerusalem and Antioch. The conversion of Gentiles was raising an urgent question for the early church: The real problem for the Jewish Christians was not whether Gentiles could be saved but whether Gentile believers also had to adhere to the laws of Moses and other Jewish traditions. The test of following these laws was circumcision. One group of Jewish Christians insisted that following the law, including submitting to the rite of circumcision, was necessary for salvation. But the Gentiles did not think they needed to become Jewish first in order to become Christians. The Jewish Christians also were worried because soon Gentile Christians would outnumber Jewish Christians. And they were afraid of weakening moral standards among believers if they did not follow Jewish laws. So Paul and Barnabas discussed this problem with the leaders of the church. Paul, Barnabas, and the other church leaders believed that the Old Testament law was very important but was not requirement for salvation. The law cannot save; only by grace through faith in Jesus Christ can a person be saved. The council upheld the conviction expressed by Paul and Barnabas that following the Jewish laws, including being circumcised, was not essential for salvation.

Acts 15:2ff It is helpful to see how the churches in Antioch and Jerusalem resolved their conflict: (1) The church in Antioch sent a delegation to help seek a solution; (2) the delegates met with the church leaders to give their reports and set another date to continue the discussion; (3) Paul and Barnabas gave their report; (4) James summarized the reports and drew up the decision; (5) everyone agreed to abide by the decision; (6) the council sent a letter with delegates back to Antioch to report the decision.

This is a wise way to handle conflicts within the church. Problems must be confronted, and all sides of the argument must be given a fair hearing. The discussion should be held in the presence of leaders who are spiritually mature and trustworthy to make wise decisions. Everyone should then abide by the decisions.

Acts 15:10 If the law was a yoke that the Jews could not bear, how did having the law help them throughout their history? Paul wrote that the law was a guide that pointed out their sins so they could repent and return to God and right living (see Gal 3:24-25). It was, and still is, impossible to obey the law completely.

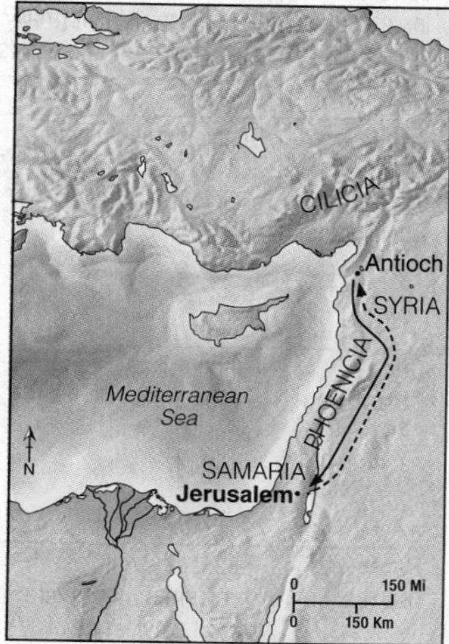

***THE JERUSALEM COUNCIL** A dispute arose when some Jewish believers taught that Gentile believers had to be circumcised to be saved. Paul and Barnabas went to Jerusalem to discuss this situation with the leaders there. After the Jerusalem council made its decision, Paul and Barnabas returned to Antioch with the news.*

Acts 15:13 This James is Jesus' half brother. He became the leader of the church in Jerusalem and wrote the book of James.

▶ **ACTS 15:1-21** ***(cont.)***

people for himself. [15]And this conversion of Gentiles
is exactly what the prophets predicted. As it is written:

16 'Afterward I will return
and restore the fallen house* of David.
I will rebuild its ruins
and restore it,
17 so that the rest of humanity might seek the LORD,
including the Gentiles—
all those I have called to be mine.
The LORD has spoken—
18 he who made these things known so long ago.'*

[19]"And so my judgment is that we should not make
it difficult for the Gentiles who are turning to God.
[20]Instead, we should write and tell them to abstain
from eating food offered to idols, from sexual immorality, from eating the meat of strangled animals,
and from consuming blood. [21]For these laws of Moses
have been preached in Jewish synagogues in every city
on every Sabbath for many generations."

Acts 15:16 Or *kingdom;* Greek reads *tent.* **Acts 15:16-18** Amos 9:11-12 (Greek version); Isa 45:21.

The Letter for Gentile Believers

ACTS 15:22-35

Then the apostles and elders together with the whole church in Jerusalem chose delegates, and they sent

THE FIRST CHURCH CONFERENCE

As long as most of the first Christians were Jewish, there was little difficulty in welcoming new believers; however, Gentiles (non-Jews) began to accept Jesus' offer of salvation. The evidence in their lives and the presence of God's Spirit in them showed that God was accepting them. Some of the early Christians believed that non-Jewish Christians needed to meet certain conditions before they could be worthy to accept Christ. The issue could have destroyed the church, so a conference was called in Jerusalem, and the issue was formally settled there, although it continued to be a problem for many years following. This chart shows an outline of the three points of view at the conference.

Group	*Position*	*Reasons*
Judaizers (some Jewish Christians)	Gentiles must become Jewish first to be eligible for salvation.	1. They were devout, practicing Jews who found it difficult to set aside a tradition of gaining merit with God by keeping the law. 2. They thought grace was too easy for the Gentiles. 3. They were afraid of seeming too non-Jewish in the practice of their new faith—which could lead to death. 4. The demands on the Gentiles were a way of maintaining control and authority in the movement.
Gentile Christians	Faith in Christ as Savior is the only requirement for salvation.	1. To submit to what the Jewish law demands would be to doubt what God had already done for them by grace alone. 2. They resisted exchanging their pagan rituals for a system of Jewish rituals—neither of which had the power to save. 3. They sought to obey Christ by baptism (rather than by circumcision) as a sign of their new faith.
Peter and James	Faith is the only requirement, but there must be evidence of change by rejecting the old lifestyle.	1. They tried to distinguish between what was true from God's Word versus what was just human tradition. 2. They had Christ's command to preach to all the world. 3. They wanted to preserve unity. 4. They saw that Christianity could never survive as just a sect within Judaism.

Acts 15:16-18 Despite the compelling experiences of Peter, Barnabas, and Paul, James turned to God's Word as the ultimate test of truth. This should be the way we evaluate events. We all have beliefs (some of them fervent), we all have experiences, and our tendency is to want to measure others by our yardstick. It is common for believers to think that their experiences and convictions are true and should be the norm. Different ideas are thought to be inferior or invalid. Ultimately what matters is what God's Word says. The more we know God's Word—the more we read it, study it, memorize it, and meditate on it—the better able we will be to discern what is right and best in times of controversy or doctrinal disagreement.

Acts 15:19-21 James's judgment was that Gentile believers did not have to be circumcised, but they should stay away from food sacrificed to idols, from sexual immorality (a common part of idol worship), and from consuming blood (reflecting the biblical teaching that the life is in the blood; Lev 17:14) or eating the meat of strangled animals. If Gentile Christians would abstain from these practices, they would please God and get along better with their Jewish brothers and sisters in Christ. Of course, other actions were inappropriate for believers, but the Jews were especially concerned about these four. This compromise helped the church grow unhindered by the cultural differences of Jews and Gentiles. When we share our message across cultural and economic boundaries, we must be sure that the requirements for faith we set up are God's, not people's.

Acts 15:19-21 The early church experienced the difficulty of bringing together diverse peoples. Jews and Gentiles had so little in common! Different histories, traditions, practices, customs, cultures, languages. How do you possibly take such dissimilar groups and make them one? One solution is to decide not to—to decide that it is impossible to accomplish. So you segregate, isolate, and study each other with suspicion. This response profoundly affects Christianity's effectiveness and attractiveness. When there is snobbery or a judgmental atmosphere, the church betrays the teachings of Christ and loses all appeal.

The other solution is to submit our prejudices and presuppositions to the greater purposes of God. When we imitate him (Eph 5:1), we become tolerant, understanding, and accepting. However, such tolerance is not

them to Antioch of Syria with Paul and Barnabas to report on this decision. The men chosen were two of the church leaders*—Judas (also called Barsabbas) and Silas. 23 This is the letter they took with them:

"This letter is from the apostles and elders, your brothers in Jerusalem. It is written to the Gentile believers in Antioch, Syria, and Cilicia. Greetings!

24 "We understand that some men from here have troubled you and upset you with their teaching, but we did not send them! 25 So we decided, having come to complete agreement, to send you official representatives, along with our beloved Barnabas and Paul, 26 who have risked their lives for the name of our Lord Jesus Christ. 27 We are sending Judas and Silas to confirm what we have decided concerning your question.

28 "For it seemed good to the Holy Spirit and to us to lay no greater burden on you than these few requirements: 29 You must abstain from eating food offered to idols, from consuming blood or the meat of strangled animals, and from sexual immorality. If you do this, you will do well. Farewell."

Acts 15:22 Greek *were leaders among the brothers.*

PAUL

No person, apart from Jesus himself, shaped the history of Christianity like the apostle Paul. Even before he was a believer, his actions were significant. His frenzied persecution of Christians following Stephen's death got the church started in obeying Christ's final command to take the gospel worldwide. • Paul was very religious. His training under Gamaliel was the finest available. His intentions and efforts were sincere. He was a good Pharisee who knew the Bible and sincerely believed that this Christian movement was dangerous to Judaism. Thus, Paul hated the Christian faith and persecuted Christians without mercy. • Paul got permission to travel to Damascus to capture Christians and bring them back to Jerusalem. But God stopped him in his hurried tracks on the Damascus road. Paul personally met Jesus Christ, and his life was never the same. • Until Paul's conversion, little had been done about carrying the gospel to non-Jews. Philip had preached in Samaria and to an Ethiopian man; Cornelius, a Gentile, was converted under Peter; and in Antioch of Syria, some Greeks had joined the believers. When Barnabas was sent from Jerusalem to check on this situation, he went to Tarsus to find Paul and bring him to Antioch, and together they worked among the believers there. They were then sent on a missionary journey, the first of three Paul would take that would carry the gospel across the Roman Empire. • The thorny issue of whether Gentile believers had to obey Jewish laws before they could become Christians caused many problems in the early church. Paul worked hard to convince the Jews that Gentiles were acceptable to God, but he spent even more time convincing the Gentiles that they were acceptable to God. The lives Paul touched were changed and challenged by meeting Christ through him. • God did not waste any part of Paul—his background, his training, his citizenship, his mind, or even his weaknesses. Are you willing to let God do the same for you? You will never know all he can do with you until you allow him to have all that you are!

Strengths and accomplishments	• Preached for Christ throughout the Roman Empire on three missionary journeys • Wrote letters to various churches, which became part of the New Testament • Was never afraid to face an issue head-on and deal with it • Was sensitive to God's leading and, despite his strong personality, always did as God directed
Weaknesses and mistakes	• Witnessed and approved of Stephen's stoning • Set out to destroy Christianity by persecuting Christians
Lessons from his life	• The Good News is that forgiveness and eternal life are available to all people and are gifts of God's grace through faith in Christ • Obedience results from a relationship with God, but obedience will never create or earn that relationship • God does not waste our time; he will use our past and present so we may serve him with our future
Vital statistics	• Where: Born in Tarsus but became a world traveler for Christ • Occupations: Trained as a Pharisee, learned the tentmaking trade, served as a missionary • Contemporaries: Gamaliel, Stephen, the apostles, Luke, Barnabas, Timothy
Key verses	"For to me, living means living for Christ, and dying is even better. But if I live, I can do more fruitful work for Christ. So I really don't know which is better. I'm torn between two desires: I long to go and be with Christ, which would be far better for me. But for your sakes, it is better that I continue to live" (Phil 1:21-24).

Paul's story is told in Acts 7:58–28:31 and throughout his New Testament letters.

meant to include sinful lifestyles. James mentioned a few laws that the Gentile believers should keep, with an understanding that basic morality and living for God would cover the rest. When believers of different races, ethnic backgrounds, and social strata come together in love and worship of the Savior, nothing gives greater glory to God or provides a more compelling witness.

Acts 15:22 Later, Silas accompanied Paul on Paul's second missionary journey in place of Barnabas, who visited different cities with John Mark.

Acts 15:23-29 This letter answered their questions and brought great joy to the Gentile Christians in Antioch (Acts 15:31). Beautifully written, it appeals to the Holy Spirit's guidance and explains what is to be done as though the readers already knew it. Believers should be careful not only in what they say but also in how they say it. We may be correct in our content, but we can lose our audience by our tone of voice or by our attitude.

▸ ACTS 15:22-35 *(cont.)*

30 The messengers went at once to Antioch, where
they called a general meeting of the believers and delivered the letter. 31 And there was great joy throughout the
church that day as they read this encouraging message.
32 Then Judas and Silas, both being prophets, spoke
at length to the believers, encouraging and strengthening their faith. 33 They stayed for a while, and then the
believers sent them back to the church in Jerusalem
with a blessing of peace.* 35 Paul and Barnabas stayed
in Antioch. They and many others taught and preached
the word of the Lord there.

Acts 15:33 Some manuscripts add verse 34, *But Silas decided to stay there.*

F. Paul Begins His Second Missionary Journey

After a little while, Paul returned to the cities that he and Barnabas had visited on their first missionary journey to encourage and strengthen the believers there, but God had even bigger plans for Paul. God sent Paul a vision and called him to push the gospel even farther into the world, and Paul obeyed by traveling across the sea to Europe. He shared the Good News about Jesus in Philippi, Thessalonica, Berea, Athens, and Corinth before finally returning home to Antioch. All along the way he faced persecution, but he also saw God working powerfully and transforming people through the power of the Holy Spirit. We don't always know where God is going to send us, but we need to be faithful to him wherever we are and be sensitive to his leading. You never know what great things God has in store for your life!

Paul and Barnabas Separate

ACTS 15:36-41

After some time Paul said to Barnabas, "Let's go back
and visit each city where we previously preached the
word of the Lord, to see how the new believers are doing." 37 Barnabas agreed and wanted to take along John
Mark. 38 But Paul disagreed strongly, since John Mark
had deserted them in Pamphylia and had not continued with them in their work. 39 Their disagreement
was so sharp that they separated. Barnabas took John
Mark with him and sailed for Cyprus. 40 Paul chose
Silas, and as he left, the believers entrusted him to the
Lord's gracious care. 41 Then he traveled throughout
Syria and Cilicia, strengthening the churches there.

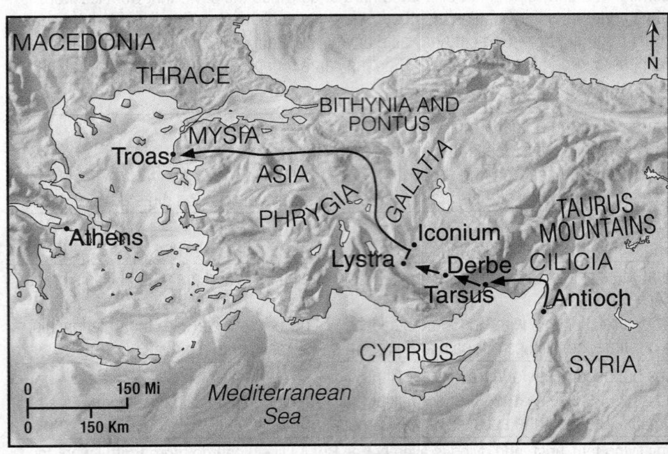

***THE SECOND JOURNEY BEGINS** Paul and Silas set out on a second missionary journey to visit the cities Paul had preached in earlier. This time they set out by land rather than sea, traveling the Roman road through Cilicia and the Cilician Gates—a gorge through the Taurus Mountains—then northwest toward Derbe, Lystra, and Iconium. The Spirit told them not to go into Asia, so they turned northward toward Bithynia. Again the Spirit said no, so they turned west through Mysia to the harbor city of Troas.*

Acts 15:31 The debate over circumcision could have split the church, but Paul, Barnabas, and the Jews in Antioch made the right decision—they sought counsel from the church leaders and from God's Word. Our differences should be settled the same way—by seeking wise counsel and abiding by the decisions. Don't let disagreements divide you from other believers.

Acts 15:36-39 Paul and Barnabas disagreed sharply over Mark. Paul didn't want to take him along because he had left them earlier (Acts 13:13). This disagreement caused the two great preachers to form two teams, opening up two missionary endeavors instead of one. God works even through conflict and disagreements. Later, Mark became vital to Paul's ministry (Col 4:10). Christians do not always agree, but problems often can be solved by agreeing to disagree and letting God work his will.

Acts 15:40 Paul's second missionary journey, this time with Silas as his co-worker, began approximately three years after his first one ended. The two visited many of the cities covered on Paul's first journey, plus others. This journey laid the groundwork for the church in Greece.

Acts 15:40 Silas had been involved in the Jerusalem council and had been one of the two men chosen to represent the Jerusalem church by taking the letter and decision back to Antioch (Acts 15:22). Paul (from the Antioch church) chose Silas (from the Jerusalem church), and they traveled together to many cities to spread the Good News. This teamwork demonstrated the church's unity after the decision at the Jerusalem council.

Acts 16:1 Timothy is the first second-generation Christian mentioned in the New Testament. His mother, Eunice, and grandmother Lois (2 Tim 1:5) had become believers and had faithfully influenced him for the Lord. Although Timothy's father apparently was not a Christian, the faithfulness of Timothy's mother and grandmother prevailed. Never underestimate the effect of godly parenting on a child.

Acts 16:2-3 Timothy and his mother, Eunice, were from Lystra. Eunice had prob-

Paul's Second Missionary Journey

ACTS 16:1-5

Paul went first to Derbe and then to Lystra, where there
was a young disciple named Timothy. His mother was
a Jewish believer, but his father was a Greek. [2]Timothy
was well thought of by the believers* in Lystra and
Iconium, [3]so Paul wanted him to join them on their
journey. In deference to the Jews of the area, he arranged for Timothy to be circumcised before they left,
for everyone knew that his father was a Greek. [4]Then
they went from town to town, instructing the believers
to follow the decisions made by the apostles and elders
in Jerusalem. [5]So the churches were strengthened in
their faith and grew larger every day.

A Call from Macedonia

ACTS 16:6-10

Next Paul and Silas traveled through the area of
Phrygia and Galatia, because the Holy Spirit had prevented them from preaching the word in the province
of Asia at that time. [7]Then coming to the borders of
Mysia, they headed north for the province of Bithynia,* but again the Spirit of Jesus did not allow
them to go there. [8]So instead, they went on through
Mysia to the seaport of Troas.

[9]That night Paul had a vision: A man from Macedonia in northern Greece was standing there, pleading
with him, "Come over to Macedonia and help us!" [10]So
we* decided to leave for Macedonia at once, having

Acts 16:2 Greek *brothers;* also in 16:40. **Acts 16:6-7** *Phrygia, Galatia, Asia, Mysia,* and *Bithynia* were all districts in what is now Turkey. **Acts 16:10** Luke, the writer of this book, here joined Paul and accompanied him on his journey.

ably heard Paul's preaching when he was there during his first missionary journey (Acts 14:6-18). Timothy was the son of a Jewish mother and Greek father—to the Jews, a half-breed like a Samaritan. So Paul asked Timothy to be circumcised to remove some of the stigma he may have had with Jewish believers. Timothy was not required to be circumcised, but he voluntarily did this to overcome any barriers to his witness for Christ. Sometimes we need to go beyond the call of duty in order to further the Kingdom of God.

Acts 16:6 We don't know how the Holy Spirit told Paul that he and his companions should not go into Asia. It may have been through a prophet, a vision, an inner conviction, or some other circumstance. To know God's will does not mean we must hear his voice. He leads in different ways. When you are seeking God's will, (1) make sure your plan is in harmony with God's Word; (2) ask mature Christians for their advice; (3) check your own motives to see if you are seeking to do what you want or what you think God wants; (4) pray for God to open and close the doors as he desires.

Acts 16:7-9 The "Spirit of Jesus" is another name for the Holy Spirit. The Holy Spirit had closed the door twice for Paul, so Paul must have wondered which geographical direction to take in spreading the Good News. Then, in a vision (Acts 16:9), Paul was given definite direction, and he and his companions obediently traveled into Macedonia. The Holy Spirit guides us to the right places, but he also guides us away from the wrong places. As we seek God's will, we need to know what God wants us to do and where he wants us to go, but we also need to know what God does *not* want us to do and where he does *not* want us to go.

Acts 16:10 The use of the pronoun *we* indicates that Luke, the author of the Gospel of Luke and of this book, joined Paul, Silas, and Timothy on their journey. He was an eyewitness to many of the remaining incidents recorded in this book.

Samothrace

Samothrace is an island in the northeastern part of the Aegean Sea off the coast of Thrace. It is a mountainous island with its central peak being the highest point in the northern part of the Aegean, second in height only to Mount Athos on the mainland. In clear weather, the island has always been an ancient landmark for seafarers sailing between Troas and Neapolis. Samothrace was about halfway between Troas and Neapolis, the seaport of Philippi. The island was a stopping place for the apostle Paul on his way to Neapolis (Acts 16:11). They must have had a fair wind because the voyage took only two days.

The words in the Irish blessing, "may the wind always be at your back," don't always come true. Half the time we are fighting against the wind as we face earthly trials. What we can count on is that God is always with us, no matter which way the winds are blowing.

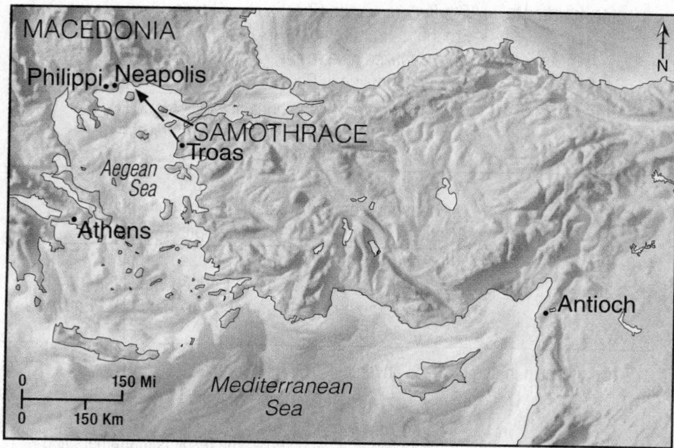

***PAUL TRAVELS TO MACEDONIA** At Troas, Paul received the Macedonian call (Acts 16:9), and he, Silas, Timothy, and Luke boarded a ship. They sailed to the island of Samothrace, then on to Neapolis, the port for the city of Philippi. Philippi sat on the Egnatian Way, a main transportation artery connecting the eastern provinces with Italy.*

▸ **ACTS 16:6-10** ***(cont.)***

concluded that God was calling us to preach the Good News there.

Lydia of Philippi Believes in Jesus

ACTS 16:11-15

We boarded a boat at Troas and sailed straight across to the island of Samothrace, and the next day we landed at Neapolis. 12From there we reached Philippi, a major city of that district of Macedonia and a Roman colony. And we stayed there several days.

13On the Sabbath we went a little way outside the city to a riverbank, where we thought people would be meeting for prayer, and we sat down to speak with some women who had gathered there. 14One of them was Lydia from Thyatira, a merchant of expensive purple cloth, who worshiped God. As she listened to us, the Lord opened her heart, and she accepted what Paul was saying. 15She was baptized along with other members of her household, and she asked us to be her guests. "If you agree that I am a true believer in the Lord," she said, "come and stay at my home." And she urged us until we agreed.

Acts 16:12 Philippi was the key city in the region of Macedonia (northern Greece today). Paul founded a church during this visit (A.D. 50–51). Later, Paul wrote a letter to that church, the book of Philippians, probably from a prison in Rome (A.D. 61). The letter was personal and tender, showing Paul's deep love for and friendship with the believers there. In it he thanked them for a gift they had sent, alerted them to a coming visit by Timothy and Epaphroditus, urged the church to clear up any disunity, and encouraged the believers not to give in to persecution.

Acts 16:13 Inscribed on the arches outside the city of Philippi was a prohibition against bringing an unrecognized religion into the city; therefore, this prayer meeting was held outside the city, beside the river.

Acts 16:13-14 After following the Holy Spirit's leading into Macedonia, Paul made his first evangelistic contact with a small group of women. Paul never allowed gender or cultural boundaries to keep him from preaching the Good News. He preached to these women, and Lydia, an influential merchant, believed. This opened the way for ministry in that region. God often worked in and through women in the early church.

Acts 16:14 Lydia was a merchant of purple cloth, so she was probably wealthy. Purple cloth was valuable and expensive. It was often worn as a sign of nobility or royalty.

Acts 16:14ff Luke highlights the stories of three individuals whose lives were changed through Paul's ministry in Philippi: Lydia, the influential businesswoman (Acts 16:14), the demon-possessed slave girl (Acts 16:16-18), and the jailer (Acts 16:27-30). The Good News was affecting all strata of society, just as it does today.

Acts 16:15 Why was Lydia's household baptized after Lydia responded in faith to the Good News? Baptism was a public sign of identification with Christ and the Christian community. Although all members of her household may not have chosen to follow Christ (we don't know), it was now a Christian home.

Acts 16:15 Lydia practically begged for the opportunity to host Paul and Silas in her home. Rather than seeing the men as a burden and their presence as a disruption of her family and business routine, Lydia laid out the welcome mat. We practice hospitality when we generously and cordially throw open the doors of our homes to care for others. In hospitality, we nurture, strengthen, and serve. The result is that others find physical, spiritual, and emotional help. When they leave us, they are healthier and more whole than when they came. Is this your practice?

LYDIA

Almost everywhere Paul and Silas traveled, they found people open to the gospel message. When they arrived in Philippi, they met just such a disciple-in-the-making. Her name was Lydia. • Lydia's business as a dealer in fine purple cloth and dye probably means she was wealthy. No husband is mentioned, but she was responsible for a household. Lydia was also a spiritual searcher. She was among the Gentile women who gathered outside Philippi on each Sabbath to pray to the God of the Jews. One eventful day, Paul and Silas visited the group. • Lydia's attendance at the prayer gathering demonstrated her willingness to respond to as much about God as she knew. God responded to her quest by providing her with more truth. When she heard the Good News about Jesus Christ, she listened and believed. She is remembered as Paul's first European convert. • Luke described with swift strokes the first two steps in Lydia's life as a disciple: (1) She was baptized, (2) she brought the rest of the members of her household to Paul and they apparently believed as well, because they were baptized. Lydia's response was both inward and outward. She immediately understood that her new faith created all kinds of opportunities for practical application. Then, as now, the gospel had life-changing effects. The first actions of new believers often indicate how deeply they have understood and received the gift of salvation. The Christian life is a gift we continue to receive by sharing it with others. • Thinking of Lydia, how would you describe the initial effects of the gospel on your life? When you accepted Christ, what changes did others notice in you? How did Christ's presence affect your behavior? To what degree has your life continued to display that gratefulness you felt when you first believed?

Strengths and accomplishments	• Successful businesswoman • The first convert to Christianity in Europe • Brought her entire household to hear about Jesus, and all were baptized as a result • Provided housing in Philippi for Paul and Silas
Lessons from her life	• God rewards those who honestly seek him • One of the marks of conversion is care for others—physically and spiritually
Vital statistics	• Where: From Thyatira, living in Philippi • Occupation: Merchant specializing in costly purple cloth • Relatives: A household that was baptized with her.
Key verse	"One of them was Lydia from Thyatira, a merchant of expensive purple cloth, who worshiped God. As she listened to us, the Lord opened her heart, and she accepted what Paul was saying" (Acts 16:14).

The events surrounding Lydia's conversion are found in Acts 16:11-40.

Paul and Silas in Prison

ACTS 16:16-40

One day as we were going down to the place of prayer, we met a demon-possessed slave girl. She was a fortune-teller who earned a lot of money for her masters. [17]She followed Paul and the rest of us, shouting, "These men are servants of the Most High God, and they have come to tell you how to be saved."

[18]This went on day after day until Paul got so exasperated that he turned and said to the demon within her, "I command you in the name of Jesus Christ to come out of her." And instantly it left her.

[19]Her masters' hopes of wealth were now shattered, so they grabbed Paul and Silas and dragged them before the authorities at the marketplace. [20]"The whole city is in an uproar because of these Jews!" they shouted to the city officials. [21]"They are teaching customs that are illegal for us Romans to practice."

SILAS

Silas first appears in Acts at the end of the first church council on the Jewish/Gentile problem. The majority of early Christians were Jews who realized that Jesus was the fulfillment of God's Old Testament promises to his people; however, the universal application of those promises had been overlooked. Thus, many felt that becoming Jewish was a prerequisite to becoming a Christian. The idea that God could accept a Gentile pagan was too incredible. But Gentiles began to accept Christ as Savior, and the transformation of their lives and the presence of God's Spirit confirmed their conversions. Some Jews were still reluctant and insisted these new Christians take on various Jewish customs. The issue came to a boiling point at the Jerusalem council but was peacefully resolved. Silas was one of the representatives from Jerusalem sent with Paul and Barnabas back to Antioch with an official letter of welcome and acceptance to the Gentile Christians. Having fulfilled this mission, Silas returned to Jerusalem. Within a short time, he was back in Antioch at Paul's request to join him on his second missionary journey. • Paul, Silas, and Timothy began a far-ranging ministry that included some exciting adventures. Paul and Silas spent a night singing in a Philippian jail after being severely beaten. An earthquake, the loosing of their chains, and the resulting panic led to the conversion of their jailer and his family. Later, they narrowly missed another beating in Thessalonica, prevented by an evening escape. In Berea there was more trouble, but Silas and Timothy stayed to teach the young believers, while Paul traveled on to Athens. The team was finally reunited in Corinth. In each place they visited, they left behind a small group of Christians. • Silas leaves the story as suddenly as he entered it. Peter mentions him at the beginning of 1 Peter, but we do not know when he joined Peter. He was an effective believer before leaving Jerusalem, and he doubtless continued to minister after his work with Paul was completed. He took advantage of opportunities to serve God and was not discouraged by the setbacks and opposition he met along the way. Silas, though not the most famous of the early missionaries, was certainly a hero worth imitating.

Strengths and accomplishments	• A leader in the Jerusalem church • Sang songs of praise to God while in jail with Paul in Philippi • Worked closely with both Paul and Peter
Lessons from his life	• Partnership is a significant part of effective ministry • God never guarantees that his servants will not suffer • Obedience to God will often mean giving up what makes us feel secure
Vital statistics	• Where: Roman citizen living in Jerusalem • Occupation: One of the first career missionaries • Contemporaries: Paul, Timothy, Peter, Mark, Barnabas
Key verses	"So we decided, having come to complete agreement, to send you official representatives, along with our beloved Barnabas and Paul, who have risked their lives for the name of our Lord Jesus Christ. We are sending Judas and Silas to confirm what we have decided concerning your question" (Acts 15:25-27).

Silas's story is told in Acts 15:22–19:10. He is also mentioned in 2 Corinthians 1:19; 1 Thessalonians 1:1; 2 Thessalonians 1:1; 1 Peter 5:12.

Acts 16:16 This girl's fortune-telling ability came from evil spirits. Fortune-telling was a common practice in Greek and Roman culture. There were many superstitious methods by which people thought they could foretell future events, from interpreting omens in nature to communicating with the spirits of the dead. This young slave girl had an evil spirit, and she made her master rich by interpreting signs and telling people their fortunes. The master was exploiting her unfortunate condition for personal gain.

Acts 16:17-18 What the slave girl said was true, although the source of her knowledge was a demon. Why did a demon announce the truth about Paul, and why did this annoy Paul? If Paul accepted the demon's words, he would appear to be linking the Good News with demon-related activities. This would damage his message about Christ. Truth and evil do not mix.

Acts 16:19 Faced with the loss of their slave girl's fortune-telling ability, the Philippian entrepreneurs were furious. Never mind that Paul and Silas were speaking eternal truths, never mind that the poor slave girl had been delivered from an awful existence; these men could only bemoan their economic loss! The gospel would also later hurt Ephesian idol makers financially (Acts 19), resulting in a citywide riot. When people care more about their own economic well-being than the glory of God and the salvation of lost souls, it is a clear sign of idolatry, greed, and worldliness.

▸ **ACTS 16:16-40** ***(cont.)***

22A mob quickly formed against Paul and Silas, and the city officials ordered them stripped and beaten with wooden rods. 23They were severely beaten, and then they were thrown into prison. The jailer was ordered to make sure they didn't escape. 24So the jailer put them into the inner dungeon and clamped their feet in the stocks.

25Around midnight Paul and Silas were praying and singing hymns to God, and the other prisoners were listening. 26Suddenly, there was a massive earthquake, and the prison was shaken to its foundations. All the doors immediately flew open, and the chains of every prisoner fell off! 27The jailer woke up to see the prison doors wide open. He assumed the prisoners had escaped, so he drew his sword to kill himself. 28But Paul shouted to him, "Stop! Don't kill yourself! We are all here!"

29The jailer called for lights and ran to the dungeon and fell down trembling before Paul and Silas. 30Then he brought them out and asked, "Sirs, what must I do to be saved?"

31They replied, "Believe in the Lord Jesus and you will be saved, along with everyone in your household." 32And they shared the word of the Lord with him and with all who lived in his household. 33Even at that hour of the night, the jailer cared for them and washed their wounds. Then he and everyone in his household were immediately baptized. 34He brought them into his house and set a meal before them, and he and his entire household rejoiced because they all believed in God.

35The next morning the city officials sent the police to tell the jailer, "Let those men go!" 36So the jailer told Paul, "The city officials have said you and Silas are free to leave. Go in peace."

37But Paul replied, "They have publicly beaten us without a trial and put us in prison—and we are Roman citizens. So now they want us to leave secretly? Certainly not! Let them come themselves to release us!"

38When the police reported this, the city officials were alarmed to learn that Paul and Silas were Roman citizens. 39So they came to the jail and apologized to them. Then they brought them out and begged them to leave the city. 40When Paul and Silas left the prison, they returned to the home of Lydia. There they met with the believers and encouraged them once more. Then they left town.

Paul Preaches in Thessalonica

ACTS 17:1-9

Paul and Silas then traveled through the towns of Amphipolis and Apollonia and came to Thessalonica, where there was a Jewish synagogue. 2As was Paul's custom, he went to the synagogue service, and for three Sabbaths in a row he used the Scriptures to reason with the people. 3He explained the prophecies and proved that the Messiah must suffer and rise from the dead. He said, "This Jesus I'm telling you about is the Messiah." 4Some of the Jews who listened were persuaded and joined Paul and Silas, along with many God-fearing Greek men and quite a few prominent women.*

Acts 17:4 Some manuscripts read *quite a few of the wives of the leading men.*

Acts 16:22-25 Paul and Silas were stripped, beaten, and placed in stocks in the inner cell. Stocks were made of two boards joined with iron clamps, leaving holes just big enough for the ankles. The prisoner's legs were placed across the lower board, and then the upper board was closed over them. Sometimes both wrists and ankles were placed in stocks. Paul and Silas, who had committed no crime and who were peaceful men, were put in stocks designed for holding the most dangerous prisoners in absolute security. Despite this dismal situation, they praised God, praying and singing as the other prisoners listened. No matter what our circumstances, we should praise God. Others may come to Christ because of our example.

Acts 16:27 The jailer drew his sword to kill himself because jailers were responsible for their prisoners and would be held accountable for their escape.

Acts 16:30-31 Paul and Silas's reputation in Philippi was well known. When the jailer realized his own condition and need, he risked everything to find the answer. The Good News of salvation is simply expressed: Believe in the Lord Jesus, and you will be saved (see Rom 10:9; 1 Cor 12:3; Eph 2:8-9; Phil 2:11). When we recognize Jesus as Lord and trust in him with our entire lives, salvation is assured to us. If you have never trusted in Jesus to save you, do so quickly. Your life can be filled with joy, just as the jailer's was (Acts 16:34).

Acts 16:31-34 Paul and Silas took the family unit seriously. So the offer of salvation was made to the jailer's entire household—family and servants. Yet it was not the jailer's faith that saved them; they all needed to come to Jesus in faith and believe in him in the same way the jailer had. His entire family did believe and all were saved. Pray that God will use you to introduce Jesus to your family and that they will come to believe in him.

Acts 16:37-38 Paul refused to take his freedom and run. He wanted to teach the city officials in Philippi a lesson and to protect the other believers from the treatment he and Silas had received. The word would spread that Paul and Silas had been found innocent and freed by the leaders, expressing the truth that believers should not be persecuted—especially if they were Roman citizens. Roman citizenship carried with it certain privileges. These Philippian authorities were alarmed because it was illegal to whip a Roman citizen. In addition, every citizen had the right to a fair trial, which Paul and Silas had not been given.

Acts 17:1 Thessalonica was one of the wealthiest and most influential cities in Macedonia. This is the first city Paul visited where his teachings attracted a large group of socially prominent citizens. The church he planted grew quickly, but from A.D. 50–51, Paul was forced out of the city by a mob (Acts 17:5-6, 10). He later sent Timothy back to Thessalonica to see how the Christians were doing. Soon afterward, Paul wrote two letters to the Thessalonian believers (the books of 1 and 2 Thessalonians), encouraging them to remain faithful and to refuse to listen to false teachers who tried to refute their beliefs.

Acts 17:1-2 A synagogue, a group of Jews who gathered for teaching and prayer, could be established wherever 10 Jewish males lived. Paul's regular practice was to preach in synagogues as long as the Jews allowed it. Often those who weren't Jews would come to these services and hear Paul's preaching. (For a description of a synagogue service, see the note on Acts 13:14-15, p. 1541.)

Acts 17:2-3 When Paul spoke in the synagogues, he wisely began by talking about Old Testament writings and explaining how the Messiah fulfilled them, moving from the known to the unknown. This is a good strategy for us. When we witness for Christ, we should begin where people are, affirming the truth they *do* know; and then we can present Christ, the one who is truth.

[5]But some of the Jews were jealous, so they gathered
some troublemakers from the marketplace to form a
mob and start a riot. They attacked the home of Jason, searching for Paul and Silas so they could drag
them out to the crowd.* [6]Not finding them there, they
dragged out Jason and some of the other believers*
instead and took them before the city council. "Paul
and Silas have caused trouble all over the world," they
shouted, "and now they are here disturbing our city,
too. [7]And Jason has welcomed them into his home.
They are all guilty of treason against Caesar, for they
profess allegiance to another king, named Jesus."
[8]The people of the city, as well as the city council,
were thrown into turmoil by these reports. [9]So the
officials forced Jason and the other believers to post
bond, and then they released them.

Paul and Silas in Berea

ACTS 17:10-15

That very night the believers sent Paul and Silas to
Berea. When they arrived there, they went to the Jewish synagogue. [11]And the people of Berea were more
open-minded than those in Thessalonica, and they
listened eagerly to Paul's message. They searched the
Scriptures day after day to see if Paul and Silas were
teaching the truth. [12]As a result, many Jews believed,
as did many of the prominent Greek women and men.
[13]But when some Jews in Thessalonica learned that
Paul was preaching the word of God in Berea, they
went there and stirred up trouble. [14]The believers
acted at once, sending Paul on to the coast, while Silas and Timothy remained behind. [15]Those escorting
Paul went with him all the way to Athens; then they
returned to Berea with instructions for Silas and Timothy to hurry and join him.

Paul Preaches in Athens

ACTS 17:16-34

While Paul was waiting for them in Athens, he was
deeply troubled by all the idols he saw everywhere in
the city. [17]He went to the synagogue to reason with the
Jews and the God-fearing Gentiles, and he spoke daily
in the public square to all who happened to be there.
[18]He also had a debate with some of the Epicurean
and Stoic philosophers. When he told them about
Jesus and his resurrection, they said, "What's this

Acts 17:5 Or *the city council.* **Acts 17:6** Greek *brothers;* also in 17:10, 14.

Acts 17:5 The Jewish leaders didn't try to refute the theology of Paul and Silas, but they were jealous of the popularity of these itinerant preachers. Their motives for causing the riot were rooted in personal jealousy, not doctrinal purity.

Acts 17:6 We don't know much about Jason except that he evidently was the local host and sponsor of Paul and Silas; thus, he took the heat for all the problems. Jason is just one of many "unsung heroes" who faithfully played their part to help spread the Good News. Because of Jason's courage, Paul and Silas were able to minister more effectively. You may not receive much attention (in fact, you may receive only grief) for your service for Christ. But God wants to use you. Lives will be changed because of your courage and faithfulness.

Acts 17:6 What a reputation these early Christians had! The power of the Good News revolutionized lives, broke down all social barriers, threw open prison doors, caused people to care deeply for one another, and stirred them to worship God. Our world needs to be turned upside down, to be transformed. The Good News doesn't merely improve programs and encourage good conduct; it dynamically transforms lives. Take courage and ask God how you can help spread his Good News throughout your world.

Acts 17:7 The Jewish leaders had to concoct charges against Paul and Silas that would be heard by the city government. The Romans did not care about theological disagreements between the Jews and these preachers. Treason, however, was a serious offense in the Roman Empire. Paul and Silas were not advocating rebellion against Roman law, but their loyalty to another king sounded suspicious.

Acts 17:8-9 Jason posted bond—putting up cash for freedom. By doing so, he promised that the trouble would cease or his own property and possibly his own life would be taken.

Acts 17:11 How do you evaluate sermons and teachings? The people in Berea searched the Scriptures for themselves to verify the message they heard. Always compare what you hear with what the Bible says. A preacher or teacher who gives God's true message will never contradict or explain away anything that is found in God's Word.

Acts 17:16 Athens, with its magnificent buildings and many gods, was a center for Greek culture, philosophy, and education. Philosophers and educated men were always ready to hear something new, so they invited Paul to speak to them at the meeting of the high council of the city (Acts 17:18-19).

Acts 17:16 Paul was filled with a combination of anger and grief by all the idols he saw in the city. Seeing people spiritually lost, blinded by Satan, and trapped in a pagan culture caused Paul to be in a state of emotional upheaval. Though highly educated, the Athenians were ignorant of the one true God. It's interesting to note that Paul turned his internal turmoil into positive action: He looked for opportunities to share the truth about Jesus. Does the lostness of people move you to action? And if so, do you seek opportunities to share the gospel?

Acts 17:18 The Epicureans and Stoics were the dominant philosophers in Greek culture. The Epicureans believed that seeking happiness or pleasure was the primary goal of life. By contrast, the Stoics placed thinking above feeling and tried to live in harmony with nature and reason, suppressing their desire for pleasure. Thus, they were very disciplined.

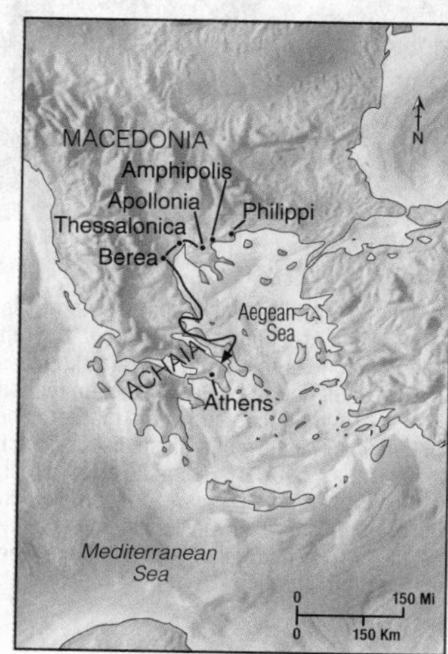

***MINISTRY IN MACEDONIA** Luke stayed in Philippi while Paul, Silas, and Timothy continued on the Egnatian Way to Amphipolis, Apollonia, and Thessalonica. But trouble arose in Thessalonica, and they fled to Berea. When their enemies from Thessalonica pursued them, Paul set out by sea to Athens, leaving Silas and Timothy to encourage the believers.*

▸ ACTS 17:16-34 ***(cont.)***

babbler trying to say with these strange ideas he's
picked up?" Others said, "He seems to be preaching
about some foreign gods."
[19]Then they took him to the high council of the
city.* "Come and tell us about this new teaching," they
said. [20]"You are saying some rather strange things, and
we want to know what it's all about." [21](It should be explained that all the Athenians as well as the foreigners
in Athens seemed to spend all their time discussing
the latest ideas.)
[22]So Paul, standing before the council,* addressed
them as follows: "Men of Athens, I notice that you are
very religious in every way, [23]for as I was walking along
I saw your many shrines. And one of your altars had
this inscription on it: 'To an Unknown God.' This God,
whom you worship without knowing, is the one I'm
telling you about.
[24]"He is the God who made the world and everything in it. Since he is Lord of heaven and earth, he
doesn't live in man-made temples, [25]and human
hands can't serve his needs—for he has no needs. He
himself gives life and breath to everything, and he
satisfies every need. [26]From one man* he created all
the nations throughout the whole earth. He decided
beforehand when they should rise and fall, and he
determined their boundaries.
[27]"His purpose was for the nations to seek after
God and perhaps feel their way toward him and find
him—though he is not far from any one of us. [28]For in
him we live and move and exist. As some of your* own
poets have said, 'We are his offspring.' [29]And since this

Acts 17:19 Or *the most learned society of philosophers in the city.* Greek reads *the Areopagus.* **Acts 17:22** Traditionally rendered *standing in the middle of Mars Hill;* Greek reads *standing in the middle of the Areopagus.* **Acts 17:26** Greek *From one;* other manuscripts read *From one blood.* **Acts 17:28** Some manuscripts read *our.*

The Areopagus

The Areopagus is a hill northwest of the Acropolis in Athens overlooking the marketplace (Acts 17:19). The Areopagus also refers to the Athenian council or court that met there. The irregular limestone outcropping was also known as Mars Hill, Mars being the Roman equivalent of the Greek god Ares. Paul had been reasoning with Jews and God-fearing Gentiles in the Athenian synagogue and in the marketplace for several days. Some Epicurean and Stoic philosophers involved in those discussions brought Paul before the council at the Areopagus (Acts 17:16-21). He spoke as an intelligent Christian believer who was able to meet the intellectual Athenians on their own ground (Acts 17:22-31). Some remained skeptical, but his address was convincing to a few who "joined him and became believers" (Acts 17:32-34). Be mindful of your audience when you share the Good News; make it pertinent to their situation.

Acts 17:19 For a time the council met on a low hill in Athens near the Acropolis. As Paul stood there and spoke about the one true God, his audience could look down on the city and see the many idols representing gods that Paul knew were worthless.

Acts 17:22 Paul was well prepared to speak to this group. He came from Tarsus, an educational center, and had the training and knowledge to present his beliefs clearly and persuasively. Paul was a rabbi, taught by the finest scholar of his day, Gamaliel, and he had spent much of his life thinking and reasoning through the Scriptures.

It is not enough to teach or preach with conviction. Like Paul, we must be prepared. The more we know about the Bible, what it means, and how to apply it to life, the more convincing our words will be. This does not mean that we should avoid presenting the Good News until we feel adequately prepared. We should use what we have learned but always seek to know more in order to be an effective witness and be able to respond to people's questions and arguments.

Acts 17:22ff Paul's address is a good example of how to communicate the Good News. Paul did not begin by reciting Jewish history, as he usually did, for this would have been meaningless to his Greek audience. He began by building a case for the one true God, using examples they understood (Acts 17:22-23). The Athenians had built an idol to the unknown god for fear of missing blessings or receiving punishment. Paul's opening statement to the men of Athens was about their unknown god. Paul was not endorsing this god but using the inscription as a point of entry for his witness to the one true God. Then he established common ground by emphasizing what they agreed on about God (Acts 17:24-29). Finally, he moved his message to the person of Christ, centering on the Resurrection (Acts 17:30-31). When you witness to others, you can follow Paul's approach: Use examples, establish common ground, and then move people toward a decision about Jesus Christ.

Gold Coin of Claudius

Claudius Caesar (who ruled A.D. 41–54) issued an edict expelling all Jews from Rome. Luke tells us that Aquila and Priscilla were among those who had been ordered to leave the imperial city (Acts 18:2). The Roman biographer and historian Suetonius wrote that "because the Jews of Rome were indulging at constant riots at the instigation of Chrestus, he [Claudius] expelled them from the city." Most scholars agree that the name Chrestus was an alternate spelling for the name Christus (Christ), viewed by Romans at that time as the founder of a movement (Christianity) that had evolved from Judaism. History tells us that God's people have often been banished from various areas, but we must remember that our true home is in heaven (see Heb 11:37-38).

is true, we shouldn't think of God as an idol designed by craftsmen from gold or silver or stone.

30"God overlooked people's ignorance about these things in earlier times, but now he commands everyone everywhere to repent of their sins and turn to
him. 31For he has set a day for judging the world with justice by the man he has appointed, and he proved to everyone who this is by raising him from the dead."
32When they heard Paul speak about the resurrection of the dead, some laughed in contempt, but others said, "We want to hear more about this later."
33That ended Paul's discussion with them, 34but some joined him and became believers. Among them were Dionysius, a member of the council,* a woman named Damaris, and others with them.

Paul Meets Priscilla and Aquila in Corinth

ACTS 18:1-11

Then Paul left Athens and went to Corinth.* 2There he
became acquainted with a Jew named Aquila, born in Pontus, who had recently arrived from Italy with his

Acts 17:34 Greek *an Areopagite.* **Acts 18:1** *Athens* and *Corinth* were major cities in Achaia, the region in the southern portion of the Greek peninsula.

Acts 17:23 Paul explained the one true God to these educated men of Athens; although these men were, in general, very religious, they did not know God. Today we have a "Christian" society, but to most people, God is still unknown. We need to proclaim who he is and make clear what he did for everyone through his Son, Jesus Christ. We cannot assume that even religious people around us truly know Jesus or understand the importance of faith in him.

Acts 17:27-28 God is in his creation and close to every one of us. But he is not trapped in his creation—he is transcendent. God is the Creator, not the creation. This means that God is sovereign and in control, while at the same time he is close and personal. Let the Creator of the universe rule your life.

Acts 17:30-31 Paul did not leave his message unfinished. He confronted his listeners with Jesus' resurrection and its meaning to all people—either blessing or punishment. The Greeks had no concept of judgment. Most of them preferred worshiping many gods instead of just one, and the concept of resurrection was unbelievable and offensive to them. Paul did not hold back the truth no matter what they might think of it. Paul often changed his approach to fit his audience, but he never changed his basic message.

Acts 17:32-34 Paul's speech received a mixed reaction: Some laughed, some wanted more information, and a few believed. Don't hesitate to tell others about Christ because you fear that some will not believe you. Don't expect a unanimously positive response to your witnessing. Even if only a few believe, it's worth the effort.

Acts 18:1 Corinth was the political and commercial center of Greece, surpassing Athens in importance. It had a reputation for great wickedness and immorality. A temple to Aphrodite, goddess of love and war, had been built on the large hill behind the city. In this popular religion, people worshiped the goddess by giving money to the temple and taking part in sexual acts with male and female temple prostitutes. Paul found Corinth a challenge and a great ministry opportunity. Later, he would write a series of letters to the Corinthians dealing in part with the problems of immorality. Two of these letters are the books of 1 and 2 Corinthians.

AQUILA & PRISCILLA

Some married couples know how to make the most of life. They complement each other, capitalize on each other's strengths, and form an effective team. Their united efforts affect those around them. Aquila and Priscilla were such a couple. They are never mentioned separately in the Bible. In marriage and ministry, they operated as one. • Priscilla and Aquila met Paul in Corinth during his second missionary journey. They had just been expelled from Rome by Emperor Claudius's decree against Jews. Their home was as movable as the tents they made to support themselves. They opened their home to Paul, and he joined them in tentmaking. He shared with them his wealth of spiritual wisdom. • Priscilla and Aquila made the most of their spiritual education. They listened carefully to sermons and evaluated what they heard. When they heard Apollos speak, they were impressed by his ability but realized that his information was not complete. Instead of open confrontation, the couple quietly took Apollos home and shared with him what he needed to know. Until then, Apollos had only been aware of John the Baptist's message about Christ. Priscilla and Aquila told him about Jesus' life, death, and resurrection, and the reality of God's indwelling Spirit. He continued to preach powerfully—but now with the full story. • As for Priscilla and Aquila, they went on using their home as a warm place for training and worship. Back in Rome years later, they hosted one of the house churches that developed. • In an age when the focus is mostly on what happens *between* a husband and wife, Aquila and Priscilla are an example of what can happen *through* a husband and wife. Their effectiveness together is the result of their good relationship with each other. Their hospitality opened the doorway of salvation to many. The Christian home is still one of the best tools for spreading the gospel. Do guests find Christ in your home?

Strengths and accomplishments	• Outstanding husband/wife team who ministered in the early church • Close friends of Paul • Explained to Apollos the full message of Christ
Lessons from their lives	• Couples can have an effective ministry together • The home is a valuable tool for evangelism
Vital statistics	• Where: Originally from Rome, moved to Corinth, then Ephesus • Occupation: Tentmakers • Contemporaries: Emperor Claudius, Paul, Timothy, Apollos
Key verses	"Give my greetings to Priscilla and Aquila, my co-workers in the ministry of Christ Jesus. In fact, they once risked their lives for me. I am thankful to them, and so are all the Gentile churches" (Rom 16:3-4).

Their story is told in Acts 18. They are also mentioned in Romans 16:3-5; 1 Corinthians 16:19; 2 Timothy 4:19.

Acts 18:2-3 Each Jewish boy learned a trade and tried to earn his living with it. Paul and Aquila had been trained in tentmaking, cutting and sewing the woven cloth of goats' hair into tents. Tents were used to house soldiers, so these tents may have been sold to the Roman army. As a tentmaker, Paul was able to go wherever God led him, carrying his livelihood with him. The word *tentmaker* in Greek was also used to describe a leatherworker.

AD 50 Romans begin using soap

▶ **ACTS 18:1-11** ***(cont.)***
wife, Priscilla. They had left Italy when Claudius Caesar
deported all Jews from Rome. 3 Paul lived and worked
with them, for they were tentmakers* just as he was.
4 Each Sabbath found Paul at the synagogue, trying
to convince the Jews and Greeks alike. 5 And after Silas
and Timothy came down from Macedonia, Paul spent
all his time preaching the word. He testified to the Jews
that Jesus was the Messiah. 6 But when they opposed
and insulted him, Paul shook the dust from his clothes
and said, "Your blood is upon your own heads—I am
innocent. From now on I will go preach to the Gentiles."
7 Then he left and went to the home of Titius Justus,
a Gentile who worshiped God and lived next door to
the synagogue. 8 Crispus, the leader of the synagogue,
and everyone in his household believed in the Lord.
Many others in Corinth also heard Paul, became believers, and were baptized.
9 One night the Lord spoke to Paul in a vision and
told him, "Don't be afraid! Speak out! Don't be silent!
10 For I am with you, and no one will attack and harm
you, for many people in this city belong to me." 11 So
Paul stayed there for the next year and a half, teaching
the word of God.

Acts 18:3 Or *leatherworkers.*

G. Paul's Letters to the Thessalonians

During Paul's year-and-a-half stay in Corinth, he heard reports about how the believers were doing in some of the other cities that he had ministered in. One of those cities was Thessalonica, and the reports he heard led him to write two letters to them to encourage them in their faith and instruct them on some matters.

1. PAUL'S FIRST LETTER TO THE THESSALONIANS

Paul wrote this letter a short time after his ministry in Thessalonica to encourage the young believers there. He wanted to assure the Thessalonian believers of his love for them, to praise them for their faithfulness in spite of persecution, and to remind them of their hope in the return of Jesus, their Lord and Savior. As you read this letter, listen carefully to Paul's practical advice for Christian living.

AD 50

Paul writes letters to the church in Thessalonica

Greetings from Paul

1 THESSALONIANS 1:1
This letter is from Paul, Silas,* and Timothy.
We are writing to the church in Thessalonica, to
you who belong to God the Father and the Lord Jesus
Christ.
May God give you grace and peace.

1 Thes 1:1 Greek *Silvanus,* the Greek form of the name.

The Faith of the Thessalonian Believers

1 THESSALONIANS 1:2-10
We always thank God for all of you and pray for you
constantly. 3 As we pray to our God and Father about
you, we think of your faithful work, your loving deeds,
and the enduring hope you have because of our Lord
Jesus Christ.

Acts 18:6 Paul told the Jews he had done all he could for them. Because they had rejected Jesus as their Messiah, he would go to the Gentiles, who would be more receptive.

Acts 18:10 In a vision, Christ told Paul that he had many people in Corinth. Sometimes we can feel alone or isolated, especially when we see wickedness all around us or are persecuted for our faith. Usually there are others in the neighborhood or community who also follow Christ. Ask God to lead you to them.

Acts 18:10-11 Others who became Christians in Corinth were Phoebe (Rom 16:1; Cenchrea was the port city of Corinth), Tertius (Rom 16:22), Erastus and Quartus (Rom 16:23), Chloe (1 Cor 1:11), Gaius (1 Cor 1:14), Stephanas and his household (1 Cor 16:15), and Fortunatus and Achaicus (1 Cor 16:17).

Acts 18:11 During the year and a half that Paul stayed in Corinth, he established a church there and wrote two letters to the believers in Thessalonica (the books of 1 and 2 Thessalonians). Although Paul had been in Thessalonica for only a short time (Acts 17:1-15), he commended the believers there for their loving deeds, strong faith, and endurance inspired by hope. While encouraging them to stay away from immorality, he dealt with the themes of salvation, suffering, and the second coming of Jesus Christ. Paul told them to continue to work hard while they awaited Christ's return.

1 Thes 1:1 Paul and his companions probably arrived in Thessalonica in the early summer of A.D. 50. They planted the first Christian church in that city, but had to leave in a hurry because their lives were threatened (Acts 17:1-10). At the first opportunity, probably when he stopped at Corinth, Paul sent Timothy back to Thessalonica to see how the new believers were doing. Timothy returned to Paul with good news: The Christians in Thessalonica were remaining firm in the faith and were unified. But the Thessalonians did have some questions about their new faith. Paul had not had time to answer all their questions during his brief visit, and in the meantime, other questions had arisen. So Paul wrote this letter to answer their questions and to commend them on their faithfulness to Christ.

1 Thes 1:1 For more information on Paul, see his Profile on p. 1571. Silas accompanied Paul on his second missionary journey (Acts 15:36–17:15). He helped Paul establish the church in Thessalonica (Acts 17:1-9). He is also mentioned in 2 Corinthians 1:19; 2 Thessalonians 1:1; 1 Peter 5:12. Silas's Profile is on p. 1575. Timothy's Profile is on p. 1727.

1 Thes 1:1 Thessalonica was the capital and largest city (about 200,000 population) of the Roman province of Macedonia. The most important Roman highway (the Egnatian Way)—extending from Rome all the way to the Orient—went through Thessalonica. This highway, along with the city's thriving seaport, made Thessalonica one of the wealthi-

4We know, dear brothers and sisters,* that God
loves you and has chosen you to be his own people.
5For when we brought you the Good News, it was not
only with words but also with power, for the Holy Spirit
gave you full assurance* that what we said was true.
And you know of our concern for you from the way
we lived when we were with you. 6So you received
the message with joy from the Holy Spirit in spite of
the severe suffering it brought you. In this way, you
imitated both us and the Lord. 7As a result, you have
become an example to all the believers in Greece—
throughout both Macedonia and Achaia.*
8And now the word of the Lord is ringing out from
you to people everywhere, even beyond Macedonia
and Achaia, for wherever we go we find people telling
us about your faith in God. We don't need to tell them
about it, 9for they keep talking about the wonderful
welcome you gave us and how you turned away from
idols to serve the living and true God. 10And they speak
of how you are looking forward to the coming of God's
Son from heaven—Jesus, whom God raised from the
dead. He is the one who has rescued us from the terrors of the coming judgment.

Paul Remembers His Visit

1 THESSALONIANS 2:1-16

You yourselves know, dear brothers and sisters,* that
our visit to you was not a failure. 2You know how badly
we had been treated at Philippi just before we came
to you and how much we suffered there. Yet our God
gave us the courage to declare his Good News to you
boldly, in spite of great opposition. 3So you can see we
were not preaching with any deceit or impure motives
or trickery.
4For we speak as messengers approved by God to
be entrusted with the Good News. Our purpose is to
please God, not people. He alone examines the motives of our hearts. 5Never once did we try to win you
with flattery, as you well know. And God is our witness
that we were not pretending to be your friends just to

1 Thes 1:4 Greek *brothers.* **1 Thes 1:5** Or *with the power of the Holy Spirit, so you can have full assurance.* **1 Thes 1:7** *Macedonia* and *Achaia* were the northern and southern regions of Greece. **1 Thes 2:1** Greek *brothers;* also in 2:9, 14, 17.

est and most flourishing trade centers in the Roman Empire. Recognized as a free city, Thessalonica was allowed self-rule and was exempt from most of the restrictions placed by Rome on other cities in the empire. With its international flavor came many pagan religions and cultural influences that challenged the faith of the young Christians there.

1 Thes 1:3 The Thessalonians had stood firm when they were persecuted (1 Thes 1:6; 3:1-4, 7-8). Paul commended these young Christians for their faithful work, loving deeds, and anticipation of the Lord's return. These characteristics are the marks of effective Christians in any age.

1 Thes 1:4 Paul reminded the Thessalonians of their status as God's "chosen" ones. Very few issues cause more confusion and even arguments among Christians than the issue of election (being chosen by God). It is difficult to simultaneously embrace God's sovereignty in choosing us and our human responsibility in choosing to follow him. Even though we may not be able to completely comprehend how these two truths can coexist, we can say the following: Being chosen comes from the heart of God (not from our minds); this should be an incentive to please God (not ignore him) and should give birth to gratitude (not complacency). Human responsibility requires that we actively confess Christ as Lord, focus on living to please him, and share the gospel with others.

God's choice of us energizes us to obey and to serve. Our choice of God challenges us to build lives worthy of him. As you consider God's divine selection of you, how do you respond?

1 Thes 1:5 The Good News came "with power"; it had a powerful effect on the Thessalonians. Whenever the Bible is heard and obeyed, lives are changed! Christianity is more than a collection of interesting facts; it is the power of God for everyone who believes. What has God's power done in your life since you first believed?

1 Thes 1:5 The Holy Spirit changes people when they believe the Good News. When we tell others about Christ, we must depend on the Holy Spirit to open their eyes and convince them that they need salvation. God's power—not our cleverness or persuasion—changes people. Without the work of the Holy Spirit, our words are meaningless. The Holy Spirit not only convicts people of sin but also assures them of the truth of the Good News. (For more information on the Holy Spirit, see John 14:23-26; 15:26-27. See also the notes on John 3:6, p. 1301; Acts 1:5, p. 1499.)

1 Thes 1:5 Paul wrote, "And you know of our concern for you from the way we lived when we were with you." The Thessalonians had seen that what Paul, Silas, and Timothy were preaching was true because these men had lived it. Does your life confirm or contradict what you say you believe?

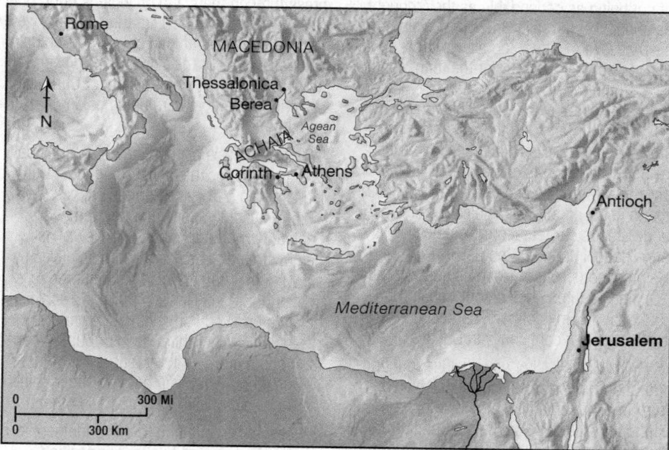

LOCATION OF THESSALONICA *Thessalonica was a seaport and trade center located on the Egnatian Way, a busy international highway. After Paul visited Thessalonica on his second missionary journey, he went on to Berea, Athens, and Corinth (Acts 17–18). Paul probably wrote his two letters to the Thessalonians from Corinth.*

▸ 1 THESSALONIANS 2:1-16 *(cont.)*

get your money! 6As for human praise, we have never
sought it from you or anyone else.
7As apostles of Christ we certainly had a right to
make some demands of you, but instead we were like
children* among you. Or we were like a mother feeding and caring for her own children. 8We loved you
so much that we shared with you not only God's Good
News but our own lives, too.
9Don't you remember, dear brothers and sisters,
how hard we worked among you? Night and day we
toiled to earn a living so that we would not be a burden
to any of you as we preached God's Good News to you.
10You yourselves are our witnesses—and so is God—
that we were devout and honest and faultless toward
all of you believers. 11And you know that we treated
each of you as a father treats his own children. 12We
pleaded with you, encouraged you, and urged you to
live your lives in a way that God would consider worthy.
For he called you to share in his Kingdom and glory.
13Therefore, we never stop thanking God that when
you received his message from us, you didn't think of
our words as mere human ideas. You accepted what
we said as the very word of God—which, of course, it
is. And this word continues to work in you who believe.
14And then, dear brothers and sisters, you suffered

1 Thes 2:7 Some manuscripts read *we were gentle.*

---

1 Thes 1:6 The message of salvation, though welcomed with great joy, brought the Thessalonians severe suffering because it led to persecution from both Jews and Gentiles (1 Thes 3:2-4; Acts 17:5). Many believers today think that pain is the exception in the Christian life. When suffering occurs, they say, "Why me?" They feel as though God deserted them, or perhaps they accuse him of not being as dependable as they thought he should be. In reality, the world is sinful, so even believers suffer. God allows some Christians to become martyrs for the faith, and he allows others to survive persecution. Rather than asking, "Why me?" we should ask, "Why not me?" Our faith and the values of this world are on a collision course. If we expect pain and suffering to come, we will not be shocked when they occur. We can take comfort in knowing that Jesus also suffered. He understands our fears, our weaknesses, and our disappointments (Heb 2:16-18; 4:14-16). He promised never to leave us (Matt 28:18-20), and he intercedes on our behalf (Heb 7:24-25). In times of pain, persecution, or suffering, trust confidently in Christ.

1 Thes 1:9-10 All of us should respond to the Good News as the Thessalonians did: Turn to God, serve him, and look forward to the return of his Son, Jesus Christ, from heaven. We should turn from sin to God because Christ is coming to judge the earth. We should be fervent in our service because we have little time before Christ returns. At all times we should be prepared for Christ to return because we don't know when he will come.

1 Thes 1:10 Paul emphasized Christ's second coming throughout this book. Because the Thessalonian church was being persecuted, Paul encouraged them to look forward to the deliverance that Christ would bring. A believer's hope is in the return of Jesus (Titus 2:13). Our perspective on life remains incomplete without this hope. Just as surely as Christ was raised from the dead and ascended into heaven, he will return (Acts 1:11).

1 Thes 2:1-2 "Our visit to you" refers to Paul's first visit to Thessalonica recorded in Acts 17:1-9. The Thessalonians knew that Paul had been imprisoned in Philippi just prior to coming to Thessalonica (see Acts 16:11–17:1). Fear of imprisonment did not keep Paul from preaching the Good News. If God wants us to do something, he will give us the strength and courage to boldly speak out for him despite any obstacles that may come our way. Boldness is not reckless impulsiveness. Boldness requires courage to press through fears and do what is right. How can we be more bold? Like the apostles, we need to pray for that kind of courage. To gain boldness, pray for the Holy Spirit's power, look for opportunities to talk about Christ, and start right where you are being bolder in even small ways.

1 Thes 2:3 This pointed statement may be a response to accusations from the Jewish leaders who had stirred up the crowds (Acts 17:5). Paul did not seek money, fame, or popularity by sharing the Good News. He demonstrated the sincerity of his motives by showing that he and Silas had suffered for sharing the Good News in Philippi. People become involved in ministry for a variety of reasons, not all of them good or pure. When their bad motives are exposed, all of Christ's work suffers. When you get involved in ministry, do so out of love for Christ and others.

1 Thes 2:4-8 In trying to persuade people, we may be tempted to alter our position just enough to make our message more palatable or to use flattery or praise. Paul never changed his message to make it more acceptable, but he did tailor his methods to each audience. Although our presentation must be altered to be appropriate to the situation, the truth of the Good News must never be compromised.

1 Thes 2:5 It's disgusting to hear a person butter up someone. Flattery is phony, and it covers up a person's real intentions. Christians should not be flatterers. Those who proclaim God's truth have a special responsibility to be honest. Are you honest and straightforward in your words and actions? Or do you tell people what *they* want to hear in order to get what *you* want or to get ahead?

1 Thes 2:6-8 When Paul was with the Thessalonians, he didn't flatter them, seek their praise, or become a burden to them. He and Silas completely focused their efforts on presenting God's message of salvation. This was important! The Thessalonian believers had their lives changed by God, not Paul; it was Christ's message they believed, not Paul's. When we witness for Christ, our focus should not be on the impression we make. As true ministers of Christ, we should point to *him*, not to ourselves.

1 Thes 2:7 That Paul and his companions "were like children" among the Thessalonians does not mean they were immature or untrained. Rather, Paul was making the point that, like children, they were honest, straightforward, and without guile in their presentation of the gospel and of their lives.

1 Thes 2:9 Although Paul had the right to receive financial support from the people he taught, he supported himself as a tentmaker (Acts 18:3) so that he wouldn't be a burden to the new Thessalonian believers.

1 Thes 2:11 No loving father would neglect the safety of his children, allowing them to walk into circumstances that might be harmful or fatal. In the same way, we must take new believers under our wing until they are mature enough to stand firm in their faith. We must help new Christians become strong enough to influence others for the sake of the Good News.

1 Thes 2:12 By his words and example, Paul encouraged the Thessalonians to live in a way God would consider worthy. Is there anything about your daily life that would embarrass God? What do people think of God from watching you?

1 Thes 2:13 Paul said that the word of God continued to work in the believers' lives. Paul knew that God's words are not mere sermons or documents but a real source of transforming power. This Bible you hold in your hands is full of real and living power. Its words are transforming lives all over the world every day. Read it. Encourage fellow believers to read it. Encourage non-Christian friends to read it. All who do so, truly seeking to learn, will be touched by its power. They will never be the same.

1 Thes 2:14 Just as the Jewish Christians in Jerusalem were persecuted by other Jews,

persecution from your own countrymen. In this way,
you imitated the believers in God's churches in Judea
who, because of their belief in Christ Jesus, suffered
from their own people, the Jews. [15]For some of the
Jews killed the prophets, and some even killed the
Lord Jesus. Now they have persecuted us, too. They
fail to please God and work against all humanity [16]as
they try to keep us from preaching the Good News of
salvation to the Gentiles. By doing this, they continue
to pile up their sins. But the anger of God has caught
up with them at last.

Timothy's Good Report about the Church

1 THESSALONIANS 2:17–3:13

Dear brothers and sisters, after we were separated
from you for a little while (though our hearts never
left you), we tried very hard to come back because
of our intense longing to see you again. [18]We wanted
very much to come to you, and I, Paul, tried again and
again, but Satan prevented us. [19]After all, what gives
us hope and joy, and what will be our proud reward
and crown as we stand before our Lord Jesus when
he returns? It is you! [20]Yes, you are our pride and joy.

3:1 Finally, when we could stand it no longer, we decided to stay alone in Athens, [2]and we sent Timothy
to visit you. He is our brother and God's co-worker* in
proclaiming the Good News of Christ. We sent him to
strengthen you, to encourage you in your faith, [3]and to
keep you from being shaken by the troubles you were
going through. But you know that we are destined
for such troubles. [4]Even while we were with you, we
warned you that troubles would soon come—and they
did, as you well know. [5]That is why, when I could bear
it no longer, I sent Timothy to find out whether your
faith was still strong. I was afraid that the tempter had
gotten the best of you and that our work had been
useless.

[6]But now Timothy has just returned, bringing us
good news about your faith and love. He reports that
you always remember our visit with joy and that you
want to see us as much as we want to see you. [7]So
we have been greatly encouraged in the midst of our
troubles and suffering, dear brothers and sisters,*
because you have remained strong in your faith. [8]It
gives us new life to know that you are standing firm
in the Lord.

1 Thes 3:2 Other manuscripts read *and God's servant;* still others read *and a co-worker,* or *and a servant and co-worker for God,* or *and God's servant and our co-worker.*
1 Thes 3:7 Greek *brothers.*

---

so the Gentile Christians in Thessalonica were persecuted by their fellow Gentiles. Persecution is discouraging, especially when it comes from your own people. When you take a stand for Christ, you may face opposition, disapproval, and ridicule from your neighbors, friends, and even family members.

1 Thes 2:14 When Paul refers to the Jews, he is talking about certain Jews who opposed his preaching of the Good News. He does not mean all Jews. Many of Paul's converts were Jewish. Paul himself was a Jew (2 Cor 11:22).

1 Thes 2:15 Having believed the Good News and accepted new life in Christ, apparently many Thessalonians thought that they would be protected from death until Christ returned. Then, when believers began to die under persecution, some Thessalonian Christians started to question their faith. Many of Paul's comments throughout this letter were addressed to these people, as he explained what happens when believers die (see 1 Thes 4:13ff).

1 Thes 2:15-16 Why were so many Jews opposed to Christianity? (1) Although the Jewish religion had been declared legal by the Roman government, it still had a tenuous relationship with the government. At this time, Christianity was viewed as a sect of Judaism. The Jews were afraid that reprisals leveled against the Christians might be expanded to include them. (2) The Jewish leaders thought Jesus was a false prophet, and they didn't want his teachings to spread. (3) The leaders feared that if many Jews were drawn away, their own political position might be weakened. (4) Jews were proud of their special status as God's chosen people and resented the fact that Gentiles could be full members within the Christian church.

1 Thes 2:18 Satan is real. He is called "the god of this world" (2 Cor 4:4) and "the commander of the powers in the unseen world" (Eph 2:2). We don't know exactly what hindered Paul from returning to Thessalonica—opposition, illness, travel complications, or a direct attack by Satan—but Satan worked in some way to keep him away. Many of the difficulties that prevent us from accomplishing God's work can be attributed to Satan (see Eph 6:12).

1 Thes 2:20 The ultimate reward for Paul's ministry was not money, prestige, or fame, but new believers whose lives had been changed by God through the preaching of the Good News. This was why he longed to see them. No matter what ministry God has given to you, your highest reward and greatest joy should be those who come to believe in Christ and are growing in him.

1 Thes 3:1-3 Some think that troubles are always caused by sin or a lack of faith. Trials may be a part of God's plan for believers. Experiencing problems and persecutions can build character (Jas 1:2-4), perseverance (Rom 5:3-5), and sensitivity toward others who also face trouble (2 Cor 1:3-7). Problems are unavoidable for God's people. Your troubles may be a sign of effective Christian living.

1 Thes 3:2-5 Because Paul could not return to Thessalonica (1 Thes 2:18), he sent Timothy as his representative. According to Acts 17:10, Paul left Thessalonica and went to Berea. When trouble broke out in Berea, some Christians took Paul to Athens, while Silas and Timothy stayed behind (Acts 17:13-15). Then Paul directed Silas and Timothy to join him in Athens. Later, Paul sent Timothy to encourage the Thessalonian Christians to be strong in their faith in the face of persecution and other troubles.

1 Thes 3:4 Some people turn to God with the hope of escaping suffering on earth. But God doesn't promise that. Instead, he gives us power to grow through our sufferings. The Christian life involves obedience to Christ despite temptations and hardships.

1 Thes 3:5 Satan ("the tempter") is the most powerful of the evil spirits. His power can affect both the spiritual world (Eph 2:1-3; 6:10-12) and the physical world (2 Cor 12:7-10). Satan even tempted Jesus (Matt 4:1-11). But Jesus defeated Satan when he died on the cross for our sins and rose again to bring us new life. At the proper time God will overthrow Satan forever (Rev 20:7-10).

1 Thes 3:7-8 During persecution or pressure, believers should encourage one another. Christians who stand firm in the Lord are an encouragement to ministers and teachers (who can see the benefit of their work in those who remain faithful) and also an encouragement to those who are new in their faith (who can learn from the steadfastness of the mature).

▸1 THESSALONIANS 2:17-3:13 *(cont.)*

[9]How we thank God for you! Because of you we have great joy as we enter God's presence. [10]Night and day we pray earnestly for you, asking God to let us see you again to fill the gaps in your faith.

[11]May God our Father and our Lord Jesus bring us to you very soon. [12]And may the Lord make your love for one another and for all people grow and overflow, just as our love for you overflows. [13]May he, as a result, make your hearts strong, blameless, and holy as you stand before God our Father when our Lord Jesus comes again with all his holy people. Amen.

Live to Please God

1 THESSALONIANS 4:1-12

Finally, dear brothers and sisters,* we urge you in the name of the Lord Jesus to live in a way that pleases God, as we have taught you. You live this way already, and we encourage you to do so even more. [2]For you remember what we taught you by the authority of the Lord Jesus.

[3]God's will is for you to be holy, so stay away from all sexual sin. [4]Then each of you will control his own body* and live in holiness and honor—[5]not in lustful passion like the pagans who do not know God and his ways. [6]Never harm or cheat a Christian brother in this matter by violating his wife,* for the Lord avenges all such sins, as we have solemnly warned you before. [7]God has called us to live holy lives, not impure lives. [8]Therefore, anyone who refuses to live by these rules is not disobeying human teaching but is rejecting God, who gives his Holy Spirit to you.

[9]But we don't need to write to you about the importance of loving each other,* for God himself has taught you to love one another. [10]Indeed, you already show your love for all the believers* throughout Macedonia. Even so, dear brothers and sisters, we urge you to love them even more.

[11]Make it your goal to live a quiet life, minding your own business and working with your hands, just as we instructed you before. [12]Then people who are not Christians will respect the way you live, and you will not need to depend on others.

The Hope of the Resurrection

1 THESSALONIANS 4:13–5:11

And now, dear brothers and sisters, we want you to know what will happen to the believers who have

1 Thes 4:1 Greek *brothers;* also in 4:10, 13. **1 Thes 4:4** Or *will know how to take a wife for himself;* or *will learn to live with his own wife;* Greek reads *will know how to possess his own vessel.* **1 Thes 4:6** Greek *Never harm or cheat a brother in this matter.* **1 Thes 4:9** Greek *about brotherly love.* **1 Thes 4:10** Greek *the brothers.*

---

1 Thes 3:9-10 It brings great joy to a Christian to see another person come to faith in Christ and mature in that faith. Paul experienced this joy countless times. He thanked God for those who had come to know Christ and for their strong faith. He also prayed for their continued growth. If new Christians have brought you joy, thank God for them and support them as they continue to grow in the faith. Likewise, have you benefited from the ministry of others? Has someone's guidance and faithfulness stimulated you to grow in Christ? Consider how you may bring that person a word of encouragement or a thoughtful gift. Let that important person know that you have followed their example by being faithful to Christ.

1 Thes 3:11 Paul wanted to return to Thessalonica. We have no record that he was able to do so; but when he was traveling through Asia on his third journey, he was joined by Aristarchus and Secundus, who were from Thessalonica (Acts 20:4-5).

1 Thes 3:12 If we are full of God's love, it will overflow to others. It's not enough merely to be courteous to others; we must actively and persistently show love to them. Our love should be growing continually. If your capacity to love has remained unchanged for some time, ask God to fill you again with his never-ending supply. Then look for opportunities to let his love spill over in refreshment to others.

1 Thes 3:13 "When our Lord Jesus comes again with all his holy people" refers to the second coming of Christ when he will establish his eternal Kingdom. At that time, Christ will gather all believers, those who have died and those who are alive, into one united family under his rule. All believers from all times, including these Thessalonian believers, will be with Christ in his Kingdom.

1 Thes 4:1-8 Sexual standards were very low in the Roman Empire, and in many societies today, they are not any higher. The temptation to engage in sexual intercourse outside the marriage relationship has always been powerful. Giving in to that temptation can have disastrous results. Sexual sins always hurt someone: individuals, families, churches. Sexual desires and activities must be placed under Christ's control. God created sex for procreation and pleasure and as an expression of love between a husband and wife. Therefore, the sexual experience must be limited to the marriage. Besides the physical consequences of sexual sin, there are also spiritual consequences. (For more on why sexual sin is so harmful, see the note on 1 Cor 6:18, p. 1604.)

1 Thes 4:3 It is God's will for you to be holy, but how can you go about doing that? The Bible teaches that holiness is not a state of being that you must manufacture on your own with hard work and good deeds and constant fear of failure. Instead, being made holy occurs in the process of living the Christian life. If you have accepted Christ's sacrifice on your behalf, then you are considered holy and complete in God's eyes. Yet you must continue to learn and grow during your time on earth. The Holy Spirit works in you, conforming you to the image of Christ (Rom 8:29).

1 Thes 4:4-5 Paul said that lustful passions should not control God's people. Some argue that if they've already sinned by having lustful thoughts, they might as well go ahead with lustful actions, too. Acting out sinful desires is harmful in several ways: (1) It causes people to excuse sin rather than to stop sinning; (2) it destroys marriages; (3) it is deliberate rebellion against God's Word; and (4) it always hurts someone else in addition to the sinner. Sinful action is more dangerous than sinful desire, so desires should not be acted out. Nevertheless, sinful desire is just as damaging to righteousness. Left unchecked, wrong desires will result in wrong actions and will turn people away from God.

1 Thes 4:11-12 Christian living is more than simply loving other Christians. We must be responsible in all areas of life. Some of the Thessalonian Christians had adopted a life of idleness, depending on others for handouts. Some Greeks looked down on manual labor. So Paul told the Thessalonians to work hard and live quiet lives. You can't be effective in sharing your faith with others if they don't respect you. Whatever you do, do it faithfully and be a positive force in society.

1 Thes 4:13ff The Thessalonians were wondering why many of their fellow believers had died and what would happen to them when Christ returned. Paul wanted the Thessalonians to understand that death is not the end of the story. The great hope for all believers is in the Resurrection. Because Jesus Christ came back to life, so will all believers, including those who have already died. Therefore, we need not despair when

died* so you will not grieve like people who have no
hope. 14For since we believe that Jesus died and was
raised to life again, we also believe that when Jesus
returns, God will bring back with him the believers
who have died.
15We tell you this directly from the Lord: We who
are still living when the Lord returns will not meet him
ahead of those who have died.* 16For the Lord himself will come down from heaven with a commanding
shout, with the voice of the archangel, and with the
trumpet call of God. First, the Christians who have
died* will rise from their graves. 17Then, together with
them, we who are still alive and remain on the earth
will be caught up in the clouds to meet the Lord in
the air. Then we will be with the Lord forever. 18So
encourage each other with these words.

5:1Now concerning how and when all this will happen, dear brothers and sisters,* we don't really need
to write you. 2For you know quite well that the day of
the Lord's return will come unexpectedly, like a thief
in the night. 3When people are saying, "Everything is
peaceful and secure," then disaster will fall on them
as suddenly as a pregnant woman's labor pains begin.
And there will be no escape.
4But you aren't in the dark about these things, dear
brothers and sisters, and you won't be surprised when
the day of the Lord comes like a thief.* 5For you are all
children of the light and of the day; we don't belong to
darkness and night. 6So be on your guard, not asleep
like the others. Stay alert and be clearheaded. 7Night
is the time when people sleep and drinkers get drunk.
8But let us who live in the light be clearheaded, protected by the armor of faith and love, and wearing as
our helmet the confidence of our salvation.
9For God chose to save us through our Lord Jesus
Christ, not to pour out his anger on us. 10Christ died
for us so that, whether we are dead or alive when he
returns, we can live with him forever. 11So encourage
each other and build each other up, just as you are
already doing.

Paul's Final Advice

1 THESSALONIANS 5:12-22

Dear brothers and sisters, honor those who are your
leaders in the Lord's work. They work hard among

1 Thes 4:13 Greek *those who have fallen asleep;* also in 4:14. **1 Thes 4:15** Greek *those who have fallen asleep.* **1 Thes 4:16** Greek *the dead in Christ.* **1 Thes 5:1** Greek *brothers;* also in 5:4, 12, 14, 25, 26, 27. **1 Thes 5:4** Some manuscripts read *comes upon you as if you were thieves.*

THE EVENTS OF CHRIST'S RETURN

While Christians have often disagreed about what events will lead up to the return of Christ, there has been less disagreement about what will happen once Christ does return.

1. Christ will return visibly, with a commanding shout.
2. There will be an unmistakable call from an angel.
3. There will be a trumpet fanfare such as has never been heard.
4. Believers in Christ who are dead will rise from their graves.
5. Believers who are alive will be caught up in the clouds to meet the Lord.

loved ones die or world events take a tragic turn. God will turn tragedy to triumph, poverty to riches, pain to glory, and defeat to victory. All believers throughout history will stand reunited in God's very presence, safe and secure. As Paul comforted the Thessalonians with the promise of the Resurrection, so we should comfort and reassure each other with this great hope.

1 Thes 4:15 What did Paul mean when he wrote, "We tell you this directly from the Lord"? Either this was something that the Lord had revealed directly to Paul, or it was a teaching of Jesus that had been passed along orally by the apostles and other Christians.

1 Thes 4:15-18 Knowing exactly *when* the dead will be raised, in relation to the other events at the Second Coming, is not as important as knowing *why* Paul wrote these words: to challenge believers to comfort and encourage one another. This passage can be a great comfort when any believer dies. The same love that should unite believers in this life (1 Thes 4:9) will unite believers when Christ returns and reigns for eternity.

1 Thes 4:16 An "archangel" is an angel with a position of authority and leadership. Michael is the only archangel mentioned in the New Testament (see Jude 1:9; Dan 10:13; 12:1).

1 Thes 5:1-3 "How and when all this will happen" refers to the knowledge of what will happen in the future, specifically at the return of Christ. Efforts to determine the date of Christ's return are foolish. Don't be misled by anyone who claims to know. We are told here that no one knows and that even believers will be surprised. The Lord will return suddenly and unexpectedly, warns Paul, so be ready! Because no one knows when Jesus will come back to earth, we should be prepared at all times. Suppose he were to return today. How would he find you living? Are you ready to meet him? Live each day prepared to welcome Christ.

1 Thes 5:2 The "day of the Lord's return" is a future time when God will intervene directly and dramatically in world affairs. Predicted and discussed often in the Old Testament (Isa 13:6-12; Joel 2:28-32; Zeph 1:14-18), the day of the Lord will include both punishment and blessing. Christ will judge sin and set up his eternal Kingdom.

1 Thes 5:4-5 It is good that we don't know exactly when Christ will return. If we knew the precise date, we might be tempted to be lazy in our work for Christ. Worse yet, we might plan to keep sinning and then turn to God right at the end. Heaven is not our only goal; we have work to do here. Christians must keep on doing God's work until death or until we see the unmistakable return of our Savior.

1 Thes 5:8 For more about the Christian's armor, see Ephesians 6:13-17.

1 Thes 5:9-11 As you near the end of a long race, your legs ache, your throat burns, and your whole body cries out for you to stop. This is when friends and fans are most valuable. Their encouragement helps you push through the pain to the finish line. In the same way, Christians are to encourage one another. Be sensitive to others' need for encouragement, and offer supportive words or actions.

1 Thes 5:12-13 "Those who are your leaders in the Lord's work" probably refers to elders and deacons in the church. How can you honor your pastor and other church leaders? Express your appreciation, tell them how you have been helped by their leadership and teaching, and thank them for their ministry in your life. If you say nothing, how will they know where you stand? Remember, they need and deserve your support and love.

▶ **1 THESSALONIANS 5:12-22** ***(cont.)***
you and give you spiritual guidance. 13Show them
great respect and wholehearted love because of their
work. And live peacefully with each other.
14Brothers and sisters, we urge you to warn those
who are lazy. Encourage those who are timid. Take
tender care of those who are weak. Be patient with
everyone.
15See that no one pays back evil for evil, but always
try to do good to each other and to all people.
16Always be joyful. 17Never stop praying. 18Be thankful in all circumstances, for this is God's will for you
who belong to Christ Jesus.
19Do not stifle the Holy Spirit. 20Do not scoff at
prophecies, 21but test everything that is said. Hold on
to what is good. 22Stay away from every kind of evil.

1 Thes 5:14 Don't loaf around with the lazy; warn them. Don't yell at the timid and weak; encourage and help them. At times it can be difficult to distinguish between idleness and timidity. Two people may be doing nothing—one out of laziness and the other out of shyness or fear of doing something wrong. The key to ministry is sensitivity: sensing the condition of each person and offering the appropriate remedy for each situation. You can't effectively help until you know the problem. You can't apply the medicine until you know where the wound is.

1 Thes 5:16-18 Our joy, prayers, and thankfulness should not fluctuate with our circumstances or feelings. Obeying these three commands—be joyful, never stop praying, and be thankful—often goes against our natural inclinations. When we make a conscious decision to do what God says, we will begin to see people in a new perspective. When we do God's will, we will find it easier to be joyful and thankful.

1 Thes 5:17 We cannot spend all our time on our knees, but it is possible to have a prayerful attitude at all times. This attitude is built upon acknowledging our dependence on God, realizing his presence within us, and determining to obey him fully. Then we will find it natural to pray frequent, spontaneous, short prayers. A prayerful attitude is not a substitute for regular times of prayer but should be an outgrowth of those times.

1 Thes 5:17 Have you ever grown tired of praying for something or someone? Paul said that believers should never stop praying. A Christian's persistence is an expression of faith that God answers prayer. Faith shouldn't die if the answers come slowly, for the delay may be God's way of working his will. When you feel tired of praying, know that God is present, always listening, always answering—in ways that he knows are best.

1 Thes 5:18 Paul was not teaching that we should thank God *for* everything that happens to us, but *in* everything. Evil does not come from God, so we should not thank him for it. But when evil strikes, we can still be thankful for God's presence and for the good that he will accomplish through the distress.

1 Thes 5:19 By warning us not to "stifle the Holy Spirit," Paul means that we should not ignore or toss aside the gifts the Holy Spirit gives. Here, he mentions prophecy (1 Thes 5:20); elsewhere, he mentions speaking in tongues (1 Cor 14:39). Sometimes spiritual gifts are controversial, and they may cause division in a church. Rather than trying to solve the problems, some Christians prefer to smother the gifts. This impoverishes the church. We should not stifle the Holy Spirit's work in anyone's life but encourage the full expression of these gifts to benefit the whole body of Christ.

1 Thes 5:20-21 We shouldn't make fun of those who are called to speak for God ("scoff at prophecies"), but we should always "test everything that is said," checking their words against the Bible. We are on dangerous ground if we laugh at a person who speaks the truth. Instead, we should carefully check out what people say, accepting what is true and rejecting what is false.

1 Thes 5:22-24 Christians cannot avoid every kind of evil because we live in a sinful world. But we can make sure that we don't give evil a foothold by avoiding tempting situations and concentrating on obeying God.

CHECKLIST FOR ENCOURAGERS

The command to "encourage" others is found throughout the Bible. In 1 Thessalonians 5:11-23, Paul gives many specific examples of how we can encourage others.

Reference	*Example*	*Suggested Application*
1 Thes 5:11	Build each other up.	Point out to someone a quality you appreciate in them.
1 Thes 5:12	Honor leaders.	Look for ways to cooperate.
1 Thes 5:13	Show leaders great respect.	Hold back your next critical comments about those in positions of responsibility. Say "thank you" to your leaders for their efforts.
1 Thes 5:13	Live in peace.	Search for ways to get along with others.
1 Thes 5:14	Warn the lazy.	Challenge someone to join you in a project.
1 Thes 5:14	Encourage the timid.	Encourage those who are timid by reminding them of God's promises.
1 Thes 5:14	Help the weak.	Support those who are weak by loving them and praying for them.
1 Thes 5:14	Be patient.	Think of a situation that tries your patience, and plan ahead of time how you can stay calm.
1 Thes 5:15	Resist revenge.	Instead of planning to get even with those who mistreat you, do good to them.
1 Thes 5:16	Be joyful.	Remember that even in the midst of turmoil, God is in control.
1 Thes 5:17	Pray continually.	God is always with you—talk to him.
1 Thes 5:18	Give thanks.	Make a list of all the gifts God has given you, giving thanks to him for each one.
1 Thes 5:19	Do not stifle the Holy Spirit.	Cooperate with the Spirit the next time he prompts you to participate in a Christian meeting.
1 Thes 5:20	Do not scoff at prophecies.	Receive God's word from those who speak for him.
1 Thes 5:22	Avoid every kind of evil.	Avoid situations where you will be drawn into temptation.
1 Thes 5:23-24	Count on God's constant help.	Realize that the Christian life is to be lived not in our own strength but through God's power.

Paul's Final Greetings

1 THESSALONIANS 5:23-28

Now may the God of peace make you holy in every way, and may your whole spirit and soul and body be kept blameless until our Lord Jesus Christ comes again. 24God will make this happen, for he who calls you is faithful.

25Dear brothers and sisters, pray for us.

26Greet all the brothers and sisters with Christian love.*

27I command you in the name of the Lord to read this letter to all the brothers and sisters.

28May the grace of our Lord Jesus Christ be with you.

1 Thes 5:26 Greek *with a holy kiss.*

2. PAUL'S SECOND LETTER TO THE THESSALONIANS

Effective communication can be difficult; even when clearly written, words can be misinterpreted or misunderstood. Paul faced this problem with the Thessalonians. Just a few months after he sent his first letter to Thessalonica, word came to him that some had misunderstood his teaching about the Second Coming. Some had taken his announcement that Jesus could return at any moment as a reason to stop working and just wait for Jesus to appear. Responding quickly, Paul sent another letter to this young church. He addresses the misunderstandings and gives further instruction about the Second Coming, but the message is essentially the same as his first letter: a call to continued courage in the face of persecution and consistent Christian conduct as we wait for Jesus to return.

Greetings from Paul

2 THESSALONIANS 1:1-2

This letter is from Paul, Silas,* and Timothy.

We are writing to the church in Thessalonica, to you who belong to God our Father and the Lord Jesus Christ.

2May God our Father* and the Lord Jesus Christ give you grace and peace.

Encouragement during Persecution

2 THESSALONIANS 1:3-12

Dear brothers and sisters,* we can't help but thank God for you, because your faith is flourishing and your love for one another is growing. 4We proudly tell God's other churches about your endurance and faithfulness in all the persecutions and hardships you are

2 Thes 1:1 Greek *Silvanus,* the Greek form of the name. **2 Thes 1:2** Some manuscripts read *God the Father.* **2 Thes 1:3** Greek *Brothers.*

---

1 Thes 5:23 The spirit, soul, and body refer not so much to the distinct parts of a person as to the entire being of a person. This expression is Paul's way of saying that God must be involved in every aspect of life. It is wrong to think that we can separate the spiritual life from everything else, obeying God only in some ethereal sense or living for him only one day each week. Christ must control all of us, not just a "religious" part.

1 Thes 5:27 For all the Christians to hear this letter, it had to be read in a public meeting—there were not enough copies to circulate. Paul wanted to make sure that everyone had the opportunity to hear his message because he was answering important questions and offering needed encouragement.

1 Thes 5:28 The Thessalonian church was young, and they needed help and encouragement. Both the persecution they faced and the temptations of their pagan culture were potential problems for these new Christians. Paul wrote to strengthen their faith and bolster their resistance to persecution and temptation. We, too, have a responsibility to help new believers—to make sure that they continue in their faith and don't become sidetracked by wrong beliefs or practices. The book of 1 Thessalonians can better equip us to help our brothers and sisters in Christ.

2 Thes 1:1 Paul wrote this letter from Corinth less than a year after he had written 1 Thessalonians. He and his companions, Timothy and Silas, had visited Thessalonica on Paul's second missionary journey (Acts 17:1-10). They established the church there, but Paul had to leave suddenly because of persecution. This prompted him to write his first letter (the book of 1 Thessalonians), which contains words of comfort and encouragement. Paul then heard how the Thessalonians had responded to this letter. The good news was that they were continuing to grow in their faith. But the bad news was that false teachings about Christ's return were spreading, leading many to quit their jobs and wait for the end of the world. So Paul wrote to them again. While the purpose of Paul's first letter was to comfort the Thessalonians with the assurance of Christ's return, the purpose of his second letter is to correct false teaching about the Second Coming.

2 Thes 1:1 Paul, Silas, and Timothy were together in Corinth (Acts 18:5). Paul wrote this letter on behalf of all three of them. Paul often included Timothy as a co-sender of his letters (see Phil 1:1; Col 1:1; 1 Thes 1:1). For more information about Paul, see his Profile on p. 1571. Silas's Profile is on p. 1575, and Timothy's Profile is on p. 1727.

2 Thes 1:1 Thessalonica was the capital and largest city of the Roman province of Macedonia. The most important Roman highway—extending from Rome to the Orient—went through Thessalonica. This highway, along with the city's thriving seaport, made Thessalonica one of the wealthiest and most flourishing trade centers in the Roman Empire. Recognized as a free city, Thessalonica was allowed self-rule and was exempt from most of the restrictions placed by Rome on other cities. Because of this open climate, the city had many pagan religions and cultural influences that challenged the Christians' faith.

2 Thes 1:3ff Regardless of the contents of Paul's letters, his style was affirming. Paul began most of his letters by stating what he most appreciated about his readers and the joy he felt because of their faith in God. We also should look for ways to encourage and build up other believers. (For more on encouragement, see the note on 1 Tim 4:12-16, p. 1732.)

2 Thes 1:4 The keys to surviving persecution and trials are endurance and faithfulness. When faced with crushing troubles, we can have faith that God is using our trials for our good and for his glory. Knowing that God is fair and just will give us patience in our suffering because we know that he has not forgotten us. In God's perfect timing, he will relieve our suffering and punish those who persecute us. Do you trust God's timing? That is the first step toward growing in endurance and faithfulness.

2 Thes 1:4-6 Paul had been persecuted during his first visit to Thessalonica (Acts 17:5-9). No doubt those who had responded to his message and had become Christians were continuing to be persecuted by both Jews and Gentiles. In Paul's first letter to the Thessalonians, he had said that Christ's return would bring deliverance from persecution for the believers and judgment on the

▸ **2 THESSALONIANS 1:3-12** ***(cont.)***

suffering. 5And God will use this persecution to show
his justice and to make you worthy of his Kingdom,
for which you are suffering. 6In his justice he will pay
back those who persecute you.
7And God will provide rest for you who are being
persecuted and also for us when the Lord Jesus appears from heaven. He will come with his mighty
angels, 8in flaming fire, bringing judgment on those
who don't know God and on those who refuse to
obey the Good News of our Lord Jesus. 9They will
be punished with eternal destruction, forever separated from the Lord and from his glorious power.
10When he comes on that day, he will receive glory
from his holy people—praise from all who believe.
And this includes you, for you believed what we told
you about him.
11So we keep on praying for you, asking our God
to enable you to live a life worthy of his call. May he
give you the power to accomplish all the good things
your faith prompts you to do. 12Then the name of our
Lord Jesus will be honored because of the way you
live, and you will be honored along with him. This is
all made possible because of the grace of our God and
Lord, Jesus Christ.*

Events prior to the Lord's Second Coming

2 THESSALONIANS 2:1-12

Now, dear brothers and sisters,* let us clarify some
things about the coming of our Lord Jesus Christ and
how we will be gathered to meet him. 2Don't be so easily shaken or alarmed by those who say that the day
of the Lord has already begun. Don't believe them,
even if they claim to have had a spiritual vision, a
revelation, or a letter supposedly from us. 3Don't be
fooled by what they say. For that day will not come
until there is a great rebellion against God and the
man of lawlessness* is revealed—the one who brings
destruction.* 4He will exalt himself and defy everything that people call god and every object of worship. He will even sit in the temple of God, claiming
that he himself is God.

2 Thes 1:12 Or *of our God and our Lord Jesus Christ.* **2 Thes 2:1** Greek *brothers*; also in 2:13, 15. **2 Thes 2:3a** Some manuscripts read *the man of sin.* **2 Thes 2:3b** Greek *the son of destruction.*

---

persecutors. But this caused the people to expect Christ's return right away to rescue and vindicate them. So Paul had to point out that while waiting for God's Kingdom, believers could and should grow in their endurance and faithfulness through the hardships they were suffering.

2 Thes 1:5 As we live for Christ, we will experience troubles because we are trying to be God's people in a perverse world. Some people say that troubles are the result of sin or lack of faith, but Paul teaches that they may be a part of God's plan for believers. Our problems can help us look upward and forward, instead of inward (Mark 13:35-36; Phil 3:13-14); they can build strong character (Rom 5:3-4); and they can provide us with opportunities to comfort others who also are struggling (2 Cor 1:3-5). Your troubles may be an indication that you are taking a stand for Christ. When you do so, you are experiencing the privilege of showing that you are worthy of God's Kingdom (see also 2 Thes 1:11).

2 Thes 1:7 The "rest" mentioned by Paul has two dimensions. We can rest in knowing that our sufferings are strengthening us, making us ready for Christ's Kingdom. We can also rest in the fact that one day everyone will stand before God. At that time, wrongs will be righted, judgment will be pronounced, and evil will be terminated.

2 Thes 1:9 The "eternal destruction" that Paul describes is the lake of fire (see Rev 20:14)—the place of eternal separation from God. Those people who will be separated from God in eternity will no longer have any hope for salvation.

2 Thes 1:11-12 As Christians, our calling from God is to become like Christ (Rom 8:29). This is a gradual, lifelong process that will be completed when we see Christ face to face (1 Jn 3:2). To be "worthy" of this calling means to *want* to do what is right and good (as Christ would). We aren't perfect yet, but we're moving in that direction as God works in us.

2 Thes 2:1ff Paul describes the end of the world and Christ's second coming. He says that great suffering and trouble lie ahead, but evil will not prevail because Christ will return to judge all people. Although Paul presents a few signs of the end times, his emphasis, like Jesus' (Mark 13), is the need for each person to prepare for Christ's return by living rightly day by day. If we are ready, we won't have to be concerned about the preceding events or the timing of Christ's return. God controls all events. (See 1 Thes 4–5 for Paul's earlier teaching on this subject.)

2 Thes 2:1-2 In the Bible, "the day of the Lord" is used in two ways: It can mean the end times (beginning with Christ's birth and continuing today), and it can mean the final judgment day (in the future). Because some false teachers were saying that judgment day had come, many believers were waiting expectantly for their vindication and for relief from suffering. But judgment day had not yet come; other events would have to happen first.

2 Thes 2:2 "A spiritual vision, a revelation, or a letter" could refer to the fact that false teaching had come from (1) someone claiming to have had a divine revelation, (2) someone passing on a teaching as though it were from Paul, or (3) someone distributing a letter supposedly written by Paul.

2 Thes 2:3 Throughout history there have been individuals who epitomized evil and who were hostile to everything Christ stands for (see 1 Jn 2:18; 4:3; 2 Jn 1:7). These antichrists have lived in every generation and will continue to work their evil. Then just before Christ's second coming, "the man of lawlessness . . . the one who brings destruction," a completely evil man, will arise. He will be Satan's tool, equipped with Satan's power (2 Thes 2:9). This lawless man will be the Antichrist.

It is dangerous to label any person as the Antichrist and to try to predict Christ's coming based on that assumption. Paul mentions a man of lawlessness, not so we might attempt to identify him, but so we might be ready for anything that threatens our faith. If our faith is strong, we don't need to be afraid of what lies ahead, because we know that this lawless man has already been defeated by God, no matter how powerful he becomes or how terrible our situation seems. God is in control, and he will be victorious. Our task is to be prepared for Christ's return and to spread the Good News so that even more people will also be prepared.

2 Thes 2:3ff When Paul first wrote to the Thessalonians, they were in danger of losing hope in the Second Coming. Then they shifted to the opposite extreme—some of them thought that Jesus would be coming at any minute and so they stopped being productive for God. Paul tried to restore the balance by describing certain events that would happen before Christ's return.

[5]Don't you remember that I told you about all this
when I was with you? [6]And you know what is holding
him back, for he can be revealed only when his time
comes. [7]For this lawlessness is already at work secretly,
and it will remain secret until the one who is holding
it back steps out of the way. [8]Then the man of lawlessness will be revealed, but the Lord Jesus will kill him
with the breath of his mouth and destroy him by the
splendor of his coming.
[9]This man will come to do the work of Satan with
counterfeit power and signs and miracles. [10]He will
use every kind of evil deception to fool those on their
way to destruction, because they refuse to love and
accept the truth that would save them. [11]So God will
cause them to be greatly deceived, and they will believe these lies. [12]Then they will be condemned for
enjoying evil rather than believing the truth.

2 Thes 2:13 Some manuscripts read *chose you from the very beginning.*

Believers Should Stand Firm

2 THESSALONIANS 2:13-17

As for us, we can't help but thank God for you, dear
brothers and sisters loved by the Lord. We are always
thankful that God chose you to be among the first* to
experience salvation—a salvation that came through
the Spirit who makes you holy and through your belief
in the truth. [14]He called you to salvation when we told
you the Good News; now you can share in the glory of
our Lord Jesus Christ.
[15]With all these things in mind, dear brothers and
sisters, stand firm and keep a strong grip on the teaching we passed on to you both in person and by letter.
[16]Now may our Lord Jesus Christ himself and God
our Father, who loved us and by his grace gave us eternal comfort and a wonderful hope, [17]comfort you and
strengthen you in every good thing you do and say.

Dear brothers and sisters, stand firm and keep a strong grip on the teaching we passed on to you both in person and by letter.
2 Thessalonians 2:15

2 Thes 2:6-7 What holds back the lawless one? We do not know for certain. Three possibilities have been suggested: (1) government and law, which help to curb evil; (2) the ministry and activity of the church and the effects of the Good News; or (3) the Holy Spirit. The Bible is not clear on who this restrainer is, only that he will not restrain forever. But we should not fear this time when the restraint is removed—God is far stronger than the man of lawlessness, and God will save his people.

2 Thes 2:7 "This lawlessness is already at work secretly" means that the work that this Antichrist will do is already going on. *Secretly* means something no one can discover but something God will reveal. *Lawlessness* is the hidden, subtle, underlying force from which all sin springs. Civilization still has a veneer of decency through law enforcement, education, science, and reason. Although we are horrified by criminal acts, we have yet to see the real horror of complete lawlessness. This will happen when "the one who is holding it back steps out of the way." Why will God allow this to happen? To show people and nations their own sinfulness, and to show them by bitter experience the true alternative to the lordship of Christ. People totally without God can act no better than vicious animals. Lawlessness, to a certain extent, is already going on, but the man of lawlessness has not yet been revealed.

2 Thes 2:9 This evil man will use "counterfeit power and signs and miracles" to deceive and draw a following. Miracles from God can help strengthen our faith and lead people to Christ, but all miracles are not necessarily from God. Christ's miracles were significant, not just because of their power, but because of their purpose—to help, to heal, and to point us to God. The man of lawlessness will have power to do amazing things, but his power will be from Satan. He will use this power to destroy and to lead people away from God and toward himself. If any religious personalities draw attention only to themselves, their work is not from God.

2 Thes 2:10-12 Does God cause people to be deceived? To understand God's allowing such deception, we must first understand his nature. (1) God himself is good (Ps 11:7). (2) God created a good world that fell because of humanity's sin (Rom 5:12). (3) Someday God will renew his creation and it will be good again (Rev 21:1). (4) God is stronger than evil (Matt 13:41-43; Rev 19:11-21). (5) God allows evil and thus has control over it. God did not create evil, and he offers help to those who wish to overcome it (Matt 11:28-30). (6) God uses everything—both good and evil—for his good purposes (Gen 50:20; Rom 8:28).

The Bible reveals a God who hates all evil and will one day do away with it completely and forever (Rev 20:10-15). God does not entice anyone to become evil. Those committed to evil may be used by God to sin even more in order to hasten their deserved judgment (see Exod 11:10). We don't need to understand every detail of how God works in order to have perfect confidence in his absolute power over evil and his total goodness toward us.

2 Thes 2:13 Paul consistently taught that salvation begins and ends with God. We can do nothing to be saved on our own merit—we must accept God's gift of salvation (see the note on Eph 1:4, p. 1705). There is no other way to receive forgiveness from sin. Paul is encouraging the Thessalonian believers by reminding them that they were chosen by God from the beginning. Being made holy is the process of Christian growth through which the Holy Spirit makes us like Christ (Rom 8:29). (See the note on 2 Thes 1:11-12, p. 1588.)

2 Thes 2:14 God worked through Paul and his companions to tell the Good News so that people could share in Christ's glory. It may seem strange that God works through us—fallible, unfaithful, untrustworthy human creatures. But he has given us the fantastic privilege of accomplishing his great mission—telling the world how to find salvation.

2 Thes 2:15 Paul knew that the Thessalonians would face pressure from persecutions, false teachers, worldliness, and apathy to waver from the truth and to leave the faith. So he urged them to "stand firm" and hold on to the truth they had been taught both through his letters and in person. We also may face persecution, false teachings, worldliness, and apathy. We should hold on to the truth of Christ's teachings because our life depends on it. Never forget the reality of Christ's life and love!

Paul's Request for Prayer

2 THESSALONIANS 3:1-5

Finally, dear brothers and sisters,* we ask you to pray for us. Pray that the Lord's message will spread rapidly and be honored wherever it goes, just as when it came to you. 2Pray, too, that we will be rescued from wicked and evil people, for not everyone is a believer. 3But the Lord is faithful; he will strengthen you and guard you from the evil one.* 4And we are confident in the Lord that you are doing and will continue to do the things we commanded you. 5May the Lord lead your hearts into a full understanding and expression of the love of God and the patient endurance that comes from Christ.

An Exhortation to Proper Living

2 THESSALONIANS 3:6-15

And now, dear brothers and sisters, we give you this command in the name of our Lord Jesus Christ: Stay away from all believers* who live idle lives and don't follow the tradition they received* from us. 7For you know that you ought to imitate us. We were not idle when we were with you. 8We never accepted food from anyone without paying for it. We worked hard day and night so we would not be a burden to any of you. 9We certainly had the right to ask you to feed us, but we wanted to give you an example to follow. 10Even while we were with you, we gave you this command: "Those unwilling to work will not get to eat."

11Yet we hear that some of you are living idle lives, refusing to work and meddling in other people's business. 12We command such people and urge them in the name of the Lord Jesus Christ to settle down and work to earn their own living. 13As for the rest of you, dear brothers and sisters, never get tired of doing good.

14Take note of those who refuse to obey what we say in this letter. Stay away from them so they will be ashamed. 15Don't think of them as enemies, but warn them as you would a brother or sister.*

Paul's Final Greetings

2 THESSALONIANS 3:16-18

Now may the Lord of peace himself give you his peace at all times and in every situation. The Lord be with you all.

17HERE IS MY GREETING IN MY OWN HANDWRITING—PAUL. I DO THIS IN ALL MY LETTERS TO PROVE THEY ARE FROM ME.

18May the grace of our Lord Jesus Christ be with you all.

2 Thes 3:1 Greek *brothers;* also in 3:6, 13. **2 Thes 3:3** Or *from evil.* **2 Thes 3:6a** Greek *from every brother.* **2 Thes 3:6b** Some manuscripts read *you received.* **2 Thes 3:15** Greek *as a brother.*

2 Thes 3:1-3 Beneath the surface of the routine of daily life, a fierce struggle among invisible spiritual powers is being waged. Our main defense is prayer that God will protect us from the evil one and that he will strengthen us. (See also Eph 6:10-19 concerning our armor for spiritual warfare.) The following guidelines can help you prepare for and survive satanic attacks: (1) Take the threat of spiritual attack seriously; (2) pray for strength and help from God; (3) study the Bible to recognize Satan's style and tactics; (4) memorize Scripture so it will be a source of help no matter where you are; (5) associate with those who speak the truth; and (6) practice what you are taught by sound spiritual leaders.

2 Thes 3:6-10 Paul was writing here about the person who is lazy. Paul explained that when he and his companions were in Thessalonica, they worked hard, buying what they needed rather than becoming a burden to any of the believers. The rule they followed was, "Those unwilling to work will not get to eat." There's a difference between leisure and laziness. Relaxation and recreation provide a necessary and much needed balance to our lives; when it is time to work, however, Christians should jump right in. We should make the most of our talents and time, doing all we can to provide for ourselves and our dependents. Rest when you should be resting, and work when you should be working.

2 Thes 3:6-15 Some people in the Thessalonian church were falsely teaching that because Christ would return any day, people should set aside their responsibilities, quit work, do no future planning, and just wait for the Lord. But their lack of activity only led them into sin. They became a burden to the church which was supporting them, they wasted time that could have been used for helping others, and they became meddlers (2 Thes 3:11). These church members may have thought that they were being more spiritual by not working, but Paul tells them to be responsible and get back to work. Being ready for Christ means obeying him in every area of life. Because we know that Christ is coming, we must live in such a way that our faith and our daily practice will please him when he arrives.

2 Thes 3:11-12 An idle person who doesn't work ends up filling their time with

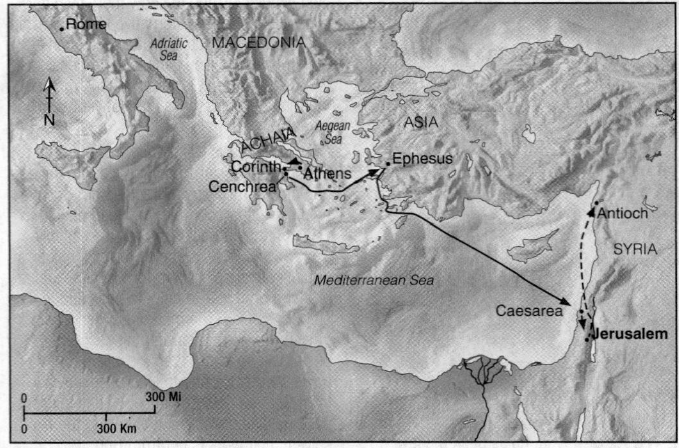

***MINISTRY IN CORINTH AND EPHESUS** Paul had been in Athens before his stay in Corinth, one of the greatest commercial centers of the empire, located on a narrow neck of land offering direct passage between the Aegean and Adriatic seas. When Paul left from the port of Corinth at Cenchrea, he visited Ephesus. He then traveled to Caesarea, from where he went on to Jerusalem to report on his trip before returning to Antioch.*

H. Paul Continues His Missionary Travels

Paul had spent a year and a half in Corinth, and he decided it was time to continue his ministry elsewhere. Paul sailed home to Antioch, and then embarked on his third missionary journey. He followed his earlier pattern of revisiting the cities where he had already planted churches, encouraging and strengthening them in their faith, and then continuing to preach the gospel in new places. On this journey he spent more than two years in Ephesus, but he also traveled again through Macedonia, Greece, and Achaia preaching the gospel and strengthening the churches. He also wrote two letters to the church in Corinth and one to believers in Rome, where he had not yet traveled.

Paul Faces More Opposition in Corinth

ACTS 18:12-17

But when Gallio became governor of Achaia, some
Jews rose up together against Paul and brought him
before the governor for judgment. 13They accused
Paul of "persuading people to worship God in ways
that are contrary to our law."
14But just as Paul started to make his defense, Gallio
turned to Paul's accusers and said, "Listen, you Jews,
if this were a case involving some wrongdoing or a
serious crime, I would have a reason to accept your
case. 15But since it is merely a question of words and
names and your Jewish law, take care of it yourselves.
I refuse to judge such matters." 16And he threw them
out of the courtroom.
17The crowd* then grabbed Sosthenes, the leader of
the synagogue, and beat him right there in the courtroom. But Gallio paid no attention.

Acts 18:17 Greek *Everyone;* other manuscripts read *All the Greeks.*

less than helpful activities, like gossip. Rumors and hearsay are tantalizing, exciting to hear, and make us feel like insiders. But they tear people down. If you often find your nose in other people's business, you may be underemployed. Look for a task to do for Christ or for your family, and get to work.

2 Thes 3:14-15 Paul counseled the church to stop supporting financially and associating with those who persisted in idleness. Hunger and loneliness can be very effective ways to make the idle person become productive. Paul was not advising coldness or cruelty, but tough love to help a person become responsible.

2 Thes 3:18 The book of 2 Thessalonians is especially meaningful for those who are being persecuted or are under pressure because of their faith. We are told what suffering can do for us (2 Thes 1); we are assured of final victory (2 Thes 2); and we are encouraged to continue living responsibly in spite of difficult circumstances (2 Thes 3). Christ's return is more than a doctrine; it is a promise. It is not just for the future; it has a vital impact on how we live now.

Acts 18:12 Gallio served as governor of Achaia (modern Greece) in A.D. 51 and was the brother of Seneca the philosopher. He became consul in A.D. 55.

Acts 18:13 Paul was charged with promoting a religion not approved by Roman law. This charge amounted to treason. Paul was not encouraging obedience to a human king other than Caesar (see Acts 17:7), nor was he speaking against the Roman Empire. Instead, he was speaking about Christ's eternal Kingdom.

Acts 18:14-16 This was an important judicial decision for the spread of the Good News in the Roman Empire. Judaism was a recognized religion under Roman law. As long as Christians were seen as part of Judaism, the court refused to hear cases brought against them. If they had claimed to be a new religion, they could easily have been outlawed by the government. In effect, Gallio was saying, "I don't understand all your terminology and finer points of theology. Handle the matter yourself and don't bother me."

Acts 18:17 Crispus had been the leader of the synagogue, but he and his family were converted and joined the Christians (Acts 18:8). Sosthenes had been chosen to take his place. The mob could have been Greeks venting their feelings against the Jews for causing turmoil, or the crowd may have included some Jews. In any case, they beat Sosthenes for losing the case and leaving the synagogue worse off than before. A person named Sosthenes is mentioned in 1 Corinthians 1:1, and many believe this was the same man who, in time, became a convert and a companion of Paul.

Caesarea

Caesarea, a city named in honor of Augustus Caesar, was built by Herod the Great from 22–10 B.C. Caesarea served as a major seaport of Judea in New Testament times. Since the southern Palestinian coastline lacked a good harbor, Herod created one by building two huge breakwaters that could shelter ships from Mediterranean storms. The 8,000-acre site lies 25 miles south of modern Haifa, in the beautiful plain of Sharon on Israel's Mediterranean coast. Known as Caesarea Maritima, it became the administrative center of the country throughout the Roman occupation. Three Roman governors of Palestine lived there: Felix (Acts 24), Festus (Acts 25:1, 4-6, 13), and Pontius Pilate, who visited Jerusalem on special occasions. Archaeologists found Pilate's name carved in stone in the theater at Caesarea.

Paul Returns to Antioch of Syria

ACTS 18:18-23

Paul stayed in Corinth for some time after that, then said good-bye to the brothers and sisters* and went to nearby Cenchrea. There he shaved his head according to Jewish custom, marking the end of a vow. Then he set sail for Syria, taking Priscilla and Aquila with him.

19They stopped first at the port of Ephesus, where Paul left the others behind. While he was there, he went to the synagogue to reason with the Jews. 20They asked him to stay longer, but he declined. 21As he left, however, he said, "I will come back later,* God willing." Then he set sail from Ephesus. 22The next stop was at the port of Caesarea. From there he went up and visited the church at Jerusalem* and then went back to Antioch.

23After spending some time in Antioch, Paul went back through Galatia and Phrygia, visiting and strengthening all the believers.*

Apollos Instructed at Ephesus

ACTS 18:24-28

Meanwhile, a Jew named Apollos, an eloquent speaker who knew the Scriptures well, had arrived in Ephesus from Alexandria in Egypt. 25He had been taught the way of the Lord, and he taught others about Jesus with an enthusiastic spirit* and with accuracy. However, he knew only about John's baptism. 26When Priscilla and Aquila heard him preaching boldly in the synagogue, they took him aside and explained the way of God even more accurately.

27Apollos had been thinking about going to Achaia, and the brothers and sisters in Ephesus encouraged him to go. They wrote to the believers in Achaia, asking them to welcome him. When he arrived there, he proved to be of great benefit to those who, by God's grace, had believed. 28He refuted the Jews with powerful arguments in public debate. Using the Scriptures, he explained to them that Jesus was the Messiah.

Acts 18:18 Greek *brothers;* also in 18:27. **Acts 18:21** Some manuscripts read *"I must by all means be at Jerusalem for the upcoming festival, but I will come back later."* **Acts 18:22** Greek *the church.* **Acts 18:23** Greek *disciples;* also in 18:27. **Acts 18:25** Or *with enthusiasm in the Spirit.*

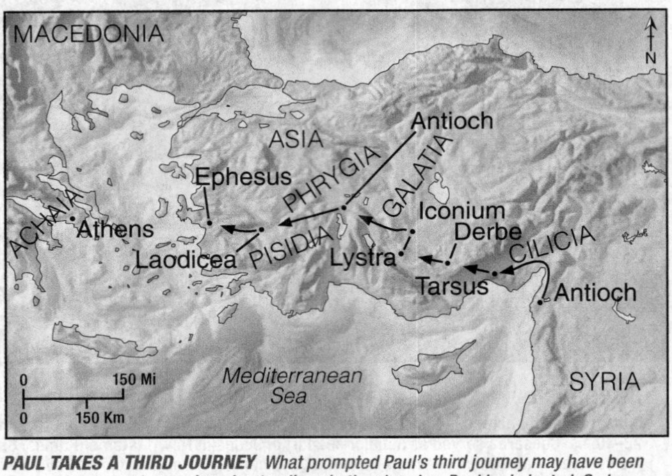

***PAUL TAKES A THIRD JOURNEY** What prompted Paul's third journey may have been the need to correct any misunderstandings in the churches Paul had planted. So he hurried north, then west, returning to many of the cities he had previously visited. This time, he stayed on a more direct westward route toward Ephesus.*

Acts 18:18 This vow Paul took was probably a temporary Nazirite vow that ended with shaving of the head and offering the hair as a sacrifice (Num 6:18).

Acts 18:22 This verse marks the end of Paul's second missionary journey and the beginning of the third, which lasted from A.D. 51–56. Leaving the church at Antioch (his home base), Paul headed toward Ephesus, but along the way he revisited the churches in Galatia and Phrygia (Acts 18:23). The heart of this trip was a lengthy stay (two to three years) in Ephesus. Before returning to Jerusalem, he also visited believers in Macedonia and Greece.

Acts 18:24-26 Apollos had heard only what John the Baptist had said about Jesus (see Luke 3:1-18), so his message was not the complete story. John focused on repentance from sin, the first step. But the whole message is to repent from sin and then believe in Christ. Apollos did not know about Jesus' life, crucifixion, and resurrection. Nor did he know about the coming of the Holy Spirit. Priscilla and Aquila explained the way of salvation to him.

Acts 18:27-28 Apollos was from Alexandria in Egypt, the second most important city in the Roman Empire, and the home of a great university. Alexandria had a thriving Jewish population. Apollos was a scholar, orator, and debater; and after his knowledge about Christ was made more complete, God greatly used these gifts to strengthen and encourage the church. Reason is a powerful tool in the right hands and in the right situation. Apollos used the gift of reason to convince many in Greece of the truth of the Good News.

As often happens, abilities sometimes cause division because of jealousy, pride, or other problems. Apollos's abilities eventually created a problem. Some of the Corinthians became more enamored with Apollos than with his message. There is no evidence to suggest that Apollos encouraged this behavior, and Paul never blamed Apollos for this development. Still, Paul eventually had to confront the Corinthians about their divisiveness (see 1 Cor 1:12-13). Be glad for God's gifts but always remember that they are given to bring honor to him. He is the point! His glory is the issue! Use the gift, but more than that, praise the Giver of the gifts and use them to his glory.

Acts 18:27-28 Not all the work of a minister or missionary is drudgery, setback, or suffering. Acts 18 is triumphant, showing victories in key cities and the addition of exciting new leaders such as Priscilla, Aquila, and Apollos to the church. Rejoice in the victories Christ brings, and don't let the hazards create a negative mind-set.

Acts 19:1 Ephesus was the capital and leading business center of the Roman province of Asia (part of present-day Turkey). A hub of sea and land transportation, it ranked with Antioch of Syria and Alexandria in Egypt as one of the great cities on the Mediterranean Sea. Paul stayed in Ephesus for a little over two years. There he wrote his first letter to the Corinthians to counter several problems the church in Corinth was facing.

Paul's Third Missionary Journey

ACTS 19:1-7

While Apollos was in Corinth, Paul traveled through the interior regions until he reached Ephesus, on the coast, where he found several believers.* 2"Did you receive the Holy Spirit when you believed?" he asked them.

"No," they replied, "we haven't even heard that there is a Holy Spirit."

3"Then what baptism did you experience?" he asked.

And they replied, "The baptism of John."

4Paul said, "John's baptism called for repentance from sin. But John himself told the people to believe in the one who would come later, meaning Jesus."

5As soon as they heard this, they were baptized in the name of the Lord Jesus. 6Then when Paul laid his hands on them, the Holy Spirit came on them, and they spoke in other tongues* and prophesied. 7There were about twelve men in all.

Acts 19:1 Greek *disciples;* also in 19:9, 30. **Acts 19:6** Or *in other languages.*

APOLLOS

Some people have an amazing natural talent for public speaking. Some even have a great message to go along with it. When Apollos arrived in Ephesus shortly after Paul's departure, he made an immediate impact. He spoke boldly in public, interpreting and applying the Old Testament Scriptures effectively. He debated opponents of Christianity forcefully and effectively. It didn't take long for Priscilla and Aquila to notice him. • The couple quickly realized that Apollos did not have the whole story. His preaching was based on the Old Testament and John the Baptist's message. He was probably urging people to repent and prepare for the coming Messiah. Priscilla and Aquila took him home with them and brought him up to speed on all that had happened. As they told him of Jesus' life, death, and resurrection, and the coming of the Holy Spirit, Apollos must have seen Scripture after Scripture become clear. He was filled with new energy and boldness now that he knew the complete gospel. • Apollos next decided to travel to Achaia. His friends in Ephesus were able to send along a glowing letter of introduction. He quickly became the verbal champion of the Christians in Corinth, debating the opponents of the gospel in public. As often happens, Apollos's abilities eventually created a problem. Some of the Corinthians began to follow Apollos rather than his message. Paul had to confront the Corinthians about their divisiveness. They had been forming little groups named after their favorite preacher. Apollos left Corinth and hesitated to return. Paul wrote warmly of Apollos as a fellow minister who had "watered" the seeds of the gospel that Paul had planted in Corinth. Paul last mentions Apollos briefly to Titus. Apollos was still a traveling representative of the gospel who deserved Titus's help. • Although his natural abilities could have made him proud, Apollos proved himself willing to learn. God used Priscilla and Aquila, fresh from months of learning from Paul, to give Apollos the complete gospel. Because Apollos did not hesitate to be a student, he became an even better teacher. How much does your willingness to learn affect God's efforts to help you become all he wants you to be?

Strengths and accomplishments	• A gifted preacher and apologist in the early church • Willing to be taught
Lessons from his life	• Effective communication of the gospel includes an accurate message delivered with God's power
Vital statistics	• Where: From Alexandria in Egypt • Occupations: Traveling preacher, apologist • Contemporaries: Priscilla, Aquila, Paul
Key verses	"He had been taught the way of the Lord, and he taught others about Jesus with an enthusiastic spirit and with accuracy. However, he knew only about John's baptism. When Priscilla and Aquila heard him preaching boldly in the synagogue, they took him aside and explained the way of God even more accurately" (Acts 18:25-26).

Apollos's story is told in Acts 18:24–19:1. He is also mentioned in 1 Corinthians 1:12; 3:4-6, 22; 4:1, 6; 16:12; Titus 3:13.

Later, while imprisoned in Rome, Paul wrote a letter to the Ephesian church (the book of Ephesians).

Acts 19:2-4 John's baptism was a sign of repentance from sin only, not a sign of new life in Christ. Like Apollos (Acts 18:24-26), these Ephesian believers needed further instruction about the message and ministry of Jesus Christ. They believed in Jesus as the Messiah, but they did not understand the significance of the work of the Holy Spirit. Becoming a Christian involves turning from sin (repentance) and turning to Christ (faith). These believers were incomplete.

In the book of Acts, believers received the Holy Spirit in a variety of ways. Usually the Holy Spirit would fill a person upon profession of faith in Christ. Here that filling happened later because these disciples' knowledge was incomplete. God was confirming to these believers, who did not initially know about the Holy Spirit, that they were a part of the church. The Holy Spirit's filling endorsed them as believers.

Pentecost was the formal outpouring of the Holy Spirit on the church. The other outpourings in the book of Acts were God's way of uniting new believers to the church. The mark of the true church is not merely right doctrine but right actions, the true evidence of the Holy Spirit's work.

Acts 19:6 When Paul laid his hands on these disciples, they received the Holy Spirit, just as the disciples had at Pentecost, resulting in outward, visible signs of the Holy Spirit's presence. This also had happened when the Holy Spirit had come on the Gentiles (non-Jews; see Acts 10:45-47). Much has been made about this passage and others in Acts that depict believers speaking in tongues. Some have uncomfortably downplayed or dismissed these historical events. Others have tried to duplicate them. Few issues have prompted more argument and confusion or split more churches. We should remember that tongues-speaking is not the central theme of the book of Acts. The point of Luke's history is the faithful communication of the gospel to the ends of the earth. If we want to be doers of the Word (Jas 1:22), we will faithfully be involved in the same process of evangelism. Seek to share your faith in the power of the Holy Spirit (Acts 1:8) and leave it up to God to give you whatever experiences he thinks you need.

Paul Ministers in Ephesus

ACTS 19:8-20

Then Paul went to the synagogue and preached boldly for the next three months, arguing persuasively about the Kingdom of God. [9]But some became stubborn, rejecting his message and publicly speaking against the Way. So Paul left the synagogue and took the believers with him. Then he held daily discussions at the lecture hall of Tyrannus. [10]This went on for the next two years, so that people throughout the province of Asia—both Jews and Greeks—heard the word of the Lord.

[11]God gave Paul the power to perform unusual miracles. [12]When handkerchiefs or aprons that had merely touched his skin were placed on sick people, they were healed of their diseases, and evil spirits were expelled.

[13]A group of Jews was traveling from town to town casting out evil spirits. They tried to use the name of the Lord Jesus in their incantation, saying, "I command you in the name of Jesus, whom Paul preaches, to come out!" [14]Seven sons of Sceva, a leading priest, were doing this. [15]But one time when they tried it, the evil spirit replied, "I know Jesus, and I know Paul, but who are you?" [16]Then the man with the evil spirit leaped on them, overpowered them, and attacked them with such violence that they fled from the house, naked and battered.

[17]The story of what happened spread quickly all through Ephesus, to Jews and Greeks alike. A solemn fear descended on the city, and the name of the Lord Jesus was greatly honored. [18]Many who became believers confessed their sinful practices. [19]A number of them who had been practicing sorcery brought their incantation books and burned them at a public bonfire. The value of the books was several million dollars.* [20]So the message about the Lord spread widely and had a powerful effect.

Acts 19:19 Greek *50,000 pieces of silver,* each of which was the equivalent of a day's wage.

I. Paul's First Letter to the Church in Corinth

AD 53

Paul writes his first letter to the church in Corinth

While Paul was in Ephesus, he got several reports about the church in Corinth that concerned him. Corinth was a very cosmopolitan city, with rampant corruption, idolatry, and immorality. It was a difficult place for a Christian to live, and the young believers there had many questions about what it meant to live for Christ. When Paul heard of their troubles, he wrote this letter to address their problems, heal their divisions, and answer their questions. Paul confronted them with their sin and their need for corrective action and a clear commitment to Christ. All Christians must live Christ-centered, blameless, loving lives that make a difference for God where we live.

1. PAUL ADDRESSES CHURCH PROBLEMS

Through various sources, Paul had received reports of problems in the Corinthian church, including jealousy, divisiveness, sexual immorality, and failure to discipline members. Churches today must also address the problems the Corinthians faced. We can learn a great deal by observing how Paul handled these delicate situations.

Greetings from Paul

1 CORINTHIANS 1:1-3

This letter is from Paul, chosen by the will of God to be an apostle of Christ Jesus, and from our brother Sosthenes.

[2]I am writing to God's church in Corinth,* to you who have been called by God to be his own holy people. He made you holy by means of Christ Jesus,* just as he did for all people everywhere who call on the name of our Lord Jesus Christ, their Lord and ours.

1 Cor 1:2a *Corinth* was the capital city of Achaia, the southern region of the Greek peninsula. **1 Cor 1:2b** Or *because you belong to Christ Jesus.*

Acts 19:9 Paul spoke in a lecture hall at this school. Such halls were used in the morning for teaching philosophy, but they were empty during the hot part of the day (about 11 a.m. to 4 p.m.). Because many people did not work during those hours, they would come to hear Paul's preaching.

Acts 19:10 "The province of Asia" refers to Asia Minor or modern-day Turkey. During this time, Paul and his co-workers spread the Good News throughout the land.

Acts 19:13 These Jews traveled from town to town making a living by claiming to heal people and drive out demons. Often they would recite a whole list of names in their incantation to be sure of including the right deity. Here they were trying to use Jesus' name in an effort to match Paul's power.

Acts 19:13-16 Some Ephesians engaged in exorcism and occult practices for profit (see Acts 19:18-19). The sons of Sceva were impressed by Paul, whose power to drive out demons came from God's Holy Spirit, not from witchcraft, and was obviously more powerful than theirs. They discovered, however, that no one can control or duplicate God's power. These men were calling on the name of Jesus without knowing him personally. The power to change people comes from Christ. It cannot be tapped by reciting his name like a magic charm. God works his power only through those he chooses.

Acts 19:18-19 Ephesus was a center for black magic and other occult practices. The people cooked up magical formulas to give them wealth, happiness, and success in marriage. Superstition and sorcery were commonplace. God clearly forbids such practices (Deut 18:9-13). You cannot be a believer and hold on to the occult, black magic, or sorcery. Once you begin to dabble in these areas, you may become obsessed by them because

3May God our Father and the Lord Jesus Christ give
you grace and peace.

Paul Gives Thanks to God

1 CORINTHIANS 1:4-9

I always thank my God for you and for the gracious
gifts he has given you, now that you belong to Christ
Jesus. 5Through him, God has enriched your church
in every way—with all of your eloquent words and all
of your knowledge. 6This confirms that what I told
you about Christ is true. 7Now you have every spiritual
gift you need as you eagerly wait for the return of our
Lord Jesus Christ. 8He will keep you strong to the end
so that you will be free from all blame on the day when

Satan is very powerful. But God's power is even greater (1 Jn 4:4; Rev 20:10). If you are mixed up in the occult, learn a lesson from the Ephesians and get rid of anything that could trap you in such practices.

1 Cor 1:1 Paul wrote this letter to the church in Corinth while he was visiting Ephesus during his third missionary journey (Acts 19:1–20:1). Corinth and Ephesus faced each other across the Aegean Sea. Paul knew the Corinthian church well because he had spent 18 months in Corinth during his second missionary journey (Acts 18:1-18). While in Ephesus, he had heard about problems in Corinth (1 Cor 1:11). About the same time, a delegation from the Corinthian church had visited Paul to ask his advice about their conflicts (1 Cor 16:17). Paul's purpose for writing was to correct those problems and to answer questions church members had asked in a previous letter (1 Cor 7:1).

1 Cor 1:1 Paul was given a special calling from God to preach about Jesus Christ. Each Christian has a job to do, a role to take, or a contribution to make. One assignment may seem more spectacular than another, but all are necessary to carry out God's greater plans for his church and for his world (1 Cor 12:12-27). Be available to God by placing your gifts at his service. Then as you discover what he calls you to do, be ready to do it.

1 Cor 1:1 Sosthenes may have been Paul's secretary who wrote down this letter as Paul dictated it. He was probably the Jewish synagogue leader in Corinth (Acts 18:17) who had been beaten during an attack on Paul and then later became a believer. Sosthenes was well known to the members of the Corinthian church, and so Paul included his familiar name in the opening of the letter.

1 Cor 1:2 Corinth, a giant cultural melting pot with a great diversity of wealth, religions, and moral standards, had a reputation for being fiercely independent and as decadent as any city in the world. The Romans had destroyed Corinth in 146 B.C. after a rebellion. But in 46 B.C., the Roman emperor Julius Caesar rebuilt it because of its strategic seaport. By Paul's day (A.D. 50), the Romans had made Corinth the capital of Achaia (present-day Greece). It was a large city, offering Rome great profits through trade as well as the military protection of its ports. But the city's prosperity made it ripe for all sorts of corruption. Idolatry flourished, and there were more than a dozen pagan temples employing at least a thousand prostitutes. Corinth's reputation was such that prostitutes in other cities began to be called "Corinthian girls."

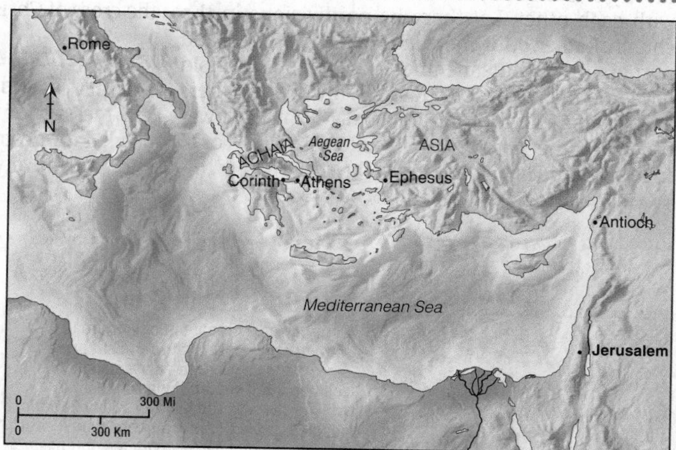

***CORINTH AND EPHESUS** Paul wrote this letter to Corinth during his three-year visit in Ephesus on his third missionary journey. The two cities sat across from each other on the Aegean Sea—both were busy and important ports. Titus may have carried this letter from Ephesus to Corinth (2 Cor 12:18).*

1 Cor 1:2 A personal invitation makes a person feel wanted and welcome. We are "called by God to be his own holy people." God personally invites us to be citizens of his eternal Kingdom. Jesus Christ, God's Son, is the only one who can bring us into this glorious Kingdom because he is the only one who removes our sins. To be made holy (or sanctified) means that we are chosen or set apart by Christ for his service. We accept God's invitation by accepting his Son, Jesus Christ, and by trusting in the work he did on the cross to forgive our sins.

1 Cor 1:2 This was probably not meant to be a private letter; rather, it may have been circulated to other churches in nearby cities. Although it deals with specific issues facing the church at Corinth, all believers can learn from it. The Corinthian church included a great cross section of believers—wealthy merchants, common laborers, former temple prostitutes, and middle-class families. Because of the wide diversity of people and backgrounds, Paul takes great pains to stress the need for both spiritual unity and Christlike character.

1 Cor 1:3 Grace is God's free gift of salvation given to us in Christ. Receiving it brings us peace (see Rom 5:1). In a world of noise, confusion, and relentless pressures, people long for peace. Many give up the search, thinking it impossible to find, but true peace of heart and mind is available to us through faith in Jesus Christ.

1 Cor 1:4-6 Paul thanked God for the Corinthian believers. During the Thanksgiving holiday, we focus on our blessings and express our gratitude to God for them. But thanks should be expressed every day. We can never say thank you enough to parents, friends, leaders, and especially to God. When thanksgiving becomes an integral part of your life, you will find that your attitude toward life will change. You will become more positive, gracious, loving, and humble. Whom do you need to thank today?

1 Cor 1:7 The Corinthian church members had all the spiritual gifts they needed to live the Christian life, to witness for Christ, and to stand against the paganism and immorality of Corinth. But instead of using what God had given them, they were arguing over which gifts were more important. Paul addresses this issue in depth in 1 Corinthians 12–14.

1 Cor 1:7-9 Before tackling the problems, Paul described his hope for the Corinthians. He guaranteed these believers that God would consider them "free from all blame" when Christ returns (see also Eph 1:7-10). This guarantee was not because of their great gifts or their shining performance but because of what Jesus Christ accomplished for them through his death and resurrection. All who believe in the Lord Jesus will be considered blameless when Jesus Christ returns (see also 1 Thes 3:13; Heb 9:28). Today's struggles, difficulties, and failures don't tell

▶ **1 CORINTHIANS 1:4-9** ***(cont.)***
our Lord Jesus Christ returns. 9God will do this, for he
is faithful to do what he says, and he has invited you
into partnership with his Son, Jesus Christ our Lord.

Divisions in the Church

1 CORINTHIANS 1:10-17
I appeal to you, dear brothers and sisters,* by the authority of our Lord Jesus Christ, to live in harmony
with each other. Let there be no divisions in the
church. Rather, be of one mind, united in thought and
purpose. 11For some members of Chloe's household
have told me about your quarrels, my dear brothers
and sisters. 12Some of you are saying, "I am a follower
of Paul." Others are saying, "I follow Apollos," or "I
follow Peter,*" or "I follow only Christ."
13Has Christ been divided into factions? Was I, Paul,
crucified for you? Were any of you baptized in the
name of Paul? Of course not! 14I thank God that I did
not baptize any of you except Crispus and Gaius, 15for
now no one can say they were baptized in my name.
16(Oh yes, I also baptized the household of Stephanas,
but I don't remember baptizing anyone else.) 17For
Christ didn't send me to baptize, but to preach the
Good News—and not with clever speech, for fear that
the cross of Christ would lose its power.

The Wisdom of God

1 CORINTHIANS 1:18-31
The message of the cross is foolish to those who are
headed for destruction! But we who are being saved
know it is the very power of God. 19As the Scriptures say,

1 Cor 1:10 Greek *brothers;* also in 1:11, 26. **1 Cor 1:12** Greek *Cephas.*

The Corinthian Canal

Corinth was a prominent city of Greece, formerly the capital of the ancient province of Achaia. Corinth was a major cosmopolitan center; it was also filled with immorality and idolatry. Many foreign people lived in Corinth, and because it sits on one side of a narrow isthmus, it functioned as a center of sea-trade. This picture shows the modern canal through Corinth, a 4-mile journey that saves a 430-mile trek around southern Greece.

In Paul's day, there was no canal; instead, ships were loaded onto large slabs and towed along a stone portage road called the *Diolkos*. Remnants of that original road can still be seen today alongside the canal.

the whole story. Keep the big picture in mind. If you have faith in Christ, even if it is weak, you are and will be saved.

1 Cor 1:10 Paul founded the church in Corinth on his second missionary journey. Eighteen months after he left, arguments and divisions arose, and some church members slipped back into an immoral lifestyle. Paul wrote this letter to address the problems and to clear up confusion about right and wrong so that they would remove the immorality from among them. The Corinthian people had a reputation for jumping from fad to fad; Paul wanted to keep Christianity from degenerating into just another fad.

1 Cor 1:10 By saying "brothers and sisters," Paul is emphasizing that all Christians are part of God's family. Believers share a unity that runs even deeper than that of blood brothers and sisters.

1 Cor 1:10-11 Like a frustrated coach watching his team bicker on the court, Paul called for a time-out. He saw the danger of divisions and arguments. The Corinthian believers' lack of unity was obvious. They may have been playing in the same "uniform," but they were doing as much as the opposition to bring about their own defeat. The problems weren't so much differences of opinion as divided allegiances. They were arguing over which position on the team was most important in a way that made them ineffective as a unit. They were on the field, but out of the game.

Divisions between Christians work like brick walls and barbed-wire fences to undermine the effectiveness of the message that believers are to proclaim. Focus on your coach, Jesus Christ, and the purpose he has for you. Strive for harmony. Keep arguments about allegiances off the team.

1 Cor 1:12ff In this large and diverse Corinthian church, the believers favored different preachers. Because there was as yet no written New Testament, the believers depended heavily on preaching and teaching for spiritual insight into the meaning of the Old Testament. Some followed Paul, who had founded their church; some who had heard Peter in Jerusalem followed him; others listened only to Apollos, an eloquent and popular preacher who had had a dynamic ministry in Corinth (Acts 18:24; 19:1). Although these three preachers were united in their message, their personalities attracted different people. At this time the church was in danger of dividing. By mentioning Jesus Christ 10 times in 1 Cor 1:1-10), Paul makes it clear who it is all preachers and teachers should emphasize. God's message is much more important than any human messenger.

1 Cor 1:12-13 Paul wondered whether the Corinthians' quarrels had "divided" Christ into factions. This is a graphic picture of what happens when the church (the body of Christ) is divided. With the many churches and styles of worship available today, we could get caught up in the same game of "my preacher is better than yours!" To do so would divide Christ again. But Christ is not divided, and his true followers should not allow anything to divide them. Don't let your appreciation for any teacher, preacher, or author lead you into pride. Our allegiance must be to Christ and to the unity that he desires.

1 Cor 1:17 When Paul said that Christ didn't send him to baptize, he wasn't minimizing the importance of baptism. Baptism was commanded by Jesus himself (Matt 28:19) and practiced by the early church (Acts 2:41). Paul was emphasizing that no one person should do everything. Paul's gift was preaching, and that's what he did. Christian ministry should be a team effort; no preacher or teacher is a complete link between God and people, and no individual can do all that the apostles did. We must be content to operate within the gifts God has given to us, and carry out his plan wholeheartedly. (For more on different gifts, see 1 Cor 12–13.)

1 Cor 1:17 Some speakers use impressive words, but they are weak on content. Paul stressed solid content and practical help for his listeners. He wanted them to be impressed with his message, not just his

"I will destroy the wisdom of the wise
and discard the intelligence of the
intelligent."*

20So where does this leave the philosophers, the
scholars, and the world's brilliant debaters? God has
made the wisdom of this world look foolish. 21Since
God in his wisdom saw to it that the world would
never know him through human wisdom, he has used
our foolish preaching to save those who believe. 22It
is foolish to the Jews, who ask for signs from heaven.
And it is foolish to the Greeks, who seek human wisdom. 23So when we preach that Christ was crucified,
the Jews are offended and the Gentiles say it's all
nonsense.
24But to those called by God to salvation, both Jews
and Gentiles,* Christ is the power of God and the
wisdom of God. 25This foolish plan of God is wiser
than the wisest of human plans, and God's weakness
is stronger than the greatest of human strength.
26Remember, dear brothers and sisters, that few
of you were wise in the world's eyes or powerful or
wealthy* when God called you. 27Instead, God chose
things the world considers foolish in order to shame
those who think they are wise. And he chose things
that are powerless to shame those who are powerful.
28God chose things despised by the world,* things
counted as nothing at all, and used them to bring to
nothing what the world considers important. 29As a
result, no one can ever boast in the presence of God.
30God has united you with Christ Jesus. For our
benefit God made him to be wisdom itself. Christ
made us right with God; he made us pure and holy,
and he freed us from sin. 31Therefore, as the Scriptures say, "If you want to boast, boast only about the
LORD."*

1 Cor 1:19 Isa 29:14. **1 Cor 1:24** Greek *and Greeks.* **1 Cor 1:26** Or *high born.* **1 Cor 1:28** Or *God chose those who are low born.* **1 Cor 1:31** Jer 9:24.

HIGHLIGHTS OF 1 CORINTHIANS

The Meaning of the Cross *1 Cor 1:18–2:16*	Be considerate of one another because of what Christ has done for us. There is no place for pride or a know-it-all attitude. We are to have the mind of Christ.
The Story of the Last Supper *1 Cor 11:23-29*	The Lord's Supper is a time of remembering Christ's final words to his disciples before he died on the cross; we must celebrate this in an orderly and correct manner.
The Poem of Love *1 Cor 13:1-13*	Love is to guide all we do. We have different gifts, abilities, likes, dislikes—but we are called, without exception, to love.
The Christian's Destiny *1 Cor 15:42-58*	Christ, who died for us, promised that as he came back to life after death, so our perishable bodies will be exchanged for heavenly bodies. Then we will live and reign with Christ.

style (see 1 Cor 2:1-5). You don't need to be a great speaker with a large vocabulary to share the Good News effectively. The persuasive power is in the story, not the storyteller. Paul was not against those who carefully prepare what they say (see 1 Cor 2:6) but against those who try to impress others with their knowledge or speaking ability.

1 Cor 1:19 Paul summarizes Isaiah 29:14 to emphasize a point Jesus often made: God's way of thinking is not like the world's way (normal human wisdom). And God offers eternal life, which the world can never give. We can spend a lifetime accumulating wisdom and yet never learn how to have a personal relationship with God. We must come to the crucified and risen Christ to receive eternal life and the joy of a personal relationship with our Savior.

1 Cor 1:22-24 Many Jews considered the Good News of Jesus Christ to be foolish because they thought the Messiah would be a conquering king accompanied by signs and miracles. Jesus had not restored David's throne as they expected. Besides, he was executed as a criminal, and how could a criminal be a savior? Greeks, too, considered the Good News foolish: They did not believe in a bodily resurrection; they did not see in Jesus the powerful characteristics of their mythological gods; and they thought no reputable person would be crucified. To them, death was defeat, not victory.

The Good News of Jesus Christ still sounds foolish to many. Our society worships power, influence, and wealth. Jesus came as a humble, poor servant, and he offers his Kingdom to those who have faith, not to those who do all kinds of good deeds to try to earn salvation. This looks foolish to the world, but Christ is the mighty power of God, the only way we can be saved. Knowing Christ personally is the greatest wisdom anyone can have.

1 Cor 1:25 The message of Christ's death for sins sounds foolish to those who don't believe. Death seems to be the end of the road, the ultimate weakness. But Jesus did not stay dead. His resurrection demonstrated his power even over death. And he will save us from eternal death and give us everlasting life if we trust him as Savior and Lord. This sounds so simple that many people won't accept it. They try other ways to obtain eternal life (being good, being wise, etc.). But all their attempts are futile. The "foolish" people who simply accept Christ's offer are actually the wisest of all, because they alone will live eternally with God.

1 Cor 1:27 Is Christianity against rational thinking? Christians clearly do believe in using their minds to weigh the evidence and make wise choices. But Paul is declaring that no amount of human knowledge can replace or bypass Christ's work on the cross. If it could, Christ would be accessible only to the intellectually gifted and well educated and not to ordinary people or to children.

1 Cor 1:28-31 Paul continues to emphasize that the way to receive salvation is so simple that any person who wants to can understand it. Skill and wisdom do not get a person into God's Kingdom—simple faith does. So no one can boast that personal achievements helped to secure eternal life. Salvation is totally from God through Jesus' death. There is nothing we can do to earn our salvation; we need only to accept what Jesus has already done for us.

1 Cor 1:30 God is our source and the reason for our personal relationship with Christ. Our union and identification with Christ results in our having God's wisdom (Col 2:3), being acceptable to God (2 Cor 5:21), being pure (1 Thes 4:3-7), and having the penalty for our sins paid by Jesus (Mark 10:45).

Paul's Message of Wisdom

1 CORINTHIANS 2:1-16

When I first came to you, dear brothers and sisters,*
I didn't use lofty words and impressive wisdom to
tell you God's secret plan.* 2For I decided that while
I was with you I would forget everything except Jesus
Christ, the one who was crucified. 3I came to you in
weakness—timid and trembling. 4And my message
and my preaching were very plain. Rather than using
clever and persuasive speeches, I relied only on the
power of the Holy Spirit. 5I did this so you would
trust not in human wisdom but in the power of God.

6Yet when I am among mature believers, I do speak
with words of wisdom, but not the kind of wisdom that
belongs to this world or to the rulers of this world,
who are soon forgotten. 7No, the wisdom we speak of
is the mystery of God*—his plan that was previously
hidden, even though he made it for our ultimate glory
before the world began. 8But the rulers of this world
have not understood it; if they had, they would not
have crucified our glorious Lord. 9That is what the
Scriptures mean when they say,

"No eye has seen, no ear has heard,
 and no mind has imagined
what God has prepared
 for those who love him."*

10But* it was to us that God revealed these things
by his Spirit. For his Spirit searches out everything
and shows us God's deep secrets. 11No one can know
a person's thoughts except that person's own spirit,
and no one can know God's thoughts except God's own
Spirit. 12And we have received God's Spirit (not the
world's spirit), so we can know the wonderful things
God has freely given us.

13When we tell you these things, we do not use
words that come from human wisdom. Instead, we
speak words given to us by the Spirit, using the Spirit's
words to explain spiritual truths.* 14But people who
aren't spiritual* can't receive these truths from God's
Spirit. It all sounds foolish to them and they can't
understand it, for only those who are spiritual can
understand what the Spirit means. 15Those who are
spiritual can evaluate all things, but they themselves
cannot be evaluated by others. 16For,

1 Cor 2:1a Greek *brothers.* **1 Cor 2:1b** Greek *God's mystery;* other manuscripts read *God's testimony.* **1 Cor 2:7** Greek *But we speak God's wisdom in a mystery.* **1 Cor 2:9** Isa 64:4. **1 Cor 2:10** Some manuscripts read *For.* **1 Cor 2:13** Or *explaining spiritual truths in spiritual language,* or *explaining spiritual truths to spiritual people.* **1 Cor 2:14** Or *who don't have the Spirit;* or *who have only physical life.*

1 Cor 2:1 Paul was referring to his first visit to Corinth during his second missionary journey (A.D. 51), when he founded the church (Acts 18:1ff).

1 Cor 2:1-5 A brilliant scholar, Paul could have overwhelmed his listeners with intellectual arguments. Instead, he shared the simple message of Jesus Christ by allowing the Holy Spirit to guide his words. In sharing the Good News with others, we should follow Paul's example and keep our message simple and basic. The Holy Spirit will give power to our words and use them to bring glory to Jesus.

1 Cor 2:4 Paul's confidence was not in his keen intellect or speaking ability but in his knowledge that the Holy Spirit was helping and guiding him. Paul is not denying the importance of study and preparation for preaching; he had a thorough education in the Scriptures. Effective preaching results from studious preparation and reliance on the work of the Holy Spirit. Don't use Paul's statement as an excuse for not studying or preparing.

1 Cor 2:7 "The mystery of God . . . that was previously hidden" was his offer of salvation to all people. Originally unknown to humanity, this plan became crystal clear when Jesus rose from the dead. His resurrection proved that he had power over sin and death and could offer us this power as well (1 Pet 1:10-12; see also the first note on Rom 16:25-27, p. 1674). God's plan is still hidden to unbelievers because they either refuse to accept it, choose to ignore it, or simply haven't heard about it.

1 Cor 2:8 Jesus was misunderstood and rejected by those whom the world considered wise and great. He was put to death by the rulers in Palestine—the high priest, King Herod, Pilate, and the Pharisees and Sadducees. Jesus' rejection by these rulers had been predicted in Isaiah 53:3; Zechariah 12:10-11.

1 Cor 2:9 We cannot imagine all that God has in store for us, both in this life and for eternity. He will create a new heaven and a new earth (Isa 65:17; Rev 21:1), and we will live with him forever. Until then, his Holy Spirit comforts and guides us. Knowing the wonderful and eternal future that awaits us gives us hope and courage to press on in this life, to endure hardship, and to avoid giving in to temptation. This world is not all there is. The best is yet to come.

1 Cor 2:10 "God's deep secrets" refers to God's unfathomable nature and his wonderful plan—Jesus' death and resurrection—and to the promise of salvation, revealed only to those who believe that what God says is true. Those who believe in Christ's death and resurrection and put their faith in him will know all they need to know to be saved. This knowledge can't be grasped by even the wisest people unless they accept God's message. All who reject God's message are foolish, no matter how wise the world thinks they are.

1 Cor 2:13 Everyone wants to be wise. Yet Paul taught the Corinthians that true wisdom or discernment requires the believer to be guided by the Holy Spirit. Because Satan's greatest impact on us occurs when he deceives us, we need the Holy Spirit's help. Spiritual discernment enables us to draw conclusions based on God's perspective, make wise decisions in difficult circumstances, recognize the activities of God's Spirit, distinguish the correct and incorrect use of Scripture, and identify and expose false teachers. Ask God to give you his discernment as you serve him. Let that discernment guide you in your daily walk.

1 Cor 2:14-15 Non-Christians cannot understand spiritual truths, and they cannot grasp the concept that God's Spirit lives in believers. Don't expect most people to approve of or understand your decision to follow Christ. It all seems so silly to them. Just as a tone-deaf person cannot appreciate fine music, the person who rejects Christ cannot understand truths from God's Spirit. With the lines of communication broken, they won't be able to hear what God is saying to them.

We must not remain silent, however, using others' difficulty in understanding as an excuse. We are still one of God's communication channels. We must be alert to opportunities. Another person's question may be evidence that God's Spirit is drawing them to the point of decision. How would you respond today if someone asked you about your faith?

1 Cor 2:15-16 No one can know what the Lord is thinking (Rom 11:34), but through the guidance of the Holy Spirit, believers have insight into some of God's plans, thoughts, and actions. They, in fact, have "the mind of Christ." Through the Holy Spirit, we can begin to know God's thoughts, talk with him, and expect his answers to our prayers. Are you spending enough time with Christ to have his very mind in you? An intimate relationship with Christ comes only from spending time consistently in his presence and in his Word. Read Philippians 2:5ff for more on the mind of Christ.

"Who can know the LORD's thoughts?
Who knows enough to teach him?"*

But we understand these things, for we have the mind of Christ.

Paul and Apollos, Servants of Christ

1 CORINTHIANS 3:1-23

Dear brothers and sisters,* when I was with you I couldn't talk to you as I would to spiritual people.* I had to talk as though you belonged to this world or as though you were infants in the Christian life.* [2]I had to feed you with milk, not with solid food, because you weren't ready for anything stronger. And you still aren't ready, [3]for you are still controlled by your sinful nature. You are jealous of one another and quarrel with each other. Doesn't that prove you are controlled by your sinful nature? Aren't you living like people of the world? [4]When one of you says, "I am a follower of Paul," and another says, "I follow Apollos," aren't you acting just like people of the world?

[5]After all, who is Apollos? Who is Paul? We are only God's servants through whom you believed the Good News. Each of us did the work the Lord gave us. [6]I planted the seed in your hearts, and Apollos watered it, but it was God who made it grow. [7]It's not important who does the planting, or who does the watering. What's important is that God makes the seed grow. [8]The one who plants and the one who waters work together with the same purpose. And both will be rewarded for their own hard work. [9]For we are both God's workers. And you are God's field. You are God's building.

[10]Because of God's grace to me, I have laid the foundation like an expert builder. Now others are building on it. But whoever is building on this foundation must be very careful. [11]For no one can lay any foundation other than the one we already have—Jesus Christ.

[12]Anyone who builds on that foundation may use a variety of materials—gold, silver, jewels, wood, hay, or straw. [13]But on the judgment day, fire will reveal what kind of work each builder has done. The fire will show if a person's work has any value. [14]If the work survives, that builder will receive a reward. [15]But if the work is burned up, the builder will suffer great loss. The builder will be saved, but like someone barely escaping through a wall of flames.

1 Cor 2:16 Isa 40:13 (Greek version). **1 Cor 3:1a** Greek *Brothers.* **1 Cor 3:1b** Or *to people who have the Spirit.* **1 Cor 3:1c** Greek *in Christ.*

1 Cor 3:1-3 Paul called the Corinthians infants in the Christian life because they were not yet spiritually healthy and mature. The proof was that they quarreled like children, allowing divisions to distract them. Immature Christians are "worldly," controlled by their own desires; mature believers are in tune with God's desires. How much influence do your desires have on your life? Your goal should be to let God's desires be yours. Being controlled by your own desires will stunt your growth.

1 Cor 3:6 Paul planted the seed of the Good News message in people's hearts. He was a missionary pioneer; he brought the message of salvation. Apollos watered the seed. He helped the believers grow stronger in the faith. Paul founded the church in Corinth, and Apollos built on that foundation. Tragically, the believers in Corinth had split into factions, pledging loyalty to different teachers (see 1 Cor 1:11-13). After the preachers' work is completed, God is the one who makes Christians grow. Our leaders should certainly be respected, but we should never place them on pedestals that create barriers between people or set them up as a substitute for Christ.

1 Cor 3:7-9 God's work involves many different individuals with a variety of gifts and abilities. There are no superstars in this task, only team members performing their own special roles. We can become useful members of God's team by setting aside our desires to receive glory for what we do. Don't seek the praise that comes from people—it is comparatively worthless. Instead, seek approval from God.

1 Cor 3:10-11 The foundation of the church—of all believers—is Jesus Christ. Nothing and no one else will do, wrote Paul. A building with no foundation, or one poorly constructed, will not last. The finest materials used to construct a home quickly rot and fall apart if they are resting on the ground, because a building is only as solid as its foundation. If we are believers, then the foundation of our lives is Jesus Christ; he is our base, our reason for being. Everything we are and do must fit into the pattern provided by him. Are you building your life on the only real and lasting foundation, or are you building on a faulty foundation, such as wealth, security, success, or fame? Be careful how you build.

1 Cor 3:10-17 While some have applied these verses to personal spiritual growth, Paul's teaching has to do with ministry to others. What do we do to build others up? Do we build on Christ as foundation? Do we build with perishable materials? The Corinthians could construct their church with lasting, eternal teaching or with the changing, temporary wisdom of the day.

Paul's words challenge our methods of discipleship. Do we attach others to ourselves as the foundation, or to Christ? Do we use our abilities and spiritual gifts to build up others in the church or keep them tied to us? Do we use Bible-based teaching or merely adaptations of worldly wisdom?

1 Cor 3:13-15 Two sure ways to destroy a building are to tamper with the foundation and to build with inferior materials. The church must be built on Christ, not on any other person or principle. Christ will evaluate each person's contribution to the life of the church, and judgment day will reveal the truth of each person's work. God will determine whether or not a person has been faithful to Jesus' instructions. Good work will be rewarded; unfaithful or inferior work will be discounted. "The builder will be saved, but like someone barely escaping through a wall of flames" means that unfaithful workers will be saved, but only by the skin of their teeth. All their accomplishments will count for nothing.

1 Cor 3:16-17 Paul wanted the Corinthians to understand that they were a unified assembly ("all of you together are the temple of God" and "the Spirit of God lives in you"). They were not to see themselves as a collection of competing interests or independent individuals. Paul was emphasizing the intent of Jesus' prayer in John 17:21-23 that believers be unified in God. What actions could you take this week to strengthen your ties to fellow Christians in the church of Jesus Christ?

▶ **1 CORINTHIANS 3:1-23** ***(cont.)***

[16]Don't you realize that all of you together are the temple of God and that the Spirit of God lives in* you? [17]God will destroy anyone who destroys this temple. For God's temple is holy, and you are that temple.

[18]Stop deceiving yourselves. If you think you are wise by this world's standards, you need to become a fool to be truly wise. [19]For the wisdom of this world is foolishness to God. As the Scriptures say,

"He traps the wise
in the snare of their own cleverness."*

[20]And again,

"The LORD knows the thoughts of the wise;
he knows they are worthless."*

[21]So don't boast about following a particular human leader. For everything belongs to you—[22]whether Paul or Apollos or Peter,* or the world, or life and death, or the present and the future. Everything belongs to you, [23]and you belong to Christ, and Christ belongs to God.

Paul's Relationship with the Corinthians

1 CORINTHIANS 4:1-21

So look at Apollos and me as mere servants of Christ who have been put in charge of explaining God's mysteries. [2]Now, a person who is put in charge as a manager must be faithful. [3]As for me, it matters very little how I might be evaluated by you or by any human authority. I don't even trust my own judgment on this point. [4]My conscience is clear, but that doesn't prove I'm right. It is the Lord himself who will examine me and decide.

[5]So don't make judgments about anyone ahead of time—before the Lord returns. For he will bring our darkest secrets to light and will reveal our private motives. Then God will give to each one whatever praise is due.

[6]Dear brothers and sisters,* I have used Apollos and myself to illustrate what I've been saying. If you pay attention to what I have quoted from the Scriptures,* you won't be proud of one of your leaders at the expense of another. [7]For what gives you the right

1 Cor 3:16 Or *among.* **1 Cor 3:19** Job 5:13. **1 Cor 3:20** Ps 94:11. **1 Cor 3:22** Greek *Cephas.* **1 Cor 4:6a** Greek *Brothers.* **1 Cor 4:6b** Or *If you learn not to go beyond "what is written."*

1 Cor 3:18-21 Paul was not telling the Corinthian believers to neglect the pursuit of knowledge. He was warning them not to glory in the wisdom of this age. God's way of thinking is far above ours; he knows all the futile thoughts of the "wise." The Corinthians were boasting about the wisdom of their leaders and teachers. Their pride made them value the messenger more than the message. We are not to put our trust in anyone but God.

1 Cor 3:22 Paul says that both life and death are ours. While nonbelievers are victims of life, swept along by its current and wondering if there is meaning to it, believers can use life well because they understand its true purpose. Nonbelievers can only fear death. For believers, death holds no terrors because Christ has conquered all fears (see 1 Jn 4:18). Death is only the beginning of eternal life with God.

1 Cor 4:1-2 Paul urged the Corinthians to think of him, Peter, and Apollos as mere servants of Christ entrusted with the secret things of God (see the note on 1 Cor 2:7, p. 1598). A servant does what his master tells him to do. We must do what God tells us to do in the Bible and through his Holy Spirit. Each day God presents us with needs and opportunities that challenge us to do what we know is right.

1 Cor 4:5 It is tempting to judge fellow Christians, evaluating whether or not they are good followers of Christ. But only God knows a person's heart, and he is the only one with the right to judge. Paul's warning to the Corinthians should also warn us. We are to confront those who are sinning (see 1 Cor 5:12-13), but we must not judge who is a better servant for Christ. When you judge someone, you invariably consider yourself better—and that is arrogant.

The Parthenon in Athens

When Paul told the Corinthians that they were the "temple of God" (1 Cor 3:16), as Greeks, they wouldn't have thought of the Jewish Temple in Jerusalem but of any number of temples that were erected throughout Greece. The Greeks strove to attain beauty in their architecture. This worthy motive found its highest expression in the 5th century B.C. In the time of Pericles (461–429 B.C.) the Parthenon and Propylaea on the Acropolis were remodeled from earlier originals, and the Erechtheum was also built there. Subsequent temples in Athens included that of Hephaestus, which was a less graceful version of the Parthenon, and the shrine of Ares. Phidias, the sculptor who designed the Parthenon, was also responsible, with his students, for many statues from the 5th century B.C.

We are God's temple. God through his Spirit inhabits us. This is a privilege and responsibility. What do you picture when you hear this?

1 Cor 4:6-7 How easy it is for us to become attached to a spiritual leader. When someone has helped us, it's natural to feel loyalty. But Paul warns against having such pride in our favorite leaders that we cause divisions in the church. True spiritual leaders are representatives of Christ and have nothing to offer that God hasn't given them. Don't let your loyalty cause strife, slander, or broken relationships. Make sure that your deepest loyalties are to Christ and not to his human agents. Those who spend more time in debating church leadership than in declaring Christ's message don't have the mind of Christ.

to make such a judgment? What do you have that God hasn't given you? And if everything you have is from God, why boast as though it were not a gift?

8You think you already have everything you need. You think you are already rich. You have begun to reign in God's kingdom without us! I wish you really were reigning already, for then we would be reigning with you. 9Instead, I sometimes think God has put us apostles on display, like prisoners of war at the end of a victor's parade, condemned to die. We have become a spectacle to the entire world—to people and angels alike.

10Our dedication to Christ makes us look like fools, but you claim to be so wise in Christ! We are weak, but you are so powerful! You are honored, but we are ridiculed. 11Even now we go hungry and thirsty, and we don't have enough clothes to keep warm. We are often beaten and have no home. 12We work wearily with our own hands to earn our living. We bless those who curse us. We are patient with those who abuse us. 13We appeal gently when evil things are said about us. Yet we are treated like the world's garbage, like everybody's trash—right up to the present moment.

14I am not writing these things to shame you, but to warn you as my beloved children. 15For even if you had ten thousand others to teach you about Christ, you have only one spiritual father. For I became your father in Christ Jesus when I preached the Good News to you. 16So I urge you to imitate me.

17That's why I have sent Timothy, my beloved and faithful child in the Lord. He will remind you of how I follow Christ Jesus, just as I teach in all the churches wherever I go.

18Some of you have become arrogant, thinking I will not visit you again. 19But I will come—and soon—if the Lord lets me, and then I'll find out whether these arrogant people just give pretentious speeches or whether they really have God's power. 20For the Kingdom of God is not just a lot of talk; it is living by God's power. 21Which do you choose? Should I come with a rod to punish you, or should I come with love and a gentle spirit?

SET AN EXAMPLE FOR OTHERS

Throughout Scripture, setting an example is stressed as an important element of discipleship. Paul told the Corinthian believers to imitate him (1 Cor 4:16). As the body of Christ, believers must show Christ to the world by being examples. Nonbelievers should be able to see Christ in believers and be so drawn to what they see that they seek Christ and his salvation. What kind of example are you?

Matt 11:29
"Take my yoke upon you."
- Jesus told his followers to learn from his example of gentleness and humility.

Phil 3:17
"Pattern your lives after mine."
- Paul urged believers to follow his example of enthusiasm, perseverance, and maturity.

1 Thes 1:6-7
"You imitated both us and the Lord. . . . You have become an example."
- The new Christians at Thessalonica received training in discipleship from Paul, and even in suffering they expressed what they had learned.

1 Tim 1:16
"But God had mercy on me so that Christ Jesus could use me as a prime example of his great patience with even the worst sinners."
- Paul used his unworthiness to receive Christ as an example of grace so that no one would hold back from coming to Christ.

1 Pet 5:3
"Don't lord it over the people assigned to your care, but lead them by your own good example."
- Peter taught Christian leaders to lead by example, not by commands.

1 Cor 4:6-13 The Corinthians had split into various cliques, each following its favorite preacher (Paul, Apollos, Peter, etc.). Each clique really believed it was the only one to have the whole truth and thus felt spiritually proud. But Paul told the groups not to boast about being tied to a particular preacher, because each preacher was simply a humble servant who had suffered for the same message of salvation in Jesus Christ. No preacher of God has more status than another.

1 Cor 4:15 Paul was calling attention to his special role as the Corinthians' spiritual father. In an attempt to unify the church, Paul appealed to his relationship with them. By *father*, he meant he was the church's founder. Because he started the church, he could be trusted to have its best interests at heart. Paul's tough words were motivated by love—like the love a good father has for his children (see also 1 Thes 2:11).

1 Cor 4:16 Paul told the Corinthians to imitate him—to follow his example. He was able to make this statement because he walked close to God, spent time meditating on God's Word and in prayer, and was aware of God's presence in his life at all times. God was Paul's example; therefore, Paul's life could be an example to other Christians. Paul wasn't expecting others to imitate everything he did, but that they should imitate those aspects of his beliefs and conduct that were modeling Christ's way of living.

1 Cor 4:17 Timothy had traveled with Paul on Paul's second missionary journey (see Acts 16:1-3) and was a key person in the growth of the early church. Timothy probably did not deliver this letter to Corinth but more likely arrived there shortly after the letter came (see 1 Cor 16:10). Timothy's role was to see that Paul's advice was read and implemented. Then he was to return to Paul and report on the church's progress.

1 Cor 4:18-20 Some people talk a lot about faith, but that's all it is—talk. They may know all the right words to say, but their lives don't reflect God's power. Paul says that the Kingdom of God is to be lived, not just discussed. There is a big difference between knowing the right words and living them out. Don't be content to have the right answers about Christ. Let your life show that God's power is really working in you.

1 Cor 4:19 It is not known whether Paul ever returned to Corinth, but it is likely. In 2 Corinthians 2:1, he writes that he decided not to make "another painful visit," implying that he had had a previous painful confrontation with the Corinthian believers (2 Cor 12:14; 13:1; see also the note on 2 Cor 2:1, p. 1627).

Paul Condemns Spiritual Pride

1 CORINTHIANS 5:1-13

I can hardly believe the report about the sexual immorality going on among you—something that even
pagans don't do. I am told that a man in your church
is living in sin with his stepmother.* [2]You are so proud
of yourselves, but you should be mourning in sorrow
and shame. And you should remove this man from
your fellowship.
[3]Even though I am not with you in person, I am
with you in the Spirit.* And as though I were there,
I have already passed judgment on this man [4]in the
name of the Lord Jesus. You must call a meeting of the
church.* I will be present with you in spirit, and so will
the power of our Lord Jesus. [5]Then you must throw
this man out and hand him over to Satan so that his
sinful nature will be destroyed* and he himself* will
be saved on the day the Lord* returns.
[6]Your boasting about this is terrible. Don't you
realize that this sin is like a little yeast that spreads
through the whole batch of dough? [7]Get rid of the old
"yeast" by removing this wicked person from among
you. Then you will be like a fresh batch of dough made
without yeast, which is what you really are. Christ, our
Passover Lamb, has been sacrificed for us.* [8]So let us
celebrate the festival, not with the old bread* of wickedness and evil, but with the new bread* of sincerity
and truth.
[9]When I wrote to you before, I told you not to associate with people who indulge in sexual sin. [10]But
I wasn't talking about unbelievers who indulge in
sexual sin, or are greedy, or cheat people, or worship
idols. You would have to leave this world to avoid
people like that. [11]I meant that you are not to associate with anyone who claims to be a believer* yet
indulges in sexual sin, or is greedy, or worships idols,
or is abusive, or is a drunkard, or cheats people. Don't
even eat with such people.

1 Cor 5:1 Greek *his father's wife.* **1 Cor 5:3** Or *in spirit.* **1 Cor 5:4** Or *In the name of the Lord Jesus, you must call a meeting of the church.* **1 Cor 5:5a** Or *so that his body will be destroyed;* Greek reads *for the destruction of the flesh.* **1 Cor 5:5b** Greek *and the spirit.* **1 Cor 5:5c** Other manuscripts read *the Lord Jesus;* still others read *our Lord Jesus Christ.* **1 Cor 5:7** Greek *has been sacrificed.* **1 Cor 5:8a** Greek *not with old leaven.* **1 Cor 5:8b** Greek *but with unleavened [bread].* **1 Cor 5:11** Greek *a brother.*

1 Cor 5:1ff The church must discipline flagrant sin among its members. Such sins left unchecked can polarize and paralyze a church. But the correction should never be vengeful. Instead, it should be given to help bring about a cure. The Corinthian believers had refused to deal with a specific sin in the church: A man was having an affair with his stepmother. The church was ignoring the situation, and Paul was saying that it had a responsibility to maintain the standards of morality found in God's commandments. God tells us not to judge others. But he also tells us not to tolerate flagrant sin because allowing such sin to go undisciplined will have a dangerous effect on other believers (1 Cor 5:6).

1 Cor 5:5 To hand this man "over to Satan" means to exclude him from the fellowship of believers. Without the spiritual support of Christians, this man would be left alone with his sin and Satan, and perhaps this would drive him to repentance. "So that his sinful nature will be destroyed" states the hope that the experience would bring him to God to destroy his sinful nature through his turning from sin. The term translated "sinful nature" could alternatively mean his body or flesh. This would imply that Satan would afflict him physically and thus bring him back to God.

Putting someone out of the church should be a last resort in disciplinary action. It should not be done out of vengeance but out of love, just as parents punish children to correct and restore them. The church's role is not to hurt but to help offenders, motivating them to repent of their sins and to return to the fellowship of the church.

1 Cor 5:6 Paul was writing to those who wanted to ignore this church problem. They didn't realize that allowing public sin to exist in the church affects all its members. Paul does not expect anyone to be sinless—all believers struggle with sin daily. Instead, he is speaking against those who deliberately sin, feel no guilt, and refuse to repent. This kind of sin cannot be tolerated in the church because it affects others. We have a responsibility to other believers. Blatant sins, left uncorrected, confuse and divide the congregation. While believers should encourage, pray for, and build up one another, they must also be intolerant of sin that jeopardizes the spiritual health of the church.

1 Cor 5:7-8 As the Hebrews prepared for their exodus from slavery in Egypt, they were commanded to prepare bread without yeast because they didn't have time to wait for it to rise. And because yeast also was a symbol of sin, they were commanded to sweep all of it out of the house (Exod 12:15; 13:7). Christ is our Passover lamb, the perfect sacrifice for our sin. Because he has delivered us from the slavery of sin, we should have nothing to do with the sins of the past ("old bread").

1 Cor 5:9 Paul is referring to an earlier letter to the Corinthian church, often called the lost letter because it has not been preserved.

1 Cor 5:10-11 Paul makes it clear that we should not disassociate ourselves from unbelievers—otherwise we could not carry out Christ's command to tell them about salvation (Matt 28:18-20). But we are to

CHURCH DISCIPLINE

The church, at times, must exercise discipline toward members who have sinned. But church discipline must be handled carefully, straightforwardly, and lovingly.

Situations	Steps (Matt 18:15-17)
Unintentional error and/or private sin Public sin and/or those done flagrantly and arrogantly	1. Go to the believer; show the fault in private. 2. If the person does not listen, go with one or two witnesses. 3. If the person refuses to listen, take the matter before the church

After these steps have been carried out, the next steps are:

1. Remove the one in error from the fellowship (1 Cor 5:2-13).
2. The church gives united disapproval, but forgiveness and comfort are in order if the person chooses to repent (2 Cor 2:5-8).
3. Do not associate with the disobedient person; and if you must, speak to that person as one who needs a warning (2 Thes 3:14-15).
4. After two warnings, reject the person from the fellowship (Titus 3:10).

12 It isn't my responsibility to judge outsiders, but it certainly is your responsibility to judge those inside the church who are sinning. 13 God will judge those on the outside; but as the Scriptures say, "You must remove the evil person from among you."*

Avoiding Lawsuits with Christians

1 CORINTHIANS 6:1-11

When one of you has a dispute with another believer, how dare you file a lawsuit and ask a secular court to decide the matter instead of taking it to other believers*! 2 Don't you realize that someday we believers will judge the world? And since you are going to judge the world, can't you decide even these little things among yourselves? 3 Don't you realize that we will judge angels? So you should surely be able to resolve ordinary disputes in this life. 4 If you have legal disputes about such matters, why go to outside judges who are not respected by the church? 5 I am saying this to shame you. Isn't there anyone in all the church who is wise enough to decide these issues? 6 But instead, one believer* sues another—right in front of unbelievers!

7 Even to have such lawsuits with one another is a defeat for you. Why not just accept the injustice and leave it at that? Why not let yourselves be cheated? 8 Instead, you yourselves are the ones who do wrong and cheat even your fellow believers.*

9 Don't you realize that those who do wrong will not inherit the Kingdom of God? Don't fool yourselves. Those who indulge in sexual sin, or who worship idols, or commit adultery, or are male prostitutes, or practice homosexuality, 10 or are thieves, or greedy people, or drunkards, or are abusive, or cheat people—none of these will inherit the Kingdom of God. 11 Some of you were once like that. But you were cleansed; you were made holy; you were made right with God by calling on the name of the Lord Jesus Christ and by the Spirit of our God.

1 Cor 5:13 Deut 17:7. **1 Cor 6:1** Greek *God's holy people;* also in 6:2. **1 Cor 6:6** Greek *one brother.* **1 Cor 6:8** Greek *even the brothers.*

distance ourselves from the person who claims to be a Christian, yet indulges in sins explicitly forbidden in Scripture by rationalizing those sinful actions. By rationalizing sin, a person harms others for whom Christ died. A church that includes such a person is hardly fit to be the light of the world. To do so would distort the picture of Christ it presents to the world. Church leaders must be ready to correct, in love, for the sake of spiritual unity.

1 Cor 5:12 The Bible consistently tells us not to criticize people by gossiping or making rash judgments. At the same time, we are to judge and deal with sin that can hurt others. Paul's instructions should not be used to handle trivial matters or to take revenge; nor should they be applied to individual problems between believers. These verses are instructions for dealing with open sin in the church by a person who claims to be a Christian and yet who sins without remorse. The church is to confront and discipline such a person in love. (See also the notes on 1 Cor 4:5, p. 1600; 1 Cor 5:1ff, p. 1602.)

1 Cor 6:1-6 In 1 Corinthians 5, Paul explained what to do with open immorality in the congregation. In 1 Corinthians 6, he teaches how the congregation should handle smaller problems between believers. Society has set up a legal system in which disagreements can be resolved in courts. But Paul declares that Christians should not have to go to a secular court to resolve their differences. As Christians, we have the Holy Spirit and the mind of Christ, so why should we turn to those who lack God's wisdom? Because of all that we have been given as believers, and because of the authority that we will have in the future to judge the world and the angels, we should be able to deal with disputes among ourselves. See John 5:22; Revelation 3:21 for more on judging the world. Judging angels is mentioned in 2 Peter 2:4; Jude 1:6.

1 Cor 6:6-8 Why did Paul say that Christians should not take their disagreements to unbelievers in secular courts? (1) If the judge and jury are not Christians, they are not likely to be sensitive to Christian values. (2) The basis for going to court is often revenge; this should never be a Christian's motive. (3) Lawsuits harm the cause of Christ and make the church look bad, causing unbelievers to focus on its problems rather than on its purpose.

1 Cor 6:9-11 Paul is describing characteristics of unbelievers. He doesn't mean that all those who have indulged in sexual sin or who have been idol worshipers, adulterers, male prostitutes, practicing homosexuals, thieves, greedy people, drunkards, abusers, and swindlers are automatically and irrevocably excluded from heaven. Christians come out of all kinds of different backgrounds, including these. They may still struggle with evil desires, but they should not continue in these practices. Paul clearly states that even those who sin in these ways can have their lives changed by Christ (1 Cor 6:11). However, those who say that they are Christians but persist in these practices with no sign of remorse will not inherit the Kingdom of God. Such people need to reevaluate their lives to see if they truly believe in Christ.

1 Cor 6:9-11 In a permissive society it is easy for Christians to overlook or tolerate some immoral behavior (greed, drunkenness, etc.) while remaining outraged at others (murder, thievery). We must not participate in sin or condone it in any way; we cannot be selective about what we condemn or excuse. Staying away from more "acceptable" forms of sin is difficult, but it is no harder for us than it was for the Corinthians. God expects his followers in any age to have high standards.

1 Cor 6:9 "Male prostitutes" refers to those who practice homosexuality. The temple of Apollo employed men whose job it was to fulfill the sexual desires of male and female worshipers.

Some people attempt to legitimize homosexual practice as an acceptable alternative lifestyle. Even some Christians say that people have a right to choose their sexual preference. But the Bible specifically calls homosexual behavior sin (see Lev 18:22-29; Rom 1:18-32; 1 Tim 1:9-11). Christians must be careful to condemn only the practice, not the people. Those who commit homosexual acts are not to be feared, ridiculed, or hated. Their lives can be transformed. The church should be a haven of forgiveness and healing for repentant homosexuals without compromising its stance against homosexual behavior.

1 Cor 6:11 Paul emphasizes God's action in making believers new people. The three aspects of God's work are all part of our salvation: Our sins were washed away, we were set apart for special use (sanctified), and we have been made right with God (justified).

Avoiding Sexual Sin

1 CORINTHIANS 6:12-20

You say, "I am allowed to do anything"—but not everything is good for you. And even though "I am allowed
to do anything," I must not become a slave to anything.
13You say, "Food was made for the stomach, and the
stomach for food." (This is true, though someday God
will do away with both of them.) But you can't say that
our bodies were made for sexual immorality. They
were made for the Lord, and the Lord cares about our
bodies. 14And God will raise us from the dead by his
power, just as he raised our Lord from the dead.
15Don't you realize that your bodies are actually parts
of Christ? Should a man take his body, which is part of
Christ, and join it to a prostitute? Never! 16And don't
you realize that if a man joins himself to a prostitute,
he becomes one body with her? For the Scriptures say,
"The two are united into one."* 17But the person who
is joined to the Lord is one spirit with him.
18Run from sexual sin! No other sin so clearly affects
the body as this one does. For sexual immorality is a
sin against your own body. 19Don't you realize that your
body is the temple of the Holy Spirit, who lives in you
and was given to you by God? You do not belong to
yourself, 20for God bought you with a high price. So
you must honor God with your body.

1 Cor 6:16 Gen 2:24.

Don't you realize that your body is the temple of the Holy Spirit, who lives in you and was given to you by God?
1 Corinthians 6:19

1 Cor 6:12 Apparently the church had been quoting and misapplying the words "I am allowed to do anything." Some Christians in Corinth were excusing their sins by saying either that Christ had taken away all sin and so they had complete freedom to live as they pleased, or what they were doing was not strictly forbidden by Scripture. Paul answered both these excuses: (1) While Christ has taken away our sin, this does not give us freedom to go on doing what we know is wrong. The New Testament specifically forbids many sins (see 1 Cor 6:9-10) that were originally prohibited in the Old Testament (see Rom 12:9-21; 13:8-10). (2) Some actions are not sinful in themselves, but they are not appropriate because they can control our lives and lead us away from God. (3) Some actions may hurt others. Anything we do that hurts rather than helps others is not right.

1 Cor 6:12-13 Many of the world's religions teach that the soul or spirit is important but the body is not. Christianity has sometimes been influenced by these ideas. In truth, Christianity takes very seriously the realm of the physical. We worship a God who created a physical world and pronounced it good. He promises us a new earth, where real people will have transformed physical lives—not a pink cloud where disembodied souls listen to harp music. At the heart of Christianity is the story of God himself taking on flesh and blood and coming to live with us, offering both physical healing and spiritual restoration.

We humans, like Adam, are a combination of dust and spirit. Just as our spirits affect our bodies, so our physical bodies affect our spirits. We cannot commit sin with our bodies without damaging our souls because our bodies and souls are inseparably joined. In the new earth we will have resurrection bodies that are not corrupted by sin. Then we will enjoy the fullness of our salvation.

1 Cor 6:12-13 Freedom is a mark of the Christian faith—freedom from sin and guilt, and freedom to use and enjoy anything that comes from God. But Christians should not abuse this freedom and hurt themselves or others. Drinking too much leads to alcoholism; gluttony leads to obesity. Be careful that what God has allowed you to enjoy doesn't grow into a bad habit that controls you. For more about Christian freedom and everyday behavior, read 1 Corinthians 8.

1 Cor 6:13 Sexual immorality is a temptation that is always before us. In movies and on television, sex outside marriage is treated as a normal, even desirable, part of life, while marriage is often shown as confining and joyless. We can even be looked down on by others if we are suspected of being pure. But God does not forbid sexual sin just to be difficult. He knows its power to destroy us physically and spiritually. No one should underestimate the power of sexual immorality. It has devastated countless lives and destroyed families, churches, communities, and even nations. God wants to protect us from damaging ourselves and others, and so he offers to fill us—our loneliness, our desires—with himself.

1 Cor 6:15-17 This teaching about sexual immorality and prostitutes was especially important for the Corinthian church because the temple of the love goddess Aphrodite was in Corinth. This temple employed more than a thousand prostitutes as priestesses, and sex was part of the worship ritual. Paul clearly stated that Christians are to have no part in sexual immorality, even if it is acceptable and popular in our culture.

1 Cor 6:18 Christians are free to be all they can be for God, but they are not free *from* God. God created sex to be a beautiful and essential ingredient of marriage, but sexual sin—sex outside the marriage relationship—always hurts someone. It hurts God because it shows that we prefer following our own desires instead of the leading of the Holy Spirit. It hurts others because it violates the commitment so necessary to a relationship. It often brings disease to our bodies. And it deeply affects our personality, which responds in anguish when we harm ourselves physically and spiritually.

1 Cor 6:19-20 What did Paul mean when he said that our body belongs to God? Many people say they have the right to do whatever they want with their own bodies. Although they think that this is freedom, they are really enslaved to their own desires. When we become Christians, the Holy Spirit comes to live in us. Therefore, we no longer own our bodies. That God bought us "with a high price" refers to slaves purchased at an auction. Christ's death freed us from sin but also obligates us to his service. Because your body belongs to God, you must not violate his standards for living.

2. PAUL ANSWERS CHURCH QUESTIONS

After discussing disorder in the church, Paul moves to the list of questions that the Corinthians had sent him, including subjects of marriage, singleness, eating meat offered to idols, propriety in worship, orderliness in the Lord's Supper, spiritual gifts, and the resurrection. Questions that plague churches today are remarkably similar to these, so we can receive specific guidance in these areas from this letter.

Instruction on Marriage

1 CORINTHIANS 7:1-40

Now regarding the questions you asked in your letter. Yes, it is good to abstain from sexual relations.* [2]But because there is so much sexual immorality, each man should have his own wife, and each woman should have her own husband.

[3]The husband should fulfill his wife's sexual needs, and the wife should fulfill her husband's needs. [4]The wife gives authority over her body to her husband, and the husband gives authority over his body to his wife.

[5]Do not deprive each other of sexual relations, unless you both agree to refrain from sexual intimacy for a limited time so you can give yourselves more completely to prayer. Afterward, you should come together again so that Satan won't be able to tempt you because of your lack of self-control. [6]I say this as a concession, not as a command. [7]But I wish everyone were single, just as I am. Yet each person has a special gift from God, of one kind or another.

[8]So I say to those who aren't married and to widows—it's better to stay unmarried, just as I am. [9]But if they can't control themselves, they should go ahead and marry. It's better to marry than to burn with lust.

[10]But for those who are married, I have a command that comes not from me, but from the Lord.* A wife must not leave her husband. [11]But if she does leave him, let her remain single or else be reconciled to him. And the husband must not leave his wife.

[12]Now, I will speak to the rest of you, though I do not have a direct command from the Lord. If a Christian man* has a wife who is not a believer and she is willing to continue living with him, he must not leave her. [13]And if a Christian woman has a husband who is not a believer and he is willing to continue living

1 Cor 7:1 Or *to live a celibate life;* Greek reads *It is good for a man not to touch a woman.* **1 Cor 7:10** See Matt 5:32; 19:9; Mark 10:11-12; Luke 16:18. **1 Cor 7:12** Greek *a brother.*

---

1 Cor 7:1 The Corinthians had written to Paul, asking him several questions relating to the Christian life and problems in the church. The first question was whether it was good to be married. Paul answers this and other questions in the remainder of this letter.

1 Cor 7:1ff Christians in Corinth were surrounded by sexual temptation. The city had a reputation even among pagans for sexual immorality and religious prostitution. It was to this kind of society that Paul delivered these instructions on sex and marriage. The Corinthians needed special, specific instructions because of their culture's immoral standards. For more on Paul's teaching about marriage, see Ephesians 5.

1 Cor 7:3-5 Sexual temptations are difficult to withstand because they appeal to the normal and natural desires that God has given us. Marriage provides God's way to satisfy these natural sexual desires and to strengthen the partners against temptation. Married couples have the responsibility to care for each other; therefore, husbands and wives should not withhold themselves sexually from one another but should fulfill each other's needs and desires. (See also the note on 1 Cor 10:13, p. 1610.)

1 Cor 7:3-11 The Corinthian church was in turmoil because of the immorality of the culture around them. Some Greeks, in rejecting immorality, rejected sex and marriage altogether. The Corinthian Christians wondered if this was what they should do also, so they asked Paul several questions: "Because sex is perverted, shouldn't we also abstain in marriage?" "If my spouse is unsaved, should I seek a divorce?" "Should unmarried people and widows remain unmarried?" Paul answered many of these questions by saying, "For now, stay put. Be content in the situation where God has placed you. If you're married, don't seek to be single. If you're single, don't seek to be married. Live God's way, one day at a time, and he will show you what to do."

1 Cor 7:4 Spiritually, our bodies belong to God when we become Christians because Jesus Christ bought us by paying the price to release us from sin (see 1 Cor 6:19-20). Physically, our bodies belong to our spouses because God designed marriage so that, through the union of husband and wife, the two become one (Gen 2:24). Paul stressed complete equality in sexual relationships. Neither male nor female should seek dominance or autonomy.

1 Cor 7:7 Both marriage and singleness are gifts from God. One is not morally better than the other, and both are valuable to accomplishing God's purposes. It is important for us, therefore, to accept our present situation. When Paul said he wished that all people were like him (unmarried), he was expressing his desire that more people would devote themselves completely to the ministry without the added concerns of a spouse and family, as he had done. He was not criticizing marriage—after all, it is God's created way of providing companionship and populating the earth.

1 Cor 7:9 Sexual pressure is not the best motive for getting married, but it is better to marry the right person than to "burn with lust." Many new believers in Corinth thought that all sex was wrong, and so engaged couples were deciding not to get married. In this passage, Paul was telling couples who wanted to marry that they should not frustrate their normal sexual drives by avoiding marriage. This does not mean that people who have trouble controlling themselves should marry the first person who comes along. It is better to deal with the pressure of desire than to deal with an unhappy marriage.

1 Cor 7:12 Paul's "command" about the permanence of marriage (1 Cor 7:10) comes from the Old Testament (Gen 2:24) and from Jesus (Mark 10:2-12). His *suggestion* in this verse is based on God's command, and Paul applies it to the situation the Corinthians were facing. Paul ranked the command above the suggestion because one is an eternal principle while the other is a specific application. Nevertheless, for people in similar situations, Paul's suggestion is the best advice they will get. Paul was a man of God, an apostle, and he had the mind of Christ.

1 Cor 7:12-14 Because of their desire to serve Christ, some people in the Corinthian church thought they ought to divorce their pagan spouses and marry Christians. But Paul affirmed the marriage commitment. God's ideal is for husbands and wives to stay together—even when one spouse is not a believer. The Christian spouse should try to win the other to Christ. It would be easy to rationalize leaving; however, Paul makes a strong case for staying with the unbelieving spouse and being a positive influence on the marriage. Paul, like Jesus, believed that marriage is permanent (see Mark 10:1-9).

▸ **1 CORINTHIANS 7:1-40** ***(cont.)***

with her, she must not leave him. [14]For the Christian wife brings holiness to her marriage, and the Christian husband* brings holiness to his marriage. Otherwise, your children would not be holy, but now they are holy. [15](But if the husband or wife who isn't a believer insists on leaving, let them go. In such cases the Christian husband or wife* is no longer bound to the other, for God has called you* to live in peace.) [16]Don't you wives realize that your husbands might be saved because of you? And don't you husbands realize that your wives might be saved because of you?

[17]Each of you should continue to live in whatever situation the Lord has placed you, and remain as you were when God first called you. This is my rule for all the churches. [18]For instance, a man who was circumcised before he became a believer should not try to reverse it. And the man who was uncircumcised when he became a believer should not be circumcised now. [19]For it makes no difference whether or not a man has been circumcised. The important thing is to keep God's commandments.

[20]Yes, each of you should remain as you were when God called you. [21]Are you a slave? Don't let that worry you—but if you get a chance to be free, take it. [22]And remember, if you were a slave when the Lord called you, you are now free in the Lord. And if you were free when the Lord called you, you are now a slave of Christ. [23]God paid a high price for you, so don't be enslaved by the world.* [24]Each of you, dear brothers and sisters,* should remain as you were when God first called you.

[25]Now regarding your question about the young women who are not yet married. I do not have a command from the Lord for them. But the Lord in his mercy has given me wisdom that can be trusted, and I will share it with you. [26]Because of the present crisis,* I think it is best to remain as you are. [27]If you have a wife, do not seek to end the marriage. If you do not have a wife, do not seek to get married. [28]But if you do get married, it is not a sin. And if a young woman gets married, it is not a sin. However, those who get married at this time will have troubles, and I am trying to spare you those problems.

[29]But let me say this, dear brothers and sisters: The time that remains is very short. So from now on, those with wives should not focus only on their marriage. [30]Those who weep or who rejoice or who buy things should not be absorbed by their weeping or their joy or their possessions. [31]Those who use the things of the

1 Cor 7:14 Greek *the brother.* **1 Cor 7:15a** Greek *the brother or sister.* **1 Cor 7:15b** Some manuscripts read *us.* **1 Cor 7:23** Greek *don't become slaves of people.* **1 Cor 7:24** Greek *brothers;* also in 7:29. **1 Cor 7:26** Or *the pressures of life.*

1 Cor 7:14 The blessings that flow to believers don't stop there but extend to others. God regards the marriage as set apart for his use by the presence of one Christian spouse. The other does not receive salvation automatically but is blessed by this relationship. The children of such a marriage have a godly influence and are set apart (because of God's blessing on the family unit) until they are old enough to make their own decision for Christ.

1 Cor 7:15-16 This verse is misused by some as a loophole to get out of marriage. But Paul's statements were given to encourage the Christian spouse to try to get along with the unbeliever and make the marriage work. If the unbelieving spouse insists on leaving, Paul said to let that person go. The only alternative would be for the Christian spouse to deny their faith to preserve the marriage, and that would be worse than dissolving the marriage. Paul's chief purpose in writing this was to urge the married couples to seek unity, not separation (see 1 Cor 7:17; 1 Pet 3:1-2).

1 Cor 7:17 Apparently the Corinthians were ready to make wholesale changes without thinking through the ramifications. Paul was writing to say that people should be Christians where they are. You can do God's work and demonstrate your faith anywhere. If you became a Christian after marriage and your spouse is not a believer, remember that you don't have to be married to a Christian to live for Christ. Don't assume that you are in the wrong place or stuck with the wrong person. You may be just where God wants you (see 1 Cor 7:20).

1 Cor 7:18-19 The ceremony of circumcision was an important part of the Jews' relationship with God. In fact, before Christ came, circumcision was commanded by God for those who claimed to follow him (Gen 17:9-14). But after Christ's death, circumcision was no longer necessary (Acts 15; Rom 4:9-11; Gal 5:2-4; Col 2:11). Pleasing God and obeying him are more important than observing traditional ceremonies.

1 Cor 7:20 We may become so concerned about what we could be doing for God somewhere else that we miss great opportunities right where we are. Paul says that when you become a Christian, you should continue on with the work you have previously been doing—provided it isn't immoral or unethical. Every job can become Christian work when you realize that it can be an opportunity to honor, serve, and speak out for Christ. Because God has placed you where you are, take advantage of every opportunity to serve him there.

1 Cor 7:22 Slavery was common throughout the Roman Empire. Some Christians in the Corinthian church were undoubtedly slaves. Paul said that although they were slaves to other human beings, they were free from the power of sin in their lives. People today are slaves to sin until they commit their lives to Christ, who alone can conquer sin's power. Sin, pride, and fear no longer have any claim over us, just as a slave owner no longer has power over the slaves he has sold. The Bible says we become Christ's slaves when we become Christians (Rom 6:18), but this actually means we gain our freedom, because sin no longer controls us.

1 Cor 7:26 Paul probably foresaw the impending persecution that the Roman government would soon bring upon Christians. He gave this practical advice because being unmarried would mean less suffering and more freedom to throw one's life into the cause of Christ (1 Cor 7:29), even to the point of fearlessly dying for him. Paul's advice reveals his single-minded devotion to spreading the Good News.

1 Cor 7:28 Many people naively think that marriage will solve all their problems. Here are some problems marriage won't solve: (1) loneliness, (2) sexual temptation, (3) one's deepest emotional needs, (4) life's difficulties. Marriage alone does not hold two people together but commitment does—commitment to Christ and to each other despite conflicts and problems. As wonderful as it is, marriage does not automatically solve every problem. Whether married or single, we must be content with our situation and focus on Christ, not on loved ones, to help address our problems.

1 Cor 7:29 Paul urges all believers to make the most of their time before Christ's return. Every person in every generation should have this sense of urgency about telling the Good News to others. Life is short—there's not much time!

1 Cor 7:29-31 Paul urges believers not to regard marriage, home, or financial security as the ultimate goals of life. As much as possible, we should live unhindered by the

world should not become attached to them. For this world as we know it will soon pass away.

32I want you to be free from the concerns of this life. An unmarried man can spend his time doing the Lord's work and thinking how to please him. 33But a married man has to think about his earthly responsibilities and how to please his wife. 34His interests are divided. In the same way, a woman who is no longer married or has never been married can be devoted to the Lord and holy in body and in spirit. But a married woman has to think about her earthly responsibilities and how to please her husband. 35I am saying this for your benefit, not to place restrictions on you. I want you to do whatever will help you serve the Lord best, with as few distractions as possible.

36But if a man thinks that he's treating his fiancée improperly and will inevitably give in to his passion, let him marry her as he wishes. It is not a sin. 37But if he has decided firmly not to marry and there is no urgency and he can control his passion, he does well not to marry. 38So the person who marries his fiancée does well, and the person who doesn't marry does even better.

39A wife is bound to her husband as long as he lives. If her husband dies, she is free to marry anyone she wishes, but only if he loves the Lord.* 40But in my opinion it would be better for her to stay single, and I think I am giving you counsel from God's Spirit when I say this.

Food Sacrificed to Idols

1 CORINTHIANS 8:1-13

Now regarding your question about food that has been offered to idols. Yes, we know that "we all have knowledge" about this issue. But while knowledge makes us feel important, it is love that strengthens the church. 2Anyone who claims to know all the answers doesn't really know very much. 3But the person who loves God is the one whom God recognizes.*

4So, what about eating meat that has been offered to idols? Well, we all know that an idol is not really a god and that there is only one God. 5There may be so-called gods both in heaven and on earth, and some people actually worship many gods and many lords. 6But we know that there is only one God, the Father, who created everything, and we live for him. And there is only one Lord, Jesus Christ, through whom God made everything and through whom we have been given life.

7However, not all believers know this. Some are accustomed to thinking of idols as being real, so

1 Cor 7:39 Greek *but only in the Lord.* **1 Cor 8:3** Some manuscripts read *the person who loves has full knowledge.*

STRONGER, WEAKER BELIEVERS

Paul advises those who are more mature in the faith about how they must care for their brothers and sisters in Christ who have more tender consciences; those "weaker" brothers and sisters are advised concerning their growth; and pastors and leaders are instructed on how to deal with the conflicts that easily could arise between these groups.

Advice to	
Stronger believers	Don't be proud of your maturity; don't flaunt your freedom. Act in love so you do not cause a weaker believer to stumble.
Weaker believers	Although you may not feel the same freedom in some areas as in others, take your time, pray to God, but do not force others to adhere to your stipulations. You would hinder other believers by making up rules and standards for how everyone ought to behave. Make sure your convictions are based on God's Word and are not simply an expression of your opinions.
Pastors and leaders	Teach correctly from God's Word, helping Christians to understand what is right and wrong in God's eyes and to see that they can have varied opinions on other issues and still be unified. Don't allow potential problems to get out of hand, causing splits and divisions.

cares of this world, not getting involved with burdensome mortgages, budgets, investments, or debts that might keep us from doing God's work. A married man or woman, as Paul points out (1 Cor 7:33-34), must take care of earthly responsibilities but should make every effort to keep them modest and manageable.

1 Cor 7:32-34 Some single people feel tremendous pressure to be married. They think their lives can be complete only with a spouse. But Paul underlines one advantage of being single—the potential of a greater focus on Christ and his work. If you are unmarried, use your special opportunity to serve Christ wholeheartedly.

1 Cor 7:38 When Paul says the unmarried person does even better, he is talking about the potential time available for service to God. The single person does not have the responsibility of caring for a spouse and raising a family. Singleness, however, does not ensure service to God; involvement in service depends on the commitment of the individual.

1 Cor 7:40 Paul's advice comes from the Holy Spirit, who guides and equips both single and married people to fulfill their roles.

1 Cor 8:1 Meat bought in the marketplace was likely to have been offered to an idol in one of the many pagan temples. Animals were brought to a temple, killed before an idol as part of a pagan religious ceremony, and eaten at a feast in the pagan temple or taken to butchers who sold the meat in the marketplace. The believers wondered if, by eating such meat, they were somehow participating in the worship of idols.

1 Cor 8:1-3 Love is more important than knowledge. Knowledge can make us look good and feel important, but we can all too easily develop an arrogant, know-it-all attitude. Many people with strong opinions are unwilling to listen to and learn from God and others. We can obtain God's knowledge only by loving him (see Jas 3:17-18). And we can know God only when we model him by showing love (1 Jn 4:7-8).

1 Cor 8:4-9 Paul addressed these words to believers who weren't bothered by eating meat that had been offered to idols. Although idols were phony, and the pagan ritual of sacrificing to them was meaningless, eating such meat offended some Christians with sensitive consciences. Paul said, therefore, that mature believers should avoid eating meat offered to idols if it would violate the conscience of weak Christians.

▸ **1 CORINTHIANS 8:1-13 *(cont.)***
when they eat food that has been offered to idols, they think of it as the worship of real gods, and their weak consciences are violated. [8]It's true that we can't win God's approval by what we eat. We don't lose anything if we don't eat it, and we don't gain anything if we do.

[9]But you must be careful so that your freedom does not cause others with a weaker conscience to stumble. [10]For if others see you—with your "superior knowledge"—eating in the temple of an idol, won't they be encouraged to violate their conscience by eating food that has been offered to an idol? [11]So because of your superior knowledge, a weak believer* for whom Christ died will be destroyed. [12]And when you sin against other believers* by encouraging them to do something they believe is wrong, you are sinning against Christ. [13]So if what I eat causes another believer to sin, I will never eat meat again as long as I live—for I don't want to cause another believer to stumble.

Paul Gives Up His Rights

1 CORINTHIANS 9:1-27
Am I not as free as anyone else? Am I not an apostle? Haven't I seen Jesus our Lord with my own eyes? Isn't it because of my work that you belong to the Lord? [2]Even if others think I am not an apostle, I certainly am to you. You yourselves are proof that I am the Lord's apostle.

[3]This is my answer to those who question my authority.* [4]Don't we have the right to live in your homes and share your meals? [5]Don't we have the right to bring a Christian wife with us as the other apostles and the Lord's brothers do, and as Peter* does? [6]Or is it only Barnabas and I who have to work to support ourselves?

[7]What soldier has to pay his own expenses? What farmer plants a vineyard and doesn't have the right to eat some of its fruit? What shepherd cares for a flock of sheep and isn't allowed to drink some of the milk? [8]Am I expressing merely a human opinion, or does the law say the same thing? [9]For the law of Moses says, "You must not muzzle an ox to keep it from eating as it treads out the grain."* Was God thinking only about oxen when he said this? [10]Wasn't he actually speaking to us? Yes, it was written for us, so that the one who plows and the one who threshes the grain might both expect a share of the harvest.

[11]Since we have planted spiritual seed among you, aren't we entitled to a harvest of physical food and drink? [12]If you support others who preach to you, shouldn't we have an even greater right to be supported? But we have never used this right. We would rather put up with anything than be an obstacle to the Good News about Christ.

[13]Don't you realize that those who work in the temple get their meals from the offerings brought to the temple? And those who serve at the altar get a share of the sacrificial offerings. [14]In the same way, the Lord ordered that those who preach the Good News should be supported by those who benefit from it. [15]Yet I have never used any of these rights. And I am not writing this to suggest that I want to start now. In fact, I would rather die than lose my right to boast about preaching without charge. [16]Yet preaching the Good News is not something I can boast about. I am

1 Cor 8:11 Greek *brother;* also in 8:13. **1 Cor 8:12** Greek *brothers.* **1 Cor 9:3** Greek *those who examine me.* **1 Cor 9:5** Greek *Cephas.* **1 Cor 9:9** Deut 25:4.

1 Cor 8:10-13 Christian freedom does not mean that anything goes. It means that our salvation is not obtained by good deeds or legalistic rules; it is the free gift of God (Eph 2:8-9). Christian freedom, then, is inseparably tied to Christian responsibility. New believers are often very sensitive to what is right or wrong, what they should or shouldn't do. Some actions may be perfectly all right for us to do but may harm a Christian brother or sister who is still young in the faith and learning what the Christian life is all about. We must be careful not to offend a sensitive or younger Christian or, by our example, cause such a one to sin. When we truly love others, our freedom is less important to us than strengthening the faith of a brother or sister in Christ.

1 Cor 9:1 Some Corinthians were questioning Paul's authority and rights as an apostle, so Paul gave his credentials: He actually had seen and talked with the resurrected Christ, who had called him to be an apostle (see Acts 9:3-18). Such credentials make the advice he gives in this letter more persuasive. In 2 Corinthians 10–13, Paul defends his apostleship in greater detail.

1 Cor 9:1 Changed lives were the evidence that God was using Paul. Does your faith have an impact on others? You can be a life-changer, helping others grow spiritually, if you dedicate yourself to being used by God and letting him make you effective.

1 Cor 9:4ff Paul uses himself as an illustration of giving up personal rights. Paul had the right to hospitality, to be married, and to be paid for his work. But he willingly gave up these rights to win people to Christ. When your focus is on living for Christ, your rights become comparatively unimportant.

1 Cor 9:4-10 Jesus said that workers deserve their wages (Luke 10:7). Paul echoes this thought and urges the church to be sure to pay their Christian workers. We have the responsibility to care for our pastors, teachers, and other spiritual leaders. It is our duty to see that those who serve us in the ministry are fairly and adequately compensated.

1 Cor 9:5 The Lord's brothers attained leadership status in the church at Jerusalem. James (one of Jesus' brothers), for example, led the way to an agreement at the Jerusalem council (Acts 15) and wrote the book of James.

1 Cor 9:13-15 As part of their pay, priests in the temple would receive a portion of the offerings as their food (see Num 18:8-24). These verses concerning Paul's rights and the church's responsibility have a two-part challenge for the church today. First, the church must support its workers in a fair and equitable way. That is the church's responsibility. It can research pay scales, examine the standard of living in its community, and do what is right and fair. Second, Christian workers must not let their attitude about pay and benefits hinder the gospel. It is too easy for the desire for more pay to enter into a person's mind and distract from serving. Ministers need Paul's attitude: a willingness not to demand their rights if to do so would hinder the gospel.

1 Cor 9:16 Preaching the Good News was Paul's gift and calling, and he said he couldn't stop preaching even if he wanted to. Paul was driven by the desire to do what God wanted, using his gifts for God's glory. What special gifts has God given you? Are you motivated, like Paul, to honor God with your gifts?

compelled by God to do it. How terrible for me if I
didn't preach the Good News!
17If I were doing this on my own initiative, I would
deserve payment. But I have no choice, for God has
given me this sacred trust. 18What then is my pay? It
is the opportunity to preach the Good News without
charging anyone. That's why I never demand my rights
when I preach the Good News.
19Even though I am a free man with no master, I
have become a slave to all people to bring many to
Christ. 20When I was with the Jews, I lived like a Jew
to bring the Jews to Christ. When I was with those
who follow the Jewish law, I too lived under that law.
Even though I am not subject to the law, I did this so
I could bring to Christ those who are under the law.
21When I am with the Gentiles who do not follow the
Jewish law,* I too live apart from that law so I can
bring them to Christ. But I do not ignore the law of
God; I obey the law of Christ.
22When I am with those who are weak, I share
their weakness, for I want to bring the weak to
Christ. Yes, I try to find common ground with everyone, doing everything I can to save some. 23I do
everything to spread the Good News and share in
its blessings.
24Don't you realize that in a race everyone runs,
but only one person gets the prize? So run to win!
25All athletes are disciplined in their training. They
do it to win a prize that will fade away, but we do it
for an eternal prize. 26So I run with purpose in every
step. I am not just shadowboxing. 27I discipline my
body like an athlete, training it to do what it should.
Otherwise, I fear that after preaching to others I
myself might be disqualified.

1 Cor 9:21 Greek *those without the law.*

WHY WE DON'T QUIT

Perseverance, persistence, the prize! The Christian life was never promised as an easy way to live; instead, Paul constantly reminds us that we must have a purpose and a plan because times will be difficult and Satan will attack. But we never persevere without the promise of a prize—a promise God will keep.

Reference	*The Purpose*	*The Plan*	*The Prize*
1 Cor 9:24-27	Run to get the prize	Discipline your body, training it	An eternal prize
Gal 6:7-10	Run with purpose in every step	Live to please the Spirit	Everlasting life
Eph 6:10-20	Don't get tired of doing good	Use every piece of God's armor to resist the enemy	Still standing firm after the battle
Phil 3:12-14	Don't give up	Forget the past; press on to reach the end of the race	The heavenly prize for which God calls you
2 Tim 2:1-13	Preach and teach the Good News	Endure suffering as a soldier, and don't get tied up in worldly affairs	We will live with Christ; we will reign with him

1 Cor 9:19-27 Paul asserts that he has freedom to do anything (1 Cor 9:19-22); but he also emphasizes a life of strict discipline (1 Cor 9:24-27). The Christian life involves both freedom and discipline. The goals of Paul's life were to glorify God and bring people to Christ. Thus, he stayed free of any philosophical position or material entanglement that might sidetrack him, while he strictly disciplined himself to carry out his goal. For Paul, both freedom and discipline were important tools to be used in God's service.

1 Cor 9:22-23 Paul gives several important principles for ministry: (1) Find common ground with those you contact; (2) avoid a know-it-all attitude; (3) make others feel accepted; (4) be sensitive to their needs and concerns; and (5) look for opportunities to tell them about Christ. These principles are just as valid for us as they were for Paul.

1 Cor 9:24-27 Winning a race requires purpose and discipline. Paul uses this illustration to explain that the Christian life takes hard work, self-denial, and grueling preparation. As Christians, we are running toward our heavenly reward. The essential disciplines of prayer, Bible study, and worship equip us to run with vigor and stamina. Don't merely observe from the grandstand; don't just turn out to jog a couple of laps each morning. Train diligently—your spiritual progress depends upon it.

1 Cor 9:25 Whatever happened to self-discipline? Many books and speakers guide wandering souls to self-fulfillment, self-satisfaction, and self-awareness. Not many tackle self-discipline.

Self-discipline requires an honest look at your strengths and weaknesses, with emphasis on the latter. It means building the will to say *no* when a powerful appetite inside you screams *yes*. For example, when you have self-discipline, you can (1) say no to friends or situations that will lead you away from Christ, (2) say no to casual sex, saving intimacy for marriage, and (3) say no to laziness in favor of "can do" and "will do." Self-discipline is a long, steady course in learning attitudes that do not come naturally, and channeling natural appetites toward God's purposes. Where are your weak points? Pray with a friend for God's help to redirect weakness into strength.

1 Cor 9:27 When Paul says he might be disqualified, he does not mean that he could lose his salvation but rather that he could lose his privilege of telling others about Christ. It is easy to tell others how to live and then not to take our own advice. We must be careful to practice what we preach.

Lessons from Israel's Idolatry

1 CORINTHIANS 10:1–11:1

I don't want you to forget, dear brothers and sisters,* about our ancestors in the wilderness long ago. All of them were guided by a cloud that moved ahead of them, and all of them walked through the sea on dry ground. [2]In the cloud and in the sea, all of them were baptized as followers of Moses. [3]All of them ate the same spiritual food, [4]and all of them drank the same spiritual water. For they drank from the spiritual rock that traveled with them, and that rock was Christ. [5]Yet God was not pleased with most of them, and their bodies were scattered in the wilderness.

[6]These things happened as a warning to us, so that we would not crave evil things as they did, [7]or worship idols as some of them did. As the Scriptures say, "The people celebrated with feasting and drinking, and they indulged in pagan revelry."* [8]And we must not engage in sexual immorality as some of them did, causing 23,000 of them to die in one day.

[9]Nor should we put Christ* to the test, as some of them did and then died from snakebites. [10]And don't grumble as some of them did, and then were destroyed by the angel of death. [11]These things happened to them as examples for us. They were written down to warn us who live at the end of the age.

[12]If you think you are standing strong, be careful not to fall. [13]The temptations in your life are no different from what others experience. And God is faithful. He will not allow the temptation to be more than you can stand. When you are tempted, he will show you a way out so that you can endure.

[14]So, my dear friends, flee from the worship of idols. [15]You are reasonable people. Decide for yourselves if what I am saying is true. [16]When we bless the cup at the Lord's Table, aren't we sharing in the

1 Cor 10:1 Greek *brothers.* **1 Cor 10:7** Exod 32:6. **1 Cor 10:9** Some manuscripts read *the Lord.*

1 Cor 10:1ff In 1 Corinthians 9, Paul used himself as an example of a mature Christian who disciplines himself to better serve God. In 1 Corinthians 10, he uses Israel as an example of spiritual immaturity, shown in their overconfidence and lack of self-discipline.

1 Cor 10:1-5 The cloud and the sea mentioned here refer to Israel's escape from slavery in Egypt when God led them by a cloud and brought them safely through the Red Sea (Exod 14). The spiritual food and water are the provisions God gave as they traveled through the wilderness (Exod 15–16).

1 Cor 10:2 "All of them were baptized" means that just as we are united in Christ by baptism, so the Israelites were united as God's children, especially seen through the events of the Exodus.

1 Cor 10:7-10 The Israelites made a gold calf and worshiped it in the wilderness (1 Cor 10:7; see Exod 32). They worshiped Baal of Peor and engaged in sexual immorality with Moabite women (1 Cor 10:8; see Num 25:1-9). They complained about their food. They put the Lord to the test by seeing how far they could go (1 Cor 10:9; see Num 21:5-6. The people complained against Moses and Aaron, and a plague resulted (1 Cor 10:10; see Num 14:2, 36; 16:41-50). The angel of death is also referred to in Exodus 12:23.

1 Cor 10:10 Paul warned the Corinthian believers not to grumble. We start to grumble when our attention shifts from what we have to what we don't have. The people of Israel didn't seem to notice what God was doing for them—setting them free, making them a nation, giving them a new land—because they were so wrapped up in what God *wasn't* doing for them. They could think of nothing but the delicious Egyptian food they had left behind (Num 11:5).

Before we judge the Israelites too harshly, it's helpful to think about what occupies our attention most of the time. Are we grateful for what God has given us, or are we always thinking about what we would like to have? Don't allow your unfulfilled desires to cause you to forget God's gifts of life, family, friends, food, health, and work.

1 Cor 10:11 Today's pressures make it easy to ignore or forget the lessons of the past. But Paul cautions us to remember the lessons the Israelites learned about God so we can avoid repeating their errors. The key to remembering is to study the Bible regularly so that these lessons remind us of how God wants us to live. We need not repeat their mistakes!

1 Cor 10:13 In a culture filled with moral depravity and sin-inducing pressures, Paul encourages us about temptation. They happen to everyone, so we don't need to feel we've been singled out. Others have resisted temptation, and so can we. We can resist any temptation because God will show us a way out. How? God will help you to: (1) recognize those people and situations that give you trouble, (2) run from anything you know is wrong, (3) choose to do only what is right, (4) pray for God's help, and (5) seek friends who love God and can offer help when you are tempted. Running from a tempting situation is your first step on the way to victory (see 2 Tim 2:22).

1 Cor 10:14 Idol worship was the major expression of religion in Corinth. There were several pagan temples in the city, and they were very popular. The statues of wood or stone were not evil in themselves, but people gave them credit for what only God could do, such as provide good weather, crops, and children. Idolatry is still a serious problem today, but it takes a different form. We don't put our trust in statues of wood and stone but in paper money and plastic cards. Putting our trust in anything but God is idolatry.

MAKING CHOICES ON SENSITIVE ISSUES

All of us make hundreds of choices every day. Most choices have no right or wrong attached to them—like what to wear or what to eat. But we also face decisions that carry a little more weight. We don't want to do wrong, and we don't want to cause others to do wrong, so how can we make such decisions?

If I choose one course of action:

. . . does it help my witness for Christ? (1 Cor 9:19-22)

. . . am I motivated by a desire to help others know Christ? (1 Cor 9:23; 10:33)

. . . does it help me do my best? (1 Cor 9:25)

. . . is it against a specific command in Scripture and would thus cause me to sin? (1 Cor 10:12)

. . . is it the best and most beneficial course of action? (1 Cor 10:23, 33)

. . . am I thinking only of myself, or do I truly care about the other person? (1 Cor 10:24)

. . . am I acting lovingly or selfishly? (1 Cor 10:28-31)

. . . does it glorify God? (1 Cor 10:31)

. . . will it cause someone else to sin? (1 Cor 10:32)

blood of Christ? And when we break the bread, aren't we sharing in the body of Christ?
17And though we are many, we all eat from one loaf of bread, showing that we are one body.
18Think about the people of Israel. Weren't they united by eating the sacrifices at the altar?

19What am I trying to say? Am I saying that food offered to idols has some significance, or that idols are real gods?
20No, not at all. I am saying that these sacrifices are offered to demons, not to God. And I don't want you to participate with demons.
21You cannot drink from the cup of the Lord and from the cup of demons, too. You cannot eat at the Lord's Table and at the table of demons, too.
22What? Do we dare to rouse the Lord's jealousy? Do you think we are stronger than he is?

23You say, "I am allowed to do anything"*—but not everything is good for you. You say, "I am allowed to do anything"—but not everything is beneficial.
24Don't be concerned for your own good but for the good of others.

25So you may eat any meat that is sold in the marketplace without raising questions of conscience.
26For "the earth is the LORD's, and everything in it."*

27If someone who isn't a believer asks you home for dinner, accept the invitation if you want to. Eat whatever is offered to you without raising questions of conscience.
28(But suppose someone tells you, "This meat was offered to an idol." Don't eat it, out of consideration for the conscience of the one who told you.
29It might not be a matter of conscience for you, but it is for the other person.) For why should my freedom be limited by what someone else thinks?
30If I can thank God for the food and enjoy it, why should I be condemned for eating it?

31So whether you eat or drink, or whatever you do, do it all for the glory of God.
32Don't give offense to Jews or Gentiles* or the church of God.
33I, too, try to please everyone in everything I do. I don't just do what is best for me; I do what is best for others so that many may be saved.
11:1And you should imitate me, just as I imitate Christ.

1 Cor 10:23 Greek *All things are lawful;* also in 10:23b. **1 Cor 10:26** Ps 24:1. **1 Cor 10:32** Greek *or Greeks.*

Our modern idols are those symbols of power, pleasure, or prestige that we so highly regard. When we understand contemporary parallels to idolatry, Paul's words to "flee from the worship of idols" become much more meaningful.

1 Cor 10:16-21 The idea of unity and fellowship with God through eating a sacrifice was strong in Judaism and Christianity as well as in paganism. In Old Testament days, when Jews offered a sacrifice, they ate a part of that sacrifice as a way of restoring unity with God, against whom they had sinned (Deut 12:17-18). Similarly, Christians participate in Christ's once-for-all sacrifice at the Lord's Table when they eat the bread and drink from the cup, signifying his body and blood. Recent converts from paganism could not help being affected if they knowingly ate meat that had been offered to idols at pagan feasts.

1 Cor 10:21 As followers of Christ we must give him our total allegiance. We cannot, as Paul explains, have a part in "the cup of the Lord and . . . the cup of demons." Eating at the Lord's Table means communing with Christ and identifying with his death. Drinking from the cup of demons means identifying with Satan by worshiping or promoting pagan (or evil) activities. Are you leading two lives, trying to follow both Christ and the crowd? The Bible says that you can't do both at the same time.

1 Cor 10:23-24 Sometimes it's hard to know when to defer to weaker believers. Paul gives a simple rule of thumb to help in making the decision: We should be sensitive and gracious. The goal here is not a general hypersensitivity that worries about what others might possibly think. Rather, it is a genuine awareness of others and a willingness to limit what we do when there is a real possibility of misunderstanding and offense. Some actions may not be wrong, but they may not be in the best interest of others. We have freedom in Christ, but we shouldn't exercise our freedom at the cost of hurting a Christian brother or sister. We are not to consider only ourselves; we must also consider the needs and perspective of others. (For more on the proper attitude toward a weak believer, see Rom 14 and the note on 1 Cor 8:10-13, p. 1608.)

1 Cor 10:25-27 Paul gave one answer to the dilemma: Buy whatever meat is sold at the market without asking whether or not it was offered to idols. It doesn't matter anyway, and no one's conscience will be bothered. When we become too worried about our every action, we become legalistic and cannot enjoy life. Everything belongs to God, and he has given us all things to enjoy. If we know something is a problem, then we can deal with it, but we don't need to go looking for problems.

1 Cor 10:28-33 Why should we be limited by another person's conscience? Simply because we are to do all things for God's glory, even our eating and drinking. Nothing we do should cause another believer to stumble. We do what is best for others so that they might be saved. We should also be sensitive to the meaning of our actions to new Christians who are sorting out how to renounce sinful ways from the past and live for Christ.

However, Christians should not make a career out of being the offended people with oversensitive consciences. Believers must not project their standards onto others. Many believers who have been Christians for years are still oversensitive and judgmental of others. Instead of being the offended weaker brothers and sisters, they are no more than offended "Pharisees."

Christian leaders and teachers should carefully teach about the freedom Christians have in matters not expressly forbidden by Scripture. New or weak Christians should not remain in a weak or sensitive state but should grow into maturity and discernment lest they prove to be an unnecessary burden on others' freedom in Christ.

1 Cor 10:31 Our actions must be motivated by God's love so that all we do will be for his glory. Keep this as a guiding principle by asking, "Is this action glorifying God?" or "How can I honor God through this action?"

1 Cor 10:33 Paul's criterion for all his actions was not what he liked best but what was best for those around him. The opposite approach would be (1) being insensitive and doing what we want, no matter who is hurt by it; (2) being oversensitive and doing nothing, for fear that someone may be displeased; (3) being a "yes person" by going along with everything, trying to gain approval from people rather than from God. In this age of "me first" and "looking out for number one," Paul's startling statement is a good standard. If we make the good of others one of our primary goals, we will develop a serving attitude that pleases God.

1 Cor 11:1 Why did Paul say, "Imitate me"? Paul wasn't being arrogant—he did not think of himself as sinless. But Paul was a committed and seasoned follower of Jesus Christ, and those in Corinth knew Paul personally. The best way to point these new Christians to Christ was to point them to a Christian whom they trusted (see also Gal 4:12; Phil 3:17; 1 Thes 1:6; 2:14; 2 Thes 3:7, 9). Paul had been in Corinth almost two years and had built a relationship of trust with many of these new believers.

Instructions for Proper Worship

1 CORINTHIANS 11:2-16

I am so glad that you always keep me in your thoughts, and that you are following the teachings I passed on to you. [3]But there is one thing I want you to know: The head of every man is Christ, the head of woman is man, and the head of Christ is God.* [4]A man dishonors his head* if he covers his head while praying or prophesying. [5]But a woman dishonors her head* if she prays or prophesies without a covering on her head, for this is the same as shaving her head. [6]Yes, if she refuses to wear a head covering, she should cut off all her hair! But since it is shameful for a woman to have her hair cut or her head shaved, she should wear a covering.*

[7]A man should not wear anything on his head when worshiping, for man is made in God's image and reflects God's glory. And woman reflects man's glory. [8]For the first man didn't come from woman, but the first woman came from man. [9]And man was not made for woman, but woman was made for man. [10]For this reason, and because the angels are watching, a woman should wear a covering on her head to show she is under authority.*

[11]But among the Lord's people, women are not independent of men, and men are not independent of women. [12]For although the first woman came from man, every other man was born from a woman, and everything comes from God.

[13]Judge for yourselves. Is it right for a woman to pray to God in public without covering her head? [14]Isn't it

1 Cor 11:3 Or *to know: The source of every man is Christ, the source of woman is man, and the source of Christ is God.* Or *to know: Every man is responsible to Christ, a woman is responsible to her husband, and Christ is responsible to God.* **1 Cor 11:4** Or *dishonors Christ.* **1 Cor 11:5** Or *dishonors her husband.* **1 Cor 11:6** Or *should have long hair.* **1 Cor 11:10** Greek *should have an authority on her head.*

Among the Lord's people, women are not independent of men, and men are not independent of women.

1 Corinthians 11:11

1 Cor 11:2ff In this section Paul's main concern is irreverence in worship. We need to read it in the context of the situation in Corinth. The matter of wearing hats or head coverings, although seemingly insignificant, had become a big problem because two cultural backgrounds were colliding. Jewish women always covered their heads in worship. For a woman to uncover her head in public was a sign of loose morals. On the other hand, Greek women may have been used to worshiping without head coverings.

In this letter Paul had already spoken about divisions and disorder in the church. Both are involved in this issue. Paul's solution came from his desire for unity among church members and for appropriateness in the worship service. He accepted God's sovereignty in creating the rules for relationships.

1 Cor 11:2-16 This section focuses primarily on proper attitudes and conduct in worship, not on the marriage relationship or on the role of women in the church. While Paul's specific instructions may be cultural (women covering their heads in worship), the principles behind them are timeless: respect for spouse, reverence and appropriateness in worship, and focus of all of life on God. If you are doing something that might easily offend members and divide the church, then change your ways to promote church unity. Paul told the women who were not wearing head coverings to wear them, not because it was a scriptural command, but because it kept the congregation from dividing over a petty issue that served only to take people's minds off Christ.

1 Cor 11:3 The phrase, "the head of every man is Christ," could mean that (1) because Christ was present at Creation, he is the Creator of every man; and (2) Christ is every believer's source of life in the new creation.

The phrase "the head of woman is man" does not indicate the man's control or supremacy but rather his being her source. Because man was created first, the woman derives her existence from man, as man does from Christ and Christ from God. Evidently Paul was correcting some excesses in worship in which the emancipated Corinthian women were engaging.

The phrase, "the head of Christ is God," does not mean that Christ was inferior to God in any way. Paul was referring to the incarnation of Christ. Through Christ's coming to earth, believers receive forgiveness and are united with God and with one another. From this theological base, then, Paul began to address the issue of head coverings.

1 Cor 11:3 The principle behind Paul's words is *submission*, which is a key element in the smooth functioning of any business, government, or family. God ordained submission in certain relationships to prevent chaos. It is essential to understand that submission is not surrender, withdrawal, or apathy. It does not mean inferiority, because God created all people in his image and all have equal value. Submission is mutual commitment and cooperation.

Thus, God calls for submission among equals. He did not make the man superior; he made a way for a husband and wife to work together. Jesus Christ, although equal with God the Father, submitted to him to carry out the plan for salvation. Likewise, although equal to man under God, the wife should submit to her husband for the sake of their marriage and family. Submission between equals is submission by choice, not by force. We serve God in these relationships by willingly submitting to others in our church, to our spouses, and to our government leaders.

1 Cor 11:9-11 God created lines of authority in order for his created world to function smoothly. Although there must be lines of authority even in marriage, there should not be lines of superiority. God created men and women with unique and complementary characteristics. One sex is not better than the other. We must not let the issue of authority and submission become a wedge to destroy oneness in marriage. Instead, we should use our unique gifts to strengthen our marriages and to glorify God.

1 Cor 11:14-15 In talking about head coverings and length of hair, Paul is saying that believers should look and behave in ways that are honorable in their own culture. In many cultures long hair on men is considered appropriate and masculine. In Corinth, it was thought to be a sign of male prostitution in the pagan temples. And women with short hair were labeled prostitutes. Paul was saying that in the Corinthian culture, Christian women should keep their hair long. If short

obvious that it's disgraceful for a man to have long hair?
15And isn't long hair a woman's pride and joy? For it has
been given to her as a covering. 16But if anyone wants
to argue about this, I simply say that we have no other
custom than this, and neither do God's other churches.

Order at the Lord's Supper

1 CORINTHIANS 11:17-34

But in the following instructions, I cannot praise you.
For it sounds as if more harm than good is done when
you meet together. 18First, I hear that there are divisions among you when you meet as a church, and to
some extent I believe it. 19But, of course, there must
be divisions among you so that you who have God's
approval will be recognized!

20When you meet together, you are not really interested in the Lord's Supper. 21For some of you hurry
to eat your own meal without sharing with others.
As a result, some go hungry while others get drunk.
22What? Don't you have your own homes for eating
and drinking? Or do you really want to disgrace God's
church and shame the poor? What am I supposed to
say? Do you want me to praise you? Well, I certainly
will not praise you for this!

23For I pass on to you what I received from the Lord
himself. On the night when he was betrayed, the Lord
Jesus took some bread 24and gave thanks to God for it.
Then he broke it in pieces and said, "This is my body,
which is given for you.* Do this to remember me." 25In
the same way, he took the cup of wine after supper, saying, "This cup is the new covenant between God and
his people—an agreement confirmed with my blood.
Do this to remember me as often as you drink it." 26For
every time you eat this bread and drink this cup, you
are announcing the Lord's death until he comes again.

27So anyone who eats this bread or drinks this cup
of the Lord unworthily is guilty of sinning against*
the body and blood of the Lord. 28That is why you

1 Cor 11:24 Greek *which is for you;* other manuscripts read *which is broken for you.* **1 Cor 11:27** Or *is responsible for.*

hair on women was a sign of prostitution, then a Christian woman with short hair would find it difficult to be a believable witness for Jesus Christ. Paul wasn't saying we should adopt all the practices of our culture but that we should avoid appearances and behavior that detract from our ultimate goal of being witnesses for Jesus Christ.

1 Cor 11:17-34 The Lord's Supper (1 Cor 11:20) is a visible representation symbolizing the death of Christ for our sins. It reminds us of Christ's death and the glorious hope of his return. Our participation in it strengthens our faith through fellowship with Christ and with other believers.

1 Cor 11:18-19 Paul acknowledges that there are differences among church members. When they develop into self-willed divisions, they are destructive to the congregation. Those who cause division only serve to highlight those who are genuine believers.

1 Cor 11:21-22 When the Lord's Supper was celebrated in the early church, it included a feast or fellowship meal. In the church in Corinth, the fellowship meal had become a time when some ate and drank excessively while others went hungry. There was little sharing and caring. This certainly did not demonstrate the unity and love that should characterize the church. Paul condemned these actions and reminded the church of the real purpose of the Lord's Supper.

1 Cor 11:24-25 What does the Lord's Supper mean? The early church remembered that Jesus instituted the Lord's Supper on the night of the Passover meal (Luke 22:13-20). Just as Passover celebrated deliverance from slavery in Egypt, so the Lord's Supper celebrates deliverance from sin by Christ's death.

Christians pose several different possibilities for what Christ meant when he said, "This is my body." (1) Some believe that the bread and wine actually become Christ's physical blood and body. (2) Others believe that the bread and wine remain unchanged, but Christ is spiritually present with the bread and wine. (3) Still others believe that the bread and wine merely symbolize Christ's body and blood. Christians generally agree that participating in the Lord's Supper is an important element in the Christian faith and that Christ's presence, however we understand it, strengthens us spiritually.

1 Cor 11:25 What is this new covenant? In the old covenant, people could approach God only through the priests and the sacrificial system. Jesus' death on the cross ushered in the new covenant or agreement between God and us. Now all people can personally approach God and communicate with him. The people of Israel first entered into this agreement after their exodus from Egypt (Exod 24), and it was designed to point to the day when Jesus Christ would come. The new covenant completes, rather than replaces, the old covenant, fulfilling everything the old covenant looked forward to (see Jer 31:31-34). Eating the bread and drinking the cup shows that we are remembering Christ's death for us and renewing our commitment to serve him.

1 Cor 11:25 Jesus said, "Do this to remember me as often as you drink it." How do we remember Christ in the Lord's Supper? By thinking about what he did and why he did it. Further, the remembering has both a backward and forward look. We remember Christ's death, and we remember that he is coming! If the Lord's Supper becomes just a ritual or a pious habit, it loses its significance. But when we appreciate what Christ has done and anticipate what he will do when he returns, the Lord's Supper takes on a profound sense of purpose. Take time to prepare yourself spiritually for Communion. Gratefully recall Christ's loving sacrifice for you. Let the reality that your sins are forgiven motivate you to love and serve him better.

1 Cor 11:27ff Paul gives specific instructions on how the Lord's Supper should be observed. (1) We should take the Lord's Supper thoughtfully because we are proclaiming that Christ died for our sins (1 Cor 11:26). (2) We should take it worthily, with due reverence and respect (1 Cor 11:27). (3) We should examine ourselves for any unconfessed sin or resentful attitude and be properly prepared (1 Cor 11:28). (4) We should be considerate of others, waiting until everyone is there and then eating in an orderly and unified manner (1 Cor 11:33).

1 Cor 11:27-34 When Paul said that no one should take the Lord's Supper unworthily, he was speaking to the church members who were participating in it without thinking of its meaning. To not honor the "body of Christ" means not understanding what the Lord's Supper means and not distinguishing it from a normal meal. Those who did so were "guilty of sinning against the body and blood of the Lord." Instead of honoring his sacrifice, they were sharing in the guilt of those who crucified Christ. If worthiness were defined as being free from sin, no one would be worthy to take the Lord's Supper. We are all sinners saved by grace. This is why we should prepare ourselves for Communion through healthy introspection, confession of sin, and resolution of differences with others. These actions remove the barriers that affect our relationship with Christ and with other believers. Awareness of your sin should not keep you away from Communion but drive you to prepare for and participate in it.

▸ **1 CORINTHIANS 11:17-34** ***(cont.)***

should examine yourself before eating the bread and drinking the cup. 29For if you eat the bread or drink the cup without honoring the body of Christ,* you are eating and drinking God's judgment upon yourself. 30That is why many of you are weak and sick and some have even died.

31But if we would examine ourselves, we would not be judged by God in this way. 32Yet when we are judged by the Lord, we are being disciplined so that we will not be condemned along with the world.

33So, my dear brothers and sisters,* when you gather for the Lord's Supper, wait for each other. 34If you are really hungry, eat at home so you won't bring judgment upon yourselves when you meet together. I'll give you instructions about the other matters after I arrive.

Spiritual Gifts

1 CORINTHIANS 12:1-11

Now, dear brothers and sisters,* regarding your question about the special abilities the Spirit gives us. I don't want you to misunderstand this. 2You know that when you were still pagans, you were led astray and swept along in worshiping speechless idols. 3So I want you to know that no one speaking by the Spirit of God will curse Jesus, and no one can say Jesus is Lord, except by the Holy Spirit.

4There are different kinds of spiritual gifts, but the same Spirit is the source of them all. 5There are different kinds of service, but we serve the same Lord. 6God works in different ways, but it is the same God who does the work in all of us.

7A spiritual gift is given to each of us so we can help each other. 8To one person the Spirit gives the ability to give wise advice*; to another the same Spirit gives a message of special knowledge.* 9The same Spirit gives great faith to another, and to someone else the one Spirit gives the gift of healing. 10He gives one person the power to perform miracles, and another the ability to prophesy. He gives someone else the ability to discern whether a message is from the Spirit of God or from another spirit. Still another person is given the ability to speak in unknown languages,* while another is given the ability to interpret what is being said. 11It is the one and only Spirit who distributes all these gifts. He alone decides which gift each person should have.

1 Cor 11:29 Greek *the body;* other manuscripts read *the Lord's body.* **1 Cor 11:33** Greek *brothers.* **1 Cor 12:1** Greek *brothers.* **1 Cor 12:8a** Or *gives a word of wisdom.* **1 Cor 12:8b** Or *gives a word of knowledge.* **1 Cor 12:10** Or *in various tongues;* also in 12:28, 30.

---

1 Cor 11:30 That some of the people had died may have been a special supernatural judgment on the Corinthian church. This type of disciplinary judgment highlights the seriousness of the Communion service. The Lord's Supper is not to be taken lightly; this new covenant cost Jesus his life. It is not a meaningless ritual, but a sacrament given by Christ to help strengthen our faith.

1 Cor 11:34 People should come to this meal desiring to fellowship with other believers and preparing for the Lord's Supper to follow, not to fill up on a big dinner. "If you are really hungry, eat at home" means that they should eat dinner beforehand so as to come to the fellowship meal in the right frame of mind.

1 Cor 12:1ff The spiritual gifts given to each person by the Holy Spirit are special abilities that are to be used to minister to the needs of the body of believers. This chapter is not an exhaustive list of spiritual gifts (see Rom 12; Eph 4; 1 Pet 4:10-11 for more examples). There are many gifts, people have different gifts, some people have more than one gift, and one gift is not superior to another. All spiritual gifts come from the Holy Spirit, and their purpose is to build up Christ's body, the church.

1 Cor 12:1ff Instead of building up and unifying the Corinthian church, the issue of spiritual gifts was splitting it. Spiritual gifts had become symbols of spiritual power, causing rivalries. Some people thought they were more "spiritual" than others because of their gifts. This was a terrible misuse of spiritual gifts because their purpose is always to help the church function more effectively, not to divide it. We can be divisive if we insist on using our gifts our own way without being sensitive to others. We must never use our gifts as a means of manipulating others or serving our own self-interests.

1 Cor 12:3 Anyone can claim to speak for God, and the world is full of false teachers. Paul gives us a test to help us discern whether or not a messenger is really from God: Does that person confess Christ as Lord? Don't naively accept the words of all who claim to speak for God; test their credentials by finding out what they teach about Christ.

1 Cor 12:6 God is completely involved in the giving, using, and empowering of gifts. Specific gifts, places of service, and activities vary, but they all have their best effects when they build up the body of Christ—the church. God creates a unique place in the body for every believer. Gifts and ministries may overlap, but each believer has a specialized, God-designed role. Part of the exciting adventure of following Christ involves discovering one's service contribution and then making it available to God. Make serving God and his people your motive as you utilize your gifts.

1 Cor 12:9 All Christians have faith. But some have the spiritual gift of faith, which is an unusual measure of trust in the power of God.

1 Cor 12:10 "The ability to prophesy" does not just refer to predicting the future; it can also mean giving a message received from God to the community of believers: "One who prophesies strengthens others, encourages them, and comforts them" (1 Cor 14:3). The prophet Joel had written the words of the Lord: "I will pour out my Spirit upon all people. Your sons and daughters will prophesy" (Joel 2:28). As with the gift of faith, the ability to speak forth with power a word from God is available to everyone (see 1 Cor 14:1-5), but to some the Spirit gives a special measure of this gift. Paul wrote in Romans, "In his grace, God has given us different gifts for doing certain things well. So if God has given you the ability to prophesy, speak out with as much faith as God has given you" (Rom 12:6). This kind of prophecy might be seen in a formal sermon or in a spontaneous, Spirit-inspired message that is given for the edification and encouragement of the body of Christ.

1 Cor 12:10 Opinions differ over exactly what Paul meant by "unknown languages." Some believe that this refers to earthly languages that a person did not know before (the same as the gift described in Acts 2:4-8). Other scholars say that this refers to an "ecstatic" language, a "heavenly" language. Most likely the second view is correct. Probably the only time that the word "tongues" refers to other earthly languages is when describing Pentecost. The rest of the time in the New Testament, the word refers to ecstatic languages unknown to anyone—languages of angels (1 Cor 13:1).

Speaking in tongues is a legitimate gift of the Spirit. The exercise of the gift demands some guidelines (as noted in 1 Cor 14) so that the purpose of the gift—to help the body of Christ—is not lost. Those who speak in tongues should follow the guidelines; those who do not speak in tongues ought not seek the gift as a sign of salvation or of special

One Body with Many Parts

1 CORINTHIANS 12:12-31

The human body has many parts, but the many parts make up one whole body. So it is with the body of Christ. 13 Some of us are Jews, some are Gentiles,* some are slaves, and some are free. But we have all been baptized into one body by one Spirit, and we all share the same Spirit.*

14 Yes, the body has many different parts, not just one part. 15 If the foot says, "I am not a part of the body because I am not a hand," that does not make it any less a part of the body. 16 And if the ear says, "I am not part of the body because I am not an eye," would that make it any less a part of the body? 17 If the whole body were an eye, how would you hear? Or if your whole body were an ear, how would you smell anything?

18 But our bodies have many parts, and God has put each part just where he wants it. 19 How strange a body would be if it had only one part! 20 Yes, there are many parts, but only one body. 21 The eye can never say to the hand, "I don't need you." The head can't say to the feet, "I don't need you."

22 In fact, some parts of the body that seem weakest and least important are actually the most necessary. 23 And the parts we regard as less honorable are those we clothe with the greatest care. So we carefully protect those parts that should not be seen, 24 while the more honorable parts do not require this special care. So God has put the body together such that extra honor and care are given to those parts that have less dignity. 25 This makes for harmony among the members, so that all the members care for each other. 26 If one part suffers, all the parts suffer with it, and if one part is honored, all the parts are glad.

27 All of you together are Christ's body, and each of you is a part of it. 28 Here are some of the parts God has appointed for the church:

first are apostles,
second are prophets,
third are teachers,
then those who do miracles,
those who have the gift of healing,
those who can help others,
those who have the gift of leadership,
those who speak in unknown languages.

29 Are we all apostles? Are we all prophets? Are we all teachers? Do we all have the power to do miracles? 30 Do we all have the gift of healing? Do we all have the ability to speak in unknown languages? Do we all have the ability to interpret unknown languages? Of course not! 31 So you should earnestly desire the most helpful gifts.

But now let me show you a way of life that is best of all.

1 Cor 12:13a Greek *some are Greeks.* **1 Cor 12:13b** Greek *we were all given one Spirit to drink.*

---

closeness with God, for it is neither. It is a gift of God, given only to whomever God chooses. A person who has not experienced the gift of tongues should not seek it but seek what gifts God has given. (For more, see the notes on 1 Cor 14, pp. 1616-1618.)

1 Cor 12:11 No matter what gift(s) a person has, all spiritual gifts are distributed by the Holy Spirit. The Holy Spirit decides which gifts each believer should have. We are responsible to use and sharpen our gifts, but we can take no credit for what God has freely given us.

Note that discussions about spiritual gifts usually create difficulties when two central points are overlooked: (1) Properly used, spiritual gifts are not self-serving but serve the whole body of Christ (1 Cor 12:7); (2) each gift becomes practically useless when used without love (1 Cor 13). As you seek to identify and utilize the gifts God has given you, make loving God and loving fellow Christians your highest motives.

1 Cor 12:12 Paul compares the body of Christ to a human body. Each part has a specific function that is necessary to the body as a whole. The parts are different for a purpose, and in their differences they must work together. Christians must avoid two common errors: (1) being proud of their abilities, or (2) thinking they have nothing to give to the body of believers. Instead of comparing ourselves to one another, we should use our different gifts together to spread the Good News of salvation.

1 Cor 12:13 The church is composed of many types of people from a variety of backgrounds with a multitude of gifts and abilities. It is easy for these differences to divide people, as was the case in Corinth. But despite the differences, all believers have one thing in common—faith in Christ. On this essential truth the church finds unity. All believers are baptized by one Holy Spirit into one body of believers, the church. We don't lose our individual identities, but we have an overriding oneness in Christ. When we become a Christian, the Holy Spirit takes up residence in us, and we are born into God's family. "We all share the same Spirit" means that each of us has received the same Holy Spirit. As members of God's family, we may have different interests and gifts, but we are united by the Spirit into one spiritual body.

1 Cor 12:23-24 Paul argued for diversity of gifts and acceptance of the full range of gifts that God gives to his people. No one should feel superior about a given gift; instead, all should use their gifts to willingly serve. Too often the up-front gifts, like speaking or teaching, are more highly regarded than the behind-the-scenes gifts, like helping and serving. No one should discount the contribution of another person, no matter how insignificant it may seem. We should not be dissatisfied with the gift God has given us but be eager to serve. Nor should we envy those who seem to have more gifts than we do. In love, treat everyone's gift, yours included, as valuable to God.

1 Cor 12:25-26 What is your response when a fellow Christian is honored? How do you respond when someone is suffering? We are to be happy with those who are happy, and if they are sad, to share their sorrow (Rom 12:15). Too often, unfortunately, we are jealous of those who rejoice and apathetic toward those who weep. Believers are in the world together—there is no such thing as private or individualistic Christianity. We need to get involved in the lives of others and not just enjoy our own relationship with God.

1 Cor 12:30 Paul discusses the subject of speaking in and interpreting unknown languages in more detail in 1 Corinthians 14. (See also the second note on 1 Cor 12:10, p. 1614.)

1 Cor 12:31 The most helpful gifts are those that are beneficial to the body of Christ. Paul has already made it clear that one gift is not superior to another, but he urges the believers to discover how they can serve Christ's body with the gifts God has given them. Your spiritual gifts are not for your own self-advancement. They were given to you for serving God and enhancing the spiritual growth of the body of believers.

Love Is the Greatest

1 CORINTHIANS 13:1-13

If I could speak all the languages of earth and of angels, but didn't love others, I would only be a noisy
gong or a clanging cymbal. 2If I had the gift of prophecy, and if I understood all of God's secret plans and
possessed all knowledge, and if I had such faith that I
could move mountains, but didn't love others, I would
be nothing. 3If I gave everything I have to the poor and
even sacrificed my body, I could boast about it;* but
if I didn't love others, I would have gained nothing.

4Love is patient and kind. Love is not jealous or
boastful or proud 5or rude. It does not demand its own
way. It is not irritable, and it keeps no record of being
wronged. 6It does not rejoice about injustice but rejoices whenever the truth wins out. 7Love never gives
up, never loses faith, is always hopeful, and endures
through every circumstance.

8Prophecy and speaking in unknown languages*
and special knowledge will become useless. But love
will last forever! 9Now our knowledge is partial and
incomplete, and even the gift of prophecy reveals only
part of the whole picture! 10But when the time of perfection comes, these partial things will become useless.

11When I was a child, I spoke and thought and
reasoned as a child. But when I grew up, I put away
childish things. 12Now we see things imperfectly, like
puzzling reflections in a mirror, but then we will see
everything with perfect clarity.* All that I know now is
partial and incomplete, but then I will know everything
completely, just as God now knows me completely.

13Three things will last forever—faith, hope, and
love—and the greatest of these is love.

The Gifts of Tongues and Prophecy

1 CORINTHIANS 14:1-25

Let love be your highest goal! But you should also desire
the special abilities the Spirit gives—especially the ability to prophesy. 2For if you have the ability to speak in
tongues,* you will be talking only to God, since people
won't be able to understand you. You will be speaking
by the power of the Spirit,* but it will all be mysterious.

1 Cor 13:3 Some manuscripts read *sacrificed my body to be burned.* **1 Cor 13:8** Or *in tongues.* **1 Cor 13:12** Greek *see face to face.* **1 Cor 14:2a** Or *in unknown languages;* also in 14:4, 5, 13, 14, 18, 22, 26, 27, 28, 39. **1 Cor 14:2b** Or *speaking in your spirit.*

---

1 Cor 13:1ff Paul gave evidence of the Corinthians' lack of love in the utilization of spiritual gifts (1 Cor 12); he then defines real love (1 Cor 13) and shows how love works (1 Cor 14). Love is more important than all the spiritual gifts exercised in the church body. Great faith, acts of dedication or sacrifice, and miracle-working power have little effect without love. Love makes our actions and gifts useful. Although people have different gifts, love is available to everyone.

1 Cor 13:4-7 Our society confuses love and lust. Unlike lust, God's kind of love is directed outward toward others, not inward toward ourselves. It is utterly unselfish. This kind of love goes against our natural inclinations. It is impossible to have this love unless God helps us set aside our own natural desires so that we can love and not expect anything in return. Thus, the more we become like Christ, the more love we will show to others.

1 Cor 13:5 Paul says that love "is not irritable." Sometimes we're irritated or angered by others, and we don't know why. Not all irritability stems from sinful or selfish motives, although the irritable treatment of others surely is wrong. Much irritability comes from a love of perfection, a deep desire that programs, meetings, and structures be run perfectly. A desire to run things perfectly can erupt into anger at events or people who get in the way or ruin that desire. Those who are easily irritated need to remember that perfection exists only in God. We need to love him and our fellow Christians, not the visions we have for perfection here on earth.

1 Cor 13:10-12 When Paul wrote of "perfect clarity," he was referring to when we see Christ face to face. God gives believers spiritual gifts for their lives on earth in order to build up, serve, and strengthen fellow Christians. The spiritual gifts are for the church. In eternity, we will be made perfect and complete and will be in the very presence of God. We will no longer need the spiritual gifts, so they will come to an end. Then, we will have a full understanding and appreciation for one another as unique expressions of God's infinite creativity. We will use our differences as a reason to praise God! Based on that perspective, let us treat each other with the same love and unity that we will one day share.

1 Cor 13:13 Paul wrote that love endures forever. In morally corrupt Corinth, love had become a mixed-up term with little meaning. Today, people are still confused about love. Love, the greatest of all human qualities, is an attribute of God himself (1 Jn 4:8); it involves unselfish service to others. *Faith* is the foundation and content of God's message; *hope* is the attitude and focus; *love* is action. When faith and hope are in line, you are free to love completely because you understand how God loves. Does your faith fully express itself in loving others?

1 Cor 14:1 The ability to prophesy may involve predicting future events, but its main purpose is to communicate God's message to people, providing insight, warning, correction, and encouragement. (See also the first note on 1 Cor 12:10, p. 1614.)

1 Cor 14:2 The gift of speaking in tongues (unknown languages) was a concern of the Corinthian church because the use of the gift had caused disorder in worship. Speaking in tongues is a legitimate gift of the Holy Spirit, but the Corinthian believers were using it as a sign of spiritual superiority rather than as

Ancient Mirror

In the biblical era, mirrors were made of copper, bronze, silver, gold, or electrum. They were highly polished so as to reflect the face as clearly as possible. Glass was in existence but was usually opaque (except Roman glass) and was not used for mirrors until after the biblical period. When Alexander the Great spread Greek culture, the use of mirrors became even more widespread in the biblical world. Archaeological excavations have unearthed bronze mirrors in Palestine along with various items of women's jewelry and clothing. Most of these date from the post-exilic era up through Roman times. These mirrors did not give a really clear reflection, as mirrors do today. This is the point of Paul's metaphor in 1 Corinthians 13:12—in the present life, this side of eternity, we see spiritual things imperfectly. In the next life, we will see with perfect clarity, like seeing someone face to face.

[3]But one who prophesies strengthens others, encourages them, and comforts them. [4]A person who speaks in tongues is strengthened personally, but one who speaks a word of prophecy strengthens the entire church.

[5]I wish you could all speak in tongues, but even more I wish you could all prophesy. For prophecy is greater than speaking in tongues, unless someone interprets what you are saying so that the whole church will be strengthened.

[6]Dear brothers and sisters,* if I should come to you speaking in an unknown language,* how would that help you? But if I bring you a revelation or some special knowledge or prophecy or teaching, that will be helpful. [7]Even lifeless instruments like the flute or the harp must play the notes clearly, or no one will recognize the melody. [8]And if the bugler doesn't sound a clear call, how will the soldiers know they are being called to battle?

[9]It's the same for you. If you speak to people in words they don't understand, how will they know what you are saying? You might as well be talking into empty space.

[10]There are many different languages in the world, and every language has meaning. [11]But if I don't understand a language, I will be a foreigner to someone who speaks it, and the one who speaks it will be a foreigner to me. [12]And the same is true for you. Since you are so eager to have the special abilities the Spirit gives, seek those that will strengthen the whole church.

[13]So anyone who speaks in tongues should pray also for the ability to interpret what has been said. [14]For if I pray in tongues, my spirit is praying, but I don't understand what I am saying.

[15]Well then, what shall I do? I will pray in the spirit,* and I will also pray in words I understand. I will sing in the spirit, and I will also sing in words I understand. [16]For if you praise God only in the spirit, how can those who don't understand you praise God along with you? How can they join you in giving thanks when they don't understand what you are saying? [17]You will be giving thanks very well, but it won't strengthen the people who hear you.

[18]I thank God that I speak in tongues more than any of you. [19]But in a church meeting I would rather speak five understandable words to help others than ten thousand words in an unknown language.

[20]Dear brothers and sisters, don't be childish in your understanding of these things. Be innocent as babies when it comes to evil, but be mature in understanding matters of this kind. [21]It is written in the Scriptures*:

"I will speak to my own people
through strange languages
and through the lips of foreigners.
But even then, they will not listen to me,"*
says the LORD.

[22]So you see that speaking in tongues is a sign, not for believers, but for unbelievers. Prophecy, however, is

1 Cor 14:6a Greek *brothers;* also in 14:20, 26, 39. **1 Cor 14:6b** Or *in tongues;* also in 14:19, 23. **1 Cor 14:15** Or *in the Spirit;* also in 14:15b, 16. **1 Cor 14:21a** Greek *in the law.* **1 Cor 14:21b** Isa 28:11-12.

a means to spiritual unity. Spiritual gifts are beneficial only when they are properly used to help everyone in the church. We should not exercise them only to make ourselves feel good. (See also the second note on 1 Cor 12:10, p. 1614.)

1 Cor 14:2-5 Paul's words to the Corinthians about tongues and prophecy have much to say to our generation. Many Christians struggle with the discussion of tongues. Paul would clearly say that no one should put down those Christians who speak in tongues, and those who speak in tongues should not disparage those who do not. Paul makes several points about speaking in tongues: (1) It is a spiritual gift from God (1 Cor 14:2); (2) it is a desirable gift even though it isn't a requirement of faith (1 Cor 12:28-31); (3) it is less important than prophecy and teaching (1 Cor 14:4). Believers need unity and love. The enemy is not each other but the sinful world system, Satan, and our selfish, sinful desires. But Paul would have another word for today: "I wish you could all prophesy." Although Paul himself spoke in tongues, he stresses prophecy (preaching) because it benefits the whole church, while speaking in tongues primarily benefits the speaker. Paul would encourage us to be so in tune with the Spirit that his messages of comfort, encouragement, and edification would be heard in our congregations today. Make sure your actions are encouraging and edifying.

1 Cor 14:7-12 As musical instruments must clearly play each note in order for the music to be recognized, so Paul says words must be preached in the hearers' language in order to be helpful. Because there are many languages in the world (1 Cor 14:10), people sometimes can't understand each other. It is the same with speaking in tongues. Although this gift is helpful to many people in private worship as well as in public worship (with interpretation), Paul says that he would rather speak a few words that his hearers can understand than many that they cannot (1 Cor 14:19).

1 Cor 14:9 Paul confronted the self-oriented use of the gift of tongues. Spiritual people must be careful not to pursue self-development at the expense of broken, lost people. When we give too much attention to our own needs, ideas, and spiritual expression, we may push aside the Spirit's true desire and abandon those who need encouragement. Follow Paul's advice and make encouraging and edifying others the highest goal.

1 Cor 14:13-20 Up to this point, Paul has been explaining that the gift of speaking in tongues was of no value to the congregation as a whole, only to the person who speaks to God in the unknown language. But if the person also has the gift of interpretation, tongues could be used in public worship if the one praying (or someone else with the gift of interpretation) would then "interpret what has been said." That way, the entire church would be edified by this gift.

1 Cor 14:15 There is a proper place for the intellect in Christianity. In praying and singing, both the mind and the spirit are to be fully engaged. When we sing, we should also think about the meaning of the words. When we pour out our feelings to God in prayer, we should not turn off our capacity to think. True Christianity is neither barren intellectualism nor thoughtless emotionalism. (See also Eph 1:17-18; Phil 1:9-11; Col 1:9.)

1 Cor 14:22-25 The way the Corinthians were speaking in tongues was helping no one because believers did not understand what was being said, and unbelievers thought that the people speaking in tongues were crazy. Speaking in tongues was supposed to be a sign to unbelievers (as it was in Acts 2). After speaking in tongues, believers were supposed to explain what was said and give the credit to God. The unsaved people would then be convinced of a spiritual reality and motivated to look further into the Christian faith. While this is one way to reach unbelievers, Paul says that clear preaching is usually better (1 Cor 14:5).

▸ **1 CORINTHIANS 14:1-25** ***(cont.)***
for the benefit of believers, not unbelievers. [23]Even so,
if unbelievers or people who don't understand these
things come into your church meeting and hear everyone speaking in an unknown language, they will think
you are crazy. [24]But if all of you are prophesying, and
unbelievers or people who don't understand these
things come into your meeting, they will be convicted
of sin and judged by what you say. [25]As they listen, their
secret thoughts will be exposed, and they will fall to
their knees and worship God, declaring, "God is truly
here among you."

A Call to Orderly Worship

1 CORINTHIANS 14:26-40
Well, my brothers and sisters, let's summarize. When
you meet together, one will sing, another will teach,
another will tell some special revelation God has
given, one will speak in tongues, and another will interpret what is said. But everything that is done must
strengthen all of you.
[27]No more than two or three should speak in
tongues. They must speak one at a time, and someone
must interpret what they say. [28]But if no one is present
who can interpret, they must be silent in your church
meeting and speak in tongues to God privately.
[29]Let two or three people prophesy, and let the
others evaluate what is said. [30]But if someone is
prophesying and another person receives a revelation
from the Lord, the one who is speaking must stop. [31]In
this way, all who prophesy will have a turn to speak,
one after the other, so that everyone will learn and be
encouraged. [32]Remember that people who prophesy
are in control of their spirit and can take turns. [33]For
God is not a God of disorder but of peace, as in all the
meetings of God's holy people.*
[34]Women should be silent during the church meetings. It is not proper for them to speak. They should
be submissive, just as the law says. [35]If they have any
questions, they should ask their husbands at home, for
it is improper for women to speak in church meetings.*
[36]Or do you think God's word originated with you
Corinthians? Are you the only ones to whom it was
given? [37]If you claim to be a prophet or think you are
spiritual, you should recognize that what I am saying is
a command from the Lord himself. [38]But if you do not
recognize this, you yourself will not be recognized.*
[39]So, my dear brothers and sisters, be eager to
prophesy, and don't forbid speaking in tongues. [40]But
be sure that everything is done properly and in order.

The Resurrection of Christ

1 CORINTHIANS 15:1-11
Let me now remind you, dear brothers and sisters,*
of the Good News I preached to you before. You welcomed it then, and you still stand firm in it. [2]It is this
Good News that saves you if you continue to believe
the message I told you—unless, of course, you believed
something that was never true in the first place.*
[3]I passed on to you what was most important and

1 Cor 14:33 The phrase *as in all the meetings of God's holy people* could instead be joined to the beginning of 14:34. **1 Cor 14:35** Some manuscripts place verses 34-35 after 14:40. **1 Cor 14:38** Some manuscripts read *If you are ignorant of this, stay in your ignorance.* **1 Cor 15:1** Greek *brothers;* also in 15:31, 50, 58. **1 Cor 15:2** Or *unless you never believed it in the first place.*

1 Cor 14:26ff Everything done in worship services must be beneficial to the worshipers, and every worshiper ought to contribute. These principles touch every aspect—singing, preaching, and the exercise of spiritual gifts. Contributions to the service (by singing, speaking, reading, praying, playing instruments, giving) must have love as their chief motivation. As you prepare to lead or participate in worship, seek to strengthen the faith of other believers.

1 Cor 14:34-35 Does this mean that women should not speak in church services today? It is clear that women prayed and prophesied in public worship (1 Cor 11:5). It is also clear that women are given spiritual gifts and are encouraged to exercise them in the body of Christ (1 Cor 12–14). Women have much to contribute and can participate in worship services.

In the Corinthian culture, women were not allowed to confront men in public. Apparently some of the women who had become Christians thought that their Christian freedom gave them the right to question the men in public worship. This was causing division in the church. In addition, women of that day did not receive formal religious education as did the men. Women may have been raising questions in the worship services that could have been answered at home without disrupting the services. Paul was asking the women not to flaunt their Christian freedom during worship. The purpose of Paul's words was to promote unity, not to teach about women's timeless roles in the church.

1 Cor 14:40 Paul stated that God is not a God of disorder but of peace (1 Cor 14:33). Note that the preferred alternative to disorder is "peace." Too often, in resisting disorder, Christians have opted for rigid, predictable, and unvarying forms of worship in which God's presence is as difficult to find as in disorderly gatherings. When there is chaos, the church is not allowing God to work among believers as he would like. Worship that "is done properly and in order" should not rule out God's creativity, joy, and unpredictability. Do your part to have worship be a joyful, peaceful, winsome experience that draws people into it.

1 Cor 15:2 Most churches contain people who do not yet believe. Some are moving in the direction of belief, and others are simply pretending. Imposters are not to be removed (see Matt 13:28-29), for that is the Lord's work alone. The Good News about Jesus Christ will save us if we continue to believe it and faithfully follow it.

1 Cor 15:3-4 The central theme of the gospel is given in these verses, a key text for the defense of Christianity. These are the three most important points:

(1) Christ died for our sins, just as the Scriptures said. Without the truth of this message, Christ's death was worthless, and those who believe in him are still in their sins and without hope. However, Christ as the sinless Son of God took the punishment of sin so that those who believe can have their sins removed. "The Scriptures" refers to Old Testament prophecies such as Psalm 16:8-11 and Isaiah 53:5-6. Christ's death on the cross was no accident or afterthought. It had been part of God's plan from all eternity in order to bring about the salvation of all who believe.

(2) He was buried. The fact of Christ's death is revealed in the fact of his burial. Many have tried to discount the actual death of Christ, but Jesus did in fact die and was buried in a tomb.

(3) He was raised from the dead on the third day, "as the Scriptures said." Christ was raised permanently, forever; his Father

WHAT THE BIBLE TEACHES ABOUT WORSHIP

Worship is first and foremost an encounter with the living and holy God.	"'Do not come any closer,' the LORD warned. 'Take off your sandals, for you are standing on holy ground'" (Exod 3:5).	God is our friend, but he is also our sovereign Lord. To approach him frivolously shows a lack of respect and sincerity. When you come to God in worship, do you approach him casually, or do you come as though you were an invited guest before a king?
Worship is only as real as the involvement of those participating.	"The LORD gave these instructions to Moses on Mount Sinai when he commanded the Israelites to present their offerings to the LORD in the wilderness of Sinai" (Lev 7:38).	All the rituals in Leviticus were meant to teach the people valuable lessons. But over time, the people became indifferent. When your church appears to be conducting dry, meaningless rituals, try rediscovering the meaning and purpose behind them. Your worship will be revitalized.
A true worship experience is often a direct result of preparation for worship.	"The LORD said to Moses, 'Give these instructions to the people of Israel: The offerings you present as special gifts are a pleasing aroma to me; they are my food. See to it that they are brought at the appointed times and offered according to my instructions'" (Num 28:1-2).	Following these rituals took time, and this gave the people the opportunity to prepare their hearts for worship. Unless your heart is ready, worship is meaningless. God is delighted when you are prepared to come before him in a spirit of thankfulness.
Believers should take advantage of every opportunity and praise God.	"Sing praises to God, our strength. Sing to the God of Jacob. Sing! Beat the tambourine. Play the sweet lyre and the harp. Blow the ram's horn at new moon, and again at full moon to call a festival!" (Ps 81:1-3).	Israel's holidays reminded the nation of God's great miracles. Remember the spiritual origin of the holidays you celebrate, and use them as opportunities to worship God for his goodness to you, your family, and your nation.
Worship and music go hand in hand.	"David and the army commanders then appointed men from the families of Asaph, Heman, and Jeduthun to proclaim God's messages to the accompaniment of lyres, harps and cymbals" (1 Chr 25:1).	David instituted music for the Temple worship services. Worship should involve the whole person, and music helps lift a person's thoughts and emotions to God. Through music you can celebrate God's greatness.
Worship is bringing the best believers have to Christ.	"They entered the house and saw the child with his mother, Mary, and they bowed down and worshiped him. Then they opened their treasure chests and gave him gifts of gold, frankincense, and myrrh" (Matt 2:11).	The wise men brought gifts and worshiped Jesus for who he was. This is the essence of true worship—honoring Christ for who he is and being willing to give to him what is valuable to you. Worship God because he is worthy of the best you have to give.
Genuine worship results in submission and obedience to Jesus.	"But even as he spoke, a bright cloud overshadowed them, and a voice from the cloud said, 'This is my dearly loved Son, who brings me great joy. Listen to him'" (Matt 17:5).	Jesus is more than just a great leader. He is the Son of God. When you understand this profound truth, the only adequate response is worship. When you have a correct understanding of Christ, you will obey him.
Everything done in corporate worship must be beneficial to the worshipers.	"Since you are so eager to have the special abilities the Spirit gives, seek those that will strengthen the whole church" (1 Cor 14:12).	This principle touches every aspect of worship. Those contributing to a worship service must speak useful words or participate in a way that will strengthen the faith of other believers.
In worship, everything must be done in harmony and with order.	"Be sure that everything is done properly and in order" (1 Cor 14:40).	Even when the gifts of the Holy Spirit are being exercised, there is no excuse for disorder. When there is chaos, the church is not allowing God to work among believers as he would like. Make sure that what you bring to worship is appropriate, but also make sure that you participate.

raised him from the dead "on the third day" as noted in the Gospels (Friday afternoon to Sunday morning—three days in Jewish reckoning of time). Jesus quoted the prophet Jonah in Matthew 12:40 (see Jon 1:17) to show the connection to "three days" as prophesied in the Old Testament. Psalms 16:8-11; 110 also foretell the resurrection of the Messiah.

▸ 1 CORINTHIANS 15:1-11 ***(cont.)***

what had also been passed on to me. Christ died for
our sins, just as the Scriptures said. 4He was buried,
and he was raised from the dead on the third day, just
as the Scriptures said. 5He was seen by Peter* and then
by the Twelve. 6After that, he was seen by more than
500 of his followers* at one time, most of whom are
still alive, though some have died. 7Then he was seen
by James and later by all the apostles. 8Last of all, as
though I had been born at the wrong time, I also saw
him. 9For I am the least of all the apostles. In fact, I'm
not even worthy to be called an apostle after the way
I persecuted God's church.

10But whatever I am now, it is all because God
poured out his special favor on me—and not without
results. For I have worked harder than any of the other
apostles; yet it was not I but God who was working
through me by his grace. 11So it makes no difference
whether I preach or they preach, for we all preach the
same message you have already believed.

1 Cor 15:5 Greek *Cephas.* **1 Cor 15:6** Greek *the brothers.*

The Resurrection of the Dead

1 CORINTHIANS 15:12-34

But tell me this—since we preach that Christ rose
from the dead, why are some of you saying there will
be no resurrection of the dead? 13For if there is no
resurrection of the dead, then Christ has not been
raised either. 14And if Christ has not been raised, then
all our preaching is useless, and your faith is useless.
15And we apostles would all be lying about God—for
we have said that God raised Christ from the grave.
But that can't be true if there is no resurrection of the
dead. 16And if there is no resurrection of the dead,
then Christ has not been raised. 17And if Christ has
not been raised, then your faith is useless and you
are still guilty of your sins. 18In that case, all who have
died believing in Christ are lost! 19And if our hope in
Christ is only for this life, we are more to be pitied than
anyone in the world.

20But in fact, Christ has been raised from the dead.
He is the first of a great harvest of all who have died.

1 Cor 15:5-8 There will always be people who say that Jesus didn't rise from the dead. Paul assures us that many people saw Jesus after his resurrection: Peter; the other apostles; more than 500 Christian believers (most of whom were still alive when Paul wrote this, although some had died); James (Jesus' half brother); and finally Paul himself. The Resurrection is a historical fact. Don't be discouraged by doubters who deny the Resurrection. Be filled with hope because of the knowledge that one day you and they will see the living proof when Christ returns. (For more evidence on the Resurrection, see the chart on p. 1490.)

1 Cor 15:7 This James is Jesus' half brother, who at first did not believe that Jesus was the Messiah (John 7:5). After seeing the resurrected Christ, he became a believer and ultimately a leader of the church in Jerusalem (Acts 15:13). James wrote the New Testament book of James.

1 Cor 15:8-9 Paul's most important credential of his apostleship was that he was an eyewitness of the risen Christ (see Acts 9:3-6). The other apostles saw Christ in the flesh. Paul was in the next generation of believers—yet Christ appeared to him.

1 Cor 15:9-10 As a zealous Pharisee, Paul had been an enemy of the Christian church—even to the point of capturing and persecuting believers (see Acts 9:1-3). Thus, he felt unworthy to be called an apostle of Christ. Though undoubtedly the most influential of the apostles, Paul was deeply humble. He knew that he had worked hard and accomplished much but only because God had poured kindness and grace upon him. True humility is not convincing yourself that you are worthless but recognizing God's work in you. It is having God's perspective on who you are and acknowledging his grace in developing your abilities.

1 Cor 15:10 Paul wrote of working harder than the other apostles. This was not an arrogant boast, because he knew that his power came from God and that it really didn't matter who worked hardest. Because of his prominent position as a Pharisee, Paul's conversion made him the object of even greater persecution than the other apostles; thus, he had to work harder to preach the same message.

1 Cor 15:12ff Most Greeks did not believe that people's bodies would be resurrected after death. They saw the afterlife as something that happened only to the soul. According to Greek philosophers, the soul was the real person, imprisoned in a physical body, and at death the soul was released. There was no immortality for the body, but the soul entered an eternal state. Christianity, by contrast, affirms that the body and soul will be united after resurrection. The church at Corinth was in the heart of Greek culture. Thus, many believers had a difficult time believing in a bodily resurrection. Paul wrote this part of his letter to clear up this confusion about the resurrection.

1 Cor 15:13-18 The bodily resurrection of Christ is the center of the Christian faith. Because Christ rose from the dead, as he promised, we know that what he said is true and that he is God. The Resurrection affirms the truthfulness of Jesus' life and words. The Resurrection confirms Jesus' unique authority to say, "I am the resurrection and the life" (John 11:25). Because he rose, we have certainty that our sins are forgiven. Because he rose, he lives and represents us before God. Because he rose and defeated death, we know we also will be raised. Christ's resurrection guaranteed both his promise to us and his authority to make that promise. We must take him at his word and believe.

1 Cor 15:19 Why does Paul say believers are "more to be pitied than anyone in the world" if there is only earthly (rather than eternal) value to Christianity? In Paul's day, Christianity often brought a person persecution, ostracism from family, and, in many cases, poverty. There were few tangible benefits from being a Christian in that society. It was certainly not a step up the social or career ladder. More important is the fact that if Christ had not been resurrected from the dead, Christians would not be forgiven of their sins or have any hope of eternal life. If what Christians believe is a lie, we would be pitiful because we would be going through such suffering for no purpose. Fortunately, that is not the case!

1 Cor 15:20 Just as the first part of the harvest was brought to the Temple as an offering (Lev 23:10ff) so Christ was the first to rise from the dead and never die again. He is our forerunner, the guarantee of our eventual resurrection to eternal life.

1 Cor 15:21 Death came into the world as a result of Adam and Eve's sin. In Romans 5:12-21, Paul explained why Adam's sin brought sin to all people, how death and sin spread to all humans because of this first sin, and the parallel between Adam's death and Christ's death.

1 Cor 15:24-28 This is not a chronological sequence of events, and no specific time for these events is given. Paul's point is that the resurrected Christ will conquer all evil, including death. (See Rev 20:14 for words about the final destruction of death.)

1 Cor 15:25-28 Although God the Father and God the Son are equal, each has a special work to do. Christ is not inferior to the Father, but his work is to defeat all evil on earth. First, he defeated sin and death on the cross, and in the end he will defeat Satan and

[21]So you see, just as death came into the world through a man, now the resurrection from the dead has begun through another man. [22]Just as everyone dies because we all belong to Adam, everyone who belongs to Christ will be given new life. [23]But there is an order to this resurrection: Christ was raised as the first of the harvest; then all who belong to Christ will be raised when he comes back.

[24]After that the end will come, when he will turn the Kingdom over to God the Father, having destroyed every ruler and authority and power. [25]For Christ must reign until he humbles all his enemies beneath his feet. [26]And the last enemy to be destroyed is death. [27]For the Scriptures say, "God has put all things under his authority."* (Of course, when it says "all things are under his authority," that does not include God himself, who gave Christ his authority.) [28]Then, when all things are under his authority, the Son will put himself under God's authority, so that God, who gave his Son authority over all things, will be utterly supreme over everything everywhere.

[29]If the dead will not be raised, what point is there in people being baptized for those who are dead? Why do it unless the dead will someday rise again?

[30]And why should we ourselves risk our lives hour by hour? [31]For I swear, dear brothers and sisters, that I face death daily. This is as certain as my pride in what Christ Jesus our Lord has done in you. [32]And what value was there in fighting wild beasts—those people of Ephesus*—if there will be no resurrection from the dead? And if there is no resurrection, "Let's feast and drink, for tomorrow we die!"* [33]Don't be fooled by those who say such things, for "bad company corrupts good character." [34]Think carefully about what is right, and stop sinning. For to your shame I say that some of you don't know God at all.

The Resurrection Body

1 CORINTHIANS 15:35-58

But someone may ask, "How will the dead be raised? What kind of bodies will they have?" [36]What a foolish question! When you put a seed into the ground, it doesn't grow into a plant unless it dies first. [37]And what you put in the ground is not the plant that will grow, but only a bare seed of wheat or whatever you are planting. [38]Then God gives it the new body he wants it to have. A different plant grows from each kind of seed. [39]Similarly there are different kinds of flesh—one kind for humans, another for animals, another for birds, and another for fish.

[40]There are also bodies in the heavens and bodies on the earth. The glory of the heavenly bodies is different from the glory of the earthly bodies. [41]The sun has one kind of glory, while the moon and stars each have another kind. And even the stars differ from each other in their glory.

[42]It is the same way with the resurrection of the dead. Our earthly bodies are planted in the ground when we die, but they will be raised to live forever. [43]Our bodies are buried in brokenness, but they will be raised in glory. They are buried in weakness, but they will be raised in strength. [44]They are buried as natural human bodies, but they will be raised as spiritual bodies. For just as there are natural bodies, there are also spiritual bodies.

[45]The Scriptures tell us, "The first man, Adam,

1 Cor 15:27 Ps 8:6. **1 Cor 15:32a** Greek *fighting wild beasts in Ephesus.* **1 Cor 15:32b** Isa 22:13.

---

all evil. World events may seem out of control, and justice may seem to have vanished. But God is in control, allowing evil to remain for a time until he sends Jesus to earth again. Then Jesus will present to God a perfect new world.

1 Cor 15:29 Some believers were baptized on behalf of others who had died unbaptized. Nothing more is known about this practice, but it obviously affirms a belief in the resurrection. Paul is not promoting baptism for the dead; he is illustrating his argument that the resurrection is a reality.

1 Cor 15:30-34 If death ends it all, enjoying the moment would be all that matters. But Christians know that life continues beyond the grave and that life on earth is only a preparation for our lives that will never end. What you do today matters for eternity. In light of eternity, sin is a foolish gamble. Your belief in the resurrection will affect your view of the future. It also ought to affect how you live today.

1 Cor 15:31-32 "I face death daily" refers to the dangers Paul encountered daily. The "wild beasts" in Ephesus referred to the savage opposition he had faced there.

1 Cor 15:33 Keeping company with those who deny the resurrection can corrupt good Christian character. Don't let your relationships with unbelievers lead you away from Christ or cause your faith to waver.

1 Cor 15:35ff Paul launches into a discussion about what our resurrected bodies will be like. If you could select your own body, what kind would you choose—strong? athletic? beautiful? Paul explains that we will be recognizable in our resurrected bodies, yet they will be better than we can imagine, for they will be made to live forever. We will still have our own personality and individuality, but these will have been perfected through Christ's work. The Bible does not reveal everything that our resurrected bodies will be able to do, but we know they will be perfect, without any infirmities (see Phil 3:21).

1 Cor 15:35ff Paul compares the resurrection with the growth of a seed in a garden. Seeds placed in the ground don't grow unless they "die" first. The plant that grows looks very different from the seed because God gives it a new "body." There are different kinds of bodies—people, animals, fish, birds. Even the angels in heaven have bodies that are different in beauty and glory. Our resurrected bodies will be very different from our earthly bodies. They will be spiritual bodies full of glory.

1 Cor 15:42-44 Our present bodies are perishable and prone to decay. Our resurrection bodies will be transformed. The spiritual body will not be limited by the laws of nature. This does not necessarily mean we'll be superpeople, but our bodies will be different from and more capable than our present earthly bodies. Our spiritual bodies will not be weak, will never get sick, and will never die.

1 Cor 15:45 Because Christ rose from the dead, he is a life-giving Spirit. This means that he entered into a new form of existence. He is the source of the spiritual life that will result in our resurrection. Christ's new glorified human body now suits his new glorified life—just as Adam's human body was suitable to his natural life. When we are resurrected, God will give us transformed, eternal bodies suited to our new eternal life.

▸ **1 CORINTHIANS 15:35-58** ***(cont.)***

became a living person."* But the last Adam—that is, Christ—is a life-giving Spirit. 46What comes first is the natural body, then the spiritual body comes later. 47Adam, the first man, was made from the dust of the earth, while Christ, the second man, came from heaven. 48Earthly people are like the earthly man, and heavenly people are like the heavenly man. 49Just as we are now like the earthly man, we will someday be like* the heavenly man.

50What I am saying, dear brothers and sisters, is that our physical bodies cannot inherit the Kingdom of God. These dying bodies cannot inherit what will last forever.

51But let me reveal to you a wonderful secret. We will not all die, but we will all be transformed! 52It will happen in a moment, in the blink of an eye, when the last trumpet is blown. For when the trumpet sounds, those who have died will be raised to live forever. And we who are living will also be transformed. 53For our dying bodies must be transformed into bodies that will never die; our mortal bodies must be transformed into immortal bodies.

54Then, when our dying bodies have been transformed into bodies that will never die,* this Scripture will be fulfilled:

"Death is swallowed up in victory.*
55 O death, where is your victory?
O death, where is your sting?*"

56For sin is the sting that results in death, and the law gives sin its power. 57But thank God! He gives us victory over sin and death through our Lord Jesus Christ.

58So, my dear brothers and sisters, be strong and immovable. Always work enthusiastically for the Lord, for you know that nothing you do for the Lord is ever useless.

The Collection for Jerusalem

1 CORINTHIANS 16:1-4

Now regarding your question about the money being collected for God's people in Jerusalem. You should follow the same procedure I gave to the churches in Galatia. 2On the first day of each week, you should each put aside a portion of the money you have earned. Don't wait until I get there and then try to collect it all at once. 3When I come, I will write letters of recommendation for the messengers you choose to deliver your gift to Jerusalem. 4And if it seems appropriate for me to go along, they can travel with me.

Paul's Final Instructions

1 CORINTHIANS 16:5-18

I am coming to visit you after I have been to Macedonia,* for I am planning to travel through Macedonia. 6Perhaps I will stay awhile with you, possibly all winter, and then you can send me on my way to my next destination. 7This time I don't want to make just a short visit and then go right on. I want to come and

1 Cor 15:45 Gen 2:7. **1 Cor 15:49** Some manuscripts read *let us be like.* **1 Cor 15:54a** Some manuscripts add *and our mortal bodies have been transformed into immortal bodies.* **1 Cor 15:54b** Isa 25:8. **1 Cor 15:55** Hos 13:14 (Greek version). **1 Cor 16:5** *Macedonia* was in the northern region of Greece.

1 Cor 15:50-53 We all face limitations. Some may have physical, mental, or emotional disabilities. Some may be blind, but they can see a new way to live. Some may be deaf, but they can hear God's Good News. Some may be lame, but they can walk in God's love. In addition, they have the encouragement that those disabilities are only temporary. Paul tells us that we all will be given new bodies when Christ returns and that these bodies will be without disabilities, never to become sick or die. This can give us hope in our suffering.

1 Cor 15:51-52 Christians alive at that day will not have to die but will be transformed immediately. A trumpet blast will usher in the new heaven and earth. The Jews would understand the significance of this because trumpets were always blown to signal the start of great festivals and other extraordinary events (Num 10:10).

1 Cor 15:54-56 Satan seemed to be victorious in the Garden of Eden (Gen 3) and at the cross of Jesus. But God turned Satan's apparent victory into defeat when Jesus Christ rose from the dead (Col 2:15; Heb 2:14-15). Thus, death is no longer a source of dread or fear. Christ overcame it, and one day we will also. The law will no longer make sinners out of us just because we cannot keep it. Death has been defeated, and we have hope beyond the grave.

1 Cor 15:58 Paul says that because of the resurrection, nothing we do is useless. Sometimes we become apathetic about serving the Lord because we don't see any results. Knowing that Christ has won the ultimate victory should affect the way we live right now. Don't let discouragement over an apparent lack of results keep you from doing the work of the Lord enthusiastically as you have opportunity.

PHYSICAL AND RESURRECTION BODIES

We all have a body—each looks different; each has different strengths and weaknesses. But as physical, earthly bodies, they are all alike. All believers are promised life after death and a body like Christ's (1 Cor 15:49), a resurrection body.

Physical Bodies	Resurrection Bodies
Perishable	Imperishable
Sown in dishonor	Raised in glory
Sown in weakness	Raised in power
Natural	Spiritual
From the dust	From heaven

1 Cor 16:1ff Paul had just said that no good deed is ever useless (1 Cor 15:58). In 1 Corinthians 16 he mentions some practical deeds that have value for all Christians.

1 Cor 16:1-4 The Christians in Jerusalem were suffering from poverty and famine, so Paul was collecting money for them (Rom 15:25-31; 2 Cor 8:4; 9:1ff). He suggested that believers set aside a certain amount each week and give it to the church until he arrived to take it to Jerusalem. Paul had planned to go straight to Corinth from Ephesus, but he changed his mind (2 Cor 1–2).

stay awhile, if the Lord will let me. [8]In the meantime, I will be staying here at Ephesus until the Festival of Pentecost. [9]There is a wide-open door for a great work here, although many oppose me.

[10]When Timothy comes, don't intimidate him. He is doing the Lord's work, just as I am. [11]Don't let anyone treat him with contempt. Send him on his way with your blessing when he returns to me. I expect him to come with the other believers.*

[12]Now about our brother Apollos—I urged him to visit you with the other believers, but he was not willing to go right now. He will see you later when he has the opportunity.

[13]Be on guard. Stand firm in the faith. Be courageous.* Be strong. [14]And do everything with love.

[15]You know that Stephanas and his household were the first of the harvest of believers in Greece,* and they are spending their lives in service to God's people. I urge you, dear brothers and sisters,* [16]to submit to them and others like them who serve with such devotion. [17]I am very glad that Stephanas, Fortunatus, and Achaicus have come here. They have been providing the help you weren't here to give me. [18]They have been a wonderful encouragement to me, as they have been to you. You must show your appreciation to all who serve so well.

Paul's Final Greetings

1 CORINTHIANS 16:19-24

The churches here in the province of Asia* send greetings in the Lord, as do Aquila and Priscilla* and all the others who gather in their home for church meetings. [20]All the brothers and sisters here send greetings to you. Greet each other with Christian love.*

[21]HERE IS MY GREETING IN MY OWN HANDWRITING—PAUL.

[22]If anyone does not love the Lord, that person is cursed. Our Lord, come!*

[23]May the grace of the Lord Jesus be with you.

[24]My love to all of you in Christ Jesus.*

1 Cor 16:11 Greek *with the brothers;* also in 16:12. **1 Cor 16:13** Greek *Be men.* **1 Cor 16:15a** Greek *in Achaia,* the southern region of the Greek peninsula. **1 Cor 16:15b** Greek *brothers;* also in 16:20. **1 Cor 16:19a** *Asia* was a Roman province in what is now western Turkey. **1 Cor 16:19b** Greek *Prisca.* **1 Cor 16:20** Greek *with a sacred kiss.* **1 Cor 16:22** From Aramaic, *Marana tha.* Some manuscripts read *Maran atha,* "Our Lord has come." **1 Cor 16:24** Some manuscripts add *Amen.*

When he finally arrived, he took the gift and delivered it to the Jerusalem church (Acts 21:18; 24:17).

1 Cor 16:10-11 Paul was sending Timothy ahead to Corinth. Paul respected Timothy and had worked closely with him (Phil 2:22; 1 Tim 1:2). Although Timothy was young, Paul encouraged the Corinthian church to welcome him because he was doing the Lord's work. God's work is not limited by age. Paul wrote two personal letters to Timothy that have been preserved in the Bible (the books of 1 and 2 Timothy).

1 Cor 16:12 Apollos, who had preached in Corinth, was doing evangelistic work in Greece (see Acts 18:24-28; 1 Cor 3:3ff). Apollos didn't go to Corinth right away, partly because he knew of the factions there and didn't want to cause any more divisions.

1 Cor 16:13-14 As the Corinthians awaited Paul's next visit, they were directed to: (1) be on guard. They were to be constantly watchful or alert for spiritual enemies that might slip in and threaten to destroy them—whether it be divisions, pride, sin, disorder, or erroneous theology; (2) stand firm in what they believed—that is, the gospel that they had been taught in the beginning, the gospel that had brought them salvation; (3) be courageous so that they could stand against false teachers, deal with sin in the congregation, and straighten out other problems; (4) be strong, with the strength given by the Holy Spirit; and (5) do everything with love because without love, they would be no more than prideful noisemakers. Today, as we wait for the return of Christ, we should follow the same instructions.

1 Cor 16:19 Aquila and Priscilla were tentmakers (or leatherworkers) whom Paul had met in Corinth (Acts 18:1-3). They followed Paul to Ephesus and lived there with him, helping to teach others about Jesus (Rom 16:3-5). Many in the Corinthian church would have known this Christian couple. They are also mentioned in Acts 18:18, 26; Romans 16:3; 2 Timothy 4:19.

1 Cor 16:21 Paul had a helper, or secretary, who wrote down this letter while he dictated. Paul wrote the final words, however, in his own handwriting. This is similar to adding a handwritten postscript (P.S.) to a typewritten letter. It also served to verify that this was a genuine letter from the apostle and not a forgery.

1 Cor 16:22 The Lord Jesus Christ is coming back to earth again. To Paul, this was a wonderful hope, the very best he could look forward to. He was not afraid of seeing Christ—he could hardly wait! Do you share Paul's eager anticipation? Those who love Christ are looking forward to that glorious time of his return (Titus 2:13). To those who do not love the Lord, Paul says, let them be cursed.

1 Cor 16:24 The church at Corinth was a church in trouble. Paul lovingly and forcefully confronted them and pointed them back to Christ. He dealt with divisions and conflicts, selfishness, inconsiderate use of freedom, disorder in worship, misuse of spiritual gifts, and wrong attitudes about the resurrection.

In every church, there are problems that create tensions and divisions. We should not ignore or gloss over problems in our churches or in our lives. Instead, like Paul, we should deal with problems head-on as they arise. The lesson for us in 1 Corinthians is that unity and love in a church are far more important than leaders and labels.

J. Paul Travels from Ephesus to Macedonia

Paul had spent over two years in Ephesus, and the Spirit was prompting him to move on to encourage the churches in Macedonia and Achaia. Before he left Ephesus, however, a riot broke out because Paul's ministry there was seen as a threat to the business of idol sales! Paul barely escaped with his life. He went on to Macedonia, where he had an urgent need to respond to the situation in the church in Corinth.

The Riot in Ephesus

ACTS 19:21-41

Afterward Paul felt compelled by the Spirit* to go over
to Macedonia and Achaia before going to Jerusalem.
"And after that," he said, "I must go on to Rome!" [22]He
sent his two assistants, Timothy and Erastus, ahead
to Macedonia while he stayed awhile longer in the
province of Asia.

[23]About that time, serious trouble developed in Ephesus concerning the Way. [24]It began with Demetrius, a
silversmith who had a large business manufacturing
silver shrines of the Greek goddess Artemis.* He kept
many craftsmen busy. [25]He called them together, along
with others employed in similar trades, and addressed
them as follows:

"Gentlemen, you know that our wealth comes from
this business. [26]But as you have seen and heard, this
man Paul has persuaded many people that handmade
gods aren't really gods at all. And he's done this not only
here in Ephesus but throughout the entire province!
[27]Of course, I'm not just talking about the loss of public
respect for our business. I'm also concerned that the
temple of the great goddess Artemis will lose its influence and that Artemis—this magnificent goddess worshiped throughout the province of Asia and all around
the world—will be robbed of her great prestige!"

[28]At this their anger boiled, and they began shouting, "Great is Artemis of the Ephesians!" [29]Soon the
whole city was filled with confusion. Everyone rushed
to the amphitheater, dragging along Gaius and Aristarchus, who were Paul's traveling companions from
Macedonia. [30]Paul wanted to go in, too, but the believers wouldn't let him. [31]Some of the officials of
the province, friends of Paul, also sent a message to
him, begging him not to risk his life by entering the
amphitheater.

[32]Inside, the people were all shouting, some one
thing and some another. Everything was in confusion. In fact, most of them didn't even know why they
were there. [33]The Jews in the crowd pushed Alexander

Acts 19:21 Or *decided in his spirit.* **Acts 19:24** *Artemis* is otherwise known as Diana.

AD 54 *Nero becomes the Roman emperor*

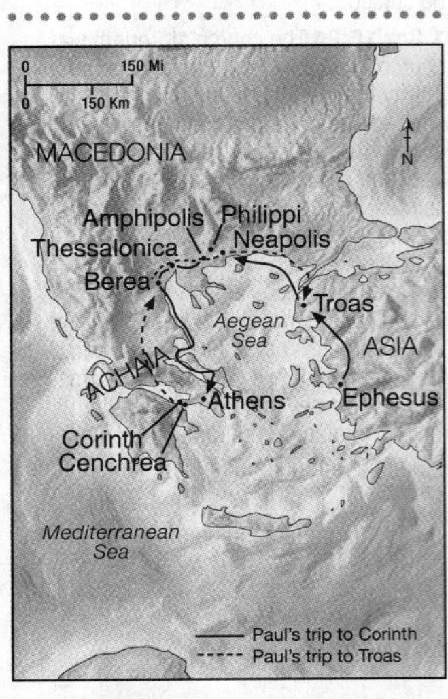

THROUGH MACEDONIA AND ACHAIA

A riot in Ephesus sent Paul to Troas, then through Macedonia to the region of Achaia. During a stay in Athens, he probably wrote the letter of 2 Corinthians before heading personally to Corinth to deal with problems there. During his three-month stay in Corinth, he wrote the book of Romans. Paul had planned to sail from Corinth straight to Antioch of Syria, but a plot against his life was discovered. So he retraced his steps through Macedonia.

Acts 19:21 Why did Paul say he had to go to Rome? Wherever he went, he could see Rome's influence. Paul wanted to take the message of Christ to the world's center of influence and power.

Acts 19:22 Paul later wrote letters to Timothy: the books of 1 and 2 Timothy. Erastus was a committed follower of Christ who was not only Paul's helpful assistant but also Corinth's city treasurer (see Rom 16:23).

Acts 19:23 "The Way" refers to those who followed the way of Christ—the Christians.

Acts 19:24 Artemis was a goddess of fertility. She was represented by a carved female figure with many breasts. A large statue of Artemis (which was said to have come from heaven; Acts 19:35) was in the great temple at Ephesus. That temple was one of the wonders of the ancient world. The festival of Artemis involved wild orgies and carousing. Obviously the religious and commercial life of Ephesus reflected the city's worship of this pagan deity.

Acts 19:25-27 When Paul preached in Ephesus, Demetrius and his fellow craftsmen did not quarrel with his doctrine. Their anger boiled because his preaching threatened their profits. They made silver shrines of the Ephesian goddess Artemis. The craftsmen knew that if people started believing in God and discarding the idols, their livelihood would suffer.

Acts 19:27 Demetrius's strategy for stirring up a riot was to appeal to his fellow workmen's love of money and then to encourage them to hide their greed behind the mask of patriotism and religious loyalty. The rioters couldn't see the selfish motives for their rioting; instead, they saw themselves as heroes for the sake of their land and beliefs.

Acts 19:29-31 Paul often sought others to help him in his work. On this occasion, his traveling companions were Aristarchus (who would accompany him on other journeys; see Acts 20:3-4; 27:1-2), and Gaius (probably not the same Gaius mentioned in Rom 16:23; 1 Cor 1:14). Paul wanted to go to the amphitheater to defend his companions, but the other believers wouldn't let him go, fearing for his safety. The officials who begged him not to risk his life were government officials responsible for the religious and political order of the region. Paul's message had reached all levels of society, crossing all social barriers and giving Paul friends in high places.

Acts 19:33-34 The mob had become anti-Jewish as well as anti-Christian. This Alexander may have been pushed forward by the Jews as a spokesman to explain that the Jews had no part in the Christian community and thus were not involved in the economic problem of the silversmiths.

forward and told him to explain the situation. He motioned for silence and tried to speak. [34]But when the crowd realized he was a Jew, they started shouting again and kept it up for about two hours: "Great is Artemis of the Ephesians! Great is Artemis of the Ephesians!"

[35]At last the mayor was able to quiet them down enough to speak. "Citizens of Ephesus," he said. "Everyone knows that Ephesus is the official guardian of the temple of the great Artemis, whose image fell down to us from heaven. [36]Since this is an undeniable fact, you should stay calm and not do anything rash. [37]You have brought these men here, but they have stolen nothing from the temple and have not spoken against our goddess.

[38]"If Demetrius and the craftsmen have a case against them, the courts are in session and the officials can hear the case at once. Let them make formal charges. [39]And if there are complaints about other matters, they can be settled in a legal assembly. [40]I am afraid we are in danger of being charged with rioting by the Roman government, since there is no cause for all this commotion. And if Rome demands an explanation, we won't know what to say." [41]*Then he dismissed them, and they dispersed.

Paul Travels to Macedonia

ACTS 20:1-2a

When the uproar was over, Paul sent for the believers* and encouraged them. Then he said good-bye and left for Macedonia. [2]While there, he encouraged the believers in all the towns he passed through.

Acts 19:41 Some translations include verse 41 as part of verse 40. **Acts 20:1** Greek *disciples.*

K. Paul's Second Letter to the Church in Corinth

Paul received some disturbing reports about how people were responding to his letter in Corinth. There were false teachers who denied Paul's authority and slandered him. Paul wrote 2 Corinthians to defend his position as an apostle and denounce those who were twisting the truth. In responding to the attacks on his character and authority, Paul explains the nature of Christian ministry and, as an example, openly shares about his ministry. This is an important letter for all who wish to be involved in any kind of Christian ministry because it has much to teach us about how we should handle our ministries today. Like Paul, those involved in ministry should be blameless, sincere, confident, caring, open, and willing to suffer for the sake of Christ.

Greetings from Paul

2 CORINTHIANS 1:1-2

This letter is from Paul, chosen by the will of God to be an apostle of Christ Jesus, and from our brother Timothy.

I am writing to God's church in Corinth and to all of his holy people throughout Greece.*

[2]May God our Father and the Lord Jesus Christ give you grace and peace.

2 Cor 1:1 Greek *Achaia,* the southern region of the Greek peninsula.

Acts 19:40 The city of Ephesus was under the domination of the Roman Empire. The main responsibility of the local city leaders was simply to maintain peace and order. If they failed to control the people, Rome would remove the appointed officials from office. The entire town could also be put under martial law, taking away many civic freedoms.

Acts 19:41 The riot in Ephesus convinced Paul that it was time to move on. But it also showed that the law still provided some protection for Christians as they challenged the worship of the goddess Artemis and the most idolatrous religion in Asia.

2 Cor 1:1 Paul visited Corinth on his second missionary journey and founded a church there (Acts 18:1ff). He later wrote several letters to the believers in Corinth, two of which are included in the Bible. Paul's first letter to the Corinthians is lost (1 Cor 5:9-11), his second letter to them is our book of 1 Corinthians, his third letter is lost (2 Cor 2:6-9; 7:12), and his fourth letter is our book of 2 Corinthians. The book of 2 Corinthians was written less than a year after 1 Corinthians.

Paul wrote 1 Corinthians to deal with divisions in the church. When his advice was not taken and their problems weren't solved, Paul visited Corinth a second time. That visit was painful both for Paul and for the church (2 Cor 2:1). He then planned a third visit but delayed it and wrote 2 Corinthians instead. After writing 2 Corinthians, Paul visited Corinth once more (Acts 20:2-3).

2 Cor 1:1 Paul had great respect for Timothy (see also Phil 2:19-20; 1 Tim 1:2), one of his traveling companions (Acts 16:1-3). Timothy had accompanied Paul to Corinth on his second missionary journey, and Paul had recently sent him there to minister (1 Cor 4:17; 16:10). Timothy's report to Paul about the crisis in the Corinthian church prompted Paul to make an unplanned visit to the church to deal with the problem in person (see 2 Cor 2:1). For more information on Timothy, see his Profile on p. 1727.

2 Cor 1:1 The Romans had made Corinth the capital of Achaia (the southern half of present-day Greece). The city was a flourishing trade center because of its seaport. With the thousands of merchants and sailors who disembarked there each year, it had developed a reputation as one of the most immoral cities in the ancient world; its many pagan temples encouraged the practice of sexual immorality along with idol worship. In fact, the Greek word "to Corinthianize" came to mean "to practice sexual immorality." A Christian church in the city would face many pressures and conflicts. (For more information on Corinth, see the first note on 1 Cor 1:2, p. 1595.)

God Offers Comfort to All

2 CORINTHIANS 1:3-11

All praise to God, the Father of our Lord Jesus Christ.
God is our merciful Father and the source of all comfort. 4He comforts us in all our troubles so that we
can comfort others. When they are troubled, we will
be able to give them the same comfort God has given
us. 5For the more we suffer for Christ, the more God
will shower us with his comfort through Christ. 6Even
when we are weighed down with troubles, it is for
your comfort and salvation! For when we ourselves
are comforted, we will certainly comfort you. Then you
can patiently endure the same things we suffer. 7We
are confident that as you share in our sufferings, you
will also share in the comfort God gives us.

8We think you ought to know, dear brothers and
sisters,* about the trouble we went through in the
province of Asia. We were crushed and overwhelmed
beyond our ability to endure, and we thought we
would never live through it. 9In fact, we expected to
die. But as a result, we stopped relying on ourselves
and learned to rely only on God, who raises the dead.
10And he did rescue us from mortal danger, and he
will rescue us again. We have placed our confidence
in him, and he will continue to rescue us. 11And you
are helping us by praying for us. Then many people
will give thanks because God has graciously answered
so many prayers for our safety.

Paul's Change of Plans

2 CORINTHIANS 1:12–2:4

We can say with confidence and a clear conscience
that we have lived with a God-given holiness* and
sincerity in all our dealings. We have depended on
God's grace, not on our own human wisdom. That is
how we have conducted ourselves before the world,
and especially toward you. 13Our letters have been
straightforward, and there is nothing written between

2 Cor 1:8 Greek *brothers.* **2 Cor 1:12** Some manuscripts read *honesty.*

DIFFERENCES BETWEEN 1 AND 2 CORINTHIANS

The two letters to the Corinthian church that we find in the Bible are very different, with different tones and focuses.

1 Corinthians **Practical**	*2 Corinthians* **Personal**
Focuses on the character of the Corinthian church	Focuses on Paul as he bares his soul and tells of his love for the Corinthian church
Deals with questions on marriage, freedom, spiritual gifts, and order in the church	Deals with the problem of false teachers, whereby Paul defends his authority and the truth of his message
Paul instructs in matters concerning the church's well-being	Paul gives his testimony because he knows that acceptance of his advice is vital to the church's well-being
Contains advice to help the church combat the pagan influences in the wicked city of Corinth	Contains testimony to help the church combat the havoc caused by false teachers

2 Cor 1:3-5 Many think that when God comforts us, our troubles should go away. But if that were always so, people would turn to God only out of a desire to be relieved of pain and not out of love for him. We must understand that being "comforted" can also mean receiving strength, encouragement, and hope to deal with our troubles. The more we suffer, the more comfort God gives us. If you are feeling overwhelmed, allow God to comfort you. Remember that every trial you endure will help you comfort other people who are suffering similar troubles.

2 Cor 1:5 Suffering for Christ refers to those afflictions we experience as we serve Christ. At the same time, Christ suffers with his people, since they are united with him. In Acts 9:4-5 Christ asked Paul why he was persecuting him. This implies that Christ suffered with the early Christians when they were persecuted.

2 Cor 1:6-7 Paul had a radically different view of suffering. Suffering—especially trials and discomfort associated with the advancement of Christ's Kingdom—is God's way of allowing Christians to become more like Jesus, to suffer for the gospel just as Jesus suffered for it (Phil 1:29; 3:10). Peter agreed with Paul: Christians should rejoice when they suffer, for in their own suffering they will in some small way experience what it meant for Jesus to suffer for their sins (1 Pet 4:12-13).

In addition to drawing people closer to Christ, suffering can also help them grow in their faith. God uses suffering to improve his people and shape them into better Christians. In fact, suffering should be thought of as the necessary pain that accompanies spiritual growth. In Romans, Paul noted that suffering produces perseverance, which in turn produces Christian character (Rom 5:3-4; see also Jas 1:3-4; 2 Pet 1:6; Rev 2:2, 19). This passage highlights another benefit to suffering: It teaches the sufferer how to encourage others who are also suffering.

2 Cor 1:8-10 Paul does not give details about their hardships in Asia, although his accounts of all three missionary journeys record many difficult trials he faced (Acts 13:2–14:28; 15:40–21:17). He does write that they felt that they were going to die and realized that they could do nothing to help themselves—they simply had to rely on God.

2 Cor 1:8-10 We often depend on our own skills and abilities when life seems easy and only turn to God when we feel unable to help ourselves. But as we realize our own powerlessness without him and our need for his constant help in our lives, we come to depend on him more and more. God is our source of power, and we receive his help by keeping in touch with him. With this attitude of dependence, problems will drive us to God rather than away from him. Learn how to rely on God daily.

2 Cor 1:11 Paul requested prayer for himself and his companions as they traveled to spread God's message. Pray for pastors, teachers, missionaries, and others who are spreading the Good News. Satan will challenge anyone making a real difference for God.

2 Cor 1:12-14 Paul knew the importance of honesty and sincerity in word and action, especially in a situation as in Corinth, where constructive criticism was necessary. So Paul did not come with impressive human wisdom. God wants us to be real and transparent in all our relationships. If we aren't, we may end up lowering ourselves to second-guessing, spreading rumors, and gossiping.

2 Cor 1:15-17 Paul had recently made a brief, unscheduled visit to Corinth that was

the lines and nothing you can't understand. I hope someday you will fully understand us, [14]even if you don't understand us now. Then on the day when the Lord Jesus* returns, you will be proud of us in the same way we are proud of you.

[15]Since I was so sure of your understanding and trust, I wanted to give you a double blessing by visiting you twice—[16]first on my way to Macedonia and again when I returned from Macedonia.* Then you could send me on my way to Judea.

[17]You may be asking why I changed my plan. Do you think I make my plans carelessly? Do you think I am like people of the world who say "Yes" when they really mean "No"? [18]As surely as God is faithful, our word to you does not waver between "Yes" and "No." [19]For Jesus Christ, the Son of God, does not waver between "Yes" and "No." He is the one whom Silas,* Timothy, and I preached to you, and as God's ultimate "Yes," he always does what he says. [20]For all of God's promises have been fulfilled in Christ with a resounding "Yes!" And through Christ, our "Amen" (which means "Yes") ascends to God for his glory.

[21]It is God who enables us, along with you, to stand firm for Christ. He has commissioned us, [22]and he has identified us as his own by placing the Holy Spirit in our hearts as the first installment that guarantees everything he has promised us.

[23]Now I call upon God as my witness that I am telling the truth. The reason I didn't return to Corinth was to spare you from a severe rebuke. [24]But that does not mean we want to dominate you by telling you how to put your faith into practice. We want to work together with you so you will be full of joy, for it is by your own faith that you stand firm.

2:1 So I decided that I would not bring you grief with another painful visit. [2]For if I cause you grief, who will make me glad? Certainly not someone I have grieved. [3]That is why I wrote to you as I did, so that when I do come, I won't be grieved by the very ones who ought to give me the greatest joy. Surely you all know that my joy comes from your being joyful. [4]I wrote that letter in great anguish, with a troubled heart and many tears. I didn't want to grieve you, but I wanted to let you know how much love I have for you.

2 Cor 1:14 Some manuscripts read *our Lord Jesus.* **2 Cor 1:16** *Macedonia* was in the northern region of Greece. **2 Cor 1:19** Greek *Silvanus.*

---

very painful for him and the church (see 2 Cor 2:1). After that visit, he told the church when he would return. But Paul changed his original travel plans. Instead of sailing from Ephesus to Corinth before going to Macedonia, he traveled from Ephesus directly to Macedonia, where he wrote a letter to the Corinthians that caused him much anguish and them much sorrow (2 Cor 7:8-9). He had made his original plans, thinking that the church would have solved its problems. When the time came for Paul's scheduled trip to Corinth, the crisis had not yet been fully resolved (although progress was being made in some areas; 2 Cor 7:11-16). So he wrote a letter instead (2 Cor 2:3-4; 7:8) because another visit might have only made matters worse. Thus, Paul stayed away from Corinth because he was concerned over the church's unity, not because he was fickle.

2 Cor 1:17-20 Paul's change of plans caused some of his accusers to say that he couldn't be trusted, hoping to undermine his authority. Paul said that he was not the type of person to say "yes" when he meant "no." Paul explained that it was not indecision but concern for their feelings that forced him to change his plans. The reason for his trip—to bring joy (2 Cor 1:24)—could not be accomplished with the present crisis. Paul didn't want to visit them only to rebuke them severely (2 Cor 1:23). Just as the Corinthians could trust God to keep his promises, they could trust Paul as God's representative to keep his. He would still visit them, but at a better time.

2 Cor 1:19-20 Instead of defending himself, Paul reminded the Corinthians of God's faithfulness. There was no duplicity in God. His promises would be fulfilled. There would be no wavering between "yes" and "no." Jesus Christ was the premier example of this. "All of God's promises have been fulfilled in Christ with a resounding 'Yes!'" Jesus is the embodiment of God's faithfulness. Because Jesus Christ is faithful, Paul (a messenger appointed by Jesus) would also be faithful in his ministry.

2 Cor 1:21-22 The Holy Spirit guarantees that we belong to God and will receive all his benefits (Eph 1:13-14). The Holy Spirit guarantees that salvation is ours now, and that we will receive so much more when Christ returns. The great comfort and power the Holy Spirit gives in this life is a foretaste or down payment ("first installment") of the benefits of our eternal life in God's presence. With the privilege of belonging to God comes the responsibility of identifying ourselves as his faithful servants. Don't be ashamed to let others know that you are his.

2 Cor 1:23 The Corinthian church had written to Paul with questions about their faith (see 1 Cor 7:1). In response, Paul had written the letter that is 1 Corinthians. But the church did not follow his instructions.

Paul had planned to visit them again, but instead, he wrote a letter that caused sorrow (2 Cor 7:8-9) but also caused them to change their ways. He had not wanted to visit and repeat the same advice for the same problems. He wrote the emotional letter to encourage them to follow the advice that he had already given in previous letters and visits.

2 Cor 1:24 Standing firm is not a way to be saved but the evidence that a person is really committed to Jesus. Endurance is not a means to earn salvation; it is the by-product of a truly devoted life. Endurance grows out of commitment to Jesus Christ. In Matthew 10:22, Jesus predicted that his followers would be severely persecuted by those who hated what he stood for. Yet in the midst of terrible persecutions they could have hope, knowing that salvation was theirs. Times of trial serve to sift true Christians from false or fair-weather Christians. When you are pressured to give up and turn your back on Christ, don't do it. Remember the benefits of standing firm and continue to live for Christ.

2 Cor 2:1 Paul's phrase "another painful visit" indicates that he had already made one difficult trip to Corinth (see the notes on 2 Cor 1:1, p. 1625; 2 Cor 1:15-17, p. 1626) since founding the church. Paul had gone there to deal with those in the church who had been attacking and undermining his authority as an apostle of Jesus Christ, thus confusing other believers.

2 Cor 2:3 Paul's last letter, referred to here, was not the book of 1 Corinthians but rather a letter written between 1 and 2 Corinthians, just after his unplanned, painful visit (2 Cor 2:1). Paul refers to this letter again (2 Cor 7:8).

2 Cor 2:4 Paul did not enjoy reprimanding his friends and fellow believers, but he cared enough about the Corinthians to confront them with their wrongdoing. Proverbs 27:6 says: "Wounds from a sincere friend are better than many kisses from an enemy." Sometimes our friends make choices that we know are wrong. If we ignore their behavior and let them continue in it, we won't be showing love to them. We show love by honestly sharing our concerns in order to help these friends be their very best for God. When we don't make any move to help, we show that we are more concerned about being well liked than about what will happen to them.

Forgiveness for the Sinner

2 CORINTHIANS 2:5-13

I am not overstating it when I say that the man who
caused all the trouble hurt all of you more than he
hurt me. 6Most of you opposed him, and that was
punishment enough. 7Now, however, it is time to forgive and comfort him. Otherwise he may be overcome
by discouragement. 8So I urge you now to reaffirm
your love for him.

9I wrote to you as I did to test you and see if you
would fully comply with my instructions. 10When
you forgive this man, I forgive him, too. And when I
forgive whatever needs to be forgiven, I do so with
Christ's authority for your benefit, 11so that Satan
will not outsmart us. For we are familiar with his
evil schemes.

12When I came to the city of Troas to preach the
Good News of Christ, the Lord opened a door of
opportunity for me. 13But I had no peace of mind
because my dear brother Titus hadn't yet arrived with
a report from you. So I said good-bye and went on to
Macedonia to find him.

Ministers of the New Covenant

2 CORINTHIANS 2:14–3:6

But thank God! He has made us his captives and
continues to lead us along in Christ's triumphal procession. Now he uses us to spread the knowledge of
Christ everywhere, like a sweet perfume. 15Our lives
are a Christ-like fragrance rising up to God. But this
fragrance is perceived differently by those who are
being saved and by those who are perishing. 16To those
who are perishing, we are a dreadful smell of death
and doom. But to those who are being saved, we are
a life-giving perfume. And who is adequate for such
a task as this?

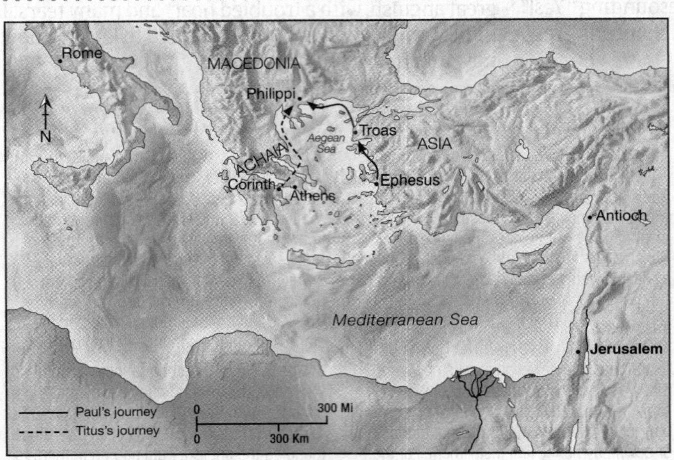

***PAUL SEARCHES FOR TITUS** Paul had searched for Titus, hoping to meet him in Troas and receive news about the Corinthian church. When he did not find Titus in Troas, he went on to Macedonia (2 Cor 2:13), most likely to Philippi, where he found Titus.*

2 Cor 2:5-11 Paul explained that it was time to forgive the man who had been punished by the church and had subsequently repented. He needed forgiveness, acceptance, and comfort. Satan would gain an advantage if they permanently separated this man from the congregation rather than forgiving and restoring him. This may have been the man who had required the disciplinary action (1 Cor 5), or he may have been the chief opponent who had caused everyone anguish (2 Cor 2:1-11). The sorrowful letter had finally brought about the repentance of the Corinthians (2 Cor 7:8-14), and their discipline of the man had led to his repentance. Church discipline should seek restoration. Two mistakes in church discipline should be avoided: being too lenient and not correcting mistakes, or being too harsh and not forgiving the repentant sinner. There is a time to confront and a time to comfort.

2 Cor 2:11 We use church discipline to help keep the church pure and to help wayward people repent. But Satan tries to harm the church by tempting it to use discipline in an unforgiving way. This causes those exercising discipline to become proud of their purity, and it causes the person who is being disciplined to become bitter and perhaps leave the church. We must remember that our purpose in discipline is to *restore* the person to the fellowship, not to destroy. We must be cautious that personal anger is not vented under the guise of church discipline.

2 Cor 2:13 Titus was a Greek convert whom Paul greatly loved and trusted (the book of Titus is a letter that Paul wrote to him). Titus was one of the men responsible for collecting the money for the poverty-stricken Jerusalem church (2 Cor 8:6). Paul may also have sent Titus with the sorrowful letter. On his way to Macedonia, Paul was supposed to meet Titus in Troas. When Paul didn't find him there, he was worried for Titus's safety and left Troas to search for him in Macedonia. There Paul found him (2 Cor 7:6), and the good news that Paul received (2 Cor 7:8-16) led to *this* letter (the book of 2 Corinthians). Paul would send Titus back to Corinth with it (2 Cor 8:16-17).

2 Cor 2:14ff In the middle of discussing his unscheduled trip to Macedonia, Paul thanked God for his ministry, his relationship with the Corinthian believers, the glory of the new covenant, and the way God had used him to help others wherever he went, despite difficulties (2 Cor 2:14–7:4). In 2 Corinthians 7:5, Paul resumes his story of his trip to Macedonia.

2 Cor 2:14-16 In a Roman triumphal procession, the Roman general would display his treasures and captives amidst a cloud of incense burned for the gods. To the victors, the aroma was sweet; to the captives in the parade, it was the smell of slavery and death. When Christians preach the Good News, it is good news to some and repulsive news to others. Believers recognize the life-giving fragrance of the message. To nonbelievers it smells foul, like death—their own.

2 Cor 2:16-17 Paul asks "who is adequate" for the task of representing Christ? Our adequacy is always from God (1 Cor 15:10; 2 Cor 3:5). He has already commissioned and sent us (see Matt 28:18-20). He has given us the Holy Spirit to enable us to speak with Christ's power. He keeps his eye on us, protecting us as we work for him. As we realize that God has equipped us, we can overcome our feelings of inadequacy. Serving Christ, therefore, requires that we focus on what he can do through us, not on what we can't do by ourselves.

2 Cor 2:17 Some preachers in Paul's day were "hucksters," preaching without understanding God's message or caring about what happened to their listeners. They weren't concerned about furthering God's Kingdom—

[17]You see, we are not like the many hucksters* who preach for personal profit. We preach the word of God with sincerity and with Christ's authority, knowing that God is watching us.

3:1 Are we beginning to praise ourselves again? Are we like others, who need to bring you letters of recommendation, or who ask you to write such letters on their behalf? Surely not! [2]The only letter of recommendation we need is you yourselves. Your lives are a letter written in our* hearts; everyone can read it and recognize our good work among you. [3]Clearly, you are a letter from Christ showing the result of our ministry among you. This "letter" is written not with pen and ink, but with the Spirit of the living God. It is carved not on tablets of stone, but on human hearts.

[4]We are confident of all this because of our great trust in God through Christ. [5]It is not that we think we are qualified to do anything on our own. Our qualification comes from God. [6]He has enabled us to be ministers of his new covenant. This is a covenant not of written laws, but of the Spirit. The old written covenant ends in death; but under the new covenant, the Spirit gives life.

The Glory of the New Covenant

2 CORINTHIANS 3:7-18

The old way,* with laws etched in stone, led to death, though it began with such glory that the people of

2 Cor 2:17 Some manuscripts read *the rest of the hucksters.* **2 Cor 3:2** Some manuscripts read *your.* **2 Cor 3:7** Or *ministry;* also in 3:8, 9, 10, 11, 12.

they just wanted money. Today there are still preachers and teachers who care only about money and not about truth. Those who truly speak for God should teach God's Word with sincerity and integrity and should never preach for selfish reasons (1 Tim 6:5-10).

2 Cor 3:1-3 Some false teachers had started carrying forged letters of recommendation to authenticate their authority. In no uncertain terms, Paul stated that he needed no such letters. The believers to whom Paul and his companions had preached were enough of a recommendation. Paul did use letters of introduction many times. He wrote them on behalf of Phoebe (Rom 16:1-2) and Timothy (1 Cor 16:10-11). These letters helped Paul's trusted companions and friends find a welcome in various churches.

2 Cor 3:3 Paul uses powerful imagery from famous Old Testament passages predicting the promised day of new hearts and new beginnings for God's people (see Jer 31:33; Ezek 11:19; 36:26). No human being can take credit for this process of conversion. It is the work of God's Spirit. We do not become believers by following some manual or using some technique. Our conversion is a result of God's implanting his Spirit in our hearts, giving us new power to live for him.

2 Cor 3:4-5 Paul was not boasting; he gave God the credit for all his accomplishments. While the false teachers boasted of their own power and success, Paul expressed his humility before God. No one can claim to be adequate without God's help. No one is competent to carry out the responsibilities of God's calling with human strength alone. Without the Holy Spirit's enabling, our natural talents can carry us only so far. As Christ's witnesses, we need the character and special strength that only God gives.

2 Cor 3:6 "The old written covenant ends in death; but under the new covenant, the Spirit gives life" means that trying to be saved by keeping the Old Testament laws will end in death. Only by believing in the Lord Jesus Christ can a person receive eternal life through the Holy Spirit. No one but Jesus has ever fulfilled the law perfectly; thus, the whole world is condemned to death. The law makes people realize their sin, but it cannot give life. Under the new covenant, eternal life comes from the Holy Spirit. The Spirit gives new life to all who believe in Christ. The law still points out sin and shows us how to obey God, but forgiveness comes only through the grace and mercy of Christ (see Rom 7:10–8:2).

2 Cor 3:7-11 Paul recalled the stone tablets on which God had written the old covenant—calling it "the old way." He identified the law, although leading to death, as nonetheless glorious because it was God's provision and proof of his intervention in the life of his people. But that which was summarized on stone is nowhere near as glorious as what came with "the new way"—life in the Holy Spirit. The Holy Spirit was present at the creation of the world as one of the agents in the origin of life itself (Gen 1:2). He is the power behind the rebirth of every Christian and the one who helps us live the Christian life. By his power, we will be transformed into Christ's perfect likeness when he returns. Thank God for the fact that the best is yet to be.

Troas

Troas was a city in Turkey on the Aegean shore, 10 miles south of the ancient site of Troy, scene of the Trojan War immortalized by the poet Homer. According to some scholars, Julius Caesar envisioned Troas as his eastern capital, and Constantine considered making it his capital before deciding on Byzantium instead. This photo shows some remains at the site of ancient Troas.

On the second missionary journey, Paul and Silas came to Troas after being forbidden by the Spirit to preach in Asia (Acts 16:6-8). Paul then sailed from Troas into Macedonia in response to a call: "Come over to Macedonia and help us!" (Acts 16:9). We know that a church must have been established in Troas because of events that are described later. After his mission in Ephesus was finished, Paul stayed and preached the gospel in Troas (2 Cor 2:12). On his way to Jerusalem for the last time, Paul stopped in Troas, where he preached until dawn (Acts 20:6-12). Paul visited Troas again and left behind a cloak and parchments, presumably when he was arrested there. In a letter to Timothy, Paul asks him to bring these to him while in prison in Rome (2 Tim 4:13).

▸ 2 CORINTHIANS 3:7-18 *(cont.)*

Israel could not bear to look at Moses' face. For his face shone with the glory of God, even though the brightness was already fading away. [8]Shouldn't we expect far greater glory under the new way, now that the Holy Spirit is giving life? [9]If the old way, which brings condemnation, was glorious, how much more glorious is the new way, which makes us right with God! [10]In fact, that first glory was not glorious at all compared with the overwhelming glory of the new way. [11]So if the old way, which has been replaced, was glorious, how much more glorious is the new, which remains forever!

[12]Since this new way gives us such confidence, we can be very bold. [13]We are not like Moses, who put a veil over his face so the people of Israel would not see the glory, even though it was destined to fade away. [14]But the people's minds were hardened, and to this day whenever the old covenant is being read, the same veil covers their minds so they cannot understand the truth. And this veil can be removed only by believing in Christ. [15]Yes, even today when they read Moses' writings, their hearts are covered with that veil, and they do not understand. [16]But whenever someone turns to the Lord, the veil is taken away. [17]For the Lord is the Spirit, and wherever the Spirit of the Lord is, there is freedom. [18]So all of us who have had that veil removed can see and reflect the glory of the Lord. And the Lord—who is the Spirit—makes us more and more like him as we are changed into his glorious image.

Treasure in Fragile Clay Jars

2 CORINTHIANS 4:1-18

Therefore, since God in his mercy has given us this new way,* we never give up. [2]We reject all shameful deeds and underhanded methods. We don't try to trick anyone or distort the word of God. We tell the truth before God, and all who are honest know this.

[3]If the Good News we preach is hidden behind a veil, it is hidden only from people who are perishing. [4]Satan, who is the god of this world, has blinded the minds of those who don't believe. They are unable to see the glorious light of the Good News. They don't understand this message about the glory of Christ, who is the exact likeness of God.

[5]You see, we don't go around preaching about

2 Cor 4:1 Or *ministry.*

2 Cor 3:13-18 When Moses came down Mount Sinai with the Ten Commandments, his face glowed from being in God's presence (Exod 34:29-35). Moses had to put on a veil to keep the people from being terrified by the brightness of his face and from seeing the radiance fade away. This veil illustrates the fading of the old system and the veiling of the people's minds because of their pride, hardness of heart, and refusal to repent. The veil kept them from understanding references to Christ in the Scriptures. When anyone becomes a Christian, the veil is taken away (2 Cor 3:16), giving eternal life and freedom from bondage. That person can then be like a mirror reflecting God's glory.

All of us who have had that veil removed can see and reflect the glory of the Lord. And the Lord—who is the Spirit—makes us more and more like him as we are changed into his glorious image.
2 Corinthians 3:18

2 Cor 3:17 Those who were trying to be saved by keeping the Old Testament law were soon tied up in rules and ceremonies. But now, through the Holy Spirit, God provides freedom from sin and condemnation (Rom 8:1). When we trust Christ to save us, he removes our heavy burden of trying to please him and our guilt for failing to do so. By trusting Christ we are loved, accepted, forgiven, and freed to live for him. "Wherever the Spirit of the Lord is, there is freedom."

2 Cor 3:18 The glory that the Spirit imparts to the believer is more excellent and lasts longer than the glory that Moses experienced. By gazing at the nature of God with unveiled minds, we can be more like him. In the Good News, we see the truth about Christ, and it transforms us morally as we understand and apply it. Through learning about Christ's life, we can understand how wonderful God is and what he is really like. As our knowledge deepens, the Holy Spirit helps us to change. Becoming Christlike is a progressive experience (see Rom 8:29; Gal 4:19; Phil 3:21; 1 Jn 3:2). The more closely we follow Christ, the more we will be like him.

2 Cor 4:2 Paul condemned those who twist God's Word. Preachers, teachers, and anyone else who talks about Jesus Christ must remember that they stand in God's presence—he hears every word. Many Christian ministers and leaders twist Scripture in their attempt to motivate audiences. Others take Scripture out of context to promote their own views. When you tell people about Christ, be careful not to distort the message to please or manipulate your audience. Proclaim the truth of God's Word.

2 Cor 4:3-4 The Good News is revealed to everyone, except to those who refuse to believe. Satan is "the god of this world." His work is to deceive, and he has blinded those who don't believe in Christ (see 2 Cor 11:14-15). The allure of money, power, and pleasure blinds people to the light of Christ's Good News. Those who reject Christ and prefer their own pursuits have unknowingly made Satan their god.

2 Cor 4:5 The focus of Paul's preaching was Christ and not himself. When you witness, tell people about what Christ has done and not about your abilities and accomplishments. People must be introduced to Christ, not to you. And if you hear someone preaching about themselves or their own ideas rather than about Christ, beware—that is a false teacher.

2 Cor 4:5 Paul willingly served the Corinthian church even though the people must have deeply disappointed him. Serving people requires a sacrifice of time and personal desires. Being Christ's follower means serving others, even when they do not measure up to our expectations.

ourselves. We preach that Jesus Christ is Lord, and
we ourselves are your servants for Jesus' sake. [6]For
God, who said, "Let there be light in the darkness,"
has made this light shine in our hearts so we could
know the glory of God that is seen in the face of Jesus
Christ.

[7]We now have this light shining in our hearts, but we
ourselves are like fragile clay jars containing this great
treasure.* This makes it clear that our great power is
from God, not from ourselves.

[8]We are pressed on every side by troubles, but we
are not crushed. We are perplexed, but not driven to
despair. [9]We are hunted down, but never abandoned by
God. We get knocked down, but we are not destroyed.
[10]Through suffering, our bodies continue to share in
the death of Jesus so that the life of Jesus may also be
seen in our bodies.

[11]Yes, we live under constant danger of death because we serve Jesus, so that the life of Jesus will be
evident in our dying bodies. [12]So we live in the face
of death, but this has resulted in eternal life for you.

[13]But we continue to preach because we have the
same kind of faith the psalmist had when he said, "I
believed in God, so I spoke."* [14]We know that God, who
raised the Lord Jesus,* will also raise us with Jesus and
present us to himself together with you. [15]All of this is
for your benefit. And as God's grace reaches more and
more people, there will be great thanksgiving, and God
will receive more and more glory.

[16]That is why we never give up. Though our bodies
are dying, our spirits are* being renewed every day.
[17]For our present troubles are small and won't last
very long. Yet they produce for us a glory that vastly
outweighs them and will last forever! [18]So we don't
look at the troubles we can see now; rather, we fix our
gaze on things that cannot be seen. For the things we
see now will soon be gone, but the things we cannot
see will last forever.

New Bodies

2 CORINTHIANS 5:1-10

For we know that when this earthly tent we live in is
taken down (that is, when we die and leave this earthly
body), we will have a house in heaven, an eternal body
made for us by God himself and not by human hands.
[2]We grow weary in our present bodies, and we long
to put on our heavenly bodies like new clothing. [3]For
we will put on heavenly bodies; we will not be spirits

2 Cor 4:7 Greek *We now have this treasure in clay jars.* **2 Cor 4:13** Ps 116:10. **2 Cor 4:14** Some manuscripts read *who raised Jesus.* **2 Cor 4:16** Greek *our inner being is.*

2 Cor 4:7 The supremely valuable message of salvation in Jesus Christ has been entrusted by God to frail and fallible human beings. Paul's focus was not on the perishable container but on its priceless contents—God's power dwelling in us. Though we are "fragile clay jars," God uses us to spread his Good News, and he gives us power to do his work. Knowing that the power is his, not ours, should keep us from pride and motivate us to keep daily contact with God, our power source. Our responsibility is to let people see God through us.

2 Cor 4:8-12 Paul reminds us that though we may think we are at the end of our rope, we are never at the end of our hope. Our perishable bodies are subject to sin and suffering, but God never abandons us. Because Christ has won the victory over death, we have eternal life. All our risks, humiliations, and trials are opportunities for Christ to demonstrate his power and presence in and through us. We must ask ourselves, "Could I handle the suffering and opposition that Paul did?" The success syndrome is a great enemy of effective ministry. From an earthly perspective, Paul was not very successful. Like Paul, we must carry out our ministry, looking to God for strength. When opposition, slander, or disappointment threaten to rob you of the victory, remember that no one can destroy what God has accomplished through you.

2 Cor 4:15-18 Paul had faced suffering, trials, and distress as he preached the Good News. But he knew that they would one day be over, and he would obtain God's rest and rewards. As we face great troubles, it's easy to focus on the pain rather than on our ultimate goal. Just as athletes concentrate on the finish line and ignore their discomfort, we must focus on the reward for our faith and the joy that lasts forever. No matter what happens to us in this life, we have the assurance of eternal life, when all suffering will end and all sorrow will flee away (Isa 35:10).

2 Cor 4:16 It is easy to lose heart and quit. We all have faced problems in our relationships or in our work that have caused us to think about giving up. Rather than quitting when persecution wore him down, Paul concentrated on the inner strength that came from the Holy Spirit (Eph 3:16). Don't let fatigue, pain, or criticism force you off the job. Renew your commitment to serve Christ. Don't forsake your eternal reward because of the intensity of today's pain. Your very weakness allows the resurrection power of Christ to strengthen you moment by moment.

2 Cor 4:17 Our troubles should not diminish our faith or disillusion us. We should realize that there is a purpose in our suffering. Problems and human limitations have several benefits: (1) They remind us of Christ's suffering for us; (2) they keep us from pride; (3) they cause us to look beyond this brief life; (4) they give us opportunities to prove our faith to others; and (5) they give God the opportunity to demonstrate his power. See your troubles as opportunities!

2 Cor 4:18 Our ultimate hope when we are experiencing terrible illness, persecution, or pain is the realization that this life is not all there is—there is life after death! Knowing that we will live forever with God in a place without sin and suffering can help us live above the pain that we face in this life.

2 Cor 5:1-10 Paul contrasts our earthly body and our future resurrection body. Paul clearly states that our present body makes us groan, but when we die we will not be spirits without bodies. We will have new bodies that will be perfect for our everlasting life.

Paul wrote as he did because the church at Corinth was surrounded by Greek culture, and many believers had difficulty with the concept of bodily resurrection because the Greeks did not believe in it. Most saw the afterlife as something that happened only to the soul, with the real person imprisoned in a physical body. They believed that at death the soul was released; there was no immortality for the body, and the soul enters an eternal state. But the Bible teaches that the body and soul are not permanently separated.

Paul describes our resurrected body in more detail in 1 Corinthians 15:46-58. We will still have personalities and recognizable characteristics in our resurrected body, but through Christ's work, our body will be better than we can imagine. The Bible does not tell us everything about our resurrected body, but we know that it will be perfect, without sickness, disease, or pain (see Phil 3:21; Rev 21:4).

▸ 2 CORINTHIANS 5:1-10 *(cont.)*

without bodies.* [4]While we live in these earthly bodies, we groan and sigh, but it's not that we want to die and get rid of these bodies that clothe us. Rather, we want to put on our new bodies so that these dying bodies will be swallowed up by life. [5]God himself has prepared us for this, and as a guarantee he has given us his Holy Spirit.

[6]So we are always confident, even though we know that as long as we live in these bodies we are not at home with the Lord. [7]For we live by believing and not by seeing. [8]Yes, we are fully confident, and we would rather be away from these earthly bodies, for then we will be at home with the Lord. [9]So whether we are here in this body or away from this body, our goal is to please him. [10]For we must all stand before Christ to be judged. We will each receive whatever we deserve for the good or evil we have done in this earthly body.

We Are God's Ambassadors

2 CORINTHIANS 5:11-6:2

Because we understand our fearful responsibility to the Lord, we work hard to persuade others. God knows we are sincere, and I hope you know this, too. [12]Are we commending ourselves to you again? No, we are giving you a reason to be proud of us,* so you can answer those who brag about having a spectacular ministry rather than having a sincere heart. [13]If it seems we are crazy, it is to bring glory to God. And if we are in our right minds, it is for your benefit. [14]Either way, Christ's love controls us.* Since we believe that Christ died for all, we also believe that we have all died to our old life.* [15]He died for everyone so that those who receive his new life will no longer live for themselves. Instead, they will live for Christ, who died and was raised for them.

[16]So we have stopped evaluating others from a human point of view. At one time we thought of Christ merely from a human point of view. How differently we know him now! [17]This means that anyone who belongs to Christ has become a new person. The old life is gone; a new life has begun!

[18]And all of this is a gift from God, who brought us back to himself through Christ. And God has given us this task of reconciling people to him. [19]For God was in Christ, reconciling the world to himself, no longer counting people's sins against them. And he

2 Cor 5:3 Greek *we will not be naked.* **2 Cor 5:12** Some manuscripts read *proud of yourselves.* **2 Cor 5:14a** Or *urges us on.* **2 Cor 5:14b** Greek *Since one died for all, then all died.*

2 Cor 5:4 Paul's knowledge that his dying body would be swallowed up by eternal life is a universal hope. According to the writer of Ecclesiastes, God "has planted eternity in the human heart" (Eccl 3:11). Human beings have an innate sense of transcendence and longing for ultimate reality experienced only in the eternal presence of God. This spiritual desire is addressed by every world religion and cult and (at least secretly) desired by every person. What occurrences in daily life can provide you an opportunity to witness God's solution to this universal spiritual search? A baby's birth, a parent's death, or the death of a dream all can be springboards for sharing the hope you have in Christ. Spread the Good News!

2 Cor 5:5 The Holy Spirit is God's "guarantee" of what will come. His work in our lives today assures us that the healing process will be thoroughly completed in Christ's presence. Each time the Holy Spirit reminds you of Scripture, convicts you of sin, restrains you from selfish behavior, or prompts you to love, you have evidence that he is present. You have the Spirit within you beginning the transformation process. Whether you deal with aches and pains or even disabling limitations, trust God that his total renovation of your body and soul is in process.

2 Cor 5:6-8 Paul was not afraid to die because he was confident of spending eternity with Christ. Of course, facing the unknown may cause us anxiety and leaving loved ones hurts deeply, but if we believe in Jesus Christ, we can share Paul's hope and confidence of eternal life with Christ. Death is only a prelude to eternal life with God. We will continue to live. Let this hope give you confidence and inspire you to faithful service.

2 Cor 5:9-10 While eternal life is a free gift given on the basis of God's grace (Eph 2:8-9), each of us will still be judged by Christ. He will reward us for how we have lived. God's gracious gift of salvation does not free us from the requirement of faithful obedience. All Christians must give an account on the day of judgment of how they have lived (see Matt 16:27; Rom 14:10-12; 1 Cor 3:10-15).

2 Cor 5:11 Having a "fearful responsibility to the Lord" does not mean that believers become paralyzed. On the contrary, knowing God's perfection and that he will judge everyone's actions (2 Cor 5:10) should spur Christians to good deeds, to what pleases our God. The fear of the Lord also frees believers from all of life's anxieties and worries. Knowing that God is "for us" (Rom 8:31) can keep believers unafraid of earthly powers—people, governments, or the forces of nature (Prov 3:25-26). God takes care of his own. The fear of God gives us uncommon courage in the face of life's troubles.

2 Cor 5:12 Those who "brag about having a spectacular ministry rather than having a sincere heart" are the false preachers (see 2 Cor 2:17), who were concerned only about getting ahead in this world. They were preaching the Good News for money and popularity, while Paul and his companions were preaching out of concern for eternity. You can identify false preachers by finding out what really motivates them. If they are more concerned about themselves than about Christ, avoid them and their message.

2 Cor 5:13-15 Everything that Paul and his companions did was to honor God. Not only did fear of God motivate them (2 Cor 5:11), but Christ's love controlled their actions. The word *controls* means "to hold fast." In other words, the love of Christ was constraining them to certain courses of action. They knew that Jesus, out of his great love, had given up his life for their sakes. He had not acted out of his own self-interest, selfishly holding on to the glory of heaven that he already possessed (Phil 2:6). Instead, Jesus had willingly "died for everyone." Because Christ died for us, we also are dead to the old life. Like Paul, we should no longer live to please ourselves; we should spend our lives pleasing Christ.

2 Cor 5:17 Christians are brand-new people on the inside. The Holy Spirit gives us new life, and we are not the same anymore. We are not reformed, rehabilitated, or reeducated—we are re-created (new creations), living in vital union with Christ (Col 2:6-7). At conversion we do not merely turn over a new leaf; we begin a new life under a new Master.

While this newness is true individually, Paul is saying much more. Not only are believers changed from within, but a whole new order of creation began with Christ. There is a new covenant, a new perspective, a new body, a new church. All of creation is being renewed. So take notice. This is not a superficial change that will be quickly superseded by another novelty. This is an entirely new order of all creation under Christ's authority. It requires a new way of looking at all people and all of creation. Does your life reflect this new perspective?

2 Cor 5:18-19 God brings us back to himself (reconciles us) by blotting out our

gave us this wonderful message of reconciliation. [20]So
we are Christ's ambassadors; God is making his appeal through us. We speak for Christ when we plead,
"Come back to God!" [21]For God made Christ, who never
sinned, to be the offering for our sin,* so that we could
be made right with God through Christ.

[6:1]As God's partners,* we beg you not to accept this
marvelous gift of God's kindness and then ignore it.
[2]For God says,

> "At just the right time, I heard you.
> On the day of salvation, I helped you."*

Indeed, the "right time" is now. Today is the day of
salvation.

Paul's Hardships

2 CORINTHIANS 6:3-13

We live in such a way that no one will stumble because of us, and no one will find fault with our ministry. [4]In everything we do, we show that we are true
ministers of God. We patiently endure troubles and
hardships and calamities of every kind. [5]We have
been beaten, been put in prison, faced angry mobs,
worked to exhaustion, endured sleepless nights, and
gone without food. [6]We prove ourselves by our purity, our understanding, our patience, our kindness,
by the Holy Spirit within us,* and by our sincere love.
[7]We faithfully preach the truth. God's power is working in us. We use the weapons of righteousness in the
right hand for attack and the left hand for defense.
[8]We serve God whether people honor us or despise
us, whether they slander us or praise us. We are honest, but they call us impostors. [9]We are ignored, even
though we are well known. We live close to death, but
we are still alive. We have been beaten, but we have
not been killed. [10]Our hearts ache, but we always have
joy. We are poor, but we give spiritual riches to others.
We own nothing, and yet we have everything.

[11]Oh, dear Corinthian friends! We have spoken
honestly with you, and our hearts are open to you.
[12]There is no lack of love on our part, but you have
withheld your love from us. [13]I am asking you to respond as if you were my own children. Open your
hearts to us!

2 Cor 5:21 Or *to become sin itself.* **2 Cor 6:1** Or *As we work together.* **2 Cor 6:2** Isa 49:8 (Greek version). **2 Cor 6:6** Or *by our holiness of spirit.*

---

sins (see also Eph 2:13-18) and making us right with him. When we trust in Christ, we are no longer God's enemies, or strangers or foreigners to him. Because we have been reconciled to God, we have the privilege of encouraging others to do the same, and thus we are those who have the "task of reconciling people to him."

2 Cor 5:20 An ambassador is an official representative of one country to another. As believers, we are Christ's ambassadors, sent with his message of reconciliation to the world. An ambassador of reconciliation has an important responsibility. We dare not take this responsibility lightly. How well are you fulfilling your commission as Christ's ambassador?

2 Cor 5:21 When we trust in Christ, we make an exchange: He takes our sin and makes us right with God. Our sin was laid on Christ at his crucifixion. His righteousness is given to us at our conversion. This is what Christians mean by Christ's atonement for sin. In the world, bartering works only when two people exchange goods of relatively equal value. But God offers to trade his righteousness for our sin—something of immeasurable worth for something completely worthless. How grateful we should be for his kindness to us.

2 Cor 6:1 How could the Corinthian believers ignore God's message? Perhaps they were doubting Paul and his words, confused by the false teachers, who taught a different message. The people heard God's message but did not let it affect what they said and did. How often do you ignore God's message?

2 Cor 6:2 God offers salvation to all people. Many people put off a decision for Christ, thinking that there will be a better time—but they could easily miss their opportunity altogether. There is no time like the present to receive God's forgiveness. Don't let anything hold you back from coming to Christ. The right time is now!

2 Cor 6:3 In everything he did, Paul always considered what his actions communicated about Jesus Christ. If you are a believer, you are a minister for God. In the course of each day, unbelievers observe you. Don't let your careless or undisciplined actions be some person's excuse for rejecting Christ.

2 Cor 6:5 Being put in jail would cause many people to become bitter or to give up, but Paul saw jail time as one more opportunity to spread the Good News of Christ. Paul realized that his circumstances weren't as important as what he did with them. Turning a bad situation into a good one, he reached out to the guards and encouraged Christians who were afraid of persecution. We may not be in prison, but we still have plenty of opportunities to be discouraged—times of indecision, financial burdens, family conflict, church conflict, or the loss of our jobs. How we act in such situations will reflect what we believe. Like Paul, look for ways to demonstrate your faith even in bad situations. Whether or not the situation improves, your faith will grow stronger.

2 Cor 6:8-10 What a difference it makes to know Jesus! He cares for us in spite of what the world thinks. Christians don't have to give in to public opinion and pressure. Paul stood faithful to God whether people praised him or slandered him. He remained joyous and content in the most difficult hardships. Don't let circumstances or people's expectations control you. Be firm as you stand true to God, and refuse to compromise his standards for living.

2 Cor 6:11-13 "Our hearts are open to you" means that Paul had told the Corinthian believers his true feelings for them, clearly revealing how much he loved them. The Corinthians were reacting coldly to Paul's words, but Paul explained that his harsh words came from his love for them. It is easy to react against those whom God has placed over us in leadership, rather than to accept their exhortations as a sign of their love for us. We need an open rather than a closed heart toward God's messengers.

The Temple of the Living God

2 CORINTHIANS 6:14–7:4

Don't team up with those who are unbelievers. How
can righteousness be a partner with wickedness?
How can light live with darkness? 15What harmony
can there be between Christ and the devil*? How can
a believer be a partner with an unbeliever? 16And
what union can there be between God's temple and
idols? For we are the temple of the living God. As
God said:

"I will live in them
and walk among them.
I will be their God,
and they will be my people.*
17 Therefore, come out from among unbelievers,
and separate yourselves from them,
says the LORD.
Don't touch their filthy things,
and I will welcome you.*
18 And I will be your Father,
and you will be my sons and daughters,
says the LORD Almighty.*"

7:1 Because we have these promises, dear friends, let us cleanse ourselves from everything that can defile our body or spirit. And let us work toward complete holiness because we fear God.

2Please open your hearts to us. We have not done
wrong to anyone, nor led anyone astray, nor taken advantage of anyone. 3I'm not saying this to condemn
you. I said before that you are in our hearts, and we
live or die together with you. 4I have the highest confidence in you, and I take great pride in you. You have
greatly encouraged me and made me happy despite
all our troubles.

2 Cor 6:15 Greek *Beliar;* various other manuscripts render this proper name of the devil as *Belian, Beliab,* or *Belial.* **2 Cor 6:16** Lev 26:12; Ezek 37:27. **2 Cor 6:17** Isa 52:11; Ezek 20:34 (Greek version). **2 Cor 6:18** 2 Sam 7:14.

Temple of Apollo at Corinth

By the mid-8th century B.C., Corinth, strategically located along east-west trade routes, was a flourishing city-state. From 350–250 B.C. it was the most prominent city in Greece. Then the Roman military machine began a relentless march to forge a vast empire. In 146 B.C. Corinth was completely destroyed and lay in ruins for a century. In 46 B.C. Julius Caesar moved a mixed group of Italians and dispossessed Greeks onto the site, and once more a magnificent city arose, this time a Roman colony. As in most Roman cities, marble temples dominated the landscape. (The picture shows remains of the temple of Apollo at Corinth.) Corinth became a cosmopolitan city attracting trades people from all over the world, though its reputation grew simultaneously as a center of luxury, indulgence, and vice. A large colony of displaced Jews (part of the Diaspora) developed in the city, the group that undoubtedly attracted the apostle Paul, where he established a church.

Christians throughout the ages have learned countless spiritual truths from reading Paul's two epistles to the church at Corinth. Take time to read these epistles, and grow in your knowledge of salvation.

2 Cor 6:14-18 Paul urges believers to not "team up," that is, form partnerships with unbelievers because this might weaken their Christian commitment, integrity, or standards. It would be a mismatch. Earlier, Paul had explained that this did not mean isolating oneself from unbelievers (see 1 Cor 5:9-10). Paul even urges Christians to stay with their unbelieving spouses (1 Cor 7:12-13). He wanted believers to be active in their witness for Christ to unbelievers but not lock themselves into personal or business relationships that could cause them to compromise their faith. Believers should do everything in their power to avoid situations that could force them to divide their loyalties.

These verses also have strong application to marriage. Paul did not want single believers to enter into marriage with unbelievers. Such marriages cannot have unity in the most important issue in life—commitment and obedience to God. Because marriage involves two people becoming one, faith may become an issue, and one spouse may have to compromise beliefs for the sake of unity. Many people discount this problem only to regret it later. Don't allow emotion or passion to bind you with someone who will not be your spiritual partner. For those who have discovered God's light, there can be no fellowship or compromise with darkness (1 Cor 10:20-21).

2 Cor 6:16 Quoting from the prophet Isaiah, Paul asserted that the church is the temple of the living God. Corinth had many temples of pagan deities, so the recipients of his letter were able to visualize the contrast the apostle intended. Those who follow Christ are not known by a building; they are known as those in whom the Spirit of God lives. The church is not where believers go, it is who they are. God is not waiting for his people in some stained-glass setting. He is always with them. That is a sobering and yet a comforting thought. How does your behavior reflect on the God you represent?

2 Cor 6:17 Separation from the world involves more than keeping our distance from sinful practices; it means staying close to God. It involves more than avoiding worldly entertainment; it extends to how we spend our time and money. There is no way to separate ourselves totally from all sinful influences. Nevertheless, we are to resist the sin around us, without either giving up or giving in. When you know what God wants you to do, make a clean break with sinful practices.

2 Cor 7:1 Cleansing is a twofold action: turning away from sin, and turning toward God. The Corinthians were to have nothing to do with paganism. They were to make a clean break with their past and give themselves to God alone. "Work toward complete holiness" literally means "perfecting holiness." It connotes becoming mature or complete. Thus, Paul wasn't suggesting that the Corinthians could become sinless in this life. Instead, he was prodding them to work at maturing in their faith. God had provided them with all the resources they needed, and Christ's Spirit would empower them to become Christlike (Rom 8:2).

Paul's Joy at the Church's Repentance

2 CORINTHIANS 7:5-16

When we arrived in Macedonia, there was no rest for us. We faced conflict from every direction, with battles on the outside and fear on the inside. [6]But God, who encourages those who are discouraged, encouraged us by the arrival of Titus. [7]His presence was a joy, but so was the news he brought of the encouragement he received from you. When he told us how much you long to see me, and how sorry you are for what happened, and how loyal you are to me, I was filled with joy!

[8]I am not sorry that I sent that severe letter to you, though I was sorry at first, for I know it was painful to you for a little while. [9]Now I am glad I sent it, not because it hurt you, but because the pain caused you to repent and change your ways. It was the kind of sorrow God wants his people to have, so you were not harmed by us in any way. [10]For the kind of sorrow God wants us to experience leads us away from sin and results in salvation. There's no regret for that kind of sorrow. But worldly sorrow, which lacks repentance, results in spiritual death.

[11]Just see what this godly sorrow produced in you! Such earnestness, such concern to clear yourselves, such indignation, such alarm, such longing to see me, such zeal, and such a readiness to punish wrong. You showed that you have done everything necessary to make things right. [12]My purpose, then, was not to write about who did the wrong or who was wronged. I wrote to you so that in the sight of God you could see for yourselves how loyal you are to us. [13]We have been greatly encouraged by this.

In addition to our own encouragement, we were especially delighted to see how happy Titus was about the way all of you welcomed him and set his mind* at ease. [14]I had told him how proud I was of you—and you didn't disappoint me. I have always told you the truth, and now my boasting to Titus has also proved true! [15]Now he cares for you more than ever when he remembers the way all of you obeyed him and welcomed him with such fear and deep respect. [16]I am very happy now because I have complete confidence in you.

A Call to Generous Giving

2 CORINTHIANS 8:1-15

Now I want you to know, dear brothers and sisters,* what God in his kindness has done through the

2 Cor 7:13 Greek *his spirit.* **2 Cor 8:1** Greek *brothers.*

---

2 Cor 7:2 Paul insisted that the Corinthians should open their hearts to him. He knew how much those in the church need one another. If fellowship was necessary in Paul's day, it is all the more crucial today. Each day holds barely enough time to care for personal and family needs, let alone to meet the needs of others. Yet the activities that occupy our time are not as important as the community described in these verses. Paul's intention is not "coffee and donuts" fellowship. Believers need accountability that comes from lives intertwined by the cords of commitment and love. If you are not in a small group Bible study, take the first steps. Offer hospitality to fellow believers; when others extend the hand of fellowship to you, grasp it enthusiastically.

2 Cor 7:5 Here Paul resumed the story that he left in 2 Corinthians 2:13, where he said he went to Macedonia to look for Titus. Though Paul had many problems and hardships yet to face, he still found comfort and joy in the progress of the ministry.

2 Cor 7:8ff "That severe letter" refers to the third letter (now lost) that Paul had written to the Corinthians. Apparently it had caused the people to begin to change. (For an explanation of the chronology of Paul's letters to the church in Corinth, see the first note on 2 Cor 1:1, p. 1625.)

2 Cor 7:10 Sorrow for our sins can result in changed behavior. Many people are sorry only for the effects of their sins or for being caught (sorrow "which lacks repentance"). Compare Peter's remorse and repentance with Judas's bitterness and act of suicide. Both denied Christ. One repented and was restored to faith and service; the other took his own life.

PRINCIPLES OF CONFRONTATION IN 2 CORINTHIANS

Sometimes rebuke is necessary, but it must be used with caution. The purpose of any rebuke, confrontation, or discipline is to help people, not hurt them.

Method	*Reference*
Be firm and bold	**2 Cor 7:9; 10:2**
Affirm all you see that is good	**2 Cor 7:4**
Be accurate and honest	**2 Cor 7:14; 8:21**
Know the facts	**2 Cor 11:22-27**
Follow up after the confrontation	**2 Cor 7:13; 12:14**
Be gentle after being firm	**2 Cor 7:15; 13:11-13**
Speak words that reflect Christ's message, not your own ideas	**2 Cor 10:3, 12-13; 12:19**
Use discipline only when all else fails	**2 Cor 13:2**

2 Cor 7:11 Paul affirmed the Corinthians for their right response to the correction he had given them. It's difficult to accept criticism, correction, or rebuke with poise and grace. It is much more natural to be defensive and then counterattack. We can accept criticism with self-pity, thinking we don't really deserve it. We can be angry and resentful. But a mature Christian should graciously accept constructive criticism, sincerely evaluate it, and grow from it.

2 Cor 8:1ff Paul, writing from Macedonia, hoped that news of the generosity of these churches would encourage the Corinthian believers and motivate them to solve their problems and unite in fellowship.

▶ **2 CORINTHIANS 8:1-15** ***(cont.)***

churches in Macedonia. [2]They are being tested by many troubles, and they are very poor. But they are also filled with abundant joy, which has overflowed in rich generosity.

[3]For I can testify that they gave not only what they could afford, but far more. And they did it of their own free will. [4]They begged us again and again for the privilege of sharing in the gift for the believers in Jerusalem.* [5]They even did more than we had hoped, for their first action was to give themselves to the Lord and to us, just as God wanted them to do.

[6]So we have urged Titus, who encouraged your giving in the first place, to return to you and encourage you to finish this ministry of giving. [7]Since you excel in so many ways—in your faith, your gifted speakers, your knowledge, your enthusiasm, and your love from us*—I want you to excel also in this gracious act of giving.

[8]I am not commanding you to do this. But I am testing how genuine your love is by comparing it with the eagerness of the other churches.

[9]You know the generous grace of our Lord Jesus Christ. Though he was rich, yet for your sakes he became poor, so that by his poverty he could make you rich.

[10]Here is my advice: It would be good for you to finish what you started a year ago. Last year you were the first who wanted to give, and you were the first to begin doing it. [11]Now you should finish what you started. Let the eagerness you showed in the beginning be matched now by your giving. Give in proportion to what you have. [12]Whatever you give is acceptable if you give it eagerly. And give according to what you have, not what you don't have. [13]Of course, I don't mean your giving should make life easy for others and hard for yourselves. I only mean that there should be some equality. [14]Right now you have plenty and can help those who are in need. Later, they will have plenty and can share with you when you need it. In this way, things will be equal. [15]As the Scriptures say,

"Those who gathered a lot had nothing left over,
and those who gathered only a little had
enough."*

Titus and His Companions

2 CORINTHIANS 8:16-24

But thank God! He has given Titus the same enthusiasm for you that I have. [17]Titus welcomed our request that he visit you again. In fact, he himself was very

2 Cor 8:4 Greek *for God's holy people.* **2 Cor 8:7** Some manuscripts read *your love for us.* **2 Cor 8:15** Exod 16:18.

2 Cor 8:2-5 During his third missionary journey, Paul had collected money for the impoverished believers in Jerusalem. The churches in Macedonia—Philippi, Thessalonica, and Berea—had given money even though they were poor, and they had sacrificially given more than Paul expected. Although they were poor themselves, they wanted to help. The amount we give is not as important as why and how we give. God does not want us to give grudgingly. Instead, he wants us to give as these churches did—out of dedication to Christ, love for fellow believers, the joy of helping those in need, as well as the fact that it was simply the good and right thing to do. How well does your giving measure up to the standards set by the Macedonian churches?

2 Cor 8:3-6 The Kingdom of God spreads through believers' concern and eagerness to help others. Here we see several churches joining to help others beyond their own circle of friends and their own city. Explore ways that you might link up with a ministry outside your city, either through your church or through a Christian organization. By joining with other believers to do God's work, you increase Christian unity and help the Kingdom grow.

2 Cor 8:7-8 The Corinthian believers excelled in everything—they had faith, gifted speakers, knowledge, enthusiasm, and love. Paul encouraged them to also excel in the grace of giving. Too often, stewardship of money is given a different status than other aspects of discipleship. Most believers would not want growth in faith, knowledge, or love to stop at a certain level. Yet many decide a fixed percentage of their money to give and stay there for life. True discipleship includes growing in the mature use of all resources, so giving should expand as well. God can give you the desire and enable you to increase your capacity to give. Don't miss this opportunity for growth.

2 Cor 8:9 There is no evidence that Jesus was any poorer than most first-century Palestinians; rather, Jesus became poor by giving up his rights as God and becoming human. In his incarnation, God voluntarily became human—the person Jesus of Nazareth. As a man, Jesus was subject to place, time, and other human limitations. He did not give up his eternal power when he became human, but he did set aside his glory and his rights (see the note on Phil 2:5-7, p. 1719). In response to the Father's will, he limited his power and knowledge. Christ became "poor" when he became human because he set aside so much. Yet by doing so, he made us "rich" because we received salvation and eternal life.

What made Jesus' humanity unique was his freedom from sin. In Jesus we can see every attribute of God's character. (The Incarnation is explained further in these Bible passages: John 1:1-14; Rom 1:2-5; Phil 2:6-11; 1 Tim 3:16; Heb 2:14; 1 Jn 1:1-3.)

2 Cor 8:10-15 The Christians in the Corinthian church had money, and apparently they had planned to collect money for the Jerusalem church a year previously (see also 2 Cor 9:2). Paul challenged them to act on their plans. Four principles of giving emerge here: (1) Your willingness to give enthusiastically is more important than the amount you give; (2) you should strive to fulfill your financial commitments; (3) if you give to others in need, they will, in turn, help you when you are in need; (4) you should give as a response to Christ, not for anything you can get out of it. How you give reflects your devotion to Christ.

2 Cor 8:12 How do you decide how much to give? What about differences in the financial resources Christians have? Paul gives the Corinthian church several principles to follow: (1) Each person should follow through on previous promises (2 Cor 8:10-11; 9:3); (2) each person should give as much as they are able (2 Cor 8:12; 9:6); (3) each must determine how much to give (2 Cor 9:7); and (4) each should give in proportion to what God has given them (2 Cor 9:10). God gives to us so that we can give to others.

2 Cor 8:12 Paul says that we should give of what we have, not what we don't have. Sacrificial giving must be responsible. Paul wants believers to give generously, but not to the extent that those who depend on the givers (their families, for example) must go without having their basic needs met. Give until it hurts, but don't give so that it hurts your family and/or relatives who need your financial support.

2 Cor 8:18-21 "Another brother" was traveling with Paul and Titus, a man who was elected by the churches to also take the large financial gift to Jerusalem. Paul explained that by traveling together there could be no suspicion and people would know that the gift was being handled honestly. The church did not need to worry that the bearers of the collection would misuse the money.

eager to go and see you. [18]We are also sending another
brother with Titus. All the churches praise him as a
preacher of the Good News. [19]He was appointed by
the churches to accompany us as we take the offering
to Jerusalem*—a service that glorifies the Lord and
shows our eagerness to help.
[20]We are traveling together to guard against any
criticism for the way we are handling this generous gift.
[21]We are careful to be honorable before the Lord, but
we also want everyone else to see that we are honorable.
[22]We are also sending with them another of our
brothers who has proven himself many times and has
shown on many occasions how eager he is. He is now
even more enthusiastic because of his great confidence in you. [23]If anyone asks about Titus, say that he
is my partner who works with me to help you. And the
brothers with him have been sent by the churches,*
and they bring honor to Christ. [24]So show them your
love, and prove to all the churches that our boasting
about you is justified.

The Collection for Christians in Jerusalem

2 CORINTHIANS 9:1-15

I really don't need to write to you about this ministry
of giving for the believers in Jerusalem.* [2]For I know
how eager you are to help, and I have been boasting
to the churches in Macedonia that you in Greece*
were ready to send an offering a year ago. In fact,
it was your enthusiasm that stirred up many of the
Macedonian believers to begin giving.
[3]But I am sending these brothers to be sure you
really are ready, as I have been telling them, and
that your money is all collected. I don't want to be
wrong in my boasting about you. [4]We would be embarrassed—not to mention your own embarrassment—if some Macedonian believers came with me
and found that you weren't ready after all I had told
them! [5]So I thought I should send these brothers
ahead of me to make sure the gift you promised is
ready. But I want it to be a willing gift, not one given
grudgingly.
[6]Remember this—a farmer who plants only a few
seeds will get a small crop. But the one who plants
generously will get a generous crop. [7]You must each
decide in your heart how much to give. And don't
give reluctantly or in response to pressure. "For God
loves a person who gives cheerfully."* [8]And God will
generously provide all you need. Then you will always
have everything you need and plenty left over to share
with others. [9]As the Scriptures say,

2 Cor 8:19 See 1 Cor 16:3-4. **2 Cor 8:23** Greek *are apostles of the churches.* **2 Cor 9:1** Greek *about the offering for God's holy people.* **2 Cor 9:2** Greek *in Achaia,* the southern region of the Greek peninsula. *Macedonia* was in the northern region of Greece. **2 Cor 9:7** See footnote on Prov 22:8.

RAISING FUNDS HONORABLY

The topic of fund-raising is not one to be avoided or one that should embarrass us, but all fund-raising efforts should be planned and conducted responsibly.

Be dedicated to God	2 Cor 8:5
Provide information	2 Cor 8:4
Show a specific purpose and goal	2 Cor 8:4
Be enthusiastic	2 Cor 8:7-8, 11
Reveal honesty and integrity	2 Cor 8:21
Be accountable	2 Cor 9:3
Let people give willingly	2 Cor 9:7
Be generous yourselves	2 Cor 8:7
Have someone to keep it moving	2 Cor 8:18-22
Be persistent, trusting God to provide	2 Cor 8:2ff

Paul used every safeguard to maintain integrity in the collection of money for the Jerusalem church. Those outside the church can view skeptically the way believers handle money in the church. Financial scandals among high-profile ministries have alerted the non-believing world to the unethical gimmicks that some Christians use. It is possible to avoid mismanagement of God's resources. Does your church or organization have a system of checks and balances that prevent wrongful behavior? Are there financial practices in your ministry that need to be reviewed? Christians must have the highest standard of financial responsibility.

2 Cor 9:1-2 By describing how their own "enthusiasm" had incited the Macedonians to give, Paul was, in effect, prodding the Corinthians to rekindle their initial enthusiasm for giving. Paul wasn't naive about human behavior. The start and end of a marathon are much more thrilling than the miles in between. It takes stubborn determination to keep going. Paul also knew that it took a community to persevere. Just as teammates will cheer their runner on in a race, so Paul was sending Titus and two other believers to the Corinthians to cheer them on.

2 Cor 9:3-5 Paul reminded the Corinthians to fulfill the commitment that they had already made (see also 2 Cor 8:10-12). They had said that they would collect a financial gift to send to the church in Jerusalem. Paul was sending a few men ahead of him to make sure their gift was ready, so it would be a real gift and not look like people had to give under pressure at the last minute. He was holding them accountable to keep their promise, so that neither Paul nor the Corinthians would be embarrassed.

2 Cor 9:6-8 People may hesitate to give generously to God because they worry about having enough money left over to meet their own needs. Paul assured the Corinthians that God was able to meet their needs. The person who gives only a little will receive only a little in return. Don't let a lack of faith keep you from giving cheerfully and generously.

2 Cor 9:7 A giving attitude is more important than the amount given. The person who can give only a small gift shouldn't be embarrassed. God is concerned about *how* a person gives from their resources (see Mark 12:41-44). According to that standard, the giving of the Macedonian churches would be difficult to match (2 Cor 8:3). God himself is a cheerful giver. Consider all he has done for us. He is pleased when we who are created in his image give generously and joyfully. Do you have a difficult time letting go of your money? It may reflect ungratefulness to God.

▸ 2 CORINTHIANS 9:1-15 ***(cont.)***

"They share freely and give generously
to the poor.
Their good deeds will be remembered
forever."*

[10]For God is the one who provides seed for the farmer
and then bread to eat. In the same way, he will provide
and increase your resources and then produce a great
harvest of generosity* in you.
[11]Yes, you will be enriched in every way so that you
can always be generous. And when we take your gifts
to those who need them, they will thank God. [12]So
two good things will result from this ministry of giving—the needs of the believers in Jerusalem* will be
met, and they will joyfully express their thanks to God.
[13]As a result of your ministry, they will give glory to
God. For your generosity to them and to all believers
will prove that you are obedient to the Good News of
Christ. [14]And they will pray for you with deep affection
because of the overflowing grace God has given to you.
[15]Thank God for this gift* too wonderful for words!

Paul Defends His Authority

2 CORINTHIANS 10:1-18

Now I, Paul, appeal to you with the gentleness and
kindness of Christ—though I realize you think I am
timid in person and bold only when I write from far
away. [2]Well, I am begging you now so that when I come
I won't have to be bold with those who think we act
from human motives.
[3]We are human, but we don't wage war as humans
do. [4]*We use God's mighty weapons, not worldly weapons, to knock down the strongholds of human reasoning and to destroy false arguments. [5]We destroy every
proud obstacle that keeps people from knowing God.
We capture their rebellious thoughts and teach them
to obey Christ. [6]And after you have become fully obedient, we will punish everyone who remains disobedient.
[7]Look at the obvious facts.* Those who say they
belong to Christ must recognize that we belong to
Christ as much as they do. [8]I may seem to be boasting
too much about the authority given to us by the Lord.
But our authority builds you up; it doesn't tear you
down. So I will not be ashamed of using my authority.
[9]I'm not trying to frighten you by my letters. [10]For
some say, "Paul's letters are demanding and forceful,
but in person he is weak, and his speeches are worthless!" [11]Those people should realize that our actions
when we arrive in person will be as forceful as what
we say in our letters from far away.
[12]Oh, don't worry; we wouldn't dare say that we
are as wonderful as these other men who tell you
how important they are! But they are only comparing

2 Cor 9:9 Ps 112:9. **2 Cor 9:10** Greek *righteousness.* **2 Cor 9:12** Greek *of God's holy people.* **2 Cor 9:15** Greek *his gift.* **2 Cor 10:4** English translations divide verses 4 and 5 in various ways. **2 Cor 10:7** Or *You look at things only on the basis of appearance.*

---

2 Cor 9:10 God gives us resources to use and invest for him. Paul uses the illustration of seed to explain that the resources God gives us are not to be hidden, foolishly devoured, or thrown away. Instead, they should be cultivated in order to produce more crops. When we invest what God has given us in his work, he will provide us with even more to give in his service.

2 Cor 9:13 Paul wanted his readers to be generous on every occasion. As he appealed to the Corinthians to give sacrificially to aid the Jerusalem congregation, he reminded them that God is the source of everything good (2 Cor 9:10). Believers are called to be generous because of the example of the Lord of life. A stingy Christian should not exist. Generosity proves that a person's heart has been cleansed of self-interest and filled with the servant spirit of Jesus himself. That is why acts of generosity result in God being praised. Do neighbors see generosity in your actions?

2 Cor 10:1-2 Paul's opponents questioned his authority. From 2 Corinthians 7:8-16 we know that the majority of Corinthian believers sided with Paul. However, a minority continued to slander him, saying that he was bold in his letters but had no authority in person. Paul's response is found in 2 Corinthians 10–13.

2 Cor 10:3-6 We, like Paul, are merely weak humans, but we don't need to use human plans and methods to win our battles. God's mighty weapons are available to us as we fight against the devil's "strongholds." The Christian must choose whose methods to use—God's or the world's. Paul assures us that God's mighty weapons—prayer, faith, hope, love, God's Word, the Holy Spirit—are powerful and effective (see Eph 6:13-18)! These weapons can break down the proud human arguments against God and the walls that Satan builds to keep people from finding God. When dealing with people's proud arguments that keep them from a relationship with Christ, we may be tempted to use our own methods. But nothing can break down these barriers like God's weapons.

2 Cor 10:5 Paul uses military terminology to describe this warfare against sin and Satan. God must be the commander in chief—even our thoughts must be submitted to his control as we live for him. Spirit-empowered believers must capture every thought and yield it to Christ. When exposed to ideas or opportunities that might lead to wrong desires, you have a choice. You can recognize the danger and turn away, or you can allow unhealthy thoughts to take you captive. You capture your fantasies and desires when you honestly admit them to the Lord and ask him to redirect your thinking. Ask God to give you the spirit of discernment to keep your thoughts focused on his truth.

2 Cor 10:7-10 Those who opposed Paul portrayed him as weak and powerless, but Paul reminded the Corinthians that he had been given authority by the Lord. False teachers were encouraging the believers to ignore Paul, but Paul explained that the advice in his letters was to be taken seriously. He had authority because he and his companions had been the first to bring the Good News to Corinth (2 Cor 10:14). Everyone knew that because of this service, their faith had been built up.

2 Cor 10:10 Some said that Paul's speaking amounted to nothing. Greece was known for its eloquent and persuasive orators. Evidently, some were judging Paul by comparing him to other speakers they had heard, and Paul was perhaps not the most powerful preacher (although he was an excellent debater). But Paul responded obediently to God's call and thus introduced Christianity to the Roman Empire. Moses and Jeremiah also had problems with speaking (see Exod 4:10-12; Jer 1:6). Preaching ability is not the first prerequisite of a great leader!

2 Cor 10:12-13 Paul criticized the false teachers who were trying to prove their goodness by comparing themselves with others rather than with God's standards. When we compare ourselves with others, we may feel proud because we think we're better. But when we measure ourselves against God's standards, it becomes obvious that we have no basis for pride. Don't worry about other people's accomplishments. Instead, ask yourself: How does my life measure up to what God wants? How does my life compare to that of Jesus Christ?

themselves with each other, using themselves as the standard of measurement. How ignorant!
[13]We will not boast about things done outside our area of authority. We will boast only about what has happened within the boundaries of the work God has given us, which includes our working with you. [14]We are not reaching beyond these boundaries when we claim authority over you, as if we had never visited you. For we were the first to travel all the way to Corinth with the Good News of Christ.
[15]Nor do we boast and claim credit for the work someone else has done. Instead, we hope that your faith will grow so that the boundaries of our work among you will be extended. [16]Then we will be able to go and preach the Good News in other places far beyond you, where no one else is working. Then there will be no question of our boasting about work done in someone else's territory. [17]As the Scriptures say, "If you want to boast, boast only about the LORD."*
[18]When people commend themselves, it doesn't count for much. The important thing is for the Lord to commend them.

2 Cor 10:17 Jer 9:24.

2 Cor 10:17-18 When we do something well, we want to tell others and be recognized. But recognition is dangerous—it can lead to inflated pride. How much better it is to seek the praise of God rather than the praise of people. Then, when we receive praise, we will be free to give God the credit. What should you change about the way you live in order to receive God's commendation?

PAUL'S CREDENTIALS

One of Paul's biggest problems with the church in Corinth was his concern that they viewed him as no more than a blustering preacher; thus, they were not taking seriously his advice in his letters and on his visits. Paul addressed this attitude in the letter of 2 Corinthians, pointing out his credentials as an apostle of Christ and why the Corinthians should take his advice.

2 Cor 1:1, 21; 4:1	Commissioned by God
2 Cor 1:12	Acted in holiness, sincerity, and dependence on God alone in his dealings with them
2 Cor 1:13-14	Was straightforward and sincere in his letters
2 Cor 1:18; 4:2	Spoke truthfully
2 Cor 1:22	Had God's Holy Spirit
2 Cor 2:4; 6:11; 11:11	Loved the Corinthian believers
2 Cor 2:17	Spoke with sincerity and Christ's authority
2 Cor 3:2-3	Worked among them and changed their lives
2 Cor 4:1, 16	Did not give up
2 Cor 4:2	Taught the Bible with integrity
2 Cor 4:5	Had Christ as the center of his message
2 Cor 4:8-12; 6:4-5, 9-10	Endured persecution as he taught the Good News
2 Cor 5:18-20	Was Christ's ambassador, called to tell the Good News
2 Cor 6:3-4	Tried to live an exemplary life so others would not be kept from God
2 Cor 6:6	Led a pure life, understood the gospel, and displayed patience with the Corinthians
2 Cor 6:7	Was truthful and filled with God's power
2 Cor 6:8	Stood true to God first and always
2 Cor 7:2; 11:7-9	Never led anyone astray or took advantage of anyone
2 Cor 8:20-21	Handled their offering for the Jerusalem believers in a responsible, blameless manner
2 Cor 10:1-6	Used God's weapons, not his own, for God's work
2 Cor 10:7-8	Was confident that he belonged to Christ
2 Cor 10:12-13	Would boast not in himself but in the Lord
2 Cor 10:14-15	Had authority because he taught them the Good News
2 Cor 11:23-33	Endured pain and danger as he fulfilled his calling
2 Cor 12:2-4	Was blessed with an astounding vision
2 Cor 12:6	Lived as an example to the believers
2 Cor 12:7-10	Was constantly humbled by a "thorn" in the flesh that God refused to take away
2 Cor 12:12	Did miracles among them
2 Cor 12:19	Was always motivated to strengthen others spiritually
2 Cor 13:4	Was filled with God's power
2 Cor 13:5-6	Passed the test
2 Cor 13:9	Was always concerned that his spiritual children become mature believers

Paul and the False Apostles

2 CORINTHIANS 11:1-15

I hope you will put up with a little more of my foolishness. Please bear with me. [2]For I am jealous for you with the jealousy of God himself. I promised you as a pure bride* to one husband—Christ. [3]But I fear that somehow your pure and undivided devotion to Christ will be corrupted, just as Eve was deceived by the cunning ways of the serpent. [4]You happily put up with whatever anyone tells you, even if they preach a different Jesus than the one we preach, or a different kind of Spirit than the one you received, or a different kind of gospel than the one you believed.

[5]But I don't consider myself inferior in any way to these "super apostles" who teach such things. [6]I may be unskilled as a speaker, but I'm not lacking in knowledge. We have made this clear to you in every possible way.

[7]Was I wrong when I humbled myself and honored you by preaching God's Good News to you without expecting anything in return? [8]I "robbed" other churches by accepting their contributions so I could serve you at no cost. [9]And when I was with you and didn't have enough to live on, I did not become a financial burden to anyone. For the brothers who came from Macedonia brought me all that I needed. I have never been a burden to you, and I never will be. [10]As surely as the truth of Christ is in me, no one in all of Greece* will ever stop me from boasting about this. [11]Why? Because I don't love you? God knows that I do.

[12]But I will continue doing what I have always done. This will undercut those who are looking for an opportunity to boast that their work is just like ours. [13]These people are false apostles. They are deceitful workers who disguise themselves as apostles of Christ. [14]But I am not surprised! Even Satan disguises himself as an angel of light. [15]So it is no wonder that his servants also disguise themselves as servants of righteousness. In the end they will get the punishment their wicked deeds deserve.

2 Cor 11:2 Greek *a virgin.* **2 Cor 11:10** Greek *Achaia,* the southern region of the Greek peninsula.

2 Cor 11:1 Paul asked the Corinthian believers to bear with him as he talked more "foolishness." In other words, Paul felt foolish rehearsing his credentials as a preacher of the Good News (2 Cor 11:16-21). But he thought that he had to do this in order to silence the false teachers (2 Cor 11:13).

2 Cor 11:2 Paul was anxious that the church's love should be for Christ alone, just as a pure bride saves her love for one man only. By "pure bride" he meant one who was unaffected by false doctrine.

2 Cor 11:3 The Corinthians' pure and simple devotion to Christ was being threatened by false teaching. Paul did not want the believers to lose their single-minded love for Christ. Keeping Christ first in your life can be very difficult when you have so many distractions threatening to sidetrack your faith. Just as Eve lost her focus by listening to the serpent, you can lose your focus by letting your life become overcrowded and confused. Is there anything that weakens your commitment to keep Christ first in your life? How can you minimize the distractions that threaten your devotion to him?

2 Cor 11:4 The Corinthian believers were falling for smooth talk and messages that sounded good and seemed to make sense. Today there are many false teachings that seem to make sense. Don't believe simply because a person sounds like an authority or says words you like to hear. Search the Bible and check those teachings against God's Word. The Bible should be your authoritative guide. The false teachers distorted the truth about Jesus and ended up preaching a different Jesus, a different spirit than the Holy Spirit, and a different way of salvation. Those who teach anything different from what God's infallible Word says are both mistaken and misleading.

2 Cor 11:5 Paul was saying that these marvelous teachers ("super apostles") were no better than he was. They may have been more eloquent speakers, but they spoke lies and were servants of Satan.

2 Cor 11:6 Paul, a brilliant thinker, was not a trained, eloquent speaker. Although his ministry was effective (see Acts 17), he had not been trained in the Greek schools of oratory and speechmaking, as many of the false teachers probably had been. Paul believed in a simple presentation of the Good News (see 1 Cor 1:17), and some people thought this showed simple-mindedness. Thus, Paul's speaking performance was often used against him by false teachers.

Content is far more important than the presentation. A simple, clear presentation that helps listeners understand will be of great value. God's Word stands on its own merit and is not dependent on imperfect human beings to create its own hearing. Many people can't sing, speak, teach, or preach as well as their idolized heroes, so they are insecure about saying or doing anything. Don't apologize for your inadequacies. Accept your limitations with the same humility that you accept the strengths God has given you.

2 Cor 11:7 The Corinthians may have thought that preachers could be judged by how much money they demanded. A good speaker would charge a large sum, a fair speaker would be a little cheaper, and a poor speaker would speak for free. The false teachers may have argued that because Paul asked no fee for his preaching, he must have been an amateur, with little authority or competence. Believers today must be careful not to assume that every preacher or evangelist who is well known or who demands a large honorarium necessarily teaches the truth.

2 Cor 11:7-12 Paul could have asked the Corinthian church for financial support. Jesus himself taught that those who minister for God should be supported by the people to whom they minister (Matt 10:10). But Paul thought that asking for support in Corinth might be misunderstood. There were many false teachers who hoped to make a good profit from preaching (2 Cor 2:17), and Paul might look like one of them. Paul separated himself completely from those false teachers in order to silence those who only claimed to do God's work.

2 Cor 11:14-15 One Jewish writing (the *Apocalypse of Moses*) says that the story of Eve's temptation includes Satan masquerading as an angel. Paul may have been thinking of this story, or he could have been referring to Satan's typical devices. In either case, nothing could be more deceitful than Satan, the prince of darkness (Eph 6:12; Col 1:13), disguising himself as an angel of light. In the same way, these false apostles were pretending to be apostles of Christ, while in reality they were agents of Satan.

2 Cor 11:14-15 Satan and his servants can deceive us by appearing to be attractive, good, and moral. Many unsuspecting people follow smooth-talking, Bible-quoting leaders into cults that alienate them from their families and lead them into the practice of immorality and deceit. Don't be fooled by external appearances. Our impressions alone are not an accurate indicator of who is or isn't a true follower of Christ; so it helps to ask these questions: (1) Do the teachings confirm Scripture (Acts 17:11)? (2) Does the teacher affirm and proclaim that Jesus Christ is God, who came into the world as a man to save people from their sins (1 Jn 4:1-3)? (3) Is the teacher's lifestyle consistent with biblical morality (Matt 12:33-37)?

2 Cor 11:15 Paul reminds the Corinthians that the false teachers and hypocritical leaders will one day "get the punishment their

Paul's Many Trials

2 CORINTHIANS 11:16-33

Again I say, don't think that I am a fool to talk like this. But even if you do, listen to me, as you would to a foolish person, while I also boast a little. [17]Such boasting is not from the Lord, but I am acting like a fool. [18]And since others boast about their human achievements, I will, too. [19]After all, you think you are so wise, but you enjoy putting up with fools! [20]You put up with it when someone enslaves you, takes everything you have, takes advantage of you, takes control of everything, and slaps you in the face. [21]I'm ashamed to say that we've been too "weak" to do that!

But whatever they dare to boast about—I'm talking like a fool again—I dare to boast about it, too. [22]Are they Hebrews? So am I. Are they Israelites? So am I. Are they descendants of Abraham? So am I. [23]Are they servants of Christ? I know I sound like a madman, but I have served him far more! I have worked harder, been put in prison more often, been whipped times without number, and faced death again and again. [24]Five different times the Jewish leaders gave me thirty-nine lashes. [25]Three times I was beaten with rods. Once I was stoned. Three times I was shipwrecked. Once I spent a whole night and a day adrift at sea. [26]I have traveled on many long journeys. I have faced danger from rivers and from robbers. I have faced danger from my own people, the Jews, as well as from the Gentiles. I have faced danger in the cities, in the deserts, and on the seas. And I have faced danger from men who claim to be believers but are not.* [27]I have worked hard and long, enduring many sleepless nights. I have been hungry and thirsty and have often gone without food. I have shivered in the cold, without enough clothing to keep me warm.

[28]Then, besides all this, I have the daily burden of my concern for all the churches. [29]Who is weak without my feeling that weakness? Who is led astray, and I do not burn with anger?

[30]If I must boast, I would rather boast about the things that show how weak I am. [31]God, the Father of our Lord Jesus, who is worthy of eternal praise, knows I am not lying. [32]When I was in Damascus, the governor under King Aretas kept guards at the city gates to catch me. [33]I had to be lowered in a basket through a window in the city wall to escape from him.

Paul's Vision and His Thorn in the Flesh

2 CORINTHIANS 12:1-10

This boasting will do no good, but I must go on. I will reluctantly tell about visions and revelations from the Lord. [2]I* was caught up to the third heaven fourteen years ago. Whether I was in my body or out of my body, I don't know—only God knows. [3]Yes, only God knows whether I was in my body or outside my body. But I do know [4]that I was caught up* to paradise and heard things so astounding that they cannot be expressed in words, things no human is allowed to tell.

[5]That experience is worth boasting about, but I'm not going to do it. I will boast only about my weaknesses. [6]If I wanted to boast, I would be no fool in doing so, because I would be telling the truth. But I won't do it, because I don't want anyone to give me credit beyond what they can see in my life or hear

2 Cor 11:26 Greek *from false brothers.* **2 Cor 12:2** Greek *I know a man in Christ who.* **2 Cor 12:3-4** Greek *But I know such a man, [4]that he was caught up.*

wicked deeds deserve." The principle of judgment applies to all who speak on God's behalf. The apostle James said that teachers will be judged by the Lord with closer scrutiny than will those who sit under their teaching (Jas 3:1). If it is not already your practice, each time you sit down with the Scriptures to prepare a lesson or a sermon, spend some quiet moments in prayer asking the Holy Spirit to guide your preparation.

2 Cor 11:22-23 Paul presented his credentials to counteract the charges that the false teachers were making against him. He felt foolish boasting like this, but his list of credentials would silence any doubts about his authority. Paul wanted to keep the Corinthians from slipping under the spell of the false teachers and turning away from the Good News. Paul also gave a list of his credentials in his letter to the Philippians (see Phil 3:4-8).

2 Cor 11:23-29 Paul was angry that the false teachers had impressed and deceived the Corinthians (2 Cor 11:13-15). Therefore, he had reestablished his credibility and authority by listing the trials he had endured in his service for Christ. Some of these trials are recorded in the book of Acts (Acts 14:19; 16:22-24). Because Paul wrote this letter during his third missionary journey (Acts 18:23–21:17), his trials weren't over. He would experience yet further difficulties and humiliations for the cause of Christ (see Acts 21:30-33; 22:24-30). Paul was sacrificing his life for the Good News, something the false teachers would never do. The trials and hurts we experience for Christ's sake build our character, demonstrate our faith, and prepare us for further service to the Lord.

2 Cor 11:25 Sea travel was not as safe as it is today. Paul had been shipwrecked three times, and he would face another accident on his voyage to Rome (see Acts 27). By this time, Paul had probably made at least eight or nine voyages.

2 Cor 11:28-29 Not only did Paul face beatings and dangers, but he also carried the daily concern for the young churches, worrying that they were staying true to the Good News and free from false teachings and inner strife. Paul was concerned for individuals in the churches he served. If God has placed you in a position of leadership and authority, treat people with Paul's kind of empathy and concern.

2 Cor 11:32-33 King Aretas, king of the Nabateans (Edomites) from 9 B.C.–A.D. 40, had appointed a governor to oversee the Nabatean segment of the population in Damascus. Somehow the Jews in Damascus had been able to enlist this governor to help them try to capture Paul (see Acts 9:22-25). Paul gave a "for instance" here, describing his escape from Damascus in a basket lowered from a window in the city wall. Paul recounted this incident to show what he had endured for Christ. The false teachers couldn't make such claims.

2 Cor 12:2-3 Paul continued his "boasting" by telling about visions and revelations he had received from the Lord. Paul explained that he didn't know if he was taken up in his body or in his spirit, but he had been in paradise ("the third heaven," perhaps referring to the place where God himself lives). This incident cannot be positively identified with a recorded event in Paul's career, although some think this may have been when he was stoned and left for dead (Acts 14:19-20). Paul told about this incident to show that God had uniquely touched him.

▸ **2 CORINTHIANS 12:1-10** ***(cont.)***

in my message, 7even though I have received such wonderful revelations from God. So to keep me from becoming proud, I was given a thorn in my flesh, a messenger from Satan to torment me and keep me from becoming proud.

8Three different times I begged the Lord to take it away. 9Each time he said, "My grace is all you need. My power works best in weakness." So now I am glad to boast about my weaknesses, so that the power of Christ can work through me. 10That's why I take pleasure in my weaknesses, and in the insults, hardships, persecutions, and troubles that I suffer for Christ. For when I am weak, then I am strong.

Paul's Concern for the Corinthians

2 CORINTHIANS 12:11-21

You have made me act like a fool—boasting like this.* You ought to be writing commendations for me, for I am not at all inferior to these "super apostles," even though I am nothing at all. 12When I was with you, I certainly gave you proof that I am an apostle. For I patiently did many signs and wonders and miracles among you. 13The only thing I failed to do, which I do in the other churches, was to become a financial burden to you. Please forgive me for this wrong!

14Now I am coming to you for the third time, and I will not be a burden to you. I don't want what you have—I want you. After all, children don't provide for their parents. Rather, parents provide for their children. 15I will gladly spend myself and all I have for you, even though it seems that the more I love you, the less you love me.

16Some of you admit I was not a burden to you. But others still think I was sneaky and took advantage of you by trickery. 17But how? Did any of the men I sent to you take advantage of you? 18When I urged Titus to visit you and sent our other brother with him, did Titus take advantage of you? No! For we have the same spirit and walk in each other's steps, doing things the same way.

19Perhaps you think we're saying these things just to defend ourselves. No, we tell you this as Christ's servants, and with God as our witness. Everything we do, dear friends, is to strengthen you. 20For I am afraid that when I come I won't like what I find, and you won't like my response. I am afraid that I will find quarreling, jealousy, anger, selfishness, slander, gossip, arrogance, and disorderly behavior. 21Yes, I am afraid that when I come again, God will humble me in your presence. And I will be grieved because many of you have not given up your old sins. You have not repented of your impurity, sexual immorality, and eagerness for lustful pleasure.

2 Cor 12:11 Some manuscripts do not include *boasting like this.*

2 Cor 12:7-8 We don't know what Paul's thorn in the flesh was because he doesn't tell us. Some have suggested that it was malaria, epilepsy, or a disease of the eyes (see Gal 4:13-15). Whatever the case, it was a chronic and debilitating problem, which at times kept him from working. This thorn was a hindrance to his ministry, and he prayed for its removal; but God refused. Paul was a very self-sufficient person, so this thorn must have been difficult for him.

Three times Paul prayed for healing and did not receive it. But he received things far greater because he received greater grace from God, a stronger character, humility, and an ability to empathize with others. In addition, it benefited those around him as they saw God at work in his life. God, according to his sovereign plan, doesn't heal some believers of their physical ailments. We don't know why some are spared and others aren't. God chooses according to his divine purposes. Our task is to pray, to believe, and to trust. Paul is living proof that holy living and courageous faith do not ensure instant physical healing. When we pray for healing, we must trust our bodies to God's care. We must recognize that nothing separates us from his love (Rom 8:35-39) and that our spiritual condition is always more important than our physical condition.

2 Cor 12:9 Although God did not remove Paul's affliction, he promised to demonstrate his power in Paul. The fact that God's power is displayed in our weaknesses should give us courage and hope. As we recognize our limitations, we will depend more on God for our effectiveness rather than on our own energy, effort, or talent. Our limitations not only help develop Christian character but also deepen our worship, because in admitting them, we affirm God's strength.

2 Cor 12:10 When we are strong in abilities or resources, we are tempted to do God's work on our own, and that can lead to pride. When we are weak, allowing God to fill us with his power, then we are stronger than we could ever be on our own. God does not intend for us to be weak, passive, or ineffective—life provides enough hindrances and setbacks without us creating them. When those obstacles come, we must depend on God. Only his power will make us effective for him and will help us do work that has lasting value.

2 Cor 12:11-15 Paul was not merely revealing his feelings; he was defending his authority as an apostle of Jesus Christ. Paul was hurt that the church in Corinth doubted and questioned him, so he defended himself for the cause of the Good News, not to satisfy his ego. When you are "put on trial," do you think only about saving your reputation or are you more concerned about what people will think about Christ?

2 Cor 12:13 Paul explained that the only thing he did in the other churches that he didn't do in Corinth was to become a burden—to ask the believers to feed and house him. When he said, "Forgive me for this wrong," he was clearly being sarcastic. He actually did more for the Corinthians than for any other church, but still they misunderstood him.

2 Cor 12:14 Paul had founded the church in Corinth on his first visit there (Acts 18:1). He subsequently made a second visit (2 Cor 2:1). He was planning what would be his third visit (see also 2 Cor 13:1). Paul explained that, as before, he didn't want to be paid, fed, or housed; he only wanted the believers to be nourished with the spiritual food he would feed them.

2 Cor 12:16-19 Although Paul asked nothing of the Corinthian believers, some doubters were still saying that Paul must have been sneaky and made money from them somehow. But Paul again explained that everything he did for the believers was for their edification, not to enrich himself.

2 Cor 12:20-21 After reading this catalog of sins, it is hard to believe that these are the people that Paul said possessed great gifts and excelled as leaders (2 Cor 8:7). Paul feared that the practices of wicked Corinth had invaded the congregation. He wrote sternly, hoping that they would straighten out their lives before he arrived. We must live differently from unbelievers, not letting society dictate how we are to treat others. Don't let culture influence your behavior.

Paul's Final Advice

2 CORINTHIANS 13:1-10

This is the third time I am coming to visit you (and as the Scriptures say, "The facts of every case must be established by the testimony of two or three witnesses"*). [2]I have already warned those who had been sinning when I was there on my second visit. Now I again warn them and all others, just as I did before, that next time I will not spare them.

[3]I will give you all the proof you want that Christ speaks through me. Christ is not weak when he deals with you; he is powerful among you. [4]Although he was crucified in weakness, he now lives by the power of God. We, too, are weak, just as Christ was, but when we deal with you we will be alive with him and will have God's power.

[5]Examine yourselves to see if your faith is genuine. Test yourselves. Surely you know that Jesus Christ is among you*; if not, you have failed the test of genuine faith. [6]As you test yourselves, I hope you will recognize that we have not failed the test of apostolic authority.

[7]We pray to God that you will not do what is wrong by refusing our correction. I hope we won't need to demonstrate our authority when we arrive. Do the right thing before we come—even if that makes it look like we have failed to demonstrate our authority. [8]For we cannot oppose the truth, but must always stand for the truth. [9]We are glad to seem weak if it helps show that you are actually strong. We pray that you will become mature.

[10]I am writing this to you before I come, hoping that I won't need to deal severely with you when I do come. For I want to use the authority the Lord has given me to strengthen you, not to tear you down.

Paul's Final Greetings

2 CORINTHIANS 13:11-14

Dear brothers and sisters,* I close my letter with these last words: Be joyful. Grow to maturity. Encourage each other. Live in harmony and peace. Then the God of love and peace will be with you.

[12]Greet each other with Christian love.* [13]All of God's people here send you their greetings.

[14]*May the grace of the Lord Jesus Christ, the love of God, and the fellowship of the Holy Spirit be with you all.

2 Cor 13:1 Deut 19:15. **2 Cor 13:5** Or *in you.* **2 Cor 13:11** Greek *Brothers.* **2 Cor 13:12** Greek *with a sacred kiss.* **2 Cor 13:14** Some English translations include verse 13 as part of verse 12, and then verse 14 becomes verse 13.

The Egnatian Way

The Romans were superb road builders. Major routes were graded and paved, making travel and commerce easier than ever before. The Egnatian Way (or Via Egnatia) extended from the Adriatic Sea on the western shore of Greece to the straits at Byzantium (later called Constantinople or Istanbul) to the east. The road was the major link between Italy and Asia; it was the main land route across northern Greece. Paul would follow this road from Neapolis to Philippi and Thessalonica. The ease of transportation in Paul's day enhanced the proclamation of the gospel. We have an even greater ability to travel today; we should appreciate its value and use it to proclaim the gospel throughout the world.

2 Cor 13:2 When Paul arrived the third time in Corinth, he would not be lenient toward unrepentant sinners. His actions could include (1) confronting and publicly denouncing their behavior, (2) exercising church discipline by calling them before the church leaders, or (3) excommunicating them from the church.

2 Cor 13:4 That we "will be alive with him and will have God's power" should be a comfort to all believers. Christians are not just playing church. We are not in this angry ocean of a world in a rubber raft with a plastic paddle. We are passengers on his Majesty's finest vessel, driven by the indwelling power of the Holy Spirit. We may be tempted to underestimate our ability to accomplish what Christ desires. We forget that Christ is on the bridge, directing the ship safely through the rough seas and finally into its eternal port.

2 Cor 13:5 The Corinthians were called to examine and test themselves to see if they really were Christians. Just as we get physical checkups, Paul urges us to give ourselves spiritual checkups. We should look for a growing awareness of Christ's presence and power in our life. Then we will know if we are true Christians or merely impostors. If we're not actively seeking to grow closer to God, we are drawing farther away from him.

2 Cor 13:8-9 Just as parents want their children to grow into mature adults, so Paul wanted the Corinthians to grow into mature believers. As we share the Good News, our goal should be not merely to see others profess faith or begin attending church but to see them become mature in their faith. Don't set your sights too low.

2 Cor 13:10 The authority Paul had received from the Lord was to strengthen the believers, not to tear them down. Paul gives good advice for our day. Fellow believers are the temple of the Holy Spirit. There is no room in the household of faith for the deprecation of a fellow worker. Before the week is over, write a note of encouragement to several people in your sphere of influence who probably aren't being built up by others in the church. Remind them how much their presence and abilities are needed in your congregation. Express how much you appreciate them.

2 Cor 13:11 Paul's closing words—what he wanted the Corinthians to remember about the needs facing their church—are still fitting for the church today. When these qualities are not present, there are problems that must be dealt with. These traits do not come to a church by glossing over problems, conflicts, and difficulties. They are not produced by neglect, denial, withdrawal, or bitterness. They are the by-products of the extremely hard work of solving problems. Just as Paul and the Corinthians had to hammer out difficulties to bring peace, so we also must apply the principles of God's Word and not just hear them.

2 Cor 13:14 Paul's farewell blessing invokes all three members of the Trinity:

1. PAUL VISITS ATHENS AND CORINTH

After writing the difficult letter to Corinth, Paul traveled down through Greece, stopping in Athens, and then stayed in Corinth to be with the believers there in person for a while.

ACTS 20:2b-3a

Then he traveled down to Greece, [3]where he stayed for three months.

L. Paul's Letter to the Romans

Paul had heard of the church at Rome, but he had not yet been there, nor had any of the other apostles. Evidently the church had been started by Jews who had come to faith during Pentecost. They had spread the gospel when they returned to Rome, and the church had grown. Paul deeply wanted to visit this church, and to go from Rome to minister in Spain and beyond, pushing the Good News to the ends of the earth. The book of Romans is somewhat of a letter of introduction. Paul was intelligent, articulate, and committed to his calling. He presented the case for the gospel clearly and forthrightly in his letter to the believers in Rome, hoping that they would be his partners in sending the Good News to Spain and beyond.

1. WHAT TO BELIEVE

Paul begins his message to the Romans by vividly portraying the sinfulness of all people, explaining how forgiveness is available through faith in Christ, and showing what believers experience in life through their new faith. In this section, we learn of the centrality of faith to becoming a Christian and to living the Christian life. Apart from faith, we have no hope in life.

Greetings from Paul

AD 54

Paul writes his letter to the church in Rome

ROMANS 1:1-7

This letter is from Paul, a slave of Christ Jesus, chosen by God to be an apostle and sent out to preach his Good News. [2]God promised this Good News long ago through his prophets in the holy Scriptures. [3]The Good News is about his Son. In his earthly life he was born into King David's family line, [4]and he was

Father (God), Son (Lord Jesus Christ), and Holy Spirit. Although the term Trinity is not explicitly used in Scripture, verses such as this one show that it was believed and experienced through knowing God's grace, love, and fellowship. See Luke 1:35—the angel Gabriel's announcement of Jesus' birth to Mary; Matthew 3:17—the Father's voice and the Holy Spirit's presence at the baptism of Jesus; and Matthew 28:19—Jesus' commission to the disciples.

2 Cor 13:14 Paul was dealing with an ongoing problem in the Corinthian church. He could have refused to communicate until they cleared up their situation, but he loved them and reached out to them again with the love of Christ. Love means that sometimes we must confront those we care about. Both authority and personal concern are needed in dealing with people who are ruining their lives with sin. But there are several wrong approaches in confronting others, and these can further break relationships rather than heal them. We can be legalistic and blast people away with the laws they should be obeying. We can turn away from them because we don't want to face the situation. We can isolate them by gossiping about their problem and turning others against them as well. Or, like Paul, we can seek to build relationships by taking a better approach—sharing, communicating, and caring. This is a difficult approach that can drain us emotionally, but it is the best way for other people, and it is the only Christlike way to deal with others' sin.

Acts 20:2-3 While in Greece, Paul spent much of his time in Corinth. From there he wrote the letter to the Romans. Although Paul had not yet been to Rome, believers had already started a church there (Acts 2:10; 18:2). Paul wrote to tell the church that he planned to visit the Roman believers. The letter to the Romans is a theological essay on the meaning of faith and salvation, an explanation of the relation between Jews and Gentiles in Christ, and a list of practical guidelines for the church.

Rom 1:1 Paul wrote this letter to the church in Rome. Neither he nor the other church leaders, James and Peter, had yet been to Rome. Most likely, the Roman church had been established by believers who had been at Jerusalem for Pentecost (Acts 2:10) and by travelers who had heard the Good News in other places and had brought it back to Rome (for example, Priscilla and Aquila; Acts 18:2; Rom 16:3-5). Paul wrote the letter to the Romans during his ministry in Corinth (at the end of his third missionary journey just before returning to Jerusalem; Acts 20:3; Rom 15:25) to encourage the believers and to express his desire to visit them someday (within three years he would). This letter may well have been the first piece of Christian literature the Roman believers had seen. Written to both Jewish and Gentile Christians, the letter to the Romans is a systematic presentation of the Christian faith.

Rom 1:1 When Paul, a devout Jew who had at first persecuted the Christians, became a believer, God used him to spread the Good News throughout the world. Although he was a prisoner, Paul did eventually preach in Rome (Acts 28), perhaps even to Caesar himself. Paul's Profile is on p. 1571.

Rom 1:1 Paul humbly calls himself a slave of Christ Jesus and an apostle ("one who is sent"). For a Roman citizen—which Paul was—to choose to be a slave was unthinkable. But Paul chose to be completely dependent on and obedient to his beloved Master. What is your attitude toward Christ, your Master? Our willingness to serve and obey Jesus Christ enables us to be useful and usable servants to do work for him—work that really matters. Obedience begins as we renounce other masters, identify ourselves with Jesus, discover his will and live according to it, and consciously turn away from conflicting interests, even if these interests have been important to us in the past.

Rom 1:2 Some of the prophecies predicting the Good News regarding Jesus Christ are found in Genesis 12:3; Psalms 16:10; 40:6-10; 118:22; Isaiah 11:1ff; Zechariah 9:9-11; 12:10; Malachi 4:1-6.

shown to be* the Son of God when he was raised
from the dead by the power of the Holy Spirit.* He
is Jesus Christ our Lord. 5Through Christ, God has
given us the privilege* and authority as apostles to
tell Gentiles everywhere what God has done for them,
so that they will believe and obey him, bringing glory
to his name.
6And you are included among those Gentiles who
have been called to belong to Jesus Christ. 7I am writing to all of you in Rome who are loved by God and are
called to be his own holy people.

May God our Father and the Lord Jesus Christ give
you grace and peace.

God's Good News

ROMANS 1:8-17

Let me say first that I thank my God through Jesus
Christ for all of you, because your faith in him is being talked about all over the world. 9God knows how
often I pray for you. Day and night I bring you and
your needs in prayer to God, whom I serve with all
my heart* by spreading the Good News about his Son.

Rom 1:4a Or *and was designated.* **Rom 1:4b** Or *by the Spirit of holiness;* or *in the new realm of the Spirit.* **Rom 1:5** Or *the grace.* **Rom 1:9** Or *in my spirit.*

Rom 1:3-4 Paul states that Jesus is the Son of God, the promised Messiah, and the resurrected Lord. Paul calls Jesus a descendant of King David to emphasize that Jesus truly had fulfilled the Old Testament Scriptures predicting that the Messiah would come from David's line. With this statement of faith, Paul declares his agreement with the teaching of all Scripture and of the apostles.

Rom 1:3-5 Here Paul summarizes the Good News about Jesus Christ, who (1) came as a human by natural descent, (2) was part of the Jewish royal line through David, (3) died and was raised from the dead, and (4) opened the door for God's grace and kindness to be poured out on us. The book of Romans is an expansion of these themes.

Rom 1:5 Christians have both a privilege and a great responsibility. Paul and the apostles received the privilege of being called, but they also received the authority and the responsibility to share with others what God has done. God also graciously forgives our sins when we believe in him as Lord. In doing this, we are committing ourselves to begin a new life. Paul's new life also involved a God-given responsibility: to witness about God's Good News to the world as a missionary. God may or may not call you to be a foreign missionary, but he does call you (and all believers) to be Christ's ambassador and to witness to the changed life that Jesus Christ has begun in you.

Rom 1:6 Jews and Christians alike stood against the idolatrous Roman religions, and Roman officials often confused the two groups. This was especially easy to do since the Christian church in Rome could have been originally composed of Jewish converts who had attended Pentecost in Jerusalem (see Acts 2:1ff). By the time Paul wrote this letter to the Romans, however, many Gentiles had joined the church. The Jews and the Gentiles needed to know the relationship between Judaism and Christianity.

Rom 1:6-7 Paul says that those who become Christians are invited by Jesus Christ to (1) belong to God's family, and (2) be his very own people. What a wonderful expression of what it means to be a Christian! In being reborn into God's family we have the greatest experience of love and the greatest inheritance. Because of all that God has done for us, we strive to be his holy people.

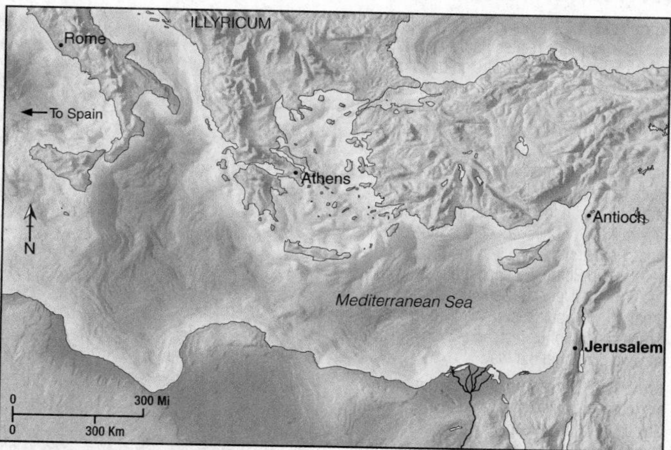

THE GOSPEL GOES TO ROME *When Paul wrote his letter to the church in Rome, he had not yet been there, but he had taken the gospel "from Jerusalem all the way to Illyricum" (Rom 15:19). He planned to visit and preach in Rome one day and hoped to continue to take the gospel farther west—even to Spain.*

Rom 1:7 Rome was the capital of the Roman Empire that had spread over most of Europe, North Africa, and the Near East. In New Testament times, Rome was experiencing a golden age. The city was wealthy, literary, and artistic. It was a cultural center, but it was also morally decadent. The Romans worshiped many pagan gods, and even some of the emperors were worshiped. In stark contrast to the Romans, the followers of Christ believed in only one God and lived by his high moral standards.

Christianity was also at odds with the Romans' dependence on military strength. Many Romans were naively pragmatic, believing that any means to accomplish the intended task was good. And for them, nothing worked better than physical might. The Romans trusted in their strong military power to protect them against all enemies. Christians in every age need to be reminded that God is the only permanent source of our security and salvation, and at the same time he is "our Father"!

Rom 1:8 Paul uses the phrase "I thank my God through Jesus Christ" to emphasize the point that Christ is the one and only mediator between us and God. Through Christ, God sends his love and forgiveness to us; through Christ, we send our thanks to God (see 1 Tim 2:5).

Rom 1:8 The Roman Christians, at the Western world's political power center, were highly visible. Fortunately, their reputation was excellent; their strong faith was making itself known around the world. When people talk about your congregation or your denomination, what do they say? Are their comments accurate? Would you rather they noticed other features? What is the best way to get the public to recognize your faith?

Rom 1:9-10 When you pray continually about a concern, don't be surprised at how God answers. Paul prayed to visit Rome so he could teach the Christians there. When he finally arrived in Rome, it was as a prisoner (see Acts 28:16). Paul prayed for a safe trip, and he did arrive safely—after getting arrested, slapped in the face, shipwrecked, and bitten by a poisonous snake. When we sincerely pray, God will answer—although in his timing and sometimes in ways we do not expect.

▶ **ROMANS 1:8-17** ***(cont.)***

[10]One of the things I always pray for is the opportunity, God willing, to come at last to see you. [11]For I
long to visit you so I can bring you some spiritual gift
that will help you grow strong in the Lord. [12]When we
get together, I want to encourage you in your faith, but
I also want to be encouraged by yours.
[13]I want you to know, dear brothers and sisters,*
that I planned many times to visit you, but I was prevented until now. I want to work among you and see
spiritual fruit, just as I have seen among other Gentiles.
[14]For I have a great sense of obligation to people in
both the civilized world and the rest of the world,* to
the educated and uneducated alike. [15]So I am eager to
come to you in Rome, too, to preach the Good News.
[16]For I am not ashamed of this Good News about
Christ. It is the power of God at work, saving everyone who believes—the Jew first and also the Gentile.*
[17]This Good News tells us how God makes us right in
his sight. This is accomplished from start to finish by
faith. As the Scriptures say, "It is through faith that a
righteous person has life."*

Rom 1:13 Greek *brothers.* **Rom 1:14** Greek *to Greeks and barbarians.* **Rom 1:16** Greek *also the Greek.* **Rom 1:17** Or *"The righteous will live by faith."* Hab 2:4.

Rom 1:11-13 A reading of the first few verses of Romans relates Paul's ardent desire to visit Rome and the sovereign hand of God that had prevented him from getting there for quite some time. The combination of these two factors—Paul's impassioned desire to go to Rome and God's sovereign "no"—resulted in his sitting down to write this letter to the Romans. This letter is a powerful exposition of the Christian faith and has helped countless millions of believers across the centuries since Paul first penned it to the group of believers in Rome. Perhaps there are some "no"s in our lives that God is planning to use greatly if we would just faithfully do what lies directly ahead of us instead of worrying about why we didn't get our way.

Rom 1:13 By the end of his third missionary journey, Paul had traveled through Syria, Galatia, Asia, Macedonia, and Achaia. The churches in these areas were made up mostly of Gentile believers.

Rom 1:14 What was Paul's obligation? After his experience with Christ on the road to Damascus (Acts 9), his whole life was consumed with spreading the Good News of salvation. His obligation was to people of the entire world. He met his obligation by proclaiming Christ's salvation to people—across all cultural, social, racial, and economic lines, both Jews and Gentiles. We also are obligated to Christ because he took the punishment we deserve for our sins. Although we cannot repay Christ for all he has done, we can demonstrate our gratitude by showing his love to others.

The Roman Coliseum

Rome had constructed impressive buildings, the one pictured being the Roman Coliseum, built by Vespasian (reigned A.D. 69–79). Vespasian had improved a number of cities in the Roman Empire that had been devastated by fire or earthquake. Then he turned his attention to Rome itself: He built the Temple of Peace after the destruction of Jerusalem and the defeat of the Jews, erected a forum, restored the Capitol, and began construction of the Coliseum. Capable of seating 50,000 spectators, the Coliseum was used for gladiatorial contests and public spectacles such as mock sea battles, reenactments of famous battles, animal hunts, and executions. Christians were martyred in the Coliseum, one of the earliest being Saint Ignatius, who was thrown to the lions. Not only should we honor such martyrs, we should be willing to face martyrdom if called upon to do so.

Rom 1:15 Paul was eager to preach the gospel. Is our Christian service done in a spirit of eagerness? Or do we serve out of habit, a feeling of obligation, or perhaps even with a feeling of reluctant duty (much like a child who has to take a bath)? When we fully understand what Christ has done for us and what he offers to others, we will be motivated to share the Good News. Ask God to rekindle that fresh, eager attitude that wants to obey him and to tell others about Christ.

Rom 1:16 Paul was not ashamed because his message was the Good News about Christ. It was a message of salvation, it had life-changing power, and it was for everyone. When you are tempted to be ashamed, remember what the Good News is all about. If you focus on God and on what God is doing in the world rather than on your own inadequacy, you won't be ashamed or embarrassed.

Rom 1:16 Why did the message go to the Jews first? They had been God's special people for more than 2,000 years, ever since God chose Abraham and promised great blessings to his descendants (Gen 12:1-3). God did not choose the Jews because they deserved to be chosen (Deut 7:7-8; 9:4-6) but because he wanted to show his love and mercy to them, for it would be through them that his Messiah would come into the world. God chose them, not to play favorites but so that they would tell the world about his plan of salvation.

For centuries the Jews had been learning about God by obeying his laws, keeping his festivals, and living according to his moral principles. Often they would forget God's promises and laws, and they would have to be disciplined; but still they had a precious heritage of belief in the one true God. Of all the people on earth, the Jews should have been the most ready to welcome the Messiah and to understand his mission and message—and some of them did (see Luke 2:25, 36-38). Of course, the disciples and the great apostle Paul were faithful Jews who recognized in Jesus God's most precious gift to the human race.

Rom 1:17 The Good News shows us both how righteous God is in his plan for us to be

God's Anger at Sin

ROMANS 1:18-32

But God shows his anger from heaven against all sinful, wicked people who suppress the truth by their wickedness.* [19]They know the truth about God because he has made it obvious to them. [20]For ever since the world was created, people have seen the earth and sky. Through everything God made, they can clearly see his invisible qualities—his eternal power and divine nature. So they have no excuse for not knowing God.

[21]Yes, they knew God, but they wouldn't worship him as God or even give him thanks. And they began to think up foolish ideas of what God was like. As a result, their minds became dark and confused. [22]Claiming to be wise, they instead became utter fools. [23]And instead of worshiping the glorious, ever-living God, they worshiped idols made to look like mere people and birds and animals and reptiles.

[24]So God abandoned them to do whatever shameful things their hearts desired. As a result, they did vile

Rom 1:18 Or *who, by their wickedness, prevent the truth from being known.*

saved and also how we may be made fit for eternal life. By trusting Christ, our relationship with God is made right. "From start to finish," God declares us to be right with him because of faith and faith alone. Paul then quotes from Habakkuk 2:4 to show that as we trust God, we are saved; we have life both now and forever.

Rom 1:18 Why is God angry at sinful people? Because they have substituted the truth about him with a lie (Rom 1:25). They have stifled the truth God naturally reveals to all people in order to believe anything that supports their own self-centered lifestyles. God cannot tolerate sin because his nature is morally perfect. He cannot ignore or condone willful rebellion. God wants to remove the sin and restore the sinner—and he is able to, as long as the sinner does not stubbornly distort or reject the truth. But God shows his anger against those who persist in sinning. Make sure you are not pursuing a lie rather than the true God. Don't suppress the truth about him merely to protect your own lifestyle.

Rom 1:18ff Romans 1:18–3:20 develops Paul's argument that no one can claim by their own efforts or merit to be good in God's sight—not the masses, not the Romans, not even the Jews. All people everywhere deserve God's condemnation for their sin.

Rom 1:18-20 In these verses, Paul answers a common objection to belief in God: How could a loving God send anyone to hell, especially someone who has never heard about Christ? In fact, says Paul, God has revealed himself plainly to all people in creation. And yet people reject even this basic knowledge of God. Also, all people have an inner sense of what God requires, but they choose not to live up to it. Put another way, people's moral standards are always better than their behavior. If people suppress God's truth in order to live their own way, they have no excuse. They know the truth, and they will have to endure the consequences of ignoring it.

Rom 1:18-20 Some people wonder why we need to send out missionaries if people can know about God through nature (the creation). The answer: (1) Although people know that God exists, their wickedness blinds them to the truth. They need someone to sensitively expose their sin and point them to Christ. (2) Although people may believe there is a God, they refuse to commit themselves to him. By sharing God's Word Christians may help persuade them of the dangerous consequences of rejecting God. (3) Our Lord commanded his followers to go and make disciples of all nations (Matt 28:19-20). (4) Most important, although nature reveals the existence of God, people need to be told about Jesus—why he came and what he did—and how, through him, they can have a personal relationship with God.

Knowing that God exists is not enough. People must learn that God is loving and that he sent his Son to demonstrate his love for us (Rom 5:8). They must be shown how to accept God's forgiveness of their sins. (See also Rom 10:14-15.)

Rom 1:19 Does anyone have an excuse for not believing in God? The Bible answers an emphatic *no.* God has revealed what he is like in and through his creation. Every person, therefore, either accepts or rejects God. Don't be fooled. When the day comes for God to judge your response to him, no excuses will be accepted. Begin today to give your devotion and worship to him.

Rom 1:20 What kind of God does nature reveal? Nature shows us a God of might, intelligence, and intricate detail; a God of order and beauty; a God who controls powerful forces. This is *general revelation.* Through *special revelation* (the Bible and the coming of Jesus), we learn about God's love and forgiveness and the promise of eternal life. God has graciously given us many sources that we might come to believe in him.

Rom 1:20 God reveals his divine nature and personal qualities through creation, even though creation's testimony has been distorted by the Fall. Adam's sin resulted in a divine curse upon the whole natural order (Gen 3:17-19); thorns and thistles were an immediate result, and natural disasters have been common from Adam's day to ours. In Romans 8:19-21, Paul says that nature itself is eagerly awaiting its own redemption from the effects of sin (see Rev 22:3).

Rom 1:21-23 How could intelligent people turn to idolatry? Idolatry begins when people reject what they know about God. Instead of looking to him as the creator and sustainer of life, they see themselves as the center of the universe. They soon invent "gods" that are convenient projections of their own selfish ideas. These gods may be wooden figures, or they may also be goals or things we pursue, such as money, power, or possessions. They may even be misrepresentations of God himself—making God in our image, instead of the reverse. The common denominator is this: Idolaters worship the things God made rather than God himself. Is there anything you feel you can't live without? Is there any priority greater than God? Do you have a dream you would sacrifice everything to realize? Does God take first place in your life? Do you worship God or idols of your own making?

Rom 1:21-32 Paul clearly portrays the inevitable downward spiral into sin. First, people reject God; next, they make up their own ideas of what a god should be and do; then they fall into every kind of wickedness: greed, hate, envy, murder, quarreling, deception, malicious behavior, and gossip. Finally, they grow to hate God and encourage others to do so. God does not cause this steady progression toward evil. Rather, when people reject him, he allows them to live as they choose. God gives them over to or permits them to experience the natural consequences of their sin. Once caught in the downward spiral, they cannot pull themselves out. Sinners must trust Christ alone to deliver them from destruction.

Rom 1:23 When Paul says that people worshiped idols made to look like people or animals instead of worshiping God, he seems to deliberately state people's wickedness in the terms used in the Genesis narrative of Adam's fall (see Gen 3:1-24). When people worship the creature instead of the Creator, they lose sight of their own identity as those who are higher than the animals—made in the image of God.

Rom 1:24-32 These people chose to reject God, and God allowed them to do it. God does not usually stop us from making wrong choices. He lets us choose independence from him, even though he knows that in time we will become slaves to our own rebellious lifestyle and lose our freedom not to sin. Does life without God look like freedom to you? Look more closely. There is no worse slavery than slavery to sin.

▶ **ROMANS 1:18-32** ***(cont.)***
and degrading things with each other's bodies. 25They
traded the truth about God for a lie. So they worshiped
and served the things God created instead of the Creator himself, who is worthy of eternal praise! Amen.
26That is why God abandoned them to their shameful
desires. Even the women turned against the natural
way to have sex and instead indulged in sex with each
other. 27And the men, instead of having normal sexual
relations with women, burned with lust for each other.
Men did shameful things with other men, and as a result
of this sin, they suffered within themselves the penalty
they deserved.
28Since they thought it foolish to acknowledge God,
he abandoned them to their foolish thinking and let
them do things that should never be done. 29Their lives
became full of every kind of wickedness, sin, greed,
hate, envy, murder, quarreling, deception, malicious
behavior, and gossip. 30They are backstabbers, haters
of God, insolent, proud, and boastful. They invent new
ways of sinning, and they disobey their parents. 31They
refuse to understand, break their promises, are heartless, and have no mercy. 32They know God's justice
requires that those who do these things deserve to die,
yet they do them anyway. Worse yet, they encourage
others to do them, too.

God's Judgment of Sin

ROMANS 2:1-16
You may think you can condemn such people, but you
are just as bad, and you have no excuse! When you say
they are wicked and should be punished, you are condemning yourself, for you who judge others do these
very same things. 2And we know that God, in his justice,
will punish anyone who does such things. 3Since you
judge others for doing these things, why do you think
you can avoid God's judgment when you do the same
things? 4Don't you see how wonderfully kind, tolerant,
and patient God is with you? Does this mean nothing
to you? Can't you see that his kindness is intended to
turn you from your sin?
5But because you are stubborn and refuse to turn

Rom 1:25 People tend to believe lies that reinforce their own selfish, personal beliefs. Today, more than ever, we need to know what the basis is for our beliefs. With TV, music, movies, and the rest of the media often presenting sinful lifestyles and unwholesome values, we find ourselves constantly bombarded by attitudes and beliefs that are totally opposed to the Bible. Be careful about what influences you use to form your opinions. The Bible is the only standard of truth. Evaluate all other opinions in light of its teachings.

Rom 1:26-27 God's plan for sexual relationships is his ideal for his creation. Unfortunately, sin distorts the natural use of God's gifts. Sin often means not only denying God but also denying the way we are made. When people say that any sex act is acceptable as long as nobody gets hurt, they are fooling themselves. In the long run (and often in the short run), sexual sin hurts people—individuals, families, whole societies. Because sex is such a powerful and essential part of what it means to be human, it must be treated with great respect. Sexual desires are of such importance that the Bible gives them special attention and counsels more careful restraint and self-control than with any other desire. One of the clearest indicators of a society or person in rebellion against God is the rejection of God's guidelines for the use of sex.

Rom 1:26-27 Homosexual practice was as widespread in Paul's day as it is in ours. God is willing to receive anyone who comes to him in faith, and Christians should love and accept others no matter what their background. Yet, homosexual activity is strictly forbidden in Scripture (Lev 18:22). It is considered an acceptable practice by many in our world today—even by some churches. But society does not set the standard for God's law. Homosexuals believe that their desires are normal and that they have a right to express them. But God does not encourage us to fulfill all our desires (even normal ones). Those desires that violate his laws must be controlled.

If you have these desires, you can and must resist acting upon them. Consciously avoid places or activities you know will kindle temptations. Don't underestimate the power of Satan to tempt you or the potential for serious harm if you continue to yield to these temptations. Remember, God can and will forgive sexual sins just as he forgives other sins. Surrender yourself to God, asking him to show you the way out of sin and into the light of his freedom and his love. Prayer, Bible study, and loving support of Christians in a Bible-believing church can help you to gain strength to resist these powerful temptations. If you are already deeply involved in homosexual behavior, seek help from a trustworthy, professional Christian counselor.

Rom 1:32 How were these people aware that God's justice would require death? All human beings are created in God's image; thus, we have a basic moral nature and a conscience. This truth is understood beyond religious circles. Psychologists, for example, say that the rare person who has no conscience has a serious personality disorder that is extremely difficult to treat. Most people instinctively know when they do wrong—but they may not care. Some people will even risk an early death for the freedom to indulge their desires now. "I know it's wrong, but I really want it," they say; or "I know it's dangerous, but it's worth the risk." For such people, part of the "fun" is knowingly going against God's law, the community's moral standards, common sense, or their own sense of right and wrong. But deep down inside they know that sin deserves the punishment of death (Rom 6:23).

Rom 2:1 Whenever we find ourselves feeling justifiably angry about someone's sin, we should be careful. We need to speak out against sin, but we must do so in a spirit of humility. Often the sins we notice most clearly in others are the ones that have taken root in us. If we look closely at ourselves, we may find that we are committing the same sins in more socially acceptable forms. For example, those who tend to gossip may be very critical of the people who gossip about them.

Rom 2:1ff When Paul's letter was read in the Roman church, no doubt many heads nodded as he condemned idol worshipers, homosexual practices, and violent people. But what surprise his listeners must have felt when he turned on them and said in effect, "You are just as bad, and you have no excuse!" Paul was emphatically stressing that we all have sinned repeatedly, and there is no way apart from Christ to be saved from sin's consequences.

Rom 2:4 In his kindness, God holds back his judgment, giving people time to turn from their sin. It is easy to mistake God's patience for approval of the wrong way we are living. Self-evaluation is difficult, and it is even more difficult to bring ourselves to God and let him tell us where we need to change. But as Christians we must ask God to point out our sins, so that he can heal them. Unfortunately, we are more likely to be amazed at God's patience with others than humbled at his patience with us.

Rom 2:5-11 Although God does not usually punish us immediately for sin, his eventual judgment is certain. We don't know exactly when it will happen, but we know that no one will escape that final encounter with the Creator. (For more on judgment, see John 12:48; Rev 20:11-15.)

Rom 2:7 Paul says that those who patiently and persistently do God's will find eternal life. He is not contradicting his previous statement

from your sin, you are storing up terrible punishment
for yourself. For a day of anger is coming, when God's
righteous judgment will be revealed. 6He will judge
everyone according to what they have done. 7He will
give eternal life to those who keep on doing good, seeking after the glory and honor and immortality that
God offers. 8But he will pour out his anger and wrath
on those who live for themselves, who refuse to obey
the truth and instead live lives of wickedness. 9There
will be trouble and calamity for everyone who keeps
on doing what is evil—for the Jew first and also for the
Gentile.* 10But there will be glory and honor and peace
from God for all who do good—for the Jew first and also
for the Gentile. 11For God does not show favoritism.
12When the Gentiles sin, they will be destroyed,
even though they never had God's written law. And
the Jews, who do have God's law, will be judged by that
law when they fail to obey it. 13For merely listening
to the law doesn't make us right with God. It is obeying the law that makes us right in his sight. 14Even
Gentiles, who do not have God's written law, show
that they know his law when they instinctively obey
it, even without having heard it. 15They demonstrate
that God's law is written in their hearts, for their own
conscience and thoughts either accuse them or tell
them they are doing right. 16And this is the message I
proclaim—that the day is coming when God, through
Christ Jesus, will judge everyone's secret life.

The Jews and the Law

ROMANS 2:17-29

You who call yourselves Jews are relying on God's law,
and you boast about your special relationship with
him. 18You know what he wants; you know what is
right because you have been taught his law. 19You are
convinced that you are a guide for the blind and a
light for people who are lost in darkness. 20You think
you can instruct the ignorant and teach children the
ways of God. For you are certain that God's law gives
you complete knowledge and truth.
21Well then, if you teach others, why don't you
teach yourself? You tell others not to steal, but do

Rom 2:9 Greek *also for the Greek;* also in 2:10.

WHAT IS FAITH?

Faith is a word with many meanings. It can mean faithfulness (Matt 24:45). It can mean absolute trust, as shown by some of the people who came to Jesus for healing (Luke 7:2-10). It can mean confident hope (Heb 11:1). Or, as James points out, it can even mean a barren belief that does not result in good deeds (Jas 2:14-26). What does Paul mean when, in Romans, he speaks of "saving faith"?

We must be very careful to understand faith as Paul uses the word because he ties faith so closely to salvation. It is not something we must do in order to earn salvation—if that were true, then faith would be just one more deed, and Paul clearly states that human deeds can never save us (Gal 2:16). Instead, faith is a gift God gives us because *he* is saving us (Eph 2:8). It is God's grace, not our faith, that saves us. In his mercy, when God saves us, he gives us faith—a relationship with his Son that helps us become like him. Through the faith he gives us, he carries us from death into life (John 5:24).

Even in Old Testament times, grace, not deeds, was the basis of salvation. As Hebrews points out, "it is not possible for the blood of bulls and goats to take away sins" (Heb 10:4). God intended for his people to look beyond the animal sacrifices to him, but all too often they instead put their confidence in fulfilling the requirements of the law—that is, performing the required sacrifices. When Jesus triumphed over death, he canceled the charges against us and opened the way to the Father (Col 2:12-15). Because he is merciful, he offers us faith. How tragic if we turn faith into a deed and try to develop it on our own! We can never come to God through our own faith any more than his Old Testament people could come through their own sacrifices. Instead, we must accept his gracious offer with thanksgiving and allow him to plant the seed of faith within us.

that salvation comes by faith alone (Rom 1:16-17). We are not saved by good deeds, but when we commit our lives fully to God, we want to please him and do his will. As such, our good deeds are a grateful response to what God has done, not a prerequisite to earning his favor.

Rom 2:12-15 People are condemned not for what they don't know but for what they do with what they know. Those who know God's written Word and his law will be judged by them. Those who have never seen a Bible still know right from wrong, and they will be judged because they violated those standards that their own consciences dictated. God's law is written within them.

Rom 2:12-15 If you traveled around the world, you would find evidence in every society and culture of God's moral law. For example, all cultures prohibit murder, and yet in all societies that law has been broken. We belong to a stubborn, sinful race. We know what is right, but we insist on doing what is wrong. It is not enough to know what is right; we must also do it. Admit to yourself and to God that you frequently fail to live up to your own standards (much less to God's standards). That's the first step to forgiveness and healing.

Rom 2:17ff Paul continues to argue that all stand guilty before God. After describing the fate of the unbelieving, pagan Gentiles, he moves to admonish God's people. Despite their knowledge of God's will, they were guilty because they, too, refuse to live by it. Those of us who have grown up in Christian families may know what God's Word says. But Paul says that if we do not live up to what we know, we are no better off than unbelievers.

Rom 2:21-22 Paul explained to the Jews that they needed to teach themselves, not others, by their law. They knew the law so well that they had learned how to excuse their own actions while criticizing others. But the law is more than a set of rules—it is a guideline for living according to God's will. It is also a reminder that we cannot please God without a proper relationship to him. As Jesus pointed out, withholding what rightfully belongs to someone else is stealing (Mark 7:9-13), and anyone who even looks at a woman with lust in his eye has committed adultery with her in his heart (Matt 5:27-28). Before we accuse others, we must look at ourselves and see if sin, in any form, exists within us.

Rom 2:21-27 These verses are a scathing criticism of hypocrisy. It is much easier to tell others how to behave than to behave properly ourselves. It is easier to say the right words than to allow them to take root in our own lives. Do you ever advise others to do something you are unwilling to do yourself? Make sure that your actions match your words.

▸ **ROMANS 2:17-29** ***(cont.)***

you steal? 22You say it is wrong to commit adultery, but
do you commit adultery? You condemn idolatry, but
do you use items stolen from pagan temples?* 23You
are so proud of knowing the law, but you dishonor
God by breaking it. 24No wonder the Scriptures say,
"The Gentiles blaspheme the name of God because
of you."*
25The Jewish ceremony of circumcision has value
only if you obey God's law. But if you don't obey
God's law, you are no better off than an uncircumcised Gentile. 26And if the Gentiles obey God's law,
won't God declare them to be his own people? 27In
fact, uncircumcised Gentiles who keep God's law
will condemn you Jews who are circumcised and
possess God's law but don't obey it.
28For you are not a true Jew just because you were
born of Jewish parents or because you have gone
through the ceremony of circumcision. 29No, a true
Jew is one whose heart is right with God. And true circumcision is not merely obeying the letter of the law;
rather, it is a change of heart produced by God's Spirit.
And a person with a changed heart seeks praise* from
God, not from people.

God Remains Faithful

ROMANS 3:1-8

Then what's the advantage of being a Jew? Is there any
value in the ceremony of circumcision? 2Yes, there are
great benefits! First of all, the Jews were entrusted with
the whole revelation of God.*
3True, some of them were unfaithful; but just because they were unfaithful, does that mean God will
be unfaithful? 4Of course not! Even if everyone else
is a liar, God is true. As the Scriptures say about him,

> "You will be proved right in what you say,
> and you will win your case in court."*

5"But," some might say, "our sinfulness serves a
good purpose, for it helps people see how righteous
God is. Isn't it unfair, then, for him to punish us?" (This
is merely a human point of view.) 6Of course not! If
God were not entirely fair, how would he be qualified to judge the world? 7"But," someone might still
argue, "how can God condemn me as a sinner if my
dishonesty highlights his truthfulness and brings him
more glory?" 8And some people even slander us by
claiming that we say, "The more we sin, the better it is!"
Those who say such things deserve to be condemned.

All People Are Sinners

ROMANS 3:9-20

Well then, should we conclude that we Jews are better
than others? No, not at all, for we have already shown
that all people, whether Jews or Gentiles,* are under
the power of sin. 10As the Scriptures say,

> "No one is righteous—
> not even one.

Rom 2:22 Greek *do you steal from temples?* **Rom 2:24** Isa 52:5 (Greek version). **Rom 2:29** Or *receives praise.* **Rom 3:2** Greek *the oracles of God.* **Rom 3:4** Ps 51:4 (Greek version). **Rom 3:9** Greek *or Greeks.*

Rom 2:24 If you claim to be one of God's people, your life should reflect what God is like. When you disobey God, you dishonor his name. People may even blaspheme or profane God's name because of you. What do people think about God as they watch your life?

Rom 2:25-29 *Circumcision* refers to the sign of God's special covenant with his people. All Jewish males were required to submit to this rite (Gen 17:9-14). According to Paul, being a circumcised Jew meant nothing if the person didn't obey God's laws. On the other hand, the uncircumcised Gentiles would receive God's love and approval if they kept God's law. Paul goes on to explain that a true Jew (one who pleases God) is not someone who has been circumcised but someone whose heart is right with God and obeys him.

Rom 2:28-29 To be a Jew meant you were in God's family, an heir to all his promises. Yet Paul made it clear that membership in God's family is based on internal, not external, qualities. All whose hearts are right with God are true Jews—that is, part of God's family (see also Gal 3:7). Attending church or being baptized, confirmed, or accepted for membership is not enough, just as submitting to circumcision was not enough for the Jews. God desires our heart-felt devotion and obedience (see also Deut 10:16; Jer 4:4).

Rom 3:1ff In Romans 3, Paul contends that everyone stands guilty before God. Paul has dismantled the common excuses of people who refuse to admit they are sinners: (1) "There is no God" or "I follow my conscience" (Rom 1:18-32); (2) "I'm not as bad as other people" (Rom 2:1-16); (3) "I'm a church member" or "I'm a religious person" (Rom 2:17-29). No one will be exempt from God's judgment of sin. We are all sinful and condemned before God; every person must accept that fact. We each need to receive God's wonderful gift of salvation.

Rom 3:1ff What a depressing picture Paul is painting! All of us—pagan Gentiles, humanitarians, and religious people—are condemned by our own actions. The law, which God gave to show us the way to live, holds up our evil deeds to public view. Is there any hope for us? Yes, says Paul. The law condemns us, it is true, but the law is not the basis of our hope. God himself is. He, in his righteousness and wonderful love, offers us eternal life. We receive our salvation not through the law but through faith in Jesus Christ. We do not—cannot—earn it; we accept it as a gift from our loving heavenly Father.

Rom 3:2 The Jewish nation had great benefits. (1) They were entrusted with God's laws ("the whole revelation of God"; Exod 19–20; Deut 4:8). (2) They were the race through whom the Messiah came to earth (Isa 11:1-10; Matt 1:1-17). (3) They were the beneficiaries of covenants with God himself (Gen 17:1-16; Exod 19:3-6). But these privileges did not make them better than anyone else (see Rom 3:9). In fact, because of them the Jews were even more responsible to live up to God's requirements.

Rom 3:5-8 Some may think they don't have to worry about sin because it's God's job to forgive, and God is so loving that he won't judge. Others may think sin isn't so bad—it teaches valuable lessons; besides, we need to stay in touch with the culture around us. It is far too easy to take God's grace for granted. But God cannot overlook sin. No matter how many excuses they make, sinners will have to answer to God for their sin.

Rom 3:10-12 Paul is referring to Psalm 14:1-3. "No one is righteous" means "no one is innocent." Every person is valuable in God's eyes because God created us in his image, and he loves us. But no one is good enough (that is, no one can earn right standing with God). Though we are valuable, we have fallen into sin. But God, through Jesus his Son, has redeemed us and offers to forgive us if we turn to him in faith.

11 No one is truly wise;
no one is seeking God.
12 All have turned away;
all have become useless.
No one does good,
not a single one."*
13 "Their talk is foul, like the stench from
an open grave.
Their tongues are filled with lies."
"Snake venom drips from their lips."*
14 "Their mouths are full of cursing and
bitterness."*
15 "They rush to commit murder.
16 Destruction and misery always follow them.
17 They don't know where to find peace."*
18 "They have no fear of God at all."*

19Obviously, the law applies to those to whom it was given, for its purpose is to keep people from having excuses, and to show that the entire world is guilty before God. 20For no one can ever be made right with God by doing what the law commands. The law simply shows us how sinful we are.

Christ Took Our Punishment

ROMANS 3:21-31

But now God has shown us a way to be made right with him without keeping the requirements of the law, as was promised in the writings of Moses* and the prophets long ago. 22We are made right with God by placing our faith in Jesus Christ. And this is true for everyone who believes, no matter who we are.

23For everyone has sinned; we all fall short of God's glorious standard. 24Yet God, with undeserved kindness, declares that we are righteous. He did this through Christ Jesus when he freed us from the penalty for our sins. 25For God presented Jesus as the sacrifice for sin. People are made right with God when they believe that Jesus sacrificed his life, shedding his blood. This sacrifice shows that God was being fair when he held back and did not punish those who sinned in times past, 26for he was looking ahead and including them in what he would do in this present time. God did this to demonstrate his righteousness, for he himself is fair and just, and he declares sinners to be right in his sight when they believe in Jesus.

Rom 3:10-12 Pss 14:1-3; 53:1-3 (Greek version). **Rom 3:13** Pss 5:9 (Greek version); 140:3. **Rom 3:14** Ps 10:7 (Greek version). **Rom 3:15-17** Isa 59:7-8. **Rom 3:18** Ps 36:1. **Rom 3:21** Greek *in the law.*

Rom 3:10-18 Paul uses these Old Testament references to show that humanity in general, in its present sinful condition, is unacceptable before God. Have you ever thought to yourself, *Well, I'm not too bad; I'm a pretty good person*? Look at these verses and see if any of them apply to you. Have you ever lied? Are you bitter toward anyone? Do you become angry with those who strongly disagree with you? In thought, word, and deed, you, like everyone else in the world, stand guilty before God. We must remember who we are in his sight—alienated sinners. Don't deny that you are a sinner. Instead, allow your desperate need to point you toward Christ.

Rom 3:19 The last time someone accused you of wrongdoing, what was your reaction? Denial, argument, and defensiveness? The entire world will be silent before God. No excuses or arguments will remain. Have you reached the point with God where you are ready to hang up your defenses and await his decision? If you haven't, stop now and admit your sin to him. If you have, the following verses are truly good news for you!

Rom 3:20, 31 In these verses we see two functions of God's law. First, the law shows us where we go wrong. Because of the law, we know that we are helpless sinners and that we must come to Jesus Christ for mercy. Second, the moral code revealed in the law can serve to guide our actions by holding up God's moral standards. We do not earn salvation by keeping the law (no one except Christ ever kept or could keep God's law perfectly), but we do please God when our life conforms to his revealed will for us.

Rom 3:21-29 After all this bad news about our sinfulness and God's condemnation, Paul gives the wonderful news. There is a way to be declared not guilty—by trusting Jesus Christ to take away our sins. Trusting means putting our confidence in Christ to forgive our sins, to make us right with God, and to empower us to live the way he taught us. God's solution is available to all of us regardless of our background or past behavior.

Rom 3:23 Some sins seem bigger than others because their obvious consequences are much more serious. Murder, for example, seems to us to be worse than hatred, and adultery seems worse than pride. But this does not mean that because we only commit "little" sins we deserve eternal life. All sins make us sinners, and all sins cut us off from our holy God. All sins, therefore, lead to death (because they disqualify us from living with God), regardless of how great or small they seem. Don't minimize "little" sins or overrate "big" sins. They all separate us from God, but they all can be forgiven.

Rom 3:24 Paul explains that God declares that we are righteous. When a judge in a court of law declares the defendant not guilty, all the charges are removed from his record. Legally, it is as if the person had never been accused. When God forgives our sins, our record is wiped clean. From his perspective, it is as though we had never sinned. He could do this because Jesus took the penalty that we deserved. Christ purchased our freedom from sin, and the price was his life.

Rom 3:25 Christ died in our place for our sins. God is justifiably angry at sinners. They have rebelled against him and cut themselves off from his life-giving power. But God declares Christ's death to be the appropriate, designated sacrifice for our sin. Christ then

For everyone has sinned; we all fall short of God's glorious standard.
Romans 3:23

stands in our place, having paid the penalty of death for our sin, and he completely satisfies God's demands. His sacrifice brings pardon, deliverance, and freedom.

Rom 3:25-26 What happened to people who lived before Christ came and died for sin? If God condemned sinners, was he being unfair? If he saved the righteous, was Christ's sacrifice unnecessary? Paul shows that God forgave all human sin at the cross of Jesus. Old Testament believers looked forward in faith to Christ's coming and were saved, even though they did not know Jesus' name or the details of his earthly life. Unlike the Old Testament believers, you know about the God who loved the world so much that he gave his own Son (John 3:16). Have you put your trust in him?

▶ **ROMANS 3:21-31** ***(cont.)***

27 Can we boast, then, that we have done anything
to be accepted by God? No, because our acquittal is
not based on obeying the law. It is based on faith. 28 So
we are made right with God through faith and not by
obeying the law.
29 After all, is God the God of the Jews only? Isn't he
also the God of the Gentiles? Of course he is. 30 There
is only one God, and he makes people right with himself only by faith, whether they are Jews or Gentiles.*
31 Well then, if we emphasize faith, does this mean
that we can forget about the law? Of course not! In
fact, only when we have faith do we truly fulfill the law.

The Faith of Abraham

ROMANS 4:1-25

Abraham was, humanly speaking, the founder of our
Jewish nation. What did he discover about being
made right with God? 2 If his good deeds had made
him acceptable to God, he would have had something
to boast about. But that was not God's way. 3 For the
Scriptures tell us, "Abraham believed God, and God
counted him as righteous because of his faith."*
4 When people work, their wages are not a gift, but
something they have earned. 5 But people are counted
as righteous, not because of their work, but because
of their faith in God who forgives sinners. 6 David
also spoke of this when he described the happiness
of those who are declared righteous without working for it:

7 "Oh, what joy for those
whose disobedience is forgiven,
whose sins are put out of sight.
8 Yes, what joy for those
whose record the LORD has cleared of sin."*

9 Now, is this blessing only for the Jews, or is it also
for uncircumcised Gentiles?* Well, we have been saying that Abraham was counted as righteous by God
because of his faith. 10 But how did this happen? Was

Rom 3:30 Greek *whether they are circumcised or uncircumcised.* **Rom 4:3** Gen 15:6. **Rom 4:7-8** Ps 32:1-2 (Greek version). **Rom 4:9** Greek *is this blessing only for the circumcised, or is it also for the uncircumcised?*

Rom 3:27-28 Most religions require specific duties that must be performed to make a person acceptable to a god. Christianity is unique in that no good deed that we do will make us right with God. No amount of human achievement or personal goodness will close the gap between God's moral perfection and our imperfect daily performance. Good deeds are important, but they will not earn us eternal life. We are saved only by trusting in what God has done for us (see Eph 2:8-10).

Rom 3:28 Why does God save us by faith alone? (1) Faith eliminates the pride of human effort, because faith is not a deed that we do. (2) Faith exalts what God has done, not what we do. (3) Faith admits that we can't keep the law or measure up to God's standards—we need help. (4) Faith is based on our relationship with God, not our performance for God.

Rom 3:31 There were some misunderstandings between the Jewish and Gentile Christians in Rome. Worried Jewish Christians were asking Paul, "Does faith wipe out everything Judaism stands for? Does it cancel our Scriptures, put an end to our customs, declare that God is no longer working through us?" (This is essentially the question used to open Rom 3.) "Of course not!" says Paul. When we understand the way of salvation through faith, we understand the Jewish religion better. We know why Abraham was chosen, why the law was given, and why God worked patiently with Israel for centuries. Faith does not wipe out the Old Testament. Rather, it makes God's dealings with the Jewish people understandable. In Romans 4, Paul will expand on this theme (see also Rom 5:20-21; 8:3-4; 13:9-10; Gal 3:24-29; 1 Tim 1:8).

Rom 4:1-3 The Jews were proud to be descendants of Abraham. Paul uses Abraham as a good example of someone who was saved by faith. By emphasizing faith, Paul is not saying that God's law is unimportant (Rom 4:13) but that it is impossible to be saved simply by obeying it. (For more about Abraham, see his Profile on p. 31.)

SALVATION'S FREEWAY

Verses in Romans that describe the way to salvation.

Rom 3:23	Everyone has sinned.
Rom 6:23	The penalty for our sin is death.
Rom 5:8	Jesus Christ died for sin.
Rom 10:8-10	To be forgiven for our sin, we must believe and confess that Jesus is Lord. Salvation comes through Jesus Christ.

Rom 4:5 When some people learn that they are saved by God through faith, they start to worry. "Do I have enough faith?" they wonder. "Is my faith strong enough to save me?" These people miss the point. It is Jesus Christ who saves us, not our feelings or actions, and he is strong enough to save us no matter how weak our faith is. Jesus offers us salvation as a gift because he loves us, not because we have earned it through our powerful faith. What, then, is the role of faith? Faith is believing and trusting in Jesus Christ and reaching out to accept his wonderful gift of salvation.

Rom 4:6-8 What can we do to get rid of guilt? King David was guilty of terrible sins—adultery, murder, lying—and yet he experienced the joy of forgiveness. We, too, can have this joy when we (1) quit denying our guilt and recognize that we have sinned, (2) admit our guilt to God and ask for his forgiveness, and (3) let go of our guilt and believe that God has forgiven us. This can be difficult when a sin has taken root in our lives over many years, when it is very serious, or when it involves others. But we must remember that Jesus is willing and able to forgive every sin. In view of the tremendous price he paid on the cross, it is arrogant to think that there is any sin too great for him to forgive. Even though our faith is weak, our conscience is sensitive, and our memory haunts us, God's Word declares that sins confessed are sins forgiven (1 Jn 1:9).

Rom 4:10-12 Circumcision was a sign to others and a personal seal or certification for the Jews that they were God's special people. Circumcision of all Jewish boys set apart the Jewish people from the nations that worshiped other gods; thus, it was a very important ceremony. God gave the blessing and the command for this ceremony to Abraham (Gen 17:9-14).

Paul's point here is that the ritual of circumcision did not earn Abraham his acceptance by God; he had been blessed long before the circumcision ceremony was introduced. Abraham found favor with God by faith alone, before he was circumcised. Genesis 12:1-3 tells of God's

he counted as righteous only after he was circumcised, or was it before he was circumcised? Clearly, God accepted Abraham before he was circumcised!
[11]Circumcision was a sign that Abraham already had faith and that God had already accepted him and declared him to be righteous—even before he was circumcised. So Abraham is the spiritual father of those who have faith but have not been circumcised. They are counted as righteous because of their faith. [12]And Abraham is also the spiritual father of those who have been circumcised, but only if they have the same kind of faith Abraham had before he was circumcised.
[13]Clearly, God's promise to give the whole earth to Abraham and his descendants was based not on his obedience to God's law, but on a right relationship with God that comes by faith. [14]If God's promise is only for those who obey the law, then faith is not necessary and the promise is pointless. [15]For the law always brings punishment on those who try to obey it. (The only way to avoid breaking the law is to have no law to break!)
[16]So the promise is received by faith. It is given as a free gift. And we are all certain to receive it, whether or not we live according to the law of Moses, if we have faith like Abraham's. For Abraham is the father of all who believe. [17]That is what the Scriptures mean when God told him, "I have made you the father of many nations."* This happened because Abraham believed in the God who brings the dead back to life and who creates new things out of nothing.
[18]Even when there was no reason for hope, Abraham kept hoping—believing that he would become the father of many nations. For God had said to him, "That's how many descendants you will have!"* [19]And Abraham's faith did not weaken, even though, at about 100 years of age, he figured his body was as good as dead—and so was Sarah's womb.
[20]Abraham never wavered in believing God's promise. In fact, his faith grew stronger, and in this he brought glory to God. [21]He was fully convinced that God is able to do whatever he promises. [22]And because of Abraham's faith, God counted him as righteous.
[23]And when God counted him as righteous, it wasn't just for Abraham's benefit. It was recorded [24]for our benefit, too, assuring us that God will also count us as righteous if we believe in him, the one who raised Jesus our Lord from the dead. [25]He was handed over to die because of our sins, and he was raised to life to make us right with God.

Rom 4:17 Gen 17:5. **Rom 4:18** Gen 15:5.

CRUCIAL CONCEPTS IN ROMANS

ELECTION	*Rom 9:10-13*	God's choice of an individual or group for a specific purpose or destiny
JUSTIFICATION	*Rom 4:25; 5:18*	God's act of declaring us "not guilty" for our sins, making us "right" with him
PROPITIATION	*Rom 3:25*	The removal of God's punishment for sin through the perfect sacrifice of Jesus Christ
REDEMPTION	*Rom 3:24; 8:23*	Jesus Christ has paid the price so we can go free. The price of sin is death; Jesus paid the price.
SANCTIFICATION	*Rom 5:2; 15:16*	Becoming more and more like Jesus Christ through the work of the Holy Spirit
GLORIFICATION	*Rom 8:18-19, 30*	The ultimate state of the believer after death when becoming like Christ (1 Jn 3:2)

call to Abraham when he was 75 years old; the circumcision ceremony was introduced when he was 99 (Gen 17:1-14). Ceremonies and rituals serve as reminders of our faith as well as instruct new or young believers, but we should not think that they give us any special merit before God. They are outward signs and seals that demonstrate inner belief and trust. The focus of our faith should be on Christ and his saving work, not on our own actions.

Rom 4:16 Paul explains that Abraham had pleased God through faith alone before he had ever heard about the rituals that would become so important to the Jewish people. We, too, are saved by faith plus nothing. It is not by loving God and doing good that we are saved; neither is it by faith plus love or by faith plus good deeds. We are saved only through faith in Christ, trusting him to forgive all our sins. (For more on Abraham, see his Profile on p. 31.)

Rom 4:17 The promise (or covenant) God gave Abraham stated that Abraham would be the father of many nations (Gen 17:2-4) and that the entire world would be blessed through him (Gen 12:3). This promise was fulfilled in Jesus Christ. Jesus was from Abraham's line, and truly the whole world was blessed through him.

Rom 4:21 Abraham never doubted that God would fulfill his promise. Abraham's life was marked by mistakes, sins, and failures as well as by wisdom and goodness, but he consistently trusted God. His faith was strengthened by the obstacles he faced, and his life was an example of faith in action. If he had looked only at his own resources for subduing Canaan and founding a nation, he would have given up in despair. But Abraham looked to God, obeyed him, and waited for God to fulfill his word.

Rom 4:25 When we accept Jesus Christ as our Savior, an exchange takes place. We give him our sins, and he forgives us and makes us right with God (see 2 Cor 5:21). There is nothing we can do to earn this. Only through Christ can we be made right in God's eyes. What an incredible bargain this is for us! But sadly, many still choose to pass up this gift to continue "enjoying" their sin.

Faith Brings Joy

ROMANS 5:1-11

Therefore, since we have been made right in God's
sight by faith, we have peace with God because of what
Jesus Christ our Lord has done for us. 2 Because of
our faith, Christ has brought us into this place of undeserved privilege where we now stand, and we confidently and joyfully look forward to sharing God's glory.
3 We can rejoice, too, when we run into problems
and trials, for we know that they help us develop endurance. 4 And endurance develops strength of character, and character strengthens our confident hope of
salvation. 5 And this hope will not lead to disappointment. For we know how dearly God loves us, because
he has given us the Holy Spirit to fill our hearts with
his love.
6 When we were utterly helpless, Christ came at just
the right time and died for us sinners. 7 Now, most
people would not be willing to die for an upright person, though someone might perhaps be willing to die
for a person who is especially good. 8 But God showed
his great love for us by sending Christ to die for us
while we were still sinners. 9 And since we have been
made right in God's sight by the blood of Christ, he
will certainly save us from God's condemnation. 10 For
since our friendship with God was restored by the
death of his Son while we were still his enemies, we
will certainly be saved through the life of his Son. 11 So
now we can rejoice in our wonderful new relationship
with God because our Lord Jesus Christ has made us
friends of God.

Adam and Christ Contrasted

ROMANS 5:12-21

When Adam sinned, sin entered the world. Adam's sin
brought death, so death spread to everyone, for every-

Rom 5:1 We are now at peace *with* God, which may differ from peaceful feelings such as calmness and tranquility. Peace with God means that we have been reconciled with him. There is no more hostility between us, no sin blocking our relationship with him. Peace with God is possible only because Jesus paid the price for our sins through his death on the cross.

Rom 5:1-5 These verses introduce a section that contains some difficult concepts. To understand Romans 5–8, it helps to keep in mind the two-sided reality of the Christian life. On the one hand, we are complete in Christ (our acceptance with him is secure). On the other hand, we are growing in Christ (we are becoming more and more like him). At one and the same time we have the status of kings and the duties of slaves. We feel both the presence of Christ and the pressure of sin. We enjoy the peace that comes from being made right with God, but we still face daily problems that often help us grow. If we remember these two sides of the Christian life, we will not grow discouraged as we face temptations and problems. Instead, we will learn to depend on the power available to us from Christ, who lives in us by the Holy Spirit.

Rom 5:2 Paul states that, as believers, we now have entered into a place of undeserved privilege. Not only has God declared us not guilty; but he also has drawn us close to himself. Instead of being enemies, we have become his friends—in fact, his own children (John 15:15; Gal 4:5).

Rom 5:3-4 For first-century Christians, suffering was the rule rather than the exception. Paul tells us that in the future we will *become*, but until then we must *overcome*. This means we will experience difficulties that help us grow. We rejoice in suffering not because we like pain or deny its tragedy but because we know God is using life's difficulties and Satan's attacks to build our character. The problems that we run into will develop our perseverance—which in turn will strengthen our character, deepen our trust in God, and give us greater confidence about the future. You probably find your patience tested in some way every day. Thank God for those opportunities to grow, and deal with them in his strength (see also Jas 1:2-4; 1 Pet 1:6-7).

WHAT WE HAVE AS GOD'S CHILDREN

What we have as Adam's children	What we have as God's children
Ruin (Rom 5:9)	Rescue (Rom 5:8)
Sin (Rom 5:12, 15, 21)	Righteousness (Rom 5:18)
Death (Rom 5:12, 17, 21)	Eternal life (Rom 5:17, 21)
Separation from God (Rom 5:18)	Relationship with God (Rom 5:11, 18)
Disobedience (Rom 5:12, 19)	Obedience (Rom 5:19)
Judgment (Rom 5:18)	Deliverance (Rom 5:10-11)
Law (Rom 5:20)	Grace (Rom 5:20)

Rom 5:5-6 All three members of the Trinity are involved in salvation. The Father loved us so much that he sent his Son to bridge the gap between us (John 3:16). The Father and the Son send the Holy Spirit to fill our lives with love and to enable us to live by his power (Acts 1:8). With all this loving care, how can we do less than serve him completely?

Rom 5:6 We were weak and helpless because we could do nothing on our own to save ourselves. Someone had to come and rescue us. Christ came at exactly the right time in history—according to God's own schedule. God controls all history, and he controlled the timing, method, and events surrounding Jesus' death.

Rom 5:8 "While we were still sinners"—these are amazing words. God sent Jesus Christ to die for us not because we were good enough but just because he loved us. Whenever you feel uncertain about God's love for you, remember that he loved you even before you turned to him.

Rom 5:9-10 The love that caused Christ to die is the same love that sends the Holy Spirit to live in us and guide us every day. The power that raised Christ from the dead is the same power that saved you and is available to you in your daily life. Be assured that, having begun a life with Christ, you have a reserve of power and love to call on each day for help to meet every challenge or trial. You can pray for God's power and love as you need it.

Rom 5:11 God is holy, and he will not be associated with sin. All people are sinful and so they are separated from God. In addition, all sin deserves punishment. Instead of punishing us with the death we deserve, however, Christ took our sins upon himself and took our punishment by dying on the cross. Now we can rejoice in God. Through faith in Christ's work, we become close to God (friends) rather than being enemies and outcasts.

Rom 5:12 How can we be declared guilty for something Adam did thousands of years ago? Many feel it isn't fair for God to judge us because of Adam's sin. Yet each of us confirms our heritage with Adam by our own sins every day. We have the same sinful nature and are prone to rebel against God, and we are judged for the sins we commit. Because we are sinners, it isn't fairness we need—it is mercy.

one sinned. [13]Yes, people sinned even before the law was given. But it was not counted as sin because there was not yet any law to break. [14]Still, everyone died—from the time of Adam to the time of Moses—even those who did not disobey an explicit commandment of God, as Adam did. Now Adam is a symbol, a representation of Christ, who was yet to come. [15]But there is a great difference between Adam's sin and God's gracious gift. For the sin of this one man, Adam, brought death to many. But even greater is God's wonderful grace and his gift of forgiveness to many through this other man, Jesus Christ. [16]And the result of God's gracious gift is very different from the result of that one man's sin. For Adam's sin led to condemnation, but God's free gift leads to our being made right with God, even though we are guilty of many sins. [17]For the sin of this one man, Adam, caused death to rule over many. But even greater is God's wonderful grace and his gift of righteousness, for all who receive it will live in triumph over sin and death through this one man, Jesus Christ.

[18]Yes, Adam's one sin brings condemnation for everyone, but Christ's one act of righteousness brings a right relationship with God and new life for everyone. [19]Because one person disobeyed God, many became sinners. But because one other person obeyed God, many will be made righteous.

[20]God's law was given so that all people could see how sinful they were. But as people sinned more and more, God's wonderful grace became more abundant. [21]So just as sin ruled over all people and brought them to death, now God's wonderful grace rules instead, giving us right standing with God and resulting in eternal life through Jesus Christ our Lord.

Sin's Power Is Broken

ROMANS 6:1-23

Well then, should we keep on sinning so that God can show us more and more of his wonderful grace? [2]Of course not! Since we have died to sin, how can we continue to live in it? [3]Or have you forgotten that when we were joined with Christ Jesus in baptism, we joined him in his death? [4]For we died and were buried with Christ by baptism. And just as Christ was raised from the dead by the glorious power of the Father, now we also may live new lives.

[5]Since we have been united with him in his death, we will also be raised to life as he was. [6]We know that

---

Rom 5:13-14 Paul has shown that keeping the law does not bring salvation. Here he adds that breaking the law is not what brings death. Death is the result of Adam's sin and of the sins we all commit, even if they don't resemble Adam's. Paul reminds his readers that for thousands of years the law had not yet been explicitly given, and yet people died. The law was added, he explains in Romans 5:20, to help people see their sinfulness, to show them the seriousness of their offenses, and to drive them to God for mercy and pardon. This was true in Moses' day, and it is still true today. Sin is a deep discrepancy between who we are and who we were created to be. The law points out our sin and places the responsibility for it squarely on our shoulders. But the law offers no remedy. When we are convicted of sin, we must turn to Jesus Christ for healing.

Rom 5:14 Adam was the counterpart of Christ. Just as Adam was a representative of created humanity, so is Christ the representative of a new spiritual humanity.

Rom 5:15-19 We were all born into Adam's physical family—the family line that leads to certain death. All of us have reaped the results of Adam's sin. We have inherited his guilt, a sinful nature (the tendency to sin), and God's punishment. Because of Jesus, we can trade judgment for forgiveness. Christ offers us the opportunity to be born into his spiritual family—the family line that begins with forgiveness and leads to eternal life. If we do nothing, we receive death through Adam; but if we come to God by faith, we receive life through Christ. To which family line do you now belong?

Rom 5:20 As a sinner, separated from God, you see his law from below, as a ladder to be climbed to get to God. Perhaps you have repeatedly tried to climb it, only to fall to the ground every time you have advanced one or two rungs. Or perhaps the sheer height of the ladder seems so overwhelming that you have never even started up it. In either case, what relief you should feel to see Jesus offering with open arms to lift you above the ladder of the law, to take you directly to God! Once Jesus lifts you into God's presence, you are free to obey—out of love, not necessity, and through God's power, not your own. You know that if you stumble, you will not fall back to the ground. Instead, you will be caught and held in Christ's loving arms.

Rom 6:1–8:39 This section deals with sanctification—the change God makes in our lives as we grow in the faith. Romans 6 explains that believers are free from sin's control. Romans 7 discusses the continuing struggle believers have with sin. Romans 8 describes how we can have victory over sin.

Rom 6:1-2 If God loves to forgive, why not give him more to forgive? If forgiveness is guaranteed, do we have the freedom to sin as much as we want to? Paul's forceful answer is: "Of course not!" Such an attitude—deciding ahead of time to take advantage of God—shows that a person does not understand the seriousness of sin. God's forgiveness does not make sin less serious; his Son's death for sin shows us the dreadful seriousness of sin. Jesus paid with his life so we could be forgiven. The availability of God's mercy must not become an excuse for careless living and moral laxness.

Rom 6:1-4 In the church of Paul's day, immersion was the usual form of baptism; that is, new Christians were completely "buried" in water. They understood baptism to symbolize the death and burial of the old way of life. Coming up out of the water symbolized resurrection to new life with Christ. If we think of our old, sinful life as dead and buried, we have a powerful motive to resist sin. We can consciously choose to treat the desires and temptations of the old nature as if they were dead. Then we can continue to enjoy our wonderful new life with Jesus (see also Gal 3:27; Col 2:12; 3:1-4).

Rom 6:5ff Our evil desires and bondage to sin died with Christ because we have been united with him in his death. Now, united by faith with him in his resurrection life, we have unbroken fellowship with God and freedom from sin's hold on us. (For more on the difference between our new life in Christ and our old sinful nature, read Eph 4:21-24; Col 3:3-15.)

Rom 6:6-7 The power of sin over us died with Christ on the cross. Our "old sinful selves," our sinful nature, died once and for all, so we are freed from its power. The "power of sin" refers to our rebellious sin-loving nature inherited from Adam. Though we often willingly cooperate with our sinful nature, it is not us but the sin in us that is evil. And it is this power of sin at work in our life that has been defeated. Paul has already stated that through faith in Christ we stand righteous before God. Here Paul emphasizes that we need no longer live under sin's power. God does not take us out of the world or make us robots—we will still feel like sinning, and sometimes we will sin. The difference is that before we were saved, we were slaves to our sinful nature; but now we can choose to live for Christ (see Gal 2:20).

▶ **ROMANS 6:1-23** ***(cont.)***

our old sinful selves were crucified with Christ so that sin might lose its power in our lives. We are no longer slaves to sin. [7]For when we died with Christ we were set free from the power of sin. [8]And since we died with Christ, we know we will also live with him. [9]We are sure of this because Christ was raised from the dead, and he will never die again. Death no longer has any power over him. [10]When he died, he died once to break the power of sin. But now that he lives, he lives for the glory of God. [11]So you also should consider yourselves to be dead to the power of sin and alive to God through Christ Jesus.

[12]Do not let sin control the way you live;* do not give in to sinful desires. [13]Do not let any part of your body become an instrument of evil to serve sin. Instead, give yourselves completely to God, for you were dead, but now you have new life. So use your whole body as an instrument to do what is right for the glory of God. [14]Sin is no longer your master, for you no longer live under the requirements of the law. Instead, you live under the freedom of God's grace.

[15]Well then, since God's grace has set us free from the law, does that mean we can go on sinning? Of course not! [16]Don't you realize that you become the slave of whatever you choose to obey? You can be a slave to sin, which leads to death, or you can choose to obey God, which leads to righteous living. [17]Thank God! Once you were slaves of sin, but now you wholeheartedly obey this teaching we have given you. [18]Now you are free from your slavery to sin, and you have become slaves to righteous living.

[19]Because of the weakness of your human nature, I am using the illustration of slavery to help you understand all this. Previously, you let yourselves be slaves to impurity and lawlessness, which led ever deeper into sin. Now you must give yourselves to be slaves to righteous living so that you will become holy.

[20]When you were slaves to sin, you were free from the obligation to do right. [21]And what was the result? You are now ashamed of the things you used to do, things that end in eternal doom. [22]But now you are free from the power of sin and have become slaves of God. Now you do those things that lead to holiness and result in eternal life. [23]For the wages of sin is death, but the free gift of God is eternal life through Christ Jesus our Lord.

Rom 6:12 Or *Do not let sin reign in your body, which is subject to death.*

Rom 6:8-9 Because of Christ's death and resurrection, his followers need never fear death. That assurance frees us to enjoy fellowship with him and to do his will. This will affect all our activities—work and worship, play, Bible study, quiet times, and times of caring for others. When you know that you don't have to fear death, you will experience a new vigor in life.

Rom 6:11 "Consider yourselves to be dead to the power of sin" means that we should regard our old sinful nature as dead and unresponsive to sin. Because of our union and identification with Christ, we no longer want to pursue our old plans, desires, and goals. Now we want to live for the glory of God. As we start this new life, the Holy Spirit will help us become all that Christ wants us to be.

Rom 6:12 How can we keep this command to not let sin control the way we live, to not give in to its desires? We can take the following steps: (1) Identify our personal weaknesses, (2) recognize the things that tempt us, (3) stay away from sources of temptation, (4) practice self-restraint, (5) consciously invest our time in good habits and service, and (6) lean on God's strength and grace.

Rom 6:13 When Paul uses the term "instrument of evil," he uses a word that can refer to a tool or a weapon. Our skills, capabilities, and bodies can serve many purposes, good or bad. In sin, every part of our bodies is vulnerable. In Christ, every part can be an instrument for service. It is the one to whom we offer our service that makes the difference. We are like lasers that can burn destructive holes in pieces of steel or do delicate cataract surgery. Will you give yourself completely to God, asking him to put you to good use for his glory?

Rom 6:14-15 If we're no longer under the law but under grace, are we now free to sin and disregard the Ten Commandments? Paul says, "Of course not!" When we were under the law, sin was our master—the law does not justify us or help us overcome sin. But now that we are bound to Christ, he is our Master, and he gives us power to do good rather than evil.

Rom 6:16-18 All people have a master to pattern themselves after. Without Jesus, we would have no choice; we would be enslaved to sin, and the results would be guilt, suffering, and separation from God. But thanks to Jesus, we can now choose God as our Master. Following him, we can enjoy new life and learn how to work for him. Are you still serving your first master, sin? Or have you chosen God?

Rom 6:17 To "wholeheartedly obey" means to give yourself fully to God, to love him "with all your heart, all your soul, and all your mind" (Matt 22:37). And yet so often our efforts to know and obey God's commands can best be described as "halfhearted." How do you rate your heart's obedience? God wants to give you the power to obey him with all your heart.

Rom 6:17 The "teaching" they were to obey refers to the Good News that Jesus died for their sins and was raised to give them new life. Many believe that this refers to the early church's statement of faith found in 1 Corinthians 15:1-11.

Rom 6:19-22 It is impossible to be neutral. Every person has a master—either God or sin. A Christian is not someone who cannot sin but someone who is no longer a slave to sin, because that person now belongs to God.

Rom 6:23 You are free to choose between two masters, but you are not free to adjust the consequences of your choice. Each of the two masters pays with a different kind of currency. The currency of sin is eternal death. That is all you can expect or hope for in life without God. Christ's currency is eternal life—new life with God that begins on earth and continues forever with God. What choice have you made?

Rom 6:23 Eternal life is a gift from God. If it is a gift, then it is not something that we earn, nor something that must be paid back. Consider the foolishness of someone who receives a gift given out of love and then offers to pay for it. A gift cannot be purchased by the recipient. A more appropriate response to a loved one who offers a gift is graceful acceptance with gratitude. Our salvation is a gift of God, not something of our own doing (Eph 2:8-9). He saved us because of his mercy, not because of any good things that we have done (Titus 3:5). How much more we should accept with thanksgiving the gift that God has freely given to us.

Rom 7:1ff Paul shows that the law is powerless to save the sinner (Rom 7:7-14), the lawkeeper (Rom 7:15-22), and even the person with a new nature (Rom 7:23-25). The sinner is condemned by the law; the lawkeeper can't live up to it; and the person with the new nature finds their obedience to the law

No Longer Bound to the Law

ROMANS 7:1-6

Now, dear brothers and sisters*—you who are familiar with the law—don't you know that the law applies only while a person is living? [2]For example, when a woman marries, the law binds her to her husband as long as he is alive. But if he dies, the laws of marriage no longer apply to her. [3]So while her husband is alive, she would be committing adultery if she married another man. But if her husband dies, she is free from that law and does not commit adultery when she remarries.

[4]So, my dear brothers and sisters, this is the point: You died to the power of the law when you died with Christ. And now you are united with the one who was raised from the dead. As a result, we can produce a harvest of good deeds for God. [5]When we were controlled by our old nature,* sinful desires were at work within us, and the law aroused these evil desires that produced a harvest of sinful deeds, resulting in death.

[6]But now we have been released from the law, for we died to it and are no longer captive to its power. Now we can serve God, not in the old way of obeying the letter of the law, but in the new way of living in the Spirit.

God's Law Reveals Our Sin

ROMANS 7:7-13

Well then, am I suggesting that the law of God is sinful? Of course not! In fact, it was the law that showed me my sin. I would never have known that coveting is wrong if the law had not said, "You must not covet."* [8]But sin used this command to arouse all kinds of covetous desires within me! If there were no law, sin would not have that power. [9]At one time I lived without understanding the law. But when I learned the command not to covet, for instance, the power of sin came to life, [10]and I died. So I discovered that the law's commands, which were supposed to bring life, brought spiritual death instead. [11]Sin took advantage

Rom 7:1 Greek *brothers;* also in 7:4. **Rom 7:5** Greek *When we were in the flesh.* **Rom 7:7** Exod 20:17; Deut 5:21.

WHAT HAS GOD DONE ABOUT SIN?

He has given us	*Reference*	*Principle*	*Importance*
New life	Rom 6:2-3	Sin's power is broken.	We can be certain that sin's power is broken.
	Rom 6:4	Sin-loving nature is buried.	
	Rom 6:6	You are no longer under sin's control.	
New nature	Rom 6:5	Now you share his new life.	We can see ourselves as unresponsive to the old power and alive to the new.
	Rom 6:11	Look upon your old self as dead; instead, be alive to God.	
New freedom	Rom 6:12	Do not let sin control you.	We can commit ourselves to obey Christ in perfect freedom.
	Rom 6:13	Give yourselves completely to God.	
	Rom 6:14	You are free.	
	Rom 6:16	You can choose your own master.	

sabotaged by the effects of the old nature. Once again Paul declares that salvation cannot be found by obeying the law. No matter who we are, only Jesus Christ can set us free.

Rom 7:2-6 Paul uses marriage to illustrate our relationship to the law. When a spouse dies, the law of marriage no longer applies. Because we have died with Christ, the law can no longer condemn us. Since we are united with Christ, his Spirit enables us to produce good deeds for God. We now serve God, not by obeying a set of rules, but out of renewed hearts and minds that overflow with love for him.

Rom 7:4 When a person dies to the old life and accepts Christ as Savior, a new life begins. An unbeliever's life is centered on personal gratification. Those who don't follow Christ have only their own self-determination as their source of power. By contrast, God is at the center of a Christian's life. God supplies the power for a Christian's daily living. Believers find that their whole way of looking at the world changes when they come to Christ.

Rom 7:6 Some people try to earn their way to God by keeping a set of rules (obeying the Ten Commandments, attending church faithfully, or doing good deeds), but all they earn for their efforts is frustration and discouragement. But because of Christ's sacrifice, the way to God is already open, and we can become his children simply by putting our faith in him. No longer trying to reach God by keeping rules, we can become more and more like Jesus as we live for him day by day. Let the Holy Spirit turn your eyes away from your own performance and toward Jesus. He will free you to serve him out of love and gratitude. This is "living in the Spirit."

Rom 7:6 Keeping the rules, laws, and customs of Christianity doesn't save us. Even if we could keep our actions pure, we would still be doomed because our hearts and minds are perverse and rebellious. Like Paul, we can find no relief in the synagogue or church until we look to Jesus Christ himself for our salvation—which he gives us freely. When we do come to Jesus, we are flooded with relief and gratitude. Will we keep the rules any better? Most likely, but we will be motivated by love and gratitude, not by the desire to get God's approval. We will not be merely submitting to an external code, but we will willingly and lovingly seek to do God's will.

Rom 7:9-11 Where there is no law, there is no sin, because people cannot know that their actions are sinful unless a law forbids those actions. God's law makes people realize that they are sinners doomed to die, yet it offers no help. Sin is real, and it is dangerous. Imagine a sunny day at the beach. You plunge into the surf; then you notice a sign on the pier: "No swimming. Sharks." Your day is ruined. Is it the sign's fault? Are you angry with the people who put it up? The law is like the sign. It is essential, and we are grateful for it—but it doesn't get rid of the sharks.

Rom 7:11-12 Sin deceives people by misusing the law. The law is holy, expressing God's nature and will for people. In the Garden of Eden (Gen 3), the serpent deceived Eve, changing her focus from the freedom she had to the one restriction God had made. Ever since then, we have all been rebels. Sin looks good to us precisely because God has said it is wrong. When we are tempted to rebel, we need to look at the law from a wider perspective—in the light of God's grace and mercy. If we focus on his great love for us, we will understand that he only restricts us from actions and attitudes that ultimately will harm us.

▸ **ROMANS 7:7-13** ***(cont.)***
of those commands and deceived me; it used the commands to kill me. 12But still, the law itself is holy, and
its commands are holy and right and good.
13But how can that be? Did the law, which is good,
cause my death? Of course not! Sin used what was
good to bring about my condemnation to death. So
we can see how terrible sin really is. It uses God's good
commands for its own evil purposes.

Struggling with Sin

ROMANS 7:14-25
So the trouble is not with the law, for it is spiritual and
good. The trouble is with me, for I am all too human,
a slave to sin. 15I don't really understand myself, for
I want to do what is right, but I don't do it. Instead, I
do what I hate. 16But if I know that what I am doing
is wrong, this shows that I agree that the law is good.
17So I am not the one doing wrong; it is sin living in
me that does it.
18And I know that nothing good lives in me, that is,
in my sinful nature.* I want to do what is right, but I
can't. 19I want to do what is good, but I don't. I don't
want to do what is wrong, but I do it anyway. 20But if
I do what I don't want to do, I am not really the one
doing wrong; it is sin living in me that does it.
21I have discovered this principle of life—that when
I want to do what is right, I inevitably do what is wrong.
22I love God's law with all my heart. 23But there is another power* within me that is at war with my mind.
This power makes me a slave to the sin that is still
within me. 24Oh, what a miserable person I am! Who
will free me from this life that is dominated by sin and
death? 25Thank God! The answer is in Jesus Christ our
Lord. So you see how it is: In my mind I really want
to obey God's law, but because of my sinful nature I
am a slave to sin.

Life in the Spirit

ROMANS 8:1-17
So now there is no condemnation for those who belong to Christ Jesus. 2And because you belong to him,
the power* of the life-giving Spirit has freed you*
from the power of sin that leads to death. 3The law of
Moses was unable to save us because of the weakness
of our sinful nature.* So God did what the law could
not do. He sent his own Son in a body like the bodies
we sinners have. And in that body God declared an end
to sin's control over us by giving his Son as a sacrifice
for our sins. 4He did this so that the just requirement
of the law would be fully satisfied for us, who no longer
follow our sinful nature but instead follow the Spirit.
5Those who are dominated by the sinful nature
think about sinful things, but those who are controlled

Rom 7:18 Greek *my flesh;* also in 7:25. **Rom 7:23** Greek *law;* also in 7:23b. **Rom 8:2a** Greek *the law;* also in 8:2b. **Rom 8:2b** Some manuscripts read *me.* **Rom 8:3** Greek *our flesh;* similarly in 8:4, 5, 6, 7, 8, 9, 12.

Rom 7:15 Paul shares three lessons that he learned in trying to deal with his sinful desires: (1) Knowledge of the rules is not the answer (Rom 7:9). Paul felt fine as long as he did not understand what the law demanded. When he learned the truth, he knew he was doomed. (2) Self-determination (struggling in one's own strength) doesn't succeed (Rom 7:15). Paul found himself sinning in ways that weren't even attractive to him. (3) Becoming a Christian does not stamp out all sin and temptation from a person's life (Rom 7:22-25).

Being born again takes a moment of faith, but becoming like Christ is a lifelong process. Paul compares Christian growth to a strenuous race or fight (1 Cor 9:24-27; 2 Tim 4:7). Thus, as Paul has been emphasizing since the beginning of this letter, no one in the world is innocent; no one deserves to be saved—not the pagan who doesn't know God's laws, not the person who knows them and tries to keep them. All of us must depend totally on the work of Christ for our salvation. We cannot earn it by our good behavior.

Rom 7:15 This is more than the cry of one desperate man; it describes the experience of all Christians struggling against sin or trying to please God by keeping rules and laws without the Spirit's help. We must never underestimate the power of sin and attempt to fight it in our own strength. Satan is a crafty tempter, and we have an amazing ability to make excuses. Instead of trying to overcome sin with our own human willpower, we must take hold of God's provision for victory over sin: the Holy Spirit, who lives within us and gives us power. And when we fall, he lovingly reaches out to help us up.

Rom 7:23-25 The "power within" is the sin nature deep within us. This is our vulnerability to sin; it refers to everything within us that is more loyal to our old way of selfish living than to God.

Rom 7:23-25 There is great tension in our daily Christian experience. The conflict is that we agree with God's commands but cannot do them. As a result, we are painfully aware of our sin. This inward struggle with sin was as real for Paul as it is for us. From Paul we learn what to do about it. Whenever he felt overwhelmed by the spiritual battle, he would return to the beginnings of his spiritual life, remembering how he had been freed from sin by Jesus Christ. When we feel confused and overwhelmed by sin's appeal, let us claim the freedom Christ gave us. His power can lift us to victory.

Rom 8:1 "Not guilty; let him go free." What would those words mean to you if you were on death row? The fact is that the whole human race is on death row, justly condemned for repeatedly breaking God's holy law. Without Jesus we would have no hope at all. But thank God! He has declared us not guilty and has offered us freedom from sin and power to do his will.

Rom 8:2 This life-giving Spirit is the Holy Spirit. He was present at the creation of the world (Gen 1:2), and he is the power behind the rebirth of every Christian. He gives us the power we need to live the Christian life. (For more about the Holy Spirit, read the notes on John 3:6, p. 1301; Acts 1:3, p. 1512; Acts 1:4-5, p. 1499; Acts 1:5, p. 1499.)

Rom 8:3 Jesus gave himself as a sacrifice for our sins. In Old Testament times, animal sacrifices were continually offered at the Temple. The sacrifices showed the Israelites the seriousness of sin: Blood had to be shed before sins could be pardoned (see Lev 17:11). But the blood of animals could not really remove sins (Heb 10:4). The sacrifices could only point to Jesus' sacrifice, which paid the penalty for all sins.

Rom 8:5-6 Paul divides people into two categories: those who are dominated by their sinful nature, and those who are controlled by the Holy Spirit. All of us would be in the first category if Jesus hadn't offered us a way out. Once we have said yes to Jesus, we will want to continue following him, because his way brings life and peace. Daily we must consciously choose to center our life on God. Use the Bible to discover God's guidelines, and then follow them. In every perplexing situation, ask yourself, "What would Jesus want me to do?" When the Holy Spirit points out what is right, do it eagerly. (For more on our sinful nature versus our new life in Christ, see Rom 6:6-8; Eph 4:22-24; Col 3:3-15.)

by the Holy Spirit think about things that please the
Spirit. [6]So letting your sinful nature control your mind
leads to death. But letting the Spirit control your mind
leads to life and peace. [7]For the sinful nature is always
hostile to God. It never did obey God's laws, and it
never will. [8]That's why those who are still under the
control of their sinful nature can never please God.

[9]But you are not controlled by your sinful nature.
You are controlled by the Spirit if you have the Spirit
of God living in you. (And remember that those who
do not have the Spirit of Christ living in them do not
belong to him at all.) [10]And Christ lives within you,
so even though your body will die because of sin, the
Spirit gives you life* because you have been made
right with God. [11]The Spirit of God, who raised Jesus
from the dead, lives in you. And just as God raised
Christ Jesus from the dead, he will give life to your
mortal bodies by this same Spirit living within you.

[12]Therefore, dear brothers and sisters,* you have no
obligation to do what your sinful nature urges you to
do. [13]For if you live by its dictates, you will die. But if
through the power of the Spirit you put to death the
deeds of your sinful nature,* you will live. [14]For all
who are led by the Spirit of God are children* of God.

[15]So you have not received a spirit that makes you
fearful slaves. Instead, you received God's Spirit when
he adopted you as his own children.* Now we call him,
"Abba, Father."* [16]For his Spirit joins with our spirit
to affirm that we are God's children. [17]And since we
are his children, we are his heirs. In fact, together with
Christ we are heirs of God's glory. But if we are to share
his glory, we must also share his suffering.

The Future Glory

ROMANS 8:18-30

Yet what we suffer now is nothing compared to the
glory he will reveal to us later. [19]For all creation is
waiting eagerly for that future day when God will reveal who his children really are. [20]Against its will, all
creation was subjected to God's curse. But with eager
hope, [21]the creation looks forward to the day when
it will join God's children in glorious freedom from
death and decay. [22]For we know that all creation has
been groaning as in the pains of childbirth right up
to the present time. [23]And we believers also groan,
even though we have the Holy Spirit within us as a
foretaste of future glory, for we long for our bodies to
be released from sin and suffering. We, too, wait with
eager hope for the day when God will give us our full
rights as his adopted children,* including the new

Rom 8:10 Or *your spirit is alive.* **Rom 8:12** Greek *brothers;* also in 8:29. **Rom 8:13** Greek *deeds of the body.* **Rom 8:14** Greek *sons;* also in 8:19. **Rom 8:15a** Greek *you received a spirit of sonship.* **Rom 8:15b** *Abba* is an Aramaic term for "father." **Rom 8:23** Greek *wait anxiously for sonship.*

Rom 8:9 Have you ever worried about whether or not you really are a Christian? A Christian is anyone who has the Spirit of God living within. If you have sincerely trusted Christ for your salvation and acknowledged him as Lord, then the Holy Spirit lives inside you and you are a Christian. You can be assured that you have the Holy Spirit because Jesus promised that he would send him. Since you now believe that Jesus Christ is God's Son and that eternal life comes through him (1 Jn 5:5), you will begin to act as Christ directs (Rom 8:5; Gal 5:22-23); you will find help in your daily problems and in your praying (Rom 8:26-27); you will be empowered to serve God and do his will (Acts 1:8; Rom 12:6ff); and you will become part of God's plan to build up his church (Eph 4:12-13).

Rom 8:11 The Holy Spirit is God's promise or guarantee of eternal life for those who believe in him. The Spirit is within us now by faith, and by faith we are certain to live with Christ forever. (See Rom 8:23; 1 Cor 6:14; 2 Cor 4:14; 1 Thes 4:14.)

Rom 8:13 When we turn away from sin's appeal in the Holy Spirit's power, regarding sin as dead, we can ignore temptation when it comes (see Rom 6:11; Gal 5:24).

Rom 8:14-17 Paul uses adoption to illustrate the believer's new relationship with God. In Roman culture, the adopted person lost all rights in their old family and gained all the rights of a legitimate child in the new family, becoming a full heir. Likewise, when a person becomes a Christian, they gain all the privileges and responsibilities of a child in God's family. One of these outstanding privileges is being led by the Spirit (see Gal 4:5-6). We may not always feel as though we belong to God, but the Holy Spirit is our witness. His inward presence reminds us of who we are and encourages us with God's love (Rom 5:5).

Rom 8:14-17 We are no longer like "fearful slaves"; instead, we are the Master's children. What a privilege! Because we are God's children, we share in great treasures as co-heirs. God has already given us his best gifts: his Son, his Holy Spirit, forgiveness, and eternal life; and he encourages us to ask him for whatever we need.

Rom 8:17 There is a price for being identified with Jesus. Along with being "heirs of God's glory," Paul also mentions the suffering that Christians must face. What kinds of suffering are we to endure? For first-century believers, there was economic and social persecution, and some even faced death. We, too, must pay a price for following Jesus. In many parts of today's world, Christians face pressures just as severe as those faced by Christ's first followers. Even in countries where Christianity is tolerated or encouraged, Christians must not become complacent. To live as Jesus did—serving others, giving up one's rights, resisting pressures to conform to the world—always exacts a price. But nothing we suffer can compare to the great price that Jesus paid to save us.

Rom 8:19-22 Sin has caused all creation to fall from the perfect state in which God created it. The world is in bondage to death and decay so that it cannot fulfill its intended purpose. One day all creation will be liberated and transformed. Until that time it waits in eager expectation for the resurrection of God's children.

Rom 8:19-22 Christians see the world as it is—physically decaying and spiritually infected with sin. But Christians do not need to be pessimistic because they have hope for future glory. They look forward to the new heaven and new earth that God has promised, and they wait for God's new order that will free the world from sin, sickness, and evil. In the meantime, Christians go with Christ into the world where they heal people's bodies and souls and fight the evil effects of sin in the world.

Rom 8:23 We will be resurrected with glorified bodies like the body Christ now has in heaven (see 1 Cor 15:25-58). We have the "foretaste," the first installment or down payment of future glory—the Holy Spirit—as a guarantee of our resurrection life (see 2 Cor 1:22; 5:5; Eph 1:14).

▸ **ROMANS 8:18-30** ***(cont.)***

bodies he has promised us. [24]We were given this hope when we were saved. (If we already have something, we don't need to hope* for it. [25]But if we look forward to something we don't yet have, we must wait patiently and confidently.)

[26]And the Holy Spirit helps us in our weakness. For example, we don't know what God wants us to pray for. But the Holy Spirit prays for us with groanings that cannot be expressed in words. [27]And the Father who knows all hearts knows what the Spirit is saying, for the Spirit pleads for us believers* in harmony with God's own will. [28]And we know that God causes everything to work together* for the good of those who love God and are called according to his purpose for them. [29]For God knew his people in advance, and he chose them to become like his Son, so that his Son would be the firstborn* among many brothers and sisters. [30]And having chosen them, he called them to come to him. And having called them, he gave them right standing with himself. And having given them right standing, he gave them his glory.

Nothing Can Separate Us from God's Love

ROMANS 8:31-39

What shall we say about such wonderful things as these? If God is for us, who can ever be against us? [32]Since he did not spare even his own Son but gave

Rom 8:24 Some manuscripts read *wait.* **Rom 8:27** Greek *for God's holy people.* **Rom 8:28** Some manuscripts read *And we know that everything works together.* **Rom 8:29** Or *would be supreme.*

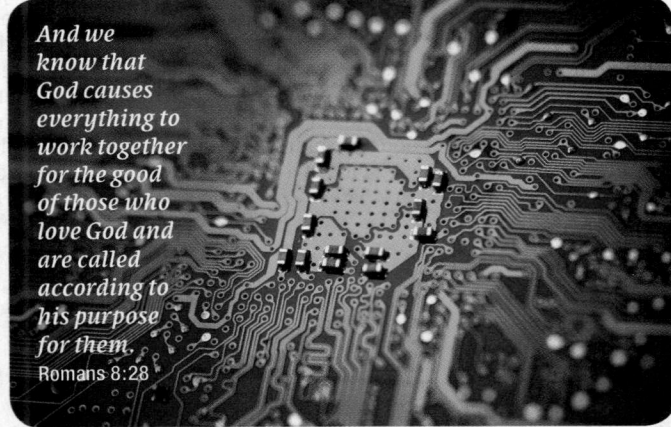

And we know that God causes everything to work together for the good of those who love God and are called according to his purpose for them.
Romans 8:28

Rom 8:24-25 It is natural for children to trust their parents, even though parents sometimes fail to keep their promises. Our heavenly Father never makes promises he won't keep. Nevertheless his plan may take more time than we expect. What are we waiting for? New bodies, a new heaven and new earth, rest and rewards, our eternal family and home, the absence of sin and suffering, and being face to face with Jesus! Rather than acting like impatient children as we wait for God's will to unfold, we need to have confidence in God's perfect timing and wisdom.

Rom 8:24-25 In Romans, Paul presents the idea that salvation is past, present, and future. It is past because we *were* saved the moment we believed in Jesus Christ as Savior (Rom 3:21-26; 5:1-11; 6:1-11, 22-23); our new life (eternal life) begins at that moment. And it is present because we *are being* saved; this is the process of sanctification (see the note on Rom 6:1–8:39, p. 1655). But at the same time, we have not fully received all the benefits and blessings of salvation that *will be* ours when Christ's new Kingdom is completely established. That's our future salvation. While we can be confident of our salvation, we still look ahead with hope and trust toward that complete change of body and personality that lies beyond this life, when we will be like Christ (1 Jn 3:2).

Rom 8:26-27 As a believer, you are not left to your own resources to cope with problems. Even when you don't know the right words to pray, the Holy Spirit prays with and for you, and God answers. With God helping you pray, you don't need to be afraid to come before him. Ask the Holy Spirit to intercede for you "in harmony with God's own will." Then, when you bring your requests to God, trust that he will always do what is best.

Rom 8:28 God works in "everything"—not just isolated incidents—for our good. This does not mean that all that happens to us is good. Evil is prevalent in our fallen world, but God is able to turn every circumstance around for our long-range good. Note that God is not working to make us happy but to fulfill his purpose. Note also that this promise is not for everybody. It can be claimed only by those who love God and are called by him, that is, those whom the Holy Spirit convinces to receive Christ. Such people have a new perspective, a new mind-set. They trust in God, not in worldly treasures; their security is in heaven, not on earth. Their faith in God does not waver in pain and persecution because they know God is with them.

Rom 8:29 God's ultimate goal for us is to make us like Christ (1 Jn 3:2). As we become more and more like him, we discover our true selves, the persons we were created to be. How can we become like Christ? By reading and heeding the Word, by studying his life on earth through the Gospels, by spending time in prayer, by being filled with his Spirit, and by doing his work in the world.

Rom 8:29-30 Some believe these verses mean that before the beginning of the world, God chose certain people to receive his gift of salvation. They point to verses such as Ephesians 1:11, which says that God "chose us in advance, and he makes everything work out according to his plan." Others believe that God knew in advance who would respond to him, and upon those he set his mark (he chose them). What is clear is that God's purpose for people was not an afterthought; it was settled before the foundation of the world. People are to serve and honor God. If you believe in Christ, you can rejoice in the fact that God has always known you would be his child. God's love is eternal. His wisdom and power are supreme. He will guide and protect you until you one day stand in his presence.

Rom 8:30 *Called* means "to be summoned or invited." For more on "right standing" (also called justification) and receiving his glory, see the chart on p. 1653.

Rom 8:31-34 Do you ever think that because you aren't good enough for God, he will not save you? Do you ever feel as if salvation is for everyone else but you? Then these verses are especially for you. If God gave his Son for you, he isn't going to hold back the gift of salvation! If Christ gave his life for you, he isn't going to turn around and condemn you! He will not withhold anything you need to live for him. The book of Romans is more than a theological explanation of God's redeeming grace—it is a letter of comfort and confidence addressed to you.

him up for us all, won't he also give us everything else? [33]Who dares accuse us whom God has chosen for his own? No one—for God himself has given us right standing with himself. [34]Who then will condemn us? No one—for Christ Jesus died for us and was raised to life for us, and he is sitting in the place of honor at God's right hand, pleading for us.

[35]Can anything ever separate us from Christ's love? Does it mean he no longer loves us if we have trouble or calamity, or are persecuted, or hungry, or destitute, or in danger, or threatened with death? [36](As the Scriptures say, "For your sake we are killed every day; we are being slaughtered like sheep."*) [37]No, despite all these things, overwhelming victory is ours through Christ, who loved us.

[38]And I am convinced that nothing can ever separate us from God's love. Neither death nor life, neither angels nor demons,* neither our fears for today nor our worries about tomorrow—not even the powers of hell can separate us from God's love. [39]No power in the sky above or in the earth below—indeed, nothing in all creation will ever be able to separate us from the love of God that is revealed in Christ Jesus our Lord.

God's Selection of Israel

ROMANS 9:1-29

With Christ as my witness, I speak with utter truthfulness. My conscience and the Holy Spirit confirm it. [2]My heart is filled with bitter sorrow and unending grief [3]for my people, my Jewish brothers and sisters.* I would be willing to be forever cursed—cut off from Christ!—if that would save them. [4]They are the people of Israel, chosen to be God's adopted children.* God revealed his glory to them. He made covenants with them and gave them his law. He gave them the privilege of worshiping him and receiving his wonderful promises. [5]Abraham, Isaac, and Jacob are their ancestors, and Christ himself was an Israelite as far as his human nature is concerned. And he is God, the one who rules over everything and is worthy of eternal praise! Amen.*

[6]Well then, has God failed to fulfill his promise to Israel? No, for not all who are born into the nation of Israel are truly members of God's people! [7]Being descendants of Abraham doesn't make them truly Abraham's children. For the Scriptures say, "Isaac is the son through whom your descendants will be counted,"* though Abraham had other children, too. [8]This means that Abraham's physical descendants are not necessarily children of God. Only the children of the promise are considered to be Abraham's children. [9]For God had promised, "I will return about this time next year, and Sarah will have a son."*

[10]This son was our ancestor Isaac. When he married Rebekah, she gave birth to twins.* [11]But before they were born, before they had done anything good or bad, she received a message from God. (This message shows that God chooses people according to his own purposes; [12]he calls people, but not according to their good or bad works.) She was told, "Your older son will serve your younger son."* [13]In the words of the Scriptures, "I loved Jacob, but I rejected Esau."*

Rom 8:36 Ps 44:22. **Rom 8:38** Greek *nor rulers.* **Rom 9:3** Greek *my brothers.* **Rom 9:4** Greek *chosen for sonship.* **Rom 9:5** Or *May God, the one who rules over everything, be praised forever. Amen.* **Rom 9:7** Gen 21:12. **Rom 9:9** Gen 18:10, 14. **Rom 9:10** Greek *she conceived children through this one man.* **Rom 9:12** Gen 25:23. **Rom 9:13** Mal 1:2-3.

Rom 8:34 Paul says that Jesus is pleading for us in heaven. God has acquitted us and has removed our sin and guilt, so it is Satan, not God, who accuses us. When he does, Jesus, our advocate, sits at God's right hand to present our case. (For more on the concept of Christ as our advocate, see the notes on Heb 4:14, p. 1766; Heb 4:15, p. 1766.)

Rom 8:35-36 These words were written to a church that would soon undergo terrible persecution. In just a few years, Paul's hypothetical situations would turn into painful realities. This passage reaffirms God's profound love for his people. No matter what happens to us, no matter where we are, we can never be separated from his love. Suffering should not drive us away from God but help us to identify with him and allow his love to heal us.

Rom 8:35-39 These verses contain one of the most comforting promises in all Scripture. Believers have always had to face hardships in many forms: persecution, illness, imprisonment, and even death. These sometimes cause them to fear that Christ has abandoned them. But Paul exclaims that it is impossible to be separated from Christ. His death for us is proof of his unconquerable love. Nothing can separate us from Christ's presence. God tells us how great his love is so that we will feel totally secure in him. If we believe these overwhelming assurances, we will not be afraid.

Rom 8:38 *Powers* are unseen forces of evil in the universe, forces like Satan and his fallen angels (see Eph 6:12). In Christ we are superconquerors, and his love will protect us from any such forces.

Rom 9:1-3 Paul expressed concern for his Jewish brothers and sisters by saying that he would willingly take their punishment if that would save them. While the only one who can save us is Christ, Paul showed a rare depth of love. Like Jesus, he was willing to sacrifice so others would be saved. How concerned are you for those who don't know Christ? Are you willing to sacrifice your time, money, energy, comfort, and safety to see them come to faith in Jesus?

Rom 9:4 The Jews viewed God's choosing of Israel in the Old Testament as being like adoption. They were undeserving and without rights as natural children. Yet God adopted them and granted them the status of his sons and daughters.

Rom 9:6 God's word in the form of beautiful covenant promises came to Abraham. Covenant people, the true children of Abraham, are not just his biological descendants. They are all those who trust in God and in what Jesus Christ has done for them (see also Rom 2:29; Gal 3:7).

Rom 9:11 The Jews were proud of the fact that their lineage came from Isaac, whose mother was Sarah (Abraham's legitimate wife), rather than Ishmael, whose mother was Hagar (Sarah's servant). But Paul asserts that no one can claim to be chosen by God because of heritage or good deeds. God freely chooses to save whomever he wills. The doctrine of election teaches that it is God's sovereign choice to save us by his goodness and mercy, not by our own merit.

Rom 9:12-14 Was it right for God to choose Jacob, the younger, to be over Esau? God chose Jacob to continue the family line of the faithful because he knew his heart was for God. But he did not exclude Esau from knowing and loving him. Keep in mind the kind of God we worship: He is sovereign; he is not arbitrary; in all things he works for our good; he is trustworthy; he will save all who believe in him. When we understand these qualities of God, we know that his choices are good even if we don't understand all his reasons.

▶ **ROMANS 9:1-29** ***(cont.)***

14 Are we saying, then, that God was unfair? Of
course not! 15 For God said to Moses,

"I will show mercy to anyone I choose,
and I will show compassion to anyone
I choose."*

16 So it is God who decides to show mercy. We can neither choose it nor work for it.

17 For the Scriptures say that God told Pharaoh, "I
have appointed you for the very purpose of displaying my power in you and to spread my fame throughout
the earth."* 18 So you see, God chooses to show mercy
to some, and he chooses to harden the hearts of others so they refuse to listen.

19 Well then, you might say, "Why does God blame people for not responding? Haven't they simply done what he makes them do?"

20 No, don't say that. Who are you, a mere human being, to argue with God? Should the thing that was created say to the one who created it, "Why have you
made me like this?" 21 When a potter makes jars out of clay, doesn't he have a right to use the same lump of clay to make one jar for decoration and another to
throw garbage into? 22 In the same way, even though God has the right to show his anger and his power, he is very patient with those on whom his anger falls, who
are destined for destruction. 23 He does this to make the riches of his glory shine even brighter on those to whom he shows mercy, who were prepared in advance
for glory. 24 And we are among those whom he selected, both from the Jews and from the Gentiles.

25 Concerning the Gentiles, God says in the prophecy of Hosea,

"Those who were not my people,
I will now call my people.
And I will love those
whom I did not love before."*

26 And,

"Then, at the place where they were told,
'You are not my people,'
there they will be called
'children of the living God.'"*

27 And concerning Israel, Isaiah the prophet cried out,

"Though the people of Israel are as numerous
as the sand of the seashore,
only a remnant will be saved.
28 For the LORD will carry out his sentence upon
the earth
quickly and with finality."*

29 And Isaiah said the same thing in another place:

"If the LORD of Heaven's Armies
had not spared a few of our children,
we would have been wiped out like Sodom,
destroyed like Gomorrah."*

Israel's Unbelief

ROMANS 9:30–10:4

What does all this mean? Even though the Gentiles were not trying to follow God's standards, they were made right with God. And it was by faith that this
took place. 31 But the people of Israel, who tried so hard to get right with God by keeping the law, never
succeeded. 32 Why not? Because they were trying to get right with God by keeping the law* instead of by

Rom 9:15 Exod 33:19. **Rom 9:17** Exod 9:16 (Greek version). **Rom 9:25** Hos 2:23. **Rom 9:26** Greek *sons of the living God.* Hos 1:10. **Rom 9:27-28** Isa 10:22-23 (Greek version). **Rom 9:29** Isa 1:9. **Rom 9:32** Greek *by works.*

Rom 9:16 The fallacy of gaining salvation by human effort remains as strong as ever—people still think good intentions are the key to unlock the door to eternal life. By the time they get to try the lock, they will find that their key does not fit. Others imagine that their efforts are building an invisible ladder to heaven made up of service, family, position, reputation, good work, and desire, although none of these rungs will support a feather. People are so busy trying to reach God that they completely miss the truth that God has already reached down to them. We cannot earn God's mercy—if we could, it would not be mercy.

Rom 9:17-18 Paul quotes from Exodus 9:16, where God foretold how Pharaoh would be used to declare God's power. Paul uses this argument to show that salvation is God's work, not people's. God's judgment on Pharaoh's choice to resist God was to confirm that sin and harden his heart. The consequences of Pharaoh's rebellion would be his own punishment.

Rom 9:21 With this illustration, Paul is not saying that some of us are worth more than others but that the Creator has control over the created object. The created object, therefore, has no right to demand anything from its Creator—its very existence depends on him. Keeping this perspective removes any temptation to have pride in personal achievement.

Rom 9:25-26 About 700 years before Jesus' birth, Hosea told of God's intention to restore his people. Paul applies Hosea's message to God's intention to bring Gentiles into his family after the Jews rejected his plan. (Rom 9:25 is a quotation from Hos 2:23; Rom 9:26 is from Hos 1:10.)

Rom 9:27-29 Isaiah prophesied that only a small number of God's original people, the Jews, would be saved. Paul saw this happening in every city where he preached. Even though he went to the Jews first, relatively few ever accepted the message. (Rom 9:27-28 are based on Isa 10:22-23; Rom 9:29 is from Isa 1:9.)

Rom 9:31-33 Sometimes we are like these people, trying to get right with God by keeping his laws. We may think that attending church, doing church work, giving offerings, and being nice will be enough. After all, we've played by the rules, haven't we? But Paul's words sting—this approach never succeeds. Paul explains that God's plan is not for those who try to earn his favor by being good; it is for those who realize that they can never be good enough and so must depend on Christ. We can be saved only by putting our faith in what Jesus Christ has done. If we do that, we will never be disappointed.

Rom 9:32 The Jews had a worthy goal—to honor God. But they tried to achieve it the wrong way—by rigid and painstaking obedience to the law. Thus, some of them became more dedicated to the law than to God. They thought that if they kept the law, God would have to accept them as his people. But God cannot be controlled. The Jews did not see that their Scriptures, the Old Testament, taught that salvation

trusting in him. They stumbled over the great rock in their path. 33God warned them of this in the Scriptures when he said,

"I am placing a stone in Jerusalem* that makes
people stumble,
a rock that makes them fall.
But anyone who trusts in him
will never be disgraced."*

10:1 Dear brothers and sisters,* the longing of my heart and my prayer to God is for the people of Israel to be saved. 2I know what enthusiasm they have for God, but it is misdirected zeal. 3For they don't understand God's way of making people right with himself. Refusing to accept God's way, they cling to their own way of getting right with God by trying to keep the law. 4For Christ has already accomplished the purpose for which the law was given.* As a result, all who believe in him are made right with God.

Salvation Is for Everyone

ROMANS 10:5-21

For Moses writes that the law's way of making a person right with God requires obedience to all of its commands.* 6But faith's way of getting right with God says, "Don't say in your heart, 'Who will go up to heaven?' (to bring Christ down to earth). 7And don't say, 'Who will go down to the place of the dead?' (to bring Christ back to life again)." 8In fact, it says,

"The message is very close at hand;
it is on your lips and in your heart."*

And that message is the very message about faith that we preach: 9If you confess with your mouth that

Rom 9:33a Greek *in Zion.* **Rom 9:33b** Isa 8:14; 28:16 (Greek version). **Rom 10:1** Greek *Brothers.* **Rom 10:4** Or *For Christ is the end of the law.* **Rom 10:5** See Lev 18:5. **Rom 10:6-8** Deut 30:12-14.

WARNING SIGNS OF DEVELOPING HARDNESS

Hardening is like a callus or like the tough bone fibers that bridge a fracture. Spiritual hardening begins with self-sufficiency, security in one's self, and self-satisfaction. The real danger is that at some point, repeated resistance to God will yield an actual inability to respond, which the Bible describes as a hardened heart. Insensitivity indicates advanced hardening. Here are some of the warning signs:

Warning Sign	*Reference*
Disobeying—Pharaoh's willful disobedience led to his hardened heart.	**Exod 4:21**
Having wealth and prosperity—Taking God's blessings for granted can cause us to feel as if they were owed to us.	**Deut 8:6-14**
Rebelling and being discontented—Suffering or discomfort can create an attitude that blames God.	**Ps 95:8**
Rejecting a deserved rebuke—Rejecting God's gift makes our necks stiff and our hearts hard.	**Prov 29:1**
Refusing to listen—Refusing to listen leads to a loss of spiritual hearing.	**Zech 7:11-13**
Failing to respond—Listening to God with no intention of obeying produces an inability to obey.	**Matt 13:11-15**

depended on faith, not on human effort (see Gen 15:6).

Rom 9:32 The "great rock" they stumbled over was Jesus. The Jews did not believe in him because he didn't meet their expectations for the Messiah. Some people still stumble over Christ because salvation by faith doesn't make sense to them. They think they must earn their way to God, or perhaps God will simply overlook their sins. Others stumble over Christ because his values are the opposite of the world's. He asks for humility, and many are unwilling to humble themselves before him. He requires obedience, and many refuse to put their wills at his disposal. Have you stumbled over this rock, or have you chosen to build your life on it?

Rom 10:1 What will happen to the Jewish people who believe in God but not in Christ? Since they believe in the same God, won't they be saved? If that were true, Paul would not have worked so hard and sacrificed so much to teach them about Christ. Because Jesus is the most complete revelation of God, we cannot fully know God apart from Christ; and because God appointed Jesus to bring God and people together, we cannot come to God by another way. The Jews, like everyone else, must find salvation through Jesus Christ (John 14:6; Acts 4:12). Like Paul, we should pray that all Jews might be saved and lovingly share the Good News with them.

Rom 10:3-5 Rather than living by faith in God, the Jews established customs and traditions (in addition to God's law) to try to make themselves acceptable in God's sight. But human effort, no matter how sincere, can never substitute for the righteousness God offers us by faith. The only way to earn salvation is to be perfect—and that is impossible. We can only hold out our empty hands and receive salvation as a gift.

Rom 10:4 Christ accomplished the purpose for which the law was given in two ways: He fulfills the purpose and goal of the law (Matt 5:17) in that he perfectly exemplified God's desires on earth. But he is also the termination of the law because in comparison to Christ, the law is powerless to save.

Rom 10:5 In order to be saved by the law, a person would have to live a perfect life, not sinning once. Then why did God give the law since he knew people couldn't keep it? According to Paul, one reason the law was given was to show people how guilty they are (Gal 3:19). The law was a shadow of Christ—that is, the sacrificial system educated the people so that when the true sacrifice came, they would be able to understand his work (Heb 10:1-4). The system of ceremonial laws was to last until the coming of Christ. The law points to our need for a Savior.

Rom 10:6-8 Paul adapts Moses' farewell challenge from Deuteronomy 30:11-14 to apply to Christ. Christ has provided our salvation through his incarnation (God in human form) and resurrection. God's salvation is right in front of us. He will come to us wherever we are. All we need to do is to respond and accept his gift of salvation.

Rom 10:8-12 Have you ever been asked, "How do I become a Christian?" These verses give you the beautiful answer: Salvation is as close as your own lips and heart. People think it must be a complicated process, but it is not. If we believe in our heart and say with our mouth that Christ is the risen Lord, we will be saved.

▸ **ROMANS 10:5-21** ***(cont.)***
Jesus is Lord and believe in your heart that God raised
him from the dead, you will be saved. 10For it is by
believing in your heart that you are made right with
God, and it is by confessing with your mouth that
you are saved. 11As the Scriptures tell us, "Anyone
who trusts in him will never be disgraced."* 12Jew
and Gentile* are the same in this respect. They have
the same Lord, who gives generously to all who call
on him. 13For "Everyone who calls on the name of
the LORD will be saved."*

14But how can they call on him to save them unless
they believe in him? And how can they believe in him
if they have never heard about him? And how can they
hear about him unless someone tells them? 15And how
will anyone go and tell them without being sent? That
is why the Scriptures say, "How beautiful are the feet
of messengers who bring good news!"*

16But not everyone welcomes the Good News, for
Isaiah the prophet said, "LORD, who has believed our
message?"* 17So faith comes from hearing, that is,
hearing the Good News about Christ. 18But I ask, have
the people of Israel actually heard the message? Yes,
they have:

> "The message has gone throughout the earth,
> and the words to all the world."*

19But I ask, did the people of Israel really understand?
Yes, they did, for even in the time of Moses, God said,

> "I will rouse your jealousy through people who
> are not even a nation.
> I will provoke your anger through the foolish
> Gentiles."*

20And later Isaiah spoke boldly for God, saying,

> "I was found by people who were not looking
> for me.
> I showed myself to those who were not asking
> for me."*

21But regarding Israel, God said,

> "All day long I opened my arms to them,
> but they were disobedient and rebellious."*

God's Mercy on Israel

ROMANS 11:1-24
I ask, then, has God rejected his own people, the nation of Israel? Of course not! I myself am an Israelite,
a descendant of Abraham and a member of the tribe
of Benjamin.

2No, God has not rejected his own people, whom he
chose from the very beginning. Do you realize what
the Scriptures say about this? Elijah the prophet complained to God about the people of Israel and said,
3"LORD, they have killed your prophets and torn down
your altars. I am the only one left, and now they are
trying to kill me, too."*

4And do you remember God's reply? He said, "No,
I have 7,000 others who have never bowed down to
Baal!"*

5It is the same today, for a few of the people of
Israel* have remained faithful because of God's
grace—his undeserved kindness in choosing them.
6And since it is through God's kindness, then it is
not by their good works. For in that case, God's grace
would not be what it really is—free and undeserved.
7So this is the situation: Most of the people of Israel

Rom 10:11 Isa 28:16 (Greek version). **Rom 10:12** Greek *and Greek.* **Rom 10:13** Joel 2:32. **Rom 10:15** Isa 52:7. **Rom 10:16** Isa 53:1. **Rom 10:18** Ps 19:4. **Rom 10:19** Deut 32:21. **Rom 10:20** Isa 65:1 (Greek version). **Rom 10:21** Isa 65:2 (Greek version). **Rom 11:3** 1 Kgs 19:10, 14. **Rom 11:4** 1 Kgs 19:18. **Rom 11:5** Greek *for a remnant.*

Rom 10:14 In telling others about Christ, an effective witness must include more than being a good example. Eventually, we will have to explain the content, the *what* and the *how* of the gospel. Modeling the Christian life is important, but we will need to connect the mind of the unbeliever and the message of the gospel. There should never be a debate between those who favor lifestyle evangelism (one's way of living proclaims the gospel) and confrontational evangelism (declaring the message). Both should be used together in promoting the gospel.

Rom 10:15 We must take God's great message of salvation to others so that they can respond to the Good News. How will your loved ones and neighbors hear it unless someone tells them? Is God calling you to take a part in making his message known in your community? Think of one person who needs to hear the Good News, and think of something you can do to help share it. Then take that step as soon as possible.

Rom 10:18-20 Many Jews who looked for the Messiah refused to believe in him when he came. God offered his salvation to the Gentiles ("people who were not looking for me"); thus, many Gentiles who didn't even know about a Messiah found and believed in him. Some religious people are spiritually blind, while those who have never been in a church are sometimes the most responsive to God's message. Because appearances are deceiving, and we can't see into people's hearts, beware of judging beforehand who will respond to the Good News and who will not.

Rom 11:1ff In Romans 11, Paul points out that not all Jews have rejected God's message of salvation. There are still a faithful few (Rom 11:5). Paul himself, after all, was a Jew, and so were Jesus' disciples and nearly all of the early Christian missionaries.

Rom 11:2 Elijah was a great reforming prophet who challenged the northern kingdom of Israel to repent. See his Profile on p. 719 for more information.

Rom 11:2 God chose the Jews ("his own people") to be the people through whom the rest of the world could find salvation. But this did not mean the entire Jewish nation would be saved; only those who were faithful to God were considered true Jews (Rom 11:5). We are saved through faith in Christ, not because we are part of a nation, religion, or family. On whom or on what are you depending for salvation?

Rom 11:6 Do you think it's easier for God to love you when you're good? Do you secretly suspect that God chose you because you deserved it? Do you think some people's behavior is so bad that God couldn't possibly save them? If you ever think this way, you don't entirely understand that salvation is by grace, a free gift. It cannot be earned, in whole or in part; it can only be accepted with thankfulness and praise.

Rom 11:7 "The hearts of the rest were hardened" was God's punishment for their sin. It was a confirmation of their own stubbornness. In judging them, God removed their ability to see and hear and to turn from sin; thus, they would experience the consequences of their rebellion. Resisting God is like saying to him, "Leave me alone!" But because God is always and everywhere present, his answer to

have not found the favor of God they are looking for so earnestly. A few have—the ones God has chosen—but the hearts of the rest were hardened.
[8]As the Scriptures say,

"God has put them into a deep sleep.
To this day he has shut their eyes so they do not see,
and closed their ears so they do not hear."*

[9]Likewise, David said,

"Let their bountiful table become a snare,
a trap that makes them think all is well.
Let their blessings cause them to stumble,
and let them get what they deserve.
[10] Let their eyes go blind so they cannot see,
and let their backs be bent forever."*

[11]Did God's people stumble and fall beyond recovery? Of course not! They were disobedient, so God made salvation available to the Gentiles. But he wanted his own people to become jealous and claim it for themselves.
[12]Now if the Gentiles were enriched because the people of Israel turned down God's offer of salvation, think how much greater a blessing the world will share when they finally accept it.

[13]I am saying all this especially for you Gentiles. God has appointed me as the apostle to the Gentiles. I stress this,
[14]for I want somehow to make the people of Israel jealous of what you Gentiles have, so I might save some of them.
[15]For since their rejection meant that God offered salvation to the rest of the world, their acceptance will be even more wonderful. It will be life for those who were dead!
[16]And since Abraham and the other patriarchs were holy, their descendants will also be holy—just as the entire batch of dough is holy because the portion given as an offering is holy. For if the roots of the tree are holy, the branches will be, too.

[17]But some of these branches from Abraham's tree—some of the people of Israel—have been broken off. And you Gentiles, who were branches from a wild olive tree, have been grafted in. So now you also receive the blessing God has promised Abraham and his children, sharing in the rich nourishment from the root of God's special olive tree.
[18]But you must not brag about being grafted in to replace the branches that were broken off. You are just a branch, not the root.

[19]"Well," you may say, "those branches were broken off to make room for me."
[20]Yes, but remember—those branches were broken off because they didn't believe in Christ, and you are there because you do believe. So don't think highly of yourself, but fear what could happen.
[21]For if God did not spare the original branches, he won't* spare you either.

[22]Notice how God is both kind and severe. He is severe toward those who disobeyed, but kind to you if you continue to trust in his kindness. But if you stop trusting, you also will be cut off.
[23]And if the people of Israel turn from their unbelief, they will be grafted in again, for God has the power to graft them back into the tree.
[24]You, by nature, were a branch cut from a wild olive tree. So if God was willing to do something contrary to nature by grafting you into his cultivated tree, he will be far more eager to graft the original branches back into the tree where they belong.

Rom 11:8 Isa 29:10; Deut 29:4. **Rom 11:9-10** Ps 69:22-23 (Greek version). **Rom 11:21** Some manuscripts read *perhaps he won't.*

that prayer might be to agree and make that person less sensitive, more hardened to him. The very possibility of that happening ought to keep us asking God specifically for ears that really hear and eyes that really see—openness and responsiveness to him.

Rom 11:8-10 These verses describe the punishment for unresponsive hearts predicted by the prophet Isaiah (Isa 6:9-13). If people refuse to hear God's Good News, they eventually will be unable to understand it. Paul saw this happening in the Jewish congregations he visited on his missionary journeys. (Rom 11:8 is based on Deut 29:4; Isa 29:10. Rom 11:9-10 are from Ps 69:22-23.)

Rom 11:11ff Paul had a vision of a church where all Jewish and Gentile believers would be united in their love of God and in obedience to Christ. While respecting God's law, this ideal church would look to Christ alone for salvation. A person's ethnic background and social status would be irrelevant (see Gal 3:28). What mattered would be their faith in Christ.

But Paul's vision has not yet been realized. For the most part, Jewish people have rejected the Good News. They have depended on their heritage for salvation, and they do not have the heart of obedience that was so important to the Old Testament prophets and to Paul. Once Gentiles became dominant in many of the Christian churches, they began rejecting Jews and even persecuting them. Unfortunately, this practice has recurred through the centuries.

True Christians should not persecute others. Both Gentiles and Jews have done so much to damage the cause of Christ, whom they claim to serve, that Paul's vision often seems impossible to fulfill. Yet God chose the Jews, just as he chose the Gentiles, and he is still working to unite all believers so they become a holy temple where God lives by his Spirit (see Eph 2:11-22).

Rom 11:13-15 Paul was appointed as an apostle to the Gentiles. He reminded his Jewish brothers and sisters of this fact, hoping that they, too, would want to be saved. The Jews rejected God's offer, and, thus, Gentiles were being offered salvation. But when a Jew comes to Christ, there is great rejoicing, as if a dead person has come back to life.

Rom 11:16-24 Speaking to Gentile Christians, Paul warns them not to feel superior because some Jews were rejected. Abraham's faith is like the root of a productive tree, and the Jewish people are the tree's natural branches. Because of faithlessness, some of the Jews have been broken off, and Gentile believers, who were branches from a wild olive tree, have been grafted in. Both Jews and Gentiles share the tree's nourishment based on faith in God; neither can rest on heritage or culture for salvation.

Rom 11:22 "Continue to trust in his kindness" refers to steadfast perseverance in faith. Steadfastness is a proof of the reality of faith and a by-product of salvation, not a means to it.

God's Mercy Is for Everyone

ROMANS 11:25-36

I want you to understand this mystery, dear brothers and sisters,* so that you will not feel proud about yourselves. Some of the people of Israel have hard hearts, but this will last only until the full number of Gentiles comes to Christ. [26]And so all Israel will be saved. As the Scriptures say,

"The one who rescues will come from Jerusalem,*
and he will turn Israel* away from
ungodliness.
[27] And this is my covenant with them,
that I will take away their sins."*

[28]Many of the people of Israel are now enemies of the Good News, and this benefits you Gentiles. Yet they are still the people he loves because he chose their ancestors Abraham, Isaac, and Jacob. [29]For God's gifts and his call can never be withdrawn. [30]Once, you Gentiles were rebels against God, but when the people of Israel rebelled against him, God was merciful to you instead. [31]Now they are the rebels, and God's mercy has come to you so that they, too, will share* in God's mercy. [32]For God has imprisoned everyone in disobedience so he could have mercy on everyone.

[33]Oh, how great are God's riches and wisdom and knowledge! How impossible it is for us to understand his decisions and his ways!

[34] For who can know the LORD's thoughts?
Who knows enough to give him advice?*
[35] And who has given him so much
that he needs to pay it back?*

[36]For everything comes from him and exists by his power and is intended for his glory. All glory to him forever! Amen.

Rom 11:25 Greek *brothers.* **Rom 11:26a** Greek *from Zion.* **Rom 11:26b** Greek *Jacob.* **Rom 11:26-27** Isa 59:20-21; 27:9 (Greek version). **Rom 11:31** Other manuscripts read *will now share;* still others read *will someday share.* **Rom 11:34** Isa 40:13 (Greek version). **Rom 11:35** See Job 41:11.

2. HOW TO BEHAVE

Moving from the theological to the practical, Paul gives guidelines for living as a redeemed people in a fallen world. We are to give ourselves to Christ as living sacrifices, obey the government, love our neighbors, and take special care of those who are weak in the faith. He closes with personal remarks. Throughout this section, we learn how to live our faith each day.

A Living Sacrifice to God

ROMANS 12:1-21

And so, dear brothers and sisters,* I plead with you to give your bodies to God because of all he has done for you. Let them be a living and holy sacrifice—the kind he will find acceptable. This is truly the way to worship him.* [2]Don't copy the behavior and customs of this world, but let God transform you into a new

Rom 12:1a Greek *brothers.* **Rom 12:1b** Or *This is your spiritual worship;* or *This is your reasonable service.*

Rom 11:26 Some say the phrase "and so all Israel will be saved" means that the majority of Jews in the final generation before Christ's return will turn to Christ for salvation. Others say that Paul is using the term *Israel* to refer to the "spiritual" nation of Israel, which is comprised of Jews and Gentiles who have received salvation through faith in Christ. Thus, "all Israel" (or all believers) will receive God's promised gift of salvation. Still others say that "all Israel" means Israel as a whole will have a role in Christ's Kingdom. The Jews' identity as a people won't be discarded. God chose the nation of Israel, and he has never rejected it. He also chose the church, through Jesus Christ, and he will never reject it, either. This does not mean, of course, that all Jews or all church members will be saved. It is possible to be Jewish or to belong to a church without ever responding in faith. But just because some people have rejected Christ does not mean that God stops working with either Israel or the church. He continues to offer salvation freely to all. Still others say that the phrase "and so" means "in this way" or "this is how," referring to the necessity of faith in Christ.

Rom 11:28-32 In this passage Paul shows how the Jews and the Gentiles benefit each other. Whenever God shows mercy to one group, the other shares the blessing. In God's original plan, the Jews would be the source of God's blessing to the Gentiles (see Gen 12:3). When the Jews neglected this mission, God blessed the Gentiles anyway through the Jewish Messiah. He still maintained his love for the Jews because of his promises to Abraham, Isaac, and Jacob. The privileges and invitation of God given to Israel will never be withdrawn. But someday all faithful Jews will share in God's mercy. God's plans will not be thwarted: He will "have mercy on everyone." (For a beautiful picture of Jews and Gentiles experiencing rich blessings, see Isa 60.)

Rom 11:34-36 The implication of these questions is that no one has fully understood the mind of the Lord. No one has been his counselor. And God owes nothing to any one of us. Isaiah and Jeremiah asked similar questions to show that we are unable to give advice to God or criticize his ways (Isa 40:13; Jer 23:18). God alone is the possessor of absolute power and absolute wisdom. In the final analysis, all of us are absolutely dependent on God. He is the source of all things, including ourselves. He is the power that sustains and rules the world that we live in. And God works out all things to bring glory to himself. The all-powerful God deserves our praise.

Rom 12:1 When sacrificing an animal according to God's law, a priest would kill the animal, cut it in pieces, and place it on the altar. Sacrifice was important, but even in the Old Testament God made it clear that obedience from the heart was much more important (see 1 Sam 15:22; Ps 40:6; Amos 5:21-24). God wants us to offer ourselves, not animals, as living sacrifices—daily laying aside our own desires to follow him, putting all our energy and resources at his disposal and trusting him to guide us. We do this out of gratitude that our sins have been forgiven.

Rom 12:1-2 God has good, pleasing, and perfect plans for his children. He wants us to be transformed people with renewed minds, living to honor and obey him. Because he wants only what is best for us, and because he gave his Son to make our new life possible, we should joyfully give ourselves as living sacrifices for his service.

Rom 12:2 Paul warned Christians: "Don't copy the behavior and customs of this world." Wise Christians decide that much worldly behavior is off-limits for them because it is usually selfish and often corrupting. Our refusal to conform to this world's values must go even deeper than just behavior and customs; it must be firmly planted in our mind:

person by changing the way you think. Then you will learn to know God's will for you, which is good and pleasing and perfect.

[3]Because of the privilege and authority* God has given me, I give each of you this warning: Don't think you are better than you really are. Be honest in your evaluation of yourselves, measuring yourselves by the faith God has given us.* [4]Just as our bodies have many parts and each part has a special function, [5]so it is with Christ's body. We are many parts of one body, and we all belong to each other.

[6]In his grace, God has given us different gifts for doing certain things well. So if God has given you the ability to prophesy, speak out with as much faith as God has given you. [7]If your gift is serving others, serve them well. If you are a teacher, teach well. [8]If your gift is to encourage others, be encouraging. If it is giving, give generously. If God has given you leadership ability, take the responsibility seriously. And if you have a gift for showing kindness to others, do it gladly.

[9]Don't just pretend to love others. Really love them. Hate what is wrong. Hold tightly to what is good. [10]Love each other with genuine affection,* and take delight in honoring each other. [11]Never be lazy, but work hard and serve the Lord enthusiastically.* [12]Rejoice in our confident hope. Be patient in trouble, and keep on praying. [13]When God's people are in need, be ready to help them. Always be eager to practice hospitality.

Rom 12:3a Or *Because of the grace;* compare 1:5. **Rom 12:3b** Or *by the faith God has given you;* or *by the standard of our God-given faith.* **Rom 12:10** Greek *with brotherly love.* **Rom 12:11** Or *but serve the Lord with a zealous spirit;* or *but let the Spirit excite you as you serve the Lord.*

"Let God transform you into a new person by changing the way you think." It is possible to avoid most worldly customs and still be proud, covetous, selfish, stubborn, and arrogant. Only when the Holy Spirit renews, reeducates, and redirects our mind are we truly transformed (see Rom 8:5).

Rom 12:3 Healthy self-esteem is important because some of us think too little of ourselves; on the other hand, some of us overestimate ourselves. The key to an honest and accurate self-evaluation is knowing the basis of our self-worth—our identity in Christ. Apart from him, we aren't capable of very much by eternal standards; in him, we are valuable and capable of worthy service. Evaluating yourself by the worldly standards of success and achievement can cause you to think too much about your worth in the eyes of others and thus miss your true value in God's eyes.

Rom 12:4-5 Paul uses the concept of the human body to teach how Christians should live and work together. Just as the parts of the body function under the direction of the brain, so Christians are to work together under the command and authority of Jesus Christ (see 1 Cor 12:12-31; Eph 4:1-16).

Rom 12:6 God gives us gifts so we can build up his church. To use them effectively, we must (1) realize that all gifts and abilities come from God; (2) understand that not everyone has the same gifts; (3) know who we are and what we do best; (4) dedicate our gifts to God's service and not to our personal success; (5) be willing to utilize our gifts wholeheartedly, not holding back anything from God's service. God's gifts differ in nature, power, and effectiveness according to his wisdom and graciousness, not according to our faith. Our role is to be faithful and to seek ways to serve others with what Christ has given us.

Rom 12:6 Prophesying in Scripture is not always predicting the future. Often it means preaching God's messages (1 Cor 14:1-3).

Rom 12:6-8 Look at this list of gifts and imagine the kinds of people who would have each gift. Prophets are often bold and articulate. Servers (those in ministry) are faithful and loyal. Teachers are clear thinkers. Encouragers know how to motivate others. Givers are generous and trusting. Leaders are good organizers and managers. Those who show kindness are caring people who are happy to give their time to others. It would be difficult for one person to embody all these gifts. An assertive prophet would not usually make a good counselor, and a generous giver might fail as a leader. When you identify your own gifts (and this list is far from complete), ask how you can use them to build up God's family. At the same time, realize that your gifts can't do the work of the church all alone. Be thankful for people whose gifts are completely different from yours. Let your strengths balance their weaknesses, and be grateful that their abilities make up for your deficiencies. Together you can build Christ's church.

Rom 12:9-10 Most of us have learned how to be courteous to others—how to speak kindly, avoid hurting their feelings, and appear to take an interest in them. We may even be skilled in pretending to show compassion when we hear of others' needs, or to become indignant when we learn of injustice. But God calls us to real and genuine love that goes far beyond being hypocritical and polite. Genuine love requires concentration and effort. It means helping others become better people. It demands our time, money, and personal involvement. No individual has the capacity to express love to a whole community, but the body of Christ in your town does. Look for people who need your love, and look for ways you and your fellow believers can love your community for Christ.

Rom 12:10 We can honor others in one of two ways. One involves ulterior motives. We honor our bosses so they will reward us, our employees so they will work harder, the wealthy so they will contribute to our cause, the powerful so they will use their power for us and not against us. God's way involves love. As Christians, we honor people because they have been created in God's image, because they are our brothers and sisters in Christ, and because they have a unique contribution to make to Christ's church. Does God's way of honoring others sound too difficult for your competitive nature? Why not try to outdo one another in showing honor? Put others first!

Don't copy the behavior and customs of this world, but let God transform you into a new person by changing the way you think.
Romans 12:2

Rom 12:13 Christian hospitality differs from social entertaining. Entertaining focuses on the host: The home must be spotless; the food must be well prepared and abundant; the host must appear relaxed and good-natured. Hospitality, by contrast, focuses on the guests' needs, such as a place to stay, nourishing food, a listening ear, or just acceptance. Hospitality can happen in a messy home. It can happen around a dinner table where the main dish is canned soup. It can even happen while the host and the guest are doing chores together. Don't hesitate to offer hospitality just because you are too tired, too busy, or not wealthy enough to entertain.

▸ **ROMANS 12:1-21** ***(cont.)***

[14]Bless those who persecute you. Don't curse them;
pray that God will bless them. [15]Be happy with those
who are happy, and weep with those who weep. [16]Live
in harmony with each other. Don't be too proud to
enjoy the company of ordinary people. And don't think
you know it all!
[17]Never pay back evil with more evil. Do things in
such a way that everyone can see you are honorable.
[18]Do all that you can to live in peace with everyone.
[19]Dear friends, never take revenge. Leave that to the
righteous anger of God. For the Scriptures say,

"I will take revenge;
I will pay them back,"*
says the LORD.

[20]Instead,

"If your enemies are hungry, feed them.
If they are thirsty, give them something
to drink.
In doing this, you will heap
burning coals of shame on their heads."*

[21]Don't let evil conquer you, but conquer evil by doing good.

Rom 12:19 Deut 32:35. **Rom 12:20** Prov 25:21-22.

Respect for Authority

ROMANS 13:1-7

Everyone must submit to governing authorities. For
all authority comes from God, and those in positions
of authority have been placed there by God. [2]So anyone who rebels against authority is rebelling against
what God has instituted, and they will be punished.
[3]For the authorities do not strike fear in people who
are doing right, but in those who are doing wrong.
Would you like to live without fear of the authorities? Do what is right, and they will honor you. [4]The
authorities are God's servants, sent for your good.
But if you are doing wrong, of course you should be
afraid, for they have the power to punish you. They
are God's servants, sent for the very purpose of punishing those who do what is wrong. [5]So you must submit to them, not only to avoid punishment, but also
to keep a clear conscience.
[6]Pay your taxes, too, for these same reasons. For
government workers need to be paid. They are serving
God in what they do. [7]Give to everyone what you owe
them: Pay your taxes and government fees to those
who collect them, and give respect and honor to those
who are in authority.

Rom 12:16 Many people use their contacts and relationships for selfish ambition. They select those people who will help them climb the social ladder. Christ demonstrated and taught that we should treat all people with respect—those of a different race, the handicapped, the poor, young and old, male and female. We must never consider others as being beneath us. Paul says we need to live in harmony with others and not be too proud to enjoy the company of ordinary people. Are you able to do humble tasks with others? Do you welcome conversation with unattractive, non-prestigious people? Are you willing to befriend newcomers and entry-level people? Or do you relate only to those who will help you get ahead?

Rom 12:17-21 These verses summarize the core of Christian living. If we love someone the way Christ loves us, we will be willing to forgive. If we have experienced God's grace, we will want to pass it on to others. And remember, grace is undeserved favor. By giving an enemy a drink, we're not excusing misdeeds; we're recognizing, forgiving, and loving that person in spite of their sins against us—just as Christ did for us.

Rom 12:19-21 In this day of lawsuits and incessant demands for legal rights, Paul's command sounds almost impossible. When people hurt you deeply, instead of giving them what they deserve, Paul says to befriend them. Why does Paul tell us to forgive our enemies? (1) Forgiveness may break a cycle of retaliation and lead to mutual reconciliation. (2) It may make the enemy feel ashamed, causing a change in that person's ways. (3) By contrast, repaying evil for evil hurts you just as much as it hurts your enemy. Even if your enemy never repents, forgiving that person will free you of a heavy load of bitterness.

Rom 12:19-21 Forgiveness involves both attitudes and actions. If you find it difficult to feel forgiving toward someone who has hurt you, try responding with kind actions. If appropriate, tell this person that you would like to heal your relationship. Lend a helping hand, send a gift, or smile. Many times you will discover that right actions lead to right feelings.

Rom 13:1 Are there times when we should not obey the government? We should never allow government to force us to disobey God. Jesus and his apostles never disobeyed the government for personal reasons; when they disobeyed, it was in order to follow God's moral standards. Their disobedience was not cheap: They were threatened, beaten, thrown into jail, tortured, or executed for their convictions. Like them, if we are compelled to disobey, we must be ready to accept the consequences.

Rom 13:1ff Christians understand Romans 13 in different ways. All Christians agree that we are to live at peace with the state as long as the state allows us to live by our religious convictions. For hundreds of years, there have been at least three interpretations of how we are to do this:

(1) Some Christians believe that the state is so corrupt that Christians should have as little to do with it as possible. Although they should be good citizens as long as they can do so without compromising their beliefs, they should not work for the government, vote in elections, or serve in the military.

(2) Others believe that God has given the state authority in certain areas and the church authority in others. Christians can be loyal to both and can work for either. They should not confuse the two. In this view, church and state are concerned with two totally different spheres—the spiritual and the physical—and thus complement each other but do not work together.

(3) Still others believe that Christians have a responsibility to make the state better. They can do this politically, by electing Christian or other high-principled leaders. They can also do this morally, by serving as an influence for good in society. In this view, church and state ideally work together for the good of all.

None of these views advocate rebelling against or refusing to obey the government's laws or regulations unless those laws clearly require you to violate the moral standards revealed by God. Wherever we find ourselves, we must be responsible citizens, as well as responsible Christians.

Rom 13:3-4 Wittingly or unwittingly, people in authority are God's servants. They are allowed their positions in order to do good. When authorities are unjust, upright people are afraid. When authorities are just, people who are doing right have nothing to fear. This provides our principal motivation to pray for our leaders. Praying for those in authority over us will also mean that we will watch them closely. If we pray diligently for our leaders, we will be functioning as God's sentinels.

Love Fulfills God's Requirements

ROMANS 13:8-14

Owe nothing to anyone—except for your obligation
to love one another. If you love your neighbor, you
will fulfill the requirements of God's law. 9For the
commandments say, "You must not commit adultery. You must not murder. You must not steal. You
must not covet."* These—and other such commandments—are summed up in this one commandment:
"Love your neighbor as yourself."* 10Love does no
wrong to others, so love fulfills the requirements
of God's law.

11This is all the more urgent, for you know how late
it is; time is running out. Wake up, for our salvation is
nearer now than when we first believed. 12The night
is almost gone; the day of salvation will soon be here.
So remove your dark deeds like dirty clothes, and put
on the shining armor of right living. 13Because we belong to the day, we must live decent lives for all to see.
Don't participate in the darkness of wild parties and
drunkenness, or in sexual promiscuity and immoral
living, or in quarreling and jealousy. 14Instead, clothe
yourself with the presence of the Lord Jesus Christ.
And don't let yourself think about ways to indulge
your evil desires.

The Danger of Criticism

ROMANS 14:1-23

Accept other believers who are weak in faith, and don't
argue with them about what they think is right or

Rom 13:9a Exod 20:13-15, 17. **Rom 13:9b** Lev 19:18.

Rom 13:8 Why is love for others called an obligation? We are permanently in debt to Christ for the lavish love he has poured out on us. The only way we can even begin to repay this debt is by fulfilling our obligation to love others in turn. Because Christ's love will always be infinitely greater than ours, we will always have the obligation to love our neighbors.

Rom 13:9 Somehow many of us have gotten the idea that self-love is wrong. But if this were the case, it would be pointless to love our neighbors as ourselves. Paul explains what he means by self-love. Even if you have low self-esteem, you probably don't willingly let yourself go hungry. You take care of your body and may even exercise. You clothe yourself reasonably well. You make sure there's a roof over your head. You try not to let yourself be cheated or injured. This is the kind of love we need to have for our neighbors. Do we see that others are fed, clothed, and housed as well as they can be? Are we concerned about issues of social justice? Loving others as ourselves means actively working to see that their needs are met. Interestingly, people who focus on others rather than on themselves rarely suffer from low self-esteem.

Rom 13:10 Christians must obey the law of love, which supersedes both religious and civil laws. How easy it is to excuse our indifference to others merely because we have no legal obligation to help them and even to justify harming them if our actions are technically legal! But Jesus does not leave loopholes in the law of love. Whenever love demands it, we are to go beyond human legal requirements and imitate the God of love. (See Jas 2:8-9; 4:11; 1 Pet 2:16-17 for more about this law of love.)

Rom 13:12-14 The "night" refers to the present evil time. The "day" refers to the time of Christ's return. Some people are surprised that Paul lists fighting and jealousy with the gross and obvious sins of drunkenness and immorality. Like Jesus in his Sermon on the Mount (Matt 5–7), Paul considers attitudes as important as actions. Just as hatred leads to murder, so jealousy leads to strife, and lust to adultery. When Christ returns, he wants to find his people clean on the inside as well as on the outside.

Rom 13:14 How do we clothe ourselves with the presence of the Lord Jesus Christ? First, we identify with Christ by being baptized (Gal 3:27). This shows our solidarity with other Christians and with the death, burial, and resurrection of Jesus Christ. Second, we exemplify the qualities Jesus showed while he was here on earth (love, humility, truth, service). In a sense, we role-play what Jesus would do in our situation (see Eph 4:24-32; Col 3:10-17). We also must avoid those situations that open the door to gratifying sinful desires.

Rom 14:1 Who is weak in faith and who is strong? We are all weak in some areas and strong in others. Our faith is strong in an area if we can survive contact with worldly people without falling into their patterns. It is weak in an area if we must avoid certain activities, people, or places in order to protect our spiritual life. It is important to take self-inventory in order to find out our strengths and weaknesses. Whenever in doubt, we should ask, Can I do that without sinning? Can I influence others for good, rather than being influenced by them?

In areas of strength, we should not fear being defiled by the world; rather we should go and serve God. In areas of weakness, we need to be cautious. If we have a strong faith but shelter it, we are not doing Christ's work in the world. If we have a weak faith but expose it, we are being extremely foolish.

Rom 14:1 This verse assumes there will be differences of opinion in the church about what is right or wrong. Paul says we are not to quarrel about issues that are matters of opinion. Differences should not be feared or avoided but accepted and handled with love. Don't expect everyone, even in the best possible church, to agree on every subject. Through sharing ideas we can come to a fuller understanding of what the Bible teaches. Accept, listen to, and respect others. Differences of opinion need not cause division. They can be a source of learning and richness in our relationships.

Rom 14:1ff What is weak faith? Paul is speaking about immature faith that has not yet developed the muscle it needs to stand against external pressures. For example, if a person who once worshiped idols became a Christian, he might understand perfectly well that Christ saved him through faith and that idols have no real power. Still, because of his past associations, he might be badly shaken if he discovered that he unknowingly had eaten meat that had been used in idol worship. If a person who once worshiped God on the required Jewish holy days became a Christian, he might well know that Christ saved him through faith, not through his keeping of the law. Still, when the festival days come, he might feel empty and unfaithful if he hasn't dedicated those days to God.

Paul responds to both weak brothers in love. Both are acting according to their consciences, but their honest convictions do not need to be made into rules for the church. Certainly some issues are central to the faith and worth fighting for, but many are based on individual differences and should not be legislated. Our principle should be: In essentials, unity; in nonessentials, liberty; in everything, love.

▶ **ROMANS 14:1-23** ***(cont.)***

wrong. [2]For instance, one person believes it's all right
to eat anything. But another believer with a sensitive
conscience will eat only vegetables. [3]Those who feel
free to eat anything must not look down on those who
don't. And those who don't eat certain foods must not
condemn those who do, for God has accepted them.
[4]Who are you to condemn someone else's servants?
Their own master will judge whether they stand or fall.
And with the Lord's help, they will stand and receive
his approval.

[5]In the same way, some think one day is more holy
than another day, while others think every day is alike.
You should each be fully convinced that whichever
day you choose is acceptable. [6]Those who worship the
Lord on a special day do it to honor him. Those who
eat any kind of food do so to honor the Lord, since
they give thanks to God before eating. And those who
refuse to eat certain foods also want to please the Lord
and give thanks to God. [7]For we don't live for ourselves
or die for ourselves. [8]If we live, it's to honor the Lord.
And if we die, it's to honor the Lord. So whether we
live or die, we belong to the Lord. [9]Christ died and
rose again for this very purpose—to be Lord both of
the living and of the dead.

[10]So why do you condemn another believer*? Why
do you look down on another believer? Remember, we
will all stand before the judgment seat of God. [11]For
the Scriptures say,

"'As surely as I live,' says the LORD,
'every knee will bend to me,
and every tongue will confess and give praise
to God.*'"

[12]Yes, each of us will give a personal account to God.
[13]So let's stop condemning each other. Decide instead
to live in such a way that you will not cause another
believer to stumble and fall.

[14]I know and am convinced on the authority of the
Lord Jesus that no food, in and of itself, is wrong to eat.
But if someone believes it is wrong, then for that person
it is wrong. [15]And if another believer is distressed by
what you eat, you are not acting in love if you eat it. Don't
let your eating ruin someone for whom Christ died.
[16]Then you will not be criticized for doing something
you believe is good. [17]For the Kingdom of God is not
a matter of what we eat or drink, but of living a life of
goodness and peace and joy in the Holy Spirit. [18]If you
serve Christ with this attitude, you will please God, and
others will approve of you, too. [19]So then, let us aim for
harmony in the church and try to build each other up.

[20]Don't tear apart the work of God over what you
eat. Remember, all foods are acceptable, but it is
wrong to eat something if it makes another person
stumble. [21]It is better not to eat meat or drink wine
or do anything else if it might cause another believer
to stumble. [22]You may believe there's nothing wrong
with what you are doing, but keep it between yourself

Rom 14:10 Greek *your brother;* also in 14:10b, 13, 15, 21. **Rom 14:11** Or *confess allegiance to God.* Isa 49:18; 45:23 (Greek version).

Rom 14:2 Eating "anything" may refer to a strong Christian being free from dietary restrictions, or it may refer to his eating meat offered to idols. The person weaker in the faith may eat only vegetables and refuse to eat meat that has been offered to idols. But how would Christians end up eating meat that had been offered to idols? The ancient system of sacrifice was at the center of the religious, social, and domestic life of the Roman world. After a sacrifice was presented to a god in a pagan temple, only part of it was burned. The remainder was often sent to the market to be sold. Thus, a Christian might easily—even unknowingly—buy such meat in the marketplace or eat it at the home of a friend. Should a Christian question the source of his meat? Some thought there was nothing wrong with eating meat that had been offered to idols because idols were worthless. Others carefully checked the source of their meat or gave up meat altogether, in order to avoid a guilty conscience. The problem was especially acute for Christians who had once been idol worshipers. For them, such a strong reminder of their pagan days might weaken their new-found faith. Paul also deals with this problem in 1 Corinthians 8.

Rom 14:10-12 Each person is accountable to Christ, not to others. While the church must be uncompromising in its stand against activities that are expressly forbidden by Scripture (adultery, murder, theft), it should not create additional rules and regulations and give them equal standing with God's law. Many times Christians base their moral judgments on opinion, personal dislikes, or cultural bias rather than on the Word of God. When they do this, they show that their own faith is weak; they do not think that God is powerful enough to guide his children. When we each stand before God and give a personal account of our lives, we won't be worried about what our Christian neighbors have done (see 2 Cor 5:10).

Rom 14:13 Both strong and weak Christians can cause their brothers and sisters to stumble. The strong but insensitive Christian may flaunt that freedom and intentionally offend others' consciences. The scrupulous but weak Christian may try to fence others in with petty rules and regulations, thus causing dissension. Paul wants his readers to be both strong in the faith and sensitive to others' needs. Because we are all strong in some areas and weak in others, we need to constantly monitor the effects of our behavior on other believers.

Rom 14:13ff Some Christians use an invisible weaker brother to support their own opinions, prejudices, or standards. "You must live by these standards," they say, "or you will be offending the weaker brother." In truth, the person would often be offending no one but the speaker. While Paul urges us to be sensitive to those whose faith may be harmed by our actions, we should not sacrifice our liberty in Christ just to satisfy the selfish motives of those who are trying to force their opinions on us. Neither fear them nor criticize them, but follow Christ as closely as you can.

Rom 14:14 At the Jerusalem council (Acts 15), the Jewish church in Jerusalem asked the Gentile church in Antioch not to eat meat that had been sacrificed to idols. Paul was at the Jerusalem council, and he accepted this request, not because he felt that eating such meat was wrong in itself, but because this practice would deeply offend many Jewish believers. Paul did not think the issue was worth dividing the church over; his desire was to promote unity. So he concludes, "If someone believes it is wrong, then for that person it is wrong." Paul's practice was to honor, as far as possible, the convictions of others.

Believers are called to accept one another without judging our varied opinions. However, when the situation has to be faced, how should we deal with those who disagree with us? Paul's response is that all believers should act in love so as to maintain peace in the church.

Rom 14:20-21 Sin is not just a private matter. Everything we do affects others, and we have to think of them constantly. God created us to be interdependent, not independent. We who are strong in our faith must, without

and God. Blessed are those who don't feel guilty for
doing something they have decided is right. 23But if
you have doubts about whether or not you should eat
something, you are sinning if you go ahead and do
it. For you are not following your convictions. If you
do anything you believe is not right, you are sinning.

Living to Please Others

ROMANS 15:1-13

We who are strong must be considerate of those who
are sensitive about things like this. We must not just
please ourselves. 2We should help others do what is
right and build them up in the Lord. 3For even Christ
didn't live to please himself. As the Scriptures say, "The
insults of those who insult you, O God, have fallen on
me."* 4Such things were written in the Scriptures long
ago to teach us. And the Scriptures give us hope and
encouragement as we wait patiently for God's promises
to be fulfilled.
5May God, who gives this patience and encouragement, help you live in complete harmony with
each other, as is fitting for followers of Christ Jesus.
6Then all of you can join together with one voice, giving praise and glory to God, the Father of our Lord
Jesus Christ.
7Therefore, accept each other just as Christ has accepted you so that God will be given glory. 8Remember
that Christ came as a servant to the Jews* to show that
God is true to the promises he made to their ancestors.
9He also came so that the Gentiles might give glory to
God for his mercies to them. That is what the psalmist
meant when he wrote:

"For this, I will praise you among the Gentiles;
I will sing praises to your name."*

10And in another place it is written,

"Rejoice with his people,
you Gentiles."*

11And yet again,

"Praise the LORD, all you Gentiles.
Praise him, all you people of the earth."*

12And in another place Isaiah said,

"The heir to David's throne* will come,
and he will rule over the Gentiles.
They will place their hope on him."*

13I pray that God, the source of hope, will fill you
completely with joy and peace because you trust in
him. Then you will overflow with confident hope
through the power of the Holy Spirit.

Paul's Reason for Writing

ROMANS 15:14-22

I am fully convinced, my dear brothers and sisters,*
that you are full of goodness. You know these things
so well you can teach each other all about them.
15Even so, I have been bold enough to write about
some of these points, knowing that all you need is this
reminder. For by God's grace, 16I am a special messenger from Christ Jesus to you Gentiles. I bring you the
Good News so that I might present you as an acceptable offering to God, made holy by the Holy Spirit.
17So I have reason to be enthusiastic about all Christ
Jesus has done through me in my service to God. 18Yet
I dare not boast about anything except what Christ
has done through me, bringing the Gentiles to God
by my message and by the way I worked among them.
19They were convinced by the power of miraculous
signs and wonders and by the power of God's Spirit.*
In this way, I have fully presented the Good News of
Christ from Jerusalem all the way to Illyricum.*
20My ambition has always been to preach the Good
News where the name of Christ has never been heard,
rather than where a church has already been started by

Rom 15:3 Greek *who insult you have fallen on me.* Ps 69:9. **Rom 15:8** Greek *servant of circumcision.* **Rom 15:9** Ps 18:49. **Rom 15:10** Deut 32:43. **Rom 15:11** Ps 117:1. **Rom 15:12a** Greek *The root of Jesse.* David was the son of Jesse. **Rom 15:12b** Isa 11:10 (Greek version). **Rom 15:14** Greek *brothers;* also in 15:30. **Rom 15:19a** Other manuscripts read *the Spirit;* still others read *the Holy Spirit.* **Rom 15:19b** *Illyricum* was a region northeast of Italy.

pride or condescension, treat others with love, patience, and self-restraint.

Rom 14:23 We try to steer clear of actions forbidden by Scripture, of course, but sometimes Scripture is silent. Then we should follow our consciences. "If you do anything you believe is not right, you are sinning" means that to go against a conviction will leave a person with a guilty or uneasy conscience. When God shows us that something is wrong for us, we should avoid it. But we should not look down on other Christians who exercise their freedom in those areas.

Rom 15:4 The knowledge of the Scriptures affects our attitude toward the present and the future. The more we know about what God has done in years past, the greater the confidence we have about what he will do in the days ahead. We need to diligently read our Bibles so we may have confidence that God's will is best for us.

Rom 15:5-7 The Roman church was a diverse community. It was made up of Jews and Gentiles, slave and free, rich and poor, strong and weak. So it was difficult for them to accept one another. *Accepting* means taking people into our homes as well as into our hearts, sharing meals and activities, avoiding racial and economic discrimination, and going out of our way to avoid favoritism. How can you accept others as Christ has accepted you? Consciously spend time greeting those you don't normally talk to, minimize differences, and seek common ground for fellowship. In this way you are giving God glory.

Rom 15:19 Illyricum was a Roman territory on the Adriatic Sea between present-day Italy and Greece. It covered much the same territory as present-day Yugoslavia. See the map on p. 1645.

Rom 15:20 Paul says that he has "ambition." Ambition can be a difficult topic for Christians because we see so many bad examples of ambitious people who claw their way to the top. But certainly that isn't the kind of ambition one sees in Paul. Instead of looking out for himself and working hard for personal advancement, he was ambitious to serve God—for Paul that meant to "preach the Good News where the name of Christ has never been heard." Are you ambitious for God? Do you want, more than anything else, to please him and to do his will? Ask God for "holy ambition."

▸ **ROMANS 15:14-22** ***(cont.)***

someone else. 21 I have been following the plan spoken
of in the Scriptures, where it says,

"Those who have never been told about him
will see,
and those who have never heard of him will
understand."*

22 In fact, my visit to you has been delayed so long because I have been preaching in these places.

Paul's Travel Plans

ROMANS 15:23-33

But now I have finished my work in these regions,
and after all these long years of waiting, I am eager
to visit you. 24 I am planning to go to Spain, and when
I do, I will stop off in Rome. And after I have enjoyed
your fellowship for a little while, you can provide for
my journey.
25 But before I come, I must go to Jerusalem to take a
gift to the believers* there. 26 For you see, the believers
in Macedonia and Achaia* have eagerly taken up an
offering for the poor among the believers in Jerusalem. 27 They were glad to do this because they feel they
owe a real debt to them. Since the Gentiles received
the spiritual blessings of the Good News from the
believers in Jerusalem, they feel the least they can do
in return is to help them financially. 28 As soon as I have
delivered this money and completed this good deed
of theirs, I will come to see you on my way to Spain.
29 And I am sure that when I come, Christ will richly
bless our time together.
30 Dear brothers and sisters, I urge you in the name
of our Lord Jesus Christ to join in my struggle by praying to God for me. Do this because of your love for me,
given to you by the Holy Spirit. 31 Pray that I will be rescued from those in Judea who refuse to obey God. Pray
also that the believers there will be willing to accept
the donation* I am taking to Jerusalem. 32 Then, by the
will of God, I will be able to come to you with a joyful
heart, and we will be an encouragement to each other.
33 And now may God, who gives us his peace, be
with you all. Amen.*

Paul Greets His Friends

ROMANS 16:1-16

I commend to you our sister Phoebe, who is a deacon
in the church in Cenchrea. 2 Welcome her in the Lord
as one who is worthy of honor among God's people.
Help her in whatever she needs, for she has been helpful to many, and especially to me.
3 Give my greetings to Priscilla and Aquila, my co-
workers in the ministry of Christ Jesus. 4 In fact, they
once risked their lives for me. I am thankful to them,
and so are all the Gentile churches. 5 Also give my
greetings to the church that meets in their home.
Greet my dear friend Epenetus. He was the first person from the province of Asia to become a follower of

Rom 15:21 Isa 52:15 (Greek version). **Rom 15:25** Greek *God's holy people;* also in 15:26, 31. **Rom 15:26** *Macedonia* and *Achaia* were the northern and southern regions of Greece. **Rom 15:31** Greek *the ministry;* other manuscripts read *the gift.* **Rom 15:33** Some manuscripts do not include *Amen.* One very early manuscript places 16:25-27 here.

Rom 15:22 Paul wanted to visit the church at Rome, but he had delayed his visit because he had heard many good reports about the believers there and knew they were doing well on their own. It was more important for him to preach in areas that had not yet heard the Good News.

Rom 15:23-24 Paul was referring to the completion of his work in Corinth, the city from which he most likely wrote this letter. Most of Paul's three-month stay in Achaia (see Acts 20:3) was probably spent in Corinth. He believed that he had accomplished what God wanted him to do there, and he was looking forward to taking the Good News to new lands west of Rome. When Paul eventually went to Rome, it was as a prisoner (see Acts 28). Tradition says that Paul was released for a time and that he used this opportunity to go to Spain to preach the Good News. This journey is not mentioned in the book of Acts.

Rom 15:28 Paul's future plan was to go to Spain because Spain was at the very western end of the civilized world. He wanted to bring Christianity there. Also, Spain had many great minds and influential leaders in the Roman world (Lucan, Martial, Hadrian), and perhaps Paul thought Christianity would advance greatly in such an atmosphere.

Rom 15:30 Too often we see prayer as a time for comfort, reflection, or making requests to God. But here Paul urges believers to join in his struggle by means of prayer. Prayer is a weapon that all believers should use in interceding for others. Many of us know believers who are living in difficult places in order to communicate the gospel. Sending them funds is part of joining them in their struggles, but prayer is also a crucial way of being with them. Missionaries and other Christian workers strongly desire the prayers of those who have sent them out. Do your prayers reflect that struggle on their behalf?

Rom 15:33 This phrase sounds like it should signal the end of the letter, and it does pronounce the end of Paul's teaching. He concludes his letter, then, with personal greetings and remarks.

Rom 16:1-2 Phoebe was known as a "deacon," or servant and helper. Apparently she was a wealthy person who helped support Paul's ministry. Phoebe was highly regarded in the church, and she may have delivered this letter from Corinth to Rome. Women had important roles in the early church. Cenchrea, the town where Phoebe lived, was the eastern port of Corinth, six miles from the city center.

Rom 16:3 Priscilla and Aquila were a married couple who had become Paul's close friends. They, along with all other Jews, had been expelled from Rome by the emperor (Acts 18:2-3) and had moved to Corinth. There they met Paul and invited him to live with them. They were Christians before they met Paul and probably told him much about the Roman church. Like Paul, Priscilla and Aquila were missionaries. They helped believers in Ephesus (Acts 18:18-28), in Rome when they were allowed to return, and again at Ephesus (2 Tim 4:19).

Rom 16:3 Priscilla and Aquila ministered effectively behind the scenes. Their tools were hospitality, friendship, and person-to-person teaching. They were not public speakers, but private evangelists. They used their home for church meetings (Rom 16:5). Priscilla and Aquila challenge us with what a couple can do together to serve Christ. Do we regard our families and homes as gifts through which God can accomplish his work? How might God want to use your home and family to serve him?

Rom 16:5ff Paul's personal greetings went to Romans and Greeks, Jews and Gentiles, men and women, prisoners and prominent citizens. The church's base was broad, crossing cultural, social, and

Christ. 6Give my greetings to Mary, who has worked so
hard for your benefit. 7Greet Andronicus and Junia,*
my fellow Jews,* who were in prison with me. They
are highly respected among the apostles and became
followers of Christ before I did. 8Greet Ampliatus, my
dear friend in the Lord. 9Greet Urbanus, our co-worker
in Christ, and my dear friend Stachys.
10Greet Apelles, a good man whom Christ approves. And give my greetings to the believers from
the household of Aristobulus. 11Greet Herodion, my
fellow Jew.* Greet the Lord's people from the household of Narcissus. 12Give my greetings to Tryphena
and Tryphosa, the Lord's workers, and to dear Persis,
who has worked so hard for the Lord. 13Greet Rufus,
whom the Lord picked out to be his very own; and
also his dear mother, who has been a mother to me.
14Give my greetings to Asyncritus, Phlegon, Hermes,
Patrobas, Hermas, and the brothers and sisters* who
meet with them. 15Give my greetings to Philologus,
Julia, Nereus and his sister, and to Olympas and all the
believers* who meet with them. 16Greet each other in
Christian love.* All the churches of Christ send you
their greetings.

Paul's Final Instructions

ROMANS 16:17-27

And now I make one more appeal, my dear brothers
and sisters. Watch out for people who cause divisions and upset people's faith by teaching things
contrary to what you have been taught. Stay away
from them. 18Such people are not serving Christ our
Lord; they are serving their own personal interests.
By smooth talk and glowing words they deceive innocent people. 19But everyone knows that you are
obedient to the Lord. This makes me very happy. I
want you to be wise in doing right and to stay innocent of any wrong. 20The God of peace will soon
crush Satan under your feet. May the grace of our
Lord Jesus* be with you.
21Timothy, my fellow worker, sends you his greetings, as do Lucius, Jason, and Sosipater, my fellow Jews.
22I, Tertius, the one writing this letter for Paul, send
my greetings, too, as one of the Lord's followers.
23Gaius says hello to you. He is my host and also
serves as host to the whole church. Erastus, the city
treasurer, sends you his greetings, and so does our
brother Quartus.*

Rom 16:7a *Junia* is a feminine name. Some late manuscripts accent the word so it reads *Junias,* a masculine name; still others read *Julia* (feminine). **Rom 16:7b** Or *compatriots;* also in 16:21. **Rom 16:11** Or *compatriot.* **Rom 16:14** Greek *brothers;* also in 16:17. **Rom 16:15** Greek *all of God's holy people.* **Rom 16:16** Greek *with a sacred kiss.* **Rom 16:20** Some manuscripts read *Lord Jesus Christ.* **Rom 16:23** Some manuscripts add verse 24, *May the grace of our Lord Jesus Christ be with you all. Amen.* Still others add this sentence after verse 27.

economic lines. From this list we learn that the Christian community was mobile. Though Paul had not yet been to Rome, he had met these people in other places on his journeys.

Rom 16:7 The statement that Andronicus and Junia were "highly respected among the apostles" could also mean they had distinguished themselves as apostles. They may have been a husband and wife team. Paul notes that they were "fellow Jews" who at one time had been in prison with him.

Rom 16:17-20 When we read books or listen to sermons, we should check the content of what is written or said so that we won't be fooled by smooth talk and glowing words. Christians who study God's Word, asking him to reveal the truth, will not be fooled, even though superficial Christians may easily be taken in. For an example of believers who carefully checked God's Word, see Acts 17:10-12.

Rom 16:21 Timothy was a key person in the growth of the early church, traveling with Paul on his second missionary journey (Acts 16:1-3). Later Paul wrote two letters to him as he worked to strengthen the churches in Ephesus—the books of 1 and 2 Timothy. See Timothy's Profile on p. 1727.

Cenchrea

Cenchrea was a seaport city that served the maritime needs of the larger city of Corinth to the west. Before the Corinthian Canal was cut through the isthmus, boat traffic to Europe from Asia often passed overland from Cenchrea, on the Aegean Sea, through Corinth to Lechaion, the ancient port city on the Corinthian Gulf (see note on the Corinthian Canal, p. 1596). Excavations begun in 1963 have located the harbor breakwater, warehouse remains dating to the early 1st century, and a large 2nd-century stone building. A 4th-century church testifies to the influence of Christianity in the city.

Cenchrea is mentioned twice in the New Testament. The apostle Paul took an oath requiring the cutting of his hair before leaving Cenchrea during his third missionary journey (Acts 18:18). In his letter to the church in Rome, Paul commended Phoebe, a deacon of the church in Cenchrea, well known for her Christian service (Rom 16:1). May each one of us also be commended for our Christian service.

▸ **ROMANS 16:17-27** ***(cont.)***

25Now all glory to God, who is able to make you
strong, just as my Good News says. This message about
Jesus Christ has revealed his plan for you Gentiles, a
plan kept secret from the beginning of time. 26But
now as the prophets* foretold and as the eternal God
has commanded, this message is made known to all
Gentiles everywhere, so that they too might believe
and obey him. 27All glory to the only wise God, through
Jesus Christ, forever. Amen.

Rom 16:26 Greek *the prophetic writings.*

M. Paul's Ministry, Imprisonment, and Journey to Rome

Paul completed his third missionary journey, traveling back through several of the cities he had previously ministered in and gathering a collection for the needy believers in Jerusalem. He then traveled to Jerusalem to deliver this generous gift from the Gentile churches, but he was arrested and thrown in prison while he was there. He was transferred to another prison in Ceasarea, but because he appealed to Caesar for judgment on his case, Paul was sent to Rome to await trial. Even while he was in prison, or being questioned by the authorities, Paul took every opportunity to share the Good News about Jesus.

Paul's Final Visit to Troas

ACTS 20:3b-12

He was preparing to sail back to Syria when he discovered a plot by some Jews against his life, so he decided
to return through Macedonia.
4Several men were traveling with him. They were
Sopater son of Pyrrhus from Berea; Aristarchus and
Secundus from Thessalonica; Gaius from Derbe; Timothy; and Tychicus and Trophimus from the province
of Asia. 5They went on ahead and waited for us at
Troas. 6After the Passover* ended, we boarded a ship
at Philippi in Macedonia and five days later joined
them in Troas, where we stayed a week.
7On the first day of the week, we gathered with the

Acts 20:6 Greek *the days of unleavened bread.*

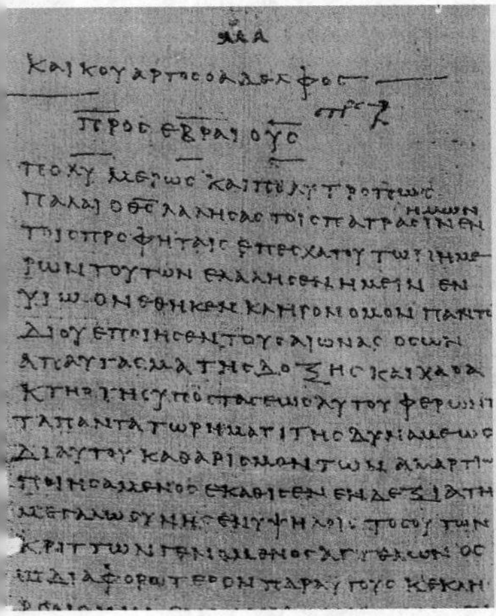

The End of Romans

Early manuscripts tell an interesting story about the end of the book of Romans. Most manuscripts have the letter in the order that it appears in modern Bibles. But P46, the earliest collection of Paul's letters (mid-2nd century), has the doxology (Rom 16:25-27) written in a different place: right between chapters 15 and 16. The picture here shows the final line of Romans in P46 (top line), which ends with the greetings from Erastus and Quartus (Rom 16:23). Some manuscripts have the doxology written between chapters 14 and 15, and a few even repeat the doxology twice, once after Romans 14:23 and then again at the end of the letter.

Several possibilities have been proposed by scholars about what this manuscript evidence could mean. Some think that Romans was originally written as one 16-chapter letter, but some of the copies that were sent out from Rome for other churches to read were shortened, omitting the final chapter that consists mostly of personal greetings specifically for the Roman church. Others have proposed that Romans 16 was originally a second letter sent with the 15-chapter Romans as a letter of recommendation for Phoebe, who carried the letter from Paul to Rome (Rom 16:1-2). When copies were made to circulate the letter for other churches, these two letters would have been combined into one longer letter as we know it today. All of this is speculation, of course. What we know for certain is that all of the book of Romans is Scripture, given by God to the church, regardless of the placement of Romans 16:25-27.

Rom 16:25-27 Paul exclaims that it is wonderful to be alive when the plan, God's secret—his way of saving the Gentiles—is becoming known throughout the world! All the Old Testament prophecies were coming true, and God was using Paul as his instrument to tell this Good News.

Rom 16:25-27 As Jerusalem was the center of Jewish life, Rome was the world's political, religious, social, and economic center. There the major governmental decisions were made, and from there the Good News spread to the ends of the earth. The church in Rome was a cosmopolitan mixture of Jews, Gentiles, slaves, free people, men, women, Roman citizens, and world travelers; therefore, it had potential for both great influence and great conflict.

Paul had not yet been to Rome to meet all the Christians there, and of course, he has not yet met us. We, too, live in a cosmopolitan setting with the entire world open to us. We also have the potential for both widespread influence and wrenching conflict. Listen carefully to Paul's teachings about unity, service, and love so you may apply them.

Acts 20:4 The men traveling with Paul represented churches that Paul had started in Asia. Each man was carrying an offering from his home church to be given to the believers in Jerusalem. Having each man deliver the gift gave the gifts a personal touch and strengthened the unity of the believers. This was also an effective way to teach the church about giving, because the men were able to report back to their churches the way God was working through their giving. Paul discussed this gift in one of his letters to the Corinthian church (see 2 Cor 8:1-21).

Acts 20:5-6 The use of *us* and *we* shows that this is where Luke again joined the group. The last *we* occurred in Acts 16.

Acts 20:6 Jewish believers celebrated the Passover (which was immediately followed by the Festival of Unleavened Bread) according to Moses' instructions (see Exod 12:43-51) even if they couldn't be at Jerusalem for the occasion.

local believers to share in the Lord's Supper.* Paul was
preaching to them, and since he was leaving the next
day, he kept talking until midnight. 8The upstairs room
where we met was lighted with many flickering lamps.
9As Paul spoke on and on, a young man named Eutychus, sitting on the windowsill, became very drowsy.
Finally, he fell sound asleep and dropped three stories
to his death below. 10Paul went down, bent over him,
and took him into his arms. "Don't worry," he said,
"he's alive!" 11Then they all went back upstairs, shared
in the Lord's Supper,* and ate together. Paul continued
talking to them until dawn, and then he left. 12Mean-
while, the young man was taken home unhurt, and
everyone was greatly relieved.

Paul Meets the Ephesian Elders

ACTS 20:13-38

Paul went by land to Assos, where he had arranged for
us to join him, while we traveled by ship. 14He joined us
there, and we sailed together to Mitylene. 15The next
day we sailed past the island of Kios. The following day
we crossed to the island of Samos, and* a day later we
arrived at Miletus.

16Paul had decided to sail on past Ephesus, for he
didn't want to spend any more time in the province of
Asia. He was hurrying to get to Jerusalem, if possible,
in time for the Festival of Pentecost. 17But when we
landed at Miletus, he sent a message to the elders of the
church at Ephesus, asking them to come and meet him.

18When they arrived he declared, "You know that
from the day I set foot in the province of Asia until
now 19I have done the Lord's work humbly and with
many tears. I have endured the trials that came to me
from the plots of the Jews. 20I never shrank back from
telling you what you needed to hear, either publicly
or in your homes. 21I have had one message for Jews
and Greeks alike—the necessity of repenting from
sin and turning to God, and of having faith in our
Lord Jesus.

22"And now I am bound by the Spirit* to go to Jerusalem. I don't know what awaits me, 23except that
the Holy Spirit tells me in city after city that jail and
suffering lie ahead. 24But my life is worth nothing to
me unless I use it for finishing the work assigned me
by the Lord Jesus—the work of telling others the Good
News about the wonderful grace of God.

25"And now I know that none of you to whom I
have preached the Kingdom will ever see me again.
26I declare today that I have been faithful. If anyone
suffers eternal death, it's not my fault,* 27for I didn't
shrink from declaring all that God wants you to know.

28"So guard yourselves and God's people. Feed and
shepherd God's flock—his church, purchased with his
own blood*—over which the Holy Spirit has appointed
you as elders.* 29I know that false teachers, like vicious
wolves, will come in among you after I leave, not spar-
ing the flock. 30Even some men from your own group
will rise up and distort the truth in order to draw a

Acts 20:7 Greek *to break bread.* **Acts 20:11** Greek *broke the bread.* **Acts 20:15** Some manuscripts read *and having stayed at Trogyllium.* **Acts 20:22** Or *by my spirit,* or *by an inner compulsion;* Greek reads *by the spirit.* **Acts 20:26** Greek *I am innocent of the blood of all.* **Acts 20:28a** Or *with the blood of his own [Son].* **Acts 20:28b** Greek *overseers.*

Acts 20:8-9 The "flickering lamps" were candles in lanterns. The combination of the heat from the candles and the number of people gathered in the upstairs room probably made the room very warm. This no doubt helped Eutychus fall asleep, as well as the fact that Paul had been speaking for a long time. Eutychus was probably between the ages of 8 to 14 years old (the age of a "young man").

Acts 20:16 Paul had missed attending the Passover in Jerusalem, so he was especially interested in arriving on time for Pentecost, which was 50 days after Passover. He was carrying with him gifts for the Jerusalem believers from churches in Asia and Greece (see Rom 15:25-26; 1 Cor 16:1ff; 2 Cor 8–9). The Jerusalem church was experiencing difficult times. Paul may have been anxious to deliver this gift to the believers at Pentecost because it was a day of celebration and thanksgiving to God for his provision.

Acts 20:18-21 The way of the believer is not an easy road; being a Christian does not solve or remove all problems. Paul served humbly and "with many tears," but he never quit, never gave up. The message of salvation was so important that he never missed an opportunity to share it. And although he preached his message in different ways to fit different audiences, the message remained the same: Repent and turn to Christ by faith. The Christian life will have its rough times, tears, and sorrows, as well as joys, but we should always be ready to tell others what good things God has done for us. His blessings far outweigh life's difficulties.

Acts 20:23 The Holy Spirit showed Paul that he would be imprisoned and experience suffering. Even knowing this, Paul did not shrink from fulfilling his mission. His strong character was a good example to the Ephesian elders, some of whom would also suffer for Christ.

Acts 20:24 We often feel that life is a failure unless we're getting a lot out of it: recognition, fun, money, success. But Paul considered life worth nothing unless he used it for God's work. What he put into life was far more important than what he got out. Which is more important to you—what you get out of life or what you put into it?

Acts 20:24 Single-mindedness is a quality needed by anyone who wishes to do God's work. The single most important goal of Paul's life was to tell others about Christ (Phil 3:7-13). It is no wonder that Paul was the greatest missionary who ever lived. God is looking for more men and women who will focus on that one great task God has given them to do.

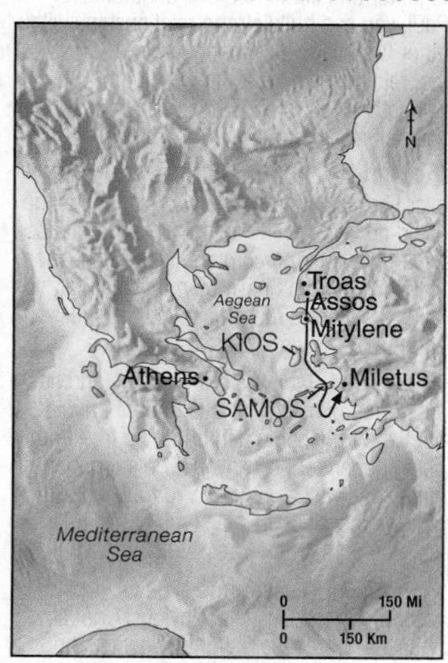

PAUL TRAVELS FROM TROAS TO MILETUS *From Troas, Paul traveled overland to Assos, then boarded a ship to Mitylene and Samos on its way to Miletus. He summoned the elders of the Ephesian church to say farewell to them, because he knew he would probably not see them again.*

▸ **ACTS 20:13-38** ***(cont.)***

following. 31Watch out! Remember the three years I was with you—my constant watch and care over you night and day, and my many tears for you.

32"And now I entrust you to God and the message of his grace that is able to build you up and give you an inheritance with all those he has set apart for himself.

33"I have never coveted anyone's silver or gold or fine clothes. 34You know that these hands of mine have worked to supply my own needs and even the needs of those who were with me. 35And I have been a constant example of how you can help those in need by working hard. You should remember the words of the Lord Jesus: 'It is more blessed to give than to receive.'"

36When he had finished speaking, he knelt and prayed with them. 37They all cried as they embraced and kissed him good-bye. 38They were sad most of all because he had said that they would never see him again. Then they escorted him down to the ship.

Paul's Journey to Jerusalem

ACTS 21:1-14

After saying farewell to the Ephesian elders, we sailed straight to the island of Cos. The next day we reached Rhodes and then went to Patara. 2There we boarded a ship sailing for Phoenicia. 3We sighted the island of Cyprus, passed it on our left, and landed at the harbor of Tyre, in Syria, where the ship was to unload its cargo.

4We went ashore, found the local believers,* and stayed with them a week. These believers prophesied through the Holy Spirit that Paul should not go on to Jerusalem. 5When we returned to the ship at the end of the week, the entire congregation, including women* and children, left the city and came down to the shore with us. There we knelt, prayed, 6and said our farewells. Then we went aboard, and they returned home.

7The next stop after leaving Tyre was Ptolemais, where we greeted the brothers and sisters* and stayed for one day. 8The next day we went on to Caesarea and stayed at the home of Philip the Evangelist, one of the seven men who had been chosen to distribute food. 9He had four unmarried daughters who had the gift of prophecy.

10Several days later a man named Agabus, who also had the gift of prophecy, arrived from Judea. 11He came over, took Paul's belt, and bound his own

Acts 21:4 Greek *disciples;* also in 21:16. **Acts 21:5** Or *wives.* **Acts 21:7** Greek *brothers;* also in 21:17.

Acts 20:31, 36-38 Paul's relationship with these believers is a beautiful example of Christian fellowship. He had cared for them and loved them, even cried over their needs. They responded with love and care for him and sorrow over his leaving. They had prayed together and comforted one another. Like Paul, you can build strong relationships with other Christians by sharing, caring, sorrowing, rejoicing, and praying with them. You will gather others around you only by giving yourself away to them.

Acts 20:33 Paul was satisfied with whatever he had, wherever he was, as long as he could do God's work. Examine your attitudes toward wealth and comfort. If you focus more on what you don't have than on what you do have, it's time to reexamine your priorities and put God's work back in first place.

Acts 20:34 Paul was a tentmaker, and he supported himself with this trade. Paul did not work to become rich but to be free from being dependent on anyone. He supported himself as well as others who traveled with him (he mentions this in some of his letters; see Phil 4:11-13; 1 Thes 2:9).

Acts 20:35 These words of Jesus are not recorded in the Gospels. Obviously, not all of Jesus' words were written down (John 21:25); this saying may have been passed on orally through the apostles.

Acts 21:4 Did Paul disobey the Holy Spirit by going to Jerusalem? No. More likely, the Holy Spirit warned these believers about the suffering that Paul would face in Jerusalem. They drew the conclusion that he should not go there because of that danger. Acts 21:10-12 supports this; the local believers, after hearing that Paul would be turned over to the Romans, begged him to turn back.

Acts 21:8 This is the Philip mentioned in Acts 6:5; 8:26-40.

Acts 21:9 Obviously the gift of prophecy was given to both men and women. Women actively participated in God's work (Acts 2:17; Phil 4:3). Other women who prophesied include Miriam (Exod 15:20), Deborah (Judg 4:4), Huldah (2 Kgs 22:14), Isaiah's wife (Isa 8:3), and Anna (Luke 2:36-38).

Acts 21:10 Fifteen years earlier, Agabus had predicted the famine in Jerusalem (Acts 11:27-29).

Temple of Athena

The photograph is the temple of Athena at Assos. Assos was a seaport of Mysia in the Roman province of Asia Minor. The apostle Paul and Luke were reunited in Assos after Paul's journey by land from Troas (Acts 20:13-14). The Roman writer Pliny identified the town as having been founded by the kings of Pergamum; they had called it Apollonia. Assos was located on the top and terraced sides of an inactive volcanic cone 770 feet in height. The Greek philosopher Aristotle lived there for several years. It was also the birthplace of Cleanthes, a Stoic poet quoted by Paul (Acts 17:28). Cleanthes wrote, "For we are his offspring." This indicates that all human beings are the children of God the *Creator.* But the way to have God as our *Father* is to believe in his Son Jesus Christ and be born again.

feet and hands with it. Then he said, "The Holy Spirit declares, 'So shall the owner of this belt be bound by the Jewish leaders in Jerusalem and turned over to the Gentiles.'" 12When we heard this, we and the local believers all begged Paul not to go on to Jerusalem.

13But he said, "Why all this weeping? You are breaking my heart! I am ready not only to be jailed at Jerusalem but even to die for the sake of the Lord Jesus." 14When it was clear that we couldn't persuade him, we gave up and said, "The Lord's will be done."

Paul Arrives at Jerusalem

ACTS 21:15-25

After this we packed our things and left for Jerusalem. 16Some believers from Caesarea accompanied us, and they took us to the home of Mnason, a man originally from Cyprus and one of the early believers. 17When we arrived, the brothers and sisters in Jerusalem welcomed us warmly.

18The next day Paul went with us to meet with James, and all the elders of the Jerusalem church were present. 19After greeting them, Paul gave a detailed account of the things God had accomplished among the Gentiles through his ministry.

20After hearing this, they praised God. And then they said, "You know, dear brother, how many thousands of Jews have also believed, and they all follow the law of Moses very seriously. 21But the Jewish believers here in Jerusalem have been told that you are teaching all the Jews who live among the Gentiles to turn their backs on the laws of Moses. They've heard that you teach them not to circumcise their children or follow other Jewish customs. 22What should we do? They will certainly hear that you have come.

23"Here's what we want you to do. We have four men here who have completed their vow. 24Go with them to the Temple and join them in the purification ceremony, paying for them to have their heads ritually shaved. Then everyone will know that the rumors are all false and that you yourself observe the Jewish laws.

25"As for the Gentile believers, they should do what we already told them in a letter: They should abstain from eating food offered to idols, from consuming blood or the meat of strangled animals, and from sexual immorality."

Acts 21:13-14 Paul knew he would be imprisoned in Jerusalem. Although his friends pleaded with him to not go there, he knew that he had to because God wanted him to. No one enjoys pain, but a faithful disciple wants above all else to please God. Our desire to please God should overshadow our desire to avoid hardship and suffering. When we really want to do God's will, we must accept all that comes with it—even the pain. Then we can say with Paul's companions, "The Lord's will be done."

Acts 21:18 James, Jesus' brother, was the leader of the Jerusalem church (Acts 15:13-21; Gal 1:19; 2:9).

Acts 21:21 The Jerusalem council (Acts 15) had settled the issue of circumcision for Gentile believers. Evidently a rumor said that Paul had gone far beyond their decision, even forbidding Jews to circumcise their children. This, of course, was not true, so Paul willingly submitted to Jewish custom to show that he was not working against the council's decision and that he was still Jewish in his lifestyle. Sometimes we must go the second mile to avoid offending others, especially when doing so would hinder God's work.

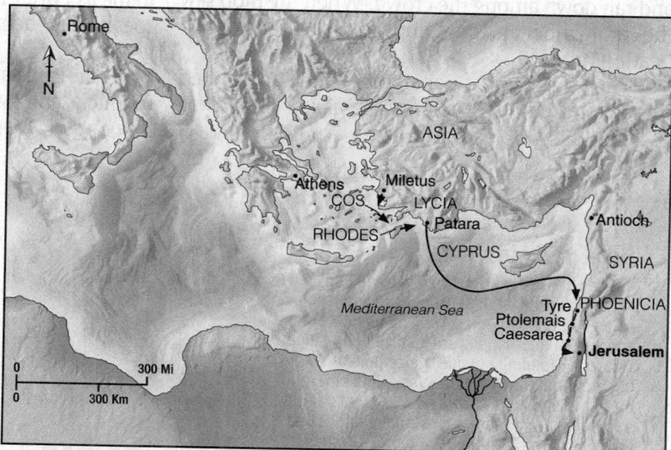

***PAUL RETURNS TO JERUSALEM** The ship sailed from Miletus to Cos, Rhodes, and Patara. Paul and his companions then boarded a cargo ship bound for Phoenicia. They passed Cyprus and landed at Tyre, then Ptolemais, and finally Caesarea, where Paul disembarked and returned by land to Jerusalem.*

Acts 21:23-24 Because Paul was going to participate with the four men in the vow (apparently he had been asked to pay for some of the required expenses), he would need to take part in the purification ceremony for entering the Temple (Num 6:9-20). Paul submitted himself to this Jewish custom to keep peace in the Jerusalem church. Although Paul was a man of strong convictions, he was willing to compromise on nonessential points, becoming all things to all people so that he might save some (1 Cor 9:19-23). Often churches split over disagreements about minor issues or traditions. Like Paul, we should remain firm on Christian essentials but flexible on nonessentials. Of course, no one should violate a true conviction, but sometimes we need to honor Christ by mutual submission for the sake of the Good News.

Acts 21:23-24 The Jewish laws can be thought of in two ways. (1) The Old Testament laws bring salvation to those who keep them. Paul rejected this idea. Salvation is freely given by God's gracious act. We receive salvation through faith. The laws are of no value for salvation except to show us our sin. (2) The Old Testament laws prepare for and teach about the coming of Jesus Christ. Paul accepted this view. Christ fulfilled the law and released us from its burden of guilt. But the law still teaches many valuable principles and provides guidelines for grateful living. Paul was not observing the laws in order to be saved. He was keeping the laws as custom to avoid offending those he wished to reach with the Good News (see Rom 3:21-31; 7:4-6; 13:9-10). (For more on the law, see Gal 3:23-29; 4:21-31; see also the chart on p. 1561.)

Paul Is Arrested

ACTS 21:26-36

So Paul went to the Temple the next day with the other
men. They had already started the purification ritual, so
he publicly announced the date when their vows would
end and sacrifices would be offered for each of them.
27The seven days were almost ended when some
Jews from the province of Asia saw Paul in the Temple
and roused a mob against him. They grabbed him,
28yelling, "Men of Israel, help us! This is the man who
preaches against our people everywhere and tells
everybody to disobey the Jewish laws. He speaks
against the Temple—and even defiles this holy place
by bringing in Gentiles.*" 29(For earlier that day they
had seen him in the city with Trophimus, a Gentile
from Ephesus,* and they assumed Paul had taken him
into the Temple.)
30The whole city was rocked by these accusations, and a great riot followed. Paul was grabbed
and dragged out of the Temple, and immediately the
gates were closed behind him. 31As they were trying
to kill him, word reached the commander of the Roman regiment that all Jerusalem was in an uproar.
32He immediately called out his soldiers and officers*
and ran down among the crowd. When the mob saw
the commander and the troops coming, they stopped
beating Paul.
33Then the commander arrested him and ordered
him bound with two chains. He asked the crowd
who he was and what he had done. 34Some shouted
one thing and some another. Since he couldn't find
out the truth in all the uproar and confusion, he ordered that Paul be taken to the fortress. 35As Paul
reached the stairs, the mob grew so violent the soldiers had to lift him to their shoulders to protect
him. 36And the crowd followed behind, shouting,
"Kill him, kill him!"

Paul Speaks to the Crowd

ACTS 21:37–22:23

As Paul was about to be taken inside, he said to the
commander, "May I have a word with you?"
"Do you know Greek?" the commander asked, surprised. 38"Aren't you the Egyptian who led a rebellion
some time ago and took 4,000 members of the Assassins out into the desert?"
39"No," Paul replied, "I am a Jew and a citizen of Tarsus in Cilicia, which is an important city. Please, let me
talk to these people." 40The commander agreed, so Paul
stood on the stairs and motioned to the people to be
quiet. Soon a deep silence enveloped the crowd, and
he addressed them in their own language, Aramaic.*

22:1"Brothers and esteemed fathers," Paul said, "listen
to me as I offer my defense." 2When they heard him
speaking in their own language,* the silence was even
greater.
3Then Paul said, "I am a Jew, born in Tarsus, a city
in Cilicia, and I was brought up and educated here in

Acts 21:28 Greek *Greeks.* **Acts 21:29** Greek *Trophimus, the Ephesian.* **Acts 21:32** Greek *centurions.* **Acts 21:40** Or *Hebrew.* **Acts 22:2** Greek *in Aramaic,* or *in Hebrew.*

Do Not Enter

Notices in Greek and Hebrew warned non-Jews not to enter the inner court of Herod's Temple on pain of death (see Acts 21:28). One whole copy and part of another, in Greek, have been found. This was standing outside the Temple at the time of Christ and the apostles. When Paul entered the Temple to help some Jewish Christians fulfill a vow, the Jews there mistakenly thought that Paul had taken Trophimus, a Gentile from Ephesus, into the Temple (Acts 21:29). This aroused great anger against Paul; a mob formed who wanted to kill him (Acts 21:30-36).

Paul was referring to this wall when he said that God broke down the wall that divided Jews and Gentiles; he did this through the crucifixion of Jesus (Eph 2:14). Now both Jews and Gentiles alike have equal access to God through Jesus Christ. Let us come to him without hesitation or fear.

Acts 21:31 Because Jerusalem was under Roman control, an uproar in the city would be investigated by Roman authorities. The commander of the troops at this time was Claudius Lysias (Acts 23:26). He was head of a regiment (a special group, part of a legion) of Roman soldiers and was the senior Roman official in Jerusalem.

Acts 21:37-38 By speaking in Greek, Paul showed that he was a cultured, educated man and not just a common rebel starting riots in the streets. The language grabbed the commander's attention and gave Paul protection and the opportunity to give his defense.

Acts 21:38 The historian Josephus wrote of an Egyptian who had led a revolt of 4,000 people in Jerusalem in A.D. 54 and then had disappeared. The commander assumed that Paul was this rebel.

Acts 21:40–22:2 Paul was speaking in Aramaic, the common language among Palestinian Jews. He used Aramaic not only to communicate in the language of his listeners but also to show that he was a devout Jew and had respect for the Jewish laws and customs. Paul spoke Greek to the Roman officials and Aramaic to the Jews.

Acts 22:3 Gamaliel was the most honored rabbi of the first century. He was well known and respected as an expert on religious law and as a voice for moderation (Acts 5:34). Paul was showing his credentials as a well-educated man trained under the most respected Jewish rabbi.

Acts 22:3-4 By saying that at one time he was as zealous for God as any of his listeners, Paul was acknowledging their sincere motives behind their desire to kill him, pointing out that he had done the same to Christian leaders a few years earlier. Paul always tried to establish common ground with his audience before launching into a full-scale defense of Christianity. When you witness for Christ, first identify yourself with your audience. They will be much more likely to listen if they feel a common bond with you.

Jerusalem under Gamaliel. As his student, I was carefully trained in our Jewish laws and customs. I became very zealous to honor God in everything I did, just like all of you today. 4And I persecuted the followers of the Way, hounding some to death, arresting both men and women and throwing them in prison. 5The high priest and the whole council of elders can testify that this is so. For I received letters from them to our Jewish brothers in Damascus, authorizing me to bring the Christians from there to Jerusalem, in chains, to be punished.

6"As I was on the road, approaching Damascus about noon, a very bright light from heaven suddenly shone down around me. 7I fell to the ground and heard a voice saying to me, 'Saul, Saul, why are you persecuting me?'

8"'Who are you, lord?' I asked.

"And the voice replied, 'I am Jesus the Nazarene,* the one you are persecuting.' 9The people with me saw the light but didn't understand the voice speaking to me.

10"I asked, 'What should I do, Lord?'

"And the Lord told me, 'Get up and go into Damascus, and there you will be told everything you are to do.'

11"I was blinded by the intense light and had to be led by the hand to Damascus by my companions. 12A man named Ananias lived there. He was a godly man, deeply devoted to the law, and well regarded by all the Jews of Damascus. 13He came and stood beside me and said, 'Brother Saul, regain your sight.' And that very moment I could see him!

14"Then he told me, 'The God of our ancestors has chosen you to know his will and to see the Righteous One and hear him speak. 15For you are to be his witness, telling everyone what you have seen and heard. 16What are you waiting for? Get up and be baptized. Have your sins washed away by calling on the name of the Lord.'

17"After I returned to Jerusalem, I was praying in the Temple and fell into a trance. 18I saw a vision of Jesus* saying to me, 'Hurry! Leave Jerusalem, for the people here won't accept your testimony about me.'

19"'But Lord,' I argued, 'they certainly know that in every synagogue I imprisoned and beat those who believed in you. 20And I was in complete agreement when your witness Stephen was killed. I stood by and kept the coats they took off when they stoned him.'

21"But the Lord said to me, 'Go, for I will send you far away to the Gentiles!'"

22The crowd listened until Paul said that word. Then they all began to shout, "Away with such a fellow! He isn't fit to live!" 23They yelled, threw off their coats, and tossed handfuls of dust into the air.

Paul Reveals His Roman Citizenship

ACTS 22:24-29

The commander brought Paul inside and ordered him lashed with whips to make him confess his crime. He wanted to find out why the crowd had become so furious. 25When they tied Paul down to lash him, Paul said to the officer* standing there, "Is it legal for you to whip a Roman citizen who hasn't even been tried?"

26When the officer heard this, he went to the commander and asked, "What are you doing? This man is a Roman citizen!"

27So the commander went over and asked Paul, "Tell me, are you a Roman citizen?"

"Yes, I certainly am," Paul replied.

28"I am, too," the commander muttered, "and it cost me plenty!"

Paul answered, "But I am a citizen by birth!"

29The soldiers who were about to interrogate Paul quickly withdrew when they heard he was a Roman citizen, and the commander was frightened because he had ordered him bound and whipped.

Paul before the High Council

ACTS 22:30–23:11

The next day the commander ordered the leading priests into session with the Jewish high council.* He wanted to find out what the trouble was all about, so he released Paul to have him stand before them.

23:1 Gazing intently at the high council,* Paul began: "Brothers, I have always lived before God with a clear conscience!"

Acts 22:8 Or *Jesus of Nazareth.* **Acts 22:18** Greek *him.* **Acts 22:25** Greek *the centurion;* also in 22:26. **Acts 22:30** Greek *Sanhedrin.* **Acts 23:1** Greek *Sanhedrin;* also in 23:6, 15, 20, 28.

Acts 22:6ff After gaining a hearing and establishing common ground with his audience, Paul gave his testimony. He shared how he had come to faith in Christ. Sound reasoning is good, but it is also important to simply share what Christ has done in our lives. No matter how we present the message, however, not everyone will accept it, as Paul knew. We must faithfully and responsibly present the Good News and leave the results to God.

Acts 22:21-22 These people listened intently to Paul, but the word *Gentiles* brought out all their anger and exposed their pride. They were supposed to be a light to the Gentiles, telling them about the one true God. But they had renounced that mission by becoming separatist and exclusive. God's plan would not be thwarted; the Gentiles were hearing the Good News through Jewish Christians, such as Paul and Peter.

Acts 22:25-28 Paul's question stopped the officer because by law a Roman citizen could not be punished until he had been proven guilty of a crime. Paul had been born a Roman citizen, whereas the commander had purchased his citizenship. Buying citizenship was a common practice and a good source of income for the Roman government. Bought citizenship was considered inferior to citizenship by birth.

Acts 22:30 Paul used his times of persecution as an opportunity to witness. Even his enemies were creating a platform for him to address the entire Jewish high council. If we are sensitive to the Holy Spirit's leading, we will see increased opportunities to share our faith, even in the face of opposition.

▸ **ACTS 22:30–23:11** *(cont.)*

[2]Instantly Ananias the high priest commanded those close to Paul to slap him on the mouth. [3]But Paul said to him, "God will slap you, you corrupt hypocrite!* What kind of judge are you to break the law yourself by ordering me struck like that?"

[4]Those standing near Paul said to him, "Do you dare to insult God's high priest?"

[5]"I'm sorry, brothers. I didn't realize he was the high priest," Paul replied, "for the Scriptures say, 'You must not speak evil of any of your rulers.'*"

[6]Paul realized that some members of the high council were Sadducees and some were Pharisees, so he shouted, "Brothers, I am a Pharisee, as were my ancestors! And I am on trial because my hope is in the resurrection of the dead!"

[7]This divided the council—the Pharisees against the Sadducees—[8]for the Sadducees say there is no resurrection or angels or spirits, but the Pharisees believe in all of these. [9]So there was a great uproar. Some of the teachers of religious law who were Pharisees jumped up and began to argue forcefully. "We see nothing wrong with him," they shouted. "Perhaps a spirit or an angel spoke to him." [10]As the conflict grew more violent, the commander was afraid they would tear Paul apart. So he ordered his soldiers to go and rescue him by force and take him back to the fortress.

[11]That night the Lord appeared to Paul and said, "Be encouraged, Paul. Just as you have been a witness to me here in Jerusalem, you must preach the Good News in Rome as well."

The Plan to Kill Paul

ACTS 23:12-22

The next morning a group of Jews* got together and bound themselves with an oath not to eat or drink until they had killed Paul. [13]There were more than forty of them in the conspiracy. [14]They went to the leading priests and elders and told them, "We have bound ourselves with an oath to eat nothing until we have killed Paul. [15]So you and the high council should ask the commander to bring Paul back to the council again. Pretend you want to examine his case more fully. We will kill him on the way."

[16]But Paul's nephew—his sister's son—heard of their plan and went to the fortress and told Paul. [17]Paul called for one of the Roman officers* and said, "Take this young man to the commander. He has something important to tell him."

[18]So the officer did, explaining, "Paul, the prisoner, called me over and asked me to bring this young man to you because he has something to tell you."

[19]The commander took his hand, led him aside, and asked, "What is it you want to tell me?"

[20]Paul's nephew told him, "Some Jews are going to ask you to bring Paul before the high council tomorrow, pretending they want to get some more information. [21]But don't do it! There are more than forty men hiding along the way ready to ambush him. They have vowed not to eat or drink anything until they have killed him. They are ready now, just waiting for your consent."

[22]"Don't let anyone know you told me this," the commander warned the young man.

Paul Is Sent to Caesarea

ACTS 23:23-35

Then the commander called two of his officers and ordered, "Get 200 soldiers ready to leave for Caesarea at nine o'clock tonight. Also take 200 spearmen and 70 mounted troops. [24]Provide horses for Paul to ride, and get him safely to Governor Felix." [25]Then he wrote this letter to the governor:

Acts 23:3 Greek *you whitewashed wall.* **Acts 23:5** Exod 22:28. **Acts 23:12** Greek *the Jews.* **Acts 23:17** Greek *centurions;* also in 23:23.

Acts 23:2-5 Josephus, a respected first-century historian, described Ananias as profane, greedy, and hot-tempered. Paul's outburst came as a result of the illegal command that Ananias had given. Ananias had violated Jewish law by assuming that Paul was guilty without a trial and ordering his punishment (see Deut 19:15). Paul didn't recognize Ananias as the high priest, probably because Ananias's command broke the law he was pledged to represent. As Christians, we are to represent Christ. If someone we know says, "I didn't know you were a Christian," we have failed to represent him as we should. We are not merely Christ's followers; we are his representatives to others.

Acts 23:6-8 The Sadducees and Pharisees were two groups of religious leaders but with strikingly different beliefs. The Pharisees believed in a bodily resurrection, but the Sadducees did not. The Sadducees adhered only to Genesis through Deuteronomy, which contain no explicit teaching on resurrection. Paul's words moved the debate away from himself and toward their festering controversy about resurrection. The Jewish council was split.

Acts 23:6-8 Paul's sudden insight that the council was a mixture of Sadducees and Pharisees is an example of the insight that Jesus promises to believers (Mark 13:9-11). God will help us when we are under fire for our faith. Like Paul, we should always be ready to present our testimony. The Holy Spirit will give us the courage to speak boldly.

Acts 23:14-15 When the Pharisee/Sadducee controversy died down, the religious leaders refocused their attention on Paul. To these leaders, politics and position had become more important than God. They were ready to plan another murder, just as they had done with Jesus. But as always, God was in control.

Acts 23:16 This is the only biblical reference to a member of Paul's family. Some scholars believe that Paul's family had disowned him when he became a Christian. Paul wrote of having suffered the loss of everything for Christ (Phil 3:8). His nephew was able to see him, even though Paul was in protective custody, because Roman prisoners were accessible to their relatives and friends, who could bring them food and other amenities.

Acts 23:16-22 It is easy to overlook children, assuming that they aren't old enough to do much for the Lord. But this young man played an important part in protecting Paul's life. God can use anyone, of any age, who is willing to yield to him. Jesus made it clear that children are important (Matt 18:2-6). Give children the importance God gives them.

Acts 23:23-24 The Roman commander ordered Paul sent to Caesarea. Jerusalem was the seat of Jewish government, but Caesarea was the Roman headquarters for the area. God works in amazing and amusing ways. God could have used any number of ways to get Paul to Caesarea, but he chose

[26]"From Claudius Lysias, to his Excellency, Governor Felix: Greetings!

[27]"This man was seized by some Jews, and they were about to kill him when I arrived with the troops. When I learned that he was a Roman citizen, I removed him to safety. [28]Then I took him to their high council to try to learn the basis of the accusations against him. [29]I soon discovered the charge was something regarding their religious law—certainly nothing worthy of imprisonment or death. [30]But when I was informed of a plot to kill him, I immediately sent him on to you. I have told his accusers to bring their charges before you."

[31]So that night, as ordered, the soldiers took Paul as far as Antipatris. [32]They returned to the fortress the next morning, while the mounted troops took him on to Caesarea. [33]When they arrived in Caesarea, they presented Paul and the letter to Governor Felix. [34]He read it and then asked Paul what province he was from. "Cilicia," Paul answered.

[35]"I will hear your case myself when your accusers arrive," the governor told him. Then the governor ordered him kept in the prison at Herod's headquarters.*

Paul Appears before Felix

ACTS 24:1-27

Five days later Ananias, the high priest, arrived with some of the Jewish elders and the lawyer* Tertullus, to present their case against Paul to the governor. [2]When Paul was called in, Tertullus presented the charges against Paul in the following address to the governor:

"You have provided a long period of peace for us Jews and with foresight have enacted reforms for us. [3]For all of this, Your Excellency, we are very grateful to you. [4]But I don't want to bore you, so please give me your attention

Acts 23:35 Greek *Herod's Praetorium.* **Acts 24:1** Greek *some elders and an orator.*

UNSUNG HEROES IN ACTS

When we think of the success of the early church, we often think of the work of the apostles. But the church could have died if it hadn't been for the unsung heroes, the men and women who through some small but committed act moved the church forward.

Hero	*Reference*	*Heroic Action*
Crippled man	Acts 3:9-12	After his healing, he praised God. As the crowds gathered to see what had happened, Peter used the opportunity to tell many about Jesus.
Five deacons	Acts 6:2-6	Everyone has heard of Stephen, and many know of Philip, but there were five other men chosen to be deacons. They not only laid the foundation for service in the church, but their hard work also gave the apostles the time they needed to preach the gospel.
Ananias	Acts 9:10-19	He had the responsibility of being the first to demonstrate Christ's love to Saul (Paul) after his conversion.
Cornelius	Acts 10:30-35	His example showed Peter that the gospel was for all people, Jews and Gentiles.
Rhoda	Acts 12:13-15	Her persistence brought Peter inside Mary's home, where he would be safe.
James	Acts 15:13-21	He took command of the Jerusalem council and had the courage and discernment to help form a decision that would affect literally millions of Christians over many generations.
Lydia	Acts 16:13-15	She opened her home to Paul, from which he led many to Christ and founded a church in Philippi.
Jason	Acts 17:5-9	He risked his life for the gospel by allowing Paul to stay in his home. He stood up for what was true and right, even though he faced persecution for it.
Paul's nephew	Acts 23:16-24	He saved Paul's life by telling officials of a murder plot.
Julius	Acts 27:1, 43	He spared Paul when the other soldiers wanted to kill him.

to use the Roman army to deliver Paul from his enemies. God's ways are not our ways. Ours are limited; his are not. Don't limit God by asking him to respond your way. When God intervenes, things will work out much better than you could ever anticipate.

Acts 23:26 Felix was the Roman governor of Judea from A.D. 52–59. This was the same position Pontius Pilate had held. While the Jews were given much freedom to govern themselves, the governor ran the army, kept the peace, and gathered the taxes.

Acts 23:26 How did Luke know what was written in the letter from Claudius Lysias? In his concern for historical accuracy, Luke used many sources to make sure that his writings were correct (see Luke 1:1-4). This letter was probably read aloud in court when Paul came before Felix to answer the Jews' accusations. Also, because Paul was a Roman citizen, a copy may have been given to him as a courtesy.

Acts 24:1 The accusers arrived: Ananias, the high priest; Tertullus, the lawyer; and several Jewish leaders. They traveled 60 miles to Caesarea, the Roman center of government, to bring their false accusations against Paul. Their murder plot had failed (Acts 23:12-15), but they were still trying to kill him. This attempt at murder was both premeditated and persistent.

Acts 24:2ff Tertullus was a special orator called to present the religious leaders' case before the Roman governor. He made three accusations against Paul: (1) He was a troublemaker, stirring up riots among the Jews around the world; (2) he was the ringleader of an unrecognized religious cult, which was against Roman law; (3) he had tried to desecrate the Temple. The religious leaders hoped that these accusations would persuade Felix to execute Paul in order to keep the peace in Palestine.

▸ **ACTS 24:1-27** ***(cont.)***
for only a moment. [5]We have found this man to be a
troublemaker who is constantly stirring up riots among
the Jews all over the world. He is a ringleader of the cult
known as the Nazarenes. [6]Furthermore, he was trying to
desecrate the Temple when we arrested him.* [8]You can
find out the truth of our accusations by examining him
yourself." [9]Then the other Jews chimed in, declaring that
everything Tertullus said was true.
[10]The governor then motioned for Paul to speak. Paul
said, "I know, sir, that you have been a judge of Jewish
affairs for many years, so I gladly present my defense
before you. [11]You can quickly discover that I arrived
in Jerusalem no more than twelve days ago to worship
at the Temple. [12]My accusers never found me arguing
with anyone in the Temple, nor stirring up a riot in any
synagogue or on the streets of the city. [13]These men
cannot prove the things they accuse me of doing.
[14]"But I admit that I follow the Way, which they call
a cult. I worship the God of our ancestors, and I firmly
believe the Jewish law and everything written in the
prophets. [15]I have the same hope in God that these
men have, that he will raise both the righteous and the
unrighteous. [16]Because of this, I always try to maintain
a clear conscience before God and all people.
[17]"After several years away, I returned to Jerusalem
with money to aid my people and to offer sacrifices to
God. [18]My accusers saw me in the Temple as I was completing a purification ceremony. There was no crowd
around me and no rioting. [19]But some Jews from the
province of Asia were there—and they ought to be
here to bring charges if they have anything against
me! [20]Ask these men here what crime the Jewish high
council* found me guilty of, [21]except for the one time
I shouted out, 'I am on trial before you today because
I believe in the resurrection of the dead!'"
[22]At that point Felix, who was quite familiar with
the Way, adjourned the hearing and said, "Wait until
Lysias, the garrison commander, arrives. Then I will
decide the case." [23]He ordered an officer* to keep Paul
in custody but to give him some freedom and allow
his friends to visit him and take care of his needs.
[24]A few days later Felix came back with his wife,
Drusilla, who was Jewish. Sending for Paul, they listened as he told them about faith in Christ Jesus. [25]As
he reasoned with them about righteousness and self-
control and the coming day of judgment, Felix became
frightened. "Go away for now," he replied. "When it
is more convenient, I'll call for you again." [26]He also
hoped that Paul would bribe him, so he sent for him
quite often and talked with him.
[27]After two years went by in this way, Felix was succeeded by Porcius Festus. And because Felix wanted to
gain favor with the Jewish people, he left Paul in prison.

Acts 24:6 Some manuscripts add an expanded conclusion to verse 6, all of verse 7, and an additional phrase in verse 8: *We would have judged him by our law, [7]but Lysias, the commander of the garrison, came and violently took him away from us, [8]commanding his accusers to come before you.* **Acts 24:20** Greek *Sanhedrin.* **Acts 24:23** Greek *a centurion.*

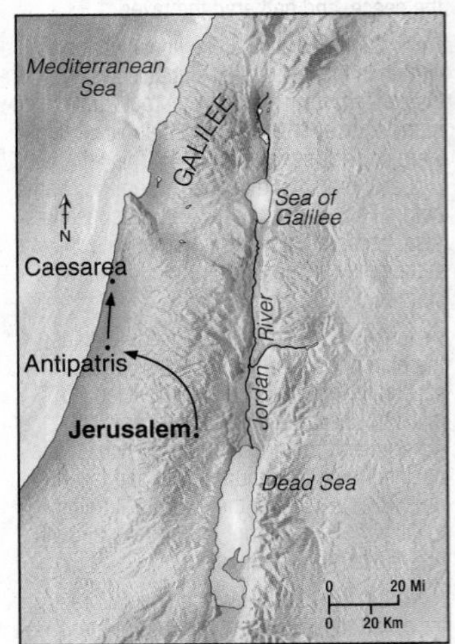

IMPRISONMENT IN CAESAREA *Paul brought news of his third journey to the elders of the Jerusalem church, who rejoiced at his ministry. But Paul's presence soon stirred up the Jews, who persuaded the Romans to arrest him. A plot to kill Paul was uncovered, so Paul was taken by night to Antipatris and then transferred to the provincial prison in Caesarea.*

Acts 24:5 While the charge that Paul was a troublemaker was insulting to Paul, it was too vague to be a substantive legal charge. "The Nazarenes" refers to the Christians—named here after Jesus' hometown of Nazareth.

Acts 24:10ff Tertullus and the religious leaders seemed to have a strong argument against Paul, but Paul refuted their accusations point by point. Paul was also able to present the Good News through his defense. Paul's accusers were unable to present specific evidence to support their general accusations. For example, Paul was accused of starting trouble among the Jews in the province of Asia (Acts 24:18-19), but the Jews in the province of Asia (western Turkey) were not present to confirm this. This is another example of Paul using every opportunity to witness for Christ (see Acts 24:14, 24).

Acts 24:22 Felix had been governor for six years and would have known about the Christians ("the Way"), a topic of conversation among the Roman leaders. The Christians' peaceful lifestyles had already proven to the Romans that Christians didn't go around starting riots.

Acts 24:25 Paul's talk with Felix became so personal that Felix grew frightened. Felix, like Herod Antipas (Mark 6:17-18), had taken another man's wife. Paul's words were interesting until they focused on "righteousness and self-control and the coming day of judgment." Many people will be glad to discuss the Good News with you as long as it doesn't touch their lives too personally. When it does, some will resist or run. But this is what the Good News is all about—God's power to change lives. The Good News is not effective until it moves from principles and doctrine into a life-changing dynamic. When someone resists or runs from your witness, you have undoubtedly succeeded in making the Good News personal.

Acts 24:27 The Jews were in the majority, and the Roman political leaders wanted to defer to them to help keep the peace. Paul seemed to incite problems among the Jews everywhere he went. By keeping him in prison, Felix left office on good terms with the Jews. Felix lost his job as governor and was called back to Rome. Porcius Festus took over as governor in late 59 or early 60. He was more just than Felix, who had kept Paul in prison for two years in the hope that perhaps Paul would bribe him and that, by detaining Paul, the Jews would be kept happy. When Festus came into office, he immediately ordered Paul's trial to resume.

Acts 24:27 Though God had promised that Paul would preach the gospel in Rome (Acts 23:11), the great apostle had to endure more than two years of Felix's refusal to decide his fate. In addition to this custody, Paul was subjected to other long stretches

Paul Appears before Festus

ACTS 25:1-22

Three days after Festus arrived in Caesarea to take over
his new responsibilities, he left for Jerusalem, 2where
the leading priests and other Jewish leaders met with
him and made their accusations against Paul. 3They
asked Festus as a favor to transfer Paul to Jerusalem
(planning to ambush and kill him on the way). 4But
Festus replied that Paul was at Caesarea and he himself
would be returning there soon. 5So he said, "Those of
you in authority can return with me. If Paul has done
anything wrong, you can make your accusations."

6About eight or ten days later Festus returned to
Caesarea, and on the following day he took his seat
in court and ordered that Paul be brought in. 7When
Paul arrived, the Jewish leaders from Jerusalem gathered around and made many serious accusations they
couldn't prove.

8Paul denied the charges. "I am not guilty of any
crime against the Jewish laws or the Temple or the
Roman government," he said.

9Then Festus, wanting to please the Jews, asked him,
"Are you willing to go to Jerusalem and stand trial
before me there?"

10But Paul replied, "No! This is the official Roman
court, so I ought to be tried right here. You know very
well I am not guilty of harming the Jews. 11If I have
done something worthy of death, I don't refuse to die.
But if I am innocent, no one has a right to turn me over
to these men to kill me. I appeal to Caesar!"

12Festus conferred with his advisers and then replied, "Very well! You have appealed to Caesar, and to
Caesar you will go!"

13A few days later King Agrippa arrived with his sister, Bernice,* to pay their respects to Festus. 14During
their stay of several days, Festus discussed Paul's case
with the king. "There is a prisoner here," he told him,
"whose case was left for me by Felix. 15When I was in
Jerusalem, the leading priests and Jewish elders pressed
charges against him and asked me to condemn him. 16I
pointed out to them that Roman law does not convict
people without a trial. They must be given an opportunity to confront their accusers and defend themselves.

17"When his accusers came here for the trial, I didn't
delay. I called the case the very next day and ordered
Paul brought in. 18But the accusations made against him
weren't any of the crimes I expected. 19Instead, it was
something about their religion and a dead man named
Jesus, who Paul insists is alive. 20I was at a loss to know
how to investigate these things, so I asked him whether

Acts 25:13 Greek *Agrippa the king and Bernice arrived.*

Caesar Nero

Nero reigned A.D. 54–68; he had been reigning more than five years when Paul, imprisoned at Caesarea, appealed to Caesar (Acts 25:11). Motives for the appeal may have been a prison release for Paul and an opportunity to seek legal recognition of Christianity. Paul's appeal to Caesar does not necessarily mean that Nero himself judged him. The emperor had made it known at the beginning of his reign that he would not be a judge. Instead, he appointed prefects of the Praetorian Guard to judge cases for him. In the early part of A.D. 62, Nero changed that rule and judged a case himself. Therefore, whether Paul stood before Nero or before one of the prefects is difficult to determine. If prosecutors failed to appear, Paul's case may not have come before the judge at all.

History seems to indicate that Paul did not face Nero during his Roman imprisonment of A.D. 60–62, but he likely did later in life (probably A.D. 66 or 67), when he met his end. Paul's goal was to glorify the Lord whether in life or in death (Phil 1:20-21). His attitude should inspire us to consider how every circumstance we find ourselves in might be an opportunity to serve God.

of time during which he could do little but trust God and wait for him to act. What do you do when it comes to the issue of waiting on God? Do you become anxious? angry? discouraged? Few things test our patience and faith like being forced to wait—which perhaps explains why our sovereign God often puts us in situations where we have no other choice.

Acts 25:1-9 Although two years had passed, the Jewish leaders still were looking for a way to kill Paul. They told Festus about Paul and tried to convince him to hold the trial in Jerusalem (so they could prepare an ambush). But God and Paul thwarted their schemes again.

Acts 25:10-11 Paul knew that he was innocent of the charges against him and could appeal to Caesar's judgment. He knew his rights as a Roman citizen and as an innocent person. Paul had met his responsibilities as a Roman, and so he had the opportunity to claim Rome's protection. Every Roman citizen had the right to appeal to Caesar. This didn't mean that Caesar himself would hear the case but that the citizen's case would be tried by the highest courts in the empire. Festus saw Paul's appeal as a way to send him out of the country and thus pacify the Jews. Paul wanted to go to Rome to preach the Good News (Rom 1:10), and he knew that his appeal would give him the opportunity. To go to Rome as a prisoner was better than not to go there at all.

Acts 25:13 This was Herod Agrippa II, son of Herod Agrippa I and a descendant of Herod the Great. He had power over the Temple, controlled the Temple treasury, and could appoint and remove the high priest. Bernice was the sister of Herod Agrippa II. She had married her uncle, Herod Chalcis, had become mistress to her brother Agrippa II, and then had become mistress to the emperor Vespasian's son, Titus. Here Agrippa and Bernice were making an official visit to Festus. Agrippa, of Jewish descent, could help clarify Paul's case for the Roman governor. Agrippa and Festus were anxious to cooperate in governing their neighboring territories.

Acts 25:19 Even though Festus knew little about Christianity, he somehow sensed that the Resurrection was central to Christian belief.

▸ **ACTS 25:1-22** ***(cont.)***
he would be willing to stand trial on these charges in
Jerusalem. 21 But Paul appealed to have his case decided
by the emperor. So I ordered that he be held in custody
until I could arrange to send him to Caesar."
22 "I'd like to hear the man myself," Agrippa said.
And Festus replied, "You will—tomorrow!"

Paul Speaks to Agrippa

ACTS 25:23–26:32
So the next day Agrippa and Bernice arrived at the
auditorium with great pomp, accompanied by military
officers and prominent men of the city. Festus ordered
that Paul be brought in. 24 Then Festus said, "King
Agrippa and all who are here, this is the man whose
death is demanded by all the Jews, both here and in
Jerusalem. 25 But in my opinion he has done nothing
deserving death. However, since he appealed his case
to the emperor, I have decided to send him to Rome.
26 "But what shall I write the emperor? For there is
no clear charge against him. So I have brought him
before all of you, and especially you, King Agrippa, so
that after we examine him, I might have something to
write. 27 For it makes no sense to send a prisoner to the
emperor without specifying the charges against him!"

26:1 Then Agrippa said to Paul, "You may speak in your
defense."
So Paul, gesturing with his hand, started his defense: 2 "I am fortunate, King Agrippa, that you are the
one hearing my defense today against all these accusations made by the Jewish leaders, 3 for I know you are
an expert on all Jewish customs and controversies.
Now please listen to me patiently!
4 "As the Jewish leaders are well aware, I was given
a thorough Jewish training from my earliest childhood among my own people and in Jerusalem. 5 If they
would admit it, they know that I have been a member
of the Pharisees, the strictest sect of our religion. 6 Now
I am on trial because of my hope in the fulfillment of
God's promise made to our ancestors. 7 In fact, that is
why the twelve tribes of Israel zealously worship God
night and day, and they share the same hope I have.

HEROD AGRIPPA II

Like great-grandfather, like grandfather, like father, like son—this tells the story of Herod Agrippa II. He inherited the character flaws of generations of powerful men. Each son followed his father in weaknesses, mistakes, and missed opportunities to know God. Each generation had a confrontation with God but failed to realize the importance of the moment. Herod Agrippa's great-uncle, Herod Antipas, actually met Jesus during his trial but failed to see Jesus for who he was. Agrippa II heard the gospel from Paul but considered the message mild entertainment. He found it humorous that Paul actually tried to convince him to become a Christian. • Like so many before and after, Agrippa II stopped within hearing distance of the Kingdom of God. He left himself without excuse. He heard the gospel but decided it wasn't worth responding to personally. Sadly, his mistake is not uncommon. Many who read his story also will not believe. Their problem, like his, is not really that the gospel isn't convincing or that they don't need to know God personally; it is that they choose not to respond. • What has been your response to the gospel? Has it turned your life around and given you the hope of eternal life, or has it been a message to resist or reject? Perhaps it has just been entertainment. It may seem like too great a price to give God control of your life, but the price is minimal compared to living apart from him for eternity because you have chosen not to be his child.

Strengths and accomplishments	• Last of the Herod dynasty that ruled parts of Palestine from 40 B.C.–A.D. 100 • Continued the family tradition of building and improving cities
Weaknesses and mistakes	• Was not convinced by the gospel and consciously rejected it • Carried on an incestuous relationship with his sister Bernice
Lessons from his life	• Families pass on both positive and negative influences to children
Vital statistics	• Occupation: Ruler of northern and eastern Palestine • Relatives: Great-grandfather: Herod the Great. Father: Herod Agrippa I. Great-uncle: Herod Antipas. Sisters: Bernice, Drusilla. • Contemporaries: Paul, Felix, Festus, Peter, Luke
Key verse	"Agrippa interrupted him. 'Do you think you can persuade me to become a Christian so quickly?'" (Acts 26:28).

Herod Agrippa II's story is told in Acts 25:13–26:32.

Acts 25:23ff Paul was in prison, but that didn't stop him from making the most of his situation. Military officers and prominent city leaders met in the auditorium with Agrippa to hear this case. Paul saw this new audience as yet another opportunity to present the Good News. Rather than complain about your present situation, look for ways to use every opportunity to serve God and share him with others. Your problems may be opportunities in disguise.

Acts 26:3ff This speech is a good example of Paul's powerful oratory. Beginning with a compliment to Agrippa, he told his story, including the resurrection of Christ, and the royal audience was spellbound.

Acts 26:17-18 Paul took every opportunity to remind his audience that the Gentiles had an equal share in God's inheritance. This inheritance is the promise and blessing of the covenant that God had made with Abraham (see Eph 2:19; 1 Pet 1:3-4). Paul's mission was to preach the Good News to the Gentiles.

Acts 26:24 Paul was risking his life for a message that was offensive to the Jews and unbelievable to the Gentiles. Jesus received the same response to his message (Mark 3:21; John 10:20). To a worldly, materialistic mind, it seems insane to risk so much to gain what seems to be so little. But as you follow Christ, you soon discover that one's most prized possessions cannot compare to even the smallest eternal reward.

Acts 26:26 Paul was appealing to the *facts:* People were still alive who had heard Jesus and seen his miracles; the empty tomb could still be seen; and the Christian message was turning the world upside down (Acts 17:6). The history of Jesus' life and the early church are facts that still confront us today. We still have eyewitness accounts of Jesus' life

Yet, Your Majesty, they accuse me for having this hope!
[8]Why does it seem incredible to any of you that God
can raise the dead?
[9]"I used to believe that I ought to do everything I
could to oppose the very name of Jesus the Nazarene.*
[10]Indeed, I did just that in Jerusalem. Authorized by
the leading priests, I caused many believers* there
to be sent to prison. And I cast my vote against them
when they were condemned to death. [11]Many times I
had them punished in the synagogues to get them to
curse Jesus.* I was so violently opposed to them that
I even chased them down in foreign cities.
[12]"One day I was on such a mission to Damascus,
armed with the authority and commission of the leading priests. [13]About noon, Your Majesty, as I was on
the road, a light from heaven brighter than the sun
shone down on me and my companions. [14]We all fell
down, and I heard a voice saying to me in Aramaic,*
'Saul, Saul, why are you persecuting me? It is useless
for you to fight against my will.*'
[15]"'Who are you, lord?' I asked.
"And the Lord replied, 'I am Jesus, the one you
are persecuting. [16]Now get to your feet! For I have
appeared to you to appoint you as my servant and
witness. You are to tell the world what you have seen
and what I will show you in the future. [17]And I will
rescue you from both your own people and the Gentiles. Yes, I am sending you to the Gentiles [18]to open
their eyes, so they may turn from darkness to light
and from the power of Satan to God. Then they will
receive forgiveness for their sins and be given a place
among God's people, who are set apart by faith in me.'
[19]"And so, King Agrippa, I obeyed that vision from
heaven. [20]I preached first to those in Damascus, then
in Jerusalem and throughout all Judea, and also to the
Gentiles, that all must repent of their sins and turn to
God—and prove they have changed by the good things
they do. [21]Some Jews arrested me in the Temple for
preaching this, and they tried to kill me. [22]But God
has protected me right up to this present time so I
can testify to everyone, from the least to the greatest.
I teach nothing except what the prophets and Moses
said would happen—[23]that the Messiah would suffer
and be the first to rise from the dead, and in this way
announce God's light to Jews and Gentiles alike."
[24]Suddenly, Festus shouted, "Paul, you are insane.
Too much study has made you crazy!"
[25]But Paul replied, "I am not insane, Most Excellent

Acts 26:9 Or *Jesus of Nazareth.* **Acts 26:10** Greek *many of God's holy people.* **Acts 26:11** Greek *to blaspheme.* **Acts 26:14a** Or *Hebrew.* **Acts 26:14b** Greek *It is hard for you to kick against the oxgoads.*

PAUL'S JOURNEY TO ROME

One of Paul's most important journeys was to Rome, but he didn't get there the way he expected. It turned out to be more of a legal journey than a missionary journey. Through a series of legal trials and transactions, Paul was delivered to Rome, where his presentation of the gospel would even penetrate the walls of the emperor's palace. Sometimes when our plans don't work out as we want them to, they work out even better than we expected.

Reference	*What Happened*
Acts 21:30-34	When Paul arrived in Jerusalem, a riot broke out. Seeing the riot, Roman soldiers put Paul into protective custody. Paul asked for a chance to defend himself to the people. His speech was interrupted by the crowd when he told about what God was doing in the lives of Gentiles.
Acts 22:24-25	A Roman commander ordered a beating to get a confession from Paul. Paul claimed Roman citizenship and escaped the whip.
Acts 22:30	Paul was brought before the Jewish high council. Because of his Roman citizenship, he was rescued from the religious leaders who wanted to kill him.
Acts 23:10	The Roman commander put Paul back under protective custody.
Acts 23:21-24	Due to a plot to kill Paul, the commander transferred him to Caesarea, which was under Governor Felix's control.
Acts 23:35	Paul was in prison until the Jews arrived to accuse him. Paul defended himself before Felix.
Acts 24:25-26	Paul was in prison for two years, speaking occasionally to Felix and Drusilla.
Acts 24:27	Felix was replaced by Festus.
Acts 25:1, 10-11	Renewed accusations were brought against Paul—Jews wanted him back in Jerusalem for a trial. Paul claimed his right to a hearing before Caesar.
Acts 25:12	Festus promised to send him to Rome.
Acts 25:13-21	Festus discussed Paul's case with Herod Agrippa II.
Acts 26:1-23	Agrippa and Festus heard Paul speak. Paul again told his story.
Acts 26:24-28	Agrippa interrupted with a sarcastic rejection of the gospel.
Acts 26:30-32	Group consensus was that Paul was guilty of nothing and could have been released if he had not appealed to Rome.
Acts 27:1-2	Paul left for Rome, courtesy of the Roman Empire.

▶ **ACTS 25:23-26:33** ***(cont.)***
Festus. What I am saying is the sober truth. 26 And King
Agrippa knows about these things. I speak boldly, for
I am sure these events are all familiar to him, for they
were not done in a corner! 27 King Agrippa, do you
believe the prophets? I know you do—"
28 Agrippa interrupted him. "Do you think you can
persuade me to become a Christian so quickly?"*
29 Paul replied, "Whether quickly or not, I pray to
God that both you and everyone here in this audience might become the same as I am, except for these
chains."
30 Then the king, the governor, Bernice, and all the
others stood and left. 31 As they went out, they talked
it over and agreed, "This man hasn't done anything to
deserve death or imprisonment."
32 And Agrippa said to Festus, "He could have been
set free if he hadn't appealed to Caesar."

Paul Sails for Rome

ACTS 27:1-12
When the time came, we set sail for Italy. Paul and
several other prisoners were placed in the custody
of a Roman officer* named Julius, a captain of the
Imperial Regiment. 2 Aristarchus, a Macedonian from
Thessalonica, was also with us. We left on a ship whose
home port was Adramyttium on the northwest coast
of the province of Asia;* it was scheduled to make
several stops at ports along the coast of the province.
3 The next day when we docked at Sidon, Julius was
very kind to Paul and let him go ashore to visit with
friends so they could provide for his needs. 4 Putting
out to sea from there, we encountered strong head-
winds that made it difficult to keep the ship on course,
so we sailed north of Cyprus between the island and
the mainland. 5 Keeping to the open sea, we passed
along the coast of Cilicia and Pamphylia, landing at
Myra, in the province of Lycia. 6 There the commanding officer found an Egyptian ship from Alexandria
that was bound for Italy, and he put us on board.
7 We had several days of slow sailing, and after great
difficulty we finally neared Cnidus. But the wind was
against us, so we sailed across to Crete and along the
sheltered coast of the island, past the cape of Salmone.
8 We struggled along the coast with great difficulty and
finally arrived at Fair Havens, near the town of Lasea.
9 We had lost a lot of time. The weather was becoming
dangerous for sea travel because it was so late in the
fall,* and Paul spoke to the ship's officers about it.
10 "Men," he said, "I believe there is trouble ahead
if we go on—shipwreck, loss of cargo, and danger to
our lives as well." 11 But the officer in charge of the

AD 59

Acts 26:28 Or *"A little more, and your arguments would make me a Christian."* **Acts 27:1** Greek *centurion;* similarly in 27:6, 11, 31, 43. **Acts 27:2** *Asia* was a Roman province in what is now western Turkey. **Acts 27:9** Greek *because the fast was now already gone by.* This fast was associated with the Day of Atonement (*Yom Kippur*), which occurred in late September or early October.

Paul's voyage to Rome

recorded in the Bible as well as historical and archaeological records of the early church to study. Examine the events and facts as verified by many witnesses. Strengthen your faith with the truth of these accounts.

Acts 26:28-29 Agrippa responded to Paul's presentation with a sarcastic remark. Paul didn't react to the brush-off but made a personal appeal to which he hoped all his listeners would respond. Paul's response is a good example for us as we tell others about God's plan of salvation. A sincere personal appeal or personal testimony can show the depth of our concern and break through hardened hearts.

Acts 26:28-29 Paul's heart is revealed here in his words: He was more concerned for the salvation of these strangers than for the removal of his own chains. Ask God to give you a burning desire to see others come to Christ—a desire so strong that it overshadows your problems.

Acts 27:1-2 Use of the pronoun *we* indicates that Luke accompanied Paul on this journey. Aristarchus is the man who had been dragged into the theater at the beginning of the riot in Ephesus (Acts 19:29; 20:4; Phlm 1:24).

Acts 27:1-3 Julius, a Roman army officer, was assigned to guard Paul. Obviously he had to remain close to Paul at all times. Through this contact, Julius developed a respect for Paul. He gave Paul a certain amount of freedom (Acts 27:3) and later spared his life (Acts 27:43). How would your character look, up close and personal?

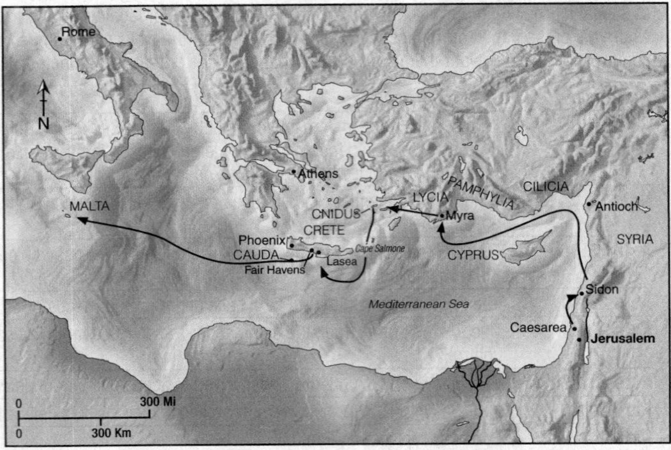

***THE TRIP TOWARD ROME** Paul began his 2,000-mile trip to Rome at Caesarea. To avoid the open seas, the ship followed the coastline. At Myra, Paul was put on a vessel bound for Italy. It arrived with difficulty at Cnidus, then went to Crete, landing at the port of Fair Havens. The next stop was Phoenix, but the ship was blown south around the island of Cauda, then drifted for two weeks until it was shipwrecked on the island of Malta.*

Acts 27:9 Ships in ancient times had no compasses, so they navigated by the stars. Overcast weather made sailing almost impossible and very dangerous. Sailing was doubtful in September and impossible by November. This event occurred in October (A.D. 59).

Acts 27:12 Although this was not the best time to sail, the ship's captain and the owner

prisoners listened more to the ship's captain and the owner than to Paul. 12And since Fair Havens was an exposed harbor—a poor place to spend the winter—most of the crew wanted to go on to Phoenix, farther up the coast of Crete, and spend the winter there. Phoenix was a good harbor with only a southwest and northwest exposure.

The Storm at Sea

ACTS 27:13-26

When a light wind began blowing from the south, the sailors thought they could make it. So they pulled up anchor and sailed close to the shore of Crete. 14But the weather changed abruptly, and a wind of typhoon strength (called a "northeaster") burst across the island and blew us out to sea. 15The sailors couldn't turn the ship into the wind, so they gave up and let it run before the gale.

16We sailed along the sheltered side of a small island named Cauda,* where with great difficulty we hoisted aboard the lifeboat being towed behind us. 17Then the sailors bound ropes around the hull of the ship to strengthen it. They were afraid of being driven across to the sandbars of Syrtis off the African coast, so they lowered the sea anchor to slow the ship and were driven before the wind.

18The next day, as gale-force winds continued to batter the ship, the crew began throwing the cargo overboard. 19The following day they even took some of the ship's gear and threw it overboard. 20The terrible storm raged for many days, blotting out the sun and the stars, until at last all hope was gone.

21No one had eaten for a long time. Finally, Paul called the crew together and said, "Men, you should have listened to me in the first place and not left Crete. You would have avoided all this damage and loss. 22But take courage! None of you will lose your lives, even though the ship will go down. 23For last night an angel of the God to whom I belong and whom I serve stood beside me, 24and he said, 'Don't be afraid, Paul, for you will surely stand trial before Caesar! What's more, God in his goodness has granted safety to everyone sailing with you.' 25So take courage! For I believe God. It will be just as he said. 26But we will be shipwrecked on an island."

The Shipwreck

ACTS 27:27-44

About midnight on the fourteenth night of the storm, as we were being driven across the Sea of Adria,* the sailors sensed land was near. 28They dropped a weighted line and found that the water was 120 feet deep. But a little later they measured again and found it was only 90 feet deep.* 29At this rate they were afraid we would soon be driven against the rocks along the shore, so they threw out four anchors from the back of the ship and prayed for daylight.

30Then the sailors tried to abandon the ship; they lowered the lifeboat as though they were going to put out anchors from the front of the ship. 31But Paul said to the commanding officer and the soldiers, "You will all die unless the sailors stay aboard." 32So the soldiers cut the ropes to the lifeboat and let it drift away.

33Just as day was dawning, Paul urged everyone to eat. "You have been so worried that you haven't touched food for two weeks," he said. 34"Please eat something now for your own good. For not a hair of your heads will perish." 35Then he took some bread, gave thanks to God before them all, and broke off a piece and ate it. 36Then everyone was encouraged

Acts 27:16 Some manuscripts read *Clauda.* **Acts 27:27** The *Sea of Adria* includes the central portion of the Mediterranean. **Acts 27:28** Greek *20 fathoms . . . 15 fathoms* [37 meters . . . 27 meters].

of the ship didn't want to spend the winter in Lasea, or Fair Havens, so the officer took a chance. At first the winds and weather were favorable, but then the deadly storm arose.

Acts 27:17 Binding ropes around the hull of the ship meant passing ropes under the ship to hold it together. Syrtis was on the northern coast of Africa.

Acts 27:21 Why would Paul talk to the crew this way? Paul was not taunting them with an "I told you so" but was reminding them that, with God's guidance, he had predicted this very problem (Acts 27:10). In the future, they listened to him (Acts 27:30-32), and their lives were spared because of it.

Acts 27:27 The Sea of Adria referred to the central part of the Mediterranean Sea between Italy, Crete, and the northern coast of Africa.

Acts 27:28 These weighted lines had marks on them so that when the weight hit the bottom, the sailors could tell the depth of the water from the marks on the line.

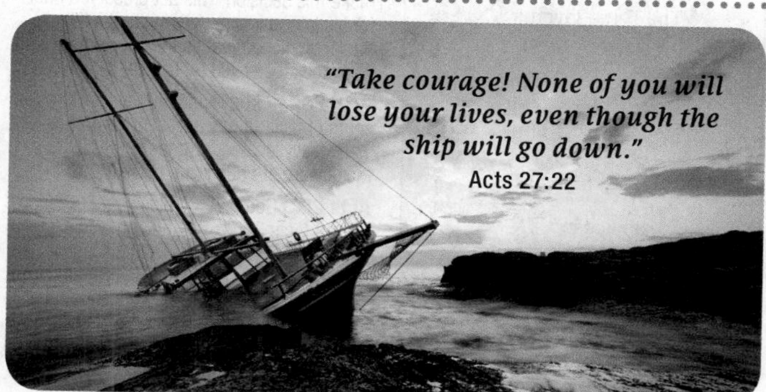
"Take courage! None of you will lose your lives, even though the ship will go down."
Acts 27:22

Acts 27:29 In the middle of a midnight squall, the passengers and crew (led by Paul) did all they could possibly do—they dropped some anchors to try to stop the runaway ship. Then they prayed. Of course, Paul was praying to the one God who could do anything about their situation. This is a good reminder for us. We must never rely solely on our own wisdom or skills. But it is equally wrong to sit and do nothing when there are still actions we can take to overcome certain problems. Do all that you can to fix the problem. And at the same time, trust God to do his part.

▸ **ACTS 27:27-44** ***(cont.)***
and began to eat—37all 276 of us who were on board.
38After eating, the crew lightened the ship further by
throwing the cargo of wheat overboard.
39When morning dawned, they didn't recognize the
coastline, but they saw a bay with a beach and wondered if they could get to shore by running the ship
aground. 40So they cut off the anchors and left them in
the sea. Then they lowered the rudders, raised the fore-
sail, and headed toward shore. 41But they hit a shoal
and ran the ship aground too soon. The bow of the ship
stuck fast, while the stern was repeatedly smashed by
the force of the waves and began to break apart.
42The soldiers wanted to kill the prisoners to make
sure they didn't swim ashore and escape. 43But the
commanding officer wanted to spare Paul, so he didn't
let them carry out their plan. Then he ordered all who
could swim to jump overboard first and make for land.
44The others held on to planks or debris from the
broken ship.* So everyone escaped safely to shore.

Paul on the Island of Malta

ACTS 28:1-10
Once we were safe on shore, we learned that we were
on the island of Malta. 2The people of the island were
very kind to us. It was cold and rainy, so they built a
fire on the shore to welcome us.
3As Paul gathered an armful of sticks and was laying
them on the fire, a poisonous snake, driven out by the
heat, bit him on the hand. 4The people of the island
saw it hanging from his hand and said to each other,
"A murderer, no doubt! Though he escaped the sea,
justice will not permit him to live." 5But Paul shook
off the snake into the fire and was unharmed. 6The
people waited for him to swell up or suddenly drop
dead. But when they had waited a long time and saw
that he wasn't harmed, they changed their minds and
decided he was a god.
7Near the shore where we landed was an estate
belonging to Publius, the chief official of the island.
He welcomed us and treated us kindly for three days.
8As it happened, Publius's father was ill with fever and
dysentery. Paul went in and prayed for him, and laying
his hands on him, he healed him. 9Then all the other
sick people on the island came and were healed. 10As
a result we were showered with honors, and when the
time came to sail, people supplied us with everything
we would need for the trip.

Paul Arrives at Rome

ACTS 28:11-16
It was three months after the shipwreck that we set sail
on another ship that had wintered at the island—an
Alexandrian ship with the twin gods* as its figure-
head. 12Our first stop was Syracuse,* where we stayed
three days. 13From there we sailed across to Rhegium.*
A day later a south wind began blowing, so the following day we sailed up the coast to Puteoli. 14There we

Acts 27:44 Or *or were helped by members of the ship's crew.* **Acts 28:11** The *twin gods* were the Roman gods Castor and Pollux. **Acts 28:12** *Syracuse* was on the island of Sicily. **Acts 28:13** *Rhegium* was on the southern tip of Italy.

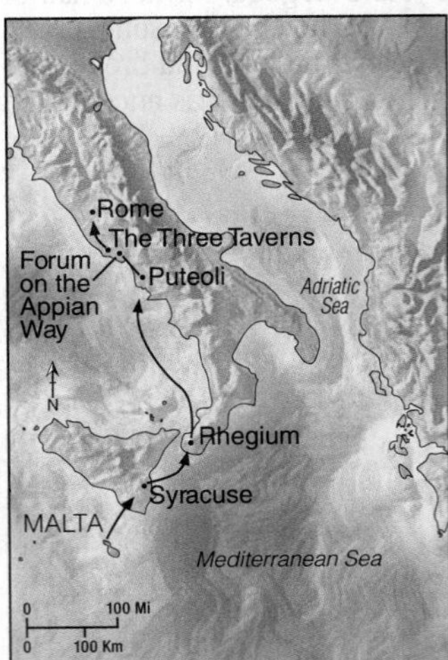

***PAUL ARRIVES IN ROME** The shipwreck occurred on Malta, where the ship's company spent three months. Finally, another ship gave them passage for the 100 miles to Syracuse, capital of Sicily, then sailed on to Rhegium, finally dropping anchor at Puteoli. Paul was taken to the Forum on the Appian Way and to The Three Taverns before arriving in Rome.*

Acts 27:42-43 The soldiers would pay with their own lives if any of their prisoners escaped. Their instinctive reaction was to kill the prisoners so they wouldn't get away. Julius, the officer, was impressed with Paul and wanted to save his life. Julius was the highest ranking official; therefore, he could make this decision. This act preserved Paul for his later ministry in Rome and fulfilled Paul's prediction that all the people on the ship would be saved (Acts 27:22).

Acts 28:1-2 The island of Malta is 60 miles south of Sicily. It had excellent harbors and was ideally located for trade. The islanders on Malta were of Phoenician ancestry.

Acts 28:3 God had promised safe passage to Paul (Acts 27:23-25), and he would let nothing stop his servant. The poisonous snake that bit Paul was unable to harm him. Our life is in God's hands, to continue on or to come to an end in his good timing. God still had work for Paul to do.

Acts 28:6 These people were very superstitious and believed in many gods. When they saw that Paul was unhurt by the poisonous snake, they thought he was a god. Acts 14:11-18 reports a similar assessment.

Acts 28:7-8 Paul continued to minister to others, even as a shipwrecked prisoner. On this trip alone, the Roman army officer, the chief official of Malta, and many others were affected. It is no wonder that the Good News spread like wildfire.

Acts 28:15 Where did the Roman believers come from? The Good News had spread to Rome by various methods. Many Jews who lived in Rome would visit Jerusalem for religious festivals. Some had been present at Pentecost (Acts 2:10), had believed in Jesus, and had brought the message back to Rome. Also, Paul had written his letter to the Romans before this time.

Acts 28:15 The Forum on the Appian Way was a town about 43 miles south of Rome; The Three Taverns was located about 35 miles south of Rome. A tavern was a shop or a place that provided food and lodging for travelers. The Christians openly went to meet Paul and encourage him.

Acts 28:17 The decree of Claudius expelling Jews from Rome (Acts 18:2) must have been temporary because Jewish leaders were back in Rome.

Acts 28:17-20 Paul wanted to preach the Good News in Rome, and he eventually got there—in chains, through shipwreck, and after many trials. Although he may have wished for an easier passage, he knew that God had blessed him greatly in allowing him to meet the believers in Rome and preach

found some believers,* who invited us to spend a week with them. And so we came to Rome.

[15]The brothers and sisters* in Rome had heard we were coming, and they came to meet us at the Forum* on the Appian Way. Others joined us at The Three Taverns.* When Paul saw them, he was encouraged and thanked God.

[16]When we arrived in Rome, Paul was permitted to have his own private lodging, though he was guarded by a soldier.

Paul Preaches in Rome under Guard

ACTS 28:17-31

Three days after Paul's arrival, he called together the local Jewish leaders. He said to them, "Brothers, I was arrested in Jerusalem and handed over to the Roman government, even though I had done nothing against our people or the customs of our ancestors. [18]The Romans tried me and wanted to release me, because they found no cause for the death sentence. [19]But when the Jewish leaders protested the decision, I felt it necessary to appeal to Caesar, even though I had no desire to press charges against my own people. [20]I asked you to come here today so we could get acquainted and so I could explain to you that I am bound with this chain because I believe that the hope of Israel—the Messiah—has already come."

[21]They replied, "We have had no letters from Judea or reports against you from anyone who has come here. [22]But we want to hear what you believe, for the only thing we know about this movement is that it is denounced everywhere."

[23]So a time was set, and on that day a large number of people came to Paul's lodging. He explained and testified about the Kingdom of God and tried to persuade them about Jesus from the Scriptures. Using the law of Moses and the books of the prophets, he spoke to them from morning until evening. [24]Some were persuaded by the things he said, but others did not believe. [25]And after they had argued back and forth among themselves, they left with this final word from Paul: "The Holy Spirit was right when he said to your ancestors through Isaiah the prophet,

[26] 'Go and say to this people:
When you hear what I say,
you will not understand.
When you see what I do,
you will not comprehend.
[27] For the hearts of these people are hardened,
and their ears cannot hear,
and they have closed their eyes—
so their eyes cannot see,
and their ears cannot hear,
and their hearts cannot understand,
and they cannot turn to me
and let me heal them.'*

[28]So I want you to know that this salvation from God has also been offered to the Gentiles, and they will accept it."*

Acts 28:14 Greek *brothers.* **Acts 28:15a** Greek *brothers.* **Acts 28:15b** *The Forum* was about 43 miles (70 kilometers) from Rome. **Acts 28:15c** *The Three Taverns* was about 35 miles (57 kilometers) from Rome. **Acts 28:26-27** Isa 6:9-10 (Greek version). **Acts 28:28** Some manuscripts add verse 29, *And when he had said these words, the Jews departed, greatly disagreeing with each other.*

The Appian Way

The Appian Way was a main highway from Rome southward to the heel of the Italian peninsula at Brundisium (a total of 350 miles). It received its name from Appius Claudius Caecus, the Roman censor who began its construction in 312 B.C. The Appian Way is referred to by ancient writers Livy, Strabo, Horace, and others in a variety of contexts. Portions of the road still exist today with the original Roman paving intact in many places. The apostle Paul traveled on the Appian Way on his journey to Rome after disembarking from a ship at Puteoli (Acts 28:13-15). This road, like many roads throughout the Roman Empire, paved the way for the spreading of the gospel. Today's ease and access of transportation should help us spread the Good News even further.

the message to both Jews and Gentiles in that great city. In all things, God worked for Paul's good (Rom 8:28). You can trust God to do the same for you. God may not make you comfortable or secure, but he will provide the opportunity to do his work.

Acts 28:22 Christians were denounced everywhere by the Romans because they were seen as a threat to the Roman establishment. They believed in one God, whereas the Romans had many gods, including Caesar. The Christians were committed to an authority higher than Caesar.

Acts 28:23 Paul used the Old Testament to teach the Jews that Jesus was the Messiah, the fulfillment of God's promises. The book of Romans, written earlier, reveals Paul's ongoing dialogue with the Jews in Rome.

▶ **ACTS 28:17-31** ***(cont.)***

30 For the next two years, Paul lived in Rome at his
own expense.* He welcomed all who visited him,
31 boldly proclaiming the Kingdom of God and teaching about the Lord Jesus Christ. And no one tried to stop him.

Acts 28:30 *Or in his own rented quarters.*

N. Paul's Letter to Philemon

While Paul was in prison in Rome, he wrote several letters to churches that he had ministered to during his missionary travels. The book of Philemon is a personal letter to a prominent man in the church at Colosse. Paul pleads on behalf of Onesimus, a runaway slave from Philemon's house. Paul's intercession for him illustrates what Christ has done for us. As Paul interceded for a slave, so Christ intercedes for us, slaves to sin. As Onesimus was reconciled to Philemon, so we are reconciled to God through Christ. As Paul offered to pay the debts of a slave, so Christ paid our debt of sin. Like Onesimus, we must return to God our Master and serve him.

Greetings from Paul

PHILEMON 1:1-3

This letter is from Paul, a prisoner for preaching the Good News about Christ Jesus, and from our brother Timothy.
I am writing to Philemon, our beloved co-worker,
2 and to our sister Apphia, and to our fellow soldier Archippus, and to the church that meets in your* house.
3 May God our Father and the Lord Jesus Christ give you grace and peace.

Phlm 2 Throughout this letter, *you* and *your* are singular except in verses 3, 22, and 25.

Paul writes several letters from prison in Rome

Acts 28:30 Paul remained in Rome under guard (Acts 28:16) in a rented house for two years. There sat the greatest apostle and spokesman for Christianity—unable to move freely and minister as he desired. However, Paul didn't complain or despair. He simply did what he could. Able to receive visitors, he taught, preached, and counseled even while he was confined to quarters. He wrote letters, commonly called his "Prison Letters," to the Ephesians, Colossians, and Philippians—letters that have impacted millions of believers down through the centuries. He also wrote personal letters, such as the one to Philemon. Luke was with Paul in Rome (2 Tim 4:11). Timothy often visited him (Phil 1:1; Col 1:1; Phlm 1:1), as did Tychicus (Eph 6:21), Epaphroditus (Phil 4:18), and Mark (Col 4:10). Paul witnessed to the whole Roman guard (Phil 1:13) and was involved with the Roman believers. If you find yourself in a negative or unpleasant situation, look for ways to redeem the circumstances. There is never a time or place in which you can't glorify and serve God.

Acts 28:30 Tradition says that Paul was released after two years of house arrest in Rome and that he then left on a fourth missionary journey. Some reasons for this tradition are as follows: (1) Luke does not give us an account of Paul's trial before Caesar, and Luke was a detailed chronicler; (2) the prosecution had two years to bring the case to trial, and time may have run out; (3) in his letter to the Philippians, written during his imprisonment in Rome, Paul implied that he would soon be released and would do further traveling; (4) Paul mentions several places where he intended to take the Good News, but he never visited those places in his first three journeys; (5) early Christian literature talks plainly about Paul's other travels.

During his time of freedom, Paul may have continued to travel extensively, even going to Spain (see Rom 15:24, 28) and back to the churches in Greece. The books of 1 Timothy and Titus were written during this time. Later, Paul was imprisoned again, probably in Rome, where he wrote his last letter (the book of 2 Timothy).

Acts 28:31 Why does the book of Acts end here and so abruptly? The book is not about the life of Paul but about the spread of the Good News, and that had been clearly presented. God apparently thought it was not necessary for someone to write an additional book describing the continuing history of the early church. Now that the Good News had been preached and established at the center of trade and government, it would spread across the world.

Acts 28:31 The book of Acts deals with the history of the Christian church and its expansion in ever-widening circles touching Jerusalem, Antioch, Ephesus, and Rome—the most influential cities in the Western world. Acts also shows the mighty miracles and testimonies of the heroes and martyrs of the early church—Peter, Stephen, James, Paul. All the ministry was prompted and held together by the Holy Spirit working in the lives of ordinary people—merchants, travelers, slaves, jailers, church leaders, males, females, Gentiles, Jews, rich, poor. Many unsung heroes of the faith continued the work, through the Holy Spirit, in succeeding generations, changing the world with a changeless message: Jesus Christ is Savior and Lord of all who call on him. Today we can be the unsung heroes in the continuing story of the spread of the Good News. It is that same message that we Christians are to take to our world so that many more may hear and believe.

Phlm 1:1 Paul wrote this letter from Rome in about A.D. 60, when he was under house arrest (see Acts 28:30-31). Onesimus was a domestic slave who belonged to Philemon, a wealthy man and a member of the church in Colosse. Onesimus had run away from Philemon and had made his way to Rome, where he met Paul, who apparently led him to Christ (Phlm 1:10). Paul convinced Onesimus that running from his problems wouldn't solve them, and he persuaded Onesimus to return to his master. Paul wrote this letter to Philemon to ask him to be reconciled with his runaway slave.

Phlm 1:1 For more information on Paul's life, see his Profile on p. 1571. Timothy's name is included with Paul's in 2 Corinthians, 1 Thessalonians, 2 Thessalonians, Philippians, Colossians, and Philemon—the last three of these letters are from a group known as the Prison Letters. Timothy was one of Paul's trusted companions; Paul wrote two letters to him—the books of 1 and 2 Timothy. See Timothy's Profile on p. 1727.

Phlm 1:1 Philemon was a Greek landowner living in Colosse. He had been converted under Paul's ministry, and the Colossian church met in his home. Onesimus was one of Philemon's slaves.

Phlm 1:2 Apphia may have been Philemon's wife. Archippus may have been Philemon's son or perhaps an elder in the Colossian church. In either case, Paul included him as a recipient of the letter, possibly so Archippus could read the letter with Philemon and encourage him to take Paul's advice.

Phlm 1:2 The early churches often would meet in people's homes. Because of sporadic

Paul's Thanksgiving and Prayer

PHILEMON 1:4-7

I always thank my God when I pray for you, Philemon,
5because I keep hearing about your faith in the Lord
Jesus and your love for all of God's people. 6And I am
praying that you will put into action the generosity
that comes from your faith as you understand and
experience all the good things we have in Christ. 7Your
love has given me much joy and comfort, my brother,
for your kindness has often refreshed the hearts of
God's people.

Paul's Appeal for Onesimus

PHILEMON 1:8-22

That is why I am boldly asking a favor of you. I could
demand it in the name of Christ because it is the right
thing for you to do. 9But because of our love, I prefer
simply to ask you. Consider this as a request from

ONESIMUS

God must have a special love for runaways. The pages of Scripture record dozens of people who were prone to flight. From Adam and Eve's attempt to elude God, through Jacob's escape from his brother, past generations of God's people on the run, to that inner circle of disciples who fled from the garden when Jesus was captured, the Bible is a collection of runaway lives. God's special love for runaways is beautifully illustrated in the life of a slave named Onesimus. • We are not told why Onesimus ran away from Philemon's house in Colosse. Eventually, he and Paul found one another in Rome. Though we might crave more details of what transpired, Paul simply wrote that Onesimus became a follower of Jesus. Later, his spiritual growth caused Paul to call him a "faithful and beloved brother" (Col 4:9). • Eventually, Paul and Onesimus decided it was time for the runaway slave to return home. Paul wrote a letter of explanation to his friend Philemon, assuring him that Onesimus would now serve him wholeheartedly. Although the culture of the day gave masters complete control over their slaves and although severe punishment usually faced a runaway, Paul challenged Philemon to think of Onesimus more as a brother than as a slave. Paul took responsibility for any restitution Philemon might require of Onesimus. As difficult as it might be for him, Onesimus, the runaway slave turned believer, had to return and face his old life as a new person. • When God finds runaways, he often sends them back to the very places and people from which they ran in the first place. As God has become real in your life, how has your past come into new perspective? Are there still situations from your past that need to be resolved? In what ways has your relationship with Christ given you new opportunities and resources to face what you used to run away from?

Strengths and accomplishments	• Grew into an able believer and assistant to Paul while in Rome • Returned to his previous master as a willing slave
Weakness and mistake	• Ran away from his master, Philemon
Lessons from his life	• God is in the radical forgiveness business • We cannot run from God and hope to escape
Vital statistics	• Where: Colosse • Occupation: Slave
Key verses	"It seems you lost Onesimus for a little while so that you could have him back forever. He is no longer like a slave to you. He is more than a slave, for he is a beloved brother, especially to me. Now he will mean much more to you, both as a man and as a brother in the Lord" (Phlm 1:15-16).

Onesimus is mentioned in Colossians 4:9 and is the subject of Paul's letter to Philemon.

persecutions and the great expense involved, churches did not construct dedicated buildings at this time.

Phlm 1:4-7 Like cold water on a long hike, this Christian brother Philemon knew how to be refreshing. He was able to revive and restore his brothers and sisters in the faith. His love and generosity had replenished and stimulated them. Philemon also encouraged Paul by his love and loyalty. Are you a refreshing influence on others, or do your attitude and temperament add to the burden they carry? Instead of draining others' energy and motivation with complaints and problems, replenish their spirits by encouragement, love, and a helpful attitude.

Phlm 1:6 Paul's prayer for Philemon was setting the stage for the request Paul would make in this letter. Philemon was active in his faith and generous in sharing its blessings. As he gained fuller understanding of all that Christ had done on his behalf, this knowledge should cause him to respond appropriately to Paul's request regarding Onesimus. Are you active and effective in sharing with others your faith, your resources, and your love?

Phlm 1:8-9 Because Paul was an elder and an apostle, he could have used his authority with Philemon, commanding him to deal kindly with his runaway slave. But Paul based his request not on his own authority but on Philemon's Christian commitment. Paul wanted Philemon's heartfelt, not grudging, obedience. When you know something is right and you have the power to demand it, do you appeal to your authority or to the other person's commitment?

Paul provides a good example of how to deal with conflict between Christians. When reconciling a separation or mediating a dispute, trust must be rebuilt between the conflicting parties. Notice the steps that Paul used to help rebuild the trust: (1) He identified with those involved, calling Philemon "brother" and Onesimus "my child." (2) He requested, not ordered, Philemon to do the right thing. (3) He sought Philemon's voluntary consent, not his submission to rules or authority. (4) He appealed to Christian love, not to power or authority. (5) He agreed to absorb the loss and pay any cost for restoration. Instead of overusing power or position, use Paul's approach to rebuild a trusting relationship.

▸ **PHILEMON 1:8-22** ***(cont.)***

me—Paul, an old man and now also a prisoner for the sake of Christ Jesus.*

[10]I appeal to you to show kindness to my child, Onesimus. I became his father in the faith while here in prison. [11]Onesimus* hasn't been of much use to you in the past, but now he is very useful to both of us. [12]I am sending him back to you, and with him comes my own heart.

[13]I wanted to keep him here with me while I am in these chains for preaching the Good News, and he would have helped me on your behalf. [14]But I didn't want to do anything without your consent. I wanted you to help because you were willing, not because you were forced. [15]It seems you lost Onesimus for a little while so that you could have him back forever. [16]He is no longer like a slave to you. He is more than a slave, for he is a beloved brother, especially to me. Now he will mean much more to you, both as a man and as a brother in the Lord.

[17]So if you consider me your partner, welcome him as you would welcome me. [18]If he has wronged you in any way or owes you anything, charge it to me. [19]I, PAUL, WRITE THIS WITH MY OWN HAND: I WILL REPAY IT. AND I WON'T MENTION THAT YOU OWE ME YOUR VERY SOUL!

[20]Yes, my brother, please do me this favor* for the Lord's sake. Give me this encouragement in Christ. [21]I am confident as I write this letter that you will do what I ask and even more! [22]One more thing—please prepare a guest room for me, for I am hoping that God will answer your prayers and let me return to you soon.

Paul's Final Greetings

PHILEMON 1:23-25

Epaphras, my fellow prisoner in Christ Jesus, sends you his greetings. [24]So do Mark, Aristarchus, Demas, and Luke, my co-workers.

[25]May the grace of the Lord Jesus Christ be with your spirit.

Phlm 9 Or *a prisoner of Christ Jesus.* **Phlm 11** *Onesimus* means "useful." **Phlm 20** Greek *onaimen,* a play on the name Onesimus.

Phlm 1:10 A master had the legal right to kill a runaway slave, so Onesimus feared for his life. Paul wrote this letter to Philemon to help him understand his new relationship with Onesimus, who was now a Christian brother, not a mere possession.

Phlm 1:10ff From his prison cell, Paul had led Onesimus to the Lord. Paul asked Philemon to forgive his runaway slave who had become a Christian and, even going beyond forgiveness, to accept Onesimus as a brother. As Christians, we should forgive as we have been forgiven (Matt 6:12; Eph 4:31-32). True forgiveness means that we treat the forgiven person as we would want to be treated. Is there someone you say you have forgiven but who still needs your kindness?

Phlm 1:11-15 *Onesimus* means "useful." Paul used a play on words, saying that Onesimus had not been much use to Philemon in the past but now had become very useful to both Philemon and Paul. Although Paul wanted to keep Onesimus with him, he was sending Onesimus back, requesting that Philemon accept him not only as a forgiven runaway servant but also as a brother in Christ.

Phlm 1:15-16 Slavery was widespread throughout the Roman Empire. In these early days, Christians did not have the political power to change the slavery system. Paul didn't condemn or condone slavery, but he worked to transform relationships. The Good News begins to change social structures by changing the *people* within those structures. (See also 1 Cor 7:20-24; Eph 6:5-9; Col 3:22–4:1 for more on master/slave relationships.)

Phlm 1:16 What a difference Onesimus's status as a Christian made in his relationship to Philemon. He was no longer merely a slave, but he was also a brother. That meant that both Onesimus and Philemon were members of God's family—equals in Christ. A Christian's status as a member of God's family transcends all other distinctions among believers. Do you look down on any fellow Christians? Remember, they are your equals before Christ (Gal 3:28). How you treat your brothers and sisters in Christ's family reflects your true Christian commitment.

Phlm 1:17 Paul called Philemon his "partner," but he did not mean a partner in the business sense of the word. Philemon was a partner in grace. Paul and Philemon shared the same experience in Jesus Christ of being saved; in that sense, they were equals. Too often our relationships in the church don't possess true partnership but reflect merely tolerance of one another. Do you have room in your heart to welcome other believers warmly? Treat them as partners in God's grace and love, not just fellow workers. Let your common interests in Christ and your common feeling of gratitude for Christ's love knit you together with others.

Phlm 1:17-19 Paul genuinely loved Onesimus. Paul showed his love by personally guaranteeing payment for any stolen goods or wrongs for which Onesimus might be responsible. Paul's investment in the life of this new believer certainly encouraged and strengthened Onesimus's faith. Are there young believers who need you to demonstrate such self-sacrifice toward them? Be grateful when you can invest in the lives of others, helping them with Bible study, prayer, encouragement, support, and friendship.

Phlm 1:19 Philemon owed his soul to Paul, meaning that Paul had led Philemon to Christ. Because Paul was Philemon's spiritual father, he was hoping that Philemon would feel a debt of gratitude that he would repay by accepting Onesimus with a spirit of forgiveness.

Phlm 1:22 Paul was released from prison soon after writing this letter, but the Bible doesn't say whether or not he returned to Colosse.

Phlm 1:23 Epaphras was well known to the Colossians because he had founded the church there (Col 1:7). He was a hero to this church, helping to hold it together in spite of growing persecution and struggles with false doctrine. His report to Paul about the problems in Colosse had prompted Paul to write his letter to the Colossians. Epaphras's greetings to the Colossian Christians reveal his deep love for them (Col 4:12-13). He may have been in prison with Paul for preaching the Good News.

Phlm 1:24 Mark, Aristarchus, Demas, and Luke are also mentioned in Colossians 4:10, 14. Mark had accompanied Paul and Barnabas on their first missionary journey (Acts 12:25ff). Mark also wrote the Gospel of Mark. Luke had accompanied Paul on his third missionary journey and was the writer of the Gospel of Luke and the book of Acts. Demas had been faithful to Paul for a while but later deserted him (see 2 Tim 4:10).

Phlm 1:25 Paul urged Philemon to be reconciled to his slave, receiving him as a brother and fellow member of God's family. *Reconciliation* means reestablishing relationship. Christ has reconciled us to God and to others. Many barriers come between people—race, social status, sex, personality differences—but Christ can break down these barriers. Jesus Christ changed Onesimus's relationship to Philemon from slave to brother. Christ can transform our most hopeless relationships into deep and loving friendships.

Col 1:1 Colossians, along with Philippians, Ephesians, and Philemon, is called a Prison Letter because Paul wrote it from prison in Rome. This prison was actually a house

O. Paul's Letter to the Church in Colosse

The book of Colossians was probably written and sent together with his personal letter to Philemon, who lived in Colosse. Writing from a prison in Rome, Paul combatted false teachings that had infiltrated the Colossian church. The problem was syncretism, combining ideas from other philosophies and religions with Christian truth. To combat these devious errors, Paul stressed Christ's deity and his sacrificial death on the cross for sin. Only by being connected to Christ by faith can anyone have eternal life, and only through a continuing connection with him can anyone have power for living.

1. WHAT CHRIST HAS DONE

Paul begins this letter with clear teaching about who Jesus Christ is and what he has done for us. Christ has paid for sin, reconciled us to God, and given us the pattern and the power to grow spiritually.

Greetings from Paul

COLOSSIANS 1:1-2

This letter is from Paul, chosen by the will of God to be an apostle of Christ Jesus, and from our brother Timothy.

[2]We are writing to God's holy people in the city of Colosse, who are faithful brothers and sisters* in Christ.

May God our Father give you grace and peace.

Col 1:2 Greek *faithful brothers.*

Paul's Thanksgiving and Prayer

COLOSSIANS 1:3-14

We always pray for you, and we give thanks to God, the Father of our Lord Jesus Christ. [4]For we have heard of your faith in Christ Jesus and your love for all of God's people, [5]which come from your confident hope of what God has reserved for you in heaven. You have had this expectation ever since you first heard the truth of the Good News.

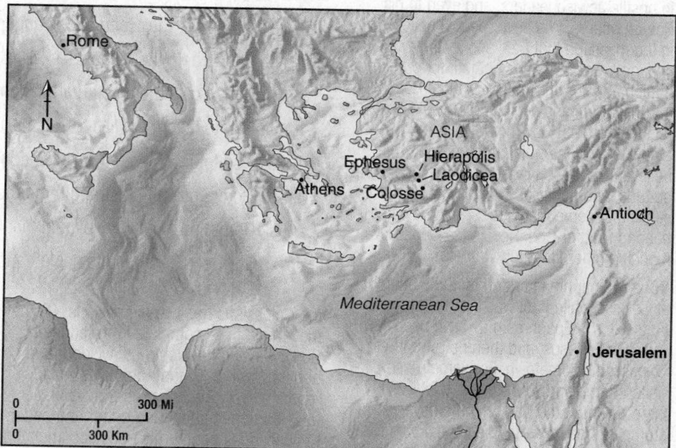

***LOCATION OF COLOSSE** Paul had no doubt been through Laodicea on his third missionary journey, as it lay on the main route to Ephesus, but he had never been to Colosse. Though a large city with a significant population, Colosse was smaller and less important than the nearby cities of Laodicea and Hierapolis.*

where Paul was kept under close guard at all times (probably chained to a soldier) but given certain freedoms not offered to most prisoners. He was allowed to write letters and to see any visitors he wanted to see.

Col 1:1 Paul was an apostle "chosen by the will of God." Paul often would establish his credentials as chosen and sent by God because he had not been one of the original 12 disciples. *Apostle* means "one sent out by God to preach the gospel." He was appointed to this task by the will of God; this was not just a matter of his own personal aspirations.

Col 1:1 Paul mentions Timothy in other New Testament letters as well: 2 Corinthians, Philippians, 1 and 2 Thessalonians, and Philemon. Paul also wrote two letters to Timothy (the books of 1 and 2 Timothy). For more information on these men, two of the greatest missionaries of the early church, see Paul's Profile on p. 1571 and Timothy's Profile on p. 1727.

Col 1:2 The city of Colosse was 100 miles east of Ephesus on the Lycus River. It was not as influential as the nearby city of Laodicea, but as a trading center, it was a crossroads for ideas and religions. Colosse had a large Jewish population—many Jews had fled there when they were forced out of Jerusalem under the persecutions of Antiochus III and IV, almost 200 years before Christ. The church in Colosse had been founded by Epaphras (Col 1:7), one of Paul's converts. Paul had not yet visited this church. His purpose in writing was to refute heretical teachings about Christ that had been causing confusion among the Christians there.

Col 1:2-3 Letters in Paul's day frequently would begin with identifying the writer and the readers, followed by a greeting of peace. Paul usually would add Christian elements to his greetings, reminding his readers of his call by God to spread the Good News, emphasizing that the authority for his words came from God, and giving thanks for God's blessings.

Col 1:4-5 Throughout this letter Paul combats a heresy similar to Gnosticism (see the notes on Col 1:9-14, p. 1694; Col 1:15-23, p. 1695; Col 2:4ff, p. 1697). Gnostics believed that it took special knowledge to be accepted by God; for them, even for those who claimed to be Christians, Christ alone was not the way of salvation (Col 1:20). In his introductory comments, therefore, Paul commended the Colossians for their faith, love, and hope as they looked forward to heaven (see 1 Cor 13:13). He deliberately omitted the word *knowledge* because of the "special knowledge" aspect of the heresy. It is not *what* we know that brings salvation but *whom* we know. Knowing Christ is knowing God.

Col 1:5 We can have "confident hope" of what God has for us in heaven because we know that our future destination and salvation are sure (1 Pet 1:3-4). We are free to live for Christ and love others. When you find yourself doubting or wavering in your faith or love, remember your destination—heaven.

▸ **COLOSSIANS 1:3-14** ***(cont.)***

6 This same Good News that came to you is going
out all over the world. It is bearing fruit everywhere by
changing lives, just as it changed your lives from the
day you first heard and understood the truth about
God's wonderful grace.
7 You learned about the Good News from Epaphras,
our beloved co-worker. He is Christ's faithful servant,
and he is helping us on your behalf.* 8 He has told
us about the love for others that the Holy Spirit has
given you.
9 So we have not stopped praying for you since
we first heard about you. We ask God to give you
complete knowledge of his will and to give you spiritual wisdom and understanding. 10 Then the way you
live will always honor and please the Lord, and your
lives will produce every kind of good fruit. All the
while, you will grow as you learn to know God better
and better.
11 We also pray that you will be strengthened with
all his glorious power so you will have all the endurance and patience you need. May you be filled with
joy,* 12 always thanking the Father. He has enabled
you to share in the inheritance that belongs to his
people, who live in the light. 13 For he has rescued us
from the kingdom of darkness and transferred us into
the Kingdom of his dear Son, 14 who purchased our
freedom* and forgave our sins.

Christ Is Supreme

COLOSSIANS 1:15-23

15 Christ is the visible image of the invisible God.
He existed before anything was created and
is supreme over all creation,*
16 for through him God created everything
in the heavenly realms and on earth.
He made the things we can see
and the things we can't see—

Col 1:7 Or *he is ministering on your behalf;* some manuscripts read *he is ministering on our behalf.* **Col 1:11** Or *all the patience and endurance you need with joy.* **Col 1:14** Some manuscripts add *with his blood.* **Col 1:15** Or *He is the firstborn of all creation.*

Col 1:6 Wherever Paul went, he preached the Good News—to Gentile audiences, to hostile Jewish leaders, and even to his Roman guards. Whenever people believed in the message that Paul spoke, they were changed. God's Word is not just for our information, it is for our transformation! Becoming a Christian means beginning a whole new relationship with God, not just turning over a new leaf or determining to do right. New believers have a changed purpose, direction, attitude, and behavior. They are no longer seeking to serve themselves, but they are bearing fruit for God. How is the Good News reaching others through your life?

HOW TO PRAY FOR OTHER CHRISTIANS

1. Be thankful for their faith and changed lives (Col 1:3-4).
2. Ask God to help them know his will (Col 1:9).
3. Ask God to give them spiritual wisdom and understanding (Col 1:9).
4. Ask God to help them live to honor and please him (Col 1:10).
5. Ask God to give them more knowledge of himself (Col 1:10).
6. Ask God to give them strength for endurance and patience (Col 1:11).
7. Ask God to fill them with joy and thankfulness (Col 1:11-12).

How many people in your life could be touched if you prayed in this way?

Col 1:7 Epaphras had founded the church at Colosse while Paul was living in Ephesus (Acts 19:10). Epaphras may have been converted in Ephesus, and then he returned to Colosse, his hometown. For some reason, he visited Rome and, while there, told Paul about the problem of the Colossian heresy. This prompted Paul to write this letter. Epaphras is also mentioned in Philemon 1:23 (the Colossian church met in Philemon's house).

Col 1:8 Because of their love for one another, Christians can have an impact that goes far beyond their neighborhoods and communities. Christian love comes from the Holy Spirit (see Gal 5:22). The Bible speaks of it as an action and attitude, not just an emotion. Love is a by-product of our new life in Christ (see Rom 5:5; 1 Cor 13). Christians have no excuse for not loving, because Christian love is a decision to act in the best interests of others.

Col 1:9-14 Paul was exposing a heresy in the Colossian church that was similar to Gnosticism (see the note on Col 2:4ff, p. 1697, for more information). Gnostics valued the accumulation of knowledge, but Paul pointed out that knowledge in itself is empty. To be worth anything, it must lead to a changed life and right living. His prayer for the Colossians has two dimensions: (1) that they might have complete knowledge of God's will and have spiritual wisdom and understanding; (2) that their lives would produce every kind of good fruit, even as they learned to know God better and better. Knowledge is not merely to be accumulated; it should give us direction for living. Paul wanted the Colossians to be wise, but he also wanted them to use their knowledge. Knowledge of God is not a secret that only a few can discover; it is open to everyone. God wants us to learn more about him, and also to put belief into practice by loving others.

Col 1:9-14 Sometimes we wonder how to pray for missionaries, leaders, and other Christians we have never met. Paul had never met the Colossians, but he faithfully prayed for them. His prayers teach us how to pray for others, whether we know them or not. We can request that they (1) understand what God wants them to do, (2) gain spiritual wisdom, (3) honor and please God, (4) produce every kind of good fruit, (5) learn to know God better and better, (6) be strengthened with God's glorious power, (7) have great endurance and patience, (8) be filled with joy, and (9) give thanks always. All believers have these same basic needs. When you don't know how to pray for someone, use Paul's prayer pattern for the Colossians.

Col 1:12-14 Paul lists five benefits God gives all believers through Christ: (1) He has enabled us to share in his inheritance (see also 2 Cor 5:21); (2) he has rescued us from Satan's kingdom of darkness and made us his children (see also Col 2:15); (3) he has brought us into his eternal Kingdom (see also Eph 1:5-6); (4) he has purchased our freedom from sin and judgment with his blood (see also Heb 9:12); and (5) he has forgiven all our sins (see also Eph 1:7). Thank God for what you have received in Christ.

Col 1:13 The Colossians feared the unseen forces of darkness, but Paul says that true believers have been transferred from darkness to light, from slavery to freedom, from guilt to forgiveness, and from the power of Satan to the power of God. We have been rescued from a rebel kingdom to serve the rightful King. Our conduct should reflect our new allegiance.

such as thrones, kingdoms, rulers, and authorities
in the unseen world.
Everything was created through him
and for him.
17 He existed before anything else,
and he holds all creation together.
18 Christ is also the head of the church,
which is his body.
He is the beginning,
supreme over all who rise from the dead.*
So he is first in everything.
19 For God in all his fullness
was pleased to live in Christ,
20 and through him God reconciled
everything to himself.
He made peace with everything in
heaven and on earth
by means of Christ's blood on the
cross.

21 This includes you who were once far away from
God. You were his enemies, separated from him by

Col 1:18 Or *the firstborn from the dead.*

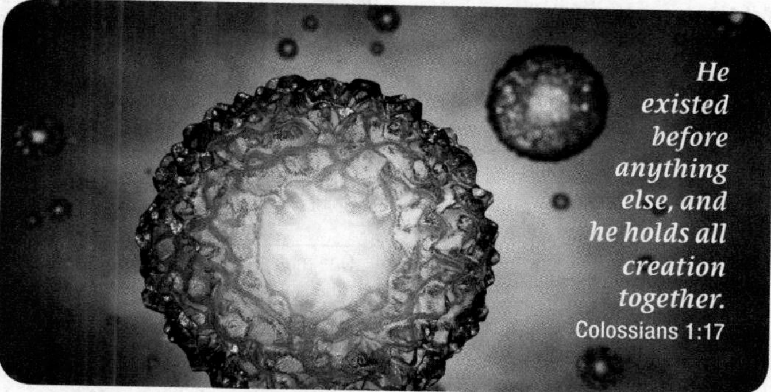
He existed before anything else, and he holds all creation together.
Colossians 1:17

Col 1:15-16 This is one of the strongest statements about the divine nature of Christ found anywhere in the Bible. Jesus is not only equal to God (Phil 2:6), he *is* God (John 10:30, 38; 12:45; 14:1-11); as the visible image of the invisible God, he is the exact representation of God. He not only reflects God, but he reveals God to us (John 1:18; 14:9); as supreme over all creation, he has all the priority and authority. He came from heaven, not from the dust of the earth (1 Cor 15:47), and he is Lord of all (Rom 9:5; 10:11-13; Rev 1:5; 17:14). He is completely holy (Heb 7:26-28; 1 Pet 1:19; 2:22; 1 Jn 3:5), and he has authority to judge the world (Rom 2:16; 2 Cor 5:10; 2 Tim 4:1). Therefore, Christ is supreme over all creation, including the spirit world. We, like the Colossian believers, must believe in the deity of Jesus Christ (that Jesus is God) or our Christian faith is hollow, misdirected, and meaningless. This is a central truth of Christianity. We must oppose those who say that Jesus was merely a prophet or a good teacher.

Col 1:15-23 In the Colossian church there were several misconceptions about Christ that Paul directly refuted: (1) Believing that matter is evil, false teachers argued that God would not have come to earth as a true human being in bodily form. Paul stated that Christ is the image—the exact likeness—of God and is himself God, and yet he died on the cross as a human being. (2) They believed that God did not create the world because he would not have created evil. Paul proclaimed that Jesus Christ, who is also God in the flesh, is the Creator of both heaven and earth. (3) They said that Christ was not the unique Son of God but rather one of many intermediaries between God and people. Paul explained that Christ existed before anything else and is the firstborn of those resurrected. (4) They refused to see Christ as the source of salvation, insisting that people could find God only through special and secret knowledge. In contrast, Paul openly proclaimed the way of salvation to be through Christ alone. Paul continued to bring the argument back to Christ. When we share the Good News, we, too, must keep the focus on Christ.

Col 1:16 Because the false teachers believed that the physical world was evil, they thought that God himself could not have created it. If Christ were God, they reasoned, he would be in charge only of the spiritual world. But Paul explained that all the thrones, kingdoms, rulers, and authorities of both the spiritual and physical worlds were created by and are under the authority of Christ himself. This includes not only the government but also the spiritual world that the heretics were so concerned about. Christ has no equal and no rival. He is the Lord of all.

Col 1:17 God is not only the creator of the world but he is also its sustainer. In him, everything is held together, protected, and prevented from g into chaos. Because Christ is the sustainer of all life, none of us is independent from him. We are all his servants who must daily trust him to protect us, care for us, and sustain us.

Col 1:18 Christ is "supreme over all who rise from the dead." Jesus was raised from death, and his resurrection proves his lordship over the material world. All who trust in Christ will also defeat death and rise again to live eternally with him (1 Cor 15:20; 1 Thes 4:14). Because of Christ's death on the cross, he has been exalted and elevated to the status that was rightfully his (see Phil 2:5-11). Because Christ is spiritually supreme in the universe, surely we should give him first place in all our thoughts and activities. (See the second note on Luke 24:6-7, p. 1491, for more about the significance of Christ's resurrection.)

Col 1:19 By this statement, Paul was refuting the Greek idea that Jesus could not be human and divine at the same time. Christ was fully human; he was also fully divine. Christ has always been God and always will be God. When we have Christ, we have all of God in human form. Don't diminish any aspect of Christ—either his humanity or his divinity.

Col 1:20 Christ's death provided a way for all people to come to God. It cleared away the sin that keeps us from having a right relationship with our creator. This does not mean that everyone has been saved but rather that the way has been cleared for anyone who will trust Christ to be saved. We can have peace with God and be reconciled to him by accepting Christ, who died in our place. Is there a distance between you and the Creator? Be reconciled to God. Come to him through Christ.

Col 1:21 Because we were alienated from God, we were strangers to his way of thinking and were "enemies." Sin corrupted our way of thinking about God. Wrong thinking leads to sin, which further perverts and destroys our thoughts about him. When we were out of harmony with God, our natural condition was to be totally hostile to his standards. (See Rom 1:21-32 for more on the perverted thinking of unbelievers.)

Col 1:21-22 We are not good enough to save ourselves—*no one* is. If we want to live eternally with Christ, we must depend totally on God's grace. This is true whether we have been murderers or honest, hardworking citizens. We have all sinned repeatedly, and *any* sin is enough to cause us to need to come to Jesus Christ for salvation and eternal life. Apart from Christ, there is no way for our sin to be forgiven and removed.

▸ **COLOSSIANS 1:15-23** ***(cont.)***

your evil thoughts and actions. 22Yet now he has reconciled you to himself through the death of Christ in
his physical body. As a result, he has brought you into
his own presence, and you are holy and blameless as
you stand before him without a single fault.
23But you must continue to believe this truth and
stand firmly in it. Don't drift away from the assurance you received when you heard the Good News.
The Good News has been preached all over the world,
and I, Paul, have been appointed as God's servant to
proclaim it.

Paul's Work for the Church

COLOSSIANS 1:24–2:5

I am glad when I suffer for you in my body, for I am
participating in the sufferings of Christ that continue
for his body, the church. 25God has given me the responsibility of serving his church by proclaiming his
entire message to you. 26This message was kept secret
for centuries and generations past, but now it has been
revealed to God's people. 27For God wanted them to
know that the riches and glory of Christ are for you
Gentiles, too. And this is the secret: Christ lives in you.
This gives you assurance of sharing his glory.

Col 1:22 In order to answer the accusation that Jesus was only a spirit and not a true human being, Paul explained that Jesus' physical body actually died. Jesus suffered death fully as a human so that we could be assured that he died in our place. Jesus faced death as God so we can be assured that his sacrifice was complete and that he truly removed our sin.

Col 1:22-23 The way to be free from sin is to trust Jesus Christ to take it away. We must stand firmly in the truth of the Good News, putting our confidence in Jesus alone to forgive our sins, to make us right with God, and to empower us to live the way he desires. When a judge in a court of law declares the defendant not guilty, the person is acquitted of all the accusations or charges. Legally, it is as if the defendant had never been accused. When God forgives our sins, our record is wiped clean. From his perspective, it is as though we had never sinned. God's solution is available to you. No matter what you have done or what you have been like, God's forgiveness is for *you.*

Col 1:24 Paul's statement, "I am participating in the sufferings of Christ that continue for his body, the church," may mean that suffering is unavoidable in bringing the Good News of Christ to the world. When we suffer, Christ feels it with us. But this suffering can be endured joyfully because it changes lives and brings people into God's Kingdom (see 1 Pet 4:1-2, 12-19). (For more about how Paul could rejoice despite his suffering, see the note on Phil 1:29, p. 1718.)

Col 1:26-27 The false teachers in the Colossian church believed that spiritual perfection was a secret and hidden plan that only a few privileged people could discover. Their secret plan was meant to be exclusive. Paul said that he was proclaiming the entire message of God, not just a part of the plan. He also called God's plan a "message . . . kept secret for centuries and generations past," not in the sense that only a few would understand, but because it was hidden until Christ came. Through Christ it was made open to all. God's secret plan is "Christ lives in you." God planned to have his Son, Jesus Christ, live in the hearts of all who believe in him, even Gentiles like the Colossians. Do you know Christ? He is not hidden if you will come to him.

THE COLOSSIAN HERESY

Paul answered the various tenets of the Colossian heresy that threatened the church. This heresy was a "mixed bag," containing elements from several different heresies, some of which contradicted each other (as the chart shows).

The Heresy	*Reference*	*Paul's Answer*
Spirit is good; matter is evil.	**Col 1:15-20**	God created heaven and earth for his glory.
One must follow ceremonies, rituals, and restrictions in order to be saved or perfected.	**Col 2:11, 16-23; 3:11**	These were only shadows that ended when Christ came. He is all you need to be saved.
One must deny the body and live in strict asceticism.	**Col 2:18-23**	Asceticism is no help in conquering evil thoughts and desires; instead, it leads to pride.
Angels must be worshiped.	**Col 2:18**	Angels are not to be worshiped; Christ alone is worthy of worship.
Christ could not be both human and divine.	**Col 1:15-20; 2:2-3**	Christ is God in the flesh; he is the eternal one, head of the body, first in everything, supreme.
One must obtain "secret knowledge" in order to be saved or perfected—and this was not available to everyone.	**Col 2:2, 18**	God's mysterious plan is Christ himself, and he has been revealed to all.
One must adhere to human wisdom, tradition, and philosophies.	**Col 2:4, 8-10; 3:15-17**	By themselves, these can be misleading and shallow because they have human origin; instead, we should remember what Christ taught and follow his words as our ultimate authority.
It is even better to combine aspects of several religions.	**Col 2:10**	You are complete through your union with Christ; he is all-sufficient.
There is nothing wrong with immorality.	**Col 3:1-11**	Get rid of sin and evil because you have been chosen by God to live a new life as a representative of the Lord Jesus.

Col 1:28-29 The word *perfect* means "mature or complete," not "flawless." Paul wanted to see each believer mature spiritually. Like Paul, we must work wholeheartedly like an athlete, but we should not strive in our own strength alone. We have the power of God's Spirit working in us. We can learn and grow daily, motivated by love and not by fear or pride, knowing that God gives the energy to become mature.

Col 1:28-29 Christ's message is for everyone; so everywhere Paul and Timothy went, they brought the Good News to all who would listen. An effective presentation of the Good

28So we tell others about Christ, warning everyone and teaching everyone with all the wisdom God has given us. We want to present them to God, perfect* in their relationship to Christ. 29That's why I work and struggle so hard, depending on Christ's mighty power that works within me.

2:1I want you to know how much I have agonized for you and for the church at Laodicea, and for many other believers who have never met me personally. 2I want them to be encouraged and knit together by strong ties of love. I want them to have complete confidence that they understand God's mysterious plan, which is Christ himself. 3In him lie hidden all the treasures of wisdom and knowledge.

Col 1:28 Or *mature.*

4I am telling you this so no one will deceive you with well-crafted arguments. 5For though I am far away from you, my heart is with you. And I rejoice that you are living as you should and that your faith in Christ is strong.

Freedom from Rules and New Life in Christ

COLOSSIANS 2:6-23

And now, just as you accepted Christ Jesus as your Lord, you must continue to follow him. 7Let your roots grow down into him, and let your lives be built on him. Then your faith will grow strong in the truth you were taught, and you will overflow with thankfulness.

SALVATION THROUGH FAITH

Salvation by faith in Christ sounds too easy for many people. They would rather think that they have done something to save themselves. Their religion becomes one of self-effort that leads either to disappointment or pride, but finally to eternal death. Christ's simple way is the only way, and it alone leads to eternal life.

	Religion by Self-Effort	*Salvation by Faith*
Goal	Please God by our own good deeds	Trust in Christ and then live to please God
Means	Practice diligent service, discipline, and obedience in hope of reward	Confess, submit, and commit ourselves to Christ's control
Power	Good, honest effort through self-determination	The Holy Spirit in us helps us do good work for Christ's Kingdom
Control	Self-motivation; self-control	Christ is in us; we are in Christ
Results	Chronic guilt, apathy, depression, failure, constant desire for approval	Joy, thankfulness, love, guidance, service, forgiveness

News includes warning and teaching. The warning is that without Christ, people are doomed to eternal separation from God. The teaching is that salvation is available through faith in Christ. As Christ works in you, tell others about him, warning and teaching them in love. Who do you know that needs to hear this message?

Col 2:1 Laodicea was located a few miles northwest of Colosse. Like the church at Colosse, the Laodicean church was probably founded by one of Paul's converts while Paul was staying in Ephesus (Acts 19:10). The city was a wealthy center of trade and commerce, but later Christ would criticize the believers at Laodicea for their lukewarm commitment (Rev 3:14-22). The fact that Paul wanted this letter to be passed on to the Laodicean church (Col 4:16) indicates that false teaching may have spread there as well. Paul was counting on ties of love to bring the churches together to stand against this heresy and to encourage each other to remain true to God's plan of salvation in Christ. Our churches should be encouraging, unified communities, committed to carrying out Christ's work.

Col 2:4ff The problem that Paul was combating in the Colossian church was similar to Gnosticism (from the Greek word for *knowledge*). This *heresy* (a teaching contrary to biblical doctrine) undermined Christianity in several basic ways: (1) It insisted that important secret knowledge was hidden from most believers; Paul, however, said that Christ provides all the knowledge we need. (2) It taught that the body was evil; Paul countered that God himself lived in a body—that is, he was embodied in Jesus Christ. (3) It contended that Christ only seemed to be human but was not; Paul insisted that Jesus was fully human and fully God.

Gnosticism became fashionable in the second century. Even in Paul's day, these ideas sounded attractive to many, and exposure to such teachings could easily seduce a church that didn't know Christian doctrine well. Similar teachings still pose significant problems for many in the church today. We combat heresy by becoming thoroughly acquainted with God's Word through personal study and sound Bible teaching.

Col 2:4 Christian faith provides a growth track into knowledge of the truth; but along the way, how do we guard against being deceived by lies masquerading as "well-crafted arguments"?

If your growth track is too narrow, you become thickheaded and insular—no one can teach you a thing. Before long, you can't teach anyone around you, for no one is listening. You are isolated. Love disappears from your life.

If your track is too wide and every idea is an exciting new possibility, you'll waste a lot of time just getting back on track and risk some dangerous detours.

The key is centering on Christ and grounding yourself in his Word. Learn daily about the Savior. Study the Bible. Develop your theological knowledge. Stay humble and curious about the amazing complexity of the world God has made. Ask lots of questions about the assumptions behind ideas new to you. Press toward wisdom. Pray for understanding. God has given us minds for learning—never quit using yours.

Col 2:6-7 Receiving Christ as Lord of your life is the beginning of life with Christ. But you must continue to follow his leadership by being rooted, built up, and strengthened in the faith. Christ wants to guide you and help you with your daily problems. You can live for Christ by (1) committing your life and submitting your will to him (Rom 12:1-2); (2) seeking to learn from him, his life, and his teachings (Col 3:16); and (3) recognizing the Holy Spirit's power in you (Acts 1:8; Gal 5:22).

Col 2:7 Paul uses the illustration of our being rooted in Christ. Just as plants draw nourishment from the soil through their roots, so we draw our life-giving strength from Christ. The more we draw our strength from him, the less we will be fooled by those who falsely claim to have life's answers. If Christ is our strength, we will be free from human regulations.

▶ **COLOSSIANS 2:6-23** ***(cont.)***
8Don't let anyone capture you with empty philosophies and high-sounding nonsense that come from
human thinking and from the spiritual powers* of this
world, rather than from Christ. 9For in Christ lives all
the fullness of God in a human body.* 10So you also
are complete through your union with Christ, who is
the head over every ruler and authority.
11When you came to Christ, you were "circumcised,"
but not by a physical procedure. Christ performed a
spiritual circumcision—the cutting away of your sinful
nature.* 12For you were buried with Christ when you
were baptized. And with him you were raised to new
life because you trusted the mighty power of God, who
raised Christ from the dead.
13You were dead because of your sins and because
your sinful nature was not yet cut away. Then God
made you alive with Christ, for he forgave all our sins.
14He canceled the record of the charges against us and
took it away by nailing it to the cross. 15In this way,

Col 2:8 Or *the spiritual principles;* also in 2:20. **Col 2:9** Or *in him dwells all the completeness of the Godhead bodily.* **Col 2:11** Greek *the cutting away of the body of the flesh.*

Col 2:8 Paul writes against any philosophy of life based only on human ideas and experiences. Paul himself was a gifted philosopher, so he is not condemning philosophy. He is condemning teaching that credits humanity, not Christ, with being the answer to life's problems. That approach becomes a false religion. There are many man-made approaches to life's problems that totally disregard God. To resist heresy you must use your mind, keep your eyes on Christ, and study God's Word.

Col 2:9 Again Paul asserts Christ's deity. "In Christ lives all the fullness of God in a human body" means that all of God was in Christ's human body. When we have Christ, we have everything we need for salvation and right living. (See the note on Col 1:15-16, p. 1695, for more on the divine nature of Christ.)

Col 2:10 Look around you. People are searching for something to give their lives a boost. Few people seem content within themselves. A strange and often hard-to-identify inner vacuum gives most people an uneasy sense of incompleteness. Christ fills that vacuum! As Jesus' person is fully divine, so we, united by faith to Jesus, find personal fulfillment in him: "You also are complete through your union with Christ."

When you know Jesus Christ, you don't need to seek God by means of other religions, cults, or unbiblical philosophies as the Colossians were doing. Christ alone holds the answers to the true meaning of life because he *is* life. Christ is the unique source of knowledge and power for the Christian life. No Christian needs anything in addition to what Christ has provided to be saved. Some days may not feel like it, but in Jesus, the vacuum is gone; the full power and presence of God have taken up residence in your mind and heart. You are a new person, equipped for life and satisfied in God. Take some risks—God will guide you. Give more generously—God will supply. Love more freely—God will energize you. Say "can do" more often—God will amaze you.

Col 2:11 Jewish males were circumcised as a sign of the Jews' covenant with God (Gen 17:9-14). With the death of Christ, circumcision was no longer necessary. So now our commitment to God is written on our hearts, not our bodies. Christ sets us free from our evil desires by a spiritual operation, not a bodily one. God removes the old nature and gives us a new nature.

FROM DEATH TO LIFE

What happens when we accept Christ?

The Bible uses many illustrations to teach what happens when we choose to let Jesus be Lord of our lives. Following are some of the most vivid pictures:

1. Because Christ died for us, we have been crucified with him.	Rom 6:2-13; 7:4-6; 2 Cor 5:14; Gal 2:20; 5:24; 6:14; Col 2:20; 3:3-5; 1 Pet 2:24
2. Our old, rebellious nature died with Christ.	Rom 6:6; 7:4-6; Col 3:9-10
3. Christ's resurrection guarantees our new life now and eternal life with him later.	Rom 6:4, 11; Col 2:12-13; 3:1, 3

This process is acted out in baptism (Col 2:12), based on our faith in Christ: (1) The old sinful nature dies (crucified). (2) We are ready to receive a new life (buried). (3) Christ gives us new life (resurrected).

Col 2:11-12 In this passage, circumcision is related to baptism; therefore, some see baptism as the New Testament sign of the covenant, identifying the person with the covenant community. Baptism parallels the death, burial, and resurrection of Christ, and it also portrays the death and burial of our sinful old way of life followed by resurrection to new life in Christ. Remembering that our old sinful life is dead and buried with Christ gives us a powerful motive to resist sin. Not wanting the desires of our past to come back to power again, we can consciously choose to treat our desires as if they were dead. Then we can continue to enjoy our wonderful new life with Christ (see Gal 3:27; Col 3:1-4).

Col 2:13-15 Before we believed in Christ, our nature was evil. We disobeyed, rebelled, and ignored God (even at our best, we did not love him with all our hearts, souls, and minds). The Christian has a new nature. God has crucified the old rebellious nature (Rom 6:6) and replaced it with a new loving nature (Col 3:9-10). The penalty of sin died with Christ on the cross. God has declared us not guilty, and we need no longer live under sin's power. God does not take us out of the world or make us robots—we will still feel like sinning, and sometimes we will sin. The difference is that before we were saved, we were slaves to our sinful nature; but now we are free to live for Christ (see Gal 2:20).

Col 2:14 The record that was canceled contained the legal demands of the Old Testament law. The law opposed us by its demands for payment for our sin. Although no one can be saved by merely keeping that record, the moral truths and principles in the Old Testament still teach and guide today.

Col 2:14 We can enjoy our new lives in Christ because we have joined him in his death and resurrection. Our evil desires, our bondage to sin, and our love of sin died with him. Now, joining him in his resurrection life, we may have unbroken fellowship with God and freedom from sin. Our debt for sin has been paid in full; our sins are swept away and forgotten by God; and we can be clean and new. (For more on the difference between our new lives in Christ and our old sinful natures, read Eph 4:23-24; Col 3:3-15.)

Col 2:15 Who are these spiritual rulers and authorities? Several suggestions have been made, including (1) demonic powers, (2) the gods of the powerful nations, (3) angels (highly regarded by the heretical teachers), or (4) the government of Rome. Since Paul did not identify who these rulers and authorities were, it could be any one of them, or all four. What Christ "disarmed" on

he disarmed* the spiritual rulers and authorities. He shamed them publicly by his victory over them on the cross.
[16]So don't let anyone condemn you for what you eat or drink, or for not celebrating certain holy days or new moon ceremonies or Sabbaths. [17]For these rules are only shadows of the reality yet to come. And Christ himself is that reality. [18]Don't let anyone condemn you by insisting on pious self-denial or the worship of angels,* saying they have had visions about these things. Their sinful minds have made them proud, [19]and they are not connected to Christ, the head of the body. For he holds the whole body together with its joints and ligaments, and it grows as God nourishes it.
[20]You have died with Christ, and he has set you free from the spiritual powers of this world. So why do you keep on following the rules of the world, such as, [21]"Don't handle! Don't taste! Don't touch!"? [22]Such rules are mere human teachings about things that deteriorate as we use them. [23]These rules may seem wise because they require strong devotion, pious self-denial, and severe bodily discipline. But they provide no help in conquering a person's evil desires.

Col 2:15 Or *he stripped off.* **Col 2:18** Or *or worshiping with angels.*

the cross was any embodiment of rebellion in the world—whether that be Satan and his demons, false idols of pagan religions, evil world governments, or even God's good angels when they become objects of worship (as in the Colossian heresy). This "disarming" occurred when Jesus died on the cross, like stripping a defeated enemy of armor on the battlefield. Evil no longer has any power over believers because Christ has disarmed it. Paul already had told the Colossians, "He has rescued us from the kingdom of darkness and transferred us into the Kingdom of his dear Son" (Col 1:13).

Col 2:16 "What you eat or drink" probably refers to the Jewish dietary laws. The festivals mentioned are Jewish holy days celebrated annually, monthly (new moon), and weekly (the Sabbath). These rituals distinguished the Jews from their pagan neighbors. Failure to observe them could be easily noticed by those who were keeping track of what others did. But we should not let ourselves be judged by the opinions of others because Christ has set us free.

Col 2:16-17 Paul told the Colossian Christians not to let others criticize their diet or their religious ceremonies. Instead of outward observance, believers should focus on faith in Christ alone. Our worship, traditions, and ceremonies can help bring us close to God, but we should never criticize fellow Christians whose traditions and ceremonies differ from ours. More important than *how* we worship is *that* we worship Christ. Don't let anyone judge you. You are responsible to Christ.

Col 2:17 Old Testament laws, holidays, and festivals pointed toward Christ. Paul calls them "shadows" of the reality that was to come—Christ himself. When Christ came, he dispelled the shadows. If we have Christ, we have what we need to know and please God.

Col 2:18 The false teachers were claiming that God was far away and could be approached only through various levels of angels. They taught that people had to worship angels in order, eventually, to reach God. This is unscriptural; the Bible teaches that angels are God's servants, and it forbids worshiping them (Exod 20:3-4; Rev 22:8-9). As you grow in your Christian faith, let God's Word be your guide, not the opinions of other people.

Col 2:19 The fundamental problem with the false teachers was that they were not connected to Christ, the head of the body of believers. If they had been joined to him, they could not have taught false doctrine or lived immorally. Anyone who teaches about God without being connected to him by faith should not be trusted.

Col 2:20 The "rules of the world" are the beliefs of pagans. (See Col 2:8 for more on Paul's view of non-Christian philosophy.)

Col 2:20; 3:1 How do we die with Christ, and how are we raised with him? When someone becomes a Christian, God gives that person new life through the power of the Holy Spirit. (See the notes on Col 2:11-12, p. 1698; Col 2:13-15, p. 1698, for further information.)

Col 2:20-23 People should be able to see a difference between the way Christians and non-Christians live. Still, we should not expect instant maturity in new Christians. Christian growth is a lifelong process. Although we have a new nature, we don't automatically think all good thoughts and have all pure attitudes when we become new people in Christ. But if we keep listening to God, we will be changing all the time. As you look over the last year, what changes for the better have you seen in your thoughts and attitudes? The maturing process may be slow, but your life will be transformed significantly if you trust God to make you like Christ.

Col 2:20-23 We cannot reach up to God by following rules of pious self-denial, by observing rituals, or by practicing religion. Paul isn't saying all rules are bad (see the note on Gal 2:15-16, p. 1559). But keeping laws or rules will not earn salvation. The Good News is that God reaches down to human beings, and he asks for our response. Man-made religions focus on human effort; Christianity focuses on Christ's work. Believers must put aside sinful desires, but doing so is the by-product of our new life in Christ, not the reason for our new life. Our salvation does not depend on our own discipline and rule keeping but on the power of Christ's death and resurrection.

Col 2:22-23 We can guard against man-made religions by asking these questions about any religious group: (1) Does it stress man-made rules and taboos rather than God's grace? (2) Does it foster a critical spirit toward others, or does it exercise discipline discreetly and lovingly? (3) Does it stress formulas, secret knowledge, or special visions more than the Word of God? (4) Does it elevate self-righteousness, honoring those who keep the rules, rather than elevating Christ? (5) Does it neglect Christ's universal church, claiming to be an elite group? (6) Does it teach humiliation of the body as a means to spiritual growth rather than focus on the growth of the whole person? (7) Does it disregard the family rather than hold it in high regard as the Bible does?

Col 2:23 To the Colossians, the discipline demanded by the false teachers seemed good, and legalism still attracts many people today. Following a long list of religious rules requires strong self-discipline and can make a person appear moral, but religious rules cannot change a person's heart. Only the Holy Spirit can do that.

2. WHAT CHRISTIANS SHOULD DO

Paul is never satisfied to simply give right teaching to the people of God; he wants to see it change the way we live. In the rest of Colossians, Paul lays out the implications of who Christ is and what he has done for how Christians should live. Because in Christ lives all the fullness of God, when we learn what he is like, we see what we need to become. Since Christ is Lord over all creation, we should crown him Lord over our lives. Since Christ is the head of the body, his church, we should nurture our vital connection to him.

Living the New Life

COLOSSIANS 3:1-17

Since you have been raised to new life with Christ, set your sights on the realities of heaven, where Christ sits in the place of honor at God's right hand. 2Think about the things of heaven, not the things of earth. 3For you died to this life, and your real life is hidden with Christ in God. 4And when Christ, who is your* life, is revealed to the whole world, you will share in all his glory.

5So put to death the sinful, earthly things lurking within you. Have nothing to do with sexual immorality, impurity, lust, and evil desires. Don't be greedy, for a greedy person is an idolater, worshiping the things of this world. 6Because of these sins, the anger of God is coming.* 7You used to do these things when your life was still part of this world. 8But now is the time to get rid of anger, rage, malicious behavior, slander, and dirty language. 9Don't lie to each other, for you have stripped off your old sinful nature and all its wicked deeds. 10Put on your new nature, and be renewed as you learn to know your Creator and become like him. 11In this new life, it doesn't matter if you are a Jew or a Gentile,* circumcised or uncircumcised, barbaric, uncivilized,* slave, or free. Christ is all that matters, and he lives in all of us.

12Since God chose you to be the holy people he loves, you must clothe yourselves with tenderhearted mercy, kindness, humility, gentleness, and patience.

Col 3:4 Some manuscripts read *our*. **Col 3:6** Some manuscripts read *is coming on all who disobey him*. **Col 3:11a** Greek *a Greek*. **Col 3:11b** Greek *Barbarian, Scythian*.

Col 3:1ff In Colossians 2, Paul exposed the wrong reasons for self-denial. In Colossians 3, he explains true Christian behavior—putting on the new nature by accepting Christ and regarding the earthly nature as dead. We change our moral and ethical behavior by letting Christ live within us, so that *he* can shape us into what we should be.

Col 3:1-2 Setting our sights on the realities of heaven means striving to put heaven's priorities into daily practice. Letting heaven fill our thoughts means concentrating on the eternal rather than the temporal. (See Col 3:15; Phil 4:7 for more on Christ's rule in our hearts and minds.)

Col 3:2-3 "For you died to this life" means that we should have as little desire for improper worldly pleasures as a dead person would have. The Christian's real home is where Christ lives (John 14:2-3). This truth provides a different perspective on our lives here on earth. To "think about the things of heaven" means to look at life from God's perspective and to seek what he desires. This provides the antidote to materialism; we gain the proper perspective on material goods when we take God's view of them. It also provides the antidote to sensuality. By seeking what Christ desires, we have the power to break our obsession with pleasure and leisure activities. But it also provides the antidote to empty religiosity because following Christ means loving and serving in this world. Regard the world around you as God does; then you will live in harmony with him.

Col 3:3 What does it mean that a believer's life is "hidden with Christ"? *Hidden* means "concealed and safe." This is not only a future hope but an accomplished fact right now. Our service and conduct do not earn our salvation, but they are results of our salvation. Take heart that your salvation is sure, and live each day for Christ.

Col 3:4 Christ gives us power to live for him now, and he gives us hope for the future—he will return. In the rest of this chapter Paul explains how Christians should act *now* in order to be prepared for Christ's return.

Col 3:5 We should consider ourselves dead and unresponsive to sexual immorality, impurity, lust, and evil desires. The warning in this verse is not against sex, but against sexual perversion. Where is the line between the two?

The Bible everywhere celebrates heterosexual, monogamous marriage as the proper situation for sexual fulfillment. Christian men and women should be open to true love—and to sexual intimacy—within the commitment to lifelong fidelity. That is God's way. The rest is dangerous and futile. Stay away. Sexual sin and perversion will drain your energies and turn your heart away from God.

Col 3:6 "The anger of God" refers to God's judgment on these kinds of behavior, culminating with future and final punishment of evil. When tempted to sin, remember that you must one day stand before God.

Col 3:8-10 We must rid ourselves of all evil practices and immorality. Then we can commit ourselves to what Christ teaches. Paul was urging the believers to remain true to their confession of faith. They were to rid themselves of the old life and put on the new nature given by Christ. If you have made such a commitment to Christ, are you remaining true to it?

Col 3:9 Lying to one another disrupts unity by destroying trust. It tears down relationships and may lead to serious conflict in a church. So don't exaggerate statistics, pass on rumors and gossip, or say things to build up your own image. Be committed to telling the truth.

Jesus wants to clean your life and your church of sexual sin and verbal sin. There is no place in the Kingdom of God for hedonistic sexual experimentation or for gossip, rage, and backbiting. In their place, witness to the world like a lighthouse on a stormy night by displaying love, faith, and hope.

Col 3:10 What does it mean to put on your new nature? It means that your conduct should match your faith. If you are a Christian, you should act like it. To be a Christian means more than just making good resolutions and having good intentions; it means taking the right actions. This is a straightforward step that is as simple as putting on your clothes. You must rid yourself of all evil practices and immorality. Then you can commit yourself to what Christ teaches. If you have made such a commitment to Christ, are you remaining true to it? What old clothes do you need to strip off?

Col 3:10 Every Christian is in a continuing education program. The more we know of Christ and his work, the more we are being changed to be like him. Because this process is lifelong, we must never stop learning and obeying. There is no justification for drifting along, but there is an incentive to find the rich treasures of growing in him. It takes practice, ongoing review, patience, and concentration to keep in line with his will.

Col 3:11 The Christian church should have no barriers of nationality, race, educational level, social standing, wealth, gender, religion, or power. Christ breaks down all barriers and accepts all people who come to him. Nothing should keep us from telling others about Christ or accepting into our fellowship any and all believers (Eph 2:14-15). Christians should be building bridges, not walls.

13Make allowance for each other's faults, and forgive
anyone who offends you. Remember, the Lord forgave
you, so you must forgive others. 14Above all, clothe
yourselves with love, which binds us all together in
perfect harmony. 15And let the peace that comes from
Christ rule in your hearts. For as members of one body
you are called to live in peace. And always be thankful.
16Let the message about Christ, in all its richness, fill
your lives. Teach and counsel each other with all the
wisdom he gives. Sing psalms and hymns and spiritual
songs to God with thankful hearts. 17And whatever you
do or say, do it as a representative of the Lord Jesus,
giving thanks through him to God the Father.

Instructions for Christian Households

COLOSSIANS 3:18–4:1

Wives, submit to your husbands, as is fitting for those
who belong to the Lord.
19Husbands, love your wives and never treat them
harshly.

SINS VS. SIGNS OF LOVE

In Colossians 3:5 Paul tells us to put to death the things found in the left column. They deal with sins of sexual attitudes and behavior, and they are particularly destructive because of what they do to destroy any group or church. In Colossians 3:8-9 he tells us to rid ourselves of the things found in the middle column. They deal with sins of speech—these are the relationship breakers. In Colossians 3:12-13 we're told to clothe ourselves with the things found in the right column. They are the relationship builders, which we are to express as members of Christ's body.

Sins of Sexual Attitude and Behavior	Sins of Speech	Signs of Love
Sexual immorality	Anger/Rage	Mercy
Impurity	Malicious behavior	Kindness
Lust	Slander	Humility
Evil desires	Dirty language	Gentleness
Greed	Lying	Patience

Col 3:12-17 Paul offers a strategy to help us live for God day by day: (1) Imitate Christ's compassionate, forgiving attitude (Col 3:12-13); (2) let love guide your life (Col 3:14); (3) let the peace of Christ rule in your heart (Col 3:15); (4) always be thankful (Col 3:15); (5) keep God's Word in you at all times (Col 3:16); (6) live as Jesus Christ's representative (Col 3:17).

Col 3:13 The key to forgiving others is remembering how much God has forgiven you. Is it difficult for you to forgive someone who has wronged you a little when God has forgiven you so much? Realizing God's infinite love and forgiveness can help you love and forgive others. Let God worry about the wrongs you've suffered. Don't quench your life in bitter feuding; live renewed in love and joy.

Col 3:14 All the virtues that Paul encourages us to develop are perfectly bound together by love. As we clothe ourselves with these virtues, the last garment we are to put on is love, which holds all of the others in place. To practice any list of virtues without practicing love will lead to distortion, fragmentation, and stagnation (1 Cor 13:3).

Col 3:14-15 Christians should live in peace. To live in peace does not mean that suddenly all differences of opinion are eliminated, but it does require that loving Christians work together despite their differences. Such love is not a feeling but a decision to meet others' needs (see 1 Cor 13). To clothe ourselves with love leads to peace between individuals and among the members of the body of believers. Do problems in your relationships with other Christians cause open conflicts or mutual silence? Consider what you can do to heal those relationships with love.

Col 3:15 The word *rule* comes from the language of athletics: Paul tells us to let Christ's peace be umpire or referee in our hearts. The heart is the center of conflict because that is where feelings and desires clash—fears and hopes, distrust and trust, jealousy and love. How can we deal with these constant conflicts and live as God wants? Paul explains that we must decide between conflicting elements by using the rule of peace. Which choice will promote peace in our souls and in our churches? (For more on the peace of Christ, see Phil 4:7.)

Col 3:16 Although the early Christians had access to the Old Testament and freely used it, they did not yet have the New Testament or any other Christian books to study. Their stories and teachings about Christ were memorized and passed on from person to person. Sometimes the teachings were set to music, and so music became an important part of Christian worship and education.

Col 3:16 Thankful people can worship wholeheartedly. Gratitude opens our hearts to God's peace and enables us to put on love. Discontented people constantly calculate what's wrong with their lot in life.

To increase your thankfulness, take an inventory of all you have (including your relationships, memories, abilities, and family, as well as material possessions). Use the inventory for prayers of gratitude. On Sunday, before worship, quit rushing around; instead, take time to reflect on reasons for thanks. Declare Sunday as your "thanks, faith, and hope" day. Celebrate God's goodness to you, and ask in prayer for all your needs for the week ahead.

Col 3:17 "Whatever you do or say, do it as a representative of the Lord Jesus" means bringing honor to Christ in every aspect and activity of daily living. As a Christian, you represent Christ at all times—wherever you go and whatever you say. What impression do people have of Christ when they see or talk with you? What changes would you make in your life in order to honor Christ?

Col 3:18–4:1 Paul gives rules for three sets of household relationships: (1) husbands and wives, (2) parents and children, and (3) slave owners and slaves. In each case there is mutual responsibility to submit and love, to obey and encourage, to work hard and be fair. Examine your family and work relationships. Do you relate to others as God intended? (See Eph 5:21–6:9 for similar instructions.)

Col 3:18-19 Why is submission of wives to husbands "fitting for those who belong to the Lord"? This may have been good advice for Christian women, newly freed in Christ, who found submission difficult. Paul told them that they should willingly follow their husbands' leadership in Christ. But Paul had words for husbands as well: "Husbands, love your wives and never treat them harshly." It may also have been true that Christian men, used to the Roman custom of giving unlimited power to the head of the family, were not used to treating their wives with respect and love. Real spiritual leadership involves service. Just as Christ served the disciples, even to the point of washing their feet, so the husband is to serve his wife. This means putting aside his own interests in order to care for his wife. A wise and Christ-honoring husband will not abuse his wife's submission. At the same time, a wise and Christ-honoring wife will not try to undermine her husband's loving service. Either approach causes disunity and friction in marriage. (For more on submission, see the notes on Eph 5:21-33, pp. 1713-1714.)

▸ **COLOSSIANS 3:18–4:1** *(cont.)*

20Children, always obey your parents, for this pleases the Lord. 21Fathers, do not aggravate your children, or they will become discouraged.

22Slaves, obey your earthly masters in everything you do. Try to please them all the time, not just when they are watching you. Serve them sincerely because of your reverent fear of the Lord. 23Work willingly at whatever you do, as though you were working for the Lord rather than for people. 24Remember that the Lord will give you an inheritance as your reward, and that the Master you are serving is Christ.* 25But if you do what is wrong, you will be paid back for the wrong you have done. For God has no favorites.

4:1Masters, be just and fair to your slaves. Remember that you also have a Master—in heaven.

An Encouragement for Prayer

COLOSSIANS 4:2-6

Devote yourselves to prayer with an alert mind and a thankful heart. 3Pray for us, too, that God will give us many opportunities to speak about his mysterious plan concerning Christ. That is why I am here in chains. 4Pray that I will proclaim this message as clearly as I should.

5Live wisely among those who are not believers, and make the most of every opportunity. 6Let your conversation be gracious and attractive* so that you will have the right response for everyone.

Col 3:24 Or *and serve Christ as your Master.* **Col 4:6** Greek *and seasoned with salt.*

Hierapolis Amphitheater

This is an ancient amphitheater at Hierapolis, a city in southwest Phrygia, located near Colosse and Laodicea. Because of its mineral springs and deep cave known as the Plutonium, Hierapolis came to be a cultic center for the worship of Phrygian gods. Lethal vapors issued from the cave, which was thought to be an entrance to the underworld. The mineral baths attracted visitors, and gradually the city developed into a leading commercial center.

Under Paul's influence, Christianity took hold there during his stay in Ephesus. Paul mentions Hierapolis in connection with the believer Epaphras, who prayed diligently for the inhabitants, as well as those in Laodicea and Colosse (Col 4:13). Even though several early Christians were martyred there, the church continued to grow. We should imitate the faith of our ancestors, standing true to the gospel, no matter what kind of opposition we might face.

Col 3:20-21 Children must be handled with care. They need firm discipline administered in love. Parents should not aggravate them by nagging, deriding, or destroying their self-respect so that they quit trying.

However, the opposite problem occurs when parents are afraid to correct a child for fear of stifling some aspect of the child's personality or losing the child's love. Single parents or parents who cannot spend much time with a child may be prone to indulgence. But such children, especially, need the security of guidance and structure. Boundaries and guidelines will not embitter a child; instead, they will set the child free to live securely within the boundaries.

Col 3:22–4:1 Paul does not condemn or condone slavery but explains that Christ transcends all divisions between people. Slaves are told to work hard as though their owner were Christ himself (Col 3:23); but owners should be just and fair (Col 4:1). Perhaps Paul was thinking specifically of Onesimus and Philemon—the slave and master whose conflict lay behind the letter to Philemon (see the book of Philemon). Philemon was a slave owner in the Colossian church, and Onesimus had been his slave (Col 4:9).

Col 3:23 Since the Creation, God has given us work to do. If we could regard our work as an act of worship or service to God, such an attitude would take some of the drudgery and boredom out of it. We could work without complaining or resentment if we would treat our job problems as the cost of discipleship.

Col 4:1 Slave owners were to provide what was just and fair. Similarly today, employers should pay fair wages and treat their employees justly. Paul's instructions encourage responsibility and integrity on the job. Christian employees should do their jobs as if Jesus Christ were their supervisor. And Christian employers should treat their employees fairly and with respect. Can you be trusted to do your best, even when the boss is not around? Do you work hard and with enthusiasm? Do you treat your employees as people, not machines? Employers should pay fair wages and treat their employees justly. Leaders should take care of their volunteers and not abuse them. If you have responsibility over others, make sure you do what is just and fair. Remember that no matter whom you work for, and no matter who works for you, the One you ultimately should want to please is your Father in heaven. You are accountable to him.

Col 4:2 Have you ever grown tired of praying for something or someone? Paul says we should "devote" ourselves to prayer and be "alert" in prayer. Our persistence is an expression of our faith that God answers our prayers. Faith shouldn't die if the answers come slowly, for the delay may be God's way of working his will in our lives. When you feel tired of praying, know that God is present, always listening, always answering—maybe not in ways you had hoped, but in ways that he knows are best.

Col 4:3 The "mysterious plan" is Christ's Good News of salvation. The whole focus of Paul's life was to tell others about Christ, explaining and preaching this wonderful mystery.

Col 4:4 Paul asked for prayer that he could proclaim the Good News about Christ clearly, and we can request prayer to do the same.

Paul's Final Instructions and Greetings

COLOSSIANS 4:7-18

Tychicus will give you a full report about how I am getting along. He is a beloved brother and faithful helper who serves with me in the Lord's work. [8]I have sent him to you for this very purpose—to let you know how we are doing and to encourage you. [9]I am also sending Onesimus, a faithful and beloved brother, one of your own people. He and Tychicus will tell you everything that's happening here.

[10]Aristarchus, who is in prison with me, sends you his greetings, and so does Mark, Barnabas's cousin. As you were instructed before, make Mark welcome if he comes your way. [11]Jesus (the one we call Justus) also sends his greetings. These are the only Jewish believers among my co-workers; they are working with me here for the Kingdom of God. And what a comfort they have been!

[12]Epaphras, a member of your own fellowship and a servant of Christ Jesus, sends you his greetings. He always prays earnestly for you, asking God to make you strong and perfect, fully confident that you are following the whole will of God. [13]I can assure you that he prays hard for you and also for the believers in Laodicea and Hierapolis.

[14]Luke, the beloved doctor, sends his greetings, and so does Demas. [15]Please give my greetings to our brothers and sisters* at Laodicea, and to Nympha and the church that meets in her house.

[16]After you have read this letter, pass it on to the church at Laodicea so they can read it, too. And you should read the letter I wrote to them.

[17]And say to Archippus, "Be sure to carry out the ministry the Lord gave you."

[18]HERE IS MY GREETING IN MY OWN HANDWRITING—PAUL.

Remember my chains.
May God's grace be with you.

Col 4:15 Greek *brothers.*

No matter what approach to evangelism we use, whether emphasizing lifestyle and example or whether building relationships, we should never obscure the message of the Good News.

Col 4:5 We should be wise in our contacts with nonbelievers, making the most of our opportunities to tell them the Good News of salvation. What opportunities do you have?

Col 4:6 When we tell others about Christ, it is important always to be gracious in what we say. No matter how much sense the message makes, we lose our effectiveness if we are not courteous. Just as we like to be respected, we must respect others if we want them to listen to what we have to say.

Col 4:7 Tychicus was one of Paul's personal representatives and probably the bearer of the letters to the Colossians and Ephesians (see also Eph 6:21-22). He accompanied Paul to Jerusalem with the collection for the church (Acts 20:4).

Col 4:10 Aristarchus was a Thessalonian who accompanied Paul on his third missionary journey. He was with Paul in the riot at Ephesus (Acts 19:29). He and Tychicus were with Paul in Greece (Acts 20:4). Aristarchus went to Rome with Paul (Acts 27:2). Mark started out with Paul and Barnabas on their first missionary journey (Acts 12:25), but he left in the middle of the trip for unknown reasons (Acts 13:13). Barnabas and Mark were relatives, and when Paul refused to take Mark on another journey, Barnabas and Mark journeyed together to preach the Good News (Acts 15:37-41). Mark also worked with Peter (Acts 12:12-13; 1 Pet 5:13). Later, Mark and Paul were reconciled (Phlm 1:24). Mark wrote the Gospel of Mark. His Profile is on p. 1541.

Col 4:12 Epaphras founded the Colossian church (see the note on Col 1:7, p. 1694), and his report to Paul in Rome caused Paul to write this letter. Epaphras was a hero of the Colossian church, one of the believers who helped keep the church together despite growing troubles. His earnest prayers for the believers show his deep love and concern for them.

Col 4:13 Laodicea was located a few miles northwest of Colosse; Hierapolis was about five miles north of Laodicea. (See the note on Col 2:1, p. 1697, for more about Laodicea.)

Col 4:14 Luke spent much time with Paul, not only accompanying him on most of his third missionary journey but sitting with him in the prison at Rome. Luke wrote the Gospel of Luke and the book of Acts. His Profile is on p. 1513. Demas was faithful for a while, but then he deserted Paul because he loved "the things of this life" (2 Tim 4:10).

Col 4:15 The early Christians often met in homes. Church buildings were not common until the third century.

Col 4:16 Some suggest that the letter from Laodicea may be the book of Ephesians, because the letter to the Ephesians was circulated to all the churches in Asia Minor. It is also possible that there was a special letter to the Laodiceans, of which we have no record today. Paul wrote several letters that have been lost (see, for example, 2 Cor 2:3).

Col 4:17 Paul's letter to Philemon is also addressed to Archippus (Phlm 1:2). Paul called him a "fellow soldier." He may have been a Roman soldier who had become a member of the Colossian church, or he may have been Philemon's son.

Col 4:17 Paul encouraged Archippus to make sure that he carried out the ministry he had received in the Lord. There are many ways for us to leave our ministries unfinished. We can easily get sidetracked morally, we can become exhausted and stop, we can get mad and quit, or we can let it slide and leave it up to others. We should see to it that we finish God's assignments, completing the work we have received.

Col 4:18 Paul usually dictated his letters to a secretary and then often ended with a short note in his own handwriting (see also 1 Cor 16:21; Gal 6:11). This assured the recipients that false teachers were not writing letters in Paul's name. It also gave the letters a personal touch.

Col 4:18 To understand the letter to the Colossians, we need to know that the church was facing pressure from a heresy that promised deeper spiritual life through secret knowledge (an early form of Gnosticism). The false teachers were destroying faith in Christ by undermining Christ's humanity and divinity.

Paul makes it clear in Colossians that Christ alone is the source of our spiritual life, the head of the body of believers. Christ is Lord of both the physical and spiritual worlds. The path to deeper spiritual life is not through religious duties, special knowledge, or secrets; it is only through a clear connection with the Lord Jesus Christ. We must never let anything come between us and our Savior.

P. Paul's Letter to the Church in Ephesus

The church in Ephesus had a special place in Paul's heart. Paul spent three years in Ephesus during his third missionary journey, and on his way back to Jerusalem he met with the elders of the Ephesian church to encourage them. He sent Timothy, his beloved partner in ministry, to serve the church in Ephesus. They even sent someone from Ephesus to visit Paul in prison when he was in Rome, and so Paul sent this letter back to the church when his visitor returned. Not written to counteract any heresy or to confront any specific problem, it is a letter of encouragement. In it Paul describes the nature and appearance of the church, and he challenges believers to function as the living body of Christ on earth.

1. UNITY IN CHRIST

After a warm greeting, Paul affirms the glorious fact that believers in Christ have been showered with God's kindness, chosen for greatness, marked with the Holy Spirit, filled with the Spirit's power, freed from sin's curse and bondage, and brought near to God. As part of God's house, we stand with the prophets, apostles, Jews, Gentiles, and Christ himself. Then, as though overcome with emotion by remembering all that God has done, Paul challenges the Ephesians to live close to Christ, and he breaks into spontaneous praise.

Greetings from Paul

EPHESIANS 1:1-2

This letter is from Paul, chosen by the will of God to be an apostle of Christ Jesus.

I am writing to God's holy people in Ephesus,* who are faithful followers of Christ Jesus.

2May God our Father and the Lord Jesus Christ give you grace and peace.

Eph 1:1 The most ancient manuscripts do not include *in Ephesus.*

Spiritual Blessings

EPHESIANS 1:3-14

All praise to God, the Father of our Lord Jesus Christ, who has blessed us with every spiritual blessing in the heavenly realms because we are united with Christ.
4Even before he made the world, God loved us and chose us in Christ to be holy and without fault in his eyes.
5God decided in advance to adopt us into his own

Eph 1:1 Paul wrote this letter to the Ephesian believers and all other believers to give them in-depth teaching about how to nurture and maintain the unity of the church. He wanted to put this important information in written form because he was in prison for preaching the Good News and could not visit the churches himself. The words "in Ephesus" are not present in some early manuscripts. Therefore, this was very likely a circular letter. It was first sent to Ephesus and then circulated to neighboring local churches. Paul mentions no particular problems or local situations, and he offers no personal greetings.

Eph 1:1 Paul had been a Christian for nearly 30 years. He had taken three missionary trips and established churches all around the Mediterranean Sea. When he wrote Ephesians, Paul was under house arrest in Rome (see Acts 28:16ff). Though a prisoner, he was free to have visitors and write letters. For more information on Paul, see his Profile on p. 1571.

Eph 1:1 Ephesus was one of the five major cities in the Roman Empire, along with Rome, Corinth, Antioch, and Alexandria. Paul first visited Ephesus on his second missionary journey (Acts 18:19-21). During his third missionary journey, he stayed there for almost three years (Acts 19). Paul later met again with the elders of the Ephesian church at Miletus (Acts 20:16-38). Ephesus was a commercial, political, and religious center for all of Asia Minor. The temple to the Greek goddess Artemis (Diana is her Roman equivalent) was located there.

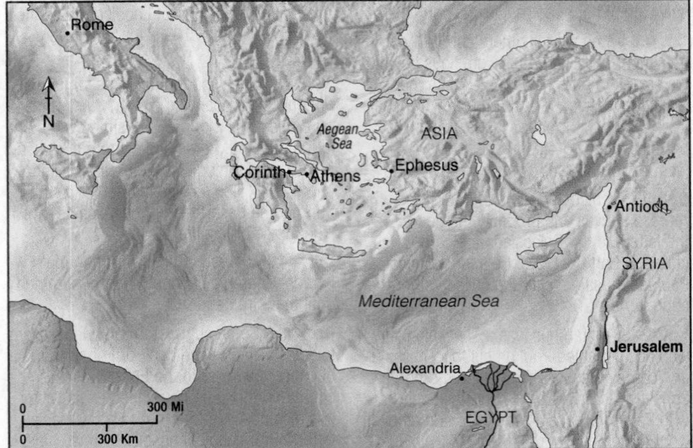

***LOCATION OF EPHESUS** Ephesus was a strategic city, ranking in importance with Alexandria in Egypt and Antioch of Syria as a port. It lay on the most western edge of Asia Minor (modern-day Turkey), the most important port on the Aegean Sea on the main route from Rome to the east.*

Eph 1:1 "Faithful followers of Christ Jesus"—what an excellent reputation! Such a label would be an honor for any believer. What would it take for others to characterize you as a faithful follower of Christ Jesus? Hold fast to your faith, one day at a time; faithfully obey God, even in the details of life. Then, like the Ephesians, you will be known as a person who is faithful to the Lord.

Eph 1:3 "Who has blessed us with every spiritual blessing in the heavenly realms" means that in Christ we have all the benefits of knowing God—being chosen for salvation, being adopted as his children, forgiveness, insight, the gifts of the Spirit, power to do God's will, the hope of living forever with Christ. Because we have an intimate relationship with Christ, we can enjoy these blessings now. The "heavenly realms" means that

family by bringing us to himself through Jesus Christ.
This is what he wanted to do, and it gave him great
pleasure. 6So we praise God for the glorious grace he
has poured out on us who belong to his dear Son.*
7He is so rich in kindness and grace that he purchased
our freedom with the blood of his Son and forgave our
sins. 8He has showered his kindness on us, along with
all wisdom and understanding.
9God has now revealed to us his mysterious plan
regarding Christ, a plan to fulfill his own good pleasure.
10And this is the plan: At the right time he will bring
everything together under the authority of Christ—
everything in heaven and on earth. 11Furthermore, because we are united with Christ, we have received an
inheritance from God,* for he chose us in advance, and
he makes everything work out according to his plan.
12God's purpose was that we Jews who were the first
to trust in Christ would bring praise and glory to God.
13And now you Gentiles have also heard the truth, the
Good News that God saves you. And when you believed

Eph 1:6 Greek *to us in the beloved.* **Eph 1:11** Or *we have become God's inheritance.*

these blessings are eternal, not temporal. The blessings come from Christ's spiritual realm, not the earthly realm of the goddess Artemis. Other references to the heavenly realms in this letter include Ephesians 1:20; 2:6; 3:10. Such passages reveal Christ in his victorious, exalted role as ruler of all.

Eph 1:4 Paul says that God "chose us" to emphasize that salvation depends totally on God. We are not saved because we deserve it but because God is gracious and freely gives salvation. We did not influence God's decision to save us; he saved us according to his plan. Thus, there is no way to take credit for our salvation or to allow room for pride. The mystery of salvation originated in the timeless mind of God long before we existed. It is hard to understand how God could accept us. But because of Christ, we are holy and blameless in his sight. God chose us, and when we belong to him through Jesus Christ, God looks at us as if we had never sinned. All we can do is express our thanks for his wonderful love.

Eph 1:5 That God "decided in advance to adopt us" is another way of saying that salvation is God's work and not our own doing. In his infinite love, God has adopted us as his own children. Through Jesus' sacrifice, he has brought us into his family and made us heirs along with Jesus (Rom 8:17). In Roman law, adopted children had the same rights and privileges as biological children, even if they had been slaves. Paul uses this term to show how strong our relationship to God is. Have you entered into this loving relationship with God? (For more on the meaning of adoption, see Gal 4:5-7.)

Eph 1:7 To speak of Jesus' blood was an important first-century way of speaking of Christ's death. His death points to two wonderful truths—redemption and forgiveness. *Redemption* was the price paid to gain freedom for a slave (Lev 25:47-54). Through his death, Jesus paid the price to release us from slavery to sin. *Forgiveness* was granted in Old Testament times on the basis of the shedding of animals' blood (Lev 17:11). Now we are forgiven on the basis of the shedding of Jesus' blood—he died as the perfect and final sacrifice (see also Rom 5:9; Eph 2:13; Col 1:20; Heb 9:22; 1 Pet 1:19).

Eph 1:7-8 God "showered his kindness on us"—this is also called God's "grace." This is his voluntary and loving favor given to those he saves. We can't earn salvation, nor do we deserve it. No religious, intellectual, or moral effort can gain it, because it comes only from God's mercy and love. Without God's grace, no person can be saved. To receive it, we must acknowledge that we cannot save ourselves, that only God can save us, and that our only way to receive this loving favor is through faith in Christ.

Eph 1:9-10 God's plan for the world could not be fully understood until Christ rose from the dead. His purpose for sending Christ was to unite Jews and Gentiles into one body with Christ as the head. Many people still do not understand God's plan; but at the right time, he will bring us together to be with him forever. Then everyone will understand. On that day, all people will bow to Jesus as Lord, either because they love him or because they fear his power (see Phil 2:10-11).

Eph 1:11 God's purpose is to offer salvation to the world, just as he planned to do long ago. God is sovereign; he is in charge. When your life seems chaotic, rest in this truth: Jesus is Lord, and God is in control. God's purpose to save you cannot be thwarted, no matter what evil Satan may bring.

Eph 1:13-14 The Holy Spirit is God's guarantee that we belong to him and that he will do what he has promised. The Holy Spirit is like a down payment, a deposit, a validating signature on the contract. The presence of the Holy Spirit in us demonstrates the genuineness of our faith, proves that we are God's children, and secures eternal life for us. His power works in us to transform us now, and what we experience now is a taste of the total change we will experience in eternity.

Ruins of Ephesus

Ephesus was the most important city of the Roman province of Asia, located on the western shore of Asia Minor (modern Turkey). Ephesus was built on a natural harbor whose waves, according to the Roman writer Pliny the Elder, "used to wash up to the temple of Diana." Ephesus was described by Strabo, an early Greek geographer, as the largest commercial center west of the Taurus Mountains. It was also well known as the "guardian" of the temple of Artemis, or as the Romans called her, Diana (Acts 19:34).

Christianity's threat to that pagan temple and to the commerce it produced for the makers of idols almost cost the apostle Paul his life (Acts 19:23-31). Priscilla and Aquila were associated with the early preaching in Ephesus (Acts 18:18-19), as was Timothy (1 Tim 1:3) and Erastus (Paul sent him from Ephesus ahead to Macedonia; Acts 19:22). Ephesus was the recipient of one of Paul's prison epistles, which he wrote around A.D. 60 while he was under house arrest in Rome. According to Irenaeus, an early Christian writer, the apostle John, after his exile on the island of Patmos (Rev 1:9), returned to live in Ephesus until the time of the emperor Trajan (A.D. 98–117). It is also believed that Mary, mother of Jesus, moved to Ephesus and was buried there. All in all, Ephesus factored very significantly in the history of the church. We have much to learn from Paul's Epistle to the Ephesians, as well as 1 John, which was written by the apostle John either to or from Ephesus.

▸ **EPHESIANS 1:3-14** ***(cont.)***
in Christ, he identified you as his own* by giving you the
Holy Spirit, whom he promised long ago. [14]The Spirit is
God's guarantee that he will give us the inheritance he
promised and that he has purchased us to be his own
people. He did this so we would praise and glorify him.

Paul's Prayer for Spiritual Wisdom

EPHESIANS 1:15-23
Ever since I first heard of your strong faith in the Lord
Jesus and your love for God's people everywhere,* [16]I
have not stopped thanking God for you. I pray for you
constantly, [17]asking God, the glorious Father of our
Lord Jesus Christ, to give you spiritual wisdom* and
insight so that you might grow in your knowledge of
God. [18]I pray that your hearts will be flooded with light
so that you can understand the confident hope he has
given to those he called—his holy people who are his
rich and glorious inheritance.*
[19]I also pray that you will understand the incredible greatness of God's power for us who believe him.
This is the same mighty power [20]that raised Christ
from the dead and seated him in the place of honor
at God's right hand in the heavenly realms. [21]Now he
is far above any ruler or authority or power or leader
or anything else—not only in this world but also in
the world to come. [22]God has put all things under the
authority of Christ and has made him head over all
things for the benefit of the church. [23]And the church
is his body; it is made full and complete by Christ, who
fills all things everywhere with himself.

Made Alive with Christ

EPHESIANS 2:1-10
Once you were dead because of your disobedience and
your many sins. [2]You used to live in sin, just like the
rest of the world, obeying the devil—the commander
of the powers in the unseen world.* He is the spirit at

Eph 1:13 Or *he put his seal on you.* **Eph 1:15** Some manuscripts read *your faithfulness to the Lord Jesus and to God's people everywhere.* **Eph 1:17** Or *to give you the Spirit of wisdom.* **Eph 1:18** Or *called, and the rich and glorious inheritance he has given to his holy people.* **Eph 2:2** Greek *obeying the commander of the power of the air.*

Eph 1:16-17 Paul prayed for the believers to know God better. How do you get to know someone? By reading biographical information or historical data? That will help you know a lot about them, but won't enable you to actually know them. If you want to get to know someone, you have to spend time with that person; there is no shortcut. The same holds true with God. Reading the Bible, great works of theology, and devotional material is wonderful, but there is no substitute for knowing God personally. What about you? Do you really *know* God, or do you just know *about* him? The difference is in spending time with him. Study Jesus' life in the Gospels to see what he was like on earth 2,000 years ago, and get to know him in prayer now. Personal knowledge of Christ will change your life.

Eph 1:19-20 The world fears the power of the atom, yet we belong to the God of the universe, who not only created that atomic power but also raised Jesus Christ from the dead. God's incomparably great power is available to help you. There is nothing too difficult for him.

Eph 1:20-22 Having been raised from the dead, Christ is now the head of the church, the ultimate authority over the world. Jesus is the Messiah, God's anointed one, the one Israel longed for, the one who would set their broken world right. As Christians we can be confident that God has won the final victory and is in control of everything. We need not fear any dictator or nation or even death or Satan himself. The contract has been signed and sealed; we are waiting just a short while for delivery. Nothing can separate us from God and his love (Rom 8:37-39).

Eph 1:22-23 Christ fills the church with gifts and blessings. The church should be the full expression of Christ, who himself fills everything (see Eph 3:19). When reading Ephesians, it is important to remember that it was written primarily to the entire church, not merely to an individual. Christ is the head, and we are the body of his church (Paul uses this metaphor in Rom 12:4-5; 1 Cor 12:12-27; Col 3:15; and throughout the book of Ephesians). The image of the body shows the church's unity. Each member is involved with all the others as they go about doing Christ's work on earth. We should not attempt to work, serve, or worship merely on our own. We need the entire body.

OUR TRUE IDENTITY IN CHRIST

Rom 3:24	We are justified (declared "righteous").
Rom 8:1	No condemnation awaits us.
Rom 8:2	We are set free from the power of sin that leads to death.
1 Cor 1:2	We are sanctified (made holy) in Jesus Christ.
1 Cor 1:30	We are pure and holy in Christ.
1 Cor 15:22	We will be given new life at the resurrection.
2 Cor 5:17	We are new persons.
2 Cor 5:21	We are made right with God.
Gal 3:28	We are one in Christ with all other believers.
Eph 1:3	We are blessed with every spiritual blessing in Christ.
Eph 1:4	We are holy and without fault.
Eph 1:5-6	We are adopted as God's children.
Eph 1:7	Our sins are taken away, and we are forgiven.
Eph 1:10-11	We will be brought under Christ's authority.
Eph 1:13	We are identified as belonging to God by the Holy Spirit.
Eph 2:6	We have been raised up to sit with Christ in the heavenly realms.
Eph 2:10	We are God's masterpiece.
Eph 2:13	We have been brought near to God.
Eph 3:6	We share in the promise of blessings through Christ.
Eph 3:12	We can come boldly and confidently into God's presence.
Eph 5:29-30	We are members of Christ's body, the church.
Col 2:10	We are made complete in Christ.
Col 2:11	We are set free from our sinful nature.
2 Tim 2:10	We will have eternal glory.

work in the hearts of those who refuse to obey God.
3All of us used to live that way, following the passionate desires and inclinations of our sinful nature. By
our very nature we were subject to God's anger, just
like everyone else.
4But God is so rich in mercy, and he loved us so
much, 5that even though we were dead because of
our sins, he gave us life when he raised Christ from
the dead. (It is only by God's grace that you have been
saved!) 6For he raised us from the dead along with
Christ and seated us with him in the heavenly realms
because we are united with Christ Jesus. 7So God can
point to us in all future ages as examples of the incredible wealth of his grace and kindness toward us, as
shown in all he has done for us who are united with
Christ Jesus.
8God saved you by his grace when you believed.
And you can't take credit for this; it is a gift from God.
9Salvation is not a reward for the good things we have
done, so none of us can boast about it. 10For we are
God's masterpiece. He has created us anew in Christ
Jesus, so we can do the good things he planned for
us long ago.

Oneness and Peace in Christ

EPHESIANS 2:11-18

Don't forget that you Gentiles used to be outsiders. You
were called "uncircumcised heathens" by the Jews,

OUR LIVES BEFORE AND AFTER CHRIST

Before	After
Dead because of sin	Made alive with Christ
Under God's anger	Shown God's mercy and given salvation
Followed the ways of the world	Stand for Christ and truth
God's enemies	God's children
Enslaved to the devil	Free in Christ to love, serve, and sit with him
Followed our evil thoughts and desires	Raised up with Christ to glory

Eph 2:1-2 Immediately after his prayer, Paul reminds the Ephesians of the reality of personal sin. Like them, we must never forget our past, the condition from which Jesus saved us. Those memories are the best fuel for our gratitude to Christ for all he has done on our behalf.

Eph 2:2 Paul describes Satan, the devil, as "the commander of the powers in the unseen world." Paul's readers believed that Satan and the evil spiritual forces inhabited the region between earth and sky. Satan is thus pictured as ruling an evil spiritual kingdom—the demons and those who are against Christ. In his resurrection, Christ was victorious over the devil and his power. Therefore, Jesus Christ is the permanent ruler of the whole world; the devil is only the temporary ruler of the part of the world that chooses to follow him.

Eph 2:3 The fact that all people, without exception, commit sin proves that without Christ we have a sinful nature. We are lost in sin and cannot save ourselves. Does this mean only Christians do good? Of course not—many people do good to others. On a relative scale, many are moral, kind, and law abiding. Comparing these people to criminals, we would say that they are very good indeed. But on God's absolute scale, no one is good enough to earn salvation ("dead because of your disobedience and your many sins" [Eph 2:1]). Only through being united with Christ's perfect life can we become good in God's sight. "Subject to God's anger" refers to those who are to receive God's wrath because of their rejection of Christ.

Eph 2:4 We were dead in our sins, *but God*. . . . We were rebels against him, *but God*. . . . We were enslaved by the devil and our sinful natures, *but God*. . . . These may be the two most welcome words in all of Scripture: "but God." God could have left us spiritually dead, in rebellion against him and in bondage to our sins. *But he didn't.* He did not save us because of, but rather in spite of, what he saw in us. In addition to thanking him for what he has done for us, we should also show humble patience and tolerance for others who seem unworthy or undeserving of our love and compassion. They may be spiritually dull, rebellious, and even antagonistic toward God. So were we; *but God loved us anyway.* Can we do less for fellow sinners?

Eph 2:4-5 In the previous verses Paul wrote about our old sinful nature (Eph 2:1-3). Here Paul emphasizes that we do not need to live any longer under sin's power. The penalty of sin and its power over us were miraculously destroyed by Christ on the cross. Through faith in Christ we stand acquitted, or not guilty, before God (Rom 3:21-22). God does not take us out of the world or make us robots—we will still feel like sinning, and sometimes we will sin. The difference is that before we became Christians, we were dead in sin and were slaves to our sinful nature. But now we are alive with Christ (see also Gal 2:20).

Eph 2:6 Because of Christ's resurrection, we know that our body will also be raised from the dead (1 Cor 15:2-23) and that we have been given the power to live as Christians now (Eph 1:19). These ideas are combined in Paul's image of sitting with Christ in "the heavenly realms" (see the note on Eph 1:3, p. 1704). Our eternal life with Christ is certain because we are united in his powerful victory.

Eph 2:8-9 When someone gives you a gift, do you say, "That's very nice—now how much do I owe you?" No, the appropriate response to a gift is "Thank you." Yet how often do Christians, even after they have been given the gift of salvation, feel obligated to try to work their way to God? Because our salvation and even our faith are gifts, we should respond with gratitude, praise, and joy.

Eph 2:8-10 We become Christians through God's unmerited favor, not as the result of any effort, ability, intelligent choice, or act of service on our part. However, out of gratitude for this free gift, we will seek to help and serve others with kindness, love, and gentleness, and not merely to please ourselves. While no action or work we do can help us obtain salvation, God's intention is that our salvation will result in acts of service. We are not saved merely for our own benefit but to serve Christ and build up the church (Eph 4:12).

Eph 2:10 We are God's masterpiece (work of art, workmanship). Our salvation is something only God can do. It is his powerful, creative work in us. If God considers us his masterpieces, we dare not treat ourselves or others with disrespect or as inferior work.

Eph 2:11-13 Pious Jews considered all non-Jews (Gentiles) ceremonially unclean. They thought of themselves as pure and clean because of their national heritage and religious ceremonies. Paul pointed out that Jews and Gentiles alike were unclean before God and needed to be cleansed by Christ. In order to realize how great a gift salvation is, we need to remember our former natural, unclean condition. Have you ever felt separate, excluded, hopeless? These verses are for you. No one is alienated from Christ's love or from the body of believers.

Eph 2:11-13 Jews and Gentiles alike could be guilty of spiritual pride—Jews for thinking their faith and traditions elevated them above everyone else, Gentiles for trusting in their achievements, power, or position. Spiritual pride blinds us to our own faults and magnifies the faults of others. Be careful not

▶ **EPHESIANS 2:11-18** ***(cont.)***

who were proud of their circumcision, even though it affected only their bodies and not their hearts. 12In those days you were living apart from Christ. You were excluded from citizenship among the people of Israel, and you did not know the covenant promises God had made to them. You lived in this world without God and without hope. 13But now you have been united with Christ Jesus. Once you were far away from God, but now you have been brought near to him through the blood of Christ.

14For Christ himself has brought peace to us. He united Jews and Gentiles into one people when, in his own body on the cross, he broke down the wall of hostility that separated us. 15He did this by ending the system of law with its commandments and regulations. He made peace between Jews and Gentiles by creating in himself one new people from the two groups. 16Together as one body, Christ reconciled both groups to God by means of his death on the cross, and our hostility toward each other was put to death.

17He brought this Good News of peace to you Gentiles who were far away from him, and peace to the Jews who were near. 18Now all of us can come to the Father through the same Holy Spirit because of what Christ has done for us.

A Temple for the Lord

EPHESIANS 2:19-22

So now you Gentiles are no longer strangers and foreigners. You are citizens along with all of God's holy people. You are members of God's family. 20Together, we are his house, built on the foundation of the apostles and the prophets. And the cornerstone is Christ Jesus himself. 21We are carefully joined together in him, becoming a holy temple for the Lord. 22Through him you Gentiles are also being made part of this dwelling where God lives by his Spirit.

God's Mysterious Plan Revealed

EPHESIANS 3:1-13

When I think of all this, I, Paul, a prisoner of Christ Jesus for the benefit of you Gentiles* . . . 2assuming, by the way, that you know God gave me the special responsibility of extending his grace to you Gentiles. 3As I briefly wrote earlier, God himself revealed his mysterious plan to me. 4As you read what I have written, you will understand my insight into this plan regarding Christ. 5God did not reveal it to previous generations, but now by his Spirit he has revealed it to his holy apostles and prophets.

6And this is God's plan: Both Gentiles and Jews who believe the Good News share equally in the riches

Eph 3:1 Paul resumes this thought in verse 14: "When I think of all this, I fall to my knees and pray to the Father."

---

to become proud of your salvation. Instead, humbly thank God for what he has done, and encourage others who might be struggling in their faith.

Eph 2:11-16 Before Christ's coming, Gentiles and Jews kept apart from one another. Jews considered Gentiles beyond God's saving power and therefore without hope. Gentiles resented Jewish claims. Christ revealed the total sinfulness of both Jews and Gentiles, and then he offered his salvation to both. Only Christ breaks down the walls of prejudice, reconciles all believers to God, and unifies us in one body.

Eph 2:14ff Christ has destroyed the barriers people build between themselves. Because these walls have been removed, we can have real unity with people who are not like us. This is true reconciliation. Because of Christ's death, we are all one (Eph 2:14); our hostility against each other has been put to death (Eph 2:16); we can all have access to the Father by the Holy Spirit (Eph 2:18); we are no longer strangers or foreigners to God (Eph 2:19); and we are all being built into a holy temple with Christ as our chief cornerstone (Eph 2:20-21).

Eph 2:14-22 There are many barriers that can divide us from other Christians: age, appearance, intelligence, political persuasion, economic status, race, theological perspective. One of the best ways to stifle Christ's love is to be friendly only with people whom we like. Fortunately, Christ has knocked down the barriers and has unified all believers into one family. His cross should be the focus of our unity. The Holy Spirit helps us look beyond the barriers to the unity we are called to enjoy.

Eph 2:15 By his death, Christ ended the angry resentment between Jews and Gentiles, caused by the Jewish laws that favored the Jews and excluded the Gentiles. Christ died to abolish that whole system of Jewish laws. Then he took the two groups that had been opposed to each other and made them parts of himself. "One new people" means that Christ made a single entity out of the two. Thus, he fused all believers together to become one in himself.

Eph 2:17-18 The Jews were near to God because they already knew of him through the Scriptures and worshiped him in their religious ceremonies. The Gentiles were far away because they knew little or nothing about God. Because neither group could be saved by good deeds, knowledge, or sincerity, both needed to hear about the salvation available through Jesus Christ. Both Jews and Gentiles are now free to come to God through Christ. You have been brought near to him (Eph 2:13).

Eph 2:19-22 A church building is sometimes called God's house. In reality, God's household is not a building but a group of people. He lives in us and shows himself to a watching world through us. People can see that God is love and that Christ is Lord as we live in harmony with each other and in accordance with what God says in his Word. We are citizens of God's Kingdom and members of his household.

Eph 2:20 What does it mean to be "built on the foundation of the apostles and prophets"? It means that the church is not built on modern ideas but rather on the spiritual heritage given to us by the early apostles and prophets of the Christian church.

Eph 3:1 Paul was under house arrest in Rome for preaching about Christ. The religious leaders in Jerusalem, who felt threatened by Christ's teachings and didn't believe he was the Messiah, pressured the Romans to arrest Paul and bring him to trial for treason and for causing rebellion among the Jews. Paul had appealed for his case to be heard by the emperor, and he was awaiting trial (see Acts 28:16-31). Even though he was under arrest, Paul maintained his firm belief that God was in control of all that happened to him. Do circumstances make you wonder if God has lost control of this world? Like Paul, remember that no matter what happens, God directs the world's affairs.

Eph 3:2-3 Paul's "special responsibility" refers to the special stewardship, trust, or commitment that Paul had been given. He had been assigned the special work of preaching the Good News to the Gentiles; God showed this to Paul in a revelation (see Acts 22:17-21).

Eph 3:5-6 God didn't reveal his plan to previous generations—not because he

inherited by God's children. Both are part of the same body, and both enjoy the promise of blessings because they belong to Christ Jesus.* 7By God's grace and mighty power, I have been given the privilege of serving him by spreading this Good News.

8Though I am the least deserving of all God's people, he graciously gave me the privilege of telling the Gentiles about the endless treasures available to them in Christ. 9I was chosen to explain to everyone* this mysterious plan that God, the Creator of all things, had kept secret from the beginning.

10God's purpose in all this was to use the church to display his wisdom in its rich variety to all the unseen rulers and authorities in the heavenly places. 11This was his eternal plan, which he carried out through Christ Jesus our Lord.

12Because of Christ and our faith in him,* we can now come boldly and confidently into God's presence. 13So please don't lose heart because of my trials here. I am suffering for you, so you should feel honored.

Paul's Prayer for Spiritual Growth

EPHESIANS 3:14-21

When I think of all this, I fall to my knees and pray to the Father,* 15the Creator of everything in heaven and on earth.* 16I pray that from his glorious, unlimited resources he will empower you with inner strength through his Spirit. 17Then Christ will make his home in your hearts as you trust in him. Your roots will grow down into God's love and keep you strong. 18And may you have the power to understand, as all God's people should, how wide, how long, how high, and how deep

Eph 3:6 Or *because they are united with Christ Jesus.* **Eph 3:9** Some manuscripts do not include *to everyone.* **Eph 3:12** Or *Because of Christ's faithfulness.* **Eph 3:14** Some manuscripts read *the Father of our Lord Jesus Christ.* **Eph 3:15** Or *from whom every family in heaven and on earth takes its name.*

wanted to keep something from his people but because he would reveal it to everyone in his perfect timing. God planned to have Jews and Gentiles comprise one body, the church. It was known in the Old Testament that the Gentiles would receive salvation (Isa 49:6); but it was never revealed in the Old Testament that all Gentile and Jewish believers would become equal in the body of Christ. This equality was accomplished when Jesus destroyed the "wall of hostility" and created "one new people" (Eph 2:14-15).

Eph 3:7 When Paul became a servant of the gospel, God gave him the ability to share the Good News of Christ effectively. You are not Paul, and you may not be an evangelist, but God will give you opportunities to tell others about Christ. And with the opportunities he will provide the ability, courage, and power. Make yourself available to God as his servant whenever an opportunity presents itself. As you focus on the other person's needs, God will communicate your caring attitude. Your words will be natural, loving, and compelling.

Eph 3:8 When Paul describes himself as "the least deserving of all God's people," he is probably referring to his history as a fierce persecutor of Christians. Yet God chose him to share the Good News with the Gentiles and gave him the power to do it. If we feel that our past limits our usefulness, we have forgotten what a difference God makes. How does God want to use you? Draw on his power, do your part, and faithfully perform the special role God has called you to play in his plan.

Eph 3:10 The "rulers and authorities in the heavenly places" are either angels who are witnesses to these events (see 1 Pet 1:12), or hostile spiritual forces opposed to God (Eph 2:2; 6:12).

Eph 3:12 It is an awesome privilege to be able to approach God with freedom and confidence. Most of us would be apprehensive in the presence of a powerful ruler. But thanks to Christ, by faith we can enter directly into God's presence through prayer. We know we'll be welcomed with open arms because we are God's children through our union with Christ. Don't be afraid of God. Talk with him about everything. He is waiting to hear from you.

Eph 3:13 Why should Paul's suffering make the Ephesians feel honored? If Paul had not preached the Good News, he would not be in jail—but then the Ephesians would not have heard the Good News and been converted, either. Just as a mother endures the pain of childbirth in order to bring new life into the world, Paul endured the pain of persecution in order to bring new believers to Christ. Obeying Christ is never easy. He calls you to take up your cross and follow him (Matt 16:24)—that is, to give up your comfort and even your life so that God's message of salvation can reach the entire world. We should feel honored that others have suffered and sacrificed for us so that we might reap the benefits.

Eph 3:14-15 The family of God includes all who have believed in him in the past, all who believe in the present, and all who will believe in the future. We are all a family because we have the same Father. He is the source of all creation, the rightful owner of everything. God promises his love and power to his family, the church (Eph 3:16-21). If we want to receive God's blessings, it is important that we stay in contact with other believers in the body of Christ. Those who isolate themselves from God's family and try to go it alone cut themselves off from God's power.

Eph 3:17-19 God's love is total, says Paul. It reaches every corner of our experience. It is *wide*—it covers the breadth of our own experience, and it reaches out to the whole world. God's love is *long*—it continues the length of our lives. It is *high*—it rises to the heights of our celebration and elation. His love is *deep*—it reaches to the depths of

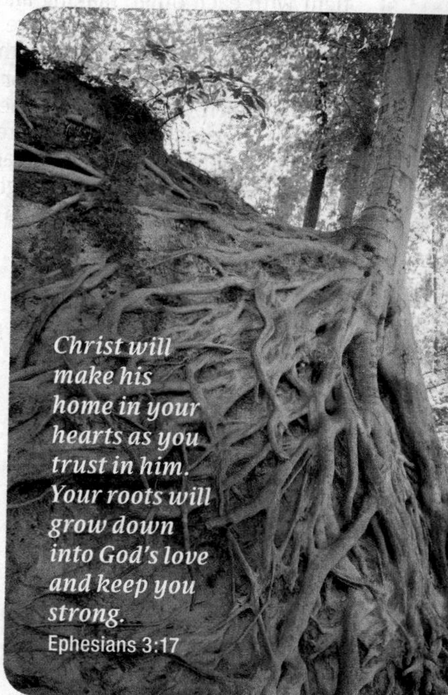
Christ will make his home in your hearts as you trust in him. Your roots will grow down into God's love and keep you strong.
Ephesians 3:17

discouragement, despair, and even death. When you feel shut out or isolated, remember that you can never be lost to God's love. (For another prayer about God's immeasurable and inexhaustible love, see Paul's words in Rom 8:38-39.)

▸ **EPHESIANS 3:14-21 *(cont.)***

his love is. 19May you experience the love of Christ,
though it is too great to understand fully. Then you
will be made complete with all the fullness of life and
power that comes from God.
20Now all glory to God, who is able, through his
mighty power at work within us, to accomplish infinitely more than we might ask or think. 21Glory to him
in the church and in Christ Jesus through all generations forever and ever! Amen.

2. UNITY IN THE BODY OF CHRIST

Paul turns his attention to the implications of being the body of Christ, the church. Believers should have unity in their commitment to Christ and their use of spiritual gifts. They should have the highest moral standards. For the individual, this means rejecting the sinful practices of those around us, and for the family, this means mutual submission and love. As you read this masterful description of the church, thank God for the diversity and unity in his family!

A Unified Body

EPHESIANS 4:1-16

Therefore I, a prisoner for serving the Lord, beg you
to lead a life worthy of your calling, for you have been
called by God. 2Always be humble and gentle. Be patient with each other, making allowance for each
other's faults because of your love. 3Make every effort to keep yourselves united in the Spirit, binding
yourselves together with peace. 4For there is one body
and one Spirit, just as you have been called to one
glorious hope for the future. 5There is one Lord, one
faith, one baptism, 6and one God and Father, who is
over all and in all and living through all.
7However, he has given each one of us a special
gift* through the generosity of Christ. 8That is why
the Scriptures say,

"When he ascended to the heights,
he led a crowd of captives
and gave gifts to his people."*

9Notice that it says "he ascended." This clearly means
that Christ also descended to our lowly world.* 10And
the same one who descended is the one who ascended
higher than all the heavens, so that he might fill the
entire universe with himself.
11Now these are the gifts Christ gave to the church:

Eph 4:7 Greek *a grace.* **Eph 4:8** Ps 68:18. **Eph 4:9** Or *to the lowest parts of the earth.*

Eph 3:19 This "fullness" is expressed only in Christ (Col 2:9-10). In union with Christ and through his empowering Spirit, we are complete. We have all the fullness of God available to us. But we must appropriate that fullness through faith and through prayer as we daily live for him. Paul's prayer for the Ephesians is also for you. You can ask the Holy Spirit to fill every aspect of your life to the fullest.

Eph 3:20-21 This doxology—prayer of praise to God—ends part 1 of Ephesians. In the first section, Paul described the timeless role of the church. In part 2 (Eph 4–6), he will explain how church members should live in order to bring about the unity God wants. As in most of his books, Paul first lays a doctrinal foundation and then makes practical applications of the truths he has presented.

Eph 4:1-2 God has chosen us to be Christ's representatives on earth. In light of this truth, Paul challenges us to live lives worthy of the calling we have received—the awesome privilege of being called Christ's very own. This includes being humble, gentle, patient, understanding, and peaceful. People are watching your life. Can they see Christ in you? How well are you doing as his representative?

Eph 4:1-6 "There is one body," says Paul. Unity does not just happen; we have to work at it. Often differences among people can lead to division, but this should not be true in the church. Instead of concentrating on what divides us, we should remember what unites us: one body, one Spirit, one future, one Lord, one faith, one baptism, one God! Have you learned to appreciate people who are different from you? Can you see how their differing gifts and viewpoints can help the church as it does God's work? Learn to enjoy the way we members of Christ's body complement one another. (See 1 Cor 12:12-13 for more on this thought.)

Eph 4:2 No one is ever going to be perfect here on earth, so we must accept and love other Christians in spite of their faults. When we see faults in fellow believers, we should be patient and gentle. Is there someone whose actions or personality really annoys you? Rather than dwelling on those weaknesses or looking for faults, pray for that person. Then do even more—spend time together and see if you can learn to like them.

Eph 4:3 To build unity is one of the Holy Spirit's important roles. He leads, but we have to be willing to be led and to do our part to keep the peace. We do that by focusing on God, not on ourselves. (For more about who the Holy Spirit is and what he does, see the notes on John 3:6, p. 1301; Acts 1:5, p. 1499; Eph 1:13-14, p. 1705.)

Eph 4:4-7 All believers in Christ belong to one body; all are united under one head, Christ himself (see 1 Cor 12:12-27). Each believer has God-given abilities that can strengthen the whole body. Your special abilities may seem small or large, but they are yours to use in God's service. Ask God to use your unique gifts to contribute to the strength and health of the body of believers.

Eph 4:6 God is "over all"—this shows his overruling care (transcendence). He is "in all" and "living through all"—this shows his active presence in the world and in the lives of believers (immanence). Any view of God that violates either his transcendence or his immanence does not paint a true picture of God.

Eph 4:8 In Psalm 68:18, God is pictured as a conqueror marching to the gates and taking tribute from the fallen city. Paul uses that picture to teach that Christ, in his crucifixion and resurrection, was victorious over Satan. When Christ ascended to heaven, he gave gifts to the church, some of which Paul discusses in Ephesians 4:11-13.

Eph 4:9 The "lowly world" may be (1) the earth itself (lowly by comparison to heaven), (2) the grave, or (3) Hades (many believe Hades is the resting place of souls between death and resurrection). However we understand it, Christ is Lord of the whole universe, past, present, and future. Nothing and no one is hidden from him. The Lord of all came to earth and faced death to rescue all people. No one is beyond his reach.

Eph 4:11-12 Our oneness in Christ does not destroy our individuality. The Holy Spirit has given each Christian special gifts for building up the church. Now that we have these gifts, it is crucial to use them. Are you spiritually mature, exercising the gifts God has given

the apostles, the prophets, the evangelists, and the
pastors and teachers. 12 Their responsibility is to equip
God's people to do his work and build up the church,
the body of Christ. 13 This will continue until we all
come to such unity in our faith and knowledge of
God's Son that we will be mature in the Lord, measuring up to the full and complete standard of Christ.
14 Then we will no longer be immature like children.
We won't be tossed and blown about by every wind of
new teaching. We will not be influenced when people
try to trick us with lies so clever they sound like the
truth. 15 Instead, we will speak the truth in love, growing in every way more and more like Christ, who is the
head of his body, the church. 16 He makes the whole
body fit together perfectly. As each part does its own
special work, it helps the other parts grow, so that the
whole body is healthy and growing and full of love.

Living as Children of Light

EPHESIANS 4:17-32

With the Lord's authority I say this: Live no longer
as the Gentiles do, for they are hopelessly confused.
18 Their minds are full of darkness; they wander far
from the life God gives because they have closed their
minds and hardened their hearts against him. 19 They
have no sense of shame. They live for lustful pleasure
and eagerly practice every kind of impurity.
20 But that isn't what you learned about Christ.
21 Since you have heard about Jesus and have learned
the truth that comes from him, 22 throw off your old

THE ONENESS OF ALL BELIEVERS

Too often believers are separated because of minor differences in doctrine. But Paul here shows those areas where Christians must agree to attain true unity. When believers have this unity of spirit, petty differences should never be allowed to dissolve that unity.

Believers are one in	*Our unity is experienced in*
Body	The fellowship of believers—the church
Spirit	The Holy Spirit, who activates the fellowship
Hope	That glorious future to which we are all called
Lord	Christ, to whom we all belong
Faith	Our singular commitment to Christ
Baptism	Baptism—the sign of entry into the church
God	God, who is our Father and keeps us for eternity

you? If you know what your gifts are, look for opportunities to serve. If you don't know, ask God to show you, perhaps with the help of your minister or Christian friends. Then, as you begin to recognize your special area of service, use your gifts to strengthen and encourage the church.

Eph 4:12-13 God has given his church an enormous responsibility—to make disciples in every nation (Matt 28:18-20). This involves preaching, teaching, healing, nurturing, giving, administering, building, and many other tasks. If we had to fulfill this command as individuals, we might as well give up without trying—it would be impossible. But God calls us as members of his body. Some of us can do one task; some can do another. Together we can obey God more fully than any of us could alone. It is a human tendency to overestimate what we can do by ourselves and to underestimate what we can do as a group. But as the body of Christ, we can accomplish more together than we would dream possible working by ourselves. Working together, the church can express the fullness of Christ (see the note on Eph 3:19, p. 1710).

Eph 4:14-16 Christ is the truth (John 14:6), and the Holy Spirit, who guides the church, is the Spirit of truth (John 16:13). Satan, by contrast, is the father of lies (John 8:44). As followers of Christ, we must be committed to the truth. This means both that our words should be honest and that our actions should reflect Christ's integrity. Speaking the truth in love is not always easy, convenient, or pleasant, but it is necessary if the church is going to do Christ's work in the world.

Eph 4:15 In describing the mature Christian, Paul says that one of the marks is the ability to "speak the truth in love." This sounds so simple, but it seems so hard for us to do. Some of us are fairly good at speaking the truth, but we forget to be loving. Some of us are good at being loving, but we don't have it in us to level with others if the truth is painful. The instruction here is to do both: Speak the truth, but do it in a loving manner. Think of the trouble we would spare ourselves if we followed this practice, especially in the church! When you have a problem with another believer, don't go to someone else with it. Go directly to that person, and speak the truth in love.

Eph 4:15-16 Some Christians fear that any mistake will destroy their witness for the Lord. They see their own weaknesses, and they know that many non-Christians seem to have stronger character than they do. How can we grow more and more like Christ? The answer is that Christ forms us into a body—into a group of individuals who are united in their purpose and in their love for one another and for the Lord. If we stumble, the rest of the group is there to pick us up and help us walk with God again. If we sin, we can find restoration through the church (Gal 6:1) even as the rest of the body continues to witness to God's truth. As part of Christ's body, do you reflect Christ's character and carry out your special role in his work?

Eph 4:17 The natural tendency of human beings is to think their way away from God—leaving them "hopelessly confused." Intellectual pride, rationalizations, and excuses all keep people from God. Don't be surprised if people can't grasp the Good News. The Good News will seem foolish to those who forsake faith and rely on their own understanding.

Eph 4:17-24 People should be able to see a difference between Christians and non-Christians because of the way Christians live. We are to live full of light (Eph 5:8). Paul told the Ephesians to leave behind the old life of sin since they were followers of Christ. Living the Christian life is a process. Although we have a new nature, we don't automatically think all good thoughts and express all right attitudes when we become new people in Christ. But if we keep listening to God, we will be changing all the time. As you look back over last year, do you see a process of change for the better in your thoughts, attitudes, and actions? Although change may be slow, it comes as you trust God to change you. (For more about our new nature as believers, see Rom 6:6; 8:9; Gal 5:16-26; Col 3:3-8.)

Eph 4:22-24 Our old way of life before we believed in Christ is completely in the past. We should put it behind us like old clothes to be thrown away. When we decide to accept Christ's gift of salvation (Eph 2:8-10), it is both a one-time decision as well as a daily conscious commitment. We are not to be driven by desire and impulse. We must put on the new nature, head in the new direction, and have the new way of thinking that the Holy Spirit gives.

▸ **EPHESIANS 4:17-32** ***(cont.)***

sinful nature and your former way of life, which is corrupted by lust and deception. [23]Instead, let the Spirit renew your thoughts and attitudes. [24]Put on your new nature, created to be like God—truly righteous and holy.

[25]So stop telling lies. Let us tell our neighbors the truth, for we are all parts of the same body. [26]And "don't sin by letting anger control you."* Don't let the sun go down while you are still angry, [27]for anger gives a foothold to the devil.

[28]If you are a thief, quit stealing. Instead, use your hands for good hard work, and then give generously to others in need. [29]Don't use foul or abusive language. Let everything you say be good and helpful, so that your words will be an encouragement to those who hear them.

[30]And do not bring sorrow to God's Holy Spirit by the way you live. Remember, he has identified you as his own,* guaranteeing that you will be saved on the day of redemption.

[31]Get rid of all bitterness, rage, anger, harsh words, and slander, as well as all types of evil behavior. [32]Instead, be kind to each other, tenderhearted, forgiving one another, just as God through Christ has forgiven you.

Living in the Light

EPHESIANS 5:1-14

Imitate God, therefore, in everything you do, because you are his dear children. [2]Live a life filled with love, following the example of Christ. He loved us* and offered himself as a sacrifice for us, a pleasing aroma to God.

[3]Let there be no sexual immorality, impurity, or greed among you. Such sins have no place among God's people. [4]Obscene stories, foolish talk, and coarse jokes—these are not for you. Instead, let there be thankfulness to God. [5]You can be sure that no immoral, impure, or greedy person will inherit the Kingdom of Christ and of God. For a greedy person is an idolater, worshiping the things of this world.

[6]Don't be fooled by those who try to excuse these sins, for the anger of God will fall on all who disobey him. [7]Don't participate in the things these people do. [8]For once you were full of darkness, but now you have light from the Lord. So live as people of light! [9]For this light within you produces only what is good and right and true.

[10]Carefully determine what pleases the Lord. [11]Take no part in the worthless deeds of evil and darkness; instead, expose them. [12]It is shameful even to talk about the things that ungodly people do in secret.

Eph 4:26 Ps 4:4. **Eph 4:30** Or *has put his seal on you.* **Eph 5:2** Some manuscripts read *loved you.*

Eph 4:25 Lying to each other disrupts unity by creating conflicts and destroying trust. It tears down relationships and leads to open warfare in a church.

Eph 4:26-27 The Bible doesn't tell us that we shouldn't feel angry, but it points out that it is important to handle our anger properly. If vented thoughtlessly, anger can hurt others and destroy relationships. If bottled up inside, it can cause us to become bitter and destroy us from within. Paul tells us to deal with our anger immediately in a way that builds relationships rather than destroys them. If we nurse our anger, we will give the devil an opportunity to divide us. Are you angry with someone right now? What can you do to resolve your differences? Don't let the day end before you begin to work on mending your relationship.

Eph 4:28-32 We can bring sorrow to the Holy Spirit by the way we live. Paul warns us against unwholesome language, bitterness, improper use of anger, harsh words, slander, and bad attitudes toward others. Instead of acting that way, we should be forgiving, just as God has forgiven us. Are you bringing sorrow or pleasing God with your attitudes and actions? Act in love toward your brothers and sisters in Christ, just as God acted in love by sending his Son to die for your sins.

Eph 4:30 The Holy Spirit within us is a guarantee that we belong to God. (For more on this thought, see the note on Eph 1:13-14, p. 1705.)

Eph 4:32 This is Christ's law of forgiveness as taught in the Gospels (Matt 6:14-15; 18:35; Mark 11:25). We also see it in the Lord's Prayer—"Forgive us our sins, as we forgive those who sin against us" (Luke 11:4). God forgives us, not because we forgive others but solely because of his great mercy. As we come to understand his mercy, we will want to be like him. Having received forgiveness, we will pass it on to others. Those who are unwilling to forgive have not become one with Christ, who was willing to forgive even those who crucified him (Luke 23:34).

Eph 5:1-2 Just as children imitate their parents, we should follow God's example. His great love for us led him to sacrifice himself so that we might live. Our love for others should be of the same kind—a love that goes beyond affection to self-sacrificing service.

Eph 5:4 Obscene stories and coarse jokes are so common that we begin to take them for granted. Paul cautions that improper language should have no place in the Christian's conversation because it does not reflect God's gracious presence in us. How can we praise God and remind others of his goodness when we are speaking coarsely?

Eph 5:5-7 Paul does not forbid all contact with unbelievers. Jesus taught his followers to befriend sinners and lead them to him (Luke 5:30-32). Instead, Paul writes against the lifestyle of people who make excuses for bad behavior and recommend its practice to others—whether they are in the church or outside of it. Such people quickly pollute the church and endanger its unity and purpose. We must befriend unbelievers if we are to lead them to Christ, but we must be wary of those who are viciously evil, immoral, or opposed to all that Christianity stands for. Such people are more likely to influence us for evil than we are to influence them for good.

Eph 5:8 As people who have light from the Lord, our actions should reflect our faith. We should live above reproach morally so that we will reflect God's goodness to others. Jesus stressed this truth in the Sermon on the Mount (Matt 5:15-16).

Eph 5:10-14 It is important to avoid the "worthless deeds of evil and darkness" (any pleasure or activity that results in sin), but we must go even further. Paul instructs us to expose these deeds because our silence may be interpreted as approval. God needs people who will take a stand for what is right. Christians must lovingly speak out for what is true and right.

[13]But their evil intentions will be exposed when the
light shines on them, [14]for the light makes everything
visible. This is why it is said,

"Awake, O sleeper,
rise up from the dead,
and Christ will give you light."

Living by the Spirit's Power

EPHESIANS 5:15-20

So be careful how you live. Don't live like fools, but
like those who are wise. [16]Make the most of every opportunity in these evil days. [17]Don't act thoughtlessly,
but understand what the Lord wants you to do. [18]Don't
be drunk with wine, because that will ruin your life.
Instead, be filled with the Holy Spirit, [19]singing psalms
and hymns and spiritual songs among yourselves, and
making music to the Lord in your hearts. [20]And give
thanks for everything to God the Father in the name
of our Lord Jesus Christ.

Spirit-Guided Relationships: Wives and Husbands

EPHESIANS 5:21-33

And further, submit to one another out of reverence
for Christ.

[22]For wives, this means submit to your husbands
as to the Lord. [23]For a husband is the head of his wife
as Christ is the head of the church. He is the Savior
of his body, the church. [24]As the church submits to
Christ, so you wives should submit to your husbands
in everything.

[25]For husbands, this means love your wives, just as

Eph 5:14 This is not a direct quote from Scripture but was probably taken from a hymn well known to the Ephesians. The hymn seems to have been based on Isaiah 26:19; 51:17; 52:1; 60:1; Malachi 4:2. Paul was appealing to the Ephesians to wake up and realize the dangerous condition into which some of them had been slipping.

Eph 5:15-16 By referring to these days as evil, Paul was communicating his sense of urgency because of evil's pervasiveness. We need the same sense of urgency because our days are also difficult. We must keep our standards high, act wisely, and do good whenever we can.

Eph 5:18 Paul contrasts getting drunk with wine, which produces a temporary "high," to being filled with the Spirit, which produces lasting joy. Getting drunk with wine is associated with the old way of life and its selfish desires. In Christ, we have a better joy, higher and longer lasting, to cure our depression, monotony, or tension. We should not be concerned with how much of the Holy Spirit we have but with how much of us the Holy Spirit has. Submit yourself daily to his leading and draw constantly on his power.

Eph 5:18-19 The effects of alcohol are obvious, but what happens when we are under the influence of the Holy Spirit? In these verses, Paul lists three by-products of the Spirit's influence in our lives: singing, making music, and giving thanks. Paul did not intend to suggest that believers only discuss religious matters, but that whatever we do or say should be permeated with an attitude of joy, thankfulness to God, and encouragement of others. Instead of whining and complaining—which our culture has raised to an art form—we are to focus on the goodness of God and his mercies toward us. How would others characterize your words and attitudes?

Eph 5:20 When you feel down, you may find it difficult to give thanks. Take heart—in all things God works for our good if we love him and are called by him (Rom 8:28). Thank God, not for your problems but for the strength he is building in you through the difficult experiences of your life. You can be sure that God's perfect love will see you through.

Eph 5:21-22 Submitting to another person is an often misunderstood concept. It does not mean becoming a doormat. Christ—at whose name "every knee should bow, in heaven and on earth and under the earth" (Phil 2:10)—submitted his will to the Father, and we honor Christ by following his example. When we submit to God, we become more willing to obey his command to submit to others, that is, to subordinate our rights to theirs. In a marriage relationship, both husband and wife are called to submit. Submission is rarely a problem in homes where both partners have a strong relationship with Christ and where each is concerned for the happiness of the other.

Eph 5:22-24 In Paul's day, women, children, and slaves were to submit to the head of the family: Slaves would submit until they were freed, male children until they grew up, and women and girls their whole lives. Paul emphasized the equality of all believers in Christ (Gal 3:28), but he did not suggest overthrowing Roman society to achieve it. Instead, he counseled all believers to submit to one another by choice—wives to husbands and also husbands to wives; slaves to masters and also masters to slaves; children to parents and also parents to children. This kind of mutual submission preserves order and harmony in the family, while it increases love and respect among family members.

Eph 5:22-24 Although some people have distorted Paul's teaching on submission by giving unlimited authority to husbands, we cannot get around it: Paul told wives to submit to their husbands. The fact that a teaching is not popular is no reason to discard it. One way to disarm the antagonism that the external culture may inject into the marriage relationship is to remember that the wife gets to submit and the husband gets to die. According to the Bible, the man is the spiritual head of the family, and his wife should acknowledge his headship. But this involves loving service (a form of dying). Just as Christ served the disciples, even to the point of washing their feet, so the husband is to serve his wife. A wise and Christ-honoring husband will not take advantage of his role, and a wise and Christ-honoring wife will not try to undermine her husband. Either approach causes disunity and friction in marriage.

Eph 5:22-28 Why did Paul tell wives to submit and husbands to love? Perhaps Christian women, newly freed in Christ, found submission difficult; perhaps Christian men, used to the Roman custom of giving unlimited power to the head of the family, were not used to treating their wives with respect and love. Of course both husbands and wives should submit to each other (Eph 5:21), just as both should love each other.

Eph 5:25ff Some Christians have thought that Paul was negative about marriage because of the counsel he gave in 1 Corinthians 7:32-38. These verses in Ephesians show a high view of marriage. Here marriage is not a practical necessity or a cure for lust, but a picture of the relationship between Christ and his church! Why the apparent difference? Paul's counsel in 1 Corinthians was designed as practical advice in response to a question. In Ephesians Paul is discussing the biblical ideal for marriage and its theological significance. Marriage, for Paul, is a holy union, a living symbol, and a precious relationship that needs tender, self-sacrificing care.

Eph 5:25-30 Paul devotes twice as many words to telling husbands to love their wives as to telling wives to submit to their husbands. How should a man love his wife? (1) He should be willing to sacrifice everything for her, (2) make her well-being of primary importance, and (3) care for her as he cares for his own body.

▸ **EPHESIANS 5:21-33** ***(cont.)***
Christ loved the church. He gave up his life for her [26]to
make her holy and clean, washed by the cleansing of
God's word.* [27]He did this to present her to himself
as a glorious church without a spot or wrinkle or any
other blemish. Instead, she will be holy and without
fault. [28]In the same way, husbands ought to love their
wives as they love their own bodies. For a man who
loves his wife actually shows love for himself. [29]No
one hates his own body but feeds and cares for it, just
as Christ cares for the church. [30]And we are members
of his body.
[31]As the Scriptures say, "A man leaves his father
and mother and is joined to his wife, and the two are
united into one."* [32]This is a great mystery, but it is an
illustration of the way Christ and the church are one.
[33]So again I say, each man must love his wife as he
loves himself, and the wife must respect her husband.

Children and Parents

EPHESIANS 6:1-4
Children, obey your parents because you belong to the
Lord,* for this is the right thing to do. [2]"Honor your
father and mother." This is the first commandment
with a promise: [3]If you honor your father and mother,
"things will go well for you, and you will have a long
life on the earth."*
[4]Fathers, do not provoke your children to anger by
the way you treat them. Rather, bring them up with the
discipline and instruction that comes from the Lord.

Eph 5:26 Greek *washed by water with the word.* **Eph 5:31** Gen 2:24. **Eph 6:1** Or *Children, obey your parents who belong to the Lord;* some manuscripts read simply *Children, obey your parents.* **Eph 6:2-3** Exod 20:12; Deut 5:16.

Eph 5:26-27 Christ's death makes the church holy and clean. He cleanses us from the old ways of sin and sets us apart for his special sacred service (Heb 10:29; 13:12). Christ cleansed the church by the washing of baptism. Through baptism we are prepared for entrance into the church just as ancient Near Eastern brides were prepared for marriage by a ceremonial bath. It is God's Word that cleanses us (John 17:17; Titus 3:5).

Eph 5:31-33 The union of husband and wife merges two persons in such a way that little can affect one without also affecting the other. Oneness in marriage does not mean losing your personality in the personality of the other. Instead, it means caring for your spouse as you care for yourself, learning to anticipate needs, helping the other person become all they can be. The creation story tells of God's plan that husband and wife should be one (Gen 2:24), and Jesus also referred to this plan (Matt 19:4-6).

Eph 6:1-2 There is a difference between obeying and honoring. To obey means to do as one is told; to honor means to respect and love. Children are not commanded to disobey God in obeying their parents. Adult children are not asked to be subservient to domineering parents. Children are to obey while under their parents' care, but the responsibility to honor parents is for life.

Eph 6:1-4 If our faith in Christ is real, it will usually prove itself in our relationships at home with those who know us best. Children and parents have a responsibility to each other. Children should honor their parents even if the parents are demanding and unfair. Parents should care gently for their children, even if the children are disobedient and unpleasant. Ideally, of course, Christian parents and Christian children will relate to each other with thoughtfulness and love. This will happen if both parents and children put the others' interests above their own—that is, if they submit to one another (Eph 5:21).

GOD'S ARMOR FOR US

We are engaged in a spiritual battle—all believers find themselves subject to the devil's attacks because they are no longer on the devil's side. Thus, Paul tells us to use every piece of God's armor to resist the devil's attacks and to stand true to God in the midst of those attacks.

Piece of Armor	*Use*	*Application*
Belt	Truth	The devil fights with lies, and sometimes his lies sound like truth; but only believers have God's truth, which can defeat the devil's lies.
Body Armor	Righteousness	The devil often attacks the heart—the seat of our emotions, self-worth, and trust. God's righteousness is the body armor that protects our hearts and ensures his approval. He approves of us because he loves us and sent his Son to die for us.
Shoes	Peace that comes from the Good News	The devil wants us to think that telling others the Good News is a worthless and hopeless task—the size of the task is too big and the negative responses are too much to handle. But the shoes God gives us are the motivation to continue to proclaim the true peace that is available in God—news everyone needs to hear.
Shield	Faith	What we see are the devil's attacks in the form of insults, setbacks, and temptations. But the shield of faith protects us from the devil's fiery arrows. With God's perspective, we can see beyond our circumstances and know that ultimate victory is ours.
Helmet	Salvation	The devil wants to make us doubt God, Jesus, and our salvation. The helmet protects our minds from doubting God's saving work for us.
Sword	Word of God	The sword is the only weapon of offense in this list of armor. There are times when we need to take the offensive against the devil. When we are tempted, we need to trust in the truth of God's Word.

Eph 6:3 Some societies honor their elders. They respect their wisdom, defer to their authority, and pay attention to their comfort and happiness. This is how Christians should act. Where elders are respected, long life is a blessing, not a burden to them.

Eph 6:4 The purpose of parental discipline is to help children grow, not to exasperate and provoke them to anger or discouragement (see also Col 3:21). Parenting is not easy—it takes lots of patience to raise children in a loving, Christ-honoring manner. But

Slaves and Masters

EPHESIANS 6:5-9

Slaves, obey your earthly masters with deep respect and fear. Serve them sincerely as you would serve Christ. [6]Try to please them all the time, not just when they are watching you. As slaves of Christ, do the will of God with all your heart. [7]Work with enthusiasm, as though you were working for the Lord rather than for people. [8]Remember that the Lord will reward each one of us for the good we do, whether we are slaves or free.

[9]Masters, treat your slaves in the same way. Don't threaten them; remember, you both have the same Master in heaven, and he has no favorites.

The Whole Armor of God

EPHESIANS 6:10-20

A final word: Be strong in the Lord and in his mighty power. [11]Put on all of God's armor so that you will be able to stand firm against all strategies of the devil. [12]For we* are not fighting against flesh-and-blood enemies, but against evil rulers and authorities of the unseen world, against mighty powers in this dark world, and against evil spirits in the heavenly places.

[13]Therefore, put on every piece of God's armor so you will be able to resist the enemy in the time of evil. Then after the battle you will still be standing firm. [14]Stand your ground, putting on the belt of truth and the body armor of God's righteousness. [15]For shoes, put on the peace that comes from the Good News so that you will be fully prepared.* [16]In addition to all of these, hold up the shield of faith to stop the fiery arrows of the devil.* [17]Put on salvation as your helmet, and take the sword of the Spirit, which is the word of God.

[18]Pray in the Spirit at all times and on every occasion. Stay alert and be persistent in your prayers for all believers everywhere.*

[19]And pray for me, too. Ask God to give me the right words so I can boldly explain God's mysterious plan

Eph 6:12 Some manuscripts read *you*. **Eph 6:15** Or *For shoes, put on the readiness to preach the Good News of peace with God.* **Eph 6:16** Greek *the evil one.* **Eph 6:18** Greek *all of God's holy people.*

Therefore, put on every piece of God's armor so you will be able to resist the enemy in the time of evil. Then after the battle you will still be standing firm.
Ephesians 6:13

frustration and anger should not be causes for discipline. Instead, parents should act in love, treating their children as Jesus treats the people he loves. This is vital to children's development and to their understanding of what Christ is like.

Eph 6:5 Slaves played a significant part in this society. There were several million of them in the Roman Empire at this time. Because many slaves and owners had become Christians, the early church had to deal straightforwardly with the question of master/slave relations. Paul's statement neither condemns nor condones slavery. Instead, it tells masters and slaves how to live together in Christian households. In Paul's day, women, children, and slaves had few rights. In the church, however, they had freedoms that society denied them. Paul tells husbands, parents, and masters to be caring.

Eph 6:6-8 Paul's instructions encourage responsibility and integrity on the job. Christian employees should do their jobs as if Jesus Christ were their supervisor. And Christian employers should treat their employees fairly and with respect. Can you be trusted to do your best, even when the boss is not around? Do you work hard and with enthusiasm? Do you treat your employees as people, not machines? Remember that no matter whom you work for, and no matter who works for you, the one you ultimately should want to please is your Father in heaven.

Eph 6:9 Although Christians may be at different levels in earthly society, we are all equal before God. He does not play favorites; no one is more important than anyone else. Paul's letter to Philemon stresses the same point: Philemon, the master, and Onesimus, his slave, were brothers in Christ.

Eph 6:10-17 In the Christian life we battle against rulers and authorities (the powerful evil forces of fallen angels headed by the devil, who is a vicious fighter; see 1 Pet 5:8). To withstand their attacks, we must depend on God's strength and use every piece of his armor. Paul is not only giving this counsel to the church, the body of Christ, but to all individuals within the church. The whole body needs to be armed. As you do battle against the "mighty powers in this dark world," fight in the strength of the church, whose power comes from the Holy Spirit.

Eph 6:12 Our actual enemies are demons over whom the devil has control. They are not mere fantasies—they are very real. We face a powerful army whose goal is to defeat Christ's church. When we believe in Christ, these beings become our enemies, and they try every device to turn us away from him and back to sin. Although we are assured of victory, we must engage in the struggle until Christ returns, because Satan is constantly battling against all who are on the Lord's side. We need supernatural power to defeat Satan, and God has provided this by giving us his Holy Spirit within us and his armor surrounding us. If you feel discouraged, remember Jesus' words to Peter: "Upon this rock I will build my church, and all the powers of hell will not conquer it" (Matt 16:18).

Eph 6:18 How can anyone pray at all times? One way is to make quick, brief prayers your habitual response to every situation you meet throughout the day. Another way is to order your life around God's desires and teachings so that your very life becomes a prayer. You don't have to isolate yourself from other people and from daily work in order to pray constantly. You can make prayer your life and your life a prayer while living in a world that needs God's powerful influence. We also should pray for all believers in Christ; so pray for the Christians you know and for the church around the world.

Eph 6:19-20 Undiscouraged and undefeated, Paul wrote powerful letters of encouragement from prison. Paul did not ask the Ephesians to pray that his chains would be removed but that he would continue to speak fearlessly for Christ in spite of them. God can use us in any circumstance to do his will. Even as we pray for a change in our circumstances, we should

▸ **EPHESIANS 6:10-20 *(cont.)***
that the Good News is for Jews and Gentiles alike.*
20I am in chains now, still preaching this message as
God's ambassador. So pray that I will keep on speaking
boldly for him, as I should.

Final Greetings

EPHESIANS 6:21-24
To bring you up to date, Tychicus will give you a full
report about what I am doing and how I am getting
along. He is a beloved brother and faithful helper in
the Lord's work. 22I have sent him to you for this very
purpose—to let you know how we are doing and to
encourage you.
23Peace be with you, dear brothers and sisters,* and
may God the Father and the Lord Jesus Christ give you
love with faithfulness. 24May God's grace be eternally
upon all who love our Lord Jesus Christ.

Eph 6:19 Greek *explain the mystery of the Good News;* some manuscripts read simply *explain the mystery.* **Eph 6:23** Greek *brothers.*

Q. Paul's Letter to the Church in Philippi

Although Paul was writing from prison, joy is a dominant theme in this letter. The secret of this joy is grounded in his relationship with Christ. People today desperately want to be happy but are tossed and turned by daily successes, failures, and inconveniences. Chistians are to be joyful in every circumstance, even when things are going badly, even when we feel like complaining, even when no one else is joyful. Christ still reigns, and we still know him, so we can rejoice at all times.

Greetings from Paul

PHILIPPIANS 1:1-2
This letter is from Paul and Timothy, slaves of Christ
Jesus.
I am writing to all of God's holy people in Philippi
who belong to Christ Jesus, including the elders* and
deacons.
2May God our Father and the Lord Jesus Christ give
you grace and peace.

Paul's Thanksgiving and Prayer

PHILIPPIANS 1:3-11
Every time I think of you, I give thanks to my God.
4Whenever I pray, I make my requests for all of you

Phil 1:1 Or *overseers;* or *bishops.*

also pray that God will accomplish his plan through us right where we are. Knowing God's eternal purpose for us will help us through the difficult times.

Eph 6:21 Tychicus is also mentioned in Acts 20:4; Colossians 4:7; 2 Timothy 4:12; Titus 3:12.

Eph 6:24 This letter was meant for circulation among other churches besides Ephesus. In this letter, Paul highlights the supremacy of Christ, gives information on both the nature of the church and on how church members should live, and stresses the unity of all believers—male, female, parent, child, master, slave—regardless of sex, nationality, or social rank. The home and the church are difficult places to live the Christian life, because our real self comes through to those who know us well. Close relationships between imperfect people can lead to trouble—or to increased faith and deepened dependence on God. We can build unity in our churches through willing submission to Christ's leadership and humble service to one another.

Phil 1:1 This is a personal letter to the Philippians, not intended for general circulation to all the churches, as was the letter to the Ephesians. Paul wanted to thank the believers for helping him when he had a need. He also wanted to tell them why he could be full of joy despite his imprisonment and upcoming trial. In this uplifting letter, Paul counseled the Philippians about humility and unity and warned them about potential problems.

Phil 1:1 On Paul's first missionary journey, he visited towns close to his headquarters in Antioch of Syria. On his second and third journeys, he traveled farther away. Because of the great distances between the congregations that Paul had founded, he could no longer personally oversee them all. Thus, he was compelled to write letters to teach and encourage the believers. Fortunately, Paul had several co-workers, including Timothy, Mark, and Epaphras, who personally delivered these letters and often remained with the congregations for a while to teach and encourage them.

Phil 1:1 For more information on Paul, see his Profile on p. 1571. Timothy's Profile is on p. 1727.

Phil 1:1 The Roman colony of Philippi was located in northern Greece (called Macedonia in Paul's day). Philip II of Macedon (the father of Alexander the Great) took the town from ancient Thrace in about 357 B.C., enlarged and strengthened it, and gave it his name. This thriving commercial center sat at the crossroads between Europe and Asia. In about A.D. 50, Paul, Silas, Timothy, and Luke crossed the Aegean Sea from Asia Minor and landed at Philippi (Acts 16:11-40). The church in Philippi consisted mostly of Gentile (non-Jewish) believers. Because they were not familiar with the Old Testament, Paul did not specifically quote any Old Testament passages in this letter.

Phil 1:1 Elders (bishops or pastors) and deacons led the early Christian churches. The qualifications and duties of the elders are explained in detail in 1 Timothy 3:1-7; Titus 1:5-9. The qualifications and duties of deacons are spelled out in 1 Timothy 3:8-13.

Phil 1:2 We get upset at children who fail to appreciate small gifts, yet we undervalue God's immeasurable gifts of grace and peace. Instead, we seek the possessions and shallow experiences the world offers. Compared to the big and bright "packages" of our culture, grace and peace appear insignificant. But when we unwrap them, we discover God's wonderful personal dealings with us. Inside the tiny package marked "grace and peace," we find an inexhaustible treasure of God's daily presence in our lives. Using these two words in his greetings to all the churches to whom he wrote, Paul wasn't offering something new. He was reminding his readers of what they already possessed in Christ. Thank God for his grace, and live in his peace.

Phil 1:4 This is the first of many times Paul used the word *joy* in this letter. The Philippians were remembered with joy and thanksgiving whenever Paul prayed. By helping Paul, they were helping Christ's cause. The Philippians were willing to be used by God for whatever he wanted them to do. When others think about you, what comes to their minds? Are you remembered with joy by them? Do your acts of kindness lift others up?

Phil 1:4-5 The Philippians first heard the Good News about 10 years earlier when Paul and his companions visited Philippi

with joy, 5for you have been my partners in spreading
the Good News about Christ from the time you first
heard it until now. 6And I am certain that God, who
began the good work within you, will continue his
work until it is finally finished on the day when Christ
Jesus returns.
7So it is right that I should feel as I do about all
of you, for you have a special place in my heart. You
share with me the special favor of God, both in my
imprisonment and in defending and confirming the
truth of the Good News. 8God knows how much I love
you and long for you with the tender compassion of
Christ Jesus.

9I pray that your love will overflow more and more,
and that you will keep on growing in knowledge and
understanding. 10For I want you to understand what
really matters, so that you may live pure and blameless
lives until the day of Christ's return. 11May you always
be filled with the fruit of your salvation—the righteous
character produced in your life by Jesus Christ*—for
this will bring much glory and praise to God.

Paul's Joy That Christ Is Preached

PHILIPPIANS 1:12-19

And I want you to know, my dear brothers and sisters,* that everything that has happened to me here

Phil 1:11 Greek *with the fruit of righteousness through Jesus Christ.* **Phil 1:12** Greek *brothers.*

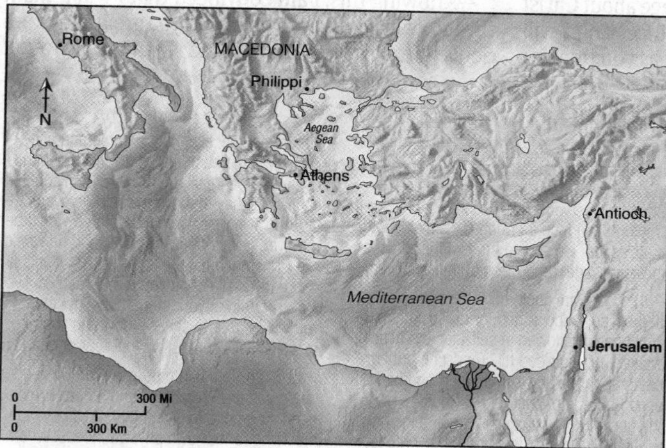

***LOCATION OF PHILIPPI** Philippi sat on the Egnatian Way, the main transportation route in Macedonia, an extension of the Appian Way, which joined the eastern empire with Italy.*

(during Paul's second missionary journey) and founded the church there.

Phil 1:5 When Paul said that the Philippians were partners in spreading the Good News, he was remembering how they contributed through their practical help when Paul was in Philippi and through their financial support when he was in prison. As we help our ministers, missionaries, and evangelists through prayer, hospitality, and financial gifts, we become partners with them in spreading the gospel message.

Phil 1:6 The God who began a good work within us continues it throughout our lifetime and will finish it when we meet him face to face. God's work *for* us began when Christ died on the cross in our place. His work *within* us began when we first believed. Now the Holy Spirit lives *in* us, enabling us to be more like Christ every day. Paul is describing the process of Christian growth and maturity that began when we accepted Jesus and continues until Christ returns.

Phil 1:6 Do you sometimes feel as though you aren't making progress in your spiritual life? When God starts a project, he completes it! As with the Philippians, God will help you grow in grace until he has completed his work in your life. When you are discouraged, remember that God won't give up on you. He promises to finish the work he has begun. When you feel incomplete, unfinished, or distressed by your shortcomings, remember God's promise and provision. Don't let your present condition rob you of the joy of knowing Christ or keep you from growing closer to him.

Phil 1:7 When he mentions his imprisonment, Paul was probably referring to his imprisonment in Philippi (see Acts16:22-36). In Philippians 1:13-14, Paul speaks of his Roman imprisonment. Wherever Paul was, even in prison, he faithfully preached the Good News. Remember Paul's inspiring example when hindrances, small or large, slow down your work for God.

Phil 1:7-8 Have you ever longed to see a friend with whom you share fond memories? Paul had such a longing to see the Christians at Philippi. His love and affection for them was based not merely on past experiences but also on the unity that comes when believers draw upon Christ's love. All Christians are part of God's family and thus share equally in the transforming power of his love. Do you feel a deep love for fellow Christians, friends and strangers alike? Let Christ's love motivate you to love other Christians and to express that love in your actions toward them.

Phil 1:9 Often the best way to influence someone is to pray for them. Paul's prayer for the Philippians was that they would be unified in love. Their love was to result in greater knowledge of Christ and deeper understanding (moral discernment). Their love was not based on feelings but on what Christ had done for them. As you grow in Christ's love, your heart and mind must grow together. Are your love and insight growing?

Phil 1:10 Paul prayed that the Philippian believers would have the ability to differentiate between right and wrong, good and bad, vital and trivial. We ought to pray for moral discernment so we can be pleasing to the Lord. (See also Heb 5:14.)

Phil 1:10 "The day of Christ's return" refers to the time when God will judge the world through Jesus Christ. We should live each day as though he might return at any moment.

Phil 1:11 The "fruit of your salvation" includes all of the character traits flowing from a right relationship with God. There is no other way for us to gain this fruit of righteousness than through Christ. (See Gal 5:22-23 for the fruit that the Spirit produces.)

Phil 1:12 In the past, missionaries—those who spread the Good News—boarded ships to go to foreign lands and did not expect to see their homeland again. Their good-byes were final, in terms of earth time. There was no turning back. While air travel, the Internet, and other technologies have greatly lessened such separation, pioneering with the Good News still requires a high sacrifice. Paul's passion was for others to discover eternal life through Jesus Christ, no matter what the cost would be. Pressing through frontiers of spiritual darkness still requires pioneers today—people who will reach neglected people or new people groups. Pray for missionaries, support them, join them.

Phil 1:12-14 Being imprisoned would cause many people to become bitter or to give up, but Paul saw it as one more opportunity to

▸ **PHILIPPIANS 1:12-19** ***(cont.)***

has helped to spread the Good News. [13]For everyone here, including the whole palace guard,* knows that I am in chains because of Christ. [14]And because of my imprisonment, most of the believers* here have gained confidence and boldly speak God's message* without fear.

[15]It's true that some are preaching out of jealousy and rivalry. But others preach about Christ with pure motives. [16]They preach because they love me, for they know I have been appointed to defend the Good News. [17]Those others do not have pure motives as they preach about Christ. They preach with selfish ambition, not sincerely, intending to make my chains more painful to me. [18]But that doesn't matter. Whether their motives are false or genuine, the message about Christ is being preached either way, so I rejoice. And I will continue to rejoice. [19]For I know that as you pray for me and the Spirit of Jesus Christ helps me, this will lead to my deliverance.

Paul's Life for Christ

PHILIPPIANS 1:20-26

For I fully expect and hope that I will never be ashamed, but that I will continue to be bold for Christ, as I have been in the past. And I trust that my life will bring honor to Christ, whether I live or die. [21]For to me, living means living for Christ, and dying is even better. [22]But if I live, I can do more fruitful work for Christ. So I really don't know which is better. [23]I'm torn between two desires: I long to go and be with Christ, which would be far better for me. [24]But for your sakes, it is better that I continue to live.

[25]Knowing this, I am convinced that I will remain alive so I can continue to help all of you grow and experience the joy of your faith. [26]And when I come to you

Phil 1:13 Greek *including all the Praetorium.* **Phil 1:14a** Greek *brothers in the Lord.* **Phil 1:14b** Some manuscripts read *speak the message.*

---

spread the Good News of Christ. Paul realized that his current circumstances weren't as important as what he did with them. Turning a bad situation into a good one, he reached out to the Roman soldiers who made up the palace guard and encouraged those Christians who were afraid of persecution. We may not be in prison, but we still have plenty of opportunities to be discouraged—times of indecision, financial burdens, family conflict, church conflict, or the loss of our jobs. How we act in such situations will reflect what we believe. Like Paul, look for ways to demonstrate your faith even in bad situations. Whether or not the situation improves, your faith will grow stronger.

Phil 1:13 How did Paul end up in chains in a Roman prison? While he was visiting Jerusalem, some Jews had him arrested for preaching the Good News, but he appealed to Caesar to hear his case (Acts 21:15–25:12). He was then escorted by soldiers to Rome, where he was placed under house arrest while awaiting trial—not a trial for breaking civil law, but for proclaiming the Good News of Christ. At that time, the Roman authorities did not consider this to be a serious charge. A few years later, Rome would take a different view of Christianity and make every effort to stamp it out of existence. Paul's house arrest allowed him some degree of freedom. He could have visitors, continue to preach, and write letters such as this one. Acts 28:11-31 gives a brief record of Paul's time in Rome. The "palace guard" refers to the elite troops housed in the emperor's palace.

Phil 1:14 When we speak fearlessly for Christ or live faithfully for him during difficult situations, we encourage others to do the same. Be an encouragement by the way that you live.

Phil 1:15-18 Paul had an amazingly selfless attitude. He knew that some were preaching to build their own reputations, taking advantage of his imprisonment to try to make a name for themselves. Regardless of the motives of these preachers, Paul rejoiced that the Good News was being preached. Some Christians serve for the wrong reasons. Paul wouldn't condone, nor does God excuse, their motives, but we should be glad if God uses their message, regardless of their motives.

Phil 1:16 Paul could have become depressed, discouraged, or disillusioned. He could have wallowed in self-pity and despair. Instead, he regarded his imprisonment as being appointed by God. In fact, God had used Paul's imprisonment in Rome to bring the gospel to the center of the empire, as well as to give Paul lots of time to write letters that would one day end up in the New Testament and help subsequent generations of believers. Do you have difficulty accepting your station in life? Do you resent where God has placed you? Although education and focused effort may enable us to take a new role or get a new job, often God puts us in a place to serve. Whether it is an actual prison or a place that feels like one, God wants you to serve him faithfully and joyfully.

Phil 1:19-21 This was not Paul's final imprisonment in Rome. But he didn't know that. Awaiting trial, he knew he could either be released or executed. However, he trusted Christ to work it out for his deliverance. Paul's prayer was that when he stood trial, he would speak courageously for Christ and not be timid or ashamed. Whether he lived or died, he wanted to exalt Christ. As it turned out, he was released from this imprisonment but arrested again a few years later. Only faith in Christ could sustain Paul in such adversity.

Phil 1:20-21 To those who don't believe in God, life on earth is all there is, and so it is natural for them to strive for this world's values: money, popularity, power, pleasure, and prestige. For Paul, to live meant to develop eternal values and to tell others about Christ, who alone could help them see life from an eternal perspective. Paul's whole purpose in life was to speak out boldly for Christ and to become more like him. Thus, Paul could confidently say that dying would be even better than living, because in death he would be removed from worldly troubles, and he would see Christ face to face (1 Jn 3:2-3). If you're not ready to die, then you're not ready to live. Make certain of your eternal destiny; then you will be free to serve—devoting your life to what really counts, without fear of death.

Phil 1:24 Paul had a purpose for living when he served the Philippians and others. We also need a purpose for living that goes beyond providing for our own physical needs. Whom can you serve or help? What is your purpose for living?

Phil 1:27 Paul encouraged the believers to be unified as they stood with "one purpose, fighting together for the faith, which is the Good News." How sad that much time and effort are lost in some churches by fighting one another instead of uniting against the real opposition! It takes a courageous church to resist infighting and to maintain the common purpose of serving Christ.

Phil 1:29 Paul considered it a privilege to suffer for Christ. We do not by nature consider suffering a privilege. Yet if we faithfully represent Christ when we suffer, our message and example affect us and others for good (see Acts 5:41). Suffering has these additional benefits: (1) It takes our eyes off of earthly comforts; (2) it weeds out superficial believers; (3) it strengthens the faith of those who endure; (4) it serves as an example to others who may follow us. When we suffer for our faith, it doesn't mean that we have done something wrong. In fact, the opposite is often true—it verifies that we have been faithful. Use suffering to build your character. Don't resent it or let it tear you down.

Phil 1:30 Throughout his life, Paul suffered for spreading the Good News. Like the Philip-

again, you will have even more reason to take pride in Christ Jesus because of what he is doing through me.

Live as Citizens of Heaven

PHILIPPIANS 1:27-30

Above all, you must live as citizens of heaven, conducting yourselves in a manner worthy of the Good News about Christ. Then, whether I come and see you again or only hear about you, I will know that you are standing together with one spirit and one purpose, fighting together for the faith, which is the Good News. 28Don't be intimidated in any way by your enemies. This will be a sign to them that they are going to be destroyed, but that you are going to be saved, even by God himself. 29For you have been given not only the privilege of trusting in Christ but also the privilege of suffering for him. 30We are in this struggle together. You have seen my struggle in the past, and you know that I am still in the midst of it.

Have the Attitude of Christ

PHILIPPIANS 2:1-11

Is there any encouragement from belonging to Christ? Any comfort from his love? Any fellowship together in the Spirit? Are your hearts tender and compassionate? 2Then make me truly happy by agreeing wholeheartedly with each other, loving one another, and working together with one mind and purpose.

3Don't be selfish; don't try to impress others. Be humble, thinking of others as better than yourselves. 4Don't look out only for your own interests, but take an interest in others, too.

5You must have the same attitude that Christ Jesus had.

---

pians, we are in conflict with anyone who would discredit the saving message of Christ. All true believers are in this fight together, uniting against the same enemy for a common cause.

Paul never urges Christians to seek suffering, as if there were virtue in pain. But we should not forget those who suffer. If your cupboard is full, share your food. If you control the wheels of power, work for justice and mercy. If you are wealthy, give generously to the poor. When life is comfortable, willingly take a share of someone else's pain, and so tell the world that the gospel is true.

Phil 2:1-5 Many people—even Christians—live only to make a good impression on others or to please themselves. But selfishness brings discord. Paul therefore stressed spiritual unity, asking the Philippians to love one another and to be one in spirit and purpose. When we work together, caring for the problems of others as if they were our problems, we demonstrate Christ's example of putting others first, and we experience unity. Don't be so concerned about making a good impression or meeting your own needs that you strain relationships in God's family.

Phil 2:3 Selfishness can ruin a church, but genuine humility can build it. Being humble involves having a true perspective about ourselves (see Rom 12:3). It does not mean that we should put ourselves down. Before God, we are sinners saved only by God's grace, but we have great worth in God's Kingdom. We are to lay aside selfishness and treat others with respect and common courtesy. Considering others' interests as more important than our own links us with Christ, who was a true example of humility.

Phil 2:4 Philippi was a cosmopolitan city. The composition of the church reflected great diversity, with people from a variety of backgrounds and walks of life. Acts 16 gives us some indication of this: The church included Lydia, a Jewish convert from Asia and a wealthy businesswoman (Acts 16:14); the slave girl (Acts 16:16-17), probably a native Greek; and the jailer serving this colony of the empire, probably a Roman (Acts 16:25-36). With so many different backgrounds among the members, unity must have been difficult to maintain. Although there is no evidence of division in the church, its unity had to be safeguarded (Phil 3:2; 4:2). Paul encourages us to guard against any selfishness, prejudice, or jealousy that might lead to dissension. Showing genuine interest in others is a positive step forward in maintaining unity among believers.

Phil 2:5 Jesus Christ was humble, willing to give up his rights in order to obey God and serve people. Like Christ, we should have a servant's attitude, serving out of love for God and for others, not out of guilt or fear. Remember, you can choose your attitude. You can approach life expecting to be served, or you can look for opportunities to serve others. (See Mark 10:45 for more on Christ's attitude of servanthood.)

Phil 2:5-7 The Incarnation was the act of the preexistent Son of God voluntarily assuming a human body and human nature. Without ceasing to be God, he became a human being, the man called Jesus. He did not give up his deity to become human, but in submission to the Father's will, Christ limited his power and knowledge. Jesus of Nazareth was subject to place, time, and many other human limitations. What made his humanity unique was his freedom from sin. In his full humanity, Jesus showed us everything about God's character that can be conveyed in human terms. (The Incarnation is explained further in these passages: John 1:1-14; Rom 1:2-5; 2 Cor 8:9; 1 Tim 3:16; Heb 2:14; 1 Jn 1:1-3.)

Phil 2:5-11 These verses are probably from a hymn sung by the early Christian church. The passage holds many parallels to the prophecy of the suffering servant in Isaiah 53. As a hymn, it was not meant to be a complete statement about the nature and work of Christ. Several key characteristics of Jesus Christ, however, are praised in this passage: (1) Christ has always existed with God; (2) Christ is equal to God because he is God (John 1:1ff; Col 1:15-19); (3) though Christ is God, he became a man in order to fulfill God's plan of salvation for all people; (4) Christ did not just have the appearance of being a man—he actually became human to identify with our sins; (5) Christ voluntarily laid aside his divine rights and privileges out of love for his Father; (6) Christ died on the cross for our sins so we wouldn't have to face eternal death; (7) God glorified Christ because of his obedience; (8) God raised Christ to his original position at the Father's right hand, where he will reign forever as our Lord and Judge. How can we do anything less than praise Christ as our Lord and dedicate ourselves to his service!

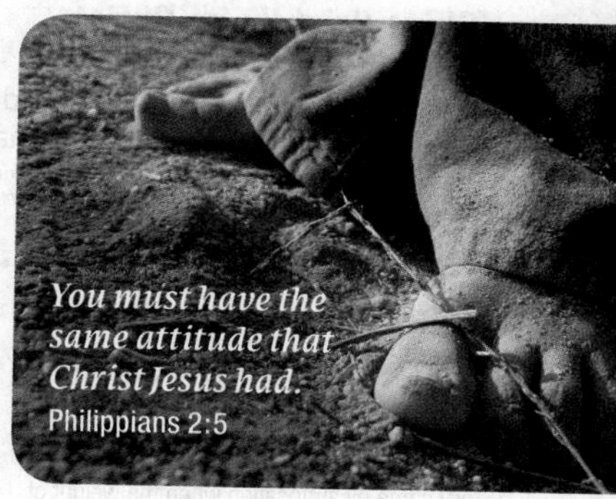

You must have the same attitude that Christ Jesus had.
Philippians 2:5

Phil 2:5-11 Often people excuse selfishness, pride, or evil by claiming their rights. They think, "I can cheat on this test; after all, I deserve to pass this class," or "I can spend all this money on myself—I worked hard for it," or "I can get an abortion; I have a right to control my own body." But as believers, we should have a different attitude, one that enables us to lay aside our rights in order to serve others. If we say we follow Christ, we must also say we want to live as he lived. We should develop his attitude of humility as we serve, even when we are not likely to get recognition for our efforts. Are you selfishly clinging to your rights, or are you willing to serve?

▶ **PHILIPPIANS 2:1-11** ***(cont.)***

6 Though he was God,*
he did not think of equality with God
as something to cling to.
7 Instead, he gave up his divine privileges*;
he took the humble position of a slave*
and was born as a human being.
When he appeared in human form,*
8 he humbled himself in obedience to God
and died a criminal's death on a cross.

9 Therefore, God elevated him to the place
of highest honor
and gave him the name above all other names,
10 that at the name of Jesus every knee should bow,
in heaven and on earth and under the earth,
11 and every tongue confess that Jesus Christ is Lord,
to the glory of God the Father.

Shine Brightly for Christ

PHILIPPIANS 2:12-18

Dear friends, you always followed my instructions
when I was with you. And now that I am away, it is
even more important. Work hard to show the results
of your salvation, obeying God with deep reverence
and fear. 13 For God is working in you, giving you the
desire and the power to do what pleases him.
14 Do everything without complaining and arguing,
15 so that no one can criticize you. Live clean, innocent
lives as children of God, shining like bright lights in
a world full of crooked and perverse people. 16 Hold
firmly to the word of life; then, on the day of Christ's
return, I will be proud that I did not run the race in
vain and that my work was not useless. 17 But I will
rejoice even if I lose my life, pouring it out like a liquid
offering to God,* just like your faithful service is an
offering to God. And I want all of you to share that
joy. 18 Yes, you should rejoice, and I will share your joy.

Paul Commends Timothy

PHILIPPIANS 2:19-24

If the Lord Jesus is willing, I hope to send Timothy to
you soon for a visit. Then he can cheer me up by telling
me how you are getting along. 20 I have no one else like
Timothy, who genuinely cares about your welfare. 21 All
the others care only for themselves and not for what

Phil 2:6 Or *Being in the form of God.* **Phil 2:7a** Greek *he emptied himself.* **Phil 2:7b** Or *the form of a slave.* **Phil 2:7c** Some English translations put this phrase in verse 8. **Phil 2:17** Greek *I will rejoice even if I am to be poured out as a liquid offering.*

Phil 2:8 Death on a cross (crucifixion) was the form of capital punishment that Romans used for notorious criminals. It was excruciatingly painful and humiliating. Prisoners were nailed or tied to a cross and left to die. Death might not come for several days, and it usually came by suffocation when the weight of the weakened body made breathing more and more difficult. Jesus died as one who was cursed (Gal 3:13). How amazing that the perfect man should die this most shameful death so that we would not have to face eternal punishment!

Phil 2:9-11 At the Last Judgment, even those who are condemned will recognize Jesus' authority and right to rule. People can choose now to commit their lives to Jesus as Lord or be forced to acknowledge him as Lord when he returns. Christ may return at any moment. Are you prepared to meet him?

Phil 2:12 "Work hard to show the results of your salvation," in light of the preceding exhortation to unity, may mean that the entire church was to work together to rid themselves of divisions and discord. The Philippian Christians needed to be especially careful to obey Christ, now that Paul wasn't there to continually remind them about what was right. We, too, must be careful about what we believe and how we live, especially when we are on our own. In the absence of cherished Christian leaders, we must focus our attention and devotion even more on Christ so that we won't be sidetracked.

Phil 2:13 What do we do when we don't feel like obeying? God has not left us alone in our struggles to do his will. He wants to come alongside us and be within us to help. God gives us the *desire* and the *power* to do what pleases him. The secret to a changed life is to submit to God's control and let him work. The next time you don't want to obey, ask God to help you desire to do his will.

Phil 2:13 To be like Christ, we must train ourselves to think like Christ. To change our desires to be more like Christ's, we need the power of the indwelling Spirit (Phil 1:19), the influence of faithful Christians, obedience to God's Word (not just exposure to it), and sacrificial service. Often it is in *doing* God's will that we gain the *desire* to do it (see Phil 4:8-9). Do what he wants and trust him to change your desires.

Phil 2:14-16 Why are complaining and arguing so harmful? If all that people know about a church is that its members constantly argue, complain, and gossip, they get a false impression of Christ and the Good News. Belief in Christ should unite those who trust him. If your church is always complaining and arguing, it lacks the unifying power of Jesus Christ. Stop arguing with other Christians or complaining about people and conditions within the church; instead, let the world see Christ.

Phil 2:14-16 Our lives should be characterized by moral purity, patience, and peacefulness, so that we will shine brightly in a dark and depraved world. A transformed life is an effective witness to the power of God's Word. Are you shining brightly, or are you clouded by complaining and arguing? Don't let dissensions snuff out your light. Shine out for God. Your role is to shine until Jesus returns and bathes the world in his radiant glory.

Phil 2:17 The drink offering was an important part of the sacrificial system of the Jews (for an explanation, see Num 28:7). Because this church had little Jewish background, the liquid offering may refer to the wine poured out to pagan deities prior to important public events. Paul regarded his life as a sacrifice.

Phil 2:17 Even if he had to die, Paul was content, knowing that he had helped the Philippians live for Christ. When you're totally committed to serving Christ, sacrificing to build the faith of others brings a joyous reward.

Phil 2:19, 22 When Paul wrote these words, most vocational training was done by fathers, and sons stayed loyal to the family business. Timothy displayed that same loyalty in his spiritual apprenticeship with Paul. Timothy was with Paul in Rome when Paul wrote this letter. He traveled with Paul on his second missionary journey when the church at Philippi was begun. (For more information on Timothy, see his Profile on p. 1727.)

Just as a skilled workman trains an apprentice, Paul was preparing Timothy to carry on the ministry in his absence. Paul encouraged younger Christians to learn, to observe, to help, and then to lead. Paul expected older Christians to teach, to model, to mentor, and then to turn over leadership. The benefits of such a process are new enthusiasm and vision, new methods and energy. Are you a teacher? Whom are you apprenticing for God's work? Are you a learner? How are you showing your eagerness to fulfill the call God has on your life?

Phil 2:21 Paul observed that most believers are too preoccupied with their own needs to

matters to Jesus Christ. 22But you know how Timothy
has proved himself. Like a son with his father, he has
served with me in preaching the Good News. 23I hope
to send him to you just as soon as I find out what is
going to happen to me here. 24And I have confidence
from the Lord that I myself will come to see you soon.

Paul Commends Epaphroditus

PHILIPPIANS 2:25-30

Meanwhile, I thought I should send Epaphroditus
back to you. He is a true brother, co-worker, and fellow soldier. And he was your messenger to help me
in my need. 26I am sending him because he has been
longing to see you, and he was very distressed that you
heard he was ill. 27And he certainly was ill; in fact, he
almost died. But God had mercy on him—and also on
me, so that I would not have one sorrow after another.
28So I am all the more anxious to send him back
to you, for I know you will be glad to see him, and
then I will not be so worried about you. 29Welcome
him with Christian love* and with great joy, and give
him the honor that people like him deserve. 30For he
risked his life for the work of Christ, and he was at the
point of death while doing for me what you couldn't
do from far away.

The Priceless Value of Knowing Christ

PHILIPPIANS 3:1-11

Whatever happens, my dear brothers and sisters,*
rejoice in the Lord. I never get tired of telling you these
things, and I do it to safeguard your faith.
2Watch out for those dogs, those people who do
evil, those mutilators who say you must be circumcised to be saved. 3For we who worship by the Spirit

Phil 2:29 Greek *in the Lord.* **Phil 3:1** Greek *brothers;* also in 3:13, 17.

Ruins of Philippi

In the Roman era, Philippi became a chief city of one of the four districts into which Macedonia was divided. But because it was about 10 miles inland from the port of Neapolis, its growth was limited. Paul visited the city on his second missionary tour. The account in Acts gives detailed attention to Paul's visit. The narrative frequently refers to the city's Roman heritage: Not only does Paul successfully employ his Roman citizenship in his defense (Acts 16:37), but the city magistrates bear the dignified Latin title *praetor* (Acts 16:20-22), usually translated in English as "magistrate." The church in Philippi began with believing Jewish women who met outside the city because there was no synagogue. Later, they convened in the home of an important woman convert named Lydia (Acts 16:14-15, 40). The church in Philippi received an epistle from Paul when he was under house arrest in Rome. Read this epistle; it has so much to teach us about Christ and our Christian life.

spend time working for Christ. Don't let your schedule and concerns crowd out your love and Christian service to others.

Phil 2:23 Paul was in prison (either awaiting his trial or its verdict) for preaching about Christ. He was telling the Philippians that when he learned of the court's decision, he would send Timothy to them with the news. Paul wanted them to know that he was ready to accept whatever came (Phil 1:21-26).

Phil 2:25 Epaphroditus delivered money from the Philippians to Paul; then he returned with this thank-you letter to Philippi. Epaphroditus may have been an elder in Philippi (Phil 2:25-30; 4:18) who, while staying with Paul, had become ill (Phil 2:27, 30). After Epaphroditus recovered, he returned home. He is mentioned only in Philippians.

Phil 2:29-30 The world honors those who are intelligent, beautiful, rich, and powerful. What kind of people should the church honor? Paul indicates that we should honor those who give their lives, sometimes literally, for the sake of Christ, going where we cannot go and doing what we cannot do ourselves.

Phil 3:1 As a safeguard, Paul reviewed the basics with these believers. The Bible is our safeguard both morally and theologically. When we read it individually and publicly in church, it alerts us to corrections we need to make in our thoughts, attitudes, and actions.

Phil 3:2-3 These "dogs" and "mutilators" were very likely Judaizers—Jewish Christians who wrongly believed that it was essential for Gentiles to follow all the Old Testament Jewish laws, especially submission to the rite of circumcision, in order to receive salvation. Many Judaizers were motivated by spiritual pride. Because they had invested so much time and effort in keeping their laws, they couldn't accept the fact that all their efforts couldn't bring them a step closer to salvation.

Paul criticized the Judaizers because they looked at Christianity backward—thinking that what they did (circumcision—cutting or mutilating the flesh) made them believers rather than the free gift of grace given by Christ. What believers do is a *result* of faith, not a *prerequisite* to faith. This had been confirmed by the early church leaders at the Jerusalem council 11 years earlier (Acts 15). Who are the Judaizers of our day? They are those who say that people must add something else to simple faith. No person should add anything to Christ's offer of salvation by grace through faith.

Phil 3:2-3 It is easy to place more emphasis on human effort than on internal faith, but God values the attitude of our heart above all else. Don't judge people's spirituality by their fulfillment of duties or by their level of human activity. And don't think that you will satisfy God by feverishly doing his work. God notices all you do for him and will reward you for it, but only if it comes as a loving response to his free gift of salvation.

▸ **PHILIPPIANS 3:1-11** *(cont.)*

of God* are the ones who are truly circumcised. We
rely on what Christ Jesus has done for us. We put no
confidence in human effort, [4]though I could have confidence in my own effort if anyone could. Indeed, if
others have reason for confidence in their own efforts,
I have even more!

[5]I was circumcised when I was eight days old. I am
a pure-blooded citizen of Israel and a member of the
tribe of Benjamin—a real Hebrew if there ever was
one! I was a member of the Pharisees, who demand
the strictest obedience to the Jewish law. [6]I was so
zealous that I harshly persecuted the church. And
as for righteousness, I obeyed the law without fault.

[7]I once thought these things were valuable, but now
I consider them worthless because of what Christ has
done. [8]Yes, everything else is worthless when compared with the infinite value of knowing Christ Jesus
my Lord. For his sake I have discarded everything else,
counting it all as garbage, so that I could gain Christ
[9]and become one with him. I no longer count on my
own righteousness through obeying the law; rather, I
become righteous through faith in Christ.* For God's
way of making us right with himself depends on faith.
[10]I want to know Christ and experience the mighty
power that raised him from the dead. I want to suffer
with him, sharing in his death, [11]so that one way or another I will experience the resurrection from the dead!

Phil 3:3 Some manuscripts read *worship God in spirit;* one early manuscript reads *worship in spirit.* **Phil 3:9** Or *through the faithfulness of Christ.*

Phil 3:4-6 At first glance, it looks like Paul is boasting about his achievements. But he is actually doing the opposite, showing that human achievements, no matter how impressive, cannot earn a person salvation and eternal life with God. Paul had impressive credentials: upbringing, nationality, family background, inheritance, orthodoxy, activity, and morality (see 2 Cor 11; Gal 1:13-24 for more of his credentials). However, his conversion to faith in Christ (Acts 9) wasn't based on what he had done but on God's grace. Paul did not depend on his deeds to please God, because even the most impressive credentials fall short of God's holy standards. Are you depending on Christian parents, church affiliation, or just being good to make you right with God? Credentials, accomplishments, or reputation cannot earn salvation. Salvation comes only through faith in Christ.

Phil 3:5 Paul belonged to the tribe of Benjamin, a heritage greatly esteemed among the Jews. From this tribe had come Israel's first king, Saul (1 Sam 10:20-24). Paul was also a Pharisee, a member of a very devout Jewish sect that scrupulously kept its own numerous rules in addition to the laws of Moses. Paul explains for these mostly-Gentile believers that his Jewish credentials were impeccable.

Phil 3:6 Why had Paul, a devout Jewish leader, persecuted the church? Agreeing with the leaders of the religious establishment, Paul had thought that Christianity was heretical and blasphemous. Because Jesus did not meet his expectations of what the Messiah would be like, Paul had assumed that Jesus' claims were false—and therefore wicked. In addition, he had seen Christianity as a political menace because it threatened to disrupt the fragile harmony between the Jews and the Roman government.

Phil 3:7 When Paul spoke of "these things," he was referring to his credentials, credits, and successes. After showing that he could beat the Judaizers at their own game (being proud of who they were and what they had done), Paul showed that it was the wrong game. Be careful of considering past achievements so important that they get in the way of your relationship with Christ.

THREE STAGES OF PERFECTION

All phases of perfection are grounded in faith in Christ and what he has done, not what we can do for him. We cannot perfect ourselves; only God can work in and through us to "continue his work until it is finally finished on the day when Christ Jesus returns" (Phil 1:6).

1. Perfect Relationship	We are perfect because of our eternal union with the infinitely perfect Christ. When we become his children, we are declared "not guilty" and thus righteous because of what Christ, God's beloved Son, has done for us. This perfection is absolute and unchangeable, and it is this perfect relationship that guarantees that we will one day be "completely perfect" (stage 3). (See Col 2:8-10; Heb 10:8-14.)
2. Perfect Progress	We can grow and mature spiritually as we continue to trust Christ, learn more about him, draw closer to him, and obey him. Our progress is changeable (in contrast to our relationship, stage 1) because it depends on our daily walk—at times in life we mature more than at other times. But we are growing toward perfection if we "press on" (Phil 3:12). These good deeds do not perfect us; rather, as God perfects us, we do good deeds for him. (See Phil 3:1-16.)
3. Completely Perfect	When Christ returns to take us into his eternal Kingdom, we will be glorified and made completely perfect. (See Phil 3:20-21.)

Phil 3:8 After Paul considered everything he had accomplished in his life, he decided to write it all off as "worthless" when compared with the greatness of knowing Christ. We should value our relationship with Christ as more important than anything else. To know Christ should be our ultimate goal. Yet how do we know him better? (1) Study the life of Christ in the Gospels. See how Christ lived and responded to people (Matt 11:29). (2) Study all the New Testament references to Christ (Col 1:15–2:15). (3) As you worship and pray, let the Holy Spirit remind you of Christ's words (John 14:26). (4) Take up Christ's mission to preach the gospel, and learn from his sufferings (Matt 28:19; Phil 3:10).

To do these things may mean that you must make major changes in your thinking and in your lifestyle. Are you willing to change your values in order to know Christ better? Will you fix or rearrange your crowded schedule in order to set aside a few minutes each day for prayer and Bible study? Will you change some of your plans, goals, and desires in order to conform with what you learn about Christ? Whatever you must change or give up, having Christ and becoming one with him will be more than worth the sacrifice.

Phil 3:9 No amount of law keeping, self-improvement, discipline, or religious effort can make us right with God. Righteousness comes only from God, and we are made righteous (receive right standing with him) by trusting in Christ. He exchanges our sin and shortcomings for his complete righteousness. (See 2 Cor 5:21 for more on Christ's gift of righteousness.)

Phil 3:9-10 Paul gave up everything—family, friendship, and freedom—in order to know Christ and his resurrection power. We, too, have access to this knowledge and this power, but we may have to make sacrifices to

Pressing toward the Goal

PHILIPPIANS 3:12–4:1

I don't mean to say that I have already achieved these
things or that I have already reached perfection. But
I press on to possess that perfection for which Christ
Jesus first possessed me. 13No, dear brothers and sisters, I have not achieved it,* but I focus on this one
thing: Forgetting the past and looking forward to what
lies ahead, 14I press on to reach the end of the race and
receive the heavenly prize for which God, through
Christ Jesus, is calling us.
15Let all who are spiritually mature agree on these
things. If you disagree on some point, I believe God
will make it plain to you. 16But we must hold on to the
progress we have already made.
17Dear brothers and sisters, pattern your lives after

Phil 3:13 Some manuscripts read *not yet achieved it.*

TRAINING FOR THE CHRISTIAN LIFE

As a great amount of training is needed for athletic activities, so we must train diligently for the Christian life. Such training takes time, dedication, energy, continued practice, and vision. We must all commit ourselves to the Christian life, but we must first know the rules as prescribed in God's Word (2 Tim 2:5).

Reference	*Metaphors*	*Training*	*Our Goal as Believers*
1 Cor 9:24-27	**Race**	Go into strict training in order to get the prize.	We train ourselves to run the race of life. So we keep our eyes on Christ—the goal—and don't get sidetracked or slowed down. When we do this, we will win a reward in Christ's Kingdom.
Phil 3:13-14	**Race**	Focus all your energies toward winning the race.	Living the Christian life demands all of our energies. We can forget the past and strain to reach the goal because we know Christ promises eternity with him at the race's end.
1 Tim 4:7-10	**Training**	Training for godliness will help you grow in faith and character.	Just as we exercise to keep physically fit, we must also train ourselves to be spiritually fit. As our faith develops, we become better Christians, living in accordance with God's will. Such a life will attract others to Christ and pay dividends in both this life and the next.
2 Tim 4:7-8	**Fight, Race**	Fighting the good fight and persevering to the end.	The Christian life is a fight against evil forces from without and temptation from within. If we stay true to God through it all, he promises an end, a rest, and a crown.

enjoy it fully. What are you willing to give up in order to know Christ? A crowded schedule in order to set aside a few minutes each day for prayer and Bible study? Your friend's approval? Some of your plans or pleasures? Whatever it is, knowing Christ is more than worth the sacrifice.

Phil 3:10 When we become one with Christ by trusting in him, we experience the power that raised him from the dead. That same mighty power will help us live morally renewed and regenerated lives. But before we can walk in newness of life, we must die to sin. Just as Christ's resurrection gives us the power to live for him, his crucifixion marks the death of our old sinful nature. We can't know the victory of the Resurrection without personally applying the Crucifixion.

Phil 3:11 When Paul wrote, "so that one way or another I will experience the resurrection from the dead," he was not implying uncertainty or doubt. He was unsure of the way that he would meet God, whether by execution or by natural death. He did not doubt that he would be raised, but attainment of it was within God's power and not his own.

Phil 3:11 Just as Christ was exalted after his resurrection, so we will one day share Christ's glory (Rev 22:1-7). Paul knew that he might die soon, but he had faith that he would be raised to life again.

Phil 3:12-14 Paul said that his goal was to know Christ, to be like Christ, and to be all Christ had in mind for him. This goal took all of Paul's energies. This is a helpful example for us. We should not let anything take our eyes off our goal—knowing Christ. With the single-mindedness of an athlete in training, we must lay aside everything harmful and forsake anything that may distract us from being effective Christians. What is holding you back?

Phil 3:13-14 Paul had reason to forget the past—he had held the coats of those who had stoned Stephen, the first Christian martyr (Acts 7:57-58; Paul was called Saul then). We have all done things for which we are ashamed, and we live in the tension of what we have been and what we want to be. Because our hope is in Christ, we can let go of past guilt and look forward to what God will help us become. Don't dwell on your past. Instead, grow in the knowledge of God by concentrating on your relationship with him *now.* Realize that you are forgiven, and then move on to a life of faith and obedience. Look forward to a fuller and more meaningful life because of your hope in Christ.

Phil 3:15-16 Sometimes trying to live a perfect Christian life can be so difficult that it leaves us drained and discouraged. We may feel so far from perfect that we think we can never please God with our lives. Paul used the term *perfection* (Phil 3:12) to mean mature or complete, not flawless in every detail. Those who are mature should press on in the Holy Spirit's power, knowing that Christ will reveal and fill in any discrepancy between what we are and what we should be. Christ's provision is no excuse for lagging devotion, but it provides relief and assurance for those who feel driven.

Phil 3:16 Christian maturity involves acting on the guidance that you have already received. We can always make excuses that we still have so much to learn. The instruction for us is to live up to what we already know and live out what we have already learned. We do not have to be sidetracked by an unending search for truth.

Phil 3:17 Paul challenged the Philippians to pursue Christlikeness by following Paul's own pattern or example. This did not mean, of course, that they should copy everything he did; he had just stated that he was not perfect (Phil 3:12). But as he focused his life on being like Christ, so should they. The Gospels were not yet in circulation, so Paul could not tell them to read the Bible to see what Christ was like. Therefore, he urged them to imitate him. That Paul could tell people to follow his example is a testimony to his character. Can you do the same? What kind of followers would new Christians become if they imitated you?

Phil 3:17-21 Paul criticized not only the Judaizers (see the first note on Phil 3:2-3, p. 1721) but also self-indulgent Christians—people who claimed to be Christians but didn't live up to Christ's model of servanthood

▸ PHILIPPIANS 3:12–4:1 *(cont.)*

mine, and learn from those who follow our example.
18For I have told you often before, and I say it again
with tears in my eyes, that there are many whose conduct shows they are really enemies of the cross of
Christ. 19They are headed for destruction. Their god
is their appetite, they brag about shameful things, and
they think only about this life here on earth. 20But we
are citizens of heaven, where the Lord Jesus Christ
lives. And we are eagerly waiting for him to return as
our Savior. 21He will take our weak mortal bodies and
change them into glorious bodies like his own, using
the same power with which he will bring everything
under his control.

4:1Therefore, my dear brothers and sisters,* stay
true to the Lord. I love you and long to see you, dear
friends, for you are my joy and the crown I receive
for my work.

Phil 4:1 Greek *brothers;* also in 4:8. **Phil 4:3** Or *loyal Syzygus.*

Words of Encouragement

PHILIPPIANS 4:2-9

Now I appeal to Euodia and Syntyche. Please, because
you belong to the Lord, settle your disagreement. 3And
I ask you, my true partner,* to help these two women,
for they worked hard with me in telling others the
Good News. They worked along with Clement and
the rest of my co-workers, whose names are written
in the Book of Life.

4Always be full of joy in the Lord. I say it again—rejoice! 5Let everyone see that you are considerate in all
you do. Remember, the Lord is coming soon.

6Don't worry about anything; instead, pray about
everything. Tell God what you need, and thank him
for all he has done. 7Then you will experience God's
peace, which exceeds anything we can understand.
His peace will guard your hearts and minds as you
live in Christ Jesus.

---

and self-sacrifice. Such people satisfy their own desires before even thinking about the needs of others. Freedom in Christ does not mean freedom to be selfish. It means taking every opportunity to serve and to become the best person you can be.

Phil 3:19 Paul gets tough with people who live to appease their appetites, who believe so strongly in their greatness that they become slaves to pride. What horrible people these must be—so concerned with earthly trivia that during worship their minds wander; so consumed with work that worship is inconvenient; so busy planning the next party that there is no time for prayer. Paul says they are headed for destruction because all they can think about is this life here on earth.

But then we must ask ourselves: Is too much of our time spent on efforts that will not endure in eternity, seeking earthly pleasures, or satisfying our physical desires? We must set our minds on knowing Christ, not on the pursuits of this world.

Phil 3:20 Citizens of a Roman colony were expected to promote the interests of Rome and maintain the dignity of the city. In the same way, citizens of heaven ought to promote heaven's interests on earth and lead lives worthy of heavenly citizenship. Too many Christians have failed to transfer their citizenship to heaven. They still seek earthly pleasures and treasures instead of heavenly ones. Paul told the Colossians to remember that they are citizens of heaven, where the Lord Jesus Christ lives. Have you transferred your citizenship? How are you promoting heaven's interests?

Phil 3:21 The phrase "weak mortal bodies" does not imply any negative attitude toward the human body. But the bodies we will receive when we are raised from the dead will be glorious, like Christ's resurrected body. Those who struggle with pain, physical limitations, or disabilities can have wonderful hope in the future resurrection. (For a more detailed discussion of our new bodies, see 1 Cor 15:35ff; 2 Cor 5:1-10.)

Phil 4:1 How do we "stay true to the Lord"? This refers to what Paul has just taught (Phil 3:20-21). The way to stay true is to keep our eyes on Christ, to remember that this world is not our home, and to focus on the fact that Christ will bring everything under his control. Staying true means steadfastly resisting the negative influences of temptation, false teaching, or persecution. It requires perseverance when we are challenged or opposed. Don't lose heart or give up. God promises to give us strength of character. With the Holy Spirit's help and with the help of fellow believers, you can stay true to the Lord.

Phil 4:2-3 Paul did not warn the Philippian church of doctrinal errors, but he did address some relational problems. These two women had been workers for Christ in the church. Their broken relationship was no small matter because many had become believers through their efforts. It is possible to believe in Christ, work hard for his Kingdom, and yet have broken relationships with others who are committed to the same cause. But there is no excuse for remaining unreconciled. Do you need to be reconciled to someone today? If you're facing a conflict you can't resolve, don't let the tension build into an explosion. Don't withdraw or resort to cruel power plays. Don't stand idly by and wait for the dispute to resolve itself. Instead, seek the help of those known for peacemaking.

Phil 4:3 The identity of this "true partner" remains a mystery. It could be Epaphroditus, the bearer of this letter, or a comrade of Paul in prison. It could also be someone named Syzygus, another way to understand the word for "partner."

Phil 4:3 Those "whose names are written in the Book of Life" are all who are marked for salvation through their faith in Christ (see also Luke 10:17-20; Rev 20:11-15).

Phil 4:4 It seems strange that a man in prison would be telling a church to rejoice. But Paul's attitude teaches us an important lesson: Our inner attitudes do not have to reflect our outward circumstances. Paul was full of joy because he knew that no matter what happened to him, Jesus Christ was with him. Several times in this letter Paul urged the Philippians to be joyful, probably because they needed to hear this. It's easy to get discouraged about unpleasant circumstances or to take unimportant events too seriously. If you haven't been joyful lately, you may not be looking at life from the right perspective.

Phil 4:4-5 Ultimate joy comes from Christ dwelling within us. Christ is near, and at his second coming we will fully realize this ultimate joy. He who lives within us will fulfill his final purposes for us.

Phil 4:5 We are to be considerate (reasonable, fair minded, and charitable) to those outside the church, and not just to fellow believers. This means we are not to seek revenge against those who treat us unfairly, nor are we to be overly vocal about our personal rights.

Phil 4:6-7 Imagine never worrying about anything! It seems like an impossibility; we all have worries on the job, in our homes, at school. But Paul's advice is to turn our worries into prayers. Do you want to worry less? Then pray more! Whenever you start to worry, stop and pray.

Phil 4:7 God's peace is different from the world's peace (see John 14:27). True peace is not found in positive thinking, in absence of conflict, or in good feelings. It comes from knowing that God is in control. Our citizenship in Christ's Kingdom is sure, our destiny is set, and we can have victory over sin. Let God's peace guard your heart against anxiety.

Phil 4:8 What we put into our mind determines what comes out in our words and actions. Paul tells us to program our mind

8And now, dear brothers and sisters, one final thing. Fix your thoughts on what is true, and honorable, and right, and pure, and lovely, and admirable. Think about things that are excellent and worthy of praise. 9Keep putting into practice all you learned and received from me—everything you heard from me and saw me doing. Then the God of peace will be with you.

Paul's Thanks for Their Gifts

PHILIPPIANS 4:10-20

How I praise the Lord that you are concerned about me again. I know you have always been concerned for me, but you didn't have the chance to help me. 11Not that I was ever in need, for I have learned how to be content with whatever I have. 12I know how to live on almost nothing or with everything. I have learned the secret of living in every situation, whether it is with a full stomach or empty, with plenty or little. 13For I can do everything through Christ,* who gives me strength. 14Even so, you have done well to share with me in my present difficulty.

15As you know, you Philippians were the only ones who gave me financial help when I first brought you the Good News and then traveled on from Macedonia. No other church did this. 16Even when I was in Thessalonica you sent help more than once. 17I don't say this because I want a gift from you. Rather, I want you to receive a reward for your kindness.

18At the moment I have all I need—and more! I am generously supplied with the gifts you sent me with Epaphroditus. They are a sweet-smelling sacrifice that is acceptable and pleasing to God. 19And this same God who takes care of me will supply all your needs from his glorious riches, which have been given to us in Christ Jesus.

20Now all glory to God our Father forever and ever! Amen.

Phil 4:13 Greek *through the one.*

---

with thoughts that are true, honorable, right, pure, lovely, admirable, excellent, and worthy of praise. Do you have problems with impure thoughts and daydreams? Examine what you are putting into your mind through television, Internet, books, conversations, movies, music, and magazines. Replace harmful input with wholesome material. Above all, read God's Word and pray. Ask God to help you focus your mind on what is good and pure. It takes practice, but it can be done.

Phil 4:9 It's not enough to hear or read the Word of God or even to know it well. We must also put it into practice. How easy it is to listen to a sermon and forget what the preacher said. How easy it is to read the Bible and not think about how to live differently. How easy it is to debate what a passage means and not live out that meaning. Exposure to God's Word is not enough. It must lead to obedience.

Phil 4:10 In 1 Corinthians 9:11-18, Paul wrote that he didn't accept gifts from the Corinthian church because he didn't want to be accused of preaching only to get money. But Paul maintained that it was a church's responsibility to support God's ministers (1 Cor 9:14). He accepted the Philippians' gift because they gave it willingly and because he was in need.

Phil 4:10-14 Are you able to get along happily (be content) in any circumstances you face? Paul knew how to be satisfied whether he had plenty or whether he was in need. The secret was drawing on Christ's power for strength. Do you have great needs, or are you dissatisfied because you don't have what you want? Learn to rely on God's promises and Christ's power to help you be content. If you always want more, ask God to remove that desire and teach you how to be satisfied in every circumstance. He will supply all your needs, but in a way that he knows is best for you. (See the note on Phil 4:19, below, for more on God supplying our needs.)

Phil 4:12-13 Paul could get along happily because he could see life from God's point of view. He focused on what he was supposed to do, not what he felt he should have. Paul had his priorities straight, and he was grateful for everything God had given him. Paul had detached himself from the nonessentials so that he could concentrate on the eternal. Often the desire for more or better possessions is really a longing to fill an empty place in a person's life. To what are you drawn when you feel empty inside? How can you find true contentment? The answer lies in your perspective, your priorities, and your source of power.

Phil 4:13 Can we really do everything? The power we receive in union with Christ is sufficient to do his will and to face the challenges that arise from our commitment to doing it. He does not grant us superhuman ability to accomplish anything *we* can imagine without regard to his interests. As we contend for the faith, we will face troubles, pressures, and trials. As they come, ask Christ to strengthen you.

Phil 4:14 The Philippians shared in Paul's financial support while he was in prison.

Phil 4:15 What makes money so magnetic and giving it away so stressful? Money measures our energy; it represents our day-to-day security. Giving money away puts our work and our futures at risk. Not every charity deserves your attention, and you're wise to scrutinize missionary appeals as well. But once you've determined that a project honors the Lord, don't hold back—give generously and joyfully. Like the Philippians, you'll be establishing an eternal partnership.

Phil 4:17 When we give to those in need, it not only benefits the receiver but it benefits us as well. It was not the Philippians' gift but their spirit of love and devotion that Paul appreciated most.

Phil 4:18 Paul was not referring to a sin offering but to a peace offering, "a sweet-smelling sacrifice that is acceptable and pleasing to God" (Lev 7:12-15 contains the instructions for such offerings of thanksgiving). Although the Greek and Roman Christians were not Jews and they had not offered sacrifices according to the Old Testament laws, they were well acquainted with the pagan rituals of offering sacrifices.

Phil 4:19 We can trust that God will always meet our needs. Whatever we need on earth he will always supply, even if it is the courage to face death as Paul did. Whatever we need in heaven he will supply. But we must remember the difference between our wants and our needs. Most people want to feel good and avoid discomfort or pain. We may not get all that we want. By trusting in Christ, our attitudes and appetites can change from wanting everything to accepting his provision and power to live for him.

Paul's Final Greetings

PHILIPPIANS 4:21-23

Give my greetings to each of God's holy people—all who belong to Christ Jesus. The brothers who are with me send you their greetings. 22 And all the rest of God's people send you greetings, too, especially those in Caesar's household.

23 May the grace of the Lord Jesus Christ be with your spirit.

R. Paul's First Letter to Timothy

Paul was released from his imprisonment in Rome, and likely had several years of ministry that were unrecorded in the Bible between writing Philippians and writing this letter to Timothy. He probably traveled back through Macedonia, Achaia, and Asia Minor visiting the churches he had founded and possibly even made his journey to Spain to spread the Good News. Paul sent Timothy to serve the church in Ephesus, and this personal letter from Paul to Timothy gives the younger leader instruction in how to deal with the particular problems he faced in leading the church in Ephesus. Paul advised Timothy on such practical topics as qualifications for church leaders, public worship practices, confronting false teaching, and how to treat various groups of people in the church. Right belief and right behavior are critical for anyone who desires to lead or serve effectively in the church.

Greetings from Paul

1 TIMOTHY 1:1-2

This letter is from Paul, an apostle of Christ Jesus, appointed by the command of God our Savior and Christ Jesus, who gives us hope.

2 I am writing to Timothy, my true son in the faith.

May God the Father and Christ Jesus our Lord give you grace, mercy, and peace.

Warnings against False Teachings

1 TIMOTHY 1:3-11

When I left for Macedonia, I urged you to stay there in Ephesus and stop those whose teaching is contrary to the truth. 4 Don't let them waste their time in endless discussion of myths and spiritual pedigrees. These things only lead to meaningless speculations,* which don't help people live a life of faith in God.*

1 Tm 1:4a Greek *in myths and endless genealogies, which cause speculation.* **1 Tm 1:4b** Greek *a stewardship of God in faith.*

AD 62 — *Paul is released from prison in Rome*

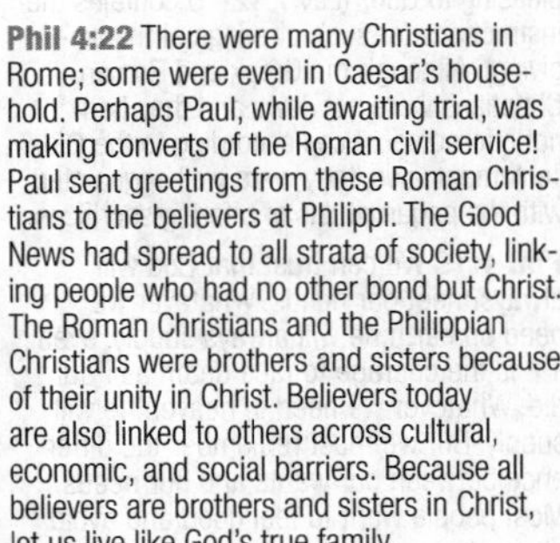

Phil 4:22 There were many Christians in Rome; some were even in Caesar's household. Perhaps Paul, while awaiting trial, was making converts of the Roman civil service! Paul sent greetings from these Roman Christians to the believers at Philippi. The Good News had spread to all strata of society, linking people who had no other bond but Christ. The Roman Christians and the Philippian Christians were brothers and sisters because of their unity in Christ. Believers today are also linked to others across cultural, economic, and social barriers. Because all believers are brothers and sisters in Christ, let us live like God's true family.

Phil 4:23 In many ways the Philippian church was a model congregation. It was made up of many different kinds of people who were learning to work together. But Paul recognized that problems could arise, so in his thank-you letter he prepared the Philippians for difficulties that could crop up within a body of believers. Although a prisoner in Rome, Paul had learned the true secret of joy and peace—imitating Christ and serving others. By focusing our minds on Christ, we will learn unity, humility, joy, and peace. We will also be motivated to live for him. We can live confidently for him because we have "the grace of the Lord Jesus Christ" with us.

1 Tim 1:1 This letter was written to Timothy in A.D. 64 or 65, after Paul's first imprisonment in Rome (Acts 28:16-31). Apparently Paul had been out of prison for a few years, and during that time he had revisited many churches in Asia and Macedonia. When he and Timothy returned to Ephesus, they found widespread false teaching in the church. Paul had warned the Ephesian elders to be on guard against the false teachers who inevitably would come after he had left (Acts 20:17-31). Paul sent Timothy to lead the Ephesian church while he moved on to Macedonia. From there Paul wrote this letter of encouragement and instruction to help Timothy deal with the difficult situation in the Ephesian church. Later, Paul was arrested again and brought back to a Roman prison.

1 Tim 1:1 Paul calls himself an *apostle*, meaning "one who is sent." Paul was sent by Jesus Christ to bring the message of salvation to the Gentiles (Acts 9:1-20). He was an apostle "by the command of God" because in Acts 13:2, the Holy Spirit, through the prophets, said, "Dedicate Barnabas and Saul [Paul] for the special work to which I have called them." From Romans 16:25-26; Titus 1:3, it is obvious that Paul regarded his commission as direct from God. For more information on Paul, see his Profile on p. 1571.

1 Tim 1:3-4 Paul first visited Ephesus on his second missionary journey (Acts 18:19-21). Later, on his third missionary journey, he stayed there for almost three years (Acts 19–20). Ephesus was one of the major cities in the Roman Empire, along with Rome, Corinth, Antioch, and Alexandria. It was a center for the commerce, politics, and religions of Asia Minor, and the location of the temple dedicated to the goddess Artemis (Diana).

1 Tim 1:3-4 The church at Ephesus may have been plagued by the same heresy that was threatening the church at Colosse—the teaching that to be acceptable to God, a person had to discover certain hidden knowledge and had to worship angels (Col 2:8, 18). The false teachers were motivated by their own interests rather than Christ's. They embroiled the church in endless and irrelevant questions and controversies, taking precious time away from the study of the truth. Stay away from religious speculation and pointless theological arguments. Such exercises may seem harmless at first, but they have a way of sidetracking us from the central message of the Good News—the person and work of Jesus Christ. They expend time we should use to share the Good News with others, and they don't help people grow in the faith. Avoid anything that keeps you from doing God's work.

1 Tim 1:3-7 Many leaders and authorities today demand allegiance, some of whom would even have us turn from Christ to follow them. When they seem to know the Bible, their influence can be dangerously subtle. They are modern-day false teachers. How can you recognize false teachers? (1) They teach what is contrary to the truth found in Scripture (1 Tim 1:3, 6-7; 4:1-3). (2) They promote trivial and divisive controversies instead of helping people come to Jesus (1 Tim 1:4). (3) They aren't concerned about personal evidence of God's presence in their lives, spending their time on "meaningless

5The purpose of my instruction is that all believers would be filled with love that comes from a pure heart, a clear conscience, and genuine faith. 6But some people have missed this whole point. They have turned away from these things and spend their time in meaningless discussions. 7They want to be known as teachers of the law of Moses, but they don't know what they are talking about, even though they speak so confidently.

8We know that the law is good when used correctly. 9For the law was not intended for people who do what is right. It is for people who are lawless and rebellious, who are ungodly and sinful, who consider nothing sacred and defile what is holy, who kill their father

TIMOTHY

Painful lessons are usually doorways to new opportunities. Even the apostle Paul had much to learn. Shortly after his disappointing experience with John Mark, Paul recruited another eager young man, Timothy, to be his assistant. Paul's intense personality may have been too much for John Mark to handle. It could easily have created the same problem for Timothy. But Paul seems to have learned a lesson in patience from his old friend Barnabas. As a result, Timothy became a "son" to Paul. • Timothy probably became a Christian after Paul's first missionary visit to Lystra (Acts 16:1-5). Timothy already had solid Jewish training in the Scriptures from his mother and grandmother. By Paul's second visit, Timothy had grown into a respected disciple of Jesus. He did not hesitate to join Paul and Silas on their journey. His willingness to be circumcised as an adult is clearly a mark of his commitment. (Timothy's mixed Greek/Jewish background could have created problems on their missionary journeys, because many of their audiences would be made up of Jews who were concerned about the strict keeping of this tradition. Timothy's submission to the rite of circumcision helped to avoid that potential problem.) • Beyond the tensions created by his mixed racial background, Timothy seemed to struggle with a naturally timid character and a sensitivity to his youthfulness. Unfortunately, many who share Timothy's character traits are quickly written off as too great a risk to deserve much responsibility. By God's grace, Paul saw great potential in Timothy. Paul demonstrated his confidence in Timothy by entrusting him with important responsibilities. Paul sent Timothy as his personal representative to Corinth during a particularly tense time (1 Cor 4:14-17). Although Timothy was apparently ineffective in that difficult mission, Paul did not give up on him. Timothy continued to travel with Paul. • Our last pictures of Timothy come from the most personal letters in the New Testament: 1 and 2 Timothy. The aging apostle Paul was near the end of his life, but his burning desire to continue his mission had not dimmed. Paul was writing to one of his closest friends—they had traveled, suffered, cried, and laughed together. They shared the intense joy of seeing people respond to the Good News and the agonies of seeing the gospel rejected and distorted. Paul left Timothy in Ephesus to oversee the young church there (1 Tim 1:3-4). He wrote to encourage Timothy and give him needed direction. These letters have provided comfort and help to countless other "Timothys" through the years. When you face a challenge that seems beyond your abilities, read 1 and 2 Timothy, and remember that others have shared your experience.

Strengths and accomplishments	• Joined Paul for his second and third missionary journeys • Was a respected Christian in his hometown • Was Paul's special representative on several occasions • Received two personal letters from Paul
Weaknesses and mistakes	• Struggled with a timid and reserved nature • Was apparently unable to correct some of the problems in the church at Corinth when Paul sent him there
Lessons from his life	• Youthfulness should not be an excuse for ineffectiveness • Our inadequacies and inabilities should not keep us from being available to God
Vital statistics	• Where: Lystra • Occupations: Missionary, pastor • Relatives: Mother: Eunice. Grandmother: Lois. Father: a Greek. • Contemporaries: Paul, Silas, Luke, Mark, Peter, Barnabas
Key verses	"I have no one else like Timothy, who genuinely cares about your welfare. All the others care only for themselves and not for what matters to Jesus Christ. But you know how Timothy has proved himself. Like a son with his father, he has served with me in preaching the Good News" (Phil 2:20-22).

Timothy's story is told in Acts, starting in chapter 16. He is also mentioned in Romans 16:21; 1 Corinthians 4:17; 16:10-11; 2 Corinthians 1:1, 19; Philippians 1:1; 2:19-23; Colossians 1:1; 1 Thessalonians 1:1-10; 2:3-4; 3:2-6; 1 and 2 Timothy; Philemon; Hebrews 13:23.

discussions" instead (1 Tim 1:6). (4) Their motivation is to make a name for themselves (1 Tim 1:7). To protect yourself from the deception of false teachers, learn what the Bible teaches and remain steadfast in your faith in Christ alone.

1 Tim 1:6 Arguing about details of the Bible can send us off on interesting but irrelevant tangents and cause us to miss the intent of God's message. The false teachers at Ephesus constructed vast speculative systems and then argued about the minor details of their wholly imaginary ideas. We should allow nothing to distract us from the Good News of salvation in Jesus Christ, the main point of Scripture. We should know what the Bible says, apply it to our lives daily, and teach it to others. When we do this, we will be able to evaluate all teachings in light of the central truth about Jesus.

1 Tim 1:7-11 The false teachers wanted to become famous as teachers of God's law, but they didn't even understand the law's purpose. The law was not meant to give believers a list of commands for every occasion but to show unbelievers their sin and bring them to God. (For more of what Paul taught about our relationship to the law, see Rom 5:20-21; 13:9-10; Gal 3:24-29.)

▸ **1 TIMOTHY 1:3-11** ***(cont.)***
or mother or commit other murders. [10]The law is for
people who are sexually immoral, or who practice
homosexuality, or are slave traders,* liars, promise
breakers, or who do anything else that contradicts the
wholesome teaching [11]that comes from the glorious
Good News entrusted to me by our blessed God.

Paul's Gratitude for God's Mercy

1 TIMOTHY 1:12-17
I thank Christ Jesus our Lord, who has given me
strength to do his work. He considered me trustworthy
and appointed me to serve him, [13]even though I used
to blaspheme the name of Christ. In my insolence,
I persecuted his people. But God had mercy on me
because I did it in ignorance and unbelief. [14]Oh, how
generous and gracious our Lord was! He filled me
with the faith and love that come from Christ Jesus.
[15]This is a trustworthy saying, and everyone should
accept it: "Christ Jesus came into the world to save
sinners"—and I am the worst of them all. [16]But God
had mercy on me so that Christ Jesus could use me
as a prime example of his great patience with even
the worst sinners. Then others will realize that they,
too, can believe in him and receive eternal life. [17]All
honor and glory to God forever and ever! He is the
eternal King, the unseen one who never dies; he alone
is God. Amen.

Timothy's Responsibility

1 TIMOTHY 1:18-20
Timothy, my son, here are my instructions for you,
based on the prophetic words spoken about you
earlier. May they help you fight well in the Lord's
battles. [19]Cling to your faith in Christ, and keep your
conscience clear. For some people have deliberately
violated their consciences; as a result, their faith has
been shipwrecked. [20]Hymenaeus and Alexander are

1 Tm 1:10 Or *kidnappers.*

1 Tim 1:10 Some attempt to legitimize "alternative lifestyles." Even some Christians say people have a right to choose their sexual preference. But the entire Bible (both in the Old and New Testaments) calls homosexual behavior sin (see Lev 18:22; Rom 1:18-32; 1 Cor 6:9-11). But we must be careful to condemn only the practice and not the people. People who live this lifestyle can be forgiven, and their lives can be transformed. The church should be a haven of forgiveness and healing for repentant homosexuals without compromising its stance against homosexual behavior. (For more on this subject, see the notes on Rom 1:26-27, p. 1648.)

"Christ Jesus came into the world to save sinners" —and I am the worst of them all.
1 Timothy 1:15

1 Tim 1:12-17 People can feel so guilt-ridden by their past that they think God could never forgive and accept them. But consider Paul's past. He had scoffed at the teachings of Jesus and had hunted down and murdered God's people before coming to faith in Christ (Acts 9:1-9). God forgave Paul and used him mightily for his Kingdom. No matter how shameful your past, God also can forgive and use you.

1 Tim 1:14 Paul's boldness in Christ can be intimidating. We may feel that our faith in God and our love for Christ and for others will always be inadequate. We will experience times of failure. But we can remain confident that Christ will help our faith and love to grow as our relationship with him deepens. Paul's prayer for the Philippians applies to us also: "I am certain that God, who began the good work within you, will continue his work until it is finally finished on the day when Christ Jesus returns" (Phil 1:6).

1 Tim 1:15 Here Paul summarizes the Good News: Jesus came into the world to save sinners, and no sinner is beyond his saving power. (See Luke 5:32 for Jesus' purpose for being on earth.) Jesus didn't come merely to show us how to live better lives or challenge us to be better people. He came to offer us salvation that leads to eternal life. Have you accepted his offer?

1 Tim 1:15 Paul was not nearly as interested in creating an image as he was in being an example. He did not hesitate to share his past, because he knew his failures would allow others to have hope. At times we hesitate to share our past struggles with others because we are afraid it will tarnish our image. Paul demonstrated that lowering our guard can be an important step in communicating the gospel. People will not believe the gospel is important if they can't see that it is crucial in your life. How has Christ shown patience with you? Did he stay with you when you doubted and rebelled? Did he remain faithful when you ignored his prior claim on your life? Did he love you when you disregarded his Word and his church? Remember that his patience is unlimited for those who love him. Don't be afraid to let others know what Christ has done for you.

1 Tim 1:18 Paul highly valued the gift of prophecy (1 Cor 14:1). Through prophecy important messages of warning and encouragement came to the church. Just as pastors are ordained and set apart for ministry in the church today, Timothy had been set apart for ministry when elders laid their hands on him (see 1 Tim 4:14). Apparently at this ceremony, several believers had prophesied about Timothy's gifts and strengths. These words from the Lord must have encouraged Timothy throughout his ministry.

1 Tim 1:19 How can you keep your conscience clear? Treasure your faith in Christ more than anything else and do what you know is right. Each time you deliberately ignore your conscience, you are hardening your heart. Over a period of time your capacity to tell right from wrong will diminish. As you walk with God, he will speak to you through your conscience, letting you know the difference between right and wrong. Be sure to act on those inner tugs so that you do what is right—then your conscience will remain clear.

1 Tim 1:20 We don't know who Alexander was—he may have been an associate of Hymenaeus. Hymenaeus's error is explained in 2 Timothy 2:17-18. He weakened people's faith by teaching that the resurrection had already occurred. Paul says that he handed both of these men over to Satan, meaning that Paul had removed them from the fellowship of the church. Paul did this so that they

two examples. I threw them out and handed them over to Satan so they might learn not to blaspheme God.

Instructions about Worship

1 TIMOTHY 2:1-15

I urge you, first of all, to pray for all people. Ask God to help them; intercede on their behalf, and give thanks for them. [2]Pray this way for kings and all who are in authority so that we can live peaceful and quiet lives marked by godliness and dignity. [3]This is good and pleases God our Savior, [4]who wants everyone to be saved and to understand the truth. [5]For there is only one God and one Mediator who can reconcile God and humanity—the man Christ Jesus. [6]He gave his life to purchase freedom for everyone. This is the message God gave to the world at just the right time. [7]And I have been chosen as a preacher and apostle to teach the Gentiles this message about faith and truth. I'm not exaggerating—just telling the truth.

[8]In every place of worship, I want men to pray with holy hands lifted up to God, free from anger and controversy.

[9]And I want women to be modest in their appearance.* They should wear decent and appropriate clothing and not draw attention to themselves by the way they fix their hair or by wearing gold or pearls or expensive clothes. [10]For women who claim to be devoted to God should make themselves attractive by the good things they do.

1 Tm 2:9 Or *to pray in modest apparel.*

---

would see their error and repent. The ultimate purpose of this punishment was correction. The church today is too often lax in disciplining Christians who deliberately sin. Deliberate disobedience should be responded to quickly and sternly to prevent the entire congregation from being affected. But discipline must be done in a way that tries to bring the offender back to Christ and into the loving embrace of the church. The definition of *discipline* includes these words: strengthening, purifying, training, correcting, perfecting. In contrast, condemnation, suspicion, withholding of forgiveness, or permanent exile should not be a part of church discipline.

1 Tim 2:1-4 Although God is all-powerful and all-knowing, he has chosen to let us help him change the world through our prayers. How this works is a mystery to us because of our limited understanding, but it is a reality. Paul based his instruction about prayer for everyone on his conviction that God's invitation for salvation extends equally to all people. The word *everyone* captures the nature of the gospel. The world that God loves includes every person (John 3:16). He loves us as individuals whom he knows intimately (Ps 139:13-18). Paul urges us to pray for "all people." Our earnest prayers will have powerful results (Jas 5:16).

1 Tim 2:2 We should pray for those in authority around the world so that their societies will be conducive to the spread of the Good News. Paul's command to pray for kings is remarkable considering that Nero, a notoriously cruel ruler, was emperor at this time (A.D. 54–68). When Paul wrote this letter, persecution was a growing threat to believers. Later, when Nero needed a scapegoat for the great fire that destroyed much of Rome in A.D. 64, he blamed the Roman Christians so as to take the focus off himself. Then persecution erupted throughout the Roman Empire. Not only were Christians denied certain privileges in society, but some were even publicly butchered, burned, or fed to animals.

1 Tim 2:4 Both Peter and Paul said that God wants everyone to be saved (see 2 Pet 3:9). This does not mean that all *will* be saved, because the Bible makes it clear that many reject Christ (Matt 25:31-46; John 12:44-50; Heb 10:26-29). The Good News has a universal scope; it is not directed only to people of one race, one gender, or one national background. God loves the whole world and sent his Son to save sinners. No one is outside God's mercy or beyond the reach of his offer of salvation.

1 Tim 2:5-6 Though some people think there are many ways to God, in practice, each person must choose a single way. We can stand on one side of a gorge and discuss the possibility of many bridges across the abyss; but if we are determined to cross, we will have to commit to one bridge. Those who insist that there are many bridges to God usually fit in one of the following categories: (1) They have not personally committed to any "bridge." They are surprised that their belief in multiple ways does not exempt them from having to choose one. (2) Their belief in "many ways to God" hides their true belief that finding God doesn't really matter at all. (3) They are convinced that arguing for "many ways to God" will insure that they won't be wrong. If there is only one way, their generalized belief will presumably have included it. (4) They have decided that believing in "many ways to God" requires less work than going to the trouble of actually considering the claims of various religious systems.

The facts remain: We human beings are separated from God by sin and we need a Savior—a way across the abyss of sin to be reconciled to God. Only one person in the universe is our Mediator and can stand between us and God and bring us together—Jesus, who is both God and man. Jesus' sacrifice brought new life to all who call on him. Have you let him bridge the gap between you and God?

1 Tim 2:7 Paul describes himself as a preacher and apostle. He was given the special privilege of announcing the Good News to the Gentiles. He gives his credentials as an apostle in 1 Corinthians 15:7-11.

1 Tim 2:8 Besides displeasing God, anger and controversy make prayer difficult. That is why Jesus said that we should interrupt our prayers, if necessary, to make peace with others (Matt 5:23-24). God wants us to obey him immediately and thoroughly. Our goal should be to have a right relationship with God and also with others.

1 Tim 2:9-10 It is not unscriptural for a woman to want to be attractive. Today, however, to what degree should women take this advice about fixing their hair or wearing gold, pearls, or expensive clothes? Paul was not prohibiting these things; he was simply saying that women should not be drawing attention to themselves through these things. Modesty and decency are the key words. All women would do well to remember that beauty begins on the inside. A gentle, modest, loving character gives a light to the face that cannot be duplicated by even the best cosmetics. A carefully groomed and well-decorated exterior is artificial and cold unless inner beauty is present. The general rule for both women and men emphasizes that both behavior and dress must express submission to and respect for Jesus Christ.

1 Tim 2:9-15 To understand these verses, we must understand the situation in which Paul and Timothy worked. In first-century Jewish culture, women were not allowed to study. When Paul said that women should "learn quietly and submissively," he was offering them an amazing new opportunity to learn God's Word. That they were to listen and learn quietly and submissively referred to an attitude of quietness and composure (not total silence). In addition, Paul himself acknowledges that women publicly prayed and prophesied (1 Cor 11:5). Apparently, however, the women in the Ephesian church were abusing their newly acquired Christian freedom. Because these women were new converts, they did not yet have the necessary experience, knowledge, or Christian maturity to teach those who already had extensive scriptural education.

▸ 1 TIMOTHY 2:1-15 ***(cont.)***

[11]Women should learn quietly and submissively.
[12]I do not let women teach men or have authority over them.* Let them listen quietly. [13]For God
made Adam first, and afterward he made Eve. [14]And
it was not Adam who was deceived by Satan. The
woman was deceived, and sin was the result. [15]But
women will be saved through childbearing,* assuming they continue to live in faith, love, holiness,
and modesty.

Leaders in the Church

1 TIMOTHY 3:1-13

This is a trustworthy saying: "If someone aspires to be
an elder,* he desires an honorable position." [2]So an
elder must be a man whose life is above reproach. He
must be faithful to his wife.* He must exercise self-
control, live wisely, and have a good reputation. He
must enjoy having guests in his home, and he must be
able to teach. [3]He must not be a heavy drinker* or be
violent. He must be gentle, not quarrelsome, and not
love money. [4]He must manage his own family well,
having children who respect and obey him. [5]For if a
man cannot manage his own household, how can he
take care of God's church?

[6]An elder must not be a new believer, because he
might become proud, and the devil would cause him
to fall.* [7]Also, people outside the church must speak
well of him so that he will not be disgraced and fall
into the devil's trap.

1 Tm 2:12 Or *teach men or usurp their authority.* **1 Tm 2:15** Or *will be saved by accepting their role as mothers,* or *will be saved by the birth of the Child.* **1 Tm 3:1** Or *an overseer,* or *a bishop;* also in 3:2, 6. **1 Tm 3:2** Or *must have only one wife,* or *must be married only once;* Greek reads *must be the husband of one wife;* also in 3:12. **1 Tm 3:3** Greek *must not drink too much wine;* similarly in 3:8. **1 Tm 3:6** Or *he might fall into the same judgment as the devil.*

1 Tim 2:12 Some interpret this passage to mean that women should never teach in the assembled church; however, commentators point out that Paul did not forbid women from ever teaching. Paul's commended co-worker Priscilla taught Apollos, the great preacher (Acts 18:24-26). Paul frequently mentioned other women who held positions of responsibility in the church. Phoebe worked in the church (Rom 16:1). Mary, Tryphena, Tryphosa and Persis were the Lord's workers (Rom 16:6, 12), as were Euodia and Syntyche (Phil 4:2). Paul was very likely prohibiting the Ephesian women, not all women, from teaching (see the note on 1 Tim 2:9-15, p. 1729).

Paul did not want the Ephesian women to teach because they didn't yet have enough knowledge or experience. The Ephesian church had a particular problem with false teachers. Evidently the women were especially susceptible to the false teachings (2 Tim 3:1-9) because they did not yet have enough biblical knowledge to discern the truth. In addition, some of the women were apparently flaunting their newfound Christian freedom by wearing inappropriate clothing (1 Tim 2:9). Paul was telling Timothy not to put anyone (in this case, women) into a position of leadership who was not yet mature in the faith (see 1 Tim 3:6; 5:22). The same principle applies to churches today (see the note on 1 Tim 3:6, below).

1 Tim 2:13-14 In previous letters Paul had discussed male/female roles in marriage (Eph 5:21-33; Col 3:18-19). Here he talks about male/female roles within the church. Some scholars see these verses about Adam and Eve as an illustration of what was happening in the Ephesian church. Just as Eve had been deceived in the Garden of Eden, so the women in the church were being deceived by false teachers. And just as Adam was the first human created by God, so the men in the church in Ephesus should be the first to speak and teach, because they had more training. This view, then, stresses that Paul's teaching here is not universal but applies to churches with similar problems. But other scholars contend that the roles Paul points out are God's design for his created order—God established these roles to maintain harmony in both the family and the church.

1 Tim 2:14 Paul is not excusing Adam for his part in the Fall (Gen 3:6-7, 17-19). On the contrary, in his letter to the Romans Paul places the primary blame for humanity's sinful nature on Adam (Rom 5:12-21).

1 Tim 2:15 The phrase "saved through childbearing" can be understood several ways: (1) Man sinned, so men were condemned to painful labor. Woman sinned, so women were condemned to pain in childbearing. Both men and women can be saved through trusting Christ and obeying him. (2) Women who fulfill their God-given roles are demonstrating true commitment and obedience to Christ. One of the most important roles for a wife and mother is to care for her family. (3) The childbearing mentioned here refers to the birth of Jesus Christ. Women (and men) are saved spiritually because of the most important birth, that of Christ himself. (4) From the lessons learned through the trials of childbearing, women can develop qualities that teach them about love, trust, submission, and service.

1 Tim 3:1 To be a church leader ("elder") is a heavy responsibility because the church belongs to the living God. The word *elder* can refer to a pastor, church leader, or presiding overseer. It is good to want to be a spiritual leader, but the standards are high. Paul enumerates some of the qualifications here. Church leaders should not be elected because they are popular, nor should they be allowed to push their way to the top. Instead, they should be chosen by the church because of their respect for the truth, both in what they believe and in how they live. Do you hold a position of spiritual leadership, or would you like to be a leader someday? Check yourself against Paul's standard of excellence. Those with great responsibility must meet high expectations.

1 Tim 3:1-13 All believers, even if they never plan to be church leaders, should strive to follow these guidelines because they are consistent with what God says is true and right. For example, some people are "able to teach" effectively but have never formally taught or led at church. Their lessons are passed on to one or two others. They become mentors of spiritual truth. Paul described this intimate kind of teaching in 2 Timothy 2:2: "You have heard me teach things that have been confirmed by many reliable witnesses. Now teach these truths to other trustworthy people who will be able to pass them on to others." More is learned through living than through lectures. If you have been able to communicate your faith clearly to another person, you have demonstrated teaching at its best. In measuring your ability to teach, don't consider how many students you have had; instead, ask how much truth you have passed on to even one student whom God has brought your way.

1 Tim 3:2 Paul's statement that each elder should be faithful to his wife prohibits both polygamy and promiscuity. This does not prohibit an unmarried person from becoming an elder or a widowed elder from remarrying.

1 Tim 3:4-5 Christian workers and volunteers sometimes make the mistake of being so involved in their work that they neglect their families, and especially the firm discipline of their children. Spiritual leadership must begin at home. If a person is not willing to care for, discipline, and teach their own children, they are not qualified to lead the church. Don't allow your volunteer activities to detract from your family responsibilities.

1 Tim 3:6 New believers should become secure and strong in the faith before taking leadership roles in the church. Too often, in a church desperate for workers, new believers are placed in positions of responsibility prematurely. New faith needs time to mature. New believers should have a place of service, but they should not be put into leadership positions until they are firmly grounded in their faith, with a solid Christian lifestyle and a knowledge of the Word of God.

8In the same way, deacons must be well respected
and have integrity. They must not be heavy drinkers
or dishonest with money. 9They must be committed
to the mystery of the faith now revealed and must live
with a clear conscience. 10Before they are appointed
as deacons, let them be closely examined. If they pass
the test, then let them serve as deacons.
11In the same way, their wives* must be respected
and must not slander others. They must exercise self-
control and be faithful in everything they do.
12A deacon must be faithful to his wife, and he must
manage his children and household well. 13Those who
do well as deacons will be rewarded with respect from
others and will have increased confidence in their
faith in Christ Jesus.

The Truths of Our Faith

1 TIMOTHY 3:14-16

14I am writing these things to you now, even though I
hope to be with you soon, 15so that if I am delayed, you
will know how people must conduct themselves in
the household of God. This is the church of the living
God, which is the pillar and foundation of the truth.
16Without question, this is the great mystery of our
faith*:

Christ* was revealed in a human body
and vindicated by the Spirit.*
He was seen by angels
and announced to the nations.
He was believed in throughout the world
and taken to heaven in glory.

1 Tm 3:11 Or *the women deacons.* The Greek word can be translated *women* or *wives.* **1 Tm 3:16a** Or *of godliness.* **1 Tm 3:16b** Greek *He who;* other manuscripts read *God.* **1 Tm 3:16c** Or *in his spirit.*

1 Tim 3:6 Younger believers who are selected for office need to beware of the damaging effects of pride. Pride can seduce emotions and cloud reason. It can make those who are immature susceptible to the influence of unscrupulous people. Pride and conceit were the devil's downfall, and he uses pride to trap others.

1 Tim 3:7 People outside the church should speak well of those who would lead in the church. The good reputation with outsiders that Paul required is realized when Christians act as dependable friends and good neighbors. How we carry out our duties as citizens, neighbors, and friends facilitates or frustrates our ability to communicate the gospel. Do you have friends who are not believers? Does your conduct help or hinder the cause of Christ? As the church carries out its mission in an increasingly secular world, the church needs those who build bridges with unbelievers in order to bring them the gospel.

1 Tim 3:8-13 *Deacon* means "one who serves." This position was possibly begun by the apostles in the Jerusalem church (Acts 6:1-6) to care for the physical needs of the congregation—at that time, the needs of the Greek-speaking widows. Deacons were leaders in the church, and their qualifications resemble those of the elders. In some churches today, the office of deacon has lost its importance. New Christians are often asked to serve in this position, but that is not the New Testament pattern. Paul says that potential deacons should have high qualifications and be very carefully chosen.

1 Tim 3:11 "Wives" can refer to women helpers or deaconesses. It could also mean wives of deacons or female leaders of the church (such as Phoebe, the deaconess mentioned in Rom 16:1). In either case, Paul expected the behavior of prominent women in the church to be just as responsible and blameless as that of prominent men.

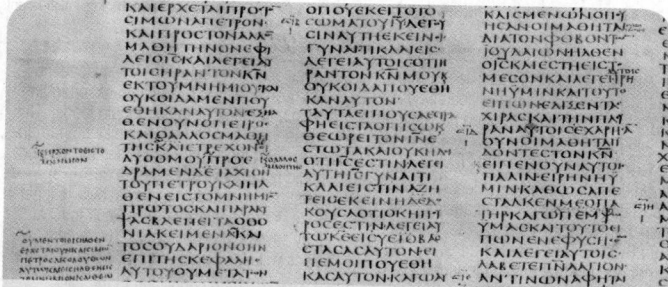

Codex Sinaiticus

This codex contains the entire Old Testament and New Testament, along with the Epistle of Barnabas and the Shepherd of Hermas. Most scholars think it was created around A.D. 350–375. This codex was discovered by Constantin von Tischendorf in Saint Catherine's Monastery (situated at the foot of Mount Sinai) in 1859. It is now housed in the British Museum in London.

In 1 Timothy 3:16, the original scribe of Codex Sinaiticus wrote, "great is the mystery of godliness: who was manifested in the flesh." This was changed by a later scribe to read, "great is the mystery of godliness: God was manifested in the flesh" (see NLT mg). The exact same thing happened in two other early manuscripts; the original reading "who" was changed to "God." Either way, the message is clear: Jesus Christ was God manifest in the flesh (cf. John 1:1, 14; Col 2:9). This is what makes the Christian faith different from all other monotheistic religions. We believe that Jesus was God incarnate. Stay true to this faith, just as Paul exhorted Timothy.

1 Tim 3:14-15 The Bible is the written form of what God expects us to know and do. God chose Paul to carry out one phase of the plan. Through Paul, the inspired teaching was written down. As such, it was passed on to Timothy. Then, it was passed on to others. Later, it was passed on to us. Times have changed, but the original authority remains. Because the Bible is from God, it must be studied seriously, understood thoroughly, and applied faithfully. Paul intended this letter to teach believers how to conduct themselves. We would do well to read carefully.

1 Tim 3:16 In this short hymn, Paul affirms the humanity and divinity of Christ. By so doing he reveals the heart of the Good News, "the great mystery of our faith" (the secret of how we become godly). "Revealed in a human body"—Jesus was a man; Jesus' incarnation is the basis of our being right with God. "Vindicated by the Spirit"—Jesus' resurrection showed that the Holy Spirit's power was in him (Rom 8:11). "Seen by angels" and "taken to heaven"—Jesus is divine. We can't please God on our own; we must depend on Christ. As a man, Jesus lived a perfect life, and so he is a perfect example of how to live. As God, Jesus gives us the power to do what is right. It is possible to live a godly life—through following Christ.

Warnings against False Teachers

1 TIMOTHY 4:1-5

Now the Holy Spirit tells us clearly that in the last
times some will turn away from the true faith; they
will follow deceptive spirits and teachings that come
from demons. 2These people are hypocrites and liars,
and their consciences are dead.*

3They will say it is wrong to be married and wrong
to eat certain foods. But God created those foods to
be eaten with thanks by faithful people who know
the truth. 4Since everything God created is good, we
should not reject any of it but receive it with thanks.
5For we know it is made acceptable* by the word of
God and prayer.

A Good Servant of Christ Jesus

1 TIMOTHY 4:6-16

If you explain these things to the brothers and sisters,*
Timothy, you will be a worthy servant of Christ Jesus,
one who is nourished by the message of faith and
the good teaching you have followed. 7Do not waste
time arguing over godless ideas and old wives' tales.
Instead, train yourself to be godly. 8"Physical training is good, but training for godliness is much better,
promising benefits in this life and in the life to come."
9This is a trustworthy saying, and everyone should
accept it. 10This is why we work hard and continue to
struggle,* for our hope is in the living God, who is the
Savior of all people and particularly of all believers.

11Teach these things and insist that everyone learn
them. 12Don't let anyone think less of you because you
are young. Be an example to all believers in what you
say, in the way you live, in your love, your faith, and
your purity. 13Until I get there, focus on reading the
Scriptures to the church, encouraging the believers,
and teaching them.

14Do not neglect the spiritual gift you received
through the prophecy spoken over you when the

1 Tm 4:2 Greek *are seared.* **1 Tm 4:5** Or *made holy.* **1 Tm 4:6** Greek *brothers.* **1 Tm 4:10** Some manuscripts read *continue to suffer.*

1 Tim 4:1 The "last times" began with Christ's resurrection and will continue until his return when he will set up his Kingdom and judge all humanity.

1 Tim 4:1-2 False teachers were and still are a threat to the church. Jesus and the apostles repeatedly warned against them (see, for example, Mark 13:21-23; Acts 20:28-31; 2 Thes 2:1-12; 2 Pet 3:3-7). It is not enough that a teacher appears to be knowledgeable, is disciplined and moral, or claims to speak for God; if the teaching contradicts the Bible, it is false. Like Timothy, we must guard against any teaching that causes believers to dilute or reject any aspect of their faith. Such false teaching can be very direct or extremely subtle. Believers ought to respond quickly when they sense false teaching being promoted. The truth does not mind honest questions. Sometimes the source may prove to be ignorant of the error and appreciate the correction. But a firm warning may at least keep potential victims from the disastrous results of apostasy that Paul described. (For how to spot false teaching, see the note on 1 Tim 1:3-7, p. 1726.)

1 Tim 4:1-5 Paul said the false teachers were hypocrites and liars who encouraged people to follow "deceptive spirits and teachings that come from demons." The danger that Timothy faced in Ephesus seems to have come from certain people in the church who were following some Greek philosophers who taught that the body was evil and that only the soul mattered. The false teachers refused to believe that the God of creation was good, because his very contact with the physical world would have soiled him. Though these Greek-influenced church members honored Jesus, they could not believe he was truly human. Paul knew that their teachings, if left unchecked, would greatly distort Christian truth.

Satan deceives people by offering a clever imitation of the real thing. The false teachers gave stringent rules (such as forbidding people to marry or to eat certain foods). This made them appear self-disciplined and righteous. But their strict disciplines for the body could not remove sin (see Col 2:20-23). We must not be unduly impressed by a teacher's style or credentials; we must look to what they say about Jesus Christ. Those conclusions will show the source of their message.

1 Tim 4:4-5 In opposition to the false teachers, Paul affirmed that everything God created is good (see Gen 1). We should ask for God's blessing on his created gifts that give us pleasure and thank him for them. But this doesn't mean that we should abuse what God has made (for example, gluttony abuses God's gift of good food, lust abuses God's gift of love, and murder abuses God's gift of life). Instead, we should enjoy these gifts by using them to serve and honor God. Have you thanked God for the good gifts he has given? Are you using the gifts in ways pleasing to you *and* to God?

1 Tim 4:7-10 Are you in shape both physically and spiritually? In our society, much emphasis is placed on physical fitness, but spiritual health is even more important. Our physical health is susceptible to disease and injury, but faith can sustain us through any tragedy. To train ourselves to be godly, we must develop our faith by using our God-given abilities in the service of the church (see 1 Tim 4:14-16). Are you developing your spiritual muscles?

1 Tim 4:10 Christ is the Savior for all, but his salvation becomes effective only for those who trust him.

1 Tim 4:12 Timothy was a young pastor. It would have been easy for older Christians to look down on him because of his youth. He had to earn the respect of his elders by setting an example in his speech, life, love, faith, and purity. Regardless of your age, God can use you. Whether you are young or old, don't think of your age as a handicap. Live so others can see Christ in you.

1 Tim 4:12-16 Apparently Timothy needed some encouragement. Most likely, so do many people around you. Each day we have many opportunities to support and inspire family members, fellow workers, and even total strangers. People need help and affirmation all along the way. Paul modeled six important principles to help us encourage others: (1) Begin with encouragement. People who know we will encourage them will be happy to work with us. (2) Expect of others only what you expect of yourself. People will resist being held to unfair standards. (3) Develop expectations of others with consideration for their skills, maturity, and experience. People will reject or fail to meet expectations that do not fit them. Be patient with distracted or slow learners. (4) Monitor your expectations of others. Changing circumstances sometimes require revised or reduced expectations. (5) Clarify your expectations with others. People are not likely to hit a target that no one has identified. (6) End with encouragement. People love to be thanked for a job well done.

1 Tim 4:13 The "Scriptures" referred to here are, in fact, the Old Testament. We must make sure to emphasize the entire Bible, both the Old and the New Testaments. There are rich rewards in studying the people, events, prophecies, and principles of the Old Testament.

1 Tim 4:14 Highly skilled and talented athletes lose their abilities if their muscles aren't toned by constant use. Likewise, we will lose our spiritual gifts if we don't put them to work. Our talents are improved by exercise, but failing to use them causes them to waste away from lack of practice and nourishment. What gifts and abilities has God given you? Use them regularly in serving God and others. (See Rom 12:1-8; 2 Tim 1:6-8 for more on using well the abilities God has given us.)

elders of the church laid their hands on you. [15]Give your complete attention to these matters. Throw yourself into your tasks so that everyone will see your progress. [16]Keep a close watch on how you live and on your teaching. Stay true to what is right for the sake of your own salvation and the salvation of those who hear you.

Advice about Widows, Elders, and Slaves

1 TIMOTHY 5:1–6:2a

Never speak harshly to an older man,* but appeal to him respectfully as you would to your own father. Talk to younger men as you would to your own brothers. [2]Treat older women as you would your mother, and treat younger women with all purity as you would your own sisters.

[3]Take care of* any widow who has no one else to care for her. [4]But if she has children or grandchildren, their first responsibility is to show godliness at home and repay their parents by taking care of them. This is something that pleases God.

[5]Now a true widow, a woman who is truly alone in this world, has placed her hope in God. She prays night and day, asking God for his help. [6]But the widow who lives only for pleasure is spiritually dead even while she lives. [7]Give these instructions to the church so that no one will be open to criticism.

[8]But those who won't care for their relatives, especially those in their own household, have denied the true faith. Such people are worse than unbelievers.

[9]A widow who is put on the list for support must be a woman who is at least sixty years old and was faithful to her husband.* [10]She must be well respected by everyone because of the good she has done. Has she brought up her children well? Has she been kind to strangers and served other believers humbly?* Has she helped those who are in trouble? Has she always been ready to do good?

[11]The younger widows should not be on the list, because their physical desires will overpower their devotion to Christ and they will want to remarry. [12]Then they would be guilty of breaking their previous pledge. [13]And if they are on the list, they will learn to be lazy and will spend their time gossiping from house to house, meddling in other people's business and talking about things they shouldn't. [14]So I advise these younger widows to marry again, have children, and take care of their own homes. Then the enemy will not be able to say anything against them. [15]For I am afraid that some of them have already gone astray and now follow Satan.

[16]If a woman who is a believer has relatives who are widows, she must take care of them and not put

1 Tm 5:1 Or *an elder.* **1 Tm 5:3** Or *Honor.* **1 Tm 5:9** Greek *was the wife of one husband.* **1 Tm 5:10** Greek *and washed the feet of God's holy people?*

---

1 Tim 4:16 We must be on constant guard against falling into sin that can so easily destroy us. Yet we must watch what we believe ("teaching") just as closely. Wrong beliefs can quickly lead us into sin and heresy. We should be on guard against those who would persuade us that how we live is more important than what we believe. We should keep a close watch on both, staying true to the faith.

1 Tim 5:1-2 Those in the ministry can avoid improper attitudes toward the people in their care by treating them as family members. If they see everyone as fellow members in God's family, they will protect them and help them grow spiritually.

1 Tim 5:3ff Paul wanted Christian families to be as self-supporting as possible. He insisted that children and grandchildren take care of the widows in their families (1 Tim 5:4); he suggested that younger widows remarry and start new families (1 Tim 5:14); he ordered the church not to support lazy members who refused to work (2 Thes 3:10). Nevertheless, when necessary, the believers pooled their resources (Acts 2:44-47); they gave generously to help disaster-ridden churches (1 Cor 16:1-4); they took care of a large number of widows (Acts 6:1-6). The church has always had limited resources and has always had to balance financial responsibility with generosity. It only makes sense for members to work as hard as they can and to be as independent as possible, so they can adequately care for themselves and for less fortunate members. When church members are both responsible and generous, everyone's needs will be met.

1 Tim 5:3-5 Because there were no pensions, no social security, no life insurance, and few honorable jobs for women, widows were usually unable to support themselves. The responsibility for caring for the helpless naturally falls first on their families—the people whose lives are most closely linked with theirs. Paul stresses the importance of each family caring for the needs of its widows and not leaving it for the church. The church can then care for those widows who have no families. A widow who had no children or other family members to support her was doomed to poverty. From the beginning, the church took care of its widows, who in turn gave valuable service to the church.

The church should support those who have no families and should also help the elderly, young, disabled, ill, or poverty-stricken with their emotional and spiritual needs. Often families who are caring for their own helpless members have heavy burdens. They may need extra money, a listening ear, a helping hand, or a word of encouragement. Interestingly, those who are helped often turn around and help others, turning the church into more of a caring community. Don't wait for people to ask. Take the initiative and look for ways to serve them.

1 Tim 5:8 Healthy homes remain the best possible training environment for children. When it comes to caring for relatives and honoring parents, children take most of their cues by watching how Mom and Dad honor the grandparents. If our children see the way we, as parents, care for our parents, they will understand the importance of such honor for us in the future. Healthy, practical honor becomes a priceless gift that one generation gives to another. Disrespect and lack of care provide harmful examples that will eventually turn on us. The warning in the verse is ominous indeed.

1 Tim 5:9-16 Apparently some older widows had been "put on the list for support," meaning that they had taken a vow committing themselves to work for the church in exchange for financial support. Paul lists a few qualifications for these church workers: These widows should be at least 60 years old, should have been faithful to their husbands, and should be well known for their kind deeds. Younger widows should not be included in this group because they might desire to marry again and thus have to break their pledge (1 Tim 5:11-12).

Three out of four wives today eventually are widowed, so many of the older women in our churches have lost their husbands. Does your church provide an avenue of service for these women? Could you help match their gifts and abilities with your church's needs? Often their maturity and wisdom can be of great service in the church.

1 Tim 5:15 "Gone astray and now follow Satan" refers to the immoral conduct that identified these women with their pagan neighbors.

▸ **1 TIMOTHY 5:1–6:2a** ***(cont.)***

the responsibility on the church. Then the church can
care for the widows who are truly alone.
17Elders who do their work well should be respected
and paid well,* especially those who work hard at both
preaching and teaching. 18For the Scripture says, "You
must not muzzle an ox to keep it from eating as it
treads out the grain." And in another place, "Those
who work deserve their pay!"*
19Do not listen to an accusation against an elder unless it is confirmed by two or three witnesses. 20Those
who sin should be reprimanded in front of the whole
church; this will serve as a strong warning to others.
21I solemnly command you in the presence of God
and Christ Jesus and the highest angels to obey these
instructions without taking sides or showing favoritism to anyone.
22Never be in a hurry about appointing a church
leader.* Do not share in the sins of others. Keep yourself pure.
23Don't drink only water. You ought to drink a little
wine for the sake of your stomach because you are
sick so often.
24Remember, the sins of some people are obvious,
leading them to certain judgment. But there are others
whose sins will not be revealed until later. 25In the
same way, the good deeds of some people are obvious. And the good deeds done in secret will someday
come to light.

6:1 All slaves should show full respect for their masters
so they will not bring shame on the name of God and
his teaching. 2If the masters are believers, that is no
excuse for being disrespectful. Those slaves should
work all the harder because their efforts are helping
other believers* who are well loved.

False Teaching and True Riches

1 TIMOTHY 6:2b-10

Teach these things, Timothy, and encourage everyone to obey them. 3Some people may contradict our
teaching, but these are the wholesome teachings of
the Lord Jesus Christ. These teachings promote a
godly life. 4Anyone who teaches something different
is arrogant and lacks understanding. Such a person
has an unhealthy desire to quibble over the meaning
of words. This stirs up arguments ending in jealousy,
division, slander, and evil suspicions. 5These people
always cause trouble. Their minds are corrupt, and
they have turned their backs on the truth. To them,
a show of godliness is just a way to become wealthy.

1 Tm 5:17 Greek *should be worthy of double honor.* **1 Tm 5:18** Deut 25:4; Luke 10:7. **1 Tm 5:22** Greek *about the laying on of hands.* **1 Tm 6:2** Greek *brothers.*

---

1 Tim 5:17 Preaching and teaching are closely related. Preaching is proclaiming the Word of God and confronting listeners with the truth of Scripture. Teaching is explaining the truth in Scripture, helping learners understand difficult passages and apply God's Word to daily life. Paul says that these elders are worthy of double honor. Unfortunately, we often take them for granted by not providing adequately for their needs or by subjecting them to heavy criticism. Think of how you can honor your leaders who work hard at preaching and teaching.

1 Tim 5:17-18 Faithful church leaders should be supported and appreciated. Too often they are targets for criticism because the congregation has unrealistic expectations. How do you treat your church leaders? Do you enjoy finding fault, or do you show your appreciation? Do they receive enough financial support to allow them to live without worry and to provide for the needs of their families? Jesus and Paul emphasized the importance of supporting those who lead and teach us (see Gal 6:6; see also the notes on Luke 10:7, p. 1394; 1 Cor 9:4-10, p. 1608). Our ministers deserve to know that we are giving to them cheerfully, gratefully, and generously.

1 Tim 5:19-21 Church leaders are not exempt from sin, faults, and mistakes. But they are often criticized for the wrong reasons—minor imperfections, failure to meet someone's expectations, personality clashes. Thus, Paul said that accusations should not even be heard unless two or three witnesses confirm them. Sometimes church leaders should be confronted about their behavior, and sometimes they should be rebuked. But all rebuking must be done fairly and lovingly and for the purpose of restoration.

1 Tim 5:21 Church leadership is a heavy responsibility. As difficult as it might be, Timothy was not to waver on any of Paul's instructions (and particularly the instructions about rebuking elders). Any needed discipline or rebuke must be administered without regard to Timothy's personal inclinations or favoritism. Likewise, leadership in the church today must be handled with maturity, faithfulness, godliness, and lack of favoritism. The health of a body of believers is far more important than playing favorites with someone who is not meeting the standards set forth here.

1 Tim 5:22, 24-25 Paul says that a church should never be in a hurry about choosing its leaders, especially the pastor, because major problems or sins might be overlooked. It is a serious responsibility to choose church leaders. They must have strong faith and be morally upright, having the qualities described in 1 Timothy 3:1-13; Titus 1:5-9. Not everyone who wants to be a church leader is eligible. Be certain of an applicant's qualifications before asking that person to take a leadership position.

1 Tim 5:23 It is unclear why Paul gave this advice to Timothy. Perhaps contaminated water had led to Timothy's indigestion, and so he should stop drinking only water. Whatever the reason, this statement is not an invitation to overindulgence or alcoholism.

1 Tim 6:1-2 In Paul's culture there was a great social and legal gulf separating masters and slaves. But as Christians, masters and slaves became spiritual equals, brothers and sisters in Christ Jesus (Gal 3:28). Paul did not speak against the institution of slavery, but he gave guidelines for Christian slaves and Christian masters. Some of his counsel for the master/slave relationship can be applied to the employer/employee relationship today. Employees should work hard, showing respect for their employers. In turn, employers should be fair (Eph 6:5-9; Col 3:22–4:15). Our work should reflect our faithfulness to and love for Christ.

1 Tim 6:3-5 Paul told Timothy to stay away from those who just wanted to make money from preaching and from those who strayed from the sound teachings of the Good News into quarrels that caused strife in the church. A person's understanding of the finer points of theology should not become the basis for lording it over others or for making money. Stay away from people who just want to argue.

[6]Yet true godliness with contentment is itself great
wealth. [7]After all, we brought nothing with us when
we came into the world, and we can't take anything
with us when we leave it. [8]So if we have enough food
and clothing, let us be content.
[9]But people who long to be rich fall into temptation
and are trapped by many foolish and harmful desires
that plunge them into ruin and destruction. [10]For the
love of money is the root of all kinds of evil. And some
people, craving money, have wandered from the true
faith and pierced themselves with many sorrows.

Paul's Final Instructions

1 TIMOTHY 6:11-21

But you, Timothy, are a man of God; so run from all
these evil things. Pursue righteousness and a godly life,
along with faith, love, perseverance, and gentleness.
[12]Fight the good fight for the true faith. Hold tightly
to the eternal life to which God has called you, which
you have confessed so well before many witnesses.
[13]And I charge you before God, who gives life to all, and
before Christ Jesus, who gave a good testimony before
Pontius Pilate, [14]that you obey this command without
wavering. Then no one can find fault with you from
now until our Lord Jesus Christ comes again. [15]For at
just the right time Christ will be revealed from heaven
by the blessed and only almighty God, the King of all
kings and Lord of all lords. [16]He alone can never die,
and he lives in light so brilliant that no human can
approach him. No human eye has ever seen him, nor
ever will. All honor and power to him forever! Amen.
[17]Teach those who are rich in this world not to be
proud and not to trust in their money, which is so
unreliable. Their trust should be in God, who richly
gives us all we need for our enjoyment. [18]Tell them
to use their money to do good. They should be rich
in good works and generous to those in need, always
being ready to share with others. [19]By doing this they
will be storing up their treasure as a good foundation
for the future so that they may experience true life.
[20]Timothy, guard what God has entrusted to you.
Avoid godless, foolish discussions with those who
oppose you with their so-called knowledge. [21]Some
people have wandered from the faith by following
such foolishness.
May God's grace be with you all.

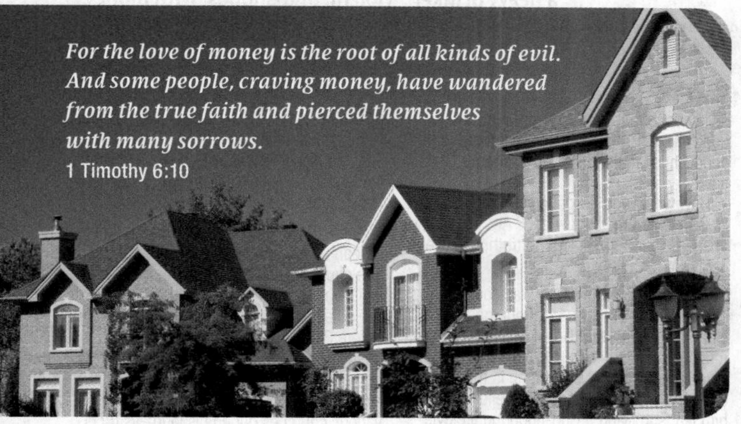

For the love of money is the root of all kinds of evil. And some people, craving money, have wandered from the true faith and pierced themselves with many sorrows.
1 Timothy 6:10

1 Tim 6:6 This statement is the key to spiritual growth and personal fulfillment. We should honor God and center our desires on him (Matt 6:33), and we should be content with what God is doing in our lives (Phil 4:11-13).

1 Tim 6:6-10 Despite overwhelming evidence to the contrary, most people still believe that money brings happiness. Rich people craving greater riches can be caught in an endless cycle that only ends in ruin and destruction. How can you keep away from the love of money? Paul gives some guidelines: (1) Realize that one day riches will all be gone (1 Tim 6:7, 17); (2) be content with what you have (1 Tim 6:8); (3) monitor what you are willing to do to get more money (1 Tim 6:9-10); (4) love people more than money (1 Tim 6:11); (5) love God's work more than money (1 Tim 6:11); (6) freely share what you have with others (1 Tim 6:18). (See Prov 30:7-9 for more on avoiding the love of money.)

1 Tim 6:8-9 "If we have enough . . . let us be content." But when is *enough* enough? How can we truly be content? There is a difference between what we need and what we want. We may have all we need to live (that is, we have enough), but we let ourselves become anxious and discontent over what we merely want. Like Paul, we can choose to be content without having all that we want. The only alternative is to be "trapped by many foolish and harmful desires" that ultimately lead only to "ruin and destruction."

1 Tim 6:11-12 Paul uses active and forceful verbs to describe the Christian life: run, pursue, fight, hold tightly. Some think Christianity is a passive religion that advocates waiting for God to act. On the contrary, we must have an active faith: training, working hard, sacrificing, and doing what we know is right. Is it time for action on your part? Christian service, like athletics, requires training and sacrifice. Our discipline and obedience largely define whether or not we will be contributors or merely spectators. How would other believers rank your contributing role on Christ's team?

1 Tim 6:13 Jesus' trial before Pilate is recorded in the Gospels: Matthew 27:11-26; Mark 15:1-15; Luke 23:1-25; John 18:28–19:16.

1 Tim 6:17-19 Ephesus was a wealthy city, and the Ephesian church probably had many wealthy members. Paul advised Timothy to deal with any potential problems by teaching that having riches carries great responsibility. If you have been blessed with wealth, then thank the Lord. Don't be proud and don't trust in your money. Use your money to do good. Be rich in good works, generous, and ready to share. No matter how much money you have, your life should demonstrate that God controls the wealth that he has placed under your care.

1 Tim 6:21 The book of 1 Timothy provides guiding principles for local churches, including rules for public worship and qualifications for elders (overseers, pastors), deacons, and special church workers (widows). Paul tells the church leaders to correct incorrect doctrine and to deal lovingly and fairly with all people in the church. The church is not organized simply for the sake of organization but so that Christ can be honored and glorified. While studying these guidelines, don't lose sight of what is most important in the life of the church—knowing God, working together in loving harmony, and taking God's Good News to the world.

S. Paul's Letter to Titus

Paul probably wrote to Titus around the same time as when he wrote 1 Timothy. Paul had sent Titus to work with the churches on the island of Crete, and this letter reflects the particular problems Titus faced in ministering there. Paul calls for church order and right living on an island known for laziness, gluttony, lying, and evil. The Christians are to be self-disciplined as individuals, and they must be orderly as people who form one body, the church. We need to obey this message in our day when discipline is not respected or rewarded by our society. Although others may not appreciate our efforts, we must live upright lives, obey the government, and control our speech. We should live together peacefully in the church and be living examples of our faith to contemporary society.

Greetings from Paul

TITUS 1:1-4

This letter is from Paul, a slave of God and an apostle of Jesus Christ. I have been sent to proclaim faith to* those God has chosen and to teach them to know the
truth that shows them how to live godly lives. [2]This
truth gives them confidence that they have eternal life, which God—who does not lie—promised them
before the world began. [3]And now at just the right time
he has revealed this message, which we announce to everyone. It is by the command of God our Savior that I have been entrusted with this work for him.
[4]I am writing to Titus, my true son in the faith that we share.

May God the Father and Christ Jesus our Savior give you grace and peace.

Titus's Work in Crete

TITUS 1:5-16

I left you on the island of Crete so you could complete our work there and appoint elders in each town as I
instructed you. [6]An elder must live a blameless life. He must be faithful to his wife,* and his children must be believers who don't have a reputation for being
wild or rebellious. [7]An elder* is a manager of God's household, so he must live a blameless life. He must not be arrogant or quick-tempered; he must not be a heavy drinker,* violent, or dishonest with money.

Ti 1:1 Or *to strengthen the faith of.* **Ti 1:6** Or *must have only one wife,* or *must be married only once;* Greek reads *must be the husband of one wife.* **Ti 1:7a** Or *An overseer,* or *A bishop.* **Ti 1:7b** Greek *must not drink too much wine.*

Titus 1:1 Paul wrote this letter between his first and second imprisonments in Rome (before he wrote 2 Timothy) to guide Titus in working with the churches on the island of Crete. Paul had visited Crete with Titus and had left him there to minister (Titus 1:5). Crete had a strong pagan influence because this island may have been a training center for Roman soldiers. Therefore, the church in Crete needed strong Christian leadership.

Titus 1:1 Paul calls himself "a slave of God"—that is, one who was committed to obeying God. This obedience led Paul to spend his life telling others about Christ. He also calls himself "an apostle." Even though Paul was not one of the original 12, he was specially called by God to bring the Good News to the Gentiles (see Acts 9:1-16 for an account of his call). The word *apostle* means "messenger or missionary." "Those God has chosen" refers to God's choice of his people, the church. For more information on Paul, see his Profile on p. 1571.

Titus 1:1 In one short phrase, Paul gives insight into his reason for living. The process begins with the proclamation of faith, continues with knowledge of the truth, which is then shown by people living godly lives. Paul wanted men and women to be mature in Jesus Christ. This was his ultimate objective by which he evaluated all he did.

How would your church evaluate its ultimate objectives? What specific goals, ministries, and service opportunities bring believers to faith, spiritual maturity, and godly living? Do established members reflect good Christian conduct and desire for Christian service?

How would you describe your purpose in life? To what are you devoted? Are you willing to share your faith, teach the truth, and live a godly life for all to see?

Titus 1:2 Apparently lying was commonplace in Crete (Titus 1:12). Paul made it clear at the start that God does not lie. The foundation of our faith is trust in God's character. Because God *is* truth, he is the source of all truth, and he cannot lie. Believing in him leads to living a God-honoring lifestyle (Titus 1:1). The eternal life that God has promised will be ours because he keeps his promises. Build your faith on the foundation of a trustworthy God who never lies.

Titus 1:3 Paul calls God "our Savior," as he does Christ Jesus (Titus 1:4). "God" here refers to the Father. Jesus did the work of salvation by dying for our sins, and therefore, he is our Savior; God planned the work of salvation, and he forgives our sins. Both the Father and the Son acted to save us from our sins.

Titus 1:4 Titus, a Greek, was one of Paul's most trusted and dependable co-workers. Paul had sent Titus to Corinth on several special missions to help the church in its troubles (2 Cor 7–8). Paul and Titus also had traveled together to Jerusalem (Gal 2:3) and Crete (Titus 1:5). Paul left Titus in Crete to lead the new churches that were springing up on the island. Paul's last mention of Titus is in his final recorded letter (2 Tim 4:10). Titus had leadership ability, so Paul gave him leadership responsibility, urging him to use his abilities well.

Titus 1:5 Crete, an island in the Mediterranean Sea, had a large population of Jews. The churches there were probably founded by Cretan Jews who had been in Jerusalem at Pentecost (Acts 2:11) more than 30 years before Paul wrote this letter. The work that needed completion refers to establishing correct teaching and appointing elders in every town. Paul had appointed elders in various churches during his journeys (Acts 14:23). He could not stay in each church, but he knew that these new churches needed strong spiritual leadership. Those appointed were to lead the churches by teaching sound doctrine, helping believers mature spiritually, and equipping them to live for Jesus Christ despite opposition.

Titus 1:5-9 Paul briefly describes some qualifications that the elders should have. Paul had given Timothy a similar set of instructions for the church in Ephesus (see 1 Tim 3:1-7; 5:22). Notice that most of the qualifications involve character, not knowledge or skill. A person's lifestyle and relationships provide a window into their character. Consider these qualifications as you evaluate a person for a position of leadership in your church. It is important to have leaders who can effectively preach God's Word; but it is even more important to have those who can

8Rather, he must enjoy having guests in his home,
and he must love what is good. He must live wisely and
be just. He must live a devout and disciplined life. 9He
must have a strong belief in the trustworthy message
he was taught; then he will be able to encourage others
with wholesome teaching and show those who oppose
it where they are wrong.
10For there are many rebellious people who engage
in useless talk and deceive others. This is especially
true of those who insist on circumcision for salvation. 11They must be silenced, because they are turning whole families away from the truth by their false
teaching. And they do it only for money. 12Even one of
their own men, a prophet from Crete, has said about
them, "The people of Crete are all liars, cruel animals,
and lazy gluttons."* 13This is true. So reprimand them
sternly to make them strong in the faith. 14They must
stop listening to Jewish myths and the commands of
people who have turned away from the truth.
15Everything is pure to those whose hearts are
pure. But nothing is pure to those who are corrupt
and unbelieving, because their minds and consciences are corrupted. 16Such people claim they
know God, but they deny him by the way they live.
They are detestable and disobedient, worthless for
doing anything good.

Ti 1:12 This quotation is from Epimenides of Knossos.

live out God's Word and be examples for others to follow.

Titus 1:8 Christian leaders must be known for their hospitality. In the early days of Christianity, believers housed and fed traveling evangelists and teachers. We would benefit from inviting people to eat with us—visitors, fellow church members, young people, those in need. Giving hospitality is very important today because so many people struggle with loneliness. In our self-centered society, we can show that we care by being hospitable. Christians were not to entertain false teachers (2 Jn 1:10), but this prohibition did not apply to non-Christians in general. God wants us to be generous, courteous, and hospitable with non-Christians; through our friendship, some may be won to Christ.

Titus 1:10 "Those who insist on circumcision for salvation" were the Judaizers, Jews who taught that the Gentiles had to obey all the Jewish laws before they could become Christians. This regulation confused new Christians and caused problems in many churches where Paul had preached the Good News. Paul wrote letters to several churches to help them understand that Gentile believers did not have to become Jews first in order to be Christians; God accepts anyone who comes to him in faith (see Rom 1:17; Gal 3:2-7). Although the Jerusalem council had dealt with this issue (see Acts 15), devout Jews who refused to believe in Jesus still tried to cause problems in the Christian churches. Church leaders must be alert and take action on anything that divides Christians.

Titus 1:10-14 Paul warns Titus to be on the lookout for people who teach wrong doctrines and lead others into error. Some false teachers are simply confused: They speak their misguided opinions without checking them against the Bible. Others have evil motives: They pretend to be Christians only because they can get more money, additional business, or a feeling of power from being a leader in the church. Jesus and the apostles repeatedly warned against false teachers (see Mark 13:22; Acts 20:29; 2 Thes 2:3-12; 2 Pet 3:3-7) because their teachings attack the foundations of truth

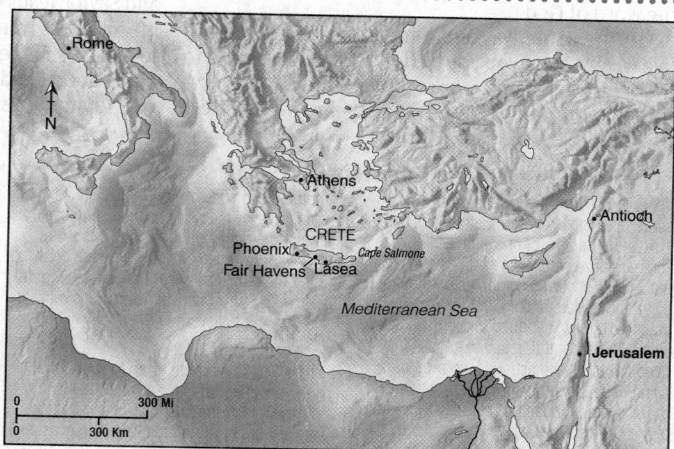

***TITUS GOES TO CRETE** Tradition says that after Paul was released from prison in Rome (before his second and final Roman imprisonment), he and Titus traveled together for a while. They stopped in Crete, and when it was time for Paul to go, he left Titus behind to help the churches there.*

and integrity upon which the Christian faith is built. You can recognize false teachers because they will (1) focus more attention on themselves than on Christ, (2) ask you to do something that will compromise or dilute your faith, (3) de-emphasize the divine nature of Christ or the inspiration of the Bible, or (4) urge believers to make decisions based more on human judgment than on prayer and biblical guidelines.

Titus 1:12 Paul is quoting a line from a poem by Epimenides, a poet and philosopher who had lived in Crete 600 years earlier. Some Cretans had a bad reputation and were known for lying. Paul used this familiar phrase to make the point that Titus's ministry and leadership were very much needed.

Titus 1:15 Some people see good all around them, while others see nothing but evil. What is the difference? Our souls become filters through which we perceive goodness or evil. The pure (those who have Christ in control of their lives) learn to see goodness and purity even in this evil world. But corrupt and unbelieving people find evil in everything because their evil minds and hearts color even the good they see and hear. Whatever you choose to fill your mind with will affect the way you think and act. Turn your thoughts to God and his Word, and you will discover more and more goodness, even in this evil world. A mind filled with good has little room for what is evil (see Phil 4:8).

Titus 1:16 Many people claim to know God. How can we know if they really do? We will not know for certain in this life, but a glance at their lifestyles will quickly tell us what they value and whether they have ordered their lives around Kingdom priorities. Our conduct speaks volumes about what we believe (see 1 Jn 2:4-6). What do people know about God and about your faith by watching your life?

Promote Right Teaching

TITUS 2:1-15

As for you, Titus, promote the kind of living that reflects wholesome teaching. 2Teach the older men to exercise self-control, to be worthy of respect, and to live wisely. They must have sound faith and be filled with love and patience.

3Similarly, teach the older women to live in a way that honors God. They must not slander others or be heavy drinkers.* Instead, they should teach others what is good. 4These older women must train the younger women to love their husbands and their children, 5to live wisely and be pure, to work in their homes,* to do good, and to be submissive to their husbands. Then they will not bring shame on the word of God.

6In the same way, encourage the young men to live wisely. 7And you yourself must be an example to them by doing good works of every kind. Let everything you do reflect the integrity and seriousness of your teaching. 8Teach the truth so that your teaching can't be criticized. Then those who oppose us will be ashamed and have nothing bad to say about us.

9Slaves must always obey their masters and do their best to please them. They must not talk back 10or steal, but must show themselves to be entirely trustworthy and good. Then they will make the teaching about God our Savior attractive in every way.

11For the grace of God has been revealed, bringing salvation to all people. 12And we are instructed to turn from godless living and sinful pleasures. We should live in this evil world with wisdom, righteousness, and devotion to God, 13while we look forward with hope to that wonderful day when the glory of our great God and Savior, Jesus Christ, will be revealed. 14He gave his life to free us from every kind of sin, to cleanse us, and to make us his very own people, totally committed to doing good deeds.

15You must teach these things and encourage the

Ti 2:3 Greek *be enslaved to much wine.* **Ti 2:5** Some manuscripts read *to care for their homes.*

Titus 2:1 Notice the emphasis on "wholesome teaching" in Paul's instructions to Titus. This is the *content* of our faith. But how can you recognize wholesome teaching? When a teaching is sound, it combines correct knowledge and understanding with consistent practice. It must be found in the Bible, keep Jesus Christ central, result in consistently good behavior and actions, and promote spiritual health in ourselves and others.

Believers must be grounded in the truths of the Bible so they won't be swayed by the powerful oratory of false teachers, the possible devastation of tragic circumstances, or the pull of emotions. Those responsible for preaching and teaching must challenge people to understand sound doctrine. Learn the Bible, study theology, apply biblical principles, and live what you learn.

Titus 2:2-8 Having people of all ages in the church makes it strong, but it also brings potential for problems. Paul gave Titus counsel on how to help various groups of people. The older people should teach the younger by words and by example. This is how values are passed on from generation to generation. Does your church carry out this basic function?

Titus 2:2, 5 Self-control is an important aspect of living the Christian life. The Christian community, then and now, is made up of people from differing backgrounds and viewpoints, making conflict inevitable. We live in a pagan and often hostile world. To stay above reproach, believers need wisdom and discernment to be discreet and to master their wills, tongues, and passions so that Christ is not dishonored. How is your self-control?

Titus 2:3-5 Women who were new Christians were to learn how to have harmony in their homes by watching older women who had been Christians for some time. We have the same need today. Young wives and mothers should learn to live in a Christian manner—loving their husbands and caring for their children—through observing exemplary women of God. If you are of an age or in a position where people look up to you, make sure that your example is motivating younger believers to live in a way that honors God.

Titus 2:6 This advice given to young men was very important. In ancient Greek society, the role of the husband/father was not viewed as a nurturing role but merely as a functional one. Many young men today have been raised in families where fathers have neglected their responsibilities to their wives and children. Husbands and fathers who are good examples of Christian living are important role models for young men who need to see how it is done.

Titus 2:7-8 Paul urges Titus to be a good example to those around him so that others might see Titus's good deeds and imitate him. Paul's life would give his words greater impact. If you want someone to act a certain way, be sure that you live that way yourself. Then you will earn the right to be heard, and your life will reinforce what you teach.

Titus 2:8 Paul counsels Titus to be above criticism in how he taught. This quality of integrity comes from careful Bible study and listening before speaking. This is especially important when teaching or confronting others about spiritual or moral issues. If we are impulsive, unreasonable, and confusing, we are likely to start arguments rather than to convince people of the truth.

Titus 2:9-10 Slavery was common in Paul's day. Paul did not condemn slavery in any of his letters, but he advised slaves and masters to be loving and responsible in their conduct (see also Eph 6:5-9). The standards set by Paul can help any employee/employer relationship. Employees should always do their best work and be trustworthy, not just when the employer is watching. Businesses lose millions of dollars a year to employee theft and time-wasting. If all Christian employees would follow Paul's advice at work, what a transformation it would make!

Titus 2:12-13 Paul brings out two aspects of Christian living that must be stressed today. "We should live in this evil world . . . while we look forward with hope." Both aspects—living and looking forward—are essential to our Christian sanity in this present evil age. The living is made bearable because we live for God—seeking to build his Kingdom with whatever gifts he has given us. And it is that very Kingdom to which we are looking forward. As we live and look forward, we anticipate three great benefits of Christ's return: (1) Christ's personal presence—we look forward to being with him. (2) Redemption from our sinful nature—we long for the end of the battle with sin and our perfection in Christ. (3) Restoration of creation—we anticipate the complete rule of grace when the image of God will be fully realized in people and when the created order will be restored.

Titus 2:14 Christ's freeing us from sin opens the way for him to cleanse us. He freed us from sin (redeemed us) by purchasing our release from the captivity of sin with a ransom (see Mark 10:45 for more on Christ as our ransom). We are not only free from the sentence of death for our sin, but we are also purified from sin's influence as we grow in Christ.

Titus 2:15 Paul tells Titus to teach the Scriptures as well as to live them. We must also teach, encourage, and correct others, when necessary. We can easily feel afraid when others are older, more influential in the community, or wealthier. Like Titus, we

believers to do them. You have the authority to correct
them when necessary, so don't let anyone disregard
what you say.

Do What Is Good

TITUS 3:1-11

Remind the believers to submit to the government and
its officers. They should be obedient, always ready to
do what is good. 2They must not slander anyone and
must avoid quarreling. Instead, they should be gentle
and show true humility to everyone.
3Once we, too, were foolish and disobedient. We
were misled and became slaves to many lusts and
pleasures. Our lives were full of evil and envy, and we
hated each other.
4But—"When God our Savior revealed his kindness
and love, 5he saved us, not because of the righteous
things we had done, but because of his mercy. He
washed away our sins, giving us a new birth and new
life through the Holy Spirit.* 6He generously poured
out the Spirit upon us through Jesus Christ our Savior.
7Because of his grace he declared us righteous and
gave us confidence that we will inherit eternal life."
8This is a trustworthy saying, and I want you to insist
on these teachings so that all who trust in God will
devote themselves to doing good. These teachings
are good and beneficial for everyone.
9Do not get involved in foolish discussions about
spiritual pedigrees* or in quarrels and fights about
obedience to Jewish laws. These things are useless
and a waste of time. 10If people are causing divisions
among you, give a first and second warning. After that,
have nothing more to do with them. 11For people like
that have turned away from the truth, and their own
sins condemn them.

Paul's Final Remarks and Greetings

TITUS 3:12-15

I am planning to send either Artemas or Tychicus to
you. As soon as one of them arrives, do your best to

Ti 3:5 Greek *He saved us through the washing of regeneration and renewing of the Holy Spirit.* **Ti 3:9** Or *spiritual genealogies.*

should not let ourselves be threatened when we are trying to minister to others or provide leadership in the church.

Titus 3:1 As Christians, our first allegiance is to Jesus as Lord, but we must obey our government and its leaders as well. Christians are not above the law. Obeying the civil law is only the beginning of our Christian responsibility; we must do what we can to be good citizens. (See Acts 5:29; Rom 13:1ff for more on the Christian's attitude toward government.)

Titus 3:2 How does one "show true humility"? Humility is a very elusive character trait, yet the Bible regards it as a highly important quality. Jesus referred to himself as "humble and gentle at heart" (Matt 11:29). In Romans 12:3, Paul wrote the clearest definition of humility apart from Jesus' own example: "Don't think you are better than you really are. Be honest in your evaluation of yourselves, measuring yourselves by the faith God has given us."

Humility, then, boils down to having an honest estimate of ourselves before God. We show false humility when we project negative worth on our abilities and efforts. We show pride when we inflate the value of our efforts or look down on others. True humility seeks to view our character and accomplishments honestly. Recognizing that we have succeeded in an effort need not be pride.

Titus 3:3 Following a life of pleasure and giving in to every sensual desire leads to slavery. Many think freedom consists of doing anything they want. But this path leads to a slavish addiction to sensual gratification; the person is no longer free but is a slave to what the body dictates (2 Pet 2:19). Christ frees us from the desires and control of sin. Have you been released?

Titus 3:4-8 Paul summarizes what Christ does for us when he saves us. We move from a life full of sin to one where we are led by God's Holy Spirit. All our sins, not merely some, are washed away. Washing refers to the water of baptism, which is a sign of salvation. In becoming a Christian, the believer acknowledges Christ as Lord and recognizes Christ's saving work. We gain eternal life with all its treasures. We have a new life through the Holy Spirit, and he continually renews our hearts. None of this occurs because we earned or deserved it; it is all God's gift.

Titus 3:4-6 All three persons of the Trinity are mentioned in these verses because all three participate in the work of salvation. Based upon the redemptive work of his Son, the Father forgives us and sends the Holy Spirit to wash away our sins and continually renew us.

Titus 3:8 In Titus 3, Paul stresses that believers must devote themselves to doing good. Paul understands good works as faithful service, acts of charity, and involvement in civil affairs. While good works can't save us or even increase God's love for us, they are true indications of our faith and love for Christ. Paul did not make this aspect of discipleship optional. Service to others is a requirement. Everyone who is a Christian should be involved. Does your church encourage everyone's involvement and service? What can your church do to help every member identify the good works they should be doing?

Titus 3:9 Paul warns Titus, as he warned Timothy, not to get involved in foolish and unprofitable arguments (2 Tim 2:14). This does not mean we should refuse to study, discuss, and examine different interpretations of difficult Bible passages. Paul is warning against petty quarrels, not honest discussion that leads to wisdom. If foolish arguments develop, it is best to turn the discussion back to a helpful direction or politely excuse yourself.

Titus 3:9 The false teachers were basing their heresies on spiritual pedigrees and speculations about the Jewish laws (see 1 Tim 1:3-4). Similar to the methods used by false teachers in Ephesus and Colosse, they were building their case on genealogies of angels. We should avoid false teachers, not even bothering to get involved in their foolish discussions. Overreaction sometimes gives more attention to their points of view.

Titus 3:10-11 A person who causes division that threatens the unity of the church must be warned. This should not be a heavy-handed action but a warning to correct the individual's divisive nature and restore them to fellowship. Anyone who refuses to be corrected should be put outside the fellowship. As Paul said, that person is self-condemned—he or she is sinning and knows it. (See also Matt 18:15-18; 2 Thes 3:14-15 for help in handling such problems in the church.)

Titus 3:12 The city of Nicopolis was on the western coast of Greece. Artemas or Tychicus would take over Titus's work on the island of Crete so Titus could meet Paul in Nicopolis. Tychicus was another of Paul's trusted companions (Acts 20:4; Eph 6:21; Col 4:7). Titus would have to leave soon because sea travel was dangerous in the winter months.

▸ **TITUS 3:12-15** ***(cont.)***
meet me at Nicopolis, for I have decided to stay there for the winter. 13Do everything you can to help Zenas the lawyer and Apollos with their trip. See that they are given everything they need. 14Our people must learn to do good by meeting the urgent needs of others; then they will not be unproductive.

15Everybody here sends greetings. Please give my greetings to the believers—all who love us.

May God's grace be with you all.

T. Paul's Second Letter to Timothy

This personal letter is the last word we have from the apostle Paul. It was probably written a few years after 1 Timothy and Titus, after Paul had been imprisoned again in Rome. This time, it looks as though Paul would not be released from prison alive, and he wrote this letter to pass the torch to a new generation of church leaders. Paul gives helpful advice to Timothy to remain solidly grounded in Christian service and to endure suffering during the difficult days to come. It is easy for us to serve Christ for the wrong reasons: because it is exciting, rewarding, or personally enriching. Without a proper foundation, however, we will find it easy to quit during difficult times. All believers need a strong foundation for their service.

Greetings from Paul

2 TIMOTHY 1:1-2

This letter is from Paul, chosen by the will of God to be an apostle of Christ Jesus. I have been sent out to tell others about the life he has promised through faith in Christ Jesus.

2I am writing to Timothy, my dear son.

May God the Father and Christ Jesus our Lord give you grace, mercy, and peace.

AD 64

Paul writes his second letter to Timothy

Encouragement to Be Faithful

2 TIMOTHY 1:3-18

Timothy, I thank God for you—the God I serve with a clear conscience, just as my ancestors did. Night and day I constantly remember you in my prayers. 4I long to see you again, for I remember your tears as we parted. And I will be filled with joy when we are together again. 5I remember your genuine faith, for you share the faith that first filled your grandmother Lois and your

Titus 3:13 Apollos was a famous Christian preacher. A native of Alexandria in North Africa, he became a Christian in Ephesus and was trained by Aquila and Priscilla (Acts 18:24-28; 1 Cor 1:12).

Titus 3:15 The letters of Paul to Titus and Timothy are his last writings and mark the end of his life and ministry. These letters are rich treasures for us today because they give vital information for church leadership. They provide a strong model for elders, pastors, and other Christian leaders as they develop younger leaders to carry on the work, following Paul's example of preparing Timothy and Titus to carry on his ministry. For practical guidelines on church leadership and problem solving, carefully study the principles found in these letters.

2 Tim 1:1 This letter has a somber tone. Paul had been imprisoned for the last time, and he knew he would soon die. Unlike Paul's first imprisonment in Rome, when he was in a house (Acts 28:16, 23, 30) where he continued to teach, this time he was probably confined to a cold dungeon, awaiting his death (2 Tim 4:6-8). Emperor Nero had begun a major persecution in A.D. 64 as part of his plan to pass the blame for the great fire of Rome from himself to the Christians. This persecution spread across the empire and included social ostracism, public torture, and murder. As Paul was waiting to die, he wrote a letter to his dear friend Timothy, a younger man who was like a son to him (2 Tim 1:2). Written in approximately A.D. 66/67, these are the last words we have from Paul.

2 Tim 1:1 When we are united with Christ, life takes on both immediate and eternal dimensions. Paul's use of the phrase, "life he has promised," can apply to the life that Jesus gives immediately to those who trust him, as well as to the life fully realized in eternity. On the one hand, Paul said, "Anyone who belongs to Christ has become a new person" (2 Cor 5:17). So new life begins at conversion. Yet on the other hand, we "wait with eager hope for the day when God will give us our full rights as his adopted children, including the new bodies he has promised us" (Rom 8:23). The present experience we enjoy provides a foretaste of our complete redemption at Christ's return. When we struggle with difficulties in this life, remember that the best is yet to come.

2 Tim 1:2 Paul's second letter to Timothy was written about two to four years after his first letter. Timothy had been Paul's traveling companion on the second and third missionary journeys, and Paul had left him in Ephesus to help the church there (1 Tim 1:3-4). For more information on Timothy, see his Profile on p. 1727. For more information on the great missionary Paul, see his Profile on p. 1571.

2 Tim 1:3 Paul consistently prayed for Timothy, his friend, his fellow traveler, his son in the faith, and a strong leader in the Christian church. Although the two men were separated from each other, their prayers provided a source of mutual encouragement. We, too, should pray consistently for others, especially for those who do God's work. On your prayer list, include your pastor, other church leaders, and missionaries around the world. They need your prayers.

2 Tim 1:4 We don't know when Paul and Timothy last parted, but it might have been when Paul was arrested and taken to Rome for his second imprisonment. The tears they shed at parting revealed the depth of their relationship.

2 Tim 1:5 Timothy's mother and grandmother, Eunice and Lois, were early Christian converts, possibly through Paul's ministry in their home city, Lystra (Acts 16:1). They had communicated their strong Christian faith to Timothy, even though his father was probably not a believer. Don't hide your light at home; our families are fertile fields for planting seeds of the Good News. Let your parents, children, spouse, brothers, and sisters know of your faith in Jesus, and be sure they see Christ's love, helpfulness, and joy in you.

2 Tim 1:6 At the time of his ordination, Timothy had received special gifts of the Spirit to enable him to serve the church (see 1 Tim 4:14). In telling Timothy to "fan into flames the spiritual gift God gave you," Paul was encouraging him to persevere. Timothy did not need new revelations or new gifts; he needed the courage and self-discipline to hang on to the truth and to use the gifts he

mother, Eunice. And I know that same faith continues strong in you. [6]This is why I remind you to fan into flames the spiritual gift God gave you when I laid my hands on you. [7]For God has not given us a spirit of fear and timidity, but of power, love, and self-discipline.

[8]So never be ashamed to tell others about our Lord. And don't be ashamed of me, either, even though I'm in prison for him. With the strength God gives you, be ready to suffer with me for the sake of the Good News. [9]For God saved us and called us to live a holy life. He did this, not because we deserved it, but because that was his plan from before the beginning of time—to show us his grace through Christ Jesus. [10]And now he has made all of this plain to us by the appearing of Christ Jesus, our Savior. He broke the power of death and illuminated the way to life and immortality through the Good News. [11]And God chose me to be a preacher, an apostle, and a teacher of this Good News.

[12]That is why I am suffering here in prison. But I am not ashamed of it, for I know the one in whom I trust, and I am sure that he is able to guard what I have entrusted to him* until the day of his return.

[13]Hold on to the pattern of wholesome teaching you learned from me—a pattern shaped by the faith and love that you have in Christ Jesus. [14]Through the power of the Holy Spirit who lives within us, carefully guard the precious truth that has been entrusted to you.

[15]As you know, everyone from the province of Asia has deserted me—even Phygelus and Hermogenes.

[16]May the Lord show special kindness to Onesiphorus and all his family because he often visited and encouraged me. He was never ashamed of me because I was in chains. [17]When he came to Rome, he searched everywhere until he found me. [18]May the Lord show him special kindness on the day of Christ's return. And you know very well how helpful he was in Ephesus.

2 Tm 1:12 Or *what has been entrusted to me.*

---

had already received (see 2 Tim 1:13-14). If Timothy would step out boldly in faith and proclaim the Good News once again, the Holy Spirit would go with him and give him power. When you use the gifts God has given you, you will find that God will give you the power you need to accomplish whatever task he gives you.

2 Tim 1:6 Clearly Timothy's spiritual gift had been given to him when Paul and the elders had laid their hands on him and set him apart for ministry (see 1 Tim 4:14). God gives all Christians gifts to use to build up the body of Christ (see 1 Cor 12:4-31), and he gives special gifts to some through church leaders, who serve as God's instruments.

2 Tim 1:6-7 Timothy was experiencing great opposition to his message and to himself as a leader. His youth, his association with Paul, and his leadership had come under fire from believers and nonbelievers alike. Paul urged him to be bold. When we allow people to intimidate us, we neutralize our effectiveness for God. The power of the Holy Spirit can help us overcome our fear of what some might say or do to us so that we can continue to do God's work.

2 Tim 1:7 Paul mentions three characteristics of the effective Christian leader: power, love, and self-discipline. These are available to us because the Holy Spirit lives in us. Follow his leading each day so that your life will more fully exhibit these characteristics. (See Gal 5:22-23 for a list of the by-products of the Holy Spirit living in us.)

2 Tim 1:8 In this time of mounting persecution, Timothy may have been afraid to continue preaching the Good News. His fears were based on fact because believers were being arrested and executed. Paul told Timothy to expect suffering—Timothy, like Paul, would be jailed for preaching the Good News (Heb 13:23). But Paul promised Timothy that God would give him strength and that he would be ready when it was his turn to suffer. Even when there is no persecution, sharing our faith in Christ can be difficult. Fortunately we, like Paul and Timothy, can rely on the Holy Spirit to give us courage. Don't be ashamed to testify of your personal faith in Jesus Christ.

2 Tim 1:9-10 In these verses Paul gives a brief summary of the Good News. God loves us, chose us, and sent Christ to die for us. We can have eternal life through faith in him because he broke the power of death with his resurrection. We do not deserve to be saved, but God offers us salvation anyway. What we must do is believe in him and accept his offer.

2 Tim 1:12 In spite of the suffering that might have caused Paul to despair, he affirmed his confidence in God's protection. This was not a claim to strong faith; rather, it was a trust in one so powerful that even a weak faith was sufficient. Paul based his confidence in Christ on his intimate relationship with him. Paul knew the one in whom he trusted with a personal knowledge; he knew Christ so well that no earthly experience could break the bond of love by which Christ held him. If your situation looks bleak, give your concerns to Christ because you know him and love him. Realize that he will guard all you have entrusted to him until the day of his return. (For more on our security in Christ, see Rom 8:38-39.)

2 Tim 1:12 The phrase "guard what I have entrusted to him" could mean: (1) Paul knew that God would protect the souls of those converted through his preaching; (2) Paul trusted God to guard his own soul until Christ's second coming; or (3) Paul was confident that, though he was in prison and facing death, God would carry out the Good News ministry through others such as Timothy. Paul may have expressed his confidence to encourage Timothy, who was undoubtedly discouraged by the problems in Ephesus and fearful of persecution. Even in prison, Paul knew that God was still in control. No matter what problems we face, we can trust fully in God.

2 Tim 1:13-14 Timothy was in a time of transition. He had been Paul's bright young helper; soon he would be on his own as leader of a church in a difficult environment. Although his responsibilities were changing, Timothy was not without help. He had everything he needed to face the future if he would hold on tightly to the Lord's resources. When you are facing difficult transitions, follow Paul's advice to Timothy and look back at your experience. Who is the foundation of your faith? How can you build on that foundation? What gifts has the Holy Spirit given you? Use the gifts you have been given.

2 Tim 1:15-16 Nothing more is known about Phygelus and Hermogenes, who evidently opposed Paul's ministry. These men serve as a warning that even leaders can fall. Onesiphorus was mentioned as a positive example in contrast to these men.

A Good Soldier of Christ Jesus

2 TIMOTHY 2:1-14

Timothy, my dear son, be strong through the grace that
God gives you in Christ Jesus. [2]You have heard me teach
things that have been confirmed by many reliable witnesses. Now teach these truths to other trustworthy
people who will be able to pass them on to others.
[3]Endure suffering along with me, as a good soldier
of Christ Jesus. [4]Soldiers don't get tied up in the affairs
of civilian life, for then they cannot please the officer
who enlisted them. [5]And athletes cannot win the prize
unless they follow the rules. [6]And hardworking farmers should be the first to enjoy the fruit of their labor.
[7]Think about what I am saying. The Lord will help you
understand all these things.
[8]Always remember that Jesus Christ, a descendant
of King David, was raised from the dead. This is the
Good News I preach. [9]And because I preach this Good
News, I am suffering and have been chained like a
criminal. But the word of God cannot be chained.
[10]So I am willing to endure anything if it will bring
salvation and eternal glory in Christ Jesus to those
God has chosen.
[11]This is a trustworthy saying:

If we die with him,
we will also live with him.
12 If we endure hardship,
we will reign with him.
If we deny him,
he will deny us.
13 If we are unfaithful,
he remains faithful,
for he cannot deny who he is.

[14]Remind everyone about these things, and command them in God's presence to stop fighting over
words. Such arguments are useless, and they can ruin
those who hear them.

---

2 Tim 2:1 How can someone be strong through grace? Grace is God's undeserved favor on our behalf. Just as we are saved by God's grace (Eph 2:8-9), we should live by it (Col 2:6). This means trusting completely in Christ and his power, and not trying to live for Christ in our strength alone. Receive and utilize Christ's power. He will give you the strength to do his work.

2 Tim 2:2 If the church were to consistently follow this advice, it would expand geometrically as well-taught believers would teach others and commission them, in turn, to teach still others. Disciples need to be equipped to pass on their faith; our work is not done until new believers are able to make disciples of others (see Eph 4:12-13).

2 Tim 2:3 The body of Christ contains all believers who have ever lived, not just those who are alive now. When we suffer, we share in a common experience not just with those alive today but with all those who have ever suffered for the sake of the gospel. All the martyrs, missionaries, and pioneers of the faith had to face what we face. Let us have the same courage, commitment, and willingness to renounce worldly pleasure in order to serve God. Can you face the challenge? "Therefore, since we are surrounded by such a huge crowd of witnesses to the life of faith, let us strip off every weight that slows us down, especially the sin that so easily trips us up. And let us run with endurance the race God has set before us" (Heb 12:1).

2 Tim 2:3-7 As Timothy preached and taught, he would face suffering, but he should be able to endure. Paul used comparisons with soldiers, athletes, and farmers who must discipline themselves and be willing to sacrifice to achieve the results they want. Like soldiers, we have to give up worldly security and endure rigorous discipline. Like athletes, we must train hard and follow the rules. Like farmers, we must work extremely hard and be patient. But we keep going despite suffering because of the thought of victory, the vision of winning, and the hope of harvest. We will see that our suffering is worthwhile when we achieve our goal of glorifying God, winning people to Christ, and one day living eternally with him.

2 Tim 2:7 Paul told Timothy to think about his words, and God would give him understanding. God speaks through the Bible, his Word, but we need to be open and receptive to him. As you read the Bible, ask God to show you his timeless truths and their application to your life. Then consider what you have read by thinking it through and meditating on it. God will give you understanding.

2 Tim 2:8 False teachers were a problem in Ephesus (see Acts 20:29-30; 1 Tim 1:3-11). At the heart of false teaching is an incorrect view of Christ. In Timothy's day many asserted that Christ was divine but not human—God but not man. These days we often hear that Jesus was human but not divine—man but not God. Either view destroys the good news that Jesus Christ has taken our sins upon himself and has reconciled us to God. In this verse, Paul firmly states that Jesus is fully man ("a descendant of King David") and fully God ("raised from the dead"). This is an important doctrine for all Christians. (For more on this key concept, see the note on Phil 2:5-7, p. 1719.)

2 Tim 2:9 Paul was in chains in prison because of the Good News he preached. The truth about Jesus is no more popular in our day than in Paul's, but it still reaches receptive hearts. When Paul said that Jesus was God, he angered the Jews who had condemned Jesus for blasphemy, but many Jews became followers of Christ (1 Cor 1:24). He angered the Romans who worshiped the emperor as god, but even some in Caesar's household turned to Jesus (Phil 4:22). When Paul said Jesus was human, he angered the Greeks, who thought divinity was soiled if it had contact with humanity, but many Greeks still accepted the faith (Acts 11:20-21). The truth that Jesus is one person with two united natures has never been easy to understand, but that doesn't make it untrue. The truth of God's Word is being believed by people every day and changing their lives for eternity. Despite the opposition, continue to proclaim Christ. Some will listen and believe.

2 Tim 2:11-13 This is probably an early Christian hymn. God is faithful to his children. Although we may suffer great hardships here, God promises that someday we will live eternally with him. What will this involve? It means believers will live in Christ's Kingdom, and that we will share in the administration of that Kingdom. This truth comforted Paul as he went through suffering and death. Are you facing hardships? Don't turn away from God—he promises you a wonderful future with him. (For more information about living eternally with God, see Matt 16:24-27; 19:28-30; Luke 22:28-30; Rom 5:17; 6:8; 8:10-11, 17; 1 Cor 15:42-58; Col 3:3-4; 1 Thes 4:13-18; Rev 3:21; 21:1–22:21.)

2 Tim 2:13 Jesus is faithful. He will stay by our side even when we have endured so much that we seem to have no faith left. We may be faithless at times, but Jesus is faithful to his promise to be with us "to the end of the age" (Matt 28:20). Refusing Christ's help will break our communication with God, but he will never turn his back on us even though we may turn our backs on him.

2 Tim 2:14-16 Paul urged Timothy to remind the believers not to argue over unimportant details ("fighting over words") or have foolish discussions because such arguments are confusing, useless, and even harmful. False teachers loved to cause strife and divisions by their meaningless quibbling over unimportant details (see 1 Tim 6:3-5). To explain the word of truth correctly, we must study what the Word of God says so we can understand what it means.

An Approved Worker

2 TIMOTHY 2:15-26

Work hard so you can present yourself to God and
receive his approval. Be a good worker, one who does
not need to be ashamed and who correctly explains
the word of truth. 16 Avoid worthless, foolish talk that
only leads to more godless behavior. 17 This kind of talk
spreads like cancer,* as in the case of Hymenaeus and
Philetus. 18 They have left the path of truth, claiming
that the resurrection of the dead has already occurred;
in this way, they have turned some people away from
the faith.

19 But God's truth stands firm like a foundation
stone with this inscription: "The LORD knows those
who are his,"* and "All who belong to the LORD must
turn away from evil."*

20 In a wealthy home some utensils are made of
gold and silver, and some are made of wood and clay.
The expensive utensils are used for special occasions,
and the cheap ones are for everyday use. 21 If you keep
yourself pure, you will be a special utensil for honorable use. Your life will be clean, and you will be ready
for the Master to use you for every good work.

22 Run from anything that stimulates youthful lusts.
Instead, pursue righteous living, faithfulness, love, and
peace. Enjoy the companionship of those who call on
the Lord with pure hearts.

23 Again I say, don't get involved in foolish, ignorant
arguments that only start fights. 24 A servant of the
Lord must not quarrel but must be kind to everyone,
be able to teach, and be patient with difficult people.
25 Gently instruct those who oppose the truth. Perhaps
God will change those people's hearts, and they will
learn the truth. 26 Then they will come to their senses
and escape from the devil's trap. For they have been
held captive by him to do whatever he wants.

2 Tm 2:17 Greek *gangrene.* **2 Tm 2:19a** Num 16:5. **2 Tm 2:19b** See Isa 52:11.

Work hard so you can present yourself to God and receive his approval.
2 Timothy 2:15

2 Tim 2:15 Because God will examine what kind of workers we have been for him, we should build our lives on his Word and build his Word into our lives. It alone tells us how to live for him and serve him. Believers who ignore the Bible will certainly be ashamed at the judgment. Consistent and diligent study of God's Word is vital; otherwise we will be lulled into neglecting God and our true purpose for living.

2 Tim 2:16 In important areas of Christian teaching, we must carefully work through our disagreements. But when we bicker long hours over words and theories that are not central to the Christian faith and life, we only provoke anger and hurt feelings. Even if "foolish talk" reaches a resolution, it gains little ground for the Kingdom. Learning and discussing are not bad unless they keep believers constantly focusing on false doctrine or unhelpful trivialities. Don't let anything keep you from service to God.

2 Tim 2:17-18 Hymenaeus was also mentioned in 1 Timothy 1:20. Paul had turned Hymenaeus over to Satan because his false teaching concerning the resurrection was destroying some people's faith.

2 Tim 2:18 The false teachers were denying the resurrection of the body. They believed that when a person became a Christian, he or she was spiritually reborn, and that was the only resurrection there would ever be. To them, resurrection was symbolic and spiritual, not physical. Paul clearly taught, however, that believers will be resurrected after they die, and that their bodies as well as their souls will live eternally with Christ (1 Cor 15:35ff; 2 Cor 5:1-10; 1 Thes 4:15-18). We should not try to shape the doctrines of Scripture to match our opinions. If we do, we are putting ourselves above God. Instead, our beliefs should be consistent with God's Word.

2 Tim 2:19 False teachers still spout lies. Some distort the truth, some dilute it, and some simply delete it by saying that God's truth no longer applies. But no matter how many people follow the liars, the solid foundation of God's truth never changes, is never shaken, and will never fade. When we follow God's truth, we will live God's way.

2 Tim 2:20-21 Here Paul urged Timothy to be the kind of person Christ could use for his noblest purposes. Don't settle for less than God's highest and best. Allow him to use you as an instrument of his will. You do this by staying close to him and keeping yourself pure so that sin and its consequences do not get in the way of what God can do in your life. While God can redeem any situation, how much better it is to stay close to Christ and ready to be used by him at a moment's notice.

2 Tim 2:22 Running away is sometimes considered cowardly. But wise people realize that removing themselves physically from temptation often can be the most courageous action to take. Timothy, a young man, was warned to run from anything that produced evil thoughts. Do you have a recurring temptation that you find difficult to resist? Remove yourself physically from any situation that stimulates your desire to sin. Knowing when to run is as important in spiritual battle as knowing when and how to fight. (See also 1 Tim 6:11.)

2 Tim 2:23-26 As a teacher, Timothy helped those who were confused about the truth. Paul's advice to Timothy, and to all who teach God's truth, is to be kind and gentle, patiently and courteously explaining the truth. Good teaching never promotes quarrels or foolish arguments. Whether you are teaching Sunday school, leading a Bible study, or preaching in church, remember to listen to people's questions and treat them respectfully, while avoiding foolish debates. If you do this, those who oppose you will be more willing to hear what you have to say and perhaps turn from their error.

The Dangers of the Last Days

2 TIMOTHY 3:1-9

You should know this, Timothy, that in the last days
there will be very difficult times. 2For people will love
only themselves and their money. They will be boastful and proud, scoffing at God, disobedient to their
parents, and ungrateful. They will consider nothing
sacred. 3They will be unloving and unforgiving; they
will slander others and have no self-control. They will
be cruel and hate what is good. 4They will betray their
friends, be reckless, be puffed up with pride, and love
pleasure rather than God. 5They will act religious, but
they will reject the power that could make them godly.
Stay away from people like that!
6They are the kind who work their way into people's
homes and win the confidence of* vulnerable women
who are burdened with the guilt of sin and controlled
by various desires. 7(Such women are forever following
new teachings, but they are never able to understand
the truth.) 8These teachers oppose the truth just as
Jannes and Jambres opposed Moses. They have depraved minds and a counterfeit faith. 9But they won't
get away with this for long. Someday everyone will
recognize what fools they are, just as with Jannes and
Jambres.

Paul's Charge to Timothy

2 TIMOTHY 3:10–4:8

But you, Timothy, certainly know what I teach, and
how I live, and what my purpose in life is. You know
my faith, my patience, my love, and my endurance.
11You know how much persecution and suffering I
have endured. You know all about how I was persecuted in Antioch, Iconium, and Lystra—but the Lord
rescued me from all of it. 12Yes, and everyone who
wants to live a godly life in Christ Jesus will suffer persecution. 13But evil people and impostors will flourish. They will deceive others and will themselves be
deceived.
14But you must remain faithful to the things you

2 Tm 3:6 Greek *and take captive.*

---

2 Tim 3:1 Paul's reference to the "last days" reveals his sense of urgency. The last days began after Jesus' resurrection when the Holy Spirit came upon the believers at Pentecost. The "last days" will continue until Christ's second coming. This means that *we* are living in the last days. So we should make the most of the time that God has given us (Eph 5:16; Col 4:5).

2 Tim 3:1ff In many parts of the world today, being a Christian is not especially difficult—people aren't typically jailed for reading the Bible or executed for preaching Christ. (This kind of persecution is very real for believers in many parts of the world even today.) Paul's descriptive list of behavior in the last days describes our society—even, unfortunately, the behavior of many Christians. Check your life against Paul's list. Don't give in to society's pressures. Don't settle for comfort without commitment. Stand up against evil by living as God would have his people live.

2 Tim 3:4 Why is it so tempting to "love pleasure rather than God"? Pleasure is something we can control; God cannot be controlled. Most pleasures can be obtained easily; love for God requires effort and sacrifice. Pleasure benefits us now; the benefits of loving God are often in the future. Pleasure has a narcotic effect—it takes our minds off ourselves and our problems. Love for God reminds us of our needs and our responsibilities. Pleasure cooperates with pride: It makes us feel good when we look good in the eyes of others. To love God we must lay aside our pride and our accomplishments. Have you chosen to love pleasure, or to love God? How do you know?

2 Tim 3:5 The "act" or appearance of being religious includes going to church, knowing Christian doctrine, using Christian clichés, and following a community's Christian traditions. Such practices can make a person look good, but if the inner attitudes of belief, love, and worship are lacking, the outer appearance is meaningless. Paul warns us not to be deceived by people who only appear to be Christians. It may be difficult to distinguish them from true Christians at first, but their daily behavior will give them away. The characteristics described in 2 Timothy 3:2-4 are unmistakable.

2 Tim 3:6-7 Because of their cultural background, women in the Ephesian church had received no formal religious training. They enjoyed their new freedom to study Christian truths, but their eagerness to learn made them a target for false teachers. Paul warned Timothy to watch out for men who would take advantage of these women. New believers need to grow in their knowledge of the Word because ignorance can make them vulnerable to deception.

2 Tim 3:7 This verse is not opposing study and learning; it is warning about ineffective learning. It is possible to be a perpetual student and never graduate to putting theory into practice. But honest seekers and true students look for answers. Remember this as you study God's Word. Seek to find God's truth and will for your life. Then do as he says.

2 Tim 3:8-9 According to tradition, Jannes and Jambres were two of the magicians who had counterfeited Moses' miracles before Pharaoh (Exod 7:11-12). Paul explained that just as Moses had exposed and defeated them (Exod 8:18-19), God would overthrow the false teachers who were plaguing the Ephesian church.

2 Tim 3:9 We can hide our sin for a while, but eventually the truth will be revealed. Sooner or later, distraction, opposition, anger, or fatigue will wear us down, and our true hearts will be exposed. The trials of life will conspire against our efforts to maintain a religious front. We can't pick when and where we will be tested by adversity. Build your character carefully because it will come out under stress. Live each day as if your actions will one day be known to everyone. It is useless, in the middle of a test, to acknowledge that you should have prepared. Now is the time to change anything you wouldn't want revealed later.

2 Tim 3:11 In Lystra, Timothy's hometown, Paul had been stoned and left for dead (Acts 14:19); and this was only one incident among many. In 2 Corinthians 11:23-33 Paul summarized his lifetime of suffering for the sake of the Good News. Paul mentioned his suffering here to contrast his experience with that of the pleasure-seeking false teachers.

2 Tim 3:12 In this charge, Paul told Timothy that people who obey God and live for Christ will be persecuted. Don't be surprised when people misunderstand, criticize, and even try to hurt you because of what you believe and how you live. Don't give up. Continue to live as you know you should. God is the only one you need to please.

2 Tim 3:13 Don't expect false teachers and evil people to reform and change on their own. Left alone, they will go from bad to worse. If you have the opportunity, correct them so as to bring them back to faith in Christ. Fight for the truth, especially to protect younger Christians.

2 Tim 3:14 Besieged by false teachers and the inevitable pressures of a growing ministry, Timothy could easily have abandoned his faith or modified his doctrine. Once again Paul counseled Timothy to look to his past and to hold to the basic teachings about Jesus that are eternally true. Like Timothy,

have been taught. You know they are true, for you know you can trust those who taught you. [15]You have been taught the holy Scriptures from childhood, and they have given you the wisdom to receive the salvation that comes by trusting in Christ Jesus. [16]All Scripture is inspired by God and is useful to teach us what is true and to make us realize what is wrong in our lives. It corrects us when we are wrong and teaches us to do what is right. [17]God uses it to prepare and equip his people to do every good work.

4:1I solemnly urge you in the presence of God and Christ Jesus, who will someday judge the living and the dead when he appears to set up his Kingdom: [2]Preach the word of God. Be prepared, whether the time is favorable or not. Patiently correct, rebuke, and encourage your people with good teaching.

[3]For a time is coming when people will no longer listen to sound and wholesome teaching. They will follow their own desires and will look for teachers who will tell them whatever their itching ears want to hear. [4]They will reject the truth and chase after myths.

[5]But you should keep a clear mind in every situation. Don't be afraid of suffering for the Lord. Work at telling others the Good News, and fully carry out the ministry God has given you.

[6]As for me, my life has already been poured out as

---

we are surrounded by false teachings. But we must not allow our society to distort or crowd out God's eternal truth. Spend time every day reflecting on the foundation of your Christian faith found in God's Word, the great truths that build up your life.

2 Tim 3:15 Timothy was one of the first second-generation Christians: He became a Christian, not because an evangelist preached a powerful sermon, but because his mother and grandmother had taught him the holy Scriptures when he was a small child (2 Tim 1:5). A parent's work is vitally important. At home and in church, we should realize that teaching small children is both an opportunity and a responsibility. Jesus wanted little children to come to him (Matt 19:13-15). Like Timothy's mother and grandmother, Eunice and Lois, do your part in leading children to Christ.

2 Tim 3:15 For Timothy, the "holy Scriptures" were the books of the Old Testament. The Old Testament is important because it is God's Word, and it points to Jesus. Faith in Christ makes the whole Bible intelligible.

2 Tim 3:16 The Bible is not a collection of stories, fables, myths, or merely human ideas about God. It is not a human book. Through the Holy Spirit, God revealed his person and plan to certain believers, who wrote down his message for his people (2 Pet 1:20-21). This process is known as *inspiration.* The writers wrote from their own personal, historical, and cultural contexts. Although they used their own minds, talents, language, and style, they wrote what God wanted them to write. Scripture is completely trustworthy because God was in control of its writing. Its words are entirely authoritative for our faith and life. The Bible is "God-breathed." Read it, and use its teachings to guide your conduct.

2 Tim 3:16-17 The whole Bible is God's inspired Word. Because it is inspired and trustworthy, we should read it and apply it to our lives. The Bible is our standard for testing everything else that claims to be true. It is our safeguard against false teaching and our source of guidance for how we should live. It is our only source of knowledge about how we can be saved. God wants to show you what is true and equip you to live for him. How much time do you spend in God's Word? Read it regularly to discover God's truth and to become confident in your life and faith. Develop a plan for reading the whole Bible, not just the familiar passages.

2 Tim 3:17 In our zeal for the truth of Scripture, we must never forget its purpose—to equip us to do good. We should not study God's Word simply to increase our knowledge or to prepare us to win arguments. We should study the Bible so that we will know how to do Christ's work in the world. Our knowledge of God's Word is not useful unless it strengthens our faith and leads us to do good.

2 Tim 4:1-2 It was important for Timothy to preach the Good News so that the Christian faith could spread throughout the world. We believe in Christ today because people like Timothy were faithful to their mission. It is still vitally important for believers to spread the Good News. Over seven billion people are alive today, and most of them do not know Christ. He is coming soon, and he wants to find his faithful believers ready for him. It may be inconvenient to take a stand for Christ or to tell others about his love, but preaching the Word of God is the most important responsibility the church and its members have been given. Be prepared for, courageous in, and sensitive to God-given opportunities to tell the Good News.

2 Tim 4:2 We should always be ready to serve God in any situation, whether or not it is convenient. Be sensitive to the opportunities God gives you.

2 Tim 4:2 Paul told Timothy to "correct, rebuke, and encourage." It is difficult to accept correction, to be told we have to change. But no matter how much the truth hurts, we must be willing to listen to it so we can more fully obey God.

2 Tim 4:3-5 Many speakers, teachers, and writers talk about the pursuit of knowledge. But often they don't want knowledge; they want power. Such people won't listen to "sound and wholesome teaching." Instead, they "reject the truth and chase after myths." You can see this everywhere—from university campuses to even some churches. People claiming to have a bit more enlightenment than what the dusty Bible has to say; people claiming to improve on God's words. Such people have several things in common: (1) *They do not tolerate the truth.* They have no interest in or respect for absolute truth or for any standard of judgment. (2) *They reject truth for sensationalism.* They want truth that fits their situation and makes sense for them. What they feel, what works for them, what seems compelling—that is their truth and they claim an absolute right to it. No one should even attempt to tell them differently. (3) *They gather viewpoints to suit their selfish desires.* Although they profess objectivity, their only defense for their viewpoints is that those viewpoints suit their desires.

Such teachers have a following because they are telling people "whatever their itching ears want to hear." These people are following myths. Be careful. False teaching can be found in many places—even inside the doors of some churches. Like Timothy, you must "keep a clear mind in every situation" and seek God's Word for the truth.

2 Tim 4:5 To keep cool when you are jarred and jolted by people or circumstances, don't react quickly. In any work of ministry that you undertake, keeping a clear mind in every situation makes you morally alert to temptation, resistant to pressure, and vigilant when facing heavy responsibility.

2 Tim 4:6-8 As he neared the end of his life, Paul could confidently say that he had been faithful to his call. Thus, he faced death calmly, knowing that he would be rewarded by Christ. Is your life preparing you for death? Do you share Paul's confident expectation of meeting Christ? The good news is that the heavenly reward is not just for giants of the faith like Paul, but for all who are eagerly looking forward to Christ's second coming. Paul gave these words to encourage Timothy and us, so that no matter how difficult the fight seems, we can keep fighting. When we are with Jesus Christ, we will discover that it was all worth it.

▸ **2 TIMOTHY 3:10–4:8** ***(cont.)***

an offering to God. The time of my death is near. [7]I
have fought the good fight, I have finished the race,
and I have remained faithful. [8]And now the prize
awaits me—the crown of righteousness, which the
Lord, the righteous Judge, will give me on the day of
his return. And the prize is not just for me but for all
who eagerly look forward to his appearing.

Paul's Final Words

2 TIMOTHY 4:9-18

Timothy, please come as soon as you can. [10]Demas has
deserted me because he loves the things of this life
and has gone to Thessalonica. Crescens has gone to
Galatia, and Titus has gone to Dalmatia. [11]Only Luke is
with me. Bring Mark with you when you come, for he
will be helpful to me in my ministry. [12]I sent Tychicus
to Ephesus. [13]When you come, be sure to bring the
coat I left with Carpus at Troas. Also bring my books,
and especially my papers.*
[14]Alexander the coppersmith did me much harm,
but the Lord will judge him for what he has done.
[15]Be careful of him, for he fought against everything
we said.
[16]The first time I was brought before the judge, no
one came with me. Everyone abandoned me. May it
not be counted against them. [17]But the Lord stood
with me and gave me strength so that I might preach
the Good News in its entirety for all the Gentiles to
hear. And he rescued me from certain death.* [18]Yes,
and the Lord will deliver me from every evil attack
and will bring me safely into his heavenly Kingdom.
All glory to God forever and ever! Amen.

Paul's Final Greetings

2 TIMOTHY 4:19-22

Give my greetings to Priscilla and Aquila and those living in the household of Onesiphorus. [20]Erastus stayed
at Corinth, and I left Trophimus sick at Miletus.
[21]Do your best to get here before winter. Eubulus
sends you greetings, and so do Pudens, Linus, Claudia,
and all the brothers and sisters.*
[22]May the Lord be with your spirit. And may his
grace be with all of you.

2 Tm 4:13 Greek *especially the parchments.* **2 Tm 4:17** Greek *from the mouth of a lion.* **2 Tm 4:21** Greek *brothers.*

AD 64

Paul martyred

Miletus Amphitheater

Miletus was an important Greek city located at the mouth of the Menderes (historically Maeander) River. It was settled by Cretans as early as 1399–1288 B.C. The Hittite Empire claimed Miletus as a vassal. Excavations indicate that Miletus, once destroyed by fire, was later surrounded by a defensive wall (13th century B.C.). The photograph shows an ancient theater in Miletus.

Miletus was well known in New Testament times, though it was not an important center to early Christianity. The apostle Paul stopped there on his third missionary journey (Acts 20:15-17). While there, he called for the Ephesian elders and exhorted them to care for the flock in their charge (Acts 20:28-35). The same admonition applies today to all those who are church leaders; they should care for their churches, the flocks of God, feeding them with the true gospel and shepherding them in the paths of righteousness.

2 Tim 4:8 In Roman athletic games, a laurel wreath would be given to each winner. A symbol of triumph and honor, it was the most coveted prize in ancient Rome. This is probably what Paul was referring to when he spoke of a "crown." But his would be a crown of righteousness. (See 2 Cor 5:10 and the note on Matt 19:27, p. 1420, for more on the rewards awaiting us for our faith and deeds.) Although Paul would not receive an earthly reward, he would be rewarded in heaven. Whatever we may face—discouragement, persecution, or death—we know we will receive our rewards from Christ in heaven.

2 Tim 4:9-10 Paul was virtually alone and probably lonely. No one had come to his trial to speak in his defense (2 Tim 4:16), and Demas had left the faith (2 Tim 4:10). Crescens and Titus had left, but not for the same reasons as Demas. Paul did not criticize or condemn them. Demas had been one of Paul's co-workers (Col 4:14; Phlm 1:24), but he had deserted Paul because he loved "the things of this life." In other words, Demas loved worldly values and worldly pleasures. There are two ways to love the world. God loves the world as he created it and as it could be if it were rescued from evil. Others, like Demas, love the world as it is, sin and all. Do you love the world as it could be if justice were done, the hungry were fed, and people loved one another? Or do you love what the world has to offer—wealth, power, pleasure—even if gaining it means hurting people and neglecting the work God has given you to do?

2 Tim 4:11-12 Mentioning Demas reminded Paul of more faithful co-workers. Luke had traveled much with Paul, writing both the Gospel of Luke and the book of Acts (much of which is a firsthand account). Tychicus, one of his most trusted companions (Acts 20:4; Eph 6:21; Col 4:7; Titus 3:12), had already left for Ephesus.

That Paul requested for Timothy to bring Mark might give us pause. Mark had left Paul and Barnabas on the first missionary journey, and this had greatly upset Paul (Acts 13:13; 15:36-41), causing a rift between Paul and Barnabas that was so severe that they parted company. Somewhere along the line, Paul had given Mark a second chance and Mark had proven to be a worthy helper. We don't have all the details in Mark's changed life or Paul's change of heart, but Paul realized that people can change.

There's a lesson in these few words. We should allow people to grow up and not hold them back from ministry or leadership for faults in the past that have now been corrected. When we encourage someone and open our minds to the possibility that they have changed and matured, we may be salvaging a significant ministry. Mark went on not only to be Paul's good friend and a trusted

U. Peter's First Letter to Christians

Peter was probably in Rome, suffering great persecution at the hands of Emperor Nero. Throughout the Roman Empire, Christians were being tortured and killed for their faith. Peter wrote to Jewish Christians who were experiencing this persecution. He wrote to comfort them with the hope of eternal life and to challenge them to continue living holy lives. Those who suffer for being Christians become partners with Christ in his suffering. As we suffer, we must remember that Christ is both our hope in the midst of suffering and our example of how to endure suffering faithfully.

Greetings from Peter

1 PETER 1:1-2

This letter is from Peter, an apostle of Jesus Christ.

I am writing to God's chosen people who are living as foreigners in the provinces of Pontus, Galatia, Cappadocia, Asia, and Bithynia.* [2]God the Father knew you and chose you long ago, and his Spirit has made you holy. As a result, you have obeyed him and have been cleansed by the blood of Jesus Christ.

May God give you more and more grace and peace.

1 Pt 1:1 *Pontus, Galatia, Cappadocia, Asia,* and *Bithynia* were Roman provinces in what is now Turkey.

Christian leader (Col 4:10; Phlm 1:24), but he also wrote the Gospel of Mark.

2 Tim 4:13 Paul's arrest probably had occurred so suddenly that he had not been allowed to return home to gather his personal belongings. Because he was a prisoner in a damp and chilly dungeon, Paul asked Timothy to bring him his coat. Even more than the coat, Paul wanted his papers (or parchments). These may have included parts of the Old Testament, copies of his own letters, or other important documents.

2 Tim 4:14-15 Alexander may have been a witness against Paul at his trial. He may have been the Alexander mentioned in 1 Timothy 1:20.

2 Tim 4:17 With his mentor in prison and his church in turmoil, Timothy was probably not feeling very brave. Paul may have been subtly telling Timothy that the Lord had called Timothy to preach and would give him the courage to continue to do so. God always gives us the strength to do what he has commanded. This strength may not be evident until we step out in faith and actually begin doing the task.

2 Tim 4:18 Here Paul was affirming his belief in eternal life after death. Paul knew the end was near, and he was ready for it. Paul was confident in God's power even as he faced death. Anyone facing a life-and-death struggle can be comforted knowing that God will bring each believer safely through death to his heavenly Kingdom.

2 Tim 4:19-20 Priscilla and Aquila were fellow Christian leaders with whom Paul had lived and worked (Acts 18:2-3). Onesiphorus visited and encouraged Paul in jail. Erastus was one of Paul's trusted companions (Acts 19:22), as was Trophimus (Acts 20:4; 21:29).

2 Tim 4:19-22 Paul ended the final chapter in his book and in his life by greeting those who were closest to him. Although Paul had spent most of his life traveling, he had developed close and lasting friendships. Too often we rush through our days, barely touching anyone's life. Do you have a Paul—a mentor or teacher who provides leadership, accountability, and encouragement? Do you have a Priscilla or Aquila—a co-worker or peer who prays with you in times of stress, loves you, and supports you? Do you have a Timothy—a younger leader whom you are helping, encouraging, and discipling? Like Paul, we should take time to weave our lives into others' through close personal relationships.

2 Tim 4:22 As Paul reached the end of his life, he could look back and know he had been faithful to God's call. Now it was time to pass the torch to the next generation, preparing leaders to take his place so that the world would continue to hear the life-changing message of Jesus Christ. Timothy was Paul's living legacy, a product of Paul's faithful teaching, discipleship, and example. Because of Paul's work with many believers, including Timothy, the world is filled with believers today who are also carrying on the work. What legacy will you leave behind? Whom are you training to carry on your work? It is our responsibility to do all we can to keep God's Good News alive for the next generation.

1 Pet 1:1 The apostle Peter wrote this letter to encourage believers who would likely face trials and persecution under Emperor Nero. During most of the first century, Christians were not hunted down and killed throughout the Roman Empire. They could expect social and economic persecution from three main sources: the Romans, the Jews, and their own families. All would very likely be misunderstood; some would be harassed; a few would be tortured and even put to death.

The legal status of Christians in the Roman Empire was unclear. Many Romans still thought of Christians as members of a Jewish sect, and because the Jewish religion was legal, they considered Christianity legal also—as long as Christians complied with the empire's laws. However, they became the target of persecution when they refused to worship the emperor as a god, refused to worship at pagan temples (so business for these moneymaking enterprises dropped wherever Christianity took hold), or exposed and rejected the horrible immorality of pagan culture.

Many Jews did not appreciate being legally associated with Christians. As the book of Acts frequently records, Jews occasionally harmed Christians physically, drove them out of town, or attempted to turn Roman officials against them. Saul, who became the great apostle Paul, was an early Jewish persecutor of Christians.

Another source of persecution was the Christian's own family. Under Roman law, the head of the household had absolute authority over all its members. Unless the ruling male became a Christian, the wife, children, and servants who were believers might well face extreme hardship. If they were sent away, they would have no place to turn but the church; if they were beaten, no court of law would uphold their interests.

Peter may have been writing especially for new Christians and those planning to be baptized. Peter wanted to warn them about what lay ahead, and they needed his encouraging words to help them face opposition. This letter is still helpful for any Christians facing trials. Many Christians around the world are living under governments more repressive than the Roman Empire of the first century. Christians everywhere are subject to misunderstanding, ridicule, and even harassment by unbelieving friends, employers, and family members. None of us is exempt from catastrophe, pain, illness, and death—trials that, like persecution, make us lean heavily on God's grace. For today's readers, as well as for Peter's original audience, the theme of this letter is *hope.*

1 Pet 1:1 Peter (also called Simon and Cephas) was one of the 12 disciples chosen by Jesus (Mark 1:16-18; John 1:42) and along with James and John was part of the inner group that Jesus singled out for special training and fellowship. Peter was one of the first to recognize Jesus as the Messiah, God's Son, and Jesus gave him a special leadership role in the church (Matt 16:16-19; Luke 22:31-32; John 21:15-19). Although during Jesus' trial Peter denied knowing Jesus, Peter repented and became a great apostle. For more information on Peter, see his Profile on p. 1473.

1 Pet 1:1 This letter is addressed to "God's chosen people who are living as foreigners" in various parts of the world—the Jewish Christians scattered throughout the world as a result of persecution against believers in and around Jerusalem. The first believers and

AD 64 *Peter writes his first letter to Christians*

The Hope of Eternal Life

1 PETER 1:3-12

All praise to God, the Father of our Lord Jesus Christ.
It is by his great mercy that we have been born again,
because God raised Jesus Christ from the dead. Now
we live with great expectation, 4and we have a priceless
inheritance—an inheritance that is kept in heaven for
you, pure and undefiled, beyond the reach of change
and decay. 5And through your faith, God is protecting
you by his power until you receive this salvation, which
is ready to be revealed on the last day for all to see.
6So be truly glad.* There is wonderful joy ahead,
even though you have to endure many trials for a
little while. 7These trials will show that your faith is

1 Pt 1:6 Or *So you are truly glad.*

leaders of the early church were Jews. When they became Christians, they didn't give up their Jewish heritage, just as you didn't give up your nationality when you became a follower of Christ. Because of persecution, these believers had been scattered throughout the Roman world (this scattering is described in Acts 8:1-4). Persecution didn't stop the spread of the Good News; instead, persecution served as a way to introduce the Good News to the whole empire. Thus, the churches to whom Peter wrote also included Gentile Christians.

1 Pet 1:2 Peter encouraged his readers by this strong declaration that they were *chosen* by God the Father. At one time, only the nation of Israel could claim to be God's chosen people; but through Christ, all believers—Jews and Gentiles—belong to God. Our salvation and security rest on God's merciful choice; no trials or persecutions can take away the eternal life he gives to those who believe in him.

1 Pet 1:2 This verse mentions all three members of the Trinity: God the Father, God the Son (Jesus Christ), and God the Holy Spirit. All members of the Trinity work to bring about our salvation. The Father chose us before we chose him (Eph 1:4). Jesus Christ, the Son, died for us while we were still sinners (Rom 5:6-10). The Holy Spirit brings us the benefits of salvation and sets us apart (makes us holy, sanctifies us) for God's service (2 Thes 2:13).

1 Pet 1:2 How did God *choose* us? Don't we make our own choices? God alone originates and accomplishes our salvation because of his grace; we do nothing to earn it. Being chosen in no way removes the necessity for people to choose to follow. The fact that God knows all events and decisions beforehand, even ordains them beforehand, does not mean that he forces the actions of his creatures or leaves them with no choice. Instead, God's foreknowledge means that he took the initiative and chose people before they had done anything to deserve it. God had intimate knowledge of these future believers; he knew who would believe, and he knew them personally. Those chosen ones were known by God the Father as a father knows his children, except that God knew about them from eternity past. God is not trapped in time—what he knows is from eternity past into eternity future. Believers are chosen, but not against their will. When the time comes, they accept the gospel message.

1 Pet 1:3 The term *born again* refers to spiritual birth (regeneration)—the Holy Spirit's act of bringing believers into God's

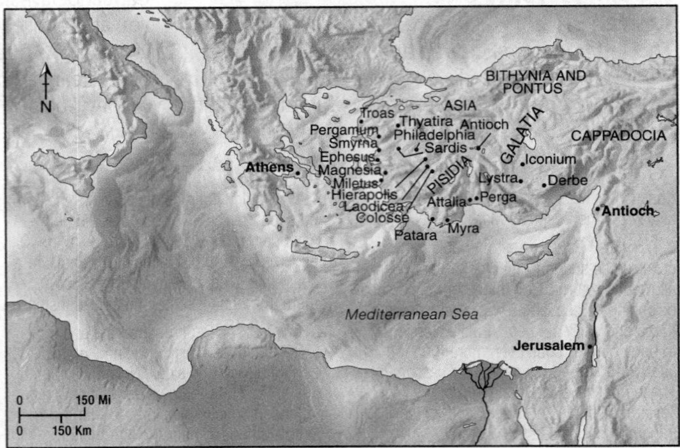

***THE CHURCHES OF PETER'S LETTER** Peter addressed his letter to the churches located throughout Bithynia, Pontus, Asia, Galatia, and Cappadocia. Paul had evangelized many of these areas; other areas had churches that were begun by the Jews who were in Jerusalem on the day of Pentecost and heard Peter's powerful sermon (see Acts 2:9-11).*

family. Jesus used this concept of new birth when he explained salvation to Nicodemus (see John 3). This term is a wonderful metaphor of new life from God. You cannot be a Christian without a fresh beginning based on the salvation Christ brings. To be born again is a magnificent gift from God.

1 Pet 1:3-5 Do you need encouragement? Peter's words offer joy and hope in times of trouble, and he bases his confidence on what God has done for us in Christ Jesus. We live with the wonderful expectation of eternal life (1 Pet 1:3). Our hope is not only for the future; eternal life begins when we trust Christ and join God's family. God will help us remain true to our faith through whatever difficult times we must face. The "last day" is the judgment day of Christ described in Romans 14:10; Revelation 20:11-15. No matter what trials or persecution you may face, your soul cannot be harmed if you have accepted Christ's gift of salvation. You will receive the promised rewards.

1 Pet 1:4 The Jews had looked forward to an inheritance in the Promised Land of Canaan (Num 32:19; Deut 2:12; 19:8). Although the nation had received that right of inheritance, eventually they defiled their faith through the influence of foreign nations. The people's sins had caused the promise to become only a fading memory. Christians now look forward to another inheritance, a "priceless" inheritance—eternal life in the eternal city of God. God has reserved the inheritance; it will never fade or decay; it will be unstained by sin. The best part is that *you* have an inheritance if you have trusted Christ as your Savior.

1 Pet 1:6 Why were Christians the target of persecution? (1) They refused to worship the emperor as a god and thus were viewed as atheists and traitors. (2) They refused to worship at pagan temples, so business for these moneymaking enterprises dropped wherever Christianity took hold. (3) They didn't support the Roman ideals of self, power, and conquest; and the Romans scorned the Christian ideal of self-sacrificing service. (4) They exposed and rejected the horrible immorality of pagan culture.

1 Pet 1:6-7 Peter mentions trials and suffering several times in this letter (1 Pet 1:6-7; 3:13-17; 4:12-19; 5:9). All believers face such trials when they let their light shine into the darkness. We must accept trials as part of the refining process that burns away impurities and prepares us to meet Christ. As gold is heated, impurities float to the top and can be skimmed off. Likewise, our trials, struggles, and persecutions refine and strengthen our faith, making us useful to God. Instead of asking, "Why me?" we should respond to suffering with a new set of responses: (1) *Confidence* that God knows,

genuine. It is being tested as fire tests and purifies gold—though your faith is far more precious than mere gold. So when your faith remains strong through many trials, it will bring you much praise and glory and honor on the day when Jesus Christ is revealed to the whole world.

8 You love him even though you have never seen him. Though you do not see him now, you trust him; and you rejoice with a glorious, inexpressible joy. 9 The reward for trusting him will be the salvation of your souls.

10 This salvation was something even the prophets wanted to know more about when they prophesied about this gracious salvation prepared for you. 11 They wondered what time or situation the Spirit of Christ within them was talking about when he told them in advance about Christ's suffering and his great glory afterward.

12 They were told that their messages were not for themselves, but for you. And now this Good News has been announced to you by those who preached in the power of the Holy Spirit sent from heaven. It is all so wonderful that even the angels are eagerly watching these things happen.

1 Pt 1:16 Lev 11:44-45; 19:2; 20:7.

A Call to Holy Living

1 PETER 1:13–2:3

So think clearly and exercise self-control. Look forward to the gracious salvation that will come to you when Jesus Christ is revealed to the world. 14 So you must live as God's obedient children. Don't slip back into your old ways of living to satisfy your own desires. You didn't know any better then. 15 But now you must be holy in everything you do, just as God who chose you is holy. 16 For the Scriptures say, "You must be holy because I am holy."*

17 And remember that the heavenly Father to whom you pray has no favorites. He will judge or reward you according to what you do. So you must live in reverent fear of him during your time as "foreigners in the land." 18 For you know that God paid a ransom to save you from the empty life you inherited from your ancestors. And the ransom he paid was not mere gold or silver. 19 It was the precious blood of Christ, the sinless, spotless Lamb of God. 20 God chose him as your ransom long before the world began, but he has now revealed him to you in these last days.

21 Through Christ you have come to trust in God.

---

plans, and directs our lives for the good. It's hard to calculate sometimes, but God always provides his love and strength for us. God leads us toward a better future. (2) *Perseverance* when facing grief, anger, sorrow, and pain. We express our grief, but we don't give in to bitterness and despair. (3) *Courage* because with Jesus as Brother and Savior, we need not be afraid. He who suffered for us will not abandon us. Jesus carries us through everything.

1 Pet 1:8-9 Jesus had said to his disciple Thomas, who came to believe after touching the resurrected Christ: "You believe because you have seen me. Blessed are those who believe without seeing me" (John 20:29). Peter, having heard those words, repeats them here: "You love him even though you have never seen him." That faith brings both salvation and the promise of a day when pain will end and perfect justice will begin. Faith will be rewarded and evil will be punished. But what should we do until then? The Bible's answer is simple but not easy: Because we know the future, we must faithfully serve God here and now. If today that means resolving a conflict, mending a hurt, working a dull job, confronting a belligerent child, rebuilding a marriage, or just waiting for guidance—do it all with the joy of God, who will return with his reward!

1 Pet 1:11 "The Spirit of Christ" is another name for the Holy Spirit. Before Jesus left his ministry on earth to return to heaven, he promised to send the Holy Spirit, the Counselor, to teach, help, and guide his followers (John 14:15-17, 26; 16:7). The Holy Spirit would tell them all about Jesus and would reveal his glory (John 15:26; 16:14). The Old Testament prophets, writing under the Holy Spirit's inspiration (2 Pet 1:20-21), described the coming of the Messiah. The New Testament apostles, through the inspiration of the same Spirit, preached the crucified and risen Lord.

1 Pet 1:13-14 The imminent return of Christ should motivate us to live for him. This means being mentally alert ("think clearly"), disciplined ("exercise self-control"), and focused ("look forward"). Are you ready to meet Christ, living as God's obedient child?

1 Pet 1:14-16 The God of Israel and of the Christian church is holy—he sets the standard for morality. Unlike the Roman gods, he is not warlike, adulterous, or spiteful. Unlike the gods of the pagan cults popular in the first century, he is not bloodthirsty or promiscuous. He is a God of mercy and justice who cares personally for each of his followers. Our holy God expects us to imitate him by following his high moral standards and by being both merciful and just.

1 Pet 1:14-16 Peter's words mean that all parts of our lives and character should be in the process of becoming conformed, both inwardly and outwardly, to God's standards. After people commit their lives to Christ, they sometimes still feel a pull back to their old ways. Peter tells us to be like our heavenly Father—holy in everything we do. *Holiness* means being totally devoted or dedicated to God, set aside for his special use and set apart from sin and its influence. We're to be set apart and different, not blending in with the crowd, yet not being different just for the sake of being different. God's qualities in our lives make us different. Our focus and priorities must be his. All this is in direct contrast to our old ways (1 Pet 1:14). We cannot become holy on our own, but God gives us his Holy Spirit to help us obey and to give us power to overcome sin. Don't use the excuse that you can't help slipping into sin. Rely on God's power to free you from sin's grip.

1 Pet 1:17 "Reverent fear" is the healthy respect a believer has for the all-powerful God. Because God is the Judge of all the earth, we dare not ignore him or treat him casually. We should not assume that our privileged status as God's children gives us freedom to do whatever we want. We should not be spoiled children but grateful children who love to show respect for our heavenly Father.

1 Pet 1:18-19 Slaves were ransomed when someone paid money to buy their freedom. God ransomed us from the tyranny of sin—not with money, but with the precious blood of his own Son (Rom 6:6-7; 1 Cor 6:20; Col 2:13-14; Heb 9:12). We cannot escape from sin on our own; only the life of God's Son can free us.

1 Pet 1:20 Christ's sacrifice for our sins was not an afterthought, not something God decided to do when the world spun out of control. This plan was set in motion by the all-knowing, eternal God long before the world was created. What a comfort it must have been to Jewish believers to know that Christ's coming and his work of salvation were planned by God long before the world began. This assured them that the law was not being scrapped because it didn't work but that both the law and the coming of Christ were part of God's eternal plan.

▸ 1 PETER 1:13–2:3 ***(cont.)***

And you have placed your faith and hope in God because he raised Christ from the dead and gave him great glory.

22You were cleansed from your sins when you obeyed the truth, so now you must show sincere love to each other as brothers and sisters.* Love each other deeply with all your heart.*

23For you have been born again, but not to a life that will quickly end. Your new life will last forever because it comes from the eternal, living word of God. 24As the Scriptures say,

"People are like grass;
  their beauty is like a flower in the field.
The grass withers and the flower fades.
25 But the word of the Lord remains forever."*

And that word is the Good News that was preached to you.

2:1So get rid of all evil behavior. Be done with all deceit, hypocrisy, jealousy, and all unkind speech. 2Like newborn babies, you must crave pure spiritual milk so that you will grow into a full experience of salvation. Cry out for this nourishment, 3now that you have had a taste of the Lord's kindness.

Living Stones for God's House

1 PETER 2:4-12

You are coming to Christ, who is the living cornerstone of God's temple. He was rejected by people, but he was chosen by God for great honor.

5And you are living stones that God is building into his spiritual temple. What's more, you are his holy priests.* Through the mediation of Jesus Christ, you offer spiritual sacrifices that please God. 6As the Scriptures say,

"I am placing a cornerstone in Jerusalem,*
  chosen for great honor,
and anyone who trusts in him
  will never be disgraced."*

7Yes, you who trust him recognize the honor God has given him. But for those who reject him,

"The stone that the builders rejected
  has now become the cornerstone."*

8And,

"He is the stone that makes people stumble,
  the rock that makes them fall."*

They stumble because they do not obey God's word, and so they meet the fate that was planned for them.

1 Pt 1:22a Greek *must have brotherly love.* **1 Pt 1:22b** Some manuscripts read *with a pure heart.* **1 Pt 1:24-25** Isa 40:6-8. **1 Pt 2:5** Greek *holy priesthood.* **1 Pt 2:6a** Greek *in Zion.* **1 Pt 2:6b** Isa 28:16 (Greek version). **1 Pt 2:7** Ps 118:22. **1 Pt 2:8** Isa 8:14.

1 Pet 1:22 "Sincere love" involves selfless giving; a self-centered person can't truly love. God's love and forgiveness free you to take your eyes off yourselves and to meet others' needs. By sacrificing his life, Christ showed that he truly loves you. Now you can love others by following his example and giving of yourself sacrificially.

1 Pet 1:24-25 Quoting Isaiah 40:6-8, Peter reminds believers that everything in this life—possessions, accomplishments, people—will eventually fade away and disappear. Only God's will, word, and work are permanent. We must stop grasping the temporary and begin focusing our time, money, and energy on the permanent: the Word of God and our eternal life in Christ.

1 Pet 2:2-3 One characteristic all children share is that they want to grow up—to be like an older sibling or like their parents. When we are born again, we become spiritual newborn babies. If we are healthy, we will yearn to grow. How sad it is that some people never grow up. The need for milk is a natural instinct for a baby, and it signals the desire for nourishment that will lead to growth. Once we see our need for God's Word and begin to find nourishment in Christ, our spiritual appetite will increase, and we will start to mature. How strong is your desire for God's Word?

1 Pet 2:4-8 In describing the church as God's spiritual temple, Peter drew on several Old Testament texts familiar to his Jewish Christian readers: Psalm 118:22; Isaiah 8:14; 28:16. Peter's readers would have understood the living stones to be Israel; then Peter applied the image of "cornerstone" to Christ. Once again Peter showed that the church does not cancel the Jewish heritage but fulfills it.

1 Pet 2:4-8 Peter portrays the church as a living, spiritual temple, with Christ as the foundation and cornerstone and each believer as a stone. Paul portrays the church as a body, with Christ as the head and each believer as a member (see, for example, Eph 4:15-16). Both pictures emphasize *community.* One stone is not a temple or even a wall; one body part is useless without the others. In our individualistic society, it is easy to forget our interdependence with other Christians. When God calls you to a task, remember that he is also calling others to work with you. Together your individual efforts will be multiplied.

1 Pet 2:5 What are the "spiritual sacrifices" that we offer to God? When sacrificing an animal according to God's law, a priest would kill the animal, cut it in pieces, and place it on the altar. Sacrifice was important, but even in the Old Testament God made it clear that obedience from the heart was much more important (see 1 Sam 15:22; Ps 40:6; Amos 5:21-24). God wants us, his "holy priests," to offer ourselves as living and spiritual sacrifices—daily laying aside our own desires and following him, putting all our energy and resources at his disposal, and trusting him to guide us.

1 Pet 2:6-8 No doubt Peter often thought of Jesus' words to him right after he confessed that Jesus was "the Messiah, the Son of the living God": "You are Peter . . . and upon this rock I will build my church, and all the powers of hell will not conquer it" (Matt 16:16, 18). What is the stone that really counts in the building of the church? Peter answers: Christ himself. Jesus Christ is called "the stone that makes people stumble, the rock that makes them fall." Some will stumble over Christ because they reject him or refuse to believe that he is who he says he is. But Psalm 118:22 says that "the stone that the builders rejected has now become the cornerstone," the most important part of God's building, the church. What are the characteristics of Christ, the cornerstone? (1) He is completely trustworthy; (2) he is precious to believers; and (3) though rejected by some, he is the most important part of the church. People who refuse to believe in Christ have made the greatest mistake of their lives. They have stumbled over the one person who could save them and give meaning to their lives, and they have fallen into God's hands for judgment.

1 Pet 2:9 Christians sometimes speak of "the priesthood of all believers." In Old Testament times, people did not approach God directly. A priest acted as intermediary between God and sinful human beings. With Christ's victory on the cross, that pattern changed. Now we can come directly into God's presence without fear (Heb 4:16), and we are given the responsibility of bringing others to him also (2 Cor 5:18-21). When we are united with Christ as members of his body, we join in his priestly work of reconciling God and people.

9 But you are not like that, for you are a chosen
people. You are royal priests,* a holy nation, God's
very own possession. As a result, you can show others
the goodness of God, for he called you out of the darkness into his wonderful light.

10 "Once you had no identity as a people;
now you are God's people.
Once you received no mercy;
now you have received God's mercy."*

11 Dear friends, I warn you as "temporary residents
and foreigners" to keep away from worldly desires that
wage war against your very souls. 12 Be careful to live
properly among your unbelieving neighbors. Then
even if they accuse you of doing wrong, they will see
your honorable behavior, and they will give honor to
God when he judges the world.*

Respecting People in Authority

1 PETER 2:13-17

For the Lord's sake, respect all human authority—
whether the king as head of state, 14 or the officials
he has appointed. For the king has sent them to punish
those who do wrong and to honor those who do right.
15 It is God's will that your honorable lives should
silence those ignorant people who make foolish accusations against you. 16 For you are free, yet you are
God's slaves, so don't use your freedom as an excuse
to do evil. 17 Respect everyone, and love your Christian
brothers and sisters.* Fear God, and respect the king.

Slaves

1 PETER 2:18-25

You who are slaves must accept the authority of your
masters with all respect.* Do what they tell you—not

1 Pt 2:9 Greek *a royal priesthood.* **1 Pt 2:10** Hos 1:6, 9; 2:23. **1 Pt 2:12** Or *on the day of visitation.* **1 Pt 2:17** Greek *love the brotherhood.* **1 Pt 2:18** Or *because you fear God.*

SUBMISSION

Submission is voluntarily cooperating with someone, first out of love and respect for God and then out of love and respect for that person. Submitting to unbelievers is difficult, but it is a vital part of leading them to Jesus Christ. We are not called to submit to nonbelievers to the point that we compromise our relationship with God, but we must look for every opportunity to humbly serve in the power of God's Spirit.

Submission is:	
Functional	a distinguishing of the work we are individually called to do
Relational	a loving acknowledgement of another's value as a person
Reciprocal	a mutual, humble cooperation with one another
Universal	an acknowledgment by the church of the all-encompassing lordship of Jesus Christ

1 Pet 2:9-10 People often base their self-concept on their accomplishments. But our relationship with Christ is far more important than our jobs, successes, wealth, or knowledge. We have been chosen by God as his very own, and we have been called to represent him to others. Remember that your value comes from being one of God's children, not from what you can achieve. You have worth because of what *God* does, not because of what you do.

1 Pet 2:11 As believers, we are "temporary residents and foreigners" in this world because our real home is with God. Heaven is not the pink-cloud-and-harp existence popular in cartoons. Heaven is where God lives. Life in heaven operates according to God's principles and values, and it is eternal and unshakable. The Kingdom of Heaven came to earth in the symbolism of the Jewish sanctuary (the Tabernacle and Temple), where God's presence dwelt. It came in a fuller way in the person of Jesus Christ: "God with us." It spread through the entire world as the Holy Spirit came to live in every believer.

Someday, after God judges and destroys all sin, the Kingdom of Heaven will rule every corner of this earth. John saw this day in a vision, and he cried out, "Look, God's home is now among his people! He will live with them, and they will be his people. God himself will be with them" (Rev 21:3). Our true loyalty should be to our citizenship in heaven, not to our citizenship here, because the earth will be destroyed. Our loyalty should be to God's truth, his way of life, and his dedicated people. Because we are loyal to God, we often will feel like strangers in a world that would prefer to ignore God.

1 Pet 2:12 Peter's advice sounds like Jesus' in Matthew 5:16: If your actions are above reproach, even hostile people will end up praising God. Peter's readers were scattered among unbelieving Gentiles who were inclined to believe and spread vicious lies about Christians. Gracious, godly, and winsome behavior on the part of Christians could show these rumors to be false and might even win some of the unsaved critics to the Lord. Don't write off people because they misunderstand Christianity; instead, show them Christ by your life. The day may come when those who criticize you will praise God with you.

1 Pet 2:13-17 When Peter told his readers to respect all human authority, he was speaking of the Roman Empire under Nero, a notoriously cruel tyrant. Obviously he was not telling believers to compromise their consciences; as Peter had told the high priest years earlier, "We must obey God rather than any human authority" (Acts 5:29). But in most aspects of daily life, it was possible and desirable for Christians to live according to the law of their land. Today, some Christians live in freedom while others live under repressive governments. All are commanded to cooperate with the rulers as far as conscience will allow. We are to do this "for the Lord's sake"—so that his Good News and his people will be respected. If we are to be persecuted, it should be for *obeying God,* not for breaking moral or civil laws. (For more about the Christian's relationship to government, see the note on Rom 13:1ff, p. 1668.)

1 Pet 2:16 Christians have freedom in Christ, but not freedom in the way people often use the word. Christians use freedom as a tool for a life of exuberant service. It's the foundation that God gives to us to reach our highest potential. Because God gives us freedom from religious rules and eternal guilt, we must not seek to indulge our own desires; instead, we should reach for the best God has for us. Let your freedom sing of power, joy, and love—accountable to God, devoted to others.

1 Pet 2:18-21 Many Christians were household slaves. It would be easy for them to submit to masters who were gentle and kind, but Peter encouraged loyalty and perseverance even in the face of unjust treatment. Similarly, we should submit to our employers, whether they are harsh or considerate. By so doing, we may win them to Christ by our good example. Paul gave similar advice in his letters (see Eph 6:5-9; Col 3:22–4:15), as did Jesus (Matt 5:46; Luke 6:32-36).

▸ 1 PETER 2:18-25 *(cont.)*

only if they are kind and reasonable, but even if they
are cruel. 19For God is pleased with you when you do
what you know is right and patiently endure unfair
treatment. 20Of course, you get no credit for being
patient if you are beaten for doing wrong. But if you
suffer for doing good and endure it patiently, God is
pleased with you.
21For God called you to do good, even if it means
suffering, just as Christ suffered* for you. He is your
example, and you must follow in his steps.

22 He never sinned,
 nor ever deceived anyone.*
23 He did not retaliate when he was insulted,
 nor threaten revenge when he suffered.
He left his case in the hands of God,
 who always judges fairly.
24 He personally carried our sins
 in his body on the cross
so that we can be dead to sin
 and live for what is right.
By his wounds
 you are healed.
25 Once you were like sheep
 who wandered away.
But now you have turned to your Shepherd,
 the Guardian of your souls.

1 Pt 2:21 Some manuscripts read *died.* **1 Pt 2:22** Isa 53:9.

Wives

1 PETER 3:1-6

In the same way, you wives must accept the authority
of your husbands. Then, even if some refuse to obey
the Good News, your godly lives will speak to them
without any words. They will be won over 2by observing your pure and reverent lives.
3Don't be concerned about the outward beauty
of fancy hairstyles, expensive jewelry, or beautiful
clothes. 4You should clothe yourselves instead with
the beauty that comes from within, the unfading
beauty of a gentle and quiet spirit, which is so precious to God. 5This is how the holy women of old
made themselves beautiful. They trusted God and
accepted the authority of their husbands. 6For instance, Sarah obeyed her husband, Abraham, and
called him her master. You are her daughters when
you do what is right without fear of what your husbands might do.

Example

The Greek word in 1 Peter 2:21 translated "example" is *hupogrammos*. Originally, the word was used to refer to a model or an example to be copied in writing. When students were being taught to write, they would copy each letter carefully by studying the *hupogrammos*, letter for letter. In the illustration a student is shown studying the alphabet. The word *hupogrammos* eventually was used metaphorically to denote how one person's actions or life served as an example for others. In 1 Peter 2:21, Peter presented Jesus as an example of one who suffered unjustly. Christ is the model for all believers when facing suffering or being mistreated for doing good, and as we follow his example we are also modeling Christ to the world around us.

1 Pet 2:21-22 We may suffer for many reasons. Some suffering is the direct result of our own sin; some happens because of our foolishness; some is the result of living in a fallen world. Peter is writing about suffering that comes as a result of doing good. Christ never sinned, and yet he suffered so that we could be set free. Jesus' suffering was part of God's plan (Matt 16:21-23; Luke 24:25-27, 44-47) and was intended to save us (Matt 20:28; 26:28). All who follow Jesus must be prepared to suffer (Mark 8:34-35). Our goal should be to face suffering as he did—with patience, calmness, and confidence that God is in control of the future.

1 Pet 2:24 Christ died for our sins, in our place, so we would not have to suffer the punishment we deserve. This is called *substitutionary atonement.*

1 Pet 3:1ff When a man became a Christian, he usually would bring his whole family into the church with him (see, for example, the story of the conversion of the Philippian jailer in Acts 16:29-34). By contrast, a woman who became a Christian usually came into the church alone. Under Roman law, the husband and father had absolute authority over all members of his household, including his wife. Demanding her rights as a free woman in Christ could endanger her marriage if her husband disapproved. Peter reassured Christian women who were married to unbelievers that they did not need to preach to their husbands. Under the circumstances, their best approach would be one of godly behavior: They should show their husbands the kind of self-giving love that Christ showed the church. By being exemplary wives, they would please their husbands. At the very least, the men might then allow them to continue practicing their faith. At best, their husbands would join them and become Christians too.

1 Pet 3:1-7 A changed life speaks loudly and clearly, and it is often the most effective way to influence a family member. Peter instructs Christian wives to develop inner beauty rather than being overly concerned about their outward appearance. Their husbands will be won over by their love. This does not mean that Christian women should be dowdy and frumpy; it is good to take care of oneself and look one's best. But far more important is the developing of an inner spirit of godliness. Live your Christian faith consistently in your home, so that your family will see Christ in you. True beauty begins inside (Prov 31:30).

1 Pet 3:5 To be submissive to another's authority means to cooperate voluntarily out of love and respect for God and for that person. Ideally, submission is mutual ("Submit to one another out of reverence for Christ"; Eph 5:21). Even when it is one-sided, the expression of submission can be an effective Christian witness. Jesus Christ submitted to death so that we could be saved; we may sometimes have to submit

Husbands

1 PETER 3:7

In the same way, you husbands must give honor to your wives. Treat your wife with understanding as you live together. She may be weaker than you are, but she is your equal partner in God's gift of new life. Treat her as you should so your prayers will not be hindered.

All Christians

1 PETER 3:8-12

Finally, all of you should be of one mind. Sympathize with each other. Love each other as brothers and sisters.* Be tenderhearted, and keep a humble attitude. [9]Don't repay evil for evil. Don't retaliate with insults when people insult you. Instead, pay them back with a blessing. That is what God has called you to do, and he will bless you for it. [10]For the Scriptures say,

"If you want to enjoy life
and see many happy days,
keep your tongue from speaking evil
and your lips from telling lies.
[11] Turn away from evil and do good.
Search for peace, and work to maintain it.
[12] The eyes of the Lord watch over those who do right,
and his ears are open to their prayers.
But the Lord turns his face
against those who do evil."*

Suffering for Doing Good

1 PETER 3:13-22

Now, who will want to harm you if you are eager to do good? [14]But even if you suffer for doing what is right, God will reward you for it. So don't worry or be afraid of their threats. [15]Instead, you must worship Christ as Lord of your life. And if someone asks about your Christian hope, always be ready to explain it. [16]But do this in a gentle and respectful way.* Keep your conscience clear. Then if people speak against you, they will be ashamed when they see what a good life you live because you belong to Christ. [17]Remember, it is better to suffer for doing good, if that is what God wants, than to suffer for doing wrong!

1 Pt 3:8 Greek *Show brotherly love.* **1 Pt 3:10-12** Ps 34:12-16. **1 Pt 3:16** Some English translations put this sentence in verse 15.

to unpleasant circumstances so that others will see Christ in us. (Christian submission never requires us to disobey God, remain in an unsafe situation, or participate in what our conscience forbids.) One-sided submission requires tremendous strength. We could not do it without the power of the Holy Spirit working in us.

1 Pet 3:7 When Peter says that women may be "weaker" than men, he was not implying moral or intellectual inferiority, but was recognizing women's physical limitations. Women in his day, if unprotected by men, were vulnerable to attack, abuse, and financial disaster. Women's lives may be easier today, but women are still vulnerable to criminal attack and family abuse. In spite of increased opportunities in the workplace, many women still earn less than men, and the vast majority of the poor in many countries are single mothers and their children. A man who honors his wife as a member of the weaker sex will protect, respect, help, and stay with her. He will not expect her to work full-time outside the home *and* full-time at home; he will lighten her load wherever he can. He will be sensitive to her needs, and he will relate to her with courtesy, consideration, insight, and tact.

1 Pet 3:7 If a man is not considerate and respectful of his wife, his prayers will not be heard, because a living relationship with God depends on right relationships with others. Jesus said that if you have a problem with a fellow believer, you must make it right with that person before coming to worship (Matt 5:23-24). This principle carries over into family relationships. If men use their position to mistreat their wives, their prayers will be hindered.

1 Pet 3:8 Peter lists five key elements that should characterize any group of believers: (1) one mind—pursuing the same goals; (2) sympathy—being responsive to others' needs; (3) love—seeing and treating each other as brothers and sisters; (4) tenderness—being affectionately sensitive and caring; and (5) humility—being willing to encourage one another and rejoice in each other's successes. These five qualities go a long way toward helping believers serve God effectively.

1 Pet 3:8-9 Where is God? How can we know God is real? Who says the Bible is any better than other holy books? To answer these questions, God sent his Son, Jesus Christ, as living evidence. God also chose Peter and others to show what a difference true faith makes in the real world. So here the once rash, belligerent, domineering, and arrogant Peter bears witness to a life of harmony, compassion, love, and humility. What a difference God makes! You, too, are God's witness to skeptical people. Let your life be evidence of God's truth. Let your pride become humility and your insensitivity give way to genuine affection for others.

1 Pet 3:9 In our fallen world, it is often deemed acceptable by some to tear people down verbally or to get back at them if we feel hurt. Peter, remembering Jesus' teaching to turn the other cheek (Matt 5:39), encourages his readers to pay back wrongs with a blessing, such as praying for the offenders. In God's Kingdom, revenge is unacceptable behavior, as is insulting a person, no matter how indirectly it is done. Rise above getting back at those who hurt you. Instead of reacting angrily to these people, pray for them.

1 Pet 3:10 For more about controlling your tongue, see the notes on James 3:2-18, pp. 1550-1551.

1 Pet 3:11 Too often we see peace as merely the absence of conflict, and we think of peacemaking as a passive role. But an effective peacemaker actively pursues peace by building good relationships, knowing that peace is a by-product of commitment. The peacemaker anticipates problems and deals with them before they occur. When conflicts arise, they are brought into the open and dealt with before they grow unmanageable. Making peace is hard work—you have to search for it and work to maintain it—but it results in God's blessing.

1 Pet 3:15 Some Christians believe that faith is a personal matter that should be kept to oneself. It is true that we shouldn't be boisterous or obnoxious in sharing our faith, but we should always be ready to give an answer, gently and respectfully, when asked about our faith, our lifestyle, or our Christian perspective. Can others see your hope in Christ? Are you prepared to tell them what Christ has done in your life?

1 Pet 3:16 You may not be able to keep people from speaking evil against you, but you can at least stop supplying them with ammunition. As long as you do what is right, their accusations will be empty and only embarrass them. Keep your conduct above criticism!

▶ **1 PETER 3:13-22** ***(cont.)***

18Christ suffered* for our sins once for all time. He never sinned, but he died for sinners to bring you safely home to God. He suffered physical death, but he was raised to life in the Spirit.*

19So he went and preached to the spirits in prison—20those who disobeyed God long ago when God waited patiently while Noah was building his boat. Only eight people were saved from drowning in that terrible flood.* 21And that water is a picture of baptism, which now saves you, not by removing dirt from your body, but as a response to God from* a clean conscience. It is effective because of the resurrection of Jesus Christ.

22Now Christ has gone to heaven. He is seated in the place of honor next to God, and all the angels and authorities and powers accept his authority.

Living for God

1 PETER 4:1-11

So then, since Christ suffered physical pain, you must arm yourselves with the same attitude he had, and be ready to suffer, too. For if you have suffered physically for Christ, you have finished with sin.* 2You won't spend the rest of your lives chasing your own desires, but you will be anxious to do the will of God. 3You have had enough in the past of the evil things that godless people enjoy—their immorality and lust, their feasting and drunkenness and wild parties, and their terrible worship of idols.

4Of course, your former friends are surprised when you no longer plunge into the flood of wild and destructive things they do. So they slander you. 5But remember that they will have to face God, who will judge everyone, both the living and the dead. 6That is why the Good News was preached to those who are now dead*—so although they were destined to die like all people,* they now live forever with God in the Spirit.*

7The end of the world is coming soon. Therefore, be earnest and disciplined in your prayers. 8Most important of all, continue to show deep love for each other, for love covers a multitude of sins. 9Cheerfully share your home with those who need a meal or a place to stay.

10God has given each of you a gift from his great

1 Pt 3:18a Some manuscripts read *died.* **1 Pt 3:18b** Or *in spirit.* **1 Pt 3:20** Greek *saved through water.* **1 Pt 3:21** Or *as an appeal to God for.* **1 Pt 4:1** Or *For the one [or One] who has suffered physically has finished with sin.* **1 Pt 4:6a** Greek *preached even to the dead.* **1 Pt 4:6b** Or *so although people had judged them worthy of death.* **1 Pt 4:6c** Or *in spirit.*

1 Pet 3:18-20 The meaning of preaching "to the spirits in prison" is not completely clear, and commentators have explained it in different ways. The traditional interpretation is that between his death and resurrection, Christ announced salvation to God's faithful followers who had been waiting for their salvation during the whole Old Testament era. Some think that this passage says that Christ's Spirit was in Noah as Noah preached to those imprisoned by sin (but now in hell). Still others say that Christ went to Hades to proclaim his victory and final condemnation to the fallen angels imprisoned there since Noah's day (see 2 Pet 2:4).

In any case, the passage shows that Christ's Good News of salvation and victory is not limited. While some Bible passages, such as this one, may remain unclear, we can discover certain truths from them along with the context of the rest of Scripture. In this passage, we discover that: (1) God speaks. While we puzzle over what, where, and how, we can see that God is communicating to the world. (2) God triumphs. Christ victoriously preached, indicating his power, control, and transcendence over all creation. (3) God saves. God exerts himself to rescue those who desire him. This mysterious passage tells us at least this much—and that is much indeed.

1 Pet 3:21 Peter says that Noah's salvation from the Flood symbolized baptism, a ceremony involving water. In baptism we identify with Jesus Christ, who separates us from the lost and gives us new life. It is not the ceremony that saves us; instead, the ceremony symbolizes our faith in Christ's death and resurrection. Baptism is a symbol of the cleansing that happens in the lives of those who believe (Rom 6:3-5; Gal 3:27; Col 2:12). By identifying themselves with Christ through baptism, Peter's readers could resist turning back, even under the pressure of persecution. Public baptism would keep them from the temptation to renounce their faith.

1 Pet 4:1-2 Suffering helps us be like Christ, yet people will do anything to avoid pain. Followers of Christ should be willing and prepared to do God's will and to suffer for it if necessary. We can overcome sin when we focus on Christ and what he wants us to do. Pain and danger reveal our true values. Anyone who suffers for doing good and still faithfully obeys in spite of suffering has made a clean break with sin.

1 Pet 4:3-4 People whose lives change radically at conversion may experience contempt from old friends. They may be scorned not only because they refuse to participate in certain activities but also because their priorities have changed and they are now heading in the opposite direction. Their lives incriminate their friends' sinful activities. Mature Christians should help new believers resist such pressures of opposition by helping them to be faithful to Christ, surrounding them as new friends, and encouraging them to develop new habits and activities that are not only enjoyable but positive for their spiritual growth.

1 Pet 4:5 The basis of salvation is our belief in Jesus (Acts 16:31), but the basis for judgment is how we have lived. All people will be judged: believers for the rewards they will receive; unbelievers for punishment. Those who inflict persecution are marked for punishment when they stand before God. All will give an account to God, so we must be ready. This may give you a new perspective on your activities and actions today. Are you prepared to explain them to God?

1 Pet 4:5-6 Many people in the early church had concerns about life after death. In Thessalonica, Christians worried that loved ones who died before Christ's return might never see Christ (1 Thes 4:13-18). Peter's readers needed to be reminded that the dead (both the faithful and their oppressors) will be judged. The judgment will be perfectly fair, he pointed out, because even the dead have heard the Good News (see also 1 Pet 3:18-19). The Good News was first announced when Jesus Christ preached on the earth, but it has been operating since before the creation of the world (Eph 1:4), and it affects all people, the dead as well as the living.

1 Pet 4:7-9 We should live expectantly because Christ is coming soon. Getting ready to meet Christ involves continually growing in love for God and for others (see Jesus' summary of the law in Matt 22:37-40). It is important to pray regularly and to reach out to needy people. Your possessions, status, and power will mean nothing in God's Kingdom, but you will spend eternity with other people. Invest your time and talents where they will make an eternal difference.

1 Pet 4:9 For more about hospitality, see the note on Romans 12:13, p. 1667.

1 Pet 4:10-11 We should use our abilities faithfully in serving others; none are for our own exclusive enjoyment. Some people, well aware of their abilities, believe that they have the right to use them as they please. Others

variety of spiritual gifts. Use them well to serve one another. 11 Do you have the gift of speaking? Then speak as though God himself were speaking through you. Do you have the gift of helping others? Do it with all the strength and energy that God supplies. Then everything you do will bring glory to God through Jesus Christ. All glory and power to him forever and ever! Amen.

Suffering for Being a Christian

1 PETER 4:12-19

Dear friends, don't be surprised at the fiery trials you are going through, as if something strange were happening to you. 13 Instead, be very glad—for these trials make you partners with Christ in his suffering, so that you will have the wonderful joy of seeing his glory when it is revealed to all the world.

14 So be happy when you are insulted for being a Christian,* for then the glorious Spirit of God* rests upon you.* 15 If you suffer, however, it must not be for murder, stealing, making trouble, or prying into other people's affairs. 16 But it is no shame to suffer for being a Christian. Praise God for the privilege of being called by his name! 17 For the time has come for judgment, and it must begin with God's household. And if judgment begins with us, what terrible fate awaits those who have never obeyed God's Good News? 18 And also,

> "If the righteous are barely saved,
> what will happen to godless sinners?"*

19 So if you are suffering in a manner that pleases God, keep on doing what is right, and trust your lives to the God who created you, for he will never fail you.

Advice for Elders and Young Men

1 PETER 5:1-11

And now, a word to you who are elders in the churches. I, too, am an elder and a witness to the sufferings of Christ. And I, too, will share in his glory when he is revealed to the whole world. As a fellow elder, I appeal to

1 Pt 4:14a Greek *for the name of Christ.* **1 Pt 4:14b** Or *for the glory of God, which is his Spirit.* **1 Pt 4:14c** Some manuscripts add *On their part he is blasphemed, but on your part he is glorified.* **1 Pt 4:18** Prov 11:31 (Greek version).

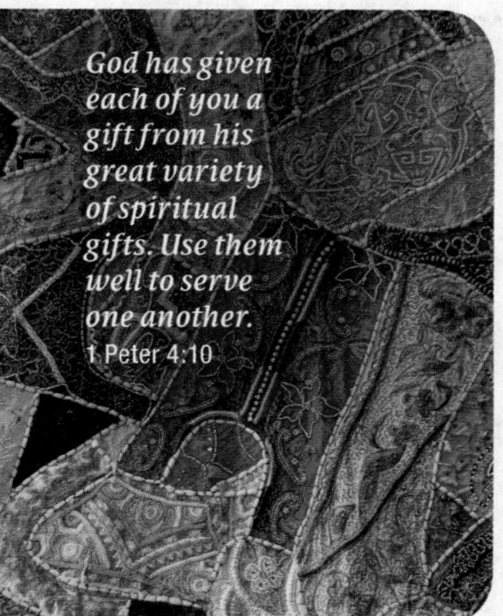
God has given each of you a gift from his great variety of spiritual gifts. Use them well to serve one another.
1 Peter 4:10

feel that they have no special talents at all. Peter addresses both groups in these verses. Everyone has some gifts; find yours and use them. Peter mentions speaking and serving. Paul lists these and other abilities (see Rom 12:6-8, 1 Cor 12:8-11; Eph 4:11). Even as you seek to discover your gifts, you might see a need in the church; look for ways to meet it. You may find gifts in areas you might not have guessed!

1 Pet 4:11 How is God glorified when we use our abilities? When we use them as he directs, to help others, they will see Jesus in us and glorify him for the help they have received. Peter may have been thinking of Jesus' words, "Let your good deeds shine out for all to see, so that everyone will praise your heavenly Father" (Matt 5:16).

1 Pet 4:14-16 Again Peter brings to mind Jesus' words: "God blesses you when people mock you and persecute you and lie about you and say all sorts of evil things against you because you are my followers" (Matt 5:11). Christ will send his Spirit to strengthen those who are persecuted for their faith. Peter creates no illusions; God's plan for your life may include pain and hardship. When trouble comes, don't be surprised.

This does not mean that all suffering is the result of good Christian conduct. Peter says to distinguish between suffering for being a believer and suffering for doing wrong things. For example, some Christians may think they are being picked on for their faith when it is obvious to everyone else that their own unpleasant behavior is the cause of their problems. It may take careful thought or wise counsel to determine the real cause of our suffering. We can be assured that whenever we suffer because of our loyalty to Christ, he will be with us all the way.

1 Pet 4:16 It is not shameful to suffer for being a Christian. When Peter and John were persecuted for preaching the Good News, they rejoiced because such persecution was a mark of God's approval of their work (Acts 5:41). Don't seek out suffering, and don't try to avoid it. Instead, keep on doing what is right whether or not it brings suffering.

1 Pet 4:17-18 This refers not to final judgment but to God's refining discipline (Heb 12:7). God often allows believers to sin and then experience the consequences. He does this for several reasons: (1) to show us our potential for sinning, (2) to encourage us to turn from sin and more constantly depend on him, (3) to prepare us to face other, even stronger temptations in the future, and (4) to help us stay faithful and keep on trusting him. If believers need earthly discipline (judgment) from God, how much more will unbelievers receive it? If the righteous are barely saved (only because of God's mercy), what chance have those who reject Christ?

1 Pet 4:19 Everywhere the Bible counsels that we trust God—in good times and bad, during sunny skies and thunderclouds, when we have a pocket full of change and a pocket full of sawdust. How does trust work? (1) *Trust overcomes fear.* Genuine trust in God says, "Whatever mess I'm in, my heavenly Father will lead me." (2) *Trust overcomes depression.* No matter how overwhelming the situation or how low it makes you feel, God can draw you back to the light. (3) *Trust overcomes hate.* When careless or cruel people hurt you, sometimes irreparably, you can hate forever or you can trust God, but you can't do both. God is there to steady even the worst situation—always with a promise, always with hope. Commit your life to him for safekeeping. Rely on him when you face your worst circumstances.

1 Pet 5:1 Elders were church officers providing supervision, protection, discipline, instruction, and direction for the other believers. *Elder* simply means "older." Both Greeks and Jews gave positions of great honor to wise older people, and the Christian church continued this pattern of leadership. Elders carried great responsibility, and they were expected to be good examples.

▸ **1 PETER 5:1-11** ***(cont.)***

you: 2Care for the flock that God has entrusted to you.
Watch over it willingly, not grudgingly—not for what
you will get out of it, but because you are eager to serve
God. 3Don't lord it over the people assigned to your
care, but lead them by your own good example. 4And
when the Great Shepherd appears, you will receive a
crown of never-ending glory and honor.

5In the same way, you younger men must accept
the authority of the elders. And all of you, serve each
other in humility, for

"God opposes the proud
but favors the humble."*

6So humble yourselves under the mighty power of
God, and at the right time he will lift you up in honor.
7Give all your worries and cares to God, for he cares
about you.

8Stay alert! Watch out for your great enemy, the
devil. He prowls around like a roaring lion, looking
for someone to devour. 9Stand firm against him, and
be strong in your faith. Remember that your Christian brothers and sisters* all over the world are going
through the same kind of suffering you are.

10In his kindness God called you to share in his
eternal glory by means of Christ Jesus. So after you
have suffered a little while, he will restore, support,
and strengthen you, and he will place you on a firm
foundation. 11All power to him forever! Amen.

Peter's Final Greetings

1 PETER 5:12-14

I have written and sent this short letter to you with
the help of Silas,* whom I commend to you as a faithful brother. My purpose in writing is to encourage
you and assure you that what you are experiencing
is truly part of God's grace for you. Stand firm in
this grace.

13Your sister church here in Babylon* sends you
greetings, and so does my son Mark. 14Greet each
other with Christian love.*

Peace be with all of you who are in Christ.

1 Pt 5:5 Prov 3:34 (Greek version). **1 Pt 5:9** Greek *your brothers.* **1 Pt 5:12** Greek *Silvanus.* **1 Pt 5:13** Greek *The elect one in Babylon.* Babylon was probably symbolic for Rome. **1 Pt 5:14** Greek *with a kiss of love.*

---

1 Pet 5:1-2 Peter, one of Jesus' original disciples, was one of the three who saw Christ's glory at the Transfiguration (Mark 9:1-13; 2 Pet 1:16-18). Often the spokesman for the apostles, Peter witnessed Jesus' death and resurrection, preached at Pentecost, and became a pillar of the Jerusalem church. But writing to the elders, he identified himself as a fellow elder, not a superior. He asked them to "care for the flock," exactly what Jesus had told him to do (John 21:15-17). Peter was taking his own advice as he worked along with the other elders in caring for God's faithful people. His identification with the elders is a good example of Christian leadership, showing that authority is based on service, not power (Mark 10:42-45).

1 Pet 5:2-5 Peter describes several characteristics of good leaders in the church: (1) They realize they are caring for God's flock, not their own; (2) they lead out of eagerness to serve, not out of obligation; (3) they are concerned for what they can give, not for what they can get; (4) they lead by example, not by force. All of us lead others in some way. Whatever our role, our leadership should be in line with these characteristics.

1 Pet 5:4 The Great Shepherd is Jesus Christ. This refers to his second coming, when he will judge all people and give rewards to his faithful followers. The "crown," while metaphorical, pictures the glory believers will receive that is eternal and unchanging. What better motivation for selfless service! What better motivation for keeping the faith in the face of suffering and temptation!

1 Pet 5:5 Both young and old can benefit from Peter's instructions. Pride often keeps older people from trying to understand young people and keeps young people from listening to those who are older. Peter told both young and old to be humble and to serve each other. Young men should follow the leadership of older men, who should lead by example. Respect those who are older than you, listen to those younger than you, and be humble enough to admit that you can learn from others.

1 Pet 5:6 We often worry about our position and status, hoping to get proper recognition for what we do. But Peter advises us to remember that God's recognition counts more than human praise. God is able and willing to bless us according to his timing. Humbly obey God regardless of present circumstances, and in his good time—either in this life or in the next—he will honor you.

1 Pet 5:7 Carrying your worries, stresses, and daily struggles by yourself shows that you have not trusted God fully with your life. It takes humility to recognize that God cares, to admit your need, and to let others in God's family help you. Sometimes we think that struggles caused by our own sin and foolishness are not God's concern. But when we turn to God in repentance, he will bear the weight even of those struggles. Letting God have your anxieties calls for action, not passivity. Don't submit to circumstances but to the Lord, who controls circumstances.

1 Pet 5:8-9 Lions attack sick, young, or straggling animals; they choose victims who are alone or not alert. Peter warns us to watch out for Satan when we are suffering or being persecuted. If you are feeling alone, weak, helpless, and cut off from other believers, or if you are so focused on your troubles that you forget to watch for danger, those are the times when you are especially vulnerable to Satan's attacks. During times of suffering, seek other Christians for support. Keep your eyes on Christ, and resist the devil. Then, says James, "he will flee from you" (Jas 4:7).

1 Pet 5:10 When we are suffering, we often feel as though our pain will never end. Peter gave these faithful Christians a broader perspective. In comparison with eternity, their suffering would last only "a little while." Some of Peter's readers would be strengthened and delivered in their own lifetimes. Others would be released from their suffering through death. All of God's faithful followers are assured of an eternal life with Christ, where there will be no suffering (Rev 21:4).

1 Pet 5:12 Silas was one of the men chosen to deliver the letter from the Jerusalem council to the church in Antioch (Acts 15:22). He accompanied Paul on his second missionary journey (Acts 15:40–18:11), is mentioned by Paul in the salutation of Paul's letters to the Thessalonians (1 Thes 1:1; 2 Thes 1:1), and ministered with Timothy in Corinth (2 Cor 1:19).

1 Pet 5:13 Mark, also called John Mark, was known to many of this letter's readers because he had traveled widely (Acts 12:25–13:13; 15:36-41) and was recognized as a leader in the church (Col 4:10; Phlm 1:24). Mark was probably with the disciples at the time of Jesus' arrest (Mark 14:51-52). Tradition says that Peter was Mark's main source of information when Mark wrote his Gospel.

1 Pet 5:14 Peter wrote this letter right around the time that the cruel emperor Nero began persecuting Christians in Rome and throughout the empire. There had been a time where, afraid for his life, Peter three times denied even knowing Jesus (John 18:15-27). But here, having learned how to stand firm in an evil world, he encouraged other Christians who were facing persecution

V. Peter's Second Letter to Christians

While Peter wrote his first letter to teach about handling persecution (trials from without), he wrote this letter to teach about handling heresy (trials from within). Peter knew that his time on earth was limited, so he wrote about what was on his heart, warning believers about how to handle false teachers when he was gone. He reminded his readers of the unchanging truth of the gospel. False teachers are often subtly deceitful. Believers today must still be vigilant against falling into false doctrine, heresy, and cult activity. This letter gives us clues to help detect false teaching and avoid it.

Greetings from Peter

2 PETER 1:1-2

This letter is from Simon* Peter, a slave and apostle
of Jesus Christ.
I am writing to you who share the same precious
faith we have. This faith was given to you because of the
justice and fairness* of Jesus Christ, our God and Savior.
2May God give you more and more grace and peace
as you grow in your knowledge of God and Jesus our
Lord.

Growing in Faith

2 PETER 1:3-11

By his divine power, God has given us everything we
need for living a godly life. We have received all of
this by coming to know him, the one who called us
to himself by means of his marvelous glory and excellence. 4And because of his glory and excellence,
he has given us great and precious promises. These
are the promises that enable you to share his divine
nature and escape the world's corruption caused by
human desires.
5In view of all this, make every effort to respond
to God's promises. Supplement your faith with a
generous provision of moral excellence, and moral
excellence with knowledge, 6and knowledge with self-
control, and self-control with patient endurance, and
patient endurance with godliness, 7and godliness with
brotherly affection, and brotherly affection with love
for everyone.
8The more you grow like this, the more productive
and useful you will be in your knowledge of our Lord
Jesus Christ. 9But those who fail to develop in this way
are shortsighted or blind, forgetting that they have
been cleansed from their old sins.
10So, dear brothers and sisters,* work hard to prove
that you really are among those God has called and
chosen. Do these things, and you will never fall away.
11Then God will give you a grand entrance into the
eternal Kingdom of our Lord and Savior Jesus Christ.

2 Pt 1:1a Greek *Symeon.* **2 Pt 1:1b** Or *to you in the righteousness.* **2 Pt 1:10** Greek *brothers.*

for their faith. Peter was eventually martyred for his faith because he lived by the words he wrote. Those who stand for Christ will be persecuted because the world is ruled by Christ's greatest enemy. But just as the small group of early believers stood against persecution, so we must be willing to stand for our faith with the patience, endurance, and courage that Peter exhibited.

2 Pet 1:1 Peter wrote this letter later than 1 Peter (perhaps between A.D. 66 and 68), after persecution had intensified. The letter of 1 Peter was encouragement to the Christians who suffered, but 2 Peter focuses on the church's internal problems, especially on the false teachers who were causing people to doubt their faith and turn away from Christianity. It combats their heresies by denouncing the evil motives of the false teachers and reaffirming Christianity's truths—the authority of Scripture, the primacy of faith, and the certainty of Christ's return.

2 Pet 1:2 Many believers want an abundance of God's grace and peace, but they are unwilling to put forth the effort to get to know him better through Bible study and prayer. To enjoy the privileges God offers us freely, we must grow in our knowledge of God and Jesus our Lord.

2 Pet 1:3-4 The power to lead a godly life comes from God. Because we don't have the resources to be truly godly, God allows us to "share his divine nature" in order to keep us from sin and help us live for him. When we are born again, God by his Spirit empowers us with his own goodness. (See John 3:6; 14:17-23; 2 Cor 5:21; 1 Pet 1:22-23.)

2 Pet 1:5-9 Faith must be more than belief in certain facts; it must result in action, growth in Christian character, and the practice of moral discipline, or it will die away (Jas 2:14-17). Peter lists several of faith's actions: learning to know God better, developing perseverance, doing God's will, loving others. These actions do not come automatically; they require hard work. They are not optional; all of them must be a continual part of the Christian life. We don't finish one and start on the next, but we work on them all together. God empowers and enables us, but he also gives us the responsibility to learn and to grow.

2 Pet 1:6 False teachers were saying that self-control was not needed because deeds do not help the believer anyway (2 Pet 2:19). It is true that deeds cannot save us, but it is absolutely false to think they are unimportant. We are saved so that we can grow to resemble Christ and serve others. God wants to produce his character in us. But to do this, he demands our discipline and effort. As we obey Christ, who guides us by his Spirit, we will develop self-control not only with respect to food and drink but also with respect to our emotions.

2 Pet 1:9 Our faith must go beyond what we believe; it must become a dynamic part of all we do, resulting in good fruit and spiritual maturity. Salvation does not *depend* on good deeds, but it *results* in good deeds. People who claim to be saved while remaining unchanged do not understand faith nor what God has done for them.

2 Pet 1:10 Peter wanted to rouse the complacent believers who had listened to the false teachers and believed that because salvation is not based on good deeds they could live any way they wanted. If you truly belong to the Lord, Peter wrote, your hard work will prove it. If you're not working to develop the qualities listed in 2 Peter 1:5-7, you may not belong to him. If you are the Lord's—and your hard work backs up your claim to be chosen by God—you will be able to resist the lure of false teaching or glamorous sin. What does your life say about your faith?

Paying Attention to Scripture

2 PETER 1:12-21

Therefore, I will always remind you about these things—even though you already know them and are standing firm in the truth you have been taught. [13]And it is only right that I should keep on reminding you as long as I live.* [14]For our Lord Jesus Christ has shown me that I must soon leave this earthly life,* [15]so I will work hard to make sure you always remember these things after I am gone.

[16]For we were not making up clever stories when we told you about the powerful coming of our Lord Jesus Christ. We saw his majestic splendor with our own eyes [17]when he received honor and glory from God the Father. The voice from the majestic glory of God said to him, "This is my dearly loved Son, who brings me great joy."* [18]We ourselves heard that voice from heaven when we were with him on the holy mountain.

[19]Because of that experience, we have even greater confidence in the message proclaimed by the prophets. You must pay close attention to what they wrote, for their words are like a lamp shining in a dark place—until the Day dawns, and Christ the Morning Star shines* in your hearts. [20]Above all, you must realize that no prophecy in Scripture ever came from the prophet's own understanding,* [21]or from human initiative. No, those prophets were moved by the Holy Spirit, and they spoke from God.

False Teachers

2 PETER 2:1-22

But there were also false prophets in Israel, just as there will be false teachers among you. They will cleverly teach destructive heresies and even deny the Master who bought them. In this way, they will bring sudden destruction on themselves. [2]Many will follow their evil teaching and shameful immorality. And because of these teachers, the way of truth will be slandered. [3]In their greed they will make up clever lies to get hold of your money. But God condemned them long ago, and their destruction will not be delayed.

[4]For God did not spare even the angels who sinned. He threw them into hell,* in gloomy pits of darkness,* where they are being held until the day of judgment.

2 Pt 1:13 Greek *as long as I am in this tent* [or *tabernacle*]. **2 Pt 1:14** Greek *I must soon put off my tent* [or *tabernacle*]. **2 Pt 1:17** Matt 17:5; Mark 9:7; Luke 9:35. **2 Pt 1:19** Or *rises.* **2 Pt 1:20** Or *is a matter of one's own interpretation.* **2 Pt 2:4a** Greek *Tartarus.* **2 Pt 2:4b** Some manuscripts read *in chains of gloom.*

2 Pet 1:12-15 Outstanding coaches constantly review the basics of the sport with their teams, and good athletes can execute the fundamentals consistently well. Believers must not neglect the basics of their faith, even as they go on to study deeper truths. Just as an athlete needs constant practice, we need constant reminders of the fundamentals of our faith and of how we came to believe in the first place. Don't allow yourself to be bored or impatient with messages on the basics of the Christian life. Instead, take the attitude of an athlete who continues to practice and refine the basics.

2 Pet 1:13-14 Peter knew that he would die soon. Many years before, Christ had prepared Peter for the kind of death he would face (see John 21:18-19). At this time, Peter knew that his death was at hand. Peter was martyred for the faith about A.D. 68. According to one tradition, he was crucified upside down, at his own request, because he did not feel worthy to die in the same manner as his Master.

2 Pet 1:16-18 Peter is referring to the Transfiguration where Jesus' divine identity was revealed to him and two other disciples, James and John (see Matt 17:1-8; Mark 9:2-8; Luke 9:28-36).

2 Pet 1:16-21 This section is a strong statement on the inspiration of Scripture. Peter affirms that the Old Testament prophets wrote God's messages. He puts himself and the other apostles in the same category because they also proclaim God's truth. The Bible is not a collection of fables or human ideas about God. It is God's very words given *through* people *to* people. Peter emphasized his authority as an eyewitness as well as the God-inspired authority of Scripture to prepare the way for his harsh words against the false teachers. If these wicked men were contradicting the apostles and the Bible, their message could not be from God.

2 Pet 1:19 Christ is a "Morning Star," and when he returns, he will shine in his full glory. Until that day we have Scripture and the Holy Spirit to illuminate it for us and guide us as we seek the truth (see also Luke 1:78; Eph 5:14; Rev 2:28; 22:16).

2 Pet 1:20-21 "Those prophets were moved by the Holy Spirit, and they spoke from God" means that Scripture did not come from the creative work of the prophets' own invention or interpretation. God inspired the writers, so their message is authentic and reliable. God used the talents, education, and cultural background of each writer (they were not mindless robots); and God cooperated with the writers in such a way to ensure that the message he intended was faithfully communicated in the very words they wrote.

2 Pet 2:1 Jesus had told the disciples that false teachers would come (Matt 24:11; Mark 13:22-23). Peter had heard these words, and at this time he was seeing them come true. Just as false prophets had contradicted the true prophets in Old Testament times (see, for example, Jer 23:16-40; 28:1-17), telling people only what they wanted to hear, so false teachers were twisting Christ's teachings and the words of his apostles. These teachers were belittling the significance of Jesus' life, death, and resurrection. Some claimed that Jesus couldn't be God; others claimed that he couldn't have been a real man. These teachers allowed and even encouraged all kinds of immorality, especially sexual sin. We must be careful to avoid false teachers today. Any book, tape series, or TV message must be evaluated in the light of God's Word. Beware of special meanings or interpretations that belittle Christ or his work.

2 Pet 2:3 Peter gives three warning signs for identifying false teachers:

(1) *Immorality.* Do their lives contain or condone immoral practices? Does the group listening to the false teachers have a lot of immoral sexual relationships?

(2) *Greed.* Teachers have a right to financial support (1 Cor 9:1-14; Gal 6:6; 1 Tim 5:17-18), but is money the teacher's or group's prime motivation? Before you send money to any cause, evaluate it carefully. Is the teacher or preacher clearly serving God or merely promoting self-interests? Will the person or organization use the money to promote valid ministry, or will it merely finance further promotions or extravagant lifestyles?

(3) *Lying.* Is the leader offended when you ask for the scriptural backing behind statements? Do facts get fudged when the leader is asked for evidence?

Believers today would do well to heed Peter's warnings against false teachers; the danger is real.

2 Pet 2:4-6 If God did not spare angels, or people who lived before the Flood, or the citizens of Sodom and Gomorrah, he would not spare these false teachers. These words that promised justice were a great comfort to those who were oppressed. God will punish all evildoers. These words also served as a warning to wanderers to not stray away from the truth. Some people would have us believe that God will save all people because he is

5And God did not spare the ancient world—except for
Noah and the seven others in his family. Noah warned
the world of God's righteous judgment. So God protected Noah when he destroyed the world of ungodly
people with a vast flood. 6Later, God condemned the
cities of Sodom and Gomorrah and turned them into
heaps of ashes. He made them an example of what will
happen to ungodly people. 7But God also rescued Lot
out of Sodom because he was a righteous man who
was sick of the shameful immorality of the wicked
people around him. 8Yes, Lot was a righteous man
who was tormented in his soul by the wickedness he
saw and heard day after day. 9So you see, the Lord
knows how to rescue godly people from their trials,
even while keeping the wicked under punishment
until the day of final judgment. 10He is especially hard
on those who follow their own twisted sexual desire,
and who despise authority.

These people are proud and arrogant, daring even
to scoff at supernatural beings* without so much as
trembling. 11But the angels, who are far greater in
power and strength, do not dare to bring from the
Lord* a charge of blasphemy against those supernatural beings.

12These false teachers are like unthinking animals,
creatures of instinct, born to be caught and destroyed.
They scoff at things they do not understand, and like
animals, they will be destroyed. 13Their destruction
is their reward for the harm they have done. They
love to indulge in evil pleasures in broad daylight.
They are a disgrace and a stain among you. They
delight in deception* even as they eat with you in
your fellowship meals. 14They commit adultery with
their eyes, and their desire for sin is never satisfied.
They lure unstable people into sin, and they are well
trained in greed. They live under God's curse. 15They
have wandered off the right road and followed the
footsteps of Balaam son of Beor,* who loved to earn
money by doing wrong. 16But Balaam was stopped
from his mad course when his donkey rebuked him
with a human voice.

17These people are as useless as dried-up springs or
as mist blown away by the wind. They are doomed to
blackest darkness. 18They brag about themselves with
empty, foolish boasting. With an appeal to twisted
sexual desires, they lure back into sin those who have
barely escaped from a lifestyle of deception. 19They
promise freedom, but they themselves are slaves of sin
and corruption. For you are a slave to whatever controls you. 20And when people escape from the wickedness of the world by knowing our Lord and Savior
Jesus Christ and then get tangled up and enslaved by
sin again, they are worse off than before. 21It would be
better if they had never known the way to righteousness than to know it and then reject the command
they were given to live a holy life. 22They prove the
truth of this proverb: "A dog returns to its vomit."*
And another says, "A washed pig returns to the mud."

2 Pt 2:10 Greek *at glorious ones,* which are probably evil angels. **2 Pt 2:11** Other manuscripts read *to the Lord;* still others do not include this phrase at all. **2 Pt 2:13** Some manuscripts read *in fellowship meals.* **2 Pt 2:15** Some manuscripts read *Bosor.* **2 Pt 2:22** Prov 26:11.

---

so loving. But it is foolish to think that God will cancel the Last Judgment. Don't ever minimize the certainty of God's judgment on those who rebel against him.

2 Pet 2:7-9 Just as God rescued Lot from Sodom, so he is able to rescue us from the temptations and trials we face in a wicked world. Lot was not sinless, but he put his trust in God and was spared when Sodom was destroyed. God also will judge those who cause temptations and trials, so we need never worry about justice being done.

2 Pet 2:10-12 The "supernatural beings" may be angels, all the glories of the unseen world, or more probably, fallen angels. A similar passage is found in Jude 1:8-10. Whoever they are, the false teachers slandered the spiritual realities they did not understand, taking Satan's power lightly and claiming to have the ability to judge evil. Many in our world today mock the supernatural. They deny the reality of the spiritual world and claim that only what can be seen and felt is real. Like the false teachers of Peter's day, they are fools who will be proven wrong in the end. Don't take Satan and his supernatural powers of evil lightly, and don't become arrogant about how defeated he will be. Although Satan will be destroyed completely, he is at work now trying to render Christians complacent and ineffective.

2 Pet 2:13-14 The fellowship meal may have been part of the celebration of the Lord's Supper—a full meal that ended with Communion. The false teachers, although they were sinning openly, took part in these meals with everyone else in the church. In one of the greatest of hypocritical acts, they attended a sacred meal designed to promote love and unity among believers, while at the same time they gossiped and slandered those who disagreed with their opinions. Paul told the Corinthians, "So anyone who eats this bread or drinks this cup of the Lord unworthily is guilty of sinning against the body and blood of the Lord" (1 Cor 11:27). These men were guilty of more than false teaching and promoting evil pleasures; they were guilty of leading others away from God's Son, Jesus.

2 Pet 2:15 Balaam was hired by a pagan king to curse Israel. He did what God told him to do for a time (Num 22–24), but eventually his evil motives and desire for money won out (Num 25:1-3; 31:16). Like the false teachers of Peter's day, Balaam used religion for personal advancement, a sin that God does not take lightly.

2 Pet 2:19 People are slaves to whatever controls them. Many believe that freedom means doing anything they want. But no one is ever completely free in that sense. If we refuse to follow God, we will follow our own sinful desires and become enslaved to what our body wants. If we submit our lives to Christ, he will free us from slavery to sin. Christ frees us to serve him, a freedom that results in our ultimate good.

2 Pet 2:20-22 Peter is speaking of people who have learned about Christ and how to be saved but then reject the truth and return to their sin. These people are worse off than before because they have rejected the only way out of sin, the only way of salvation. Like someone sinking in quicksand who refuses to grab a rescue rope, the person who turns away from Christ rejects the only means of escape (see the note on Luke 11:24-26, p. 1343).

The Day of the Lord Is Coming

2 PETER 3:1-16

This is my second letter to you, dear friends, and in both
of them I have tried to stimulate your wholesome thinking and refresh your memory. 2 I want you to remember
what the holy prophets said long ago and what our Lord
and Savior commanded through your apostles.
3 Most importantly, I want to remind you that in
the last days scoffers will come, mocking the truth
and following their own desires. 4 They will say, "What
happened to the promise that Jesus is coming again?
From before the times of our ancestors, everything has
remained the same since the world was first created."
5 They deliberately forget that God made the heavens by the word of his command, and he brought the
earth out from the water and surrounded it with water. 6 Then he used the water to destroy the ancient
world with a mighty flood. 7 And by the same word,
the present heavens and earth have been stored up
for fire. They are being kept for the day of judgment,
when ungodly people will be destroyed.
8 But you must not forget this one thing, dear
friends: A day is like a thousand years to the Lord,
and a thousand years is like a day. 9 The Lord isn't really
being slow about his promise, as some people think.
No, he is being patient for your sake. He does not want
anyone to be destroyed, but wants everyone to repent.
10 But the day of the Lord will come as unexpectedly as
a thief. Then the heavens will pass away with a terrible
noise, and the very elements themselves will disappear
in fire, and the earth and everything on it will be found
to deserve judgment.*
11 Since everything around us is going to be destroyed like this, what holy and godly lives you should
live, 12 looking forward to the day of God and hurrying
it along. On that day, he will set the heavens on fire, and
the elements will melt away in the flames. 13 But we are
looking forward to the new heavens and new earth he
has promised, a world filled with God's righteousness.
14 And so, dear friends, while you are waiting for these
things to happen, make every effort to be found living
peaceful lives that are pure and blameless in his sight.
15 And remember, our Lord's patience gives people
time to be saved. This is what our beloved brother
Paul also wrote to you with the wisdom God gave
him— 16 speaking of these things in all of his letters.
Some of his comments are hard to understand, and
those who are ignorant and unstable have twisted his
letters to mean something quite different, just as they
do with other parts of Scripture. And this will result
in their destruction.

Peter's Final Words

2 PETER 3:17-18

I am warning you ahead of time, dear friends. Be on
guard so that you will not be carried away by the errors
of these wicked people and lose your own secure footing. 18 Rather, you must grow in the grace and knowledge of our Lord and Savior Jesus Christ.
All glory to him, both now and forever! Amen.

2 Pt 3:10 Other manuscripts read *will be burned up;* still others read *will be found destroyed.*

2 Pet 3:3-4 "In the last days" scoffers will say that Jesus is never coming back, but Peter refutes their argument by explaining God's mastery over time. The "last days" is the time between Christ's first and second comings; thus, we, like Peter, live in the last days. We must do the work to which God has called us and believe that he will return as he promised.

2 Pet 3:7 In Noah's day the earth was judged by water; at the Second Coming it will be judged by fire. This fire is described in Revelation 19:20; 20:10-15.

2 Pet 3:8-9 God may have seemed slow to these believers as they faced persecution every day and longed to be delivered. But God is not slow; he just is not on *our* timetable (Ps 90:4). Jesus is waiting so that more sinners will repent and turn to him. We must not sit and wait for Christ to return, but we should realize that time is short and we have important work to do. Be ready to meet Christ any time, even today; yet plan your course of service as though he may not return for many years.

2 Pet 3:10-11 The day of the Lord is the day of God's judgment on the earth. Here it is used in reference to Christ's return. Christ's second coming will be sudden and terrible for those who do not believe in him. But if we are spiritually alert, it won't come as a surprise. (For other prophetic pictures of the day of the Lord, see Isa 34:4; Joel 3:15-16; Matt 24; Mark 13; Luke 21; Rev 6:12-17.) Realizing that the earth is going to be burned up, we should put our confidence in what is lasting and eternal and not be bound to earth and its treasures or pursuits. Do you spend more of your time piling up possessions or striving to develop Christlike character?

2 Pet 3:13 God's purpose for people is not destruction but re-creation (see Isa 66:22; Rev 21–22). God will purify the heavens and earth with fire; then he will create them anew. We can joyously look forward to the restoration of God's good world.

2 Pet 3:14 We should not become lazy and complacent because Christ has not yet returned. Instead, we should live in eager expectation of his coming. What would you like to be doing when Christ returns? That is how you should be living each day.

2 Pet 3:15-16 By the time of Peter's writing, Paul's letters already had a widespread reputation. Notice that Peter spoke of Paul's letters as if they were on a level with "other parts of Scripture." Already the early church was thinking of Paul's letters as inspired by God.

2 Pet 3:15-18 Peter and Paul had very different backgrounds and personalities, and they preached from different viewpoints. Paul emphasized salvation by grace, not law, while Peter preferred to talk about Christian life and service. The two men's ideas did not contradict each other, and they always held each other in high esteem. The false teachers intentionally misused Paul's writings by distorting them to condone lawlessness. No doubt this made the teachers popular, because people always like to have their favorite sins justified, but the net effect was to totally destroy Paul's message. Paul may have been thinking of teachers like these when he wrote in Romans 6:15: "Since God's grace has set us free from the law, does that mean we can go on sinning? Of course not!" Peter warned his readers to avoid the mistakes of those wicked teachers by growing in the special favor and knowledge of Jesus. The better we know Jesus, the less attractive false teaching will be.

2 Pet 3:18 Peter concludes this brief letter as he began, urging his readers to grow in the grace and knowledge of the Lord and Savior Jesus Christ; that is, they were to get to know him better and better. This is the best way to discern false teaching. No matter where we are in our spiritual journey, no matter how mature we are in our faith, the sinful world will always challenge our faith. We still have much room for growth. Every day we need to draw closer to Christ so that we will be prepared to stand for truth in any and all circumstances.

W. The Book of Hebrews

The book of Hebrews is difficult to date chronologically because we don't know who wrote it or precisely who it was intended for. However, it does appear to be from later in the era of the early church but before the Temple was destroyed by the Roman army in A.D. 70. The audience was likely a group of Jewish Christians who were undergoing fierce persecution socially and physically both from Jews and from Romans. The people needed to be assured that Christianity was true and that Jesus was indeed the Messiah. Hebrews is a masterful document, full of complex arguments and beautiful language. The message is that Jesus is better than any other religious figure, Christianity is superior, and Christ is supreme and completely sufficient for salvation. It is a message that has timeless application.

1. THE SUPERIORITY OF CHRIST

The relationship of Christianity to Judaism was a critical issue in the early church. The author clears up confusion by carefully explaining how Christ is superior to angels, Moses, and high priests. The new covenant is shown to be far superior to the old. This can be a great encouragement to us and help us avoid drifting away from our faith in Christ.

Jesus Christ Is God's Son

HEBREWS 1:1-4

Long ago God spoke many times and in many ways
to our ancestors through the prophets. 2And now in
these final days, he has spoken to us through his Son.
God promised everything to the Son as an inheritance, and through the Son he created the universe.
3The Son radiates God's own glory and expresses the

Heb 1:1 The book of Hebrews describes in detail how Jesus Christ not only fulfills the promises and prophecies of the Old Testament but is better than everything in the Jewish system of thought. The Jews accepted the Old Testament, but most of them rejected Jesus as the long-awaited Messiah. The recipients of this letter seem to have been Jewish Christians. They were well versed in Scripture, and they had professed faith in Christ. Whether through doubt, persecution, or false teaching, they may have been in danger of giving up their Christian faith and returning to Judaism.

The authorship of this book is uncertain. Several names have been suggested, including Luke, Barnabas, Apollos, Priscilla, and Paul. Most scholars do not believe that Paul was the author, because the writing style of Hebrews is quite different from that of his letters. In addition, Paul identified himself in his other letters and appealed to his authority as an apostle, whereas this writer of Hebrews, who never gives a name, appeals to eyewitnesses of Jesus' ministry for authority.

Heb 1:1-2 God used many approaches to send his messages to people in Old Testament times. He spoke to Isaiah in visions (Isa 6), to Jacob in a dream (Gen 28:10-22), and to Abraham and Moses personally (Gen 18; Exod 31:18). Jewish people familiar with these stories would not have found it hard to believe that God was still revealing his will, but it was astonishing for them to think that God had revealed *himself* by speaking through his Son, Jesus Christ. Jesus is the fulfillment and culmination of God's revelation through the centuries. When we know him, we have all we need to be saved from our sin and to have a perfect relationship with God.

Heb 1:2 Jesus was God's agent in creating the world: "For through him God created everything" (Col 1:16). As followers of Christ, we may give easy assent to this truth but deny it in practice. We may believe that Christ knows and controls the laws of heaven (pertaining to salvation and spiritual growth), but we may act each day as though our financial, family, or medical problems are beyond his reach. If Jesus created the universe, then no part of life is out of his control. Do not exclude Jesus' wisdom and the Bible's guidance in your complex problems of life. No expert, professor, doctor, lawyer, or financial adviser knows more about your ultimate security and well-being than Jesus does. Go first to God for advice. Talk to him in prayer and listen to him in his Word. He can sustain you in times of stress. From that perspective you can evaluate all the other wisdom and help made available to you.

Heb 1:3 Not only is Jesus the exact representation of God, but he is God himself—the very God who spoke in Old Testament times. He is eternal; he worked with the Father in creating the world (John 1:3; Col 1:16). He is the full revelation of God. You can have no clearer view of God than by looking at Christ. Jesus Christ is the complete expression of God in a human body.

Heb 1:3 The book of Hebrews links God's saving power with his creative power. In other words, the power that brought the universe into being and that keeps it operating is the very power that cleanses our sins. How mistaken we would be to ever think that God couldn't forgive us. No sin is too big for the Ruler of the universe to handle. He can and will forgive us when we come to him through his Son. That Jesus *sat down* means that the work was complete. Christ's sacrifice was final.

But we are looking forward to the new heavens and new earth he has promised, a world filled with God's righteousness.

2 Peter 3:13

▸ **HEBREWS 1:1-4** ***(cont.)***

very character of God, and he sustains everything by the mighty power of his command. When he had cleansed us from our sins, he sat down in the place of honor at the right hand of the majestic God in heaven. [4]This shows that the Son is far greater than the angels, just as the name God gave him is greater than their names.

The Son Is Greater Than the Angels

HEBREWS 1:5-14

For God never said to any angel what he said to Jesus:

"You are my Son.
Today I have become your Father.*"

God also said,

"I will be his Father,
and he will be my Son."*

[6]And when he brought his supreme* Son into the
world, God said,*

"Let all of God's angels worship him."*

[7]Regarding the angels, he says,

"He sends his angels like the winds,
his servants like flames of fire."*

[8]But to the Son he says,

"Your throne, O God, endures forever and ever.
You rule with a scepter of justice.
[9] You love justice and hate evil.
Therefore, O God, your God has anointed you,
pouring out the oil of joy on you more than on anyone else."*

[10]He also says to the Son,

"In the beginning, Lord, you laid the foundation of the earth
and made the heavens with your hands.
[11] They will perish, but you remain forever.
They will wear out like old clothing.
[12] You will fold them up like a cloak
and discard them like old clothing.
But you are always the same;
you will live forever."*

Heb 1:5a Or *Today I reveal you as my Son.* Ps 2:7. **Heb 1:5b** 2 Sam 7:14. **Heb 1:6a** Or *firstborn.* **Heb 1:6b** Or *when he again brings his supreme Son* [or *firstborn Son*] *into the world, God will say.* **Heb 1:6c** Deut 32:43. **Heb 1:7** Ps 104:4 (Greek version). **Heb 1:8-9** Ps 45:6-7. **Heb 1:10-12** Ps 102:25-27.

Heb 1:4 The "far greater" name that was given to Jesus is "Son." This name given to him by his Father is greater than the names and titles of the angels.

Heb 1:4ff False teachers in many of the early churches taught that God could be approached only through angels. Instead of worshiping God directly, followers of these heretics revered angels. Hebrews clearly denounces such teaching as false. Some thought of Jesus as the highest angel of God. But Jesus is not a superior angel, and in any case, angels are not to be worshiped (see Col 2:18; Rev 19:1-10). We should not regard any intermediaries or authorities as greater than Christ. Jesus is God. He alone deserves our worship.

Heb 1:5-6 Jesus is God's honored, firstborn Son. In Jewish families the firstborn son held the place of highest privilege and responsibility. The Jewish Christians reading this message would understand that as God's firstborn, Jesus was superior to any created being.

Heb 1:10-12 The author of Hebrews quotes Psalm 102:25-27. In the quotation, he regards God as the speaker and applies the words to the Son, Jesus. The earth and the heavens folded up like a cloak reveals that the earth is not permanent or indestructible (a position held by many Greek and Roman philosophies). Jesus' authority is established over all of creation, so we dare not treat any created object or earthly resource as more important than he is. When we spend more time on ourselves than on serving Christ, we treat ourselves (his creation) as being more important than our Creator. When we regard our finances, rather than our faith in Christ, as the basis for security, we give higher status to an earthly resource than we do to God. Rather than trusting in changeable and temporary resources, trust in God, who is eternal.

CHRIST AND THE ANGELS

The writer of Hebrews quotes from the Old Testament repeatedly in demonstrating Christ's greatness in comparison to the angels. This audience of first-century Jewish Christians had developed an imbalanced belief in angels and their role. Christ's lordship is affirmed without disrespect to God's valued angelic messengers.

Hebrews Passage	*Old Testament Passage*	*How Christ Is Superior to Angels*
Heb 1:5-6	Ps 2:7	Christ is called "Son" of God, a title never given to an angel.
Heb 1:7, 14	Ps 104:4	Angels are important but are still only servants under God.
Heb 1:8-9	Ps 45:6	Christ's Kingdom is forever.
Heb 1:10	Ps 102:25	Christ is the Creator of the world.
Heb 1:13	Ps 110:1	Christ is given unique honor by God.

Heb 1:11-12 Because the readers of Hebrews (Jewish Christians) had experienced the rejection of their fellow Jews, they often felt isolated. Many were tempted to exchange the changeless Christ for their familiar old faith. The writer of Hebrews warned them not to do this: Christ is our *only* security in a changing world. Whatever may happen in this world, Christ remains forever changeless. If we trust him, we are absolutely secure, because we stand on the firmest foundation in the universe—Jesus Christ. A famous hymn captures this truth: "On Christ the solid rock I stand, all other ground is sinking sand."

Heb 1:12 What does it mean that Christ is changeless ("you are always the same")? It means that Christ's character will never change. He persistently shows his love to us. He is always fair, just, and merciful to us who are so undeserving. Be thankful that Christ is changeless; he will always help you when you need it and offer forgiveness when you fall.

Heb 1:14 Angels are God's messengers, spiritual beings created by God and under his authority (Col 1:16). They have several functions: serving believers (Heb 1:14), pro-

13 And God never said to any of the angels,

"Sit in the place of honor at my right hand
until I humble your enemies,
making them a footstool under your feet."*

14 Therefore, angels are only servants—spirits sent to
care for people who will inherit salvation.

A Warning against Drifting Away

HEBREWS 2:1-4

So we must listen very carefully to the truth we have
heard, or we may drift away from it. 2 For the message God delivered through angels has always stood
firm, and every violation of the law and every act of
disobedience was punished. 3 So what makes us think
we can escape if we ignore this great salvation that
was first announced by the Lord Jesus himself and
then delivered to us by those who heard him speak?
4 And God confirmed the message by giving signs and
wonders and various miracles and gifts of the Holy
Spirit whenever he chose.

Jesus, the Man

HEBREWS 2:5-18

And furthermore, it is not angels who will control the
future world we are talking about. 6 For in one place
the Scriptures say,

"What are mere mortals that you should
think about them,
or a son of man* that you should care
for him?
7 Yet you made them only a little lower than
the angels
and crowned them with glory and
honor.*
8 You gave them authority over all things."*

Now when it says "all things," it means nothing is left
out. But we have not yet seen all things put under their
authority. 9 What we do see is Jesus, who was given a
position "a little lower than the angels"; and because
he suffered death for us, he is now "crowned with glory
and honor." Yes, by God's grace, Jesus tasted death

Heb 1:13 Ps 110:1. **Heb 2:6** Or *the Son of Man.* **Heb 2:7** Some manuscripts add *You gave them charge of everything you made.* **Heb 2:6-8** Ps 8:4-6 (Greek version).

LESSONS FROM CHRIST'S HUMANITY

God, in Christ, became a living, breathing human being. Hebrews points out many reasons why this is so important.

Christ is the perfect human		
	leader	and he wants to lead you
	model	and he is worth imitating
	sacrifice	and he died for you
	conqueror	and he conquered death to give you eternal life
	High Priest	and he is merciful, loving, and understanding

tecting the helpless (Matt 18:10), proclaiming God's messages (Rev 14:6-12), and executing God's judgment (Acts 12:1-23; Rev 20:1-3).

Heb 2:1-3 The author called on readers to pay attention to the truth they had heard so that they wouldn't drift away into false teachings. Paying careful attention is hard work. It involves focusing mind, body, and senses. Listening to Christ means not merely hearing but also obeying (see Jas 1:22-25). We must listen carefully and be ready to carry out his instructions.

Heb 2:1 These early believers were in danger of falling away from following Jesus. They had heard the words of the gospel, but those words had not sunk in. People raised in believing families and churches risk the same danger today. They hear the words and more or less agree, but mental assent to Christ's leadership is insufficient to be Christ's disciple. Are you a Sunday school teacher, a small group leader, or a club leader? Don't assume that people who comply and conform are truly committed to Christ. Get to know each person who attends your group and challenge each with the truth and implications of commitment to Christ. Don't surrender anyone to casual belief.

Heb 2:2-3 "The message God delivered through angels" refers to the teaching that angels, as messengers for God, had brought the law to Moses (see Gal 3:19). A central theme of Hebrews is that Christ is infinitely greater than all other proposed ways to God. The author was saying that the faith of his Jewish readers was good, but faith must point to Christ. Just as Christ is greater than angels, so Christ's message is more important than theirs. No one will escape God's punishment if indifferent to the salvation offered by Christ.

Heb 2:3 Eyewitnesses to Jesus' ministry had handed down his teachings to the readers of this book. These readers were second-generation believers who had not seen Christ in the flesh. They are like us; we have not seen Jesus personally. We base our belief in Jesus on the eyewitness accounts recorded in the Bible. See John 20:29 for Jesus' encouragement to those who believe without ever having seen him.

Heb 2:4 "God confirmed the message" continues the thought from Hebrews 2:3. Those who had heard Jesus speak and then had passed on his words also had the truth of their words confirmed by "signs and wonders and various miracles and gifts of the Holy Spirit." In the book of Acts, miracles and gifts of the Spirit authenticated the Good News wherever it was preached (see Acts 9:31-42; 14:1-20). Paul taught that the purpose of spiritual gifts is to build up the church, making it strong and mature (see Rom 12; 1 Cor 12–14; Eph 4). When we see the gifts of the Spirit in an individual or a congregation, we know that God is truly present. As we receive God's gifts, we should thank him and put them to use in the church.

Heb 2:8-9 God put Jesus in charge of everything, and Jesus revealed himself to us. We do not yet see Jesus reigning on earth, but we can picture him in his heavenly glory. When you are confused by present events and anxious about the future, remember Jesus' true position and authority. He is Lord of all, and one day he will rule on earth as he does now in heaven. This truth can give stability to your decisions day by day.

Heb 2:9-10 God's grace to us led Christ to his death. Jesus did not come into the world to gain status or political power, but to suffer and die so that we could have eternal life ("bring many children into glory"). If it is difficult for us to identify with Christ's servant attitude, perhaps we need to evaluate our own motives. Are we more interested in power or participation, domination or service, getting or giving?

▶ **HEBREWS 2:5-18** ***(cont.)***

for everyone. 10God, for whom and through whom
everything was made, chose to bring many children
into glory. And it was only right that he should make
Jesus, through his suffering, a perfect leader, fit to
bring them into their salvation.
11So now Jesus and the ones he makes holy have the
same Father. That is why Jesus is not ashamed to call
them his brothers and sisters.* 12For he said to God,

"I will proclaim your name to my brothers
and sisters.
I will praise you among your assembled
people."*

13He also said,

"I will put my trust in him,"
that is, "I and the children God has
given me."*

14Because God's children are human beings—made
of flesh and blood—the Son also became flesh and
blood. For only as a human being could he die, and
only by dying could he break the power of the devil,
who had* the power of death. 15Only in this way could
he set free all who have lived their lives as slaves to the
fear of dying.
16We also know that the Son did not come to help
angels; he came to help the descendants of Abraham.
17Therefore, it was necessary for him to be made in
every respect like us, his brothers and sisters,* so that
he could be our merciful and faithful High Priest before God. Then he could offer a sacrifice that would
take away the sins of the people. 18Since he himself
has gone through suffering and testing, he is able to
help us when we are being tested.

Jesus Is Greater Than Moses

HEBREWS 3:1-19

And so, dear brothers and sisters who belong to God
and* are partners with those called to heaven, think
carefully about this Jesus whom we declare to be God's
messenger* and High Priest. 2For he was faithful to
God, who appointed him, just as Moses served faithfully when he was entrusted with God's entire* house.
3But Jesus deserves far more glory than Moses, just
as a person who builds a house deserves more praise

Heb 2:11 Greek *brothers;* also in 2:12. **Heb 2:12** Ps 22:22. **Heb 2:13** Isa 8:17-18. **Heb 2:14** Or *has.* **Heb 2:17** Greek *like the brothers.* **Heb 3:1a** Greek *And so, holy brothers who.* **Heb 3:1b** Greek *God's apostle.* **Heb 3:2** Some manuscripts do not include *entire.*

Heb 2:10 How was Jesus made a perfect leader through suffering? Jesus' suffering made him a perfect leader, or pioneer, of our salvation (see the notes on Heb 5:8, p. 1767; Heb 5:9, p. 1767). Jesus did not need to suffer for his own salvation, because he was God in human form. His perfect obedience (which led him down the road of suffering) demonstrates that he was the complete sacrifice for us. Through suffering, Jesus completed the work necessary for our salvation. Our suffering can make us more sensitive servants of God. People who have known pain are able to reach out with compassion to others who hurt. If you have suffered, ask God how your experience can be used to help others.

Heb 2:11-13 We who have been set apart for God's service, cleansed, and made holy (sanctified) by Jesus now have the same Father he has, so he has made us his brothers and sisters. Various psalms look forward to Christ and his work in the world. Here the writer quotes a portion of Psalm 22, a messianic psalm. Because God has adopted all believers as his children, Jesus calls them his brothers and sisters.

Heb 2:14-15 Jesus had to become human so that he could die and rise again in order to destroy the devil's power over death (Rom 6:5-11). Only then could Christ deliver those who had lived in constant fear of death and free them to live for him. When we belong to God, we need not fear death, because we know that death is only the doorway into eternal life (1 Cor 15).

Heb 2:14-15 Christ's death and resurrection set us free from the fear of death because death has been defeated. Every person must die, but death is not the end; instead, it is the doorway to a new life. All who dread death should have the opportunity to know the hope that Christ's victory brings. How can you share this truth with those close to you?

Heb 2:16-17 In the Old Testament, the high priest was the mediator between God and his people. His job was to regularly offer animal sacrifices according to the law and to intercede with God for forgiveness of the people's sins. Jesus Christ is now our High Priest. He came to earth as a human being; therefore, he understands our weaknesses and shows mercy to us. He has once and for all paid the penalty for our sins by his own sacrificial death (atonement), and he can be depended on to restore our broken relationship with God. We are released from sin's domination over us when we commit ourselves fully to Christ, trusting completely in what he has done for us (see the note on Heb 4:14, p. 1766, for more about Jesus as the great High Priest).

Heb 2:18 Knowing that Christ suffered pain and faced temptation helps us face our trials. Jesus understands our struggles because he faced them as a human being. We can trust Christ to help us survive suffering and overcome temptation. When you face trials, go to Jesus for strength and patience. He understands your needs and is able to help (see Heb 4:14-16).

Heb 3:1 This verse would have been especially meaningful to Jewish Christians. For Jews, the highest human authority was the high priest. For Christians, the highest human authorities were God's messengers, the apostles. Jesus, God's messenger and High Priest, is the ultimate authority in the church.

Heb 3:1 The writer says to "think carefully about this Jesus"—to fix our minds, ponder carefully, and focus on the true significance of Jesus. How much do we do that? In our age of sound bites, fast food, and quick-fix solutions, very few people take time to think about anything or anyone. In Jesus we have one to whom we should listen (God's messenger), through whom we come to the Father (High Priest), and to whom we give obedience (he is entrusted with God's entire house). When you think about the significance and superiority of Jesus, how does it affect your life today? Your decisions? Your actions?

Heb 3:2-3 To the Jewish people, Moses was a great hero; he had led their ancestors, the Israelites, from Egyptian bondage to the border of the Promised Land. He also had written the first five books of the Old Testament, and he was the prophet through whom God had given the law; therefore, Moses was the greatest prophet in the Scriptures. But Jesus is worthy of greater honor, as the central figure of faith, than Moses, who was merely a human servant. Jesus is more than human; he is God himself (Heb 1:3). As Moses led the people of Israel out of Egyptian bondage, so Christ leads us out of sin's slavery. Why settle for Moses, the author of Hebrews asks, when you can have Jesus Christ, who appointed Moses?

Heb 3:5 Moses was faithful to God's calling not only to deliver Israel but also to prepare the way for the Messiah ("his work was an

than the house itself. [4]For every house has a builder, but the one who built everything is God.

[5]Moses was certainly faithful in God's house as a servant. His work was an illustration of the truths God would reveal later. [6]But Christ, as the Son, is in charge of God's entire house. And we are God's house, if we keep our courage and remain confident in our hope in Christ.*

[7]That is why the Holy Spirit says,

"Today when you hear his voice,
8 don't harden your hearts
as Israel did when they rebelled,
when they tested me in the wilderness.
9 There your ancestors tested and tried my patience,
even though they saw my miracles for forty years.
10 So I was angry with them, and I said,
'Their hearts always turn away from me.
They refuse to do what I tell them.'
11 So in my anger I took an oath:
'They will never enter my place of rest.'"*

[12]Be careful then, dear brothers and sisters.* Make sure that your own hearts are not evil and unbelieving, turning you away from the living God. [13]You must warn each other every day, while it is still "today," so that none of you will be deceived by sin and hardened against God. [14]For if we are faithful to the end, trusting God just as firmly as when we first believed, we will share in all that belongs to Christ. [15]Remember what it says:

"Today when you hear his voice,
don't harden your hearts
as Israel did when they rebelled."*

[16]And who was it who rebelled against God, even though they heard his voice? Wasn't it the people Moses led out of Egypt? [17]And who made God angry for forty years? Wasn't it the people who sinned, whose corpses lay in the wilderness? [18]And to whom was God speaking when he took an oath that they would never enter his rest? Wasn't it the people who disobeyed him? [19]So we see that because of their unbelief they were not able to enter his rest.

Promised Rest for God's People

HEBREWS 4:1-13

God's promise of entering his rest still stands, so we ought to tremble with fear that some of you might fail to experience it. [2]For this good news—that God has prepared this rest—has been announced to us just as it was to them. But it did them no good because they didn't share the faith of those who listened to God.* [3]For only we who believe can enter his rest. As for the others, God said,

Heb 3:6 Some manuscripts add *faithful to the end.* **Heb 3:7-11** Ps 95:7-11. **Heb 3:12** Greek *brothers.* **Heb 3:15** Ps 95:7-8. **Heb 4:2** Some manuscripts read *they didn't combine what they heard with faith.*

illustration of the truths God would reveal later"). All the Old Testament believers also served to prepare the way. Thus, knowing the Old Testament is the best foundation for understanding the New Testament. If you include the Old Testament in your regular Bible reading, the New Testament will grow clearer and more meaningful to you.

Heb 3:6 Because Christ lives in us as believers, we can remain courageous and hopeful to the end. We are not saved by being steadfast and firm in our faith, but our courage and hope do reveal that our faith is real. Without this enduring faithfulness, we could easily be blown away by the winds of temptation, false teaching, or persecution (see also Heb 3:14).

Heb 3:7-15 This passage refers to the Israelites who had hardened their hearts in the wilderness. A hardened heart is as useless as a hardened lump of clay or a hardened loaf of bread. Nothing can restore it and make it useful. The writer of Psalm 95 warns against hardening our hearts as Israel did in the wilderness by continuing to resist God's will (Exod 17:7; Num 13; 14; 20). The people were so convinced that God couldn't deliver them that they simply lost their faith in him. People with hardened hearts are so stubbornly set in their ways that they cannot turn to God. This does not happen suddenly or all at once; it is the result of a series of choices to disregard God's will. Let people know: For those who resist God long enough, God will toss them aside like hardened bread, useless and worthless.

Heb 3:11 God's *rest* has several meanings in Scripture: (1) the seventh day of creation and the weekly Sabbath commemorating it (Gen 2:2; Heb 4:4-9); (2) the Promised Land of Canaan (Deut 12:8-12; Ps 95); (3) peace with God now because of our relationship with Christ through faith (Matt 11:28; Heb 4:1, 3, 8-11); and (4) our future eternal life with Christ (Heb 4:8-11). All of these meanings were probably familiar to the Jewish Christian readers of the book of Hebrews. We can apply the verses as a warning about God's anger in the face of human rebellion against his Kingdom. By rejecting God's provision (Christ) and not enduring in our faith, we miss the opportunity for spiritual rest.

Heb 3:12-14 Our hearts turn away from the living God when we stubbornly refuse to believe him. If we persist in our unbelief, God will eventually leave us alone in our sin. But God can give us new hearts, new desires, and new spirits (Ezek 36:22-27). To prevent having an unbelieving heart, stay in fellowship with other believers, talk daily about your mutual faith, be aware of the deceitfulness of sin (it attracts but also destroys), and encourage each other with love and concern.

Heb 3:15-19 The Israelites failed to enter the Promised Land because they did not believe in God's protection, and they did not believe that God would help them conquer the giants in the land (see Num 14–15). So God sent them into the wilderness to wander for 40 years. This was an unhappy alternative to the wonderful gift he had planned for them. Lack of trust in God always prevents us from receiving his best.

Heb 4:1-3 Some of the Jewish Christians who received this letter may have been on the verge of turning back from their promised rest in Christ, just as the people in Moses' day had turned back from the Promised Land. In both cases, the difficulties of the present moment overshadowed the reality of God's promise, and the people doubted that God would fulfill his promises. When we trust our own efforts instead of Christ's power, we, too, are in danger of turning back. Our own efforts are never adequate; only Christ can see us through.

Heb 4:2 The Israelites of Moses' day illustrate a problem facing many who fill our churches today. They know a great deal about Christ, but they do not know him personally—they don't combine their knowledge with faith. Let the Good News about Christ benefit your life. Believe in him and then act on what you know. Trust in Christ and do what he says.

▸ **HEBREWS 4:1-13** ***(cont.)***

"In my anger I took an oath:
'They will never enter my place of rest,'"*

even though this rest has been ready since he made the world. 4We know it is ready because of the place in the Scriptures where it mentions the seventh day: "On the seventh day God rested from all his work."* 5But in the other passage God said, "They will never enter my place of rest."*

6So God's rest is there for people to enter, but those who first heard this good news failed to enter because they disobeyed God. 7So God set another time for entering his rest, and that time is today. God announced this through David much later in the words already quoted:

"Today when you hear his voice,
don't harden your hearts."*

8Now if Joshua had succeeded in giving them this rest, God would not have spoken about another day of rest still to come. 9So there is a special rest* still waiting for the people of God. 10For all who have entered into God's rest have rested from their labors, just as God did after creating the world. 11So let us do our best to enter that rest. But if we disobey God, as the people of Israel did, we will fall.

12For the word of God is alive and powerful. It is sharper than the sharpest two-edged sword, cutting between soul and spirit, between joint and marrow. It exposes our innermost thoughts and desires. 13Nothing in all creation is hidden from God. Everything is naked and exposed before his eyes, and he is the one to whom we are accountable.

Christ Is Our High Priest

HEBREWS 4:14–5:10

So then, since we have a great High Priest who has entered heaven, Jesus the Son of God, let us hold firmly to what we believe. 15This High Priest of ours understands our weaknesses, for he faced all of the same testings we do, yet he did not sin. 16So let us come

Heb 4:3 Ps 95:11. **Heb 4:4** Gen 2:2. **Heb 4:5** Ps 95:11. **Heb 4:7** Ps 95:7-8. **Heb 4:9** Or *a Sabbath rest.*

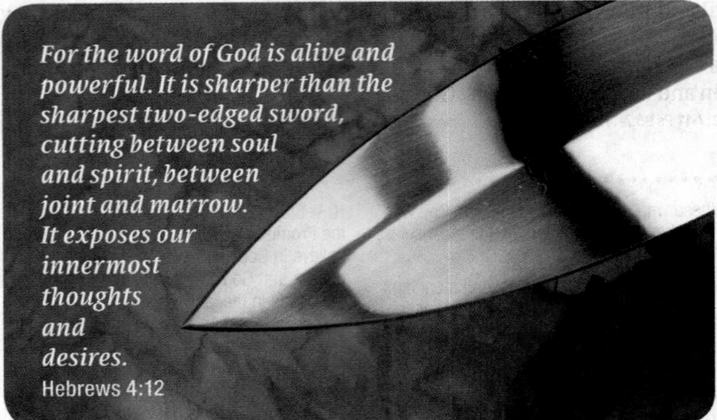
For the word of God is alive and powerful. It is sharper than the sharpest two-edged sword, cutting between soul and spirit, between joint and marrow. It exposes our innermost thoughts and desires.
Hebrews 4:12

Heb 4:4 God rested on the seventh day not because he was tired but to indicate the completion of creation. The world was perfect, and God was well satisfied with it. This rest is a foretaste of our eternal joy when creation will be renewed and restored, every mark of sin will be removed, and the world will be made perfect again. Our Sabbath rest in Christ begins when we trust him to complete his good and perfect work in us (see the note on Heb 3:11, p. 1765).

Heb 4:6-7 God had given the Israelites the opportunity to enter Canaan, but they disobeyed and failed to enter (Num 13–14). Now God offers us the opportunity to enter his ultimate place of rest—he invites us to come to Christ. To enter his rest, you must believe that God has this relationship in mind for you; you must stop trying to create it; you must trust in Christ for it; and you must determine to obey him. *Today* is the best time to find peace with God. Tomorrow may be too late.

Heb 4:8-11 God wants us to enter his rest. For the Israelites of Moses' time, this rest was the earthly rest to be found in the Promised Land. For Christians, it is peace with God now and eternal life on a new earth later. We do not need to wait for the next life to enjoy God's rest and peace; we may have it daily now! Our daily rest in the Lord will not end with death but will become an eternal rest in the place that Christ is preparing for us (John 14:1-4).

Heb 4:11 If Jesus has provided for our rest through faith, why must we "do our best to enter that rest"? This is not the struggle of doing good in order to obtain salvation, nor is it a mystical struggle to overcome selfishness. It refers to making every effort to appreciate and benefit from what God has already provided. Salvation is not to be taken for granted; to appropriate the gift God offers requires decision and commitment.

Heb 4:12 The Word of God is not simply a collection of words from God, a vehicle for communicating ideas; it is living, life-changing, and dynamic as it works in us. With the incisiveness of a surgeon's knife, God's Word reveals who we are and what we are not. It penetrates the core of our moral and spiritual life. It discerns what is within us, both good and evil. The demands of God's Word require decisions. We must not only listen to the Word; we must also let it shape our lives.

Heb 4:13 Nothing can be hidden from God. He knows about everyone everywhere, and everything about us is wide open to his all-seeing eyes. God sees all we do and knows all we think. Even when we are unaware of his presence, he is there. When we try to hide from him, he sees us. We can have no secrets from God. It is comforting to realize that although God knows us intimately, he still loves us.

Heb 4:14 Christ is superior to the priests, and his priesthood is superior to their priesthood. To the Jews, the high priest was the highest religious authority in the land. He alone entered the Most Holy Place in the Temple once a year to make atonement for the sins of the whole nation (Lev 16). Like the high priest, Jesus mediates between God and us. As humanity's representative, he intercedes for us before God. As God's representative, he assures us of God's forgiveness. Jesus has more authority than the Jewish high priests because he is truly God and truly man. Unlike the high priest, who could go before God only once a year, Christ is always at God's right hand, interceding for us. He is always available to hear us when we pray.

Heb 4:15 Jesus is like us because he experienced a full range of temptations throughout his life as a human being. We

boldly to the throne of our gracious God. There we will receive his mercy, and we will find grace to help us when we need it most.

5:1Every high priest is a man chosen to represent other people in their dealings with God. He presents their gifts to God and offers sacrifices for their sins. 2And he is able to deal gently with ignorant and wayward people because he himself is subject to the same weaknesses. 3That is why he must offer sacrifices for his own sins as well as theirs.

4And no one can become a high priest simply because he wants such an honor. He must be called by God for this work, just as Aaron was. 5That is why Christ did not honor himself by assuming he could become High Priest. No, he was chosen by God, who said to him,

> "You are my Son.
> Today I have become your Father.*"

6And in another passage God said to him,

> "You are a priest forever in the order of
> Melchizedek."*

7While Jesus was here on earth, he offered prayers and pleadings, with a loud cry and tears, to the one who could rescue him from death. And God heard his prayers because of his deep reverence for God. 8Even though Jesus was God's Son, he learned obedience from the things he suffered. 9In this way, God qualified him as a perfect High Priest, and he became the source of eternal salvation for all those who obey him. 10And God designated him to be a High Priest in the order of Melchizedek.

A Call to Spiritual Growth

HEBREWS 5:11–6:12

There is much more we would like to say about this, but it is difficult to explain, especially since you are spiritually dull and don't seem to listen. 12You have been believers so long now that you ought to be teaching others. Instead, you need someone to teach you again the basic things about God's word.* You are like babies who need milk and cannot eat solid food. 13For someone who lives on milk is still an infant and doesn't know how to do what is right. 14Solid food is for those who are mature, who through training have

Heb 5:5 Or *Today I reveal you as my Son.* Ps 2:7. **Heb 5:6** Ps 110:4. **Heb 5:12** Or *about the oracles of God.*

---

can be comforted knowing that Jesus faced temptation—he can sympathize with us. We can be encouraged knowing that Jesus faced temptation without giving in to sin. He shows us that we do not have to sin when facing the seductive lure of temptation. Jesus is the only perfect human being who has ever lived.

Heb 4:16 Prayer is our approach to God, and we are to come "boldly." Some Christians approach God meekly with heads hung low, afraid to ask him to meet their needs. Others pray flippantly, giving little thought to what they say. Come with reverence because he is your King. But also come with bold assurance because he is your Friend and Counselor.

Heb 5:4-6 Hebrews 5 stresses both Christ's divine appointment and his humanity. The writer uses two Old Testament verses to show Christ's divine appointment: Psalms 2:7; 110:4. At the time this book was written, the Romans selected the high priest in Jerusalem. In the Old Testament, God chose Aaron, and only Aaron's descendants could be high priests. Christ, like Aaron, was chosen and called by God.

Heb 5:6 Melchizedek was a priest of Salem (now called Jerusalem). His Profile is on p. 35. Hebrews 7 explains Melchizedek's position.

Heb 5:7 Jesus was in great agony as he prepared to face death (Luke 22:41-44). Although Jesus cried out to God, asking to be delivered, he was prepared to suffer humiliation, separation from his Father, and death in order to do God's will. At times we will undergo trials not because we want to suffer but because we want to obey God. Let Jesus' obedience sustain and encourage you in times of trial. You will be able to face anything if you know that Jesus Christ is with you.

Heb 5:7 Have you ever felt that God didn't hear your prayers? Be sure you are praying with reverent submission, willing to do what God wants. God responds to his obedient children.

Heb 5:8 Jesus' human life was not a script that he passively followed. It was a life that he chose freely (John 10:17-18). It was a continuous process of making the will of God the Father his own. Jesus chose to obey, even though obedience led to suffering and death. Because Jesus obeyed perfectly, even under great trial, he can help us obey, no matter how difficult obedience seems to be.

Heb 5:9 Christ was always morally perfect. By obeying, he demonstrated his perfection to us, not to God or to himself. In the Bible, *perfect* usually means completeness or maturity. By sharing our experience of suffering, Christ shared our human experience completely. He is now able to offer eternal salvation to those who obey him. (See Phil 2:5-11 for Christ's attitude as he became human.)

Heb 5:9 The "eternal salvation" we have been offered means the elimination of a verdict on our sin, the setting aside of judgment, and the award of undeserved membership in God's family. It is a change in destiny, an awakening of hope, an overcoming of death. Salvation turns a person toward heaven and inaugurates a life of discipleship with the living Christ. It is God's invitation to you, God's energy invested in you. Salvation is the reason you can smile in the morning and rest in the evening. God loves you, and you belong to him.

Heb 5:12-13 These Jewish Christians were immature. Some of them should have been teaching others, but they had not even applied the basics to their own lives. They were reluctant to move beyond age-old traditions, established doctrines, and discussion of the basics. They wouldn't be able to understand the high-priestly role of Christ unless they moved out of their comfortable position, cut some of their Jewish ties, and stopped trying to blend in with their culture. Commitment to Christ moves people out of their comfort zones.

Heb 5:12-14 In order to grow from infant Christians to mature Christians, we must learn discernment. We must train our consciences, our senses, our minds, and our bodies to distinguish good from evil. Can you recognize temptation before it traps you? Can you tell the difference between a correct use of Scripture and a mistaken one?

Heb 5:14 Our capacity to feast on deeper knowledge of God ("solid food") is determined by our spiritual growth. Too often we want God's banquet before we are spiritually capable of digesting it. As you grow in the Lord and put into practice what you have learned, your capacity to understand will also grow.

▸ HEBREWS 5:11–6:12 ***(cont.)***

the skill to recognize the difference between right
and wrong.

6:1So let us stop going over the basic teachings about
Christ again and again. Let us go on instead and become mature in our understanding. Surely we don't
need to start again with the fundamental importance
of repenting from evil deeds* and placing our faith in
God. 2You don't need further instruction about baptisms, the laying on of hands, the resurrection of the
dead, and eternal judgment. 3And so, God willing, we
will move forward to further understanding.

4For it is impossible to bring back to repentance
those who were once enlightened—those who have
experienced the good things of heaven and shared in
the Holy Spirit, 5who have tasted the goodness of the
word of God and the power of the age to come—6and
who then turn away from God. It is impossible to bring
such people back to repentance; by rejecting the Son
of God, they themselves are nailing him to the cross
once again and holding him up to public shame.

7When the ground soaks up the falling rain and
bears a good crop for the farmer, it has God's blessing.
8But if a field bears thorns and thistles, it is useless.
The farmer will soon condemn that field and burn it.

9Dear friends, even though we are talking this way,
we really don't believe it applies to you. We are confident that you are meant for better things, things that
come with salvation. 10For God is not unjust. He will
not forget how hard you have worked for him and how
you have shown your love to him by caring for other
believers,* as you still do. 11Our great desire is that you
will keep on loving others as long as life lasts, in order
to make certain that what you hope for will come true.
12Then you will not become spiritually dull and indifferent. Instead, you will follow the example of those
who are going to inherit God's promises because of
their faith and endurance.

God's Promises Bring Hope

HEBREWS 6:13-20

For example, there was God's promise to Abraham.
Since there was no one greater to swear by, God took
an oath in his own name, saying:

Heb 6:1 Greek *from dead works.* **Heb 6:10** Greek *for God's holy people.*

Heb 6:1-2 Certain basic teachings are essential for all believers to understand. These basics include the importance of faith, the foolishness of trying to be saved by good deeds, the meaning of baptism and spiritual gifts, and the facts of resurrection and eternal life. To go on to maturity in our understanding, we need to move beyond (but not away from) the basic teachings to a more complete understanding of the faith. Mature Christians should be teaching new Christians the basics. Then, acting on what they know, the mature will learn even more from God's Word.

Heb 6:3 These Christians needed to move beyond the basics of their faith to an understanding of Christ as the perfect High Priest and the fulfillment of all the Old Testament prophecies. Rather than arguing about the respective merits of Judaism and Christianity, they needed to depend on Christ and live effectively for him.

Heb 6:4-6 In the first century, a pagan who investigated Christianity and then went back to paganism made a clean break with the church. But for Jewish Christians who decided to return to Judaism, the break was less obvious. Their lifestyle remained relatively unchanged. But by deliberately turning away from Christ, they were cutting themselves off from God's forgiveness. Those who persevere in believing are true saints; those who continue to reject Christ are unbelievers, no matter how well they behave.

Heb 6:6 This verse points to the danger of the Hebrew Christians' returning to Judaism and thus committing apostasy. Some apply this verse today to superficial believers who renounce their Christianity or to unbelievers who come close to salvation and then turn away. Either way, those who reject Christ will not be saved. Christ died once for all. He will not be crucified again. Apart from his cross, there is no other possible way of salvation. However, the author does not indicate that his readers were in danger of renouncing Christ (see Heb 6:9). He is warning against hardness of heart that would make repentance inconceivable for the sinner.

Heb 6:7-8 The writer uses an analogy from agriculture to make a simple point. Real seeds (the gospel) given genuine care by the farmer (God) and planted in a fertile field (your heart and life) will produce a bountiful crop (spiritual maturity). Weeds (temptations) threaten to overwhelm the crop. If the field produces only weeds, then the seeds are lost and the field ruined.

An unproductive Christian life falls under God's condemnation. You have been watered by God's grace with clear and abundant teaching and preaching. What excuse do you have for a useless or unproductive life? Don't be a Christian in name only. Make sure your life bears fruit.

Heb 6:10 It's easy to get discouraged, thinking that God has forgotten us. But God is never unjust. He never forgets or overlooks our hard work for him. Presently you may not be receiving rewards and acclaim, but God knows your efforts of love and ministry. Let God's love for you and his intimate knowledge of your service for him bolster you as you face disappointment and rejection here on earth.

THE CHOICES OF MATURITY

One way to evaluate spiritual maturity is by looking at the choices we make. The writer of Hebrews notes many of the ways these choices change with personal growth.

Mature Choices	*Versus*	Immature Choices
Teaching others	rather than	just being taught
Developing depth of understanding	rather than	struggling with the basics
Self-evaluation	rather than	self-criticism
Seeking unity	rather than	promoting disunity
Desiring spiritual challenges	rather than	desiring entertainment
Careful study and observation	rather than	opinions and halfhearted efforts
Active faith	rather than	cautious apathy and doubt
Confidence	rather than	fear
Feelings and experiences evaluated in the light of God's Word	rather than	experiences evaluated according to feelings

14 "I will certainly bless you,
and I will multiply your descendants beyond
number."*
15Then Abraham waited patiently, and he received
what God had promised.
16Now when people take an oath, they call on someone greater than themselves to hold them to it. And
without any question that oath is binding. 17God also
bound himself with an oath, so that those who received the promise could be perfectly sure that he
would never change his mind. 18So God has given
both his promise and his oath. These two things are
unchangeable because it is impossible for God to lie.
Therefore, we who have fled to him for refuge can
have great confidence as we hold to the hope that

Heb 6:14 Gen 22:17.

ABRAHAM IN THE NEW TESTAMENT

Abraham was an ancestor of Jesus Christ.	Matt 1:1-2, 17; Luke 3:23, 34	Jesus Christ was human; he was born into the line of Abraham, whom God had chosen to be the father of a great nation through which the whole world would be blessed. We are blessed because of what Jesus Christ, Abraham's descendant, did for us.
Abraham was the father of the Jewish nation.	Matt 3:9; Luke 3:8; Acts 13:26; Rom 4:1; 11:1; 2 Cor 11:22; Heb 6:13-14	God wanted to set apart a nation for himself, a nation that would tell the world about him. He began with a man of faith who, though old and childless, believed God's promise of innumerable descendants. We can trust God to do the impossible when we have faith.
Abraham, because of his faith, now sits in the Kingdom with Christ.	Matt 8:11; Luke 13:28; 16:23-31	Abraham followed God, and now he is enjoying his reward—eternity with God. We will one day meet Abraham because we have been promised eternity as well.
God is Abraham's God; thus, Abraham is alive with God.	Matt 22:32; Mark 12:26; Luke 20:37; Acts 7:32	As Abraham lives forever, we will live forever, because we, like Abraham, have chosen the life of faith.
Abraham received great promises from God.	Luke 1:55, 72-73; Acts 3:25; 7:17-18; Gal 3:6, 14-16; Heb 6:13-15	Many of the promises God made to Abraham seemed impossible to be realized, but Abraham trusted God. The promises to believers in God's Word also seem too incredible to believe, but we can trust God to keep all his promises.
Abraham followed God.	Acts 7:2-8; Heb 11:8, 17-19	Abraham followed God's leading from his homeland to an unknown territory, which became the Jews' Promised Land. When we follow God, even before he makes all his plans clear to us, we will never be disappointed.
God blessed Abraham because of his faith.	Rom 4; Gal 3:6-9, 14-19; Heb 11:8, 17-19; Jas 2:21-24	Abraham showed faith in times of disappointment, trial, and testing. Because of Abraham's faith, God counted him righteous and called him his "friend." God accepts us because of our faith.
Abraham is the father of all those who come to God by faith.	Rom 9:6-8; Gal 3:6-9, 14-29	The Jews are Abraham's children, and Christ was his descendant. We are Christ's brothers and sisters; thus, all believers are Abraham's children and God's children. Abraham was righteous because of his faith; we are made righteous through faith in Christ. The promises made to Abraham apply to us because of Christ.

Heb 6:11-12 Hope keeps the Christian from becoming lazy or feeling bored. Like an athlete, train hard and run well, remembering the reward that lies ahead (Phil 3:14).

Heb 6:15 Abraham waited patiently; it was 25 years from the time God had promised him a son (Gen 12:7; 13:14-16; 15:4-5; 17:16) to Isaac's birth (Gen 21:1-3). Because our trials and temptations are often so intense, they seem to last for an eternity. Both the Bible and the testimony of mature Christians encourage us to wait for God to act in *his* timing, even when our needs seem too great to wait any longer.

Heb 6:17 God's promises are unchanging and trustworthy because God is unchanging and trustworthy. When promising Abraham a son, God took an oath in his own name. The oath was as good as God's name, and God's name was as good as his divine nature.

Heb 6:18-19 These two unchangeable things are God's promise and his oath. God embodies all truth; therefore, he cannot lie. Because God is truth, you can be secure in his promises; you don't need to wonder if he will change his plans. Our hope is secure and immovable, anchored in God, just as a ship's anchor holds firmly to the seabed. To the true seeker who comes to God in belief, God gives an unconditional promise of acceptance. When you ask God with openness, honesty, and sincerity to save you from your sins, *he will do it.* This truth should give you encouragement, assurance, and confidence.

▸ **HEBREWS 6:13-20** ***(cont.)***

lies before us. 19This hope is a strong and trustworthy anchor for our souls. It leads us through the curtain into God's inner sanctuary. 20Jesus has already gone in there for us. He has become our eternal High Priest in the order of Melchizedek.

Melchizedek Is Greater Than Abraham

HEBREWS 7:1-14

This Melchizedek was king of the city of Salem and also a priest of God Most High. When Abraham was returning home after winning a great battle against the kings, Melchizedek met him and blessed him. 2Then Abraham took a tenth of all he had captured in battle and gave it to Melchizedek. The name Melchizedek means "king of justice," and king of Salem means "king of peace." 3There is no record of his father or mother or any of his ancestors—no beginning or end to his life. He remains a priest forever, resembling the Son of God.

4Consider then how great this Melchizedek was. Even Abraham, the great patriarch of Israel, recognized this by giving him a tenth of what he had taken in battle. 5Now the law of Moses required that the priests, who are descendants of Levi, must collect a tithe from the rest of the people of Israel,* who are also descendants of Abraham. 6But Melchizedek, who was not a descendant of Levi, collected a tenth from Abraham. And Melchizedek placed a blessing upon Abraham, the one who had already received the promises of God. 7And without question, the person who has the power to give a blessing is greater than the one who is blessed.

8The priests who collect tithes are men who die, so Melchizedek is greater than they are, because we are told that he lives on. 9In addition, we might even say that these Levites—the ones who collect the tithe—paid a tithe to Melchizedek when their ancestor Abraham paid a tithe to him. 10For although Levi wasn't born yet, the seed from which he came was in Abraham's body when Melchizedek collected the tithe from him.

11So if the priesthood of Levi, on which the law was based, could have achieved the perfection God intended, why did God need to establish a different priesthood, with a priest in the order of Melchizedek instead of the order of Levi and Aaron?*

12And if the priesthood is changed, the law must also be changed to permit it. 13For the priest we are talking about belongs to a different tribe, whose members have never served at the altar as priests. 14What I mean is, our Lord came from the tribe of Judah, and Moses never mentioned priests coming from that tribe.

Jesus Is like Melchizedek

HEBREWS 7:15-28

This change has been made very clear since a different priest, who is like Melchizedek, has appeared. 16Jesus became a priest, not by meeting the physical requirement of belonging to the tribe of Levi, but by the power of a life that cannot be destroyed. 17And the psalmist pointed this out when he prophesied,

> "You are a priest forever in the order of
> Melchizedek."*

18Yes, the old requirement about the priesthood was set aside because it was weak and useless. 19For the law never made anything perfect. But now we have confidence in a better hope, through which we draw near to God.

20This new system was established with a solemn oath. Aaron's descendants became priests without

Heb 7:5 Greek *from their brothers.* **Heb 7:11** Greek *the order of Aaron?* **Heb 7:17** Ps 110:4.

Heb 6:19-20 A curtain hung between the Holy Place and the Most Holy Place, "God's inner sanctuary." This curtain prevented anyone from entering, gazing into, or even getting a fleeting glimpse of the interior of the Most Holy Place (see also Heb 9:1-8). The high priest could enter there only once a year to stand in God's presence and atone for the sins of the entire nation. But Christ is in God's presence at all times, not just once a year, as the High Priest who can continually intercede for us.

Heb 7:2ff The writer uses this story from Genesis 14:18-20 to show that Christ is even greater than Abraham (father of the Jewish nation) and Levi (Abraham's descendant). Therefore, the Jewish priesthood (made up of Levi's descendants) was inferior to Melchizedek's priesthood (a type of Christ's priesthood).

Heb 7:3-10 Melchizedek was a priest of God Most High (see the note on Gen 14:18, p. 34, and his Profile on p. 35). He is said to remain a priest forever (see also Ps 110:4), because his priesthood has no record of beginning or ending. He was a priest of God in Salem (Jerusalem) long before the nation of Israel and the regular priesthood began.

Heb 7:11-17 Jesus' high-priestly role was superior to that of any priest of Levi, because the Messiah was a priest of a higher order (Ps 110:4). If the Jewish priests and their laws had been able to save people, why would God need to send Christ as a priest, who came not from the tribe of Levi (the priestly tribe) but from the tribe of Judah? The animal sacrifices had to be repeated, and they offered only temporary forgiveness; but Christ's sacrifice was offered once, and it offers total and permanent forgiveness. Under the new covenant, the Levitical priesthood was canceled in favor of Christ's role as High Priest. Because Christ is our High Priest, we need to pay attention to him. No minister, leader, or Christian friend can substitute for Christ's work and for his role in our salvation.

Heb 7:18-19 The law was not intended to save people or to make them perfect, but to point out sin (see Rom 3:20; 5:20) and to point toward Christ (see Gal 3:24-25). Salvation comes through Christ, whose sacrifice brings forgiveness for our sins. Being ethical, working diligently to help others, and giving to charitable causes are all commendable, but all of our good deeds cannot save us or make us right with God.

Heb 7:19 How can you draw near to God? The Bible makes it clear that your own body is God's temple. Your spirit needs and wants closeness with God. You want to know the living God personally, not as an idea or concept, not as a distant monarch. You can draw near to God through prayer, worship, and Bible meditation. You need not live like a monk, but you probably need more prayer in your life. The habit of worship has become a convenience to be wedged between sports and other recreations. Instead, make worship your top priority. Bible meditation may include verse memory, songs, and quiet personal reading. The Bible is the word of God for you. Use it every day and you will draw nearer and nearer to God.

such an oath, [21]but there was an oath regarding Jesus. For God said to him,

"The LORD has taken an oath and will not break his vow:
'You are a priest forever.'"*

[22]Because of this oath, Jesus is the one who guarantees this better covenant with God.

[23]There were many priests under the old system, for death prevented them from remaining in office. [24]But because Jesus lives forever, his priesthood lasts forever. [25]Therefore he is able, once and forever, to save* those who come to God through him. He lives forever to intercede with God on their behalf.

[26]He is the kind of high priest we need because he is holy and blameless, unstained by sin. He has been set apart from sinners and has been given the highest place of honor in heaven.* [27]Unlike those other high priests, he does not need to offer sacrifices every day. They did this for their own sins first and then for the sins of the people. But Jesus did this once for all when he offered himself as the sacrifice for the people's sins. [28]The law appointed high priests who were limited by human weakness. But after the law was given, God appointed his Son with an oath, and his Son has been made the perfect High Priest forever.

Christ Is Our High Priest

HEBREWS 8:1-13

Here is the main point: We have a High Priest who sat down in the place of honor beside the throne of the majestic God in heaven. [2]There he ministers in the heavenly Tabernacle,* the true place of worship that was built by the Lord and not by human hands.

[3]And since every high priest is required to offer gifts and sacrifices, our High Priest must make an offering, too. [4]If he were here on earth, he would not even be a priest, since there already are priests who offer the gifts required by the law. [5]They serve in a system of worship that is only a copy, a shadow of the real one in heaven. For when Moses was getting ready to build the Tabernacle, God gave him this warning: "Be sure that you make everything according to the pattern I have shown you here on the mountain."*

[6]But now Jesus, our High Priest, has been given a ministry that is far superior to the old priesthood, for he is the one who mediates for us a far better covenant with God, based on better promises.

[7]If the first covenant had been faultless, there would have been no need for a second covenant to replace it. [8]But when God found fault with the people, he said:

Heb 7:21 Ps 110:4. **Heb 7:25** Or *is able to save completely.* **Heb 7:26** Or *has been exalted higher than the heavens.* **Heb 8:2** Or *tent;* also in 8:5. **Heb 8:5** Exod 25:40; 26:30.

Heb 7:22-24 Jesus has a permanent priesthood. He should be everyone's ultimate authority for spiritual life. In our culture today, many people have advisers and counselors whom they elevate almost to the role of priest. People look to political leaders, lawyers, physicians, insurance agents, and financial advisers to provide hope, long life, and security against all disasters. Many Christians regard the advice of priests and ministers, Christian friends, and even pop musicians before they consider the words of Jesus written in the Bible. Make sure your first allegiance and priority is to know and follow the advice given by Jesus.

Heb 7:25 No one can add to what Jesus did to save us; our past, present, and future sins are all forgiven, and Jesus is with the Father as a sign that our sins are forgiven. As our High Priest, Christ is our Advocate, the mediator between us and God. He looks after our interests and intercedes for us with God. The Old Testament high priest went before God once a year to plead for the forgiveness of the nation's sins; Christ makes perpetual intercession before God for us. Christ's continuous presence in heaven with the Father assures us that our sins have been paid for and forgiven (see Rom 8:33-34; Heb 2:17-18; 4:15-16; 9:24). This wonderful assurance frees us from guilt and from fear of failure. If you are a Christian, remember that Christ has paid the price for your sins once and for all (see also Heb 9:24-28).

Heb 7:27 In Old Testament times when animals were sacrificed, they were cut into pieces, the parts were washed, the fat was burned, the blood was sprinkled, and the meat was boiled. Blood was demanded as atonement for sin, and God accepted animal blood to cover the people's sin (Lev 17:11). Because of the sacrificial system, the Israelites were generally aware that sin costs someone something and that they themselves were sinful. Many people take Christ's work on the cross for granted. They don't realize how costly it was for Jesus to secure our forgiveness—it cost him his life and painful, temporary separation from his Father (Matt 27:46; 1 Pet 1:18-19).

Because Jesus died *once for all,* he brought the sacrificial system to an end. He forgave sins—past, present, and future. The Jews did not need to go back to the old system because Christ, the perfect sacrifice, completed the work of redemption. You don't have to look for another way to have your sins forgiven—Christ is the final sacrifice for you.

Heb 7:28 So much is attributed to Jesus in this chapter that it might appear that there is nothing you need to do, or can do, to make salvation a reality for you. And that is true. Jesus has done it all. Nothing you do can improve his work. Nothing you do adds to God's acceptance of Jesus' sacrifice.

So how do the benefits of Jesus' sacrifice become yours? You accept the gift of salvation by faith, trusting entirely in Jesus for salvation. You can do that now through a simple prayer: "Dear God, I trust in Jesus alone. Please forgive my sins through him, and give me the eternal life secured by him. Amen."

Heb 8:4 Under the old Jewish system, priests were chosen only from the tribe of Levi, and sacrifices were offered daily on the altar for forgiveness of sins (see Heb 7:12-14). This system would not have allowed Jesus to be a priest because he was from the tribe of Judah. But his perfect sacrifice ended all need for further priests and sacrifices.

Heb 8:5 The pattern for the Tabernacle built by Moses was given by God. It was a pattern of the spiritual reality of Christ's sacrifice, and thus it looked forward to the future reality. There is no Tabernacle in heaven of which the earthly one is a copy, but rather the earthly Tabernacle was an expression of eternal, theological principles. Because the Temple at Jerusalem had not yet been destroyed, using the worship system there as an example would have had a great impact on this original audience.

Heb 8:8-12 This passage is a quotation of Jeremiah 31:31-34, which compares the new covenant with the old. The old covenant was the covenant of law between God and Israel. The new and better way is the covenant of grace—Christ's offer to forgive our sins and bring us to God through his sacrificial death. This covenant is new in extent—it goes beyond Israel and Judah to include all the Gentile nations. It is new in application because it is written on our hearts and in our minds. It offers a new way to forgiveness, not through animal sacrifice but through faith. Have you entered into this new covenant and begun walking in the better way?

▸ **HEBREWS 8:1-13** ***(cont.)***

"The day is coming, says the LORD,
when I will make a new covenant
with the people of Israel and Judah.
9 This covenant will not be like the one
I made with their ancestors
when I took them by the hand
and led them out of the land of Egypt.
They did not remain faithful to my covenant,
so I turned my back on them, says the LORD.
10 But this is the new covenant I will make
with the people of Israel on that day,* says
the LORD:
I will put my laws in their minds,
and I will write them on their hearts.
I will be their God,
and they will be my people.
11 And they will not need to teach their neighbors,
nor will they need to teach their relatives,*
saying, 'You should know the LORD.'
For everyone, from the least to the greatest,
will know me already.
12 And I will forgive their wickedness,
and I will never again remember their sins."*

13When God speaks of a "new" covenant, it means he
has made the first one obsolete. It is now out of date
and will soon disappear.

Old Rules about Worship

HEBREWS 9:1-10

That first covenant between God and Israel had regulations for worship and a place of worship here on earth.
2There were two rooms in that Tabernacle.* In the first
room were a lampstand, a table, and sacred loaves of
bread on the table. This room was called the Holy Place.
3Then there was a curtain, and behind the curtain was
the second room* called the Most Holy Place. 4In that
room were a gold incense altar and a wooden chest
called the Ark of the Covenant, which was covered with
gold on all sides. Inside the Ark were a gold jar containing manna, Aaron's staff that sprouted leaves, and the
stone tablets of the covenant. 5Above the Ark were the
cherubim of divine glory, whose wings stretched out
over the Ark's cover, the place of atonement. But we
cannot explain these things in detail now.

6When these things were all in place, the priests
regularly entered the first room* as they performed
their religious duties. 7But only the high priest ever
entered the Most Holy Place, and only once a year. And
he always offered blood for his own sins and for the
sins the people had committed in ignorance. 8By these
regulations the Holy Spirit revealed that the entrance
to the Most Holy Place was not freely open as long as
the Tabernacle* and the system it represented were
still in use.

9This is an illustration pointing to the present time.
For the gifts and sacrifices that the priests offer are
not able to cleanse the consciences of the people who
bring them. 10For that old system deals only with food
and drink and various cleansing ceremonies—physical regulations that were in effect only until a better
system could be established.

Christ Is the Perfect Sacrifice

HEBREWS 9:11-28

So Christ has now become the High Priest over all
the good things that have come.* He has entered that

Heb 8:10 Greek *after those days.* **Heb 8:11** Greek *their brother.* **Heb 8:8-12** Jer 31:31-34. **Heb 9:2** Or *tent;* also in 9:11, 21. **Heb 9:3** Greek *second tent.* **Heb 9:6** Greek *first tent.* **Heb 9:8** Or *the first room;* Greek reads *the first tent.* **Heb 9:11** Some manuscripts read *that are about to come.*

Heb 8:10 If our hearts are not changed, following God's rules will be unpleasant and difficult. We will rebel against being told how to live. The Holy Spirit gives us new desires, helping us *want* to obey God (see Phil 2:12-13). With new hearts, we find that serving God is our greatest joy.

Heb 8:10-11 Under God's new covenant, God's law is *inside* us. It is no longer an external set of rules and principles. The Holy Spirit reminds us of Christ's words, activates our consciences, influences our motives and desires, and makes us want to obey. Now doing God's will is something we desire with all our hearts and minds.

Heb 8:13 Some of the Jewish believers were clinging to the obsolete old ways instead of embracing Christ's new covenant. All the joy of newfound faith and all the relief of fresh forgiveness had given way to a kind of boredom that was never supposed to be. Growth had stopped. What should be done if this happens to you?

Realize that life in Christ is never complete. Heaven promises completeness; until then, growth is the normal pattern. Growth often endures seasons of drought and drabness. That's also normal. Think about what you are doing that might be spiritually ineffective or obsolete. The key to growth includes daily devotion to Christ through Bible study and prayer. Perhaps you need to intensify your study and find helps that provide more substance. Perhaps you need to grow by engaging in new areas of service that express your faith. Seek God for how he would have you keep growing in your faith.

Heb 9:5 *Cherubim* are mighty angels. One of the functions of the cherubim was to serve as guardians. These angels guarded the entrances to both the tree of life (Gen 3:24) and the Most Holy Place (Exod 26:31-33). With their wings "stretched out over the Ark's cover, the place of atonement," these two gold statues were believed to support God's invisible presence (Ezek 9:3; 10:4, 18). Here they are called "the cherubim of divine glory," referring to God's glory which hovered over the Ark of the Covenant (Exod 40:34-36; Lev 16:2).

Heb 9:6-8 The high priest could enter the Most Holy Place (Heb 9:3), the innermost room of the Tabernacle, one day each year to atone for the nation's sins. The Most Holy Place was a small room that contained the Ark of the Covenant (a gold-covered chest containing the original stone tablets on which the Ten Commandments were written, a jar of manna, and Aaron's staff). The top of the chest served as the atonement cover (the altar) on which the blood would be sprinkled by the high priest on the Day of Atonement. The Most Holy Place was the most sacred spot on earth for the Jews and only the high priest could enter it. The other priests and the common people were forbidden to come into the room. Their only access to God was through the high priest, who would offer sacrifice, using the animals' blood to atone first for his own sins and then for the people's sins (see also Heb 10:19).

Heb 9:10 The people had to keep the Old Testament dietary laws and ceremonial cleansing laws until Christ came with God's new and better way.

greater, more perfect Tabernacle in heaven, which was not made by human hands and is not part of this created world.
12With his own blood—not the blood of goats and calves—he entered the Most Holy Place once for all time and secured our redemption forever.
13Under the old system, the blood of goats and bulls and the ashes of a young cow could cleanse people's bodies from ceremonial impurity.
14Just think how much more the blood of Christ will purify our consciences from sinful deeds* so that we can worship the living God. For by the power of the eternal Spirit, Christ offered himself to God as a perfect sacrifice for our sins.
15That is why he is the one who mediates a new covenant between God and people, so that all who are called can receive the eternal inheritance God has promised them. For Christ died to set them free from the penalty of the sins they had committed under that first covenant.
16Now when someone leaves a will,* it is necessary to prove that the person who made it is dead.*
17The will goes into effect only after the person's death. While the person who made it is still alive, the will cannot be put into effect.
18That is why even the first covenant was put into effect with the blood of an animal.
19For after Moses had read each of God's commandments to all the people, he took the blood of calves and goats,* along with water, and sprinkled both the book of God's law

Heb 9:14 Greek *from dead works.* **Heb 9:16a** Or *covenant;* also in 9:17. **Heb 9:16b** Or *Now when someone makes a covenant, it is necessary to ratify it with the death of a sacrifice.* **Heb 9:19** Some manuscripts do not include *and goats.*

THE OLD AND NEW COVENANTS

Like pointing out the similarities and differences between the photograph of a person and the actual person, the writer of Hebrews shows the connection between the old Mosaic covenant and the new Messianic covenant. He proves that the old covenant was a shadow of the real Christ.

Reference	*The Old Covenant under Moses*	*The New Covenant in Christ*	*Application*
Heb 8:3-4	Gifts and sacrifices by those guilty of sin	Self-sacrifice by the guiltless Christ	Christ died for you
Heb 8:5-6, 10-12	Focused on a physical building where one goes to worship	Focuses on the reign of Christ in believers' hearts	God is directly involved in your life
Heb 8:5-6, 10-12	A shadow	A reality	Not temporal, but eternal
Heb 8:6	Limited promises	Limitless promises	We can trust God's promises to us
Heb 8:8-9	Failed agreement by people	Faithful agreement by Christ	Christ has kept the agreement where people couldn't
Heb 9:1	External standards and rules	Internal standards—a new heart	God sees both actions and motives—we are accountable to God, not rules
Heb 9:7	Limited access to God	Unlimited access to God	God is personally available
Heb 9:9-10	Legal cleansing	Personal cleansing	God's cleansing is complete
Heb 9:11-14; 24-28	Continual sacrifice	Conclusive sacrifice	Christ's sacrifice was perfect and final
Heb 9:22	Forgiveness earned	Forgiveness freely given	We have true and complete forgiveness
Heb 9:24-28	Repeated yearly	Completed by Christ's death	Christ's death can be applied to our sin
Heb 9:26	Available to some	Available to all	Available to you

Heb 9:12 This imagery comes from the Day of Atonement rituals described in Leviticus 16. Through his own death, Christ freed us from the slavery of sin forever.

Heb 9:12-14 Though you know Christ, you may believe that you have to work hard to make yourself good enough for God. But rules and rituals have never cleansed people's hearts. By Jesus' blood alone (1) we have our consciences cleansed, (2) we are freed from death's sting and can live to serve God, and (3) we are freed from sin's power. If you are carrying a load of guilt because you are finding that you can't be good enough for God, take another look at Jesus' death and what it means for you. Christ can heal your conscience and deliver you from the frustration of trying to earn God's favor. Bring your guilt-ridden life to Christ, confess your inability to clean up your own conscience, ask him to forgive you. Thank him for his deliverance. God can forgive you and clear your record.

Heb 9:13-14 When the people sacrificed animals, God considered the people's faith and obedience, cleansed them from sin, and made them ceremonially acceptable according to Old Testament law. But Christ's sacrifice transforms our lives and hearts and makes us clean on the inside. His sacrifice is infinitely more effective than animal sacrifices. No barrier of sin or weakness on our part can stifle his forgiveness.

Heb 9:14 Sinful deeds are more than just wrong actions; ironically, these also include our attempts to reach God by being good enough! Our culture glorifies self-effort and personal achievement. It defines a successful person as one who obtains certain goals: financial security, health and fitness, and the respect of others. But here the Bible gives us a different picture of successful living: accept Jesus' sacrifice for your sin, abandon the futility of sinful deeds, and let the blood of Christ purify your conscience (see Heb 10:19-22).

Heb 9:15 People in Old Testament times were saved through Christ's sacrifice, although that sacrifice had not yet happened. In offering unblemished animal sacrifices, they were anticipating Christ's coming and his death for sin. There was no point in returning to the sacrificial system now that Christ had come and had become the final, perfect sacrifice.

▸ **HEBREWS 9:11-28** ***(cont.)***

and all the people, using hyssop branches and scarlet wool. 20Then he said, "This blood confirms the covenant God has made with you."* 21And in the same way, he sprinkled blood on the Tabernacle and on everything used for worship. 22In fact, according to the law of Moses, nearly everything was purified with blood. For without the shedding of blood, there is no forgiveness.

23That is why the Tabernacle and everything in it, which were copies of things in heaven, had to be purified by the blood of animals. But the real things in heaven had to be purified with far better sacrifices than the blood of animals.

24For Christ did not enter into a holy place made with human hands, which was only a copy of the true one in heaven. He entered into heaven itself to appear now before God on our behalf. 25And he did not enter heaven to offer himself again and again, like the high priest here on earth who enters the Most Holy Place year after year with the blood of an animal. 26If that had been necessary, Christ would have had to die again and again, ever since the world began. But now, once for all time, he has appeared at the end of the age* to remove sin by his own death as a sacrifice.

27And just as each person is destined to die once and after that comes judgment, 28so also Christ died once for all time as a sacrifice to take away the sins of many people. He will come again, not to deal with our sins, but to bring salvation to all who are eagerly waiting for him.

Christ's Sacrifice Once for All

HEBREWS 10:1-18

The old system under the law of Moses was only a shadow, a dim preview of the good things to come, not the good things themselves. The sacrifices under that system were repeated again and again, year after year, but they were never able to provide perfect cleansing for those who came to worship. 2If they could have provided perfect cleansing, the sacrifices would have stopped, for the worshipers would have been purified once for all time, and their feelings of guilt would have disappeared.

3But instead, those sacrifices actually reminded them of their sins year after year. 4For it is not possible for the blood of bulls and goats to take away sins. 5That is why, when Christ* came into the world, he said to God,

> "You did not want animal sacrifices or sin
> offerings.
> But you have given me a body to offer.

Heb 9:20 Exod 24:8. **Heb 9:26** Greek *the ages.* **Heb 10:5** Greek *he;* also in 10:8.

Heb 9:22 Why does forgiveness require the shedding of blood? This is no arbitrary decree on the part of a bloodthirsty God, as some have suggested. There is no greater symbol of life than blood; blood keeps us alive. Jesus shed his blood—gave his life—for our sins so that we wouldn't have to experience spiritual death, eternal separation from God. Jesus is the source of life, not death. He gave his own life to pay our penalty for us so that we might live. After shedding his blood for us, Christ rose from the grave and proclaimed victory over sin and death.

Heb 9:23 In a way that we don't fully understand, the earthly Tabernacle was a copy and symbol of heavenly realities. This purification of the heavenly things can best be understood as referring to Christ's spiritual work for us in heaven (see the note on Heb 8:5, p. 1771).

Heb 9:24 Among references to priests, Tabernacles, sacrifices, and other ideas unfamiliar to us, we come to this description of Christ appearing in God's presence on our behalf. We can relate to this role and be encouraged by it. Christ is on our side at God's side. He is our Lord and Savior. He is not there to convince or remind God that our sins are forgiven but to present both our needs and our service for him as an offering (see Heb 7:25).

Heb 9:24-28 All people die physically, but Christ died so that we would not have to die spiritually. We can have wonderful confidence in his saving work for us, doing away with sin—past, present, and future. He has forgiven our past sin—when he died on the cross, he sacrificed himself once for all (Heb 9:26). He has given us the Holy Spirit to help us deal with present sin; he appears before God for us now in heaven (Heb 9:24). He promises to return (Heb 9:28) and raise us to eternal life in a world where sin will be banished.

Heb 9:26 The "end of the age" refers to the time of Christ's coming to earth in fulfillment of the Old Testament prophecies. Christ ushered in the new era of grace and forgiveness. We are still living in the "end of the age." The day of the Lord has begun and will be completed at Christ's return.

Heb 9:27 Judgment is not a popular theme today, but the Bible teaches that judgment is coming. Do you look forward to Christ's return, or do you see it as a threat? As sure as death itself, judgment awaits. At God's judgment there will be no higher court of appeal should the verdict not be to your liking. If you hope for a favorable verdict in this court, put your hope entirely on Jesus. Pray today—now if you haven't before—for the freedom and pardon Jesus has won for you. Then rejoice that God's judgment of you will be based on the perfect life of his Son, Jesus. After that, tell others, for many will face an unfavorable judgment without Jesus.

Heb 10:3 When people gathered for the offering of sacrifices on the Day of Atonement, they were reminded of their sins, and they undoubtedly felt guilty all over again. What they needed most was forgiveness—the permanent, powerful, sin-destroying forgiveness we have from Christ. When we confess a sin to him, we need never think of it again. Christ has forgiven us, and the sin no longer exists. (See 1 Jn 1:9.)

Heb 10:4 Animal sacrifices could not take away sins; they provided only a temporary way to deal with sin until Jesus came to deal with sin permanently. How, then, were people forgiven in Old Testament times? Because Old Testament believers were following God's command to offer sacrifices, he graciously forgave them when, by faith, they made their sacrifices. But that practice looked forward to Christ's perfect sacrifice. Christ's way was superior to the Old Testament way because the old way only pointed to what Christ would do to take away sins.

Heb 10:5-10 This quotation is not cited in any other New Testament book. However, it is a central teaching of the Old Testament that God desires obedience and a right heart, not empty compliance with the sacrifice system (see the chart on p. 809). The writer of Hebrews applies to Christ the words of the psalmist in Psalm 40:6-8. Christ came to offer his body on the cross for us as a sacrifice that is completely acceptable to God. God's new and living way for us to please him is not by keeping laws or even by abstaining from sin. It is by coming to him in faith to be forgiven, and then following him in loving obedience.

Heb 10:5-10 The costly sacrifice of an animal's life impressed upon the sinner the seriousness of one's own sin before God. Because Jesus shed his own blood for us, his

6 You were not pleased with burnt offerings
or other offerings for sin.
7 Then I said, 'Look, I have come to do your will,
O God—
as is written about me in the Scriptures.'"*

8First, Christ said, "You did not want animal sacrifices
or sin offerings or burnt offerings or other offerings
for sin, nor were you pleased with them" (though
they are required by the law of Moses). 9Then he said,
"Look, I have come to do your will." He cancels the first
covenant in order to put the second into effect. 10For
God's will was for us to be made holy by the sacrifice
of the body of Jesus Christ, once for all time.
11Under the old covenant, the priest stands and
ministers before the altar day after day, offering the
same sacrifices again and again, which can never take
away sins. 12But our High Priest offered himself to
God as a single sacrifice for sins, good for all time.
Then he sat down in the place of honor at God's right
hand. 13There he waits until his enemies are humbled
and made a footstool under his feet. 14For by that one
offering he forever made perfect those who are being
made holy.
15And the Holy Spirit also testifies that this is so.
For he says,

16 "This is the new covenant I will make
with my people on that day,* says the LORD:
I will put my laws in their hearts,
and I will write them on their minds."*

17Then he says,

"I will never again remember
their sins and lawless deeds."*

18And when sins have been forgiven, there is no need
to offer any more sacrifices.

Heb 10:5-7 Ps 40:6-8 (Greek version). **Heb 10:16a** Greek *after those days.* **Heb 10:16b** Jer 31:33a. **Heb 10:17** Jer 31:34b.

2. THE SUPERIORITY OF FAITH

Moving from argument to instruction, the author cites many examples of those who have demonstrated faith throughout history. Living by faith is far better than merely fulfilling rituals and rules. This can challenge us to grow in faith and to live in obedience to God each day.

A Call to Persevere

HEBREWS 10:19-39

And so, dear brothers and sisters,* we can boldly enter heaven's Most Holy Place because of the blood of Jesus. 20By his death,* Jesus opened a new and life-giving way through the curtain into the Most Holy Place. 21And since we have a great High Priest who rules over God's house, 22let us go right into the

Heb 10:19 Greek *brothers.* **Heb 10:20** Greek *Through his flesh.*

sacrifice is infinitely greater than any Old Testament offering. Considering the immeasurable gift he gave us, we should respond by giving him our devotion and service.

Heb 10:9 Canceling the first covenant in order to put into effect a far better one meant doing away with the system of sacrifices contained in the ceremonial law. It didn't mean eliminating God's *moral* law. The ceremonial law prepared people for Christ's coming. With Christ's death and resurrection, that system was no longer needed. And through Christ we can fulfill the moral law as we let him live in us.

Heb 10:11-12 Christ's work is contrasted with the work of the Jewish priests. The priests' work was never finished, so they had to stand day after day and offer sacrifices; Christ's sacrifice (dying in our place) is finished, so he is seated. The priests repeated the sacrifices often; Christ sacrificed once for all. The sacrifice system couldn't completely remove sin; Christ's sacrifice effectively cleansed us.

Heb 10:12 If the Jewish readers of this book were to return to the old Jewish system, they would be implying that Christ's sacrifice wasn't enough to forgive their sins. Adding anything to his sacrifice or taking anything from it denies its validity. Any system to gain salvation through good deeds is essentially rejecting the significance of Christ's death and spurning the Holy Spirit's work. Beware of anyone who tells you that Christ's sacrifice still leaves you incomplete or that something else is needed to make you acceptable to God. When we believe in Christ, he makes us completely right with God. Our loving relationship leads us to follow him in willing obedience and service. He is pleased with our service, but we cannot be saved by our good deeds.

Heb 10:14 We have been made perfect, yet we are being made holy. Through his death and resurrection, Christ, once for all, made his believers perfect in God's sight. At the same time, he is making them holy (progressively cleansed and set apart for his special use) in their daily pilgrimage here. We should not be surprised, ashamed, or shocked that we still need to grow. God is not finished with us. We can encourage this growth process by deliberately applying Scripture to all areas of our life, by accepting the discipline and guidance Christ provides, and by giving him control of our desires and goals.

Heb 10:17 The writer concludes his argument with this powerful statement that God will never again remember our sins. Christ forgives completely, so there is no need to confess our past sins repeatedly. As believers, we can be confident that the sins we confess and renounce are forgiven and forgotten.

Heb 10:19 The Most Holy Place in the Temple was sealed from view by a curtain (Heb 10:20). Only the high priest could enter this holy room, and he did so only once a year on the Day of Atonement when he offered the sacrifice for the nation's sins. But Jesus' death removed the curtain, and all believers may walk into God's presence at any time (see also Heb 6:19-20).

Heb 10:21-22 How is it possible for us to go right into the presence of God? We come not halfheartedly or with improper motives or pretense, but with pure, individual, and sincere worship. We can know that we have "sincere hearts" if we evaluate our thoughts and motives according to his Word (see Heb 4:12). Christians can approach God boldly, free from our "guilty consciences" and in full assurance because of the work of Jesus Christ. We can go to God without doubting, knowing that he will hear and answer us. Under the new covenant, our hearts and consciences are cleansed completely, not partially or temporarily (see Heb 9:14). Our clean consciences allow us to enter God's presence with boldness. Finally, the imagery of our bodies having been "washed with pure water" actually pictures an inward cleansing. Just as baptism is an outward sign that represents the purification that Christ does inside us, so this washing speaks of an internal

▸ **HEBREWS 10:19-39** ***(cont.)***

presence of God with sincere hearts fully trusting him. For our guilty consciences have been sprinkled with Christ's blood to make us clean, and our bodies have been washed with pure water.

23Let us hold tightly without wavering to the hope we affirm, for God can be trusted to keep his promise. 24Let us think of ways to motivate one another to acts of love and good works. 25And let us not neglect our meeting together, as some people do, but encourage one another, especially now that the day of his return is drawing near.

26Dear friends, if we deliberately continue sinning after we have received knowledge of the truth, there is no longer any sacrifice that will cover these sins. 27There is only the terrible expectation of God's judgment and the raging fire that will consume his enemies. 28For anyone who refused to obey the law of Moses was put to death without mercy on the testimony of two or three witnesses. 29Just think how much worse the punishment will be for those who have trampled on the Son of God, and have treated the blood of the covenant, which made us holy, as if it were common and unholy, and have insulted and disdained the Holy Spirit who brings God's mercy to us. 30For we know the one who said,

"I will take revenge.
I will pay them back."*

He also said,

"The LORD will judge his own people."*

31It is a terrible thing to fall into the hands of the living God.

32Think back on those early days when you first learned about Christ.* Remember how you remained faithful even though it meant terrible suffering. 33Sometimes you were exposed to public ridicule and were beaten, and sometimes you helped others who were suffering the same things. 34You suffered along with those who were thrown into jail, and when all you owned was taken from you, you accepted it with joy. You knew there were better things waiting for you that will last forever.

35So do not throw away this confident trust in the Lord. Remember the great reward it brings you! 36Pa-

Heb 10:30a Deut 32:35. **Heb 10:30b** Deut 32:36. **Heb 10:32** Greek *when you were first enlightened.*

cleansing from sin. Once cleansed, we can approach God.

Heb 10:22-25 We have significant privileges associated with our new life in Christ: (1) We have personal access to God through Christ and can draw near to him without an elaborate system (Heb 10:22); (2) we may grow in faith, overcome doubts and questions, and deepen our relationship with God (Heb 10:23); (3) we may enjoy motivation from one another (Heb 10:24); (4) we may worship together (Heb 10:25).

Heb 10:25 To neglect Christian meetings is to give up the encouragement and help of other Christians. We gather together to share our faith and to strengthen one another in the Lord. As we get closer to the day when Christ will return, we will face many spiritual struggles, and even times of persecution. Anti-Christian forces will grow in strength. Difficulties should never be excuses for missing church services. Rather, as difficulties arise, we should make an even greater effort to meet together.

Heb 10:26 When people deliberately reject Christ's offer of salvation, they reject God's most precious gift. They ignore the leading of the Holy Spirit, the one who communicates to us God's saving love. This warning was given to Jewish Christians who were tempted to reject Christ for Judaism, but it applies to anyone who rejects Christ for another religion or, having understood Christ's atoning work, deliberately turns away from it (see also Num 15:30-31 and Mark 3:28-30). The point is that there is no acceptable sacrifice for sin other than the death of Christ on the cross. If someone deliberately rejects the sacrifice of Christ after clearly understanding the Good News teaching about it, then there is no way for that person to be saved, because God has not provided any other name in all of heaven for people to call on to save them (see Acts 4:12).

Heb 10:29 How have people "insulted and disdained the Holy Spirit"? The sacrifice of Christ is tied with the Holy Spirit; therefore, to scorn Christ's sacrifice is to insult and disdain the Holy Spirit by arrogantly rejecting him. The Holy Spirit is a person, not just a force or influence. To reject him is to cut off the means of God's acceptance. This is equivalent to blasphemy against the Holy Spirit (see Matt 12:31-32). Insulting the Holy Spirit who brings God's mercy is deserving of great punishment.

Heb 10:31 God's power is awesome, and his punishment terrible. These words give us a glimpse into the holiness of God. He is sovereign; his power is unlimited; he will do as he promises. This judgment is for those who have rejected God's mercy. For them, falling into God's hands will be a dreadful experience. They will have no more excuses. They will discover that they were wrong, but it will be too late. For those who accept Christ's love and his salvation, the coming judgment is no cause for worry. Being saved through his grace, they have nothing to fear (see 1 Jn 4:18).

Heb 10:32-36 Hebrews encourages believers to persevere in their Christian faith and conduct when facing persecution and pressure. We don't usually think of suffering as good for us, but it can build our character and our patience. During times of great stress, we may feel God's presence more clearly and find help from Christians we never thought would care. Knowing that Jesus is with us in our suffering and that he will return one day to put an end to all pain helps us grow in our faith and our relationship with him (see Rom 5:3-5).

Heb 10:35-38 The Bible gives us a clear choice between two life directions. Because life often forks off in two directions, you must take the higher road, even though it looks more difficult and treacherous. That road gets steep in places. The climb takes a toll on your energy. It gets lonely. Not many on it, but more than you imagined, and some because of your example. It gets slippery; the devil blows ice on the narrow passages. Despite its dangers, the higher road is bound for the peak, and you'll make it—God has a lifeline around you. When you are tempted to falter in your faith or to turn back from following Christ, keep focused on what he has done for you and what he offers in the future (see Rom 8:12-25; Gal 3:10-13). Then keep climbing.

Heb 10:36 For the time being, these believers needed "patient endurance"—to remain steadfast, to hold firm. Because Christ lives in us, we can have that kind of endurance. Jesus predicted that his followers would be severely persecuted by those who hated him (Matt 10:22). But in the midst of terrible persecution, they could have hope knowing that salvation was theirs. Times of trial serve to sift true Christians from false or fair-weather Christians. When you are pressured to give up and turn your back on Christ, remember the benefits of standing firm and continue to live for Christ. Patient endurance is not a way to be saved but the evidence that you are really committed to Jesus.

tient endurance is what you need now, so that you will continue to do God's will. Then you will receive all that he has promised.

37 "For in just a little while,
the Coming One will come and not delay.
38 And my righteous ones will live by faith.*
But I will take no pleasure in anyone who
turns away."*

39 But we are not like those who turn away from God to their own destruction. We are the faithful ones, whose souls will be saved.

Great Examples of Faith

HEBREWS 11:1-40

Faith is the confidence that what we hope for will actually happen; it gives us assurance about things we
cannot see. 2 Through their faith, the people in days
of old earned a good reputation.
3 By faith we understand that the entire universe was
formed at God's command, that what we now see did
not come from anything that can be seen.
4 It was by faith that Abel brought a more acceptable
offering to God than Cain did. Abel's offering gave evidence that he was a righteous man, and God showed
his approval of his gifts. Although Abel is long dead,
he still speaks to us by his example of faith.
5 It was by faith that Enoch was taken up to heaven
without dying—"he disappeared, because God took
him."* For before he was taken up, he was known as
a person who pleased God. 6 And it is impossible to
please God without faith. Anyone who wants to come
to him must believe that God exists and that he rewards those who sincerely seek him.
7 It was by faith that Noah built a large boat to save
his family from the flood. He obeyed God, who warned
him about things that had never happened before. By
his faith Noah condemned the rest of the world, and
he received the righteousness that comes by faith.
8 It was by faith that Abraham obeyed when God
called him to leave home and go to another land that
God would give him as his inheritance. He went without knowing where he was going. 9 And even when he
reached the land God promised him, he lived there
by faith—for he was like a foreigner, living in tents.
And so did Isaac and Jacob, who inherited the same
promise. 10 Abraham was confidently looking forward
to a city with eternal foundations, a city designed and
built by God.
11 It was by faith that even Sarah was able to have

Heb 10:38 Or *my righteous ones will live by their faithfulness;* Greek reads *my righteous one will live by faith.* **Heb 10:37-38** Hab 2:3-4. **Heb 11:5** Gen 5:24.

Heb 11:1 Do you remember how you felt when you were very young and your birthday approached? You were excited and anxious. You knew you would certainly receive gifts and other special treats. But some things would be a surprise. Birthdays combine assurance and anticipation, and so does faith! Faith is the confidence based on past experience that God's new and fresh surprises will surely be ours.

Heb 11:1 The beginning point of faith is believing in God's character: He *is* who he says. The end point is believing in God's promises: He *will do* what he says. When we believe that God will fulfill his promises even though we don't see those promises materializing yet, we demonstrate true faith (see John 20:24-31).

Heb 11:3 God called the universe into existence out of nothing; he declared that it was to be, and it was. Our faith is in the God who created the entire universe by his word. God's word has awesome power. When he speaks, do you listen and respond? How can you better prepare yourself to respond to God's word?

Heb 11:4 Cain and Abel were Adam and Eve's first two sons. Abel offered a sacrifice that pleased God, while Cain's sacrifice was unacceptable. Abel's Profile is on p. 14. Cain's Profile is on p. 15. Abel's sacrifice (an animal substitute) was more acceptable to God, both because it was a blood sacrifice and, most important, because of Abel's attitude when he offered it.

Heb 11:6 Believing that God exists is only the beginning; even the demons believe that much (Jas 2:19-20). God will not settle for mere acknowledgment of his existence. He wants your faith that leads to a personal, dynamic relationship with him.

But does faith make sense, really? Do you believe because faith makes sense, or because faith doesn't need to make sense? Some Christians think people cannot understand God and should not try. Others believe that nothing true is irrational, including true faith. The truth is, God gave us minds that should be developed and used. To ignore intellectual growth is to live a stunted and naive life. God wants our trust and faith, even while we ponder and wonder about so many matters mysterious to us. Even so, we do not believe in a void nor leap into the dark. Faith is reasonable, though reason alone cannot explain the whole of it. So use your mind to think things through. But leave room for the unexplainable works of God.

Heb 11:6 Sometimes we wonder about the fate of those who haven't heard of Christ and have not even had a Bible to read. God assures us that all who honestly seek him—who act in faith on the knowledge of God that they do possess—will be rewarded. When you tell others the Good News, encourage them to be honest and diligent in their search for truth. Those who hear the Good News are responsible for what they have heard (see 2 Cor 6:1-2).

Heb 11:7 Noah experienced rejection because he was different from his neighbors. God commanded him to build a huge boat in the middle of dry land, and although God's command seemed foolish, Noah obeyed. Noah's obedience made him appear strange to his neighbors, just as the new beliefs of Jewish Christians undoubtedly made them stand out. As you obey God, don't be surprised if others regard you as "different." Your obedience makes their disobedience stand out. Remember, if God asks you to do something, he will give you the necessary strength to carry out that task. For more information on Noah, see his Profile on p. 19.

Heb 11:8-10 Abraham's life was filled with faith. At God's command, he left home and went to another land—obeying without question (Gen 12:1ff). He believed the covenant that God made with him (Gen 12:2-3; 13:14-16; 15:1-6). In obedience to God, Abraham was even willing to sacrifice his son Isaac (Gen 22:1-19). Do not be surprised if God asks you to give up secure, familiar surroundings in order to carry out his will. For further information on Abraham, see his Profile on p. 31.

Heb 11:11-12 Sarah was Abraham's wife. They were unable to have children through many years of their marriage. God promised Abraham a son, but Sarah doubted that she could become pregnant in her old age. At first she laughed, but afterward, she believed (Gen 18). For more information on Sarah, see her Profile on p. 38.

▶ **HEBREWS 11:1-40** ***(cont.)***

a child, though she was barren and was too old. She
believed* that God would keep his promise. 12And so
a whole nation came from this one man who was as
good as dead—a nation with so many people that, like
the stars in the sky and the sand on the seashore, there
is no way to count them.

13All these people died still believing what God had
promised them. They did not receive what was promised, but they saw it all from a distance and welcomed
it. They agreed that they were foreigners and nomads
here on earth. 14Obviously people who say such things
are looking forward to a country they can call their
own. 15If they had longed for the country they came
from, they could have gone back. 16But they were looking for a better place, a heavenly homeland. That is
why God is not ashamed to be called their God, for
he has prepared a city for them.

17It was by faith that Abraham offered Isaac as a
sacrifice when God was testing him. Abraham, who
had received God's promises, was ready to sacrifice
his only son, Isaac, 18even though God had told him,
"Isaac is the son through whom your descendants will
be counted."* 19Abraham reasoned that if Isaac died,
God was able to bring him back to life again. And in a
sense, Abraham did receive his son back from the dead.

20It was by faith that Isaac promised blessings for
the future to his sons, Jacob and Esau.

21It was by faith that Jacob, when he was old and
dying, blessed each of Joseph's sons and bowed in
worship as he leaned on his staff.

22It was by faith that Joseph, when he was about to
die, said confidently that the people of Israel would
leave Egypt. He even commanded them to take his
bones with them when they left.

23It was by faith that Moses' parents hid him for
three months when he was born. They saw that God
had given them an unusual child, and they were not
afraid to disobey the king's command.

24It was by faith that Moses, when he grew up, refused to be called the son of Pharaoh's daughter. 25He
chose to share the oppression of God's people instead
of enjoying the fleeting pleasures of sin. 26He thought
it was better to suffer for the sake of Christ than to own
the treasures of Egypt, for he was looking ahead to his
great reward. 27It was by faith that Moses left the land

Heb 11:11 Or *It was by faith that he [Abraham] was able to have a child, even though Sarah was barren and he was too old. He believed.* **Heb 11:18** Gen 21:12.

Heb 11:13 That we are "foreigners and nomads" on earth may be an awareness forced on us by circumstances. It may come late in life or as the result of difficult times. But this world is not our home. We cannot live here forever (see also 1 Pet 1:1). It is best for us not to be so attached to this world's desires and possessions that we can't move out at God's command.

Heb 11:13-16 These people of faith died without receiving all that God had promised, but they never lost their vision of heaven ("a better place, a heavenly homeland"). Many Christians become frustrated and defeated because their needs, wants, expectations, and demands are not immediately met when they accept Christ as Savior. They become impatient and want to quit. Are you discouraged because the achievement of your goal seems far away? Take courage from these heroes of faith, who lived and died without seeing the fruit of their faith on earth and yet continued to believe (see Heb 11:36-39).

Heb 11:17-19 Abraham was willing to give up his son when God commanded him to do so (Gen 22:1-19). God did not let Abraham take Isaac's life because God had given the command in order to test Abraham's faith. Instead of taking Abraham's son, God gave Abraham a whole nation of descendants through Isaac. If you are afraid to trust God with the possession, dream, or person you treasure most, pay attention to Abraham's example. Because Abraham was willing to give up everything for God, he received back more than he could have imagined. What we receive is not always immediate or in the form of material possessions. Material things should be among the least satisfying of rewards. Our best and greatest rewards await us in eternity.

Heb 11:20 Isaac was the son who had been promised to Abraham and Sarah in their old age. It was through Isaac that God fulfilled his promise to eventually give Abraham countless descendants. Isaac had twin sons, Jacob and Esau. God chose the younger son, Jacob, through whom to continue the fulfillment of his promise to Abraham. For more information on Isaac, see his Profile on p. 44.

Heb 11:21 Jacob was Isaac's son and Abraham's grandson. Jacob's sons became the fathers of Israel's 12 tribes. Even when Jacob (also called "Israel") was dying in a strange land, he believed the promise that Abraham's descendants would be like the sand on the seashore and that Israel would become a great nation (Gen 48:1-22). True faith helps us see beyond the grave. For more information on Jacob and Esau, see their Profiles on pp. 55 and 52.

Heb 11:22 Joseph, one of Jacob's sons, was sold into slavery by his jealous brothers (Gen 37). Then Joseph was sold again, this time to an official of the Pharaoh of Egypt. But eventually, because of Joseph's faithfulness to God, he was given a top-ranking position in Egypt. Although Joseph could have used that position to build a personal empire, he remembered God's promise to Abraham. After he had been reconciled to his brothers, Joseph brought his family to be near him and requested that his bones be taken to the Promised Land when the Jews eventually left Egypt (Gen 50:24-25). Faith means trusting in God and doing what he wants, regardless of the circumstances or consequences. For more information on Joseph, see his Profile on p. 71.

Heb 11:23 Moses' parents trusted God to protect their son's life. They were not merely proud parents; they were believers who had faith that God would care for him. As a parent, have you trusted God enough to take care of your children? God has a plan for every person, and your important task is to pray for your children and prepare them to do the work God has planned for them to do. Faith allows us to entrust even our children to God.

Heb 11:24-28 Moses became one of Israel's greatest leaders, a prophet and a lawgiver. But when he was born, his people were slaves in Egypt, and the Egyptian officials had ordered that all Hebrew baby boys be killed. Moses was spared, and Pharaoh's daughter raised Moses in Pharaoh's own household (Exod 1–2)! It took faith for Moses to give up his place in the palace, but he could do it because he saw the fleeting nature of great wealth and prestige. It is easy to be deceived by the temporary benefits of wealth, popularity, status, and achievement, and to be blind to the long-range benefits of God's Kingdom. Faith helps us look beyond the world's value system to see the eternal values of God's Kingdom. For more information on Moses, see his Profile on p. 148.

Heb 11:26 True wealth is eternal. Consider the most powerful or well-known people in our world—how many got where they are by being humble, self-effacing, and gentle? Not many! But in the life to come, the last will be first—if they got in last place by choosing to follow Jesus. Hebrews has a critical message for earth-loving Christians. Don't forfeit eternal rewards for temporary benefits. Like Moses, be willing to make sacrifices now for greater rewards later (Matt 6:19-21).

of Egypt, not fearing the king's anger. He kept right on going because he kept his eyes on the one who is invisible. 28 It was by faith that Moses commanded the people of Israel to keep the Passover and to sprinkle blood on the doorposts so that the angel of death would not kill their firstborn sons.

29 It was by faith that the people of Israel went right through the Red Sea as though they were on dry ground. But when the Egyptians tried to follow, they were all drowned.

30 It was by faith that the people of Israel marched around Jericho for seven days, and the walls came crashing down.

31 It was by faith that Rahab the prostitute was not destroyed with the people in her city who refused to obey God. For she had given a friendly welcome to the spies.

32 How much more do I need to say? It would take too long to recount the stories of the faith of Gideon, Barak, Samson, Jephthah, David, Samuel, and all the prophets. 33 By faith these people overthrew kingdoms, ruled with justice, and received what God had promised them. They shut the mouths of lions, 34 quenched the flames of fire, and escaped death by the edge of the sword. Their weakness was turned to strength. They became strong in battle and put whole armies to flight. 35 Women received their loved ones back again from death.

But others were tortured, refusing to turn from God in order to be set free. They placed their hope in a better life after the resurrection. 36 Some were jeered at, and their backs were cut open with whips. Others were chained in prisons. 37 Some died by stoning, some were sawed in half,* and others were killed with the sword. Some went about wearing skins of sheep and goats, destitute and oppressed and mistreated. 38 They were too good for this world, wandering over deserts and mountains, hiding in caves and holes in the ground.

39 All these people earned a good reputation because of their faith, yet none of them received all that God had promised. 40 For God had something better in mind for us, so that they would not reach perfection without us.

Heb 11:37 Some manuscripts add *some were tested.*

Heb 11:31 When Joshua planned the conquest of Jericho, he sent spies to investigate the fortifications of the city. The spies met Rahab, who had two strikes against her—she was a Gentile and a prostitute. But she showed that she had faith in God by welcoming the spies and by trusting God to spare her and her family when the city was destroyed. Faith helps us turn around and do what is right regardless of our past or the disapproval of others. For more information on Rahab, see her Profile on p. 345.

Heb 11:32-35 The Old Testament records the lives of the various people who experienced these great victories. Joshua and Deborah overthrew kingdoms (the book of Joshua; Judg 4–5). Nehemiah ruled with justice (the book of Nehemiah). Daniel was saved from the mouths of lions (Dan 6). Shadrach, Meshach, and Abednego were kept from harm in the flames of a blazing furnace (Dan 3). Elijah escaped the swords of evil Queen Jezebel's henchmen (1 Kgs 19:2ff). Hezekiah regained strength after sickness (2 Kgs 20). Gideon was strong in battle (Judg 7). A widow's son was brought back to life by the prophet Elisha (2 Kgs 4:8-37).

We, too, can experience victory through faith in Christ. Our victories over oppressors may be like those of the Old Testament saints, but more likely, our victories will be directly related to the role God wants us to play. Even though our body deteriorates and dies, we will live forever because of Christ. In the promised resurrection, even death will be defeated, and Christ's victory will be made complete.

Heb 11:32-40 These verses summarize the lives of other great men and women of faith. Some experienced outstanding victories, even over the threat of death. But others were severely mistreated, tortured, and even killed. Having a steadfast faith in God does not guarantee a happy, carefree life. On the contrary, our faith almost guarantees us some form of abuse from the world. While we are on earth, we may never see the purpose of our suffering. But we know that God will keep his promises to us. Do you believe that God will keep his promises to *you*?

Heb 11:35-39 Many think that pain is the exception in the Christian life. When suffering occurs, they say, "Why me?" They feel as though God deserted them, or perhaps they accuse him of not being as dependable as they thought. In reality, we live in an evil world filled with suffering, even for believers. But God is still in control. He allows some Christians to become martyrs for the faith, and he allows others to survive persecution. Rather than asking, "Why me?" it is much more helpful to ask, "Why not me?" Our faith and the values of this world are on a collision course. If we expect pain and suffering to come, we will not be shocked when they hit. But we can take comfort in knowing that Jesus also suffered. He understands our fears, our weaknesses, and our disappointments (see Heb 2:16-18; 4:14-16). He promised never to leave us (Matt 28:18-20), and he intercedes on our behalf (Heb 7:24-25). In times of pain, persecution, or suffering, we should trust confidently in Christ.

Heb 11:39-40 Hebrews 11 has been called faith's hall of fame. No doubt the author surprised his readers by this conclusion: These mighty Jewish heroes did not receive all that God had promised because they died before Christ came. In God's plan, they and the Christian believers (who were also enduring much testing) would be rewarded together. Once again Hebrews shows that Christianity offers a better way than Judaism.

Heb 11:40 There is a solidarity among believers (see Heb 12:23). Old and New Testament believers will be glorified together. Not only are we one in the body of Christ with all those now alive, but we are also one with all those who have ever lived. It takes all of us to be perfect in him.

God's Discipline Proves His Love

HEBREWS 12:1-13

Therefore, since we are surrounded by such a huge crowd of witnesses to the life of faith, let us strip off every weight that slows us down, especially the sin that so easily trips us up. And let us run with endurance the race God has set before us. 2We do this by keeping our eyes on Jesus, the champion who initiates and perfects our faith.* Because of the joy* awaiting him, he endured the cross, disregarding its shame. Now he is seated in the place of honor beside God's throne. 3Think of all the hostility he endured from sinful people;* then you won't become weary and give up. 4After all, you have not yet given your lives in your struggle against sin.

5And have you forgotten the encouraging words God spoke to you as his children?* He said,

"My child,* don't make light of the LORD's
 discipline,
and don't give up when he corrects you.
6 For the LORD disciplines those he loves,
and he punishes each one he accepts
 as his child."*

7As you endure this divine discipline, remember that God is treating you as his own children. Who ever heard of a child who is never disciplined by its father? 8If God doesn't discipline you as he does all of his children, it means that you are illegitimate and are not really his children at all. 9Since we respected our earthly fathers who disciplined us, shouldn't we submit even more to the discipline of the Father of our spirits, and live forever?*

10For our earthly fathers disciplined us for a few years, doing the best they knew how. But God's discipline is always good for us, so that we might share in his holiness. 11No discipline is enjoyable while it is happening—it's painful! But afterward there will be a peaceful harvest of right living for those who are trained in this way.

12So take a new grip with your tired hands and

Heb 12:2a Or *Jesus, the originator and perfecter of our faith.* **Heb 12:2b** Or *Instead of the joy.* **Heb 12:3** Some manuscripts read *Think of how people hurt themselves by opposing him.* **Heb 12:5a** Greek *sons;* also in 12:7, 8. **Heb 12:5b** Greek *son;* also in 12:6, 7. **Heb 12:5-6** Prov 3:11-12 (Greek version). **Heb 12:9** Or *and really live?*

Heb 12:1 This "huge crowd of witnesses" is composed of the people described in Hebrews 11. Their faithfulness is a constant encouragement to us. We do not struggle alone, and we are not the first to struggle with the problems we face. Others have run the race and won, and their witness stirs us to run and win also. What an inspiring heritage we have!

Heb 12:1 Long-distance runners work hard to build endurance and strength. On race day, their clothes are lightweight and their bodies lean. To run the race that God has set before us, we must also strip off the excess weight that slows us down. How can we do that? (1) Choose friends who are also committed to the race. Wrong friends will have values and activities that may deter you from the course. Much of your own weight may result from the crowd you run with. Make wise choices. (2) Drop certain activities. That is, for you at this time these may be excess weight. Try dropping them for a while; then check the results in your life. (3) Get help for addictions that disable you. If you have a secret "weight" such as pornography, gambling, or alcohol, admit your need and get help today.

Heb 12:1-4 The Christian life involves hard work. It requires us to give up whatever endangers our relationship with God, to run with endurance, and to struggle against sin with the power of the Holy Spirit. To live effectively, we must keep our eyes on Jesus. We will stumble if we look away from him to stare at ourselves or at the circumstances surrounding us. We should be running for Christ, not ourselves, and we must always keep him in sight.

Heb 12:3 When we face hardship and discouragement, it is easy to lose sight of the big picture. But we're not alone; there is help. Many have already made it through life, enduring far more difficult circumstances than we have experienced. Suffering is the training ground for Christian maturity. It develops our patience and makes our final victory sweet.

Let us strip off every weight that slows us down, especially the sin that so easily trips us up. And let us run with endurance the race God has set before us.
Hebrews 12:1

Heb 12:4 These readers were facing difficult times of persecution, but none of them had yet died for their faith. Because they were still alive, the writer urged them to continue to run their race. Just as Christ did not give up, neither should they.

Heb 12:5-11 Who loves his children more—the father who allows the children to do what will harm them, or the one who corrects, trains, and even punishes the children to help them learn what is right? It's never pleasant to be corrected and disciplined by God, but his discipline is a sign of his deep love for us. When God corrects you, see it as proof of his love, and ask him what he is trying to teach you.

Heb 12:11 We may respond to discipline in several ways: (1) We can accept it with resignation; (2) we can accept it with self-pity, thinking we really don't deserve it; (3) we can be angry and resentful toward God; or (4) we can accept it gratefully, as the appropriate response we owe a loving Father.

Heb 12:12-13 God is not only a disciplining parent but also a demanding coach who pushes us to our limits and requires our lives to be disciplined. Although we may not feel strong enough to push on to victory, we will be able to accomplish it as we follow Christ and draw on his strength. Then we can use our growing strength to help those around us who are weak and struggling.

strengthen your weak knees. 13Mark out a straight path for your feet so that those who are weak and lame will not fall but become strong.

A Call to Listen to God

HEBREWS 12:14-29

Work at living in peace with everyone, and work at living a holy life, for those who are not holy will not see the Lord. 15Look after each other so that none of you fails to receive the grace of God. Watch out that no poisonous root of bitterness grows up to trouble you, corrupting many. 16Make sure that no one is immoral or godless like Esau, who traded his birthright as the firstborn son for a single meal. 17You know that afterward, when he wanted his father's blessing, he was rejected. It was too late for repentance, even though he begged with bitter tears.

18You have not come to a physical mountain,* to a place of flaming fire, darkness, gloom, and whirlwind, as the Israelites did at Mount Sinai. 19For they heard an awesome trumpet blast and a voice so terrible that they begged God to stop speaking. 20They staggered back under God's command: "If even an animal touches the mountain, it must be stoned to death."* 21Moses himself was so frightened at the sight that he said, "I am terrified and trembling."*

22No, you have come to Mount Zion, to the city of the living God, the heavenly Jerusalem, and to countless thousands of angels in a joyful gathering. 23You have come to the assembly of God's firstborn children, whose names are written in heaven. You have come to God himself, who is the judge over all things. You have come to the spirits of the righteous ones in heaven who have now been made perfect. 24You have come to Jesus, the one who mediates the new covenant between God and people, and to the sprinkled blood, which speaks of forgiveness instead of crying out for vengeance like the blood of Abel.

25Be careful that you do not refuse to listen to the One who is speaking. For if the people of Israel did not escape when they refused to listen to Moses, the earthly messenger, we will certainly not escape if we reject the One who speaks to us from heaven! 26When God spoke from Mount Sinai his voice shook the earth, but now he makes another promise: "Once again I will shake not only the earth but the heavens also."* 27This means that all of creation will be shaken and removed, so that only unshakable things will remain.

28Since we are receiving a Kingdom that is unshakable, let us be thankful and please God by worshiping him with holy fear and awe. 29For our God is a devouring fire.

Heb 12:18 Greek *to something that can be touched.* **Heb 12:20** Exod 19:13. **Heb 12:21** Deut 9:19. **Heb 12:26** Hag 2:6.

Heb 12:12-13 We must not live with only our own survival in mind. Others will follow our example, and we have a responsibility to them if we are living for Christ, as we claim to be. Does your example make it easier for others to believe in and follow Christ, and to mature in him? Or would those who follow you end up confused and misled?

Heb 12:14 The readers were familiar with the ceremonial cleansing ritual that prepared them for worship, and they knew that they had to be holy or clean in order to enter the Temple. Sin always blocks our vision of God; so if we want to see God, we must renounce sin and obey him (see Ps 24:3-4). Holiness is coupled with living in peace. A right relationship with God leads to right relationships with fellow believers. Although we will not always feel loving toward all other believers, we must pursue peace as we become more Christlike.

Heb 12:15 Like a small root that grows into a great tree, bitterness springs up in our hearts and overshadows even our deepest Christian relationships. A "poisonous root of bitterness" comes when we allow disappointment to grow into resentment, or when we nurse grudges over past hurts. Bitterness brings with it jealousy, dissension, and immorality. When the Holy Spirit fills us, he can heal the hurt that causes bitterness.

Heb 12:16-17 Esau's story shows us that mistakes and sins sometimes have lasting consequences (Gen 25:29-34; 27:36). Even repentance and forgiveness do not always eliminate sin's consequences. How often do you make decisions based on what you want now, rather than on what you need in the long run? Evaluate the long-range effects of your decisions and actions.

Heb 12:18-24 What a contrast between the people's terrified approach to God at Mount Sinai and their joyful approach at Mount Zion! What a difference Jesus has made! Before Jesus came, God seemed distant and threatening. After Jesus came, God welcomes us through Christ into his presence. Accept God's invitation!

Heb 12:22 As Christians, we are citizens of the heavenly Jerusalem right now; because Christ rules our lives, the Holy Spirit is always with us, and we experience close fellowship with other believers. (The full and ultimate rewards and the reality of the heavenly Jerusalem are depicted in Rev 21.)

Heb 12:27-29 Eventually the world will crumble, and only God's Kingdom will last. Those who follow Christ are part of this unshakable Kingdom, and they will withstand the shaking, sifting, and burning. When we feel unsure about the future, we can take confidence from these verses. No matter what happens here, our future is built on a solid foundation that cannot be destroyed. Don't put your confidence in what will be destroyed; instead, build your life on Christ and his unshakable Kingdom. (See Matt 7:24-27 for the importance of building on a solid foundation.)

Heb 12:28 Here are five ways we can be thankful: (1) We can be thankful that God answers our prayers (Isa 65:24; John 11:41). (2) We can be thankful for God's provision (1 Thes 5:17-18; 1 Tim 4:4-5). (3) We can be thankful for God's blessings (1 Chr 16:34; Phil 4:6). (4) We can be thankful for God's character and wondrous works (Ps 7:17; 2 Cor 9:15; Rev 11:17). (5) We can be thankful for our brothers and sisters in Christ (1 Cor 1:4; Eph 1:16; Phil 1:3-5).

Heb 12:29 There is a big difference between the flame of a candle and the roaring blast of a forest fire. We cannot even stand near a raging fire. Even with sophisticated firefighting equipment, a devouring fire is often beyond human control. God is not within our control, either. We cannot force him to do anything for us through our prayers. He cannot be contained. Yet, he is a God of compassion. He has saved us from sin, and he will save us from death. But everything that is worthless and sinful will be devoured by the fire of his wrath. Only what is good, dedicated to God, and righteous will remain.

Concluding Words

HEBREWS 13:1-25

Keep on loving each other as brothers and sisters.*
2Don't forget to show hospitality to strangers, for some
who have done this have entertained angels without
realizing it! 3Remember those in prison, as if you were
there yourself. Remember also those being mistreated,
as if you felt their pain in your own bodies.
4Give honor to marriage, and remain faithful to one
another in marriage. God will surely judge people who
are immoral and those who commit adultery.
5Don't love money; be satisfied with what you have.
For God has said,

"I will never fail you.
I will never abandon you."*

6So we can say with confidence,

"The LORD is my helper,
so I will have no fear.
What can mere people do to me?"*

7Remember your leaders who taught you the word
of God. Think of all the good that has come from their
lives, and follow the example of their faith.
8Jesus Christ is the same yesterday, today, and forever. 9So do not be attracted by strange, new ideas.
Your strength comes from God's grace, not from
rules about food, which don't help those who follow them.
10We have an altar from which the priests in the
Tabernacle* have no right to eat. 11Under the old system, the high priest brought the blood of animals into
the Holy Place as a sacrifice for sin, and the bodies of
the animals were burned outside the camp. 12So also
Jesus suffered and died outside the city gates to make
his people holy by means of his own blood. 13So let us
go out to him, outside the camp, and bear the disgrace
he bore. 14For this world is not our permanent home;
we are looking forward to a home yet to come.
15Therefore, let us offer through Jesus a continual
sacrifice of praise to God, proclaiming our allegiance

Heb 13:1 Greek *Continue in brotherly love.* **Heb 13:5** Deut 31:6, 8. **Heb 13:6** Ps 118:6. **Heb 13:10** Or *tent.*

Heb 13:1-5 Real love for others produces tangible actions: (1) hospitality to strangers (Heb 13:2); (2) empathy for those who are in prison and for those who have been mistreated (Heb 13:3); (3) respect for your marriage vows (Heb 13:4); and (4) contentment with what you have (Heb 13:5). Make sure that your love runs deep enough to affect your hospitality, empathy, fidelity, and contentment.

Heb 13:2 Three Old Testament people "entertained angels without realizing it": (1) Abraham (Gen 18:1ff), (2) Gideon (Judg 6:11ff), and (3) Manoah (Judg 13:2ff). Some people say they cannot be hospitable because their homes are not large enough or nice enough. But even if you have no more than a table and two chairs in a rented room, there are people who would be grateful to spend time in your home. Are there visitors to your church with whom you could share a meal? Do you know single people who would enjoy an evening of conversation? Is there any way your home could meet the needs of traveling missionaries? Hospitality simply means making other people feel comfortable and at home.

Heb 13:3 We are to have empathy for those in prison, especially for (but not limited to) Christians imprisoned for their faith. Jesus said that his true followers would represent him as they visit those in prison (Matt 25:36). Prisons are a mission field—believers can send in evangelists and Bible teachers. Prison systems are political projects—Christian voices are needed regarding justice and mercy in funding, staff training, and rehabilitative programs. Prisons are an international problem—through multinational Christian agencies, believers can help victims in other countries. Compassion for suffering people demands no less. There is a wide open field of ways to obey this command to "remember those in prison."

Heb 13:4 Giving honor to marriage will require the utmost in Christian conviction and sensitivity. Modern social theory may redefine the family, and the new definitions may be far from its biblical foundation. What can you do? Witness to the depth of God's love for you by keeping your marriage happy and strong. Remain faithful—in body and in mind. Pray for your spouse. Honor biblical marriage (man–woman unions) by resisting political pressure to recognize and legalize other sexual preferences. Teach children the biblical meaning of marriage. Pray early for their own eventual spouses and families. Make marriage enrichment the goal of your small group discussions and study. Encourage the marriages around you to stay strong as well.

Heb 13:5-6 How can we learn to be satisfied with what we have? Strive to live with less rather than desiring more; give away out of your abundance rather than accumulating more; relish what you have rather than resent what you're missing. We become satisfied when we realize God's sufficiency for our needs. Christians who become materialistic are saying by their actions that God can't take care of them—or at least that he won't take care of them the way they want. Insecurity can lead to the love of money, whether we are rich or poor. The only antidote is to trust God to meet all our needs. See God's love expressed in what he has provided, and remember that money and possessions will all pass away. (See Phil 4:11 for more on contentment, and 1 Jn 2:17 for the futility of earthly desires.)

Heb 13:7 If you are a Christian, you owe much to others who have taught you and modeled for you what you needed to know about the Good News and Christian living. Continue following the good examples of those who have invested themselves in you by investing in your life through evangelism, service, and Christian education.

Heb 13:8 Though human leaders have much to offer, we must keep our eyes on Christ, our ultimate leader. Unlike any human leaders, he will never change. Christ has been and will be the same forever. In a changing world, we can trust our unchanging Lord.

Heb 13:9 Apparently some were teaching that keeping the Old Testament ceremonial laws and rituals (such as not eating certain foods) was important for salvation. But these laws were useless for conquering a person's evil thoughts and desires (Col 2:23). The laws could influence conduct, but they could not change the heart. Lasting changes in conduct begin when the Holy Spirit lives in each person.

Heb 13:13 The Jewish Christians were being ridiculed and persecuted by Jews who didn't believe in Jesus the Messiah. Most of the book of Hebrews tells them how Christ is greater than the sacrificial system. Here the writer drives home the point of his lengthy argument: It may be necessary to leave the "camp" and suffer with Christ. To be outside the camp meant to be unclean—in the days of the Exodus, those who were ceremonially unclean had to stay outside the camp. Jesus suffered humiliation and uncleanness outside the Jerusalem gates on their behalf. The time had come for Jewish Christians to declare their loyalty to Christ above any other loyalty, to choose to follow the Messiah whatever suffering that might entail. They needed to move outside the safe confinement of their past, their

to his name. [16]And don't forget to do good and to
share with those in need. These are the sacrifices
that please God.
[17]Obey your spiritual leaders, and do what they say.
Their work is to watch over your souls, and they are
accountable to God. Give them reason to do this with
joy and not with sorrow. That would certainly not be
for your benefit.
[18]Pray for us, for our conscience is clear and we
want to live honorably in everything we do. [19]And especially pray that I will be able to come back to you
soon.

20 Now may the God of peace—
who brought up from the dead our
Lord Jesus,
the great Shepherd of the sheep,
and ratified an eternal covenant with his
blood—
21 may he equip you with all you need
for doing his will.
May he produce in you,*
through the power of Jesus Christ,
every good thing that is pleasing to him.
All glory to him forever and ever! Amen.

[22]I urge you, dear brothers and sisters,* to pay attention to what I have written in this brief exhortation.
[23]I want you to know that our brother Timothy has
been released from jail. If he comes here soon, I will
bring him with me to see you.
[24]Greet all your leaders and all the believers there.*
The believers from Italy send you their greetings.
[25]May God's grace be with you all.

Heb 13:21 Some manuscripts read *in us.* **Heb 13:22** Greek *brothers.* **Heb 13:24** Greek *all of God's holy people.*

---

traditions, and their ceremonies to live for Christ. What holds you back from complete loyalty to Jesus Christ?

Heb 13:14 Christians love their families, spouses, jobs, and churches—but their sights should be set ahead beyond the horizon. Christians are activists, invested in witnessing to a needy world—but they take frequent glances toward a promised community still to come. Christians are gardeners and builders, shaping environments, turning weed pits into floral splendor, painting and patching and clearing—but they know God is building something far more beautiful and breathtaking just for them. Christians should be characterized by looking forward to the future. We should not be attached to this world, because all that we are and have here is temporary. We should not love our present home so much that we lose sight of God's future blessing. Don't store up your treasures here; store them in heaven (Matt 6:19-21).

Heb 13:15 Our lips should confess God's name in praise. Yet, in your typical day, how many times do you hear God's name used profanely? Christians should turn their frequency toward praise! Praise God early in the day before the rush, then again in the hurried middle, and at the end as business winds down. Offer Jesus a continual sacrifice of praise.

Heb 13:15-16 Since these Jewish Christians, because of their witness to the Messiah, no longer worshiped with other Jews, they should consider praise and acts of service their sacrifices—ones they could offer anywhere, anytime. This must have reminded them of the prophet Hosea's words, "Forgive all our sins and graciously receive us, so that we may offer you our praises" (Hos 14:2). A "sacrifice of praise" today would include thanking Christ for his sacrifice on the cross and telling others about it. Acts of kindness and sharing are particularly pleasing to God, even when they go unnoticed by others.

Heb 13:17 The task of church leaders is to help people mature in Christ. Cooperative followers greatly ease the burden of leadership. Does your conduct give your leaders reason to report joyfully about you?

Heb 13:18-19 The writer recognizes the need for prayer. Christian leaders are especially vulnerable to criticism from others, pride (if they succeed), depression (if they fail), and Satan's constant efforts to destroy their work for God. The leaders in your church have been placed in that position by a loving God who has entrusted them with the responsibility of caring for you. Your leaders need your prayers! For whom should you regularly pray?

Heb 13:20-21 These verses include two significant results of Christ's death and resurrection. God works in us to make us the kind of people that would please him, and he equips us to do the kind of work that would please him. Let God change you from within and then use you to help others.

Heb 13:23 We have no record of Timothy's imprisonment, but we know that he had been in prison because it states here that he had been released. For more about Timothy, see his Profile on p. 1727.

Heb 13:24-25 Hebrews is a call to Christian maturity. It was addressed to first-century Jewish Christians, but it applies to Christians of any age or background. Christian maturity means making Christ the beginning and end of our faith. To grow in maturity, we must center our lives on him, not depending on religious ritual, not falling back into sin, not trusting in ourselves, and not letting anything come between us and Christ. Christ is sufficient and superior.

X. Jude's Letter to Christians

Jude was the brother of James, and Jesus' half brother. Like James, he didn't believe in Jesus until after the Resurrection, but then he became a leader in the church. Jude wrote to motivate Christians everywhere to action. He wanted them to recognize the dangers of false teaching, to protect themselves and other believers, and to win back those who had already been deceived. Jude was writing against godless teachers who were saying that Christians could do as they pleased without fear of God's punishment. While few teach this heresy openly in the church today, many in the church act as though this were true. This letter warns against living a nominal Christian life.

Greetings from Jude

JUDE 1:1-2

This letter is from Jude, a slave of Jesus Christ and a
brother of James.
I am writing to all who have been called by God the
Father, who loves you and keeps you safe in the care
of Jesus Christ.*
2May God give you more and more mercy, peace,
and love.

The Danger of False Teachers

JUDE 1:3-16

Dear friends, I had been eagerly planning to write to
you about the salvation we all share. But now I find
that I must write about something else, urging you
to defend the faith that God has entrusted once for
all time to his holy people. 4I say this because some
ungodly people have wormed their way into your
churches, saying that God's marvelous grace allows
us to live immoral lives. The condemnation of such
people was recorded long ago, for they have denied
our only Master and Lord, Jesus Christ.
5So I want to remind you, though you already know
these things, that Jesus* first rescued the nation of Israel from Egypt, but later he destroyed those who did
not remain faithful. 6And I remind you of the angels
who did not stay within the limits of authority God
gave them but left the place where they belonged. God
has kept them securely chained in prisons of darkness, waiting for the great day of judgment. 7And don't

Jude 1 Or *keeps you for Jesus Christ.* **Jude 5** As in the best manuscripts; various other manuscripts read *[the] Lord,* or *God,* or *Christ;* one reads *God Christ.*

Jude 1:1 Jude's letter focuses on *apostasy*—when people turn away from God's truth and embrace false teachings. Jude reminded his readers of God's judgment on those who had left the faith. This letter warns against false teachers—in this case, probably Gnostic teachers (see the note on Col 2:4ff, p. 1697, for a description of the Gnostic heresy). Gnostics opposed two of the basic tenets of Christianity—the incarnation of Christ and the call to Christian ethics. Jude wrote to combat these false teachings and to encourage true doctrine and right conduct.

Jude 1:1 Jude was a brother of James, who was one of the leaders in the early church. Both of these men were Jesus' half brothers. Mary was their mother, and Joseph was their father. Although Mary was Jesus' true mother, God was Jesus' true Father.

Jude 1:3 Jude emphasizes the important relationship between correct doctrine and true faith. The truth of the Bible must not be compromised because it gives us the real facts about Jesus and salvation. The Bible is inspired by God and should never be twisted or manipulated; when it is, we can become confused over right and wrong and lose sight of the only path that leads to eternal life. Before writing about salvation, then, Jude felt he had to set his readers back on the right track, calling them back to the basics of their faith. Then the way of salvation would be clearer. "His holy people" refers to all believers.

Jude 1:3 How do ordinary Christians "defend the faith" today? Think about these ideas:

(1) We can defend the faith by knowing the truth. We do that by studying the Bible. Don't ever imagine that pastors and seminary professors hold a monopoly on this task. Without study, you cannot know what to defend. You must understand the basic doctrines of the faith so that you can recognize false doctrines and prevent wrong teaching from undermining your faith and hurting others.

(2) We can defend the faith as we grow personally with Christ. While knowledge is important, your personal relationship with Christ is essential. Through that relationship, God has given you the Holy Spirit as a teacher. Unattached to God, you may know everything, but understand nothing. Attached to Christ, you are given spiritual understanding as well as experiences with Christ that underscore your faith.

(3) We can defend the faith by remaining unified on the essentials. While Christians can certainly disagree on many nonessentials (music in worship, methods of worship, methods of outreach), we must always defend the truth of the basics of our faith as found in God's Word.

Jude 1:4 Even some of our churches today have false ("ungodly") teachers who have "wormed" their way in and are twisting the Bible's teachings to justify their own opinions, lifestyle, or wrong behavior. In doing this, they may gain temporary freedom to do as they wish; but they will discover that in distorting Scripture they are playing with fire. God will judge them for excusing, tolerating, and promoting sin.

Jude 1:4 Many first-century false teachers were teaching that Christians could do whatever they liked without fear of God's punishment. They had a light view of God's holiness and his justice. Paul refuted this same kind of false teaching in Romans 6:1-23. Even today, some Christians minimize the sinfulness of sin, believing that how they live has little to do with their faith. But what a person truly believes will show up in how that person acts. Those who truly have faith will show it by their deep respect for God and their sincere desire to live according to the principles in his Word.

Jude 1:5-7 Jude gives three examples of rebellion: (1) the nation of Israel—who, although they were delivered from Egypt, refused to trust God and enter the Promised Land (Num 14:26-39); (2) the angels—although they were once pure, holy, and living in God's presence, some gave in to pride and joined Satan to rebel against God (2 Pet 2:4); (3) the cities of Sodom and Gomorrah—the inhabitants were so full of sin that God wiped them off the face of the earth (Gen 19:1-29). If the chosen people, angels, and sinful cities were punished, how much more would these false teachers be severely judged?

Jude 1:7 Many people don't want to believe that God sentences people to "eternal fire" for rejecting him. But this is clearly taught in Scripture. Sinners who don't seek forgiveness from God will face eternal separation from him. Jude warns all who rebel against, ignore, or reject God.

forget Sodom and Gomorrah and their neighboring towns, which were filled with immorality and every kind of sexual perversion. Those cities were destroyed by fire and serve as a warning of the eternal fire of God's judgment.

[8]In the same way, these people—who claim authority from their dreams—live immoral lives, defy
authority, and scoff at supernatural beings.* [9]But
even Michael, one of the mightiest of the angels,* did not dare accuse the devil of blasphemy, but simply said, "The Lord rebuke you!" (This took place when Michael was arguing with the devil about
Moses' body.) [10]But these people scoff at things
they do not understand. Like unthinking animals, they do whatever their instincts tell them, and
so they bring about their own destruction. [11]What
sorrow awaits them! For they follow in the footsteps of Cain, who killed his brother. Like Balaam, they deceive people for money. And like Korah, they perish in their rebellion.

[12]When these people eat with you in your fellowship meals commemorating the Lord's love, they are like dangerous reefs that can shipwreck you.* They are like shameless shepherds who care only for themselves. They are like clouds blowing over the land without giving any rain. They are like trees in autumn that are doubly dead, for they bear no fruit and have
been pulled up by the roots. [13]They are like wild waves
of the sea, churning up the foam of their shameful deeds. They are like wandering stars, doomed forever to blackest darkness.

[14]Enoch, who lived in the seventh generation after Adam, prophesied about these people. He said, "Listen! The Lord is coming with countless thousands of
his holy ones [15]to execute judgment on the people
of the world. He will convict every person of all the ungodly things they have done and for all the insults that ungodly sinners have spoken against him."*

[16]These people are grumblers and complainers, living only to satisfy their desires. They brag loudly about themselves, and they flatter others to get what they want.

A Call to Remain Faithful

JUDE 1:17-23

But you, my dear friends, must remember what the
apostles of our Lord Jesus Christ said. [18]They told you
that in the last times there would be scoffers whose purpose in life is to satisfy their ungodly desires.
[19]These people are the ones who are creating divisions among you. They follow their natural instincts because they do not have God's Spirit in them.
[20]But you, dear friends, must build each other up
in your most holy faith, pray in the power of the Holy

Jude 8 Greek *at glorious ones,* which are probably evil angels. **Jude 9** Greek *Michael, the archangel.* **Jude 12** Or *they are contaminants among you;* or *they are stains.* **Jude 14-15** The quotation comes from intertestamental literature: Enoch 1:9.

AD 66

Painting on canvas

Jude 1:8 The "supernatural beings" here are probably evil angels. Just as the men of Sodom insulted angels (Gen 19), these false teachers scoffed at any authority. (For information on the danger of insulting even the fallen angels, see the note on 2 Pet 2:10-12, p. 1759.)

Jude 1:9 This incident is not recorded in any other place in Scripture. Moses' death is recorded in Deuteronomy 34. Here Jude may have been making use of an ancient book called *The Assumption of Moses*.

Jude 1:10 False teachers claimed to possess secret knowledge that gave them authority. Their "knowledge" of God was esoteric—mystical and beyond human understanding. The nature of God *is* beyond our understanding, but God, in his grace, has chosen to reveal himself to us—in his Word and supremely in Jesus Christ. Therefore, we must seek to know all we can about what he *has* revealed, even though we cannot fully comprehend God with our finite human minds. Beware of those who claim to have all the answers and who belittle what they do not understand.

Jude 1:11 Jude gives three examples of men who did whatever they wanted (Jude 1:10): Cain, who murdered his brother out of vengeful jealousy (Gen 4:1-16); Balaam, who prophesied out of greed, not out of obedience to God's command (Num 22–24); Korah, who rebelled against God's divinely appointed leaders, wanting the power for himself (Num 16:1-35). These stories illustrate attitudes that are typical of false teachers—pride, selfishness, jealousy, greed, lust for power, and disregard of God's will.

Jude 1:12 When the Lord's Supper was celebrated in the early church, believers would eat a full meal before taking part in Communion with the sharing of the bread and wine. The meal was called a "fellowship meal," and it was designed to be a sacred time of fellowship to prepare their hearts for Communion. In several of the churches, however, this meal had turned into a time of gluttony and drunken revelry. In Corinth, for example, some people hastily gobbled food while others went hungry (1 Cor 11:20-22). No church function should be an occasion for selfishness, gluttony, greed, disorder, or other sins that destroy unity or take one's mind away from the real purpose for gathering together.

Jude 1:12 The false teachers were "doubly dead." They were useless "trees" because they weren't producing fruit. They weren't even believers, so they would be rooted up and burned.

Jude 1:14 Enoch is mentioned briefly in Genesis 5:21-24. This quotation is from an apocryphal book called the book of Enoch.

Jude 1:14 Jesus is also mentioned as coming with angels ("holy ones") in Matthew 16:27; 24:31. Daniel 7:10 speaks of God judging humanity in the presence of millions of angels.

Jude 1:17 Other apostles also warned about false teachers. (See Acts 20:29; 1 Tim 4:1-2; 2 Tim 3:1-5; 2 Pet 2:1-3; 2 Jn 7.)

Jude 1:18 The "last times" is a common phrase referring to the time between Jesus' first and second comings. We live in the last times.

▶ **JUDE 1:17-23** ***(cont.)***

Spirit,* [21]and await the mercy of our Lord Jesus Christ, who will bring you eternal life. In this way, you will keep yourselves safe in God's love.

[22]And you must show mercy to* those whose faith is wavering. [23]Rescue others by snatching them from the flames of judgment. Show mercy to still others,* but do so with great caution, hating the sins that contaminate their lives.*

A Prayer of Praise

JUDE 1:24-25

Now all glory to God, who is able to keep you from falling away and will bring you with great joy into his glorious presence without a single fault. [25]All glory to him who alone is God, our Savior through Jesus Christ our Lord. All glory, majesty, power, and authority are his before all time, and in the present, and beyond all time! Amen.

Jude 20 Greek *pray in the Holy Spirit.* **Jude 22** Some manuscripts read *must reprove.* **Jude 22-23a** Some manuscripts have only two categories of people: (1) those whose faith is wavering and therefore need to be snatched from the flames of judgment, and (2) those who need to be shown mercy. **Jude 23b** Greek *with fear, hating even the clothing stained by the flesh.*

Y. John's Letters to Christians

At this point in history, John was the elder statesman of the early church. He was probably the last of the 12 disciples that was still alive, and he lived in Ephesus. The three letters that we have from him all came from near the end of his life but before he was exiled to the island of Patmos, where he received a vision from the Lord and recorded it in the book of Revelation.

1. JOHN'S FIRST LETTER

John didn't write this letter to any particular church, but instead seems to have meant it to be read to several congregations that he had served throughout the region. He wrote about the most vital aspects of faith so that his readers would know Christian truth from error. He emphasizes the basics of faith so that we can be confident in our faith. In our dark world, God is light. In our cold world, God brings the warmth of love. In our dying world, God brings life. When we lack confidence, these truths can bring us certainty.

Introduction

1 JOHN 1:1-4

We proclaim to you the one who existed from the beginning,* whom we have heard and seen. We saw him with our own eyes and touched him with our own hands. He is the Word of life. [2]This one who is life itself was revealed to us, and we have seen him. And now we testify and proclaim to you that he is the one

1 Jn 1:1 Greek *What was from the beginning.*

Jude 1:21 John, too, warns his readers to live close to God and his people, not listening to false teachers who would try to pull us away from him (see John 15:9-10).

Jude 1:22-23 Bringing people to Jesus saves them from God's judgment. We can do this through compassion and kindness. We are to hate the sin, but we must witness to and love the sinner. Unbelievers, no matter how successful they seem by worldly standards, are lost and in need of salvation. We should not take witnessing lightly—it is a matter of life and death.

Jude 1:23 In trying to find common ground with those to whom we witness, we must be careful not to fall into the quicksand of compromise. When reaching out to others, we must be sure that our own footing is safe and secure. Be careful not to become so much like non-Christians that no one can tell who you are or what you believe. Influence them for Christ—don't allow them to influence you to sin!

Jude 1:24 As the letter begins, so it ends—with assurance. God keeps believers from falling prey to false teachers. Although false teachers are widespread and dangerous, we don't have to be afraid if we trust God and are rooted and grounded in him.

Jude 1:24 To be sinless and perfect ("without a single fault") will be the ultimate condition of all believers when they finally see Christ face to face. When Christ appears and we are given our new bodies, we will be like Christ (1 Jn 3:2). Coming into Christ's presence will be more wonderful than we could ever imagine!

Jude 1:25 The audience to whom Jude wrote was vulnerable to heresies and to temptations toward immoral living. Jude encouraged the believers to remain firm in their faith and trust in God's promises for their futures. This was all the more important because they were living in a time of increased apostasy. We, too, are living in the last days, much closer to the end than were the original readers of this letter. We, too, are vulnerable to doctrinal error. We, too, are tempted to give in to sin. Although much false teaching is around us, we need not be afraid or give up in despair—God can keep us from falling, and he guarantees that if we remain faithful, he will bring us into his presence and give us everlasting joy.

1 Jn 1:1 The letter of 1 John was written by John, one of Jesus' original 12 disciples. He was probably "the disciple Jesus loved" (John 21:20), and along with Peter and James, he had a special relationship with Jesus. This letter was written between A.D. 85 and 90 from Ephesus, before John's exile to the island of Patmos (see Rev 1:9). Jerusalem had been destroyed in A.D. 70, and Christians were scattered throughout the empire. By the time John wrote this letter, Christianity had been around for more than a generation. It had faced and survived severe persecution. The main problem confronting the church at this time was declining commitment: Many believers were conforming to the world's standards, failing to stand up for Christ, and compromising their faith. False teachers were plentiful, and they were accelerating the church's downward slide away from the Christian faith.

John wrote this letter to put believers back on track, to show the difference between light and darkness (truth and error), and to encourage the church to grow in genuine love for God and for one another. He also wrote to assure true believers that they possessed eternal life and to help them know that their faith was genuine—so they could enjoy all

who is eternal life. He was with the Father, and then
he was revealed to us. [3]We proclaim to you what we
ourselves have actually seen and heard so that you may
have fellowship with us. And our fellowship is with the
Father and with his Son, Jesus Christ. [4]We are writing
these things so that you may fully share our joy.*

Living in the Light

1 JOHN 1:5–2:6

This is the message we heard from Jesus* and now
declare to you: God is light, and there is no darkness
in him at all. [6]So we are lying if we say we have fellowship with God but go on living in spiritual darkness;
we are not practicing the truth. [7]But if we are living
in the light, as God is in the light, then we have fellowship with each other, and the blood of Jesus, his Son,
cleanses us from all sin.
[8]If we claim we have no sin, we are only fooling
ourselves and not living in the truth. [9]But if we confess our sins to him, he is faithful and just to forgive
us our sins and to cleanse us from all wickedness.
[10]If we claim we have not sinned, we are calling God

1 Jn 1:4 Or *so that our joy may be complete;* some manuscripts read *your joy.* **1 Jn 1:5** Greek *from him.*

JOHN COUNTERS FALSE TEACHINGS

John counters two major threads in the false teachings of the heretics in this letter:

1 Jn 1:6, 8, 10	They denied the reality of sin. John says that if we continue in sin, we can't claim to belong to God. If we say we have no sin, we are only fooling ourselves and refusing to live according to the truth.
1 Jn 2:22; 4:1-3	They denied that Jesus was the Messiah—God in the flesh. John said that if we believe that Jesus is God incarnate and trust him for our salvation, we are children of God.

the benefits of being God's children. For more about John, see his Profile on p. 1459.

1 Jn 1:1-5 John opens his first letter to the churches similarly to the way he began the Gospel of John, emphasizing that Christ ("the Word of life") is eternal, that God came into the world as a human, and that he, John, was an eyewitness to Jesus' life. John had lived with Jesus, having personal, physical contact with Jesus. He knew beyond any doubt that Jesus brings light and life.

1 Jn 1:3 As an eyewitness to Jesus' ministry, John was qualified to teach the truth about him. The readers of this letter had not seen and heard Jesus themselves, but they could trust that what John wrote was accurate. We are like those second- and third-generation Christians. Though we have not personally seen, heard, or touched Jesus, we have the New Testament record of his eyewitnesses, and we can trust that they spoke the truth about him. (See John 20:29.)

1 Jn 1:3-4 John writes about having fellowship with other believers. There are three principles behind true Christian fellowship: (1) Our fellowship is grounded in the testimony of God's Word. Without this underlying strength, togetherness is impossible. (2) It is mutual, depending on the unity of believers. (3) It is renewed daily through the Holy Spirit. True fellowship combines social and spiritual interaction, and it is made possible only through a living relationship with Christ.

1 Jn 1:5-6 Light represents what is good, pure, true, holy, and reliable. Darkness represents what is sinful and evil. The statement "God is light" means that God is perfectly holy and true and that he alone can guide us out of the darkness of sin. Light is also related to truth in that light exposes whatever exists, whether it is good or bad. In the dark, good and evil look alike; in the light, they can be clearly distinguished. Just as darkness cannot exist in the presence of light, sin cannot exist in the presence of a holy God. If we want to have a relationship with God, we must put aside our sinful ways of living. To claim that we belong to him but then to go out and live for ourselves is hypocrisy. Christ will expose and judge such deceit.

1 Jn 1:6 Here John was confronting the first of three claims of the false teachers: that we can have fellowship with God and go on living in spiritual darkness. False teachers who thought that the physical body was evil or worthless taught one of two approaches to behavior: They insisted on denying bodily desires through rigid discipline, or they approved of gratifying every physical lust because the body was going to be destroyed anyway. Obviously the second approach was more popular! Here John is saying that no one can claim to be a Christian and still live in evil and immorality. We can't love God and court sin at the same time.

1 Jn 1:7 How does Jesus' blood cleanse us from all sin? In Old Testament times, believers symbolically transferred their sins to an animal, which they then sacrificed (see a description of this ceremony in Lev 4). The animal died in their place to pay for their sin and to allow them to continue living in God's favor. God graciously forgave them because of their faith in him and because they obeyed his commandments concerning the sacrifice. Those sacrifices anticipated the day when Christ would completely remove sin. Real cleansing from sin came with Jesus, "the Lamb of God who takes away the sin of the world" (John 1:29). Sin, by its very nature, brings death—that is a fact as certain as the law of gravity. Jesus did not die for his own sins; he had none. Instead, by a transaction that we may never fully understand, he died for the sins of the world. When we commit our lives to Christ and thus identify ourselves with him, his death becomes ours. He has paid the penalty for our sins, and his blood has purified us. Just as Christ rose from the grave, we rise to a new life of fellowship with him (Rom 6:4).

1 Jn 1:8 Here John was attacking the second claim of the false teachers: that people had no natural tendency toward sin, that they had "no sin," and that they were then incapable of sinning. This is a lie. The false teachers refused to take sin seriously. They wanted to be considered Christians, but they saw no need to confess and repent. The death of Christ did not mean much to them because they didn't think they needed it. Instead of repenting and being purified by Christ's blood, they were encouraging sin among believers. In this life we are always capable of sinning. Never let down your guard.

1 Jn 1:8-10 The false teachers not only denied that sin breaks fellowship with God (1 Jn 1:6) and that they had a sinful nature (1 Jn 1:8), but they also denied that their conduct involved any sin at all (1 Jn 1:10). That lie ignores one basic truth: All people are sinners by nature and by practice. At conversion all our sins are forgiven—past, present, and future. Yet even after we become Christians, we still sin and still need to confess. This kind of confession is not offered to gain God's acceptance but to remove the barrier to fellowship that our sin has put between us and him. It is difficult for many people to admit their faults and shortcomings, even to God. It takes humility and honesty to recognize our weaknesses, and most of us would rather pretend that we are strong. But we need not fear revealing our sins to God—he knows them already. He will not push us away, no matter what we've done. Instead, he will draw us to himself.

1 Jn 1:9 Confession is supposed to free us to enjoy fellowship with Christ. It should ease our consciences and lighten our cares. But some Christians do not understand how it works. They feel so guilty that they confess

AD 70 *Rome destroys Jerusalem*

▸ **1 JOHN 1:5–2:6** ***(cont.)***
a liar and showing that his word has no place in our hearts.

2:1My dear children, I am writing this to you so that you will not sin. But if anyone does sin, we have an advocate who pleads our case before the Father. He is Jesus Christ, the one who is truly righteous. 2He himself is the sacrifice that atones for our sins—and not only our sins but the sins of all the world.

3And we can be sure that we know him if we obey his commandments. 4If someone claims, "I know God," but doesn't obey God's commandments, that person is a liar and is not living in the truth. 5But those who obey God's word truly show how completely they love him. That is how we know we are living in him. 6Those who say they live in God should live their lives as Jesus did.

A New Commandment

1 JOHN 2:7-14
Dear friends, I am not writing a new commandment for you; rather it is an old one you have had from the very beginning. This old commandment—to love one another—is the same message you heard before. 8Yet it is also new. Jesus lived the truth of this commandment, and you also are living it. For the darkness is disappearing, and the true light is already shining.

9If anyone claims, "I am living in the light," but hates

---

the same sins over and over; then they wonder if they might have forgotten something. Other Christians believe that God forgives them when they confess, but if they died with unconfessed sins, they would be forever lost. These Christians do not understand that God *wants* to forgive us. He allowed his beloved Son to die just so he could offer us pardon. When we come to Christ, he forgives all the sins we have committed or will ever commit. We don't need to confess the sins of the past all over again, and we don't need to fear that God will reject us if we don't keep our slate perfectly clean. Of course we should continue to confess our sins, but not because failure to do so will make us lose our salvation. Our relationship with Christ is secure. Instead, we should confess so that we can enjoy complete fellowship and joy with him.

True confession also involves a commitment not to continue in sin. We wouldn't be genuinely confessing our sins to God if we planned to commit them again and just wanted temporary forgiveness. We should also pray for strength to defeat temptation the next time we face it.

1 Jn 1:9 If God has forgiven us for our sins because of Christ's death, why must we confess our sins? In admitting our sins and receiving Christ's cleansing, we are (1) agreeing with God that our sin truly is sin and that we are willing to turn from it, (2) ensuring that we don't conceal our sins from him and consequently from ourselves, and (3) recognizing our tendency to sin and relying on his power to overcome it.

1 Jn 2:1 John uses "dear children" in a warm, fatherly way. He is not talking down to his readers but is showing affection for them. At this writing, John was a very old man. He had spent almost all his life in ministry, and many of his readers were indeed his spiritual children.

1 Jn 2:1-2 To people who are feeling guilty and condemned, John offers reassurance. They know they have sinned, and Satan (called "the accuser" in Rev 12:10) is demanding the death penalty. When you feel this way, don't give up hope—the best defense attorney in the universe is pleading your case. Jesus Christ, your advocate, your defender, is the Judge's Son. He has already suffered your penalty in your place. You can't be tried for a case that is no longer on the docket. United with Christ, you are as safe as he is. Don't be afraid to ask Christ to plead your case—he has already won it (see Rom 8:33-34; Heb 7:24-25).

A BOOK OF CONTRASTS

One of the distinct features of John's writing style was his habit of noting both sides of a conflict. He wrote to show the difference between real Christianity and anything else. Here are some of his favorite contrasts.

Contrast between	*Passage*
Light and darkness	**1 Jn 1:5**
The new commandment and the old commandment	**1 Jn 2:7-8**
Loving the Father and loving the world	**1 Jn 2:15-16**
Christ and Antichrist	**1 Jn 2:18, 22**
Truth and lies	**1 Jn 2:20-21**
Children of God and children of the devil	**1 Jn 3:1-10**
Eternal life and eternal death	**1 Jn 3:14**
Love and hatred	**1 Jn 3:15-16**
True prophecy and false prophecy	**1 Jn 4:1-3**
Love and fear	**1 Jn 4:18-19**
Having life and not having life	**1 Jn 5:11-12**

1 Jn 2:2 Jesus Christ is the atoning sacrifice for our sins (see also 1 Jn 4:10). He is our defense attorney. He can stand before God as our mediator because his death satisfied the wrath of God against sin and paid the death penalty for our sin. Thus, Christ both satisfies God's requirement and removes our sin. In him we are forgiven and purified.

1 Jn 2:2 Sometimes it is difficult to forgive those who wrong us. Imagine how hard it would be to forgive all people, no matter what they had done! This is what God has done in Jesus. No one, no matter what sin has been committed, is beyond forgiveness. All a person has to do is turn from sin, receive Christ's forgiveness, and live a committed life to Christ.

1 Jn 2:3-6 How can you be sure that you belong to Christ? This passage gives two ways to know: if you do what Christ says and live as Christ wants. What does Christ tell us to do? John answers in 1 John 3:23: "Believe in the name of his Son, Jesus Christ, and love one another." True Christian faith results in loving behavior; that is why John says that the way we act can give us assurance that we belong to Christ.

1 Jn 2:6 To live as Jesus lived doesn't mean choosing 12 disciples, performing great miracles, and being crucified. We cannot merely copy Christ's life; much of what Jesus did had to do with his identity as God's Son, the fulfillment of his special role in dying for sin, and the cultural context of the first-century Roman world. To walk today as Christ did, we must obey his teachings and follow his example of complete obedience to God and loving service to people.

1 Jn 2:7-8 The commandment to love others is both old and new. It is old because it comes from the Old Testament (Lev 19:18). It is new because Jesus interpreted it in a radically new way (John 13:34-35). In the Christian church, love is not only expressed by showing respect; it is also expressed through self-sacrifice and servanthood (John 15:13). In fact, it can be defined as selfless giving, reaching beyond friends to enemies

a Christian brother or sister,* that person is still living
in darkness. 10Anyone who loves another brother or
sister* is living in the light and does not cause others
to stumble. 11But anyone who hates another brother
or sister is still living and walking in darkness. Such
a person does not know the way to go, having been
blinded by the darkness.

12 I am writing to you who are God's children
because your sins have been forgiven through
Jesus.*
13 I am writing to you who are mature in the faith*
because you know Christ, who existed from
the beginning.
I am writing to you who are young in the faith
because you have won your battle with the
evil one.
14 I have written to you who are God's children
because you know the Father.
I have written to you who are mature in the faith
because you know Christ, who existed from
the beginning.
I have written to you who are young in the faith
because you are strong.
God's word lives in your hearts,
and you have won your battle with the
evil one.

Do Not Love This World

1 JOHN 2:15-17

Do not love this world nor the things it offers you, for
when you love the world, you do not have the love of
the Father in you. 16For the world offers only a craving
for physical pleasure, a craving for everything we see,
and pride in our achievements and possessions. These
are not from the Father, but are from this world. 17And
this world is fading away, along with everything that
people crave. But anyone who does what pleases God
will live forever.

Warning about Antichrists

1 JOHN 2:18-29

Dear children, the last hour is here. You have heard
that the Antichrist is coming, and already many such
antichrists have appeared. From this we know that the
last hour has come. 19These people left our churches,
but they never really belonged with us; otherwise they

1 Jn 2:9 Greek *hates his brother;* similarly in 2:11. **1 Jn 2:10** Greek *loves his brother.* **1 Jn 2:12** Greek *through his name.* **1 Jn 2:13** Or *to you fathers;* also in 2:14.

---

and persecutors (Matt 5:43-48). Love should be the unifying force and the identifying mark of the Christian community. Love is the key to walking in the light, because we cannot grow spiritually while we hate others. Our growing relationship with God will result in growing relationships with others.

1 Jn 2:9-11 Does this mean that if you dislike someone you aren't a Christian? These verses are not talking about disliking a disagreeable Christian brother or sister. There will always be people we will not like as well as others. John's words focus on the attitude that causes us to ignore or despise others, to treat them as irritants, competitors, or enemies. Christian love is not a feeling but a choice. We can choose to be concerned with people's well-being and treat them with respect, whether or not we feel affection toward them. If we choose to love others, God will help us express our love.

1 Jn 2:12-14 John was writing to believers of all ages. The "children" had experienced forgiveness through Jesus. Those who were "mature in the faith" had a long-standing relationship with Christ. The "young in the faith" had battled with Satan's temptations and had won. Each stage of life in the Christian pilgrimage builds upon the other. As children learn about Christ, they grow in their ability to win battles with temptation. As young adults move from victory to victory, they grow in their relationship with Christ. Older adults, having known Christ for years, have developed the wisdom needed to teach young people and start the cycle all over again. Has your Christian growth reached the maturity level appropriate for your stage in life?

1 Jn 2:15-16 Some people think that worldliness is limited to external behavior—the people we associate with, the places we go, the activities we enjoy. Worldliness is also internal because it begins in the heart and is characterized by three attitudes: (1) craving for physical pleasure—preoccupation with gratifying physical desires; (2) craving for everything we see—coveting and accumulating things, bowing to the god of materialism; and (3) pride in our achievements and possessions—obsession with one's status or importance. When the serpent tempted Eve (Gen 3:6), he tempted her in these areas. Also, when the devil tempted Jesus in the wilderness, these were his three areas of attack (see Matt 4:1-11).

By contrast, God values self-control, a spirit of generosity, and a commitment to humble service. It is possible to give the impression of avoiding worldly pleasures while still harboring worldly attitudes in one's heart. It is also possible, like Jesus, to love sinners and spend time with them while maintaining a commitment to the values of God's Kingdom. What values are most important to you? Do your actions reflect the world's values or God's values?

1 Jn 2:17 When the desire for possessions and sinful pleasures feels so intense, we probably doubt that these objects of desire will all one day pass away. It may be even more difficult to believe that the person who does the will of God will live forever. But this was John's conviction based on the facts of Jesus' life, death, resurrection, and promises. Knowing that this evil world will end can give you the courage to deny yourself temporary pleasures in this world in order to enjoy what God has promised for eternity.

1 Jn 2:18-23 John is talking about the last days, the time between Christ's first and second comings. The first-century readers of John's letter lived in the last days, and so do we. During this time, antichrists (false teachers who pretend to be Christians and who lure weak members away from Christ) will appear. Finally, just before the end of the age, one great Antichrist will arise (Rev 13; 19:20; 20:10). We do not need to fear these evil people. The Holy Spirit shows us their errors, so we will not be deceived. However, we must teach God's Word clearly and carefully to the peripheral, weak members among us so that they won't fall prey to these teachers who "come disguised as harmless sheep but are really vicious wolves" (Matt 7:15).

1 Jn 2:19 The antichrists were not total strangers to the church; they once had been in the church, but they did not really belong to it. John does not say why they left; it is clear that their reasons for joining in the first place were wrong. Some people may call themselves Christians for less than the best reasons. Perhaps going to church is a family tradition. Maybe they like the social and business contacts they make there. Or possibly going to church is a long-standing habit, and they have never stopped to ask themselves why they do it. What is your main reason for being a Christian? Unless it is a Christ-centered reason, you may not really belong. You don't have to settle for less than the best. You can become personally acquainted with Jesus Christ and become a loyal, trustworthy follower.

▸ **1 JOHN 2:18-29 *(cont.)***

would have stayed with us. When they left, it proved
that they did not belong with us.
[20]But you are not like that, for the Holy One has
given you his Spirit,* and all of you know the truth.
[21]So I am writing to you not because you don't know
the truth but because you know the difference between truth and lies. [22]And who is a liar? Anyone who
says that Jesus is not the Christ.* Anyone who denies
the Father and the Son is an antichrist.* [23]Anyone
who denies the Son doesn't have the Father, either. But
anyone who acknowledges the Son has the Father also.
[24]So you must remain faithful to what you have
been taught from the beginning. If you do, you will
remain in fellowship with the Son and with the Father.
[25]And in this fellowship we enjoy the eternal life he
promised us.
[26]I am writing these things to warn you about those
who want to lead you astray. [27]But you have received
the Holy Spirit,* and he lives within you, so you don't
need anyone to teach you what is true. For the Spirit*
teaches you everything you need to know, and what he
teaches is true—it is not a lie. So just as he has taught
you, remain in fellowship with Christ.
[28]And now, dear children, remain in fellowship with
Christ so that when he returns, you will be full of courage and not shrink back from him in shame.
[29]Since we know that Christ is righteous, we also
know that all who do what is right are God's children.

Living as Children of God

1 JOHN 3:1-10

See how very much our Father loves us, for he calls us
his children, and that is what we are! But the people
who belong to this world don't recognize that we are
God's children because they don't know him. [2]Dear

1 Jn 2:20 Greek *But you have an anointing from the Holy One.* **1 Jn 2:22a** Or *not the Messiah.* **1 Jn 2:22b** Or *the antichrist.* **1 Jn 2:27a** Greek *the anointing from him.* **1 Jn 2:27b** Greek *the anointing.*

See how very much our Father loves us, for he calls us his children, and that is what we are!
1 John 3:1

1 Jn 2:20 Upon becoming a Christian, a person receives the Holy Spirit. One way the Holy Spirit helps the believer and the church is by communicating truth. Jesus is the truth (John 14:6), and the Holy Spirit guides believers to him (John 16:13). People who are opposed to Christ are also opposed to his truth, and the Holy Spirit is not working in their lives. When we are led by the Spirit, we can stand against false teachers and the Antichrist. Ask the Spirit to guide you each day (see 1 Jn 2:27).

1 Jn 2:22-23 Apparently the antichrists in John's day were claiming faith in God while denying and opposing Christ. To do so, John firmly states, is impossible. Because Jesus is God's Son and the Messiah, to deny Christ is to reject God's way of revealing himself to the world. A person who accepts Christ as God's Son accepts God the Father at the same time. The two are one and cannot be separated. Many cultists today call themselves Christians, but they deny that Jesus is divine. We must expose these heresies and oppose such teachings so that the weak believers among us do not succumb to their teachings.

1 Jn 2:24 These Christians had heard the Good News, very likely from John himself. They knew that Christ is God's Son, that he died for their sins and was raised to give them new life, and that he would return and establish his Kingdom in its fullness. But their fellowship was being infiltrated by teachers who denied these basic doctrines of the Christian faith, and some of the believers were in danger of succumbing to false arguments. John encouraged them to hold on to the Christian truth they heard at the beginning of their walk with Christ. It is important to grow in our knowledge of the Lord, to deepen our understanding through careful study, and to teach these truths to others. But no matter how much we learn, we must never abandon the basic truths about Christ. Jesus will always be God's Son, and his sacrifice for our sins is permanent. No truth will ever contradict these teachings in the Bible.

1 Jn 2:26-27 Christ had promised to send the Holy Spirit to teach his followers and to remind them of all that Christ had taught (John 14:26). As a result, Christians have the Holy Spirit within them to keep them from going astray. In addition, they have the God-inspired Scriptures, against which they can test questionable teachings. To stay true to Christ, we must follow his Word and his Spirit. Let the Holy Spirit help you discern truth from error. (For more about who the Holy Spirit is and what he does, see the notes on John 3:6, p. 1301; Acts 1:5, p. 1499; Eph 1:13-14, p. 1705.)

1 Jn 2:27 Christ lives in us through the Holy Spirit, and we also live in Christ. This means that we place our total trust in him, rely on him for guidance and strength, and live as he wants us to live. It implies a personal, life-giving relationship. John uses the same idea in John 15:5, where he speaks of Christ as the vine and his followers as the branches (see also 1 Jn 3:24; 4:15).

1 Jn 2:28-29 The visible proof of being a Christian is right behavior. Many people do good deeds but don't have faith in Jesus Christ, while others claim to have faith but rarely produce good deeds. A deficit in either faith or right behavior will be a cause for shame when Christ returns. Because true faith always results in good deeds, those who claim to have faith *and* who consistently do what is right are true believers. Good deeds cannot produce salvation (see Eph 2:8-9), but they are necessary proof that true faith is actually present (Jas 2:14-17).

1 Jn 3:1 As believers, our self-worth is based on the fact that God loves us and calls us his children. We are his children now, not just sometime in the distant future. Knowing that we are his children should encourage us to live as Jesus did. (For other references about being part of God's family, see Rom 8:14-17; Gal 3:26-27; 4:6-7.)

1 Jn 3:1ff Who are we? Members of God's family, his children (1 Jn 3:1). Who are we becoming? Reflections of God (1 Jn 3:2). The rest of 1 John 3 tells us what we have as we grow to resemble God: (1) victory over sin (1 Jn 3:4-9); (2) love for others (1 Jn 3:10-18); and (3) confidence before God (1 Jn 3:19-24).

1 Jn 3:2-3 The Christian life is a process of becoming more and more like Christ (see Rom

friends, we are already God's children, but he has not yet shown us what we will be like when Christ appears. But we do know that we will be like him, for we will see him as he really is. 3And all who have this eager expectation will keep themselves pure, just as he is pure.

4Everyone who sins is breaking God's law, for all sin is contrary to the law of God. 5And you know that Jesus came to take away our sins, and there is no sin in him. 6Anyone who continues to live in him will not sin. But anyone who keeps on sinning does not know him or understand who he is.

7Dear children, don't let anyone deceive you about this: When people do what is right, it shows that they are righteous, even as Christ is righteous. 8But when people keep on sinning, it shows that they belong to the devil, who has been sinning since the beginning. But the Son of God came to destroy the works of the devil. 9Those who have been born into God's family do not make a practice of sinning, because God's life* is in them. So they can't keep on sinning, because they are children of God. 10So now we can tell who are children of God and who are children of the devil. Anyone who does not live righteously and does not love other believers* does not belong to God.

Love One Another

1 JOHN 3:11-24

This is the message you have heard from the beginning: We should love one another. 12We must not be like Cain, who belonged to the evil one and killed his brother. And why did he kill him? Because Cain had been doing what was evil, and his brother had been doing what was righteous. 13So don't be surprised, dear brothers and sisters,* if the world hates you.

14If we love our Christian brothers and sisters,* it proves that we have passed from death to life. But a person who has no love is still dead. 15Anyone who hates another brother or sister* is really a murderer at heart. And you know that murderers don't have eternal life within them.

16We know what real love is because Jesus gave up his life for us. So we also ought to give up our lives for our brothers and sisters. 17If someone has enough money to live well and sees a brother or sister* in need

1 Jn 3:9 Greek *because his seed.* **1 Jn 3:10** Greek *does not love his brother.* **1 Jn 3:13** Greek *brothers.* **1 Jn 3:14** Greek *the brothers;* similarly in 3:16. **1 Jn 3:15** Greek *hates his brother.* **1 Jn 3:17** Greek *sees his brother.*

8:29). This process will not be complete until we see Christ face to face (1 Cor 13:12; Phil 3:21), but knowing that it is our ultimate destiny should motivate us to purify ourselves. To keep pure means to keep morally straight, free from the corruption of sin. God purifies us, but we also must take action to remain morally fit (see 1 Tim 5:22; Jas 4:8; 1 Pet 1:22).

1 Jn 3:4ff There is a difference between committing a sin and continuing to sin. Even the most faithful believers sometimes commit sins, but they do not cherish a particular sin or continually choose to commit it. A believer who commits a sin can repent, confess it, and find forgiveness. A person who continues to sin, by contrast, is not sorry for doing so. Thus, this person never confesses and never receives forgiveness. Such a person is in opposition to God, no matter what religious claims to the contrary.

1 Jn 3:5 Under the Old Testament sacrificial system, a lamb without blemish was offered as a sacrifice for sin. Jesus is "the Lamb of God who takes away the sin of the world" (John 1:29). Because Jesus lived a perfect life and sacrificed himself for our sins, we can be completely forgiven (1 Jn 2:2). We can look back to his death for us and know that we need never suffer eternal death (1 Pet 1:18-20).

1 Jn 3:8-9 We all have areas where temptation is strong and habits are hard to conquer. These weaknesses give the devil a foothold, so we must deal with our areas of vulnerability. If we are struggling with a particular sin, these verses are not directed at us, even if for the time we seem to keep on sinning. John is not talking about people whose victories are still incomplete; he is talking about people who make a practice of sinning and look for ways to justify it.

Three steps are necessary to find victory over prevailing sin: (1) Seek the power of the Holy Spirit and God's Word; (2) stay away from tempting situations; and (3) seek the help of the body of Christ—be open to their willingness to hold you accountable and to pray for you.

1 Jn 3:9 "They can't keep on sinning" means that true believers do not make a practice of sinning, nor do they become indifferent to God's moral law. All believers still sin, but they are working to gain victory over sin.

1 Jn 3:9 We are "born into God's family" when the Holy Spirit lives in us and gives us Jesus' new life. Being born again is more than a fresh start; it is a rebirth, receiving a new family name based on Christ's death for us. When this happens, God forgives us and totally accepts us; the Holy Spirit gives us a new mind and heart, lives in us, and begins helping us to become like Christ. Our perspective changes, too, because we have a mind that is renewed day by day by the Holy Spirit (see Rom 12:2; Eph 4:22-24). So we must begin to think and act differently. (See John 3:1-21 for more on being born again.)

1 Jn 3:12-13 Cain killed his brother, Abel, when God accepted Abel's offering and not his (Gen 4:1-16). Abel's offering showed that Cain was not giving his best to God, and Cain's jealous anger drove him to murder. People who are morally upright expose and shame those who aren't. If we live for God, the world will often hate us because we make them painfully aware of their immoral way of living.

1 Jn 3:15 John echoes Jesus' teaching that whoever hates another person is a murderer at heart (Matt 5:21-22). Christianity is a religion of the heart; outward compliance alone is not enough. Bitterness against someone who has wronged you is an evil cancer within you and will eventually destroy you. Don't let a "poisonous root of bitterness" (Heb 12:15) grow in you or your church.

1 Jn 3:16 Real love is an action, not a feeling. It produces selfless, sacrificial giving. The greatest act of love is giving oneself for others. How can we "give up our lives"? By serving others with no thought of receiving anything in return. Sometimes it is easier to say we'll die for others than to truly live for them—this involves putting others' desires first. Jesus taught this same principle of love in John 15:13.

1 Jn 3:17-18 These verses give an example of how to give up our lives for others—to help those in need. This is strikingly similar to James's teaching (Jas 2:14-17). How clearly do your actions say you really love others? Are you as generous as you should be with your money, possessions, and time?

▸ **1 JOHN 3:11-24** ***(cont.)***
but shows no compassion—how can God's love be in
that person?
18Dear children, let's not merely say that we love
each other; let us show the truth by our actions. 19Our
actions will show that we belong to the truth, so we
will be confident when we stand before God. 20Even
if we feel guilty, God is greater than our feelings, and
he knows everything.
21Dear friends, if we don't feel guilty, we can come
to God with bold confidence. 22And we will receive
from him whatever we ask because we obey him and
do the things that please him.
23And this is his commandment: We must believe in
the name of his Son, Jesus Christ, and love one another,
just as he commanded us. 24Those who obey God's
commandments remain in fellowship with him, and
he with them. And we know he lives in us because the
Spirit he gave us lives in us.

Discerning False Prophets

1 JOHN 4:1-6
Dear friends, do not believe everyone who claims
to speak by the Spirit. You must test them to see if
the spirit they have comes from God. For there are
many false prophets in the world. 2This is how we
know if they have the Spirit of God: If a person claiming to be a prophet* acknowledges that Jesus Christ
came in a real body, that person has the Spirit of God.
3But if someone claims to be a prophet and does not
acknowledge the truth about Jesus, that person is
not from God. Such a person has the spirit of the

1 Jn 4:2 Greek *If a spirit;* similarly in 4:3.

1 Jn 3:19-20 Many are afraid that they don't love others as they should. They feel guilty because they think they are not doing enough to show proper love to Christ. Their consciences bother them. John has these people in mind in this letter. How do we escape the gnawing accusations of our consciences? Not by ignoring them or rationalizing our behavior but by setting our heart on God's love. When we feel guilty, we should remind ourselves that God knows our motives as well as our actions. His voice of assurance is stronger than the accusing voice of our conscience. If we are in Christ, he will not condemn us (Rom 8:1; Heb 9:14-15). So if you are living for the Lord but feeling that you are not good enough, remind yourself that God is greater than your conscience.

1 Jn 3:21-22 If your conscience is clear, you can come to God without fear, confident that your requests will be heard. John reaffirms Jesus' promise that whatever we ask for will be given to us (Matt 7:7; see also Matt 21:22; John 9:31; 15:7). You will receive if you obey and do what pleases him because you will then be asking in line with God's will. Of course this does not mean that you can have anything you want, like instant riches. If you are truly seeking God's will, there are some requests you will not make.

1 Jn 3:23 All throughout Scripture, the *names* of people stand for their character. The names represent who they really are. We are to believe not only in Jesus' words, but also in his very person as the Son of God. Moreover, to believe "in the name" means to pattern your life after Christ's, to become more like him by uniting yourself with him. And if we are living like Christ, we will "love one another."

1 Jn 3:24 This mutual relationship, living in Christ as he lives in us, shows itself in Christians who keep these three essential commands: (1) Believe in Christ, (2) love the brothers and sisters, and (3) live morally upright lives by obeying his commands. The Spirit's presence is not only spiritual and mystical, but it is also practical. Our conduct verifies his presence.

HERESIES

Most of the eyewitnesses to Jesus' ministry had died by the time John composed this letter. Some of the second- or third-generation Christians began to have doubts about what they had been taught about Jesus. Some Christians with a Greek background had a hard time believing that Jesus was human as well as divine, because in Platonic thought the spirit was all-important—the body was only a prison from which one desired to escape. Heresies developed from a uniting of this kind of Platonic thought and Christianity.

A particularly widespread false teaching, later called *Docetism* (from a Greek word meaning "to seem"), held that Jesus was actually a spirit who only appeared to have a body. Therefore he cast no shadow and left no footprints; he was God but not man. Another heretical teaching, related to *Gnosticism* (from a Greek word meaning "knowledge"), held that all physical matter was evil, the spirit was good, and only the intellectually enlightened could enjoy the benefits of religion. Both groups found it hard to believe in a Savior who was fully human.

John answers these false teachers as an eyewitness to Jesus' life on earth. He saw Jesus, talked with him, touched him—he knew that Jesus was more than a mere spirit. In the very first sentence of his letter, John establishes that Jesus had been alive before the world began and also that he lived as a man among men and women. In other words, he was both divine and human.

Through the centuries, many heretics have denied that Jesus was both God and man. In John's day people had trouble believing he was human; today more people have problems seeing him as God. But Jesus' divine–human nature is the pivotal issue of Christianity. Before you accept what religious teachers say about any topic, listen carefully to what they believe about Jesus. To deny either his divinity or his humanity is to consider him less than Christ, the Savior.

1 Jn 4:1-2 "Do not believe everyone who claims to speak by the Spirit. You must test them to see if the spirit they have comes from God" means that we shouldn't believe everything we hear just because someone says it is a message from God. There are many ways to test teachers to see if their message is truly from the Lord. One is to check to see if their words match what God says in the Bible. Other tests include their commitment to the body of believers (1 Jn 2:19), their lifestyles (1 Jn 3:23-24), and the fruit of their ministries (1 Jn 4:6). But the most important test of all, says John, is what they believe about Christ. Do they teach that Jesus is fully God and fully man? Our world is filled with voices claiming to speak for God. Give them these tests to see if they are indeed speaking God's truth.

1 Jn 4:3 The Antichrist will be a person who epitomizes all that is evil, and he will be readily received by an evil world. He is more fully described in 2 Thessalonians 2:3-12; Revelation 13. The "spirit of the Antichrist" is already here (see the note on 1 Jn 2:18-23, p. 1789). Those who reject Christ are either unknowingly or consciously siding with the spirit of the Antichrist.

Antichrist, which you heard is coming into the world and indeed is already here.
[4]But you belong to God, my dear children. You have already won a victory over those people, because the Spirit who lives in you is greater than the spirit who lives in the world.
[5]Those people belong to this world, so they speak from the world's viewpoint, and the world listens to them.
[6]But we belong to God, and those who know God listen to us. If they do not belong to God, they do not listen to us. That is how we know if someone has the Spirit of truth or the spirit of deception.

Loving One Another

1 JOHN 4:7-21

Dear friends, let us continue to love one another, for love comes from God. Anyone who loves is a child of God and knows God.
[8]But anyone who does not love does not know God, for God is love.

[9]God showed how much he loved us by sending his one and only Son into the world so that we might have eternal life through him.
[10]This is real love—not that we loved God, but that he loved us and sent his Son as a sacrifice to take away our sins.
[11]Dear friends, since God loved us that much, we surely ought to love each other.
[12]No one has ever seen God. But if we love each other, God lives in us, and his love is brought to full expression in us.
[13]And God has given us his Spirit as proof that we live in him and he in us.
[14]Furthermore, we have seen with our own eyes and now testify that the Father sent his Son to be the Savior of the world.
[15]All who confess that Jesus is the Son of God have God living in them, and they live in God.
[16]We know how much God loves us, and we have put our trust in his love.

God is love, and all who live in love live in God, and God lives in them.
[17]And as we live in God, our love

1 Jn 4:4 It is easy to be frightened by the wickedness we see all around us and to be overwhelmed by the problems we face. Evil is obviously much stronger than we are. John assures us that God is even stronger. He will conquer all evil—and his Spirit and his Word live in our hearts!

1 Jn 4:6 False teachers are popular with the world because, like the false prophets of the Old Testament, they tell people what they want to hear. John warns that Christians who faithfully teach God's Word will not win any popularity contests in the world. People don't want to hear their sins denounced; they don't want to listen to demands that they change their behavior.

1 Jn 4:7ff Everyone believes that love is important, but love is usually thought of as a feeling. In reality, love is a choice and an action, as 1 Corinthians 13:4-7 shows. God is the source of our love. He loved us enough to sacrifice his Son for us. Jesus is our example of what it means to love; everything he did in life and death was supremely loving. The Holy Spirit gives us the power to love; he lives in our hearts and makes us more and more like Christ. God's love always involves a choice and an action, and our love should be like his. How well do you display your love for God in the choices you make and the actions you take?

1 Jn 4:8 John says, "God is love," not "Love is God." Our world, with its shallow and selfish view of love, has turned these words around and contaminated our understanding of love. The world thinks that love is what makes a person feel good and that it is all right to sacrifice moral principles and others' rights in order to obtain such "love." But that isn't real love; it is the exact opposite—selfishness. And God is not that kind of "love." Real love is like God, who is holy, just, and perfect. If we truly know God, we will love as he does.

1 Jn 4:9 Jesus is God's *only* Son. While all believers are sons and daughters of God, only Jesus lives in this special, unique relationship (see John 1:18; 3:16).

1 Jn 4:9-10 Love explains: (1) why God creates—because he loves, he creates people to love; (2) why God cares—because he loves them, he cares for sinful people; (3) why we are free to choose—God wants a loving response from us; (4) why Christ died—his love for us caused him to offer a solution to the problem of sin; and (5) why we receive eternal life—God's love expresses itself to us forever.

1 Jn 4:10 Nothing sinful or evil can exist in God's presence. He is absolute goodness. He cannot overlook, condone, or excuse sin as though it never happened. He loves us, but his love does not make him morally lax. If we trust in Christ, we will not have to bear the penalty for our sins (1 Pet 2:24). We will be acquitted (Rom 5:18) by his atoning sacrifice.

1 Jn 4:12 If no one has ever seen God, how can we ever know him? John in his Gospel said, "The unique One, who is himself God, is near to the Father's heart. He has revealed God to us" (John 1:18). Jesus is the complete expression of God in human form, and he has revealed God to us. When we love one another, the invisible God reveals himself to others through us, and his love is made complete.

1 Jn 4:12 Some people simply enjoy being with others. They make friends with strangers easily and always are surrounded by friends. Other people are shy or reserved. They have a few friends, are frequently uncomfortable talking with people they don't know or mingling in crowds. Shy people don't need to become extroverts in order to love others. John isn't telling us how many people to love, but how much to love the people we already know. Our job is to love faithfully the people God has given us to love, whether there are two or 200 of them. If God sees that we are ready to love others, he will bring them to us. No matter how shy we are, we don't need to be afraid of the love commandment. God provides us the strength to do what he asks.

1 Jn 4:13 When we become Christians, we receive the Holy Spirit. God's presence in our life is proof that we really belong to him. He also gives us the power to love (Rom 5:5; 8:9; 2 Cor 1:22). Rely on that power as you reach out to others. As you do so, you will gain confidence. (See also Rom 8:16.)

Sign of the Fish

Early Christians used the sign of the fish as a special insignia of Jesus' names or titles. The symbol came into use because the Greek word meaning "fish," ***ichthus*****, is an anagram for the phrase, "Jesus Christ, God's Son, Savior." Early Christians would use the sign of the fish in times of persecution (when they had to be discrete) to identify themselves to each other as believers. Today, it is popular to have the sign of the fish on jewelry or on car bumpers. These should remind us to be true believers in God's Son, Jesus Christ, and confess him daily as our Savior and Lord.**

1 Jn 4:17 The day of judgment is that time when all people will appear before Christ and be held accountable for their actions. With God living in us through Christ, we have no reason to fear this day because we have been saved from punishment. Instead, we can look forward to the day of judgment because it will mean the end of sin and the beginning of a face-to-face relationship with Jesus Christ.

▸ **1 JOHN 4:7-21** ***(cont.)***

grows more perfect. So we will not be afraid on the day of judgment, but we can face him with confidence because we live like Jesus here in this world.

18 Such love has no fear, because perfect love expels all fear. If we are afraid, it is for fear of punishment, and this shows that we have not fully experienced his perfect love. 19 We love each other* because he loved us first.

20 If someone says, "I love God," but hates a Christian brother or sister,* that person is a liar; for if we don't love people we can see, how can we love God, whom we cannot see? 21 And he has given us this command: Those who love God must also love their Christian brothers and sisters.*

Faith in the Son of God

1 JOHN 5:1-12

Everyone who believes that Jesus is the Christ* has become a child of God. And everyone who loves the Father loves his children, too. 2 We know we love God's children if we love God and obey his commandments. 3 Loving God means keeping his commandments, and his commandments are not burdensome. 4 For every child of God defeats this evil world, and we achieve this victory through our faith. 5 And who can win this battle against the world? Only those who believe that Jesus is the Son of God.

6 And Jesus Christ was revealed as God's Son by his baptism in water and by shedding his blood on the cross*—not by water only, but by water and blood. And the Spirit, who is truth, confirms it with his testimony. 7 So we have these three witnesses*—8 the Spirit, the water, and the blood—and all three agree. 9 Since we believe human testimony, surely we can believe the greater testimony that comes from God. And God has testified about his Son. 10 All who believe in the Son of God know in their hearts that this testimony is true. Those who don't believe this are actually calling God a liar because they don't believe what God has testified about his Son.

11 And this is what God has testified: He has given us eternal life, and this life is in his Son. 12 Whoever has the Son has life; whoever does not have God's Son does not have life.

Conclusion

1 JOHN 5:13-21

I have written this to you who believe in the name of the Son of God, so that you may know you have eternal life. 14 And we are confident that he hears us whenever we ask for anything that pleases him. 15 And since we know he hears us when we make our requests, we also know that he will give us what we ask for.

16 If you see a Christian brother or sister* sinning in a way that does not lead to death, you should pray, and God will give that person life. But there is a sin that

1 Jn 4:19 Greek *We love.* Other manuscripts read *We love God;* still others read *We love him.* **1 Jn 4:20** Greek *hates his brother.* **1 Jn 4:21** Greek *The one who loves God must also love his brother.* **1 Jn 5:1** Or *the Messiah.* **1 Jn 5:6** Greek *This is he who came by water and blood.* **1 Jn 5:7** A few very late manuscripts add *in heaven—the Father, the Word, and the Holy Spirit, and these three are one. And we have three witnesses on earth.* **1 Jn 5:16** Greek *a brother.*

1 Jn 4:18 If we ever are afraid of the future, eternity, or God's judgment, we can remind ourselves of God's love. We know that he loves us perfectly (Rom 8:38-39). We can resolve our fears first by focusing on his immeasurable love for us, and then by allowing him to love others through us. His love will quiet our fears and give us confidence.

1 Jn 4:19 God's love is the source of all human love, and it spreads like fire. In loving his children, God kindles a flame in their hearts. In turn, they love others, who are warmed by God's love through them.

1 Jn 4:20-21 It is easy to say we love God when that love doesn't cost us anything more than weekly attendance at religious services. But the real test of our love for God is how we treat the people right in front of us—our family members and fellow believers. We cannot truly love God while neglecting to love those who are created in his image.

1 Jn 5:1-2 When we become Christians, we become part of God's family, with fellow believers as our brothers and sisters. It is God who determines who the other family members are, not us. We are simply called to accept and love them. How well do you treat your fellow family members?

1 Jn 5:3-4 Jesus never promised that obeying him would be easy. But the hard work and self-discipline of serving Christ is no burden to those who love him. And if our load starts to feel heavy, we can always trust Christ to help us bear it (see Matt 11:28-30).

1 Jn 5:6-8 At this time, there was a false teaching in circulation that said Jesus was "the Christ" only between his baptism and his death—that is, he was merely human until he was baptized, at which time "the Christ" then descended upon him but then later left him before his death on the cross. But if Jesus died only as a man, he could not have taken upon himself the sins of the world, and Christianity would be an empty religion. Only an act of God could take away the punishment that we deserve for our sin.

1 Jn 5:7-9 The Gospels twice record God's clear declaration that Jesus was his Son—at Jesus' baptism (Matt 3:16-17) and at his transfiguration (Matt 17:5).

1 Jn 5:12 Whoever believes in God's Son has eternal life. He is all you need. You don't need to *wait* for eternal life because it begins the moment you believe. You don't need to *work* for it because it is already yours. You don't need to *worry* about it because you have been given eternal life by God himself—and it is guaranteed.

1 Jn 5:13 Some people *hope* that they will receive eternal life. John says we can *know* we have it. Our certainty is based on God's promise that he has given us eternal life through his Son. This is true whether you feel close to God or far away from him. Eternal life is not based on feelings but on facts. You can know that you have eternal life if you believe God's truth. If you aren't sure that you are a Christian, ask yourself: Have I honestly committed my life to him as my Savior and Lord? If so, you know by faith that you are indeed a child of God.

1 Jn 5:14-15 The emphasis here is on God's will, not our will. When we communicate with God, we don't demand what we want; rather we discuss with him what *he* wants for us. If we align our prayers to his will, he will listen; and we can be certain that if he listens, he will give us a definite answer. Start praying with confidence!

1 Jn 5:16-17 Commentators differ widely in their thoughts about what this sin that leads to death is and whether the death it causes is physical or spiritual. Paul wrote that some Christians had died because they took Communion unworthily (1 Cor 11:27-30), and Ananias and Sapphira were struck dead when they lied to God (Acts 5:1-11). Blasphemy against the Holy Spirit results in spiritual death (Mark 3:29), and the book of Hebrews describes the spiritual death of the person who turns against Christ (Heb 6:4-6). John was probably referring to the people who had left the Christian fellowship and joined the

leads to death, and I am not saying you should pray
for those who commit it. [17]All wicked actions are sin,
but not every sin leads to death.
[18]We know that God's children do not make a practice of sinning, for God's Son holds them securely, and
the evil one cannot touch them. [19]We know that we
are children of God and that the world around us is
under the control of the evil one.
[20]And we know that the Son of God has come, and
he has given us understanding so that we can know
the true God.* And now we live in fellowship with
the true God because we live in fellowship with his
Son, Jesus Christ. He is the only true God, and he is
eternal life.
[21]Dear children, keep away from anything that
might take God's place in your hearts.*

1 Jn 5:20 Greek *the one who is true.* **1 Jn 5:21** Greek *keep yourselves from idols.*

2. JOHN'S SECOND LETTER

This letter seems to be written to a local church, referred to as a "chosen lady" and her children. John was warning about false teachers who were becoming prevalent among some churches at that time. False teachers were a dangerous problem for this church. His warning against showing hospitality to false teachers may sound harsh and unloving to many today. Yet these people were teaching heresies that could seriously harm many others for eternity.

Greetings

2 JOHN 1:1-3

This letter is from John, the elder.*
I am writing to the chosen lady and to her children,*
whom I love in the truth—as does everyone else who
knows the truth—[2]because the truth lives in us and
will be with us forever.
[3]Grace, mercy, and peace, which come from God
the Father and from Jesus Christ—the Son of the
Father—will continue to be with us who live in truth
and love.

Live in the Truth

2 JOHN 1:4-11

How happy I was to meet some of your children and
find them living according to the truth, just as the
Father commanded.
[5]I am writing to remind you, dear friends,* that we

2 Jn 1a Greek *From the elder.* **2 Jn 1b** Or *the church God has chosen and its members.* **2 Jn 5** Greek *I urge you, lady.*

antichrists. By rejecting the only way of salvation, these people were putting themselves out of reach of prayer. In most cases, even if we knew what the terrible sin was, we would have no sure way of knowing whether a certain person had committed it. Therefore, we should continue praying for our loved ones and for our Christian brothers and sisters, leaving the judgment up to God. Note that John says, "I am not saying you should pray for those who commit it," rather than, "You cannot pray for them." He recognized the lack of certainty.

1 Jn 5:18-19 Christians commit sins, of course, but they ask God to forgive them, and then they continue serving him. God has freed believers from their slavery to Satan, and he keeps them safe from Satan's continued attacks. The rest of the world does not have the Christian's freedom to obey God. Unless they come to Christ in faith, they have no choice but to obey Satan. There is no middle ground; people either belong to God and obey him, or they live under Satan's control.

1 Jn 5:21 Many things can take God's place in our lives. This includes anything that substitutes for the true faith, anything that denies Christ's full deity and humanity, any human idea that claims to be more authoritative than the Bible, any loyalty that replaces God at the center of our lives.

1 Jn 5:21 John presents a clear picture of Christ. What we think about Jesus Christ is central to our teaching, preaching, and living. Jesus is the God-man, fully God and fully human at the same time. He came to earth to die in our place for our sins. Through faith in him, we are given eternal life and the power to do his will. What is your answer to the most important question you could ever ask: Who is Jesus Christ?

2 Jn 1:1 The "elder" is John, one of Jesus' 12 disciples and the writer of the Gospel of John, three letters, and the book of Revelation. For more information about John, see his Profile on p. 1459. This letter was written shortly after the letter that is the book of 1 John to warn about false teachers. The salutation "to the chosen lady and to her children" could refer to a specific woman or to a church whose identity is no longer known. John may have written this from Ephesus.

2 Jn 1:1-2 John wrote this second letter (which probably fit on one sheet of papyrus) to warn believers against inadvertently supporting false teachers. The number of itinerant evangelists and teachers had grown by the end of the first century; mixed in with the legitimate missionaries were others who were promoting heretical ideas about Christ and the gospel. Little has changed in 2,000 years. Advocates of unorthodox beliefs still exist and still attempt to confuse and deceive the people of God. This letter, 2 John, should serve as a wake-up call to believers to be alert, to be careful, and to be solidly grounded in the faith. Are you prepared to recognize false doctrine?

2 Jn 1:3-4 The "truth" is the truth about Jesus Christ, as opposed to the lies of the false teachers (see 1 Jn 2:21-23). John refers to truth five times in the first four verses of this brief letter. In contrast to so many in our culture who dogmatically deny truth ("There are no ultimate realities") or absurdly define it according to personal preference ("Your truth is your truth and my truth is my truth"), John declared the existence of an Absolute. God is that ultimate standard by which all else can be judged. God is true, his words and ways are true, and whatever or whoever contradicts or opposes him is false, deceptive, and dangerous. Christian leaders, teachers, and parents must engage now in the difficult but critical battle for truth. To paraphrase a familiar saying: "All that is required for deception to triumph is for the people of the Truth to do nothing." Begin an intentional campaign to teach those under your care how to distinguish between truth and error.

2 Jn 1:5-6 The statement that Christians should love one another is a recurrent New Testament theme. Yet love for one's neighbor is an old command, first appearing in the third book of Moses (Lev 19:18). We can show love in many ways: by avoiding prejudice and discrimination; by accepting people; by listening, helping, giving, serving, and refusing to judge. Knowing God's command is not enough. We must put it into practice, "doing what God has commanded us" (see also Matt 22:37-39; 1 Jn 2:7-8).

AD 79 Mount Vesuvius erupts

▸ **2 JOHN 1:4-11** ***(cont.)***
should love one another. This is not a new commandment, but one we have had from the beginning. [6]Love means doing what God has commanded us, and he has commanded us to love one another, just as you heard from the beginning.

[7]I say this because many deceivers have gone out into the world. They deny that Jesus Christ came* in a real body. Such a person is a deceiver and an antichrist. [8]Watch out that you do not lose what we* have worked so hard to achieve. Be diligent so that you receive your full reward. [9]Anyone who wanders away from this teaching has no relationship with God. But anyone who remains in the teaching of Christ has a relationship with both the Father and the Son.

[10]If anyone comes to your meeting and does not teach the truth about Christ, don't invite that person into your home or give any kind of encouragement. [11]Anyone who encourages such people becomes a partner in their evil work.

John's Closing Remarks

2 JOHN 1:12-13
I have much more to say to you, but I don't want to do it with paper and ink. For I hope to visit you soon and talk with you face to face. Then our joy will be complete.

[13]Greetings from the children of your sister,* chosen by God.

2 Jn 7 Or *will come.* **2 Jn 8** Some manuscripts read *you.* **2 Jn 13** Or *from the members of your sister church.*

3. JOHN'S THIRD LETTER

John's third letter was written to Gaius, a leader in one of the churches John knew well. John wrote to commend Gaius, who was taking care of traveling teachers and missionaries, and to warn against people like Diotrephes, who was proud and refused to listen to spiritual leaders in authority. If we are to live in the truth of the gospel, we must look for ways to support pastors, Christian workers, and missionaries today. All Christians should work together to support God's work both at home and around the world.

Greetings

3 JOHN 1:1-4
This letter is from John, the elder.*

I am writing to Gaius, my dear friend, whom I love in the truth.

[2]Dear friend, I hope all is well with you and that you are as healthy in body as you are strong in spirit. [3]Some of the traveling teachers* recently returned and made me very happy by telling me about your faithfulness and that you are living according to the truth. [4]I could have no greater joy than to hear that my children are following the truth.

3 Jn 1 Greek *From the elder.* **3 Jn 3** Greek *the brothers;* also in verses 5 and 10.

---

2 Jn 1:7 In John's day, many false teachers (deceivers) taught that spirit was good and matter was evil; therefore, they reasoned that Jesus could not have been both God and man. In strong terms, John warns against this kind of teaching. Many false teachers still promote an understanding of Jesus that is not biblical. These teachers are dangerous because they distort the truth and undermine the foundations of the Christian faith. They may use the right words but change the meanings.

2 Jn 1:7 The term translated "deceivers" can also be translated "impostors"; it carries the idea of leading another astray. Notice that the verse refers to "many" such charlatans and pretenders. The great danger of deceitful leaders is that they seem so sincere and believable. They are not easy to spot in a crowd. Usually they are winsome and attractive; otherwise, how would they gather people to themselves? We do not want to become paranoid and suspicious about everyone we meet, but we do need to be wise in evaluating the character and conduct of those who would seek to influence people. The way your teachers live shows a lot about what they believe about Christ. (For more on testing teachers, see 1 Jn 4:1.)

2 Jn 1:8 To "receive your full reward" refers not to salvation but to the rewards of loyal service. All who value the truth and persistently hold to it will win their full reward. Those who live for themselves and justify their self-centeredness by teaching false doctrines will lose that reward (see Matt 7:21-23).

2 Jn 1:10 John instructs the believers not to show hospitality to false teachers. They were to do nothing that would encourage the heretics in their propagation of falsehoods. In addition, if believers were to invite them in, such action would show that they were approving of what the false teachers said and did. John is condemning the support of those who are dedicated to opposing the true teachings of God, not condemning hospitality to unbelievers. John adds that a person who supports a false teacher in any way shares in the teacher's evil work.

2 Jn 1:10 False teaching is serious business, and we dare not overlook it. It is so serious that John wrote this letter to warn against it. Because our world has so many false teachings, we might be tempted to take many of them lightly. Instead, we should realize the dangers they pose and actively refuse to give heresies any foothold.

3 Jn 1:1 This letter provides us an important glimpse into the life of the early church. Addressed to Gaius, 3 John highlights the need for showing hospitality to traveling preachers and other believers. It also warns against a would-be church dictator.

3 Jn 1:1 The "elder," John, was one of Jesus' 12 disciples and the writer of the Gospel of John, three letters, and the book of Revelation. For more information about John, see his Profile on p. 1459. We have no further information about Gaius, but he is someone whom John loved dearly. Perhaps Gaius had shared his home and hospitality with John at some time during John's travels. If so, John would have appreciated his actions because traveling preachers depended on expressions of hospitality to survive (see Matt 10:11-16).

3 Jn 1:2 John was concerned for Gaius's physical and spiritual well-being. This was the opposite of the popular heresy that taught the separation of spirit and matter and despised the physical side of life. Today, many people still fall into this way of thinking. This non-Christian attitude logically leads to one of two responses: neglect of the body and physical health, or indulgence of the body's sinful desires. God is concerned for both your body and your

Caring for the Lord's Workers

3 JOHN 1:5-12

Dear friend, you are being faithful to God when you care for the traveling teachers who pass through, even though they are strangers to you. 6They have told the church here of your loving friendship. Please continue providing for such teachers in a manner that pleases God. 7For they are traveling for the Lord,* and they accept nothing from people who are not believers.* 8So we ourselves should support them so that we can be their partners as they teach the truth.

9I wrote to the church about this, but Diotrephes, who loves to be the leader, refuses to have anything to do with us. 10When I come, I will report some of the things he is doing and the evil accusations he is making against us. Not only does he refuse to welcome the traveling teachers, he also tells others not to help them. And when they do help, he puts them out of the church.

11Dear friend, don't let this bad example influence you. Follow only what is good. Remember that those who do good prove that they are God's children, and those who do evil prove that they do not know God.*

12Everyone speaks highly of Demetrius, as does the truth itself. We ourselves can say the same for him, and you know we speak the truth.

John's Closing Remarks

3 JOHN 1:13-15

I have much more to say to you, but I don't want to write it with pen and ink. 14For I hope to see you soon, and then we will talk face to face.

15*Peace be with you.

Your friends here send you their greetings. Please give my personal greetings to each of our friends there.

3 Jn 7a Greek *They went out on behalf of the Name.* **3 Jn 7b** Greek *from Gentiles.* **3 Jn 11** Greek *they have not seen God.* **3 Jn 15** Some English translations combine verses 14 and 15 into verse 14.

soul. As a responsible Christian, you should neither neglect nor indulge yourself but care for your physical needs and discipline your body so that you are at your best for God's service.

3 Jn 1:4 John writes about "my children" because, as a result of his preaching, he was the spiritual father of many, including Gaius.

3 Jn 1:5-6 In the church's early days, traveling prophets, evangelists, and teachers were helped on their way by people like Gaius, who housed and fed them. Hospitality is a lost art in many churches today. We would do well to invite more people for meals—fellow church members, young people, traveling missionaries, those in need, visitors. This is an active and much-appreciated way to show your love. In fact, it is probably more important today. Because of our individualistic, self-centered society, many lonely people wonder if anyone cares whether they live or die. If you find such a lonely person, show that you care!

3 Jn 1:7 The traveling missionaries neither asked for nor accepted anything from nonbelievers. This was not intended to be a criticism of unbelievers, but a statement of how things ought to be. Imagine the awkwardness of a Christian worker's requesting funds or lodging from the very people he or she was trying to reach! Instead, it is the responsibility of churches and Christian individuals to support those who are called by God to full-time vocational ministry. In that way, unbelievers will not be questioning the missionaries' motives for preaching. God's true preachers do not preach to make money but to fulfill their calling and express their love for God. It is the church's responsibility to care for Christian workers; this should never be left to nonbelievers. Don't just automatically discard the next missionary fund-raising letter you receive. That appeal may be God's invitation for you to become a partner in a new gospel venture.

3 Jn 1:8 When you help someone who is spreading the Good News, you are in a very real way a partner in the ministry. This is the other side of the principle in 2 John 1:10 (see the note on 2 Jn 1:10, p. 1796). Not everyone should go to the mission field; those who work for Christ at home are vital to the ministry of those who go and who need support. We can support missionaries by praying for them and by giving our money, hospitality, and time.

3 Jn 1:9 This letter to which John refers was neither 1 nor 2 John but another letter that no longer exists.

3 Jn 1:9-10 All we know about Diotrephes is that he wanted to control the church. John denounced (1) his refusal to have anything to do with other spiritual leaders, (2) his slander of the leaders, (3) his bad example in refusing to welcome any teachers, and (4) his attempt to excommunicate those who opposed his leadership. Sins such as pride, jealousy, and slander are still present in the church, and when a leader makes a habit of encouraging sin and discouraging right actions, they must be stopped. If no one speaks up, great harm can come to the church. We must confront sin in the church; if we ignore it, it will continue to grow. A true Christian leader is a servant, not an autocrat!

3 Jn 1:12 We know nothing about Demetrius except that he may have carried this letter from John to Gaius. The book of Acts mentions an Ephesian silversmith named Demetrius, who opposed Paul (Acts 19:24ff), but this is probably another man. In contrast to the corrupt Diotrephes, Demetrius had a high regard for truth. John personified truth as a witness to Demetrius's character and teaching. In other words, if truth could speak, it would speak on Demetrius's behalf. When Demetrius arrived, Gaius certainly opened his home to him.

3 Jn 1:14 Whereas 2 John emphasizes the need to refuse hospitality to false teachers, 3 John urges continued hospitality to those who teach the truth. Hospitality is a strong sign of support for people and their work. It means giving of your resources to them so their stay will be comfortable and their work and travel easier. Actively look for creative ways to show hospitality to God's workers. It may be in the form of a letter of encouragement, a gift, financial support, an open home, or prayer.

AD 81 **Domitian becomes the Roman emperor**

Z. The Book of Revelation

Most scholars believe that the seven churches of Asia to whom John writes were experiencing the persecution that took place under Emperor Domitian (A.D. 90–95). It seems that the Roman authorities had exiled John to the island of Patmos. John, who had been an eyewitness to the incarnate Christ, had a vision of the glorified Christ. God also revealed to John what would take place in the future: judgment and the ultimate triumph of God over evil.

1. LETTERS TO THE CHURCHES

The vision John received opens with instructions for him to write to seven churches. He both commends them for their strengths and warns them about their flaws. Each letter was directed to a church then in existence but also speaks to conditions in the church throughout history. Both in the church and in our individual lives, we must constantly fight against the temptation to become loveless, immoral, lenient, compromising, lifeless, or casual about our faith. The letters make it clear how our Lord feels about such qualities.

Prologue

REVELATION 1:1-3

This is a revelation from* Jesus Christ, which God
gave him to show his servants the events that must
soon* take place. He sent an angel to present this revelation to his servant John, 2who faithfully reported
everything he saw. This is his report of the word of
God and the testimony of Jesus Christ.
3God blesses the one who reads the words of this
prophecy to the church, and he blesses all who listen
to its message and obey what it says, for the time is
near.

Rv 1:1a Or *of.* **Rv 1:1b** Or *suddenly,* or *quickly.*

Rev 1:1 Revelation is a book about the future *and* about the present. It offers future hope to all believers, especially those who have suffered for their faith, by proclaiming Christ's final victory over evil and the reality of eternal life with him. It also gives present guidance as it teaches us about Jesus Christ and how we should live for him now. Through graphic pictures we learn that (1) Jesus Christ is coming again, (2) evil will be judged, and (3) the dead will be raised to judgment, resulting in either eternal life or eternal destruction.

Rev 1:1 According to tradition, John, the author, was the only one of Jesus' original 12 disciples who was not killed for the faith. He also wrote the Gospel of John and three letters. When he wrote Revelation, John was in exile on the island of Patmos in the Aegean Sea, sent there by the Romans for his witness about Jesus Christ. For more information on John, see his Profile on p. 1459.

Rev 1:1 This book is the revelation *from, concerning,* and *of* Jesus Christ. God gave the revelation of his plan to Jesus Christ, who, in turn, revealed it to John. The book of Revelation unveils Christ's full identity and God's plan for the end of the world, and it focuses on Jesus Christ, his second coming, his victory over evil, and the establishment of his Kingdom. As you read and study Revelation, don't focus so much on the timetable of the events or the details of John's imagery that you miss the main message—the infinite love, power, and justice of the Lord Jesus Christ.

Rev 1:1 The book of Revelation is *apocalyptic* in style. This style of ancient literature usually featured spectacular and mysterious imagery, and such literature was often written under the name of an ancient hero. John was acquainted with Jewish apocalyptic works, but his book is different in several ways: (1) He uses his own name rather than the name of an ancient hero; (2) he denounces evil and exhorts people to high Christian standards; (3) he offers hope rather than gloom. John was not a psychic attempting to predict the future; he was a prophet of God describing what God had shown him.

Rev 1:1 For more about angels, see the note on Revelation 5:11, p. 1810.

Rev 1:1 Jesus gave his message to John in a revelation (or vision), allowing John to see and record certain future events so they could be an encouragement to all believers. The vision includes many signs and symbols that convey the essence of what is to happen. What John saw, in most cases, was indescribable, so he used illustrations to show what it was *like.* When reading this symbolic language, we don't have to understand every detail—John himself didn't. Instead, realize that John's imagery shows us that Christ is indeed the glorious and victorious Lord of all.

Rev 1:1-3 The book of Revelation reveals future events, but there is not the gloomy pessimism we might expect. The drama of these unfolding events is spectacular, but there is nothing to fear if you are on the winning side. When you think about the future, walk with confidence because Christ, the Victor, walks with you.

Rev 1:3 Revelation is a book of prophecy that is both prediction (foretelling future events) and proclamation (preaching about who God is and what he will do). Prophecy is more than telling the future. Behind the predictions are important principles about God's character and promises. As we read, we will get to know God better so that we can trust him completely.

Rev 1:3 The typical news reports—filled with violence, scandal, and political haggling—are depressing, and we may wonder where the world is heading. God's plan for the future provides inspiration and encouragement because we know he will intervene in history to conquer evil. John encourages churches to read this book aloud so everyone can hear it, apply it ("obey" it), and be assured of the fact that God will triumph.

Rev 1:3 When John says that "the time is near," he is urging his readers to be ready at all times for the Last Judgment and the establishment of God's Kingdom. We do not know when these events will occur, but we must always be prepared. They will happen quickly, and there will be no second chance to change sides.

Rev 1:4 Jesus told John to write to seven churches (see Rev 1:11) that knew and trusted him and had read his earlier letters (1–3 Jn). These letters to the seven churches were addressed so that they could be read and passed on in a systematic fashion, following the main Roman road clockwise around the province of Asia (now called Turkey).

Rev 1:4 The "sevenfold Spirit" is another name for the Holy Spirit. The number seven is used throughout Revelation to symbolize completeness and perfection. (For more about the Holy Spirit, see the notes on John 3:6, p. 1301; Acts 1:5, p. 1499.)

Rev 1:4-6 The Trinity—the Father ("the one who is, who always was, and who is still to come"), the Holy Spirit ("the sevenfold

John's Greeting to the Seven Churches

REVELATION 1:4-8

This letter is from John to the seven churches in the province of Asia.*

Grace and peace to you from the one who is, who always was, and who is still to come; from the sevenfold Spirit* before his throne; 5and from Jesus Christ. He is the faithful witness to these things, the first to rise from the dead, and the ruler of all the kings of the world.

All glory to him who loves us and has freed us from our sins by shedding his blood for us. 6He has made us a Kingdom of priests for God his Father. All glory and power to him forever and ever! Amen.

Rv 1:4a *Asia* was a Roman province in what is now western Turkey. **Rv 1:4b** Greek *the seven spirits.*

A JOURNEY THROUGH THE BOOK OF REVELATION

Revelation is a complex book, and it has baffled interpreters for centuries. We can avoid a great deal of confusion by understanding the literary structure of this book. This approach will allow us to understand the individual scenes within the overall structure of Revelation and keep us from getting unnecessarily bogged down in the details of each vision. John gives hints throughout the book to indicate a change of subject, or a flashback to an earlier scene.

First, John relates the circumstances that led to the writing of this book (Rev 1:1-20). Next, Jesus gives special messages to the seven churches of Asia Minor (Rev 2:1–3:22).

Suddenly, John is caught up into heaven, where he sees a vision of God Almighty on his throne. All of Christ's followers and the heavenly angels are worshiping God (Rev 4:1-11). John watches as God gives a scroll with seven seals to the worthy Lamb, Jesus Christ (Rev 5:1-14). The Lamb begins to open the seals one by one. As each seal is opened, a new vision appears.

As the first four seals are opened, riders appear on horses of different colors: war, famine, disease, and death (Rev 6:1-8). As the fifth seal is opened, John sees those in heaven who have been martyred for their faith in Christ (Rev 6:9-11).

A set of contrasting images appears at the opening of the sixth seal. On one side, there is a great earthquake, stars fall from the sky, and the sky rolls up like a scroll (Rev 6:12-17). On the other side, multitudes are before the throne, worshiping and praising God and the Lamb (Rev 7:1-17).

Then, the seventh seal is opened (Rev 8:1-5), unveiling a series of God's judgments announced by seven angels with seven trumpets. The first four angels bring hail, fire, a mountain of fire, and a falling star—the sun and moon are darkened (Rev 8:6-13). The fifth trumpet announces the coming of locusts with the power to sting (Rev 9:1-12). The sixth trumpet heralds the coming of an army of warriors on horses (Rev 9:13-21). Then, John is given a small scroll to eat (Rev 10:1-11). Following this, John is commanded to measure the Temple of God (Rev 11:1-2). He sees two witnesses, who proclaim God's judgment on the earth for three and a half years (Rev 11:3-14).

Finally, the seventh trumpet sounds, calling the rival forces of good and evil to the final battle. On one side is Satan and his forces; on the other side stands Jesus Christ with his forces (Rev 11:15–13:18). In the midst of this call to battle, John sees three angels announcing the final judgment (Rev 14:6-13). Two angels begin to reap this harvest of judgment on the earth (Rev 14:14-20). Following on the heels of these two angels are seven more angels, who pour out God's judgment on the earth from seven bowls (Rev 15:1–16:21). One of these angels from the group of seven reveals to John a vision of a "great prostitute" called Babylon (symbolizing the Roman Empire), riding a scarlet beast (Rev 17:1-18). After the defeat of Babylon (Rev 18:1-24), a great multitude in heaven shouts praise to God for his mighty victory (Rev 19:1-10).

The final three chapters of the book of Revelation catalog the events that finalize Christ's victory over the enemy: Satan's 1,000-year imprisonment (Rev 20:1-10), the final judgment (Rev 20:11-15), and the creation of a new earth and a new Jerusalem (Rev 21:1–22:6). An angel then gives John final instructions concerning the visions John has seen and what to do once he has written them all down (Rev 22:7-11).

Revelation concludes with the promise of Christ's soon return, an offer to drink of the water of life that flows through the great street of the new Jerusalem, and a warning to those who read the book (Rev 22:12-21). May we pray with John, "Amen! Come, Lord Jesus!" (Rev 22:20).

The Bible ends with a message of warning and hope for men and women of every generation. Christ is victorious, and all evil has been done away with. As you read the book of Revelation, marvel at God's grace in the salvation of the saints and his power over the evil forces of Satan, and remember the hope of this victory to come.

Spirit"), and the Son (Jesus Christ)—is the source of all truth (John 14:6, 17; 1 Jn 2:27; Rev 19:11). Thus, we can be assured that John's message is reliable and is God's word to us.

Rev 1:5 Others had risen from the dead—people whom the prophets, Jesus, and the apostles brought back to life during their ministries—but later those people died again. Jesus was the first who rose from the dead in an imperishable body (1 Cor 15:20), never to die again. He is the "first to rise from the dead."

Rev 1:5-6 Many hesitate to witness about their faith in Christ because they don't feel the change in their lives has been spectacular enough. But you qualify as a witness for Jesus because of what he has done for you, not because of what you have done for him. Christ demonstrated his great love by setting us free from our sins through his death on the cross ("freed us from our sins by shedding his blood for us"), guaranteeing us a place in his Kingdom, and making us priests to administer God's love to others. The fact that the all-powerful God has offered eternal life to you is nothing short of spectacular.

▸ **REVELATION 1:4-8** ***(cont.)***

7 Look! He comes with the clouds of heaven.
And everyone will see him—
even those who pierced him.
And all the nations of the world
will mourn for him.
Yes! Amen!

8"I am the Alpha and the Omega—the beginning
and the end,"* says the Lord God. "I am the one who
is, who always was, and who is still to come—the Almighty One."

Vision of the Son of Man

REVELATION 1:9-20

I, John, am your brother and your partner in suffering
and in God's Kingdom and in the patient endurance
to which Jesus calls us. I was exiled to the island of
Patmos for preaching the word of God and for my testimony about Jesus. 10It was the Lord's Day, and I was
worshiping in the Spirit.* Suddenly, I heard behind
me a loud voice like a trumpet blast. 11It said, "Write
in a book* everything you see, and send it to the seven
churches in the cities of Ephesus, Smyrna, Pergamum,
Thyatira, Sardis, Philadelphia, and Laodicea."

12When I turned to see who was speaking to me,
I saw seven gold lampstands. 13And standing in the
middle of the lampstands was someone like the Son
of Man.* He was wearing a long robe with a gold sash
across his chest. 14His head and his hair were white
like wool, as white as snow. And his eyes were like
flames of fire. 15His feet were like polished bronze
refined in a furnace, and his voice thundered like
mighty ocean waves. 16He held seven stars in his right

Rv 1:8 Greek *I am the Alpha and the Omega*, referring to the first and last letters of the Greek alphabet. **Rv 1:10** Or *in spirit*. **Rv 1:11** Or *on a scroll*. **Rv 1:13** Or *like a son of man*. See Dan 7:13. "Son of Man" is a title Jesus used for himself.

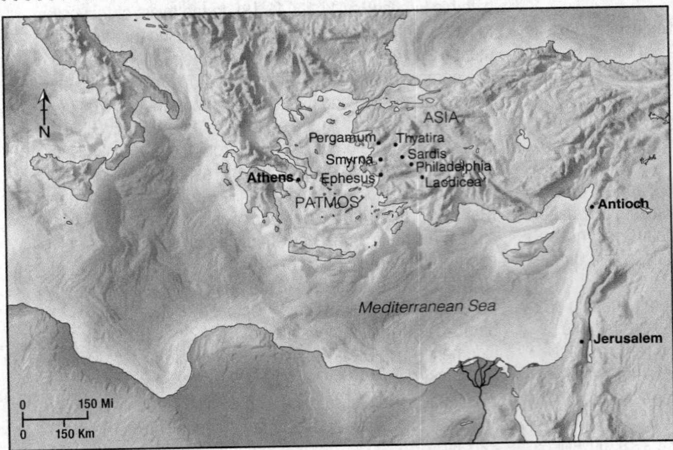

THE SEVEN CHURCHES *The seven churches were located on a major Roman road. A letter carrier would leave the island of Patmos (where John was exiled), arriving first at Ephesus. He would travel north to Smyrna and Pergamum, turn southeast to Thyatira, and continue on to Sardis, Philadelphia, and Laodicea—in the exact order in which the letters were dictated.*

Rev 1:5-7 Jesus is portrayed as the all-powerful King, victorious in battle, glorious in peace. He is not just a humble earthly teacher; he is the glorious God. When you read John's description of the vision, keep in mind that his words are not just good advice; they are truth from the King of kings. Don't just read his words for their interesting and amazing portrayal of the future. Let the truth about Christ penetrate your life, deepen your faith in him, and strengthen your commitment to follow him no matter what the cost.

Rev 1:7 John is announcing the return of Jesus to earth (see also Matt 24; Mark 13; 1 Thes 4:15-18). Jesus' second coming will be visible and victorious. All people will see him arrive (Mark 13:26), and they will *know* it is Jesus. When he comes, he will conquer evil and judge all people according to their deeds (Rev 20:11-15).

Rev 1:7 "Those who pierced him" could refer to the Roman soldiers who pierced Jesus' side as he hung on the cross or to the Jews who were responsible for his death. John saw Jesus' death with his own eyes, and he never forgot the horror of it (see John 19:34-35; see also Zech 12:10).

Rev 1:8 Alpha and Omega are the first and last letters of the Greek alphabet. The Lord God is the beginning and the end. God the Father is the eternal Lord and Ruler of the past, present, and future (see also Rev 4:8; Isa 44:6; 48:12-15). Without him you have nothing that is eternal, nothing that can change your life, nothing that can save you from sin. Is the Lord your reason for living, "the Alpha and the Omega" of your life? Honor the one who is the beginning and the end of all existence, wisdom, and power.

Rev 1:9 Patmos was a small rocky island in the Aegean Sea, about 50 miles offshore from the city of Ephesus on the Asia Minor seacoast (see the map above).

Rev 1:9 The Christian church was facing severe persecution. Almost all believers were socially, politically, or economically suffering because of this empire-wide persecution, and some were even being killed for their faith. John was exiled to Patmos because he refused to stop preaching the Good News. We may not face persecution for our faith as the early Christians did, but even with our freedom few of us have the courage to share God's Word with others. If we hesitate to share our faith during easy times, how will we do during times of persecution?

Rev 1:12-13 The seven gold lampstands are the seven churches in Asia (Rev 1:11, 20), and Jesus stands among them. No matter what the churches face, Jesus protects them with his all-encompassing love and reassuring power. Through his Spirit, Jesus Christ is still among the churches today. When a church faces persecution, it should remember Christ's deep love and compassion. When a church is troubled by internal strife and conflict, it should remember Christ's concern for purity and his intolerance of sin.

Rev 1:13-14 This "Son of Man" is Jesus himself. The title *Son of Man* occurs many times in the New Testament in reference to Jesus as the Messiah. John recognized Jesus because he lived with him for three years and had seen him both as the Galilean preacher and as the glorified Son of God at the Transfiguration (Matt 17:1-8). Here Jesus appears as the mighty Son of Man. His white hair indicates his wisdom and divine nature (see also Dan 7:9); his bright eyes symbolize judgment of all evil; the gold sash across his chest reveals him as the High Priest, who goes into God's presence to obtain forgiveness of sin for those who have believed in him.

hand, and a sharp two-edged sword came from his
mouth. And his face was like the sun in all its brilliance.
17When I saw him, I fell at his feet as if I were dead.
But he laid his right hand on me and said, "Don't be
afraid! I am the First and the Last. 18I am the living
one. I died, but look—I am alive forever and ever! And
I hold the keys of death and the grave.*
19"Write down what you have seen—both the things
that are now happening and the things that will happen.* 20This is the meaning of the mystery of the seven
stars you saw in my right hand and the seven gold
lampstands: The seven stars are the angels* of the
seven churches, and the seven lampstands are the
seven churches.

The Message to the Church in Ephesus

REVELATION 2:1-7

"Write this letter to the angel* of the church in Ephesus. This is the message from the one who holds the
seven stars in his right hand, the one who walks among
the seven gold lampstands:

Rv 1:18 Greek *and Hades*. **Rv 1:19** Or *what you have seen and what they mean—the things that have already begun to happen*. **Rv 1:20** Or *the messengers*. **Rv 2:1** Or *the messenger*; also in 2:8, 12, 18.

Patmos

Patmos is a small island in the Aegean Sea, located about 35 miles west of the city of Miletus off the coast of Asia Minor. Consisting of rocky volcanic hills, Patmos is about ten miles long and six miles wide at its northern end. The Roman historian Tacitus informs us that the Romans used some of the Aegean islands as places of banishment and exile during the 1st century (*Annals* 3.68; 4.30; 15.71). Thus, the language of the author of Revelation and the evidence of Tacitus, joined to Christian traditions from the 2nd and 3rd centuries about John's banishment, support the likelihood that Patmos was a place of exile or political confinement.

In Revelation 1:9, John says that he was "exiled to the island of Patmos for preaching the word of God and for my testimony about Jesus." He also indicates that he was a fellow participant in suffering. If our faith ever causes us to suffer, let us stay faithful to Jesus, as John did.

Revelation will challenge your mental picture of Jesus Christ. What forms your impression of him right now—famous paintings, movies, Sunday school art? Do you ever picture Jesus with a gold sash and snow white, woolly hair? Do his eyes flash fire and his feet glow like bronze? When you imagine Jesus speaking to you, does his voice thunder like mighty ocean waves? Reevaluate the way you think of Jesus as you read and study Revelation. Allow his powerful presence to transform your life.

Rev 1:16 The sword in Jesus' mouth symbolizes the power and force of his message. His words of judgment are as sharp as swords (Isa 49:2; Heb 4:12).

Rev 1:17-18 As the Roman government stepped up its persecution of Christians, John must have wondered if the church could survive and stand against the opposition. But Jesus appeared in glory and splendor, reassuring John that he and his fellow believers had access to God's strength to face these trials. If you are facing difficult problems, remember that the power available to John and the early church is also available to you (see 1 Jn 4:4).

Rev 1:17-18 Our sins have convicted and sentenced us, but Jesus holds the keys of death and the grave. He alone can free us from eternal bondage to Satan. He alone has the power and authority to set us free from sin's control. Believers don't have to fear death or the grave because Christ holds the keys to both. All we must do is turn from sin and turn to him in faith. When we attempt to control our lives and disregard God, we set a course that leads directly to hell. But when we place our lives in Christ's hands, he restores us now and resurrects us later to an eternal, peaceful relationship with him.

Rev 1:20 Who are the "angels of the seven churches"? Some say that they are angels designated to guard the churches; others say that they are elders or pastors of the local churches. Because the seven letters in Revelation 2–3 contain reprimands, it is doubtful that these angels are heavenly messengers. If these are earthly leaders or messengers, they are accountable to God for the churches they represent.

Rev 2:1 Ephesus was the capital of Asia Minor, a center of land and sea trade, and, along with Alexandria and Antioch in Syria, one of the three most influential cities in the eastern part of the Roman Empire. The temple to Artemis, one of the ancient wonders of the world, was located in this city, and a major industry was the manufacture of images of this goddess (see Acts 19:21-41). Paul ministered in Ephesus for three years and warned the Ephesians that false teachers would come and try to draw people away from the faith (see Acts 20:29-31). False teachers did indeed cause problems in the Ephesian church, but the church resisted them, as we can see from Paul's letter to the Ephesians. John spent much of his ministry in this city and knew that they had resisted false teaching (Rev 2:2).

Rev 2:1 The one who "walks among the seven gold lampstands" (the seven churches) is Jesus (Rev 1:11-13). He holds the "seven stars in his right hand" (messengers of the churches), indicating his power and authority over the churches and their leaders. Ephesus had become a large, proud church, and Jesus' message would remind them that he alone is the head of the body of believers.

Rev 2:1ff Does God care about your church? If you are tempted to doubt it, look more closely at these seven letters. The Lord of the universe knew each of these churches and its precise situation. In each letter, Jesus told John to write about specific people, places, and events. He praised believers for their successes and told them how to correct their failures. Just as Jesus cared for each of these churches, he cares for yours. He wants it to reach its greatest potential. The group of believers with whom you worship and serve is God's vehicle for changing the world. Take it seriously—God does.

▸ **REVELATION 2:1-7** ***(cont.)***

[2]"I know all the things you do. I have seen
your hard work and your patient endurance.
I know you don't tolerate evil people. You have
examined the claims of those who say they are
apostles but are not. You have discovered they
are liars. [3]You have patiently suffered for me
without quitting.
[4]"But I have this complaint against you. You
don't love me or each other as you did at first!*
[5]Look how far you have fallen! Turn back to me
and do the works you did at first. If you don't
repent, I will come and remove your lampstand
from its place among the churches. [6]But this
is in your favor: You hate the evil deeds of the
Nicolaitans, just as I do.
[7]"Anyone with ears to hear must listen to the
Spirit and understand what he is saying to the
churches. To everyone who is victorious I will give
fruit from the tree of life in the paradise of God.

The Message to the Church in Smyrna

REVELATION 2:8-11

"Write this letter to the angel of the church in Smyrna. This is the message from the one who is the First and the Last, who was dead but is now alive:

Rv 2:4 Greek *You have lost your first love.*

Rev 2:2 Over a long period of time, the church in Ephesus had steadfastly refused to tolerate sin among its members. This was not easy in a city noted for immoral sexual practices associated with the worship of the goddess Artemis. We also are living in times of widespread sin and sexual immorality. It is popular to be open-minded toward many types of sin, calling them personal choices or alternative lifestyles. But when the body of believers begins to tolerate sin in the church, it is lowering the standards and compromising the church's witness. Remember that God's approval is infinitely more important than the world's. Use God's Word, not what people around you are willing to accept, to set the standards for what is right or wrong.

Rev 2:2-3 Christ commended the church at Ephesus for (1) working hard, (2) patiently enduring, (3) not tolerating evil people, (4) critically examining the claims of false apostles, and (5) suffering without quitting. Every church should have these characteristics. But these good efforts should spring from our love for Jesus Christ. Both Jesus and John stressed love for one another as an authentic proof of the Good News (John 13:34; 1 Jn 3:18-19). In the battle to maintain sound teaching and moral and doctrinal purity, it is possible to lose a charitable spirit. Prolonged conflict can weaken or destroy our patience and affection. In defending the faith, guard against any structure or rigidity that weakens love.

Rev 2:4 Paul had once commended the church at Ephesus for its love for God and others (Eph 1:15), but many of the church founders had died, and many of the second-generation believers had lost their zeal for God. They were a busy church—the members did much to benefit themselves and the community—but they were acting out of the wrong motives. Work for God must be motivated by love for God, or it will not last.

Rev 2:4-5 Just as when a man and woman fall in love, so also new believers rejoice at their newfound forgiveness. But when we lose sight of the seriousness of sin, we begin to lose the thrill of our forgiveness (see 2 Pet 1:9). In the first steps of your Christian life, you may have had enthusiasm without knowledge. Do you now have knowledge without enthusiasm? Both are necessary if we are to keep love for God intense and untarnished (see Heb 10:32, 35). Do you love God with the same fervor as when you were a new Christian?

Rev 2:5 For Jesus to "remove your lampstand from its place" would mean the church would cease to be an effective church. Just as the seven-branched candlestick in the Temple gave light for the priests to see, the churches were to give light to their surrounding communities. But Jesus warned them that their lights could go out. In fact, Jesus himself would extinguish any light that did not fulfill its purpose. The church needed to repent of its sins.

Rev 2:6 The Nicolaitans were believers who compromised their faith in order to enjoy some of the sinful practices of Ephesian society. Some hold that their name is roughly the Greek equivalent of the Hebrew word for "Balaamites." Balaam was a prophet who had induced the Israelites to carry out their lustful desires (see Rev 2:14; Num 31:16). When we want to take part in an activity that we know is wrong, we may make excuses to justify our behavior, saying that it isn't as bad as it seems or that it won't hurt our faith. Christ has strong words for those who look for excuses to sin.

Rev 2:6 Through John, Jesus commended the church at Ephesus for hating the wicked practices of the Nicolaitans. Note that they didn't hate the people, just their sinful actions. We should accept and love all people but refuse to tolerate any evil. God cannot tolerate sin, and he expects us to stand against it. The world needs Christians who will stand for God's truth and point people toward right living.

Rev 2:7 Two trees had been in the Garden of Eden—the tree of life and the tree of the knowledge of good and evil (see Gen 2:9). Eating from the tree of life brought eternal life with God; eating from the tree of knowledge brought realization of good and evil. When Adam and Eve ate from the tree of knowledge, they disobeyed God's command. So they were excluded from Eden and barred from eating from the tree of life. Eventually, evil will be destroyed and believers will be brought into a restored paradise. In the new earth, everyone will eat from the tree of life and live forever.

Rev 2:8 The city of Smyrna was about 25 miles north of Ephesus. It was nicknamed "Port of Asia" because it had an excellent harbor on the Aegean Sea. The church in

THE NAMES OF JESUS IN REVELATION

Scattered among the vivid images of the book of Revelation is a large collection of names for Jesus. Each one tells something of his character and highlights a particular aspect of his role within God's plan of redemption.

Reference	*Jesus' Name*	*Reference*	*Jesus' Name*
Rev 1:13	The Son of Man	**Rev 12:10**	Christ
Rev 1:17	The First and the Last	**Rev 19:11**	Faithful and True
Rev 1:18	The living one	**Rev 19:13**	The Word of God
Rev 2:18	The Son of God	**Rev 19:16**	King of all kings
Rev 3:14	The faithful and true witness	**Rev 19:16**	Lord of all lords
Rev 5:5	The Lion of the tribe of Judah	**Rev 22:13**	The Alpha and the Omega
Rev 5:5	The heir to David's throne	**Rev 22:13**	The Beginning and the End
Rev 5:6	Lamb	**Rev 22:16**	The bright morning star
Rev 7:17	Shepherd		

9"I know about your suffering and your poverty—
but you are rich! I know the blasphemy of those
opposing you. They say they are Jews, but they are
not, because their synagogue belongs to Satan.
10Don't be afraid of what you are about to suffer.
The devil will throw some of you into prison to
test you. You will suffer for ten days. But if you
remain faithful even when facing death, I will
give you the crown of life.
11"Anyone with ears to hear must listen to
the Spirit and understand what he is saying to
the churches. Whoever is victorious will not be
harmed by the second death.

The Message to the Church in Pergamum

REVELATION 2:12-17

"Write this letter to the angel of the church in Pergamum. This is the message from the one with the sharp two-edged sword:

13"I know that you live in the city where Satan has
his throne, yet you have remained loyal to me.

this city struggled against two hostile forces: a Jewish population strongly opposed to Christianity, and a non-Jewish population that was loyal to Rome and supported emperor worship. Persecution and suffering were inevitable in an environment like this.

Rev 2:9-10 Persecution comes from Satan, not from God. Satan, the devil, will cause believers to be thrown into prison and even killed. But believers need not fear death, because it will only result in their receiving the crown of life. Satan may harm their earthly bodies, but he can do them no spiritual harm. That their "synagogue belongs to Satan" means that these Jews were serving Satan's purposes, not God's, when they gathered to worship. "Ten days" means that although persecution would be intense, it would be relatively short. It would have a definite beginning and end, and God would remain in complete control.

Rev 2:9-11 Pain is part of life, but it is never easy to suffer, no matter what the cause. Jesus commended the church at Smyrna for its faith in suffering. He then encouraged the believers that they need not fear the future if they remained faithful. If you are experiencing difficult times, don't let them turn you away from God. Instead, let them draw you toward greater faithfulness. Trust God and remember your heavenly reward (see also Rev 22:12-14).

Rev 2:10 Smyrna was famous for its athletic games. A crown was the victory wreath, the trophy for the champion at the games. If we have been faithful, we will receive the prize of victory—eternal life (Jas 1:12). The message to the Smyrna church was to remain faithful during suffering because God is in control and his promises are reliable. Jesus never says that by being faithful to him we will avoid troubles, suffering, and persecution. Rather, we must be faithful to him *in* our sufferings. Only then will our faith prove to be genuine. We remain faithful by keeping our eyes on Christ and on what he promises us now and in the future (see Phil 3:13-14; 2 Tim 4:8).

Rev 2:11 Believers and unbelievers alike experience physical death. All people will be resurrected. But believers will be resurrected to eternal life with God, while unbelievers will be resurrected to be punished with a second death—eternal separation from God (see also Rev 20:14; 21:8, 27; 22:15).

Rev 2:12 The city of Pergamum was built on a hill 1,000 feet above the surrounding countryside, creating a natural fortress. It was a sophisticated city, a center of Greek culture and education, with a 200,000-volume library. But it was also the center of four cults, and it rivaled Ephesus in its worship of idols. The city's chief god was Asclepius, whose symbol was a serpent and who was considered the god of healing. People came to Pergamum from all over the world to seek healing from this god.

Rev 2:12 Just as the Romans used their swords for authority and judgment, Jesus' sharp two-edged sword represents God's ultimate authority and judgment. It may also represent God's future separation of believers from unbelievers. Unbelievers cannot experience the eternal rewards of living in God's Kingdom.

Rev 2:13 As the center for four idolatrous cults (Zeus, Dionysius, Asclepius, and Athena), Pergamum was called the city "where Satan has his throne." Surrounded by worship of Satan and the Roman emperor as god, the church at Pergamum refused to renounce its faith, even when Satan's worshipers martyred one of its members. Standing firm against the strong pressures and temptations of society is never easy, but the alternative is deadly (Rev 2:11).

Rev 2:13-15 It was not easy to be a Christian in Pergamum. Believers experienced great pressure to compromise or leave the faith. (For information on the Nicolaitans, see the first note on Rev 2:6, p. 1802.) Nothing is known about Antipas except that he did not compromise. He was faithful, and he died for his faith. Apparently, some in the church were tolerating those who taught or practiced what Christ opposed. *Compromise* can be defined as a blending of the qualities of two different things or a concession of principles. Cooperate with people as much as you can, but avoid any alliance, partnership, or participation that could lead to immoral practices.

Pergamum Library

Pergamum was a city just north of the Caicus River, in the southern part of Mysia (western Turkey), and one of the greatest cultural centers of the Hellenistic era. The early geographer Strabo (63 B.C.–A.D. 24?) called the area around Pergamum the richest land in Mysia. The city had a lovely fountain, theater, pool, medical building, temples, and large library. Pliny the Elder (1st century A.D.) said that King Eumenes of Pergamum wanted to build a rival to the famous library at Alexandria but was hindered by an Egyptian embargo on the export of papyrus. Thereupon he chose parchment as the material for the manuscripts in his library. Pergamum, therefore, became well-known for the production of a particularly good quality of parchment. The photo shows the remains of the ancient library at Pergamum, second in size to the great Alexandrian library.

Pergamum is mentioned only twice in the Bible (Rev 1:11; 2:12), both times referring to one of the seven churches in Asia to which the last book of the New Testament was written. Among those at Pergamum was one called Antipas, who lost his life for the sake of Christ (Rev 2:13). Let us ask God for the grace to do the same if we are ever called to martyrdom.

▸ **REVELATION 2:12-17** ***(cont.)***

You refused to deny me even when Antipas, my
faithful witness, was martyred among you there
in Satan's city.
[14]"But I have a few complaints against you. You
tolerate some among you whose teaching is like
that of Balaam, who showed Balak how to trip up
the people of Israel. He taught them to sin by eating
food offered to idols and by committing sexual
sin. [15]In a similar way, you have some Nicolaitans
among you who follow the same teaching. [16]Repent
of your sin, or I will come to you suddenly and fight
against them with the sword of my mouth.
[17]"Anyone with ears to hear must listen to the
Spirit and understand what he is saying to the
churches. To everyone who is victorious I will give
some of the manna that has been hidden away in
heaven. And I will give to each one a white stone,
and on the stone will be engraved a new name
that no one understands except the one who
receives it.

The Message to the Church in Thyatira

REVELATION 2:18-29

"Write this letter to the angel of the church in Thyatira. This is the message from the Son of God, whose eyes are like flames of fire, whose feet are like polished bronze:

[19]"I know all the things you do. I have seen
your love, your faith, your service, and your
patient endurance. And I can see your constant
improvement in all these things.
[20]"But I have this complaint against you. You
are permitting that woman—that Jezebel who
calls herself a prophet—to lead my servants
astray. She teaches them to commit sexual sin
and to eat food offered to idols. [21]I gave her time

THE LETTERS TO THE SEVEN CHURCHES

This summary of the letters to the seven churches shows us the qualities our churches should seek and those we should avoid.

Church	*Reference*	*Commendation*	*Rebuke*	*Action*
Ephesus	Rev 2:1-7	Hard work, endurance	They do not love as at first	Remember and repent
Smyrna	Rev 2:8-11	Suffered persecution, poverty	None	Don't fear; be faithful
Pergamum	Rev 2:12-17	Remained loyal	Tolerate compromise	Repent
Thyatira	Rev 2:18-29	Love, faith, service, endurance	Tolerate immorality	Repent
Sardis	Rev 3:1-6	Effective	Superficial	Wake up; repent
Philadelphia	Rev 3:7-13	Faithful	None	Hold on
Laodicea	Rev 3:14-22	None	Lukewarm	Be diligent and repent

Rev 2:14 There is room for differences of opinion among Christians in some areas, but there is no room for heresy and moral impurity. Your town might not participate in idol feasts, but it probably has pornography, sexual sin, cheating, gossiping, and lying. Don't tolerate sin by bowing to the pressure to be open-minded.

Rev 2:14-16 Balak was a king who feared the large number of Israelites traveling through his country, so he hired Balaam to pronounce a curse on them. Balaam refused at first to do it, but an offer of money made him willing (Num 22–24). Later Balaam influenced the Israelites to turn to idol worship (Num 31:16; also see 2 Pet 2:15; Jude 1:11). Here Christ rebuked the church for tolerating those who, like Balaam, were leading people away from God.

Rev 2:16 This sword is God's judgment against rebellious nations (Rev 19:15, 21) and all forms of sin. (See also the note on Rev 1:16, p. 1801, and the second note on Rev 2:12, p. 1803.)

Rev 2:17 This "manna that has been hidden away in heaven" suggests the spiritual nourishment that the faithful believers will receive. As the Israelites traveled toward the Promised Land, God provided manna from heaven for their physical nourishment (Exod 16:13-18). Jesus, as the bread of life (John 6:51), provides spiritual nourishment that satisfies our deepest hunger.

Rev 2:17 It is unclear what the white stones are or exactly what the name on each will be. Because they relate to the hidden manna, they may be symbols of the believer's eternal nourishment or eternal life. The stones are significant because each will bear the new name of every person who truly believes in Christ. They are the evidence that a person has been accepted by God and declared worthy to receive eternal life. A person's name represented his or her character. God will give each of us a new name and a new heart.

Rev 2:18 Thyatira was a working person's town, with many trade guilds for cloth making, dyeing, and pottery. Lydia, Paul's first convert in Philippi, was a merchant from Thyatira (Acts 16:14). The city was basically secular, with no focus on any particular religion.

Rev 2:19 The believers in Thyatira were commended for growing in good deeds. We should not only take comfort in gathering for worship or rejoice when people give their lives to Christ in our church. We should also seek to grow in love, faith, and acts of service. Because the times are critical, we must spend our days wisely and faithfully.

Rev 2:20 A woman in the church in Thyatira was teaching that immorality was not a serious matter for believers. Her name may have been Jezebel, or John may have used the name Jezebel to symbolize the kind of evil she was promoting. Jezebel, a pagan queen of Israel, was considered the most evil woman who ever lived (see 1 Kgs 19:1-2; 21:1-15; 2 Kgs 9:7-10, 30-37; see also her Profile on p. 724).

Rev 2:20 Why is sexual immorality serious? Sex outside marriage always hurts someone. It hurts God because it shows that we prefer to satisfy our desires our own way instead of according to God's Word or to satisfy them immediately instead of waiting for his timing. It hurts others because it violates the commitment so necessary to a relationship. It hurts us because it often brings disease to our bodies and adversely affects our personalities. Sexual immorality has tremendous power to destroy families, churches, and communities

to repent, but she does not want to turn away
from her immorality.
[22]"Therefore, I will throw her on a bed of
suffering,* and those who commit adultery with
her will suffer greatly unless they repent and
turn away from her evil deeds. [23]I will strike her
children dead. Then all the churches will know
that I am the one who searches out the thoughts
and intentions of every person. And I will give to
each of you whatever you deserve.
[24]"But I also have a message for the rest of
you in Thyatira who have not followed this false
teaching ('deeper truths,' as they call them—
depths of Satan, actually). I will ask nothing more
of you [25]except that you hold tightly to what you
have until I come. [26]To all who are victorious, who
obey me to the very end,
To them I will give authority over all the
nations.
[27] They will rule the nations with an iron rod
and smash them like clay pots.*
[28]They will have the same authority I received
from my Father, and I will also give them the
morning star!
[29]"Anyone with ears to hear must listen to the
Spirit and understand what he is saying to the
churches.

The Message to the Church in Sardis

REVELATION 3:1-6

"Write this letter to the angel* of the church in Sardis. This is the message from the one who has the sevenfold Spirit* of God and the seven stars:

Rv 2:22 Greek *a bed.* **Rv 2:26-27** Ps 2:8-9 (Greek Version). **Rv 3:1a** Or *the messenger;* also in 3:7, 14. **Rv 3:1b** Greek *the seven spirits.*

Sardis

Sardis was an important city in the Roman province of Asia and was once the capital of the ancient kingdom of Lydia. It lay astride great highways linking it to the coastal regions to the west and to eastern Asia Minor. It was a cultural, religious, and commercial center. Christianity took root here before the end of the 1st century. After the Arab invasion of A.D. 716, the city declined. Extensive excavations in recent years have identified many Roman buildings: an amphitheater, a temple of Artemis, a gymnasium, and an impressive late-Jewish synagogue (pictured here), suggesting it had become an important center for the Jewish Diaspora.

The New Testament letter to the church in Sardis (Rev 1:11; 3:1-6) gives insight into the condition of the church at that time. Sadly, they had a reputation for being alive, but they were really spiritually dead (Rev 3:1). We should learn from them that we can't live on a reputation; we need to have ongoing spiritual reality, connected to our head, Jesus Christ.

because it destroys the integrity on which these relationships are built. God wants to protect us from hurting ourselves and others; thus, we are to have no part in sexual immorality, even if our culture accepts it.

Rev 2:20 In pagan temples, meat was often offered to idols. Then the meat that wasn't burned was sold to shoppers in the temple marketplace. Eating food offered to idols wasn't wrong in itself, but it could violate the conscience of weaker Christian brothers and sisters who would be bothered by it (see 1 Cor 8 and the note on Rom 14:2, p. 1670). Jezebel was obviously more concerned about her own selfish pleasure and freedom than about the needs and concerns of fellow believers.

Rev 2:21 Jezebel was unwilling to repent. *Repent* means "to change one's mind and to turn from sin"—to turn from sin's disastrous consequences and turn to God and eternal life. In his mercy, God has given us time to decide to follow him. Only our stubborn willfulness stands in the way.

Rev 2:23 We cannot hide from Christ; he knows what is in our hearts and minds, and still he loves us. The sins we try to hide from God need to be confessed to him.

Rev 2:24-25 The "deeper truths" of Satan were either false teachings advocated by heretics, or secret insights by so-called believers supposedly guaranteed to promote deeper spiritual life. What was the appeal of such teaching? It may have been appealing to hear that what happens in the body is inconsequential; therefore, it is not sinful to fulfill sexual desires outside of marriage. Another appeal may have been the sense of pride that such knowledge stimulated in those seeking it. We should hold tightly to the basics of our Christian faith and view with extreme caution any new teaching that turns us away from the Bible, the fellowship of our church, or our basic confession of faith.

Rev 2:26-27 Christ says that those who are victorious (those who remain faithful until the end and continue to please God) will rule over Christ's enemies and reign with him as he judges evil (see also Ps 2:8-9; Isa 30:14; Jer 19:11; 1 Cor 6:2-3; Rev 12:5; 19:15; 20:3-4).

Rev 2:28 Christ is also called the "morning star" in Revelation 22:16. A morning star appears just before dawn, when the night is coldest and darkest. When the world is at its bleakest point, Christ will burst onto the scene, exposing evil with his light of truth and bringing his promised reward.

Rev 3:1 The wealthy city of Sardis was actually in two locations. The older section of the city was on a mountain, and when its population outgrew the spot, a newer section was built in the valley below.

Rev 3:1 The "sevenfold Spirit" is another name for the Holy Spirit (see the second note on Rev 1:4, p. 1798). The seven stars are the messengers, or leaders, of the churches (see Rev 1:16, 20; see also the note on Rev 1:20, p. 1801, and the second note on Rev 2:1, p. 1801).

Rev 3:1 The problem in the Sardis church was not heresy but spiritual death. In spite of its reputation for being active, Sardis was infested with sin. Its deeds were evil and its clothes soiled. The Spirit has no words of

▸ REVELATION 3:1-6 *(cont.)*

"I know all the things you do, and that you have a reputation for being alive—but you are dead.
[2]Wake up! Strengthen what little remains, for even what is left is almost dead. I find that your actions do not meet the requirements of my God.
[3]Go back to what you heard and believed at first; hold to it firmly. Repent and turn to me again. If you don't wake up, I will come to you suddenly, as unexpected as a thief.

[4]"Yet there are some in the church in Sardis who have not soiled their clothes with evil. They will walk with me in white, for they are worthy.
[5]All who are victorious will be clothed in white. I will never erase their names from the Book of Life, but I will announce before my Father and his angels that they are mine.

[6]"Anyone with ears to hear must listen to the Spirit and understand what he is saying to the churches.

Rv 3:7 Isa 22:22.

The Message to the Church in Philadelphia

REVELATION 3:7-13

"Write this letter to the angel of the church in Philadelphia.

This is the message from the one who is holy
and true,
the one who has the key of David.
What he opens, no one can close;
and what he closes, no one can open:*

[8]"I know all the things you do, and I have opened a door for you that no one can close. You have little strength, yet you obeyed my word and did not deny me.
[9]Look, I will force those who belong to Satan's synagogue—those liars who say they are Jews but are not—to come and bow down at your feet. They will acknowledge that you are the ones I love.

commendation for this church that looked so good on the outside but was so corrupt on the inside.

Even though Christ called Sardis a dead church, he also affirmed the handful of people who were faithful believers. Christ loves to defeat death. If you find yourself in a dead church, make sure you preserve your own faithfulness. Ask God to intervene. Ask God to help you find other believers, and pray together for an awakening of your church.

Rev 3:3 The church at Sardis was urged to go back to what they first heard and believed, to get back to the basics of the faith. It is important to grow in our knowledge of the Lord, to deepen our understanding through careful study. But no matter how much we learn, we must never abandon the basic truths. No new truth from God will ever contradict these fundamental biblical teachings.

The church was also told to "wake up." Their wealth and comfort had lulled them to sleep. Their self-satisfaction caused them to die spiritually. Not only had they wandered from the apostles' teaching, but they were no longer growing in faith or evangelism. They lacked compassionate service to others and had no unity or love. Are you watchful and alert? If God has given you a place of responsibility to teach, lead, or serve, use that position to encourage those around you to be spiritually awake and morally prepared.

Rev 3:5 To be "clothed in white" means to be set apart for God and made pure. Christ promises future honor and eternal life to those who stand firm in their faith. The names of all believers are registered in the Book of Life. This book symbolizes God's knowledge of who belongs to him. All such people are guaranteed a listing in the Book of Life and are introduced to the hosts of heaven as belonging to Christ (see Luke 12:8-9).

Laodicea Water Pipe

Laodicea stood where the Lycus Valley joined the Maeander River. The water supply to the city (see Rev 3:15-16) came principally via an aqueduct from springs six miles to the north in the direction of Hierapolis. Fragments of the aqueduct can be seen today (see photograph), the conduit badly narrowed by thick deposits of calcium carbonate. Laodicea also had a medical school. It was probably the medical school of Laodicea that developed the Phrygian eye powder, famous in the ancient world (see Rev 3:18). It is a fair guess that this was dried mud of the Hierapolis thermal springs, which could be mixed with water to form a kaolin poultice, an effective remedy for inflammation. The spiritual lesson here is that we need the eyes of our hearts spiritually enlightened so that we can see all the spiritual blessings we have in Christ Jesus.

Rev 3:7 Philadelphia was founded by the citizens of Pergamum. The community was built in a frontier area as a gateway to the central plateau of Asia Minor. Philadelphia's residents kept barbarians out of the region and brought in Greek culture and language. The city was destroyed by an earthquake in A.D. 17, and aftershocks kept the people so worried that most of them lived outside the city limits.

Rev 3:7 The "key of David" represents Christ's authority to open the door into his future Kingdom. After the door is opened, no one can close it—salvation is assured. Once it is closed, no one can open it—judgment is certain.

Rev 3:10 Some believe that "I will protect you from the great time of testing" means there will be a future time of great tribulation

10 “Because you have obeyed my command to
persevere, I will protect you from the great time
of testing that will come upon the whole world to
test those who belong to this world. 11 I am coming
soon.* Hold on to what you have, so that no one
will take away your crown. 12 All who are victorious
will become pillars in the Temple of my God, and
they will never have to leave it. And I will write
on them the name of my God, and they will be
citizens in the city of my God—the new Jerusalem
that comes down from heaven from my God. And
I will also write on them my new name.
13 “Anyone with ears to hear must listen to the
Spirit and understand what he is saying to the
churches.

The Message to the Church in Laodicea

REVELATION 3:14-22

“Write this letter to the angel of the church in Laodicea. This is the message from the one who is the
Amen—the faithful and true witness, the beginning*
of God's new creation:
15 “I know all the things you do, that you are
neither hot nor cold. I wish that you were one
or the other! 16 But since you are like lukewarm
water, neither hot nor cold, I will spit you out of
my mouth! 17 You say, ‘I am rich. I have everything
I want. I don't need a thing!’ And you don't
realize that you are wretched and miserable and
poor and blind and naked. 18 So I advise you to
buy gold from me—gold that has been purified
by fire. Then you will be rich. Also buy white
garments from me so you will not be shamed by
your nakedness, and ointment for your eyes so
you will be able to see. 19 I correct and discipline
everyone I love. So be diligent and turn from
your indifference.
20 “Look! I stand at the door and knock.
If you hear my voice and open the door,

Rv 3:11 Or *suddenly*, or *quickly*. **Rv 3:14** Or *the ruler*, or *the source*.

from which true believers will be spared. Others interpret this to mean that the church will go through the time of tribulation and that God will keep them strong in the midst of it. Still others believe this refers to times of great distress in general, the church's suffering through the ages. We cannot interpret from this verse when or for how long Christians will experience the “great time of testing.” Today, millions of Christians are suffering and dying at the hands of godless tyrants throughout the world. To them, the time of testing has already begun. Whenever Christians suffer, Christ promises protection of their eternal souls (see Luke 21:17-19).

Rev 3:11 Christians have differing gifts, abilities, experience, and maturity. God doesn't expect us all to be and act the same, but he does expect us to “hold on” to what we have, to persevere in using our resources for him. The Philadelphians are commended for their effort to obey (Rev 3:8) and encouraged to hold tightly to whatever strength they have. You may be a new believer and feel that your faith and spiritual strength are little. Use what you have to live for Christ, and God will commend you.

Rev 3:12 The new Jerusalem is the future dwelling of the people of God (Rev 21:2). We will have a new citizenship in God's future Kingdom. Everything will be new, pure, and secure.

Rev 3:15 Laodicea was the wealthiest of the seven cities, known for its banking industry, manufacture of wool, and a medical school that produced eye ointment. But the city had always had a problem with its water supply. At one time an aqueduct was built to bring water to the city from hot springs. But by the time the water reached the city, it was neither hot nor refreshingly cool—only lukewarm. The church had become as bland as the tepid water that came into the city.

Rev 3:16 Lukewarm water makes a disgusting drink. The church in Laodicea had become lukewarm and thus distasteful and repugnant. The believers didn't take a stand for anything; indifference had led to idleness. By neglecting to do anything for Christ, the church had become hardened and self-satisfied, and it was destroying itself. There is nothing more disgusting than a halfhearted, nominal Christian who is self-sufficient. Don't settle for following God halfway. Let Christ fire up your faith and get you into the action.

Rev 3:17 Some believers assume that numerous material possessions are a sign of God's spiritual blessing. Laodicea was a wealthy city, and the church was also wealthy. But what the Laodiceans could see and buy had become more valuable to them than what is unseen and eternal. Wealth, luxury, and ease can make people feel confident, satisfied, and complacent. But no matter how much you possess or how much money you make, you have nothing if you don't have a vital relationship with Christ. How does your current level of wealth affect your spiritual desire? Instead of centering your life primarily on comfort and luxury, find your true riches in Christ.

Rev 3:18 Laodicea was known for its great wealth; Christ told the Laodiceans to buy their gold from him (real spiritual treasures). The city was proud of its cloth and dyeing industries; Christ told them to buy white garments from him (his righteousness). Laodicea prided itself on its precious eye ointment that healed many eye problems; Christ told them to buy ointment for their eyes so they could see the truth (John 9:39). Christ was showing the Laodiceans that true value was not in material possessions but in a right relationship with God. Their possessions and achievements were worthless compared with the everlasting future of Christ's Kingdom.

Rev 3:19 God would discipline this lukewarm church unless it turned from its indifference toward him. God's purpose in discipline is not to punish but to bring people back to him. Are you lukewarm in your devotion to God? God may discipline you to help you out of your uncaring attitude, but he uses only loving discipline. You can avoid God's discipline by drawing near to him again through confession, service, worship, and studying his Word. Just as the spark of love can be rekindled in marriage, so the Holy Spirit can reignite our zeal for God when we allow him to work in our hearts.

Rev 3:20 The Laodicean church was complacent and rich. They felt self-satisfied, but they didn't have Christ's presence among them. Christ knocked at the door of their hearts, but they were so busy enjoying worldly pleasures that they didn't notice that he was trying to enter. The pleasures of this world—money, security, material possessions—can be dangerous, because their temporary satisfaction makes us indifferent to God's offer of lasting satisfaction. If you find yourself feeling indifferent to church, to God, or to the Bible, you have begun to shut God out of your life. Leave the door of your heart constantly open to God, and you won't need to worry about hearing his knock. Letting him in is your only hope for lasting fulfillment.

Rev 3:20 Jesus knocks at the door of our hearts because he wants to save us and have fellowship with us. He is patient and persistent in trying to get through to us—not breaking and entering, but knocking. He allows us to decide whether or not to open our lives to him. Do you intentionally keep his life-changing presence and power on the other side of the door?

▸ **REVELATION 3:14-22** ***(cont.)***

I will come in, and we will share a meal
together as friends. [21]Those who are victorious
will sit with me on my throne, just as I was
victorious and sat with my Father on his throne.
[22]"Anyone with ears to hear must listen to the
Spirit and understand what he is saying to the
churches."

2. MESSAGE FOR THE CHURCH

Moving from the conditions within the churches in Asia to the future of the universal church, John sees the course of coming events in a way similar to Daniel and Ezekiel. Many of these passages contain clear spiritual teachings, but others seem beyond our ability to understand. The clear teaching of this book is that God will defeat all evil in the end. We must live in obedience to Jesus Christ, the coming Conqueror and Judge.

Worshiping God in Heaven

REVELATION 4:1-11

Then as I looked, I saw a door standing open in heaven,
and the same voice I had heard before spoke to me like
a trumpet blast. The voice said, "Come up here, and
I will show you what must happen after this." [2]And
instantly I was in the Spirit,* and I saw a throne in
heaven and someone sitting on it. [3]The one sitting on
the throne was as brilliant as gemstones—like jasper
and carnelian. And the glow of an emerald circled
his throne like a rainbow. [4]Twenty-four thrones surrounded him, and twenty-four elders sat on them.
They were all clothed in white and had gold crowns on
their heads. [5]From the throne came flashes of lightning and the rumble of thunder. And in front of the
throne were seven torches with burning flames. This
is the sevenfold Spirit* of God. [6]In front of the throne
was a shiny sea of glass, sparkling like crystal.
In the center and around the throne were four living
beings, each covered with eyes, front and back. [7]The
first of these living beings was like a lion; the second
was like an ox; the third had a human face; and the
fourth was like an eagle in flight. [8]Each of these living
beings had six wings, and their wings were covered all
over with eyes, inside and out. Day after day and night
after night they keep on saying,

"Holy, holy, holy is the Lord God, the Almighty—
the one who always was, who is, and who is still to come."

[9]Whenever the living beings give glory and honor and
thanks to the one sitting on the throne (the one who
lives forever and ever), [10]the twenty-four elders fall
down and worship the one sitting on the throne (the
one who lives forever and ever). And they lay their
crowns before the throne and say,

Rv 4:2 Or *in spirit.* **Rv 4:5** Greek *They are the seven spirits.*

Rev 3:22 At the end of each letter to these churches, the believers were urged to listen and understand what was written to them. Although a different message was addressed to each church, all the messages contain warnings and principles for everyone. Which letter speaks most directly to your church? Which has the greatest bearing on your own spiritual condition at this time? How will you respond?

Rev 4:1 Revelation 4–5 records glimpses into Christ's glory. Here we see into the throne room of heaven. God is on the throne and orchestrating all the events that John will record. The world is not spinning out of control; the God of creation will carry out his plans as Christ initiates the final battle with the forces of evil. John shows us heaven before showing us earth so that we will not be frightened by future events.

Rev 4:1 The voice John had first heard that sounded like a trumpet blast was the voice of Christ (see Rev 1:10-11).

Rev 4:2 Four times in the book of Revelation John says he was "in the Spirit" (Rev 1:10; 4:2; 17:3; 21:10). This expression means that the Holy Spirit was giving him a vision—showing him situations and events he could not have seen with mere human eyesight. All true prophecy comes from God through the Holy Spirit (2 Pet 1:20-21).

Rev 4:4 Who are these 24 elders? Because there were 12 tribes of Israel in the Old Testament and 12 apostles in the New Testament, the 24 elders in this vision probably represent all the redeemed of God for all time (both before and after Christ's death and resurrection). They symbolize all those—both Jews and Gentiles—who are now part of God's family. The 24 elders show us that all the redeemed of the Lord are worshiping him.

Rev 4:5 In Revelation, lightning and thunder are connected with significant events in heaven. They remind us of the lightning and thunder at Mount Sinai when God gave the people his laws (Exod 19:16). The Old Testament often uses such imagery to reflect God's power and majesty (Ps 77:18).

Rev 4:5 The "sevenfold Spirit of God" is another name for the Holy Spirit. (See also Zech 4:2-6, where seven lamps—like the seven torches here—are equated with the one Spirit.)

Rev 4:6 Glass was very rare in New Testament times, and crystal-clear glass was virtually impossible to find (see 1 Cor 13:12). The "sea of glass" highlights both the magnificence and holiness of God.

Rev 4:6-7 Just as the Holy Spirit is seen symbolically in the seven lighted lamps, so the "four living beings" represent the attributes (the qualities and character) of God. These creatures are not real animals. Like the cherubim (the highest order of the angels), they guard God's throne, lead others in worship, and proclaim God's holiness. God's attributes symbolized in the animal-like appearance of these four creatures are majesty and power (the lion), faithfulness (the ox), intelligence (the human), and sovereignty (the eagle). The Old Testament prophet Ezekiel saw four similar creatures in one of his visions (Ezek 1:5-10).

Rev 4:9 John describes these scenes in such detail because Christians in the first century came from many backgrounds. Not all of them understood Jewish history or knew the glory of the Temple. Revelation instructs us in worship. It shows us where, why, and how to praise God. Worship takes our minds off our problems and focuses them on God. Worship leads us from individual meditation to corporate praise. Worship causes us to consider and appreciate God's character. Worship lifts our perspective from the earthly to the heavenly.

11 "You are worthy, O Lord our God,
to receive glory and honor and power.
For you created all things,
and they exist because you created what you pleased."

The Lamb Opens the Scroll

REVELATION 5:1-14

Then I saw a scroll* in the right hand of the one who
was sitting on the throne. There was writing on the
inside and the outside of the scroll, and it was sealed
with seven seals. 2And I saw a strong angel, who
shouted with a loud voice: "Who is worthy to break
the seals on this scroll and open it?" 3But no one in
heaven or on earth or under the earth was able to open
the scroll and read it.
4Then I began to weep bitterly because no one was
found worthy to open the scroll and read it. 5But one
of the twenty-four elders said to me, "Stop weeping!
Look, the Lion of the tribe of Judah, the heir to David's
throne,* has won the victory. He is worthy to open the
scroll and its seven seals."
6Then I saw a Lamb that looked as if it had been
slaughtered, but it was now standing between the
throne and the four living beings and among the
twenty-four elders. He had seven horns and seven
eyes, which represent the sevenfold Spirit* of God that
is sent out into every part of the earth. 7He stepped

Rv 5:1 Or *book;* also in 5:2, 3, 4, 5, 7, 8, 9. **Rv 5:5** Greek *the root of David.* See Isa 11:10. **Rv 5:6** Greek *which are the seven spirits.*

Rev 4:11 The point of Revelation 4 is summed up in this verse: All creatures in heaven and earth will praise and honor God because he is the creator and sustainer of everything.

Rev 5:1ff Revelation 5 continues the glimpse into heaven begun in Revelation 4.

Rev 5:1 In John's day, books were written on scrolls—pieces of papyrus or vellum up to 30 feet long, rolled up and sealed with clay or wax. The scroll that John sees contains the full account of what God has in store for the world. The seven seals indicate the importance of its contents. The seals are located throughout the scroll so that as each one is broken, more of the scroll can be read to reveal another phase of God's plan for the end of the world. Only Christ is worthy to break the seals and open the scroll (Rev 5:3-5).

Rev 5:5 The Lion, Jesus, proved himself worthy to break the seals and open the scroll by living a perfect life of obedience to God, dying on the cross for the sins of the world, and rising from the dead to show his power and authority over evil and death. Only Christ conquered sin, death, hell, and Satan himself; so only he can be trusted with the world's future. "Heir to David's throne" refers to Jesus being from David's family line, thus fulfilling the promise of the Messiah in the Old Testament.

Rev 5:5-6 Jesus Christ is pictured as both a Lion (symbolizing his authority and power) and a Lamb (symbolizing his submission to God's will). One of the elders calls John to look at the Lion, but when John looks he sees a Lamb. Christ the Lamb was the perfect sacrifice for the sins of all; therefore, only he can save us from the terrible events revealed by the scroll. Christ the Lamb won the greatest battle of all. He defeated all the forces of evil by dying on the cross. The role of Christ the Lion will be to lead the battle where Satan is finally defeated (Rev 19:19-21). Christ the Lion is victorious because of what Christ the Lamb has already done. We will participate in his victory, not because of our effort or goodness, but because he has promised eternal life to all who believe in him.

Rev 5:6 John says the Lamb "had been slaughtered"; the wounds inflicted on Jesus' body during his trial and crucifixion could still be seen (see John 20:24-31). Jesus was called the Lamb of God by John the Baptist (John 1:29). In the Old Testament, lambs were sacrificed to atone for sins; the Lamb of God died as the final sacrifice for all sins (see Isa 53:7; Heb 10:1-12, 18).

Rev 5:6 The horns symbolize strength and power (see 1 Kgs 22:11; Zech 1:18). Although Christ is a sacrificial lamb, he is in no way weak. He was killed, but now he lives in God's strength and power. In Zechariah 4:2-10, the eyes are equated with the seven lamps and the one Spirit.

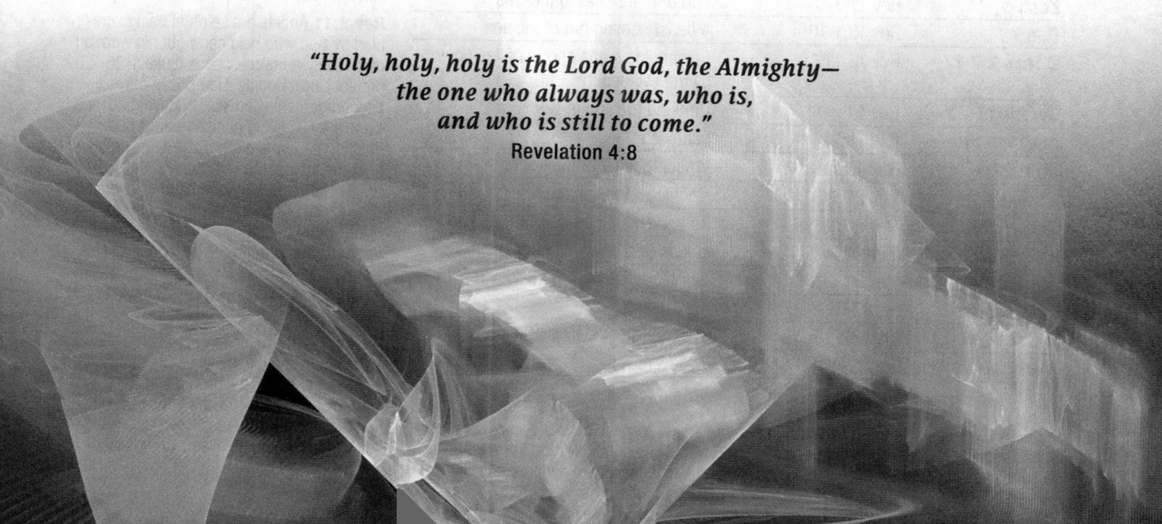

"Holy, holy, holy is the Lord God, the Almighty— the one who always was, who is, and who is still to come."
Revelation 4:8

▶ **REVELATION 5:1-14** ***(cont.)***

forward and took the scroll from the right hand of
the one sitting on the throne. [8]And when he took the
scroll, the four living beings and the twenty-four elders
fell down before the Lamb. Each one had a harp, and
they held gold bowls filled with incense, which are the
prayers of God's people. [9]And they sang a new song
with these words:

"You are worthy to take the scroll
and break its seals and open it.
For you were slaughtered, and your blood has
ransomed people for God
from every tribe and language and people
and nation.
[10] And you have caused them to become
a Kingdom of priests for our God.
And they will reign* on the earth."

[11]Then I looked again, and I heard the voices of
thousands and millions of angels around the throne
and of the living beings and the elders. [12]And they
sang in a mighty chorus:

"Worthy is the Lamb who was slaughtered—
to receive power and riches
and wisdom and strength
and honor and glory and blessing."

[13]And then I heard every creature in heaven and on
earth and under the earth and in the sea. They sang:

Rv 5:10 Some manuscripts read *they are reigning.*

EVENTS IN REVELATION DESCRIBED ELSEWHERE IN THE BIBLE

Other Reference	*Reference*	*Event*
Ezek 1:22-28	Rev 4:2-3; 10:1-3	Glowing rainbow around God's throne
Isa 53:7	Rev 5:6-8	Christ is pictured as a Lamb
Ps 96	Rev 5:9-14	New song
Zech 1:7-11; 6:1-8	Rev 6:1-8	Horses and riders
Isa 2:19-22	Rev 6:12; 8:5; 11:13	Earthquake
Joel 2:28-32; Acts 2:14-21	Rev 6:12	Moon turns red as blood
Mark 13:21-25	Rev 6:13	Stars falling from the sky
Isa 34:1-4	Rev 6:14	Sky rolled up like a scroll
Zeph 1:14-18; 1 Thes 5:1-3	Rev 6:15-17	God's inescapable wrath
Jer 49:35-39	Rev 7:1	Four winds of judgment
Luke 8:26-33	Rev 9:1-2; 17:3-8	Bottomless pit
Joel 1:2–2:11	Rev 9:3-11	Plague of locusts
Luke 21:20-24	Rev 11:1-2	Trampling of the holy city of Jerusalem
Zech 4	Rev 11:3-6	Two olive trees as witnesses
Dan 7	Rev 13:1-10	A beast coming out of the sea
2 Thes 2:7-12	Rev 13:11-15	Astounding signs and miracles done by the evil beast
Jer 25:15-29	Rev 14:9-11	Drinking the cup of God's wrath
Isa 21:1-10	Rev 18:2-3	"Babylon" falls
Matt 22:1-14	Rev 19:5-8	Wedding feast of the Lamb
Ezek 38–39	Rev 20:7-9	Conflict with Gog and Magog
John 5:19-30	Rev 20:11-15	Judging of all people
Ezek 37:21-28	Rev 21:3	God lives among his people
Isa 25:1-8	Rev 21:4	Our tears will be wiped away forever
Gen 2:8-14	Rev 22:1-2	Tree of life
1 Cor 13:11-12	Rev 22:3-5	We will see God face to face
Dan 7:18-28	Rev 22:5	Believers will reign with God forever

Rev 5:9-10 People from every nation are praising God before his throne. God's message of salvation and eternal life is not limited to a specific culture, race, or country. Anyone who comes to God in repentance and faith is accepted by him and will be part of his Kingdom. Don't allow prejudice or bias to keep you from sharing Christ with others. Christ welcomes all people into his Kingdom.

Rev 5:9-10 The song of God's people praises Christ's work. He (1) was killed, (2) ransomed them with his blood, (3) gathered them into a Kingdom, (4) made them priests, and (5) appointed them to reign on the earth. Jesus has already died and paid the penalty for sin. He is now gathering us into his Kingdom and making us priests. In the future we will reign with him. Worship God and praise him for what he has done, what he is doing, and what he will do for all who trust in him. When we realize the glorious future that awaits us, we will find the strength to face our present difficulties.

Rev 5:10 The believers' song praises Christ for bringing his redeemed into the Kingdom and making them rulers and priests. While now we are sometimes despised and mocked for our faith (John 15:17-27), in the future we will reign over all the earth (Luke 22:29-30). Christ's death made all believers priests of God—the channels of blessing between God and people (1 Pet 2:5-9).

Rev 5:11 Angels are spiritual beings created by God who help carry out his work on earth. They bring messages (Luke 1:26-28), protect God's people (Dan 6:22), offer encouragement (Gen 16:7ff), give guidance (Exod 14:19), bring punishment (2 Sam 24:16), patrol the earth (Ezek 1:9-14), and fight the forces of evil (2 Kgs 6:16-18; Rev 20:1). There are both good and evil angels (Rev 12:7), but because evil angels are allied with Satan, they have considerably less power and authority than good angels. Eventually, the main role of the good angels will be to offer continuous praise to God (see also Rev 19:1-3).

Rev 5:14 The scene in Revelation 5 shows us that only the Lamb, Jesus Christ, is worthy to open the scroll (the events of history). Jesus, not Satan, holds the future. Jesus Christ is in control, and he alone is worthy to set into motion the events of the last days of history.

"Blessing and honor and glory and power
belong to the one sitting on the throne
and to the Lamb forever and ever."
[14]And the four living beings said, "Amen!" And the
twenty-four elders fell down and worshiped the Lamb.

The Lamb Breaks the First Six Seals

REVELATION 6:1-17

As I watched, the Lamb broke the first of the seven
seals on the scroll.* Then I heard one of the four living
beings say with a voice like thunder, "Come!" [2]I looked
up and saw a white horse standing there. Its rider
carried a bow, and a crown was placed on his head.
He rode out to win many battles and gain the victory.
[3]When the Lamb broke the second seal, I heard the
second living being say, "Come!" [4]Then another horse
appeared, a red one. Its rider was given a mighty sword
and the authority to take peace from the earth. And
there was war and slaughter everywhere.
[5]When the Lamb broke the third seal, I heard the
third living being say, "Come!" I looked up and saw a
black horse, and its rider was holding a pair of scales
in his hand. [6]And I heard a voice from among the four
living beings say, "A loaf of wheat bread or three loaves
of barley will cost a day's pay.* And don't waste* the
olive oil and wine."
[7]When the Lamb broke the fourth seal, I heard the
fourth living being say, "Come!" [8]I looked up and saw a
horse whose color was pale green. Its rider was named
Death, and his companion was the Grave.* These two
were given authority over one-fourth of the earth, to
kill with the sword and famine and disease* and wild
animals.
[9]When the Lamb broke the fifth seal, I saw under

Rv 6:1 Or *book.* **Rv 6:6a** Greek *A choinix* [1 quart or 1 liter] *of wheat for a denarius, and 3 choinix of barley for a denarius.* A denarius was equivalent to a laborer's full day's wage. **Rv 6:6b** Or *harm.* **Rv 6:8a** Greek *was Hades.* **Rv 6:8b** Greek *death.*

Rev 6:1ff This is the first of three seven-part judgments. The trumpets (Rev 8–9) and the bowls (Rev 16) are the other two. As each seal is opened, Christ the Lamb sets in motion events that will bring about the end of human history. This scroll is not completely opened until the seventh seal is broken (Rev 8:1). The contents of the scroll reveal humanity's depravity and portray God's authority over the events of human history.

Rev 6:2ff Four horses appear as the first four seals are opened. The horses represent God's judgment of people's sin and rebellion. God is directing human history—even using his enemies to accomplish his purposes. The four horses are a foretaste of the final judgments yet to come. Some view this chapter as a parallel to the Olivet Discourse (see Matt 24). The imagery of four horses is also found in Zechariah 6:1-8.

Rev 6:2-8 Each of the four horses is a different color. Some assume that the white horse represents victory and that its rider must be Christ (because Christ later rides to victory on a white horse; Rev 19:11). But because the other three horses relate to judgment and destruction, this rider on a white horse would most likely not be Christ. The four are part of the unfolding judgment of God, and it would be premature for Christ to ride forth as conqueror. The other horses represent different kinds of judgment: red for warfare and bloodshed; black for famine; pale green for death. The high prices of wheat and barley illustrate famine conditions. But the worst is yet to come.

Rev 6:4 Complete peace will only come when Christ returns. The picture in Revelation of the coming persecutions and natural disasters is gloomy, but ultimately it is cause for great joy. When believers see these events happening, they will know that their Messiah's return is coming soon, and they can look forward to his reign of justice and peace. Rather than being terrified by what is happening in our world, we should confidently await Christ's return to bring justice and restoration to his people.

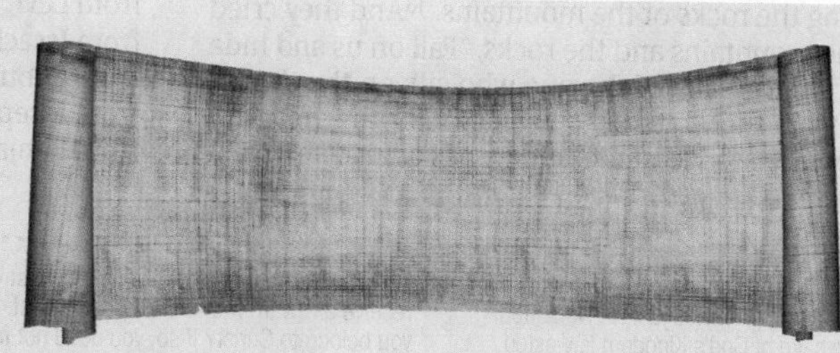

Papyrus Scroll

Many scholars think the book in Christ's hand is a scroll (Rev 5:1), whether made of papyrus (as in the photo) or made of vellum (animal hide). Some scholars think the book is a codex (a book made of separate leaves, stitched at the spine). One of the main reasons that some scholars think it is a codex is because one seal can be loosened at a time, revealing a new page or two each time one of the seven seals is broken; whereas, with a scroll, all the seals would have to be broken before the scroll could be opened. Either way, the book in Christ's hand will be opened and the revelation will be unveiled for all of us to read, understand, and apply.

Rev 6:8 It is not clear whether "the Grave" was on a separate horse or merely rode along with Death, but the riders described in Revelation 6:2-8 are commonly referred to as the four horsemen of the Apocalypse. The four riders are given power over one-fourth of the earth, indicating that God is still limiting his judgment—it is not yet complete. With these judgments there is still time for unbelievers to turn away from their sin and turn to Christ. In this case, the limited punishment not only demonstrates God's wrath on sin but also his merciful love in giving people yet another opportunity to turn to him before he brings final judgment. We must not presume upon God's patience. Our repentance must be visible and authentic. In what ways does your life reflect new and different behavior?

Rev 6:9 The altar represents the altar of sacrifice in the Temple, where animals were sacrificed to atone for sins. Instead of the animals' blood at the base of the altar, John saw the souls of martyrs who had died for preaching the Good News. These martyrs were told that still more would lose their lives for their belief in Christ (Rev 6:11). In the face of warfare, famine, persecution, and death, Christians will be called on to stand firmly for what they believe. Only those who endure to the end will be rewarded by God (Mark 13:13).

Rev 6:9-11 The martyrs are eager for God to bring justice to the earth, but they are told to wait. God is not waiting until a certain number is reached; he is promising that those who suffer and die for their faith will not be forgotten. Rather, they will be singled out by God for special honor. We may wish for justice immediately, as these martyrs did, but we must be

▶ REVELATION 6:1-17 ***(cont.)***

the altar the souls of all who had been martyred for the
word of God and for being faithful in their testimony.
10They shouted to the Lord and said, "O Sovereign
Lord, holy and true, how long before you judge the
people who belong to this world and avenge our blood
for what they have done to us?" 11Then a white robe
was given to each of them. And they were told to rest
a little longer until the full number of their brothers
and sisters*—their fellow servants of Jesus who were
to be martyred—had joined them.
12I watched as the Lamb broke the sixth seal, and
there was a great earthquake. The sun became as dark
as black cloth, and the moon became as red as blood.
13Then the stars of the sky fell to the earth like green
figs falling from a tree shaken by a strong wind. 14The
sky was rolled up like a scroll, and all of the mountains
and islands were moved from their places.
15Then everyone—the kings of the earth, the rulers,
the generals, the wealthy, the powerful, and every slave
and free person—all hid themselves in the caves and
among the rocks of the mountains. 16And they cried
to the mountains and the rocks, "Fall on us and hide
us from the face of the one who sits on the throne
and from the wrath of the Lamb. 17For the great day
of their wrath has come, and who is able to survive?"

Rv 6:11 Greek *their brothers.*

God's People Will Be Preserved

REVELATION 7:1-8

Then I saw four angels standing at the four corners
of the earth, holding back the four winds so they did
not blow on the earth or the sea, or even on any tree.
2And I saw another angel coming up from the east,
carrying the seal of the living God. And he shouted to
those four angels, who had been given power to harm
land and sea, 3"Wait! Don't harm the land or the sea
or the trees until we have placed the seal of God on
the foreheads of his servants."
4And I heard how many were marked with the seal of
God—144,000 were sealed from all the tribes of Israel:

5 from Judah 12,000
from Reuben 12,000
from Gad 12,000
6 from Asher 12,000
from Naphtali 12,000
from Manasseh 12,000
7 from Simeon 12,000
from Levi 12,000
from Issachar 12,000
8 from Zebulun 12,000
from Joseph 12,000
from Benjamin 12,000

---

patient. God works according to his own timetable, and he promises justice. No suffering for the sake of God's Kingdom is wasted.

Rev 6:10 The martyrs call out to God, "How long before you judge the people who belong to this world and avenge our blood for what they have done to us?" As we see the world's wickedness, we, too, may cry out to God, "How long?" In the following chapters, the judgment comes at last. We may be distressed and impatient, but God has his plan and his timing, and we must learn to trust him to know what is best. Judgment is coming—be sure of that. Thank God for the time he has given you to turn from sin. Use the available time working to help others turn to him.

Rev 6:12 The sixth seal changes the scene back to the physical world. The first five judgments were directed toward specific areas, but this judgment is universal. Everyone will be afraid when the earth itself trembles.

Rev 6:15-17 At the sight of God sitting on the throne, all human beings, great and small, will be terrified, calling for the mountains to fall on them so that they will not have to face the judgment of the Lamb. This vivid picture was not intended to frighten believers. For them, the Lamb is a gentle Savior. But those kings, rulers, generals, and other powerful people who previously showed no fear of God and arrogantly flaunted their unbelief will find that they were wrong, and in that day they will have to face God's wrath. No one who has rejected God can survive the day of his wrath, but those who belong to Christ will receive a reward rather than punishment. Do you belong to Christ? If so, you need not fear these final days.

Rev 7:1ff The sixth seal has been opened, and the people of the earth have tried to hide from God, saying, "Who is able to survive?" (Rev 6:12-17). Just when all hope seems lost, four angels hold back the four winds of judgment until God's people are sealed as his own. Only then will God open the seventh seal (Rev 8:1).

Rev 7:2 A seal on a scroll or document identified and protected its contents. God places his own seal on his followers, identifying them as his own and guaranteeing his protection over their souls. This shows how valuable we are to him. Our physical bodies may be beaten, maimed, or even destroyed, but nothing can harm our souls when we have been sealed by God. (See Eph 1:13 for the seal of the Holy Spirit.)

Rev 7:3 God's seal is placed on the foreheads of his servants. This seal is the exact opposite of the mark of the beast explained in Revelation 13:16. These two marks place people in two distinct categories—those owned by God and those owned by Satan.

Rev 7:4-8 The number 144,000 is 12 x 12 x 1,000, symbolizing completeness—all God's followers will be brought safely to him; not one will be overlooked or forgotten. God seals these believers either by withdrawing them from the earth (this is called the Rapture) or by giving them special strength and courage to make it through this time of great persecution. Even though many believers have to undergo persecution, the seal does not necessarily guarantee protection from physical harm—many will die (see Rev 6:11)—but God will protect them from spiritual harm. No matter what happens, they will be brought to their reward of eternal life. Their destiny is secure. These believers will not fall away from God even though they may undergo intense persecution.

This is not saying that 144,000 individuals must be sealed before the persecution comes, but that when persecution begins, the faithful will have already been sealed (marked by God), and they will remain true to him until the end.

Rev 7:4-8 This is a different list from the usual listing of the 12 tribes in the Old Testament, because it is a symbolic list of God's true followers. (1) Judah is mentioned first because Judah is both the tribe of David and of Jesus the Messiah (Gen 49:8-12; Matt 1:1). (2) Levi had no tribal allotment because of the Levites' work for God in the Temple (Deut 18:1), but here the tribe is given a place as a reward for faithfulness. (3) Dan is not mentioned because it was known for rebellion and idolatry, traits unacceptable for God's followers (Gen 49:17). (4) The two tribes representing Joseph (usually called Ephraim and Manasseh, after Joseph's sons) are here called Joseph and Manasseh because of Ephraim's rebellion. (See Gen 49 for the story of the beginning of these 12 tribes.)

Praise from the Great Crowd

REVELATION 7:9-17

After this I saw a vast crowd, too great to count, from every nation and tribe and people and language, standing in front of the throne and before the Lamb. They were clothed in white robes and held palm branches in their hands. 10And they were shouting with a great roar,

"Salvation comes from our God who sits
on the throne
and from the Lamb!"

11And all the angels were standing around the throne and around the elders and the four living beings. And they fell before the throne with their faces to the ground and worshiped God. 12They sang,

"Amen! Blessing and glory and wisdom
and thanksgiving and honor
and power and strength belong to our God
forever and ever! Amen."

13Then one of the twenty-four elders asked me, "Who are these who are clothed in white? Where did they come from?"

14And I said to him, "Sir, you are the one who knows."
Then he said to me, "These are the ones who died in* the great tribulation.* They have washed their robes in the blood of the Lamb and made them white.

15 "That is why they stand in front of God's throne
and serve him day and night in his Temple.
And he who sits on the throne
will give them shelter.
16 They will never again be hungry or thirsty;
they will never be scorched by the heat
of the sun.
17 For the Lamb on the throne*
will be their Shepherd.
He will lead them to springs of life-giving water.
And God will wipe every tear from their eyes."

The Lamb Breaks the Seventh Seal

REVELATION 8:1-5

When the Lamb broke the seventh seal on the scroll,*
there was silence throughout heaven for about half an
hour. 2I saw the seven angels who stand before God,
and they were given seven trumpets.
3Then another angel with a gold incense burner
came and stood at the altar. And a great amount of
incense was given to him to mix with the prayers of
God's people as an offering on the gold altar before
the throne. 4The smoke of the incense, mixed with
the prayers of God's holy people, ascended up to God

Rv 7:14a Greek *who came out of.* **Rv 7:14b** Or *the great suffering.* **Rv 7:17** Greek *on the center of the throne.* **Rv 8:1** Or *book.*

Rev 7:9 Who is this vast crowd? While some interpreters identify it as the martyrs described in Revelation 6:9, it may also be the same group as the 144,000 just mentioned (Rev 7:4-8). The 144,000 were sealed by God before the great time of persecution; the vast crowd was brought to eternal life, as God had promised. Before, they were being prepared; now, they are victorious. This crowd in heaven is composed of all those who remained faithful to God throughout the generations. No true believer ever need worry: God includes and protects each of us, and we are guaranteed a place in his presence forever.

Rev 7:10 People try many methods to remove the guilt of sin—good deeds, intellectual pursuits, and even casting blame on others. The crowd in heaven praises God, saying that salvation comes from him and from the Lamb. Salvation from sin's penalty can come only through Jesus Christ. Have you had the guilt of sin removed in the only way possible?

Rev 7:11 More information about the elders is found in the note on Revelation 4:4, p. 1808. The four living beings are explained further in the note on Revelation 4:6-7, p. 1808.

Rev 7:14 "The great tribulation" has been explained in several ways. Some believe it refers to the suffering of believers through the ages; others believe that there is a specific time of intense tribulation yet to come. In either case, these believers come through their times of suffering by remaining loyal to God. Because they remain faithful, God will give them eternal life with him (Rev 7:17).

Rev 7:14 It is difficult to imagine how blood could make any cloth white, but the blood of Jesus Christ is the world's greatest purifier because it removes the stain of sin. White symbolizes sinless perfection or holiness, which can be given to people only by the death of the sinless Lamb of God on our behalf. This is a picture of how we are saved through faith (see Isa 1:18; Rom 3:21-26).

Rev 7:16-17 God will provide for his children's needs in their eternal home where there will be no hunger, thirst, or pain, and he will wipe away all tears. When you are suffering or torn apart by sorrow, take comfort in this promise of complete protection and relief.

Rev 7:17 In Revelation 7:1-8 we see the believers receiving a seal to protect them through a time of great tribulation and suffering; in Revelation 7:9-17 we see the believers finally with God in heaven. All who have been faithful through the ages are singing before God's throne. Their tribulations and sorrows are over: no more tears for sin, for all sins are forgiven; no more tears for suffering, for all suffering is over; no more tears for death, for all believers have been resurrected to die no more.

Rev 8:1 There was silence in heaven for about half an hour. With all the activity, this dramatic pause must have seemed to last for an eternity. During this time, the only activity was the prayers of the saints (Rev 8:3-4). We must seek God in times of silence. How proper for us to be quiet and honor God for his power and might. Take time each day to be silent and exalt God. Silence also conveys trust and confidence in God (see Isa 30:15). We can trust that God will give us strength and provide the justice against oppressors that we seek.

Rev 8:1-2 When the seventh seal is opened, the seven trumpet judgments are revealed. In the same way, the seventh trumpet will announce the seven bowl judgments (Rev 11:15; 16:1-21). The trumpet judgments, like the seal judgments, are only partial. God's final and complete judgment has not yet come.

Rev 8:3-5 An incense burner filled with live coals was used in Temple worship. Incense was poured on the coals, and the sweet-smelling smoke drifted upward, symbolizing believers' prayers ascending to God (see Exod 30:7-9).

The angel then threw the incense burner down upon the earth. This symbolizes the judgment of God released on earth in answer to the prayers of the saints for justice on those who had oppressed and killed them. This shows that judgment, vindication, and revenge are in God's hands, not ours (see Matt 5:38; Rom 12:9; 1 Pet 3:9). No matter how strong the desire to exact revenge and retaliate at our enemies, our work is to pray to God for his justice.

▸ REVELATION 8:1-5 *(cont.)*

from the altar where the angel had poured them out.
5Then the angel filled the incense burner with fire
from the altar and threw it down upon the earth; and
thunder crashed, lightning flashed, and there was a
terrible earthquake.

The First Four Trumpets

REVELATION 8:6-13

Then the seven angels with the seven trumpets prepared to blow their mighty blasts.
7The first angel blew his trumpet, and hail and fire
mixed with blood were thrown down on the earth.
One-third of the earth was set on fire, one-third of the
trees were burned, and all the green grass was burned.
8Then the second angel blew his trumpet, and a
great mountain of fire was thrown into the sea. One-
third of the water in the sea became blood, 9one-third
of all things living in the sea died, and one-third of all
the ships on the sea were destroyed.
10Then the third angel blew his trumpet, and a great
star fell from the sky, burning like a torch. It fell on
one-third of the rivers and on the springs of water.
11The name of the star was Bitterness.* It made one-
third of the water bitter, and many people died from
drinking the bitter water.
12Then the fourth angel blew his trumpet, and one-
third of the sun was struck, and one-third of the moon,
and one-third of the stars, and they became dark. And
one-third of the day was dark, and also one-third of
the night.
13Then I looked, and I heard a single eagle crying
loudly as it flew through the air, "Terror, terror, terror
to all who belong to this world because of what will
happen when the last three angels blow their trumpets."

The Fifth Trumpet Brings the First Terror

REVELATION 9:1-12

Then the fifth angel blew his trumpet, and I saw a star
that had fallen to earth from the sky, and he was given
the key to the shaft of the bottomless pit.* 2When he
opened it, smoke poured out as though from a huge
furnace, and the sunlight and air turned dark from
the smoke.
3Then locusts came from the smoke and descended
on the earth, and they were given power to sting like
scorpions. 4They were told not to harm the grass or
plants or trees, but only the people who did not have
the seal of God on their foreheads. 5They were told not
to kill them but to torture them for five months with
pain like the pain of a scorpion sting. 6In those days
people will seek death but will not find it. They will
long to die, but death will flee from them!
7The locusts looked like horses prepared for battle.
They had what looked like gold crowns on their heads,
and their faces looked like human faces. 8They had
hair like women's hair and teeth like the teeth of a lion.
9They wore armor made of iron, and their wings roared
like an army of chariots rushing into battle. 10They had
tails that stung like scorpions, and for five months they
had the power to torment people. 11Their king is the
angel from the bottomless pit; his name in Hebrew
is *Abaddon,* and in Greek, *Apollyon*—the Destroyer.
12The first terror is past, but look, two more terrors
are coming!

Rv 8:11 Greek *Wormwood.* **Rv 9:1** Or *the abyss,* or *the underworld;* also in 9:11.

Rev 8:6 The trumpet blasts have three purposes: (1) to warn that judgment is certain, (2) to call the forces of good and evil to battle, and (3) to announce the return of the King, the Messiah. These warnings urge us to make sure our faith is firmly fixed on Christ.

Rev 8:7-12 Since only one-third of the earth is destroyed by these trumpet judgments, this is only a partial judgment from God. His full wrath is yet to be unleashed.

Rev 8:13 Habakkuk used the image of an eagle to symbolize swiftness and destruction (see Hab 1:8). The picture here is also of an eagle flying over all the earth, warning of the terrors yet to come. While both believers and unbelievers experience the terrors described in Revelation 8:7-12, those "who belong to this world" are the unbelievers who will meet spiritual harm through the next three trumpet judgments. God has guaranteed believers protection from spiritual harm (Rev 7:2-3).

Rev 9:1 It is not known whether this "star" that fell from the sky is Satan, a fallen angel, Christ, or a good angel. Most likely it is a good angel, because the key to the shaft of the bottomless pit is normally held by Christ (Rev 1:17-18), and it was temporarily given to this other being from heaven (see also Rev 20:1). This being, whoever he may be, is still under God's control and authority. The bottomless pit represents the place of the demons and of Satan, the king of demons (Rev 9:11). See also Luke 8:31 for another reference to the bottomless pit.

Rev 9:3 The prophet Joel described a locust plague as a foreshadowing of the "day of the LORD," meaning God's coming judgment (Joel 2:1-10). In the Old Testament, locusts were symbols of destruction because they destroyed vegetation. Here they symbolize an invasion of demons called to torture people who do not believe in God. The limitations placed on the demons (they could only torment people for five months) show that they are under God's authority.

Rev 9:3ff Most likely these locusts are demons—evil spirits ruled by Satan who tempt people to sin. They were not created by Satan, because God is the Creator of all; rather, they are fallen angels who joined Satan in his rebellion. God limits what they can do; they can do nothing without his permission. Their main purpose on earth is to prevent, distort, or destroy people's relationships with God. Because they are corrupt and degenerate, their appearance reflects the distortion of their spirits. While it is important to recognize their evil activity so we can stay away from them, we must avoid any curiosity about or involvement with demonic forces or with the occult.

Rev 9:11 The locust-demons have a leader whose name in Hebrew and in Greek means "Destroyer." It may be a play on words by John to show that those who worshiped the great god Apollo worshiped only a demon.

Rev 9:13 The altar in the Temple had four projections, one at each corner, and these were called the horns of the altar (see Exod 27:2).

Rev 9:14 The word *angels* here means fallen angels or demons. These four unidentified demons will be exceedingly evil and destructive. But note that they do not have the power

The Sixth Trumpet Brings the Second Terror

REVELATION 9:13-21

Then the sixth angel blew his trumpet, and I heard a voice speaking from the four horns of the gold altar that stands in the presence of God. 14And the voice said to the sixth angel who held the trumpet, "Release the four angels who are bound at the great Euphrates River." 15Then the four angels who had been prepared for this hour and day and month and year were turned loose to kill one-third of all the people on earth. 16I heard the size of their army, which was 200 million mounted troops.

17And in my vision, I saw the horses and the riders sitting on them. The riders wore armor that was fiery red and dark blue and yellow. The horses had heads like lions, and fire and smoke and burning sulfur billowed from their mouths. 18One-third of all the people on earth were killed by these three plagues—by the fire and smoke and burning sulfur that came from the mouths of the horses. 19Their power was in their mouths and in their tails. For their tails had heads like snakes, with the power to injure people.

20But the people who did not die in these plagues still refused to repent of their evil deeds and turn to God. They continued to worship demons and idols made of gold, silver, bronze, stone, and wood—idols that can neither see nor hear nor walk! 21And they did not repent of their murders or their witchcraft or their sexual immorality or their thefts.

The Angel and the Small Scroll

REVELATION 10:1-11

Then I saw another mighty angel coming down from heaven, surrounded by a cloud, with a rainbow over his head. His face shone like the sun, and his feet were like

INTERPRETING THE BOOK OF REVELATION

Over the centuries, four main approaches to interpreting the book of Revelation have developed. Each approach has had capable supporters, but none has proved itself the only way to read this book. However, the most basic application question for each approach can be summarized by asking yourself, "Will this help me become a better follower of Jesus Christ today?"

Approach	*Description*	*Challenge*	*Caution*
Preterist View	John is writing to encourage Christians in his own day who are experiencing persecution from the Roman Empire.	To gain the same kind of encouragement John's first readers gained from the vivid images of God's sovereignty	Do not forget that most biblical prophecy has both an immediate and a future application.
Futurist View	Except for the first three chapters, John is describing events that will occur at the end of history.	To see in contemporary events many of the characteristics John describes and realize that the end could come at any time	Do not assume that we have "figured out" the future, since Jesus said that no one will know the day of his return before it happens.
Historicist View	The book of Revelation is a presentation of history from John's day until the second coming of Christ and beyond.	To note the consistency of human evil throughout history and recognize that names may change but the rebellion against God has not	Be careful before identifying current events or leaders as fulfilling aspects of the book of Revelation.
Idealist View	The book of Revelation is a symbolic representation of the continual struggle of good and evil. It does not refer to any particular historical events. It is applicable at any point in history.	To gain insight into the past, to prepare for the future, and to live obediently and confidently in the present	Do not avoid the book because it is difficult. Try to understand Revelation within its broader literary context.

to release themselves and do their evil work on earth. Instead, they are held back by God and will be released at a specific time, doing only what he allows them to do.

Rev 9:15 Here one-third of all people are killed. Previously, one-fourth of all people were killed (Rev 6:7-8). Thus, one-half of the people in the world will have been killed by God's great judgments. Even more would have been killed if God had not set limits on the destruction.

Rev 9:16 In John's day, this number of mounted troops in an army was inconceivable, but today there are countries and alliances that could easily amass this many soldiers. This huge army, led by the four demons, will be sent out to destroy one-third of the earth's population. But the judgment is still not complete.

Rev 9:20-21 These people were so hard-hearted that even plagues did not drive them to God. People don't usually fall into immorality and evil suddenly—they slip into it a little bit at a time until, hardly realizing what has happened, they are irrevocably mired in their wicked ways. Any person who allows sin to take root will end up in this predicament. Temptation entertained today becomes sin tomorrow, a habit the next day, then death and separation from God forever (see Jas 1:15). To think you could never become this evil is the first step toward a hard heart. Acknowledge your need to confess your sin before God.

Rev 10:1-6 The purpose of this mighty angel is clear—to announce the final judgments on the earth. His right foot on the sea and left foot on the land (Rev 10:2) indicate that his words deal with all creation, not just a limited part as did the seal and trumpet judgments. The seventh trumpet (Rev 11:15) will usher in the seven bowl judgments, which will bring an end to the present world. When this universal judgment comes, God's truth will prevail.

▶ **REVELATION 10:1-11** ***(cont.)***
pillars of fire. [2]And in his hand was a small scroll* that
had been opened. He stood with his right foot on the
sea and his left foot on the land. [3]And he gave a great
shout like the roar of a lion. And when he shouted, the
seven thunders answered.

[4]When the seven thunders spoke, I was about to
write. But I heard a voice from heaven saying, "Keep
secret* what the seven thunders said, and do not write
it down."

[5]Then the angel I saw standing on the sea and on
the land raised his right hand toward heaven. [6]He
swore an oath in the name of the one who lives forever
and ever, who created the heavens and everything in
them, the earth and everything in it, and the sea and
everything in it. He said, "There will be no more delay.
[7]When the seventh angel blows his trumpet, God's
mysterious plan will be fulfilled. It will happen just as
he announced it to his servants the prophets."

[8]Then the voice from heaven spoke to me again: "Go
and take the open scroll from the hand of the angel
who is standing on the sea and on the land."

[9]So I went to the angel and told him to give me
the small scroll. "Yes, take it and eat it," he said. "It
will be sweet as honey in your mouth, but it will turn
sour in your stomach!" [10]So I took the small scroll
from the hand of the angel, and I ate it! It was sweet
in my mouth, but when I swallowed it, it turned sour
in my stomach.

[11]Then I was told, "You must prophesy again about
many peoples, nations, languages, and kings."

The Two Witnesses

REVELATION 11:1-14
Then I was given a measuring stick, and I was told,
"Go and measure the Temple of God and the altar, and
count the number of worshipers. [2]But do not measure
the outer courtyard, for it has been turned over to the
nations. They will trample the holy city for 42 months.
[3]And I will give power to my two witnesses, and they
will be clothed in burlap and will prophesy during
those 1,260 days."

[4]These two prophets are the two olive trees and
the two lampstands that stand before the Lord of all

Rv 10:2 Or *book;* also in 10:8, 9, 10. **Rv 10:4** Greek *Seal up.*

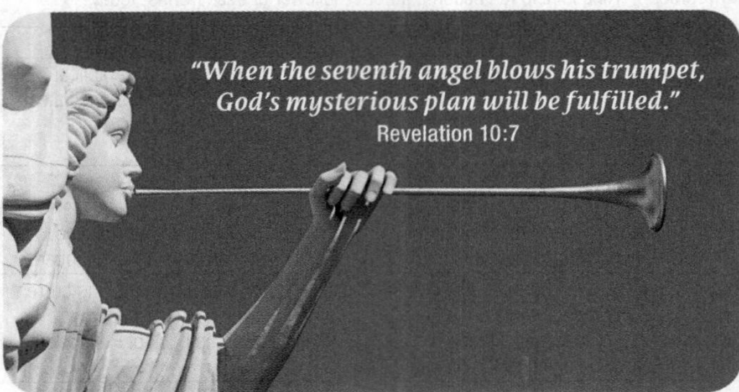
"When the seventh angel blows his trumpet, God's mysterious plan will be fulfilled."
Revelation 10:7

Rev 10:2 We see two scrolls in Revelation. The first contains a revelation of judgments against evil (Rev 5:1ff). The contents of the second small scroll are not indicated, but it also may contain a revelation of judgment.

Rev 10:2 This powerful angel conveyed his high rank and his authority from God by straddling the land and the sea. His huge size contrasts with the smallness of God's enemies. When things are going badly in your life, remember that this angel represents the kind of power that is on your side. God's angelic forces are with you (Matt 18:10; Heb 1:14). Keep your problems in their proper perspective by remembering that God's power is available to you to deal with your problems.

Rev 10:4 Throughout history people have wanted to know what would happen in the future, and God reveals some of it in this book. But John was stopped from revealing certain parts of his vision. An angel also told the prophet Daniel that some visions he saw were not to be revealed yet to everyone (Dan 12:9), and Jesus told his disciples that the time of the end is known by no one but God (Mark 13:32-33). God has revealed all we need to know to live for him now. In our desire to be ready for the end, we must not place more emphasis on speculation about the last days than on living for God while we wait.

Rev 10:7 By saying that "God's mysterious plan will be fulfilled," John was pointing to God's removal of all evil and the final exaltation of Christ as Lord. This pronouncement would bring fear to God's enemies. For God's chosen ones, it would bring hope and peace. Do you really long for Christ's return? Do you long for God and his people to be vindicated? Believers ought to pray for God's justice to be carried out and his plan fulfilled. We should want Christ to come because of the triumph of his Kingdom—not because things are bad or because we want out of our struggles. Pray expectantly for the fulfillment of God's plan.

Rev 10:9-10 The prophet Ezekiel also had a vision in which he was told to eat a scroll filled with judgments against the nation of Israel (Ezek 3:1ff). The taste was sweet in his mouth, but the scroll's contents brought destruction—just like the scroll John was told to eat. God's Word is sweet to us as believers because it brings encouragement, but it sours our stomach because of the coming judgment we must pronounce on unbelievers.

Rev 11:1ff This Temple is most likely a symbol of the church (all true believers), because there will be no Temple in the new Jerusalem (Rev 21:22). John measured the Temple to show that God is building walls of protection around his people to spare them from spiritual harm, and that there is a place reserved for all believers who remain faithful to God.

Rev 11:1-2 Those worshiping inside the Temple will be protected spiritually, but those outside will face great suffering. This is a way of saying that true believers will be protected through persecution, but those who refuse to believe will be destroyed.

Rev 11:3 These two witnesses bear strong resemblance to Moses and Elijah, two of God's mighty prophets. With God's power, Moses called plagues down upon the nation of Egypt (see Exod 7–11). Elijah defeated the prophets of Baal (1 Kgs 18). Both of these men appeared with Christ at his transfiguration (see Matt 17:1-7).

Rev 11:3 In the book of Revelation, numbers are likely to have symbolic rather than literal meanings. The 42 months or 1,260 days equal 3½ years. As half of the perfect number 7, 3½ can indicate incompletion, imperfection, or even evil. Notice the events predicted for this time period: there is trouble (Dan 12:7), the holy city is trampled (Rev 11:2), the

the earth. 5If anyone tries to harm them, fire flashes
from their mouths and consumes their enemies. This
is how anyone who tries to harm them must die.
6They have power to shut the sky so that no rain will
fall for as long as they prophesy. And they have the
power to turn the rivers and oceans into blood, and
to strike the earth with every kind of plague as often
as they wish.
7When they complete their testimony, the beast
that comes up out of the bottomless pit* will declare
war against them, and he will conquer them and kill
them. 8And their bodies will lie in the main street of
Jerusalem,* the city that is figuratively called "Sodom"
and "Egypt," the city where their Lord was crucified.
9And for three and a half days, all peoples, tribes, languages, and nations will stare at their bodies. No one
will be allowed to bury them. 10All the people who
belong to this world will gloat over them and give
presents to each other to celebrate the death of the
two prophets who had tormented them.
11But after three and a half days, God breathed life
into them, and they stood up! Terror struck all who
were staring at them. 12Then a loud voice from heaven
called to the two prophets, "Come up here!" And they
rose to heaven in a cloud as their enemies watched.
13At the same time there was a terrible earthquake
that destroyed a tenth of the city. Seven thousand
people died in that earthquake, and everyone else
was terrified and gave glory to the God of heaven.
14The second terror is past, but look, the third terror
is coming quickly.

The Seventh Trumpet Brings the Third Terror

REVELATION 11:15-19

Then the seventh angel blew his trumpet, and there
were loud voices shouting in heaven:

"The world has now become the Kingdom of our
Lord and of his Christ,*
and he will reign forever and ever."

16The twenty-four elders sitting on their thrones
before God fell with their faces to the ground and
worshiped him. 17And they said,

"We give thanks to you, Lord God, the Almighty,
the one who is and who always was,
for now you have assumed your great power
and have begun to reign.
18 The nations were filled with wrath,
but now the time of your wrath has come.
It is time to judge the dead
and reward your servants the prophets,
as well as your holy people,
and all who fear your name,
from the least to the greatest.
It is time to destroy
all who have caused destruction on the earth."

19Then, in heaven, the Temple of God was opened
and the Ark of his covenant could be seen inside the
Temple. Lightning flashed, thunder crashed and
roared, and there was an earthquake and a terrible
hailstorm.

Rv 11:7 Or *the abyss,* or *the underworld.* **Rv 11:8** Greek *the great city.* **Rv 11:15** Or *his Messiah.*

woman takes refuge in the wilderness (Rev 12:6), and the devil-inspired beast exercises his authority (Rev 13:5). Some commentators link the 3½ years with the period of famine in the days of Elijah (Luke 4:25; Jas 5:17). Since Malachi predicted the return of Elijah before the Last Judgment (Mal 4:5), and since the events in Daniel and Revelation pave the way for the Second Coming, perhaps John was making this connection. It is possible, of course, that the 3½ years are literal. If so, we will clearly recognize when the 3½ years are over! Whether symbolic or literal, they indicate that evil's reign will have a definite end.

Rev 11:7 This beast could be Satan or an agent of Satan.

Rev 11:8-9 Jerusalem, once the great city and the capital of Israel, is now enemy territory. It is compared with Sodom and with Egypt, both well known for their evil. By the time of John's writing, Jerusalem had been destroyed by the Romans in A.D. 70, nearly a million Jews had been slaughtered, and the Temple treasures had been carried off to Rome.

Rev 11:10 As representatives of every believer who has witnessed for Jesus Christ, the two final, faithful witnesses are a picture of both invincibility and vulnerability. They win, they lose, they win again. Truth remains victorious, even though human channels fall. Their message—and God's plan—march on in spite of death, for even death proves to be a defeated foe.

Seldom do we face the possibility of death when we share our faith. Why should Satan threaten our lives when fear of embarrassment or rejection is enough to keep us silent? But if Jesus has truly changed our lives, we will find a way to let others know. Not to witness represents more than just fear; it also reveals selfishness. Have those near you heard what Jesus has done for you?

Rev 11:13 The ultimate goal of God's saving plan is that everything in creation will glorify him. "Glory" refers to the splendor, radiance, and magnificence of God. It refers not only to God in his essential nature but to the praiseworthy effects of what God has accomplished. We glorify God because his glory is true and real, and we acknowledge his greatness. In so doing, we see our rightful position as his servants. When we glorify him in our singing, our speaking, and our living, we experience some of his transcendence and thus edify and uplift our own spirits. Glorifying God prompts us to moral action and loving service.

Rev 11:15 The seventh trumpet is sounded, announcing the arrival of the King. There is now no turning back. The coming judgments are no longer partial but complete in their destruction. God is in control, and he unleashes his full wrath on the evil world that refuses to turn to him (Rev 9:20-21). When his wrath begins, there will be no escape.

Rev 11:16 For more on the 24 elders, see the note on Revelation 4:4, p. 1808.

Rev 11:18 In the Bible, God gives rewards to his people according to what they deserve. Throughout the Old Testament, obedience often brought reward in this life (Deut 28), but obedience and immediate reward are not always linked. If they were, good people would always be rich, and suffering would always be a sign of sin. If we were quickly rewarded for every faithful deed, we would soon think we were pretty good. Before long, we would be doing many good deeds for purely selfish reasons. While it is true that God will reward us for our earthly deeds (see Rev 20:12), our greatest reward will be eternal life in his presence.

Rev 11:19 In Old Testament days, the Ark of the Covenant was the most sacred treasure of the Israelite nation. (For more information about the Ark, see the note on Exod 37:1, p. 191.)

The Woman and the Dragon

REVELATION 12:1-18

Then I witnessed in heaven an event of great significance. I saw a woman clothed with the sun, with the
moon beneath her feet, and a crown of twelve stars
on her head. 2She was pregnant, and she cried out because of her labor pains and the agony of giving birth.
3Then I witnessed in heaven another significant
event. I saw a large red dragon with seven heads and
ten horns, with seven crowns on his heads. 4His tail
swept away one-third of the stars in the sky, and he
threw them to the earth. He stood in front of the
woman as she was about to give birth, ready to devour
her baby as soon as it was born.
5She gave birth to a son who was to rule all nations
with an iron rod. And her child was snatched away
from the dragon and was caught up to God and to
his throne. 6And the woman fled into the wilderness,
where God had prepared a place to care for her for
1,260 days.
7Then there was war in heaven. Michael and his
angels fought against the dragon and his angels. 8And
the dragon lost the battle, and he and his angels were
forced out of heaven. 9This great dragon—the ancient
serpent called the devil, or Satan, the one deceiving
the whole world—was thrown down to the earth with
all his angels.
10Then I heard a loud voice shouting across the
heavens,

"It has come at last—
salvation and power
and the Kingdom of our God,
and the authority of his Christ.*
For the accuser of our brothers and sisters*
has been thrown down to earth—
the one who accuses them
before our God day and night.
11 And they have defeated him by the blood
of the Lamb
and by their testimony.
And they did not love their lives so much
that they were afraid to die.
12 Therefore, rejoice, O heavens!
And you who live in the heavens, rejoice!
But terror will come on the earth and the sea,
for the devil has come down to you
in great anger,
knowing that he has little time."

Rv 12:10a Or *his Messiah.* **Rv 12:10b** Greek *brothers.*

Rev 12:1–14:20 The seventh trumpet (Rev 11:15) ushers in the bowl judgments (Rev 15:1–16:21), but in the intervening chapters (Rev 12–14), John sees the conflict between God and Satan. He sees the source of all sin, evil, persecution, and suffering on the earth, and he understands why the great battle between the forces of God and Satan must soon take place. In these chapters the nature of evil is exposed, and Satan is seen in all his wickedness.

Rev 12:1-6 The woman represents God's faithful people who have been waiting for the Messiah; the crown of 12 stars represents the 12 tribes of Israel. God set apart the Jews for himself (Rom 9:4-5), and that nation gave birth to the Messiah. The son (Rev 12:5) is Jesus, born to a devout Jewish girl named Mary (Luke 1:26-33). Evil King Herod immediately tried to destroy the infant Jesus (Matt 2:13-20). Herod's desire to kill this newborn king, whom he saw as a threat to his throne, was motivated by Satan (the red dragon), who wanted to kill the world's Savior. The heavenly pageant of Revelation 12 shows that Christ's lowly birth in the town of Bethlehem had cosmic significance.

Rev 12:3-4 The large red dragon, Satan, has seven heads, ten horns, and seven crowns, representing his power and the kingdoms of the world over which he rules. The stars that plunged to earth with him are usually considered to be the angels who fell with Satan and became his demons. According to Hebrew tradition, one-third of all the angels in heaven fell with Satan. (For more on demons, see the notes on Rev 9:3ff, p. 1814; Mark 5:1-2, p. 1351.)

Rev 12:6 The wilderness represents a place of spiritual refuge and protection from Satan. Because God aided the woman's escape into the wilderness, we can be sure that he offers security to all true believers. Satan always attacks God's people, but God keeps them spiritually secure. Some will experience physical harm, but all will be protected from spiritual harm. God will not let Satan take the souls of God's true followers. When Satan's attacks seem overpowering, remember that God is ruler over all. Trust him.

Rev 12:6 The 1,260 days (3½ years) is the same length of time that the dragon is allowed to exercise his authority (Rev 13:5) and that the holy city is trampled (see the second note on Rev 11:3, p. 1816).

Rev 12:7 This event fulfills Daniel 12:1ff. Michael is a high-ranking angel. One of his responsibilities is to guard God's community of believers.

Rev 12:7ff Much more happened at Christ's birth, death, and resurrection than most people realize. A war between the forces of good and evil was under way. With Christ's resurrection, Satan's ultimate defeat was assured. Some believe that Satan's fall to earth took place at Jesus' resurrection or ascension and that the 1,260 days (3½ years) is a symbolic way of referring to the time between Christ's first and second comings. Others say that Satan's defeat will occur in the middle of a literal seven-year tribulation period, following the rapture of the church and preceding the second coming of Christ and the beginning of Christ's 1,000-year reign. Whatever the case, we must remember that Christ is victorious—Satan has already been defeated because of Christ's death on the cross (Rev 12:10-12).

Rev 12:9 The devil is not a symbol or legend; he is very real. Originally Satan was an angel of God, but through his own pride, he became corrupt. The devil is God's enemy, and he constantly tries to hinder God's work, but he is limited by God's power and can do only what he is permitted to do (Job 1:6–2:8). The name *Satan* means "accuser" (Rev 12:10). He actively looks for people to attack (1 Pet 5:8-9). Satan likes to pursue believers who are vulnerable in their faith, who are spiritually weak, or who are isolated from other believers.

Even though God permits the devil to do his work in this world, God is still in control. And Jesus has complete power over Satan—he defeated Satan when he died and rose again for the sins of everyone. One day Satan will be bound forever, never again to do his evil work (see Rev 20:10).

Rev 12:10 Many believe that until this time, Satan still had access to God (see the note on Job 1:7ff, p. 95). But here his access is forever barred (see also Rev 9:1). He can no longer accuse people before God (see how Satan made accusations about Job before God in Job 1:6ff).

Rev 12:11 The critical blow to Satan came when the Lamb, Jesus Christ, shed his blood for our sins. The victory is won by sacrifice—Christ's death in our place to pay the penalty for our sin. As we face the battle with Satan, we should not fear it or try to escape from it, but we should loyally serve Christ, who alone brings victory (see Rom 8:34-39).

[13]When the dragon realized that he had been thrown down to the earth, he pursued the woman who had given birth to the male child. [14]But she was given two wings like those of a great eagle so she could fly to the place prepared for her in the wilderness. There she would be cared for and protected from the dragon* for a time, times, and half a time.

[15]Then the dragon tried to drown the woman with a flood of water that flowed from his mouth. [16]But the earth helped her by opening its mouth and swallowing the river that gushed out from the mouth of the dragon. [17]And the dragon was angry at the woman and declared war against the rest of her children—all who keep God's commandments and maintain their testimony for Jesus.

[18]Then the dragon took his stand* on the shore beside the sea.

The Beast out of the Sea

REVELATION 13:1-10

Then I saw a beast rising up out of the sea. It had seven heads and ten horns, with ten crowns on its horns. And written on each head were names that blasphemed God. [2]This beast looked like a leopard, but it had the feet of a bear and the mouth of a lion! And the dragon gave the beast his own power and throne and great authority.

[3]I saw that one of the heads of the beast seemed wounded beyond recovery—but the fatal wound was healed! The whole world marveled at this miracle and gave allegiance to the beast. [4]They worshiped the dragon for giving the beast such power, and they also worshiped the beast. "Who is as great as the beast?" they exclaimed. "Who is able to fight against him?"

[5]Then the beast was allowed to speak great

Rv 12:14 Greek *the serpent;* also in 12:15. See 12:9. **Rv 12:18** Greek *Then he took his stand;* some manuscripts read *Then I took my stand.* Some translations put this entire sentence into 13:1.

SATAN'S WORK IN THE WORLD

His hatred for Christ	**Rev 12:4, 13-15**
His hatred for God's people	**Rev 12:17**
His power and authority	**Rev 13:2**
His popularity among unbelievers	**Rev 13:3-4**
His blasphemy against God	**Rev 13:6**
His war against believers	**Rev 13:7**
His ability to deceive	**Rev 13:14**

Rev 12:12 The devil begins to step up his persecution because he knows that "he has little time." We are living in the last days, and Satan's work has become more intense. Even though the devil is very powerful, as we can see by the condition of our world, he is always under God's control. One of the reasons God allows Satan to work evil and bring temptation is so that those who pretend to be Christ's followers will be weeded out from Christ's true believers. Knowing that the last great confrontation with Jesus is near, Satan is desperately trying to recruit as great an enemy force as possible for this final battle.

Rev 12:17 While the woman (Rev 12:1) represents faithful Jews and the son (Rev 12:5) represents Christ, the rest of her children could be either Jewish believers or, more likely, all believers.

Rev 12:17 The apostle Paul tells us that we are in a spiritual battle (Eph 6:10-12). John says that the war is still being waged, but the outcome has already been determined. Satan and his followers have been defeated and will be destroyed. Nevertheless Satan is battling daily to bring more into his ranks and to keep his own from defecting to God's side. Those who belong to Christ have gone into battle on God's side, and he has guaranteed them victory. God will not lose the war, but we must make certain not to lose the battle for our own souls. Don't waver in your commitment to Christ. A great spiritual battle is being fought, and there is no time for indecision.

Rev 13:1 This beast was initially identified with Rome because the Roman Empire, in its early days, encouraged an evil lifestyle, persecuted believers, and opposed God and his followers. But the beast also symbolizes the Antichrist—not Satan, but someone under Satan's power and control. This Antichrist looks like a combination of the four beasts that Daniel saw centuries earlier in a vision (Dan 7). As the dragon (Rev 12:17) is in opposition to God, so the beast from the sea is against Christ and may be seen as Satan's false messiah. The early Roman Empire was strong and also anti-Christ (against Christ's standards); many other individual powers throughout history have been anti-Christ. Many Christians believe that Satan's evil will culminate in a final Antichrist who will focus all the powers of evil against Jesus Christ and his followers.

Rev 13:1ff Revelation 13 introduces Satan's (the dragon's) two evil accomplices: the beast out of the sea (Rev 13:1ff) and the beast out of the earth (Rev 13:11ff). Together, the three evil beings form an unholy trinity in direct opposition to the Holy Trinity of God the Father, God the Son, and God the Holy Spirit.

When Satan tempted Jesus in the wilderness, he wanted Jesus to show his power by turning stones into bread, to do miracles by jumping from a high place, and to gain political power by worshiping him (see Matt 4:1-11). Satan's plan was to rule the world through Jesus, but Jesus refused to do Satan's bidding. Thus, Satan turns to the fearsome beasts described in Revelation. To the beast out of the sea he gives political power. To the beast out of the earth he gives power to do miracles. Both beasts work together to capture the control of the whole world. This unholy trinity—the dragon, the beast out of the sea, and the beast out of the earth (later identified as "the false prophet"; see Rev 16:13)—unite in a desperate attempt to overthrow God, but their efforts are doomed to failure. (See what becomes of them in Rev 19:19-21; 20:10.)

Rev 13:3ff Because the beast, the Antichrist, is a false messiah, he will be a counterfeit of Christ and will even stage a false resurrection (Rev 13:14). People will follow and worship him because they will be awed by his power and miracles (Rev 13:3-4). He will unite the world under his leadership (Rev 13:7-8), and he will control the world economy (Rev 13:16-17). People are impressed by power and will follow those who display it forcefully or offer it to their followers. But those who follow the beast will only be fooling themselves: He will use his power to manipulate others, to point to himself, and to promote evil plans. God, by contrast, uses his infinitely greater power to love and to build up. Don't be misled by claims of great miracles or reports about a resurrection or reincarnation of someone claiming to be Christ. When Jesus returns, he will reveal himself to everyone (Matt 24:23-28).

Rev 13:5 The power given to the beast will be limited by God. He will allow the beast to exercise authority only for a short time. Even while the beast is in power, God will still be in control (Rev 11:15; 12:10-12).

▸ **REVELATION 13:1-10 *(cont.)***

blasphemies against God. And he was given authority to do whatever he wanted for forty-two months.
6 And he spoke terrible words of blasphemy against
God, slandering his name and his dwelling—that is,
those who dwell in heaven.* 7 And the beast was allowed to wage war against God's holy people and to
conquer them. And he was given authority to rule
over every tribe and people and language and nation. 8 And all the people who belong to this world
worshiped the beast. They are the ones whose names
were not written in the Book of Life before the world
was made—the Book that belongs to the Lamb who
was slaughtered.*

9 Anyone with ears to hear
should listen and understand.
10 Anyone who is destined for prison
will be taken to prison.
Anyone destined to die by the sword
will die by the sword.

This means that God's holy people must endure persecution patiently and remain faithful.

The Beast out of the Earth

REVELATION 13:11-18

Then I saw another beast come up out of the earth. He
had two horns like those of a lamb, but he spoke with
the voice of a dragon. 12 He exercised all the authority
of the first beast. And he required all the earth and its
people to worship the first beast, whose fatal wound
had been healed. 13 He did astounding miracles, even
making fire flash down to earth from the sky while
everyone was watching. 14 And with all the miracles
he was allowed to perform on behalf of the first beast,
he deceived all the people who belong to this world. He
ordered the people to make a great statue of the first
beast, who was fatally wounded and then came back to
life. 15 He was then permitted to give life to this statue
so that it could speak. Then the statue of the beast commanded that anyone refusing to worship it must die.
16 He required everyone—small and great, rich and
poor, free and slave—to be given a mark on the right
hand or on the forehead. 17 And no one could buy or sell
anything without that mark, which was either the name
of the beast or the number representing his name.
18 Wisdom is needed here. Let the one with under-

Rv 13:6 Some manuscripts read *and his dwelling and all who dwell in heaven.* **Rv 13:8** Or *not written in the Book of Life that belongs to the Lamb who was slaughtered before the world was made.*

Rev 13:7 The beast will conquer God's people and rule over them, but he will not be able to harm them spiritually. He will establish worldwide dominance and demand that everyone worship him. And many *will* worship him—everyone except true believers. Refusal to worship the beast will result in temporary suffering for God's people, but they will be rewarded with eternal life in the end.

Rev 13:8 See the note on Revelation 3:5, p. 1806, for more information on the Book of Life.

Rev 13:10 In this time of persecution, being faithful to Christ could bring imprisonment and even execution. Some believers will be hurt or killed. But all that the beast and his followers will be able to do to believers is harm them physically; no spiritual harm will come to those whose faith in God is sincere. All believers will enter God's presence perfected and purified by the blood of the Lamb (Rev 7:9-17).

Rev 13:10 The times of great persecution that John saw will provide an opportunity for believers to exercise patient endurance and faithfulness. The tough times we face right now are also opportunities for spiritual growth. Don't fall into Satan's trap and turn away from God when hard times come. Instead, use those tough times as opportunities for testifying about God (see Phil 1:28-29).

Rev 13:11ff The first beast came out of the sea (Rev 13:1), but this second beast comes out of the earth. Later identified as the false prophet (Rev 16:13; 19:20), he is a counterfeit of the Holy Spirit. He seems to do good, but the purpose of his miracles is to deceive.

Rev 13:14 Throughout the Bible we see miracles performed as proofs of God's power, love, and authority. But here we see counterfeit miracles performed to deceive. This is a reminder of Pharaoh's magicians, who duplicated Moses' signs in Egypt. True signs and miracles point us to Jesus Christ, but miracles alone can be deceptive. That is why we must ask with respect to each miracle we see: Is this consistent with what God says in the Bible? The second beast here gains influence through the signs and wonders that he can perform on behalf of the first beast. The second beast orders the people to worship a statue in honor of the first beast—a direct flouting of the second commandment (Exod 20:4-6). Allowing the Bible to guide our faith and practice will keep us from being deceived by false signs, however convincing they appear to be. Any teaching that contradicts God's Word is false.

Rev 13:16-17 In every generation, Christians need to maintain a healthy skepticism about society's pleasures and rewards. In our educational, economic, and civic structures, there are incentives and rewards. Cooperating Christians must always support what is good and healthy about our society, but we must stand against sin. In some cases, such as Satan's system described here, the system or structure becomes so evil that there is no way to cooperate with it.

Rev 13:16-18 This mark of the beast is designed to mock the seal that God places on his followers (Rev 7:2-3). Just as God marks his people to save them, so Satan's beast marks his people to save them from the persecution that Satan will inflict upon God's followers. Identifying this particular mark is not as important as identifying the purpose of the mark. Those who accept it show their allegiance to Satan, their willingness to operate within the economic system he promotes, and their rebellion against God. To refuse the mark means to commit oneself entirely to God, preferring death to compromising one's faith in Christ.

Rev 13:18 The meaning of this number has been discussed more than that of any other part of the book of Revelation. The three sixes have been said to represent many things, including the number of a man or the unholy trinity of Satan, the first beast, and the false prophet (Rev 16:13). If the number seven is considered to be the perfect number in the Bible, and if three sevens represent complete perfection, then the number 666 falls completely short of perfection. The first readers of this book probably applied the number to the emperor Nero, who symbolized all the evils of the Roman Empire. (The Greek letters of Nero's name represent numbers that total 666.) Whatever specific application the number is given, the number symbolizes the worldwide dominion and complete evil of this unholy trinity designed to undo Christ's work and overthrow him.

Rev 14:1ff Revelation 13 described the onslaught of evil that will occur when Satan and his helpers control the world. Revelation 14 gives a glimpse into eternity to show believers what awaits them if they endure. The Lamb is the Messiah. Mount Zion, often another name for Jerusalem, the capital of Israel, is contrasted with the worldly empire. The 144,000 represent believers who have endured persecutions on earth and now are ready to enjoy the eternal benefits and bless-

standing solve the meaning of the number of the beast, for it is the number of a man.* His number is 666.*

The Lamb and the 144,000

REVELATION 14:1-5

Then I saw the Lamb standing on Mount Zion, and with him were 144,000 who had his name and his Father's name written on their foreheads. [2]And I heard a sound from heaven like the roar of mighty ocean waves or the rolling of loud thunder. It was like the sound of many harpists playing together.

[3]This great choir sang a wonderful new song in front of the throne of God and before the four living beings and the twenty-four elders. No one could learn this song except the 144,000 who had been redeemed from the earth. [4]They have kept themselves as pure as virgins,* following the Lamb wherever he goes. They have been purchased from among the people on the earth as a special offering* to God and to the Lamb. [5]They have told no lies; they are without blame.

The Three Angels

REVELATION 14:6-13

And I saw another angel flying through the sky, carrying the eternal Good News to proclaim to the people who belong to this world—to every nation, tribe, language, and people. [7]"Fear God," he shouted. "Give glory to him. For the time has come when he will sit as judge. Worship him who made the heavens, the earth, the sea, and all the springs of water."

[8]Then another angel followed him through the sky, shouting, "Babylon is fallen—that great city is fallen—because she made all the nations of the world drink the wine of her passionate immorality."

[9]Then a third angel followed them, shouting, "Anyone who worships the beast and his statue or who accepts his mark on the forehead or on the hand [10]must drink the wine of God's anger. It has been poured full strength into God's cup of wrath. And they will be tormented with fire and burning sulfur in the presence of the holy angels and the Lamb. [11]The smoke of their torment will rise forever and ever, and they will have no relief day or night, for they have worshiped the beast and his statue and have accepted the mark of his name."

[12]This means that God's holy people must endure persecution patiently, obeying his commands and maintaining their faith in Jesus.

[13]And I heard a voice from heaven saying, "Write this down: Blessed are those who die in the Lord from now on. Yes, says the Spirit, they are blessed indeed, for they will rest from their hard work; for their good deeds follow them!"

Rv 13:18a Or *of humanity.* **Rv 13:18b** Some manuscripts read *616.* **Rv 14:4a** Greek *They are virgins who have not defiled themselves with women.* **Rv 14:4b** Greek *as firstfruits.*

ings of life with God forever. The three angels contrast the destiny of believers with that of unbelievers.

Rev 14:4 These people are true believers whose robes have been washed and made white in Christ's blood (Rev 7:14) through his death ("purchased from among the people on the earth"). In the Old Testament, idolatry was often portrayed as spiritual adultery (see the book of Hosea). Their being "pure as virgins" is best understood symbolically, meaning that they are free from involvement with the pagan world system. To remain spiritually pure means resisting the seductions and idolatries of the present world—power, wealth, and sexual immorality. To do so requires daily application of God's Word, for it has a purifying effect on the mind and heart. It requires great resolution not to give in to these temptations.

Following Christ, the Lamb, "wherever he goes" requires heroic effort to carry out Christ's commission to face oppression and even death if required. Too many shrink back when the work is difficult or the future looks bleak. Join those who take their stand with Christ and against sin.

The "special offering" refers to the act of dedicating the first part of the harvest as holy to God (Exod 23:19; see also Jas 1:18).

Rev 14:6-7 Some believe that this is a final, worldwide appeal to all people to recognize the one true God. No one will have the excuse of never hearing God's truth. Others see this as an announcement of judgment rather than as an appeal. The people of the world have had their chance to proclaim their allegiance to God, and now God's great judgment is about to begin. If you are reading this, you have already heard God's truth. You know that God's final judgment will not be put off forever. Have you joyfully received the everlasting Good News? Have you confessed your sins and trusted in Christ to save you? If so, you have nothing to fear from God's judgment. The Judge of all the earth is your Savior!

Rev 14:8 Babylon was the name of both an evil city and an immoral empire, a world center for idol worship. Babylon ransacked Jerusalem and carried the people of Judah into captivity (see 2 Kgs 25; 2 Chr 36). Just as Babylon was the Jews' worst enemy, the Roman Empire was the early Christians' worst enemy. John, who probably did not dare speak against Rome openly, applied the name Babylon to this enemy of God's people (Rome)—and, by extension, to all God's enemies of all times.

Rev 14:9-11 Those who worship the beast, accept his mark, and operate according to his world economic system will ultimately face God's judgment. Our world values money, power, and pleasure over God's leadership. To get what the world values, many people deny God and violate Christian principles. Thus, they must drink of the wine of God's anger (see Ps 75; Isa 51:17).

Rev 14:11 The ultimate result of sin is unending separation from God. Because human beings are created in God's image with an inborn thirst for fellowship with him, separation from God will be the ultimate torment and misery. Sin always brings misery, but in this life we can choose to repent and restore our relationship with God. In eternity there will no longer be opportunity for repentance. If in this life we choose to be independent of God, in the next life we will be separated from him forever. Nobody is forced to choose eternal separation from God, and nobody suffers this fate by accident. Jesus invites all of us to open the door of our hearts to him (Rev 3:20). If we do this, we will enjoy everlasting fellowship with him.

Rev 14:12 This news about God's ultimate triumph should encourage God's people to remain faithful through every trial and persecution. They can do this, God promises, by trusting in Jesus and obeying the commands found in his Word. The secret to enduring, therefore, is trust and obedience. Trust God to give you patience to endure even the small trials you face daily; obey him even when obedience is unattractive or dangerous.

Rev 14:13 While it is true that money, fame, and belongings can't be taken with us from this life, God's people can produce fruit that survives even death. God will remember our love, kindness, and faithfulness, and those who accept Christ through our witness will join us on the new earth. Be sure that your values are in line with God's values, and decide today to produce fruit that lasts forever.

The Harvest of the Earth

REVELATION 14:14-20

Then I saw a white cloud, and seated on the cloud was someone like the Son of Man.* He had a gold crown on his head and a sharp sickle in his hand.
15 Then another angel came from the Temple and shouted to the one sitting on the cloud, "Swing the sickle, for the time of harvest has come; the crop on earth is ripe."
16 So the one sitting on the cloud swung his sickle over the earth, and the whole earth was harvested.
17 After that, another angel came from the Temple in heaven, and he also had a sharp sickle.
18 Then another angel, who had power to destroy with fire, came from the altar. He shouted to the angel with the sharp sickle, "Swing your sickle now to gather the clusters of grapes from the vines of the earth, for they are ripe for judgment."
19 So the angel swung his sickle over the earth and loaded the grapes into the great winepress of God's wrath.
20 The grapes were trampled in the winepress outside the city, and blood flowed from the winepress in a stream about 180 miles* long and as high as a horse's bridle.

The Song of Moses and of the Lamb

REVELATION 15:1-4

Then I saw in heaven another marvelous event of great significance. Seven angels were holding the seven last plagues, which would bring God's wrath to completion.
2 I saw before me what seemed to be a glass sea mixed with fire. And on it stood all the people who had been victorious over the beast and his statue and the number representing his name. They were all holding harps that God had given them.
3 And they were singing the song of Moses, the servant of God, and the song of the Lamb:

"Great and marvelous are your works,
O Lord God, the Almighty.
Just and true are your ways,
O King of the nations.*
4 Who will not fear you, Lord,
and glorify your name?
For you alone are holy.
All nations will come and worship before you,
for your righteous deeds have been revealed."

The Seven Bowls of the Seven Plagues

REVELATION 15:5–16:21

Then I looked and saw that the Temple in heaven, God's Tabernacle, was thrown wide open.
6 The seven angels who were holding the seven plagues came out of the Temple. They were clothed in spotless white linen* with gold sashes across their chests.
7 Then one of the four living beings handed each of the seven angels a gold bowl filled with the wrath of God, who lives forever and ever.
8 The Temple was filled with smoke from God's glory and power. No one could enter the Temple until the seven angels had completed pouring out the seven plagues.

16:1 Then I heard a mighty voice from the Temple say to the seven angels, "Go your ways and pour out on the earth the seven bowls containing God's wrath."
2 So the first angel left the Temple and poured out his bowl on the earth, and horrible, malignant sores

Rv 14:14 Or *like a son of man.* See Dan 7:13. "Son of Man" is a title Jesus used for himself. **Rv 14:20** Greek *1,600 stadia* [296 kilometers]. **Rv 15:3** Some manuscripts read *King of the ages.* **Rv 15:6** Other manuscripts read *white stone;* still others read *white [garments] made of linen.*

Rev 14:14-16 This is an image of judgment: Christ is separating the faithful from the unfaithful like a farmer harvesting his crops. This is a time of joy for the Christians who have been persecuted and martyred—they will receive their long-awaited reward. Christians should not fear the Last Judgment. Jesus said, "I tell you the truth, those who listen to my message and believe in God who sent me have eternal life. They will never be condemned for their sins, but they have already passed from death into life" (John 5:24).

Rev 14:19 A winepress was a large vat or trough where grapes were collected and then crushed. The juice flowed out of a duct that led into a large holding vat. The winepress is often used in the Bible as a symbol of God's wrath and judgment against sin (Isa 63:3-6; Lam 1:15; Joel 3:12-13). The distance of 180 miles is approximately the north-south length of Palestine.

To those unaccustomed to vivid descriptions of God's anger in judgment, these are disturbing images. People dislike the idea of other people, even evil ones, being trampled like grapes. The depth and length of the blood flow provides a sickening scene of the immensity of God's judgment. But unless we face the necessity of God's judgment, we will never see our desperate need for his mercy. A god with only a grandfatherly kindness would not inspire our repentance, obedience, or worship. God has promised a harsh harvest for those who reject him. Those who know God well enough to fear his wrath know God well enough to desire his grace. The crushing wrath of God is coming. Blessed are those who have had their sins forgiven, and blessed are those who lead others to God's mercy.

Rev 15:1 The seven last plagues are also called the seven bowl judgments. They actually begin in Revelation 16. Unlike the previous plagues, these are universal, and they will culminate in the abolition of all evil and the end of the world.

Rev 15:3-4 The song of Moses celebrated Israel's deliverance from Egypt (Exod 15). The song of the Lamb celebrates the ultimate deliverance of God's people from the power of Satan.

Rev 15:5-8 This imagery brings us back to the time of the Exodus in the wilderness when the Ark of the Covenant (the symbol of God's presence among his people) resided in the Tabernacle. The angels' garments are reminiscent of the high priest's clothing, showing that they are free from corruption, immorality, and injustice. The smoke that fills the Temple is the manifestation of God's glory and power. There is no escape from this judgment.

Rev 15:8 John saw the Temple filled with the glory and power of God. The key to God's eternal glory and power is his holiness (Rev 4:8). God's glory is not only his strength but also his perfect moral character. God will never do anything that is not morally perfect. This reassures us that we can trust him, yet it places a demand on us. Our desire to be holy (dedicated to God and morally pure) is our only suitable response. Our eternal reign with Christ won't begin until all evil is destroyed by his judgment. We must wait for his timetable to be revealed.

Rev 16:1ff The bowl judgments are God's final and complete judgments on the earth. The end has come. There are many similarities between the bowl judgments and the trumpet judgments (Rev 8:6–11:19), but there are three main differences: (1) These judgments are complete whereas the trumpet judgments are partial; (2) the trumpet judgments still give unbelievers the opportunity to

broke out on everyone who had the mark of the beast
and who worshiped his statue.
3Then the second angel poured out his bowl on
the sea, and it became like the blood of a corpse. And
everything in the sea died.
4Then the third angel poured out his bowl on the rivers and springs, and they became blood. 5And I heard
the angel who had authority over all water saying,

"You are just, O Holy One, who is and who
always was,
because you have sent these judgments.
6 Since they shed the blood
of your holy people and your prophets,
you have given them blood to drink.
It is their just reward."

7And I heard a voice from the altar,* saying,

"Yes, O Lord God, the Almighty,
your judgments are true and just."

8Then the fourth angel poured out his bowl on
the sun, causing it to scorch everyone with its fire.
9Everyone was burned by this blast of heat, and they
cursed the name of God, who had control over all these
plagues. They did not repent of their sins and turn to
God and give him glory.
10Then the fifth angel poured out his bowl on the
throne of the beast, and his kingdom was plunged into
darkness. His subjects ground their teeth in anguish,
11and they cursed the God of heaven for their pains
and sores. But they did not repent of their evil deeds
and turn to God.
12Then the sixth angel poured out his bowl on
the great Euphrates River, and it dried up so that the
kings from the east could march their armies toward
the west without hindrance. 13And I saw three evil*
spirits that looked like frogs leap from the mouths of
the dragon, the beast, and the false prophet. 14They
are demonic spirits who work miracles and go out to
all the rulers of the world to gather them for battle
against the Lord on that great judgment day of God
the Almighty.

15"Look, I will come as unexpectedly as a thief!
Blessed are all who are watching for me, who

Rv 16:7 Greek *I heard the altar.* **Rv 16:13** Greek *unclean.*

BLESSINGS IN REVELATION

Seven times in Revelation, God promises blessings upon the believers.

Reference	*Verse*
Rev 1:3	"God blesses the one who reads the words of this prophecy to the church, and he blesses all who listen to its message and obey what it says."
Rev 14:13	"Blessed are those who die in the Lord from now on. Yes, says the Spirit, they are blessed indeed, for they will rest from their hard work; for their good deeds follow them!"
Rev 16:15	"Blessed are all who are watching for me, who keep their clothing ready so they will not have to walk around naked and ashamed."
Rev 19:9	"Blessed are those who are invited to the wedding feast of the Lamb."
Rev 20:6	"Blessed and holy are those who share in the first resurrection. For them the second death holds no power, but they will be priests of God and of Christ and will reign with him a thousand years."
Rev 22:7	"Blessed are those who obey the words of prophecy written in this book."
Rev 22:14	"Blessed are those who wash their robes. They will be permitted to enter through the gates of the city and eat the fruit from the tree of life."

repent, but the bowl judgments do not; and (3) people are indirectly affected by several of the trumpet judgments but directly attacked by all the bowl judgments.

Rev 16:6 The angel acclaimed God for his justice in dealing with those who had killed the martyrs. God's wrath may be hard for us to accept. In a moral universe, God must ultimately oppose and destroy evil. Those who join the revolt against God suffer with their leaders.

We must avoid the misconception that God must be fair and kind in his dealings with humanity. This view of justice is merely a projection of a human idea. People who believe this notion appeal to tolerance and forgiveness and assume that God must play by our rules. In reality, God sets his own standard of justice. He uses his power according to his own moral perfection. Thus, whatever he chooses or decrees is fair, even if we don't understand it or like it. Those who rebel and reject God are not rejecting a "lifestyle option"; they are rejecting truth and justice itself.

Rev 16:7 The significance of the altar itself responding is that *everyone and everything* will be praising God, acknowledging his righteousness and perfect justice.

Rev 16:9-21 We know that the people realize that these judgments come from God because they curse him for sending them. But they still refuse to recognize God's authority and repent of their sins. Christians should not be surprised at the hostility and hardness of heart of unbelievers. Even when the power of God is fully and completely revealed, many will still refuse to repent. Don't wait until "just the right time" before turning to God. Do it now while you still have the chance. If you continually ignore God's warnings, you will eventually be unable to hear him at all.

Rev 16:12 The Euphrates River was a natural protective boundary against the empires to the east (Babylon, Assyria, Persia). If it dried up, nothing could hold back invading armies. The armies from the east symbolize unhindered judgment.

Rev 16:13-14 These evil spirits performing miraculous signs, who come out of the mouths of the unholy trinity, unite the rulers of the world for battle against God. The imagery of the demons coming out of the mouths of the three evil rulers signifies the verbal enticements and propaganda that will draw many people to their evil cause. (For more about demons, see the note on Rev 9:3ff, p. 1814.)

Rev 16:15 Christ will return unexpectedly (1 Thes 5:1-6), so we must always be ready for his return. We can prepare ourselves by standing firm in temptation and by being committed to God's moral standards. In what ways does your life show either your readiness or your lack of preparation for Christ's return?

▸ **REVELATION 15:5–16:21** ***(cont.)***

keep their clothing ready so they will not have to walk around naked and ashamed."

[16]And the demonic spirits gathered all the rulers and their armies to a place with the Hebrew name *Armageddon.**

[17]Then the seventh angel poured out his bowl into the air. And a mighty shout came from the throne in the Temple, saying, "It is finished!" [18]Then the thun-
der crashed and rolled, and lightning flashed. And a great earthquake struck—the worst since people were placed on the earth. [19]The great city of Babylon split into three sections, and the cities of many nations fell into heaps of rubble. So God remembered all of Babylon's sins, and he made her drink the cup that was filled with the wine of his fierce wrath. [20]And every island disappeared, and all the mountains were leveled. [21]There was a terrible hailstorm, and hailstones weighing as much as seventy-five pounds* fell from the sky onto the people below. They cursed God because of the terrible plague of the hailstorm.

The Great Prostitute

REVELATION 17:1-18

One of the seven angels who had poured out the seven bowls came over and spoke to me. "Come with me," he said, "and I will show you the judgment that is going to come on the great prostitute, who rules over many waters. [2]The kings of the world have committed adultery with her, and the people who belong to this world have been made drunk by the wine of her immorality."

[3]So the angel took me in the Spirit* into the wilder-
ness. There I saw a woman sitting on a scarlet beast that had seven heads and ten horns, and blasphemies against God were written all over it. [4]The woman wore purple and scarlet clothing and beautiful jewelry made of gold and precious gems and pearls. In her hand she held a gold goblet full of obscenities and the impurities of her immorality. [5]A mysterious name was written on her forehead: "Babylon the Great, Mother of All Prostitutes and Obscenities in the World." [6]I
could see that she was drunk—drunk with the blood of God's holy people who were witnesses for Jesus. I stared at her in complete amazement.

[7]"Why are you so amazed?" the angel asked. "I will tell you the mystery of this woman and of the beast with seven heads and ten horns on which she sits. [8]The
beast you saw was once alive but isn't now. And yet he will soon come up out of the bottomless pit* and go to eternal destruction. And the people who belong to this world, whose names were not written in the Book of Life before the world was made, will be amazed at the reappearance of this beast who had died.

[9]"This calls for a mind with understanding: The seven heads of the beast represent the seven hills

Rv 16:16 Or *Harmagedon.* **Rv 16:21** Greek *1 talent* [34 kilograms]. **Rv 17:3** Or *in spirit.* **Rv 17:8** Or *the abyss,* or *the underworld.*

Rev 16:16 This battlefield called Armageddon is near the city of Megiddo (southeast of the modern port of Haifa), which guarded a large plain in northern Israel. It is a strategic location near a prominent international highway leading north from Egypt through Israel, along the coast, and on to Babylon. Megiddo overlooked the entire plain southward toward Galilee and westward toward the mountains of Gilboa.

Rev 16:16 Sinful people will unite to fight against God in a final display of rebellion. Opposing truth, peace, justice, and morality, many are already united against Christ and his people. Your personal battle with evil foreshadows the great battle pictured here, where God will meet evil and destroy it once and for all. Be strong and courageous as you battle against sin and evil: You are fighting on the winning side.

Rev 16:17-21 For more information on Babylon and what it represents in Revelation, see the note on Revelation 14:8, p. 1821. The city's division into three sections is a symbol of its complete destruction.

Rev 17:1ff The destruction of Babylon mentioned in Revelation 16:17-21 is now described in greater detail. The "great prostitute," called Babylon, represents the early Roman Empire with its many gods and the blood of Christian martyrs on its hands. The water stands for either sea commerce or a well-watered (well-provisioned) city. The great prostitute represents the seductiveness of the governmental system that uses immoral means to gain its own pleasure, prosperity, and advantage. In contrast to the prostitute, Christ's bride, the church, is pure and obedient (Rev 19:6-9). The wicked city of Babylon contrasts with the heavenly city of Jerusalem (Rev 21:10–22:5). The original readers probably rather quickly identified Babylon with Rome, but Babylon also symbolizes any system that is hostile to God (see Rev 17:5).

Rev 17:3 The angel took John into the wilderness to see the prostitute in her reality. (The scarlet beast is either the dragon of Rev 12:3 or the beast out of the sea described in Rev 13:1.) Sometimes we can only get a clear view of reality when we step back from our daily lives and see the patterns of evil and sin around us. Retreats, conferences, and days of prayer and fasting can help us extricate ourselves from jobs, newspapers, and television and bring us to new spiritual heights. Take time to view the reality of your life and evaluate its direction and activities. Do these glorify God and renew you to serve others?

Rev 17:6 Throughout history, people have been killed for their faith. Over the last century, millions have been killed by oppressive governments, and many of those victims were believers. The woman's drunkenness shows her pleasure in her evil accomplishments and her false feeling of triumph over the church. But every martyr who has fallen before her sword has only served to strengthen the faith of the church. Persecution is by no means a thing of the past. Christians in many parts of the world know that faith in Christ amounts to a death sentence. Believers who live in places free of such persecution must not forget to pray for their brothers and sisters in Christ in those difficult parts of the world.

Rev 17:8 We met the dragon, Satan (Rev 12); we saw the beast from the sea and the power he received from Satan (Rev 13); we saw God's great judgments (Rev 14–16). In Revelation 17, a scarlet beast similar to the beast and the dragon appears as an ally of the great prostitute. The beast was alive, died, and then came back to life. The beast's resurrection symbolizes the persistence of evil. This resurgence of evil power will convince many to join forces with the beast, but those who choose the side of evil condemn themselves to the devil's fate—eternal torment.

Rev 17:8 For more information on the Book of Life, see the note on Revelation 3:5, p. 1806.

Rev 17:9-11 Here John is referring to Rome, the city famous for its seven hills. Many say that this city also symbolized all evil in the world—any person, religion, group, government, or structure that opposed Christ. Whatever view is taken of the seven hills and seven kings, this section indicates

where the woman rules. They also represent seven
kings. [10]Five kings have already fallen, the sixth now
reigns, and the seventh is yet to come, but his reign
will be brief.

[11]"The scarlet beast that was, but is no longer, is the
eighth king. He is like the other seven, and he, too, is
headed for destruction. [12]The ten horns of the beast
are ten kings who have not yet risen to power. They will
be appointed to their kingdoms for one brief moment
to reign with the beast. [13]They will all agree to give
him their power and authority. [14]Together they will
go to war against the Lamb, but the Lamb will defeat
them because he is Lord of all lords and King of all
kings. And his called and chosen and faithful ones
will be with him."

[15]Then the angel said to me, "The waters where
the prostitute is ruling represent masses of people
of every nation and language. [16]The scarlet beast and
his ten horns all hate the prostitute. They will strip
her naked, eat her flesh, and burn her remains with
fire. [17]For God has put a plan into their minds, a plan
that will carry out his purposes. They will agree to give
their authority to the scarlet beast, and so the words
of God will be fulfilled. [18]And this woman you saw in
your vision represents the great city that rules over
the kings of the world."

The Fall of Babylon

REVELATION 18:1-24

After all this I saw another angel come down from
heaven with great authority, and the earth grew bright
with his splendor. [2]He gave a mighty shout:

"Babylon is fallen—that great city is fallen!
She has become a home for demons.
She is a hideout for every foul* spirit,
a hideout for every foul vulture
and every foul and dreadful animal.*
3 For all the nations have fallen*
because of the wine of her passionate
immorality.
The kings of the world
have committed adultery with her.
Because of her desires for extravagant luxury,
the merchants of the world have
grown rich."

[4]Then I heard another voice calling from heaven,

"Come away from her, my people.
Do not take part in her sins,
or you will be punished with her.
5 For her sins are piled as high as heaven,
and God remembers her evil deeds.

Rv 18:2a Greek *unclean;* also in each of the two following phrases. **Rv 18:2b** Some manuscripts condense the last two lines to read *a hideout for every foul [unclean] and dreadful vulture.* **Rv 18:3** Some manuscripts read *have drunk.*

HOW CAN A PERSON KEEP AWAY FROM THE EVIL SYSTEM?

Here are some suggestions:

1. People must always be more important than products.
2. Keep away from pride in your own programs, plans, and successes.
3. Remember that God's will and Word must never be compromised.
4. People must always be considered above the making of money.
5. Do what is right, no matter what the cost.
6. Be involved in businesses that provide worthwhile products or services—not just things that feed the world's desires.

the climax of Satan's struggle against God. Evil's power is limited, and its destruction is on the horizon.

Rev 17:12 As we ponder the identity of the seven kings and the emergence of the ten kings, we must see John's theme of worldly power and its ultimate ineffectiveness against God and his people. Their authority only lasts "for one brief moment," symbolizing its brevity and ultimate destruction. As Christians, have we become infatuated with the worldly power of movie stars, sports celebrities, political coalitions, and world economic forces? Are you craving the power and prestige that position, wealth, and connections offer? If so, you are an easy target for Satan's great deception. Worldly power is Satan's trap; the desire for it can turn us away from God. Worship only God and make it your strongest desire to serve him.

Rev 17:16 In a dramatic turn of events, the prostitute's allies turn on her and destroy her. This is how evil operates. Destructive by its very nature, it discards its own adherents when they cease to serve its purposes. An unholy alliance is an uneasy alliance because each partner puts its own interests first.

Rev 17:17 No matter what happens, we must trust that God is still in charge, that God overrules all the plans and intrigues of the evil one, and that God's plans will happen just as he says. God even uses people opposed to him as tools to execute his will. Although he allows evil to permeate this present world, the new earth will never know sin.

Rev 18:1ff This chapter shows the complete destruction of Babylon, John's metaphorical name for the evil world power and all it represents. Everything that tries to block God's purposes will come to a violent end. (For more information on how the book of Revelation uses the name Babylon, see the note on Rev 14:8, p. 1821.)

Rev 18:2-3 Merchants in the Roman Empire grew rich by exploiting the sinful pleasures of their society. Many businesspeople today do the same thing. Businesses and governments are often based on greed, money, and power. Many bright individuals are tempted to take advantage of an evil system to enrich themselves. Christians are warned to stay free from the lure of money, status, and the good life. We are to live according to the values Christ exemplified: service, giving, self-sacrifice, obedience, and truth.

Rev 18:4-8 The people of Babylon had lived in luxury and pleasure. The city boasted, "I am queen on my throne. . . . I have no reason to mourn." The powerful, wealthy people of this world are susceptible to this same attitude. A person who is financially comfortable often feels invulnerable, secure, and in control, feeling no need for God or anyone else. This kind of attitude defies God, and his judgment against it is harsh. We are told to avoid Babylon's sins. If you are financially secure, don't become complacent and deluded by the myth of self-sufficiency. Use your resources to help others and advance God's Kingdom.

▸ **REVELATION 18:1-24** ***(cont.)***

6 Do to her as she has done to others.
Double her penalty* for all her evil deeds.
She brewed a cup of terror for others,
so brew twice as much* for her.
7 She glorified herself and lived in luxury,
so match it now with torment and sorrow.
She boasted in her heart,
'I am queen on my throne.
I am no helpless widow,
and I have no reason to mourn.'
8 Therefore, these plagues will overtake her
in a single day—
death and mourning and famine.
She will be completely consumed by fire,
for the Lord God who judges her is mighty."

9 And the kings of the world who committed adultery with her and enjoyed her great luxury will mourn
for her as they see the smoke rising from her charred
remains. 10 They will stand at a distance, terrified by
her great torment. They will cry out,

"How terrible, how terrible for you,
O Babylon, you great city!
In a single moment
God's judgment came on you."

11 The merchants of the world will weep and mourn
for her, for there is no one left to buy their goods.
12 She bought great quantities of gold, silver, jewels,
and pearls; fine linen, purple, silk, and scarlet cloth;
things made of fragrant thyine wood, ivory goods, and
objects made of expensive wood; and bronze, iron,
and marble. 13 She also bought cinnamon, spice, incense, myrrh, frankincense, wine, olive oil, fine flour,
wheat, cattle, sheep, horses, chariots, and bodies—that
is, human slaves.

14 "The fancy things you loved so much
are gone," they cry.
"All your luxuries and splendor
are gone forever,
never to be yours again."

15 The merchants who became wealthy by selling
her these things will stand at a distance, terrified by
her great torment. They will weep and cry out,

16 "How terrible, how terrible for that great city!
She was clothed in finest purple and scarlet
linens,
decked out with gold and precious stones
and pearls!
17 In a single moment
all the wealth of the city is gone!"

And all the captains of the merchant ships and their
passengers and sailors and crews will stand at a distance. 18 They will cry out as they watch the smoke ascend, and they will say, "Where is there another city as
great as this?" 19 And they will weep and throw dust on
their heads to show their grief. And they will cry out,

"How terrible, how terrible for that great city!
The shipowners became wealthy
by transporting her great wealth on the seas.
In a single moment it is all gone."

20 Rejoice over her fate, O heaven
and people of God and apostles and prophets!
For at last God has judged her
for your sakes.

21 Then a mighty angel picked up a boulder the size
of a huge millstone. He threw it into the ocean and
shouted,

"Just like this, the great city Babylon
will be thrown down with violence
and will never be found again.
22 The sound of harps, singers, flutes, and trumpets
will never be heard in you again.

Rv 18:6a Or *Give her an equal penalty.* **Rv 18:6b** Or *brew just as much.*

Rev 18:9-10 Those who are tied to the world's system will lose everything when it collapses. What they have worked for a lifetime to build up will be destroyed in one hour. Those who work only for material rewards will have nothing when they die or when their possessions are destroyed. What can we take with us to the new earth? Our faith, our Christian character, and our relationships with other believers. These are more important than any amount of money, power, or pleasure.

Rev 18:9-19 Those who are in control of various parts of the economic system will mourn at Babylon's fall. The political leaders will mourn because they were the overseers of Babylon's wealth and were in a position to enrich themselves greatly. The merchants will mourn because Babylon, the greatest customer for their goods, will be gone. The sea captains will no longer have anywhere to bring their goods because the merchants will have nowhere to sell them. The fall of the evil world system affects all who enjoyed and depended on it. No one will remain unaffected by Babylon's fall.

Rev 18:11-14 The voice from heaven (Rev 18:4) continued to prophesy against the greedy merchants. "The fancy things you loved" and the "luxuries and splendor" were gone. This list of merchandise illustrates the extreme materialism of this society. Few of these goods were necessities—most are luxuries. Even people had become commodities—sold as slaves to Babylon. The desire for nonessential luxuries had driven these merchants. Yet, how many of these luxuries listed are in your home? Most people will find that they own almost everything on this list. We are people who truly live in great luxury. We, too, are in danger of being absorbed in possessions and pleasure. Make sure that your desires lead you in the right direction. Put boundaries on them. Don't go after everything you see. Keep your desires on serving God and building his Kingdom by helping others.

Rev 18:11-19 God's people should not live for money, because money will be worthless in eternity. And they should keep on guard constantly against greed, a sin that is always ready to take over their lives. God wants us to work and to provide for our families, and he commands the proper use of money. But when the desire for money fills our lives, it becomes a false god. Don't be enslaved by the desire for wealth.

No craftsmen and no trades
will ever be found in you again.
The sound of the mill
will never be heard in you again.
23 The light of a lamp
will never shine in you again.
The happy voices of brides and grooms
will never be heard in you again.
For your merchants were the greatest in the world,
and you deceived the nations with your sorceries.
24 In your* streets flowed the blood of the prophets
and of God's holy people
and the blood of people slaughtered all over the world."

Songs of Victory in Heaven

REVELATION 19:1-10

After this, I heard what sounded like a vast crowd in heaven shouting,

"Praise the LORD!*
Salvation and glory and power belong
to our God.
2 His judgments are true and just.
He has punished the great prostitute
who corrupted the earth with her immorality.
He has avenged the murder of his servants."

3 And again their voices rang out:

"Praise the LORD!
The smoke from that city ascends forever
and ever!"

4 Then the twenty-four elders and the four living beings fell down and worshiped God, who was sitting on the throne. They cried out, "Amen! Praise the LORD!"
5 And from the throne came a voice that said,

"Praise our God,
all his servants,
all who fear him,
from the least to the greatest."

6 Then I heard again what sounded like the shout of a vast crowd or the roar of mighty ocean waves or the crash of loud thunder:

"Praise the LORD!
For the Lord our God,* the Almighty, reigns.
7 Let us be glad and rejoice,
and let us give honor to him.
For the time has come for the wedding feast
of the Lamb,
and his bride has prepared herself.
8 She has been given the finest of pure white linen
to wear."
For the fine linen represents the good deeds
of God's holy people.

Rv 18:24 Greek *her.* **Rv 19:1** Greek *Hallelujah;* also in 19:3, 4, 6. *Hallelujah* is the transliteration of a Hebrew term that means "Praise the LORD." **Rv 19:6** Some manuscripts read *the Lord God.*

Rev 19:1ff Praise is the heartfelt response to God by those who love him. The more you get to know God and realize what he has done, the more you will respond with praise. Praise is at the heart of true worship. Let your praise of God flow out of your realization of who he is and how much he loves you.

Rev 19:1-8 A vast crowd in heaven initiates the chorus of praise to God for his victory (Rev 19:1-3). Then the 24 elders (identified in the note on Rev 4:4, p. 1808) join the chorus (Rev 19:4). Finally, the great choir of heaven once again praises God—the wedding of the Lamb has come (Rev 19:6-8). (See Matt 25:1-13 where Christ compares the coming of his Kingdom to a wedding for which we must be prepared.)

Rev 19:2 The identity of this great prostitute is explained in the note on Revelation 17:1ff, p. 1824.

Rev 19:7-8 This is the culmination of human history—the judgment of the wicked and the wedding of the Lamb and his bride, the church. The church consists of all faithful believers from all time. The bride's clothing stands in sharp contrast to the gaudy clothing of the great prostitute (Rev 17:4; 18:16). The bride's clothing represents the good deeds of the believers. These good deeds are not done to earn merit, but they reflect the work of Christ to save us (Rev 7:9, 14).

Hallelujah

"Hallelujah" is an important Christian acclamation used extensively in the church's worship and liturgy from early times. *Hallelujah* is a transliteration into Greek and then into English of two Hebrew words that mean "Praise the Lord." "Hallelujah" does not appear anywhere in the New Testament except Revelation 19:1-8. There it is a chant of the saints in heaven. It was taken over into the liturgy and hymnody of the church at an early date. It became the characteristic expression of joy and was therefore sung especially at Easter, as was witnessed by Saint Augustine. You are continuing a long tradition from the early church by singing "Hallelujah" to our Lord Jesus Christ!

▸ **REVELATION 19:1-10** ***(cont.)***

9And the angel said to me, "Write this: Blessed
are those who are invited to the wedding feast of the
Lamb." And he added, "These are true words that
come from God."
10Then I fell down at his feet to worship him, but
he said, "No, don't worship me. I am a servant of God,
just like you and your brothers and sisters* who testify about their faith in Jesus. Worship only God. For
the essence of prophecy is to give a clear witness for
Jesus.*"

The Rider on the White Horse

REVELATION 19:11-21

Then I saw heaven opened, and a white horse was
standing there. Its rider was named Faithful and True,
for he judges fairly and wages a righteous war. 12His
eyes were like flames of fire, and on his head were
many crowns. A name was written on him that no one
understood except himself. 13He wore a robe dipped
in blood, and his title was the Word of God. 14The
armies of heaven, dressed in the finest of pure white
linen, followed him on white horses. 15From his mouth
came a sharp sword to strike down the nations. He will
rule them with an iron rod. He will release the fierce
wrath of God, the Almighty, like juice flowing from a
winepress. 16On his robe at his thigh* was written this
title: King of all kings and Lord of all lords.
17Then I saw an angel standing in the sun, shouting
to the vultures flying high in the sky: "Come! Gather
together for the great banquet God has prepared.
18Come and eat the flesh of kings, generals, and strong
warriors; of horses and their riders; and of all humanity, both free and slave, small and great."
19Then I saw the beast and the kings of the world
and their armies gathered together to fight against the
one sitting on the horse and his army. 20And the beast
was captured, and with him the false prophet who did

Rv 19:10a Greek *brothers.* **Rv 19:10b** Or *is the message confirmed by Jesus.* **Rv 19:16** Or *On his robe and thigh.*

Rev 19:10 The angel did not accept John's homage and worship because only God is worthy of worship. Like John, it would be easy for us to become overwhelmed by this prophetic pageant. But Jesus is the central focus of God's revelation and his redemptive plan (as announced by the prophets). As you read the book of Revelation, don't get bogged down in all the details of the awesome visions; remember that the overarching theme in all the visions is the ultimate victory of Jesus Christ over evil.

Rev 19:11 The name "Faithful and True" contrasts with the faithless and deceitful Babylon described in Revelation 18.

Rev 19:11-21 John's vision shifts again. Heaven opens, and Jesus appears—this time not as a Lamb but as a warrior on a white horse (symbolizing victory). Jesus came first as a Lamb to be a sacrifice for sin, but he will return as a conqueror and king to execute judgment (2 Thes 1:7-10). Jesus' first coming brought forgiveness; his second will bring judgment. The battle lines have been drawn between God and evil, and the world is waiting for the King to ride onto the field.

Rev 19:12 Although Jesus is called "Faithful and True" (Rev 19:11), "Word of God" (Rev 19:13), and "King of all kings and Lord of all lords" (Rev 19:16), this verse implies that no name can do him justice. He is greater than any description or expression the human mind can devise.

Rev 19:13 For more about the symbolism of Jesus' robe being dipped in blood, see the second note on Revelation 7:14, p. 1813.

Rev 19:15 This scene provides a graphic display of the wrath of God. It shows God's anger and judgment against sin and against those who have constantly rejected Christ as the means of forgiveness and reconciliation. God's wrath exists alongside his mercy. In each generation, there must be balanced preaching and teaching about God's grace and his anger against sin.

In our day, teaching about God's love and tolerance have become so predominant that God's anger seems to be mythical. Such a portrayal of God hardly warns people away from sin. Teaching about God's wrath may be watered down by some, but it is nevertheless real and will be terrible for those who have steadfastly refused him (1 Thes 1:10). In your study and teaching, do not emphasize God's mercy to the exclusion of his wrath.

Rev 19:16 This title indicates our God's sovereignty. Most of the world is worshiping the beast, the Antichrist, whom they believe has all power and authority. Then suddenly out of heaven ride Christ and his army of angels—the "King of all kings and Lord of all lords." His entrance signals the end of the false powers.

Rev 19:17 This "great banquet" is a grim contrast to the wedding feast of the Lamb (Rev 19:9). One is a celebration; the other is devastation.

Rev 19:19 The beast is identified in the note on Revelation 13:1, p. 1819.

Rev 19:19-21 The battle lines have been drawn, and the greatest confrontation in the history of the world is about to begin. The beast (the Antichrist) and the false prophet have gathered the governments and armies of the earth under the Antichrist's rule. The enemy armies believe they have come of their own volition; in reality, God has summoned them to battle in order to defeat them. That they would even presume to fight against God shows how their pride and rebellion have distorted their thinking. There really is no fight, however, because the victory was won when Jesus died on the cross for sin and rose from the dead. Thus, the evil leaders are immediately captured and sent to their punishment, and the forces of evil are annihilated.

THE BEGINNING AND THE END

The Bible records for us the beginning of the world and the end of the world. The story of mankind, from beginning to end—from the fall into sin to redemption and God's ultimate victory over evil—is found in the pages of the Bible.

Genesis	Revelation
The sun is created.	The sun is not needed.
Satan is victorious.	Satan is defeated.
Sin enters the human race.	Sin is banished.
People run and hide from God.	People are invited to live with God forever.
People are cursed.	The curse is removed.
Tears are shed, with sorrow for sin.	No more sin; no more tears or sorrow.
The garden and earth are cursed.	God's city is glorified; the earth is made new.
Paradise is lost.	Paradise is regained.
People are doomed to death.	Death is defeated; believers live forever with God.

mighty miracles on behalf of the beast—miracles that deceived all who had accepted the mark of the beast and who worshiped his statue. Both the beast and his false prophet were thrown alive into the fiery lake of burning sulfur. [21]Their entire army was killed by the sharp sword that came from the mouth of the one riding the white horse. And the vultures all gorged themselves on the dead bodies.

The Thousand Years

REVELATION 20:1-6

Then I saw an angel coming down from heaven with the key to the bottomless pit* and a heavy chain in his hand. [2]He seized the dragon—that old serpent, who is the devil, Satan—and bound him in chains for a thousand years. [3]The angel threw him into the bottomless pit, which he then shut and locked so Satan could not deceive the nations anymore until the thousand years were finished. Afterward he must be released for a little while.

[4]Then I saw thrones, and the people sitting on them had been given the authority to judge. And I saw the souls of those who had been beheaded for their testimony about Jesus and for proclaiming the word of God. They had not worshiped the beast or his statue, nor accepted his mark on their foreheads or their hands. They all came to life again, and they reigned with Christ for a thousand years.

[5]This is the first resurrection. (The rest of the dead did not come back to life until the thousand years had ended.) [6]Blessed and holy are those who share in the first resurrection. For them the second death holds no power, but they will be priests of God and of Christ and will reign with him a thousand years.

The Defeat of Satan

REVELATION 20:7-10

When the thousand years come to an end, Satan will be let out of his prison. [8]He will go out to deceive the nations—called Gog and Magog—in every corner of the earth. He will gather them together for battle—a mighty army, as numberless as sand along the seashore. [9]And I saw them as they went up on the broad plain of the earth and surrounded God's people and the beloved city. But fire from heaven came down on the attacking armies and consumed them.

Rv 20:1 Or *the abyss,* or *the underworld;* also in 20:3.

Rev 19:20 The fiery lake of burning sulfur is the final destination of the wicked. This lake is different from the bottomless pit referred to in Revelation 9:1. The Antichrist and the false prophet are thrown into the fiery lake. Then their leader, Satan himself, will later be thrown into that lake (Rev 20:10), and finally death and the grave (Rev 20:14). Afterward, everyone whose name is not recorded in the Book of Life will be thrown into the fiery lake (Rev 20:15).

Rev 20:1 The angel and the bottomless pit are explained in the notes on Revelation 9:1, p. 1814; Revelation 19:20, above.

Rev 20:2 The dragon, Satan, is discussed in more detail in the notes on Revelation 12:3-4, p. 1818; Revelation 12:9, p. 1818. The dragon is not bound as punishment at this time (that occurs in Rev 20:10) but so that he cannot deceive the nations.

Rev 20:2-4 The 1,000 years are often referred to as the Millennium (Latin for 1,000). Just how and when this 1,000 years takes place is understood differently among Christian scholars. The three major positions on this issue are called postmillennialism, premillennialism, and amillennialism.

(1) *Postmillennialism* looks for a literal 1,000-year period of peace on earth ushered in by the church. At the end of the 1,000 years, Satan will be unleashed once more, but then Christ will return to defeat him and reign forever. Christ's second coming will not occur until after the 1,000-year period.

(2) *Premillennialism* also views the 1,000 years as a literal time period but holds that Christ's second coming initiates his 1,000-year reign and that this reign occurs before the final removal of Satan.

(3) *Amillennialism* understands the 1,000-year period to be symbolic of the time between Christ's ascension and his return. This Millennium is the reign of Christ in the hearts of believers and in his church; thus, it is another way of referring to the church age. This period will end with the second coming of Christ.

These different views about the Millennium need not cause division and controversy in the church because each view acknowledges what is most crucial to Christianity: Christ will return, defeat Satan, and reign forever! Whatever and whenever the Millennium is, Jesus Christ will unite all believers; therefore, we should not let this issue divide us.

Rev 20:3 John doesn't say why God releases Satan for a little while, but it is part of God's plan for judging the world. Perhaps it is to expose those who rebel against God in their hearts and confirm those who are truly faithful to God. Whatever the reason, Satan's release results in the final destruction of all evil (Rev 20:12-15).

Rev 20:4 The beast's mark is explained in the note on Revelation 13:16-18, p. 1820.

Rev 20:5-6 Christians hold two basic views concerning this first resurrection: (1) Some believe that the first resurrection is spiritual (in our hearts at salvation) and that the Millennium is our spiritual reign with Christ between his first and second comings. During this time, we are priests of God because Christ reigns in our hearts. In this view, the second resurrection is the bodily resurrection of all people for judgment. (2) Others believe that the first resurrection occurs after Satan has been set aside. It is a physical resurrection of believers, who then reign with Christ on the earth for a literal 1,000 years. The second resurrection occurs at the end of this Millennium in order to judge unbelievers who have died.

Rev 20:6 The second death is spiritual death—everlasting separation from God (see Rev 21:8).

Rev 20:7-9 Gog and Magog symbolize all the forces of evil that band together to battle God. Noah's son Japheth had a son named Magog (Gen 10:2). Ezekiel presents Gog as a leader of forces against Israel (Ezek 38–39).

Rev 20:9 This is not a typical battle where the outcome is in doubt during the heat of the conflict. Here again, there is no contest. Two mighty forces of evil—those of the beast (Rev 19:19) and of Satan (Rev 20:8)—unite to do battle against God. The Bible uses just two verses to describe each battle: The evil beast and his forces are captured and thrown into the fiery lake (Rev 19:20-21), and fire from heaven consumes Satan and his attacking armies (Rev 20:9-10). For God, it is as easy as that. There will be no doubt, no worry, no second thoughts for believers about whether they have chosen the right side. If you are with God, you will experience this tremendous victory with Christ.

▸ **REVOLUTION 20:7-10** ***(cont.)***

[10]Then the devil, who had deceived them, was
thrown into the fiery lake of burning sulfur, joining
the beast and the false prophet. There they will be
tormented day and night forever and ever.

The Final Judgment

REVELATION 20:11-15

And I saw a great white throne and the one sitting
on it. The earth and sky fled from his presence, but
they found no place to hide. [12]I saw the dead, both
great and small, standing before God's throne. And
the books were opened, including the Book of Life.
And the dead were judged according to what they had
done, as recorded in the books. [13]The sea gave up its
dead, and death and the grave* gave up their dead.
And all were judged according to their deeds. [14]Then
death and the grave were thrown into the lake of fire.
This lake of fire is the second death. [15]And anyone
whose name was not found recorded in the Book of
Life was thrown into the lake of fire.

The New Jerusalem

REVELATION 21:1-22:6

Then I saw a new heaven and a new earth, for the old
heaven and the old earth had disappeared. And the
sea was also gone. [2]And I saw the holy city, the new
Jerusalem, coming down from God out of heaven like
a bride beautifully dressed for her husband.

[3]I heard a loud shout from the throne, saying, "Look,
God's home is now among his people! He will live with
them, and they will be his people. God himself will be
with them.* [4]He will wipe every tear from their eyes,
and there will be no more death or sorrow or crying
or pain. All these things are gone forever."

[5]And the one sitting on the throne said, "Look, I
am making everything new!" And then he said to me,
"Write this down, for what I tell you is trustworthy
and true." [6]And he also said, "It is finished! I am the
Alpha and the Omega—the Beginning and the End. To
all who are thirsty I will give freely from the springs
of the water of life. [7]All who are victorious will inherit
all these blessings, and I will be their God, and they
will be my children.

[8]"But cowards, unbelievers, the corrupt, murderers, the immoral, those who practice witchcraft, idol
worshipers, and all liars—their fate is in the fiery lake
of burning sulfur. This is the second death."

[9]Then one of the seven angels who held the seven
bowls containing the seven last plagues came and said
to me, "Come with me! I will show you the bride, the
wife of the Lamb."

Rv 20:13 Greek *and Hades;* also in 20:14. **Rv 21:3** Some manuscripts read *God himself will be with them, their God.*

Rev 20:10 Satan's power is not eternal—he will meet his doom. He began his evil work in people at the beginning (Gen 3:1-6) and continues it today, but he will be destroyed when he is thrown into the fiery lake of burning sulfur. The devil will be released from the bottomless pit ("his prison"; Rev 20:7), but he will never be released from the fiery lake. He will never be a threat to anyone again.

Rev 20:12-15 At the judgment, the books will be opened. The Book of Life contains the names of those who have put their trust in Christ to save them. These books also contain the recorded deeds of everyone, good or evil. Everyone's life will be reviewed and evaluated. No one is saved by deeds, but deeds are seen as clear evidence of a person's actual relationship with God. Jesus will look at how we have handled gifts, opportunities, and responsibilities. God's gracious gift of salvation does not free us from the requirement of faithful obedience and service. Each of us must serve Christ in the best way we know and live each day knowing the books will one day be opened.

Rev 20:14 Death and the grave are thrown into the lake of fire. God's judgment is finished. The lake of fire is the ultimate destination of everything wicked—Satan, the beast, the false prophet, the demons, death, the grave, and all those whose names are not recorded in the Book of Life because they did not place their faith in Jesus Christ. John's vision does not permit any gray areas in God's judgment. If by faith we have not identified with Christ, confessing him as Lord, there will be no hope, no second chance, no other appeal.

Rev 21:1 The earth as we know it will not last forever, but after God's great judgment, he will create a new earth (see Rom 8:18-21; 2 Pet 3:7-13). God had also promised Isaiah that he would create a new and eternal earth (Isa 65:17; 66:22). The sea is gone as well; in John's time, the sea was viewed as dangerous and changeable. It was also the source of the beast (Rev 13:1). We don't know how the new earth will look or where it will be, but God and his followers—those whose names are written in the Book of Life—will be united to live there forever. Will you be there?

Rev 21:2-3 The new Jerusalem is where God lives among his people. Instead of our going up to meet him, he comes down to be with us, just as God became man in Jesus Christ and lived among us (John 1:14). Wherever God reigns, there is peace, security, and love.

Rev 21:3-4 Have you ever wondered what eternity will be like? The "holy city, the new Jerusalem" is described as the place where God will remove all sorrows. Forevermore, there will be no death, sorrow, crying, or pain. What a wonderful truth! No matter what you are going through, it's not the last word—God has written the final chapter, and it is about true fulfillment and eternal joy for those who love him. We do not know as much as we would like, but it is enough to know that eternity with God will be more wonderful than we could ever imagine.

Rev 21:5 God is the Creator. The Bible begins with the majestic story of his creation of the universe, and it concludes with his creation of a new heaven and a new earth. This is a tremendous hope and encouragement for the believer. When we are with God, our sins forgiven and our future secure, we will be like Christ. We will be made perfect like him.

Rev 21:6 Just as God finished the work of creation (Gen 2:1-3) and Jesus finished the work of redemption (John 19:30), so the Trinity will finish the entire plan of salvation by inviting the redeemed into a new creation.

Rev 21:6 For more about the water of life, see the note on Revelation 22:1, p. 1832.

Rev 21:7-8 The "cowards" are the fearful ones who abandon Christ at the threats of the beast. They fear persecution so badly that they choose temporary safety over eternal life. They are put in the same list as the unbelieving, the corrupt, the murderers, the immoral, the idolaters, the liars, and those practicing magic arts.

By contrast, people who are victorious "endure to the end" (Mark 13:13). They will receive the blessings that God promised: To follow Christ requires boldness and bravery to stand for him when oppression occurs. Pray for courage to do what is right no matter what pressure you face. Those who can endure the testing of evil and remain faithful will be rewarded by God.

Rev 21:8 The lake is explained in the notes on Revelation 19:20, p. 1829; Revelation 20:14, above. The second death is spiritual

[10]So he took me in the Spirit* to a great, high mountain, and he showed me the holy city, Jerusalem, descending out of heaven from God. [11]It shone with the
glory of God and sparkled like a precious stone—like
jasper as clear as crystal. [12]The city wall was broad and
high, with twelve gates guarded by twelve angels. And
the names of the twelve tribes of Israel were written
on the gates. [13]There were three gates on each side—
east, north, south, and west. [14]The wall of the city had
twelve foundation stones, and on them were written
the names of the twelve apostles of the Lamb.
[15]The angel who talked to me held in his hand a
gold measuring stick to measure the city, its gates,
and its wall. [16]When he measured it, he found it was
a square, as wide as it was long. In fact, its length and
width and height were each 1,400 miles.* [17]Then he
measured the walls and found them to be 216 feet
thick* (according to the human standard used by
the angel).
[18]The wall was made of jasper, and the city was pure
gold, as clear as glass. [19]The wall of the city was built on
foundation stones inlaid with twelve precious stones:*
the first was jasper, the second sapphire, the third
agate, the fourth emerald, [20]the fifth onyx, the sixth
carnelian, the seventh chrysolite, the eighth beryl,
the ninth topaz, the tenth chrysoprase, the eleventh
jacinth, the twelfth amethyst.
[21]The twelve gates were made of pearls—each gate
from a single pearl! And the main street was pure gold,
as clear as glass.
[22]I saw no temple in the city, for the Lord God Almighty and the Lamb are its temple. [23]And the city has
no need of sun or moon, for the glory of God illuminates the city, and the Lamb is its light. [24]The nations
will walk in its light, and the kings of the world will
enter the city in all their glory. [25]Its gates will never
be closed at the end of day because there is no night
there. [26]And all the nations will bring their glory and
honor into the city. [27]Nothing evil* will be allowed to
enter, nor anyone who practices shameful idolatry and
dishonesty—but only those whose names are written
in the Lamb's Book of Life.

Rv 21:10 Or *in spirit.* **Rv 21:16** Greek *12,000 stadia* [2,220 kilometers]. **Rv 21:17** Greek *144 cubits* [65 meters]. **Rv 21:19** The identification of some of these gemstones is uncertain. **Rv 21:27** Or *ceremonially unclean.*

WHAT WE KNOW ABOUT ETERNITY

The Bible devotes much less space to describing eternity than it does to convincing people that eternal life is available as a free gift from God. Most of the brief descriptions of eternity would be more accurately called hints, since they use terms and ideas from present experience to describe what we cannot fully grasp until we are there ourselves. These references hint at aspects of what our future will be like if we have accepted Christ's gift of eternal life.

Description	*Reference*
A place prepared for us	**John 14:2-3**
Unlimited by physical properties	**John 20:19, 26**
Like Jesus	**1 Jn 3:2**
New bodies	**1 Cor 15:35-49**
A wonderful experience	**1 Cor 2:9**
A new environment	**Rev 21:1**
A new experience of God's presence	**1 Cor 13:12; Rev 21:3**
New emotions	**Rev 21:4**
No more death	**Rev 21:4**

death, meaning either eternal torment or destruction. In either case, it is permanent separation from God.

Rev 21:10ff The rest of the chapter is a stunning description of the new city of God. The vision is symbolic and shows us that our new home with God will defy description. We will not be disappointed by it in any way.

Rev 21:12-14 The new Jerusalem is a picture of God's future home for his people. The 12 tribes of Israel (Rev 21:12) probably represent all the faithful in the Old Testament; the 12 apostles (Rev 21:14) represent the church. Thus, both believing Gentiles and Jews who have been faithful to God will live together on the new earth.

Rev 21:15-17 The city's measurements are symbolic of a place that will hold all God's people. These measurements are all multiples of 12, the number for God's people: There were 12 tribes in Israel, and 12 apostles who started the church. The walls are 144 (12 x 12) cubits (216 feet) thick. There are 12 layers in the walls, and 12 gates in the city; and the length, width, and height are all the same, 12,000 stadia (1,400 miles). The new Jerusalem is a perfect cube, the same shape as the Most Holy Place in the Temple (1 Kgs 6:20). These measurements illustrate that this new home will be perfect for us.

Rev 21:18-21 The picture of walls made of jewels reveals that the new Jerusalem will be a place of purity and durability—it will last forever.

Rev 21:22-24 The Temple, the center of God's presence among his people, was the primary place of worship. No temple is needed in the new city because God's presence will be everywhere. God will be the light in the new Jerusalem. Light represents what is good, pure, true, holy, and reliable. Darkness represents what is sinful and evil. That God's glory illuminates the city means that the city will be enveloped by him, who is perfectly holy and true. Light is also related to truth in that it exposes whatever exists. Just as darkness cannot exist in the presence of light, so sin cannot exist in the presence of a holy God. The city will be completely without sin and evil. We will be able to worship God throughout the city; nothing will hinder us from being with him.

Rev 21:25-27 Not everyone will be allowed into the new Jerusalem, but "only those whose names are written in the Lamb's Book of Life." (The Book of Life is explained in the notes on Rev 3:5, p. 1806; Rev 20:12-15, p. 1830.) Don't think that you will get in because of your background, personality, or good behavior. Eternal life is available to you only because of what Jesus, the Lamb, has done. Trust him today to secure your citizenship in his new creation.

▶ **REVELATION 21:1–22:6** ***(cont.)***

22:1 Then the angel showed me a river with the water of life, clear as crystal, flowing from the throne of God and of the Lamb. [2]It flowed down the center of the main street. On each side of the river grew a tree of life, bearing twelve crops of fruit,* with a fresh crop each month. The leaves were used for medicine to heal the nations.

[3]No longer will there be a curse upon anything. For the throne of God and of the Lamb will be there, and his servants will worship him. [4]And they will see his face, and his name will be written on their foreheads. [5]And there will be no night there—no need for lamps or sun—for the Lord God will shine on them. And they will reign forever and ever.

[6]Then the angel said to me, "Everything you have heard and seen is trustworthy and true. The Lord God, who inspires his prophets,* has sent his angel to tell his servants what will happen soon.*"

Jesus Is Coming

REVELATION 22:7-21

"Look, I am coming soon! Blessed are those who obey the words of prophecy written in this book.*"

[8]I, John, am the one who heard and saw all these things. And when I heard and saw them, I fell down to worship at the feet of the angel who showed them to me. [9]But he said, "No, don't worship me. I am a servant of God, just like you and your brothers the prophets, as well as all who obey what is written in this book. Worship only God!"

[10]Then he instructed me, "Do not seal up the prophetic words in this book, for the time is near. [11]Let the one who is doing harm continue to do harm; let the one who is vile continue to be vile; let the one who is righteous continue to live righteously; let the one who is holy continue to be holy."

[12]"Look, I am coming soon, bringing my reward with me to repay all people according to their deeds. [13]I am the Alpha and the Omega, the First and the Last, the Beginning and the End."

[14]Blessed are those who wash their robes. They will be permitted to enter through the gates of the city and eat the fruit from the tree of life. [15]Outside the city are the dogs—the sorcerers, the sexually immoral, the murderers, the idol worshipers, and all who love to live a lie.

Rv 22:2 Or *twelve kinds of fruit.* **Rv 22:6a** Or *The Lord, the God of the spirits of the prophets.* **Rv 22:6b** Or *suddenly,* or *quickly;* also in 22:7, 12, 20. **Rv 22:7** Or *scroll;* also in 22:9, 10, 18, 19.

Rev 22:1 The water of life is a symbol of eternal life. Jesus used this same image with the Samaritan woman (John 4:7-14). It pictures the fullness of life with God and the eternal blessings that come when we believe in him and allow him to satisfy our spiritual thirst (see Rev 22:17).

Rev 22:2 This tree of life is like the tree of life in the Garden of Eden (Gen 2:9). After Adam and Eve sinned, they were forbidden to eat from the tree of life because they could not have eternal life as long as they were under sin's control. But because of the forgiveness of sin through the blood of Jesus, there will be no evil or sin in this city. We will be able to eat freely from the tree of life when sin's control over us is destroyed and our eternity with God is secure.

Rev 22:2 Why would the nations need to be healed if all evil is gone? John is quoting from Ezekiel 47:12, where water flowing from the Temple produces trees with healing leaves. He is not implying that there will be illness in the new earth; he is emphasizing that the water of life produces health and strength wherever it goes.

Rev 22:3 "No longer will there be a curse upon anything" means that nothing accursed will be in God's presence. This fulfills Zechariah's prophecy (see Zech 14:11).

Rev 22:8-9 The first of the Ten Commandments is "You must not have any other god but me" (Exod 20:3). Jesus said that the greatest command of Moses' laws was "You must love the LORD your God with all your heart, all your soul, and all your mind" (Matt 22:37). Here, at the end of the Bible, this truth is reiterated. The angel instructs John to worship God, and worship is a major emphasis in Revelation. The first step toward meaningful worship is a desire to know God. If we thirst for him, the Bible promises that he will provide for us and satisfy our needs. Would you like your worship to be completely transformed? Confess any sins that might be hindering your fellowship with God. Then ask God to stir your heart, to instill within you an unquenchable thirst to know him. Meditate upon how God has revealed himself in the Bible, and ask him to reveal himself to you again. When you see God in a new way, worship will be your only fitting response.

Rev 22:10-11 The angel tells John what to do after his vision is over. Instead of sealing up what he has written, as Daniel was commanded to do (Dan 12:4-12), the book is to be left open so that all can read and understand. Daniel's message was sealed because it was not a message for Daniel's time. But the book of Revelation was a message for John's time, and it is relevant today. As Christ's return gets closer, there is a greater polarization between God's followers and Satan's followers. We must read the book of Revelation, hear its message, and be prepared for Christ's imminent return.

Rev 22:12-14 Those who wash their robes are those who seek to purify themselves from a sinful way of life. They strive daily to remain faithful and ready for Christ's return. (This concept is also explained in the second note on Rev 7:14, p. 1813.)

Rev 22:14 In Eden, Adam and Eve were barred from any access to the tree of life because of their sin (Gen 3:22-24). In the new earth, God's people will eat from the tree of life because their sins have been removed by Christ's death and resurrection. Those who eat the fruit of this tree will live forever. If Jesus has forgiven your sins, you will have the right to eat from this tree. (For more on this concept, see the first note on Rev 22:2, above.)

Rev 22:15 Jesus will exclude from the holy city those "who love to live a lie." These are people whose lives have gone so wrong that they resemble Satan, who deceived the whole world (Rev 12:9; 13:13-15; 16:14). They are hypocrites, trying to live one way while pretending to believe another. They are like the Nicolaitans (mentioned in Rev 2:15), who were among the believers but compromised their faith in order to also include worship of the Roman emperor. John records Jesus' statement that Satan is the father of lies (John 8:44).

Today we see leaders who twist the truth to serve their purposes. Many people have lost the ability to distinguish what's true from what they wish was true. Dishonest people soon begin to believe the lies they construct around themselves. Then they lose the ability to tell the difference between truth and lies. By believing your own lies, you deceive yourself, you alienate yourself from God, and you lose credibility in all your relationships. In the long run, honesty wins out.

16"I, Jesus, have sent my angel to give you this
message for the churches. I am both the source of
David and the heir to his throne.* I am the bright
morning star."

17The Spirit and the bride say, "Come." Let anyone
who hears this say, "Come." Let anyone who is thirsty
come. Let anyone who desires drink freely from the
water of life. 18And I solemnly declare to everyone who
hears the words of prophecy written in this book: If
anyone adds anything to what is written here, God
will add to that person the plagues described in this
book. 19And if anyone removes any of the words from
this book of prophecy, God will remove that person's
share in the tree of life and in the holy city that are
described in this book.

20He who is the faithful witness to all these things
says, "Yes, I am coming soon!"

Amen! Come, Lord Jesus!

21May the grace of the Lord Jesus be with God's
holy people.*

Rv 22:16 Greek *I am the root and offspring of David.* **Rv 22:21** Other manuscripts read *be with all;* still others read *be with all of God's holy people.* Some manuscripts add *Amen.*

Rev 22:16 Jesus is both David's "source" and "heir." As the Creator of all, Jesus existed long before David. As a human, he was one of David's direct descendants (see Isa 11:1-5; Matt 1:1-17). As the Messiah, he is the "bright morning star," the light of salvation to all.

Rev 22:17 Both the Holy Spirit and the bride, the church, extend the invitation to all the world to come to Jesus and experience the joys of salvation in Christ.

Rev 22:17 When Jesus met the Samaritan woman at the well, he told her of the living water that he could supply (John 4:10-15). This image is used again as Christ invites anyone to come and drink of the water of life. The Good News is unlimited in scope—all people everywhere may come. Salvation cannot be earned, but God gives it freely. We live in a world desperately thirsty for living water, and many are dying of thirst. But it's still not too late. Let us invite everyone to come and drink.

Rev 22:18-19 This warning is given to those who might purposefully distort the message in this book. Moses gave a similar warning in Deuteronomy 4:1-4. We, too, must handle the Bible with care and great respect so that we do not distort its message, even unintentionally. We should be quick to put its principles into practice in our life. No human explanation or interpretation of God's Word should be elevated to the same authority as the text itself.

Rev 22:20 We don't know the day or the hour, but Jesus is coming soon and unexpectedly. This is good news to those who trust him, but a terrible message for those who have rejected him and stand under judgment. Soon means "at any moment," and we must be ready for him, always prepared for his return. Would Jesus' sudden appearance catch you off guard?

Rev 22:21 Revelation closes human history as Genesis opened it—in paradise. But there is one distinct difference in Revelation—evil is gone forever. Genesis describes Adam and Eve walking and talking with God; Revelation describes people worshiping God face to face. Genesis describes a garden with an evil serpent; Revelation describes a perfect city with no evil. The Garden of Eden was destroyed by sin; but paradise is re-created in the new Jerusalem.

The book of Revelation ends with an urgent plea: "Come, Lord Jesus!" In a world of problems, persecution, evil, and immorality, Christ calls us to endure in our faith. Our efforts to better our world are important, but their results cannot compare with the transformation that Jesus will bring about when he returns. He alone controls human history, forgives sin, and will re-create the earth and bring lasting peace.

Revelation is, above all, a book of hope. It shows that no matter what happens on earth, God is in control. It promises that evil will not last forever. And it depicts the wonderful reward that is waiting for all those who believe in Jesus Christ as Savior and Lord.

On each side of the river grew a tree of life,
bearing twelve crops of fruit, with a fresh crop each month.
The leaves were used for medicine to heal the nations.
Revelation 22:2

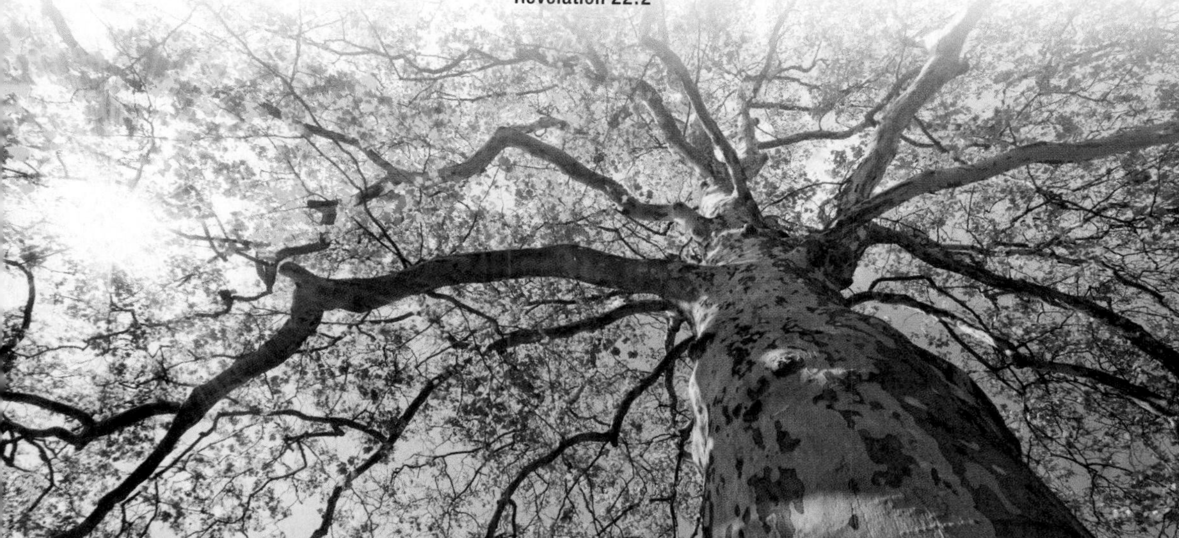

A CHRISTIAN WORKER'S RESOURCE

This section includes:

How to Become a Christian

As a believer, you will have the opportunity to talk to others about your faith. At times you will find a person who wants to know how to become a Christian. Following is a guide you can use to help a person understand what it means to begin a relationship with Christ.

FACT: You were created by a loving God. You have great value. God loves you and wants to have a personal relationship with you.

SET-UP: Explain to the person that the world tells us that we are accidents of nature. We began as ooze in a pond, evolved into apes, and finally into humans. We live, we die, so we should grab for all we can get in this life—after all, that's the only way to fulfillment. In contrast, the Bible tells us that we are *not* accidents. We were created by a loving God who knew about us before we were born. We are here for a purpose, and we can find ultimate fulfillment by finding a relationship with him.

Read the following verses and make the following points:

God created you.

Psalm 139:13-16. *You made all the delicate, inner parts of my body and knit me together in my mother's womb. Thank you for making me so wonderfully complex! Your workmanship is marvelous—how well I know it. You watched me as I was being formed in utter seclusion, as I was woven together in the dark of the womb. You saw me before I was born. Every day of my life was recorded in your book. Every moment was laid out before a single day had passed.*

God knew you before you were born—even while you were in your mother's womb. He knows all about your family and your life until now. [Be sensitive that some people have had difficult circumstances in their lives. Explain that God loves them deeply, even if we can't understand everything that has happened to us.] He wants to give you a brand new start and a new way of living. He can do that when you give him your life. Why would you do that? Because . . .

God wants to have a personal relationship with you.

John 17:3. *And this is the way to have eternal life—to know you, the only true God, and Jesus Christ, the one you sent to earth.*

God is not some "force," an unspeaking or unseeing idol, or merely another name for your own self-esteem. Instead, God is a person, your Creator, who created you to be in relationship with him. Why? Because . . .

God loves you.

John 3:16. *For God loved the world so much that he gave his one and only Son, so that everyone who believes in him will not perish but have eternal life.*

You can turn your life over to God's control because he loves you and wants the very best for you. In fact, he loves you so much that he gave his Son, Jesus, to die on the cross for you. I'll explain more about that in a minute. I just want you to realize that when you trust God, you are actually trusting the One who created you. When you turn your life over to him, you are giving your life to the One who knows you inside out. Don't you think that's a good place to put your trust?

FACT: Your sin keeps you from having a personal relationship with God.

SET-UP: Most people don't understand the concept of sin. We live in a fairly amoral world that believes each person can decide what is right, what is true, and what is "moral"—whatever that might mean. Television and movies don't help with their portrayals of happy people blatantly living sinful lives. You will probably need to explain that God has set some standards about right and wrong, and that there is such a thing as "sin."

What is sin?

James 4:17. *Remember, it is sin to know what you ought to do and then not do it.*

1 John 3:4. *Everyone who sins is breaking God's law, for all sin is contrary to the law of God.*

God is holy and perfect; people are sinful. You probably know that for yourself—if you tried to be perfect for a day, you'd quickly discover that you couldn't do it. [Here, you can draw a picture of a chasm, with a stick figure on one side and the word "God" on the other. Put the word "sin" in the chasm and explain further.] Sin means not understanding or even caring about what is "right." You defy God when you know what is right and then refuse to do it.

Who has sinned?

Romans 3:23. *For everyone has sinned; we all fall short of God's glorious standard.*

Romans 5:17. *For the sin of this one man, Adam, caused death to rule over many.*

The Bible says "everyone has sinned." We simply cannot help it—we're human. When Adam sinned (way back in the Garden of Eden in the book of Genesis), sin entered the human race and sinfulness is now part of our natures. You might be asking, "So what?"

What's so bad about sin?

Romans 6:23. *For the wages of sin is death.*

Isaiah 59:2. *It's your sins that have cut you off from God.*

Sin leads to death. That's a big problem! Because God is perfect, he cannot have anything to do with us because we are sinners. He wants to have a personal relationship with us but our sin prevents it! So what did God do?

FACT: Only through Jesus Christ can you have a personal relationship with God.

SET-UP: Sometimes people don't understand the concept of having a "relationship" with a being they cannot see or touch. Yet it is a reality. That's why Jesus Christ came. He was a human being who lived on this earth so that we could understand what God is like. At this point you may discover that the person has lots of questions (for example, "How can God be God and also Jesus?"), the details of which can send you off the point. If that happens, explain that you don't have all of the answers to some of those kinds of questions—in fact, some questions are simply unanswerable because we humans cannot completely understand God and how he works. Explain that having a relationship with Christ is a spiritual reality that must be experienced, and that doing so will answer a lot of questions. The key questions to deal with at this point in the discussion include:

Why Jesus Christ?

John 14:6. *Jesus told him, "I am the way, the truth, and the life. No one can come to the Father except through me."*

God decided to deal with our sin. However, he had made it clear throughout the Old Testament that sin leads to death. In the Old Testament, God asked people to sacrifice animals as a way to show that their sins required payment by death, and he allowed the animals to substitute for the people asking forgiveness. But that was only temporary. God's plan all along was to send his Son, Jesus—a perfect human being—to be the final and ultimate sacrifice.

Why did Jesus have to die?

1 Peter 3:18. *Christ suffered for our sins once for all time. He never sinned, but he died for sinners to bring you safely home to God. He suffered physical death, but he was raised to life in the Spirit.*

Jesus died to take the penalty our sins deserved. In essence, he took our punishment so that we wouldn't have to! Now, because of Jesus, the way is prepared for us to be able to have a personal relationship with a holy God. [At this point, you can draw a cross in the chasm, connecting the two sides. On the cross, write the word "Jesus." This visually shows that Jesus is the only way to God. Also add that Jesus did not stay dead. He rose from the dead, which is a promise to us that we will also rise from the dead and go to heaven to be with him.] So what do you need to do next?

FACT: You must personally respond by trusting Jesus Christ as Savior and Lord.

SET-UP: The fact of salvation means nothing unless a person accepts it personally. Emphasize that even if the person grew up in church, it is still necessary to accept Jesus personally. Also emphasize that even if the person has led a terrible life, no one is too bad for God—a person does not have to "clean up their act" before coming to Christ. In fact, Jesus died to take away all that sin and to help the person start anew. So emphasize that being good is not good enough, yet no one is too bad to be able to be forgiven—God wants all people to come to him. All people need to trust in Jesus in order to be saved. So what kind of response should a person have? Talk about the following:

You respond with belief in Christ.

Romans 10:9-10. *If you confess with your mouth that Jesus is Lord and believe in your heart that God raised him from the dead, you will be saved. For it is by believing in your heart that you are made right with God, and it is by confessing with your mouth that you are saved.*

You simply need to believe. That doesn't mean that you don't have any questions or that you understand everything. It simply means recognizing that you are indeed a sinner in need of a Savior. You recognize that you cannot be good enough on your own. And you understand that God loved you so much that he sent Jesus to save you. If you believe that, say so.

You respond by receiving Christ.

John 1:12. *But to all who believed him and accepted him, he gave the right to become children of God.*

"Receiving Christ" means acknowledging your belief in Christ, inviting him to come into your life, turning to God from your present way of living (repentance), and then beginning the adventure of letting God direct your life! And the moment you ask, it's done. Jesus has come in!

QUESTION: Would you like to accept Jesus as your Savior?

SET-UP: If the person is ready, explain that a person can express belief and trust in Christ through prayer. Prayer is simply talking to God. He knows what a person means even when it is difficult to express. Tell the person to pray spontaneously, or to repeat the following prayer after you:

Dear God, I know that my sin has separated me from you. Thank you that Jesus Christ died in my place. I ask Jesus to forgive my sin and to come into my life. Please begin to direct my life. Thank you for giving me eternal life. In Jesus' name, Amen.

That's it! You can officially welcome this person into God's family—your new brother or sister in Christ!

Just as a baby is not born and then left to fend for themselves, so a newborn believer in God's family needs some guidance. As the one who introduced this person to Christ, you should attempt to help this new believer grow. The following pages will show you how.

■ How to Follow Up with a New Believer

Helping a New Believer Take the Next Steps in the Christian Life

If you have had the privilege of helping someone make the step of faith and accept Jesus as Savior, you want to continue that relationship if possible by offering some help to that new believer about the basics of the Christian faith. Your friend may wonder: "What does 'being a Christian' mean? How does it make a difference in my life? What should I be doing differently from now on?" This section gives you fourteen discussion points to use with a new believer. You don't need to (and shouldn't) cover all of these points in one sitting. These are designed to be discussion points that you can use over the course of several weeks as part of discipling someone in understanding the basic tenets of the Christian faith and ways they can keep growing.

Tell your friend that you would like to get together regularly (in person, by phone, by e-mail, by instant messaging, whatever works) over the next few weeks to talk about the next steps in walking with God. After you've worked out a schedule, give the person a first assignment—to get a Bible (if the person doesn't already have one—or doesn't have one in an easy-to-read translation). You might offer to go with the person, as the first trip to a Christian bookstore and its wide array of Bibles can be a bit daunting. Or even better—purchase a Bible yourself and give it as a gift. Also ask the person to get a journal in which to record some of the material you will be sharing as well as some of the person's own thoughts.

You can use each numbered point below as a basis for each meeting, or divide up the material as you wish. Read the Bible verses. As you meet together, help your friend find the verses in the Bible and underline them. Encourage your friend to ask whatever questions come to mind. You may not know all the answers. If you don't, be honest and say, "I don't know the answer to that question, but I'll do some research and see what I can find out." Then do what you can to try to answer that question to the best of your ability.

Also realize that God will do his work in his timing. Don't expect a new believer to suddenly get rid of all vices (not swear anymore and change their wardrobe, for example) the very next day after accepting Christ. Part of your discipleship process will be to help this person learn how to be sensitive to God's leading. You will need to be sensitive as well—to know what to say and when to say it, and what not to say until the time is right. Commit yourself to praying daily for this new believer!

Here are the points to discuss:

1. You can be assured of your salvation.
You recently became a Christian, but you may have experienced doubts about what really happened to you. So I want to share with you some assurances that God gives in the Bible.

God assures you that Jesus Christ has come into your life.

John 14:20. *When I am raised to life again, you will know that I am in my Father, and you are in me, and I am in you.*

God assures you that your sins have been forgiven.

Colossians 2:13-14. *God made you alive with Christ, for he forgave all our sins. He canceled the record of the charges against us and took it away by nailing it to the cross.*

God assures you that you have eternal life.

1 John 5:13. *I have written this to you who believe in the name of the Son of God, so that you may know you have eternal life.*

Assignment: In your journal, write a description of when, where, and how you became a Christian. Make a note of the assurances that God has given you today.

2. You can know that you are loved unconditionally.
No matter what else may be going on in your life, no matter what acceptance or rejection you may be facing from others, you can know that God has completely accepted you and loves you unconditionally.

God loves you, chose you, and adopts you into his own family.

Ephesians 1:4-5. *Even before he made the world, God loved us and chose us in Christ to be holy and without fault in his eyes. God decided in advance to adopt us into his own family by bringing us to himself through Jesus Christ. This is what he wanted to do, and it gave him great pleasure.*

Assignment: Write about what it means to you to be a part of God's family and to be loved unconditionally.

3. You have a new life in Christ.
What's next? God has given you a new life, but don't expect to be different all at once. Just as a new baby has to grow and learn, so God is going to work in you and help you to grow.

You have begun a relationship that will continue the rest of your life.

Colossians 2:6-7. *And now, just as you accepted Christ Jesus as your Lord, you must continue to follow him. Let your roots grow down into him, and let your lives be built on him. Then your faith will grow strong in the truth you were taught, and you will overflow with thankfulness.*

Assignment: Write how it feels to know that God has given you a new life. What does that mean to you personally?

4. You have the privilege of prayer.
Just as good friends can talk to each other, so God, your heavenly Father, wants you to talk to him. And, while you may not understand it right now, you'll find that he "talks" to you as well.

You can pray to God about anything and everything. He wants to hear from you.

Philippians 4:6. *Don't worry about anything; instead, pray about everything. Tell God what you need, and thank him for all he has done.*

Assignment: Commit yourself to getting used to talking to God. Start out with about three minutes a day of focused time talking to God. Talk to him as you would to a friend. In your journal, begin a list of the things you're talking to God about and the concerns that you're bringing to him.

5. You have the treasure of God's Word.
When you buy a new gadget, you usually get an instruction manual. With your new life in Christ, you need God's instruction manual, the Bible. In fact, the communication you "hear" from God will often come as you read his Word.

You can trust God's Word.

2 Timothy 3:16. *All Scripture is inspired by God and is useful to teach us what is true and to make us realize what is wrong in our lives. It corrects us when we are wrong and teaches us to do what is right.*

Assignment: Commit yourself to spending five minutes a day reading the Bible. Begin in section 9 (the Gospels in the New Testament) and read about Jesus. As a result of something you read, write in your journal something you learned or something you need to do.

6. You have a great friend in Jesus, so get to know him!
As you're reading in the book of Mark, you've been learning more about Jesus. In essence, Jesus is God put into focus for human eyes. Jesus came in order to show us God and then to take the punishment for our sins.

Only because of Jesus do you have a personal relationship with God.

Colossians 1:19-20. *For God in all his fullness was pleased to live in Christ, and through him God reconciled everything to himself. He made peace with everything in heaven and on earth by means of Christ's blood on the cross.*

Assignment: Write a prayer to Jesus, thanking him for all he did for you.

7. You have a new lifestyle.
A good foundation is essential for a house to stand strong. Jesus wants you to know that obeying God will give your life a solid foundation.

You show your love for Jesus by doing as he says.

John 14:15. *If you love me, obey my commandments.*

Philippians 2:13. *For God is working in you, giving you the desire and the power to do what pleases him.*

Assignment: In your journal, write one area of your life where you are obeying God and one where you think you are not. Ask God to show you what he wants you to do and to give you the strength to do it.

8. God will help you to follow and obey him.
As a Christian, you have been given the Holy Spirit. He will give you insight into what God is like and what he wants you to do.

God gives you his Holy Spirit to enable you to live the Christian life.

John 14:26. *But when the Father sends the Advocate as my representative—that is, the Holy Spirit—he will teach you everything and will remind you of everything I have told you.*

Assignment: Write down one question that you'd like the Holy Spirit to help you with. Now take a couple of minutes and just talk to God about it.

9. You can resist temptation.
Becoming a Christian is like switching sides in a battle. You used to be on Satan's side and now you're on God's side—and Satan isn't happy about it! He wants to try to trip you up and tempt you to disobey God.

> **You're not alone in temptation. God promises to show the way out.**
>
> 1 Corinthians 10:13. *The temptations in your life are no different from what others experience. And God is faithful. He will not allow the temptation to be more than you can stand. When you are tempted, he will show you a way out so that you can endure.*

Assignment: List three temptations that Satan often uses on you. Now thank God ahead of time that he will show you how not to give in next time.

10. You can continue to receive forgiveness.
As a child in God's family, you'll still mess up. But God's love for you is so great that he will continue to forgive you.

> **When you mess up, go to God and ask him to forgive you.**
>
> 1 John 1:9. *But if we confess our sins to him, he is faithful and just to forgive us our sins and to cleanse us from all wickedness.*

Assignment: Write down ways that you have disobeyed God recently. Look at each one and confess it through prayer. Then cross out each sin. Let this remind you of God's loving forgiveness. Commit to obey him in the future.

11. You have the privilege of worship.
When you became a Christian, you joined a family—called "the body of Christ," which means you're now "related" to Christians all over the world! You need to join a portion of that family by beginning to attend a local church.

> **You need the church to help you continue to grow.**
>
> Hebrews 10:25. *And let us not neglect our meeting together, as some people do, but encourage one another, especially now that the day of his return is drawing near.*

Assignment: Go with some friends or family to church this week. List two ways you worshiped God.

12. You can let others know about what Christ has done for you.
If you found a really great doctor, or a helpful mechanic, or even a terrific diet, you probably would tell your closest friend about it. Since you've found the One who forgives sin and gives you a new life, don't you think that's something you ought to share?

> **The news you have to share is the best news anyone could hear!**
>
> Romans 1:16. *For I am not ashamed of this Good News about Christ. It is the power of God at work, saving everyone who believes—the Jew first and also the Gentile.*

Assignment: Write down the name of one person who needs to know Jesus Christ. Start praying for that person to become a Christian. Ask a Christian friend to pray with you for the person and to help you learn how to share your faith.

13. Take time to memorize Scripture.
To fight a battle you need powerful equipment. The Holy Spirit will use the power of God's Word like a sword to defeat Satan. A great strategy is to memorize Scripture so you always have it with you.

> **Memorized verses will give you comfort and help you in temptation.**
>
> Ephesians 6:17. *Take the sword of the Spirit, which is the word of God.*

Assignment: Review the verses you've underlined in your Bible. Choose one or two favorites and begin to memorize them.

14. Realize your long-term goal—to be like Christ.
You've been a Christian for a short time now, and you're learning that you have a lifelong relationship with Christ. So what's your long-range goal? Becoming like Christ!

> **Fortunately, you don't do this alone. God works in you to help you become more like his Son.**

Philippians 1:6. *And I am certain that God, who began the good work within you, will continue his work until it is finally finished on the day when Christ Jesus returns.*

Psalm 119:105. *Your word is a lamp to guide my feet and a light for my path.*

Assignment: Make a list of at least five ways you want to become more like Jesus. Spend time asking God to help you. Remind yourself to read this part of your journal in one month to check on your spiritual growth.

Mining the Treasures of the *Chronological Life Application Study Bible*

As a believer in Christ, you will often be asked questions about your faith—sometimes these are from honest seekers with tough questions that have bothered them; sometimes they're questions used by the questioners in hopes of tripping you up. In either case, it helps to be prepared with answers, or at least to know where to find the answers. The *Chronological Life Application Study Bible* notes were written not only to help explain the contents of the Bible and to get people started in thinking about application, but also to answer some of these key questions.

The treasures are here, and so we have mined them for you by guiding you to the notes that best answer questions in the following twenty-five categories. The references noted after each question are for the note(s) that will best help you to answer that question. (A number in parentheses indicates that there is more than one note on that particular Scripture.)

BELIEF

Why should I believe? *See notes on Gen 15:6, p. 35; Exod 9:12, p. 153.*
What does it mean to "believe" in Jesus? *See note on John 3:16 (3), p. 1302.*

BIBLE

Why should I read the Bible? *See notes on 2 Chr 17:7-9, p. 714; 2 Chr 34:31, p. 972; Ps 119:19, p. 878.*
Why should I trust the Bible? *See notes on Ps 33:4, p. 858; Prov 16:22, p. 651; 2 Pet 1:16-21, p. 1758.*
Why do you call the Bible God's Word? *See note on 2 Tim 3:16-17, p. 1745.*
How is the Bible different from other religious literature? *See note on 2 Tim 3:16, p. 1745.*

CHURCH

How should I choose a church? *See notes on 1 Cor 3:10-11, p. 1599; 1 Pet 5:8-9, p. 1756.*
If eternal life is free, what's this 10 percent I keep hearing about? *See notes on Deut 14:22-23, p. 304; 2 Cor 8:10-15, p. 1636; 2 Cor 8:12 (1 and 2), p. 1636.*
Isn't participation in church optional? *See note on Heb 10:25, p. 1776*

DEATH

What happens when people die? *See notes on Heb 2:14-15 (1 and 2), p. 1764; 1 Thes 4:15-18, p. 1585.*
How can I be ready to die? *See notes on Gen 50:24, p. 93; Ps 23:4, p. 558.*

DEVIL

Is the devil real? *See notes on Job 1:6-12, p. 94; Matt 4:1, p. 1294.*
What does the devil do? *See notes on Gen 3:5, p. 11; Gen 3:6, p. 11.*
How powerful is the devil? *See note on Josh 6:2-5, p. 343.*

FAITH

How strong does my faith have to be? *See notes on Matt 17:17-20, p. 1381; Luke 17:6, p. 1413; Rom 14:1ff, p. 1669.*
Is faith enough? That seems too easy. *See notes on 2 Kgs 5:12, p. 744; Matt 3:9-10, p. 1288; Phil 3:2-3 (2), p. 1721; Jas 2:1ff, p. 1548.*
How can I tell others about my faith? *See notes on Exod 3:16-17, p. 144; Rev 1:5-6, p. 1799.*

FORGIVENESS

How can I know that God forgives me? *See notes on Ps 32:1-2, p. 564; Isa 1:18, p. 824; Heb 10:17, p. 1775; 1 Jn 1:9 (1), p. 1787.*

FUTURE
What can God tell me about the future? *See notes on Job 19:25-27, p. 112; Matt 24:3ff, p. 1446; John 14:19-21, p. 1462; Rev 21:7-8, p. 1830; Rev 22:20, p. 1833.*
How is the world going to end? *See notes on Mark 13:5-7, p. 1448; Luke 12:40, p. 1401; 1 Jn 2:18-23, p. 1789.*

GOD
What is God really like? *See notes on Gen 1:1, p. 6; Gen 18:14, p. 40; Num 14:17-20, p. 253; Deut 27:15-26, p. 316; Ps 34:9-10, p. 458; Ps 36:5-8, p. 566; Ps 99:5, p. 865; John 14:5-6, p. 1461; 2 Thes 2:10-12, p. 1589.*
What are idols and what's wrong with them? *See notes on Exod 20:1-6, p. 169; Exod 32:4-5, p. 184; 1 Kgs 18:29, p. 717.*
Isn't God only all about rules? *See note on Isa 5:11-13, p. 829.*

GOSPEL
What is the gospel? *See notes on Matt 4:23-24, p. 1310; John 3:16 (1), p. 1302; Rom 1:3-5, p. 1645; 1 Cor 15:3-4, p. 1618.*

GRACE
What is grace? *See note on Eph 1:7-8, p. 1705.*
How important it is to have God's grace? *See note on Neh 9:28-31, p. 1217.*

HEAVEN/HELL
What does the Bible really say about heaven? *See notes on Mark 12:24, p. 1440; 1 Cor 2:9, p. 1598; 1 Pet 2:11, p. 1751.*
What does the Bible really say about hell? *See notes on Matt 25:46, p. 1453; 2 Thes 1:9, p. 1588; Jude 1:7, p. 1784; Rev 20:14, p. 1830.*

HOLY SPIRIT
Who is the Holy Spirit? *See notes on Ps 48:14, p. 853; John 14:15-16, p. 1462; John 14:17ff, p. 1462; Acts 1:5, p. 1499.*

JESUS
How do we know Jesus wasn't just a really great teacher? *See notes on Matt 17:5, p. 1379; Luke 24:6-7 (2), p. 1491; John 5:31ff, p. 1319; Phil 2:5-11 (1), p. 1719.*
What do you mean when you say Jesus is God? *See notes on Heb 1:1-2, p. 1761; Heb 1:3 (1), p. 1761.*
What did Jesus do for me? *See notes on Mark 15:31, p. 1483; 2 Cor 5:21, p. 1633; Col 1:12-14, p. 1694; Heb 9:22, p. 1774.*

LIFE
What does God really want from me? *See notes on Num 9:23, p. 202; Judg 21:25, p. 409; Prov 13:6, p. 646; Eccl 1:8-11, p. 673; 1 Jn 4:20-21, p. 1794.*
Doesn't God want me to be perfect? How can I do that? *See notes on Matt 5:48, p. 1330; Rom 5:20, p. 1655; Heb 10:14, p. 1775.*
How can I "commit" my life to God? *See notes on Prov 16:3, p. 650; 1 Pet 1:14-16 (2), p. 1749.*
If I am a Christian, how am I supposed to live? *See notes on Exod 23:24-25, p. 174; Josh 1:5, p. 336; John 17:18, p. 1467; Rom 13:1ff, p. 1668; 1 Pet 1:8-9, p. 1749.*

OLD TESTAMENT
The Old Testament seems so—*old*. How much of it really applies to me today? *See notes on Deut 4:8, p. 290; Matt 5:17-20, p. 1327; Acts 21:23-24 (2), p. 1677.*
How do the Old and New Testaments relate? *See notes on Lev 1:2 (2), p. 203; Matt 13:52, p. 1349; Heb 3:5, p. 1764.*

ONLY ONE WAY
How can Christians insist that Jesus is the only way to God? *See notes on John 6:67-68, p. 1369; Acts 4:12, p. 1519; 1 Tim 2:5-6, p. 1729; 2 Tim 4:3-5, p. 1745; Heb 10:26, p. 1776.*
Why isn't just being "good" good enough? *See note on Col 1:21-22, p. 1695; Heb 7:28, p. 1771; Heb 9:14, p. 1773.*

OTHER RELIGIONS
How can you say that devout people who follow other religions are wrong? *See notes on Col 2:20-23 (2), p. 1699; Col 2:22-23, p. 1696; 2 Jn 1:1-2, p. 1795; 2 Jn 1:3-4, p. 1795.*
What makes Christianity any different from the rest of religions? *See notes on Heb 7:25, p. 1771; 1 Jn 5:12, p. 1794; 1 Jn 5:13, p. 1794.*

PRAYER
What good does prayer do? *See notes on 2 Chr 6:19-42, p. 621; Ps 4:3, p. 546; Mark 9:29, p. 1382.*
If God knows everything, why pray? *See notes on Isa 38:1-5, p. 920; Acts 1:12-13, p. 1512.*
How should I pray? *See notes on Jon 2:1ff, p. 767; Mark 11:22-23, p. 1435; Heb 4:16, p. 1767; 1 Jn 5:14-15, p. 1794.*

REPENTANCE/CONFESSION
Why are confession and repentance necessary? *See notes on Lev 5:5, p. 207; 2 Sam 12:14 (1), p. 507; Matt 3:1-2 (1), p. 1287; 1 Jn 1:9 (1 and 2), p. 1787.*

SIN
What is sin? *See note on Jas 4:17, p. 1552.*
Why is sin dangerous? What's the big deal? *See notes on 2 Sam 11:1ff, p. 503; 1 Kgs 11:9-10, p. 671; 1 Chr 21:13-14, p. 530; 1 Chr 21:14, p. 531; 1 Cor 6:12-13 (1), p. 1604; 1 Thes 4:4-5, p. 1584; Rev 9:20-21, p. 1815.*
Why should I call myself a sinner when I can think of a lot of people who are *really* bad? *See note on Rom 3:23, p. 1651.*
How could a loving God send sincere people to hell? *See notes on Deut 7:2, p. 295; Rom 1:18-20 (1 and 2), p. 1647.*
Can someone be too sinful to be saved? *See notes on 2 Chr 33:12-13, p. 956; Ps 51:1ff, p. 505; Ps 51:1-7, p. 505.*

SPIRITUAL GIFTS
What are spiritual gifts? Does everyone have one? *See notes on Rom 12:6 (1), p. 1667; Rom 12:6-8, p. 1667; Eph 4:11-12, p. 1710.*

SUFFERING
Why do bad things happen to good people? *See notes on Job 1:1ff, p. 94; Job 2:10, p. 96; Acts 12:2-11, p. 1537; Rom 8:28, p. 1660.*
How does God help me deal with the problems in my life? *See notes on Exod 5:22-23, p. 147; Job 5:17-26, p. 100; Ps 106:40-42, p. 871; Phil 1:29, p. 1718; 1 Thes 3:1-3, p. 1583; Heb 11:35-39, p. 1779.*

TEMPTATION
How does the devil tempt me? *See notes on Luke 4:3 (1 and 2), p. 1296.*
Why does the devil tempt me? *See notes on Gen 3:1-6, p. 11.*
At what point does temptation become sin? *See note on Matt 4:1ff (1), p. 1294.*
How do I handle temptation? *See notes on Matt 26:40-41, p. 1468; Luke 4:1-13, p. 1296; 1 Cor 10:13, p. 1610.*

TRINITY
Why isn't the Trinity like believing in three gods? *See notes on Matt 3:16-17, p. 1293; Mark 1:10-11, p. 1294; Acts 1:4-5, p. 1499.*

So You've Been Asked to Speak . . .

Chances are you're going to find yourself faced with the task of leading a Bible study, giving a devotional, offering a short talk, or teaching a Sunday school class. Or perhaps you will be given the responsibility for leading a small group study and you won't know where to begin.

The *Chronological Life Application Study Bible* is an inexhaustible resource of information. If you follow some of the steps and hints below, you'll be able to put together a talk that is both informative and challenging—to any audience, at any time.

Ways to Use the Chronological Life Application Study Bible *as a Research Tool*

Using the Master Index
If you need to cover a topic, take a quick trip to the Master Index (p. 1924) and look up the topic. There you will find notes on that topic (with a phrase that gives you an idea of the content of the note)

as well as any charts or personality profiles on that topic. (See the Sample Lesson below to get an idea how this would work.)

Focusing on a Book of the Bible
For studying a Bible book, the *Chronological Life Application Study Bible* has plenty of overview material to help. Simply start at the beginning of the book you're studying. For example, if you're working through Jonah with your Bible study group or preparing to speak about that book, go to the Bible Book-by-Book feature in the index and read the introductory paragraph to get a feel for the message of the book, study the Blueprint to understand how the book is organized, and read the Megathemes to discover the main themes of that book and their importance. Next, go to the page in the section introduction that contains the Vital Statistics like author, audience, and date (in this case, Jonah is found on p. 688 in the Splintered Nation introduction). Read the section introduction thoroughly to get a handle on the time period where the book falls, paying careful attention to details that will help understand the book you are studying. Finally, use the Canonical Table of Contents in the front of the Bible to find where the text and study notes for your book are placed in the chronological arrangement.

Focusing on a Particular Passage
If you have been assigned a verse or passage of Scripture to discuss, use the life application notes and section headings to help you put the passage into context. If you don't find a note on that particular verse, consider the topic that you want to discuss and go to the index to look up the topic and other notes that will give further insight.

Studying the Personality Profiles
The Personality Profiles are a great resource of study ideas. For instance, in a women's Bible study, you could work your way through the profiles of women. Or you could study the profiles ahead of time and do a topical study based on the life lessons for various women (using them like case studies). You can study all the people in a particular book, compare various kings or apostles, or even study the Bible characters by age (for example, choosing some of the more elderly faithful followers, such as Simeon and Anna, for an older group).

Employing the Charts as Visual Aids
The charts are designed to be simple and to summarize Bible data and teachings. They will give you an overview of a topic either from a specific book or the Bible as a whole. You could do an entire study from one chart or series of charts. For example, the charts in Proverbs pull together scattered verses on similar topics. These would be helpful in discussing key topics covered in Proverbs. In addition, this Bible includes several large charts that give sweeping overviews on various topics.

Giving a Wider Perspective by Teaching the Text in Historical Order
Use the chronological arrangement of the text of Scripture in this Bible to help the people in your group understand how various books of the Bible work together. Help them to think about how it helps us to understand the letter of Galatians better when we understand when and why it was written. Show them how the prophets Haggai and Zechariah worked together with leaders like Zerubbabel (whose story is found in Ezra 2–5) to encourage the people to finish the work of rebuilding the Temple. Find other places where the organization of the *Chronological Life Application Study Bible* will help others understand God's Word better, and then show them how the different books of the Bible are all telling the same story.

Sampling the Maps
If your group is interested in maps, use the maps in the Gospels to trace Jesus' steps throughout his ministry. Use the maps of Paul's journeys and follow his footsteps across Asia Minor and on to Rome. Use the maps in Genesis to help your readers visualize the whereabouts of the people they are studying.

Those are just a few suggestions for using the resources in the *Chronological Life Application Study Bible*. The following section takes you through steps for planning a topical talk using the Master Index.

A Sample Lesson in Six Easy Steps
You've been given the assignment to give a talk to a group about the importance of prayer in a Christian's life.

STEP ONE: Pray.
Begin by asking God to guide you as you put together your talk. Ask him to give you insight and wisdom. Ask him to guide the process and give you the right words to say.

STEP TWO: Anticipate questions.
List questions your group might have about this topic, focusing on particular issues that may be

important to them at this time. (For example, if a family is facing a difficult illness and God doesn't seem to be answering their request, you will need to be prepared to discuss the issue of unanswered prayer or prayer answered in a way we don't understand.)

STEP THREE: Prepare an outline.
Keeping in mind the questions from step two, begin an outline. Three points are usually good. Give an introduction (an anecdote, a question, an example). List the three points you want to make about prayer. Give an application-oriented conclusion (see the article, "Taking the Step to Application" below).

STEP FOUR: Go to the Master Index.
Look up "Prayer" in the Master Index. You'll find a long list of notes on various verses. Whittle it down by looking at the topic sentence for each note; then jot down the locations of notes you think might fit into your outline. Also notice that the Master Index lists several charts and Profiles that touch on the topic of prayer. Make a note of the page numbers for these.

STEP FIVE: Read the passages, notes, and other helpful materials.
Now refer to your jotted list and read the notes, charts, and profiles. When you find Bible verses and significant points in the notes that you want to use, write them on your three-point outline.

STEP SIX: Put it all together.
Now make your points flow together. Write transition sentences between points. Finally, add a conclusion that challenges your listeners to take the message to heart and let it make a difference in their lives.

■ Taking the Step to Application

Whether you are studying the Bible for yourself or teaching it to others, moving toward application is the most important part of the studying and teaching process. You see, just having information about what is in the Bible is not enough (even Satan knew enough of the Bible to be able to quote it; see Matthew 4:1-11). Understanding the context or the concepts is not enough. Even being able to see that it is relevant to today's world is not enough. For the Bible to really make a difference in our lives, we need to (1) receive the message personally, (2) reflect on our lives and identify what needs to change as a result of God's Word, and (3) lay out a plan to make that change. Taking the step to application means that we finish our Bible study or go away from a lesson asking:

> Now that I know what God wants me to do, how am I going to start doing it?

Application is the step between *knowing* what the Bible says and *doing* what it says. While the truths of the Bible never change, people's life situations are different and are constantly changing. You must continue to study the Bible and learn the new things God wants you to learn. And when you teach, you may be able to tell your listeners how *you* are applying certain principles from God's Word, but at the same time you need to give them the tools and the opportunity to apply the Bible to *their own* life situations. So how do you do that? We have developed a Bible study system called the Pyramid. Using the nine sets of questions in the Pyramid, you will be able to study the Bible and then apply its principles more practically and thoroughly to your personal life situations.

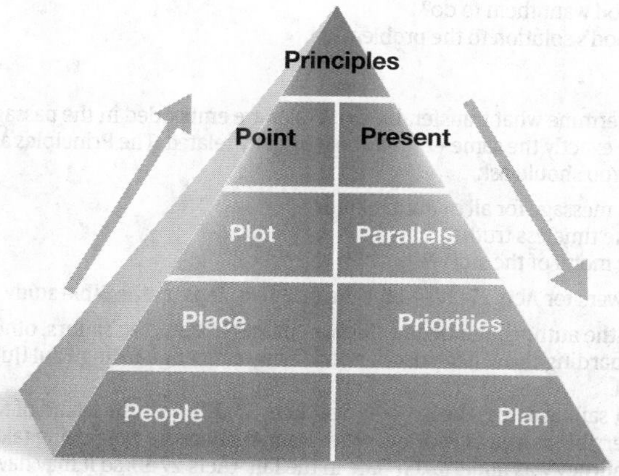

LIFE APPLICATION PYRAMID

Each step is described in detail below, followed by the questions you should ask yourself as you work your way over the Pyramid toward application. After point 5, at the top of the Pyramid, we offer an example of how your study might look. Then follow points 6 to 9 down the other side of the Pyramid. We have provided an example here as well although these points will vary greatly for each individual.

1. People
Begin by identifying the people in the passage, the characters who are actively involved. Sometimes no specific individuals or groups will be named (such as when you're reading Proverbs or Romans). But don't forget the author and the original audience. Note the people and learn something about them. (For example, if you're reading Isaiah's message to Moab, look up the "Moabites" in the Master Index and read the notes to better understand the people in this passage.) So you should ask,

- Who are all the people in this passage?
- How are these people like people in my world?
- What characteristics of these people do I see in myself?

2. Place
Next, consider Place. This step puts the passage in its original setting, the historical and cultural context. You can learn about Place by again using the Master Index and looking up the notes (and often the maps or archaeological notes). The more you know about the culture, history, and problems of the people in the passage, the more you will be able to find parallels to your life today. Ask,

- What is the setting of this passage?
- What are the significant details in the history, culture, and geography?
- What are the similarities to my world?

3. Plot
This step answers "What's happening?" Usually you can discover this by the context of the passage and book. The notes in the section you're reading will also help you to unravel the plot of a particular passage. Ask,

- What is happening in this passage?
- What is the conflict or tension?
- What would I have done in this situation?
- How is this similar to what is happening in my life or in the world today?

4. Point
Before you can determine what something in the Bible means for you today, you must first ascertain the meaning for the original audience. The events recorded in the Bible happened to real people at specific times in history. Real audiences heard the parables, and real churches received the epistles. Therefore, carefully consider the cultural context (what you learned in the first three steps) to find the particular lessons that God wanted to teach these people. A clear understanding of the Point can prevent damaging misapplication and is invaluable for determining the timeless truths in the passage. To determine the Point, ask,

- What was the intended message for the original audience?
- What did the people in the passage learn?
- What did God want them to do?
- What was God's solution to the problem?

5. Principles
The next step is to determine what transferable principles are embedded in the passage. The Point and Principles may be exactly the same—or may be indirectly related. The Principles are the distilled essence of a passage. You should ask,

- What is the message for all of humankind?
- What are the timeless truths?
- What is the moral of the story?

Here are possible answers for Acts 27:27-44 for the first five steps up the Bible study Pyramid.

PEOPLE: Luke (the author, included in the "we" passage), Paul, the sailors, other prisoners, soldiers guarding the other prisoners, the army officer guarding Paul (Julius, see Acts 27:1), God.

PLACE: on ship, sailing across the Adriatic Sea (Acts 27:27), near the island of Malta (Acts 28:1), during a terrible storm, as Paul and other Roman prisoners were being taken to Rome for trial; the journey was undertaken "late in the fall" (Acts 27:9), so it may have been October, a time when dangerous storms could arise suddenly.

PLOT: Paul had warned that the trip would be disastrous (Acts 27:9-10), but the pilot and officer didn't listen and determined to sail anyway. When the terrible storm arose, Paul encouraged everyone (Acts 27:22) and told them what to do; this time the Roman crew listened (Acts 27:31-38). Paul also thanked God in front of everyone (Acts 27:35). When the ship began to break up, the soldiers were about to kill their prisoners (so they wouldn't escape), but the officer guarding Paul stopped them (Acts 27:43).

POINT: Paul was confident of God's protection and care, even during a life-threatening storm. This confidence freed Paul to encourage others, even his captors, and to give a clear testimony of his faith in Christ.

PRINCIPLES: God is present and in control of all our "storms"; we can take courage and have hope because we know that God is with us and he cares for us. Even when we are going through difficult times, we should encourage and help others and give clear evidence of our faith.

Now you've made it up one side of the Pyramid. The path to the top of the Pyramid narrows to a single point and a few principles, but the paths going down the other side are diverse and varied for each person and for each situation. Points 6 to 9 are as follows:

6. Present

This step expands the areas of application for the Point and Principles that you have extracted so far. A different kind of thinking is required because you are expanding possibilities and adding your life to the Principles. Here you describe the significant implications of these timeless truths for life at home, school, job, and in your neighborhood. This step brings the truth into your context, into today's world, here and now. The meaning for the original audience may be clear, but the implications for the Present may be rich and varied. Ask,

- What do these Principles mean for my society and culture?
- How is this relevant?
- What back then is similar to today?
- How can I make the timeless truth timely?

7. Parallels

This step is similar to Present, except that it is very personal, addressing specific life situations, fears, hopes, and relationships. This is the time to explore all the areas of life where the truth might apply. Thus, you should ask,

- What does this truth mean for me?
- Where are my areas of need, conviction, and opportunity?
- Where in my life might this truth possibly apply?

8. Priorities

After surfacing application areas, select one that you consider to be most important—one that God is nudging you about. This is one of the more difficult steps—it can be easy to start rationalizing or to make excuses. But to truly get God's Word into your life and grow as a believer, you need to listen when God speaks. In taking this step, you are answering the question, "So what?"; that is, what does this passage say about how I should change? This involves asking these tough questions:

- How should I adjust my Priorities?
- What should I change about my values, beliefs, attitudes, or character?
- What about my thoughts and motives should change?
- What kind of person does God want me to become?

9. Plan

After pinpointing what needs to change, you need to take action. You need to answer the question, "Now what?" and put truth into practice by determining to change and then making plans to live differently. Planning involves selecting a goal, breaking it down into bite-size pieces, and getting moving! These questions will help:

- What does God want me to do about what I have learned?
- What steps will get me to that goal?
- What should be my first step? How should I get started?

Here are possible answers for Acts 27:27-44 for the last four steps down the Bible study Pyramid. While the answers in Steps 1 through 5 are pretty straightforward, the answers in Steps 6 through 9 will vary greatly from person to person, so these are merely suggestions:

PRESENT: I'm not a prisoner of a foreign government being taken to trial by ship in a terrible storm, but I do have rough seas in my life. I have a conflict with my daughter's teacher, a problem with one of my company's clients, and other difficult situations.

PARALLELS: The main parallel to my life is Paul's attitude in the middle of the crisis—he remained calm, gave instructions, encouraged everyone, and was a positive example of a follower of Christ. In both the problem at school and the one at work, I need to explain my case calmly and confidently. But in doing this, I should be positive and helpful, not negative, hateful, or divisive.

PRIORITIES: My natural tendency is to get angry and tell someone off when I think that person is wrong, or to shout orders without being sensitive to the feelings of others. I think that God wants me to be more patient and understanding. Perhaps through the *way* I communicate, I can be a positive witness for Christ.

PLAN: With the conflict at school, I need to speak directly to the teacher (not write a letter) and explain my position carefully, calmly, and with concern for the feelings of the teacher. I will make an appointment, write out my points beforehand so I won't get off on tangents and get upset, and carefully explain my position while making it clear that I have respect for the teacher.

Remember, a big difference stands between *knowing* and *doing*, and another big difference between *teaching* and *doing*. So as you begin taking the steps to application in both your personal study and in your teaching, ask yourself:

Am I doing what God wants me to do?
Am I obeying him?

Be honest in your self-evaluation. Applying the Bible begins *now*, with *you*. James wrote:

> But don't just listen to God's word. You must do what it says. Otherwise, you are only fooling yourselves. For if you listen to the word and don't obey, it is like glancing at your face in a mirror. You see yourself, walk away, and forget what you look like. But if you look carefully into the perfect law that sets you free, and if you do what it says and don't forget what you heard, then God will bless you for doing it (Jas 1:22-25).

This article is adapted from Dave Veerman, *How to Apply the Bible* (Carol Stream, Ill.: Tyndale House Publishers, 1993). Books are available at www.lifeapplicationbible.com.

THE BIBLE **BOOK-BY-BOOK**

Because the *Chronological Life Application Study Bible* is designed to give you the experience of reading through God's redemptive story in historical order, it isn't arranged in sixty-six books like a traditional canonically arranged Bible. As a result, some of the information from the helpful book introductions in the *Life Application Study Bible* wasn't able to be included without interrupting the story. Nonetheless, it is important to remember that God's Word was given to us in sixty-six books, and each has its own story to tell in a particular way. This index gives you the overview paragraph, Blueprint, and Megathemes for every individual book in the Bible, along with a reference to the page in the section introductions where you can find the Vital Statistics such as author, audience, and date.

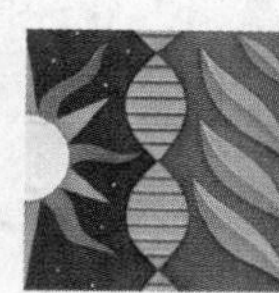

Beginnings God's Chosen Family

For Vital Statistics, see p. 4

GENESIS

BEGIN . . . open . . . start. . . . There's something refreshing and optimistic about these words, whether they refer to the dawn of a new day, the birth of a child, the prelude of a symphony, or the first miles of a family vacation. Free of problems and full of promise, beginnings stir hope and imaginative visions of the future. Genesis means "beginnings" or "origin," and it unfolds the record of the beginning of the world, of human history, of family, of civilization, of salvation. It is the story of God's purpose and plan for his creation. As the book of beginnings, Genesis sets the stage for the entire Bible. It reveals the person and nature of God (Creator, Sustainer, Judge, Redeemer); the value and dignity of human beings (made in God's image, saved by grace, used by God in the world); the tragedy and consequences of sin (the Fall, separation from God, judgment); and the promise and assurance of salvation (covenant, forgiveness, promised Messiah).

God. That's where Genesis begins. All at once we see him creating the world in a majestic display of power and purpose, culminating with a man and woman made like himself (Gen 1:26-27). But before long, sin entered the world, and Satan was unmasked. Bathed in innocence, creation was shattered by the Fall (the willful disobedience of Adam and Eve). Fellowship with God was broken, and evil began weaving its destructive web. In rapid succession, we read how Adam and Eve were expelled from the beautiful garden, their first son turned murderer, and evil bred evil until God finally destroyed everyone on earth except a small family led by Noah, the only godly person left.

As we come to Abraham on the plains of Canaan, we discover the beginning of God's covenant people and the broad strokes of his salvation plan: Salvation comes by faith, Abraham's descendants will be God's people, and the Savior of the world will come through this chosen nation. The stories of Isaac, Jacob, and Joseph that follow are more than interesting biographies. They emphasize the promises of God and the proof that he is faithful. The people we meet in Genesis are simple, ordinary people, yet through them, God did great things. These are vivid pictures of how God can and does use all kinds of people to accomplish his good purposes—even people like you.

Read Genesis and be encouraged. There is hope! No matter how dark the world situation seems, God has a plan. No matter how insignificant or useless you feel, God loves you and wants to use you in his plan. No matter how sinful and separated from God you are, his salvation is available. Read Genesis . . . and hope!

THE BLUEPRINT

A. THE STORY OF CREATION (1:1–2:4)

God created the sky, seas, and land. He created the plants, animals, fish, and birds. But he created human beings in his own image. At times, others may treat us disrespectfully. But we can be certain of our dignity and worth because we have been created in the image of God.

B. THE STORY OF ADAM (2:4–5:32)
1. Adam and Eve
2. Cain and Abel
3. Adam's descendants

When Adam and Eve were created by God, they were without sin. But they became sinful when they disobeyed God and ate some fruit from the tree. Through Adam and Eve we learn about the destructive power of sin and its bitter consequences.

C. THE STORY OF NOAH (6:1–11:32) 1. The Flood 2. Repopulating the earth 3. The tower of Babel	Noah was spared from the destruction of the Flood because he obeyed God and built the boat. Just as God protected Noah and his family, he still protects those who are faithful to him today.
D. THE STORY OF ABRAHAM (12:1–25:18) 1. God promises a nation to Abram 2. Abram and Lot 3. God promises a son to Abram 4. Sodom and Gomorrah 5. Birth and near sacrifice of Isaac 6. Isaac and Rebekah 7. Abraham dies	Abraham was asked to leave his country, wander in Canaan, wait years for a son, and then sacrifice him as a burnt offering. Through these periods of sharp testing, Abraham remained faithful to God. His example teaches us what it means to live a life of faith.
E. THE STORY OF ISAAC (25:19–28:9) 1. Jacob and Esau 2. Isaac and Abimelech 3. Jacob gets Isaac's blessing	Isaac did not demand his own way. He did not resist when he was about to be sacrificed, and he gladly accepted a wife chosen for him by others. Like Isaac, we must learn to put God's will ahead of our own.
F. THE STORY OF JACOB (28:10–36:43) 1. Jacob starts a family 2. Jacob returns home	Jacob did not give up easily. He faithfully served Laban for over 14 years. Later, he wrestled with God. Although Jacob made many mistakes, his hard work teaches us about living a life of service for our Lord.
G. THE STORY OF JOSEPH (37:1–50:26) 1. Joseph is sold into slavery 2. Judah and Tamar 3. Joseph is thrown into prison 4. Joseph is placed in charge of Egypt 5. Joseph and his brothers meet in Egypt 6. Jacob's family moves to Egypt 7. Jacob and Joseph die in Egypt	Joseph was sold into slavery by his brothers and unjustly thrown into prison by his master. Through the life of Joseph, we learn that suffering, no matter how unfair, can develop strong character in us.

MEGATHEMES

THEME	EXPLANATION	IMPORTANCE
Beginnings	Genesis explains the beginning of many important realities: the universe, the earth, people, sin, and God's plan of salvation.	Genesis teaches us that the earth is well made and good. People are special to God and unique. God creates and sustains all life.
Disobedience	People are always facing great choices. Disobedience occurs when people choose not to follow God's plan of living.	Genesis explains why people are evil: They choose to do wrong. Even great Bible heroes failed God and disobeyed.
Sin	Sin ruins people's lives. It happens when we disobey God.	Living God's way makes life productive and fulfilling.
Promises	God makes promises to help and protect people. This kind of promise is called a "covenant."	God kept his promises then, and he keeps them now. He promises to love us, accept us, forgive us.
Obedience	The opposite of sin is obedience. Obeying God restores our relationship to him.	The only way to enjoy the benefits of God's promises is to obey him.
Prosperity	Prosperity is deeper than mere material wealth. True prosperity and fulfillment come as a result of obeying God.	When people obey God, they find peace with him, with others, and with themselves.
Israel	God started the nation of Israel in order to have a dedicated people who would (1) keep his ways alive in the world, (2) proclaim to the world what he is really like, and (3) prepare the world for the birth of Christ.	God is looking for people today to follow him. We are to proclaim God's truth and love to all nations, not just our own. We must be faithful to carry out the mission God has given us.

Birth of Israel

For Vital Statistics, see p. 137

EXODUS

GET UP . . . leave . . . take off—these words sound good to those trapped or enslaved. Some resist their marching orders, however, preferring present surroundings to a new, unknown environment. It's not easy to trade the comfortable security of the known for an uncertain future. But what if God gives the order to move? Will we follow his lead? Exodus describes a series of God's calls and the responses of his people.

Four hundred years had passed since Joseph moved his family to Egypt. These descendants of Abraham had now grown to over two million strong. To Egypt's new pharaoh, the Hebrews were foreigners, and their numbers were frightening. Pharaoh decided to make them slaves so they wouldn't upset his balance of power. As it turned out, that was his biggest mistake, for God then came to the rescue of his people.

Through a series of strange events, a Hebrew boy named Moses became a prince in Pharaoh's palace and then an outcast in a wilderness land. God visited Moses in the mysterious flames of a burning bush, and, after some discussion, Moses agreed to return to Egypt to lead God's people out of slavery. Pharaoh was confronted, and through a cycle of plagues and promises made and broken, Israel was torn from his grasp.

Mobilizing this mass of humanity was no easy task, but they marched out of Egypt, through the Red Sea, and into the wilderness behind Moses and the pillars of cloud and fire. Despite continual evidence of God's love and power, the people complained and began to yearn for their days in Egypt. God provided for their physical and spiritual needs with food and a place to worship, but he also judged their disobedience and unbelief. Then in the dramatic Sinai meeting with Moses, God gave his laws for right living.

God led Moses and the nation of Israel, and he wants to lead us as well. Is he preparing you, like Moses, for a specific task? He will be with you; obey and follow. Is he delivering you from an enemy or a temptation? Trust him, and do what he says. Have you heard his clear moral directions? Read, study, and obey his Word. Is he calling you to true worship? Discover God's presence in your life, in your home, and in the body of assembled believers. Exodus is the exciting story of God's guidance. Read with the determination to follow God wherever he leads.

THE BLUEPRINT

A. ISRAEL IN EGYPT (1:1–12:30)
1. Slavery in Egypt
2. God chooses Moses
3. God sends Moses to Pharaoh
4. Plagues strike Egypt
5. The Passover

When the Israelites were enslaved in Egypt, God heard their cries and rescued them. We can be confident that God still hears the cries of his people. Just as he delivered the Israelites from their captors, he delivers us from sin, death, and evil.

B. ISRAEL IN THE WILDERNESS (12:31–18:27)
1. The Exodus
2. Crossing the sea
3. Complaining in the wilderness

After crossing the Red Sea, the Israelites became quarrelsome and discontent. Like the Israelites, we find it easy to complain and be dissatisfied. Christians still have struggles, but we should never allow difficulties and unpleasant circumstances to turn us away from trusting God.

C. ISRAEL AT SINAI (19:1–40:38)
1. Giving the law
2. Tabernacle instructions
3. Breaking the law
4. Tabernacle construction

God revealed his law to the Israelites at Sinai. Through the law, they learned more about what God is like and how he expected his people to live. The law is still instructional for us, for it exposes our sin and shows us God's standard for living.

MEGATHEMES

THEME	EXPLANATION	IMPORTANCE
Slavery	During the Israelites' 400-year stay in the land of Egypt, they became enslaved to the Egyptians. Pharaoh, the king of Egypt, oppressed them cruelly. They prayed to God for deliverance from this situation.	Like the Israelites, we need both human and divine leadership to escape from the slavery of sin. After their escape, the memory of slavery helped the Israelites learn to treat others generously. We need to stand against those who oppress others.
Rescue/ Redemption	God rescued Israel through the leader Moses and through mighty miracles. The Passover celebration was an annual reminder of their escape from slavery.	God delivers us from the slavery of sin. Jesus Christ celebrated the Passover with his disciples at the Last Supper and then went on to rescue us from sin by dying in our place.
Guidance	God guided Israel out of Egypt by using the plagues, Moses' heroic courage, the miracle of the Red Sea, and the Ten Commandments. God is a trustworthy guide.	Although God is all-powerful and can do miracles, he normally leads us by wise leadership and team effort. His Word gives us the wisdom to make daily decisions and govern our lives.
Ten Commandments	God's law system can be thought of in three parts. The Ten Commandments were the first part, containing the absolutes of spiritual and moral life. The civil law was the second part, giving the people rules to manage their lives. The ceremonial law was the third part, showing them patterns for building the Tabernacle and for regular worship.	God was teaching Israel the importance of choice and responsibility. When they obeyed the conditions of the law, he blessed them; if they forgot or disobeyed, he punished them or allowed calamities to come. Many great countries of the world base their laws on the moral system set up in the book of Exodus.
The Nation	God founded the nation of Israel to be the source of truth and salvation to all the world. His relationship to his people was loving yet firm. The Israelites had no army, schools, governors, mayors, or police when they left Egypt. God had to instruct them in their constitutional laws and daily practices. He showed them how to worship and how to have national holidays.	Israel's newly formed nation had all the behavioral characteristics of Christians today. We are often disorganized, sometimes rebellious, and sometimes victorious. God's Person and Word are still our only guides. If our churches reflect his leadership, they will be effective in serving him.

Birth of Israel

For Vital Statistics, see p. 137

LEVITICUS

"GOD seems so far away . . . if only I could see or hear him." Have you ever felt this way—struggling with loneliness, burdened by despair, riddled with sin, overwhelmed by problems? Made in God's image, we were created to have a close relationship with him; thus, when fellowship is broken, we are incomplete and need restoration. Communion with the living God is the essence of worship. It is vital, touching the very core of our lives. Perhaps this is why a whole book of the Bible is dedicated to worship. After Israel's dramatic exit from Egypt, the nation was camped at the foot of Mount Sinai for two years to listen to God (Exodus 19 to Numbers 10). It was a time of resting, teaching, building, and meeting with him face to face. Redemption in Exodus is the foundation for cleansing, worship, and service in Leviticus.

The overwhelming message of Leviticus is the holiness of God—"You must be holy because I, the LORD your God, am holy" (Lev 19:2). But how can unholy people approach a holy God? The answer—first sin must be dealt with. Thus the opening chapters of Leviticus give detailed instructions for offering sacrifices, which were the active symbols of repentance and obedience. Whether bulls, grain, goats, or sheep, the sacrificial offerings had to be perfect, with no defects or bruises—pictures of the ultimate sacrifice to come, Jesus, the Lamb of God. Jesus has come and opened the way to God by giving up his life as the final sacrifice in our place. True worship and oneness with God begin as we confess our sin and accept Christ as the only one who can redeem us from sin and help us approach God.

In Leviticus, sacrifices, priests, and the sacred Day of Atonement opened the way for the Israelites to come to God. God's people were also to worship him with their lives. Thus we read of purity laws (Lev 11–15) and rules for daily living, concerning family responsibilities, sexual conduct, relationships, worldliness (Lev 18–20), and vows (Lev 27). These instructions involve one's holy walk with God, and the patterns of spiritual living still apply today. Worship, therefore, has a horizontal aspect—that is, God is honored by our lives as we relate to others.

The final emphasis in Leviticus is celebration. The book gives instructions for the festivals. These were special, regular, and corporate occasions for remembering what God had done, giving thanks to him, and rededicating lives to his service (Lev 23). Our Christian traditions and holidays are different, but they are necessary ingredients of worship. We, too, need special days of worship and celebration with our spiritual brothers and sisters to remember God's goodness in our lives.

As you read Leviticus, rededicate yourself to holiness, worshiping God in private confession, public service, and group celebration.

THE BLUEPRINT

A. WORSHIPING A HOLY GOD (1:1–17:16) 1. Instructions for the offerings 2. Instructions for the priests 3. Instructions for the people 4. Instructions for the altar	God provided specific directions for the kind of worship that would be pleasing to him. These instructions teach us about the nature of God and can help us develop a right attitude toward worship. Through the offerings we learn of the seriousness of sin and the importance of bringing our sins to God for forgiveness.
B. LIVING A HOLY LIFE (18:1–27:34) 1. Standards for the people 2. Rules for priests 3. Seasons and festivals 4. Receiving God's blessing	God gave clear standards to the Israelites for living a holy life. They were to be separate and distinct from the pagan nations around them. In the same way, all believers should be separated from sin and dedicated to God. God still wants to remove sin from the lives of his people.

MEGATHEMES

THEME	EXPLANATION	IMPORTANCE
Sacrifice/ Offering	There are five kinds of offerings that fulfill two main purposes: one to show praise, thankfulness, and devotion; the other for atonement, the covering and removal of guilt and sin. Animal offerings demonstrated that the person was giving his or her life to God by means of the life of the animal.	The sacrifices (offerings) were for worship and forgiveness of sin. Through them we learn about the cost of sin, for we see that we cannot forgive ourselves. God's system says that a life must be given for a life. In the Old Testament, an animal's life was given to save the life of a person. But this was only a temporary measure until Jesus' death paid the penalty of sin for all people forever.
Worship	Seven festivals were designated as religious and national holidays. They were often celebrated in family settings. These events teach us much about worshiping God in both celebration and quiet dedication.	God's rules about worship set up an orderly, regular pattern of fellowship with him. They allowed times for celebration and thanksgiving as well as for reverence and rededication. Our worship should demonstrate our deep devotion.
Health	Civil rules for handling food, disease, and sex were taught. In these physical principles, many spiritual principles were suggested. Israel was to be different from the surrounding nations. God was preserving Israel from disease and community health problems.	We are to be different morally and spiritually from the unbelievers around us. Principles for healthy living are as important today as in Moses' time. A healthy environment and a healthy body make our service to God more effective.

Holiness	Holy means "separated" or "devoted." God removed his people from Egypt; now he was removing Egypt from the people. He was showing them how to exchange Egyptian ways of living and thinking for his ways.	We must devote every area of life to God. God desires absolute obedience in motives as well as practices. Though we do not observe all the worship practices of Israel, we are to have the same spirit of preparation and devotion.
Levites	The Levites and priests instructed the people in their worship. They were the ministers of their day. They also regulated the moral, civil, and ceremonial laws and supervised the health, justice, and welfare of the nation.	The Levites were servants who showed Israel the way to God. They provide the historical backdrop for Christ, who is our High Priest and yet our Servant. God's true servants care for all the needs of their people.

Birth of Israel

For Vital Statistics, see p. 137

NUMBERS

EVERY parent knows the shrill whine of a young child—a slow, high-pitched complaint that grates on the eardrums and aggravates the soul. The tone of voice is difficult to bear, but the real irritation is the underlying cause—discontentment and disobedience. As the "children" of Israel journeyed from the foot of Mount Sinai to the land of Canaan, they grumbled, whined, and complained at every turn. They focused on their present discomforts. Faith had fled, and they added an extra 40 years to their trip.

Numbers, which records the tragic story of Israel's unbelief, should serve as a dramatic lesson for all of God's people. God loves us and wants the very best for us. He can and should be trusted. Numbers also gives a clear portrayal of God's patience. Again and again he withholds judgment and preserves the nation. But his patience must not be taken for granted. His judgment will come. We must obey.

As Numbers begins, the nation of Israel was camped at the foot of Mount Sinai. The people had received God's laws and were preparing to move. A census was taken to determine the number of men fit for military service. Next, the people were set apart for God. God was making the people, both spiritually and physically, ready to receive their inheritance.

But then the complaining began. First, the people complained about the food. Next, it was over Moses' authority. God punished some people but spared the nation because of Moses' prayers. The nation then arrived at Kadesh, and spies were sent into Canaan to assess its strength. Ten returned with fearful stories of giants. Only Caleb and Joshua encouraged the nation to "go at once to take the land" (Num 13:30). The minority report fell on deaf ears full of the ominous message of the majority. Because of their unbelief, God declared that the present generation would not live to see the Promised Land. Thus the "wanderings" began. These wilderness wanderings featured a continuous pattern of grumbling, defiance, discipline, and death. How much better it would have been to have trusted God and entered his land! Then the terrible waiting began—waiting for the old generation to die off and waiting to see if the new generation could faithfully obey God.

Numbers ends as it begins, with preparation. This new generation of Israelites was numbered and sanctified. After defeating numerous armies, they settled on the east side of the Jordan River. Then they faced their greatest test: to cross the river and possess the beautiful land God had promised to them.

The lesson is clear. God's people must trust him, moving ahead by faith if they are to claim his promises.

THE BLUEPRINT

A. PREPARING FOR THE JOURNEY (1:1–10:10) 1. The first census of the nation 2. The role of the Levites 3. The purity of the camp 4. Receiving guidance for the journey	As part of their preparations, the Lord gave strict guidelines to the Israelites regarding purity in the camp. He wanted them to have a lifestyle distinct from the nations around them. He wanted them to be a holy people. Similarly, we should concern ourselves with purity in the church.
B. FIRST APPROACH TO THE PROMISED LAND (10:11–14:45) 1. The people complain 2. Miriam and Aaron oppose Moses 3. The scouts incite rebellion	The Israelites were prevented from entering the Promised Land because of their unbelief. Throughout history, God's people have continued to struggle with lack of faith. We must prevent unbelief from gaining a foothold in our lives, for it will keep us from enjoying the blessings that God has promised.
C. WANDERING IN THE WILDERNESS (15:1–21:35) 1. Additional regulations 2. Many leaders rebel against Moses 3. Duties of priests and Levites 4. The new generation	When the people complained against God and criticized Moses, they were severely punished. Over 14,000 people died as a result of rebellion against Moses. As a result of Korah's rebellion, Korah, Dathan, and Abiram and their households died, along with 250 false priests. Dissatisfaction and discontent, if allowed to remain in our lives, can easily lead to disaster. We should refrain from complaining and criticizing our leaders.

D. SECOND APPROACH TO THE PROMISED LAND (22:1–36:13)
1. The story of Balaam
2. The second census of the nation
3. Instructions concerning offerings
4. Vengeance on the Midianites
5. The Transjordan tribes
6. Camped on the plains of Moab

The Moabites and Midianites could not get Balaam to curse Israel, but they did get him to give advice on how to draw the Israelites to idol worship. Balaam knew what was right, but he gave in to the temptation of material rewards and sinned. Knowing what is right alone is never enough. We must also do what is right.

MEGATHEMES

THEME	EXPLANATION	IMPORTANCE
Census	Moses counted the Israelites twice. The first census organized the people into marching units to better defend themselves. The second prepared them to conquer the country east of the Jordan River.	People have to be organized, trained, and led to be effective in great movements. It is always wise to count the cost before setting out on some great undertaking. When we are aware of the obstacles before us, we can more easily avoid them.
Rebellion	At Kadesh, 12 scouts were sent out into the land of Canaan to report on the fortifications of the enemies. When the scouts returned, 10 said that they should give up and go back to Egypt. As a result, the people refused to enter the land. Faced with a choice, Israel rebelled against God. Rebellion did not start with an uprising, but with griping and murmuring against Moses and God.	Rebellion against God is always a serious matter. It is not something to take lightly, for God's punishment for sin is often very severe. Our rebellion does not usually begin with all-out warfare, but in subtle ways—with griping and criticizing. Make sure your negative comments are not the product of a rebellious spirit.
Wandering	Because they rebelled, the Israelites wandered 40 years in the wilderness. This shows how severely God can punish sin. Forty years was enough time for all those who held on to Egypt's customs and values to die off. It gave time to train up a new generation in the ways of God.	God judges sin harshly because he is holy. The wanderings in the wilderness demonstrate how serious God considers flagrant disobedience of his commands. Purging our lives of sin is vital to God's purpose.
Canaan	Canaan is the Promised Land. It was the land God had promised to Abraham, Isaac, and Jacob—the land of the covenant. Canaan was to be the dwelling place of God's people, those set apart for true spiritual worship.	Although God's punishment for sin is often severe, he offers reconciliation and hope—his love is truly amazing. Just as God's love and law led Israel to the Promised Land, God desires to give purpose and destiny to our lives.

DEUTERONOMY

Birth of Israel

For Vital Statistics, see p. 137

CLASS reunions, photo albums, familiar songs, and old neighborhoods—like long-time friends they awaken our memories and stir our emotions. The past is a kaleidoscope of promises, failures, victories, and embarrassments. Sometimes we want to forget memories that are too painful. As the years pass, however, remembrances of unpleasant events usually fade into our subconscious. But there is a time to remember: Mistakes should not be repeated; commitments made must be fulfilled; and the memory of special events can encourage us and move us to action.

The book of Deuteronomy is written in the form of a treaty between a king and his vassal state typical of the second millennium B.C. It calls Israel to remember who God is and what he has done. Lacking faith, the old generation had wandered for 40 years and had died in the wilderness. They left Egypt behind, but never knew the Promised Land. Then on the east bank of the Jordan River, Moses prepared the sons and daughters of that faithless generation to possess the land. After a brief history lesson emphasizing God's great acts on behalf of his people, Moses reviewed the law. Then he restated the covenant—God's contract with his people.

The lessons are clear. Because of what God has done, Israel should have hope and follow him; because of what he expects, they should listen and obey; because of who he is, they should love him completely. Learning these lessons will prepare them to possess the Promised Land.

As you hear the message of Deuteronomy, remember how God has expressed his kindness in your life, and then commit yourself anew to trust, love, and obey him.

THE BLUEPRINT

A. WHAT GOD HAS DONE FOR US: MOSES' FIRST ADDRESS (1:1–4:43)

Moses reviewed the mighty acts of God for the nation of Israel. Remembering God's special involvement in our lives gives us hope and encouragement for the future.

B. PRINCIPLES FOR GODLY LIVING: MOSES' SECOND ADDRESS (4:44–29:1) 1. The Ten Commandments 2. Love the Lord your God 3. Laws for proper worship 4. Laws for ruling the nation 5. Laws for human relationships 6. Consequences of obedience and disobedience	Obeying God's laws brought blessings to the Israelites and disobeying brought misfortune. This was part of the written agreement God made with his people. Although we are not part of this covenant, the principle holds true: Obedience and disobedience carry inevitable consequences in this life and the next.
C. A CALL FOR COMMITMENT TO GOD: MOSES' THIRD ADDRESS (29:2–30:20)	Moses called the people to commitment. God still calls us to be committed to love him with all our heart, soul, mind, and strength.
D. THE CHANGE IN LEADERSHIP: MOSES' LAST DAYS (31:1–34:12)	Although Moses made some serious mistakes, he had lived uprightly and carried out God's commands. Moses died with integrity. We too may make some serious mistakes, but that should not stop us from living with integrity and godly commitment.

MEGATHEMES

THEME	EXPLANATION	IMPORTANCE
History	Moses reviewed the mighty acts of God whereby he liberated Israel from slavery in Egypt. He recounted how God had helped them and how the people had disobeyed.	By reviewing God's promises and mighty acts in history, we can learn about his character. We come to know God more intimately through understanding how he has acted in the past. We can also avoid mistakes in our own lives by learning from Israel's failures.
Laws	God reviewed his laws for the people. The legal contract between God and his people had to be renewed by the new generation about to enter the Promised Land.	Commitment to God and his truth cannot be taken for granted. Each generation and each person must respond afresh to God's call for obedience.
Love	God's faithful and patient love is portrayed more often than his punishment. God shows his love by being faithful to his people and his promises. In response, God desires love from the heart, not merely a legalistic keeping of his law.	God's love forms the foundation for our trust in him. We trust him because he loves us. Because God loves us, we should maintain justice and respect.
Choices	God reminded his people that in order to ratify his covenant, they must choose the path of obedience. A personal decision to obey would bring benefits to their lives; rebellion would bring severe calamity.	Our choices make a difference. Choosing to follow God benefits us and improves our relationships with others. Choosing to abandon God's ways brings harm to ourselves and others.
Teaching	God commanded the Israelites to teach their children his ways. They were to use ritual, instruction, and memorization to make sure their children understood God's principles and passed them on to the next generation.	Quality teaching for our children must be a priority. It is important to pass on God's truth to future generations in our traditions. But God desires that his truth be in our hearts and minds and not merely in our traditions.

Possessing the Land

For Vital Statistics, see p. 332

JOSHUA

REMEMBER "follow the leader"? The idea was to mimic the antics of the person in front of you in the line of boys and girls winding through the neighborhood. Being a follower was all right, but being leader was the most fun, creating imaginative routes and tasks for everyone else to copy. In real life, great leaders are rare. Often, men and women are elected or appointed to leadership positions but then falter or fail to act. Others abuse their power to satisfy their egos, crushing their subjects and squandering resources. But without faithful, ethical, and effective leaders, people wander.

For 40 years, Israel had journeyed a circuitous route through the wilderness, but not because they were following their leader. Quite the opposite was true—with failing faith, they had refused to obey God and to conquer Canaan. So they wandered. Finally, the new generation was ready to cross the Jordan and possess the land. Having distinguished himself as a man of faith and courage (he and Caleb had given the minority scout report recorded in Num 13:30–14:9), Joshua was chosen to be Moses' successor. This book records Joshua's leadership of the people of God as they finished their march and conquered the Promised Land.

Joshua was a brilliant military leader and a strong spiritual influence. But the key to his success was his submission to God. When God spoke, Joshua listened and obeyed. Joshua's obedience served as a model. As a result, Israel remained faithful to God throughout Joshua's lifetime.

The book of Joshua is divided into two main parts. The first narrates the events surrounding the conquest of Canaan. After crossing the Jordan River on dry ground, the Israelites camped near the mighty city of Jericho. God commanded the people to conquer Jericho by marching around the city 13 times, blowing trumpets and shouting. Because they followed God's unique battle strategy, they won (Josh 6). After the destruction of Jericho, they set out against the small town of Ai. Their first attack was driven back because one of the Israelites (Achan) had sinned (Josh 7). After the men of

Israel stoned Achan and his family—purging the community of its sin—the Israelites succeeded in capturing Ai (Josh 8). In their next battle against the Amorites, God even provided extended daylight to aid them in their victory (Josh 10). Finally, after defeating other assorted Canaanites led by Jabin and his allies (Josh 11), they possessed most of the land.

Part two of the book of Joshua records the assignment and settlement of the captured territory (Josh 13–22). The book concludes with Joshua's farewell address and his death (Josh 23–24).

Joshua was committed to obeying God, and this book is about obedience. Whether conquering enemies or settling the land, God's people were required to do it God's way. In his final message to the people, Joshua underscored the importance of obeying God. "So be very careful to love the LORD your God" (Josh 23:11), and "choose today whom you will serve. . . . But as for me and my family, we will serve the LORD" (Josh 24:15). Read Joshua and make a fresh commitment to obey God today. Decide to follow your Lord wherever he leads and whatever it costs.

THE BLUEPRINT

A. ENTERING THE PROMISED LAND (1:1–5:12)
1. Joshua leads the nation
2. Crossing the Jordan

Joshua demonstrated his faith in God as he took up the challenge to lead the nation. The Israelites reaffirmed their commitment to God by obediently setting out across the Jordan River to possess the land. As we live the Christian life, we need to cross over from the old life to the new, put off our selfish desires, and press on to possess all God has planned for us. Like Joshua and Israel, we need courageous faith to live the new life.

B. CONQUERING THE PROMISED LAND (5:13–12:24)
1. Joshua attacks the center of the land
2. Joshua attacks the southern kings
3. Joshua attacks the northern kings
4. Summary of conquests

Joshua and his army moved from city to city, cleansing the land of its wickedness by destroying every trace of idol worship. Conflict with evil is inevitable, and we should be as merciless as Israel in destroying sin in our lives.

C. DIVIDING THE PROMISED LAND (13:1–24:33)
1. The tribes receive their land
2. Special cities are set aside
3. Eastern tribes return home
4. Joshua's farewell to Israel

Joshua urged the Israelites to continue to follow the Lord and worship him alone. The people had seen God deliver them from many enemies and miraculously provide for all their needs, but they were prone to wander from the Lord. Even though we may have experienced God at work in our lives, we, too, must continually renew our commitment to obey him above all other authority and to worship him alone.

MEGATHEMES

THEME	EXPLANATION	IMPORTANCE
Success	God gave success to the Israelites when they obeyed his master plan, not when they followed their own desires. Victory came when they trusted in him rather than in their military power, money, muscle, or mental capacity.	God's work done in God's way will bring his success. The standard for success, however, is not to be set by the society around us but by God's Word. We must adjust our minds to God's way of thinking in order to see his standard for success.
Faith	The Israelites demonstrated their faith by trusting God daily to save and guide them. By noticing how God fulfilled his promises in the past, they developed strong confidence that he would be faithful in the future.	Our strength to do God's work comes from trusting him. His promises reassure us of his love and that he will be there to guide us in the decisions and struggles we face. Faith begins with believing he can be trusted.
Guidance	God gave instructions to Israel for every aspect of their lives. His law guided their daily living, and his specific marching orders gave them victory in battle.	Guidance from God for daily living can be found in his Word. By staying in touch with God, we will have the needed wisdom to meet the great challenges of life.
Leadership	Joshua was an example of an excellent leader. He was confident in God's strength, courageous in the face of opposition, and willing to seek God's advice.	To be a strong leader like Joshua, we must be ready to listen and to move quickly when God instructs us. Once we have his instructions, we must be diligent in carrying them out. Strong leaders are led by God.
Conquest	God commanded his people to conquer the Canaanites and take all their land. Completing this mission would have fulfilled God's promise to Abraham and brought judgment on the evil people living there. Unfortunately, Israel never finished the job.	The Israelites were faithful in accomplishing their mission at first, but their commitment faltered. To love God means more than being enthusiastic about him. We must complete all the work he gives us and apply his instructions to every corner of our lives.

Possessing the Land

For Vital Statistics, see p. 332

JUDGES

REAL heroes are hard to find these days. Modern research and the media have made the foibles and weaknesses of our leaders very apparent; we search in vain for men and women to emulate. The music, movie, and sports industries produce a steady stream of "stars" who shoot to the top and then quickly fade from view. Judges is a book about heroes—12 men and women who delivered Israel from its oppressors. These judges were not perfect; in fact, they included an assassin, a sexually promiscuous man, and a person who broke all the laws of hospitality. But they were submissive to God, and God used them.

Judges is also a book about sin and its consequences. Like a minor cut or abrasion that becomes infected when left untreated, sin grows and soon poisons the whole body. The book of Joshua ends with the nation taking a stand for God, ready to experience all the blessings of the Promised Land. After settling in Canaan, however, the Israelites lost their spiritual commitment and motivation. When Joshua and the elders died, the nation experienced a leadership vacuum, leaving them without a strong central government. Instead of enjoying freedom and prosperity in the Promised Land, Israel entered the dark ages of her history.

Simply stated, the reason for this rapid decline was sin—individual and corporate. The first step away from God was incomplete obedience (Judg 1:11–2:5); the Israelites refused to eliminate the enemy completely from the land. This led to intermarriage and idolatry (Judg 2:6–3:7) and everyone doing "whatever seemed right" (Judg 17:6). Before long the Israelites became captives. Out of their desperation they begged God to rescue them. In faithfulness to his promise and out of his loving-kindness, God would raise up a judge to deliver his people, and for a time there would be peace. Then complacency and disobedience would set in, and the cycle would begin again.

The book of Judges spans a period of over 275 years, recording several cycles of oppression and deliverance, and the careers of 12 deliverers. Their captors included the Mesopotamians, Moabites, Philistines, Canaanites, Midianites, and Ammonites. God used a variety of deliverers—from Othniel to Samson—to lead his people to freedom and true worship. God's deliverance through the judges is a powerful demonstration of his love and mercy toward his people.

As you read the book of Judges, take a good look at these heroes from Jewish history. Note their dependence on God and obedience to his commands. Observe Israel's repeated downward spiral into sin, refusing to learn from history and living only for the moment. But most of all, stand in awe of God's mercy as he delivers his people over and over again.

THE BLUEPRINT

A. THE MILITARY FAILURE OF ISRAEL (1:1–3:6) 1. Incomplete conquest of the land 2. Disobedience and defeat	The tribes had compromised God's command to drive out the inhabitants of the land. Incomplete removal of evil often means disaster in the end. We must beware of compromising with wickedness.
B. THE RESCUE OF ISRAEL BY THE JUDGES (3:7–16:31) 1. First period: Othniel 2. Second period: Ehud and Shamgar 3. Third period: Deborah and Barak 4. Fourth period: Gideon, Tola, and Jair 5. Fifth period: Jephthah, Ibzan, Elon, and Abdon 6. Sixth period: Samson	Repeatedly we see the nation of Israel sinning against God and God allowing suffering to come upon the land and the people. Sin always has its consequences. Where there is sin we can expect suffering to follow. Rather than living in an endless cycle of abandoning God and then crying out to him for rescue, we should seek to live a consistent life of faithfulness.
C. THE MORAL FAILURE OF ISRAEL (17:1–21:25) 1. Idolatry in the tribe of Dan 2. War against the tribe of Benjamin	Despite the efforts of Israel's judges, the people still would not turn wholeheartedly to God. They all did whatever they thought was best for themselves. The result was the spiritual, moral, and political decline of the nation. Our lives will also fall into decline and decay unless we live by the guidelines God has given us.

MEGATHEMES

THEME	EXPLANATION	IMPORTANCE
Decline/ Compromise	Whenever a judge died, the people faced decline and failure because they compromised their high spiritual purpose in many ways. They abandoned their mission to drive all the people out of the land, and they adopted the customs of the people living around them.	Society has many rewards to offer those who compromise their faith: wealth, acceptance, recognition, power, and influence. When God gives us a mission, it must not be polluted by a desire for approval from society. We must keep our eyes on Christ, who is our Judge and Deliverer.
Decay/ Apostasy	Israel's moral downfall had its roots in the fierce independence that each tribe cherished. It led to everyone doing whatever seemed right in his own eyes. There was no unity in government or in worship. Law and order broke down. Finally, idol worship and man-made religion led to the complete abandoning of faith in God.	We can expect decay when we value anything more highly than God. If we value our own independence more than dedication to God, we have placed an idol in our hearts. Soon our lives become temples to that god. We must constantly regard God's first claim on our lives and all our desires.

Defeat/ Oppression	God used evil oppressors to punish the Israelites for their sin, to bring them to the point of repentance, and to test their allegiance to him.	Rebellion against God leads to disaster. God may use defeat to bring wandering hearts back to him. When all else is stripped away, we recognize the importance of serving only him.
Repentance	Decline, decay, and defeat caused the people to cry out to God for help. They vowed to turn from idolatry and to turn to God for mercy and deliverance. When they repented, God delivered them.	Idolatry gains a foothold in our hearts when we make anything more important than God. We must identify modern idols in our hearts, renounce them, and turn to God for his love and mercy.
Deliverance/ Heroes	Because Israel repented, God raised up heroes to deliver his people from their path of sin and the oppression it brought. He used many kinds of people to accomplish this purpose by filling them with his Holy Spirit.	God's Holy Spirit is available to all people. Anyone who is dedicated to God can be used for his service. Real heroes recognize the futility of human effort without God's guidance and power.

Possessing the Land

For Vital Statistics, see p. 333

RUTH

WHEN someone says, "Let me tell you about my mother-in-law," we expect some kind of negative statement or humorous anecdote because the mother-in-law caricature has been a standard centerpiece of ridicule or comedy. The book of Ruth, however, tells a different story. Ruth loved her mother-in-law, Naomi. Recently widowed, Ruth begged to stay with Naomi wherever she went, even though it would mean leaving her homeland. In heartfelt words, Ruth said, "Your people will be my people, and your God will be my God" (Ruth 1:16). Naomi agreed, and Ruth traveled with her to Bethlehem.

Not much is said about Naomi except that she loved and cared for Ruth. Obviously, Naomi's life was a powerful witness to the reality of God. Ruth was drawn to her—and to the God she worshiped. In the succeeding months, God led this young Moabite widow to a man named Boaz, whom she eventually married. As a result, she became the great-grandmother of David and an ancestor in the line of the Messiah. What a profound impact Naomi's life made!

The book of Ruth is also the story of God's grace in the midst of difficult circumstances. Ruth's story occurred during the time of the judges—a period of disobedience, idolatry, and violence. Even in times of crisis and deepest despair, there are those who follow God and through whom God works. No matter how discouraging or antagonistic the world may seem, there are always people who follow God. He will use anyone who is open to him to achieve his purposes. Ruth was a Moabite, and Boaz was a descendant of Rahab, a former prostitute from Jericho. Nevertheless, their offspring continued the family line through which the Messiah came into our world.

Read this book and be encouraged. God is at work in the world, and he wants to use you. God could use you, as he used Naomi, to bring family and friends to him.

THE BLUEPRINT

1. Ruth remains loyal to Naomi (1:1-22)
2. Ruth gleans in Boaz's field (2:1-23)
3. Ruth follows Naomi's plan (3:1-18)
4. Ruth and Boaz are married (4:1-22)

When we first meet Ruth, she is a destitute widow. We follow her as she joins God's people, gleans in the grain fields, and risks her honor at the threshing floor of Boaz. In the end, we see Ruth becoming the wife of Boaz. What a picture of how we come to faith in Christ. We begin with no hope and are rebellious aliens with no part in the kingdom of God. Then as we risk everything by putting our faith in Christ, God saves us, forgives us, rebuilds our lives, and gives us blessings that will last through eternity. Boaz's redeeming of Ruth is a picture of Christ redeeming us.

MEGATHEMES

THEME	EXPLANATION	IMPORTANCE
Faithfulness	Ruth's faithfulness to Naomi as a daughter-in-law and friend is a great example of love and loyalty. Ruth, Naomi, and Boaz are also faithful to God and his laws. Throughout the story we see God's faithfulness to his people.	Ruth's life was guided by faithfulness toward God and showed itself in loyalty toward the people she knew. To be loyal and loving in relationships, we must imitate God's faithfulness in our relationships with others.
Kindness	Ruth showed great kindness to Naomi. In turn, Boaz showed kindness to Ruth—a despised Moabite woman with no money. God showed his kindness to Ruth, Naomi, and Boaz by bringing them together for his purposes.	Just as Boaz showed his kindness by buying back land to guarantee Ruth and Naomi's inheritance, so Christ showed his kindness by dying for us to guarantee our eternal life. God's kindness should motivate us to love and honor him.
Integrity	Ruth showed high moral character by being loyal to Naomi, by her clean break from her former land and customs, and by her hard work in the fields. Boaz showed integrity in his moral standards, his honesty, and by following through on his commitments.	When we have experienced God's faithfulness and kindness, we should respond by showing integrity. Just as the values by which Ruth and Boaz lived were in sharp contrast to those of the culture portrayed in Judges, so our lives should stand out from the world around us.

Protection	We see God's care and protection over the lives of Naomi and Ruth. His supreme control over circumstances brings them safety and security. He guides the minds and activities of people to fulfill his purposes.	No matter how devastating our present situation may be, our hope is in God. His resources are infinite. We must believe that he can work in the life of any person—whether that person is a king or a stranger in a foreign land. Trust his protection.
Prosperity/ Blessing	Ruth and Naomi came to Bethlehem as poor widows, but they soon became prosperous through Ruth's marriage to Boaz. Ruth became the great-grandmother of King David. Yet the greatest blessing was not the money, the marriage, or the child; it was the quality of love and respect between Ruth, Boaz, and Naomi.	We tend to think of blessings in terms of prosperity rather than the high-quality relationships God makes possible for us. No matter what our economic situation, we can love and respect the people God has brought into our lives. In so doing, we give and receive blessings. Love is the greatest blessing.

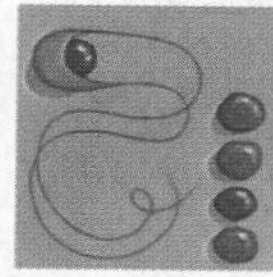

Possessing the Land
United Monarchy
For Vital Statistics, see p. 430

1 SAMUEL

"RUNNERS, take your marks," the starter barks his signal, and the crowd turns quiet attention to the athletes walking toward the line. "Get set" . . . in position now, muscles tense, nervously anticipating the sound of the gun. It resounds! And the race begins. In any contest, the start is important, but the finish is even more crucial. Often a front-runner will lose strength and fade to the middle of the pack. And there is the tragedy of the brilliant beginner who sets the pace for a time, but does not even finish. He quits the race burned out, exhausted, or injured.

First Samuel is a book of great beginnings . . . and tragic endings. It begins with Eli as high priest during the time of the judges. As a religious leader, Eli certainly must have begun his life with a close relationship to God. In his communication with Hannah, and in his training of her son Samuel, he demonstrated a clear understanding of God's purposes and call (1 Sam 1; 3). But his life ended in ignominy as his sacrilegious sons were judged by God, and the sacred Ark of the Covenant fell into enemy hands (1 Sam 4). Eli's death marked the decline of the influence of the priesthood and the rise of the prophets in Israel.

Samuel was dedicated to God's service by his mother, Hannah. He became one of Israel's greatest prophets. He was a man of prayer who finished the work of the judges, began the school of the prophets, and anointed Israel's first kings. But even Samuel was not immune to finishing poorly. Like Eli's family, Samuel's sons turned away from God, taking bribes and perverting justice. The people rejected the leadership of the judges and priests and clamored for a king "like all the other nations have" (1 Sam 8:5).

Saul also started quickly. A striking figure, this handsome (1 Sam 9:2) and humble (1 Sam 9:21; 10:22) man was God's choice as Israel's first king (1 Sam 10:24). His early reign was marked by leadership (1 Sam 11) and bravery (1 Sam 14:46-48). But he disobeyed God (1 Sam 15), became jealous and paranoid (1 Sam 18–19), and finally had his kingship taken away from him by God (1 Sam 16). Saul's life continued steadily downward. Obsessed with killing David (1 Sam 19–30), he consulted a medium (1 Sam 28) and finally committed suicide (1 Sam 31).

Among the events of Saul's life stands another great beginner—David. A man who followed God (1 Sam 13:14; 16:7), David ministered to Saul (1 Sam 16), killed Goliath (1 Sam 17), and became a great warrior. But we'll have to wait until the book of 2 Samuel to see how David finished.

As you read 1 Samuel, note the transition from theocracy to monarchy; exult in the classic stories of David and Goliath, David and Jonathan, David and Abigail; and watch the rise of the influence of the prophets. But in the midst of reading all the history and adventure, determine to run your race as God's person from start to finish.

THE BLUEPRINT

A. ELI AND SAMUEL (1:1–7:17)
1. Samuel's birth and childhood
2. War with the Philistines

We see a vivid contrast between young Samuel and Eli's sons. Eli's sons were selfish, but Samuel was helpful. Eli's sons defrauded people, but Samuel grew in wisdom and gave the people messages from God. As an adult, Samuel became a prophet, priest, and judge over Israel. A person's actions reflect his character. This was true of Samuel and of Eli's sons. It is also true of us. Strive, like Samuel, to keep your heart pure before God.

B. SAMUEL AND SAUL (8:1–15:35)
1. Saul becomes king of Israel
2. God rejects Saul for disobedience

Saul showed great promise. He was strong, tall, and modest. God's Spirit came upon him, and Samuel was his counselor. But Saul deliberately disobeyed God and became an evil king. We must not base our hopes or future on our potential. Instead, we must consistently obey God in all areas of life. God evaluates obedience, not potential.

C. SAUL AND DAVID (16:1–31:13)
1. Samuel anoints David
2. David and Goliath
3. David and Jonathan become friends
4. Saul pursues David
5. Saul's defeat and death

David quickly killed Goliath but waited patiently for God to deal with Saul. Although David was anointed to be Israel's next king, he had to wait years to realize this promise. The difficult circumstances in life and the times of waiting often refine, teach, and prepare us for the future responsibilities God has for us.

MEGATHEMES

THEME	EXPLANATION	IMPORTANCE
King	Because Israel suffered from corrupt priests and judges, the people wanted a king. They wanted to be organized like the surrounding nations. Though it was against his original purpose, God chose a king for them.	Establishing a monarchy did not solve Israel's problems. What God desires is the genuine devotion of each person's mind and heart to him. No government or set of laws can substitute for the rule of God in your heart and life.
God's Control	Israel prospered as long as the people regarded God as their true king. When the leaders strayed from God's law, God intervened in their personal lives and overruled their actions. In this way, God maintained ultimate control over Israel's history.	God is always at work in this world, even when we can't see what he is doing. No matter what kinds of pressures we must endure or how many changes we must face, God is ultimately in control of our situation. Being confident of God's sovereignty, we can face the difficult situations in our lives with boldness.
Leadership	God guided his people using different forms of leadership: judges, priests, prophets, kings. Those whom he chose for these different offices, such as Eli, Samuel, Saul, and David, portrayed different styles of leadership. Yet the success of each leader depended on his devotion to God, not his position, leadership style, wisdom, age, or strength.	When Eli, Samuel, Saul, and David disobeyed God, they faced tragic consequences. Sin affected what they accomplished for God and how some of them raised their children. Being a real leader means letting God guide all aspects of your activities, values, and goals, including the way you raise your children.
Obedience	For God, "obedience is better than sacrifice" (1 Sam 15:22). God wanted his people to obey, serve, and follow him with a whole heart rather than to maintain a superficial commitment based on tradition or ceremonial systems.	Although we are free from the sacrificial system of the Jewish law, we may still rely on outward observances to substitute for inward commitment. God desires that all our work and worship be motivated by genuine, heartfelt devotion to him.
God's Faithfulness	God faithfully kept the promises he made to Israel. He responded to his people with tender mercy and swift justice. In showing mercy, he faithfully acted in the best interest of his people. In showing justice, he was faithful to his word and perfect moral nature.	Because God is faithful, he can be counted on to be merciful toward us. Yet God is also just, and he will not tolerate rebellion against him. His faithfulness and unselfish love should inspire us to dedicate ourselves to him completely. We must never take his mercy for granted.

United Monarchy

For Vital Statistics, see p. 430

2 SAMUEL

THE CHILD enters the room with long gown flowing, trailing well behind her high-heeled shoes. The wide-brimmed hat rests precariously atop her head, tilted to the right, and the long necklace swings like a pendulum as she walks. Following close is the "man." His fingertips peek out of the coat sleeves that are already pushed upward six inches. With feet shuffling in the double-sized boots, his unsteady steps belie his confident smile. Children at play, dressing up—they copy Mom and Dad, having watched them dress and walk. Models . . . everyone has them . . . people we emulate, people who are our ideals. Unconsciously, perhaps, we copy their actions and adopt their ideas.

Among all the godly role models mentioned in the Bible, probably no one stands out more than King David. He was God's leader for all of Israel and the ancestor of the Messiah. David was "a man after [God's] own heart" (1 Sam 13:14). What are the personal qualities that David possessed that pleased God?

The book of 2 Samuel tells David's story. As you read, you will be filled with excitement as he is crowned king over Judah and then king over all of Israel (2 Sam 5:1-5), praising God as he brings the Ark of the Covenant back to the Tabernacle (2 Sam 6:1-23) and exulting as he leads his armies to victory over all their enemies and completes the conquest of the Promised Land begun by Joshua (2 Sam 8–10). David accomplished much.

But David was human, and during dark times he stumbled and fell into sin. The record of lust, adultery, and murder is not easy to read (2 Sam11–13) and reveals that even great people who try to follow God are susceptible to temptation and sin.

Godliness does not guarantee an easy and carefree life. David had family problems—his own son incited the entire nation to rebellion and crowned himself king (2 Sam 14:1–18:33). And greatness can cause pride, as we see in David's sinful act of taking a census in order to glory in the strength of his nation (2 Sam 24:1–25). But the story of this fallen hero does not end in tragedy. Through repentance, his fellowship and peace with God were restored, but he had to face the consequences of the sins he committed (2 Sam 12–20). These consequences stayed with him the rest of his life as a reminder of his sinful deeds and his need for God.

As you read 2 Samuel, look for David's god-like characteristics—his faithfulness, patience, courage, generosity, commitment, honesty—as well as other God-honoring characteristics, such as modesty and penitence. Valuable lessons can be learned from his sins and from his repentance. You, like David, can become a person after God's own heart.

THE BLUEPRINT

A. DAVID'S SUCCESSES (1:1–10:19) 1. David becomes king over Judah 2. David becomes king over Israel 3. David conquers the surrounding nations	David took the fractured kingdom that Saul had left behind and built a strong, united power. Forty years later, David would turn this kingdom over to his son Solomon. David had a heart for God. He was a king who governed God's people by God's principles, and God blessed him greatly. We may not have David's earthly success, but following God is, ultimately, the most successful decision we can make.
B. DAVID'S STRUGGLES (11:1–24:25) 1. David and Bathsheba 2. Turmoil in David's family 3. National rebellion against David 4. The later years of David's rule	David sinned with Bathsheba and then tried to cover his sin by having her husband killed. Although he was forgiven for his sin, the consequences remained—he experienced trouble and distress, both with his family and with the nation. God is always ready to forgive, but we must live with the consequences of our actions. Covering up our sin will only multiply sin's painful consequences.

MEGATHEMES

THEME	EXPLANATION	IMPORTANCE
Kingdom Growth	Under David's leadership, Israel's kingdom grew rapidly. With the growth came many changes: from tribal independence to centralized government, from the leadership of judges to a monarchy, from decentralized worship to worship at Jerusalem.	No matter how much growth or how many changes we experience, God provides for us if we love him and highly regard his principles. God's work done in God's way never lacks God's supply of wisdom and energy.
Personal Greatness	David's popularity and influence increased greatly. He realized that the Lord was behind his success because he wanted to pour out his kindness on Israel. David regarded God's interests as more important than his own.	God graciously pours out his favor on us because of what Christ has done. God does not regard personal greatness as something to be used selfishly, but as an instrument to carry out his work among his people. The greatness we should desire is to love others as God loves us.
Justice	King David showed justice, mercy, and fairness to Saul's family, enemies, rebels, allies, and close friends alike. His just rule was grounded in his faith in and knowledge of God. God's perfect moral nature is the standard for justice.	Although David was the most just of all Israel's kings, he was still imperfect. His use of justice offered hope for a heavenly, ideal kingdom. This hope will never be satisfied in our hearts until Christ, the Son of David, comes to rule in perfect justice forever.
Consequences of Sin	David abandoned his purpose as leader and king in time of war. His desire for prosperity and ease led him from triumph to trouble. Because David committed adultery with Bathsheba, he experienced consequences of his sin that destroyed both his family and the nation.	Temptation quite often comes when a person's life is aimless. We sometimes think that sinful pleasures and freedom from God's restraint will bring us a feeling of vitality; but sin creates a cycle of suffering that is not worth the fleeting pleasures it offers.
Feet of Clay	David not only sinned with Bathsheba, he murdered an innocent man. He neglected to discipline his sons when they got involved in rape and murder. This great hero showed a lack of character in some of his most important personal decisions. The man of iron had feet of clay.	Sin should never be considered as a mere weakness or flaw. Sin is fatal and must be eradicated from our lives. David's life teaches us to have compassion for all people, including those whose sinful nature leads them into sinful acts. It serves as a warning to us not to excuse sin in our own lives, even in times of success.

United Monarchy Splintered Nation

For Vital Statistics, see p. 687

1 KINGS

"I DON'T CARE what anyone says, I'm going to do it!" the boy yells at his mother as he storms out of the house. This is a familiar scene in our society. The words change, but the essential message is the same: A person is not open to advice because his or her mind is closed. Some advice may be sought, but it is heeded only if it reinforces the decision already made or is an easier path to take. It is human nature to reject help and to do things our way.

A much wiser approach is to seek, hear, and heed the advice of good counselors. Solomon, the world's wisest man, urges this in Proverbs (see Prov 11:14; 15:22; 24:6). How ironic that his son and successor, Rehoboam, listened instead to foolish advice, with devastating results. At Rehoboam's inauguration, he was petitioned by the people to be a kind and generous ruler. The older men counseled him to "be a servant . . . and give them a favorable answer" (1 Kgs 12:7). But Rehoboam agreed to the cruel advice of his peers who urged him to be harsh. As a result, Rehoboam split the kingdom. Learn from Rehoboam's mistake. Commit yourself to seeking and following wise counsel.

The main events of 1 Kings are David's death, Solomon's reign, the division of the kingdom, and Elijah's ministry. As Solomon ascended the throne, David charged him to obey God's laws and to "follow all his ways" (1 Kgs 2:3). This Solomon did; and when given the choice of gifts from God, he humbly asked for wisdom (1 Kgs 3:9). As a result, Solomon's reign began with great success, including the construction of the Temple—his greatest achievement. Unfortunately, Solomon took many pagan wives and concubines who eventually turned his heart away from the Lord to their false gods (1 Kgs 11:1-4).

Rehoboam succeeded Solomon and had the opportunity to be a wise, compassionate, and just king. Instead, he accepted the poor advice of his young friends and attempted to rule with an iron hand. But the people rebelled, and the kingdom split with 10 tribes in the north (Israel) ruled by Jeroboam, and only Judah and Benjamin remaining with Rehoboam. Both kingdoms wove a path through the reigns of corrupt and idolatrous kings with only the clear voice of the prophets continuing to warn and call the nation back to God.

Elijah is surely one of the greatest prophets, and chapters 17 through 22 feature his conflict with wicked Ahab and Jezebel in Israel. In one of the most dramatic confrontations in history, Elijah defeated the prophets of Baal at Mount Carmel. In spite of incredible opposition, Elijah stood for God and proved that one plus God is a majority. If God is on our side, no one can stand against us (Rom 8:31).

THE BLUEPRINT

A. THE UNITED KINGDOM (1:1–11:43)
1. Solomon becomes king
2. Solomon's wisdom
3. Solomon builds the Temple
4. Solomon's greatness and downfall

Solomon was a botanist, zoologist, architect, poet, and philosopher. He was the wisest king in the history of Israel, but his wives led to the introduction of false gods and false worship in Israel. It is good for us to have wisdom, but that is not enough. The highest goal in life is to obey the Lord. Patient obedience to God should characterize our lives.

B. THE DIVIDED KINGDOM (12:1–22:53)
1. Revolt of the northern tribes
2. Kings of Israel and Judah
3. Elijah's ministry
4. Kings of Israel and Judah

When the northern kingdom of Israel was being led by wicked kings, God raised up a prophet to proclaim his messages. Elijah single-handedly challenged the priesthood of the state religion and had them removed in one day. Through the dividing of the kingdom and the sending of Elijah, God dealt with the people's sin in powerful ways. Sin in our lives is graciously forgiven by God. However, the sin of an unrepentant person will be handled harshly. We must turn from sin and turn to God to be saved from judgment.

MEGATHEMES

THEME	EXPLANATION	IMPORTANCE
The King	Solomon's wisdom, power, and achievements brought honor to the Israelite nation and to God. All the kings of Israel and Judah were told to obey God and to govern according to his laws. But their tendency to abandon God's commands and to worship other gods led them to change the religion and government to meet their personal desires. This neglect of God's law led to their downfall.	Wisdom, power, and achievement do not ultimately come from any human source; they are from God. No matter what we lead or govern, we can't do well when we ignore God's guidelines. Whether or not we are leaders, effectiveness depends upon listening and obeying God's Word. Don't let your personal desires distort God's Word.
The Temple	Solomon's Temple was a beautiful place of worship and prayer. This sanctuary was the center of Jewish religion. It was the place of God's special presence and housed the Ark of the Covenant containing the Ten Commandments.	A beautiful house of worship doesn't always guarantee heartfelt worship of God. Providing opportunities for true worship doesn't ensure that it will happen. God wants to live in our hearts, not just meet us in a sanctuary.
Other Gods	Although the Israelites had God's law and experienced his presence among them, they became attracted to other gods. When this happened, their hearts became cold to God's law, resulting in the ruin of families and government, and eventually leading to the destruction of the nation.	Through the years, the people took on the false qualities of the false gods they worshiped. They became cruel, power-hungry, and sexually perverse. We tend to become what we worship. Unless we serve the true God, we will become slaves to whatever takes his place.
The Prophet's Message	The prophet's responsibility was to confront and correct any deviation from God's law. Elijah was a bolt of judgment against Israel. His messages and miracles were a warning to the evil and rebellious kings and people.	The Bible, the truth in sermons, and the wise counsel of believers are warnings to us. Anyone who points out how we deviate from obeying God's Word is a blessing to us. Changing our lives in order to obey God and get back on track often takes painful discipline and hard work.
Sin and Repentance	Each king had God's commands, a priest or prophet, and the lessons of the past to draw him back to God. All the people had the same resources. Whenever they repented and returned to God, God heard their prayers and forgave them.	God hears and forgives us when we pray—if we are willing to trust him and turn from sin. Our desire to forsake our sin must be heartfelt and sincere. Then he will give us a fresh start and a desire to live for him.

2 KINGS

Splintered Nation
Exile

For Vital Statistics, see p. 687

SPARKLING as it crashes against boulders along its banks, the river swiftly cascades toward the sea. The current grabs, pushes, and tugs at leaves and logs, carrying them along for the ride. Here and there a sportsman is spotted in a kayak or a canoe, going with the flow. Gravity pulls the water, and the river pulls the rest . . . downward. Suddenly, a silver missile breaks the surface and darts upstream, and then another. Oblivious to the swirling opposition, the shining salmon swim against the stream. They must go upstream, and nothing will stop them from reaching their destination.

The current of society's river is flowing fast and furious, pulling downward everything in its way. It would be easy to float along with the current. But God calls us to swim against the flow. It will not be easy, and we may be alone, but it will be right.

In the book of 2 Kings, we read of evil rulers, rampant idolatry, and a complacent populace—certainly pulling downward. Despite the pressure to conform, to turn from the Lord and to serve only self, a minority of chosen people moved in the opposite direction, toward God. The Bethel prophets and others, as well as two righteous kings, spoke God's word and stood for him. As you read 2 Kings, watch these courageous individuals. Catch the strength and force of Elijah and Elisha and the commitment of Hezekiah and Josiah, and determine to be one who swims against the current!

Second Kings continues the history of Israel, halfway between the death of David and the death of the nation. Israel had been divided (1 Kgs 12), and the two kingdoms had begun to slide into idolatry and corruption toward collapse and captivity. Second Kings relates the sordid stories of the 12 kings of the northern kingdom (called Israel) and the 16 kings of the southern kingdom (called Judah). For 130 years Israel endured the succession of evil rulers until they were conquered by Shalmaneser of Assyria and led into captivity in 722 B.C. (2 Kgs 17:6). Of all the kings in both the north and south, only two—Hezekiah and Josiah—were called good. Because of their obedience to God and the spiritual revivals during their reigns, Judah stood for an additional 136 years until falling to Nebuchadnezzar and the Babylonians in 586 B.C.

Throughout this dark period, the Bible mentions 30 prophets who proclaimed God's message to the people and their leaders. Most notable of these fearless people of God are Elijah and Elisha. As Elijah neared the end of his earthly ministry, Elisha asked that he might become Elijah's rightful successor (2 Kgs 2:9). Soon after, Elijah was taken to heaven in a whirlwind (2 Kgs 2:11), and Elisha became God's spokesman to the northern kingdom. Elisha's life was filled with signs, proclamations, warnings, and miracles. Four of the most memorable are the flowing oil (2 Kgs 4:1-7), the healing of the Shunammite woman's son (2 Kgs 4:8-37), the healing of Naaman's leprosy (2 Kgs 5:1-27), and the floating ax head (2 Kgs 6:1-7).

Even in the midst of terrible situations, God will have his faithful minority, his remnant (2 Kgs 19:31). He desires courageous men and women to proclaim his truth.

THE BLUEPRINT

A. THE DIVIDED KINGDOM (1:1–17:41)
1. Elisha's ministry
2. Kings of Israel and Judah
3. Israel is exiled to Assyria

Although Israel had the witness and power of Elisha, the nation turned from God and was exiled to Assyria. Assyria filled the northern kingdom with people from other lands. There has been no return from this captivity—it was permanent. Such is the end of all who shut God out of their lives.

B. THE SURVIVING KINGDOM (18:1–25:30)
1. Kings of Judah
2. Judah is exiled to Babylon

The northern kingdom was destroyed, and prophets were predicting the same fate for Judah. What more could cause the nation to repent? Hezekiah and Josiah were able to stem the tide of evil. They both repaired the Temple and gathered the people for the Passover. Josiah eradicated idolatry from the land, but as soon as these good kings were gone, the people returned again to living their own way instead of God's way. Each individual must believe and live for God in his or her family, church, and nation.

MEGATHEMES

THEME	EXPLANATION	IMPORTANCE
Elisha	The purpose of Elisha's ministry was to restore respect for God and his message, and he stood firmly against the evil kings of Israel. By faith, with courage and prayer, he revealed not only God's judgment on sin but also his mercy, love, and tenderness toward faithful people.	Elisha's mighty miracles showed that God controls not only great armies but also events in everyday life. When we listen to and obey God, he shows us his power to transform any situation. God's care is for all who are willing to follow him. He can perform miracles in our lives.
Idolatry	Every evil king in both Israel and Judah encouraged idolatry. These false gods represented war, cruelty, power, and sex. Although they had God's law, priests, and prophets to guide them, these kings sought priests and prophets whom they could manipulate to their own advantage.	An idol is any idea, ability, possession, or person that we regard more highly than God. We condemn Israel and Judah for foolishly worshiping idols, but we also worship other gods—power, money, physical attractiveness. Those who believe in God must resist the lure of these attractive idols.

Evil Kings/ Good Kings	Only a few of Israel and Judah's kings followed God. The evil kings were shortsighted. They thought they could control their nations' destinies by importing other religions, forming alliances with pagan nations, and enriching themselves. The good kings had to spend most of their time undoing the evil done by their predecessors.	Although the evil kings led the people into sin, the priests, princes, heads of families, and military leaders all had to cooperate with the evil plans and practices in order for them to be carried out. We cannot discharge our responsibility to obey God by blaming our leaders. We are responsible to know God's Word and obey it.
God's Patience	God told his people that if they obeyed him, they would live successfully; if they disobeyed, they would be judged and destroyed. God had been patient with the people for hundreds of years. He sent many prophets to guide them. And he gave ample warning of coming destruction. But even God's patience has limits.	God is patient with us. He gives us many chances to hear his message, to turn from sin, and to believe him. His patience does not mean he is indifferent to how we live, nor does it mean we can ignore his warnings. His patience should make us want to come to him now.
Judgment	After King Solomon's reign, Israel lasted 209 years before the Assyrians destroyed it; Judah lasted 345 years before the Babylonians took Jerusalem. After repeated warnings to his people, God used these evil nations as instruments for his justice.	The consequences of rejecting God's commands and purpose for our lives are severe. He will not ignore unbelief or rebellion. We must believe in him and accept Christ's sacrificial death on our behalf, or we will be judged also.

United Monarchy
Return & Diaspora

For Vital Statistics, see p. 430

1 CHRONICLES

IN THE WIDE shade of the ageless oak, a mother watches her toddler discover acorns, leaves, and dandelions. Nearby, her mother, aunt, and uncle spread the checkerboard cloth over park tables and cover it with bowls and platters of fried chicken, potato salad, baked beans, and assorted family recipes. The clanging of Grandpa's and Dad's horseshoes against stakes regularly pierces the air and mixes with the cheers, laughs, and shouts of teenagers playing a game of touch football. A family reunion—a sunny afternoon filled with four generations of miscellaneous kids, parents, and second cousins once removed.

Reunions are important. They are times for touching and connecting with others from branches of the family tree, tracing one's personal history back through time and culture, seeing physical reminders (her eyes, his nose), recalling warm traditions. Knowing one's genetic and relational path gives a sense of identity, heritage, and destiny.

With this same high purpose, the writer of Chronicles begins his unifying work with an extensive genealogy. He traces the roots of the nation in a literary family reunion from Adam onward, recounting its royal line and the loving plan of a personal God. We read 1 Chronicles and gain a glimpse of God at work through his people for generations. If you are a believer, these people are your ancestors, too. As you approach this part of God's Word, read their names with awe and respect, and gain new security and identity in your relationship with God.

The previous book, 2 Kings, ends with both Israel and Judah in captivity, surely a dark age for God's people. Then follows Chronicles (1 and 2 Chronicles were originally one book). Written after the Captivity, it summarizes Israel's history, emphasizing the Jewish people's spiritual heritage in an attempt to unify the nation. The chronicler is selective in his history telling. Instead of writing an exhaustive work, he carefully weaves the narrative, highlighting spiritual lessons and teaching moral truths. In Chronicles the northern kingdom is virtually ignored, David's triumphs—not his sins—are recalled, and the Temple is given great prominence as the vital center of national life.

First Chronicles begins with Adam, and for nine chapters, the writer gives us a "Who's Who" of Israel's history with special emphasis on David's royal line. The rest of the book tells the story of David—the great man of God, Israel's king—who served God and laid out the plans for the construction of and worship in the Temple.

First Chronicles is an invaluable supplement to 2 Samuel and a strong reminder of the necessity for tracing our roots and thus rediscovering our spiritual foundation. As you read 1 Chronicles, trace your own godly heritage, thank God for your spiritual forefathers, and recommit yourself to passing on God's truth to the next generation.

THE BLUEPRINT

A. THE GENEALOGIES OF ISRAEL (1:1–9:44) 1. Ancestry of the nation 2. The tribes of Israel 3. Returnees from exile in Babylon	The long list of names that follows presents a history of God's work in the world from Adam through Zerubbabel. Some of these names remind us of stories of great faith, and others, of tragic failure. About most of the people named, however, we know nothing. But those who died unknown to us are known by God. God will also remember us when we die.
B. THE REIGN OF DAVID (10:1–29:30) 1. David becomes king over all of Israel 2. David brings the Ark to Jerusalem 3. David's military exploits 4. David arranges for the building of the Temple	David loved the Lord and wanted to build a Temple to replace the Tabernacle, but God denied his request. David's greatest contribution to the Temple would not be the construction but the preparation. We may be unable to see the results of our labors for God in our lifetime, but David's example helps us understand that we serve God so he will see his results, not so we will see ours.

MEGATHEMES

THEME	EXPLANATION	IMPORTANCE
Israel's History	By retelling Israel's history in the genealogies and the stories of the kings, the writer laid down the true spiritual foundation for the nation. God kept his promises, and we are reminded of them in the historical record of his people, leaders, prophets, priests, and kings.	Israel's past formed a reliable basis for reconstructing the nation after the Exile. Because God's promises are revealed in the Bible, we can know God and trust him to keep his word. Like Israel, we should have no higher goal in life than devoted service to God.
God's People	By listing the names of people in Israel's past, God established Israel's true heritage. They were all one family in Adam, one nation in Abraham, one priesthood under Levi, and one kingdom under David. The national and spiritual unity of the people was important to the rebuilding of the nation.	God is always faithful to his people. He protects them in every generation and provides leaders to guide them. Because God has been at work throughout the centuries, his people can trust him to work in the present. You can rely on his presence today.
David, the King	The story of David's life and his relationship with God showed that he was God's appointed leader. David's devotion to God, the law, the Temple, true worship, the people, and justice sets the standard for what God's chosen king should be like.	Jesus Christ came to earth as a descendant of David. One day he will rule as King over all the earth. His strength and justice will fulfill God's ideal for the king. He is our hope. We can experience God's Kingdom now by giving Christ complete control of our lives.
True Worship	David brought the Ark of the Covenant to the Tabernacle at Jerusalem to restore true worship to the people. God gave the plans for building the Temple, and David organized the priests to make worship central to all Israel.	The Temple stood as the throne of God on earth, the place of true worship. God's true throne is in the hearts of his people. When we acknowledge him as the true King over our lives, true worship takes place.
The Priests	God ordained the priests and Levites to guide the people in faithful worship according to his law. By leading the people in worship according to God's design, the priests and Levites were an important safeguard to Israel's faith.	For true worship to remain central in our lives, God's people need to take a firm stand for the ways of God recorded in the Bible. Today, all believers are priests for one another, and we should encourage each other to faithful worship.

United Monarchy
Splintered Nation
Return & Diaspora
For Vital Statistics, see p. 687

2 CHRONICLES

THE SLIDE clicks, and our eyes focus on the image flashed onto the screen in the darkened sanctuary. "This idol," explains the missionary, "is made of stone and is worshiped daily. The natives believe that this will guarantee good crops and healthy children." With condescending smiles, we wonder at their ignorance. How could anyone worship an object? Idols are for the naive and the superstitious! But after the presentation, we return home to our idols of wealth, prestige, or self-fulfillment. Whatever we put in God's place, we worship—despite what we profess.

Our experience parallels Israel's. They were chosen by God to represent him on earth. But too often they forgot the truth and their calling, stumbling blindly after idols as the neighboring nations did. Then prophets, priests, and judgment would push them abruptly back to the one true God. Second Chronicles relates this sordid history of Judah's corrupt and idolatrous kings. Here and there a good king would arise in Judah, and for a time revival would follow, but the downward spiral would continue—ending in chaos, destruction, and captivity.

The chronicler writes this volume to bring the people of Israel back to God by reminding them of their past. Only by following God would they prosper! As you read 2 Chronicles, you will catch a vivid glimpse of Judah's history (the history of Israel, the northern kingdom, is virtually ignored), and you will see the tragic results of idolatry. Learn the lessons of the past: Determine to get rid of any idols in your life and to worship God alone.

Second Chronicles continues the history of 1 Chronicles. David's son Solomon was inaugurated as king. Solomon built the magnificent Temple in Jerusalem, thus fulfilling his father's wish and last request (2 Chr 2–5). Solomon enjoyed a peaceful and prosperous reign of 40 years that made him world famous. After Solomon died, his son Rehoboam assumed the throne, and his immaturity divided the kingdom.

In Judah there were a few good kings and many evil ones. The writer of Chronicles faithfully records their achievements and failures, noting how each king measured up to God's standard for success. Clearly a good king obeyed God's laws, eliminated the places of idol worship, and made no alliances with other nations. Judah's good kings include Asa, Jehoshaphat, Uzziah, Hezekiah, and Josiah. Of its many evil ones, Ahaz and Manasseh were perhaps the worst. Eventually the nation was conquered and taken captive, and the Temple was destroyed.

The writer's purpose was to reunite the nation around the true worship of God after the Captivity. In these pages, he reminds the people of their past. He clearly broadcasts his message through one of the best-known verses in Scripture, "Then if my people who are called by my name will humble themselves and pray and seek my face and turn from their wicked ways, I will hear from heaven and will forgive their sins and restore their land" (2 Chr 7:14). As you read 2 Chronicles, listen to God's voice and obey him; and receive his redemptive, healing touch.

THE BLUEPRINT

A. THE REIGN OF SOLOMON (1:1–9:31) 1. Solomon asks for wisdom 2. Solomon builds the Temple 3. Solomon dedicates the Temple 4. Solomon's riches and wisdom	Solomon achieved much in business and government, but most important, he was the man God used to build the glorious Temple. This beautiful building was the religious center of the nation. It symbolized the unity of all the tribes, the presence of God among them, and the nation's high calling. We may achieve great things in life, but we must not neglect any effort that will help nurture God's people or bring others into God's Kingdom. It is easy for us to get the wrong perspective on what's really important in life.
B. THE KINGDOM OF JUDAH (10:1–36:23) 1. The northern tribes revolt 2. History of apostasy and reform 3. Judah is exiled to Babylon	Throughout the reigns of 20 kings, the nation of Judah wavered between obedience to God and apostasy. The reigning king's response to God determined the spiritual climate of the nation and whether or not God would send judgment upon his people. Our personal history is shaped by our response to God. Just as Judah's failure to repent brought them captivity in Babylon, so the abuse of our high calling by sinful living will ultimately bring us catastrophe and destruction.

MEGATHEMES

THEME	EXPLANATION	IMPORTANCE
Temple	The Temple was the symbol of God's presence and the place set aside for worship and prayer. Built by Solomon from the plans God gave to David, the Temple was the spiritual center of the nation.	As Christians meet together to worship God, they experience the presence of God in a way that no individual believer can, for the dwelling place of God is the people of God. The body of Christ is God's temple.
Peace	As Solomon and his descendants were faithful to God, they experienced victory in battle, success in government, and peace with other nations. Peace was the result of the people being unified and loyal to God and his law.	Only God can bring true peace. God is greater than any enemy, army, or nation. Just as Israel's faithful response was key to her peace and survival as a nation, so our obedience to God as individuals and nations is vital to peace today.
Prayer	After Solomon died, David's kingdom was divided. When a king led the Israelites into idolatry, the nation suffered. When the king and his people prayed to God for deliverance and they turned from their sinful ways, God delivered them.	God still answers prayer today. We have God's promise that if we humble ourselves, seek him, turn from our sin, and pray, God will hear, restore, and forgive us. If we are alert, we can pray for God's guidance before we get into trouble.
Reform	Although idolatry and injustice were common, some kings turned to God and led the people in spiritual revival—renewing their commitment to God and reforming their society. Revival included the destruction of idols, obedience to the law, and the restoration of the priesthood.	We must constantly commit ourselves to obeying God. We are never secure in what others have done before us. Believers in each generation must dedicate themselves to the task of carrying out God's will in their own lives as well as in society.
National Collapse	In 586 B.C. the Babylonians completely destroyed Solomon's beautiful Temple. The formal worship of God was ended. The Israelites had abandoned God. As a result, God brought judgment upon his people, and they were carried off into captivity.	Although our disobedience may not be as blatant as Israel's, quite often our commitment to God is insincere and casual. When we forget that all our power, wisdom, and wealth come from God and not ourselves, we are in danger of the same spiritual and moral collapse that Israel experienced.

Return & Diaspora

For Vital Statistics, see p. 1147

EZRA

NAME the truly great men and women of your lifetime. Celebrities, including politicians, war heroes, sports figures, and maybe your parents and special friends come to mind. You remember them because of certain acts or character qualities. Now, name some biblical heroes—figures etched in your mind through countless sermons and church school lessons. This list undoubtedly includes many who served God faithfully and courageously. Does your list include Ezra? Far from being well known, this unheralded man of God deserves to be mentioned in any discussion of greatness.

Ezra was a priest, a scribe, and a great leader. His name means "help," and his whole life was dedicated to serving God and God's people. Tradition says that Ezra wrote most of 1 and 2 Chronicles, Ezra, Nehemiah, and Psalm 119 and that he led the council of 120 men who compiled the Old Testament canon. The narrative of the book of Ezra is centered on God and his promise that the Jews would return to their land, as prophesied by Jeremiah (see the third note on Ezra 1:1). This message formed the core of Ezra's life. The last half of the book gives a very personal glimpse of Ezra. His knowledge of Scripture and his God-given wisdom were so obvious to the king that he appointed Ezra to lead the second emigration to Jerusalem, to teach the people God's Word, and to administer national life (Ezra 7:14-26).

Ezra not only knew God's Word, he believed and obeyed it. Upon learning of the Israelites' sins of intermarriage and idolatry, Ezra fell in humility before God and prayed for the nation (Ezra 9:1-15). Their disobedience touched him deeply (Ezra 10:1). His response helped lead the people back to God.

Second Chronicles ends with Cyrus, king of Persia, asking for volunteers to return to Jerusalem to build a house for God. Ezra continues this account (Ezra 1:1-3 is almost identical to 2 Chr 36:22-23) as two caravans of God's people were returning to Jerusalem. Zerubbabel, the leader of the first trip, was joined by 42,360 pilgrims who journeyed homeward (Ezra 2). After arriving, they began to build the altar and the Temple foundations (Ezra 3). But opposition arose from the local inhabitants, and a campaign of accusations and rumors temporarily halted the project (Ezra 4). During this time, the prophets Haggai and Zechariah encouraged the people (Ezra 5). Finally, Darius decreed that the work should proceed unhindered (Ezra 6).

After a 58-year gap, Ezra led a group of Jews from Persia. Armed with decrees and authority from Artaxerxes I, Ezra's task was to administer the affairs of the land (Ezra 7–8). Upon arriving, he learned of intermarriage between God's people and their pagan neighbors. He wept and prayed for the nation (Ezra 9). Ezra's example of humble confession led to national revival (Ezra 10). Ezra, a man of God and a true hero, was a model for Israel, and he is a fitting model for us.

Read Ezra, the book, and remember Ezra, the man—a humble, obedient helper. Commit yourself to serving God as he did, with your whole life.

THE BLUEPRINT

A. THE RETURN LED BY ZERUBBABEL (1:1–6:22) 1. The first group of exiles returns to the land 2. The people rebuild the Temple	Finally given the chance to return to their homeland, the people started to rebuild the Temple, only to be stopped by opposition from their enemies. God's work in the world is not without opposition. We must not get discouraged and quit, as the returning people did at first, but continue on boldly in the face of difficulties, as they did later with encouragement from the prophets.
B. THE RETURN LED BY EZRA (7:1–10:44) 1. The second group of exiles returns to the land 2. Ezra opposes intermarriage	Ezra returned to Jerusalem almost 80 years after Zerubbabel, only to discover that the people had married pagan or foreign spouses. This polluted the religious purity of the people and endangered the future of the nation. Believers today must be careful not to threaten their walk with God by taking on the practices of unbelievers.

MEGATHEMES

THEME	EXPLANATION	IMPORTANCE
The Jews Return	By returning to the land of Israel from Babylon, the Jews showed their faith in God's promise to restore them as a people. They returned not only to their homeland but also to the place where their forefathers had promised to follow God.	God shows his mercy to every generation. He compassionately restores his people. No matter how difficult our present "captivity," we are never far from his love and mercy. He restores us when we return to him.
Rededication	In 536 B.C., Zerubbabel led the people in rebuilding the altar and laying the Temple foundation. They reinstated daily sacrifices and annual festivals, and rededicated themselves to a new spiritual worship of God.	In rededicating the altar, the people were recommitting themselves to God and his service. To grow spiritually, our commitment must be reviewed and renewed often. As we rededicate ourselves to God, our lives become altars to him.
Opposition	Opposition came soon after the altar was built and the Temple foundation laid. Enemies of the Jews used deceit to hinder the building for over six years. Finally, there was a decree to stop the building altogether. This opposition severely tested their wavering faith.	There will always be adversaries who oppose God's work. The life of faith is never easy. But God can overrule all opposition to his service. When we face opposition, we must not falter or withdraw, but keep active and patient.
God's Word	When the people returned to the land, they were also returning to the influence of God's Word. The prophets Haggai and Zechariah helped encourage them, while Ezra's preaching of Scripture built them up. God's Word gave them what they needed to do God's work.	We also need the encouragement and direction of God's Word. We must make it the basis for our faith and actions to finish God's work and fulfill our obligations. We must never waver in our commitment to hear and obey his Word.
Faith and Action	The urging of Israel's leaders motivated the people to complete the Temple. Over the years they had intermarried with idol worshipers and adopted their pagan practices. Their faith, tested and revived, also led them to remove these sins from their lives.	Faith led them to complete the Temple and to remove sin from their society. As we trust God with our hearts and minds, we must also act by completing our daily responsibilities. It is not enough to say we believe; we must make the changes God requires.

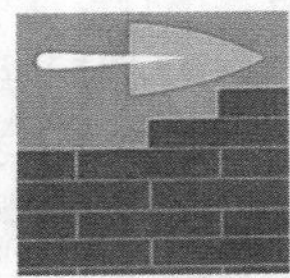

Return & Diaspora

For Vital Statistics, see p. 1147

NEHEMIAH

"WHAT this church needs is . . . !" "I can't believe our government officials. If I were there I would . . . !" "Our schools are really in bad shape. Someone ought to do something!" Gripers, complainers, self-proclaimed prophets, and "armchair quarterbacks" abound. It is easy to analyze, scrutinize, and talk about all the problems in the world. But what we really need are people who will not just discuss a situation but who will do something about it!

Nehemiah saw a problem and was distressed. Instead of complaining or wallowing in self-pity and grief, he took action. Nehemiah knew that God wanted him to motivate the Jews to rebuild Jerusalem's walls, so he left a responsible position in the Persian government to do what God wanted. Nehemiah knew God could use his talents to get the job done. From the moment he arrived in Jerusalem, everyone knew who was in charge. He organized, managed, supervised, encouraged, met opposition, confronted injustice, and kept going until the walls were built. Nehemiah was a man of action.

The story begins with Nehemiah talking with fellow Jews who reported that the walls and gates of Jerusalem were in disrepair. This was disturbing news, and rebuilding those walls became Nehemiah's burden. At the appropriate time, Nehemiah asked King Artaxerxes for permission to go to Jerusalem to rebuild its fallen walls. The king approved.

Armed with royal letters, Nehemiah traveled to Jerusalem. He organized the people into groups and assigned them to specific sections of the wall (Neh 3). The construction project was not without opposition, however. Sanballat, Tobiah, and others tried to halt the work with insults, ridicule, threats, and sabotage. Some of the workers became fearful; others became weary. In each case, Nehemiah employed a strategy to frustrate the enemies—prayer, encouragement, guard duty, consolidation (Neh 4). But a different problem arose—an internal one. Rich Jews were profiteering off the plight of their working countrymen. Hearing of their oppression and greed, Nehemiah confronted the extortioners face to face (Neh 5). Then, with the walls almost complete, Sanballat, Tobiah, and company tried one last time to stop Nehemiah. But Nehemiah stood firm, and the wall was finished in just 52 days. What a tremendous monument to God's love and faithfulness. Enemies and friends alike knew that God had helped (Neh 6).

After building the walls, Nehemiah continued to organize the people, taking a registration and appointing gatekeepers, Levites, and other officials (Neh 7). Ezra led the city in worship and Bible instruction (Neh 8–9). This led to a reaffirmation of faith and religious revival as the people promised to serve God faithfully (Neh 10–11).

Nehemiah closes with the listing of the clans and their leaders, the dedication of the new wall of Jerusalem, and the purging of sin from the land (Neh 12–13). As you read this book, watch Nehemiah in action—and determine to be a person on whom God can depend to act for him in the world.

THE BLUEPRINT

A. REBUILDING THE WALL (1:1–7:73)
1. Nehemiah returns to Jerusalem
2. Nehemiah leads the people

Nehemiah's life is an example of leadership and organization. Giving up a comfortable and wealthy position in Persia, he returned to the fractured homeland of his ancestors and rallied the people to rebuild Jerusalem's wall. In the face of opposition, he used wise defense measures to care for the people and to keep the project moving. To accomplish more for the sake of God's Kingdom, we must pray, persevere, and sacrifice, as did Nehemiah.

B. REFORMING THE PEOPLE (7:73–13:31)
1. Ezra renews the covenant
2. Nehemiah establishes policies

After the wall was rebuilt, Ezra read the law to the people, bringing about national repentance. Nehemiah and Ezra were very different people, yet God used them both to lead the nation. Remember, there is a place for you in God's work even if you're different from most other people. God uses each person in a unique way to accomplish his purposes.

MEGATHEMES

THEME	EXPLANATION	IMPORTANCE
Vision	Although the Jews completed the Temple in 515 B.C., the city walls remained in shambles for the next 70 years. These walls represented power, protection, and beauty to the city of Jerusalem. They were also desperately needed to protect the Temple from attack and to ensure the continuity of worship. God put the desire to rebuild the walls in Nehemiah's heart, giving him a vision for the work.	Does God have a vision for us? Are there "walls" that need to be built today? God still wants his people to be united and trained to do his work. As we recognize deep needs in our world, God can give us the vision and desire to "build." With that vision, we can mobilize others to pray and put together a plan of action.
Prayer	Both Nehemiah and Ezra responded to problems with prayer. When Nehemiah began his work, he recognized the problem, immediately prayed, and then acted on the problem.	Prayer is still God's mighty force in solving problems today. Prayer and action go hand in hand. Through prayer, God guides our preparation, teamwork, and diligent efforts to carry out his will.

Leadership	Nehemiah demonstrated excellent leadership. He was spiritually ready to heed God's call. He used careful planning, teamwork, problem solving, and courage to get the work done. Although he had tremendous faith, he never avoided the extra work necessary for good leadership.	Being God's leader is not just gaining recognition or being the boss. It requires planning, hard work, courage, and perseverance. Positive expectations are never a substitute for doing the difficult work. And in order to lead others, you need to listen for God's direction in your own life.
Problems	After the work began, Nehemiah faced scorn, slander, and threats from enemies, as well as fear, conflict, and discouragement from his own workers. Although these problems were difficult, they did not stop Nehemiah from finishing the work.	When difficulties come, there is a tendency for conflict and discouragement to set in. We must recognize that there are no triumphs without troubles. When problems arise, we must face them squarely and press on to complete God's work.
Repentance/ Revival	Although God had enabled them to build the wall, the work wasn't complete until the people rebuilt their lives spiritually. Ezra instructed the people in God's Word. As they listened, they recognized the sin in their lives, admitted it, and took steps to remove it.	Recognizing and admitting sin are not enough; revival must result in reform, or it is merely the expression of enthusiasm. God does not want halfhearted measures. We must not only remove sin from our lives but also ask God to move into the center of all we do.

Return & Diaspora

For Vital Statistics, see p. 1147

ESTHER

DRAMA, power, romance, intrigue—this is the stuff of which best-selling novels are made. But far from a modern piece of fiction, those words describe a true story, lived and written centuries ago. More than entertaining reading, it is a story of the profound interplay of God's sovereignty and human will. God prepared the place and the opportunity, and his people, Esther and Mordecai, chose to act. The book of Esther begins with Queen Vashti refusing to obey an order from her husband, King Xerxes. She was subsequently banished, and the search began for a new queen. The king sent out a decree to gather together all the beautiful young women in the empire and bring them into the royal harem. Esther, a young Jewish woman, was one of those chosen. King Xerxes was so pleased with Esther that he made her his queen.

Meanwhile, Mordecai, Esther's older cousin, became a government official and during his tenure foiled an assassination plot. But the ambitious and self-serving Haman was appointed second-in-command in the empire. When Mordecai refused to bow in reverence to him, Haman became furious and determined to destroy Mordecai and all the Jews along with him.

To accomplish his vengeful deed, Haman deceived the king and persuaded him to issue an edict condemning the Jews to death. Mordecai told Queen Esther about this edict, and she decided to risk her life to save her people. Esther asked King Xerxes and Haman to be her guests at a banquet. During the feast, the king asked Esther what she really wanted, and he promised to give her anything. Esther simply invited both men to another banquet the next day.

That night, unable to sleep, the king was flipping through some records in the royal archives when he read of the assassination plot that Mordecai had thwarted. Surprised to learn that Mordecai had never been rewarded for this deed, the king asked Haman what should be done to properly thank a hero. Haman thought the king must be talking about him, and so he described a lavish reward. The king agreed, but to Haman's shock and utter humiliation, he learned that Mordecai was the person to be so honored.

During the second banquet, the king again asked Esther what she desired. She replied that someone had plotted to destroy her and her people, and she named Haman as the culprit. Immediately the king sentenced Haman to die on the impaling pole that he had set up for Mordecai.

In the final act of this true-life drama, Mordecai was appointed to Haman's position, and the Jews were guaranteed protection throughout the land. To celebrate this historic occasion, the Festival of Purim was established.

Because of Queen Esther's courageous act, a whole nation was saved. Seeing her God-given opportunity, she seized it! Her life made a difference. Read Esther and watch for God at work in your life. Perhaps he has prepared you to act in "such a time as this" (Esth 4:14).

THE BLUEPRINT

1. Esther becomes queen (1:1–2:23)
2. The Jews are threatened (3:1–4:17)
3. Esther intercedes for the Jews (5:1–8:17)
4. The Jews are delivered (9:1–10:3)

The book of Esther is an example of God's divine guidance and care over our lives. God's sovereignty and power are seen throughout this book. Although we may question certain circumstances in our lives, we must have faith that God is in control, working through both the pleasant and difficult times so that we can serve him effectively.

MEGATHEMES

THEME	EXPLANATION	IMPORTANCE
God's Sovereignty	The book of Esther tells of the circumstances that were essential to the survival of God's people in Persia. These "circumstances" were not the result of chance but of God's grand design. God is sovereign over every area of life.	With God in charge, we can take courage. He can guide us through the circumstances we face in our lives. We should expect God to display his power in carrying out his will. As we unite our life's purposes to God's purpose, we benefit from his sovereign care.
Racial Hatred	The Jews in Persia had been a minority since their deportation from Judah 100 years earlier. Haman was a descendant of King Agag, an enemy of the Jews. Lust for power and pride drove Haman to hate Mordecai, Esther's cousin. Haman convinced the king to kill all the Jews.	Racial hatred is always sinful. We must never condone it in any form. Every person on earth has intrinsic worth because God created people in his own image. Therefore, God's people must stand against racism whenever and wherever it occurs.
Deliverance	In February or March, the Jews celebrate the Festival of Purim, which symbolizes God's deliverance. Purim means "lots," such as those used by Haman to set the date for the extermination of all Jews from Persia. But God overruled, using Queen Esther to intercede on behalf of the Jews.	Because God is in control of history, he is never frustrated by any turn of events. He is able to save us from the evil of this world and deliver us from sin and death. Because we trust God, we are not to fear what people may do to us; instead, we are to be confident in God's control.
Action	Faced with death, Esther and Mordecai set aside their own fear and took action. Esther risked her life by asking King Xerxes to save the Jews.	When outnumbered and powerless, it is natural for us to feel helpless. Esther and Mordecai resisted this temptation and acted with courage. It is not enough to know that God is in control; we must act with self-sacrifice and courage to follow God's guidance.
Wisdom	The Jews were a minority in a world hostile to them. It took great wisdom for Mordecai to survive. Serving as a faithful official of the king, Mordecai took steps to understand and work within the Persian law. Yet he did not compromise his integrity.	It takes great wisdom to survive in a non-believing world. In a setting which is for the most part hostile to Christianity, we can demonstrate wisdom by giving respect to what is true and good and by humbly standing against what is wrong.

God's Chosen Family

For Vital Statistics, see p. 28

JOB

TREES snap like toothpicks or fly upward, wrenched from the earth. Whole rooftops sail, cars tumble like toys, houses collapse, and a wall of water obliterates the shore and inundates the land. A hurricane cuts and tears, and only solid foundations survive its unbridled fury. But those foundations can be used for rebuilding after the storm.

For any building, the foundation is critical. It must be deep enough and solid enough to withstand the weight of the building and other stresses. Lives are like buildings, and the quality of each one's foundation will determine the quality of the whole. Too often inferior materials are used, and when tests come, lives crumble.

Job was tested. With a life filled with prestige, possessions, and people, he was suddenly assaulted on every side, devastated, stripped down to his foundation. But his life had been built on God, and he endured.

Job, the book, tells the story of Job, the man of God. It is a gripping drama of riches-to-rags-to-riches, a theological treatise about suffering and divine sovereignty, and a picture of faith that endures. As you read Job, analyze your life and check your foundation. May you be able to say that when all is gone but God, he is enough.

Job was a prosperous farmer living in the land of Uz. He had thousands of sheep, camels, and other livestock, a large family, and many servants. Suddenly, Satan the Accuser came before God claiming that Job was trusting God only because he was wealthy and everything was going well for him. And thus the testing of Job's faith began.

Satan was allowed to destroy Job's children, servants, livestock, herdsmen, and home; but Job continued to trust in God. Next Satan attacked Job physically, covering him with painful sores. Job's wife told him to curse God and die (Job 2:9), but Job suffered in silence.

Three of Job's friends, Eliphaz, Bildad, and Zophar, came to visit him. At first they silently grieved with Job. But when they began to talk about the reasons for Job's tragedies, they told him that sin had caused his suffering. They told him to confess his sins and turn back to God. But Job maintained his innocence.

Unable to convince Job of his sin, the three men fell silent (Job 32:1). At this point, another voice—the young Elihu—entered the debate. Although his argument also failed to convince Job, it prepared the way for God to speak.

Finally, God spoke out of a mighty storm. Confronted with the great power and majesty of God,

Job fell in humble reverence before him—speechless. God rebuked Job's friends (and Job), and the drama ended with Job restored to happiness and wealth.

It is easy to think that we have all the answers. In reality, only God knows exactly why events unfold as they do, and we must submit to him as our Sovereign. As you read this book, emulate Job and decide to trust God no matter what happens.

THE BLUEPRINT

A. JOB IS TESTED (1:1–2:13)	Job, a wealthy and upright man, lost his possessions, his children, and his health. Job did not understand why he was suffering. Why does God allow his children to suffer? Although there is an explanation, we may not know it while we are here on earth. In the meantime, we must always be ready for testing in our lives.
B. THREE FRIENDS ANSWER JOB (3:1–31:40) 1. First round of discussion 2. Second round of discussion 3. Third round of discussion	Job's friends wrongly assumed that suffering always came as a result of sin. With this in mind, they tried to persuade Job to repent of his sin. But the three friends were wrong. Suffering is not always a direct result of personal sin. When we experience severe suffering, it may not be our fault, so we don't have to add to our pain by feeling guilty that some hidden sin is causing our trouble.
C. A YOUNG MAN ANSWERS JOB (32:1–37:24)	A young man named Elihu, who had been listening to the entire conversation, criticized the three friends for being unable to answer Job. He said that although Job was a good man, he had allowed himself to become proud, and God was punishing him in order to humble him. This answer was partially true because suffering does purify our faith. But God is beyond our comprehension, and we cannot know why he allows each instance of suffering to come into our lives. Our part is simply to remain faithful.
D. GOD ANSWERS JOB (38:1–41:34)	God himself finally answered Job. God is in control of the world, and only he understands why the good are allowed to suffer. This only becomes clear to us when we see God for who he is. We must courageously accept what God allows to happen in our lives and remain firmly committed to him.
E. JOB IS RESTORED (42:1-17)	Job finally learned that when nothing else was left, he had God, and that was enough. Through suffering, we learn that God is enough for our lives and our future. We must love God regardless of whether he allows blessing or suffering to come to us. Testing is difficult, but the result is often a deeper relationship with God. Those who endure the testing of their faith will experience God's great rewards in the end.

MEGATHEMES

THEME	EXPLANATION	IMPORTANCE
Suffering	Through no fault of his own, Job lost his wealth, children, and health. Even his friends were convinced that Job had brought this suffering upon himself. For Job, the greatest trial was not the pain or the loss; it was not being able to understand why God allowed him to suffer.	Suffering can be, but is not always, a penalty for sin. In the same way, prosperity is not always a reward for being good. Those who love God are not exempt from trouble. Although we may not be able to understand fully the pain we experience, it can lead us to rediscover God.
Satan's Attacks	Satan attempted to drive a wedge between Job and God by getting Job to believe that God's governing of the world was not just and good. Satan had to ask God for permission to take Job's wealth, children, and health away. Satan was limited to what God allowed.	We must learn to recognize but not fear Satan's attacks because Satan cannot exceed the limits that God sets. Don't let any experience drive a wedge between you and God. Although you can't control how Satan may attack, you can always choose how you will respond when it happens.
God's Goodness	God is all-wise and all-powerful. His will is perfect, yet he doesn't always act in ways that we understand. Job's suffering didn't make sense because everyone believed good people were supposed to prosper. When Job was at the point of despair, God spoke to him, showing him his great power and wisdom.	Although God is present everywhere, at times he may seem far away. This may cause us to feel alone and to doubt his care for us. We should serve God for who he is, not what we feel. He is never insensitive to our suffering. Because God is sufficient, we must hold on to him.
Pride	Job's friends were certain that they were correct in their judgment of him. God rebuked them for their pride and arrogance. Human wisdom is always partial and temporary, so undue pride in our own conclusions is sin.	We must be careful not to judge others who are suffering. We may be demonstrating the sin of pride. We must be cautious in maintaining the certainty of our own conclusions about how God treats us. When we congratulate ourselves for being right, we become proud.
Trusting	God alone knew the purpose behind Job's suffering, and yet he never explained it to Job. In spite of this, Job never gave up on God—even in the midst of suffering. He never placed his hope in his experience, his wisdom, his friends, or his wealth. Job focused on God.	Job showed the kind of trust we are to have. When everything is stripped away, we are to recognize that God is all we ever really had. We should not demand that God explain everything. God gives us himself, but not all the details of his plans. We must remember that this life, with all its pain, is not our final destiny.

PSALMS

Birth of Israel
United Monarchy
Splintered Nation
Exile
Return & Diaspora

For Vital Statistics, see p. 430-31

"HI, how are you?" "Fine." Not exactly an "in-depth" discussion, this brief interchange is normal as friends and acquaintances pass and briefly touch each other with a cliché or two. Actually, clichés are a way of life, saturating sentences and permeating paragraphs. But if this is the essence of our communication, our relationships will stall on a superficial plateau. Facts and opinions also fill our verbiage. These words go deeper, but the true person still lies hidden beneath them. In reality, only when honest feelings and emotions are shared can real people be known, loved, and helped.

Often, patterns of superficial communication spill over into our talks with God. We easily slide through well-worn lines recited for decades, or we quickly toss a cliché or two at God and call it prayer. Certainly God hears and understands these feeble attempts, but by limiting the depth of our communication, we become shallow in our relationship with him. But God knows us, and he wants to have genuine communication with us.

At the center of the Bible is the book of Psalms. This great collection of songs and prayers expresses the heart and soul of humanity. In them we find the whole range of human experiences expressed. This book holds no clichés. Instead, David and the other writers honestly poured out their true feelings, reflecting a dynamic, powerful, and life-changing friendship with God. The psalmists confess their sins, express their doubts and fears, ask God for help in times of trouble, and praise and worship him.

As you read the book of Psalms, you will hear believers crying out to God from the depths of despair, and you will hear them singing to him in the heights of celebration. But whether the psalm writers are despairing or rejoicing, you will always hear them sharing honest feelings with their God. Because of the honesty expressed by these writers, men and women throughout history have come, again and again, to the book of Psalms for comfort during times of struggle and distress. And through the psalms, they have risen from the depths of despair to new heights of joy and praise as they also discovered the power of God's everlasting love and forgiveness. Let the honesty of the psalms guide you into a deep and genuine relationship with God.

THE BLUEPRINT

BOOK ONE PSALMS 1:1–41:13

While the psalms are not organized by topic, it is helpful to compare the dominant themes in each section of the Psalms to the five books of Moses. This first collection of psalms, mainly written by David, is similar to the book of Genesis. Just as Genesis tells how mankind was created, fell into sin, and was then promised redemption, many of these psalms discuss humans as blessed, fallen, and redeemed by God.

BOOK TWO PSALMS 42:1–72:20

This collection of psalms, mainly written by David and the sons of Korah, is similar to the book of Exodus. Just as Exodus describes the nation of Israel, many of these psalms describe the nation as ruined and then recovered. As God rescued the nation of Israel, he also rescues us. We do not have to work out solutions first, but we can go to God with our problems and ask him to help.

BOOK THREE PSALMS 73:1–89:52

This collection of psalms, mainly written by Asaph or Asaph's descendants, is similar to the book of Leviticus. Just as Leviticus discusses the Tabernacle and God's holiness, many of these psalms discuss the Temple and God's enthronement. Because God is almighty, we can turn to him for deliverance. These psalms praise God because he is holy, and his perfect holiness deserves our worship and reverence.

BOOK FOUR PSALMS 90:1–106:48

This collection of psalms, mainly written by unknown authors, is similar to the book of Numbers. Just as Numbers discusses the relationship of the nation of Israel to surrounding nations, these psalms often mention the relationship of God's overruling Kingdom to the other nations. Because we are citizens of the Kingdom of God, we can keep the events and troubles of earth in their proper perspective.

BOOK FIVE PSALMS 107:1–150:6

This collection of psalms, mainly written by David, is similar to the book of Deuteronomy. Just as Deuteronomy was concerned with God and his Word, these psalms are anthems of praise and thanksgiving for God and his Word. Most of the psalms were originally set to music and used in worship. We can use these psalms today as they were used in the past, as a hymnbook of praise and worship. This is a book that ought to make our hearts sing.

MEGATHEMES

THEME	EXPLANATION	IMPORTANCE
Praise	Psalms are songs of praise to God as our Creator, Sustainer, and Redeemer. Praise is recognizing, appreciating, and expressing God's greatness.	Focusing our thoughts on God moves us to praise him. The more we know him, the more we can appreciate what he has done for us.
God's power	God is all-powerful; and he always acts at the right time. He is sovereign over every situation. God's power is shown by the ways he reveals himself in creation, history, and his Word.	When we feel powerless, God can help us. His strength can overcome the despair of any pain or trial. We can always pray that he will deliver, protect, and sustain us.
Forgiveness	Many psalms are intense prayers asking God for forgiveness. God forgives us when we confess our sin and turn from it.	Because God forgives us, we can pray to him honestly and directly. When we receive his forgiveness, we move from alienation to intimacy, from guilt to love.

Thankfulness	We are grateful to God for his personal concern, help, and mercy. Not only does he protect, guide, and forgive us, but his creation provides everything we need.	When we realize how we benefit from knowing God, we can fully express our thanks to him. By thanking him often, we develop spontaneity in our prayer life.
Trust	God is faithful and just. When we put our trust in him, he quiets our hearts. Because he has been faithful throughout history, we can trust him in times of trouble.	People can be unfair and friends may desert us. But we can trust God. Knowing God intimately drives away doubt, fear, and loneliness.

United Monarchy
Splintered Nation

For Vital Statistics, see p. 431

PROVERBS

ALPHABET letters, vowels, and consonants formed into words, sentences, paragraphs, and books—spoken, signed, whispered, written, and printed. From friendly advice to impassioned speeches and from dusty volumes to daily tabloids, messages are sent and received, with each sender trying to impart knowledge . . . and wisdom.

Woven into human fabric is the desire to learn and understand. Our mind sets us apart from animals, and we analyze, conceptualize, theorize, discuss, and debate everything from science to the supernatural. We build schools, institutes, and universities, where learned professors can teach us about the world and about life.

Knowledge is good, but a vast difference stands between "knowledge" (having the facts) and "wisdom" (applying those facts to life). We may amass knowledge, but without wisdom our knowledge is useless. We must learn how to live out what we know.

The wisest man who ever lived, Solomon, left us a legacy of written wisdom in three volumes—Proverbs, Ecclesiastes, and Song of Songs. In these books, under the inspiration of the Holy Spirit, he gives practical insights and guidelines for life.

In the first of these three volumes, Solomon passes on his practical advice in the form of proverbs. A proverb is a short, concise sentence that conveys moral truth. The book of Proverbs is a collection of these wise statements. The main theme of Proverbs, as we might expect, is the nature of true wisdom. Solomon writes, "Fear of the LORD is the foundation of true knowledge, but fools despise wisdom and discipline" (Prov 1:7). He then proceeds to give hundreds of practical examples of how to live according to godly wisdom.

Proverbs covers a wide range of topics, including youth and discipline, family life, self-control and resisting temptation, business matters, words and the tongue, knowing God, marriage, seeking the truth, wealth and poverty, immorality, and, of course, wisdom. These proverbs are short poems (usually in couplet form), containing a holy mixture of common sense and timely warnings. Although they are not meant to teach doctrine, a person who follows their advice will walk closely with God. The word proverb comes from a Hebrew word that means "to rule or to govern," and these sayings, reminders, and admonitions provide profound advice for governing our lives.

As you read Proverbs, understand that knowing God is the key to wisdom. Listen to the thoughts and lessons from the world's wisest man, and apply these truths to your life. Don't just read these proverbs; act on them!

THE BLUEPRINT

A. WISDOM FOR YOUNG PEOPLE (1:1–9:18)	Solomon instructed the young people of his day like a father giving advice to his child. While many of these proverbs are directed toward young people, the principles supporting them are helpful to all believers, male and female, young and old. Anyone beginning his or her journey to discover more of wisdom will benefit greatly from these wise sayings.
B. WISDOM FOR ALL PEOPLE (10:1–24:34)	Solomon wanted to impart wisdom to all people, regardless of their age, sex, or position in society. These short, wise sayings give us practical wisdom for daily living. We should study them diligently and integrate them into our lives.
C. WISDOM FOR THE LEADERS (25:1–31:31)	In addition to the proverbs that Solomon collected, the advisers of Hezekiah collected many proverbs that Solomon and others wrote. While most of these are general in nature, many are directed specifically to the king and those who dealt with the king. These are particularly useful for leaders or those who aspire to be leaders.

MEGATHEMES

THEME	EXPLANATION	IMPORTANCE
Wisdom	God wants his people to be wise. Two kinds of people portray two contrasting paths of life. The fool is the wicked, stubborn person who hates or ignores God. The wise person seeks to know and love God.	When we choose God's way, he grants us wisdom. His Word, the Bible, leads us to live right, have right relationships, and make right decisions.

Relationships	Proverbs gives us advice for developing our personal relationships with friends, family members, and co-workers. In every relationship, we must show love, dedication, and high moral standards.	To relate to people, we need consistency, tact, and discipline to use the wisdom God gives us. If we don't treat others according to the wisdom God gives, our relationships will suffer.
Speech	What we say shows our real attitude toward others. How we talk reveals what we're really like. Our speech is a test of how wise we have become.	To be wise in our speech we need to use self-control. Our words should be honest and well chosen.
Work	God controls the final outcome of all we do. We are accountable to carry out our work with diligence and discipline, not laziness.	Because God evaluates how we live, we should work purposefully. We must never be lax or self-satisfied in using our skills.
Success	Although people work very hard for money and fame, God views success as having a good reputation, moral character, and the spiritual devotion to obey him.	A successful relationship with God counts for eternity. Everything else is perishable. All our resources, time, and talents come from God. We should strive to use them wisely.

United Monarchy

For Vital Statistics, see p. 431

ECCLESIASTES

THE CHOCOLATE bunny lies in the basket, surrounded by green paper "grass." With Easter morning eyes wide with anticipation, the little boy carefully lifts the candy figure and bites into one of the long ears. But the sweet taste fades quickly, and the child looks again at the candy in his hand. It's hollow!

Empty, futile, hollow, nothing—the words have a ring of disappointment and disillusionment. Yet this is the life experience of many. Grasping the sweet things—possessions, experience, power, and pleasure—they find nothing inside. Life is empty, meaningless—and they sink into despair.

Almost 3,000 years ago, Solomon spoke of this human dilemma; but the insights and applications of his message are relevant to our time. Ecclesiastes, Solomon's written sermon, is an analysis of life's experiences and a critical essay about life's true meaning. In this profound book, Solomon takes us on a reflective journey through his life, explaining how everything he had tried, tested, or tasted had been "meaningless"—useless, irrational, pointless, foolish, and empty—an exercise in futility. And remember, these words are from one who "had it all"—tremendous intellect, power, and wealth. After this biographical tour, Solomon made his triumphant conclusion: "Fear God and obey his commands, for this is everyone's duty. God will judge us for everything we do, including every secret thing, whether good or bad" (Eccl 12:13-14).

When Solomon became king, he asked God for wisdom (2 Chr 1:7-12), and he became the wisest man in the world (1 Kgs 4:29-34). Solomon studied, taught, judged, and wrote. Kings and leaders from other nations came to Jerusalem to learn from him. But with all of his practical insight on life, Solomon failed to heed his own advice, and he began a downward spiral. Near the end of his life, Solomon looked back with an attitude of humility and repentance. He took stock of his life, hoping to spare his readers the bitterness of learning through personal experience that everything apart from God is empty, hollow, and meaningless.

Although the tone of Ecclesiastes is negative and pessimistic, we must not conclude that the only chapter worth reading and applying is the last one, where he draws his conclusions. In reality, the entire book is filled with practical wisdom (how to accomplish things in the world and stay out of trouble) and spiritual wisdom (how to find and know eternal values).

Solomon had a very honest approach. All of his remarks relating to the futility of life are there for a purpose: to lead us to seek fulfillment and happiness in God alone. He was not trying to destroy all hope, but to direct our hopes to the only one who can truly fulfill them and give our life meaning. Solomon affirms the value of knowledge, relationships, work, and pleasure, but only in their proper place. Everything temporal must be seen in light of the eternal.

Read Ecclesiastes and learn about life. Hear the stern warnings and dire predictions, and commit yourself to remember your Creator now (Eccl 12:1).

THE BLUEPRINT

1. Solomon's personal experience (1:1–2:26)
2. Solomon's general observations (3:1–5:20)
3. Solomon's practical counsel (6:1–8:17)
4. Solomon's final conclusion (9:1–12:14)

Ecclesiastes shows that certain paths in life lead to emptiness. This profound book also helps us discover true purpose in life. Such wisdom can spare us from the emptiness that results from a life without God. Solomon teaches that people will not find meaning in life through knowledge, money, pleasure, work, or popularity. True satisfaction comes from knowing that what we are doing is part of God's purpose for our life. This is a book that can help free us from our scramble for power, approval, and money, and draw us closer to God.

MEGATHEMES

THEME	EXPLANATION	IMPORTANCE
Searching	Solomon searched for satisfaction almost as though he was conducting a scientific experiment. He discovered that life without God is a long and fruitless search for enjoyment, meaning, and fulfillment. True happiness is not within our grasp because we always want more than we can have. In addition, there are circumstances beyond our control that can snatch away our possessions or attainments.	People are still searching. Yet the more they try to get, the more they realize how little they really have. No pleasure or happiness is possible without God. Without him, satisfaction is a lost search. Above everything we should strive to know and love God. He gives wisdom, knowledge, and joy.
Emptiness	Solomon shows how empty it is to pursue the pleasures that this life has to offer rather than seek to have a relationship with the eternal God. The search for pleasure, wealth, and success is ultimately disappointing. Nothing in the world can fill the emptiness and satisfy the deep longings in our restless hearts.	The cure for emptiness is to center on God. His love also can fill the emptiness of human experience. Fear God throughout your life, and fill your life with serving God and others rather than with selfish pleasures.
Work	Solomon tried to shake people's confidence in their own efforts, abilities, and wisdom and to direct them to faith in God as the only sound basis for living. Without God, there is no lasting reward or benefit in hard work.	Work done with the wrong attitude will leave us empty. But work accepted as an assignment from God can be seen as a gift. Examine what you expect from your efforts. God gives you abilities and opportunities to work so that you can use your time well.
Death	The certainty of death makes all human achievements futile. God has a plan for each one of us that goes beyond life and death. The reality of aging and dying reminds each individual of the end to come when God will judge each person's life.	Because life is short, we need wisdom that is greater than this world can offer. We need the words of God so we can live right. If we listen to him, his wisdom spares us the bitterness of futile human experience and gives us a hope that goes beyond death.
Wisdom	Human wisdom doesn't contain all the answers. Knowledge and education have their limits. To understand life and make right choices, we need the wisdom that can be found only in God's Word—the Bible.	When we realize that God will evaluate all that we do, we should learn to live wisely, remembering that he is present each day, and learn to obey his guidelines for living. But in order to have God's wisdom, we must first get to know and honor him.

United Monarchy

For Vital Statistics, see p. 431

SONG OF SONGS

SATURATED with stories of sexual escapades, secret rendezvous, and extramarital affairs, today's media teach that immorality means freedom, perversion is natural, and commitment is old-fashioned. Sex, created by God and pronounced good in Eden, has been twisted, exploited, and turned into an urgent, illicit, casual, and self-gratifying activity. Love has turned into lust, giving into getting, and lasting commitment into "no strings attached."

In reality, sexual intercourse, the physical and emotional union of male and female, should be a holy means of celebrating love, producing children, and experiencing pleasure, protected by the commitment of marriage.

God thinks sex is important, and Scripture contains numerous guidelines for its use and warnings about its misuse. And sex is only proper in the context of a loving relationship between husband and wife. Perhaps the highlight of this is Song of Songs, the intimate story of a man and a woman, their love, courtship, and marriage. Solomon probably wrote this "song" in his youth, before being overtaken by his own obsession with women, sex, and pleasure.

A moving story, drama, and poem, Song of Songs features the love dialogue between a simple Jewish maiden (the young woman) and her lover (Solomon, the king). They describe in intimate detail their feelings for each other and their longings to be together. Throughout the dialogue, sex and marriage are put in their proper, God-given perspective.

Much debate has raged over the meaning of this song. Some say it is an allegory of God's love for Israel or for the church. Others say it is a literal story about married love. In reality, it is both—a historical story with two layers of meaning. On one level, we learn about love, marriage, and sex; and on the other level, we see God's overwhelming love for his people. As you read Song of Songs, remember that you are loved by God, and commit yourself to seeing life, sex, and marriage from his point of view.

THE BLUEPRINT

1. The wedding day (1:1–2:7)
2. Memories of courtship (2:8–3:5)
3. Memories of engagement (3:6–5:1)
4. A troubling dream (5:2–6:3)
5. Praising the bride's beauty (6:4–7:9)
6. The bride's tender appeal (7:10–8:4)
7. The power of love (8:5-14)

Song of Songs is a wedding song honoring marriage. The most explicit statements on sex in the Bible can be found in this book. It has often been criticized down through the centuries because of its sensuous language. The purity and sacredness of love represented here, however, are greatly needed in our day in which distorted attitudes about love and marriage are commonplace. God created sex and intimacy, and they are holy and good when enjoyed within marriage. A husband and wife honor God when they love and enjoy each other.

MEGATHEMES

THEME	EXPLANATION	IMPORTANCE
Sex	Sex is God's gift to his creatures. He endorses sex but restricts its expression to a man and a woman who are committed to each other in marriage.	God wants sex to be motivated by love and commitment, not lust. It is for mutual pleasure, not selfish enjoyment.
Love	As the relationship developed, the beauty and wonder of a romance unfolded between Solomon and his bride. The intense power of love affected the hearts, minds, and bodies of the two lovers.	Because love is such a powerful expression of feeling and commitment between a man and a woman, it is not to be regarded casually. We are not to manipulate others into loving us, and love should not be prematurely encouraged in a relationship.
Commitment	The power of love requires more than the language of feeling to protect it. Sexual expression is such an integral part of our selfhood that we need the boundary of marriage to safeguard our love. Marriage is the celebration of daily commitment between a husband and wife.	While romance keeps a marriage interesting, commitment keeps romance from dwindling away. The decision to commit yourself to your spouse alone begins at the marriage altar. It must be maintained day by day.
Beauty	The two lovers praise the beauty they see in each other. The language they use shows the spontaneity and mystery of love. Praise should not be limited to physical beauty; beautiful personality and moral purity should also be praised.	Our love for someone makes him or her appear beautiful to us. As you consider marriage, don't just look for physical attractiveness in a person. Look for the inner qualities that don't fade with time—spiritual commitment, integrity, sensitivity, and sincerity.
Problems	Over time, feelings of loneliness, indifference, and isolation came between Solomon and his bride. During those times, love grew cold, and barriers were raised.	Through careful communication, lovers can be reconciled, commitment can be renewed, and romance refreshed. Don't let walls come between you and your spouse. Take care of problems while they are still small.

Splintered Nation

For Vital Statistics, see p. 687

ISAIAH

SLOWLY he rose, and the crowd fell silent. Those at the back leaned forward, straining to hear. The atmosphere was electric. He spoke, and his carefully chosen words flew like swift arrows and found their mark. The great man, a spokesman for God, was warning—and condemning. The crowd became restless—shifting positions, clenching fists, and murmuring. Some agreed with his message, nodding their heads and weeping softly. But most were angry, and they began to shout back insults and threats.

Such was the life of a prophet.

The "office" of prophet was instituted during the days of Samuel, the last of the judges. Prophets stood with the priests as God's special representatives. The prophet's role was to speak for God, confronting the people and their leaders with God's commands and promises. Because of this confrontational stance and the continuing tendency of people to disobey God, true prophets usually were not very popular. But though their message often went unheeded, they faithfully and forcefully proclaimed the truth.

The book of Isaiah comes first in the writings of the prophets in the Bible, and Isaiah, the author, is generally considered to be the greatest prophet. He was probably reared in an aristocratic home and was married to a prophet. In the beginning of his ministry he was well liked. But, like most prophets, he soon became unpopular because his messages were so difficult to hear. He called the people to turn from their lives of sin and warned them of God's judgment and punishment. Isaiah had an active ministry for 60 years before he was executed during Manasseh's reign (according to tradition). As God's special messenger to Judah, Isaiah prophesied during the reigns of several of its rulers. Many of those messages are recorded in his book: Uzziah and Jotham, chapters 1–6; Ahaz, chapters 7–14; and Hezekiah, chapters 15–39.

The first half of the book of Isaiah (Isa 1–39) contains scathing denunciations and pronouncements as he calls Judah, Israel, and the surrounding nations to repent of their sins. The last 27 chapters (Isa 40–66), however, are filled with consolation and hope as Isaiah unfolds God's promise of future blessings through his Messiah.

As you read Isaiah, imagine this strong and courageous man of God, fearlessly proclaiming God's word, and listen to his message in relation to your own life—return, repent, and be renewed. Then trust in God's redemption through Christ and rejoice. Your Savior has come, and he's coming again!

THE BLUEPRINT

A. WORDS OF JUDGMENT (1:1–39:8) 1. The sins of Israel and Judah 2. Judgment against heathen nations 3. God's purpose in judgment 4. Jerusalem's true and false hopes 5. Events during the reign of Hezekiah	The 39 chapters in the first half of Isaiah generally carry the message of judgment for sin. Isaiah brings the message of judgment to Judah, Israel, and the surrounding pagan nations. The people of Judah had a form of godliness, but in their hearts they were corrupt. Isaiah's warnings were intended to purify the people by helping them understand God's true nature and message. However, they ignored the repeated warnings that Isaiah brought. We need to heed the prophetic voice and not repeat their error.
B. WORDS OF COMFORT (40:1–66:24) 1. Israel's release from captivity 2. The future Redeemer 3. The future Kingdom	The 27 chapters in the second half of Isaiah generally bring a message of forgiveness, comfort, and hope. This message of hope looks forward to the coming of the Messiah. Isaiah speaks more about the Messiah than does any other Old Testament prophet. He describes the Messiah as both a suffering Servant and a sovereign Lord. The fact that the Messiah was to be both a suffering Servant and a sovereign Lord would not be understood clearly until New Testament times. Based on what Jesus Christ has done, God freely offers forgiveness to all who turn to him in faith. This is God's message of comfort to us because those who need it find eternal peace and fellowship with him.

MEGATHEMES

THEME	EXPLANATION	IMPORTANCE
Holiness	God is highly exalted above all his creatures. His moral perfection stands in contrast to evil people and nations. God is perfect and sinless in all his motives and actions, so he is in perfect control of his power, judgment, love, and mercy. His holy nature is our standard for morality.	Because God is without sin, he alone can help us with our sin. It is only right that we regard him as supreme in power and moral perfection. We must never treat God as common or ordinary. He alone deserves our devotion and praise. He is always truthful, fair, and just.
Punishment	Because God is holy, he requires his people to treat others justly. He promised to punish Israel, Judah, and other nations for faithless immorality and idolatry. True faith had degenerated into national pride and empty religious rituals.	We must trust in God alone and fulfill his commands. We cannot forsake justice nor give in to selfishness. If we harden our hearts against his message, punishment will surely come to us.
Salvation	Because God's judgment is coming, we need a Savior. No person or nation can be saved without God's help. Christ's perfect sacrifice for our sins is foretold and portrayed in Isaiah. All who trust God can be freed from their sin and restored to him.	Christ died to save us from our sin. We cannot save ourselves. He is willing to save all those who turn from their sin and come to him. Salvation is from God alone. No amount of good works can earn it.
Messiah	God will send the Messiah to save his people. He will set up his own Kingdom as the faithful Prince of Peace, who rules with righteousness. He will come as sovereign Lord, but he will do so as a servant who will die to take away sins.	Our trust must be in the Messiah, not in ourselves or in any nation or power. There is no hope unless we believe in him. Trust Christ fully and let him rule in your life as your sovereign Lord.
Hope	God promises comfort, deliverance, and restoration in his future Kingdom. The Messiah will rule over his faithful followers in the age to come. Hope is possible because Christ is coming.	We can be refreshed because there is compassion for those who repent. No matter how bleak our situation or how evil the world is, we must continue to be God's faithful people who hope for his return.

Splintered Nation
Exile

For Vital Statistics, see p. 687

JEREMIAH

WHAT is success? Most definitions include references to achieving goals and acquiring wealth, prestige, favor, and power. "Successful" people enjoy the good life—being financially and emotionally secure, being surrounded by admirers, and enjoying the fruits of their labors. They are leaders, opinion makers, and trendsetters. Their example is emulated; their accomplishments are noticed. They know who they are and where they are going, and they stride confidently to meet their goals.

By these standards, Jeremiah was a miserable failure. For 40 years he served as God's spokesman to Judah, but when Jeremiah spoke, nobody listened. Consistently and passionately he urged them to act, but nobody moved. And he certainly did not attain material success. He was poor and underwent severe deprivation to deliver his prophecies. He was thrown into prison (Jer 37) and into a cistern (Jer 38), and he was taken to Egypt against his will (Jer 43). He was rejected by his neighbors

(Jer 11:19–21), his family (Jer 12:6), the false priests and prophets (Jer 20:1-2; 28:1-17), friends (Jer 20:10), his audience (Jer 26:8), and the kings (Jer 36:23). Throughout his life, Jeremiah stood alone, declaring God's messages of doom, announcing the new covenant, and weeping over the fate of his beloved country. In the eyes of the world, Jeremiah was not a success.

But in God's eyes, Jeremiah was one of the most successful people in all of history. Success, as measured by God, involves obedience and faithfulness. Regardless of opposition and personal cost, Jeremiah courageously and faithfully proclaimed the word of God. He was obedient to his calling. Jeremiah's book begins with his call to be a prophet. The next 38 chapters are prophecies about Israel (the nation united) and Judah (the southern kingdom). Chapters 2–20 are general and undated, and chapters 21–39 are particular and dated. The basic theme of Jeremiah's message is simple: "Repent and turn to God, or he will punish." Because the people rejected this warning, Jeremiah then began predicting the destruction of Jerusalem. This terrible event is described in chapter 39. Chapters 40–45 describe events following Jerusalem's fall. The book concludes with prophecies concerning a variety of nations (Jer 46–52).

As you read Jeremiah, feel with him as he agonizes over the message he must deliver, pray with him for those who refuse to respond to the truth, and watch his example of faith and courage. Then commit yourself to being successful in God's eyes.

THE BLUEPRINT

A. GOD'S JUDGMENT ON JUDAH (1:1–45:5) 1. The call of Jeremiah 2. Jeremiah condemns Judah for its sins 3. Jeremiah prophesies destruction 4. Jeremiah accuses Judah's leaders 5. Restoration is promised 6. God's promised judgment arrives	Jeremiah confronts many people with their sins: kings, false prophets, those at the temples, and those at the gates. A lack of response made Jeremiah wonder if he was doing any good at all. He often felt discouraged and sometimes bitter. To bring such gloomy messages to these people was a hard task. We, too, have a responsibility to bring this news to a fallen world: Those who continue in their sinful ways are eternally doomed. Although we may feel discouraged at the lack of response, we must press on to tell others about the consequences of sin and the hope that God offers. Those who tell people only what they want to hear are being unfaithful to God's message.
B. GOD'S JUDGMENT ON THE NATIONS (46:1–52:34) 1. Prophecies about foreign nations 2. The fall of Jerusalem	Jeremiah lived to see many of his prophecies come true—most notably the fall of Jerusalem. The fulfillment of this and other prophecies against the foreign nations came as a result of sin. Those who refuse to confess their sin bring judgment upon themselves.

MEGATHEMES

THEME	EXPLANATION	IMPORTANCE
Sin	King Josiah's reformation failed because the people's repentance was shallow. They continued in their selfishness and worship of idols. All the leaders rejected God's law and will for the people. Jeremiah lists all their sins, predicts God's judgment, and begs for repentance.	Judah's deterioration and disaster came from a callous disregard and disobedience of God. When we ignore sin and refuse to listen to God's warning, we invite disaster. Don't settle for half measures in removing sin.
Punishment	Because of sin, Jerusalem was destroyed, the Temple was ruined, and the people were captured and carried off to Babylon. The people were responsible for their destruction and captivity because they refused to listen to God's message.	Unconfessed sin brings God's full punishment. It is useless to blame anyone else for our sin; we are accountable to God before anyone else. We must answer to him for how we live.
God Is Lord of All	God is the righteous Creator. He is accountable to no one but himself. He wisely and lovingly directs all creation to fulfill his plans, and he brings events to pass according to his timetable. He is Lord over all the world.	Because of God's majestic power and love, our only duty is to submit to his authority. By following his plans, not our own, we can have a loving relationship with him and serve him with our whole hearts.
New Hearts	Jeremiah predicted that after the destruction of the nation, God would send a new shepherd, the Messiah. He would lead them into a new future, a new covenant, and a new day of hope. He would accomplish this by changing their sinful hearts into hearts of love for God.	God still transforms people by changing their hearts. His love can eliminate the problems created by sin. We can have assurance of a new heart by loving God, trusting Christ to save us, and repenting of our sin.
Faithful Service	Jeremiah served God faithfully for 40 years. During that time the people ignored, rejected, and persecuted him. Jeremiah's preaching was unsuccessful by human standards, yet he did not fail in his task. He remained faithful to God.	People's acceptance or rejection of us is not the measure of our success. God's approval alone should be our standard for service. We must bring God's message to others even when we are rejected. We must do God's work even if it means suffering for it.

Exile

For Vital Statistics, see p. 1092

LAMENTATIONS

TEARS are defined simply as "drops of salty fluid flowing from the eyes." They can be caused by irritation or laughter but are usually associated with weeping, sorrow, and grief. When we cry, friends wonder what's wrong and try to console us. Babies cry for food; children cry at the loss of a pet; adults cry when confronted with trauma and death. Jeremiah's grief ran deep. He is remembered as the "weeping prophet," and his tears flowed from a broken heart. As God's spokesman, he knew what lay ahead for Judah, his country, and for Jerusalem, the capital and "the city of God." God's judgment would fall and destruction would come. So Jeremiah wept. His tears were not self-centered, mourning over personal suffering or loss. He wept because the people had rejected their God—the God who had made them, loved them, and sought repeatedly to bless them. Jeremiah's heart was broken because he knew that the selfishness and sinfulness of the people would bring them much suffering and an extended exile. Jeremiah's tears were tears of empathy and sympathy. His heart was broken with those things that break God's heart.

Jeremiah's two books focus on one event—the destruction of Jerusalem. The book of Jeremiah predicts it, and Lamentations looks back on it. Known as the book of tears, Lamentations is a dirge, a funeral song written for the fallen city of Jerusalem.

What makes a person cry says a lot about that person—whether he or she is self-centered or God-centered. The book of Lamentations allows us to see what made Jeremiah sorrowful. As one of God's choice servants, he stands alone in the depth of his emotions, broken by his care for the people, his love for the nation, and his devotion to God.

What causes your tears? Do you weep because your selfish pride has been wounded or because the people around you lead sinful lives and reject the God who loves them dearly? Do you weep because you have lost something of value or because people all around you will suffer for their sinfulness? Our world is filled with injustice, poverty, war, and rebellion against God, all of which should move us to tears and to action. Read Lamentations and learn what it means to grieve with God.

THE BLUEPRINT

1. Jeremiah mourns for Jerusalem (1:1-22)
2. God's anger at sin (2:1-22)
3. Hope in the midst of affliction (3:1-66)
4. God's anger is satisfied (4:1-22)
5. Jeremiah pleads for restoration (5:1-22)

Jeremiah grieves deeply because of the destruction of Jerusalem and the devastation of his nation. But in the middle of the book, in the depths of his grief, there shines a ray of hope. God's compassion is ever present. His faithfulness is great. Jeremiah realizes that it is only the Lord's mercy that has prevented total annihilation. This book shows us the serious consequences of sin and how we can still have hope in the midst of tragedy because God is able to turn it around for good. We see the timeless importance of prayer and confession of sin. We will all face tragedy in our lives. But in the midst of our afflictions, there is hope in God.

MEGATHEMES

THEME	EXPLANATION	IMPORTANCE
Destruction of Jerusalem	Lamentations is a sad funeral song for the great capital city of the Jews. The Temple has been destroyed, the king is gone, and the people are in exile. God had warned that he would destroy them if they abandoned him. Now, afterward, the people realize their condition and confess their sin.	God's warnings are justified. He does what he says he will do. His punishment for sin is certain. Only by confessing and renouncing our sin can we turn to him for deliverance. How much better to do so before his warnings are fulfilled.
God's Mercy	God's compassion was at work even when the Israelites were experiencing the affliction of their Babylonian conquerors. Although the people had been unfaithful, God's faithfulness was great. He used this affliction to bring his people back to him.	God will always be faithful to his people. His merciful, refining work is evident even in affliction. At those times, we must pray for forgiveness and then turn to him for deliverance.
Sin's Consequences	God was angry at the prolonged rebellion by his people. Sin was the cause of their misery, and destruction was the result of their sin. The destruction of the nation shows the vanity of human glory and pride.	To continue in rebellion against God is to invite disaster. We must never trust our own leadership, resources, intelligence, or power more than God. If we do, we will experience consequences similar to Jerusalem's.
Hope	God's mercy in sparing some of the people offers hope for better days. One day, the people will be restored to a true and fervent relationship with God.	Only God can deliver us from sin. Without him there is no comfort or hope for the future. Because of Christ's death for us and his promise to return, we have a bright hope for tomorrow.

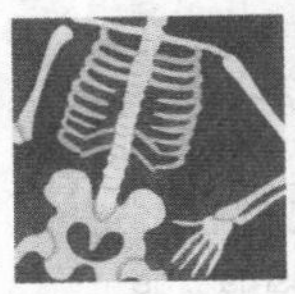

Splintered Nation
Exile

For Vital Statistics, see p. 687

EZEKIEL

A COMPUTER can be programmed to respond at your command. And by conditioning a dog with rewards and punishments, you can teach it to obey. But as every parent knows, children are not so easily taught. People have wills and must choose to submit, to follow the instructions of those who have authority over them. Surely discipline is part of the process—boys and girls should know that they will reap the consequences of disobedience.

God's children must learn to obey their heavenly Father. Created in his image, they have a choice, and God allows them to choose.

Ezekiel was a man who chose to obey God. Although he was a priest (Ezek 1:3), he served as a Jewish "street preacher" in Babylon for 22 years, telling everyone about God's judgment and salvation, and calling them to repent and obey. And Ezekiel lived what he preached. During his ministry God told him to illustrate his messages with dramatic object lessons. Some of these acts included (1) lying on his side for 390 days during which he could eat only one eight-ounce meal a day cooked over manure, (2) shaving his head and beard, and (3) showing no sorrow when his wife died. He obeyed and faithfully proclaimed God's word.

God may not ask you to do anything quite so dramatic or difficult; but if he did, would you do it?

The book of Ezekiel chronicles the prophet's life and ministry. Beginning with his call as a prophet and commissioning as a "watchman for Israel" (Ezek 1–3), Ezekiel immediately began to preach and demonstrate God's truth, as he predicted the approaching siege and destruction of Jerusalem (Ezek 4–24). This devastation would be God's judgment for the people's idolatry. Ezekiel challenged them to turn from their wicked ways. In the next section, he spoke to the surrounding nations, prophesying that God would judge them for their sins as well (Ezek 25–32). The book concludes with a message of hope, as Ezekiel proclaimed the faithfulness of God and foretold the future blessings for God's people (Ezek 33–48).

As you read this exciting record, observe how Ezekiel fearlessly preached the word of God to the exiled Jews in the streets of Babylon, and hear the timeless truth of God's love and power. Think about each person's responsibility to trust God and about the inevitability of God's judgment against idolatry, rebellion, and indifference. Then commit yourself to obey God, whatever, wherever, and whenever he asks.

THE BLUEPRINT

A. MESSAGES OF DOOM (1:1–24:27) 1. Ezekiel's call 2. Visions of sin and judgment 3. Punishment is certain	While Jeremiah was prophesying in Jerusalem that the city would soon fall to the Babylonians, Ezekiel was giving the same message to the captives who were already in Babylon. Like those in Jerusalem, the captives stubbornly believed that Jerusalem would not fall and that they would soon return to their land. Ezekiel warned them that punishment was certain because of their sins and that God was purifying his people. God will always punish sin, whether we believe it or not.
B. MESSAGES AGAINST FOREIGN NATIONS (25:1–32:32)	Ezekiel condemns the sinful actions of seven nations. The people in these nations were saying that God was obviously too weak to defend his people and the city of Jerusalem. But God was allowing his people to be defeated in order to punish them for their sins. These pagan nations, however, would face a similar fate, and then they would know that God is all-powerful. Those who dare to mock God today will also face a terrible fate.
C. MESSAGES OF HOPE (33:1–48:35) 1. Restoring the people of God 2. Restoring the worship of God	After the fall of Jerusalem, Ezekiel delivered messages of future restoration and hope for the people. God is holy, but Jerusalem and the Temple had become defiled. The nation had to be cleansed through 70 years of captivity. Ezekiel gives a vivid picture of the unchangeable holiness of God. We, too, must gain a vision of the glory of God, a fresh sense of his greatness, as we face the struggles of daily life.

MEGATHEMES

THEME	EXPLANATION	IMPORTANCE
God's Holiness	Ezekiel saw a vision that revealed God's absolute moral perfection. God was spiritually and morally superior to members of Israel's corrupt and compromising society. Ezekiel wrote to let the people know that God in his holiness was also present in Babylon, not just in Jerusalem.	Because God is morally perfect, he can help us live above our tendency to compromise with this world. When we focus on his greatness, he gives us the power to overcome sin and to reflect his holiness.
Sin	Israel had sinned, and God's punishment came. The fall of Jerusalem and the Babylonian exile were used by God to correct the rebels and draw them back from their sinful way of life. Ezekiel warned them that not only was the nation responsible for sin but each individual was also accountable to God.	We cannot excuse ourselves from our responsibilities before God. We are accountable to God for our choices. Rather than neglect him, we must recognize sin for what it is—rebellion against God—and choose to follow him instead.

Restoration	Ezekiel consoles the people by telling them that the day will come when God will restore those who turn from sin. God will be their King and shepherd. He will give his people a new heart to worship him, and he will establish a new government and a new Temple.	The certainty of future restoration encourages believers in times of trial. But we must be faithful to God because we love him, not merely for what he can do for us. Is our faith in him or merely in our future benefits?
Leaders	Ezekiel condemned the shepherds (unfaithful priests and leaders), who led the people astray. By contrast, he served as a caring shepherd and a faithful watchman to warn the people about their sin. One day God's perfect shepherd, the Messiah, will lead his people.	Jesus is our perfect leader. If we truly want him to lead us, our devotion must be more than talk. If we are given the responsibility of leading others, we must take care of them even if it means sacrificing personal pleasure, happiness, time, or money. We are responsible for those we lead.
Worship	An angel gave Ezekiel a vision of the Temple in great detail. God's holy presence had departed from Israel and the Temple because of sin. The building of a future Temple portrays the return of God's glory and presence. God will cleanse his people and restore true worship.	All of God's promises will be fulfilled under the rule of the Messiah. The faithful followers will be restored to perfect fellowship with God and with one another. To be prepared for this time, we must focus on God. We do this through regular worship. Through worship we learn about God's holiness and the changes we must make in how we live.

Splintered Nation
Exile
Return & Diaspora
For Vital Statistics, see p. 1092

DANIEL

AN EARTHQUAKE shakes the foundation of our security; a tornado blows away a lifetime of treasures; an assassin's bullet changes national history; a drunk driver claims an innocent victim; a divorce shatters a home; terrorism frightens a nation. International and personal tragedies make our world seem a fearful place, overflowing with evil and seemingly out of control. And the litany of bombings, coups, murders, and natural disasters could cause us to think that God is absent or impotent. "Where is God?" we cry, engulfed by sorrow and despair.

Twenty-five centuries ago, Daniel could have despaired. He and thousands of his countrymen had been deported to a foreign land after Judah was conquered. Daniel found himself facing an egocentric despot and surrounded by idolaters. Instead of giving in or giving up, this courageous young man held fast to his faith in his God. Daniel knew that despite the circumstances, God was sovereign and was working out his plan for nations and individuals. The book of Daniel centers around this profound truth—the sovereignty of God.

After a brief account of Nebuchadnezzar's siege and defeat of Jerusalem, the scene quickly shifts to Daniel and his three friends, Hananiah, Mishael, and Azariah (Shadrach, Meshach, and Abednego). These men held prominent positions within the Babylonian government. Daniel, in particular, held such a position because of his ability to interpret the king's dreams that tell of God's unfolding plan (Dan 2; 4). Sandwiched between the dreams is the fascinating account of Daniel's three friends and the furnace (Dan 3). Because they refused to bow down to an image of gold, they were condemned to a fiery death. But God intervened and spared their lives.

Belshazzar ruled Babylon after Nebuchadnezzar, and chapter 5 tells of his encounter with God's message written on a wall. Daniel, who was summoned to interpret the message, predicted Babylon's fall to the Medes and Persians. This prediction came true that very night, and Darius the Mede conquered the Babylonian kingdom.

Daniel became one of Darius's most trusted advisers. His privileged position angered other administrators, who plotted his death by convincing the king to outlaw prayer. In spite of the law, Daniel continued to pray to his sovereign Lord. As a result, he was condemned to die in a den of hungry lions. Again, God intervened, saving him, and shutting the mouths of the lions (Dan 6).

The book concludes with a series of visions that Daniel had during the reigns of Belshazzar (Dan 7–8), Darius (Dan 9), and Cyrus (Dan 10–12). These dreams dramatically outline God's future plans, beginning with Babylon and continuing to the end of the age. They give a preview of God's redemption and have been called the key to all biblical prophecy.

God is sovereign. He was in control in Babylon, and he has been moving in history, controlling the destinies of people ever since. And he is here now! Despite news reports or personal stress, we can be confident that God is in control. As you read Daniel, watch God work and find your security in his sovereignty.

THE BLUEPRINT

A. DANIEL'S LIFE (1:1–6:28)	Daniel and his three friends chose not to eat the king's food. They did not bow down to the king's image, even under penalty of death. Daniel continued to pray even though he knew he might be noticed and sentenced to death. These men are inspiring examples for us of how to live godly lives in a sinful world. When we face trials, we can expect God to also be with us through them. May God grant us similar courage to remain faithful under pressure.

B. DANIEL'S VISIONS (7:1–12:13)	These visions gave the captives added confidence that God is in control of history. They were to wait patiently in faith and not worship the gods of Babylon or accept that society's way of life. God still rules over human activities. Evil will be overcome, so we should wait patiently and not give in to the temptations and pressures of the sinful way of life around us.

MEGATHEMES

THEME	EXPLANATION	IMPORTANCE
God Is in Control	God is all-knowing, and he is in charge of world events. God overrules and removes rebellious leaders who defy him. God will overcome evil; no one is exempt. But he will deliver the faithful who follow him.	Although nations vie for world control now, one day Christ's Kingdom will replace and surpass the kingdoms of this world. Our faith is sure because our future is secure in Christ. We must have courage and put our faith in God, who controls everything.
Purpose in Life	Daniel and his three friends are examples of dedication and commitment. They determined to serve God regardless of the consequences. They did not give in to pressures from an ungodly society because they had a clear purpose in life.	It is wise to make trusting and obeying God alone our true purpose in life. This will give us direction and peace in spite of the circumstances or consequences. We should disobey anyone who asks us to disobey God. Our first allegiance must be to God.
Perseverance	Daniel served for 70 years in a foreign land that was hostile to God, yet he did not compromise his faith in God. He was truthful, persistent in prayer, and disinterested in power for personal glory.	In order to fulfill your life's purpose, you need staying power. Don't let your Christian distinctness become blurred. Be relentless in your prayers, maintain your integrity, and be content to serve God wherever he puts you.
God's Faithfulness	God was faithful in Daniel's life. He delivered him from execution, from a den of lions, and from enemies who hated him. God cares for his people and deals patiently with them.	We can trust God to be with us through any trial. Because he has been faithful to us, we should remain faithful to him.

Splintered Nation

For Vital Statistics, see p. 688

HOSEA

GROOMSMEN stand at attention as the music swells and the bride begins her long walk down the aisle, arm in arm with her father. The smiling, but nervous, husband-to-be follows every step, his eyes brimming with love. Then happy tears are shed, vows stated, and families merged. A wedding is a joyous celebration of love. It is the holy mystery of two becoming one, of beginning life together, and of commitment. Marriage is ordained by God and illustrates his relationship with his people. Thus, there is perhaps no greater tragedy than the violation of those sacred vows.

God told Hosea to find a wife and revealed to him ahead of time that she would be unfaithful to him. Although she would bear many children, some of these offspring would be fathered by others. In obedience to God, Hosea married Gomer. His relationship with her, her adultery, and their children became living, prophetic examples to Israel.

The book of Hosea is a love story—real, tragic, and true. Transcending the tale of a young man and wife, it tells of God's love for his people and the response of his "bride." A covenant had been made, and God had been faithful. His love was steadfast, and his commitment unbroken. But Israel, like Gomer, was adulterous and unfaithful, spurning God's love and turning instead to false gods. Then after warning of judgment, God reaffirmed his love and offered reconciliation. His love and mercy were overflowing, but justice would be served.

The book begins with God's marriage instructions to Hosea. After Hosea's marriage, children were born, and each given a name signifying a divine message (Hos 1). Then, as predicted, Gomer left Hosea to pursue her lusts (Hos 2). But Hosea (whose name means "salvation") found her, redeemed her, and brought her home again, fully reconciled (Hos 3). Images of God's love, judgment, grace, and mercy were woven into their relationship. Next, God outlined his case against the people of Israel: Their sins would ultimately cause their destruction (Hos 4; 6–7; 12) and would rouse his anger, resulting in punishment (Hos 5; 8–10; 12–13). But even in the midst of Israel's immorality, God was merciful and offered hope, expressing his infinite love for his people (Hos 11) and the fact that their repentance would bring about blessing (Hos 14).

The book of Hosea dramatically portrays our God's constant and persistent love. As you read this book, watch the prophet submit himself willingly to his Lord's direction; grieve with him over the unfaithfulness of his wife and his people; and hear the clear warning of judgment. Then reaffirm your commitment to being God's person, faithful in your love and true to your vows.

THE BLUEPRINT

A. HOSEA'S WAYWARD WIFE (1:1–3:5)	Hosea was commanded by God to marry a woman who would be unfaithful to him and would cause him many heartaches. Just as Gomer lost interest in Hosea and ran after other lovers, we, too, can easily lose appreciation for our special relationship with God and pursue dreams and goals that do not include him. When we compromise our Christian lifestyles and adopt the ways of the world, we are being unfaithful.
B. GOD'S WAYWARD PEOPLE (4:1–14:9) 1. Israel's sinfulness 2. Israel's punishment 3. God's love for Israel	God wanted the people in the northern kingdom to turn from their sin and return to worshiping him alone, but they persisted in their wickedness. Throughout the book, Israel is described as ignorant of God, with no desire to please him. Israel did not understand God at all, just as Gomer did not understand Hosea. Like a loving husband or patient father, God wants people to know him and to turn to him daily.

MEGATHEMES

THEME	EXPLANATION	IMPORTANCE
The Nation's Sin	Just as Hosea's wife, Gomer, was unfaithful to him, so the nation of Israel had been unfaithful to God. Israel's idolatry was like adultery. They sought illicit relationships with Assyria and Egypt in pursuit of military might, and they mixed Baal worship with the worship of God.	Like Gomer, we can chase after other loves—love of power, pleasure, money, or recognition. The temptations in this world can be very seductive. Are we loyal to God, remaining completely faithful, or have other loves taken his rightful place?
God's Judgment	Hosea solemnly warned Judah against following Israel's example. Because Judah broke the covenant, turned away from God, and forgot her Maker, she experienced a devastating invasion and exile. Sin has terrible consequences.	Disaster surely follows ingratitude toward God and rebellion. The Lord is our only true refuge. If we harden our hearts against him, there is no safety or security anywhere else. We cannot escape God's judgment.
God's Love	Just as Hosea went after his unfaithful wife to bring her back, so the Lord pursues us with his love. His love is tender, loyal, unchanging, and undying. No matter what, God still loves us.	Have you forgotten God and become disloyal to him? Don't let prosperity diminish your love for him or let success blind you to your need for his love.
Restoration	Although God will discipline his people for sin, he encourages and restores those who have repented. True repentance opens the way to a new beginning. God forgives and restores.	There is still hope for those who turn back to God. No loyalty, achievement, or honor can be compared to loving him. Turn to the Lord while the offer is still good. No matter how far you have strayed, God is willing to forgive you.

Return & Diaspora

For Vital Statistics, see p. 1147

JOEL

A SINGLE bomb devastates a city, and the world is ushered into the nuclear age. A split atom—power and force such as we had never seen. At a launch site, rockets roar and a payload is thrust into space. Discoveries dreamed of for centuries are ours as we begin to explore the edge of the universe. Volcanos, earthquakes, tsunamis, hurricanes, and tornados unleash uncontrollable and unstoppable force. And we can only avoid them and then pick up the pieces.

Power, strength, might—we stand in awe at the natural and human-made display. But these forces cannot touch the power of omnipotent God. Creator of galaxies, atoms, and natural laws, the Sovereign Lord rules all there is and ever will be. How silly to live without him; how foolish to run and hide from him; how ridiculous to disobey him. But we do. Since Eden, we have sought independence from his control, as though we were gods and could plot our destiny. And he has allowed our rebellion. But soon the day of the Lord will come.

It is about this day that the prophet Joel speaks, and it is the theme of his book. On this day God will judge all unrighteousness and disobedience—all accounts will be settled and the crooked made straight.

We know very little about Joel—only that he was a prophet and the son of Pethuel. He may have lived in Jerusalem. Whoever he was, Joel speaks forthrightly and forcefully in this short and powerful book. His message is one of foreboding and warning, but it is also filled with hope. Joel states that our Creator, the omnipotent Judge, is also merciful, and he wants to bless all those who trust him.

Joel begins by describing a terrible plague of locusts that covers the land and devours the crops. The devastation wrought by these creatures is but a foretaste of the coming judgment of God, the "day of the LORD." Joel, therefore, urges the people to turn from their sin and turn back to God. Woven into this message of judgment and the need for repentance is an affirmation of God's kindness and the blessings he promises for all who follow him. In fact, "everyone who calls on the name of the LORD will be saved" (Joel 2:32).

As you read Joel, catch his vision of the power and might of God and of God's ultimate judgment of sin. Choose to follow, obey, and worship God alone as your sovereign Lord.

THE BLUEPRINT

1. The day of the locusts (1:1–2:27) 2. The day of the Lord (2:28–3:21)	The locust plague was only a foretaste of the judgment to come in the day of the Lord. This is a timeless call to repentance with the promise of blessing. Just as the people faced the tragedy of their crops being destroyed, we, too, will face tragic judgment if we live in sin. But God's grace is available to us both now and in that coming day.

MEGATHEMES

THEME	EXPLANATION	IMPORTANCE
Punishment	Like a destroying army of locusts, God's punishment for sin is overwhelming, dreadful, and unavoidable. When it comes, there will be no food, no water, no protection, and no escape. The day for settling accounts with God for how we have lived is fast approaching.	God is the one with whom we all must reckon—not nature, the economy, or a foreign invader. We can't ignore or offend God forever. We must pay attention to his message now, or we will face his anger later.
Forgiveness	God stood ready to forgive and restore all those who would come to him and turn away from sin. God wanted to shower his people with his love and restore them to a proper relationship with him.	Forgiveness comes by turning from sin and turning toward God. It is not too late to receive God's forgiveness. God's greatest desire is for you to come to him.
Promise of the Holy Spirit	Joel predicts the time when God will pour out his Holy Spirit on all people. It will be the beginning of new and fresh worship of God by those who believe in him, as well as the beginning of judgment on all who reject him.	God is in control. Justice and restoration are in his hands. The Holy Spirit confirms God's love for us just as he did for the first Christians (Acts 2). We must be faithful to God and place our life under the guidance and power of his Holy Spirit.

Splintered Nation

For Vital Statistics, see p. 688

AMOS

WHEN we hear, "He's a man of God," we think of some famous evangelist, a "Reverend," a missionary, or the campus minister—professionals, Christian workers, those who preach and teach the Word as a vocation. Surely Amos was a man of God, a person whose life was devoted to serving the Lord and whose lifestyle reflected this devotion—but he was a layperson. Herding sheep and tending sycamore-fig trees in the Judean countryside, Amos was not the son of a prophet; he was not the son of a priest. As a humble shepherd, he could have stayed in Tekoa, doing his job, providing for his family, and worshiping his God. But God gave Amos a vision of the future (Amos 1:1) and told him to take his message to Israel, the northern kingdom (Amos 7:15). Amos obeyed and thus proved he was a man of God.

Amos's message has impacted God's people throughout the centuries, and it needs to be heard today by individuals and nations. Though divided from their southern brothers and sisters in Judah, the northern Israelites were still God's people. But they were living beneath a pious veneer of religion, worshiping idols and oppressing the poor. Amos, a fiery, fearless, and honest shepherd from the south, confronted them with their sin and warned them of the impending judgment.

The book of Amos opens with this humble shepherd watching his sheep. God then gave him a vision of what was about to happen to the nation of Israel. God condemned all the nations who had sinned against him and harmed his people. Beginning with Aram, he moved quickly through Philistia, Tyre, Edom, Ammon, and Moab. All were condemned, and we can almost hear the Israelites shouting, "Amen!" And then, even Judah, Amos's homeland, was included in God's scathing denunciation (Amos 2:4-5). How Amos's listeners must have enjoyed hearing those words! Suddenly, however, Amos turned to the people of Israel and pronounced God's judgment on them. The next four chapters enumerate and describe their sins. It is no wonder that Amaziah the priest intervened and tried to stop the preaching (Amos 7:10-13). Fearlessly, Amos continued to relate the visions of future judgment that God gave to him (Amos 8–9). After all the chapters on judgment, the book concludes with a message of hope. Eventually God will restore his people and make them great again (Amos 9:8-15).

As you read Amos's book, put yourself in the place of those Israelites and listen to God's message. Have you grown complacent? Have other concerns taken God's place in your life? Do you ignore those in need or oppress the poor? Picture yourself as Amos, faithfully doing what God calls you to do. You, too, can be God's person. Listen for his clear call and do what he says, wherever it leads.

THE BLUEPRINT

1. Announcement of judgment (1:1–2:16) 2. Reasons for judgment (3:1–6:14) 3. Visions of judgment (7:1–9:15)	Amos speaks with brutal frankness in denouncing sin. He collided with the false religious leaders of his day and was not intimidated by priest or king. He continued to speak his message boldly. God requires truth and goodness, justice and righteousness, from all people and nations today as well. Many of the conditions in Israel during Amos's time are evident in today's society. We need Amos's courage to ignore danger and stand against sin.

MEGATHEMES

THEME	EXPLANATION	IMPORTANCE
Everyone Answers to God	Amos pronounced judgment from God on all the surrounding nations. Then he included Judah and Israel. God is in supreme control of all the nations. Everyone is accountable to him.	All people will have to account for their sin. When those who reject God seem to get ahead, don't envy their prosperity or feel sorry for yourself. Remember that we all must answer to God for how we live.
Complacency	Everyone was optimistic, business was booming, and people were happy (except for the poor and oppressed). With all the comfort and luxury came self-sufficiency and a false sense of security. But prosperity brought corruption and destruction.	A complacent present leads to a disastrous future. Don't congratulate yourself for the blessings and benefits you now enjoy. They are from God. If you are more satisfied with yourself than with God, remember that everything is meaningless without him. A self-sufficient attitude may be your downfall.
Oppressing the Poor	The wealthy and powerful people of Samaria, the capital of Israel, had become prosperous, greedy, and unjust. Illegal and immoral slavery came as the result of over-taxation and land-grabbing. There was also cruelty and indifference toward the poor. God is weary of greed and will not tolerate injustice.	God made all people; therefore, to ignore the poor is to ignore those whom God loves and whom Christ came to save. We must go beyond feeling bad for the poor and oppressed. We must act compassionately to stop injustice and to help care for those in need.
Superficial Religion	Although many people had abandoned real faith in God, they still pretended to be religious. They were carrying on superficial religious exercises instead of having spiritual integrity and practicing heartfelt obedience toward God.	Merely participating in ceremony or ritual falls short of true religion. God wants simple trust in him, not showy external actions. Don't settle for impressing others with external rituals when God wants heartfelt obedience and commitment.

Exile

For Vital Statistics, see p. 1092

OBADIAH

WRINKLED face, tiny hands with fingernail chips, folds of new skin, and miniature eyes, nose, and mouth—she's a newborn. After months of formation, she burst forth into the world and into her family. "She has her mother's eyes." "I can sure tell who her parents are." "Now that's your nose." Relatives and friends gaze into the little face and see her mom and dad. Mother and Father rejoice in their daughter, a miracle, a new member of the family. As loving parents, they will feed, protect, nurture, guide, and discipline her. This is their duty and joy.

God, too, has children—men and women whom he has chosen as his very own. There have always been individuals marked as his, but with Abraham he promised to build a nation. Israel was to be God's country, and her people, the Jews, his very own sons and daughters. Down through the centuries, God meted out discipline and punishment, but always with love and mercy. God, the eternal Father, protected and cared for his children.

Obadiah, the shortest book in the Old Testament, is a dramatic example of God's response to anyone who would harm his children. Edom was a mountainous nation, occupying the region southeast of the Dead Sea including Petra, the spectacular city discovered by archaeologists a few decades ago. As descendants of Esau (Gen 25:19–27:45), the Edomites were blood relatives of Israel, and like their father, they were rugged, fierce, and proud warriors with a seemingly invincible mountain home. Of all people, they should have rushed to the aid of their northern brothers. Instead, however, they gloated over Israel's problems, captured and delivered fugitives to the enemy, and even looted Israel's countryside.

Obadiah gave God's message to the Edomites. Because of their indifference to and defiance of God, their cowardice and pride, and their treachery toward their relatives in Judah, they stood condemned and would be destroyed. The book begins with the announcement that disaster was coming to Edom (Obad 1:1-9). Despite their "impregnable" cliffs and mountains, they would not be able to escape God's judgment. Obadiah then gave the reasons for their destruction (Obad 1:10-14)—their blatant arrogance toward God and their persecution of God's children. This concise prophecy ends with a description of the day of the Lord, when judgment will fall on all who have harmed God's people (Obad 1:15-21).

Today, God's holy nation is his church—all who have trusted Christ for their salvation and have given their lives to him. These men and women are God's born-again and adopted children. As you read Obadiah, catch a glimpse of what it means to be God's child, under his love and protection. See how the heavenly Father responds to all who would attack those whom he loves.

THE BLUEPRINT

1. Edom's destruction (1:1-16) 2. Israel's restoration (1:17-21)	The book of Obadiah shows the outcome of the ancient feud between Edom and Israel. Edom was proud of its high position, but God would bring her down. Those who are high and powerful today should not be overconfident in themselves, whether they are a nation, a corporation, a church, or a family. Just as Edom was destroyed for its pride, so will anyone be who lives in defiance of God.

MEGATHEMES

THEME	EXPLANATION	IMPORTANCE
Justice	Obadiah predicted that God would destroy Edom as punishment for standing by when Babylon invaded Judah. Because of their treachery, Edom's land would be given to Judah in the day when God rights the wrongs against his people.	God will judge and fiercely punish all who harm his people. We can be confident in God's final victory. He is our champion, and we can trust him to bring about true justice.
Pride	Because of their seemingly invincible rock fortress, the Edomites were proud and self-confident. But God humbled them and their nation disappeared from the face of the earth.	All those who defy God will meet their doom as Edom did. Any nation who trusts in its power, wealth, technology, or wisdom more than in God will be brought low. All who are proud will one day be shocked to discover that no one is exempt from God's justice.

Splintered Nation

For Vital Statistics, see p. 688

JONAH

SIN runs rampant in society—daily headlines and overflowing prisons bear dramatic witness to that fact. With child abuse, pornography, serial killings, terrorism, anarchy, and ruthless dictatorships, the world seems to be filled to overflowing with violence, hatred, and corruption. Reading and hearing about these tragedies—and perhaps even experiencing them—we begin to understand the necessity of God's judgment. We may even find ourselves wishing for vengeance by any means upon the violent perpetrators. Surely they are beyond redemption! But suppose that in the midst of such thoughts, God told you to take the gospel to the worst of the offenders—how would you respond?

Jonah was given such a task. Assyria—a great but evil empire—was Israel's most dreaded enemy. The Assyrians flaunted their power before God and the world through numerous acts of heartless cruelty. So when Jonah heard God tell him to go to Assyria and call the people to repentance, he ran in the opposite direction.

The book of Jonah tells the story of this prophet's flight and how God stopped him and turned him around. But it is much more than a story of a man and a great fish. Jonah's story is a profound illustration of God's mercy and grace. No one deserved God's favor less than the people of Nineveh, Assyria's capital. Jonah knew this. But he knew that God would forgive and bless them if they would turn from their sin and worship him. Jonah also knew the power of God's message, that even through his own weak preaching, they would respond and be spared God's judgment. But Jonah hated the Assyrians, and he wanted vengeance, not mercy. So he ran the other way. Eventually, Jonah obeyed and preached in the streets of Nineveh, and the people repented and were delivered from judgment. Then Jonah sulked and complained to God, "Didn't I say before I left home that you would do this, LORD? That is why I ran away to Tarshish! I knew that you are a merciful and compassionate God, slow to get angry and filled with unfailing love. You are eager to turn back from destroying people" (Jon 4:2). In the end, God confronted Jonah about his self-centered values and lack of compassion, saying, "But Nineveh has more than 120,000 people living in spiritual darkness, not to mention all the animals. Shouldn't I feel sorry for such a great city?" (Jon 4:11).

As you read Jonah, see the full picture of God's love and compassion and realize that no one is beyond redemption. The gospel is for all who will repent and believe. Begin to pray for those who seem to be farthest from the Kingdom, and look for ways to tell them about God. Learn from the story of this reluctant prophet and determine to obey God, doing whatever he asks and going wherever he leads.

THE BLUEPRINT

1. Jonah forsakes his mission (1:1–2:10) 2. Jonah fulfills his mission (3:1–4:11)	Jonah was a reluctant prophet given a mission he found distasteful. He chose to run away from God rather than obey him. Like Jonah, we may have to do things in life that we don't want to do. Sometimes we find ourselves wanting to turn and run. But it is better to obey God than to defy him or run away. Often, in spite of our defiance, God in his mercy will give us another chance to serve him when we return to him.

MEGATHEMES

THEME	EXPLANATION	IMPORTANCE
God's Sovereignty	Although the prophet Jonah tried to run away from God, God was in control. By controlling the stormy seas and a great fish, God displayed his absolute, yet loving guidance.	Rather than running from God, trust him with your past, present, and future. Saying no to God quickly leads to disaster. Saying yes brings new understanding of God and his purpose in the world.
God's Message to All the World	God had given Jonah a purpose—to preach to the great Assyrian city of Nineveh. Jonah hated Nineveh, and so he responded with anger and indifference. Jonah had to learn that God loves all people. Through Jonah, God reminded Israel of its missionary purpose.	We must not limit our focus to our own people. God wants his people to proclaim his love in words and actions to the whole world. He wants us to be his missionaries wherever we are, wherever he sends us.
Repentance	When the reluctant preacher went to Nineveh, there was a great response. The people repented and turned to God. This was a powerful rebuke to the people of Israel, who thought they were better but refused to respond to God's message. God will forgive all those who turn from their sin.	God doesn't honor sham or pretense. He wants the sincere devotion of each person. It is not enough to share the privileges of Christianity; we must ask God to forgive us and to remove our sin. Refusing to repent shows that we still love our sin.
God's Compassion	God's message of love and forgiveness was not for the Jews alone. God loves all the people of the world. The Assyrians didn't deserve it, but God spared them when they repented. In his mercy, God did not reject Jonah for aborting his mission. God has great love, patience, and forgiveness.	God loves each of us, even when we fail him. But he also loves other people, including those not of our group, background, race, or denomination. When we accept his love, we must also learn to accept all those whom he loves. We will find it much easier to love others when we truly love God.

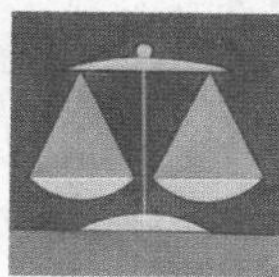

Splintered Nation

For Vital Statistics, see p. 688

MICAH

"I HATE YOU!" she screams and runs from the room. Words from a child thrown as emotional darts. Perhaps she learned the phrase from Mom and Dad, or maybe it just burst forth from that inner well of "sinful nature." Whatever the case, hate and love have become society's bywords, almost tired clichés, tossed carelessly at objects, situations, and even people.

The casual use of such words as love and hate has emptied them of their meaning. We no longer understand statements that describe a loving God who hates sin. So we picture God as gentle and kind—a cosmic pushover, and our concept of what he hates is tempered by our misconceptions and wishful thinking.

The words of the prophets stand in stark contrast to such misconceptions. God's hatred is real—burning, consuming, and destroying. He hates sin, and he stands as the righteous Judge, ready to mete out just punishment to all who defy his rule. God's love is also real. So real that he sent his Son, the Messiah, to save and accept judgment in the sinner's place. Love and hate are together—both unending, irresistible, and unfathomable.

In seven short chapters, Micah presents this true picture of God—the almighty Lord who hates sin and loves the sinner. Much of the book is devoted to describing God's judgment on Israel (the northern kingdom), on Judah (the southern kingdom), and on all the earth. This judgment will come "because of the rebellion of Israel—yes, the sins of the whole nation" (Mic 1:5). And the prophet lists their despicable sins, including fraud (Mic 2:2), theft (Mic 2:8), greed (Mic 2:9), debauchery (Mic 2:11), oppression (Mic 3:3), hypocrisy (Mic 3:4), heresy (Mic 3:5), injustice (Mic 3:9), extortion and lying (Mic 6:12), murder (Mic 7:2), and other offenses. God's judgment will come.

In the midst of this overwhelming prediction of destruction, Micah gives hope and consolation because he also describes God's love. The truth is that judgment comes only after countless opportunities to repent, to turn back to true worship and obedience—"to do what is right, to love mercy, and to walk humbly with your God " (Mic 6:8). But even in the midst of judgment, God promises to deliver the small minority who have continued to follow him. He states, "Your king will lead you; the LORD himself will guide you" (Mic 2:13). The king, of course, is Jesus; and we read in Micah 5:2 that he will be born as a baby in Bethlehem, an obscure Judean village.

As you read Micah, catch a glimpse of God's anger in action as he judges and punishes sin. See God's love in action as he offers eternal life to all who repent and believe. And then determine to join the faithful remnant of God's people, who live according to his will.

THE BLUEPRINT

1. The trial of the capitals (1:1–2:13) 2. The trial of the leaders (3:1–5:15) 3. The trial of the people (6:1–7:20)	Micah emphasized the need for justice and peace. Like a lawyer, he set forth God's case against Israel and Judah, their leaders, and their people. Throughout the book are prophecies about Jesus, the Messiah, who will gather the people into one nation. He will be their King and Ruler, acting mercifully toward them. Micah makes it clear that God hates unkindness, idolatry, injustice, and empty ritual—and he still hates these today. But God is very willing to pardon the sins of any who repent.

MEGATHEMES

THEME	EXPLANATION	IMPORTANCE
Perverting Faith	God will judge the false prophets, dishonest leaders, and selfish priests in Israel and Judah. While they publicly carried out religious ceremonies, they were privately seeking to gain money and influence. To mix selfish motives with an empty display of religion is to pervert faith.	Don't try to mix your own selfish desires with true faith in God. One day God will reveal how foolish it is to substitute anything for loyalty to him. Coming up with your own private blend of religion will pervert your faith.
Oppression	Micah predicted ruin for all nations and leaders who were oppressive toward others. The upper classes oppressed and exploited the poor. Yet no one was speaking against them or doing anything to stop them. God will not put up with such injustice.	We dare not ask God to help us while we ignore those who are needy and oppressed, or while we silently condone the actions of those who oppress them.
The Messiah—King of Peace	God promised to provide a new King to bring strength and peace to his people. Hundreds of years before Christ's birth, God promised that the eternal King would be born in Bethlehem. It was God's great plan to restore his people through the Messiah.	Christ our King leads us just as God promised. But until his final judgment, his leadership is only visible among those who welcome his authority. We can have God's peace now by giving up our sins and welcoming him as King.
Pleasing God	Micah preached that God's greatest desire was not the offering of sacrifices at the Temple. God delights in faith that produces justice, love for others, and obedience to him.	True faith in God generates kindness, compassion, justice, and humility. We can please God by seeking these attributes in our work, our family, our church, and our neighborhood.

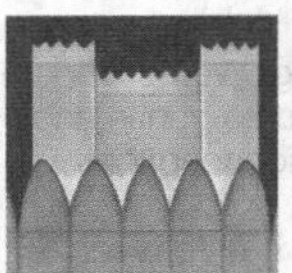

Splintered Nation

For Vital Statistics, see p. 688

NAHUM

THE SHRILL whistle pierces the air, and all the action on the court abruptly stops. Pointing to the offending player, the referee shouts, "Foul!" Rules, fouls, and penalties are part of any game and are regulated and enforced vigorously by referees, umpires, judges, and other officials. Every participant knows that boundaries must be set and behavior monitored, or the game will degenerate into chaos.

The world also has laws—boundaries and rules for living established by God. But men and women regularly flaunt these regulations, hiding their infractions or overpowering others and declaring that might makes right. God calls this sin—willful disobedience, rebellion against his control, or apathy. And at times it seems as though the violators succeed—no whistles blow, no fouls are called, and individual dictators rule. The truth is, however, that ultimately justice will be served in the world. God will settle all accounts.

Assyria was the most powerful nation on earth. Proud in their self-sufficiency and military might, they plundered, oppressed, and slaughtered their victims. One hundred years earlier, Jonah had preached in the streets of the great city Nineveh; the people had heard God's message and had turned from their evil. But generations later, evil was again reigning, and the prophet Nahum pronounced judgment on this wicked nation. Nineveh is called a "city of murder" (Nah 3:1), a city of cruelty (Nah 3:19), and the Assyrians are judged for their pride (Nah 2:13), idolatry (Nah 1:14), murder, lies, treachery, and social injustice (Nah 3:1-19). Nahum predicted that this proud and powerful nation would be utterly destroyed because of its sins. The end came within 50 years.

In this judgment of Assyria and its capital city, Nineveh, God is judging a sinful world. And the message is clear: Disobedience, rebellion, and injustice will not prevail but will be punished severely by a righteous and holy God, who rules over all the earth.

As you read Nahum, sense God's wrath as he avenges sin and brings about justice. Then decide to live under his guidance and within his rules, commands, and guidelines for life.

THE BLUEPRINT

1. Nineveh's judge (1:1-15) 2. Nineveh's judgment (2:1–3:19)	Nineveh, the capital of the Assyrian Empire, is the subject of Nahum's prophecy. The news of its coming destruction was a relief for Judah, who was subject to Assyrian domination. No longer would Judah be forced to pay tribute as insurance against invasions. Judah was comforted to know that God was still in control. Nineveh is an example to all rulers and nations of the world today. God is sovereign over even those who are seemingly invincible. We can be confident that God's power and justice will one day conquer all evil.

MEGATHEMES

THEME	EXPLANATION	IMPORTANCE
God Judges	God would judge the city of Nineveh for its idolatry, arrogance, and oppression. Although Assyria was the leading military power in the world, God would completely destroy this "invincible" nation. God allows no person or power to usurp or scoff at his authority.	Anyone who remains arrogant and resists God's authority will face his anger. No ruler or nation will get away with rejecting him. No individual will be able to hide from his judgment. Yet those who keep trusting God will be kept safe forever.
God Rules	God rules over all the earth, even over those who don't acknowledge him. God is all-powerful, and no one can thwart his plans. God will overcome any who attempt to defy him. Human power is futile against God.	If you are impressed by or afraid of any weapons, armies, or powerful people, remember that God alone can truly rescue you from fear or oppression. We must place our confidence in God because he alone rules all of history, all the earth, and our life.

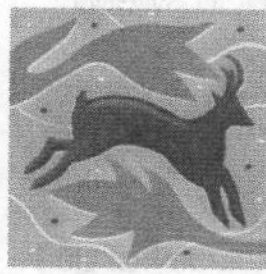

Splintered Nation

For Vital Statistics, see p. 688

HABAKKUK

FROM innocent childhood queries to complex university discussions, life is filled with questions. Asking how and why and when, we probe beneath the surface to find satisfying answers. But not all questions have answers wrapped and neatly tied. These unanswered interrogations create more questions and nagging, spirit-destroying doubt. Some choose to live with their doubts, ignoring them and moving on with life. Others become cynical and hardened. But many reject those options and continue to ask, looking for answers.

Habakkuk was a man who sought answers. Troubled by what he observed, he asked difficult questions. These questions were not merely intellectual exercises or bitter complaints. Habakkuk saw a dying world, and it broke his heart. Why is there evil in the world? Why do the wicked seem to be winning? He boldly and confidently took his complaints directly to God. And God answered with an avalanche of proof and prediction.

The prophet's questions and God's answers are recorded in this book. As we turn the pages, we are immediately confronted with his urgent cries, "How long, O LORD, must I call for help? But you do not listen! 'Violence is everywhere!' I cry, but you do not come to save" (Hab 1:2). In fact, most of the first chapter is devoted to his questions. As chapter two begins, Habakkuk declares that he will wait to hear God's answers to his complaints. Then God begins to speak, telling the prophet to write his answer plainly so that all will see and understand. It may seem, God says, as though the wicked triumph, but eventually they will be judged, and righteousness will prevail. Judgment may not come quickly, but it will come. God's answers fill chapter two. Then Habakkuk concludes his book with a prayer of triumph. With questions answered and a new understanding of God's power and love, Habakkuk rejoices in who God is and in what he will do. "Yet I will rejoice in the LORD! I will be joyful in the God of my salvation! The Sovereign LORD is my strength! He makes me as surefooted as a deer, able to tread upon the heights" (Hab 3:18-19).

Listen to the profound questions that Habakkuk boldly brings to God, and realize that you can also bring your complaints and inquiries to him. Listen to God's answers and rejoice that he is at work in the world and in your life.

THE BLUEPRINT

1. Habakkuk's complaints (1:1–2:20)
2. Habakkuk's prayer (3:1-19)

When Habakkuk was troubled, he brought his concerns directly to God. After receiving God's answers, he responded with a prayer of faith. Habakkuk's example is one that should encourage us as we struggle to move from doubt to faith. We don't have to be afraid to ask questions of God. The problem is not with God and his ways but with our limited understanding of him.

MEGATHEMES

THEME	EXPLANATION	IMPORTANCE
Struggle and Doubt	Habakkuk asked God why the wicked in Judah were not being punished for their sin. He couldn't understand why a just God would allow such evil to exist. God promised to use the Babylonians to punish Judah. When Habakkuk cried out for answers in his time of struggle, God answered him with words of hope.	God wants us to come to him with our struggles and doubts. His answers may not be what we expect, however. God sustains us by revealing himself to us. Trusting him leads to quiet hope, not bitter resignation.
God's Sovereignty	Habakkuk asked God why he would use the wicked Babylonians to punish his people. God said that he would also punish the Babylonians after they had fulfilled his purpose.	God is still in control of this world in spite of the apparent triumph of evil. God doesn't overlook sin. One day he will rule the whole earth with perfect justice.

Hope	God is the Creator; he is all-powerful. He has a plan, and he will carry it out. He will punish sin. He is our strength and our place of safety. We can have confidence that he will love us and guard our relationship with him forever.	Hope means going beyond our unpleasant daily experiences to the joy of knowing God. We live by trusting in him, not by the benefits, happiness, or success we may experience in this life. Our hope comes from God.

Splintered Nation

For Vital Statistics, see p. 688

ZEPHANIAH

OVERWHELMING grief, prolonged distress, incessant abuse, continual persecution, and imminent punishment breed hopelessness and despair. "If only," we cry, as we search our mind for a way out and look to the skies for rescue. With just a glimmer of hope, we would take courage and carry on. Hope is the silver shaft of sun breaking through the storm-darkened sky, words of comfort in the intensive care unit, the first spring bird perched on a snow-covered twig, and the finish line in sight. It is a rainbow, a song, a loving touch. Hope is knowing God and resting in his love.

As God's prophet, Zephaniah was bound to speak the truth. This he did clearly, thundering certain judgment and horrible punishment for all who would defy the Lord. God's awful wrath would sweep away everything in the land and destroy it. " 'I will sweep away people and animals alike. I will sweep away the birds of the sky and the fish in the sea. I will reduce the wicked to heaps of rubble, and I will wipe humanity from the face of the earth,' says the LORD" (Zeph 1:3). No living thing in the land would escape. And that terrible day was coming soon: "That terrible day of the LORD is near. Swiftly it comes—a day of bitter tears, a day when even strong men will cry out. It will be a day when the LORD's anger is poured out—a day of terrible distress and anguish, a day of ruin and desolation, a day of darkness and gloom, a day of clouds and blackness" (Zeph 1:14-15). We can sense the oppression and depression his listeners must have felt. They were judged guilty, and they were doomed.

But in the midst of this terrible pronouncement, there is hope. The first chapter of Zephaniah's prophecy is filled with terror. In chapter two, however, a whispered promise appears. "Seek the LORD, all who are humble, and follow his commands. Seek to do what is right and to live humbly. Perhaps even yet the LORD will protect you—protect you from his anger" (Zeph 2:3). And a few verses later we read of "the remnant of the tribe of Judah" (Zeph 2:7) who will be restored.

Finally in chapter three, the quiet refrain grows to a crescendo as God's salvation and deliverance for those who are faithful to him is declared. "Sing, O daughter of Zion; shout aloud, O Israel! Be glad and rejoice with all your heart, O daughter of Jerusalem! For the LORD will remove his hand of judgment and will disperse the armies of your enemy. And the LORD himself, the King of Israel, will live among you! At last your troubles will be over, and you will never again fear disaster" (Zeph 3:14-15). This is true hope, grounded in the knowledge of God's justice and in his love for his people.

As you read Zephaniah, listen carefully to the words of judgment. God does not take sin lightly, and it will be punished. But be encouraged by the words of hope—our God reigns, and he will rescue his own. Decide to be part of that faithful remnant of souls who humbly worship and obey the living Lord.

THE BLUEPRINT

1. The day of judgment (1:1–3:8)
2. The day of hope (3:9-20)

Zephaniah warned the people of Judah that if they refused to repent, the entire nation, including the beloved city of Jerusalem, would be lost. The people knew that God would eventually bless them, but Zephaniah made it clear that there would be judgment first, then blessing. This judgment would not be merely punishment for sin, but it would also be a means of purifying the people. Though we live in a fallen world surrounded by evil, we can hope in the perfect Kingdom of God to come, and we can allow any punishment that touches us now to purify us from sin.

MEGATHEMES

THEME	EXPLANATION	IMPORTANCE
Day of Judgment	Destruction was coming because Judah had forsaken the Lord. The people worshiped Baal, Molech, and the stars in heaven. Even the priests mixed pagan practices with faith in God. God's punishment for sin was on the way.	To escape God's judgment we must listen to him, accept his correction, trust him, and seek his guidance. If we accept him as our Lord, we can escape his condemnation.
Indifference to God	Although there had been occasional attempts at renewal, Judah had no sorrow for its sins. The people were prosperous, and they no longer cared about God. God's demands for righteous living seemed irrelevant to the people, whose security and wealth made them complacent.	Don't let material comfort be a barrier to your commitment to God. Prosperity can lead to an attitude of proud self-sufficiency. We need to admit that money won't save us and that we cannot save ourselves. Only God can save us.
Day of Cheer	The day of judgment will also be a day of cheer. God will judge all those who mistreat his people. He will purify his people, purging away all sin and evil. God will restore his people and give them hope.	When people are purged of sin, there is great relief and hope. No matter how difficult our experience now, we can look forward to the day of celebration when God will completely restore us. It will truly be a day to rejoice!

Return & Diaspora

For Vital Statistics, see p. 1147

HAGGAI

PRESSURES, demands, expectations, and tasks push in from all sides and assault our schedules. Do this! Be there! Finish that! Call them! Everyone seems to want something from us—family, friends, employer, school, church, clubs. Soon we have little left to give as we run out of energy and time. We find ourselves rushing through life, attending to the necessary, the immediate, and the urgent. The important is all too often left in the dust. Our problem is not the volume of demands or lack of scheduling skills, but values—what is truly important to us.

Our values and priorities are reflected in how we use our resources—time, money, strength, and talent. Often our actions belie our words. We say God is number one, but then we relegate him to a lesser number on our "to do" lists.

Twenty-six centuries ago, a voice was heard, calling men and women to the right priorities. Haggai knew what was important and what had to be done, and he challenged God's people to respond.

In 586 B.C., the armies of Babylon had destroyed the Temple in Jerusalem—God's house, the symbol of his presence. In 538 B.C. King Cyrus decreed that Jews could return to their beloved city and rebuild the Temple. So they traveled to Jerusalem and began the work. But then they forgot their purpose and lost their priorities, as opposition and apathy brought the work to a standstill (Ezra 4:4-5). Then Haggai spoke, calling them back to God's values: "Why are you living in luxurious houses while my house lies in ruins?" (Hag 1:4). The people were more concerned with their own needs than with doing God's will, and, as a result, they suffered. Then Haggai called them to action: "This is what the LORD of Heaven's Armies says: Look at what's happening to you! Now go up into the hills, bring down timber, and rebuild my house. Then I will take pleasure in it and be honored, says the LORD" (Hag 1:7-8). And God's message through his servant Haggai became the catalyst for finishing the work.

Although Haggai is a small book, it is filled with challenge and promise, reminding us of God's claim on our lives and our priorities. As you read Haggai, imagine him walking the streets and alleys of Jerusalem, urging the people to get back to doing God's work. And listen to Haggai speaking to you, urging you to reorder your priorities in accordance with God's will. What has God told you to do? Put all else aside and obey him.

THE BLUEPRINT

1. The call to rebuild the Temple (1:1-15)
2. Encouragement to complete the Temple (2:1-23)

When the exiles first returned from Babylon, they set about rebuilding the Temple right away. Although they began with the right attitudes, they slipped back into wrong behavior, and the work came to a standstill. We need to be on guard to keep our priorities straight. Remain active in your service to God and continue to put first things first.

MEGATHEMES

THEME	EXPLANATION	IMPORTANCE
Right Priorities	God had given the Jews the assignment to finish the Temple in Jerusalem when they returned from captivity. After 15 years, they still had not completed it. They were more concerned about building their own homes than finishing God's work. Haggai told them to get their priorities straight.	It is easy to make other priorities more important than doing God's work. But God wants us to follow through and build up his Kingdom. Don't stop and don't make excuses. Set your heart on what is right and do it. Get your priorities straight.
God's Encouragement	Haggai encouraged the people as they worked. He assured them of the divine presence of the Holy Spirit and of final victory, and instilled in them the hope that the Messiah would reign.	If God gives you a task, don't be afraid to get started. His resources are infinite. God will help you complete it by giving you encouragement from others along the way.

Return & Diaspora

For Vital Statistics, see p. 1147

ZECHARIAH

THE FUTURE—that vast uncharted sea of the unknown, holding joy or terror, comfort or pain, love or loneliness. Some people fear the days to come, wondering what evils lurk in the shadows; others consult seers and future-telling charlatans, trying desperately to discover its secrets. But tomorrow's story is known only to God and to those special messengers called prophets, to whom God has revealed a chapter or two. A prophet's primary task was to proclaim the word of the Lord, pointing out sin, explaining its consequences, and calling men and women to repentance and obedience. Elijah, Elisha, Isaiah, Jeremiah, Ezekiel, Hosea, and Amos stand with scores of others who faithfully delivered God's message despite rejection, ridicule, and persecution. And at times they were given prophetic visions foretelling coming events.

Nestled near the end of the Old Testament, among what are known as "minor prophets," is the book of Zechariah. As one of the postexilic prophets, along with Joel, Haggai, and Malachi,

Zechariah ministered to the small remnant of Jews who had returned to Judah to rebuild the Temple and their nation. Like Haggai, he encouraged the people to finish rebuilding the Temple, but his message went far beyond those physical walls and contemporary issues. With spectacular apocalyptic imagery and graphic detail, Zechariah told of the Messiah, the one whom God would send to rescue his people and to reign over all the earth. Zechariah is one of our most important prophetic books, giving detailed messianic references that were clearly fulfilled in the life of Jesus Christ. The rebuilding of the Temple, he says, was just the first act in the drama of the end times and the ushering in of the messianic age. Zechariah proclaimed a stirring message of hope to these ex-captives and exiles—their King was coming!

Jesus is Messiah, the promised "great deliverer" of Israel. Unlike Zechariah's listeners, we can look back at Christ's ministry and mission. As you study Zechariah's prophecy, you will see details of Christ's life that were written 500 years before their fulfillment. Read and stand in awe of our God, who keeps his promises. But there is also a future message that has not yet been fulfilled—the return of Christ at the end of the age. As you read Zechariah, think through the implications of this promised event. Your King is coming, and he will reign forever and ever.

God knows and controls the future. We may never see more than a moment ahead, but we can be secure if we trust in him. Read Zechariah and strengthen your faith in God—he alone is your hope and security.

THE BLUEPRINT

A. MESSAGES WHILE REBUILDING THE TEMPLE (1:1–8:23) 1. Zechariah's night visions 2. Zechariah's words of encouragement	Zechariah encouraged the people to put away the sin in their lives and to continue rebuilding the Temple. His visions described the judgment of Israel's enemies, the blessings to Jerusalem, and the need for God's people to remain pure—avoiding hypocrisy, superficiality, and sin. Zechariah's visions provided hope for the people. We also need to carefully follow the instruction to remain pure until Christ returns.
B. MESSAGES AFTER COMPLETING THE TEMPLE (9:1–14:21)	Besides encouragement and hope, Zechariah's messages were also a warning that God's messianic Kingdom would not begin as soon as the Temple was complete. Israel's enemies would be judged and the King would come, but God's people would themselves face many difficult circumstances before experiencing the blessing of the messianic Kingdom. We, too, may face much sorrow, disappointment, and distress before coming into Christ's eternal Kingdom.

MEGATHEMES

THEME	EXPLANATION	IMPORTANCE
God's Jealousy	God was angry at his people for ignoring his prophets through the years, and he was concerned that they not follow the careless and false leaders who exploited them. Disobedience was the root of their problems and the cause of their misery. God was jealous for their devotion to him.	God is jealous for our devotion. To avoid Israel's ruin, don't walk in their steps. Don't reject God, follow false teachers, or lead others astray. Turn to God, faithfully obey his commands, and make sure you are leading others correctly.
Rebuild the Temple	The Jews were discouraged. They were free from exile, yet the Temple was not completed. Zechariah encouraged them to rebuild it. God would both protect his workmen and empower them by his Holy Spirit to carry out his work.	More than the rebuilding of the Temple was at stake—the people were staging the first act in God's wonderful drama of the end times. Those of us who love God must complete his work. To do so we must have the Holy Spirit's help. God will empower us with his Spirit.
The King Is Coming	The Messiah will come both to rescue people from sin and to reign as King. He will establish his Kingdom, conquer all his enemies, and rule over all the earth. Everything will one day be under his loving and powerful control.	The Messiah came as a servant to die for us. He will return as a victorious King. At that time, he will usher in peace throughout the world. Submit to his leadership now to be ready for the King's triumphant return.
God's Protection	There was opposition to God's plan in Zechariah's day, and he prophesied future times of trouble. But God's Word endures. God remembers the covenants he makes with his people. He cares for his people and will deliver them from all the world powers that oppress them.	Although evil is still present, God's infinite love and personal care have been demonstrated through the centuries. God keeps his promises. Although our bodies may be destroyed, we need never fear our ultimate destiny if we love and obey him.

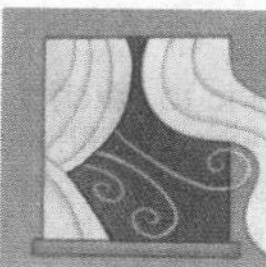

Return & Diaspora

For Vital Statistics, see p. 1148

MALACHI

A VASE shatters, brushed by a careless elbow; a toy breaks, handled roughly by young fingers; fabric rips, pulled by strong and angry hands. Spills and rips take time to clean up, effort to repair, and money to replace, but far more costly are shattered relationships. Unfaithfulness, untruths, hateful words, and forsaken vows tear delicate personal bonds and inflict wounds not easily healed. Most tragic, however, is a broken relationship with God.

God loves perfectly and completely. And his love is a love of action—giving, guiding, and guarding. He is altogether faithful, true to his promises to his chosen people. But consistently they spurn their loving God, breaking the covenant, following other gods, and living for themselves. So their relationship with him is shattered.

But the breach is not irreparable; all hope is not lost. God can heal and mend and reweave the fabric. Forgiveness is available. And that is grace.

This is the message of Malachi, God's prophet in Jerusalem. His words reminded the Jews, God's chosen nation, of their willful disobedience, beginning with the priests (Mal 1:1–2:9) and then including every person (Mal 2:10–3:15). They had shown contempt for God's name (Mal 1:6), offered defiled sacrifices (Mal 1:7-14), led others into sin (Mal 2:7-9), broken God's laws (Mal 2:11-16), called evil "good" (Mal 2:17), kept God's tithes and offerings for themselves (Mal 3:8-9), and become arrogant (Mal 3:13-15). The relationship was broken, and judgment and punishment would be theirs. In the midst of this wickedness, however, a faithful few—the remnant—still loved and honored God. God would shower his blessings upon these men and women (Mal 3:16-18).

Malachi paints a stunning picture of Israel's unfaithfulness that clearly shows the people to be worthy of punishment, but woven throughout this message is hope—the possibility of forgiveness. This is beautifully expressed in Malachi 4:2—"But for you who fear my name, the Sun of Righteousness will rise with healing in his wings. And you will go free, leaping with joy like calves let out to pasture."

Malachi concludes with a promise of the coming of "the prophet Elijah," who will offer God's forgiveness to all people through repentance and faith (Mal 4:5-6).

The book of Malachi forms a bridge between the Old Testament and the New Testament. As you read Malachi, see yourself as the recipient of this word of God to his people. Evaluate the depth of your commitment, the sincerity of your worship, and the direction of your life. Then allow God to restore your relationship with him through his love and forgiveness.

THE BLUEPRINT

1. The sinful priests (1:1–2:9)
2. The sinful people (2:10–3:15)
3. The faithful few (3:16–4:6)

Malachi rebuked the people and the priests for neglecting the worship of God and failing to live according to his will. The priests were corrupt; how could they lead the people? They had become stumbling blocks instead of spiritual leaders. The men were divorcing their wives and marrying pagan women; how could they have godly children? Their relationship to God had become inconsequential. If our relationship with God is unimportant, we need to take stock of ourselves by setting aside our sinful habits, putting the Lord first, and giving God our best each day.

MEGATHEMES

THEME	EXPLANATION	IMPORTANCE
God's Love	God loves his people even when they ignore or disobey him. He has great blessings to bestow on those who are faithful to him. His love never ends.	Because God loves us so much, he hates hypocrisy and careless living. This kind of living denies him the relationship he wants to have with us. What we give and how we live reflects the sincerity of our love for God.
The Sin of the Priests	Malachi singled out the priests for condemnation. They knew what God required, yet their sacrifices were unworthy and their service was insincere; they were lazy, arrogant, and insensitive. They had a casual attitude toward the worship of God and observance of God's standards.	If religious leaders go wrong, how will the people be led? We are all leaders in some capacity. Don't neglect your responsibilities or be ruled by what is convenient. Neglect and insensitivity are acts of disobedience. God wants leaders who are faithful and sincere.
The Sin of the People	The people had not learned the lesson of the Exile, nor had they listened to the prophets. Men were divorcing their wives to marry pagan women. This was against God's law because it disobeyed his commands about marriage and threatened the religious training of the children. But pride had hardened the hearts of the people.	God deserves our very best honor, respect, and faithfulness. But sin hardens our heart to our true condition. Pride is unwarranted self-esteem; it is setting your own judgment above God's and looking down on others. Don't let pride keep you from giving God your devotion, money, marriage, and family.
The Lord's Coming	God's love for his faithful people is demonstrated by the Messiah's coming. The Messiah will lead the people to the realization of all their fondest hopes. The day of the Lord's coming will be a day of comfort and healing for a faithful few, and a day of judgment for those who reject him.	At Christ's first coming, he refined and purified all those who believed in him. Upon his return, he will expose and condemn those who are proud, insensitive, or unprepared. Yet God is able to heal and forgive. Forgiveness is available to all who come to him.

Jesus Christ

For Vital Statistics, see p. 1257

MATTHEW

AS the motorcade slowly winds through the city, thousands pack the sidewalks hoping to catch a glimpse. Marching bands with great fanfare announce the arrival, and protective agents scan the crowd and run alongside the limousine. Pomp, ceremony, protocol—modern symbols of position and evidences of importance—herald the arrival of a head of state. Whether they are leaders by birth or election, we honor and respect them.

The Jews waited for a leader who had been promised centuries before by prophets. They believed that this leader—the Messiah ("anointed one")—would rescue them from their Roman oppressors and establish a new kingdom. As their king, he would rule the world with justice. Many Jews, however, overlooked prophecies that also spoke of this king as a suffering servant who would be rejected and killed. It is no wonder, then, that few recognized Jesus as the Messiah. How could this humble carpenter's son from Nazareth be their king? But Jesus was and is the King of all the earth!

Matthew (Levi) was one of Jesus' 12 disciples. Once he was a despised tax collector, but his life was changed by this man from Galilee. Matthew wrote this Gospel to his fellow Jews to prove that Jesus is the Messiah and to explain God's Kingdom.

Matthew begins his account by giving Jesus' genealogy. He then tells of Jesus' birth and early years, including the family's escape to Egypt from the murderous Herod and their return to Nazareth. Following Jesus' baptism by John (Matt 3:16-17) and his defeat of Satan in the wilderness, Jesus began his public ministry by calling his first disciples and giving the Sermon on the Mount (Matt 5–7). Matthew shows Christ's authority by reporting his miracles of healing the sick and the demon-possessed, and even raising the dead.

Despite opposition from the Pharisees and others in the religious establishment (Matt 12–15), Jesus continued to teach concerning the Kingdom of Heaven (Matt 16–20). During this time, Jesus spoke with his disciples about his imminent death and resurrection (Matt 16:21) and revealed his true identity to Peter, James, and John (Matt 17:1-5). Near the end of his ministry, Jesus entered Jerusalem in a triumphant procession (Matt 21:1-11). But soon opposition mounted, and Jesus knew that his death was near. So he taught his disciples about the future—what they could expect before his return (Matt 24) and how to live until then (Matt 25).

In Matthew's finale (Matt 26–28), he focuses on Jesus' final days on earth—the Last Supper, his prayer in Gethsemane, the betrayal by Judas, the flight of the disciples, Peter's denial, the trials before Caiaphas and Pilate, Jesus' final words on the cross, and his burial in a borrowed tomb. But the story does not end there, for the Messiah rose from the dead—conquering death and then telling his followers to continue his work by making disciples in all nations.

As you read this Gospel, listen to Matthew's clear message: Jesus is the Christ, the King of kings and Lord of lords. Celebrate his victory over evil and death, and make Jesus the Lord of your life.

THE BLUEPRINT

A. BIRTH AND PREPARATION OF JESUS, THE KING (1:1–4:11)

The people of Israel were waiting for the Messiah, their king. Matthew begins his book by showing how Jesus Christ was a descendant of David. But Matthew goes on to show that God did not send Jesus to be an earthly king but a heavenly King. His Kingdom would be much greater than David's because it would never end. Even at Jesus' birth, many recognized him as a King. Herod, the ruler, as well as Satan, was afraid of Jesus' kingship and tried to stop him, but others worshiped him and brought royal gifts. We must be willing to recognize Jesus for who he really is and worship him as King of our life.

B. MESSAGE AND MINISTRY OF JESUS, THE KING (4:12–25:46)

1. Jesus begins his ministry
2. Jesus gives the Sermon on the Mount
3. Jesus performs many miracles
4. Jesus teaches about the Kingdom
5. Jesus encounters differing reactions to his ministry
6. Jesus faces conflict with the religious leaders
7. Jesus teaches on the Mount of Olives

Jesus gave the Sermon on the Mount, directions for living in his Kingdom. He also told many parables about the difference between his Kingdom and the kingdoms of earth. Forgiveness, peace, and putting others first are some of the characteristics that make one great in the Kingdom of God. And to be great in God's Kingdom, we must live by God's standards right now. Jesus came to show us how to live as faithful subjects in his Kingdom.

C. DEATH AND RESURRECTION OF JESUS, THE KING (26:1–28:20)

Jesus was formally presented to the nation of Israel but was rejected. How strange for the King to be accused, arrested, and crucified. But Jesus demonstrated his power, even over death, through his resurrection and gained access for us into his Kingdom. With all this evidence that Jesus is God's Son, we, too, should accept him as our Lord.

MEGATHEMES

THEME	EXPLANATION	IMPORTANCE
Jesus Christ, the King	Jesus is revealed as the King of kings. His miraculous birth, his life and teaching, his miracles, and his triumph over death show his true identity.	Jesus cannot be equated with any person or power. He is the supreme ruler of time and eternity, heaven and earth, humans and angels. We should give him his rightful place as King of our lives.
The Messiah	Jesus was the Messiah, the one for whom the Jews had waited to deliver them from Roman oppression. Yet, tragically, they didn't recognize him when he came because his kingship was not what they expected. The true purpose of God's anointed deliverer was to die for all people to free them from sin's oppression.	Because Jesus was sent by God, we can trust him with our lives. It is worth everything we have to acknowledge him and give ourselves to him, because he came to be our Messiah, our Savior.
Kingdom of God	Jesus came to earth to begin his Kingdom. His full Kingdom will be realized at his return and will be made up of anyone who has faithfully followed him.	The way to enter God's Kingdom is by faith—believing in Christ to save us from sin and change our lives. We must do the work of his Kingdom now to be prepared for his return.
Teachings	Jesus taught the people through sermons, illustrations, and parables. Through his teachings, he showed the true ingredients of faith and how to guard against a fruitless and hypocritical life.	Jesus' teachings show us how to prepare for life in his eternal Kingdom by living properly right now. He lived what he taught, and we, too, must practice what we preach.
Resurrection	When Jesus rose from the dead, he rose in power as the true King. In his victory over death, he established his credentials as King and his power and authority over evil.	The Resurrection shows Jesus' all-powerful life for us—not even death could stop his plan of offering eternal life. Those who believe in Jesus can hope for a resurrection like his. Our role is to tell his story to all the earth so that everyone may share in his victory.

Jesus Christ

For Vital Statistics, see p. 1257

MARK

WE'RE number one! . . . The greatest, strongest, prettiest . . . champions! Daily such proclamations boldly assert claims of supremacy. Everyone wants to be associated with a winner. Losers are those who finish less than first. In direct contrast are the words of Jesus: "And whoever wants to be first among you must be the slave of everyone else. For even the Son of Man came here not to be served but to serve others and to give his life as a ransom for many" (Mark 10:44-45). Jesus is the greatest—God incarnate, our Messiah—but he entered history as a servant.

This is the message of Mark. Written to encourage Roman Christians and to prove beyond a doubt that Jesus is the Messiah, Mark presents a rapid succession of vivid pictures of Jesus in action—his true identity revealed by what he does, not necessarily by what he says. It is Jesus on the move.

Omitting the birth of Jesus, Mark begins with John the Baptist's preaching. Then, moving quickly past Jesus' baptism, temptation in the wilderness, and call of the disciples, Mark takes us directly into Jesus' public ministry. We see Jesus confronting a demon, healing a man with leprosy, and forgiving and healing the paralyzed man lowered into Jesus' presence by friends.

Next, Jesus calls Matthew (Levi) and has dinner with him and his questionable associates. This initiates the conflict with the Pharisees and other religious leaders, who condemn Jesus for eating with sinners and breaking the Sabbath.

In chapter 4, Mark pauses to give a sample of Jesus' teaching—the parable of the farmer and the illustration of the mustard seed—and then plunges back into the action. Jesus calms the waves, drives out demons, and raises Jairus's daughter from the dead.

After returning to Nazareth for a few days and experiencing rejection in his hometown, Jesus commissions the disciples to spread the Good News everywhere. Opposition from Herod and the Pharisees increases, and John the Baptist is beheaded. But Jesus continues to move, feeding 5,000, reaching out to the woman from Syrian Phoenicia, healing the deaf man, and feeding 4,000.

Finally, it is time to reveal his true identity to the disciples. Do they really know who Jesus is? Peter proclaims him Messiah but then promptly shows that he does not understand Jesus' mission. After the Transfiguration, Jesus continues to teach and heal, confronting the Pharisees about divorce and the rich young man about eternal life. Blind Bartimaeus is healed.

Events move rapidly toward a climax. The Last Supper, the betrayal, the Crucifixion, and the Resurrection are dramatically portrayed, along with more examples of Jesus' teachings. Mark shows us Jesus—moving, serving, sacrificing, and saving! As you read Mark, be ready for action, be open for God's move in your life, and be challenged to move into your world to serve.

THE BLUEPRINT

A. BIRTH AND PREPARATION OF JESUS, THE SERVANT (1:1-13)	Jesus did not arrive unannounced or unexpected. The Old Testament prophets had clearly predicted the coming of a great one, sent by God himself, who would offer salvation and eternal peace to Israel and the entire world. Then came John the Baptist, who announced that the long-awaited Messiah had finally come and would soon be among the people. In God's work in the world today, Jesus does not come unannounced or unexpected. Yet many still reject him. We have the witness of the Bible, but some choose to ignore it, just as many ignored John the Baptist in his day.
B. MESSAGE AND MINISTRY OF JESUS, THE SERVANT (1:14–13:37) 1. Jesus' ministry in Galilee 2. Jesus' ministry beyond Galilee 3. Jesus' ministry in Jerusalem	Jesus had all the power of God: He raised the dead, gave sight to the blind, restored deformed bodies, and quieted stormy seas. But with all this power, Jesus came to humanity as a servant. We can use his life as a pattern for how to live today. As Jesus served God and others, so should we.
C. DEATH AND RESURRECTION OF JESUS, THE SERVANT (14:1–16:20)	Jesus came as a servant, so many did not recognize or acknowledge him as the Messiah. We must be careful that we also don't reject God or his will because he doesn't quite fit our image of what God should be.

MEGATHEMES

THEME	EXPLANATION	IMPORTANCE
Jesus Christ	Jesus Christ alone is the Son of God. In Mark, Jesus demonstrates his divinity by overcoming disease, demons, and death. Although he had the power to be king of the earth, Jesus chose to obey the Father and die for us.	When Jesus rose from the dead, he proved that he was God, that he could forgive sin, and that he has the power to change our lives. By trusting in him for forgiveness, we can begin a new life with him as our guide.
Servant	As the Messiah, Jesus fulfilled the prophecies of the Old Testament by coming to earth. He did not come as a conquering king; he came as a servant. He helped people by telling them about God and healing them. Even more, by giving his life as a sacrifice for sin, he performed the ultimate act of service.	Because of Jesus' example, we should be willing to serve God and others. Real greatness in Christ's Kingdom is shown by service and sacrifice. Ambition or love of power or position should not be our motive; instead, we should do God's work because we love him.
Miracles	Mark records more of Jesus' miracles than sermons. Jesus is clearly a man of power and action, not just words. Jesus did miracles to convince the people who he was and to confirm to the disciples his true identity—God.	The more convinced we become that Jesus is God, the more we will see his power and his love. His mighty works show us he is able to save anyone regardless of his or her past. His miracles of forgiveness bring healing, wholeness, and changed lives to those who trust him.
Spreading the Gospel	Jesus directed his public ministry to the Jews first. When the Jewish leaders opposed him, Jesus also went to the non-Jewish world, healing and preaching. Roman soldiers, Syrians, and other Gentiles heard the Good News. Many believed and followed him. Jesus' final message to his disciples challenged them to go into all the world and preach the gospel of salvation.	Jesus crossed national, racial, and economic barriers to spread his Good News. Jesus' message of faith and forgiveness is for the whole world—not just our church, neighborhood, or nation. We must reach out beyond our own people and needs to fulfill the worldwide vision of Jesus Christ so that people everywhere may hear this great message and be saved from sin and death.

Jesus Christ

For Vital Statistics, see p. 1257

LUKE

EVERY birth is a miracle, and every child is a gift from God. But 20 centuries ago, the miracle of miracles occurred. A baby was born, but he was the Son of God. The Gospels tell of this birth, but Dr. Luke, as though he were the attending physician, provides most of the details surrounding this awesome occasion. Jesus entered history—God in the flesh.

Luke affirms Jesus' divinity, but the real emphasis of his book is on Jesus' humanity—Jesus, the Son of God, is also the Son of Man. As a doctor, Luke was a man of science, and as a Greek, he was a man of detail. It is not surprising, then, that he begins by outlining his extensive research and explaining that he is reporting the facts (Luke 1:1-4). Luke also was a close friend and traveling companion of Paul, so he could interview the other disciples, had access to other historical accounts, and was an eyewitness to the birth and growth of the early church. His Gospel and book of Acts are reliable, historical documents.

Luke's story begins with angels appearing to Zechariah and then to Mary, telling them of the upcoming births of their sons. From Zechariah and Elizabeth would come John the Baptist, who would prepare the way for Christ. And Mary would conceive a child by the Holy Spirit and bear Jesus, the Son of God. Soon after John's birth, Caesar Augustus declared a census, and so Mary and Joseph traveled to Bethlehem, the town of David, their ancient ancestor. There the child was born. Angels announced the joyous event to shepherds, who rushed to the manger. When the shepherds left, they went praising God and spreading the news. Eight days later, Jesus was circumcised and then dedicated to God in the Temple, where Simeon and Anna confirmed Jesus' identity as the Savior, their Messiah.

Luke gives us a glimpse of Jesus at age 12—discussing theology with the teachers of the Jewish law at the Temple (Luke 2:41-52). Eighteen years later Jesus went out in the wilderness to be baptized by John the Baptist before beginning his public ministry (Luke 3:1-23). At this point, Luke traces Jesus' genealogy on his stepfather Joseph's side, through David and Abraham back to Adam, underscoring Jesus' identity as the Son of Man (Luke 3:23-38).

After the Temptation (Luke 4:1-13), Jesus returned to Galilee to preach, teach, and heal (Luke 4:14ff). During this time, he began gathering his group of 12 disciples (Luke 5:1-11, 27-29). Later Jesus commissioned the disciples and sent them out to proclaim the Kingdom of God. When they returned, Jesus revealed to them his mission, his true identity, and what it meant to be his disciple (Luke 9:18-62). His mission would take him to Jerusalem (Luke 9:51-53), where he would be rejected, tried, and crucified.

While Jesus carried his own cross to Golgotha, some women in Jerusalem wept for him, but Jesus told them to weep for themselves and for their children (Luke 23:28). Luke's Gospel does not end in sadness, however. It concludes with the thrilling account of Jesus' resurrection from the dead, his appearances to the disciples, and his promise to send the Holy Spirit (Luke 24:1-53). Read Luke's beautifully written and accurate account of the life of Jesus, Son of Man and Son of God. Then praise God for sending the Savior—our risen and triumphant Lord—for all people.

THE BLUEPRINT

A. BIRTH AND PREPARATION OF JESUS, THE SAVIOR (1:1–4:13)	From an infant who could do nothing on his own, Jesus grew to become completely able to fulfill his mission on earth. He was fully human, developing in all ways like us. Yet he remained fully God. He took no shortcuts and was not isolated from the pressures and temptations of life. There are no shortcuts for us either as we prepare for lives of service to God.
B. MESSAGE AND MINISTRY OF JESUS, THE SAVIOR (4:14–21:38) 1. Jesus' ministry in Galilee 2. Jesus' ministry on the way to Jerusalem 3. Jesus' ministry in Jerusalem	Jesus taught great crowds of people, especially through parables, which are stories that illustrate great truths. But only those with ears to hear will understand. We should pray that God's Spirit would help us understand the implications of these truths for our lives so we can become more and more like Jesus.
C. DEATH AND RESURRECTION OF JESUS, THE SAVIOR (22:1–24:53)	The Savior of the world was arrested and executed. But death could not destroy him, and Jesus came back to life and ascended to heaven. In Luke's careful, historical account, we receive the facts about Jesus' resurrection. We must not only believe that these facts are true, but we must also trust Christ as our Savior. It is shortsighted to neglect the facts, but how sad it is to accept the facts and neglect the forgiveness that Jesus offers to each of us.

MEGATHEMES

THEME	EXPLANATION	IMPORTANCE
Jesus Christ, the Savior	Luke describes how God's Son entered human history. Jesus lived as the perfect example of a human. After a perfect ministry, he provided a perfect sacrifice for our sin so we could be saved.	Jesus is our perfect leader and Savior. He offers forgiveness to all who will accept him as Lord of their lives and believe that what he says is true.
History	Luke was a medical doctor and historian. He put great emphasis on dates and details, connecting Jesus to events and people in history.	Luke gives details so we can believe in the reliability of the history of Jesus' life. Even more important, we can believe with certainty that Jesus is God.
People	Jesus was deeply interested in people and relationships. He showed warm concern for his followers and friends—men, women, and children.	Jesus' love for people is good news for everyone. His message is for all people in every nation. Each one of us has an opportunity to respond to him in faith.
Compassion	As a perfect human, Jesus showed tender sympathy to the poor, the despised, the hurt, and the sinful. No one was rejected or ignored by him.	Jesus is more than a good teacher—he cares for you. Because of his deep love for you, he can satisfy your needs.
Holy Spirit	The Holy Spirit was present at Jesus' birth, baptism, ministry, and resurrection. As a perfect example for us, Jesus lived in dependence on the Holy Spirit.	The Holy Spirit was sent by God as confirmation of Jesus' authority. The Holy Spirit is given to enable people to live for Christ. By faith we can have the indwelling Holy Spirit's presence and power to witness and to serve.

Jesus Christ

For Vital Statistics, see p. 1257

JOHN

HE SPOKE, and galaxies whirled into place, stars burned the heavens, and planets began orbiting their suns—words of awesome, unlimited, unleashed power. He spoke again, and the waters and lands were filled with plants and creatures, running, swimming, growing, and multiplying—words of animating, breathing, pulsing life. Again he spoke, and man and woman were formed, thinking, speaking, and loving—words of personal and creative glory. Eternal, infinite, unlimited—he was, is, and always will be the Maker and Lord of all that exists.

And then he came in the flesh to a speck in the universe called planet Earth. The mighty Creator became a part of the creation, limited by time and space and susceptible to aging, sickness, and death. But love propelled him, and so he came to rescue and save those who were lost and to give them the gift of eternity. He is the Word; he is Jesus, the Messiah.

It is this truth that the apostle John brings to us in this book. John's Gospel is not a life of Christ; it is a powerful argument for the incarnation, a conclusive demonstration that Jesus was, and is, the very heaven-sent Son of God and the only source of eternal life.

John discloses Jesus' identity with his very first words, "In the beginning the Word already existed. The Word was with God, and the Word was God. He existed in the beginning with God" (John 1:1-2); and the rest of the book continues the theme. John, the eyewitness, chose eight of Jesus' miracles (or miraculous signs, as he calls them) to reveal his divine/human nature and his life-giving mission. These signs are (1) turning water to wine (John 2:1-11), (2) healing the official's son (John 4:46-54), (3) healing the lame man at the pool of Bethesda (John 5:1-9), (4) feeding the 5,000 with just a few loaves and fish (John 6:1-14), (5) walking on the water (John 6:15-21), (6) restoring sight to the blind man (John 9:1-41), (7) raising Lazarus from the dead (John 11:1-44), and, after the Resurrection, (8) giving the disciples an overwhelming catch of fish (John 21:1-14).

In every chapter Jesus' deity is revealed. And Jesus' true identity is underscored through the titles he is given—the Word, the only Son, Lamb of God, Son of God, true bread, life, resurrection, vine. And the formula is "I am." When Jesus uses this phrase, he affirms his preexistence and eternal deity. Jesus says, I am the bread of life (John 6:35); I am the light of the world (John 8:12; 9:5); I am the gate (John 10:7); I am the good shepherd (John 10:11, 14); I am the resurrection and the life (John 11:25); I am the way, the truth, and the life (John 14:6); and I am the true grapevine (John 15:1).

The greatest sign, of course, is the Resurrection, and John provides a stirring eyewitness account of finding the empty tomb. Then he records various post-Resurrection appearances by Jesus.

John, the devoted follower of Christ, has given us a personal and powerful look at Jesus Christ, the eternal Son of God. As you read his story, commit yourself to believe in and follow him.

THE BLUEPRINT

A. BIRTH AND PREPARATION OF JESUS, THE SON OF GOD (1:1–2:12)	John makes it clear that Jesus is not just a man; he is the eternal Son of God. He is the light of the world because he offers this gift of eternal life to all people. How blind and foolish to call Jesus nothing more than an unusually good man or moral teacher. Yet we sometimes act as if this were true when we casually toss around his words and go about living our own way. If Jesus is the eternal Son of God, we should pay attention to his divine identity and life-giving message.
B. MESSAGE AND MINISTRY OF JESUS, THE SON OF GOD (2:13–12:50) 1. Jesus encounters belief and unbelief from the people 2. Jesus encounters conflict with the religious leaders 3. Jesus encounters crucial events in Jerusalem	Jesus meets with individuals, preaches to great crowds, trains his disciples, and debates with the religious leaders. The message that he is the Son of God receives a mixed reaction. Some worship him, some are puzzled, some shrink back, and some move to silence him. We see the same varied reactions today. Times have changed, but people's hearts remain hard. May we see ourselves in these encounters Jesus had with people, and may our response be to worship and follow him.
C. DEATH AND RESURRECTION OF JESUS, THE SON OF GOD (13:1–21:25) 1. Jesus teaches his disciples 2. Jesus completes his mission	Jesus carefully instructed the disciples how to continue to believe even after his death, yet they could not take it in. After he died and the first reports came back that Jesus was alive, the disciples could not believe it. Thomas is especially remembered as one who refused to believe even when he heard the eyewitness accounts from other disciples. May we not be like Thomas, demanding a physical face-to-face encounter, but may we accept the eyewitness testimony of the disciples that John has recorded in this Gospel.

MEGATHEMES

THEME	EXPLANATION	IMPORTANCE
Jesus Christ, Son of God	John shows us that Jesus is unique as God's special Son, yet he is fully God. Because he is fully God, Jesus is able to reveal God to us clearly and accurately.	Because Jesus is God's Son, we can perfectly trust what he says. By trusting him, we can gain an open mind to understand God's message and fulfill his purpose in our lives.

Eternal Life	Because Jesus is God, he lives forever. Before the world began, he lived with God, and he will reign forever with him. In John we see Jesus revealed in power and magnificence even before his resurrection.	Jesus offers eternal life to us. We are invited to begin living in a personal, eternal relationship with him now. Although we must grow old and die, by trusting him we can have a new life that lasts forever.
Belief	John records eight specific signs, or miracles, that show the nature of Jesus' power and love. We see his power over everything created, and we see his love of all people. These signs encourage us to believe in him.	Believing is active, living, and continuous trust in Jesus as God. When we believe in his life, his words, his death, and his resurrection, we are cleansed from sin and receive power to follow him. But we must respond to him by believing.
Holy Spirit	Jesus taught his disciples that the Holy Spirit would come after he ascended from earth. The Holy Spirit would then indwell, guide, counsel, and comfort those who follow Jesus. Through the Holy Spirit, Christ's presence and power are multiplied in all who believe.	Through God's Holy Spirit, we are drawn to him in faith. We must know the Holy Spirit to understand all Jesus taught. We can experience Jesus' love and guidance as we allow the Holy Spirit to do his work in us.
Resurrection	On the third day after he died, Jesus rose from the dead. This was verified by his disciples and many eyewitnesses. This reality changed the disciples from frightened deserters to dynamic leaders in the new church. This fact is the foundation of the Christian faith.	We can be changed as the disciples were and have confidence that our bodies will one day be raised to live with Christ forever. The same power that raised Christ to life can give us the ability to follow Christ each day.

ACTS

Jesus Christ
The Church

For Vital Statistics, see p. 1505

WITH a flick of a match, friction occurs and a spark leaps from match to tinder. A small flame burns the edges and grows, fueled by wood and air. Heat builds, and soon the kindling is licked by reddish orange tongues. Higher and wider it spreads, consuming the wood. The flame has become a fire.

Nearly 2,000 years ago, a match was struck in Palestine. At first, just a few in that corner of the world were touched and warmed, but the fire spread beyond Jerusalem and Judea out to the world and to all people. Acts provides an eyewitness account of the flame and fire—the birth and spread of the church. Beginning in Jerusalem with a small group of disciples, the message traveled across the Roman Empire. Empowered by the Holy Spirit, this courageous band preached, taught, healed, and demonstrated love in synagogues, schools, homes, marketplaces, and courtrooms, and on streets, hills, ships, and desert roads—wherever God sent them, lives and history were changed.

Written by Luke as a sequel to his Gospel, Acts is an accurate historical record of the early church. But Acts is also a theological book, with lessons and living examples of the work of the Holy Spirit, church relationships and organization, the implications of grace, and the law of love. And Acts is an apologetic work, building a strong case for the validity of Christ's claims and promises.

The book of Acts begins with the outpouring of the promised Holy Spirit and the commencement of the proclamation of the gospel of Jesus Christ. This Spirit-inspired evangelism began in Jerusalem and eventually spread to Rome, covering most of the Roman Empire. The gospel first went to the Jews, but they, as a nation, rejected it. A remnant of Jews, of course, gladly received the Good News. But the continual rejection of the gospel by the vast majority of the Jews led to the ever-increasing proclamation of the gospel to the Gentiles. This was according to Jesus' plan: The gospel was to go from Jerusalem, to Judea, to Samaria, and to the ends of the earth (Acts 1:8). This, in fact, is the pattern that the Acts narrative follows. The glorious proclamation began in Jerusalem (Acts 1–7), went to Judea and Samaria (Acts 8 and following), and to the countries beyond Judea (Acts 11:19; 13:4 and on to the end of Acts). The second half of Acts is focused primarily on Paul's missionary journeys to many countries north of the Mediterranean Sea. He, with his companions, took the gospel first to the Jews and then to the Gentiles. Some of the Jews believed, and many of the Gentiles received the Good News with joy. New churches were started, and new believers began to grow in the Christian life.

As you read Acts, put yourself in the place of the disciples: Identify with them as they are filled with the Holy Spirit, and experience the thrill of seeing thousands respond to the gospel message. Sense their commitment as they give every ounce of talent and treasure to Christ. And as you read, watch the Spirit-led boldness of these first-century believers, who through suffering and in the face of death take every opportunity to tell of their crucified and risen Lord. Then decide to be a twenty-first-century version of those men and women of God.

THE BLUEPRINT

A. PETER'S MINISTRY (1:1–12:25)
1. Establishment of the church
2. Expansion of the church

After the resurrection of Jesus Christ, Peter preached boldly and performed many miracles. Peter's actions demonstrate vividly the source and effects of Christian power. Because of the Holy Spirit, God's people were empowered so they could accomplish their tasks. The Holy Spirit still empowers believers today. We should turn to the Holy Spirit to give us the strength, courage, and insight to accomplish our work for God.

B. PAUL'S MINISTRY (13:1–28:31) 1. First missionary journey 2. The council at Jerusalem 3. Second missionary journey 4. Third missionary journey 5. Paul on trial	Paul's missionary adventures show us the progress of Christianity. The gospel could not be confined to one corner of the world. This was a faith that offered hope to all humanity. We, too, should venture forth and share in this heroic task to witness for Christ in all the world.

MEGATHEMES

THEME	EXPLANATION	IMPORTANCE
Church Beginnings	Acts is the history of how Christianity was founded and organized and solved its problems. The community of believers began by faith in the risen Christ and in the power of the Holy Spirit, who enabled them to witness, to love, and to serve.	New churches are continually being founded. By faith in Jesus Christ and through the power of the Holy Spirit, the church can be a vibrant agent for change. As we face new problems, Acts gives important remedies for solving them.
Holy Spirit	The church did not start or grow by its own power or enthusiasm. The disciples were empowered by God's Holy Spirit. He was the promised Advocate and Guide sent when Jesus went to heaven.	The Holy Spirit's work demonstrated that Christianity was supernatural. Thus, the church became more Holy Spirit conscious than problem conscious. By faith, any believer can do Christ's work by the power of the Holy Spirit.
Church Growth	Acts presents the history of a dynamic, growing community of believers from Jerusalem to Syria, Africa, Asia, and Europe. In the first century, Christianity spread from believing Jews to non-Jews in 39 cities and 30 countries, islands, or provinces.	When the Holy Spirit works, there is movement, excitement, and growth. He gives us the motivation, energy, and ability to get the gospel to the whole world. How are you fitting into God's plan for spreading Christianity? What is your place in this movement?
Witnessing	Peter, John, Philip, Paul, Barnabas, and thousands more witnessed to their new faith in Christ. By personal testimony, preaching, or defense before authorities, they told the story with boldness and courage to groups of all sizes.	We are God's people, chosen to be part of his plan to reach the world. In love and by faith, we can have the Holy Spirit's help as we witness or preach. Witnessing is also beneficial to us because it strengthens our faith as we confront those who challenge it.
Opposition	Through imprisonment, beatings, plots, and riots, Christians were persecuted by both Jews and Gentiles. But the opposition became a catalyst for the spread of Christianity. Growth during times of oppression showed that Christianity was not the work of humans, but of God.	God can work through any opposition. When persecution from hostile unbelievers comes, realize that it has come because you have been a faithful witness and you have looked for the opportunity to present the Good News about Christ. Seize the opportunities that opposition brings.

The Church

For Vital Statistics, see p. 1505

ROMANS

KNOWLEDGEABLE and experienced, the district attorney makes his case. Calling key witnesses to the stand, he presents the evidence. After discrediting the testimonies of witnesses for the defense by skillfully cross-examining them, he concludes with an airtight summary and stirring challenge for the jury. The announced verdict is no surprise. "Guilty" states the foreman, and justice is served. The apostle Paul was intelligent, articulate, and committed to his calling. Like a skilled lawyer, he presented the case for the gospel clearly and forthrightly in his letter to the believers in Rome.

Paul had heard of the church at Rome, but he had not yet been there, nor had any of the other apostles. Evidently the church had been started by Jews who had come to faith during Pentecost (Acts 2). They had spread the gospel on their return to Rome, and the church had grown.

Although many barriers separated them, Paul felt a bond with these believers in Rome. They were his brothers and sisters in Christ, and he longed to see them face to face. He had never met most of the believers there, yet he loved them. He sent this letter to introduce himself and to make a clear declaration of the faith.

After a brief introduction, Paul presents the facts of the gospel (Rom 1:3) and declares his allegiance to it (Rom 1:16-17). He continues by building an airtight case for the lostness of humanity and the necessity for God's intervention (Rom 1:18–3:20).

Then Paul presents the Good News: Salvation is available to all, regardless of a person's identity, sin, or heritage. We are saved by grace (unearned, undeserved favor from God) through faith (complete trust) in Christ and his finished work. Through him we can stand before God justified, "not guilty" (Rom 3:21–5:21). With this foundation Paul moves directly into a discussion of the freedom that comes from being saved—freedom from the power of sin (Rom 6:1-23), freedom from the domination of the law (Rom 7:1-25), freedom to become like Christ and discover God's limitless love (Rom 8:1-39).

Speaking directly to his Jewish brothers and sisters, Paul shares his concern for them and explains how they fit into God's plan (Rom 9:1–11:12). God has made the way for Jews and Gentiles to be united in the body of Christ; both groups can praise God for his wisdom and love (Rom 11:13-36).

Paul explains what it means to live in complete submission to Christ: Use spiritual gifts to serve others (Rom 12:3-8), genuinely love others (Rom 12:9-21), and be good citizens (Rom 13:1-14). Freedom must be guided by love as we build each other up in the faith, being sensitive and helpful to those who are weak (Rom 14:1–15:4). Paul stresses unity, especially between Gentiles and Jews (Rom 15:5-13). He concludes by reviewing his reasons for writing, outlining his personal plans (Rom 15:22-33), greeting his friends, and giving a few final thoughts and greetings from his traveling companions (Rom 16:1-27).

As you read Romans, reexamine your commitment to Christ, and reconfirm your relationships with other believers in Christ's body.

THE BLUEPRINT

A. WHAT TO BELIEVE (1:1–11:36) 1. Sinfulness of humanity 2. Forgiveness of sin through Christ 3. Freedom from sin's grasp 4. Israel's past, present, and future	Paul clearly sets forth the foundations of the Christian faith. All people are sinful; Christ died to forgive sin; we are made right with God through faith; this begins a new life with a new relationship with God. Like a sports team that constantly reviews the basics, we will be greatly helped in our faith by keeping close to these foundations. If we study Romans carefully, we will never be at a loss to know what to believe.
B. HOW TO BEHAVE (12:1–16:27) 1. Personal responsibility 2. Personal notes	Paul gives clear, practical guidelines for the believers in Rome. The Christian life is not abstract theology unconnected with life, but it has practical implications that will affect how we choose to behave each day. It is not enough merely to know the gospel; we must let it transform our life and let God impact every aspect of our lives.

MEGATHEMES

THEME	EXPLANATION	IMPORTANCE
Sin	Sin means refusing to do God's will and failing to do all that God wants. Since Adam's rebellion against God, our nature is to disobey him. Our sin cuts us off from God. Sin causes us to want to live our own way rather than God's way. Because God is morally perfect, just, and fair, he is right to condemn sin.	Each person has sinned, either by rebelling against God or by ignoring his will. No matter what our background or how hard we try to live good and moral lives, we cannot earn salvation or remove our sin. Only Christ can save us.
Salvation	Our sin points out our need to be forgiven and cleansed. Although we don't deserve it, God, in his kindness, reached out to love and forgive us. He provides the way for us to be saved. Christ's death paid the penalty for our sin.	It is good news that God saves us from our sin. But in order to enter into a wonderful new relationship with God, we must believe that Jesus died for us and that he forgives all our sin.
Growth	By God's power, believers are sanctified—made holy. This means we are set apart from sin, enabled to obey and to become more like Christ. When we are growing in our relationship with Christ, the Holy Spirit frees us from the demands of the law and from fear of judgment.	Because we are free from sin's control, the law's demands, and fear of God's punishment, we can grow in our relationship with Christ. By trusting in the Holy Spirit and allowing him to help us, we can overcome sin and temptation.
Sovereignty	God oversees and cares about his people—past, present, and future. God's ways of dealing with people are always fair. Because God is in charge of all creation, he can save whomever he wills.	Because of God's mercy, both Jews and Gentiles can be saved. We all must respond to his mercy and accept his gracious offer of forgiveness. Because he is sovereign, let him reign in your heart.
Service	When our purpose is to give credit to God for his love, power, and perfection in all we do, we can serve him properly. Serving him unifies all believers and enables them to show love and sensitivity to others.	None of us can be fully Christlike by ourselves—it takes the entire body of Christ to fully express Christ. By actively and vigorously building up other believers, Christians can be a symphony of service to God.

The Church

For Vital Statistics, see p. 1505

1 CORINTHIANS

ON A BED of grass, a chameleon's skin turns green. On the earth, it becomes brown. The animal changes to match the environment. Many creatures blend into nature with God-given camouflage suits to aid their survival. It's natural to fit in and adapt to the environment. But followers of Christ are new creations, born from above and changed from within, with values and lifestyles that confront the world and clash with accepted morals. True believers don't blend in very well.

The Christians in Corinth were struggling with their environment. Surrounded by corruption and every conceivable sin, they felt the pressure to adapt. They knew they were free in Christ, but what did this freedom mean? How should they view idols or sexuality? What should they do about marriage, women in the church, and the gifts of the Spirit? These were more than theoretical questions—the church was being undermined by immorality and spiritual immaturity. The believers' faith was being tried in the crucible of immoral Corinth, and some of them were failing the test.

Paul heard of their struggles and wrote this letter to address their problems, heal their divisions, and answer their questions. Paul confronted them with their sin and their need for corrective action and clear commitment to Christ.

After a brief introduction (1 Cor 1:1-9), Paul immediately turns to the question of unity (1 Cor 1:10–4:21). He emphasizes the clear and simple gospel message around which all believers should rally, he explains the role of church leaders, and he urges them to grow up in their faith.

Paul then deals with the immorality of certain church members and the issue of lawsuits among Christians (1 Cor 5:1–6:8). He tells the believers to exercise church discipline and to settle their internal matters themselves. Because so many of the problems in the Corinthian church involved sex, Paul denounces sexual sin in the strongest possible terms (1 Cor 6:9-20).

Next, Paul answers some of the Corinthians' questions. Because prostitution and immorality were pervasive, marriages in Corinth were in shambles, and Christians weren't sure how to react. Paul gives pointed and practical answers (1 Cor 7:1-40). Concerning the question of meat sacrificed to idols, Paul suggests that they show complete commitment to Christ and sensitivity to other believers, especially weaker brothers and sisters (1 Cor 8:1–11:1).

Paul goes on to talk about worship, and he carefully explains the role of women, the Lord's Supper, and spiritual gifts (1 Cor 11:2–14:40). Sandwiched in the middle of this section is his magnificent description of the greatest gift—love (1 Cor 13). Then Paul concludes with a discussion of the resurrection (1 Cor 15:1-58), some final thoughts, greetings, and a benediction (1 Cor 16:1-24).

This letter confronts the Corinthians about their sins and shortcomings. And 1 Corinthians calls all Christians to be careful not to blend in with the world and accept its values and life-styles. We must live Christ-centered, blameless, loving lives that make a difference for God. As you read 1 Corinthians, examine your values in light of complete commitment to Christ.

THE BLUEPRINT

A. PAUL ADDRESSES CHURCH PROBLEMS (1:1–6:20)
1. Divisions in the church
2. Disorder in the church

Without Paul's presence, the Corinthian church had fallen into divisiveness and disorder. This resulted in many problems, which Paul addressed squarely. We must be concerned for unity and order in our local churches, but we should not mistake inactivity for order and cordiality for unity. We, too, must squarely address problems in our churches.

B. PAUL ANSWERS CHURCH QUESTIONS (7:1–16:24)
1. Instruction on Christian marriage
2. Instruction on Christian freedom
3. Instruction on public worship
4. Instruction on resurrection

The Corinthians had sent Paul a list of questions, and he answered them in a way meant to correct abuses in the church and to show how important it is that they live what they believe. Paul gives us a Christian approach to problem solving. He analyzed the problem thoroughly to uncover the underlying issue and then highlighted the biblical values that should guide our actions.

MEGATHEMES

THEME	EXPLANATION	IMPORTANCE
Loyalties	The Corinthians were rallying around various church leaders and teachers—Peter, Paul, and Apollos. These loyalties led to intellectual pride and created a spirit of division in the church.	Our loyalty to human leaders or human wisdom must never divide Christians into camps. We must care for our fellow believers, not fight with them. Your allegiance must be to Christ. Let him lead you.
Immorality	Paul received a report of uncorrected sexual sin in the church at Corinth. The people had grown indifferent to immorality. Others had misconceptions about marriage. We are to live morally, keeping our bodies for God's service at all times.	Christians must never compromise with sinful ideas and practices. We should not blend in with people around us. You must live up to God's standard of morality and not condone immoral behavior, even if society accepts it.
Freedom	Paul taught freedom of choice on practices not expressly forbidden in Scripture. Some believers felt certain actions—like eating the meat of animals used in pagan rituals—were corrupt by association. Others felt free to participate in such actions without feeling that they had sinned.	We are free in Christ, yet we must not abuse our Christian freedom by being inconsiderate and insensitive to others. We must never encourage others to do something they feel is wrong just because we have done it. Let love guide your behavior.
Worship	Paul addressed disorder in worship. People were taking the Lord's Supper without first confessing sin. There was misuse of spiritual gifts and confusion over women's roles in the church.	Worship must be carried out properly and in an orderly manner. Everything we do to worship God should be done in a manner worthy of his high honor. Make sure that worship is harmonious, useful, and edifying to all believers.
Resurrection	Some people denied that Christ rose from the dead. Others felt that people would not physically be resurrected. Christ's resurrection assures us that we will have new, living bodies after we die. The hope of the Resurrection forms the secret of Christian confidence.	Since we will be raised again to life after we die, our life is not in vain. We must stay faithful to God in our morality and our service. We are to live today knowing we will spend eternity with Christ.

The Church

For Vital Statistics, see p. 1505

2 CORINTHIANS

SLITHERING through the centuries, the serpent whispers his smooth-tongued promises, beguiling, deceiving, and tempting—urging men and women to reject God and to follow Satan. Satan's emissaries have been many—false prophets contradicting God's ancient spokesmen, "pious" leaders hurling blasphemous accusations, and heretical teachers infiltrating churches. And the deception continues. Our world is filled with cults, "isms," and ideologies, all claiming to provide the way to God.

Paul constantly struggled with those who would mislead God's people, and he poured his life into spreading the Good News to the uttermost parts of the world. During three missionary trips and other travels, he proclaimed Christ, made converts, and established churches. But often young believers were easy prey for false teachers, who were a constant threat to the gospel and the early church. So Paul had to spend much time warning and correcting these new Christians.

The church at Corinth was weak. Surrounded by idolatry and immorality, they struggled with their Christian faith and life-style. Through personal visits and letters, Paul tried to instruct them in the faith, resolve their conflicts, and solve some of their problems. First Corinthians was sent to deal with specific moral issues in the church and to answer questions about sex, marriage, and tender consciences. That letter confronted the issues directly and was well received by most. But there were false teachers who denied Paul's authority and slandered him. Paul then wrote 2 Corinthians to defend his position and to denounce those who were twisting the truth.

Second Corinthians must have been a difficult letter for Paul to write because he had to list his credentials as an apostle. Paul was reluctant to do so as a humble servant of Christ, but he knew it was necessary. Paul also knew that most of the believers in Corinth had taken his previous words to heart and were beginning to mature in their faith. He affirmed their commitment to Christ.

Second Corinthians begins with Paul reminding his readers of (1) his relationship to them—Paul had always been honest and straightforward with them (2 Cor 1:12-14), (2) his itinerary—he was planning to visit them again (2 Cor 1:15–2:2), and (3) his previous letter (2 Cor 2:3-11). Paul then moves directly to the subject of false teachers (2 Cor 2:17), and he reviews his ministry among the Corinthians to demonstrate the validity of his message and to urge them not to turn away from the truth (2 Cor 3:1–7:16).

Paul next turns to the issue of collecting money for the poor Christians in Jerusalem. He tells them how others have given, and he urges them to show their love in a tangible way as well (2 Cor 8:1–9:15). Paul then gives a strong defense of his authority as a genuine apostle while pointing out the deceptive influence of the false apostles (2 Cor 10:1–13:10).

As you read this intensely personal letter, listen to Paul's words of love and exhortation, and be committed to the truth of God's Word and prepared to reject all false teaching.

THE BLUEPRINT

1. Paul explains his actions (1:1–2:11)
2. Paul defends his ministry (2:12–7:16)
3. Paul defends the collection (8:1–9:15)
4. Paul defends his authority (10:1–13:14)

In responding to the attacks on his character and authority, Paul explains the nature of Christian ministry and, as an example, openly shares about his ministry. This is an important letter for all who wish to be involved in any kind of Christian ministry, because it has much to teach us about how we should handle our ministries today. Like Paul, those involved in ministry should be blameless, sincere, confident, caring, open, and willing to suffer for the sake of Christ.

MEGATHEMES

THEME	EXPLANATION	IMPORTANCE
Trials	Paul experienced great suffering, persecution, and opposition in his ministry. He even struggled with a personal weakness—a "thorn" in the flesh. Through it all, Paul affirmed God's faithfulness.	God is faithful. His strength is sufficient for any trial. When trials come, they keep us from pride and teach us dependence on God. He comforts us so we can comfort others.
Church Discipline	Paul defends his role in church discipline. Neither immorality nor false teaching could be ignored. The church was to be neither too lax nor too severe in administering discipline. The church was to restore the corrected person when he or she repented.	The goal of all discipline in the church should be correction, not vengeance. For churches to be effective, they must confront and solve problems, not ignore them. In everything, we must act in love.
Hope	To encourage the Corinthians as they faced trials, Paul reminded them that they would receive new bodies in heaven. This would be a great victory in contrast to their present suffering.	To know we will receive new bodies offers us hope. No matter what adversity we face, we can keep going. Our faithful service will result in triumph.
Giving	Paul organized a collection of funds for the poor in the Jerusalem church. Many of the Asian churches gave money. Paul explains and defends his beliefs about giving, and he urges the Corinthians to follow through on their previous commitment.	Like the Corinthians, we should follow through on our financial commitments. Our giving must be generous, sacrificial, well planned, and based on need. Our generosity not only helps those in need but enables them to thank God.

Sound Doctrine	False teachers were challenging Paul's ministry and authority as an apostle. Paul asserts his authority in order to preserve correct Christian doctrine. His sincerity, his love for Christ, and his concern for the people were his defense.	We should share Paul's concern for correct teaching in our churches. But in so doing, we must share his motivation—love for Christ and people—and his sincerity.

The Church

For Vital Statistics, see p. 1505

GALATIANS

A FAMILY, executing their carefully planned escape at midnight, dashing for the border . . . a man standing outside prison walls, gulping fresh air, awash in the new sun . . . a young woman with every trace of the ravaging drug gone from her system . . . they are FREE! With fresh anticipation, they can begin life anew. Whether fleeing oppression, stepping out of prison, or breaking a strangling habit, freedom means life. There is nothing so exhilarating as knowing that the past is forgotten and that new options await. People yearn to be free.

The book of Galatians is the charter of Christian freedom. In this profound letter, Paul proclaims the reality of our liberty in Christ—freedom from the law and the power of sin, and freedom to serve our living Lord.

Most of the first converts and early leaders in the church were Jewish Christians who proclaimed Jesus as their Messiah. As Jewish Christians, they struggled with a dual identity: Their Jewishness constrained them to be strict followers of the law; their newfound faith in Christ invited them to celebrate a holy liberty. They wondered how Gentiles (non-Jews) could be part of the Kingdom of Heaven.

This controversy tore the early church. Judaizers—an extremist Jewish faction within the church—taught that Gentile Christians had to submit to Jewish laws and traditions in addition to believing in Christ. As a missionary to the Gentiles, Paul had to confront this issue many times.

Galatians was written, therefore, to refute the Judaizers and to call believers back to the pure gospel. The Good News is for all people—Jews and Gentiles alike. Salvation is by God's grace through faith in Christ Jesus and nothing else. Faith in Christ means true freedom.

After a brief introduction (Gal 1:1-5), Paul addresses those who were accepting the Judaizers' perverted gospel (Gal 1:6-9). He summarizes the controversy, including his personal confrontation with Peter and other church leaders (Gal 1:10–2:16). He then demonstrates that salvation is by faith alone by alluding to his conversion (Gal 2:17-21), appealing to his readers' own experience of the gospel (Gal 3:1-5), and showing how the Old Testament teaches about grace (Gal 3:6-20). Next, he explains the purpose of God's laws and the relationship between law, God's promises, and Christ (Gal 3:21–4:31).

Having laid the foundation, Paul builds his case for Christian liberty. We are saved by faith, not by keeping the law (Gal 5:1-12); our freedom means that we are free to love and serve one another, not to do wrong (Gal 5:13-26); and Christians should carry each other's burdens and be kind to each other (Gal 6:1-10). In 6:11-18, Paul takes the pen into his own hand and shares his final thoughts.

As you read Galatians, try to understand this first-century conflict between grace and law, or faith and deeds, but also be aware of modern parallels. Like Paul, defend the truth of the gospel and reject all those who would add to or twist this truth. You are free in Christ—step into the light and celebrate!

THE BLUEPRINT

1. Authenticity of the gospel (1:1–2:21)
2. Superiority of the gospel (3:1–4:31)
3. Freedom of the gospel (5:1–6:18)

In response to attacks from false teachers, Paul wrote to defend his apostleship and the authority of the gospel. The Galatians were beginning to turn from faith to legalism. The struggle between the gospel and legalism is still a relevant issue. Many today would have us return to trying to earn God's favor through following rituals or obeying a set of rules. As Christians, we are not boxed in but set free. To preserve our freedom, we must stay close to Christ and resist any who promote subtle ways for us to earn our salvation.

MEGATHEMES

THEME	EXPLANATION	IMPORTANCE
Law	A group of Jewish teachers insisted that non-Jewish believers must obey Jewish law and traditional rules. They believed a person was saved by following the law of Moses (with emphasis on circumcision, the sign of the covenant), in addition to faith in Christ. Paul opposed them by showing that the law can't save anyone.	We can't be saved by keeping the Old Testament law, even the Ten Commandments. The law served as a guide to point out our need to be forgiven. Christ fulfilled the obligations of the law for us. We must turn to him to be saved. He alone can make us right with God.
Faith	We are saved from God's judgment and penalty for sin by God's gracious gift to us. We receive salvation by faith—trusting in him—not in anything else. Becoming a Christian is in no way based on our initiative, wise choice, or good character. We can be right with God only by believing in him.	Your acceptance with God comes by believing in Christ alone. You must never add to or twist this truth. We are saved by faith, not by the good that we do. Have you placed your whole trust and confidence in Christ? He alone can forgive you and bring you into a relationship with God.

Freedom	Galatians is our charter of Christian freedom. We are not under the jurisdiction of Jewish laws and traditions nor under the authority of Jerusalem. Faith in Christ brings true freedom from sin and from the futile attempt to be right with God by keeping the law.	We are free in Christ, and yet freedom is a privilege. We are not free to disobey Christ or practice immorality, but we are free to serve the risen Christ. Let us use our freedom to love and to serve, not to do wrong.
Holy Spirit	We become Christians through the work of the Holy Spirit. He brings new life; even our faith to believe is a gift from him. The Holy Spirit instructs, guides, leads, and gives us power. He ends our bondage to evil desires, and he creates in us love, joy, peace, and many other wonderful changes.	When the Holy Spirit leads us, he produces his fruit in us. Just as we are saved by faith, not deeds, we also grow by faith. By believing, we can have the Holy Spirit within us, helping us live for Christ. Obey Christ by following the Holy Spirit's leading.

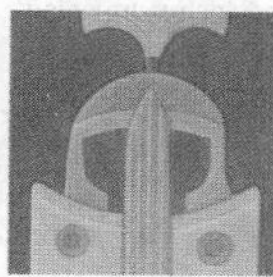

The Church

For Vital Statistics, see p. 1505

EPHESIANS

OUR churches come in all styles and shapes—secret meetings in homes; wide-open gatherings in amphitheaters; worship services packing thousands into a sanctuary while an overflow crowd watches on closed-circuit television; handfuls who kneel in urban storefronts. Buildings will vary, but the church is not confined to four walls. The church of Jesus Christ is people, his people, of every race and nation, who love Christ and are committed to serving him.

The "church age" began at Pentecost (Acts 2). Born in Jerusalem, the church spread rapidly through the ministry of the apostles and the early believers. Fanned by persecution, the gospel flame then spread to other cities and nations. On three courageous journeys, Paul and his associates established local assemblies in scores of Gentile cities.

One of the most prominent of those churches was at Ephesus. It was established in A.D. 53 on Paul's homeward journey to Jerusalem. But Paul returned a year later, on his third missionary trip, and stayed there for three years, preaching and teaching with great effectiveness (Acts 19:1-20). At another time, Paul met with the Ephesian elders, and he sent Timothy to serve as their leader (1 Tim 1:3). Just a few years later, Paul was sent as a prisoner to Rome. There, he was visited by messengers from various churches, including Tychicus of Ephesus. Paul wrote this letter to the church and sent it with Tychicus. Not written to counteract heresy or to confront any specific problem, Ephesians is a letter of encouragement. In it Paul describes the nature and appearance of the church, and he challenges believers to function as the living body of Christ on earth.

After a warm greeting (Eph 1:1-2), Paul affirms the nature of the church—the glorious fact that believers in Christ have been showered with God's kindness (Eph 1:3-8), chosen for salvation (Eph 1:9-12), marked with the Holy Spirit (Eph 1:13-14), filled with the Spirit's power (Eph 1:15-23), freed from sin's curse and bondage (Eph 2:1-10), and brought near to God (Eph 2:11-18). As part of God's "house," we stand with the prophets, apostles, Jews, Gentiles, and Christ himself (Eph 2:19–3:13). Then, as though overcome with emotion by remembering all that God has done, Paul challenges the Ephesians to live close to Christ, and he breaks into spontaneous praise (Eph 3:14-21).

Paul then turns his attention to the implications of being in the body of Christ, the church. Believers should have unity in their commitment to Christ and their use of spiritual gifts (Eph 4:1-16). They should have the highest moral standards (Eph 4:17–6:9). For the individual, this means rejecting pagan practices (Eph 4:17–5:20), and for the family, this means mutual submission and love (Eph 5:21–6:9).

Paul then reminds believers that the church is in a constant battle with the forces of darkness and that they should use every spiritual weapon at their disposal (Eph 6:10-17). He concludes by asking for their prayers, commissioning Tychicus, and giving a benediction (Eph 6:18-24).

As you read this masterful description of the church, thank God for the diversity and unity in his family, pray for your brothers and sisters across the world, and draw close to those in your local church.

THE BLUEPRINT

1. Unity in Christ (1:1–3:21) 2. Unity in the body of Christ (4:1–6:24)	In this letter, Paul explains the wonderful things that we have received through Christ and refers to the church as a body to illustrate unity of purpose and show how each individual member is a part that must work together with all the other parts. In our own life, we should work to eradicate all backbiting, gossip, criticism, jealousy, anger, and bitterness, because these are barriers to unity in the church.

MEGATHEMES

THEME	EXPLANATION	IMPORTANCE
God's Purpose	According to God's eternal, loving plan, he directs, carries out, and sustains our salvation.	When we respond to Christ's love by trusting in him, his purpose becomes our mission. Have you committed yourself to fulfilling God's purpose?

Christ the Center	Christ is exalted as the center of the universe and the focus of history. He is the head of the body, the church. He is the Creator and sustainer of all creation.	Because Christ is central to everything, his power must be central in us. Begin by placing all your priorities under his control.
Living Church	Paul describes the nature of the church. The church, under Christ's control, is a living body, a family, a dwelling. God gives believers special abilities by his Holy Spirit to build the church.	We are part of Christ's body, and we must live in vital union with him. Our conduct must be consistent with this living relationship. Use your God-given abilities to equip believers for service. Fulfill your role in the living church.
New Family	Because God through Christ paid our penalty for sin and forgave us, we have been reconciled—brought near to him. We are a new society, a new family. Being united with Christ means we are to treat one another as family members.	We are one family in Christ, so there should be no barriers, no divisions, no basis for discrimination. We all belong to him, so we should live in harmony with one another.
Christian Conduct	Paul encourages all Christians to wise, dynamic Christian living, for with privileges goes family responsibility. As a new community, we are to live by Christ's new standards.	God provides his Holy Spirit to enable us to live his way. To utilize the Spirit's power, we must lay aside our evil desires and draw on the power of his new life. Submit your will to Christ, and seek to love others.

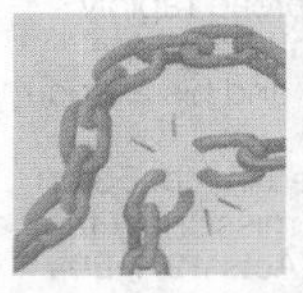

The Church
For Vital Statistics, see p. 1506

PHILIPPIANS

THE WORD happiness evokes visions of unwrapping gifts on Christmas morning, strolling hand in hand with the one you love, being surprised on your birthday, responding with unbridled laughter to a comedian, or vacationing in an exotic locale. Everyone wants to be happy; we make chasing this elusive ideal a lifelong pursuit: spending money, collecting things, and searching for new experiences. But if happiness depends on our circumstances, what happens when the toys rust, loved ones die, health deteriorates, money is stolen, and the party's over? Often happiness flees and despair sets in.

In contrast to happiness stands joy. Running deeper and stronger, joy is the quiet, confident assurance of God's love and work in our lives—that he will be there no matter what! Happiness depends on happenings, but joy depends on Christ.

Philippians is Paul's joy letter. The church in that Macedonian city had been a great encouragement to Paul. The Philippian believers had enjoyed a very special relationship with him, so he wrote them a personal expression of his love and affection. They had brought him great joy (Phil 4:1). Philippians is also a joyful book because it emphasizes the real joy of the Christian life. The concept of rejoicing or joy appears sixteen times in four chapters, and the pages radiate this positive message, culminating in the exhortation to "always be full of joy in the Lord. I say it again—rejoice!" (Phil 4:4).

In a life dedicated to serving Christ, Paul had faced excruciating poverty, abundant wealth, and everything in between. He even wrote this joyful letter from prison. Whatever the circumstances, Paul had learned to be content (Phil 4:11-12), finding real joy as he focused all of his attention and energy on knowing Christ (Phil 3:8) and obeying him (Phil 3:12-13).

Paul's desire to know Christ above all else is wonderfully expressed in the following words: "Yes, everything else is worthless when compared with the infinite value of knowing Christ Jesus my Lord. For his sake I have discarded everything else, counting it all as garbage, so that I could gain Christ and become one with him. . . . I want to know Christ and experience the mighty power that raised him from the dead. I want to suffer with him, sharing in his death" (Phil 3:8-10). May we share Paul's aspiration and seek to know Jesus Christ more and more. Rejoice with Paul in Philippians, and rededicate yourself to finding joy in Christ.

THE BLUEPRINT

1. Joy in suffering (1:1-30)
2. Joy in serving (2:1-30)
3. Joy in believing (3:1–4:1)
4. Joy in giving (4:2-23)

Although Paul was writing from prison, joy is a dominant theme in this letter. The secret of his joy is grounded in his relationship with Christ. People today desperately want to be happy but are tossed and turned by daily successes, failures, and inconveniences. Christians are to be joyful in every circumstance, even when things are going badly, even when we feel like complaining, even when no one else is joyful. Christ still reigns, and we still know him, so we can rejoice at all times.

MEGATHEMES

THEME	EXPLANATION	IMPORTANCE
Humility	Christ showed true humility when he laid aside his rights and privileges as God to become human. He poured out his life to pay the penalty we deserve. Laying aside self-interest is essential to all our relationships.	We are to take Christ's attitude in serving others. We must renounce personal recognition and merit. When we give up our self-interest, we can serve with joy, love, and kindness.

Self-Sacrifice	Christ suffered and died so we might have eternal life. With courage and faithfulness, Paul sacrificed himself for the ministry. He preached the gospel even while he was in prison.	Christ gives us power to lay aside our personal needs and concerns. To utilize his power, we must imitate those leaders who show self-denying concern for others. We dare not be self-centered.
Unity	In every church, in every generation, there are divisive influences (issues, loyalties, and conflicts). In the midst of hardships, it is easy to turn on one another. Paul encouraged the Philippians to agree with one another, stop complaining, and work together.	As believers, we should not contend with one another but unite against a mutual enemy. When we are unified in love, Christ's strength is most abundant. Keep before you the ideals of teamwork, consideration of others, and unselfishness.
Christian Living	Paul shows us how to live successful Christian lives. We can become mature by being so identified with Christ that his attitude of humility and self-sacrifice becomes ours. Christ is both our source of power and our guide.	Developing our character begins with God's work in us. But growth also requires self-discipline, obedience to God's Word, and concentration on our part.
Joy	Believers can have profound contentment, serenity, and peace no matter what happens. This joy comes from knowing Christ personally and from depending on his strength rather than our own.	We can have joy, even in hardship. Joy does not come from outward circumstances but from inward strength. As Christians, we must not rely on what we have or what we experience to give us joy but on Christ within us.

The Church

For Vital Statistics, see p. 1506

COLOSSIANS

REMOVE the head coach, and the team flounders; break the fuel line, and the car won't run; unplug the electrical appliance, and it has no power. Whether for leadership, power, or life, connections are vital! Colossians is a book of connections. Writing from prison in Rome, Paul combatted false teachings, which had infiltrated the Colossian church. The problem was "syncretism," combining ideas from other philosophies and religions (such as paganism, strains of Judaism, and Greek thought) with Christian truth. The resulting heresy later became known as "Gnosticism," emphasizing special knowledge (*gnosis* in Greek) and denying Christ as God and Savior. To combat this devious error, Paul stressed Christ's deity—his connection with the Father—and his sacrificial death on the cross for sin. Only by being connected with Christ through faith can anyone have eternal life, and only through a continuing connection with him can anyone have power for living. Christ is God incarnate and the only way to forgiveness and peace with God the Father. Paul also emphasized believers' connections with each other as Christ's body on earth.

Paul's introduction to the Colossians includes a greeting, a note of thanksgiving, and a prayer for spiritual wisdom and strength for these brothers and sisters in Christ (Col 1:1-12). He then moves into a doctrinal discussion of the person and work of Christ (Col 1:13-23), stating that Christ is "the visible image of the invisible God" (Col 1:15), the Creator (Col 1:16), "the head of the church, which is his body" (Col 1:18), and "supreme over all who rise from the dead" (Col 1:18). His death on the cross makes it possible for us to stand in the presence of God (Col 1:22).

Paul then explains how the world's teachings are totally empty when compared with God's plan, and he challenges the Colossians to reject shallow answers and to live in union with Christ (Col 1:24–2:23).

Against this theological backdrop, Paul turns to practical considerations—what the divinity, death, and resurrection of Jesus should mean to all believers (Col 3:1–4:6). Because our eternal destiny is sure, heaven should fill our thoughts (Col 3:1-4), sexual impurity and other worldly lusts should not be named among us (Col 3:5-8), and truth, love, and peace should mark our lives (Col 3:9-15). Our love for Christ should also translate into love for others—friends, fellow believers, spouses, children, parents, slaves, and masters (Col 3:16–4:1). We should constantly communicate with God through prayer (Col 4:2-4), and we should take every opportunity to tell others the Good News (Col 4:5-6). In Christ we have everything we need for salvation and for living the Christian life.

Paul had probably never visited Colosse, so he concludes this letter with personal comments about their common Christian associations, providing a living lesson of the connectedness of the body of Christ.

Read Colossians as a book for an embattled church in the first century, but read it also for its timeless truths. Gain a fresh appreciation for Christ as the fullness of God and the only source for living the Christian life. Know that he is your leader, head, and power source, and make sure of your connection to him.

THE BLUEPRINT

1. What Christ has done (1:1–2:23) 2. What Christians should do (3:1–4:18)	In this letter Paul clearly teaches that Christ has paid for sin, that Christ has reconciled us to God, and that Christ gives us the pattern and the power to grow spiritually. Because in Christ lives all the fullness of God, when we learn what he is like, we see what we need to become. Since Christ is Lord over all creation, we should crown him Lord over our lives. Since Christ is the head of the body, his church, we should nurture our vital connection to him.

MEGATHEMES

THEME	EXPLANATION	IMPORTANCE
Christ Is God	Jesus Christ is God in the flesh, Lord of all creation, and Lord of the new creation. He is the visible image of the invisible God. He is eternal, preexistent, omnipotent, equal with the Father. He is supreme and complete.	Because Christ is supreme, our lives must be Christ-centered. To recognize him as God means to regard our relationship with him as most vital and to make his interests our top priority.
Christ Is Head of the Church	Because Christ is God, he is the head of the church, his true believers. Christ is the founder, the leader, and the highest authority on earth. He requires first place in all our thoughts and activities.	To acknowledge Christ as our head, we must welcome his leadership in all we do and think. No person, group, or church can regard any loyalty as more critical than that of loyalty to Christ.
Union with Christ	Because our sin has been forgiven and we have been reconciled to God, we have a union with Christ that can never be broken. In our faith connection with him, we identify with his death, burial, and resurrection.	We should live in constant contact and communication with God. When we do, we all will be unified with Christ and with one another.
Heresy	False teachers were promoting a heresy that stressed self-made rules (legalism). They also sought spiritual growth by discipline of the body (asceticism) and visions (mysticism). This search created pride in their self-centered efforts.	We must not cling to our own ideas and try to blend them into Christianity. Nor should we let our hunger for a more fulfilling Christian experience cause us to trust in a teacher, a group, or a system of thought more than in Christ himself. Christ is our hope and our true source of wisdom.

The Church

For Vital Statistics, see p. 1506

1 THESSALONIANS

SLOWLY they walk, one by one, scattering the leaves and trampling the grass under measured and heavy steps. The minister's words still echoing in their minds, they hear workmen moving toward the terrible place, preparing to cover the casket of their loved one. Death, the enemy, has torn the bonded relationships of family and friends, leaving only memories . . . and tears . . . and loneliness. But like a golden shaft of sun piercing the winter sky, a singular truth shatters the oppressive gloom: Death is not the end! Christ is the victor over death, and there is the hope of resurrection through him.

As with every member of the human family, first-century Christians came face to face with their mortality. Many of them met early deaths at the hands of those who hated Christ and all allied with him. Whether at the hands of zealous Jews (like Paul before his conversion), angry Greeks, or ruthless Roman authorities, persecution included stonings, beatings, crucifixions, torture, and death. To be a follower of Christ meant to give up everything.

Paul established the church in Thessalonica during his second missionary journey (about A.D. 50). He wrote this letter a short time later to encourage the young believers there. He wanted to assure them of his love, to praise them for their faithfulness during persecution, and to remind them of their hope—the sure return of their Lord and Savior.

Paul begins this letter with a note of affirmation, thanking God for the strong faith and good reputation of the Thessalonians (1 Thes 1:1-10). Then Paul reviews their relationship—how he and his companions brought the gospel to them (1 Thes 2:1-12), how they accepted the message (1 Thes 2:13-16), and how he longed to be with them again (1 Thes 2:17-20). Because of his concern, he had sent Timothy to encourage them in their faith (1 Thes 3:1-13).

Paul then presents the core of his message—exhortation and comfort. He challenges them to please God in their daily living by avoiding sexual immorality (1 Thes 4:1-8), loving each other (1 Thes 4:9-10), and living as good citizens in a sinful world (1 Thes 4:11-12).

Paul comforts the Thessalonians by reminding them of the hope of resurrection (1 Thes 4:13-18). Then he warns them to be prepared at all times, for Jesus Christ could return at any moment. When Christ returns, those Christians who are alive and those who have died will be raised to new life (1 Thes 5:1-11).

Paul then gives the Thessalonians a handful of reminders on how to prepare themselves for the Second Coming (1 Thes 5:14-22): Warn the lazy, encourage the timid, help the weak, be patient with everyone, be kind to everyone, be joyful always, pray continually, give thanks, test everything that is taught, and avoid evil. Paul concludes his letter with two benedictions and a request for prayer.

As you read this letter, listen carefully to Paul's practical advice for Christian living. And when burdened by grief and overwhelmed by sorrow, take hope in the reality of Christ's return, resurrection, and eternal life!

THE BLUEPRINT

1. Faithfulness to the Lord (1:1–3:13) 2. Watchfulness for the Lord (4:1–5:28)	Paul and his companions were faithful to bring the gospel to the Thessalonians in the midst of persecution. The Thessalonians had only recently become Christians, and yet they had remained faithful to the Lord, despite the fact that the apostles were not with them. Others have been faithful in bringing God's Word to us. We must remain faithful and live in the expectation that Christ will return at any time.

MEGATHEMES

THEME	EXPLANATION	IMPORTANCE
Persecution	Paul and the new Christians at Thessalonica experienced persecution because of their faith in Christ. We can expect trials and troubles as well. We need to stand firm in our faith in the midst of trials, being strengthened by the Holy Spirit.	The Holy Spirit helps us to remain strong in faith, able to show genuine love to others and maintain our moral character even when we are being persecuted, slandered, or oppressed.
Paul's Ministry	Paul expressed his concern for this church even while he was being slandered. Paul's commitment to share the gospel in spite of difficult circumstances is a model we should follow.	Paul not only delivered his message, but gave of himself. In our ministries, we must become like Paul—faithful and bold, yet sensitive and self-sacrificing.
Hope	One day all believers, both those who are alive and those who have died, will be united with Christ. To those Christians who die before Christ's return, there is hope—the hope of the resurrection of the body.	If we believe in Christ, we will live with him forever. All those who belong to Jesus Christ from throughout history will be present with him at his second coming. We can be confident that we will be with loved ones who have trusted in Christ.
Being Prepared	No one knows the time of Christ's return. We are to live moral and holy lives, ever watchful for his coming. Believers must not neglect daily responsibilities, but always work and live to please the Lord.	The gospel is not only what we believe but also what we must live. The Holy Spirit leads us in faithfulness, so we can avoid lust and fraud. Live as though you expect Christ's return at any time. Don't be caught unprepared.

The Church

For Vital Statistics, see p. 1506

2 THESSALONIANS

"BUT I thought he said, . . ." "I'm sure he meant, . . ." "It is clear to me that we should, . . ." "I disagree. I think we must . . ."

Effective communication is difficult; often the message sent is not the message received in the home, marketplace, neighborhood, or church. Even when clearly stated or written, words can be misinterpreted and misunderstood, especially when filtered through the sieve of prejudices and preconceptions.

Paul faced this problem with the Thessalonians. He had written them earlier to help them grow in the faith, comforting and encouraging them by affirming the reality of Christ's return. Just a few months later, however, word came from Thessalonica that some had misunderstood Paul's teaching about the Second Coming. His announcement that Christ could come at any moment had caused some to stop working and just wait, rationalizing their idleness by pointing to Paul's teaching. Adding fuel to this fire was the continued persecution of the church. Many felt that indeed this must be the "day of the Lord."

Responding quickly, Paul sent a second letter to this young church. In it he gave further instruction concerning the Second Coming and the day of the Lord (2 Thes 2:1-2). Second Thessalonians, therefore, continues the subject of 1 Thessalonians and is a call to continued courage and consistent conduct.

The letter begins with Paul's trademark—a personal greeting and a statement of thanksgiving for their faith (2 Thes 1:1-3). He mentions their perseverance in spite of their persecution and trials (2 Thes 1:4) and uses this situation to broach the subject of Christ's return. At that time, Christ will vindicate the righteous who endure and will punish the wicked (2 Thes 1:5-12).

Paul then directly answers the misunderstanding concerning the timing of the events of the end times. He tells them not to listen to rumors and reports that the day of the Lord has already begun (2 Thes 2:1-2) because a number of events must occur before Christ returns (2 Thes 2:3-12). Meanwhile, they should stand firm for Christ's truth (2 Thes 2:13-15), receive God's encouragement and hope (2 Thes 2:16-17), pray for strength and for the spread of the Lord's message (2 Thes 3:1-5), and warn those who are idle (2 Thes 3:6-15). Paul ends with personal greetings and a benediction (2 Thes 3:16-18).

Almost 2,000 years later, we stand much closer to the time of Christ's return; but we also would be wrong to see his imminent appearance as an excuse for idle waiting and heavenward gazing. Being prepared for his coming means spreading the gospel, reaching out to those in need, and building the church, his body. As you read 2 Thessalonians, then, see clearly the reality of his return and your responsibility to live for him until that day.

THE BLUEPRINT

1. The bright hope of Christ's return (1:1–2:17) 2. Living in the light of Christ's return (3:1-18)	Paul wrote to encourage those who were facing persecution and to correct a misunderstanding about the timing of Christ's return. The teaching about the Lord's return promoted idleness in this young church. The imminent coming of Christ should never make us idle; we should be even more busy—living purely, using our time well, and working for his Kingdom. We must work not only during easy times when it is convenient but also during difficult times. Christians must patiently watch for Christ's return and work for him while they wait.

MEGATHEMES

THEME	EXPLANATION	IMPORTANCE
Persecution	Paul encouraged the church to persevere in spite of troubles and trials. God will bring victory to his faithful followers and judge those who persecute them.	God promises to reward our faith by giving us his power and helping us bear persecution. Suffering for our faith will strengthen us to serve Christ. We must be faithful to him.
Christ's Return	Since Paul had said that the Lord could come at any moment, some of the Thessalonian believers had stopped working in order to wait for Christ.	Christ will return and bring total victory to all who trust in him. If we are ready, we need not be concerned about when he will return. We should stand firm, keep working, and wait for Christ.
Great Rebellion	Before Christ's return, there will be a great rebellion against God led by the man of lawlessness (the Antichrist). God will remove all the restraints on evil before he brings judgment on the rebels. The Antichrist will attempt to deceive many.	We should not be afraid when we see evil increase. God is in control, no matter how evil the world becomes. God guards us during Satan's attacks. We can have victory over evil by remaining faithful to God.
Persistence	Because church members had quit working and become disorderly and disobedient, Paul chastised them for their idleness. He called on them to show courage and true Christian conduct.	We must never get so tired of doing right that we quit. We can be persistent by making the most of our time and talents. Our endurance will be rewarded.

The Church

For Vital Statistics, see p. 1506

1 TIMOTHY

WITHOUT trying, we model our values. Parents in particular demonstrate to their children what they consider important and valuable. "Like father, like son" is not just a well-worn cliché; it is a truth repeated in our homes. And experience proves that children often follow the life-styles of their parents, repeating their successes and mistakes.

Timothy is a prime example of one who was influenced by godly relatives. His mother, Eunice, and grandmother Lois were Jewish believers who helped shape his life and promote his spiritual growth (2 Tim 1:5; 3:15). The first "second generation" Christian mentioned in the New Testament, Timothy became Paul's protégé and pastor of the church at Ephesus. As a young minister, Timothy faced all sorts of pressures, conflicts, and challenges from the church and his surrounding culture. To counsel and encourage Timothy, Paul sent this very personal letter.

Paul wrote 1 Timothy in about A.D. 62, not long after he had been released from his first Roman imprisonment. Because he had appealed to Caesar, Paul had been sent as a prisoner to Rome (see Acts 25–28). Most scholars believe that Paul was released about A.D. 62 (possibly because the "statute of limitations" had expired), and that during the next few years he was able to travel. During this time, he wrote 1 Timothy and Titus. Soon, however, Emperor Nero began his campaign to eliminate Christianity. It is believed that during this time Paul was imprisoned again and eventually executed. During this second Roman imprisonment, Paul wrote 2 Timothy. Titus and the two letters to Timothy comprise what are called the "Pastoral Letters."

Paul's first letter to Timothy affirms their relationship (1 Tim 1:2). Paul begins his fatherly advice, warning Timothy about false teachers (1 Tim 1:3-11) and urging him to hold on to his faith in Christ (1 Tim 1:12-20). Next, Paul considers public worship, emphasizing the importance of prayer (1 Tim 2:1-7) and order in church meetings (1 Tim 2:8-15). This leads to a discussion of the qualifications of church leaders—elders and deacons. Here Paul lists specific criteria for each office (1 Tim 3:1-16).

Paul speaks again about false teachers, telling Timothy how to recognize them and respond to them (1 Tim 4:1-16). Next, he gives practical advice on pastoral care to the young and old (1 Tim 5:1-2), widows (1 Tim 5:3-16), elders (1 Tim 5:17-25), and slaves (1 Tim 6:1-2). Paul concludes by exhorting Timothy to guard his motives (1 Tim 6:3-10), to stand firm in his faith (1 Tim 6:11-12), to live above reproach (1 Tim 6:13-16), and to minister faithfully (1 Tim 6:17-21).

First Timothy holds many lessons. If you are a church leader, take note of Paul's relationship with this young disciple—his careful counsel and guidance. Measure yourself against the qualifications that Paul gives for elders and deacons. If you are young in the faith, follow the example of godly Christian leaders like Timothy, who imitated Paul's life. If you are a parent, remind yourself of the profound effect a Christian home can have on family members. A faithful mother and grandmother led Timothy to Christ, and Timothy's ministry helped change the world.

THE BLUEPRINT

1. Instructions on right belief (1:1-20) 2. Instructions for the church (2:1–3:16) 3. Instructions for elders (4:1–6:21)	Paul advised Timothy on such practical topics as qualifications for church leaders, public worship, confronting false teaching, and how to treat various groups of people within the church. Right belief and right behavior are critical for anyone who desires to lead or serve effectively in the church. We should all believe rightly, participate in church actively, and minister to one another lovingly.

MEGATHEMES

THEME	EXPLANATION	IMPORTANCE
Sound Doctrine	Paul instructed Timothy to preserve the Christian faith by teaching sound doctrine and modeling right living. Timothy had to oppose false teachers, who were leading church members away from belief in salvation by faith in Jesus Christ alone.	We must know the truth in order to defend it. We must cling to the belief that Christ came to save us. We should stay away from those who twist the words of the Bible for their own purposes.
Public Worship	Prayer in public worship must be done with a proper attitude toward God and fellow believers.	Christian character must be evident in every aspect of worship. We must rid ourselves of any anger, resentment, or offensive behavior that might disrupt worship or damage church unity.
Church Leadership	Paul gives specific instructions concerning the qualifications for church leaders so that the church might honor God and operate smoothly.	Church leaders must be wholly committed to Christ. If you are a new or young Christian, don't be anxious to become a leader in the church. Seek to develop your Christian character first. Be sure to seek God, not your own ambition.
Personal Discipline	It takes discipline to be a leader in the church. Timothy, like all pastors, had to guard his motives, minister faithfully, and live above reproach. Any pastor must keep morally and spiritually fit.	To stay in good spiritual shape, you must discipline yourself to study God's Word and to obey it. Put your spiritual abilities to work!
Caring Church	The church has a responsibility to care for the needs of all its members, especially the sick, the poor, and the widowed. Caring must go beyond good intentions.	Caring for the family of believers demonstrates our Christlike attitude and exhibits genuine love to non-believers.

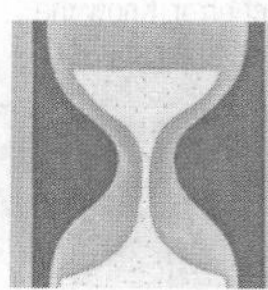

The Church

For Vital Statistics, see p. 1506

2 TIMOTHY

"FAMOUS last words" is more than a cliché. When notable men and women of influence are about to die, the world waits to hear their final words of insight and wisdom. Then those quotes are repeated worldwide. This is also true with a dying loved one. Gathered at his or her side, the family strains to hear every whispered syllable of blessing, encouragement, and advice, knowing that this will be the final message.

One of the most knowledgeable, influential, and beloved men of history is the apostle Paul. And we have his famous last words.

Paul was facing death. He was not dying of a disease in a sterile hospital with loved ones gathered nearby. He was very much alive, but his condition was terminal. Convicted as a follower of Jesus of Nazareth, Paul sat in a cold Roman prison, cut off from the world, with just a visitor or two and his writing materials. Paul knew that soon he would be executed (2 Tim 4:6), so he wrote his final thoughts to his "son" Timothy, passing to him the torch of leadership, reminding him of what was truly important, and encouraging him in the faith. Imagine how Timothy must have read and reread every word; this was the last message from his beloved mentor, Paul. Because of the situation and the recipient, this is the most intimate and moving of Paul's letters—and his last.

Paul's introduction is tender, and every phrase exudes the love he has for Timothy (2 Tim 1:1-5). He then reminds Timothy of the qualities necessary for a faithful minister of Jesus Christ (2 Tim 1:6–2:13). Timothy should remember his call and use his gifts with boldness (2 Tim 1:6-12), keep to the truth (2 Tim 1:13-18), prepare others to follow him in the ministry (2 Tim 2:1-2), be disciplined and ready to endure suffering (2 Tim 2:3-7), and keep his eyes and mind focused on Christ (2 Tim 2:8-13). Paul challenges Timothy to hold to sound doctrine, reject error and avoid foolish talk, correctly explain the word of truth (2 Tim 2:14-19), and keep his life pure (2 Tim 2:20-26).

Next, Paul warns Timothy of the opposition that he and other believers would face in the last days from self-centered people who use the church for their own gain and teach false doctrines (2 Tim 3:1-9). Paul tells Timothy to be prepared for these unfaithful people by remembering his example (2 Tim 3:10-11), understanding the real source of the opposition (2 Tim 3:12-13), and finding strength and power in the Word of God (2 Tim 3:14-17). Then Paul gives Timothy a stirring charge: to preach the Word (2 Tim 4:1-4) and to fulfill his ministry until the end (2 Tim 4:5-8).

Paul concludes with personal requests and items of information. In these final words, he reveals his loneliness and his strong love for his brothers and sisters in Christ (2 Tim 4:9-22).

There has never been another person like Paul, the missionary apostle. He was a man of deep faith, undying love, constant hope, tenacious conviction, and profound insight. And he was inspired by the Holy Spirit to give us God's message. As you read 2 Timothy, know that you are reading the last words of this great man of God—his last words to Timothy and to all who would claim to follow Christ. Recommit yourself to stand courageously for the truth, knowing the Word and being empowered by the Holy Spirit.

THE BLUEPRINT

1. Foundations of Christian service (1:1–2:26) 2. Difficult times for Christian service (3:1–4:22)	Paul gives helpful advice to Timothy to remain solidly grounded in Christian service and to endure suffering during the difficult days to come. It is easy for us to serve Christ for the wrong reasons: because it is exciting, rewarding, or personally enriching. Without a proper foundation, however, we will find it easy to quit during difficult times. All believers need a strong foundation for their service, because Christian service does not get easier as we grow older, and it will become no easier as the time of Christ's return grows closer.

MEGATHEMES

THEME	EXPLANATION	IMPORTANCE
Boldness	In the face of opposition and persecution, Timothy was to carry out his ministry without fear or shame. Paul urged him to utilize boldly the gifts of preaching and teaching that the Holy Spirit had given him.	The Holy Spirit helps us to be wise and strong. God honors our confident testimony even when we suffer. To get over our fear of what people might say or do, we must take our eyes off of people and look only to God.
Faithfulness	Christ was faithful to all of us in dying for our sin. Paul was a faithful minister even when he was in prison. Paul urged Timothy to maintain not only sound doctrine but also loyalty, diligence, and endurance.	We can count on opposition, suffering, and hardship as we serve Christ. But this shows that our faithfulness is having an effect on others. As we trust Christ, he counts us worthy to suffer, and he will give us the strength we need to be steadfast.
Preaching and Teaching	Paul and Timothy were active in preaching and teaching the Good News about Jesus Christ. Paul encouraged Timothy not only to carry the torch of truth but also to train others, passing on to them sound doctrine and enthusiasm for Christ's mission.	We must prepare people to transmit God's Word to others so that they in turn might pass it on. Does your church carefully train others to teach?
Error	In the final days before Christ returns, there will be false teachers, spiritual dropouts, and heretics. The remedy for error is to have a solid program for teaching Christians.	Because of deception and false teaching, we must be disciplined and ready to reject error. Know the Word of God as your sure defense against error and confusion.

TITUS

The Church

For Vital Statistics, see p. 1506

THE VACUUM produced when a strong leader departs can devastate a movement, organization, or institution. Having been dependent on his or her skill, style, and personality, associates and subordinates flounder or vie for control. Soon efficiency and vitality are lost, and decline and demise follow. Often this pattern is repeated in churches. A great speaker or teacher gathers a following, and soon a church is flourishing. It is alive, vital, and effective. Lives are being changed and people led into the Kingdom. But when this person leaves or dies, with him or her goes the drive and the heart of the organization.

People flocked to hear Paul's teaching. Educated, articulate, motivated, and filled with the Holy Spirit, this man of God faithfully proclaimed the Good News throughout the Roman Empire; lives were changed and churches begun. But Paul knew that the church must be built on Christ, not on a person. And he knew that eventually he would not be there to build, encourage, discipline, and teach. So he trained young pastors to assume leadership in the churches after he was gone. Paul urged them to center their lives and preaching on the Word of God (2 Tim 3:16-17) and to train others to carry on the ministry (2 Tim 2:2).

Titus was a Greek believer. Taught and nurtured by Paul, he stood before the leaders of the church in Jerusalem as a living example of what Christ was doing among the Gentiles (Gal 2:1-3). Like Timothy, he was one of Paul's trusted traveling companions and closest friends. Later he became Paul's special ambassador (2 Cor 7:5-16) and eventually the overseer of the churches on Crete (Titus 1:5). Slowly and carefully, Paul developed Titus into a mature Christian and a responsible leader. The letter to Titus was a step in this discipleship process. As with Timothy, Paul told Titus how to organize and lead the churches.

Paul begins his letter with a longer than usual greeting and introduction, outlining the leadership progression: Paul's ministry (Titus 1:1-3), Titus's responsibilities (Titus 1:4-5), and those leaders whom Titus would appoint and train (Titus 1:5). Paul then lists pastoral qualifications (Titus 1:6-9) and contrasts faithful elders with the false leaders and teachers (Titus 1:10-16).

Next, Paul emphasizes the importance of good deeds in the life of the Christian, telling Titus how to relate to the various age groups in the church (Titus 2:2-6). He urges Titus to be a good example of a mature believer (Titus 2:7-8) and to teach with courage and conviction (Titus 2:9-15). He then discusses the general responsibilities of Christians in society: Titus should remind the people of these (Titus 3:1-8), and he should avoid divisive arguments (Titus 3:9-11). Paul concludes with a few matters of itinerary and personal greetings (Titus 3:12-15).

Paul's letter to Titus is brief, but it is an important link in the discipleship process, helping a young man grow into leadership in the church. As you read this pastoral letter, you will gain insight into the organization and life of the early church, and you will find principles for structuring contemporary churches. But you should also see how to be a responsible Christian leader. Read the letter to Titus and determine, like Paul, to train men and women to lead and teach others.

THE BLUEPRINT

1. Leadership in the church (1:1-16) 2. Right living in the church (2:1-15) 3. Right living in society (3:1-15)	Paul calls for church order and right living on an island known for laziness, gluttony, lying, and evil. The Christians are to be self-disciplined as individuals, and they must be orderly as people who form one body, the church. We need to obey this message in our day when discipline is not respected or rewarded by our society. Although others may not appreciate our efforts, we must live upright lives, obey the government, and control our speech. We should live together peacefully in the church and be living examples of our faith to contemporary society.

MEGATHEMES

THEME	EXPLANATION	IMPORTANCE
A Good Life	The Good News of salvation is that we can't be saved by living a good life; we are saved only by faith in Jesus Christ. But the gospel transforms people's lives, so that they eventually perform good deeds. Our service won't save us, but we are saved to serve.	A good life is a witness to the gospel's power. As Christians, we must have commitment and discipline to serve. Are you putting your faith into action by serving others?
Character	Titus's responsibility in Crete was to appoint elders to maintain proper organization and discipline, so Paul listed the qualities needed for the eldership. Their conduct in their homes revealed their fitness for service in the church.	It's not enough to be educated or to have a loyal following to be Christ's kind of leader. You must have self-control, spiritual and moral fitness, and Christian character. Who you are is just as important as what you can do.
Church Relationships	Church teaching must relate to various groups. Older Christians were to teach and to be examples to younger men and women. People of every age and group have a lesson to learn and a role to play.	Right living and right relationships go along with right doctrine. Treat relationships with other believers as an outgrowth of your faith.
Citizenship	Christians must be good citizens in society, not just in church. Believers must obey the government and work honestly.	How you fulfill your civic duties is a witness to the watching world. Your community life should reflect Christ's love as much as your church life does.

PHILEMON

The Church

For Vital Statistics, see p. 1507

AT THE foreman's signal, the giant ball is released, and with dynamite force and a reverberating crash, it meets the wall, snapping bricks like twigs and scattering pieces of mortar. Repeatedly, the powerful pendulum works, and soon the barrier has been reduced to rubble. Then it is carted away so that construction can begin.

Life has many walls and fences that divide, separate, and compartmentalize. Not made of wood or stone, they are personal obstructions, blocking people from each other and from God. But Christ came as the great wall remover, tearing down the sin partition that separates us from God and blasting the barriers that keep us from each other. His death and resurrection opened the way to eternal life to bring all who believe into the family of God (see Eph 2:14-18).

Roman, Greek, and Jewish cultures were littered with barriers, as society assigned people to classes and expected them to stay in their place—men and women, slave and free, rich and poor, Jews and Gentiles, Greeks and barbarians, pious and pagan. But with the message of Christ, the walls came down, and Paul could declare, "In this new life, it doesn't matter if you are a Jew or a Gentile, circumcised or uncircumcised, barbaric, uncivilized, slave, or free. Christ is all that matters, and he lives in all of us" (Col 3:11).

This life-changing truth forms the backdrop for the letter to Philemon. One of three personal letters in the Bible, the letter to Philemon is Paul's personal plea for a slave. Onesimus "belonged" to Philemon, a member of the Colossian church and Paul's friend. But Onesimus, the slave, had stolen from his master and had run away. He had run to Rome, where he had met Paul, and there he had responded to the Good News and had come to faith in Christ (Phlm 1:10). So Paul wrote to Philemon and reintroduced Onesimus to him, explaining that he was sending him back, not just as a slave but as a brother (Phlm 1:11-12, 16). Tactfully he asked Philemon to accept and forgive his brother (Phlm 1:10, 14-15, 20). The barriers of the past and the new ones erected by Onesimus's desertion and theft should divide them no longer—they are one in Christ.

This small book is a masterpiece of grace and tact and a profound demonstration of the power of Christ and of true Christian fellowship in action. What barriers stand in your home, neighborhood, and church? What separates you from fellow believers? Race? Status? Wealth? Education? Personality? As with Philemon, God calls you to seek unity, breaking down those walls and embracing your brothers and sisters in Christ.

THE BLUEPRINT

1. Paul's appreciation of Philemon (1:1-7) 2. Paul's appeal for Onesimus (1:8-25)	Paul pleads on behalf of Onesimus, a runaway slave. Paul's intercession for him illustrates what Christ has done for us. As Paul interceded for a slave, so Christ intercedes for us, slaves to sin. As Onesimus was reconciled to Philemon, so we are reconciled to God through Christ. As Paul offered to pay the debts of a slave, so Christ paid our debt of sin. Like Onesimus, we must return to God our Master and serve him.

MEGATHEMES

THEME	EXPLANATION	IMPORTANCE
Forgiveness	Philemon was Paul's friend and the legal owner of the slave Onesimus. Paul asked Philemon not to punish Onesimus but to forgive and restore him as a new Christian brother.	Christian relationships must be full of forgiveness and acceptance. Can you forgive those who have wronged you?
Barriers	Slavery was widespread in the Roman Empire, but no one is lost to God or beyond his love. Slavery was a barrier between people, but Christian love and fellowship are to overcome such barriers.	In Christ we are one family. No walls of racial, economic, or political differences should separate us. Let Christ work through you to remove barriers between Christian brothers and sisters.
Respect	Paul was a friend of both Philemon and Onesimus. He had the authority as an apostle to tell Philemon what to do. Yet Paul chose to appeal to his friend in Christian love rather than to order him what to do.	Tactful persuasion accomplishes a great deal more than commands when dealing with people. Remember to exhibit courtesy and respect in your relationships.

The Church

For Vital Statistics, see p. 1507

HEBREWS

CONSCIENTIOUS consumers shop for value, the best products for the money. Wise parents desire only the best for their children, nourishing their growing bodies, minds, and spirits. Individuals with integrity seek the best investment of time, talents, and treasures. In every area, to settle for less would be wasteful, foolish, and irresponsible. Yet it is a natural pull to move toward what is convenient and comfortable.

Judaism was not second-rate or easy. Divinely designed, it was the best religion, expressing true worship and devotion to God. The commandments, the rituals, and the prophets described God's promises and revealed the way to forgiveness and salvation. But Christ came, fulfilling the Law and the Prophets, conquering sin, shattering all barriers to God, freely providing eternal life.

This message was difficult for Jews to accept. Although they had sought the Messiah for centuries, they were entrenched in thinking and worshiping in traditional forms. Following Jesus seemed to repudiate their marvelous heritage and Scriptures. With caution and questions they listened to the gospel, but many rejected it and sought to eliminate this "heresy." Those who did accept Jesus as the Messiah often found themselves slipping back into familiar routines, trying to live a hybrid faith.

Hebrews is a masterful document written to Jews who were evaluating Jesus or struggling with this new faith. The message of Hebrews is that Jesus is better, Christianity is superior, Christ is supreme and completely sufficient for salvation.

Hebrews begins by emphasizing that the old (Judaism) and the new (Christianity) are both religions revealed by God (Heb 1:1-3). In the doctrinal section that follows (Heb 1:4–10:18), the writer shows how Jesus is superior to angels (Heb 1:4–2:18), superior to their leaders (Heb 3:1–4:13), and superior to their priests (Heb 4:14–7:28). Christianity surpasses Judaism because it has a better covenant (Heb 8:1-13), a better sanctuary (Heb 9:1-10), and a more sufficient sacrifice for sins (Heb 9:11–10:18).

Having established the superiority of Christianity, the writer moves on to the practical implications of following Christ. The readers are exhorted to hold on to their new faith, encourage each other, and look forward to Christ's return (Heb 10:19-25). They are warned about the consequences of rejecting Christ's sacrifice (Heb 10:26-31) and reminded of the rewards for faithfulness (Heb 10:32-39). Then the author explains how to live by faith, giving illustrations of the faithful men and women in Israel's history (Heb 11:1-40) and giving encouragement and exhortation for daily living (Heb 12:1-17). This section ends by comparing the old covenant with the new (Heb 12:18-29). The writer concludes with moral exhortations (Heb 13:1-17), a request for prayer (Heb 13:18-19), and a benediction and greetings (Heb 13:20-25).

Whatever you are considering as the focus of life, Christ is better. He is the perfect revelation of God, the final and complete sacrifice for sin, the compassionate and understanding mediator, and the only way to eternal life. Read Hebrews and begin to see history and life from God's perspective. Then give yourself unreservedly and completely to Christ.

THE BLUEPRINT

A. THE SUPERIORITY OF CHRIST (1:1–10:18) 1. Christ is greater than the angels 2. Christ is greater than Moses 3. Christ is greater than the Old Testament priesthood 4. The new covenant is greater than the old	The superiority of Christ over everyone and everything is clearly demonstrated by the author. Christianity supersedes all other religions and can never be surpassed. Where can one find anything better than Christ? Living in Christ is having the best there is in life. All competing religions are deceptions or cheap imitations.
B. THE SUPERIORITY OF FAITH (10:19–13:25)	Jews who had become Christians in the first century were tempted to fall back into Judaism because of uncertainty, the security of custom, and persecution. Today believers are also tempted to fall back into legalism, fulfilling minimum religious requirements rather than pressing on in genuine faith. We must strive to live by faith each day.

MEGATHEMES

THEME	EXPLANATION	IMPORTANCE
Christ Is Superior	Hebrews reveals Jesus' true identity as God. Jesus is the ultimate authority. He is greater than any religion or any angel. He is superior to any Jewish leader (such as Abraham, Moses, or Joshua) and superior to any priest. He is the complete revelation of God.	Jesus alone can forgive our sin. He has secured our forgiveness and salvation by his death on the cross. We can find peace with God and real meaning for life by believing in Christ. We should not accept any alternative to or substitute for him.
High Priest	In the Old Testament, the high priest represented the Jews before God. Jesus Christ links us with God. There is no other way to reach God. Because Jesus Christ lived a sinless life, he is the perfect substitute to die for our sin. He is our perfect representative with God.	Jesus guarantees our access to God the Father. He intercedes for us so we can boldly come to the Father with our needs. When we are weak, we can come confidently to God for forgiveness and ask for his help.
Sacrifice	Christ's sacrifice was the ultimate fulfillment of all that the Old Testament sacrifices represented—God's forgiveness for sin. Because Christ is the perfect sacrifice for our sin, our sins are completely forgiven—past, present, and future.	Christ removed sin, which barred us from God's presence and fellowship. But we must accept his sacrifice for us. By believing in him, we are no longer guilty but cleansed and made whole. His sacrifice clears the way for us to have eternal life.
Maturity	Though we are saved from sin when we believe in Christ, we are given the task of going on and growing in our faith. Through our relationship with Christ, we can live blameless lives, be set apart for his special use, and develop maturity.	The process of maturing in our faith takes time. Daily commitment and service produce maturity. When we are mature in our faith, we are not easily swayed or shaken by temptations or worldly concerns.
Faith	Faith is confident trust in God's promises. God's greatest promise is that we can be saved through Jesus.	If we trust in Jesus Christ for our complete salvation, he will transform us completely. A life of obedience and complete trust is pleasing to God.
Endurance	Faith enables Christians to face trials. Genuine faith includes the commitment to stay true to God when we are under fire. Endurance builds character and leads to victory.	We can have victory in our trials if we don't give up or turn our back on Christ. Stay true to Christ and pray for endurance.

The Church

For Vital Statistics, see p. 1507

JAMES

"MIRACULOUS!" . . . "Revolutionary!" . . . "Greatest ever!" We are inundated by a flood of extravagant claims as we channel surf the television or flip magazine pages. The messages leap out at us. The products assure that they are new, improved, fantastic, and capable of changing our lives. For only a few dollars, we can have "cleaner clothes," "whiter teeth," "glamorous hair," and "tastier food." Automobiles, perfume, diet drinks, and mouthwash are guaranteed to bring happiness, friends, and the good life. And just before an election, no one can match the politicians' promises. But talk is cheap, and too often we soon realize that the boasts were hollow, quite far from the truth.

"Jesus is the answer!" . . . "Believe in God!" . . . "Follow me to church!" Christians also make great claims but are often guilty of belying them with their actions. Professing to trust God and to be his people, they cling tightly to the world and its values. Possessing all the right answers, they contradict the gospel with their lives.

With energetic style and crisp, well-chosen words, James confronts this conflict head-on. It is not enough to talk the Christian faith, he says; we must live it. "What good is it, dear brothers and sisters, if you say you have faith but don't show it by your actions? Can that kind of faith save anyone?" (Jas 2:14). The proof of the reality of our faith is a changed life.

Genuine faith will inevitably produce good deeds. This is the central theme of James' letter, around which he supplies practical advice on living the Christian life.

James begins his letter by outlining some general characteristics of the Christian life (Jas 1:1-27). Next, he exhorts Christians to act justly in society (Jas 2:1-13). He follows this practical advice with a theological discourse on the relationship between faith and action (Jas 2:14-26). Then James shows the importance of controlling one's speech (Jas 3:1-12). In 3:13-18, James distinguishes two kinds of wisdom—earthly and heavenly. Then he encourages his readers to turn from evil desires and obey God (Jas 4:1-12). James reproves those who trust in their own plans and possessions (Jas 4:13–5:6). Finally, he exhorts his readers to be patient with each other (Jas 5:7-11), to be straightforward in their promises (Jas 5:12), to pray for each other (Jas 5:13-18), and to help each other remain faithful to God (Jas 5:19-20).

This letter could be considered a how-to book on Christian living. Confrontation, challenges, and a call to commitment await you. Read James and become a doer of the Word (Jas 1:22-25).

THE BLUEPRINT

1. Genuine religion (1:1-27)
2. Genuine faith (2:1–3:12)
3. Genuine wisdom (3:13–5:20)

James wrote to Jewish Christians who had been scattered throughout the Mediterranean world because of persecution. In their hostile surroundings they were tempted to let intellectual agreement pass for true faith. This letter can have rich meaning for us as we are reminded that genuine faith transforms lives. We are encouraged to put our faith into action. It is easy to say we have faith, but true faith will produce loving actions toward others.

MEGATHEMES

THEME	EXPLANATION	IMPORTANCE
Living Faith	James wants believers not only to hear the truth but also to put it into action. He contrasts empty faith (claims without conduct) with faith that works. Commitment to love and to serve others is evidence of true faith.	Living faith makes a difference. Make sure your faith is more than just a statement; it should also result in action. Seek ways of putting your faith to work.
Trials	In the Christian life there are trials and temptations. Successfully overcoming these adversities produces maturity and strong character.	Don't resent troubles when they come. Pray for wisdom; God will supply all you need to face persecution or adversity. He will give you patience and keep you strong in times of trial.
Law of Love	We are saved by God's gracious mercy, not by keeping the law. But Christ gave us a special command: "Love your neighbor as yourself" (Matt 19:19). We are to love and serve those around us.	Keeping the law of love shows that our faith is vital and real. When we show love to others, we are overcoming our own selfishness.
Wise Speech	Wisdom shows itself in wise speech. God holds us responsible for the results of our destructive words. The wisdom of God that helps control the tongue can help control all our actions.	Accepting God's wisdom will affect your speech. Your words will convey true humility and lead to peace. Think before you speak and allow God to give you self-control.
Wealth	James taught Christians not to compromise with worldly attitudes about wealth. Because the glory of wealth fades, Christians should store up God's treasures through sincere service. Christians must not show partiality to the wealthy or be prejudiced against the poor.	All of us are accountable for how we use what we have. We should not hoard wealth but be generous toward others. In addition, we should not be impressed by the wealthy nor look down on those who are poor.

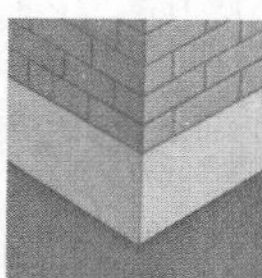

The Church

For Vital Statistics, see p. 1507

1 PETER

CRUSHED, overwhelmed, devastated, torn—these waves of feelings wash over those who suffer, obliterating hope and threatening to destroy them. Suffering has many forms—physical abuse, debilitating disease, social ostracism, persecution. The pain and anguish tempt a person to turn back, to surrender, to give in.

Many first-century followers of Christ were suffering and being abused and persecuted for believing in and obeying Jesus. Beginning in Jerusalem at the hands of their Jewish brothers, the persecution spread to the rest of the world—wherever Christians gathered. It climaxed when Rome determined to rid the empire of the "Christ-ones"—those who would not bow to Caesar.

Peter knew persecution firsthand. Beaten and jailed, he had been threatened often. He had seen fellow Christians die and the church scattered. But he knew Christ, and nothing could shake his confidence in his risen Lord. So Peter wrote to the church scattered and suffering for the faith, giving comfort and hope, and urging continued loyalty to Christ.

Peter begins by thanking God for salvation (1 Pet 1:2-6). He explains to his readers that trials will refine their faith (1 Pet 1:7-9). They should believe in spite of their circumstances; for many in past ages believed in God's plan of salvation, even the prophets of old who wrote about it but didn't understand it. But now salvation has been revealed in Christ (1 Pet 1:10-13).

In response to such a great salvation, Peter commands them to live holy lives (1 Pet 1:14-16), to reverently fear and trust God (1 Pet 1:17-21), to be honest and loving (1 Pet 1:22–2:1), and to become like Christ (1 Pet 2:1-3).

Jesus Christ, as "the living cornerstone" upon whom the church is to be built (1 Pet 2:4, 6), is also the stone that was rejected, causing those who are disobedient to stumble and fall (1 Pet 2:7-8). But the church, built upon this stone, is to be God's royal priesthood (1 Pet 2:9-10).

Next, Peter explains how believers should live during difficult times (1 Pet 2:11–4:11). Christians should be above reproach (1 Pet 2:12-17), imitating Christ in all their social roles—masters and servants, husbands and wives, church members and neighbors (1 Pet 2:18–3:17). Christ should be our model for obedience to God in the midst of great suffering (1 Pet 3:18–4:11).

Peter then outlines the right attitude to have about persecution: Expect it (1 Pet 4:12), be thankful for the privilege of suffering for Christ (1 Pet 4:13-18), and trust God for deliverance (1 Pet 4:19).

Next, Peter gives some special instructions: Elders should care for God's flock (1 Pet 5:1-4), younger men should be submissive to those who are older (1 Pet 5:5-6), and everyone should trust God and resist Satan (1 Pet 5:7-11).

Peter concludes by introducing Silas and by sending personal greetings, possibly from the church in Rome, and from Mark (1 Pet5:12-14).

When you suffer for doing what is right, remember that following Christ is a costly commitment. When persecuted for your faith, rejoice that you have been counted worthy to suffer for your Lord. He suffered for us; as his followers, we should expect nothing less. As you read 1 Peter, remember that trials will come to refine your faith. When they come, remain faithful to God.

THE BLUEPRINT

1. God's great blessings to his people (1:1–2:10)
2. The conduct of God's people in the midst of suffering (2:11–4:19)
3. The shepherding of God's people in the midst of suffering (5:1-14)

Peter wrote to Jewish Christians who were experiencing persecution for their faith. He wrote to comfort them with the hope of eternal life and to challenge them to continue living holy lives. Those who suffer for being Christians become partners with Christ in his suffering. As we suffer, we must remember that Christ is both our hope in the midst of suffering and our example of how to endure suffering faithfully.

MEGATHEMES

THEME	EXPLANATION	IMPORTANCE
Salvation	Our salvation is a gracious gift from God. God chose us out of his love for us, Jesus died to pay the penalty for our sin, and the Holy Spirit cleansed us from sin when we believed. Eternal life is a wonderful gift for those who trust in Christ.	Our safety and security are in God. If we experience joy in relationship with Christ now, how much greater will our joy be when he returns and we see him face to face. Such a hope should motivate us to serve Christ with greater commitment.
Persecution	Peter offers faithful believers comfort and hope. We should expect ridicule, rejection, and suffering because we are Christians. Persecution makes us stronger because it refines our faith. We can face persecution victoriously, as Christ did, if we rely on him.	Christians still suffer for what they believe. We should expect persecution, but we don't have to be terrified by it. The fact that we will live eternally with Christ should give us the confidence, patience, and hope to stand firm even when we are persecuted.
God's Family	We are privileged to belong to God's family, a community with Christ as the founder and foundation. Everyone in this community is related—we are all brothers and sisters, loved equally by God.	Because Christ is the foundation of our family, we must be devoted, loyal, and faithful to him. By obeying him, we show that we are his children. We must accept the challenge to live differently from the society around us.

Family Life	Peter encouraged the wives of unbelievers to submit to their husbands' authority as a means of winning them to Christ. He urged all family members to treat others with sympathy, love, compassion, and humility.	We must treat our families lovingly. Though it's never easy, willing service is the best way to influence loved ones. To gain the strength we need for self-discipline and submission, we need to pray for God's help.
Judgment	God will judge everyone with perfect justice. We all will face God. He will punish evildoers and those who persecute God's people. Those who love him will be rewarded with life forever in his presence.	Because all are accountable to God, we can leave judgment of others to him. We must not hate or resent those who persecute us. We should realize that we will be held responsible for how we live each day.

The Church

For Vital Statistics, see p. 1507

2 PETER

WARNINGS have many forms: lights, signs, sights, sounds, smells, feelings, and written words. With varied focus, their purpose is the same—to advise alertness and give notice of imminent danger. Responses to these warnings will also vary—from disregard and neglect to evasive or corrective action. How a person reacts to a warning is usually determined by the situation and the source. One reacts differently to an impending storm than to an onrushing automobile, and the counsel of a trusted friend is heeded more than advice from a stranger or the fearful imaginings of a child.

Second Peter is a letter of warning—from an authority none other than the courageous, experienced, and faithful apostle. And it is the last communication from this great warrior of Christ. Soon thereafter he would die, martyred for his faith.

Previously Peter had written to comfort and encourage believers in the midst of suffering and persecution—an external onslaught. But later, in this letter containing his last words, he wrote to warn them of an internal attack—complacency and heresy. He spoke of holding fast to the nonnegotiable facts of the faith, of growing and maturing in the faith, and of rejecting all who would distort the truth. To follow this advice would ensure Christ-honoring individuals and Christ-centered churches.

After a brief greeting (2 Pet 1:1), Peter gives the antidote for stagnancy and shortsightedness in the Christian life (2 Pet 1:2-11). Then he explains that his days are numbered (2 Pet 1:12-15) and that the believers should listen to his messages and the words of Scripture (2 Pet 1:16-21).

Next, Peter gives a blunt warning about false teachers (2 Pet 2:1-22). They will become prevalent in the last days (2 Pet 2:1-2); they will do or say anything for money (2 Pet 2:3); they will despise the things of God (2 Pet 2:2, 10-11); they will do whatever they feel like doing (2 Pet 2:12-17); they will be proud and boastful (2 Pet 2:18-19); they will be judged and punished by God (2 Pet 2:3-10, 20-22).

Peter concludes his brief letter by explaining why he has written it (2 Pet 3:1-18): to remind them of the words of the prophets and apostles that predicted the coming of false teachers, to give the reasons for the delay in Christ's return (2 Pet 3:1-13), and to encourage them to beware of heresies and to grow in their faith (2 Pet 3:14-18).

Addressed to those who "share the same precious faith," 2 Peter could have been written to us. Our world is filled with false prophets and teachers who claim to have the truth and who clamor for attention and allegiance. Listen carefully to Peter's message and heed his warning. Determine to grow in your knowledge of Christ and to reject all those who preach anything inconsistent with God's Word.

THE BLUEPRINT

1. Guidance for growing Christians (1:1-21)
2. Danger to growing Christians (2:1-22)
3. Hope for growing Christians (3:1-18)

While Peter wrote his first letter to teach about handling persecution (trials from without), he wrote this letter to teach about handling heresy (trials from within). False teachers are often subtly deceitful. Believers today must still be vigilant against falling into false doctrine, heresy, and cult activity. This letter gives us clues to help detect false teaching.

MEGATHEMES

THEME	EXPLANATION	IMPORTANCE
Diligence	If our faith is real, it will be evident in our godly behavior. If people are diligent in Christian growth, they won't backslide or be deceived by false teachers.	Growth is essential. It begins with faith and culminates in love for others. To keep growing we need to know God, keep on following him, and remember what he taught us. We must remain diligent in faithful obedience and Christian growth.
False Teachers	Peter warns the church to beware of false teachers. These teachers were proud of their position, promoted sexual sin, and advised against keeping the Ten Commandments. Peter countered them by pointing to the Spirit-inspired Scriptures as our authority.	Christians need discernment to be able to resist false teachers. God can rescue us from their lies if we stay true to his Word, the Bible, and reject those who distort the truth.

Christ's Return	One day Christ will create a new heaven and earth, where we will live forever. As Christians, our hope is in this promise. But with Christ's return comes his judgment on all who refuse to believe.	The cure for complacency, lawlessness, and heresy is found in the confident assurance that Christ will return. God is still giving unbelievers time to repent. To be ready, Christians must keep on trusting and resist the pressure to give up waiting for Christ's return.

The Church

For Vital Statistics, see p. 1508

1 JOHN

"A GOOD man . . . yes . . . perhaps one of the best who ever lived . . . but just a man," say many. Others disagree, claiming that he suffered from delusions of grandeur—a "messiah complex." And the argument rages over the true identity of this man called Jesus. Suggestions have ranged from "simple teacher" to "egomaniac" and "misguided fool." Whoever he was, all would agree that Jesus left his mark on history.

Hearing these discussions, even Christians can begin to wonder and doubt. Is Jesus really God? Did he come to save sinners like us? Does God care about me?

First John was written to dispel doubts and to build assurance by presenting a clear picture of Christ. Entering history, Jesus was and is God in the flesh and God in focus—seen, heard, and touched by the author of this letter, John the apostle. John walked and talked with Jesus, saw him heal, heard him teach, watched him die, met him arisen, and saw him ascend. John knew God—he had lived with him and had seen him work. And John enjoyed fellowship with the Father and the Son all the days of his life.

The elder statesman in the church, John wrote this letter to his "dear children." In it he presented God as light, as love, and as life. He explained in simple and practical terms what it means to have fellowship with God.

At the same time, false teachers had entered the church, denying the incarnation of Christ. John wrote to correct their serious errors. So John's letter is a model for us to follow as we combat modern heresies.

John opens this letter by presenting his credentials as an eyewitness of the Incarnation and by stating his reason for writing (1 Jn 1:1-4). He then presents God as "light," symbolizing absolute purity and holiness (1 Jn 1:5-7), and he explains how believers can walk in the light and have fellowship with God (1 Jn 1:8-10). If they do sin, Christ is their advocate (1 Jn 2:1-2). John urges them to obey Christ fully and to love all the members of God's family (1 Jn 2:3-17). He warns his readers of "antichrists" and the Antichrist who will try to lead them away from the truth (1 Jn 2:18-29).

In the next section, John presents God as "love"—giving, dying, forgiving, and blessing (1 Jn 3:1–4:21). God is love, and because God loves us, he calls us his children and makes us like Christ (1 Jn 3:1-2). This truth should motivate us to live close to him (1 Jn 3:3-6). We can be sure of our family relationship with God when our lives are filled with good deeds and love for others (1 Jn 3:7-24). Again, John warns of false teachers who twist the truth. We should reject these false teachers (1 Jn 4:1-6) as we continue to live in God's love (1 Jn 4:7-21).

In the last section, John presents God as "life" (1 Jn 5:1-21). God's life is in his Son. To have his Son is to have eternal life.

Do you know God? Do you know Christ? Do you know that you have eternal life? First John was written to help you know the reality of God in your life through faith in Christ, to assure you that you have eternal life, and to encourage you to remain in fellowship with the God who is light and love. Read this letter written by one overwhelmed by God's love, and with renewed confidence, pass on his love to others.

THE BLUEPRINT

1. God is light (1:1–2:29) 2. God is love (3:1–4:21) 3. God is life (5:1-21)	John wrote about the most vital aspects of faith so that his readers would know Christian truth from error. He emphasizes the basics of faith so that we can be confident in our faith. In our dark world, God is light. In our cold world, God brings the warmth of love. In our dying world, God brings life. When we lack confidence, these truths bring us certainty.

MEGATHEMES

THEME	EXPLANATION	IMPORTANCE
Sin	Even Christians sin. Sin requires God's forgiveness, and Christ's death provides it for us. Determining to live according to God's standards in the Bible shows that our life is being transformed.	We cannot deny our sin nature, maintain that we are "above" sinning, or minimize the consequences of sin in our relationship with God. We must resist the attraction of sin, yet we must confess when we do sin.

Love	Christ commands us to love others as he loved us. This love is evidence that we are truly saved. God is the Creator of love; he cares that his children love each other.	Love means putting others first and being unselfish. Love is action—showing others we care—not just saying it. To show love we must give sacrificially of our time and money to meet the needs of others.
Family of God	We become God's children by believing in Christ. God's life in us enables us to love our fellow family members.	How we treat others shows who our Father is. Live as a faithful, loving family member.
Truth and Error	Teaching that the physical body does not matter, false teachers encouraged believers to throw off moral restraints. They also taught that Christ wasn't really a man and that we must be saved by having some special mystical knowledge. The result was that people became indifferent to sin.	God is truth and light, so the more we get to know him, the better we can keep focused on the truth. Don't be led astray by any teaching that denies Christ's deity or humanity. Check the message; test the claims.
Assurance	God is in control of heaven and earth. Because his word is true, we can have assurance of eternal life and victory over sin. By faith we can be certain of our eternal destiny with him.	Assurance of our relationship with God is a promise, but it is also a way of life. We build our confidence by trusting in God's Word and in Christ's provision for our sin.

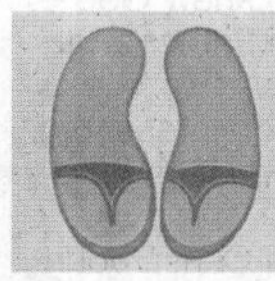
The Church

For Vital Statistics, see p. 1508

2 JOHN

TRUTH and love are frequently discussed in our world but seldom practiced. From politicians to marketers, people conveniently ignore or conceal facts and use words to enhance positions or sell products. Perjury is common, and integrity and credibility are endangered species. Words, twisted in meaning and torn from context, have become mere tools for ego building. It is not surprising that we have to "swear" to tell the truth.

And what about love? Our world is filled with its words: Popular songs, greeting cards, media counselors, and romantic novels shower us with notions and dreams of ethereal, idyllic relationships and feelings. Real love, however, is scarce—selfless giving, caring, sharing, and even dying. We yearn to love and be loved, but we see few living examples of real love. Plentiful are those who grasp, hoard, and watch out for "number one."

Christ is the antithesis of society's prevailing values, that is, falsehood and self-centeredness—for he is truth and love in person. Therefore, all who claim loyalty to him must be committed to these ideals—following the truth and living the truth, reflecting love and acting with love toward one another.

The apostle John had seen Truth and Love firsthand—he had been with Jesus. So affected was this disciple that all of his writings, from the Gospel to the book of Revelation, are filled with this theme: Truth and love are vital to the Christian and are inseparable in the Christian life. Second John, his brief letter to a dear friend, is no different. John says to live in the truth and obey God (2 Jn 1:4), watch out for deceivers (2 Jn 1:7), and love God and each other (2 Jn 1:6).

Second John will take just a few minutes to read, but its message should last a lifetime. As you reflect on these few paragraphs penned by the wise and aged follower of Christ, recommit yourself to being a person of truth, of love, and of obedience.

THE BLUEPRINT

1. Watch out for false teachers (1:1-11) 2. John's final words (1:12-13)	False teachers were a dangerous problem for the church to which John was writing. His warning against showing hospitality to false teachers may sound harsh and unloving to many today. Yet these men were teaching heresy that could seriously harm many believers—for eternity.

MEGATHEMES

THEME	EXPLANATION	IMPORTANCE
Truth	Following God's Word, the Bible, is essential to Christian living because God is truth. Christ's true followers consistently obey his truth.	To be loyal to Christ's teaching, we must seek to know the Bible, but we may never twist its message to our own needs or purposes or encourage others who misuse it.
Love	Christ's command is for Christians to love one another. This is the basic ingredient of true Christianity.	To obey Christ fully, we must believe his command to love others. Helping, giving, and meeting needs put love into practice.
False Leaders	We must be wary of religious leaders who are not true to Christ's teaching. We should not give them a platform to spread false teaching.	Don't encourage those who are opposed to Christ. Politely remove yourself from association with false leaders. Be aware of what is being taught in your church.

The Church

For Vital Statistics, see p. 1508

3 JOHN

BY SPECIAL invitation or with a surprise knock, company arrives and with them comes the promise of soiled floors, extra laundry, dirty dishes, altered schedules, personal expense, and inconvenience. From sharing a meal to providing a bed, hospitality costs . . . in time, energy, and money. But how we treat others reflects our true values—what is really important to us. Do we see people as objects or inconveniences, or as unique creations of a loving God? And which is more important to God, a person or a carpet? Perhaps the most effective way to demonstrate God's values and Christ's love to others is to invite and welcome guests into our homes.

For Gaius, hospitality was a habit, and his reputation for friendship and generosity, especially to traveling teachers and missionaries (3 Jn 1:5), had spread. To affirm and thank Gaius for his Christian lifestyle, and to encourage him in his faith, John wrote this personal note.

John's format for this letter centers around three men: Gaius, the example of one who follows Christ and loves others (3 Jn 1:1-8); Diotrephes, the self-proclaimed church leader who does not reflect God's values (3 Jn 1:9-11); and Demetrius, who also follows the truth (3 Jn 1:12). John encourages Gaius to practice hospitality, continue to walk in the truth, and do what is right.

Although this is a personal letter, we can look over the shoulder of Gaius and apply its lessons to our life. As you read 3 John, with which man do you identify? Are you a Gaius, generously giving to others? a Demetrius, loving the truth? or a Diotrephes, looking out for yourself and your things? Determine to reflect Christ's values in your relationships, opening your home and touching others with his love.

THE BLUEPRINT

1. God's children live by the standards of the gospel (1:1-12)
2. John's final words (1:13-15)

John wrote to commend Gaius, who was taking care of traveling teachers and missionaries, and to warn against people like Diotrephes, who was proud and refused to listen to spiritual leaders in authority. If we are to live in the truth of the gospel, we must look for ways to support pastors, Christian workers, and missionaries today. All Christians should work together to support God's work both at home and around the world.

MEGATHEMES

THEME	EXPLANATION	IMPORTANCE
Hospitality	John wrote to encourage those who were kind to others. Genuine hospitality for traveling Christian workers was needed then and is still important today.	Faithful Christian teachers and missionaries need our support. Whenever you can extend hospitality to others, it will make you a partner in their ministry.
Pride	Diotrephes not only refused to offer hospitality but also set himself up as a church boss. Pride disqualified him from being a real leader.	Christian leaders must shun pride and its effects on them. Be careful not to misuse your position of leadership.
Faithfulness	Gaius and Demetrius were commended for their faithful work in the church. They were held up as examples of faithful, selfless servants.	Don't take for granted Christian workers who serve faithfully. Be sure to encourage them so they won't grow weary of serving.

The Church

For Vital Statistics, see p. 1508

JUDE

TO PROTECT from harm, to guard from attack, to repulse enemies—for centuries rugged defenders have built walls, launched missiles, and waged wars, expending material and human resources in the battle to save nations and cities. And with total commitment and courageous abandon, individuals have fought for their families. It is a rule of life that we fight for survival, defending with all our strength what is most precious to us, from every real or imagined attack.

God's Word and the gift of eternal life have infinite value and have been entrusted to Christ's faithful followers. Many people live in opposition to God and his followers. They twist God's words, seeking to deceive and destroy the unwary. But God's truth must go forth, carried and defended by those who have committed their lives to his Son. It is an important task, an awesome responsibility, and a profound privilege to have this commission.

This was Jude's message to Christians everywhere. Opposition would come and godless teachers would arise, but Christians should "defend the faith" (Jude 1:3) by rejecting all falsehood and immorality (Jude 1:4-19), remembering God's mighty acts of rescue and punishment (Jude 1:5-11, 14-16) and the warnings of the apostles (Jude 1:17-19). His readers are to build up their own faith through prayer (Jude 1:20), keeping close to Christ (Jude 1:21), helping others (Jude 1:22-23), and hating sin (Jude 1:23). Then Jude concludes with a glorious benediction of praise to God (Jude 1:24-25).

How much do you value God's Word, the fellowship of the church, and obedience to Jesus Christ? Many false teachers are waiting to destroy your Christ-centered life, the credibility of God's Word, and the unity of the body of Christ. Read Jude and determine to stand firm in your faith and defend God's truth at all costs. Nothing is more valuable.

THE BLUEPRINT

1. The danger of false teachers (1:1-16) 2. The duty to fight for God's truth (1:17-25)	Jude wrote to motivate Christians everywhere to action. He wanted them to recognize the dangers of false teaching, to protect themselves and other believers, and to win back those who had already been deceived. Jude was writing against godless teachers who were saying that Christians could do as they pleased without fear of God's punishment. While few teach this heresy openly in the church today, many in the church act as though this were true. This letter contains a warning against living a nominal Christian life.

MEGATHEMES

THEME	EXPLANATION	IMPORTANCE
False Teachers	Jude warns against false teachers and leaders who reject the lordship of Christ, undermine the faith of others, and lead them astray. These leaders and any who follow them will be punished.	We must staunchly defend Christian truth. Make sure that you avoid leaders and teachers who distort the Bible to suit their own purposes. Genuine servants of God will faithfully portray Christ in their words and conduct.
Apostasy	Jude also warns against apostasy—turning away from Christ. We are to remember that God punishes rebellion against him. We must be careful not to drift away from a faithful commitment to Christ.	Those who do not seek to know the truth in God's Word are susceptible to apostasy. Christians must guard against any false teachings that would distract them from the truth preached by the apostles and written in God's Word.

The Church

For Vital Statistics, see p. 1508

REVELATION

WITH tiny wrinkles and cries, he entered the world and, wrapped in strips of cloth, took his first nap on a bed of straw. Subject to time and to parents, he grew to manhood in Roman-occupied Palestine, his gentle hands becoming strong and calloused in Joseph's woodworking shop. As a man, he walked through the countryside and city, touching individuals, preaching to crowds, and training 12 men to carry on his work. At every step he was hounded by those seeking to rid the world of his influence. Finally, falsely accused and tried, he was condemned to a disgraceful execution by foreign hands. And he died—spat upon, cursed, pierced by nails, and hung heavenward for all to deride. Jesus, the God-man, gave his life completely so that all might live.

At God's appointed time, the risen and ascended Lord Jesus will burst onto the world scene. Then everyone will know that Jesus is Lord of the universe! Those who love him will rejoice, greeting their Savior with hearts overflowing into songs of praise. But his enemies will be filled with fear. Allied with Satan, the enemies of Christ will marshal their legions against Christ and his armies. But who can withstand God's wrath? Christ will win the battle and reign victorious forever! Jesus, the humble suffering servant, is also the powerful, conquering King and Judge.

Revelation is a book of hope. John, the beloved apostle and eyewitness of Jesus, proclaimed that the victorious Lord would surely return to vindicate the righteous and judge the wicked. But Revelation is also a book of warning. Things were not as they should have been in the churches, so Christ called the members to commit themselves to live in righteousness.

Although Jesus gave this revelation of himself to John nearly 2,000 years ago, it still stands as a comfort and challenge to God's people today. We can take heart as we understand John's vision of hope: Christ will return to rescue his people and settle accounts with all who defy him.

John begins this book by explaining how he received this revelation from God (Rev 1:1-20). He then records specific messages from Jesus to the seven churches in Asia (Rev 2:1–3:22). Suddenly, the scene shifts as a mosaic of dramatic and majestic images bursts into view before John's eyes. This series of visions portrays the future rise of evil, culminating in the Antichrist (Rev 4:1–18:24). Then follows John's recounting of the triumph of the King over all kings, the wedding of the Lamb, the final judgment, and the coming of the new Jerusalem (Rev 19:1–22:5). Revelation concludes with the promise of Christ's soon return (Rev 22:6-21), and John breathes a prayer that has been echoed by Christians through the centuries: "Amen! Come, Lord Jesus!" (Rev 22:20).

As you read the book of Revelation, marvel with John at the wondrous panorama of God's revealed plan. Listen as Christ warns the churches, and root out any sin that blocks your relationship with him. Be full of hope, knowing that God is in control, Christ's victory is assured, and all who trust him will be saved.

THE BLUEPRINT

A. LETTERS TO THE CHURCHES (1:1–3:22)	The vision John received opens with instructions for him to write to seven churches. He both commends them for their strengths and warns them about their flaws. Each letter was directed to a church then in existence but also speaks to conditions in the church throughout history. Both in the church and in our individual lives, we must constantly fight against the temptation to become loveless, immoral, lenient, compromising, lifeless, or casual about our faith. The letters make it clear how our Lord feels about these qualities.

B. MESSAGE FOR THE CHURCH (4:1–22:21) 1. Worshiping God in heaven 2. Opening the seven seals 3. Sounding the seven trumpets 4. Observing the great conflict 5. Pouring out the seven plagues 6. Seizing the final victory 7. Making all things new	This revelation is both a warning to Christians who have grown apathetic and an encouragement to those who are faithfully enduring the struggles in this world. It reassures us that good will triumph over evil, gives us hope as we face difficult times, and gives guidance when we are wavering in our faith. Christ's message to the church is a message of hope for all believers in every generation.

MEGATHEMES

THEME	EXPLANATION	IMPORTANCE
God's Sovereignty	God is sovereign. He is greater than any power in the universe. God is not to be compared with any leader, government, or religion. He controls history for the purpose of uniting true believers in loving fellowship with him.	Though Satan's power may temporarily increase, we are not to be led astray. God is all-powerful. He is in control. He will bring his true family safely into eternal life. Because he cares for us, we can trust him with our very life.
Christ's Return	Christ came to earth as a "Lamb," the symbol of his perfect sacrifice for our sin. He will return as the triumphant "Lion," the rightful ruler and conqueror. He will defeat Satan, settle accounts with all those who reject him, and bring his faithful people into eternity.	Assurance of Christ's return gives suffering Christians the strength to endure. We can look forward to his return as king and judge. Since no one knows the time when he will appear, we must be ready at all times by keeping our faith strong.
God's Faithful People	John wrote to encourage the church to resist the demands to worship the Roman emperor. He warns all God's faithful people to be devoted only to Christ. Revelation identifies who the faithful people are and what they should be doing until Christ returns.	You can take your place in the ranks of God's faithful people by believing in Christ. Victory is sure for those who resist temptation and make loyalty to Christ their top priority.
Judgment	One day God's anger toward sin will be fully and completely unleashed. Satan will be defeated with all of his agents. False religion will be destroyed. God will reward the faithful with eternal life, but all who refuse to believe in him will face eternal punishment.	Evil and injustice will not prevail forever. God's final judgment will put an end to these. We need to be certain of our commitment to Jesus if we want to escape this great final judgment. No one who rejects Christ will escape God's punishment.
Hope	One day God will create a new heaven and a new earth. All believers will live with him forever in perfect peace and security. Those who have already died will be raised to life. These promises for the future bring us hope.	Our great hope is that what Christ promises will come true. When we have confidence in our final destination, we can follow Christ with unwavering dedication no matter what we must face. We can be encouraged by hoping in Christ's return.

Following is a list of abbreviations in the Master Index:

BOOKS OF THE BIBLE

Genesis	Gn
Exodus	Ex
Leviticus	Lv
Numbers	Nm
Deuteronomy	Dt
Joshua	Jos
Judges	Jgs
Ruth	Ru
1 Samuel	1 Sm
2 Samuel	2 Sm
1 Kings	1 Kgs
2 Kings	2 Kgs
1 Chronicles	1 Chr
2 Chronicles	2 Chr
Ezra	Ezr
Nehemiah	Neh
Esther	Est
Job	Jb
Psalms	Ps
Proverbs	Prv
Ecclesiastes	Eccl
Song of Songs	Song
Isaiah	Is
Jeremiah	Jer
Lamentations	Lam
Ezekiel	Ez
Daniel	Dn
Hosea	Hos
Joel	Jl
Amos	Am
Obadiah	Ob
Jonah	Jon
Micah	Mi
Nahum	Na
Habakkuk	Hb
Zephaniah	Zep
Haggai	Hg
Zechariah	Zec
Malachi	Mal
Matthew	Mt
Mark	Mk
Luke	Lk
John	Jn
Acts	Acts
Romans	Rom
1 Corinthians	1 Cor
2 Corinthians	2 Cor
Galatians	Gal
Ephesians	Eph
Philippians	Phil
Colossians	Col
1 Thessalonians	1 Thes
2 Thessalonians	2 Thes
1 Timothy	1 Tm
2 Timothy	2 Tm
Titus	Ti
Philemon	Phlm
Hebrews	Heb
James	Jas
1 Peter	1 Pt
2 Peter	2 Pt
1 John	1 Jn
2 John	2 Jn
3 John	3 Jn
Jude	Jude
Revelation	Rv

MASTER INDEX

This is an index to the features of the *Chronological Life Application Study Bible.* Every entry concerning a study note has a Bible reference and a page number; every entry concerning a chart, map, personality profile, or archaeology note has a page number. In some instances, a Bible reference is followed by a number in parentheses to indicate that there is more than one note on that particular Scripture. For example, Rv 1:1(2) means that the reader should look up the second note on that verse. Additionally, features from the section introductions, Scripture outline, and the images throughout the Bible are indexed by page number. Following the general index are special indexes: Index to Charts, Index to Maps, Index to Personality Profiles, Index to Archaeological Notes and Index to Illustrations. Because of the emphasis on application in the *Chronological Life Application Study Bible*, these indexes are helpful guides for personal and group Bible study, sermon preparation, or teaching.

FEATURES INDEX

INDEX TO CHARTS

FEATURES INDEX . . . 2040

INDEX TO MAPS

INDEX TO PERSONALITY PROFILES

INDEX TO ARCHAEOLOGICAL NOTES

INDEX TO ILLUSTRATIONS

NLT DICTIONARY/CONCORDANCE

AARON First high priest of Israel; elder brother and spokesman of Moses (Exod 4:14-31, p. 145; 7:1-2, p. 149); confronted Pharaoh with Moses (Exod 5–12, p. 146); held up Moses' hands during battle (Exod 17:8-15, p. 165); led Israel while Moses was absent (Exod 24:14, p. 175); priestly clothing and accessories (Exod 28, p. 178); his ordination (Exod 29, p. 180; Lev 8, p. 210); his failure with the gold calf (Exod 32, p. 184; Acts 7:40, p. 1525); spoke against Moses, then interceded on behalf of sister, Miriam (Num 12:1-16, p. 249); helped stop the plague (Num 16:45-48, p. 258); priesthood confirmed (Num 17, p. 258; Heb 5:1-4, p. 1767); failed at Meribah and was denied entry to Promised Land (Num 20:1-13, p. 261); died (Num 20:22-29, p. 262; 33:38-39, p. 281).

ABANDON, ABANDONED, ABANDONS (v) to desert or forsake
Josh 1:5 *will not fail you or **a** you*..........336
Josh 24:16 *We would never **a** the LORD*......370
Ezra 9:9 *God did not **a** us in our slavery*.....1200
Neh 9:31 *completely or **a** them forever*......1217
Ps 22:1 *why have you **a-ed** me?*..........556
Ps 37:25 *never seen the godly **a-ed***..........568
Ps 37:28 *he will never **a** the godly.*..........568
Prov 15:10 *Whoever **a-s** the right path*.......648
Matt 27:46 *why have you **a-ed** me?*.........1485
John 16:1 *you won't **a** your faith.*..........1464
Rom 1:24 *So God **a-ed** them to do*..........1647
Rom 1:28 ***a-ed** them to their foolish*.........1648
2 Cor 4:9 *down, but never **a-ed** by God.*...1631
Heb 13:5 *I will never **a** you.*..........1782

ABASED (KJV)
Ezek 21:26 *mighty will be **brought down***..........1068
Matt 23:12 *themselves will be **humbled***...1443
Phil 4:12 *how to **live on almost nothing***..1725

ABEL Son of Adam and Eve, brother of Cain (Gen 4:1-2, p. 14); his offering accepted (Gen 4:4, p. 14; Heb 11:4, p. 1777); murdered by Cain (Gen 4:8, p. 14; Matt 23:35, p. 1445; Luke 11:51, p. 1399; Heb 12:24, p. 1781; 1 Jn 3:11-12, p. 1791; Jude 1:11, p. 1785); replaced by Seth (Gen 4:25, p. 16).

ABHOR (v) to hate or loathe
Ps 119:163 *I hate and **a** all falsehood,*........881

ABIDE(TH), ABIDING (KJV)
Luke 2:8 *shepherds **staying** in the fields*...1281
John 12:46 *no longer **remain** in the dark*..1435
John 15:4 *be fruitful unless you **remain***....1463

ABILITY, ABILITIES (n) talent, aptitude, or skill
Exod 35:34 *the **a** to teach their skills*..........190
Dan 6:3 *because of Daniel's great **a,***........1140
Acts 2:4 *Spirit gave them this **a.***..........1514
1 Cor 12:1 *special **a-ies** the Spirit gives*...1614
1 Cor 14:1 *special **a-ies** the Spirit gives—*..........1616
1 Cor 14:12 *special **a-ies** the Spirit gives,*..........1617
2 Cor 1:8 *beyond our **a** to endure,*..........1626

ABLE (adj) marked by power, intelligence, competence, skill, giftedness
Deut 16:17 *must give as they are **a,***..........306
Dan 3:17 *whom we serve is **a** to save*.......1006
Rom 8:39 *ever be **a** to separate us from*...1661
Rom 16:25 *to God, who is **a** to*..........1674
Eph 3:20 *all glory to God, who is **a,***..........1710
Eph 6:13 *you will be **a** to resist*..........1715
2 Tim 1:12 *that he is **a** to guard*..........1741
2 Tim 2:24 *be **a** to teach, and*..........1743
Jude 1:24 *to God, who is **a** to keep*..........1786

ABOLISH (v) to destroy; to annul
Matt 5:17 *did not come to **a** the law*.........1327

ABOUND(ED) (KJV)
Prov 28:20 *person will **get a rich reward***...844
Matt 24:12 *Sin will **be rampant everywhere***..........1446
Rom 5:15 ***even greater** is God's wonderful grace*..........1655
Rom 5:20 *grace **became more abundant***..........1655
2 Cor 8:7 ***excel** also in this gracious act*...1636

ABOVE (adv or prep) in a higher position, superior
Ps 95:3 *a great King **a** all gods*..........863
Ps 99:2 *exalted **a** all the nations*..........865
Luke 12:31 *Seek the Kingdom of God **a** all*..........1401
Eph 1:21 *far **a** any ruler or authority*.........1706
Phil 2:9 *the name **a** all other names,*.........1720
1 Tim 3:2 *a man whose life is **a** reproach*..1730
Jas 3:17 *wisdom from **a** is first of all pure*..........1551

ABRAHAM (ABRAM) Father of the nation of Israel (Isa 51:2, p. 938; John 8:37-59, p. 1393); friend of God (Isa 41:8, p. 925); father of all people of faith (Gen 12–25, p. 30; Rom 4, p. 1652; Heb 11, p. 1777); made covenant with the LORD (Gen 12:1-3, p. 30; 13:14-17, p. 32; 15:12-21, p. 35; 22:15-18, p. 46; 50:24, p. 93; Exod 2:24, p. 143; 32:13, p. 185; Lev 26:42, p. 236; 2 Kgs 13:23, p. 760; 1 Chr 16:16, p. 493; Neh 9:7-8, p. 1216; Ps 105:9, p. 868; Luke 1:73, p. 1276; Acts 3:25, p. 1518; Gal 3:17-20, p. 1561; Heb 6:13, p. 1768); descendant of Terah from Ur (Gen 11:27-31, p. 24); husband of Sarah (Sarai) (Gen 11:29, p. 24); called to leave home (Gen 12:1-9, p. 30; Acts 7:2-4, p. 1524; Heb 11:8-10, p. 1777); went to Egypt and deceived the Pharaoh (Gen 12:10-20, p. 31); chose Canaan over the Jordan Plain (Gen 13, p. 32); rescued Lot from enemies (Gen 14:11-16, p. 33); blessed by Melchizedek (Gen 14:18-24, p. 34; Heb 7:1, p. 1770); covenant restated by God (Gen 15, p. 34); faith counted as righteousness (Gen 15:6, p. 35; Rom 4:3, p. 1652; Gal 3:6-9, p. 1561; Jas 2:21-23, p. 1550); given son (Ishmael) by Hagar (Gen 16, p. 36); circumcision commanded (Gen 17, p. 37; Rom 4:9-12, p. 1652); name changed to "Abraham" (Gen 17:5, p. 38; Neh 9:7, p. 1216); son promised to Sarah (Gen 17:16, p. 39; 18:10, p. 39); welcomed heavenly visitor (Gen 18:1-15, p. 39); bargained to save Sodom and Gomorrah (Gen 18:16-33, p. 40); deceived Abimelech (Gen 20, p. 42); named as a prophet (Gen 20:7, p. 42); given son (Isaac) by Sarah (Gen 21:1-7, p. 43; Heb 11:11-12, p. 1777); sent Hagar and Ishmael away (Gen 21:9-14, p. 43; Gal 4:21-31, p. 1564); offered Isaac as test (Gen 22:1-19, p. 45; Heb 11:17-19, p. 1778; Jas 2:21, p. 1550); secured burial ground for Sarah (Gen 23, p. 46); found a wife for Isaac (Gen 24, p. 47); descendants through wife Keturah (Gen 25:1-6, p. 50); died (Gen 25:7-11, p. 50).

ABSTAIN (v) to refrain from, forgo
Exod 19:15 *then **a** from having sexual intercourse*..........168
Acts 15:20 ***a** from eating food offered to idols,*..........1570

ABUNDANCE (n) great quantity, affluence; more than ample
Job 36:31 *giving them food in **a.***..........126
Ps 66:12 *a place of great **a.***..........859
Jer 31:14 *The priests will enjoy **a,***..........1033
Matt 13:12 *have an **a** of knowledge*..........1345
Matt 25:29 *they will have an **a.***..........1452
John 1:16 *From his **a** we have all*..........1272

ABUNDANT (adj) marked by great plenty, abounding
Deut 28:11 *livestock, and **a** crops*..........318
Ps 68:9 *You sent **a** rain, O God*..........576
Jer 31:12 *good gifts—the **a** crops*..........1033
John 16:24 *you will have **a** joy*..........1465
2 Cor 8:2 *are also filled with **a** joy,*..........1636

ABUSE (n) strong condemnation or disapproval
Mark 15:29 *shouted **a,** shaking their heads*..........1483

ABUSE (v) to injure or damage physically or verbally
1 Cor 4:12 *patient with those who **a** us*.....1601

ABUSIVE (adj) using harsh, insulting language; characterized by wrong or improper use or action
1 Cor 5:11 *worships idols, or is **a,***..........1602
1 Cor 6:10 *drunkards, or are **a,** or*..........1603
Eph 4:29 *use foul or **a** language*..........1712

ABYSS (KJV)
Luke 8:31 *send them into the **bottomless pit***..........1353
Rev 9:1 *the shaft of the **bottomless pit***....1814
Rev 9:11 *the angel from the **bottomless pit***..........1814

ACACIA (n) several species of shrubs and trees, some of which are found in the Holy Land, yielding highly durable wood
Exod 25:10 *make an Ark of **a** wood*..........176
Exod 27:1 ***a** wood, construct a square altar*.177
Josh 2:1 *the Israelite camp at **A** Grove*........337

ACCEPT, ACCEPTED, ACCEPTS (v) to receive willingly
Gen 4:4 *The LORD **a-ed** Abel*..........14
Gen 4:7 *be **a-ed** if you do what is right*.........14
Deut 16:19 *Never **a** a bribe, for bribes*........306

Job 42:8 *I will **a** his prayer*..........132
Job 42:9 *the LORD **a-ed** Job's prayer.*..........132
Eccl 5:18 *to **a** their lot in life*..........677
Luke 4:24 *no prophet is **a-ed** in his*..........1357
Luke 10:16 *who **a-s** your message*..........1394
John 1:12 *believed him and **a-ed** him,*..........1271
John 17:8 *They **a-ed** it and know that*..........1467
Rom 11:12 *when they finally **a** it*..........1665
Gal 2:9 *they **a-ed** Barnabas and me*..........1558
Col 2:6 *just as you **a-ed** Christ Jesus*..........1697
1 Tim 1:15 *everyone should **a** it:*..........1728
1 Tim 4:9 *everyone should **a** it.*..........1732
Jas 1:21 ***a** the word God has planted*..........1548

ACCEPTABLE (adj) capable or worthy of being accepted; welcome, pleasing, favorable
Mark 7:19 *every kind of food is **a***..........1371
Rom 4:2 *had made him **a** to God,*..........1652
Rom 12:1 *the kind he will find **a**.*..........1666
Rom 14:20 *all foods are **a**, but it is*..........1670
2 Cor 8:12 *is **a** if you give it eagerly.*..........1636
1 Tim 4:5 *made **a** by the word of God*..........1732

ACCIDENTALLY (adv) unintentionally, by mistake
Josh 20:9 *who **a** killed another person*..........365
Matt 23:24 *so you won't **a** swallow a gnat,*..........1444

ACCOMPLISH, ACCOMPLISHES (v) perform, do to completion
Eccl 2:11 *to **a**, it was all so meaningless*..........674
Isa 55:11 *fruit. It will **a** all I want it to,*..........942
Matt 5:17 *No, I came to **a** their purpose.*..........1327
John 6:63 *Human effort **a-es** nothing.*..........1368
Eph 3:20 *within us, to **a** infinitely more*..........1710
2 Thes 1:11 *power to **a** all the good things*..........1588

ACCOUNT (n) description of facts, conditions, or events; a report
Gen 2:4 *This is the **a** of the creation*..........9
Gen 5:1 *written **a** of the descendants*..........16
Gen 6:9 *the **a** of Noah and his family*..........17
Gen 10:1 *This is the **a** of the families*..........22
Gen 37:2 *This is the **a** of Jacob and*..........72
Rom 14:12 *give a personal **a** to God.*..........1670

ACCOUNTABLE (adj) subject to giving an account; answerable
Heb 4:13 *the one to whom we are **a**.*..........1766
Heb 13:17 *and they are **a** to God.*..........1783

ACCURATE (adj) conforming exactly to truth or to a standard; free from error, correct
Lev 19:36 *and weights must be **a**.*..........226
Deut 25:13 *You must use **a** scales.*..........315
Prov 11:1 *delights in **a** weights.*..........643
Prov 22:21 *take an **a** report to those*..........660
John 21:24 *account of these things is **a**.*..........1497

ACCURSED (KJV)
Deut 21:23 *anyone who is hung is **cursed***..........311
Josh 6:18 *things **set apart for destruction***..........344
1 Cor 12:3 *will **curse** Jesus, and no one*..........1614
Gal 1:9 *let that person be **cursed***..........1556

ACCUSATION, ACCUSATIONS (n) a charge of wrongdoing, often false
Ps 4:2 *will you make groundless **a-s?***..........547
Luke 3:14 *extort money or make false **a-s**.*..........1291
1 Tim 5:19 *Do not listen to an **a***..........1734

ACCUSE, ACCUSED, ACCUSES, ACCUSING (v) to charge with fault or offense; to blame
Job 22:4 ***a-s** you and brings judgment*..........115
Ps 27:12 *For they **a** me of things*..........561
Dan 6:5 *grounds for **a-ing** Daniel*..........1140
Luke 23:14 ***a-ing** him of leading a revolt.*..........1480
John 5:45 *it isn't I who will **a***..........1319
John 7:7 *because I **a** it of doing evil*..........1386
John 8:46 *can truthfully **a** me of sin?*..........1393
Acts 18:13 ***a-d** Paul of "persuading*..........1591
Rom 2:15 *and thoughts either **a** them*..........1649
Rom 8:33 *Who dares **a** us whom God*..........1661
Rev 12:10 *who **a-s** them before our God*..........1818

ACCUSER, ACCUSERS (n) one who charges another of wrongdoing
Deut 19:18 *If the **a** has brought false*..........309
Isa 50:8 *Where are my **a-s?***..........937
Luke 12:58 *the way to court with your **a**,*..........1402
Rev 12:10 *the **a** of our brothers*..........1818

ACKNOWLEDGE, ACKNOWLEDGES (v) to express a gratitude of debt; to recognize as valid; to confess (wrongdoing)
Jer 3:13 *Only **a** your guilt. Admit*..........963
Matt 10:32 *Everyone who **a-s** me*..........1360
Luke 12:8 *Son of Man will also **a***..........1399
Rom 1:28 *thought it foolish to **a** God,*..........1648
1 Jn 2:23 *anyone who **a-s** the Son*..........1790
1 Jn 4:3 *and does not **a** the truth*..........1792

ACQUAINTED (v) to make familiar; to know firsthand
Isa 53:3 *sorrows, **a** with deepest grief*..........940
Acts 18:2 ***a** with a Jew named Aquila,*..........1579

ACQUIT, ACQUITTING (v) to free from the penalty of a guilty action; (used theologically) to justify or make right with God
2 Chr 6:23 ***A** the innocent because of*..........621
Prov 17:15 ***A-ting** the guilty and*..........652

ACT (v) to behave; to take action or do something
Ps 119:126 *it is time for you to **a**,*..........881
Eccl 6:8 *how to **a** in front of others?*..........678

ACTION, ACTIONS (n) a thing done, deed; an exercise of will
Jer 4:18 *Your own **a-s** have brought*..........965
Phlm 1:6 *put into **a** the generosity*..........1691
Rev 3:2 ***a-s** do not meet the requirements*..........1806

ACTIVITY (n) a pursuit in which a person is active; quality or state of being active
Eccl 3:1 *for every **a** under heaven*..........675

ADAM First man (Gen 1:26–2:25, p. 8; Rom 5:14, p. 1655; 1 Tim 2:13-14, p. 1730); son of God (Luke 3:38, p. 1280); sinned (Gen 3:1-19, p. 11; Hos 6:7, p. 809; Rom 5:12-21, p. 1654); descendants of (Gen 5, p. 16); died (Gen 5:5, p. 16; 1 Cor 15:22-49, p. 1621).

ADD, ADDED (v) to make or serve as an addition
Deut 4:2 *Do not **a** to or subtract from*..........289
Deut 12:32 *You must not **a** anything to*..........302
Prov 30:6 *Do not **a** to his words,*..........846
Eccl 3:14 *Nothing can be **a-ed** to it*..........676
Matt 6:27 *worries **a** a single moment*..........1332
Luke 12:25 *worries **a** a single moment*..........1400
Acts 2:47 *each day the Lord **a-ed** to their*..........1516
Rev 22:18 *God will **a** to that person*..........1833

ADEQUATE (adj) suitable for a task; suitable
2 Cor 2:16 *who is **a** for such a task as this?*..........1628

ADMIT (v) to acknowledge, confess
Hos 5:15 *until they **a** their guilt*..........808
John 12:42 *But they wouldn't **a** it*..........1435

ADMINISTRATOR
Num 3:32 *chief **a** over all the Levites*..........241
Isa 37:2 *sent Eliakim the palace **a***..........916

ADMONISH(ED) (KJV)
Eccl 12:12 *give you **some further advice***..........683
Jer 42:19 *Don't forget this **warning** I*..........1106
2 Thes 3:15 ***warn** them as you would*..........1590
Heb 8:5 *God gave him this **warning***..........1771

ADMONITION (KJV)
1 Cor 10:11 *written down **to warn us***..........1610
Eph 6:4 ***instruction** that comes from the Lord*..........1714
Titus 3:10 *a first and second **warning***..........1739

ADOPT, ADOPTED (v) to take another's child into one's own family
Rom 8:15 *when he **a-ed** you as his own*..........1659
Rom 8:23 *rights as his **a-ed** children,*..........1659
Rom 9:4 *to be God's **a-ed** children.*..........1661
Gal 4:5 *so that he could **a** us as*..........1563
Eph 1:5 *decided in advance to **a** us*..........1704

ADULTERER, ADULTERERS (n) one who commits adultery
Job 24:15 *The **a** waits for the twilight,*..........116
Jas 4:4 *You **a-s!** Don't you realize*..........1551

ADULTEROUS (adj) prone to adultery or idolatry
Mark 8:38 *in these **a** and sinful days,*..........1378

ADULTERY (n) unlawful sexual relations between a married and an unmarried person; symbolic of idolatry
Exod 20:14 *You must not commit **a**.*..........170
Deut 5:18 *You must not commit **a**.*..........293
Prov 6:32 *who commits **a** is an utter fool,*..........639
Matt 5:27 *You must not commit **a**.*..........1328
Matt 19:18 *You must not commit **a**.*..........1420
Mark 10:11 *someone else commits **a***..........1419
Luke 18:20 *You must not commit **a**.*..........1422
John 8:4 *caught in the act of **a**.*..........1391
1 Cor 6:9 ***a**, or are male prostitutes,*..........1603

ADVANTAGE (n) benefit; upper hand
Exod 17:11 *in his hand, the Israelites had the **a**.*..........165
Lev 25:17 *not taking **a** of each other.*..........233
Rom 3:1 *Then what's the **a** of being a Jew?*..........1650
Rom 7:11 *Sin took **a** of those commands*..........1657
2 Cor 7:2 *astray, nor taken **a** of anyone.*..........1634

ADVERSARY, ADVERSARIES (n) enemy, opponent
2 Sam 19:22 *Why have you become my **a***..........521
Esth 7:6 *Haman is our **a** and our enemy.*..........1191
Ps 89:23 *beat down his **a-ies** before him*..........592
Matt 5:25 *on the way to court with your **a**,*..........1328

ADVERSITY (n) affliction, misfortune, woe
Job 36:15 *gets their attention through **a**.*..........126
Isa 30:20 *gave you **a** for food and suffering*..........900

ADVICE (n) recommendation regarding a decision or course of conduct; counsel
1 Kgs 12:8 *rejected the **a** of*..........696
2 Chr 10:8 *rejected the **a** of*..........698
Prov 12:5 ***a** of the wicked is*..........645
Prov 12:26 *godly give good **a** to their*..........646
Prov 15:22 *Plans go wrong for lack of **a**;*..........650
Isa 44:25 *I cause the wise to give bad **a**,*..........931
Rom 11:34 *enough to give him **a?***..........1666

ADVISE (v) to give advice; to counsel
Ps 32:8 *I will **a** you and watch over*..........565

1 Tim 5:14 *I **a** these younger widows*........1733
Rev 3:18 *I **a** you to buy gold from me—*...1807

ADVISERS (n) those who give advice; counselors
1 Sam 28:23 *his **a** joined the woman in*......471
1 Kgs 12:14 *counsel of his younger **a.***........696
Esth 1:13 *consulted with his wise **a,***.........1183
Prov 11:14 *safety in having many **a.***...........643
Prov 29:12 *all his **a** will be wicked.*............845

ADVOCATE (n) one who pleads the cause of another; defender
see also HOLY SPIRIT, COUNSELOR
Job 16:19 *My **a** is there on high.*...............110
John 14:16 *he will give you another **A,***.....1462
John 14:26 *the Father sends the **A***...........1462
John 15:26 *I will send you the **A**—*..........1464
John 16:7 *if I don't, the **A** won't come.*.....1465
1 Jn 2:1 *an **a** who pleads our case*...........1788

AFFECTION (n) tender attachment; a positive feeling
Rom 12:10 *each other with genuine **a,***.....1667
2 Pet 1:7 *godliness with brotherly **a,***.........1757

AFFIRM (v) to validate; to confirm
John 3:33 *can **a** that God is true.*............1303
Rom 8:16 ***a** that we are God's children.*....1659
Heb 10:23 *hope we **a,** for God can*...........1776

AFFLICT, AFFLICTED (v) relating to, characterized by, or given to persistent suffering or anguish
Deut 28:61 *LORD will **a** you*............................319
1 Sam 5:12 *were **a-ed** with tumors;*...........425

AFFORD (v) to have enough money or other assets for
Lev 5:7 *cannot **a** to bring a sheep,*.............207
2 Cor 8:3 *they could **a,** but far more.*.........1636

AFRAID (adj) fearful or apprehensive about an unwanted or uncertain situation
Gen 3:10 *I was **a** because I was naked.*........12
Gen 26:24 *Do not be **a,** for I am*...................53
Exod 3:6 *he was **a** to look at God*...............144
Deut 1:21 *Don't be **a!***..............................285
Deut 20:1 *your own, do not be **a.***...............310
Ps 23:4 *I will not be **a,** for you are*.............558
Isa 10:24 *do not be **a** of the Assyrians*........795
Isa 41:10 *Don't be **a,** for I am*....................925
Isa 43:1 *Do not be **a,** for I have*.................928
Matt 8:26 *Why are you **a?***........................1350
Matt 10:31 *So don't be **a;***.........................1360
Mark 5:36 *Don't be **a.***............................1354
John 14:27 *don't be troubled or **a.***...........1463
2 Tim 4:5 *Don't be **a** of suffering*.............1745
1 Pet 3:14 *don't worry or be **a***.................1753

AFRESH (adv) from a fresh beginning; anew, again
Lam 3:23 *his mercies begin **a** each*..........1098

AGAINST (prep) in opposition or hostility to; contrary to
Ps 41:9 *has turned **a** me*...........................571
Ps 78:19 *even spoke **a** God himself,*...........598
Matt 6:12 *those who sin **a** us.*..................1331
Matt 10:35 *to set a man **a** his father,*........1361
Matt 12:30 *actually working **a** me*............1341
Acts 26:14 *for you to fight **a** my will*..........1685
Rom 11:30 *Gentiles were rebels **a** God,*....1666
1 Cor 8:12 *you are sinning **a** Christ*...........1608
1 Pet 5:9 *Stand firm **a** him,*.......................1756

AGED (adj) showing the effects or characteristics of increasing age
Job 12:12 *Wisdom belongs to the **a,***..........106
Prov 17:6 *crowning glory of the **a;***.............652

AGES (n) long period of time; a generation; a measure of history, geology, or culture
Prov 8:23 *I was appointed in **a** past,*...........640
Jer 23:40 *infamous throughout the **a.***........1029
Eph 2:7 *in all future **a** as examples*...........1707

AGGRAVATE (v) to cause anger by persistent goading; to produce inflammation in
Col 3:21 *do not **a** your children,*................1702

AGONY (n) extreme pain and suffering
Ps 6:2 *LORD, for my bones are in **a.***............548
Luke 22:44 *he was in such **a** of spirit that*...1469

AGREE, AGREED, AGREEING (v) to admit, concede
Matt 18:19 *If two of you **a** here on*............1385
Luke 7:29 ***a-d** that God's way was right,*...1338
Rom 7:16 *that I **a** that the law is good*.......1658
Phil 2:2 *make me truly happy by **a-ing***.....1719

AID (v) to give assistance
Acts 24:17 *with money to **a** my people*.....1682

AIM (v) to direct to or toward a specified object or goal
Rom 14:19 ***a** for harmony in the church*....1670

AIR (n) empty space, nothingness; atmosphere
1 Thes 4:17 *meet the Lord in the **a.***..........1585

ALABASTER (adj) a compact, fine-textured, usually white and translucent plaster often carved into vases and ornaments
Matt 26:7 *with a beautiful **a** jar*.................1427
Mark 14:3 *with a beautiful **a** jar*................1428
Luke 7:37 *she brought a beautiful **a** jar*.....1340

ALARM (n) a signal that warns or alerts
Num 10:9 *sound the **a** with the trumpets.*...202
2 Cor 7:11 *such indignation, such **a,***.......1635

ALCOHOL (n) drink (as wine or beer) containing ethanol
Prov 20:1 ***a** leads to brawls.*.........................655
Isa 5:22 *boast about all the **a** they*.............829

ALCOHOLIC (adj) containing alcohol
Num 6:3 *give up wine and other **a***.............244

ALERT (adj) quick to perceive and act
Isa 21:7 *the watchman be fully **a.***...............891
Mark 13:33 *be on guard! Stay **a!***..............1449
1 Pet 5:8 *Stay **a!** Watch out for*..................1756

ALIEN (KJV)
Exod 18:3 *a **foreigner** in a foreign*.............166
Job 19:15 *I am like a **foreigner** to them*.....112
Eph 2:12 *were **excluded from citizenship***..1708

ALIENATED (KJV)
Ezek 48:14 *traded or **used by others***.......1132
Eph 4:18 ***wander far from** the life God*.....1711
Col 1:21 *were **once far away from God***...1695

ALIVE (adj) animate, having life; active; aware
Gen 45:7 *keep you and your families **a***.........86
Ps 41:2 *them and keeps them **a.***................571
Luke 24:23 *Jesus is **a!***................................1494
Acts 1:3 *ways that he was actually **a.***.......1512
Rom 6:11 *the power of sin and **a** to God*......1656
Rev 2:8 *who was dead but is now **a:***.........1802

ALLELUIA (KJV)
Rev 19:1 *shouting, **"Praise the Lord!***.......1827
Rev 19:3 *rang out: **"Praise the Lord!***.......1827
Rev 19:4 *"Amen! **Praise the Lord!"***.........1827
Rev 19:6 ***"Praise the Lord!** For the Lord*...1827

ALLOTMENT, ALLOTMENTS (n) share, portion, provision
Num 18:21 *Instead of an **a** of land, I will*.....259
Josh 13:32 *These are the **a-s** Moses had*...357
Jer 13:25 *your **a,** the portion I have assigned*...1017

ALLOWANCE (n) the act of admitting or conceding; permission
Eph 4:2 ***a** for each other's faults*..............1710

ALLOW, ALLOWED (v) to admit or concede; to permit
1 Cor 6:12 *though "I am **a-ed** to*..............1604
1 Cor 10:23 *I am **a-ed** to do anything*.......1611
2 Cor 12:4 *no human is **a-ed** to tell*..........1641

ALMIGHTY (n) having absolute power over all; God
see also (HEAVEN'S) ARMIES
Gen 17:1 *I am El-Shaddai—'God **A.'***...........37
Exod 6:3 *as El-Shaddai—'God **A'**—*...........148
Ruth 1:20 ***A** has made life very bitter*.........411
Job 6:14 *without any fear of the **A.***...........101
Job 33:4 *breath of the **A** gives me life*.........123
Ps 91:1 *rest in the shadow of the **A.***...........861
Rev 4:8 *the **A**—the one who always was,*.1808
Rev 15:3 *O Lord God, the **A.***.....................1822
Rev 19:6 *our God, the **A,** reigns*................1827

ALONE (adj) isolated or solitary; solely or exclusively; without aid or support
John 5:44 *the one who **a** is God.*..............1319

ALONGSIDE (adv) at the side; in parallel position, close by
Gal 3:19 *It was given **a** the promise*.........1562

ALPHA (n) first letter of Greek alphabet; figurative of beginning or first one
Rev 1:8 *I am the **A** and the Omega—*.......1800
Rev 21:6 *I am the **A** and the Omega—*.....1830
Rev 22:13 *I am the **A** and the Omega,*......1832

ALTAR, ALTARS (n) high places of worship on which sacrifices are offered or incense is burned
Gen 8:20 *Noah built an **a** to the LORD,*...........20
Gen 12:7 *Abram built an **a** there*..................30
Gen 22:9 *Abraham built an **a** and*................45
Gen 26:25 *Isaac built an **a** there*..................53
Exod 30:1 *make another **a** of acacia*...........181
Exod 37:25 *incense **a** of acacia wood.*.........192
Josh 8:30 *Joshua built an **a** to the LORD,*.....348
Josh 22:10 *a large and imposing **a.***............367
1 Sam 7:17 *Samuel built an **a** to the*...........427
2 Chr 4:1 *made a bronze **a** 30 feet long,*.....614
2 Chr 4:19 *Temple of God: the gold **a;***........617
2 Chr 32:12 *only at the **a** at the Temple*......916
2 Chr 33:16 *restored the **a** of the LORD*.......956
Ezra 3:2 *rebuilding the **a** of the God*..........1155
Isa 6:6 *coal he had taken from the **a***...........784
Matt 5:23 *presenting a sacrifice at the **a***...1328
Acts 17:23 *your **a-s** had this inscription*....1578
Heb 13:10 *an **a** from which the priests*.....1782
Rev 6:9 *I saw under the **a** the souls*..........1811

ALTERED (v) to make change or become different; to modify
John 10:35 *the Scriptures cannot be **a.***.....1406

ALWAYS (adv) at all times; forever, perpetually
1 Kgs 2:4 *will **a** sit on the throne*................545
Ps 16:8 *the LORD is **a** with me.*...................553
Ps 52:8 *will **a** trust in God's unfailing*..........462
Ps 102:27 *But you are **a** the same;*............867
Ps 106:3 *and **a** do what is right*..................870
Prov 23:7 *They are **a** thinking about*...........661
Isa 16:5 *He will **a** do what is just*................833
Matt 28:20 *I am with you **a,** even to*.........1498
Mark 14:7 *You will **a** have the poor*...........1428

John 12:8 *you will not* ***a*** *have me.* 1429
1 Pet 3:15 ***a*** *be ready to explain it.* 1753

AMAZED (v) to fill with wonder, astound
Matt 7:28 *were* ***a*** *at his teaching* 1335
Mark 7:37 *They were completely* ***a*** *and* 1372
Mark 10:24 *This* ***a*** *them. But Jesus* 1421
Luke 2:33 *Jesus' parents were* ***a*** *at* 1282
Acts 2:7 *They were completely* ***a.*** 1514

AMAZING (adj) causing amazement, great wonder, or surprise
1 Chr 16:24 *about the* ***a*** *things he does.* 493
Ps 96:3 *about the* ***a*** *things he does* 864
Ps 126:2 *What* ***a*** *things the* LORD *has* 1154

AMBASSADOR, AMBASSADORS (n) an authorized representative or messenger
2 Cor 5:20 *So we are Christ's* ***a-s;*** 1633
Eph 6:20 *this message as God's* ***a.*** 1716

AMBITION (n) aspiration to achieve a particular goal, good or bad
Gal 5:20 *anger, selfish* ***a,*** *dissension,* 1566
Phil 1:17 *They preach with selfish* ***a,*** 1718
Jas 3:14 *there is selfish* ***a*** *in your heart,* 1550

ANCESTOR, ANCESTORS (n) one from whom a person is descended; forefather
Exod 3:15 *God of your* ***a-s*** *—the God of* 144
Deut 19:14 *markers your* ***a-s*** *set up* 309
Isa 9:7 *throne of his* ***a*** *David for all* 793
Isa 43:27 *your first* ***a*** *sinned against me;* 929
Mark 11:10 *Kingdom of our* ***a*** *David!* 1430
Luke 1:32 *the throne of his* ***a*** *David.* 1274
Rom 9:5 *Abraham, Isaac, and Jacob are their* ***a-s,*** 1661
Gal 1:14 *for the traditions of my* ***a-s.*** 1557
Heb 1:1 *to our* ***a-s*** *through the prophets.* ..1761

ANCHOR (n) a reliable or principal support; mainstay
Heb 6:19 *trustworthy* ***a*** *for our souls.* 1770

ANCIENT (adj) having the qualities of age or long existence; old
Dan 7:22 *until the* ***A*** *One—the Most High—* 1136
Mark 7:3 *required by their* ***a*** *traditions.* 1370

ANDREW One of the 12 disciples; listed second (Matt 10:2, p. 1358; Luke 6:14, p. 1323) and fourth (Mark 3:18, p. 1323; 13:3, p. 1447; Acts 1:13, p. 1512); came from Bethsaida (John 1:44, p. 1298); brother of Simon Peter (Matt 4:18, p. 1307); former fisherman (Mark 1:16, p. 1308); follower of John the Baptist who introduced Peter to Jesus (John 1:40-44, p. 1298).

ANGEL, ANGELS (n) human or superhuman agent or messenger of God
Exod 23:20 *I am sending an* ***a*** 174
2 Sam 24:16 *and said to the death* ***a,*** 530
Ps 91:11 *will order his* ***a-s*** *to protect* 861
Matt 4:6 *will order his* ***a-s*** *to protect* 1295
Matt 28:2 *an* ***a*** *of the Lord came down* 1489
Luke 1:26 *God sent the* ***a*** *Gabriel* 1274
Luke 2:9 *an* ***a*** *of the Lord appeared* 1281
Luke 20:36 *they will be like* ***a-s.*** 1441
Acts 12:7 *The* ***a*** *struck him on the side* 1537
1 Cor 6:3 *we will judge* ***a-s?*** 1603
2 Cor 11:14 *disguises himself as an* ***a*** 1640
Gal 1:8 *or even an* ***a*** *from heaven,* 1556
Heb 1:6 *all of God's* ***a-s*** *worship him.* 1762
Heb 2:7 *a little lower than the* ***a-s*** 1763
Heb 13:2 *entertained* ***a-s*** *without* 1782
1 Pet 1:12 *the* ***a-s*** *are eagerly watching* ...1749
2 Pet 2:4 *even the* ***a-s*** *who sinned.* 1758
Jude 1:6 *I remind you of the* ***a-s*** 1784

ANGELIC (adj) having or displaying characteristics of an angel
2 Sam 22:11 *on a mighty* ***a*** *being, he flew,* 526
Ps 18:10 *on a mighty* ***a*** *being, he flew,* 528

ANGER (n) a strong feeling of displeasure
Exod 34:6 *slow to* ***a*** *and filled with* 187
Num 14:18 *slow to* ***a*** *and filled with* 253
Deut 9:19 *furious* ***a*** *of the* LORD, ...298
Deut 29:28 *In great* ***a*** *and fury* 321
2 Kgs 22:13 LORD*'s great* ***a*** *is burning* 969
Ps 30:5 *his* ***a*** *lasts only a moment,* 563
Ps 78:38 *Many times he held back his* ***a*** 599
Rom 1:18 *God shows his* ***a*** *from heaven* ...1647
Rom 2:5 *a day of* ***a*** *is coming,* 1648
Eph 4:26 *by letting* ***a*** *control you.* 1712
1 Thes 5:9 *pour out his* ***a*** *on us.* 1585
Jas 1:20 *Human* ***a*** *does not produce* 1548
Rev 14:10 *the wine of God's* ***a.*** 1821

ANGRY (adj) feeling or showing anger; wrathful
Exod 32:11 *so* ***a*** *with your own people* 185
Neh 9:17 *merciful, slow to become* ***a,*** 1216
Ps 103:8 *merciful, slow to get* ***a*** 580
Prov 22:24 *Don't befriend* ***a*** *people* 660
Jonah 4:2 *slow to get* ***a*** *and filled* 769
Matt 5:22 *if you are even* ***a*** *with* 1328
Mark 10:14 *he was* ***a*** *with his disciples* 1419
John 3:36 *under God's* ***a*** *judgment.* 1303
Acts 4:25 *Why were the nations so* ***a?*** 1519
Jas 1:19 *to speak, and slow to get* ***a.*** 1547

ANGUISH (n) extreme pain, distress, or anxiety
Isa 53:11 *by his* ***a,*** *he will be satisfied.* 940
Zeph 1:15 *of terrible distress and* ***a,*** 984
Matt 24:21 *greater* ***a*** *than at any time* 1446
Luke 16:24 *I am in* ***a*** *in these flames.* 1412
Rev 16:10 *ground their teeth in* ***a,*** 1823

ANIMAL, ANIMALS (n) any of a kingdom of living things that typically differ from plants
Gen 1:24 *livestock, small* ***a-s*** *that scurry* 7
Gen 6:19 *a pair of every kind of* ***a*** *—* 18
Gen 7:8 *all the various kinds of* ***a-s*** *—* 18
Deut 14:4 *These are the* ***a-s*** *you may eat:* ..303
1 Kgs 4:33 ***a-s,*** *birds, small creatures,* 629
Job 12:7 *ask the* ***a-s,*** *and they will teach* 106
Ps 73:22 *like a senseless* ***a*** *to you.* 594
Isa 43:20 *The wild* ***a-s*** *in the fields* 929

ANNIHILATED (v) to cause to cease to exist; to kill
Esth 3:13 *and* ***a*** *on a single day.* 1187

ANNOUNCE, ANNOUNCED, ANNOUNCING (v) to proclaim; to tell news
Jer 51:10 *let us* ***a*** *in Jerusalem* 1037
Matt 9:35 *and* ***a-ing*** *the Good News* 1357
Mark 15:26 ***a-ed*** *the charge against him.* .1483
Acts 26:23 ***a*** *God's light to Jews and* 1685
Rev 10:7 *as he* ***a-d*** *it to his servants the prophets.* 1816

ANNUAL (adj) occurring or happening every year or once a year
Exod 30:10 *a regular,* ***a*** *event* 182
Judg 21:19 *the* ***a*** *festival of the* LORD 409
1 Sam 1:21 *their* ***a*** *trip to offer a sacrifice* ...418
1 Sam 20:6 *for an* ***a*** *family sacrifice.* 455
2 Chr 8:13 *the three* ***a*** *festivals—* 625

ANOINT, ANOINTED, ANOINTING (v) to smear or rub with oil; used for healing or consecration to sacred duty; used for grooming or burial; figurative for divine appointment
see also ANOINTED ONE
Exod 30:26 *oil to* ***a*** *the Tabernacle,* 182
Exod 30:30 ***A*** *Aaron and his sons* 182
Lev 8:12 ***a-ing*** *him and making him holy* 211
1 Sam 15:1 *told me to* ***a*** *you as king* 445
2 Sam 2:4 *David and* ***a-ed*** *him king over* 478
2 Sam 23:1 *man* ***a-ed*** *by the God of Jacob,* 480
Ps 23:5 *honor me by* ***a-ing*** *my head* 558
Ps 92:10 *You have* ***a-ed*** *me with* 862
Isa 61:1 *the* LORD *has* ***a-ed*** *me* 948
Dan 9:24 *and to* ***a*** *the Most Holy Place.* 1143
Acts 10:38 *you know that God* ***a-ed*** *Jesus* 1534
Heb 1:9 *your God has* ***a-ed*** *you,* 1762
Jas 5:14 *over you,* ***a-ing*** *you with oil* 1553

ANOINTED ONE (n) one chosen by divine election
see also MESSIAH
1 Sam 2:10 *the strength of his* ***a."*** 419
1 Sam 26:9 *attacking the* LORD*'s* ***a?*** 468
Ps 132:17 *my* ***a*** *will be a light for* 884
Isa 45:1 *the* LORD *says to Cyrus, his* ***a*** 931
Dan 9:25 *a ruler—the* ***A*** *—comes.* 1143

ANSWER, ANSWERED (v) to reply to a question; to solve a problem
Ps 6:9 *the* LORD *will* ***a*** *my prayer.* 548
Ps 34:4 LORD, *and he* ***a-ed*** *me.* 458
Jonah 2:2 *trouble, and he* ***a-ed*** *me.* 767

ANTICHRIST, ANTICHRISTS (n) opponent of Christ; the personification of evil
1 Jn 2:18 *heard that the* ***A*** *is coming,* 1789
1 Jn 2:18 *many such* ***a-s*** *have appeared.* .1789
1 Jn 4:3 *has the spirit of the* ***A,*** 1792
2 Jn 1:7 *deceiver and an* ***a.*** 1796

ANTS (n) any of a family of colonial hymenopterous insects
Prov 6:6 *from the* ***a,*** *you lazybones.* 638

ANXIETY, CARE(S) (KJV)
Ps 139:23 *know my* ***anxious thoughts*** 586
Phil 4:6 *Don't* ***worry*** *about anything* 1724
1 Pet 5:7 *your* ***worries and cares*** *to God,* 1756

APOSTLE, APOSTLES (n) messengers or "sent ones"; generally but not exclusively applied to the original twelve followers of Christ and to Paul
Mark 3:14 *and called them his* ***a-s.*** 1322
Acts 1:26 *selected to become an* ***a*** 1513
Acts 5:2 *part of the money to the* ***a-s,*** 1520
Acts 8:18 ***a-s*** *laid their hands on* 1528
Rom 11:13 *the* ***a*** *to the Gentiles.* 1665
1 Cor 9:1 *Am I not an* ***a?*** 1608
1 Cor 9:2 *I am the Lord's* ***a.*** 1608
1 Cor 12:28 *first are* ***a-s,*** *second are,* 1615
2 Cor 12:12 *I am an* ***a.*** 1642
Eph 2:20 *on the foundation of the* ***a-s*** 1708
Eph 4:11 *the* ***a-s,*** *the prophets,* 1710
2 Tim 1:11 *to be a preacher, an* ***a,*** 1741
Rev 21:14 *of the twelve* ***a-s*** *of the Lamb.* .1831

APPEAR, APPEARED, APPEARING, APPEARS (v) to come out of hiding and show up in public view; to make one's presence known
Gen 1:9 *so dry ground may* ***a.*** 7
Num 14:10 *presence of the* LORD ***a-ed*** 252
Deut 33:16 ***a-ed*** *in the burning bush.* 327
Mal 3:2 *and face him when he* ***a-s?*** 1247
Matt 1:20 *angel of the Lord* ***a-ed*** *to him* ...1277
Matt 24:30 *will* ***a*** *in the heavens,* 1447

Luke 2:9 *angel of the Lord* ***a-ed*** *among*....1281
Luke 16:15 *You like to* ***a*** *righteous*............1412
Phil 2:7 *When he* ***a-ed*** *in human form,*.....1720
2 Thes 1:7 *the Lord Jesus* ***a-s*** *from*..........1588
2 Tim 1:10 *by the* ***a-ing*** *of Christ Jesus,*...1741
2 Tim 4:1 ***a-s*** *to set up his Kingdom:*.........1745
Heb 9:24 ***a*** *now before God on our*...........1774
Heb 9:26 ***a-ed*** *at the end of the age*........1774
1 Pet 5:4 *when the Great Shepherd* ***a-s,***...1756
1 Jn 3:2 *will be like when Christ* ***a-s.***........1790

APPEARANCE (n) external show; the outward or visible aspect
Isa 53:2 *or majestic about his* ***a,***.................940

APPETITE (n) the desire to eat; an inherent craving
Prov 13:2 *have an* ***a*** *for violence*................646
Prov 16:26 *good for workers to have*
an ***a;***...651
Phil 3:19 *Their god is their* ***a,***..................1724

APPLES (n) the fleshy, usually rounded, red, yellow, or green edible fruit of a tree
Prov 25:11 *golden* ***a*** *in a silver basket*.........839

APPLY (v) to bring into action; to put to use especially for some practical purpose
Prov 22:17 ***a*** *your heart to my instruction*....660

APPOINT, APPOINTED, APPOINTING (v) to ordain or designate; to name officially
Deut 1:15 ***a-ed*** *them to serve as judges*.....285
2 Sam 7:11 *the time I* ***a-ed*** *judges to rule*..495
Prov 8:23 *I was* ***a-ed*** *in ages past,*.............640
John 15:16 *I chose you. I* ***a-ed*** *you*..........1464
Rom 11:13 *God has* ***a-ed*** *me as the*........1665
1 Tim 5:22 *about* ***a-ing*** *a church leader*....1734
Titus 1:5 *work there and* ***a*** *elders*.............1736

APPOINTED (adj) marked by being fixed or set officially
Exod 23:15 *annually at the* ***a*** *time*.............173
Lev 23:2 *the LORD's* ***a*** *festivals,*...................229
Dan 11:27 *come at the* ***a*** *time*...................1160
Matt 8:29 *before God's* ***a*** *time?"*...............1351
Acts 3:20 *Jesus, your* ***a*** *Messiah.*.............1518

APPRECIATE (v) to value or admire highly
Prov 28:23 *people* ***a*** *honest criticism*..........844

APPRECIATION (n) an expression of admiration, approval, or gratitude
1 Cor 16:18 *must show your* ***a*** *to all*.........1623

APPROACH (v) to draw closer to; to come very near to
1 Tim 6:16 *no human can* ***a*** *him*...............1735

APPROPRIATE (adj) especially suitable or compatible; fitting
Deut 25:2 *lashes* ***a*** *to the crime*..................314
1 Tim 2:9 *wear decent and* ***a*** *clothing*.......1729

APPROVAL (n) an act or instance of approving
Ps 90:17 *LORD our God show us his* ***a***.........326
John 6:27 *the seal of his* ***a.***.......................1367
Rom 14:4 *stand and receive his* ***a.***...........1670
1 Cor 11:19 *you who have God's* ***a***...........1613
2 Tim 2:15 *and receive his* ***a.***......................1743
Heb 11:4 *God showed his* ***a*** *of his gifts.*....1777

APPROVE, APPROVED, APPROVES (v) to have or express a favorable opinion of; to attest
Gen 7:2 *animal I have* ***a-ed*** *for eating*...........18
Prov 12:2 *LORD* ***a-s*** *of those who*................644
Rom 14:18 *and others will* ***a*** *of you,*..........1670
Rom 16:10 *a good man whom Christ* ***a-s.*** 1673
1 Thes 2:4 *speak as messengers* ***a-ed***.....1581

ARARAT (n) a mountain on the far east border of modern Turkey; the mountain Noah's ark rested on after the Flood
Gen 8:4 *to rest on the mountains of* ***A.***..........19

ARCHANGEL, ARCHANGELS (n) a leader and chief angel; biblically designated as Michael
Dan 10:13 *one of the* ***a-s,*** *came to help*...1158
Dan 12:1 *At that time Michael, the* ***a***.........1161
1 Thes 4:16 *with the voice of the* ***a,***..........1585

ARCHER (n) one who uses a bow and arrow
Prov 26:10 *an* ***a*** *who shoots at random*.......841

ARCHITECT (n) a person who designs buildings and advises in their construction; a person who designs and guides a plan or undertaking
Prov 8:30 *I was the* ***a*** *at his side*................641

ARGUE, ARGUING (v) to contend or disagree in words; to dispute
Job 13:8 *Will you* ***a*** *God's case*..................107
Job 40:2 *to* ***a*** *with the Almighty?*...............130
Prov 25:9 ***a-ing*** *with your neighbor,*...........839
Isa 45:9 *those who* ***a*** *with their Creator.*......931
Rom 14:1 *and don't* ***a*** *with them*.............1669
1 Cor 11:16 *anyone wants to* ***a***................1613

ARGUMENT, ARGUMENTS (n) the act or process of arguing; discourse intended to persuade
Job 32:3 *to answer Job's* ***a-s.***....................122
Job 36:3 *I will present profound* ***a-s***...........125
Prov 26:17 *in someone else's* ***a***..................841
1 Tim 6:4 *This stirs up* ***a-s***......................1734
2 Tim 2:14 *Such* ***a-s*** *are useless,*..............1742

ARK (n) commonly, a portable wooden chest, box, or coffer; specifically, of Noah, a ship the size of a light cruiser; of the Covenant, a sacred housing for the Law of Moses
Exod 25:21 *inside the* ***A*** *the stone*.............176
Deut 10:5 *tablets in the* ***A*** *of the*...............299
1 Kgs 8:9 *Nothing was in the* ***A*** *except*........617
1 Chr 13:9 *his hand to steady the* ***A.***..........488
Rev 11:19 *the* ***A*** *of his covenant*...............1817

ARM, ARMS (n) upper limb of the body; extension or projection of; lineage; figurative of power or might
Num 11:23 *Has my* ***a*** *lost its power?*..........248
Deut 4:34 *a powerful* ***a,*** *and terrifying*.........291
Deut 7:19 *strong hand and powerful* ***a***........296
Deut 33:27 *everlasting* ***a-s*** *are under*.........327
Ps 44:3 *it was not their own strong* ***a***..........850
Ps 98:1 *his holy* ***a*** *has shown*....................865
Isa 40:11 *carry the lambs in his* ***a-s,***..........924
Isa 65:2 *opened my* ***a-s*** *to a rebellious*........951
Jer 27:5 *powerful* ***a*** *I made the earth*........1049
Mark 10:16 *took the children in his* ***a-s***....1420

ARMAGEDDON (n) the gathering place for the final battle between God's forces and Satan's forces associated with Christ's second coming
Rev 16:16 *with the Hebrew name* ***A.***.........1824

ARMOR (n) weapons of war or self-defense; figurative of spiritual resources
Ps 91:4 *are your* ***a*** *and protection*..............861
Isa 59:17 *righteousness as his body* ***a***........946
Jer 46:4 *and prepare your* ***a.***.......................997
Rom 13:12 *put on the shining* ***a***...............1669
Eph 6:11 *Put on all of God's* ***a***..................1715
Eph 6:13 *put on every piece of God's* ***a*****.....1715
1 Thes 5:8 *protected by the* ***a*** *of faith*.......1585

ARMY, ARMIES (n) large band of men organized and armed for war; any large multitude devoted to a cause
Ps 33:16 *best-equipped* ***a*** *cannot save*.......858
Ps 84:12 *LORD of Heaven's* ***A-ies,***.............855
Isa 6:3 *LORD of Heaven's* ***A-ies!***.................783
Isa 45:13 *LORD of Heaven's* ***A-ies,***............932
Isa 51:15 *the LORD of Heaven's* ***A-ies.***........939
Joel 2:2 *great and mighty* ***a*** *appears*.........1240
Joel 2:5 *like a mighty* ***a*** *moving into*..........1240
Joel 2:11 *This is his mighty* ***a,***..................1241
Hag 1:5 *LORD of Heaven's* ***A-ies*** *says:*.......1162
Zech 8:6 *LORD of Heaven's* ***A-ies*** *says:*.....1173
Rev 19:14 *The* ***a-ies*** *of heaven,*...............1828
Rev 19:19 *the horse and his* ***a.***.................1828

AROMA (n) a distinctive, pervasive, and usually pleasant or savory smell; a distinctive quality or atmosphere
Gen 8:21 *LORD was pleased with the* ***a***..........20
Exod 29:18 *it is a pleasing* ***a,***....................180
Lev 3:16 *a special gift of food, a*
pleasing ***a***...205
Eph 5:2 *a pleasing* ***a*** *to God.*....................1712

ARREST, ARRESTED, ARRESTING (v) to take or keep in custody by authority of law
Dan 6:16 *orders for Daniel to be* ***a-ed***......1141
Matt 10:19 *When you are* ***a-ed,*** *don't*......1360
Mark 14:44 ***a*** *when I greet him with a*
kiss....1470
Mark 14:49 *Why didn't you* ***a*** *me in*
the Temple?..1470
Luke 20:20 *so he would* ***a*** *Jesus.*.............1439
Acts 22:4 *to death,* ***a-ing*** *both men*.........1679

ARROGANCE (n) a feeling or an impression of superiority manifested in an overbearing manner or presumptuous claims
1 Sam 2:3 *Don't speak with such* ***a!***...........418
Prov 8:13 *I hate pride and* ***a,***.......................640
Isa 16:6 *its pride and* ***a*** *and rage.*...............833
2 Cor 12:20 *slander, gossip,* ***a,***.................1642

ARROGANT (adj) exaggerating or disposed to exaggerate one's own worth or importance in an overbearing manner
Ps 31:23 *harshly punishes the* ***a.***...............564
Ps 119:78 *upon the* ***a*** *people who lied*........879
1 Tim 6:4 *is* ***a*** *and lacks understanding.*....1734
Titus 1:7 *not be* ***a*** *or quick-tempered;*.......1736

ARROW, ARROWS (n) a missile weapon shot from a bow and usually having a slender shaft, a pointed head, and feathers at the butt
Ps 64:3 *their bitter words like* ***a-s.***.............574
Ps 64:7 *with his* ***a-s,*** *suddenly striking*.......575
Ps 91:5 *the* ***a*** *that flies in the day*...............861
Ps 127:4 *like* ***a-s*** *in a warrior's hands*.........631
Eph 6:16 *the fiery* ***a-s*** *of the devil*............1715

ASCEND, ASCENDED (v) to go or move up
Ps 68:18 *When you* ***a-ed*** *to the heights,*.....576
Isa 14:13 *I will* ***a*** *to heaven*.......................832
John 6:62 *Son of Man* ***a*** *to heaven again?*..1368
John 20:17 *I haven't yet* ***a-ed*** *to the*
Father....1493
Acts 2:34 *never* ***a-ed*** *into heaven,*............1516
Eph 4:8 *When he* ***a-ed*** *to the heights,*......1710

ASHAMED (adj) feeling shame, guilt, or disgrace
Ps 69:6 *be* ***a*** *because of me,*......................577
Jer 31:19 *I was thoroughly* ***a*** *of all I did*....1033
Jer 48:13 *were* ***a*** *of their gold calf*.............989
Mark 8:38 *If anyone is* ***a*** *of me*................1378
Luke 9:26 *If anyone is* ***a*** *of me*.................1378
Rom 1:16 *I am not* ***a*** *of this Good News*....1646
2 Tim 1:8 *So never be* ***a*** *to tell others*.......1741
2 Tim 2:15 *who does not need to be* ***a***......1743

ASHES (n) burnt residue or remains of the dead, or anything ruined; denotes grief, repentance, or humiliation
Job 42:6 *sit in dust and **a*** ... 132
Matt 11:21 *throwing **a** on their heads* ... 1339

ASK, ASKED, ASKING, ASKS (v) to seek information; to call on for an answer; to make a request
1 Sam 10:22 *So they **a-ed** the LORD,* ... 438
Prov 18:6 *they are **a-ing** for a beating.* ... 653
Isa 8:19 *Let's **a** the mediums* ... 792
Matt 7:7 ***a-ing,** and you will receive* ... 1334
Luke 6:30 *Give to anyone who **a-s;*** ... 1330
Luke 11:9 *will receive what you **a** for.* ... 1398
John 17:15 *I'm not **a-ing** you to take them* ... 1467
Eph 3:20 *more than we might **a** or* ... 1710
Phlm 1:21 *do what I **a** and even more!* ... 1692
1 Jn 5:14 *whenever we **a** for anything* ... 1794

ASLEEP (adj) state of bodily rest; figurative for physical death or spiritual dullness
see also DIE, SLEEP
Judg 4:21 *Sisera fell **a** from exhaustion,* ... 380
1 Kgs 18:27 *away on a trip, or is **a** and.* ... 717
Matt 9:24 *isn't dead; she's only **a."*** ... 1353
Matt 26:40 *disciples and found them **a**.* ... 1468
John 11:11 *Lazarus has fallen **a,** but* ... 1414
1 Thes 5:6 *be on your guard, not **a** like* ... 1585

ASSEMBLY (n) a company of persons gathered for deliberation and legislation, worship, or entertainment
Ps 35:18 *in front of the great **a.*** ... 566
Ps 149:1 *praises in the **a** of the faithful.* ... 887

ASSIGN, ASSIGNED (v) to transfer (property) to another, especially in trust or for the benefit of creditors; to appoint to a duty or task
Gen 47:11 *So Joseph **a-ed** the best land.* ... 89
Deut 32:8 *the Most High **a-ed** lands.* ... 323
Josh 13:14 *Moses did not **a** any allotment* ... 356

ASSOCIATE (v) to join as a partner, friend, or companion; to keep company with
Prov 13:20 ***a** with fools and get in* ... 646
Prov 22:24 *or **a** with hot-tempered* ... 660
Prov 24:21 *Don't **a** with rebels,* ... 663
Acts 10:28 *like this or to **a** with you.* ... 1533
1 Cor 5:9 *not to **a** with people who* ... 1602
1 Cor 5:11 *are not to **a** with anyone.* ... 1602

ASSURANCE (n) the act or action of giving confidence to or making sure or certain
Col 1:27 *This gives you **a** of sharing* ... 1696
1 Thes 1:5 *full **a** that what we said* ... 1581

ASSURE (v) to make certain or reassure
Mark 10:29 *I **a** you that everyone who has* ... 1421
Luke 23:43 *I **a** you, today you will be with* ... 1484
John 3:5 *I **a** you, no one can enter* ... 1301
John 5:25 *I **a** you that the time is coming,* ... 1318

ASTRAY (adv) off the right path or route; in error, away from what is desirable or proper
Prov 20:1 *Those led **a** by drink* ... 655
Isa 47:10 *'knowledge' have led you **a,*** ... 934
Jer 50:6 *shepherds have led them **a*** ... 1035
1 Jn 2:26 *who want to lead you **a**.* ... 1790

ASTROLOGERS (n) those who study the stars and planets to foresee or foretell future events by their positions and aspects
Isa 47:13 *all your **a,** those stargazers* ... 934
Dan 2:2 *enchanters, sorcerers, and **a,*** ... 1002

ATE (v) to partake of food
see also EAT
Gen 3:6 *some of the fruit and **a** it.* ... 11
Ezek 3:3 *And when I **a** it, it tasted as* ... 1046
Matt 15:37 ***a** as much as they wanted.* ... 1373
Rev 10:10 *I **a** it! It was sweet* ... 1816

ATHLETE, ATHLETES (n) a person who is trained or skilled in exercises, sports, or games requiring physical strength, agility, or stamina
Ps 19:5 *like a great **a** eager to run* ... 554
1 Cor 9:25 *All **a-s** are disciplined* ... 1609
1 Cor 9:27 *body like an **a,** training it* ... 1609
2 Tim 2:5 ***a-s** cannot win the prize unless* ... 1742

ATONE, ATONES (v) to supply satisfaction for; to make amends; to reconcile
see also FORGIVE
Dan 9:24 *their sin, to **a** for their guilt,* ... 1143
1 Jn 2:2 *sacrifice that **a-s** for our sins—* ... 1788

ATONEMENT (n) reconciliation; reparation for an offense or injury; cleansing
see also FORGIVENESS
Exod 25:17 *cover—the place of **a**—* ... 176
Lev 23:27 *Day of **A** on the tenth day* ... 231
2 Chr 29:24 *to make **a** for the sins* ... 835
Prov 16:6 *faithfulness make **a** for sin.* ... 651

ATTACK, ATTACKED (v) to set upon or work against forcefully; to assail with unfriendly or bitter words
1 Sam 17:48 *Goliath moved closer to **a,*** ... 451
Joel 3:19 *they **a-ed** the people of Judah* ... 1244
Zech 10:2 ***a-ed** because they have no* ... 1176
2 Tim 4:18 *deliver me from every evil **a*** ... 1746

ATTENTION (n) the act or state of applying the mind to an object or thought
Exod 23:13 *Pay close **a** to all my* ... 173
Prov 4:20 *pay **a** to what I say.* ... 636
Prov 5:1 *My son, pay **a** to my wisdom;* ... 637
Acts 18:17 *Gallio paid no **a**.* ... 1591
1 Tim 4:15 *Give your complete **a** to* ... 1733

ATTITUDE, ATTITUDES (n) a mental position with regard to a fact or state; a feeling or emotion toward a fact or state
Eph 4:23 *your thoughts and **a-s**.* ... 1712
Phil 2:5 *have the same **a** that Christ* ... 1719
1 Pet 3:8 *keep a humble **a**.* ... 1753
1 Pet 4:1 *with the same **a** he had,* ... 1754

ATTRACT, ATTRACTED (v) to pull to or draw toward oneself or itself; to draw by appeal to natural or excited interest, emotion, or aesthetic sense
Isa 53:2 *nothing to **a** us to him.* ... 940
Heb 13:9 ***a-ed** by strange, new ideas.* ... 1782

ATTRACTIVE (adj) arousing interest or pleasure; having the power to attract
Prov 19:22 *Loyalty makes a person **a**.* ... 655
Col 4:6 *conversation be gracious and **a*** ... 1702
1 Tim 2:10 *make themselves **a** by the* ... 1729
Titus 2:10 *God our Savior **a** in every* ... 1738

AUTHORITY, AUTHORITIES (n) the right to govern; the freedom or ability to act; one entrusted with the right to govern
Matt 28:18 *been given all **a** in heaven* ... 1497
Luke 10:19 *have given you **a** over* ... 1395
John 5:22 *absolute **a** to judge,* ... 1318
Acts 1:7 ***a** to set those dates and times,* ... 1500
Rom 13:1 *submit to governing **a-ies**.* ... 1668
Rom 13:1 *For all **a** comes from God,* ... 1668
Rom 13:2 *anyone who rebels against **a*** ... 1668
Rom 13:3 *without fear of the **a-ies?*** ... 1668
1 Cor 4:3 *by any human **a**.* ... 1600
1 Cor 15:24 *ruler and **a** and power.* ... 1621
Eph 1:22 *things under the **a** of Christ.* ... 1706
Eph 3:10 *all the unseen rulers and **a-ies*** ... 1709
Eph 6:12 *against evil rulers and **a-ies*** ... 1715
Col 2:10 *every ruler and **a**.* ... 1698
Col 2:15 *the spiritual rulers and **a-ies**.* ... 1698
1 Tim 2:2 *all who are in **a** so that* ... 1729
Titus 2:15 *You have the **a** to correct.* ... 1738
1 Pet 2:18 *accept the **a** of your masters* ... 1751
1 Pet 3:1 *accept the **a** of your husbands.* ... 1752
1 Pet 3:22 *the angels and **a-ies** and* ... 1754
1 Pet 5:5 *accept the **a** of the elders.* ... 1756
Jude 1:6 *the limits of **a** God gave them* ... 1784

AVENGE, AVENGES (v) to take revenge or punish
Deut 32:43 ***a** the blood of his servants;* ... 325
1 Thes 4:6 *the Lord **a-s** all such sins,* ... 1584
Rev 6:10 ***a** our blood for what they* ... 1812

AVENGER (n) one who seeks revenge or to punish an evildoer
Num 35:27 ***a** finds him outside the city* ... 283

AVOID, AVOIDING (v) to keep away from; to depart or withdraw from
Prov 4:24 ***A** all perverse talk;* ... 637
Prov 14:16 *are cautious and **a** danger;* ... 648
Prov 16:6 *By fearing the LORD, people **a*** ... 651
Prov 20:3 ***A-ing** a fight is a mark* ... 656
Eccl 7:18 *fears God will **a** both* ... 679
Rom 2:3 *think you can **a** God's* ... 1648

AWAKE (v) to cease sleeping; to become aroused or active again
see also WAKE
Ps 17:15 *When I **a,** I will see* ... 554
Eph 5:14 *"**A,** O sleeper, rise up.* ... 1713

AWARE (adj) having or showing realization, perception, or knowledge
Exod 34:29 *he wasn't **a** that* ... 188

AWARENESS (n) the state of realization or perception
Hab 2:14 *filled with an **a** of the glory* ... 980

AWAY (adv) in another direction; by a long distance or interval
1 Thes 4:3 *stay **a** from all sexual sin.* ... 1584
2 Tim 3:5 *Stay **a** from people like that!* ... 1744
1 Pet 2:11 *keep **a** from worldly desires* ... 1751

AWE (n) an emotion variously combining dread, respect, and wonder that is inspired by authority or the sacred
see also FEAR, REVERENCE
1 Kgs 3:28 *people were in **a** of the king,* ... 608
Ps 119:120 *I stand in **a** of your* ... 880
Luke 5:26 *with great wonder and **a,*** ... 1314
Acts 2:43 *sense of **a** came over them* ... 1516
Heb 12:28 *holy fear and **a**.* ... 1781

AWESOME (adj) characterized by reverential fear; expressive of or inspiring awe
see also MARVELOUS, WONDERFUL
Exod 34:10 *the **a** power I will display* ... 187
Deut 7:21 *a great and **a** God.* ... 296
2 Sam 7:23 *You performed **a** miracles* ... 496
Neh 1:5 *the great and **a** God* ... 1203
Job 10:16 *display your **a** power.* ... 104
Ps 47:2 *Most High is **a**.* ... 852
Ps 65:5 *answer our prayers with **a*** ... 575
Ps 99:3 *your great and **a** name.* ... 865
Ps 106:22 *such **a** deeds at the Red Sea.* ... 870
Ps 131:1 *too **a** for me to grasp.* ... 584
Dan 9:4 *a great and **a** God!* ... 1142

AX (n) a cutting tool that is used especially for felling trees and chopping and splitting wood
2 Kgs 6:6 *Then the **a** head floated*..............745
Prov 25:18 *hitting them with an **a**,*..............840

BAAL (n) a fertility and nature god of the Canaanites and Phoenicians
1 Kgs 18:25 *said to the prophets of **B**,*.........717
1 Kgs 19:18 *bowed down to **B** or kissed*.....720
Rom 11:4 *have never bowed down to **B**!*...1664

BABY, BABIES (n) infant child; youngest of a group; figurative of new or immature Christians
Exod 2:7 *women to nurse the **b** for you?*.....142
Luke 1:44 ***b** in my womb jumped for*........1275
Luke 2:12 *find a **b** wrapped snugly*...........1281
Luke 2:16 *the **b**, lying in the manger*.........1281
Acts 7:19 *abandon their newborn **b-ies***....1525
1 Cor 14:20 *Be innocent as **b-ies** when*...1617
1 Pet 2:2 *Like newborn **b-ies**, you must*...1750

BABYLON (n) capital city of the Babylonian Empire; a city devoted to materialism and sensual pleasure; biblical writers used as model of paganism and idolatry
Ps 137:1 *Beside the rivers of **B**, we sat*.....1118
Jer 29:10 *will be in **B** for seventy years*.....1030
Jer 51:37 ***B** will become a heap of ruins,*..1039
Rev 14:8 *shouting, "**B** is fallen—*.............1821

BACKSLIDERS, BACKSLIDING (KJV)
Prov 14:14 ***Backsliders** get what they deserve*..647
Jer 3:22 *I will heal your **wayward** hearts*....963
Jer 31:22 *wander, my **wayward** daughter*..1033
Hos 14:4 *heal you of your **faithlessness***.....817

BAD (adj) poor, inadequate; morally objectionable; disagreeable, unpleasant
Job 2:10 *of God and never anything **b**?*........96
Eccl 12:14 *thing, whether good or **b**.*..........683
Isa 45:7 *good times and **b** times*................931

BALAAM Pagan prophet, summoned to curse the Israelites but instead blessed them (Num 22–24 p. 265; also Deut 23:3-5, p. 313; 2 Pet 2:15-16, p. 1759; Jude 1:11, p. 1785; Rev 2:14, p. 1804); died (Num 31:8, p. 277; Josh 13:22, p. 357).

BALANCES (n) an instrument for weighing; a means of judging or deciding
see also SCALES
Dan 5:27 *you have been weighed on the **b***..1139

BALD (adj) lacking a natural or usual covering (as of hair or vegetation); bare, unadorned
Mic 1:16 *yourselves as **b** as a vulture,*.........788

BALDY (n) a derogatory nickname for someone who is bald
2 Kgs 2:23 *"Go away, **b**!" they chanted.*......740

BANNER (n) a piece of cloth attached by one edge to a staff and used by a leader as his emblem
Exod 17:15 *"the LORD is my **b**")*..................165
Isa 11:10 *will be a **b** of salvation*................796

BANQUET, BANQUETS (n) a sumptuous feast, especially a ceremonious meal in honor of a person, occasion, or achievement
Song 2:4 *He escorts me to the **b** hall;*.........664
Matt 24:38 *enjoying **b-s** and parties*.........1447

BAPTISM, BAPTISMS (n) a Christian ordinance; a washing with water to demonstrate cleansing from sin, linked with repentance and admission into the community of faith; figurative of an ordeal or initiation
Matt 3:16 *After his **b**, as Jesus came up*...1293
Luke 3:7 *crowds came to John for **b**,*.........1290
Acts 19:3 *what **b** did you experience?*.......1593
Rom 6:3 *joined with Christ Jesus in **b**,*......1655
Gal 3:27 *united with Christ in **b***................1562
Eph 4:5 *one Lord, one faith, one **b**,*...........1710
Heb 6:2 *further instruction about **b-s**,*.......1768
1 Pet 3:21 *that water is a picture of **b**,*......1754

BAPTIST (n) one who baptizes
Matt 11:11 *greater than John the **B**.*.........1338
Mark 1:4 *messenger was John the **B**.*.........1289

BAPTIZE, BAPTIZED, BAPTIZING (v) to engage in the ordinance of baptism (see above)
see also WASH
Matt 3:13 *River to be **b-d** by John*............1293
Matt 28:19 *of all the nations, **b-ing***..........1498
Mark 1:4 *that people should be **b-d***...........1289
Mark 1:8 *will **b** you with the Holy Spirit!*.....1290
Mark 10:38 *suffering I must be **b-d** with?*...1424
Luke 3:3 *that people should be **b-d***...........1279
Luke 3:16 *I **b** you with water;*.....................1292
Luke 3:21 *Jesus himself was **b-d**.*..............1294
John 1:28 *where John was **b-ing**.*...............1293
John 1:31 *I have been **b-ing** with water*....1297
John 1:33 *is the one who will **b** with*..........1297
John 3:22 *with them there, **b-ing** people*..1302
John 3:26 *is also **b-ing** people*...................1302
John 4:1 *was **b-ing** and making more*.........1303
John 4:2 *Jesus himself didn't **b** them—*....1303
John 10:40 *where John was first **b-ing***....1407
Acts 1:5 *be **b-d** with the Holy Spirit.*.........1499
Acts 1:22 *time he was **b-d** by John*...........1513
Acts 2:41 ***b-d** and added to the church*....1516
Acts 8:12 *and women were **b-d**.*................1527
Acts 8:38 *water, and Philip **b-d** him*...........1529
Acts 11:16 *will be **b-d** with the Holy*.........1535
Acts 16:15 *She was **b-d** along with*...........1574
Acts 16:33 *were immediately **b-d**.*.............1576
Acts 19:5 ***b-d** in the name of the Lord*......1593
1 Cor 1:13 *you **b-d** in the name of Paul?*..1596
1 Cor 1:14 *I did not **b** any of you*...............1596
1 Cor 1:16 ***b-d** the household of*...............1596
1 Cor 10:2 *were **b-d** as followers*..............1610
1 Cor 15:29 ***b-d** for those who are dead?*...1621
Col 2:12 *when you were **b-d**.*....................1698

BARN (n) a usually large building for the storage of farm products, feed, animals, and/or equipment
Matt 13:30 *the wheat in the **b**.*..................1348

BARNABAS Levite believer from Cyprus, generous giver of property (Acts 4:36-37, p. 1520); encourager of Paul (Acts 9:26-29, p. 1531); missionary with Paul (Acts 11:22-30, p. 1536; 12:25, p. 1539; 13:1-3, p. 1539); at Jerusalem council (Acts 15:1-2, 12, p. 1568, 1569); disagreed with Paul over John Mark (Acts 15:36-40, p. 1572; *see also* 1 Cor 9:6, p. 1608; Col 4:10, p. 1703).

BARREN (adj) unproductive, unfruitful, especially in childbearing
Heb 11:11 *she was **b** and was too old.*......1777

BASKET (n) a receptacle made of interwoven material; any of various lightweight, usually wood, containers
Exod 2:3 *she got a **b** made of papyrus*........141
Acts 9:25 *lowered him in a large **b***...........1531
2 Cor 11:33 *in a **b** through a window*........1641

BATCH (n) the quantity baked at one time
Rom 11:16 *the entire **b** of dough is holy*...1665
1 Cor 5:6 *through the whole **b** of dough?*..1602
1 Cor 5:7 *like a fresh **b** of dough*..............1602
Gal 5:9 *through the whole **b** of dough!*......1565

BATH (n) a washing or soaking (as in water or steam) of all or part of the body
2 Sam 11:2 *unusual beauty taking a **b**.*........502

BATHED (v) to take a bath; to give a bath to
John 13:10 *A person who has **b** all over*...1456

BATHSHEBA Committed adultery with King David, widow of Uriah the Hittite (2 Sam 11–12, p. 502); mother of Solomon, her second son with David (1 Kgs 1–2, p. 542; 1 Chr 3:5, p. 1229).

BATTLE, BATTLES (n) a combat between two persons; a general encounter between armies, ships of war, aircraft; an extended contest, struggle, or controversy
1 Sam 17:47 *This is the LORD's **b**,*..............451
1 Sam 18:17 *the LORD's **b-s**.*......................453
1 Sam 25:28 *the LORD's **b-s**.*......................467
2 Kgs 14:8 *Come and meet me in **b**!*.........761
2 Chr 32:8 *to fight our **b-s** for us!*..............913
Ps 24:8 *LORD, invincible in **b**.*....................559
Rev 16:14 *gather them for **b** against*.........1823
Rev 20:8 *gather them together for **b**—*......1829

BEAR (v) to carry or support; to give as testimony; to give birth to or produce
see also BORN
Gen 4:13 *too great for me to **b**!*.....................15
Ps 38:4 *too heavy to **b**.*................................568
John 15:2 *branches that do **b** fruit*............1463
Heb 13:13 *and **b** the disgrace he bore.*......1782

BEAR, BEARS (n) a large heavy mammal with shaggy hair, rudimentary tail, and plantigrade feet
2 Kgs 2:24 *Then two **b-s** came out*............740
Isa 11:7 *cow will graze near the **b**.*.............796
Dan 7:5 *it looked like a **b**.*.........................1135

BEARD, BEARDS (n) the hair that grows on a man's face often excluding the mustache
Lev 19:27 *or trim your **b-s**.*..........................226
Isa 50:6 *who pulled out my **b**.*.....................937

BEAST, BEASTS (n) devilish creature(s) ravishing the earth during the Tribulation; animals, as distinguished from plants or humans; a contemptible person
Dan 7:3 *Then four huge **b-s** came up*.......1135
Dan 7:6 *authority was given to this **b**.*........1135
1 Cor 15:32 *fighting wild **b-s**—those*.......1621
Rev 13:18 *number of the **b**, for it is*..........1820
Rev 16:2 *had the mark of the **b***................1822
Rev 19:20 *accepted the mark of the **b***.......1828

BEATEN (v) to be stricken repeatedly so as to inflict pain
see also FLOGGED, WHIPPED
Acts 16:23 *They were severely **b**,*.............1576
2 Cor 11:25 *Three times I was **b***..............1641
1 Pet 2:20 *if you are **b** for doing wrong.*....1752

BEAUTIFUL (adj) lovely, handsome, or pleasing to the eye; excellent
Gen 2:9 *trees that were **b***............................10
Gen 6:2 *sons of God saw the **b***.....................17
Prov 11:22 *A **b** woman who lacks*..............644
Eccl 3:11 *everything **b** for its own time*........675
Isa 53:2 *was nothing **b** or majestic*.............940
Lam 2:15 *the city called 'Most **B***..............1097
Acts 3:2 *the one called the **B** Gate,*...........1516
Rom 10:15 *How **b** are the feet of*..............1664

BEAUTY (n) a particularly graceful, ornamental, or excellent quality; the quality in a person or thing that gives pleasure to the senses
2 Sam 11:2 *a woman of unusual **b***............502
Ps 50:2 *the perfection of **b**, God shines*......593
Prov 31:30 *and **b** does not last;*..................848
Isa 28:1 *but its glorious **b** will fade*............818
Jas 1:11 *and its **b** fades away.*.................1547
1 Pet 1:24 *their **b** is like a flower*..............1750
1 Pet 3:4 ***b** of a gentle and quiet spirit,*.....1752

BED (n) a piece of furniture on or in which to lie and sleep; a place for sleeping
Deut 6:7 *when you are going to **b***..............295
Song 3:1 *as I lay in **b**, I yearned*.................665
Luke 17:34 *will be asleep in one **b**;*..........1417

BEDROCK (n) the solid rock underlying loosely arranged surface materials (as soil)
Matt 7:25 *it is built on **b**.*..........................1335

BEG, BEGGED, BEGGING (v) to ask for charity or mercy; to ask earnestly for
Ps 37:25 *their children **b-ging** for bread*.....568
Ps 80:14 *Come back, we **b** you,*.................601
Mal 1:9 *Go ahead, **b** God to*......................1245
2 Cor 12:8 *different times I **b-ged** the Lord*...1642

BEGINNING (n) the point at which something starts; the first part; the origin, source
Gen 1:1 *In the **b** God created*...........................6
John 1:1 *In the **b** the Word already*...........1270
Rom 16:25 *secret from the **b** of time.*........1674
1 Jn 1:1 *one who existed from the **b**,*........1786
Rev 21:6 *the **B** and the End.*...................1830
Rev 22:13 *the **B** and the End.*...................1832

BEHEMOTH (n) Hebrew word that could mean elephant, crocodile, hippopotamus, water buffalo, or mythological monster; a mighty animal created as an example of the power of God
Job 40:15 *a look at **B**, which I made,*..........130

BELIEF (n) the content of one's conviction on a matter; confidence in or reliance upon the truth of a matter
1 Thes 2:14 *because of their **b** in Christ*....1582
2 Thes 2:13 *through your **b** in the truth*.....1589
Titus 1:9 ***b** in the trustworthy message*.....1737

BELIEVE, BELIEVED, BELIEVES, BELIEVING (v) to trust in; to hold a firm conviction about; to accept as true, genuine, or real
see also FAITH, TRUST
Gen 15:6 *Abram **b-d** the LORD,*.....................35
Prov 14:15 *simpletons **b** everything*............647
Isa 53:1 *Who has **b-d** our message?*..........940
Matt 27:42 *we will **b** in him!*...................1483
Mark 9:23 *is possible if a person **b-s**.*.........1381
Mark 9:24 *I do **b**, but help me*.....................1381
Mark 15:32 *we can see it and **b** him!*.......1483
Luke 8:12 *prevent them from **b-ing***.........1347
Luke 24:25 *You find it so hard to **b***...........1494
John 1:7 *so that everyone might **b***............1271
John 1:12 *all who **b-d** him and accepted*..1271
John 3:16 *everyone who **b-s** in him*..........1302
John 4:41 *hear his message and **b**.*...........1306
John 5:38 *because you do not **b** me—*.....1319
John 6:69 *We **b**, and we know you are*......1369
John 7:5 *his brothers didn't **b** in him*.......1386
John 7:39 *to everyone **b-ing** in him*..........1390
John 9:35 *asked, "Do you **b** in the Son*.....1404
John 9:38 *Yes, Lord, I **b**!*...........................1404
John 10:37 *Don't **b** me unless*..................1406
John 11:25 *Anyone who **b-s** in me.*...........1414
John 11:27 ***b-d** you are the Messiah,*.......1414
John 11:40 *see God's glory if you **b**?*.........1415
John 12:37 *did not **b** in him.*.....................1434
John 12:38 *who has **b-d** our message?*...1434
John 13:19 *you will **b** that I AM.*...............1456
John 14:11 *Or at least **b** because of the*...1462
John 14:12 *anyone who **b-s** in me*............1462
John 16:30 ***b** that you came from God.*.....1465
John 17:21 *world will **b** you sent me.*........1467
John 19:35 *so that you also can **b**.*.........1487
John 20:8 *and he saw and **b-d**—*............1492
John 20:29 ***b** because you have seen*.......1496
John 20:31 *and that by **b-ing** in him*..........1496
Acts 10:43 *that everyone who **b-s** in him*...1534
Acts 13:8 *keep the governor from **b-ing**.*..1540
Acts 16:31 ***B** in the Lord Jesus and*.........1576
Acts 19:4 ***b** in the one who would come*...1593
Acts 26:27 *do you **b** the prophets?*...........1686
Acts 27:25 *For I **b** God. I will be just*.........1687
Rom 1:16 *saving everyone who **b-s**—*.....1646
Rom 3:22 *for everyone who **b-s**, no*.........1651
Rom 3:25 ***b** that Jesus sacrificed his life,*..1651
Rom 4:3 *tell us, "Abraham **b-d** God,*.........1652
Rom 4:20 *never wavered in **b-ing** God's*...1653
Rom 10:9 ***b** in your heart that God.*...........1663
Rom 10:10 *For it is by **b-ing** in your heart*..1664
Rom 10:14 *unless they **b** in him?*............1664
Rom 14:23 *anything you **b** is not right,*......1671
Rom 16:26 *they too might **b** and obey*......1674
1 Cor 1:21 *to save those who **b**.*...............1597
1 Cor 15:2 ***b-d** something that was never*...1618
2 Cor 5:7 *by **b-ing** and not by seeing.*......1632
2 Cor 5:14 *Since we **b** that Christ*............1632
Gal 3:2 *because you **b-d** the message.*.....1560
Gal 3:6 *same way, "Abraham **b-d** God,*.....1561
Eph 2:8 *his grace when you **b-d**.*..............1707
Col 1:23 *continue to **b** this truth*..............1696
1 Thes 4:14 *For since we **b** that Jesus*......1585
2 Thes 2:11 *and they will **b** these lies.*......1589
2 Thes 2:12 *enjoying evil rather than **b-ing***..1589
1 Tim 3:16 *He was **b-d** in throughout the*..1731
Heb 3:14 *firmly as when we first **b-d**,*.......1765
Heb 11:6 *must **b** that God exists*.............1777
Heb 11:13 *still **b-ing** what God had*..........1778
Jas 2:19 *you **b** that there is one God.*.........1549
1 Jn 3:23 *We must **b** in the name*............1792
1 Jn 4:1 *friends, do not **b** everyone*..........1792
1 Jn 5:1 *Everyone who **b-s** that Jesus is*..1794
1 Jn 5:10 *All who **b** in the Son*.................1794

BELIEVER, BELIEVERS (n) one who accepts something as true, genuine, or real; one who trusts in or has a firm conviction about
Matt 18:15 *If another **b** sins*.......................1385
Acts 2:44 *all the **b-s** met together*............1516
Acts 4:32 *All the **b-s** were united*.............1520
Acts 6:1 *as the **b-s** rapidly multiplied,*........1522
Acts 6:7 *number of **b-s** greatly increased*...1523
Acts 13:48 *for eternal life became **b-s**.*.....1543
Acts 14:22 *they strengthened the **b-s**.*.....1545
Acts 15:2 *accompanied by some local **b-s**,*..1568
Acts 15:23 *to the Gentile **b-s** in Antioch,*....1571
Acts 15:32 *to the **b-s**, encouraging*.........1572
Acts 16:15 *I am a true **b** in the Lord,*........1574
Acts 20:2 *there, he encouraged the **b-s***....1625
Acts 21:25 *As for the Gentile **b-s**,*...........1677
Rom 8:27 *the Spirit pleads for us **b-s***.......1660
Rom 14:13 *cause another **b** to stumble*....1670
Rom 14:15 *if another **b** is distressed*........1670
Rom 14:21 *cause another **b** to stumble.*....1670
Rom 15:27 *the **b-s** in Jerusalem,*.............1672
1 Cor 6:2 *someday we **b-s** will judge*.........1603
1 Cor 10:27 *who isn't a **b** asks you*...........1611
1 Cor 14:22 *tongues is a sign, not for **b-s**,*..1617
2 Cor 6:15 *can a **b** be a partner with an*....1634
2 Cor 11:26 *claim to be **b-s** but are not*....1641
Col 4:5 *among those who are not **b-s**,*......1702
2 Thes 3:6 *away from all **b-s** who live idle*..1590
1 Tim 3:6 *An elder must not be a new **b**,*..1730
1 Tim 4:12 *Be an example to all **b-s***..........1732
1 Tim 5:16 *a woman who is a **b***..................1733
1 Jn 3:10 *and does not love other **b-s***......1791

BELITTLE (v) to cause (a person or thing) to seem little or less; to speak slightingly of
Prov 11:12 *foolish to **b** one's neighbor;*.......643
Prov 14:21 *a sin to **b** one's neighbor;*.........648

BELLY (n) abdomen; the stomach and its adjuncts
Gen 3:14 *crawl on your **b**, groveling*.............13
Dan 2:32 *its **b** and thighs were bronze,*.....1004
Matt 12:40 *in the **b** of the great fish*.........1343

BELONG, BELONGED, BELONGS (v) to be the property of a person or thing
Lev 25:55 *people of Israel **b** to me.*............234
Lev 27:30 ***b-s** to the LORD and*...................237
Ps 22:28 *royal power **b-s** to the LORD.*.........557
John 8:47 *Anyone who **b-s** to God*...........1393
John 15:19 *if you **b-ed** to it, but you*........1464
Rom 1:6 *called to **b** to Jesus*....................1645
Rom 12:5 *we all **b** to each other.*..............1667
2 Cor 10:7 *who say they **b** to Christ*.........1638
Gal 5:24 *Those who **b** to Christ*...............1567
1 Thes 5:5 *we don't **b** to darkness*...........1585
2 Tim 2:19 *All who **b** to the LORD*..............1743
1 Pet 3:16 *because you **b** to Christ.*..........1753
1 Jn 4:6 *If they do not **b** to God,*..............1793

BELOVED (adj) dearly loved; dear to the heart
Ps 60:5 *rescue your **b** people.*.....................499
Matt 12:18 *He is my **B**, who pleases me.*..1322
1 Cor 4:14 *as my **b** children.*.....................1601
1 Cor 4:17 *Timothy, my **b** and faithful*.......1601
Eph 6:21 *a **b** brother and faithful helper*....1716
Col 1:7 *Epaphras, our **b** co-worker.*...........1694
Col 4:9 *a faithful and **b** brother,*................1703
Col 4:14 *Luke, the **b** doctor,*.......................1703
Phlm 1:1 *to Philemon, our **b** co-worker,*....1690
Phlm 1:16 *he is a **b** brother,*......................1692
2 Pet 3:15 *our **b** brother Paul also wrote*...1760
Rev 20:9 *God's people and the **b** city.*........1829

BENEFICIAL (adj) conferring benefits; conducive to personal or social well-being
Titus 3:8 *good and **b** for everyone.*.............1739

BENEFIT, BENEFITS (n) advantages or blessings; something that promotes well-being
Prov 12:14 *Wise words bring many **b-s**,*......645
Acts 18:27 *he proved to be of great **b** to*...1592
2 Cor 4:15 *this is for your **b**.*....................1631

BENEFIT, BENEFITS (v) to be useful or profitable to; to favor (another) or gain (for oneself)
Job 36:28 *and everyone **b-s**.*.......................126
Prov 9:12 *you will be the one to **b**.*...............641
Luke 9:25 *what do you **b** if you gain*..........1378
1 Cor 9:14 *by those who **b** from it.*............1608

BENJAMIN Second son of Jacob and Rachel, the youngest of Jacob's 12 sons; never knew his mother (Gen 35:16-20, p. 70); taken to Egypt against Jacob's wishes (Gen 43:3-17, p. 83); gave his name to a tribe of Israel; his tribe was blessed (Gen 49:27, p. 92; Deut 33:12,

p. 327), numbered (Num 1:36-37, p. 238), allotted land and cities (Josh 18:11-28, p. 362); civil war nearly wiped them out (Judg 20–21, p. 407); 12,000 will be marked by God (Rev 7:8, p. 1812).

BESEECH(ING), BESOUGHT (KJV)
Deut 3:23 *I **pleaded with** the* L*ORD*............289
Ps 118:25 L*ORD*, ***please** give us success*....876
Jon 1:14 ***pleaded**, "don't make us die*........767
Matt 8:5 *came and **pleaded with** him*......1335
2 Cor 12:8 ***begged** the Lord to take it away*.........1642

BESIDE (prep) by the side of
Ps 16:8 *he is right **b** me*..........553
Ps 109:31 *he stands **b** the needy,*..........582

BEST (adj) excelling all others
Ps 122:9 *seek what is **b** for you,*..........584
1 Cor 12:31 *life that is **b** of all*..........1615
Heb 4:11 *do our **b** to enter that rest*..........1766

BESTOWED (KJV)
Isa 63:7 *he has **granted** according*..........949

BETHLEHEM (n) a city about five miles south of Jerusalem in the hill country of Judah; the ancestral home of King David and the birthplace of Jesus Christ
Ruth 1:19 *When they came to **B**,*..........410
1 Sam 16:1 *go to **B**. Find a man named*......447
2 Sam 23:15 *the well by the gate in **B**.*.......480
Mic 5:2 ***B** Ephrathah, are only a small*.........908
Matt 2:1 *Jesus was born in **B** in Judea,*....1283
Matt 2:6 *you, O **B** in the land of Judah,*.....1284

BETRAY, BETRAYED (v) to turn your back on a friend; to deliver to an enemy by treachery; to lead astray, seduce
Num 5:6 *men or women—**b** the* L*ORD*.........243
Deut 32:51 *both of you **b-ed** me*..........325
Jer 38:22 *They have **b-ed** and misled*......1043
Mal 2:10 *Then why do we **b** each other,*....1246
Matt 10:21 *A brother will **b** his brother*......1360
Matt 24:10 *and **b** and hate each other.*......1446
Matt 26:21 *one of you will **b** me.*..........1456
Matt 27:4 *I have **b-ed** an innocent man*....1475
Luke 6:16 *(who later **b-ed** him).*..........1323
John 18:5 *Judas, who **b-ed** him,*..........1470

BETRAYER (n) one who violates a trust or loyalty
Matt 26:46 *Look, my **b** is here!*..........1468
John 18:2 *Judas, the **b**, knew this place,*..1470

BETTER (adj) more attractive, favorable, or commendable; more advantageous or effective
Ps 63:3 *unfailing love is **b** than life*..........517
Matt 5:20 *unless your righteousness is **b***..1328
Phil 1:21 *and dying is even **b**.*..........1718

BEWARE (v) to take heed or be careful
Mark 8:15 ***B** of the yeast of the Pharisees.*1374

BIRD, BIRDS (n) any of a class of warm-blooded vertebrates distinguished by having the body more or less completely covered with feathers and the forelimbs modified as wings
Prov 27:8 ***b** that strays from its nest.*..........842
Eccl 10:20 ***b** might deliver your*..........682
Matt 8:20 *and **b-s** have nests,*..........1387
Luke 9:58 *and **b-s** have nests,*..........1387

BIRTH (n) the emergence of a new individual from the body of its parent; beginning, start
Gen 25:24 *the time came to give **b**,*..........51
Ps 58:3 *even from **b** they have lied*..........573
Matt 24:8 *only the first of the **b** pains,*......1446
John 3:6 *Spirit gives **b** to spiritual life*........1301
Titus 3:5 *giving us a new **b** and new life*....1739
Jas 1:15 *it gives **b** to death.*..........1547

BIRTHRIGHT (KJV)
Gen 25:31 *your **rights as the firstborn son***..51
1 Chr 5:1 ***birthright** was given to the*........1231
Heb 12:16 ***birthright as the firstborn son***..........1781

BITTER (adj) expressive of severe pain, grief, or regret; distasteful
Exod 12:8 *eat it along with **b** salad greens*..156
Prov 27:7 ***b** food tastes sweet to the*..........842
Prov 30:23 *a **b** woman who finally gets*.......847
Jas 3:11 *both fresh water and **b** water?*....1550

BITTERNESS (n) an intense or severe expression or feeling of pain, grief, or regret; exhibiting intense animosity
Prov 14:10 *Each heart knows its own **b**,*.....647
Prov 17:25 ***b** to the one who gave them*......653
Rom 3:14 *full of cursing and **b**.*..........1651
Eph 4:31 *Get rid of all **b**, rage,*..........1712

BLACK (adj) of the color black; very dark in color
Zech 6:6 *The chariot with **b** horses*..........1170
Rev 6:5 *I looked up and saw a **b** horse,*.....1811

BLAME (n) an expression of disapproval or reproach; responsibility for something believed to deserve censure
1 Cor 1:8 *free from all **b** on the day*..........1595
Rev 14:5 *they are without **b**.*..........1821

BLAMELESS (adj) characterized by being free from sin and fault
see also INTEGRITY, RIGHTEOUS
Gen 6:9 *only **b** person living on earth*..........17
Job 1:8 ***b**—a man of complete integrity*........95
Ps 18:23 *I am **b** before God;*..........528
Prov 13:6 *guards the path of the **b**,*..........646
Prov 29:10 *The bloodthirsty hate **b***..........845
Phil 1:10 *live pure and **b** lives*..........1717
Col 1:22 *and you are holy and **b***..........1696
1 Thes 5:23 *kept **b** until our Lord*..........1587
Titus 1:6 *must live a **b** life.*..........1736
2 Pet 3:14 *pure and **b** in his sight*..........1760

BLASPHEME, BLASPHEMED, BLASPHEMES, BLASPHEMING (v) to dishonor or revile God; to speak of or address with irreverence
Lev 24:11 *son of an Israelite woman **b-ed***..232
Lev 24:16 *Anyone who **b-s** the Name*.........232
Num 15:30 *have **b-ed** the* L*ORD*,..........255
Isa 52:5 *My name is **b-ed** all day long.*........939
Dan 11:36 *even **b-ing** the God of gods*.....1160
Mark 3:29 *who **b-s** the Holy Spirit*..........1342
Luke 12:10 *who **b-s** the Holy Spirit*..........1400
Acts 6:11 *We heard him **b** Moses,*..........1523
Rom 2:24 *Gentiles **b** the name of God*......1650
1 Tim 1:13 *to **b** the name of Christ.*..........1728
1 Tim 1:20 *learn not to **b** God*..........1728
Rev 13:1 *were names that **b-ed** God.*........1819

BLASPHEMER (n) one who dishonors or reviles God; one who speaks or addresses with irreverence
Lev 24:14 *Take the **b** outside the camp,*......232
Lev 24:23 *took the **b** outside the camp*.......232

BLASPHEMOUS (adj) impiously irreverent; profane
2 Kgs 19:6 *by this **b** speech against me*.....915
Isa 37:6 *by this **b** speech against me*..........917

BLASPHEMY, BLASPHEMIES (n) the words or actions that dishonor God; the act of insulting or showing contempt or lack of reverence for God
Neh 9:18 *They committed terrible **b-ies**.*..1216
Mark 3:28 *all sin and **b** can be forgiven,*...1342
Mark 14:64 *You have all heard his **b**.*........1473
John 10:33 *for any good work, but for **b**!*..1406
2 Pet 2:11 *a charge of **b** against those*.....1759
Rev 13:5 *speak great **b-ies** against God*...1819
Rev 13:6 *words of **b** against God,*..........1820
Rev 17:3 *and **b-ies** against God were*......1824

BLESS, BLESSED, BLESSES (v) to confer prosperity or happiness upon; to honor in worship; to offer approval or encouragement; to bring pleasure or divine favor
Gen 1:22 *Then God **b-ed** them,*..........7
Gen 12:3 *I will **b** those who **b** you*..........30
Gen 22:18 *of the earth will be **b-ed**—*.........46
Ps 16:7 *I will **b** the* L*ORD who guides*..........553
Prov 31:28 *Her children stand and **b***..........848
Matt 5:3 *God **b-es** those who are poor*.....1323
Matt 5:7 ***b-es** those who are merciful,*.......1326
Matt 5:9 *God **b-es** those who work for*.....1326
Matt 5:11 *God **b-es** you when people*........1326
Jas 1:12 *God **b-es** those who patiently*.....1547
Rev 22:7 ***B-ed** are those who obey*..........1832
Rev 22:14 ***B-ed** are those who wash*........1832

BLESSING, BLESSINGS (n) happiness; praise; divine favor or heavenly reward; the antidote to cursings
Josh 8:34 ***b-s** and curses Moses*..........348
Prov 13:21 ***b-s** reward the righteous.*.........647
John 12:13 ***B-s** on the one who comes in*..1431
Acts 4:33 *God's great **b** was upon them*...1520
Acts 11:23 *evidence of God's **b**,*..........1536
Rom 15:27 *spiritual **b-s** of the Good*.........1672
Eph 3:6 *both enjoy the promise of **b-s***......1708
Rev 7:12 ***B** and glory and wisdom*..........1813

BLIND (adj) sightless; lacking spiritual discernment
Matt 11:5 *the **b** see, the lame walk,*..........1337
Matt 15:14 ***b** guides leading the **b**,*..........1370
Mark 10:46 ***b** beggar named*..........1425
Luke 6:39 *Can one **b** person lead*..........1333

BLINDED (v) to withhold light from; to be without sight
John 12:40 *The Lord has **b** their eyes*.......1434
2 Cor 4:4 *god of this world, has **b** the*......1630

BLINK (n) glimpse, glance; a usually involuntary shutting and opening of the eye
1 Cor 15:52 *moment, in the **b** of an eye,*...1622

BLOOD (n) fluid in the circulatory system; signifies human life; kinfolk; of animals, used in priestly sacrifices; of Christ, effective for the forgiveness of sins; on hands or head, symbolic of guilt
Exod 12:13 *When I see the **b**, I will pass*.....156
Deut 12:23 *But never consume the **b**,*........302
Isa 1:11 *no pleasure from the **b** of bulls*......823
Mark 14:24 *my **b**, which confirms the*......1458
John 6:53 *and drink his **b**, you cannot*......1368
Acts 15:20 *and from consuming **b**.*..........1570
1 Cor 11:25 *confirmed with my **b**.*..........1613
Eph 1:7 *with the **b** of his Son*..........1705
Eph 2:13 *through the **b** of Christ*..........1708
Heb 9:7 *offered **b** for his own sins*..........1772
Heb 9:20 *This **b** confirms the covenant*.....1774
1 Pet 1:2 *cleansed by the **b** of Jesus*........1747
1 Pet 1:19 *the precious **b** of Christ,*..........1749
1 Jn 1:7 *the **b** of Jesus, his Son, cleanses*...1787
Rev 1:5 *by shedding his **b** for us*..........1799

Rev 5:9 *your **b** has ransomed people* ... 1810
Rev 7:14 *in the **b** of the Lamb* ... 1813
Rev 12:11 *by the **b** of the Lamb* ... 1818
Rev 19:13 *He wore a robe dipped in **b**,* ... 1828

BLOT (v) to wipeout, destroy; to erase or cover up
Ps 51:1 ***b** out the stain of my sins* ... 505
Isa 43:25 *I alone—will **b** out your sins* ... 929

BOAST, BOASTED, BOASTING (v) to puff oneself up in speech, brag
Isa 20:5 ***b-ed** of their allies in Egypt!* ... 890
Jer 9:23 *the wise **b** in their wisdom,* ... 1012
Rom 2:17 ***b** about your special* ... 1649
1 Cor 1:31 ***b, b** only about the Lord* ... 1597
2 Cor 8:24 *our **b-ing** about you is justified* ... 1637
2 Cor 10:13 *We will **b** only about* ... 1639
Gal 6:14 ***b** about anything except* ... 1568
Eph 2:9 *none of us can **b** about it.* ... 1707
Jas 1:9 *have something to **b** about,* ... 1546
Jas 4:16 ***b-ing** about your own plans,* ... 1552

BOASTFUL (adj) bragging, overproud, vainglorious
Ps 12:3 *and silence their **b** tongues.* ... 550
1 Cor 13:4 *Love is not jealous or **b** or proud* ... 1616

BOAT, BOATS (n) a small vessel for travel on water; ship
Gen 6:14 *Build a large **b** from cypress* ... 18
Luke 5:3 *Stepping into one of the **b-s**,* ... 1308

BOAZ
1. Family redeemer and husband of the widow Ruth; ancestor of David in the family line of Jesus (Ruth 2–4 p. 411; especially 4:1-10, 18-21, p. 414, 415; *see also* 1 Chr 2:12-15, p. 1227; Matt 1:5, p. 1278; Luke 3:32, p. 1280).
2. Pillar's name at front of the Jerusalem Temple (1 Kgs 7:15-22, p. 613).

BODILY (adj) of or relating to the body
Col 2:23 *and severe **b** discipline.* ... 1699

BODY, BODIES (n) one's physical essence; a corpse; a group of people
see also FLESH
Job 19:26 *in my **b** I will see God!* ... 112
Ps 49:14 *Their **b-ies** will rot in the grave,* ... 854
Isa 26:19 *their **b-ies** will rise again!* ... 897
Matt 26:41 *willing, but the **b** is weak!* ... 1468
Mark 14:22 *Take it, for this is my **b**.* ... 1457
Rom 12:4 *our **b-ies** have many parts* ... 1667
1 Cor 6:15 *that your **b-ies** are actually* ... 1604
1 Cor 6:19 *that your **b** is the temple* ... 1604
1 Cor 6:20 *honor God with your **b**.* ... 1604
1 Cor 11:24 *my **b**, which is given for* ... 1613
1 Cor 12:13 *into one **b** by one Spirit,* ... 1615
1 Cor 15:44 *be raised as spiritual **b-ies**.* ... 1621
2 Cor 5:1 *eternal **b** made for us by God* ... 1631
2 Cor 5:2 *to put on our heavenly **b-ies*** ... 1631
2 Cor 5:4 *so that these dying **b-ies** will* ... 1632
Eph 1:23 *the church is his **b**;* ... 1706
Eph 3:6 *Both are part of the same **b**,* ... 1708
Eph 5:28 *love their own **b-ies**.* ... 1714
Eph 5:30 *are members of his **b**.* ... 1714
Col 1:24 *for his **b**, the church* ... 1696

BOLD (adj) fearless before danger; self-assured, confident; prominent
2 Sam 7:27 *been **b** enough to pray* ... 497
1 Chr 17:25 *been **b** enough to pray* ... 497
Phil 1:20 *continue to be **b** for Christ,* ... 1718

BOLDLY (adv) showing a fearless, daring spirit
Acts 26:26 *I speak **b**, for I am sure* ... 1686
Eph 3:12 ***b** and confidently into God's* ... 1709
Heb 4:16 *let us come **b** to the throne* ... 1766
Heb 10:19 ***b** enter heaven's Most Holy* ... 1775

BOLDNESS (n) fearlessness before danger; self-assurance; confidence; prominence
Acts 4:13 *they saw the **b** of Peter* ... 1519
Acts 4:29 *give us, your servants, great **b**.* ... 1519

BONE, BONES (n) one of the hard parts of the skeleton
Gen 2:23 *This one is **b** from my **b**,* ... 10
Ps 22:14 *all my **b-s** are out of joint* ... 556
Ps 22:17 *I can count all my **b-s**.* ... 556
Ezek 37:1 *a valley filled with **b-s**.* ... 1113
John 19:36 *Not one of his **b-s** will be* ... 1487

BOOK, BOOKS (n) a long written or printed literary composition; written records, register, or accounting
Josh 1:8 *Study this **B** of Instruction* ... 337
Ps 69:28 *names from the **B** of Life;* ... 578
Ps 139:16 *recorded in your **b**.* ... 586
Eccl 12:12 *for writing **b-s** is endless* ... 683
Dan 7:10 *and the **b-s** were opened.* ... 1136
Dan 12:1 *name is written in the **b**.* ... 1161
John 21:25 *could not contain the **b-s*** ... 1497
Phil 4:3 *are written in the **B** of Life* ... 1724
Rev 3:5 *names from the **B** of Life,* ... 1806
Rev 20:12 *including the **B** of Life.* ... 1830
Rev 20:12 *as recorded in the **b-s**.* ... 1830
Rev 21:27 *in the Lamb's **B** of Life.* ... 1831

BORN (v) to give birth to or produce; to be productive; spiritually, to renew or confirm a commitment of faith
see also BEAR
Ps 51:5 *For I was **b** a sinner—* ... 506
Eccl 3:2 *time to be **b** and a time to die.* ... 675
Isa 9:6 *For a child is **b** to us,* ... 793
Luke 2:11 *the Lord—has been **b** today* ... 1281
John 3:3 *unless you are **b** again,* ... 1301
John 3:7 *You must be **b** again.* ... 1301
1 Pet 1:3 *we have been **b** again,* ... 1748
1 Pet 1:23 *you have been **b** again,* ... 1750

BORROWER, BORROWERS (n) one who takes with the implied or expressed intention of returning the same; to borrow (money) with the intention of returning the same plus interest
Prov 22:7 *the **b** is servant to the lender.* ... 659
Isa 24:2 *lenders and **b-s**, bankers and* ... 894

BOSS (n) one who directs or supervises workers
Eccl 10:4 *If your **b** is angry at you,* ... 681
Luke 16:3 *Now what? My **b** has fired me* .. 1411

BOTTOMLESS (adj) unfathomable; boundless, unlimited
Luke 8:31 *into the **b** pit* ... 1353
Rev 9:1 *shaft of the **b** pit* ... 1814
Rev 9:11 *the angel from the **b** pit;* ... 1814
Rev 11:7 *up out of the **b** pit* ... 1817
Rev 17:8 *up out of the **b** pit* ... 1824
Rev 20:1 *the key to the **b** pit* ... 1829
Rev 20:3 *into the **b** pit,* ... 1829

BOUGHT (v) to purchase; to obtain by way of sacrifice or expenditure
see also BUY
Job 28:15 *It cannot be **b** with gold.* ... 119
1 Cor 6:20 *God **b** you with a high price.* ... 1604
2 Pet 2:1 *the Master who **b** them.* ... 1758

BOUND (v) to confine, restrain, or restrict as if with bonds; to put under an obligation
Acts 20:22 *now I am **b** by the Spirit* ... 1675
Rev 20:2 *and **b** him in chains* ... 1829

BOUNDARY (n) border, limit; dividing line
Num 34:3 *The southern **b** will begin* ... 281
Prov 22:28 *moving the ancient **b** markers* ... 660

BOUNTIFUL (adj) given or provided abundantly; generous
Ps 65:11 *year with a **b** harvest;* ... 575
Ps 68:10 *with a **b** harvest, O God,* ... 576

BOUNTY (n) crop yield; generosity
Deut 33:16 *gifts of the earth and its **b**,* ... 327

BOW, BOWED, BOWS (v) to bend the head, body, or knee in reverence, submission, or shame
Gen 47:31 *Jacob **b-ed** humbly* ... 89
Deut 5:9 *You must not **b** down to them* ... 292
1 Kgs 1:16 *Bathsheba **b-ed** down before* ... 543
1 Kgs 19:18 *never **b-ed** down to Baal* ... 720
2 Chr 29:29 *everyone with him **b-ed** down* ... 836
2 Chr 29:30 *and **b-ed** down in worship.* ... 836
Esth 3:2 *would **b** down before Haman* ... 1186
Ps 72:9 *nomads will **b** before him;* ... 630
Ps 95:6 *let us worship and **b** down.* ... 863
Isa 44:15 *an idol and **b-s** down in front* ... 930
Mic 6:6 *Should we **b** before God* ... 910
Rom 11:4 *never **b-ed** down to Baal!* ... 1664
Phil 2:10 *every knee should **b**, in heaven* .. 1720

BOWL (n) a concave vessel often used for holding food or liquids
Prov 15:17 *A **b** of vegetables with* ... 649
Luke 8:16 *covers it with a **b** or hides* ... 1347

BOY, BOYS (n) a male child from birth to puberty
Gen 21:17 *God has heard the **b** crying* ... 44
Gen 22:12 *Don't lay a hand on the **b**!* ... 46
Exod 1:18 *you allowed the **b-s** to live?* ... 140
1 Sam 2:11 *the **b** served the LORD* ... 419
1 Sam 3:8 *who was calling the **b**.* ... 422
Matt 17:18 *rebuked the demon in the **b**,* ... 1381

BRAG (v) to talk boastfully
Prov 27:1 *Don't **b** about tomorrow,* ... 842
Amos 4:5 *so you can **b** about it* ... 774
2 Cor 5:12 *you can answer those who **b*** ... 1632

BRANCH, BRANCHES (n) limb of a (family) tree; part of a complex body (of knowledge); figurative of offspring and of disciples (of Christ and his disciples)
Isa 4:2 *the **b** of the LORD will be beautiful* ... 828
Dan 4:21 *nested in its **b-es**.* ... 1121
Zech 3:8 *bring my servant, the **B**.* ... 1168
Matt 13:32 *make nests in its **b-es**."* ... 1348
John 15:2 ***b** of mine that doesn't* ... 1463
John 15:4 *a **b** cannot produce fruit if* ... 1463
John 15:5 *you are the **b-es**.* ... 1463
Rom 11:20 *those **b-es** were broken off* ... 1665
Rom 11:21 *not spare the original **b-es**,* ... 1665

BREAD (n) basic staple in diet of ancient Israel, usually baked using flour or meal; signifies livelihood
see also FOOD
Exod 23:15 *Festival of Unleavened **B**.* ... 173
Prov 20:17 *Stolen **b** tastes sweet,* ... 657
Mark 14:22 *Jesus took some **b** and* ... 1457
Luke 4:3 *stone to become a loaf of **b**.* ... 1296
Luke 9:13 *only five loaves of **b*** ... 1364
John 6:48 *Yes, I am the **b** of life!* ... 1368
John 6:51 *I am the living **b*** ... 1368

1 Cor 10:16 *when we break the **b**,* 1610
1 Cor 11:23 *the Lord Jesus took some **b*** ..1613
1 Cor 11:26 *eat this **b** and drink*..............1613

BREAK, BREAKING (v) to fracture; to shatter; to violate or transgress; to burst forth; to separate into parts
see also BROKE
Lev 26:15 *and if you **b** my covenant* 235
Prov 25:15 *soft speech can **b** bones*...........840
Matt 5:33 *You must not **b** your vows;*.........1329
1 Cor 10:16 *And when we **b** the bread,* 1610
1 Jn 3:4 *who sins is **b-ing** God's law,*.......1791

BREAKFAST (n) first meal of the day, especially taken in the morning
Prov 31:15 *to prepare **b** for her*..................847

BREATH (n) air inhaled and exhaled in breathing; a spoken sound, utterance; a slight indication, suggestion
Gen 2:7 *He breathed the **b** of life*....................9
Exod 15:8 *At the blast of your **b**,*...............162
Ps 18:15 *at the blast of your **b**,* 528
Ps 144:4 *we are like a **b** of air;*..................589

BREATHED (v) to inhale and exhale freely; to blow softly
Gen 2:7 *He **b** the breath of life* 9
Mark 15:37 *and **b** his last.*.......................1486
John 20:22 *Then he **b** on them* 1495

BREVITY (n) shortness of duration
Ps 90:12 *to realize the **b** of life,*.................326

BRIBE (n) something that serves to induce or influence
Deut 16:19 *Never accept a **b**,* 306

BRIBERY (n) the act or practice of giving or taking a bribe
Job 15:34 *homes, enriched through **b**,* 110

BRICKS (n) units for building or paving, made of mud and often a binding agent such as straw; in the ancient world bricks were baked or sun dried
Gen 11:3 *Let's make **b** and harden*...............23
Exod 5:7 *any more straw for making **b**.*........147
Exod 5:13 *Meet your daily quota of **b**,*.........147
Isa 9:10 *the broken **b** of our ruins*...............793
Nah 3:14 *making **b** to repair the walls*.........977

BRIDE (n) a woman just married or about to be married
2 Cor 11:2 *as a pure **b** to one husband*— 1640
Rev 19:7 ***b** has prepared herself*...............1827
Rev 21:2 *like a **b** beautifully dressed*.........1830
Rev 21:9 *the **b**, the wife of the Lamb.* 1830
Rev 22:17 *Spirit and the **b** say, "Come."*....1833

BRIDEGROOM (n) a man just married or about to be married
Ps 19:5 *like a radiant **b** after*.......................554
Matt 25:1 *and went to meet the **b**.* 1451
Matt 25:5 *When the **b** was delayed,*..........1451

BRIDESMAIDS (n) women attendants of a bride
Matt 25:1 *will be like ten **b** who*................1451

BRIDLE (n) the headgear consisting of a bit and reins with which a horse or other animal is governed
Prov 26:3 *a donkey with a **b**, and a fool*......841

BRIGHTNESS (n) the quality or state of being bright; luminance; radiance
Ps 18:12 *shielded the **b** around him*...........528
Isa 24:23 *the **b** of the sun will fade,*............895

BRILLIANT (adj) very bright, glittering; striking, distinctive
Hab 3:4 *His coming is as **b** as*....................981
1 Tim 6:16 *he lives in light so **b** that*.........1735

BROAD (adj) extending far and wide; spacious
Matt 7:13 *highway to hell is **b**,*...................1334

BROKE, BROKEN (v) *see also* BREAK
Josh 9:20 *if we **b** our oath.*.........................349
1 Kgs 19:10 *have **b-n** their covenant*..........720
Ps 34:20 *not one of them is **b-n!***..............459
Ps 51:17 *not reject a **b-n** and repentant*.....506
Eccl 4:12 *braided cord is not easily **b-n**.*.....676
Eccl 12:6 *the golden bowl is **b-n**.*...............683
Matt 26:26 *Then he **b** it in pieces*............1457
Mark 14:22 *Then he **b** it in pieces*............1457
Luke 20:18 *stone will be **b-n** to pieces,* 1438
John 19:36 *of his bones will be **b-n**,* 1487
Rom 11:20 *those branches were **b-n** off* ..1665
1 Cor 11:24 *Then he **b** it in pieces* 1613
2 Tim 1:10 *He **b** the power of death.*.........1741
Jas 2:10 *who has **b-n** all of God's laws*....1549

BROKENHEARTED (n) those who are overcome by grief or despair
Ps 34:18 *The LORD is close to the **b**;*..........459
Ps 109:16 *he hounded the **b** to death*.........582
Ps 147:3 *He heals the **b** and*...................1154

BROTHER, BROTHERS (n) male family members with the same parents; kinsmen in the extended family, church, or nation; co-workers in ministry; fellow believers, followers, or friends in Christ
Ps 133:1 ***b-s** live together in harmony!*.......584
Prov 18:24 *friend sticks closer than a **b**.*.....654
Prov 27:10 *to ask your **b** for assistance.* 842
Mark 3:33 *Who are my **b-s?***...................1344
Mark 10:29 *given up house or **b-s** or* 1421
John 7:5 *even his **b-s** didn't believe* 1386
Heb 2:11 *ashamed to call them his **b-s*** 1764
Heb 13:1 *each other as **b-s** and sisters.* ...1782
Jas 2:15 *you see a **b** or sister* 1549
Jas 4:11 *against each other, dear **b-s*** 1552
1 Pet 1:22 *each other as **b-s** and sisters.* .1750
1 Pet 3:8 *Love each other as **b-s** and*.......1753
1 Jn 2:9 *a Christian **b** or sister,*.................1788
1 Jn 3:16 *for our **b-s** and sisters.*.............1791
1 Jn 3:17 *sees a **b** or sister in need.*..........1791
1 Jn 4:20 *hates a Christian **b** or sister,*.......1794
1 Jn 4:21 *love their Christian **b-s** and*.......1794
Rev 12:10 *the accuser of our **b-s** and* 1818

BROTHERLY (adj) natural or becoming to brothers; affectionate
2 Pet 1:7 *godliness with **b** affection,*.........1757

BROUGHT (v) to carry, lead, or otherwise cause something to move toward an end
Jer 40:2 *has **b** this disaster on this land,*...1086
Rom 5:12 *Adam's sin **b** death, so death*....1654
Eph 2:17 *He **b** this Good News*...............1708

BUILD, BUILDING, BUILDS, BUILT (v) to erect or construct; to edify or encourage; to increase, enlarge
Gen 6:14 ***B** a large boat from cypress*...........18
1 Kgs 6:14 *Solomon finished **b-ing** the* 612
Neh 4:17 *who were **b-ing** the wall.* 1209
Ps 127:1 *Unless the LORD **b-s** a house,*.......631
Prov 14:1 *A wise woman **b-s** her home,* 647
Prov 16:12 *his rule is **b-t** on justice.*...........651
Hag 1:9 ***b-ing** your own fine houses*.........1163
Matt 7:24 *who **b-s** a house on solid rock*..1335
Matt 16:18 *rock I will **b** my church,*...........1375
Rom 14:19 *try to **b** each other up.*............1670
1 Cor 3:10 *Now others are **b-ing** on it.*....1599
1 Cor 3:12 *Anyone who **b-s** on that*..........1599
2 Cor 10:8 *But our authority **b-s** you up;*...1638
Eph 2:20 ***b-t** on the foundation of the*.......1708
Eph 4:12 *work and **b** up the church,*.........1711
Col 2:7 *let your lives be **b-t** on him.*..........1697
1 Thes 5:11 *and **b** each other up, just as*..1585
Heb 3:3 *as a person who **b-s** a house* 1764
1 Pet 2:5 *God is **b-ing** into his spiritual* 1750
Jude 1:20 *friends, must **b** each other up*...1785

BUILDER, BUILDERS (n) one who builds
Ps 118:22 *The stone that the **b-s** rejected* 876
Mark 12:10 *stone that the **b-s** rejected* 1438
Acts 4:11 *The stone that you **b-s** rejected*...1519
1 Cor 3:10 *foundation like an expert **b**.*.....1599
1 Cor 3:14 *that **b** will receive a reward.*.....1599
Heb 3:4 *For every house has a **b**,*...............1765
1 Pet 2:7 *The stone that the **b-s** rejected*..1750

BUILDING (n) a walled structure built for permanent use; figurative of the Church
1 Cor 3:9 *You are God's **b**.*.........................1599

BULL, BULLS (n) a male, adult, uncastrated bovine
Lev 4:3 *a young **b** with no defects.* 205
Heb 10:4 *the blood of **b-s** and goats* 1774

BURDEN, BURDENS (n) a (usually) heavy load to be borne—physically, emotionally, or spiritually
Ps 38:4 *a **b** too heavy to bear.*......................568
Matt 11:28 *weary and carry heavy **b-s**,* 1339
Matt 11:30 *the **b** I give you is light*...........1340
Acts 15:28 *to lay no greater **b** on you*.......1571
2 Cor 11:9 *a financial **b** to anyone.*...........1640
2 Cor 11:28 *the daily **b** of my concern*......1641
2 Cor 12:14 *I will not be a **b** to you.*..........1642
Gal 6:2 *Share each other's **b-s**,*.................1567
1 Thes 2:9 *so that we would not be a **b*** 1582
2 Thes 3:8 *so we would not be a **b***...........1590

BURDENED (v) to load; to oppress
Isa 43:23 *I have not **b** and wearied you.*.....929
Isa 43:24 *Instead, you have **b** me*..............929
2 Tim 3:6 *are **b** with the guilt of sin* 1744

BURGLAR (n) one who enters a building with the intent to commit a crime
Luke 12:39 *when a **b** was coming,* 1401

BURLAP (n) a coarse, heavy, plain-woven fabric usually of jute or hemp used for bagging and wrapping
Dan 9:3 *I also wore rough **b***......................1142
Matt 11:21 *clothing themselves in **b***.........1339

BURN, BURNED, BURNING (v) to consume by fire; to be emotionally excited or agitated; to produce or undergo discomfort or pain
see also BURNING, BURNT
Exod 27:20 *keep the lamps **b-ing***..............178
Lev 6:9 *must be kept **b-ing** all night*...........208
Deut 7:5 *Asherah poles and **b** their idols*.....296
Ps 79:5 *will your jealousy **b** like fire?* 600
Isa 30:27 *far away, **b-ing** with anger,* 901
Jer 23:29 *Does not my word **b** like fire?*....1028
Luke 24:32 *"Didn't our hearts **b** within us*...1494
Rom 1:27 ***b-ed** with lust for each other*.....1648
1 Cor 7:9 *to marry than to **b** with lust*........1605

BURNER, BURNERS (n) the part of a fuel-burning device where the flame or heat is produced
Lev 16:12 *an incense **b** with burning coals* ...222
Num 16:6 *prepare your incense **b-s**.* 256

BURNING (adj) being on fire
see also BURN, BURNT
Prov 25:22 *heap **b** coals of shame* 840
Rom 12:20 *heap **b** coals of shame* 1668
Rev 19:20 *fiery lake of **b** sulfur.* 1828

BURNISHED (adj) shiny or lustrous from rubbing; polished
1 Kgs 7:45 *these things of **b** bronze* 614
Ezek 1:7 *shone like **b** bronze.* 1045

BURNT (adj) marked by alteration or destruction by fire
see also BURN
Gen 22:2 *sacrifice him as a **b** offering* 45
Exod 18:12 *brought a **b** offering* 166
Lev 1:3 *present as a **b** offering* 202
Josh 8:31 *they presented **b** offerings* 348
Judg 6:26 *Sacrifice the bull as a **b*** 384
Judg 13:16 *a **b** offering as a sacrifice* 397
1 Kgs 3:4 *sacrificed 1,000 **b** offerings.* 606
Ezra 3:2 *to sacrifice **b** offerings* 1155

BURY, BURIED (v) to deposit in the earth or in a tomb; figurative of denying oneself and submitting to Christ
Deut 34:6 *The LORD **b-ied** him* 328
Ruth 1:17 *and there I will be **b-ied.*** 410
Mark 6:29 *get his body and **b-ied** it in* 1362
Luke 9:60 *dead **b** their own dead!* 1388
Luke 23:30 *plead with the hills, '**B** us.'* 1482
Rom 6:4 *and were **b-ied** with Christ* 1655
1 Cor 15:4 ***b-ied,** and he was raised* 1620
Col 2:12 *For you were **b-ied** with Christ* ...1698

BUSH (n) a low, densely branched shrub
Exod 3:2 *fire from the middle of a **b.*** 143
Mark 12:26 *story of the burning **b?*** 1440
Luke 20:37 *wrote about the burning **b.*** 1441
Acts 7:35 *him in the burning **b,*** 1525

BUSINESS (n) economic dealings; affair or matter
Gen 40:8 *Interpreting dreams is God's **b,*** 78
Ps 112:5 *conduct their **b** fairly.* 873
1 Thes 4:11 *minding your own **b** and* 1584
2 Thes 3:11 *meddling in other people's **b.*** 1590
1 Tim 5:13 *meddling in other people's **b*** ...1733

BUSY (adj) engaged in action; occupied
1 Kgs 20:40 *I was **b** doing something* 723
Eccl 11:6 *keep **b** all afternoon,* 682
Hag 1:9 ***b** building your own fine houses* ...1163

BUY, BUYS (v) to purchase; to redeem; to hire, bribe
see also BOUGHT
Prov 31:16 *to inspect a field and **b-s** it;* 847
Gal 4:5 *sent him to **b** freedom for us* 1563
Rev 13:17 *no one could **b** or sell* 1820

CAESAR (n) a title applied to several emperors of the Roman Empire
Matt 22:21 *to **C** what belongs to **C,*** 1439

CALF (n) the young of a domestic cow
Exod 32:4 *it into the shape of a **c.*** 184
Luke 15:23 *kill the **c** we have been* 1411
Acts 7:41 *made an idol shaped like a **c,*** 1525

CALL, CALLED, CALLING, CALLS (v) to make a request or demand; to designate or name
see also CHOSE, CHOSEN
Gen 2:23 *She will be **c-ed** 'woman,'* 10
1 Kgs 18:24 ***c** on the name of your god,* 717
2 Kgs 5:11 *leprosy and **c** on the name* 744
2 Chr 7:14 *who are **c-ed** by my name* 623
Ps 147:4 *stars and **c-s** them all by name.* .1154
Isa 40:26 ***c-ing** each by its name* 924
Isa 45:3 *the one who **c-s** you by name.* 931
Isa 56:7 *Temple will be **c-ed** a house of* 943
Hos 11:1 *I **c-ed** my son out of Egypt* 814
Joel 2:32 *everyone who **c-s** on the name* ...1242
Matt 2:15 *I **c-ed** my Son out of Egypt.* 1285
Matt 9:13 *I have come to **c** not those* 1315
Matt 22:14 *many are **c-ed,** but few are* 1438
Matt 22:43 ***c** the Messiah 'my Lord'?* 1442
Mark 2:17 *I have come to **c** not those* 1315
Mark 10:49 *Come on, he's **c-ing** you!* 1425
Luke 1:32 ***c-ed** the Son of the Most High.* ..1274
Luke 23:15 *this man has done **c-s*** 1480
Acts 2:21 *everyone who **c-s** on the name* .1515
Acts 2:39 *have been **c-ed** by the Lord* 1516
Acts 9:14 *arrest everyone who **c-s** upon* ...1530
Acts 22:16 *sins washed away by **c-ing** on* 1679
Rom 1:6 ***c-ed** to belong to Jesus* 1645
Rom 8:28 ***c-ed** according to his purpose* ..1660
Rom 10:12 *to all who **c** on him* 1664
Rom 10:13 *Everyone who **c-s** on the* 1664
Rom 11:29 ***c** can never be withdrawn* 1666
1 Cor 1:2 *who have been **c-ed** by God* 1594
1 Cor 1:2 ***c** on the name of our Lord* 1594
1 Cor 1:24 ***c-ed** by God to salvation,* 1597
1 Cor 7:17 *when God first **c-ed** you* 1606
Gal 1:6 *so soon from God, who **c-ed*** 1555
Gal 5:13 *been **c-ed** to live in freedom,* 1565
Eph 1:18 *to those he **c-ed**—his holy* 1706
Col 3:15 *you are **c-ed** to live in peace.* 1701
1 Thes 2:12 ***c-ed** you to share in his* 1582
1 Thes 4:7 *God has **c-ed** us to live holy* 1584
1 Thes 5:24 *he who **c-s** you is faithful* 1587
2 Tim 2:22 *those who **c** on the Lord* 1743
Heb 9:15 *all who are **c-ed** can receive* 1773
1 Pet 2:9 *he **c-ed** you out of the darkness* ..1751
1 Pet 3:9 *what God has **c-ed** you to do,* 1753
1 Pet 5:10 *God **c-ed** you to share in his* ...1756
2 Pet 1:10 *are among those God has **c-ed*** 1757

CALLING (n) a strong inner impulse toward a particular course of action; an occupation or vocation
Eph 4:1 *to lead a life worthy of your **c,*** 1710

CALM (v) to make still; to free from agitation, excitement, or disturbance
Zeph 3:17 *he will **c** all your fears.* 986

CALVARY (KJV)
Luke 23:33 *place called **The Skull,*** 1483

CAME (v) to originate or proceed from
see also COME
John 1:17 *faithfulness **c** through Jesus* 1272
Heb 7:14 *our Lord **c** from the tribe of* 1770

CAMEL (n) either of two large ruminant mammals used as draft and saddle animals in desert regions especially of Africa and Asia
Matt 19:24 *easier for a **c** to go through* 1420
Matt 23:24 *but you swallow a **c!*** 1444

CANAAN (n) region along the Mediterranean Sea taken and settled by the Israelites
Num 33:51 *Jordan River into the land of **C,*** ...281
1 Chr 16:18 ***C** as your special possession* ...493
Ps 105:11 ***C** as your special possession* 869
Acts 13:19 *destroyed seven nations in **C*** ...1541

CANCEL, CANCELED (v) to destroy the force, effectiveness, or validity of; to annul
Deut 15:1 *year you must **c** the debts* 305
Matt 15:6 *so you **c** the word of God* 1369
Col 2:14 ***c-ed** the record of the charges* ...1698

CANDLE (n) a usually molded or dipped mass of wax or tallow containing a wick that may be burned
Isa 42:3 *or put out a flickering **c.*** 926
Matt 12:20 *or put out a flickering **c.*** 1322

CANDLESTICK(S) (KJV)
Exod 25:31 *Make a **lampstand** of pure,* 176
Dan 5:5 *palace, near the **lampstand.*** 1138
Matt 5:15 *a lamp is placed on a **stand*** 1327
Heb 9:2 *a **lampstand,** a table, and* 1772
Rev 1:12 *I saw seven gold **lampstands*** 1800

CANOPY (n) a cover (as of cloth) fixed or carried above a person of high rank or a sacred object; a protective covering
2 Kgs 16:18 *he also removed the **c** that* 798
Isa 4:5 *He will provide a **c** of cloud* 828
Isa 51:16 *stretched out the sky like a **c*** 939
Jer 43:10 *spread his royal **c** over them.* 1107

CAPSTONE, HEADSTONE (KJV)
Ps 118:22 *become the **cornerstone*** 876
Zech 4:7 *the **final stone** of the Temple* 1169
Matt 21:42 *now become the **cornerstone.*** ..1437
Luke 20:17 *now become the **cornerstone.*** 1438

CAPTIVE (adj) (people) taken and held against their will
Prov 5:22 *is held **c** by his own sins;* 637
Acts 8:23 *and are held **c** by sin.* 1528
2 Tim 2:26 *they have been held **c.*** 1743

CAPTIVES (n) prisoners
Ps 68:18 *you led a crowd of **c.*** 576
Isa 60:11 *led as **c** in a victory* 947
Isa 61:1 *that **c** will be released* 948
Luke 4:18 *that **c** will be released,* 1357

CAPTIVITY (n) imprisonment, exile; subjection or subservience
Deut 28:41 *they will be led away into **c.*** 318

CAPTURE, CAPTURED (v) an act of catching, winning, or gaining control by force, stratagem, or guile
1 Sam 4:11 *The Ark of God was **c-ed,*** 423
2 Sam 5:7 *David **c-ed** the fortress of Zion,* 487
Song 4:9 *You have **c-ed** my heart,* 666
2 Cor 10:5 *We **c** their rebellious* 1638
Col 2:8 ***c** you with empty philosophies* 1698

CARCASS (n) a dead body; corpse
Judg 14:9 *honey from the **c** of the lion* 398
Matt 24:28 *vultures shows there is a **c*** 1446

CARE, CARED, CARES, CARING (v) to feel interest or concern; to attend to or provide for the needs, operation, or treatment of
Deut 1:31 *LORD your God **c-d** for you* 286
Ps 8:4 *human beings that you should **c.*** 548
Ps 37:17 *LORD takes **c** of the godly.* 567
Ps 65:9 *take **c** of the earth and* 575
Ps 116:15 ***c-s** deeply when his loved* 875
Ps 138:6 *is great, he **c-s** for the humble,* 585
Prov 12:10 *godly **c** for their animals,* 645
Prov 27:23 *into **c-ing** for your herds,* 842
Isa 53:8 ***c-d** that he died without* 940
Jer 23:2 *Instead of **c-ing** for my flock* 1027
Matt 6:30 *if God **c-s** so wonderfully for* 1332
Matt 25:36 *sick, and you **c-d** for me.* 1453
Luke 10:34 *an inn, where he took **c** of* 1396
John 10:13 *really **c** about the sheep.* 1405
John 12:25 *who **c** nothing for their life* 1432

John 21:16 *Then take* ***c*** *of my sheep,*.......1497
Eph 5:29 *just as Christ* ***c-s*** *for the church.*........1714
Phil 2:21 *others* ***c*** *only for themselves*......1720
1 Thes 2:7 ***c-ing*** *for her own children*.......1582
1 Tim 5:14 *take* ***c*** *of their own homes*.......1733
1 Tim 5:16 *she must take* ***c*** *of them and*...1733
Heb 2:6 *that you should* ***c*** *for him?*...........1763
1 Pet 5:2 ***C*** *for the flock that God*............1756
1 Pet 5:7 *and cares to God, for he* ***c-s***......1756

CAREFUL (adj) marked by wary caution; meticulous
Exod 34:12 ***c*** *never to make a treaty*..........187
Lev 18:4 *and be* ***c*** *to obey my decrees,*.......224
Lev 22:2 *be very* ***c*** *with the sacred gifts*......229
Lev 26:3 *are* ***c*** *to obey my commands,*.......234
Deut 4:9 *But watch out! Be* ***c*** *never to*.........290
Deut 6:3 *and be* ***c*** *to obey.*........................294
Deut 8:1 *Be* ***c*** *to obey all the commands*.....296
Deut 12:1 ***c*** *to obey when you live in*..........301
Deut 12:28 *Be* ***c*** *to obey all my*.................302
Josh 1:7 *and very courageous. Be* ***c***...........336
Josh 23:11 *be very* ***c*** *to love the LORD*.........368
2 Kgs 21:8 *Israelites will be* ***c*** *to obey*.........954
1 Cor 8:9 *be* ***c*** *so that your freedom*.........1608
1 Cor 10:12 *strong, be* ***c*** *not to fall.*..........1610
Eph 5:15 *So be* ***c*** *how you live*.................1713

CAREFULLY (adv) scrupulously attentive
Deut 11:13 ***c*** *obey all the commands*..........300
2 Kgs 18:6 *he* ***c*** *obeyed all the commands*..800
Prov 5:1 *to my wisdom; listen* ***c***..................637
1 Cor 15:34 ***c*** *about what is right, and stop*........1621
Heb 2:1 *must listen very* ***c*** *to the truth*......1763
Heb 3:1 *think* ***c*** *about this Jesus*..............1764

CARNAL(LY) (KJV)
Rom 7:14 ***all too human,*** *a slave to sin*....1658
Rom 8:6 *letting your* ***sinful nature*** *control*..1659
1 Cor 3:3 *still* ***controlled by your sinful nature***........1599
2 Cor 10:4 *not* ***worldly*** *weapons*.............1638

CAROUSE, CAROUSING (v) to drink liquor freely or excessively
Prov 23:20 *Do not* ***c*** *with drunkards*...........661
Luke 21:34 *your hearts be dulled by* ***c-ing***........1451

CARPENTER (n) a worker who builds or repairs wooden structures or their structural parts
Matt 13:55 *He's just the* ***c's*** *son,*...............1356
Mark 6:3 *He's just a* ***c,*** *the son of Mary*.....1357

CARRY, CARRIED, CARRIES (v) to transport or convey; to sustain the weight of; to bring to a successful end
Exod 19:4 *how I* ***c-ied*** *you on eagles'*.........167
Lev 16:22 *will* ***c*** *all the people's sins*...........222
Deut 32:11 *to take them up and* ***c-ied***.......324
Ps 68:19 *For each day he* ***c-ies*** *us in his*....576
Ps 103:20 *ones who* ***c*** *out his plans,*..........580
Isa 40:11 ***c*** *the lambs in his arms,*...............924
Isa 53:4 *it was our weaknesses he* ***c-ied;***...940
Isa 63:9 *He lifted them up and* ***c-ied***..........950
Luke 14:27 *do not* ***c*** *your own cross*.........1409
Col 4:17 *Be sure to* ***c*** *out the ministry*.......1703
1 Pet 2:24 *He personally* ***c-ied*** *our sins*.....1752
2 Pet 3:17 *not be* ***c-ied*** *away by the errors*........1760

CAST, CASTING (v) to toss (dice); to drive out
Lev 16:8 *He is to* ***c*** *sacred lots to*...............221
Matt 10:1 *authority to* ***c*** *out evil spirits*......1358
Matt 12:26 *if Satan is* ***c-ing*** *out Satan,*......1341

CATCH (v) to entangle; to seize and hold firmly
see also CAUGHT
Luke 5:4 *let down your nets to* ***c*** *some fish.* 1308

CATTLE (n) bovine animals on a farm or ranch
Ps 50:10 *I own the* ***c*** *on a thousand*...........593

CAUGHT (v) to get entangled; to seize and hold firmly
see also CATCH
Gen 22:13 *saw a ram* ***c*** *by its horns*............46
Prov 6:2 *and are* ***c*** *by what you said—*.......638
2 Cor 12:2 *I was* ***c*** *up to the third heaven*....1641
1 Thes 4:17 *will be* ***c*** *up in the clouds*.......1585

CAUTION (n) prudent forethought to minimize risk; precaution; warning
Jude 1:23 *with great* ***c,*** *hating the sins*.....1786

CEASE (v) to come to an end; to discontinue
Lam 3:22 *His mercies never* ***c.***................1098

CELEBRATE, CELEBRATED, CELEBRATING (v) to perform (a sacrament or ceremony) publicly and with appropriate rites; to observe a notable occasion with festivities
Exod 10:9 *together in* ***c-ing*** *a festival*.........154
Exod 12:47 *Israel must* ***c*** *this Passover*.......158
Exod 13:5 *You must* ***c*** *this event in this*.......158
Exod 23:14 ***c*** *three festivals in my*.............173
Exod 34:18 ***c*** *the Festival of Unleavened*.....188
Exod 34:22 ***c*** *the Festival of the Final*.........188
Num 9:2 ***c*** *the Passover at the*..................200
Deut 16:1 *your God,* ***c*** *the Passover*...........305
2 Sam 6:21 *so I* ***c*** *before the LORD*.............494
2 Kgs 23:21 ***c*** *the Passover to the LORD*......973
2 Chr 30:1 *Jerusalem to* ***c*** *the Passover*......836
2 Chr 30:13 ***c*** *the Festival of Unleavened*....837
2 Chr 30:23 ***c-d*** *joyfully for another*...........837
Neh 8:12 *to* ***c*** *with great joy*....................1215
Esth 8:15 *people of Susa* ***c-d*** *the new*......1192
Esth 9:19 *villages* ***c*** *an annual festival*.......1193
Esth 9:21 *to* ***c*** *an annual festival*..............1193
Matt 25:21 *Let's* ***c*** *together!*...................1452
Luke 15:23 *We must* ***c*** *with a feast,*..........1411
Luke 15:32 *We had to* ***c*** *this happy day*.....1411
John 18:28 *to* ***c*** *the Passover.*.................1477
Col 2:16 *for not* ***c-ing*** *certain holy days*....1699
Rev 11:10 *to* ***c*** *the death of the two prophets*........1817

CELEBRATION, CELEBRATIONS (n) a party or festival in honor of a religious ceremony or holiday; the observation of a notable occasion with festivities
Num 9:3 *regulations concerning this* ***c.***........200
2 Sam 6:12 *City of David with a great* ***c.***.....491
Esth 8:17 *had a great* ***c*** *and declared*.......1192
Jer 31:13 *young—will join in the* ***c.***..........1033
Joel 1:16 *No joyful* ***c-s*** *are held in the*......1240
Zech 8:19 ***c*** *for the people of Judah.*.........1174
John 11:55 *for the Jewish Passover* ***c,***.....1415

CENSUS (n) count of population, sometimes including assessment of property value
2 Sam 24:1 *to harm them by taking a* ***c.***.....529
Luke 2:1 *that a* ***c*** *should be taken*............1280

CENTURION (KJV)
Matt 8:5 ***Roman officer*** *came and*...........1335
Luke 7:2 *slave of a* ***Roman officer*** *was sick*........1336
Acts 10:1 ***Roman army officer*** *named Cornelius*........1532

CEPHAS (n) rock; Aramaic name of Simon Peter, given to him by Christ
John 1:42 *called* ***C"*** *(which means*...........1298

CEREMONIAL (adj) marked by, involved in, or belonging to ceremony; stressing careful attention to form and detail
Lev 14:2 *seeking* ***c*** *purification from a*........218
John 2:6 *used for Jewish* ***c*** *washing.*........1299
John 3:25 *Jew over* ***c*** *cleansing.*.............1302
Heb 9:13 *bodies from* ***c*** *impurity.*.............1773

CEREMONIALLY (adv) in accordance with law and custom
Lev 4:12 *the camp that is* ***c*** *clean,*..............206
Lev 6:11 *to a place that is* ***c*** *clean.*............208
Lev 10:14 *eaten in any place that is* ***c*** *clean.*........214
Lev 12:2 *she will be* ***c*** *unclean for seven*.....216
Lev 13:3 *pronounce the person* ***c*** *unclean*...216
Lev 15:13 *water, and he will be* ***c*** *clean*.......220
Lev 15:33 *intercourse with a woman who is* ***c*** *unclean*........221
Lev 21:1 ***c*** *unclean by touching*...............227
Lev 22:3 *any of your descendants is* ***c***........228
Num 5:2 *who has become* ***c*** *unclean by*.......243
Num 9:6 *the men had been* ***c*** *defiled*..........200
Num 18:11 *your family who is* ***c*** *clean*........259
Num 19:7 ***c*** *unclean until evening*...............260
Num 19:18 *someone who is* ***c*** *clean must*..261
Deut 12:22 *whether* ***c*** *clean or unclean,*......302
Deut 14:7 *so they are* ***c*** *unclean for you.*......304
1 Sam 20:26 *made David* ***c*** *unclean.*...........456

CEREMONY, CEREMONIES (n) a formal act or series of acts prescribed by ritual, protocol, or convention
Exod 12:25 *continue to observe this* ***c.***......156
Exod 12:26 *ask, 'What does this* ***c*** *mean?'*........156
Neh 12:27 *to assist in the* ***c-ies.***.............1221
Acts 24:18 *completing a purification* ***c.***......1682
Heb 9:10 *and various cleansing* ***c-ies—***..1772

CERTAIN (adj) assured in mind or action; dependable, reliable; known or proved to be true, indisputable
Josh 23:13 *know for* ***c*** *that the LORD*..........368
Eccl 7:14 *nothing is* ***c*** *in this life.*...............679
Luke 1:4 *so you can be* ***c*** *of the truth*........1270
Phil 1:6 ***c*** *that God, who began the good work*........1717
Heb 6:11 *to make* ***c*** *that what you hope*....1768

CHAFF (n) the seed coverings and other debris separated from the seed in threshing grain; something comparatively worthless
Ps 1:4 ***c,*** *scattered by the wind.*................856
Ps 35:5 *Blow them away like* ***c*** *in the*..........565
Dan 2:35 *like* ***c*** *on a threshing floor*..........1004
Matt 3:12 *separate the* ***c*** *from the*............1289

CHAIN, CHAINS (n) metal links or rings connected to one another and used for various purposes
Prov 1:9 *a* ***c*** *of honor around your neck*.......632
Acts 26:29 *as I am, except for these* ***c-s."***........1686
Eph 6:20 *I am in* ***c-s*** *now, still preaching*........1716
Col 4:18 *Remember my* ***c-s.***....................1703
2 Tim 1:16 *because I was in* ***c-s.***............1741

CHAINED (v) to fasten, bind, or connect with or as with a chain; to obstruct
2 Tim 2:9 *the word of God cannot be* ***c.***.....1742
Jude 1:6 ***c*** *in prisons of darkness,*............1784

CHALLENGE (v) to put to a test or trial; to dispute with
Jer 49:19 *like me, and who can* ***c*** *me?*.....1025

CHANCE (n) something that happens unpredictably without discernible human intention or cause, luck; a situation favoring some purpose, opportunity
1 Sam 18:21 *another **c** to see him killed*.....453
Eccl 9:11 *all decided by **c**, by being*............681
Jer 15:6 *giving you another **c**.*..................1018
Phil 4:10 *didn't have the **c** to help*..............1725

CHANGE, CHANGED, CHANGES (v) to make different or transform; to shift, exchange, or transfer
Exod 32:14 *the LORD **c-d** his mind about*....185
1 Sam 10:6 *be **c-d** into a different person.*...437
1 Sam 15:29 *human that he should **c***.........447
Ps 93:5 *Your royal laws cannot be **c-d**.*.......862
Isa 14:27 *who can **c** his plans?*.................832
Jer 33:25 *than I would **c** my laws*...............1081
Jonah 3:9 *even yet God will **c** his mind*.......768
Mal 3:6 *I am the LORD, and I do not **c**.*........1248
2 Cor 3:18 *we are **c-d** into his glorious*.....1630
Heb 6:17 *he would never **c** his mind*.........1769
Jas 1:17 *never **c-s** or casts a shifting*.........1547

CHARACTER (n) moral excellence and firmness; main or essential nature
Rom 5:4 *develops strength of **c**,*..............1654
1 Cor 15:33 *corrupts good **c**.*....................1621
Heb 1:3 *expresses the very **c** of God,*........1761

CHARGE, CHARGES (n) management, supervision; obligation, requirement; a formal assertion of illegality or statement of complaint
Deut 19:18 *brought false **c-s** against*.........309
Ps 8:6 *gave them **c** of everything you*.........548
Prov 23:11 *bring their **c-s** against you.*.......661
Isa 50:8 *dare to bring **c-s** against me*.........937
Mic 6:2 *will bring **c-s** against Israel.*...........909
1 Cor 4:1 *in **c** of explaining God's*............1600
1 Cor 4:2 *in **c** as a manager must be*........1600

CHARGE, CHARGED, CHARGING (v) to impose a financial burden on; to command, instruct, or exhort with authority
Ps 119:4 ***c-d** us to keep your commandments*.......................................877
1 Cor 9:18 *the Good News without **c-ing***..1609
Phlm 1:18 *owes you anything, **c** it to me*...1692

CHARIOT, CHARIOTS (n) a two-wheeled horse-drawn battle car of ancient times used also in processions and races
2 Kgs 2:11 *suddenly a **c** of fire appeared,*...739
2 Kgs 6:17 *with horses and **c-s** of fire*........745
Ps 20:7 *boast of their **c-s** and horses,*........555
Ps 68:17 *thousands of **c-s**, the LORD came*...576
Ps 104:3 *You make the clouds your **c**;*........867

CHARITY (KJV)
1 Cor 8:1 ***love** that strengthens the church*..1607
1 Cor 13:1 *but didn't **love** others, I would*...1616
Col 3:14 *clothe yourselves with **love**,*........1701
1 Tim 4:12 *in your **love**, your faith, and*.....1732
2 Pet 1:7 *with **love** for everyone*..............1757

CHARM (n) something worn about the person to ward off evil or ensure good fortune; a trait that fascinates, allures, or delights
Prov 17:8 *A bribe is like a lucky **c**;*.............652
Prov 31:30 ***C** is deceptive, and beauty*........848

CHASTE (KJV)
2 Cor 11:2 *a **pure** bride to one husband—*...1640
Titus 2:5 *to live wisely and be **pure***...........1738
1 Pet 3:2 ***pure** and reverent lives*.............1752

CHASTEN(ED) (KJV)
Ps 6:1 *or **discipline** me in your rage*...........548
Prov 19:18 ***Discipline** your children*...........655
1 Cor 11:32 ***being disciplined** so that we*..1614
Heb 12:11 *No **discipline** is enjoyable*.......1780
Rev 3:19 *I correct and **discipline**.*.............1807

CHEAT, CHEATED, CHEATING, CHEATS (v) to deprive of something valuable by deceit or fraud; to practice fraud or trickery
Gen 31:7 *he has **c-ed** me, changing my*.......63
1 Sam 12:3 *Have I ever **c-ed** any of you?*...440
1 Sam 12:4 *have never **c-ed** or oppressed*...440
Amos 8:5 *get back to **c-ing** the helpless*.....779
Mal 3:8 *You have **c-ed** me of the tithes*....1248
Mark 10:19 *You must not **c** anyone.*........1421
Mark 12:40 *they shamelessly **c** widows*.......1443
1 Cor 5:10 *are greedy, or **c** people,*...........1602
1 Cor 5:11 *is a drunkard, or **c-s** people.*...1602
1 Cor 6:7 *not let yourselves be **c-ed**?*.......1603
1 Cor 6:8 *who do wrong and **c** even*...........1603
1 Cor 6:10 *abusive, or **c** people—*..............1603

CHEEK (n) the fleshy side of the face below the eye and above and to the side of the mouth
Matt 5:39 *slaps you on the right **c**,*..........1329
Luke 6:29 *offer the other **c** also.*...............1330

CHEERFUL (adj) full of good spirits; merry, ungrudging
Prov 15:30 *A **c** look brings joy*...................650
Prov 17:22 *A **c** heart is good medicine,*.......653

CHEERFULLY (adv) marked by or suggestive of lighthearted ease of mind and spirit; cheerily, gladly
2 Cor 9:7 *loves a person who gives **c**.*.......1637
1 Pet 4:9 ***C** share your home with those*....1754

CHEERS (v) to instill with hope, joy, hilarity, or comfort
Prov 12:25 *encouraging word **c** a person*....645

CHERISH (v) to hold dear; to feel or show affection for
Ps 102:14 ***c** even the dust in her streets*....866
Prov 19:8 *people who **c** understanding*.......654

CHERUBIM (n) winged angelic beings, often associated with worship and praise of God
Gen 3:24 *God stationed mighty **c** to the*........13
Exod 25:19 *Mold the **c** on each end*...........176
1 Sam 4:4 *enthroned between the **c**.*..........423
1 Kgs 6:23 *He made two **c** of wild olive*......612
Isa 37:16 *between the mighty **c**!*................917
Ezek 10:1 *over the heads of the **c**.*...........1056

CHEST (n) a wooden box or container; the trunk or rib cage of the human body
Exod 25:10 *a sacred **c** 45 inches long,*.......176
2 Kgs 12:9 *a hole in the lid of a large **c**.*......756
Zech 13:6 *those wounds on your **c**?*..........1179
Rev 1:13 *with a gold sash across his **c**.*....1800

CHESTPIECE (n) a breastplate attached to the front of an ephod worn by the high priest
Exod 28:15 *make a **c** to be worn for*...........179

CHILD, CHILDREN (n) an unborn or recently born person; a young person between infancy and youth, not yet of age; offspring or descendants
see also SON(S)
Exod 20:5 *family is affected—even **c-ren***..168
Deut 24:16 *sins of their **c-ren**, nor **c-ren***...314
Deut 32:46 *as a command to your **c-ren***....325
1 Kgs 3:26 *Give her the **c**—please do*........608
Job 1:5 *Perhaps my **c-ren** have sinned*........94
Ps 8:2 *have taught **c-ren** and infants*..........548
Prov 20:7 *blessed are their **c-ren** who*........656
Prov 23:13 *discipline your **c-ren**.*...............661
Prov 29:15 *To discipline a **c** produces*.........845
Prov 31:28 *Her **c-ren** stand and bless*........848
Isa 7:14 *The virgin will conceive a **c**!*..........790
Isa 9:6 *For a **c** is born to us,*......................793
Isa 54:13 *I will teach all your **c-ren**,*...........941
Mal 4:6 *hearts of **c-ren** to their fathers*.....1249
Matt 1:23 *The virgin will conceive a **c**!*......1278
Matt 5:9 *will be called the **c-ren** of God*....1326
Matt 18:3 *and become like little **c-ren**,*.....1383
Mark 9:37 *welcomes a little **c** like this*......1383
Mark 10:14 *Let the **c-ren** come to me*......1419
Mark 10:16 *took the **c-ren** in his arms*.....1420
Luke 1:42 *and your **c** is blessed.*..............1275
Luke 6:35 *as **c-ren** of the Most High,*........1330
Luke 18:15 *their little **c-ren** to Jesus.*.......1420
John 1:12 *to become **c-ren** of God.*..........1271
John 12:36 *become **c-ren** of the light.*......1434
Acts 2:39 *to your **c-ren**, and even to the*....1516
Rom 9:26 *called '**c-ren** of the living God.'*...1662
1 Cor 13:11 *and reasoned as a **c**.*............1616
Gal 3:26 *you are all **c-ren** of God*.............1562
Eph 3:6 *riches inherited by God's **c-ren**.*...1708
Eph 6:1 ***C-ren**, obey your parents*............1714
Eph 6:4 *not provoke your **c-ren** to anger*..1714
Col 3:21 *do not aggravate your **c-ren**,*.......1702
1 Tim 3:4 *having **c-ren** who respect and*..1730
1 Tim 3:12 *manage his **c-ren** and*............1731
1 Tim 5:10 *brought up her **c-ren** well?*.....1733
Heb 12:7 *treating you as his own **c-ren**.*...1780
1 Jn 4:7 *who loves is a **c** of God*...............1793
1 Jn 5:4 *every **c** of God defeats this evil*....1794
1 Jn 5:18 *God's **c-ren** do not make a*.......1795

CHILDISH (adj) of, relating to, or befitting a child; marked by or suggestive of immaturity
1 Cor 13:11 *I put away **c** things*...............1616
1 Cor 14:20 *brothers and sisters, don't be **c**.*...1617

CHILDLESS (adj) a person characterized by lack of children; barren
Ps 113:9 *He gives the **c** woman a family,*....874
Isa 54:1 *Sing, O **c** woman, you who*...........941
Gal 4:27 *Rejoice, O **c** woman, you who*.....1564

CHILDLIKE (adj) resembling, suggesting, or appropriate to a child; marked by innocence, trust, and ingenuousness
Ps 116:6 *protects those of **c** faith;*.............875
Matt 11:25 *revealing them to the **c**.*..........1339

CHOOSE, CHOOSES (v) to decide; to have a preference for; to select freely and after consideration
see also CALL, CHOSE
Deut 30:19 *Oh, that you would **c** life, so*......321
Josh 24:15 ***c** today whom you will serve.*....370
Eccl 10:2 *A wise person **c-s** the right road;*...681
Jer 27:5 *things of mine to anyone I **c**.*.......1049
Dan 4:25 *gives them to anyone he **c-s**.*...1121
John 15:16 *You didn't **c** me. I chose you*...1464
Rom 9:11 *God **c-s** people according to*....1661
Rom 9:18 *he **c-s** to harden the hearts of*..1662

CHOSE, CHOSEN (v) to decide; to have a preference for
see also CALL, CHOOSE, CHOSEN
Matt 22:14 *called, but few are **c-n**.*..........1438
John 15:16 *You didn't choose me. I **c** you.*1464
Rom 1:1 ***c-n** by God to be an apostle*.......1644
Rom 8:29 ***c** them to become like his*.........1660
1 Cor 1:1 *Paul, **c-n** by the will of God*.......1594
1 Cor 1:27 ***c** things that are powerless*.....1597

Eph 1:4 *loved us and **c** us in Christ*...........1704
Eph 1:11 *God, for he **c** us in advance,*.......1705
2 Thes 2:13 *thankful that God **c** you*.........1589
1 Pet 1:15 *as God who **c** you is holy.*........1749
2 Pet 1:10 *God has called and **c-n**.*..........1757

CHOSEN (adj) selected or marked for special favor or privilege
see also CALLED
1 Chr 16:22 *Do not touch my **c** people,*.......493
Isa 41:8 *my **c** one, descended from Abraham*..925
Mark 13:20 *for the sake of his **c** ones*.......1449
Luke 23:35 *God's Messiah, the **C** One.*.....1484
John 1:34 *that he is the **C** One of God.*.....1297
1 Pet 1:1 *writing to God's **c** people*..........1747
1 Pet 2:9 *for you are a **c** people*...............1751

CHRIST (n) Son of God, Messiah, Anointed One
see also JESUS, MESSIAH
John 1:17 *faithfulness came through Jesus **C**.*..1272
Rom 1:4 *He is Jesus **C** our Lord.*..............1644
Rom 3:22 *by placing our faith in Jesus **C**.*.1651
Rom 5:1 *Jesus **C** our Lord has done*.........1654
Rom 5:6 ***C** came at just the right time*.......1654
Rom 5:11 ***C** has made us friends of God*...1654
Rom 6:4 *as **C** was raised from the dead*....1655
Rom 6:23 *eternal life through **C** Jesus*......1656
Rom 7:4 *when you died with **C**.*...............1657
Rom 8:1 *who belong to **C** Jesus.*..............1658
Rom 8:34 ***C** Jesus died for us and*............1661
Rom 8:35 *separate us from **C's** love?*.......1661
Rom 14:9 ***C** died and rose again for this*...1670
Rom 15:5 *fitting for followers of **C** Jesus*...1671
Rom 15:20 *where the name of **C** has never*..1671
1 Cor 1:2 *the name of our Lord Jesus **C**,*...1594
1 Cor 1:13 *Has **C** been divided into*...........1596
1 Cor 1:17 *cross of **C** would lose its power.*...1596
1 Cor 1:23 *preach that **C** was crucified,*....1597
1 Cor 1:30 *God has united you with **C***.......1597
1 Cor 5:7 ***C**, our Passover Lamb,*.............1602
1 Cor 6:15 *his body, which is part of **C**,*.....1604
1 Cor 8:12 *you are sinning against **C**.*.......1608
1 Cor 9:19 *to bring many to **C**.*................1609
1 Cor 10:4 *that rock was **C**.*....................1610
1 Cor 10:9 *Nor should we put **C** to the test,*...1610
1 Cor 11:3 *and the head of **C** is God.*........1612
1 Cor 12:27 *you together are **C's** body,*.....1615
1 Cor 15:3 ***C** died for our sins,*...............1618
2 Cor 1:5 *the more we suffer for **C**, the*.....1626
2 Cor 3:3 *you are a letter from **C***.............1629
2 Cor 3:14 *removed only by believing in **C**.*...1630
2 Cor 5:10 *stand before **C** to be judged.*...1632
2 Cor 5:14 ***C's** love controls us*................1632
2 Cor 5:20 *we are **C's** ambassadors;*........1633
Gal 1:7 *twist the truth concerning **C**.*.........1556
Gal 2:4 *the freedom we have in **C** Jesus.*..1558
Gal 2:21 *need for **C** to die.*.......................1560
Gal 3:13 *But **C** has rescued us*................1561
Gal 4:19 *continue until **C** is fully developed*..1563
Gal 5:4 *you have been cut off from **C**!*.......1565
Gal 5:24 *Those who belong to **C** Jesus*.....1567
Eph 1:3 *because we are united with **C**.*.....1704
Eph 1:10 *under the authority of **C**—*.........1705
Eph 1:20 *that raised **C** from the dead*.......1706
Eph 2:10 *created us anew in **C** Jesus,*.......1707
Eph 2:20 *the cornerstone is **C** Jesus*.........1708
Eph 4:7 *through the generosity of **C**.*.........1710
Eph 4:32 *God through **C** has forgiven you.*..1712
Eph 5:21 *out of reverence for **C**.*...............1713
Eph 5:23 *head of his wife as **C** is*.............1713
Eph 5:25 *wives, just as **C** loved the*...........1713
Phil 1:21 *living means living for **C**,*............1718
Phil 1:23 *with **C**, which would be far better*..1718
Phil 1:29 *the privilege of trusting in **C***.......1719
Phil 2:5 *same attitude that **C** Jesus had.*...1719
Phil 3:18 *enemies of the cross of **C**.*.........1724
Col 1:22 *through the death of **C***................1696
Col 2:2 *mysterious plan, which is **C***..........1697
Col 2:6 *accepted **C** Jesus as your Lord,*....1697
Col 2:13 *God made you alive with **C**,*.........1698
Col 3:1 *raised to new life with **C**,*..............1700
Col 3:3 *life is hidden with **C** in God.*..........1700
Col 3:15 *peace that comes from **C***...........1701
1 Thes 5:9 *through our Lord Jesus **C**,*.......1585
1 Tim 1:15 ***C** Jesus came into the world*...1728
1 Tim 2:5 *humanity—the man **C** Jesus*.....1729
2 Tim 1:10 *by the appearing of **C** Jesus,*...1741
2 Tim 2:3 *as a good soldier of **C** Jesus*......1742
2 Tim 2:10 *eternal glory in **C** Jesus*...........1742
2 Tim 3:12 *a godly life in **C** Jesus will*.......1744
2 Tim 3:15 *by trusting in **C** Jesus.*............1745
2 Tim 4:1 *of God and **C** Jesus, who will*.....1745
Titus 2:13 *and Savior, Jesus **C**, will be*......1738
Heb 3:14 *share in all that belongs to **C**.*....1765
Heb 6:1 *teachings about **C** again and*.......1768
Heb 9:14 *the blood of **C** will purify*............1773
Heb 9:28 ***C** died once for all time*............1774
Heb 10:10 *body of Jesus **C**, once for all*....1775
Heb 13:8 *Jesus **C** is the same yesterday,*..1782
1 Pet 1:11 *the Spirit of **C** within them*.......1749
1 Pet 1:19 *blood of **C**, the sinless,*............1749
1 Pet 2:21 *just as **C** suffered for you*.........1752
1 Pet 3:15 *you must worship **C** as Lord*.....1753
1 Pet 4:13 *partners with **C** in his suffering,*...1755
2 Pet 1:16 *coming of our Lord Jesus **C**.*....1758
1 Jn 2:1 *He is Jesus **C**, the one who is*.....1788
1 Jn 2:22 *says that Jesus is not the **C**.*.....1790
1 Jn 4:2 *that Jesus **C** came in a real*.........1792
1 Jn 5:1 *Jesus is the **C** has become*.........1794
1 Jn 5:20 *fellowship with his Son, Jesus **C**.*...1795
Rev 1:1 *from Jesus **C**, which God gave*.....1798
Rev 1:5 *his throne; and from Jesus **C**.*......1799
Rev 20:4 *and they reigned with **C** for*........1829
Rev 20:6 *God and of **C** and will reign*........1829

CHRISTIAN, CHRISTIANS (n) one who professes belief in and follows the teachings of Jesus Christ; believer
Acts 11:26 *believers were first called **C-s**.*...1536
Acts 26:28 *persuade me to become a **C***...1686
Gal 2:4 *some so-called **C-s***.....................1558
1 Thes 4:12 *people who are not **C-s***.........1584
1 Pet 4:14 *insulted for being a **C**,*............1755
1 Pet 4:16 *to suffer for being a **C**.*............1755
1 Pet 5:9 *your **C** brothers and sisters*........1756

CHURCH, CHURCHES (n) "assembly" or "called ones"; the body of believers gathered to worship Jesus (not the building in which they meet)
Matt 16:18 *this rock I will build my **c**,*.......1375
Matt 18:17 *take your case to the **c**.*..........1385
Acts 16:5 *the **c-es** were strengthened*......1573
Acts 20:28 *shepherd God's flock—his **c**,*..1675
1 Cor 15:9 *way I persecuted God's **c**.*.......1620
Gal 1:13 *I violently persecuted God's **c**.*.....1556
Eph 5:23 *Christ is the head of the **c**.*.........1713
Col 1:18 *head of the **c**, which is his*..........1695
Col 1:24 *continue for his body, the **c**.*.........1696
2 Thes 1:4 *tell God's other **c-es** about your*...1587
Rev 1:20 *angels of the seven **c-es**,*..........1801

CIRCUMCISE, CIRCUMCISED, CIRCUMCISING (v) to cut off the foreskin of a male child
Gen 17:10 *among you must be **c-d**.*.............38
Gen 17:12 ***c-d** on the eighth day after his*.....38
Josh 5:3 *made flint knives and **c-d***............342
John 7:23 *correct time for **c-ing** your son*..1390
Acts 21:21 *not to **c** their children*.............1677
Rom 4:11 *even before he was **c-d**.*............1653
1 Cor 7:19 *or not a man has been **c-d**.*.......1606

CIRCUMCISION (n) the condition of being circumcised; the ceremony signifying Israel's covenant with God; act symbolic of cleansing
Rom 2:25 ***c** has value only if you obey*......1650
Rom 2:29 *true **c** is not merely*..................1650
Gal 5:2 *If you are counting on **c** to make*...1565

CIRCUMSTANCES (n) conditions, facts, or events accompanying, conditioning, or determining another
1 Thes 5:18 *Be thankful in all **c**, for this*....1586

CITIZEN, CITIZENS (n) a person owing allegiance to and deriving protection from a sovereign state
Acts 22:28 *But I am a **c** by birth!*..............1679
Eph 2:19 *You are **c-s** along with*..............1708
Phil 3:20 *But we are **c-s** of heaven,*..........1724

CITIZENSHIP (n) the status of being a citizen; membership in a community
Eph 2:12 *excluded from **c** among*.............1708

CLAIM, CLAIMS (v) to assert in the face of possible contradiction; to take as the rightful owner
Eccl 8:17 *no matter what they **c**.*................680
Song 7:10 *and he **c-s** me as his own.*.........669
Isa 62:4 *delights in you and will **c** you*.........948
Jas 1:26 ***c** to be religious but don't*..........1548
1 Jn 1:10 *If we **c** we have not sinned,*.......1787
1 Jn 2:9 *If anyone **c-s**, "I am living in*.......1788

CLAP, CLAPPED (v) to strike (the hands) together repeatedly usually in applause
2 Kgs 11:12 *everyone **c-ped** their hands*....754
Ps 47:1 *everyone! **C** your hands!*...............852
Ps 98:8 *Let the rivers **c** their hands*...........865
Isa 55:12 *trees of the field will **c**.*..............942
Nah 3:19 *hear of your destruction will **c***......978

CLAY (n) an earthy material that is pliable when moist but hard when fired and is used for brick, tile, and pottery
Isa 45:9 *Does the **c** dispute with the one*.....931
Isa 64:8 ***c**, and you are the potter.*..............951
Lam 4:2 *are now treated like pots of **c***......1099
Dan 2:33 *of iron and baked **c**.*..................1004
Rom 9:21 *to use the same lump of **c***........1662
2 Cor 4:7 ***c** jars containing this great*........1631
2 Tim 2:20 *are made of wood and **c**.*........1743

CLEAN (adj) unadulterated, pure; without guilt or moral corruption; without ceremonial defilement
see also PURE
Lev 10:10 *unclean and what is **c**.*...............213
Ps 51:2 *Wash me **c** from my guilt*..............505
Ps 51:7 *and I will be **c**; wash me,*...............506

Ps 51:10 *Create in me a **c** heart, O God*.....506
John 13:10 *you disciples are **c,** but not all*.....1456
Acts 10:15 *if God has made it **c.***.....1533
2 Tim 2:21 *Your life will be **c,***.....1743

CLEANSE, CLEANSED, CLEANSES (v) to make clean, pure, holy
see also PURIFY, WASH
Ps 19:12 ***C** me from these hidden*.....555
Prov 20:9 *Who can say, "I have **c-d** my*.....656
Jer 4:14 *O Jerusalem, **c** your heart*.....964
Acts 15:9 *he **c-d** their hearts through*.....1569
1 Cor 6:11 *were **c-d;** you were made holy;*.....1603
2 Cor 7:1 *let us **c** ourselves from*.....1634
Titus 2:14 ***c** us, and to make us his*.....1738
Heb 1:3 *he had **c-d** us from our sins,*.....1761
Heb 9:13 *of a young cow could **c***.....1773
1 Pet 1:2 *and have been **c-d** by the blood*.....1747
1 Pet 1:22 *You were **c-d** from your sins*.....1750
2 Pet 1:9 *that they have been **c-d***.....1757
1 Jn 1:7 *blood of Jesus, his Son, **c-s** us*.....1787
1 Jn 1:9 *to **c** us from all wickedness*.....1787

CLEAR, CLEARED (v) to free from what obstructs or is unneeded
Ps 32:2 *whose record the LORD has **c-ed***.....564
John 1:23 ***C** the way for the Lord's coming!*.....1293
Rom 4:8 *whose record the LORD has **c-ed***.....1652

CLEARHEADED (adj) having or showing a clear understanding; able to think clearly
1 Thes 5:6 *Stay alert and be **c.***.....1585

CLEVER (adj) mentally quick and resourceful; marked by wit or ingenuity
Job 15:5 *are based on **c** deception*.....109
Isa 5:21 *and think themselves so **c.***.....829
Eph 4:14 *so **c** they sound like the truth*.....1711
2 Pet 1:16 *we were not making up **c** stories*.....1758

CLEVERNESS (n) the state of being mentally quick and resourceful; showing wit or ingenuity
1 Cor 3:19 *in the snare of their own **c.***.....1600

CLING (v) to adhere as if glued firmly; to hold or hold on tightly or tenaciously
Deut 10:20 *worship him and **c** to him.*.....300
Deut 13:4 *listen to his voice, and **c** to*.....303
Matt 10:39 *If you **c** to your life,*.....1361
Luke 8:15 *who hear God's word, **c** to it,*.....1347
John 20:17 *"Don't **c** to me," Jesus*.....1493
Phil 2:6 *as something to **c** to.*.....1720

CLOSE, CLOSED, CLOSES (v) to draw near; to contract, fold, swing, or slide so as to leave no opening
Gen 7:16 *Then the LORD **c-d** the door*.....19
Prov 28:27 *who **c** their eyes to poverty*.....844
Isa 22:22 *no one will be able to **c** them;*.....893
Acts 28:27 *and they have **c-d** their eyes—*.....1689
Rev 3:7 *what he **c-s,** no one can open:*.....1806
Rev 21:25 *Its gates will never be **c-d***.....1831

CLOSE, CLOSER (adv) being near in time, space, effect, or degree
Exod 3:5 *Do not come any **c-r,***.....143
Ps 34:18 *is **c** to the brokenhearted;*.....459
Ps 148:14 *of Israel who are **c** to him.*.....887
Prov 18:24 *sticks **c-r** than a brother.*.....654
Isa 40:11 *in his arms, holding them **c***.....924

CLOTHED (v) to dress; to endow especially with power or a quality
Ps 30:11 *mourning and **c** me with joy,*.....563
Prov 31:25 *She is **c** with strength*.....848
Rev 7:9 *They were **c** in white robes*.....1813
Rev 7:13 *these who are **c** in white?*.....1813

CLOTHES (n) cloth articles of personal use that can be worn and washed
Deut 8:4 *years your **c** didn't wear out,*.....297
Isa 50:9 *old **c** that have been eaten by*.....937
Matt 6:25 *food and drink, or enough **c***.....1332
Matt 27:35 *soldiers gambled for his **c***.....1482
John 19:23 *they divided his **c** among*.....1484
Gal 3:27 *like putting on new **c.***.....1562

CLOTHING (n) garments in general; covering
Gen 3:21 *God made **c** from animal skins*.....13
Deut 22:5 *must not put on men's **c,***.....312
Ps 22:18 *and throw dice for my **c.***.....556
Matt 6:28 *And why worry about your **c?***.....1332
1 Tim 6:8 *food and **c,** let us be content.*.....1735

CLOUD, CLOUDS (n) a visible mass of particles of condensed vapor suspended in the atmosphere
1 Kgs 18:44 *I saw a little **c** about the*.....718
Ps 68:4 *praises to him who rides the **c-s.***.....576
Ps 108:4 *faithfulness reaches to the **c-s.***.....581
Isa 19:1 *Egypt, riding on a swift **c.***.....889
Dan 7:13 *coming with the **c-s** of heaven*.....1136
Mark 13:26 *coming on the **c-s** with great*.....1449
Luke 21:27 *Son of Man coming on a **c***.....1450
1 Thes 4:17 *up in the **c-s** to meet the Lord*.....1585
Rev 1:7 *comes with the **c-s** of heaven.*.....1800
Rev 14:14 *I saw a white **c,** and seated on*.....1822

COALS (n) a piece of glowing carbon or charred wood; ember
Prov 25:22 *heap burning **c** of shame*.....840
Rom 12:20 *heap burning **c** of shame*.....1668

COARSE (adj) crude or unrefined in taste, manners, or language; harsh, raucous, or rough in tone
Eph 5:4 ***c** jokes—these are not for you.*.....1712

COAT (n) an outer garment worn on the upper body
Matt 5:40 *give your **c,** too.*.....1329
Luke 6:29 *your **c,** offer your shirt*.....1330

COIN, COINS (n) a usually flat piece of metal issued by governmental authority as money
Mark 12:15 *Show me a Roman **c,***.....1439
Mark 12:42 *dropped in two small **c-s.***.....1445
Luke 12:6 *sparrows—two copper **c-s?***.....1399
Luke 15:8 *woman has ten silver **c-s***.....1410

COLLAPSE (v) to cave or fall in or give way
Matt 7:25 *it won't **c** because it is built*.....1335
Luke 6:49 *it will **c** into a heap of ruins*.....1335

COLLECTED (v) to bring together into one body or place
Hos 13:12 *Ephraim's guilt has been **c,***.....816
1 Cor 16:1 *about the money being **c***.....1622

COLT (n) a young male animal of the horse family
Zech 9:9 *riding on a donkey's **c.***.....1175

COME, COMES, COMING (v) to originate, arise; to move or journey to a vicinity with a specified purpose; to happen, occur
see also CAME
Ps 121:1 *does my help **c** from there?*.....882
Prov 12:21 *No harm **c-s** to the godly,*.....645
1 Thes 3:13 *our Lord Jesus **c-s** again*.....1584
Heb 9:28 *He will **c** again,*.....1774
Heb 13:7 *good that has **c** from their*.....1782
Jas 5:8 *for the **c-ing** of the Lord*.....1553
Rev 7:10 *Salvation **c-s** from our God*.....1813

COMFORT (n) consolation in time of trouble or worry; solace
Gen 24:67 *she was a special **c** to him*.....50
Job 10:20 *I may have a moment of **c.***.....104
Ps 94:19 *your **c** gave me renewed hope*.....863
Zech 10:2 *falsehoods that give no **c.***.....1176
2 Cor 1:5 *shower us with his **c***.....1626
2 Cor 1:7 *share in the **c** God gives us.*.....1626
Col 4:11 *And what a **c** they have been!*.....1703

COMFORT, COMFORTED, COMFORTS (v) to give strength and hope to; to console
Gen 37:35 *he refused to be **c-ed.***.....74
Ruth 2:13 *You have **c-ed** me by speaking*.....412
Job 2:11 *traveled from their homes to **c***.....96
Job 42:11 *consoled him and **c-ed** him*.....132
Ps 69:20 *one would turn and **c** me.*.....578
Ps 86:17 *O LORD, help and **c** me*.....579
Ps 119:50 *it **c-s** me in all my troubles.*.....879
Ps 119:52 *O LORD, they **c** me.*.....879
Isa 40:1 ***C, c** my people,*.....923
Isa 49:13 *the LORD has **c-ed** his people*.....936
Isa 51:3 *The LORD will **c** Israel again*.....938
Isa 51:12 *yes I, am the one who **c-s** you*.....938
Isa 51:19 *Who is left to **c** you?*.....939
Isa 52:9 *the LORD has **c-ed** his people.*.....939
Isa 61:1 *to **c** the brokenhearted*.....948
Isa 66:13 *as a mother **c-s** her child*.....953
Lam 1:2 *there is no one left to **c** her*.....1094
Lam 1:17 *but no one **c-s** her*.....1095
Zech 1:17 *the LORD will again **c** Zion*.....1166
Matt 5:4 *mourn, for they will be **c-ed.***.....1323
1 Cor 14:3 *encourages them, and **c-s***.....1617
2 Cor 1:4 *He **c-s** us in all our troubles*.....1626
2 Cor 1:4 *so that we can **c** others.*.....1626
2 Cor 1:6 *when we ourselves are **c-ed,***.....1626
2 Cor 1:6 *we will certainly **c** you.*.....1626
2 Cor 2:7 *forgive and **c** him.*.....1628

COMFORTER (KJV)
John 14:16 *another **Advocate,** who will*.....1462
John 14:26 *sends the **Advocate** as my*.....1462
John 15:26 *the **Advocate**—the Spirit of*.....1464
John 16:7 *if I don't, the **Advocate** won't*.....1465

COMMAND, COMMANDS (n) an order given; religious instruction
see also COMMANDMENT
Exod 20:6 *who love me and obey my **c-s.***.....169
Exod 24:12 *the instructions and **c-s***.....175
Lev 22:31 *keep all my **c-s***.....229
Num 15:39 *and obey all the **c-s***.....255
Deut 4:2 *or subtract from these **c-s***.....289
Deut 6:6 *wholeheartedly to these **c-s***.....295
Deut 7:9 *who love him and obey his **c-s.***.....296
Deut 8:1 *Be careful to obey all the **c-s***.....296
Deut 11:1 *decrees, regulations, and **c-s.***.....300
Deut 11:27 *if you obey the **c-s** of the*.....301
Deut 28:1 *keep all his **c-s** that I am giving*.....317
Deut 32:46 *as a **c** to your children*.....325
Josh 1:9 *my **c**—be strong and*.....337
1 Kgs 8:58 *obey all the **c-s,** decrees,*.....622
1 Kgs 8:61 *obey his decrees and **c-s,***.....622
1 Chr 28:7 *if he continues to obey my **c-s***.....539
Neh 1:5 *who love him and obey his **c-s,***.....1203
Job 36:10 ***c-s** that they turn from evil*.....125
Ps 33:9 *It appeared at his **c.***.....858
Ps 78:7 *and obeying his **c-s.***.....598
Ps 103:20 *listening for each of his **c-s.***.....580

Ps 112:1 *and delight in obeying his **c-s**.*.....873
Ps 119:32 *I will pursue your **c-s**,*...............878
Ps 119:47 *How I delight in your **c-s!***..........879
Ps 119:73 *the sense to follow your **c-s**.*.......879
Ps 119:96 *your **c-s** have no limit.*...............880
Ps 119:127 *I love your **c-s** more than.*........881
Ps 119:143 *I find joy in your **c-s**.*..............881
Ps 119:172 *all your **c-s** are right.*...............882
Ps 119:176 *I have not forgotten your **c-s**.*...882
Prov 3:1 *Store my **c-s** in your heart.*...........634
Prov 6:23 *For their **c** is a lamp*..................638
Eccl 12:13 *Fear God and obey his **c-s**,*.......683
Isa 48:18 *you had listened to my **c-s!***........935
Dan 9:4 *who love you and obey your **c-s**.*...1142
Matt 28:20 *disciples to obey all the **c-s***....1498
John 15:17 *my **c:** Love each other.*...........1464
Acts 17:30 *he **c-s** everyone every-where to*...........1579
Rom 7:8 *sin used this **c** to arouse*............1657
Rom 7:9 *I learned the **c** not to covet,*........1657
Rom 7:12 *law itself is holy, and its **c-s** are*..1658
1 Cor 14:37 *saying is a **c** from the Lord*....1618
Gal 5:14 *summed up in this one **c:***..........1566
2 Thes 3:6 *we give you this **c***...................1590
2 Pet 2:21 *reject the **c** they were given*.....1759

COMMAND, COMMANDED, COMMANDING (v) to issue a charge or directive
Gen 7:5 *everything as the LORD **c-ed***...........18
Exod 7:6 *did just as the LORD had **c-ed***.......150
Exod 19:7 *everything the LORD had **c-ed***.....168
Deut 6:1 *your God **c-ed** me to teach*..........294
Deut 6:24 *our God **c-ed** us to obey*............295
Deut 15:11 *why I am **c-ing** you to share*.....305
John 15:14 *my friends if you do what I **c**.*....1464
2 Tim 2:14 ***c** them in God's presence*.......1742
2 Pet 3:2 *Savior **c-ed** through your*...........1760
1 Jn 3:23 *just as he **c-ed** us*....................1792
2 Jn 1:4 *just as the Father **c-ed**.*..............1795

COMMANDER (n) one in an official position of command or control
Eph 2:2 ***c** of the powers in the unseen*......1706

COMMANDMENT, COMMANDMENTS (n) a gracious provision of God's law or covenant, obeyed as an act of love and devotion
see also COMMAND
Exod 34:28 *Ten **C-s**—on the stone*............188
Deut 4:13 *his covenant—the Ten **C-s***.........290
Deut 10:4 *LORD wrote the Ten **C-s** on*..........299
Ps 103:18 *of those who obey his **c-s!***........580
Ps 111:7 *all his **c-s** are trustworthy.*...........873
Ps 111:10 *who obey his **c-s** will grow*........873
Ps 119:93 *I will never forget your **c-s**,*........880
Prov 19:16 *the **c-s** and keep your life;*........655
Matt 5:19 *if you ignore the least **c***............1327
Matt 19:17 *eternal life, keep the **c-s**.*........1420
Matt 22:36 *the most important **c***..............1441
Matt 22:38 *the first and greatest **c**.*..........1441
Mark 10:19 *you know the **c-s:***....................1421
Mark 12:28 ***c-s**, which is the most*...........1441
Luke 18:20 *you know the **c-s:***...................1422
John 13:34 *a new **c:** Love each other.*.......1461
John 14:15 *If you love me, obey my **c-s**.*..1462
Rom 13:9 *in this one **c:** "Love your*...........1669
1 Cor 7:19 *is to keep God's **c-s**.*...............1606
Eph 2:15 *law with its **c-s** and regulations*....1708
Eph 6:2 *the first **c** with a promise:*............1714
Heb 9:19 *had read each of God's **c-s***.......1773
1 Jn 2:3 *know him if we obey his **c-s**.*.......1788
1 Jn 3:24 *Those who obey God's **c-s***........1792
1 Jn 5:3 *God means keeping his **c-s**,*.......1794
Rev 12:17 *who keep God's **c-s** and*..........1819

COMMEND, COMMENDING (v) to entrust for care or preservation; to praise
Rom 16:1 *I **c** to you our sister Phoebe,*......1672
2 Cor 5:12 *Are we **c-ing** ourselves to you*...1632
2 Cor 10:18 *When people **c** themselves,*....1639

COMMENDATIONS (n) praiseworthy citations
2 Cor 12:11 *ought to be writing **c** for me,* .1642

COMMIT, COMMITS, COMMITTED, COMMITTING (v) to carry into action deliberately, perpetrate; to obligate or pledge oneself
Deut 30:20 ***c-ting** yourself firmly to him*.....321
2 Chr 16:9 *hearts are fully **c-ted** to him*......711
2 Chr 17:6 *deeply **c-ted** to the ways*..........714
Prov 6:32 *the man who **c-s** adultery*...........639
Prov 29:22 *a hot-tempered person **c-s***.......845
Matt 5:28 *has already **c-ted** adultery*.......1328
Matt 5:32 *causes her to **c** adultery*............1329
Matt 19:9 *someone else **c-s** adultery—*...1418
Mark 10:11 *someone else **c-s** adultery*.....1419
Mark 10:19 *You must not **c** adultery.*........1421
Luke 16:18 *her husband **c-s** adultery.*......1412
Rom 13:9 *You must not **c** adultery.*...........1669
Titus 2:14 *totally **c-ted** to doing good*.......1738
Jas 2:11 *You must not **c** adultery,*.............1549
Rev 18:3 *world have **c-ted** adultery with* ..1825
Rev 18:9 *the world who **c-ted** adultery*.....1826

COMMON (adj) characterized by a lack of privilege or special status; belonging to or shared by two or more individuals or things or all members of a group
Lev 10:10 *what is sacred and what is **c**,*.....213
1 Cor 9:22 *I try to find **c** ground with*........1609

COMMUNITY (n) a unified body of individuals
Num 20:1 *whole **c** of Israel arrived*.............261

COMPANION , COMPANIONS (n) a close friend or fellow participant
Ps 55:13 *my **c** and close friend.*.................572
Ps 55:20 *As for my **c**, he betrayed his*........572
Prov 16:29 *mislead their **c-s**, leading*.........652

COMPANY (n) association with another, fellowship; companions, associates
Prov 21:16 *end up in the **c** of the dead.*.......658
Prov 24:1 *or desire their **c**.*.........................662
Rom 12:16 *to enjoy the **c** of ordinary*........1668
1 Cor 15:33 *for "bad **c** corrupts good*.......1621

COMPASSION (n) sympathy, usually granted because of unusual or distressing circumstances
Exod 34:6 *The God of **c** and mercy!*...........187
Ps 51:1 *Because of your great **c**,*................505
Ps 86:15 *a God of **c** and mercy, slow to*......579
Ps 145:9 *He showers **c** on all*....................589
Isa 49:13 *and will have **c** on them*.............936
Isa 63:15 *your mercy and **c** now?*..............950
Lam 3:32 *brings grief, he also shows **c***.....1098
Hos 2:19 *unfailing love and **c**.*..................804
Mic 7:19 *you will have **c** on us.*.................911
Zech 10:6 *because of my **c***.....................1176
Mark 1:41 *Moved with **c**, Jesus reached*...1312
Mark 6:34 *and he had **c** on them*............1363
Luke 15:20 *with love and **c**, he ran to*.......1410
Rom 9:15 *show **c** to anyone I choose.*........1662

COMPASSIONATE (adj) having or showing compassion; sympathetic
Ps 103:13 *tender and **c** to those who*.........580
Ps 112:4 *They are generous, **c**,*..................873
Ps 145:8 *is merciful and **c**, slow to*............589
Joel 2:13 *he is merciful and **c**, slow to*......1241
Luke 6:36 *You must be **c**, just as your*......1330
Phil 2:1 *Are your hearts tender and **c**?*......1719

COMPELLED (v) to drive or urge forcefully or irresistibly
1 Cor 9:16 *I am **c** by God to do it.*............1608

COMPENSATION (n) something that constitutes an equivalent or recompense
Prov 6:35 *He will accept no **c**,*...................639

COMPLACENCY (n) self-satisfaction especially when accompanied by unawareness of actual dangers or deficiencies
Prov 1:32 *destroyed by their own **c**.*............633
Isa 32:11 *throw off your **c**.*........................902

COMPLACENT (adj) self-satisfied; unconcerned
Jer 49:31 *attack that **c** nation,*.................1026
Zeph 1:12 *who sit **c** in their sins.*................983

COMPLAINED, COMPLAINING (v) to express grief, pain, or discontent; to make a formal accusation or charge
Exod 15:24 *the people **c** and turned*...........162
Num 14:2 *in the wilderness!" they **c**.*..........251
Num 14:29 *Because you **c** against me,*.......253
John 6:43 *Jesus replied, "Stop **c-ing***.......1367
Phil 2:14 *Do everything without **c-ing***.......1720

COMPLAINERS (n) those who complain
Jude 1:16 *grumblers and **c**, living only*......1785

COMPLAINT (n) a formal allegation against a party
Mic 6:2 *listen to the LORD's **c!***....................909

COMPLETE (adj) having all necessary parts, elements, or steps
Eph 4:13 *full and **c** standard of Christ.*......1711
Jas 2:22 *made his faith **c**.*........................1550
2 Jn 1:12 *joy will be **c**.*.............................1796

COMPREHEND (v) to grasp the nature, significance, or meaning of
Matt 13:14 *I do, you will not **c**.*.................1345

COMPREHENSION (n) the act or action of grasping with the intellect; understanding
Ps 147:5 *is beyond **c!***.............................1154

CONCEAL, CONCEALED (v) to prevent disclosure or recognition of; to place out of sight
Prov 25:2 *God's privilege to **c***....................839
Prov 28:13 *People who **c** their sins will*.......844
Luke 8:17 *everything that is **c-ed** will be* ..1347

CONCEIT (n) excessive appreciation of one's own worth or virtue
Ps 36:2 *In their blind **c**, they cannot*............566

CONCEITED (adj) having or showing an excessively high opinion of oneself
Gal 5:26 *us not become **c**, or provoke*......1567

CONCEIVE, CONCEIVED (v) to become pregnant; to devise or imagine
Gen 29:31 *Rachel could not **c**.*.....................61
Ps 7:14 *The wicked **c** evil; they are*............524
Matt 1:20 *was **c-d** by the Holy Spirit*.........1277
Luke 1:7 *Elizabeth was unable to **c**,*..........1272
Luke 1:31 *You will **c** and give birth*...........1274

CONCERN, CONCERNS (n) affair or business; an uneasy state of blended interest, uncertainty, and apprehension
Job 19:4 *that is my **c**, not yours.*..................112
1 Cor 7:32 *free from the **c-s** of this life*.....1607
2 Cor 7:11 *such **c** to clear yourselves,*......1635
2 Cor 11:28 *the daily burden of my **c**.*........1641

CONCERN, CONCERNED (v) to involve; to be a care, trouble, or distress to
1 Sam 23:21 *someone is **c-ed** about me!*...463
Ps 131:1 *I don't **c** myself with matters*........584

1 Cor 10:24 *be **c-ed** for your own good*....1611
Phil 4:10 *have always been **c-ed** for me,*..1725

CONCUBINE, CONCUBINES (n) a woman living in a man's household, though not married; of lower family status than the wife
Judg 19:1 *in Judah to be his **c.***....405
2 Sam 3:7 *one of his father's **c-s,***....482
2 Sam 5:13 *David married more **c-s** and*....487
2 Sam 16:22 *sex with his father's **c-s.***....515
2 Sam 21:11 *what Rizpah, Saul's **c,** had*....524
1 Chr 1:32 *Keturah, Abraham's **c,***....1226
1 Chr 7:13 *of Jacob's **c** Bilhah.*....1235

CONDEMN, CONDEMNED, CONDEMNING, CONDEMNS (v) to declare guilty; to sentence or doom
Job 15:6 *Your own mouth **c-s** you, not I*....109
Job 40:8 *my justice and **c** me just to*....130
Ps 37:33 *or let the godly be **c-ed***....568
Ps 102:20 *to release those **c-ed** to die.*....867
Prov 12:2 ***c-s** those who plan wickedness.*...644
Prov 17:15 *guilty and **c-ing** the innocent—*..652
Isa 53:8 *Unjustly **c-ed,** he was led away.*...940
Matt 12:7 *not have **c-ed** my innocent*....1320
Matt 12:37 *acquit you or **c** you.*....1342
Matt 12:41 *on judgment day and **c** it,*....1343
Matt 27:3 *Jesus had been **c-ed** to die,*....1475
Luke 11:31 *on judgment day and **c** it,*....1344
John 8:10 *even one of them **c** you?*....1392
Rom 2:1 *think you can **c** such people,*....1648
Rom 2:1 *you are **c-ing** yourself,*....1648
Rom 3:7 *how can God **c** me as a sinner*....1650
Rom 3:8 *deserve to be **c-ed.***....1650
Rom 8:34 *Who then will **c** us? No one—*..1661
Rom 14:3 *foods must not **c** those who*....1670
Rom 14:13 *So let's stop **c-ing** each other.*....1670
1 Cor 4:9 *a victor's parade, **c-ed** to die*....1601
2 Cor 7:3 *saying this to **c** you.*....1634
Col 2:16 *So don't let anyone **c** you*....1699
Jas 5:6 *You have **c-ed** and killed*....1553
Jas 5:12 *not sin and be **c-ed.***....1553

CONDEMNATION (n) conviction of guilt; censure or blame
Rom 5:9 *save us from God's **c.***....1654
Rom 5:18 *Adam's one sin brings **c***....1655
Rom 7:13 *bring about my **c** to death.*....1658
Rom 8:1 *there is no **c** for those who*....1658
2 Cor 3:9 *which brings **c,** was glorious,*....1630

CONDUCT (n) a mode or standard of personal behavior especially as based on moral principles
Prov 20:11 *act, whether their **c** is pure,*....656
Jer 32:19 *You see the **c** of all people,*....1079
Gal 6:5 *responsible for our own **c.***....1567

CONDUCT, CONDUCTED, CONDUCTING (v) to cause (oneself) to act or behave in a particular and controlled manner; to direct or take part in the management or operation of
Exod 18:20 *them how to **c** their lives.*....167
Ps 112:5 *lend money generously and **c***....873
2 Cor 1:12 *how we have **c-ed** ourselves*...1626
Phil 1:27 *of heaven, **c-ing** yourselves in a*....1719
1 Tim 3:15 ***c** themselves in the*....1731

CONFESS, CONFESSED, CONFESSES, CONFESSING (v) to admit or acknowledge (sin or faith)
1 Sam 7:6 ***c-ed** that they had sinned*....427
Ezra 10:11 *So now **c** your sin to*....1201
Ps 32:3 *I refused to **c** my sin,*....564
Ps 32:5 *Finally, I **c-ed** all my sins*....565
Ps 38:18 *But I **c** my sins;*....569
Ps 66:18 *If I had not **c-ed** the sin in my*....859
Dan 9:4 *to the LORD my God and **c-ed:***....1142
Dan 9:20 *praying and **c-ing** my sin*....1143
Matt 18:15 ***c-es** it, you have won*....1385
Mark 1:5 *And when they **c-ed** their sins,*..1290
Rom 10:10 *by **c-ing** with your mouth*....1664
Rom 14:11 *every tongue will **c** and give*....1670
Phil 2:11 *and every tongue **c** that Jesus*....1720
1 Tim 6:12 *which you have **c-ed** so well*....1735
Jas 5:16 ***C** your sins to each other.*....1554
1 Jn 1:9 *But if we **c** our sins to him,*....1787

CONFESSION, CONFESSIONS (n) a disclosure of one's sins; a formal statement of religious beliefs
Ezra 10:1 *and made this **c,** weeping*....1200
Hos 14:2 *your **c-s,** and return*....817

CONFIDENCE (n) faith or belief that one will act in a right, proper, or effective way; a feeling or consciousness of one's powers; a quality or state of being certain
Ps 146:3 *Don't put your **c** in powerful*....886
Isa 30:15 *In quietness and **c** is your*....900
2 Cor 8:22 *of his great **c** in you.*....1637
Phil 1:14 *believers here have gained **c***....1718
Phil 2:24 *And I have **c** from the Lord*....1721
Phil 3:4 *I could have **c** in my own*....1722
Col 2:2 *want them to have complete **c***....1697
1 Thes 5:8 *as our helmet the **c** of our*....1585
Titus 1:2 *This truth gives them **c.***....1736
Heb 11:1 *Faith is the **c** that what we*....1777
2 Pet 1:19 *we have even greater **c***....1758
1 Jn 4:17 *but we can face him with **c***....1793

CONFIDENT (adj) full of conviction, certain; trustful
Ps 27:13 *Yet I am **c** I will see the*....561
Ps 57:7 *My heart is **c** in you, O God;*....460
2 Cor 3:4 *We are **c** of all this*....1629
Eph 1:18 *can understand the **c** hope*....1706
Col 1:5 ***c** hope of what God has reserved*..1693
Col 4:12 *fully **c** that you are following*....1703
2 Thes 3:4 *And we are **c** in the Lord*....1590
Heb 3:6 *keep our courage and remain **c***...1765

CONFIDENTLY (adv) acting with confidence
Ps 112:7 *they **c** trust the LORD.*....873
Rom 5:2 *we **c** and joyfully look forward*....1654
Eph 3:12 *boldly and **c** into God's*....1709

CONFIRM, CONFIRMED, CONFIRMING, CONFIRMS (v) to strengthen; to remove doubt by authoritative statement or action
Gen 6:18 *I will **c** my covenant with you.*....18
Gen 9:17 *sign of the covenant I am **c-ing***....21
Gen 17:21 *will be **c-ed** with Isaac,*....39
Heb 9:20 *This blood **c-s** the covenant*....1774

CONFLICT (n) fight, battle, war
Prov 13:10 *Pride leads to **c;***....646
Prov 17:1 *filled with feasting—and **c.***....652
Gal 3:21 *Is there a **c,** then, between*....1562

CONFUSED (v) to confound, stupefy, perplex
Gen 11:9 *where the LORD **c** the people*....23

CONFUSED (adj) the state of being confounded, stupefied, perplexed
Matt 9:36 *they were **c** and helpless,*....1357
Rom 1:21 *their minds became dark and **c.***..1647

CONGRATULATE (v) to express pleasure to (a person) on the occasion of success or good fortune
2 Sam 19:7 *go out there and **c** your troops,*....520

CONGREGATION (n) an assembly or gathering (not church)
Ps 107:32 *exalt him publicly before the **c***...872

CONQUER, CONQUERED, CONQUERING (v) to gain or acquire by force of arms
see also OVERCOME
Gen 22:17 *descendants will **c** the cities*....46
Num 13:30 *We can certainly **c** it!*....251
Prov 16:32 *than to **c** a city.*....652
Dan 2:44 *never be destroyed or **c-ed.***....1005
Matt 16:18 *of hell will not **c** it.*....1375
Rom 12:21 *Don't let evil **c** you,*....1668
Col 2:23 *no help in **c-ing** a person's evil*...1699

CONQUEROR (n) one who subdues, defeats, or vanquishes
Mic 1:15 *I will bring a **c** to capture*....788

CONSCIENCE, CONSCIENCES (n) one's moral sensitivity or scruples
2 Sam 24:10 *census, David's **c** began to*....530
Acts 24:16 *maintain a clear **c** before God*...1682
Rom 14:2 *with a sensitive **c** will eat*....1670
1 Cor 8:7 *their weak **c-s** are violated.*....1607
1 Cor 8:10 *to violate their **c** by eating*....1608
1 Cor 10:25 *raising questions of **c.***....1611
1 Tim 1:5 *a clear **c,** and genuine faith.*....1727
1 Tim 1:19 *and keep your **c** clear.*....1728
Titus 1:15 *minds and **c-s** are corrupted.*...1737
Heb 9:9 *are not able to cleanse the **c-s***....1772
Heb 9:14 *will purify our **c-s** from sinful*....1773
Heb 10:22 *guilty **c-s** have been sprinkled*...1775
Heb 13:18 *for our **c** is clear*....1783
1 Pet 3:16 *Keep your **c** clear.*....1753
1 Pet 3:21 *to God from a clean **c.***....1754

CONSCIENTIOUS (adj) scrupulous, meticulous, careful
2 Chr 29:34 *been more **c** about purifying*....836

CONSECRATE, CONSECRATED (v) to devote irrevocably to God by a solemn ceremony; to make or declare sacred
see also DEDICATE, DEVOTE, ORDAINED
Exod 40:9 *all its furnishings to **c** them*....195
Lev 19:24 *the entire crop must be **c-d***....225
2 Chr 29:31 *you have **c-d** yourselves*....836

CONSIDER (v) to think about carefully; to come to judge or classify; to regard
Job 37:14 *Stop and **c** the wonderful*....127
Rom 6:11 ***c** yourselves to be dead*....1656
Jas 1:2 *troubles come your way, **c** it*....1546

CONSIDERATE (adj) thoughtful of the rights and feelings of others
Phil 4:5 *see that you are **c** in all you*....1724

CONSOLE, CONSOLING (v) to alleviate the grief or sense of loss; to offer just reward
John 11:19 *come to **c** Martha and Mary*...1414
John 11:31 *at the house **c-ing** Mary*....1414

CONSTANT (adj) marked by steadfast faithfulness; continually occurring or recurring
Ps 119:98 *they are my **c** guide*....880
Prov 27:15 *is as annoying as **c** dripping*....842
Luke 18:5 *with her **c** requests!*....1417

CONSTRUCT (v) to build
1 Kgs 6:1 *he began to **c** the Temple.*....611

CONSULT (v) to ask the advice or opinion of; to confer
Gal 1:16 *rush out to **c** with any human*....1557

CONSUME, CONSUMED (v) to engage fully, engross
Ps 69:9 *Passion for your house has **c-d***....577

John 2:17 *Passion for God's house will **c***.....1300

CONTAIN (v) to keep within limits; to restrain or control
1 Kgs 8:27 *heavens cannot **c** you*.....619
John 21:25 *world could not **c** the books*...1497

CONTAMINATE (v) to soil, corrupt, or infect
Jude 1:23 *the sins that **c** their lives*.....1786

CONTEMPT (n) the state of despising; displaying disgust, scorn, or disdain
Gen 25:34 *showed **c** for his rights*.....52
Ps 119:51 *The proud hold me in utter **c,***.....879
Prov 18:3 *scandalous behavior brings **c.***.....653
Mal 1:6 *ever shown **c** for your name?*.....1245

CONTENT, CONTENTED (adj) feeling or showing satisfaction with one's possessions, status, or situation; pleased
Josh 7:7 *If only we had been **c***.....345
1 Kgs 4:20 *They were very **c-ed,***.....629
Prov 13:25 *godly eat to their hearts' **c,***.....647
Luke 3:14 *And be **c** with your pay*.....1291
Phil 4:11 *I have learned how to be **c***.....1725
1 Tim 6:8 *food and clothing, let us be **c.***...1735

CONTENTMENT (n) the quality or state of being contented
1 Tim 6:6 *godliness with **c** is*.....1735

CONTINUAL (adj) continuing indefinitely in time
Prov 15:15 *life is a **c** feast*.....649

CONTINUALLY (adv) in continual or steadily recurring manner
1 Chr 16:11 ***c** seek him.*.....493

CONTINUE, CONTINUED, CONTINUES (v) to maintain without interruption a condition, course, or action
Ps 100:5 *unfailing love **c-s** forever,*.....866
Jer 32:20 *have **c-d** to do*.....1079
Acts 13:43 ***c** to rely on*.....1542
Acts 14:22 *encouraged them to **c***.....1545
Rom 11:22 *if you **c** to trust in*.....1665
Col 1:23 *But you must **c** to believe*.....1696
Col 2:6 *you must **c** to follow*.....1697
1 Tim 2:15 *assuming they **c** to live in*.....1730
1 Jn 3:6 *who **c-s** to live in him*.....1791
Rev 22:11 ***c** to be holy.*.....1832

CONTRACT (n) a binding agreement between two or more persons or parties
Exod 21:8 *who broke the **c** with her.*.....171

CONTRIBUTIONS (n) payments imposed by authorities for a special purpose; giving to a common fund or store
Mark 12:43 *who are making **c.***.....1445

CONTRITE (adj) feeling or showing sorrow or remorse for a sin
see also HUMBLE, REPENTANT
Isa 66:2 *have humble and **c** hearts,*.....952

CONTROL, CONTROLS (v) to exercise restraining or directing influence over; to rule
Job 37:15 *know how God **c-s** the storm*.....127
Rom 6:12 *Do not let sin **c***.....1656
Rom 8:6 *letting the Spirit **c** your mind*.....1659
Rom 8:8 *still under the **c** of*.....1659
1 Cor 7:9 *they can't **c** themselves,*.....1605
1 Cor 7:37 *and he can **c** his passion,*.....1607
2 Cor 5:14 *Christ's love **c-s** us.*.....1632
Jas 1:26 *but don't **c** your tongue,*.....1548
Jas 3:2 *could also **c** ourselves*.....1550
2 Pet 2:19 *a slave to whatever **c-s** you.*....1759

CONTROVERSY, CONTROVERSIES (n) a dispute or quarrel
Acts 26:3 *customs and **c-ies.***.....1684
1 Tim 2:8 *from anger and **c.***.....1729

CONVERTED (v) to bring over from one belief, view, or party to another
Acts 6:7 *priests were **c,** too*.....1523
Acts 15:3 *the Gentiles, too, were being **c.***.1569

CONVICT, CONVICTED (v) to find or prove guilty of an offense
Prov 24:25 *for those who **c** the guilty;*.....663
John 7:51 *Is it legal to **c** a man*.....1391
John 16:8 *he will **c** the world of*.....1465
1 Cor 14:24 *they will be **c-ed** of sin*.....1618
Jude 1:15 *He will **c** every person*.....1785

CONVICTIONS (n) strongly held beliefs or principles
Rom 14:23 *you are not following your **c.***...1671

CONVINCE, CONVINCED, CONVINCING (v) to persuade to a belief, consent, or course of action
Exod 4:31 *people of Israel were **c-d***.....146
Acts 18:4 *to **c** the Jews and Greeks*.....1580
Rom 2:19 *are **c-d** that you are a guide*.....1649
Rom 8:38 *I am **c-d** that nothing*.....1661
Rom 14:14 *I know and am **c-d.***.....1670
Rom 15:14 *I am fully **c-d,***.....1671
Phil 1:25 *I am **c-d** that I will*.....1718

COPY (n) an imitation or reproduction of an original work; a duplicate
Heb 8:5 *that is only a **c,***.....1771
Heb 9:24 *was only a **c** of*.....1774

COPY (v) to duplicate; to model oneself on
Deut 17:18 *he must **c** for himself*.....307
Rom 12:2 *Don't **c** the behavior and*.....1666

CORD (n) a long, slender, flexible material usually consisting of several strands woven together
Eccl 4:12 *for a triple-braided **c***.....676

CORNERSTONE (n) a stone forming a corner or angle in a wall; foundation
Ps 118:22 *now become the **c.***.....876
Mark 12:10 *now become the **c.***.....1438
Acts 4:11 *now become the **c.***.....1519
Eph 2:20 *And the **c** is Christ*.....1708
1 Pet 2:7 *now become the **c.***.....1750

CORRECT, CORRECTED, CORRECTING, CORRECTS (v) to set right with remedies, revisions, or reforms
Job 5:17 *joy of those **c-ed** by God!*.....99
Ps 141:5 *If they **c** me,*.....588
Prov 3:12 *For the LORD **c-s** those*.....635
Prov 9:8 *don't bother **c-ing** mockers;*.....641
Prov 19:25 *if you **c** the wise,*.....655
Jer 5:3 *refused to be **c-ed.***.....965
Jer 10:24 *Do not **c** me in anger,*.....1013
2 Tim 3:16 *It **c-s** us when we*.....1745
2 Tim 4:2 *Patiently **c,** rebuke,*.....1745
Titus 2:15 *the authority to **c** them*.....1738
Heb 12:5 *give up when he **c-s** you.*.....1780

CORRECTION (n) a rebuke or punishment; the action of making right
Prov 10:17 *those who ignore **c***.....642
Prov 12:1 *it is stupid to hate **c.***.....644
Prov 15:5 *learns from **c** is wise.*.....648
Prov 15:10 *whoever hates **c** will die*.....648
Prov 15:32 *if you listen to **c,***.....650
Zeph 3:2 *it refuses all **c.***.....985

CORRUPT (adj) morally degenerate and perverted; depraved
Gen 6:11 *the earth had become **c***.....17
Ps 14:1 *They are **c,***.....551
Ps 14:3 *all have become **c.***.....552
Prov 19:28 *A **c** witness*.....655
Luke 9:41 *faithless and **c** people!*.....1382

CORRUPT, CORRUPTED, CORRUPTS (v) to change from good to bad, physically or morally
Eccl 7:7 *and bribes **c** the heart.*.....678
1 Cor 15:33 *bad company **c-s** good*.....1621
Titus 1:15 *and consciences are **c-ed.***.....1737
Jas 1:27 *let the world **c** you.*.....1548

CORRUPTION (n) impairment of integrity, virtue, or moral principle; depravity, decay
2 Pet 1:4 *the world's **c** caused*.....1757
2 Pet 2:19 *slaves of sin and **c.***.....1759

CORRUPTLY (adv) marked by moral perversion and degeneracy
Deut 32:5 *they have acted **c***.....323

COST (n) loss or penalty incurred especially in gaining something; price
Num 16:38 *sinned at the **c** of their lives,*.....257
Luke 14:28 *calculating the **c***.....1409

COST (v) to require effort, suffering, or loss
Prov 7:23 *it would **c** him his life.*.....640
Rev 6:6 *barley will **c** a day's pay.*.....1811

COUNCIL (n) a group elected or appointed as an advisory or legislative body
Acts 17:19 *to the high **c** of the city.*.....1578
Acts 17:22 *standing before the **c,***.....1578
Acts 17:34 *a member of the **c,***.....1579

COUNSEL (n) advice; policy, plan, or action
Ps 37:30 *godly offer good **c;***.....568
Ps 73:24 *guide me with your **c,***.....594
Ps 107:11 *scorning the **c** of the*.....872
Prov 27:9 *The heartfelt **c** of a friend*.....842
1 Cor 7:40 *I am giving you **c***.....1607

COUNSEL (v) to advise
Col 3:16 *Teach and **c** each other*.....1701

COUNSELOR (n) one who gives advice or wisdom
see also ADVOCATE, HOLY SPIRIT
Isa 9:6 *Wonderful **C,** Mighty God,*.....793

COUNT, COUNTED, COUNTING, COUNTS (v) to number; to consider
Gen 15:6 *and the LORD **c-ed** him as*.....35
Ps 22:17 *I can **c** all my bones.*.....556
Ps 130:5 *yes, I am **c-ing** on him.*.....884
Ps 147:4 *He **c-s** the stars*.....1154
Prov 20:25 *and only later **c-ing** the cost.*....657
Acts 5:41 ***c-ed** them worthy to suffer*.....1522
Rom 4:9 *Abraham was **c-ed** as righteous*...1652
Rom 4:24 *that God will also **c** us*.....1653
Rom 5:13 *it was not **c-ed** as sin*.....1655
2 Cor 5:19 *no longer **c-ing** people's sins*..1632
Gal 3:6 *and God **c-ed** him as righteous*...1561
Jas 2:23 *and God **c-ed** him as righteous*..1550

COUNTENANCE (KJV)
Gen 4:6 *Why do you **look** so dejected*.....14
Num 6:26 *LORD **show you his favor***.....245
1 Sam 16:7 *Don't judge by his **appearance***.....448
Prov 15:13 *glad heart makes a happy **face***...649
Luke 9:29 ***appearance of his face** was transformed*.....1380

COURAGE (n) mental or moral strength
Judg 5:21 *March on with **c,** my soul!*.....381

2 Chr 15:8 *he took **c** and removed*............708
Dan 11:25 *stir up his **c** and raise a*...........1160
Mark 6:50 *Take **c!** I am here!*...................1366
Acts 27:22 *But take **c!***.............................1687
Heb 3:6 *if we keep our **c***..........................1765
Jas 5:8 *Take **c,** for the coming*...............1553
1 Jn 2:28 *be full of **c** and not shrink*.........1790

COURAGEOUS (adj) having or characterized by courage; brave
Deut 31:6 *So be strong and **c!***.................322
Josh 1:6 *Be strong and **c,***.........................336
2 Sam 10:12 *Be **c!** Let us fight*.................501
2 Chr 32:7 *Be strong and **c!***.......................913
Ps 31:24 *be strong and **c,***...........................564
1 Cor 16:13 *Be **c.** Be strong*.......................1623

COURT, COURTS (n) a place for the administration of justice; an open space enclosed by buildings
Ps 82:1 *presides over heaven's **c;***.............602
Ps 84:10 *single day in your **c-s***..................855
Ps 96:8 *come into his **c-s.***..........................864
Ps 100:4 *go into his **c-s***.............................866
Prov 22:22 *exploit the needy in **c.***...............660
Prov 25:8 *to go to **c.***...................................839
Isa 3:13 *takes his place in **c***.......................827
Amos 5:15 ***c-s** into true halls of justice*.......775
Zech 8:16 *verdicts in your **c-s***.................1174
Matt 5:25 *are on the way to **c***..................1328

COURTROOM (n) a room in which a court of law is held
Eccl 3:16 *evil in the **c.***...............................676

COURTYARD (n) enclosed area adjacent to a building
Exod 27:9 *make the **c** for the Tabernacle,*....178
Exod 27:18 *the entire **c** will be 150 feet long*...178
Matt 26:69 *sitting outside in the **c.***...........1473

COVENANT, COVENANTS (n) a mutual agreement or contract (between persons, between nations, or between God and humanity) with conditions and consequences spelled out
see also PROMISE, VOW
Gen 9:9 *hereby confirm my **c***........................21
Gen 17:2 *I will make a **c** with you,*................38
Exod 19:5 *and keep my **c,***...........................167
Deut 4:13 *He proclaimed his **c**—*...................290
Judg 2:1 *never break my **c***............................373
1 Kgs 8:21 *which contains the **c***.................619
2 Kgs 23:2 *Book of the **C** that had been*......971
2 Chr 6:14 *You keep your **c***...........................620
Neh 1:5 *keeps his **c** of unfailing love*.........1203
Ps 105:8 *stands by his **c**—*...........................868
Prov 2:17 *and ignores the **c***.........................634
Isa 61:8 *an everlasting **c** with them.*............948
Jer 31:31 *make a new **c** with the people*..1034
Hos 10:4 *make **c-s** they don't intend*............813
Mal 3:1 *messenger of the **c,***......................1247
Mark 14:24 *confirms the **c** between God*..1458
Luke 22:20 *new **c** between God and his*...1458
Rom 9:4 *He made **c-s** with them*..............1661
1 Cor 11:25 *new **c** between God and his*..1613
2 Cor 3:6 *under the new **c,***........................1629
Heb 8:6 *a far better **c** with God,*...............1771
Heb 9:15 *mediates a new **c** between*........1773
Heb 12:24 *the new **c** between God and*....1781

COVER (n) something that is placed over or about another thing; lid or top piece
Exod 25:17 *make the Ark's **c**—*.................176
Exod 25:21 *put the atonement **c***..................176
Lev 16:2 *the atonement **c.***..........................221

COVER, COVERED, COVERS (v) to hide from sight or knowledge; to lay or spread something over; to lie over
Gen 3:7 *to **c** themselves.*...............................12
Exod 33:22 *and **c** you with my hand*...........186
Job 29:14 *Righteousness **c-ed** me*............120
Ps 85:2 *you **c-ed** all their sins*...................855
Ps 91:4 *He will **c** you with*...........................861
Isa 6:2 *they **c-ed** their faces,*......................783
Matt 10:26 *everything that is **c-ed***...........1360
1 Cor 11:4 *if he **c-s** his head while*...........1612
2 Cor 3:15 *their hearts are **c-ed***...............1630
Jas 3:14 *don't **c** up the truth*......................1550
1 Pet 4:8 *love **c-s** a multitude of sins*........1754

COVERING (n) something that covers or conceals
1 Cor 11:5 *without a **c** on her head,*.........1612
1 Cor 11:15 *given to her as a **c.***..............1613

COVET, COVETED, COVETING (v) to inordinately desire unjust gain or another's property
see also DESIRE
Exod 20:17 *not **c** your neighbor's wife,*.......170
Exod 34:24 *so no one will **c** and conquer*....188
Deut 7:25 *must not **c** the silver or gold*.......296
Acts 20:33 ***c-ed** anyone's silver or gold*....1676
Rom 7:7 *known that **c-ing** is wrong*.........1657
Rom 13:9 *You must not **c.***........................1669

COWARDS (n) those who show disgraceful fear or timidity
Rev 21:8 *But **c,** unbelievers, the*..............1830

COWS (n) the mature female of cattle
Gen 41:2 *he saw seven fat, healthy **c***..........79

CRAFTSMAN, CRAFTSMEN (n) a worker who practices a trade or handicraft
Isa 45:16 *All **c-en** who make idols*.............932
Jer 10:3 *and a **c** carves an idol.*..............1012

CRAFTSMANSHIP (n) the product of a craftsman that demonstrates his skill
Ps 19:1 *the skies display his **c.***..................554

CRAVE, CRAVED, CRAVES (v) to want greatly; to yearn for
Num 11:4 *began to **c** the good things*.........247
Num 11:34 *people who had **c-d** meat*........249
Ps 78:18 *the foods they **c-d.***.......................598
Ps 78:29 *gave them what they **c-d.***.............598
Prov 31:4 *should not **c** alcohol.*...................847
Gal 5:16 *your sinful nature **c-s.***...............1566
1 Pet 2:2 ***c** pure spiritual milk*....................1750
1 Jn 2:17 *everything that people **c.***...........1789

CRAVING (n) an intense, urgent, or abnormal desire or longing
Ps 78:30 *they satisfied their **c,***...................598
Prov 10:3 *satisfy the **c** of the wicked*..........642
1 Jn 2:16 *world offers only a **c***..................1789

CREATE, CREATED, CREATING (v) to bring into being; to form, make, or produce
see also FORMED, MADE, MAKE
Gen 1:1 *God **c-d** the heavens*..........................6
Gen 1:27 *male and female he **c-d** them;*........8
Gen 6:7 *human race I have **c-d** from*...........17
Ps 51:10 ***C** in me a clean heart*.....................506
Ps 104:30 *life is **c-d,** and you renew*...........868
Prov 8:22 *before he **c-d** anything else.*.......640
Isa 43:1 *the* L*ORD* *who **c-d** you.*.......................928
Isa 43:7 *I who **c-d** them*...............................928
Isa 45:8 *I, the* L*ORD*, ***c-d** them.*.......................931
Isa 54:16 *I have **c-d** the blacksmith*...........941
Isa 65:17 *I am **c-ing** new heavens and*.......952
John 1:3 ***c-d** everything through him,*.......1270

Rom 1:20 *since the world was **c-d,***............1647
Rom 1:25 *served the things God **c-d***........1648
Rom 9:20 *the thing that was **c-d** say*..........1662
Eph 2:10 *He has **c-d** us anew*....................1707
Eph 2:15 *by **c-ing** in himself*......................1708
Eph 4:24 ***c-d** to be like God—*....................1712
Col 1:16 *Everything was **c-d** through*.........1694
1 Tim 4:3 *But God **c-d** those foods*............1732
Heb 1:2 *through the Son he **c-d***...............1761
1 Pet 4:19 *to the God who **c-d** you,*..........1755
Rev 4:11 *For you **c-d** all things,*................1809
Rev 10:6 *who **c-d** the heavens*....................1816

CREATION (n) something that is created; the world; the act of bringing the world into existence
Gen 2:3 *from all his work of **c.***.........................9
Mark 10:6 *from the beginning of **c.***...........1419
Rom 8:19 *For all **c** is waiting*.......................1659
Rom 8:39 *nothing in all **c** will ever*.............1661
Gal 6:15 *into a new **c.***.................................1568
Col 1:17 *holds all **c** together.*.......................1695
Heb 12:27 *all of **c** will be shaken*..............1781
Jas 1:18 *we, out of all **c,***............................1547
Rev 3:14 *of God's new **c:***...........................1807

CREATOR (n) maker; one who creates
see also MAKER
Gen 14:19 *God Most High, **C** of heaven*........34
Job 40:19 *only its **C** can threaten*...............130
Eccl 12:1 *to forget your **C.***..........................682
Isa 40:28 *the **C** of all the earth.*....................925
Isa 45:9 *argue with their **C.***..........................931
Isa 51:13 *the* L*ORD*, *your **C,***..........................938
Jer 51:19 *He is the **C** of everything*...........1038
Rom 1:25 *instead of the **C** himself,*............1648
Eph 3:9 *the **C** of all things,*.........................1709
Eph 3:15 *the **C** of everything*......................1709

CREATURE, CREATURES (n) something created either animate or inanimate
Lev 17:14 *the life of any **c** is in*....................223
Ps 104:24 *full of your **c-s.***...........................868

CREDIT (n) honor, recognition, or acknowledgment
Luke 6:33 *should you get **c?***.....................1330
1 Pet 2:20 *no **c** for being patient*...............1752

CRETE (n) an island in the Mediterranean Sea
Acts 27:12 *up the coast of **C,***.....................1686
Titus 1:12 *The people of **C** are all liars,*......1737

CRIME, CRIMES (n) a grave offense; criminal activity
Deut 22:26 *no **c** worthy of death*................313
Judg 19:30 *Such a horrible **c** has*...............407
1 Sam 20:1 *What is my **c?** How have I*.......455
Job 31:11 *lust is a shameful sin, a **c***...........121
Ps 52:1 *about your **c-s,** great warrior?*.......462
Luke 11:48 *join in their **c** by*.......................1399
Luke 23:41 *deserve to die for our **c-s,***.......1484

CRIMINAL, CRIMINALS (n) one who has broken the law
Ps 59:2 *Rescue me from these **c-s;***............454
Isa 53:9 *he was buried like a **c;***..................940
Luke 23:32 *Two others, both **c-s,***.............1483

CRIMSON (n) any of several deep purplish reds
Isa 1:18 *Though they are red like **c,***.............824

CRIPPLED (adj) lame, physically disabled
2 Sam 9:3 *He is **c** in both feet.*....................500
Luke 14:13 *invite the poor, the **c,** the lame,*...1408
Acts 14:8 *came upon a man with **c** feet.*...1544

CRITIC (n) one who expresses an opinion on a matter involving a judgment of its value, truth, righteousness, beauty, or technique
Job 40:2 *You are God's **c**, but do you*..........130

CRITICISM (n) a critical observation or remark; critique
Prov 15:31 *listen to constructive **c**,*............650
Prov 25:12 *valid **c** is like a gold*..................839
Prov 28:23 *people appreciate honest **c***........844
Prov 29:1 *refuses to accept **c**.*....................844
2 Cor 8:20 *guard against any **c***...............1637

CRITICIZE, CRITICIZED, CRITICIZING (v) to find fault with; to point out the faults of
Job 34:29 *who can **c** him?*.......................125
Eccl 7:5 *be **c-d** by a wise person*..............678
Rom 14:16 *not be **c-d** for doing*...............1670
Phil 2:15 *no one can **c** you*......................1720
Titus 2:8 *teaching can't be **c-d.***..............1738
Jas 4:11 ***c-ing** and judging God's law*.......1552

CROOKED (adj) not straight, twisted; dishonest, evil
Ps 125:5 *those who turn to **c** ways,*............883
Prov 5:6 *staggers down a **c** trail*.................637
Prov 8:8 *nothing devious or **c** in it.*.............640
Prov 10:9 *those who follow **c** paths*...........642
Prov 21:8 *The guilty walk a **c** path;*.............657
Eccl 7:13 *what he has made **c**?*.................679
Isa 59:8 *have mapped out **c** roads,*.............945

CROP, CROPS (n) the product or yield after a harvest
Exod 23:16 *bring me the first **c-s***..............173
Prov 28:3 *that destroys the **c-s.***................843
Hos 10:12 *harvest a **c** of love.*.....................813
Matt 13:8 *they produced a **c** that was*.......1345
Matt 21:41 *his share of the **c***...................1437

CROSS (n) an upright post used as an instrument of death in ancient times; the means by which atonement was made between God and humanity
Mark 8:34 *take up your **c**,*.......................1377
Luke 9:23 *take up your **c** daily,*.................1378
Acts 2:23 *you nailed him to a **c***...............1515
Acts 5:30 *hanging him on a **c**.*................1521
1 Cor 1:18 *message of the **c** is*................1596
Gal 3:1 *death on the **c**.*..........................1560
Gal 6:12 *that the **c** of Christ alone*............1568
Phil 2:8 *criminal's death on a **c**.*...............1720
Col 1:20 *Christ's blood on the **c**.*...............1695
Heb 12:2 *he endured the **c**,*........................1780
1 Pet 2:24 *his body on the **c***....................1752

CROSSED (v) to fold one (arm) over the other
Gen 48:14 *But Jacob **c** his arms*.................90

CROSSROADS (n) the place of intersection of two or more roads
Jer 6:16 *Stop at the **c** and look*.................968

CROUCHING (v) to lie close to the ground with the legs bent
Gen 4:7 *Sin is **c** at the door,*........................14

CROW, CROWED, CROWS (v) to make the loud shrill sound characteristic of a rooster
Matt 26:34 *before the rooster **c-s**,*...........1460
Matt 26:74 *the rooster **c-ed.***...................1474

CROWD, CROWDS (n) a large number of persons especially when collected together
Exod 23:2 *by the **c** to twist justice.*..............173
Matt 9:36 *When he saw the **c-s**,*.............1357
Heb 12:1 *such a huge **c** of witnesses*.......1780
Rev 19:1 *like a vast **c** in heaven*..............1827

CROWDED (v) to push or force
Mark 4:19 *the message is **c** out*..............1346

CROWN, CROWNS (n) top of the head; a cap or headdress worn by victors, priests, or royalty
Prov 16:31 *Gray hair is a **c** of glory;*............652
Song 3:11 *He wears the **c** his mother*.........666
Isa 61:3 *will give a **c** of beauty*..................948
Isa 62:3 *a splendid **c** in the hand*...............948
Zech 9:16 *like jewels in a **c**.*.......................1176
Matt 27:29 *thorn branches into a **c***.........1481
Mark 15:17 *thorn branches into a **c***..........1482
John 19:2 *wove a **c** of thorns*..................1480
John 19:5 *wearing the **c** of thorns*............1480
Phil 4:1 *and the **c** I receive*.......................1724
1 Thes 2:19 *our proud reward and **c***.........1583
Jas 1:12 *will receive the **c** of life*.............1547
Rev 2:10 *will give you the **c** of life*............1803
Rev 3:11 *take away your **c**.*........................1807
Rev 4:4 *had gold **c-s** on their heads.*........1808
Rev 4:10 *lay their **c-s** before the throne*....1808
Rev 12:3 *with seven **c-s** on his heads*.......1818
Rev 14:14 *He had a gold **c** on his head*.....1822
Rev 19:12 *on his head were many **c-s**.*....1828

CROWNED, CROWNS (v) to place a crown on the head of; to bless or adorn
Ps 8:5 *and **c-ed** them with*.......................548
Ps 149:4 *he **c-s** the humble*.......................887
Prov 14:18 *are **c-ed** with knowledge.*..........648
Isa 51:11 ***c-ed** with everlasting joy.*...........938
Heb 2:7 *and **c-ed** them with*...................1763
Heb 2:9 ***c-ed** with glory and honor.*..........1763

CRUCIFIXION (n) the execution or death of a person on a cross
Matt 23:34 *you will kill some by **c**,*............1445
John 19:41 *The place of **c** was near*.........1489

CRUCIFY, CRUCIFIED (v) to execute or nail to the cross; to put to death
Matt 26:2 *handed over to be **c-ied.***...........1453
Matt 27:22 *"**C** him!"*...................................1478
Matt 27:44 *who were **c-ied** with him*........1483
Mark 15:13 *"**C** him!"*..................................1479
Mark 15:27 *revolutionaries were **c-ied***.....1483
Mark 15:32 *who were **c-ied** with Jesus*....1483
Mark 16:6 *who was **c-ied**.*.......................1490
Luke 23:21 *"**C** him! **C** him!"*.....................1480
Luke 23:23 *that Jesus be **c-ied**,*.............1480
Luke 23:33 *criminals were also **c-ied**—*..1483
Luke 24:20 *and they **c-ied** him.*..............1493
John 19:6 *"**C** him! **C** him!"*......................1481
John 19:10 *to release you or **c** you?*.........1481
John 19:20 *where Jesus was **c-ied***.........1484
John 19:32 *the two men **c-ied** with Jesus.*...1487
Acts 4:10 *the man you **c-ied***..................1519
Rom 6:6 *were **c-ied** with Christ*..............1655
1 Cor 1:13 *Was I, Paul, **c-ied** for you?*......1596
1 Cor 1:23 *preach that Christ was **c-ied**,*...1597
1 Cor 2:8 *would not have **c-ied***..............1598
2 Cor 13:4 *he was **c-ied** in weakness,*.....1643
Gal 5:24 *and **c-ied** them there*................1567
Rev 11:8 *where their Lord was **c-ied**.*.......1817

CRUEL (adj) disposed to inflict pain or suffering; devoid of human feelings
2 Tim 3:3 *They will be **c** and hate*............1744
1 Pet 2:18 *even if they are **c**.*.....................1751

CRUELTY (n) the quality or state of being cruel; inhuman treatment
Prov 11:17 *your **c** will destroy you.*............643

CRUSH, CRUSHED (v) to squeeze or force by pressure so as to alter or destroy; to oppress or burden grievously
Ps 34:18 *whose spirits are **c-ed**.*..............459
Prov 31:8 *justice for those being **c-ed**.*.......847
Isa 42:3 *will not **c** the weakest reed*...........926
Isa 42:13 *and **c** all his enemies.*.................927
Isa 53:5 ***c-ed** for our sins.*.........................940
Matt 26:38 *My soul is **c-ed** with grief*.......1468
Luke 10:19 *scorpions and **c** them*............1395
Rom 16:20 *will soon **c** Satan*....................1673
2 Cor 1:8 *were **c-ed** and overwhelmed*.....1626
2 Cor 4:8 *but we are not **c-ed**.*.................1631

CRY, CRIES (n) entreaty, appeal; an inarticulate utterance of distress, rage, or pain
Exod 2:23 *their **c** rose up to God.*...............143
Ps 5:2 *Listen to my **c** for help,*......................547
Ps 34:15 *open to their **c-ies** for help.*.........459
Ps 40:1 *and heard my **c**.*............................570
Ps 142:6 *Hear my **c**, for I am*.......................460
Prov 21:13 *to the **c-ies** of the poor*...........658

CRY, CRIED (v) to shout; to beg or beseech; to shed tears often noisily
Exod 14:10 *They **c-ied** out to the LORD,*......160
Josh 24:7 *When your ancestors **c-ied** out*..369
Judg 3:9 *people of Israel **c-ied** out*............376
Judg 4:3 *people of Israel **c-ied** out*............378
Judg 6:6 *Then the Israelites **c-ied** out*........382
Judg 10:12 *you **c-ied** out to me*...............392
Ps 18:6 *in my distress I **c-ied** out*..............528
Eccl 3:4 *A time to **c** and a time*...................675
Lam 2:18 ***C** aloud before the LORD,*..........1097
Hab 2:11 *walls **c** out against you,*..............980

CULTIVATE (v) to foster the growth of; to encourage
Job 4:8 *plant trouble and **c** evil*....................98

CUP (n) a drinking vessel; figurative of human vessel; token of tangible consolation, salvation of Christ, wrath of God, drunkenness, or fate
Ps 23:5 *My **c** overflows.*...............................558
Matt 26:39 *let this **c** of suffering*..............1468
Matt 26:42 *If this **c** cannot be*.................1468
Mark 10:39 *drink from my bitter **c***...........1424
Mark 14:23 *And he took a **c** of wine*..........1458
Mark 14:36 *take this **c** of suffering*...........1468
Luke 22:20 *This **c** is the new covenant*.....1458
John 18:11 *from the **c** of suffering*...........1470
1 Cor 10:16 *When we bless the **c***............1610
1 Cor 10:21 *from the **c** of the Lord*...........1611
1 Cor 11:25 *took the **c** of wine after*.........1613
1 Cor 11:25 *This **c** is the new covenant*....1613

CUP-BEARER (n) one who tasted and served wine to a king
Gen 40:1 *Pharaoh's chief **c***..........................78
Neh 1:11 *I was the king's **c**.*......................1204

CURE (n) recovery or relief from a disease; a complete or permanent solution
Jer 30:15 *wound that has no **c**?*..............1032
Luke 8:43 *she could find no **c**.*.................1355

CURE, CURED (v) to restore to health, soundness, or normality
Isa 30:26 *and **c** the wounds*.......................900
Matt 11:5 *the lepers are **c-d**,*..................1337
John 5:10 *said to the man who was **c-d**,*..1317

CURSE, CURSES, CURSING (n) a condemnation or judgment
Num 5:23 *priest will write these **c-s***..........244
Josh 8:34 *blessings and **c-s** Moses had*.....348
Rom 3:14 *full of **c-ing** and bitterness.*.......1651

Rom 8:20 *was subjected to God's **c**.*.........1659
Gal 3:10 *right with God are under his **c**,*....1561
Gal 3:13 *the **c** for our wrongdoing.*...........1561
Jas 3:10 *and **c-ing** come pouring out*......1550
Rev 22:3 *No longer will there be a **c***.........1832

CURSE, CURSES (v) to pronounce a sentence; to afflict; to call upon a supernatural power to bring injury upon; to utter profane language against
Gen 8:21 *will never again **c** the ground*.........20
Gen 12:3 ***c** those who treat you*...................30
Prov 3:33 ***c-s** the house of the wicked,*.......635
Matt 5:22 *And if you **c** someone,*.............1328
Rom 12:14 *Don't **c** them;*.......................1668
1 Cor 12:3 *will **c** Jesus, and no one*..........1614
Jas 3:9 *and sometimes it **c-s** those who*...1550

CURSED (adj) being under or deserving a curse
Gen 3:17 *the ground is **c** because*...............13
Deut 21:23 *anyone who is hung is **c***...........311
Deut 27:16 ***C** is anyone who dishonors*.......317
Deut 27:18 ***C** is anyone who leads*..............317
Deut 27:20 ***C** is anyone who has sexual*......317
Deut 27:24 ***C** is anyone who attacks a*........317
Deut 27:26 ***C** is anyone who does not*.........317
Prov 28:27 *poverty will be **c**.*........................844
Gal 3:10 ***C** is everyone who does not*........1561
Gal 3:13 ***C** is everyone who is hung*..........1561

CURTAIN (n) a hanging screen usually capable of being drawn back or up
Isa 40:22 *the heavens like a **c***...................924
Mark 15:38 *And the **c** in the sanctuary*.....1486

CUT OFF (v) separated; isolated
Gen 17:14 *fails to be circumcised will be **c***..39
Ps 31:22 *"I am **c** from the LORD!"*..............564
Prov 21:28 *false witness will be **c**, but a*.....658
Ezek 21:4 *will **c** both the righteous*...........1067
Hos 10:7 *Samaria and its king will be **c***......813
Zech 13:8 *in the land will be **c** and die*......1179
Rom 9:3 ***c** from Christ!—if that*...............1661
Gal 5:4 *the law, you have been **c***..............1565

DAILY (adv) every day
Deut 17:19 *read it **d** as long as he*..............307
Acts 17:17 *spoke **d** in the public square*...1577

DAN

1. First son of Jacob and Bilhah (Gen 30:3-6, p. 61), who gave his name to a tribe of Israel; his tribe was blessed (Gen 49:16-17, p. 92; Deut 33:22, p. 327), numbered (Num 1:38-39, p. 238), allotted land and cities (Josh 19:40-47, p. 363); took the town of Laish and renamed it Dan (Judg 18, p. 403).
2. Town at the northern boundary of Israel (Judg 20:1, p. 407), earlier known as Laish; captured and renamed by Danites (Josh 19:47, p. 364); became a center for idolatry (1 Kgs 12:28-30, p. 699); attacked by Ben-hadad (1 Kgs 15:20, p. 709).

DANCE, DANCING (n) a series of rhythmic bodily movements usually performed to music
Ps 30:11 *into joyful **d-ing**.*..........................563
Mark 6:22 *a **d** that greatly pleased*...........1362

DANCE, DANCED (v) to move in a rhythmic manner, usually to music
2 Sam 6:14 *David **d-d** before the LORD*......491
Eccl 3:4 *and a time to **d**.*............................675
Matt 11:17 *and you didn't **d**,*...................1338

DANGER (n) harm or damage
Ps 57:1 *until the **d** passes by*......................459
Prov 22:3 *prudent person foresees **d***..........659
Matt 5:22 *in **d** of being brought*................1328
Rom 8:35 *or in **d**, or threatened*..............1661
2 Cor 1:10 *did rescue us from mortal **d**,*...1626
2 Cor 11:26 *I have faced **d** from rivers*......1641

DANGEROUS (adj) able or likely to inflict injury or harm
Prov 29:25 *Fearing people is a **d** trap,*........846

DANIEL

1. Prophet of Judah (southern kingdom), exiled to Babylon; also called "Belteshazzar" (Dan 1:6-7, p. 1001); refused food of the Babylonian court (Dan 1:8-17, p. 1001); interpreted dreams (Dan 2, p. 1002) and writing on a wall (Dan 5:12-29, p. 1139); survived in lion's den (Dan 6:1-23, p. 1140); recorded visions (Dan 7–12, p. 1135); identified as a hero of renown (Ezek 14:14, 20, p. 1060; 28:3, p. 1084).
2. Son of David (1 Chr 3:1, p. 1229), also called "Kileab" (2 Sam 3:3, p. 480).

DARK, DARKEST (adj) devoid or partially devoid of light; wholly or partially black
Exod 20:21 *approached the **d** cloud*...........170
Ps 23:4 *walk through the **d-est** valley,*........558
Song 1:6 *because I am **d**—*.........................664
Song 5:10 *My lover is **d** and dazzling,*.........667
Joel 2:31 *The sun will become **d**,*.............1242
Acts 2:20 *The sun will become **d**,*.............1515
2 Pet 1:19 *lamp shining in a **d** place—*....1758

DARKENED (v) to make dark
Matt 24:29 *the sun will be **d**,*...................1446

DARKNESS (n) the state of being devoid of light; nightfall; in spiritual terms, secret, closed, blinded, or evil; place of punishment (hell)
Gen 1:2 *and **d** covered the deep waters*..........6
Gen 1:4 *the light from the **d**.*.............................6
Ps 18:28 *my God, lights up my **d**.*..............528
Matt 4:16 *people who sat in **d***.................1306
Luke 23:44 *it was about noon, and **d** fell*...1486
John 1:5 *light shines in the **d**,*.................1271
John 3:19 *people loved the **d** more*...........1302
John 12:35 *the **d** will not overtake*............1434
2 Cor 4:6 *Let there be light in the **d**,*.........1631
2 Cor 6:14 *can light live with **d**?*..............1634
Eph 5:8 *once you were full of **d**,*..............1712
Eph 5:11 *deeds of evil and **d**;*....................1712
1 Pet 2:9 *called you out of the **d***..............1751
1 Jn 1:5 *there is no **d** in him at all.*...........1787
1 Jn 2:9 *is still living in **d**.*........................1788
Jude 1:6 *chained in prisons of **d**,*..............1784

DARLING (n) a dearly loved person
Song 2:10 *Rise up, my **d**!*..........................665
Jer 31:20 *my son, my **d** child?" says*........1033

DAUGHTER, DAUGHTERS (n) the female offspring or adopted offspring of parents
Gen 19:36 *Lot's **d-s** became pregnant*.........42
Num 36:10 *The **d-s** of Zelophehad*.............284
Judg 11:40 *the fate of Jephthah's **d**.*..........395
Esth 2:7 *raised her as his own **d**.*..............1184
Joel 2:28 *sons and **d-s** will prophesy*.........1242
Mark 5:34 *said to her, "**D**, your faith*..........1354
Mark 7:29 *the demon has left your **d**.*........1372

DAVID King of Israel (united kingdom); son of Jesse, in the family line of Jesus (Ruth 4:17-22, p. 415; Matt 1:1, p. 1278; Luke 3:31, p. 1280); anointed king (1 Sam 16:1-13, p. 447); skillful musician to Saul (1 Sam 16:14-23, p. 448; 18:10, p. 452); David and Goliath (1 Sam 17, p. 449); faithful friendship with Jonathan (1 Sam 18:1-4, p. 452); envied by Saul, but loved by the people (1 Sam 18:5-16, p. 452); married Michal (1 Sam 18:17-30, p. 453); wives and children (2 Sam 3:2-5, p. 480; 5:13-16, p. 487; 1 Chr 3:1-9, p. 1229); fled from Saul (1 Sam 19–23, p. 453); ate used "Bread of the Presence" (1 Sam 21:1-6, p. 457; Matt 12:3-4, p. 1319); dealings with the Philistines (1 Sam 21:10-14, p. 457; 27–30, p. 469); spared Saul twice (1 Sam 22–24, p. 459; 26, p. 467); married widow Abigail (1 Sam 25:2-42, p. 465); lamented death of Saul and Jonathan (2 Sam 1, p. 476); contended with Saul's dynasty (2 Sam 2–4, p. 478); anointed king of Judah (2 Sam 2:1-7, p. 478); lamented Abner's death (2 Sam 3:31-39, p. 484); made king over all Israel (2 Sam 5:1-5, p. 485); victories over the Philistines (2 Sam 5:17-25, p. 489; 21:15-22, p. 524; 1 Chr 14:8-17, p. 490; 20:4-8, p. 525); made Jerusalem the royal city (2 Sam 5:6-16, p. 487); moved Ark to Jerusalem (2 Sam 6, p. 487); eternal covenant with God (2 Sam 7, p. 495; 1 Chr 17, p. 496); showed loyal love to Mephibosheth (2 Sam 9, p. 500); committed adultery with Bathsheba (2 Sam 11–12, p. 502; Pss 32, p. 564; 51, p. 505); plotted Uriah's death (2 Sam 11:14-25, p. 504); rebuked by Nathan (2 Sam 12:1-12, p. 505); repented of affair and intrigue (2 Sam 12:13, p. 507); rebellion and death of Absalom (2 Sam 14–18, p. 510); lamented Absalom's death (2 Sam 18:33–19:8, p. 520); rebellion and death of Sheba (2 Sam 20, p. 522); judged for taking census (2 Sam 24:1-25, p. 529); made Solomon next king (1 Kgs 1:28–2:9, p. 544); final words to Solomon (1 Kgs 2:1-9, p. 545); died (1 Kgs 2:10-12, p. 546); preparations for the Temple (1 Chr 22–29, p. 532).

DAWN (n) first appearance of light in the morning followed by sunrise
Exod 14:24 *But just before **d** the LORD*........160
Ps 37:6 *radiate like the **d**, and the*.............567
Prov 4:18 *gleam of **d**, which shines ever*.....636
Prov 31:15 *gets up before **d** to prepare*......847
Amos 4:13 *the light of **d** into darkness*........774
Acts 20:11 *talking to them until **d**,*............1675

DAWNS (v) to begin to grow light as the sun rises
Hos 10:15 *day of judgment **d**, the king*.......814
2 Pet 1:19 *until the Day **d**, and Christ*.......1758

DAY, DAYS (n) the time of light between one night and the next; a specified time or period; a 24-hour time period
Gen 1:5 *called the light "**d**" and the*................6
Gen 2:2 *On the seventh **d** God had*..................9
Exod 16:30 *any food on the seventh **d**.*........164
Lev 23:28 *it is the **D** of Atonement,*.............231
Josh 1:8 *Meditate on it **d** and night so*........337
2 Kgs 7:9 *This is a **d** of good news,*............746
Ps 23:6 *all the **d-s** of my life,*.....................558
Ps 84:10 *A single **d** in your*..........................855
Ps 118:24 *This is the **d** the LORD has*..........876
Isa 13:9 *coming—the terrible **d** of his*........831
Jer 46:10 *this is the **d** of the LORD,*.............997
Jer 50:31 *Your **d** of reckoning*.....................1036
Hos 3:5 *In the last **d-s**, they will*..................805

Joel 1:15 *How terrible that* ***d*** *will be!*.........1240
Joel 2:31 *great and terrible* ***d*** *of the*..........1242
Amos 5:20 *Yes, the* ***d*** *of the* LORD..............776
Zeph 1:14 *That terrible* ***d*** *of the*..................984
Zech 14:1 *Watch, for the* ***d*** *of the* LORD.....1179
Zech 14:7 *there will be continuous* ***d!***.......1180
Mal 4:5 *great and dreadful* ***d*** *of the* 1249
Matt 24:38 *In those* ***d-s*** *before the*...........1447
Luke 11:3 *Give us each* ***d*** *the food we*......1344
Acts 2:17 *'In the last* ***d-s,'*** *God says,*........1514
Rom 14:5 *some think one* ***d*** *is more holy*..1670
1 Cor 5:5 *be saved on the* ***d*** *the Lord*.........1602
2 Cor 4:16 *renewed every* ***d.***....................1631
1 Thes 5:2 *the* ***d*** *of the Lord's return*.........1585
1 Thes 5:4 *surprised when the* ***d*** *of the*.....1585
2 Thes 2:2 *say that the* ***d*** *of the Lord*........1588
2 Tim 3:1 *in the last* ***d-s*** *there will be*.......1744
Heb 1:2 *now in these final* ***d-s,*** *he has*.....1761
2 Pet 3:3 *in the last* ***d-s*** *scoffers will*........1760
2 Pet 3:10 *But the* ***d*** *of the Lord*..............1760
Rev 16:14 *that great judgment* ***d*** *of God*...1823

DAZZLING (adj) characterized by shining brilliantly or arousing admiration
Job 37:22 *is clothed in* ***d*** *splendor.* 127
Song 5:10 *My lover is dark and* ***d,***..............667
Mark 9:3 *his clothes became* ***d*** *white,*........1379

DEACON, DEACONS (n) a servant; an officer of the church
see also ELDERS
Phil 1:1 *the elders and* ***d-s.***......................1716
1 Tim 3:8 ***d-s*** *must be well respected.*......1731
1 Tim 3:10 *they are appointed as* ***d-s,***......1731
1 Tim 3:12 *A* ***d*** *must be faithful*................1731
1 Tim 3:13 *Those who do well as* ***d-s***.......1731

DEAD (n) Those who have died (physically or spiritually)
Matt 8:22 *the spiritually* ***d*** *bury their*.........1387
Luke 24:46 *rise from the* ***d*** *on the third*.....1498
1 Cor 15:29 *If the* ***d*** *will not be raised*.......1621
Rev 20:12 *I saw the* ***d,*** *both great and*......1830

DEAD (adj) without (physical or spiritual) life; fatal; useless; unresponsive
Rom 6:11 *be* ***d*** *to the power of sin.*...........1656
Eph 2:1 *Once you were* ***d*** *because of*.........1706
Jas 2:17 *good deeds, it is* ***d*** *and useless*...1549
1 Pet 2:24 *that we can be* ***d*** *to sin and*.....1752
Rev 2:8 *Last, who was* ***d*** *but is now*..........1802

DEAF (adj) lacking or deficient in the sense of hearing
Ps 94:9 *Is he* ***d****—the one who made*..........862

DEAR (adj) highly valued; precious
1 Cor 10:14 *my* ***d*** *friends, flee from*..........1610
2 Cor 7:1 *these promises,* ***d*** *friends,*..........1634
Eph 5:1 *you are his* ***d*** *children.*.................1712
2 Tim 1:2 *to Timothy, my* ***d*** *son.*...............1740
Jas 1:16 *don't be misled, my* ***d*** *brothers*...1547
1 Jn 4:4 *to God, my* ***d*** *children.*...............1793
3 Jn 1:1 *to Gaius, my* ***d*** *friend, whom I*......1796
Jude 1:20 *But you,* ***d*** *friends, must*...........1785

DEATH (n) the cessation of (physical or spiritual) life; personification and consequence of evil
Exod 21:12 *must be put to* ***d.***......................171
Ruth 1:17 *anything but* ***d*** *to separate*..........410
Prov 11:19 *evil people find* ***d.***....................644
Prov 14:12 *it ends in* ***d.***.............................647
Prov 23:14 *save them from* ***d.***....................661
Song 8:6 *love is as strong as* ***d,***..................669
Isa 38:17 *have rescued me from* ***d***..............921
Acts 2:24 *for* ***d*** *could not keep him*..........1515
Rom 5:12 *brought* ***d,*** *so* ***d*** *spread to*.........1654
Rom 6:23 *the wages of sin is* ***d,***...............1656
Rom 7:24 *dominated by sin and* ***d?***..........1658
1 Cor 15:21 *see, just as* ***d*** *came into the*...1621
1 Cor 15:26 *enemy to be destroyed is* ***d.***..1621
2 Cor 3:6 *written covenant ends in* ***d;***.......1629
Gal 3:1 *the meaning of Jesus Christ's* ***d***....1560
2 Tim 1:10 *power of* ***d*** *and illuminated*......1741
Heb 2:14 *who had the power of* ***d.***............1764
Heb 9:17 *after the person's* ***d.***..................1773
1 Jn 5:16 *there is a sin that leads to* ***d,***.....1794
Rev 2:11 *by the second* ***d.***........................1803
Rev 20:6 *them the second* ***d*** *holds no*.......1829
Rev 20:14 *of fire is the second* ***d.***.............1830
Rev 21:4 *be no more* ***d*** *or sorrow or*.........1830
Rev 21:8 *This is the second* ***d.***.................1830

DEBATERS (n) those who contend or argue
1 Cor 1:20 *world's brilliant* ***d?***.................1597

DEBAUCHERY (KJV)
Rom 13:13 *promiscuity and* ***immoral living***..1669
2 Cor 12:21 ***eagerness for lustful pleasure***...1642
Gal 5:19 *impurity,* ***lustful pleasures***.........1566
1 Pet 4:3 *their* ***immorality*** *and lust, their*..1754

DEBT, DEBTS (n) what is owing; sense of obligation
Deut 15:1 *cancel the* ***d-s*** *of everyone*.........305
Deut 15:3 *This release from* ***d,*** *however,*.....305
Deut 15:9 *year for canceling* ***d-s*** *is close*....305
1 Sam 22:2 *trouble or in* ***d*** *or who were*......459
2 Kgs 4:7 *pay your* ***d-s,*** *and*......................740
Neh 10:31 *will cancel all* ***d-s*** *owed to us*...1218
Prov 22:26 *another person's* ***d*** *or put up*.....660
Matt 18:25 *to pay the* ***d.***..........................1386
Matt 18:27 *and forgave his* ***d.***..................1386
Matt 18:30 *in prison until the* ***d*** *could*.......1386
Matt 18:32 *you that tremendous* ***d***...........1386
Luke 7:42 *canceling their* ***d-s.***.................1340
Luke 7:43 *canceled the larger* ***d.***..............1340

DEBTORS (n) those who owe a debt
Hab 2:7 *Suddenly, your* ***d*** *will take*.............980

DECAY (n) a wasting or wearing away
Rom 8:21 *freedom from death and* ***d.***.......1659
1 Pet 1:4 *the reach of change and* ***d.***........1748

DECAY, DECAYED (v) to undergo decomposition
Job 19:26 *my body has* ***d-ed,*** *yet in my*.....112
Acts 13:37 *whose body did not* ***d.***............1542

DECEIT (n) fraud; trickery; lying
Mark 7:22 *greed, wickedness,* ***d,*** *lustful*....1371
Acts 13:10 *of every sort of* ***d*** *and fraud,*....1540
1 Pet 2:1 *done with all* ***d,*** *hypocrisy,*..........1750

DECEITFUL (adj) not honest; misleading, deceptive
Isa 59:13 *planning our* ***d*** *lies.*....................945
2 Cor 11:13 *They are* ***d*** *workers who*........1640

DECEIVE, DECEIVED, DECEIVES, DECEIVING (v) to lead astray; to cause to accept as true what is false
Gen 3:13 *"The serpent* ***d-d*** *me," she*...........12
Prov 10:31 *the tongue that* ***d-s*** *will be*........643
Prov 14:8 *but fools* ***d*** *themselves.*...............647
Prov 26:24 *but they're* ***d-ing*** *you.* 841
Matt 24:24 *so as to* ***d,*** *if possible, even*.....1446
Mark 13:6 *They will* ***d*** *many.* 1448
Rom 7:11 *those commands and* ***d-d*** *me;*..1657
Rom 16:18 *they* ***d*** *innocent people.* 1673
1 Cor 3:18 *Stop* ***d-ing*** *yourselves.*............1600
2 Cor 11:3 *as Eve was* ***d-d*** *by the cunning*..1640
Col 2:4 *so no one will* ***d*** *you with*.............1697
1 Tim 2:14 *The woman was* ***d-d,*** *and sin*..1730
2 Tim 3:13 *They will* ***d*** *others and will*.......1744
2 Tim 3:13 *will themselves be* ***d-d.***...........1744
Heb 3:13 *you will be* ***d-d*** *by sin*...............1765
Rev 20:3 *Satan could not* ***d*** *the nations*.....1829
Rev 20:10 *devil, who had* ***d-d*** *them, was*..1830

DECEIVER, DECEIVERS (n) one who leads astray; one who causes another to accept as true what is false
Ps 101:7 *will not allow* ***d-s*** *to serve in*........580
Matt 27:63 *remember what that* ***d*** *once said*..1489
2 Jn 1:7 *because many* ***d-s*** *have gone*.....1796
2 Jn 1:7 *Such a person is a* ***d*** *and an*.......1796

DECENT (adj) conforming to the standards of propriety or morality; modest
1 Tim 2:9 *should wear* ***d*** *and appropriate*..1729

DECEPTION (n) something that deceives; trick; the act of deceiving
Isa 28:15 *refuge made of lies and* ***d.***..........819
Dan 8:25 *He will be a master of* ***d***...........1138
Rom 1:29 *quarreling,* ***d,*** *malicious*...........1648
Eph 4:22 *corrupted by lust and* ***d.***.............1711
2 Thes 2:10 *kind of evil* ***d*** *to fool those*......1589
1 Jn 4:6 *truth or spirit of* ***d.***......................1793

DECEPTIVE (adj) tending or having power to deceive; misleading
Prov 31:30 *Charm is* ***d,*** *and beauty* 848
1 Tim 4:1 *will follow* ***d*** *spirits and*.............1732

DECIDE, DECIDED, DECIDES (v) to make a final choice or judgment about; to select as a course of action
1 Sam 14:7 *whatever you* ***d.***......................443
Job 14:5 *You have* ***d-d*** *the length of*...........108
Ps 75:7 *he* ***d-s*** *who will rise and*................596
Rom 14:13 ***D*** *instead to live*....................1670
Rom 14:22 *they have* ***d-d*** *is right.*............1670
1 Cor 2:2 *For I* ***d-d*** *that while I*.................1598
1 Cor 6:2 *can't you* ***d*** *even these*.............1603
1 Cor 12:11 *He alone* ***d-s*** *which gift*.........1614
2 Cor 9:7 *You must each* ***d*** *in your heart*...1637

DECISION, DECISIONS (n) a determination arrived at after consideration; conclusion
Joel 3:14 *waiting in the valley of* ***d.***...........1243
Mic 3:11 *You rulers make* ***d-s*** *based on*......907
Rom 11:33 *to understand his* ***d-s*** *and his*.1666

DECLARE, DECLARED, DECLARING (v) to make known formally, officially, or explicitly; to state emphatically, affirm; to make evident, show
Deut 25:1 *and the judges* ***d*** *that one is*.......314
Ps 71:8 *praising you; I* ***d*** *your glory.*............860
Ps 92:15 *They will* ***d,*** *"The* LORD..................862
Prov 31:31 *deeds publicly* ***d*** *her praise.* 848
Dan 4:24 *what the Most High has* ***d-d***......1121
Mark 7:19 *saying this, he* ***d-d*** *that every*......1371
Acts 20:27 *didn't shrink from* ***d-ing*** *all*.....1675
Rom 4:6 *who are* ***d-d*** *righteous without*....1652
Heb 3:1 *Jesus whom we* ***d*** *to be God's*.....1764

DECREE, DECREES (n) an order usually having the force of law; a foreordaining will
Exod 15:25 *them the following* ***d***................162
Exod 15:26 *and keeping all his* ***d-s,*** *then I*..162
Exod 18:20 *Teach them God's* ***d-s,***............167
Lev 18:4 *to obey my* ***d-s,*** *for I am the*........224
Num 15:15 *to the same* ***d-s.***.....................254
Deut 4:1 *to these* ***d-s*** *and regulations*.........289
1 Kgs 3:3 *and followed all the* ***d-s*** *of his*.....606
1 Chr 16:17 *it to Jacob as a* ***d,***..................493

Ps 2:7 *proclaims the LORD's **d:***....857
Ps 119:12 *LORD; teach me your **d-s.***....878
Ps 119:54 *Your **d-s** have*....879
Ps 148:6 *His **d** will never be*....887

DECREED (v) to determine or order judicially; to command by or as if by decree
Dan 9:24 *sets of seven has been **d***....1143
Luke 2:1 *Augustus, **d** that a census*....1280

DEDICATE, DEDICATED (v) to devote to the worship of a divine being; to set apart to a definite use
see also CONSECRATE, DEVOTE, ORDAINED
Exod 13:2 ***D** to me every firstborn*....158
Num 6:9 *the hair they have **d-d** will be*....244
Num 6:18 *the hair that had been **d-d***....245
Num 18:6 *a gift to you, **d-d** to the LORD*....259
1 Kgs 8:63 *Israel **d-d** the Temple*....622
Neh 3:1 *which they **d-d,** and the Tower*....1206
Luke 2:23 *he must be **d-d** to the LORD*....1282

DEDICATION (n) an act or rite of dedicating to a diving being or to sacred use
John 10:22 *the Festival of **D.***....1406

DEED, DEEDS (n) a signed instrument containing some legal transfer, bargain, or contract; a usually illustrious act or action; feat, exploit
see also WORKS
Ps 45:4 *perform awe-inspiring **d-s!***....851
Ps 66:3 *awesome are your **d-s!***....859
Ps 71:24 *your righteous **d-s** all day*....860
Ps 88:12 *your wonderful **d-s?***....591
Ps 96:3 *his glorious **d-s** among the*....864
Ps 105:2 *his wonderful **d-s.***....868
Prov 31:31 *Let her **d-s** publicly declare*....848
Isa 64:6 *our righteous **d-s,** they are*....950
Jer 32:10 *and sealed the **d** of purchase*....1079
Matt 5:16 *let your good **d-s** shine out for*..1327
Rom 4:2 *If his good **d-s** had made him*....1652
2 Cor 9:9 *Their good **d-s** will be*....1637
Col 3:9 *all its wicked **d-s.***....1700
Jas 2:18 *my faith by my good **d-s.***....1549
Jas 2:20 *without good **d-s** is useless?*....1550

DEEP, DEEPER (adj) extending far downward from some surface or area; situated well within the boundaries; difficult to penetrate or comprehend
Gen 1:2 *covered the **d** waters*....6
Rom 6:19 *which led ever **d-er** into sin.*....1656
1 Cor 2:10 *shows us God's **d** secrets*....1598

DEEPLY (adv) in an intense, profound manner
Ps 116:15 *The LORD cares **d***....875
Isa 66:11 *Drink **d** of her glory*....953

DEER (n) a mammal with usually brownish fur and antlers borne by the males
Ps 42:1 *As the **d** longs for streams of*....848

DEFEAT (n) an overthrow especially of an army in battle; loss, destruction
Ps 25:2 *enemies rejoice in my **d.***....559
1 Cor 6:7 *with one another is a **d***....1603

DEFEAT, DEFEATED, DEFEATS (v) to destroy; to win victory over
Ps 129:2 *they have never **d-d** me.*....883
1 Jn 5:4 *child of God **d-s** this evil*....1794
Rev 12:11 *And they have **d-d** him by the*..1818
Rev 17:14 *the Lamb will **d** them*....1825

DEFEND, DEFENDING, DEFENDS (v) to maintain or support in the face of argument or hostile criticism; to drive danger or attack away from
Deut 33:7 *strength to **d** their cause;*....326
Ps 10:14 *You **d** the orphans.*....857
Ps 34:7 *he surrounds and **d-s** all who*....458
Ps 72:4 *Help him to **d** the poor,*....630
Ps 106:8 *saved them—to **d** the honor of*....870
Phil 1:7 *and in **d-ing** and confirming*....1717
Phil 1:16 *been appointed to **d** the Good*....1718
Jude 1:3 *urging you to **d** the faith*....1784

DEFENDER (n) one who guards and protects
Ps 68:5 *the fatherless, **d** of widows—*....576
Prov 22:23 *the LORD is their **d.***....660
Isa 51:22 *your God and **D,** says:*....939

DEFENSE (n) the act of defending
Ps 35:23 *Rise to my **d!***....566

DEFILE, DEFILED, DEFILING (v) to make unclean—either physically, sexually, ethically, or ceremonially
Num 6:7 *must not **d** themselves,*....244
Num 15:39 *desires and **d-ing** yourselves,*..255
Ezek 23:7 *idols and **d-ing** herself.*....1070
Ezek 44:7 *In this way, you **d-d** my Temple.*1127
Matt 15:11 *you are **d-d** by the words*....1369
Mark 7:23 *they are what **d** you.*....1371
Acts 21:28 *even **d-s** this holy place.*....1678
2 Cor 7:1 *that can **d** our body or*....1634

DEFLECTS (v) to turn aside; deviate
Prov 15:1 *A gentle answer **d** anger,*....648

DEFY, DEFIED, DEFYING (v) to challenge to combat, dare; to disregard
1 Sam 17:10 *I **d** the armies of Israel*....449
1 Sam 17:45 *whom you have **d-ied.***....451
Isa 37:23 *Whom have you been **d-ing***....919

DELAY (n) the state of being delayed; putting off; wait
Rev 10:6 *There will be no more **d.***....1816

DELAY, DELAYED (v) to put off; to postpone
Eccl 5:4 *don't **d** in following through,*....677
Matt 25:5 *the bridegroom was **d-ed,***....1451
Heb 10:37 *will come and not **d.***....1777

DELIBERATE (adj) characterized by awareness of the consequences
Ps 19:13 *servant from **d** sins!*....555

DELICACIES (n) indulgences; something pleasing to eat that is considered rare or luxurious
Ps 141:4 *share in the **d** of those who*....588
Prov 23:6 *don't desire their **d.***....661

DELIGHT, DELIGHTS (n) source of great pleasure; joy
Ps 36:8 *your river of **d-s.***....566
Ps 40:6 *You take no **d** in sacrifices*....570
Ps 119:111 *they are my heart's **d.***....880
Prov 8:30 *I was his constant **d,***....641
Isa 58:13 *and speak of it with **d***....945
Jer 15:16 *my joy and my heart's **d,***....1019
Mal 3:12 *your land will be such a **d,***....1248
Mark 12:37 *to him with great **d.***....1443

DELIGHT, DELIGHTED, DELIGHTING, DELIGHTS (v) to enjoy
Exod 4:14 *He will be **d-ed** to see you.*....145
2 Sam 22:20 *because he **d-s** in me.*....526
Ps 1:2 *But they **d** in the law of*....856
Ps 18:19 *he rescued me because he **d-s***...528
Ps 27:4 ***d-ing** in the LORD's*....561
Ps 37:4 *Take **d** in the LORD,*....567
Ps 119:70 *I **d** in your instructions.*....879
Prov 3:12 *a child in whom he **d-s.***....635
Prov 11:1 *he **d-s** in accurate weights.*....643
Prov 11:20 *he **d-s** in those with integrity.*....644
Song 8:10 *he is **d-ed** with what he sees.*....670
Isa 11:3 *He will **d** in obeying*....796
Isa 65:19 *and **d** in my people.*....952
Isa 66:3 ***d-ing** in their detestable sins—*....953
Jer 9:24 *I **d** in these things.*....1012

DELIGHTFUL (adj) highly pleasing
Prov 3:17 *guide you down **d** paths;*....635
Song 2:3 *sit in his **d** shade and taste*....664

DELIVER (v) to save, liberate, set free from
Ps 82:4 ***d** them from the grasp of evil*....602
2 Tim 4:18 ***d** me from every evil attack*....1746

DELIVERANCE (n) freedom from harm, salvation
Esth 4:14 ***d** and relief for the Jews will arise*....1188
Isa 51:1 *"Listen to me, all who hope for **d***...938
Phil 1:19 *this will lead to my **d.***....1718

DEMON-POSSESSED (adj) characterized by the possession or control of demons
Matt 4:24 *if they were **d** or epileptic*....1311
Matt 8:16 *That evening many **d** people*....1309
Matt 8:33 *happened to the **d** men.*....1351
Matt 9:32 *When they left, a **d** man who*....1356
Matt 12:22 *Then a **d** man, who was*....1341
Mark 1:32 *many sick and **d** people were*...1310
Mark 5:16 *about the **d** man and*....1352
Luke 8:36 *others how the **d** man had*....1353

DEMON, DEMONS (n) an agent of the Devil; an evil spirit
Deut 32:17 *They offered sacrifices to **d-s,***....324
Matt 8:31 *So the **d-s** begged, "If you cast*...1351
Matt 9:34 *by the prince of **d-s.***....1356
Matt 11:18 *He's possessed by a **d.***....1338
Matt 12:24 *he can cast out **d-s.***....1341
Matt 12:28 *if I am casting out **d-s** by the*..1341
Matt 17:18 *Jesus rebuked the **d.***....1381
Mark 1:34 *But because the **d-s** knew who*....1310
Mark 5:15 *by the legion of **d-s.***....1351
Mark 5:18 *been **d** possessed begged*....1352
Mark 7:29 *the **d** has left your daughter.*....1372
Mark 9:38 *to cast out **d-s,** but we told*....1383
Mark 16:9 *cast out seven **d-s.***....1492
Mark 16:17 *will cast out **d-s** in my name,*.1498
Luke 4:33 *possessed by a **d**—an evil*....1309
Luke 7:33 *He's possessed by a **d.***....1339
Luke 8:2 *he had cast out seven **d-s;***....1341
Luke 8:30 *with many **d-s.***....1353
Luke 8:33 *Then the **d-s** came out of the*...1353
Luke 8:38 *freed from the **d-s** begged*....1353
Luke 9:49 *to cast out **d-s,** but we told*....1384
Luke 10:17 *Lord, even the **d-s** obey us*....1394
Luke 11:14 *Jesus cast out a **d** from*....1342
Luke 11:19 *They cast out **d-s,** too, so they.*....1342
Luke 11:20 *casting out **d-s** by the power*..1342
John 8:49 *Jesus said, "I have no **d** in me.*.1393
John 10:21 *possessed by a **d!***....1406
Rom 8:38 *neither angels nor **d-s,***....1661
1 Cor 10:20 *to participate with **d-s.***....1611
1 Cor 10:21 *the cup of **d-s,** too.*....1611
1 Cor 10:21 *the table of **d-s,** too.*....1611
1 Tim 4:1 *teachings that come from **d-s.***..1732
Rev 9:20 *to worship **d-s** and idols made*...1815
Rev 18:2 *become a home for **d-s.***....1825

DEMONIC (adj) of, relating to, or suggestive of a demon
Jas 3:15 *unspiritual, and **d.***....1550
Rev 16:14 *They are **d** spirits who work*....1823

DEMONSTRATE (v) to show clearly
Ezek 39:21 ***d** my glory to the nations.*....1115
Rom 3:26 *to **d** his righteousness,*....1651

DEN (n) the lair of a wild, usually predatory, animal; a center of secret activity
Dan 6:16 *thrown into the **d** of lions.* ... 1141
Matt 21:13 *into a **d** of thieves!* ... 1432

DENY, DENIED, DENIES (v) to disavow or refuse to accept as true; to refuse to grant
Exod 23:6 *you must not **d** justice to the* ... 173
Deut 27:19 *is anyone who **d-ies** justice* ... 317
Prov 30:9 *I may **d** you and say,* ... 846
Matt 10:33 *everyone who **d-ies** me* ... 1360
Matt 26:35 *I will never **d** you!* ... 1460
Matt 26:70 *But Peter **d-ied** it* ... 1474
Luke 12:9 *anyone who **d-ies** me* ... 1400
Luke 22:34 *you will **d** three times* ... 1460
John 18:25 *He **d-ied** it, saying,* ... 1474
Acts 4:16 *We can't **d** that they* ... 1519
1 Tim 5:8 *have **d-ied** the true faith.* ... 1733
2 Tim 2:12 ***d** him, he will **d** us.* ... 1742
Titus 1:16 ***d** him by the way they live.* ... 1737
2 Pet 2:1 *and even **d** the Master who* ... 1758
1 Jn 2:22 *Anyone who **d-ies** the Father* ... 1790
1 Jn 2:23 *Anyone who **d-ies** the Son* ... 1790
Jude 1:4 *they have **d-ied** our only Master.* 1784
Rev 3:8 *and did not **d** me.* ... 1806

DEPEND (v) to place reliance or trust
Prov 3:5 *do not **d** on your own* ... 634
Jer 49:11 *widows, too, can **d** on me* ... 1025
Gal 3:10 *But those who **d** on the law* ... 1561

DEPOSIT (v) to place especially for safekeeping
Matt 25:27 *why didn't you **d** my money in* 1452

DEPRAVED (adj) characterized by moral corruption or evil; perverted
2 Tim 3:8 *They have **d** minds and* ... 1744

DEPRESSION (n) a state of feeling sad; dejection
Ps 143:7 *answer me, for my **d** deepens.* ... 588

DEPRIVE (v) to withhold something from; to remove
Isa 10:2 *They **d** the poor* ... 794
1 Cor 7:5 *Do not **d** each other of* ... 1605

DEPTHS (n) deep places in a body of water; the quality of being deep
Ps 130:1 *From the **d** of despair,* ... 884
Mic 7:19 *them into the **d** of the ocean!* ... 911

DESCENDANT, DESCENDANTS (n) those who came or originated from; offspring, children
see also OFFSPRING, SON(S)
Gen 12:7 *give this land to your **d-s**.* ... 30
Gen 13:16 *will give you so many **d-s** that,* ... 33
Gen 17:9 *You and all your **d-s** have this* ... 38
Deut 30:19 *you and your **d-s** might live!* ... 321
Isa 53:8 *he died without **d-s**, that his* ... 940
Isa 53:10 *he will have many **d-s**.* ... 940
Jer 23:5 *I will raise up a righteous **d*** ... 1027
Matt 1:1 *the Messiah, a **d** of David and* ... 1278
Acts 3:25 *Through your **d-s** all the* ... 1518
Rom 4:18 *That's how many **d-s** you will* ... 1653
Rom 9:8 *Abraham's physical **d-s** are not* ... 1661

DESCEND, DESCENDED, DESCENDING (v) to pass from a higher place or level to a lower one
Matt 3:16 *Spirit of God **d-ing** like a dove* ... 1293
Mark 1:10 *the Holy Spirit **d-ing** on him* ... 1294
Eph 4:9 *that Christ also **d-ed** to our* ... 1710

DESECRATE, DESECRATED (v) to profane something holy or treat it with contempt
Neh 13:18 *Sabbath to be **d-d** in this way!* 1223
Isa 56:6 *and do not **d** the Sabbath day* ... 943

DESECRATION (n) violation of something sacred; profanation; blasphemy
Dan 11:31 *object that causes **d**.* ... 1160
Dan 12:11 *object that causes **d** is set* ... 1162
Matt 24:15 *causes **d** standing in the* ... 1446

DESERT, DESERTS (n) arid land with usually sparse vegetation
see also WILDERNESS
Prov 21:19 *better to live alone in the **d*** ... 658
Isa 32:2 *like streams of water in the **d*** ... 902
Isa 43:20 *giving them water in the **d**.* ... 929
2 Cor 11:26 *cities, in the **d-s**, and on the* ... 1641

DESERTED (v) to abandon
Matt 26:56 *all the disciples **d** him and* ... 1469
2 Tim 1:15 *of Asia has **d** me—even* ... 1741

DESERVE, DESERVED, DESERVES (v) to be worthy, fit, or suitable for some reward or requital; to merit
Judg 9:16 *the honor he **d-s** for all he* ... 389
2 Sam 12:5 *do such a thing **d-s** to die!* ... 505
Neh 9:33 *gave us only what we **d-d**.* ... 1217
Ps 103:10 *with us, as we **d**.* ... 580
Prov 14:14 *Backsliders get what they **d**;* ... 647
Dan 9:18 *not because we **d** help,* ... 1142
Zech 1:6 *received what we **d-d** from the* ... 1164
Luke 7:4 *If anyone **d-s** your help,* ... 1336
Acts 26:31 *done anything to **d** death or* ... 1686
Rom 3:8 *who say such things **d** to be* ... 1650
Rom 11:9 *get what they **d**.* ... 1665
2 Cor 11:15 *their wicked deeds **d**.* ... 1640
1 Tim 5:18 *Those who work **d** their pay!* ... 1734
Heb 3:3 *But Jesus **d-s** far more* ... 1764

DESIRABLE (adj) attractive; worth seeking or doing
Ps 19:10 *They are more **d** than gold,* ... 555

DESIRE, DESIRES (n) conscious impulse toward something that promises enjoyment or satisfaction in its attainment; longing, craving
Job 17:11 *My heart's **d-s** are broken.* ... 111
Ps 10:3 *brag about their evil **d-s**;* ... 857
Ps 37:4 *give you your heart's **d-s**.* ... 567
Ps 145:19 *He grants the **d-s** of those who* ... 590
Song 6:12 *my strong **d-s** had taken me* ... 668
Mark 4:19 *wealth, and the **d** for other* ... 1346
Rom 1:26 *to their shameful **d-s**.* ... 1648
Rom 6:12 *not give in to sinful **d-s**.* ... 1656
Rom 7:5 *sinful **d-s** were at work* ... 1657
Rom 13:14 *indulge your evil **d-s**.* ... 1669
Gal 5:24 *the passions and **d-s** of their* ... 1567
Phil 2:13 *you the **d** and the power* ... 1720
Col 2:23 *a person's evil **d-s**.* ... 1699
Col 3:5 *lust, and evil **d-s**.* ... 1700
1 Tim 6:9 *and harmful **d-s** that plunge* ... 1735
2 Tim 4:3 *follow their own **d-s** and will* ... 1745
Jas 1:14 *from our own **d-s**, which entice* ... 1547
Jas 4:1 *from the evil **d-s** at war within* ... 1551
1 Pet 2:11 *from worldly **d-s** that wage* ... 1751
1 Pet 4:2 *chasing your own **d-s**,* ... 1754
2 Pet 2:10 *their own twisted sexual **d**,* ... 1759
2 Pet 2:18 *twisted sexual **d-s**, they lure* ... 1759
2 Pet 3:3 *following their own **d-s**.* ... 1760
Jude 1:18 *their ungodly **d-s**.* ... 1785

DESIRE, DESIRED, DESIRES (v) to long or hope for; to wish or request
see also COVET
Gen 3:16 *And you will **d** to control* ... 13
Ps 51:6 *But you **d** honesty from* ... 506
Ps 51:16 *You do not **d** a sacrifice,* ... 506
Prov 8:11 *Nothing you **d** can compare* ... 640
Prov 21:10 *Evil people **d** evil;* ... 657
Rom 1:24 *things their hearts **d-d**.* ... 1647
1 Cor 12:31 *earnestly **d** the most* ... 1615
1 Cor 14:1 *you should also **d** the special* ... 1616
1 Tim 3:1 *an elder, he **d-s** an honorable* ... 1730
Jas 1:20 *righteousness God **d-s**.* ... 1548
Rev 22:17 *Let anyone who **d-s** drink* ... 1833

DESOLATE (adj) deserted; joyless; alone; barren
Isa 54:1 *For the **d** woman now has* ... 941
Gal 4:27 *For the **d** woman now has* ... 1564

DESPAIR (n) utter loss of hope
Ps 40:2 *out of the pit of **d**,* ... 570
Ps 79:8 *on the brink of **d**.* ... 600
Ps 130:1 *the depths of **d**, O LORD,* ... 884
Isa 61:3 *praise instead of **d**.* ... 948
2 Cor 4:8 *but not driven to **d**.* ... 1631

DESPISE, DESPISED, DESPISES (n) to scorn or regard as unworthy, sometimes with malice or outrage
2 Sam 12:9 *you **d-d** the word of the LORD* ... 505
Job 5:17 *Do not **d** the discipline* ... 99
Job 9:21 *to me—I **d** my life.* ... 103
Ps 22:6 *I am scorned and **d-d** by all!* ... 556
Prov 1:7 *but fools **d** wisdom and* ... 632
Prov 12:8 *a warped mind is **d-d**.* ... 645
Prov 15:5 *Only a fool **d-s** a parent's* ... 648
Prov 15:20 *foolish children **d** their* ... 650
Prov 29:27 *The righteous **d** the unjust;* ... 846
Prov 30:17 *and **d-s** a mother's* ... 846
Isa 53:3 *He was **d-d**, and we did not* ... 940
Mic 7:6 *For the son **d-s** his father.* ... 911
Luke 16:13 *to one and **d** the other.* ... 1412
Gal 4:14 *you did not **d** me or* ... 1563
2 Pet 2:10 *and who **d** authority.* ... 1759

DESTINED (v) to decree beforehand; to predetermine
Luke 2:34 *This child is **d** to cause* ... 1282
Heb 9:27 *each person is **d** to die once* ... 1774

DESTINY (n) a predetermined course of events; fate or fortune
Ps 73:17 *understood the **d** of the* ... 594
Eccl 9:2 *The same **d** ultimately awaits* ... 680

DESTITUTE (adj) lacking possessions and resources; suffering extreme poverty
Ps 82:3 *of the oppressed and the **d**.* ... 602
Ps 102:17 *prayers of the **d**.* ... 866
Rom 8:35 *or hungry, or **d**, or in* ... 1661
Heb 11:37 ***d** and oppressed* ... 1779

DESTROY, DESTROYED, DESTROYING, DESTROYS (v) to kill; to cause devastation or ruin
see also PERISH
Gen 6:17 *that will **d** every living* ... 18
Gen 9:11 *will a flood **d** the earth.* ... 21
Num 32:15 *responsible for **d-ing** this* ... 279
Deut 28:63 *find pleasure in **d-ing** you.* ... 319
Josh 10:40 *He completely **d-ed** everyone* ... 351
Prov 6:32 *fool, for he **d-s** himself.* ... 639
Prov 10:21 *fools are **d-ed** by their lack* ... 642
Prov 10:29 *but it **d-s** the wicked.* ... 643
Prov 11:3 *dishonesty **d-s** treacherous* ... 643
Prov 11:9 *the godless **d** their friends,* ... 643
Prov 18:9 *as someone who **d-s** things* ... 653
Prov 18:24 *"friends" who **d** each other,* ... 654
Prov 29:1 *will suddenly be **d-ed** beyond* ... 844
Isa 11:4 *his mouth will **d** the wicked.* ... 796
Dan 2:44 *never be **d-ed** or conquered.* ... 1005
Jonah 3:9 *fierce anger from **d-ing** us.* ... 768
Jonah 4:2 *turn back from **d-ing** people.* ... 769
Matt 10:28 *God, who can **d** both soul* ... 1360

Luke 9:25 *but are yourself lost or* ***d-ed?***...1378
John 10:10 *and kill and* ***d.***...............1405
Rom 2:12 *they will be* ***d-ed,*** *even though*...1649
1 Cor 3:17 *anyone who* ***d-s*** *this temple*....1600
1 Cor 5:5 *nature will be* ***d-ed*** *and he*.......1602
1 Cor 8:11 *died will be* ***d-ed.***................1608
1 Cor 15:24 ***d-ed*** *every ruler and*...........1621
1 Cor 15:26 *enemy to be* ***d-ed*** *is death*....1621
2 Cor 4:9 *are not* ***d-ed.***........................1631
Gal 5:15 *Beware of* ***d-ing*** *one another*......1566
Heb 7:16 *that cannot be* ***d-ed.***...............1770
2 Pet 2:12 *be caught and* ***d-ed.***...............1759
2 Pet 3:7 *people will be* ***d-ed.***................1760
Jude 1:5 *but later he* ***d-ed*** *those who did*...1784
Rev 11:18 *It is time to* ***d*** *all who have*.......1817

DESTRUCTION (n) the state or fact of being destroyed, ruin; place of punishment (hell)
Ps 1:6 *of the wicked leads to* ***d.***.................856
Prov 16:18 *Pride goes before* ***d,***...............651
1 Cor 1:18 *are headed for* ***d!***....................1596
2 Thes 1:9 *punished with eternal* ***d,***..........1588
2 Thes 2:3 *the one who brings* ***d.***..............1588
1 Tim 6:9 *into ruin and* ***d.***........................1735
2 Pet 2:3 *their* ***d*** *will not be delayed*..........1758
Rev 17:8 *and go to eternal* ***d.***...................1824

DESTRUCTIVE (adj) designed or tending to hurt or destroy; ruinous
1 Pet 4:4 *and* ***d*** *things they do*.................1754
2 Pet 2:1 *cleverly teach* ***d*** *heresies and*.....1758

DETERMINE, DETERMINED, DETERMINES (v) to decide; to resolve
Exod 28:30 *objects used to* ***d*** *the* LORD*'s*.....179
Ezra 7:10 *because Ezra had* ***d-d*** *to study*..1196
Ps 17:3 *I am* ***d-d*** *not to sin in*....................553
Ps 119:30 *I have* ***d-d*** *to live by*.................878
Ps 119:112 *I am* ***d-d*** *to keep your*.............880
Prov 4:23 *it* ***d-s*** *the course of your life*........636
Prov 16:9 *but the* LORD ***d-s*** *our steps*..........651
Dan 1:8 *But Daniel was* ***d-d*** *not to*............1001
Dan 11:36 *what has been* ***d-d*** *will surely*..1160
Matt 12:34 *heart* ***d-s*** *what you say*...........1341
Luke 22:22 *it has been* ***d-d*** *that the Son*..1458
Acts 4:28 *was* ***d-d*** *beforehand according*...1519

DETEST, DETESTS (v) to loathe; to denounce
Prov 8:7 *the truth and* ***d*** *every kind of*.........640
Prov 12:22 *The* LORD ***d-s*** *lying lips,*............645
Prov 15:8 *The* LORD ***d-s*** *the sacrifice*..........648
Prov 15:26 *The* LORD ***d-s*** *evil plans,*............650
Prov 16:5 *The* LORD ***d-s*** *the proud;*.............651
Prov 20:10 *the* LORD ***d-s*** *double*...................656
Prov 24:9 *everyone* ***d-s*** *a mocker*..................662

DETESTABLE (adj) arousing or meriting intense dislike; abominable
Lev 11:10 *They are* ***d*** *to you*........................214
Prov 3:32 *wicked people are* ***d*** *to the*..........635
Prov 17:15 *both are* ***d*** *to the* LORD...............652
Prov 21:27 *an evil person is* ***d,***....................658
Luke 16:15 *What this world honors is* ***d***....1412

DEVIL (n) Satan; enemy of God and of everything good; destroyer, tempter, adversary
see also SATAN
Matt 4:1 *tempted there by the* ***d.***..............1294
Matt 4:11 *Then the* ***d*** *went away,*................1295
Matt 13:39 *among the wheat is the* ***d.***......1349
Matt 25:41 *prepared for the* ***d*** *and his*......1453
Luke 4:2 *tempted by the* ***d*** *for forty*..........1296
Luke 4:13 *When the* ***d*** *had finished*..........1296
Luke 8:12 *to have the* ***d*** *come and take*....1347
John 6:70 *twelve of you, but one is a* ***d.***....1369
John 13:2 ***d*** *had already prompted*..........1456
Eph 4:27 *foothold to the* ***d.***.....................1712
Eph 6:11 *strategies of the* ***d.***....................1715
Eph 6:16 *fiery arrows of the* ***d.***.................1715
2 Tim 2:26 *escape from the* ***d****'s trap.*........1743
Jas 4:7 *Resist the* ***d,*** *and he*....................1551
1 Jn 3:8 *the works of the* ***d.***.....................1791
1 Jn 3:10 *children of the* ***d.***......................1791
Jude 1:9 *accuse the* ***d*** *of blasphemy,*........1785
Rev 12:9 *called the* ***d,*** *or Satan,*................1818

DEVOTE, DEVOTED (v) to commit by a solemn act
see also CONSECRATE, DEDICATE
2 Chr 31:4 *could* ***d*** *themselves fully*...........838
Acts 2:42 *the believers* ***d-d*** *themselves to*..1516
Col 4:2 ***D*** *yourselves to prayer*...................1702

DEVOTED (adj) characterized by loyalty and devotion
1 Kgs 18:3 *(Obadiah was a* ***d*** *follower of*.....716
Ps 86:2 *for I am* ***d*** *to you*...........................579
Matt 6:24 *you will be* ***d*** *to one and*...........1332
1 Tim 2:10 *claim to be* ***d*** *to God should*.....1729

DEVOTION (n) religious fervor; being ardently dedicated and loyal
1 Chr 29:3 *of my* ***d*** *to the Temple*..............540
2 Chr 32:32 *his acts of* ***d*** *are recorded*.......923
2 Chr 35:26 *his acts of* ***d*** *(carried out*.........988
1 Cor 16:16 *serve with such* ***d.***...............1623
2 Cor 11:3 *and undivided* ***d*** *to Christ*........1640
Col 2:23 *they require strong* ***d,*** *pious*......1699
1 Tim 5:11 *overpower their* ***d*** *to Christ*......1733

DEVOUR, DEVOURED, DEVOURING, DEVOURS (v) to consume by eating; to destroy (as if by eating); to enjoy avidly
2 Sam 11:25 *The sword* ***d-s*** *this one*.........504
Isa 66:24 *the worms that* ***d*** *them will*..........954
Jer 15:16 *your words, I* ***d-ed*** *them*..........1019
Jer 30:16 *you will be* ***d-ed,*** *and all your*....1032
Gal 5:15 *biting and* ***d-ing*** *one another,*......1566
1 Pet 5:8 *for someone to* ***d.***.....................1756

DEVOURING (adj) characterized by consuming or destroying ravenously
Deut 4:24 *your God is a* ***d*** *fire; he is a*........290
Heb 12:29 *our God is a* ***d*** *fire.*..................1781

DEVOUT (adj) very religious; devoted
Luke 2:25 *was righteous and* ***d*** *and was*...1282
Acts 2:5 *time there were* ***d*** *Jews from*......1514
Acts 10:2 *He was a* ***d,*** *God-fearing man,*...1532
Acts 10:7 *servants and a* ***d*** *soldier,*..........1533
Acts 13:43 *Many Jews and* ***d*** *converts to*..1542
Titus 1:8 *must live a* ***d*** *and disciplined*......1737

DEW (n) moisture condensed upon cool surfaces especially at night
Judg 6:37 *is wet with* ***d*** *in the morning*.......384

DICE (n) small cubes marked on each face with numbers and used usually for games and gambling by being shaken and thrown
Ps 22:18 *throw* ***d*** *for my clothing*...............556
Matt 27:35 *his clothes by throwing* ***d.***.......1482

DIE, DIED, DIES (v) to pass from physical life; to cease from existence
see also DYING, PERISH
Gen 2:17 *you are sure to* ***d.***..........................10
Gen 3:3 *if you do, you will* ***d.***........................11
Esth 4:16 *If I must* ***d,*** *I must* ***d.***...............1188
Job 2:9 *Curse God and* ***d.***...............................96
Prov 5:23 *He will* ***d*** *for lack of*....................637
Prov 11:7 *When the wicked* ***d,*** *their*............643
Prov 11:10 *when the wicked* ***d.***....................643
Prov 23:13 *They won't* ***d*** *if you*...................661
Eccl 7:2 *After all, everyone* ***d-s—***..............678
Isa 22:13 *drink, for tomorrow we* ***d!***............892
Isa 66:24 *that devour them will never* ***d,***.....954
Jer 31:30 *All people will* ***d*** *for their*...........1034
Matt 26:52 *will* ***d*** *by the sword.*...................1469
Mark 9:48 *the maggots never* ***d*** *and the*...1384
Luke 16:22 *The rich man also* ***d-d*** *and*.....1412
John 13:37 *I'm ready to* ***d*** *for you*.............1461
Rom 4:25 *handed over to* ***d*** *because of*.....1653
Rom 5:6 *the right time and* ***d-d*** *for us*......1654
Rom 5:7 *be willing to* ***d*** *for a person*.........1654
Rom 5:8 *by sending Christ to* ***d*** *for us*.......1654
Rom 5:14 *Still, everyone* ***d-d—****from the*...1655
Rom 6:7 *when we* ***d-d*** *with Christ we*.......1656
Rom 6:10 *When he* ***d-d,*** *he* ***d-d*** *once*........1656
Rom 7:2 *But if he* ***d-s,*** *the laws of*............1657
Rom 7:6 *the law, for we* ***d-d*** *to it and*.......1657
Rom 14:8 *whether we live or* ***d,*** *we*...........1670
1 Cor 7:39 *If her husband* ***d-s,*** *she is free*1607
1 Cor 9:15 *I would rather* ***d*** *than lose*.........1608
1 Cor 15:6 *though some have* ***d-d.***............1620
1 Cor 15:18 *all who have* ***d-d*** *believing in*.1620
1 Cor 15:22 *Just as everyone* ***d-s*** *because*.......................................1621
1 Cor 15:32 *for tomorrow we* ***d!***..................1621
1 Cor 15:36 *plant unless it* ***d-s*** *first*.........1621
1 Cor 15:42 *in the ground when we* ***d,***......1621
1 Cor 15:51 *will not all* ***d,*** *but we will*........1622
2 Cor 5:15 *for Christ, who* ***d-d*** *and was*....1632
Col 2:20 *You have* ***d-d*** *with Christ,*...........1699
1 Thes 4:16 *who have* ***d-d*** *will rise from*...1585
1 Thes 5:10 *Christ* ***d-d*** *for us so*..............1585
1 Tim 6:16 *He alone can never* ***d,***.............1735
2 Tim 2:11 *saying: If we* ***d*** *with him,*.........1742
Heb 9:27 *is destined to* ***d*** *once and*..........1774
1 Pet 3:18 *sinned, but he* ***d-d*** *for sinners*..1754

DIFFERENCE (n) the quality or state of being different; a significant change in or affect on a situation
2 Chr 12:8 *know the* ***d*** *between serving*......704
Ezek 22:26 *teach my people the* ***d.***..........1069
Gal 2:6 *leaders made no* ***d*** *to me,*.............1558

DIFFERENT (adj) not the same as; dissimilar; another
Lev 19:19 *woven from two* ***d*** *kinds of*.........225
1 Sam 10:6 *into a* ***d*** *person*........................437
Dan 7:24 *king will arise,* ***d*** *from the*..........1136
Rom 12:6 *God has given us* ***d*** *gifts for*......1667
1 Cor 12:4 *There are* ***d*** *kinds of*................1614
1 Cor 12:6 *God works in* ***d*** *ways, but it*.....1614
2 Cor 11:4 *if they preach a* ***d*** *Jesus than*..1640
Gal 1:8 *who preaches a* ***d*** *kind of Good*.....1556

DIFFICULT (adj) hard to understand; hard to do or carry out; hard to manage or overcome
Deut 30:11 ***d*** *for you to understand,*...........321
2 Kgs 2:10 *have asked a* ***d*** *thing," Elijah*.....739
Acts 15:19 *should not make it* ***d*** *for the*.....1570
2 Tim 3:1 *will be very* ***d*** *times*...................1744

DIFFICULTY (n) the quality or state of being difficult; trouble
Phil 4:14 *in my present* ***d.***.........................1725

DIGNITY (n) the quality or state of being worthy, honored, or esteemed
Prov 31:25 *with strength and* ***d,*** *and she*.....848

DILIGENT (adj) characterized by steady, earnest, and energetic effort; painstaking
Ezra 4:22 *Be* ***d,*** *and don't*.............................1195
Prov 12:27 *but the* ***d*** *make use of*..............646

DILIGENTLY (adv) in a diligent manner
Deut 6:17 *You must* ***d*** *obey the*..................295

DINING (v) to take or give a dinner
Prov 23:1 *While **d** with a ruler,*....................661

DINNER (n) the principal meal of the day
1 Cor 10:27 *believer asks you home for **d**,*..1611

DIRECT, DIRECTED, DIRECTS (v) to regulate the activities or course of
Gen 18:19 *that he will **d** his sons and*...........40
Gen 24:51 *as the LORD has **d-ed**.*.................50
Job 38:31 *Can you **d** the movement of*.......128
Prov 20:24 *The LORD **d-s** our steps,*...........657
Jer 13:2 *as the LORD **d-ed** me, and I put*...1016
Gal 5:18 *you are **d-ed** by the Spirit,*..........1566

DISAPPEAR, DISAPPEARED, DISAPPEARING (v) to pass from view; to cease to be
1 Kgs 20:40 *the prisoner **d-ed!***.................723
Job 17:11 *My hopes have **d-ed**.*................111
Ps 37:20 *they will **d** like smoke.*................567
Prov 26:20 *and quarrels **d** when gossip*......841
Isa 29:14 *of the intelligent will **d**.*...............898
Isa 51:6 *the skies will **d** like smoke,*...........938
Matt 5:18 *until heaven and earth **d**,*..........1327
Matt 24:35 *Heaven and earth will **d**,*..........1447
Mark 13:31 *Heaven and earth will **d**,*........1449
Luke 16:17 *and earth to **d** than for the*.....1412
John 5:13 *for Jesus had **d-ed** into the*......1317
Heb 8:13 *and will soon **d**.*.......................1772
1 Jn 2:8 *the darkness is **d-ing**, and the*....1788

DISAPPOINTED (v) to fail to meet the expectation or hope of; to frustrate
Prov 23:18 *hope will not be **d**.*....................661

DISAPPOINTMENT (n) the state or emotion of being frustrated, failed, or let down
Rom 5:5 *this hope will not lead to **d**.*.........1654

DISARMED (v) to make harmless
Col 2:15 *this way, he **d** the spiritual*..........1698

DISASTER, DISASTERS (n) a sudden calamitous event bringing great damage, loss, or destruction; a sudden or great misfortune or failure
Exod 32:12 *this terrible **d** you have*.............185
Deut 31:17 *will say, 'These **d-s** have come*...322
Deut 31:21 *when great **d-s** come down*......322
Ps 91:6 *nor the **d** that strikes at*.................861
Prov 3:25 *not be afraid of sudden **d***............635
Prov 27:10 *When **d** strikes,*........................842
Jer 17:17 *my hope in the day of **d**.*...........1022
Jer 29:11 *plans for good and not for **d**,*.....1030
1 Thes 5:3 *then **d** will fall on them*............1585

DISCERNMENT (n) the quality of being able to grasp and comprehend what is obscure
Ps 119:125 *Give **d** to me,*..........................881
Prov 1:4 *knowledge and **d** to the young*.......631
Prov 5:2 *you will show **d**, and your*.............637
Prov 8:12 *knowledge and **d**.*.......................640
Prov 28:11 *a poor person with **d** can see*....844

DISCIPLE, DISCIPLES (n) student or follower of some doctrine or teacher
Matt 28:19 *go and make **d-s** of all the*.....1498
Mark 16:20 *the **d-s** went everywhere and*..1499
Luke 6:13 *all of his **d-s** and chose twelve*...1323
Luke 14:26 *you cannot be my **d**.*..............1409
Luke 14:33 *become my **d** without*...........1409
John 6:66 *many of his **d-s** turned away*....1369
John 8:31 *are truly my **d-s** if you remain*..1393
John 13:5 *to wash the **d-s'** feet, drying*....1456
John 13:23 *The **d** Jesus loved*................1459
John 15:8 *fruit, you are my true **d-s**.*........1464
John 19:26 *there beside the **d** he loved,*...1485
John 21:7 *Then the **d** Jesus loved*............1496
John 21:20 *the **d** Jesus loved—*..............1497

DISCIPLINE (n) punishment; instruction
Deut 11:2 *the **d** of the LORD*.......................300
Prov 10:17 *People who accept **d** are on*......642
Prov 13:1 *child accepts a parent's **d;***..........646
Prov 13:24 *spare the rod of **d** hate their*......647
Prov 15:32 *If you reject **d**, you only*............650
Heb 12:5 *of the LORD's **d**, and don't*..........1780
Heb 12:11 *No **d** is enjoyable*...................1780

DISCIPLINE, DISCIPLINED, DISCIPLINES (v) to punish or correct with love; to exercise self-control
Deut 8:5 *as a parent **d-s** a child,*................297
Deut 8:5 *your God **d-s** you for your*............297
Ps 38:1 *in your anger or **d** me in your*.........568
Ps 39:11 *When you **d** us for our*.................569
Ps 119:67 *wander off until you **d-d** me;*.....879
Ps 119:75 *you **d-d** me because I needed*...879
Prov 15:10 *right path will be severely **d-d;***..648
Jer 30:11 *I will **d** you, but with*................1031
Jer 31:18 *saying, 'You **d-d** me severely,*....1033
1 Cor 9:25 *All athletes are **d-d** in their*......1609
1 Cor 9:27 *I **d** my body like an athlete*.........1609
1 Cor 11:32 *we are being **d-d** so that we*...1614
Heb 12:6 *For the LORD **d-s** those he*.........1780
Heb 12:7 *who is never **d-d** by its father?*..1780
Heb 12:9 *fathers who **d-d** us, shouldn't*....1780
1 Pet 4:7 *be earnest and **d-d** in your*.......1754

DISCOURAGED (v) to dissuade or hinder; to deprive of courage or confidence
Deut 31:8 *be afraid or **d**, for the LORD*.........322
2 Sam 11:25 *not to be **d**," David said.*........504
1 Chr 28:20 *afraid or **d**, for the LORD*..........540
Isa 41:10 *Don't be **d**, for I am*...................925
2 Cor 7:6 *who are **d**, encouraged us by*....1635
Col 3:21 *will become **d**.*.........................1702

DISCOURAGEMENT (n) the state of being discouraged
2 Cor 2:7 *may be overcome by **d**.*.............1628

DISCRETION (n) cautious reserve in speech; prudent or modest in behavior and dress
Prov 11:22 *woman who lacks **d** is like a*.....644

DISCRIMINATION (n) prejudiced outlook, action, or treatment
see also FAVORITISM, PARTIALITY
Jas 2:4 *doesn't this **d** show that your*.......1548

DISEASE, DISEASES (n) sickness, malady
Exod 4:6 *a severe skin **d**.*.........................145
2 Chr 16:12 *a serious foot **d**.*....................713
Ps 91:6 *not dread the **d** that stalks*............861
Ps 103:3 *heals all my **d-s**.*........................580
Matt 9:35 *every kind of **d** and illness.*.......1357
Matt 10:1 *every kind of **d** and illness.*.......1358
Luke 4:40 *matter what their **d-s** were,*......1310

DISGRACE (n) loss of grace, favor, or honor; source of shame
Prov 11:2 *Pride leads to **d**, but with*............643
Prov 14:34 *but sin is a **d** to any people.*.......648
Acts 5:41 *worthy to suffer **d** for the*..........1522
Heb 13:13 *and bear the **d** he bore.*............1782

DISGRACE, DISGRACED (v) to cause to lose favor or standing; to be a source of shame to
Ps 25:3 *trusts in you will ever be **d-d**,*........559
Ps 37:19 *will not be **d-d** in hard times;*.......567
Prov 29:15 *but a mother is **d-d** by an*.........845
Matt 1:19 *did not want to **d** her*...............1277
Rom 9:33 *in him will never be **d-d**.*..........1663
Rom 10:11 *in him will never be **d-d**.*........1664
1 Tim 3:7 *will not be **d-d** and fall into*.......1730

DISGRACEFUL (adj) bringing or involving disgrace
Prov 12:4 *a **d** woman is like cancer*...........644
Prov 17:2 *over the master's **d** son and*........652
1 Cor 11:14 *it's **d** for a man to have*.........1612

DISGUISES (v) to mask the identity of; to use pretense or deception
2 Cor 11:14 *Even Satan **d** himself as an*...1640

DISGUSTS (v) provokes loathing, repugnance, or aversion
Isa 1:13 *of your offerings **d** me!*.................824

DISHONEST (adj) characterized by lack of truth, honesty, or trustworthiness
Lev 19:35 *Do not use **d** standards when*.....226
Prov 20:23 *not pleased by **d** scales.*...........657
Luke 16:8 *to admire the **d** rascal for*.........1411
Luke 16:10 *But if you are **d** in little*...........1412

DISHONESTLY (adv) in a shameful, unfair, or deceptive manner
Hab 2:9 *houses with money gained **d!***........980

DISHONESTY (n) lack of honesty or integrity
Jer 22:17 *eyes only for greed and **d!***..........992
Jer 23:14 *commit adultery and love **d**.*......1027
Rom 3:7 *sinner if my **d** highlights his*........1650
Rev 21:27 *idolatry and **d**—but only*..........1831

DISHONOR, DISHONORED, DISHONORING, DISHONORS (v) to degrade or bring shame upon
Exod 21:17 *Anyone who **d-s** father or*.......171
Exod 22:28 *You must not **d** God or*.............173
Lev 20:19 *This would **d** a close*..................227
Deut 27:16 *is anyone who **d-s** father or*......317
Ezra 4:14 *see the king **d-ed** in this way,*...1195
Lam 2:2 ***d-ing** the kingdom and its*...........1096
John 8:49 *my Father—and you **d** me.*......1393
Rom 2:23 *the law, but you **d** God by*.........1650
1 Cor 11:4 *A man **d-s** his head if*............1612
1 Cor 11:5 *a woman **d-s** her head if*.........1612
Jas 2:6 *But you **d** the poor!*......................1548

DISMAYED (v) to cause to lose courage or resolution; to be upset or perturbed
Ps 49:16 *So don't be **d** when the wicked*....854

DISOBEDIENCE (n) refusal or neglect to obey
Ps 32:1 *those whose **d** is forgiven,*.............564
Rom 11:32 *imprisoned everyone in **d**.*.......1666

DISOBEDIENT (adj) refusing or neglecting to obey
Neh 9:26 *they were **d** and rebelled*...........1216
2 Cor 10:6 *everyone who remains **d**.*........1638
Titus 1:16 *detestable and **d**, worthless*......1737

DISOBEY, DISOBEYED, DISOBEYING (v) to fail to obey
Judg 2:2 *But you **d-ed** my command*..........373
1 Kgs 13:26 *man of God who **d-ed** the*.......701
2 Chr 24:20 *says: Why do you **d** the*...........758
Neh 9:29 *and obstinate and **d-ed** your*.....1216
Esth 3:3 *Why are you **d-ing** the king's*......1186
Dan 9:11 *Israel has **d-ed** your instruction*.1142
Acts 7:53 *You deliberately **d-ed** God's*......1526
Rom 1:30 *and they **d** their parents*............1648
Rom 5:19 *Because one person **d-ed** God,*..1655
Eph 5:6 *fall on all who **d** him.*..................1712
Heb 3:18 *the people who **d-ed** him?*.........1765
Heb 4:6 *enter because they **d-ed** God.*.....1766
Heb 4:11 *But if we **d** God, as the*.............1766
1 Pet 3:20 *those who **d-ed** God long ago*.1754

DISORDER (n) lack of order; confusion
1 Cor 14:33 *not a God of **d** but of peace,*...1618
Jas 3:16 *you will find **d** and evil of*...1551

DISORDERLY (adj) in a manner that lacks order; turbulent
2 Cor 12:20 *arrogance, and **d** behavior.*...1642

DISPLAY (n) a presentation of something in open view; exhibition
1 Cor 4:9 *apostles on **d,** like prisoners*...1601

DISPLAYED, DISPLAYING (v) to put or spread before the view; to make evident
Neh 9:10 *You **d** miraculous signs*...1216
Isa 5:16 *The holiness of God will be **d***...829
Isa 63:12 *power was **d** when Moses*...950
Rom 9:17 *purpose of **d-ing** my power*...1662

DISPLEASED (v) to incur the disapproval or dislike of
2 Sam 11:27 *But the LORD was **d** with*...505
Prov 24:18 *LORD will be **d** with you and*...662

DISPUTE, DISPUTES (n) verbal controversy; quarrel or debate
Prov 18:18 *it settles **d-s** between*...654
1 Cor 6:1 *you has a **d** with another*...1603

DISSENSION (n) disagreement; discord
Gal 5:20 *selfish ambition, **d,** division,*...1566

DISTINCTION (n) the distinguishing of a difference; division
Acts 15:9 *He made no **d** between us and*...1569

DISTORT (v) to twist out of the true meaning or proportion
Acts 20:30 *rise up and **d** the truth in*...1675

DISTRACTED (v) to divert one's attention
Luke 10:40 *But Martha was **d** by the big*...1397

DISTRACTIONS (n) something that distracts
1 Cor 7:35 *with as few **d** as possible.*...1607

DISTRESS (n) a troubling or painful situation; a state of danger or desperate need
Exod 3:7 *their cries of **d** because of*...144
Job 36:16 *to a place free from **d.***...126
Ps 18:6 *But in my **d** I cried out*...528
Ps 118:5 *In my **d** I prayed to*...876
Ps 143:11 *bring me out of this **d.***...589
Jas 1:27 *and widows in their **d***...1548

DISTRESSED (v) to subject one to grief or misery
Rom 14:15 *another believer is **d** by*...1670

DISTURB (v) to interfere with; to interrupt
Ezra 6:7 *Do not **d** the construction of*...1172

DIVIDE, DIVIDED (v) to separate into parts; to distribute; to make distinctions
Ps 22:18 *They **d** my garments*...556
Luke 12:51 *have come to **d** people*...1402
1 Cor 1:13 *Has Christ been **d-d** into*...1596
Jas 4:8 *loyalty is **d-d** between God*...1551

DIVINATION (n) the attempt through ritual means to know the future or other hidden knowledge
Num 24:1 *he did not resort to **d** as before*...268
2 Kgs 21:6 *He practiced sorcery and **d,***...954

DIVINE (adj) of, relating to, or preceding directly from God or a god
Prov 29:18 *not accept **d** guidance,*...845
Rom 1:20 *power and **d** nature.*...1647
2 Pet 1:4 *to share his **d** nature*...1757

DIVISION, DIVISIONS (n) act or process of dividing, separating, distributing; a portion, part, grouping, or distinction
1 Cor 1:10 *there be no **d-s** in the church.*...1596
1 Cor 11:18 *that there are **d-s** among*...1613
Gal 5:20 *selfish ambition, dissension, **d,***...1566
Titus 3:10 *are causing **d-s** among you,*...1739

DIVORCE (n) the action or an instance of legally dissolving a marriage
Deut 24:1 *a letter of **d,** hands it to*...314
Mal 2:16 *"For I hate **d!"** says the*...1247
Matt 19:8 *Moses permitted **d** only as a*...1418

DIVORCE, DIVORCED, DIVORCES (v) to dissolve a marriage; to end a relationship
Lev 21:7 *a woman who is **d-d** from her*...228
Lev 21:14 *who is **d-d,** or a woman*...228
Lev 22:13 *a widow or is **d-d** and has no*...229
Num 30:9 *is a widow or is **d-d,** she must*...276
Deut 22:19 *and he may never **d** her.*...312
1 Chr 8:8 *After Shaharaim **d-d** his wives*...1236
Jer 3:1 *If a man **d-s** a woman and*...962
Jer 3:8 *saw that I **d-d** faithless Israel*...962
Matt 5:31 *A man can **d** his wife by*...1329
Matt 5:32 *a man who **d-s** his wife, unless*...1329
Matt 5:32 *who marries a **d-d** woman also*...1329
Mark 10:2 *be allowed to **d** his wife?*...1419
Mark 10:11 *Whoever **d-s** his wife and*...1419
Mark 10:12 *if a woman **d-s** her husband*...1419
Luke 16:18 *a man who **d-s** his wife and*...1412
Luke 16:18 *marries a woman **d-d** from*...1412

DOCTOR, DOCTORS (n) a person skilled or specializing in healing arts
Matt 9:12 *don't need a **d**—sick people*...1315
Mark 5:26 *great deal from many **d-s,***...1354

DOG, DOGS (n) a carnivorous (usually domestic) mammal similar to wolves and coyotes
Prov 26:11 *As a **d** returns to its*...841
Eccl 9:4 *to be a live **d** than a dead*...680
Matt 15:26 *throw it to the **d-s.***...1371
Phil 3:2 *Watch out for those **d-s,***...1721
2 Pet 2:22 *this proverb: "A **d** returns to*...1759

DONKEY (n) a domestic mammal smaller than the horse and having long ears
Num 22:30 *same **d** you have ridden*...266
Matt 21:5 *riding on a **d**—riding on a*...1429
2 Pet 2:16 *when his **d** rebuked him*...1759

DOOMED (adj) condemned; certain to be destroyed
Isa 6:5 *I am **d,** for I am*...784

DOOR, DOORS (n) a barrier by which an entry is closed and opened; a means of access or participation
Ps 24:7 *Open up, ancient **d-s,** and let*...559
Matt 7:7 *the **d** will be opened to you.*...1334
Luke 13:24 *enter the narrow **d** to God's*...1407
Acts 14:27 *had opened the **d** of faith to*...1546
1 Cor 16:9 *is a wide-open **d** for a great*...1623
2 Cor 2:12 *opened a **d** of opportunity*...1628
Rev 3:20 *stand at the **d** and knock.*...1807

DOORPOSTS (n) the two sides of a doorway, similar to a door frame
Deut 6:9 *Write them on the **d** of*...295

DOUBLE-EDGED (adj) having two cutting edges
Prov 5:4 *dangerous as a **d** sword*...637

DOUBT, DOUBTS (n) uncertainty of belief or opinion; lack of confidence; distrust
Mark 11:23 *have no **d** in your heart.*...1435
Luke 24:38 *hearts filled with **d?***...1495
Rom 14:23 *if you have **d-s** about whether*...1671

DOUBT (v) to distrust; to be uncertain
Matt 14:31 *Why did you **d** me?*...1365
Matt 21:21 *faith and don't **d,** you*...1435

DOVE, DOVES (n) a small wild pigeon, often symbolic of gentleness
Gen 8:8 *also released a **d** to see if*...20
Matt 3:16 *like a **d** and settling on him.*...1293
Matt 10:16 *snakes and harmless as **d-s.***...1359

DOWNTRODDEN (adj) suffering oppression
Ps 74:21 *Don't let the **d** be humiliated*...595

DRAGON (n) a huge serpent
Rev 12:7 *fought against the **d** and his*...1818
Rev 20:2 *He seized the **d**—that old*...1829

DRAW, DRAWING, DRAWS (v) to pull; to bring in or gather; to come steadily or gradually
John 6:44 *who sent me **d-s** them to me,*...1367
John 12:32 *I will **d** everyone to myself.*...1434
Heb 10:25 *day of his return is **d-ing** near.*...1776

DREAD (n) great fear; extreme uneasiness in the face of a disagreeable prospect
Isa 51:13 *remain in constant **d** of human*...938

DREADFUL (adj) causing great and oppressive fear; inspiring awe or reverence
Job 25:2 *powerful and **d.***...117

DREAM, DREAMS (n) a strongly desired goal or purpose; a series of thoughts, images, or emotions occurring during sleep
Prov 13:12 *sick, but a **d** fulfilled is a*...646
Prov 13:19 *pleasant to see **d-s** come true,*...646
Eccl 5:3 *gives you restless **d-s;***...677

DREAM (v) to have a dream
Joel 2:28 *old men will **d** dreams,*...1242
Acts 2:17 *old men will **d** dreams.*...1514

DRESSED (v) to put on clothing
Exod 12:11 *Be fully **d,** wear your*...156
Ps 104:2 *You are **d** in a robe*...867
Isa 61:10 *For he has **d** me with the*...948

DRINK, DRINKING, DRINKS (v) to swallow; to partake of alcoholic beverages
1 Sam 1:13 *she had been **d-ing.***...417
Isa 5:22 *who are heroes at **d-ing** wine*...829
Isa 12:3 *you will **d** deeply from*...797
Matt 26:27 *Each of you **d** from it,*...1457
Mark 16:18 ***d** anything poisonous,*...1498
John 4:13 *Anyone who **d-s** this water*...1304
John 6:54 *my flesh and **d-s** my blood has*...1368
Rom 14:17 *we eat or **d,** but of living a*...1670
1 Cor 11:27 *this bread or **d-s** this cup of*...1613
Rev 14:10 ***d** the wine of God's anger.*...1821
Rev 22:17 *who desires **d** freely from*...1833

DRINKER, DRINKERS (n) a person who drinks alcoholic beverages
1 Tim 3:3 *not be a heavy **d** or be violent.*...1730
1 Tim 3:8 *not be heavy **d-s** or dishonest*...1731
Titus 2:3 *or be heavy **d-s.***...1738

DRIVE (v) to exert inescapable or coercive pressure on; to force
Exod 23:30 *I will **d** them out a little*...174
Num 33:52 *you must **d** out all the people.*...281
Josh 13:13 *failed to **d** out the people of*...356
Josh 23:13 *will no longer **d** them out of*...368

DROUGHT (n) a period of prolonged dryness
1 Kgs 18:1 *in the third year of the **d,***...716
Jer 17:8 *by long months of **d.***...1021

DROWNED (v) to suffocate by submersion especially in water
Exod 15:4 *officers are **d** in the Red*.............161
Matt 18:6 *neck and be **d** in the depths*.....1384
Heb 11:29 *they were all **d.***......................1779

DRUNK (adj) having the faculties impaired by alcohol; intoxicated
Acts 2:15 *These people are not **d,** as*........1514

DRUNKARD, DRUNKARDS (n) one who is habitually drunk
Prov 23:20 *not carouse with **d-s** or feast*....661
Matt 11:19 *glutton and a **d,** and a friend*...1338
1 Cor 5:11 *or is a **d,** or cheats people*.......1602
1 Cor 6:10 *greedy people, or **d-s,** or are*...1603

DRUNKENNESS
Ezek 23:33 ***D** and anguish will fill you,*......1071
Rom 13:13 *darkness of wild parties and **d***...1669

DRY (adj) free or relatively free from a liquid, especially water
Gen 1:9 *so **d** ground may appear*....................7
Exod 14:16 *of the sea on **d** ground*.............160
Josh 3:17 *Covenant stood on **d** ground*.......340
Isa 53:2 *a root in **d** ground*.........................940

DULL (adj) slow in action, sluggish; slow in perception or sensibility
Heb 6:12 *not become spiritually **d** and*......1768

DUST (n) specks or clumps of earthy matter; ground or earth
Gen 2:7 *man from the **d** of the ground*...........9
Gen 3:19 *were made from **d,** and to **d***..........13
Ps 22:15 *laid me in the **d** and left me*.........556
Eccl 3:20 *they return to **d.***..........................676
Matt 10:14 *shake its **d** from your feet*.......1358
1 Cor 15:47 *from the **d** of the earth,*........1622

DUTY, DUTIES (n) moral or legal obligation; assigned service or task
Eccl 8:3 *to avoid doing your **d,***..................679
Eccl 12:13 *is everyone's **d.***.......................683
Dan 8:27 *performed my **d-ies** for the*.......1138

DWELLING (n) a shelter (as a house) in which one lives; residence
see also HOME, HOUSE
Exod 15:17 *your own **d,** the sanctuary,*......162
Eph 2:22 *made part of this **d** where God*...1708

DWELLS (v) to stay for a time; to live as a resident
see also LIVE(S)
Ps 26:8 *glorious presence **d.***......................560

DYING (v) *see also* DIE
John 11:25 *even after **d.***..........................1414
2 Cor 4:16 *our bodies are **d,** our spirits*.....1631
Phil 1:21 *for Christ, and **d** is even*............1718

DYNASTY (n) a succession of rulers of the same line of descent
see also HOUSE
2 Sam 3:1 *Saul's **d** became weaker and*.....480
1 Chr 17:17 *your servant a lasting **d!***.........497

EAGER (adj) marked by enthusiastic or impatient desire or interest
Rom 15:23 *I am **e** to visit you*..................1672
1 Cor 14:39 *sisters, be **e** to prophesy,*.......1618
1 Pet 5:2 *because you are **e** to serve*........1756

EAGERLY (adv) in an enthusiastic or impatient manner
Rom 8:19 *creation is waiting **e** for that*......1659

EAGERNESS (n) the state or quality of enthusiasm for a desire or interest
Ps 119:36 *Give me an **e** for your laws*........878

EAGLE, EAGLES (n) any of various large diurnal birds of prey noted for their strength, size, keenness of vision, and powers of flight
Deut 32:11 *Like an **e** that rouses her chicks*..324
Isa 40:31 *soar high on wings like **e-s.***........925
Rev 4:7 *was like an **e** in flight*....................1808
Rev 12:14 *wings like those of a great **e***...1819

EARN, EARNED (v) to receive as return for effort or work done
2 Thes 3:12 ***e** their own living*..................1590
Heb 11:2 ***e-ed** a good reputation*.............1777

EARNEST (adj) characterized by or proceeding from an intense and serious state of mind; ardent or fervent
Jas 5:16 *The **e** prayer of a righteous*.........1554
1 Pet 4:7 *be **e** and disciplined*.................1754

EARNESTLY (adv) in a manner that is intense and serious; fervently
2 Chr 15:15 *they **e** sought after God,*..........709
Col 4:12 *He always prays **e** for you,*..........1703

EARNINGS (n) pay; wages
Prov 31:16 *with her **e** she plants a vineyard*...847

EARRING, EARRINGS (n) an ornament for the ear and especially the earlobe
Exod 35:22 *gold—brooches, **e-s,** rings*......189
Prov 25:12 *valid criticism is like a gold **e***.....839

EARS (n) the external organs for hearing, expressing the entire faculty of understanding
Prov 2:2 *Tune your **e** to wisdom,*.................633
Eccl 5:1 ***e** open and your mouth shut*.........677
2 Tim 4:3 *whatever their itching **e** want*.....1745

EARTH (n) The ground; the planet on which we live
Gen 1:1 *created the heavens and the **e.***..........6
Gen 7:24 *floodwaters covered the **e***............19
Gen 14:19 *Creator of heaven and **e.***............34
Job 26:7 *and hangs the **e** on nothing*..........117
Job 38:4 *I laid the foundations of the **e?***.....127
Ps 24:1 *The **e** is the* Lord*'s, and*.................558
Ps 108:5 *your glory shine over all the **e.***.....581
Prov 8:23 *first, before the **e** began*.............640
Prov 8:26 *had made the **e** and fields*............640
Isa 6:3 *whole **e** is filled with his glory!*.........783
Isa 40:22 *God sits above the circle of the **e.***924
Isa 44:23 *O depths of the **e!***.......................930
Isa 55:9 *higher than the **e,** so my ways*........942
Isa 65:17 *new heavens and a new **e,***...........952
Isa 66:1 *and the **e** is my footstool*...............952
Jer 23:24 *in all the heavens and **e?***..........1028
Hab 2:20 *Let all the **e** be silent*....................981
Matt 5:18 *until heaven and **e** disappear,*....1327
Matt 5:35 *do not say, 'By the **e!'***..............1329
Matt 6:10 *your will be done on **e,***.............1331
Matt 16:19 *Whatever you forbid on **e***........1375
Matt 28:18 *in heaven and on **e.***..................1497
Luke 2:14 *and peace on **e***.........................1281
Acts 4:24 *Creator of heaven and **e,***..........1519
Acts 7:49 *the **e** is my footstool*..................1526
Rom 8:39 *or in the **e** below—*......................1661
1 Cor 10:26 *the **e** is the Lord's,*..................1611
Eph 3:15 *in heaven and on **e.***....................1709
Phil 2:10 *in heaven and on **e** and under*....1720
Col 3:2 *not the things of **e.***........................1700
Heb 1:10 *laid the foundation of the **e***........1762
2 Pet 3:13 *and new **e** he has promised,*....1760
Rev 20:11 *The **e** and sky fled*....................1830
Rev 21:1 *a new heaven and a new **e,***.......1830
Rev 21:1 *the old **e** had disappeared*..........1830

EARTHLY (adj) belonging to the earth; mundane or worldly; temporal or temporary; human
Rom 1:3 *In his **e** life he was born*..............1644
Col 3:5 *put to death the sinful, **e** things*.....1700

EARTHQUAKE, EARTHQUAKES (n) a shaking or trembling of the earth
Matt 24:7 *There will be famines and **e-s***...1446
Matt 28:2 *there was a great **e!***................1489
Rev 6:12 *there was a great **e.***..................1812

EAST (n) the general direction of the sunrise
Gen 2:8 *a garden in Eden in the **e,***..................9
Ps 103:12 *far from us as the **e** is from*........580

EASTERN (adj) coming from the east
Matt 2:1 *wise men from **e** lands arrived*....1283

EASY (adj) causing or involving little difficulty or discomfort
Matt 11:30 *For my yoke is **e** to bear,*..........1340

EAT, EATEN, EATING, EATS (v) to ingest, chew, and swallow in turn
see also ATE
Gen 2:16 *You may freely **e** the fruit*..............10
Gen 3:11 *Have you **e-en** from the tree*..........12
Deut 14:4 *the animals you may **e:***.............303
Isa 65:25 *The lion will **e** hay*.......................952
Jer 31:29 *parents have **e-en** sour grapes,*..1033
Matt 26:26 *Take this and **e** it,*...................1457
Luke 15:2 *sinful people—even **e-ing** with*...1409
John 6:52 *give us his flesh to **e?***.............1368
John 6:54 *anyone who **e-s** my flesh and*....1368
Acts 10:13 *"Get up, Peter; kill and **e** them*...1533
Acts 10:14 *I have never **e-en** anything*.......1533
Rom 14:15 *Don't let your **e-ing** ruin*...........1670
1 Cor 8:4 *So, what about **e-ing** meat that*...1607
1 Cor 8:10 ***e-ing** in the temple of an idol,*...1608
1 Cor 10:31 *So whether you **e** or drink,*.......1611
1 Cor 11:26 *every time you **e** this bread*.....1613
1 Cor 11:27 *anyone who **e-s** this bread or*..1613

EDEN (n) the garden where Adam and Eve first lived
Gen 2:8 *a garden in **E** in the east,*..................9
Ezek 28:13 *in **E,** the garden of God*...........1084

EDIFY, EDIFYING (KJV)
1 Cor 10:23 *but not everything is **beneficial***...1611
1 Cor 14:5 *will be **strengthened***...............1617
1 Cor 14:17 *won't **strengthen** the people*..1617
Eph 4:12 *work and **build up** the church,*...1711

EFFORT, EFFORTS (n) conscious exertion of power; hard work; a serious attempt
2 Chr 31:21 ***e-s** to follow God's laws*..........839
Ps 90:17 *make our **e-s** successful*............326
Gal 3:3 *by your own human **e?***................1560
Eph 4:3 *Make every **e** to keep*..................1710
2 Pet 1:5 *make every **e** to respond*...........1757
2 Pet 3:14 *make every **e** to be found*........1760

EGYPT (n) the country in the northeast corner of Africa that extended from the Mediterranean Sea on the north to the Nile River on the south
Gen 46:6 *his entire family went to **E—***.........88
Exod 3:11 *people of Israel out of **E?***...........144
Exod 12:40 *Israel had lived in **E.***................158
Hos 11:1 *I called my son out of **E.***..............814

Matt 2:15 *I called my Son out of **E.***...........1285
Heb 11:27 *Moses left the land of **E,***..........1778

ELDER, ELDERS (n) older, wise man; ruling body of decision makers invested with authority by virtue of their age, character, or experience
see also DEACONS
Acts 14:23 *appointed **e-s** in every church.*1545
Acts 15:2 *talk to the apostles and **e-s***......1568
Acts 20:17 *a message to the **e-s** of the*....1675
Acts 20:28 *appointed you as **e-s.***............1675
Phil 1:1 *including the **e-s** and deacons.*....1716
1 Tim 3:1 *aspires to be an **e,** he desires.*...1730
1 Tim 3:2 ***e** must be a man whose life is*...1730
1 Tim 4:14 ***e-s** of the church laid their*......1732
1 Tim 5:19 *against an **e** unless it is*..........1734
Titus 1:6 *An **e** must live a blameless life.*...1736
Titus 1:7 *An **e** is a manager of God's*........1736
Jas 5:14 *call for the **e-s** of the church*.......1553
1 Pet 5:1 *a word to you who are **e-s.***........1755
1 Pet 5:1 *I, too, am an **e** and a witness*.....1755
1 Pet 5:5 *the authority of the **e-s.***...............1756
2 Jn 1:1 *letter is from John, the **e.***............1795
3 Jn 1:1 *letter is from John, the **e.***............1796
Rev 4:10 *the twenty-four **e-s** fall down*....1808

ELDERLY (n) people of advanced age
Lev 19:32 *the **e,** and show respect*.............226

ELECT (KJV)
Isa 42:1 ***chosen one,** who pleases me*.......926
Matt 24:31 *gather his **chosen ones** from all*...1447
Rom 8:33 ***us whom God has chosen** for*.1661
Col 3:12 ***chose** you to be the holy people*.1700
2 Tim 2:10 *Jesus to **those God has chosen***...1742

ELEMENTS (n) any of four substances air, water, fire, and earth
2 Pet 3:10 *the very **e** themselves*.............1760
2 Pet 3:12 *the **e** will melt away*.................1760

ELIJAH Powerful prophet in Israel (northern kingdom); proclaimed drought (1 Kgs 17:1, p. 715; Jas 5:17, p. 1554); hid and was fed by ravens (1 Kgs 17:2-6, p. 715); performed miracles for widow (1 Kgs 17:8-24, p. 715; Luke 4:25, p. 1357); proclaimed truth to King Ahab (1 Kgs 18:1-15, p. 716); defeated Baal and his prophets on Mount Carmel (1 Kgs 18:16-40, p. 717); brought rain (1 Kgs 18:41-46, p. 718; Jas 5:17, p. 1554); ran for his life (1 Kgs 19:3, p. 719); served by angels (1 Kgs 19:1-9, p. 719); given assurance by God (1 Kgs 19:9-18, p. 720); put mantle on Elisha (1 Kgs 19:19-21, p. 720); condemned by Ahab (1 Kgs 21:17-29, p. 724); whirlwind and fire took him into heaven (2 Kgs 2:11, p. 739); return prophesied and expected (Mal 4:5-6, p. 1249; Matt 11:14, p. 1338; Luke 1:17, p. 1273; John 1:25, p. 1293); compared to John the Baptist (Matt 17:9-13, p. 1379; Mark 9:9-13, p. 1379; Luke 1:17, p. 1273); appeared at Jesus' Transfiguration (Matt 17:1-8, p. 1378; Mark 9:2-13, p. 1379).

ELISHA Powerful prophet in Israel (northern kingdom) who replaced Elijah (1 Kgs 19:16-21, p. 720); inherited Elijah's cloak (2 Kgs 2:1-18, p. 738); asked for double measure of spirit (2 Kgs 2:9, p. 739); witnessed Elijah's departure (2 Kgs 2:11-12, p. 739); healed bad water (2 Kgs 2:19-22, p. 739); cursed 42 mockers (2 Kgs 2:23-25, p. 740); prophesied victory over Moab (2 Kgs 3:11-27, p. 735); provided abundant oil for widow (2 Kgs 4:1-7, p. 740); raised child to life (2 Kgs 4:32-37, p. 742); made stew edible (2 Kgs 4:38-41, p. 742); fed a multitude with few loaves (2 Kgs 4:42-44, p. 743); healed Naaman's leprosy (2 Kgs 5:14-15, p. 744); made an ax head float (2 Kgs 6:1-7, p. 744); prophesied the availability of food (2 Kgs 7:1, p. 746); prophesied death of Ben-hadad (2 Kgs 8:7-15, p. 747); died (2 Kgs 13:20, p. 760); bones produced miracle after death (2 Kgs 13:21, p. 760).

ELIZABETH Mother of John the Baptist, cousin of Mary the mother of Jesus (Luke 1:5-66, p. 1272).

EMBARRASSED (v) to become anxiously self-conscious
Luke 14:9 *you will be **e,** and you will*........1408

EMBARRASSMENT (n) the state of being anxiously self-conscious
2 Cor 9:4 *not to mention your own **e**—*.....1637

EMPLOYER (n) one who provides with a job that pays wages
Luke 16:5 *owed money to his **e** to come*...1411

EMPOWER, EMPOWERED (v) to give official authority or legal power to; to enable
Luke 11:18 *You say I am **e-ed** by Satan.*...1342
Eph 3:16 *resources he will **e** you with*.......1709

EMPTINESS (n) a void; containing nothing
Job 15:31 *for **e** will be their only*...............109
Isa 40:17 *nothing—mere **e** and froth*.........924

EMPTY (adj) containing nothing; having no purpose or result; destitute of effect or force
Gen 1:2 *formless and **e,** and darkness*............6
Deut 32:47 *not **e** words—they are your life!*...325
Job 26:7 *the northern sky over **e** space*......117
Isa 45:18 *not to be a place of **e** chaos.*........932
Jer 4:23 *and it was **e** and formless.*.............965
Luke 1:53 *the rich away with **e** hands.*......1276
1 Cor 14:9 *be talking into **e** space.*...........1617
1 Pet 1:18 *to save you from the **e** life*.......1749
2 Pet 2:18 *with **e,** foolish boasting.*...........1759

EMPTY-HANDED (adj) having, bringing, or gaining nothing
Eccl 5:15 *as naked and **e** as on the day*......677

ENABLE, ENABLED (v) to make possible, provide an opportunity for
2 Cor 3:6 ***e-ed** us to be ministers of his.*...1629
2 Thes 1:11 *to **e** you to live a life worthy*...1588
2 Pet 1:4 ***e** you to share his divine*...........1757

ENCOURAGE, ENCOURAGED, ENCOURAGES, ENCOURAGING (v) to inspire with courage or hope; to spur on
Isa 41:7 *The carver **e-s** the goldsmith,*........925
Acts 11:23 *and he **e-d** the believers*.........1536
Acts 15:32 *length to the believers, **e-ing***..1572
Acts 20:1 *sent for the believers and **e-d***...1625
Acts 28:15 *he was **e-d** and thanked God.*...1689
Rom 1:12 *I also want to be **e-d** by yours*...1646
Rom 12:8 *your gift is to **e** others,*.............1667
1 Cor 8:12 *other believers by **e-ing***..........1608
1 Cor 14:3 *strengthens others, **e-s** them,*...1617
2 Cor 7:6 *who **e-s** those who are*............1635
2 Cor 7:6 ***e-d** us by the arrival of Titus.*.....1635
2 Cor 7:13 *have been greatly **e-d** by this.*...1635
Eph 6:22 *how we are doing and to **e.***........1716
Col 4:8 *how we are doing and to **e** you.*....1703
1 Thes 2:12 *pleaded with you, **e-d** you,*....1582
1 Thes 3:2 *to strengthen you, to **e** you*......1583
1 Thes 3:7 *we have been greatly **e-d** in*....1583
1 Thes 5:11 *So **e** each other and build*......1585
1 Thes 5:14 ***E** those who are timid*............1586
Titus 1:9 *he will be able to **e** others*..........1737
Heb 12:5 *you forgotten the **e-ing** words*...1780
1 Pet 5:12 *purpose in writing is to **e** you*...1756
2 Jn 1:11 *Anyone who **e-s** such people*....1796

ENCOURAGEMENT (n) the act of encouraging; the state of being encouraged
Rom 15:5 *who gives this patience and **e,***..1671
1 Cor 16:18 *a wonderful **e** to me,*.............1623
2 Cor 7:13 *In addition to our own **e,***..........1635
Eph 4:29 *an **e** to those who hear them.*......1712
Phil 2:1 *any **e** from belonging to Christ?*...1719
Phlm 1:20 *Give me this **e** in Christ.*...........1692

END, ENDS (n) the point where something ceases to exist; death and destruction; the goal or result toward which some action or agent is heading
Ps 65:8 *live at the **e-s** of the earth stand*....575
Eccl 3:11 *work from beginning to **e.***...........675
Isa 30:8 *stand until the **e** of time*...............900
Isa 49:6 *bring my salvation to the **e-s***.........936
Matt 24:13 *the one who endures to the **e***...1446
Matt 24:14 *and then the **e** will come.*..........1446
Matt 24:31 *farthest **e-s** of the earth*...........1447
1 Cor 15:24 *After that the **e** will come,*........1621
Phil 3:14 *press on to reach the **e** of*............1723
Rev 21:6 *the Beginning and the **E.***............1830
Rev 22:13 *the Beginning and the **E.***...........1832

END, ENDING, ENDS (v) to come to an end; to die
1 Sam 12:23 *sin against the* LORD *by **e-ing***...441
Prov 14:12 *but it **e-s** in death.*....................647
Prov 14:13 *the laughter **e-s,** the grief*.........647
Prov 29:23 *Pride **e-s** in humiliation,*............845
Isa 9:7 *its peace will never **e.***......................793
Eph 2:15 *by **e-ing** the system of law*........1708

ENDANGER (v) to bring into danger or peril
Prov 22:25 *be like them and **e** your soul.*....660

ENDLESS (adj) being or seeming to be without end
Eccl 12:12 *writing books is **e,***......................683
Amos 5:24 *an **e** river of righteous*...............776
Eph 3:8 *the **e** treasures available*..............1709

ENDURANCE (n) the ability to withstand hardship or adversity
see also PERSEVERANCE
Rom 5:3 *they help us develop **e.***..............1654
Col 1:11 *have all the **e** and patience*.........1694
2 Thes 1:4 *your **e** and faithfulness*.............1587
Heb 12:1 *let us run with **e** the race*...........1780
Jas 1:3 *your faith is tested, your **e***............1546
2 Pet 1:6 *self-control with patient **e,***.........1757
Rev 1:9 *in the patient **e** to which Jesus*.....1800

ENDURE, ENDURED, ENDURES, ENDURING (v) to withstand, suffer, or persevere
see also PERSEVERE
Ps 89:2 *Your faithfulness is as **e-ing** as*......591
Ps 136:1 *faithful love **e-s** forever.*..............886
Matt 10:22 *everyone who **e-s** to the end*..1360
Mark 13:13 *one who **e-s** to the end*.........1448
1 Cor 13:7 ***e-s** through every*....................1616
2 Cor 1:6 *Then you can patiently **e***...........1626
2 Cor 6:4 *patiently **e** troubles and*.............1633
2 Tim 2:3 ***E** suffering along with me,*..........1742
2 Tim 2:12 *If we **e** hardship,*.......................1742
2 Tim 3:11 *suffering I have **e-d.***.................1744
Heb 12:2 *he **e-d** the cross,*..........................1780

Heb 12:3 *hostility he **e-d** from sinful*......1780
Heb 12:7 *As you **e** this divine discipline,*....1780
Jas 1:12 *who patiently **e** testing and*......1547
Jas 5:11 *those who **e** under suffering.*......1553
1 Pet 2:19 *patiently **e** unfair treatment.*......1752
Rev 13:10 *must **e** persecution patiently*....1820

ENEMY, ENEMIES (n) foe—personal, national, or spiritual
Ps 23:5 *the presence of my **e-ies.***......558
Ps 62:7 *rock where no **e** can reach me.*......574
Prov 16:7 *even their **e-ies** are at peace*......651
Prov 24:17 *rejoice when your **e-ies** fall;*......662
Prov 25:21 *If your **e-ies** are hungry,*......840
Prov 27:6 *than many kisses from an **e.***......842
Isa 51:13 *fear the anger of your **e-ies?***......938
Isa 59:18 *repay his **e-ies** for their evil*......946
Matt 5:44 *love your **e-ies!** Pray for those*..1330
Luke 6:35 *Love your **e-ies!** Do good to*.....1330
Luke 10:19 *over all the power of the **e,***.....1395
Rom 5:10 *while we were still his **e-ies,***....1654
Rom 12:20 *If your **e-ies** are hungry,*......1668
1 Cor 15:25 *until he humbles all his **e-ies***......1621
1 Cor 15:26 *the last **e** to be destroyed*......1621
Phil 3:18 *they are really **e-ies** of the cross*..1724
Jas 4:4 *makes you an **e** of God?*......1551
1 Pet 5:8 *Watch out for your great **e,***......1756

ENERGY (n) vigorous exertion of power; effort
Ezra 5:8 *with great **e** and success.*......1171
John 6:27 *your **e** seeking the eternal*......1367

ENGAGED (adj) pledged to be married; betrothed
Matt 1:18 *His mother, Mary, was **e** to*......1277

ENGAGEMENT (n) a pledge to marry; betrothal
Matt 1:19 *to break the **e** quietly.*......1277

ENJOY, ENJOYED, ENJOYING (v) to have a good time; to experience; to take pleasure in
see also HAPPY, JOY
Deut 6:2 *you will **e** a long life.*......294
Neh 9:25 *grew fat and **e-ed** themselves*...1216
Eccl 5:19 *good health to **e** it.*......677
Eccl 5:20 *so busy **e-ing** life that*......678
Eccl 8:15 *eat, drink, and **e** life.*......680
2 Tim 2:6 *the first to **e** the fruit*......1742
Heb 11:25 ***e-ing** the fleeting pleasures*....1778
1 Pet 3:10 *If you want to **e** life*......1753

ENJOYABLE (adj) of or relating to having a good time; pleasurable
Heb 12:11 *No discipline is **e** while*......1780

ENJOYMENT (n) an attitude, circumstance, or favorable response to a stimulus that tends to make one gratified or happy; delight; joy
1 Tim 6:17 *all we need for our **e.***......1735

ENQUIRE (KJV)
1 Sam 28:7 *a medium, so I can go and **ask***470
2 Kgs 1:2 *the god of Ekron, to **ask***......733

ENRICH, ENRICHED (v) to make rich or richer; to enhance
Prov 31:11 *she will greatly **e** his life*......847
2 Cor 9:11 *you will be **e-ed** in every way*..1638

ENSLAVE, ENSLAVED (v) to reduce to slavery; to subjugate
Gal 2:4 *wanted to **e** us and force us*......1558
2 Pet 2:20 *get tangled up and **e-d** by sin*..1759

ENSURE (v) to make sure, certain, or safe; to guarantee
Prov 31:8 ***e** justice for those being crushed*......847

ENTER, ENTERED, ENTERING, ENTERS (v) to go or come in
Ps 100:4 ***E** his gates with thanksgiving*......866
Matt 5:20 *you will never **e** the Kingdom*....1328
Matt 7:13 ***e** God's Kingdom only*......1334
Matt 19:23 *rich person to **e** the*......1420
Mark 9:43 ***e** eternal life with only*......1384
Mark 10:23 *for the rich to **e** the*......1421
Luke 11:52 *prevent others from **e-ing.***.....1399
Luke 13:24 *Work hard to **e** the narrow*......1407
Luke 18:17 *like a child will never **e** it.*......1420
John 3:5 *no one can **e** the Kingdom*......1301
John 10:2 *who **e-s** through the gate.*......1405
Rom 5:12 *When Adam sinned, sin **e-ed***....1654
Heb 3:11 *will never **e** my place of rest.*......1765
Heb 4:1 *God's promise of **e-ing** his rest*...1765
Heb 4:11 *do our best to **e** that rest.*......1766
Heb 9:12 *of goats and calves—he **e-ed***...1773

ENTERTAIN, ENTERTAINS (v) to provide entertainment for; to amuse
Ps 45:8 *music of strings **e-s** you.*......851
Hos 7:3 *The people **e** the king*......809

ENTERTAINMENT (n) amusement or diversion provided especially by performers
Dan 6:18 *refused his usual **e***......1141

ENTHRONED (v) to seat ceremonially on a throne or in a place associated with power and authority
1 Sam 4:4 ***e** between the cherubim.*......423
2 Kgs 19:15 ***e** between the mighty*......916
1 Chr 13:6 ***e** between the cherubim*......488
Ps 22:3 *you are holy, **e** on the praises*......556
Ps 113:5 *God, who is **e** on high?*......874
Isa 37:16 *God of Israel, you are **e***......917

ENTHUSIASM (n) strong excitement of feeling; zeal, fervor, passion
Neh 4:6 *the people had worked with **e.***.....1208
Prov 19:2 ***E** without knowledge*......654
Rom 10:2 *I know what **e** they have*......1663
2 Cor 8:7 *your **e,** and your love*......1636
2 Cor 8:16 *Titus the same **e** for you*......1636
2 Cor 9:2 *your **e** that stirred up*......1637
Eph 6:7 *Work with **e,** as though*......1715

ENTHUSIASTIC (adj) filled with or marked by zeal, fervor, or passion
Ps 45:15 *a joyful and **e** procession*......851
Acts 18:25 *about Jesus with an **e** spirit*....1592
Rom 15:17 *I have reason to be **e** about*....1671

ENTICE, ENTICED, ENTICES (v) to tempt; to lure
Deut 13:6 *someone secretly **e-s** you—*......303
Job 31:27 *secretly **e-d** in my heart*......122
Prov 1:10 *if sinners **e** you, turn your back*...632
Prov 7:21 *and **e-d** him with her flattery*......640
Jas 1:14 *our own desires, which **e** us*......1547

ENTRUST, ENTRUSTED (v) to commit to another with confidence
Ps 31:5 *I **e** my spirit into your hand*......563
Luke 12:48 *has been **e-ed** with much,*.....1401
Luke 23:46 *I **e** my spirit into your*......1486
Acts 15:40 *left, the believers **e-ed** him*.....1572
Acts 20:32 *And now I **e** you to God*......1676
Rom 3:2 *Jews were **e-ed** with the whole*......1650
1 Thes 2:4 *to be **e-ed** with the Good News*......1581
1 Tim 1:11 *Good News **e-ed** to me*......1728
2 Tim 1:14 *truth that has been **e-ed** to you*......1741
1 Pet 5:2 *flock that God has **e-ed** to you*...1756

ENVY (n) discontent or resentment because of another's success, advantages, or superiority
see also JEALOUSY
Mark 7:22 *lustful desires, **e,** slander,*......1371
Rom 1:29 *sin, greed, hate, **e,** murder,*......1648
Gal 5:21 ***e,** drunkenness, wild parties,*......1566
Titus 3:3 *full of evil and **e,** and we hated*...1739
Jas 4:5 *within us is filled with **e?***......1551

ENVY (v) to feel or show envy; to begrudge
Prov 3:31 *Don't **e** violent people*......635
Prov 24:1 *Don't **e** evil people*......662

EPILEPTIC (adj) relating to, affected with, or having characteristics of epilepsy
Matt 4:24 *were demon-possessed or **e** or*...1311

EQUAL (adj) like in quantity, quality, nature, or status
John 5:18 *making himself **e** with God.*......1318
2 Cor 8:14 *In this way, things will be **e.***.....1636

EQUIP (v) to prepare; to furnish for service or action
Eph 4:12 *to **e** God's people to do*......1711
2 Tim 3:17 *to prepare and **e** his people*.....1745
Heb 13:21 ***e** you with all you need*......1783

ERASE (v) to blot out, cause to disappear
Ps 34:16 ***e** their memory from the earth.*....459
Rev 3:5 ***e** their names from the Book*......1806

ESCAPE (n) evasion of something undesirable
1 Thes 5:3 *there will be no **e.***......1585

ESCAPE, ESCAPED, ESCAPING (v) to avoid; to get free of or break away from
Ps 89:48 *can **e** the power of the grave*......592
Ps 139:7 *I can never **e** from your Spirit!*......586
Matt 23:33 *will you **e** the judgment*......1445
1 Cor 3:15 *barely **e-ing** through a wall of*...1599
Heb 2:3 *think we can **e** if we ignore*......1763
Heb 12:25 *we will certainly not **e** if we*......1781
2 Pet 2:18 *those who have barely **e-d***......1759
2 Pet 2:20 ***e** from the wickedness*......1759

ESTABLISH, ESTABLISHED (v) to institute permanently; to set up; to bring into existence
1 Kgs 9:5 ***e** the throne of your dynasty*......623
Ps 89:4 *I will **e** your descendants as kings*..591
Prov 8:28 *when he **e-ed** springs*......640
Isa 16:5 *God will **e** one of David's*......833

ESTEEM (n) the regard in which one is held; worth; value
2 Chr 18:1 *great riches and high **e,***......725
Prov 22:1 *being held in high **e** is better*......658

ESTHER Jewish exile who became queen of Persia, also known as "Hadassah" (Esth 1:1, p. 1182); cousin of Mordecai (Esth 2:7, p. 1184); brought into king's harem (Esth 2:8-9, p. 1184); crowned queen (Esth 2:17, p. 1185); agreed to help Jews (Esth 4:14-17, p. 1188); invited king to a banquet (Esth 5:1-8, p. 1188); revealed Haman's plan (Esth 7:3-6, p. 1190); rescued the Jews (Esth 8:8, p. 1192); established Festival of Purim (Esth 9:18-32, p. 1193).

ETERNAL (adj) having infinite duration; valid or existing at all times
see also EVERLASTING, FOREVER
Gen 9:16 *will remember the **e** covenant*......21
Exod 3:15 *my **e** name, my name to*......144
Lev 24:8 *a requirement of the **e***......232
Num 18:19 *an **e** and unbreakable*......259
Ps 119:142 *Your justice is **e,***......881
Jer 50:5 *with an **e** covenant*......1035
Dan 4:34 *and his kingdom is **e.***......1121

Dan 7:14 *His rule is* **e**—....1136
Matt 18:8 *better to enter* **e** *life with*....1384
Matt 19:16 *must I do to have* **e** *life?*....1420
Matt 25:41 *into the* **e** *fire prepared*....1453
Matt 25:46 *away into* **e** *punishment,*....1453
Mark 3:29 *a sin with* **e** *consequences.*....1342
Luke 10:25 *should I do to inherit* **e** *life?*....1395
Luke 18:18 *should I do to inherit* **e** *life?*....1422
John 3:15 *in him will have* **e** *life.*....1302
John 3:16 *not perish but have* **e** *life.*....1302
John 3:36 *believes in God's Son has* **e**....1303
John 5:29 *will rise to experience* **e** *life,*....1319
John 5:39 *you think they give you* **e** *life.*....1319
John 6:68 *the words that give* **e** *life.*....1369
John 12:50 *his commands lead to* **e** *life;*....1435
John 17:2 *He gives* **e** *life prepared for*....1466
Rom 1:20 **e** *power and divine nature*....1647
Rom 5:21 *resulting in* **e** *life through*....1655
Rom 6:23 *free gift of God is* **e** *life*....1656
Rom 9:5 *is worthy of* **e** *praise! Amen*....1661
Rom 16:26 *the* **e** *God has commanded,*....1674
Eph 3:11 *This was his* **e** *plan,*....1709
2 Thes 1:9 *punished with* **e** *destruction,*....1588
1 Tim 6:12 *Hold tightly to the* **e** *life*....1735
Titus 3:7 *we will inherit* **e** *life.*....1739
Heb 5:9 *source of* **e** *salvation*....1767
Heb 9:15 **e** *inheritance God has*....1773
Heb 13:20 *an* **e** *covenant with his blood—*....1783
1 Pet 1:23 *from the* **e,** *living word*....1750
1 Pet 5:10 *to share in his* **e** *glory*....1756
1 Jn 1:2 *he is the one who is* **e** *life.*....1786
1 Jn 2:25 *we enjoy the* **e** *life he*....1790
1 Jn 5:20 *and he is* **e** *life.*....1795
Jude 1:7 *the* **e** *fire of God's judgment.*....1784
Jude 1:21 *who will bring you* **e** *life*....1786

ETERNALLY (adv) in an endless, infinite manner
Eph 6:24 *May God's grace be* **e** *upon all*....1716

ETERNITY (n) immortality; infinite time
Eccl 3:11 *has planted* **e** *in the human*....675
Isa 57:15 *who lives in* **e,** *the Holy One,*....944
John 12:25 *will keep it for* **e.**....1432

EUNUCH, EUNUCHS (n) male attendant, often castrated, implying singular devotion to a master
Isa 56:4 *I will bless those* **e-s** *who keep*....942
Matt 19:12 *some have been made* **e-s** *by*....1419
Acts 8:27 *The* **e** *had gone to Jerusalem*....1529

EVALUATE, EVALUATED (v) to determine the significance, worth, or value of
1 Cor 2:15 *Those who are spiritual can* **e**....1598
1 Cor 2:15 *cannot be* **e-d** *by others.*....1598
1 Cor 4:3 **e-d** *by you or by any human*....1600
1 Cor 14:29 *let the others* **e** *what is said*....1618

EVALUATION (n) the determination of the significance, worth, or value of
Rom 12:3 *in your* **e** *of yourselves,*....1667

EVANGELIST, EVANGELISTS (n) preacher of the gospel
Acts 21:8 *Philip the* **E,** *one of the seven*....1676
Eph 4:11 *apostles, the prophets, the* **e-s,**....1710

EVE First woman and mother of all people; created from Adam's rib (Gen 2:21-23, p. 10; 1 Tim 2:13, p. 1730); deceived by the serpent (Gen 3:1-13, p. 11; 2 Cor 11:3, p. 1640); named "Eve" by Adam (Gen 3:20, p. 13); cursed with painful childbirth (Gen 3:16, p. 13; 4:1, p. 14); descendants of (Gen 5, p. 16).

EVENING (n) the latter part and close of the day
Gen 1:5 **e** *passed and morning came,*....6

EVER-LIVING (adj) eternal; immortal
Rom 1:23 *the glorious,* **e** *God,*....1647

EVER (adv) always; at any time
Exod 15:18 *will reign forever and* **e!**....162
Ps 145:1 *praise your name forever and* **e.**....589
Dan 7:18 *they will rule forever and* **e.**....1136
John 1:18 *No one has* **e** *seen God.*....1272
Phil 4:20 *forever and* **e!** *Amen.*....1725
2 Tim 4:18 *glory to God forever and* **e!**....1746
Heb 1:8 *endures forever and* **e.**....1762
1 Pet 4:11 *to him forever and* **e!** *Amen.*....1755
1 Jn 4:12 *No one has* **e** *seen God.*....1793
Rev 1:6 *to him forever and* **e!** *Amen.*....1799
Rev 1:18 *I am alive forever and* **e!**....1801
Rev 22:5 *they will reign forever and* **e.**....1832

EVERLASTING (adj) continuing indefinitely
see also ETERNAL, FOREVER
Gen 17:7 *This is the* **e** *covenant:*....38
Gen 48:4 *as an* **e** *possession.*....90
2 Sam 23:5 *made an* **e** *covenant with*....546
Ps 139:24 *lead me along the path of* **e** *life.*....586
Isa 9:6 *God,* **E** *Father, Prince of Peace.*....793
Isa 35:10 *crowned with* **e** *joy.*....905
Isa 40:28 *The LORD is the* **e** *God,*....925
Isa 54:8 *But with* **e** *love*....941
Isa 55:3 *an* **e** *covenant with you.*....942
Isa 60:19 *God will be your* **e** *light,*....947
Isa 60:20 *the LORD will be your* **e** *light.*....947
Isa 61:7 *and* **e** *joy will be yours.*....948
Isa 61:8 *an* **e** *covenant with them.*....948
Jer 10:10 *the living God and the* **e** *King!*....1013
Jer 31:3 *with an* **e** *love.*....1032
Ezek 16:60 *establish an* **e** *covenant with*....1062
Dan 4:34 *His rule is* **e,**....1121
Dan 9:24 *to bring in* **e** *righteousness,*....1143
Dan 12:2 *to* **e** *life and some to shame*....1161
Gal 6:8 *will harvest* **e** *life from the*....1567

EVERYTHING (n) all that exists; all that relates to the subject
Ps 145:17 *is righteous in* **e** *he does;*....590
Matt 6:6 *your Father, who sees* **e,**....1331
Mark 12:44 *has given* **e** *she had to live on.*....1445
Acts 2:44 *and shared* **e** *they had.*....1516
2 Cor 1:22 **e** *he has promised*....1627
2 Cor 6:10 *and yet we have* **e.**....1633
Heb 13:18 *to live honorably in* **e** *we do.*....1783

EVIDENCE (n) an outward sign; proof
Acts 11:23 **e** *of God's blessing,*....1536
Heb 11:4 **e** *that he was a righteous man,*....1777

EVIL-MINDED (adj) having an evil disposition or evil thoughts
Ps 119:115 *out of my life, you* **e** *people,*....880

EVIL (adj) bad, sinful, or morally reprehensible; of the devil
Gen 6:5 *was consistently and totally* **e.**....17
Exod 32:22 *know how* **e** *these people*....185
Ps 51:4 *what is* **e** *in your sight.*....506
Ps 140:8 *not let* **e** *people have their way.*....587
Prov 15:26 *The LORD detests* **e** *plans,*....650
Matt 6:13 *rescue us from the* **e** *one.*....1331
Matt 12:45 *spirits more* **e** *than itself,*....1343
Matt 15:19 *from the heart come* **e**....1370
Mark 7:21 *heart, come* **e** *thoughts,*....1371
Luke 11:24 *When an* **e** *spirit leaves*....1343
John 17:15 *them safe from the* **e** *one.*....1467
Acts 19:13 *casting out* **e** *spirits.*....1594
Rom 2:9 *keeps on doing what is* **e**—....1649
Rom 13:14 *to indulge your* **e** *desires.*....1669
1 Cor 5:13 *remove the* **e** *person from*....1603
Eph 5:16 *in these* **e** *days.*....1713
Col 3:5 *lust, and* **e** *desires.*....1700
2 Thes 3:3 *guard you from the* **e** *one.*....1590
1 Tim 6:4 *slander, and* **e** *suspicions.*....1734
2 Tim 3:13 **e** *people and impostors*....1744
1 Jn 2:13 *your battle with the* **e** *one.*....1789
1 Jn 3:12 *who belonged to the* **e** *one.*....1791
1 Jn 5:18 *the* **e** *one cannot touch*....1795

EVIL (n) something that brings sorrow, distress, or misfortune
Gen 2:9 *the knowledge of good and* **e.**....10
Gen 3:5 *knowing both good and* **e.**....11
Judg 6:1 *The Israelites did* **e**....382
Ps 5:5 *for you hate all who do* **e.**....547
Ps 14:4 *those who do* **e** *never learn?*....552
Ps 34:13 *tongue from speaking* **e**....459
Ps 37:27 *Turn from* **e** *and do good,*....568
Ps 45:7 *You love justice and hate* **e.**....851
Ps 53:4 *those who do* **e** *never learn?*....571
Ps 92:15 *There is no* **e** *in him!*....862
Ps 101:4 *and stay away from every* **e.**....580
Ps 125:5 *with those who do* **e.**....883
Prov 6:18 *a heart that plots* **e,**....638
Prov 8:13 *fear the LORD will hate* **e.**....640
Prov 11:27 *search for* **e,** *it will find you!*....644
Prov 13:6 *but the* **e** *are misled by sin.*....646
Prov 17:13 *repay good with* **e, e** *will*....652
Prov 20:30 *cleanses away* **e;** *such*....657
Isa 5:20 *those who say that* **e** *is good*....829
Isa 13:11 *punish the world for its* **e**....831
Jer 23:14 *who are doing* **e** *so that*....1027
Hab 1:13 *cannot stand the sight of* **e.**....979
Mal 3:15 *those who do* **e** *get rich,*....1248
Matt 5:45 *to both the* **e** *and the good,*....1330
Luke 13:27 *all you who do* **e.**....1407
John 3:20 *All who do* **e** *hate the light.*....1302
Rom 12:21 *Don't let* **e** *conquer you,*....1668
1 Cor 14:20 *babies when it comes to* **e,**....1617
1 Thes 5:15 *no one pays back* **e** *for* **e,**....1586
1 Thes 5:22 *away from every kind of* **e.**....1586
1 Tim 6:10 *the root of all kinds of* **e.**....1735
2 Tim 2:19 *must turn away from* **e.**....1743
Heb 1:9 *You love justice and hate* **e.**....1762
Jas 1:21 *get rid of all the filth and* **e**....1548
Jas 3:8 *It is restless and* **e,**....1550
1 Pet 2:16 *as an excuse to do* **e.**....1751
1 Pet 3:9 *Don't repay* **e** *for* **e.**....1753
1 Pet 3:11 *Turn away from* **e** *and do*....1753
3 Jn 1:11 *those who do* **e** *prove that they*....1797

EVILDOERS (n) those who do evil
Ps 92:7 *like weeds and* **e** *flourish,*....862
Ps 92:9 *perish; all* **e** *will be scattered.*....862
Ps 94:16 *will stand up for me against* **e?**....863
Prov 21:15 *it terrifies* **e.**....658
Prov 24:19 *Don't fret because of* **e;**....663

EXALT, EXALTED, EXALTING, EXALTS (v) to elevate; to glorify; to raise in rank or power
see also GLORIFY, HONOR
Exod 15:2 *and I will* **e** *him!*....161
2 Sam 22:47 *of my salvation, be* **e-ed!**....527
Neh 9:5 *be* **e-ed** *above all blessing*....1215
Job 36:7 *kings and* **e-s** *them forever.*....125
Ps 18:46 *God of my salvation be* **e-ed!**....529
Ps 30:1 *I will* **e** *you, LORD,*....562
Ps 92:8 *O LORD, will be* **e-ed** *forever.*....862
Ps 97:9 *you are* **e-ed** *far above all gods.*....864
Ps 107:32 *Let them* **e** *him publicly*....872
Ps 145:1 *I will* **e** *you, my God and King,*....589

Dan 11:36 *as he pleases,* ***e-ing*** *himself* ...1160
Luke 14:11 *those who* ***e*** *themselves will* ...1408
Acts 2:33 *is* ***e-ed*** *to the place of highest* ..1516
2 Thes 2:4 *He will* ***e*** *himself*....................1588

EXAMINE, EXAMINED, EXAMINES, EXAMINING (v) to test the condition of; to inspect closely
1 Chr 29:17 *you* ***e*** *our hearts*......................541
Ps 11:4 ***e-ing*** *every person on earth.* 550
Ps 11:5 *The* *LORD* ***e-s*** *both*..........................550
Ps 17:3 ***e-d*** *my heart in the night*..............553
Ps 139:1 *LORD, you have* ***e-d*** *my heart* 586
Prov 5:21 ***e-ing*** *every path he takes*...........637
Prov 21:2 *the* *LORD* ***e-s*** *their heart*. 657
Jer 11:20 *you* ***e*** *the deepest thoughts*.......1015
Jer 17:10 *and* ***e*** *secret motives*. 1021
Lam 3:40 *let us test and* ***e*** *our ways*. 1099
1 Cor 4:4 *Lord himself who will* ***e*** 1600
1 Cor 11:28 *you should* ***e*** *yourself*............1613
2 Cor 13:5 ***E*** *yourselves to see*.................1643
1 Thes 2:4 *He alone* ***e-s*** *the motives* 1581

EXAMPLE, EXAMPLES (n) one that serves as a pattern to be or not to be imitated
John 13:15 *given you an* ***e*** *to*...................1456
1 Cor 10:11 *happened to them as* ***e-s*** *for*...1610
2 Thes 3:9 *give you an* ***e*** *to follow*............1590
Titus 2:7 ***e*** *to them by doing good*.............1738
Heb 13:7 *and follow the* ***e*** *of their faith*......1782
Jas 5:10 *For* ***e-s*** *of patience in suffering*,..1553
1 Pet 2:21 *He is your* ***e****, and you must*......1752

EXCEEDS (v) to be greater than or superior to
Phil 4:7 ***e*** *anything we can understand*......1724

EXCEL (v) to surpass in accomplishment or achievement
2 Cor 8:7 ***e*** *also in this gracious act of*......1636

EXCELLENCE (n) something that gives special worth or value
2 Pet 1:5 *generous provision of moral* ***e****,*...1757

EXCELLENT (adj) very good of its kind; superior
Phil 4:8 *Think about things that are* ***e***........1725

EXCHANGE (n) the act of giving or taking one thing for another
Lev 17:11 *blood, given in* ***e*** *for a life,* 223

EXCHANGED (v) to part with for a substitute
Job 28:19 *cannot be* ***e*** *for it*........................119
Jer 2:11 *have* ***e*** *their glorious God*..............960
Hos 4:7 *They have* ***e*** *the glory of God*..........806

EXCUSE (n) the apology or justification offered
John 15:22 *they have no* ***e*** *for their sin*.....1464
Rom 1:20 *no* ***e*** *for not knowing God*..........1647
Rom 2:1 *and you have no* ***e!*** 1648
1 Pet 2:16 *your freedom as an* ***e***.............1751

EXCUSE (v) to overlook, justify, or make an apology for
Exod 34:7 *But I do not* ***e*** *the guilty*..............187
Eph 5:6 *those who try to* ***e*** *these sins*,.......1712

EXECUTED (v) to put to death
Num 35:16 *the murderer must be* ***e.*** 283
Deut 21:22 *and is* ***e*** *and hung on a tree*,.....311

EXECUTION (n) a putting to death especially as a legal penalty
Num 35:31 *murder and subject to* ***e;*** 283

EXHAUST (v) to consume entirely
Isa 7:13 *you* ***e*** *the patience of my God*........790

EXHAUSTION (n) fatigue, tiredness, collapse
2 Cor 6:5 *worked to* ***e****, endured*...............1633

EXHORT(ATION) (KJV)
Rom 12:8 *If your gift is to* ***encourage***.......1667
1 Thes 2:3 *not* ***preaching*** *with any deceit*...1581
Heb 3:13 *You must* ***warn*** *each other* 1765

EXILE, EXILES (n) the state of forced absence from one's country or home; a person who is in exile
2 Kgs 25:11 *took as* ***e-s*** *the rest of*..........1087
2 Kgs 25:21 *sent into* ***e*** *from their land*.....1088
Ezra 2:1 *the Jewish* ***e-s*** *of the provinces*...1152
Jer 52:27 *sent into* ***e*** *from their land*.........1089

EXILED (v) to banish or expel
2 Kgs 17:6 *of Israel were* ***e*** *to Assyria*. 820
2 Kgs 17:23 *So Israel was* ***e*** *from their land*..821

EXISTS (v) to have real being whether material or spiritual
Heb 11:6 *must believe that God* ***e***............1777

EXORCISTS (n) one who expels evil spirits
Luke 11:19 *what about your own* ***e?***.........1342

EXPELLED, EXPELS (v) to force to leave
Ezek 28:16 *I* ***e*** *you, O mighty guardian,*.....1084
1 Jn 4:18 *perfect love* ***e-s*** *all fear*.............1794

EXPENSES (n) financial costs
1 Cor 9:7 *has to pay his own* ***e?***..............1608

EXPENSIVE (adj) involving high cost
Mark 14:3 *alabaster jar of* ***e*** *perfume*........1428
Luke 7:25 *a man dressed in* ***e*** *clothes?*.....1338
John 12:3 *a twelve-ounce jar of* ***e*** *perfume*...1428
1 Tim 2:9 *gold or pearls or* ***e*** *clothes*.........1729

EXPERIENCE (v) to learn by or have direct observation or participation
Deut 28:2 *You will* ***e*** *all these blessings*.......317
Eph 3:19 *May you* ***e*** *the love of Christ,*......1710

EXPLAIN, EXPLAINED, EXPLAINS (v) to make plain or understandable; to give the reason or cause
Gen 2:24 *This* ***e-s*** *why a man leaves his*.......11
Neh 8:8 *and clearly* ***e-ed*** *the meaning*......1214
Matt 19:5 *This* ***e-s*** *why a man leaves his*....1418
Acts 17:3 *He* ***e-ed*** *the prophecies*...........1576
Acts 18:28 ***e-ed*** *to them that Jesus was* ..1592
Eph 6:19 ***e*** *God's mysterious plan*............1715
2 Tim 2:15 *correctly* ***e-s*** *the word of*.........1743
1 Pet 3:15 *always be ready to* ***e*** *it*............1753

EXPLOIT (v) to make use of meanly or unfairly for one's own advantage
Exod 22:22 *not* ***e*** *a widow or an orphan*. 172
Prov 22:22 *or* ***e*** *the needy in court*.............660

EXPLOITED (n) one unfairly used for another's advantage
Isa 11:4 *fair decisions for the* ***e.*** 796

EXPLORE (v) to investigate, study, or analyze
Num 13:2 *Send out men to* ***e*** *the land* 250
Num 32:8 *to* ***e*** *the land.* 278

EXPOSE, EXPOSED, EXPOSES, EXPOSING (v) to make known; to display
Prov 20:27 ***e-ing*** *every hidden motive*........657
Lam 4:22 *your many sins will be* ***e-d.***.......1101
John 3:20 *fear their sins will be* ***e-d.*** 1302
Eph 5:11 *instead,* ***e*** *them*. 1712
Heb 4:12 *It* ***e-s*** *our innermost thoughts* 1766
Heb 4:13 *naked and* ***e-d*** *before his eyes*,..1766

EXTENDS (v) to stretch out to the fullest length; to proffer
Ps 119:90 *faithfulness* ***e*** *to every* 880
Prov 31:20 *She* ***e*** *a helping hand*................848

EXTINGUISH (v) to cause to cease burning
John 1:5 *the darkness can never* ***e*** *it*. 1271

EXTOL(LED) (KJV)
Ps 30:1 *will* ***exalt*** *you,* *LORD*, *for you*............562
Ps 66:17 *to him for help,* ***praising*** *him* 859
Ps 68:4 ***Sing loud praises*** *to him who* 576
Isa 52:13 *he will be* ***highly exalted***...........940

EXTORTION (n) the act or practice of obtaining money or property by illegal power
Lev 6:4 *or the money you took by* ***e****,* 208

EXTREME
Josh 15:21 *of Edom in the* ***e*** *south* 359
Ezek 46:19 *a place at the* ***e*** *west end* 1130
Ezek 48:1 *Dan is in the* ***e*** *north*................1132

EXTREMES (n) something situated at or marking one end or the other of a range
Eccl 7:18 *will avoid both* ***e.***........................679

EXULT (v) to be extremely joyful; to rejoice
Ps 89:16 *They* ***e*** *in your righteousness*........591

EYE, EYES (n) organ of (physical and spiritual) sight
Exod 21:24 *an* ***e*** *for an* ***e****,* 171
Deut 16:19 *bribes blind the* ***e-s*** *of*..............306
Job 36:7 *never takes his* ***e-s*** *off the* 125
Ps 119:18 *Open my* ***e-s*** *to see* 878
Ps 119:37 *Turn my* ***e-s*** *from worthless*.......878
Ps 123:1 *I lift my* ***e-s*** *to you,*.....................882
Prov 4:25 *and fix your* ***e-s*** *on what*.............637
Matt 5:29 ***e****—causes you to lust,* 1328
Matt 5:38 *An* ***e*** *for an* ***e****,* 1329
Matt 6:22 *When your* ***e*** *is good,*................1332
1 Cor 2:9 *when they say, "No* ***e*** *has seen,* ...1598
Heb 12:2 *by keeping our* ***e-s*** *on Jesus,*.....1780
2 Pet 1:16 *with our own* ***e-s*** 1758
Rev 21:4 *wipe every tear from their* ***e-s****,* ...1830

EYELIDS (n) the movable folds of skin and muscle that close over the eyeballs
2 Kgs 9:30 *painted her* ***e*** *and fixed her hair*...751

EYEWITNESS (n) one who sees an occurrence or object
Luke 1:2 *They used the* ***e*** *reports* 1270

EZEKIEL Prophet of Judah (southern kingdom) and priest (Ezek 1:3, p. 1044); exiled to Babylon near the Kebar River (Ezek 3:15, p. 1047).

EZRA Postexilic priestly reformer in time of Artaxerxes (Ezra 7, p. 1195; 10, p. 1200; Neh 8, p. 1214; 12, p. 1221); descendant of Seraiah (Ezra 7:1, p. 1195); skillful, learned teacher of the Law (Ezra 7:6, p. 1196); determined to study and obey the Law (Ezra 7:10, p. 1196); served as priest (Ezra 7:11, p. 1196); restored Temple and its worship (Ezra 7–8, p. 1195); corrected pagan intermarriage (Ezra 9–10, p. 1199); dedicated Jerusalem's repaired walls (Neh 12, p. 1221).

FACE (n) in or into direct contact or confrontation (as in "face to face"); countenance; presence; the front part of the head
Gen 32:30 *I have seen God* ***f*** *to* ***f****,*..................66
Exod 33:11 *speak to Moses* ***f*** *to* ***f****,* 186
Exod 34:29 *his* ***f*** *had become radiant*..........188
Num 12:8 *I speak to him* ***f*** *to* ***f****,*.................250
Deut 31:17 *hiding my* ***f*** *from them,* 322
Judg 6:22 *angel of the* *LORD* ***f*** *to* ***f!*** 384
2 Chr 7:14 *and seek my* ***f*** *and turn from* 623

Ps 4:6 Let your f smile on us, ...547
Ps 17:15 I will see you f to f.......................554
Ps 67:1 May his f smile with favor 859
Luke 9:29 appearance of his f was...........1380
2 Cor 3:7 For his f shone with the glory 1629
Rev 1:16 And his f was like the sun..........1800
Rev 22:4 they will see his f, ...1832

FACE, FACED, FACING (v) to confront; to be confronted by
Ps 112:8 f their foes triumphantly...........873
Ps 116:6 I was f-ing death, and he saved ..875
2 Cor 6:5 f-d angry mobs, ...1633

FADE, FADING (v) to lose freshness, strength, or vitality
Isa 40:7 and the flowers f 924
1 Cor 9:25 to win a prize that will f...........1609
2 Cor 3:7 brightness was already f-ing.....1629
2 Cor 3:13 it was destined to f away.........1630
Jas 1:11 the rich will f away.....................1547
1 Jn 2:17 this world is f-ing away, ...1789

FAIL, FAILED, FAILS (v) to disappoint; to fall short; to weaken; to miss performing an expected service; to be unsuccessful
Num 23:19 spoken and f-ed to act?...........267
Deut 31:6 He will neither f you 322
Josh 23:14 Not a single one has f-ed! 369
1 Kgs 8:56 Not one word has f-ed 622
Ps 77:8 his promises permanently f-ed?....597
Luke 13:24 try to enter but will f..............1407
Luke 22:32 faith should not f. 1460
Rom 9:6 has God f-ed to fulfill his promise..1661
2 Cor 13:5 if not, you have f-ed the test...1643
2 Cor 13:6 we have not f-ed the test.........1643
Heb 12:15 none of you f-s to receive........1781
Heb 13:5 I will never f you.......................1782
1 Pet 4:19 he will never f you. 1755

FAINT (adj) lacking strength or vigor
Jonah 4:8 grew f and wished to die. 769

FAINT (v) to become weak or lose courage in body or spirit
Isa 40:31 will walk and not f.......................925

FAIR (adj) free from self-interest, prejudice, or favoritism; beautiful
Prov 1:3 do what is right, just, and f............631
Song 2:13 away with me, my f one!............665
Isa 11:4 make f decisions for the................796
Rom 3:25 God was being f when he 1651
Rom 3:26 he himself is f and just, ...1651
Col 4:1 be just and f to your slaves. 1702

FAIRNESS (n) the quality of being free from self-interest, prejudice, or favoritism
Ps 9:8 rule the nations with f.....................549
Ps 98:9 and the nations with f...................865
Ps 99:4 you have established f..................865
Isa 9:7 will rule with f and justice................793

FAITH (n) reliance, loyalty, or complete trust in God; a system of religious beliefs
see also BELIEVE, FAITHLESS, TRUST
Exod 14:31 They put their f in the LORD.......161
Isa 7:9 Unless your f is firm, ...790
Matt 9:2 Seeing their f, Jesus said 1312
Matt 9:29 Because of your f, it will 1356
Matt 15:28 your f is great. 1371
Matt 17:20 f even as small as a mustard ..1381
Matt 21:22 if you have f, you will receive ..1435
Mark 10:52 for your f has healed you. 1425
Luke 5:20 Seeing their f, Jesus said.........1314
Luke 7:50 Your f has saved you;...............1341
Luke 8:48 your f has made you well..........1355
Luke 12:28 Why do you have so little f?....1401
Luke 17:6 f even as small as a mustard....1413
Luke 18:8 find on the earth who have f?....1417
John 16:1 won't abandon your f...............1464
Acts 6:5 full of f and the Holy Spirit...........1522
Acts 14:9 he had f to be healed................1544
Acts 14:27 opened the door of f to the......1546
Acts 16:5 strengthened in their f and.........1573
Acts 24:24 told them about f in Christ.......1682
Rom 1:8 f in him is being talked about......1645
Rom 1:12 to encourage you in your f, ...1646
Rom 1:17 from start to finish by f. 1646
Rom 1:17 through f that a righteous 1646
Rom 3:28 right with God through f............1652
Rom 3:30 right with himself only by f,........1652
Rom 3:31 only when we have f 1652
Rom 4:5 because of their f in God 1652
Rom 4:9 righteous because of his f............1652
Rom 4:12 same kind of f Abraham had.....1653
Rom 4:13 with God that comes by f..........1653
Rom 4:14 then f is not necessary 1653
Rom 4:16 the promise is received by f......1653
Rom 4:16 if we have f like Abraham's. 1653
Rom 4:19 Abraham's f did not weaken,.....1653
Rom 4:20 In fact, his f grew stronger, ...1653
Rom 5:1 made right in God's sight by f, ...1654
Rom 5:2 Because of our f, Christ has........1654
Rom 10:8 message about f that we preach:..1663
Rom 10:17 So f comes from hearing, ...1664
Rom 12:6 speak out with as much f as.....1667
Rom 14:1 believers who are weak in f, ...1669
1 Cor 12:9 gives great f to another, ...1614
1 Cor 13:13 f, hope, and love—..............1616
1 Cor 15:14 and your f is useless. 1620
1 Cor 16:13 Stand firm in the f.................1623
2 Cor 1:24 put your f into practice. 1627
2 Cor 13:5 failed the test of genuine f.......1643
Gal 1:23 the very f he tried to destroy! 1557
Gal 3:9 all who put their f in Christ............1561
Gal 3:11 f that a righteous person 1561
Gal 3:12 This way of f is very different......1561
Gal 3:14 Holy Spirit through f. 1561
Gal 3:23 way of f in Christ was available ...1562
Gal 3:24 made right with God through f. ...1562
Gal 3:25 the way of f has come, ...1562
Gal 3:26 of God through f in Christ 1562
Gal 5:5 eagerly wait to receive by f............1565
Eph 1:15 of your strong f in the Lord.........1706
Eph 4:5 one Lord, one f, one baptism,.......1710
Eph 6:16 hold up the shield of f................1715
Phil 1:25 experience the joy of your f. 1718
Phil 3:9 righteous through f in Christ.........1722
Col 1:4 have heard of your f in Christ........1693
1 Thes 1:8 telling us about your f in God. ..1581
1 Thes 3:5 your f was still strong. 1583
1 Thes 3:10 fill the gaps in your f. 1584
2 Thes 1:3 because your f is flourishing....1587
1 Tim 1:4 live a life of f in God. 1726
1 Tim 1:19 Cling to your f in Christ, ...1728
1 Tim 3:9 mystery of the f now..................1731
1 Tim 4:1 will turn away from the true f;....1732
1 Tim 6:10 have wandered from the true f...1735
1 Tim 6:12 good fight for the true f. 1735
2 Tim 1:5 remember your genuine f,.........1740
2 Tim 2:18 away from the f. 1743
2 Tim 3:10 You know my f, my patience,...1744
Titus 1:1 have been sent to proclaim f 1736
Titus 1:13 make them strong in the f. 1737
Titus 2:2 must have sound f and be filled..1738
Phlm 1:5 about your f in the Lord 1691
Phlm 1:6 that comes from your f 1691
Heb 4:2 they didn't share the f.................1765
Heb 6:1 and placing our f in God. 1768
Heb 6:12 their f and endurance. 1768
Heb 10:38 righteous ones will live by f......1777
Heb 11:5 It was by f that Enoch................1777
Heb 11:7 It was by f that Noah 1777
Heb 11:8 It was by f that Abraham............1777
Heb 11:23 It was by f that Moses' parents 1778
Heb 11:29 It was by f that the people 1779
Heb 12:2 initiates and perfects our f. 1780
Jas 1:3 when your f is tested,...................1546
Jas 2:5 this world to be rich in f? 1548
Jas 2:14 Can that kind of f save anyone?..1549
Jas 2:17 f by itself isn't enough.................1549
Jas 2:18 Some people have f; 1549
Jas 2:20 f without good deeds 1550
Jas 2:22 made his f complete. 1550
Jas 2:24 what we do, not by f alone..........1550
Jas 2:26 so also f is dead without good 1550
Jas 5:15 prayer offered in f will heal..........1553
1 Pet 1:21 have placed your f and hope....1749
2 Pet 1:1 the same precious f we have. 1757
Jude 1:3 defend the f that God.................1784
Jude 1:20 in your most holy f, ...1785

FAITHFUL (adj) firm in adherence, utterly loyal
see also LOYAL, TRUSTWORTHY, UNFAILING
Deut 7:9 He is the f God who keeps his.......296
1 Sam 2:9 will protect his f ones, ...419
1 Sam 20:14 me with the f love of the........456
2 Sam 22:26 you show yourself f; to those ...526
1 Kgs 8:61 you be completely f to the.........622
1 Kgs 15:14 remained completely f to 705
2 Kgs 20:3 have always been f to you.........919
Ps 18:25 you show yourself f; 528
Ps 71:22 because you are f to your 860
Ps 89:8 You are entirely f. 591
Ps 89:49 to David with a f pledge. 592
Ps 143:1 you are f and righteous...............588
Isa 38:3 have always been f to you and 920
Hos 11:12 God and is f to the Holy One. 815
Zech 8:3 be called the F City;....................1173
Zech 8:8 I will be f and just toward...........1174
Matt 24:45 A f, sensible servant is one.....1447
Matt 25:21 You have been f in handling....1452
Matt 25:23 my good and f servant............1452
Luke 12:42 Lord replied, "A f, sensible 1401
Luke 16:10 If you are f in little things, ...1412
1 Cor 4:17 my beloved and f child in the...1601
2 Cor 1:18 as God is f, our word to you.....1627
Eph 1:1 who are f followers of Christ 1704
Phil 2:17 just like your f service is 1720
Col 4:7 brother and f helper who 1703
Col 4:9 Onesimus, a f and beloved 1703
1 Thes 1:3 we think of your f work,............1580
1 Thes 5:24 for he who calls you is f. 1587
2 Thes 3:3 But the Lord is f; he will 1590
1 Tim 3:2 He must be f to his wife. 1730
1 Tim 3:11 and be f in everything they......1731
1 Tim 5:9 old and was f to her husband. ...1733
2 Tim 4:7 I have remained f. 1746
Heb 2:17 merciful and f High Priest..........1764
Heb 3:2 For he was f to God, who.............1764
Heb 8:9 They did not remain f to my.........1772
Heb 13:4 marriage, and remain f to one....1782
1 Jn 1:9 to him, he is f and just to 1787
Rev 1:5 He is the f witness to these..........1799
Rev 2:10 But if you remain f even when....1803
Rev 3:14 is the Amen—the f and true 1807
Rev 17:14 chosen and f ones will be 1825

FAITHFUL (n) those who practice faith
Ps 149:1 *assembly of the **f***. 887
Ps 149:5 *Let the **f** rejoice that he* 887

FAITHFULLY (adv) in a manner that is firm, regular, and steady
Deut 7:12 *regulations and **f** obey them,* 296
1 Kgs 8:25 *and **f** follow me* 619
2 Chr 32:1 *Hezekiah had **f** carried out*.........912
Neh 13:14 *all that I have **f** done for* 1223
Isa 61:8 *I will **f** reward my people for* 948

FAITHFULNESS (n) the quality of steadfast loyalty or firm adherence to promises
Exod 34:6 *unfailing love and **f***. 187
Ps 25:10 *with unfailing love and **f***..............560
Ps 36:5 *your **f** reaches beyond*...................566
Ps 57:10 *Your **f** reaches to the clouds*.........460
Ps 92:2 *your **f** in the evening,*....................862
Ps 100:5 ***f** continues to each*.....................866
Prov 14:22 *unfailing love and **f***..................648
Prov 16:6 *love and **f** make atonement*.........651
Prov 20:28 *love and **f** protect the king;* 657
Isa 38:18 *no longer hope in your **f***. 921
Lam 3:23 *Great is his **f**;* 1098
Gal 5:22 *kindness, goodness, **f**,*................1566
Eph 6:23 *give you love with **f***....................1716
2 Thes 1:4 *your endurance and **f***..............1587
2 Tim 2:22 *pursue righteous living, **f**,*........1743

FAITHLESS (adj) disloyal; lacking trust
Ps 78:57 *and were as **f** as their parents*.....599
Jer 3:8 *I divorced **f** Israel because* 962
Jer 3:11 *Even **f** Israel is less guilty than* 963
Jer 3:12 *Israel, my **f** people, come home* 963
Matt 17:17 *You **f** and corrupt people!*.......1381
Mark 9:19 *You **f** people!*...........................1381
John 20:27 *Don't be **f** any longer*..............1495

FALL, FALLEN, FALLING (v) to collapse; to drop down (wounded or dead); to become lower in degree or level; to come by assignment or inheritance; to descend; to stumble or stray (morally)
2 Sam 1:19 *the mighty heroes have* ***f-en!***..477
Ps 37:24 *they will never **f**,*..........................567
Ps 69:9 *who insult you have **f-en** on*..........577
Prov 10:8 *babbling fools **f** flat on their* 642
Prov 24:17 *when your enemies **f**;*..............662
Isa 14:12 *How you are **f-en** from heaven,*...832
Matt 13:21 *They **f** away as soon as*..........1345
Luke 10:18 *I saw Satan **f** from heaven*......1395
Rom 3:23 *we all **f** short of God's glorious*..1651
Rom 14:13 *believer to stumble and **f***. 1670
Gal 5:4 ***f-en** away from God's grace*. 1565
2 Pet 1:10 *and you will never **f** away*.........1757
Jude 1:24 *to keep you from **f-ing** away*....1786

FALSE (adj) intentionally untrue; dishonest; misleading; unwise; faithless
Prov 12:17 *a **f** witness tells lies*. 645
Isa 44:25 *I expose the **f** prophets as* 931
Matt 24:11 *And many **f** prophets will* 1446
Mark 13:22 *For **f** messiahs and **f** prophets* 1449
2 Cor 11:13 *These people are **f** apostles*...1640
Titus 1:11 *by their **f** teaching*...................1737
2 Pet 2:1 *were also **f** prophets in Israel,* 1758
1 Jn 4:1 *many **f** prophets in the world*.......1792
Rev 16:13 *and the **f** prophet*.....................1823
Rev 19:20 *beast and his **f** prophet were*....1828
Rev 20:10 *the beast and the **f** prophet*......1830

FALSEHOOD (n) a lie; the practice of lying
Ps 119:163 *hate and abhor all **f**,* 881

FALSELY (adv) in an untrue, deceptive, or misleading manner
Exod 20:16 *must not testify **f** against*..........170
Mark 10:19 *You must not testify **f***. 1421

FAME (n) popular acclaim
Exod 9:16 *spread my **f** throughout the earth*..153
Ps 49:12 *but their **f** will not last*.................854
Ps 102:12 *Your **f** will endure* 866
Isa 66:19 *heard of my **f** or seen my glory*. ...953

FAMILY, FAMILIES (n) a household unit of related people, as in a clan
see also HOUSEHOLD
Josh 24:15 *my **f**, we will serve the* LORD......370
Ps 68:6 *God places the lonely in **f-ies**;*.......576
Mark 3:25 *a **f** splintered by feuding* 1342
Luke 9:61 *let me say good-bye to my **f***.....1388
Luke 12:52 ***f-ies** will be split apart,* 1402
Gal 6:10 *to those in the **f** of faith*. 1567
Eph 2:19 *members of God's **f***...................1708
1 Tim 3:4 *manage his own **f** well,* 1730
Titus 1:11 *whole **f-ies** away from the truth*...1737
1 Jn 3:9 *have been born into God's **f*** 1791

FAMINE (n) extreme scarcity of food
Gen 12:10 *a severe **f** struck the land*...........31
Gen 26:1 *A severe **f** now struck the*.............52
Gen 41:30 *seven years of **f** so great*...........80
Ruth 1:1 *a severe **f** came upon the land*......409
1 Kgs 18:2 *the **f** had become very*..............716
Amos 8:11 *I will send a **f** on the land—*......779

FAMOUS (adj) widely known; honored for achievement
Gen 11:4 *This will make us **f***........................23
Gen 12:2 *bless you and make you **f**,*.............30
Isa 63:12 *making himself **f** forever?*............950

FANCY (adj) not plain; ornamental
1 Pet 3:3 *outward beauty of **f** hairstyles,* ...1752

FANTASIES (n) unrealistic or improbable mental images
Prov 12:11 *who chases **f** has no sense*.......645

FAR (adv) at a considerable distance in space or degree
Ps 22:19 LORD, *do not stay **f** away!*............556
Ezek 11:15 *are **f** away from the Lord*........1057
Eph 2:13 *you were **f** away from God,* 1708
Col 1:21 *were once **f** away from God*........1695

FARMER (n) one who cultivates crops or raises animals for food
Isa 28:24 *Does a **f** always plow and*............819
Isa 55:10 *producing seed for the **f***.............942
Matt 13:18 *the parable about the **f** planting*...1345
2 Cor 9:6 *a **f** who plants only a few seeds*...1637
2 Cor 9:10 *seed for the **f** and then bread*..1638

FARTHEST (adj) most distant, especially in space or time
Acts 13:47 *bring salvation to the **f** corners*..1543

FAST, FASTING (v) to abstain from food
Ps 35:13 *denied myself by **f-ing** for*...........565
Matt 6:16 *when you **f**, don't make it*.........1332
Acts 13:2 *worshiping the Lord and **f-ing**,*.1539

FASTING (n) the practice of abstaining, usually from food
Joel 2:12 *Come with **f-ing**, weeping,*........1241
Acts 14:23 *prayer and **f-ing**, they turned*..1545

FATE (n) an inevitable and often adverse outcome or end
Prov 1:19 *the **f** of all who are greedy* 632
Eccl 9:3 *suffers the same **f***........................680
1 Pet 2:8 *the **f** that was planned for them*. 1750

FATHER, FATHERS (n) male parent; ancestor(s); characteristic of a mentor or provider relationship; name and role for God in relation to the children he fosters/adopts; originator or creator
see also PARENT
Gen 2:24 *a man leaves his **f** and mother*.......11
Gen 17:4 *make you the **f** of a multitude* 38
Exod 20:12 *Honor your **f** and mother*...........169
Exod 21:15 *Anyone who strikes **f** or*...........171
Deut 32:6 *he your **F** who created you?*........323
2 Sam 7:14 *I will be his **f**, and he* 495
Ps 2:7 *Today I have become your **F***. 857
Ps 89:26 *You are my **F**, my God,*................592
Prov 10:1 *wise child brings joy to a **f**;* 641
Prov 23:22 *Listen to your **f**, who gave you*...661
Isa 9:6 *Everlasting **F**, Prince of Peace*. 793
Isa 63:16 *you would still be our **F***...............950
Jer 3:19 *forward to your calling me '**F**,'* 963
Ezek 22:10 *sleep with their **f-s'** wives* 1069
Mal 2:10 *children of the same **F**?*.............1246
Mal 4:6 *will turn the hearts of **f-s*** 1249
Matt 5:16 *will praise your heavenly **F***. 1327
Matt 6:9 *Our **F** in heaven, may your*..........1331
Matt 6:14 *heavenly **F** will forgive* 1331
Matt 10:37 *If you love your **f** or mother*.....1361
Matt 11:27 *no one truly knows the **F*** 1339
Matt 15:4 *Honor your **f** and mother,* 1369
Matt 16:27 *in the glory of his **F*** 1377
Matt 19:5 *a man leaves his **f** and mother*..1418
Matt 19:29 *or **f** or mother or children*........1421
Matt 23:9 *is your spiritual **F***. 1443
Luke 1:17 *hearts of the **f-s** to their*...........1273
Luke 9:59 *return home and bury my **f**."* 1388
John 4:21 *you worship the **F** on this* 1304
John 5:17 *My **F** is always working,* 1318
John 5:20 *For the **F** loves the Son* 1318
John 6:44 *come to me unless the **F***..........1367
John 6:65 *unless the **F** gives them* 1369
John 8:19 *you don't know who my **F** is*. 1392
John 8:41 *God himself is our true **F***. 1393
John 10:38 *understand that the **F** is in me,*..1406
John 14:6 *come to the **F** except through*...1461
John 14:21 *love me, my **F** will love*...........1462
John 15:8 *brings great glory to my **F***........1464
John 15:23 *also hates my **F***. 1464
John 20:17 *ascending to my **F** and*...........1493
Acts 13:33 *Today I have become your **F***. ...1542
Rom 4:11 *Abraham is the spiritual **f***..........1653
Rom 4:16 *Abraham is the **f** of all who*.......1653
Rom 8:15 *we call him, "Abba, **F**."* 1659
2 Cor 6:18 *I will be your **F**, and you*...........1634
Eph 5:31 *man leaves his **f** and mother*......1714
Eph 6:2 *Honor your **f** and mother*. 1714
Eph 6:4 ***F-s**, do not provoke*.....................1714
Phil 2:11 *to the glory of God the **F***............1720
Col 3:21 ***F-s**, do not aggravate*.................1702
Heb 12:7 *is never disciplined by its **f**?*.......1780
Heb 12:9 *earthly **f-s** who disciplined*.........1780
1 Jn 1:3 *fellowship is with the **F** and*.........1787
1 Jn 2:15 *the love of the **F** in you*. 1789
1 Jn 2:22 *who denies the **F** and the Son*...1790
1 Jn 3:1 *See how very much our **F** loves*...1790
Rev 3:21 *sat with my **F** on his throne*. 1808

FATHERLESS (adj) without a father; orphaned
see also ORPHAN
Ps 68:5 *Father to the **f**, defender of*............576

FATTENING (v) to feed (as a stock animal) and make fat for slaughter
Luke 15:23 *calf we have been f.* 1411

FAULT (n) lack or error; moral weakness less serious than a vice
1 Sam 29:3 *never found a single f in*...........471
Prov 17:9 *when a f is forgiven,*....................652
Acts 20:26 *eternal death, it's not my f,* 1675
2 Cor 6:3 *no one will find f with our*..........1633
Eph 5:27 *she will be holy and without f.*....1714
Jude 1:24 *without a single f.*....................1786

FAULTLESS (adj) having no fault; irreproachable
1 Thes 2:10 *honest and f toward all of you*..1582

FAVOR, FAVORS (n) gracious kindness; approval from a superior; a special privilege or right granted or conceded
see also GRACE
Gen 6:8 *Noah found f with the LORD*.............17
Exod 34:9 *if it is true that I have found f*......187
1 Sam 2:26 *and grew in f with the LORD*......420
Prov 3:4 *you will find f with both God*..........634
Prov 18:22 *receives f from the LORD.* 654
Prov 19:6 *Many seek f-s from a ruler;* 654
Zech 11:7 *named one F and the other*......1177
Luke 1:30 *you have found f with God!*.......1274
Luke 2:40 *and God's f was on him*............1286
Luke 2:52 *and in f with God*.....................1287
Luke 4:19 *the time of the LORD's f*............1357
Rom 11:7 *have not found the f of God*......1664
Phil 1:7 *with me the special f of God,*........1717

FAVOR, FAVORING (v) to show partiality toward
Lev 19:15 *justice in legal matters by f-ing*....225
Jas 2:9 *But if you f some people over*.......1549

FAVORITE (adj) specially favored or liked
Gen 27:4 *Prepare my f dish,*.........................54

FAVORITES (n) persons specially loved, trusted, or provided with favors
see also PARTIALITY
Job 32:21 *I won't play f.*...........................123
Matt 22:16 *and don't play f.*......................1439
Gal 2:6 *for God has no f.*.........................1558
Eph 6:9 *he has no f.*...............................1715
Col 3:25 *For God has no f.*........................1702

FAVORITISM (n) the showing of special favor; partiality
see also DISCRIMINATION, PARTIALITY
Prov 24:23 *f when passing judgment*..........663
Mal 2:9 *f in the way you carry out*............1246
Acts 10:34 *that God shows no f.* 1534
Rom 2:11 *God does not show f.* 1649
Jas 3:17 *It shows no f and is always*.........1551

FEAR, FEARS (n) dread or alarm in facing danger; profound reverence and awe
2 Sam 23:3 *who rules in the f of God,*.........482
Ps 2:11 *Serve the LORD with reverent f,*.......857
Ps 34:4 *freed me from all my f-s.*...............458
Prov 1:33 *untroubled by f of harm.* 633
Heb 13:6 *will have no f.*...........................1782

FEAR, FEARED, FEARING, FEARS (v) to have reverential awe of God; to be afraid or apphrehensive
Deut 6:13 *You must f the LORD your*............295
Deut 8:6 *walking in his ways and f-ing*.......297
Deut 13:4 *your God and f him alone.* 303
Deut 31:12 *learn to f the LORD your God*......322
Josh 4:24 *might f the LORD your God*..........341
1 Sam 12:14 *if you f and worship*...............440
2 Chr 26:5 *taught him to f God*....................764
Neh 5:15 *But because I f-ed God,* 1210
Neh 7:2 *a faithful man who f-ed God*...........1211
Job 1:1 *He f-ed God and stayed*...................94
Job 1:8 *f-s God and stays away from* 95
Ps 34:7 *and defends all who f him*...............458
Ps 46:2 *not f when earthquakes come*........851
Ps 61:5 *for those who f your name.* 573
Ps 76:7 *you are greatly f-ed!*......................596
Ps 103:17 *with those who f him.*..................580
Ps 128:1 *joyful are those who f the* 883
Prov 8:13 *All who f the LORD will*.................640
Prov 28:14 *those who f to do wrong,* 844
Prov 31:30 *a woman who f-s the LORD*.......848
Isa 25:3 *nations will f you*..........................895
Jer 2:19 *your God and not to f him.* 961
Mal 3:16 *those who f-ed the LORD spoke*..1248
Mal 4:2 *for you who f my name,* 1249
2 Cor 7:1 *because we f God.*......................1634
Rev 11:18 *and all who f your name,*..........1817

FEARFUL (adj) very great—used as an intensive
2 Cor 5:11 *our f responsibility to the Lord,* 1632

FEAST (n) an elaborate meal; banquet
Ps 23:5 *You prepare a f for me*...................558
Prov 15:15 *life is a continual f.*...................649
Luke 15:29 *goat for a f with my friends*.....1411

FEAST, FEASTING (v) to enjoy a good meal
Esth 9:17 *a day of f-ing and gladness.*.....1193
Prov 17:1 *a house filled with f-ing—and*....652
Prov 23:20 *or f with gluttons,* 661
Isa 22:13 *You f on meat and drink wine.* 892

FED (v) gave food to
see also FEED
Deut 8:16 *He f you with manna* 297
Ezek 3:2 *mouth, and he f me the scroll.* 1046
John 6:26 *want to be with me because I f*...1367

FEED, FEEDS (v) to give food to; to eat; to provide something essential to the development, sustenance, maintenance, or operation of
see also FED
Prov 15:14 *while the fool f-s on trash*.........649
Prov 22:9 *because they f the poor*..............660
Jer 50:19 *own land, to f in the fields*..........1036
Matt 6:26 *your heavenly Father f-s them.* ...1332
Matt 14:16 *necessary—you f them."*..........1363
Matt 25:42 *and you didn't f me*..................1453
John 6:57 *anyone who f-s on me will live*...1368
John 21:15 *"Then f my lambs,"*..................1497
John 21:17 *"Then f my sheep."*..................1497
Rom 12:20 *enemies are hungry, f them.* ...1668

FEEL (v) to perceive by physical sensation
Ps 115:7 *have hands but cannot f,*.............874

FEET (n) *see also* FOOT
Ps 22:16 *pierced my hands and f.*..............556
Ps 40:2 *He set my f on solid ground*...........570
Ps 73:2 *My f were slipping,*.........................594
Ps 119:105 *a lamp to guide my f*................880
Isa 52:7 *are the f of the messenger*............939
Matt 10:14 *shake its dust from your f*.......1358
Luke 24:39 *Look at my f.*..........................1495
John 13:5 *began to wash the disciples' f,* .1456
John 13:14 *wash each other's f.* 1456
Rom 10:15 *beautiful are the f of*...............1664
Rom 16:20 *crush Satan under your f.* 1673
1 Cor 15:25 *his enemies beneath his f.* 1621
Heb 1:13 *a footstool under your f.* 1763
Heb 12:13 *a straight path for your f*..........1781

FELLOWSHIP (n) friendship; association; company; partnership
Gen 5:24 *walking in close f with God.* 16
1 Cor 5:2 *remove this man from your f.* 1602
2 Cor 13:14 *and the f of the Holy Spirit*.....1643
1 Jn 1:3 *you may have f with us.*..............1787
1 Jn 1:3 *our f is with the Father and*.........1787
1 Jn 1:6 *we say we have f with God but*....1787
1 Jn 2:27 *remain in f with Christ.* 1790

FEMALE (adj) of, relating to, or being a woman
Gen 1:27 *male and f he created them*.............8
Gen 5:2 *He created them male and f,* 16
Mark 10:6 *God made them male and f* 1419
Gal 3:28 *slave or free, male and f.*............1562

FERTILE (adj) capable of sustaining abundant growth; productive
Mark 4:8 *other seeds fell on f soil,*............1346

FESTIVAL, FESTIVALS (n) a time of celebration marked by special observances
Lev 23:2 *the LORD's appointed f-s,* 229
Isa 30:29 *at the holy f-s.* 901
Amos 5:21 *religious f-s and solemn*...........776
Zech 14:18 *of Egypt refuse to attend the f,*...1180
1 Cor 5:8 *let us celebrate the f,*.................1602

FESTIVE (adj) joyful, happy
Isa 61:3 *f praise instead of despair.* 948

FEVER (n) a rise of body temperature above the normal
Job 30:30 *my bones burn with f.*................121
Matt 8:14 *sick in bed with a high f.*..........1309
Luke 4:38 *very sick with a high f.* 1310
John 4:52 *his f suddenly disappeared!*.......1307
Acts 28:8 *was ill with f and dysentery.* 1688

FEW (adj) not many; a low number of
Prov 17:27 *wise person uses f words;* 653
Matt 9:37 *is great, but the workers are f.*..1357
Matt 22:14 *many are called, but f are*.......1438

FIANCÉE (n) a woman engaged to be married
1 Cor 7:36 *treating his f improperly*..........1607

FIELD, FIELDS (n) an open land area free of woods and buildings; an area of cleared land used for cultivation
Lev 19:9 *along the edges of your f-s,* 225
Ruth 2:2 *into the harvest f-s to pick* 411
Isa 40:6 *the flowers in a f.* 924
Matt 6:28 *Look at the lilies of the f*...........1332
Matt 13:44 *discovered hidden in a f.* 1349
Luke 2:8 *staying in the f-s nearby,*............1281
John 4:35 *The f-s are already ripe* 1305
1 Cor 3:9 *And you are God's f.* 1599
1 Pet 1:24 *like a flower in the f.* 1750

FIERY (adj) consisting of fire
Eph 6:16 *stop the f arrows of the devil*......1715

FIG, FIGS (n) an oblong or pear-shaped syconium fruit of a tree of the mulberry family; a fruit-producing plant which could be either a tall tree or a low-spreading shrub
Gen 3:7 *they sewed f leaves together* 12
Judg 9:10 *they said to the f tree,*................389
Prov 27:18 *workers who tend a f tree* 842
Mic 4:4 *grapevines and f trees,* 907
Zech 3:10 *grapevine and f tree.*..................1168
Matt 21:19 *a f tree beside the road.* 1435
Luke 13:6 *man planted a f tree in his* 1402
Jas 3:12 *Does a f tree produce olives,* 1550
Jas 3:12 *or a grapevine produce f-s?*.......1550

FIGHT, FIGHTS (n) a hostile encounter; a struggle for a goal or an objective
Prov 15:18 *hot-tempered person starts* ***f-s;*** ... 650
Prov 20:3 *Avoiding a* ***f*** *is a mark of* ... 656
Prov 29:22 *An angry person starts* ***f-s;*** ... 845
2 Tim 4:7 *fought the good* ***f,*** ... 1746
Jas 4:1 *causing the quarrels and* ***f-s*** ... 1551

FIGHT, FIGHTING, FIGHTS (v) to actively oppose or combat, as with weapons; to gain by struggle
see also FOUGHT
Exod 14:14 *LORD himself will* ***f*** *for you.* ... 160
Josh 23:10 *LORD your God* ***f-s*** *for you,* ... 368
1 Sam 17:32 *I'll go* ***f*** *him!* ... 450
1 Sam 25:28 *are* ***f-ing*** *the LORD's battles.* ... 467
Neh 4:20 *our God will* ***f*** *for us!* ... 1209
Ps 35:1 ***F*** *those who* ***f*** *against me.* ... 565
Prov 28:25 *Greed causes* ***f-ing;*** ... 844
Isa 49:25 *I will* ***f*** *those who* ***f*** *you,* ... 937
1 Cor 15:32 *value was there in* ***f-ing*** *wild* ... 1621
Phil 1:27 *one purpose,* ***f-ing*** *together for* ... 1719
1 Tim 6:12 ***F*** *the good fight* ... 1735
Jas 4:2 *so you* ***f*** *and wage war* ... 1551

FILL, FILLED, FILLS (v) to occupy the whole of; to supply fully; to spread through
Gen 1:28 ***F*** *the earth and govern it.* ... 8
Exod 34:6 ***f-ed*** *with unfailing love* ... 187
1 Kgs 8:11 *presence of the LORD* ***f-ed*** ... 617
Ps 81:10 *and I will* ***f*** *it with good things.* ... 602
Ps 107:9 *the thirsty and* ***f-s*** *the hungry* ... 872
Ps 119:64 *unfailing love* ***f-s*** *the earth;* ... 879
Ps 123:3 *have had our* ***f*** *of contempt.* ... 883
Isa 6:3 *earth is* ***f-ed*** *with his glory!* ... 783
Joel 2:13 *and* ***f-ed*** *with unfailing love.* ... 1241
Jonah 4:2 *and* ***f-ed*** *with unfailing love.* ... 769
Hag 2:7 *I will* ***f*** *this place with glory,* ... 1164
Luke 1:15 *be* ***f-ed*** *with the Holy Spirit,* ... 1273
Luke 1:41 *was* ***f-ed*** *with the Holy Spirit.* ... 1275
Luke 1:67 ***f-ed*** *with the Holy Spirit* ... 1276
Luke 2:40 *He was* ***f-ed*** *with wisdom,* ... 1286
Luke 24:49 *Holy Spirit comes and* ***f-s*** ... 1498
Acts 2:4 *was* ***f-ed*** *with the Holy Spirit* ... 1514
Acts 2:28 *you will* ***f*** *me with the joy* ... 1516
Acts 4:8 ***f-ed*** *with the Holy Spirit,* ... 1518
Acts 4:31 *all* ***f-ed*** *with the Holy Spirit* ... 1520
Acts 9:17 *be* ***f-ed*** *with the Holy Spirit.* ... 1530
Acts 13:9 *was* ***f-ed*** *with the Holy Spirit,* ... 1540
Rom 5:5 *Holy Spirit to* ***f*** *our hearts* ... 1654
Rom 15:13 ***f*** *you completely with joy* ... 1671
Eph 1:23 *by Christ, who* ***f-s*** *all things* ... 1706
Eph 5:18 *be* ***f-ed*** *with the Holy Spirit,* ... 1713
Col 3:16 *in all its richness,* ***f*** *your lives.* ... 1701

FILTH (n) moral corruption or defilement
Isa 4:4 *wash the* ***f*** *from beautiful Zion* ... 828

FILTHY (adj) covered with, containing, or characterized by foul or putrid matter or moral corruption
Isa 6:5 *I have* ***f*** *lips, and I live* ... 784
Isa 64:6 *they are nothing but* ***f*** *rags.* ... 950
Zech 3:4 *Take off his* ***f*** *clothes.* ... 1168
2 Cor 6:17 *Don't touch their* ***f*** *things,* ... 1634

FINANCIAL (adj) relating to money
2 Cor 11:9 *did not become a* ***f*** *burden* ... 1640

FIND, FINDS (v) to attain or reach (a goal or conclusion); to discover by searching or effort; to experience
see also FOUND
1 Chr 28:9 *seek him, you will* ***f*** *him.* ... 540
Job 23:3 *knew where to* ***f*** *God,* ... 115
Prov 3:13 *the person who* ***f-s*** *wisdom,* ... 635
Prov 8:17 *who search will surely* ***f*** *me.* ... 640
Prov 8:35 *For whoever* ***f-s*** *me* ***f-s*** *life.* ... 641
Prov 11:27 *you will* ***f*** *favor;* ... 644
Prov 31:10 *Who can* ***f*** *a virtuous and* ... 847
Isa 55:6 *while you can* ***f*** *him.* ... 942
Jer 6:16 *will* ***f*** *rest for your souls.* ... 968
Matt 7:7 *seeking, and you will* ***f.*** ... 1334
Matt 7:8 *Everyone who seeks,* ***f-s.*** ... 1334
Matt 10:39 *your life for me, you will* ***f*** *it.* ... 1361
Luke 11:9 *and you will* ***f.*** ... 1398
Luke 11:10 *Everyone who seeks,* ***f-s.*** ... 1398
Luke 15:4 *that is lost until he* ***f-s*** *it?* ... 1410
Luke 15:8 *search carefully until she* ***f-s*** *it?* ... 1410

FINEST (adj) superior in kind, quality, or appearance
Isa 55:2 *will enjoy the* ***f*** *food.* ... 942
Jer 3:19 *the* ***f*** *possession in the world.* ... 963

FINGER, FINGERS (n) any of the five terminating members of the hand; figurative for the power of God
Exod 8:19 *This is the* ***f*** *of God!* ... 152
Exod 31:18 *written by the* ***f*** *of God.* ... 183
Deut 9:10 *had written with his own* ***f*** ... 298
Luke 16:24 *dip the tip of his* ***f*** *in water.* ... 1412
John 8:6 *wrote in the dust with his* ***f.*** ... 1391
John 20:25 *in his hands, put my* ***f-s*** *into* ... 1495

FINISH (n) the end
Rom 1:17 *from start to* ***f*** *by faith.* ... 1646

FINISH, FINISHED, FINISHING (v) to bring to completion; to bring to an end
Gen 2:2 *had* ***f-ed*** *his work of creation,* ... 9
John 4:34 *and from* ***f-ing*** *his work.* ... 1305
John 19:30 *he said, "It is* ***f-ed!"*** ... 1487
Acts 20:24 *I use it for* ***f-ing*** *the work.* ... 1675
2 Cor 8:11 *Now you should* ***f*** *what you* ... 1636
2 Tim 4:7 *I have* ***f-ed*** *the race,* ... 1746
Rev 20:3 *the thousand years were* ***f-ed.*** ... 1829

FIRE, FIRES (n) hot flame and burning light; symbolic of hell; severe trial or ordeal
Exod 3:2 ***f*** *from the middle of a bush.* ... 143
Exod 13:21 *at night with a pillar of* ***f.*** ... 159
Dan 3:25 *walking around in the* ***f.*** ... 1007
Matt 3:11 *the Holy Spirit and with* ***f.*** ... 1289
Matt 5:22 *are in danger of the* ***f-s*** *of hell.* ... 1328
Matt 18:8 *be thrown into eternal* ***f*** ... 1384
Mark 9:43 *the unquenchable* ***f-s*** *of hell* ... 1384
Mark 9:49 *be tested with* ***f.*** ... 1384
Luke 3:16 *with the Holy Spirit and with* ***f.*** ... 1292
Acts 2:3 *tongues of* ***f*** *appeared and* ... 1514
1 Cor 3:13 *The* ***f*** *will show* ... 1599
Heb 12:29 *God is a devouring* ***f.*** ... 1781
Jas 3:6 *it is set on* ***f*** *by hell itself.* ... 1550

FIRM (adj) securely or solidly fixed in place; not weak or uncertain
Isa 7:9 *Unless your faith is* ***f,*** ... 790
2 Cor 1:21 *to stand* ***f*** *for Christ.* ... 1627
2 Cor 1:24 *own faith that you stand* ***f.*** ... 1627
Eph 6:13 *will still be standing* ***f.*** ... 1715
1 Thes 3:8 *you are standing* ***f*** *in the Lord.* ... 1583
2 Thes 2:15 *brothers and sisters, stand* ***f*** ... 1589
1 Pet 5:9 *Stand* ***f*** *against him,* ... 1756

FIRMAMENT (KJV)
Gen 1:7 ***space*** *to separate the waters* ... 6
Ps 19:1 ***skies*** *display his craftsmanship* ... 554
Ezek 1:22 *surface like the* ***sky,*** *glittering* ... 1045
Dan 12:3 *will shine as bright as the* ***sky.*** ... 1161

FIRST (adj) preceding all others in time, order, or importance
Gen 1:5 *came, marking the* ***f*** *day.* ... 6
Isa 44:6 *I am the* ***F*** *and the Last;* ... 930
Isa 48:12 *God, the* ***F*** *and the Last.* ... 935
Matt 22:38 *the* ***f*** *and greatest* ... 1441
Mark 9:35 *wants to be* ***f*** *must take last* ... 1383
Mark 13:10 *Good News must* ***f*** *be* ... 1448
Rom 1:16 *Jew* ***f*** *and also the Gentile.* ... 1646
Rom 2:9 *Jew* ***f*** *and also for the Gentile.* ... 1649
1 Cor 15:45 *The* ***f*** *man, Adam,* ... 1621
Eph 6:2 *the* ***f*** *commandment with a* ... 1714
1 Tim 2:13 *God made Adam* ***f,*** ... 1730
Heb 10:9 *He cancels the* ***f*** *covenant* ... 1775
1 Jn 4:19 *because he loved us* ***f.*** ... 1794
Rev 1:17 *I am the* ***F*** *and the Last.* ... 1801
Rev 22:13 *and the Omega, the* ***F*** *and the* ... 1832

FIRSTBEGOTTEN (KJV)
Heb 1:6 *his* ***supreme Son*** *into the world* ... 1762

FIRSTBORN (adj) eldest; the most prominent; the rightful heir
Exod 11:5 *All the* ***f*** *sons will die* ... 155
Exod 34:20 *buy back every* ***f*** *son.* ... 188
Ps 89:27 *I will make him my* ***f*** *son,* ... 592
Mic 6:7 *sacrifice our* ***f*** *children to pay* ... 910
Heb 12:23 *assembly of God's* ***f*** *children* ... 1781

FIRSTBORN (n) the eldest offspring; one possessing special rights of inheritance
Gen 25:34 *for his rights as the* ***f.*** ... 52
Exod 13:2 *every* ***f*** *among the Israelites.* ... 158
Exod 34:19 *The* ***f*** *of every animal* ... 188

FIRSTFRUITS (KJV)
Exod 23:16 *the* ***first crops*** *of your harvest* ... 173
Exod 23:19 *bring the* ***very best*** *of* ... 174
Lev 2:14 ***first portion*** *of your harvest* ... 204
Lev 23:10 *you harvest its* ***first crops,*** ... 230
Num 28:26 *the* ***first*** *of your new grain* ... 275
Rev 14:4 *as a* ***special offering*** *to God.* ... 1821

FISH (n) any of numerous cold-blooded aquatic vertebrates
Jonah 1:17 *had arranged for a great* ***f*** ... 767
Matt 12:40 *in the belly of the great* ***f.*** ... 1343
Luke 9:13 *loaves of bread and two* ***f,*** ... 1364
John 6:9 *five barley loaves and two* ***f.*** ... 1365

FISH, FISHED, FISHING (v) to attempt to catch fish
Mark 1:16 *for they* ***f-ed*** *for a living.* ... 1308
Mark 1:17 *how to* ***f*** *for people!* ... 1308
Luke 5:10 *you'll be* ***f-ing*** *for people!* ... 1308

FISHERMEN (n) those who engage in fishing as an occupation
Ezek 26:5 *a rock in the sea, a place for* ***f*** ... 1082

FISHERS (KJV)
Isa 19:8 ***fishermen*** *will lament for lack of work* ... 889
Jer 16:16 ***fishermen*** *who will catch* ... 1020
Matt 4:19 ***how to fish*** *for people* ... 1307

FLAME, FLAMES (n) a state of blazing combustion; burning zeal or passion
Isa 5:24 *and dry grass shrivels in the* ***f,*** ... 830
1 Cor 3:15 *escaping through a wall of* ***f-s.*** ... 1599
2 Tim 1:6 *fan into* ***f-s*** *the spiritual gift* ... 1741
Rev 1:14 *his eyes were like* ***f-s*** *of fire.* ... 1800

FLAMING (adj) blazing; intense
Isa 4:5 *and smoke and* ***f*** *fire at night,* ... 828
2 Thes 1:8 *in* ***f*** *fire, bringing judgment on* ... 1588
Heb 12:18 *to a place of* ***f*** *fire, darkness,* ... 1781

FLASHED (v) to break forth in or like a sudden flame; to give off light suddenly
1 Kgs 18:38 *the fire of the LORD **f** down*......718
Dan 10:6 *His face **f** like lightning,*.............1158

FLATTER (v) to praise excessively out of self-interest
Job 32:21 *or try to **f** anyone.*......................123
Prov 29:5 *To **f** friends is*............................845
Dan 11:32 *He will **f** and win over those*.....1160
Jude 1:16 ***f** others to get what they want.*.1785

FLATTERING (adj) characterized by excessive praise out of self-interest
Ps 12:2 *speaking with **f** lips*........................550
Ps 12:3 *cut off their **f** lips.*.........................550
Prov 26:28 *and **f** words cause ruin.*...........842

FLATTERY (n) insincere or excessive praise
Job 32:22 *For if I tried **f**, my Creator*...........123
Ps 5:9 *tongues are filled with **f**.*..................547
Prov 28:23 *criticism far more than **f**.*..........844
1 Thes 2:5 *try to win you with **f**,*..............1581

FLEE (v) to run away; to shun
1 Cor 10:14 ***f** from the worship of idols.*....1610
Jas 4:7 *and he will **f** from you.*................1551

FLEECE (n) the wool obtained from a sheep at one shearing
Judg 6:37 *If the **f** is wet with dew*..............384

FLEETING (adj) passing swiftly
Ps 39:4 *how **f** my life is.*............................569

FLESH (n) the meaty part of animal and human bodies
see also BODY, HUMAN
Gen 2:23 *and **f** from my **f**!*..........................10
John 6:51 *so the world may live, is my **f**.*....1368
1 Cor 15:39 *different kinds of **f**—*............1621

FLIGHT (n) an act or instance of running away
Deut 32:30 *put ten thousand to **f**,*..............325

FLIRTING (v) to behave amorously without serious intent
Isa 3:16 ***f** with her eyes,*..............................827

FLOCK, FLOCKS (n) a group of animals assembled or herded together; a group under the guidance of a leader
Isa 40:11 *feed his **f** like a shepherd.*...........924
Jer 10:21 *and their **f-s** are scattered.*........1013
Jer 31:10 *as a shepherd does his **f**.*...........1033
Zech 11:17 *who abandons the **f**!*...............1178
Matt 26:31 *the **f** will be scattered.*............1460
Luke 2:8 *guarding their **f-s** of sheep.*.........1281
Luke 12:32 *don't be afraid, little **f**.*............1401
John 10:16 *one **f** with one shepherd.*.........1405
Acts 20:28 *shepherd God's **f**—*..................1675

FLOGGED (v) to beat with a rod or whip
Deut 25:2 *is sentenced to be **f**,*..................314
John 19:1 *Pilate had Jesus **f**.*.....................1480
Acts 5:40 *and had them **f**.*.........................1522

FLOOD, FLOODS (n) a rising and overflowing of a body of water; the destruction of the world by water during the time of Noah
Gen 7:7 *the boat to escape the **f**—*...............18
Prov 27:4 *cruel, and wrath is like a **f**,*..........842
Matt 24:38 *In those days before the **f**,*......1447
Luke 6:49 *the **f-s** sweep down against*.......1335
2 Pet 2:5 *ungodly people with a vast **f**.*.....1759

FLOUR (n) a product consisting of finely milled wheat
Lev 2:1 *must consist of choice **f**.*...............204
Num 7:13 ***f** moistened with olive oil.*...........196
Luke 17:35 *grinding **f** together at the mill;* 1417

FLOURISH, FLOURISHING (v) to grow luxuriantly; to prosper or thrive
Ps 72:7 *all the godly **f** during his reign.*........630
Ps 92:7 *and evildoers **f**, they will be*............862
Ps 92:12 *the godly will **f** like palm trees*......862
Prov 14:11 *the tent of the godly will **f**.*.........647
Prov 28:28 *meet disaster, the godly **f**.*..........844
Isa 35:7 *reeds and rushes will **f**.*.................905
2 Thes 1:3 *your faith is **f-ing***..................1587

FLOW, FLOWING, FLOWS (v) to proceed smoothly and readily; to abound
Exod 3:8 ***f-ing** with milk and honey—*..........144
Exod 33:3 *land that **f-s** with milk and*.........186
Num 13:27 ***f-ing** with milk and honey.*........251
Josh 5:6 ***f-ing** with milk and honey.*............342
Ps 119:171 *Let praise **f** from my lips,*.........882
Jer 32:22 ***f-ing** with milk and honey.*..........1079
Lam 1:16 *tears **f** down my cheeks.*...............1095
John 7:38 *living water will **f** from his.*........1390
Rev 22:1 ***f-ing** from the throne of God.*.....1832

FLOWER, FLOWERS (n) the blossom of a plant
Job 14:2 *We blossom like a **f** and then*.......108
Isa 40:6 *as quickly as the **f-s** in a field.*.......924
Isa 40:7 ***f-s** fade beneath the breath*..........924
Jas 1:10 *like a little **f** in the field.*..............1547

FOCUS (v) to concentrate attention or effort
1 Tim 4:13 ***f** on reading the Scriptures*......1732

FOES (n) adversaries, opponents, or enemies
Ps 112:8 *face their **f** triumphantly.*..............873

FOLLOW, FOLLOWED, FOLLOWING, FOLLOWS (v) to pursue or run after; to imitate; to obey
Deut 1:36 *because he has **f-ed** the LORD*....286
Deut 5:32 ***f-ing** his instructions*.................294
Josh 14:14 *he wholeheartedly **f-ed** the*......358
1 Kgs 3:3 *loved the LORD and **f-ed***............606
2 Chr 10:14 *and **f-ed** the counsel*.............698
Prov 4:27 *feet from **f-ing** evil.*......................637
Prov 10:9 *those who **f** crooked paths*..........642
Isa 57:2 *For those who **f** godly paths*..........943
Isa 65:2 *But they **f** their own evil paths*.......951
Matt 4:20 *at once and **f-ed** him.*..................1307
Matt 7:24 *listens to my teaching and **f-s***...1335
Matt 8:19 *I will **f** you wherever you go.*.......1387
Matt 8:22 ***F** me now. Let the*.......................1387
Matt 9:9 *got up and **f-ed** him.*....................1314
Matt 16:24 *take up your cross, and **f***.........1377
Matt 19:27 *given up everything to **f** you.*...1420
Matt 26:58 *Meanwhile, Peter **f-ed** him*.....1472
Mark 1:17 *Come, **f** me, and I will show*.....1308
Luke 9:23 *your cross daily, and **f** me.*........1378
Luke 17:23 *go out and **f** them.*.................1416
Luke 18:43 ***f-ed** Jesus, praising God.*......1426
John 8:12 *If you **f** me, you won't have to*...1392
John 10:4 *they **f** him because they know*..1405
John 10:27 *know them, and they **f** me.*.....1406
John 12:26 *to be my disciple must **f** me,*..1434
John 21:19 *Jesus told him, "**F** me."*..........1497
1 Cor 1:12 *or "I **f** only Christ."*..................1596
1 Cor 4:17 *of how I **f** Christ Jesus,*...........1601
Gal 5:7 *you back from **f-ing** the truth?*......1565
Gal 5:25 ***f** the Spirit's leading*....................1567
Phil 2:12 *always **f-ed** my instructions*.......1720
Phil 3:17 *those who **f** our example.*...........1723
2 Thes 3:6 *and don't **f** the tradition.*.........1590
1 Pet 2:21 *must **f** in his steps.*....................1752
Rev 14:4 *as virgins, **f-ing** the Lamb*............1821

FOLLOWER, FOLLOWERS (n) one who follows the teachings of another; a disciple
1 Kgs 18:3 *was a devoted **f** of the LORD.*......716
Matt 10:42 *one of the least of my **f-s**,*........1361
Matt 18:20 *together as my **f-s**, I am there*1385
Acts 9:21 *Jesus' **f-s** in Jerusalem?*..........1531

FOLLY (KJV)
Prov 14:18 *clothed with **foolishness***..........648
Prov 26:11 *a fool repeats his **foolishness***...841
Eccl 2:13 *is better than **foolishness***...........674
Isa 9:17 *they all speak **foolishness***............793
2 Tim 3:9 *recognize what **fools** they are*...1744

FOOD (n) something that nourishes, sustains, or supplies energy and vitality
see also BREAD
Lev 11:2 *the ones you may use for **f**.*..........214
Prov 25:21 *hungry, give them **f** to eat.*........840
Isa 58:7 *Share your **f** with the hungry,*........944
Dan 1:8 *defile himself by eating the **f**.*.......1001
Matt 6:11 *today the **f** we need,*..................1331
Matt 6:25 *Isn't life more than **f**,*.................1332
Mark 7:19 *every kind of **f** is acceptable.*.....1371
John 6:55 *my flesh is true **f**, and my.*..........1368
John 13:18 *eats my **f** has turned against*..1456
Acts 15:20 *abstain from eating **f***..............1570
Rom 14:6 *kind of **f** do so to honor*..............1670
1 Tim 6:8 *have enough **f** and clothing,*.......1735
Jas 2:15 *who has no **f** or clothing,*.............1549

FOOL, FOOLS (n) one deficient in intellectual, practical, or moral sense
1 Sam 25:25 *He is a **f**, just as his name*.....466
Ps 14:1 *Only **f-s** say in their hearts,*............551
Prov 6:32 *commits adultery is an utter **f**,*.....639
Prov 10:8 *babbling **f-s** fall flat on*...............642
Prov 10:23 *wrong is fun for a **f**,*.....................643
Prov 17:7 *are not fitting for a **f**;*....................652
Prov 17:16 *to pay tuition to educate a **f**,*......652
Prov 26:1 *associated with **f-s** than snow*....840
Prov 26:7 *A proverb in the mouth of a **f***......841
Prov 29:11 ***F-s** vent their anger,*.................845
Prov 29:20 *more hope for a **f** than for*.........845
Rom 1:22 *became utter **f-s**.*...........................1647
1 Cor 3:18 *need to become a **f** to be*.........1600
2 Cor 11:21 *I'm talking like a **f** again—*.....1641
Eph 5:15 *Don't live like **f-s**,*.........................1713
2 Tim 3:9 *recognize what **f-s** they are,*......1744

FOOL, FOOLED, FOOLING (v) to trick or deceive
Ps 119:118 *are only **f-ing** themselves.*........880
Jer 7:4 *don't be **f-ed** by those who*..........1008
1 Cor 15:33 *Don't be **f-ed** by those who.*...1621
Gal 6:3 *you are only **f-ing** yourself.*...........1567
Eph 5:6 *Don't be **f-ed** by those who try*....1712
2 Thes 2:3 *Don't be **f-ed** by what they say.*...1588
Jas 1:22 *are only **f-ing** yourselves.*............1548
Jas 1:26 *you are **f-ing** yourself,*..................1548
1 Jn 1:8 *we are only **f-ing** ourselves*........1787

FOOLISH (adj) lacking in sense, judgment, or discretion; irreverent
Prov 26:4 *the **f** arguments of fools,*............841
Prov 26:17 *else's argument is as **f**.*..............841
Rom 1:28 *abandoned them to their **f***........1648
1 Cor 1:18 *the cross is **f** to those who*......1596
1 Cor 1:27 *world considers **f** in order to*....1597
1 Cor 2:14 *It all sounds **f** to them*...............1598
Eph 5:4 *Obscene stories, **f** talk,*...............1712
1 Tim 6:20 *Avoid godless, **f** discussions*....1735
Titus 3:9 *not get involved in **f** discussions*....1739

FOOLISHNESS (n) aimless behavior befitting a fool
Prov 19:3 *ruin their lives by their own **f***.......654
Prov 22:15 *heart is filled with **f**,*...................660

Eccl 10:1 *so a little **f** spoils great*................681
Mark 7:22 *envy, slander, pride, and **f.***........1371

FOOT (n) the end of the leg upon which an individual stands
see also FEET
Josh 1:3 *Wherever you set **f,***.......................336
Matt 18:8 *with only one hand or one **f***......1384
Luke 4:11 *won't even hurt your **f***.............1296
1 Cor 12:15 *If the **f** says,*.........................1615
Rev 10:2 *and his left **f** on the land.*...........1816

FOOTHOLD (n) a strategic position enabling further advance or advantage
Eph 4:27 *anger gives a **f** to the devil.*........1712

FOOTSTOOL (n) a low stool used to support the feet
Ps 110:1 *making them a **f** under*...............582
Isa 66:1 *throne, and the earth is my **f.***........952
Matt 5:35 *the earth is his **f.***.......................1329
Acts 7:49 *the earth is my **f.***.......................1526
Heb 1:13 *making them a **f** under*..............1763
Heb 10:13 *and made a **f** under*...............1775

FORBID, FORBIDDEN (v) to command against
Matt 16:19 *Whatever you **f** on earth*.........1375
Matt 16:19 *will be **f-den** in heaven,*..........1375
Matt 18:18 *whatever you **f** on earth*..........1385
1 Cor 14:39 *don't **f** speaking in*...............1618

FORCE (n) violence, compulsion, or constraint exerted upon or against a person or thing
Zech 4:6 *is not by **f** nor by strength,*.........1169

FORCE, FORCED (v) to compel by physical, moral, or intellectual means
Matt 27:32 *soldiers **f-d** him to carry*.........1482
John 6:15 *were ready to **f** him to be*.........1365

FORCEFUL (adj) possessing or filled with force; effective
2 Cor 10:10 *letters are demanding and **f,***.1638

(FORE)FATHERS (KJV)
Exod 10:6 ***ancestors** seen a plague like*.....154
Num 11:12 *swore to give their **ancestors***.....248
Jer 11:10 *the sins of their **forefathers***......1014
Matt 23:32 *what your **ancestors** started*...1445

FOREHEAD, FOREHEADS (n) the part of the face above the eyes
Exod 13:9 *on your hand or your **f.***...............158
Deut 6:8 *wear them on your **f***....................295
1 Sam 17:49 *hit the Philistine in the **f.***........451
Rev 9:4 *seal of God on their **f-s.***...............1814
Rev 13:16 *right hand or on the **f.***..............1820
Rev 14:1 *written on their **f-s.***...................1821

FOREIGN (adj) related to or dealing with other nations; pagan
see also STRANGE
2 Chr 14:3 *He removed the **f** altars and*......706
2 Chr 33:15 *also removed the **f** gods and*...956
Isa 28:11 *through **f** oppressors*..................818

FOREIGNER, FOREIGNERS (n) nonresident, alien, or sojourner
see also STRANGER
Exod 22:21 *not mistreat or oppress **f-s***.......172
Exod 23:9 *must not oppress **f-s.***...............173
Lev 24:22 *to the **f-s** living among you*..........232
Neh 9:2 *separated themselves from all **f-s***...1215
Ps 119:19 *I am only a **f** in the land*............878
Hos 7:8 *mingle with godless **f-s,***..................810
Luke 17:18 *glory to God except this **f?***.....1416
1 Cor 14:11 *I will be a **f** to someone*.........1617
Eph 2:19 *no longer strangers and **f-s.***.......1708
1 Pet 1:1 *living as **f-s** in the provinces*......1747
1 Pet 2:11 *temporary residents and **f-s***....1751

FOREKNOW, FOREKNEW, FOREKNOWLEDGE (KJV)
Acts 2:23 *God **knew what would happen***...1515
Rom 8:29 *God knew his people **in advance***...1660
Rom 11:2 *whom he **chose from the very beginning***..................................1664
1 Pet 1:2 *Father **knew you and chose you***...1747

FOREORDAINED (KJV)
1 Pet 1:20 *chose him **as** your ransom*......1749

FORESKIN (n) flap of skin covering the tip of the penis
Gen 17:11 *cut off the flesh of your **f** as*.........38
Exod 4:25 *touched his feet with the **f** and*...146
Lev 12:3 *boy's **f** must be circumcised.*........216

FORETASTE (n) a small anticipatory sample
Rom 8:23 *as a **f** of future glory,*................1659

FORETOLD (v) to tell beforehand; to predict
Rom 16:26 *as the prophets **f.***...................1674

FOREVER (adv) for a limitless time; continually
see also ETERNAL, EVERLASTING
Gen 3:22 *they will live **f!***..............................13
Gen 17:8 *be their possession **f,***...................38
2 Sam 7:26 *name be honored **f***.................497
1 Chr 17:24 *be established and honored **f***..497
1 Chr 29:10 *be praised **f** and ever!*............541
Ezra 9:12 *prosperity to your children **f.***......1200
Ps 9:7 *the LORD reigns **f,***............................549
Ps 21:4 *of his life stretch on **f.***....................555
Ps 28:9 *in your arms **f.***..................................562
Ps 37:28 *keep them safe **f,***.........................568
Ps 61:8 *sing praises to your name **f***..........574
Ps 73:26 *he is mine **f.***...................................594
Ps 79:13 *will thank you **f** and ever,*............600
Ps 86:12 *glory to your name **f,***...................579
Ps 92:8 *will be exalted **f.***..........................862
Ps 100:5 *unfailing love continues **f,***...........866
Ps 103:17 *the LORD remains **f** with*............580
Ps 107:1 *faithful love endures **f.***.................871
Ps 110:4 *are a priest **f***..................................582
Ps 111:8 *They are **f** true,*..............................873
Ps 112:9 *be remembered **f.***..........................873
Ps 119:152 *laws will last **f.***.........................881
Ps 146:6 *every promise **f.***...........................887
Isa 32:17 *and confidence **f.***.........................902
Isa 51:6 *but my salvation lasts **f.***.................938
Isa 60:15 *make you beautiful **f,***.................947
Isa 63:12 *making himself famous **f?***...........950
Jer 25:5 *you and your ancestors **f.***.............994
Dan 2:44 *and it will stand **f.***.......................1005
Dan 4:3 *kingdom will last **f,** his rule*..........1119
Dan 7:27 *kingdom will last **f,***......................1136
John 6:51 *eats this bread will live **f;***...........1368
1 Cor 13:8 *But love will last **f!***....................1616
1 Cor 13:13 *Three things will last **f**—*.......1616
1 Cor 15:42 *will be raised to live **f.***...........1621
1 Cor 15:50 *inherit what will last **f.***...........1622
2 Cor 4:17 *and will last **f!***............................1631
2 Cor 4:18 *cannot see will last **f.***...............1631
1 Thes 4:17 *will be with the Lord **f.***............1585
2 Thes 1:9 *destruction, **f** separated*..........1588
Heb 5:6 *a priest **f** in the order*..................1767
Heb 7:17 *a priest **f** in the order*................1770
Heb 7:24 *Jesus lives **f,***...............................1771
Heb 9:12 *secured our redemption **f.***.........1773
Heb 13:8 *yesterday, today, and **f.***..............1782
1 Pet 1:25 *word of the Lord remains **f.***.....1750
1 Jn 2:17 *will live **f.***.....................................1789
Rev 22:5 *they will reign **f** and ever.*...........1832

FORGAVE (v) to pardon or acquit of guilt
see also FORGIVE
Ps 78:38 *was merciful and **f** their sins*........599
Luke 7:42 *so he kindly **f** them both,*..........1340
Eph 1:7 *his Son and **f** our sins.*...................1705
Col 1:14 *our freedom and **f** our sins*..........1694
Col 2:13 *with Christ, for he **f** all our*..........1698

FORGET, FORGETTING (v) to slip from remembrance; to disregard intentionally; to cease from remembering
see also FORGOT
Deut 4:9 *careful never to **f***.........................290
Ps 78:7 *hope anew on God, not **f-ting***........598
Ps 119:16 *and not **f** your word.*.................878
Prov 3:1 *My child, never **f***..........................634
Eccl 12:1 *cause you to **f** your Creator.*.........682
Jer 2:32 *a young woman **f** her jewelry?*......962
Luke 12:6 *God does not **f** a single one*......1399
Rom 3:31 *we can **f** about the law?*...........1652
Phil 3:13 ***F-ting** the past and looking*.......1723
Heb 13:16 *And don't **f** to do good.*.............1783
Jas 1:24 *walk away, and **f***...........................1548
Jas 1:25 *and don't **f** what you heard,*........1548
2 Pet 1:9 ***f-ting** that they have been*........1757
2 Pet 3:8 *must not **f** this one thing,*...........1760

FORGIVE, FORGIVEN, FORGIVES, FORGIVING (v) to pardon or acquit of sins
see also ATONE, FORGAVE
Gen 50:17 *Please **f** your brothers*.................93
Exod 23:21 *he will not **f** your rebellion*.........174
Exod 34:7 *I **f** iniquity, rebellion,*..................187
Exod 34:9 *but please **f** our iniquity and*.......187
Num 14:18 ***f-ing** every kind of sin*................253
Num 14:19 *just as you have **f-n** them*.......253
1 Sam 3:14 *never be **f-n** by sacrifices*........422
1 Kgs 8:34 *hear from heaven and **f***...........620
Ps 65:3 *by our sins, you **f** them all.*............575
Ps 79:9 *Save us and **f** our sins*.................600
Ps 86:5 *so good, so ready to **f,***..................579
Ps 103:3 *He **f-s** all my sins*..........................580
Prov 17:9 *when a fault is **f-n,***.......................652
Isa 22:14 *you will never be **f-n** for this*.......892
Isa 38:17 *and **f-n** all my sins*.......................921
Isa 55:7 *for he will **f** generously.*................942
Jer 31:34 *I will **f** their wickedness,*..............1034
Dan 9:19 *O Lord, hear. O Lord, **f.***...............1143
Hos 14:2 ***F** all our sins and*..........................817
Matt 6:12 *and **f** us our sins,*.........................1331
Matt 6:14 *If you **f** those who sin*..................1331
Matt 6:15 *if you refuse to **f** others,*..............1331
Matt 9:6 *authority on earth to **f** sins.*..........1312
Matt 18:21 *how often should I **f***................1385
Matt 26:28 *to **f** the sins of many.*...............1457
Mark 2:7 *Only God can **f** sins!*...................1314
Mark 2:10 *authority on earth to **f** sins.*......1314
Mark 3:29 *will never be **f-n.***...........................1342
Mark 11:25 *first **f** anyone you are*............1436
Mark 11:25 *will **f** your sins,*...........................1436
Luke 5:21 *Only God can **f** sins!*.................1314
Luke 5:24 *authority on earth to **f** sins*.........1314
Luke 6:37 ***F** others, and you will be*..........1333
Luke 7:47 *a person who is **f-n** little*..........1340
Luke 7:49 *he goes around **f-ing** sins?*......1340
Luke 11:4 ***f** us our sins, as we*...................1397
Luke 17:3 *if there is repentance, **f.***............1413
Luke 17:4 *asks forgiveness, you must **f.***...1413
Luke 23:34 *Father, **f** them,*.........................1484
John 20:23 *If you **f** anyone's sins,*.............1495

Acts 5:31 *repent of their sins and be **f-n.***...1521
Acts 8:22 *Perhaps he will **f** your evil*...1528
Rom 4:5 *faith in God who **f-s** sinners*...1652
Rom 4:7 *whose disobedience is **f-n,***...1652
2 Cor 2:7 *time to **f** and comfort*...1628
2 Cor 2:10 *When you **f** this man,*...1628
Col 3:13 *so you must **f** others*...1701
Heb 8:12 *I will **f** their wickedness,*...1772
1 Jn 1:9 *is faithful and just to **f** us*...1787

FORGIVENESS (n) aquittal or pardon of sins
see also ATONEMENT, MERCY
Neh 9:17 *you are a God of **f,***...1216
Luke 24:47 *There is **f** of sins for all*...1498
Acts 13:38 *this man Jesus there is **f.***...1542
Rom 5:15 *his gift of **f** to many*...1655
Heb 9:22 *of blood, there is no **f.***...1774
Jas 5:20 *bring about the **f** of many sins.*...1554

FORGOT, FORGOTTEN (v) see also FORGET
Deut 32:18 ***f** the God who had given*...324
Ps 44:20 *If we had **f-ten** the name*...850
Ps 78:11 *They **f** what he had done—*...598
Ps 106:13 *how quickly they **f***...870
Ps 119:176 *not **f-ten** your commands*...882
Isa 17:10 *You have **f-ten** the Rock*...797
Isa 51:13 *Yet you have **f-ten** the LORD,*...938
Hos 8:14 *Israel has **f-ten** its Maker*...811

FORMED (v) to create, fashion, or give shape to something
see also CREATE(D), MADE, MAKE
Gen 2:7 *the LORD God **f** the man*...9
Gen 2:19 *LORD God **f** from the ground*...10
Ps 94:9 *the one who **f** your eyes?*...862
Isa 49:5 *the one who **f** me*...936
Jer 1:5 *knew you before I **f** you*...958
Heb 11:3 *universe was **f** at God's*...1777

FORMLESS (adj) lacking order or arrangement; having no physical existence
Gen 1:2 *The earth was **f** and empty,*...6
Jer 4:23 *and it was empty and **f.***...965

FORNICATION (KJV)
Isa 23:17 ***be a prostitute** to all kingdoms*...894
Matt 19:9 *wife has been **unfaithful***...1418
1 Cor 5:1 ***sexual immorality** going on*...1602
1 Cor 6:18 ***sexual immorality** is a sin*...1604
Jude 1:7 *were filled with **immorality***...1784

FORSAKE (v) to renounce or turn away from entirely
1 Chr 28:9 *But if you **f** him, he will*...540
Job 28:28 *to **f** evil is real understanding*...119

FORTRESS (n) a fortified place; a place of security or survival
see also REFUGE
2 Sam 22:2 *my **f,** and my savior;*...526
Ps 27:1 *The LORD is my **f,***...561
Ps 71:3 *my rock and my **f.***...860
Ps 144:2 *and my **f,** my tower of safety,*...589
Prov 18:10 *LORD is a strong **f;***...653
Zeph 3:6 *devastating their **f** walls and*...986

FORTUNE-TELLER, FORTUNE-TELLERS (n) one who professes to foretell future events
Jer 29:8 *your prophets and **f-s** who are*...1030
Acts 16:16 *She was a **f** who earned a lot*...1575

FORTUNE-TELLING (n) the act of one foretelling future events by occultic means
Lev 19:26 *not practice **f** or witchcraft*...226

FORTY (adj) the number 40
Gen 7:4 *for **f** days and **f** nights,*...18
Exod 16:35 *Israel ate manna for **f** years*...164
Exod 24:18 ***f** days and **f** nights.*...175
Num 14:34 *wilderness for **f** years—*...253
Matt 4:2 *For **f** days and **f** nights*...1294
Acts 1:3 *the **f** days after his crucifixion,*...1512
Acts 13:18 ***f** years of wandering*...1541

FOUGHT (v) *see also* FIGHT
Gen 32:28 *because you have **f** with God*...66
Josh 10:14 *Surely the LORD **f** for Israel*...350
2 Tim 4:7 *I have **f** the good fight,*...1746

FOUND (v) *see also* FIND
2 Kgs 22:8 *I have **f** the Book of the Law*...969
2 Kgs 23:24 *Hilkiah the priest had **f***...973
2 Chr 15:15 *after God, and they **f***...709
Luke 15:6 *I have **f** my lost sheep.*...1410
Luke 15:9 *because I have **f** my lost coin*...1410
Luke 15:24 *but now he is **f.***...1411
Jas 2:8 *the royal law as **f** in the*...1549
Rev 5:4 *because no one was **f** worthy*...1809

FOUNDATION (n) basis upon which something is built, supported, or added to; substructure
Prov 1:7 *Fear of the LORD is the **f***...632
Prov 9:10 *the LORD is the **f** of wisdom.*...641
Isa 28:16 *placing a **f** stone in Jerusalem,*...819
Luke 6:49 *a house without a **f.***...1335
Eph 2:20 *built on the **f** of the apostles*...1708
1 Tim 3:15 *pillar and **f** of the truth.*...1731
2 Tim 2:19 *stands firm like a **f** stone*...1743
Heb 1:10 *you laid the **f** of the earth*...1762

FOUNTAIN (n) source; spring of water
Isa 12:3 *from the **f** of salvation!*...797
Zech 13:1 *a **f** to cleanse them*...1179

FOXES (n) any of various carnivorous mammals of the dog family with shorter legs, pointed muzzles, and long bushy tails
Song 2:15 *Catch all the **f,** those little **f,***...665
Luke 9:58 ***F** have dens to live in,*...1387

FRAGRANCE (n) a sweet or delicate odor
see also PERFUME
2 Cor 2:15 *are a Christ-like **f** rising up*...1628

FRANKINCENSE (n) an aromatic gum resin obtained from the Boswellia tree
Matt 2:11 *gifts of gold, **f,** and myrrh*...1285

FRAUD (n) an act of deceiving or misrepresenting; trickery
Lev 6:2 *you steal or commit **f,***...208
Acts 13:10 *every sort of deceit and **f,***...1540

FREE (adj) not bound, confined, or detained by force; without restraint, inhibition, or cost; possessing the rights of citizenship
John 8:32 *the truth will set you **f.***...1393
John 8:36 *sets you **f,** you are truly **f.***...1393
Rom 6:7 *we were set **f** from the power*...1656
Rom 6:18 *you are **f** from your slavery*...1656
Gal 3:28 *slave or **f,** male and female.*...1562
Jas 1:25 *the perfect law that sets you **f,***...1548
1 Pet 2:16 *For you are **f,** yet*...1751

FREED, FREES (v) to relieve or rid of what restrains, confines, restricts, or embarrasses
Ps 116:16 ***f-d** me from my chains*...875
Ps 146:7 *The LORD **f-s** the prisoners*...887
Isa 61:1 *prisoners will be **f-d.***...948
Rom 3:24 *he **f-d** us from the penalty*...1651
1 Cor 1:30 *and he **f-d** us from sin.*...1597
Rev 1:5 *and has **f-d** us from our sins*...1799

FREEDOM (n) liberation from slavery, restraint, or the power of another
Ps 119:45 *I will walk in **f,** for I have*...879
2 Cor 3:17 *the Lord is, there is **f.***...1630
Gal 2:4 *the **f** we have in Christ*...1558
Gal 4:5 *sent him to buy **f** for us*...1563
Gal 5:13 *don't use your **f** to satisfy*...1565
Eph 1:7 *purchased our **f** with the blood*...1705
1 Pet 2:16 *don't use your **f** as an excuse*...1751

FRIEND, FRIENDS (n) intimate associate; a favored companion
Prov 16:28 *separates the best of **f-s.***...652
Prov 17:9 *on it separates close **f-s.***...652
Prov 20:6 *will say they are loyal **f-s,***...656
Prov 27:6 *Wounds from a sincere **f** are*...842
Prov 28:7 *with wild **f-s** bring shame*...843
Prov 29:5 *To flatter **f-s** is to lay a trap*...845
Isa 41:8 *from Abraham my **f,***...925
Zech 13:6 *was wounded at my **f-s'** house!*...1179
John 11:3 *Lord, your dear **f** is very sick*...1413
John 15:13 *one's life for one's **f-s.***...1464
John 15:14 *You are my **f-s** if you do*...1464
John 15:15 *Now you are my **f-s,***...1464
John 19:12 *you are no '**f** of Caesar.'*...1481
Jas 2:23 *even called the **f** of God.*...1550
Jas 4:4 *want to be a **f** of the world,*...1551

FRIENDSHIP (n) association of familiarity and companionship
Prov 3:32 *he offers his **f** to the godly.*...635
Rom 5:10 *since our **f** with God was*...1654
Jas 4:4 *you realize that **f** with the world*...1551

FRIGHTENED (v) to terrify; to make afraid
Heb 12:21 *was so **f** at the sight*...1781

FRINGE (n) the edge; the threads hanging from cut or raveled edges
Matt 9:20 *touched the **f** of his robe,*...1353

FROGS (n) leaping aquatic amphibians with smooth moist skin, long hind legs, and webbed feet
Exod 8:2 *I will send a plague of **f***...151
Rev 16:13 *spirits that looked like **f***...1823

FRUIT (n) a product of plant growth; product or result
Ps 1:3 *bearing **f** each season.*...856
Isa 11:1 *new Branch bearing **f** from*...795
Dan 4:12 *loaded with **f** for all to eat.*...1119
Matt 3:10 *not produce good **f** will be*...1288
Matt 7:20 *can identify a tree by its **f,***...1334
Matt 12:33 *is bad, its **f** will be bad*...1341
John 15:2 *that doesn't produce **f,***...1463
John 15:16 *go and produce lasting **f,***...1464
Gal 5:22 *produces this kind of **f***...1566
Phil 1:11 *the **f** of your salvation—*...1717
2 Tim 2:6 *first to enjoy the **f***...1742
Rev 22:2 *bearing twelve crops of **f,***...1832

FRUITFUL (adj) bearing fruit (product of a tree or plant); abundant (at producing work or in bearing children)
Gen 1:22 *Be **f** and multiply.*...7
Gen 9:1 *Be **f** and multiply.*...20
Gen 35:11 *Be **f** and multiply.*...70
Ps 128:3 *will be like a **f** grapevine,*...883
Jer 2:7 *brought you into a **f** land*...960
Phil 1:22 *do more **f** work for Christ.*...1718

FRUSTRATES (v) to impede or obstruct; to make invalid or with no effect
Ps 33:10 *The LORD **f** the plans*...858

FULFILL, FULFILLED, FULFILLS (v) to complete or perform as promised; to measure up or satisfy
Ps 57:2 *to God who will **f** his purpose*...459
Dan 9:4 *You always **f** your covenant*...1142
Matt 2:15 *This **f-ed** what the Lord had*...1285

Matt 2:23 *This* ***f-ed*** *what the prophets*.....1286
Matt 13:35 ***f-ed*** *what God had spoken*.....1348
Matt 27:9 *This* ***f-ed*** *the prophecy of*.........1476
Luke 4:21 *has been* ***f-ed*** *this very day!*.....1357
Luke 24:44 *Psalms must be* ***f-ed.***............1498
John 18:9 *this to* ***f*** *his own statement:*......1470
John 19:28 *and to* ***f*** *Scripture he said,*......1486
Acts 1:16 *Scriptures had to be* ***f-ed***.........1512
Rom 3:31 *do we truly* ***f*** *the law*.................1652
Rom 13:8 *you will* ***f*** *the requirements*........1669
Rom 13:10 *love* ***f-s*** *the requirements*.......1669
Eph 1:9 *to* ***f*** *his own good pleasure*...........1705

FULFILLMENT (n) the act of bringing to completion as promised
John 19:36 *happened in* ***f*** *of the Scriptures*...1487

FULL (adj) possessing or containing a great amount
Deut 34:9 *was* ***f*** *of the spirit of wisdom,*......328
Luke 4:1 *Then Jesus,* ***f*** *of the Holy Spirit,* ..1295
Acts 6:3 ***f*** *of the Spirit and wisdom.*.........1522
Acts 6:5 *Stephen (a man* ***f*** *of faith and*......1522
Acts 7:55 *Stephen,* ***f*** *of the Holy Spirit,*......1526
Acts 11:24 *man,* ***f*** *of the Holy Spirit*..........1536

FULLNESS (n) the quality or state of containing all that is wanted, needed, or possible
Eph 3:19 *with all the* ***f*** *of life and*.............1710
Col 1:19 *God in all his* ***f*** *was pleased*........1695
Col 2:9 *lives all the* ***f*** *of God*....................1698

FUN (n) providing entertainment, amusement, or enjoyment
Prov 10:23 *Doing wrong is* ***f*** *for a fool,*........643
Prov 14:9 *Fools make* ***f*** *of guilt,*.................647

FUNDAMENTAL (adj) primary; basic; central
Heb 6:1 *the* ***f*** *importance of repenting*.......1768

FUNERAL (adj) of, relating to, or constituting the observances held for a dead person
2 Sam 1:17 *David composed a* ***f*** *song*........477
Luke 7:32 *so we played* ***f*** *songs,*.............1339

FUNERALS (n) observances held for dead people
Eccl 7:2 *Better to spend your time at* ***f***........678

FURIOUS (adj) exhibiting or goaded by anger
Judg 14:19 *But Samson was* ***f***..................399
2 Sam 12:5 *David was* ***f.***............................505
Jer 21:5 *You have made me* ***f!***................1076

FURNACE (n) an enclosed structure in which heat is produced
Dan 3:6 *be thrown into a blazing* ***f.***...........1005
Matt 13:42 *throw them into the fiery* ***f,*** 1349

FURY (n) wrath; fierceness; rage
Exod 15:7 *You unleash your blazing* ***f;***.........162
Deut 29:28 *In great anger and* ***f***.................321
Ps 7:6 *against the* ***f*** *of my enemies!*...........523
Jer 32:37 *will scatter them in my* ***f.***..........1080
Zeph 2:2 *the fierce* ***f*** *of the Lord.*................984

FUTILITY the state of having no hope of success
Job 7:3 *months of* ***f,*** *long and weary*...........101

FUTURE (adj) existing or occurring at a later time
Deut 29:15 *also with the* ***f*** *generations*........320
Rom 8:19 *waiting eagerly for that* ***f*** *day*.....1659
Eph 2:7 *can point to us in all* ***f*** *ages*..........1707
Heb 2:5 *will control the* ***f*** *world*................1763

FUTURE (n) time that is to come; what is going to happen
Num 24:14 *do to your people in the* ***f.***.........268
Ps 31:15 *My* ***f*** *is in your hands.*..................564
Ps 37:37 *a wonderful* ***f*** *awaits those*...........568
Isa 42:9 *tell you the* ***f*** *before it happens.* 927
Isa 46:10 *can tell you the* ***f*** *before it*...........933
Jer 29:11 *to give you a* ***f*** *and a hope*.........1030
Jer 31:17 *There is hope for your* ***f,***...........1033

GABRIEL Angel who stands in God's presence; seen in Daniel's visions (Dan 8:16-18, p. 1137; 9:21, p. 1143); announced birth of John the Baptist (Luke 1:11-20, p. 1272); announced birth of Jesus (Luke 1:26-28, p. 1274).

GAIN (n) winnings or profits
Isa 56:11 *intent on personal* ***g.***..................943

GAIN, GAINED, GAINS (v) to acquire or win; to profit or increase
Prov 3:13 *one who* ***g-s*** *understanding.*........635
Prov 11:16 *gracious woman* ***g-s*** *respect,*....643
Mark 8:36 ***g*** *the whole world but lose*.......1378
Luke 9:25 ***g*** *the whole world but are*.........1378
1 Cor 13:3 *I would have* ***g-ed*** *nothing*.......1616

GALILEE (n) a Roman province of Palestine during the time of Jesus
Isa 9:1 *a time in the future when* ***G***.............792
Matt 4:15 *beyond the Jordan River, in* ***G***....1306
Matt 26:32 *I will go ahead of you to* ***G***.......1460
Matt 28:10 *my brothers to leave for* ***G,***......1492

GARBAGE (n) food waste; discarded or useless material
1 Cor 4:13 *treated like the world's* ***g,***........1601
Phil 3:8 *counting it all as* ***g,***.....................1722

GARDEN (n) a planted area where fruits, vegetables, and flowers are cultivated
Gen 2:8 *God planted a* ***g*** *in Eden*.....................9
Gen 2:15 *God placed the man in the* ***G***.........10
1 Kgs 4:25 *had its own home and* ***g.***..........629
Song 4:12 *my private* ***g,*** *my treasure,*.........666
Isa 58:11 *will be like a well-watered* ***g,***.......945
Jer 31:12 *life will be like a watered* ***g,*** 1033
Ezek 28:13 *in Eden, the* ***g*** *of God*.............1084

GARDENER (n) one who takes care of a garden
John 15:1 *my Father is the* ***g.***.................1463
John 20:15 *She thought he was the* ***g.***......1492

GARMENT, GARMENTS (n) an article of clothing
Exod 28:2 *Make sacred* ***g-s*** *for Aaron*.........178
Lev 16:23 *he must take off the linen* ***g-s***....222
Lev 16:24 *put on his regular* ***g-s,*** *and go*....222
Ps 102:26 *You will change them like a* ***g***.....867
John 19:24 *divided my* ***g-s*** *among*...........1484

GATE, GATES (n) opening in a (city) wall or fence, consisting of a door and protected by defensive structures (as towers); the place of judicial decisions, town criers, and marketplace trade; entrance
Esth 6:10 *sits at the* ***g*** *of the palace*..........1190
Ps 24:7 *Open up, ancient* ***g-s!***.....................559
Ps 100:4 *his* ***g-s*** *with thanksgiving;*............866
Isa 62:10 *Go out through the* ***g-s!***.............949
Matt 7:13 *only through the narrow* ***g.***.........1334
John 10:1 *going through the* ***g,***.................1405
John 10:2 *who enters through the* ***g***.........1405
John 10:7 *I am the* ***g*** *for the sheep*...........1405
Heb 13:12 *died outside the city* ***g-s***..........1782
Rev 21:21 ***g-s*** *were made of pearls—*.....1831
Rev 21:21 *each* ***g*** *from a single pearl!* 1831

GATEKEEPER (n) one who guards or tends a gate
Ps 84:10 *a* ***g*** *in the house of my God*..........855

GATHER, GATHERED, GATHERING (v) to bring together; to reap or harvest; to assemble
Exod 16:18 *Those who* ***g-ed*** *a lot*..............164
Jer 23:3 *will* ***g*** *together the remnant*.........1027
Zech 14:2 *I will* ***g*** *all the nations*..............1179
Matt 24:31 *they will* ***g*** *his chosen ones*.....1447
Matt 25:26 ***g-ed*** *crops I didn't cultivate,*...1452
Matt 25:32 *the nations will be* ***g-ed*** *in his*...1452
Mark 13:27 *to* ***g*** *his chosen ones*............1449
Luke 3:17 ***g-ing*** *the wheat into his barn*...1292
Luke 13:34 *wanted to* ***g*** *your children*.......1407
2 Cor 8:15 *say, "Those who* ***g-ed*** *a lot*.....1636
2 Thes 2:1 *we will be* ***g-ed*** *to meet him*....1588
Rev 16:16 *demonic spirits* ***g-ed*** *all*...........1824

GAVE (v) to suffer the loss of
see also GIVE
John 3:16 *he* ***g*** *his one and only Son,*.......1302
Rom 8:32 ***g*** *him up for us all,*...................1660
Gal 2:20 *loved me and* ***g*** *himself for me*....1560
1 Tim 2:6 *He* ***g*** *his life to purchase*...........1729

GENERATION, GENERATIONS (n) the whole body of individuals born about the same time (nation or racial group); the period of time during which those individuals lived (also, age or era); offspring
Gen 17:7 *after you, from* ***g*** *to* ***g.***...................38
Exod 20:6 *love for a thousand* ***g-s***.............169
Num 32:13 *the entire* ***g*** *that sinned*.............279
Judg 2:10 *After that* ***g*** *died,*........................374
1 Chr 16:15 *to a thousand* ***g-s.***..................493
Ps 71:18 *your power to this new* ***g,***............860
Ps 100:5 *continues to each* ***g.***....................866
Ps 102:12 *endure to every* ***g.***......................866
Ps 102:18 *recorded for future* ***g-s,***..............866
Ps 105:8 *to a thousand* ***g-s.***........................868
Ps 119:90 *extends to every* ***g,***......................880
Ps 145:4 *Let each* ***g*** *tell its children*............589
Ps 146:10 *throughout the* ***g-s.***........................887
Prov 27:24 *not be passed to the next* ***g.***.......842
Isa 41:4 *summoning each new* ***g***...................925
Lam 5:19 *continues from* ***g*** *to* ***g.***.............1101
Joel 1:3 *the story down from* ***g*** *to* ***g.***.........1239
Matt 12:39 *Only an evil, adulterous* ***g***.......1343
Mark 13:30 *this* ***g*** *will not pass*.................1449
Luke 1:48 *all* ***g-s*** *will call me blessed.*......1275
Luke 11:29 *This evil* ***g*** *keeps asking me*...1344
Acts 2:40 *from this crooked* ***g!***.....................1516
Eph 3:5 *not reveal it to previous* ***g-s,***........1708
Eph 3:21 *all* ***g-s*** *forever and ever!*..............1710

GENEROSITY (n) the quality or fact of being magnanimous, kindly, or openhanded; abundance
Acts 2:46 *meals with great joy and* ***g—***....1516
2 Cor 9:10 *a great harvest of* ***g*** *in you*.......1638
Eph 4:7 *through the* ***g*** *of Christ*.................1710
Phlm 1:6 *put into action the* ***g*** *that*............1691

GENEROUS (adj) magnanimous, kindly; liberal in giving; abundant
Deut 15:8 *Instead, be* ***g*** *and lend*................305
Ps 37:26 *godly always give* ***g*** *loans to*........568
2 Cor 9:6 *will get a* ***g*** *crop*.......................1637
1 Tim 6:18 ***g*** *to those in need,*..................1735

GENTILE, GENTILES (n) non-Jewish individuals or nations, often connoting heathens or pagans
see also NATION(S)
Isa 49:6 *make you a light to the* ***G-s,***..........936
Luke 21:24 *period of the* ***G-s*** *comes*........1450
Acts 10:45 *out on the* ***G-s,*** *too.*................1534
Acts 14:27 *faith to the* ***G-s,*** *too.*................1546
Acts 15:14 *God first visited the* ***G-s***..........1569

Acts 21:25 *As for the **G** believers,*1677
Acts 28:28 *also been offered to the **G-s,***1689
Rom 1:16 *Jews first and also the **G.***1646
Rom 2:9 *Jews first and also for the **G.***1649
Rom 3:9 *people, whether Jews or **G-s,***1650
Rom 3:29 *God of the **G-s?***1652
Rom 10:12 *Jew and **G** are the same*1664
Rom 11:11 *available to the **G-s.***1665
Rom 15:9 *the **G-s** might give glory*1671
Rom 15:27 ***G-s** received the spiritual*1672
Gal 2:2 *preaching to the **G-s.***1558
Gal 2:8 *apostle to the **G-s.***1558
Gal 2:9 *keep preaching to the **G-s,***1558
Gal 3:8 *God would declare the **G-s***1561
Gal 3:14 *blessed the **G-s** with the same*1561
Gal 3:28 *no longer Jew or **G,** slave or*1562
Eph 3:8 *the privilege of telling the **G-s***1709
Col 3:11 *a Jew or a **G,** circumcised or*1700

GENTLE (adj) kind; mild-mannered; soft
1 Kgs 19:12 *sound of a **g** whisper.*720
Prov 15:1 *A **g** answer deflects anger,*648
Prov 15:4 ***G** words are a tree of life;*648
Matt 11:29 *am humble and **g** at heart,*1339
1 Cor 4:21 *love and a **g** spirit?*1601
Eph 4:2 *be humble and **g.** Be patient*1710
1 Tim 3:3 *must be **g,** not quarrelsome,*1730
Titus 3:2 *be **g** and show true humility*1739
Jas 3:17 ***g** at all times,*1551

GENTLENESS (n) mildness of manners or disposition
Gal 5:23 ***g,** and self-control*1566
Col 3:12 *kindness, humility, **g,** and*1700
1 Tim 6:11 *perseverance, and **g.***1735

GENUINE (adj) actual, true, authentic, sincere
John 1:47 *here is a **g** son of Israel—*1298
2 Cor 8:8 *I am testing how **g** your love*1636
Phil 1:18 *motives are false or **g,***1718
2 Tim 1:5 *I remember your **g** faith,*1740

GETHSEMANE (n) the garden where Jesus often went for prayer, rest, or fellowship; the site where Judas betrayed Jesus before the crucifixion
Matt 26:36 *to the olive grove called **G,***1468
Mark 14:32 *to the olive grove called **G,***1468

GHOST, GHOSTS (n) the soul of a dead person believed to appear to the living in bodily likeness
Luke 24:39 *I am not a **g,** because **g-s***1495

GIDEON Judge of Israel, also called "Jerub-baal" (Judg 6–8, p. 382; 7:1, p. 385; Heb 11:32, p. 1779); called by angel of the LORD (Judg 6:11-16, p. 382); cut down Baal's altar (Judg 6:25-32, p. 384); used fleece for guidance (Judg 6:36-40, p. 384); led Israel against Midianite oppressors (Judg 7:1–8:21, p. 385); refused kingship (Judg 8:22-23, p. 388); made an ephod (Judg 8:24-28, p. 388); died (Judg 8:29-35, p. 388).

GIFT, GIFTS (n) a present from people to people (often a bribe); a sacrifice from people to God; anything given voluntarily or at no cost; that which is given from God, enabling or empowering his people
Prov 18:16 *Giving a **g** can open doors;*654
Matt 2:11 *and gave him **g-s** of gold,*1285
Luke 11:13 *how to give good **g-s** to your*1398
Rom 4:16 *given as a free **g.***1653
Rom 5:15 *and God's gracious **g.***1655
Rom 6:23 *free **g** of God is eternal*1656
Rom 11:29 *For God's **g-s** and his call*1666
1 Cor 12:4 *kinds of spiritual **g-s,***1614
1 Cor 12:7 *A spiritual **g** is given*1614
1 Cor 12:31 *the most helpful **g-s.***1615
2 Cor 9:5 *I want it to be a willing **g,***1637
2 Cor 9:15 *Thank God for this **g***1638
Gal 2:9 *recognized the **g** God had*1558
Eph 2:8 *it is a **g** from God.*1707
Eph 4:8 *and gave **g-s** to his people.*1710
2 Tim 1:6 *the spiritual **g** God gave you*1741
Heb 2:4 ***g-s** of the Holy Spirit*1763
1 Pet 3:7 *equal partner in God's **g***1753
1 Pet 4:10 *of spiritual **g-s.***1754

GIRL (n) a female child from birth to adulthood
2 Kgs 5:2 *was a young **g** who had been*743
Mark 5:41 *which means "Little **g,** get up!"*1354

GIVE, GIVEN, GIVES, GIVING (v) to grant, bestow, convey, offer, provide, or designate; to yield or produce; to suffer the loss of (life)
Exod 30:15 *poor must not **g** less.*182
1 Sam 1:28 ***g-ing** him to the LORD,*418
Ps 112:9 *share freely and **g** generously*873
Ps 119:130 *your word **g-s** light,*881
Prov 21:26 *the godly love to **g!***658
Prov 23:26 *O my son, **g** me your heart.*661
Isa 9:6 *a son is **g-n** to us.*793
Matt 7:11 *heavenly Father **g** good gifts*1334
Matt 16:19 *And I will **g** you the keys*1375
Matt 22:30 *marry nor be **g-n** in marriage*1440
Mark 6:7 *by two, **g-ing** them authority*1358
Luke 11:13 *know how to **g** good gifts to*1398
Luke 14:33 *my disciple without **g-ing** up*1409
Luke 22:19 *body, which is **g-n** for you.*1458
John 1:17 *the law was **g-n** through Moses,*1272
John 5:21 *so the Son **g-s** life to anyone*1318
John 13:34 *So now I am **g-ing** you a new*1461
John 14:27 *And the peace I **g** is a gift*1463
Acts 5:32 *Spirit, who is **g-n** by God*1521
Acts 14:3 *was true by **g-ing** them power*1544
Acts 15:8 *by **g-ing** them the Holy Spirit*1569
Acts 20:35 *is more blessed to **g** than to*1676
Rom 2:7 *He will **g** eternal life.*1649
Rom 5:5 *because he has **g-n** us the Holy*1654
Rom 8:32 *won't he also **g** us everything*1660
Rom 10:12 *Lord, who **g-s** generously.*1664
Rom 12:8 *is giving, **g** generously.*1667
Rom 14:12 *each of us will **g** a personal*1670
1 Cor 9:17 *God has **g-n** me this sacred*1609
1 Cor 11:24 *body, which is **g-n** for you.*1613
1 Cor 15:57 *thank God! He **g-s** us victory*1622
2 Cor 3:6 *the Spirit **g-s** life.*1629
2 Cor 8:6 *this ministry of **g-ing.***1636
2 Cor 9:7 *how much to **g.***1637
Eph 4:7 *he has **g-n** each one of us.*1710
Eph 4:28 *and then **g** generously to*1712
1 Thes 4:8 *rejecting God, who **g-s.***1584
1 Tim 6:17 *God, who richly **g-s** us all we*1735
1 Jn 4:13 *And God has **g-n** us his Spirit*1793

GLAD (adj) joyful or happy, often with shouts
Ps 16:9 *my heart is **g,** and I rejoice.*553
Ps 32:11 *LORD and be **g,** all you who*565
Ps 69:32 *at work and be **g.***578
Ps 97:1 *coastlands be **g.***864
Ps 104:15 *wine to make them **g,***867
Ps 118:24 *will rejoice and be **g** in it.*876
Prov 10:8 *The wise are **g** to be*642
Prov 27:11 *make my heart **g.***842
Isa 35:1 *and desert will be **g***904
Zeph 3:14 *O Israel! Be **g** and rejoice*986
Matt 5:12 *Be very **g!***1326
John 11:15 *for your sakes, I'm **g** I wasn't*1414
Acts 13:48 *they were very **g.***1543
1 Cor 12:26 *the parts are **g.***1615
2 Cor 2:2 *will make me **g?***1627
Rev 19:7 *Let us be **g** and rejoice,*1827

GLADNESS (n) the quality or state of joy or delight; happiness
Ps 40:16 *with joy and **g** in you.*570
Ps 90:15 *Give us **g** in proportion to*326
Isa 35:10 *filled with joy and **g.***905
Jer 48:33 *Joy and **g** are gone*990
Zeph 3:17 *in you with **g.***986

GLEAMING (adj) shining with or as if with moderate brightness
Ezek 1:27 *he looked like **g** amber,*1045

GLORIFY, GLORIFIED, GLORIFIES, GLORIFYING (v) to bestow honor or praise (as in worship); to magnify
see also EXALT, HONOR
Ps 147:12 ***G** the LORD, O Jerusalem!*1155
Isa 26:8 *desire is to **g** your name.*896
Isa 42:12 *the whole world **g** the LORD;*927
Dan 4:37 *praise and **g** and honor the*1121
Luke 2:20 *flocks, **g-ing** and praising*1281
John 8:50 *no wish to **g** myself, God is*1393
John 13:31 *God will be **g-ied***1460
John 17:1 ***G** your Son so*1466
John 21:19 *of death he would **g** God.*1497
2 Cor 8:19 *a service that **g-ies** the Lord*1637
Eph 1:14 *would praise and **g** him.*1706
Rev 15:4 *you, Lord, and **g** your name?*1822

GLORIOUS (adj) possessing or deserving special honor; splendid or magnificent
Exod 15:6 *O LORD, is **g** in power.*161
Exod 33:18 *show me your **g** presence.*186
Deut 32:3 *the LORD; how **g** is our God!*323
1 Chr 16:28 *the LORD is **g** and strong.*493
Neh 9:5 *prayed: "May your **g** name be*1215
Job 37:5 *God's voice is **g** in the*127
Ps 45:3 *You are so **g,** so majestic!*851
Ps 76:4 *You are **g** and more majestic*596
Ps 96:3 *Publish his **g** deeds among the*864
Ps 149:9 *This is the **g** privilege of*887
Isa 55:5 *of Israel, have made you **g.***942
Isa 63:15 *from your holy, **g** home,*950
Dan 8:9 *east and toward the **g** land of*1137
Dan 11:45 *between the **g** holy mountain*1161
Matt 19:28 *sits upon his **g** throne,*1420
Acts 2:20 *that great and **g** day of the*1515
Acts 7:2 *Our **g** God appeared to*1524
Rom 1:23 *worshiping the **g,** ever-living*1647
Rom 3:23 *of God's **g** standard.*1651
Rom 8:21 *children in **g** freedom from*1659
2 Cor 3:9 *how much more **g** is the new*1630
2 Cor 3:10 *first glory was not **g** at all*1630
2 Cor 3:18 *into his **g** image.*1630
Eph 1:6 *God for the **g** grace he has*1705
Eph 1:17 *asking God, the **g** Father of*1706
Eph 3:16 *that from his **g,** unlimited*1709
Eph 5:27 *himself as a **g** church without*1714
Phil 3:21 *them into **g** bodies like his*1724
Phil 4:19 *from his **g** riches, which have*1725
Col 1:11 *with all his **g** power so you*1694
Jas 2:1 *faith in our **g** Lord Jesus*1548
1 Pet 1:8 *with a **g,** inexpressible joy.*1749
1 Pet 4:14 *for then the **g** Spirit of God*1755
Jude 1:24 *into his **g** presence without a*1786

GLORY (n) honor bestowed; splendor or magnificence; a distinguishing quality, asset, or attribute
Exod 16:10 *awesome **g** of the LORD*163

Num 14:21 *filled with the* LORD's ***g,*** 253
Josh 7:19 *My son, give* ***g*** *to the* LORD,.........346
1 Sam 4:21 *said, "Israel's* ***g*** *is gone."* 424
Ps 8:5 *them with* ***g*** *and honor*....................548
Ps 19:1 *proclaim the* ***g*** *of God*.......................554
Ps 29:1 LORD *for his* ***g*** *and strength*. 562
Ps 44:8 *O God, we give* ***g*** *to you*...............850
Ps 57:11 *May your* ***g*** *shine over all the* 460
Ps 71:8 *I declare your* ***g*** *all day* 860
Ps 86:12 *I will give* ***g*** *to your name*.............579
Ps 108:5 *May your* ***g*** *shine over all the* 581
Ps 145:12 *the majesty and* ***g*** *of your* 590
Prov 16:31 *is a crown of* ***g;*** *it is gained*.......652
Isa 6:3 *earth is filled with his* ***g!***.................783
Isa 24:16 *songs that give* ***g*** *to the*..............895
Isa 35:2 *display his* ***g,*** *the splendor*............905
Isa 42:8 *not give my* ***g*** *to anyone else,* 927
Isa 48:11 *not share my* ***g*** *with idols!* 935
Isa 66:11 *Drink deeply of her* ***g*** *even* 953
Isa 66:19 *they will declare my* ***g*** *to the*..........953
Ezek 44:4 *saw that the* ***g*** *of the* LORD 1127
Matt 16:27 *angels in the* ***g*** *of his Father* ...1377
Matt 25:31 *comes in his* ***g,*** *and all the*......1452
Mark 13:26 *great power and* ***g.***.....................1449
Luke 2:14 ***G*** *to God in highest heaven,*.......1281
Luke 9:26 *and in the* ***g*** *of the Father*.........1378
Luke 9:32 *they saw Jesus'* ***g*** *and the two* ...1380
Luke 21:27 *power and great* ***g.*** 1450
John 1:14 *have seen his* ***g,*** *the* ***g*** *of*..........1271
John 7:39 *not yet entered into his* ***g.*** 1390
John 11:40 *you would see God's* ***g*** *if*...........1415
John 12:23 *enter into his* ***g.***..........................1432
John 12:41 *the Messiah's* ***g.***..........................1435
John 14:13 *the Son can bring* ***g*** *to the*......1462
John 16:14 *will bring me* ***g*** *by telling*.........1465
John 17:22 *given them the* ***g*** *you gave* 1467
Acts 3:13 *who has brought* ***g*** *to his* 1517
Rom 2:7 *seeking after the* ***g*** *and honor*.....1649
Rom 2:10 *there will be* ***g*** *and honor and* ...1649
Rom 3:7 *and brings him more* ***g?***............1650
Rom 4:20 *in this he brought* ***g*** *to God*. 1653
Rom 8:17 *heirs of God's* ***g.*** 1659
Rom 8:18 *compared to the* ***g*** *he will*..........1659
Rom 8:30 *gave them his* ***g.***..........................1660
Rom 9:4 *God revealed his* ***g*** *to them*..........1661
Rom 9:23 *riches of his* ***g*** *shine even*.........1662
Rom 9:23 *in advance for* ***g.***...........................1662
Rom 15:6 *giving praise and* ***g*** *to God,*.......1671
Rom 15:9 *Gentiles might give* ***g*** *to God*.....1671
Rom 16:27 *All* ***g*** *to the only wise God* 1674
1 Cor 2:7 *for our ultimate* ***g*** *before the*.......1598
1 Cor 10:31 *all for the* ***g*** *of God*..............1611
1 Cor 15:43 *will be raised in* ***g.*** 1621
2 Cor 1:20 *to God for his* ***g.*** 1627
2 Cor 3:7 *shone with the* ***g*** *of God, even* ...1629
2 Cor 3:10 *In fact, that first* ***g*** *was not*.......1630
2 Cor 4:4 *about the* ***g*** *of Christ, who is*.......1630
2 Cor 4:17 *for us a* ***g*** *that vastly* 1631
Eph 1:12 *bring praise and* ***g*** *to God*. 1705
Phil 1:11 *will bring much* ***g*** *and praise*......1717
Phil 2:11 *is Lord, to the* ***g*** *of God the*.........1720
Phil 4:20 *Now all* ***g*** *to God our*...................1725
1 Thes 2:12 *Kingdom and* ***g.***........................1582
2 Thes 2:14 *share in the* ***g*** *of our Lord*.......1589
1 Tim 1:17 *All honor and* ***g*** *to God*...............1728
1 Tim 3:16 *to heaven in* ***g.***..........................1731
2 Tim 4:18 *All* ***g*** *to God forever*.....................1746
Titus 2:13 *when the* ***g*** *of our great God*.....1738
Heb 1:3 *God's own* ***g*** *and expresses the* ...1761
Heb 2:9 *crowned with* ***g*** *and honor*..........1763
Heb 3:3 *far more* ***g*** *than Moses, just*.........1764
1 Pet 1:7 *much praise and* ***g*** *and honor*....1748
1 Pet 1:21 *gave him great* ***g.***..................1749
1 Pet 5:4 *of never-ending* ***g*** *and honor*......1756
2 Pet 1:3 *means of his marvelous* ***g*** *and*...1757
2 Pet 1:17 *from the majestic* ***g*** *of God*......1758
Jude 1:25 *All* ***g,*** *majesty, power,*...............1786
Rev 4:9 *beings give* ***g*** *and honor and*........1808
Rev 4:11 *God, to receive* ***g*** *and honor*.......1809
Rev 5:12 *honor and* ***g*** *and blessing*...........1810
Rev 5:13 *and honor and* ***g*** *and power*.......1810
Rev 11:13 *terrified and gave* ***g*** *to the*........1817
Rev 16:9 *God and give him* ***g.*** 1823
Rev 21:11 *shone with the* ***g*** *of God and*....1831
Rev 21:23 *for the* ***g*** *of God*......................1831
Rev 21:26 *will bring their* ***g*** *and honor* 1831

GLUTTON, GLUTTONS (n) one given habitually to greedy and voracious eating and drinking

Prov 23:20 *or feast with* ***g-s,*** 661
Matt 11:19 *He's a* ***g*** *and a drunkard,* 1338
Titus 1:12 *cruel animals, and lazy* ***g-s.*** 1737

GNASHING (v) to grate or grind one's teeth together as an expression of hatred, scorn, or utter despair

Matt 8:12 *be weeping and* ***g*** *of teeth*. 1336

GNAT, GNATS (n) any of various small usually biting dipteran flies

Exod 8:16 *swarms of* ***g-s*** *throughout the*....152
Matt 23:24 *swallow a* ***g,*** *but you swallow*..1444

GOAL (n) the end toward which effort is directed; aim

1 Cor 14:1 *be your highest* ***g!*** 1616
2 Cor 5:9 *our* ***g*** *is to please him*. 1632
1 Thes 4:11 *Make it your* ***g*** *to live a*..........1584

GOAT, GOATS (n) any of various hollow-horned ruminant mammals with backwardly arching horns, a short tail, and usually straight hair

Gen 15:9 *a three-year-old female* ***g,***............35
Gen 30:32 *all the sheep and* ***g-s*** *that are* 62
Gen 37:31 *killed a young* ***g*** *and dipped*.........74
Lev 16:9 *sin offering the* ***g*** *chosen by*.........221
Num 7:16 *and a male* ***g*** *for a sin*..............196
Num 7:17 *rams, five male* ***g-s,*** *and five*.....196
Isa 11:6 *with the baby* ***g.*** 796
Dan 8:5 *a male* ***g*** *appeared from the* 1137
Matt 25:32 *the sheep from the* ***g-s.*** 1452
Heb 10:4 *blood of bulls and* ***g-s***...............1774

GOD, GODS (n) eternal, infinite Spirit; Creator, Redeemer, sovereign Lord; impotent pagan diety; image of pagan diety (made of wood, metal, or stone)
see also IDOL(S)

Gen 1:1 *In the beginning* ***G*** *created*................6
Gen 1:27 *In the image of* ***G*** *he created*............8
Gen 3:1 *Did* ***G*** *really say you must not*...........11
Gen 6:2 *The sons of* ***G*** *saw the*....................17
Gen 14:18 *a priest of* ***G*** *Most High,*...............34
Gen 17:1 *El-Shaddai—'****G*** *Almighty.'* 37
Gen 22:12 *I know that you truly fear* ***G.***.........46
Gen 50:20 ***G*** *intended it all for good*. 93
Exod 20:5 *am a jealous* ***G*** *who will not*........168
Exod 22:28 *must not dishonor* ***G*** *or curse* ...173
Exod 32:4 *these are the* ***g-s*** *who brought*...184
Exod 34:6 *The* ***G*** *of compassion* 187
Deut 6:4 LORD *is our* ***G,*** *the* LORD................294
Deut 23:5 LORD *your* ***G*** *loves you*................313
Deut 32:16 *by worshiping foreign*
g-s; *they*...324
Deut 32:39 *There is no other* ***g*** *but me!* 325
Deut 33:27 *The eternal* ***G*** *is* 327
Josh 24:19 *a holy and jealous* ***G.***................370
1 Kgs 8:23 *there is no* ***G*** *like you*................619
1 Kgs 18:21 *if Baal is* ***G,*** *then follow*..........717
2 Kgs 19:15 *You alone are* ***G*** *of all*..............916
Ezra 9:9 *unfailing love our* ***G*** *did not*..........1200
Neh 1:5 *awesome* ***G*** *who keeps* 1203
Ps 19:1 *proclaim the glory of* ***G.*** 554
Ps 22:1 *My* ***G,*** *my* ***G,*** *why have*..................556
Ps 42:2 *I thirst for* ***G,*** *the living* ***G.***...........848
Ps 42:8 *praying to* ***G*** *who gives* 849
Ps 51:10 *a clean heart, O* ***G.*** 506
Ps 82:6 *say, 'You are* ***g-s;*** *you are all*..........603
Ps 100:3 *the* LORD *is* ***G!*** 865
Ps 139:23 *Search me, O* ***G,*** *and know* 586
Prov 24:12 *For* ***G*** *understands all* 662
Eccl 12:13 *conclusion: Fear* ***G*** *and obey*......683
Isa 9:6 *Mighty* ***G,*** *Everlasting Father,* 793
Isa 43:10 *I alone am* ***G.***..............................928
Dan 6:16 *May your* ***G,*** *whom you*.............1141
Jonah 4:2 *compassionate* ***G,*** *slow to*...........769
Mic 6:8 *walk humbly with your* ***G.***...............910
Mic 7:18 *Where is another* ***G*** *like you,*.........911
Nah 1:2 *a jealous* ***G,*** *filled with* 974
Mark 2:7 *Only* ***G*** *can forgive*........................1314
Mark 3:35 *Anyone who does* ***G's*** *will is*.....1344
Mark 15:34 *My* ***G,*** *my* ***G,*** *why*..................1486
Luke 2:14 *Glory to* ***G*** *in highest* 1281
Luke 10:9 *The Kingdom of* ***G*** *is near*.........1394
Luke 16:13 *cannot serve both* ***G*** *and*........1412
Luke 20:38 *So he is the* ***G*** *of the living,*.....1441
John 1:1 *Word was with* ***G***..........................1270
John 1:18 *One, who is himself* ***G,*** *is near*..1272
John 1:29 *The Lamb of* ***G*** *who* 1297
John 3:16 *For* ***G*** *loved the world so*............1302
John 10:34 *I say, you are* ***g-s!*** 1406
John 14:1 *Trust in* ***G,*** *and trust also* 1461
Acts 5:29 *We must obey* ***G*** *rather than*......1521
Acts 12:24 *word of* ***G*** *continued to*............1539
Acts 19:26 *aren't really* ***g-s*** *at all*. 1624
Rom 1:16 *the power of* ***G*** *at work,* 1646
Rom 3:23 *short of* ***G's*** *glorious*..................1651
Rom 5:1 *have peace with* ***G*** *because* 1654
Rom 5:5 *know how dearly* ***G*** *loves us,*........1654
Rom 6:23 *free gift of* ***G*** *is eternal*..............1656
Rom 8:17 *are heirs of* ***G's*** *glory*. 1659
Rom 12:2 *learn to know* ***G's*** *will for you,* ...1666
1 Cor 1:18 *the very power of* ***G.***..................1596
1 Cor 1:25 *foolish plan of* ***G*** *is wiser* 1597
1 Cor 6:20 *you must honor* ***G*** *with your*.....1604
1 Cor 14:33 *not a* ***G*** *of disorder but* 1618
2 Cor 10:4 *We use* ***G's*** *mighty weapons,*.....1638
Gal 3:6 *believed* ***G,*** *and* ***G*** *counted him* 1561
Eph 2:10 *For we are* ***G's*** *masterpiece*. 1707
Eph 5:1 *Imitate* ***G,*** *therefore, in*................1712
Phil 2:6 *equality with* ***G*** *as something*........1720
Phil 4:7 *you will experience* ***G's*** *peace,* 1724
Col 2:9 *the fullness of* ***G*** *in a human* 1698
1 Thes 5:18 *for this is* ***G's*** *will* 1586
1 Tim 2:5 *is only one* ***G*** *and one* 1729
Titus 1:2 ***G****—who does not lie—*...................1736
Heb 6:18 *is impossible for* ***G*** *to lie*. 1769
Heb 7:19 *we draw near to* ***G.***.....................1770
Heb 11:6 *believe that* ***G*** *exists* 1777
Jas 2:19 *there is one* ***G.***...............................1549
Jas 2:23 *Abraham believed* ***G,*** *and* ***G***........1550
Jas 4:8 *Come close to* ***G,*** *and* ***G*** 1551
1 Pet 2:15 *It is* ***G's*** *will that your*..............1751
1 Pet 5:5 *for "****G*** *opposes the proud*..........1756
1 Jn 1:5 *declare to you:* ***G*** *is light,*..............1787
1 Jn 4:21 *Those who love* ***G*** *must also*......1794
Rev 19:6 *the Lord our* ***G,*** *the Almighty,*......1827
Rev 21:23 *glory of* ***G*** *illuminates the* 1831

GOD-BREATHED (KJV)

2 Tim 3:16 *Scripture is* ***inspired by God***...1745

GOD-FEARING (adj) having a reverent feeling toward God; devout
Acts 10:2 *was a devout, **G** man,*...1532
Acts 10:22 *is a devout and **G** man,*...1533
Acts 13:26 *and also you **G** Gentiles—this*...1542
Acts 17:4 *along with many **G** Greek men*...1576
Acts 17:17 *Jews and the **G** Gentiles,*...1577

GODDESS (n) a female god
Acts 19:27 *of the great **g** Artemis will*...1624

GODLESS (adj) not acknowledging a deity or divine law
see also UNGODLY
Job 20:5 *joy of the **g** has been only*...113
Hos 7:8 *mingle with **g** foreigners,*...810
1 Tim 6:20 *Avoid **g**, foolish*...1735
2 Tim 2:16 *to more **g** behavior.*...1743
Titus 2:12 *to turn from **g** living and*...1738
1 Pet 4:3 *things that **g** people enjoy—*...1754
1 Pet 4:18 *will happen to **g** sinners?*...1755

GODLINESS (n) devotion to God; piety
see also RIGHTEOUSNESS
Prov 16:8 *Better to have little, with **g**,*...651
1 Tim 4:8 *but training for **g** is much*...1732
1 Tim 5:4 *to show **g** at home*...1733
1 Tim 6:6 *Yet true **g** with contentment*...1735

GODLY (adj) marked by or showing reverence for God and devotion to worship
see also RIGHTEOUS, UPRIGHT
Ps 31:23 *LORD, all you **g** ones!*...564
Ps 34:9 *LORD, you his **g** people,*...458
Prov 16:31 *by living a **g** life.*...652
Prov 23:24 *The father of **g** children has*...661
Acts 22:12 *He was a **g** man, deeply*...1679
Gal 6:1 *you who are **g** should gently*...1567
1 Tim 6:3 *promote a **g** life.*...1734
2 Tim 3:12 *to live a **g** life in Christ*...1744
Titus 1:1 *how to live **g** lives.*...1736
2 Pet 2:9 *how to rescue **g** people from*...1759
2 Pet 3:11 *what holy and **g** lives you*...1760

GODLY (n) people who are righteous or devout
Ps 1:5 *no place among the **g**.*...856
Ps 37:21 *but the **g** are generous givers.*...567
Ps 37:30 *The **g** offer good counsel;*...568
Ps 68:3 *But let the **g** rejoice.*...575
Ps 118:20 *LORD, and the **g** enter there.*...876
Prov 3:32 *friendship to the **g**.*...635
Prov 10:11 *The words of the **g** are a*...642
Prov 10:20 *The words of the **g** are like*...642
Prov 10:28 *The hopes of the **g** result in*...643
Prov 11:5 *The **g** are directed by*...643
Prov 11:28 *But the **g** flourish like*...644
Prov 13:9 *The life of the **g** is full of*...646
Prov 20:7 *The **g** walk with*...656
Prov 21:15 *Justice is a joy to the **g**,*...658
Prov 28:1 *the **g** are as bold as lions.*...843

GOLD (n) a valuable yellow malleable metal especially used in coins and jewelry
1 Kgs 20:3 *Your silver and **g** are mine,*...721
Ps 19:10 *more desirable than **g**,*...555
Ps 119:127 *even the finest **g**.*...881
Prov 3:14 *are better than **g**.*...635
Matt 2:11 *gifts of **g**, frankincense,*...1285
Rev 3:18 *advise you to buy **g** from me—*...1807

GOLGOTHA (n) a hill just outside Jerusalem; the place where Jesus was crucified
Matt 27:33 *a place called **G***...1482
Mark 15:22 *a place called **G***...1483
John 19:17 *(in Hebrew, **G**)*...1484

GOLIATH Great Philistine warrior killed by David (1 Sam 17:4, 8, 23, p. 449, 450; 21:9, p. 457; 22:10, p. 461; 2 Sam 21:19, p. 525; 1 Chr 20:5, p. 525).

GOMORRAH (n) one of the five "cities of the plain" located in the Valley of Siddim; God destroyed this city by fire for its extreme wickedness
Gen 19:24 *on Sodom and **G**.*...42
Matt 10:15 *and **G** will be better*...1358
2 Pet 2:6 *of Sodom and **G** and turned*...1759
Jude 1:7 *forget Sodom and **G** and their*...1784

GOOD (adj) kind; profitable; excellent; fitting or appropriate; morally right
Gen 1:4 *that the light was **g**.*...6
Gen 1:31 *it was very **g**!*...9
Gen 2:18 *It is not **g** for the man to*...10
2 Chr 7:3 *He is **g**! His faithful*...622
2 Chr 31:20 *was pleasing and **g** in the*...839
Ps 34:8 *see that the LORD is **g**.*...458
Ps 119:68 *You are **g** and do only*...879
Eccl 7:20 *earth is always **g** and never*...679
Isa 5:20 *that evil is **g** and **g** is*...829
Isa 45:7 *I send **g** times and*...931
Mic 6:8 *told you what is **g**, and this is*...910
Matt 5:29 *eye—even your **g** eye—causes*...1328
Matt 19:17 *is only One who is **g**.*...1420
Matt 22:10 *they could find, **g** and bad*...1438
Matt 25:21 *Well done, my **g** and*...1452
Mark 3:4 *the law permit **g** deeds on the*...1321
Mark 10:18 *God is truly **g**.*...1421
Luke 6:45 *person produces **g** things from*...1335
Luke 6:45 *treasury of a **g** heart,*...1335
Luke 8:15 *seeds that fell on the **g** soil*...1347
Luke 14:34 *Salt is **g** for seasoning*...1409
Luke 18:19 *God is truly **g**.*...1422
Luke 19:17 *You are a **g** servant.*...1427
John 10:11 *I am the **g** shepherd*...1405
Rom 7:12 *and right and **g**.*...1658
Rom 7:16 *that the law is **g**.*...1658
Rom 7:18 *know that nothing **g** lives in*...1658
Rom 7:19 *do what is **g**, but I don't.*...1658
Rom 12:2 *you, which is **g** and pleasing*...1666
Rom 12:9 *Hold tightly to what is **g**.*...1667
1 Cor 6:12 *not everything is **g** for you.*...1604
1 Cor 7:1 *Yes, it is **g** to abstain*...1605
1 Cor 15:33 *corrupts **g** character.*...1621
Gal 6:9 *doing what is **g**.*...1567
Eph 2:10 *so we can do the g things he*...1707
Phil 1:6 *who began the **g** work within*...1717
1 Thes 5:21 *Hold on to what is **g**.*...1586
1 Tim 4:4 *everything God created is **g**,*...1732
1 Tim 6:12 *Fight the **g** fight.*...1735
2 Tim 3:17 *people to do every **g** work.*...1745
2 Tim 4:7 *I have fought the **g** fight,*...1746
Titus 3:8 *These teachings are **g***...1739
Heb 10:24 *of love and **g** works.*...1776
Heb 12:10 *is always **g** for us,*...1780
Jas 2:8 *indeed, it is **g** when you obey*...1549

GOOD (n) something that is excellent, profitable, or morally right; advancement of prosperity or well-being; something useful or beneficial
Gen 2:9 *the knowledge of **g** and evil.*...10
Gen 3:22 *knowing both **g** and evil*...13
Gen 50:20 *God intended it all for **g**.*...93
1 Sam 26:23 *reward for doing **g** and for*...468
Ps 14:1 *not one of them does **g**!*...551
Ps 53:3 *No one does **g**, not a single*...571
Prov 3:27 *Do not withhold **g** from those*...635
Prov 11:27 *If you search for **g**, you will*...644
Prov 31:12 *She brings him **g**, not harm,*...847
Isa 55:2 *does you no **g**?*...942
Jer 13:23 *you start doing **g**, for you*...1017
Jer 32:39 *for their own **g** and for the*...1080
Matt 5:45 *evil and the **g**, and he sends*...1330
Rom 3:12 *No one does **g**, not a single*...1651
Rom 8:28 *together for the **g** of those*...1660
Rom 13:4 *sent for your **g**.*...1668
1 Cor 10:24 *but for the **g** of others.*...1611
Gal 6:10 *we should do **g** to everyone—*...1567
Eph 6:8 *each one of us for the **g** we do,*...1715
1 Tim 5:10 *because of the **g** she has*...1733
Heb 13:16 *forget to do **g** and to share*...1783
1 Pet 2:20 *suffer for doing **g** and endure*...1752
1 Pet 3:17 *suffer for doing **g**, if that*...1753

GOODNESS (n) the beneficial quality of something; kindness
Ps 145:7 *the story of your wonderful **g**;*...589
Isa 63:7 *in his great **g** to Israel,*...949
Rom 14:17 *a life of **g** and peace and joy*...1670
Rom 15:14 *that you are full of **g**.*...1671

GOSPEL (KJV)
Mark 1:1 *the **Good News** about Jesus*...1270
Luke 4:18 *anointed me to bring **Good News***...1357
Rom 1:16 *not ashamed of this **Good News***...1646
Rom 10:15 *feet of messengers who bring **good news***...1664
Gal 3:8 *proclaimed this **good news***...1561

GOSSIP (n) rumor or report revealing personal or sensational facts about others
Prov 16:28 *of strife; **g** separates the*...652
Prov 26:20 *disappear when **g** stops.*...841
2 Cor 12:20 *slander, **g**, arrogance,*...1642

GOSSIP, GOSSIPING (v) to relate rumors or reports about others
Ps 15:3 *who refuse to **g** or harm their*...552
1 Tim 5:13 *spend their time **g-ing***...1733

GOVERN (v) to exercise continuous sovereign authority over; to control or rule
Gen 1:16 *larger one to **g** the day,*...7
Gen 1:28 *the earth and **g** it.*...8
Gen 49:16 *Dan will **g** his people, like*...92
Job 34:17 *Could God **g** if he hated*...124
Ps 67:4 *because you **g** the nations*...859

GOVERNMENT (n) the organization or agency through which a political unit exercises authority
Isa 9:6 *The **g** will rest on his*...793
Rom 13:6 *For **g** workers need*...1668
Titus 3:1 *to submit to the **g** and its*...1739

GRACE (n) God's free and unmerited favor toward sinful humanity
see also FAVOR
Acts 6:8 *full of God's **g** and power,*...1523
Acts 14:3 *about the **g** of the Lord.*...1544
Acts 15:11 *by the undeserved **g** of the*...1569
Acts 20:32 *message of his **g** that is able*...1676
Rom 5:15 *is God's wonderful **g** and his*...1655
Rom 5:21 *now God's wonderful **g** rules*...1655
Rom 6:1 *of his wonderful **g**?*...1655
Rom 11:5 *of God's **g**—his undeserved*...1664
Rom 12:6 *In his **g**, God has given us*...1667
1 Cor 3:10 *Because of God's **g** to me,*...1599
1 Cor 16:23 *May the **g** of the Lord*...1623
2 Cor 4:15 *And as God's **g** reaches more*...1631
2 Cor 9:14 *of the overflowing **g** God has*...1638
Gal 1:15 *by his marvelous **g**.*...1557
Gal 2:21 *do not treat the **g** of God as*...1560
Gal 5:4 *away from God's **g**.*...1565
Eph 1:7 *in kindness and **g** that he*...1705
Eph 2:5 *only by God's **g** that you have*...1707

Eph 2:7 *wealth of his **g** and kindness*........1707
Eph 2:8 *saved you by his **g** when you*.......1707
Eph 3:2 *of extending his **g** to you*.............1708
Eph 3:7 *By God's **g** and mighty*.................1709
Phil 4:23 *May the **g** of the Lord*...............1726
2 Thes 1:12 *because of the **g** of our God*....1588
2 Thes 2:16 *and by his **g** gave us eternal*....1589
1 Tim 1:2 *Lord give you **g**, mercy,*............1726
2 Tim 1:9 *show us his **g** through Christ*.....1741
2 Tim 2:1 *strong through the **g** that God*...1742
2 Tim 4:22 *And may his **g** be with all of*....1746
Titus 2:11 *For the **g** of God has*................1738
Titus 3:7 *Because of his **g** he declared*......1739
Titus 3:15 *May God's **g** be with you*..........1740
Heb 4:16 *and we will find **g** to help us*......1766
Heb 12:15 *to receive the **g** of God.*...........1781
Heb 13:9 *comes from God's **g**, not from*...1782
Heb 13:25 *May God's **g** be with you all.*....1783
Jas 4:6 *gives us even more **g** to stand*.......1551
1 Pet 5:12 *Stand firm in this **g**.*...............1756
2 Pet 3:18 *grow in the **g** and knowledge*...1760
Rev 22:21 *May the **g** of the Lord*.............1833

GRACIOUS (adj) abounding in grace and kindness; merciful, compassionate
2 Kgs 13:23 *the Lord was **g** and merciful*...760
Ps 145:13 *he is **g** in all he*.........................590
Prov 11:16 *A **g** woman gains*.....................643
John 1:16 *received one **g** blessing after*....1272
2 Cor 8:7 *also in this **g** act of giving*..........1636
Col 4:6 *your conversation be **g** and*..........1702
1 Tim 1:14 *generous and **g** our Lord was!*...1728
1 Pet 1:10 *about this **g** salvation*..............1749
1 Pet 1:13 *to the **g** salvation that will*........1749

GRAFTED (v) to unite a shoot or bud with a growing plant so they grow as one
Rom 11:18 *not brag about being **g** in to*....1665

GRANDCHILDREN (n) children of one's son or daughter
1 Tim 5:4 *children or **g**, their first*............1733

GRANDMOTHER (n) the mother of one's father or mother
2 Tim 1:5 *first filled your **g** Lois and*..........1740

GRANT (n) property transferred by deed or writing
Josh 14:3 *already given a **g** of land to*........357

GRANT, GRANTED (v) to permit as a right, privilege, or favor; to consent to carry out for a person
Prov 10:24 *of the godly will be **g-ed**.*..........643
Isa 26:12 *Lord, you will **g** us peace;*...........896
Matt 15:28 *Your request is **g-ed**." And her*...1371
John 15:7 *and it will be **g-ed!***..................1464

GRAPES (n) a smooth-skinned juicy greenish-white to deep red or purple berry
Gen 40:10 *it produced clusters of ripe **g***.......78
Lev 19:10 *not pick up the **g** that fall*...........225
Num 6:3 *not eat **g** or raisins*.......................244
Num 13:23 *single cluster of **g** so large*.......251
Deut 32:32 *Their **g** are poison*...................325
Job 15:33 *a vine whose **g** are harvested*....109
Isa 5:4 *expected sweet **g**, why did*.............828
Isa 63:3 *my enemies as if they were **g***........949
Matt 7:16 ***g** from thornbushes, or figs*........1334
Rev 14:19 ***g** into the great winepress*.......1822

GRAPEVINE (n) the vine on which grapes grow
Ps 128:3 *a fruitful **g**, flourishing*.................883
Isa 36:16 *from your own **g** and fig tree*.......914
John 15:1 *am the true **g**, and my Father*...1463

GRASS (n) green plants that grow from the ground and are suitable for grazing animals
Isa 40:6 *people are like the **g**.*...................924
1 Pet 1:24 *The **g** withers and*..................1750

GRAVE, GRAVES (n) burial place; euphemism for Hades, hell, or Sheol
Ps 5:9 *from an open **g**.*.............................547
Ps 49:15 *power of the **g**.*..........................854
John 5:28 *dead in their **g-s** will hear the*..1319
Acts 2:27 *rot in the **g**.*.............................1515
Rom 3:13 *from an open **g**.*........................1651
Rev 20:13 *death and the **g** gave up their*..1830

GRAVECLOTHES (n) strips of cloth wrapped around a corpse in preparation for burial
John 11:44 *and feet bound in **g**, his face*..1415

GREAT, GREATER, GREATEST (adj) huge; remarkable in magnitude, degree, or effectiveness
Deut 10:17 *He is the **g** God, the mighty*......300
2 Sam 24:14 *his mercy is **g**.*......................530
Ps 107:8 *Lord for his **g** love and for*...........872
Ps 147:5 *How **g** is our Lord!*...................1154
Dan 9:4 *you are a **g** and awesome God!*...1142
Matt 12:41 *someone **g-er** than Jonah is*...1343
Matt 12:42 ***g-er** than Solomon*................1343
Matt 19:30 *who are the **g-est** now will be*..1421
Matt 22:38 *first and **g-est** commandment.*................................1441
John 3:30 *He must become **g-er***............1303
John 15:13 *There is no **g-er** love than to*..1464
1 Cor 13:13 *and the **g-est** of these is love.*..1616
Rev 20:11 *I saw a **g** white throne and*.......1830

GREED (n) a selfish and excessive desire for more of something (as money) than is needed
Prov 15:27 ***G** brings grief*.........................650
Rom 1:29 *of wickedness, sin, **g**, hate,*.......1648
2 Pet 2:3 *In their **g** they will make up*........1758
2 Pet 2:14 *well trained in **g**.*....................1759

GREEDY (adj) having or showing a selfish desire for wealth and possessions
1 Sam 8:3 *for they were **g** for money.*.........434
Prov 1:19 *all who are **g** for money;*............632
Prov 21:26 *people are always **g***.................658
1 Cor 6:10 *are thieves, or **g** people,*..........1603
Eph 5:5 *For a **g** person is an*..................1712
Col 3:5 *Don't be **g**, for a **g***.....................1700

GREEKS (n) natives or inhabitants of Greece
1 Cor 1:22 *And it is foolish to the **G**,*.........1597

GREEN (adj) of the color green; pleasantly alluring
Ps 23:2 *lets me rest in **g** meadows;*............558

GREET (v) to address with expressions of kind wishes upon meeting or arrival
Rom 16:16 ***G** each other in Christian*........1673
1 Cor 16:20 ***G** each other with*................1623
2 Cor 13:12 ***G** each other with*................1643
1 Thes 5:26 ***G** all the brothers*.................1587
1 Pet 5:14 ***G** each other with*...................1756

GREW (v) to increase; to develop in maturity
see also GROW
Luke 1:80 *John **g** up and became*...........1277
Luke 2:52 *Jesus **g** in wisdom*...................1287
Acts 9:31 *Spirit, it also **g** in numbers.*.......1531
Acts 16:5 *faith and **g** larger every day.*......1573

GRIEF (n) deep and poignant distress due to bereavement; a cause of suffering
Job 16:5 *take away your **g**.*........................110
Ps 10:14 *the trouble and **g** they cause.*.......857
Prov 10:1 *a foolish child brings **g** to a*.........641
Prov 15:27 *Greed brings **g** to the*...............650
John 16:20 *your **g** will suddenly turn*........1465
Rom 9:2 *sorrow and unending **g**.*..............1661

GRIEVE, GRIEVED (v) to feel, show, or cause distress, vexation, sorrow, or regret
Eccl 3:4 *A time to **g** and a time*....................675
Isa 63:10 *rebelled against him and **g-d***......950
Lam 3:20 *time, as I **g** over my loss.*...........1098
1 Thes 4:13 *so you will not **g** like people*...1584

GROAN, GROANING, GROANINGS (n) a deep moan indicative of pain, grief, or annoyance
Exod 2:24 *God heard their **g-ing**, and he*....143
Ps 90:9 *ending our years with a **g**.*.............326
Rom 8:26 *for us with **g-ings** that cannot*..1660

GROAN, GROANING (v) to utter a deep moan indicative of pain, grief, or annoyance
Job 35:9 *They **g** beneath the power*...........125
Rom 8:22 *creation has been **g-ing** as*......1659
Rom 8:23 *believers also **g**, even though*....1659
2 Cor 5:4 *bodies, we **g** and sigh,*..............1632

GROUND (n) soil, earth, or territory
Gen 1:10 *called the dry **g** "land" and*.............7
Gen 3:17 *the **g** is cursed because of you.*....13
Gen 4:2 *Cain cultivated the **g**.*....................14
Gen 4:10 *cries out to me from the **g!***............15
Exod 3:5 *standing on holy **g**.*....................143
Exod 15:19 *sea on dry **g!***..........................162
Isa 53:2 *like a root in dry **g**.*......................940
Matt 10:29 *fall to the **g** without your*.........1360

GROW, GROWING, GROWS (v) to become; to spring up and develop to maturity
see also GREW
Isa 40:31 *run and not **g** weary.*..................925
1 Cor 3:6 *God who made it **g**.*...................1599
Eph 4:16 *is healthy and **g-ing** and full of*....1711
Phil 1:25 *all of you **g** and experience*........1718
Col 2:19 *it **g-s** as God nourishes it.*...........1699
2 Thes 1:3 *one another is **g-ing**.*.............1587
Jas 1:15 *when sin is allowed to **g**,*............1547
2 Pet 3:18 *Rather, you must **g** in the*.........1760

GRUDGE (n) a feeling of deep-seated resentment or ill will
Mark 11:25 *you are holding a **g** against,*...1436

GRUMBLE (v) to mutter in discontent
1 Cor 10:10 *And don't **g** as some*.............1610
Jas 5:9 *Don't **g** about each other.*.............1553

GRUMBLERS (n) those who mutter in discontent
Jude 1:16 *people are **g** and complainers,*..1785

GUARANTEE (n) an assurance for the fulfillment of a condition
2 Cor 5:5 *and as a **g** he has given us*........1632

GUARANTEED, GUARANTEEING, GUARANTEES (v) to assure that some agreement or condition will be fulfilled; to give security for
Ps 111:9 *He has **g** his covenant*.................873
2 Cor 1:22 *first installment that **g-s***...........1627
Eph 4:30 ***g-ing** that you will be saved*.......1712
Heb 7:22 *is the one who **g-s** this better*....1771

GUARD (adj) defensively watchful; alert
2 Pet 3:17 *Be on **g** so that you*.................1760

GUARD, GUARDING, GUARDS (v) to protect by watchful attention; to watch over
see also KEEP
Prov 4:23 ***G** your heart*...............................636
Prov 7:2 *as you **g** your own eyes.*...............639

Prov 24:12 *He who **g-s** your soul knows*....662
Luke 2:8 *fields nearby, **g-ing** their flocks*..1281
Phil 4:7 *His peace will **g** your hearts*......1724
2 Thes 3:3 *and **g** you from*.......................1590

GUARDIAN (n) one caring for another person or the property of another
Gen 4:9 *Am I my brother's **g?***....................15
Gal 3:25 *the law as our **g.***........................1562
1 Pet 2:25 *your Shepherd, the **G** of your*...1752

GUIDANCE (n) direction or counsel provided by another person
2 Chr 26:5 *as the king sought **g** from*.........764
Prov 24:6 *go to war without wise **g;***............662
Prov 29:18 *do not accept divine **g,***.............845

GUIDE, GUIDED, GUIDES, GUIDING (v) to direct, supervise, or influence usually to a particular end
Exod 13:21 *He **g-d** them during the*...........159
Exod 15:13 *In your might, you **g** them*.........162
Deut 1:33 ***g-ing** you with a pillar of fire*........286
Job 10:10 ***g-d** my conception and formed*..104
Ps 16:7 *bless the LORD who **g-s** me;*.........553
Ps 23:3 *He **g-s** me along*............................558
Ps 32:8 *I will **g** you along*..........................565
Ps 139:10 *your hand will **g** me,*..................586
John 16:13 *he will **g** you into all*..............1465
Gal 5:16 *let the Holy Spirit **g** your lives*......1566
Jas 2:4 *are **g-d** by evil motives?*...............1548

GUIDES (n) those who lead or direct another's way
Matt 23:16 *Blind **g! What sorrow***...............1444
Matt 23:24 *Blind **g!** You strain*..................1444

GUILT (n) the state or feeling of one who has committed an offense
Job 6:29 *Stop assuming my **g,** for I*............101
Ps 32:2 *the LORD has cleared of **g,***............564
Ps 38:4 *My **g** overwhelms me—*..................568
Ps 51:2 *Wash me clean from my **g.***............505
Isa 6:7 *Now your **g** is removed,*..................784
Dan 9:24 *atone for their **g,** to bring*..........1143

GUILTY (adj) justly chargeable with wrong-doing
Lev 19:17 *not be held **g** for their sin.*.........225
Rom 3:19 *entire world is **g** before God.*......1651
1 Cor 11:27 ***g** of sinning against*...............1613
1 Jn 3:20 *if we feel **g,** God is greater*.......1792
1 Jn 3:21 *we don't feel **g,** we can come*.......1792

HAGAR Sarah's Egyptian servant and rival, mother of Ishmael (Gen 16, p. 36); sent away by Abraham, son's cries heard by God (Gen 21:9-21, p. 43); Paul's analogy using Hagar and Sarah (Gal 4:24-25, p. 1564).

HAIL (n) precipitation in the form of small balls of ice and snow
Exod 9:19 *die when the **h** falls*....................153
Ps 18:12 *rained down **h** and*........................528
Rev 8:7 *his trumpet, and **h** and fire*..........1814

HAIR, HAIRS (n) a slender threadlike outgrowth of the skin of an animal or human
Lev 19:27 *Do not trim off the **h** on your*......226
2 Sam 18:9 *his **h** got caught in the tree.*......518
Matt 10:30 *And the very **h-s** on your head*.......................................1360
1 Cor 11:6 *to have her **h** cut or her head*..1612
1 Cor 11:14 *man to have long **h?***............1612
1 Cor 11:15 *And isn't long **h** a woman's*...1613
Rev 1:14 *His head and his **h** were white*...1800

HAIRSTYLES (n) a way of wearing the hair
1 Pet 3:3 *outward beauty of fancy **h,***........1752

HAIRY (adj) covered with hair
Gen 27:11 *Esau, is a **h** man, and my skin*.....55

HALF, HALVES (n) either of two equal parts that compose something
Gen 15:17 *between the **h** of the carcasses.*..36
Exod 30:13 *(This payment is **h** a shekel,*.....182
1 Kgs 3:25 *to one woman and **h** to the*.......608
1 Kgs 10:7 *not heard the **h** of it!*................626
Esth 5:3 *if it is **h** the kingdom!*..................1189
Jer 34:18 *between its **h** to solemnize*.......1075
Dan 7:25 *a time, times, and **h** a time.*.......1136
Mark 6:23 *ask, up to **h** my kingdom!*........1362

HALLELUJAH (KJV)
Rev 19:1 *shouting, **"Praise the Lord!***.......1827
Rev 19:3 *rang out: **"Praise the Lord!***.......1827
Rev 19:4 *"Amen! **Praise the Lord!"***.........1827
Rev 19:6 ***"Praise the Lord!** For the Lord*...1827

HALLOW(ED) (KJV)
Exod 20:11 *Sabbath day and **set it apart as holy***......................................169
Lev 25:10 *Set this year **apart as holy***.........232
1 Kgs 9:3 *set this Temple **apart to be holy***...623
Matt 6:9 *may your name **be kept holy***......1331

HAND, HANDS (n) the end of the arm that serves as a grasping and handling tool for humans; symbolic of power
Gen 47:29 *Put your **h** under my*....................89
Exod 15:6 *Your right **h,** O LORD,*..................161
Exod 29:10 *will lay their **h-s** on its head.*....180
Exod 33:22 *cover you with my **h** until*..........186
1 Kgs 13:4 *king's **h** became paralyzed*........701
Ps 22:16 *have pierced my **h-s** and feet.*.....556
Ps 24:4 *those whose **h-s** and hearts*..........558
Ps 32:4 *your **h** of discipline*........................564
Ps 44:3 *It was your right **h** and*..................850
Ps 63:4 *my **h-s** to you in prayer.*..................517
Ps 75:8 *a cup in his **h** that is full*................596
Ps 110:1 *at my right **h** until I humble*..........582
Ps 137:5 *let my right **h** forget how to*........1118
Ps 145:16 *you open your **h,** you satisfy*.......590
Isa 40:12 *the oceans in his **h?***....................924
Isa 41:13 *by your right **h**—I, the LORD*.........925
Isa 55:12 *will clap their **h-s!***......................942
Isa 64:8 *formed by your **h.***.........................951
Dan 10:10 *Just then a **h** touched me*..........1158
Matt 5:30 *And if your **h**—even your*..........1328
Matt 6:3 *don't let your left **h** know what*....1330
Matt 18:8 *with only one **h** or one foot*.........1384
Matt 26:64 *at God's right **h** and coming*.....1472
Mark 12:36 *at my right **h** until I humble*....1442
Acts 6:6 *they laid their **h-s** on them*..........1523
Acts 7:55 *at God's right **h.***........................1526
Acts 8:18 *laid their **h-s** on people,*............1528
Acts 13:3 *men laid their **h-s** on them*.........1540
Acts 19:6 *Paul laid his **h-s** on them,*...........1593
Acts 28:8 *and laying his **h-s** on him,*..........1688
1 Thes 4:11 *working with your **h-s,***...........1584
1 Tim 2:8 *pray with holy **h-s** lifted up*........1729
1 Tim 4:14 *church laid their **h-s** on you.*.....1732
2 Tim 1:6 *when I laid my **h-s** on you*...........1741
Heb 1:13 *at my right **h** until I humble*.........1763
Rev 13:16 *mark on the right **h** or on the*.....1820

HANDED (v) to yield control of
Rom 4:25 *He was **h** over to die*...................1653
1 Tim 1:20 *them out and **h** them over*........1728

HANDFUL (n) a small quantity or number
Eccl 4:6 *to have one **h** with quietness*.........676

HANDSOME (adj) having a pleasing and unusually impressive appearance; beautiful
Gen 39:6 *Joseph was a very **h** and*...............77
1 Sam 16:12 *dark and **h,** with beautiful*......448
2 Sam 14:25 *as the most **h** man in all Israel.*...510
1 Kgs 1:6 *he was very **h.***............................542
Ezek 23:6 *commanders dressed in **h** blue,*...1070

HANGED, HANGING, HANGS (v) to suspend; to execute (on a tree or gallows)
see also HUNG
Job 26:7 ***h-s** the earth on nothing.*..............117
Matt 27:5 *went out and **h-ed** himself.*......1476
Acts 10:39 *death by **h-ing** him on a cross,*...1534

HAPPINESS (n) a state of well-being and contentment; joy
Deut 24:5 ***h** to the wife he has married.*.......314
Job 7:7 *never again feel **h.***.........................102
Job 9:25 *a glimpse of **h.***............................104
Ps 86:4 *Give me **h,** O LORD,*.........................579
Ps 119:35 *that is where my **h** is found*........878
Eccl 8:15 ***h** along with all the hard work*......680
Isa 65:18 *Jerusalem as a place of **h.***...........952
Luke 6:24 *you have your only **h** now.*.........1327

HAPPY (adj) expressing, reflecting, or suggestive of happiness
see also BLESSED
Deut 16:14 *festival will be a **h** time*............306
Ps 113:9 *making her a **h** mother.*...............874
Prov 15:13 *A glad heart makes a **h** face;*....649
Prov 15:15 *for the **h** heart, life is*...............649
Prov 23:25 *she who gave you birth be **h.***.....661
Eccl 9:7 *drink your wine with a **h** heart,*.......680
Zech 10:7 *will be made **h** as if by wine.*....1176
Rom 12:15 *Be **h** with those who are **h,***.......1668
Phil 2:2 *make me truly **h** by agreeing*........1719
Jas 5:13 *Are any of you **h?***......................1553

HARBOR (n) a part of a body of water where ships dock; a place of security and comfort
Ps 107:30 *brought them safely into **h!***........872

HARD (adj) lacking in responsiveness, unfeeling; demanding the exertion of energy
Rom 11:25 *of Israel have **h** hearts,*...........1666
Rev 2:2 *I have seen your **h** work and*.........1802

HARD, HARDER (adv) with great or utmost effort or energy
Prov 13:4 *those who work **h***.........................646
Acts 20:35 *in need by working **h.***..............1676
Rom 16:12 *has worked so **h***......................1673
1 Cor 15:10 *worked **h-er** than any of*..........1620
2 Cor 11:23 *worked **h-er,** been put in*.......1641
1 Thes 5:12 *They work **h** among you*.........1585
2 Thes 3:8 *We worked **h** day and night*......1590

HARD-HEARTED (adj) lacking in sympathetic understanding; unfeeling
Deut 15:7 *do not be **h** or tightfisted*............305

HARDEN, HARDENED (v) to make callous or unfeeling
Exod 4:21 *But I will **h** his heart*...................146
Exod 10:20 *LORD **h-ed** Pharaoh's heart*.......154
Ps 95:8 *Don't **h** your hearts as Israel did*.....863
Isa 6:10 ***H** the hearts of these people*..........785
Matt 13:15 *hearts of these people are **h-ed,***...1345
John 12:40 *and **h-ed** their hearts—*.........1434
Eph 4:18 *minds and **h-ed** their hearts*......1711
Heb 3:8 *don't **h** your hearts as Israel did*...1765

HARDSHIPS (n) things that cause or entail suffering or privation
Acts 14:22 *must suffer many* ***h*** *to enter*....1545
2 Cor 6:4 *troubles and* ***h*** *and calamities*....1633
2 Thes 1:4 *and* ***h*** *you are suffering.*...........1587
Jas 5:13 *Are any of you suffering* ***h?***........1553

HARLOT (KJV)
Gen 38:15 *thought she was a* ***prostitute***......75
Josh 2:1 *a* ***prostitute*** *named Rahab*...........337
Hos 4:15 *you, Israel, are a* ***prostitute***..........807
Matt 21:31 ***prostitutes*** *will get into the Kingdom*...1437
Rev 17:5 *Mother of All* ***Prostitutes*** *and*.....1824

HARM (n) physical or mental damage; injury, hurt
Ps 37:8 *it only leads to* ***h.***..........................567
Prov 3:29 *Don't plot* ***h*** *against your*............635
Prov 19:23 *and protection from* ***h.***.............655
Prov 31:12 *brings him good, not* ***h,*** *all*........847
1 Cor 11:17 *more* ***h*** *than good is done*.....1613

HARM, HARMED, HARMS (v) to injure or hurt
Ps 121:6 *sun will not* ***h*** *you by day,*............882
Jer 10:5 *they can neither* ***h*** *you nor do*.....1012
Zech 2:8 *who* ***h-s*** *you* ***h-s*** *my most*.........1167
Rev 2:11 *will not be* ***h-ed*** *by the second*...1803

HARMLESS (adj) lacking capacity or intent to injure
Matt 10:16 *shrewd as snakes and* ***h*** *as*....1359

HARMONY (n) tranquility; agreement; unity
Zech 6:13 *will be perfect* ***h*** *between his*....1170
Rom 12:16 *Live in* ***h*** *with each other.*........1668
Rom 14:19 *aim for* ***h*** *in the church*...........1670
Rom 15:5 *live in complete* ***h*** *with each*......1671
1 Cor 12:25 *This makes for* ***h.***.................1615
2 Cor 6:15 *What* ***h*** *can there be*..............1634
2 Cor 13:11 *Live in* ***h*** *and peace.*.............1643
Col 3:14 *together in perfect* ***h.***................1701

HARP, HARPS (n) a plucked stringed instrument
Gen 4:21 *all who play the* ***h*** *and flute.*...........16
1 Sam 16:23 *would play the* ***h.***..................448
Ps 33:2 *on the ten-stringed* ***h.***...................858
Ps 98:5 *with the* ***h*** *and melodious song,*......865
Ps 137:2 *our* ***h-s,*** *hanging them*.............1118
Ps 144:9 *a ten-stringed* ***h.***.........................589
Ps 147:7 *praises to our God with a* ***h.***.......1154
Ps 150:3 *praise him with the lyre and* ***h!***.....888
Rev 5:8 *Each one had a* ***h,*** *and they*..........1810

HARSH (adj) causing a disagreeable reaction; unduly exacting
Prov 15:1 ***h*** *words make tempers flare*........648
Eph 4:31 *rage, anger,* ***h*** *words,*.................1712

HARVEST, HARVESTS (n) the time or fruit of reaping or gathering in a crop—physically or spiritually
Deut 16:15 *blesses you with bountiful* ***h-s***....306
Matt 9:37 *The* ***h*** *is great, but*.....................1357
John 4:35 *fields are already ripe for* ***h.***......1305
1 Cor 15:23 *raised as the first of the* ***h;***....1621
2 Cor 9:10 *great* ***h*** *of generosity*..............1638
Gal 6:9 *we will reap a* ***h*** *of blessing*..........1567
Heb 12:11 *peaceful* ***h*** *of right living*..........1780
Jas 3:18 *reap a* ***h*** *of righteousness*...........1551
Rev 14:15 *the time of* ***h*** *has come;*...........1822

HARVEST, HARVESTS (v) to gather in (a crop); to reap
Gen 8:22 *there will be planting and* ***h,***..........20
Job 4:8 *and cultivate evil will* ***h***.....................98
Prov 10:5 *wise youth* ***h-s*** *in the summer,*....642
Gal 6:8 *sinful nature will* ***h*** *decay and*.......1567

HARVESTER, HARVESTERS (n) one who gathers in (a crop)
Ruth 2:3 *to gather grain behind the* ***h-s.***.....412
John 4:36 *planter and the* ***h*** *alike!*............1305

HASTE (n) rash or headlong action; swiftness
Prov 19:2 ***h*** *makes mistakes.*.....................654

HASTY (adj) done or made in a hurry; impatient; speedy
Prov 21:5 ***h*** *shortcuts lead to poverty.*..........657
Eccl 5:2 *don't be* ***h*** *in bringing matters*.......677

HATE, HATED, HATES, HATING (v) to feel extreme enmity toward; to have a strong aversion to
Ps 45:7 *love justice and* ***h*** *evil.*...................851
Prov 1:22 *you fools* ***h*** *knowledge?*.............632
Prov 6:16 *six things the* L*ORD* ***h-s—***...........638
Prov 13:5 *The godly* ***h*** *lies;*........................646
Prov 15:27 *those who* ***h*** *bribes will live.*.......650
Prov 26:28 *A lying tongue* ***h-s*** *its victims,*...842
Prov 28:16 *but one who* ***h-s*** *corruption*......844
Mal 2:16 *"For I* ***h*** *divorce!"*.......................1247
Matt 5:43 *and* ***h*** *your enemy.*....................1330
Matt 24:9 *be* ***h-d*** *all over the world*..........1446
Luke 6:22 *when people* ***h*** *you*.................1327
John 3:20 *All who do evil* ***h*** *the light*.........1302
John 15:18 *remember that it* ***h-d*** *me*.......1464
2 Tim 3:3 *be cruel and* ***h*** *what is good.*.....1744
Heb 1:9 *You love justice and* ***h*** *evil.*..........1762
1 Jn 2:9 ***h-s*** *a Christian brother or sister,*..1788
1 Jn 4:20 ***h-s*** *a Christian brother or*.........1794
Jude 1:23 ***h-ing*** *the sins that contaminate.*...1786

HATERS (n) those who feel or express enmity or aversion
Rom 1:30 *are backstabbers,* ***h*** *of God,*......1648

HATRED (n) strong emotional aversion
Lev 19:17 *Do not nurse* ***h*** *in your heart*.......225
Prov 26:24 *People may cover their* ***h***..........841

HAUGHTY (adj) blatantly and disdainfully proud
Prov 6:17 ***h*** *eyes, a lying tongue,*...............638
Prov 21:24 *are proud and* ***h;*** *they act*.........658

HAY (n) herbage and especially grass mowed and cured for fodder
1 Cor 3:12 *jewels, wood,* ***h,*** *or straw.*.........1599

HEAD, HEADS (n) top part of the body that contains the brain; one in charge; person, individual
Gen 3:15 *He will strike your* ***h,*** *and*..............13
Lev 26:13 *walk with your* ***h-s*** *held high.*......235
Ps 22:7 *shake their* ***h-s,*** *saying,*.................556
Ps 23:5 *by anointing my* ***h*** *with oil.*.............558
Ps 133:2 *over Aaron's* ***h,*** *that ran*..............584
Prov 25:22 *coals of shame on their* ***h-s,***.....840
Matt 27:39 *shaking their* ***h-s*** *in mockery.*..1482
John 19:2 *thorns and put it on his* ***h,***........1480
Acts 18:6 *your own* ***h-s****—I am innocent.*...1580
Rom 12:20 *coals of shame on their* ***h-s.***....1668
Eph 1:22 *and has made him* ***h*** *over all*......1706
Eph 5:23 *as Christ is the* ***h*** *of the*............1713
Rev 4:4 *crowns on their* ***h-s.***....................1808
Rev 14:14 *He had a gold crown on his* ***h***...1822
Rev 19:12 *on his* ***h*** *were many crowns.*....1828

HEADCLOTH (n) portion of burial garb covering the head and face
John 11:44 *wrapped in a* ***h.***.....................1415

HEAL, HEALED, HEALING, HEALS (v) to mend, cure, make whole; to restore to health
Gen 20:17 *and God* ***h-ed*** *Abimelech,*............43
Exod 15:26 *I am the* L*ORD who* ***h-s*** *you.*......162
Num 12:13 *I beg you, please* ***h*** *her!*............250
Deut 32:39 *one who wounds and* ***h-s;***........325
2 Chr 30:20 *prayer and* ***h-ed*** *the people.*....837
Job 5:18 *his hands also* ***h.***.........................100
Ps 6:2 ***H*** *me,* L*ORD,*....................................548
Ps 103:3 *and* ***h-s*** *all my diseases.*.............580
Ps 107:20 *his word and* ***h-ed*** *them,*............872
Prov 3:8 *will have* ***h-ing*** *for your body*........635
Prov 13:17 *messenger brings* ***h-ing.***..........646
Isa 6:10 *and turn to me for* ***h-ing.***..............785
Isa 30:26 L*ORD begins to* ***h*** *his people*.........900
Isa 57:18 *but I will* ***h*** *them anyway!*.............944
Isa 57:19 *the* L*ORD, who* ***h-s*** *them.*..............944
Jer 8:18 *My grief is beyond* ***h-ing;***..........1011
Jer 17:14 *O* L*ORD, if you* ***h*** *me, I will*..........1021
Jer 17:14 *I will be truly* ***h-ed;***....................1021
Jer 30:13 *No medicine can* ***h*** *you.*............1032
Hos 6:1 *now he will* ***h*** *us.*...........................808
Hos 7:1 *I want to* ***h*** *Israel, but its*...............809
Hos 14:4 *Then I will* ***h*** *you of your*..............817
Zech 11:16 *nor* ***h*** *the injured,*....................1178
Mal 4:2 *with* ***h-ing*** *in his wings.*................1249
Matt 4:23 *And he* ***h-ed*** *every kind*............1311
Matt 8:7 *will come and* ***h*** *him.*...................1335
Matt 8:16 *and he* ***h-ed*** *all the sick.*...........1309
Matt 9:35 *he* ***h-ed*** *every kind of disease*...1357
Matt 10:8 ***H*** *the sick, raise the*.................1358
Matt 15:30 *Jesus, and he* ***h-ed*** *them all*...1372
Matt 17:16 *they couldn't* ***h*** *him.*...............1381
Mark 1:34 *So Jesus* ***h-ed*** *many people*....1310
Mark 3:2 *If he* ***h-ed*** *the man's*.................1321
Mark 3:10 *He had* ***h-ed*** *many people*.......1322
Mark 5:28 *touch his robe, I will be* ***h-ed.***..1354
Mark 6:5 *sick people and* ***h*** *them.*............1357
Mark 6:13 *and* ***h-ed*** *many sick*................1359
Mark 6:56 *who touched him were* ***h-ed.***....1367
Mark 10:52 *your faith has* ***h-ed*** *you.*.........1425
Luke 4:23 *Physician,* ***h*** *yourself*................1357
Luke 4:40 *his hand* ***h-ed*** *every one.*.........1310
Luke 6:7 *If he* ***h-ed*** *the man's*...................1321
Luke 8:50 *faith, and she will be* ***h-ed.***......1355
Luke 10:9 ***H*** *the sick, and tell them.*..........1394
Luke 13:14 *indignant that Jesus had* ***h-ed***...1403
Luke 14:3 ***h*** *people on the Sabbath*...........1408
Luke 14:4 *the sick man and* ***h-ed*** *him*......1408
Luke 17:19 *Your faith has* ***h-ed*** *you.*........1416
Luke 18:42 *Your faith has* ***h-ed*** *you.*........1426
Luke 22:51 *man's ear and* ***h-ed*** *him.*........1470
John 4:47 *to Capernaum to* ***h*** *his son,*......1307
John 7:23 *angry with me for* ***h-ing*** *a man*..1390
John 12:40 *and have me* ***h*** *them.*..............1434
Acts 3:16 *this man was* ***h-ed—***................1517
Acts 4:9 *to know how he was* ***h-ed?***........1518
Acts 4:14 *see the man who had been* ***h-ed***...1519
Acts 4:22 *sign—the* ***h-ing*** *of a man*.........1519
Acts 8:7 *or lame were* ***h-ed.***.....................1527
Acts 9:34 *Jesus Christ* ***h-s*** *you! Get up,*....1532
Acts 10:38 *and* ***h-ing*** *all who were*...........1534
Acts 28:8 *his hands on him, he* ***h-ed***........1688
Acts 28:27 *turn to me and let me* ***h***..........1689
1 Cor 12:28 *the gift of* ***h-ing,***....................1615
1 Cor 12:30 *have the gift of* ***h-ing?***...........1615
Jas 5:16 *so that you may be* ***h-ed.***...........1554
1 Pet 2:24 *By his wounds you are* ***h-ed.***....1752
Rev 13:3 *fatal wound was* ***h-ed!***..............1819
Rev 13:12 *wound had been* ***h-ed.***.............1820

HEALING (adj) marked by restoring to original purity or integrity
Luke 6:19 ***h*** *power went out from him,*.....1322
Acts 4:30 *your hand with* ***h*** *power;*...........1519

HEALTH (n) the general condition of the body
Ps 38:3 my **h** is broken because of............568
Ps 38:7 and my **h** is broken.......................568
Prov 15:30 makes for good **h.**....................650
Isa 38:16 You restore my **h**........................921
Jer 30:17 I will give you back your **h**.........1032

HEALTHY, HEALTHIER (adj) enjoying good health and vigor of body, mind, or spirit
Ps 73:4 bodies are so **h** and strong. 594
Prov 16:24 the soul and **h** for the body........651
Dan 1:15 friends looked **h-ier** and better..1002
Zech 11:16 nor feed the **h.** Instead,...........1178
Matt 9:12 he said, "**H** people don't need...1315
Mark 2:17 **H** people don't need..................1315
Luke 5:31 answered them, "**H** people 1316
Eph 4:16 whole body is **h** and growing......1711
3 Jn 1:2 that you are as **h** in body as........1796

HEAP (v) to pile in great quantity; to load heavily
Prov 25:22 You will **h** burning coals of........840
Rom 12:20 you will **h** burning coals of......1668

HEAR, HEARD, HEARING (v) to perceive sound; to listen with attention; to be informed of; to take testimony from and make a legal decision
see also LISTEN
Gen 3:8 and his wife **h-d** the LORD God.........12
Exod 2:24 God **h-d** their groaning,..............143
Deut 1:16 judges, 'You must **h** the cases 285
Josh 7:9 people living in the land **h**.............345
1 Kgs 8:30 May you **h** the humble.............619
2 Chr 7:14 I will **h** from heaven and will......623
Neh 1:11 O LORD, please **h** my prayer! 1204
Ps 5:1 O LORD, **h** me as I pray;....................547
Ps 89:1 Young and old will **h** of your...........591
Isa 29:18 the deaf will **h** words read...........898
Isa 30:21 own ears will **h** him........................900
Isa 40:28 Have you never **h-d?**....................925
Isa 59:1 too deaf to **h** you call. 945
Dan 10:12 has been **h-d** in heaven. 1158
Matt 5:21 have **h-d** that our ancestors 1328
Matt 5:43 You have **h-d** the law 1330
Matt 11:5 cured, the deaf **h,** the dead.......1337
Matt 13:14 When you **h** what I say,...........1345
Mark 4:12 When they **h** what I say,...........1346
Luke 7:22 cured, the deaf **h,** the dead 1338
John 8:26 what I have **h-d** from the one...1392
Acts 2:6 When they **h-d** the loud noise, ...1514
Acts 13:7 he wanted to **h** the word of.......1540
Rom 10:14 how can they **h** about him 1664
Rom 10:17 faith comes from **h-ing,** 1664
1 Cor 2:9 no ear has **h-d,** and no mind.....1598
1 Cor 12:17 how would you **h?** 1615
Heb 3:7 Today when you **h** his voice, ...1765
2 Jn 1:6 just as you **h-d** from the.............1796
Rev 3:20 If you **h** my voice and.................1807
Rev 22:8 I, John, am the one who **h-d**......1832

HEART, HEARTS (n) figuratively, the seat of emotions, thoughts, and intentions; personality, disposition; courage; love, affection; central or most vital part of something
Gen 6:6 It broke his **h.** 17
Exod 4:21 will harden his **h** so he 146
Exod 35:21 All whose **h-s** were stirred 189
Deut 6:5 LORD your God with all your **h,**.......294
Deut 9:10 from the **h** of the fire..................298
Deut 20:3 Do not lose **h** or panic 310
Deut 28:65 will cause your **h** to tremble,.....319
Josh 22:5 with all your **h** and all your..........366
Josh 23:14 Deep in your **h-s** you know.......369
1 Sam 1:15 pouring out my **h**.....................417
1 Sam 10:9 God gave him a new **h,**............437
1 Sam 12:20 the LORD with all your **h,** 440
1 Sam 13:14 a man after his own **h.** 442
1 Sam 16:7 but the LORD looks at the **h.** 448
1 Kgs 8:48 with their whole **h** and soul.......620
1 Kgs 11:2 turn your **h-s** to their gods.........671
1 Kgs 11:3 turn his **h** away from the LORD...671
1 Kgs 14:8 followed me with all his **h** 702
2 Kgs 23:3 with all his **h** and soul. 971
1 Chr 22:19 God with all your **h** and soul. ...533
2 Chr 6:38 with their whole **h** and soul 622
2 Chr 22:9 sought the LORD with all his **h.** ...752
2 Chr 34:31 with all his **h** and soul. 972
Ezra 1:5 stirred the **h-s** of the priests........1151
Job 4:5 trouble strikes, you lose **h.** 98
Ps 9:1 praise you, LORD, with all my **h;** 549
Ps 14:1 say in their **h-s,** "There is no..........551
Ps 19:14 meditation of my **h**.......................555
Ps 24:4 whose hands and **h-s** are pure, ...558
Ps 27:8 my **h** responds, "LORD,...................561
Ps 36:1 within their **h-s.** They have no........566
Ps 42:11 Why is my **h** so sad?...................849
Ps 45:1 Beautiful words stir my **h.** 850
Ps 51:10 Create in me a clean **h,** O God. 506
Ps 57:7 my **h** is confident...........................460
Ps 73:7 everything their **h-s** could ever 594
Ps 73:26 the strength of my **h;**...................594
Ps 108:1 with all my **h!**..................................581
Ps 111:1 thank the LORD with all my **h** 873
Ps 119:2 with all their **h-s.** 877
Ps 119:11 hidden your word in my **h,** 878
Ps 119:58 With all my **h** I want your 879
Ps 119:145 I pray with all my **h;**................881
Ps 139:23 and know my **h;** test me and......586
Prov 3:3 deep within your **h.**.........................634
Prov 4:23 Guard your **h** above all else,........636
Prov 13:12 deferred makes the **h** sick,........646
Prov 14:30 A peaceful **h** leads to a 648
Prov 15:13 a broken **h** crushes the.............649
Prov 15:30 look brings joy to the **h;** 650
Prov 17:22 A cheerful **h** is good 653
Prov 20:9 have cleansed my **h;** I am pure ...656
Prov 23:15 wise, my own **h** will rejoice! 661
Prov 27:23 and put your **h** into caring.........842
Song 4:9 captured my **h,** my treasure,.........666
Song 5:2 I slept, but my **h** was awake,........667
Song 5:4 and my **h** thrilled within me...........667
Song 8:6 like a seal over your **h,**.................669
Isa 1:5 and your **h** is sick. 823
Isa 6:10 Harden the **h-s** of these people. 785
Isa 42:4 or lose **h** until justice......................926
Jer 3:15 shepherds after my own **h,** 963
Jer 3:22 your wayward **h-s.**........................963
Jer 9:26 have uncircumcised **h-s.**............1012
Jer 20:9 burns in my **h** like a fire................999
Jer 32:39 will give them one **h** and one 1080
Ezek 44:7 who have no **h** for God. 1127
Joel 2:12 Give me your **h-s.** Come with....1241
Matt 5:8 those whose **h-s** are pure,..........1326
Matt 5:28 adultery with her in his **h.** 1328
Matt 11:29 I am humble and gentle at **h,** ..1339
Matt 12:34 whatever is in your **h**..............1341
Matt 15:19 For from the **h** come evil.........1370
Matt 18:35 and sisters from your **h.**.........1386
Matt 22:37 God with all your **h,** all your.....1441
Mark 11:23 have no doubt in your **h.** 1435
Mark 12:30 God with all your **h,** all your.....1441
Mark 12:33 love him with all my **h** and 1442
Luke 6:45 treasury of a good **h,**................1335
Luke 10:27 God with all your **h,** all your....1396
Luke 12:34 desires of your **h** will also.......1401
Luke 24:38 Why are your **h-s** filled with ...1495
John 5:38 your **h-s,** because you do not...1319
Acts 1:24 you know every **h.** Show us.......1513
Acts 4:32 were united in **h** and mind. 1520
Acts 8:21 this, for your **h** is not right.........1528
Acts 15:8 God knows people's **h-s,** and....1569
Acts 16:14 Lord opened her **h,** and she 1574
Acts 28:27 hear, and their **h-s** cannot.......1689
Rom 1:9 with all my **h** by spreading............1645
Rom 2:15 written in their **h-s,** for their......1649
Rom 2:29 changed **h** seeks praise............1650
Rom 10:9 believe in your **h** that God 1663
2 Cor 2:4 with a troubled **h** and many.......1627
2 Cor 7:2 Please open your **h-s** to us........1634
2 Cor 9:7 decide in your **h** how much to....1637
Eph 1:18 I pray that your **h-s** will be 1706
Eph 3:13 don't lose **h** because of my........1709
Eph 5:19 music to the Lord in your **h-s.**....1713
Eph 6:6 of God with all your **h.** 1715
Phil 1:7 place in my **h.** You share with.......1717
1 Tim 1:5 comes from a pure **h,** a clear 1727

HEARTLESS (adj) lacking feeling; cruel
Rom 1:31 promises, are **h,** and have no....1648

HEATHEN, HEATHENS (n) one who does not worship the true God; uncivilized; without religion
Acts 7:51 You are **h** at heart and deaf to...1526
Eph 2:11 called "uncircumcised **h-s**" by...1707

HEAVEN, HEAVENS (n) sky and stars above; God's dwelling place; abode of eternal bliss
Deut 30:12 is not kept in **h,** so distant 321
Job 41:11 Everything under **h** is mine.........131
Ps 18:16 down from **h** and rescued me; 528
Ps 71:19 to the highest **h-s.** You have 860
Ps 108:4 than the **h-s.** Your faithfulness 581
Matt 11:25 Father, Lord of **h** and earth,......1339
Matt 24:30 appear in the **h-s,** and there...1447
Rom 10:6 go up to **h?**' (to bring Christ......1663
2 Cor 12:2 to the third **h** fourteen years 1641
Heb 9:24 He entered into **h** itself to 1774

HEAVENLY (adj) celestial; of or pertaining to God in the highest
Ps 29:1 the LORD, you **h** beings; 562

HEIR, HEIRS (n) one who succeeds to a hereditary title; one who inherits
see also INHERIT(ANCE)
Isa 11:10 In that day the **h** to David's..........796
Rom 8:17 with Christ we are **h-s** of God's...1659

HELL (n) abode of the dead; place of punishment; personification of evil; lowest place one can go
see also UNDERWORLD
Matt 5:22 of the fires of **h.** 1328
Matt 16:18 all the powers of **h** will not......1375
Matt 23:33 judgment of **h?** 1445
Mark 9:43 fires of **h** with two hands..........1384
Luke 12:5 throw you into **h.** 1399
Jas 3:6 on fire by **h** itself..........................1550
2 Pet 2:4 threw them into **h,** in gloomy 1758

HELMET (n) any of various protective head coverings usually made of hard metal
Isa 59:17 and placed the **h** of salvation.......946
Eph 6:17 salvation as your **h,** and take.....1715

HELP (n) aid, assistance
2 Sam 22:36 your **h** has made me great.....527
Ps 30:2 I cried to you for **h,** and you..........563
Ps 33:20 He is our **h** and our shield............858
Ps 108:12 for all human **h** is useless..........581
Isa 30:18 wait for his **h.**............................900
Isa 38:14 looking to heaven for **h.** I am.......921
Phil 4:16 you sent **h** more than once.........1725

HELP, HELPED, HELPING, HELPS (v) to give assistance or support; to rescue or save
Exod 23:5 *Instead, stop and* **h.** 173
Deut 2:36 *our God also* **h-ed** *us conquer* 288
1 Sam 7:12 *the LORD has* **h-ed** *us!* 427
Ps 46:1 *always ready to* **h** *in times of* 851
Ps 72:12 *he will* **h** *the oppressed,* 630
Ps 145:14 *The LORD* **h-s** *the fallen* 590
Prov 11:4 *Riches won't* **h** *on the* 643
Prov 14:31 *their Maker, but* **h-ing** *the poor* 648
Prov 19:17 *If you* **h** *the poor,* 655
Isa 41:10 *strengthen you and* **h** *you.* 925
Isa 44:10 *that cannot* **h** *him one bit?* 930
Jer 51:9 *We would have* **h-ed** *her if we* 1037
Lam 4:16 *he no longer* **h-s** *them.* 1100
Mark 9:24 *but* **h** *me overcome* 1381
Acts 9:36 *for others and* **h-ing** *the poor.* 1532
Acts 16:9 *to Macedonia and* **h** *us!* 1573
Rom 12:13 *be ready to* **h** *them.* 1667
1 Cor 12:28 *those who can* **h** *others,* 1615
2 Cor 6:2 *salvation, I* **h-ed** *you.* 1633
Gal 6:1 *and humbly* **h** *that person back* 1567
1 Tim 5:10 *Has she* **h-ed** *those who* 1733
2 Tim 2:7 *Lord will* **h** *you understand* 1742
Heb 10:33 *you* **h-ed** *others who* 1776
1 Pet 4:11 *the gift of* **h-ing** *others?* 1755

HELPER (n) one who gives aid; co-worker
Gen 2:18 *I will make a* **h** *who is just* 10
Ps 70:5 *You are my* **h** *and my savior;* 579
Ps 115:9 *He is your* **h** *and your shield.* 875
Heb 13:6 *The LORD is my* **h,** *so I will* 1782

HELPFUL (adj) of service or assistance; useful
Job 22:2 *Can even a wise person be* **h** 114
Prov 10:32 *the godly speak* **h** *words,* 643
1 Cor 12:31 *desire the most* **h** *gifts.* 1615
Eph 4:29 *be good and* **h,** *so that your* 1712

HELPLESS (adj) without any aid, comfort, protection, or chance of success
Ps 9:12 *cares for the* **h.** *He does not* 549
Ps 10:12 *not ignore the* **h!** 857
Ps 34:2 *let all who are* **h** *take heart.* 458
Ps 35:10 *Who else protects the* **h** 565
Amos 2:7 *They trample* **h** *people in the* 772
Matt 9:36 *confused and* **h,** *like sheep* 1357
Rom 5:6 *were utterly* **h,** *Christ came* 1654

HEN (n) a female chicken especially over a year old
Matt 23:37 *together as a* **h** *protects her* 1407
Luke 13:34 *together as a* **h** *protects her* 1407

HEROD
1. Herod the Great, ruler of Palestine at birth of John the Baptist and Jesus (Luke 1:5, p. 1272); tried to kill baby Jesus (Matt 2:1-18, p. 1283); died (Matt 2:19, p. 1285).
2. Herod Antipas, tetrarch of Galilee (Luke 3:1, p. 1290), son of Herod the Great; arrested and beheaded John the Baptist (Matt 14:1-12, p. 1361; Mark 1:14, p. 1303; 6:14-29, p. 1363; Luke 3:19-20, p. 1303; 9:7-9, p. 1363); tried Jesus (Luke 23:7-15, p. 1476).
3. Herod Agrippa I, grandson of Herod the Great; killed the apostle James (Acts 12:1-2, p. 1537); arrested Peter (Acts 12:3-19, p. 1537); died (Acts 12:21-23, p. 1538).
4. Herod Agrippa II, great grandson of Herod the Great; spoke at Paul's trial (Acts 25–26, p. 1683).

HEROES (n) greatly admired persons
Ps 16:3 *in the land are my true* **h!** 552

HEZEKIAH King of Judah (southern kingdom) (2 Kgs 18–20, p. 799; 2 Chr 29–32, p. 800); reformed the Temple and its worship (2 Chr 29:20-36, p. 835); offered effective prayer during war against Assyria (2 Kgs 19:14-19, p. 916; 2 Chr 32:1-23, p. 912; Isa 36:14-20, p. 914); became sick but was healed (2 Kgs 20:1-11, p. 919; 2 Chr 32:24-26, p. 920; Isa 38:1-22, p. 920); showed kingdom's treasures to Babylonians (2 Kgs 20:12-19, p. 922; 2 Chr 32:31, p. 920; Isa 39, p. 922); died (2 Kgs 20:20-21, p. 923; 2 Chr 32:32-33, p. 923).

HID, HIDDEN (v) to remain out of sight; unrevealed
see also HIDE
Ps 119:11 *I have* **h-den** *your word.* 878
Matt 13:35 *explain things* **h-den** *since the* 1348
Matt 13:44 *discovered* **h-den** *in a field.* 1349
Matt 13:44 *he* **h** *it again and* 1349
Matt 25:25 *your money, so I* **h** *it in the* 1452
Mark 4:22 *that is* **h-den** *will eventually be* 1347
1 Cor 2:7 *was previously* **h-den,** *even* 1598
Col 3:3 *real life is* **h-den** *with Christ in* 1700
Heb 11:23 *that Moses' parents* **h** *him* 1778

HIDE, HIDING (v) to shield; to seek protection; to put or remain out of sight
see also HID
Deut 31:17 *abandon them,* **h-ing** *my face* 322
1 Sam 10:22 *"He is* **h-ing** *among the* 438
Ps 27:5 *he will* **h** *me in his* 561
Ps 57:1 *I will* **h** *beneath the shadow* 459
Ps 143:9 *run to you to* **h** *me.* 588
Jer 16:17 *cannot hope to* **h** *from me.* 1020
Matt 11:25 *thank you for* **h-ing** *these* 1339

HIGH, HIGHER, HIGHEST (adj) foremost in rank, dignity, or standing; having large extension upward; of greater degree or value than average, usual, or expected
Gen 14:18 *of God Most* **H,** *brought Abram* 34
Gen 14:22 *LORD, God Most* **H,** *Creator of* 34
Ps 113:4 *glory is* **h-er** *than the heavens.* 874
Isa 14:14 *be like the Most* **H.** 832
Dan 4:17 *that the Most* **H** *rules over* 1120
Mark 5:7 *Son of the Most* **H** *God?* 1351
Phil 2:9 *the place of* **h-est** *honor and* 1720
Heb 7:1 *a priest of God Most* **H.** 1770

HIGHLIGHTS (v) to throw a strong light on
Rom 3:7 *sinner if my dishonesty* **h** *his* 1650

HIGHWAY (n) a main direct road
Isa 40:3 *Make a straight* **h** *through the* 923
Matt 7:13 *The* **h** *to hell is broad.* 1334

HILLS (n) usually rounded, natural elevations of land lower than mountains
1 Kgs 20:23 *are gods of the* **h;** 722
Ps 50:10 *the cattle on a thousand* **h.** 593
Isa 40:4 *mountains and* **h.** *Straighten* 923
Hos 10:8 *plead with the* **h,** *"Fall on* 813
Matt 24:16 *Judea must flee to the* **h.** 1446
Luke 3:5 *mountains and* **h** *made level.* 1290
Luke 23:30 *plead with the* **h,** *'Bury us.'* 1482
Rev 17:9 *the seven* **h** *where the woman* 1824

HILLTOP (n) the highest part of a hill
Matt 5:14 *a city on a* **h** *that cannot be* 1327

HINDER, HINDERED (v) to delay, impede, or prevent action
1 Sam 14:6 *for nothing can* **h** *the LORD.* 443
1 Pet 3:7 *will not be* **h-ed.** 1753

HIRE(v) to engage the personal services of for pay
Luke 15:15 *a local farmer to* **h** *him,* 1410

HOARD, HOARDING (v) to keep something to oneself
Prov 11:26 *those who* **h** *their grain,* 644
Eccl 5:13 **H-ing** *riches harms* 677

HOLD, HOLDING, HOLDS (v) to keep under restraint; to have or maintain in the grasp; to keep from falling or moving; to have in the mind or express as a judgment, opinion, or belief; to maintain control of
2 Kgs 4:16 *you will be* **h-ing** *a son in* 741
Ps 3:3 *the one who* **h-s** *my head high.* 517
Ps 37:24 *for the LORD* **h-s** *them by the* 567
Ps 39:1 *I will* **h** *my tongue when* 569
Ps 63:8 *right hand* **h-s** *me securely.* 518
Prov 27:16 **h** *something with greased* 842
Isa 40:11 **h-ing** *them close to his heart.* 924
Isa 48:9 *name, I will* **h** *back my anger* 935
Matt 4:6 *And they will* **h** *you up with* 1295
Mark 11:25 *forgive anyone you are* **h-ing** 1436
Col 1:17 *and he* **h-s** *all creation* 1695
Col 2:19 *For he* **h-s** *the whole body* 1699
Heb 4:14 *God, let us* **h** *firmly to what* 1766
Heb 10:23 *Let us* **h** *tightly without* 1776

HOLINESS (n) sanctity or purity
Exod 15:11 *glorious in* **h,** *awesome in* 162
Deut 32:51 *to demonstrate my* **h** *to the* 325
Ps 29:2 *the splendor of his* **h.** 562
Luke 1:75 *in* **h** *and righteousness for* 1276
1 Cor 7:14 *wife brings* **h** *to her* 1606
2 Cor 1:12 *a God-given* **h** *and sincerity* 1626
1 Thes 4:4 *and live in* **h** *and honor—* 1584
1 Tim 2:15 *faith, love,* **h,** *and modesty* 1730
Heb 12:10 *share in his* **h.** 1780

HOLY (adj) consecrated or set aside for sacred use (as opposed to pagan or common use); standing apart from sin and evil; characteristic of God, especially the third person of the Trinity
see also PURE
Gen 2:3 *and declared it* **h,** *because it* 9
Exod 3:5 *are standing on* **h** *ground.* 143
Exod 19:6 *priests, my* **h** *nation.* 168
Exod 26:33 *separate the* **H** *Place* 177
Exod 29:37 *be absolutely* **h,** 181
Exod 30:10 *LORD's most* **h** *altar.* 182
Exod 31:13 *the LORD, who makes you* **h.** 183
Lev 11:45 *you must be* **h** *because I am* 215
Lev 19:8 *for defiling what is* **h** *to the* 225
Lev 20:7 *set yourselves apart to be* **h,** 226
Lev 20:26 *You must be* **h** *because I,* 227
Lev 21:12 *for he has been made* **h** *by the* 228
Lev 22:32 *the LORD who makes you* **h.** 229
Lev 27:9 *LORD will be considered* **h.** 236
Deut 5:12 *by keeping it* **h,** *as the LORD* 293
Josh 5:15 *where you are standing is* **h.** 343
Josh 24:19 *he is a* **h** *and jealous God.* 370
1 Chr 16:35 *we can thank your* **h** *name* 493
Neh 11:1 *in Jerusalem, the* **h** *city.* 1220
Ps 22:3 *Yet you are* **h,** *enthroned on* 556
Ps 30:4 *Praise his* **h** *name.* 563
Ps 99:3 *Your name is* **h!** 865
Ps 105:3 *Exult in his* **h** *name; rejoice,* 868
Ps 111:9 *What a* **h,** *awe-inspiring name* 873
Prov 9:10 *of the* **H** *One results in good* 641
Isa 6:3 *to each other, "***H, h, h** 783
Isa 40:25 *my equal?" asks the* **H** *One.* 924
Isa 54:5 *your Redeemer, the* **H** *One of* 941
Isa 66:20 *them to my* **h** *mountain in* 953
Dan 7:18 *But in the end, the* **h** *people* 1136

Dan 9:24 *anoint the Most **H** Place*.............1143
Zech 14:5 *and all his **h** ones with him*.......1180
Matt 24:15 *standing in the **H** Place*...........1446
Mark 1:24 *you are—the **H** One of God*.....1309
Luke 1:35 *baby to be born will be **h**,*.........1274
Luke 1:49 *Mighty One is **h**, and he has*.....1276
Luke 4:34 *you are—the **H** One of God*......1309
Luke 11:2 *may your name be kept **h**.*........1342
John 6:69 *you are the **H** One of God!"*.......1369
John 17:17 *Make them **h** by your*...............1467
Acts 13:35 *not allow your **H** One to rot*.....1542
Rom 7:12 *the law itself is **h**, and its*........1658
Rom 14:5 *day is more **h** than another*.......1670
Rom 15:16 *made **h** by the **H** Spirit*............1671
1 Cor 1:2 *be his own **h** people*...................1594
1 Cor 1:30 *made us pure and **h**,*...............1597
1 Cor 3:17 *God's temple is **h**, and you*.........1600
1 Cor 6:11 *you were made **h**; you were*.....1603
1 Cor 7:14 *children would not be **h**, but*....1606
Eph 1:4 *in Christ to be **h** and without*........1704
Eph 2:21 *becoming a **h** temple for*.............1708
Eph 4:24 *righteous and **h**.*..........................1712
Eph 5:26 *to make her **h** and clean,*...........1714
Col 1:22 *and you are **h** and blameless*......1696
1 Thes 3:13 *blameless, and **h** as you*.........1584
1 Thes 4:7 *called us to live **h** lives,*...........1584
1 Thes 5:23 *make you **h** in every*...............1587
2 Thes 1:10 *from his **h** people—praise*.....1588
1 Tim 2:8 *to pray with **h** hands lifted*.........1729
2 Tim 1:9 *called us to live a **h** life.*............1741
2 Tim 3:15 *taught the **h** Scriptures from*....1745
Heb 2:11 *ones he makes **h** have the same*..1764
Heb 10:14 *those who are being made **h**.*..1775
Heb 10:19 *heaven's Most **H** Place*.............1775
Heb 10:29 *which made us **h**, as if it*..........1776
Heb 13:12 *make his people **h** by means*...1782
1 Pet 1:16 *You must be **h** because I am*....1749
1 Pet 2:5 *you are his **h** priests*..................1750
1 Pet 2:9 *priests, a **h** nation, God's*...........1751
1 Pet 3:5 *is how the **h** women of old*.........1752
2 Pet 1:18 *on the **h** mountain*...................1758
2 Pet 2:21 *to live a **h** life.*..........................1759
2 Pet 3:11 *like this, what **h** and godly*.......1760
Rev 3:7 *one who is **h** and true,*...................1806
Rev 4:8 *on saying, "**H**, **h**, **h** is*...................1808
Rev 15:4 *you alone are **h**. All nations*........1822
Rev 20:6 *Blessed and **h** are those who*.....1829
Rev 22:11 *continue to be **h**.*.....................1832

HOLY GHOST (KJV)
Matt 1:18 *the power of the **Holy Spirit***......1277
Matt 3:11 *baptize you with the **Holy Spirit***...1289
Matt 28:19 *the Son and the **Holy Spirit***....1498
Luke 3:22 ***Holy Spirit**, in bodily form,*.......1294
1 Jn 5:7-8 *three witnesses—the **Spirit***....1794

HOLY SPIRIT the third person of the Holy Trinity
see ADVOCATE, COUNSELOR
Luke 11:13 *give the **H** to those*.................1398
2 Cor 5:5 *he has given us his **H**.*...............1632
Eph 1:13 ***H**, whom he promised*...............1705
Eph 4:30 *sorrow to God's **H***.......................1712
1 Thes 4:8 *gives his **H** to you*...................1584

HOME (n) one's place of residence; place of origin, destiny, or comfort; family-style social unit
see also DWELLING, HOUSE
Deut 11:19 *when you are at **h** and*.............301
1 Chr 16:43 *turned and went **h** to bless*......495
Ps 46:4 *God, the sacred **h** of the Most*........851
Prov 3:33 *but he blesses the **h** of the*..........635
Prov 27:8 *person who strays from **h***...........842
Matt 10:11 *stay in his **h** until you leave*......1358
Luke 10:7 *move around from **h***...............1394
Luke 19:9 *has come to this **h** today,*............1426
John 14:2 *in my Father's **h**. If this*.............1461
John 14:23 *make our **h** with each*...............1462
Acts 16:15 *come and stay at my **h**.*...........1574
Rom 16:5 *meets in their **h**. Greet my*........1672
Eph 3:17 *will make his **h** in your*...............1709
1 Tim 5:4 *show godliness at **h***...................1733
Heb 13:14 *not our permanent **h**; we are*...1782
1 Pet 4:9 *share your **h** with those who*.......1754

HOMELAND (n) area set aside to be a state for a people of a particular national, cultural, or racial origin
2 Sam 7:10 *And I will provide a **h** for my*......495

HOMETOWN (n) the city or town where one was born or grew up
Matt 13:57 *in his own **h** and among his*....1356
Luke 4:24 *is accepted in his own **h**.*...........1357
John 4:44 *is not honored in his own **h**.*......1307

HOMOSEXUALITY (n) erotic activity with another of the same sex
1 Cor 6:9 *prostitutes, or practice **h**,*..........1603
1 Tim 1:10 *or who practice **h**, or are*..........1728

HONEST (adj) truthful; genuine; reputable; marked by integrity
Exod 18:21 *some capable, **h** men*..............167
2 Kgs 12:15 *were **h** and trustworthy*...........757
Ps 37:37 *those who are **h** and good,*..........568
Prov 12:17 *An **h** witness tells*.....................645
Prov 28:6 *Better to be poor and **h** than*.......843
Jer 5:1 *even one just and **h** person,*............965
Matt 22:16 *we know how **h** you are*...........1439
1 Thes 2:10 *devout and **h** and faultless*.....1582

HONESTY (n) fairness and straightforwardness of conduct; sincerity
Ps 51:6 *But you desire **h** from the*..............506
Prov 11:5 *are directed by **h**; the wicked*......643
Jer 5:3 *searching for **h**. You struck*.............965

HONEY (n) a sweet liquid substance produced by bees; symbolic of abundance or delight in God's word
Exod 3:8 *with milk and **h**—the land*............144
1 Sam 14:26 *They didn't dare touch the **h***...444
Ps 19:10 *sweeter than **h**, even **h***..............555
Ps 119:103 *they are sweeter than **h**.*..........880
Isa 7:15 *eating yogurt and **h**.*.......................790
Rev 10:9 *be sweet as **h** in your mouth,*.....1816

HONEYCOMB (n) a mass of hexagonal wax cells in a honeybee nest that stores honey
Song 5:1 *and eat **h** with my honey.*.............667

HONOR, HONORS (n) having a renowned reputation or social standing; physical or spiritual blessing (from God); a showing of merited respect
Ps 8:5 *crowned them with glory and **h**.*........548
Ps 104:1 *are robed with **h** and majesty.*.......867
Prov 3:35 *The wise inherit **h**, but fools*........635
Prov 15:33 *humility precedes **h**.*.................650
Prov 25:27 *not good to seek **h-s***...................840
Isa 53:12 *I will give him the **h-s** of a*...........941
Isa 55:13 *will bring great **h** to the*..............942
Luke 14:8 *don't sit in the seat of **h**.*..........1408
Eph 1:20 *the place of **h** at God's right*.......1706
Heb 13:4 *Give **h** to marriage,*.....................1782
1 Pet 2:6 *chosen for great **h**, and*............1750
1 Pet 2:12 *they will give **h** to God when*....1751
1 Pet 3:7 *husbands must give **h** to*............1753
2 Pet 1:17 *when he received **h** and glory*..1758
Rev 4:9 *give glory and **h** and thanks*..........1808
Rev 19:7 *and let us give **h** to him.*............1827

HONOR, HONORED, HONORING, HONORS (v) of God, to reverence his majesty; of man, to respect or esteem; to confer honor upon
Exod 20:12 ***H** your father and mother*.........169
1 Kgs 8:43 *Temple I have built **h-s***.............620
Neh 1:11 *who delight in **h-ing** you.*...........1204
Ps 29:1 ***H** the* L*ORD*, *you*...............................562
Ps 45:11 ***h** him, for he is your* L*ORD*. 851
Ps 46:10 *I will be **h-ed** by every nation*.......852
Ps 47:9 *He is highly **h-ed** everywhere*.......852
Prov 14:31 *helping the poor **h-s** him.*..........648
Isa 66:5 *the* L*ORD* *be **h-ed!***.................................953
Matt 15:4 *God says, '**H** your father and*.....1369
Mark 6:4 *A prophet is **h-ed** everywhere*....1357
Luke 16:15 *What this world **h-s***...............1412
John 5:23 *that everyone will **h** the Son,*.......1318
John 12:26 *the Father will **h** anyone who*..1434
Rom 12:10 *delight in **h-ing** each other.*......1667
Rom 13:3 *and they will **h** you.*....................1668
1 Cor 6:20 *So you must **h** God with your*...1604
1 Cor 12:26 *if one part is **h-ed**, all the*.....1615
Eph 6:2 ***H** your father and mother*..............1714
Col 1:10 *the way you live will always **h***......1694
1 Thes 5:12 *and sisters, **h** those who are*..1585
2 Thes 1:12 *be **h-ed** along with him*..........1588
Titus 2:3 *a way that **h-s** God*......................1738

HONORABLE (adj) characterized by integrity; upright
Rom 12:17 *everyone can see you are **h**.*...1668
2 Cor 8:21 *to see that we are **h**.*................1637
Phil 4:8 *is true, and **h**, and right,*................1725
1 Pet 2:12 *will see your **h** behavior,*..........1751

HOOKS (n) poles bearing curved blades for pruning plants
Isa 2:4 *into pruning **h**. Nation will*...............825
Joel 3:10 *your pruning **h** into spears*..........1243
Mic 4:3 *into pruning **h**. Nation will*...............907

HOPE, HOPES (n) confident trust with the expectation of fulfillment
1 Sam 9:20 *focus of all Israel's **h-s**.*.............436
Job 31:16 *crushed the **h-s** of widows?*.......121
Ps 10:17 L*ORD*, *you know the **h-s** of the*.......858
Ps 42:5 *I will put my **h** in God!*...................848
Ps 112:10 *slink away, their **h-s** thwarted*....873
Ps 119:49 *to me; it is my only **h**.*...................879
Ps 119:74 *I have put my **h** in your word*......879
Prov 10:24 *the **h-s** of the godly will be*.......643
Prov 13:12 ***H** deferred makes the heart*.......646
Zech 9:12 *prisoners who still have **h**!*........1175
Rom 5:4 *our confident **h** of salvation*.........1654
Rom 8:20 *curse. But with eager **h**,*............1659
Rom 12:12 *Rejoice in our confident **h**.*.......1667
Rom 15:4 *give us **h** and encouragement*...1671
Rom 15:13 *God, the source of **h**, will*.........1671
1 Cor 13:13 *faith, **h**, and love—*...............1616
1 Cor 15:19 *And if our **h** in Christ is*..........1620
Eph 2:12 *without God and without **h**.*.........1708
1 Thes 1:3 *and the enduring **h** you have*...1580
1 Tim 4:10 *struggle, for our **h** is in the*......1732
Heb 10:23 *wavering to the **h** we affirm,*.....1776
1 Pet 3:15 *about your Christian **h**,*.............1753

HOPE (v) to desire with expectation of obtainment
Rom 8:24 *don't need to **h** for it*..................1660

HOPEFUL (adj) full of or inclined to hope
1 Cor 13:7 *is always **h**, and endures*.........1616

HORN, HORNS (n) a bony material arising from the head of many animals; a projection on the four corners of the altar in the tabernacle and Temple; a symbol of power and might
Exod 19:13 *when the ram's **h** sounds a* 168
Exod 27:2 *so that the **h-s** and altar are*.......177
Judg 7:19 *blew the rams' **h-s** and broke*....385
Dan 7:8 *This little **h** had eyes*..................1135
Dan 7:24 *Its ten **h-s** are ten kings*...........1136
Amos 2:2 *and the ram's **h** sounds.*............771
Zech 9:14 *sound the ram's **h** and attack*...1176
Rev 5:6 *He had seven **h-s** and seven*........1809
Rev 12:3 *heads and ten **h-s,** with seven*...1818
Rev 13:1 *heads and ten **h-s,** with ten*.......1819
Rev 17:3 *and ten **h-s,** and blasphemies*....1824

HORROR (n) painful and intense fear, dread, or aversion
Jer 2:12 *shrink back in **h** and dismay,*.........960

HORSE (n) a large solid-hoofed herbivorous mammal often used for working or riding
Ps 147:10 *strength of a **h** or in human*.....1155
Prov 26:3 *Guide a **h** with a*.........................841
Zech 1:8 *on a red **h** that was standing*......1166
Rev 6:2 *saw a white **h** standing there.* 1811
Rev 6:4 *Then another **h** appeared,*...........1811
Rev 6:5 *saw a black **h,** and its rider*.........1811
Rev 6:8 *and saw a **h** whose color was* 1811
Rev 19:11 *and a white **h** was standing* 1828

HOSANNA (KJV)
Matt 21:9 ***Praise God** in highest heaven!*..1429
Matt 21:15 ***Praise God** for the Son of David*...1432
Mark 11:9 ***Praise God!** Blessings on the*...1430
Mark 11:10 ***Praise God** in highest heaven*...1430
John 12:13 ***Praise God!** Blessings on the*...1431

HOSPITALITY (n) generous and cordial treatment, reception, or disposition
Matt 25:38 *and show you **h?***...................1453
Luke 10:7 *Don't hesitate to accept **h,*** 1394
Rom 12:13 *be eager to practice **h.*** 1667

HOSTILE (adj) openly opposed or resisting
Rom 8:7 *nature is always **h** to God.* 1659

HOSTILITY (n) deep-seated ill will; enmity
Gen 3:15 *I will cause **h** between you*............13
Lev 26:28 *I will give full vent to my **h.*** 235
Gal 5:20 *sorcery, **h,** quarreling,*.................1566
Eph 2:14 *the wall of **h** that separated* 1708
Eph 2:16 *our **h** toward each other was*......1708
Heb 12:3 *of all the **h** he endured from* 1780

HOUR (n) a (short) unit or passage of time; moment
John 12:27 *save me from this **h**'?*...........1434
John 13:1 *knew that his **h** had come*........1455
John 17:1 *Father, the **h** has come*............1466

HOUSE, HOUSES (n) living quarters; a family including ancestors, descendants, and kindred extended family unit, including ancestors and descendants
see also DWELLING, DYNASTY, HOME, TEMPLE
Exod 12:22 *doorframes of your **h-s.*** 156
Exod 12:27 *he passed over the **h-s** of the*...156
Exod 20:17 *your neighbor's **h.***....................170
2 Sam 7:11 *he will make a **h** for you—*......495
Ps 23:6 *live in the **h** of the LORD* 558
Ps 27:4 *to live in the **h** of the LORD*.............561
Ps 69:9 *for your **h** has consumed me,* 577
Ps 127:1 *Unless the LORD builds a **h,*** 631
Isa 54:2 *Enlarge your **h;** build an*................941
Amos 5:11 *beautiful stone **h-s,** you will*......775
Matt 7:24 *who builds a **h** on solid rock*......1335
Matt 19:29 *given up **h-s** or brothers or*.....1421
Mark 11:17 *be called a **h** of prayer for*......1432
John 2:17 *for God's **h** will consume me.* ...1300

HOUSEHOLD (n) a social unit composed of those living together in the same dwelling; family
see also FAMILY
Exod 12:3 *one animal for each **h.*** 155
Acts 16:31 *everyone in your **h.***................1576
1 Tim 3:5 *manage his own **h,***......................1730
1 Tim 3:12 *children and **h** well.* 1731
1 Tim 3:15 *themselves in the **h** of God.*......1731
1 Pet 4:17 *begin with God's **h.***...................1755

HOUSETOPS (n) roofs
Matt 10:27 *shout from the **h** for all to* 1360

HUMAN (adj) of, relating to, or characteristic of men and women collectively; mortal; finite
see also FLESH
Gen 1:26 *Let us make **h** beings in our* 8
Gen 3:22 *Look, the **h** beings have*..................13
Gen 9:6 *If anyone takes a **h** life,* 21
Ps 9:20 *they are merely **h.***........................550
Ps 33:13 *sees the whole **h** race.* 858
Ps 89:47 *futile this **h** existence!*..................592
John 1:14 *So the Word became **h.***............1271
John 2:24 *because he knew **h** nature.* 1300
John 8:15 *judge me by **h** standards,*..........1392
Rom 6:19 *weakness of your **h** nature,*.......1656
1 Cor 2:5 *trust not in **h** wisdom but in*.......1598
1 Cor 2:13 *come from **h** wisdom.* 1598
2 Cor 3:3 *of stone, but on **h** hearts.*..........1629
2 Cor 10:3 *We are **h,** but we*.....................1638
Gal 3:3 *by your own **h** effort?* 1560
Col 2:9 *of God in a **h** body.*........................1698
1 Thes 2:13 *words as mere **h** ideas.*..........1582
Heb 7:28 *limited by **h** weakness.*..............1771
2 Pet 1:21 *or from **h** initiative.*...................1758

HUMAN, HUMANS (n) a homo sapien; mankind
Gen 6:3 *Spirit will not put up with **h-s***...........17
Isa 2:22 *trust in mere **h-s.** They are as*.......826
Jer 17:5 *trust in mere **h-s,** who rely on*.....1021

HUMANITY (n) the quality or state of being human; the human race
Job 14:1 *How frail is **h!** How short*..............108
Zech 2:13 *Be silent before the LORD, all **h,*** 1167

HUMBLE (adj) not proud or haughty; can imply lower social or economic status; meek or gentle
Num 12:3 *Moses was very **h**—*.....................249
Ps 138:6 *cares for the **h,** but he keeps*.......585
Ps 149:4 *he crowns the **h** with victory.*.........887
Zech 9:9 *yet he is **h,** riding on a* 1175
Matt 5:5 *those who are **h,***...........................1326
Matt 11:29 *I am **h** and gentle at*..............1339
Matt 21:5 *He is **h,** riding on a*....................1429
Eph 4:2 *Always be **h** and gentle.*..............1710
Phil 2:3 *Be **h,** thinking of*...........................1719
Jas 4:6 *but favors the **h.***...........................1551
1 Pet 3:8 *and keep a **h** attitude.* 1753

HUMBLE, HUMBLED, HUMBLES (v) to not think too highly of oneself; to bring low or prostrate
Isa 26:5 *He **h-s** the proud and*...................896
Luke 14:11 *themselves will be **h-d,***..........1408
Luke 18:14 *will be **h-d,** and those who*.....1418
2 Cor 11:7 *wrong when I **h-d** myself* 1640
Phil 2:8 *he **h-d** himself in obedience* 1720
Jas 1:10 *that God has **h-d** them*..............1547
Jas 4:10 ***H** yourselves before the Lord,* 1552
1 Pet 5:6 *So **h** yourselves under*..............1756

HUMBLY (adv) in an unhaughty, unproud manner; in an insignificant or unpretentious manner
Zeph 2:3 *and to live **h.** Perhaps even*..........984
Acts 20:19 *I have done the Lord's work **h***...1675
1 Tim 5:10 *served other believers **h?***........1733

HUMILIATE, HUMILIATED (v) to shame or mortify
Deut 21:14 *for you have **h-ed** her*..............311
2 Sam 22:28 *watch the proud and **h*** 526
Ps 18:27 *but you **h** the proud*.....................528

HUMILIATION (n) shame, mortification, disgrace, dishonor
Job 19:5 *using my **h** as evidence* 112
Ps 44:15 *the constant **h;** shame is* 850
Prov 29:23 *ends in **h,** while humility*..........845

HUMILITY (n) show of meekness; quality of being humble
Prov 11:2 *but with **h** comes wisdom.*..........643
Prov 15:33 ***h** precedes honor.* 650
Prov 22:4 *True **h** and fear* 659
Col 3:12 *kindness, **h,** gentleness,* 1700
Jas 3:13 *works with the **h** that comes* 1550
1 Pet 5:5 *each other in **h,** for "God* 1756

HUNDRED (n) the number 100
Matt 13:8 *and even a **h** times as much as* ..1345
Luke 8:8 *that was a **h** times as much as*...1346

HUNG (v) to suspend
see also HANG
Deut 21:23 *anyone who is **h** is cursed*........311
Luke 19:48 *all the people **h** on every word*..1432
Gal 3:13 *When he was **h** on the cross,*.......1561

HUNGER (n) a craving or urgent need for food
Ps 145:16 *you satisfy the **h** and thirst*........590

HUNGRY (adj) feeling a strong desire for food; a craving for anything
Prov 25:21 *If your enemies are **h,***...............840
Matt 15:32 *to send them away **h,***............1372
Matt 25:35 *For I was **h,** and you fed me*....1453
Luke 1:53 *He has filled the **h** with good* 1276
Luke 6:21 *you who are **h** now, for you* 1326
John 6:35 *never be **h** again*......................1367
Rom 8:35 *or are persecuted, or **h,** or*........1661
Rom 12:20 *enemies are **h,** feed them*.......1668
Rev 7:16 *never again be **h** or thirsty;* 1813

HUNT, HUNTED (v) to pursue with intent to capture
Ps 119:86 *from those who **h** me* 880
2 Cor 4:9 *We are **h-ed** down,*....................1631

HURT, HURTING, HURTS (v) to wound, injure, or damage
1 Chr 16:22 *and do not **h** my prophets.* 493
Ps 15:4 *promises even when it **h-s.*** 552
Eccl 8:9 *the power to **h** each other*..............680
Lam 3:33 *he does not enjoy **h-ing** people* 1098
Matt 4:6 *you won't even **h** your foot on*.....1295
Mark 16:18 *it won't **h** them*......................1498

HUSBAND, HUSBANDS (n) male partner in a marriage; head of family; protector and provider; figurative of Christ
Ruth 1:8 *kindness to your **h-s** and to me.* ...410
Prov 12:4 *is a crown for her **h,*** 644
Prov 31:28 *Her **h** praises her:*.....................848
Jer 3:20 *wife who leaves her **h.***..................963
Rom 7:2 *binds her to her **h** as long as* 1657
1 Cor 7:3 *The **h** should fulfill* 1605

1 Cor 7:10 *not leave her **h.*** 1605
1 Cor 7:39 *is bound to her **h** as long as*....1607
2 Cor 11:2 *bride to one **h**—Christ.*............1640
Gal 4:27 *lives with her **h!***........................1564
Eph 5:22 *submit to your **h-s** as to the*.......1713
Eph 5:23 *For a **h** is the head*...................1713
Eph 5:25 *For **h-s,** this means*...................1713
Eph 5:28 *same way, **h-s** ought to love*......1714
Col 3:18 *submit to your **h-s,** as is* 1701
Col 3:19 ***H-s,** love your*..........................1701
1 Tim 5:9 *faithful to her **h.***.......................1733
Titus 2:4 *to love their **h-s** and their*...........1738
1 Pet 3:1 *the authority of your **h-s.***...........1752
1 Pet 3:7 *same way, you **h-s** must give* 1753

HYMN, HYMNS (n) a song of praise to God
Ps 40:3 *to sing, a **h** of praise to our*...........570
Matt 26:30 *they sang a **h** and went out* 1457
Mark 14:26 *they sang a **h** and went out*....1458
Acts 16:25 *praying and singing **h-s***..........1576
Eph 5:19 *psalms and **h-s** and spiritual* 1713
Col 3:16 *psalms and **h-s** and spiritual* 1701

HYPOCRISY (n) feigning to be what one is not; pretense of piety
Matt 23:28 *your hearts are filled with **h*** 1445
Mark 12:15 *saw through their **h***.............1439
Gal 2:13 *followed Peter's **h,** and even*.......1559
Gal 2:13 *led astray by their **h.***.................1559
1 Pet 2:1 *all deceit, **h,** jealousy,*..............1750

HYPOCRITE, HYPOCRITES (n) a person who portrays a false appearance of religion; a pretender
Matt 6:16 *make it obvious, as the **h-s*** 1332
Matt 7:5 ***H!** First get rid of the log*............1333
Matt 23:13 *and you Pharisees. **H-s!***.........1444
Luke 6:42 *the log in your own eye? **H!***......1333
Luke 13:15 *Lord replied, "You **h-s!***...........1403
1 Tim 4:2 *These people are **h-s** and liars,*...1732

HYSSOP (n) an aromatic shrub of the species of marjoram and a member of the mint family that has clusters of yellow flowers
Exod 12:22 *Brush the **h** across the*............156
John 19:29 *put it on a **h** branch, and held it*...1486

IDEAS (n) formulated thoughts or opinions; notions or concepts
Ps 73:20 *you will laugh at their silly **i***..........594
Ps 81:12 *living according to their own **i.*** 602

IDENTIFY, IDENTIFIED (v) to establish the distinguishing character or personality of; to relate to in solidarity
Matt 7:16 *You can **i** them by their fruit,*.....1334
Matt 12:33 *A tree is **i-ied** by its fruit*..........1341
Eph 1:13 *believed in Christ, he **i-ied** you* ..1705

IDLE (adj) not employed or useful for work; inactive, lazy
2 Thes 3:6 *believers who live **i** lives*..........1590
2 Thes 3:7 *not **i** when we were with you.* ..1590
2 Thes 3:11 *you are living **i** lives,*.............1590

IDLENESS (n) a state of unemployment, inactivity, or laziness
Prov 19:15 *but **i** leaves them hungry*...........655
Eccl 10:18 ***i** leads to a leaky house*.............682

IDOL, IDOLS (n) a representation or symbol of a false god
Exod 20:4 *make for yourself an **i***................168
Deut 27:15 *who carves or casts an **i***...........316
1 Sam 15:23 *as bad as worshiping **i-s.***.......446
Isa 40:19 *Can he be compared to an **i***........924
Isa 44:9 *who worship **i-s** don't know*..........930
Isa 44:15 *makes an **i** and bows down*.........930
Isa 44:17 *and makes his god: a carved **i!***....930
Isa 44:19 *who made the **i** never stops to*.....930
Hab 2:18 *What good is an **i** carved*.............981
Acts 15:20 *eating food offered to **i-s,***.......1570
Rom 1:23 *worshiped **i-s** made to look*......1647
1 Cor 6:9 *or who worship **i-s,** or commit*...1603
1 Cor 8:1 *has been offered to **i-s.*** 1607
1 Cor 8:4 *an **i** is not really a god*..............1607
Rev 2:14 *sin by eating food offered to **i-s***....1804

IDOLATER (n) worshiper of idols; one who worships an undeserving object blindly
Eph 5:5 *a greedy person is an **i,***..............1712
Col 3:5 *a greedy person is an **i,***...............1700

IDOLATRY (n) the worship of a physical object as a god; immoderate attachment or devotion to something
Gal 5:20 *pleasures, **i,** sorcery,*.................1566

IGNORANT (adj) resulting from or showing lack of knowledge, comprehension, or intelligence; unaware, uninformed
Job 38:2 *questions my wisdom with such **i***...127
Heb 5:2 *with **i** and wayward people*..........1767
1 Pet 2:15 *lives should silence those **i***......1751
2 Pet 3:16 *are **i** and unstable have twisted*..1760

IGNORE (v) to refuse to take notice of
Ps 9:12 *He does not **i** the cries of*.............549
Ps 9:17 *all the nations who **i** God.* 550
Ps 10:12 *Do not **i** the helpless!*...............857
Prov 13:18 *If you **i** criticism,*......................646
Heb 2:3 *if we **i** this great salvation*............1763

ILL-TEMPERED (adj) having a cross or surly disposition; quarrelsome
1 Sam 25:17 *He's so **i** that no*..................466

ILLEGITIMATE (adj) not recognized as lawful offspring
Heb 12:8 *means that you are **i** and*............1780

ILLUMINATES (v) to supply or brighten with light
Rev 21:23 *the glory of God **i** the city,* 1831

IMAGE (n) a God-given likeness or reflection; a tangible or visible representation
Gen 1:26 *make human beings in our **i,*** 8
Gen 1:27 *human beings in his own **i.***...........8
Gen 9:6 *made human beings in his own **i.***.....21
Col 1:15 *Christ is the visible **i** of the*..........1694
Jas 3:9 *made in the **i** of God.*...................1550

IMAGINE, IMAGINED (v) to form a mental image of; to suppose or guess
Gen 6:5 ***i-d** was consistently and totally*........17
Job 37:5 *can't even **i** the greatness*............127
1 Cor 2:9 *no mind has **i-ed** what God has* ..1598

IMITATE, IMITATED (v) to follow as a pattern, model, or example; to resemble; to mimic
1 Cor 4:16 *I urge you to **i** me*...................1601
1 Cor 11:1 *should **i** me, just as I **i***............1611
1 Thes 1:6 *you **i-d** both us and the Lord*...1581
1 Thes 2:14 *you **i-d** the believers*............1582
2 Thes 3:7 *that you ought to **i** us.* 1590

IMMANUEL (n) Hebrew name meaning "God is with us"
Isa 7:14 *to a son and will call him **I.***............790
Isa 8:8 *one end to the other, O **I.***...............791
Matt 1:23 *a son, and they will call him **I,***...1278

IMMATURE (adj) lacking complete growth, development, or maturity
Eph 4:14 *no longer be **i** like children.*.........1711

IMMORAL (adj) characterized by conflicting with traditionally (biblically) held moral principles; sinful or impure
Prov 2:16 *save you from the **i** woman,*........634
Prov 6:24 *keep you from the **i** woman,*........638
Prov 22:14 *an **i** woman is a dangerous*.......660
Luke 7:37 *a certain **i** woman from*...........1340
Rom 13:13 *promiscuity and **i** living,*...........1669
Eph 5:5 *be sure that no **i,** impure,*............1712
1 Tim 1:10 *people who are sexually **i,***.......1728
Jude 1:4 *grace allows us to live **i** lives.* 1784
Rev 22:15 *the sorcerers, the sexually **i,***.....1832

IMMORALITY (n) the quality or state of being immoral; an immoral act or practice
Matt 15:19 *all sexual **i,** theft, lying,*...........1370
Acts 15:29 *animals, and from sexual **i.*** 1571
1 Cor 6:13 *made for sexual **i.***..................1604
1 Cor 6:18 ***i** is a sin against*......................1604
1 Cor 7:2 *there is so much sexual **i,***...........1605
Gal 5:19 *very clear: sexual **i,** impurity,*.......1566
2 Pet 2:7 *who was sick of the shameful **i***..1759
Jude 1:7 *towns, which were filled with **i***....1784

IMMORTAL (adj) exempt from death; imperishable
1 Cor 15:53 *transformed into **i** bodies*.......1622

IMMORTALITY (n) unending existence; lasting fame
Rom 2:7 *and honor and **i***...........................1649
2 Tim 1:10 *the way to life and **i***................1741

IMMOVABLE (adj) incapable of being moved; steadfast, unyielding
1 Cor 15:58 *be strong and **i.** Always work*...1622

IMPALED (v) to torture or kill by fixing on a sharp stake
Esth 7:10 *they **i** Haman on the pole*..........1191

IMPARTIAL (adj) not partial or biased; treating all equally
Deut 1:17 *and **i** in your judgments.*.............285
Matt 22:16 ***i** and don't play favorites.*........1439

IMPATIENT (adj) restless or short of temper especially under irritation, delay, or opposition
Zech 11:8 *I became **i** with these sheep,*....1177

IMPORTANT (adj) marked by or indicative of significant worth or consequence
Matt 23:23 *ignore the more **i** aspects of*...1444
Matt 23:23 *do not neglect the more **i***........1444
Mark 12:29 *The most **i** commandment*.....1441
Mark 12:33 *I know it is **i** to love him*.........1442
1 Cor 7:19 *The **i** thing is to keep God's*.....1606
1 Cor 15:3 *what was most **i** and what*.......1618
Gal 5:6 *What is **i** is faith expressing*..........1565

IMPOSSIBLE (adj) incapable of being or occurring
Zech 8:6 *this may seem **i** to you now,*.......1173
Luke 1:37 *For nothing is **i** with God.*..........1274
Heb 6:4 *it is **i** to bring back*......................1768
Heb 11:6 *it is **i** to please God*...................1777

IMPOSTORS (n) those who assume false identity or title for the purpose of deception
2 Cor 6:8 *are honest, but they call us **i.***.....1633
2 Tim 3:13 *evil people and **i** will flourish*....1744

IMPRESS, IMPRESSED (v) to gain the admiration or interest of
Dan 1:19 ***i-ed** him as much as Daniel,*......1002
Phil 2:3 *don't try to **i** others. Be humble*....1719

IMPRESSION (n) an often indistinct or imprecise notion or remembrance
Luke 19:11 *correct the **i** that the Kingdom*.........1426

IMPRESSIVE (adj) having the power to excite attention, awe, or admiration
Ps 107:24 *his **i** works on the deepest seas*. . .872

IMPURE (adj) ritually unclean; lewd, unchaste
Acts 11:8 *have declared **i** or unclean*........1535
Eph 5:5 *no immoral, **i**, or greedy person*....1712
1 Thes 2:3 *with any deceit or **i** motives*.....1581
1 Thes 4:7 *live holy lives, not **i** lives*. 1584

IMPURITY, IMPURITIES (n) something that is impure or makes something else impure; the quality or state of being impure
Prov 25:4 *Remove the **i-ies** from silver,* 839
Gal 5:19 *clear: sexual immorality, **i**,* 1566
Col 3:5 *to do with sexual immorality, **i**,* 1700

INCENSE (n) material used to produce a fragrant odor when burned
Exod 30:1 *acacia wood for burning **i**.* 181
Exod 30:38 *Anyone who makes **i***...............183
Exod 40:5 *Place the gold **i** altar*...................195
Ps 141:2 *Accept my prayer as **i** offered*......588
Heb 9:4 *In that room were a gold **i** altar*....1772
Rev 5:8 *held gold bowls filled with **i**,*.........1810
Rev 8:3 *great amount of **i** was given*.........1813
Rev 8:4 *smoke of the **i**, mixed with the* 1813

INCORRUPTIBLE (KJV)
1 Cor 15:52 *will be raised **to live forever**.*...............1622
1 Pet 1:4 *beyond the reach of change and **decay**.*...............1748

INCREASE, INCREASED, INCREASES (v) to become progressively greater (as in size, amount, number, or intensity)
1 Sam 2:10 *he **i-s** the strength of his anointed*..........................419
Ps 62:10 *if your wealth **i-s**, don't* 574
Luke 17:5 *Show us how to **i** our faith*........1413
Acts 6:7 *number of believers greatly **i-d*** 1523

INCREDIBLE (adj) too extraordinary and improbable to be believed; amazing, extraordinary
Acts 26:8 *does it seem **i** to any of you* 1685
Eph 2:7 *examples of the **i** wealth of*..........1707

INCURABLE (adj) unlikely to be changed or corrected
Jer 30:12 *Your injury is **i**—a terrible*.........1031

INDEPENDENT (adj) not requiring or relying on others; not subject to control by others
1 Cor 11:11 *women are not **i** of men,* 1612
1 Cor 11:11 *men are not **i** of women*. 1612

INDULGE, INDULGED, INDULGES (v) to take unrestrained pleasure in
Rom 1:26 ***i-d** in sex with each other*. 1648
Rom 13:14 *ways to **i** your evil desires*.......1669
1 Cor 5:9 *people who **i** in sexual sin*. 1602
1 Cor 5:11 *claims to be a believer yet **i-s***..1602

INEXPRESSIBLE (adj) not capable of being expressed; indescribable
1 Pet 1:8 *rejoice with a glorious, **i** joy*........1749

INFANTS (n) a child in the first period of (physical or spiritual) life
Ps 8:2 *and **i** to tell of your strength,* 548
Matt 21:16 *and **i** to give you praise*............1432
1 Cor 3:1 *were **i** in the Christian life*..........1599

INFINITE (adj) subject to no limitation or external determination
Phil 3:8 *compared with the **i** value*...........1722

INFLUENCE, INFLUENCED (v) to sway; to affect or modify
Luke 20:21 ***i-d** by what others think*.........1439
3 Jn 1:11 *bad example **i** you*. 1797

INFLUENTIAL (adj) exerting or possessing the power or capacity of causing an effect in indirect ways
Ruth 2:1 *there was a wealthy and **i** man* 411

INHERIT, INHERITED (v) to receive as a legacy or promise; to take possession as a rightful heir
Matt 5:5 *they will **i** the whole earth*. 1326
Matt 25:34 ***i** the Kingdom prepared*..........1453
Mark 10:17 *I do to **i** eternal life?*..............1421
1 Cor 6:9 *will not **i** the Kingdom* 1603
Eph 3:6 *share equally in the riches **i-ed***....1708
Eph 5:5 *impure, or greedy person will **i***.....1712
Rev 21:7 *All who are victorious will **i***.........1830

INHERITANCE (n) the acquisition of a possession, condition, or trait from past generations; something that is or may be inherited
Ps 16:6 *What a wonderful **i**!*......................553
Ps 33:12 *people he has chosen as his **i**.* 858
Ps 61:5 *an **i** reserved for those who* 573
Gal 4:30 *will not share the **i*** 1565
Eph 1:14 *give us the **i** he promised*..........1706
Col 3:24 *give you an **i** as your reward,* 1702
Heb 9:15 *receive the eternal **i** God has* 1773

INIQUITY, INIQUITIES (KJV)
Ps 51:9 *Remove the stain of my **guilt***.........506
Isa 6:7 *your **guilt** is removed,*........................784
Isa 53:6 *laid on him the **sins** of us all*..........940
1 Cor 13:6 *not rejoice about **injustice*** 1616
Rev 18:5 *God remembers her **evil deeds***..1825

INJURE, INJURED (v) to do an injustice to; to harm or impair
Prov 8:36 *who miss me **i** themselves*..........641
Ezek 34:16 *I will bandage the **i-ed** and*.....1110
Zech 11:16 *nor heal the **i-ed**, nor feed*.....1178

INJUSTICE (n) unfairness; wrongs
1 Cor 6:7 *accept the **i** and leave it*............1603
1 Cor 13:6 *It does not rejoice about **i***........1616

INK (n) a colored, usually liquid, material for writing and printing
2 Cor 3:3 *is written not with pen and **i**,* 1629

INNOCENCE (n) freedom from guilt or sin through being unacquainted with evil; blamelessness
Gen 20:5 *I acted in complete **i**!* 42
2 Sam 22:25 *He has seen my **i**.* 526
Hos 8:5 *will you be incapable of **i**?* 811

INNOCENT (adj) regarded as righteous; free from guilt or sin; unaware or ignorant
Job 13:18 *I will be proved **i**.*.......................107
Job 34:5 *Job also said, 'I am **i**,*..................124
Ps 7:8 *for I am **i**, O Most High!*...................523
Ps 26:1 *Declare me **i**, O Lord, for I*............560
Ps 143:2 *no one is **i** before you*. 588
Matt 27:4 *I have betrayed an **i** man*. 1475
Matt 27:24 *I am **i** of this man's blood*........1478
Rom 16:18 *they deceive **i** people*.............1673

INQUIRE (v) to ask about or look into
Deut 12:30 *Do not **i** about their gods,* 302
Deut 32:7 ***I** of your elders* 323
1 Chr 21:30 *to go there to **i** of God*............532

INSIGHT (n) the power or act of seeing into a situation; discernment
Ps 19:8 *are clear, giving **i** for living*. 554
Prov 7:4 *make **i** a beloved member*............639
Eph 1:17 *and **i** so that you might grow*......1706

INSOLENCE (n) the quality or state of being overbearing or impudent
1 Tim 1:13 *In my **i**, I persecuted his people*. 1728

INSPECT (v) to view closely in critical appraisal
Prov 31:16 *She goes to **i** a field*..................847

INSPIRATION (n) guidance by divine influence
Matt 22:43 *under the **i** of the Spirit*..........1442

INSPIRED (adj) Influenced, moved; guided or created by divine influence
2 Tim 3:16 *All Scripture is **i** by God*...........1745

INSTINCT, INSTINCTS (n) a natural or inherent aptitude, impulse, or capacity
2 Pet 2:12 *creatures of **i**, born to be caught*...............1759
Jude 1:10 *whatever their **i-s** tell them,* 1785
Jude 1:19 *They follow their natural **i-s***......1785

INSTITUTED (v) to originate and get established; to set going
Rom 13:2 *against what God has **i**,*............1668

INSTRUCT, INSTRUCTED, INSTRUCTS (v) to provide with authoritative information or advice; to teach, train, or direct
Exod 4:12 *I will **i** you in what to say*............145
Deut 2:1 *just as the Lord had **i-ed** me,*........286
Deut 4:36 *so he could **i** you*........................291
Josh 11:9 *chariots, as the Lord had **i-ed***....352
Josh 11:23 *as the Lord had **i-ed** Moses*.....353
Ps 105:22 *He could **i** the king's aides*.........869
Prov 9:9 ***I** the wise, and they will be*...........641
Prov 10:8 *The wise are glad to be **i-ed**,* 642
Prov 21:11 *if you **i** the wise,*.......................657
Acts 8:31 *unless someone **i-s** me?* 1529
2 Tim 2:25 *Gently **i** those who oppose* 1743
Titus 2:12 ***i-ed** to turn from godless living*.1738

INSTRUCTION, INSTRUCTIONS (n) a command or principle intended especially as a general rule of action; an order; directions; the action, practice, or profession of teaching
see also COMMANDMENT(S), LAW(S)
Exod 34:32 *Moses gave them all the **i-s***.....188
Deut 31:11 *you must read this Book of **I***.....322
Josh 1:7 *Be careful to obey all the **i-s***.........336
Josh 1:8 *Study this Book of **I***......................337
Ps 19:7 *The **i-s** of the Lord are perfect,*......554
Ps 40:8 ***i-s** are written on my heart*. 570
Ps 119:97 *Oh, how I love your **i-s**!* 880
Prov 4:13 *Take hold of my **i-s**;* 636
Prov 7:2 *Guard my **i-s** as you guard*...........639
Prov 8:33 *Listen to my **i** and be wise*. 641
Prov 23:12 *Commit yourself to **i**;* 661
Isa 40:14 *need **i** about what is good?*.........924
Jer 31:33 *put my **i-s** deep within* 1034
Zech 7:12 *they could not hear the **i-s***.......1173
1 Tim 1:5 *purpose of my **i** is that all*..........1727
1 Tim 1:18 *here are my **i-s** for you,* 1728

INSTRUMENT, INSTRUMENTS (n) a device used to produce music; one used by another as a means or aid; a means whereby something is achieved, performed, or furthered
Dan 3:7 *at the sound of the musical **i-s**,*...1005
Hab 3:19 *accompanied by stringed **i-s**.)* 982
Acts 9:15 *Saul is my chosen **i*** 1530
Rom 6:13 *part of your body become an **i***..1656

INSULT, INSULTS (n) a gross indignity
Job 20:3 *I've had to endure your **i-s**,* 113
Ps 69:7 *For I endure **i-s** for your sake;* 577
Ps 69:9 *the **i-s** of those who insult you* 577
Ps 69:20 *Their **i-s** have broken my heart,* ...578
Prov 9:7 *will get an **i** in return.* 641
Prov 22:10 *and **i-s** will disappear.* 660
Rom 15:3 *The **i-s** of those who insult you,* 1671
2 Cor 12:10 *and in the **i-s**, hardships,* 1642
Jude 1:15 *all the **i-s** that ungodly sinners* .1785

INSULT, INSULTED (v) to treat with insolence, indignity, or contempt
Prov 12:16 *stays calm when **i-ed**.* 645
Prov 20:20 ***i** your father or mother,* 657
Prov 30:9 *and thus **i** God's holy name.* 846
Heb 10:29 *have **i-ed** and disdained* 1776
1 Pet 2:23 *not retaliate when he was **i-ed**,* 1752
1 Pet 3:9 *insults when people **i** you.* 1753
1 Pet 4:14 *be happy when you are **i-ed*** 1755

INTEGRITY (n) honesty; without compromise or corruption
Job 2:3 *a man of complete **i**.* 96
Job 2:9 *still trying to maintain your **i**?* 96
Job 27:5 *I will defend my **i** until I die.* 117
Ps 25:21 *May **i** and honesty protect me,* 560
Ps 26:11 *I live with **i**. So redeem* 561
Ps 111:8 *faithfully and with **i**.* 873
Ps 119:1 *Joyful are people of **i**,* 876
Prov 2:7 *shield to those who walk with **i**.* 633
Prov 10:9 *People with **i** walk safely,* 642
Titus 2:7 *you do reflect the **i*** 1738

INTELLIGENCE (n) the ability to learn or understand; mental acuteness
Isa 29:14 *the **i** of the intelligent will* 898
1 Cor 1:19 *the **i** of the intelligent.* 1596

INTELLIGENT (adj) having or indicating a high or satisfactory degree of mental capacity
Job 32:8 *that makes them **i**.* 122
Prov 17:28 *mouths shut, they seem **i**.* 653

INTERCEDE, INTERCEDED (v) to mediate or plead another's case for justice or mercy
Isa 53:12 *of many and **i-d** for rebels.* 941
1 Tim 2:1 ***i** on their behalf, and* 1729
Heb 7:25 *lives forever to **i** with God* 1771

INTEREST, INTERESTS (n) a charge for borrowed money; the profit in goods or money that is made on invested capital; a feeling that accompanies or causes special attention to an object
Lev 25:36 *Do not charge **i** or make a profit* ...234
Deut 23:20 *You may charge **i** to foreigners,* ...313
Deut 23:20 *not charge **i** to Israelites,* 313
Neh 5:10 *stop this business of charging **i**.* .1210
Ps 15:5 *lend money without charging **i**,* 552
Prov 28:8 *Income from charging high **i*** 843
Matt 25:27 *I could have gotten some **i*** 1452
1 Cor 7:34 *His **i-s** are divided.* 1607
Phil 2:4 *look out only for your own **i-s**,* 1719

INTERMARRY, INTERMARRYING (v) to marry across a group boundaries
Deut 7:3 *You must not **i** with them.* 296
Ezra 9:14 ***i-ing** with people who* 1200

INTERPRET, INTERPRETS (v) to explain; to translate
Gen 41:15 *a dream you can **i** it.* 79
Matt 16:3 *how to **i** the weather* 1373
1 Cor 12:30 *to **i** unknown languages?* 1615
1 Cor 14:5 *unless someone **i-s** what you* 1617
1 Cor 14:13 ***i** what has been said.* 1617
1 Cor 14:26 *another will **i** what is said.* 1618
1 Cor 14:27 *must **i** what they say.* 1618
1 Cor 14:28 *is present who can **i**,* 1618

INTIMIDATED (v) to make timid or fearful
Phil 1:28 *Don't be **i** in any way* 1719

INVADED (v) to enter for conquest or plunder
2 Kgs 17:5 *king of Assyria **i** the entire* 818
2 Kgs 24:1 *Nebuchadnezzar of Babylon **i*** 994

INVENT (v) to devise by thinking; to find or discover
Rom 1:30 *They **i** new ways of sinning,* 1648

INVISIBLE (adj) hidden; imperceptible
Rom 1:20 *see his **i** qualities—* 1647
Col 1:15 *visible image of the **i** God* 1694
Heb 11:27 *his eyes on the one who is **i**.* 1778

INVITATION (n) an often formal request to be present or participate
1 Cor 10:27 *accept the **i** if you want to.* 1611

INVITE, INVITED (v) to request the presence or participation of; to welcome
Matt 25:35 *a stranger, and you **i-d** me* 1453
Luke 14:12 *For they will **i** you back,* 1408
Rev 19:9 *Blessed are those who are **i-d*** ...1828

IRON (n) metal used in instruments of war, farming, and building; symbolic of strength for both security and destruction
Ps 2:9 *break them with an **i** rod* 857
Prov 27:17 *As **i** sharpens **i**, so* 842
Dan 2:33 *its legs were **i**, and its feet* 1004
Rev 2:27 *rule the nations with an **i** rod* 1805
Rev 12:5 *nations with an **i** rod.* 1818
Rev 19:15 *rule them with an **i** rod.* 1828

IRRITABLE (adj) easily exasperated or excited
1 Cor 13:5 *It is not **i**, and it keeps* 1616

ISAAC Patriarch, son of Abraham; promised by God (Gen 17:16-22, p. 39; 18:14, p. 40); born (Gen 21:1-7, p. 43; 1 Chr 1:28, p. 1226; Acts 7:8, p. 1524); recipient of divine covenant (Gen 17:21, p. 39; 26:2-5, p. 52); offered to God by Abraham (Gen 22:1-19, p. 45; Heb 11:17-19, p. 1778); took Rebekah as wife (Gen 24:67, p. 50); inherited wealth (Gen 25:5, p. 50); prayed for wife to have children (Gen 25:20-21, p. 51); father of twins, Esau and Jacob (Gen 25:24, p. 51; 1 Chr 1:34, p. 1226); preferred Esau (Gen 25:28, p. 51); dealings with Abimelech (Gen 26:1-31, p. 52); tricked into blessing Jacob (Gen 27:1-29, p. 54); died (Gen 35:27-29, p. 70); father of a nation (Deut 29:13, p. 320; Rom 9:7, 10, p. 1661); often mentioned in NT (Luke 3:34, p. 1280; Gal 4:28, p. 1564; Heb 11:9, 17-20, p. 1777; Jas 2:21, p. 1550).

ISAIAH Prophet of Judah (southern kingdom) who prophesied during the reigns of four consecutive kings (Isa 1:1, p. 822); called by God in a vision (Isa 6, p. 783); prophesied Immanuel's coming (Isa 7–11, p. 790); prophesied to Hezekiah (2 Kgs 19–20, p. 915; Isa 36–38, p. 913); recorded history of kings (2 Chr 26:22, p. 782; 32:32, p. 923); often quoted in NT (Matt 3:3, p. 1287; 4:14, p. 1306; 8:17, p. 1309; 12:17, p. 1322; 13:14, p. 1345; 15:7, p. 1369; Luke 4:17, p. 1357; John 12:38, p. 1434; Acts 8:28, p. 1529; 28:25, p. 1689; Rom 9:27, p. 1662; 10:16, 20, p. 1664).

ISLAND (n) small tract of land surrounded by water
Rev 1:9 *I was exiled to the **i** of Patmos* 1800
Rev 16:20 *And every **i** disappeared,* 1824

ISRAEL
1. Another name for Jacob (Gen 32:28, p. 66)
2. The united kingdom of Israel, including all twelve tribes, as ruled by Saul, David, and Solomon.
3. The northern kingdom of Israel, including the ten northern tribes, in contrast to Judah (southern kingdom) (*see* 2 Sam 19:41-43, p. 522).

Exod 3:9 *cry of the people of **I** has* 144
Exod 12:37 ***I** left Rameses and started* 158
Exod 16:1 ***I** set out from Elim* 163
Exod 28:29 ***I** on the sacred chestpiece* 179
Exod 31:16 ***I** must keep the Sabbath day* 183
Exod 39:42 ***I** followed all of the Lord's* 194
Lev 25:55 *the people of **I** belong to me.* 234
Num 6:23 ***I** with this special blessing:* 245
Num 9:17 ***I** would break camp and follow* ...201
Num 20:22 *community of **I** left Kadesh* 262
Num 27:12 *I have given the people of **I**.* 273
Num 35:10 *instructions to the people of **I**.* ...282
Deut 10:12 ***I**, what does the Lord your* 300
Josh 21:3 ***I** gave the Levites the following* ...365
Judg 17:6 *In those days **I** had no king;* 403
1 Sam 3:20 *And all **I**, from Dan* 422
1 Sam 4:21 *said, "**I**'s glory is gone."* 424
1 Sam 15:26 *rejected you as king of **I**.* 447
1 Sam 18:16 *all **I** and Judah loved David* 453
2 Sam 14:25 *handsome man in all **I**.* 510
1 Kgs 1:35 *him to be ruler over **I*** 545
1 Kgs 12:1 ***I** had gathered to make him king.* 696
1 Kgs 19:18 *preserve 7,000 others in **I*** 720
2 Kgs 17:24 *replacing the people of **I**.* 821
1 Chr 11:4 *and all **I** went to Jerusalem* 482
1 Chr 21:1 *Satan rose up against **I*** 530
2 Chr 9:8 *Because God loves **I*** 626
Ps 73:1 *Truly God is good to **I**,* 593
Ps 98:3 *to love and be faithful to **I**.* 865
Isa 44:6 *says—**I**'s King and Redeemer,* 930
Isa 44:21 *you are my servant, O **I**.* 930
Jer 2:3 *In those days **I** was holy* 960
Jer 31:2 *give rest to the people of **I**.* 1032
Jer 31:9 *For I am **I**'s father,* 1032
Jer 31:31 *covenant with the people of **I*** 1034
Ezek 3:17 *as a watchman for **I**.* 1047
Hos 1:10 ***I**'s people will be like the sands* 802
Hos 3:1 *Lord still loves **I**, even though* 804
Amos 4:12 *in judgment, you people of **I**!* 774
Amos 8:2 *Like this fruit, **I** is ripe* 779
Mic 5:2 *a ruler of **I** will come from you,* 908
Mal 1:5 *far beyond **I**'s borders!* 1244
Matt 2:6 *the shepherd for my people **I**.* 1284
Matt 10:6 *people of **I**—God's lost sheep* ...1358
Matt 15:24 *lost sheep—the people of **I**.* 1371
Mark 12:29 *Listen, O **I**!* 1441
Acts 1:6 *time come for you to free **I*** 1500
Acts 9:15 *as well as to the people of **I**.* 1530
Rom 9:4 ***I**, chosen to be God's adopted* 1661
Rom 9:6 ***I** are truly members of God's* 1661
Rom 9:27 ***I** are as numerous as the sand* ..1662
Rom 9:31 ***I**, who tried so hard to get* 1662
Rom 10:1 *the people of **I** to be saved* 1663
Rom 11:7 ***I** have not found the favor* 1664
Rom 11:26 *And so all **I** will be saved.* 1666
Eph 2:12 *citizenship among the people of **I**,* 1708
Phil 3:5 *a pure-blooded citizen of **I** and* 1722

Heb 8:8 *covenant with the people of **I***.......1771
Rev 7:4 *sealed from all the tribes of **I**:*.......1812
Rev 21:12 ***I** were written on the gates*.......1831

ISRAELITE, ISRAELITES (n) members of the nation of Israel
see also JEW(S)
Exod 1:7 *the **I-s,** had many children*...........140
Exod 16:12 *heard the **I-s'** complaints*.........163
Lev 25:46 *never treat your fellow **I-s** this*....234
Num 10:12 ***I-s** set out from the wilderness*..246
Josh 1:2 *lead these people, the **I-s,***............336
Josh 7:1 *was very angry with the **I-s.***.........344
Judg 2:7 ***I-s** served the LORD throughout*....371
Judg 3:12 ***I-s** did evil in the LORD's sight,*....377
Judg 6:1 ***I-s** did evil in the LORD's sight*.......382
Judg 10:16 ***I-s** put aside their foreign*.........392
Rom 11:1 *I myself am an **I,** a descendant*.....................................1664
2 Cor 11:22 *Are they **I-s?** So am I*............1641

ITALY (n) a long boot-shaped country that juts into the Mediterranean Sea
Acts 27:1 *we set sail for **I.***.......................1686
Heb 13:24 *believers from **I** send*..............1783

JACOB Patriarch, son of Isaac, grandson of Abraham; younger twin son of Issac and Rebekah (Gen 25:23–35:26, p. 51; 48–49, p. 90); also known as "Israel" (Gen 32:28, p. 66); favored by Rebekah (Gen 25:28, p. 51); bought Esau's birthright for a meal (Gen 25:29-34, p. 51); deceived Isaac to receive his blessing (Gen 27:1-29, p. 54); fled from Esau (Gen 27:41-45, p. 56); married inside of clan (Gen 28:1-5, p. 57); Jacob's ladder (Gen 28:12, p. 57); covenant extended to Jacob in a dream (Gen 28:13-15, p. 57); wives and concubines, Rachel favored (Gen 29:1-30, p. 59); children (Gen 29:31–30:24, p. 61; 35:16-26, p. 70); prospered at his uncle Laban's expense (Gen 30:25-43, p. 62); fled from Laban (Gen 31, p. 63); name changed to "Israel" (Gen 32:22-32, p. 66); reconciled with Esau (Gen 33, p. 67); favored Rachel's oldest son Joseph (Gen 37:3, p. 72); overwhelmed by loss of Joseph (Gen 37:33-35, p. 74); migrated to Egypt (Gen 46:5-7, p. 87); blessed Joseph's sons (Gen 48, p. 90); blessed his own sons (Gen 49:1-28, p. 91); died (Gen 49:33, p. 92); buried (Gen 50:1-14, p. 92); often mentioned in NT (John 4:5-6, 12, p. 1304; Acts 7:8-15, p. 1524; Rom 9:13, p. 1661; Heb 11:20-21, p. 1778).
see ISRAEL

JAMES
1. One of the 12 disciples, brother of John, son of Zebedee (Matt 10:2, p. 1358; Mark 3:17, p. 1323); called by Jesus (Matt 4:21, p. 1308; Luke 5:10, p. 1308); zealous for the Lord (Luke 9:54, p. 1387); wanted honor (Mark 10:35-45, p. 1424); witnessed the Transfiguration (Matt 17:1-9, p. 1378; Mark 9:2-8, p. 1379; Luke 9:28-36, p. 1380); killed by Herod Agrippa I (Acts 12:2, p. 1537).
2. One of the 12 disciples, son of Alphaeus (Matt 10:3, p. 1358; Mark 3:18, p. 1323; Luke 6:15, p. 1323); called "the younger" (Mark 15:40, p. 1486).
3. Half-brother of Jesus (Matt 13:55, p. 1356; Mark 6:3, p. 1357; Luke 24:10, p. 1491; 1 Cor 15:7, p. 1620; Gal 1:19, p. 1557; 2:9, 12, p. 1558), brother of Jude (Jude 1:1, p. 1784); leader of Jerusalem Council (Acts 15:13, p. 1569; 21:18, p. 1677); with select group before Pentecost (Acts 1:13, p. 1512); wrote letter (Jas 1:1, p. 1546).
4. Father of the apostle Judas, not Iscariot (Luke 6:16, p. 1323).
5. Son of a certain Mary, perhaps the same as the "son of Alphaeus" (Matt 27:56, p. 1486).

JAR, JARS (n) an open container, typically made of clay in the ancient world
John 12:3 ***j** of expensive perfume*............1428
John 19:29 *A **j** of sour wine was*...............1486
2 Cor 4:7 *like fragile clay **j-s** containing*....1631

JAVELIN (n) a light spear thrown as a weapon of war or in hunting
1 Sam 17:45 *sword, spear, and **j,** but I*.......451

JAWBONE (n) either of two bony structures that border the mouth
Judg 15:15 ***j** of a recently killed donkey.*.....400

JEALOUS (adj) intolerant of rivalry or unfaithfulness; hostile toward a rival
Exod 20:5 *am a **j** God who will not*.............168
Exod 34:14 *whose very name is **J,***............188
Prov 6:34 ***j** husband will be furious,*............639
Nah 1:2 *a **j** God, filled with vengeance*........974
Rom 11:14 ***j** of what you Gentiles have,*....1665
1 Cor 13:4 *Love is not **j** or boastful*...........1616
Gal 5:26 *provoke one another, or be **j***.......1567
Jas 3:14 *if you are bitterly **j** and there is*...1550

JEALOUSY (n) a jealous feeling, disposition, or attitude
Prov 27:4 *but **j** is even more dangerous.*......842
Rom 10:19 *I will rouse your **j***...................1664
Rom 13:13 *or in quarreling and **j.***.............1669
1 Cor 10:22 *dare to rouse the Lord's **j?***....1611
2 Cor 11:2 *you with the **j** of God*..............1640
Gal 5:20 ***j,** outbursts of anger,*..................1566
1 Tim 6:4 *arguments ending in **j,***.............1734
1 Pet 2:1 *with all deceit, hypocrisy, **j,***........1750

JEERED, JEERS (v) to scoff; to taunt
Job 27:23 ***j-s** at them and mocks them.*......118
Heb 11:36 *Some were **j-ed** at,*.................1779

JEHOVAH (KJV)
Exod 6:3 *did not reveal my name, **Yahweh,** to them*....................................148
Ps 83:18 *you alone are called **the LORD***......603
Isa 12:2 *The LORD **GOD** is my strength*.........797
Isa 26:4 *the LORD **GOD** is the eternal*..........896

JEREMIAH Prophet of Judah (southern kingdom) from Anathoth (Jer 11:18-23, p. 1014); never married (Jer 16:2, p. 1019); put in stocks (Jer 20:1-6, p. 999); threatened by priests and prophets (Jer 26:8, p. 993); brought death to false prophet (Jer 28:16-17, p. 1050); writings burned (Jer 36, p. 995); imprisoned in dungeon (Jer 37:15, p. 1042); removed from the dungeon by King Zedekiah (Jer 37:21, p. 1042); lowered into cistern (Jer 38:1-6, p. 1042); set free by invaders (Jer 39:11–40:6, p. 1086); taken to Egypt (Jer 43, p. 1107); mentioned in NT (Matt 2:17, p. 1285; 27:9, p. 1476).

JERICHO (n) a city in the plain of the Jordan Valley at the foot of the ascent to the Judean mountains
Num 22:1 *across from **J.***..........................265
Josh 3:16 *near the town of **J.***....................340
Josh 5:10 *at Gilgal on the plains of **J,***.........342
Luke 10:30 *from Jerusalem down to **J,***.....1396
Heb 11:30 *around **J** for seven days,*.........1779

JERUSALEM (n) sacred city and well-known capital of Palestine during Bible times
Josh 10:1 *Adoni-zedek, king of **J,** heard*.....349
Josh 15:8 *where the city of **J** is located.*.....358
Judg 1:8 *attacked **J** and captured it,*..........372
2 Sam 5:5 ***J** he reigned over all Israel*.........486
2 Sam 11:1 *David stayed behind in **J.***........502
1 Kgs 9:15 *terraces, the wall of **J,***.............624
1 Kgs 10:26 *and some near him in **J.***.........628
1 Kgs 14:25 *came up and attacked **J.***........703
2 Kgs 8:17 *he reigned in **J** eight years.*........737
2 Kgs 12:1 *He reigned in **J** forty years.*........755
2 Kgs 14:2 *reigned in **J** twenty-nine years.* .760
2 Kgs 15:2 *he reigned in **J** fifty-two years.* ..763
2 Kgs 16:2 *he reigned in **J** sixteen years.*......788
2 Kgs 18:2 *reigned in **J** twenty-nine years.* .799
2 Kgs 19:31 *will spread out from **J,***............918
2 Kgs 21:12 *I will bring such disaster on **J.***.955
2 Kgs 22:1 *reigned in **J** thirty-one years.*......957
2 Kgs 23:31 *he reigned in **J** three months.* .990
2 Kgs 24:8 *he reigned in **J** three months.* .1026
2 Kgs 24:14 *Nebuchadnezzar took all of **J.***.1041
2 Kgs 24:20 *anger against the people of **J.***.1041
2 Kgs 25:9 *and all the houses of **J.***..........1087
1 Chr 21:16 *reaching out over **J.***................531
2 Chr 3:1 *the Temple of the LORD in **J***.........611
2 Chr 9:1 *she came to **J** to test him.*...........626
2 Chr 20:15 *all you people of Judah and **J!***...732
2 Chr 29:8 *has fallen upon Judah and **J.***....834
2 Chr 36:19 *tore down the walls of **J,***.......1088
Ezra 2:1 *but now they returned to **J***..........1152
Ezra 4:12 *came here to **J** from Babylon*....1195
Ezra 6:12 *who has chosen the city of **J***.....1172
Ezra 9:9 *a protective wall in Judah and **J.***...1200
Neh 1:3 *The wall of **J** has been torn*.........1203
Neh 3:8 *They left out a section of **J***..........1206
Neh 11:1 *of the people were living in **J,***....1220
Neh 12:43 *joy of the people of **J** could be*.1222
Ps 9:11 *the LORD who reigns in **J.***...............549
Ps 51:18 *rebuild the walls of **J.***..................506
Ps 74:2 *remember **J,** your home here.*........595
Ps 79:1 *made **J** a heap of ruins.*.................600
Ps 87:2 *He loves the city of **J** more than*.....855
Ps 102:13 *arise and have mercy on **J**—*.....866
Ps 122:2 *standing inside your gates, O **J.***...584
Ps 122:6 *Pray for peace in **J.***.....................584
Ps 125:2 ***J,** so the LORD surrounds*............883
Ps 128:5 *May you see **J** prosper*...............883
Ps 137:3 *Sing us one of those songs of **J!***...1118
Ps 137:5 *If I forget you, O **J,***...................1118
Ps 147:2 *The LORD is rebuilding **J***............1154
Ps 147:12 *Glorify the LORD, O **J!***..............1155
Isa 1:1 *saw concerning Judah and **J.***..........822
Isa 3:1 *take away from **J** and Judah*...........826
Isa 4:3 *who survive the destruction of **J***......828
Isa 27:13 *return to **J** to worship the LORD*....897
Isa 31:5 *will hover over **J** and protect it*.......901
Isa 40:2 *Speak tenderly to **J.***......................923
Isa 51:11 *They will enter **J** singing,*............938
Isa 52:1 *clothes, O holy city of **J,***...............939
Isa 52:8 *see the LORD returning to **J.***..........939
Isa 62:7 *makes **J** the pride of the earth.*.......949
Jer 2:2 *Go and shout this message to **J.***.....959
Jer 4:5 *to Judah, and broadcast to **J!***.........964
Jer 6:6 *ramps against the walls of **J.***..........967
Jer 9:11 *will make **J** into a heap of ruins,*..1012
Jer 23:14 *prophets of **J** are even worse!*...1027
Jer 26:18 ***J** will be reduced to ruins!*...........993
Jer 39:1 *came with his army to besiege **J.***..1072
Jer 51:50 *think about your home in **J.***......1039

Lam 1:7 ***J** remembers her ancient splendor*...1094
Dan 6:10 *windows open toward **J**.*............1140
Dan 9:2 ***J** must lie desolate for seventy*.....1142
Dan 9:12 *a disaster as happened in **J**.*.........1142
Dan 9:25 *command is given to rebuild **J***...1143
Joel 3:16 *from Zion and thunder from **J**,*...1243
Amos 2:5 *fortresses of **J** will be destroyed.*.772
Obad 1:11 *and cast lots to divide up **J**,*.....1103
Mic 4:2 *his word will go out from **J**.*............907
Zeph 3:16 *the announcement to **J** will be,*...986
Zech 1:17 *Zion and choose **J** as his own.*.1166
Zech 2:4 ***J** will someday be so full*............1167
Zech 8:8 *home again to live safely in **J**.*....1174
Zech 8:22 *nations will come to **J** to seek*..1174
Zech 9:10 *and the warhorses from **J**.*........1175
Zech 12:10 *and on the people of **J**.*..........1178
Zech 14:8 *waters will flow out from **J**,*......1180
Matt 20:18 *going up to **J**, where the Son*..1423
Matt 21:10 *city of **J** was in an uproar*.......1429
Matt 23:37 ***J**, the city that kills the*...........1407
Mark 10:33 *going up to **J**, where the Son*...1423
Luke 2:22 *parents took him to **J***...............1282
Luke 2:41 *Jesus' parents went to **J***..........1286
Luke 4:9 *Then the devil took him to **J**,*......1296
Luke 9:31 *about to be fulfilled in **J**.*...........1380
Luke 13:34 *O **J**, **J**, the city that kills*.........1407
Luke 18:31 *to **J**, where all the predictions*...1423
Luke 21:20 *you see **J** surrounded*............1450
Luke 24:47 *nations, beginning in **J**:*..........1498
Acts 1:8 *about me everywhere—in **J**,*.......1500
Acts 6:7 *believers greatly increased in **J**,*..1523
Acts 20:22 *bound by the Spirit to go to **J**.*.1675
Acts 23:11 *a witness to me here in **J**,*.......1680
Rom 9:33 *I am placing a stone in **J***..........1663
Rom 11:26 *rescues will come from **J**,*.......1666
Rom 15:19 *from **J** all the way to Illyricum*....1671
Gal 4:25 ***J** is just like Mount Sinai*............1564
Gal 4:26 *represents the heavenly **J**.*..........1564
Heb 12:22 *living God, the heavenly **J**,*.......1781
Rev 21:10 *he showed me the holy city, **J**,*.1831

JESUS see also CHRIST, MESSIAH
Family line (Matt 1:1-17, p. 1277; Luke 3:23-38, p. 1279); birth announced (Matt 1:18-25, p. 1277; Luke 1:26-38, p. 1274); born in Bethlehem (Luke 2:1-20, p. 1280); circumcised, officially named, and presented at Temple (Luke 2:21-40, p. 1282); visited by Magi (Matt 2:1-12, p. 1283); escape to and return from Egypt (Matt 2:13-23, p. 1285); amazed the Temple scholars (Luke 2:41-50, p. 1286); summary of youth (Luke 2:51-52, p. 1287); baptized by John (Matt 3:13-17, p. 1293; Mark 1:9-11, p. 1294; Luke 3:21-22, p. 1294; John 1:32-34, p. 1297); tempted by Satan (Matt 4:1-11, p. 1294; Mark 1:12-13, p. 1295; Luke 4:1-13, p. 1295); ministered in Galilee (Matt 4:12–18:35, p. 1303; Mark 1:14–9:50, p. 1303); transfigured on a mountain (Matt 17:1-13, p. 1378; Mark 9:2-13, p. 1379; Luke 9:28-36, p. 1380; 2 Pet 1:16-18, p. 1758); triumphal entry (Matt 21:1-11, p. 1429; Mark 11:1-11, p. 1430; Luke 19:28-44, p. 1430; John 12:12-19, p. 1431); the Last Supper (Matt 26:17-35, p. 1455; Mark 14:12-31, p. 1455; Luke 22:7-38, p. 1455; John 13–17, p. 1455); betrayed and tried (Matt 26:36–27:31, p. 1468; Mark 14:32–15:20, p. 1468; Luke 22:39–23:25, p. 1469; John 18:1–19:16, p. 1470); crucified, died, and was buried (Matt 27:32-66, p. 1482; Mark 15:21-47, p. 1482; Luke 23:26-56, p. 1482; John 19:17-42, p. 1484); rose again and appeared to followers (Matt 28, p. 1489; Mark 16, p. 1490; Luke 24, p. 1491; John 20–21, p. 1492; Acts 1:1-11, p. 1500; 7:55-56, p. 1526; 9:3-6, p. 1530; 1 Cor 15:1-8, p. 1618; Rev 1:1-20, p. 1798); ascended to heaven (Mark 16:19, p. 1499; Luke 24:50-53, p. 1500; John 1:51, p. 1298; Acts 1:9, p. 1500; Eph 4:8, p. 1710).

JEW, JEWS (n) a name applied first to the people living in the southern kingdom of Judah; broadly, a descendant of Abraham
see also ISRAELITE(S)
Esth 3:13 *property of the **J-s** would be*.....1187
Zech 8:23 *clutch at the sleeve of one **J**.*....1174
Matt 2:2 *the newborn king of the **J-s?***......1283
John 19:3 *Hail! King of the **J-s!***...............1480
Acts 20:21 *message for **J-s** and Greeks*....1675
Acts 21:39 *I am a **J** and a citizen of*..........1678
Rom 1:16 *everyone who believes—the **J**.*.1646
Rom 2:28 *you are not a true **J**.*.................1650
Rom 9:24 *from the **J-s** and from*...............1662
Rom 10:12 ***J** and Gentile are the same*.....1664
1 Cor 9:20 *with the **J-s**, I lived like a **J***.....1609
1 Cor 12:13 ***J-s**, some are Gentiles,*.........1615
Gal 2:8 *Peter as the apostle to the **J-s***......1558
Gal 2:14 ***J** by birth, have discarded*..........1559
Gal 3:28 *There is no longer **J** or Gentile,*...1562
Eph 3:6 *Gentiles and **J-s** who believe*.......1708
Col 3:11 ***J** or a Gentile, circumcised or*.....1700

JEWEL, JEWELS (n) a precious stone; gem
Prov 3:22 *They are like **j-s** on a necklace*....635
Song 4:9 *with a single **j** of your necklace*.....666
Isa 61:10 *or a bride with her **j-s**.*................948
Zech 9:16 *in his land like **j-s** in a crown*....1176
1 Cor 3:12 *gold, silver, **j-s**, wood, hay,*......1599

JEWELRY (n) objects of precious metal worn for personal adornment
Prov 25:12 *earring or other gold **j**.*..............839
Jer 2:32 *a young woman forget her **j?***........962
Ezek 16:11 *I gave you lovely **j**, bracelets,*..1061

JEWISH (adj) of, relating to, or characteristic of the Jews
Esth 2:5 *a **J** man in the fortress of Susa*....1184
John 3:10 *You are a respected **J** teacher,*..1302

JEZEBEL Queen of Israel (northern kingdom), daughter of Ethbaal, king of Sidon; evil, influential wife of King Ahab (1 Kgs 21:25, p. 725); Baal worshiper (1 Kgs 16:31-33, p. 712); tried to kill all the LORD's prophets (1 Kgs 18:4, 13, p. 716); vowed to kill Elijah (1 Kgs 19:1-2, p. 719); arranged murder to get vineyard for Ahab (1 Kgs 21:1-16, p. 723); death foretold and fulfilled (1 Kgs 21:23, p. 725; 2 Kgs 9:10, 30-37, p. 749, 751).

JOB Man who feared God and had integrity (Job 1:1-5, p. 94); slandered and attacked by Satan (Job 1:6–2:10, p. 94); debated suffering with his "friends" (Job 3–37, p. 97); enlightened by vision of the LORD (Job 38–41, p. 127); restored to peace and prosperity (Job 42, p. 132); example of righteousness (Ezek 14:14, 20, p. 1060); example of endurance in suffering (Jas 5:11, p. 1553).

JOHN
1. The Baptist, son of Zechariah and Elizabeth (Luke 1:5-25, 57-80, p. 1272, 1276); called to prepare the way for the Messiah (Isa 40:3-5, p. 923; Luke 3:1-6, p. 1290; John 1:19-28, p. 1292); called to preach and baptize (Matt 3:1-12, p. 1287; Mark 1:1-8, p. 1270, 1289); preached repentance (Luke 3:7-20, p. 1290); baptized Jesus (Matt 3:13-17, p. 1293; Luke 3:21-22, p. 1294); confirmed Jesus' ministry (Matt 3:11-12, p. 1289; Mark 1:7-8, p. 1290; Luke 3:15-18, p. 1291; John 3:22-36, p. 1302; 5:33, p. 1319); ministry compared to Elijah (Mal 4:5, p. 1249; Matt 11:11-19, p. 1338; Mark 9:11-13, p. 1379; Luke 7:24-35, p. 1338); arrested and beheaded by Herod Antipas (Matt 14:1-12, p. 1361; Mark 6:14-29, p. 1363; Luke 9:7-9, p. 1363).
2. One of the 12 disciples, brother of James, son of Zebedee (Matt 10:2, p. 1358; Mark 3:17, p. 1323); witnessed the Transfiguration (Matt 17:1-9, p. 1378; Mark 9:2-8, p. 1379; Luke 9:28-36, p. 1380); inner circle of Jesus' followers (Matt 17:1, p. 1378; Mark 5:37, p. 1354; 9:2, p. 1379; 13:3, p. 1447; Luke 8:51, p. 1355; 9:28, p. 1380; Gal 2:9, p. 1558); with Peter, healed a man and was arrested (Acts 3–4, p. 1516); with Peter, rebuked sorcerer (Acts 8:14-25, p. 1528); wrote fourth Gospel (John 13:23-25; *see also* 20:2, p. 1625; 21:20-25, p. 1677), letters of John (the "elder," 2 Jn 1:1, p. 1795; 3 Jn 1:1, p. 1796), and Revelation (the "servant," Rev 1:1, 9, p. 1798; 22:8, p. 1832).
3. *See* MARK, also known as John Mark.

JOIN, JOINED, JOINS (v) to put or bring into close association or relationship; to take part in a collective activity
Ps 26:5 *I refuse to **j** in with the wicked*........560
Dan 11:34 *who **j** them will not be sincere.* 1160
Zech 2:11 *will **j** themselves to the LORD*.....1167
Matt 19:6 *what God has **j-ed** together.*......1418
Mark 10:9 *what God has **j-ed** together.*.....1419
Rom 6:3 ***j-ed** with Christ Jesus in baptism,*...1655
Rom 8:16 *his Spirit **j-s** with our spirit*........1659
Rom 15:30 ***j** in my struggle by praying*......1672
1 Cor 6:16 *if a man **j-s** himself to*............1604
Eph 2:21 *carefully **j-ed** together in him,*....1708

JOINT (n) the point of contact between bone and the parts surrounding and supporting it
Ps 22:14 *all my bones are out of **j**.*.............556
Heb 4:12 *between **j** and marrow*...............1766

JOKE, JOKES (n) something said or done to provoke laughter
Ps 44:14 *made us the butt of their **j-s**;*.......850
Ps 89:41 *he has become a **j** to his*.............592
Eph 5:4 *coarse **j-s**—these are not*...........1712

JOKING (v) to jest; to kid
Gen 19:14 *men thought he was only **j**.*..........41
Prov 26:19 *and then says, "I was only **j**."*....841

JONAH Prophet of Israel (northern kingdom), in the days of Jeroboam II (2 Kgs 14:25, p. 762); swallowed by great fish (Jonah 1:17, p. 767); survived and then preached to Nineveh (Jon 3, p. 768); mentioned by Jesus as a sign (Matt 12:39-41, p. 1343; 16:4, p. 1373; Luke 11:29-32, p. 1344).

JORDAN (n) the longest and most important river in Palestine
Josh 4:22 *crossed the **J** on dry ground.*......341
Matt 3:6 *them in the **J** River.*....................1288
Matt 4:15 *sea, beyond the **J** River, in*........1306
Mark 1:9 *him in the **J** River.*.....................1294

JOSEPH
1. Oldest son of Jacob and Rachel (Gen 30:24, p. 62); loved by Jacob—hated by brothers

(Gen 37:3-4, p. 72); dreamer of dreams (Gen 37:5-11, p. 73); captured to be killed, but sold into slavery (Gen 37:20, 27-28, p. 73); faithfully served Egyptian master (Gen 39:3, p. 76); wrongfully accused and imprisoned (Gen 39, p. 76); interpreted dreams of royal staff (Gen 40, p. 78); interpreted dreams of Pharaoh, then ruled Egypt (Gen 41:4-44, p. 79); prepared Egypt for famine (Gen 41:46-57, p. 81); tested brothers, revealed identity, and reconciled with them (Gen 42–45, p. 81); brought his father Jacob and family to Egypt (Gen 46–47, p. 87); sons, Ephraim and Manasseh, blessed by Jacob (Gen 48, p. 90); Joseph blessed by Jacob (Gen 49:22-26, p. 92; Deut 33:13-17, p. 327); reassured his brothers (Gen 50:15-21, p. 93); died (Gen 50:22-26, p. 93; Heb 11:22, p. 1778); remembered as one chosen and helped by God (Acts 7:9-18, p. 1524); 12,000 descendants will be marked by God (Rev 7:8, p. 1812).

2. Husband of Mary the mother of Jesus; accepted supernatural pregnancy of Mary (Matt 1:16-25, p. 1279); had no relations with Mary until birth of Jesus (Matt 1:25, p. 1278); was present at birth and dedication of Jesus (Luke 2:4-38, p. 1280); fled to Egypt, then Nazareth (Matt 2:13-22, p. 1285); descendant of David in the family line of Jesus (Luke 3:23, p. 1279); Jesus called his son (Luke 4:22, p. 1357; John 1:45, p. 1298; 6:42, p. 1367).

JOSHUA Son of Nun, who led Israel into Promised Land (Acts 7:45, p. 1526; Heb 4:8, p. 1766); commanded by Moses to fight Amalek (Exod 17:8-16, p. 165); assistant to Moses (Exod 24:13, p. 175); explored Canaan (Num 13:8, p. 250); demonstrated faith in his report (Num 14:6-9, p. 252); allowed to enter Promised Land (Num 14:30, p. 253; Deut 1:38, p. 286); became Israel's leader after Moses (Num 27:18-23, p. 273; Deut 31:1-18, p. 322); went with Moses up the mountain of God (Exod 24:13, p. 175); assumed command (Josh 1, p. 336); sent spies to Jericho (Josh 2, p. 337); led Israel across the Jordan (Josh 3–4, p. 339); established memorial stones (Josh 4, p. 340); circumcised the people (Josh 5:2-9, p. 342); conquered Jericho (Josh 6, p. 343) and Ai (Josh 7–8, p. 344); uncovered Achan's sin (Josh 7:10-26, p. 346); made pact with the Gibeonites (Josh 9, p. 348); sun stood still (Josh 10:1-15, p. 349); conquered southern Canaan (Josh 10:28-43, p. 351); conquered northern Canaan (Josh 11–12, p. 352); divided the land (Josh 13–22, p. 355); gave final words to Israel (Josh 23, p. 368); made covenant at Shechem (Josh 8:30-35, p. 348; 24:1-28, p. 369); died (Josh 24:29-30, p. 370).

JOURNEY (n) an act or instance of traveling from one place to another
Judg 18:6 *LORD is watching over your **j**.* 404
Ezra 8:21 *give us a safe **j*** 1198
Rom 15:24 *provide for my **j**.* 1672

JOY, JOYS (n) the emotion evoked by well-being, success, or good fortune
Deut 16:15 *be a time of great **j** for all.* 306
1 Sam 18:6 *danced for **j** with tambourines*..452
1 Chr 16:27 *and **j** fill his dwelling.* 493
1 Chr 29:22 *with great **j** that day.* 541
Ezra 3:12 *however, were shouting for **j**.*.....1156
Neh 8:10 ***j** of the LORD is your strength!* 1215
Neh 8:17 *they were all filled with great **j**!*..1215
Esth 9:22 *and their mourning into **j**.*...........1193
Job 3:22 *with **j** when they finally die,* 98
Job 8:21 *your lips with shouts of **j**.* 103
Ps 1:1 ***j-s** of those who do not follow*..........856
Ps 2:12 ***j** for all who take refuge in him!*......857
Ps 9:2 *filled with **j** because of you*..............549
Ps 19:8 *bringing **j** to the heart.* 554
Ps 21:1 *He shouts with **j*** 555
Ps 28:7 *my heart is filled with **j**.* 562
Ps 30:11 *and clothed me with **j**,* 563
Ps 32:2 *what **j** for those whose record*........564
Ps 33:12 ***j** for the nation whose God*...........858
Ps 41:1 ***j-s** of those who are kind*..............571
Ps 42:4 *singing for **j** and giving thanks* 848
Ps 45:7 *pouring out the oil of **j** on you*.........851
Ps 46:4 *A river brings **j** to the city*..............851
Ps 51:12 *to me the **j** of your salvation,*.........506
Ps 65:8 *you inspire shouts of **j**.* 575
Ps 65:13 *They all shout and sing for **j**!*........575
Ps 71:23 *I will shout for **j** and sing*.............860
Ps 92:4 *I sing for **j** because of what*............862
Ps 98:4 *in praise and sing for **j**!*..................865
Ps 105:43 *his people out of Egypt with **j**,* 869
Ps 106:5 *Let me rejoice in the **j*** 870
Ps 119:92 *hadn't sustained me with **j**,*........880
Ps 126:2 *laughter, and we sang for **j**.*........1154
Ps 132:9 *loyal servants sing for **j**.*...............884
Ps 132:16 *servants will sing for **j**.*..............884
Ps 145:7 ***j** about your righteousness.*..........589
Prov 10:1 *A wise child brings **j*** 641
Prov 11:10 ***j** when the wicked die.*..............643
Prov 14:10 *no one else can fully share its **j**.* 647
Prov 15:20 *Sensible children bring **j** to*........650
Prov 21:15 *Justice is a **j** to the godly,*..........658
Prov 23:25 *your father and mother **j**!*..........661
Prov 29:6 *righteous escape, shouting for **j**.*....845
Isa 12:6 *shout his praise with **j**!*..................797
Isa 16:9 *no more shouts of **j** over your*........834
Isa 16:10 *gone the **j** of harvest.*..................834
Isa 26:19 *will rise up and sing for **j**!*............897
Isa 35:10 *crowned with everlasting **j**.*..........905
Isa 42:11 *Let the people of Sela sing for **j**;* 927
Isa 49:13 *Sing for **j**, O heavens!* 936
Isa 51:11 *filled with **j** and gladness*.............938
Isa 52:8 *watchmen shout and sing with **j**,* ...939
Isa 56:7 *fill them with **j** in my house*............943
Isa 60:15 *beautiful forever, a **j** to all*............947
Isa 61:7 *everlasting **j** will be yours.* 948
Isa 65:14 *My servants will sing for **j**, but*.....952
Jer 31:13 *young women will dance for **j**,*...1033
Jer 31:13 *turn their mourning into **j**.* 1033
Jer 33:11 *the sounds of **j** and laughter*......1081
Jer 48:33 *treads the grapes with shouts of **j**.* 990
Jer 49:25 *a city of **j**, will be forsaken!* 1025
Joel 1:12 *the people's **j** has dried up* 1240
Matt 2:10 *they were filled with **j**!* 1284
Matt 28:8 *but also filled with great **j**,*.........1490
Mark 1:11 *Son, and you bring me great **j**.* ...1294
Mark 4:16 *receive it with **j**.*.......................1346
Luke 1:14 *have great **j** and gladness,* 1273
Luke 1:44 *in my womb jumped for **j**.* 1275
Luke 2:10 *bring great **j** to all people*..........1281
Luke 6:23 *be happy! Yes, leap for **j**!*..........1327
Luke 10:21 *with the **j** of the Holy Spirit,*.....1395
Luke 24:41 *filled with **j** and wonder.* 1495
John 15:11 *you will be filled with my **j**.* 1464
John 16:20 *turn to wonderful **j**.* 1465
John 16:24 *and you will have abundant **j**.*.1465
John 20:20 ***j** when they saw the Lord!*......1495
Acts 2:28 *you will fill me with the **j*** 1516
Acts 2:46 *their meals with great **j***.............1516
Acts 11:23 *he was filled with **j**,*................1536
Acts 13:52 *believers were filled with **j***.......1543
Acts 15:3 *much to everyone's **j**—*...........1569
Rom 14:17 *and **j** in the Holy Spirit.* 1670
Rom 15:13 *with **j** and peace because*.......1671
2 Cor 1:24 *so you will be full of **j**,* 1627
2 Cor 2:3 *ought to give me the greatest **j**.*...1627
2 Cor 2:3 ***j** comes from your being joyful*...1627
2 Cor 6:10 *but we always have **j**.* 1633
2 Cor 7:7 *I was filled with **j**!*......................1635
Gal 5:22 *fruit in our lives: love, **j**, peace,*....1566
Phil 1:4 *requests for all of you with **j**,* 1716
Phil 1:25 *experience the **j** of your faith.* 1718
Phil 4:1 *you are my **j** and the crown*..........1724
1 Thes 1:6 *received the message with **j***....1581
1 Thes 2:19 *what gives us hope and **j**,*......1583
1 Thes 2:20 *Yes, you are our pride and **j**.*..1583
1 Thes 3:9 *we have great **j***......................1584
2 Tim 1:4 *with **j** when we are together*......1740
Heb 10:34 *you accepted it with **j**.* 1776
Heb 12:2 *Because of the **j** awaiting him,* ...1780
Heb 13:17 *reason to do this with **j***............1783
Jas 1:2 *it an opportunity for great **j**.*..........1546
1 Pet 1:8 *a glorious, inexpressible **j**.* 1749
1 Pet 4:13 *the wonderful **j** of seeing his*....1755
1 Jn 1:4 *you may fully share our **j**.*............1787

JOYFUL (adj) characterized by gladness or delight
Ps 30:11 *my mourning into **j** dancing*..........563
Ps 66:1 *Shout **j** praises to God, all the* 859
Ps 98:6 *a **j** symphony before the LORD,* 865
Ps 137:3 *insisted on a **j** hymn:*..................1118
Rom 15:32 *come to you with a **j** heart,* 1672
Gal 4:15 *that **j** and grateful spirit*..............1563
Gal 4:27 *Break into a **j** shout, you who*......1564
1 Thes 5:16 *Always be **j**.*..........................1586
Heb 12:22 *angels in a **j** gathering*.............1781

JOYOUS (adj) characterized by gladness or delight
2 Chr 29:30 *offered **j** praise and bowed*......836
Neh 12:43 *were offered on that **j** day,*.......1222
Isa 61:3 *for ashes, a **j** blessing instead*.......948
Jer 33:11 *with the **j** songs of people*.........1081

JUBILEE (n) a year of celebration, emancipation, and restoration
Lev 25:11 *fiftieth year will be a **j***.................232

JUDAH

1. Fourth son of Jacob and Leah (Gen 29:35, p. 61), who gave his name to a tribe of Israel; interceded for Joseph (Gen 37:26-27, p. 74); failed to uphold daughter-in-law Tamar's rights (Gen 38:1-30, p. 74); offered himself as slave and ransom (Gen 44:18-34, p. 85); given the family birthright by Jacob (Gen 49:3-10, p. 91); his tribe was numbered (Num 1:26-27, p. 238), allotted land and cities (Josh 15:1-63, p. 358), led the conquest of Canaan (Judg 1:2, p. 371); 12,000 will be marked by God (Rev 7:5, p. 1812).
2. The southern kingdom of Judah, including the tribes of Judah and Benjamin, in contrast to Israel (northern kingdom) (*see* 2 Sam 12:8, p. 505).

JUDAISM (n) the cultural, social, and religious beliefs and practices of the Jews
Acts 13:43 *converts to **J** followed Paul* 1542

JUDAS
1. One of the 12 disciples, also known as "Iscariot" (Mark 3:19, p. 1323; Luke 6:16, p. 1323); criticized Mary (John 12:3-6, p. 1428); foretold as betrayer (John 6:70-71, p. 1369; 13:21-30, p. 1459); made deal for 30 pieces of silver (Matt 26:14-15; *see also* Mark 14:10, p. 1454); identified as a thief (John 12:6, p. 1429); entered by Satan (Luke 22:3, p. 1454; John 13:27, p. 1459); betrayed Jesus with kiss (Mark 14:43-45, p. 1469); had remorse and committed suicide (Matt 27:3-10, p. 1475; Acts 1:18, p. 1512); his position refilled (Acts 1:20-26, p. 1513).
2. One of the 12 disciples, son of James, likely also called Thaddaeus (Matt 10:3, p. 1358; Mark 3:18, p. 1323), not Iscariot (John 14:22, p. 1462); *see also* Luke 6:16, p. 1323; Acts 1:13, p. 1512.
3. Brother of James and half-brother of Jesus, also known as "Jude" (Matt 13:55, p. 1356; Mark 6:3, p. 1357; Jude 1:1, p. 1784).

JUDEA (n) the Greco-Roman name for the land of Judah
Matt 2:1 *was born in Bethlehem in **J**,* 1283
Matt 24:16 *in **J** must flee to the hills*.........1446
Luke 3:1 *Pilate was governor over **J**;* 1290
Acts 1:8 *throughout **J**, in Samaria,*............1500
Acts 9:31 *had peace throughout **J**,*...........1531
1 Thes 2:14 *in God's churches in **J***..........1582

JUDGE, JUDGES (n) a public official authorized to decide issues brought before a court; one of a cycle of charismatic deliverers of ancient Israel
Deut 17:12 *to reject the verdict of the **j***.......307
Judg 2:16 *LORD raised up **j-s** to rescue*.......375
Judg 2:18 *the LORD raised up a **j***...............375
1 Sam 7:6 *Samuel became Israel's **j**.)*........427
1 Sam 7:15 *continued as Israel's **j***.............427
Ps 50:6 *God himself will be the **j**.* 593
Isa 33:22 *the LORD is our **j**, our lawgiver,* 903
Acts 7:35 *you a ruler and **j** over us?*........1525
Acts 10:42 ***j** of all—the living and*............1534
Rev 14:7 *he will sit as **j**.*..........................1821

JUDGE, JUDGED, JUDGES, JUDGING (v) to form an evaluation of; to decide as a judge; to govern or rule; to punish or condemn; to form a negative opinion about
1 Sam 16:7 *Don't **j** by his appearance or*....448
1 Sam 24:12 *the LORD **j** between us.* 464
2 Chr 19:7 ***j** with integrity, for the LORD* 730
Ps 7:8 *The LORD **j-s** the nations.*...............523
Ps 9:4 *For you have **j-d** in my favor;* 549
Ps 9:8 *He will **j** the world.*..........................549
Ps 82:8 *Rise up, O God, and **j** the earth,*......603
Ps 96:10 *He will **j** all peoples fairly.*..............864
Ps 96:13 *will **j** the world with justice,*...........864
Prov 16:10 *he must never **j** unfairly.*............651
Prov 29:14 *If a king **j-s** the poor fairly,*.......845
Isa 11:3 *He will not **j** by appearance*............796
Isa 66:16 *He will **j** the earth,*........................953
Matt 7:1 *Do not **j** others, and you.*............1333
Matt 16:27 *will **j** all people according.*........1377
Matt 19:28 *thrones, **j-ing** the twelve* 1420
John 3:18 *been **j-d** for not believing*.........1302
John 5:22 *the Father **j-s** no one.*.............1318
John 5:22 *absolute authority to **j**,*.............1318
John 5:27 *authority to **j** everyone.*...........1318
John 5:30 *I **j** as God tells me.*...................1319
John 12:31 *time for **j-ing** this world*..........1434
John 12:47 *not **j** those who hear me* 1435
Acts 17:31 *he has set a day for **j-ing*** 1579
Rom 2:16 *Jesus, will **j** everyone's secret*...1649
Rom 3:6 *be qualified to **j** the world?*..........1650
1 Cor 6:2 *we believers will **j** the world?*.....1603
1 Cor 11:31 *we would not be **j-d***...............1614
2 Cor 5:10 *stand before Christ to be **j-d**.* ..1632
2 Tim 4:1 *Jesus, who will someday **j***.........1745
Heb 10:30 *The LORD will **j** his own* 1776
Heb 13:4 ***j** people who are immoral*..........1782
Jas 2:13 *will be merciful when he **j-s*** 1549
Jas 3:1 *we who teach will be **j-d** more* 1550
Jas 4:11 *criticizing and **j-ing** God's law.* ...1552
Jas 4:12 *So what right do you have to **j*** 1552
1 Pet 1:17 *He will **j** or reward you.*............1749
1 Pet 2:23 *God, who always **j-s** fairly.*........1752
Rev 19:11 ***j-s** fairly and wages a righteous*...1828
Rev 20:4 *given the authority to **j**.*...............1829
Rev 20:12 *the dead were **j-d** according to*..1830

JUDGMENT, JUDGMENTS (n) a ruling or decision by a ruler, a judge, or an individual; the process of forming an opinion or evalution by discerning and comparing
see also JUSTICE
Deut 1:17 *impartial in your **j-s**.*...................285
1 Sam 3:13 *warned him that **j** is coming*.....422
Ps 1:5 *be condemned at the time of **j**.* 856
Ps 37:13 *he sees their day of **j** coming.* 567
Ps 51:4 *your **j** against me is just*................506
Prov 4:1 *Pay attention and learn good **j**,*......636
Prov 4:7 *else you do, develop good **j**.*...........636
Prov 9:10 *results in good **j**.* 641
Isa 3:14 *comes forward to pronounce **j***.......827
Jer 11:20 *you make righteous **j-s**,*............1015
Jer 25:31 *His cry of **j** will reach*..................995
Dan 9:11 *curses and **j-s** written in* 1142
Hos 6:5 *with **j-s** as inescapable as light.*.....808
Joel 3:12 *LORD, will sit to pronounce **j***.......1243
Matt 5:21 *murder, you are subject to **j**.* 1328
Matt 11:24 *will be better off on **j** day*........1339
Matt 12:36 *on **j** day for every idle word*.....1341
Matt 12:41 *this generation on **j** day*..........1343
John 5:30 ***j** is just, because I carry out*......1319
John 8:16 *if I did, my **j** would be correct*...1392
John 16:8 *and of the coming **j**.*................1465
Acts 24:25 *coming day of **j**,* 1682
1 Cor 4:3 *I don't even trust my own **j***........1600
1 Cor 4:5 *don't make **j-s** about anyone.*....1600
1 Cor 11:29 *eating and drinking God's **j***....1614
2 Thes 1:8 ***j** on those who don't know.*......1588
Heb 9:27 *and after that comes **j**,* 1774
1 Pet 4:17 *And if **j** begins with us,*............1755
2 Pet 2:9 *until the day of final **j**.*................1759
2 Pet 3:7 *being kept for the day of **j**,*.........1760
Jude 1:6 *waiting for the great day of **j**.*.......1784
Rev 16:7 *your **j-s** are true and just.* 1823

JUST (adj) conforming to a standard of correctness; faithful to the original design; honest, fair, upright
see also RIGHT, RIGHTEOUS
Gen 18:19 *by doing what is right and **j**.*.........40
Deut 32:4 *Everything he does is **j***..............323
2 Sam 8:15 *did what was **j** and right*..........498
Neh 9:13 *and instructions that were **j**,* 1216
Job 37:23 *he is **j** and righteous,*.................127
Ps 33:5 *loves whatever is **j** and good;*.........858
Ps 92:15 *The LORD is **j**! He is* 862
Ps 119:121 *I have done what is **j*** 880
Prov 1:3 *do what is right, **j**, and fair.*...........631
Prov 2:9 *will understand what is right, **j**,*......634
Prov 12:5 *The plans of the godly are **j**;*.......645
Isa 16:5 *He will always do what is **j***............833
Isa 59:8 *or what it means to be **j***...............945
Jer 22:3 *Be fair-minded and **j**.*.....................991
Ezek 18:5 *and does what is **j** and right*......1064
Dan 4:37 *All his acts are **j** and true,*..........1121
Matt 5:45 *rain on the **j** and the unjust*.......1330
1 Jn 1:9 *he is faithful and **j** to forgive*........1787
Rev 15:3 ***J** and true are your ways,*...........1822
Rev 16:5 *You are **j**, O Holy One,*...............1823
Rev 16:7 *your judgments are true and **j**.* ...1823
Rev 19:2 *His judgments are true and **j**.* 1827

JUSTICE (n) the administration of law that determines what is right, based on principles of equity and correctness, and rewards accordingly; the quality of being just, impartial, or fair
see also JUDGMENT, RIGHTEOUSNESS
Exod 23:2 *by the crowd to twist **j**.*...............173
Lev 19:15 *Do not twist **j** in legal matters*.....225
Deut 16:19 *never twist **j** or show partiality*...306
Deut 32:36 *LORD will give **j** to his*................325
1 Sam 8:3 *bribes and perverted **j**.* 434
1 Kgs 3:11 *governing my people with **j***.......606
1 Kgs 7:7 *Hall of **J**, where he sat to hear*....613
2 Chr 9:8 *so you can rule with **j***..................626
Job 8:3 *Does God twist **j**?*..........................102
Job 19:7 *I protest, but there is no **j**.*............112
Job 31:6 *weigh me on the scales of **j**,*.........121
Job 34:17 *God govern if he hated **j**?*..........124
Ps 9:8 *He will judge the world with **j***..........549
Ps 10:18 *You will bring **j** to the orphans*......858
Ps 36:6 *your **j** like the ocean depths.*..........566
Ps 45:4 *defending truth, humility, and **j**.*......851
Ps 45:7 *You love **j** and hate evil.*.................851
Ps 72:1 *Give your love of **j** to the king,* 630
Ps 82:3 *Give **j** to the poor.*..........................602
Ps 96:13 *He will judge the world with **j**,* 864
Ps 98:9 ***j**, and the nations with fairness*.......865
Ps 99:4 *You have acted with **j*** 865
Ps 103:6 ***j** to all who are treated*................580
Ps 146:7 *He gives **j** to the oppressed*..........887
Prov 16:12 *his rule is built on **j**.*................651
Prov 19:28 *makes a mockery of **j**;*..............655
Prov 29:26 *but **j** comes from the LORD.* 846
Prov 31:9 *and see that they get **j**.*..............847
Isa 1:17 *Seek **j**. Help the oppressed*............824
Isa 1:27 *Zion will be restored by **j**;*...............824
Isa 5:16 *will be exalted by his **j**.*...................829
Isa 10:2 *They deprive the poor of **j***..............794
Isa 28:17 *with the measuring line of **j***.........819
Isa 33:5 *make Jerusalem his home of **j***........903
Isa 42:1 *He will bring **j** to the nations.* 926
Isa 51:4 *my **j** will become a light*.................938
Isa 59:9 *there is no **j** among us,* 945
Isa 59:14 ***j** is nowhere to be found*..............946
Isa 61:8 *I, the LORD, love **j**.*..........................948
Jer 4:2 *you could do so with truth, **j**,*...........964
Jer 9:24 *who brings **j** and righteousness*...1012
Jer 21:12 *Give **j** each morning* 1076
Jer 30:11 *discipline you, but with **j**;*.........1031
Lam 3:36 *if they twist **j** in the courts—*.....1098
Hos 2:19 *righteousness and **j**,*.....................804
Amos 5:7 *You twist **j**, making it a bitter*.......775
Amos 5:15 *courts into true halls of **j**.* 775
Amos 6:12 *when you turn **j** into poison*.......777
Mic 3:8 *I am filled with **j** and strength*.........907
Hab 1:4 *there is no **j** in the courts.*...............978
Zeph 3:5 *Day by day he hands down **j**,* 986
Mal 2:17 *Where is the God of **j**?*...................1247
Matt 5:6 *who hunger and thirst for **j**,*...........1326
Matt 12:18 *proclaim **j** to the nations.* 1322
Matt 23:23 *aspects of the law—**j**,*..............1444
Luke 11:42 *ignore **j** and the love of God.*...1398
Luke 18:3 *Give me **j** in this dispute*...........1417

Acts 8:33 *humiliated and received no **j.*** 1529
Acts 17:31 ***j** by the man he has appointed*....1579
Rom 2:2 *God, in his **j**, will punish*....1648
2 Thes 1:5 *persecution to show his **j***....1588
2 Thes 1:6 *In his **j** he will pay back*....1588
Heb 1:8 *You rule with a scepter of **j.*** 1762
Heb 7:2 *Melchizedek means "king of **j,"*** 1770
Heb 11:33 *ruled with **j**, and received*....1779

JUSTIFY, JUSTIFIED (v) to prove to be just, right, or reasonable; to acquit or absolve
see also RIGHT, RIGHTEOUS
Luke 10:29 *wanted to **j** his actions,*....1396
Luke 18:14 *returned home **j-ied***....1418
2 Cor 8:24 *boasting about you is **j-ied.***....1637

KEEP, KEEPING, KEEPS, KEPT (v) to be faithful to; to have in control; to refrain from granting, giving, or allowing; to cause to remain in a given place, situation, or condition; to refrain from revealing; to maintain or preserve
see also GUARD, OBEY, PROTECT
Exod 12:42 *the LORD **k-pt** his promise*....158
Exod 20:8 *Sabbath day by **k-ing** it holy*....169
Exod 31:13 *Be careful to **k** my Sabbath*....183
Deut 5:12 *Sabbath day by **k-ing** it holy,*....293
Deut 7:8 ***k-ing** the oath he had sworn*....296
Deut 7:9 *God who **k-s** his covenant for a*....296
Deut 7:12 *your God will **k** his covenant*....296
2 Chr 6:14 *You **k** your covenant*....620
2 Chr 34:31 *to obey the LORD by **k-ing***....972
Neh 1:5 *God who **k-s** his covenant of*....1203
Ps 15:4 ***k** their promises even when*....552
Ps 116:14 *I will **k** my promises to*....875
Ps 119:100 ***k-pt** your commandments.*....880
Ps 121:7 *The LORD **k-s** you from*....882
Ps 130:3 *LORD, if you **k-pt** a record of*....884
Ps 146:6 *He **k-s** every promise*....887
Prov 10:19 *and **k** your mouth shut*....642
Prov 15:3 ***k-ing** his eye on*....648
Prov 21:23 *your tongue and **k***....658
Eccl 3:6 *A time to **k** and a time to*....675
John 17:6 *and they have **k-pt** your word.* .1466
Acts 2:24 *death could not **k** him in its*....1515
Rom 10:3 *by trying to **k** the law.*....1663
Rom 14:22 ***k** it between yourself*....1670
1 Cor 1:8 *He will **k** you strong*....1595
1 Cor 7:19 ***k** God's commandments.*....1606
1 Cor 13:5 *it **k-s** no record*....1616
Eph 4:3 *effort to **k** yourselves united*....1710
1 Tim 5:22 ***K** yourself pure.*....1734
2 Tim 4:5 *But you should **k** a clear mind*....1745
Heb 11:27 *going because he **k-pt** his eyes*....1778
Jas 2:10 *the person who **k-s** all of the*....1549
1 Pet 1:4 ***k-pt** in heaven for you, pure*....1748
1 Jn 5:3 ***k-ing** his commandments,*....1794
Jude 1:21 ***k** yourselves safe in God's love.* 1786
Rev 12:17 ***k** God's commandments*....1819

KEY, KEYS (n) instrument that opens (or locks) doors or gates; symbolic of authority, power, and control
Matt 16:19 *the **k-s** of the Kingdom*....1375
Rev 1:18 *And I hold the **k-s** of death and*..1801
Rev 20:1 *with the **k** to the bottomless*....1829

KILL, KILLED, KILLING, KILLS (v) to take or deprive of life
Gen 4:8 *Abel, and **k-ed** him.*....14
Exod 2:12 *Moses **k-ed** the Egyptian*....142
Exod 21:12 *assaults and **k-s** another*....171
Lev 24:21 *whoever **k-s** another person*....232
2 Sam 2:26 *always be **k-ing** each other?*....479
Neh 9:26 *they **k-ed** your prophets*....1216
Job 13:15 *God might **k** me, but I*....107
Ps 44:22 *for your sake we are **k-ed***....850
Prov 6:17 *hands that **k** the innocent,*....638
Eccl 3:3 *A time to **k** and a time to*....675
Matt 10:28 *who want to **k** your body;*....1360
Matt 16:21 *He would be **k-ed,***....1376
Mark 10:34 *flog him with a whip, and **k***....1423
Luke 11:48 *They **k-ed** the prophets,*....1399
Acts 3:15 *You **k-ed** the author*....1517
Rom 8:36 *For your sake we are **k-ed***....1661
1 Tim 1:9 *who **k** their father or mother*....1727
1 Jn 3:12 *evil one and **k-ed** his brother.*...1791

KIND (adj) affectionate, loving; of a sympathetic or helping nature; gentle
Luke 6:35 *for he is **k** to those who are*....1330
1 Cor 13:4 *is patient and **k.** Love is not*....1616
Eph 4:32 *Instead, be **k** to each other,*....1712
2 Tim 2:24 *but must be **k** to everyone,*....1743

KIND, KINDS (n) nature, family, type, or category
Gen 1:12 *and trees of the same **k.***....7
1 Cor 12:4 *different **k-s** of spiritual gifts,*..1614
1 Tim 6:10 *root of all **k-s** of evil.*....1735

KINDNESS (n) a kind deed; affection; the quality or state of being kind
Ps 106:7 *his many acts of **k** to them.*....870
Rom 2:4 *his **k** is intended to turn you*....1648
Rom 3:24 *with undeserved **k,** declares*....1651
Rom 12:8 *gift for showing **k** to others,*....1667
2 Cor 6:1 *marvelous gift of God's **k***....1633
2 Cor 8:1 *God in his **k** has done through*...1635
2 Cor 10:1 *gentleness and **k** of Christ—*..1638
Gal 5:22 *peace, patience, **k,** goodness,*....1566
Eph 2:7 *his grace and **k** toward us,*....1707
Col 3:12 *mercy, **k,** humility,*....1700
Titus 3:4 *revealed his **k** and love,*....1739
1 Pet 2:3 *a taste of the Lord's **k.***....1750

KING, KINGS (n) a sovereign ruler (often God); chief among competitors
Deut 17:14 *We should select a **k** to rule*....307
Judg 17:6 *In those days Israel had no **k;***....403
1 Sam 8:5 *Give us a **k** to judge us*....434
1 Sam 11:15 *they made Saul **k.***....440
2 Sam 2:4 *and anointed him **k** over the*....478
2 Kgs 19:15 *of all the **k-s** of the earth.*....916
Ps 44:4 *You are my **K** and my God.*....850
Ps 68:32 *to God, you **k-s** of the earth.*....577
Ps 72:11 *All **k-s** will bow*....630
Ps 97:1 *The LORD is **k!***....864
Isa 32:1 *a righteous **k** is coming!*....902
Isa 37:16 *of all the **k-s** of the earth.*....917
Dan 2:21 *he removes **k-s** and sets*....1003
Dan 4:17 *Most High rules over the **k-s***....1120
Dan 4:37 *and honor the **K** of heaven.*....1121
Dan 7:24 *Its ten horns are ten **k-s.***....1136
Zeph 3:8 *to gather the **k-s** of the earth*....986
Zech 9:9 *Look, your **k** is coming to you.*....1175
Matt 27:11 *Are you the **k** of the Jews?*....1476
John 1:49 *Son of God—the **K** of Israel!*....1298
John 12:13 *Hail to the **K** of Israel!*....1431
Acts 17:7 *to another **k,** named Jesus.*....1577
1 Tim 1:17 *is the eternal **K,** the unseen*....1728
1 Tim 6:15 *the **K** of all **k-s** and*....1735
1 Pet 2:13 *the **k** as head of state,*....1751
Rev 1:5 *of all the **k-s** of the world.*....1799
Rev 17:14 *all lords and **K** of all **k-s.***....1825
Rev 19:16 ***K** of all **k-s** and Lord*....1828

KINGDOM (n) rule or realm; dominion of a king
Exod 19:6 *will be my **k** of priests,*....168
1 Kgs 11:31 *to tear the **k** from the hand*....672
1 Chr 28:7 *make his **k** last forever.*....539
Ps 145:11 *glory of your **k;***....589
Matt 3:2 *for the **K** of Heaven is near.*....1287
Matt 4:23 *Good News about the **K.***....1311
Matt 5:10 *right, for the **K** of Heaven is*....1326
Matt 5:19 *great in the **K** of Heaven.*....1327
Matt 6:10 *May your **K** come soon.*....1331
Matt 7:21 *will enter the **K** of Heaven.*....1334
Matt 8:12 *for whom the **K** was prepared—*....1336
Matt 10:7 *them that the **K** of Heaven is*....1358
Matt 11:12 *until now, the **K** of Heaven*....1338
Matt 12:26 *His own **k** will not*....1341
Matt 13:11 *secrets of the **K** of Heaven,*....1345
Matt 13:38 *represents the people of the **K.***....1349
Matt 13:43 *their Father's **K.** Anyone with* ..1349
Matt 13:45 *Again, the **K** of Heaven is*....1349
Matt 13:52 *a disciple in the **K** of Heaven*...1349
Matt 16:28 *Son of Man coming in his **K.*** ...1377
Matt 18:4 *greatest in the **K** of Heaven.*....1383
Matt 19:12 *sake of the **K** of Heaven*....1419
Matt 19:23 *to enter the **K** of Heaven.*....1420
Matt 20:1 *For the **K** of Heaven is*....1422
Matt 21:43 *I tell you, the **K** of God will*....1437
Matt 23:13 *shut the door of the **K** of Heaven*....1444
Matt 24:14 *Good News about the **K** will be*....1446
Matt 25:34 *inherit the **K** prepared for*....1453
Mark 3:24 *A **k** divided by*....1342
Mark 4:11 *secret of the **K** of God.*....1346
Mark 4:30 *I describe the **K** of God?*....1348
Mark 9:1 *they see the **K** of God arrive*....1378
Mark 10:15 *doesn't receive the **K** of God*..1420
Mark 10:24 *to enter the **K** of God.*....1421
Mark 11:10 *on the coming **K** of our*....1430
Mark 13:8 *and **k** against **k.***....1448
Mark 15:43 *waiting for the **K** of God to*....1487
Luke 4:43 *Good News of the **K** of God in*...1311
Luke 7:28 *least person in the **K** of God*....1338
Luke 8:10 *secrets of the **K** of God.*....1347
Luke 9:11 *taught them about the **K** of God,*....1364
Luke 9:60 *preach about the **K** of God.*....1388
Luke 10:9 *tell them, 'The **K** of God is*....1394
Luke 10:11 *know this—the **K** of God is*....1394
Luke 11:17 *he said, "Any **k** divided*....1342
Luke 11:20 *the **K** of God has arrived*....1342
Luke 12:31 *Seek the **K** of God.*....1401
Luke 13:18 *What is the **K** of God like?*....1348
Luke 14:15 *a banquet in the **K** of God!*....1408
Luke 17:20 *When will the **K** of God*....1416
Luke 17:21 *For the **K** of God is*....1416
Luke 18:24 *to enter the **K** of God!*....1422
Luke 18:29 *for the sake of the **K** of God,*...1422
Luke 21:10 *and **k** against **k.***....1450
Luke 22:16 *fulfilled in the **K** of God.*....1458
Luke 22:29 *granted me a **K,** I now grant*...1459
Luke 23:42 *come into your **K.***....1484
John 3:3 *you cannot see the **K** of God.*....1301
John 3:5 *no one can enter the **K** of God*....1301
John 18:36 *But my **K** is not of*....1478
Acts 1:3 *talked to them about the **K** of God.*....1512
Acts 1:6 *restore our **k?***....1500
Acts 8:12 *News concerning the **K** of God*..1527
Acts 19:8 *about the **K** of God.*....1594
Acts 28:23 *testified about the **K** of God*....1689

Rom 14:17 *For the **K** of God is*................1670
1 Cor 4:20 *For the **K** of God is*................1601
1 Cor 6:10 *will inherit the **K** of God.*..........1603
1 Cor 15:24 *will turn the **K** over to God*.....1621
1 Cor 15:50 *cannot inherit the **K** of God*....1622
Gal 5:21 *will not inherit the **K** of God*.........1566
Eph 5:5 *will inherit the **K** of Christ*............1712
Col 4:11 *with me here for the **K** of God.*....1703
1 Thes 2:12 *to share in his **K** and glory.*....1582
2 Thes 1:5 *worthy of his **K,** for which*........1588
2 Tim 4:18 *his heavenly **K.** All glory to*......1746
Heb 12:28 *we are receiving a **K** that is*......1781
Jas 2:5 *inherit the **K** he promised to*.........1548
2 Pet 1:11 *into the eternal **K** of our*...........1757
Rev 1:6 *made us a **K** of priests for*...........1799
Rev 5:10 *to become a **K** of priests for*.......1810
Rev 11:15 *now become the **K** of our Lord*...1817
Rev 12:10 *power and the **K** of our God,* 1818
Rev 16:10 ***k** was plunged into darkness*....1823

KINSMAN-REDEEMER (KJV)
Ruth 3:9 *my **family redeemer***...................414
Ruth 3:12 *of your **family redeemers***...........414
Ruth 4:1 *the **family redeemer** he had*........414

KISS, KISSES (n) a greeting or caress with the lips; an expression of affection
Prov 27:6 *better than many **k-es** from an*...842
Song 7:9 *May your **k-es** be as*..................669
Mark 14:45 *and gave him the **k.***..............1470
Luke 22:48 *the Son of Man with a **k?***.......1470

KISS, KISSING (v) to caress with the lips
Song 1:2 ***K** me and **k** me again,*.................663
Song 8:1 *Then I could **k** you no matter*........669
Luke 7:38 *Then she kept **k-ing** his feet*....1340

KNEE, KNEES (n) the joint in the middle part of the leg; when bent, symbolic of submission or defeat
Isa 35:3 *those who have weak **k-s.***...........905
Isa 45:23 *Every **k** will bend to me,*.............932
Luke 5:8 *he fell to his **k-s** before Jesus*....1308
Rom 14:11 *every **k** will bend to me,* 1670
Eph 3:14 *I fall to my **k-s** and pray to*.........1709
Phil 2:10 *at the name of Jesus every **k***.....1720
Heb 12:12 *strengthen your weak **k-s.*** 1780

KNEEL, KNELT (v) to bend the knee; to fall or rest on the knees; usually a gesture of submission, defeat, or reverence
2 Chr 6:13 *then he **k-lt** in front of*..............620
Ps 95:6 *Let us **k** before the LORD*................863
Dan 6:10 *went home and **k-lt** down*..........1140
Matt 8:2 *approached him and **k-lt***............1311
Matt 9:18 *came and **k-lt** before him.*.........1353
Matt 17:14 *came and **k-lt** before Jesus* ...1381
Matt 27:29 ***k-lt** before him in mockery*.....1481
Luke 22:41 *stone's throw, and **k-lt** down*...1469
Acts 20:36 *speaking, he **k-lt** and prayed*..1676
Acts 21:5 *There we **k-lt,** prayed,*.............1676

KNEW (v) to be familiar with
see also KNOW
Matt 7:23 *reply, 'I never **k** you.*................1334
John 2:24 *because he **k** human nature*.....1300
John 19:28 *Jesus **k** that his mission*.........1486
Acts 2:23 *But God **k** what would*..............1515
Rom 1:21 *Yes, they **k** God,*.......................1647
Rom 8:29 *God **k** his people in advance,*....1660
1 Pet 1:2 *God the Father **k** you and*..........1747

KNIT (v) to link firmly or closely
Ps 139:13 ***k** me together in my mother's*....586
Col 2:2 *encouraged and **k** together by*......1697

KNOCK, KNOCKING, KNOCKS (v) to strike sharply
Matt 7:7 *Keep on **k-ing,** and the door*......1334
Matt 7:8 *to everyone who **k-s,** the door*....1334
Luke 11:9 *Keep on **k-ing,** and the door*....1398
Rev 3:20 *I stand at the door and **k.***...........1807

KNOW, KNOWING, KNOWN, KNOWS (v) to be intimately familiar with; to discern, recognize, regard, acknowledge, pay heed to, approve, learn
see also KNEW
Gen 3:5 *like God, **k-ing** both good and*.........11
Gen 3:22 *like us, **k-ing** both good and*.........13
Gen 22:12 *for now I **k** that you truly*.............46
Exod 6:7 *Then you will **k** that I am the* 148
Deut 18:21 *How will we **k** whether or not*....309
Deut 29:29 *God has secrets **k-n** to no*.........321
Josh 23:14 *Deep in your hearts you **k** that*..369
Job 19:25 *for me, I **k** that my Redeemer*......112
Ps 9:10 *Those who **k** your name trust*.........549
Ps 19:2 *after night they make him **k-n.*** 554
Ps 44:21 *for he **k-s** the secrets of*..............850
Ps 46:10 *Be still, and **k** that I am*...............852
Ps 94:10 *doesn't he also **k** what you*..........862
Ps 94:11 *The LORD **k-s** people's thoughts;*..862
Ps 103:14 *For he **k-s** how weak we are;* 580
Ps 119:168 *you **k** everything I do.*.............881
Ps 139:2 *You **k** when I sit*..........................586
Ps 139:23 *O God, and **k** my heart;* 586
Isa 12:4 *Let them **k** how mighty*.................797
Jer 9:24 *that they truly **k** me and* 1012
Jer 31:34 *will **k** me already,*.......................1034
Dan 11:32 *the people who **k** their God*......1160
Matt 6:3 *don't let your left hand **k** what* 1330
Matt 10:29 *without your Father **k-ing** it*....1360
Matt 11:27 *no one truly **k-s** the Father*.....1339
Mark 12:24 *you don't **k** the Scriptures,*.....1440
Luke 11:13 *if you sinful people **k** how to*...1398
Luke 13:25 *will reply, 'I don't **k** you*..........1407
Luke 16:15 *but God **k-s** your hearts.*........1412
Luke 23:34 *they don't **k** what they are*......1484
John 3:11 *you what we **k** and have seen,* ...1302
John 4:42 *Now we **k** that he*.....................1306
John 6:69 *we **k** you are the Holy One* 1369
John 7:28 *Yes, you **k** me, and you*............1390
John 8:14 *For I **k** where I came*................1392
John 8:32 *And you will **k** the truth,* 1393
John 10:4 *because they **k** his voice.*..........1405
John 10:27 *I **k** them, and they follow*........1406
John 13:17 *Now that you **k** these things,* ..1456
John 14:7 *If you had really **k-n** me,*..........1461
John 16:30 *we understand that you **k***.......1465
John 17:23 *the world will **k** that you sent*..1467
John 21:15 *Peter replied, "you **k** I love*......1497
Acts 1:24 *O Lord, you **k** every heart*..........1513
Rom 1:19 *They **k** the truth*.........................1647
Rom 7:18 *And I **k** that nothing good* 1658
Rom 8:26 *we don't **k** what God wants us*..1660
Rom 8:27 *the Father who **k-s** all hearts*....1660
Rom 11:34 *For who can **k** the LORD's*........1666
Rom 12:16 *And don't think you **k** it all!*.....1668
Rom 16:26 *message is made **k-n** to all*.....1674
1 Cor 2:11 *no one can **k** God's thoughts*...1598
1 Cor 13:12 *All that I **k** now is partial*........1616
2 Cor 4:6 *so we could **k** the glory of*.........1631
Gal 4:9 *now that you **k** God (or should*......1563
Phil 3:10 *I want to **k** Christ and*................1722
Col 1:10 *you learn to **k** God better and*......1694
1 Thes 3:3 *But you **k** that we*....................1583
1 Thes 5:2 *For you **k** quite well*.................1585
2 Thes 1:8 *on those who don't **k** God*.......1588
1 Tim 1:7 *but they don't **k** what they*........1727
1 Tim 3:15 *you will **k** how people must*.....1731
2 Tim 1:12 *I **k** the one in whom I trust,*......1741
2 Tim 2:19 *The LORD **k-s** those who are*....1743
Heb 8:11 *greatest, will **k** me already.*.........1772
Heb 11:8 *without **k-ing** where he*.............1777
Jas 1:3 *For you **k** that when your faith*......1546
Jas 4:14 *How do you **k** what your life* 1552
Jas 4:17 *it is sin to **k** what you ought*.........1552
1 Pet 2:19 *do what you **k** is right and*.......1752
2 Pet 2:21 *they had never **k-n** the way to*...1759
1 Jn 2:3 *we can be sure that we **k** him*.....1788
1 Jn 2:4 *claims, "I **k** God," but*..................1788
1 Jn 2:5 *is how we **k** we are living in*........1788
1 Jn 2:11 *person does not **k** the way to*....1789
1 Jn 2:29 *Since we **k** that Christ*..............1790
1 Jn 3:1 *they don't **k** him.*........................1790
1 Jn 3:2 *But we do **k** that we will be*.........1790
1 Jn 3:24 *And we **k** he lives in us*.............1792
1 Jn 4:6 *is how we **k** if someone has*.........1793
1 Jn 4:7 *is a child of God and **k-s** God*......1793
1 Jn 4:8 *does not **k** God, for God*..............1793
1 Jn 5:13 *you may **k** you have eternal*......1794
1 Jn 5:15 *And since we **k** he hears us*......1794
1 Jn 5:20 *And we **k** that the Son of*..........1795
Rev 3:15 *I **k** all the things you do,*.............1807

KNOWLEDGE (n) the fact or condition of being aware of something, of having information, or of being learned; information, wisdom
Gen 2:9 *the tree of the **k** of good and*...........10
Gen 2:17 *the tree of the **k** of good and*.........10
Prov 1:7 *foundation of true **k,** but fools*.......632
Prov 2:6 *From his mouth come **k** and*.........633
Prov 3:20 *By his **k** the deep*.......................635
Prov 8:10 ***k** rather than pure gold.*..............640
Prov 14:6 ***k** comes easily to those with*.......647
Prov 18:15 *Their ears are open for **k.*** 654
Isa 11:2 *the Spirit of **k** and the fear* 795
Luke 11:52 *remove the key to **k** from* 1399
Rom 2:20 *gives you complete **k***...............1649
1 Cor 12:8 *gives a message of special **k.***..1614
1 Cor 13:2 *and possessed all **k,***...............1616
1 Cor 13:9 *Now our **k** is partial.*................1616
2 Cor 2:14 *to spread the **k** of Christ.*.........1628
Eph 1:17 *grow in your **k** of God.* 1706
Eph 4:13 *our faith and **k** of God's Son.*......1711
Phil 1:9 *will keep on growing in **k** and.*......1717
Col 1:9 *to give you complete **k** of his*.......1694
Col 2:3 *treasures of wisdom and **k.*** 1697
Heb 10:26 *we have received **k** of the*........1776
2 Pet 1:5 *and moral excellence with **k,*** 1757
2 Pet 1:8 ***k** of our Lord Jesus Christ.*.........1757
2 Pet 3:18 *the grace and **k** of our Lord*.....1760

LABOR (adj) of or relating to manual labor; of or relating to the physical activities of giving birth
1 Kgs 12:4 *Lighten the harsh **l** demands*.....696
Gal 4:19 *I'm going through **l** pains for*.......1563

LABOR (n) work that produces goods and services; the physical activities of giving birth
Ps 128:2 *enjoy the fruit of your **l.***................883
Isa 54:1 *you who have never been in **l.*** 941
Gal 4:27 *have never been in **l!***..................1564

LACK (n) the fact or state of being wanting or deficient; absence
Prov 5:23 *die for **l** of self-control;* 637
Prov 15:22 *go wrong for **l** of advice;* 650
1 Cor 7:5 *because of your **l** of self-control.*1605

LACK, LACKED, LACKING (v) to be deficient, missing, or short; to have need of something
Deut 2:7 *and you have **l-ed** nothing*............287

Deut 28:48 *naked, and **l-ing** in everything*.....319
Neh 9:21 *and they **l-ed** nothing*.....1216
Prov 28:27 *the poor will **l** nothing,*.....844

LAID (v) to place or set down
see also LAY
Isa 53:6 *Yet the LORD **l** on him the*.....940
Acts 6:6 *as they **l** their hands on them*.....1523
Acts 8:18 *the apostles **l** their hands on*.....1528
1 Tim 4:14 *elders of the church **l** their*.....1732
2 Tim 1:6 *when I **l** my hands on*.....1741

LAKE (n) a considerable inland body of standing water
Matt 8:24 *a fierce storm struck the **l**,*.....1349
Luke 8:33 *into the **l** and drowned.*.....1353
John 6:25 *on the other side of the **l***.....1367
Rev 19:20 *into the fiery **l** of burning*.....1828
Rev 20:14 *This **l** of fire is*.....1830

LAKESHORE (n) the land bordering a lake
Mark 4:1 *Jesus began teaching by the **l***....1346

LAMB, LAMBS (n) a young sheep that is less than one year old; symbolic name of Jesus
Exod 12:21 *pick out a **l** or young goat*.....156
Isa 53:7 *He was led like a **l** to the*.....940
Mark 14:12 *the Passover **l** is sacrificed,*.....1455
Luke 10:3 *out as **l-s** among wolves.*.....1394
John 1:29 *and said, "Look! The **L** of God*.....1297
John 21:15 *"Then feed my **l-s**," Jesus*.....1497
Acts 8:32 *And as a **l** is silent before*.....1529
1 Pet 1:19 *sinless, spotless **L** of God.*.....1749
Rev 5:6 *Then I saw a **L** that looked as*.....1809
Rev 5:12 *Worthy is the **L** who was*.....1810
Rev 7:14 *robes in the blood of the **L***.....1813
Rev 15:3 *the song of the **L**:*.....1822
Rev 17:14 *to war against the **L**, but the*....1825
Rev 19:9 *to the wedding feast of the **L**.*....1828
Rev 21:23 *and the **L** is its light.*.....1831

LAME (adj) having a disabled body part as to impair freedom of movement
Isa 33:23 *Even the **l** will take*.....903
Isa 35:6 *The **l** will leap like a*.....905
Matt 11:5 *blind see, the **l** walk,*.....1337
Matt 15:31 *the **l** were walking,*.....1372
Luke 14:21 *the blind, and the **l**.*.....1409
Heb 12:13 *weak and **l** will not fall*.....1781

LAMP, LAMPS (n) a source of intellectual or spiritual illumination; any of various devices for producing light
2 Sam 22:29 *O LORD, you are my **l**.*.....527
Ps 18:28 *You light a **l** for me.*.....528
Ps 119:105 *Your word is a **l** to guide my*.....880
Prov 6:23 *For their command is a **l***.....638
Prov 31:18 *her **l** burns late*.....847
Matt 6:22 *Your eye is a **l** that*.....1332
Matt 25:1 *who took their **l-s***.....1451
Matt 25:7 *got up and prepared their **l-s**.*...1451
Luke 8:16 *No one lights a **l** and then*.....1347
Luke 12:35 *and keep your **l-s** burning,*.....1401
Rev 22:5 *no need for **l-s** or sun—for the*..1832

LAMPSTAND, LAMPSTANDS (n) a support that holds a lamp
Exod 25:31 *Make the entire **l** and its*.....176
2 Chr 4:7 *cast ten gold **l-s** according to*.....616
Zech 4:2 *a solid gold **l** with a bowl of*.....1168
Zech 4:11 *on each side of the **l**,*.....1169
Heb 9:2 *In the first room were a **l**,*.....1772
Rev 1:12 *I saw seven gold **l-s**.*.....1800
Rev 1:20 *the seven gold **l-s**:*.....1801
Rev 2:5 *and remove your **l** from its*.....1802

LAND (n) the solid part of the surface of the earth; a portion of the earth's solid surface distinguishable by boundaries or ownership
Gen 1:10 *the dry ground "**l**" and the*.....7
Gen 15:18 *I have given this **l** to your*.....36
Exod 6:8 *you into the **l** I swore to*.....148
Deut 8:7 *you into a good **l** of flowing*.....297
Ps 37:11 *will possess the **l** and will*.....567

LANGUAGE, LANGUAGES (n) means of communication peculiar to a certain people; a special language gift given by the Holy Spirit
see also TONGUE(S)
Gen 11:9 *the people with different **l-s**.*.....23
Isa 28:11 *speak a strange **l**!*.....818
Mark 16:17 *they will speak in new **l-s**.*.....1498
Acts 2:4 *speaking in other **l-s**, as the*.....1514
1 Cor 12:28 *speak in unknown **l-s**.*.....1615
1 Cor 12:30 *to interpret unknown **l-s**?*.....1615
1 Cor 13:8 *in unknown **l-s** and special*.....1616
1 Cor 14:19 *in an unknown **l**.*.....1617
Eph 4:29 *or abusive **l**. Let everything*.....1712
Col 3:8 *slander, and dirty **l**.*.....1700
Rev 5:9 *every tribe and **l** and people*.....1810
Rev 7:9 *and tribe and people and **l**,*.....1813
Rev 14:6 *nation, tribe, **l**, and people*.....1821

LAP (v) to take in food or drink with the tongue
Judg 7:5 *and **l** it up with their tongues*.....385

LASCIVIOUSNESS (KJV)
Mark 7:22 *deceit, **lustful desires**, envy,*.....1371
2 Cor 12:21 *and **eagerness for lustful pleasure***.....1642
Gal 5:19 *impurity, **lustful pleasures***.....1566
Eph 4:19 *They live for **lustful pleasure***.....1711
1 Pet 4:3 *their **immorality** and lust,*.....1754

LAST, LASTING (adj) following all the rest; being the only remaining; belonging to the final stage; of or relating to being continuous in time; existing or continuing a long while
Prov 10:25 *have a **l-ing** foundation.*.....643
Matt 20:16 *who are **l** now will be first*.....1423
John 15:16 *to go and produce **l-ing** fruit,*.1464
Acts 2:17 *'In the **l** days,' God says,*.....1514
1 Cor 15:26 *And the **l** enemy to be*.....1621
1 Cor 15:52 ***l** trumpet is blown.*.....1622
2 Tim 3:1 *that in the **l** days there will*.....1744
2 Pet 3:3 *that in the **l** days scoffers*.....1760
Jude 1:18 *you that in the **l** times there*.....1785
Rev 1:17 *I am the First and the **L**.*.....1801
Rev 22:13 *the Omega, the First and the **L**,*.....1832

LAST (n) the one who is at or endures to the end
Isa 41:4 *First and the **L**. I alone*.....925
Isa 44:6 *First and the **L**; there is no*.....930
Isa 48:12 *God, the First and the **L**.*.....935

LAST, LASTS (v) to continue in time
Ps 30:5 *For his anger **l** only a moment,*.....563
1 Cor 13:13 ***l** forever—faith, hope, and*....1616

LAUGH, LAUGHED, LAUGHS (v) to show mirth or joy or to despise or mock something with a chuckle or explosive vocal sound
Gen 17:17 ***l-ed** to himself in disbelief.*.....39
Gen 18:12 *So she **l-ed** silently to herself*.....39
Ps 2:4 *one who rules in heaven **l-s**.*.....856
Ps 37:13 *the LORD just **l-s**, for he sees*.....567
Ps 59:8 *But LORD, you **l** at them.*.....454
Prov 31:25 *and she **l-s** without fear of*.....848
Eccl 3:4 *and a time to **l**. A time to*.....675
Luke 6:21 *for in due time you will **l**.*.....1326
Luke 6:25 *awaits you who **l** now,*.....1327

LAUGHTER (n) a chuckle or explosive vocal sound; cause for merriment
Gen 21:6 *God has brought me **l**.*.....43
Ps 126:2 *We were filled with **l**, and we*.....1154
Eccl 2:2 *So I said, "**L** is silly.*.....674
Jer 7:34 *happy singing and **l** in the*.....1009
Jas 4:9 *instead of **l**, and gloom*.....1552

LAVER(S) (KJV)
Exod 30:18 *Make a bronze **washbasin***.....182
Lev 8:11 ***washbasin** and its stand,*.....211
1 Kgs 7:38 *ten smaller bronze **basins***.....614
2 Chr 4:14 *carts holding the **basins***.....616

LAVISH (v) to expend or bestow with profusion
Exod 34:7 *I **l** unfailing love*.....187

LAW, LAWS (n) words of Moses; a binding decree; a universal principle; governing authority
see also COMMANDMENT(S), INSTRUCTION(S), REGULATIONS, TEACHING(S)
2 Chr 17:9 *the Book of the **L***.....714
Ps 1:2 *delight in the **l** of the LORD,*.....856
Ps 93:5 *Your royal **l-s** cannot be*.....862
Ps 119:14 *rejoiced in your **l-s** as much as*..878
Ps 119:36 *for your **l-s** rather than a love*....878
Ps 119:125 *I will understand your **l-s**.*.....881
Ps 119:152 *days that your **l-s** will last*.....881
Matt 5:17 *to abolish the **l** of Moses or*.....1327
Matt 5:19 *who obeys God's **l-s**.*.....1327
Matt 22:40 *The entire **l** and all the*.....1441
Matt 23:23 *of the **l**—justice, mercy,*.....1444
Mark 7:8 *ignore God's **l** and substitute*.....1370
Luke 11:52 *experts in religious **l**!*.....1399
Luke 23:56 *rested as required by the **l**.*.....1488
Luke 24:44 *written about me in the **l***.....1498
John 1:17 *For the **l** was given*.....1272
Rom 2:12 *be judged by that **l** when they*...1649
Rom 2:15 *that God's **l** is written in*.....1649
Rom 2:20 *that God's **l** gives you*.....1649
Rom 2:25 *if you don't obey God's **l**,*.....1650
Rom 3:19 *Obviously, the **l** applies to*.....1651
Rom 3:21 *requirements of the **l**, as was*....1651
Rom 3:28 *not by obeying the **l**.*.....1652
Rom 4:13 *his obedience to God's **l**,*.....1653
Rom 4:16 *according to the **l** of Moses,*.....1653
Rom 5:13 *was not yet any **l** to break.*.....1655
Rom 6:15 *has set us free from the **l**,*.....1656
Rom 7:4 *power of the **l** when you died*.....1657
Rom 7:5 *the **l** aroused these evil desires*...1657
Rom 7:8 *If there were no **l**, sin would*.....1657
Rom 7:12 *But still, the **l** itself is*.....1658
Rom 7:22 *I love God's **l** with all my*.....1658
Rom 7:25 *I really want to obey God's **l**,*.....1658
Rom 8:3 *did what the **l** could not do*.....1658
Rom 8:4 *requirement of the **l** would be*.....1658
Rom 8:7 *did obey God's **l-s**, and it*.....1659
Rom 9:4 *gave them his **l**. He gave them*.....1661
Rom 9:31 *with God by keeping the **l**,*.....1662
Rom 10:4 *for which the **l** was given.*.....1663
Rom 13:10 *requirements of God's **l**.*.....1669
1 Cor 9:9 *For the **l** of Moses*.....1608
1 Cor 9:21 *I obey the **l** of Christ.*.....1609
2 Cor 3:6 *not of written **l-s**, but of the*.....1629
Gal 2:16 *by obeying the **l**. And we have*....1559
Gal 2:19 *So I died to the **l**—I stopped*.....1560
Gal 3:2 *by obeying the **l** of Moses?*.....1560
Gal 3:5 *because you obey the **l**?*.....1560
Gal 3:11 *by trying to keep the **l**.*.....1561
Gal 3:19 *But the **l** was designed*.....1562
Gal 3:21 *If the **l** could give us*.....1562
Gal 3:23 *placed under guard by the **l**.*.....1562
Gal 4:21 *live under the **l**, do you know*.....1564
Gal 5:3 *in the whole **l** of Moses*.....1565

Gal 5:14 *the whole **l** can be summed*........1566
Gal 6:2 *this way obey the **l** of Christ*..........1567
Eph 2:15 *the system of **l** with its*...............1708
Phil 3:6 ***l** obeyed the **l** without fault*...........1722
1 Tim 1:8 *know that the **l** is good when*.....1727
Heb 10:1 *under the **l** of Moses*................1774
Jas 1:25 *into the perfect **l** that sets*..........1548
Jas 2:8 *obey the royal **l** as found in*..........1549
Jas 2:10 *all of the **l-s** except one is as*.....1549

LAWGIVER (n) one who gives a code of laws to a people
Isa 33:22 *is our judge, our **l**, and our*..........903

LAWLESS (adj) not regulated by law; not restrained or controlled by law; unruly
Acts 2:23 *the help of **l** Gentiles,*................1515
Heb 10:17 *their sins and **l** deeds.*.............1775

LAWLESSNESS (n) the quality or state of not being restrained or controlled by law
2 Thes 2:3 *the man of **l** is revealed—*.......1588
2 Thes 2:7 *For this **l** is already*..................1589
2 Thes 2:8 *Then the man of **l** will be*.........1589

LAWSUITS (n) acts or instances of suing
1 Cor 6:7 *Even to have such **l** with one*.....1603

LAY, LAYING (v) to put or set down
see also LAID
Exod 29:10 *his sons will **l** their hands*.........180
Lev 1:4 ***L** your hand on*............................203
Lev 4:15 *must then **l** their hands on*...........206
Num 8:10 *of Israel must **l** their hands*.........200
Num 27:18 *in him, and **l** your hands on*......273
Acts 8:19 *so that when I **l** my hands on*....1528
Heb 6:2 *the **l-ing** on of hands,*................1768
Rev 4:10 *And they **l** their crowns*.............1808

LAZINESS (n) a disinclination to activity or exertion
Prov 31:27 *suffers nothing from **l**.*..............848
Ezek 16:49 *gluttony, and **l**, while the*.........1062

LAZY (adj) disinclined to activity or exertion; not energetic or vigorous
Prov 12:27 ***L** people don't*............................646
Prov 20:4 *Those too **l** to plow in the*............656
Rom 12:11 *Never be **l**, but work*..............1667
1 Tim 5:13 *they will learn to be **l**.*.............1733
Titus 1:12 *animals, and **l** gluttons.*.............1737

LAZYBONES (n) a lazy person
Prov 6:6 *from the ants, you **l**.*.....................638

LEAD, LEADING, LEADS (v) to guide by direction or example; to go at the head of; to result in
see also LED
Deut 27:18 *anyone who **l-s** a blind*............317
Deut 31:2 *no longer able to **l** you.*..............322
Josh 1:6 *one who will **l** these people*..........336
2 Chr 1:10 *knowledge to **l** them*.................608
Ps 25:9 *He **l-s** the humble in*....................560
Ps 73:24 *with your counsel, **l-ing** me to a*....594
Prov 6:22 *counsel will **l** you.*.......................638
Prov 14:30 *A peaceful heart **l-s** to a*..........648
Prov 19:23 *Fear of the LORD **l-s** to life,*........655
Isa 11:6 *little child will **l** them all.*................796
Matt 15:14 *blind guides **l-ing** the blind,*.....1370
John 10:3 *by name and **l-s** them out*........1405
Rom 6:16 *to sin, which **l-s** to death,*.........1656
Rom 6:22 *things that **l** to holiness and*......1656
1 Tim 5:24 ***l-ing** them to certain judgment.*.1734
Rev 7:17 *He will **l** them to*.......................1813

LEADER, LEADERS (n) a person who has commanding authority or influence; chief among others
1 Sam 13:14 *to be the **l** of his people,*........442
Prov 17:26 *to flog **l-s** for being honest*........653
Jer 51:46 ***l-s** fight against each other.*......1039
Matt 20:26 *a **l** among you must be*...........1424
Mark 10:43 *a **l** among you must be*..........1424
Luke 22:26 ***l** should be like a servant.*.......1458
Acts 13:27 *Jerusalem and their **l-s** did not*..1542
1 Thes 5:12 *who are your **l-s** in the Lord's*..1585
Heb 13:7 *Remember your **l-s** who taught*...1782
Heb 13:17 *Obey your spiritual **l-s**, and do*...1783
3 Jn 1:9 *to be the **l**, refuses to have*.........1797

LEADERSHIP (n) the office or position of a leader; capacity to lead
Num 33:1 *under the **l** of Moses*.................280
1 Cor 12:28 *those who have the gift of **l**,*..1615

LEAP, LEAPED (v) to spring from (or as if from) the ground
Isa 35:6 *The lame will **l** like a deer,*.............905
Luke 1:41 *Elizabeth's child **l-ed** within*......1275

LEARN, LEARNED, LEARNS (v) to come to know or realize; to acquire knowledge, skill, or behavioral tendency
Deut 4:10 *Then they will **l** to fear me*..........290
Deut 5:1 *so you may **l** them and obey*.........292
Prov 9:9 *and they will **l** even more.*.............641
Prov 18:15 *are always ready to **l**.*...............654
Isa 1:17 ***L** to do good.*..............................824
Isa 26:9 *will people **l** what is right.*.............896
Isa 29:13 *man-made rules **l-ed** by rote.*.......898
Matt 2:7 *and he **l-ed** from them the time*..1284
John 6:45 *listens to the Father and **l-s***.....1368
Phil 4:9 *all you **l-ed** and received from*.....1725
Phil 4:11 *have **l-ed** how to be content*.......1725
Col 1:10 *grow as you **l** to know God.*.........1694
1 Tim 2:11 *Women should **l** quietly and*....1730
2 Tim 1:13 *teaching you **l-ed** from me—*.1741
Heb 5:8 *he **l-ed** obedience from the*.........1767

LEAST (adj) lowest in importance or position
Matt 19:30 *will be **l** important then,*..........1421
Mark 10:31 *will be **l** important then,*.........1421

LEATHER (adj) of or relating to animal skin dressed for use
2 Kgs 1:8 *he wore a **l** belt around his*..........733
Matt 3:4 *he wore a **l** belt around his*.........1288

LEAVEN (KJV)
Exod 12:20 *anything made with **yeast***........156
Exod 13:7 *any **yeast** at all found within*........158
Matt 13:33 *of Heaven is like the **yeast***......1348
Matt 16:6 *the **yeast** of the Pharisees*..........1374
1 Cor 5:6 *this sin is like a little **yeast***.........1602

LED (v) to guide by direction or example
see also LEAD
Ps 68:18 *the heights, you **l** a crowd of*........576
Isa 53:7 *He was **l** like a lamb*.....................940
Jer 11:19 *like a lamb being **l** to the*...........1014
Luke 4:1 *He was **l** by the Spirit*.................1295
Acts 8:32 *He was **l** like a sheep*................1529
Rom 8:14 *all who are **l** by the Spirit*............1659
Eph 4:8 *the heights, he **l** a crowd of*..........1710

LEFT (adj) of, relating to, situated on, or being the side of the body in which the heart is mostly located
Matt 6:3 *don't let your **l** hand know*..........1330

LEFT (n) the location or direction of the left side
Josh 1:7 *or to the **l**. Then you will be*..........336
Josh 23:6 *either to the right or to the **l**.*.......368
Isa 30:21 *to the right or to the **l**.*.................900
Matt 25:33 *and the goats at his **l**.*.............1453
Matt 25:41 *those on the **l** and say, 'Away*..1453

LEFT (v) to depart from; to allow to remain
Isa 53:6 *We have **l** God's paths*..................940
Ezek 34:8 *and **l** the sheep to starve.*..........1110

LEFTOVERS (n) something that remains unused or unconsumed
Matt 14:20 *picked up twelve baskets of **l**.*.1363

LEGION (n) a very large number; multitude
Mark 5:9 *My name is **L**, because there*.....1351

LEND, LENDING (v) to give for temporary use on condition that the same or its equivalent be returned
Lev 25:37 *interest on money you **l***..............234
Deut 15:8 *and **l** them whatever*..................305
Ps 15:5 *Those who **l** money without*...........552
Prov 19:17 *you are **l-ing** to the LORD—*.......655
Luke 6:34 *Even sinners will **l** to other*........1330

LENDER, LENDERS (n) one who loans to another
Exod 22:25 *as a money **l** would*..................173
Prov 22:7 *borrower is servant to the **l**.*.........659
Isa 24:2 *and sellers, **l-s** and borrowers,*......894

LENGTHENS (v) to make longer; to extend
Prov 10:27 *of the LORD **l** one's life,*..............643

LEPERS (n) one who suffers from a severe contagious skin and nerve disease
Matt 11:5 *lame walk, the **l** are cured,*........1337
Luke 17:12 *ten **l** stood at a distance,*.........1416

LEPROSY (n) a chronic infectious disease affecting the skin and peripheral nerves which causes loss of sensation, paralysis, and deformities
Num 12:10 *as white as snow from **l**.*...........250
2 Kgs 5:1 *he suffered from **l**.*.......................743
2 Kgs 7:3 *four men with **l** sitting at*.............746
2 Chr 26:21 *King Uzziah had **l** until the*.......764

LESSON (n) something learned by study or experience; an instructive example
Lev 26:23 *to learn the **l** and continue*..........235
Prov 6:6 *Take a **l** from the ants,*...................638

LETTER, LETTERS (n) a piece of written communication
Deut 24:1 *he writes her a **l** of divorce,*........314
2 Cor 3:2 *Your lives are a **l** written in*.........1629
2 Cor 10:10 *Paul's **l-s** are demanding*......1638
2 Thes 3:14 *obey what we say in this **l**.*....1590
2 Pet 3:16 *have twisted his **l-s** to mean*....1760

LEVEL (v) to make flat
Isa 40:4 *valleys, and **l** the mountains*..........923

LEVI

1. Third son of Jacob and Leah (Gen 29:34, p. 61), who gave his name to a tribe of Israel; violently avenged his sister Dinah (Gen 34, p. 67); cursed for his violent temper (Gen 49:5-7, p. 91); his tribe was blessed (Deut 33:8-11, p. 326), chosen for priestly service (Num 3–4, p. 240), numbered (Num 3:39, p. 241; 26:62, p. 272), allotted cities, but not land (Josh 13:14, p. 356; *see also* Num 18:21-32, p. 259); 12,000 will be marked by God (Rev 7:7, p. 1812).
2. *See* MATTHEW, also known as Levi.

LEVIATHAN (n) a sea monster represented as a cruel enemy defeated by God
Job 41:1 *Can you catch **L** with a hook*........131
Ps 74:14 *crushed the heads of **L** and*.........595
Isa 27:1 *and punish **L**, the swiftly*...............897

LEWDNESS that which lacks legal or moral restraints; sexual obscenity or vulgarity
Ezek 23:27 *stop to the **l** and prostitution* ...1071
Ezek 24:13 *impurity is your **l** and* ...1073

LIAR, LIARS (n) a person who deceives by telling untruths or falsehoods
Ps 63:11 *while **l-s** will be silenced* ...518
Ps 116:11 *These people are all **l-s!*** ...875
Prov 17:4 ***l-s** pay close attention to* ...652
Prov 29:12 *pays attention to **l-s,** all his* ...845
Prov 30:6 *expose you as a **l.*** ...846
Isa 57:4 *of sinners and **l-s!*** ...943
John 8:44 *a **l** and the father of lies.* ...1393
Rom 3:4 *else is a **l,** God is true* ...1650
1 Tim 1:10 *are slave traders, **l-s,** promise* ...1728
Titus 1:12 *are all **l-s,** cruel animals,* ...1737
1 Jn 1:10 *calling God a **l** and showing* ...1787
1 Jn 2:4 *that person is a **l** and is not* ...1788
1 Jn 4:20 *that person is a **l;** for if we* ...1794
1 Jn 5:10 *calling God a **l** because they* ...1794
Rev 3:9 *synagogue—those **l-s** who say* ...1806
Rev 21:8 *and all **l-s**—their fate is in* ...1830

LIBERATORS (n) those who free or set at liberty
Neh 9:27 *you sent them **l** who rescued* ...1216

LICK (v) to draw the tongue over
Isa 49:23 *before you and **l** the dust* ...937

LIE, LIES (n) an untrue or inaccurate statement; something that misleads or deceives
Ps 7:14 *give birth to **l-s.*** ...524
Ps 24:4 *and never tell **l-s.*** ...558
Ps 34:13 *lips from telling **l-s!*** ...459
Prov 12:17 *a false witness tells **l-s.*** ...645
Prov 30:8 *never to tell a **l.*** ...846
John 8:44 *the father of **l-s.*** ...1393
Rom 1:25 *about God for a **l.*** ...1648
Rom 3:13 *filled with **l-s.*** ...1651
Eph 4:14 *to trick us with **l-s** so clever* ...1711
Eph 4:25 *So stop telling **l-s.*** ...1712
2 Thes 2:11 *they will believe these **l-s.*** ...1589
1 Pet 3:10 *and your lips from telling **l-s.*** ...1753
2 Pet 2:3 *make up clever **l-s** to get hold* ...1758
1 Jn 2:21 *between truth and **l-s.*** ...1790
Rev 14:5 *They have told no **l-s;*** ...1821

LIE, LIED, LIES (v) to make an untrue statement with intent to deceive; to create a false or misleading impression
see also LYING
Lev 6:3 *lost property and **l** about it,* ...208
Job 31:5 *Have I **l-d** to anyone or* ...121
Ps 58:3 *even from birth they have **l-d*** ...573
Ps 89:35 *in my holiness I cannot **l:*** ...592
Prov 24:28 *don't **l** about them.* ...663
Prov 26:19 *who **l-s** to a friend.* ...841
Jer 7:9 *commit adultery, **l,** and burn* ...1008
Matt 5:11 *persecute you and **l*** ...1326
Col 3:9 *Don't **l** to each other,* ...1700
Titus 1:2 *God—who does not **l*** ...1736

LIFE (n) the quality that distinguishes a vital and functional being from a dead body; period from birth to death; a way or manner of living; spiritual existence transcending death; salvation
see also LIVES
Gen 1:30 *everything that has **l.*** ...9
Gen 2:7 *He breathed the breath of **l*** ...9
Gen 2:9 *the tree of **l** and the tree of* ...10
Gen 9:5 *who takes another person's **l.*** ...21
Gen 9:6 *a human **l,** that person's **l*** ...21
Exod 21:23 *the injury: a **l** for a **l,*** ...171
Num 35:31 *payment for the **l** of someone* ...283
Deut 19:21 *be **l** for **l,** eye for eye,* ...310
Deut 30:19 *choice between **l** and death,* ...321
Deut 32:39 *kills and gives **l;** I am the* ...325
1 Sam 2:6 *both death and **l;** he brings* ...418
Ps 23:6 *the days of my **l,** and I will* ...558
Ps 69:28 *the Book of **L;** don't let them* ...578
Ps 91:16 *with a long **l** and give them* ...861
Ps 139:24 *the path of everlasting **l.*** ...586
Prov 3:2 *your **l** will be satisfying* ...634
Prov 6:26 *will cost you your **l.*** ...639
Prov 13:3 *have a long **l;** opening your* ...646
Prov 15:4 *Gentle words are a tree of **l;*** ...648
Prov 21:21 *will find **l,** righteousness,* ...658
Prov 28:16 *will have a long **l.*** ...844
Isa 53:8 *that his **l** was cut short in* ...940
Isa 55:3 *you will find **l.** I will make* ...942
Lam 3:58 *you have redeemed my **l.*** ...1099
Dan 12:2 *to everlasting **l** and some to* ...1161
Matt 7:14 *But the gateway to **l** is very* ...1334
Matt 18:8 *to enter eternal **l** with only* ...1384
Matt 20:28 *and to give his **l** as a ransom* ...1424
Mark 8:35 *to hang on to your **l,*** ...1378
Mark 10:45 *and to give his **l** as a ransom* ...1425
Luke 6:9 *a day to save **l** or to destroy* ...1321
Luke 9:24 *give up your **l** for my sake,* ...1378
Luke 12:25 *single moment to your **l?*** ...1400
John 1:4 *The Word gave **l** to everything* ...1271
John 3:15 *will have eternal **l.*** ...1302
John 4:14 *giving them eternal **l.*** ...1304
John 5:24 *passed from death into **l.*** ...1318
John 5:39 *they give you eternal **l.*** ...1319
John 6:27 *the eternal **l** that the Son of* ...1367
John 6:35 *I am the bread of **l.*** ...1367
John 6:47 *who believes has eternal **l.*** ...1368
John 6:53 *have eternal **l** within you.* ...1368
John 6:68 *the words that give eternal **l.*** ...1369
John 10:10 *a rich and satisfying **l.*** ...1405
John 10:15 *So I sacrifice my **l** for the* ...1405
John 10:28 *give them eternal **l,** and they* ...1406
John 12:25 *nothing for their **l** in this* ...1432
John 14:6 *the truth, and the **l.*** ...1461
John 17:2 *He gives eternal **l** to each* ...1466
John 20:31 *you will have **l** by the power* ...1496
Acts 3:15 *You killed the author of **l,*** ...1517
Rom 1:17 *a righteous person has **l.*** ...1646
Rom 2:7 *will give eternal **l** to those* ...1649
Rom 4:25 *he was raised to **l** to make us* ...1653
Rom 5:10 *be saved through the **l** of his* ...1654
Rom 5:18 *God and new **l** for everyone.* ...1655
Rom 5:21 *in eternal **l** through Jesus* ...1655
Rom 6:13 *now you have new **l.*** ...1656
Rom 6:22 *result in eternal **l.*** ...1656
Rom 6:23 *is eternal **l** through Christ* ...1656
Rom 8:6 *mind leads to **l** and peace.* ...1659
Rom 8:11 *he will give **l** to your mortal* ...1659
Rom 8:38 *death nor **l,** neither angels* ...1661
2 Cor 3:6 *the Spirit gives **l.*** ...1629
2 Cor 4:10 *so that the **l** of Jesus may* ...1631
Gal 3:11 *a righteous person has **l.*** ...1561
Gal 3:21 *give us new **l,** we could be* ...1562
Gal 6:8 *harvest everlasting **l** from* ...1567
Eph 2:5 *he gave us **l** when he raised* ...1707
Eph 4:1 *to lead a **l** worthy of your* ...1710
Phil 2:16 *Hold firmly to the word of **l;*** ...1720
Phil 4:3 *written in the Book of **L.*** ...1724
Col 3:3 *and your real **l** is hidden* ...1700
1 Tim 1:16 *and receive eternal **l.*** ...1728
1 Tim 4:8 *and in the **l** to come.* ...1732
1 Tim 6:19 *may experience true **l.*** ...1735
2 Tim 1:9 *called us to live a holy **l.*** ...1741
2 Tim 3:12 *to live a godly **l** in Christ* ...1744
Titus 3:5 *new **l** through the Holy Spirit* ...1739
Heb 7:16 *power of a **l** that cannot be* ...1770
Jas 1:12 *the crown of **l** that God has* ...1547
1 Pet 3:7 *God's gift of new **l.*** ...1753
1 Pet 3:10 *want to enjoy **l** and see many* ...1753
1 Pet 3:16 *see what a good **l** you live* ...1753
2 Pet 1:3 *for living a godly **l.*** ...1757
1 Jn 1:1 *He is the Word of **l.*** ...1786
1 Jn 3:14 *have passed from death to **l.*** ...1791
1 Jn 3:16 *gave up his **l** for us.* ...1791
1 Jn 5:20 *God, and he is eternal **l.*** ...1795
Jude 1:21 *bring you eternal **l.*** ...1786
Rev 3:5 *names from the Book of **L,*** ...1806
Rev 13:8 *in the Book of **L** before the* ...1820
Rev 17:8 *in the Book of **L** before the* ...1824
Rev 20:12 *the Book of **L.** And the dead* ...1830
Rev 21:27 *in the Lamb's Book of **L.*** ...1831
Rev 22:1 *with the water of **l,** clear as* ...1832
Rev 22:2 *a tree of **l,** bearing twelve* ...1832
Rev 22:14 *eat the fruit from the tree of **l.*** ...1832
Rev 22:17 *from the water of **l.*** ...1833
Rev 22:19 *in the tree of **l** and in the* ...1833

LIFE-GIVING (adj) giving or having power to give life and spirit; invigorating
Prov 10:11 *the godly are a **l** fountain;* ...642
Prov 16:22 *Discretion is a **l** fountain to* ...651
Rom 8:2 *the power of the **l** Spirit has* ...1658
1 Cor 15:45 *Christ—is a **l** Spirit.* ...1621
2 Cor 2:16 *we are a **l** perfume.* ...1628
Rev 7:17 *to springs of **l** water.* ...1813

LIFETIME (n) the duration of the existence of a living being or thing
Ps 30:5 *his favor lasts a **l!*** ...563
Ps 39:5 *My entire **l** is just a* ...569
Luke 16:25 *that during your **l** you had* ...1412

LIFT, LIFTED, LIFTING, LIFTS (v) to raise from a lower to a higher position; to raise in rank or condition
Lev 23:11 *the priest will **l** it up* ...230
1 Sam 2:7 *some down and **l-s** others up.* ...418
Neh 8:6 *as they **l-ed** their hands.* ...1214
Ps 28:2 *I **l** my hands toward your holy* ...562
Ps 63:4 ***l-ing** up my hands to you in prayer.* ...517
Ps 89:13 *Your right hand is **l-ed** high in* ...591
Ps 113:7 *He **l-s** the poor from the dust* ...874
Ps 123:1 *I **l** my eyes to you, O God* ...882
Ps 134:2 ***L** up holy hands* ...885
Lam 1:9 *no one to **l** her out.* ...1094
Lam 3:41 *Let us **l** our hearts and* ...1099
John 3:14 *Son of Man must be **l-ed** up,* ...1302
John 8:28 *When you have **l-ed** up the Son* ...1392
John 12:32 *And when I am **l-ed** up* ...1434
1 Tim 2:8 *holy hands **l-ed** up to God,* ...1729
Jas 4:10 *he will **l** you up in honor.* ...1552
1 Pet 5:6 *he will **l** you up in honor.* ...1756

LIGHT, LIGHTS (n) daylight; brightness; illumination; celestial body; spiritual enlightenment; exposure to the truth and justice
Gen 1:3 *"Let there be **l,**" and there* ...6
Gen 1:14 *said, "Let **l-s** appear in the sky* ...7
Exod 13:21 *and he provided **l** at night* ...159
Job 38:19 *Where does **l** come from,* ...128
Ps 27:1 *The LORD is my **l** and my* ...561
Ps 56:13 *in your life-giving **l.*** ...472
Ps 119:105 *my feet and a **l** for my path* ...880
Ps 132:17 *will be a **l** for my people* ...884
Ps 139:12 *Darkness and **l** are the* ...586
Isa 2:5 *us walk in the **l** of the LORD!* ...825
Isa 42:6 *you will be a **l** to guide the* ...927

Isa 45:7 *I create the **l** and make the*............931
Isa 49:6 *make you a **l** to the Gentiles,*.........936
Matt 5:14 *You are the **l** of the world—*......1327
Luke 2:32 *He is a **l** to reveal God to*..........1282
Luke 11:33 *its **l** can be seen by all*...........1398
John 1:4 *life brought **l** to everyone*............1271
John 1:9 *who is the true **l,** who gives*........1271
John 3:20 *All who do evil hate the **l***...........1302
John 3:21 *come to the **l** so others can*........1302
John 8:12 *I am the **l** of the world.*............1392
John 9:5 *I am the **l** of the world.*..............1403
John 12:46 *I have come as a **l** to shine*.....1435
Acts 13:47 *made you a **l** to the Gentiles,*...1543
2 Cor 4:6 *said, "Let there be **l** in the*.........1631
2 Cor 6:14 *can **l** live with darkness?*.........1634
2 Cor 11:14 *as an angel of **l.***.....................1640
Eph 1:18 *be flooded with **l** so that you*......1706
Eph 5:8 *live as people of **l!***......................1712
Phil 2:15 *like bright **l-s** in a world*.............1720
1 Thes 5:5 *children of the **l** and of the*.......1585
1 Tim 6:16 *he lives in **l** so brilliant*............1735
1 Pet 2:9 *into his wonderful **l.***....................1751
1 Jn 1:5 *God is **l,** and there is*....................1787
1 Jn 1:7 *living in the **l,** as God is in*............1787
1 Jn 2:9 *I am living in the **l,***......................1788
Rev 21:23 *city, and the Lamb is its **l.***........1831

LIGHT, LIGHTS (v) to brighten; to ignite something
Ps 18:28 *The LORD, my God, **l-s** up my*.......528
Luke 8:16 *No one **l-s** a lamp and*.............1347

LIGHTNING (n) the flashing of light produced by a discharge of atmospheric electricity
Exod 9:23 ***l** flashed toward the earth*..........153
Exod 20:18 *saw the flashes of **l** and the*......170
Dan 10:6 *face flashed like **l,** and his*.........1158
Matt 24:27 *For as the **l** flashes in the*.......1446
Matt 28:3 *face shone like **l,** and his*...........1489
Luke 10:18 *from heaven like **l!***.................1395
Rev 4:5 *came flashes of **l** and the*.............1808

LIKE (prep) similar in appearance, character, quality
Gen 1:26 *to be **l** us. They will*.........................8
Ps 86:8 *No pagan god is **l** you, O LORD*........579
Isa 14:14 *and be **l** the Most High*................832
Luke 13:18 *Kingdom of God **l?***.................1348
Rom 8:3 *Son in a body **l** the bodies we*.....1658
Rom 8:29 *to become **l** his Son,*.................1660

LIKENESS (n) copy; resemblance; appearance
2 Cor 4:4 *is the exact **l** of God.*................1630

LINEN (adj) made of flax
Lev 16:4 ***l** undergarments worn next to*.......221
Prov 31:24 *makes belted **l** garments*..........848
Mark 15:46 *a long sheet of **l** cloth.*............1487
John 20:6 *noticed the **l** wrappings lying*....1492

LINEN (n) cloth made of flax and noted for its strength, coolness, and luster
Prov 31:22 *dresses in fine **l** and purple*.......848
Rev 15:6 *in spotless white **l** with gold*.......1822
Rev 19:8 *of pure white **l** to wear.*..............1827

LION, LIONS (n) a wild beast with a threatening roar; symbolic of a strong and fierce enemy
Isa 11:7 *The **l** will eat hay like a cow.*..........796
Isa 65:25 *The **l** will eat hay like a cow.*........952
Dan 6:7 *thrown into the den of **l-s.***...........1140
Dan 7:4 *was like a **l** with eagles'*..............1135
1 Pet 5:8 *like a roaring **l,** looking for*.........1756
Rev 5:5 *Look, the **L** of the tribe of*.............1809

LIPS (n) the fleshy, muscular folds that surround the mouth; symbolic of speech
Ps 140:3 *drips from their **l.***.........................587
Prov 12:22 *The LORD detests lying **l,***...........645
Isa 6:5 *I have filthy **l,** and I live*....................784
Matt 15:8 *honor me with their **l,***...............1369
Rom 3:13 *venom drips from their **l.***..........1651
1 Pet 3:10 *evil and your **l** from telling*.......1753

LISTEN, LISTENED, LISTENING (v) to hear something with thoughtful attention
see also HEAR
Deut 6:4 ***L,** O Israel! The LORD*...................294
Deut 18:15 *You must **l** to him.*......................308
1 Sam 3:9 *LORD, your servant is **l-ing.***.........422
Neh 8:3 *All the people **l-ed** closely to*.......1214
Ps 95:7 *If only you would **l** to his voice*........863
Prov 12:15 *but the wise **l** to others.*............645
Prov 18:13 *Spouting off before **l-ing** to*......654
Isa 6:9 *to this people, '**L** carefully,*...............785
Dan 9:6 *We have refused to **l** to your*........1142
Mark 9:7 *dearly loved Son. **L** to him.*.........1379
Luke 10:39 *the Lord's feet, **l-ing** to*..........1397
Luke 16:31 *If they won't **l** to Moses and*...1413
John 10:27 *My sheep **l** to my*..................1406
John 15:20 *And if they had **l-ed** to me,*....1464
Rom 2:13 *For merely **l-ing** to the law*.......1649
1 Tim 2:12 *Let them **l** quietly.*...................1730
Jas 1:19 *be quick to **l,** slow to speak,*.......1547
1 Jn 4:6 *they do not **l** to us.*.....................1793
Rev 1:3 *he blesses all who **l** to its*.............1798
Rev 2:7 *to hear must **l** to the Spirit*...........1802

LIVE, LIVED, LIVES, LIVING (v) to be alive or come to life; to endure a period of time (a life span); to attain eternal life; to dwell; to subsist; to continue alive; to conduct or pass one's life
see also DWELLS
Gen 3:22 *Then they will **l** forever!*.................13
Exod 20:12 *Then you will **l** a long, full*.........169
Lev 26:11 *I will **l** among you,*.......................235
Deut 6:2 *as long as you **l.***.............................294
Deut 8:3 *that people do not **l** by bread*........297
Job 14:14 *Can the dead **l** again?*................108
Job 19:25 *that my Redeemer **l-s,** and he*....112
Ps 23:6 *and I will **l** in the house of*..............558
Ps 37:3 *Then you will **l** safely in the*............567
Ps 61:4 *Let me **l** forever in your*..................573
Ps 104:33 *as long as I **l.** I will praise*...........868
Prov 21:19 *It's better to **l** alone in the*.........658
Isa 33:14 *Who can **l** with this*.....................903
Isa 45:18 *He made the world to be **l-d** in,*...932
Amos 5:6 *to the LORD and **l!***.......................775
Hab 2:4 *the righteous will **l** by their*.............980
Zech 2:11 *I will **l** among you,*...................1167
Matt 4:4 *People do not **l** by bread*.............1294
John 14:19 *Since I **l,** you also will **l.***..........1462
Acts 17:28 *For in him we **l** and move*........1578
Rom 2:8 *on those who **l** for themselves,*....1649
Rom 6:10 *he **l-s,** he **l-s** for the glory*........1656
Rom 8:11 *same Spirit **l-ing** within you*......1659
Rom 13:13 *we must **l** decent lives*............1669
Rom 14:7 *For we don't **l** for ourselves*......1670
1 Cor 3:16 *Spirit of God **l-s** in you?*..........1600
2 Cor 5:7 *For we **l** by believing*.................1632
2 Cor 6:16 *said: "I will **l** in them and*.........1634
Gal 2:20 *no longer I who **l,** but Christ*........1560
Gal 5:25 *Since we are **l-ing** by the Spirit,*..1567
Col 1:19 *was pleased to **l** in Christ,*...........1695
Col 2:5 *you are **l-ing** as you should*..........1697
1 Thes 4:11 *your goal to **l** a quiet life,*........1584
1 Thes 5:13 *And **l** peacefully with*.............1586
1 Tim 2:2 *so that we can **l** peaceful and*....1729
1 Tim 4:16 *close watch on how you **l***........1733
2 Tim 3:12 *who wants to **l** a godly life*.......1744
Heb 10:38 *righteous ones will **l** by faith*.....1777
Heb 12:14 *and work at **l-ing** a holy life,*....1781
1 Pet 1:17 *So you must **l** in reverent*.........1749
1 Jn 1:7 *But if we are **l-ing** in the light,*....1787
1 Jn 4:16 *God, and God **l-s** in them.*.........1793

LIVES (n) way or manner of living
see also LIFE
Exod 23:26 *I will give you long, full **l.***..........174
1 Thes 2:8 *but our own **l,** too.*...................1582
1 Tim 2:2 *and quiet **l** marked by*..................1729
1 Pet 3:2 *pure and reverent **l.***.....................1752
1 Pet 4:2 *rest of your **l** chasing your*..........1754

LIVING (adj) having life; active, functioning
Gen 2:7 *man became a **l** person.*.......................9
Gen 6:17 *destroy every **l** thing that*...............18
Jer 2:13 *the fountain of **l** water.*....................960
Matt 22:32 *God of the **l,** not the dead.*.......1440
John 4:10 *would give you **l** water.*.............1304
John 6:51 *I am the **l** bread that came*.......1368
Rom 12:1 *Let them be a **l** and holy*...........1666
Heb 10:31 *the hands of the **l** God.*............1776
Rev 1:18 *I am the **l** one.*............................1801

LIVING (n) conduct or manner of life
Phil 1:21 *to me, **l** means living for*............1718
2 Tim 2:22 *righteous **l,** faithfulness,*..........1743

LOAF, LOAVES (n) a shaped or molded mass of bread
Mark 6:41 *took the five **l-ves** and two fish,*.1364
Mark 8:6 *the seven **l-ves,** thanked God*....1373
Luke 11:5 *to borrow three **l-ves** of bread.*.1397
1 Cor 10:17 *all eat from one **l** of bread,*....1611

LOAN, LOANS (n) money lent at interest
Deut 15:2 *must cancel the **l-s** they have.*....305
Deut 15:9 *refuse someone a **l***.....................305
Deut 24:6 *as security for a **l,** for the*...........314
Ps 37:26 *give generous **l-s** to others,*.........568

LOANED (v) to give for temporary use
Luke 7:41 *A man **l** money to two*..............1340

LOCKED (v) fastened in or out or made secure or inaccessible by means of locks
Job 38:10 *For I **l** it behind barred*...............128
John 20:26 *doors were **l;** but suddenly,*.....1495

LOCUSTS (n) short-horned grasshoppers
Exod 10:4 *a swarm of **l** on your country.*......154
Joel 2:25 *and the cutting **l.** It was I*............1242
Matt 3:4 *he ate **l** and wild honey.*...............1288
Rev 9:3 *Then **l** came from*............................1814

LODGING (n) a temporary place to stay
Luke 2:7 *there was no **l** available for*.........1280

LOFTY (adj) elevated in character, spirit, and status; rising to a great height
Isa 6:1 *sitting on a **l** throne,*.........................783
Isa 57:15 *The high and **l** one who lives*.......944

LOG (n) a usually bulky piece or length of a tree
Matt 7:3 *you have a **l** in your own?*............1333
Luke 6:41 *you have a **l** in your own?*...........1333

LONG (adj) extending over a considerable time or space
Deut 5:33 *will live **l** and prosperous*............294
1 Cor 11:14 *man to have **l** hair?*................1612
Eph 3:18 *how wide, how **l,** how high,*.........1709

LONG, LONGING, LONGS (v) to feel a strong desire or craving; to yearn
Job 7:2 *a worker who **l-s** for the shade,*......101
Ps 42:1 *As the deer **l-s** for streams of*........848
Ps 42:1 *of water, so I **l** for you,*....................848
Ps 63:1 *my whole body **l-s** for you in*..........517
Ps 119:131 ***l-ing** for your commands*.........881

Luke 16:21 *lay there **l-ing** for scraps from* 1412
Phil 1:8 *I love you and **l** for you with*....1717
Phil 2:26 *he has been **l-ing** to see you,* 1721

LONGING (n) a strong desire especially for something unattainable; craving
Rom 10:1 *the **l** of my heart and*....1663
2 Cor 7:11 *such alarm, such **l** to see me,*..1635
1 Thes 2:17 *of our intense **l** to see you* 1583

LONGSUFFERING (KJV)
Exod 34:6 *I am **slow to anger** and filled* 187
Num 14:18 *LORD is **slow to anger***....253
Ps 86:15 *mercy, **slow to get angry***....579
Gal 5:22 *love, joy, peace, **patience,*** 1566
Eph 4:2 *Be **patient** with each other* 1710

LOOK (n) glance
Prov 15:30 *A cheerful **l** brings joy to*....650

LOOK, LOOKED, LOOKING, LOOKS (v) to direct the eyes; to examine; to see; to make sure or take care (that something is done); to regard with contempt; to seem; to search
Gen 19:17 *And don't **l** back or*....41
Gen 19:26 *But Lot's wife **l-ed** back as she*....42
Exod 3:6 *was afraid to **l** at God*....144
1 Sam 6:19 *they **l-ed** into the Ark* 426
1 Sam 16:7 *LORD **l-s** at the heart*....448
Ps 34:5 *Those who **l** to him for*....458
Ps 113:6 *He stoops to **l** down on heaven* 874
Ps 123:2 *We keep **l-ing** to the LORD*....882
Isa 65:1 *but no one was **l-ing** for me*....951
Dan 10:5 *I **l-ed** up and saw a man*....1158
Hab 3:6 *When he **l-s,** the nations*....981
Zech 12:10 *They will **l** on me* 1178
Matt 5:28 *who even **l-s** at a woman*....1328
Mark 16:6 *You are **l-ing** for Jesus*....1490
Luke 9:62 *plow and then **l-s** back is not*...1388
Luke 22:61 *turned and **l-ed** at Peter*....1474
John 4:23 *The Father is **l-ing** for those* 1305
John 17:1 *Jesus **l-ed** up to heaven* 1466
Rom 14:10 *Why do you **l** down*....1670
Phil 2:4 *Don't **l** out only*....1719
Heb 11:16 *they were **l-ing** for a better*.....1778
Jas 1:25 *But if you **l** carefully into*....1548
2 Pet 3:12 ***l-ing** forward to the day* 1760
Rev 5:6 *I saw a Lamb that **l-ed** as if it*......1809

LOOSE (adv) in an unrigidly fastened or unsecure manner
Isa 33:23 *sails hang **l** on broken masts*....903

LORD (n) traditionally rendered Jehovah (Hebrew *Yahweh*); the sovereign God Almighty
see also YAHWEH
Gen 2:4 *When the **L** God made* 9
Gen 4:4 *The **L** accepted Abel* 14
Gen 15:6 *Abram believed the **L,** and*....35
Gen 22:14 *the **L** will provide*....46
Gen 31:49 *May the **L** keep watch* 65
Exod 6:2 *I am Yahweh—'the **L.**'* 148
Exod 15:26 *I am the **L** who heals you*....162
Exod 40:34 *the glory of the **L** filled* 196
Lev 20:26 *because I, the **L,** am holy*....227
Lev 23:4 *these are the **L's** appointed* 229
Num 6:24 *May the **L** bless you and*....245
Num 14:18 *The **L** is slow to anger*....253
Num 14:21 *filled with the **L's** glory,*....253
Num 14:41 *disobeying the **L's** orders*....254
Deut 5:9 *I, the **L** your God, am a jealous*......292
Deut 6:5 *love the **L** your God with all*....294
Deut 6:18 *good in the **L's** sight,*....295
Deut 10:13 *obey the **L's** commands* 300
Deut 10:20 *must fear the **L** your God*....300
Deut 11:1 *must love the **L** your God*....300
Deut 29:29 *The **L** our God has secrets*....321
Deut 30:20 *obey the **L,** you will live* 321
Josh 23:11 *to love the **L** your God.* 368
2 Sam 22:2 *sang: "The **L** is my rock,* 526
2 Sam 22:31 *All the **L's** promises prove*......527
2 Kgs 22:2 *pleasing in the **L's** sight* 957
2 Kgs 22:8 *Law in the **L's** Temple!*....969
1 Chr 17:1 *Ark of the **L's** Covenant is*....496
2 Chr 16:9 *The eyes of the **L** search*....711
Neh 9:6 *You alone are the **L.*** 1215
Job 38:1 *Then the **L** answered Job*....127
Ps 1:6 *For the **L** watches over* 856
Ps 12:6 *The **L's** promises are pure,*....551
Ps 18:30 *All the **L's** promises prove*....528
Ps 23:1 *The **L** is my shepherd;* 558
Ps 24:1 *The earth is the **L's,***....558
Ps 34:3 *tell of the **L's** greatness;* 458
Ps 34:8 *see that the **L** is good*....458
Ps 89:1 *sing of the **L's** unfailing love*....591
Ps 92:13 *to the **L's** own house.* 862
Ps 95:6 *kneel before the **L** our maker,* 863
Ps 97:1 *The **L** is king!*....864
Ps 99:5 *Exalt the **L** our God!*....865
Ps 100:5 *For the **L** is good.* 866
Ps 107:1 *thanks to the **L,** for he is*....871
Ps 118:8 *better to take refuge in the **L***....876
Ps 118:23 *This is the **L's** doing,*....876
Ps 121:2 *help comes from the **L,** who* 882
Ps 145:3 *Great is the **L!***....589
Ps 145:17 *The **L** is righteous* 590
Ps 146:7 *The **L** frees the prisoners*....887
Ps 147:11 *No, the **L's** delight is*....1155
Prov 3:5 *Trust in the **L** with all your*....634
Prov 3:9 *Honor the **L** with your* 635
Prov 3:11 *reject the **L's** discipline,* 635
Prov 12:22 *The **L** detests lying* 645
Prov 15:33 *Fear of the **L*** 650
Prov 19:21 *the **L's** purpose will prevail.*....655
Prov 21:2 *the **L** examines their heart*....657
Prov 31:30 *a woman who fears the **L** will*....848
Isa 6:3 *holy is the **L** of Heaven's* 783
Isa 24:14 *praise the **L's** majesty*....895
Isa 30:9 *to the **L's** instructions*....900
Isa 42:8 *I am the **L;** that is my name!*....927
Isa 43:11 *I, am the **L,** and there is* 928
Isa 49:4 *leave it all in the **L's** hand;*....936
Isa 53:6 *Yet the **L** laid on him* 940
Isa 53:10 *was the **L's** good plan* 940
Isa 55:13 *honor to the **L's** name;* 942
Isa 61:2 *time of the **L's** favor* 948
Isa 66:15 *See, the **L** is coming* 953
Jer 8:7 *do not know the **L's** laws.* 1010
Jer 17:10 *But I, the **L,** search all*....1021
Jer 31:11 *For the **L** has redeemed*....1033
Jer 48:10 *to do the **L's** work,*....989
Jer 51:7 *cup in the **L's** hands,* 1037
Ezek 7:19 *day of the **L's** anger*....1053
Ezek 44:4 *the glory of the **L** filled*....1127
Joel 1:15 *The day of the **L** is near,* 1240
Joel 3:18 *from the **L's** Temple, watering*....1244
Jonah 2:9 *salvation comes from the **L***....768
Mic 4:1 *mountain of the **L's** house* 907
Mic 6:2 *listen to the **L's** complaint!* 909
Nah 1:2 *The **L** is a jealous God,* 974
Nah 1:7 *The **L** is good, a strong*....975
Hab 2:16 *cup of the **L's** judgment,* 981
Zeph 2:3 *yet the **L** will protect* 984
Matt 3:3 *way for the **L's** coming!* 1287
Matt 4:7 *not test the **L** your God.* 1295
Matt 4:10 *must worship the **L** your God* 1295
Matt 22:37 *must love the **L** your God*....1441
Mark 1:3 *way for the **L's** coming!*....1289
Mark 12:11 *This is the **L's** doing,*....1438
John 1:23 *way for the **L's** coming!*....1293
Acts 2:21 *name of the **L** will be saved*....1515
Rom 10:13 *name of the **L** will be saved.* ...1664
Rom 11:34 *can know the **L's** thoughts?* 1666
1 Cor 10:26 *the earth is the **L's,*** 1611
Heb 12:5 *of the **L's** discipline,* 1780

LORD, LORDS (n) honored one or a superior; master (to a slave); king or ruler; God or Jesus
see also LORD
Deut 10:17 *of gods and **L** of **l-s.*** 300
Neh 4:14 *Remember the **L,** who is* 1209
Isa 6:1 *I saw the **L.** He was sitting* 783
Dan 9:19 *O **L,** listen and act!*....1143
Matt 12:8 *Son of Man is **L,** even*....1320
Luke 1:38 *I am the **L's** servant.* 1275
Acts 10:36 *Christ, who is **L** of all.* 1534
Acts 16:31 *Believe in the **L** Jesus*....1576
Rom 10:9 *that Jesus is **L** and believe*....1663
1 Cor 8:6 *only one **L,** Jesus Christ,* 1607
1 Cor 11:26 *announcing the **L's** death* 1613
1 Cor 12:3 *say Jesus is **L,** except*....1614
Eph 4:5 *There is one **L,** one faith,* 1710
Phil 2:11 *Jesus Christ is **L,***....1720
Col 2:6 *Jesus as your **L,** you must*....1697
1 Thes 5:2 *day of the **L's** return*....1585
1 Tim 6:15 *kings and **L** of all **l-s.*** 1735
Jas 5:8 *the coming of the **L** is near.* 1553
1 Pet 2:3 *taste of the **L's** kindness.* 1750
1 Pet 3:15 *worship Christ as **L** of*....1753
Rev 4:8 *holy, holy is the **L** God,* 1808
Rev 4:11 *are worthy, O **L** our God,* 1809
Rev 19:16 *kings and **L** of all **l-s.*** 1828
Rev 22:20 *Amen! Come, **L** Jesus!*....1833

LOSE, LOSES (v) to fail to keep, sustain, or maintain; to damn
Matt 10:39 *cling to your life, you will **l***.......1361
Mark 8:36 *whole world but **l** your own* 1378
Luke 15:8 *silver coins and **l-s** one*....1410
Luke 17:33 *cling to your life, you will **l*** 1416
John 6:39 *I should not **l** even one of*....1367
2 Jn 1:8 *you do not **l** what we have* 1796

LOSS (n) the act of losing possession; deprivation
1 Cor 3:15 *the builder will suffer great **l.***...1599

LOST (adj) no longer possessed or known; lacking assurance of eternal salvation
Jer 50:6 *have been **l** sheep*....1035
Ezek 34:16 *will search for my **l** ones*....1110
Luke 15:4 *and one of them gets **l,*** 1410
Luke 15:6 *I have found my **l** sheep.* 1410
Luke 15:9 *have found my **l** coin*....1410
Luke 15:24 *He was **l,** but now he* 1411

LOTS (n) small stones or other devices used for making choices, much like throwing dice or drawing straws
Josh 18:10 *Joshua cast sacred **l** in the*....362
Obad 1:11 *wealth and cast **l** to divide* 1103
Acts 1:26 *they cast **l,** and Matthias was*....1513

LOUD (adj) marked by intensity or volume of sound
Isa 54:1 *Break into **l** and joyful song,* 941

LOVE (n) the ultimate expression of God's loyalty, purity, and mercy extended toward his people—to be reflected in human relationships of brotherly concern, marital fidelity, and adoration of God; a beloved person
Gen 24:12 *unfailing **l** to my master,* 48
Gen 32:10 *unfailing **l** and faithfulness*....66

Gen 34:3 he fell in l with her, and he.............68
Gen 39:21 showed him his faithful l...............78
Exod 20:6 unfailing l for a thousand............169
Exod 34:6 filled with unfailing l and 187
Num 14:18 with unfailing l, forgiving 253
Num 14:19 unfailing l, please pardon 253
Deut 5:10 unfailing l for a thousand..............292
Deut 7:9 his unfailing l on those who 296
Deut 10:15 the objects of his l. 300
Deut 10:18 He shows l to the......................300
Deut 10:19 must show l to foreigners, ...300
Judg 16:4 Samson fell in l with a woman....400
1 Sam 18:20 had fallen in l with David,.......453
1 Kgs 8:23 and show unfailing l to all 619
1 Kgs 10:9 LORD's eternal l for Israel,..........626
1 Chr 16:41 for "his faithful l endures.........494
1 Chr 29:18 See to it that their l..................541
2 Chr 5:13 His faithful l endures...................618
2 Chr 20:21 faithful l endures forever! 732
Ezra 3:11 His faithful l for Israel................1156
Job 37:13 to show his unfailing l. 127
Ps 6:4 because of your unfailing l...............548
Ps 13:5 I trust in your unfailing l................551
Ps 18:50 you show unfailing l to your 529
Ps 21:7 The unfailing l of the 555
Ps 23:6 and unfailing l will pursue 558
Ps 25:6 and unfailing l, which you...............560
Ps 25:10 leads with unfailing l and...............560
Ps 26:3 of your unfailing l, and I 560
Ps 31:7 in your unfailing l, for you 564
Ps 31:16 your unfailing l, rescue me..............564
Ps 32:10 but unfailing l surrounds 565
Ps 33:5 the unfailing l of the 858
Ps 33:18 who rely on his unfailing l. 858
Ps 33:22 your unfailing l surround us,..........858
Ps 36:5 Your unfailing l, O LORD, is 566
Ps 36:10 Pour out your unfailing l on 566
Ps 40:10 of your unfailing l and.....................570
Ps 40:11 Let your unfailing l and..................570
Ps 42:8 his unfailing l upon me, ...849
Ps 48:9 on your unfailing l as we..................853
Ps 51:1 your unfailing l. Because of............505
Ps 57:3 send forth his unfailing l and............459
Ps 57:10 For your unfailing l is as...............460
Ps 59:10 In his unfailing l, my God 454
Ps 59:16 your unfailing l. For you 454
Ps 59:17 shows me unfailing l. 454
Ps 62:12 unfailing l, O LORD, is yours............574
Ps 66:20 his unfailing l from me.....................859
Ps 69:16 LORD, for your unfailing l is..............578
Ps 77:8 his unfailing l gone forever?............597
Ps 85:7 us your unfailing l, O LORD, ...855
Ps 86:5 full of unfailing l for all 579
Ps 86:15 filled with unfailing l and..................579
Ps 88:11 your unfailing l?...............................591
Ps 89:1 LORD's unfailing l forever!.................591
Ps 89:14 Unfailing l and truth........................591
Ps 89:49 is your unfailing l?...........................592
Ps 90:14 with your unfailing l, so we 326
Ps 92:2 your unfailing l in the........................862
Ps 100:5 His unfailing l continues.................866
Ps 101:1 sing of your l and justice,...............579
Ps 103:4 crowns me with l and tender...........580
Ps 103:11 his unfailing l toward those 580
Ps 103:17 But the l of the LORD......................580
Ps 106:1 His faithful l endures 870
Ps 106:45 because of his unfailing l..............871
Ps 107:31 for his great l and for the..............872
Ps 107:43 the faithful l of the LORD................873
Ps 108:4 your unfailing l is higher 581
Ps 109:26 because of your unfailing l...........582
Ps 115:1 for your unfailing l and....................874
Ps 118:1 His faithful l endures 876
Ps 119:41 give me your unfailing l, ...879
Ps 119:76 let your unfailing l comfort 879
Ps 119:124 deal with me in unfailing l,.........880
Ps 130:7 LORD there is unfailing l. 884
Ps 138:2 unfailing l and faithfulness; 585
Ps 143:12 your unfailing l, silence all 589
Ps 147:11 hope in his unfailing l. 1155
Prov 5:19 be captivated by her l..................637
Prov 14:22 will receive unfailing l and.........648
Prov 16:6 Unfailing l and...............................651
Prov 20:28 is made secure through l. 657
Prov 21:21 and unfailing l will find...............658
Prov 27:5 better than hidden l!......................842
Song 1:4 We praise your l even more...........663
Song 1:7 Tell me, my l, where are you 664
Song 1:16 so handsome, my l, pleasing......664
Song 2:7 not to awaken l until the 664
Song 2:17 to me, my l, like a gazelle 665
Song 3:4 I found my l! 665
Song 4:10 Your l delights me,.......................666
Song 4:16 your garden, my l; taste its.........667
Song 5:5 door for my l, and my hands 667
Song 5:8 tell him I am weak with l. 667
Song 7:6 How pleasing, my l, how full..........669
Song 7:12 will give you my l..........................669
Song 8:4 not to awaken l until the 669
Song 8:6 for l is as strong as death 669
Song 8:7 cannot quench l, nor can..............670
Song 8:14 Come away, my l!.........................670
Isa 55:3 the unfailing l I promised to............942
Isa 63:7 LORD's unfailing l. 949
Isa 63:9 In his l and mercy he 950
Jer 2:25 I'm in l with these 961
Jer 9:24 demonstrates unfailing l and.......1012
Jer 16:5 taken away my unfailing l 1020
Jer 31:3 with an everlasting l. 1032
Jer 33:11 His faithful l endures 1081
Lam 3:22 The faithful l of the......................1098
Lam 3:32 the greatness of his unfailing l. .1098
Dan 9:4 of unfailing l to those who 1142
Hos 1:7 I will show l to the people 802
Hos 2:19 and justice, unfailing l and 804
Hos 2:23 I will show l to those I....................804
Hos 6:4 For your l vanishes like the 808
Hos 6:6 want you to show l, not offer...........809
Hos 11:4 my ropes of kindness and l...........814
Hos 12:6 Act with l and justice, ...815
Joel 2:13 filled with unfailing l....................1241
Jonah 4:2 filled with unfailing l.....................769
Zeph 3:17 With his l, he will..........................986
Zech 8:17 Stop your l of telling.....................1174
Mark 10:21 Jesus felt genuine l for him....1421
John 5:42 have God's l within you. 1319
John 15:9 Remain in my l. 1464
John 15:10 remain in his l. 1464
John 15:13 is no greater l than to lay 1464
John 17:26 Then your l for me will 1467
Rom 5:5 fill our hearts with his l. 1654
Rom 5:8 showed his great l for us by.........1654
Rom 8:35 us from Christ's l?........................1661
Rom 8:39 us from the l of God that is 1661
Rom 13:10 L does no wrong.........................1669
Rom 13:10 to others, so l fulfills the 1669
Rom 14:15 not acting in l if you eat............1670
Rom 15:30 because of your l for me,..........1672
1 Cor 4:21 I come with l and a gentle 1601
1 Cor 8:1 it is l that strengthens the............1607
1 Cor 13:13 faith, hope, and l—and the ...1616
1 Cor 13:13 the greatest of these is l.........1616
2 Cor 2:4 know how much l I have for........1627
2 Cor 2:8 to reaffirm your l for him. 1628
2 Cor 5:14 Either way, Christ's l controls...1632
2 Cor 8:7 and your l from us—I want.......1636
2 Cor 8:24 show them your l, and prove ...1637
Gal 5:22 l, joy, peace, patience, ...1566
Eph 1:15 Jesus and your l for God's 1706
Eph 3:17 down into God's l and keep........1709
Eph 3:18 how deep his l is. 1709
Eph 4:15 the truth in l, growing in 1711
Eph 5:2 filled with l, following the 1712
Eph 6:23 give you l with faithfulness..........1716
Phil 1:9 that your l will overflow 1717
Col 1:4 Jesus and your l for all of 1693
Col 1:8 told us about the l for others.........1694
Col 2:2 strong ties of l..................................1697
1 Thes 3:6 your faith and l. 1583
1 Thes 3:12 the Lord make your l for one....1584
1 Thes 5:13 and wholehearted l
because of...1586
2 Thes 3:5 expression of the l of God.........1590
1 Tim 1:5 be filled with l that comes 1727
1 Tim 2:15 in faith, l, holiness, ...1730
1 Tim 4:12 live, in your l, your faith,............1732
1 Tim 6:10 For the l of money is the 1735
1 Tim 6:11 with faith, l, perseverance, ...1735
2 Tim 1:7 but of power, l, and......................1741
2 Tim 1:13 the faith and l that you have....1741
2 Tim 2:22 living, faithfulness, l, and.........1743
2 Tim 3:10 my patience, my l, and my......1744
Titus 2:2 filled with l and patience............1738
Titus 3:4 revealed his kindness and l, ...1739
Heb 10:24 to acts of l and good works......1776
1 Pet 4:8 for l covers a multitude..............1754
1 Pet 5:14 with Christian l. 1756
1 Jn 3:14 who has no l is still dead...........1791
1 Jn 3:16 know what real l is because......1791
1 Jn 4:7 for l comes from God..................1793
1 Jn 4:8 for God is l.....................................1793
1 Jn 4:10 This is real l—not that we 1793
1 Jn 4:16 put our trust in his l. 1793
1 Jn 4:16 God is l, and all who..................1793
1 Jn 4:17 live in God, our l grows more.....1793
1 Jn 4:18 because perfect l expels all.......1794
Jude 1:12 commemorating the Lord's l,....1785
Jude 1:21 safe in God's l. 1786
Rev 2:19 have seen your l, your faith, ...1804

LOVE, LOVED, LOVES, LOVING (v) to hold dear; to feel a lover's passion, devotion, or tenderness for; to feel affection or experience desire; to like or desire actively

Gen 22:2 Isaac, whom you l so much— 45
Gen 29:32 my husband will l me. 61
Exod 21:5 may declare, 'I l my master,........171
Lev 19:34 as you l yourself. 226
Deut 4:37 Because he l-d your ancestors, ..291
Deut 6:5 And you must l the LORD your 294
Deut 7:8 that the LORD l-s you, and he.........296
Deut 7:13 He will l you and 296
Deut 11:13 and if you l the LORD your 300
Deut 13:3 if you truly l him with all 303
Deut 15:16 because he l-s you and............305
Deut 21:15 son of the wife he does not l.....311
Deut 23:5 LORD your God l-s you.................313
Deut 30:6 that you will l him with all 321
Deut 30:16 to l the LORD 321
Deut 30:20 this choice by l-ing the LORD 321
Deut 30:20 And if you l and obey the..........321
Deut 33:3 Indeed, he l-s his people;..........326
Josh 23:11 be very careful to l the LORD 368
Judg 14:16 said, "You don't l me;...............399
Judg 16:15 tell me, 'I l you,' when you.........401
1 Sam 18:1 for Jonathan l-d David.............452
2 Sam 12:24 The LORD l-d the child 507

2 Sam 19:6 You seem to **l** those who hate ..520
1 Kgs 3:3 Solomon **l-d** the LORD and..........606
1 Kgs 11:1 Solomon **l-d** many foreign 671
2 Chr 2:11 the LORD **l-s** his people 610
2 Chr 19:2 the wicked and **l** those who............729
Neh 1:5 with those who **l** him and obey.......1203
Neh 13:26 **l-d** him and made him king.....1223
Ps 11:5 those who **l** violence......................550
Ps 11:7 righteous LORD **l-s** justice..............550
Ps 18:1 I **l** you, LORD;.................................527
Ps 26:8 I **l** your sanctuary,..........................560
Ps 36:10 on those who **l** you;......................566
Ps 40:16 those who **l** your salvation............570
Ps 44:3 helped them, for you **l-d** them........850
Ps 45:7 You **l** justice and.............................851
Ps 52:3 You **l** evil more 462
Ps 52:4 You **l** to destroy 462
Ps 70:4 those who **l** your salvation..............579
Ps 78:68 Mount Zion, which he **l-d.** 599
Ps 89:28 I will **l** him and be.........................592
Ps 89:33 I will never stop **l-ing** him nor......592
Ps 91:14 rescue those who **l** me. 861
Ps 97:10 You who **l** the LORD,.....................864
Ps 98:3 his promise to **l** and be..................865
Ps 119:48 I honor and **l** your commands.....879
Ps 119:97 how I **l** your instructions!............880
Ps 119:113 but I **l** your instructions. 880
Ps 119:119 no wonder I **l** to obey your........880
Ps 119:127 I **l** your commands more..........881
Ps 119:140 that is why I **l** them so much. ...881
Ps 122:6 May all who **l** this city..................584
Ps 145:20 all those who **l** him, but he.........590
Ps 146:8 The LORD **l-s** the godly. 887
Prov 3:12 corrects those he **l-s,** just as 635
Prov 8:17 I **l** all who **l** me. 640
Prov 8:21 Those who **l** me inherit 640
Prov 8:36 All who hate me **l** death. 641
Prov 9:8 and they will **l** you.........................641
Prov 12:1 you must **l** discipline; it is............644
Prov 15:17 with someone you **l** is better 649
Prov 17:19 Anyone who **l-s** to quarrel..........653
Prov 18:21 those who **l** to talk....................654
Prov 19:8 wisdom is to **l** oneself;..................654
Prov 21:17 Those who **l** pleasure 658
Prov 22:11 Whoever **l-s** a pure 660
Prov 30:19 how a man **l-s** a woman...........846
Eccl 3:8 A time to **l** and a time....................675
Eccl 9:9 the woman you **l** through all 680
Song 1:3 the young women **l** you!...............663
Song 3:2 search for the one I **l.** 665
Song 3:3 Have you seen the one I **l?**...........665
Isa 1:23 All of them **l** bribes and.................824
Isa 56:6 serve him and **l** his name, who......943
Isa 61:8 I, the LORD, **l** justice......................948
Jer 2:2 long ago, how you **l-d** me and 959
Jer 8:2 my people have **l-d,** served, ...1009
Jer 31:20 to punish him, but I still **l** him, ...1033
Hos 2:1 Ruhamah—'The ones I **l.'**..............802
Hos 2:4 I will not **l** her children, ...803
Hos 2:23 to those I called 'Not **l-d.'**............804
Hos 9:15 I will **l** them no 812
Hos 11:1 was a child, I **l-d** him, and I..........814
Hos 12:7 scales—they **l** to cheat...............815
Amos 4:5 you Israelites **l** to do," says..........774
Amos 5:15 Hate evil and **l** what is good; 775
Mic 6:8 is right, to **l** mercy, and to..............910
Mal 1:2 "I have always **l-d** you," says 1244
Matt 5:43 that says, '**L** your neighbor'.......1330
Matt 5:44 But I say, **l** your enemies!..........1330
Matt 5:46 If you **l** only those.....................1330
Matt 6:24 hate one and **l** the other; 1332
Matt 10:37 If you **l** your father or.............1361
Matt 19:19 **L** your neighbor.........................1420
Matt 22:37 You must **l** the LORD your 1441
Mark 12:6 his son whom he **l-d** dearly.......1437
Mark 12:30 you must **l** the LORD your........1441
Mark 12:33 it is important to **l** him with 1442
Mark 12:33 and to **l** my neighbor as..........1442
Luke 6:27 I say, **l** your enemies! 1330
Luke 6:32 If you **l** only those who 1330
Luke 6:35 **L** your enemies!.........................1330
Luke 10:27 You must **l** the LORD your..........1396
Luke 10:27 And, '**L** your neighbor..............1396
Luke 16:13 hate one and **l** the other; 1412
John 3:16 For God **l-d** the world so...........1302
John 3:35 The Father **l-s** his Son 1303
John 5:20 For the Father **l-s** the Son and....1318
John 8:42 you would **l** me, because I..........1393
John 10:17 The Father **l-s** me because I ..1405
John 11:36 See how much he **l-d** him!.....1415
John 12:25 Those who **l** their life 1432
John 12:43 For they **l-d** human praise more 1435
John 13:1 He had **l-d** his disciples during..1455
John 13:34 **L** each other. Just as I have....1461
John 13:34 as I have **l-d** you, you should..1461
John 14:21 are the ones who **l** me. 1462
John 14:28 If you really **l-d** me, you 1463
John 14:31 know that I **l** the Father...........1463
John 17:23 and that you **l** them as much..1467
John 17:24 gave me because you **l-d** me.1467
John 19:26 beside the disciple he **l-d,**......1485
John 20:2 one whom Jesus **l-d.**...............1492
John 21:15 do you **l** me more than..........1497
John 21:16 son of John, do you **l** me?......1497
John 21:20 the disciple Jesus **l-d**— the one...1497
Rom 8:28 of those who **l** God and are.......1660
Rom 8:37 through Christ, who **l-d** us........1661
Rom 9:13 Scriptures, "I **l-d** Jacob, but I 1661
Rom 9:25 And I will **l** those whom I did 1662
Rom 12:10 **L** each other with genuine 1667
1 Cor 2:9 for those who **l** him...................1598
1 Cor 13:2 but didn't **l** others, I would.......1616
1 Cor 16:22 anyone does not **l** the Lord, ...1623
2 Cor 9:7 For God **l-s** a person.................1637
2 Cor 12:15 the more I **l** you, the less.......1642
Gal 2:20 of God, who **l-d** me and gave 1560
Eph 1:4 God **l-d** us and chose us 1704
Eph 2:4 mercy, and he **l-d** us so much,.....1707
Eph 5:25 this means **l** your wives, just 1713
Eph 5:25 just as Christ **l-d** the church.......1713
Eph 5:28 their wives as they **l** their own 1714
Eph 5:28 a man who **l-s** his wife actually..1714
Eph 5:33 love his wife as he **l-s** himself, ...1714
Phil 1:16 preach because they **l** me,.........1718
Phil 2:2 each other, **l-ing** one another, ...1719
1 Thes 1:4 God **l-s** you and has chosen....1581
1 Thes 4:10 urge you to **l** them even.........1584
2 Thes 2:10 they refuse to **l** and accept 1589
2 Thes 2:16 our Father, who **l-d** us and 1589
1 Tim 3:3 and not **l** money.........................1730
1 Tim 6:2 believers who are well **l-d.**.........1734
2 Tim 3:2 people will **l** only themselves 1744
Titus 1:8 and he must **l** what is good. 1737
Titus 2:4 women to **l** their husbands 1738
Titus 3:15 believers—all who **l** us.............1740
Heb 12:6 disciplines those he **l-s,** 1780
Heb 13:1 Keep on **l-ing** each other as......1782
Heb 13:5 Don't **l** money; 1782
Jas 2:5 to those who **l** him? 1548
1 Pet 1:8 You **l** him even though...............1749
1 Pet 2:17 Respect everyone, and **l** your ...1751
1 Pet 3:8 **L** each other as brothers............1753
2 Pet 2:15 **l-d** to earn money by doing 1759
1 Jn 2:5 how completely they **l** him.............1788
1 Jn 2:10 Anyone who **l-s** another 1789
1 Jn 3:1 very much our Father **l-s** us,........1790
1 Jn 3:14 If we **l** our Christian..................1791
1 Jn 4:9 how much he **l-d** us by sending..1793
1 Jn 4:10 not that we **l-d** God, but that.....1793
1 Jn 4:11 since God **l-d** us that much,......1793
1 Jn 4:11 surely ought to **l** each other.......1793
1 Jn 4:19 We **l** each other because he **l-d**..1794
1 Jn 4:20 someone says, "I **l** God," but 1794
1 Jn 4:20 how can we **l** God, whom we 1794
1 Jn 5:1 everyone who **l-s** the Father 1794
Jude 1:1 God the Father, who **l-s** you and...1784
Rev 1:5 glory to him who **l-s** us and has...1799
Rev 2:4 You don't **l** me or each other 1802
Rev 3:9 you are the ones I **l.**......................1806
Rev 3:19 discipline everyone I **l.** 1807
Rev 12:11 they did not **l** their lives so 1818
Rev 22:15 and all who **l** to live a lie...........1832

LOVE, LOVED, LOVING (adj) of or relating to a strong affection for another; affectionate, painstaking
Ps 88:18 my companions and **l-d** ones.......591
Ps 127:2 gives rest to his **l-d** ones. 631
Ezek 33:32 who sings **l** songs with a 1109
Mark 1:11 are my dearly **l-d** Son, and you..1294
Mark 9:7 is my dearly **l-d** Son. 1379
1 Thes 1:3 work, your **l-ing** deeds, and the...1580

LOVELY (adj) eliciting love by moral or ideal worth; beautiful
Phil 4:8 pure, and **l,** and admirable. 1725

LOVER, LOVERS (n) one who loves; two persons in love with each other; a person with whom one has sexual relations
Ps 99:4 Mighty King, **l** of justice,.................865
Song 2:9 My **l** is like a 665
Song 5:2 I heard my **l** knocking and............667
Ezek 16:33 gifts to your **l-s,** bribing them .1062
Ezek 16:39 who are your **l-s,** and they will..1062
Hos 2:5 run after other **l-s** and sell.............803

LOVINGKINDNESS (KJV)
Ps 25:6 **unfailing love,** which you have 560
Ps 40:11 Let your **unfailing love** and 570
Ps 63:3 **unfailing love** is better than life.....517
Ps 143:8 **unfailing love** each morning........588
Isa 63:7 according to his **mercy and love**...949

LOWER, LOWEST (adj) of lesser position, rank, or order
Ps 8:5 only a little **l** than God and 548
Luke 14:10 Instead, take the **l-est** place at..1408
Heb 2:7 them only a little **l** than the 1763

LOWLY (adj) humble in manner or spirit; of or relating to a low social or economic rank
Ps 37:11 The **l** will possess........................567
Ezek 21:26 Now the **l** will be 1068

LOYAL (adj) unswerving in allegiance; faithful
see also FAITHFUL, TRUSTWORTHY
1 Sam 26:23 and for being **l,** 468
2 Sam 2:6 May the LORD be **l** to you in........478
1 Chr 12:33 and completely **l** to David. 486
Ps 31:23 those who are **l** to him,................564
Ps 51:10 Renew a **l** spirit within 506
Prov 17:17 A friend is always **l,** and a.........652
Prov 20:6 say they are **l** friends, ...656

LOYALTY, LOYALTIES (n) the quality or state or an instance of being loyal
Judg 8:35 *Nor did they show any **l** to*..........388
Ps 119:113 *I hate those with divided **l-ies,***..........880
Prov 19:22 ***L** makes a person*..........655

LUKE The beloved doctor (Col 4:14, p. 1703); faithful co-worker of Paul (2 Tim 4:11, p. 1746; Phlm 1:23-24, p. 1692); noted fact-gatherer and writer of the third Gospel and the book of Acts.

LURE (n) enticement, appeal, attraction
Mark 4:19 *the **l** of wealth,*..........1346

LURE (v) to draw with a hint of pleasure or gain
2 Pet 2:18 *they **l** back into sin those*..........1759

LUST, LUSTS (n) unbridled sexual desire; an intense longing
1 Cor 7:9 *than to burn with **l.***..........1605
Eph 4:22 *corrupted by **l** and deception*..........1711
Col 3:5 *immorality, impurity, **l,** and*..........1700
2 Tim 2:22 *stimulates youthful **l-s.***..........1743
Titus 3:3 *to many **l-s** and pleasures*..........1739

LUST, LUSTED (v) to have an intense (sexual) desire
Prov 6:25 *Don't **l** for her*..........638
Ezek 23:5 *Then Oholah **l-ed** after other*..........1070

LUSTFUL (adj) excited by lust; lecherous
Mark 7:22 *deceit, **l** desires, envy,*..........1371
Gal 5:19 *impurity, **l** pleasures,*..........1566
Eph 4:19 *They live for **l** pleasure and*..........1711

LUXURY (n) a condition of abundance or great ease and comfort
Prov 21:17 *those who love wine and **l***..........658
Jas 5:5 *your years on earth in **l,***..........1553

LYING (adj) marked by or containing falsehoods; false
Prov 6:17 *haughty eyes, a **l** tongue,*..........638
Prov 12:22 *The LORD detests **l** lips,*..........645
Prov 21:6 *Wealth created by a **l** tongue*..........657
Prov 26:28 *A **l** tongue hates*..........842

LYING (v) to make an untrue statement with the intent to deceive
see also LIE
Mic 6:12 *are so used to **l** that their*..........910
Matt 15:19 *immorality, theft, **l,** and*..........1370
Acts 5:4 *You weren't **l** to us but*..........1520
1 Cor 15:15 *would all be **l** about God—*..........1620

MACEDONIA (n) a mountainous country north of Greece in the Balkan Peninsula
Acts 16:9 *A man from **M** in northern*..........1573

MAD (adj) insane; carried away by intense anger
Deut 28:34 *You will go **m** because of*..........318

MADE (v) to create, prepare, or fashion; to bring about
see also CREATE(D), FORMED, MAKE
Gen 1:7 *God **m** this space to separate*..........6
Gen 1:16 *He also **m** the stars.*..........7
Gen 1:25 ***m** all sorts of wild animals,*..........7
Gen 1:31 *God looked over all he had **m,***..........9
Gen 2:4 *LORD God **m** the earth and*..........9
Gen 2:22 *LORD God **m** a woman*..........10
Gen 6:6 *LORD was sorry he had ever **m***..........17
Gen 9:6 *God **m** human beings in his*..........21
Exod 20:11 *the LORD **m** the heavens,*..........169
Deut 32:6 *Has he not **m** you and*..........323
2 Chr 2:12 ***m** the heavens and*..........610
Job 10:9 *that you **m** me from dust—*..........104
Ps 95:5 *sea belongs to him, for he **m** it.*..........863
Ps 115:15 *who **m** heaven and earth.*..........875
Prov 22:2 *The LORD **m** them both.*..........658
Eccl 3:11 *God has **m** everything*..........675
Isa 27:11 *the one who **m** them will*..........897
Isa 43:7 *I have **m** them for my glory.*..........928
Isa 57:16 *all the souls I have **m.***..........944
Jer 51:15 *The LORD **m** the earth*..........1038
Jonah 1:9 *God of heaven, who **m** the sea*..........766
Matt 19:4 ***m** them male and female.*..........1418
Matt 19:28 *when the world is **m** new.*..........1420
1 Cor 11:9 *man was not **m** for woman,*..........1612
2 Cor 5:1 *an eternal body **m** for us by*..........1631
1 Tim 2:13 *For God **m** Adam first,*..........1730
Heb 4:3 *since he **m** the world.*..........1765
Rev 13:8 *before the world was **m**—*..........1820
Rev 14:7 *him who **m** the heavens,*..........1821

MAGIC (adj) having seemingly supernatural qualities or powers
Ezek 13:20 *all your **m** charms,*..........1059

MAGICIANS (n) ones skilled in extraordinary power or influence seemingly from a supernatural source; sorcerers
Exod 7:11 *Egyptian **m** did the same*..........150
Dan 2:2 *called in his **m,** enchanters,*..........1002

MAGNIFICENT (adj) grand or lavish; strikingly beautiful or impressive
Num 14:19 *In keeping with your **m,***..........253
1 Chr 22:5 *must be a **m** structure,*..........532
Ps 48:2 *It is high and **m;***..........852
Isa 63:14 *and gained a **m** reputation.*..........950

MAJESTIC (adj) having or exhibiting majesty; grand, stately
Ps 8:1 *your **m** name fills the earth!*..........548
Ps 29:4 *the voice of the LORD is **m.***..........562
Ps 145:5 *I will meditate on your **m,***..........589
Isa 53:2 *nothing beautiful or **m** about*..........940
Heb 1:3 *hand of the **m** God in heaven.*..........1761
Heb 8:1 *the throne of the **m** God*..........1771
2 Pet 1:16 *saw his **m** splendor with our*..........1758
2 Pet 1:17 *from the **m** glory of God*..........1758

MAJESTY (n) greatness or splendor of quality or character; sovereign power, authority, or dignity
Exod 15:7 *In the greatness of your **m,***..........162
1 Chr 16:27 *and **m** surround him;*..........493
Job 40:10 *splendor, your honor and **m.***..........130
Ps 21:5 *with splendor and **m.***..........555
Ps 68:34 *His **m** shines down on Israel;*..........577
Ps 93:1 *is king! He is robed in **m.***..........862
Ps 145:12 *about the **m** and glory of*..........590
Isa 2:10 *and the glory of his **m.***..........826
Isa 26:10 *no notice of the LORD's **m.***..........896
Jude 1:25 *All glory, **m,** power, and*..........1786

MAKE, MAKES, MAKING (v) to create, prepare, or fashion; to force; to bring about; to render
see also CREATE(D), FORMED, MADE
Gen 1:26 *Let us **m** human beings in our*..........8
Gen 2:18 *will **m** a helper who is just*..........10
Exod 4:11 *Who **m-s** a person's mouth?*..........145
Exod 25:40 *you **m** everything*..........176
Lev 16:34 ***m-ing** them right with the*..........223
Ps 19:7 ***m-ing** wise the simple.*..........554
Ps 139:14 ***m-ing** me so wonderfully*..........586
Prov 13:12 *Hope deferred **m-s** the heart*..........646
Isa 8:14 *stone that **m-s** people stumble,*..........791
Isa 29:16 *"He didn't **m** me"?*..........898
Isa 44:10 *fool would **m** his own god—*..........930
Jer 18:4 *he was **m-ing** did not turn out*..........1022
Jer 23:16 ***m-ing** up everything they say.*..........1028
Jer 31:31 *when I will **m** a new covenant*..........1034
Matt 28:19 ***m** disciples of all*..........1498
John 5:18 ***m-ing** himself equal with God.*..........1318
Rom 14:20 *it **m-s** another person stumble.*..........1670
1 Cor 3:7 *that God **m-s** the seed grow.*..........1599
Heb 8:5 *you **m** everything according to*..........1771
1 Pet 2:8 *stone that **m-s** people stumble,*..........1750

MAKER (n) one who makes; God
see also CREATOR
Ps 95:6 *before the LORD our **m,***..........863
Ps 149:2 *Israel, rejoice in your **M.***..........887
Prov 17:5 *mock the poor insult their **M;***..........652
Isa 45:9 *clay pot argue with its **m?***..........931
Hos 8:14 *Israel has forgotten its **M***..........811

MALE (adj) of, relating to, or being of the masculine sex
Gen 1:27 ***m** and female he created them.*..........8
Matt 19:4 *God made them **m** and female.*..........1418
Gal 3:28 *slave or free, **m** and female.*..........1562

MALICIOUS (adj) given to, marked by, or arising from a desire to cause pain, injury, or distress to another
Rom 1:29 *deception, **m** behavior,*..........1648
Col 3:8 *of anger, rage, **m** behavior,*..........1700

MAMMON (KJV)
Matt 6:24 *serve both God and **money***..........1332
Luke 16:9 ***worldly resources** to benefit*..........1411
Luke 16:11 *untrustworthy about **worldly wealth,***..........1412

MAN (n) an adult male human; individual, person
Gen 2:7 *the **m** from the dust*..........9
Gen 2:15 *the **m** in the Garden*..........10
Gen 2:18 *for the **m** to be alone.*..........10
Gen 2:23 *she was taken from '**m.**'*..........10
Gen 2:25 ***m** and his wife were both*..........11
Gen 3:9 *God called to the **m,** "Where*..........12
Isa 53:3 *rejected—a **m** of sorrows,*..........940
1 Cor 11:3 *of every **m** is Christ,*..........1612
1 Cor 11:3 *the head of woman is **m,***..........1612
1 Cor 15:45 *The first **m,** Adam,*..........1621
Eph 5:31 *A **m** leaves his father and*..........1714
1 Tim 2:5 *the **m** Christ Jesus.*..........1729

MAN-MADE (adj) manufactured, created, or constructed by human beings
Matt 15:9 *teach **m** ideas as commands*..........1369

MANAGE, MANAGING (v) to handle or direct with a degree of skill
Luke 12:42 *of **m-ing** his other household*..........1401
1 Tim 3:4 ***m** his own family well,*..........1730
1 Tim 3:12 *he must **m** his children*..........1731

MANAGER (n) a person who conducts business or household affairs
Luke 16:1 *a **m** handling his affairs.*..........1411
1 Cor 4:2 *as a **m** must be faithful.*..........1600
Titus 1:7 *a **m** of God's household,*..........1736

MANGER (n) a trough or open box in a stable designed to hold feed for livestock
Luke 2:7 *cloth and laid him in a **m,***..........1280
Luke 2:12 *strips of cloth, lying in a **m.***..........1281

MANNA (n) miraculous supply of food given to Israel in the wilderness; symbolic of spiritual nourishment
Exod 16:31 *Israelites called the food **m.***..........164
Deut 8:16 *He fed you with **m** in the*..........297

John 6:49 *Your ancestors ate* ***m*** *in the*......1368
Rev 2:17 *some of the* ***m*** *that has been*.....1804

MANNER (n) a mode of procedure or way of acting
Phil 1:27 *a* ***m*** *worthy of the Good News*....1719

MANSIONS (n) very large houses
Isa 5:9 *beautiful* ***m*** *will be empty.*...............828
Amos 3:15 *their winter* ***m*** *and their*...........774

MARANATHA (KJV)
1 Cor 16:22 ***Our Lord, come!***................1623

MARCH (v) to move along steadily usually with a rhythmic stride and in step with others; to advance or proceed
Josh 6:4 *you are to* ***m*** *around the town*.......343
Isa 42:13 *The LORD will* ***m*** *forth*................927

MARK Son of Mary of Jerusalem (Acts 12:12, p. 1537); traveled with Barnabas and Paul (Acts 12:25, p. 1539; 13:5, p. 1540); returned to Jerusalem (Acts 13:13, p. 1540); went to Cyprus with Barnabas (Acts 15:37-39, p. 1572); in Paul's greetings (Col 4:10, p. 1703; 2 Tim 4:11, p. 1746; Phlm 1:24, p. 1692); Peter's "son" (1 Pet 5:13, p. 1756).

MARK (n) an impression (as a scratch, scar, or stain) made on something; a distinguishing trait or quality
Gen 4:15 *LORD put a* ***m*** *on Cain*...................15
Rev 13:16 *given a* ***m*** *on the right hand or*...1820

MARKETPLACE, MARKETPLACES (n) an open square or place in town where markets or public sales are held
Matt 23:7 *as they walk in the* ***m-s,***...........1443
John 2:16 *my Father's house into a* ***m!***.....1300

MARRIAGE (adj) of or relating to marriage
Gen 49:4 *you defiled my* ***m*** *couch.*...............91
Mal 2:14 *the wife of your* ***m*** *vows*............1247

MARRIAGE (n) the state of being lawfully united to a person of the opposite sex as husband or wife; an act of marrying
Matt 22:30 *marry nor be given in* ***m.***........1440
Rom 7:2 *laws of* ***m*** *no longer apply*...........1657
1 Cor 7:14 *brings holiness to her* ***m,***.........1606
1 Cor 7:27 *do not seek to end the* ***m.***.......1606
Heb 13:4 *Give honor to* ***m,*** *and remain*.....1782

MARRY, MARRIED, MARRIES, MARRYING (v) to take a spouse according to law or custom
Exod 21:10 *who has* ***m-ied*** *a slave wife*.....171
Deut 24:4 *first husband may not* ***m*** *her*.......314
Deut 24:5 *newly* ***m-ied*** *man must not be*...314
Deut 25:5 *husband's brother should* ***m***.......315
Ezra 10:10 *By* ***m-ing*** *pagan women,*........1201
Hos 1:2 *Go and* ***m*** *a prostitute, so that*........801
Matt 1:18 *to be* ***m-ied*** *to Joseph*.............1277
Matt 19:9 *divorces his wife and* ***m-ies***.....1418
Matt 22:30 *will neither* ***m*** *nor be given*......1440
Mark 12:23 *all seven were* ***m-ied*** *to her.*..1440
Luke 16:18 *his wife and* ***m-ies*** *someone*..1412
Rom 7:2 *when a woman* ***m-ies,*** *the law*...1657
1 Cor 7:9 *better to* ***m*** *than to burn*............1605
1 Cor 7:28 *if you do get* ***m-ied,*** *it is not*....1606
1 Cor 7:33 *a* ***m-ied*** *man has to think*.......1607
1 Tim 5:14 *these younger widows to* ***m***.....1733

MARTYRED (v) to put to death for adhering to a belief, faith, or profession
Rev 6:9 *who had been* ***m*** *for the word*......1811

MARVELING (v) to become filled with surprise, wonder, or amazed curiosity
Luke 9:43 *everyone was* ***m*** *at*.................1382

MARVELOUS (adj) astonishing; miraculous, supernatural
Ps 9:1 *tell of all the* ***m*** *things*.....................549
Rev 15:1 *heaven another* ***m*** *event*...........1822
Rev 15:3 *Great and* ***m*** *are your works,*......1822

MARY
1. Mother of Jesus, the foretold virgin (Matt 1:16-25, p. 1279, 1277; Luke 1:26-38, p. 1274); psalmist of the Magnificat (Luke 1:46-56, p. 1275); gave birth in Bethlehem (Luke 2:5-20, p. 1280); at first sign (miracle) of Jesus (John 2:1-5, p. 1299); at the cross (John 19:25-27, p. 1485); Jesus assigned her care to John (John 19:25-27, p. 1485); in upper room after the ascension (Acts 1:14, p. 1512).
2. Mary Magdalene, former demoniac, supporter of Jesus (Luke 8:1-3, p. 1341); at the cross and Jesus' burial (Matt 27:55-61, p. 1486; Mark 15:40-47, p. 1486; John 19:25, p. 1485); saw angel after resurrection (Matt 28:1-10, p. 1489; Mark 16:1-9, p. 1490; Luke 24:10, p. 1491); saw Jesus after resurrection (John 20:1-18, p. 1492).
3. Sister of Martha and Lazarus (Luke 10:38-42, p. 1397; John 11, p. 1413; 12:1-8, p. 1428).
4. Mother of James and Joseph (Matt 27:56, p. 1486; Mark 15:40, 47, p. 1486; 16:1, p. 1490).
5. Mother of John Mark (Acts 12:12, p. 1537).
6. A woman in Rome greeted by Paul (Rom 16:6, p. 1673).

MASTER, MASTERS (n) one in authority or leadership; employer; teacher; lord or Lord
Jer 3:14 *the LORD, "for I am your* ***m.***...........963
Matt 10:24 *are not greater than their* ***m.***...1360
Luke 16:13 *No one can serve two* ***m-s.***....1412
Rom 6:14 *Sin is no longer your* ***m,***..........1656
Eph 6:5 *obey your earthly* ***m-s*** *with*..........1715
Col 3:22 *Slaves, obey your earthly* ***m-s***.....1702
1 Tim 6:1 *full respect for their* ***m-s***...........1734
1 Tim 6:2 *If the* ***m-s*** *are believers,*............1734
2 Tim 2:21 *ready for the* ***M*** *to use you*......1743
Titus 2:9 *always obey their* ***m-s*** *and do*....1738
1 Pet 2:18 *the authority of your* ***m-s***.........1751
2 Pet 2:1 *deny the* ***M*** *who bought them.*...1758
Jude 1:4 *denied our only* ***M*** *and Lord,*.........1784

MAT (n) a large thick pad or cushion
Mark 2:9 *pick up your* ***m,*** *and walk'?*........1314
Acts 9:34 *and roll up your sleeping* ***m!***.....1532

MATTHEW One of the 12 disciples (Matt 10:3, p. 1358; Mark 3:18, p. 1323; Luke 6:15, p. 1323; Acts 1:13, p. 1512); former tax collector who followed Jesus (Matt 9:9-10, p. 1314); also known as "Levi" (Mark 2:14, p. 1315).

MATURE (adj) of or relating to a condition of full development or to attaining a desired or final state
1 Cor 2:6 *I am among* ***m*** *believers,*...........1598
1 Cor 14:20 *but be* ***m*** *in understanding*....1617
2 Cor 13:9 *that you will become* ***m.***..........1643
Eph 4:13 *we will be* ***m*** *in the Lord,*...........1711
Phil 3:15 *all who are spiritually* ***m*** *agree*....1723
Heb 6:1 ***m*** *in our understanding.*..............1768
1 Jn 2:13 *who are* ***m*** *in the faith*.............1789

MATURITY (n) the quality or state of being fully developed
Luke 8:14 *so they never grow into* ***m.***........1347
2 Cor 13:11 *Grow to* ***m.*** *Encourage each*...1643

MEADOWS (n) grassy land areas
Ps 23:2 *He lets me rest in green* ***m;***...........558

MEAL, MEALS (n) a portion of food eaten usually at designated times in the day to satisfy appetite; an act or time of eating
Matt 26:18 *I will eat the Passover* ***m***.........1455
Heb 12:16 *firstborn son for a single* ***m.***.....1781
Jude 1:12 *in your fellowship* ***m-s***.............1785

MEAN-SPIRITED (adj) exhibiting or characterized by meanness of spirit
Deut 15:9 *not be* ***m*** *and refuse someone*....305

MEAN, MEANS (v) to serve or intend to convey, show, or indicate
Gen 41:16 *God can tell you what it* ***m-s.***.......79
Rom 3:3 *that* ***m*** *God will be unfaithful?*.....1650

MEANING (n) the thing that is conveyed especially by language
Neh 8:8 *and clearly explained the* ***m***.........1214

MEANINGLESS (adj) having no meaning; lacking any significance
Eccl 1:2 ***m,"*** *says the Teacher,*..................673
Eccl 8:14 *not all that is* ***m*** *in our world.*.......680
1 Tim 1:6 *their time in* ***m*** *discussions*........1727

MEASURE, MEASURED, MEASURING (v) to gauge or regulate the specific dimensions of; to have a specified measurement; to regulate by a standard
Ps 145:3 *No one can* ***m*** *his greatness.*.......589
Isa 40:28 *No one can* ***m*** *the depths*............925
Jer 31:37 *heavens cannot be* ***m-d*** *and*.....1034
Ezek 45:3 *area,* ***m*** *out a portion of land*.....1128
Dan 5:27 *balances and have not* ***m-d*** *up.*.1139
Zech 2:2 *I am going to* ***m*** *Jerusalem,*........1166
Luke 12:15 *Life is not* ***m-d*** *by how much*...1400
Eph 4:13 *mature in the Lord,* ***m-ing*** *up*....1711
Rev 11:1 *Go and* ***m*** *the Temple*...............1816

MEASURES (n) instruments or utensils for measuring; a system of standard units of measure
Deut 25:14 *must use full and honest* ***m.***......315
Prov 20:10 *unequal* ***m****—the LORD detests*...656

MEAT (n) animal tissue considered especially as food
Rom 14:21 *better not to eat* ***m*** *or drink*.....1670
1 Cor 8:13 *sin, I will never eat* ***m*** *again*.....1608
1 Cor 10:25 *may eat any* ***m*** *that is sold*.....1611

MEDDLING (v) to interest oneself in what is not one's concern; to interfere without right or propriety
2 Thes 3:11 *refusing to work and* ***m*** *in*......1590
1 Tim 5:13 ***m*** *in other people's*................1733

MEDIATE, MEDIATES (v) to act as an intermediary agent in bringing, effecting, or communicating; to interpose
Job 16:21 *to* ***m*** *between God and me,*........110
Isa 2:4 *LORD will* ***m*** *between nations*..........825
Heb 8:6 *the one who* ***m-s*** *for us a far*.......1771
Heb 9:15 *who* ***m-s*** *a new covenant*..........1773
Heb 12:24 *Jesus, the one who* ***m-s***..........1781

MEDIATOR (n) one who mediates
Job 9:33 *If only there were a* ***m*** *between*....104
1 Tim 2:5 *one God and one* ***M*** *who can*.....1729

MEDICINE (n) a substance or preparation used in treating disease; something that affects well-being
Prov 17:22 *A cheerful heart is good* ***m,***.......653
Jer 8:22 *Is there no* ***m*** *in Gilead?*.............1011
Rev 22:2 *The leaves were used for* ***m***.......1832

MEDITATE, MEDITATING (v) to contemplate, reflect, or ponder
see also PONDER, THINK
Gen 24:63 ***m-ing*** *in the fields,*......................50
Ps 1:2 ***m-ing*** *on it day and night.*...............856
Ps 48:9 *O God, we* ***m*** *on your unfailing*.......853
Ps 63:6 ***m-ing*** *on you through the night.*....518
Ps 119:23 *but I will* ***m*** *on your decrees.*.......878
Ps 119:27 ***m*** *on your wonderful deeds*........878
Ps 119:48 *I* ***m*** *on your decrees.*...............879
Ps 145:5 *I will* ***m*** *on your majestic,*............589

MEDITATION (n) the act or process of meditating
Ps 19:14 *words of my mouth and the* ***m***....555

MEDIUMS (n) psychics; those through whom it is thought the dead communicate with the living
Lev 20:27 *who act as* ***m*** *or who consult*......227

MELCHIZEDEK King of Salem, priest of God Most High (Gen 14:18, p. 34); blessed Abram and accepted his tithe (Gen 14:19-20, p. 34); associated with mysterious priesthood (Ps 110:4, p. 582; Heb 7:11, p. 1770).

MELODIOUS (adj) having a pleasant melody
Ps 98:5 *the harp and* ***m*** *song,*...................865

MELODY (n) a sweet succession or arrangement of sounds
Ps 92:3 *harp and the* ***m*** *of the lyre.* 862

MELT, MELTS (v) to dissolve or disintegrate; to disappear as if by dissolving
Jer 9:7 ***m*** *them down in a crucible*..........1011
Amos 9:5 *touches the land and it* ***m-s,***.....780

MEMBERS (n) the individuals composing a group; parts of a whole
see also PARTS
Eph 5:30 *And we are* ***m*** *of his body.*..........1714
Col 3:15 *For as* ***m*** *of one body*................1701

MERCIFUL (adj) compassionate; forgiving
Deut 4:31 *your God is a* ***m*** *God;*.................291
Ps 78:38 *Yet he was* ***m*** *and forgave*...........599
Dan 4:27 *and be* ***m*** *to the poor.*................1121
Dan 9:9 *our God is* ***m*** *and forgiving,*..........1142
Matt 5:7 *God blesses those who are* ***m,***....1326
Luke 1:54 *and remembered to be* ***m.***........1276
Heb 2:17 ***m*** *and faithful High Priest*..........1764
Jas 2:13 *God will be* ***m*** *when he judges*....1549

MERCY, MERCIES (n) a blessing that is an act of divine favor or compassion; withholding of the punishment or judgment our sins deserve
see also COMPASSION, FORGIVENESS
Exod 34:6 *God of compassion and* ***m!***........187
2 Sam 24:14 *for his* ***m*** *is great.*..................530
Neh 9:27 *In your great* ***m,*** *you sent*...........1216
Job 41:3 *beg you for* ***m*** *or implore*.............131
Ps 28:6 *he has heard my cry for* ***m.***............562
Ps 103:4 *me with love and tender* ***m-ies.***...580
Ps 119:77 *with your tender* ***m-ies*** *so I*.......879
Ps 119:156 *how great is your* ***m;***...............881
Isa 14:1 *LORD will have* ***m*** *on*......................831
Isa 49:10 *LORD in his* ***m*** *will lead*................936
Isa 60:10 *I will now have* ***m*** *on you*............947
Lam 3:22 *His* ***m-ies*** *never cease.* 1098
Lam 3:23 ***m-ies*** *begin afresh each morning.*...1098
Dan 9:18 *because of your* ***m.***..................1142
Jonah 2:8 *their backs on all God's* ***m-ies.***...767
Mic 6:8 *do what is right, to love* ***m,***............910
Matt 5:7 *for they will be shown* ***m.***............1326
Matt 9:13 *I want you to show* ***m,***..............1315
Matt 18:33 *just as I had* ***m*** *on you?*..........1386
Matt 23:23 *law—justice,* ***m,*** *and faith.*.....1444
Rom 9:15 *I will show* ***m*** *to anyone*...........1662
Rom 9:18 *God chooses to show* ***m***...........1662
Rom 11:32 *have* ***m*** *on everyone.*..............1666
2 Cor 4:1 *God in his* ***m*** *has given us*.........1630
Gal 1:6 *through the loving* ***m*** *of Christ.*......1555
Eph 2:4 *But God is so rich in* ***m,*** *and*.........1707
1 Tim 1:13 *But God had* ***m*** *on me.*............1728
Titus 3:5 *but because of his* ***m.***...............1739
Heb 4:16 *we will receive his* ***m,***..............1766
Heb 10:29 *who brings God's* ***m*** *to us.*........1776
Jas 2:13 *will be no* ***m*** *for those*..............1549
Jas 3:17 *It is full of* ***m*** *and good*...............1551
1 Pet 1:3 *by his great* ***m*** *that we*.............1748
Jude 1:22 *show* ***m*** *to those whose faith*....1786

MERCYSEAT (KJV)
Heb 9:5 *the* ***Ark's cover, the place of atonement.***...1772

MESSAGE (n) a communication in writing, in speech, or by signals; an underlying theme or idea
Isa 53:1 *Who has believed our* ***m?***............940
Isa 62:11 *LORD has sent this* ***m***.................949
John 12:38 *who has believed our* ***m?***.......1434
Acts 5:20 *give the people this* ***m*** *of life!*....1521
Acts 10:36 *This is the* ***m*** *of Good News*....1534
Rom 10:16 *who has believed our* ***m?***.......1664
1 Cor 1:18 *The* ***m*** *of the cross*................1596
2 Cor 5:19 *wonderful* ***m*** *of reconciliation*...1632
Titus 1:9 *belief in the trustworthy* ***m***..........1737
2 Pet 1:19 *confidence in the* ***m*** *proclaimed.*..1758

MESSENGER, MESSENGERS (n) one who bears a message or does an errand
Prov 13:17 *a reliable* ***m*** *brings healing.*.......646
Prov 25:13 *Trustworthy* ***m-s*** *refresh like*.....840
Isa 52:7 *feet of the* ***m*** *who brings good*.......939
Isa 66:19 *who survive to be* ***m-s*** *to the*.......953
Mal 3:1 *my* ***m,*** *and he will prepare*...........1247
Matt 11:10 *am sending my* ***m*** *ahead*..........1337
Rom 10:15 *feet of* ***m-s*** *who bring good*....1664
Rom 15:16 *a special* ***m*** *from Christ*..........1671
2 Cor 12:7 ***m*** *from Satan to torment*..........1642
Phil 2:25 *he was your* ***m*** *to help me*.........1721
1 Thes 2:4 *speak as* ***m-s*** *approved by God.*...1581
Heb 3:1 *to be God's* ***m*** *and High Priest.*.....1764

MESSIAH, MESSIAHS (n) the one anointed by God to deliver His people and establish His kingdom
see also ANOINTED ONE, CHRIST, JESUS
Matt 24:24 *false* ***m-s*** *and false*...............1446
Mark 13:22 *false* ***m-s*** *and false*..............1449
John 1:41 *him, "We have found the* ***M"***....1298
John 4:25 *I know the* ***M*** *is coming—*........1305

METHUSELAH The oldest man, who lived 969 years; the son of Enoch, who never died (Gen 5:21-24, p. 16); the father of Lamech (Gen 5:25-27, p. 16).

MICHAEL Ruling angel (Jude 1:9, p. 1785; Rev 12:7, p. 1818); great defender-prince in the visions of Daniel (Dan 10:13, 21, p. 1158; 11:1, p. 1159; 12:1, p. 1161).

MIDNIGHT (n) the middle of the night
Exod 12:29 *at* ***m,*** *the Lord struck down*.....157
Acts 16:25 *Around* ***m*** *Paul and Silas were* 1576

MIDWIVES (n) those who assist women in childbirth
Exod 1:17 *because the* ***m*** *feared God,*........140

MIGHT (n) the power, energy, or intensity of which one is capable
Josh 9:9 *heard of the* ***m*** *of the LORD*..........348
2 Sam 6:14 *the LORD with all his* ***m,***...........491
Ps 54:1 *Defend me with your* ***m.***...............464
Isa 11:2 *the Spirit of counsel and* ***m,***..........795
Isa 63:15 *and the* ***m*** *you used to show*.......950

MIGHTY, MIGHTIER, MIGHTIEST (adj) powerful; great or imposing in size or extent
Gen 49:24 *hands of the* ***M*** *One of Jacob,*......92
Deut 10:17 *God, the* ***m*** *and awesome*.........300
Deut 34:12 *With* ***m*** *power, Moses*..............328
2 Sam 23:8 *David's* ***m-iest*** *warriors*...........480
2 Chr 20:6 *You are powerful and* ***m;***...........732
Neh 9:32 *and* ***m*** *and awesome God,*.........1217
Job 9:4 *For God is so wise and so* ***m.***.........103
Job 36:5 *He is* ***m*** *in both power and*............125
Ps 24:8 *LORD, strong and* ***m;***......................559
Ps 47:5 *ascended with a* ***m*** *shout*...............852
Ps 50:1 *LORD, the* ***M*** *One, is God,* 593
Ps 71:16 *I will praise your* ***m*** *deeds,*...........860
Ps 77:12 *thinking about your* ***m*** *works.*........597
Ps 89:27 *son, the* ***m-iest*** *king on earth.* 592
Ps 93:4 ***m-ier*** *than the violent raging*.........862
Ps 93:4 *LORD above is* ***m-ier*** *than these!*....862
Ps 95:4 *and the* ***m-iest*** *mountains.*............863
Ps 145:4 *children of your* ***m*** *acts;*...............589
Ps 145:12 *will tell about your* ***m*** *deeds*......590
Ps 150:2 *Praise him for his* ***m*** *works;*.........888
Prov 24:5 *wise are* ***m-ier*** *than the strong,* ..662
Isa 9:6 *Wonderful Counselor,* ***M*** *God,*.........793
Isa 60:16 *your Redeemer, the* ***M*** *One of*......947
Zeph 3:17 *He is a* ***m*** *savior.*........................986
Eph 1:19 *This is the same* ***m*** *power*..........1706
Eph 6:10 *in the Lord and in his* ***m.***............1715
Heb 1:3 *sustains everything by the* ***m***.......1761
1 Pet 5:6 *yourselves under the* ***m***.............1756
Jude 1:9 *Michael, one of the* ***m-iest*** *of the angels,*.......................................1785

MILE (n) In the Roman Empire, a unit of distance equal to 5,280 feet
Matt 5:41 *gear for a* ***m,*** *carry it two*..........1329

MILK (n) from goats, cows, or sheep, used for food and drink; figurative of abundant produce, prosperity, spiritual food, or salvation
Exod 3:8 *flowing with* ***m*** *and honey—* 144
1 Cor 3:2 *feed you with* ***m,*** *not with*..........1599
1 Pet 2:2 *must crave pure spiritual* ***m***.......1750

MILLSTONE (n) either of two circular stones used for grinding
Luke 17:2 *into the sea with a* ***m*** *hung*.......1413

MIND, MINDS (n) the part of humans that engages in conscious thinking, feeling, and decision making; in the Bible, mind is akin to the heart, not the brain
Num 23:19 *he does not change his* ***m.***........267
1 Sam 15:29 *nor will he change his* ***m,*** 447
Mark 12:30 *all your soul, all your* ***m,***.........1441
Luke 24:45 *opened their* ***m-s***.................1498
Acts 4:32 *were united in heart and* ***m.***......1520
Rom 8:6 *Spirit control your* ***m***..................1659
1 Cor 1:10 *be of one* ***m,*** *united in*.............1596
1 Cor 2:9 *heard, and no* ***m*** *has imagined*..1598
2 Cor 4:4 *has blinded the* ***m-s*** *of those* 1630
Col 2:18 *sinful* ***m-s*** *have made them*.........1699
2 Tim 4:5 *clear* ***m*** *in every situation.*.........1745
Heb 8:10 *I will put my laws in their* ***m-s,***...1772
Heb 10:16 *I will write them on their* ***m-s.***...1775

MINDING (v) to be concerned about
1 Thes 4:11 *live a quiet life,* ***m*** *your own*...1584

MINISTERS (n) agents; those who serve or assist others of higher rank
2 Cor 3:6 *to be **m** of his new covenant*......1629

MINISTRY (n) exercise of one's gifts and resources
2 Cor 9:12 *from this **m** of giving—*..........1638
2 Cor 9:13 *As a result of your **m,** they*......1638
Heb 8:6 *a **m** that is far superior to*...........1771

MIRACLE, MIRACLES (n) an extraordinary event manifesting divine intervention in human affairs
Exod 3:20 *performing all kinds of **m-s***........144
Exod 7:9 *demand, 'Show me a **m.'***............150
Deut 13:1 *they promise you signs or **m-s,***..302
Job 9:10 *He performs countless **m-s.***........103
Ps 105:5 *he has performed, his **m-s,***.........868
Ps 106:2 *the glorious **m-s** of the LORD?*......870
Jer 32:19 *and do great and mighty **m-s.***..1079
Matt 7:22 *and performed many **m-s***.........1334
Matt 13:54 *and the power to do **m-s?***......1356
Mark 6:2 *power to perform such **m-s?***.....1356
Mark 9:39 *No one who performs a **m***.......1383
Luke 19:37 *wonderful **m-s** they had*.........1430
Luke 23:8 *to see him perform a **m.***..........1478
John 7:21 *I did one **m** on the Sabbath,*.....1390
Acts 2:22 *by doing powerful **m-s,***............1515
Acts 8:13 ***m-s** Philip performed.*..............1528
Acts 19:11 *to perform unusual **m-s.***.........1594
1 Cor 12:28 *those who do **m-s,** those*......1615
2 Cor 12:12 *and **m-s** among you.*...............1642
Gal 3:5 *and work **m-s** among you*............1560
Heb 2:4 *and various **m-s** and gifts of*........1763

MIRACULOUS (adj) working or able to work miracles; supernatural
Ps 106:7 *the LORD's **m** deeds*.....................870
Matt 12:39 *would demand a **m***................1343
John 9:16 *sinner do such **m** signs?*..........1404
John 12:37 *despite all the **m** signs Jesus*.1434
John 20:30 *do many other **m** signs*..........1496
Acts 2:43 *performed many **m** signs*..........1516
Acts 4:16 *have performed a **m** sign,*.........1519
Rom 15:19 *of **m** signs and wonders*.........1671

MIRROR (n) a polished or smooth surface (as of glass) that forms images by reflection
1 Cor 13:12 *puzzling reflections in a **m,***....1616
Jas 1:23 *glancing at your face in a **m.***.......1548

MISERABLE (adj) being in a pitiable state of distress or unhappiness
Rom 7:24 *Oh, what a **m** person I am!*.........1658

MISERY (n) a state of suffering or discomfort; a state of great unhappiness and emotional distress
Judg 10:16 *And he was grieved by their **m.***..392
Rom 3:16 *Destruction and **m** always*.........1651

MISFORTUNE (n) bad luck; a distressing or unfortunate incident or event
Prov 17:5 *who rejoice at the **m** of others*.....652
Obad 1:12 *Judah suffered such **m.***..........1103

MISLEAD, MISLED (v) to lead astray; to deceive
Prov 13:6 *the evil are **m-ed** by sin*.............646
Prov 16:29 ***m** their companions,*.................652
Matt 24:4 *Don't let anyone **m** you,*............1446
Gal 6:7 *Don't be **m-ed**—you cannot*........1567
Jas 1:16 *So don't be **m-ed,** my dear*........1547

MISTREAT, MISTREATED (v) to treat badly; to abuse
Exod 22:21 *You must not **m** or oppress*.......172
Prov 19:26 *Children who **m** their father*......655
Heb 13:3 *those being **m-ed,** as if you*.......1782

MISUSE (v) to use incorrectly; to mistreat or abuse
Exod 20:7 *must not **m** the name of*............169
Deut 5:11 *must not **m** the name of*............292
Ps 139:20 *your enemies **m** your name*........586

MOCK, MOCKED, MOCKS (v) to treat with contempt or ridicule; to mimic in sport or derision
Job 11:3 *When you **m** God, shouldn't*.........105
Ps 22:7 *Everyone who sees me **m-s** me.*....556
Ps 89:51 *Your enemies have **m-ed** me,*......592
Prov 3:34 *The LORD **m-s** the mockers*.........635
Prov 30:17 *The eye that **m-s** a father and*..846
Mic 6:16 *with contempt, **m-ed** by all*..........910
Matt 5:11 *blesses you when people **m***......1326
Matt 27:41 *the elders also **m-ed** Jesus.*...1483
Mark 10:34 *They will **m** him, spit on*.........1423
Luke 6:22 *and exclude you and **m** you*......1327
Gal 6:7 *cannot **m** the justice of God.*.........1567

MOCKER, MOCKERS (n) one who mocks
Ps 1:1 *sinners, or join in with **m-s.***............856
Prov 3:34 *The LORD mocks the **m-s***...........635
Prov 9:7 *Anyone who rebukes a **m** will*........641
Prov 20:1 *Wine produces **m-s;** alcohol*.......655

MOCKERY (n) a subject of laughter, derision, or sport; insulting or contemptuous action or speech
1 Kgs 9:7 *object of **m** and ridicule*.............623
Isa 50:6 *not hide my face from **m** and*........937
Joel 2:17 *become an object of **m.***............1241
Matt 27:29 *in **m** and taunted,*...................1481

MODEL (n) an example for imitation or emulation
Ezek 28:12 *were the **m** of perfection,*.......1084

MODESTY (n) propriety in dress, speech, or conduct; freedom from conceit or vanity
1 Tim 2:15 *faith, love, holiness, and **m.***...1730

MOLTEN (adj) made by melting and casting
Exod 34:17 *not make any gods of **m** metal*...188

MOMENT (n) a comparatively brief period of time; instant
Ps 30:5 *lasts only a **m,** but his favor*..........563
Prov 11:18 *get rich for the **m,***...................644
Isa 54:7 *For a brief **m** I abandoned you,*......941
Isa 66:8 *come forth in a mere **m?***.............953
Matt 6:27 *your worries add a single **m***......1332
Gal 2:5 *give in to them for a single **m.***......1558

MONEY (n) officially coined currency
see also POSSESSIONS, RICHES, TREASURE(S), WEALTH
2 Chr 24:10 *gladly brought their **m** and*.......757
Eccl 5:10 *who love **m** will never have*..........677
Matt 6:24 *serve both God and **m.***.............1332
Luke 3:14 *Don't extort **m** or make false*....1291
1 Tim 3:3 *and not love **m.***........................1730
1 Tim 6:10 *love of **m** is the root of all*.........1735
1 Tim 6:17 *and not to trust in their **m,***......1735
1 Jn 3:17 *If someone has enough **m***........1791

MONTH, MONTHS (n) a measure of time corresponding nearly to the period of the moon's revolution and amounting to approximately 4 weeks or 30 days
Ezek 47:12 *will be a new crop every **m,***....1131
Gal 4:10 *certain days or **m-s** or seasons*..1563
Rev 11:2 *trample the holy city for 42 **m-s.***1816
Rev 13:5 *he wanted for forty-two **m-s.***.....1819
Rev 22:2 *fruit, with a fresh crop each **m.***..1832

MOON (n) a celestial body that orbits the earth
Josh 10:13 *and the **m** stayed in place*........350
Ps 121:6 *harm you by day, nor the **m** at*.....882
Ps 148:3 *Praise him, sun and **m!***..............887
Joel 2:31 *the **m** will turn blood red*..........1242
Hab 3:11 *The sun and **m** stood still*.............981
Matt 24:29 *the **m** will give no light,*...........1446
Acts 2:20 *the **m** will turn blood red*..........1515
Col 2:16 *or new **m** ceremonies*..................1699
Rev 21:23 *city has no need of sun or **m,***...1831

MORE (adv) to a greater or higher degree
Ps 73:25 *I desire you **m** than anything*.......594
1 Pet 1:2 *give you **m** and **m** grace*...........1747

MORNING (n) the time from sunrise to noon
Gen 1:5 *evening passed and **m** came,*............6
Ps 5:3 *Listen to my voice in the **m,***.............547
Lam 3:23 *mercies begin afresh each **m.***...1098

MORNING STAR (n) a bright planet (Venus) seen in the eastern sky before or at sunrise
2 Pet 1:19 *and Christ the **M** shines*..........1758
Rev 2:28 *give them the **m!***........................1805
Rev 22:16 *I am the bright **m.***....................1833

MORTAL (adj) subject to death
Gen 6:3 *for they are only **m** flesh.*................17
Rom 8:11 *will give life to your **m** bodies*....1659
1 Cor 15:53 *our **m** bodies must be*...........1622

MORTALS (n) human beings
Ps 8:4 *mere **m** that you should think*..........548
Ps 144:3 *mere **m** that you should think*......589

MOSES Deliverer of Israel from Egypt, lawgiver, servant of God; "drawn out" of the Nile, raised in Pharaoh's house (Exod 2:1-10, p. 141); killed an Egyptian and fled to Midian (Exod 2:11-15, p. 142; Acts 7:24, p. 1525); married Zipporah and had a child (Exod 2:16-22, p. 142); saw the LORD at the burning bush (Exod 3:1–4:17, p. 143); returned to Egypt (Exod 4:18-31, p. 145); conflict with Pharaoh and the 10 plagues (Exod 5–11, p. 146); brother of Aaron and Miriam (1 Chr 6:3, p. 1232); Passover and the Exodus (Exod 12–14, p. 155; 1 Cor 10:2, p. 1610); song of salvation and praise (Exod 15:1-21, p. 161; Rev 15:3, p. 1822); heavenly provisions (Exod 15:22–17:7, p. 162); raised arms to defeat enemies (Exod 17:8-16, p. 165); delegated judgeships (Exod 18, p. 166); received the law at Sinai (Exod 19–23, p. 167; John 1:17, p. 1272; Heb 12:21, p. 1781); received Tabernacle plans (Exod 25–31, p. 175); broke tablets at gold calf incident (Exod 32, p. 184); received new tablets (Exod 33–34, p. 186); face glowed with the LORD's glory (Exod 34:29-35, p. 188; 2 Cor 3:13-15, p. 1630); directed the building of the Tabernacle (Exod 35–40, p. 188); anointed Tabernacle and Aaronic priesthood (Lev 8–9, p. 210); opposed by Aaron and Miriam, interceded for sister (Num 12, p. 249); interceded for Israel when they refused to enter Canaan (Num 14:11-25, p. 252); Korah's rebellion (Num 16, p. 255); water at Meribah (Num 20:1-13, p. 261); denied entrance to Promised Land (Num 20:12, p. 262; Deut 1:37, p. 286; 3:23-28, p. 289); bronze snake healed (Num 21:4-9, p. 263; John 3:14, p. 1302); succeeded by Joshua (Num 27:12-23, p. 273; Deut 31:1-8, p. 322); received additional laws (Num 28–30, p. 273); gave concluding messages to Israel (Deut 1–33, p. 284); gave final blessings to the tribes (Deut 33, p. 326; *see also* Gen 49, p. 91); died and was exalted

(Deut 34, p. 328; Heb 3:2, p. 1764); wrote a psalm (Ps 90, p. 325); recorded book of the law (Ezra 3:2, p. 1155; Neh 13:1, p. 1222; Luke 24:44, p. 1498); appeared with Elijah at the Transfiguration (Luke 9:30, p. 1380).

MOTHER (n) a female parent; a woman in authority
see also PARENT
Gen 2:24 *a man leaves his father and* **m**.......11
Gen 3:20 *she would be the* **m** *of all who*.......13
Exod 20:12 *Honor your father and* **m.**.........169
Deut 21:18 *not obey his father or* **m,**..........311
Judg 5:7 *Deborah arose as a* **m**..................381
Prov 10:1 *brings grief to a* **m.**....................641
Prov 23:22 *don't despise your* **m**.................661
Isa 66:13 *as a* **m** *comforts her child*............953
Matt 10:35 *a daughter against her* **m,**......1361
Matt 10:37 *father or* **m** *more than you*.......1361
Matt 12:48 *Who is my* **m?**..............................1344
Mark 10:19 *Honor your father and* **m.**........1421
John 19:27 *disciple, "Here is your* **m."**.....1485
Eph 5:31 *A man leaves his father and* **m**...1714
Eph 6:2 *Honor your father and* **m.**.............1714

MOTHER-IN-LAW (n) the mother of one's spouse
Ruth 2:19 *Ruth told her* **m** *about the man*...413
Matt 10:35 *daughter-in-law against her* **m.**..1361

MOTHS (n) insects whose larvae eat wool, fur, or feathers
Matt 6:19 *on earth, where* **m** *eat them*......1332

MOTIVES (n) something (as a need or desire) that causes a person to act
1 Chr 29:17 *all this with good* **m,**..............541
Ps 26:2 *Test my* **m** *and my heart*...............560
Prov 16:2 *LORD examines their* **m.**.............650
Jer 17:10 *hearts and examine secret* **m.**...1021
1 Cor 4:5 *will reveal our private* **m.**...........1600
Phil 1:18 *Whether their* **m** *are false or*......1718
1 Thes 2:3 *with any deceit or impure* **m**....1581
1 Thes 2:4 *He alone examines the* **m** *of*....1581
Jas 4:3 *your* **m** *are all wrong—*...............1551

MOUNT (n) a high hill; mountain
Exod 17:6 *on the rock at* **M** *Sinai*................165
Exod 19:18 **M** *Sinai was covered with smoke*..168
Zech 14:4 *the* **M** *of Olives will split*...........1180
Matt 24:3 *Jesus sat on the* **M** *of Olives*.....1446
Luke 22:39 *as usual to the* **M** *of Olives*.....1469

MOUNTAIN, MOUNTAINS (n) a landmass that projects conspicuously above its surroundings and is higher than a hill
Exod 24:18 *on the* **m** *forty days*...................175
Deut 5:4 *At the* **m** *the LORD*........................292
Ps 36:6 *is like the mighty* **m-s,**....................566
Ps 121:1 *I look up to the* **m-s—**...................882
Isa 14:13 *preside on the* **m** *of the gods*.......832
Matt 17:20 *say to this* **m,** *'Move*...............1381
Mark 9:2 *led them up a high* **m**................1379
Mark 9:9 *went back down the* **m,**..............1379
Luke 23:30 *beg the* **m-s,** *'Fall on us,'*.......1482
1 Cor 13:2 *faith that I could move* **m-s,**....1616
2 Pet 1:18 *with him on the holy* **m.**...........1758
Rev 6:16 *they cried to the* **m-s** *and*..........1812

MOUNTAINTOPS (n) the summits of mountains
Isa 42:11 *shout praises from the* **m!**...........927

MOURN (v) to feel or express grief or sorrow
Gen 50:11 *watched them* **m**........................93
Zech 12:10 *have pierced and* **m** *for him*...1178
Matt 5:4 *God blesses those who* **m,**..........1323

MOURNING (n) the act of sorrowing; a period of time during which signs of grief are shown
Ps 30:11 *my clothes of* **m** *and clothed*........563
Isa 60:20 *Your days of* **m** *will come to*.........947
Isa 61:3 *instead of* **m,** *festive praise*...........948
Jer 31:13 *I will turn their* **m** *into joy*..........1033
Zech 8:19 *times of* **m** *you have kept*.........1174

MOUTH, MOUTHS (n) the natural opening through which food passes into the body of an animal; voice, speech
Ps 10:7 *Their* **m-s** *are full of cursing,*.........857
Ps 19:14 *words of my* **m** *and*.....................555
Prov 13:3 *opening your* **m** *can ruin*.............646
Isa 51:16 *have put my words in your* **m**......939
Isa 53:7 *he did not open his* **m.**..................940
Isa 59:3 *and your* **m** *spews corruption.*........945
Jer 31:29 *their children's* **m-s** *pucker*.......1033
Matt 4:4 *word that comes from the* **m**.......1294
Rom 3:14 *Their* **m-s** *are full of cursing*.....1651
Rom 10:9 **m** *that Jesus is Lord*................1663
Rev 2:16 *with the sword of my* **m.**............1804

MOVE, MOVED, MOVES, MOVING (v) to change the place or position of; to go from one place to another in continuous motion; to carry on one's life or activities in a specified environment; to stir the emotions or passions of; to prompt to the doing of something
Exod 35:21 *and whose spirits were* **m-d**.....189
Deut 19:14 *steal anyone's land by* **m-ing**...309
Deut 23:14 *LORD your God* **m-s** *around*........313
Prov 4:15 *Turn away and keep* **m-ing.**........636
Prov 23:10 *cheat your neighbor by* **m-ing**..661
Isa 54:10 *For the mountains may* **m**...........941
Acts 17:28 *For in him we live and* **m**.........1578
1 Cor 13:2 *faith that I could* **m**...............1616
2 Pet 1:21 *were* **m-d** *by the Holy Spirit,*....1758

MUD (n) soft, wet earth
Ps 40:2 *pit of despair, out of the* **m**............570
John 9:6 *spread the* **m** *over the blind*.......1403

MUDDYING (v) to soil or stain with or as if with mud
Prov 25:26 *a fountain or* **m** *a spring*...........840

MULTIPLY, MULTIPLIED (v) to increase greatly in extent or number
Gen 1:22 *Be fruitful and* **m.**............................7
Acts 6:1 *the believers rapidly* **m-ied,**........1522

MULTITUDE (n) a great number
1 Pet 4:8 *love covers a* **m** *of sins*.............1754

MURDER (n) the personal, intentional killing of another person
Matt 5:21 *If you commit* **m,**.......................1328
Rom 1:29 *hate, envy,* **m,** *quarreling,*.........1648

MURDER, MURDERED, MURDERS (v) to kill (a human being) unlawfully and with premeditated malice
Gen 9:5 **m-s** *a fellow human must die*..........21
Exod 20:13 *You must not* **m.**.......................170
Deut 5:17 *You must not* **m.**........................293
Matt 23:31 *who* **m-ed** *the prophets*..........1445
Acts 7:52 *whom you betrayed and* **m-ed.**.1526
Rom 13:9 *You must not* **m.**.......................1669
Jas 2:11 *You must not* **m.**..........................1549

MURDERER, MURDERERS (n) one who commits the crime of murder
Num 35:16 **m** *must be executed.*...............283
Ps 5:6 *LORD detests* **m-s** *and deceivers.*.....547
Ps 26:9 *condemn me along with* **m-s.**.........560
Ps 59:2 *save me from these* **m-s.**..............454
Ezek 18:10 *a robber or* **m** *and refuses*......1064
1 Jn 3:15 *brother or sister is really a* **m**....1791
Rev 21:8 *the corrupt,* **m-s,** *the immoral,*....1830
Rev 22:15 *the sexually immoral, the* **m-s,**...1832

MUSIC (n) vocal, instrumental, or mechanical sounds having rhythm, melody, or harmony
Judg 5:3 *I will make* **m** *to the LORD,*............380
1 Chr 6:31 *lead the* **m** *at the house of*......1233
Neh 12:27 *and with the* **m** *of cymbals,*......1221
Ps 45:8 *the* **m** *of strings entertains*.............851
Amos 5:23 *to the* **m** *of your harps.*.............776
Eph 5:19 *and making* **m** *to the Lord*..........1713

MUSICAL (adj) of or relating to music
1 Chr 23:5 *praise the LORD with the* **m**........533
2 Chr 23:13 *with* **m** *instruments*..................754
Neh 12:36 *the* **m** *instruments*..................1222
Dan 3:5 *and other* **m** *instruments,*............1005
Dan 3:15 *of the* **m** *instruments*.................1006

MUSICIAN, MUSICIANS (n) a composer, conductor, or performer of music; instrumentalist
1 Chr 6:33 *Heman the* **m** *was from*...........1233
1 Chr 9:33 **m-s,** *all prominent Levites,*......1238
1 Chr 15:16 *were singers and* **m-s** *to sing*....491
1 Chr 15:19 *The* **m-s** *Heman, Asaph,*...........491
2 Chr 9:11 *lyres and harps for the* **m-s.**.......626
2 Chr 34:12 *were skilled* **m-s,**......................970
2 Chr 35:15 **m-s,** *descendants of*................974

MUSTARD (n) a plant whose seeds are used as a condiment and for oil; in Jesus' time, the smallest seed known
Matt 13:31 *is like a* **m** *seed planted*..........1348
Matt 17:20 *as small as a* **m** *seed,*.............1381
Mark 4:31 *is like a* **m** *seed planted*...........1348

MUTILATORS (n) those who cripple or maim
Phil 3:2 **m** *who say you must be*...............1721

MUZZLE (v) to fit with a fastening or covering for the mouth of an animal to prevent eating or biting
Deut 25:4 *You must not* **m** *an ox*................315
1 Tim 5:18 *You must not* **m** *an ox*.............1734

MYRRH (n) an aromatic extract from a stiff-branched tree with white flowers and plum-like fruit
Song 1:13 *My lover is like a sachet of* **m**.....664
Matt 2:11 *gold, frankincense, and* **m.**........1285
Mark 15:23 *wine drugged with* **m,**.............1483
John 19:39 *ointment made from* **m** *and*.....1488
Rev 18:13 *incense,* **m,** *frankincense,*.........1826

MYSTERIOUS (adj) exciting wonder, curiosity, or surprise while baffling efforts to comprehend or identify; of, relating to, or constituting mystery
1 Cor 14:2 *Spirit, but it will all be* **m.**.........1616
Eph 1:9 *now revealed to us his* **m** *plan*......1705
Eph 3:3 *revealed his* **m** *plan to me*............1708
Eph 6:19 *explain God's* **m** *plan that the*.....1715
Col 2:2 *they understand God's* **m** *plan,*......1697
Col 4:3 *about his* **m** *plan concerning*..........1702
Rev 10:7 *God's* **m** *plan will be fulfilled*......1816

MYSTERY, MYSTERIES (n) something not understood or beyond understanding; a religious truth that one can know only by revelation and cannot fully understand
see also SECRET(S)
Dan 4:9 *and that no* **m** *is too great*..........1119
Rom 11:25 *to understand this* **m,**.............1666
1 Cor 2:7 *speak of is the* **m** *of God—*.......1598
1 Cor 4:1 *explaining God's* **m-ies.**.............1600

1 Tim 3:9 *to the **m** of the faith*.................1731
1 Tim 3:16 *the great **m** of our faith:*..........1731
Rev 1:20 *the **m** of the seven stars*............1801
Rev 17:7 *tell you the **m** of this woman*......1824

MYTHS (n) popular beliefs or traditions that have grown up around something or someone
1 Tim 1:4 *in endless discussion of **m***........1726
2 Tim 4:4 *and chase after **m.***....................1745
Titus 1:14 *listening to Jewish **m***..............1737

NAILED, NAILING (v) to fasten with or as if with a nail
Matt 27:35 *had **n** him to the cross,*...........1482
Mark 15:24 *soldiers **n** him to the*.............1483
Acts 2:23 *you **n** him to a cross*................1515
Col 2:14 *away by **n-ing** it to the cross.*.....1698
Heb 6:6 *are **n-ing** him to the cross*..........1768

NAKED (adj) not covered by clothing; nude
Gen 2:25 *man and his wife were both **n,***.......11
Job 1:21 *and I will be **n** when I leave.*...........96
Eccl 5:15 *the end of our lives as **n***..............677

NAME, NAMES (n) a word or phrase that constitutes the distinctive designation of a person or thing; reputation
see also REPUTATION
Gen 2:19 *the man chose a **n** for each*...........10
Exod 3:15 *my **n** to remember*.....................144
Exod 28:9 *on them the **n-s** of the tribes*......178
Exod 34:14 *whose very **n** is Jealous,*..........188
Lev 24:11 *blasphemed the **N***.....................232
Deut 18:5 *minister in the LORD's **n***.............308
Deut 28:58 *awesome **n** of the LORD*............319
1 Chr 17:8 *will make your **n** as famous*.......496
2 Chr 7:14 *called by my **n** will humble*........623
Ps 8:1 *your majestic **n** fills the earth!*..........548
Ps 23:3 *paths, bringing honor to his **n.***.......558
Ps 34:3 *let us exalt his **n** together.*..............458
Ps 66:2 *Sing about the glory of his **n!***.........859
Ps 103:1 *I will praise his holy **n.***................580
Ps 138:2 *I praise your **n** for your*................585
Ps 147:4 *stars and calls them all by **n.***......1154
Isa 40:26 *calling each by its **n.***...................924
Isa 42:8 *I am the LORD; that is my **n!***...........927
Jer 15:16 *I bear your **n,** O LORD*................1019
Dan 12:1 *people whose **n** is written in*......1161
Joel 2:32 *calls on the **n** of the LORD*..........1242
Mic 5:4 *majesty of the **n** of the LORD*...........908
Zech 14:9 *one LORD—his **n** alone*............1180
Mal 1:6 *shown contempt for my **n!***...........1245
Matt 24:5 *come in my **n,** claiming, 'I am*...1446
Matt 28:19 *baptizing them in the **n** of*.......1498
Luke 10:20 *your **n-s** are registered*..........1395
Luke 11:2 *may your **n** be kept holy.*...........1342
John 16:24 *Ask, using my **n,** and you*.......1465
Acts 2:21 *calls on the **n** of the LORD*..........1515
Acts 4:12 *no other **n** under heaven*...........1519
Rom 10:13 *calls on the **n** of the LORD*.......1664
Phil 2:9 *gave him the **n** above all*.............1720
Phil 2:10 *that at the **n** of Jesus every*........1720
Phil 4:3 *whose **n-s** are written in the Book of Life*..1724
Heb 12:23 ***n-s** are written in heaven.*........1781
Jas 5:14 *with oil in the **n** of the Lord*.........1553
Rev 2:17 *stone will be engraved a new **n***..1804
Rev 3:5 *erase their **n-s** from the Book*......1806
Rev 3:12 *write on them the **n***....................1807
Rev 20:15 *whose **n** was not found*............1830
Rev 21:27 ***n-s** are written in the Lamb's*...1831

NAME (v) to give a name to; to call
Matt 1:21 *you are to **n** him Jesus,*............1277

NARROW (adj) of slender width
Matt 7:13 *only through the **n** gate*............1334
Matt 7:14 *the gateway to life is very **n***......1334

NATION, NATIONS (n) group of people defined by geography or ethnicity
see also GENTILE(S), PEOPLE(S)
Gen 12:2 *I will make you into a great **n.***........30
Gen 17:4 *father of a multitude of **n-s!***..........38
Gen 17:16 *the mother of many **n-s.***.............39
Gen 25:23 *will become two **n-s.***..................51
Gen 28:3 *and become many **n-s!***................57
Exod 19:6 *of priests, my holy **n.***..................168
Deut 15:6 *You will rule many **n-s,** but*.........305
Deut 28:10 *the **n-s** of the world will see*.....318
Ps 2:8 *you the **n-s** as your inheritance,*........857
Ps 22:28 *He rules all the **n-s.***.....................557
Ps 46:10 *I will be honored by every **n.***........852
Ps 66:7 *every movement of the **n-s;***...........859
Ps 68:30 *Scatter the **n-s** that delight in*.......577
Ps 87:6 *the LORD registers the **n-s,***............855
Ps 99:2 *exalted above all the **n-s.***................865
Ps 113:4 *LORD is high above the **n-s;***.........874
Prov 14:34 *Godliness makes a **n** great,*.......648
Isa 11:10 *The **n-s** will rally to him,*..............796
Isa 34:1 *listen, O **n-s** of the earth.*..............904
Isa 40:15 *for all the **n-s** of the world.*..........924
Isa 42:1 *He will bring justice to the **n-s.***......926
Isa 52:15 *And he will startle many **n-s.***.......940
Isa 56:7 *a house of prayer for all **n-s.***.........943
Isa 60:12 *the **n-s** that refuse to serve.*........947
Isa 66:8 *Has a **n** ever been born in a*..........953
Ezek 37:22 *divided into two **n-s** or into*.....1113
Joel 3:2 *my people among the **n-s,***..........1243
Amos 9:12 ***n-s** I have called to be mine.*......780
Mic 4:3 *disputes between strong **n-s***..........907
Mic 5:7 *take their place among the **n-s.***......909
Zeph 3:8 *stand and accuse these evil **n-s.***....986
Hag 2:7 *I will shake all the **n-s,***................1164
Zech 8:13 *Among the other **n-s,** Judah*.......1174
Zech 12:2 *makes the nearby **n-s** stagger*...1178
Matt 12:18 *proclaim justice to the **n-s.***.....1322
Matt 24:14 *so that all **n-s** will hear it;*.......1446
Matt 28:19 *make disciples of all the **n-s,***..1498
Mark 11:17 *house of prayer for all **n-s,***....1432
Acts 4:25 *Why were the **n-s** so angry?*.....1519
Gal 3:8 *All **n-s** will be blessed through*......1561
1 Pet 2:9 *royal priests, a holy **n,***..............1751
Rev 5:9 *language and people and **n.***..........1810
Rev 14:6 *to every **n,** tribe, language,*..........1821
Rev 21:24 *The **n-s** will walk in its light,*.....1831
Rev 22:2 *for medicine to heal the **n-s.***.......1832

NATIVITY (KJV)
Gen 11:28 *the land of his **birth***....................24
Jer 46:16 *to the land of our **birth.***................998

NATURAL (adj) having a physical existence as contrasted with one that is spiritual
1 Cor 15:44 *as there are **n** bodies,*...........1621

NATURE (n) inherent character or essence
Rom 1:20 *eternal power and divine **n.***.......1647
Rom 8:4 *follow our sinful **n***......................1658
Rom 8:7 *For the sinful **n** is always*............1659
Gal 5:19 *the desires of your sinful **n,***........1566
Gal 5:24 *desires of their sinful **n** to*...........1567
2 Pet 1:4 *share his divine **n** and escape*....1757

NAZARENE, NAZARENES (n) a native or resident of Nazareth; an early name given to followers of Jesus
Matt 2:23 *He will be called a **N.***................1286
Acts 24:5 *of the cult known as the **N-s.***....1682
Acts 26:9 *the very name of Jesus the **N.***....1685

NAZARETH (n) a town of lower Galilee where Jesus spent his boyhood years
Matt 4:13 *He went first to **N,***....................1306
Mark 14:67 *those with Jesus of **N.***...........1474
Mark 16:6 *looking for Jesus of **N,** who*......1490
John 1:46 *anything good come from **N?***...1298

NAZIRITE (n) a person consecrated to God by a vow to avoid drinking wine, cutting the hair, and being defiled by the presence of a corpse
Num 6:2 *take the special vow of a **N,***..........244
Judg 13:7 *be dedicated to God as a **N***........396

NECK (n) the part of the body that connects the head and the torso
Prov 6:21 *Tie them around your **n.***..............638
Matt 18:6 *millstone tied around your **n***......1384

NECKLACE (n) an ornament worn around the neck
Prov 3:22 *They are like jewels on a **n.***.........635

NEED, NEEDS (n) a condition requiring supply or relief; poverty; obligation; a lack of something requisite, desirable, or useful
1 Kgs 8:59 *according to each day's **n-s.***.....622
Ps 79:8 *quickly meet our **n-s,***....................600
Ps 112:9 *give generously to those in **n.***......873
Prov 11:26 *who sells in time of **n.***...............644
Prov 30:8 *just enough to satisfy my **n-s.***.....846
Matt 6:2 *give to someone in **n,***...................1330
Acts 2:45 *the money with those in **n.***........1516
Acts 20:35 *you can help those in **n** by*......1676
Rom 12:13 *God's people are in **n,***............1667
1 Cor 7:3 *fulfill his wife's sexual **n-s,***.........1605
Eph 4:28 *give generously to others in **n.***...1712
Phil 4:19 *supply all your **n-s** from his*.......1725
Titus 3:14 *by meeting the urgent **n-s***.......1740

NEED, NEEDED, NEEDING (v) to require; to be necessary; to be in want
Ps 34:9 *fear him will have all they **n.***..........458
Ps 119:75 *disciplined me because I **n-ed***.....879
Phil 4:6 *Tell God what you **n,** and*.............1724
Heb 4:16 *grace to help us when we **n** it*....1766
Jas 1:4 *complete, **n-ing** nothing.*.............1546
Jas 1:5 *If you **n** wisdom, ask our*.............1546

NEEDLE (n) a small slender instrument that has an eye for thread at one end and is used for sewing
Matt 19:24 *go through the eye of a **n***.......1420

NEEDY (adj) poverty-stricken; marked by want of affection, attention, or emotional support
1 Sam 2:8 ***n** from the garbage dump.*..........419
Ps 9:18 *the **n** will not be ignored*...............550
Ps 68:10 *you provided for your **n***...............576
Ps 69:33 *LORD hears the cries of the **n;***.......578
Prov 22:22 *or exploit the **n** in court.*...........660
Prov 31:20 *opens her arms to the **n.***..........848

NEGLECT (v) to disregard; to overlook; to ignore
Deut 12:19 *careful never to **n** the Levites*....302
Deut 14:27 *And do not **n** the Levites.*..........304
Ezra 4:22 *and don't **n** this matter,*............1195
Neh 10:39 *together not to **n** the Temple*....1218
Luke 11:42 *do not **n** the more important*...1398
1 Tim 4:14 *Do not **n** the spiritual*.............1732

NEHEMIAH Cup-bearer of the Persian king Artaxerxes (Neh 1:11, p. 1204); governor of Israel (Neh 5:14, p. 1210; 8:9, p. 1214); prayed for restoration (Neh 1:4, p. 1203); king commissioned him to rebuild Jerusalem's walls (Neh 2:8, p. 1205); rebuilt walls over opposition (Neh 2:9–6:19, p. 1205); reestablished worship

(Neh 8:1-18, p. 1214); prayer of praise and confession (Neh 9, p. 1215); dedicated wall of Jerusalem (Neh 12:27-43, p. 1221).

NEIGHBOR, NEIGHBORS (n) one living or located near another; fellow man
Lev 19:18 *but love your **n** as yourself*..........225
Ps 15:3 *to gossip or harm their **n-s***..........552
Prov 24:28 *your **n-s** without cause;*..........663
Prov 27:10 *better to go to a **n** than*..........842
Jer 31:34 *not need to teach their **n-s,***......1034
Mark 12:31 *Love your **n** as yourself*..........1441
Luke 10:29 *And who is my **n?***..........1396
Rom 13:8 *If you love your **n,** you will*..........1669
Gal 5:14 *Love your **n** as yourself*..........1566
Eph 4:25 *Let us tell our **n-s** the truth,*.......1712
Heb 8:11 *not need to teach their **n-s,***.......1772
Jas 2:8 *Love your **n** as yourself.* 1549

NET, NETS (n) a meshed fabric made of ropes used for catching fish, birds, insects, or other animals
Ps 66:11 *You captured us in your **n***..........859
Ps 141:10 *wicked fall into their own **n-s,***....588
Hab 1:15 *caught in their **n-s** while they*......979
Matt 4:20 *they left their **n-s** at once and*...1307
Matt 13:47 *is like a fishing **n** that was*......1349
John 21:6 *Throw out your **n** on the*..........1496

NEVER (adv) at no time; not in any degree; not under any condition
1 Chr 29:18 *their love for you **n** changes.*....541
Ps 89:33 *But I will **n** stop loving him*..........592
Ps 111:3 *His righteousness **n** fails.*..........873
John 14:16 *who will **n** leave you*..........1462
Rom 11:29 *his call can **n** be withdrawn.*....1666
Rom 12:11 ***N** be lazy, but work hard*..........1667
1 Cor 15:2 *something that was **n** true*.......1618

NEVER-ENDING (adj) unceasing
1 Chr 16:17 *of Israel as a **n** covenant:*........493
Ps 105:10 *of Israel as a **n** covenant:*..........868
Luke 3:17 *burning the chaff with **n** fire*......1292

NEW (adj) fresh; original; different than before; unfamiliar
Ps 98:1 *Sing a **n** song to the* L*ORD*,..........865
Jer 31:31 *I will make a **n** covenant with*....1034
Ezek 36:26 *I will give you a **n** heart,*..........1112
Mark 16:17 *will speak in **n** languages*.......1498
Luke 22:20 *cup is the **n** covenant*..........1458
Rom 6:4 *we also may live **n** lives.*..........1655
Rom 12:2 *you into a **n** person*..........1666
1 Cor 11:25 *cup is the **n** covenant*..........1613
2 Cor 3:6 *but under the **n** covenant,*..........1629
2 Cor 5:17 *is gone; a **n** life has begun!*.....1632
Gal 6:15 *into a **n** creation*..........1568
Eph 4:24 *Put on your **n** nature,*..........1712
Col 3:10 *Put on your **n** nature,*..........1700
Heb 8:8 *when I will make a **n** covenant*.....1771
Heb 9:15 *mediates a **n** covenant*..........1773
Heb 12:24 *the **n** covenant*..........1781
2 Pet 3:13 ***n** heavens and **n** earth he*........1760
Rev 2:17 *a **n** name that no one*..........1804
Rev 21:1 ***n** heaven and a **n** earth,*..........1830

NEWBORN (adj) recently born
1 Pet 2:2 *Like **n** babies, you must crave*....1750

NEWS (n) a report of recent events; "Good News": the Gospel of Jesus Christ
Isa 40:9 *of good **n,** shout from the*..........924
Matt 4:23 *the Good **N** about*..........1311
Mark 1:15 *sins and believe the Good **N!***....1306
Luke 4:43 *I must preach the Good **N***.........1311
Acts 13:32 *to bring you this Good **N.***........1542
Acts 14:21 *preaching the Good **N***..........1545
Rom 1:16 *not ashamed of this Good **N***......1646
Rom 10:17 *the Good **N** about Christ.*..........1664
Rom 15:16 *I bring you the Good **N***..........1671
Rom 16:25 *just as my Good **N** says.*..........1674
1 Cor 1:17 *to preach the Good **N**—*..........1596
1 Cor 9:12 *an obstacle to the Good **N***.......1608
1 Cor 9:16 *preach the Good **N!***..........1608
1 Cor 9:23 *to spread the Good **N***..........1609
1 Cor 15:1 *the Good **N** I preached*..........1618
2 Cor 4:4 *glorious light of the Good **N.***......1630
2 Cor 9:13 *obedient to the Good **N***..........1638
2 Cor 11:7 *preaching God's Good **N***..........1640
Gal 1:7 *is not the Good **N** at all.*..........1556
Eph 6:15 *comes from the Good **N***..........1715
Phil 1:27 *worthy of the Good **N***..........1719
Col 1:5 *heard the truth of the Good **N.***......1693
Col 1:23 *Good **N** has been preached*..........1696
1 Thes 2:4 *entrusted with the Good **N.***......1581
2 Thes 1:8 *obey the Good **N** of our Lord*....1588
2 Tim 1:10 *through the Good **N.***..........1741
2 Tim 4:5 *telling others the Good **N,***..........1745
Rev 14:6 *the eternal Good **N***..........1821

NIGHT, NIGHTS (n) period of darkness between sunset and sunrise; figurative of suffering and sorrow or the reign of sin and immorality
Gen 1:16 *smaller one to govern the **n.***..........7
Exod 13:21 *provided light at **n***..........159
Job 35:10 *who gives songs in the **n?***..........125
Ps 1:2 *meditating on it day and **n.***..........856
Ps 19:2 ***n** after **n** they make him*..........554
Ps 77:6 *my **n-s** were filled with joyful*..........597
Jonah 1:17 *for three days and three **n-s.***....767
Matt 4:2 *days and forty **n-s** he fasted*.......1294
Matt 12:40 *for three days and three **n-s.***..1343
Luke 2:8 *That **n** there were shepherds*......1281
2 Cor 6:5 *endured sleepless **n-s,** and*.......1633
1 Thes 5:2 *like a thief in the **n.***..........1585
1 Thes 5:5 *belong to darkness and **n.***.......1585
Rev 21:25 *there is no **n** there.*..........1831

NINETY-NINE (n) the number 99
Matt 18:13 *than over the **n** that didn't*.......1385
Luke 15:7 *to God than over **n** others*..........1410

NOAH Builder of great boat, survivor of the Flood (Gen 6–9, p. 17; Matt 24:37-38, p. 1447; Luke 17:26-27, p. 1416; Heb 11:7, p. 1777; 1 Pet 3:20, p. 1754; 2 Pet 2:5, p. 1759); family line (Gen 5:25-32, p. 16); found favor with God (Gen 6:8, p. 17); enacted covenant between God and all creatures (Gen 9:1-17, p. 20); made wine and became drunk (Gen 9:18-23, p. 21); gave blessings and curse to descendants (Gen 9:24-27, p. 21); considered righteous (Ezek 14:14, 20, p. 1060).

NONSENSE (n) words or language having no meaning or intelligible ideas; things of no importance or value
Luke 24:11 *sounded like **n** to the men,*......1492
1 Cor 1:23 *the Gentiles say it's all **n.***........1597
Col 2:8 *high-sounding **n** that come*..........1698

NOOSE (n) a loop with a slipknot that binds closer the more it is drawn
Job 41:1 *or put a **n** around its jaw?*..........131

NORMAL (adj) occurring naturally
Rom 1:27 ***n** sexual relations with women,*.1648

NOSTRILS (n) the external openings of the nose
Gen 2:7 *breath of life into the man's **n,***..........9

NOTES (n) melody, song; tones
1 Cor 14:7 *harp must play the **n** clearly,*....1617

NOTHING (pron) not any thing
Neh 9:21 *wilderness, and they lacked **n.***....1216
Eccl 5:5 *better to say **n** than to make*..........677
Jas 1:4 *and complete, needing **n.***..........1546

NOTICE (n) a warning or intimation of something; announcement
Matt 5:31 *a written **n** of divorce*..........1329

NOTICED (v) to treat with attention
Job 1:8 *Satan, "Have you **n** my servant*.........95
Job 2:3 *Satan, "Have you **n** my servant*.........96

NOTORIOUS (adj) generally known and talked of; infamous
Hab 1:7 *They are **n** for their cruelty*..........979

NOURISHMENT (n) food, nutriment; sustenance
John 4:34 *my **n** comes from doing the*......1305
Rom 11:17 *in the rich **n** from the root*.......1665

NUMBERED (v) to restrict to a definite number
Ps 39:4 *Remind me that my days are **n**—*..569
Matt 10:30 *hairs on your head are all **n.***...1360

NUMEROUS (adj) consisting of great numbers; many
Ps 40:5 *plans for us are too **n** to list.*..........570

OATH (n) an appeal to God to witness the truth of some statement
Ps 95:11 *in my anger I took an **o:***..........864
Ps 110:4 L*ORD has taken an **o***..........582
Ezek 20:42 *I promised with a solemn **o***.....1067
Heb 6:16 *people take an **o,** they call*.........1769
Heb 7:20 *established with a solemn **o.***......1770
Heb 7:21 *was an **o** regarding Jesus.*..........1771
Jas 5:12 *never take an **o,** by heaven*........1553

OBEDIENCE (n) an act or instance of obeying; the quality or state of being obedient
Judg 2:17 *who had walked in **o** to the*........375
1 Sam 15:22 ***O** is better than sacrifice,*.......446
Phil 2:8 *humbled himself in **o** to God*........1720
Heb 5:8 *learned **o** from the things he*........1767

OBEDIENT (adj) submissive to authority; willing to obey
Luke 2:51 *with them and was **o** to them.*..1287
Rom 16:19 *that you are **o** to the Lord.*......1673
2 Cor 9:13 *that you are **o** to the Good*.......1638
2 Cor 10:6 *you have become fully **o,***.........1638
1 Pet 1:14 *as God's **o** children.*..........1749

OBEY, OBEYED, OBEYING, OBEYS (v) to follow the commands or guidance of; to conform to or comply with
see also KEEP
Gen 22:18 *because you have **o-ed** me.*........46
Exod 20:6 *love me and **o** my commands.*....169
Lev 18:4 *be careful to **o** my decrees,*..........224
Lev 25:18 *decrees and **o** my regulations.*....233
Deut 4:2 *Just **o** the commands of the*.........289
Deut 5:27 *we will listen and **o.***..........294
Deut 6:17 *diligently **o** the commands of*......295
Deut 6:25 *when we **o** all the commands*.....295
Deut 11:1 *and **o** all his requirements,*.........300
Deut 11:22 *Be careful to **o** all these.*..........301
Deut 13:4 ***O** his commands, listen to his*.....303
Deut 26:16 *to **o** them wholeheartedly.*.........316
Deut 28:1 *If you fully **o** the* L*ORD*..........317
Deut 30:2 *if you **o** with all your heart*..........321
Deut 30:12 *so we can hear it and **o?***..........321
Deut 30:20 *love and **o** the* L*ORD*,..........321
Josh 1:7 *to **o** all the instructions Moses*......336
Josh 22:5 *all his ways, **o** his commands,*....366
1 Sam 7:3 *to **o** only the* L*ORD*;..........427

1 Kgs 8:61 *May you always **o** his decrees*...622
2 Kgs 17:13 ***O** my commands and*.............820
2 Kgs 18:6 ***o-ed** all the commands*...........800
2 Kgs 23:3 *pledged to **o** the LORD*..............971
Neh 1:5 *love him and **o** his commands,*....1203
Job 36:11 *they listen and **o** God,*................125
Ps 111:10 *All who **o** his commandments*....873
Ps 119:17 *I may live and **o** your word.*........878
Ps 119:129 *No wonder I **o** them!*...............881
Eccl 8:2 ***O** the king since you vowed*...........679
Eccl 12:13 *and **o** his commands,*................683
Isa 11:3 *delight in **o-ing** the LORD*..............796
Jer 32:33 *not receive instruction or **o**.* 1080
Jer 42:6 *For if we **o** him, everything*..........1106
Jer 43:4 *refused to **o** the LORD's*..............1107
Dan 9:4 *love you and **o** your commands*....1142
Dan 9:10 *We have not **o-ed** the LORD*.......1142
Jonah 3:3 *This time Jonah **o-ed** the LORD's*..768
Mic 5:15 *nations that refuse to **o** me.* 909
Matt 5:19 *anyone who **o-s** God's laws*......1327
Matt 8:27 *the winds and waves **o** him!* 1350
Matt 19:20 ***o-ed** all these commandments,*...1420
Matt 28:20 *to **o** all the commands*............1498
Luke 8:21 *hear God's word and **o** it.* 1344
John 3:36 *who doesn't **o** the Son*............1303
John 8:51 *anyone who **o-s** my teaching*...1393
John 14:15 ***o** my commandments.* 1462
Acts 4:19 *to **o** you rather than him?*..........1519
Acts 5:29 *We must **o** God rather than*.......1521
Rom 1:5 *believe and **o** him,*......................1645
Rom 2:27 *possess God's law but don't **o***..1650
Rom 3:28 *and not by **o-ing** the law.* 1652
Rom 6:16 *of whatever you choose to **o**?*...1656
Rom 6:17 *wholeheartedly **o** this* 1656
Rom 15:31 *in Judea who refuse to **o** God.* 1672
2 Cor 10:5 *teach them to **o** Christ*.............1638
Gal 2:16 *Christ, not by **o-ing** the law.*........1559
Gal 3:2 *by **o-ing** the law of Moses?*..........1560
Gal 3:10 *and **o** all the commands*.............1561
Eph 2:2 *who refuse to **o** God.* 1706
Eph 6:1 *Children, **o** your parents*...............1714
Eph 6:5 *Slaves, **o** your earthly masters*......1715
2 Thes 3:14 *who refuse to **o** what we*.......1590
1 Tim 3:4 *who respect and **o** him.* 1730
Titus 2:9 *Slaves must always **o** their*.........1738
Heb 11:8 *that Abraham **o-ed** when God*...1777
Heb 11:31 *who refused to **o** God.*.............1779
Jas 2:8 *good when you **o** the royal law*.....1549
1 Pet 1:2 *you have **o-ed** him and have*.....1747
1 Pet 1:22 *when you **o-ed** the truth,*..........1750
1 Pet 2:8 *they do not **o** God's word,*..........1750
1 Jn 3:22 *because we **o** him and do*.........1792
Rev 22:7 *Blessed are those who **o** the*......1832

OBLIGATION (n) something one is bound to do; duty, responsibility
Rom 1:14 *a great sense of **o** to people*.....1646
Rom 8:12 *no **o** to do what your sinful*........1659
Rom 13:8 *except for your **o** to love one*.....1669

OBSERVE, OBSERVES (v) to notice or consider; to keep or comply with; to watch carefully
Exod 12:24 *descendants must **o** forever*......156
Lev 25:2 *the land itself must **o** a Sabbath*...232
Deut 5:12 ***O** the Sabbath day by keeping*....293
Deut 16:13 ***o** the Festival of Shelters*..........306
Ps 33:14 *From his throne he **o-s** all who*....858
Acts 21:24 ***o** the Jewish laws*..................1677
Gal 3:10 *everyone who does not **o***............1561

OBSOLETE (adj) no longer in use or no longer useful
Heb 8:13 *he has made the first one **o**.*......1772

OBSTINATE (adj) unreasonably persistent; stubborn
Isa 48:4 *how stubborn and **o** you are*..........934
Ezek 3:8 *as **o** and hard-hearted as*...........1046

OCCUPY (v) to take or hold possession or control of; to reside in as an owner or tenant
Deut 1:8 *Go in and **o** it, for it is*..................285
Deut 4:14 *are about to enter and **o**.*............290

OFFEND, OFFENDED, OFFENDS (v) to violate, wrong, insult, or hurt; to cause difficulty, discomfort, or injury
Ps 139:24 *anything in me that **o-s** you,*......586
1 Cor 1:23 *the Jews are **o-ed** and the*......1597
Gal 5:11 *Christ, no one would be **o-ed**.* 1565
Col 3:13 *forgive anyone who **o-s** you*........1701

OFFENSE, OFFENSES (n) a cause or occasion of sin; the act of displeasing
Isa 44:22 *I have scattered your **o-s***.............930
Matt 18:15 *and point out the **o**.*................1385
1 Cor 10:32 *Don't give **o** to Jews or*.........1611

OFFER, OFFERED, OFFERING (v) to present for acceptance as an act of worship or devotion; to sacrifice
Ps 4:5 ***O** sacrifices in the right spirit,*...........547
Ps 116:12 *What can I **o** the LORD*...............875
Mic 6:7 *Should we **o** him thousands of*.......910
1 Cor 10:20 *sacrifices are **o-ed** to demons,*...1611
Eph 5:2 *He loved us and **o-ed** himself*......1712
Heb 7:27 *when he **o-ed** himself*.............1771
Heb 9:14 *Christ **o-ed** himself to God*........1773
Heb 9:25 *to **o** himself again and again,*.....1774
Heb 10:11 ***o-ing** the same sacrifices again*..1775
Heb 11:17 *that Abraham **o-ed** Isaac*.......1778
Heb 13:15 *let us **o** through Jesus*............1782
Jas 5:15 *a prayer **o-ed** in faith will heal*...1553

OFFERING, OFFERINGS (n) a sacrifice ceremonially offered as a part of worship; a contribution to the support of a church
Gen 22:8 *a sheep for the burnt **o**,*.................45
1 Sam 13:9 *Bring me the burnt **o***..............441
1 Sam 15:22 *burnt **o-s** and sacrifices*........446
Ps 40:6 *no delight in sacrifices or **o-s**.*........570
Ps 141:2 *hands as an evening **o**.* 588
Isa 53:10 *his life is made an **o** for sin,*........940
Hos 6:6 *more than I want burnt **o-s**.*...........809
Mal 3:8 *of the tithes and **o-s***...................1248
Mark 12:33 *all of the burnt **o-s***..............1442
Rom 15:26 *taken up an **o** for the poor*......1672
Phil 2:17 *faithful service is an **o***...............1720
Heb 10:5 *animal sacrifices or sin **o-s**.* 1774
Heb 10:14 *that one **o** he forever made*......1775
Heb 11:4 *Abel's **o** gave evidence that he*...1777

OFFICER (n) one who holds a position of authority or command in the armed forces
Matt 8:5 *a Roman **o** came and pleaded*....1335
Luke 7:2 *slave of a Roman **o** was sick*......1336
Acts 10:1 *army **o** named Cornelius,*..........1532
Acts 27:1 *a Roman **o** named Julius,* 1686

OFFSPRING (n) children or descendants
see also DESCENDANT(S)
Gen 3:15 *between your **o** and her **o**.*............13
Acts 17:28 *said, 'We are his **o**.'*................1578

OIL (n) liquid produced from olives used in biblical times for lamp fuel, anointing, and dressing wounds; often symbolic of the Holy Spirit
Exod 29:7 *anointing **o** over his head.*...........180
Exod 30:25 *to make a holy anointing **o**.* 182
1 Sam 10:1 ***o** and poured it over Saul's*......436
1 Sam 16:13 ***o** he had brought and*............448
Ps 23:5 *anointing my head with **o**.*.............558
Ps 133:2 *as precious as the anointing **o***.....584
Heb 1:9 *pouring out the **o** of joy*..............1762

OINTMENT, OINTMENTS (n) a salve for application to the skin
Isa 1:6 *any soothing **o-s** or bandages.*........823
Rev 3:18 *and **o** for your eyes so you*.........1807

OLD, OLDER (adj) dating from the remote past; advanced in years or age
1 Kgs 12:8 *rejected the advice of the **o-er***....696
2 Cor 3:11 *So if the **o** way, which*.............1630
1 Tim 5:2 *Treat **o-er** women as you would*..1733
Titus 2:2 *Teach the **o-er** men to exercise*..1738

OLIVE, OLIVES (n) a Mediterranean evergreen tree with berries that ripen black; the berries of an olive tree
Gen 8:11 *evening with a fresh **o** leaf*............20
Jer 11:16 *a thriving **o** tree, beautiful*.........1014
Zech 4:3 *And I see two **o** trees,*................1169
Zech 14:4 *the Mount of **O-s** will split*........1180
Matt 24:3 *Jesus sat on the Mount of **O-s**.*...1446
Rom 11:17 *of God's special **o** tree.*...........1665
Rom 11:24 *cut from a wild **o** tree.* 1665
Jas 3:12 *Does a fig tree produce **o-s**, or*...1550
Rev 11:4 *prophets are the two **o** trees*.......1816

OMEGA (n) the last letter of the Greek alphabet
Rev 1:8 *I am the Alpha and the **O**—*.........1800
Rev 21:6 *I am the Alpha and the **O**—*.......1830
Rev 22:13 *I am the Alpha and the **O**,*.........1832

ONE (adj) being a single unit or thing; being in agreement or union
2 Chr 30:12 *giving them all **o** heart*............837
Phil 2:2 *working together with **o** mind*.......1719

ONE (n) a single person or thing
Gen 2:24 *the two are united into **o**.*...............11
Jas 2:10 *all of the laws except **o***.............1549

ONIONS (n) a plant with a large pungent, edible bulb
Num 11:5 *melons, leeks, **o**, and garlic*........248

OPEN-MINDED (adj) receptive to arguments or ideas
Acts 17:11 *people of Berea were more **o***..1577

OPENED (v) to spread out; to unfold
Isa 65:2 *All day long I **o** my arms*................951
Rom 10:21 *All day long I **o** my arms*.........1664

OPINIONS (n) a view, judgment, or appraisal formed in the mind about a particular matter
1 Kgs 18:21 *hobbling between two **o**?*........717

OPPONENTS (n) those who take an opposite position; adversaries
Prov 18:18 *disputes between powerful **o**.*....654

OPPORTUNITY (n) a favorable circumstance or advantage
2 Cor 11:12 *looking for an **o** to boast*........1640
Gal 6:10 *have the **o**, we should do good*...1567
Col 4:5 *make the most of every **o**.* 1702

OPPOSE, OPPOSED, OPPOSES (v) to set oneself against or opposite someone or something; to resist
Exod 23:22 ***o** those who **o** you.* 174
Ps 8:2 *enemies and all who **o** you*..............548

Ps 35:1 *o those who **o** me.*...............565
Acts 26:11 *was so violently **o-d** to them*...1685
Gal 2:11 *I had to **o** him to his face,*...........1559
1 Tim 6:20 *with those who **o***...................1735
2 Tim 2:25 *instruct those who **o***..............1743
Titus 1:9 *show those who **o** it*.................1737
Titus 2:8 *who **o** us will be ashamed*..........1738
Jas 4:6 *God **o-s** the proud but favors*.......1551
1 Pet 5:5 *God **o-s** the proud but favors*.....1756

OPPRESS, OPPRESSES, OPPRESSING (v) to crush or burden by abuse of power or authority
Exod 22:21 *not mistreat or **o** foreigners*......172
Prov 22:16 *gets ahead by **o-ing** the poor*...660
Prov 28:16 *no understanding will **o***............844
Isa 3:5 *People will **o** each other—*..............827
Isa 58:3 *you keep **o-ing** your workers*.........944
Ezek 18:12 ***o-es** the poor and helpless,*....1064
Dan 7:25 *defy the Most High and **o** the*.....1136
Amos 5:12 ***o** good people by taking*............775
Zech 7:10 *Do not **o** widows, orphans,*.......1173
Jas 2:6 *the rich who **o** you and drag*.........1548

OPPRESSED (n) those subject to the abuse of another's power or authority
Ps 9:9 *a shelter for the **o**, a refuge*............549
Ps 14:6 *frustrate the plans of the **o**,*............552
Ps 82:3 *uphold the rights of the **o***..............602
Ps 146:7 *He gives justice to the **o***.............887
Prov 31:5 *not give justice to the **o**.*..............847
Isa 1:17 *Seek justice. Help the **o**.*...............824
Amos 2:7 *shove the **o** out of the way.* 772
Luke 4:18 *that the **o** will be set free,*.........1357

OPPRESSION (n) unjust or cruel exercise of power or authority
Judg 2:18 *burdened by **o** and suffering*.......375
Ps 72:14 *redeem them from **o** and*............630
Ps 119:134 *Ransom me from the **o** of*........881
Isa 58:9 *Remove the heavy yoke of **o**.*.........945
Heb 11:25 *chose to share the **o** of God's*..1778

OPPRESSORS (n) those who abuse power or authority to crush or burden others
Ps 72:4 *and to crush their **o**.*......................630
Eccl 4:1 *The **o** have great power,*...............676
Jer 22:3 *rescue them from their **o**.*..............991

ORDAINED (v) to appoint someone to a specific duty or office
see also CONSECRATE(D), DEDICATE(D)
Ezek 28:14 *I **o** and anointed you*..............1084

ORDER, ORDERS (n) a rank, class, or special group in a community or society; a command
Ps 110:4 *in the **o** of Melchizedek*...............582
Joel 2:11 *they follow his **o-s**.*...................1241
Mark 1:27 *spirits obey his **o-s!***................1309
Heb 5:10 *in the **o** of Melchizedek*...............1767

ORDER (v) to command
Ps 91:11 *For he will **o** his angels*...............861
Matt 4:6 *He will **o** his angels*...................1295

ORPHAN, ORPHANS (n) a child deprived by death of one or usually both parents
see also FATHERLESS
Exod 22:22 *not exploit a widow or an **o**.*.......172
Deut 10:18 ***o-s** and widows receive*...........300
Deut 24:17 *among you and to **o-s**,*............314
Deut 24:19 ***o-s**, and widows.*......................314
Ps 10:14 *in you. You defend the **o-s**.*..........857
Ps 82:3 *justice to the poor and the **o**;*.........602
Prov 23:10 *the land of defenseless **o-s**.*......661
John 14:18 *will not abandon you as **o-s**—*...1462
Jas 1:27 *caring for **o-s** and widows in*......1548

OUTSIDE (prep) located on the outer side of
1 Tim 3:7 *Also, people **o** the church*..........1730

OUTSMART (v) to get the better of; to outwit
2 Cor 2:11 *Satan will not **o** us.*.................1628

OUTWARD, OUTWARDLY (adj or adv) superficial, having to do with external appearance or circumstance only
1 Sam 16:7 *People judge by **o** appearance,*..448
Matt 23:28 ***o-ly** you look like righteous*.....1445
1 Pet 3:3 *concerned about the **o** beauty*....1752

OUTWEIGHS (v) to exceed in weight, value, or importance
2 Cor 4:17 *glory that vastly **o** them and*....1631

OVERCOME (v) to get the better of; to overwhelm
see also CONQUER, VICTORIOUS, VICTORY
Ps 119:133 *will not be **o** by evil*..................881
Mark 9:24 *but help me **o** my unbelief!*......1381
John 16:33 *because I have **o** the world*.....1466
2 Cor 2:7 *may be **o** by discouragement*.....1628

OVERFLOW, OVERFLOWED, OVERFLOWS (v) to fill a space to capacity and spread beyond its limits; to flow over bounds
Ps 23:5 *My cup **o-s** with blessings.*............558
Ps 65:11 *even the hard pathways **o** with*.....575
Prov 3:10 *vats will **o** with good wine.*..........635
John 15:11 *Yes, your joy will **o!***...............1464
Rom 15:13 *you will **o** with confident*.........1671
2 Cor 8:2 *joy, which has **o-ed** in rich*........1636
Phil 1:9 *I pray that your love will **o***............1717
Col 2:7 *you will **o** with thankfulness.*.........1697

OVERJOYED (adj) feeling great joy
Dan 6:23 *The king was **o** and ordered*......1141
Acts 12:14 *she was so **o** that,*.................1538

OVERLOOKING (v) to look past; to ignore or excuse
Prov 19:11 *they earn respect by **o** wrongs.*...654
Mic 7:18 ***o** the sins of his special people?*...911

OVERSEER(S) (KJV)
2 Chr 2:18 *and 3,600 as **foremen***............611
Neh 11:22 ***chief officer** of the Levites*......1220
Prov 6:7 *or **governor** or ruler to make*........638
Acts 20:28 *appointed you as **elders***.........1675
1 Tim 3:1 *an **elder** must be a man whose*...1730
1 Pet 2:25 *Shepherd, the **Guardian** of*......1752

OVERSHADOW (v) to cast a shadow over
Luke 1:35 *power of the Most High will **o***...1274

OVERWHELMED, OVERWHELMING, OVERWHELMS (v) to overpower in thought or feeling; to submerge; to overthrow
2 Sam 22:5 *waves of death **o-ed** me;*........526
Job 19:27 *I am **o-ed** at the thought!*..........112
Ps 38:4 *My guilt **o-s** me—it is*..................568
Ps 65:3 *we are **o-ed** by our sins,*...............575
Ps 90:7 *we are **o-ed** by your fury.*.............326
Isa 61:10 *I am **o-ed** with joy in*..................948
Mark 9:15 *they were **o-ed** with awe,*........1381
2 Cor 1:8 *We were crushed and **o-ed***.......1626
2 Cor 3:10 *with the **o-ing** glory*................1630

OWE (v) to be under obligation to pay or repay in return for something received
Rom 13:7 *Give to everyone what you **o***.....1668
Phlm 1:19 *that you **o** me your very soul!*...1692

OWN (adj) belonging to oneself or itself
Luke 18:9 *in their **o** righteousness*...........1418
1 Cor 13:5 *does not demand its **o** way.*.....1616
Titus 2:14 *to make us his very **o** people,*....1738

OWN (v) to have or hold as property
Gen 28:4 *May you **o** this land*.........................57

OX, OXEN (n) a domestic bovine mammal
Deut 25:4 *not muzzle an **o** to keep it*...........315
1 Kgs 7:25 *base of twelve bronze **o-en**,*.....613
1 Kgs 19:20 *Elisha left the **o-en***................720
Isa 1:3 ***o** knows its owner, and a*................823
Ezek 1:10 *the face of an **o** on the left*........1045
1 Cor 9:9 *not muzzle an **o** to keep it*.........1608
1 Tim 5:18 *not muzzle an **o** to keep it*.......1734
Rev 4:7 *the second was like an **o**;*............1808

PACT (n) an agreement or covenant between two or more parties
1 Sam 23:18 *renewed their solemn **p** before*...463

PAGAN (adj) of or relating to a pagan
1 Sam 17:26 *Who is this **p** Philistine*..........450

PAGAN, PAGANS (n) a follower of a false god or religion; one who delights in sensual pleasures and material goods
Ps 106:35 *they mingled among the **p-s***......871
Isa 2:6 *have made alliances with **p-s**.*.........825
Matt 5:47 *Even **p-s** do that.*.....................1330
Matt 18:17 *treat that person as a **p***..........1385
1 Cor 5:1 *something that even **p-s** don't*...1602
1 Cor 12:2 *when you were still **p-s**, you*....1614

PAID (v) to render payment or due return
see also PAY
1 Cor 7:23 *God **p** a high price for you,*......1606
Col 3:25 *be **p** back for the wrong*.............1702
1 Tim 5:17 *should be respected and **p***......1734

PAIN, PAINS (n) physical, mental, or emotional suffering; the spasms of childbirth
Job 6:10 *Despite the **p**, I have not*.............101
Ps 73:14 *every morning brings me **p**.*.........594
Jer 4:19 *my heart—I writhe in **p!***...............965
Matt 24:8 *only the first of the birth **p-s**,*....1446
John 16:21 *suffering the **p-s** of labor*........1465
Rom 8:22 *in the **p-s** of childbirth*..............1659
Gal 4:19 *going through labor **p-s** for*........1563
1 Thes 5:3 *woman's labor **p-s** begin*.........1585
Heb 13:3 *as if you felt their **p** in your*........1782
Rev 21:4 *death or sorrow or crying or **p**.*...1830

PAINFUL (adj) feeling or giving pain
Gen 5:29 *the **p** labor of farming*......................17
Prov 17:21 ***p** to be the parent of a fool;*.......653
2 Cor 2:1 *grief with another **p** visit*...........1627
Heb 12:11 *while it is happening—it's **p!***...1780

PALACE, PALACES (n) the official residence of a chief of state (as a monarch or president)
2 Sam 7:2 *living in a beautiful cedar **p**,*.......495
Jer 22:6 *concerning Judah's royal **p**:*..........991
Matt 11:8 *expensive clothes live in **p-s**.*....1337
Luke 7:25 *live in luxury are found in **p-s**.*..1338

PALM, PALMS (n) a long feathery leaf from any of various mostly tropical or subtropical trees; the part of the human hand between the base of the fingers and wrist
Isa 49:16 *on the **p-s** of my hands*..............936
John 12:13 *took **p** branches and went*......1431
Rev 7:9 *and held **p** branches*....................1813

PAMPERED (v) to treat with extreme or excessive care and attention
Prov 29:21 *A servant **p** from childhood*.......845

PANIC (n) a sudden unreasoning terror often accompanied by mass flight
1 Sam 14:15 *Suddenly, **p** broke out*............443
Zech 14:13 *by the LORD with great **p.***.......1180

PANIC (v) to be affected with panic
Deut 20:3 *Do not lose heart or **p***................310
Mark 13:7 *threats of wars, but don't **p.***.....1448

PAPERS (n) pieces of paper containing writing or print; documents
Jer 32:16 *had given the **p** to Baruch,*........1079
2 Tim 4:13 *books, and especially my **p.*** 1746

PARABLE, PARABLES (n) a brief narrative story told with earthly analogies to illustrate a spiritual truth
Ps 78:2 *I will speak to you in a **p.*** 598
Matt 13:35 *I will speak to you in **p-s.***........1348
Luke 8:10 *I use **p-s** to teach the* 1347

PARADE (n) a public procession
1 Cor 4:9 *at the end of a victor's **p,***...........1601

PARADISE (n) an intermediate place where the souls of the righteous await resurrection and the final judgment
Luke 23:43 *you will be with me in **p.*** 1484
2 Cor 12:4 *that I was caught up to **p***.........1641

PARALYZED (adj) characterized by the inability to move
Matt 9:2 *Jesus said to the **p** man,* 1312
Mark 2:3 *men arrived carrying a **p** man* 1313
John 5:3 *blind, lame, or **p**—* 1317

PARDON, PARDONED (v) to allow (an offense) to pass without punishment; to forgive
Num 14:19 ***p** the sins of this people,* 253
Deut 29:20 *LORD will never **p** such*.............320
2 Kgs 5:18 *may the LORD **p** me*..................744
2 Chr 30:18 *LORD, who is good, **p***...............837
Isa 40:2 *gone and her sins are **p-ed.***..........923
Jer 5:7 *How can I **p** you?*..........................966
Joel 3:21 *I will **p** my people's crimes,*........1244
Joel 3:21 *which I have not yet **p-ed;***.........1244

PARENT, PARENTS (n) one who produces and cares for offspring
see also FATHER, MOTHER
Exod 20:5 *I lay the sins of the **p-s** upon*......168
Prov 13:1 *child accepts a **p's** discipline;* 646
Jer 31:29 ***p-s** have eaten sour grapes,*.....1033
Ezek 18:19 *child pay for the **p's** sins?*.......1064
Matt 10:21 *will rebel against their **p-s***......1360
Rom 1:30 *and they disobey their **p-s.***........1648
Eph 6:1 *Children, obey your **p-s***..............1714
Col 3:20 *always obey your **p-s,***................1702

PART, PARTS (n) portion or segment; role
see also MEMBER(S)
Rom 12:5 *We are many **p-s** of one body,* ..1667
1 Cor 6:15 *are actually **p-s** of Christ?*.......1604
1 Cor 12:18 *each **p** just where he wants*...1615
1 Cor 12:28 ***p-s** God has appointed for* 1615
Gal 5:25 *leading in every **p** of our*.............1567
Eph 4:25 *we are all **p-s** of the same body.* 1712

PARTIAL (adj) inclined to favor one party more than the other; of or relating to a part rather than the whole
Lev 19:15 *or being **p** to the rich* 225
1 Cor 13:10 ***p** things will become*............1616

PARTIALITY (n) the quality or state of being partial
see also FAVORITES, FAVORITISM
Deut 10:17 *God, who shows no **p** and* 300
Deut 16:19 *twist justice or show **p.***............306
2 Chr 19:7 *perverted justice, **p,***...................730

PARTICIPATE (v) to have a part or share in something; to take part
1 Cor 10:20 *to **p** with demons.*................1611
Eph 5:7 ***p** in the things these people*.........1712

PARTNER, PARTNERS (n) a person with whom one shares an intimate relationship; one associated with another, especially in action
Mal 2:14 *she remained your faithful **p,***......1247
2 Cor 6:14 *can righteousness be a **p***........1634
Phil 1:5 ***p-s** in spreading the Good*...........1717
1 Pet 3:7 *but she is your equal **p** in*..........1753
1 Pet 4:13 *trials make you **p-s** with*..........1755
3 Jn 1:8 *be their **p-s** as they teach*...........1797
Rev 1:9 *your **p** in suffering and in God's Kingdom*....................................1800

PARTNERSHIP (n) the state of being a partner
1 Cor 1:9 *into **p** with his Son,* 1596

PARTY, PARTIES (n) a social gathering
Luke 15:24 *So the **p** began.*.....................1411
Rom 13:13 *of wild **p-ies** and drunkenness,* 1669
1 Pet 4:3 *drunkenness and wild **p-ies,*** 1754

PASS, PASSED (v) to move, proceed, go; to go away; to move past
Exod 12:13 *the blood, I will **p** over you.* 156
Exod 33:22 *my hand until I have **p-ed***........186
1 Kgs 19:11 *there, the LORD **p-ed*** 720
1 Cor 7:31 *it will soon **p** away.*..................1606
2 Pet 3:10 *the heavens will **p** away* 1760

PASSION, PASSIONS (n) intense, driving, or overmastering feeling or conviction; ardent affection; sexual desire
Isa 59:17 *himself in a cloak of divine **p.*** 946
Zech 8:2 *with **p** for Jerusalem!*................1173
1 Cor 7:37 *he can control his **p,** he does*...1607
Gal 5:24 *Jesus have nailed the **p-s*** 1567
1 Thes 4:5 *lustful **p** like the pagans* 1584

PASSIONATE (adj) capable of, affected by, or expressing intense feeling
2 Kgs 19:31 ***p** commitment of the LORD*......918
Isa 9:7 ***p** commitment of the LORD* 793
Isa 37:32 ***p** commitment of the LORD* 919
Zech 1:14 *Mount Zion is **p** and strong.*......1166
Zech 8:2 *Mount Zion is **p** and strong;* 1173

PASSOVER (n) a festival that commemorated the Hebrew departure from Egypt in haste
Num 9:2 *celebrate the **P***...........................200
Deut 16:1 *celebrate the **P** each year*...........305
Ezra 6:19 *returned exiles celebrated **P.***......1181
Mark 14:12 ***P** lamb is sacrificed,* 1455
Heb 11:28 *to keep the **P** and to sprinkle* ...1779

PASTORS (n) spiritual overseers
Eph 4:11 *and the **p** and teachers.*.............1710

PASTURE, PASTURES (n) land or a plot of land used for grazing
Ps 100:3 *his people, the sheep of his **p.*** 865
John 10:9 *freely and will find good **p-s.***.....1405

PATH, PATHS (n) course, route; a way of life, conduct, or thought
1 Kgs 8:36 *follow the right **p,*** 620
Ps 23:3 *He guides me along right **p-s,*** 558
Ps 27:11 *Lead me along the right **p,***...........561
Prov 2:13 *to walk down dark **p-s.***...............634
Prov 3:6 *show you which **p** to take.*............634
Prov 5:21 *examining every **p** he takes.*........637
Prov 8:20 *in **p-s** of justice.*.........................640
Prov 14:12 *a **p** before each person that*......647
Isa 48:17 *leads you along the **p-s*** 935
Hos 14:9 ***p-s** of the LORD are true.*..............817
2 Tim 2:18 *have left the **p** of truth,*............1743
Heb 12:13 *Mark out a straight **p***...............1781

PATHWAY (n) path, course
Ps 32:8 *along the best **p** for your life.* 565

PATIENCE (n) the power or capacity to endure without complaint something difficult or disagreeable; forbearance, longsuffering
Rom 15:5 *May God, who gives this **p***........1671
Gal 5:22 *joy, peace, **p,** kindness,* 1566
Col 1:11 *endurance and **p** you need.* 1694
Col 3:12 *humility, gentleness, and **p.***.........1700
2 Tim 3:10 *my faith, my **p,** my love,* 1744
Titus 2:2 *and be filled with love and **p.***......1738
Jas 5:10 *examples of **p** in suffering,* 1553
2 Pet 3:15 *Lord's **p** gives people time*.......1760

PATIENT (adj) bearing pains or trials calmly or without complaint; steadfast despite opposition, difficulty, or adversity; not hasty or impetuous
Rom 2:4 *and **p** God is with you?*..............1648
Rom 12:12 *Be **p** in trouble,* 1667
1 Cor 4:12 *We are **p** with those who*.........1601
1 Cor 13:4 *Love is **p** and kind.*..................1616
1 Thes 5:14 *Be **p** with everyone.* 1586
Jas 5:8 *You, too, must be **p.***......................1553

PATIENTLY (adv) in a patient manner
Ps 40:1 *I waited **p** for the LORD*..................570
1 Pet 3:20 *God waited **p** while Noah*.........1754
Rev 14:12 *endure persecution **p,***..............1821

PATTERN (n) a form or model proposed for imitation
Exod 25:40 *according to the **p.***...................176
Exod 26:30 *the **p** you were shown*.............177
2 Tim 1:13 *Hold on to the **p***......................1741
Heb 8:5 *according to the **p***.......................1771

PAUL Pharisee and Roman citizen (Acts 22:3, p. 1678); from city of Tarsus (Acts 9:11, p. 1530; Phil 3:5, p. 1722); became apostle (Gal 1, p. 1554) to the Gentiles (Rom 11:13, p. 1665); also known as "Saul" (Acts 7:58, p. 1526; 13:9, p. 1540); supported stoning of Stephen (Acts 8:1, p. 1526); attacked early Christians (Acts 8:1-3, p. 1527; 9:1-2, p. 1529; Gal 1:13, p. 1556); converted on road to Damascus (Acts 9:1-9, p. 1529; 22:6-16, p. 1679; 26:12-18, p. 1685); preached in Damascus (Acts 9:20-22, p. 1530); escaped over the wall in basket (Acts 9:23-25, p. 1531); escaped to Jerusalem, then on to Tarsus (Acts 9:26-30, p. 1531); saw visions in Arabia (Gal 1:17, p. 1557); with Barnabas in Antioch (Acts 11:22-26, p. 1536); sent to Jerusalem (Acts 11:27-30, p. 1536); first missionary journey: Cyprus and Galatia (Acts 13–14, p. 1539); advocate for Gentile believers (Acts 15:1-5, p. 1568); testified at Jerusalem Council (Acts 15:12, p. 1569); split with Barnabas over John Mark (Acts 15:36-41, p. 1572); second missionary journey with Silas: northern and southern Greece, western Asia (Acts 15:36–18:22, p. 1572); received call to Macedonia (Acts 16:6-10, p. 1573); Philippi, Thessalonica, Berea (Acts 16–17, p. 1573); Athens, Corinth (Acts 17–18, p. 1576); third missionary journey: returned to northern and southern Greece, western Asia (Acts 18:23–21:14, p. 1592); Corinth, Ephesus, Macedonia, Troas—to Jerusalem (Acts 18–21, p. 1579); farewell to Ephesian elders

(Acts 20:13-38, p. 1675); journey to Rome (Acts 21–28, p. 1676); falsely arrested and in hands of mob (Acts 21:26–22:21, p. 1678); saved by Roman custody (Acts 22:22-29, p. 1679; 23:10, p. 1680); before the Jewish high council (Acts 23:1-11, p. 1679); relocated to Caesarea (Acts 23:12-35, p. 1680); trial before Felix (Acts 24, p. 1681); appealed to Caesar before Festus (Acts 25:1-12, p. 1683), before Herod Agrippa (Acts 25:13–26:32, p. 1683); sailed to Rome, was shipwrecked (Acts 27, p. 1686); arrived in Rome (Acts 28, p. 1688); pattern of self-denial (1 Cor 9, p. 1608); his gospel message (Rom 1–5, p. 1644; Gal 3–6, p. 1560); catalog of trials (2 Cor 11:22-33, p. 1641); his goal (Phil 3:7-15, p. 1722); last known written words (2 Tim 4, p. 1745); intervened for returning slave (Phlm 1:8-22, p. 1691); wrote letters: Romans through Philemon (see the first verse of each book).

PAVEMENT (n) a surface covered firmly and solidly with material (as asphalt or concrete)
John 19:13 *that is called the Stone **P*** 1481

PAY (n) something paid for a purpose and especially as a salary or wage
1 Tim 5:18 *who work deserve their **p**!* 1734

PAY, PAYS (v) to suffer the consequences of an act; to requite according to what is deserved; to make due return to for services or goods rendered
see also PAID
Exod 22:3 *A thief who is caught must **p*** 172
Deut 32:35 *I will **p** them back.* 325
Ps 137:8 *Happy is the one who **p-s** you* 1119
Matt 22:17 *to **p** taxes to Caesar or not?* 1439
Rom 12:19 *I will **p** them back,* 1668
1 Thes 5:15 *no one **p-s** back evil* 1586
2 Thes 1:6 *he will **p** back those who* 1588

PAYMENT (n) the act of paying; something that is paid
Deut 15:2 *must not demand **p**.* 305
Deut 27:25 *anyone who accepts **p*** 317
Hos 9:7 *the day of **p** is here.* 812

PEACE (n) a state of tranquility or quiet; a pact or agreement to end hostilities between those who have been at war or in a state of enmity; harmony in personal relations, especially with God; a state of security or order within a community; freedom from disquieting or oppressive thoughts or emotions
Exod 20:24 *and **p** offerings, your sheep* 170
Lev 26:6 *I will give you **p** in the land,* 235
Num 6:26 *his favor and give you his **p**.* 245
Deut 20:10 *offer its people terms for **p**.* 310
1 Sam 7:14 *there was **p** between Israel* 427
1 Kgs 5:4 *God has given me **p** on every* 609
1 Chr 22:9 *a son who will be a man of **p**.* 532
2 Chr 14:7 *has given us **p** on every side.* 706
Job 3:26 *I have no **p**, no quietness.* 98
Job 25:2 *He enforces **p** in the heavens.* 117
Ps 34:14 *Search for **p**, and work to* 459
Ps 37:37 *awaits those who love **p**.* 568
Ps 120:7 *I search for **p**; but when I* 882
Ps 147:14 *He sends **p** across your nation* 1155
Prov 12:20 *hearts that are planning **p**!* 645
Eccl 3:8 *for war and a time for **p**.* 675
Isa 9:6 *Everlasting Father, Prince of **P**.* 793
Isa 32:17 *righteousness will bring **p**.* 902
Isa 48:22 *there is no **p** for the wicked,* 935
Isa 52:7 *good news of **p** and salvation,* 939
Jer 6:14 *give assurances of **p** when* 968
Jer 46:27 *return to a life of **p** and quiet,* 998
Ezek 34:25 *I will make a covenant of **p*** 1110
Zech 8:19 *So love truth and **p**.* 1174
Matt 5:9 *blesses those who work for **p**,* 1326
Mark 9:50 *live in **p** with each other.* 1384
Luke 1:79 *guide us to the path of **p**.* 1277
John 16:33 *you may have **p** in me.* 1466
Rom 5:1 *by faith, we have **p** with God* 1654
Rom 8:6 *your mind leads to life and **p**.* 1659
1 Cor 14:33 *God of disorder but of **p**,* 1618
Gal 5:22 *love, joy, **p**, patience,* 1566
Eph 2:14 *Christ himself has brought **p*** 1708
Eph 2:15 *made **p** between Jews and* 1708
Eph 2:17 *Good News of **p** to you Gentiles.* 1708
Eph 6:15 *put on the **p** that comes from* 1715
Phil 4:7 *experience God's **p**,* 1724
1 Thes 5:23 *God of **p** make you holy.* 1587
2 Thes 3:16 *Lord of **p** himself give you* 1590
2 Tim 2:22 *faithfulness, love, and **p**.* 1743
Heb 13:20 *the God of **p**—who brought* 1783
Jas 3:17 *It is also **p** loving, gentle* 1551
1 Pet 3:11 *Search for **p**, and work to* 1753

PEACEFUL (adj) quiet, tranquil; devoid of violence or force; of or relating to a state or time of peace
Ps 23:2 *leads me beside **p** streams.* 558
Prov 14:30 *A **p** heart leads to a healthy* 648
1 Thes 5:3 *Everything is **p** and secure,* 1585
1 Tim 2:2 *we can live **p** and quiet lives.* 1729
Heb 12:11 *a **p** harvest of right living* 1780
2 Pet 3:14 *effort to be found living **p**.* 1760

PEACEMAKER, PEACEMAKERS (n) one who makes peace especially by reconciling parties at variance
Acts 7:26 *He tried to be a **p**.* 1525
Jas 3:18 ***p-s** will plant seeds of peace.* 1551

PEARL, PEARLS (n) a white translucent jewel created within certain species of mollusks
Matt 7:6 *throw your **p-s** to pigs!* 1333
Matt 13:45 *on the lookout for choice **p-s**.* 1349
1 Tim 2:9 *or by wearing gold or **p-s*** 1729
Rev 21:21 *were made of **p-s**—* 1831
Rev 21:21 *each gate from a single **p**!* 1831

PENALTY (n) disadvantage, loss, or hardship due to some action
Job 34:36 *you deserve the maximum **p*** 125
Rom 3:24 *freed us from the **p*** 1651

PENNY (n) the smallest monetary unit
Matt 5:26 *you have paid the last **p**.* 1328
Luke 12:59 *paid the very last **p**.* 1402

PENTECOST (n) a Jewish feast celebrated on the 50th day after the Feast of Unleavened Bread; the day God sent the Holy Spirit after Christ's resurrection
Acts 2:1 *the day of **P** all the believers* 1513
Acts 20:16 *in time for the Festival of **P**.* 1675
1 Cor 16:8 *until the Festival of **P**.* 1623

PEOPLE, PEOPLES (n) human beings making up a group or assembly or linked by a common interest; clan or nation; humanity
see also NATION(S)
Exod 5:1 *says: Let my **p** go* 146
Exod 8:23 *between my **p** and your **p**.* 152
Exod 19:5 *among all the **p-s** on earth;* 167
Exod 19:8 *all the **p** responded together,* 168
Exod 33:13 *nation is your very own **p**.* 186
Lev 26:12 *and you will be my **p**.* 235
Num 14:11 *How long will these **p*** 252
Deut 7:6 *you are a holy **p**, who belong* 296
Deut 14:1 *are the **p** of the* LORD 303
Deut 32:9 *For the **p** of Israel belong* 324
Deut 33:29 ***p** saved by the* LORD*?* 328
Ruth 1:16 *Your **p** will be my **p**,* 410
2 Chr 7:20 *uproot the **p** from this land* 624
Neh 1:10 *The **p** you rescued by your* 1204
Neh 8:1 *the **p** assembled with a unified* 1214
Ps 33:12 *whose **p** he has chosen* 858
Ps 53:6 *When God restores his **p**,* 571
Ps 94:14 *will not reject his **p**;* 863
Ps 96:10 *He will judge all **p-s** fairly.* 864
Ps 135:14 *will give justice to his **p*** 885
Isa 2:2 ***p** from all over the world* 825
Isa 6:10 *Harden the hearts of these **p**.* 785
Isa 40:1 *Comfort, comfort my **p**,* 923
Isa 49:13 LORD *has comforted his **p*** 936
Isa 52:6 *I will reveal my name to my **p**,* 939
Isa 53:8 *for the rebellion of my **p**.* 940
Isa 55:4 *my power among the **p-s**.* 942
Jer 2:11 *Yet my **p** have exchanged their* 960
Jer 2:32 *my **p** have forgotten me.* 962
Jer 7:16 *Pray no more for these **p**,* 1008
Jer 32:27 *of all the **p-s** of the world.* 1080
Dan 8:24 *and devastate the holy **p**.* 1138
Dan 9:24 *decreed for your **p*** 1143
Hos 1:10 *You are not my **p**,* 802
Hos 2:23 *Now you are my **p**.* 804
Mic 4:1 ***p** from all over the world* 907
Mic 4:3 LORD *will mediate between **p-s*** 907
Matt 4:19 *show you how to fish for **p**!* 1307
Mark 7:6 ***p** honor me with their lips,* 1370
Mark 8:27 *Who do **p** say I am?* 1376
Luke 1:68 *visited and redeemed his **p**.* 1276
John 11:50 *should die for the **p*** 1415
John 18:14 *should die for the **p**.* 1471
Rom 9:25 *Those who were not my **p**,* 1662
Rom 11:1 ***p**, the nation of Israel?* 1664
2 Cor 6:16 *and they will be my **p**.* 1634
Gal 6:16 *they are the new **p** of God.* 1568
Eph 1:14 *purchased us to be his own **p**.* 1706
Eph 1:18 *he called—his holy **p*** 1706
Eph 2:15 *creating in himself one new **p*** 1708
Eph 4:8 *and gave gifts to his **p**.* 1710
2 Tim 2:2 *trustworthy **p** who will* 1742
2 Tim 3:17 *and equip his **p** to do every* 1745
Titus 2:11 *bringing salvation to all **p**.* 1738
Titus 2:14 *make us his very own **p**,* 1738
Heb 4:9 *waiting for the **p** of God.* 1766
1 Pet 2:9 *for you are a chosen **p**.* 1751
1 Pet 2:10 *now you are God's **p**.* 1751
Rev 5:8 *prayers of God's **p**.* 1810
Rev 10:11 *again about many **p-s**,* 1816
Rev 18:4 *from her, my **p**.* 1825
Rev 19:8 *of God's holy **p**.* 1827
Rev 21:3 *home is now among his **p**!* 1830

PERFECT (adj) being entirely without fault or defect; corresponding to an ideal standard or abstract concept; mature, pure, complete
Deut 32:4 *the Rock; his deeds are **p**.* 323
Ps 19:7 *instructions of the* LORD *are **p**,* 554
Ps 119:138 *laws are **p** and completely* 881
Matt 5:48 *you are to be **p**, even as* 1330
John 17:23 *experience such **p** unity* 1467
Gal 3:3 *become **p** by your* 1560
Col 4:12 *God to make you strong and **p**,* 1703
Heb 2:10 *suffering, a **p** leader,* 1764
Heb 5:9 *as a **p** High Priest,* 1767
Heb 7:19 *law never made anything **p**.* 1770
Heb 9:11 *greater, more **p** Tabernacle* 1772
Heb 9:14 *as a **p** sacrifice for our sins.* 1773
Heb 10:14 *he forever made **p** those* 1775
Heb 12:23 *who have now been made **p**.* 1781

Jas 1:25 *look carefully into the **p** law*........1548
1 Jn 4:18 *because **p** love expels all fear*....1794

PERFECT, PERFECTED, PERFECTS (v) to bring to final form; to refine or improve
Ezek 16:14 *splendor and **p-ed** your beauty,*..1061
Heb 12:2 *champion who initiates and **p-s***...1780

PERFECTION (n) flawlessness; maturity; an exemplification of supreme excellence
Job 37:16 *with wonderful **p** and skill?*.........127
Ps 50:2 *Mount Zion, the **p** of beauty,* 593
1 Cor 13:10 *when the time of **p** comes,*....1616
Phil 3:12 *I have already reached **p**.*...........1723
Heb 7:11 *achieved the **p** God intended,*.....1770
Heb 11:40 *not reach **p** without us*............1779

PERFORM, PERFORMED, PERFORMING (v) to carry out; to do
Exod 3:20 ***p-ing** all kinds of miracles* 144
2 Sam 7:23 *You **p-ed** awesome miracles* ...496
John 10:41 *John didn't **p** miraculous*........1407

PERFUME (n) a substance that emits a pleasant odor
Eccl 7:1 *more valuable than costly **p**.*..........678
Mark 14:3 *poured the **p** over his head.*.....1428
2 Cor 2:14 *everywhere, like a sweet **p**.*.....1628
2 Cor 2:16 *saved, we are a life-giving **p**.*...1628

PERISH, PERISHING (v) to become destroyed or ruined physically or spiritually; to die
see also DESTROY, DIE
Ps 102:26 *They will **p**, but you remain*........867
John 3:16 *believes in him will not **p** but*....1302
John 10:28 *they will never **p**.* 1406
2 Cor 2:15 *by those who are **p-ing**.* 1628
2 Cor 4:3 *from people who are **p-ing**.*.......1630
Jude 1:11 *they **p** in their rebellion*............1785

PERMANENT (n) continuing or enduring without fundamental or marked change; lasting
Num 25:13 *a **p** right to the priesthood,* 270

PERMIT, PERMITTED (v) to consent to; to authorize; to make possible
Matt 16:19 *whatever you **p** on earth*.........1375
Matt 18:18 *whatever you **p** on earth*.........1385
Matt 19:8 *"Moses **p-ted** divorce* 1418

PERPLEXED (adj) unable to grasp something clearly; puzzled
Luke 21:25 ***p** by the roaring seas and*.......1450
2 Cor 4:8 ***p**, but not driven to despair.*.......1631

PERSECUTE, PERSECUTED, PERSECUTING (v) to harass or punish in a manner designed to injure, grieve, or afflict; to cause to suffer because of belief
Ps 140:12 *help those they **p**;* 587
Matt 5:10 *blesses those who are **p-d*** 1326
Matt 5:11 *when people mock you and **p*** ...1326
Matt 5:12 *prophets were **p-d***...................1326
Matt 5:44 *Pray for those who **p** you!*.........1330
Matt 13:21 ***p-d** for believing God's*...........1345
John 15:20 *they **p-d** me, naturally they will **p** you.*..1464
Acts 9:4 *Why are you **p-ing** me?*.............1530
Rom 8:35 *or are **p-d**, or hungry,*...............1661
Rom 12:14 *Bless those who **p** you.*...........1668
1 Cor 15:9 *the way I **p-d** God's church.* 1620
2 Thes 1:7 *for you who are being **p-d***.......1588

PERSECUTION, PERSECUTIONS (n) the condition of being persecuted, harassed, or annoyed
Mark 10:30 *along with **p**.*........................1421
2 Cor 12:10 *insults, hardships, **p-s**,* 1642
2 Thes 1:4 *all the **p-s** and hardships*.........1587
2 Thes 1:5 *God will use this **p** to show*.......1588
2 Tim 3:11 *You know how much **p** and*.....1744
2 Tim 3:12 *in Christ Jesus will suffer **p**.*....1744
Rev 13:10 *must endure **p** patiently*...........1820

PERSECUTORS (n) those who persecute
Ps 142:6 *Rescue me from my **p**,*................460

PERSEVERANCE (n) enduring hardships with patience; steadfastness
see also ENDURANCE
1 Tim 6:11 *along with faith, love, **p**, and*....1735

PERSEVERE (v) to persist in a state, enterprise, or undertaking in spite of opposition or discouragement
see also ENDURE
Rev 3:10 *obeyed my command to **p**,*.........1807

PERSISTENCE (n) the action, quality, or state of continuing resolutely in the face of obstacles
Luke 11:8 *because of your shameless **p**.*..1398

PERSON (n) human, individual
Ps 119:9 *How can a young **p** stay pure?*.....878
2 Cor 5:17 *to Christ has become a new **p**.*...1632
Heb 9:27 *just as each **p** is destined to die*...1774

PERSUADE, PERSUADED (v) to move by argument or entreaty to a belief, position, or course of action
Prov 25:15 *Patience can **p** a prince,* 840
Acts 19:26 *Paul has **p-d** many people*......1624
Acts 28:23 *tried to **p** them about Jesus* 1689
Acts 28:24 *were **p-d** by the things he*.......1689

PERSUASIVE (adj) tending to persuade
Prov 16:21 *and pleasant words are **p**.*.........651
Prov 16:23 *the words of the wise are **p**.*.........651
1 Cor 2:4 *clever and **p** speeches,* 1598

PERVERSE (adj) corrupt; improper, incorrect; perverted
Lev 18:23 *This is a **p** act*..........................224
Lev 20:12 *They have committed a **p** act* 227
Phil 2:15 *a world full of crooked and **p***......1720

PERVERT, PERVERTED (v) to cause to turn aside or away from what is good, true, or morally right; to corrupt
1 Sam 8:3 *bribes and **p-ed** justice.* 434
Prov 17:23 *secret bribes to **p** the course*.....653

PETER Leader of the twelve disciples, also known as "Simon son of John" (John 21:17, p. 1497) and "Cephas" (John 1:42, p. 1298); called to "fish for people" (Matt 4:18-20, p. 1307; Mark 1:16-20, p. 1308; Luke 5:1-11, p. 1308; *see also* John 21:3, p. 1496); mother-in-law healed (Matt 8:14-15, p. 1309; Mark 1:29-31, p. 1310; Luke 4:38-39, p. 1310); called to preach (Mark 1:36-39, p. 1311); brother of Andrew (Matt 10:2, p. 1358; Mark 3:16, p. 1322; Luke 6:14, p. 1323; Acts 1:13, p. 1512); present at raising of the dead (Mark 5:37, p. 1354; Luke 8:51, p. 1355); walked on water (Matt 14:22-33, p. 1365; Mark 6:45-52, p. 1366; John 6:16-21, p. 1366); identified Jesus as the Christ (Matt 16:13-20, p. 1375; Mark 8:27-30, p. 1376; Luke 9:18-20, p. 1376; *see also* John 6:68-69, p. 1369); rebuked by Jesus for lack of heavenly perspective (Matt 16:21-23, p. 1376; Mark 8:32-33, p. 1377; *see also* John 13:6-11, p. 1456); witnessed the Transfiguration (Matt 16:28–17:8, p. 1377, 1378; Mark 9:1-13, p. 1378, 1379; Luke 9:28-36, p. 1380; 2 Pet 1:16-20, p. 1758); noticed the withered fig tree (Mark 11:21, p. 1435; *see also* Matt 21:20, p. 1435); his denial predicted by Jesus (Matt 26:31-35, p. 1460; Mark 14:27-31, p. 1460; Luke 22:31-34, p. 1460; John 13:36-38, p. 1461); in Gethsemane (Matt 26:36-46, p. 1468; Mark 14:32-42, p. 1468; Luke 22:39-46, p. 1469); cut off ear of Malchus (Matt 26:51, p. 1469; Mark 14:47, p. 1470; Luke 22:50, p. 1470); denied Jesus—then wept (Matt 26:69-75, p. 1473; Mark 14:66-72, p. 1474; Luke 22:54-62, p. 1474; John 18:15-27, p. 1471); visited empty tomb (Luke 24:12, p. 1492; John 20:1-10, p. 1492; *see also* Matt 28:1-8, p. 1489); saw Jesus (Luke 24:34, p. 1494; 1 Cor 15:5, p. 1620); told by Jesus to shepherd his flock (John 21:15-19, p. 1497); in upper room before Pentecost (Acts 1:13, p. 1512); preached at Pentecost (Acts 2, p. 1513); performed miracles (Acts 3:1-10, p. 1516; 5:14-16, p. 1521; 9:32-43, p. 1531); preached at Temple (Acts 3:11-26, p. 1517); preached before Jewish high council (Acts 4:1-22, p. 1518); prophesied death of Ananias and Sapphira (Acts 5:1-11, p. 1520); preached again before Jewish high council (Acts 5:29-32, p. 1521); rebuked power seeker (Acts 8:14-25, p. 1528); healed sick (Acts 9:32-34, p. 1531); raised dead (Acts 9:36-43, p. 1532); introduced Gentiles to gospel (Acts 10–11, p. 1532); rescued by angel from prison (Acts 12:3-19, p. 1537); preached grace at Jerusalem Council (Acts 15, p. 1568); became pillar of the church (Gal 2:9, p. 1558); was correctable (Gal 2:14, p. 1559); wrote letters (1 Pet 1:1, p. 1747; 2 Pet 1:1, p. 1757); had believing wife (1 Cor 9:5, p. 1608).

PHARAOH (n) the ruler of the ancient Egyptians
Gen 12:15 *praises to **P**, their king,* 31
Gen 41:14 *went in and stood before **P**.*..........79
Exod 14:4 *to display my glory through **P*** 159
Exod 14:17 *will be displayed through **P***.......160

PHARISEE, PHARISEES (n) a religious and political party in Palestine in New Testament times known for strict observance of rites and ceremonies of the written law and for insistence on the validity of their own oral traditions concerning the law
Matt 5:20 ***P-s**, you will never enter*...........1328
Matt 16:6 *of the yeast of the **P-s***.............1374
Matt 23:13 *and you **P-s**. Hypocrites!* 1444
John 3:1 *religious leader who was a **P**.*......1300
Acts 23:6 ***P**, as were my ancestors!* 1680

PHILIP
1. One of the twelve disciples (Matt 10:3, p. 1358; Mark 3:18, p. 1323; Luke 6:14, p. 1323; John 1:43-48, p. 1298; 12:21-22, p. 1432; 14:8, p. 1461; Acts 1:13, p. 1512).
2. Deacon and evangelist (Acts 6:5, p. 1522; Acts 8:5-25, p. 1527); with the Ethiopian eunuch (Acts 8:26-40, p. 1529); hosted Paul in Caesarea (Acts 21:8-9, p. 1676).
3. Son of Herod the Great and Cleopatra of Jerusalem, half-brother of Antipas and Archelaus; tetrarch of the regions north of Galilee (Luke 3:1, p. 1290).
4. Son of Herod the Great and Mariamne; first husband of Herodias, who left him for Herod Antipas (Matt 14:3, p. 1361; Mark 6:17, p. 1361). (He also was half-brother to Archelaus and Antipas.)

PHILISTINE, PHILISTINES (n) a native or inhabitant of ancient Philistia
Judg 16:20 *"Samson! The **P-s** have come* 402
1 Sam 4:1 *was at war with the **P-s**.* 423
1 Sam 17:1 ***P-s** now mustered their* 449
1 Sam 17:26 *get for killing this **P*** 450
1 Sam 31:1 *the **P-s** attacked Israel,* 474

PHILOSOPHERS (n) persons who seeks wisdom or enlightenment
1 Cor 1:20 *leave the **p**, the scholars,* 1597

PHILOSOPHIES (n) theories underlying or regarding a sphere of activity or thought
Col 2:8 *capture you with empty **p*** 1698

PHYSICAL (adj) having material existence; of or relating to the body
John 1:13 *reborn—not with a **p** birth* 1271
Col 1:22 *of Christ in his **p** body.* 1696
1 Tim 4:8 ***P** training is good, but* 1732
1 Tim 5:11 ***p** desires will overpower.* 1733
1 Jn 2:16 *a craving for **p** pleasure* 1789

PICTURE (n) a representation, image, or copy
1 Pet 3:21 *water is a **p** of baptism,* 1754

PIERCE, PIERCED (v) to make a hole through; to stab
Exod 21:6 *and publicly **p** his ear* 171
Ps 22:16 *have **p-d** my hands and feet.* 556
Zech 12:10 *me whom they have **p-d*** 1178
Luke 2:35 *sword will **p** your very soul.* 1282
John 19:37 *look on the one they **p-d**.* 1487
Rev 1:7 *even those who **p-d** him.* 1800

PIG, PIGS (n) a wild or domestic swine
Matt 7:6 *Don't throw your pearls to **p-s!*** ... 1333
Mark 5:11 *a large herd of **p-s** feeding* 1351
Luke 15:15 *his fields to feed the **p-s**.* 1410
2 Pet 2:22 *washed **p** returns to the mud.* .. 1759

PIGEONS (n) any of the family of birds with a stout body, rather short legs, and smooth and compact plumage
Lev 5:11 *turtledoves or two young **p**,* 207
Luke 2:24 *turtledoves or two young **p**.* 1282

PILATE The procurator (Roman governor) in Palestine at the time of the crucifixion of Christ (Luke 3:1, p. 1290). "Pontius" was his family name; he questioned Jesus found him innocent; later, influenced by the Jewish leaders, he sentenced him to execution (Matt 27, p. 1475; Mark 15, p. 1475; Luke 23, p. 1476; John 18–19, p. 1470).

PILGRIMS (KJV)
Heb 11:13 ***nomads** here on earth* 1778
1 Pet 2:11 *as "temporary residents and **foreigners"*** 1751

PILLAR, PILLARS (n) a column or shaft standing alone as a monument or supporting a superstructure; miraculous cloud by day and fire by night; memorial pile of stones; a supporting, integral, or upstanding member of a group
Gen 19:26 *she turned into a **p** of salt.* 42
Exod 13:21 *night with a **p** of fire.* 159
Exod 24:4 *set up twelve **p-s**, one for* 174
Deut 1:33 *by night and a **p** of cloud by* 286
Judg 16:26 *my hands against the **p-s*** 402
Gal 2:9 *known as **p-s** of the church,* 1558
1 Tim 3:15 ***p** and foundation of* 1731
Rev 3:12 *victorious will become **p-s*** 1807

PINIONS (n) the tips of a bird's wings
Deut 32:11 *carried them safely on his **p**.* 324

PIOUS (adj) marked by or showing reverence for God and devotion to worship; religious
Isa 58:2 *Yet they act so **p!*** 944
Col 2:18 *insisting on **p** self-denial* 1699
Col 2:23 *strong devotion, **p** self-denial,* 1699

PIT (n) a hole, shaft, or cavity in the ground; a place or situation of misery, futility, or degradation
Ps 40:2 *me out of the **p** of despair,* 570
Luke 14:5 *or your cow falls into a **p**,* 1408

PITCH (n) a black or dark sticky substance
Exod 2:3 *waterproofed it with tar and **p**.* 141

PITIED (v) to feel pity for
1 Cor 15:19 *we are more to be **p** than* 1620

PITY (n) sympathetic sorrow for one suffering, distressed, or unhappy
Judg 2:18 *For the LORD took **p** on* 375
Ps 17:10 *They are without **p**.* 553
Ps 69:20 *would show some **p**;* 578
Ps 72:13 *He feels **p** for the weak* 630
Isa 27:11 *show them no **p** or mercy* 897
Hos 13:14 *I will not take **p** on them.* 816

PLAGUE, PLAGUES (n) a disastrous evil, affliction, or epidemic of infectious disease, issued by God in judgment
2 Chr 6:28 *or a **p** or crop disease* 621
Luke 21:11 *will be famines and **p-s*** 1450
Rev 21:9 *the seven last **p-s** came* 1830
Rev 22:18 *add to that person the **p-s*** 1833

PLAGUED (v) to smite, infest, or afflict with disease, calamity, or natural evil
Ps 73:5 *they're not **p** with problems* 594

PLAN, PLANS (n) a detailed formulation of a program of action; goal, aim
see also PURPOSE
Ps 2:1 *waste their time with futile **p-s?*** 856
Ps 33:10 *frustrates the **p-s** of the* 858
Ps 40:5 ***p-s** for us are too numerous* 570
Isa 30:1 *You make **p-s** that are contrary* 899
Isa 32:6 *and make evil **p-s**.* 902
Jer 29:11 *I know the **p-s** I have for you* 1030
Acts 2:23 *his prearranged **p** was carried* ... 1515
Acts 4:25 *waste their time with futile **p-s?*** 1519
Acts 7:44 *according to the **p** God had* 1526
Rom 16:25 ***p** kept secret from* 1674
Eph 3:9 *this mysterious **p** that God,* 1709
Eph 3:11 *This was his eternal **p**,* 1709
2 Tim 1:9 ***p** from before the beginning* 1741

PLANNED, PLANNING (v) to devise or project the realization or achievement of
Prov 12:20 *hearts that are **p-ning** peace!* ... 645
Isa 25:1 *You **p-ed** them long ago,* 895
Jer 23:20 *has finished all he has **p-ed**.* 1028
Eph 2:10 *do the good things he **p-ed*** 1707

PLANT (n) a young tree, vine, shrub, or herb planted or suitable for planting
Matt 15:13 ***p** not planted by* 1370
1 Cor 15:36 *it doesn't grow into a **p*** 1621

PLANT, PLANTED, PLANTING, PLANTS (v) to put or set (seeds or plants) in the ground for growth; to establish or settle
Gen 2:8 *the LORD God **p-ed** a garden* 9
Gen 8:22 *there will be **p-ing** and harvest,* 20
Ps 1:3 *like trees **p-ed** along the riverbank,* 856
Ps 126:5 *who **p** in tears will harvest* 1154
Prov 22:8 *who **p** injustice will harvest* 659
Prov 31:16 *earnings she **p-s** a vineyard.* 847
Hos 10:12 ***P** the good seeds* 813
Amos 9:15 *I will firmly **p** them there* 781
Matt 6:26 *They don't **p** or harvest or* 1332
Matt 13:3 *A farmer went out to **p** some* 1345
Matt 13:18 *about the farmer **p-ing*** 1345
1 Cor 3:6 ***p-ed** the seed in your hearts,* 1599
1 Cor 3:7 *who does the **p-ing**,* 1599
1 Cor 9:7 *What farmer **p-s** a vineyard* 1608
1 Cor 15:42 *earthly bodies are **p-ed**.* 1621
2 Cor 9:6 *a farmer who **p-s** only a few* 1637
Jas 1:21 *accept the word God has **p-ed*** ... 1548
Jas 3:18 *will **p** seeds of peace* 1551

PLANTER (n) one who cultivates plants
John 4:36 *What joy awaits both the **p** and* 1305

PLAY, PLAYED (v) to perform music; to engage in sport or recreation
1 Sam 16:23 *David would **p** the harp* 448
Ps 87:7 *The people will **p** flutes* 855
Ps 137:5 *forget how to **p** the harp.* 1118
Isa 11:8 *baby will **p** safely near the hole.* 796
Luke 7:32 *so we **p-ed** funeral songs,* 1339

PLEA, PLEAS (n) an earnest entreaty; appeal
1 Kgs 8:28 *prayer and my **p**, O LORD.* 619
Ps 102:17 *He will not reject their **p-s**.* 866

PLEAD, PLEADING, PLEADS (v) to entreat or appeal earnestly; to argue a case or cause
Job 9:15 *I could only **p** for mercy.* 103
Lam 3:56 *Listen to my **p-ing!*** 1099
Hos 10:8 *and **p** with the hills,* 813
Acts 16:9 ***p-ing** with him, "Come over* 1573
Rom 8:27 *the Spirit **p-s** for us* 1660
Rom 8:34 *right hand, **p-ing** for us.* 1661
2 Cor 5:20 *speak for Christ when we **p**,* 1633

PLEASANT (adj) having qualities that tend to give pleasure; agreeable
Gen 49:15 *and how **p** the land,* 91
Ps 16:6 *given me is a **p** land.* 553
Prov 16:21 *and **p** words are persuasive.* 651
Isa 5:7 *of Judah are his **p** garden.* 828

PLEASE, PLEASED, PLEASES (v) to make glad; to satisfy; to like or wish; to be the will or pleasure of
Deut 12:25 *doing what **p-s** the LORD* 302
Ps 135:6 *The LORD does whatever **p-s**.* 885
Prov 16:7 *people's lives **p** the LORD,* 651
Isa 42:1 *my chosen one, who **p-s** me.* 926
Matt 12:18 *my Beloved, who **p-s** me.* 1322
Luke 2:14 *those with whom God is **p-d**.* ... 1281
Luke 10:21 *Yes, Father, it **p-d** you to do.* ... 1395
John 8:29 *I always do what **p-s** him.* 1392
Rom 8:8 *sinful nature can never **p** God.* 1659
Rom 14:18 *this attitude, you will **p** God,* 1670
2 Cor 5:9 *our goal is to **p** him.* 1632
Gal 6:8 *live to **p** the Spirit will harvest* 1567
Eph 5:10 *determine what **p-s** the* 1712
Phil 2:13 *power to do what **p-s** him.* 1720
Col 1:10 *always honor and **p** the Lord,* 1694
Col 1:19 *God in all his fullness was **p-d*** 1695
1 Thes 2:4 *Our purpose is to **p** God,* 1581
1 Thes 2:15 *They fail to **p** God* 1583
1 Tim 2:3 *is good and **p-s** God our* 1729
1 Tim 5:4 *is something that **p-s** God.* 1733
Heb 10:6 *not **p-d** with burnt offerings.* 1775
Heb 11:6 *to **p** God without faith.* 1777
Heb 13:16 *sacrifices that **p** God.* 1783
1 Pet 2:19 *God is **p-d** with you when* 1752
1 Jn 2:17 *does what **p-s** God will live* 1789
Rev 4:11 *you created what you **p-d**.* 1809

PLEASING (adj) giving pleasure; agreeable
Lev 1:9 *a special gift, a **p** aroma* 203
Ps 19:14 *of my heart be **p** to you,* 555

Ps 104:34 *my thoughts be **p** to him,* 868
Eccl 7:26 *who are **p** to God will escape* 679
Rom 12:2 *is good and **p** and perfect.* 1666
Phil 4:18 *is acceptable and **p** to God.* 1725

PLEASURE, PLEASURES (n) desire, inclination; a source of delight or joy; sensual gratification
Ps 5:4 *you take no **p** in wickedness;* 547
Ps 16:3 *I take **p** in them!* 552
Ps 16:11 *the **p-s** of living with you* 553
Isa 1:11 *I get no **p** from the blood of* 823
Luke 8:14 *cares and riches and **p-s*** 1347
Eph 1:9 *a plan to fulfill his own good **p.*** 1705
1 Tim 5:6 *widow who lives only for **p*** 1733
2 Tim 3:4 *and love **p** rather than God.* 1744
Titus 2:12 *living and sinful **p-s.*** 1738
Titus 3:3 *slaves to many lusts and **p-s.*** 1739
Heb 11:25 *the fleeting **p-s** of sin.* 1778
Jas 4:3 *only what will give you **p.*** 1551

PLEDGE (n) a binding promise or agreement to do or forbear
1 Tim 5:12 *breaking their previous **p.*** 1733

PLENTY (n) the full or more-than-adequate amount or supply
Ps 17:14 *May their children have **p,*** 554
Prov 12:11 *A hard worker has **p** of food,* 645
2 Cor 8:14 *now you have **p** and can help* ..1636
2 Cor 9:8 ***p** left over to share with others.* .1637

PLOT, PLOTS (v) to plan or contrive especially secretly; to scheme
Prov 3:29 ***p** harm against your neighbor* 635
Prov 6:14 *perverted hearts **p** evil,* 638
Prov 6:18 *a heart that **p-s** evil,* 638

PLOWS (v) to turn, break up, or work with a plow
1 Cor 9:10 *the one who **p** and the one* 1608

PLOWSHARES (n) a part of a plow that cuts the furrow
Isa 2:4 *hammer their swords into **p.*** 825
Joel 3:10 *Hammer your **p** into swords.* 1243
Mic 4:3 *hammer their swords into **p*** 907

PLUNDER (v) to take by force (as in war)
Matt 12:29 *like Satan and **p** his goods?* 1341

PLUNGE (v) to cause to enter a state or course of action usually suddenly, unexpectedly, or violently; to act with reckless haste
1 Tim 6:9 *desires that **p** them into ruin* 1735
1 Pet 4:4 *no longer **p** into the flood of* 1754

POINT (n) a particular place; a particular step, stage, or degree in development
Matt 4:5 *the highest **p** of the Temple,* 1295
Matt 26:38 *grief to the **p** of death.* 1468

POINT (v) to indicate the fact or probability of something specified
John 5:39 *But the Scriptures **p** to me!* 1319

POISON (n) a substance that usually kills, injures, or impairs an organism; something destructive or harmful
2 Kgs 4:40 *there's **p** in this stew!* 743
Jas 3:8 *and evil, full of deadly **p.*** 1550

POISONOUS (adj) destructive, harmful; venomous
Mark 16:18 ***p,** it won't hurt them.* 1498

POLISHED (adj) smooth or glossy; burnished
Dan 10:6 *feet shone like **p** bronze,* 1158
Rev 1:15 *feet were like **p** bronze refined* ...1800
Rev 2:18 *feet are like **p** bronze:* 1804

POLLUTE, POLLUTES, POLLUTING (v) to make ceremonially, physically, or morally impure
Num 35:33 *for murder **p-s** the land.* 283
Prov 25:26 *it's like **p-ing** a fountain* 840
Isa 41:24 *who choose you **p** themselves.* 926

POMEGRANATES (n) red fruit about the size of an orange with a thick, leathery skin and many tartish seeds
Exod 28:33 *Make **p** out of blue, purple,* 179
Song 4:3 *Your cheeks are like rosy **p*** 666

PONDER, PONDERED (v) to think or consider especially quietly, soberly, and deeply
see also MEDITATE
Ps 111:2 *delight in him should **p*** 873
Ps 119:59 *I **p-ed** the direction of my life,* 879
Ps 143:5 *I **p** all your great works* 588

POOR (adj) characterized by poverty or insufficient resources; humble
Deut 15:4 *should be no **p** among you,* 305
Deut 15:11 *some in the land who are **p.*** 305
Deut 24:12 *If your neighbor is **p*** 314
1 Sam 2:7 *The Lord makes some **p.*** 418
Prov 10:4 *Lazy people are soon **p;*** 642
Prov 13:7 *Some who are **p** pretend* 646
Mark 12:42 *Then a **p** widow came and* 1445
2 Cor 8:9 *for your sakes he became **p,*** 1636
Jas 2:2 *another comes in who is **p*** 1548

POOR (n) those characterized by poverty or insufficient resources
Lev 19:10 *Leave them for the **p.*** 225
Job 5:16 *at last the **p** have hope,* 99
Ps 35:10 *protects the helpless and **p*** 565
Ps 41:1 *those who are kind to the **p!*** 571
Ps 82:3 *Give justice to the **p** and the* 602
Prov 14:21 *those who help the **p.*** 648
Prov 17:5 *mock the **p** insult* 652
Prov 21:13 *cries of the **p** will be ignored* 658
Prov 22:2 *rich and **p** have this* 658
Prov 22:22 *Don't rob the **p** just because* 660
Prov 28:27 *Whoever gives to the **p** will* 844
Prov 31:20 *helping hand to the **p*** 848
Isa 3:14 *things stolen from the **p.*** 827
Isa 14:30 *I will feed the **p** in my pasture;* 833
Isa 32:7 *They lie to convict the **p,*** 902
Isa 61:1 *to bring good news to the **p.*** 948
Jer 22:16 *help to the **p** and needy,* 992
Amos 4:1 *who oppress the **p** and crush* 774
Amos 5:11 *trample the **p,** stealing their* 775
Zech 7:10 *foreigners, and the **p.*** 1173
Matt 11:5 *is being preached to the **p.*** 1337
Matt 19:21 *and give the money to the **p,*** ...1420
Mark 14:7 *You will always have the **p*** 1428
Luke 4:18 *to bring Good News to the **p.*** 1357
Luke 14:13 *Instead, invite the **p,** the* 1408
John 12:8 *You will always have the **p*** 1429
Rom 15:26 *an offering for the **p** among* 1672
Jas 2:6 *you dishonor the **p!*** 1548

PORTIONS (n) an often limited part set off or abstracted from a whole; share
Num 18:29 *give to the Lord the best **p*** 260

POSITION (n) social or official rank or status; job
Ps 109:8 *let someone else take his **p.*** 581
Acts 1:20 *Let someone else take his **p.*** 1513
1 Tim 3:1 *he desires an honorable **p.*** 1730

POSSESS, POSSESSED (v) to seize, gain, or take (control of); to own
see also INHERIT
Ps 37:11 *The lowly will **p** the land* 567
Ps 37:29 *The godly will **p** the land* 568
John 7:20 *You're demon **p-ed!*** 1388
John 8:48 *you were **p-ed** by a demon?* 1393
John 8:52 *you are **p-ed** by a demon.* 1393
John 10:20 *He's demon **p-ed** and out* 1406
John 10:21 *like a man **p-ed** by a demon!* .1406
Phil 3:12 *press on to **p** that perfection* 1723

POSSESSION, POSSESSIONS (n) something owned, occupied, or controlled
see also INHERITANCE, RICHES, TREASURE(S), WEALTH
Exod 6:8 *as your very own **p.*** 148
Deut 4:20 *and his special **p,*** 290
Deut 32:9 *is his special **p.*** 324
Zech 2:12 *the Lord's special **p*** 1167
Matt 19:21 *sell all your **p-s** and* 1420
Mark 10:22 *for he had many **p-s.*** 1421
1 Pet 2:9 *God's very own **p.*** 1751

POSSIBLE (adj) being within the limits of ability, capacity, or realization
Matt 19:26 *with God everything is **p.*** 1420
Matt 26:39 ***p,** let this cup of suffering* 1468
Mark 9:23 *Anything is **p** if a person* 1381
Mark 10:27 *Everything is **p** with God.* 1421
Mark 14:35 *if it were **p,** the awful hour* 1468
Heb 10:4 *it is not **p** for the blood* 1774

POTTER (n) one who makes pottery
Isa 29:16 ***p** who made me is stupid"?* 898
Isa 64:8 *the clay, and you are the **p.*** 951
Zech 11:13 *threw them to the **p*** 1177
Matt 27:7 *to buy the **p's** field,* 1476
Rom 9:21 *a **p** makes jars out of clay,* 1662

POUR, POURED, POURING, POURS (v) to move or come continuously; to supply or produce freely
Ps 42:8 *Lord **p-s** his unfailing love* 849
Ps 45:7 ***p-ing** out the oil of joy on* 851
Isa 32:15 *Spirit is **p-ed** out on us* 902
Isa 44:3 *I will **p** out my Spirit* 929
Ezek 39:29 *I will **p** out my Spirit* 1116
Joel 2:28 *I will **p** out my Spirit* 1242
Zech 12:10 *I will **p** out a spirit of* 1178
Mal 3:10 *I will **p** out a blessing* 1248
Luke 22:20 *blood, which is **p-ed** out* 1458
Acts 2:17 *I will **p** out my Spirit* 1514
Acts 2:33 *the Holy Spirit to **p** out* 1516
Acts 10:45 *Holy Spirit had been **p-ed*** 1534
Eph 1:6 *grace he has **p-ed** out on us* 1705
Phil 2:17 ***p-ing** it out like a liquid* 1720
Titus 3:6 *generously **p-ed** out the Spirit* 1739

POVERTY (n) the state of one who lacks money or material possessions
Prov 6:11 ***p** will pounce on you like* 638
Prov 13:18 *end in **p** and disgrace;* 646
Prov 21:5 *hasty shortcuts lead to **p.*** 657
Prov 24:34 ***p** will pounce on you like* 663
Prov 31:7 *drink to forget their **p*** 847
2 Cor 8:9 *by his **p** he could make you* 1636
Rev 2:9 *your suffering and your **p**—* 1803

POWER, POWERS (n) ability to act or produce an effect; possession of control, authority, or influence over others; physical might; mental or moral efficacy; a controlling group
see also STRENGTH
Exod 15:6 *Lord, is glorious in **p.*** 161
Deut 8:18 *one who gives you **p** to be* 297
Ps 89:7 *angelic **p-s** stand in awe* 591
Isa 40:26 *great **p** and incomparable* 924
Jer 9:23 *the powerful boast in their **p,*** 1012
Mic 3:8 *I am filled with **p**—* 907
Matt 16:18 *all the **p-s** of hell will not* 1375

Matt 22:29 *don't know the **p** of God.* 1440
Luke 1:35 *the **p** of the Most High will*........1274
Luke 4:14 *the Holy Spirit's **p**.*....................1306
Luke 9:1 *gave them **p** and authority*............1359
Luke 10:19 *over all the **p** of the enemy,* 1395
Luke 11:20 *demons by the **p** of God,*........1342
Acts 1:8 *receive **p** when the Holy Spirit*.....1500
Rom 1:16 *the **p** of God at work,*...................1646
Rom 1:20 *his eternal **p** and divine*...............1647
Rom 6:9 *Death no longer has any **p** over*...1656
Rom 7:23 *another **p** within me that is*.......1658
Rom 8:38 *not even the **p-s** of hell can*......1661
Rom 15:13 *the **p** of the Holy Spirit*............1671
1 Cor 1:18 *is the very **p** of God*.................1596
1 Cor 6:14 *from the dead by his **p**,*............1604
1 Cor 15:24 *ruler and authority and **p**.*......1621
2 Cor 4:7 *our great **p** is from God,*............1631
2 Cor 13:4 *now lives by the **p** of God.*........1643
Eph 6:10 *Lord and in his mighty **p**.*...........1715
Phil 3:10 *and experience the mighty **p***.......1722
Col 1:11 *with all his glorious **p***..................1694
Col 1:29 *on Christ's mighty **p***......................1697
1 Thes 1:5 *words but also with **p**,*...............1581
2 Tim 1:7 *but of **p**, love, and*......................1741
2 Tim 3:5 *reject the **p** that could make*.......1744
Heb 2:14 *break the **p** of the devil,*...............1764
Jas 5:16 *righteous person has great **p***.......1554
1 Pet 1:5 *is protecting you by his **p***...........1748
1 Pet 3:22 ***p-s** accept his authority*...........1754
1 Pet 4:11 *All glory and **p** to him*..............1755
2 Pet 1:3 ***p**, God has given us everything*..1757
Jude 1:25 ***p**, and authority are his*............1786
Rev 4:11 *receive glory and honor and **p**.*...1809
Rev 5:12 *receive **p** and riches and*............1810
Rev 19:1 *glory and **p** belong to our God.* ...1827
Rev 20:6 *the second death holds no **p**,* 1829

POWERFUL (adj) having great power, prestige, or influence
Exod 6:6 *will redeem you with a **p** arm*........148
Deut 5:15 *strong hand and **p** arm*...............293
Job 25:2 *God is **p** and dreadful.* 117
Ps 29:4 *the LORD is **p**;*..................................562
Ps 136:12 *strong hand and **p** arm*..............886
Jer 9:23 *the **p** boast in their power,* 1012
Jer 27:5 *my great strength and **p** arm* 1049
Luke 24:19 *who did **p** miracles,*....................1493
1 Cor 1:27 *to shame those who are **p**.*........1597

POWERLESS (adj) devoid of strength or resources; lacking the authority or capacity to act
Num 24:13 *would be **p** to do anything*........268
1 Cor 1:27 *things that are **p** to shame* 1597

PRACTICE, PRACTICING (v) to do or perform often, habitually, or customarily; to carry out, apply
Lev 19:26 *Do not **p** fortune-telling*..............226
Matt 23:3 *they don't **p** what they teach*.....1407
Rom 12:13 *eager to **p** hospitality.* 1667
Phil 4:9 *putting into **p** all you learned*........1725
1 Jn 1:6 *we are not **p-ing** the truth.* 1787
1 Jn 5:18 *not make a **p** of sinning,* 1795

PRAISE, PRAISES (n) worship; commendation; value, merit
Deut 26:19 ***p**, honor, and renown.* 316
2 Sam 22:4 *LORD, who is worthy of **p**,*..........526
2 Chr 29:30 *So they offered joyous **p***..........836
Ps 7:17 *I will sing **p** to the name* 524
Ps 18:49 *I will sing **p-s** to your name*..........529
Ps 34:1 *will constantly speak his **p-s**.*..........458
Ps 65:1 *What mighty **p**, O God,* 575
Ps 81:1 *Sing **p-s** to God,* 602
Ps 100:4 *into his courts with **p**.*...................866
Ps 108:1 *your **p-s** with all my heart!*............581
Ps 145:3 *He is most worthy of **p**!* 589
Ps 149:6 *Let the **p-s** of God be in* 887
John 12:43 *loved human **p** more than* 1435
Rom 2:29 *heart seeks **p** from God,* 1650
Rom 15:9 *will sing **p-s** to your name.* 1671
1 Thes 2:6 *As for human **p**,*.........................1582
2 Thes 1:10 *his holy people—**p** from all*...1588
Jas 5:13 *You should sing **p-s**.*....................1553

PRAISE, PRAISED, PRAISES, PRAISING (v) to worship, commend, or give honor to
Exod 15:2 *and I will **p** him—*..........................161
1 Chr 16:35 *name and rejoice and **p** you.* ...493
2 Chr 5:13 *together in unison to **p** and* 618
2 Chr 20:21 ***p-ing** him for his holy*.............732
Neh 9:5 *Stand up and **p** the LORD* 1215
Ps 9:1 *I will **p** you, LORD,* 549
Ps 12:8 *evil is **p-d** throughout the land.* 551
Ps 34:1 *I will **p** the LORD*..............................458
Ps 42:5 *I will **p** him again—*..........................848
Ps 45:17 *nations will **p** you forever*.............851
Ps 51:15 *my mouth may **p** you*.....................506
Ps 63:3 *how I **p** you!*.....................................517
Ps 71:8 *I can never stop **p-ing** you;* 860
Ps 71:14 *I will **p** you more and*......................860
Ps 74:21 *and needy **p** your name.*..............595
Ps 89:5 *angels will **p** you for your*..............591
Ps 96:2 *LORD; **p** his name.* 864
Ps 102:18 *not yet born will **p** the*...............866
Ps 104:1 *all that I am **p** the*..........................867
Ps 115:18 *But we can **p** the LORD*...............875
Ps 135:20 *LORD, **p** the LORD!* 885
Ps 144:1 ***P** the LORD, who is*........................589
Ps 148:13 *Let them all **p** the name*.............887
Ps 150:2 ***p** his unequaled greatness!*..........888
Prov 27:2 *Let someone else **p** you,*..............842
Prov 27:21 *person is tested by being **p-d**.* 842
Isa 63:7 *I will **p** the LORD*............................949
Dan 2:19 *Daniel **p-d** the God of heaven.*....1003
Dan 2:20 *He said, "**P** the name* 1003
Dan 4:34 ***p-d** and worshiped the Most* 1121
Matt 5:16 *will **p** your heavenly Father*........1327
Mark 11:9 *were shouting, "**P** God!* 1430
Luke 1:46 *how my soul **p-s** the Lord.* 1275
Luke 2:13 *armies of heaven—**p-ing** God*...1281
Luke 2:20 *glorifying and **p-ing** God for*.....1281
Luke 18:43 *all who saw it **p-d** God, too*.....1426
Luke 19:37 ***p-ing** God for all the wonderful*..1430
Acts 2:47 *and all the while **p-ing** God*............1516
Acts 10:46 *in other tongues and **p-ing** God*...1534
1 Cor 14:16 *if you **p** God only in*...............1617
Gal 1:24 *they **p-d** God because of me.* 1558
Eph 1:6 *we **p** God for the glorious*.............1705
Jas 3:9 *Sometimes it **p-s** our Lord* 1550
Rev 19:1 *heaven shouting, "**P** the LORD!* 1827

PRAY, PRAYED, PRAYING, PRAYS (v) to address God with adoration, confession, supplication, or thanksgiving; to intercede
Gen 24:45 *I had finished **p-ing** in my*..........49
1 Sam 1:12 *she was **p-ing** to the LORD,*.......417
2 Chr 7:14 *humble themselves and **p** and*...623
2 Chr 30:18 *King Hezekiah **p-ed** for*.........837
Neh 4:9 *we **p-ed** to our God and*..............1208
Job 42:8 *servant Job will **p** for you,*............132
Job 42:10 *When Job **p-ed** for his friends,*...132
Ps 5:2 *I **p** to no one but you.* 547
Ps 32:6 *all the godly **p** to you*......................565
Ps 34:6 *In my desperation I **p-ed**,* 458
Dan 6:10 *He **p-ed** three times a day,*........1140
Dan 9:4 *I **p-ed** to the LORD*.........................1142
Jonah 2:1 *Jonah **p-ed** to the LORD*...............767
Matt 6:5 *When you **p**, don't be like*...........1331
Matt 6:9 ***P** like this: Our Father in* 1331
Matt 26:39 *face to the ground, **p-ing**,* 1468
Mark 11:24 *you can **p** for anything,* 1436
Mark 11:25 *when you are **p-ing**, first*.......1436
Luke 3:21 ***p-ing**, the heavens opened,*.....1294
Luke 9:29 *he was **p-ing**, the appearance*...1380
Luke 11:1 *teach us to **p**, just as John*.......1342
Luke 22:41 *and knelt down and **p-ed**,*......1469
John 17:20 *I am **p-ing** not only for these*....1467
Acts 6:6 *apostles, who **p-ed** for them*.......1523
Acts 9:11 *He is **p-ing** to me right now.*.....1530
Acts 16:25 *Paul and Silas were **p-ing*** 1576
Rom 8:26 *the Holy Spirit **p-s** for us* 1660
Rom 12:12 *and keep on **p-ing**.*..................1667
Rom 15:30 *join in my struggle by **p-ing*** ...1672
1 Cor 14:14 *For if I **p** in tongues,*..............1617
1 Cor 14:14 *my spirit is **p-ing**,*....................1617
2 Cor 13:9 *We **p** that you will become* 1643
Eph 1:18 *I **p** that your hearts will be*..........1706
Eph 3:16 *I **p** that from his glorious,*...........1709
Phil 4:6 *instead, **p** about everything*..........1724
1 Thes 1:3 *As we **p** to our God and*...........1580
1 Thes 5:17 *Never stop **p-ing**.*...................1586
2 Thes 1:11 *we keep on **p-ing** for you,*.....1588
1 Tim 2:8 *to **p** with holy hands* 1729
Jas 5:13 *You should **p**.* 1553
Jas 5:16 ***p** for each other so that*..............1554
Jude 1:20 ***p** in the power of the Holy* 1785

PRAYER, PRAYERS (n) conversation with God—in praise, thanksgiving, or intercession
2 Chr 30:27 *God heard their **p** from*............837
Ps 4:1 *mercy on me and hear my **p**.* 547
Ps 17:1 *Pay attention to my **p**,* 553
Ps 20:5 *LORD answer all your **p-s**.* 555
Ps 86:6 *Listen closely to my **p**,*....................579
Prov 15:8 *in the **p-s** of the upright*..............648
Isa 1:15 *Though you offer many **p-s**,* 824
Isa 56:7 *will be called a house of **p***.............943
Matt 11:25 *Jesus prayed this **p**:*.................1339
John 17:9 *My **p** is not for the world,* 1467
Acts 1:14 *were constantly united in **p**,* 1512
Acts 4:31 *After this **p**, the meeting* 1520
Acts 6:4 *can spend our time in **p***...............1522
Acts 10:31 *your **p** has been heard,*...........1534
Acts 13:3 *So after more fasting and **p**,*......1540
Eph 6:18 *persistent in your **p-s** for all*.......1715
Col 4:2 *Devote yourselves to **p** with an*......1702
1 Pet 3:7 *your **p-s** will not be hindered.* 1753
1 Pet 3:12 *ears are open to their **p-s**.*........1753
Rev 5:8 *are the **p-s** of God's people*..........1810

PREACH, PREACHED, PREACHES, PREACHING (v) to deliver a sermon; to exhort an idea or course of action
see also PROCLAIM, TEACH
Luke 9:6 ***p-ing** the Good News and*..........1359
Luke 9:60 *go and **p** about the Kingdom* 1388
Acts 5:42 *teach and **p** this message:*........1522
Acts 9:20 *he began **p-ing** about Jesus*.....1530
Acts 16:10 *to **p** the Good News*................1573
Acts 18:5 *all his time **p-ing** the word*........1580
Rom 1:15 *to **p** the Good News*....................1646
1 Cor 2:4 *my message and my **p-ing***.......1598
1 Cor 9:27 *I fear that after **p-ing** to*..........1609
1 Cor 15:1 *Good News I **p-ed** to you* 1618
2 Cor 4:5 *We **p** that Jesus Christ is Lord,*..1630
2 Cor 11:4 *Jesus than the one we **p**,*........1640
Gal 1:8 ***p-es** a different kind of Good*........1556

Gal 1:8 *than the one we **p-ed** to you*.........1556
Gal 1:9 ***p-es** any other Good News*...........1556
Gal 5:11 *no longer **p-ing** salvation*...........1565
Phil 1:18 *Christ is being **p-ed** either way,*..1718
Col 1:23 *Good News has been **p-ed** all*.....1696
1 Tim 5:17 *work hard at both **p-ing** and*...1734
2 Tim 4:17 *might **p** the Good News*..........1746
1 Pet 1:25 *Good News that was **p-ed** to*...1750
1 Pet 3:19 *went and **p-ed** to the spirits*....1754

PREACHER (n) one who delivers sermons or proclaims the gospel
1 Tim 2:7 *chosen as a **p** and apostle*........1729
2 Tim 1:11 *God chose me to be a **p,***.........1741

PRECEPT(S) (KJV)
Ps 119:15 *study your **commandments***......878
Ps 119:159 *I love your **commandments,***...881
Mark 10:5 *this **commandment** only as a*..1419
Heb 9:19 *each of God's **commandments***..1773

PRECIOUS (adj) of great value or high price; highly esteemed or cherished
Prov 31:10 *She is more **p** than rubies*.........847
Isa 28:16 *It is a **p** cornerstone*....................819
1 Pet 1:19 *was the **p** blood of Christ,*........1749
2 Pet 1:4 *great and **p** promises*...............1757

PREDICTED (v) to declare or indicate in advance; to foretell
Isa 43:12 *First I **p** your rescue,*...................928
John 12:38 *the prophet had **p:***.................1434
Acts 7:52 ***p** the coming of*........................1526

PREDICTIONS (n) something that is predicted; forecast
Isa 44:26 *I carry out the **p** of my*.................931
Jer 28:9 *Only when his **p** come true*.........1050

PREGNANCY (n) the condition of being pregnant
Gen 3:16 *sharpen the pain of your **p,***............13

PREGNANT (adj) containing a developing unborn offspring within the body
Gen 11:30 *was unable to become **p***.............24
Matt 24:19 *How terrible it will be for **p***......1446
1 Thes 5:3 *as a **p** woman's labor*.............1585

PREPARE, PREPARED (v) to make ready beforehand for some purpose, use, or activity; to get ready
Exod 23:20 *to the place I have **p-d** for*........174
Ps 23:5 *You **p** a feast for me*......................558
Zeph 1:7 *LORD has **p-d** his people*.............983
Mal 3:1 *he will **p** the way before me*. 1247
Matt 3:3 *'**P** the way for the Lord's*.............1287
Matt 25:34 *inherit the Kingdom **p-d***.........1453
John 14:2 *I am going to **p** a place*...........1461
1 Cor 2:9 *has **p-d** for those who love*.......1598
2 Cor 5:5 *God himself has **p-d** us for*......1632
2 Tim 4:2 *the word of God. Be **p-d,***..........1745

PRESBYTERY (KJV)
1 Tim 4:14 ***elders of the church** laid their hands*...1732

PRESENCE (n) company; nearness; (symbolic of) God-with-us
Exod 25:30 *Bread of the **P** on the table*.......176
1 Sam 6:20 *in the **p** of the LORD,*...............427
Ps 15:1 *enter your **p** on your holy hill?*........552
Ps 21:6 *given him the joy of your **p.***............555
Ps 23:5 *in the **p** of my enemies*.................558
Ps 31:20 *in the shelter of your **p,***...............564
Ps 89:15 *walk in the light of your **p,***............591
Ps 114:7 *at the **p** of the God of Jacob*.........874
Ps 139:7 *never get away from your **p!***........586
Isa 53:2 *grew up in the LORD's **p***................940
Jer 5:22 *tremble in my **p?***.........................967
Matt 18:10 *always in the **p** of my heavenly*...1384
1 Thes 3:9 *joy as we enter God's **p.***..........1584

PRESENT (adj) being in view or at hand; now existing or in progress
Lev 16:2 *I myself am **p** in the cloud*............221
1 Cor 7:26 *Because of the **p** crisis,*...........1606

PRESENT, PRESENTED, PRESENTING (v) to give or bestow formally
Gen 28:22 *I will **p** to God a tenth*.................58
Matt 5:23 *you are **p-ing** a sacrifice*..........1328
Rom 3:25 ***p-ed** Jesus as the sacrifice*......1651
Rom 15:19 *fully **p-ed** the Good News*.......1671
Eph 5:27 *did this to **p** her to himself*.........1714
2 Tim 2:15 *Work hard so you can **p***..........1743

PRESERVE, PRESERVES (v) to keep safe from injury, harm, or destruction
see also SAVE
Gen 45:5 *ahead of you to **p** your lives*. 86
Deut 33:12 ***p-s** them from every harm*. 327
1 Kgs 19:18 *I will **p** 7,000 others*..............720
Jer 10:12 *he **p-s** it by his wisdom*. 1013

PRESS (v) to follow through (a course of action)
Phil 3:12 *I **p** on to possess that*...............1723
Phil 3:14 *I **p** on to reach the end*..............1723

PRESSURE (n) the burden of physical or mental distress
Prov 24:10 ***p,** your strength is too small*......662

PRETEND, PRETENDED (v) to give a false appearance of being, possessing, or performing
1 Sam 21:13 *So he **p-ed** to be insane,*.......457
Zech 13:4 *No one will **p** to be a prophet*....1179
Rom 12:9 *Don't just **p** to love*..................1667

PRETENSE (n) professed rather than real intention or purpose
Amos 5:21 *I hate all your show and **p**—*.......776

PREVAIL, PREVAILS (v) to triumph
Prov 19:21 *LORD's purpose will **p.***..............655
Isa 42:4 *lose heart until justice **p-s***............926

PRICE (n) the quantity of one thing that is exchanged or demanded in barter or sale for another
Job 28:18 ***p** of wisdom is far above*............119
1 Cor 6:20 *bought you with a high **p.***........1604

PRIDE (n) inordinate self-esteem or conceit; disdainful behavior or treatment of others
Ps 101:5 *will not endure conceit and **p.***......580
Prov 6:3 *Now swallow your **p;***....................638
Prov 8:13 *I hate **p** and arrogance,*..............640
Mark 7:22 *envy, slander, **p,** and*................1371
1 Jn 2:16 ***p** in our achievements and*........1789

PRIEST, PRIESTS (n) one authorized to perform the sacred rites of sacrifice and worship; a mediator between God and humans
Exod 19:6 *will be my kingdom of **p-s,***.........168
Ps 110:4 *You are a **p** forever*.......................582
Mal 1:6 *Armies says to the **p-s:***...............1245
Heb 4:14 *since we have a great High **P***.....1766
Heb 5:6 *You are a **p** forever*......................1767
Heb 6:20 *our eternal High **P***.......................1770
Heb 8:1 *a High **P** who sat down*................1771
1 Pet 2:5 *you are his holy **p-s.***..................1750
1 Pet 2:9 *You are royal **p-s,***......................1751
Rev 5:10 *Kingdom of **p-s** for our God*. 1810
Rev 20:6 *but they will be **p-s** of God*.........1829

PRIESTHOOD (n) the office, dignity, or character of a priest
Heb 7:24 *his **p** lasts forever*.......................1771

PRINCE, PRINCES (n) a son of a king; the ruler of a principality or state; a man of high rank or high standing in his class or profession
Ps 118:9 *LORD than to trust in **p-s.***.............876
Prov 25:15 *Patience can persuade a **p,***.......840
Isa 9:6 *Everlasting Father, **P** of Peace*..........793
Ezek 34:24 *David will be a **p** among*.........1110
Dan 8:25 *take on the **P** of **p-s***.................1138
Matt 10:25 *called the **p** of demons,*..........1360
Luke 11:15 *the **p** of demons*. 1342
Acts 5:31 *at his right hand as **P** and*.........1521

PRINCESS (n) the daughter of a king; a woman having sovereign power
Ps 45:13 *The bride, a **p,** looks glorious*.......851

PRINCIPLE, PRINCIPLES (n) a comprehensive and fundamental law, doctrine, or assumption
Gal 4:9 *spiritual **p-s** of this world?*...........1563
Gal 6:16 *all who live by this **p;***.................1568

PRISON, PRISONS (n) a state of confinement or captivity; jail
Ps 142:7 *Bring me out of **p***.........................460
Isa 42:7 *will free the captives from **p,***.........927
Matt 25:36 *I was in **p,** and you visited*......1453
2 Cor 11:23 *been put in **p** more often,*......1641
Heb 11:36 *were chained in **p-s.***...............1779
Heb 13:3 *Remember those in **p,***...............1782
1 Pet 3:19 *preached to the spirits in **p**—*..1754
Jude 1:6 *chained in **p-s** of darkness,*.........1784
Rev 20:7 *Satan will be let out of his **p.***......1829

PRISONER, PRISONERS (n) a person deprived of liberty and kept under involuntary restraint, confinement, or custody
Ps 79:11 *to the moaning of the **p-s.***...........600
Ps 146:7 *The LORD frees the **p-s.***...............887
Zech 9:12 *you **p-s** who still have hope!*....1175
Gal 3:22 *we are all **p-s** of sin,*.................1562
Eph 3:1 *I, Paul, a **p** of Christ Jesus*...........1708

PRIVATE, PRIVATELY (adj) secret, not to be seen by others
Matt 6:4 *Give your gifts in **p,** and*.............1331
Matt 6:6 *and pray to your Father in **p.***.......1331
Matt 18:15 *go **p-ly** and point out the*........1385
1 Cor 4:5 *and will reveal our **p** motives*. 1600

PRIVILEGE (n) a right or immunity held as a peculiar benefit, advantage, or favor
Prov 25:2 *God's **p** to conceal things*.........839
Rom 5:2 *into this place of undeserved **p***...1654
2 Cor 8:4 *for the **p** of sharing in*...............1636

PRIZE (n) something offered or striven for in competitions or in contests
1 Cor 9:24 *one person gets the **p?***..........1609
1 Cor 9:25 *we do it for an eternal **p.***.........1609
Phil 3:14 *heavenly **p** for which God,*.........1723
2 Tim 2:5 *cannot win the **p** unless*............1742
2 Tim 4:8 ***p** awaits me—the crown*...........1746

PRIZE (v) to value highly, esteem
Prov 4:8 *If you **p** wisdom,*...........................636

PROBLEMS (n) sources of perplexity, distress, or vexation
Matt 13:21 *as soon as they have **p***...........1345
Rom 5:3 *we run into **p** and trials,*..............1654

PROCESSION (n) a group of individuals moving along in an orderly often and ceremonial way
Ps 68:24 *O God—the **p** of my God*.............577
2 Cor 2:14 *in Christ's triumphal **p.***............1628

PROCLAIM, PROCLAIMING, PROCLAIMS (v) to declare publicly
see also PREACH
Lev 25:10 *a time to **p** freedom*..........232
Deut 32:3 *I will **p** the name of*..........323
1 Chr 16:8 *and **p** his greatness.*..........493
Ps 2:7 *king **p-s** the LORD's decree:*..........857
Ps 50:6 *heavens **p** his justice,*..........593
Ps 97:6 *heavens **p** his righteousness;*..........864
Ps 145:4 *let them **p** your power.*..........589
Isa 61:1 *to **p** that captives will be*..........948
Acts 28:31 ***p-ing** the Kingdom of God*..........1690
Col 1:25 ***p-ing** his entire message to you.*..........1696
1 Thes 3:2 *in **p-ing** the Good News*..........1583
Titus 1:1 *I have been sent to **p** faith*..........1736
1 Jn 1:1 ***p** to you the one who existed*..........1786

PRODUCE, PRODUCES (v) to yield, make, or manufacture
Prov 3:9 *best part of everything you **p.***..........635
Isa 55:11 *and it always **p-s** fruit.*..........942
Matt 7:18 *good tree can't **p** bad fruit,*..........1334
Luke 3:9 *tree that does not **p** good fruit*..........1291
John 15:8 *When you **p** much fruit,*..........1464
John 15:16 *to go and **p** lasting fruit,*..........1464
Rom 7:4 ***p** a harvest of good deeds*..........1657
Eph 5:9 *light within you **p-s** only what*..........1712
Col 1:10 *lives will **p** every kind of good*..........1694
Jas 2:17 *Unless it **p-s** good deeds, it is*..........1549

PRODUCTIVE (adj) yielding results, benefits, or profits
2 Pet 1:8 *the more **p** and useful you will*..........1757

PROFANING (v) to treat (something sacred) with abuse, irreverence, or contempt
Neh 13:17 *Why are you **p** the Sabbath*..........1223

PROFESSIONAL (adj) of, relating to, or characteristic of a profession
Amos 7:14 *I'm not a **p** prophet,*..........778

PROFIT (n) gain, benefit, or usefulness
Prov 14:23 *Work brings **p,** but*..........648
2 Cor 2:17 *who preach for personal **p.***..........1629

PROFITABLE (adj) yielding advantageous returns or results
Prov 31:18 *her dealings are **p;***..........847

PROGRESS (n) a forward or onward movement (as to an objective or goal)
Phil 3:16 *hold on to the **p** we have.*..........1723
1 Tim 4:15 *everyone will see your **p.***..........1733

PROLONG (v) to lengthen in time, extent, scope, or range
Ps 85:5 *Will you **p** your wrath to all*..........855

PROMISCUITY (n) sexual excesses
see also IMMORALITY
Rom 13:13 ***p** and immoral living,*..........1669

PROMISCUOUS (adj) not restricted to one sexual partner
Prov 23:27 *a **p** woman is as dangerous*..........661

PROMISE, PROMISES (n) a declaration that one will do or refrain from doing something specified
see also COVENANT, VOW
2 Sam 7:25 *a **p** that will last forever.*..........497
Neh 5:13 *If you fail to keep your **p,***..........1210
Ps 91:4 *faithful **p-s** are your armor.*..........861
Ps 116:14 *keep my **p-s** to the LORD.*..........875
Ps 145:13 *LORD always keeps his **p-s;***..........590
Ps 146:6 *He keeps every **p** forever.*..........887
Rom 4:20 *in believing God's **p.***..........1653
Rom 9:4 *receiving his wonderful **p-s.***..........1661
Rom 15:4 *patiently for God's **p-s** to be*..........1671
2 Cor 1:20 ***p-s** have been fulfilled*..........1627
2 Cor 7:1 *Because we have these **p-s,***..........1634
Eph 2:12 *covenant **p-s** God had made.*..........1708
Heb 6:13 *God's **p** to Abraham.*..........1768
Heb 8:6 *based on better **p-s.***..........1771
Heb 10:23 *be trusted to keep his **p.***..........1776
Heb 11:11 *that God would keep his **p.***..........1777
2 Pet 3:4 ***p** that Jesus is coming again?*..........1760
2 Pet 3:9 *being slow about his **p,***..........1760

PROMISED, PROMISES, PROMISING (v) to pledge to do, bring about, or provide
Exod 3:17 *I have **p-d** to rescue you*..........144
Deut 15:6 *bless you as he has **p-d.***..........305
Josh 23:15 *the good things he **p-d,***..........369
Luke 24:49 *as my Father **p-d.***..........1498
Acts 1:4 *sends you the gift he **p-d,***..........1499
Rom 4:21 *able to do whatever he **p-s.***..........1653
Gal 3:14 *blessing he **p-d** to Abraham,*..........1561
1 Tim 4:8 ***p-ing** benefits in this life.*..........1732
Titus 1:2 *God—who does not lie—**p-d.***..........1736
Heb 10:36 *receive all that he has **p-d.***..........1776
Jas 1:12 *of life that God has **p-d***..........1547
Jas 2:5 *inherit the Kingdom he **p-d***..........1548
2 Pet 3:13 *new earth he has **p-d,***..........1760
1 Jn 2:25 *eternal life he **p-d** us.*..........1790

PROMOTE (v) to further; to advance
Titus 2:1 ***p** the kind of living that*..........1738

PRONOUNCE (v) to declare officially or ceremoniously
1 Chr 23:13 *to **p** blessings in his name.*..........534

PROOF (n) something that induces certainty or establishes validity
John 10:25 *The **p** is the work I do*..........1406

PROPERTY (n) a piece of real estate owned or possessed
Acts 5:1 *wife, Sapphira, sold some **p.***..........1520

PROPHECY, PROPHECIES (n) the spoken or written word from God; may forthtell (consoling or corrective) and/or foretell (predicative)
Matt 13:14 *fulfills the **p** of Isaiah*..........1345
Acts 13:29 *all that the **p-ies** said about*..........1542
Acts 17:3 ***p-ies** and proved that the Messiah*..........1576
Acts 21:9 *who had the gift of **p.***..........1676
Acts 21:10 *who also had the gift of **p,***..........1676
1 Cor 13:2 *If I had the gift of **p,***..........1616
1 Cor 13:9 *gift of **p** reveals only part*..........1616
1 Cor 14:6 *knowledge or **p** or teaching,*..........1617
Rev 22:18 *words of **p** written in*..........1833

PROPHESY, PROPHESIED, PROPHESIES, PROPHESYING (v) to issue a prophecy
Num 11:25 *upon them, they **p-ied.***..........248
1 Sam 19:24 *day and all night, **p-ing** in*..........455
Isa 42:9 *Everything I **p-ied** has come true,*..........927
Joel 2:28 *sons and daughters will **p.***..........1242
Matt 7:22 *We **p-ied** in your name and*..........1334
Acts 2:17 *sons and daughters will **p.***..........1514
Acts 19:6 *in other tongues and **p-ied.***..........1593
Rom 12:6 *the ability to **p,***..........1667
1 Cor 11:4 *head while praying or **p-ing.***..........1612
1 Cor 12:10 *the ability to **p.***..........1614
1 Cor 14:1 *the ability to **p.***..........1616
1 Cor 14:3 *one who **p-ies** strengthens*..........1617
1 Cor 14:39 *be eager to **p,***..........1618

PROPHET, PROPHETS (n) an interpreter of the times and people's hearts; one who issues divinely inspired revelations
Exod 7:1 *Aaron, will be your **p.***..........149
Exod 15:20 *Miriam the **p,** Aaron's*..........162
Deut 13:1 *there are **p-s** among you*..........302
Deut 18:18 *I will raise up a **p** like you*..........308
1 Sam 9:9 ***p-s** used to be called seers.*..........436
1 Kgs 18:36 *Elijah the **p** walked up to*..........718
2 Kgs 5:8 *a true **p** here in Israel.*..........743
2 Kgs 6:12 *Elisha, the **p** in Israel,*..........745
Isa 44:26 *the predictions of my **p-s!***..........931
Hos 9:7 *you say, "The **p-s** are crazy*..........812
Amos 7:14 *I'm not a professional **p,***..........778
Hab 1:1 *that the **p** Habakkuk received*..........978
Zech 7:12 *through the earlier **p-s.***..........1173
Mal 4:5 *the **p** Elijah before the great*..........1249
Matt 5:17 *or the writings of the **p-s.***..........1327
Matt 7:12 *in the law and the **p-s.***..........1334
Matt 10:41 *the same reward as a **p.***..........1361
Matt 11:9 *Yes, and he is more than a **p.***..........1337
Matt 12:39 *sign of the **p** Jonah.*..........1343
Matt 23:37 *the city that kills the **p-s***..........1407
Matt 26:56 *fulfill the words of the **p-s.***..........1469
Luke 4:24 *no **p** is accepted in his own*..........1357
Luke 7:16 *A mighty **p** has risen*..........1337
Luke 11:49 *will send **p-s** and apostles*..........1399
Luke 24:19 ***p** who did powerful*..........1493
Luke 24:25 *all that the **p-s** wrote in*..........1494
Luke 24:44 *law of Moses and the **p-s***..........1498
John 1:21 *you the **P** we are expecting?*..........1292
Acts 7:37 *a **P** like me from among your*..........1525
Acts 10:43 *all the **p-s** testified about,*..........1534
Acts 13:1 *Among the **p-s** and teachers*..........1539
Rom 1:2 *long ago through his **p-s***..........1644
Rom 3:21 *Moses and the **p-s** long ago.*..........1651
Rom 11:3 *they have killed your **p-s***..........1664
1 Cor 12:28 *second are **p-s,** third are*..........1615
1 Cor 14:37 *If you claim to be a **p** or*..........1618
Eph 2:20 *of the apostles and the **p-s.***..........1708
Eph 3:5 *to his holy apostles and **p-s.***..........1708
Eph 4:11 *the apostles, the **p-s,** the*..........1710
1 Pet 1:10 *the **p-s** wanted to know*..........1749
2 Pet 1:19 *proclaimed by the **p-s.***..........1758
2 Pet 1:21 *those **p-s** were moved by*..........1758
2 Pet 3:2 *what the holy **p-s** said long*..........1760
Rev 11:10 *death of the two **p-s** who*..........1817
Rev 18:20 *God and apostles and **p-s!***..........1826

PROPHETIC (adj) of, relating to, or characteristic of a prophet or prophecy
Ezek 37:4 ***p** message to these bones*..........1113
Dan 9:24 *to confirm the **p** vision,*..........1143
1 Tim 1:18 *based on the **p** words*..........1728

PROPITIATION (KJV)
Rom 3:25 *Jesus as the **sacrifice** for sin*..........1651
1 Jn 2:2 *the **sacrifice that atones***..........1788
1 Jn 4:10 ***sacrifice to take away** our sins*..........1793

PROSELYTE(S) (KJV)
Matt 23:15 *and sea to make one **convert***..........1444
Acts 2:11 *Jews and **converts to Judaism***..........1514
Acts 6:5 ***convert to the Jewish faith***..........1522
Acts 13:43 *devout converts **to Judaism***..........1542

PROSPER, PROSPERS (v) to achieve economic success; to become strong and flourishing
Deut 28:63 *pleasure in causing you to **p***..........319
Ps 37:3 *safely in the land and **p.***..........567
Ps 73:3 ***p** despite their wickedness.*..........594
Prov 16:20 *listen to instruction will **p;***..........651
Prov 17:9 *Love **p-s** when a fault is forgiven,*..........652
Prov 19:8 *cherish understanding will **p.***..........654
Isa 53:10 *LORD's good plan will **p.***..........940

Isa 55:11 *it will **p** everywhere I send it.* 942
Dan 4:27 *then you will continue to **p**.* 1121

PROSPERITY (n) the condition of being successful or thriving
Gen 41:29 *will be a period of great **p*** 80
Deut 28:11 *LORD will give you **p*** 318
Deut 30:15 *life and death, between **p*** 321
1 Sam 25:6 *Peace and **p** to you,* 465
Ps 41:2 *He gives them **p** in the land* 571
Prov 21:5 *and hard work lead to **p**,* 657
Prov 28:25 *trusting the LORD leads to **p**.* 844
Jer 33:6 *give it **p** and true peace.* 1081
Mic 4:4 *will live in peace and **p**,* 907

PROSPEROUS (adj) marked by success or economic well-being; flourishing
Deut 5:33 *live long and **p** lives* 294
Ps 30:6 *When I was **p**, I said,* 563
Ps 34:12 *a life that is long and **p**?* 459
Ps 128:2 *How joyful and **p** you will be!* 883
Ps 132:15 *bless this city and make it **p**;* 884
Jer 12:1 *Why are the wicked so **p**?* 1015

PROSTITUTE, PROSTITUTES (n) a person who engages in promiscuous sexual relations, especially for money
Josh 6:17 *Rahab the **p** and* 344
Prov 6:26 *a **p** will bring you to poverty,* 639
Prov 29:3 *hangs around with **p-s**,* 844
Ezek 16:15 *as a **p** to every man* 1061
Ezek 23:3 *They became **p-s** in Egypt.* 1070
Matt 21:31 ***p-s** will get into the* 1437
Luke 15:30 *your money on **p-s**,* 1411
1 Cor 6:16 *if a man joins himself to a **p**,* ...1604
Rev 17:1 *going to come on the great **p**,* 1824

PROSTITUTING (v) to devote to corrupt or unworthy purposes
Ezek 20:30 ***p** yourselves by worshiping* 1066

PROSTITUTION (n) the act or practice of engaging in promiscuous sexual relations especially for money
Lev 20:6 *who commit spiritual **p** by* 226
Hos 3:3 *days and stop your **p**.* 804

PROTECT, PROTECTED, PROTECTING, PROTECTS (v) to cover or shield from exposure, injury, damage, or destruction; to defend
see also KEEP
Gen 15:1 *for I will **p** you,* 34
Num 6:24 *bless you and **p** you.* 245
Josh 6:17 *for she **p-ed** our spies.* 344
1 Sam 2:9 *He will **p** his faithful ones,* 419
Ps 23:4 *your staff **p** and comfort me.* 558
Ps 27:1 *fortress, **p-ing** me from danger,* 561
Ps 41:2 *LORD **p-s** them and keeps* 571
Ps 116:6 *LORD **p-s** those of childlike* 875
Ps 127:1 *Unless the LORD **p-s** a city,* 631
Ps 145:20 *LORD **p-s** all those who love* 590
Ps 146:9 *LORD **p-s** the foreigners* 887
Prov 2:8 ***p-s** those who are faithful* 633
Isa 31:5 *like a bird **p-ing** its nest* 901
Isa 57:1 *God is **p-ing** them from the* 943
John 17:11 *now **p** them by the power of* ...1467
Acts 26:22 *But God has **p-ed** me* 1685
Gal 3:24 ***p-ed** us until we could be* 1562
1 Pet 1:5 *God is **p-ing** you by his power* ...1748
Rev 3:10 *I will **p** you from the great* 1807

PROTECTION (n) the act of protecting; the state of being protected
see also REFUGE
2 Sam 22:3 *my rock, in whom I find **p**.* 526
2 Sam 22:31 *look to him for **p**.* 527
Ps 5:11 *Spread your **p** over them,* 548
Ps 31:2 *Be my rock of **p**,* 563
Ps 71:1 *I have come to you for **p**;* 860
Ps 91:4 *promises are your armor and **p**.* 861
Prov 19:23 *security and **p** from harm.* 655

PROTECTIVE (adj) of or relating to protection or defense
Ezra 9:9 *He has given us a **p** wall* 1200

PROUD (adj) having or displaying excessive self-esteem
Ps 5:5 ***p** may not stand in your* 547
Prov 21:4 *Haughty eyes, a **p** heart,* 657
Rom 1:30 *haters of God, insolent, **p**,* 1648
1 Cor 13:4 *not jealous or boastful or **p*** 1616
1 Tim 3:6 *he might become **p**,* 1730
1 Tim 6:17 *rich in this world not to be **p*** 1735
2 Tim 3:2 *They will be boastful and **p**,* 1744

PROUD (n) those having or displaying excessive self-esteem
Prov 16:5 *LORD detests the **p**;* 651
Dan 4:37 *he is able to humble the **p**.* 1121
Jas 4:6 *God opposes the **p** but favors* 1551
1 Pet 5:5 *God opposes the **p** but favors* 1756

PROVE, PROVED, PROVING (v) to test or establish the truth, validity, or genuineness of
Ps 51:4 ***p-d** right in what you say,* 506
Isa 44:25 *thus **p-ing** them to be fools.* 931
John 13:35 *love for one another will **p*** 1461
Acts 1:3 *he **p-d** to them in many ways* 1512
Acts 17:3 ***p-d** that the Messiah* 1576
Acts 17:31 ***p-d** to everyone who this is* 1579
Acts 26:20 ***p** they have changed by* 1685
Rom 3:4 ***p-d** right in what you say,* 1650

PROVIDE, PROVIDED, PROVIDES (v) to furnish or supply, implying foresight in making provision for the future
Gen 22:8 *God will **p** a sheep* 45
Gen 22:14 *means "the LORD will **p**"* 46
Ps 68:10 *O God, you **p-d** for your needy* 576
Isa 4:5 *the LORD will **p** shade* 828
Jer 5:28 *refuse to **p** justice to orphans* 967
Ezek 18:7 *and **p-s** clothes for the needy.* ...1064
2 Cor 9:8 *God will generously **p** all you* 1637
2 Cor 9:10 *he will **p** and increase your* 1638

PROVOKE (v) to incite to anger; to stir up purposely
Eph 6:4 *do not **p** your children to anger* 1714

PROWLS (v) to roam over in a predatory manner
1 Pet 5:8 ***p** around like a roaring lion,* 1756

PRUDENT (adj) marked by wisdom or judiciousness; discreet
Prov 14:8 ***p** understand where they are* 647
Prov 14:18 *the **p** are crowned with* 648
Prov 22:3 *A **p** person foresees danger* 659

PRUNES (v) to cut back or off for better shape or more fruitful growth
John 15:2 *and he **p** the branches* 1463

PRUNING HOOKS (n) poles bearing curved blades for pruning plants
Isa 2:4 *their spears into **p**.* 825
Joel 3:10 *your **p** into spears.* 1243

PSALMS (n) sacred songs or poems used in worship
Ps 95:2 *Let us sing **p** of praise* 863
Eph 5:19 *singing **p** and hymns and* 1713
Col 3:16 *Sing **p** and hymns and spiritual* ...1701

PSYCHICS (n) those who claim to have sensitivity to knowledge and forces that lie outside the normal human experience
Deut 18:11 *function as mediums or **p**,* 308
2 Kgs 21:6 *with mediums and **p**.* 954
2 Kgs 23:24 *rid of the mediums and **p**,* 973

PUBLICAN(S) (KJV)
Matt 5:46 *Even **corrupt tax collectors*** 1330
Matt 9:10 *with many **tax collectors*** 1314
Matt 10:3 *Matthew (the **tax collector**),* 1358
Luke 5:30 *and drink with **such scum?*** 1316
Luke 18:11 *not like that **tax collector*** 1418

PUNISH, PUNISHED, PUNISHES, PUNISHING (v) to impose a penalty to fit the crime: from corrective measures (fines or scolding) and corporal punishment (spanking or whipping) to capital punishment and eternal damnation
Gen 15:14 *But I will **p** the nation* 35
1 Kgs 8:32 ***P** the guilty as they deserve.* 619
Prov 11:21 *people will surely be **p-ed**,* 644
Jer 25:14 *I will **p** them in proportion* 994
Lam 3:39 *when we are **p-ed** for our sins?* 1099
Mark 12:40 *will be more severely **p-ed**.* ...1443
Acts 7:7 *But I will **p** the nation* 1524
Rom 2:2 *God, in his justice, will **p*** 1648
Rom 13:4 *they have the power to **p** you.* ...1668
Rom 13:4 *the very purpose of **p-ing*** 1668
2 Thes 1:9 ***p-ed** with eternal destruction,* 1588
Heb 2:2 *act of disobedience was **p-ed**.* 1763
Heb 12:6 *he **p-es** each one he accepts* 1780
1 Pet 2:14 *sent them to **p** those who* 1751
Rev 19:2 *has **p-ed** the great prostitute* 1827

PUNISHMENT (n) suffering, pain, or loss that serves as retribution
Isa 53:4 *troubles were a **p** from God,* 940
Jer 2:19 *will bring its own **p**.* 961
Jer 4:18 *This **p** is bitter, piercing* 965
Hos 5:9 *On your day of **p**, you will* 808
Matt 25:46 *will go away into eternal **p**,* 1453
Rom 13:5 *not only to avoid **p**, but also* 1668
2 Pet 2:9 *keeping the wicked under **p*** 1759

PURCHASE, PURCHASED (v) to gain or acquire; to buy
see also REDEEM
Acts 20:28 ***p-d** with his own blood—* 1675
Eph 1:7 ***p-d** our freedom with the* 1705
Eph 1:14 ***p-d** us to be his own people.* 1706
Col 1:14 *who **p-d** our freedom* 1694
1 Tim 2:6 *gave his life to **p** freedom* 1729
Rev 14:4 *have been **p-d** from among* 1821

PURE (adj) free of contamination or impurities; ritually clean; guileless; faultless; guiltless; chaste
see also CLEAN, HOLY
Ps 19:9 *Reverence for the LORD is **p**,* 554
Prov 20:9 *I am **p** and free* 656
Matt 5:8 *those whose hearts are **p**,* 1326
1 Cor 1:30 *he made us **p** and holy,* 1597
Phil 4:8 *right, and **p**, and lovely,* 1725
1 Tim 5:22 *Keep yourself **p**.* 1734
2 Tim 2:21 *If you keep yourself **p**,* 1743
Titus 1:15 *Everything is **p** to those* 1737
Titus 2:5 *to live wisely and be **p**,* 1738
Jas 1:27 ***P** and genuine religion* 1548
1 Pet 3:2 *your **p** and reverent* 1752
2 Pet 3:14 *are **p** and blameless* 1760
1 Jn 3:3 *will keep themselves **p**, just as* 1791

PURIFICATION (n) the act or an instance of purifying or of being purified
Lev 16:30 *offerings of **p** will be made* 222
Acts 21:24 *join them in the **p** ceremony,* ...1677

PURIFY, PURIFIED (v) to make pure or remove (physical or moral) blemishes; to make ritually clean
see also CLEANSE
Exod 30:10 *offering made to **p** the people*...182
Exod 30:15 *given to the LORD to **p***...182
Num 25:13 ***p-ied** the people of Israel,*...270
1 Chr 15:12 *You must **p** yourselves and*...491
2 Chr 30:17 *had not **p-ied** themselves,*...837
Neh 12:30 *Levites first **p-ied** themselves;*.1221
Isa 52:11 *and **p** yourselves,*...939
John 15:3 *pruned and **p-ied** by the*...1463
Heb 9:14 *Christ will **p** our consciences*...1773
Heb 9:22 *was **p-ied** with blood.*...1774
Jas 4:8 *you sinners; **p** your hearts,*...1551

PURIM (n) a Jewish holiday in commemoration of the deliverance of the Jews from the massacre plotted by Haman
Esth 9:26 *this celebration is called **P**,*...1193

PURITY (n) the quality or state of being pure
Job 14:4 *Who can bring **p** out of an*...108
Ps 86:11 *Grant me **p** of heart,*...579
2 Cor 6:6 *by our **p**, our understanding,*...1633
1 Tim 4:12 *love, your faith, and your **p**.*...1732
1 Tim 5:2 *younger women with all **p***...1733

PURPLE (adj) of the color purple; symbolic of royalty and wealth
Prov 31:22 *fine linen and **p** gowns.*...848
Mark 15:17 *They dressed him in a **p** robe,*..1482
Acts 16:14 *merchant of expensive **p** cloth,*..1574

PURPOSE, PURPOSES (n) something set up as an object or end to be attained; resolution, determination
see also PLAN
Exod 9:16 *I have spared you for a **p**—*...153
Prov 19:21 *the LORD's **p** will prevail.*...655
Rom 8:28 *according to his **p** for them.*...1660
Rom 9:11 *according to his own **p-s**;*...1661
Rom 9:17 *for the very **p** of displaying.*...1662
1 Cor 3:8 *with the same **p**.*...1599
1 Cor 9:26 *I run with **p** in every step.*...1609
Phil 2:2 *together with one mind and **p**.*...1719

PURSUE, PURSUES (v) to follow in order to overtake, capture, kill, or defeat; to seek
Ps 23:6 *unfailing love will **p** me*...558
Ps 119:32 *I will **p** your commands,*...878
Prov 15:9 *those who **p** godliness.*...648
Prov 21:21 *Whoever **p-s** righteousness*...658
1 Tim 6:11 ***P** righteousness and a godly*...1735
2 Tim 2:22 *Instead, **p** righteous living,*...1743

QUAIL (n) in Palestine, a migrating bird that arrives in droves along the shores of the Mediterranean Sea
Exod 16:13 *vast numbers of **q** flew*...164
Num 11:31 *there were **q** flying*...249

QUAKE (v) to shake or vibrate
Ps 99:1 *the whole earth **q**!*...865

QUALIFICATION (n) a condition or standard that must be complied with (as for the attainment of a privilege)
2 Cor 3:5 *Our **q** comes from God.*...1629

QUALIFIED (adj) to declare competent or adequate
2 Cor 3:5 *not that we think we are **q***...1629

QUALITIES (n) distinguishing attributes; characteristics; nature
Rom 1:20 *clearly see his invisible **q**—*...1647

QUARREL, QUARRELS (n) a usually verbal conflict between antagonists
Prov 10:12 *Hatred stirs up **q-s**,*...642
Prov 17:14 *Starting a **q** is like opening*...652
Prov 26:20 ***q-s** disappear when gossip*...841
Prov 30:33 *anger causes **q-s**.*...847
Titus 3:9 ***q-s** and fights about*...1739
Jas 4:1 *causing the **q-s** and fights*...1551

QUARREL, QUARRELING (v) to find fault; to contend or dispute actively
Exod 21:18 *"Now suppose two men **q**,*...171
Prov 17:19 *Anyone who loves to **q** loves*...653
Prov 20:3 *fools insist on **q-ing**.*...656
Isa 58:4 *keep on fighting and **q-ing**?*...944
Rom 13:13 *or in **q-ing** and jealousy.*...1669
1 Cor 3:3 *and **q** with each other.*...1599
2 Cor 12:20 *will find **q-ing**, jealousy,*...1642

QUARRELSOME (adj) apt or disposed to quarrel in an often petty manner; contentious
Prov 19:13 ***q** wife is as annoying as*...655
Prov 21:9 *than with a **q** wife in a lovely*...657
Prov 26:21 *A **q** person starts fights.*...841
1 Tim 3:3 *He must be gentle, not **q**,*...1730

QUEEN (n) the wife or widow of a king; a female monarch
1 Kgs 10:1 ***q** of Sheba heard*...626
Ps 45:9 *your right side stands the **q**,*...851
Matt 12:42 *The **q** of Sheba will*...1343

QUENCH (v) to put out or extinguish
Song 8:7 *Many waters cannot **q** love,*...670

QUICK (KJV)
Heb 4:12 *word of God is **alive** and*...1766
1 Pet 4:5 *the **living** and the dead.*...1754

QUICKEN (KJV)
Ps 80:18 ***Revive** us so we can call on*...601
Ps 119:37 *give me **life** through your*...878
Rom 8:11 *he will **give life** to your mortal*...1659

QUIET (adj) calm; gentle; peaceful, still; free from noise
Prov 11:12 *a sensible person keeps **q**.*...643
Eccl 3:7 *A time to be **q** and a time*...675
Eccl 9:17 *to hear the **q** words of a wise*...681
Luke 19:40 *If they kept **q**, the stones*...1431
1 Thes 4:11 *to live a **q** life,*...1584
1 Tim 2:2 *peaceful and **q** lives marked*...1729

QUIETNESS (n) the state of being quiet; calmness; stillness
Eccl 4:6 *one handful with **q** than two*...676
Isa 30:15 ***q** and confidence is*...900
Isa 32:17 *it will bring **q** and confidence*...902

QUIT, QUITTING (v) to cease action; to give up
Prov 23:4 *wise enough to know when to **q**.*...661
Eccl 10:4 *boss is angry at you, don't **q**!*...681
Rev 2:3 *suffered for me without **q-ting**.*...1802

QUIVER (n) a case for carrying or holding arrows
Ps 127:5 *joyful is the man whose **q** is*...631

RABBI (n) a title of honor and respect given by the Jews to a teacher of the Law
Matt 23:8 *anyone call you '**R**,'*...1443
John 3:2 *"**R**," he said, "we all know*...1300

RACE (n) an athletic contest; an ethnic classification
Ps 19:5 *athlete eager to run the **r**.*...554
Eccl 9:11 *doesn't always win the **r**,*...681
Dan 7:14 *people of every **r** and nation*...1136
1 Cor 9:24 *that in a **r** everyone runs,*...1609
Gal 2:2 *running the **r** for nothing.*...1558
Gal 5:7 *were running the **r** so well.*...1565
2 Tim 4:7 *I have finished the **r**,*...1746
Heb 12:1 *run with endurance the **r** God*...1780

RACE (v) to go, move, or function at top speed or out of control
Prov 6:18 *feet that **r** to do wrong,*...638

RADIANCE (n) the quality or state of being radiant
Isa 60:3 *will come to see your **r**.*...946
Luke 2:9 *and the **r** of the Lord's*...1281

RADIANT (adj) vividly bright and shining; marked by or expressive of love, confidence, or happiness
Exod 34:29 *face had become **r** because*...188
Ps 34:5 *help will be **r** with joy;*...458
Ps 80:1 *display your **r** glory*...600

RADIATES (v) to spread abroad or around as if from a center; to shine brightly
Heb 1:3 *The Son **r** God's own glory*...1761

RAGE (n) violent and uncontrolled anger
Isa 14:6 *with endless blows of **r***...832
Col 3:8 *rid of anger, **r**, malicious*...1700

RAGING (adj) violent, wild
Ps 42:7 *tumult of the **r** seas as your*...849
Ps 65:7 *You quieted the **r** oceans*...575

RAGS (n) clothes usually in poor or ragged condition
Isa 64:6 *are nothing but filthy **r**.*...950

RAIMENT (KJV)
Exod 12:35 ***clothing** and articles of silver*...158
Deut 8:4 *your **clothes** didn't wear out*...297
Luke 9:29 *his **clothes** became dazzling*...1380

RAIN, RAINS (n) water falling in drops from the sky
Deut 11:14 *will send the **r-s** in their*...300
1 Kgs 17:1 *no dew or **r** during the next*...715
1 Kgs 18:1 *that I will soon send **r**!*...716
Prov 16:15 *refreshes like a spring **r**.*...651
Matt 5:45 *and he sends **r** on the just*...1330
Jas 5:17 *earnestly that no **r** would fall,*...1554
Jude 1:12 *land without giving any **r**.*...1785

RAIN (v) to fall as water in drops from the clouds
Gen 7:4 *And it will **r** for forty days.*...18

RAINBOW (n) an arch of colors in the sky caused by light passing through moisture in the air
Gen 9:13 *I have placed my **r** in the*...21

RAISE, RAISED (v) to recall from death
see also RESURRECTION
Judg 2:16 *the LORD **r-d** up judges*...375
Luke 7:22 *the dead are **r-d** to life,*...1338
John 6:39 *that I should **r** them up*...1367
Acts 2:32 *God **r-d** Jesus from the dead,*...1516
Acts 24:15 *that he will **r** both the*...1682
Rom 1:4 *he was **r-d** from the dead*...1644
Rom 6:5 *we will also be **r-d** to life*...1655
Rom 10:9 *God **r-d** him from the dead,*...1663
1 Cor 15:4 *he was **r-d** from the dead*...1620
Phil 3:10 *mighty power that **r-d** him*...1722
1 Thes 4:14 *died and was **r-d** to life*...1585
1 Pet 1:3 *because God **r-d** Jesus Christ*...1748

RALLY (v) to join in a common cause
Isa 11:10 *The nations will **r** to him,*...796

RAM, RAMS (n) a male sheep
Gen 22:13 he took the r and sacrificed.........46
1 Sam 15:22 offering the fat of r-s.............446
Dan 8:3 I saw a r with two long.................1137
Mic 6:7 him thousands of r-s and ten.........910

RANSOM (n) price paid or demanded to release someone or something from captivity
Matt 20:28 his life as a r for many...........1424
Mark 10:45 his life as a r for many...........1425
1 Pet 1:18 that God paid a r to save.........1749

RANSOM, RANSOMED (v) to deliver especially from sin or its penalty; to free from captivity or punishment by paying a price
see also REDEEM(ED)
Ps 44:26 Help us! R us because of.............850
Ps 71:23 for you have r-ed me....................860
Isa 35:10 have been r-ed by the LORD........905
Hos 13:14 Should I r them from.................816
Rev 5:9 your blood has r-ed people..........1810

RAVEN, RAVENS (n) a large, black, corvine bird
Gen 8:7 and released a r. The bird................20
1 Kgs 17:6 The r-s brought him bread and .715
Job 38:41 provides food for the r-s............129
Ps 147:9 feeds the young r-s when they...1155
Luke 12:24 Look at the r-s. They don't.....1400

READ, READING, READS (v) to receive and interpret letters or symbols by sight
Deut 17:19 with him and r it daily...............307
Josh 8:34 Joshua then r to them................348
2 Kgs 23:2 There the king r to them...........971
Acts 8:28 carriage, he was r-ing aloud.....1529
2 Cor 3:2 everyone can r it and................1629
1 Tim 4:13 focus on r-ing the Scriptures..1732
Rev 1:3 the one who r-s the words of.......1798

READY (adj) prepared mentally or physically for some experience or action
1 Tim 6:18 always being r to share...........1735
1 Pet 3:15 always be r to explain.............1753

REAL (adj) not artificial, fraudulent, or illusory; genuine
1 Kgs 3:26 who was the r mother of...........608
1 Jn 4:2 Christ came in a r body,..............1792

REALITY (n) a real event, entity, or state of affairs
Col 2:17 shadows of the r yet to come......1699

REALIZATION (n) the state of being fully aware of
Mark 5:33 trembling at the r of what........1354

REALIZE, REALIZED, REALIZING (v) to be fully aware of; to conceive vividly as real
2 Chr 33:13 Manasseh finally r-d that........956
Job 38:18 Do you r the extent of................128
Ps 64:9 and r all the amazing things...........575
Song 6:12 Before I r-d it, my strong...........668
Isa 61:9 Everyone will r that they are..........948
Heb 13:2 angels without r-ing it!.............1782
Jas 4:4 Don't you r that friendship............1551

REALMS (n) kingdoms; spheres, domains
Eph 1:3 in the heavenly r because we.......1704
Eph 2:6 in the heavenly r because we.......1707

REAP (v) to harvest or gather; to obtain
see also HARVEST, GATHER
Gal 6:9 will r a harvest of blessing............1567
Jas 3:18 r a harvest of righteousness. 1551

REAPERS (KJV)
Ruth 2:3 grain behind the harvesters.........412
2 Kgs 4:18 working with the harvesters.....741
Matt 13:30 the harvesters to sort out......1348
Matt 13:39 the harvesters are the angels...1349

REBEL, REBELLED, REBELLING, REBELS (v) to oppose or disobey one in authority or control
Num 14:9 Do not r against the.................252
Num 27:14 of Israel r-led, you failed to......273
1 Sam 12:14 if you do not r against the......440
Ps 78:56 testing and r-ling against God.....599
Isa 63:10 But they r-led against him..........950
Matt 10:21 children will r against their.....1360
Rom 13:2 So anyone who r-s against........1668

REBELLION (n) opposition to one in authority or dominance; defiance
Exod 34:7 forgive iniquity, r, and sin............187
Ps 32:5 I will confess my r to the................565
Ps 39:8 Rescue me from my r. 569
Ps 51:3 I recognize my r; it haunts 505
Isa 53:5 was pierced for our r,...................940
Isa 53:8 for the r of my people....................940
Dan 9:24 to finish their r, to put an...........1143
2 Thes 2:3 is a great r against God...........1588

REBELLIOUS (adj) given to or engaged in rebellion
Isa 65:2 opened my arms to a r people.......951
Luke 1:17 those who are r to accept.........1273
Rom 10:21 were disobedient and r. 1664
1 Tim 1:9 people who are lawless and r, ...1727
Titus 1:6 reputation for being wild or r.......1736

REBELS (n) those who rebel or participate in a rebellion
Ps 51:13 will teach your ways to r, ...506
Isa 53:12 He was counted among the r.......941
Luke 22:37 was counted among the r.......1460
Rom 11:30 Gentiles were r against God,...1666
Rom 11:31 they are the r, and God's 1666

REBUILD, REBUILT (v) to reconstruct; to restore to a previous state
Ezra 5:2 again to r the Temple of God 1165
Neh 2:17 Let us r the wall of....................1205
Ps 102:16 the LORD will r Jerusalem............866
Amos 9:14 and they will r their ruined..........781
Zech 1:16 My Temple will be r-t, says the.1166
Acts 15:16 I will r its ruins and.................1570

REBUKE (n) an expression of strong disapproval; reprimand
see also CORRECT, DISCIPLINE
Prov 17:10 A single r does more for 652
Prov 27:5 An open r is better than.............842

REBUKE, REBUKED (v) to criticize sharply; to reprimand
Prov 30:6 or he may r you and expose........846
Mark 16:14 He r-d them for their.............1494
Luke 17:3 believer sins, r that person; 1413
2 Tim 4:2 Patiently correct, r, and.............1745
Jas 1:5 He will not r you for asking. 1546

RECEIVE, RECEIVED, RECEIVES (v) to acquire or take possession of; to welcome
Matt 7:8 For everyone who asks, r-s.........1334
Matt 19:17 you want to r eternal life, ...1420
John 20:22 said, "R the Holy Spirit............1495
Acts 1:8 But you will r power when the 1500
Acts 2:38 Then you will r the gift of 1516
Acts 8:17 they r-d the Holy Spirit..............1528
Acts 10:47 they have r-d the Holy............1534
Acts 19:2 Did you r the Holy Spirit 1593
Rom 8:15 Instead, you r-d God's Spirit 1659
1 Tim 1:16 in him and r eternal life...........1728
Rev 4:11 our God, to r glory and honor 1809

RECKONING (n) a settling of accounts
Jer 51:18 On the day of r they will all 1038

RECOGNIZE, RECOGNIZED (v) to admit as being lord or sovereign; to acknowledge or take notice of in some definite way; to perceive to be something or someone previously known
1 Chr 16:28 of the world, r the LORD, ...493
Ps 96:7 of the world, r the LORD;.................864
Jer 24:7 give them hearts that r me...........1029
Hos 4:6 refuse to r you as my priests..........806
John 1:26 is someone you do not r. 1293
1 Cor 14:38 But if you do not r this,..........1618
1 Cor 14:38 yourself will not be r-d. 1618
2 Cor 3:2 read it and r our good work........1629

RECOMMEND (v) to endorse; to advise
Eccl 8:15 So I r having fun, because...........680

RECOMMENDATION (n) something that expresses commendation
2 Cor 3:1 to bring you letters of r, ...1629

RECONCILED, RECONCILING (v) to restore to friendship or harmony, especially between God and human beings
2 Cor 5:18 task of r-ing people to him......1632
Eph 2:16 Christ r-d both groups to God 1708
Col 1:20 God r-d everything to himself......1695
Col 1:22 now he has r-d you to himself 1696

RECONCILIATION (n) the action of reconciling; the state of being reconciled
Prov 14:9 acknowledge it and seek r. 647
2 Cor 5:19 this wonderful message of r. ...1632

RECORD (n) an official body of known or recorded facts about someone
1 Cor 13:5 keeps no r of being wronged. ..1616
Col 2:14 canceled the r of the charges 1698

RECORDED (v) to set down in writing
John 20:30 to the ones r in this book.........1496

RED (adj) of the color red
Exod 15:4 are drowned in the R Sea. 161
Ps 106:9 He commanded the R Sea to 870
Prov 23:31 wine, seeing how r it is, ...662
Isa 1:18 they are r like crimson, ...824
Isa 63:1 with his clothing stained r? 949

REDEDICATE (v) to devote or commit oneself or one's possessions again
Num 6:12 They must r themselves to 244

REDEEM, REDEEMED, REDEEMS (v) to buy back; to save by payment of a ransom; to free from the consequences of sin
see also PURCHASE, RANSOM, RESCUE
Exod 6:6 I will r you with a powerful............148
2 Sam 7:23 have you r-ed from slavery......496
Ps 34:22 the LORD will r those.....................459
Ps 49:15 God will r my life. 854
Ps 74:2 the tribe you r-ed as your own.......595
Ps 103:4 He r-s me from death and...........580
Ps 107:2 Has the LORD r-ed you?...............871
Ps 130:8 He himself will r Israel from 884
Isa 35:9 Only the r-ed will walk..................905
Isa 63:9 love and mercy he r-ed them. 950
Hos 7:13 I wanted to r them, but they........810

REDEEMER (n) one who frees or delivers another from difficulty, danger, or bondage, usually by the payment of a ransom price
Ruth 3:9 for you are my family r..................414
Ruth 4:14 has now provided a r for............415
Job 19:25 I know that my R lives,...............112
Ps 19:14 LORD, my rock and my r. 555
Prov 23:11 For their R is strong;.................661

Isa 44:6 *Israel's King and **R**, the LORD*.......930
Isa 48:17 *your **R**, the Holy One of Israel:*......935
Isa 59:20 *The **R** will come to Jerusalem*......946

REDEMPTION (n) the act, process, or an instance of redeeming
Ps 130:7 *love. His **r** overflows.*..................884
Eph 4:30 *be saved on the day of **r**.*...........1712
Heb 9:12 *and secured our **r** forever*..........1773

REEDS (n) any of various tall grasses that grow in wet places
Exod 2:5 *basket among the **r**,*.....................142
Isa 35:7 ***r** and rushes will flourish*...............905
Isa 58:5 *bowing your heads like **r***..............944
Ezek 29:6 *a staff made of **r***.....................1076

REFINE, REFINED (v) to remove impurities from metal; figurative of purifying God's people of sin
Isa 48:10 *I have **r-d** you in the furnace*.......935
Zech 13:9 *I will **r** them like silver*.............1179

REFINER (n) someone or something that refines
Mal 3:3 *will sit like a **r** of silver,*.................1247

REFLECT, REFLECTS (v) to make manifest or apparent; to think quietly and calmly
Ps 119:5 *consistently **r** your decrees!*.........877
Ps 119:15 *and **r** on your ways.*...................878
Prov 27:19 *the heart **r-s** the real person.*....842
Isa 44:19 *never stops to **r**, "Why, it's*...........930
Titus 2:7 *Let everything you do **r** the*.........1738

REFRESH, REFRESHED, REFRESHES, REFRESHING (v) to restore strength and animation to; to replenish, arouse, or stimulate
Prov 9:17 *Stolen water is **r-ing;** food*..........641
Prov 11:25 *will themselves be **r-ed.***...........644
Prov 16:15 *favor **r-es** like a spring rain.*......651
Phlm 1:7 *has often **r-ed** the hearts*...........1691

REFUGE (n) shelter or protection from danger or distress
see also FORTRESS, PROTECTION, SHELTER
Deut 33:27 *eternal God is your **r**,*................327
2 Sam 22:3 *He is my **r**, my savior,*..............526
Ps 2:12 *for all who take **r** in him!*................857
Ps 5:11 *But let all who take **r** in you.*...........548
Ps 17:7 *those who seek **r** from their*...........553
Ps 34:8 *those who take **r** in him!*.................458
Ps 46:1 *God is our **r** and strength,*.............851
Ps 91:2 *He alone is my **r**, my place*............861

REFUSE, REFUSED, REFUSING (v) to show or express unwillingness to do or comply with
Lev 26:15 *and **r-ing** to obey*......................235
Num 14:22 *tested me by **r-ing** to listen to*..253
Josh 24:15 *But if you **r** to serve the*............370
Prov 13:19 *fools **r** to turn from evil*............646
Eccl 11:10 *So **r** to worry, and keep*............682
Luke 15:29 *never once **r-d** to do a single*....1411
Rom 14:6 *And those who **r** to eat*.............1670
2 Thes 2:10 *because they **r** to love*...........1589
2 Thes 3:14 *of those who **r** to obey*...........1590
Heb 12:25 *escape when they **r-d** to listen.*1781

REFUTE (v) to prove wrong by argument or evidence
Luke 21:15 *be able to reply or **r** you!*........1450
Acts 9:22 *couldn't **r** his proofs that*...........1531

REGARDED (v) to consider and appraise
Ps 106:31 *has been **r** as a righteous*.........871

REGENERATION (KJV)
Matt 19:28 *world is **made new** and the*....1420
Titus 3:5 *giving us a **new birth** and new*...1739

REGISTERED (v) to make or secure official entry of in a register
Luke 10:20 *your names are **r** in heaven.*...1395

REGRET (v) to be very sorry for
Nah 3:7 *Does anyone **r** your destruction?*....977

REGULAR (adj) formed, built, arranged, or ordered according to some established rule, law, principle, or type
2 Kgs 25:30 *gave him a **r** food allowance*...1134

REGULATIONS (n) authoritative rules dealing with details or procedure
see also LAW(S)
Exod 21:1 *These are the **r** you must*...........170
Deut 33:10 *They teach your **r** to Jacob;*......327
Ps 119:30 *determined to live by your **r**.*.......878
Ps 119:43 *for your **r** are my only hope.*.......879
Ps 119:120 *I stand in awe of your **r**.*...........880
Ps 119:164 *because all your **r** are just*........881
Ps 119:175 *and may your **r** help me.*..........882

REIGN, REIGNED, REIGNING, REIGNS (v) to possess or exercise sovereign power; to rule
Exod 15:18 *The LORD will **r** forever.*............162
Ps 9:7 *But the LORD **r-s** forever,*................549
Ps 29:10 *LORD **r-s** as king forever.*.............562
Ps 96:10 *The LORD **r-s!***.............................864
Ps 146:10 *The LORD will **r** forever.*.............887
Isa 52:7 *that the God of Israel **r-s!***.............939
1 Cor 4:8 *we would be **r-ing** with you.*.......1601
1 Cor 15:25 *For Christ must **r** until he.*......1621
Rev 5:10 *And they will **r** on the earth.*.......1810
Rev 11:15 *and he will **r** forever.*.................1817
Rev 19:6 *our God, the Almighty, **r-s.***.........1827
Rev 20:4 *and they **r-ed** with Christ*...........1829
Rev 22:5 *And they will **r** forever.*...............1832

REIGNS (n) the time during which one (as a sovereign) rules
Dan 2:44 *During the **r** of those kings,*.......1005

REJECT, REJECTED, REJECTING, REJECTS (v) to refuse to accept, consider, submit to, or take for some purpose, or use; to refuse to hear, receive, or admit
1 Sam 8:7 *me they are **r-ing**, not you.*........434
Ps 51:17 *not **r** a broken and repentant*.......506
Ps 118:22 *stone that the builders **r-ed***.......876
Prov 3:11 *My child, don't **r** the LORD's*.........635
Mal 1:3 *but I **r-ed** his brother,*.................1244
Matt 21:42 *stone that the builders **r-ed***....1437
Luke 10:16 *who **r-s** me is **r-ing** God,*.......1394
John 6:37 *I will never **r** them.*..................1367
John 12:48 *But all who **r** me and my*.........1435
Rom 9:13 *loved Jacob, but I **r-ed** Esau.*....1661
1 Thes 4:8 *teaching but is **r-ing** God,*.......1584
1 Tim 4:4 *we should not **r** any of it.*..........1732
2 Tim 3:5 *but they will **r** the power.*...........1744
Heb 6:6 *by **r-ing** the Son of God, they*......1768
1 Pet 2:4 *He was **r-ed** by people,*.............1750
1 Pet 2:7 *stone that the builders **r-ed***.......1750

REJECTION (n) the action of rejecting
Rom 11:15 *For since their **r** meant that*....1665

REJOICE, REJOICED, REJOICES, REJOICING (v) to feel joy or great delight; to gladden
1 Chr 16:31 *glad, and the earth **r!***...............493
1 Chr 29:17 ***r** when you find integrity.*.........541
Esth 8:17 *decree arrived, the Jews **r-d***.....1192
Ps 5:11 *who take refuge in you **r;***...............548
Ps 13:5 *I will **r** because you*.........................551
Ps 35:9 *I will **r** in the LORD.*.........................565
Ps 48:2 *the whole earth **r-s** to see it!*..........852
Ps 58:10 *The godly will **r** when they*..........573
Ps 66:6 *There we **r-d** in him.*........................859
Ps 68:4 *LORD—**r** in his presence!*..............576
Ps 119:14 *I have **r-d** in your laws.*..............878
Ps 119:162 *I **r** in your word like one*..........881
Prov 8:31 *I **r-d** with the human family!*........641
Prov 17:5 *who **r** at the misfortune*..............652
Prov 29:2 *in authority, the people **r**.*.............844
Isa 9:3 *and its people will **r**.*........................792
Isa 35:1 *wasteland will **r** and blossom.*........904
Isa 62:5 ***r** over you as a bridegroom **r-s***.......948
Jer 51:48 *the heavens and earth will **r**,*.....1039
Lam 4:21 *Are you **r-ing** in the land*..........1101
Hab 1:15 *while they **r** and celebrate?*..........979
Zeph 3:17 *He will **r** over you.*.....................986
Zech 2:10 *Shout and **r**, O beautiful*...........1167
Luke 1:14 *and many will **r** at his birth,*......1273
Luke 1:47 *How my spirit **r-s** in God my*.....1275
Luke 1:58 *everyone **r-d** with her.*.............1276
Luke 10:20 *But don't **r** because evil*.........1395
Luke 13:17 *but all the people **r-d** at the*....1403
Acts 5:41 *high council **r-ing** that God*......1522
Acts 16:34 *his entire household **r-d**.*..........1576
1 Cor 13:6 ***r** about injustice but **r-s***............1616
Phil 2:18 *you should **r**, and I will*..............1720
Phil 3:1 *and sisters, **r** in the Lord.*............1721
Phil 4:4 *I say it again—**r!***..........................1724
Col 2:5 *I **r** that you are living as*...............1697
Rev 19:7 *Let us be glad and **r**, and*..........1827

RELATIONSHIP (n) a state of affairs existing between those having relations or dealings
Rom 5:11 *our wonderful new **r** with God*...1654
2 Jn 1:9 *teaching has no **r** with God.*........1796

RELATIVES (n) a person connected with another by blood or affinity
Lev 19:17 *your heart for any of your **r**.*........225
Mark 6:4 *among his **r** and his own*...........1357
Luke 21:16 *parents, brothers, **r**, and*.........1450
1 Tim 5:8 *who won't care for their **r**,*.........1733

RELEASE (n) relief or deliverance from restraint, sorrow, suffering, or trouble
Deut 31:10 *the Year of **R**, during the*.............322
Job 14:14 *eagerly await the **r** of death.*.......108

RELEASED (v) to set free from restraint, confinement, or servitude
Isa 61:1 *that captives will be **r***....................948
Matt 18:27 *and he **r** him and forgave*.......1386
Matt 27:50 *and he **r** his spirit.*..................1485
Luke 4:18 *that captives will be **r**,*..............1357
John 19:30 *his head and **r** his spirit.*.........1487
Rom 7:6 *we have been **r** from the law,*......1657
Rom 8:23 *bodies to be **r** from sin and*.......1659

RELENT, RELENTED (v) to become less severe, harsh, or strict; to give in
Ps 106:45 ***r-ed** because of his unfailing*.....871
Joel 2:13 *eager to **r** and not punish.*........1241

RELIABLE (adj) dependable
1 Chr 9:22 *they were **r** men.*....................1238
Prov 13:17 *but a **r** messenger brings*..........646
Prov 20:6 *find one who is truly **r?***...............656
2 Tim 2:2 *by many **r** witnesses.*...............1742

RELIEF (n) removal or lightening of something oppressive, painful, or distressing
Gen 5:29 *he bring us **r** from our work*...........17
Ps 94:13 *You give them **r** from troubled*......863

RELIEVED, RELIEVING (v) to free from a burden; to discharge the bladder or bowels
1 Kgs 18:27 *or is **r-ing** himself.*................717
Acts 20:12 *and everyone was greatly **r-d.***..1675

RELIGION, RELIGIONS (n) a personal set or institutionalized system of religious attitudes, beliefs, and practices; the service and worship of God or the supernatural
Matt 6:7 *as people of other **r-s** do.*...........1331
Acts 25:19 *something about their **r** and*...........1683
Acts 26:5 *the strictest sect of our **r.***...........1684
Gal 1:13 *I followed the Jewish **r**—*...........1556
Jas 1:26 *and your **r** is worthless.*...........1548

RELIGIOUS (adj) relating to or manifesting faithful devotion to God or a god
Luke 11:46 *with unbearable **r** demands,*...1398
Acts 13:50 *the influential **r** women and*....1543
Jas 1:26 *you claim to be **r** but don't*.........1548

RELY, RELIED, RELIES (v) to be dependent
2 Chr 16:8 *time you **r-ied** on the LORD,*........710
Ps 22:8 *one who **r-ies** on the LORD?*...........556
Ps 33:18 *those who **r** on his unfailing*.........858
Prov 11:7 *for they **r** on their own feeble*......643
Isa 50:10 *the LORD and **r** on your God.*.........937
2 Cor 1:9 *and learned to **r** only on God,*.....1626

REMAIN, REMAINED, REMAINS (v) to stay in the same place or with the same person or group; to continue unchanged
2 Kgs 18:6 *He **r-ed** faithful to the LORD*........800
John 15:7 *But if you **r** in me and my*........1464
John 15:9 *loved me. **R** in my love.*...........1464
Rom 11:5 *of Israel have **r-ed** faithful*........1664
2 Tim 2:13 *unfaithful, he **r-s** faithful,*.........1742
2 Tim 3:14 *But you must **r** faithful*............1744
2 Tim 4:7 *and I have **r-ed** faithful.*............1746
Heb 7:3 *He **r-s** a priest forever,*...............1770
Heb 10:32 *how you **r-ed** faithful even*.......1776
Heb 13:4 *and **r** faithful to one another*......1782
1 Pet 1:25 *word of the Lord **r-s***...............1750
1 Jn 2:27 ***r** in fellowship with Christ.*..........1790

REMARRY, REMARRIES (v) to marry again after divorce or being widowed
Rom 7:3 *commit adultery when she **r-ies.***...........1657
1 Tim 5:11 *Christ and they will want to **r.***...........1733

REMEMBER, REMEMBERED, REMEMBERING, REMEMBERS (v) to bring to mind or think of again; to keep in mind for attention or consideration; to retain in the memory
Gen 9:15 *I will **r** my covenant with*................21
Exod 2:24 ***r-ed** his covenant promise*.........143
1 Chr 16:12 ***R** the wonders he has*............493
Ps 49:13 *though they are **r-ed** as being*......854
Ps 103:14 *he **r-s** we are only dust*..............580
Ps 106:45 ***r-ed** his covenant with them*.......871
Ps 111:5 *he always **r-s** his covenant.*..........873
Ps 136:23 *He **r-ed** us in our weakness.*........886
Jer 31:34 *never again **r** their sins.*............1034
Jer 32:20 *things still **r-ed** to this day!*.......1079
Hab 3:2 *in your anger, **r** your mercy.*...........981
Matt 26:13 *will be **r-ed** and discussed*......1428
Luke 1:72 ***r-ing** his sacred covenant—*....1276
Luke 22:19 *Do this to **r** me.*....................1458
1 Cor 11:24 *Do this to **r** me.*....................1613
2 Tim 2:8 *Always **r** that Jesus*..................1742
Heb 8:12 *never again **r** their sins.*.............1772
2 Pet 1:15 *you always **r** these things*........1758

REMIND, REMINDING (v) to cause to remember
John 14:26 *will **r** you of everything*...........1462
2 Pet 1:12 *I will always **r** you about*..........1758
2 Pet 1:13 *keep on **r-ing** you as long*.......1758

REMINDER, REMINDERS (n) something that causes to remember
Deut 6:8 *them on your forehead as **r-s.***......295
Prov 7:3 *Tie them on your fingers as a **r.***.....639

REMISSION (KJV)
Matt 26:28 *as a sacrifice **to forgive***.........1457
Acts 10:43 *sins **forgiven** through his*........1534
Rom 3:25 *he **held back and did not punish***...........1651
Heb 9:22 *blood, there is no **forgiveness***...1774

REMNANT (n) a usually small part, member, or trace remaining; the few people left who gathered together after God scattered them into exile
Ezra 9:8 *few of us to survive as a **r.***..........1200
Isa 6:13 *a tenth—a **r**—survive,*.................786
Isa 11:11 *to bring back the **r** of his*............796
Jer 23:3 *gather together the **r** of my*.........1027
Zech 8:12 *will cause the **r** in Judah*..........1174

REMOVE, REMOVED (v) to get rid of; to eliminate
Ps 103:12 *He has **r-d** our sins as far*..........580
Isa 6:7 *Now your guilt is **r-d**, and your*........784
1 Cor 5:13 *You must **r** the evil person*.......1603

RENEW, RENEWED, RENEWS (v) to restore to freshness, vigor, or perfection; to make new spiritually
Ps 23:3 *He **r-s** my strength.*.......................558
Ps 51:10 ***R** a loyal spirit within me.*............506
Isa 57:10 *Desire gave you **r-ed** strength,*....943
Eph 4:23 *let the Spirit **r** your thoughts.*......1712
Col 3:10 *be **r-ed** as you learn to know*.....1700

RENOWN (KJV)
Gen 6:4 *the **heroes** and famous warriors*......17
Isa 14:20 *will never again **receive honor***....832
Ezek 16:14 ***fame** soon spread.*..................1061
Ezek 39:13 *a **glorious victory** for Israel*....1115

REPAY, REPAYS (v) to give or inflict in return or requital; to pay back (money)
Ps 62:12 *Surely you **r** all people*................574
Prov 17:13 *If you **r** good with evil,*...............652
Prov 19:17 *and he will **r** you!*.....................655
Jer 51:6 *he will **r** her in full.*....................1037
Jer 51:56 *he always **r-s** in full.*..................1040
Luke 6:34 *to those who can **r** you,*............1330
Luke 7:42 *neither of them could **r** him,*.....1340
1 Tim 5:4 ***r** their parents by taking*............1733
1 Pet 3:9 *Don't **r** evil for evil.*...................1753

REPENT, REPENTED, REPENTING, REPENTS (v) to turn from sin and change one's heart and behavior; to feel regret and contrition
Matt 3:2 ***R** of your sins and turn*..............1287
Matt 3:8 *that you have **r-ed** of your sins*...1288
Matt 4:17 *began to preach, "**R** of your*......1306
Matt 11:21 *people would have **r-ed** of*......1339
Luke 3:8 *that you have **r-ed** of your sins*...1291
Luke 15:7 *sinner who **r-s** and returns*.......1410
Luke 15:10 *when even one sinner **r-s.***.....1410
Acts 2:38 *you must **r** of your sins*............1516
Acts 17:30 *everywhere to **r** of their sins*....1579
Acts 20:21 *necessity of **r-ing** from sin*......1675
Heb 6:1 *importance of **r-ing** from evil*.......1768
2 Pet 3:9 *but wants everyone to **r.***............1760
Rev 2:5 *If you don't **r**, I will come*.............1802

REPENTANCE (n) a turning away from sin, disobedience, or rebellion, and a turning back to God
1 Kgs 8:47 *to you in **r** and pray,*..................620
Job 42:6 *dust and ashes to show my **r.***........132
Luke 17:3 *if there is **r**, forgive.*...................1413
2 Cor 7:10 *sorrow, which lacks **r**,*.............1635

REPENTANT (adj) penitent; expressive of repentance
see also CONTRITE
Ps 51:17 *a broken and **r** heart, O God.*........506

REPORT (n) a usually detailed account or statement
Luke 16:2 *Get your **r** in order,*...................1411

REPRESENTATIVE (n) one that represents another as an agent or delegate usually being invested with the authority of the principal
Col 3:17 *do it as a **r** of the Lord*................1701

REPRIMAND, REPRIMANDED (v) to reprove sharply or censure formally
see also CORRECT, REBUKE
1 Tim 5:20 *sin should be **r-ed** in front*......1734
Titus 1:13 *So **r** them sternly to make*........1737

REPROACH (n) a cause or occasion of blame, discredit, or disgrace
1 Tim 3:2 *man whose life is above **r.***..........1730

REPUTATION (n) overall quality or character as seen or judged by people in general
see also NAME
Ps 109:21 *the sake of your own **r!***.............582
Prov 3:4 *you will earn a good **r.***..................634
Prov 22:1 *Choose a good **r** over great*.........658
Eccl 7:1 *A good **r** is more valuable*............678
1 Tim 3:2 *wisely, and have a good **r.***.........1730
Heb 11:39 *good **r** because of their*...........1779

REQUIRE, REQUIRED, REQUIRES (v) to demand as necessary or essential; to feel or be obliged
Ps 40:6 *you don't **r** burnt offerings*.............570
Mic 6:8 *this is what he **r-s** of you:*...............910
Luke 12:48 *much will be **r-d** in return;*.....1401
Luke 23:56 *they rested as **r-d** by the law.*...........1488
Rom 1:32 *God's justice **r-s** that those*.......1648
Heb 8:3 *high priest is **r-d** to offer*............1771

REQUIREMENTS (n) things that are required conditions
Rom 13:8 *will fulfill the **r** of God's*............1669
Rom 13:10 *love fulfills the **r** of God's*........1669

RESCUE, RESCUED, RESCUES, RESCUING (v) to save or deliver
see also REDEEM, SAVE
2 Kgs 13:5 *someone to **r** the Israelites*........758
Ps 9:14 *rejoice that you have **r-d** me.*..........549
Ps 17:7 *mighty power you **r** those who*.......553
Ps 22:8 *let the LORD **r** him!*.........................556
Ps 31:2 *listen to me; **r** me quickly.*.............563
Ps 37:39 *The LORD **r-s** the godly;*...............568
Ps 37:40 *LORD helps them, **r-ing** them*.......568
Ps 68:20 *The Sovereign LORD **r-s** us*...........576
Ps 72:12 *He will **r** the poor when*................630
Ps 145:19 *cries for help and **r-s** them.*........590
Prov 11:8 *godly are **r-d** from trouble,*..........643
Isa 56:1 *coming soon to **r** you and*.............942
Dan 6:27 *He **r-s** and saves his people;*.....1141
Zech 8:7 *that I will **r** my people from*.........1173
Matt 6:13 *but **r** us from the evil one*..........1331
Rom 11:26 *The one who **r-s** will come*.....1666
2 Cor 1:10 *And he did **r** us from mortal*.....1626
Gal 1:4 *in order to **r** us from this*..............1555
Gal 3:13 *But Christ has **r-d** us from the*....1561
Col 1:13 *For he has **r-d** us from the*.........1694
1 Thes 1:10 *the one who has **r-d** us*.........1581
2 Pet 2:9 *knows how to **r** godly people*.....1759

RESCUER (n) one who frees from confinement, danger, or evil
Judg 3:9 *raised up a **r** to save them*..........376
Judg 3:15 *raised up a **r** to save them*..........377
Ps 144:2 *my tower of safety, my **r**.*..........589

RESIST (v) to withstand the force or effect of; to counteract or defeat
Dan 11:32 *will be strong and will **r** him*.....1160
Matt 5:39 *do not **r** an evil person!*..........1329
Jas 4:7 ***R** the devil, and he will flee*..........1551

RESPECT (n) a high or special regard; esteem
see also AWE, REVERENCE
Prov 11:16 *A gracious woman gains **r**,*..........643
Mal 1:6 *the honor and **r** I deserve?*..........1245
Titus 2:2 *be worthy of **r**, and to live*..........1738

RESPECT, RESPECTED (v) to consider worthy of high regard; to esteem
Eph 5:33 *the wife must **r** her husband.*.....1714
1 Tim 3:4 *children who **r** and obey him.*.....1730
1 Tim 3:8 *deacons must be well **r-ed***.....1731
1 Tim 3:11 *their wives must be **r-ed***.....1731
1 Tim 5:17 *work well should be **r-ed***.....1734
1 Pet 2:17 *Fear God, and **r** the king.*.....1751

RESPECTFUL (adj) marked by or showing respect or deference
1 Pet 3:16 *a gentle and **r** way.*..........1753

RESPONSIBILITY (n) moral, legal, or mental accountability
1 Cor 5:12 *certainly is your **r** to judge*.....1603
1 Tim 5:16 *not put the **r** on the church*.....1733

RESPONSIBLE (adj) marked by or involving responsibility or accountability; liable to be called to account as the primary cause, motive, or agent
Exod 32:34 *hold them **r** for their sins.*..........186
Num 1:53 *The Levites are **r** to stand*..........239
Ezek 33:6 *he is **r** for their captivity.*..........1118
Jonah 1:14 *And don't hold us **r** for his*..........767
Gal 6:5 *For we are each **r** for our own*.....1567

REST (n) freedom from activity or labor; peace of mind or spirit; repose, sleep
see also SABBATH
Exod 31:15 *day of complete **r**, a holy*..........183
Exod 33:14 *and I will give you **r**—*..........186
Ps 91:1 *Most High will find **r** in the*..........861
Ps 127:2 *for God gives **r** to his loved*..........631
Jer 6:16 *you will find **r** for your*..........968
Matt 11:28 *and I will give you **r**.*..........1339
2 Thes 1:7 *God will provide **r** for you*..........1588
Heb 4:3 *even though this **r** has been*..........1765
Heb 4:9 *a special **r** still waiting*..........1766
Heb 4:10 *who have entered into God's **r***...1766

REST, RESTED, RESTING, RESTS (v) to sit or lie on; to cease from action or motion; to take relief or respite
Gen 2:2 *of creation, so he **r-ed** from all*..........9
Ps 16:9 *My body **r-s** in safety.*..........553
Ps 23:2 *He lets me **r** in green*..........558
Isa 11:2 *Spirit of the LORD will **r***..........795
Isa 30:15 *and **r-ing** in me will you*..........900
John 1:32 *from heaven and **r-ing** upon*....1297
Heb 4:4 *seventh day God **r-ed** from all*.....1766
Rev 14:13 *will **r** from their hard work;*.......1821

RESTITUTION (n) a making good of or giving an equivalent for some injury
Lev 6:5 *You must make **r** by paying*..........208
Num 5:8 *relatives to whom **r** can be*..........243

RESTLESS (adj) continuously moving
Isa 57:20 *are like the **r** sea, which is*..........944

RESTORE, RESTORED, RESTORES, RESTORING (v) to give back, return; to renew
Ps 14:7 *When the LORD **r-s** his people,*.......552
Ps 30:2 *and you **r-d** my health.*..........563
Isa 58:11 *dry and **r-ing** your strength*..........945
Jer 30:3 *when I will **r** the fortunes of*..........1031
Jer 30:18 *from captivity and **r** their*..........1032
Jer 31:18 *Turn me again to you and **r***..........1033
Hos 6:2 *a short time he will **r** us,*..........808
Nah 2:2 *but he will **r** its splendor.*..........976
Rom 5:10 *friendship with God was **r-d**.*.....1654
1 Pet 5:10 *will **r**, support, and strengthen*..1756

RESURRECTION (n) the state of one risen from the dead; the rising again to life of all the human dead before the final judgment
see also RAISE, RISE
Matt 27:53 *cemetery after Jesus' **r**,*..........1485
Mark 12:23 *will she be in the **r**?*..........1440
Luke 20:36 *children of the **r**.*..........1441
John 11:25 *I am the **r** and the life.*..........1414
Acts 1:22 *as a witness of Jesus' **r**.*..........1513
Acts 2:31 *speaking of the Messiah's **r**.*.......1516
Acts 4:2 *there is a **r** of the dead.*..........1518
Acts 4:33 *powerfully to the **r** of*..........1520
Acts 17:32 *Paul speak about the **r** of*.......1579
1 Cor 15:13 *if there is no **r** of the*..........1620
1 Cor 15:42 *way with the **r** of the dead.*....1621
Phil 3:11 *experience the **r** from the*..........1722
2 Tim 2:18 *claiming that the **r** of the*..........1743
Heb 6:2 *of hands, the **r** of the dead,*..........1768
Heb 11:35 *a better life after the **r**.*..........1779
1 Pet 3:21 *because of the **r** of Jesus*..........1754
Rev 20:5 *This is the first **r**.*..........1829

RETALIATE (v) to repay (as an injury) in kind; to get revenge
1 Pet 2:23 *He did not **r** when he*..........1752

RETURN, RETURNED, RETURNING, RETURNS (v) to go or come back again; to go back in thought, practice, or condition; to repent
2 Sam 12:23 *but he cannot **r** to me.*..........507
2 Chr 30:9 *if you **r** to the LORD,*..........836
Neh 1:9 *But if you **r** to me and obey*..........1204
Ps 35:13 *my prayers **r-ed** unanswered.*.......565
Ps 51:13 *and they will **r** to you.*..........506
Ps 126:6 *they sing as they **r** with the*..........1154
Isa 52:8 *the LORD **r-ing** to Jerusalem*..........939
Jer 24:7 *for they will **r** to me*..........1029
Hos 6:1 *let us **r** to the LORD.*..........808
Amos 4:6 *you would not **r** to me,*..........774
Matt 24:46 *If the master **r-s** and finds*......1447

REVEAL, REVEALED (v) to make known through divine inspiration; to make (something secret or hidden) publicly or generally known; to display
Exod 6:3 *did not **r** my name, Yahweh,*..........148
Deut 29:29 *all that he has **r-ed** to us,*..........321
Isa 40:5 *the LORD will be **r-ed**,*..........923
Isa 53:1 *the LORD **r-ed** his powerful*..........940
Matt 10:26 *is covered will be **r-ed**,*..........1360
Matt 11:27 *Son chooses to **r** him*..........1339
Luke 2:32 *He is a light to **r** God*..........1282
John 12:38 *the LORD **r-ed** his powerful*.....1434
John 14:21 *love them and **r** myself*..........1462
John 17:6 *I have **r-ed** you to the*..........1466
Rom 8:18 *glory he will **r** to us*..........1659
Rom 16:25 *Christ has **r-ed** his plan*..........1674
1 Cor 2:10 *that God **r-ed** these things*......1598
Gal 1:16 *to **r** his Son to me so that*..........1557
Gal 2:2 *because God **r-ed** to me*..........1558
Eph 3:3 *himself **r-ed** his mysterious*..........1708
Col 1:26 *it has been **r-ed** to God's*..........1696
2 Thes 2:3 *man of lawlessness is **r-ed***.....1588
Titus 2:13 *Christ, will be **r-ed**.*..........1738
Heb 9:8 *the Holy Spirit **r-ed** that*..........1772
1 Pet 1:7 *when Jesus Christ is **r-ed***..........1748

REVELATION, REVELATIONS (n) something that is revealed by God to humans; an act of revealing or communicating divine truth
1 Cor 14:6 *bring you a **r** or some*..........1617
1 Cor 14:30 *person receives a **r** from*.......1618
2 Cor 12:1 *visions and **r-s** from the*..........1641
2 Cor 12:7 *wonderful **r-s** from God.*..........1642
Gal 1:12 *by direct **r** from Jesus*..........1556
Rev 1:1 *This is a **r** from Jesus*..........1798

REVELRY (n) noisy partying or merrymaking
Exod 32:6 *they indulged in pagan **r**.*..........184
1 Cor 10:7 *they indulged in pagan **r**.*..........1610

REVENGE (n) an act or instance of retaliating in order to get even
Lev 19:18 *Do not seek **r** or bear*..........225
Num 31:3 *war of **r** against Midian*..........277
Deut 32:35 *I will take **r**; I will*..........325
Josh 20:3 *relatives seeking **r** for*..........364
Judg 20:10 *will take **r** on Gibeah*..........407
Isa 34:8 *day of the LORD's **r**,*..........904
Heb 10:30 *I will take **r**. I will*..........1776

REVERENCE (n) profound, adoring, awed respect
see also AWE, FEAR, RESPECT
Lev 19:30 *of rest, and show **r** toward*..........226
Job 15:4 *fear of God, no **r** for him?*..........109
Job 37:24 *who are wise show him **r**.*..........127
Eph 5:21 *another out of **r** for Christ*..........1713
Heb 5:7 *of his deep **r** for God.*..........1767

REVERENT (adj) expressing or characterized by reverence; worshipful
Col 3:22 *because of your **r** fear*..........1702
1 Pet 1:17 *must live in **r** fear*..........1749
1 Pet 3:2 *your pure and **r** lives.*..........1752

REVIVE, REVIVES, REVIVING (v) to become active or flourishing again; to restore from a depressed, inactive, or unused state
Ps 19:7 *are perfect, **r-ing** the soul*..........554
Ps 85:6 *Won't you **r** us again,*..........855
Ps 119:25 *lie in the dust; **r** me*..........878
Ps 119:50 *Your promise **r-s** me;*..........879
Prov 25:13 *They **r** the spirit of*..........840

REVOLUTIONARIES (n) those who engage in a revolution
Mark 15:27 *Two **r** were crucified with*.......1483

REWARD, REWARDS (n) something that is given in return for good or evil done or received or that is offered or given for some service or attainment
Gen 15:1 *and your **r** will be*..........34
1 Sam 26:23 *gives his own **r** for doing*..........468
Prov 12:14 *and hard work brings **r-s**.*..........645
Isa 49:4 *I will trust God for my **r**.*..........936
Matt 5:12 *For a great **r** awaits you*..........1326
Matt 6:5 *all the **r** they will ever*..........1331
Luke 6:23 *For a great **r** awaits you*..........1327
Luke 6:35 *your **r** from heaven will*..........1330
Phil 4:17 *you to receive a **r** for your*..........1725
1 Thes 2:19 *be our proud **r** and crown*......1583
Heb 10:35 *the great **r** it brings you!*..........1776
1 Pet 1:9 *The **r** for trusting him*..........1749

REWARD, REWARDED, REWARDS (v) to give a reward to or for; to recompense
2 Sam 22:21 *The LORD **r-ed** me for*..........526
Prov 13:21 *while blessings **r** the*..........647

Prov 25:22 the LORD will **r** you. ... 840
Jer 31:16 for I will **r** you," says ... 1033
Matt 6:18 sees everything, will **r** you ... 1332
Luke 12:37 for his return will be **r-ed.** ... 1401
Luke 14:14 God will **r** you for ... 1408
1 Cor 3:8 both will be **r-ed** for their ... 1599
Eph 6:8 the Lord will **r** each one ... 1715
1 Tim 3:13 will be **r-ed** with respect ... 1731
Heb 11:6 that he **r-s** those who ... 1777
Rev 11:18 the dead and **r** your servants ... 1817

RICH (adj) having abundant possessions and especially material wealth
Job 34:19 no more attention to the **r** ... 124
Ps 49:16 the wicked grow **r** and ... 854
Prov 10:4 poor; hard workers get **r.** ... 642
Prov 11:18 Evil people get **r** for ... 644
Prov 13:7 are poor pretend to be **r;** ... 646
Prov 21:17 and luxury will never be **r.** ... 658
Prov 22:2 The **r** and poor have this ... 658
Prov 23:4 yourself out trying to get **r.** ... 661
Prov 28:6 than to be dishonest and **r.** ... 843
Prov 28:22 Greedy people try to get **r** ... 844
Eccl 5:12 But the **r** seldom get a ... 677
Isa 53:9 put in a **r** man's grave ... 940
Matt 19:23 hard for a **r** person to enter ... 1420
Luke 1:53 and sent the **r** away with ... 1276
Luke 6:24 you who are **r,** for you have ... 1327
Luke 16:1 was a certain **r** man who had ... 1411
Luke 21:1 watched the **r** people ... 1445
2 Cor 8:9 Though he was **r,** yet for your ... 1636
1 Tim 6:9 who long to be **r** fall into ... 1735
1 Tim 6:17 who are **r** in this world ... 1735
Jas 1:10 those who are **r** should boast ... 1547
Jas 2:3 seat to the **r** person, but you ... 1548
Jas 5:1 Look here, you **r** people: ... 1553

RICHES (n) things that make one rich; wealth
see also MONEY, POSSESSIONS, TREASURE(S), WEALTH
2 Chr 1:11 ask for wealth, **r,** fame, ... 608
Ps 49:6 wealth and boast of great **r.** ... 853
Prov 27:24 for **r** don't last forever, ... 842
Eccl 5:13 Hoarding **r** harms the ... 677
Jer 9:23 rich boast in their **r.** ... 1012
Luke 8:14 cares and **r** and pleasures ... 1347
Rom 11:33 great are God's **r** and ... 1666
2 Cor 6:10 give spiritual **r** to others ... 1633
Col 1:27 know that the **r** and glory ... 1696

RIDER (n) one who sits and travels on the back of an animal
Rev 6:2 Its **r** carried a bow, and a ... 1811
Rev 19:11 Its **r** was named Faithful and ... 1828

RIDICULED, RIDICULING (v) to make fun of
2 Kgs 19:22 you been defying and **r-ing?** ... 917
1 Cor 4:10 are honored, but we are **r.** ... 1601

RIDING (v) to sit and travel on the back of an animal that one directs
Zech 9:9 is humble, **r** on a donkey— ... 1175
Matt 21:5 is humble, **r** on a donkey— ... 1429

RIGHT (adj) being in accordance with what is good, just, or proper; being in a correct or proper state; located opposite of left; acting or judging in accordance with truth or fact
see also JUST, JUSTIFY, RIGHTEOUS, UPRIGHT
Gen 4:7 do what is **r,** then watch out! ... 14
Gen 18:19 by doing what is **r** and just ... 40
Exod 15:26 do what is **r** in his sight, ... 162
Num 25:13 making them **r** with me. ... 270
Deut 6:18 Do what is **r** and good ... 295
Deut 25:1 that one is **r** and the other ... 314
Josh 1:7 either to the **r** or to the ... 336
Judg 17:6 whatever seemed **r** in their ... 403
1 Sam 12:23 what is good and **r.** ... 441
1 Kgs 3:9 difference between **r** and ... 606
2 Chr 12:6 The LORD is **r** in doing ... 704
Ps 19:8 LORD are **r,** bringing joy ... 554
Ps 24:5 have a **r** relationship with ... 559
Ps 25:8 does what is **r;** he shows the ... 560
Ps 37:30 they teach **r** from wrong. ... 568
Ps 64:10 do what is **r** will praise him. ... 575
Ps 71:2 do what is **r.** Turn your ear ... 860
Ps 84:11 from those who do what is **r.** ... 855
Ps 97:11 on those whose hearts are **r.** ... 864
Ps 106:3 and always do what is **r.** ... 870
Ps 119:144 laws are always **r;** help me ... 881
Prov 1:3 do what is **r,** just, and fair. ... 631
Prov 2:13 men turn from the **r** way ... 634
Prov 14:2 who follow the **r** path ... 647
Prov 14:12 person that seems **r,** but ... 647
Prov 15:21 stays on the **r** path. ... 650
Prov 15:23 to say the **r** thing at the ... 650
Prov 18:17 in court sounds **r**—until ... 654
Eccl 8:5 and a way to do what is **r,** ... 679
Eccl 9:11 being in the **r** place at the ... 681
Isa 7:15 choose what is **r** and reject ... 790
Isa 16:5 be eager to do what is **r.** ... 833
Isa 26:7 who does what is **r,** and you ... 896
Jer 23:5 is just and **r** throughout the ... 1027
Ezek 18:5 and does what is just and **r.** ... 1064
Ezek 18:21 and do what is just and **r,** ... 1064
Hos 14:9 are true and **r,** and righteous ... 817
Mic 3:1 to know **r** from wrong, ... 906
Mic 6:8 do what is **r,** to love mercy, ... 910
Zeph 2:3 to do what is **r** and to live ... 984
Matt 6:3 hand know what your **r** hand ... 1330
Matt 22:44 of honor at my **r** hand until ... 1442
Acts 2:34 the place of honor at my **r** hand ... 1516
Acts 7:55 honor at God's **r** hand. ... 1526
Acts 13:39 is declared **r** with God— ... 1542
Rom 1:17 God makes us **r** in his sight ... 1646
Rom 2:13 doesn't make us **r** with God. ... 1649
Rom 3:4 will be proved **r** in what you ... 1650
Rom 3:20 ever be made **r** with God by ... 1651
Rom 3:22 We are made **r** with God by ... 1651
Rom 3:28 So we are made **r** with God ... 1652
Rom 3:30 makes people **r** with himself ... 1652
Rom 4:13 but on a **r** relationship with ... 1653
Rom 4:25 life to make us **r** with God. ... 1653
Rom 5:1 we have been made **r** in God's ... 1654
Rom 5:16 being made **r** with God, ... 1655
Rom 6:13 to do what is **r** for the glory ... 1656
Rom 8:10 have been made **r** with God. ... 1659
Rom 8:30 given them **r** standing, ... 1660
Rom 9:30 they were made **r** with God ... 1662
Rom 10:3 way of getting **r** with God by ... 1663
Rom 10:10 you are made **r** with God, ... 1664
1 Cor 6:11 you were made **r** with God ... 1603
2 Cor 3:9 which makes us **r** with God! ... 1630
2 Cor 5:21 be made **r** with God ... 1633
Gal 2:16 person is made **r** with God by ... 1559
Gal 2:17 to be made **r** with God through ... 1560
Gal 2:21 law could make us **r** with God, ... 1560
Gal 3:11 can be made **r** with God by ... 1561
Gal 3:21 could be made **r** with God by ... 1562
Gal 3:24 could be made **r** with God ... 1562
Gal 5:4 to make yourselves **r** with God ... 1565
Eph 5:9 what is good and **r** and true. ... 1712
Phil 4:8 honorable, and **r,** and pure, ... 1725
2 Tim 3:16 teaches us to do what is **r.** ... 1745
Heb 2:10 it was only **r** that he should ... 1764
Heb 12:11 harvest of **r** living for those ... 1780
Jas 2:24 are shown to be **r** with God by ... 1550
1 Jn 2:29 who do what is **r** are God's ... 1790

RIGHT, RIGHTS (n) correct or moral behavior; something to which one has a just claim
Job 27:2 has taken away my **r-s,** by ... 117
Ps 25:9 in doing **r,** teaching them his ... 560
Ps 34:15 those who do **r;** his ears are ... 459
Ps 82:3 the **r-s** of the oppressed ... 602
Prov 29:7 about the **r-s** of the poor; ... 845
Isa 1:17 Fight for the **r-s** of widows. ... 824
Isa 10:2 and deny the **r-s** of the needy ... 794
Lam 3:35 others of their **r-s** in ... 1098
Matt 5:10 for doing **r,** for the Kingdom ... 1326
John 1:12 he gave the **r** to become ... 1271
Rom 9:21 he have a **r** to use the same ... 1662
1 Cor 9:4 have the **r** to live in your ... 1608
1 Pet 3:12 those who do **r,** and his ears ... 1753

RIGHTEOUS (adj) acting in accord with divine or moral law; free from guilt or sin; morally right or justifiable
see also JUST, JUSTIFY, RIGHT, UPRIGHT
Gen 6:9 Noah was a **r** man, the only ... 17
Gen 15:6 counted him as **r** because of ... 35
Gen 18:23 sweep away both the **r** and ... 40
Ps 7:8 Declare me **r,** O LORD, for ... 523
Ps 17:15 Because I am **r,** I will see ... 554
Ps 106:31 regarded as a **r** man ever ... 871
Ps 119:7 I learn your **r** regulations, ... 877
Ps 119:137 O LORD, you are **r,** ... 881
Ps 145:17 The LORD is **r** in everything ... 590
Prov 4:18 The way of the **r** is like the ... 636
Prov 9:9 Teach the **r,** and they ... 641
Prov 29:6 but the **r** escape, shouting ... 845
Isa 26:2 to all who are **r;** allow the ... 896
Isa 42:21 Because he is **r,** the LORD ... 927
Isa 64:6 we display our **r** deeds, ... 950
Jer 11:20 you make **r** judgments, and ... 1015
Jer 23:5 raise up a **r** descendant from ... 1027
Ezek 3:20 None of their **r** acts will be ... 1047
Amos 5:24 river of **r** living. ... 776
Hab 2:4 But the **r** will live ... 980
Mal 3:18 between the **r** and the wicked, ... 1249
Matt 9:13 think they are **r,** but those ... 1315
Matt 13:43 Then the **r** will shine ... 1349
Matt 25:37 Then these **r** ones will ... 1453
Luke 1:6 and Elizabeth were **r** in God's ... 1272
Luke 16:15 like to appear **r** in public, ... 1412
Rom 1:17 faith that a **r** person has ... 1646
Rom 3:5 people see how **r** God is. ... 1650
Rom 3:10 No one is **r**—not even one ... 1650
Rom 4:3 counted him as **r** because of ... 1652
Rom 4:6 who are declared **r** without ... 1652
Rom 4:22 God counted him as **r.** ... 1653
Rom 6:19 be slaves to **r** living so that ... 1656
Gal 3:6 counted him as **r** because of ... 1561
Eph 4:24 like God—truly **r** and holy. ... 1712
Phil 1:11 salvation—the **r** character ... 1717
2 Tim 2:22 Instead, pursue **r** living, ... 1743
Titus 3:7 he declared us **r** and gave us ... 1739
Jas 2:23 counted him as **r** because of ... 1550
Jas 5:16 prayer of a **r** person has ... 1554
1 Jn 2:1 the one who is truly **r.** ... 1788
1 Jn 3:7 that they are **r,** even as ... 1791

RIGHTEOUSNESS (n) the state or quality of being righteous
see also GODLINESS, JUSTICE
Ps 36:6 Your **r** is like the mighty ... 566
Ps 71:15 tell everyone about your **r.** ... 860
Ps 85:10 **R** and peace have kissed! ... 855
Ps 98:2 has revealed his **r** to every ... 865
Ps 111:3 His **r** never fails. ... 873
Prov 21:21 Whoever pursues **r** and ... 658
Isa 11:5 He will wear **r** like a belt ... 796

Isa 42:6 *you to demonstrate my **r.*** 927
Isa 45:8 *so salvation and **r** can sprout*.........931
Isa 56:1 *to display my **r** among you.* 942
Isa 59:17 *He put on **r** as his body*..............946
Jer 9:24 *brings justice and **r** to the*.............1012
Jer 23:6 *Lord Is Our **R.*** 1027
Hos 10:12 *come and shower **r** upon*..............813
Mic 7:9 *and I will see his **r.*** 911
Mal 4:2 *the Sun of **R** will rise*......................1249
Matt 5:20 *unless your **r** is better*..............1328
John 16:8 *and of God's **r,** and of the*...........1465
Acts 24:25 *about **r** and self-control*..........1682
Rom 3:26 *to demonstrate his **r,** for he*.......1651
Rom 5:18 *one act of **r** brings a right*.........1655
2 Cor 6:7 *the weapons of **r** in the*..............1633
Eph 6:14 *the body armor of God's **r.*** 1715
Phil 3:6 *And as for **r,** I obeyed the*..........1722
2 Tim 4:8 *the crown of **r,** which*.................1746
Heb 11:7 *he received the **r** that comes*.....1777
Jas 3:18 *and reap a harvest of **r.*** 1551
2 Pet 3:13 *filled with God's **r.*** 1760

RIPE (adj) fully grown and developed
John 4:35 *are already **r** for harvest.*..........1305
Rev 14:15 *the crop on earth is **r.*** 1822

RISE, RISEN, RISES (v) to ascend or extend above other objects; to return from death; to assume an upright position
see also RESURRECTION
Num 24:17 *A star will **r** from Jacob;*...........268
Isa 26:19 *bodies will **r** again!*......................897
Mal 4:2 *of Righteousness will **r** with*..........1249
Matt 22:30 *when the dead **r,** they will*.......1440
Matt 27:63 *I will **r** from the dead.*.............1489
Matt 28:6 *He is **r-n** from the dead,*...........1490
Mark 8:31 *later he would **r** from the*.........1377
Mark 16:6 *He is **r-n** from the dead!*..........1490
Luke 18:33 *day he will **r** again*....................1423
Luke 24:34 *The Lord has really **r-n!***.........1494
John 5:29 *and they will **r** again*..................1319
John 11:24 *when everyone else **r-s,** at*.....1414
John 20:9 *said Jesus must **r** from the*.......1492
Acts 17:3 *must suffer and **r** from the*........1576
1 Thes 4:16 *have died will **r** from*.............1585

RIVER (n) a natural stream of water; large or overwhelming quantities
Isa 66:12 *give Jerusalem a **r** of peace*........953
Ezek 47:8 *"This **r** flows east through*.........1130
Amos 5:24 *an endless **r** of righteous*..........776
Rev 22:1 *showed me a **r** with the water*....1832

RIVERBANK (n) the ground serving as an edge of a river
Ps 1:3 *along the **r,** bearing fruit*..................856

ROAD (n) an open way for vehicles, persons, and animals; a route or way to an end, conclusion, or circumstance
Ps 25:4 *point out the **r** for me to*.................559
Prov 22:5 *treacherous **r;** whoever values*.....659
Isa 35:8 *And a great **r** will go through*.........905
Matt 3:3 *Clear the **r** for him!*.....................1287

ROARING (adj) making or characterized by a sound resembling a roar
1 Pet 5:8 *around like a **r** lion, looking*.........1756

ROB (v) to steal from by force
Ezek 22:29 *oppress the poor, **r** the needy,*...1070

ROBBERS (n) those who steal usually by violence or threat
John 10:8 *before me were thieves and **r.***..1405

ROBBERY (n) the act or practice of stealing by violence or threat
Isa 61:8 *I hate **r** and wrongdoing.*..............948

ROBE (n) a long, flowing outer garment
Gen 37:3 *for Joseph—a beautiful **r.*** 72
Isa 6:1 *the train of his **r** filled the*................783

ROBED (v) clothed or covered with or as if with a robe
Ps 93:1 *Lord is **r** in majesty*........................862

ROCK (n) a stone; a cliff; foundation, support; refuge
Exod 17:6 *Moses struck the **r** as he was*.....165
Num 20:8 *speak to the **r** over there,*...........261
Deut 32:13 *honey from the **r** and olive*........324
2 Sam 22:2 *Lord is my **r,** my*.......................526
Ps 18:2 *God is my **r,** in whom I*...................527
Ps 19:14 *Lord, my **r** and my redeemer.*........555
Ps 61:2 *to the towering **r** of safety,*............573
Ps 62:7 *my refuge, a **r** where no enemy*......574
Ps 92:15 *He is my **r!*** 862
Isa 26:4 *God is the eternal **R.*** 896
Matt 7:24 *builds a house on solid **r.*** 1335
Matt 16:18 *upon this **r** I will build*............1375
Rom 9:33 *stumble, a **r** that makes them*...1663
1 Cor 10:4 *and that **r** was Christ.*..............1610
1 Pet 2:8 *stumble, the **r** that makes.*..........1750

ROD, RODS (n) a straight, slender stick used as a walking stick, a club or weapon, a shepherd's crook, a paddling stick, a royal scepter, or a measuring stick; figurative of divine authority
see also STAFF
2 Sam 7:14 *him with the **r,** like any*............495
Ps 2:9 *will break them with an iron **r.*** 857
Ps 23:4 *Your **r** and your staff*......................558
Prov 13:24 *spare the **r** of discipline*............647
2 Cor 11:25 *times I was beaten with **r-s.***..1641
Rev 2:27 *the nations with an iron **r***...........1805
Rev 12:5 *rule all nations with an iron **r.*** 1818
Rev 19:15 *rule them with an iron **r.*** 1828

ROMAN (adj) of or relating to Rome or the people of Rome
Acts 16:37 *and we are **R** citizens*..............1576
Acts 22:25 *you to whip a **R** citizen*............1679

ROMAN OFFICER (n) a person of some authority in the Roman military
Matt 8:5 *a **R** came and pleaded*.................1335
Luke 23:47 *the **R** overseeing the execution*...1486
Acts 10:22 *sent by Cornelius, a **R***.............1533

ROMAN SOLDIERS (n) those actively involved in the Roman military
Mark 15:15 *over to the **R** to be crucified*...1479
John 18:3 *given Judas a contingent of **R***..1470

ROOSTER (n) an adult male domestic chicken
Matt 26:34 *before the **r** crows, you will*.....1460

ROOT, ROOTS (n) the part of a plant usually found underground; something that is an origin or source (as of a condition or quality)
Isa 11:1 *bearing fruit from the old **r.*** 795
Isa 53:2 *green shoot, like a **r** in dry*............940
Matt 3:10 *to sever the **r-s** of the trees.*......1288
Matt 13:21 *don't have deep **r-s,** they*........1345
Eph 3:17 *Your **r-s** will grow down*...............1709
1 Tim 6:10 *money is the **r** of all kinds*.......1735
Jude 1:12 *have been pulled up by the **r-s.***1785

ROPE, ROPES (n) a large stout cord of strands twisted or braided together
Josh 2:18 *this scarlet **r** hanging from*..........338
Prov 5:22 *they are **r-s** that catch*...............637
Hos 11:4 *with my **r-s** of kindness*...............814

ROT (v) to undergo decomposition
Ps 16:10 *holy one to **r** in the grave.*............553
Acts 2:27 *Holy One to **r** in the grave.*........1515
Acts 13:35 *Holy One to **r** in the grave.*......1542

ROYAL (adj) of, relating to, or subject to the crown
Ps 93:5 *Your **r** laws cannot be*...................862
Isa 63:1 *this in **r** robes, marching*...............949
Jas 2:8 *you obey the **r** law as found*.........1549
1 Pet 2:9 *You are **r** priests,*......................1751

RUDDER (n) an underwater blade that steers a boat or ship
Jas 3:4 *a small **r** makes a huge ship*.........1550

RUDE (adj) offensive in manner or action
1 Cor 13:5 *or **r.** It does not demand*..........1616

RUIN (n) physical, moral, economic, or social collapse
Eccl 4:5 *idle hands, leading them to **r.*** 676
1 Tim 6:9 *them into **r** and destruction.*.......1735

RUIN, RUINED, RUINING, RUINS (v) to damage irreparably; to subject to frustration, failure, or disaster
Prov 19:3 *People **r** their lives by*................654
Prov 19:18 *you will **r** their lives*..................655
Prov 22:23 *He will **r** anyone who **r-s***............660
Isa 3:14 *You have **r-ed** Israel,*......................827
Matt 9:17 *the wine and **r-ing** the skins*.....1316
2 Tim 2:14 *they can **r** those who hear*.......1742

RULE, RULES (n) a prescribed guide for conduct or action
Isa 29:13 *but man-made **r-s** learned by*.....898
2 Tim 2:5 *unless they follow the **r-s.*** 1742
Heb 13:9 *not from **r-s** about food,*............1782

RULE, RULED, RULES (v) to exert control, direction, or influence on; to exercise authority or power over
Gen 3:16 *but he will **r** over you*......................13
Ps 2:4 *But the one who **r-s** in heaven*.........856
Ps 11:4 *Lord still **r-s** from heaven.*.............550
Ps 55:19 *God, who has **r-d** forever,*............572
Ps 66:7 *great power he **r-s** forever.*............859
Ps 89:9 *You **r** the oceans.*............................591
Ps 103:19 *there he **r-s** over everything*......580
Prov 17:2 *wise servant will **r** over the*..........652
Isa 9:7 *He will **r** with fairness*......................793
Isa 40:10 *He will **r** with a powerful*.............924
Jer 23:5 *a King who **r-s** with wisdom*........1027
Zech 6:13 *honor and will **r** as king*............1170
Rom 5:21 *as sin **r-d** over all people*..........1655
Rom 15:12 *come, and he will **r** over*.........1671
Col 3:15 *comes from Christ **r** in your*........1701
Rev 19:15 *He will **r** them with*..................1828

RULER, RULERS (n) person with authority; tribal chief; prince or king; city magistrate; powerful spiritual beings; God himself
Judg 8:22 *to Gideon, "Be our **r!***...................388
1 Sam 10:1 *to be the **r** over Israel,*.............436
Prov 19:6 *favors from a **r;** everyone is*........654
Prov 23:1 *with a **r,** pay attention to*.............661
Jer 30:21 *have their own **r** again,*..............1032
Dan 7:27 *all **r-s** will serve and obey him.*..1136
Dan 9:25 *until a **r**—the Anointed One—*......1143
Mic 5:2 *a **r** of Israel will come from*.............908
Matt 2:6 *for a **r** will come from*...................1284
Matt 20:25 *that the **r-s** in this world*.........1424
John 12:31 *when Satan, the **r** of this*..........1434
1 Cor 2:6 *or to the **r-s** of this world,*..........1598
Eph 1:21 *far above any **r** or authority*........1706
Eph 3:10 *the unseen **r-s** and authorities*......1709
Eph 6:12 *but against evil **r-s** and*.................1715
Col 1:16 *as thrones, kingdoms, **r-s,** and*...1694

Col 2:15 *disarmed the spiritual* ***r-s*** *and*.....1698
Rev 1:5 *and the* ***r*** *of all the kings*.............1799

RUMORS (n) statements or reports without known authority for being true
Exod 23:1 *must not pass along false* ***r.***........173
Prov 18:8 ***R*** *are dainty morsels that*............653
Jer 51:46 *For* ***r*** *will keep coming year*.......1039

RUN, RUNNING (v) to go faster than a walk; to flee
Ps 19:5 *athlete eager to* ***r*** *the race.* 554
Prov 4:12 *when you* ***r,*** *you won't*................636
Isa 40:31 *will* ***r*** *and not grow weary.* 925
1 Cor 9:26 *So I* ***r*** *with purpose in*.............1609
Gal 2:2 *and I was* ***r-ning*** *the race for*........1558
Gal 5:7 *You were* ***r-ning*** *the race so*.........1565
Phil 2:16 *that I did not* ***r*** *the race in*...........1720
1 Tim 6:11 *so* ***r*** *from all these evil* 1735
2 Tim 2:22 ***R*** *from anything that*..............1743
Heb 12:1 *let us* ***r*** *with endurance*.............1780

RUNNER (n) a messenger
Hab 2:2 *so that a* ***r*** *can carry*.....................979

RUST (n) the reddish brittle coating formed on iron
Matt 6:19 *them and* ***r*** *destroys them,*.........1332

RUTH Moabitess (Ruth 1:4, p. 410); widowed daughter-in-law of Naomi (Ruth 1:18, p. 410); later married Boaz (Ruth 4:10, p. 415); ancestor of David and Jesus (Ruth 4:13, 21-22, p. 415; Matt 1:5, p. 1278).

RUTHLESS (adj) having no pity; cruel
Prov 11:16 *gains respect, but* ***r*** *men gain*....643
Isa 25:3 ***r*** *nations will fear you*...................895

SABAOTH (KJV)
Rom 9:29 *the* Lord *of* ***Heaven's Armies***...1662
Jas 5:4 *the* Lord *of* ***Heaven's Armies***.......1553

SABBATH, SABBATHS (n) cessation of activity; a holy day set aside to honor God through rest and worship
see also REST
Exod 20:8 *to observe the* ***S*** *day by*.............169
Exod 31:14 *must keep the* ***S*** *day, for it*........183
Lev 25:2 *must observe a* ***S*** *rest before*........232
Deut 5:12 *Observe the* ***S*** *day by*................293
2 Chr 2:4 *and evening, on the* ***S-s,***............610
Isa 56:2 *who honor my* ***S*** *days of rest*.........942
Isa 56:6 *do not desecrate the* ***S*** *day*...........943
Isa 58:13 *Honor the* ***S*** *in everything*............945
Matt 12:1 *some grainfields on the* ***S.***.........1319
Luke 13:10 *One* ***S*** *day as Jesus was*........1402
Col 2:16 *new moon ceremonies or* ***S-s.***....1699

SACKCLOTH (KJV)
Gen 37:34 *dressed himself in* ***burlap.***...........74
Esth 4:1 *put on* ***burlap*** *and ashes,*............1187
Job 16:15 *I wear* ***burlap*** *to show my grief*...110
Ps 30:11 *my* ***clothes of mourning*** *and*......563
Luke 10:13 ***burlap*** *and throwing ashes*....1394

SACRED (adj) dedicated or set apart for the service or worship of a deity; entitled to reverence and respect
Lev 10:13 *eat it in a* ***s*** *place, for*.................214
Num 4:15 *and all the* ***s*** *articles*...................242
2 Tim 3:2 *They will consider nothing* ***s.***.....1744

SACRIFICE, SACRIFICES (n) worship or atonement offering; something given up or lost
Exod 12:27 *It is the Passover* ***s*** *to the*.........156
1 Sam 15:22 *Obedience is better than* ***s,***....446
Ps 40:6 *no delight in* ***s-s*** *or offerings.*..........570
Ps 51:16 *do not desire a* ***s,*** *or I would*.........506
Ps 51:17 *The* ***s*** *you desire is*......................506
Ps 107:22 *offer* ***s-s*** *of thanksgiving*............872
Prov 15:8 Lord *detests the* ***s*** *of*.................648
Hos 6:6 *to show love, not offer* ***s-s.***............809
Matt 9:13 *to show mercy, not offer* ***s-s.***....1315
Rom 3:25 *Jesus as the* ***s*** *for sin.* 1651
Rom 8:3 *Son as a* ***s*** *for our sins*................1658
Rom 12:1 *a living and holy* ***s***—*the* 1666
Eph 5:2 *himself as a* ***s*** *for us,*...................1712
Heb 5:3 *he must offer* ***s-s*** *for his own* 1767
Heb 7:27 *need to offer* ***s-s*** *every day.*........1771
Heb 9:28 *time as a* ***s*** *to take away*............1774
Heb 10:5 *did not want animal* ***s-s*** *or sin*...1774
Heb 10:10 *holy by the* ***s*** *of the body of*......1775
Heb 13:15 *Jesus a continual* ***s*** *of praise*...1782
Heb 13:16 *These are the* ***s-s*** *that please*..1783
1 Pet 2:5 *offer spiritual* ***s-s*** *that please*.....1750
1 Jn 2:2 *himself is the* ***s*** *that atones*.........1788
1 Jn 4:10 *his Son as a* ***s*** *to take away*......1793

SACRIFICE, SACRIFICED, SACRIFICES (v) to suffer loss of, give up, renounce, injure, kill, or destroy, especially for an ideal, belief, or end
Gen 22:2 *Go and* ***s*** *him as a*.........................45
John 10:11 *good shepherd* ***s-s*** *his life*......1405
John 10:15 *I* ***s*** *my life for the sheep.*.........1405
1 Cor 5:7 *Lamb, has been* ***s-d*** *for us.*.......1602
1 Cor 13:3 *poor and even* ***s-d*** *my body,*....1616

SACRILEGIOUS (adj) of, relating to, or characterized by a violation of or gross irreverence toward something holy or sacred
Dan 11:31 *and set up the* ***s*** *object that*.....1160
Dan 12:11 *stopped and the* ***s*** *object that*..1162
Matt 24:15 *about—the* ***s*** *object that*.......1446
Mark 13:14 *will see the* ***s*** *object that*........1448

SAD (adj) affected with or expressive of grief or unhappiness
Ps 42:5 *Why is my heart so* ***s?***..................848
Luke 18:23 ***s,*** *for he was very rich*............1422

SADDUCEES (n) members of a Jewish faction that rejected doctrines not in the law (as resurrection, retribution in a future life, and the existence of angels)
Matt 16:6 *yeast of the Pharisees and* ***S.***....1374
Mark 12:18 ***S***—*religious leaders*.............1440
Acts 23:8 *for the* ***S*** *say there is no*...........1680

SADNESS (n) grief or unhappiness
Ps 31:10 *my years are shortened by* ***s.***.......564
Eccl 7:3 ***s*** *has a refining influence*............678
Jas 4:9 ***s*** *instead of laughter*..................1552

SAFE (adj) free from harm or risk; secure from threat of danger, harm, or loss
Deut 29:19 *I am* ***s,*** *even though I am*..........320
1 Sam 30:23 *has kept us* ***s*** *and helped*.......473
Ps 4:8 *O* Lord, *will keep me* ***s.*** 547
Ps 28:8 *He is a* ***s*** *fortress for his*...............562
Prov 2:11 *will keep you* ***s.***..........................634
Prov 4:26 *stay on the* ***s*** *path*......................637
Prov 18:10 *run to him and are* ***s.***...............653
Prov 28:26 *who walks in wisdom is* ***s.***........844
John 17:15 *keep them* ***s*** *from the evil*.......1467

SAFETY (n) the condition of being safe from undergoing or causing hurt, injury, or loss
Deut 33:12 *and live in* ***s*** *beside him.*.........327
2 Sam 23:5 *ensure my* ***s*** *and success.* 546
Ps 16:9 *My body rests in* ***s.***.......................553
Ps 59:16 *my refuge, a place of* ***s***..............454
Prov 11:14 *is* ***s*** *in having many advisers*......643
Prov 29:25 *trusting the* Lord *means* ***s.***........846
Hos 2:18 *live unafraid in peace and* ***s.***........804

SAINTS (KJV)
Ps 34:9 *you his* ***godly people,*** *for*..............458
Ps 97:10 *the lives of his* ***godly people***........864
Dan 7:18 ***holy people*** *of the Most High*....1136
Rom 8:27 *Spirit pleads for* ***us believers***....1660
1 Cor 6:2 ***we believers*** *will judge the*.......1603

SAKE (n) personal or social welfare, safety, or benefit; the good, advantage, or enhancement of some entity
Rom 8:36 *say, "For your* ***s*** *we are*............1661
2 Tim 1:8 *for the* ***s*** *of the Good News.*.......1741
Heb 11:26 *to suffer for the* ***s*** *of Christ*.......1778

SALT (n) the mineral sodium chloride used mainly for seasoning and as a preservative
Gen 19:26 *she turned into a pillar of* ***s.***.........42
Matt 5:13 *You are the* ***s*** *of the earth*..........1327

SALVATION (n) deliverance from the power and effects of sin, danger, or difficulty by God's intervention
see also SAVE
2 Sam 22:47 *Rock of my* ***s,*** *be exalted!* 527
2 Chr 6:41 *be clothed with* ***s;*** *may your*.......622
Ps 18:46 *God of my* ***s*** *be exalted!*...............529
Ps 27:1 *light and my* ***s***—*so why should*......561
Ps 40:16 *love your* ***s*** *repeatedly shout,*........570
Ps 51:12 *joy of your* ***s,*** *and make me*...........506
Ps 62:2 *rock and my* ***s,*** *my fortress*............574
Ps 69:13 *my prayer with your sure* ***s.*** 578
Ps 74:12 *ages past, bringing* ***s*** *to*...............595
Ps 85:4 *us again, O God of our* ***s.***...............855
Ps 89:26 *and the Rock of my* ***s.*** 592
Ps 91:16 *long life and give them my* ***s.***........861
Ps 95:1 *joyfully to the Rock of our* ***s.***...........863
Isa 25:9 *rejoice in the* ***s*** *he brings!*...............896
Isa 26:18 *We have not given* ***s*** *to the*..........896
Isa 33:6 *rich store of* ***s,*** *wisdom,*..................903
Isa 45:8 *wide so* ***s*** *and righteousness*..........931
Isa 45:22 *the world look to me for* ***s!***.............932
Isa 49:6 *will bring my* ***s*** *to the ends*............936
Isa 51:6 *but my* ***s*** *lasts forever.*.....................938
Isa 52:7 *of peace and* ***s,*** *the news that*.......939
Isa 59:17 *the helmet of* ***s*** *on his head.*..........946
Isa 62:1 *dawn, and her* ***s*** *blazes like*..........948
Lam 3:26 *wait quietly for* ***s*** *from the*........1098
Jonah 2:9 *For my* ***s*** *comes from the* 768
Luke 1:77 *to find* ***s*** *through forgiveness*....1276
Luke 2:30 *I have seen your* ***s,*** 1282
Luke 3:6 *will see the* ***s*** *sent from*...............1290
Luke 21:28 *up, for your* ***s*** *is near!*............1451
John 4:22 *him, for* ***s*** *comes through the*...1305
Acts 13:26 *this message of* ***s*** *has been*....1542
Acts 13:47 *Gentiles, to bring* ***s*** *to the*........1543
Acts 28:28 *know that this* ***s*** *from God*.......1689
Rom 11:11 *so God made* ***s*** *available to*.....1665
Rom 13:11 *for our* ***s*** *is nearer now*............1669
2 Cor 6:2 *the day of* ***s,*** *I helped you.*........1633
2 Cor 7:10 *from sin and results in* ***s.***........1635
Eph 6:17 *Put on* ***s*** *as your helmet,*............1715
Phil 2:12 *show the results of your* ***s,***.........1720
2 Thes 2:13 *to experience* ***s***—*a* ***s***............1589
Titus 2:11 *bringing* ***s*** *to all people.*............1738
Heb 2:3 *if we ignore this great* ***s*** *that*........1763
Heb 5:9 *source of eternal* ***s*** *for all*............1767
Heb 9:28 *but to bring* ***s*** *to all who*.............1774
1 Pet 1:9 *will be the* ***s*** *of your souls.*.........1749
1 Pet 1:13 *to the gracious* ***s*** *that will*.........1749
1 Pet 2:2 *into a full experience of* ***s.***..........1750
Rev 7:10 *a great roar, "****S*** *comes from* 1813

SAMARIA (n) the capital city of the northern kingdom of Israel; a region in the uplands of central Palestine between Galilee and Judea
1 Kgs 16:24 *hill now known as **S** from*........712
2 Kgs 17:6 *Hoshea's reign, **S** fell,*..............820
John 4:4 *to go through **S** on the way*.........1304

SAMARITAN (n or adj) a native or inhabitant of Samaria
Luke 10:33 *a despised **S** came along,*......1396
Luke 17:16 *man was a **S**.*..........................1416
John 4:5 *he came to the **S** village of*.........1304
John 4:7 *a **S** woman came to draw*..........1304

SAMSON Judge of Israel from tribe of Dan; defeated oppressing Philistines (Judg 14–15, p. 398); killed lion with bare hands (Judg 14:6, p. 398); set 300 fox tails on fire (Judg 15:4, p. 399); killed 1,000 men (Judg 15:15, p. 400); carried large gates to top of hill (Judg 16:3, p. 400); seduced and deceived by Delilah (Judg 16:1-22, p. 400); died as he destroyed many Philistines (Judg 16:23-31, p. 402).

SAMUEL Judge and prophet of Israel (Heb 11:32, p. 1779); prophet's birth and dedication (1 Sam 1, p. 416); raised by Eli in the Temple (1 Sam 2:11, 18-21, p. 419); called as a prophet (1 Sam 3, p. 421); served as judge over Israel (1 Sam 7:15, p. 427); warned Israel of the tyranny of kingship (1 Sam 8:10-18, p. 435); anointed Saul (1 Sam 10:1, p. 436); rejected Saul (1 Sam 15:23, p. 446); anointed David (1 Sam 16:13, p. 448); protected David from Saul (1 Sam 19:18-24, p. 455); died (1 Sam 25:1, p. 465); ghost of Samuel rebuked Saul (1 Sam 28:14-19, p. 470).

SANCTIFY, SANCTIFIED (KJV)
Gen 2:3 *and **declared it holy***.........................9
Exod 31:13 *LORD, who **makes you holy***......183
Deut 5:12 *Sabbath day by **keeping it holy***...293
John 17:19 *myself as a **holy sacrifice***......1467
Heb 10:10 *for us to **be made holy** by*.......1775

SANCTUARY (n) a holy place set apart for worship of God or refuge from danger
see also TABERNACLE, TEMPLE
Exod 25:8 *build me a holy **s** so I can*...........175
Lev 19:30 *show reverence toward my **s**.*......226
Ps 27:5 *he will hide me in his **s**.*.................561
Ps 63:2 *you in your **s** and gazed upon*........517
Ps 68:35 *God is awesome in his **s**.*.............577
Ps 150:1 *Praise God in his **s;** praise*..........888
Heb 6:19 *curtain into God's inner **s**.*..........1770

SAND (n) fine grains of rock that are worn away by wind and rain
Gen 22:17 *in the sky and the **s** on*.................46
Matt 7:26 *who builds a house on **s**.*...........1335

SANDAL, SANDALS (n) a shoe consisting of a sole strapped to the foot
Exod 3:5 *Take off your **s-s,** for you are*.......143
Exod 12:11 *wear your **s-s,** and carry*..........156
Deut 25:9 *elders, pull his **s** from his*...........315
Josh 5:15 *Take off your **s-s,** for the*............343
Ruth 4:7 *to remove his **s** and hand it*..........415
Matt 3:11 *his slave and carry his **s-s**.*........1289

SANG (v) to produce musical tones by means of the voice
see also SING
Exod 15:1 *people of Israel **s** this*.................161
Exod 15:21 *And Miriam **s** this song:*...........162
Num 21:17 *the Israelites **s** this song:*..........264
Judg 5:1 *son of Abinoam **s** this song:*.........380
2 Sam 22:1 *David **s** this song to*...............526
Ezra 3:11 *and thanks, they **s** this song*......1156
Job 38:7 *morning stars **s** together and*.......128
Ps 106:12 *Then they **s** his praise.*..............870
Matt 26:30 *Then they **s** a hymn*..............1457
Rev 5:9 *And they **s** a new song*................1810
Rev 5:13 *They **s:** "Blessing and*...............1810
Rev 14:3 *great choir **s** a wonderful*...........1821

SAPS (v) to gradually diminish the supply or intensity of
Prov 17:22 *broken spirit **s** a person's*..........653

SARAH (SARAI) Wife of Abraham (Abram) (Gen 11:30-31, p. 24); was infertile (Gen 11:30, p. 24; Rom 4:19, p. 1653) and very beautiful (Gen 12:11, p. 31); with Abraham, deceived Pharaoh (Gen 12:10-20, p. 31); dealings with Hagar and Ishmael (Gen 16, p. 36); name changed (Gen 17:15, p. 39); Isaac promised (Gen 18:10-15, p. 39; Rom 9:9, p. 1661); example of faith (Heb 11:11, p. 1777); with Abraham, deceived Abimelech (Gen 20, p. 42); Isaac born (Gen 21:1-7, p. 43); Hagar and Ishmael sent away (Gen 21:8-21, p. 43); died and was buried (Gen 23, p. 46); Paul's analogy using Sarah and Hagar (Gal 4:25-26, p. 1564).

SARDIS (n) the capital city of Lydia in the province of Asia, in western Asia Minor (modern Turkey)
Rev 3:1 *the angel of the church in **S**.*........1805

SAT (v) to place (the buttocks) on or in a seat
see also SIT
Dan 7:9 *and the Ancient One **s** down to*....1135
Mark 16:19 *into heaven and **s** down in*.....1499
Heb 8:1 *High Priest who **s** down in the*......1771
Heb 10:12 *Then he **s** down in the*............1775

SATAN (n) "adversary" of God and man; the personal name of the devil
see also DEVIL
Job 1:6 *and the Accuser, **S,** came with*.........94
Zech 3:2 *your accusations, **S.** Yes,*............1168
Matt 12:26 *if **S** is casting out **S,** he*...........1341
Matt 16:23 *Get away from me, **S!***............1377
Mark 4:15 *only to have **S** come at once*....1346
Luke 10:18 *told them, "I saw **S** fall from*...1395
Luke 22:3 *Then **S** entered into Judas*........1454
Rom 16:20 *soon crush **S** under your*.........1673
1 Cor 5:5 *him over to **S** so that his*...........1602
2 Cor 11:14 *Even **S** disguises himself as*..1640
2 Cor 12:7 *from **S** to torment*....................1642
1 Tim 1:20 *them over to **S** so they might*...1728
Rev 12:9 *the devil, or **S,** the one*.............1818
Rev 20:2 *is the devil, **S**—and bound*.........1829
Rev 20:7 *come to an end, **S** will be let*......1829

SATISFY, SATISFIED, SATISFIES, SATISFYING (v) to make happy; to gratify to the full
Josh 22:33 *Israelites were **s-ied** and*.........368
Ps 17:14 *But **s** the hunger of your*.............554
Ps 17:15 *you face to face and be **s-ied**.*......554
Ps 22:26 *poor will eat and be **s-ied**.*...........557
Ps 63:5 *You **s** me more than the richest*......517
Ps 105:40 *quail; he **s-ied** their hunger*.......869
Ps 107:9 *he **s-ies** the thirsty and fills*.........872
Ps 145:16 *your hand, you **s** the hunger*......590
Ps 147:14 *and **s-ies** your hunger with the*...1155
Prov 5:19 *Let her breasts **s** you always.*......637
Prov 30:8 *just enough to **s** my needs.*..........846
Prov 30:15 *that are never **s-ied**—no, four*....846
Isa 9:12 *LORD's anger will not be **s-ied**.*.......793
Mic 7:1 *be found to **s** my hunger.*...............910
Luke 6:21 *now, for you will be **s-ied**.*........1326
Heb 13:5 *be **s-ied** with what you have.*....1782
Jas 5:5 *luxury, **s-ing** your every desire.*....1553

SAUL

1. First king of Israel (united kingdom), from tribe of Benjamin (1 Sam 9–11, p. 435); anointed by Samuel (1 Sam 10:1, p. 436); made unlawful sacrifices (1 Sam 13:1-14, p. 441); warrior in battles (1 Sam 13:15–14:52, p. 442); rejected as king (1 Sam 15:26, p. 447); troubled by evil spirit (1 Sam 16:14-23, p. 448); resentful of David and tried to kill him (1 Sam 18:5–19:22, p. 452); gave Michal as wife to David (1 Sam 18:17-30, p. 453); hunted David (1 Sam 22–24, p. 459; 26, p. 467); had priests at Nob killed (1 Sam 22:6-23, p. 461); consulted medium at Endor, rebuked by Samuel's ghost (1 Sam 28:3-25, p. 470); wounded in battle, then killed himself (1 Sam 31:4-6, p. 474; *see also* 2 Sam 1:4-16, p. 476); body desecrated, burned, and buried (1 Sam 31:12-13, p. 474).
2. *See* PAUL, also known as Saul.

SAVE, SAVED, SAVES, SAVING (v) to rescue or deliver from danger or harm; to deliver from sin; to preserve or guard from injury, destruction, or loss; to maintain or preserve
see also PRESERVE, RESCUE, SALVATION
2 Sam 22:3 *the power that **s-s** me,*............526
1 Chr 16:23 *good news that he **s-s**.*...........493
Ps 7:10 *is my shield, **s-ing** those whose*.....524
Ps 18:48 *you **s** me from violent*.................529
Ps 22:8 *let the LORD **s** him!*.......................556
Ps 25:5 *you are the God who **s-s** me*..........559
Ps 33:16 *army cannot **s** a king, nor*...........858
Ps 34:6 *LORD listened; he **s-d** me*..............458
Ps 44:6 *not count on my sword to **s**.*..........850
Ps 68:20 *Our God is a God who **s-s!***..........576
Ps 109:31 *the needy, ready to **s** them*.........582
Ps 116:6 *death, and he **s-d** me*...................875
Prov 2:16 *Wisdom will **s** you from*..............634
Prov 10:2 *right living can **s** your*................641
Isa 25:9 *trusted in him, and he **s-d** us!*.......896
Isa 30:15 *resting in me will you be **s-d**.*......900
Isa 35:4 *He is coming to **s** you*....................905
Isa 59:1 *arm is not too weak to **s**.*...............945
Isa 63:1 *who has the power to **s!***..................949
Jer 4:14 *your heart that you may be **s-d**.*.......964
Jer 17:14 *if you **s** me, I will*......................1021
Jer 51:9 *nothing can **s** her now.*................1037
Dan 3:17 *we serve is able to **s** us*..............1006
Joel 2:32 *name of the LORD will be **s-d,***.....1242
Mic 7:7 *wait confidently for God to **s***..........911
Zeph 1:18 *gold will not **s** you*........................984
Matt 1:21 *he will **s** his people*....................1277
Matt 16:25 *my sake, you will **s** it.*..............1377
Matt 24:13 *to the end will be **s-d**.*..............1446
Luke 17:33 *life go, you will **s** it*..................1416
Luke 19:10 *seek and **s** those who are*......1426
John 10:9 *in through me will be **s-d**.*.........1405
John 12:47 *I have come to **s** the world*.....1435
Acts 2:21 *name of the LORD will be **s-d**.*....1515
Acts 4:12 *by which we must be **s-d**.*..........1519
Acts 15:11 *we are all **s-d** the same way,*..1569
Acts 16:30 *what must I do to be **s-d?***.......1576
Rom 1:16 *God at work, **s-ing** everyone*....1646
Rom 5:9 *he will certainly **s** us from*...........1654
Rom 10:9 *the dead, you will be **s-d**.*..........1663
Rom 10:13 *of the LORD will be **s-d**.*............1664
1 Cor 1:18 *we who are being **s-d** know*....1596
1 Cor 5:5 *himself will be **s-d** on the*..........1602

1 Cor 7:16 *wives might be **s-d** because* ...1606
1 Cor 10:33 *so that many may be **s-d.***.....1611
1 Cor 15:2 *this Good News that **s-s***..........1618
Eph 1:13 *Good News that God **s-s** you.* 1705
1 Thes 5:9 *God chose to **s** us through*.......1585
1 Tim 1:15 *the world to **s** sinners*............1728
1 Tim 2:4 *wants everyone to be **s-d** and*...1729
1 Tim 2:15 *women will be **s-d** through*.....1730
2 Tim 1:9 *For God **s-d** us and called*.........1741
Titus 3:5 *he **s-d** us, not because of the*.....1739
Heb 7:25 *and forever, to **s** those who*........1771
Jas 5:20 *sinner back will **s** that person*.....1554
2 Pet 3:15 *gives people time to be **s-d.***....1760

SAVING (adj) of or relating to delivering or rescuing
Ps 40:10 *faithfulness and **s** power.*............570
Ps 67:2 *the earth, your **s** power*...............859
Ps 69:29 *God, by your **s** power.*.................578
Ps 71:15 *proclaim your **s** power,* 860
Ps 98:1 *has shown his **s** power!*..................865

SAVIOR (n) one who delivers from trouble, sin, or judgment
2 Sam 22:2 *my fortress, and my **s;***............526
Ps 38:22 *help me, O LORD my **s.***................569
Ps 40:17 *You are my helper and my **s.***........570
Ps 106:21 *They forgot God, their **s,***............870
Isa 43:11 *and there is no other **S.***...............928
Isa 45:21 *a righteous God and **S.***...............932
Isa 49:26 *the LORD, am your **S** and*............937
Isa 62:11 *Look, your **S** is coming.*...............949
Jer 14:8 *Hope of Israel, our **S** in* 1017
Hos 13:4 *for there is no other **s.***................816
Zeph 3:17 *He is a mighty **s.***.........................986
Luke 1:47 *rejoices in God my **S!***...............1275
Luke 1:69 *He has sent us a mighty **S.***.......1276
John 4:42 *he is indeed the **S** of the*..........1306
Acts 5:31 *right hand as Prince and **S.***.......1521
Acts 13:23 *God's promised **S** of Israel!*.....1541
Eph 5:23 *He is the **S** of his body,*................1713
1 Tim 2:3 *good and pleases God our **S,***.....1729
1 Tim 4:10 *who is the **S** of all people*........1732
Titus 2:10 *about God our **S** attractive*..........1738
Titus 3:4 *When God our **S** revealed his*......1739
2 Pet 3:2 *Lord and **S** commanded*..............1760
1 Jn 4:14 *Son to be the **S** of the world.*.....1793

SAVOUR (KJV)
2 Cor 2:16 *a dreadful **smell** of death*........1628
Eph 5:2 *for us, a pleasing **aroma** to God*...1712

SAW (v) to percieve using the eye
see also SEE
Ps 139:16 *You **s** me before I was born*........586

SCALES (n) the outer covering of fish or reptiles; an instrument for weighing
see also BALANCES
Lev 11:9 *fins and **s,** whether taken*.............214
Lev 19:36 *Your **s** and weights*....................226
Deut 25:13 *must use accurate **s** when you*...315
Prov 11:1 *use of dishonest **s,** but he*...........643
Rev 6:5 *a pair of **s** in his hand.*..................1811

SCAPEGOAT (n) a goat upon whose head the sins of the people are symbolically placed, after which he is sent into the wilderness on the Day of Atonement
Lev 16:10 *other goat, the **s** chosen by*........221

SCARLET (adj) of the color of any various bright reds
Josh 2:21 *leaving the **s** rope hanging*.........338
Isa 1:18 *sins are like **s,** I will make*.............824
Matt 27:28 *and put a **s** robe on him*..........1481

SCARS (n) marks left (as in the skin) by the healing of injured tissue
Gal 6:17 *on my body the **s** that show*........1568

SCATTER, SCATTERED (v) to separate and go in various directions; to disperse
Deut 4:27 *the LORD will **s** you*....................291
Neh 1:8 *to me, I will **s** you among*.............1204
Isa 11:12 *will gather the **s-ed** people* 796
Jer 9:16 *I will **s** them around*...................1012
Jer 30:11 *where I have **s-ed** you, but I*.....1031
Jer 31:10 *LORD, who **s-ed** his people,*.......1033
Ezek 34:21 *flock until you **s-ed** them to*....1110
Zech 2:6 *for I have **s-ed** you to the four*....1167
Zech 10:9 *Though I have **s-ed** them like*..1176
Zech 13:7 *sheep will be **s-ed,** and I will* 1179
Matt 26:31 *of the flock will be **s-ed.***.......1460
John 11:52 *children of God **s-ed** around* ..1415
Acts 8:4 *were **s-ed** preached the Good* 1527
Jas 1:1 *Jewish believers **s-ed** abroad*.......1546

SCEPTER (n) the official staff of a ruler, symbolizing his authority and power
Gen 49:10 *The **s** will not depart from*............91
Num 24:17 *a **s** will emerge from Israel.* 268
Heb 1:8 *rule with a **s** of justice.*................1762

SCHEME (v) to make crafty or secret plans
Zech 8:17 *Don't **s** against each*................1174

SCHEMERS (n) those who plot or scheme
Job 5:12 *He frustrates the plans of **s***............99
Prov 14:17 *things, and **s** are hated.*............648

SCHEMES (n) crafty or secret plans
Job 5:13 *cunning **s** are thwarted.*.................99
Ps 37:7 *or fret about their wicked **s.***...........567
Ps 140:8 *let their evil **s** succeed,*................587
Prov 13:11 *from get-rich-quick **s***................646
2 Cor 2:11 *familiar with his evil **s.*** 1628

SCOFF (v) to show contempt by derisive acts or language; to mock
Lam 2:15 *They **s** and insult*......................1097
1 Thes 5:20 *Do not **s** at prophecies,*.........1586
2 Pet 2:12 *They **s** at things they do not*.....1759
Jude 1:8 *defy authority, and **s** at*..............1785

SCOFFERS (n) those who scoff
2 Pet 3:3 *the last days **s** will come,*...........1760

SCORN (n) open dislike, disrespect, or derision often mixed with indignation
Ps 109:25 *they shake their heads in **s.*** 582
Isa 51:7 *not be afraid of people's **s,***............938

SCORN, SCORNED (v) to reject or dismiss as contemptible or unworthy
Ps 22:6 *I am **s-ed** and despised by all!*.......556
Ps 119:22 *Don't let them **s** and insult*.........878
Prov 9:12 *If you **s** wisdom, you will*............641
Jer 6:10 *They **s** the word of the LORD.*.........968

SCORNFUL (adj) full of scorn; contemptuous
Ezek 28:24 *will Israel's **s** neighbors* 1085

SCORPION (n) a small crawling animal with eight legs, two sets of pincers, and a tail with a poisonous stinger
Luke 11:12 *give them a **s?** Of course*.......1398
Rev 9:5 *pain of a **s** sting.*.........................1814

SCRIPTURE, SCRIPTURES (n) the law; the writings of Moses; the entire collection of sacred books
Matt 21:16 *you ever read the **S-s?***...........1432
Matt 22:29 *you don't know the **S-s,*** 1440
Luke 24:27 *from all the **S-s** the things*......1494
Luke 24:45 *to understand the **S-s.***...........1498
John 2:22 *believed both the **S-s** and*.......1300
John 5:39 *You search the **S-s** because*.......1319
John 7:42 *the **S-s** clearly state that*..........1390
John 10:35 *know that the **S-s** cannot*.......1406
Acts 8:32 *The passage of **S** he had*..........1529
1 Cor 4:6 *quoted from the **S-s,** you won't*..1600
1 Tim 4:13 *focus on reading the **S-s** to*.....1732
2 Tim 3:16 *All **S** is inspired by God*...........1745
Heb 10:7 *written about me in the **S-s.*** 1775
2 Pet 1:20 *no prophecy in **S** ever came* 1758
2 Pet 3:16 *do with other parts of **S.*** 1760

SCROLL (n) a roll (as of papyrus, leather, or parchment) for writing a document
Isa 34:4 *disappear like a rolled-up **s.***..........904
Ezek 3:1 *giving you—eat this **s!***...............1046
Rev 6:14 *sky was rolled up like a **s,***..........1812
Rev 10:8 *take the open **s** from the hand*...1816

SEA, SEAS (n) a great body of salt water that covers much of the earth; a large basin used in the Temple
Exod 14:16 *middle of the **s** on dry*.............160
Deut 30:13 *not kept beyond the **s,***.............321
1 Kgs 7:23 *rim to rim, called the **S.***.............613
Job 11:9 *and wider than the **s.***....................105
Ps 93:4 *violent raging of the **s-s,*** 862
Ps 95:5 *The **s** belongs to him,*....................863
Eccl 11:1 *your grain across the **s-s,*** 682
Isa 57:20 *like the restless **s,** which*............944
Jonah 1:4 *wind over the **s,** causing a*...........765
Hab 2:14 *waters fill the **s,** the earth*...........980
Matt 18:6 *in the depths of the **s.***..............1384
Jas 1:6 *wave of the **s** that is blown*............1546
Jude 1:13 *waves of the **s,** churning up*.....1785
Rev 10:2 *right foot on the **s** and*..............1816
Rev 13:1 *rising up out of the **s.***................1819
Rev 20:13 *The **s** gave up its dead,*............1830
Rev 21:1 *And the **s** was also gone.*...........1830

SEAL, SEALS (n) a piece of wax or clay impressed with a device such as a signet ring or cylinder engraved with the owner's name, a design, or both that certifies or authenticates a document
Rev 5:2 *break the **s-s** on this scroll*..........1809
Rev 6:1 *the seven **s-s** on the scroll.*..........1811
Rev 6:3 *broke the second **s,** I heard*..........1811
Rev 6:5 *broke the third **s,** I heard*..............1811
Rev 6:7 *broke the fourth **s,** I heard*............1811
Rev 6:9 *Lamb broke the fifth **s,** I saw*.........1811
Rev 6:12 *broke the sixth **s,** and there*..........1812
Rev 8:1 *broke the seventh **s** on the*............1813
Rev 9:4 *did not have the **s** of God*..............1814

SEAL, SEALED (v) to confirm or make secure by or as if by a seal
Dan 12:4 *secret; **s** up the book until*.........1161
Rev 5:1 *and it was **s-ed** with seven*...........1809
Rev 22:10 *Do not **s** up the prophetic*.........1832

SEARCH, SEARCHES (v) to investigate or examine thoroughly in an effort to find or verify something
Ps 34:14 ***S** for peace, and work* 459
Ps 139:23 ***S** me, O God, and know*.............586
Eccl 3:6 *A time to **s** and a time to*...............675
Jer 17:10 *I, the LORD, **s** all hearts* 1021
1 Cor 2:10 *Spirit **s-es** out everything*........1598
1 Pet 3:11 ***S** for peace, and work* 1753

SEASHORE (n) land adjacent to the sea
Josh 11:4 *like the sand on the **s.***................352
1 Kgs 4:29 *vast as the sands of the **s.*** 629

SEASON, SEASONS (n) the period normally characterized by a particular kind of weather; a period associated with some phase or activity of agriculture (as growth or harvesting)
Gen 1:14 *signs to mark the **s-s**, days,*........7
Ps 1:3 *bearing fruit each **s**.*........856
Gal 4:10 *or months or **s-s** or years.*........1563

SEASONAL (adj) of, relating to, or varying in occurrence according to the season
Lev 26:4 *send you the **s** rains.*........234

SEAT, SEATS (n) a chair, stool, or bench intended to be sat in or on
Luke 11:43 *to sit in the **s-s** of honor*........1398
Luke 14:9 *to take whatever **s** is left*........1408

SEATED (v) to put into a sitting position; to take one's seat or place
Matt 26:64 *Son of Man **s** in the place*........1472
Luke 22:69 *of Man will be **s** in the place*........1475
Eph 1:20 *the dead and **s** him in the*........1706
Eph 2:6 *with Christ and **s** us with him*........1707
Heb 12:2 *Now he is **s** in the place of*........1780
Rev 14:14 *a white cloud, and **s** on the*........1822

SECOND (adj) next to the first in place or time
Job 42:12 *Job in the **s** half of his life*........132
Rev 20:14 *lake of fire is the **s** death*........1830

SECRET (adj) kept from knowledge or view; hidden
Ps 90:8 *before you—our **s** sins—*........326
Jer 23:24 *from me in a **s** place?*........1028
Matt 10:26 *all that is **s** will be*........1360
Rom 2:16 *judge everyone's **s** life*........1649
Rom 16:25 *a plan kept **s** from the*........1674
1 Cor 13:2 *all of God's **s** plans*........1616
1 Cor 14:25 *their **s** thoughts will be*........1618
Col 1:26 *was kept **s** for centuries and*........1696

SECRET, SECRETS (n) something kept hidden or unexplained; something kept from the knowledge of others or shared only confidentially with a few
see also MYSTERY
Deut 29:29 *God has **s-s** known to no*........321
Judg 16:15 *don't share your **s-s** with*........401
Ps 44:21 *he knows the **s-s** of every*........850
Prov 11:13 *goes around telling **s-s**,*........643
Dan 2:28 *heaven who reveals **s-s**, and*........1004
Dan 2:29 *who reveals **s-s** has shown*........1004
Mark 4:11 *to understand the **s***........1346
Mark 4:22 *and every **s** will be brought*........1347
Luke 8:10 *to understand the **s-s** of*........1347
1 Cor 15:51 *reveal to you a wonderful **s**.*........1622
Phil 4:12 *have learned the **s** of living*........1725
Col 1:27 *the **s**: Christ lives in you.*........1696

SECURE (adj) easy in mind; free from danger or the risk of loss; trustworthy, dependable
Job 31:24 *felt **s** because of my gold?*........121
Ps 30:7 *made me as **s** as a mountain.*........563
Prov 14:26 *fear the LORD are **s**;*........648
1 Thes 5:3 *is peaceful and **s**," then*........1585
2 Pet 3:17 *your own **s** footing.*........1760

SECURE, SECURED (v) to make fast, safe, or steady
Matt 27:65 *Take guards and **s** it the*........1489
Heb 9:12 *and **s-d** our redemption*........1773

SECURITY (n) something given, deposited, or pledged to make certain the fulfillment of an obligation; freedom from danger; protection
Deut 24:17 *widow's garment as **s** for*........314
Ezra 9:8 *has given us **s** in this holy*........1200
Prov 3:26 *the LORD is your **s**.*........635
Prov 19:23 *bringing **s** and protection*........655

SEDUCE, SEDUCED (v) to persuade to disobedience or disloyalty; to entice
Deut 4:19 *don't be **s-d** into*........290
Job 31:9 *has been **s-d** by a woman,*........121
Job 36:18 *you may be **s-d** by wealth.*........126
Prov 6:25 *her coy glances **s** you.*........638

SEE, SEEING, SEES (v) to perceive by the eye; to understand or recognize; to come to know
see also SAW
Ps 34:8 *Taste and **s** that the*........458
Ps 36:2 *they cannot **s** how wicked*........566
Ps 90:8 *sins—and you **s** them*........326
Ps 119:82 *straining to **s** your promises*........879
Prov 5:21 *For the LORD **s-s** clearly*........637
Prov 13:19 *pleasant to **s** dreams come*........646
Eccl 3:11 *people cannot **s** the whole*........675
Matt 6:18 *Father, who **s-s** everything,*........1332
John 12:45 *you are **s-ing** the one who*........1435
Rom 1:20 *can clearly **s** his invisible*........1647
Rom 7:13 *So we can **s** how terrible sin*........1658
1 Cor 13:12 *we will **s** everything with*........1616
2 Cor 4:18 *things we cannot **s** will last*........1631
2 Cor 5:7 *by believing and not by **s-ing**.*........1632
2 Cor 8:21 *everyone else to **s** that we*........1637
Phil 4:5 *Let everyone **s** that you are*........1724
Col 1:16 *things we can't **s**—such as*........1694
Rev 1:7 *everyone will **s** him—even*........1800

SEED, SEEDS (n) the grains of plants used for sowing
Gen 1:11 *These **s-s** will then produce*........7
Prov 11:30 *The **s-s** of good deeds*........644
Matt 13:3 *went out to plant some **s-s**.*........1345
Matt 13:31 *like a mustard **s** planted in*........1348
Matt 17:20 *as a mustard **s**, you could say*...1381
Mark 4:15 *The **s** that fell on*........1346
Luke 8:12 *The **s-s** that fell on*........1347
1 Cor 3:6 *I planted the **s** in your*........1599
2 Cor 9:6 *few **s-s** will get a small*........1637
2 Cor 9:10 *one who provides **s** for the*........1638

SEED-BEARING (adj) a plant that produces seeds
Gen 1:11 *every sort of **s** plant,*........7

SEEK, SEEKING, SEEKS (v) to go in search of; to try to acquire or gain
see also SOUGHT
2 Chr 7:14 *pray and **s** my face and*........623
2 Chr 15:2 *Whenever you **s** him,*........708
Prov 3:6 ***S** his will in all you do,*........634
Prov 25:27 *not good to **s** honors*........840
Prov 29:26 *Many **s** the ruler's favor,*........846
Isa 55:6 ***S** the LORD while you can*........942
Hos 10:12 *time to **s** the LORD,*........813
Zeph 2:3 ***S** the LORD, all who are*........984
Matt 6:33 ***S** the Kingdom of God above*........1332
Matt 7:7 *Keep on **s-ing**, and you*........1334
Matt 7:8 *Everyone who **s-s**, finds.*........1334
Luke 12:31 ***S** the Kingdom of God*........1401
Luke 19:10 *Son of Man came to **s** and*........1426
Rom 3:11 *no one is **s-ing** God.*........1651
1 Cor 7:27 *have a wife, do not **s** to get*........1606
Heb 11:6 *those who sincerely **s** him.*........1777

SEER (n) one who practices divination and predicts events or developments
1 Sam 9:9 *ask the **s**," for prophets*........436

SELF-CONTROL (n) restraint exercised over one's own impulses, emotions, or desires
Prov 5:23 *He will die for lack of **s**;*........637
Prov 16:32 *better to have **s** than to*........652
Acts 24:25 *righteousness and **s** and the*........1682
Gal 5:23 *gentleness, and **s**. There is no*........1566
1 Tim 3:2 *must exercise **s**, live wisely,*........1730
1 Tim 3:11 *They must exercise **s** and be*........1731
Titus 2:2 *older men to exercise **s**,*........1738
1 Pet 1:13 *think clearly and exercise **s**.*........1749
2 Pet 1:6 *and knowledge with **s**, and*........1757

SELF-DENIAL (n) a restraint or limitation of one's own desires or interests
Col 2:18 *insisting on pious **s** or the*........1699
Col 2:23 *devotion, pious **s**, and severe*........1699

SELF-DISCIPLINE (n) correction or regulation of oneself for the sake of improvement
2 Tim 1:7 *but of power, love, and **s**.*........1741

SELF-INDULGENCE (n) excessive or unrestrained gratification of one's own appetites, desires, or whims
Matt 23:25 *full of greed and **s**!*........1444

SELFISH (adj) seeking or concentrating on one's own advantage, pleasure, or well-being without regard for others
Matt 16:24 *turn from your **s** ways,*........1377
Luke 9:23 *turn from your **s** ways,*........1378
Gal 5:20 *of anger, **s** ambition,*........1566
Phil 1:17 *They preach with **s** ambition,*........1718
Jas 3:14 *and there is **s** ambition in*........1550
Jas 3:16 *is jealousy and **s** ambition,*........1551

SELFISHNESS (n) the act of being concerned only with oneself
2 Cor 12:20 *jealousy, anger, **s**, slander*........1642
Jas 3:15 *jealousy and **s** are not God's*........1550

SELL, SELLING (v) to give up (property) to another for something of value (as money)
see also SOLD
Prov 23:23 *truth and never **s** it;*........661
Prov 31:24 *and sashes to **s** to the*........848
Mark 10:21 *and **s** all your possessions*........1421
Luke 17:28 *buying and **s-ing**, farming and*........1416
Rev 13:17 *could buy or **s** anything*........1820

SEND, SENDING (v) to direct, order, or request to go
see also SENT
Isa 6:8 *Here I am. **S** me.*........785
Isa 55:11 *with my word. I **s** it out,*........942
Mal 3:1 *I am **s-ing** my messenger,*........1247
Matt 9:38 *ask him to **s** more workers*........1357
Mark 1:2 *I am **s-ing** my messenger*........1289
1 Cor 1:17 *For Christ didn't **s** me to*........1596

SENSE (n) sound and prudent judgment based on a simple perception of the situation or facts; intelligence
Prov 3:21 *common **s** and discernment.*........635
Prov 8:14 *Common **s** and success.*........640
Prov 12:11 *chases fantasies has no **s**.*........645
Prov 15:21 *brings joy to those with no **s**;*........650
Prov 18:1 *they lash out at common **s**.*........653
Prov 24:30 *of one with no common **s**.*........663

SENSIBLE (adj) having, containing, or indicative of good sense or reason; rational, reasonable
Prov 10:23 *brings pleasure to the **s**.*........643
Prov 11:12 *a **s** person keeps quiet.*........643
Prov 15:21 ***s** person stays on the right.*........650
Matt 24:45 *A faithful, **s** servant is one*........1447

SENSITIVE (adj) highly responsive or susceptible
Rom 15:1 *those who are **s** about things*........1671

SENT (v) to direct, order, or request to go
see also SEND
Exod 3:14 *I AM has **s** me*...144
Matt 10:40 *the Father who **s** me.*...1361
Luke 10:16 *God, who **s** me.*...1394
John 3:17 *God **s** his Son into the*...1302
John 20:21 *As the Father has **s** me, so*...1495
Rom 8:3 *He **s** his own Son in a*...1658
Rom 10:15 *them without being **s?***...1664
Gal 4:4 *time came, God **s** his Son,*...1562

SEPARATE, SEPARATED, SEPARATES (v) to set or keep apart; to sort
Prov 17:9 *on it **s-s** close friends.*...652
Matt 25:32 *a shepherd **s-s** the sheep.*...1452
Rom 8:35 *Can anything ever **s** us*...1661
Eph 2:14 *of hostility that **s-d** us.*...1708
Col 1:21 *his enemies, **s-d** from him.*...1695

SERAPHIM (n) six-winged angels standing in God's presence
Isa 6:2 *were mighty **s,** each having*...783
Isa 6:6 *Then one of the **s** flew to me*...784

SERIOUSNESS (n) a sober attitude
Titus 2:7 *the integrity and **s** of your*...1738

SERPENT (n) a snake or crawling reptile often associated with temptation, sin, and evil; Satan
Gen 3:1 *The **s** was the shrewdest of*...11
Isa 27:1 ***s,** the coiling, writhing **s.***...897
2 Cor 11:3 *the cunning ways of the **s.***...1640
Rev 12:9 *the ancient **s** called the devil,*...1818
Rev 20:2 *that old **s,** who is the devil,*...1829

SERVANT, SERVANTS (n) one who performs tasks under the direction of another
see also SLAVE(S)
Exod 14:31 *LORD and in his **s** Moses.*...161
Lev 25:55 *They are my **s-s,** whom I*...234
1 Sam 3:10 *Speak, your **s** is listening.*...422
2 Kgs 17:13 *my **s-s** the prophets.*...820
Job 1:8 *Have you noticed my **s** Job?*...95
Ps 19:13 *Keep your **s** from deliberate*...555
Ps 31:16 *your favor shine on your **s.***...564
Ps 89:3 *with David, my chosen **s.***...591
Ps 104:4 *flames of fire are your **s-s.***...867
Prov 14:35 *king rejoices in wise **s-s***...648
Prov 17:2 *A wise **s** will rule*...652
Prov 22:7 *so the borrower is **s** to the*...659
Prov 31:15 *work for her **s** girls.*...847
Eccl 7:21 *may hear your **s** curse you.*...679
Eccl 10:7 *seen **s-s** riding horseback*...681
Isa 53:11 *my righteous **s** will make it*...940
Isa 65:8 *I still have true **s-s** there.*...951
Zech 3:8 *to bring my **s,** the Branch.*...1168
Mal 1:6 *father, and a **s** respects his*...1245
Matt 20:26 *among you must be your **s,***...1424
Matt 24:45 *faithful, sensible **s** is one*...1447
Luke 1:48 *of his lowly **s** girl, and*...1275
Luke 17:10 *We are unworthy **s-s** who*...1413
Luke 22:26 *leader should be like a **s.***...1458
John 12:26 *because my **s-s** must be*...1434
Rom 13:4 *authorities are God's **s-s,***...1668
1 Cor 3:5 *are only God's **s-s** through*...1599
Col 1:23 *God's **s** to proclaim it.*...1696
1 Tim 4:6 *be a worthy **s** of Christ.*...1732
Heb 1:7 *his **s-s** like flames of fire.*...1762
Heb 1:14 *angels are only **s-s**—spirits*...1763

SERVE, SERVED, SERVES, SERVING (v) to meet the needs of and subject one's will to that of another
Deut 10:12 *love him and **s** him with*...300
Deut 11:13 *your God and **s** him with*...300
Deut 28:47 *If you do not **s** the LORD*...319
Deut 30:17 *drawn away to **s** and*...321
Josh 24:15 *family, we will **s** the LORD.*...370
2 Chr 12:8 *between **s-ing** me and*...704
Ps 34:22 *redeem those who **s** him.*...459
Ps 101:6 *be allowed to **s** me.*...580
Ps 103:21 *of angels who **s** him and do*...580
Isa 38:3 *have **s-d** you single-mindedly*...920
Dan 3:17 *the God whom we **s** is able to*...1006
Matt 4:10 *your God and **s** only him.*...1295
Matt 6:24 *No one can **s** two masters.*...1332
Matt 20:28 *not to be **s-d** but to **s***...1424
Luke 22:27 *among you as one who **s-s.***...1459
John 12:2 *Martha **s-d,** and Lazarus was*...1428
John 12:26 *honor anyone who **s-s** me.*...1434
Acts 17:25 *hands can't **s** his needs—*...1578
Rom 1:25 *worshiped and **s-d** the things*...1648
Rom 12:7 *your gift is **s-ing** others, **s***...1667
Rom 12:11 *work hard and **s** the Lord.*...1667
Rom 13:6 *They are **s-ing** God in what*...1668
Rom 14:18 *If you **s** Christ with*...1670
Rom 16:18 *people are not **s-ing** Christ.*...1673
1 Cor 16:18 *to all who **s** so well.*...1623
Gal 5:13 *your freedom to **s** one another*...1565
Col 3:24 *Master you are **s-ing** is Christ.*...1702
1 Tim 5:10 *kind to strangers and **s-d** other*...1733
1 Pet 5:5 *all of you, **s** each other in*...1756

SERVICE (n) employment as a servant; the work performed by one that serves
Num 8:11 *dedicating them to the LORD's **s.***...200
Luke 12:35 *Be dressed for **s** and keep*...1401
Rom 15:17 *through me in my **s** to God.*...1671
1 Cor 12:5 *different kinds of **s,** but we*...1614

SET APART (v) to designate or preserve for a particular use
Exod 16:23 *holy Sabbath day **s** for the Lord*...164
Deut 14:2 ***s** as holy to the Lord*...303
Heb 7:26 *been **s** from sinners*...1771

SEVEN (adj) of or relating to the number 7
Josh 6:4 *around the town **s** times, with*...343
Prov 6:16 *LORD hates—no, **s** things*...638
Prov 24:16 *godly may trip **s** times,*...662
Isa 4:1 *so few men will be left that **s***...828
Luke 11:26 *spirit finds **s** other spirits*...1343
Rev 1:4 *John to the **s** churches in the*...1799
Rev 6:1 *first of the **s** seals on the*...1811
Rev 8:2 *were given **s** trumpets.*...1813
Rev 10:4 *what the **s** thunders said,*...1816
Rev 15:7 *handed each of the **s** angels*...1822

SEVEN (n) the number 7
Dan 9:26 *period of sixty-two sets of **s,***...1143

SEVENFOLD (adj) having seven units or members
Rev 4:5 *This is the **s** Spirit of God.*...1808

SEVENTH (adj) of or relating to the position of the number seven
Gen 2:2 *On the **s** day God*...9
Exod 20:10 *the **s** day is a Sabbath day*...169
Exod 23:11 *uncultivated during the **s***...173
Exod 23:12 *but on the **s** day you must*...173
Heb 4:4 *On the **s** day God rested.*...1766

SEVENTY (adj) of or relating to the number 70
Dan 9:24 *A period of **s** sets of seven*...1143
Matt 18:22 *Jesus replied, "but **s** times.*...1385

SEVERE (adj) strict in judgment, discipline, or government; inflicting physical discomfort or hardship
Rom 11:22 *God is both kind and **s.***...1665
1 Thes 1:6 *in spite of the **s** suffering.*...1581

SEWED (v) united or fastened by stitches
Gen 3:7 *So they **s** fig leaves together.*...12

SEXUAL (adj) of, relating to, or associated with sex or the sexes; having or involving sex
Exod 22:19 *who has **s** relations with.*...172
Lev 18:6 *never have **s** relations with.*...224
Num 25:1 *by having **s** relations with*...269
Matt 1:25 *did not have **s** relations with*...1278
Matt 15:19 *adultery, all **s** immorality,*...1370
Acts 15:20 *to idols, from **s** immorality,*...1570
1 Cor 5:1 *about the **s** immorality going*...1602
1 Cor 5:11 *yet indulges in **s** sin*...1602
1 Cor 6:9 *who indulge in **s** sin, or who*...1603
1 Cor 6:18 *Run from **s** sin! No other*...1604
1 Cor 7:1 *to abstain from **s** relations.*...1605
1 Cor 10:8 *not engage in **s** immorality*...1610
2 Cor 12:21 *impurity, **s** immorality,*...1642
Eph 5:3 *be no **s** immorality, impurity,*...1712
Col 3:5 *to do with **s** immorality,*...1700
1 Thes 4:3 *stay away from all **s** sin*...1584
2 Pet 2:10 *own twisted **s** desire, and*...1759
2 Pet 2:18 *to twisted **s** desires,*...1759
Rev 2:14 *and by committing **s** sin.*...1804
Rev 2:20 *teaches them to commit **s** sin*...1804

SEXUALLY (adv)
1 Tim 1:10 *is for people who are **s** immoral*...1728
Rev 22:15 *the sorcerers, the **s** immoral,*...1832

SHADE (n) a place sheltered from the sun
Ps 121:5 *you as your protective **s.***...882

SHADOW, SHADOWS (n) shelter from danger or observation; an imperfect and faint representation; partial darkness or obscurity within a part of space
Ps 17:8 *me in the **s** of your wings.*...553
Ps 36:7 *shelter in the **s** of your*...566
Ps 39:6 *are merely moving **s-s,** and*...569
Ps 91:1 *find rest in the **s** of the*...861
Col 2:17 *these rules are only **s-s** of*...1699
Heb 8:5 *only a copy, a **s** of the real*...1771
Heb 10:1 *was only a **s,** a dim preview.*...1774

SHADOWBOXING (v) to box with an imaginary opponent especially as a form of training
1 Cor 9:26 *I am not just **s.***...1609

SHAKE, SHAKEN, SHAKING (v) to move to and fro or up and down; to cause to quake, quiver, or tremble; to weaken
Ps 16:8 *I will not be **s-n,** for he*...553
Ps 22:7 *They sneer and **s** their heads,*...556
Ps 62:2 *where I will never be **s-n.***...574
Ps 64:8 *see them will **s** their heads*...575
Isa 28:16 *believes need never be **s-n.***...819
Ezek 38:19 *I promise a mighty **s-ing** in the.*...1114
Hag 2:6 *I will again **s** the heavens*...1164
Matt 24:29 *the heavens will be **s-n.***...1446
Mark 15:29 *abuse, **s-ing** their heads*...1483
Luke 6:38 *pressed down, **s-n** together to*...1333
Acts 2:25 *I will not be **s-n,** for he is*...1515
2 Thes 2:2 *be so easily **s-n** or alarmed.*...1588
Heb 12:26 *again I will **s** not only.*...1781
Heb 12:27 *will be **s-n** and removed,*...1781

SHAME (n) a condition or feeling of humiliating disgrace or disrepute; something that brings censure and reproach
Lev 19:12 *Do not bring **s** on the name*...225
Ps 34:5 *no shadow of **s** will darken*...458
Prov 28:7 *wild friends bring **s** to*...843
Dan 12:2 *some to **s** and everlasting*...1161
Titus 2:5 *not bring **s** on the word*...1738

Heb 6:6 *holding him up to public **s.*** 1768
1 Jn 2:28 *shrink back from him in **s.*** 1790

SHAME (v) to disgrace
1 Cor 1:27 *in order to **s** those who* 1597
1 Cor 11:22 *church and **s** the poor?*.........1613

SHAMEFUL (adj) bringing shame
Prov 18:13 *facts is both **s** and foolish.* 654
Hab 2:15 *over their **s** nakedness.* 981
Rom 1:24 *do whatever **s** things their* 1647
Rom 1:27 *Men did **s** things with*...............1648
2 Cor 4:2 *We reject all **s** deeds* 1630
2 Pet 2:2 *teaching and **s** immorality.*..........1758

SHARE (n) a portion belonging to or due to
Deut 10:9 *Levites have no **s** of property*......299
2 Kgs 2:9 *inherit a double **s** of your* 739
Matt 21:34 *to collect his **s** of the crop.*......1437
Rev 22:19 *remove that person's **s** in*.........1833

SHARE, SHARED, SHARING (v) to grant or give a share in; to partake of, use, experience, occupy, or enjoy with others; to have in common
Gen 21:10 *to **s** the inheritance* 43
1 Sam 30:24 *We **s** and **s** alike—* 473
Ps 41:9 *the one who **s-d** my food,*.............571
Luke 3:11 *If you have food, **s** it with*.........1291
Acts 2:42 *fellowship, and to **s-ing** in* 1516
Acts 2:45 *possessions and **s-d** the*...........1516
Rom 8:17 *we must also **s** his suffering.* 1659
Rom 11:31 *they, too, will **s** in God's*..........1666
1 Cor 10:16 *aren't we **s-ing** in the blood.*.1610
1 Cor 12:13 *we all **s** the same Spirit.*........1615
2 Cor 1:7 *as you **s** in our sufferings,* 1626
2 Cor 9:8 *left over to **s** with others.*...........1637
Gal 4:30 *will not **s** the inheritance.*............1565
Gal 6:6 *teachers, **s-ing** all good things*.....1567
Phil 3:10 *suffer with him, **s-ing** in his*.......1722
Col 1:12 *has enabled you to **s** in the*.........1694
1 Thes 2:8 *much that we **s-d** with you.*......1582
2 Thes 2:14 *you can **s** in the glory*............1589
1 Tim 6:18 *ready to **s** with others.* 1735
Heb 6:4 *and **s-d** in the Holy Spirit,*...........1768
Heb 12:10 *we might **s** in his holiness.*.........1780
Heb 13:16 *to **s** with those in need.*..............1783
Rev 3:20 *and we will **s** a meal together.*.....1807

SHARPENS (v) to make sharp or sharper
Prov 27:17 *As iron **s** iron, so a*..................842

SHAVED, SHAVING (v) to sever the hair from (the skin) close to the roots
Judg 16:17 *my head were **s,** my strength*...401
1 Cor 11:5 *the same as **s-ing** her head.*...1612
1 Cor 11:6 *her hair cut or her head **s,***.......1612

SHEARERS (n) those who cut or clip (as hair or wool) from someone or something
Isa 53:7 *silent before the **s,** he did*.............940
Acts 8:32 *silent before the **s,** he did* 1529

SHED, SHEDDING (v) to spill; to cause to flow
1 Chr 22:8 *you have **s** so much blood*.........532
Ps 106:38 *They **s** innocent blood,*..............871
Rom 3:25 *his life, **s-ding** his blood*...........1651
Heb 9:22 *without the **s-ding** of blood,* 1774
1 Jn 5:6 *by **s-ding** his blood on the cross*...1794
Rev 16:6 *they **s** the blood of your holy people*..1823

SHEEP (n) a small domesticated animal, representing wealth and livelihood for many Israelites; figurative of God's people
Gen 22:8 *God will provide a **s** for*.................45
Num 27:17 *not be like **s** without a*.............273
Deut 17:1 *defective cattle, **s,** or*..................306
1 Sam 15:14 *bleating of **s** and goats*..........446
Ps 44:22 *being slaughtered like **s.***..............850
Ps 78:52 *people like a flock of **s,***..............599
Ps 100:3 *We are his people, the **s*** 865
Ps 119:176 *wandered away like a lost **s;***....882
Isa 53:7 *as a **s** is silent before*...................940
Jer 50:6 *people have been lost **s.***...........1035
Matt 7:15 *disguised as harmless **s** but* 1334
Matt 9:36 *like **s** without a shepherd.*..........1357
Matt 10:16 *you out as **s** among wolves.*....1359
Matt 12:11 *a **s** that fell into a well* 1320
Matt 25:32 *separates the **s** from the*.........1452
John 10:3 *calls his own **s** by name*...........1405
John 10:7 *I am the gate for the **s.*** 1405
John 10:15 *sacrifice my life for the **s.***........1405
John 21:17 *Then feed my **s.*** 1497
1 Pet 2:25 *were like **s** who wandered*........1752

SHEEPFOLD (n) a pen or shelter for sheep
John 10:1 *sneaks over the wall of a **s,*** 1405

SHELTER, SHELTERS (n) something that covers or affords protection
see also REFUGE
Lev 23:34 *the Festival of **S-s** on the*...........231
Deut 16:16 *the Festival of **S-s.***...............306
Ps 9:9 *Lord is a **s** for the* 549
Ps 31:20 *hide them in the **s** of your*...........564
Ps 36:7 *All humanity finds **s** in the*............566
Ps 61:4 *safe beneath the **s** of your* 573
Isa 4:6 *will be a **s** from daytime heat* 828
Isa 32:2 *be like a **s** from the wind*..............902
Isa 58:7 *give **s** to the homeless.* 944
Zech 14:16 *the Festival of **S-s.*** 1180

SHEPHERD, SHEPHERDS (n) a person who tends sheep; figurative of political and religious leaders, especially those who care for God's people
Gen 48:15 *has been my **s** all my life,*............90
Gen 49:24 *by the **S,** the Rock of Israel.*.........92
Num 27:17 *be like sheep without a **s.***..........273
2 Sam 7:7 *tribal leaders, the **s-s** of my*......495
1 Kgs 22:17 *like sheep without a **s.***...........727
Ps 23:1 *The Lord is my **s;*** 558
Ps 28:9 *Lead them like a **s,** and*..................562
Isa 40:11 *feed his flock like a **s.*** 924
Jer 23:1 *my people—the **s-s** of my* 1027
Jer 31:10 *as a **s** does his flock.*..................1033
Ezek 34:5 *scattered without a **s,** and* 1109
Ezek 34:8 *you were my **s-s,** you didn't*.....1110
Ezek 34:12 *like a **s** looking for his* 1110
Zech 11:9 *won't be your **s** any longer.* 1177
Zech 13:7 *Strike down the **s,** and*............1179
Matt 2:6 *will be the **s** for my people*..........1284
Matt 9:36 *like sheep without a **s.***.............1357
Matt 26:31 *God will strike the **S,*** 1460
John 10:11 *I am the good **s.*** 1405
Acts 20:28 *Feed and **s** God's flock—*.........1675
Heb 13:20 *Jesus, the great **S** of the*..........1783
Jude 1:12 *are like shameless **s-s** who care* 1785
Rev 7:17 *on the throne will be their **S.*** 1813

SHEWBREAD (KJV)
Exod 25:30 *Place the **Bread of the Presence*** 176
Num 4:7 *the **Bread of the Presence** is*........242
1 Chr 23:29 *in charge of the **sacred bread*** 534
Matt 12:4 *the **sacred loaves of bread*** 1319
Heb 9:2 *and **sacred loaves of bread*** 1772

SHIELD (n) a broad piece of defensive armor carried on the arm; one who protects or defends
2 Sam 22:3 *He is my **s,** the power that*.......526
2 Sam 22:36 *me your **s** of victory;*..............527
Ps 3:3 *Lord, are a **s** around me;*...................517
Ps 5:12 *them with your **s** of love.*...............548
Ps 7:10 *God is my **s,** saving those*.............524
Ps 18:2 *He is my **s,** the power that*............527
Ps 28:7 *Lord is my strength and **s.***..............562
Ps 33:20 *is our help and our **s.*** 858
Ps 35:2 *armor, and take up your **s.*** 565
Ps 84:11 *God is our sun and our **s.*** 855
Ps 119:114 *are my refuge and my **s;***..........880
Ps 144:2 *He is my **s,** and I take refuge* 589
Prov 2:7 *He is a **s** to those who walk* 633
Eph 6:16 *hold up the **s** of faith* 1715

SHINE, SHINES, SHINING (v) to emit rays of light; to be eminent, conspicuous, or distinguished; to have a bright, glowing appearance
see also SHONE
Ps 37:6 *of your cause will **s** like* 567
Ps 50:2 *God **s-s** in glorious radiance.*..........593
Ps 112:4 *Light **s-s** in the darkness for*.........873
Ps 118:27 *Lord is God, **s-ing** upon us.*........876
Isa 60:1 *Let your light **s** for all* 946
Ezek 1:27 *like a burning flame, **s-ing*** 1045
Dan 12:3 *righteousness will **s** like* 1161
Matt 13:43 *the righteous will **s** like*...........1349
John 1:5 *The light **s-s** in the darkness,* 1271
2 Cor 4:6 *has made this light **s** in*.............1631
Phil 2:15 *of God, **s-ing** like bright lights*....1720

SHIP (n) a large seagoing vessel
Prov 31:14 *a merchant's **s,** bringing*...........847

SHIPWRECK, SHIPWRECKED (v) to destroy (a ship) by grounding or foundering
2 Cor 11:25 *Three times I was **s-ed.***........1641
1 Tim 1:19 *their faith has been **s-ed.*** 1728
Jude 1:12 *reefs that can **s** you.* 1785

SHONE (v) to have a bright, glowing appearance
see also SHINE
Matt 17:2 *his face **s** like the sun,*..............1378
Rev 21:11 *It **s** with the glory of God*..........1831

SHOP (n) a handicraft establishment; workshop
Jer 18:2 *Go down to the potter's **s,***............1022

SHORT (adj) brief; not coming up to a measure or requirement
Ps 89:47 *Remember how **s** my life is,*.........592
Rom 3:23 *all fall **s** of God's glorious*...........1651
1 Cor 7:29 *time that remains is very **s.*** 1606

SHORT-LIVED (adj) not living or lasting long
Job 20:5 *of the wicked has been **s*** 113

SHORT-TEMPERED (adj) having a quick temper
Prov 14:17 ***S** people do foolish things,* 648

SHOULDERS (n) the place on the human body where the arm is joined to the trunk
Isa 9:6 *government will rest on his **s.***..........793
Luke 15:5 *carry it home on his **s.*** 1410

SHOUT, SHOUTED, SHOUTING (v) to utter a loud cry or in a loud voice
Job 38:7 *all the angels **s-ed** for joy?* 128
Ps 95:1 *Let us **s** joyfully to*........................863
Ps 100:1 ***S** with joy to the Lord,* 865
Isa 12:6 *people of Jerusalem **s** his* 797
Isa 40:3 *someone **s-ing,** "Clear the way*.....923
Isa 40:9 ***s** from the mountaintops!*..............924
Isa 42:2 *He will not **s** or raise his*...............926
Zech 9:9 *people of Zion! **S** in triumph,* 1175
Matt 3:3 *a voice **s-ing** in the wilderness,* ..1287
Matt 10:27 ***s** from the housetops for* 1360

SHOW (n) an impressive display
Matt 23:5 *Everything they do is for* ***s.***........1443

SHOW, SHOWED, SHOWN, SHOWS (v) to cause or permit to be seen; to point out; to reveal or demonstrate; to bestow
Exod 33:18 *Then* ***s*** *me your glorious*..........186
2 Sam 22:26 *To the faithful you* ***s***..............526
Neh 9:19 *pillar of fire* ***s-ed*** *them the*.........1216
Ps 4:6 *Who will* ***s*** *us better times?*..............547
Ps 16:11 *You will* ***s*** *me the way*...................553
Ps 119:132 *Come and* ***s*** *me your*..............881
Prov 3:6 *he will* ***s*** *you which path*..............634
Prov 24:23 *wrong to* ***s*** *favoritism*..............663
Eccl 9:1 *God will* ***s*** *them favor*....................680
Isa 30:18 *so he can* ***s*** *you his love*.............900
Hos 6:6 *I want you to* ***s*** *love, not*................809
Zech 7:9 *Judge fairly, and* ***s*** *mercy*..........1173
Luke 24:40 ***s-ed*** *them his hands and his*....1495
Acts 2:28 *You have* ***s-n*** *me the way*........1516
Acts 10:34 *that God* ***s-s*** *no favoritism*.......1534
Rom 3:20 *The law simply* ***s-s*** *us how*.......1651
Rom 3:21 *But now God has* ***s-n*** *us a way*...1651
Rom 5:8 *God* ***s-ed*** *his great love for us*....1654
Rom 9:22 *the right to* ***s*** *his anger*............1662
Eph 2:7 *as* ***s-n*** *in all he has done*............1707
Jas 2:18 *I will* ***s*** *you my faith*...................1549
1 Jn 4:9 *God* ***s-ed*** *how much he loved*.....1793

SHOWER, SHOWERED (v) to give in abundance
Hos 10:12 *come and* ***s*** *righteousness*.........813
2 Cor 1:5 *more God will* ***s*** *us with*............1626
Eph 1:8 *He has* ***s-ed*** *his kindness*............1705

SHOWERS (n) something resembling a rain shower
Ezek 34:26 *will be* ***s*** *of blessing*...............1110

SHREWD, SHREWDEST (adj) marked by clever discerning awareness and hardheaded acumen
Gen 3:1 *serpent was the* ***s-est*** *of all*............11
Matt 10:16 *So be as* ***s*** *as snakes* 1359

SHRINK (v) to become smaller or more compacted
Matt 9:16 *new patch would* ***s*** *and rip*........1316

SHUT (v) to close
Isa 6:10 *their ears and* ***s*** *their eyes*............785
Dan 6:22 *his angel to* ***s*** *the lions'* 1141
Amos 5:13 *keep their mouths* ***s,*** *for it*........775
Heb 11:33 *They* ***s*** *the mouths of lions,*......1779

SICK (adj) affected with disease or ill health; lacking vigor
Ps 41:3 *when they are* ***s*** *and restores*.........571
Prov 13:12 *deferred makes the heart* ***s,***......646
Matt 9:12 *need a doctor—****s*** *people do.* 1315
Matt 10:8 *Heal the* ***s,*** *raise the dead,*........1358
Matt 25:36 *I was* ***s,*** *and you cared for* 1453
Mark 3:10 *all the* ***s*** *people eagerly*............1322
1 Cor 11:30 *many of you are weak and* ***s***..1614
Jas 5:14 *Are any of you* ***s?***.....................1553

SICKLE (n) a small hand tool with a curved metal blade used for cutting stalks of grain
Joel 3:13 *Swing the* ***s,*** *for the* 1243
Rev 14:14 *a sharp* ***s*** *in his hand.*.............1822

SICKNESS, SICKNESSES (n) a disordered, weakened, or unsound condition; illness
Matt 4:24 *whatever their* ***s*** *or disease,*......1311
Matt 8:17 *He took our* ***s-es*** *and removed* .1309

SIDE (n) the right or left part of the trunk of the body
John 20:20 *in his hands and his* ***s.***...........1495

SIGHT (n) mental or spiritual perception
Ps 51:4 *done what is evil in your* ***s.***...........506
Hab 1:13 *cannot stand the* ***s*** *of evil*............979
Jas 1:27 *religion in the* ***s*** *of God*...............1548

SIGN, SIGNS (n) something indicating the presence or existence of something else; something material or external that stands for or signifies something spiritual
Gen 9:12 *you a* ***s*** *of my covenant* 21
Gen 17:11 *your foreskin as a* ***s*** *of*..................38
Ps 105:27 *performed miraculous* ***s-s***........869
Isa 55:13 *be an everlasting* ***s*** *of*................942
Dan 6:27 *he performs miraculous* ***s-s***......1141
Matt 12:38 *a miraculous* ***s*** *to prove*..........1343
Matt 24:3 *What* ***s*** *will signal your*............1446
Matt 24:30 *the* ***s*** *that the Son of Man*.......1447
Mark 16:17 *These miraculous* ***s-s*** *will*......1498
Luke 11:29 *them is the* ***s*** *of Jonah.* 1344
John 3:2 *Your miraculous* ***s-s*** *are*...........1300
John 20:30 *do many other miraculous* ***s-s***..1496
1 Cor 14:22 *in tongues is a* ***s,*** *not for*.......1617
2 Cor 12:12 *did many* ***s-s*** *and wonders*.....1642
2 Thes 2:9 *counterfeit power and* ***s-s***.......1589

SIGNAL (n) something (as a sound, gesture, or object) that conveys notice or warning
Num 10:5 *you sound the* ***s*** *to move on,*.......202

SILENCE (n) absence of speech, sound, or noise
Ps 39:2 *I stood there in* ***s****—not even*..........569
Rev 8:1 *there was* ***s*** *throughout heaven*....1813

SILENCE, SILENCED, SILENCING (v) to compel or reduce to silence; to cause to cease criticism
Ps 8:2 *strength,* ***s-ing*** *your enemies*...........548
Titus 1:11 *They must be* ***s-d,***
because they......................................1737
1 Pet 2:15 *honorable lives should* ***s***.........1751

SILENT (adj) mute, speechless; still
Ps 30:12 *praises to you and not be* ***s.***.........563
Isa 53:7 *as a sheep is* ***s*** *before the*............940
Isa 62:1 *Jerusalem, I cannot remain* ***s.*** 948
Hab 2:20 *the earth be* ***s*** *before him.* 981
Acts 8:32 *And as a lamb is* ***s*** *before*.........1529
Acts 18:9 *Speak out! Don't be* ***s!***..............1580
1 Cor 14:34 *Women should be* ***s*** *during*....1618

SILVER (adj) made of silver
Prov 25:11 *apples in a* ***s*** *basket*.................839
Dan 2:32 *and arms were* ***s,*** *its belly*..........1004

SILVER (n) a shiny gray metal valued next to gold, capable of a high polish; coin made of silver
Ps 66:10 *have purified us like* ***s.***...............859
Prov 3:14 *is more profitable than* ***s,***..........635
Prov 8:10 *instruction rather than* ***s,***............640
Prov 22:1 *is better than* ***s*** *or gold*...............658
Isa 48:10 *but not as* ***s*** *is refined.*...............935
Zech 11:12 *wages thirty pieces of* ***s.***........1177
Zech 13:9 *refine them like* ***s*** *and*...............1179
Matt 25:15 *two bags of* ***s*** *to another,* 1451
Matt 26:15 *gave him thirty pieces of* ***s.***.....1454
Luke 7:41 *500 pieces of* ***s*** *to one*............1340
Acts 3:6 *don't have any* ***s*** *or gold* 1517
1 Cor 3:12 *materials—gold,* ***s,*** *jewels,*......1599

SILVERSMITH (n) an artisan who makes articles of silver
Acts 19:24 *with Demetrius, a* ***s*** *who had*...1624

SIMON
1. One of the twelve disciples, Simon Peter (Matt 16:16, p. 1375); *see* PETER.
2. One of the twelve disciples, Simon the Zealot (Matt 10:4, p. 1358; Mark 3:18, p. 1323; Luke 6:15, p. 1323; Acts 1:13, p. 1512).
3. Simon the sorcerer, rebuked by Peter (Acts 8:9-24, p. 1527).
4. Simon who had leprosy (Matt 26:6, p. 1427; Mark 14:3, p. 1428).

SIMPLE (n) a person lacking in knowledge or expertise
Ps 19:7 *trustworthy, making wise the* ***s.***......554

SIMPLEMINDED (adj) foolish
Prov 19:25 *the* ***s*** *will learn a lesson;* 655

SIN, SINS (n) moral evil; transgression of or rebellion against God's laws
Gen 4:7 ***S*** *is crouching at the door,*..............14
Lev 5:5 *ways, you must confess your* ***s.***......207
Num 32:23 *be sure that your* ***s*** *will find* 279
Deut 24:16 *to death for the* ***s-s*** *of their*......314
Ps 19:13 *servant from deliberate* ***s-s!***.........555
Ps 32:1 *whose* ***s*** *is put out of sight!*..........564
Ps 38:18 *I confess my* ***s-s;*** *I am deeply*......569
Ps 51:1 *blot out the stain of my* ***s-s.***..........505
Ps 51:2 *Purify me from my* ***s.***......................505
Ps 65:3 *are overwhelmed by our* ***s-s,***.........575
Ps 79:9 *Save us and forgive our* ***s-s***...........600
Ps 103:12 *removed our* ***s-s*** *as far from*......580
Prov 5:22 *held captive by his own* ***s-s;***.......637
Prov 10:19 *Too much talk leads to* ***s.***..........642
Prov 14:21 ***s*** *to belittle one's neighbor;*.......648
Prov 17:19 *who loves to quarrel loves* ***s;***.....653
Prov 28:13 *who conceal their* ***s-s*** *will*.........844
Prov 29:22 *commits all kinds of* ***s.***..............845
Isa 1:18 *your* ***s-s*** *are like scarlet,* 824
Isa 53:6 *laid on him the* ***s-s*** *of us all*...........940
Isa 59:2 *Because of your* ***s-s,*** *he has*.........945
Jer 31:30 *die for their own* ***s-s****—* 1034
Jer 31:34 *again remember their* ***s-s.***........1034
Ezek 18:19 *pay for the parent's* ***s-s?***........1064
Matt 1:21 *save his people from their* ***s-s.*** .1277
Matt 6:12 *forgive us our* ***s-s,*** *as we*..........1331
Matt 26:28 *to forgive the* ***s-s*** *of many*.......1457
Mark 3:29 *This is a* ***s*** *with eternal*.............1342
Luke 5:24 *on earth to forgive* ***s-s.*** 1314
John 1:29 *takes away the* ***s*** *of the world!*..1297
John 20:23 *forgive anyone's* ***s-s,*** *they*......1495
Acts 2:38 *repent of your* ***s-s*** *and turn*.......1516
Rom 4:25 *because of our* ***s-s,*** *and he*.......1653
Rom 6:2 *we have died to* ***s,*** *how can* 1655
Rom 6:11 *the power of* ***s*** *and alive to*........1656
Rom 6:23 *the wages of* ***s*** *is death,* 1656
Rom 7:7 *law that showed me my* ***s.***..........1657
Rom 7:25 *nature I am a slave to* ***s.***...........1658
1 Cor 6:18 *is a* ***s*** *against your own body*....1604
1 Cor 15:3 *died for our* ***s-s,*** *just as*...........1618
1 Cor 15:56 *the law gives* ***s*** *its power.* 1622
Gal 1:4 *gave his life for our* ***s-s,*** *just*.........1555
Gal 6:1 *believer is overcome by some* ***s,*** ...1567
Eph 2:5 *were dead because of our* ***s-s,*** 1707
1 Tim 5:22 *share in the* ***s-s*** *of others*........1734
Heb 2:17 *would take away the* ***s-s*** *of* 1764
Heb 9:28 *to take away the* ***s-s*** *of many* 1774
Heb 10:12 *sacrifice for* ***s-s,*** *good for*.........1775
Heb 12:1 *the* ***s*** *that so easily trips*............1780
Jas 1:15 *when* ***s*** *is allowed to grow,* 1547
Jas 4:17 *is* ***s*** *to know what you ought*.......1552
Jas 5:16 *Confess your* ***s-s*** *to each other*...1554
1 Pet 2:24 *carried our* ***s-s*** *in his body*.......1752
1 Pet 3:18 *suffered for our* ***s-s*** *once for*....1754
1 Jn 1:8 *claim we have no* ***s,*** *we are* 1787
1 Jn 1:9 *to forgive us our* ***s-s*** *and to* 1787
1 Jn 2:1 *if anyone does* ***s,*** *we have*..........1788

1 Jn 3:5 *take away our **s-s,** and*...1791
1 Jn 3:5 *there is no **s** in him*...1791
1 Jn 5:16 *a **s** that leads to death,*...1794
Rev 1:5 *from our **s-s** by shedding his*...1799

SIN, SINNED, SINNING, SINS (v) to commit an offense or fault against God; to break God's law
Exod 20:20 *will keep you from **s-ning!***...170
2 Sam 12:13 *I have **s-ned** against the*...507
2 Chr 6:37 *We have **s-ned,** done evil,*...622
Job 1:5 *my children have **s-ned***...94
Ps 51:4 *and you alone, have I **s-ned;***...506
Ps 119:11 *I might not **s** against you*...878
Jer 14:20 *all have **s-ned** against you.*...1018
Dan 9:5 *have **s-ned** and done wrong.*...1142
Mark 9:43 *causes you to **s,** cut it off*...1384
Luke 15:18 *I have **s-ned** against both*...1410
Luke 17:3 *another believer **s-s,** rebuke*...1413
John 8:7 *who has never **s-ned** throw*...1391
John 8:11 *Go and **s** no more.*...1392
Rom 1:30 *invent new ways of **s-ning,***...1648
Rom 3:23 *everyone has **s-ned;** we all*...1651
Rom 5:12 *When Adam **s-ned,** sin entered*...1654
Rom 14:23 *is not right, you are **s-ning.***...1671
1 Cor 15:34 *is right, and stop **s-ning.***...1621
Heb 4:15 *we do, yet he did not **s.***...1766
Heb 10:26 *deliberately continue **s-ning***...1776
1 Pet 2:22 *He never **s-ned,** nor ever*...1752
1 Jn 1:10 *we have not **s-ned,** we are*...1787
1 Jn 3:6 *who keeps on **s-ning** does not*...1791
1 Jn 5:18 *not make a practice of **s-ning,***...1795

SINCERE (adj) genuine, having no intention to deceive
Prov 27:6 *Wounds from a **s** friend are*...842
2 Cor 6:6 *within us, and by our **s** love.*...1633
Jas 3:17 *no favoritism and is always **s.***...1551
1 Pet 1:22 *show **s** love to each other*...1750

SINFUL (adj) tainted with, marked by, or full of sin; wicked
Lev 5:1 *is **s** to refuse to testify,*...207
1 Sam 15:23 *is as **s** as witchcraft,*...446
Luke 11:13 *So if you **s** people know*...1398
Rom 5:20 *could see how **s** they were.*...1655
Rom 7:5 *harvest of **s** deeds, resulting*...1657
Rom 7:18 *is, in my **s** nature.*...1658
Rom 7:25 *because of my **s** nature I am*...1658
Rom 8:4 *follow our **s** nature but*...1658
Rom 8:13 *deeds of your **s** nature,*...1659
Gal 5:13 *to satisfy your **s** nature.*...1565
Col 2:11 *away of your **s** nature.*...1698

SING, SINGING (v) to produce musical tones by means of the voice
Exod 15:1 *I will **s** to the LORD,*...161
Ps 5:11 *let them **s** joyful praises*...548
Ps 13:6 *I will **s** to the LORD*...551
Ps 47:6 *to our King, **s** praises!*...852
Ps 51:14 *I will joyfully **s** of*...506
Ps 63:7 *my helper, I **s** for joy*...518
Ps 69:30 *praise God's name with **s-ing,***...578
Ps 89:1 *I will **s** of the LORD's unfailing*...591
Ps 95:1 *let us **s** to the LORD!*...863
Ps 96:1 ***S** a new song to the LORD!*...864
Ps 98:4 *praise and **s** for joy!*...865
Ps 100:2 *Come before him, **s-ing** with*...865
Ps 101:1 *I will **s** of your love.*...579
Ps 108:1 *can **s** your praises with all*...581
Ps 147:1 *How good to **s** praises to*...1154
Isa 35:10 *enter Jerusalem **s-ing***...905
Jer 16:9 *to the happy **s-ing** and laughter*...1020
Acts 16:25 *praying and **s-ing** hymns*...1576
1 Cor 14:15 *I will also **s** in words*...1617
1 Cor 14:26 *one will **s,** another will*...1618
Col 3:16 ***S** psalms and hymns and*...1701
Rev 15:3 *And they were **s-ing** the song*...1822

SINGERS (n) those who sing
2 Chr 5:13 *trumpeters and **s** performed*...618
Rev 18:22 *of harps, **s,** flutes,*...1826

SINLESS (adj) having no moral blemish; having done nothing to incur the wrath of God
1 Pet 1:19 *the **s,** spotless Lamb of God.*...1749

SINNER, SINNERS (n) those guilty of sin
Ps 51:5 *I was born a **s**—yes,*...506
Prov 1:10 *if **s-s** entice you, turn*...632
Prov 23:17 *Don't envy **s-s,** but*...661
Eccl 9:18 *one **s** can destroy much that*...681
Isa 59:12 *we know what **s-s** we are.*...945
Isa 64:5 *We are constant **s-s;** how*...950
Matt 9:13 *who know they are **s-s.***...1315
Luke 5:8 *I'm too much of a **s** to be*...1308
Luke 15:7 *over one lost **s** who repents*...1410
Luke 18:13 *to me, for I am a **s.***...1418
Rom 4:5 *faith in God who forgives **s-s.***...1652
Rom 5:6 *time and died for us **s-s.***...1654
1 Tim 1:15 *into the world to save **s-s***...1728
Jas 5:20 *whoever brings the **s** back*...1554
1 Pet 3:18 *he died for **s-s** to bring*...1754

SISTER, SISTERS (n) a female who has one or both parents in common with another; a female fellow Christian
Lev 18:9 *relations with your **s** or half*...224
Matt 19:29 *or brothers or **s-s** or father*...1421
Mark 3:35 *my brother and **s** and*...1344
1 Tim 5:2 *as you would your own **s-s.***...1733
Jas 2:1 *dear brothers and **s-s,** how can*...1548

SIT, SITS, SITTING (v) to place (the buttocks) on or in a seat
Ps 110:1 *to my Lord, "**S** in the place*...582
Matt 19:28 *Son of Man **s-s** upon his*...1420
Matt 20:23 *to say who will **s** on my right*...1424
Col 3:1 *heaven, where Christ **s-s** in*...1700
Rev 3:21 *are victorious will **s** with me*...1808
Rev 4:9 *to the one **s-ting** on the throne*...1808

SKILL (n) a developed aptitude or ability
Heb 5:14 *have the **s** to recognize*...1767

SKILLED (adj) having acquired mastery of or skill in something
Ps 71:15 *I am not **s** with words.*...860

SKILLFUL (adj) possessed of or displaying skill
1 Kgs 7:14 *was extremely **s** and talented*...613
Ps 45:1 *the pen of a **s** poet.*...850
Ps 78:72 *led them with **s** hands.*...600

SKY, SKIES (n) the upper atmosphere appearing as a great vault or arch above the earth
Gen 1:8 *God called the space "**s.**"*...7
Deut 33:26 *across the **s-ies** in majestic*...327
Ps 19:1 ***s-ies** display his craftsmanship*...554
Prov 30:19 *eagle glides through the **s,***...846
Isa 34:4 *fall from the **s** like withered*...904
Jer 33:22 *the stars of the **s** cannot*...1081
Matt 24:29 *will fall from the **s,***...1446
Rev 20:11 *The earth and **s** fled from*...1830

SLANDER (n) the utterance of false charges or misrepresentations that defame and damage another's reputation
Matt 15:19 *theft, lying, and **s.***...1370
Mark 7:22 *desires, envy, **s,** pride,*...1371
2 Cor 12:20 *selfishness, **s,** gossip,*...1642
Eph 4:31 *harsh words, and **s,** as*...1712
Col 3:8 *malicious behavior, **s,***...1700

SLANDER, SLANDERED, SLANDERING (v) to utter slander; to malign or defame
Prov 10:18 ***s-ing** others makes you a*...642
1 Tim 3:11 *must not **s** others.*...1731
2 Tim 3:3 *they will **s** others*...1744
Titus 2:3 *They must not **s** others*...1738
Titus 3:2 *They must not **s** anyone*...1739
2 Pet 2:2 *way of truth will be **s-ed.***...1758

SLANDEROUS (adj) of, relating to, or marked by slander
Lev 19:16 *Do not spread **s** gossip*...225

SLAUGHTER (n) the butchering of livestock for market or sacrifice
Isa 53:7 *led like a lamb to the **s.***...940
Jer 11:19 *lamb being led to the **s.***...1014
Acts 8:32 *led like a sheep to the **s.***...1529

SLAUGHTER, SLAUGHTERED (v) to discredit, defeat, or demolish completely; to kill in a bloody or violent manner
Hos 6:5 *to **s** you with my words,*...808
Rev 5:6 *looked as if it had been **s-ed,***...1809
Rev 5:12 *is the Lamb who was **s-ed***...1810

SLAVE, SLAVES (n) a person bound in servitude; one who has lost his liberty and has no rights
see also SERVANT(S)
Matt 20:27 *must become your **s.***...1424
John 8:34 *who sins is a **s** of sin.*...1393
John 15:15 *longer call you **s-s,** because*...1464
Rom 1:1 *is from Paul, a **s** of Christ*...1644
Rom 6:6 *are no longer **s-s** to sin.*...1655
Rom 6:16 *you become the **s** of whatever*...1656
Rom 6:22 *and have become **s-s** of God.*...1656
Rom 7:23 *makes me a **s** to the sin*...1658
1 Cor 6:12 *not become a **s** to anything.*...1604
1 Cor 9:19 *have become a **s** to all*...1609
1 Cor 12:13 *some are **s-s,** and some*...1615
Gal 3:28 *Jew or Gentile, **s** or free,*...1562
Gal 4:7 *no longer a **s** but God's own*...1563
Gal 4:8 *you were **s-s** to so-called gods*...1563
Gal 4:30 *rid of the **s** and her son,*...1565
Eph 6:5 ***S-s,** obey your earthly masters*...1715
Phil 2:7 *position of a **s** and was born*...1720
Col 3:11 *barbaric, uncivilized, **s,** or*...1700
Col 4:1 *be just and fair to your **s-s.***...1702
1 Tim 1:10 *or are **s** traders, liars,*...1728
Titus 3:3 *became **s-s** to many lusts*...1739
Phlm 1:16 *no longer like a **s** to you.*...1692
2 Pet 2:19 *For you are a **s** to whatever*...1759

SLAVERY (n) submission to a dominating influence; the practice of slaveholding
Exod 2:23 *under their burden of **s.***...143
Rom 6:19 *the illustration of **s** to help*...1656

SLEEP (n) natural or induced state of rest; a state of lazy inactivity
Gen 2:21 *man to fall into a deep **s.***...10
Gen 15:12 *Abram fell into a deep **s,***...35
Prov 20:13 *If you love **s,** you will*...656
Prov 23:21 *too much **s** clothes them*...661
Rom 11:8 *has put them into a deep **s.***...1665

SLEEP, SLEEPING, SLEEPS (v) to rest in a state of natural unconsciousness
Gen 28:11 *against and lay down to **s.***...57
Ps 4:8 *peace I will lie down and **s,***...547
Ps 121:4 *Israel never slumbers or **s-s.***...882
Prov 6:9 *how long will you **s?***...638
Eccl 5:12 *who work hard **s** well,*...677
Mark 13:36 *find you **s-ing** when he*...1449

SLEEPER (n) one that sleeps
Eph 5:14 *said, "Awake, O **s,** rise up*..........1713

SLEEPLESS (adj) affording no sleep
2 Cor 6:5 *exhaustion, endured **s** nights,*....1633

SLING (n) an instrument for throwing stones; slingshot
1 Sam 17:50 *with only a **s** and a stone,*......451

SLOTHFUL(NESS) (KJV)
Prov 15:19 ***lazy** person's way is blocked*.....650
Prov 21:25 *the **lazy** will come to ruin,*.........658
Eccl 10:18 ***Laziness** leads to a sagging roof*...682
Rom 12:11 *Never be **lazy,** but work hard* ..1667
Heb 6:12 ***spiritually dull and indifferent***..1768

SLUGGARD (KJV)
Prov 6:6 *a lesson from the ants, you **lazybones***...638
Prov 10:26 ***Lazy people** irritate their employers*..643
Prov 13:4 ***Lazy people** want much but*.......646
Prov 20:4 ***Those too lazy** to plow*..............656
Prov 26:16 ***Lazy people** consider themselves smarter*..............................841

SLUMBER (n) sleep
Prov 6:10 *a little more **s,** a little*...............638

SLY (adj) clever in concealing one's aims or ends
Prov 7:10 *dressed and **s** of heart*................639

SMALLEST (adj) of little consequence
Matt 5:18 *not even the **s** detail*................1327

SMASH, SMASHES (v) to break or crush by violence
Ps 2:9 *rod and **s** them like clay* 857
Jer 23:29 *hammer that **s-es** a rock*..........1028

SMILE (v) to bestow approval
Num 6:25 *May the LORD **s** on you and*.........245
Ps 4:6 *Let your face **s** on us, LORD*. 547
Ps 67:1 *May his face **s** with favor on* 859

SMOKE (n) the gaseous products of burning materials
Exod 19:18 *The **s** billowed into the sky*.......168
Isa 6:4 *building was filled with **s.***................783
Joel 2:30 *and fire and columns of **s.***..........1242
Acts 2:19 *and fire and clouds of **s.*** 1515
Rev 9:2 *air turned dark from the **s.***...........1814
Rev 15:8 *filled with **s** from God's*.............1822

SMOKE (v) to emit smoke
Ps 104:32 *the mountains **s** at his touch*.......868

SMOOTH (adj) having a continuous, even surface
Jer 31:9 ***s** paths where they will not*.........1032
Luke 3:5 *and the rough places made **s.***....1290

SMOOTH (v) to make smooth
Isa 26:7 *you **s** out the path ahead*..............896
Isa 40:4 *and **s** out the rough places*.............923

SNAKE, SNAKES (n) any of numerous limbless scaled reptiles
Num 21:8 *replica of a poisonous **s** and*.......263
Prov 23:32 *it bites like a poisonous **s;***.........662
Matt 10:16 *shrewd as **s-s** and harmless*...1359
Luke 3:7 *You brood of **s-s!** Who warned*...1290
John 3:14 *lifted up the bronze **s** on a*........1302
Rom 3:13 ***S** venom drips from their*..........1651

SNARE, SNARES (n) something by which one is entangled, involved in difficulties, or impeded
Josh 23:13 *they will be a **s** and a trap* 368
Eccl 7:26 *passion is a **s,** and her soft*..........679
Lam 4:20 *was caught in their **s-s***.............1100
Rom 11:9 *table become a **s,** a trap that*....1665

SNOUT (n) a long projecting nose (as of swine)
Prov 11:22 *gold ring in a pig's **s.***................644

SNOW (n) precipitation in the form of small white ice crystals
Prov 25:13 *refresh like **s** in summer*............840
Isa 1:18 *will make them as white as **s.*** 824
Dan 7:9 *clothing was as white as **s,***..........1135

SNUFFED (v) to extinguish
Prov 13:9 *wicked will be **s** out*. 646

SOAP (n) a cleansing and emulsifying agent
Mal 3:2 *like a strong **s** that bleaches* 1247

SOAR, SOARING (v) to sail or hover in the air often at a great height
2 Sam 22:11 *flew, **s-ing** on the wings*........526
Isa 40:31 *will **s** high on wings*...................925

SODOM (n) a city at the southern end of the Dead Sea destroyed because of its wickedness
Gen 13:12 *to a place near **S** and settled*.......32
Gen 19:24 *the sky on **S** and Gomorrah.* 42
Isa 1:9 *have been wiped out like **S,***.............823
Luke 10:12 *you, even wicked **S** will be*......1394
Rom 9:29 *have been wiped out like **S,***......1662
Rev 11:8 *figuratively called "**S**"*................1817

SOIL (n) firm land, earth
Matt 13:23 *on good **s** represents those* 1345

SOJOURN (KJV)
Gen 12:10 *where he **lived as a foreigner***.....31
Acts 7:6 *descendants would **live in a foreign land***..1524

SOJOURNER (KJV)
Gen 23:4 *a stranger and a **foreigner***...........46
Num 35:15 ***foreigners** living among you*.....283
Ps 39:12 *a **traveler** passing through* 569

SOLD (v) to give up (property) to another in exchange for something of value
see also SELL
1 Kgs 21:25 ***s** himself to what was evil*.......725
Matt 13:44 *and **s** everything he owned*.....1349

SOLDIER (n) one engaged in military service
1 Cor 9:7 *What **s** has to pay his own* 1608
2 Tim 2:3 *a good **s** of Christ Jesus*............1742

SOLID (adj) firm; not liquid
Ps 40:2 *set my feet on **s** ground*.................570
Heb 5:12 *and cannot eat **s** food*...............1767

SOLOMON King of Israel (united kingdom), second son of David and Bathsheba (2 Sam 12:24-25, p. 507); chosen as successor by David (1 Kgs 1:28-40, p. 544); given final advice by David (1 Kgs 2:1-9, p. 545); enemies of his rule removed (1 Kgs 2:13-46, p. 604); prayed for wisdom (1 Kgs 3:3-15, p. 606; 4:29-34, p. 629); demonstrated wisdom (1 Kgs 3:16-28, p. 608); built and dedicated the Temple (1 Kgs 5–8, p. 609); the LORD's second appearance (1 Kgs 9:1-9, p. 623); became famous and powerful (1 Kgs 9:10–10:29, p. 624); visited by the queen of Sheba (1 Kgs 10:1-13, p. 626); practiced idolatry and warned by God (1 Kgs 11:1-13, p. 671); troubled by enemies (1 Kgs 11:14-40, p. 672); died (1 Kgs 11:41-43, p. 673); wrote many things (1 Kgs 4:32, p. 629; Ps 72, p. 630; 127, p. 631; Prov 1:1, p. 631; 10:1, p. 641; 25:1, p. 839; Eccl 1:1, p. 673; Song 1:1, p. 663); often mentioned in NT (Matt 6:29, p. 1332; 12:42, p. 1343; Luke 11:31, p. 1344; 12:27, p. 1401; Acts 7:47, p. 1526).

SON, SONS (n) a parent's male child or descendant further removed; spiritual heir; relationship of Jesus to the heavenly Father
see also CHILD(REN), DESCENDANT(S)
Gen 17:19 *birth to a **s** for you*.......................39
Gen 21:10 *slave-woman and her **s.***..............43
Gen 22:2 *Take your **s,** your only* 45
Ruth 4:15 *better to you than seven **s-s!***......415
Ps 2:7 *You are my **s.** Today I have*..............857
Isa 7:14 *birth to a **s** and will call*.................790
Dan 7:13 *someone like a **s** of man* 1136
Hos 11:1 *I called my **s** out of Egypt*.............814
Joel 2:28 ***s-s** and daughters will* 1242
Matt 1:21 *will have a **s,** and you are*.........1277
Matt 2:15 *I called my **S** out of Egypt*. 1285
Matt 3:17 *my dearly loved **S,** who brings* ..1293
Matt 4:3 *you are the **S** of God, tell* 1294
Matt 11:27 *truly knows the **S** except the*...1339
Matt 13:55 *the carpenter's **s,** and we* 1356
Matt 14:33 *really are the **S** of God!*...........1366
Matt 16:16 *are the Messiah, the **S** of*.........1375
Matt 17:5 *my dearly loved **S,** who brings* ..1379
Matt 21:9 *God for the **S** of David!* 1429
Matt 27:54 *truly was the **S** of God!* 1485
Matt 28:19 *Father and the **S** and the*.........1498
Mark 14:62 *will see the **S** of Man seated* ..1473
Luke 1:32 *be called the **S** of the Most*.........1274
Luke 2:7 *first child, a **s.** She wrapped*.......1280
Luke 9:35 *This is my **S,** my Chosen One*...1380
Luke 12:8 *on earth, the **S** of Man will*.........1399
Luke 15:20 *ran to his **s,** embraced him,*.....1410
John 3:16 *his one and only **S,** so that*.......1302
John 3:36 *doesn't obey the **S** will never*....1303
John 17:1 *Glorify your **S** so he*..................1466
Acts 13:33 *You are my **S.** Today I have* 1542
Rom 1:4 *shown to be the **S** of God* 1644
Rom 5:10 *death of his **S** while we* 1654
Rom 8:3 *He sent his own **S** in a body*........1658
Rom 8:29 *to become like his **S,** so* 1660
Rom 8:32 *even his own **S** but gave him* 1660
1 Cor 15:28 *who gave his **S** authority*.......1621
2 Cor 6:18 *be my **s-s** and daughters,* 1634
Gal 4:4 *God sent his **S,** born of a* 1562
Gal 4:30 *slave and her **s,** for the **s***............1565
Heb 1:2 *and through the **S** he created* 1761
Heb 1:5 *You are my **S.** Today I have* 1762
Heb 7:28 *God appointed his **S** with an* 1771
Heb 10:29 *trampled on the **S** of God,*.........1776
1 Jn 2:23 *acknowledges the **S** has the* 1790
1 Jn 4:9 *one and only **S** into the world*......1793
1 Jn 5:5 *Jesus is the **S** of God*..................1794
Rev 1:13 *someone like the **S** of Man*.........1800

SONG, SONGS (n) a short musical composition of words and music; the act of singing
Exod 15:2 *my strength and my **s;***..............161
Job 35:10 *who gives **s-s** in the night?*........125
Ps 40:3 *given me a new **s** to sing,*..............570
Ps 63:5 *praise you with **s-s** of joy*...............517
Ps 96:1 *Sing a new **s** to the LORD!* 864
Ps 119:54 *theme of my **s-s** wherever*.........879
Ps 137:3 *of those **s-s** of Jerusalem!*..........1118
Ps 149:1 *Sing to the LORD a new **s.*** 887
Isa 49:13 *Burst into **s,** O mountains!*............936
Isa 55:12 *and hills will burst into **s,***.............942
Rev 5:9 *they sang a new **s** with these*..........1810
Rev 15:3 *God, and the **s** of the Lamb:*.......1822

SOON (adv) before long
John 13:32 *Son, he will **s** give glory to*......1460
2 Cor 4:18 *see now will **s** be gone,*...........1631

SORCERER, SORCERERS (n) a person who practices sorcery
Exod 7:11 *his own wise men and **s-s,*** 150
Acts 8:9 *a **s** there for many years,* 1527
Acts 13:6 *a Jewish **s,** a false prophet* 1540
Rev 22:15 *the dogs—the **s,** the sexually* 1832

SORCERY (n) the use of power gained from the assistance or control of evil spirits, especially for divining
Gal 5:20 *idolatry, **s,** hostility, quarreling,* 1566

SORROW, SORROWS (n) deep distress, sadness, or regret
Ps 116:3 *I saw only trouble and **s.*** 875
Isa 65:14 *will cry in **s** and despair.* 952
Jer 31:12 *all their **s-s** will be gone.* 1033
Ezek 34:2 *What **s** awaits you* 1109
Amos 5:18 *What **s** awaits you* 776
Matt 18:7 *What **s** awaits the* 1384
Matt 23:13 *What **s** awaits you.* 1444
Luke 11:46 *what **s** also awaits* 1398
Rom 9:2 *with bitter **s** and unending* 1661
2 Cor 7:10 *the kind of **s** God wants* 1635
Eph 4:30 *do not bring **s** to God's Holy* 1712
1 Tim 6:10 *themselves with many **s-s.*** 1735
Heb 13:17 *with joy and not with **s.*** 1783
Jude 1:11 *What **s** awaits them!* 1785
Rev 21:4 *more death or **s** or crying.* 1830

SORRY (adj) feeling sorrow, regret, or penitence; inspiring pity
Gen 6:6 *So the Lord was **s** he had* 17
2 Chr 21:20 *No one was **s** when he died.* 748
Ps 38:18 *I am deeply **s** for what I have* 569
Mal 3:14 *that we are **s** for our sins?* 1248
Matt 15:32 *I feel **s** for these people.* 1372
Matt 20:34 *Jesus felt **s** for them and* 1425
Mark 8:2 *I feel **s** for these people.* 1373

SOUGHT (v) to search or look for
see also SEEK
2 Chr 26:5 *the king **s** guidance from* 764
2 Chr 31:21 *Hezekiah **s** his God* 839
2 Chr 33:12 *Manasseh **s** the Lord* 956
Eccl 12:10 *The Teacher **s** to find just* 683
1 Thes 2:6 *we have never **s** it from* 1582

SOUL, SOULS (n) the inner life of a human being, the seat of emotions, and the center of human personality
Deut 6:5 *heart, all your **s,** and all* 294
Deut 28:65 *fail, and your **s** to despair.* 319
Deut 30:6 *your heart and **s** and so you* 321
Josh 22:5 *all your heart and all your **s.*** 366
2 Kgs 23:25 *heart and **s** and strength,* 973
Prov 3:22 *for they will refresh your **s.*** 635
Prov 16:24 *sweet to the **s** and healthy* 651
Jer 6:16 *you will find rest for your **s-s.*** 968
Matt 10:28 *can destroy both **s** and body* 1360
Matt 11:29 *you will find rest for your **s-s.*** 1339
Matt 22:37 *all your heart, all your **s,*** 1441
Mark 8:37 *worth more than your **s?*** 1378
Mark 12:30 *heart, all your **s,** all your* 1441
Luke 16:23 *his **s** went to the place of* 1412
Luke 21:19 *firm, you will win your **s-s.*** 1450
John 12:27 *my **s** is deeply troubled.* 1434
Heb 4:12 *cutting between **s** and spirit,* 1766

SOUND (adj) free from error, fallacy, or misapprehension
see also WHOLESOME
2 Tim 4:3 *listen to **s** and wholesome.* 1745

SOUND (n) a particular auditory impression
Job 39:25 *snorts at the **s** of the horn.* 129
Ps 98:6 *trumpets and the **s** of the* 865
Dan 3:10 *they hear the **s** of the horn,* 1005
Acts 2:2 *there was a **s** from heaven.* 1513

SOUND (v) to give a summons by sound
Num 10:6 *When you **s** the signal a* 202
1 Cor 14:8 *the bugler doesn't **s** a clear* 1617

SOUR (adj) having an unpleasant, acidic taste
Ezek 18:2 *parents have eaten **s** grapes,* 1064

SOVEREIGN (adj) possessed of supreme power; unlimited in extent
Ps 71:16 *your mighty deeds, O **S** Lord* 860
Isa 25:8 ***S** Lord will wipe away all* 895
Isa 40:10 *the **S** Lord is coming* 924
Isa 50:4 ***S** Lord has given me his* 937
Isa 61:1 *Spirit of the **S** Lord is upon* 948

SOVEREIGNTY (n) supreme power especially over a body politic
Dan 5:18 *God gave **s,** majesty, glory,* 1139
Dan 7:27 *the **s,** power, and greatness* 1136

SOW(ED), SOWING (KJV)
Lev 25:3 *you may **plant** your fields* 232
Ps 126:5 *Those who **plant** in tears* 1154
Matt 13:4 *As he **scattered** them across* 1345
Luke 12:24 *the ravens. They don't **plant*** 1400
Luke 19:21 *crops you didn't **plant*** 1427

SOWER (KJV)
Isa 55:10 *producing seed for the **farmer*** 942
Jer 50:16 *all **those who plant crops*** 1036
Matt 13:18 *the **farmer planting seeds*** 1345
2 Cor 9:10 *provides seed for the **farmer*** 1638

SPACE (n) a blank or empty area; expanse
Gen 1:8 *God called the **s** "sky."* 7

SPANK (v) to strike especially on the buttocks with the open hand
Prov 23:13 *won't die if you **s** them.* 661

SPARE, SPARED, SPARES (v) to hold back from destroying, punishing, or harming; to have left over or as margin; to rescue from the necessity of doing or undergoing something
Esth 7:3 *lives of my people will be **s-d.*** 1190
Prov 13:24 *Those who **s** the rod of* 647
Isa 54:2 *your home, and **s** no expense!* 941
Mal 3:17 *as a father **s-s** an obedient* 1249
Rom 8:32 *did not **s** even his own Son* 1660
Rom 11:21 *if God did not **s** the original* 1665
2 Pet 2:4 *God did not **s** even the angels* 1758
2 Pet 2:5 *And God did not **s** the ancient* 1759

SPARKLED (v) to glitter or shine
Rev 21:11 ***s** like a precious stone—* 1831

SPARROW, SPARROWS (n) any of several species of birds that eat grain and insects and gather in noisy flocks
Ps 84:3 *Even the **s** finds a home,* 854
Matt 10:31 *than a whole flock of **s-s.*** 1360
Luke 12:6 *What is the price of five **s-s*** 1399

SPEAK, SPEAKING, SPEAKS (v) to express thoughts, opinions, or feelings orally; to talk
see also SPOKE
Deut 18:22 *If the prophet **s-s** in the* 309
Ps 15:3 *or **s** evil of their friends.* 552
Ps 78:2 *will **s** to you in a parable.* 598
Isa 3:8 *because they **s** out against* 827
Isa 32:4 *stammer will **s** out plainly.* 902
Matt 12:34 *men like you **s** what is good* 1341
Matt 15:18 *the words you **s** come from* 1370
Acts 2:11 *hear these people **s-ing** in our* 1514
1 Cor 14:2 *ability to **s** in tongues,* 1616
1 Cor 14:19 *I would rather **s** five* 1617
1 Pet 3:16 *if people **s** against you,* 1753

SPEAKERS (n) one who makes a public speech
2 Cor 8:7 *in your faith, your gifted **s,*** 1636

SPECK (n) a small particle
Matt 7:3 *why worry about a **s** in your* 1333

SPEECH (n) the communication of thoughts in spoken words
Prov 16:23 *a wise mind comes wise **s;*** 651
Prov 22:11 *gracious **s** will have the king* 660
Prov 25:15 *soft **s** can break bones.* 840
Zeph 3:9 *I will purify the **s** of all* 986
1 Cor 1:17 *not with clever **s,** for* 1596

SPELL (n) a state of enchantment
Gal 3:1 *cast an evil **s** on you?* 1560

SPEND, SPENT (v) to use up or pay out; to exhaust or wear out
Prov 21:20 *but fools **s** whatever they* 658
Isa 55:2 *Why **s** your money on food* 942
Mark 5:26 *she had **s-t** everything she had* 1354
2 Cor 12:15 *I will gladly **s** myself* 1642

SPINS (v) to draw out and twist into yarns or threads
Prov 31:13 *flax and busily **s** it* 847

SPIRIT, SPIRITS (n) "wind" or "breath"; a supernatural being; the third member of the Trinity, with God the Father and Jesus the Son; an attitude, mood, or disposition; an evil presence that can possess or influence a person; invisible, nonmaterial part of humans (as opposed to body or flesh)
see also ADVOCATE, HOLY SPIRIT
Gen 1:2 *the **S** of God was hovering* 6
Gen 6:3 *My **S** will not put up with* 17
Exod 31:3 *filled him with the **S** of God,* 183
Num 11:25 ***S** rested upon them, they* 248
Deut 34:9 *full of the **s** of wisdom,* 328
Judg 13:25 *And the **S** of the Lord* 398
1 Sam 16:13 *And the **S** of the Lord* 448
1 Sam 16:14 *a tormenting **s** that filled* 448
2 Kgs 2:9 *double share of your **s** and* 739
Job 33:4 *the **S** of God has made me,* 123
Ps 31:5 *I entrust my **s** into your* 563
Ps 34:18 *those whose **s-s** are crushed.* 459
Ps 51:10 *Renew a loyal **s** within me.* 506
Ps 51:17 *you desire is a broken **s.*** 506
Ps 139:7 *can never escape from your **S!*** 586
Isa 11:2 ***S** of the Lord will rest* 795
Isa 44:3 *I will pour out my **S** on your* 929
Isa 63:10 *him and grieved his Holy **S.*** 950
Ezek 11:19 *put a new **s** within them.* 1057
Joel 2:28 *I will pour out my **S** upon all* 1242
Zech 4:6 *by my **S,** says the Lord* 1169
Matt 3:11 *baptize you with the Holy **S*** 1289
Matt 3:16 *and he saw the **S** of God* 1293
Matt 4:1 *was led by the **S** into the* 1294
Matt 28:19 *and the Son and the Holy **S.*** 1498
Mark 1:8 *baptize you with the Holy **S!*** 1290
Mark 5:12 *pigs," the **s-s** begged.* 1351
Luke 1:35 *The Holy **S** will come upon* 1274
John 3:5 *born of water and the **S.*** 1301
John 6:63 ***S** alone gives eternal life.* 1368
John 14:26 *the Holy **S**—he will teach* 1462
John 16:13 *When the **S** of truth comes,* 1465
Acts 1:8 *when the Holy **S** comes* 1500
Acts 2:4 *as the Holy **S** gave them this* 1514
Acts 2:17 *will pour out my **S** upon all* 1514
Acts 5:3 *You lied to the Holy **S,** and* 1520
Acts 6:3 *full of the **S** and wisdom.* 1522
Acts 8:15 *to receive the Holy **S.*** 1528

Acts 9:17 *and be filled with the Holy **S.***.....1530
Acts 11:16 *be baptized with the Holy **S.***....1535
Acts 19:2 *receive the Holy **S** when you*.....1593
Rom 8:5 *controlled by the Holy **S** think*......1658
Rom 8:9 *do not have the **S** of Christ*.........1659
Rom 8:26 *the Holy **S** prays for us*.............1660
1 Cor 2:10 *For his **S** searches out*.............1598
1 Cor 12:1 *abilities the **S** gives us*............1614
1 Cor 12:13 *one body by one **S,** and we*...1615
1 Cor 14:1 *abilities the **S** gives—*..............1616
2 Cor 3:6 *covenant, the **S** gives life*...........1629
2 Cor 3:17 *and wherever the **S** of the*.......1630
2 Cor 5:3 *not be **s-s** without bodies*..........1631
Gal 3:2 *receive the Holy **S** by obeying*.......1560
Gal 5:22 *But the Holy **S** produces this*.......1566
Eph 4:4 *body and one **S,** just as you*.........1710
Eph 4:30 *to God's Holy **S** by the way*.........1712
Eph 6:12 *and against evil **s-s** in the*.........1715
Eph 6:17 *sword of the **S,** which is the*.......1715
1 Thes 5:19 *Do not stifle the Holy **S.***.........1586
1 Tim 3:16 *vindicated by the **S.***................1731
2 Tim 1:7 *not given us a **s** of fear*.............1741
1 Pet 3:4 *gentle and quiet **s,** which*..........1752
1 Jn 4:1 *who claims to speak by the **S.***......1792

SPIRITUAL (adj) having to do with the spirit, usually God's Spirit
Jonah 4:11 *living in **s** darkness, not*............769
Rom 7:14 *for it is **s** and good.*...................1658
1 Cor 2:14 *who are **s** can understand*.........1598
1 Cor 14:37 *think you are **s,** you should*....1618
1 Cor 15:44 *there are also **s** bodies*...........1621
Eph 5:19 *and hymns and **s** songs among*...1713
1 Pet 2:5 *you offer **s** sacrifices that*..........1750

SPIT (v) to eject (as saliva) from the mouth
Matt 27:30 *And they **s** on him and*...........1481
Rev 3:16 *I will **s** you out of my mouth*.......1807

SPLENDOR (n) great brightness or luster; magnificence
2 Chr 20:21 *him for his holy **s.***....................732
Ps 29:2 *the LORD in the **s** of*........................562
Ps 145:5 *majestic, glorious **s** and*...............589
Prov 20:29 *experience is the **s** of*...............657
Isa 33:17 *see the king in all his **s,***.............903
Hab 3:3 *brilliant **s** fills the heavens,*.............981

SPLINTERS (n) thin pieces split or broken off lengthwise; slivers
Num 33:55 *will be like **s** in your eyes*...........281

SPLIT (v) to tear or rend apart
Matt 19:6 *let no one **s** apart what God*......1418

SPOKE, SPOKEN (v) to orally express thoughts, opinions, or feeling
see also SPEAK
Isa 40:5 *The LORD has **s-n!***........................923
Acts 19:37 *and have not **s-n** against our*....1625
2 Pet 1:21 *Spirit, and they **s** from God.*......1758

SPOT, SPOTS (n) a small area visibly different (as in color, finish, or material) from the surrounding area; a taint on character or reputation
Jer 13:23 *leopard take away its **s-s?***.......1017
Eph 5:27 *church without a **s** or wrinkle*.....1714

SPOTLESS (adj) free from impurity; unblemished
1 Pet 1:19 *the sinless, **s** Lamb of God.*......1749

SPREAD (v) to stretch out; to become distributed, dispersed, or scattered
Isa 25:6 *Armies will **s** a wonderful*.............895
Acts 6:7 *God's message continued to **s.***...1523
Acts 13:49 *Lord's message **s** throughout*..1543
Acts 19:20 *about the Lord **s** widely and*....1594
Phil 1:12 *helped to **s** the Good News.*........1717
2 Thes 3:1 *message will **s** rapidly and*......1590

SPRING, SPRINGS (n) a source of water issuing from the ground
Ps 107:33 *and **s-s** of water into dry,*...........872
Jas 3:12 *fresh water from a salty **s.***...........1550
2 Pet 2:17 *useless as dried-up **s-s** or*.......1759

SPRINKLE, SPRINKLED (v) to scatter in drops or particles
Lev 8:30 *and he **s-d** them on Aaron*...........211
Lev 16:14 *He must **s** blood seven*...............222
Heb 10:22 *have been **s-d** with Christ's*.....1775

STAFF (n) a long stick used for walking or a weapon, often a symbol of authority and protection
see also ROD
Gen 49:10 *nor the ruler's **s** from his*............91
Exod 7:12 *then Aaron's **s** swallowed up*......150
Num 17:6 *Aaron, brought Moses a **s.***..........258
2 Kgs 4:29 *travel; take my **s** and go!*..........741
Ps 23:4 *Your rod and your **s** protect*............558

STAGGER (v) to totter
Isa 63:6 *and made them **s** and fall*.............949

STAIN (n) a soiled or discolored spot
2 Pet 2:13 *disgrace and a **s** among you.*...1759

STAINED (v) to discolor, soil
Isa 63:1 *with his clothing **s** red?*.................949

STAIRWAY (n) one or more flights of stairs
Gen 28:12 *dreamed of a **s** that reached*........57

STAND, STANDING, STANDS (v) to remain stationary; to remain erect; to maintain one's position; to endure successfully
see also STOOD
Exod 3:5 *you are **s-ing** on holy ground.*......143
Josh 5:15 *where you are **s-ing** is holy.*.......343
Josh 10:12 *Let the sun **s** still*......................350
2 Chr 20:17 *then **s** still and*.........................732
Ps 24:3 *Who may **s** in his holy*...................558
Ps 33:11 *LORD's plans **s** firm*......................858
Ps 76:7 *Who can **s** before you*...................596
Ps 119:89 *word, O LORD, **s-s** firm*..............880
Prov 12:7 *family of the godly **s-s** firm.*........645
Isa 40:8 *word of our God **s-s** forever*...........924
Mal 3:2 *be able to **s** and face him*............1247
Luke 6:48 *that house, it **s-s** firm because*...1335
Rom 14:10 *all **s** before the judgment*........1670
1 Cor 10:12 *think you are **s-ing** strong,*....1610
1 Cor 10:13 *to be more than you can **s.***....1610
2 Cor 5:10 *we must all **s** before Christ*......1632
Eph 6:14 ***S** your ground, putting on the*.....1715
Phil 1:27 *you are **s-ing** together with*.......1719
2 Tim 2:19 *But God's truth **s-s** firm like*....1743
1 Pet 5:9 ***S** firm against him, and*............1756
Rev 3:20 *I **s** at the door and knock.*...........1807

STANDARD, STANDARDS (n) something established by authority, custom, or general consent as a model or example; criterion
Lev 24:22 *This same **s** applies both to*........232
Prov 20:23 *LORD detests double **s-s;***..........657

STANDING (n) a position or condition
Rom 8:33 *us right **s** with himself.*.............1661

STAR, STARS (n) a natural luminous body visible in the sky especially at night; sometimes symbolic for angels
Gen 1:16 *He also made the **s-s.***.......................7
Num 24:17 *A **s** will rise from Jacob;*...........268
Job 38:7 *morning **s-s** sang together*..........128
Isa 14:12 *O shining **s,** son of the*...............832
Dan 12:3 *shine like the **s-s** forever.*.........1161
Matt 2:2 *We saw his **s** as it rose,*..............1283
2 Pet 1:19 *the Morning **S** shines in*...........1758
Rev 2:28 *also give them the morning **s!***....1805
Rev 22:16 *I am the bright morning **s.***........1833

STARLIGHT (n) light given by the stars
Ps 74:16 *you made the **s** and the sun*.........595

STARVE, STARVING (v) to suffer extreme hunger
Job 24:10 *they themselves are **s-ing.***.........116
Prov 6:30 *who steals because he is **s-ing.***...639
Luke 15:14 *the land, and he began to **s.***...1410

STATUE (n) a three-dimensional representation usually of a person, animal, or mythical being that is produced by sculpturing, modeling, or casting
Dan 3:1 *made a gold **s** ninety feet*............1005
Rev 13:14 *make a great **s** of the*..............1820

STATURE (n) quality or status gained by growth, development, or achievement
Luke 2:52 *wisdom and in **s** and in favor*....1287

STATUTES (KJV)
Exod 15:26 *keeping all his* ***decrees***............162
Deut 4:40 *If you obey all the* ***decrees*** *and*...291
1 Kgs 3:14 ***decrees*** *and my commands*.....607
Ps 19:8 ***commandments*** *of the LORD*..........554
Ps 119:112 *to keep your* ***decrees***..............880

STAY, STAYED (v) to continue in a place or condition
Ps 119:9 *can a young person **s** pure?*.........878
Luke 2:43 *but Jesus **s-ed** behind in*.........1286
Luke 22:28 *You have **s-ed** with me*..........1459
Gal 5:1 *make sure that you **s** free,*............1565

STEAL, STEALING, STEALS (v) to take the property of another wrongfully
see also STOLE
Exod 20:15 *You must not **s.***.......................170
Lev 19:11 *Do not **s.***......................................225
Deut 5:19 *You must not **s.***..........................293
Prov 28:24 *who **s-s** from his father*............844
Matt 19:18 *You must not **s.***.......................1420
Matt 27:64 *coming and **s-ing** his body*.......1489
Rom 13:9 *You must not **s.***..........................1669
*Eph 4:28 If you are a thief, quit **s-ing.**......1712*
1 Pet 4:15 *not be for murder, **s-ing,***...........755

STEDFAST (KJV)
Ps 78:37 *They did not* ***keep*** *his covenant*....599
1 Cor 15:58 *be* ***strong*** *and immovable.*.....1622
Heb 3:14 *if we are* ***faithful*** *to the end,*.....1765
1 Pet 5:9 *and be* ***strong*** *in your faith*........1756

STEPS (n) course, way
Ps 37:23 *LORD directs the **s** of*....................567
Prov 20:24 *LORD directs our **s,***....................657
1 Pet 2:21 *you must follow in his **s.***...........1752

STIFFHEARTED (KJV)
Ezek 2:4 *stubborn and* ***hard-hearted***.........1046

STIFFNECKED (KJV)
Exod 32:9 *how* ***stubborn and rebellious***....185
Exod 34:9 ***stubborn and rebellious*** *people*..187
Deut 10:16 *stop being* ***stubborn***...............300
2 Chr 30:8 *not be* ***stubborn,*** *as they*...........836
Acts 7:51 *You* ***stubborn*** *people! You are*...1526

STILL (adj) devoid of or abstaining from motion; quiet, calm
Ps 46:10 *Be **s,** and know that I am*............852
Isa 57:20 *never **s** but continually*...............944
Mark 4:39 *Silence! Be **s!***.........................1350

STILL (adv) without motion
Exod 14:13 *Just stand **s** and watch*............160
Josh 10:13 *sun stood **s** and the moon*........350
2 Chr 20:17 *then stand **s** and watch*............732

STILLNESS (n) the quality or state of being still
Ps 107:30 *What a blessing was that **s***........872

STING (n) a wound or pain caused by or as if by stinging
1 Cor 15:55 *where is your **s?***..................1622

STIRS (v) to provoke
Prov 10:12 *Hatred **s** up quarrels,*..................642

STOLE (v) to wrongfully take the property of another
see also STEAL
Lev 6:4 *give back whatever you **s,***.............208

STOMACH (n) the digestive tract of the body
1 Cor 6:13 ***s,** and the **s** for food.*..............1604
Phil 4:12 *with a full **s** or empty,*................1725

STONE (adj) of, relating to, or made of stone
Deut 4:13 *he wrote on two **s** tablets.*..........290

STONE, STONES (n) hardened mineral or rock; figurative of Christ or of hardened hearts
Exod 28:10 *Six names will be on each **s,***....179
Josh 4:3 *Take twelve **s-s** from the very*.......340
1 Sam 17:40 *picked up five smooth **s-s***.....451
Ps 91:12 *even hurt your foot on a **s.***..............861
Ps 118:22 ***s** that the builders rejected*........876
Isa 8:14 *a **s** that makes people stumble,*.....791
Isa 28:16 *a foundation **s** in Jerusalem,*.......819
Isa 50:7 *face like a **s,** determined to*...........937
Jer 51:26 *Even your **s-s** will never again*..1038
Matt 3:9 *Abraham from these very **s-s.***....1288
Matt 7:9 *give them a **s** instead?*...............1334
Matt 21:42 ***s** that the builders rejected*.....1437
Matt 24:2 *Not one **s** will be left*.................1445
Mark 16:3 *roll away the **s** for us from*.......1490
Luke 4:3 *tell this **s** to become a loaf*.........1296
John 8:7 *sinned throw the first **s!***............1391
1 Pet 2:5 *you are living **s-s** that God*.........1750

STONED, STONING (v) to kill by pelting with stones
2 Cor 11:25 *with rods. Once I was **s-d.***....1641
Heb 11:37 *Some died by **s-ing,** some were*..1779

STONY (adj) insensitive to pity or human feeling
Ezek 11:19 *away their **s,** stubborn heart*...1057

STOOD (v) to maintain one's position
see also STAND
Josh 10:13 *So the sun **s** still and*................350
2 Tim 4:17 *But the Lord **s** with me*............1746

STOP, STOPS (v) to cease activity or operation; to pause or hesitate; to restrain or prevent
Job 37:14 ***S** and consider the wonderful*.....127
Prov 15:18 *cool-tempered person **s-s***........650
Jer 7:5 *only if you **s** your evil*...................1008
Jer 32:40 *I will never **s** doing good*...........1080
Lam 3:49 *flow endlessly; they will not **s***....1099
Dan 4:35 *No one can **s** him or say to*........1121
Matt 19:14 *come to me. Don't **s** them!*.....1419
Eph 6:16 *shield of faith to **s** the*...............1715

STORE (n) a large quantity, supply, or number
Isa 33:6 *a rich **s** of salvation,*......................903

STORE, STORED (v) to lay away; to accumulate
Matt 6:19 *Don't **s** up treasures*.................1332
Matt 6:26 *plant or harvest or **s** food*..........1332
Luke 2:51 *And his mother **s-d** all these*....1287

STORIES (n) fictional narratives
2 Pet 1:16 *making up clever **s** when*.........1758

STORM (n) a heavy fall of rain, snow, or hail sometimes accompanied by thunder and lightning; a disturbed or agitated state
see also WHIRLWIND, WIND
Ps 50:3 *and a great **s** rages around*...........593
Ps 55:8 *from this wild **s** of hatred*..............572
Ps 107:29 *He calmed the **s** to a whisper*.....872
Luke 8:24 ***s** stopped and all was calm.*.....1350

STRAIN (v) to exert (as oneself) to the utmost; to filter
Ps 119:123 *My eyes **s** to see your*.............880
Jer 14:6 *They **s** their eyes*.......................1017
Matt 23:24 *You **s** your water so*...............1444

STRANGE (adj) foreign; not before known, heard, or seen
see also FOREIGN
Isa 28:11 *who speak a **s** language!*............818
1 Cor 14:21 *people through **s** languages*..1617
1 Pet 4:12 *something **s** were happening*...1755

STRANGER, STRANGERS (n) a person who is unknown or with whom one is unacquainted
see also FOREIGNER(S)
Job 31:32 *turned away a **s** but have*...........122
Matt 25:35 *I was a **s,** and you invited*.......1453
John 10:5 *They won't follow a **s;***.............1405
1 Tim 5:10 *been kind to **s-s** and served*....1733
Heb 13:2 *to show hospitality to **s-s,** for*.....1782

STRANGLED (adj) characterized by choking to death
Acts 15:29 *or the meat of **s** animals,*........1571

STRATEGIES (n) a careful and clever plan or method
Eph 6:11 *against all **s** of the devil.*...........1715

STRAW (n) stalks of grain after threshing
1 Cor 3:12 *jewels, wood, hay, or **s.***...........1599

STRAYED (v) to wander
Isa 53:6 *like sheep, have **s** away*................940
Ezek 34:16 *lost ones who **s** away, and*......1110

STREAMS (n) bodies of running water (as a river or brook)
Ps 23:2 *leads me beside peaceful **s.***..........558
Jer 31:9 *walk beside quiet **s** and*.............1032

STRENGTH (n) capacity for exertion or endurance; support; the power of a person or of God, measured variously in terms of wealth, wisdom, military might, or physical prowess
Exod 15:2 *LORD is my **s** and my*.................161
Deut 6:5 *your soul, and all your **s.***.............294
2 Kgs 23:25 *his heart and soul and **s,***..........973
1 Chr 16:11 *LORD and for his **s;***.................493
Neh 8:10 *of the LORD is your **s!***...............1215
Ps 23:3 *He renews my **s.** He guides me*......558
Ps 28:7 *LORD is my **s** and shield.*...............562
Ps 33:16 *nor is great **s** enough to save*.......858
Ps 46:1 *God is our refuge and **s,***...............851
Ps 59:17 *O my **S,** to you I sing*..................454
Ps 65:6 *armed yourself with mighty **s.***.........575
Ps 84:5 *for those whose **s** comes from*.......854
Ps 139:10 *your **s** will support me.*..............586
Isa 31:1 *depending on the **s** of human*........901
Isa 40:26 *power and incomparable **s,***.........924
Jer 27:5 *With my great **s** and powerful*.....1049
Mic 5:4 *with the LORD's **s,** in*......................908
Hab 3:19 *LORD is my **s!***............................982
Zech 4:6 *nor by **s,** but by my Spirit,*..........1169
Mark 12:30 *your mind, and all your **s.***.......1441
1 Cor 1:25 *the greatest of human **s.***..........1597
Phil 4:13 *Christ, who gives me **s.***..............1725
Heb 11:34 *weakness was turned to **s.***.......1779
Heb 13:9 *Your **s** comes from God's*.............1782

STRENGTHEN, STRENGTHENED, STRENGTHENS (v) to make or become stronger
2 Chr 16:9 *in order to **s** those whose*..........711
Isa 41:10 *I will **s** you and help you.*.............925
1 Cor 8:1 *is love that **s-s** the church*..........1607
1 Cor 14:4 *in tongues is **s-ed** personally,*..1617
1 Cor 14:4 *word of prophecy **s-s** the*........1617
1 Cor 14:5 *whole church will be **s-ed.***......1617
1 Cor 14:12 *seek those that will **s** the*.......1617
1 Cor 14:17 *but it won't **s** the people*........1617
1 Cor 14:26 *is done must **s** all of you.*......1618
2 Cor 13:10 *has given me to **s** you, not*....1643
Heb 12:12 *tired hands and **s** your weak*....1780
1 Pet 5:10 *support, and **s** you, and he*......1756

STRIKE (v) to aim and deliver a blow, stroke, or thrust (as with the hand, a weapon, or a tool); to inflict
see also STRUCK
Zech 13:7 ***S** down the shepherd, and*.......1179
Matt 26:31 *God will **s** the Shepherd,*.........1460
Rev 19:15 *sword to **s** down the nations.*...1828

STRIP (v) to remove extraneous or superficial matter from
Heb 12:1 *let us **s** off every weight*............1780

STRIPES (KJV)
Acts 16:33 *washed their **wounds***............1576
2 Cor 11:24 *gave me thirty-nine **lashes***....1641
1 Pet 2:24 *By his **wounds** you are healed*...1752

STRIPS (n) Long, narrow pieces of a material
Luke 2:12 *wrapped snugly in **s** of cloth,*....1281

STRONG, STRONGER, STRONGEST (adj) having or marked by great physical power, moral or intellectual power, or great resources (as of wealth or talent); firm
Exod 6:1 *force of my **s** hand, he*................148
Deut 5:15 *you out with his **s** hand*..............293
Deut 7:8 *with such a **s** hand from your*........296
Deut 31:6 *So be **s** and courageous!*............322
Josh 1:6 *Be **s** and courageous,*....................336
Judg 16:5 *makes him so **s** and how he*.......400
2 Sam 22:33 *God is my **s** fortress, and*.......527
1 Kgs 8:42 *and your **s** hand and your*..........620
1 Chr 28:20 *Be **s** and courageous, and*.......540
Ezra 10:4 *so be **s** and take action.*............1201
Ps 24:8 *The LORD, **s** and mighty;*................559
Ps 96:7 *LORD is glorious and **s.***....................864
Prov 18:10 *LORD is a **s** fortress;*...................653
Prov 24:5 *wise are mightier than the **s,***.......662
Prov 30:25 *Ants—they aren't **s,** but*..............847
Prov 31:17 *She is energetic and **s,** a*..........847
Eccl 9:11 ***s-est** warrior doesn't always*.......681
Isa 35:4 *Be **s,** and do not fear,*....................905
Jer 50:34 *one who redeems them is **s.***.....1036
Zeph 1:14 *when even **s** men will cry*...........984
Luke 1:80 *and became **s** in spirit*.............1277
Luke 2:40 *grew up healthy and **s.***.............1286
Luke 11:22 *someone even **s-er** attacks*....1342
1 Cor 1:8 *keep you **s** to the end*..............1595
1 Cor 1:25 *God's weakness is **s-er** than*...1597
1 Cor 16:13 *Be courageous. Be **s.***............1623
Eph 6:10 *final word: Be **s** in the Lord*........1715
1 Thes 3:13 *your hearts **s,** blameless,*.......1584
2 Tim 2:1 *dear son, be **s** through the*........1742

STRUCK (v) to inflict
see also STRIKE
Job 2:7 *presence, and he* **s** *Job with* 96
Isa 53:8 *But he was* **s** *down for the*............940

STRUGGLE (n) strife; a violent effort or exertion
Rom 15:30 *to join in my* **s** *by praying*........1672
Heb 12:4 *lives in your* **s** *against sin*...........1780

STRUGGLE (v) to proceed with difficulty or with great effort; to make strenuous or violent efforts in the face of difficulties or opposition
Gen 3:17 *will* **s** *to scratch a living*.................13
Col 1:29 *why I work and* **s** *so hard,*...........1697
1 Tim 4:10 *and continue to* **s,** *for our*........1732

STUBBORN (adj) unreasonably or perversely unyielding
Exod 33:5 *You are a* **s** *and rebellious*..........186
Exod 34:9 *this is a* **s** *and rebellious*.............187
Lev 26:41 *at last their* **s** *hearts will*............236
Deut 10:16 *hearts and stop being* **s.**...........300
2 Chr 36:13 *a hard and* **s** *man, refusing*...1041
Ps 78:8 *ancestors—***s,** *rebellious,*..................598
Prov 28:14 *the* **s** *are headed for serious*.....844
Ezek 36:26 *out your stony,* **s** *heart and*......1112
Rom 2:5 *because you are* **s** *and refuse*.....1648

STUDENTS (n) those who study
Matt 10:24 **S** *are not greater than*...........1360

STUDY (n) application of the mental faculties to the acquisition of knowledge
Eccl 12:12 *and much* **s** *wears you*.............683

STUDY (v) to read in detail, especially with the intention of learning
Josh 1:8 **S** *this Book of Instruction*.............337
Ezra 7:10 *had determined to* **s** *and obey*...1196

STUMBLE, STUMBLES, STUMBLING (v) to trip or walk unsteadily; to fall into sin or waywardness
Lev 19:14 *or cause the blind to* **s.** 225
Ps 37:24 *Though they* **s,** *they will*...............567
Ps 66:9 *he keeps our feet from* **s-ing.**.........859
Ps 119:165 *great peace and do not* **s.**.........881
Ps 121:3 *He will not let you* **s;**....................882
Prov 3:23 *and your feet will not* **s.** 635
Prov 24:17 *don't be happy when they* **s.**.....662
Isa 8:14 *stone that makes people* **s,** 791
Jer 13:16 *causing you to* **s** *and fall*...........1016
Hos 14:9 *paths sinners* **s** *and fall*...............817
Mal 2:8 *caused many to* **s** *into sin.* 1246
Matt 21:44 *Anyone who* **s-s** *over that*.......1437
John 11:10 *is danger of* **s-ing** *because*....1414
Rom 9:33 *that makes people* **s,**...............1663
Rom 14:13 *believer to* **s** *and fall.*.............1670
Rom 14:20 *makes another person* **s.**........1670
1 Cor 8:9 *weaker conscience to* **s.**...........1608
2 Cor 6:3 *no one will* **s** *because of us,*......1633
1 Jn 2:10 *does not cause others to* **s.**.......1789

STUMP (n) the part of a tree remaining attached to the root after the trunk is cut
Isa 6:13 *so Israel's* **s** *will be a*....................786
Isa 11:1 *Out of the* **s** *of David's*..................795

STUPID (adj) lacking intelligence or reason
Ps 119:70 *hearts are dull and* **s,** 879
Prov 12:1 *is* **s** *to hate correction.*................644

STUPIDITY (n) the quality or state of being stupid
Jer 31:19 *kicked myself for my* **s!** 1033

SUBMISSION (n) the condition of being submissive, humble, or compliant
1 Sam 15:22 **s** *is better than offering*.........446

SUBMISSIVE (adj) submitting to others
1 Cor 14:34 *They should be* **s,** *just*...........1618
Titus 2:5 *be* **s** *to their husbands*...............1738

SUBMIT, SUBMITS (v) to yield to authority or be accountable to another—God, society, or fellow believers
Ps 2:12 **S** *to God's royal son,*....................857
Rom 13:1 *Everyone must* **s** *to governing*...1668
Rom 13:5 *So you must* **s** *to them, not*.......1668
Eph 5:21 **s** *to one another out of*.............1713
Eph 5:24 *As the church* **s-s** *to Christ,*.......1713
Col 3:18 *Wives,* **s** *to your husbands,*.........1701
Heb 12:9 *shouldn't we* **s** *even more*..........1780

SUBTRACT (v) to take away
Deut 4:2 *Do not add to or* **s** *from*................289
Deut 12:32 *to them or* **s** *anything*..............302

SUBVERT (KJV)
Lam 3:36 *they* ***twist*** *justice in the courts*..1098
Titus 1:11 *turning whole families* ***away from the truth***....................................1737

SUCCEED (v) to turn out well; to attain a desired end
Gen 39:23 *everything he did to* **s.**................78
Josh 1:8 *prosper and* **s** *in all you*...............337
1 Sam 2:9 *No one will* **s** *by strength*..........419
1 Sam 18:14 *continued to* **s** *in*....................453
2 Chr 20:20 *prophets, and you will* **s.**..........732
Ps 20:4 *and make all your plans* **s.**............555
Prov 11:10 *celebrates when the godly* **s;**.....643
Prov 13:13 *respect a command will* **s.**........646
Prov 16:3 *and your plans will* **s.**..................650
Prov 20:18 *Plans* **s** *through good*..................657
Prov 28:12 *When the godly* **s,** *everyone*......844
Eccl 10:10 *wisdom; it helps you* **s.** 681

SUCCESS (n) the attainment of wealth, favor, or eminence; favorable or desired outcome
1 Chr 12:18 *and* **s** *to all who help*..............461
2 Chr 26:5 *LORD, God gave him* **s.** 764
Prov 15:22 *many advisers bring* **s.**..............650

SUCCESSFUL (adj) resulting or terminating in success; gaining or having gained success
Deut 8:18 *gives you power to be* **s,**............297
Deut 30:9 *make you* **s** *in everything*...........321
1 Kgs 2:3 *that you will be* **s** *in all*..............545
2 Kgs 18:7 *Hezekiah was* **s** *in* 800
1 Chr 22:13 *For you will be* **s** *if you* 533
2 Chr 31:21 *result, he was very* **s.**..............839
Ps 90:17 *and make our efforts* **s.** 326
Prov 1:3 *disciplined and* **s** *lives,*.................631
Eccl 9:11 *don't always lead* **s** *lives*.............681

SUES (v) to seek justice or right from (a person) by legal process
1 Cor 6:6 *one believer* **s** *another—* 1603

SUFFER, SUFFERED, SUFFERING, SUFFERS (v) to endure death, pain, distress, or loss
Job 36:15 *rescues those who* **s.**..................126
Mark 8:31 *Son of Man must* **s** *many*.........1377
Luke 24:26 *would have to* **s** *all these*........1494
Luke 24:46 *Messiah would* **s** *and die*........1498
Rom 8:18 *Yet what we* **s** *now is nothing*....1659
1 Cor 12:26 *If one part* **s-s,** *all the parts*...1615
2 Cor 1:5 *the more we* **s** *for Christ,*...........1626
2 Cor 12:10 *troubles that I* **s** *for Christ*......1642
Phil 3:10 *I want to* **s** *with him, sharing* 1722
2 Thes 1:4 *and hardships you are* ***s-ing.***...1587
Heb 11:26 *better to* **s** *for the sake*............1778
1 Pet 2:21 *just as Christ* **s-ed** *for you.* 1752
1 Pet 4:1 *since Christ* **s-ed** *physical pain,* .1754
1 Pet 4:16 *is no shame to* **s** *for being*.......1755
1 Pet 5:10 *So after you have* **s-ed** *a little*...1756
Rev 2:3 *You have patiently* **s-ed** *for me*.....1802

SUFFERING, SUFFERINGS (n) the state or experience of one that suffers; pain, distress
Deut 16:3 *the bread of* **s***—so that*..............305
Job 36:15 *means of their* **s,** *he rescues*......126
Ps 119:71 *My* **s** *was good for me,*..............879
Isa 48:10 *you in the furnace of* **s.**...............935
Isa 49:13 *on them in their* **s.**.......................936
Lam 1:12 *if there is any* **s** *like mine,*.........1095
Luke 22:15 *you before my* **s** *begins*..........1458
2 Cor 1:7 *as you share in our* **s-s,** *you*......1626
Phil 1:29 *the privilege of* **s** *for him.* 1719
Col 1:24 *participating in the* **s-s** *of*............1696
2 Tim 2:3 *Endure* **s** *along with me,* 1742
2 Tim 4:5 *afraid of* **s** *for the Lord.* 1745
Heb 2:10 *through his* **s,** *a perfect*.............1764
Heb 2:18 *gone through* **s** *and testing,*.......1764
1 Pet 1:11 *about Christ's* **s** *and his*............1749
1 Pet 4:13 *Christ in his* **s,** *so that*............1755

SUMMED (v) to summarize
Rom 13:9 *commandments—are* **s** *up in*...1669
Gal 5:14 *whole law can be* **s** *up in this*......1566

SUN (n) the star that sustains life on the earth, being the source of heat and light
Josh 10:13 *So the* **s** *stood still and*............350
Judg 5:31 *rise like the* **s** *in all its*...............382
Ps 84:11 *God is our* **s** *and our shield.* 855
Ps 121:6 *The* **s** *will not harm you* 882
Ps 136:8 *the* **s** *to rule the day,*...................886
Eccl 1:9 *Nothing under the* **s** *is truly* 673
Isa 60:19 *you need the* **s** *to shine by* 947
Mal 4:2 *name, the* **S** *of Righteousness*......1249
Matt 13:43 *shine like the* **s** *in their* 1349
Matt 17:2 *shone like the* **s,** *and his*...........1378
Luke 23:45 *light from the* **s** *was gone.*.......1486
Eph 4:26 *Don't let the* **s** *go down while*.....1712
Rev 1:16 *was like the* **s** *in all its* 1800
Rev 21:23 *has no need of* **s** *or moon,* 1831

SUNDAY (n) the first day of the week
Matt 28:1 *Early on* **S** *morning, as*.............1489

SUNLIGHT (n) the light of the sun; sunshine
Matt 5:45 *he gives his* **s** *to both the*..........1330

SUPERIOR (adj) of higher rank, quality, or importance
Heb 8:6 *that is far* **s** *to the old*.................1771

SUPERNATURAL (adj) of or relating to God, a spirit, or the devil
2 Pet 2:10 *scoff at* **s** *beings without*..........1759
Jude 1:8 *and scoff at* **s** *beings*.................1785

SUPPER (n) meal eaten toward the end of the day; communion (i.e., Lord's Supper)
Luke 22:20 *After* **s** *he took another cup of*..1458
Acts 2:42 *meals (including the Lord's* **S***)* ...1516
1 Cor 11:33 *gather for the Lord's* **S,** 1614

SUPPORT, SUPPORTS (v) to pay the costs of; to assist or help
Lev 25:35 *and cannot* **s** *himself,* **s**.............234
Ps 18:35 *Your right hand* **s-s** *me;*...............529
Ps 139:10 *your strength will* **s** *me.* 586
Ps 147:6 *The LORD* **s-s** *the humble,*..........1154
1 Pet 5:10 *he will restore,* **s,** *and*.............1756
3 Jn 1:8 *we ourselves should* **s** *them*........1797

SUPPRESS (v) to stop or prohibit the revelation of
Rom 1:18 *wicked people who* **s** *the truth* ..1647

SUPREME (adj) highest in rank, authority, degree, or quality
Col 1:15 *was created and is **s** over all*.......1694
Col 1:18 *is the beginning, **s** over all*..........1695

SURE (adj) admitting of no doubt; careful to remember, attend to, or find out something
Num 32:23 *you may be **s** that your sin* 279
1 Sam 12:24 *But be **s** to fear the* 441
2 Cor 1:15 *Since I was so **s** of your* 1627
2 Cor 9:5 *of me to make **s** the gift you*......1637
Eph 5:5 *You can be **s** that no immoral,*......1712
2 Tim 1:12 *trust, and I am **s** that he is* 1741

SURETY (KJV)
Gen 43:9 *I **personally guarantee** his safety* 83
Prov 17:18 ***put up security** for a friend* 652
Heb 7:22 *Jesus is the one who **guarantees*** 1771

SURFACE (n) the external or superficial aspect of something
John 7:24 *Look beneath the **s** so you can*..1390

SURGING (adj) characterized by tossing and swelling
Ps 42:7 *your waves and **s** tides sweep*........849

SURPASS (v) to become better, greater, or stronger than
Prov 31:29 *world, but you **s** them all!*..........848

SURPLUS (n) the amount that remains when use or need is satisfied
Luke 21:4 *part of their **s**, but she,*.............1445

SURPRISED (v) to take unawares; to strike with wonder or amazement especially because it is unexpected
1 Thes 5:4 *you won't be **s** when the day*...1585
1 Pet 4:4 *former friends are **s** when you*...1754
1 Jn 3:13 *So don't be **s**, dear brothers* 1791

SURRENDERED (v) to yield to the power, control, or possession of another upon compulsion or demand
2 Sam 10:19 *by Israel, they **s** to Israel*........501
1 Chr 19:19 *by Israel, they **s** to David*.........502

SURROUND, SURROUNDED, SURROUNDS (v) to envelop; to encircle
Deut 33:12 *He **s-s** them continuously*.........327
Ps 5:12 *O LORD; you **s** them with*...................548
Ps 32:10 *unfailing love **s-s** those who*........565
Ps 33:22 *unfailing love **s** us, LORD,*.............858
Ps 89:7 *than all who **s** his throne*...............591
Ps 125:2 *the mountains **s** Jerusalem,*.........883
Ps 125:2 *the LORD **s-s** his people,* 883
Heb 12:1 *we are **s-ed** by such a huge*......1780

SUSTAINS (v) to keep up or prolong
Heb 1:3 *God, and he **s** everything by* 1761

SWADDLED, SWADDLING (KJV)
Ezek 16:4 *salt, and **wrapped in cloth***.......1061
Luke 2:7 *wrapped him **snugly in strips of cloth*** 1280
Luke 2:12 *baby **wrapped snugly** in strips* 1281

SWALLOW, SWALLOWED (v) to take through the mouth and esophagus into the stomach; to envelop or absorb
Isa 25:8 *He will **s** up death*.........................895
Jonah 1:17 *a great fish to **s** Jonah.* 767
Hab 1:13 *while the wicked **s** up people*.......979
Matt 23:24 *a gnat, but you **s** a camel!* 1444
1 Cor 15:54 *fulfilled: "Death is **s-ed** up*.....1622
2 Cor 5:4 *bodies will be **s-ed** up by life*.....1632

SWEAR (v) to affirm by a solemn oath or binding commitment
see also SWORE, SWORN
Lev 19:12 *using it to **s** falsely.*...................225
Isa 54:9 *earth, so now I **s** that I will*............941
Heb 6:13 *one greater to **s** by, God took*.....1768

SWEET, SWEETER (adj) pleasing to the taste; agreeable, gratifying
Job 20:12 *They enjoyed the **s** taste of* 113
Ps 19:10 *They are **s-er** than honey,*.........555
Ps 119:103 *How **s** your words taste* 880
Ps 119:103 *they are **s-er** than honey.* 880
Prov 20:17 *Stolen bread tastes **s**, but*........657
Prov 24:14 *wisdom is **s** to your soul.* 662
Prov 27:9 *friend is as **s** as perfume* 842
Song 1:2 *your love is **s-er** than wine*...........663
Song 4:11 *lips are as **s** as nectar,*...............666
Isa 5:20 *bitter is **s** and **s** is bitter*...............829
Ezek 3:3 *it tasted as **s** as honey in my* 1046

SWEET-SMELLING (adj) of or relating to a pleasant scent
Phil 4:18 *They are a **s** sacrifice that*..........1725

SWEETNESS (n) the quality or state of being sweet
Song 5:16 *His mouth is **s** itself;*..................668

SWEPT (adj) cleaned with a broom or brush
Matt 12:44 *former home empty, **s**, and in*...1343

SWORD, SWORDS (n) a handheld weapon with a long blade; figurative of war or persecution by government, also of God's word in spiritual warfare
Gen 3:24 *a flaming **s** that flashed*..................13
Deut 32:41 *my flashing **s** and begin* 325
1 Sam 17:45 *come to me with **s**, spear,*......451
1 Sam 31:4 *Take your **s** and kill me*............474
2 Sam 12:10 *live by the **s** because you*........505
1 Kgs 20:11 *putting on his **s** for battle*........722
Ps 44:6 *not count on my **s** to save me.* 850
Ps 45:3 *Put on your **s**, O mighty*.................851
Ps 64:3 *their tongues like **s-s** and aim* 574
Joel 3:10 *plowshares into **s-s** and your* 1243
Amos 9:4 *I will command the **s** to kill*..........780
Mic 4:3 *will hammer their **s-s** into*.............907
Matt 10:34 *not to bring peace, but a **s**.*.....1361
Matt 26:52 *who use the **s** will die by* 1469
Luke 2:35 *a **s** will pierce your very*...........1282
Eph 6:17 *take the **s** of the Spirit,* 1715
Heb 4:12 *sharpest two-edged **s**, cutting* ...1766
Rev 1:16 *sharp two-edged **s** came* 1800
Rev 19:15 *came a sharp **s** to strike* 1828

SWORE, SWORN (v) to affirm by a solemn oath or binding commitment
see also SWEAR
Exod 33:1 *up to the land I **s** to give*............186
Deut 7:8 *the oath he had **s-n** to your*............296
Deut 30:20 *land the LORD **s** to give* 321
Isa 45:23 *I have **s-n** by my own* 932

SYCAMORE-FIG (n) a fig tree that has edible fruit similar but inferior to the common fig
Amos 7:14 *take care of **s** trees*....................778
Luke 19:4 *and climbed a **s** tree beside* 1426

SYMBOL (n) something that stands for or suggests something else
Rom 5:14 *Adam is a **s**, a representation* ...1655

SYMPATHIZE (v) to share in suffering or grief
1 Pet 3:8 ***S** with each other. Love each* 1753

SYNAGOGUE (n) the house of worship and communal center of a Jewish congregation
Luke 4:16 *to the **s** on the Sabbath*............1357
John 12:42 *expel them from the **s**.*..........1435
Acts 17:2 *he went to the **s** service,*..........1576
Rev 3:9 *who belong to Satan's **s**—*............1806

TABERNACLE (n) portable shrine or tent designated for the worship of God; metaphor for God dwelling among his people
see also SANCTUARY, TEMPLE
Exod 27:21 *stand in the **T**, in front of*...........178
Exod 40:2 *Set up the **T** on the first.*.............195
Exod 40:34 *cloud covered the **T**, and* 196
Exod 40:34 *of the LORD filled the **T**.*............196
Num 3:29 *area south of the **T** for their*........241
Heb 8:5 *to build the **T**, God gave him* 1771
Heb 9:11 *more perfect **T** in heaven,*..........1772
Heb 9:21 *blood on the **T** and on* 1774
Rev 15:5 *heaven, God's **T**, was thrown*.......1822

TABLE, TABLES (n) a piece of furniture consisting of a smooth flat slab fixed on legs
Exod 25:23 *Then make a **t** of acacia*...........176
John 2:15 *and turned over their **t-s**.*.........1300

TABLETS (n) flat slabs or plaques suited for or bearing an inscription
Exod 31:18 *two stone **t** inscribed with*.........183
Deut 10:5 *and placed the **t** in the Ark*..........299
2 Cor 3:3 *carved not on **t** of stone,* 1629

TAKE, TAKEN, TAKES (v) to exploit; to seize or capture physically; to remove; to move onto or into; to feel or experience; to lead, carry, or cause to go along to another place; to grasp or grip; to accept; to derive
see also TOOK
Gen 2:23 *she was **t-n** from 'man.'*................10
Gen 9:6 *life will also be **t-n** by human*...........21
Lev 25:14 *you must not **t** advantage of*.......233
Num 13:30 *go at once to **t** the land,*.............251
Num 19:3 *it will be **t-n** outside the camp*.....260
1 Chr 17:13 *I will never **t** my favor*...............496
Ps 2:12 *for all who **t** refuge in him!*...............857
Ps 5:4 *O God, you **t** no pleasure in*...............547
Ps 49:17 *they die, they **t** nothing with*.........854
Ps 51:11 *and don't **t** your Holy Spirit*............506
Prov 3:6 *show you which path to **t**.*..............634
Jer 25:10 *I will **t** away your happy* 994
Zech 3:4 *See, I have **t-n** away your sins,*...1168
Matt 10:38 *refuse to **t** up your cross*..........1361
Matt 11:29 ***T** my yoke upon you. Let me*...1339
Matt 16:24 *selfish ways, **t** up your cross,*..1377
Matt 24:40 *one will be **t-n**, the other*........1447
Matt 26:26 ***T** this and eat it, for this*..........1457
Matt 26:39 *cup of suffering be **t-n** away*...1468
Mark 14:36 *Please **t** this cup of suffering*..1468
Mark 16:19 *he was **t-n** up into heaven*.....1499
John 1:29 *Lamb of God who **t-s** away the* 1297
John 10:18 *No one can **t** my life from me.* 1405
Acts 1:9 *he was **t-n** up into a cloud*..........1500
1 Tim 3:16 *and **t-n** to heaven in glory.*.......1731

TALK (n) speech; pointless or fruitless discussion
Ps 5:9 *Their **t** is foul, like*............................547
Prov 10:19 *Too much **t** leads to*.................642
2 Tim 2:16 *worthless, foolish **t** that*...........1743

TALK BACK (v) to answer impertinently
Titus 2:9 *They must not **t***.........................1738

TALL, TALLER (adj) of a specified or considerable height
1 Sam 2:26 *boy Samuel grew **t-er** and*.......420
1 Sam 9:2 *and shoulders **t-er** than anyone*.435
1 Sam 17:4 *He was over nine feet **t**!*...........449
1 Chr 11:23 *was 7½ feet **t** and whose*........482

TAME (v) to domesticate; to harness
Jas 3:7 *People can* ***t*** *all kinds of* ... 1550
Jas 3:8 *no one can* ***t*** *the tongue.* ... 1550

TANGLED (v) to involve so as to hamper, obstruct, or embarrass; to entrap
Exod 4:10 *and my words get* ***t.*** ... 145
2 Pet 2:20 *Christ and then get* ***t*** *up and* ... 1759

TASK (n) duty, function
2 Cor 2:16 *for such a* ***t*** *as this?* ... 1628
2 Cor 5:18 *us this* ***t*** *of reconciling* ... 1632

TASTE (n) the act of tasting; a sample experience
Prov 24:13 *honeycomb is sweet to the* ***t.*** ... 662
1 Pet 2:3 *a* ***t*** *of the Lord's kindness.* ... 1750

TASTE, TASTED, TASTES (v) to become acquainted with by experience; to ascertain the flavor of by taking a little into the mouth
Ps 34:8 ***T*** *and see that the* LORD ... 458
Prov 9:17 *eaten in secret* ***t-s*** *the best!* ... 641
Song 2:3 *and* ***t*** *his delicious fruit* ... 664
Ezek 3:3 *I ate it, it* ***t-d*** *as sweet as* ... 1046
Col 2:21 *Don't handle! Don't* ***t!*** ... 1699

TATTOOS (n) indelible marks or figures fixed upon the body
Lev 19:28 *not mark your skin with* ***t.*** ... 226

TAX, TAXES (n) a charge usually of money imposed by authority on persons or property for public purposes
Matt 17:24 *teacher pay the Temple* ***t?*** ... 1382
Matt 22:17 *right to pay* ***t-es*** *to Caesar* ... 1439
Rom 13:7 *Pay your* ***t-es*** *and* ... 1668

TAX COLLECTOR, TAX COLLECTORS (n) one who collects tax or custom on behalf of the government
Matt 5:46 *corrupt* ***t-s*** *do that* ... 1330
Matt 9:10 *along with many* ***t-s*** *and* ... 1314
Matt 11:19 *a friend of* ***t-s*** *and other sinners* ... 1338
Matt 21:31 ***t-s*** *and prostitutes will get* ... 1437
Luke 5:27 *he saw a* ***t*** *named Levi* ... 1316
Luke 18:11 *I'm certainly not like that* ***t!*** ... 1418

TEACH, TEACHES, TEACHING (v) to cause to know something; to instruct by precept, example, or experience
see also INSTRUCT, PREACH, TRAIN
Lev 10:11 *you must* ***t*** *the Israelites* ... 214
Deut 6:1 *commanded me to* ***t*** *you* ... 294
2 Chr 17:9 *of Judah,* ***t-ing*** *the people.* ... 714
Job 21:22 *who can* ***t*** *a lesson to God,* ... 114
Ps 37:30 *they* ***t*** *right from wrong.* ... 568
Ps 51:13 *Then I will* ***t*** *your ways* ... 506
Prov 15:33 *the* LORD ***t-es*** *wisdom;* ... 650
Isa 2:3 *he will* ***t*** *us his ways,* ... 825
Matt 5:19 *obeys God's laws and* ***t-es*** ... 1327
Matt 11:29 *Let me* ***t*** *you, because* ... 1339
Matt 15:9 *they* ***t*** *man-made ideas* ... 1369
Matt 22:16 *You* ***t*** *the way of God* ... 1439
Matt 28:20 ***T*** *these new disciples to* ... 1498
Mark 10:1 *as usual he was* ***t-ing*** *them.* ... 1387
Luke 11:1 *Lord,* ***t*** *us to pray,* ... 1342
Luke 12:12 *Holy Spirit will* ***t*** *you* ... 1400
John 14:26 *he will* ***t*** *you everything* ... 1462
Acts 6:4 *in prayer and* ***t-ing*** *the word.* ... 1522
Rom 15:4 *Scriptures long ago to* ***t*** ... 1671
Rom 15:14 *you can* ***t*** *each other all* ... 1671
1 Cor 2:16 *knows enough to* ***t*** *him?* ... 1598
1 Cor 14:26 *another will* ***t,*** *another* ... 1618
1 Tim 2:12 *do not let women* ***t*** *men* ... 1730
1 Tim 3:2 *he must be able to* ***t.*** ... 1730
2 Tim 3:16 *is useful to* ***t*** *us what* ... 1745
2 Tim 3:16 ***t-es*** *us to do what is right.* ... 1745
Titus 2:15 *You must* ***t*** *these things* ... 1738
Heb 5:12 *you ought to be* ***t-ing*** *others* ... 1767
1 Jn 2:27 *need anyone to* ***t*** *you what* ... 1790

TEACHER, TEACHERS (n) one who teaches
Job 36:22 *Who is a* ***t*** *like him?* ... 126
Prov 5:13 *didn't I listen to my* ***t-s?*** ... 637
Eccl 1:1 *words of the* ***T,*** *King David's* ... 673
Matt 10:24 *not greater than their* ***t,*** ... 1360
Matt 23:10 *only one* ***t,*** *the Messiah.* ... 1443
Luke 6:40 *will become like the* ***t.*** ... 1333
Luke 20:46 *these* ***t-s*** *of religious law!* ... 1443
John 13:14 *Lord and* ***T,*** *have washed* ... 1456
Rom 12:7 *If you are a* ***t,*** *teach well.* ... 1667
1 Cor 12:28 *third are* ***t-s,*** *then those* ... 1615
Gal 6:6 *should provide for their* ***t-s,*** ... 1567
Eph 4:11 *and the pastors and* ***t-s.*** ... 1710
2 Tim 4:3 *look for* ***t-s*** *who will tell* ... 1745
Jas 3:1 *of you should become* ***t-s*** ... 1550
3 Jn 1:10 *the traveling* ***t-s,*** *he also* ... 1797

TEACHING, TEACHINGS (n) something taught; doctrine
see also INSTRUCTION(S), LAW(S)
Isa 8:20 *to God's instructions and* ***t-s!*** ... 792
Luke 6:47 *listens to my* ***t,*** *and then* ... 1335
John 7:17 *whether my* ***t*** *is from God* ... 1388
John 8:31 *remain faithful to my* ***t-s.*** ... 1393
Acts 2:42 *themselves to the apostles'* ***t,*** ... 1516
Eph 4:14 *about by every wind of new* ***t.*** ... 1711
1 Thes 4:8 *not disobeying human* ***t*** *but* ... 1584
2 Thes 2:15 *grip on the* ***t*** *we passed on* ... 1589
1 Tim 1:3 *those whose* ***t*** *is contrary to* ... 1726
1 Tim 1:10 *contradicts the wholesome* ***t.*** ... 1728
1 Tim 4:6 *and the good* ***t*** *you have* ... 1732
1 Tim 4:16 *how you live and on your* ***t.*** ... 1733
1 Tim 6:3 *people may contradict our* ***t,*** ... 1734
2 Tim 4:2 *your people with good* ***t.*** ... 1745
Titus 1:9 *with wholesome* ***t*** *and show* ... 1737
Titus 3:8 *insist on these* ***t-s*** *so that* ... 1739
Heb 6:1 *stop going over the basic* ***t-s*** ... 1768

TEAR, TEARS (n) a drop of clear saline fluid secreted from the eye
Job 16:20 *I pour out my* ***t-s*** *to God* ... 110
Isa 25:8 *will wipe away all* ***t-s.*** ... 895
Rev 7:17 *will wipe every* ***t*** *from their* ... 1813
Rev 21:4 *will wipe every* ***t*** *from their* ... 1830

TELL, TELLING, TELLS (v) to divulge or reveal; to give information to
Ps 26:7 *thanksgiving and* ***t-ing*** *of all* ... 560
Ps 71:16 *I will* ***t*** *everyone that* ... 860
Ps 118:17 *live to* ***t*** *what the* LORD ... 876
Jer 1:7 *and say whatever I* ***t*** *you.* ... 958
Jer 1:17 *Go out and* ***t*** *them everything* ... 959
John 2:25 *No one needed to* ***t*** *him what* ... 1300
Acts 20:20 *shrank back from* ***t-ing*** *you* ... 1675
Rom 10:14 *him unless someone* ***t-s*** *them?* ... 1664
2 Cor 10:12 *these other men who* ***t*** *you* ... 1638

TEMPER (n) disposition; characteristic state of mind or of emotion; proneness to anger
Ps 37:8 *Do not lose your* ***t****—it only* ... 567
Prov 14:29 ***t*** *shows great foolishness* ... 648
Prov 19:11 *people control their* ***t;*** ... 654
Eccl 7:9 *Control your* ***t,*** *for anger* ... 678

TEMPLE, TEMPLES (n) first built in Solomon's reign as a permanent worship center, which was destroyed then rebuilt under Herod's reign; figurative of the human body and of Christ
see also HOUSE, SANCTUARY, TABERNACLE
1 Kgs 6:1 *to construct the* ***T*** *of the* ... 611
1 Kgs 8:10 *cloud filled the* ***T*** *of the* ... 617
1 Chr 29:16 *to build a* ***T*** *to honor your* ... 541
2 Chr 36:19 *his army burned the* ***T*** ... 1088
Ps 27:4 *meditating in his* ***T.*** ... 561
Isa 6:1 *train of his robe filled the* ***T.*** ... 783
Jer 7:8 *suffer because the* ***T*** *is here* ... 1008
Joel 3:18 *forth from the* LORD'S ***T,*** ... 1244
Hab 2:20 LORD *is in his holy* ***T.*** ... 981
Hag 2:18 *of the* LORD'S ***T*** *began.* ... 1165
Matt 12:6 *is even greater than the* ***T!*** ... 1319
Matt 26:61 *able to destroy the* ***T*** *of God* ... 1472
Matt 27:51 *sanctuary of the* ***T*** *was torn* ... 1485
Luke 21:5 *stonework of the* ***T*** *and the* ... 1449
John 2:14 *the* ***T*** *area he saw merchants* ... 1300
Acts 5:20 *Go to the* ***T*** *and give the* ... 1521
Acts 17:24 *live in man-made* ***t-s,*** ... 1578
1 Cor 3:16 *together are the* ***t*** *of God* ... 1600
1 Cor 6:19 *body is the* ***t*** *of the Holy* ... 1604
Eph 2:21 *becoming a holy* ***t*** *for the* ... 1708
1 Pet 2:5 *building into his spiritual* ***t.*** ... 1750
Rev 21:22 *and the Lamb are its* ***t.*** ... 1831

TEMPT, TEMPTED, TEMPTING (v) to entice to do wrong by promise of pleasure or gain; to test
Isa 13:17 *They cannot be* ***t-ed*** *by silver* ... 831
Matt 4:1 *wilderness to be* ***t-ed*** *there by* ... 1294
Luke 4:2 *where he was* ***t-ed*** *by the devil* ... 1296
Luke 4:13 *finished* ***t-ing*** *Jesus, he left* ... 1296
1 Cor 7:5 *be able to* ***t*** *you because* ... 1605
1 Cor 10:13 *When you are* ***t-ed,*** *he will* ... 1610
Jas 1:13 *you are being* ***t-ed,*** *do not say,* ... 1547
Jas 1:13 *God is never* ***t-ed*** *to do wrong,* ... 1547

TEMPTATION, TEMPTATIONS (n) a cause or occasion of enticement
Matt 6:13 *don't let us yield to* ***t,*** ... 1331
Matt 18:7 ***T-s*** *are inevitable, but what* ... 1384
Matt 26:41 *will not give in to* ***t.*** ... 1468
Luke 8:13 *fall away when they face* ***t.*** ... 1347
1 Cor 10:13 *The* ***t-s*** *in your life are* ... 1610
1 Cor 10:13 *not allow the* ***t*** *to be* ... 1610
Gal 6:1 *fall into the same* ***t*** *yourself* ... 1567
1 Tim 6:9 *to be rich fall into* ***t*** *and* ... 1735
Jas 1:12 *endure testing and* ***t.*** ... 1547

TEN (n) the number 10
Exod 34:28 *the* ***T*** *Commandments—* ... 188
Deut 10:4 *wrote the* ***T*** *Commandments* ... 299
Luke 15:8 *a woman has* ***t*** *silver coins* ... 1410
Rev 12:3 *seven heads and* ***t*** *horns, with* ... 1818

TENDERHEARTED (adj) easily moved to love, pity, or sorrow; compassionate
Deut 28:54 *The most* ***t*** *man among you* ... 319
Eph 4:32 *each other,* ***t,*** *forgiving one* ... 1712
Col 3:12 *yourselves with* ***t*** *mercy,* ... 1700

TENDERNESS (n) the quality or state of being gentle, fond, or loving
Jas 5:11 *is full of* ***t*** *and mercy.* ... 1553

TENTH (n) one-tenth of any property or produce
see also TITHE
Gen 14:20 *gave Melchizedek a* ***t*** *of all* ... 34
Heb 7:2 *Abraham took a* ***t*** *of all he* ... 1770

TENTMAKERS (n) those who make tents
Acts 18:3 *for they were* ***t*** *just as he* ... 1580

TENTS (n) portable housing made of cloth or skins
see also TABERNACLE
Gen 13:12 *Lot moved his* ***t*** *to a place* ... 32

TERRIBLE (adj) extremely bad; terrifying
Jer 8:6 *What a* ***t*** *thing I have done* ... 1010

Zeph 1:15 *a day of **t** distress and*...............984
Heb 10:31 *It is a **t** thing to fall into*...........1776

TERRIFY, TERRIFIED, TERRIFIES (v) to scare, deter, or intimidate; to fill with terror
Deut 2:25 *the earth **t-ied** because of you.*..287
Deut 28:67 *you will be **t-ied** by the awful*...319
1 Sam 12:18 *were **t-ied** of the LORD*..........440
Prov 21:15 *but it **t-ies** evildoers.*...............658
Isa 13:8 *and people are **t-ied.** Pangs of*......831
Zeph 2:11 *The LORD will **t** them*.................985
Matt 14:26 *on the water, they were **t-ied.***...1365
Matt 17:6 *disciples were **t-ied** and fell*.....1379
Matt 27:54 *the crucifixion were **t-ied***.......1485
Mark 4:41 *disciples were absolutely **t-ied.***...1350
Luke 21:26 *will be **t-ied** at what they*.......1450

TERRIFYING (adj) causing terror or apprehension
Deut 4:34 *powerful arm, and **t** acts?*...........291
Deut 34:12 *Moses performed **t** acts in the*...328
Judg 13:6 *of God's angels, **t** to see*.............396

TERRITORY (n) an indeterminate geographic area
2 Cor 10:16 *done in someone else's **t.***.......1639

TERROR, TERRORS (n) a state of intense fear; a frightening aspect
Deut 7:19 *Remember the great **t-s** the*.......296
Job 9:34 *no longer live in **t** of his*...............104
Ps 53:5 *will grip them, **t** like they*...............571
Ps 91:5 *afraid of the **t-s** of the night,*...........861
Prov 22:8 *their reign of **t** will come to*.........659
Isa 51:17 *the cup of **t,** tipping out its*..........939
Mic 7:17 *trembling in **t** at his*.......................911
Luke 9:34 *them, and **t** gripped them*.........1380
Acts 7:32 *Moses shook with **t** and did*......1525

TEST, TESTINGS, TESTS (n) a critical examination, observation, or evaluation
see also TRIAL(S), TROUBLE(S)
Deut 29:3 *all the great **t-s** of strength,*.........320
1 Cor 10:9 *should we put Christ to the **t,***...1610
1 Tim 3:10 *If they pass the **t,** then let*........1731
Heb 4:15 *of the same **t-ings** we do, yet*...1766

TEST, TESTED, TESTING, TESTS (v) to put to test or proof
Gen 22:1 *God **t-ed** Abraham's faith.*.............45
Deut 6:16 *You must not **t** the LORD your*......295
Judg 3:1 *land to **t** those Israelites*...............376
1 Kgs 10:1 *she came to **t** him with hard*.....626
Job 23:10 *when he **t-s** me, I will come*.......116
Ps 17:3 *You have **t-ed** my thoughts*............553
Ps 66:10 *You have **t-ed** us,*.......................859
Ps 78:18 *They stubbornly **t-ed** God in*........598
Ps 106:14 *ran wild, **t-ing** God's patience*....870
Ps 139:23 ***t** me and know my anxious*........586
Prov 17:3 *the LORD **t-s** the heart*.................652
Luke 4:12 *You must not **t** the LORD your*....1296
Acts 5:9 *of conspiring to **t** the Spirit*..........1520
1 Thes 5:21 *but **t** everything that is said*....1586
Heb 2:18 *suffering and **t-ing,** he is able*...1764
Heb 2:18 *us when we are being **t-ed.***.......1764
Heb 3:8 *they **t-ed** me in the wilderness.*...1765
Heb 11:17 *when God was **t-ing** him*.........1778
Jas 1:3 *when your faith is **t-ed,** your*........1546
Jas 1:12 *who patiently endure **t-ing** and*..1547
1 Pet 1:7 *It is being **t-ed** as fire tests*........1748
1 Jn 4:1 *You must **t** them to see if*............1792
Rev 2:10 *you into prison to **t** you.*.............1803
Rev 3:10 *great time of **t-ing** that will*........1807

TESTIFY, TESTIFIED, TESTIFIES, TESTIFYING (v) to make a statement based on personal knowledge or belief; to give evidence or proof
Exod 20:16 *must not **t** falsely against*.........170
Deut 5:20 *must not **t** falsely against*...........293
Prov 24:28 *Don't **t** against your*..................663
Luke 18:20 *You must not **t** falsely.*............1422
John 1:34 *Jesus, so I **t** that he is*.............1297
John 5:32 *else is also **t-ing** about me,*.....1319
John 15:26 *Father and will **t** all about*.......1464
John 18:37 *the world to **t** to the truth*........1478
John 21:24 *one who **t-ies** to these events*...1497
Acts 4:33 *The apostles **t-ied** powerfully*....1520
Acts 10:43 *the prophets **t-ied** about,*........1534
1 Jn 4:14 *own eyes and now **t** that the*.....1793

TESTIMONY (n) the evidence given by a witness
see also TESTIFY
Num 35:30 *to death on the **t** of only*...........283
John 1:7 *might believe because of his **t.***...1271
1 Tim 6:13 *gave a good **t** before Pontius*...1735
1 Jn 5:9 *Since we believe human **t,***..........1794
Rev 12:11 *of the Lamb and by their **t.***..........1818

THANK, THANKING (v) to express gratitude to; to acknowledge God's goodness
Ps 35:18 *Then I will **t** you in front*..............566
Ps 79:13 *pasture, will **t** you forever*............600
Ps 145:10 *works will **t** you, LORD,*...............589
Isa 12:4 *sing: "**T** the LORD!*.........................797
1 Cor 10:30 *If I can **t** God for the food*......1611
Phil 4:6 *and **t** him for all he has done*........1724
1 Thes 2:13 *we never stop **t-ing** God*.......1582
1 Thes 3:9 *How we **t** God for you!*............1584

THANKFUL (adj) conscious of benefit received; expressive of thanks
Col 3:15 *And always be **t.***........................1701
Col 3:16 *to God with **t** hearts*...................1701
1 Thes 5:18 *Be **t** in all circumstances,*......1586
Heb 12:28 *let us be **t** and please God by*...1781

THANKFULNESS (n) the quality or state of being thankful
Col 2:7 *you will overflow with **t.***................1697

THANKS (n) kindly or grateful thoughts; gratitude
1 Chr 16:4 *to give **t,** and to praise*.............492
Ps 30:12 *I will give you **t** forever!*...............563
Ps 107:1 *Give **t** to the LORD,*.......................871
Rom 1:21 *as God or even give him **t.***........1647
1 Cor 11:24 *gave **t** to God for it.*..............1613
Phil 1:3 *of you, I give **t** to my God.*............1716
1 Tim 2:1 *behalf, and give **t** for them.*.......1729
1 Tim 4:3 *be eaten with **t** by faithful*..........1732
Rev 4:9 *and honor and **t** to the one*............1808

THANKSGIVING (n) a prayer expressing gratitude; a public acknowledgment or celebration of God's goodness
Ps 26:7 *singing a song of **t** and telling*........560
Ps 28:7 *I burst out in songs of **t.***.................562
Ps 100:4 *Enter his gates with **t;** go*............866
Isa 51:3 *Songs of **t** will fill the air.*..............938

THIEF, THIEVES (n) one who steals, especially stealthily or secretly
Prov 6:30 *might be found for a **t***................639
Prov 29:24 *If you assist a **t,** you only*...........845
Jer 7:11 *has become a den of **t-ves?***......1008
Matt 6:19 *where **t-ves** break in and steal.*1332
Luke 19:46 *turned it into a den of **t-ves.***..1432
John 10:1 *surely be a **t** and a robber!*.......1405
John 10:8 *me were **t-ves** and robbers*......1405
1 Cor 6:10 *or are **t-ves,** or greedy people,*..1603
1 Thes 5:2 *unexpectedly, like a **t** in the*.....1585
Rev 16:15 *as unexpectedly as a **t!***............1823

THINK, THINKING, THINKS (v) to reflect, ponder, or remember; to subject to the processes of logical thought; to have as an opinion; to conceive or reason
see also MEDITATE, THOUGHT
1 Sam 12:24 ***T** of all the wonderful*.............441
2 Chr 19:6 *Always **t** carefully before*...........729
Ps 8:4 *you should **t** about them,*...................548
Ps 63:6 *I lie awake **t-ing** of you,*.................518
Ps 77:12 *I cannot stop **t-ing** about your*.....597
Ps 119:97 *I **t** about them all day long*..........880
Ps 119:148 *the night, **t-ing** about your*........881
Prov 13:16 *Wise people **t** before they*.........646
Prov 15:28 *godly **t-s** carefully before*..........650
Prov 21:29 *the virtuous **t** before they*..........658
Prov 23:7 *are always **t-ing** about how*........661
Prov 29:20 *who speaks without **t-ing.***.........845
Isa 44:18 *are shut, and they cannot **t.***.........930
Matt 22:42 *What do you **t** about the*.........1442
Rom 11:20 *So don't **t** highly of*.................1665
Phil 1:3 *Every time I **t** of you, I give*...........1716
Phil 2:3 *Be humble, **t-ing** of others as*.......1719
Phil 3:19 *they **t** only about this life*...........1724
Heb 10:24 *Let us **t** of ways to motivate*.....1776
1 Pet 1:13 *So **t** clearly and exercise*..........1749

THINKING (n) opinion, judgment
Rom 1:28 *them to their foolish **t***..............1648
2 Pet 3:1 *wholesome **t** and refresh*...........1760

THIRST (v) to crave vehemently and urgently
Ps 42:2 *I **t** for God, the living God.*.............848
Matt 5:6 *who hunger and **t** for justice,*.......1326

THIRSTY (adj) feeling a desire for liquids; having a strong desire
Ps 107:9 *he satisfies the **t** and fills*.............872
Prov 25:21 *If they are **t,** give them*.............840
Isa 55:1 *Is anyone **t?** Come and drink—*.....942
Matt 25:35 *I was **t,** and you gave*.............1453
John 4:14 *will never be **t** again*..................1304
John 19:28 *Scripture he said, "I am **t.**"*.....1486
Rom 12:20 *If they are **t,** give them*...........1668
2 Cor 11:27 *been hungry and **t** and*..........1641
Rev 7:16 *never again be hungry or **t;***........1813
Rev 22:17 *Let anyone who is **t** come.*.........1833

THOMAS One of the twelve disciples, also known as "the Twin" (Matt 10:3, p. 1358; Mark 3:18, p. 1323; Luke 6:15, p. 1323; Acts 1:13, p. 1512); willing to die with Jesus (John 11:16, p. 1414); queried Jesus (John 14:5, p. 1461); doubted Jesus' resurrection but was convinced by his appearance (John 20:24-28, p. 1495).

THORN, THORNS (n) a woody plant bearing sharp impeding prickles or spines; something that causes distress or irritation
Gen 3:18 *It will grow **t-s** and thistles*............13
Num 33:55 *in your eyes and **t-s** in your*.......281
Matt 13:7 *seeds fell among **t-s** that*.........1345
Matt 27:29 *wove **t** branches into a*.............1481
2 Cor 12:7 *I was given a **t** in my flesh,*.......1642
Heb 6:8 *a field bears **t-s** and thistles,*.........1768

THORNBUSHES (n) any of various spiny or thorny shrubs or small trees
Luke 6:44 *never gathered from **t,** nor*.......1335

THOUGHT, THOUGHTS (n) the action or process of thinking; a developed intention or plan; recollection, remembrance
Ps 77:12 *They are constantly in my **t-s.***.......597
Ps 92:5 *And how deep are your **t-s.***............862

Ps 94:11 *LORD knows people's* ***t-s;***.............862
Ps 104:34 *May all my* ***t-s*** *be pleasing*........868
Ps 139:23 *and know my anxious* ***t-s.***..........586
Ps 142:4 *no one gives me a passing* ***t!***.......460
Isa 26:3 *whose* ***t-s*** *are fixed on you!*...........896
Isa 55:8 *My* ***t-s*** *are nothing like your*..........942
Matt 9:4 *you have such evil* ***t-s*** *in your*.....1312
Matt 15:19 *heart come evil* ***t-s,*** *murder,*...1370
1 Cor 14:25 *their secret* ***t-s*** *will be*...........1618
Eph 4:23 *renew your* ***t-s*** *and attitudes*.....1712
Rev 2:23 *searches out the* ***t-s*** *and*...........1805

THOUGHT (v) to reflect, ponder, or remember
see also THINK
Ps 39:3 *The more I* ***t*** *about it,*.....................569
Luke 2:19 *in her heart and* ***t*** *about them*...1281
1 Cor 13:11 *I spoke and* ***t*** *and reasoned*...1616

THOUSAND (adj) of the number 1,000
Ps 90:4 *For you, a* ***t*** *years are as*...............326
Rev 20:7 *When the* ***t*** *years come to an*.....1829

THOUSANDS (n) a very large number
Joel 3:14 ***T*** *upon* ***t*** *are waiting*.................1243

THREATS (n) expressions of intention to inflict evil, injury, or damage
Matt 24:6 *of wars and* ***t*** *of wars,*...............1446

THREE (adj) of the number 3
Deut 19:15 *of two or* ***t*** *witnesses*...............309
Jonah 1:17 ***t*** *days and* ***t*** *nights*..................767
Matt 12:40 ***t*** *days and* ***t*** *nights,*................1343
Matt 18:20 *where two or* ***t*** *gather*............1385
Matt 26:34 *you will deny* ***t*** *times that*.........1460
Mark 8:31 *but* ***t*** *days later he would rise*...1377
1 Jn 5:7 *have these* ***t*** *witnesses—*............1794

THRILL (v) to cause to experience a sudden sharp feeling of excitement
Ps 92:4 *You* ***t*** *me, LORD,*............................862
Isa 60:5 *your heart will* ***t*** *with joy,*...............946

THRIVING (adj) characterized by success, prosperity, or growth
Ps 52:8 *olive tree,* ***t*** *in the house*................462

THROAT (n) the front part of the neck
Prov 23:2 *put a knife to your* ***t;***..................661

THRONE, THRONES (n) seat of power for a king or deity; symbolic of royal authority and the king's role as a judge
Deut 17:18 *he sits on the* ***t*** *as king,*...........307
2 Sam 7:16 *and your* ***t*** *will be secure*..........496
1 Chr 17:12 *will secure his* ***t*** *forever*...........496
Job 36:7 *sets them on* ***t-s*** *with kings*..........125
Ps 45:6 *Your* ***t,*** *O God, endures*..................851
Ps 47:8 *nations, sitting on his holy* ***t.***..........852
Ps 89:14 *are the foundation of your* ***t.***.........591
Ps 99:1 *He sits on his* ***t*** *between the*...........865
Ps 102:12 *sit on your* ***t*** *forever*...................866
Ps 103:19 *has made the heavens his* ***t;***......580
Isa 6:1 *He was sitting on a lofty* ***t,***...............783
Isa 66:1 *Heaven is my* ***t,*** *and the*...............952
Dan 7:9 *on a fiery* ***t*** *with wheels*..............1135
Matt 19:28 *upon his glorious* ***t,*** *you who*...1420
Matt 19:28 *sit on twelve* ***t-s,*** *judging*........1420
Acts 7:49 *Heaven is my* ***t,*** *and the*............1526
Rom 15:12 *heir to David's* ***t*** *will come,*.......1671
Col 1:16 *such as* ***t-s,*** *kingdoms, rulers,*....1694
Heb 12:2 *place of honor beside God's* ***t.***....1780
Rev 3:21 *sat with my Father on his* ***t.***........1808
Rev 4:2 *and I saw a* ***t*** *in heaven*................1808
Rev 4:4 *Twenty-four* ***t-s*** *surrounded*.........1808
Rev 5:5 *heir to David's* ***t,*** *has won*.............1809
Rev 20:11 *a great white* ***t*** *and the*.............1830
Rev 22:3 *the* ***t*** *of God and of the Lamb*.....1832

THROUGH (prep) by way of
Eph 2:18 *to the Father* ***t*** *the same Holy*.....1708

THROUGHOUT (prep) in or to every part of; during the whole course or period of
Gen 1:29 *seed-bearing plant* ***t*** *the*.................8
Jer 23:40 *be infamous* ***t*** *the ages*.............1029
Rom 10:18 *message has gone* ***t*** *the earth,*..1664

THROW, THROWING (v) to propel through the air by a forward motion of the hand or arm; to discard
Ps 22:18 *themselves and* ***t*** *dice for my*.......556
Prov 16:33 *We may* ***t*** *the dice,*...................652
Isa 41:9 *and will not* ***t*** *you away*.................925
Matt 27:35 *his clothes by* ***t-ing*** *dice*.........1482
John 8:7 *has never sinned* ***t*** *the first*.........1391
John 19:24 *apart, let's* ***t*** *dice for it*...........1484
Heb 10:35 *do not* ***t*** *away this confident*.....1776

THUNDER, THUNDERS (n) the sound that follows a flash of lightning
Job 37:5 *voice is glorious in the* ***t.***..............127
Mark 3:17 *nicknamed them "Sons of* ***T"***...1323
Rev 10:3 *the seven* ***t-s*** *answered*..............1816

THUNDER, THUNDERS (v) to give forth a sound that resembles thunder
Ps 29:3 *The God of glory* ***t-s.***....................562
Amos 1:2 *from Zion and* ***t*** *from Jerusalem*..770

TIE, TIED (v) to fasten, attach, or close by means of a tie
Prov 3:3 ***T*** *them around your neck as*..........634
Matt 18:6 *large millstone* ***t-d*** *around your*...1384

TIES (n) bonds of kinship or affection
Col 2:2 *together by strong* ***t*** *of love*...........1697

TIME, TIMES (n) occasion; an opportune or suitable moment; an appointed, fixed, or customary moment or hour for something to happen, begin, or end; duration; conditions at present or at some specified period; added or accumulated quantities or instances
Esth 4:14 *just such a* ***t*** *as this?"*................1188
Ps 9:9 *a refuge in* ***t-s*** *of trouble*..................549
Ps 62:8 *trust in him at all* ***t-s.***...................574
Eccl 3:1 *a* ***t*** *for every activity under*............675
Eccl 7:14 *when hard* ***t-s*** *strike,*.................679
Eccl 8:5 *wise will find a* ***t*** *and a way*............679
Dan 12:7 *at* ***t, t-s,*** *and half a* ***t.***................1161
Hos 10:12 *for now is the* ***t*** *to seek the*........813
Amos 5:13 *shut, for it is an evil* ***t.***...............775
Matt 16:3 *interpret the signs of the* ***t-s!***....1373
Matt 18:21 *sins against me? Seven* ***t-s?***..1385
Luke 12:40 *ready all the* ***t,*** *for the Son*......1401
John 4:53 *was the very* ***t*** *Jesus had told*...1307
John 12:23 *the* ***t*** *has come for the Son*.....1432
Acts 1:7 *those dates and* ***t-s,*** *and they*.....1500
Acts 18:5 *spent all his* ***t*** *preaching*...........1580
1 Cor 7:29 *The* ***t*** *that remains is very*........1606
2 Cor 6:2 *the "right* ***t"*** *is now*.....................1633
Gal 6:9 *just the right* ***t*** *we will reap*...........1567
2 Tim 1:9 *the beginning of* ***t****—to show*......1741
Heb 9:28 *once for all* ***t*** *as a sacrifice*.........1774
Heb 10:12 *for sins, good for all* ***t.***..............1775
1 Pet 4:17 *For the* ***t*** *has come for*...............1755
Rev 12:14 *for a time,* ***t-s,*** *and half a*.........1819

TIMID (adj) lacking in courage or self-confidence
1 Thes 5:14 *Encourage those who are* ***t.***...1586

TIMIDITY (n) the quality or state of being timid
2 Tim 1:7 *of fear and* ***t,*** *but of power,*........1741

TIMOTHY Paul's student and traveling companion from Lystra (Acts 16:1-3, p. 1573); raised by devout Jewish mother (2 Tim 1:5, p. 1740; 3:15, p. 1745); joined Paul on second missionary journey (Acts 16–20, p. 1573); sent to serve NT churches (1 Cor 4:17, p. 1601; 16:10, p. 1623; Phil 2:19, p. 1720; 1 Thes 3:5-6, p. 1583; 1 Tim 1:3, p. 1726); wrote letters with Paul (2 Cor 1:1, p. 1625; Phil 1:1, p. 1716; Col 1:1, p. 1693; 1 Thes 1:1, p. 1580; 2 Thes 1:1, p. 1587; Phlm 1:1, p. 1690); letters written to him by Paul (1 Tim 1:2, p. 1726; 2 Tim 1:2, p. 1740).

TIRED (adj) drained of strength and energy
Exod 17:12 *became so* ***t*** *he could no*..........165
Isa 35:3 *those who have* ***t*** *hands,*...............905
Gal 6:9 *let's not get* ***t*** *of doing what*..........1567
2 Thes 3:13 *never get* ***t*** *of doing good*.......1590
Heb 12:12 *new grip with your* ***t*** *hands*......1780

TITHE, TITHES (n) one-tenth of any property or produce
see also TENTH
Num 18:21 *give them the* ***t-s*** *from the*.......259
Deut 12:17 *neither the* ***t*** *of your grain*.........302
2 Chr 31:12 *brought all the* ***t-s*** *and*...........838
Amos 4:4 *bring your* ***t-s*** *every three*...........774
Mal 3:8 *of the* ***t-s*** *and offerings due*.........1248
Mal 3:10 *Bring all the* ***t-s*** *into the*............1248

TITHE (v) to pay or give a tenth of as an offering to God
Matt 23:23 *You should* ***t,*** *yes,*....................1444
Luke 11:42 *you are careful to* ***t*** *even the*...1398

TITTLE (KJV)
Matt 5:18 *the* ***smallest detail*** *of God's law*..1327
Luke 16:17 *the* ***smallest point*** *of God's law*..1412

TITUS Young Gentile pastor and helper of Paul (Gal 2:1-3, p. 1558; 2 Tim 4:10, p. 1746); sent to Corinth (2 Cor 2:13, p. 1628; 7:6-14, p. 1635; 8:6-23, p. 1636; 12:18, p. 1642); sent to Crete (Titus 1:4-5, p. 1736).

TODAY (adv) on or for this day; at the present time
Ps 2:7 ***T*** *I have become your Father*............857
Ps 95:7 *listen to his voice* ***t!***......................863
Matt 6:11 *Give us* ***t*** *the food we*...............1331
Luke 2:11 *born* ***t*** *in Bethlehem,*................1281
Luke 23:43 *I assure you,* ***t*** *you will be*.......1484
Heb 1:5 ***T*** *I have become your Father*........1762
Heb 3:7 ***T*** *when you hear his voice,*...........1765
Heb 13:8 *is the same yesterday,* ***t,*** *and*.....1782

TOGETHER (adv) with each other; as a unit; in or into one place, mass, collection, or group
Ps 133:1 *brothers live* ***t*** *in harmony!*...........584
Jer 3:18 *will return* ***t*** *from exile*..................963
Zeph 3:9 *can worship the LORD* ***t.***...............986
Acts 1:14 *They all met* ***t*** *and were*............1512
Rom 1:12 *When we get* ***t,*** *I want to*...........1646
Eph 1:10 *bring everything* ***t*** *under the*.......1705

TOLERANT (adj) marked by forbearance and endurance
Rom 2:4 *how wonderfully kind,* ***t,*** *and*.......1648

TOLERATE (v) to put up with
Rev 2:2 *know you don't* ***t*** *evil people*..........1802

TOMORROW (n) the day after the present; the future
Prov 27:1 *Don't brag about* ***t,*** *since you*......842
Isa 22:13 *and drink, for* ***t*** *we die!*................892
Rom 8:38 *our worries about* ***t****—not even*..1661
1 Cor 15:32 *and drink, for* ***t*** *we die!*..........1621

TONGUE, TONGUES (n) part of the mouth that enables speech; dialect or language of a people; a special gift of speech given by the Holy Spirit
see also LANGUAGE(S)
Ps 5:9 *Their **t-s** are filled*....................547
Ps 34:13 *keep your **t** from speaking*............459
Ps 39:1 *I will hold my **t** when*.....................569
Ps 45:1 *king, for my **t** is like*.....................850
Ps 78:36 *lied to him with their **t-s**.*..............599
Ps 119:172 *Let my **t** sing about*.................882
Ps 137:6 *May my **t** stick to the*...............1118
Prov 13:3 *who control their **t** will have*.......646
Prov 15:4 *a deceitful **t** crushes the*.............648
Prov 17:20 *the lying **t** tumbles into*............653
Prov 21:23 *Watch your **t** and keep*.............658
Luke 16:24 *in water and cool my **t**.*...........1412
Acts 2:3 *like flames or **t-s** of fire*.............1514
Acts 10:46 *speaking in other **t-s** and*.........1534
Acts 19:6 *in other **t-s** and prophesied*.......1593
Rom 14:11 *me, and every **t** will confess*....1670
1 Cor 14:2 *to speak in **t-s,** you will*...........1616
1 Cor 14:4 *speaks in **t-s** is strengthened*..1617
1 Cor 14:5 *speak in **t-s,** but even more*....1617
1 Cor 14:13 *speaks in **t-s** should pray*......1617
1 Cor 14:18 *I speak in **t-s** more than*........1617
1 Cor 14:27 *three should speak in **t-s**.*......1618
1 Cor 14:39 *forbid speaking in **t-s**.*.........1618
Phil 2:11 *and every **t** confess that*............1720
Jas 3:2 *if we could control our **t-s,** we*......1550
Jas 3:5 *same way, the **t** is a small*............1550

TOOK (v) to seize, grasp, or carry
see also TAKE
Matt 8:17 *He **t** our sicknesses and*...........1309
Matt 26:26 *eating, Jesus **t** some bread and*...........1457
Matt 26:27 *And he **t** a cup of wine and*......1457
1 Cor 11:23 *the Lord Jesus **t** some bread*...1613
1 Cor 11:25 *the same way, he **t** the cup of*..........1613
Phil 2:7 *he **t** the humble position of*.........1720

TOOTH (n) a bonelike structure in the mouth used for chewing
Exod 21:24 *eye for an eye, a **t** for a **t**,*.........171
Matt 5:38 *eye for an eye, and a **t** for a **t**.*...1329

TORMENT (n) extreme pain or anguish of body or mind
Luke 16:28 *end up in this place of **t**.*.........1412

TORMENT, TORMENTED (v) to cause severe usually persistent or recurrent distress of body or mind
2 Cor 12:7 *messenger from Satan to **t**.*.....1642
Rev 20:10 *they will be **t-ed** day and night*..........1830

TORMENTORS (n) those who torment
Ps 137:3 *Our **t** insisted on a joyful*............1118

TORTURED (v) to punish or coerce by inflicting excruciating pain
Matt 18:34 *prison to be **t** until he*.............1386
Heb 11:35 *others were **t**, refusing to*........1779

TOSSED (v) to fling or heave continuously about
Jas 1:6 *blown and **t** by the wind.*.............1546

TOUCH, TOUCHED, TOUCHES (v) to reach out or come in contact with; to lay hands upon; to have an influence upon
Gen 3:3 *must not eat it or even **t** it;*..............11
Exod 19:12 *or even **t** its boundaries*............168
Exod 19:12 *Anyone who **t-es** the mountain*..168
Isa 6:7 *this coal has **t-ed** your lips*.............784
Matt 9:21 *If I can just **t** his robe,*..............1353
Matt 14:36 *who **t-ed** him were healed*..........1366
Luke 8:45 *"Who **t-ed** me?" Jesus asked*...1355
Luke 18:15 *so he could **t** and bless*..........1420
Luke 24:39 ***T** me and make sure that*.......1495
2 Cor 6:17 *Don't **t** their filthy things,*.........1634
Col 2:21 *Don't taste! Don't **t!**"?*....................1699
1 Jn 1:1 ***t-ed** him with our own hands*.......1786
1 Jn 5:18 *evil one cannot **t** them.*...............1795

TOWER (n) a tall building or structure typically higher than its surroundings
Gen 11:4 *with a **t** that reaches into*..............23

TRADE, TRADED (v) to give one thing in exchange for another
Gen 25:31 *Jacob replied, "but **t** me your*......51
Ps 106:20 *They **t-d** their glorious God*........870
Rom 1:25 *They **t-d** the truth about God*....1648

TRADERS (n) persons whose business is buying and selling
1 Tim 1:10 *are slave **t**, liars, promise*.......1728

TRADITION, TRADITIONS (n) an inherited, customary, or established pattern of thought, action, or behavior
Matt 15:6 *for the sake of your own **t**.*........1369
Mark 7:5 *disciples follow our age-old **t?***...1370
Mark 7:8 *law and substitute your own **t**.*...1370
Mark 7:13 *to hand down your own **t**.*........1371
Gal 1:14 *in my zeal for the **t-s** of my*........1557

TRAGEDY (n) a disastrous event; misfortune
Eccl 9:12 *are caught by sudden **t**.*..............681

TRAGIC (adj) of, marked by, or expressive of tragedy
Eccl 1:13 *has dealt a **t** existence to*...........673

TRAIN (n) a part of a gown that trails behind the wearer
Isa 6:1 *throne, and the **t** of his robe*............783

TRAIN, TRAINED (v) to form by or undergo instruction or discipline
see also TEACH
Isa 2:4 *against nation, nor **t** for war*..........825
Luke 6:40 *who is fully **t-ed** will become*....1333
John 7:15 *when he hasn't been **t-ed?***......1388
Acts 22:3 *I was carefully **t-ed** in our*.........1678
1 Tim 4:7 ***t** yourself to be godly*.................1732
Titus 2:4 *women must **t** the younger*.........1738
Heb 12:11 *those who are **t-ed** in this way.*1780

TRAINING (n) acquired skill, knowledge, or experience; the act, process, or method of one who trains
Acts 4:13 *men with no special **t** in the*......1519
1 Tim 4:8 *Physical **t** is good, but*...............1732

TRAITORS (n) those who betray another's trust, are false to an obligation or duty, or commit treason
Ps 59:5 *Show no mercy to wicked **t**.*..........454
Ps 119:158 *Seeing these **t** makes me*.........881

TRAMPLE, TRAMPLED (v) to crush, injure, or destroy by or as if by treading
Ps 60:12 *for he will **t** down our foes*...........500
Ps 91:13 *You will **t** upon lions*.....................861
Amos 5:11 *You **t** the poor,*..........................775
Amos 8:4 *rob the poor and **t** down the*........779
Mic 4:13 *so you can **t** many nations to*........908
Mic 7:19 *You will **t** our sins under*..............911
Matt 7:6 *They will **t** the pearls,*.................1333
Luke 21:24 *Jerusalem will be **t-d** down*....1450
Heb 10:29 *who have **t-d** on the Son*..........1776
Rev 14:20 *The grapes were **t-d** in the*......1822

TRANCE (n) a sleeplike state (as of deep hypnosis)
Acts 10:10 *prepared, he fell into a **t**.*........1533
Acts 11:5 *I went into a **t** and saw a*..........1535
Acts 22:17 *the Temple and fell into a **t**.*....1679

TRANSFIGURED (KJV)
Matt 17:2 *Jesus' appearance was **transformed***..........1378
Mark 9:2 *Jesus' appearance was **transformed***..........1379

TRANSFORM, TRANSFORMED (v) to change the outward appearance of; to change in character or condition
see also CHANGE(D)
Matt 17:2 *appearance was **t-ed** so that*....1378
Rom 12:2 *let God **t** you into a new*............1666
1 Cor 15:51 *but we will all be **t-ed!***..........1622

TRANSGRESSED, TRANSGRESSION (KJV)
Josh 7:11 *and **broken** my covenant*...........346
1 Chr 5:25 *tribes were **unfaithful***..............1232
1 Chr 10:13 *because he was **unfaithful***.......475
Rom 4:15 *to avoid **breaking** the law*.........1653
1 Jn 3:4 *sin is **contrary to** the law*...........1791

TRAP, TRAPS (n) something by which one is caught or stopped unawares; a position or situation from which it is difficult or impossible to escape; a device for taking game or other animals
Deut 7:25 *will become a **t** to you,*...............296
Deut 12:30 *fall into the **t** of following*..........302
Ps 91:3 *you from every **t** and protect*..........861
Prov 1:17 *a bird sees a **t** being set,*..............632
Prov 3:26 *foot from being caught in a **t**.*......635
Prov 28:10 *into their own **t**, but the*............843
Prov 29:5 *is to lay a **t** for their feet*.............845
Prov 29:25 *a dangerous **t**, but trusting*........846
Isa 8:14 *he will be a **t** and a snare*.............791
Isa 24:17 *Terror and **t-s** and snares will*......895
Matt 16:23 *are a dangerous **t** to me.*.........1377
Rom 11:9 *a snare, a **t** that makes them*....1665
1 Tim 3:7 *into the devil's **t**.*......................1730
2 Tim 2:26 *from the devil's **t**.*....................1743

TRAP, TRAPPED, TRAPS (v) to catch or take in or as if in a trap
Ps 7:15 *a deep pit to **t** others, then*.............524
Ps 9:16 *wicked are **t-ped** by their own*.......550
Prov 6:2 *if you have **t-ped** yourself by*........638
Prov 12:13 *wicked are **t-ped** by their*.........645
Prov 18:7 *they **t** themselves with*...............653
Matt 22:15 *to plot how to **t** Jesus into*.......1439
1 Cor 3:19 *He **t-s** the wise in the snare*....1600
1 Tim 6:9 *temptation and are **t-ped** by*.....1735

TREACHEROUS (adj) characterized by or manifesting treachery
Prov 11:6 *ambition of **t** people traps*..........643
Prov 13:2 *but **t** people have an appetite*......646
Prov 13:15 *a **t** person is headed for*...........646
Prov 22:12 *ruins the plans of the **t**.*............660
Jer 3:8 *But that **t** sister Judah had*...........962

TREACHERY (n) violation of allegiance or of faith and confidence
Acts 1:18 *he received for his **t**.*..................1512

TREAD, TREADING, TREADS (v) to beat or press with the feet
Deut 25:4 *eating as it **t-s** out the grain.*......315
Isa 63:2 *have been **t-ing** out grapes?*.........949
Joel 3:13 *Come, **t** the grapes,*..................1243
1 Cor 9:9 *from eating as it **t-s** out*............1608
1 Tim 5:18 *from eating as it **t-s** out*..........1734

TREASURE, TREASURES (n) wealth or a collection of precious things; something of great value
Exod 19:5 *my own special **t** from*................167
Deut 7:6 *to be his own special **t**.* 296
1 Chr 29:3 *my own private **t-s** of gold*........540
Ps 119:111 *Your laws are my **t**; they*..........880
Ps 135:4 *Israel for his own special **t**.*..........885
Prov 2:4 *seek them like hidden **t-s**.*............633
Prov 18:22 *finds a wife finds a **t**,*................654
Song 4:10 *delights me, my **t**, my bride*........666
Isa 10:3 *Where will your **t-s** be safe?*..........794
Hag 2:7 *the **t-s** of all the nations*..............1164
Mal 3:17 *they will be my own special **t**.*.....1249
Matt 6:19 *Don't store up **t-s** here on*........1332
Matt 6:21 *Wherever your **t** is, there the*.....1332
Matt 13:44 *Heaven is like a **t** that a man*...1349
Luke 12:33 *will store up **t** for you in*..........1401
2 Cor 4:7 *jars containing this great **t**.*........1631
Eph 3:8 *the endless **t-s** available to*..........1709
Col 2:3 *hidden all the **t-s** of wisdom*.........1697
1 Tim 6:19 *storing up their **t** as a good*.....1735
Heb 11:26 *to own the **t-s** of Egypt, for*......1778

TREASURE, TREASURED (v) to hold or keep as precious
Job 23:12 *but have **t-d** his words more*........116
Prov 2:1 *I say, and **t** my commands.*............633
Prov 7:1 *always **t** my commands.*.................639
Prov 10:14 *Wise people **t** knowledge,*..........642

TREASURY (n) a place in which stores of wealth are kept
Deut 28:12 *time from his rich **t** in the*.........318
Luke 6:45 *things from the **t** of a good*.......1335

TREAT, TREATED, TREATING (v) to regard and deal with in a specified manner
Gen 18:25 ***t-ing** the righteous*......................40
Eccl 8:14 *people are often **t-ed** as though*....680
Matt 18:17 ***t** that person as a pagan*.........1385
Eph 6:9 *Masters, **t** your slaves in the*........1715
Heb 10:29 *God, and have **t-ed** the blood*....1776
1 Pet 3:7 ***T** your wife with understanding*....1753
Heb 12:7 *God is **t-ing** you as his own*.......1780

TREATY, TREATIES (n) an agreement or arrangement made by negotiation
Exod 34:12 *to make a **t** with the people*......187
Deut 7:2 *Make no **t-ies** with them and*.........295
Dan 9:27 *will make a **t** with the people*......1143

TREE, TREES (n) woody perennial plants, many of which produce crops; highly treasured natural resource; often linked with worship of pagan gods; symbolic of a growing believer
Gen 2:9 *he placed the **t** of life and*.................10
Deut 21:23 *from the **t** overnight*..................311
Judg 9:8 *the **t-s** decided to choose*...........389
2 Sam 18:9 *got caught in the **t**.*..................518
1 Kgs 14:23 *and under every green **t**.*.........702
Ps 1:3 *They are like **t-s** planted along*.........856
Ps 52:8 *like an olive **t**, thriving in*...............462
Ps 92:12 *like palm **t-s** and grow*...............862
Ps 96:12 *Let the **t-s** of the forest*..............864
Prov 3:18 *Wisdom is a **t** of life to*................635
Prov 11:30 *deeds become a **t** of life;*...........644
Isa 55:12 *and the **t-s** of the field*...............942
Isa 65:22 *people will live as long as **t-s**,*.....952
Jer 17:8 *They are like **t-s** planted along*....1021
Dan 4:10 *saw a large **t** in the middle*........1119
Mic 4:4 *and fig **t-s**, for there will be*...........907
Matt 3:10 *sever the roots of the **t-s**.*..........1288
Matt 3:10 *every **t** that does not produce*...1288
Matt 12:33 ***t** is identified by its fruit.*.........1341
Mark 8:24 *look like **t-s** walking*................1375
Luke 19:4 *a sycamore-fig **t** beside the*......1426
Rom 11:24 *cut from a wild olive **t**.*............1665
Gal 3:13 *everyone who is hung on a **t**.*......1561
Jas 3:12 *Does a fig **t** produce olives,*........1550
Jude 1:12 *They are like **t-s** in autumn*......1785
Rev 22:2 *the river grew a **t** of life,*.............1832
Rev 22:14 *the fruit from the **t** of life.*.........1832
Rev 22:19 *share in the **t** of life and*...........1833

TREMBLE, TREMBLED, TREMBLES, TREMBLING (v) to be affected with great fear or anxiety; to shake involuntarily
Exod 15:14 *hear and **t**; anguish grips*............162
Exod 19:16 *horn, and all the people **t-d**.*......168
Exod 20:18 *a distance, **t-ing** with fear.*.......170
2 Sam 22:8 *the earth quaked and **t-d**.*..........526
1 Chr 16:30 *all the earth **t** before him*..........493
Ps 2:11 *fear, and rejoice with **t-ing**.*.............857
Ps 97:4 *The earth sees and **t-s**.*...................864
Ps 102:15 *the earth will **t** before his*...........866
Ps 104:32 *The earth **t-s** at his glance;*.......868
Isa 66:2 *contrite hearts, who **t** at my*...........952
Jer 10:10 *whole earth **t-s** at his anger.*.....1013
Dan 10:10 *and lifted me, still **t-ing**,*..........1158
Joel 2:1 *Let everyone **t** in fear*...................1240
Nah 1:5 *hills melt away; the earth **t-s**,*........974
Hab 3:6 *the nations **t**. He shatters*.............981
Heb 4:1 *we ought to **t** with fear that*..........1765
Heb 12:21 *I am terrified and **t-ing**.*...........1781

TRESPASS(ES) (KJV)
Lev 19:21 *a ram as a **guilt** offering*..............225
2 Chr 24:18 *Because of this **sin**, divine*.......758
Matt 6:15 *Father will not forgive your **sins***...1331
Matt 18:15 *believer **sins** against you,*..........1385
Eph 2:1 *because of your **disobedience***.....1706

TRIAL, TRIALS (n) a legal proceeding based in court; a test of faith, patience, or stamina through subjection to suffering or temptation
see also TEMPTATION(S), TEST(S), TROUBLE(S)
Job 42:11 *all the **t-s** the LORD had*.............132
Ps 26:2 *Put me on **t**, LORD,*.........................560
Ps 37:33 *when they are put on **t**.*...............568
Ps 143:2 *Don't put your servant on **t**,*..........588
Mark 13:11 *and stand **t**, don't worry in*.....1448
Luke 22:28 *with me in my time of **t**.*..........1459
John 16:33 *have many **t-s** and sorrows*....1466
Rom 5:3 *into problems and **t-s**, for we*.....1654
1 Pet 1:7 *through many **t-s**, it will*............1748
1 Pet 4:12 *the fiery **t-s** you are going*.......1755
2 Pet 2:9 *from their **t-s**, even while*..........1759

TRIBE, TRIBES (n) family divisions, usually within Israel, but also of other ethnic peoples
Gen 49:28 *are the twelve **t-s** of Israel,*..........92
Matt 19:28 *the twelve **t-s** of Israel*............1420
Heb 7:13 *a different **t**, whose members*....1770
Rev 5:5 *Lion of the **t** of Judah,*..................1809
Rev 5:9 *God from every **t** and language*....1810
Rev 11:9 *all peoples, **t-s**, languages,*........1817
Rev 14:6 *to every nation, **t**, language,*.......1821

TRIBULATION (n) a period of unparalleled suffering in the last days
Rev 7:14 *who died in the great **t**.*..............1813

TRIBUTE (n) a gift or service showing respect, gratitude, or affection
Ps 76:11 *Let everyone bring **t** to the*...........597

TRICK, TRICKED (v) to deceive or cheat
Gen 27:35 *and he **t-ed** me*..........................56
Gen 29:25 *Why have you **t-ed** me*................60
Jer 29:31 *has **t-ed** you into believing*.......1031
2 Cor 4:2 *We don't try to **t** anyone*............1630
Eph 4:14 *people try to **t** us with lies*..........1711

TRICKERY (n) deception
Isa 29:21 *those who use **t** to pervert*...........899
2 Cor 12:16 *advantage of you by **t**.*...........1642

TRIED (v) to make an attempt at; to put to test
Ps 73:16 *So I **t** to understand*......................594
Ps 95:9 *tested and **t** my patience,*..............863
Ps 119:10 *I have **t** hard to find*...................878
Heb 3:9 *tested and **t** my patience,*...........1765

TRIUMPH (n) the joy or exultation of victory or success
Ps 118:7 *I will look in **t** at those*...................876

TRIUMPH, TRIUMPHED (v) to obtain victory
1 Sam 17:50 *So David **t-ed** over the*..........451
Ps 54:7 *and helped me to **t** over my*...........464

TRIUMPHAL (adj) of, relating to, or marked by triumph
2 Cor 2:14 *in Christ's **t** procession*............1628

TRIUMPHANT (adj) victorious, conquering
Deut 33:29 *shield and your **t** sword!*...........328

TROUBLE, TROUBLES (n) a state, condition, or cause of distress, annoyance, difficulty, or inconvenience
see also TEST(S), TRIAL(S)
Gen 41:51 *made me forget all my **t-s***...........81
Josh 7:25 *have you brought **t** on us?*..........346
2 Chr 15:4 *they were in **t** and turned*..........708
Job 5:7 *are born for **t** as readily as*..............99
Ps 7:14 *they are pregnant with **t**.*...............524
Ps 9:9 *a refuge in times of **t**.*......................549
Ps 10:14 *you see the **t** and grief*.................857
Ps 22:11 *from me, for **t** is near,*...................556
Ps 27:5 *me there when **t-s** come;*...............561
Ps 32:7 *you protect me from **t**.*....................565
Ps 34:17 *them from all their **t-s**.*.................459
Ps 37:39 *their fortress in times of **t**.*............568
Ps 40:12 *For **t-s** surround me—*...................570
Ps 41:1 *them when they are in **t**.*.................571
Ps 46:1 *ready to help in times of **t**.*............851
Ps 49:5 *I fear when **t** comes, when*.............853
Ps 50:15 *when you are in **t**, and I will*.........593
Ps 54:7 *have rescued me from my **t-s***........464
Ps 55:3 *They bring **t** on me*..........................572
Ps 66:14 *I was in deep **t**.*...........................859
Ps 81:7 *cried to me in **t**, and*.......................602
Ps 86:7 *whenever I'm in **t**, and*...................579
Ps 91:15 *I will be with them in **t**.*.................861
Ps 107:6 *they cried in their **t**,*......................872
Ps 107:41 *rescues the poor from **t***............872
Ps 116:3 *I saw only **t** and sorrow*.................875
Ps 120:1 *took my **t-s** to the LORD;*..............882
Ps 138:7 *I am surrounded by **t-s**, you*.........585
Prov 6:14 *they constantly stir up **t**.*.............638
Prov 10:10 *who wink at wrong cause **t**,*......642
Prov 11:8 *godly are rescued from **t**,*............643
Prov 11:29 *Those who bring **t** on their*........644
Prov 12:13 *the godly escape such **t**.*...........645
Prov 12:21 *wicked have their fill of **t**.*.........645
Prov 13:20 *with fools and get in **t**.*..............646
Prov 25:19 *in times of **t** is like chewing*.......840
Eccl 4:10 *falls alone is in real **t**.*..................676
Isa 38:14 *I am in **t**, LORD. Help me!*.............921
Isa 53:4 *And we thought his **t-s** were*.........940
Isa 58:10 *and help those in **t**.*.....................945
Hos 5:15 *as soon as **t** comes, they*...............808
Nah 1:7 *strong refuge when **t** comes.*..........975
Matt 6:34 *Today's **t** is enough*....................1333
Rom 8:35 *if we have **t** or calamity,*..............1661

1 Cor 7:28 *at this time will have* ***t-s,***.........1606
2 Cor 4:17 *our present* ***t-s*** *are small*........1631
2 Cor 6:4 *We patiently endure* ***t-s*** *and*......1633
2 Cor 7:4 *me happy despite all our* ***t-s.*** 1634
2 Cor 8:2 *being tested by many* ***t-s,***........1636
1 Thes 3:3 *shaken by the* ***t-s*** *you were*.....1583
1 Tim 6:5 *These people always cause* ***t.***.....1734
Jas 1:2 *when* ***t-s*** *come your way,*.............1546
Jas 5:1 *all the terrible* ***t-s*** *ahead*..............1553

TROUBLE (v) to worry or disturb
Luke 7:6 *Lord, don't* ***t*** *yourself by*.............1336

TROUBLED (adj) concerned, worried
Dan 6:14 *the king was deeply* ***t,*** *and he*....1140
Mark 14:33 *and he became deeply* ***t*** *and*..1468
John 14:1 *Don't let your hearts be* ***t.***..........1461
John 14:27 *So don't be* ***t*** *or afraid.*...........1463

TROUBLEMAKERS (n) those who consciously or unconsciously cause trouble
Judg 19:22 *crowd of* ***t*** *from the town*..........406

TRUE (adj) fully realized or fulfilled; accurate; properly so called; steadfast, loyal, honest, and just; ideal, essential; being in accordance with the actual state of affairs; legitimate, rightful
Num 11:23 *my word comes* ***t!***....................248
Deut 18:22 *does not happen or come* ***t,***......309
Josh 23:14 *your God has come* ***t.***...............369
1 Sam 9:6 *everything he says comes* ***t.*** 436
1 Kgs 10:6 *and wisdom is* ***t!***.......................626
2 Chr 15:3 *without the* ***t*** *God,*....................708
Ps 7:10 *hearts are* ***t*** *and right.*....................524
Ps 19:9 *laws of the* LORD *are* ***t;***......................554
Ps 119:142 *instructions are perfectly* ***t.***......881
Ps 119:151 *your commands are* ***t.***..............881
Isa 45:19 *speak only what is* ***t*** *and*.............932
Jer 10:10 *is the only* ***t*** *God.*.......................1013
Jer 26:15 *it is absolutely* ***t*** *that*....................993
Jer 28:9 *when his predictions come* ***t***.......1050
Luke 16:11 *the* ***t*** *riches of heaven?*...........1412
Luke 18:31 *Son of Man will come* ***t.***..........1423
John 1:9 *one who is the* ***t*** *light,*..................1271
John 3:33 *can affirm that God is* ***t.***..........1303
John 4:23 ***t*** *worshipers will worship*..........1305
John 6:32 *offers you the* ***t*** *bread.*.............1367
John 6:55 *my flesh is* ***t*** *food, and*..............1368
John 7:28 *one who sent me is* ***t,***..............1390
John 15:1 *I am the* ***t*** *grapevine,*...............1463
John 17:3 *know you, the only* ***t*** *God,*.........1466
Rom 3:4 *else is a liar, God is* ***t.***................1650
Rom 15:8 *God is* ***t*** *to the promises*...........1671
Eph 5:9 *is good and right and* ***t.***...............1712
Phil 4:1 *stay* ***t*** *to the Lord.*.........................1724
Phil 4:8 *thoughts on what is* ***t,***..................1725
Jas 1:18 *giving us his* ***t*** *word.*......................1547
1 Jn 2:8 *the* ***t*** *light is already*.....................1788
1 Jn 2:27 *to teach you what is* ***t.***..............1790
1 Jn 5:20 *He is the only* ***t*** *God,*..................1795
Rev 19:9 *These are* ***t*** *words that come*......1828
Rev 22:6 *seen is trustworthy and* ***t.***...........1832

TRUMPET, TRUMPETS (n) a wind instrument made of metal or an animal horn used to rally troops on the battlefield or by priests during sacrifices
Isa 27:13 *the great* ***t*** *will sound.*.................897
Matt 24:31 *blast of a* ***t,*** *and they will*.........1447
1 Cor 15:52 *when the last* ***t*** *is blown.*.......1622
1 Thes 4:16 *with the* ***t*** *call of God.*............1585
Rev 8:2 *they were given seven* ***t-s.***...........1813
Rev 8:7 *angel blew his* ***t,*** *and hail*............1814
Rev 18:22 *flutes, and* ***t-s*** *will never*..........1826

TRUST (n) assured reliance on the character, ability, strength, or truth of someone or something; hope
see also BELIEVE, FAITH
Job 31:24 *Have I put my* ***t*** *in money*...........121
Ps 40:3 *put their* ***t*** *in the* LORD...................570
Ps 56:3 *I will put my* ***t*** *in you.*....................472
Isa 2:22 *Don't put your* ***t*** *in mere*...............826
Jer 13:25 *putting your* ***t*** *in false*................1017
Jer 17:5 *who put their* ***t*** *in mere*..............1021
John 12:46 *who put their* ***t*** *in me*............1435
Heb 2:13 *will put my* ***t*** *in him,*...................1764
1 Jn 4:16 *have put our* ***t*** *in his love*...........1793

TRUST, TRUSTED, TRUSTING, TRUSTS (v) to place confidence or depend; to commit or place in one's care or keeping; to rely on the truthfulness or accuracy of
see also BELIEVE, FAITH
Gen 39:8 *master* ***t-s*** *me with everything*.......77
Deut 1:32 *refused to* ***t*** *the* LORD................286
Deut 28:52 *walls you* ***t-ed*** *to protect*..........319
2 Kgs 18:5 *Hezekiah* ***t-ed*** *in the*..................800
2 Kgs 18:19 *What are you* ***t-ing*** *in that*......913
1 Chr 5:20 *because they* ***t-ed*** *in him.*........1232
2 Chr 13:18 *they* ***t-ed*** *in the* LORD,............705
Job 4:18 *God does not* ***t*** *his own angels*.......99
Job 15:31 *fool themselves by* ***t-ing*** *in*........109
Ps 13:5 *I* ***t*** *in your unfailing love.*...............551
Ps 21:7 *the king* ***t-s*** *in the* LORD..................555
Ps 25:2 *I* ***t*** *in you, my God!*........................559
Ps 25:3 *No one who* ***t-s*** *in you will*..............559
Ps 31:14 *I am* ***t-ing*** *you, O* LORD,...............564
Ps 33:4 *we can* ***t*** *everything he*....................858
Ps 37:3 ***T*** *in the* LORD *and do*........................567
Ps 41:9 *the one I* ***t-ed*** *completely,*..............571
Ps 44:6 *I do not* ***t*** *in my bow;*.......................850
Ps 55:23 *but I am* ***t-ing*** *you to save*...........573
Ps 62:8 *O my people,* ***t*** *in him at*.................574
Ps 71:5 *I've* ***t-ed*** *you, O* LORD,......................860
Ps 84:12 *for those who* ***t*** *in you.*...................855
Ps 86:2 *serve you and* ***t*** *you.*.........................579
Ps 112:7 *confidently* ***t*** *the* LORD....................873
Ps 115:8 *as are all who* ***t*** *in them.*..............874
Ps 118:8 LORD *than to* ***t*** *in*..............................876
Ps 119:42 *for I* ***t*** *in your word.*.....................879
Prov 3:5 ***T*** *in the* LORD *with*...........................634
Prov 21:22 *fortress in which they* ***t.***............658
Prov 28:25 ***t-ing*** *the* LORD *leads to*..............844
Prov 28:26 *who* ***t*** *their own insight*..............844
Prov 29:25 ***t-ing*** *the* LORD *means safety.*.....846
Prov 31:11 *Her husband can* ***t*** *her,*..............847
Isa 12:2 *I will* ***t*** *in him and*...........................797
Isa 25:9 *We* ***t-ed*** *in him, and he saved*.......896
Isa 26:3 *peace all who* ***t*** *in you,*..................896
Isa 31:1 *for help,* ***t-ing*** *their horses,*...........901
Isa 40:31 *who* ***t*** *in the* LORD...........................925
Jer 7:14 *this Temple that you* ***t*** *in*..............1008
Jer 12:6 *Do not* ***t*** *them, no matter*...........1015
Jer 48:7 *Because you have* ***t-ed*** *in your*.....989
Dan 3:28 *his servants who* ***t-ed*** *in him.*.....1007
Dan 6:23 *for he had* ***t-ed*** *in his God.*........1141
Nah 1:7 *to those who* ***t*** *in him.*....................975
Hab 2:4 *They* ***t*** *in themselves,*.....................980
Hab 2:18 *foolish to* ***t*** *in your own*...............981
Matt 18:6 *little ones who* ***t-s*** *in me to*.......1384
John 2:24 *Jesus didn't* ***t*** *them,*....................1300
John 12:44 *you are* ***t-ing*** *not only me,*.....1435
John 14:1 *in God, and* ***t*** *also in me.*..........1461
Rom 9:32 *instead of by* ***t-ing*** *in him.*..........1662
Rom 9:33 *But anyone who* ***t-s*** *in him will*..1663
Rom 10:11 *Anyone who* ***t-s*** *in him will*.....1664
Rom 15:13 *peace because you* ***t*** *in*...........1671
1 Cor 2:5 *so you would* ***t*** *not in*..................1598
1 Cor 7:25 *wisdom that can be* ***t-ed,***.........1606
Eph 3:17 *hearts as you* ***t*** *in him.*................1709
Phil 1:29 *the privilege of* ***t-ing*** *in Christ*....1719
Col 2:12 *because you* ***t-ed*** *the mighty*......1698
1 Tim 6:17 *not to* ***t*** *in their money,*............1735
2 Tim 1:12 *the one in whom I* ***t,***.................1741
2 Tim 3:15 *that comes by* ***t-ing*** *in Christ*..1745
Heb 10:22 *hearts fully* ***t-ing*** *him.*.............1775
Heb 10:23 *God can be* ***t-ed*** *to keep his*....1776
1 Pet 1:9 *reward for* ***t-ing*** *him will be*.......1749
1 Pet 2:6 *anyone who* ***t-s*** *in him will*.........1750
1 Pet 2:7 *you who* ***t*** *him recognize*............1750

TRUSTWORTHY (adj) worthy of confidence; dependable
see also FAITHFUL, LOYAL
2 Kgs 22:7 *honest and* ***t*** *men.*......................969
Ps 19:7 *of the* LORD *are* ***t,***...........................554
Ps 119:86 *All your commands are* ***t.***............880
Ps 119:138 *perfect and completely* ***t.***..........881
Prov 11:13 *those who are* ***t*** *can keep*..........643
Dan 6:4 *responsible, and completely* ***t.***......1140
Titus 2:10 *to be entirely* ***t*** *and good*...........1738
Heb 6:19 *a strong and* ***t*** *anchor*..................1770

TRUTH, TRUTHS (n) the property (as of a statement) of being in accord with fact or reality (natural and spiritual); sincerity in action, character, and utterance
Ps 15:2 *speaking the* ***t*** *from sincere*...........552
Ps 25:5 *Lead me by your* ***t*** *and teach*..........559
Ps 26:3 *lived according to your* ***t.***.................560
Ps 43:3 *light and your* ***t;*** *let them*..................849
Ps 45:4 *defending* ***t,*** *humility, and*..............851
Ps 86:11 *live according to your* ***t!***.................579
Ps 119:160 *essence of your words is* ***t;***.......881
Prov 8:7 *for I speak the* ***t*** *and detest*..........640
Prov 12:17 *honest witness tells the* ***t;***.........645
Prov 12:22 *in those who tell the* ***t.***..............645
Prov 23:23 *Get the* ***t*** *and never sell*.............661
Isa 45:23 *I have spoken the* ***t,***......................932
Isa 59:15 *Yes,* ***t*** *is gone,*..............................946
Jer 4:2 *do so with* ***t,*** *justice,*..........................964
Jer 9:3 *to stand up for the* ***t.***.......................1011
Dan 10:21 *written in the Book of* ***T.***...........1159
Dan 11:2 *I will reveal the* ***t*** *to you.*...........1159
Amos 5:10 *people who tell the* ***t!***.................775
Zech 8:16 *Tell the* ***t*** *to each other.*..............1174
Zech 8:19 *So love* ***t*** *and peace.*.................1174
Luke 1:4 *can be certain of the* ***t.***.................1270
John 4:23 *Father in spirit and in* ***t.***............1305
John 7:18 *him speaks* ***t,*** *not lies.*..................1388
John 8:32 *the* ***t*** *will set you free.*.................1393
John 8:44 *there is no* ***t*** *in him.*.....................1393
John 14:6 *way, the* ***t,*** *and the life.*................1461
John 14:17 *who leads into all* ***t.***..................1462
John 15:26 *Advocate—the Spirit of* ***t.***.........1464
John 16:13 *the Spirit of* ***t*** *comes,*.................1465
John 17:17 *your word, which is* ***t.***................1467
John 18:37 *to testify to the* ***t.***......................1478
Acts 20:30 *distort the* ***t*** *in order*.................1675
Acts 21:34 *find out the* ***t*** *in all*.....................1678
Acts 24:8 *can find out the* ***t*** *of our*...............1682
Rom 1:18 *who suppress the* ***t*** *by their*.........1647
Rom 1:25 *They traded the* ***t*** *about God*.......1648
Rom 2:8 *to obey the* ***t*** *and instead*...............1649
Rom 2:20 *complete knowledge and* ***t.***..........1649
1 Cor 2:13 *to explain spiritual* ***t-s.***...............1598
2 Cor 6:7 *We faithfully preach the* ***t.***............1633
2 Cor 13:8 *always stand for the* ***t.***..............1643
Gal 2:5 *wanted to preserve the* ***t.***..................1558
Gal 5:7 *back from following the* ***t?***...............1565
Eph 1:13 *also heard the* ***t,*** *the Good*............1705

Eph 4:15 *will speak the **t** in love,* 1711
Eph 6:14 *the belt of **t** and the body* 1715
2 Thes 2:10 ***t** that would save them* 1589
2 Thes 2:12 *rather than believing the **t*** 1589
1 Tim 2:4 *and to understand the **t*** 1729
1 Tim 3:15 *and foundation of the **t*** 1731
1 Tim 4:3 *people who know the **t*** 1732
1 Tim 6:5 *their backs on the **t*** 1734
2 Tim 2:15 *explains the word of **t*** 1743
2 Tim 3:7 *able to understand the **t*** 1744
Titus 1:14 *turned away from the **t*** 1737
Heb 10:26 *received knowledge of the **t**,* 1776
Jas 3:14 *don't cover up the **t** with* 1550
Jas 5:19 *wanders away from the **t*** 1554
1 Pet 1:22 *you obeyed the **t**, so now* 1750
2 Pet 1:12 *standing firm in the **t*** 1758
2 Pet 2:2 *the way of **t** will be* 1758
1 Jn 1:8 *and not living in the **t*** 1787
1 Jn 2:20 *all of you know the **t*** 1790
1 Jn 3:19 *belong to the **t**, so we* 1792
1 Jn 4:6 *Spirit of **t** or the spirit* 1793
1 Jn 5:6 *Spirit, who is **t**, confirms* 1794
2 Jn 1:2 *because the **t** lives* 1795
2 Jn 1:3 *who live in **t** and love* 1795
3 Jn 1:3 *living according to the **t*** 1796
3 Jn 1:8 *partners as they teach the **t*** 1797

TRUTHFUL (adj) telling or disposed to tell the truth
Ps 5:9 *cannot speak a **t** word* 547
Prov 12:19 ***T** words stand the test* 645
John 8:26 *and he is completely **t*** 1392

TRUTHFULNESS (n) the quality or state of being truthful
Rom 3:7 *highlights his **t** and brings* 1650
Rom 9:1 *I speak with utter **t*** 1661

TURMOIL (n) a state or condition of extreme confusion, agitation, or commotion
Prov 15:16 *treasure and inner **t*** 649

TURN, TURNED, TURNING, TURNS (v) to convert or change allegiance; to return or change direction; to face toward or away; to divert one's attention from; to become or transform; to shape or bend
Deut 28:14 *You must not **t** away from* 318
Deut 30:10 *if you **t** to the LORD* 321
1 Kgs 11:4 *old age, they **t-ed** his heart* 671
2 Chr 7:14 *seek my face and **t** from* 623
2 Chr 34:33 *they did not **t** away from* 973
Esth 9:22 *sorrow was **t-ed** into gladness* 1193
Ps 14:3 *no, all have **t-ed** away; all* 552
Ps 30:11 *You have **t-ed** my mourning* 563
Ps 40:1 *and he **t-ed** to me and* 570
Ps 119:59 *I **t-ed** to follow your* 879
Ps 119:102 *I haven't **t-ed** away from* 880
Prov 3:7 *fear the LORD and **t** away* 634
Prov 28:13 *confess and **t** from them,* 844
Isa 17:7 *Creator and **t** their eyes to* 797
Isa 54:8 *anger I **t-ed** my face away* 941
Isa 55:7 *Let them **t** to the LORD* 942
Isa 59:2 *he has **t-ed** away and will* 945
Jer 14:7 *We have **t-ed** away from you* 1017
Jer 31:13 *I will **t** their mourning into* 1033
Jer 31:19 *I **t-ed** away from God,* 1033
Lam 3:40 *Let us **t** back to the LORD* 1099
Mal 4:6 *preaching will **t** the hearts* 1249
Matt 3:8 *your sins and **t-ed** to God* 1288
Matt 18:3 *truth, unless you **t** from your* 1383
Mark 4:12 *Otherwise, they will **t** to me* 1346
Mark 8:34 *must **t** from your selfish* 1377
Luke 1:17 *He will **t** the hearts of* 1273
Luke 17:4 ***t-s** again and asks forgiveness* 1413
Luke 22:32 *you have repented and **t-ed*** 1460
John 12:40 *and they cannot **t** to me* 1434
John 16:20 *will suddenly **t** to wonderful* 1465
Acts 3:19 *of your sins and **t** to God,* 1517
Acts 7:42 *Then God **t-ed** away from* 1525
Acts 26:18 *so they may **t** from darkness* 1685
Rom 1:26 *Even the women **t-ed** against* 1648
Rom 2:4 *to **t** you from your sin?* 1648
Rom 3:12 *All have **t-ed** away;* 1651
Gal 1:6 *that you are **t-ing** away so* 1555
2 Tim 2:19 *LORD must **t** away from* 1743
Titus 2:12 *instructed to **t** from godless* 1738
Heb 10:38 *in anyone who **t-s** away* 1777
1 Pet 2:25 *But now you have **t-ed** to* 1752

TURTLEDOVES (n) any of several small wild pigeons noted for plaintive cooing
Lev 12:8 *must bring two **t** or two young* 216
Luke 2:24 *a pair of **t** or two young* 1282

TWELVE (adj) of or relating to the number 12
Gen 35:22 *names of the **t** sons of Jacob:* 70
Gen 49:28 *These are the **t** tribes of* 92
Matt 10:1 *Jesus called his **t** disciples* 1358
Luke 9:17 *picked up **t** baskets of* 1364
Rev 21:12 *names of the **t** tribes of* 1831
Rev 21:14 *names of the **t** apostles of* 1831
Rev 21:21 *The **t** gates were made of* 1831

TWINS (n) two offspring produced at a birth
Gen 25:24 *she did indeed have **t!*** 51

TWIST, TWISTED (v) to distort or pervert
Exod 14:25 *He **t-ed** their chariot wheels,* 160
Exod 23:8 *righteous person **t** the truth.* 173
Deut 16:19 *You must never **t** justice or* 306
Job 34:12 *will not **t** justice.* 124
Isa 24:5 *have **t-ed** God's instructions,* 894
Lam 3:36 *if they **t** justice in the courts—* 1098
Ezek 7:13 *whose life is **t-ed** by sin* 1053
Gal 1:7 *who deliberately **t** the truth* 1556
2 Pet 3:16 *unstable have **t-ed** his letters* 1760

TWO-EDGED (adj) marked by having two cutting edges
Heb 4:12 *sharpest **t** sword, cutting* 1766
Rev 1:16 *a sharp **t** sword came from* 1800
Rev 2:12 *with the sharp **t** sword:* 1803

UNAFRAID (adv) in a manner not filled with fear
Hos 2:18 *you can live **u** in peace* 804

UNBELIEF (n) incredulity or skepticism in matters of religious truth
see also UNFAITHFUL
Matt 13:58 *there because of their **u**.* 1356
Mark 6:6 *he was amazed at their **u*** 1357
Mark 9:24 *help me overcome my **u!*** 1381
Mark 16:14 *them for their stubborn **u*** 1494
Rom 11:23 *Israel turn from their **u**,* 1665
1 Tim 1:13 *it in ignorance and **u**.* 1728
Heb 3:19 *because of their **u** they* 1765

UNBELIEVER, UNBELIEVERS (n) one who does not believe; a non-Christian
Matt 6:32 *dominate the thoughts of **u-s**,* 1332
Luke 12:30 *the thoughts of **u-s** all over* 1401
1 Cor 6:6 *right in front of **u-s!*** 1603
1 Cor 14:22 *for believers, but for **u-s**.* 1617
2 Cor 6:15 *a partner with an **u?*** 1634
1 Tim 5:8 *people are worse than **u-s**.* 1733
Rev 21:8 *But cowards, **u-s**, the corrupt,* 1830

UNBELIEVING (adj) marked by unbelief
1 Pet 2:12 *among your **u** neighbors* 1751

UNBREAKABLE (adj) not capable of being broken
Num 18:19 *an eternal and **u** covenant* 259

UNCHANGEABLE (adj) not changing or to be changed; immutable
Heb 6:18 *two things are **u** because* 1769

UNCIRCUMCISED (adj) not circumcised; spiritually impure
Jer 9:26 *of Israel also have **u** hearts.* 1012
1 Cor 7:18 *man who was **u** when he* 1606
Gal 5:6 *being circumcised or being **u**.* 1565
Col 3:11 *circumcised or **u**, barbaric,* 1700

UNCLEAN (adj) morally or spiritually impure; prohibited by ritual law for use or contact
Lev 10:10 *is ceremonially **u** and what is* 213
Lev 11:4 *it is ceremonially **u** for you* 214
Lev 17:15 *remain ceremonially **u** until* 223
Lev 27:11 *vow involves an **u** animal—* 236
Isa 52:11 *everything you touch is **u**.* 939
Acts 10:14 *have declared impure and **u**.* 1533
Acts 10:15 *not call something **u** if God* 1533

UNDERGROUND (adj) beneath the surface of the earth
Gen 8:2 *The **u** waters stopped.* 19

UNDERMINE (v) to weaken or ruin by degrees
Jer 38:4 *will **u** the morale of* 1043
Ezek 13:11 *A heavy rainstorm will **u** it* 1059

UNDERSTAND (v) to grasp the meaning or reasonableness of; to be thoroughly familiar with
see also UNDERSTOOD
Job 5:9 *things too marvelous to **u*** 99
Job 36:26 *is greater than we can **u**.* 126
Ps 73:16 *tried to **u** why the wicked* 594
Ps 119:27 *Help me **u** the meaning of* 878
Ps 119:125 *then I will **u** your laws* 881
Ps 119:130 *so even the simple can **u**.* 881
Prov 2:5 *will **u** what it means to fear* 633
Prov 2:9 *you will **u** what is right,* 634
Prov 28:5 *the LORD **u** completely* 843
Prov 30:18 *things that I don't **u:*** 846
Eccl 7:25 *and to **u** the reason* 679
Isa 6:9 *carefully, but do not **u**.* 785
Isa 40:21 *you heard? Don't you **u?*** 924
Jer 9:24 *truly know me and **u** that* 1012
Hos 14:9 *who are wise **u** these things* 817
Matt 13:11 *permitted to **u** the secrets* 1345
Matt 13:23 *truly hear and **u** God's* 1345
Luke 19:42 *people would **u** the way* 1431
Luke 24:45 *minds to **u** the Scriptures.* 1498
Acts 8:30 *Do you **u** what you are* 1529
Rom 7:15 *I don't really **u** myself,* 1658
Rom 15:21 *never heard of him will **u**.* 1672
1 Cor 2:14 *and they can't **u** it,* 1598
1 Cor 14:14 *but I don't **u** what I am* 1617
2 Cor 3:14 *they cannot **u** the truth* 1630
Gal 1:11 *you to **u** that the gospel* 1556
Eph 1:18 *you can **u** the confident* 1706
Eph 5:17 *thoughtlessly, but **u** what* 1713
Phil 1:10 *want you to **u** what really* 1717
Phil 4:7 *exceeds anything we can **u**.* 1724
Col 2:2 *that they **u** God's mysterious* 1697
1 Tim 2:4 *saved and to **u** the truth* 1729
2 Tim 2:7 *will help you **u** all these* 1742
Heb 11:3 *By faith we **u** that the entire* 1777
2 Pet 3:16 *are hard to **u**, and those* 1760

UNDERSTANDABLE (adj) marked by being able to understand; comprehendible
1 Cor 14:19 *rather speak five **u** words*......1617

UNDERSTANDING (n) comprehension; explanation, interpretation; sympathy
Job 28:12 *Where can they find **u**?*............119
Job 28:28 *to forsake evil is real **u**.*..............119
Ps 119:32 *for you expand my **u**.*..................878
Ps 119:34 *Give me **u** and I will*.....................878
Ps 119:104 *commandments give me **u**;*.....880
Prov 3:5 *not depend on your own **u**.*..........634
Prov 10:13 *lips of people with **u**,*................642
Prov 14:29 *People with **u** control*...............648
Prov 15:32 *correction, you grow in **u**.*.........650
Prov 16:21 *wise are known for their **u**,*.......651
Prov 18:2 *Fools have no interest in **u**;*........653
Prov 19:8 *who cherish **u** will prosper.*.........654
Prov 20:5 *a person with **u** will draw*...........656
Prov 28:16 *ruler with no **u** will oppress*.......844
Isa 40:28 *the depths of his **u**.*....................925
Isa 50:4 *opens my **u** to his will.*..................937
Jer 10:12 *With his own **u** he stretched*.....1013
Mark 12:33 *heart and all my **u** and all*.....1442
Luke 2:47 *were amazed at his **u** and his*...1286
1 Cor 14:20 *but be mature in **u** matters*....1617
2 Cor 6:6 *purity, our **u**, our patience,*.......1633
Eph 1:8 *along with all wisdom and **u**.*........1705
Phil 1:9 *growing in knowledge and **u**.*.......1717
Col 1:9 *you spiritual wisdom and **u**.*..........1694
2 Thes 3:5 *a full **u** and expression*.............1590
1 Tim 6:4 *is arrogant and lacks **u**.*.............1734
1 Pet 3:7 *your wife with **u** as you live*........1753
2 Pet 1:20 *from the prophet's own **u**,*.........1758
1 Jn 5:20 *he has given us **u** so that*..........1795

UNDERSTOOD (v) comprehended the meaning of
see also UNDERSTAND
Neh 8:12 *God's words and **u** them*............1215
Ps 73:17 *I finally **u** the destiny*...................594
1 Cor 13:2 *and if I **u** all of God's*..............1616

UNDERWORLD (n) place of destruction (Hebrew *Sheol*)
see also HELL
Job 26:6 *The **u** is naked in God's*...............117

UNDESERVED (adj) of, relating to, or being that which one does not deserve
Rom 5:2 *place of **u** privilege where*...........1654

UNDISCIPLINED (adj) marked by or possessing no discipline
Prov 29:15 *disgraced by an **u** child*.............845

UNDIVIDED (adj) not directed or moved toward conflicting interests, states, or objects
2 Chr 19:9 *faithfulness and an **u** heart*........730
2 Cor 11:3 *your pure and **u** devotion*.........1640

UNFADING (adj) not losing freshness, value, or effectiveness
1 Pet 3:4 *the **u** beauty of a gentle*............1752

UNFAILING (adj) constant, everlasting, inexhaustible, sure
see also FAITHFUL
Exod 15:13 *With your **u** love you*...............162
Ps 6:4 *because of your **u** love*.....................548
Ps 13:5 *trust in your **u** love.*.......................551
Ps 17:7 *Show me your **u** love in*.................553
Ps 18:50 *you show **u** love to your*...............529
Ps 25:6 *compassion and **u** love,*.................560
Ps 31:16 *In your **u** love, rescue*...................564
Ps 32:10 *but **u** love surrounds*.....................565
Ps 33:5 *the **u** love of the LORD*...................858
Ps 33:22 *Let your **u** love surround*.............858
Ps 36:7 *precious is your **u** love,*..................566
Ps 36:10 *Pour out your **u** love*....................566
Ps 48:9 *meditate on your **u** love*..................853
Ps 51:1 *because of your **u** love*.....................505
Ps 52:8 *trust in God's **u** love*.......................462
Ps 57:10 *For your **u** love is*..........................460
Ps 85:7 *Show us your **u** love,*.........................855
Ps 90:14 *morning with your **u** love,*...............326
Ps 117:2 *he loves us with **u** love;*..................875
Ps 119:41 *give me your **u** love,*.....................879
Ps 119:76 *let your **u** love comfort*...................879
Ps 143:8 *me hear of your **u** love*....................588
Ps 147:11 *hope in his **u** love*.....................1155
Isa 55:3 *the **u** love I promised*.....................942
Isa 63:7 *the LORD's **u** love*............................949
Lam 3:32 *greatness of his **u** love*...............1098
Mic 7:18 *in showing **u** love*...........................911

UNFAIR (adj) marked by injustice, partiality, or deception
Job 31:13 *If I have been **u** to my male*........121
Rom 3:5 *Isn't it **u**, then, for him*................1650
Rom 9:14 *then, that God was **u**?*...............1662
1 Pet 2:19 *endure **u** treatment.*..................1752

UNFAITHFUL (adj) marked by stubborn disbelief and disloyalty; adulterous
see also TREACHEROUS, UNBELIEF
Ps 78:8 *rebellious, and **u**, refusing*...............598
Prov 23:28 *eager to make more men **u**.*.......662
Jer 3:20 *you have been **u** to me,*...................963
Matt 5:32 *unless she has been **u**,*...............1329
Rom 3:3 *some of them were **u**; but*...........1650
2 Tim 2:13 *If we are **u**, he remains*..............1742

UNFORGIVING (adj) unwilling or unable to forgive
2 Tim 3:3 *will be unloving and **u**;*...............1744

UNGODLY (adj) sinful, wicked
see also GODLESS, WICKED
Eph 5:12 *the things that **u** people do*........1712
2 Pet 2:6 *will happen to **u** people.*............1759
Jude 1:15 *of all the **u** things they*............1785

UNHOLY (adj) showing disregard for what is holy; wicked
Matt 7:6 *people who are **u**. Don't throw*....1333
Heb 10:29 *were common and **u**, and have*...1776

UNION (n) an act or instance of uniting two or more things into one
2 Cor 6:16 *And what **u** can there be*.........1634
Col 2:10 *through your **u** with Christ,*...........1698

UNITED (v) to become one or as if one; in one accord or spirit
Gen 2:24 *the two are **u** into one.*....................11
Mark 10:8 *the two are **u** into one*..............1419
Rom 6:5 *we have been **u** with him*............1655
Rom 7:4 *now you are **u** with the one*.........1657
1 Cor 6:16 *The two are **u** into one.*............1604
Eph 4:3 *to keep yourselves **u** in the*..........1710
Eph 5:31 *the two are **u** into one."*.............1714

UNITY (n) the quality or state of oneness or harmony
John 17:23 *perfect **u** that the world*..........1467
Eph 4:13 *come to such **u** in our faith*........1711

UNIVERSE (n) the whole body of things created; cosmos
Eph 4:10 *the entire **u** with himself.*...........1710
Heb 1:2 *the Son he created the **u**.*............1761
Heb 11:3 *the entire **u** was formed at*.........1777

UNJUST (adj) characterized by injustice
Ps 82:2 *you hand down **u** decisions*............602
Matt 5:45 *the just and the **u** alike.*............1330

UNKIND (adj) harsh, cruel
1 Pet 2:1 *and all **u** speech.*.......................1750

UNKNOWN (adj) not known or well-known
1 Cor 12:28 *who speak in **u** languages*.....1615

UNLEAVENED (adj) characterized by being without yeast
Exod 12:17 *this Festival of **U** Bread,*...........156
Deut 16:16 *the Festival of **U** Bread,*............306

UNLOVING (adj) characterized by lack of affection
2 Tim 3:3 *be **u** and unforgiving;*................1744

UNMARRIED (adj) not married
1 Cor 7:8 *it's better to stay **u**,*...................1605
1 Cor 7:32 *An **u** man can spend his*.........1607

UNPUNISHED (adj) to not pay the consequences for a fault, offense, or violation
Exod 20:7 *let you go **u** if you misuse*...........169
Deut 5:11 *let you go **u** if you misuse*...........292
Prov 6:29 *embraces her will not go **u**.*.........639
Prov 19:5 *false witness will not go **u**,*..........654
Jer 49:12 *You will not go **u**!*......................1025
Amos 1:3 *will not let them go **u**!*..................770

UNRELIABLE (adj) not dependable
Prov 25:19 *confidence in an **u** person*.........840
1 Tim 6:17 *money, which is so **u**.*.............1735

UNSTABLE (adj) not firm, fixed, or constant; unsteady
2 Pet 2:14 *They lure **u** people into sin,*......1759
2 Pet 3:16 *ignorant and **u** have twisted*.....1760

UNTHANKFUL (adj) showing no gratitude
Luke 6:35 *those who are **u** and wicked.*....1330

UNTHINKING (adj) not having the power of thought
2 Pet 2:12 *like **u** animals, creatures,*..........1759

UNTIE (v) to free from something that ties, fastens, or restrains
Mark 1:7 *a slave and **u** the straps*............1290
Luke 13:15 *Don't you **u** your ox or*............1403

UNTRUSTWORTHY (adj) not worthy of confidence; undependable
Luke 16:11 *if you are **u** about worldly*.......1412

UNWORTHILY (adv) in an undeserving manner
1 Cor 11:27 *this cup of the Lord **u***...........1613

UPHOLD (v) to give support to
Ps 82:3 ***u** the rights of the oppressed*.........602

UPRIGHT (adj) marked by strong moral integrity
see also GODLY, RIGHT, RIGHTEOUS
Deut 32:4 *how just and **u** he is!*..................323
Prov 3:33 *blesses the home of the **u**.*..........635
Prov 15:8 *in the prayers of the **u**.*...............648

UPROOT (v) to displace from a country or traditional habitat
Ps 52:5 *and **u** you from the land of*............462
Matt 13:29 *'you'll **u** the wheat if you do.*....1348

UPSET (adj) emotionally disturbed or agitated
Prov 3:11 *and don't be **u** when he*.............635
Luke 10:41 *worried and **u** over all*...........1397

URGE (n) a continuing impulse
Deut 12:20 *you have the **u** to eat meat,*......302

URGE, URGED, URGES (v) to solicit or entreat; to impel
Job 32:18 *spirit within me **u-s** me on.*........123

Matt 15:23 *__u-d__ him to send her away.*......1371
Rom 15:30 *I __u__ you in the name of our*.......1672
1 Cor 4:16 *I __u__ you to imitate me.*..............1601
1 Thes 2:12 *encouraged you, and __u-d__ you.*.1582
2 Tim 4:1 *I solemnly __u__ you in the*.............1745

URGENCY (n) a force or impulse that impels
Exod 12:11 *meal with __u,__ for this is*.............156

USE (v) to put into action or service
2 Tim 2:21 *for the Master to __u__ you*...........1743
1 Pet 2:16 *don't __u__ your freedom as an*......1751

USEFUL (adj) serviceable for an end or purpose
2 Tim 3:16 *inspired by God and is __u__ to*......1745
2 Pet 1:8 *productive and __u__ you will be*......1757

USELESS (adj) having or being of no use; ineffectual, inept
John 15:6 *thrown away like a __u__ branch*.....1463
Acts 26:14 *It is __u__ for you to fight*.............1685
1 Cor 13:s8 *knowledge will become __u.__*.....1616
1 Cor 15:14 *__u,__ and your faith is __u.__*...........1620
1 Cor 15:58 *do for the Lord is ever __u.__*.........1622
2 Tim 2:14 *Such arguments are __u,__ and*......1742
Titus 1:10 *who engage in __u__ talk and*.........1737
Heb 7:18 *because it was weak and __u.__*......1770

UTTERMOST (KJV)
Isa 24:16 *songs of praise from the __ends of the earth__*..895
Acts 1:8 *and to the __ends of the earth__*......1500

VAIN (adj) marked by futility or ineffectualness
Isa 65:23 *will not work in __v,__ and*.................952

VALID (adj) well-grounded or justifiable
John 8:14 *claims are __v__ even though*.........1392

VALLEY, VALLEYS (n) a depression in the earth's surface between ranges of mountains, hills, or other uplands
Ps 23:4 *through the darkest __v,__ I will*............558
Song 2:1 *lily of the __v.__*................................664
Isa 40:4 *Fill in the __v-s,__ and level*.................923
Joel 3:14 *waiting in the __v__ of decision.*........1243
Luke 3:5 *The __v-s__ will be filled, and*...........1290

VALUABLE (adj) having desirable or esteemed characteristics or qualities; of great use or service
Job 28:17 *Wisdom is more __v__ than gold*.......119
Ps 119:72 *instructions are more __v__*..............879
Prov 8:11 *is far more __v__ than rubies.*............640
Prov 20:15 *words are more __v__ than*.............656
Matt 10:31 *you are more __v__ to God than*....1360
Luke 12:24 *are far more __v__ to him than*......1400
Phil 3:7 *these things were __v,__ but now*.........1722

VALUE (n) monetary worth of something; relative worth, utility, or importance
Matt 13:46 *a pearl of great __v,__ he sold*.......1349
1 Cor 3:13 *a person's work has any __v.__*......1599
Phil 3:8 *the infinite __v__ of knowing*..............1722

VALUED (v) to estimate or assign the monetary worth of
Zech 11:13 *sum at which they __v__ me!*........1177

VANISHING (adj) disappearing
Prov 21:6 *lying tongue is a __v__ mist*..............657

VANITY, VANITIES (KJV)
Deut 32:21 *with their __useless idols__*...........324
Ps 144:4 *For we are like __a breath of air__*.....589
Eccl 12:8 *Everything is __meaningless__*.........683
Acts 14:15 *turn from these __worthless things__*...1544

Eph 4:17 *they are __hopelessly confused__*..1711

VEGETABLES (n) plants or their edible parts
Rom 14:2 *conscience will eat only __v.__*.........1670

VEIL (n) a facial covering
Exod 34:33 *covered his face with a __v.__*.........188
2 Cor 3:14 *same __v__ covers their minds*......1630
2 Cor 3:18 *have had that __v__ removed can*..1630

VENGEANCE (n) punishment inflicted in retaliation for an injury or offense
1 Sam 25:26 *taking __v__ into your own*...........466
1 Sam 25:33 *carrying out __v__ with my*..........467
Ps 94:1 *O LORD, the God of __v,__*.....................862
Isa 66:6 *the LORD taking __v__ against*.............953
Luke 21:22 *be days of God's __v,__ and the*....1450

VENOM (n) poisonous matter secreted by some animals
Ps 140:3 *a snake; the __v__ of a viper*.............587
Rom 3:13 *Snake __v__ drips from their*..........1651

VERILY (KJV)
Ps 58:11 *There __truly__ is a reward*...............573
John 16:20 *__I tell you the truth__*...............1465

VICIOUS (adj) dangerously aggressive
Matt 7:15 *but are really __v__ wolves.*............1334
Acts 20:29 *teachers, like __v__ wolves,*...........1675

VICTORIOUS (adj) of, relating to, or characteristic of victory; having won a victory
see also OVERCOME
2 Sam 8:6 *made David __v__ wherever he*........498
Isa 53:12 *of a __v__ soldier, because he*............941
Matt 12:20 *cause justice to be __v.__*..............1322
Rev 2:11 *Whoever is __v__ will not be*............1803
Rev 2:17 *everyone who is __v__ I will give*.......1804
Rev 2:26 *To all who are __v,__ who obey*.........1805
Rev 3:5 *All who are __v__ will be clothed*.........1806
Rev 3:21 *Those who are __v__ will sit with*......1808
Rev 21:7 *All who are __v__ will inherit*............1830

VICTORY, VICTORIES (n) the overcoming of an enemy, antagonist, or struggle
see also OVERCOME
Exod 15:2 *he has given me __v.__*.....................161
2 Sam 22:51 *You give great __v-ies__ to your*...527
Ps 18:50 *You give great __v-ies__ to your*..........529
Ps 20:5 *we hear of your __v__ and*......................555
Ps 21:1 *because you give him __v.__*..................555
Ps 35:3 *I will give you __v!__*..............................565
Ps 44:4 *You command __v-ies__ for Israel.*.........850
Ps 45:4 *majesty, ride out to __v,__*........................851
Ps 48:10 *right hand is filled with __v.__*................853
Ps 62:1 *for my __v__ comes from him.*..................574
Ps 98:3 *have seen the __v__ of our God.*.............865
Ps 118:14 *he has given me __v.__*.....................876
Ps 149:4 *crowns the humble with __v.__*..............887
Isa 12:2 *he has given me __v.__*.........................797
Isa 52:10 *see the __v__ of our God.*.....................939
Rom 8:37 *overwhelming __v__ is ours.*...............1661
1 Cor 15:54 *Death is swallowed up in __v.__*...1622
Col 2:15 *publicly by his __v__ over them*..........1698
Rev 5:5 *David's throne, has won the __v.__*......1809

VILLAGE (n) a settlement usually smaller than a town
Mark 6:6 *Jesus went from __v__ to __v,__*.............1358

VINDICATED (v) shown to be without blame; prove right
1 Tim 3:16 *body and __v__ by the Spirit.*..........1731

VINE (KJV)
Gen 49:11 *He ties his foal to a __grapevine__*.....91
Deut 8:8 *and barley; of __grapevines__*............297

Ps 80:8 *from Egypt like a __grapevine__*...........601
John 15:5 *I am the __vine;__ you are the branches*...1463

VINEGAR (n) a liquid made from wine that has been soured or overfermented
Prov 10:26 *employers, like __v__ to the*.............643

VINEYARD (n) a plantation of grapevines
1 Kgs 21:1 *who owned a __v__ in Jezreel*..........723
Prov 31:16 *earnings she plants a __v.__*............847
Song 1:6 *for myself—my own __v.__*.................664
Isa 5:1 *beloved had a __v__ on a rich*...............828
1 Cor 9:7 *farmer plants a __v__ and*................1608

VIOLATE, VIOLATED, VIOLATES, VIOLATING (v) to do harm to the person or especially the chastity of; to fail to show proper respect for; to break or disregard
Lev 18:7 *Do not __v__ your father*......................224
Lev 18:8 *for this would __v__ your father.*...........224
Lev 18:10 *this would __v__ yourself.*..................224
Lev 18:14 *Do not __v__ your uncle,*....................224
Lev 18:16 *this would __v__ your brother.*............224
Lev 20:11 *If a man __v-s__ his father by*...........227
Lev 20:20 *he has __v-d__ his uncle.*..................227
Lev 20:21 *He has __v-d__ his brother, and*.........227
Num 15:30 *who brazenly __v__ the LORD's*.........255
Deut 22:30 *for this would __v__ his father.*.........313
Deut 27:20 *for he has __v-d__ his father.*...........317
Isa 24:5 *instructions, __v-d__ his laws,*.............894
Mal 2:10 *each other, __v-ing__ the covenant*..1246

VIOLATION (n) infringement, transgression
Heb 2:2 *firm, and every __v__ of the law*.........1763

VIOLENCE (n) exertion of physical force so as to injure or abuse
Gen 6:11 *and was filled with __v.__*.......................17
Ps 12:5 *I have seen __v__ done to the*...............551
Ps 72:14 *them from oppression and __v,__*.......630
Isa 60:18 *__V__ will disappear from your*............947
Jonah 3:8 *and stop all their __v.__*.....................768
Mic 2:2 *take it by fraud and __v.__*.....................905

VIOLENT (adj) emotionally agitated to the point of loss of self-control
1 Tim 3:3 *a heavy drinker or be __v.__*.............1730
Titus 1:7 *not be a heavy drinker, __v,__*............1736

VIPER (n) a particular species of venomous snakes
Ps 140:3 *venom of a __v__ drips from*...............587

VIRGIN (n) an unmarried woman who has not had sexual intercourse
Gen 24:16 *but she was still a __v.__*....................48
Isa 7:14 *The __v__ will conceive a child!*............790
Matt 1:18 *while she was still a __v,__ she*........1277
Matt 1:23 *The __v__ will conceive a child!*.........1278
Luke 1:34 *this happen? I am a __v.__*..............1274

VIRGINITY (n) the quality or state of being virgin
Deut 22:15 *proof of her __v__ to the elders*.......312

VIRTUE (KJV)
Phil 4:8 *things that are __excellent__*.............1725
2 Pet 1:5 *provision of __moral excellence__*...1757

VIRTUOUS (adj) morally excellent; righteous
Ruth 3:11 *you are a __v__ woman*.....................414
Prov 31:10 *Who can find a __v__ and*...............847
Prov 31:29 *There are many __v__ and*...............848

VISION, VISIONS (n) a visual form of divine revelation, including dreams, that consists of symbolic images, often accompanied by their interpretation
Num 12:6 *would reveal myself in __v-s.__*..........250

2 Sam 7:17 *LORD had said in this **v.***............496
Dan 9:24 *the prophetic **v,** and to*..............1143
Dan 10:1 *that the **v** concerned events*......1158
Joel 2:28 *your young men will see **v-s.***.....1242
Hab 2:3 *This **v** is for a future time.*..........980
Acts 2:17 *Your young men will see **v-s,***....1514
Acts 26:19 *I obeyed that **v** from heaven.*...1685
Col 2:18 *they have had **v-s** about these*...1699

VOICE (n) verbal communication by human and divine means
Isa 40:3 *the **v** of someone shouting,*...........923
Mark 1:3 *He is a **v** shouting in the*............1289
John 10:3 *sheep recognize his **v** and*........1405
John 12:28 *a **v** spoke from heaven,*..........1434
Rev 3:20 *If you hear my **v** and open*..........1807

VOMIT (n) matter disgorged from the stomach
Prov 26:11 *returns to its **v,** so a fool*..........841
2 Pet 2:22 *A dog returns to its **v.***.............1759

VOMIT (v) to eject violently or abundantly
Lev 18:28 *it will **v** out the people*................225

VOW, VOWS (n) a binding promise or pledge
see also COVENANT, PROMISE
Num 6:2 *the special **v** of a Nazirite,*...........244
Judg 11:30 *Jephthah made a **v** to the*........394
Ps 110:4 *and will not break his **v:***..............582
Matt 5:34 *do not make any **v-s!***...............1329
Heb 7:21 *and will not break his **v:***.............1771

VOWED (v) to promise solemnly
Eccl 8:2 *since you **v** to God that*.................679
Mark 7:11 *For I have **v** to give to*.............1370

VULGAR (adj) lewdly or profanely indecent
Ps 101:3 *at anything vile and **v.***.................580

VULNERABLE (adj) capable of being physically or emotionally wounded
2 Tim 3:6 *the confidence of **v** women*.......1744

VULTURES (n) any of various large birds that subsist chiefly or entirely on dead flesh
Matt 24:28 *gathering of **v** shows there*.....1446
Rev 19:17 *shouting to the **v** flying high*.....1828

WAGE, WAGES (n) payment for labor or services; compensation
Hag 1:6 *Your **w-s** disappear as though*.....1162
Zech 11:12 *give me my **w-s,** whatever*.....1177
Mal 3:5 *cheat employees of their **w-s,***......1247
Matt 20:2 *the normal daily **w** and*............1422
Rom 4:4 *their **w-s** are not a gift,*..............1652
Rom 6:23 *For the **w-s** of sin is death,*.......1656

WAGE (v) to engage in or carry on
2 Cor 10:3 *but we don't **w** war*................1638

WAILING (v) the act of expressing sorrow audibly
Amos 5:17 *There will be **w** in every*............776

WAIT, WAITED, WAITING (v) to look forward expectantly; to stay in place in expectation of
Ps 40:1 *I **w-ed** patiently for the LORD*..........570
Ps 62:5 *that I am **w** quietly before*.............574
Ps 69:3 ***w-ing** for my God to help me.*........577
Isa 30:18 *Blessed are those who **w** for*.......900
Mic 7:7 *I **w** confidently for God to*..............911
Hab 3:16 *I will **w** quietly for the*..................982
Luke 12:37 *who are ready and **w-ing***......1401
Rom 8:19 *all creation is **w-ing** eagerly*.....1659
Rom 8:23 *We, too, **w** with eager hope*......1659
Heb 9:28 *are eagerly **w-ing** for him.*........1774

WAKE (v) to rouse from or as if from sleep
see also AWAKE
Prov 6:22 *When you **w** up, they will*...........638
Rev 3:3 *If you don't **w** up, I will*.................1806

WAKENS (v) to wake
Isa 50:4 *by morning he **w** me and*.............937

WALK, WALKED, WALKING (v) to roam, traverse, or advance by steps; to pursue a course of action or way of life
Gen 3:8 *God **w-ing** about in the garden.* 12
Lev 26:12 *I will **w** among you;*....................235
Deut 11:22 *God by **w-ing** in his ways*........301
Deut 26:17 *promised to **w** in his ways,*.......316
Josh 22:5 *God, **w** in all his ways,*...............366
Ps 23:4 *when I **w** through the*....................558
Ps 89:15 *they will **w** in the light*.................591
Prov 4:12 *When you **w,** you won't*..............636
Prov 6:22 *When you **w,** their counsel*..........638
Isa 2:3 *we will **w** in his paths*......................825
Isa 40:31 *They will **w** and not*....................925
Isa 43:2 *When you **w** through the*..............928
Jer 6:16 *godly way, and **w** in it.*..................968
Dan 3:25 ***w-ing** around in the fire*...........1007
Amos 3:3 *two people **w** together*...............773
Mic 6:8 *to **w** humbly with your God*............910
Mal 2:6 *they **w-ed** with me, living good*....1246
Matt 14:29 *boat and **w-ed** on the water*...1365
Mark 2:9 *pick up your mat, and **w***.............1314
John 8:12 *have to **w** in darkness,*.............1392

WALL, WALLS (n) a thick, high, continuous structure of stones or brick that formed a defensive barricade around an ancient city
Josh 6:20 *Suddenly, the **w-s** of Jericho*......344
Neh 2:17 *rebuild the **w** of Jerusalem*........1205
Isa 58:12 *as a rebuilder of **w-s** and*............945
Heb 11:30 *and the **w-s** came crashing*.....1779
Rev 21:12 *city **w** was broad and high,*......1831

WANDER, WANDERED, WANDERS (v) to follow a winding course; to stray
Num 32:13 *them **w** in the wilderness*..........279
Ps 119:10 *don't let me **w** from your*...........878
Ps 119:67 *I used to **w** off until you*.............879
Ps 119:176 *I have **w-ed** away like a*..........882
Matt 18:12 *one of them **w-s** away*...........1385
Eph 4:18 ***w** far from the life God*..............1711
1 Tim 6:10 *have **w-ed** from the true*.........1735
Jas 5:19 *someone among you **w-s***..........1554
1 Pet 2:25 *like sheep who **w-ed** away.*......1752
2 Pet 2:15 *They have **w-ed** off the*...........1759

WANT, WANTED, WANTS (v) to desire or wish
Gen 3:6 *she **w-ed** the wisdom it would*........11
Job 23:13 *Whatever he **w-s** to do,*.............116
Ps 51:16 *do not **w** a burnt offering.*...........506
Ps 119:58 *heart I **w** your blessings.*............879
Prov 13:4 *Lazy people **w** much but*.............646
Eccl 6:2 *they could ever **w,** but then*...........678
Mic 7:3 *get what they **w,** and together*........910
Matt 5:42 *from those who **w** to borrow.* 1329
Matt 14:20 *as they **w-ed,** and afterward,* ...1363
Matt 19:21 *If you **w** to be perfect,* 1420
Matt 23:37 *I have **w-ed** to gather your*.....1407
Luke 19:14 *We do not **w** him to be*...........1427
John 3:8 *blows wherever it **w-s.*** 1302
John 7:17 *Anyone who **w-s** to do the*.......1388
John 15:7 *ask for anything you **w,***............1464
Acts 20:27 *all that God **w-s** you to know*.....1675
Rom 7:15 *I **w** to do what is right,*..............1658
1 Cor 12:18 *part just where he **w-s** it*.......1615
2 Cor 8:5 *just as God **w-ed** them to do*.....1636
2 Cor 8:10 *the first who **w-ed** to give,* 1636
2 Cor 12:14 *you have—I **w** you.* 1642
Eph 1:5 *This is what he **w-ed** to do,*.........1704
Eph 5:17 *what the Lord **w-s** you to do.*........1713
1 Tim 2:4 *who **w-s** everyone to be saved.*.1729
Heb 10:5 *did not **w** animal sacrifices*.......1774
Heb 13:18 *is clear and we **w** to live*..........1783
1 Pet 1:10 *the prophets **w-ed** to know*.....1749
1 Pet 3:17 *if that is what God **w-s,***..........1753

WAR, WARS (n) armed conflict with an opposing military force; a state of hostility, conflict, or antagonism
Josh 11:23 *finally had rest from **w.*** 353
Ps 46:9 *He causes **w-s** to end*...................852
Ps 68:30 *nations that delight in **w.***............577
Ps 120:7 *peace, they want **w!***...................882
Ps 144:1 *He trains my hands for **w***............589
Isa 2:4 *nor train for **w** anymore.* 825
2 Cor 10:3 *we don't wage **w** as humans*...1638
1 Pet 2:11 *that wage **w** against your*........1751
Rev 12:7 *Then there was **w** in heaven.* 1818
Rev 19:11 *and wages a righteous **w.***........1828

WARN, WARNED, WARNING (v) to give notice to beforehand especially of danger or evil; to counsel
Gen 2:16 *God **w-ed** him, "You may*..............10
Gen 31:24 *told him, "I'm **w-ing** you—*.........64
Gen 31:29 *to me last night and **w-ed** me,*....64
Exod 19:21 *down and **w** the people*............168
Num 16:40 *This would **w** the Israelites*.......257
1 Sam 8:9 *but solemnly **w** them about*.......434
1 Kgs 2:42 *LORD and **w** you not to*.............606
2 Kgs 17:13 *and seers to **w** both Israel*.......820
2 Chr 19:10 *must **w** them not to sin*...........730
Ezek 3:18 *If I **w** the wicked,* 1047
Ezek 33:3 *the alarm to **w** the people*.........1109
Matt 16:6 *"Watch out!" Jesus **w-ed** them*...1374
Luke 16:28 *I want him to **w** them so*........1412
Acts 4:17 *must **w** them not to speak*........1519
1 Cor 4:14 *to **w** you as my beloved*..........1601
1 Cor 10:11 *written down to **w** us who*.....1610
Col 1:28 ***w-ing** everyone and teaching*.....1697
1 Thes 4:6 *solemnly **w-ed** you before*.......1584
1 Thes 5:14 *urge you to **w** those who*.......1586
2 Thes 3:15 *but **w** them as you would*......1590
Heb 3:13 *You must **w** each other.*............1765

WARNING, WARNINGS (n) something that warns or serves to warn; the act of warning
Ps 19:11 *They are a **w** to your servant,*.......555
Ps 81:8 *while I give you stern **w-s.***...........602
Jer 6:8 *Listen to this **w,** Jerusalem,*............967
Jer 42:19 *Don't forget this **w** I have*..........1106
Zeph 3:7 *they will listen to my **w-s.***............986
1 Cor 10:6 *happened as a **w** to us,*...........1610
1 Tim 5:20 *as a strong **w** to others.*..........1734
Titus 3:10 *give a first and second **w.***........1739

WARRIOR, WARRIORS (n) a man engaged or experienced in warfare
Gen 6:4 *and famous **w-s** of ancient*..............17
Exod 15:3 *LORD is a **w;** Yahweh*.................161
Josh 1:14 *strong **w-s,** fully armed,*.............337
1 Chr 28:3 *for you are a **w** and*..................539
Ps 45:3 *your sword, O mighty **w!***.................851
Jer 20:11 *beside me like a great **w.***...........999

WASH, WASHED (v) to cleanse—of physical, ceremonial, or spiritual significance
see also BAPTIZE(D), CLEANSE
Ps 51:7 ***w** me, and I will be whiter*.............506
John 13:5 *he began to **w** the disciples'*.....1456
John 13:10 *does not need to **w,** except*....1456
Acts 22:16 *Have your sins **w-ed** away*......1679

Eph 5:26 *holy and clean, **w-ed** by the* 1714
Titus 3:5 *He **w-ed** away our sins,* 1739
Heb 10:22 *bodies have been **w-ed*** 1775
Jas 4:8 ***W** your hands, you sinners;* 1551
2 Pet 2:22 ***w-ed** pig returns to the mud*....1759
Rev 7:14 *They have **w-ed** their robes in*...1813
Rev 22:14 *those who **w** their robes.* 1832

WASHBASIN (n) a large bowl for water that is used to wash
Exod 30:18 *Make a bronze **w** with a*...........182

WASTE, WASTED (v) to spend or use carelessly or inefficiently
Ps 127:1 *work of the builders is **w-d.***.........631
Prov 29:3 *prostitutes, his wealth is **w-d.***........844
Prov 31:3 *do not **w** your strength* 847
Luke 15:13 *there he **w-d** all his money*....1410
John 6:12 *so that nothing is **w-d.*** 1365
Gal 2:2 *all my efforts had been **w-d*** 1558

WATCH (n) the act of keeping awake to guard, protect, or attend
Matt 24:42 *you, too, must keep **w!***...........1447
Acts 20:31 *my constant **w** and care* 1676

WATCH, WATCHES, WATCHING (v) to diligently wait or keep guard; to observe closely
Judg 18:6 *the* LORD *is **w-ing** over* 404
Job 14:16 *my steps, instead of **w-ing***........108
Job 34:21 *God **w-es** how people live;* 124
Ps 1:6 *For the* LORD ***w-es** over the* 856
Ps 17:11 *and surround me, **w-ing** for*........553
Ps 61:7 *faithfulness **w** over him.* 574
Ps 121:3 *one who **w-es** over you will*.........882
Prov 2:11 *Wise choices will **w** over*...............634
Prov 31:27 *carefully **w-es** everything* 848
Eccl 11:4 *If they **w** every cloud,* 682
Jer 24:6 *I will **w** over and care for* 1029
Jer 31:10 *gather them and **w** over* 1033
Acts 1:9 *while they were **w-ing,** and*........1500
Eph 6:6 *just when they are **w-ing** you.* 1715
Heb 13:17 *is to **w** over your souls,*.............1783
1 Pet 1:12 *eagerly **w-ing** these things* 1749
1 Pet 3:12 *eyes of the Lord **w** over*...........1753

WATCHER (n) one who watches
Job 7:20 *you, O **w** of all humanity?*.............102

WATCHMAN (n) a person who keeps watch; guard
Ezek 3:17 *you as a **w** for Israel.*................1047
Ezek 33:6 *hold the **w** responsible*.............1118
Ezek 33:7 *you a **w** for the people* 1118

WATER, WATERS (n) precious resource for drink and irrigation, usually associated with blessing; a body of water
Exod 7:20 *struck the **w** of the Nile.* 150
Exod 17:1 *there was no **w** there for*...........165
Num 20:2 *was no **w** for the people.*............261
2 Sam 23:15 *good **w** from the well* 480
Ps 42:1 *streams of **w,** so I long* 848
Prov 25:21 *give them **w** to drink.*................840
Song 8:7 *Many **w-s** cannot quench.*............670
Isa 11:9 *for as the **w-s** fill the sea,*.............796
Isa 32:2 *like streams of **w** in the.*................902
Isa 43:2 *through deep **w-s,** I will be* 928
Isa 49:10 *lead them beside cool **w-s.***.........936
Jer 17:8 *reach deep into the **w.***...................1021
Jonah 2:3 *The mighty **w-s** engulfed me;*.....767
Hab 2:14 *For as the **w-s** fill the sea,*...........980
Zech 14:8 *life-giving **w-s** will flow*...........1180
Matt 14:25 *them, walking on the **w.*** 1365
John 3:5 *born of **w** and the Spirit.* 1301
John 4:10 *would give you living **w.*** 1304
John 7:38 *Rivers of living **w** will* 1390
1 Jn 5:6 *his baptism in **w** and by.*............1794
Rev 7:17 *springs of life-giving **w.*** 1813
Rev 21:6 *springs of the **w** of life.*..............1830

WATERED, WATERING (v) to moisten, sprinkle, or soak with water
Joel 3:18 ***w-ing** the arid valley of acacias.*...1244
1 Cor 3:6 *hearts, and Apollos **w-ed** it,* 1599
1 Cor 3:7 *planting, or who does the **w-ing.*** 1599

WATERPROOF (v) to cover or treat with a material to prevent permeation by water
Gen 6:14 *cypress wood and **w** it with* 18

WAVE, WAVES (n) a moving ridge or swell on the surface of a liquid (as of the sea)
Matt 8:27 *the winds and **w-s** obey him!*...1350
Jas 1:6 *unsettled as a **w** of the* 1546

WAVER, WAVERED, WAVERING (v) to fluctuate in opinion, allegiance, or direction
Rom 4:20 *Abraham never **w-ed** in believing*..1653
Jude 1:22 *to those whose faith is **w-ing.***..1786

WAY, WAYS (n) characteristic, regular, or habitual manner or mode of being, behaving, or happening; manner or method of doing or happening; a course of action; route; early name for Christianity
Exod 33:13 *let me know your **w-s***.............186
Deut 26:17 *to walk in his **w-s,** and* 316
Deut 30:16 *by walking in his **w-s.***..............321
Josh 22:5 *walk in all his **w-s,** obey* 366
2 Sam 22:31 *God's **w** is perfect.* 527
Ps 77:13 *O God, your **w-s** are holy.*...........597
Ps 86:11 *Teach me your **w-s,** O* LORD,.........579
Prov 2:9 *find the right **w** to go.* 634
Prov 4:11 *teach you wisdom's **w-s***............636
Eccl 8:6 *and a **w** for everything,* 679
Isa 2:3 *teach us his **w-s,** and we will*..........825
Isa 40:3 *Clear the **w** through the* 923
Jer 6:16 *old, godly **w,** and walk in* 968
Mic 4:2 *teach us his **w-s,** and we will*.........907
Mal 3:1 *prepare the **w** before me.* 1247
Matt 3:3 *Prepare the **w** for the* 1287
Matt 3:8 *Prove by the **w** you live.*..............1288
Luke 7:27 *prepare your **w** before you.* 1338
John 14:6 *I am the **w,** the truth,* 1461
Acts 9:2 *followers of the **W** he*.................1529
Acts 24:14 *I follow the **W,** which*...............1682
Rom 1:30 *invent new **w-s** of sinning,* 1648
1 Cor 10:13 *will show you a **w** out* 1610
1 Cor 12:31 *show you a **w** of life*..............1615
Col 1:10 *Then the **w** you live will* 1694
Heb 10:20 *and life-giving **w** through*.........1775

WAYWARD (adj) following one's own capricious, wanton, or depraved inclinations
Jer 3:14 *Return home, you **w** children,* 963
Jer 3:22 *will heal your **w** hearts.*.................963

WEAK, WEAKER, WEAKEST (adj) lacking strength; not able to withstand temptation or persuasion
Ps 72:13 *pity for the **w** and the* 630
Ps 103:14 *he knows how **w** we are;* 580
Isa 59:1 *arm is not too **w** to save.*...............945
Matt 12:20 *will not crush the **w-est** reed.*.1322
Matt 26:41 *but the body is **w!***..................1468
Rom 14:1 *who are **w** in faith,*....................1669
1 Cor 8:9 *others with a **w-er** conscience*..1608
1 Cor 9:22 *bring the **w** to Christ.* 1609
1 Cor 11:30 *many of you are **w** and*...........1614
1 Cor 12:22 *of the body that seem **w-est.***1615
2 Cor 12:10 *For when I am **w,** then*..........1642
1 Thes 5:14 *care of those who are **w.***........1586

WEAKNESS, WEAKNESSES (n) the quality or state of being weak
Ps 136:23 *He remembered us in our **w.*** 886
Isa 53:4 *it was our **w-es** he carried;*.........940
Rom 8:3 *the **w** of our sinful nature.*...........1658
Rom 8:26 *Spirit helps us in our **w.***............1660
1 Cor 1:25 *God's **w** is stronger than* 1597
1 Cor 2:3 *I came to you in **w**—timid.*........1598
2 Cor 12:5 *boast only about my **w-es.*** 1641
2 Cor 12:10 *take pleasure in my **w-es,*** 1642
2 Cor 13:4 *he was crucified in **w,*** 1643
Heb 5:2 *is subject to the same **w-es.*** 1767

WEALTH (n) abundance of valuable material possessions or resources
see also MONEY, POSSESSIONS, RICHES, TREASURE(S)
2 Chr 1:11 *not ask for **w,** riches,* 608
Job 36:18 *you may be seduced by **w.***.........126
Ps 39:6 *We heap up **w,** not knowing.*..........569
Ps 62:10 *if your **w** increases, don't* 574
Prov 3:9 *the* LORD *with your **w*** 635
Prov 10:2 *Tainted **w** has no lasting*.............641
Prov 13:11 ***w** from hard work grows*...........646
Prov 21:20 *wise have **w** and luxury,*...........658
Prov 29:3 *prostitutes, his **w** is wasted.*.........844
Eccl 4:8 *gain as much **w** as he can.* 676
Luke 19:8 *give half my **w** to the poor,* 1426
Eph 2:7 *of the incredible **w** of his* 1707
1 Tim 6:6 *contentment is itself great **w.*** 1735
Jas 5:3 *The very **w** you were counting*......1553

WEALTHY (adj) characterized by abundance
Prov 11:24 *freely and become more **w;*** 644
Eccl 2:26 *sinner becomes **w,** God takes*......675
1 Cor 1:26 *or **w** when God called you.* 1597

WEAPON, WEAPONS (n) something used to injure, defeat, or destroy
Prov 26:18 *shooting a deadly **w*** 841
Eccl 9:18 *have wisdom than **w-s** of war,*.....681
2 Cor 6:7 *use the **w-s** of righteousness*....1633

WEARY (adj) exhausted in strength, endurance, or vigor
Isa 40:31 *They will run and not grow **w.***.......925
Isa 50:4 *know how to comfort the **w.***...........937
Matt 11:28 *you who are **w** and carry*.........1339
2 Cor 5:2 *We grow **w** in our present*.........1631
Heb 12:3 *won't become **w** and give up.*....1780

WEDDING, WEDDINGS (n) a marriage ceremony usually with its accompanying festivities
Matt 11:17 *We played **w** songs, and*.........1338
Matt 22:11 *the proper clothes for a **w.***......1438
Matt 24:38 *parties and **w-s** right up*.........1447
Rev 19:7 *for the **w** feast of the Lamb,*........1827

WEEDS (n) undesirable growth surrounding a plant
Matt 13:25 *and planted **w** among the*.......1348

WEEK (n) a seven-day cycle
1 Cor 16:2 *of each **w,** you should*............1622

WEEP, WEEPING (v) to cry aloud, often linked with prayer and repentance
2 Sam 1:26 *How I **w** for you,*.......................477
Ps 126:6 *They **w** as they go to*................1154
Jer 31:16 *Do not **w** any longer,* 1033
Jer 50:4 *will come **w-ing** and seeking.*.......1035
Matt 2:18 *heard in Ramah—**w-ing** and*...1285
Matt 8:12 *will be **w-ing** and gnashing*......1336
Luke 6:21 *blesses you who **w** now,*...........1326
Luke 22:62 *the courtyard, **w-ing** bitterly.*..1474

Luke 23:28 *don't **w** for me, but **w***...........1482
Rom 12:15 *and **w** with those who **w.***........1668

WEEPING (n) shedding of tears out of grief or sadness
Jer 31:15 *deep anguish and bitter **w.***.......1033
Matt 2:18 *heard in Ramah—**w** and*..........1285
Matt 8:12 *will be **w** and gnashing*............1336

WEIGHED, WEIGHS (v) to oppress or depress; to measure weight
Ps 146:8 *up those who are **w-ed** down.*.....887
Prov 12:25 *Worry **w-s** a person down;*.......645
Isa 53:4 *our sorrows that **w-ed** him*...........940
Dan 5:27 *Tekel means '**w-ed**'—you*........1139

WEIGHT, WEIGHTS (n) a piece of material (as metal) of known specified weight for use in weighing articles; burden, hindrance
Lev 19:36 *Your scales and **w-s** must be*.....226
Prov 11:1 *he delights in accurate **w-s.***.......643
Heb 12:1 *strip off every **w** that slows*........1780

WELCOME (n) the state of being accepted with pleasure
Prov 25:17 *you will wear out your **w.***..........840

WELCOMED, WELCOMES, WELCOMING (v) to greet hospitably and with courtesy or cordiality
Matt 18:5 *And anyone who **w-s** a little*.....1383
Mark 9:37 *Anyone who **w-s** a little child*...1383
John 13:20 *who **w-s** my messenger*.........1456
John 13:20 ***w-s** me is **w-ing** the Father*..1456
Acts 28:7 *He **w-d** us and treated us*.........1688

WELL (adj) completely cured or healed (physically or spiritually)
Isa 38:9 *King Hezekiah was **w** again,*..........921
Matt 15:31 *the crippled were made **w,***.....1372
Matt 17:18 *that moment the boy was **w.***...1381
Mark 5:34 *your faith has made you **w.***......1354
Jas 5:15 *the Lord will make you **w.***..........1553

WELL (adv) in a prosperous or affluent manner; in a kindly or friendly manner
Deut 6:18 *all will go **w** with you.*................295
Eph 6:3 *things will go **w** for you,*..............1714
1 Tim 3:7 *church must speak **w** of him*.....1730

WEPT (v) to cry aloud
see also WEEP
Ps 137:1 *we sat and **w** as we thought*......1118
John 11:35 *Then Jesus **w.***......................1415

WEST (n) the general direction of the sunset
Ps 103:12 *as the east is from the **w.***..........580
Ps 107:3 *from east and **w,** from north*........871

WHEAT (n) a cereal grain that yields a fine white flour
Matt 3:12 *gathering the **w** into his barn*....1289
Matt 13:25 *among the **w,** then slipped*.....1348
Mark 4:28 *the heads of **w** are formed,*......1348
Luke 22:31 *sift each of you like **w.***...........1460
John 12:24 *a kernel of **w** is planted in*......1432

WHEELS (n) circular frames of hard material capable of turning on an axle
Ezek 1:16 *All four **w** looked alike*.............1045

WHIPPED (v) to strike with a lash or rod
2 Cor 11:23 *been **w** times without*...........1641

WHIRLWIND (n) a small rotating windstorm, sometimes violent and destructive
see also STORM, WIND
2 Kgs 2:1 *to heaven in a **w,***.........................738
Job 38:1 *answered Job from the **w:***..........127
Hos 8:7 *and will harvest the **w.***..................811
Nah 1:3 *in the **w** and the storm.*................974

WHISPER (n) a minor or softer reflection of the original noise; hint, trace
1 Kgs 19:12 *sound of a gentle **w.***..............720
Job 26:14 *merely a **w** of his power.*............117
Ps 107:29 *calmed the storm to a **w***...........872

WHISPER (v) to speak softly with little or no vibration of the vocal cords
Matt 10:27 *What I **w** in your ear,*...............1360

WHITE, WHITER (adj) free from color; of the color white
Ps 51:7 *I will be **w-r** than snow.*................506
Isa 1:18 *make them as **w** as snow.*............824
Dan 7:9 *clothing was as **w** as snow,*........1135
Matt 28:3 *clothing was as **w** as snow.*......1489
Rev 1:14 *like wool, as **w** as snow.*............1800
Rev 6:2 *saw a **w** horse standing*...............1811
Rev 19:11 *a **w** horse was standing*...........1828
Rev 20:11 *saw a great **w** throne*...............1830

WHITE (n) the absence of color; free from spot or blemish
Rev 3:4 *will walk with me in **w,***...............1806
Rev 7:13 *who are clothed in **w?***..............1813

WHITEWASHED (adj) glossed over with whitewash
Matt 23:27 *are like **w** tombs—*................1444

WHOLE (adj) entire; complete, unmodified; undivided
1 Sam 1:28 *LORD his **w** life.*......................418
1 Sam 17:46 *the **w** world will know*...........451
1 Chr 28:9 *him with your **w** heart*..............540
Ps 72:19 *Let the **w** earth be filled*..............630
Ps 103:1 *with my **w** heart, I will*................580
Prov 4:22 *healing to their **w** body.*.............636
Eccl 12:13 *That's the **w** story.*..................683
Isa 6:3 *The **w** earth is filled*.......................783
Isa 14:26 *plan for the **w** earth,*....................832
Dan 2:35 *covered the **w** earth.*..................1004
Zeph 1:18 *For the **w** land will be*................984
Matt 6:22 *eye is good, your **w** body*..........1332
Matt 16:26 *gain the **w** world but lose*.......1377
Matt 24:14 *throughout the **w** world,*.........1446
John 21:25 *I suppose the **w** world*...........1497
Acts 17:26 *throughout the **w** earth.*..........1578
1 Cor 12:17 *Or if your **w** body were*..........1615
Gal 5:3 *regulation in the **w** law of*............1565

WHOLEHEARTEDLY (adv) in a completely and sincerely devoted, determined, or enthusiastic manner
Num 32:11 *they have not obeyed me **w.***....279
Deut 11:18 *commit yourselves **w** to.*..........301
Deut 26:16 *careful to obey them **w.***..........316
Josh 14:8 *For my part, I **w** followed*............358
Josh 24:14 *LORD and serve him **w.***............370
1 Chr 29:9 *had given freely and **w.***...........541
2 Chr 25:2 *sight, but not **w.***.......................761
2 Chr 31:21 *sought his God **w.***..................839
Jer 29:13 *look for me **w,** you will.*............1030
Jer 32:41 *faithfully and **w** replant*.............1080
Phil 2:2 *happy by agreeing **w** with*............1719

WHOLESOME (adj) promoting health or well-being of mind or spirit
see also SOUND
1 Tim 1:10 *contradicts the **w** teaching*......1728
1 Tim 6:3 *these are the **w** teachings*.........1734
Titus 1:9 *others with **w** teaching and*........1737
Titus 2:1 *that reflects **w** teaching.*............1738
2 Pet 3:1 *stimulate your **w** thinking*...........1760

WHORE (KJV)
Lev 21:7 *woman **defiled by prostitution***....228
Deut 23:18 *the earnings of a **prostitute***......313
Prov 23:27 ***prostitute** is a dangerous trap*....661
Hos 4:14 *sinning with **whores***.....................807
Rev 17:1 ***prostitute,** who rules over*..........1824

WICKED (adj) morally very bad
Gen 13:13 *area were extremely **w** and*.........32
Ps 7:9 *those who are **w,** and defend*...........523
Prov 10:7 *name of a **w** person rots*.............642
Prov 26:23 *may hide a **w** heart, just*...........841
Jer 35:15 *Turn from your **w** ways,*............1024
Ezek 18:21 *But if **w** people turn away*.......1064
Ezek 21:25 *you corrupt and **w** prince*.......1068
Ezek 33:8 *that some **w** people are sure*....1118
Hos 10:9 *not right that the **w** men of*.........813
Jonah 1:2 *I have seen how **w** its people*......765
Luke 6:35 *who are unthankful and **w.***.......1330
1 Jn 5:17 *All **w** actions are sin,*................1795

WICKED (n) those who practice evil
2 Sam 22:27 *but to the **w** you show*...........526
Ps 1:1 *the advice of the **w,** or stand*...........856
Ps 10:13 *Why do the **w** get away with*........857
Ps 12:8 *though the **w** strut about,*.............551
Ps 14:6 *The **w** frustrate the plans*..............552
Ps 18:26 *but to the **w** you show*...................528
Ps 37:1 *worry about the **w** or envy*.............567
Ps 82:2 *by favoring the **w?***........................602
Ps 101:8 *ferret out the **w** and free*.............580
Ps 139:19 *you would destroy the **w!***..........586
Ps 146:9 *the plans of the **w.***.........................887
Prov 4:14 *Don't do as the **w** do,*.................636
Prov 9:7 *who corrects the **w** will*..................641
Prov 10:28 *expectations of the **w** come*......643
Prov 12:5 *of the **w** is treacherous.*..............645
Prov 29:7 *the **w** don't care at all*..................845
Isa 5:23 *to let the **w** go free,*........................830
Isa 11:4 *mouth will destroy the **w.***...............796
Isa 26:10 *the **w** keep doing wrong*..............896
Isa 48:22 *no peace for the **w,***........................935
Mal 4:1 *arrogant and the **w** will be*...........1249

WICKEDNESS (n) the quality or state of being wicked; something wicked
Lev 16:21 *it all the **w,** rebellion,*..................222
Lev 19:29 *with prostitution and **w.***...............226
Deut 9:4 *because of the **w** of the other*......298
Ps 73:3 *them prosper despite their **w.***.........594
Jer 3:2 *your prostitution and your **w.***.........962
Jer 14:16 *out their own **w** on them.*...........1018
Jer 14:20 *we confess our **w** and that*.......1018
Ezek 33:19 *turn from their **w** and do*........1118
Luke 11:39 *of greed and **w!***.......................1398
Rom 1:18 *the truth by their **w.***....................1647
Rom 1:29 *every kind of **w,** sin, greed,*.......1648
Rom 2:8 *and instead live lives of **w.***..........1649
2 Cor 6:14 *be a partner with **w?***................1634
Heb 8:12 *I will forgive their **w,***....................1772

WIDE-OPEN (adj) having virtually no limits or restrictions
1 Cor 16:9 *a **w** door for a great*...................1623

WIDE (adj) fully opened; having great extent
Ps 81:10 *Open your mouth **w,** and I*...........602
Matt 7:13 *its gate is **w** for the*....................1334
Eph 3:18 *should, how **w,** how long,*...........1709

WIDOW, WIDOWS (n) a woman whose husband has died
Deut 10:18 *orphans and **w-s** receive*.........300
Ps 68:5 *defender of **w-s**—this is God,*.......576
Ps 146:9 *for the orphans and **w-s,** but*........887
Isa 1:17 *Fight for the rights of **w-s.***.............824
Luke 21:2 *Then a poor **w** came by and*.....1445
Acts 6:1 *that their **w-s** were being*...........1522
1 Cor 7:8 *aren't married and to **w-s**—*.....1605

1 Tim 5:3 *Take care of any* **w** *who*............1733
1 Tim 5:16 *care for the* **w-s** *who are*........1733
Jas 1:27 *for orphans and* **w-s** *in their*.......1548

WIFE (n) the female partner in a marriage
see also WIVES
Gen 2:24 *and is joined to his* **w,**..................11
Gen 19:26 *But Lot's* **w** *looked back*.............42
Exod 20:17 *covet your neighbor's* **w,**.........170
Lev 20:10 *his neighbor's* **w,** *both*...............227
Deut 5:21 *not covet your neighbor's* **w.**.......293
Deut 24:5 *happiness to the* **w** *he has*.........314
Prov 5:18 *Rejoice in the* **w** *of your*.............637
Prov 12:4 *A worthy* **w** *is a crown*...............644
Prov 18:22 *man who finds a* **w**.....................654
Prov 19:13 *a quarrelsome* **w** *is as*.............655
Prov 21:9 *a quarrelsome* **w** *in a*..................657
Prov 31:10 *a virtuous and capable* **w?**.........847
Mal 2:14 *vows you and your* **w** *made*........1247
Matt 1:20 *to take Mary as your* **w.**..........1277
Matt 19:3 *to divorce his* **w** *for just*..........1418
Luke 17:32 *happened to Lot's* **w!**.............1416
Luke 18:29 *up house or* **w** *or brothers*......1422
1 Cor 7:2 *should have his own* **w,**.............1605
1 Cor 7:15 *the husband or* **w** *who isn't*.....1606
1 Cor 7:33 *and how to please his* **w.** 1607
Eph 5:23 *head of his* **w** *as Christ*.............1713
Eph 5:33 *love his* **w** *as he loves*...............1714
1 Tim 3:12 *be faithful to his* **w,**...............1731
Titus 1:6 *be faithful to his* **w,**....................1736
1 Pet 3:7 *Treat your* **w** *with*.......................1753
Rev 21:9 *bride, the* **w** *of the Lamb*............1830

WILD (adj) not tame or domesticated; growing without human aid; uncontrolled, unruly
Gen 1:25 *made all sorts of* **w** *animals,*............7
Gen 8:1 *and all the* **w** *animals*.......................19
Luke 15:13 *his money in* **w** *living.*..........1410
Rom 11:17 *branches from a* **w** *olive*.........1665

WILDERNESS (n) any desolate, barren, or unpopulated area, usually linked with danger
see also DESERT
Num 16:13 *kill us here in this* **w,**...............256
Num 26:65 *all die in the* **w.**.........................272
Num 32:13 *wander in the* **w** *for forty*..........279
Deut 8:16 *manna in the* **w,** *a food*..............297
Deut 29:5 *led you through the* **w,**...............320
Ps 78:19 *give us food in the* **w.**...................598
Ps 78:52 *safely through the* **w.**.....................599
Isa 32:15 **w** *will become a fertile*.................902
Isa 35:6 *will gush forth in the* **w,**..................905
Matt 3:3 *the* **w,** *'Prepare the way*.............1287
Luke 5:16 *withdrew to the* **w** *for*...............1312
Rev 12:6 *fled into the* **w,** *where God*.........1818

WILDFLOWERS (n) the flower of a wild or uncultivated plant
Ps 103:15 *like grass; like* **w,** *we bloom*.......580
Matt 6:30 *so wonderfully for* **w** *that are*......1332

WILL (n) desire, wish
Ps 40:8 *in doing your* **w,** *my God,*...............570
Ps 143:10 *me to do your* **w,** *for you*............588
Prov 3:6 *Seek his* **w** *in all you do,*...............634
Matt 6:10 *May your* **w** *be done on*............1331
Matt 7:21 *who actually do the* **w**..............1334
Matt 12:50 *does the* **w** *of my Father*.........1344
Matt 18:14 *heavenly Father's* **w** *that*.........1385
Matt 26:39 *want your* **w** *to be done,*..........1468
Matt 26:42 *I drink it, your* **w** *be done.*........1468
John 5:30 *carry out the* **w** *of the one*........1319
John 6:38 *heaven to do the* **w** *of God*.......1367
Rom 12:2 *learn to know God's* **w**.............1666
1 Thes 5:18 *this is God's* **w** *for you*...........1586

Heb 10:7 *come to do your* **w,** *O God—*.....1775
Heb 13:21 *need for doing his* **w.**..............1783
1 Pet 4:2 *to do the* **w** *of God.*...................1754

WILLING (adj) inclined or favorably disposed in mind; done, borne, or accepted by choice or without reluctance
1 Chr 28:9 *heart and a* **w** *mind.*.................540
Ps 51:12 *and make me* **w** *to obey you*........506
Dan 3:28 *command and were* **w** *to die*.....1007
Matt 26:41 *spirit is* **w,** *but the body*..........1468
Rom 9:3 *I would be* **w** *to be forever*..........1661

WIN (v) to be the victor in
1 Jn 5:5 *who can* **w** *this battle*.................1794
Rev 6:2 *rode out to* **w** *many battles*..........1811

WIND, WINDS (n) a natural movement of air
see also STORM, WHIRLWIND
Ps 1:4 *chaff, scattered by the* **w.**................856
Eccl 2:11 *like chasing the* **w.**......................674
Hos 8:7 *have planted the* **w** *and*..................811
Mark 4:41 *Even the* **w** *and waves*............1350
John 3:8 *The* **w** *blows wherever*..............1302
Eph 4:14 *blown about by every* **w**............1711
Heb 1:7 *his angels like the* **w-s,**...............1762
Jas 1:6 *and tossed by the* **w.** 1546

WINDOW, WINDOWS (n) an opening in the wall of a building
Josh 2:21 *rope hanging from the* **w.**...........338
Mal 3:10 *will open the* **w-s** *of heaven*........1248
2 Cor 11:33 *a basket through a* **w**.............1641

WINDOWSILL (n) the edge at the bottom of a window opening
Acts 20:9 *sitting on the* **w,** *became*..........1675

WINE (n) the fermented juice of grapes, linked positively with blessings and negatively with drunkenness
Ps 104:15 **w** *to make them glad,* 867
Prov 31:6 *and* **w** *for those in bitter* 847
Song 1:2 *love is sweeter than* **w.**................663
Isa 28:7 *who reel with* **w** *and stagger*.........818
Mark 15:36 *with sour* **w,** *holding it*...........1486
John 2:3 *The* **w** *supply ran out*................1299
Rom 14:21 *to eat meat or drink* **w**...........1670
Eph 5:18 *Don't be drunk with* **w,**.............1713
1 Tim 5:23 *drink a little* **w** *for*...................1734
Rev 16:19 *was filled with the* **w**...............1824

WINEBIBBER(S) (KJV)
Prov 23:20 *not carouse with* **drunkards**.......661
Matt 11:19 *glutton and a* **drunkard,** *and*....1338
Luke 7:34 *glutton and a* **drunkard,** *and*....1339

WINEPRESS (n) a vat in which the juice from grapes is pressed in the process of making wine
Rev 19:15 *juice flowing from a* **w.** 1828

WINESKINS (n) a bag used for holding wine, made from the skin of an animal
Matt 9:17 *stored in new* **w** *so that*..........1316
Luke 5:37 *new wine into old* **w.**...............1317

WINGS (n) feathered appendages of a bird, figurative of freedom, strength, and protection from God
Exod 19:4 *carried you on eagles'* **w**...........167
Ps 17:8 *in the shadow of your* **w.** 553
Ps 91:4 *shelter you with his* **w.**....................861
Isa 6:2 *each having six* **w.**............................783
Isa 40:31 *high on* **w** *like eagles.*....................925
Mal 4:2 *rise with healing in his* **w.** 1249
Luke 13:34 *chicks beneath her* **w,**...........1407
Rev 4:8 *living beings had six* **w,**.................1808

WIPE, WIPED (v) to clean or dry by rubbing; to expunge completely
Isa 25:8 *will* **w** *away all tears*......................895
Luke 7:38 *she* **w-d** *them off with her* 1340
Acts 3:19 *your sins may be* **w-d** *away.* 1517
Rev 7:17 *And God will* **w** *every tear*..........1813
Rev 21:4 *He will* **w** *every tear*...................1830

WISDOM (n) knowledge, insight, judgment
Gen 3:6 *she wanted the* **w** *it would*...............11
1 Kgs 4:29 *gave Solomon very great* **w**.......629
1 Kgs 10:24 *to hear the* **w** *God had*...........627
2 Chr 1:10 *Give me the* **w** *and*...................608
Job 11:6 **w,** *for true* **w** *is not*......................105
Job 42:3 *that questions my* **w** *with such*......132
Ps 51:6 *teaching me* **w** *even there.*............506
Prov 2:6 *the LORD grants* **w!**.......................633
Prov 3:13 *the person who finds* **w,**..............635
Prov 8:11 **w** *is far more valuable*...............640
Prov 11:2 *with humility comes* **w.**................643
Prov 16:16 *better to get* **w** *than gold,*..........651
Prov 23:23 *also get* **w,** *discipline,*..............661
Prov 29:3 *man who loves* **w** *brings joy*.........844
Eccl 10:10 *the value of* **w;** *it helps*.............681
Isa 11:2 *on him—the Spirit of* **w**................795
Isa 50:4 *me his words of* **w,** *so that*............937
Luke 2:52 *Jesus grew in* **w** *and in*............1287
Acts 6:3 *full of the Spirit and* **w.** 1522
1 Cor 1:21 *him through human* **w,** *he*.......1597
Eph 1:17 *you spiritual* **w** *and insight*.........1706
Col 2:3 *treasures of* **w** *and knowledge.*......1697
Col 3:16 *with all the* **w** *he gives*................1701
2 Tim 3:15 *given you the* **w** *to receive* 1745
Titus 2:12 *world with* **w,** *righteousness,* 1738
Jas 1:5 *If you need* **w,** *ask our*...................1546
Rev 5:12 *riches and* **w** *and strength* 1810

WISE, WISER, WISEST (adj) marked by deep understanding, keen discernment, and a capacity for sound judgment
1 Kgs 3:12 *you a* **w** *and understanding*.......606
Job 9:4 *God is so* **w** *and so mighty.*............103
Ps 14:2 *anyone is truly* **w,** *if anyone*...........552
Ps 19:7 *are trustworthy, making* **w** *the*........554
Ps 119:100 *I am even* **w-r** *than my*............880
Prov 4:7 *wisdom is the* **w-st** *thing*...............636
Prov 9:8 *correct the* **w,** *and they*..................641
Prov 10:1 *A* **w** *child brings joy to*.................641
Prov 11:30 *a* **w** *person wins friends*............644
Prov 12:16 *a* **w** *person stays calm*...............645
Prov 12:18 *of the* **w** *bring healing*................645
Prov 13:1 *A* **w** *child accepts a parent's*.......646
Prov 13:10 *who take advice are* **w.**..............646
Prov 13:20 *Walk with the* **w** *and*..................646
Prov 15:5 *learns from correction is* **w.** 648
Prov 16:23 *From a* **w** *mind comes* **w**..........651
Prov 18:4 *wisdom flows from the* **w**............653
Prov 19:25 *they will be all the* **w-r.**..............655
Prov 24:5 **w** *are mightier than the*..............662
Prov 28:7 *who obey the law are* **w;**..............843
Eccl 8:5 *who are* **w** *will find a time*..............679
Eccl 9:17 *quiet words of a* **w** *person*...........681
Matt 2:1 *some* **w** *men from eastern*..........1283
Matt 11:25 *who think themselves* **w**..........1339
Matt 25:2 *foolish, and five were* **w.**...........1451
Rom 3:11 *No one is truly* **w;** *no one*..........1651
1 Cor 1:19 *wisdom of the* **w** *and*................1596
1 Cor 1:25 *plan of God is* **w-r** *than*.............1597
1 Cor 12:8 *ability to give* **w** *advice;*...........1614
Jas 3:13 *If you are* **w** *and understand*.........1550

WITCHCRAFT (n) the use of sorcery or magic
Lev 19:26 *practice fortune-telling or* **w.** 226

Deut 18:10 *omens, or engage in* **w,** ...308
Rev 21:8 *those who practice* **w,** *idol* ...1830

WITHDRAW, WITHDREW (v) to remove; to retreat
Ps 66:20 *or* **w** *his unfailing love from* ...859
Luke 5:16 *But Jesus often* **w-ew** *to the* ...1312

WITHER, WITHERS (v) to shrivel and lose vitality, force, or freshness
Job 14:2 *like a flower and then* **w.** ...108
Ps 1:3 *leaves never* **w,** *and they* ...856
Isa 40:7 *grass* **w-s** *and the flowers* ...924
Isa 64:6 *autumn leaves, we* **w** *and fall,* ...950
1 Pet 1:24 *grass* **w-s** *and the flower* ...1750

WITHHELD (v) to refrain from granting, giving, or allowing
Gen 22:12 *You have not* **w** *from me* ...46

WITNESS, WITNESSES (n) a person who gives testimony; one asked to be present at a transaction so as to be able to testify to its having taken place
Deut 19:15 *of two or three* **w-es.** ...309
Prov 19:5 *A false* **w** *will not go* ...654
Prov 21:28 *but a credible* **w** *will be* ...658
Matt 18:16 *by two or three* **w-es.** ...1385
John 1:8 *simply a* **w** *to tell about* ...1271
Acts 1:8 *will be my* **w-es,** *telling people* ...1500
1 Tim 5:19 *by two or three* **w-es.** ...1734
1 Jn 5:7 *we have these three* **w-es—** ...1794

WITNESSED (v) had personal or direct cognizance of
Mal 2:14 *the* L*ORD* **w** *the vows* ...1247

WIVES (n) the female partner in marriage
see also WIFE
Eph 5:22 *For* **w,** *this means submit* ...1713
Eph 5:25 *this means love your* **w,** ...1713
1 Pet 3:1 *way, you* **w** *must accept* ...1752

WOE (KJV)
Isa 6:5 ***It's all over!*** *I am doomed* ...784
Matt 18:7 ***What sorrow awaits*** *the world.* ...1384
Matt 23:13 ***What sorrow awaits*** *you* ...1444
1 Cor 9:16 ***How terrible*** *for me if I didn't* ...1608
Rev 8:13 ***Terror, terror, terror*** *to all who* ...1814

WOLVES (n) any of several wild, predatory animals that resemble large dogs
Matt 7:15 *but are really vicious* **w.** ...1334
Matt 10:16 *you out as sheep among* **w.** ...1359

WOMAN (n) an adult female person
see also WOMEN
Gen 2:22 *God made a* **w** *from the rib,* ...10
Gen 3:6 *The* **w** *was convinced* ...11
Gen 3:12 *It was the* **w** *you gave me* ...12
Gen 3:16 *he said to the* **w,** *"I will* ...13
Exod 3:22 *Every Israelite* **w** *will ask* ...144
Lev 12:2 *If a* **w** *becomes pregnant* ...216
Lev 15:19 *a* **w** *has her menstrual* ...220
Lev 15:25 *a* **w** *has a flow of blood* ...220
Num 5:29 *If a* **w** *goes astray and defiles* ...244
Judg 4:9 *be at the hands of a* **w.** ...379
Judg 16:4 *love with a* **w** *named Delilah,* ...400
Ruth 3:11 *knows you are a virtuous* **w.** ...414
2 Sam 11:2 *he noticed a* **w** *of unusual* ...502
2 Sam 20:16 *But a wise* **w** *in the town* ...523
Prov 11:16 *A gracious* **w** *gains respect,* ...643
Prov 11:22 *A beautiful* **w** *who lacks* ...644
Prov 14:1 *A wise* **w** *builds her* ...647
Prov 30:19 *how a man loves a* **w.** ...846
Prov 30:23 *a bitter* **w** *who finally gets* ...847
Prov 31:30 **w** *who fears the* L*ORD* ...848
Matt 5:28 *looks at a* **w** *with lust* ...1328
Matt 9:20 *Just then a* **w** *who had* ...1353
Matt 26:7 *was eating, a* **w** *came in* ...1427
Mark 7:25 *Right away a* **w** *who had* ...1372
Luke 7:39 *what kind of* **w** *is touching* ...1340
John 4:7 *Soon a Samaritan* **w** *came to* ...1304
John 8:3 *Pharisees brought a* **w** *who* ...1391
Rom 7:2 *when a* **w** *marries, the law* ...1657
1 Cor 7:2 *and each* **w** *should have* ...1605
1 Cor 7:34 *a married* **w** *has to think* ...1607
1 Cor 11:3 *the head of* **w** *is man, and* ...1612
1 Cor 11:6 *shameful for a* **w** *to have* ...1612
1 Cor 11:13 *it right for a* **w** *to pray* ...1612
Gal 4:4 *born of a* **w,** *subject to the* ...1562
Gal 4:31 *are children of the free* **w.** ...1565
Rev 12:1 *I saw a* **w** *clothed with the* ...1818
Rev 12:13 *he pursued the* **w** *who had* ...1819
Rev 17:3 *There I saw a* **w** *sitting on a* ...1824

WOMB (n) uterus
Ps 139:13 *together in my mother's* **w.** ...586
Prov 31:2 *O son of my* **w,** *O son* ...847
Jer 1:5 *you in your mother's* **w.** ...958
Luke 1:44 *baby in my* **w** *jumped for joy.* ...1275
John 3:4 *into his mother's* **w** *and be* ...1301

WOMEN (n) adult female persons
see also WOMAN
Gen 6:2 *saw the beautiful* **w** *and took* ...17
Song 1:3 *all the young* **w** *love you!* ...663
Mark 15:41 *Many other* **w** *who had* ...1486
Luke 1:42 *you above all* **w,** *and your* ...1275
Luke 23:27 *many grief-stricken* **w.** ...1482
Rom 1:26 *Even the* **w** *turned against* ...1648
1 Cor 7:25 *the young* **w** *who are not* ...1606
1 Tim 2:9 *I want* **w** *to be modest in* ...1729
2 Tim 3:6 *of vulnerable* **w** *who are* ...1744
Titus 2:3 *teach the older* **w** *to live in* ...1738
Titus 2:4 *train the younger* **w** *to love* ...1738
1 Pet 3:5 *how the holy* **w** *of old made* ...1752

WON (v) to gain victory
see also WIN
1 Kgs 20:11 *warrior who has already* **w.** ...722
1 Pet 3:1 *They will be* **w** *over* ...1752
1 Jn 2:13 *you have* **w** *your battle* ...1789

WONDERFUL (adj) marked by a marvelous, amazing, or extraordinary quality
1 Chr 16:9 *about his* **w** *deeds.* ...493
Job 37:14 *consider the* **w** *miracles* ...127
Ps 16:6 *What a* **w** *inheritance!* ...553
Ps 17:7 *unfailing love in* **w** *ways.* ...553
Ps 71:17 *about the* **w** *things you* ...860
Ps 72:18 *does such* **w** *things.* ...630
Ps 75:1 *tell of your* **w** *deeds.* ...595
Ps 105:2 *about his* **w** *deeds.* ...868
Ps 118:23 *it is* **w** *to see.* ...876
Ps 119:18 *to see the* **w** *truths in* ...878
Ps 119:27 *meditate on your* **w** *deeds.* ...878
Ps 119:129 *Your laws are* **w.** ...881
Ps 139:6 *knowledge is too* **w** *for* ...586
Ps 145:5 *and your* **w** *miracles.* ...589
Eccl 11:9 *Young people, it's* **w** *to be* ...682
Isa 9:6 *be called:* **W** *Counselor,* ...793
Isa 12:5 *he has done* **w** *things.* ...797
Isa 25:1 *You do such* **w** *things!* ...895
Matt 21:15 *saw these* **w** *miracles* ...1432
Matt 21:42 *and it is* **w** *to see.* ...1437
Luke 13:17 *rejoiced at the* **w** *things* ...1403
Acts 2:11 *about the* **w** *things God has* ...1514
Acts 20:24 *News about the* **w** *grace of* ...1675
2 Cor 10:12 *we are as* **w** *as these* ...1638
Titus 2:13 *hope to that* **w** *day when* ...1738

WONDERS (n) mighty works, miracles
1 Chr 16:12 *Remember the* **w** *he has* ...493
Ps 26:7 *and telling of all your* **w.** ...560
Ps 31:21 *has shown me the* **w** *of his* ...564
Ps 77:14 *are the God of great* **w!** ...597
Ps 89:5 *your great* **w,** L*ORD;* ...591
Mark 13:22 *perform signs and* **w** *so* ...1449
Acts 2:19 *will cause* **w** *in the heavens* ...1515
Acts 5:12 *signs and* **w** *among the people.* ...1520
2 Cor 12:12 *signs and* **w** *and miracles* ...1642
Heb 2:4 *signs and* **w** *and various* ...1763

WORD, WORDS (n) something that is said; special revelation from God; commands
Deut 8:3 *live by every* **w** *that comes* ...297
Deut 11:18 *to these* **w-s** *of mine. Tie* ...301
Job 38:2 *with such ignorant* **w-s?** ...127
Ps 19:3 *speak without a sound or* **w;** ...554
Ps 52:4 *others with your* **w-s,** *you liar!* ...462
Ps 119:9 *pure? By obeying your* **w.** ...878
Ps 119:11 *hidden your* **w** *in my heart,* ...878
Ps 119:103 *How sweet your* **w-s** *taste* ...880
Ps 119:160 *essence of your* **w-s** *is* ...881
Ps 119:162 *I rejoice in your* **w** *like* ...881
Prov 12:19 *Truthful* **w-s** *stand the test.* ...645
Prov 12:25 *an encouraging* **w** *cheers* ...645
Prov 16:24 *Kind* **w-s** *are like honey—* ...651
Prov 17:27 *wise person uses few* **w-s;** ...653
Prov 26:23 *Smooth* **w-s** *may hide a* ...841
Isa 40:21 *deaf to the* **w-s** *of God—* ...924
Jer 15:16 *your* **w-s,** *I devoured* ...1019
Jer 23:29 *Does not my* **w** *burn like* ...1028
Amos 8:13 *for the* L*ORD's* **w.** ...779
Matt 4:4 *but by every* **w** *that comes* ...1294
Matt 15:6 *you cancel the* **w** *of God* ...1369
Matt 24:35 **w-s** *will never disappear* ...1447
John 1:1 *the beginning the* **W** *already* ...1270
John 6:68 *the* **w-s** *that give eternal life.* ...1369
John 15:7 *and my* **w-s** *remain in you,* ...1464
John 17:17 *teach them your* **w,** *which* ...1467
Rom 10:18 *the* **w-s** *to all the world.* ...1664
1 Cor 2:1 *use lofty* **w-s** *and impressive* ...1598
1 Cor 2:13 *do not use* **w-s** *that come* ...1598
1 Cor 14:9 *to people in* **w-s** *they don't* ...1617
1 Cor 14:19 *than ten thousand* **w-s** *in* ...1617
2 Cor 2:17 *We preach the* **w** *of God* ...1629
2 Cor 4:2 *or distort the* **w** *of God.* ...1630
Eph 6:17 *which is the* **w** *of God.* ...1715
Phil 2:16 *firmly to the* **w** *of life;* ...1720
2 Tim 2:15 *explains the* **w** *of truth.* ...1743
Titus 2:5 *shame on the* **w** *of God.* ...1738
Heb 4:12 *For the* **w** *of God is* ...1766
Heb 5:12 *things about God's* **w.** ...1767
Jas 1:22 *listen to God's* **w.** ...1548
1 Pet 1:23 *eternal, living* **w** *of God.* ...1750
1 Pet 2:8 *not obey God's* **w,** *and so* ...1750
1 Pet 3:1 *to them without any* **w-s.** ...1752
2 Pet 3:5 *the heavens by the* **w** *of* ...1760
Rev 19:13 *title was the* **W** *of God.* ...1828
Rev 22:19 *of the* **w-s** *from this book* ...1833

WORK, WORKS (n) one's occupation; physical or creative effort
see also DEEDS
Gen 2:2 *finished his* **w** *of creation,* ...9
Exod 20:9 *week for your ordinary* **w,** ...169
Deut 5:13 *week for your ordinary* **w,** ...293
Ps 77:12 *about your mighty* **w-s.** ...597
Ps 107:24 *impressive* **w-s** *on the* ...872
Ps 127:1 **w** *of the builders is wasted.* ...631
Ps 150:2 *Praise him for his mighty* **w-s;** ...888
Prov 21:5 *planning and hard* **w** *lead* ...657
Eccl 2:19 *my skill and hard* **w** *under* ...675
Eccl 5:19 *To enjoy your* **w** *and accept* ...677
John 4:34 *and from finishing his* **w.** ...1305

John 5:36 *Father gave me these* ***w-s*** *to*...1319
John 10:32 *have done many good* ***w-s.***...1406
Acts 13:2 *for the special* ***w*** *to which*.........1539
Acts 20:24 *finishing the* ***w*** *assigned*.........1675
Rom 4:5 *not because of their* ***w,*** *but*.........1652
1 Cor 3:5 *the* ***w*** *the Lord gave us.* 1599
Gal 6:4 *attention to your own* ***w,*** *for*..........1567
Eph 4:12 *people to do his* ***w*** *and build*......1711
Eph 4:16 *part does its own special* ***w,***.......1711
Eph 4:28 *your hands for good hard* ***w,***......1712
Phil 1:6 *began the good* ***w*** *within you,* 1717
1 Tim 6:18 *rich in good* ***w-s*** *and*..............1735
2 Tim 3:17 *people to do every good* ***w.***.....1745
Heb 10:24 *acts of love and good* ***w-s.***......1776
Jas 2:26 *faith is dead without good* ***w-s.***..1550
Rev 15:3 *marvelous are your* ***w-s,***...........1822

WORK, WORKED, WORKING (v) to exert oneself physically or mentally
Prov 13:4 *but those who* ***w*** *hard will*...........646
Eccl 5:12 *who* ***w*** *hard sleep well,* 677
Matt 6:28 *They don't* ***w*** *or make their*.......1332
Matt 12:30 *anyone who isn't* ***w-ing*** *with*..1341
Luke 10:7 *who* ***w*** *deserve their pay.* 1394
Luke 13:24 ***W*** *hard to enter the narrow*....1407
Rom 4:6 *righteous without* ***w-ing*** *for*........1652
Rom 8:28 *to* ***w*** *together for the good*........1660
Rom 12:11 *Never be lazy, but* ***w*** *hard*.......1667
1 Cor 15:10 *I have* ***w-ed*** *harder than*.......1620
1 Cor 15:58 *Always* ***w*** *enthusiastically*......1622
2 Cor 11:27 *I have* ***w-ed*** *hard and*..........1641
Eph 6:7 *you were* ***w-ing*** *for the Lord*........1715
1 Thes 4:11 *and* ***w-ing*** *with your hands,*..1584
2 Thes 3:10 *unwilling to* ***w*** *will not* 1590
1 Tim 5:18 *Those who* ***w*** *deserve their*.....1734
1 Tim 6:2 *slaves should* ***w*** *all the harder*...1734
Heb 6:10 *how hard you have* ***w-ed*** *for*.....1768
2 Pet 1:10 ***w*** *hard to prove that you* 1757

WORKER, WORKERS (n) one who works; laborer
Prov 10:4 *poor; hard* ***w-s*** *get rich*..............642
Prov 12:11 *A hard* ***w*** *has plenty of*..............645
Prov 22:29 *see any truly competent* ***w-s?***....660
Prov 27:18 ***w-s*** *who protect*.......................842
Prov 31:17 *and strong, a hard* ***w.***...............847
Matt 9:37 *great, but the* ***w-s*** *are few.*........1357
Matt 20:1 *one morning to hire* ***w-s*** *for*......1422
1 Cor 3:9 *For we are both God's* ***w-s.***........1599
2 Tim 2:15 *Be a good* ***w,*** *one who does*.......1743

WORLD (n) the earth and its inhabitants; the human race; the current age and its value system
Ps 33:9 *he spoke, the* ***w*** *began!*.................858
Ps 50:12 *for all the* ***w*** *is mine* 593
Ps 96:13 *judge the* ***w*** *with justice,*.............864
Isa 13:11 *will punish the* ***w*** *for its*..............831
Matt 16:26 *you gain the whole* ***w*** *but*........1377
John 1:29 *away the sin of the* ***w!*** 1297
John 3:16 *God loved the* ***w*** *so much*.........1302
John 8:12 *I am the light of the* ***w.***............1392
John 13:35 *prove to the* ***w*** *that you* 1461
John 16:33 *I have overcome the* ***w.***...........1466
John 17:5 *shared before the* ***w*** *began.* 1466
John 17:14 *And the* ***w*** *hates them* 1467
John 18:36 *Kingdom is not of this* ***w.***........1478
Rom 3:19 *the entire* ***w*** *is guilty*................1651
1 Cor 1:27 *things the* ***w*** *considers*............1597
1 Cor 2:7 *glory before the* ***w*** *began.* 1598
1 Cor 3:1 *you belonged to this* ***w*** *or*.........1599
1 Cor 3:19 *of this* ***w*** *is foolishness*............1600
1 Cor 6:2 *to judge the* ***w,*** *can't you*...........1603
2 Cor 5:19 *reconciling the* ***w*** *to himself,*....1632
Eph 2:12 *lived in this* ***w*** *without God*.........1708
Eph 4:9 *also descended to our lowly* ***w.***....1710
Phil 2:15 *lights in a* ***w*** *full of crooked*........1720
Titus 1:2 *them before the* ***w*** *began.*...........1736
Heb 9:26 *ever since the* ***w*** *began.* 1774
Jas 2:5 *poor in this* ***w*** *to be rich*..............1548
Jas 4:4 *a friend of the* ***w,*** *you make*..........1551
1 Jn 2:2 *the sins of all the* ***w.***...................1788
1 Jn 2:15 *Do not love this* ***w*** *nor* 1789
1 Jn 5:4 *defeats this evil* ***w,*** *and*...............1794

WORLDLY (adj) belonging to the sphere of human existence only; affected by sin; corrupt
Luke 16:9 *Use your* ***w*** *resources to benefit*...1411
2 Cor 7:10 ***w*** *sorrow, which lacks repentance,*...1635
2 Cor 10:4 *not* ***w*** *weapons, to knock down*..1638
1 Pet 2:11 ***w*** *desires that wage war* 1751

WORRY, WORRIES (n) mental distress or agitation resulting from concern; anxiety
Prov 12:25 ***W*** *weighs a person down;*.........645
Matt 6:27 *Can all your* ***w-ies*** *add a single* 1332
Luke 21:34 *and by the* ***w-ies*** *of this life.* ..1451
1 Pet 5:7 *Give all your* ***w-ies*** *and cares*....1756

WORRY, WORRIED, WORRYING (v) to feel or experience concern or anxiety
Deut 20:8 *anyone here afraid or* ***w-ied?***.....310
Ps 37:1 *Don't* ***w*** *about the wicked*.............567
Isa 7:4 *Tell him to stop* ***w-ing.*** 790
Matt 6:25 *I tell you not to* ***w*** *about*...........1332
Matt 10:19 *don't* ***w*** *about how to*............1360
Luke 6:41 *And why* ***w*** *about a speck in*.....1333
Acts 27:33 *You have been so* ***w-ied*** *that*..1687
Phil 4:6 *Don't* ***w*** *about anything;*..............1724

WORSE (adj) of more inferior condition
Matt 12:45 *that person is* ***w*** *off than*.........1343
2 Pet 2:20 *they are* ***w*** *off than*.................1759

WORSHIP (n) reverent devotion and allegiance pledged to God or a god
1 Cor 10:14 *flee from the* ***w*** *of idols.* 1610

WORSHIP, WORSHIPED, WORSHIPING, WORSHIPS (v) to regard with great respect, honor, or devotion
Gen 12:8 *and he* ***w-ed*** *the* L*ORD*...................30
Gen 13:4 *and there he* ***w-ed*** *the* L*ORD*..........32
Gen 21:33 *and there he* ***w-ed*** *the* L*ORD,*.......44
Gen 26:25 *there and* ***w-ed*** *the* L*ORD*.............53
Deut 12:30 *and* ***w-ing*** *their gods.*..............302
2 Kgs 17:36 *But* ***w*** *only the* L*ORD,*...............822
Ps 29:2 ***W*** *the* L*ORD* *in the splendor* 562
Ps 95:6 *Come, let us* ***w*** *and bow down.* 863
Ps 105:3 *rejoice, you who* ***w*** *the* L*ORD*.........868
Isa 44:19 *bow down to* ***w*** *a piece of*...........930
Jer 16:11 ***w-ed*** *other gods and served*....1020
Dan 3:28 *die rather than serve or* ***w*** *any*...1007
Hos 9:1 *like prostitutes,* ***w-ing*** *other*..........811
Hos 9:10 *as vile as the god they* ***w-ed.*** 812
Hos 13:1 *Ephraim sinned by* ***w-ing*** *Baal*.....816
Zeph 3:9 *everyone can* ***w*** *the* L*ORD*............986
Zech 14:17 *to Jerusalem to* ***w*** *the King,*....1180
Matt 2:2 *we have come to* ***w*** *him.* 1283
Matt 4:9 *kneel down and* ***w*** *me.*................1295
Matt 15:25 *she came and* ***w-ed*** *him,* 1371
Matt 28:9 *grasped his feet, and* ***w-ed***......1492
Luke 23:47 *he* ***w-ed*** *God and said,* 1486
John 4:24 ***w*** *in spirit and in truth*.............1305
1 Cor 5:11 *is greedy, or* ***w-s*** *idols,*............1602
Heb 9:14 *we can* ***w*** *the living God.* 1773

WORST (adj) most corrupt, bad, or evil
1 Tim 1:15 *I am the* ***w*** *of them all*............1728

WORTHLESS (adj) valueless, useless, contemptible
1 Sam 12:21 *worshiping* ***w*** *idols that*..........441
Prov 6:12 ***w*** *and wicked people*..................638
1 Cor 3:20 *he knows they are* ***w.***..............1600
Eph 5:11 *part in the* ***w*** *deeds of evil* 1712
Titus 1:16 ***w*** *for doing anything good*........1737
Jas 5:3 *and silver have become* ***w.***...........1553

WORTHY (adj) having sufficient merit or importance; estimable, honorable
Gen 32:10 *I am not* ***w*** *of all the*...................66
Prov 12:4 *A* ***w*** *wife is a crown*....................644
Matt 8:8 *Lord, I am not* ***w*** *to have*............1335
Matt 10:37 *are not* ***w*** *of being mine;* 1361
Matt 22:8 *I invited aren't* ***w*** *of the*............1438
Luke 15:19 *I am no longer* ***w*** *of being*......1410
1 Cor 15:9 *I'm not even* ***w*** *to be called*.....1620
Eph 4:1 *lead a life* ***w*** *of your calling,* 1710
Phil 1:27 *a manner* ***w*** *of the Good News*...1719
Rev 5:5 *He is* ***w*** *to open the scroll* 1809

WOUNDS (n) injuries to the body
Isa 30:26 *and cure the* ***w*** *he gave them.*.....900
Zech 13:6 *what about those* ***w*** *on your*.....1179
John 20:20 *he showed them the* ***w*** *in*.......1495
1 Pet 2:24 *By his* ***w*** *you are healed.* 1752

WRAP (v) to fold cloth, paper, etc. around something, especially in order to cover it
Exod 29:9 ***W*** *the sashes around*................180
Num 4:12 ***w*** *them in a blue cloth* 242

WRAPPINGS (n) something used to wrap an object
John 20:5 *saw the linen* ***w*** *lying there,*......1492

WRATH (n) extreme displeasure, anger, or hostility; God's response to sin
Isa 13:13 *Armies displays his* ***w*** *in* 831
Rev 6:16 *and from the* ***w*** *of the Lamb*.......1812
Rev 16:19 *the wine of his fierce* ***w.***...........1824

WREATH (n) a band of intertwined flowers or leaves worn as a mark of honor or victory
Prov 4:9 *will place a lovely* ***w*** *on your*..........636

WRESTLED (v) to engage in a violent or determined struggle
Gen 32:24 *man came and* ***w*** *with him*..........66

WRITE, WRITING (v) to inscribe or engrave; to record
see also WRITTEN
Deut 10:2 *I will* ***w*** *on the tablets*.................299
Prov 3:3 ***W*** *them deep within your*.............634
Prov 7:3 ***W*** *them deep within your*.............639
Eccl 12:12 *for* ***w-ing*** *books is endless,*........683
Jer 31:33 *I will* ***w*** *them on their hearts*......1034
1 Tim 3:14 *I am* ***w-ing*** *these things to* 1731
Heb 8:10 *I will* ***w*** *them on their hearts*.......1772
Rev 3:12 *I will* ***w*** *on them the name of*......1807

WRITHE (v) to twist (the body or body part) in pain
Jer 4:19 *my heart—I* ***w*** *in pain!* 965

WRITTEN (v) to inscribe or engrave; to record
see also WRITE
Deut 28:58 *that are* ***w*** *in this book,*.............319
Josh 1:8 *to obey everything* ***w*** *in it.* 337
Isa 49:16 *See, I have* ***w*** *your name*.............936
Dan 12:1 *whose name is* ***w*** *in the book*....1161
Mal 3:16 *scroll of remembrance was* ***w***....1248
Luke 24:44 *everything* ***w*** *about me in*.......1498
John 20:31 *these are* ***w*** *so that you* 1496

John 21:25 *the books that would be* ***w.*** 1497
Rom 2:15 *law is* ***w*** *in their hearts,* 1649
1 Cor 10:11 *They were* ***w*** *down to warn* ...1610
Heb 12:23 *names are* ***w*** *in heaven.* 1781
Rev 21:27 *whose names are* ***w*** *in the* 1831

WRONG (adj) incorrect, sinful, immoral, or improper
Prov 14:2 *who take the* ***w*** *path* 647
Rom 7:19 *don't want to do what is* ***w,*** 1658
Rom 12:9 *Hate what is* ***w.*** *Hold tightly* 1667
Rom 14:14 *of itself, is* ***w*** *to eat* 1670
2 Tim 3:16 *make us realize what is* ***w*** 1745

WRONG (adv) in an unsuccessful or unfortunate way
Prov 15:22 *Plans go* ***w*** *for lack* 650

WRONG (n) an injurious, unfair, or unjust act; something wrong, immoral, or unethical
Exod 23:2 *the crowd in doing* ***w.*** 173
Deut 32:4 *faithful God who does no* ***w;*** 323
Job 34:10 *The Almighty can do no* ***w.*** 124
Ps 141:9 *snares of those who do* ***w.*** 588
Isa 53:9 *done no* ***w*** *and had never* 940
Rom 13:10 *Love does no* ***w*** *to others,* 1669
Rom 16:19 *to stay innocent of any* ***w.*** 1673
1 Cor 6:9 *those who do* ***w*** *will not* 1603
Jas 1:13 *God is never tempted to do* ***w,*** 1547
1 Pet 3:17 *to suffer for doing* ***w!*** 1753

WRONGDOING (n) evil or improper behavior or action
Prov 26:26 *their* ***w*** *will be exposed* 841
Isa 61:8 *justice. I hate robbery and* ***w.*** 948
Acts 18:14 *some* ***w*** *or serious crime,* 1591
Gal 3:13 *the curse for our* ***w.*** 1561

WRONGED (v) to injure or harm; to malign or discredit
Num 5:7 *to the person who was* ***w.*** 243
Isa 42:3 *to all who have been* ***w.*** 926
1 Cor 13:5 *keeps no record of being* ***w.*** 1616

XERXES Persian king (486–465 B.C.); mentioned in the books of Ezra, Esther, and Daniel (9:1, where he is called Ahasuerus)
Ezra 4:6 *later when* ***X*** *began his reign,* 1181
Esth 1:1 *in the days of King* ***X,*** *who* 1182
Esth 1:9 *in the royal palace of King* ***X.*** 1182
Esth 1:19 *from the presence of King* ***X,*** 1183
Esth 2:16 *Esther was taken to King* ***X*** 1185
Esth 3:1 *later King* ***X*** *promoted Haman* 1186
Esth 6:2 *plotted to assassinate King* ***X.*** 1190
Esth 8:7 *King* ***X*** *said to Queen Eshter* 1192
Esth 10:3 *with authority next to that of King* ***X*** *himself* 1194

YAHWEH (n) "I AM WHO I AM" or "I WILL BE WHAT I WILL BE"; the personal name of God revealed to Moses in the burning bush
see also LORD
Gen 22:14 *named the place* ***Y****-Yireh* 46
Exod 3:15 ***Y,*** *the God of your ancestors* 144
Exod 6:2 *I am* ***Y****—'the* LORD' 148
Exod 15:3 *warrior;* ***Y*** *is his name!* 161
Exod 17:15 *there and named it* ***Y****-nissi* 165
Exod 33:19 *I will call out my name,* ***Y,*** 186
Exod 34:5 *called out his own name,* ***Y.*** 187
Judg 6:24 *there and named it* ***Y****-Shalom* 384

YEAR, YEARS (n) the period of about 365 days; a period having special significance; a measure of age or duration
Gen 1:14 *the seasons, days, and* ***y-s.*** 7
Exod 12:40 *lived in Egypt for 430* ***y-s.*** 158
Exod 16:35 *manna for forty* ***y-s*** *until* 164
Exod 34:23 *Three times each* ***y*** *every* 188
Lev 16:34 *the* LORD *once each* ***y.*** 223
Lev 25:11 *During that* ***y*** *you must* 232
Job 36:26 *His* ***y-s*** *cannot be counted.* 126
Ps 90:4 *a thousand* ***y-s*** *are as a* 326
Luke 3:23 *about thirty* ***y-s*** *old when* 1279
Heb 10:1 *again and again,* ***y*** *after* ***y,*** 1774
Heb 10:3 *of their sins* ***y*** *after* ***y.*** 1774
2 Pet 3:8 *like a thousand* ***y-s*** *to the* 1760
Rev 20:2 *in chains for a thousand* ***y-s.*** 1829

YEAST (n) a fungus used for making alcohol and bread
Exod 12:8 *and bread made without* ***y.*** 156
Exod 12:15 *bread made with* ***y*** *during* 156
Matt 16:6 *Beware of the* ***y*** *of the* 1374
1 Cor 5:6 *a little* ***y*** *that spreads* 1602

YESTERDAY (adv) on the day preceding today
Heb 13:8 *same* ***y,*** *today, and forever.* 1782

YIELD, YIELDS (v) to produce; to surrender or submit
Prov 30:33 *beating of cream* ***y-s*** *butter* 847
Matt 6:13 *don't let us* ***y*** *to temptation,* 1331
Luke 11:4 *don't let us* ***y*** *to temptation.* 1397
Jas 3:17 *willing to* ***y*** *to others.* 1551

YOKE (n) a wooden crossbar linking two load-pulling animals together; figurative of bondage or linkage between people
Hos 11:4 *lifted the* ***y*** *from his neck,* 814
Matt 11:29 *Take my* ***y*** *upon you.* 1339

YOUNG, YOUNGER (adj) being in the first or an early stage of life, growth, or development
2 Chr 10:14 *counsel of his* ***y-er*** *advisers.* ...698
Ps 119:9 *How can a* ***y*** *person stay pure?* 878
Prov 20:29 *The glory of the* ***y*** *is their* 657
Joel 2:28 *your* ***y*** *men will see visions.* 1242
Acts 2:17 *Your* ***y*** *men will see visions,* 1514
Acts 7:58 *feet of a* ***y*** *man named Saul.* 1526
1 Tim 5:1 *Talk to* ***y-er*** *men as you* 1733
Titus 2:4 *must train the* ***y-er*** *women to* 1738
Titus 2:6 *encourage the* ***y*** *men to live* 1738
1 Pet 5:5 *same way, you* ***y-er*** *men must* ...1756
1 Jn 2:13 *you who are* ***y*** *in the faith* 1789

YOUTH (n) the period between childhood and maturity
Ps 103:5 *My* ***y*** *is renewed like the* 580
Eccl 12:1 *Honor him in your* ***y*** *before* 682

YOUTHFUL (adj) of, relating to, or characteristic of youth
2 Tim 2:22 *that stimulates* ***y*** *lusts.* 1743

ZEAL (n) eagerness and ardent interest in pursuit of something
Num 25:13 *in his* ***z*** *for me, his God,* 270
Rom 10:2 *but it is misdirected* ***z.*** 1663
Gal 1:14 ***z*** *for the traditions of my ancestors* 1557

ZEALOT (n) a Jewish revolutionary who sought liberation from Roman rule near and during the time of Christ
Matt 10:4 *Simon (the* ***z****), Judas Iscariot,* 1358
Mark 3:18 *Thaddaeus, Simon (the* ***z****),* 1323
Acts 1:13 *Simon (the* ***Z****), and Judas (son* 1512

IMAGE CREDITS

Section introduction icons © Sodafish bvba/iStockphoto.
Maps © 2001 Tyndale House Publishers, Inc.
Drawings of the Tabernacle, Solomon's Temple, Herod's Temple, Jesus' Tomb, Jerusalem in the Time of David, Jerusalem from Solomon to Hezekiah, Jerusalem in the Time of Nehemiah, and Jerusalem in the First Century © Leen Ritmeyer.

Timeline
Noah's Ark © photostockam/iStockphoto.
Horse © Giorgio Fochesato/iStockphoto.
Stonehenge © Lee Pettet/iStockphoto.
Shackels © Charles Schug/iStockphoto.
Sun Pyramid © rockdrigo68/iStockphoto.
Boat wake © Kim Bunker/iStockphoto.
King Tut statue © Greg Nicholas/iStockphoto.
Trojan Horse © bumihills/Shutterstock.
Boat at sunset © topal/Shutterstock.
Stone in hand © Benjamin Howell/iStockphoto.
Mayan ruin © Dmitry Rukhlenko/iStockphoto.
The Iliad © justasc/Shutterstock.
Whale © sweetlifephotos/iStockphoto.
Olympic statue © tomml/iStockphoto.
Otorii Gate © Karen Grieve/iStockphoto.
Scrolls in jar © John Barnett/iStockphoto.
Stone ruins © Arkady/Shutterstock.
Temple model © dominiquelandau/iStockphoto.
Art of War © fenghui/Shutterstock.
Feathers © Lee Pettet/iStockphoto.
Great Wall © Subbotina Anna/Shutterstock.
Egyptian Papyrus © ewg3d/iStockphoto.
Baby's hand © gmvozd/iStockphoto.
Saddle © DNY59/iStockphoto.
London © franckreporter/iStockphoto.
Sailing ship © Spectral-Design/iStockphoto.
Paintbrush © Kemal Baş/iStockphoto.
Colosseum © Keith Binns/iStockphoto.

Beginnings
Wenzel Peter's "Adam and Eve in the Garden of Eden" © Eishier/Bigstock.com.
Nebula © Stocktrek Images, Inc./Alamy.
Elephants © EcoPrint/Shutterstock.
Rainbow © garloon/Shutterstock.
Ziggurat © Barry Beitzel.

God's Chosen Family
Camels © Kurt Drubbel/iStockphoto.
Old Bible engraving © John Butterfield/iStockphoto.
Ziggurat used with permission under terms of the GNU Free Documentation License.
Ram © Mary Lane/Shutterstock.
People on escalator © Losevsky Pavel/Alamy.
Wrestlers © Nicholas Piccillo/Shutterstock.
Spider web © Paul Aniszewski/Shutterstock.
Gavel © ericsphotography/iStockphoto.
Blacksmith © Valeriy Lebedev/Shutterstock.
Lightning © Anettphoto/Shutterstock.
Sheep © Richard Semik/Shutterstock.
Hebron, Beersheba, Qumran, and Mount Ebal © Barry Beitzel.

Birth of Israel
Sphinx © R Gombarik/Shutterstock.
Tetragrammaton © Tyndale House Publishers, Inc.
Grasshoppers © Prill Mediendesign & Fotografie/iStockphoto.
Red Sea © Mayovsky Andrew/Shutterstock.
Illustrations of atonement cover, washbasin, lampstand, incense altar, altar for burnt offerings and high Priest's chest piece © Tyndale House Publishers, Inc.
Wide Antelope Canyon © Keith Kiska/iStockphoto.
Fire © David Mantel/iStockphoto.
Doves © XAOC/Shutterstock.
Plate © Tom Young/iStockphoto.
Leper's feet © Karen Low Phillips/iStockphoto.
wild goat © kavram/iStockphoto.
Somali girl © ranplett/iStockphoto.
Fireworks © David Virtser/iStockphoto.
Sunrise © Mycola/Shutterstock.
Incense © David Lovere/iStockphoto.
Snake fresco © alessandro0770/Shutterstock.
Dead Sea coastline © Nickolay Vinokurov/iStockphoto.
Doorpost © Mikhail Levit/Shutterstock.
Kite © Graham De'ath/Shutterstock.
Musician © Form Advertising/Alamy.
Great Pyramids, Desert of Sinai, Qumran, Mount Ebal, Mount Nebo, and Mt. Sinai © Barry Beitzel.

Possessing the Land
Sunflare © photovideostock/iStockphoto.
Hiker © Marek Szumlas/iStockphoto.
Cupped hands © gaspr13/iStockphoto.
Bees © Charles Hough/Shutterstock.
Barley © Alexander Chernyakov/iStockphoto.
Wedding © Nadav/Shutterstock.com.
Newborn © Katseyepho/Dreamstime.com.
Jordan River, Jericho, Hazor, Mount Hermon, Beth-shemesh, Arad, Mount Gilboa, Ashkelon, and Dan © Barry Beitzel.

United Monarchy
Lyre © Maria Toutoudaki/iStockphoto.
Man worshipping © digitalskillet/iStockphoto.
Slingshot © James SteidlIDreamstime.com.
Dog © Art_man/Shutterstock.
Baby © LP7/iStockphoto.
Olive tree © Royster/Shutterstock.
Pouch © michelle compton/iStockphoto.
Hyssop © ruhrpix/iStockphoto.
Man with stick © isgaby/iStockphoto.
Fort © Samot/Shutterstock.
Mountain climber © fototravel/iStockphoto.
Aurora Borealis © Pi-Lens/Shutterstock.
Stream © David Sucsy/iStockphoto.
Abstract rushing © Maciej Noskowski/iStockphoto.
Fire © Luis Sandoval Mandujano/iStockphoto.
Child on road © mshep2/iStockphoto.
Kids at sunset © Galina Barskaya/iStockphoto.
Knitting © Victoria Rayu/iStockphoto.
Ornate atrium © shao weiwei/iStockphoto.
Tambourine © kali9/iStockphoto.
Lighthouse © floridastock/Shutterstock.
Feet © Catherine Yeulet/iStockphoto.
Doves © Dhoxax/Shutterstock.
Rope © Sergiy Goruppa/iStockphoto.
Trophies © DNY59/iStockphoto.
Library © zen jung/iStockphoto.
Jezreel Valley, Beth-shan, Kidron Valley, Joppa, and Zion © Barry Beitzel.

Splintered Nation
White-necked raven © Hedrus/Shutterstock.
Family at sunset © Aldo Murillo/iStockphoto.
Wild horses © Sofiaworld/Dreamstime.com.
Man splashing in water © Lipik/Shutterstock.
Treasure chest © Chris Curtis/Shutterstock.
Viking ship © J. Helgason/Shutterstock.
Cairo © Steve Heap/Shutterstock.
Stream © Maxim Petrichuk/Shutterstock.
St. Peter's © nadirco/Shutterstock.
Walkers © Özgür Donmaz/iStockphoto.
Wedding © Heike Hofstaetter/iStockphoto.
Shofar © Moti Meiri/iStockphoto.
Snow © Kuttelvaserova/Shutterstock.
Underground cave © Sergios/Shutterstock.
Portrait of woman © Blend Images/Shutterstock.
Man at dusk © Zack Clothier/Shutterstock.
Apple tree © Christian Mueller/Shutterstock.
Orchestra © Ferenc Szelepcsenyi/Shutterstock.
Chariot relief © Kamira/Shutterstock.
Hezekiah's Tunnel © Tamar Hayardeni, used under Creative Commons Attribution license.
Wine press © by Nicola Aravecchia , "Marea," Ancient World Image Bank (New York: Institute for the Study of the Ancient World, 2009) <http://www.flickr.com/photos/isawnyu/5613580338/>, used under Creative Commons Attribution license.
Ship's wheel © galoczka/Shutterstock.
Partridge © Natursports/Shutterstock.
Blueprints © doram/iStockphoto.
Man in field © Chesterf/Dreamstime.com.
Stone wall © Shipov Oleg/Shutterstock.

Mareshah, Mount Carmel, threshing grain, millstone, Sharon Plain, almond tree, Megiddo, Elephantine, and Negev © Barry Beitzel.
Man with load © pavelsvoboda/Shutterstock.

Exile
Sandstorm and pyramid © Tulay Over/iStockphoto.
Skull and bones © Robert Ridder/iStockphoto.
Road construction lights © Kellie L. Folkerts/Shutterstock.
Weeping willow © Taushia Jackson/Shutterstock.
Stream © Blyg/Bigstock.
Throwing fishing net © noomhh/Shutterstock.
Old city © Wim Claes/Shutterstock.

Return & Diaspora
Ancient city wall © Nick Pavlakis/Shutterstock.
Snowstorm © Igumnova Irina/Shutterstock.
Hikers at sunset © Andrushko Galyna/Bigstock.
INRI, metal Jesus © Michal Ninger/Shutterstock.
Bride © Tatiana Morozova/Shutterstock.
Construction worker © Yula Zubritsky/iStockphoto.
Torah scroll © Carly Rose Hennigan/Shutterstock.
Man hiking in mountains © Photo_Concepts/iStockphoto.
Abstract background © Barauskaite/Shutterstock.
Breeze in an open window © Diane Diederich/iStockphoto.
Olive press, Gaza, Mount of Olives, Scribes at Qumran, Dor, and Petra © Barry Beitzel.
Ancient tomb © Ariel Palmon.

Jesus Christ
Parthenon © Ricardo demattos/iStockphoto.
Christ painting © Iconotec/Alamy.
Jerusalem © photostockar/Shutterstock.
Sheep © Claude Dagenais/iStockphoto.
Jordan River © Torsten Stahlberg/iStockphoto.
Village © Alexeys/Dreamstime.
Funeral © Gertan/Shutterstock.
Oxen © Lit Liu/iStockphoto.
Grain © Masson/Shutterstock.
Stormy sea © Andrejs Pidjass/iStockphoto.
Loaves and fishes © Anyka/iStockphoto.
Child at sunset © Roberto A Sanchez/iStockphoto.
Man holding lamb © Alexander Frolov/Alamy.
Birdhouse © Maridav/Shutterstock.
Oil lamp © John Said/Shutterstock.
Grapes © N. Frey Photography/Shutterstock.
Illustration of whip © Tyndale House Publishers, Inc.
Fig tree © Geanina Bechea/Shutterstock.
Wailing wall © Mikhail Levit/Shutterstock.
Goats on hill © Andrei Yarygin/iStockphoto.
Bridge © Carsten Medom Madsen/Shutterstock.
Grapevine © Ricardo Miguel Silva Saraiva/Shutterstock.
Centurion © William Attard mccarthy/Shutterstock.
Illustration of cross inscription © Tyndale House Publishers, Inc.
Crucifixion © Lisa Thornberg/iStockphoto.
Sunrise © Andrii Ospishchev/Shutterstock.
Flags © Mike Tan C. T./Shutterstock.
Nazareth, Samaria, Capernaum, Masada, Egypt, fishing boats, millstone, and Sea of Galilee © Barry Beitzel.

The Church
Colosseum © mary416/Shutterstock.
Twin Beaches of Patmos © Sarikosta/Shutterstock.
Candles © Kartouchken/Shutterstock.
Rosetta Stone © Vladimir Korostyshevskiy/Shutterstock.
Clothesline © Maurice van der Velden/iStockphoto.
Farmer praying © Mojca Odar/Shutterstock.
Old ink pot © Anneka/Shutterstock.
Man rockclimbing © Scott Hailstone/iStockphoto.
Hands © S. Dashkevych/Shutterstock.
Senior couple © Abel Mitja Varela/iStockphoto.
Cloud reflections © Andrea Zanchi/iStockphoto.
Arrows © naphtalina/iStockphoto.
Electronic background texture © Stefan Glebowski/Shutterstock.
Butterfly © Sergey Goruppa/Shutterstock.
Shipwreck © Kurt Paris/iStockphoto.
Appian Way © millsrymer/iStockphoto.
Zygote © nobeastsofierce/iStockphoto.
Tree roots © Joyfnp/Dreamstime.
Armor © Masson/Shutterstock.
Dirty feet © Andrew Munoz/iStockphoto.
Snake © Nuno Silva/iStockphoto.
Houses © Tony Tremblay/iStockphoto.
Carpenter © rtem/Shutterstock.
Quilt © hainaultphoto/Shutterstock.
Sunrise © Daniel Bendjy/iStockphoto.
Sword © James Pauls/iStockphoto.
Sprinter © Jim Parkin/iStockphoto.
Little boy © Elena Elisseeva/Shutterstock.
Sign of the fish © Martin Pietak/iStockphoto.
Green fractal © Tyler Boyes/Shutterstock.
Papyrus scroll © Natalia Lukiyanova/iStockphoto.
Angel © xtremerx/iStockphoto.
Illustration of Hallelujah © Timothy R. Botts.
Tree © Tobias Helbig/iStockphoto.
Syria and Cilicia, Samothrace, Areopagus, Caesarea, Corinthian Canal, Parthenon, Troas, Temple of Apollo, Egnatian Way, Coliseum, Temple of Athena, Hierapolis Amphitheater, Ephesus, Philippi, Miletus Amphitheater, Patmos, Pergamum Library, Sardis, Cenchrea, and Laodicea water pipe © Barry Beitzel.

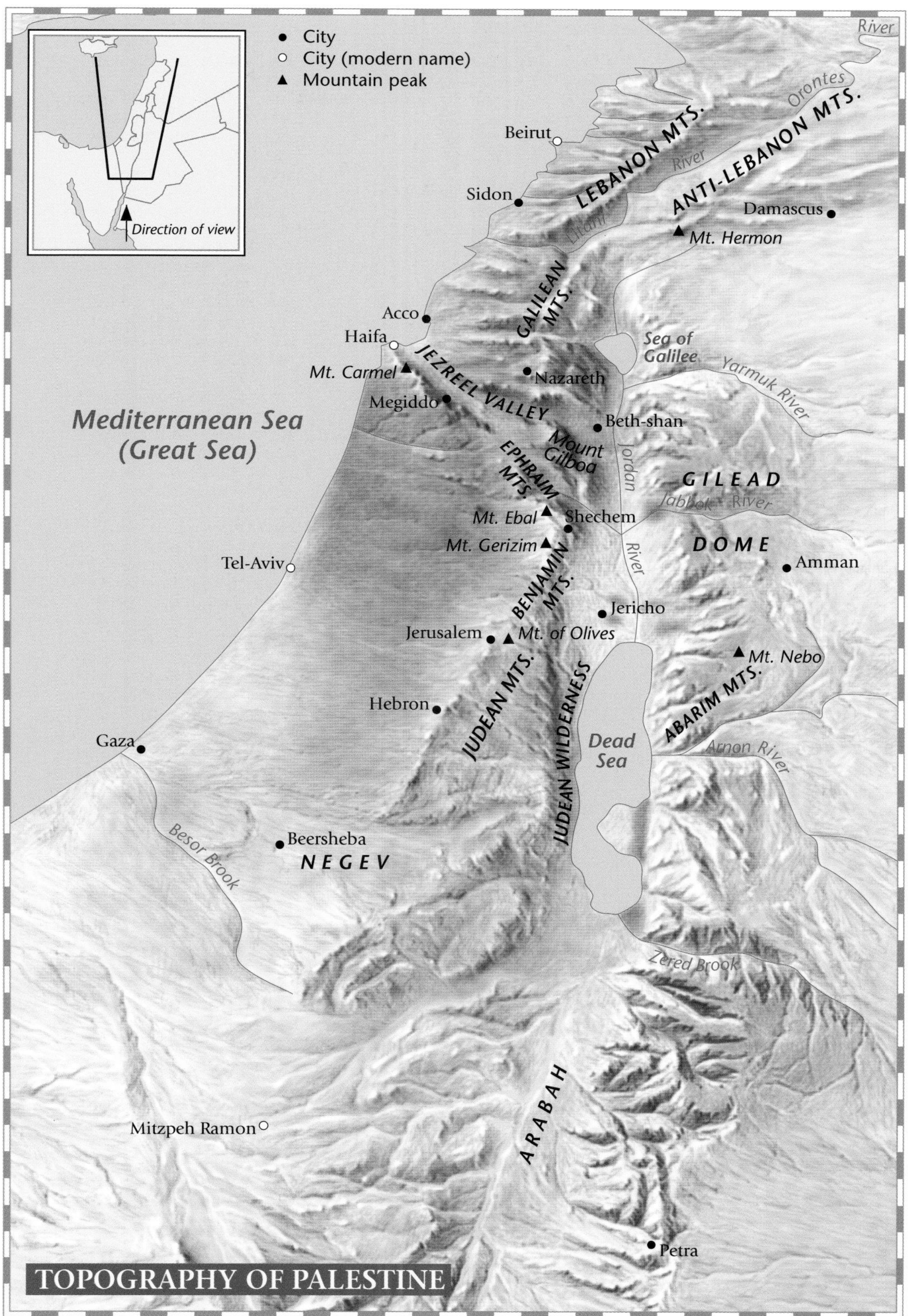
City
City (modern name)
Mountain peak
Direction of view
River
Orontes
LEBANON MTS.
ANTI-LEBANON MTS.
Beirut
River
Sidon
Litani
Damascus
Mt. Hermon
GALILEAN MTS.
Acco
Haifa
Sea of Galilee
Yarmuk River
Mt. Carmel
JEZREEL VALLEY
Nazareth
Megiddo
Mediterranean Sea (Great Sea)
Beth-shan
Mount Gilboa
EPHRAIM MTS.
Jordan
GILEAD
Jabbok River
Mt. Ebal
Shechem
Mt. Gerizim
DOME
River
Tel-Aviv
Amman
BENJAMIN MTS.
Jericho
Jerusalem
Mt. of Olives
Mt. Nebo
JUDEAN MTS.
JUDEAN WILDERNESS
ABARIM MTS.
Hebron
Dead Sea
Gaza
Arnon River
Besor Brook
Beersheba
NEGEV
Zered Brook
ARABAH
Mitzpeh Ramon
Petra
TOPOGRAPHY OF PALESTINE

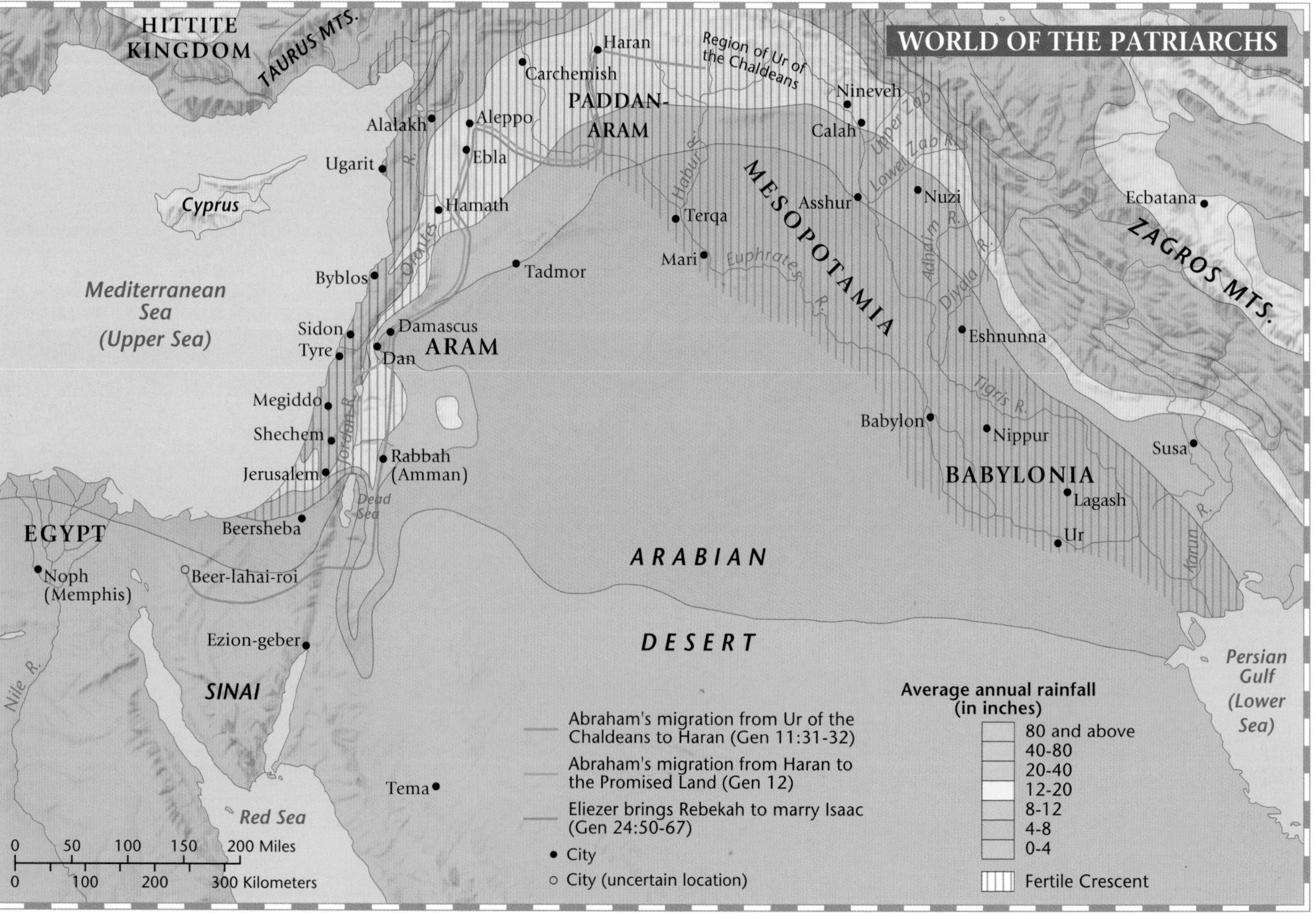
WORLD OF THE PATRIARCHS
HITTITE KINGDOM
TAURUS MTS.
Haran
Region of Ur of the Chaldeans
Carchemish
PADDAN-ARAM
Nineveh
Calah
Alalakh
Aleppo
Ebla
Ugarit
Upper Zab R.
Lower Zab R.
Cyprus
Hamath
Habur R.
MESOPOTAMIA
Asshur
Nuzi
Terqa
Ecbatana
ZAGROS MTS.
Mari
Euphrates R.
Adhaim R.
Diyala R.
Orontes R.
Byblos
Tadmor
Mediterranean Sea (Upper Sea)
Sidon
Tyre
Damascus
Dan
ARAM
Eshnunna
Tigris R.
Megiddo
Jordan R.
Shechem
Babylon
Nippur
Susa
Rabbah (Amman)
Jerusalem
Dead Sea
BABYLONIA
Lagash
Beersheba
EGYPT
Ur
Karun R.
ARABIAN DESERT
Noph (Memphis)
Beer-lahai-roi
Ezion-geber
Nile R.
SINAI
Persian Gulf (Lower Sea)
Tema
Red Sea
Abraham's migration from Ur of the Chaldeans to Haran (Gen 11:31-32)
Abraham's migration from Haran to the Promised Land (Gen 12)
Eliezer brings Rebekah to marry Isaac (Gen 24:50-67)
City
City (uncertain location)
Average annual rainfall (in inches)
80 and above
40-80
20-40
12-20
8-12
4-8
0-4
Fertile Crescent
0 50 100 150 200 Miles
0 100 200 300 Kilometers

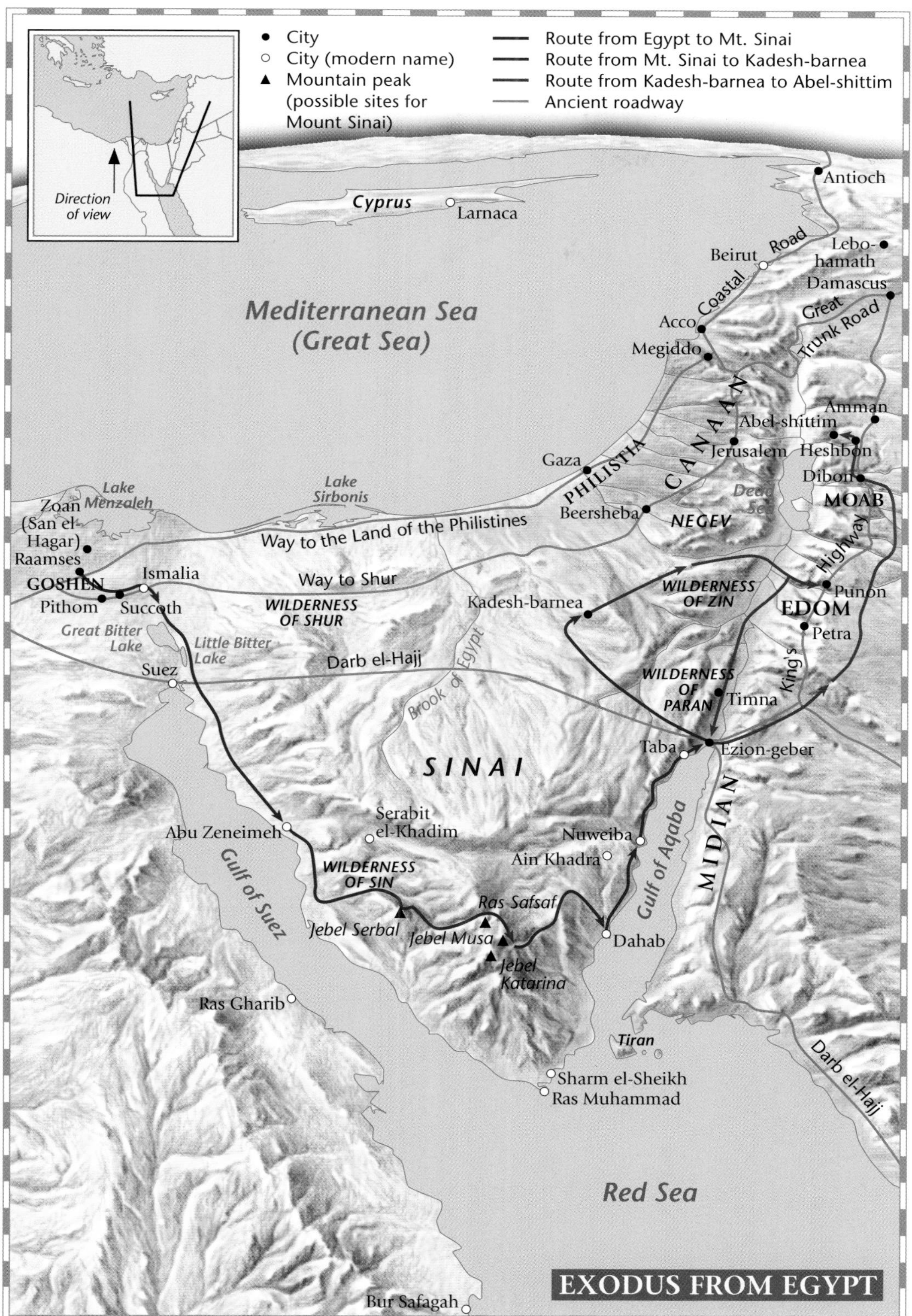

City
City (modern name)
Mountain peak (possible sites for Mount Sinai)
Route from Egypt to Mt. Sinai
Route from Mt. Sinai to Kadesh-barnea
Route from Kadesh-barnea to Abel-shittim
Ancient roadway
Direction of view
Cyprus
Larnaca
Antioch
Mediterranean Sea (Great Sea)
Beirut
Coastal Road
Lebo-hamath
Damascus
Great Trunk Road
Acco
Megiddo
CANAAN
Amman
Abel-shittim
Jerusalem
Heshbon
Gaza
PHILISTIA
Dibon
Dead Sea
MOAB
Beersheba
NEGEV
Lake Menzaleh
Lake Sirbonis
Zoan (San el-Hagar)
Raamses
GOSHEN
Pithom
Succoth
Ismalia
Way to the Land of the Philistines
Way to Shur
WILDERNESS OF SHUR
Kadesh-barnea
WILDERNESS OF ZIN
Punon
EDOM
Petra
King's Highway
Great Bitter Lake
Little Bitter Lake
Suez
Darb el-Hajj
Brook of Egypt
WILDERNESS OF PARAN
Timna
Taba
Ezion-geber
SINAI
MIDIAN
Serabit el-Khadim
Abu Zeneimeh
Nuweiba
Ain Khadra
Gulf of Aqaba
Gulf of Suez
WILDERNESS OF SIN
Ras Safsaf
Jebel Serbal
Jebel Musa
Jebel Katarina
Dahab
Ras Gharib
Tiran
Sharm el-Sheikh
Ras Muhammad
Darb el-Hajj
Red Sea
EXODUS FROM EGYPT
Bur Safagah

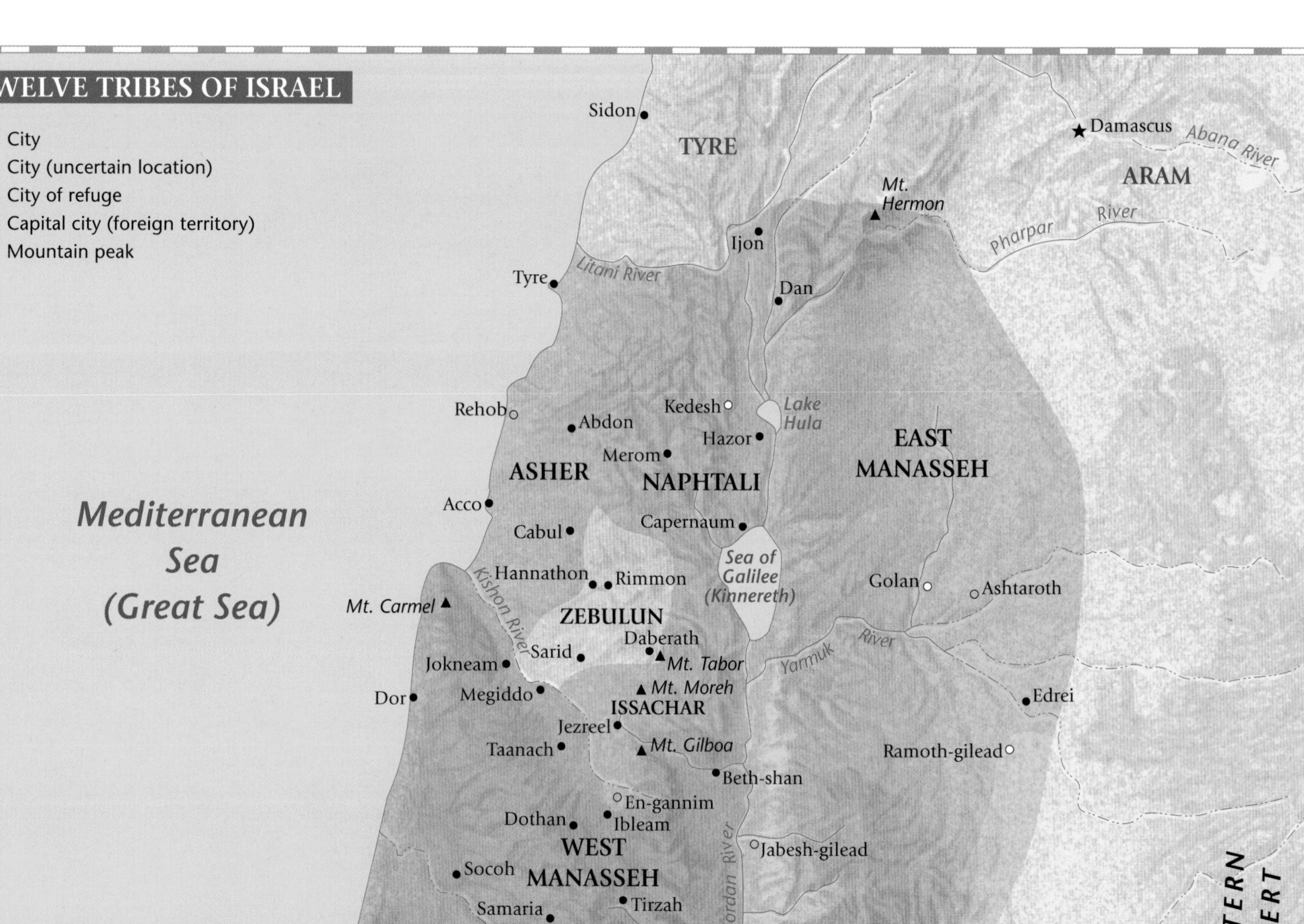

TWELVE TRIBES OF ISRAEL
City
City (uncertain location)
City of refuge
Capital city (foreign territory)
Mountain peak
Mediterranean Sea (Great Sea)
Sidon
TYRE
Damascus
Abana River
ARAM
Mt. Hermon
Pharpar River
Ijon
Tyre
Litani River
Dan
Rehob
Abdon
Kedesh
Lake Hula
Hazor
EAST MANASSEH
Merom
ASHER
NAPHTALI
Acco
Cabul
Capernaum
Sea of Galilee (Kinnereth)
Hannathon
Rimmon
Golan
Ashtaroth
Mt. Carmel
Kishon River
ZEBULUN
Daberath
Sarid
Mt. Tabor
Yarmuk River
Jokneam
Mt. Moreh
Dor
Megiddo
ISSACHAR
Edrei
Jezreel
Mt. Gilboa
Taanach
Ramoth-gilead
Beth-shan
En-gannim
Dothan
Ibleam
WEST MANASSEH
Jordan River
Jabesh-gilead
Socoh
Samaria
Tirzah
Mt. Ebal
Mt. Gerizim
Shechem
Succoth
Penuel
Mahanaim
AMMON
Jabbok River
EASTERN DESERT

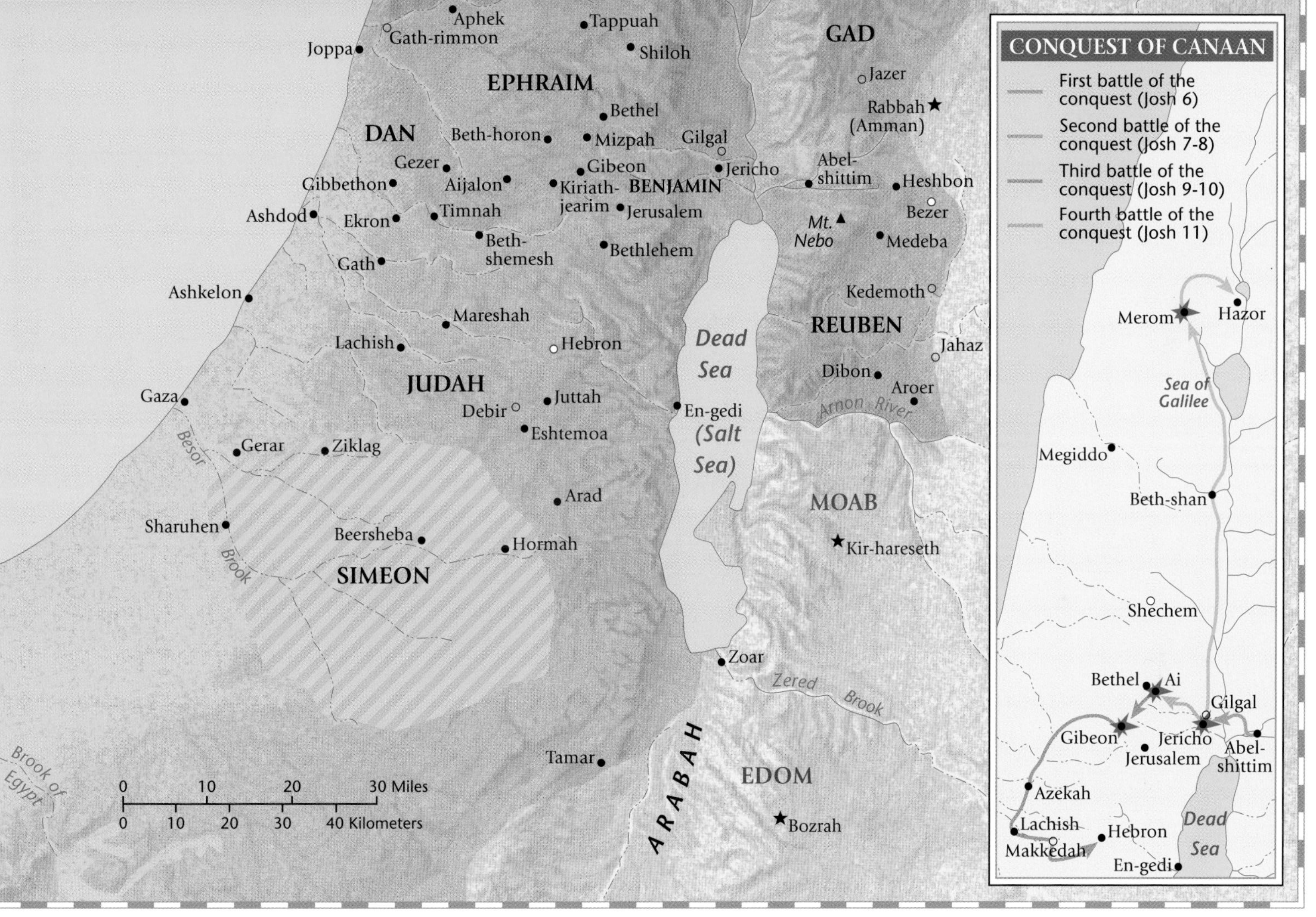
CONQUEST OF CANAAN
First battle of the conquest (Josh 6)
Second battle of the conquest (Josh 7-8)
Third battle of the conquest (Josh 9-10)
Fourth battle of the conquest (Josh 11)
Merom
Hazor
Sea of Galilee
Megiddo
Beth-shan
Shechem
Bethel
Ai
Gilgal
Gibeon
Jericho
Jerusalem
Abel-shittim
Azekah
Lachish
Makkedah
Hebron
Dead Sea
En-gedi
Aphek
Gath-rimmon
Joppa
Tappuah
Shiloh
GAD
Jazer
EPHRAIM
Bethel
Rabbah (Amman)
DAN
Beth-horon
Mizpah
Gilgal
Gezer
Gibeon
Jericho
Abel-shittim
Heshbon
Gibbethon
Aijalon
Kiriath-jearim
BENJAMIN
Ashdod
Ekron
Timnah
Jerusalem
Bezer
Mt. Nebo
Beth-shemesh
Medeba
Bethlehem
Gath
Ashkelon
Kedemoth
Mareshah
REUBEN
Lachish
Hebron
Dead Sea
Jahaz
Dibon
JUDAH
Aroer
Gaza
Juttah
Debir
En-gedi
Arnon River
(Salt Sea)
Eshtemoa
Besor
Gerar
Ziklag
Arad
MOAB
Sharuhen
Beersheba
Hormah
Kir-hareseth
Brook
SIMEON
Zoar
Zered Brook
Tamar
EDOM
Brook of Egypt
ARABAH
Bozrah
0 10 20 30 Miles
0 10 20 30 40 Kilometers

UNITED KINGDOM
Kingdom of Saul
Kingdom of David
Kingdom of Solomon
0 40 Miles
0 40 Kilometers
Aleppo
YAMHAD
Euphrates R.
Tiphsah
Cyprus
Hamath
HAMATH
Arvad
Tadmor
Byblos
Lebo-hamath
PHOENICIA
Mediterranean Sea (Great Sea)
Damascus
ARAM
Tyre
Dan
Hazor
Sea of Galilee (Kinnereth)
Dor
Megiddo
Shechem
Jordan R.
AMMON
Joppa
Gezer
Rabbah (Amman)
PHILISTIA
Gaza
Jerusalem
Dead Sea (Salt Sea)
Raphia
MOAB
Beersheba
EASTERN DESERT
AMALEK
Petra
Kadesh-barnea
EDOM
Ezion-geber
Gulf of Aqaba
SINAI
DIVIDED KINGDOM
0 25 50 Miles
0 25 50 Kilometers
AMURRU
Great Trunk Road
Hamath
HAMATH
Mediterranean Sea (Great Sea)
Arvad
Qatna
Kadesh
Orontes R.
PHOENICIA
Coastal Road
Byblos
Sadad
Lebo-hamath
Berothai
Sidon
Damascus
Litani R.
Tyre
Dan
Kedesh
ARAM
Hazor
Acco
Sea of Galilee (Kinnereth)
Dor
Ashtaroth
Megiddo
Ramoth-gilead
Salecah
Beth-shan
Road
Jordan R.
Jabbok R.
Shechem
Joppa
ISRAEL
Rabbah (Amman)
Gezer
Gibeah
AMMON
Ashdod
Jerusalem
Gath
Medeba
Lachish
Dead Sea (Salt Sea)
Highway
Gaza
Hebron
Aroer
Trunk
Raphia
JUDAH
MOAB
Beersheba
Kir-hareseth (Kir-moab)
Great
PHILISTIA
NEGEV
Brook of Egypt
King's
Kadesh-barnea
Bozrah
EDOM
Petra
Territory periodically contested by Edom and Judah
WILDERNESS OF ZIN
EASTERN DESERT
Ezion-geber
Gulf of Aqaba
SINAI

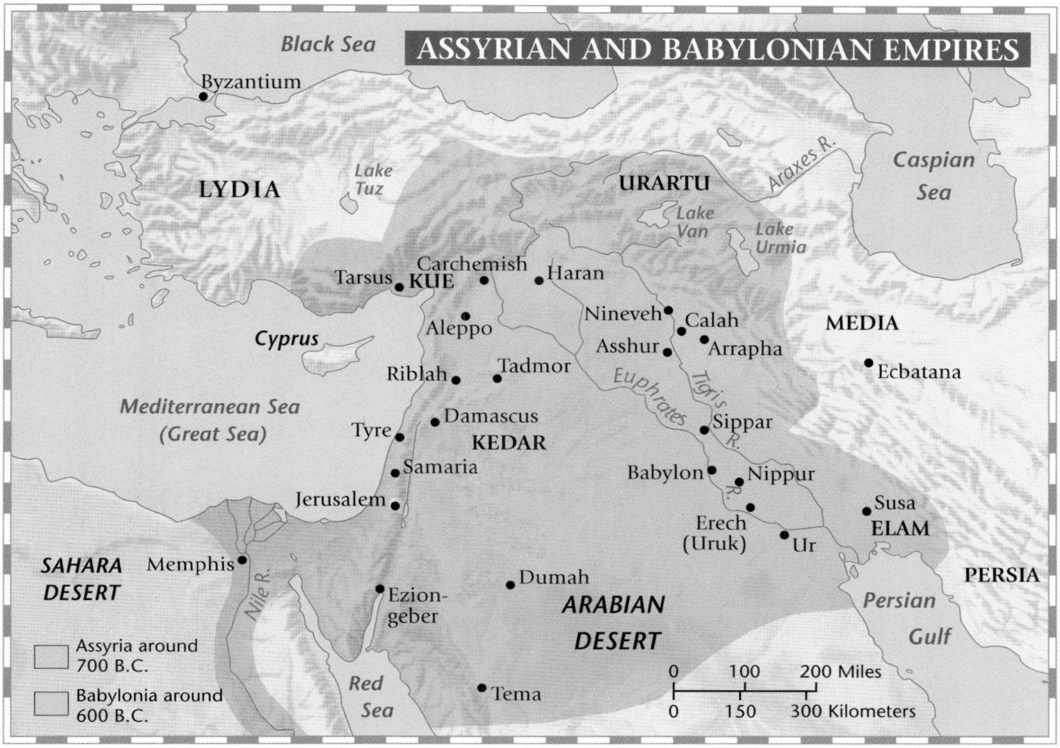

ASSYRIAN AND BABYLONIAN EMPIRES

Black Sea
Byzantium
LYDIA
Lake Tuz
URARTU
Araxes R.
Caspian Sea
Lake Van
Lake Urmia
Tarsus
KUE
Carchemish
Haran
Nineveh
Calah
Aleppo
Cyprus
Asshur
Arrapha
MEDIA
Riblah
Tadmor
Ecbatana
Mediterranean Sea (Great Sea)
Euphrates R.
Tigris R.
Damascus
Sippar
Tyre
KEDAR
Samaria
Babylon
Nippur
Jerusalem
Susa
Erech (Uruk)
ELAM
Ur
SAHARA DESERT
Memphis
PERSIA
Nile R.
Dumah
Ezion-geber
ARABIAN DESERT
Persian Gulf
Red Sea
Tema
Assyria around 700 B.C.
Babylonia around 600 B.C.
0 100 200 Miles
0 150 300 Kilometers

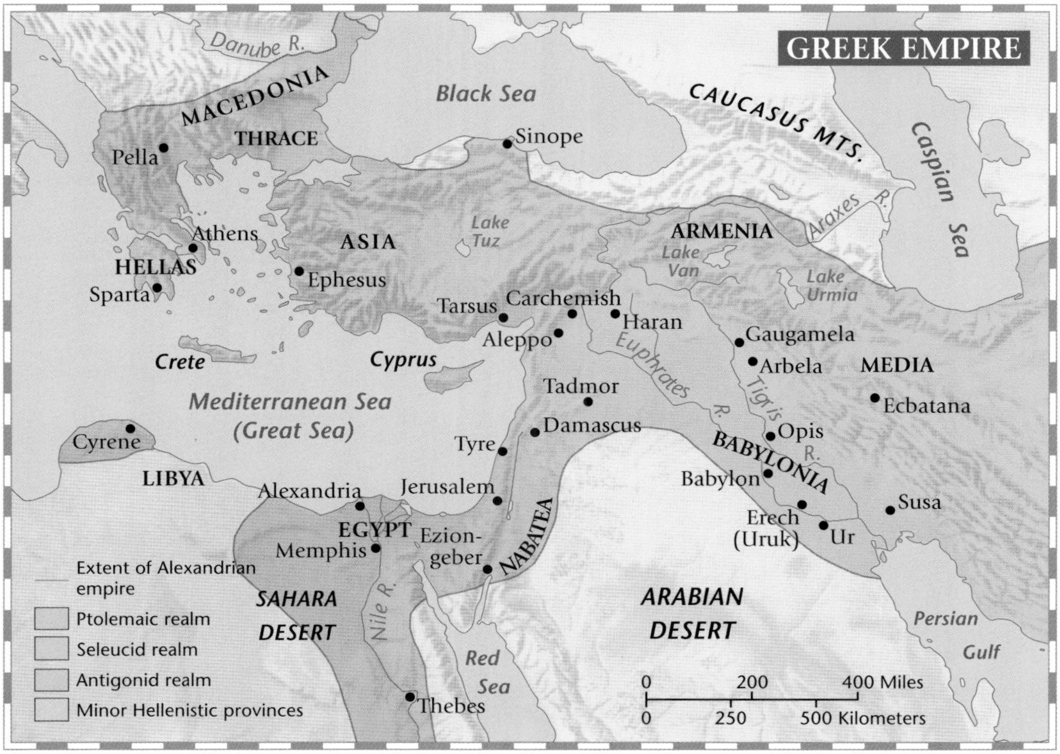

GREEK EMPIRE

Danube R.
MACEDONIA
Black Sea
CAUCASUS MTS.
Caspian Sea
THRACE
Sinope
Pella
Athens
ASIA
Lake Tuz
ARMENIA
Araxes R.
HELLAS
Lake Van
Lake Urmia
Ephesus
Sparta
Tarsus
Carchemish
Haran
Aleppo
Euphrates R.
Gaugamela
Crete
Cyprus
Arbela
MEDIA
Tadmor
Tigris R.
Ecbatana
Mediterranean Sea (Great Sea)
Damascus
Opis
Cyrene
Tyre
BABYLONIA
LIBYA
Babylon
Alexandria
Jerusalem
Susa
EGYPT
Erech (Uruk)
Ur
Memphis
Ezion-geber
NABATEA
Extent of Alexandrian empire
SAHARA DESERT
ARABIAN DESERT
Ptolemaic realm
Nile R.
Persian Gulf
Seleucid realm
Red Sea
Antigonid realm
0 200 400 Miles
Minor Hellenistic provinces
Thebes
0 250 500 Kilometers

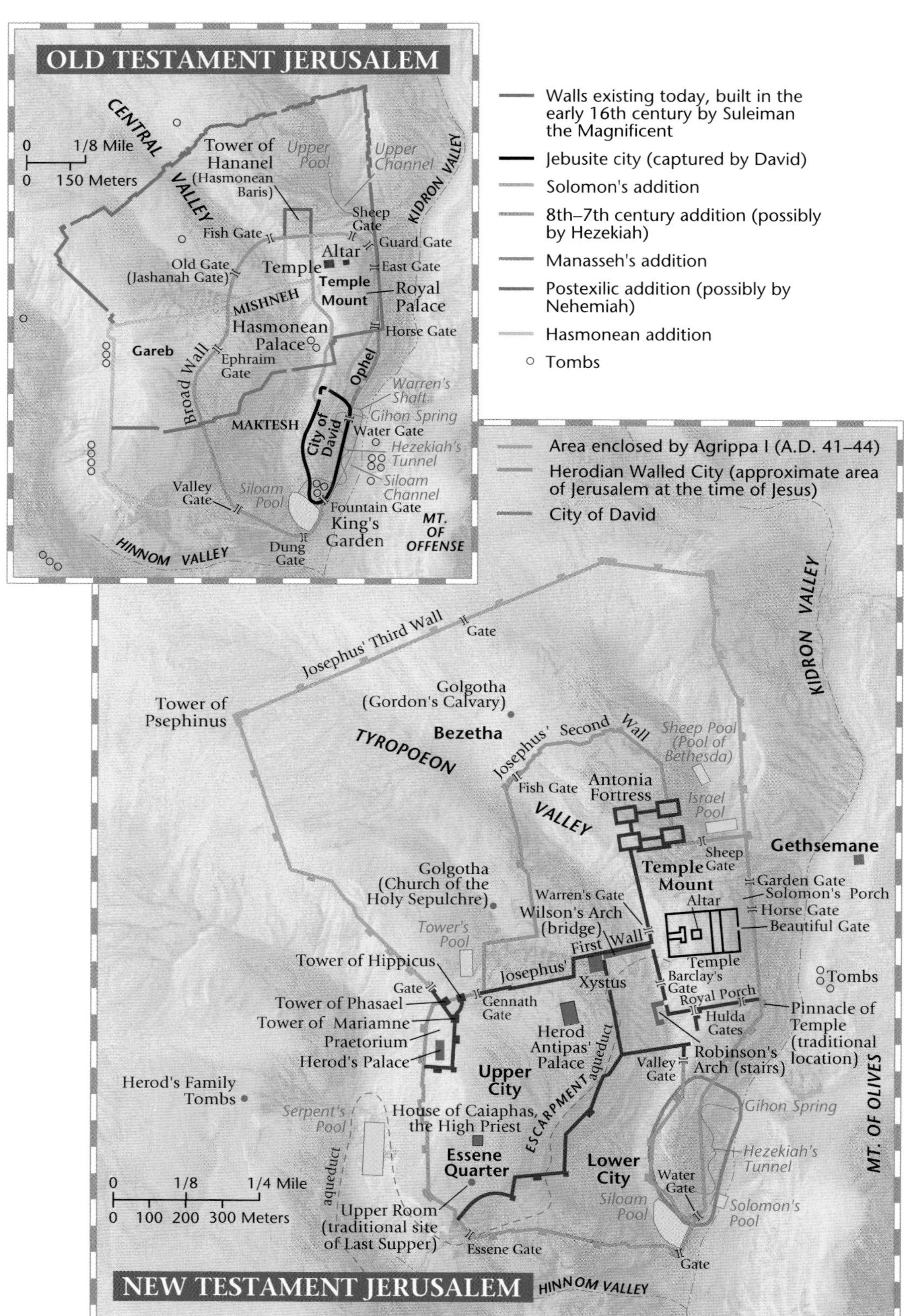
OLD TESTAMENT JERUSALEM
Walls existing today, built in the early 16th century by Suleiman the Magnificent
Jebusite city (captured by David)
Solomon's addition
8th–7th century addition (possibly by Hezekiah)
Manasseh's addition
Postexilic addition (possibly by Nehemiah)
Hasmonean addition
Tombs
0 1/8 Mile
0 150 Meters
CENTRAL VALLEY
KIDRON VALLEY
Tower of Hananel (Hasmonean Baris)
Upper Pool
Upper Channel
Sheep Gate
Fish Gate
Guard Gate
Altar
Old Gate (Jashanah Gate)
Temple
East Gate
Temple Mount
Royal Palace
MISHNEH
Hasmonean Palace
Horse Gate
Gareb
Broad Wall
Ephraim Gate
Ophel
Warren's Shaft
Gihon Spring
MAKTESH
City of David
Water Gate
Hezekiah's Tunnel
Siloam Channel
Valley Gate
Siloam Pool
Fountain Gate
King's Garden
MT. OF OFFENSE
HINNOM VALLEY
Dung Gate
NEW TESTAMENT JERUSALEM
Area enclosed by Agrippa I (A.D. 41–44)
Herodian Walled City (approximate area of Jerusalem at the time of Jesus)
City of David
Josephus' Third Wall
Gate
KIDRON VALLEY
Golgotha (Gordon's Calvary)
Tower of Psephinus
Bezetha
TYROPOEON
Josephus' Second Wall
Sheep Pool (Pool of Bethesda)
Fish Gate
Antonia Fortress
VALLEY
Israel Pool
Gethsemane
Sheep Gate
Golgotha (Church of the Holy Sepulchre)
Temple Mount
Garden Gate
Solomon's Porch
Warren's Gate
Altar
Horse Gate
Wilson's Arch (bridge)
Beautiful Gate
Tower's Pool
Josephus' First Wall
Tower of Hippicus
Temple
Xystus
Barclay's Gate
Tombs
Gate
Royal Porch
Tower of Phasael
Gennath Gate
Pinnacle of Temple (traditional location)
Tower of Mariamne
Hulda Gates
Praetorium
Herod Antipas' Palace
Herod's Palace
aqueduct
Robinson's Arch (stairs)
Valley Gate
Upper City
Herod's Family Tombs
ESCARPMENT
Serpent's Pool
House of Caiaphas, the High Priest
Gihon Spring
MT. OF OLIVES
Essene Quarter
Hezekiah's Tunnel
Lower City
aqueduct
Water Gate
0 1/8 1/4 Mile
0 100 200 300 Meters
Siloam Pool
Solomon's Pool
Upper Room (traditional site of Last Supper)
Essene Gate
Gate
HINNOM VALLEY

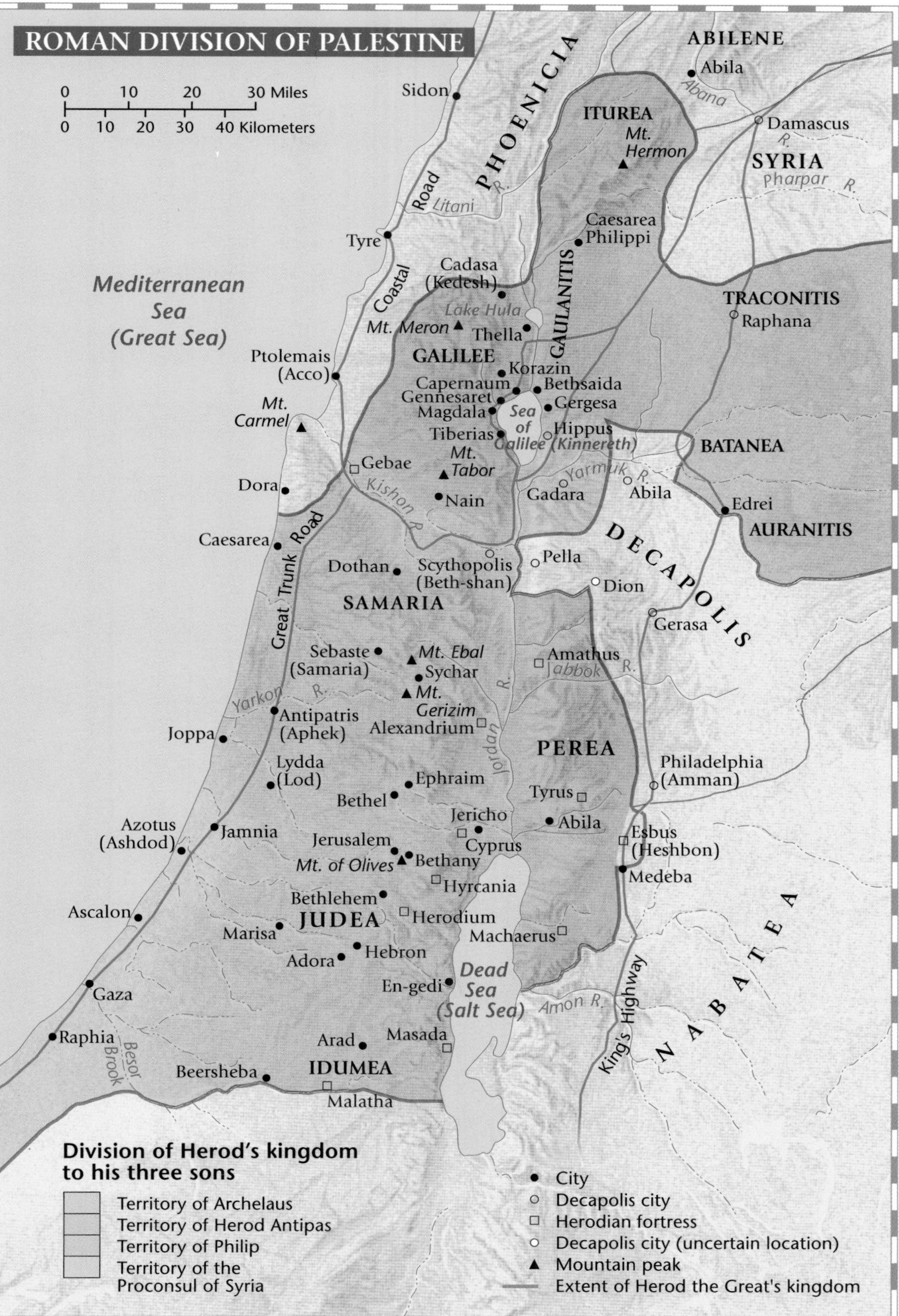
ROMAN DIVISION OF PALESTINE
0 10 20 30 Miles
0 10 20 30 40 Kilometers
Mediterranean Sea (Great Sea)
PHOENICIA
ABILENE
Abila
Abana
ITUREA
Mt. Hermon
Damascus
SYRIA
Pharpar R.
Sidon
Coastal Road
Litani
Tyre
Caesarea Philippi
GAULANITIS
Cadasa (Kedesh)
Lake Hula
Mt. Meron
Thella
TRACONITIS
Raphana
Ptolemais (Acco)
GALILEE
Korazin
Capernaum
Bethsaida
Gennesaret
Gergesa
Magdala
Sea of Galilee (Kinnereth)
Tiberias
Hippus
Mt. Carmel
Mt. Tabor
BATANEA
Gebae
Kishon R.
Yarmuk R.
Dora
Nain
Gadara
Abila
Edrei
AURANITIS
Caesarea
Great Trunk Road
DECAPOLIS
Pella
Dothan
Scythopolis (Beth-shan)
Dion
SAMARIA
Gerasa
Sebaste (Samaria)
Mt. Ebal
Sychar
Amathus
Jabbok R.
Mt. Gerizim
Yarkon R.
Antipatris (Aphek)
Alexandrium
Joppa
Jordan R.
PEREA
Lydda (Lod)
Ephraim
Philadelphia (Amman)
Bethel
Tyrus
Jericho
Abila
Azotus (Ashdod)
Jamnia
Jerusalem
Cyprus
Esbus (Heshbon)
Mt. of Olives
Bethany
Medeba
Hyrcania
Bethlehem
Ascalon
JUDEA
Herodium
Marisa
Machaerus
Hebron
Adora
NABATEA
En-gedi
Dead Sea (Salt Sea)
Gaza
Arnon R.
King's Highway
Raphia
Arad
Masada
Besor Brook
Beersheba
IDUMEA
Malatha
Division of Herod's kingdom to his three sons
Territory of Archelaus
Territory of Herod Antipas
Territory of Philip
Territory of the Proconsul of Syria
City
Decapolis city
Herodian fortress
Decapolis city (uncertain location)
Mountain peak
Extent of Herod the Great's kingdom

MINISTRY OF JESUS

Chronologically speaking, it is not possible to sequentially arrange the events in the life of Christ in any definitive way; none of the New Testament Gospels follows an overtly chronological pattern. Accordingly, the arrangement here follows a geographic order, basically proceeding from north to south on the map. Because the Gospel of Matthew most frequently contains information cited here, and because it is the most geographically particularistic Gospel, synoptic passages are keyed to the book of Matthew, except where they are unattested there or where more pertinent information about the event cited is available in another Gospel.

A. *Region of Tyre:* Gentile woman's daughter healed (Mt 15:21-28)

B. *Caesarea Philippi:* Peter's great declaration (Mt 16:13-20)

C. *Mt. Meron/Mt. Tabor/Mt. Hermon:* (1) possible location of Transfiguration (Mt 17:1-13); (2) demon-possessed boy healed nearby (Mt 17:14-21)

D. *Cana of Galilee:* (1) water changed to wine (Jn 2:1-11); (2) Capernaum official's son healed (Jn 4:46-54)

E. *Gennesaret:* (1) possible location of feeding of multitudes (Mt 14:13-21; 15:32-39); (2) many healings (Mk 6:53-56)

F. *Area of Korazin:* (1) judgment pronounced on the cities of Korazin, Bethsaida, and Capernaum (Mt 11:20-24); (2) possible area of Sermon on the Mount (Mt 5–7)

G. *Capernaum:* (1) catch of fish (Lk 5:1-11); (2) evil spirit cast out (Mk 1:21-28); (3) Sermon on the Mount (Mt 5–7); (4) Peter's mother-in-law healed (Mt 8:14-15); (5) Roman officer's servant healed (Mt 8:5-13); (6) paralyzed man healed (Mk 2:1-12); (7) woman with a hemorrhage healed (Mk 5:25-34); (8) Jairus's daughter raised (Lk 8:40-56); (9) two blind men healed (Mt 9:27-31); (10) a mute, demon-possessed man healed (Mt 9:32-34); (11) the twelve apostles sent out (Mt 10:1-15); (12) man with deformed hand healed (Mt 12:9-13); (13) another demon-possessed man healed (Mt 12:22-37); (14) Temple tax provided (Mt 17:24-27); (15) Bread of Life discourse (Jn 6:22-59)

H. *Bethsaida:* (1) possible location of feeding of multitudes (Mt 14:13-21; 15:32-39); (2) blind man healed (Mk 8:22-26)

I. *Sea of Galilee near Bethsaida:* walking on water (Mt 14:22-33)

J. *Sea of Galilee:* storm quieted (Mt 8:23-27)

K. *Gergesa/Gadara:* possible location of casting out demons, which enter pigs; the pigs then rush down a steep bank and drown (Lk 8:26-39)

L. *Nazareth:* (1) childhood home (Mt 2:19-23); (2) rejected by townspeople (Lk 4:16-30)

M. *Nain:* widow's son raised (Lk 7:11-17)

N. *Region of Galilee:* (1) leper cleansed (Mk 1:40-45); (2) post-resurrection appearances to the disciples (Mt 28:16-20)

O. *Decapolis (Region of Ten Towns):* many healings (Mt 15:29-31; Mk 7:31-37)

P. *Region between Galilee and Samaria:* (1) refused entry into village (Lk 9:51-56); (2) ten lepers healed (Lk 17:11-19)

Q. *Sychar:* woman at the well of Samaria (Jn 4:1-42)

R. *Ephraim:* enters into seclusion with the disciples (Jn 11:54)

S. *Region of Perea:* (1) teaching on marriage (Mt 19:1-12); (2) possible location of healing of woman with infirmity (Lk 13:10-13); (3) possible location of healing of man with swollen limbs (Lk 14:1-6); (4) possible location of the rich young ruler (Lk 18:18-30)

T. *Jericho:* (1) Bartimaeus healed (Mk 10:46-52); (2) Zacchaeus converted (Lk 19:1-10)

U. *Bethany:* (1) Lazarus raised (Jn 11:1-44); (2) anointing by Mary (Jn 12:1-11)

V. *Jerusalem:* (1) taken to Temple (Lk 2:41-52); (2) discourse with Nicodemus

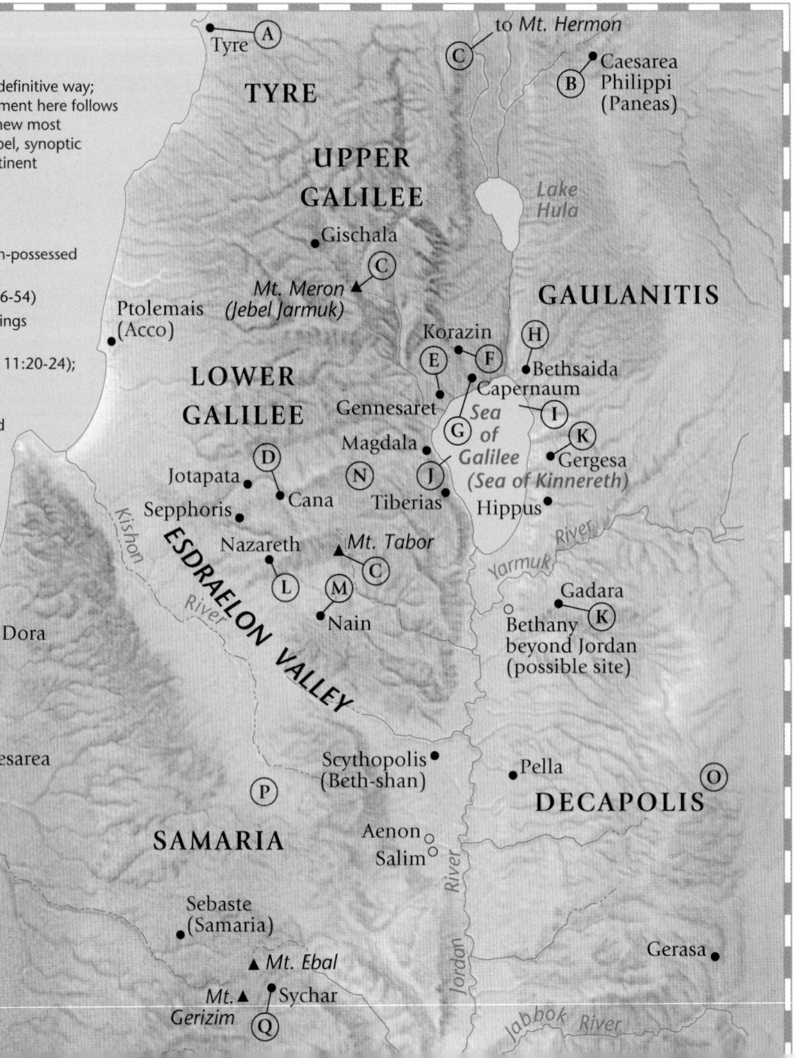

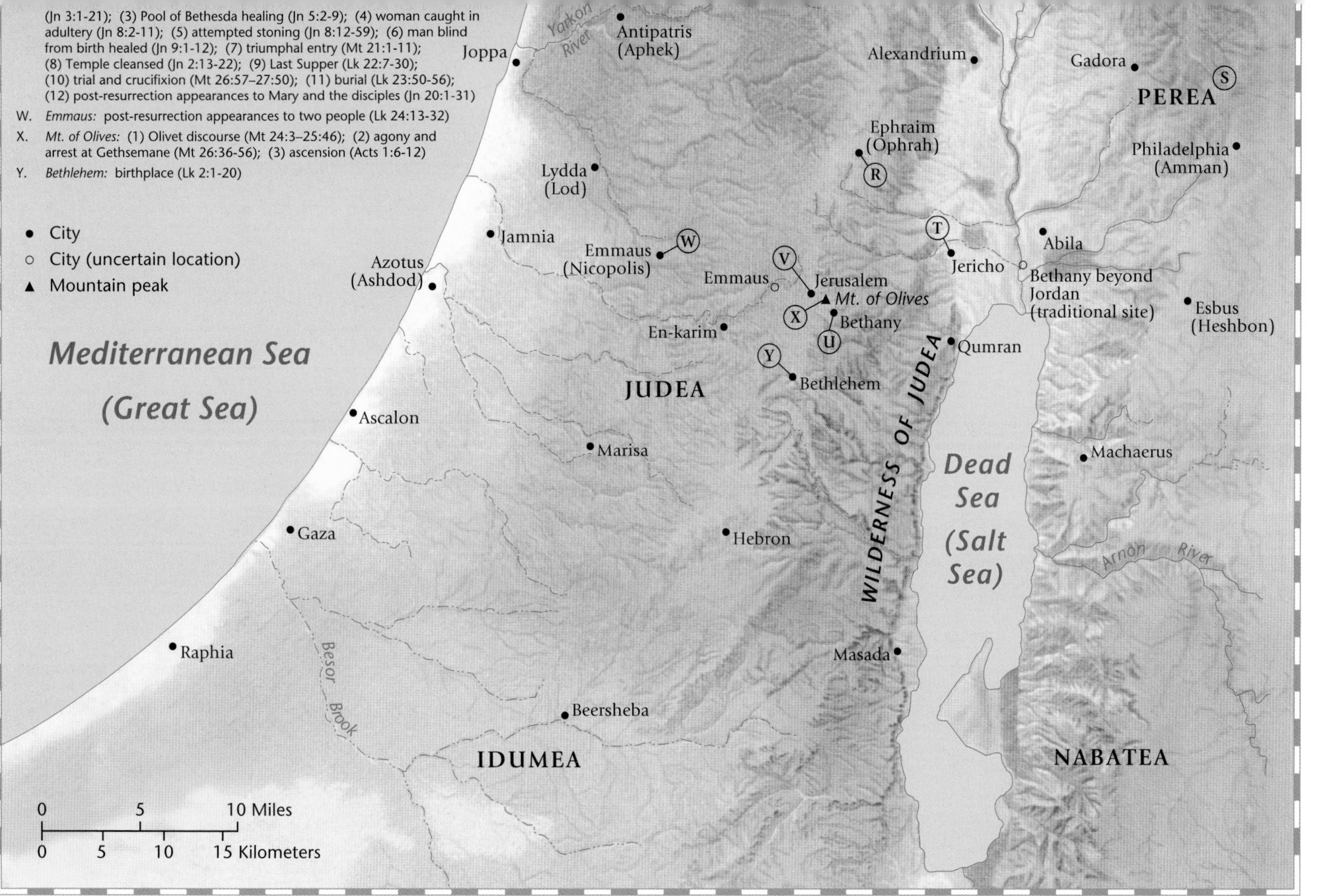
(Jn 3:1-21); (3) Pool of Bethesda healing (Jn 5:2-9); (4) woman caught in adultery (Jn 8:2-11); (5) attempted stoning (Jn 8:12-59); (6) man blind from birth healed (Jn 9:1-12); (7) triumphal entry (Mt 21:1-11); (8) Temple cleansed (Jn 2:13-22); (9) Last Supper (Lk 22:7-30); (10) trial and crucifixion (Mt 26:57–27:50); (11) burial (Lk 23:50-56); (12) post-resurrection appearances to Mary and the disciples (Jn 20:1-31)
W. *Emmaus:* post-resurrection appearances to two people (Lk 24:13-32)
X. *Mt. of Olives:* (1) Olivet discourse (Mt 24:3–25:46); (2) agony and arrest at Gethsemane (Mt 26:36-56); (3) ascension (Acts 1:6-12)
Y. *Bethlehem:* birthplace (Lk 2:1-20)
● City
○ City (uncertain location)
▲ Mountain peak
Joppa
Yarkon River
Antipatris (Aphek)
Alexandrium
Gadora
S
PEREA
Ephraim (Ophrah)
R
Philadelphia (Amman)
Lydda (Lod)
Jamnia
T
Abila
Emmaus (Nicopolis)
W
V
Jericho
Azotus (Ashdod)
Emmaus
Jerusalem
Mt. of Olives
Bethany beyond Jordan (traditional site)
Esbus (Heshbon)
X
Bethany
En-karim
U
Qumran
Mediterranean Sea
(Great Sea)
Y
Bethlehem
JUDEA
WILDERNESS OF JUDEA
Ascalon
Marisa
Machaerus
Dead Sea (Salt Sea)
Gaza
Hebron
Arnon River
Raphia
Besor Brook
Masada
Beersheba
IDUMEA
NABATEA
0 5 10 Miles
0 5 10 15 Kilometers

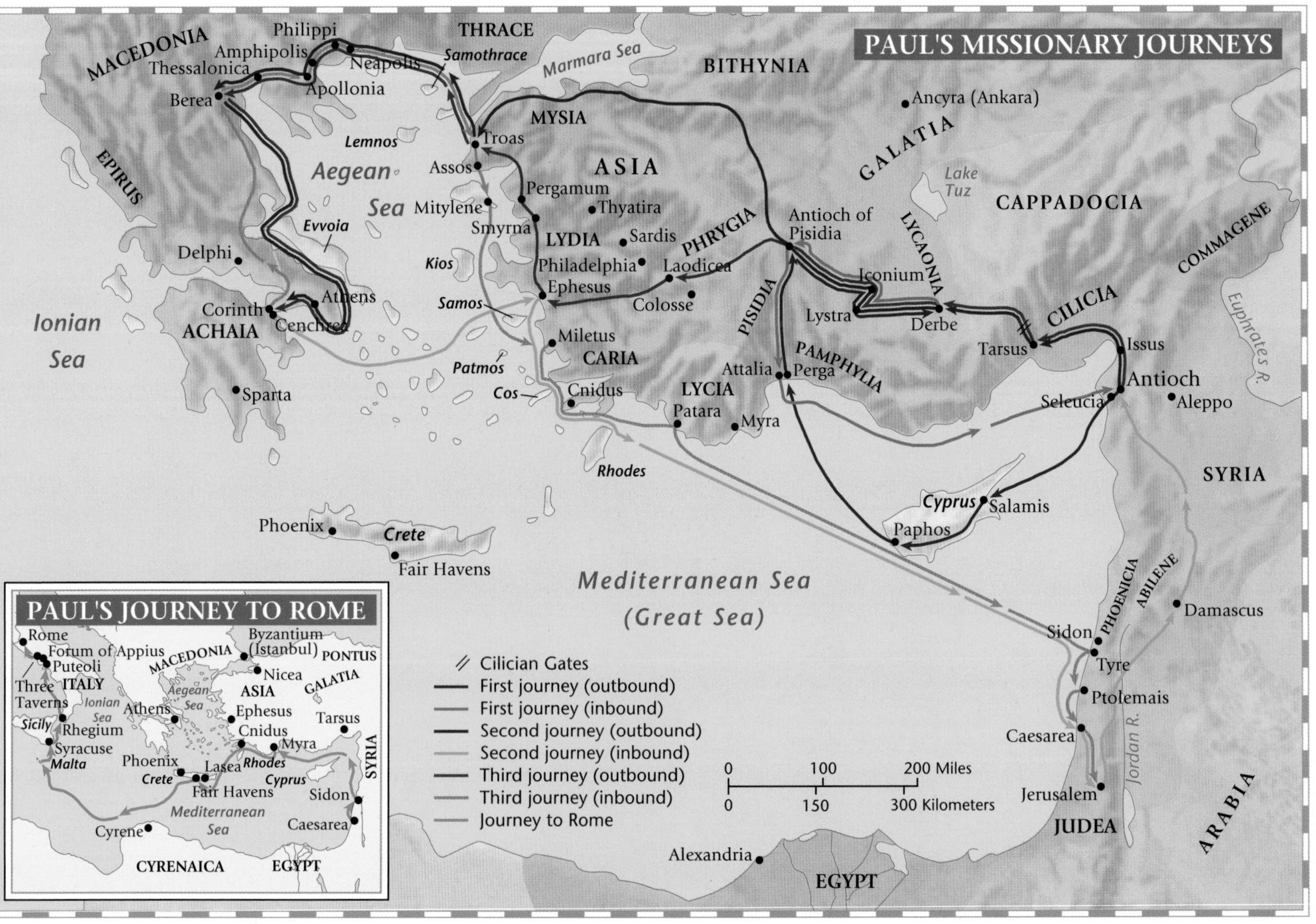

PAUL'S MISSIONARY JOURNEYS
MACEDONIA
THRACE
EPIRUS
ACHAIA
MYSIA
ASIA
LYDIA
CARIA
LYCIA
PHRYGIA
PISIDIA
PAMPHYLIA
LYCAONIA
GALATIA
BITHYNIA
CAPPADOCIA
CILICIA
COMMAGENE
SYRIA
PHOENICIA
ABILENE
JUDEA
ARABIA
EGYPT
Euphrates R.
Jordan R.
Lake Tuz
Marmara Sea
Aegean Sea
Ionian Sea
Mediterranean Sea
(Great Sea)
Samothrace
Lemnos
Evvoia
Kios
Samos
Patmos
Cos
Rhodes
Crete
Cyprus
Berea
Thessalonica
Amphipolis
Apollonia
Philippi
Neapolis
Troas
Assos
Mitylene
Pergamum
Smyrna
Thyatira
Sardis
Philadelphia
Ephesus
Miletus
Cnidus
Colosse
Laodicea
Patara
Myra
Attalia
Perga
Antioch of Pisidia
Iconium
Lystra
Derbe
Ancyra (Ankara)
Tarsus
Issus
Antioch
Seleucia
Aleppo
Salamis
Paphos
Sidon
Tyre
Ptolemais
Caesarea
Jerusalem
Damascus
Alexandria
Delphi
Athens
Corinth
Cenchrea
Sparta
Phoenix
Fair Havens
Cilician Gates
First journey (outbound)
First journey (inbound)
Second journey (outbound)
Second journey (inbound)
Third journey (outbound)
Third journey (inbound)
Journey to Rome
0 100 200 Miles
0 150 300 Kilometers
PAUL'S JOURNEY TO ROME
Rome
Forum of Appius
Puteoli
Three Taverns
ITALY
Ionian Sea
Rhegium
Syracuse
Sicily
Malta
MACEDONIA
Aegean Sea
Athens
Byzantium (Istanbul)
Nicea
PONTUS
GALATIA
ASIA
Ephesus
Cnidus
Rhodes
Myra
Tarsus
Cyprus
SYRIA
Sidon
Caesarea
Phoenix
Crete
Lasea
Fair Havens
Mediterranean Sea
CYRENAICA
Cyrene
EGYPT

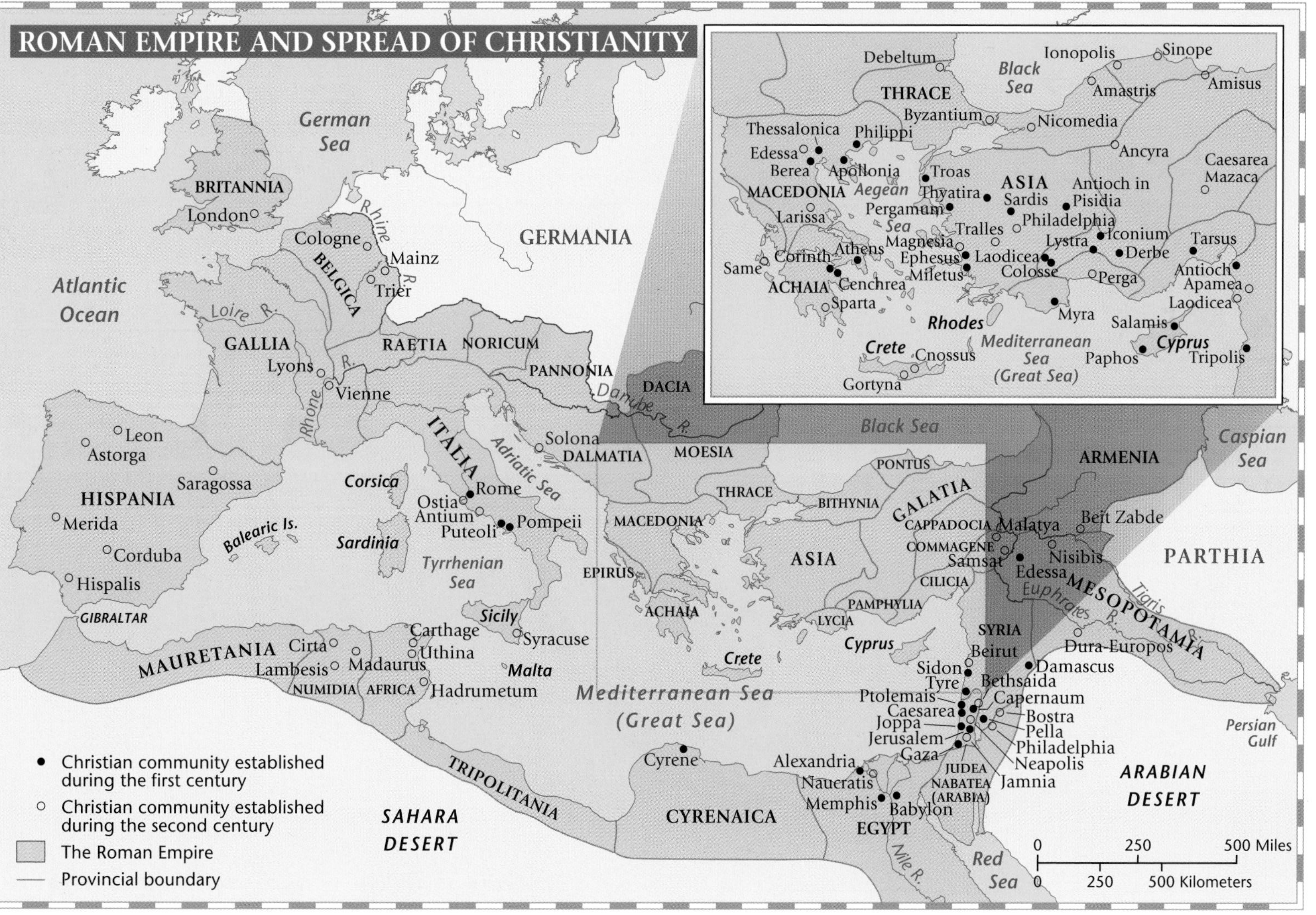
ROMAN EMPIRE AND SPREAD OF CHRISTIANITY
German Sea
BRITANNIA
London
GERMANIA
Cologne
Mainz
Rhine R.
BELGICA
Trier
Atlantic Ocean
Loire R.
GALLIA
Lyons
Vienne
Rhone R.
RAETIA
NORICUM
PANNONIA
DACIA
Danube R.
Leon
Astorga
HISPANIA
Saragossa
Merida
Corduba
Hispalis
GIBRALTAR
Balearic Is.
Corsica
Sardinia
ITALIA
Rome
Ostia
Antium
Puteoli
Pompeii
Adriatic Sea
Tyrrhenian Sea
Sicily
Syracuse
Malta
Solona
DALMATIA
MOESIA
THRACE
MACEDONIA
EPIRUS
ACHAIA
Crete
Black Sea
PONTUS
BITHYNIA
GALATIA
ASIA
CAPPADOCIA
COMMAGENE
CILICIA
PAMPHYLIA
LYCIA
Cyprus
Malatya
Samsat
Edessa
Nisibis
Beit Zabde
ARMENIA
Caspian Sea
PARTHIA
MESOPOTAMIA
Euphrates R.
Tigris R.
Dura-Europos
SYRIA
Beirut
Sidon
Tyre
Ptolemais
Caesarea
Joppa
Jerusalem
Gaza
Damascus
Bethsaida
Capernaum
Bostra
Pella
Philadelphia
Neapolis
Jamnia
JUDEA
NABATEA (ARABIA)
Persian Gulf
ARABIAN DESERT
MAURETANIA
Cirta
Lambesis
Madaurus
NUMIDIA
AFRICA
Carthage
Uthina
Hadrumetum
Mediterranean Sea (Great Sea)
Cyrene
Alexandria
Naueratis
Memphis
Babylon
EGYPT
Nile R.
Red Sea
TRIPOLITANIA
CYRENAICA
SAHARA DESERT
Christian community established during the first century
Christian community established during the second century
The Roman Empire
Provincial boundary
0 250 500 Miles
0 250 500 Kilometers
Debeltum
Black Sea
Ionopolis
Sinope
Amastris
Amisus
THRACE
Byzantium
Nicomedia
Thessalonica
Philippi
Ancyra
Edessa
Berea
Apollonia
Troas
Caesarea Mazaca
MACEDONIA
Aegean Sea
Thyatira
ASIA
Antioch in Pisidia
Larissa
Pergamum
Sardis
Philadelphia
Tralles
Iconium
Tarsus
Athens
Magnesia
Lystra
Derbe
Same
Corinth
Ephesus
Laodicea
Antioch
Miletus
Colosse
Perga
Apamea
ACHAIA
Cenchrea
Laodicea
Sparta
Myra
Rhodes
Salamis
Crete
Cnossus
Mediterranean Sea (Great Sea)
Paphos
Cyprus
Tripolis
Gortyna

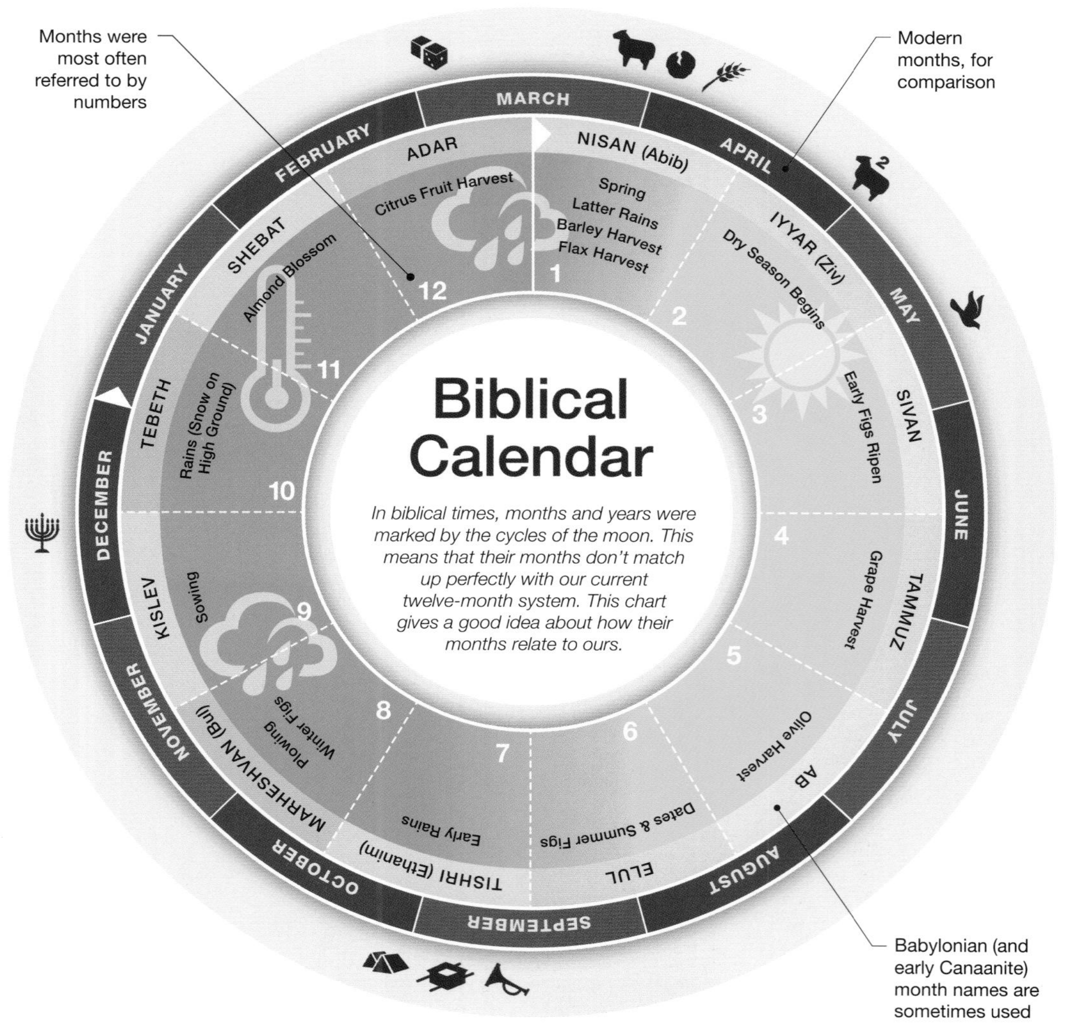

Biblical Calendar

In biblical times, months and years were marked by the cycles of the moon. This means that their months don't match up perfectly with our current twelve-month system. This chart gives a good idea about how their months relate to ours.

Months were most often referred to by numbers

Modern months, for comparison

Babylonian (and early Canaanite) month names are sometimes used

1 NISAN (Abib) — MARCH/APRIL: Spring; Latter Rains; Barley Harvest; Flax Harvest

2 IYYAR (Ziv) — APRIL/MAY: Dry Season Begins

3 SIVAN — MAY/JUNE: Early Figs Ripen

4 TAMMUZ — JUNE/JULY: Grape Harvest

5 AB — JULY/AUGUST: Olive Harvest

6 ELUL — AUGUST/SEPTEMBER: Dates & Summer Figs

7 TISHRI (Ethanim) — SEPTEMBER/OCTOBER: Early Rains

8 MARHESHVAN (Bul) — OCTOBER/NOVEMBER: Plowing; Winter Figs

9 KISLEV — NOVEMBER/DECEMBER: Sowing

10 TEBETH — DECEMBER/JANUARY: Rains (Snow on High Ground)

11 SHEBAT — JANUARY/FEBRUARY: Almond Blossom

12 ADAR — FEBRUARY/MARCH: Citrus Fruit Harvest

FESTIVALS

Passover (Lev 23:5)
14th day of the 1st month. This one-day festival celebrates God's deliverance of the Israelites from Egypt.

Unleavened Bread (Lev 23:6-8)
15th-21st days of the 1st month. All Jews traveled to Jerusalem to commemorate their departure from Egypt in this seven-day festival.

First Harvest (Lev 23:9-14)
Day after the Sabbath during the Festival of Unleavened Bread. Celebrates the beginning of the grain harvest.

Later Passover (Num 9:4-12)
14th day of the 2nd month. God provided an opportunity for those who were prevented from celebrating Passover at the normal time to celebrate one month later.

Harvest (Lev 23:15-22)
50th day after the Festival of First Harvest. Also called Pentecost, this festival celebrates God's provision in the harvest season.

Trumpets (Lev 23:23-25)
1st day of the 7th month. This day of complete rest was set aside for a solemn assembly and the blast of trumpets.

Day of Atonement (Lev 23:26-32)
10th day of the 7th month. The year's most solemn day. A special fast and Sabbath accompanied by the high priest's sacrifice to make atonement for all Israel's sins.

Shelters (Lev 23:33-43)
15th-21st days of the 7th month. All Jews traveled to Jerusalem and lived in temporary shelters to celebrate the final harvest and remember God's provision when they wandered in the wilderness.

Dedication (John 10:22)
8 days, beginning the 25th day of the 9th month. Also called Hanukkah, this festival commemorates the Temple's rededication in 164 B.C. during the Intertestamental period.

Purim (Esth 9:1-32)
14th or 15th day of the 12th month. Commemorates God's protection of the Jews from their enemies through Esther and Mordecai.

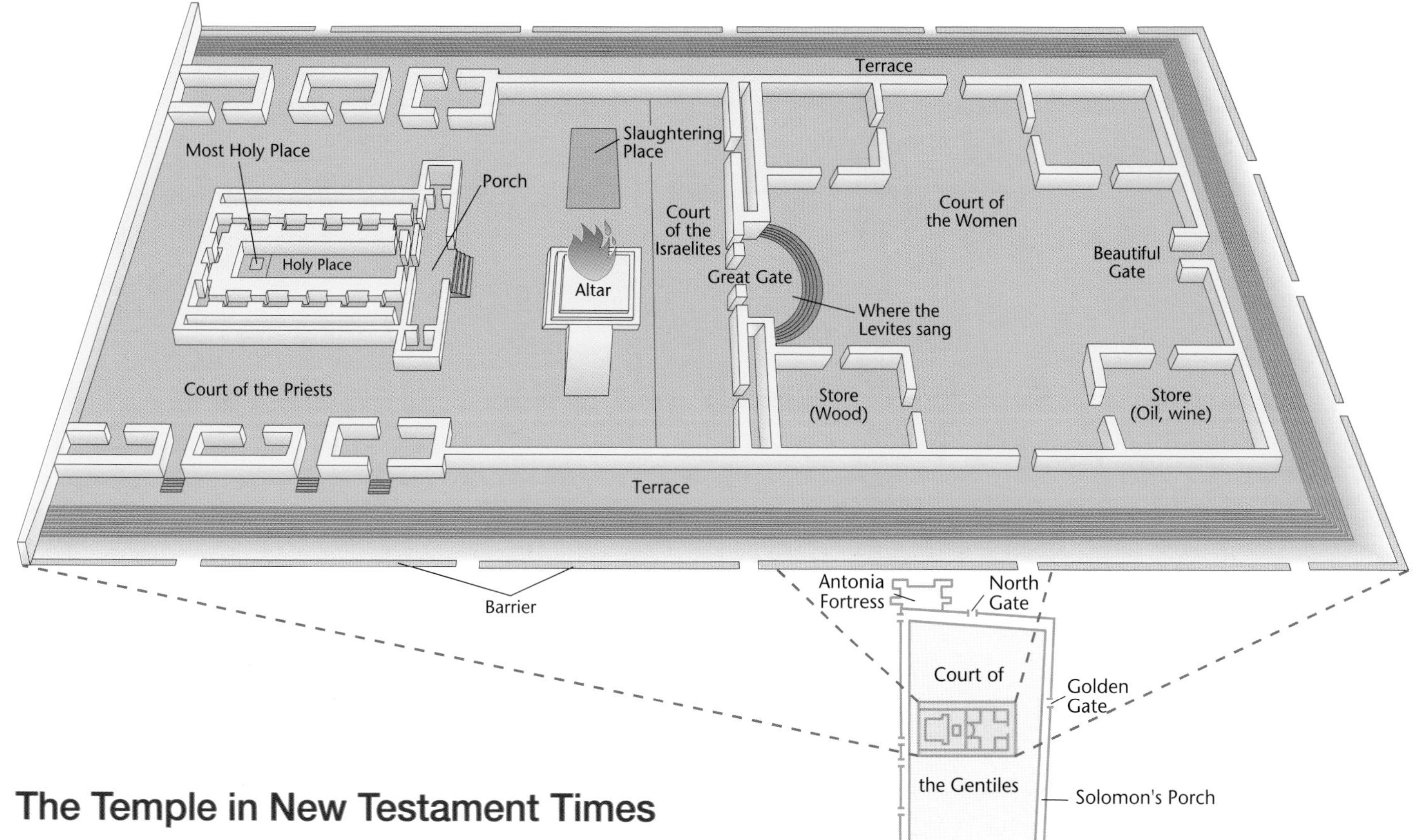

The Temple in New Testament Times

ISRAEL AND THE MIDDLE EAST TODAY
ROMANIA
Odessa
UKRAINE
Bucharest
Sofia
BULGARIA
Black Sea
RUSSIA
KAZAKHSTAN
UZBEKISTAN
Caspian Sea
GEORGIA
Istanbul
AZERBAIJAN
ARMENIA
Baku
TURKMENISTAN
Oxus R.
GREECE
Ankara
Halys R.
Mt. Ararat
Izmir (Smyrna)
TURKEY
Tabriz
Maimana
Tehran
Aleppo
Mosul
Tigris R.
AFGHANISTAN
CYPRUS
SYRIA
Euphrates R.
LEBANON
Beirut
Damascus
IRAN
Mediterranean Sea
Baghdad
Jerusalem
Amman
IRAQ
PAKISTAN
Alexandria
Cairo
JORDAN
Basra
Shiraz
Kuwait City
Bandar Abbas
SINAI
KUWAIT
SAHARA DESERT
Persian Gulf
Nile R.
SAUDI ARABIA
EGYPT
Doha
QATAR
Riyadh
Arabian Sea
Medina
Aswan
Red Sea
SUDAN
ERITREA
Khartoum
ETHIOPIA
0 200 400 Miles
0 200 400 600 Kilometers
LEBANON
Mt. Hermon
Tyre
SYRIA
Kiryat Shemona
GOLAN HEIGHTS
Safed
Acco
Mediterranean Sea
Sea of Galilee
Haifa
Tiberias
Nazareth
Megiddo
Jenin
Beth-shan
Netanya
Tulkarm
Jordan R.
Nablus
Tel Aviv
WEST BANK
Amman
Ramallah
Jericho
Jerusalem
Qumran
Dead Sea
Gaza
Hebron
En-gedi
Khan Yunis
GAZA STRIP
Beersheba
El-Arish
Dimona
ISRAEL
JORDAN
Mizpe Ramon
Petra
EGYPT
SINAI
Eilat
Red Sea
AL
GA
SC
Atlantic Ocean
FL
Gulf of Mexico

Note the comparative size of Israel to the state of Florida